DOMI MINA
NVS TIO
ILLV MEA

THE OXFORD ENGLISH DICTIONARY

SECOND EDITION

THE OXFORD ENGLISH DICTIONARY

First Edited by

JAMES A. H. MURRAY, HENRY BRADLEY, W. A. CRAIGIE
and C. T. ONIONS

COMBINED WITH

A SUPPLEMENT TO THE OXFORD ENGLISH DICTIONARY

Edited by

R. W. BURCHFIELD

AND RESET WITH CORRECTIONS, REVISIONS
AND ADDITIONAL VOCABULARY

THE OXFORD ENGLISH DICTIONARY

SECOND EDITION

Prepared by

J. A. SIMPSON *and* E. S. C. WEINER

VOLUME XVIII

Thro–Unelucidated

CLARENDON PRESS · OXFORD

3 3210 0515466

Oxford University Press, Great Clarendon Street, Oxford OX2 6DP
Oxford New York
Athens Auckland Bangkok Bogotá Buenos Aires Calcutta
Cape Town Chennai Dar es Salaam Delhi Florence Hong Kong Istanbul
Karachi Kuala Lumpur Madrid Melbourne Mexico City Mumbai
Nairobi Paris São Paulo Singapore Taipei Tokyo Toronto Warsaw
and associated companies in
Berlin Ibadan

Oxford is a registered trade mark of Oxford University Press

© Oxford University Press 1989

First published 1989
Reprinted 1991 (with corrections), 1998

All rights reserved. No part of this publication may be reproduced, stored in a retrieval system, or transmitted, in any form or by any means, without the prior permission in writing of Oxford University Press. Within the UK, exceptions are allowed in respect of any fair dealing for the purpose of research or private study, or criticism or review, as permitted under the Copyright, Designs and Patents Act, 1988, or in the case of reprographic reproduction in accordance with the terms of the licences issued by the Copyright Licensing Agency. Enquiries concerning reproduction outside these terms and in other countries should be sent to the Rights Department, Oxford University Press, at the address above

British Library Cataloguing in Publication Data
Oxford English dictionary.—2nd ed.
1. English language—Dictionaries
I. Simpson, J. A. (John Andrew), 1953-
II. Weiner, Edmund S. C., 1950-
423
ISBN 0-19-861230-3 (vol. XVIII)
ISBN 0-19-861186-2 (set)

Library of Congress Cataloging-in-Publication Data
The Oxford English dictionary.—2nd ed.
prepared by J. A. Simpson and E. S. C. Weiner
Bibliography: p.
ISBN 0-19-861230-3 (vol. XVIII)
ISBN 0-19-861186-2 (set)
1. English language—Dictionaries. I. Simpson, J. A.
II. Weiner, E. S. C. III. Oxford University Press.
PE1625.087 1989
423—dc19 88-5330

Data capture by ICC, Fort Washington, Pa.
Text-processing by Oxford University Press
Typesetting by Pindar Graphics Origination, Scarborough, N. Yorks.
Manufactured in the United States of America by
World Color Book Services, Taunton, Mass.

KEY TO THE PRONUNCIATION

THE pronunciations given are those in use in the educated speech of southern England (the so-called 'Received Standard'), and the keywords given are to be understood as pronounced in such speech.

I. *Consonants*

b, d, f, k, l, m, n, p, t, v, z *have their usual English values*

g as in *go* (gəʊ)
h ... *ho!* (həʊ)
r ... *run* (rʌn), *terrier* ('tɛrɪə(r))
(r) ... *her* (hɜː(r))
s ... *see* (siː), *success* (sək'sɛs)
w ... *wear* (wɛə(r))
hw ... *when* (hwɛn)
j ... *yes* (jɛs)

θ as in *thin* (θɪn), *bath* (bɑːθ)
ð ... *then* (ðɛn), *bathe* (beɪð)
ʃ ... *shop* (ʃɒp), *dish* (dɪʃ)
tʃ ... *chop* (tʃɒp), *ditch* (dɪtʃ)
ʒ ... *vision* ('vɪʒən), *déjeuner* (deʒøne)
dʒ ... *judge* (dʒʌdʒ)
ŋ ... *singing* ('sɪŋɪŋ), *think* (θiŋk)
ŋg ... *finger* ('fɪŋgə(r))

(FOREIGN AND NON-SOUTHERN)

ʎ as in It. *serraglio* (ser'raʎo)
ɲ ... Fr. *cognac* (kɔɲak)
x ... Ger. *ach* (ax), Sc. *loch* (lɒx), Sp. *frijoles* (fri'xoles)
ç ... Ger. *ich* (ıç), Sc. *nicht* (nıçt)
ɣ ... North Ger. *sagen* ('zaːɣən)
c ... Afrikaans *baardmannetjie* ('baːrtmanəci)
ɥ ... Fr. *cuisine* (kɥizin)

Symbols in parentheses are used to denote elements that may be omitted either by individual speakers or in particular phonetic contexts: e.g. *bottle* ('bɒt(ə)l), *Mercian* ('mɜːʃ(ɪ)ən), *suit* (s(j)uːt), *impromptu* (ɪm'prɒm(p)tjuː), *father* ('fɑːðə(r)).

II. *Vowels and Diphthongs*

SHORT

ɪ as in *pit* (pɪt), *-ness*, (-nɪs)
ɛ ... *pet* (pɛt), Fr. *sept* (sɛt)
æ ... *pat* (pæt)
ʌ ... *putt* (pʌt)
ɒ ... *pot* (pɒt)
ʊ ... *put* (pʊt)
ə ... *another* (ə'nʌðə(r))
(ə) ... *beaten* ('biːt(ə)n)
i ... Fr. *si* (si)
e ... Fr. *bébé* (bebe)
a ... Fr. *mari* (mari)
ɑ ... Fr. *bâtiment* (bɑtimɑ̃)
ɔ ... Fr. *homme* (ɔm)
o ... Fr. *eau* (o)
ø ... Fr. *peu* (pø)
œ ... Fr. *boeuf* (bœf) *coeur* (kœr)
u ... Fr. *douce* (dus)
ʏ ... Ger. *Müller* ('mʏlər)
y ... Fr. *du* (dy)

LONG

iː as in *bean* (biːn)
ɑː ... *barn* (bɑːn)
ɔː ... *born* (bɔːn)
uː ... *boon* (buːn)
ɜː ... *burn* (bɜːn)
eː ... Ger. *Schnee* (ʃneː)
ɛː ... Ger. *Fähre* ('fɛːrə)
aː ... Ger. *Tag* (taːk)
oː ... Ger. *Sohn* (zoːn)
øː ... Ger. *Goethe* ('gøːtə)
yː ... Ger. *grün* (gryːn)

NASAL

ɛ̃, æ̃ as in Fr. *fin* (fɛ̃, fæ̃)
ɑ̃ ... Fr. *franc* (frɑ̃)
ɔ̃ ... Fr. *bon* (bɔ̃)
œ̃ ... Fr. *un* (œ̃)

DIPHTHONGS, etc.

eɪ as in *bay* (beɪ)
aɪ ... *buy* (baɪ)
ɔɪ ... *boy* (bɔɪ)
əʊ ... *no* (nəʊ)
aʊ ... *now* (naʊ)
ɪə ... *peer* (pɪə(r))
ɛə ... *pair* (pɛə(r))
ʊə ... *tour* (tʊə(r))
ɔə ... *boar* (bɔə(r))

aɪə as in *fiery* ('faɪərɪ)
aʊə ... *sour* (saʊə(r))

The incidence of main stress is shown by a superior stress mark (') preceding the stressed syllable, and a secondary stress by an inferior stress mark (ˌ), e.g. *pronunciation* (prəˌnʌnsɪ'eɪʃ(ə)n).

For further explanation of the transcription used, see *General Explanations*, Volume I.

LIST OF ABBREVIATIONS, SIGNS, ETC.

Some abbreviations listed here in italics are also in certain cases printed in roman type, and vice versa.

a. (in Etym.)	adoption of, adopted from
a (as *a* 1850)	*ante*, 'before', 'not later than'
a.	adjective
abbrev.	abbreviation (of)
abl.	ablative
absol.	absolute, -ly
Abstr.	(in titles) *Abstract, -s*
acc.	accusative
Acct.	(in titles) *Account*
A.D.	*Anno Domini*
ad. (in Etym.)	adaptation of
Add.	Addenda
adj.	adjective
Adv.	(in titles) *Advance, -d, -s*
adv.	adverb
advb.	adverbial, -ly
Advt.	advertisement
Aeronaut.	(as label) in Aeronautics; (in titles) *Aeronautic, -al, -s*
AF., AFr.	Anglo-French
Afr.	Africa, -n
Agric.	(as label) in Agriculture; (in titles) *Agriculture, -al*
Alb.	Albanian
Amer.	American
Amer. Ind.	American Indian
Anat.	(as label) in Anatomy; (in titles) *Anatomy, -ical*
Anc.	(in titles) *Ancient*
Anglo-Ind.	Anglo-Indian
Anglo-Ir.	Anglo-Irish
Ann.	Annals
Anthrop., Anthropol.	(as label) in Anthropology; (in titles) *Anthropology, -ical*
Antiq.	(as label) in Antiquities; (in titles) *Antiquity*
aphet.	aphetic, aphetized
app.	apparently
Appl.	(in titles) *Applied*
Applic.	(in titles) *Application, -s*
appos.	appositive, -ly
Arab.	Arabic
Aram.	Aramaic
Arch.	in Architecture
arch.	archaic
Archæol.	in Archæology
Archit.	(as label) in Architecture; (in titles) *Architecture, -al*
Arm.	Armenian
assoc.	association
Astr.	in Astronomy
Astrol.	in Astrology
Astron.	(in titles) *Astronomy, -ical*
Astronaut.	(in titles) *Astronautic, -s*
attrib.	attributive, -ly
Austral.	Australian
Autobiogr.	(in titles) *Autobiography, -ical*
A.V.	Authorized Version
B.C.	Before Christ
B.C.	(in titles) British Columbia
bef.	before
Bibliogr.	(as label) in Bibliography; (in titles) *Bibliography, -ical*
Biochem.	(as label) in Biochemistry; (in titles) *Biochemistry, -ical*
Biol.	(as label) in Biology; (in titles) *Biology, -ical*
Bk.	*Book*
Bot.	(as label) in Botany; (in titles) *Botany, -ical*
Bp.	Bishop
Brit.	(in titles) *Britain, British*
Bulg.	Bulgarian
Bull.	(in titles) *Bulletin*
c (as *c* 1700)	*circa*, 'about'
c. (as 19th c.)	century
Cal.	(in titles) *Calendar*
Cambr.	(in titles) *Cambridge*
Canad.	Canadian
Cat.	Catalan
catachr.	catachrestically
Catal.	(in titles) *Catalogue*
Celt.	Celtic
Cent.	(in titles) *Century, Central*
Cent. Dict.	*Century Dictionary*
Cf., cf.	*confer*, 'compare'
Ch.	Church
Chem.	(as label) in Chemistry; (in titles) *Chemistry, -ical*
Chr.	(in titles) *Christian*
Chron.	(in titles) *Chronicle*
Chronol.	(in titles) *Chronology, -ical*
Cinemat., Cinematogr.	in Cinematography
Clin.	(in titles) *Clinical*
cl. L.	classical Latin
cogn. w.	cognate with
Col.	(in titles) *Colonel, Colony*
Coll.	(in titles) *Collection*
collect.	collective, -ly
colloq.	colloquial, -ly
comb.	combined, -ing
Comb.	Combinations
Comm.	in Commercial usage
Communic.	in Communications
comp.	compound, composition
Compan.	(in titles) *Companion*
compar.	comparative
compl.	complement
Compl.	(in titles) *Complete*
Conc.	(in titles) *Concise*
Conch.	in Conchology
concr.	concrete, -ly
Conf.	(in titles) *Conference*
Congr.	(in titles) *Congress*
conj.	conjunction
cons.	consonant
const.	construction, construed with
contr.	contrast (with)
Contrib.	(in titles) *Contribution*
Corr.	(in titles) *Correspondence*
corresp.	corresponding (to)
Cotgr.	R. Cotgrave, *Dictionarie of the French and English Tongues*
cpd.	compound
Crit.	(in titles) *Criticism, Critical*
Cryst.	in Crystallography
Cycl.	(in titles) *Cyclopædia, -ic*
Cytol.	(in titles) *Cytology, -ical*
Da.	Danish
D.A.	*Dictionary of Americanisms*
D.A.E.	*Dictionary of American English*
dat.	dative
D.C.	District of Columbia
Deb.	(in titles) *Debate, -s*
def.	definite, -ition
dem.	demonstrative
deriv.	derivative, -ation
derog.	derogatory
Descr.	(in titles) *Description, -tive*
Devel.	(in titles) *Development, -al*
Diagn.	(in titles) *Diagnosis, Diagnostic*
dial.	dialect, -al
Dict.	Dictionary; *spec.*, the *Oxford English Dictionary*
dim.	diminutive
Dis.	(in titles) *Disease*
Diss.	(in titles) *Dissertation*
D.O.S.T.	*Dictionary of the Older Scottish Tongue*
Du.	Dutch
E.	East
Eccl.	(as label) in Ecclesiastical usage; (in titles) *Ecclesiastical*
Ecol.	in Ecology
Econ.	(as label) in Economics; (in titles) *Economy, -ics*
ed.	edition
E.D.D.	*English Dialect Dictionary*
Edin.	(in titles) *Edinburgh*
Educ.	(as label) in Education; (in titles) *Education, -al*
EE.	Early English
e.g.	*exempli gratia*, 'for example'
Electr.	(as label) in Electricity; (in titles) *Electricity, -ical*
Electron.	(in titles) *Electronic, -s*
Elem.	(in titles) *Element, -ary*
ellipt.	elliptical, -ly
Embryol.	in Embryology
e.midl.	east midland (dialect)
Encycl.	(in titles) *Encyclopædia, -ic*
Eng.	England, English
Engin.	in Engineering
Ent.	in Entomology
Entomol.	(in titles) *Entomology, -logical*
erron.	erroneous, -ly
esp.	especially
Ess.	(in titles) *Essay, -s*
et al.	*et alii*, 'and others'
etc.	et cetera
Ethnol.	in Ethnology
etym.	etymology
euphem.	euphemistically
Exam.	(in titles) *Examination*
exc.	except
Exerc.	(in titles) *Exercise, -s*
Exper.	(in titles) *Experiment, -al*
Explor.	(in titles) *Exploration, -s*
f.	feminine
f. (in Etym.)	formed on
f. (in subordinate entries)	form of
F.	French
fem. (*rarely* f.)	feminine
fig.	figurative, -ly
Finn.	Finnish
fl.	*floruit*, 'flourished'
Found.	(in titles) *Foundation, -s*
Fr.	French
freq.	frequent, -ly
Fris.	Frisian
Fund.	(in titles) *Fundamental, -s*
Funk or *Funk's Stand. Dict.*	*Funk and Wagnalls Standard Dictionary*
G.	German
Gael.	Gaelic
Gaz.	(in titles) *Gazette*
gen.	genitive
gen.	general, -ly
Geogr.	(as label) in Geography; (in titles) *Geography, -ical*

Geol.	(as label) in Geology; (in titles) *Geology, -ical*
Geom.	in Geometry
Geomorphol.	in Geomorphology
Ger.	German
Gloss.	Glossary
Gmc.	Germanic
Godef.	F. Godefroy, *Dictionnaire de l'ancienne langue française*
Goth.	Gothic
Govt.	(in titles) *Government*
Gr.	Greek
Gram.	(as label) in Grammar; (in titles) *Grammar, -tical*
Gt.	Great
Heb.	Hebrew
Her.	in Heraldry
Herb.	among herbalists
Hind.	Hindustani
Hist.	(as label) in History; (in titles) *History, -ical*
hist.	historical
Histol.	(in titles) *Histology, -ical*
Hort.	in Horticulture
Househ.	(in titles) *Household*
Housek.	(in titles) *Housekeeping*
Ibid.	*Ibidem*, 'in the same book or passage'
Icel.	Icelandic
Ichthyol.	in Ichthyology
id.	*idem*, 'the same'
i.e.	*id est*, 'that is'
IE.	Indo-European
Illustr.	(in titles) *Illustration, -ted*
imit.	imitative
Immunol.	in Immunology
imp.	imperative
impers.	impersonal
impf.	imperfect
ind.	indicative
indef.	indefinite
Industr.	(in titles) *Industry, -ial*
inf.	infinitive
infl.	influenced
Inorg.	(in titles) *Inorganic*
Ins.	(in titles) *Insurance*
Inst.	(in titles) *Institute, -tion*
int.	interjection
intr.	intransitive
Introd.	(in titles) *Introduction*
Ir.	Irish
irreg.	irregular, -ly
It.	Italian
J., (J.)	(quoted from) Johnson's *Dictionary*
(Jam.)	Jamieson, *Scottish Dict.*
Jap.	Japanese
joc.	jocular, -ly
Jrnl.	(in titles) *Journal*
Jun.	(in titles) *Junior*
Knowl.	(in titles) *Knowledge*
l.	line
L.	Latin
lang.	language
Lect.	(in titles) *Lecture, -s*
Less.	(in titles) *Lesson, -s*
Let., Lett.	letter, letters
LG.	Low German
lit.	literal, -ly
Lit.	Literary
Lith.	Lithuanian
LXX	Septuagint
m.	masculine
Mag.	(in titles) *Magazine*
Magn.	(in titles) *Magnetic, -ism*
Mal.	Malay, Malayan
Man.	(in titles) *Manual*
Managem.	(in titles) *Management*
Manch.	(in titles) *Manchester*
Manuf.	in Manufacture, -ing
Mar.	(in titles) *Marine*

masc. (*rarely* m.)	masculine
Math.	(as label) in Mathematics; (in titles) *Mathematics, -al*
MDu.	Middle Dutch
ME.	Middle English
Mech.	(as label) in Mechanics; (in titles) *Mechanics, -al*
Med.	(as label) in Medicine; (in titles) *Medicine, -ical*
med.L.	medieval Latin
Mem.	(in titles) *Memoir, -s*
Metaph.	in Metaphysics
Meteorol.	(as label) in Meteorology; (in titles) *Meteorology, -ical*
MHG.	Middle High German
midl.	midland (dialect)
Mil.	in military usage
Min.	(as label) in Mineralogy; (in titles) *Ministry*
Mineral.	(in titles) *Mineralogy, -ical*
MLG.	Middle Low German
Misc.	(in titles) *Miscellany, -eous*
mod.	modern
mod.L	modern Latin
(Morris),	(quoted from) E. E. Morris's *Austral English*
Mus.	(as label) in Music; (in titles) *Music, -al; Museum*
Myst.	(in titles) *Mystery*
Mythol.	in Mythology
N.	North
n.	neuter
N. Amer.	North America, -n
N. & Q.	*Notes and Queries*
Narr.	(in titles) *Narrative*
Nat.	(in titles) *Natural*
Nat. Hist.	in Natural History
Naut.	in nautical language
N.E.	North East
N.E.D.	*New English Dictionary*, original title of the *Oxford English Dictionary* (first edition)
Neurol.	in Neurology
neut. (*rarely* n.)	neuter
NF., NFr.	Northern French
No.	Number
nom.	nominative
north.	northern (dialect)
Norw.	Norwegian
n.q.	no quotations
N.T.	New Testament
Nucl.	Nuclear
Numism.	in Numismatics
N.W.	North West
N.Z.	New Zealand
obj.	object
obl.	oblique
Obs., obs.	obsolete
Obstetr.	(in titles) *Obstetrics*
occas.	occasionally
OE.	Old English (= Anglo-Saxon)
OF., OFr.	Old French
OFris.	Old Frisian
OHG.	Old High German
OIr.	Old Irish
ON.	Old Norse
ONF.	Old Northern French
Ophthalm.	in Ophthalmology
opp.	opposed (to), the opposite (of)
Opt.	in Optics
Org.	(in titles) *Organic*
orig.	origin, -al, -ally
Ornith.	(as label) in Ornithology; (in titles) *Ornithology, -ical*
OS.	Old Saxon
OSl.	Old (Church) Slavonic
O.T.	Old Testament
Outl.	(in titles) *Outline*
Oxf.	(in titles) *Oxford*
p.	page
Palæogr.	in Palæography

Palæont.	(as label) in Palæontology; (in titles) *Palæontology, -ical*
pa. pple.	passive participle, past participle
(Partridge),	(quoted from) E. Partridge's *Dictionary of Slang and Unconventional English*
pass.	passive, -ly
pa.t.	past tense
Path.	(as label) in Pathology; (in titles) *Pathology, -ical*
perh.	perhaps
Pers.	Persian
pers.	person, -al
Petrogr.	in Petrography
Petrol.	(as label) in Petrology; (in titles) *Petrology, -ical*
(Pettman),	(quoted from) C. Pettman's *Africanderisms*
pf.	perfect
Pg.	Portuguese
Pharm.	in Pharmacology
Philol.	(as label) in Philology; (in titles) *Philology, -ical*
Philos.	(as label) in Philosophy; (in titles) *Philosophy, -ic*
phonet.	phonetic, -ally
Photogr.	(as label) in Photography; (in titles) *Photography, -ical*
phr.	phrase
Phys.	physical; (*rarely*) in Physiology
Physiol.	(as label) in Physiology; (in titles) *Physiology, -ical*
Pict.	(in titles) *Picture, Pictorial*
pl., plur.	plural
poet.	poetic, -al
Pol.	Polish
Pol.	(as label) in Politics; (in titles) *Politics, -al*
Pol. Econ.	in Political Economy
Polit.	(in titles) *Politics, -al*
pop.	popular, -ly
Porc.	(in titles) *Porcelain*
poss.	possessive
Pott.	(in titles) *Pottery*
ppl. a., pple. adj.	participial adjective
pple.	participle
Pr.	Provençal
pr.	present
Pract.	(in titles) *Practice, -al*
prec.	preceding (word or article)
pred.	predicative
pref.	prefix
pref., Pref.	preface
prep.	preposition
pres.	present
Princ.	(in titles) *Principle, -s*
priv.	privative
prob.	probably
Probl.	(in titles) *Problem*
Proc.	(in titles) *Proceedings*
pron.	pronoun
pronunc.	pronunciation
prop.	properly
Pros.	in Prosody
Prov.	Provençal
pr. pple.	present participle
Psych.	in Psychology
Psychol.	(as label) in Psychology; (in titles) *Psychology, -ical*
Publ.	(in titles) *Publications*
Q.	(in titles) *Quarterly*
quot(s).	quotation(s)
q.v.	*quod vide*, 'which see'
R.	(in titles) *Royal*
Radiol.	in Radiology
R.C.Ch.	Roman Catholic Church
Rec.	(in titles) *Record*
redupl.	reduplicating
Ref.	(in titles) *Reference*
refash.	refashioned, -ing
refl.	reflexive
Reg.	(in titles) *Register*

reg.	regular
rel.	related to
Reminisc.	(in titles) *Reminiscence, -s*
Rep.	(in titles) *Report, -s*
repr.	representative, representing
Res.	(in titles) *Research*
Rev.	(in titles) *Review*
rev.	revised
Rhet.	in Rhetoric
Rom.	Roman, -ce, -ic
Rum.	Rumanian
Russ.	Russian
S.	South
S.Afr.	South Africa, -n
sb.	substantive
sc.	*scilicet*, 'understand' or 'supply'
Sc., Scot.	Scottish
Scand.	(in titles) *Scandinavia, -n*
Sch.	(in titles) *School*
Sc. Nat. Dict.	*Scottish National Dictionary*
Scotl.	(in titles) *Scotland*
Sel.	(in titles) *Selection, -s*
Ser.	Series
sing.	singular
Sk.	(in titles) *Sketch*
Skr.	Sanskrit
Slav.	Slavonic
S.N.D.	*Scottish National Dictionary*
Soc.	(in titles) *Society*
Sociol.	(as label) in Sociology; (in titles) *Sociology, -ical*
Sp.	Spanish
Sp.	(in titles) *Speech, -es*
sp.	spelling
spec.	specifically
Spec.	(in titles) *Specimen*
St.	Saint
Stand.	(in titles) *Standard*
Stanf.	(quoted from) *Stanford Dictionary of Anglicised Words & Phrases*
str.	strong
Struct.	(in titles) *Structure, -al*
Stud.	(in titles) *Studies*
subj.	subject
subord. cl.	subordinate clause
subseq.	subsequent, -ly
subst.	substantively
suff.	suffix
superl.	superlative
Suppl.	Supplement
Surg.	(as label) in Surgery; (in titles) *Surgery, Surgical*
s.v.	*sub voce*, 'under the word'
Sw.	Swedish
s.w.	south-western (dialect)
Syd. Soc. Lex.	Sydenham Society, *Lexicon of Medicine & Allied Sciences*
syll.	syllable
Syr.	Syrian
Syst.	(in titles) *System, -atic*
Taxon.	(in titles) *Taxonomy, -ical*
techn.	technical, -ly
Technol.	(in titles) *Technology, -ical*
Telegr.	in Telegraphy
Teleph.	in Telephony
(Th.),	(quoted from) Thornton's *American Glossary*
Theatr.	in the Theatre, theatrical
Theol.	(as label) in Theology; (in titles) *Theology, -ical*
Theoret.	(in titles) *Theoretical*
Tokh.	Tokharian
tr., transl.	translated, translation
Trans.	(in titles) *Transactions*
trans.	transitive
transf.	transferred sense
Trav.	(in titles) *Travel(s)*
Treas.	(in titles) *Treasury*
Treat.	(in titles) *Treatise*
Treatm.	(in titles) *Treatment*
Trig.	in Trigonometry
Trop.	(in titles) *Tropical*
Turk.	Turkish
Typog., Typogr.	in Typography
ult.	ultimately
Univ.	(in titles) *University*
unkn.	unknown
U.S.	United States
U.S.S.R.	Union of Soviet Socialist Republics
usu.	usually
v., vb.	verb
var(r)., vars.	variant(s) of
vbl. sb.	verbal substantive
Vertebr.	(in titles) *Vertebrate, -s*
Vet.	(as label) in Veterinary Science; (in titles) *Veterinary*
Vet. Sci.	in Veterinary Science
viz.	*videlicet*, 'namely'
Voy.	(in titles) *Voyage, -s*
v.str.	strong verb
vulg.	vulgar
v.w.	weak verb
W.	Welsh; West
wd.	word
Webster	*Webster's* (*New International*) *Dictionary*
Westm.	(in titles) *Westminster*
WGmc.	West Germanic
Wks.	(in titles) *Works*
w.midl.	west midland (dialect)
WS.	West Saxon
(Y.),	(quoted from) Yule & Burnell's *Hobson-Jobson*
Yrs.	(in titles) *Years*
Zoogeogr.	in Zoogeography
Zool.	(as label) in Zoology; (in titles) *Zoology, -ical*

Signs and Other Conventions

Before a word or sense

† = obsolete
|| = not naturalized, alien
¶ = catachrestic and erroneous uses

In the listing of Forms

1 = before 1100
2 = 12th c. (1100 to 1200)
3 = 13th c. (1200 to 1300), etc.
5–7 = 15th to 17th century
20 = 20th century

In the etymologies

* indicates a word or form not actually found, but of which the existence is inferred
:— = normal development of

The printing of a word in SMALL CAPITALS indicates that further information will be found under the word so referred to.

.. indicates an omitted part of a quotation.

- (in a quotation) indicates a hyphen doubtfully present in the original; (in other text) indicates a hyphen inserted only for the sake of a line-break.

PROPRIETARY NAMES

THIS Dictionary includes some words which are or are asserted to be proprietary names or trade marks. Their inclusion does not imply that they have acquired for legal purposes a non-proprietary or general significance nor any other judgement concerning their legal status. In cases where the editorial staff have established in the records of the Patent Offices of the United Kingdom and of the United States that a word is registered as a proprietary name or trade mark this is indicated, but no judgement concerning the legal status of such words is made or implied thereby.

†**thro, thra**, *sb.* *Obs.* Forms: 4 **þro**, 4–5 **thro, throo**, 5–6 *Sc.* **thra**. [ME. a. ON. *þrá*, neut. obstinacy, persistence in opposition, contrariety, 'hard struggle' (Vigf.); perh. confounded with *þrá* fem., painful or violent longing, eager yearning (cognate with OE. *þrawu* painful pressure): see Falk and Torp s.v. *traa*[2].]

1. Struggle, contest; trouble.

1303 R. BRUNNE *Handl. Synne* 10570 Þat tyme was mykyl þro, And ofte was boþe werre and wo. *c* **1330** —— *Chron. Wace* (Rolls) 54 In sclaundire & threte, & in thro. *Ibid.* 13925 Mikel was þe pres, ful þykke þe þro. *a* **1400–50** *Alexander* 2282 He..Thringis to þe thrid time & þe thra [*Dubl. MS.* thro] wynnys [in wrestling].

2. Anger, wrath.

13.. *E.E. Allit. P.* B. 754 Ȝet for þretty in þrong I schal my þro steke. *a* **1400** *Sir Perc.* 376, I hafe spokene with thame, I wene, Wordes in throo.

3. Eagerness, keenness, haste.

c **1470** HENRY *Wallace* VIII. 237 Our men on him thrang forthwart in to thra. *c* **1475** *Rauf Coilȝear* 801 He sa cummand in thra The maist man of all tha, That euer he had sene. **1513** DOUGLAS *Æneis* VIII. Prol. 17 Thochtis thretis in thra our breistis ourthwort.

†**thro, thra**, *a.*[1] (*adv.*) *Obs.* Forms: 3–4 **þra**, (5–7 *Sc.*) **thra**, 4–5 **þro, thro, throo** (5 **throe**). [ME. a. ON. *þrá-r* 'stubborn, obstinate, unyielding, refractory, persistent, zealous, eager, keen', adj. cognate with *þrá* sb.: see prec.]

1. Stubborn, obstinate, persistent; reluctant to give way, or accede to a request.

(The spelling *throw* in quot. *c* 1500 is app. due to confusion with other words.)

a **1300** *Cursor M.* 5803 (Cott.) King pharaon..es ful thra [*Trin.* þro], Lath sal him think to let þam ga. **13..** *Ibid.* 28092 (Cott.) Vn-buxum haf i bene, and thra A-gayn my gastly fader al-sa. *c* **1400** *Destr. Troy* 5246 Þat were þro men in threpe, & thre-tyms mo. ?*a* **1500** *Chester Pl.* (Shaks. Soc.) II. 11 In this place, be you never so throe, Shall you no longer dwell. *c* **1500** *Smyth & his Dame* 317 in Hazl. *E.P.P.* III. 213 Be thov neuer so throw, I shal amende the sonne, I trow. *c* **1560** A. SCOTT *Poems* (S.T.S.) xiii. 31 Than be not thra ȝour scherwand to confort. **1603** *Philotus* xl, Scho is sa ackwart and sa thra, That with refuse I come hir fra.

b. Of a corpse: Stiff, rigid.

a **1400–50** *Alexander* 4452 Graffis garnyscht of gold & gilten tombis Thurghis to thrawyn in quen ȝe þraa worthe.

2. Stubborn in fight, sturdy, bold; fierce. Also *fig.*

c **1320** *Sir Tristr.* 777 Þei þou be þro, Lat mo men wiþ þe ride On rowe. ?*a* **1400** *Morte Arth.* 3757 They..thristis to þe erthe Of the thraeste mene thre hundrethe. *c* **1400** *Ywaine & Gaw.* 3570 Thir wordes herd the knyghtes twa, It made tham forto be mor thra. *c* **1400** *Destr. Troy* 6422 Merion..With þre thousand þro men þrong hym vnto. *Ibid.* 6446, 6462, etc. *c* **1470** HENRY *Wallace* IX. 846 Wallace with him had fourty archarys thra. **1513** DOUGLAS *Æneis* VIII. xii. 128 And Gelones, thai pepill of Sithya, In archery the quhilk ar wonder thra. **1535** STEWART *Cron. Scot.* (Rolls) I. 250 The Albionis, thocht tha war neuir sa thra, Out of the feild on force wer maid to ga.

3. Angry, wroth, furious, violent.

13.. *E.E. Allit. P.* A. 344 Anger gaynez þe not a cresse, Who nedez schal þole be not so þro. *c* **1375** *Sc. Leg. Saints* ii. (*Paulus*) 504 As he, þat firste wes cristis fa, And in thra will his men can sla. *c* **1380** *Sir Ferumb.* 3968 Wan þay come to þe dupe Ryuer, þat wilde was & thro, Entrye þanne ne darst hy noȝt. *c* **1400** *Destr. Troy* 147 He bethought hym full thicke in his throo hert. *c* **1440** *Bone Flor.* 2075 Sche dyd me oonys an evyll dede, My harte was wondur throo. *c* **1475** *Sqr. Lowe Degre* 1017 With egre mode, and herte full throwe, The stewardes throte he cut in two.

4. Keen, eager, zealous, earnest.

a **1300** *Cursor M.* 14392 (Cott.) Ful deueli war þai Iuus thra þair blisced lauerd for to sla. *c* **1320** *Sir Tristr.* 615 Rohand was ful þra Of tristrem for to frain. *c* **1350** *Will Palerne* 3264 Þre M. of men þat þro were to fiȝt. **1400** *Destr. Troy* 470 Mony thoughtes full thro thrange in hir brest. *c* **1425** WYNTOUN *Cron.* V. vi. 1198 Sancte Gregor..Made special and thra oryson þat God walde grant his saule to be ..fre. ?*a* **1500** *Chester Pl.* (E.E.T.S.) 451 Falsehed to further he was euer throe. [**1775** JOHN WATSON *Hist. Halifax* 547 A person is said to be thro about any thing, who is very keen or intent about it.]

b. *fig.* Of a thing: Ready, apt, disposed.

a **1425** *Cursor M.* 16560 (Trin.) Þei..cut þis tre in two.. What þei wolde þerof shape: þerto hit was ful þro.

B. *adv.* Obstinately; vigorously; boldly.

a **1425** *Cursor M.* 5997 (Trin.) Ȝitt þe kyng hem helde ful þro For wolde he not lete hem go. *c* **1450** *St. Cuthbert* (Surtees) 6032 Oxen twenty and twa War drawand þis bell full thra. *c* **1470** *Golagros & Gaw.* 60 The berne bovnit to the burgh..and thrang in full thra.

†**thro**, *a.*[2] *Obs.* Origin, status, and meaning uncertain; occurs in the alliterative phrase ***thriven and thro***, always commendatory or honorific, and apparently meaning something like 'excellent'.

(It is not impossible that this may originally have been the same word as THRO *a.*[1] 2, and that 'thriven and thro' became a stock phrase which was vaguely used; cf. 'a þro knight, þrivand in armys', *c* 1400 in THRIVING *ppl. a.* 1, and the other references there given. But there seems also to have been connexion in sense with THRO *v.*, as if it had been taken as 'grown, become great'; cf. the phrases 'throd and thriven' [*v.r.* 'wele þriuen'] *c* 1300 in THRIVEN *ppl. a.* 1, 'thryven ant thowen' [from THEE *v.*[1]] *a* 1310 *ibid.* 2.)

a **1310** in Wright *Lyric P.* 26 He is thrustle thryven in [? and] thro that singeth in sale. *Ibid.* 39 Wel were him that wiste hire thoht, That thryven ant þro. **13..** *E.E. Allit. P.* A. 867, I seghe, says Iohan, þe loumbe hym stande, On þe mount of syon ful þryuen & þro. *a* **1450** *Le Morte Arth.* 589 There is no lady of flesshe ne bone In this world so thryve or thro, Thoughe hyr herte were stele or stone, That might hyr loue hald hym fro.

†**thro**, *v.* *Obs.* Pa. pple. **throd, throdd, (throded)**. [Northern ME., app. ad. ON. *þróa-sk* refl. to thrive, wax, grow: cf. *þroskr* adj. full-grown, *þroska-sk* vb. to grow up to manhood; also dial. Ger. *drûhen, trûhen* (Grimm), *drôen, trühen* to thrive, prosper, grow.] *intr.* To grow, wax, increase in size or stature; to grow up.

Cf. dial. *Throdden* ppl. adj., fat, well-grown, in good condition, well-fed (Brockett, and E.D.D. Northumb., Yorksh.).

c **1325** *Metr. Hom.* 112 That ilke childe Was sa unthewed and sa wilde, That alle the schathe that he moht do, He did quen he bigan to thro. *c* **1330** R. BRUNNE *Chron.* (1810) 240 Now [MS. no] gynnes Dauid to thro. For now bigynnes Dauid to wax a werreour. **13..** *Cursor M.* 3077 (Cott.) For quen [ysmael] throded [*v.r.* waxyn] was to yoman. *Ibid.* 5641 Quen it [the child Moses] was throd [*F.* waxen, *G.* thriuen] and sumdel ald To kinges doghter sco it yald. *Ibid.* 14806 Fast es he [Jesus] throd [*G.* throdd] and thriuen, And mikel grace ai es him giuen.

b. ? To advance. (Perh. a different word.)

c **1330** R. BRUNNE *Chron. Wace* (Rolls) 10058 Al softly he bad hem go, þat non schulde byfore oþer þro Til þey come vnto þe bataille.

thro, thro', early form and contraction of THROUGH.

throale, obs. form of THRALL *sb.*[3]

throat (θrəʊt), *sb.* Forms: 1 **ð-, þrote, þrotu**, 2–5 **þ-**, 2–7 **throte**, (3 **þorte**), 4–9 (mainly *Sc.*) **throt**, 5–6 (8 *Naut.*) **thrott**, (5 **troht**, 5–6 **throthe**, *Sc.* **throit**), 6–7 **throate**, 6– **throat**. [OE. *þrote, -u*, wk. fem., = OHG. *drozza* wk. f., MHG. *drozze* wk. f. or m. (whence mod.Ger. *drossel* wk. f., throat, THROTTLE); app. from OTeut. root **þrut-*, Indo-Eur. **trud-*: cf. OE. *þrútian* to swell, *þrútung* swelling, ON. *þrútna* to swell, *þrútinn* swollen, *þroti* a swelling; the name may have had reference to the external appearance of the throat. Beside this an OTeut. **strut-* is evidenced by OLG. *strota* wk. f., throat (MLG., LG. *strotte*, MDu. *strote*, Du. *strot* throat); cf. OFris. *strotbolla*, beside OE. *þrotbolla*, THROAT-BOLL; also MHG. *strozze* wk. f. (whence It. *strozza* throat). The original relations between the stems *þrut-* and *strut-* are not determined, but both may have had the sense 'thrust out, project, swell'.]

I. The part of the body.

1. The front of the neck beneath the chin and above the collar-bones, containing the passages from the mouth and nose to the lungs and stomach. Also the corresponding part in vertebrates generally, and sometimes the analogous part in insects, etc.

(As 'round the neck' necessarily includes 'round the throat', 'throat' is sometimes said with the wider sense of the 'neck': cf. quot. 13..[2].)

a **700**, etc. [implied in THROAT-BOLL]. *c* **1000** ÆLFRIC *Hom.* II. 250 Iudas..hine sylfne aheng sona mid grine, and rihtlice ȝewrað ða forwyrhtan ðrotan. *a* **1154** *O.E. Chron.* an. 1137, Me..diden an scærp iren abuton þa mannes throte. *c* **1290** *S. Eng. Leg.* I. 16/525 In þe þrote with a swerd he smot þe suete rode. **13..** *K. Alis.* 5952 He ne had noiþere nekke ne þrote His heued was in his body yshote. **13..** *Sir Beues* (A.) 218 Þow schelt ben hanged be þe þrote. **1340** *Ayenb.* 14 Þet bodi of þe beste wes ase lipard, þe uet weren of bere, þe þrote of lioun. *a* **1450** MYRC *Festial* 79 By ryght dome, þat þrote þat spake þe wordes of traytery aȝeynys his Lord, þat þrote was ystrangled wyth þe grynne of a rope. **1553** EDEN *Treat. Newe Ind.* (Arb.) 15 [The Elephant] his mouth is vnder his throte. **1573** *Satir. Poems Reform.* xxxix. 142 Thay schot gude Manfrild in athort the throit. **1741** RICHARDSON *Pamela* (1824) I. 84 His throat sticking out like a wen. **1826** KIRBY & SP. *Entomol.* III. 367 External Anatomy of Insects... 2. *Jugulum* (the Throat). That part of the subface that lies between the temples. **1860** TYNDALL *Glac.* I. xxii. 156 The cold smote my naked throat bitterly. **1878** VILLARI *Machiavelli* (1898) I. III. viii. 143 Her throat is well turned but seems to me somewhat thin.

2. a. The passage in the anterior part of the neck, leading from the mouth and nose to the gullet and windpipe; also, either of these passages considered separately.

c **888** K. ÆLFRED *Boeth.* xxii. § 1 He is swiðe biter on muðe, & he þe tirð on ða þrotan. *c* **1000** ÆLFRIC *Voc.* in Wr.-Wülcker 157/41 *Guttur*, þrotu. *c* **1220** *Bestiary* 507 in *O.E. Misc.* 16 Vt of his ðrote it [whale] smit an onde, Ðe swetteste ðing ðat is o londe. *c* **1375** *Sc. Leg. Saints* xx. (*Blasius*) 344 Quha-sa-euire in þare throt seknes has. **1398** TREVISA *Barth. De P.R.* V. xxiv. (Bodl. MS.) The þrote is þe pipes of þe lunges..þe substaunce of þis pipe is grustely and hard. *c* **1425** *Voc.* in Wr.-Wülcker 635/17 *Nomina membrorum*... *Hec gula*, troht. *c* **1475** *Pict. Voc.* ibid. 748/13 *Hec gula*, *Hoc guttur*, *Hic jugulus*, a throthe. **1527** ANDREW *Brunswyke's Distyll. Waters* A iij b, The same water.. gargoled in the throte..withdryueth the payne of the throte. **1602** MARSTON *Ant. & Mel.* III. Wks. 1856 I. 31 Thou..choakst their throts with dust. **1769** COOK *Voy. round World* I. v. (1773) 56 A sound exactly like that which we make to clear the throat when any thing happens to obstruct it. **1897** 'TIVOLI' (H. W. Bleakley) *Short Innings* v. 76 A huge piece of cake went down the wrong throat, and Carrots had to belabour him lustily to persuade it to take the right direction.

b. A sore throat. *colloq.*

1885 A. EDWARDES *Girton Girl* I. iii. 68 That reasonless creature..has one of her throats again, and I did so want her to take some of my globules. **1915** LD. FISHER *Let.* 2 Apr. in M. Gilbert *Winston S. Churchill* (1972) III. Compan. I. 764, I thought I had a throat coming on but drastic measures have relieved it. **1979** M. SOAMES *Clementine Churchill* xiii. 201 In the last year she had been subject to 'throats' and coughs.

3. This part with its passages, considered in various capacities, whence various expressions.

a. Viewed as the entrance to the stomach; hence in figurative expressions, as

(*to fill, full*) ***up to the throat***, to the limit of capacity; ***to pour*** (also ***send***) ***down the throat***, to waste or squander (property or money) in eating and drinking; ***to cram, ram, thrust down one's throat***, to force (an opinion or the like) upon one's acceptance; ***to jump down one's throat***, † (*a*) to be excessively attentive to one; also, to accept one with alacrity as prospective husband (*obs.*); (*b*) to reprimand or contradict one fiercely.

a **1225** *Ancr. R.* 216 Ȝif þe gulchecuppe weallinde bres to drincken, & ȝeot in his wide þrote. **1340–70** *Alex. & Dind.* 677 Bacus þe bollere..Ȝe callen him kepere of þe þrote. **1500–20** DUNBAR *Poems* xxvi. 65 Ay as thay tomit thame of schot, Ffyendis fild thame new vp to the thrott. **1606** SHAKS. *Ant. & Cl.* II. v. 36 The Gold I giue thee, will I melt and powr Downe thy ill vttering throate. **1610** HOLLAND *Camden's Brit.* (1637) 543 Who..delight to send their estates downe the throat. **1724** RAMSAY *Vision* viii, Quha rammed, and crammed, That bargin down thair throts. **1829** FONBLANQUE *Eng. under Seven Administr.* (1837) I. 232 Since the Duke of Wellington..thrust the Emancipation Bill down his [Geo. IV's] royal throat. **1861** DICKENS *Lett.* 3 Dec., A place already full to the throat. **1871** *Monthly Packet* Sept. 287 The small boat held only three... 'Just as well,' Hugh said... 'We don't want *all* to jump down her throat in a moment.' **1879** TROLLOPE *Cousin Henry* I. iii. 52 Was she to jump down your throat when you asked her? **1883** MRS. KENNARD *Right Sort* ix, I might have jumped down this gentleman's throat in my foolish admiration for his powers of equitation. **1916** E. F. BENSON *David Blaize* xi. 215 He simply jumped down my throat the other day in your defence. **1940** 'N. BLAKE' *Malice in Wonderland* I. vii. 88 There's no need to jump down my throat. I was only trying to be helpful.

b. Considered as containing the vocal organs; hence *transf.* the voice.

† ***to lay, set out,*** (***set up***) ***a*** or ***one's throat***, to raise one's voice; † (***to speak***) ***with a full throat***, (to speak) loudly; hence *fig.* plainly, roundly; ***at the top of one's throat***, at the top of one's voice: see TOP *sb.*

a **1250** *Owl & Night.* 1721 Þe wrenne..hadde stefne small Heo hadde gode þrote [*v.r.* þorte] & schille. *c* **1369** CHAUCER *Dethe Blaunche* 320 To fynde out of mery crafty notys They ne spared nat her throtes. *a* **1450** [see sense 1]. **1535** COVERDALE *Ps.* cxiii. [cxv.] 7 Fete haue they, but they can not go, nether can they speake thorow their throte. **1567** *Gude & Godlie B.* (S.T.S.) 110 Thay can pronunce na voce furth of thair throtis. **1600** HOLLAND *Livy* VII. ix. 255 As lowd as ever he could set out a throate, maketh this challenge. **1686** tr. *Chardin's Coronat. Solyman* 94 These Women made such a noise..set up their throats as they did before. **1742** GRAY *Spring* i, The Attic warbler pours her throat, Responsive to the cuckow's note. **1819** SCOTT *Leg. Montrose* xi, Men..talking Earse at the top of their throats. **1869** RUSKIN *Q. of Air* § 65 Into the throat of the bird is given the voice of the air.

c. In the repudiation of a statement as false, in phr. (*to give*, etc. ***one the lie***) ***in*** (†***down***) ***one's throat***, regarded as the place of issue, to which the assertion is thrown back; also, with merely intensive force, ***to lie in one's throat***, to lie foully or infamously.

1588 SHAKS. *Tit. A.* II. i. 55 Till I haue..Thrust these reprochfull speeches downe his throat, That he hath breath'd in my dishonour heere. **1601** —— *Twel. N.* III. iv. 172 Thou lyest in thy throat. **1602** —— *Ham.* II. ii. 600 Who ..giues me the Lye i'th' Throate, As deepe as to the Lungs? **1616** J. LANE *Cont. Sqr.'s T.* IX. 198 Gave him home the lie, adowne his throte. *a* **1648** LD. HERBERT *Hen. VIII* (1683) 227 We say unto you, that you have lyed in your throat. **1805** SCOTT *Last Minstr.* V. xx, He lyes most foully in his throat. **1824** BYRON *Let. to Murray* Wks. (1846) 433/1 Whoever asserts that I am the author.., lies in his throat.

d. Regarded as a vital part, and the most vulnerable point of attack; esp. in the phrase ***to cut the throat***, to kill by this method; also *fig.*

Hence, ***to cut one's own throat*** (***with one's own knife***), to be the means of one's own defeat or destruction; ***to cut the throat of*** (a project, etc.), to defeat, destroy, put an end to: see CUT *v.* 47; ***to cut one another's throats***, to be desperately at variance, quarrel violently; *mod. colloq.*, to engage in ruinous competition (cf. CUTTHROAT 6, quot. 1886); also ***to have, hold, catch, take by the throat*** (also *fig.*), † ***to pull out, to fly at***, † ***start into*** (***unto***) ***one's throat***; ***to be at each other's throats***, to quarrel violently; ***to have*** (***got***) ***the game*** or ***it by the throat*** (Austral. slang), to have the situation under control.

c **1380** WYCLIF *Sel. Wks.* III. 423 Þes apes..done more harm to men þen þof þei cutted hor throtes. *c* **1385** CHAUCER *L.G.W.* 1803 (*Lucrece*) That hast hire by the throte with a swerd at herte. *a* **1400–50** *Alexander* 1812 Þai suld titly þam take & by þe toȝe throtis, And for þaire souerayne sake þam send to þe galawis. *c* **1400** *Brut* 22 She come to here sone.. wiþ ij knyfes, and þerwiþ cotte his þrote. **1583** GOLDING *Calvin on Deut.* lxxx. 490 They cut their own throtes with their own knife. **1596** DALRYMPLE tr. *Leslie's Hist. Scot.* IX. (S.T.S.) II. 197 Quha committis a sworde til an vnskilful persone, quhairwith, quhither he cut his awne throt, or hurt the cuntrie [etc.]. **1631** R. BYFIELD *Doctr. Sabb.* 111 That.. cuts the throat of your solution. **1685** DK. BUCKHM. *Reason. Relig.* in *Phenix* (1708) II. 526 Perpetually quarrelling amongst themselves, and cutting one another's Throats. *a* **1722** FOUNTAINHALL *Decis.* (1759) I. 7 This interlocutor.. knocked his cause..in the head, and cutted its throat. **1824**,

1867 [see CUT *v.* 47]. **1884** RIDER HAGGARD *Dawn* xii, He had let him die; he had effectually and beyond redemption cut his own throat. *a* **1912** *Mod.* Ready to fly at each other's throats. **1947** J. MORRISON *Sailors belong Ships* 15 We're sailors, see? Two sailors. We got the game by the throat. **1949** D. M. DAVIN *Roads from Home* I. i. 21 'The old fellow's gone at last.' 'You don't say.' 'Yes, and a hard fight he made of it, they say, with the sons hardly waiting for him to go before they were at one another's throats over who was to have his leavings.' **1960** R. TULLIPAN *Follow the Sun* 105 'Think we'll get it done to-day?' 'Can't miss... We have it by the throat now all right.' **1978** I. B. SINGER *Shosha* 265 The women are at each other's throats.

†**4.** *fig.* The devouring capacity of any destructive agency, as death, war, etc.; cf. JAW *sb.*[1] 5, MAW *sb.*[1] 1 b, TEETH. *Obs.*

a **1578** LINDESAY (Pitscottie) *Chron. Scot* (S.T.S.) I. 55 The maist walliezand men in the throt of the battell. **1594** SHAKS. *Rich. III*, v. iv. 5 He fights, Seeking for Richmond in the throat of death. **1730–46** THOMSON *Seasons, Autumn* 937 Calm and intrepid in the very throat Of sulphurous war.

II. Transferred senses.

5. A narrow passage, esp. in or near the entrance of something; a narrow part in a passage.

a **1584** MONTGOMERIE *Cherrie & Slae* 1551 A prettie spring: Quhois throt, sir, I wot, sir, ȝe may stap with ȝour neive. **1814** SCOTT *Diary* 17 Aug., in *Lockhart*, The access through this strait would be easy, were it not for the Island of Græmsay, lying in the very throat of the passage. **1823** BUCKLAND *Reliq. Diluv.* 141 The throat of the cave, by which we ascend from the mouth to the interior. **1837** EMERSON *Address Amer. Schol.* Wks. (Bohn) II. 186 One central fire, which flaming now out of the..throat of Vesuvius, illuminates the towers..of Naples. **1838** J. L. STEPHENS *Trav. Russia* 70/1 Field-pieces, whose throats once poured their iron hail against the walls within which they now repose as trophies. **1899** A. GRIFFITHS in *Fortn. Rev.* LXV. 312 Lang's Nek, the throat of the passage into the Transvaal.

6. *spec.* in technical use. **a.** *Archit.*, *Building*, etc. †(*a*) The narrowest part of the shaft of a column, immediately below the capital; the hypotrachelium. (*b*) The neck of an outwork: = GORGE *sb.*[1] 6. (*c*) The part in a chimney, furnace, or furnace-arch immediately above the fire-place, which narrows down to the neck or 'gathering'. (*d*) A groove or channel on the under side of a coping or projecting moulding to keep the drip from reaching the wall.

1663 GERBIER *Counsel* 32 The Freese, Gul or Throat. **1727–41** CHAMBERS *Cycl.*, *Throat*, in architecture, fortification, &c., see *Gorge*, and *Gula*. **1815** J. SMITH *Panorama Sc. & Art.* I. 246 The throat is that part of the opening immediately above the fire, and contained between the mantle and the back. **1838** *Civil Eng. & Arch. Jrnl.* I. 364/1 The smoke..ascends vertically by the throat of the chimney into the flue. **1868** JOYNSON *Metals* 16 The opening at the top of the furnace, called the throat or trunnel-hole. **1895** *Jrnl. Roy. Instit. Brit. Archit.* 14 Mar. 351 If brick sills be used, see that they have a good, clean throat.

b. *Shipbuilding* and *Naut.* (*a*) The hollow of the bend of a knee-timber. (*b*) The outside curve of the jaws of a gaff; hence, the forward upper corner of a fore-and-aft sail; see also quot. 1867. (*c*) The amidships part of a floor-timber, esp. if it bulges and then tapers into the kelson. (*d*) The curve of the flukes of an anchor where they join the shank.

1711 W. SUTHERLAND *Shipbuild. Assist.* 165 *Throat*, the inward bending of Knee-timber. **1776** FALCONER *Dict. Marine*, *Throat*, a name given to the inner end of a gaff, or to that part which is next to the mast. It is opposed to *peek*, which implies the outer extremity of the said gaff. *c* **1850** *Rudim. Navig.* (Weale) 142 They must be deeper in the throat or at the cutting-down. *Ibid.* 155 *Throat*,..the midship part of the floor-timbers. *c* **1860** H. STUART *Seaman's Catech.*, It is..bolted through the throat of each floor. **1867** SMYTH *Sailor's Word-bk.*, *Throt*, that part of the mizen-yard close to the mast. **1882** NARES *Seamanship* (ed. 6) 81 Hooked to a bolt in the throat of the gaff.

c. *Mech.*, etc. (*a*) Of a plough: see quot. 1807. (*b*) In a threshing-machine, the passage from the feed-board to the threshing-cylinder (Knight *Dict. Mech.* 1877). (*c*) The opening in the stock of a plane, in which the iron is set, and through which the shavings pass. (*d*) A contracted part of a spoke near the hub (Knight). (*e*) The angle between the running surface of a railway or tramcar wheel and its flange. *U.S.* (*f*) A tapered pipe connecting two tubes or sections of different diameters (*Cent. Dict.*, *Suppl.* 1909).

1807 A. YOUNG *Agric. Essex* I. 132 *The throat*,..the space from the share point to the junction or approach of the breast to the beam. **1805** DICKSON *Pract. Agric.* I. 4 The throat and breast, or that part which enters, perforates, and breaks up the ground.

7. *Bot.* The throat-like opening of a gamopetalous corolla at which the tube and the petals unite.

1847 W. E. STEELE *Field Bot.* 8 Florets all tubular, with an inflated throat, generally spreading into a hemispherical head. **1880** GRAY *Struct. Bot.* vi. §5 (ed. 6) 246 The line, or sometimes a manifest or conspicuous portion, between the limb and the tube..is called the Throat, in Latin Faux, pl. fauces. **1882** *Garden* 28 Jan. 66/3 The throat of the flower is unbearded.

8. *attrib.* and *Comb.* **a.** attrib. 'of, pertaining to, or affecting the throat', as ***throat-ache, -disease, -muscle, -performer, -roar***, etc.; in sense 6 b (*b*), as ***throat-bolt, -brail, cringle, -downhaul, halyard, lashing*** (see these words, and quots. here); **b.** 'that is on, around, or near the throat', as ***throat-bar, button, -cloth, -feather, -fringe, -patch, -wattle***; **c.** objective, obj. genitive, locative, etc., as ***throat-clearing*** sb. and adj., ***-catching, -clutching, -slitting***; ***throat-bursten, -cracking, -swollen*** adjs. **d.** Special combs.: †**throat-brisk**, ? part of the brisket near the throat; **throat-chain**, in whaling, a chain passed through the throat and tongue of the whale; **throat-clutch**, a guttural catch or momentary closure; **throat-deafness**, deafness caused by a diseased condition of the throat; **throat-flap**, the epiglottis; **throat-full** *a.*, full to the throat, stuffed, crammed; **throat-jaws**, jaw-like pharyngeal bones in the lower vertebrates; **throat-letter**, a guttural; **throat-mane**, a growth of hair on the front of an animal's neck; **throat microphone**, (*colloq.*) **mike**, a microphone attached to a speaker's throat and actuated directly by his larynx; **throat-piece**, (*a*) in mediæval armour, a part of the helm protecting the throat; (*b*) the neck of a racket, where the ends of the rim are brought together upon the handle (*Cent. Dict.*, *Suppl.* 1909); **throat-pipe**, the windpipe; also, the steam supply pipe in a steam-engine; **throat-pit**, a triangular depression at the front of the neck, between the collar-bones at the point where they articulate with the breastbone; **throat-plate**, the forward exterior plate of a locomotive fire-box (*Cent. Dict.*, *Suppl.*); **throat-pouch**, a gular sac in certain birds and animals; **throat-register**, the lowest register of the voice; **throat-ring**, Waldeyer's name for the circular group of lymphatic bodies surrounding the beginning of the respiratory tract; **throat-room**, room for shouting; **throat-root**, an American hairy species of Avens, *Geum virginianum*; **throat-rupture**, goitre; **throat-seizing**, *Naut.*: see quot.; **throat-stopper**, the epiglottis: cf. *throat-flap*; **throat-strap** = THROAT-LATCH; **throat-sweetbread**, butcher's name for the thymus gland; also called *neck-sweetbread*; **throat-thong** = THROAT-LATCH; **throat-toggle**, a toggle with which the *throat-chain* is secured; **throat-vent**, the opening in a coking-oven for the escape of smoke, etc.; **throat-wash**, a medicinal gargle. See also THROAT-BAND, THROAT-BOLL, etc.

1898 J. ARCH *Story of Life* x. 247 Head-aches and heart-aches and *throat-aches. **1872** COUES *N. Amer. Birds* 180 Chuck-will's-widow..a whitish *throatbar. **1867** SMYTH *Sailor's Word-bk.*, **Throat-bolts*, eye-bolts fixed in the lower parts of the tops, and the jaw-ends of gaffs for hooking the throat-halliards to. **1815** BURNEY *Falconer's Dict. M.*, **Throat-Brails*,..are those which are attached to the gaff close to the mast. **1615** CHAPMAN *Odyss.* III. 620 Apart flew either thie: That with the fat they dubd with art alone; The *throte-briske, and the sweet-bread pricking on. **1890** 'R. BOLDREWOOD' *Miner's Right* xxxiv, One button was missing between the upper or *throat button and the third. **1958** *Times Lit. Suppl.* 1 Aug. 438/4 Everything about Happy Knoll that inspires such back-slapping, *throat-catching loyalty in its members. **1811** L. M. HAWKINS *C'tess & Gertr.* I. 78 A vast deal of *throat-clearing, face-stroking, and awkward hesitation. **1958** B. HAMILTON *Too Much of Water* iv. 80 Tremendous expectorations and shattering throat-clearings. **1973** T. PYNCHON *Gravity's Rainbow* I. 31 Relaxation, chairs squeaking, sighs and throatclearings. **1871** *Routledge's Ev. Boy's Ann.* Dec. 2 He invariably wore a white *throat-cloth or neckerchief. **1895** F. OSGOOD in *Forum* (N.Y.) June 507 Nerve-strain tends to the prevalence of the high vocal pitch and to the American fault—the *throat-clutch. **1895** *Outing* (U.S.) XXVI. 47/1 To bend a mainsail, shackle the *throat cringle to the eyebolt under the jaws of the gaff [etc.]. **1897** *Allbutt's Syst. Med.* IV. 778 Adult patients suffering since childhood from '*throat-deafness'. *Ibid.* 750 The so-called 'lithæmic diathesis' is a much more frequent cause of *throat-disease than is generally believed. **1877** KNIGHT *Dict. Mech.*, **Throat-down-hauls*.., ropes for rousing down the throat of a gaff. **1872** COUES *N. Amer. Birds* 162 Ravens, with *throat-feathers acute, lengthened, disconnected. **1683** A. SNAPE *Anat. Horse* IV. x. (1686) 165 The Epiglottis or *Throat-flap, that covers the chink of the Larynx. **1896** *Proc. Zool. Soc. Lond.* 1 Dec. 932 The narrowness and banded coloration of the *throat-fringe must likewise be noted. **1681** W. ROBERTSON *Phraseol. Gen.* (1693) 475 To dine, or eat till he be *throat-full. *a* **1800** COWPER *On Receipt of Hamper*, A bottle green Throat-full. **1762** FALCONER *Shipwr.* II. 389 The halyards *thrott and peek are next apply'd. **1776**— *Dict. Marine* s.v. *Throat*, The ropes employed to hoist up, and lower a gaff,..are called the throat or peek haliards. **1893** PEMBERTON *Iron Pirate* 39 There being..no hand either at the peak halyards or the throat halyards. **1873** MIVART *Lessons Elem. Anat.* viii. §18. 318 Moving those '*throat-jaws', the pharyngeal bones, which exist in so many of the lowest Vertebrate class. **1893** *Times* 13 June 12/1 A *throat lashing of steel rope. **1847** *Proc. Philol. Soc.* III. 116 A similar interchange between lip and *throat letters. **1908** H. JOHNSTON *George Grenfell & Congo* II. xxiv. 618 The larger, taller domestic sheep of East and South Africa.. changes its *throat-mane into a dewlap. **1948** A. L. RAND *Mammals Eastern Rockies* 213 Mountain caribou... Neck greyish brown with a small white throat mane. **1945** N. M. COOKE *Electronics Dict.* 391 *Throat microphone. **1972** K. BENTON *Spy in Chancery* i. 13 He began to talk quietly through his throat microphone, which connected with a transmitter in his pocket. **1965** P. O'DONNELL *Modest Blaise* xvi. 170 The sensitive *throat-mike would pick up the vibration of his vocal chords and relay them. **1875** HUXLEY & MARTIN *Elem. Biol.* (1877) 203 The *throat-muscles: through the broad thin muscle in front (mylo-hyoid) is seen the hypoglossal nerve. **1872** COUES *N. Amer. Birds* 195 Young birds lack..the crimson *throat-patch. **1776** BURNEY *Hist. Mus.* I. 340 The vociferous Stentor..the most illustrious *Throat-performer, or herald of antiquity. **1869** BOUTELL *Arms & Arm.* v. (1874) 79 His helm is ornamented ..; the *throat-piece has thunderbolts..in hammer work. **1600** J. PORY tr. *Leo's Africa* III. 185 The inhabitants of this region haue the balles of their *throat-pipes very great. **1632** J. HAYWARD tr. *Biondi's Eromena* 29 She..stab'd her husband..in the face, thinking to strike him in the throat-pipes. **1824** R. STUART *Hist. Steam Engine* 72 The regulator valve [the 'throttle'], which opens or shuts the communication between the cylinder and boiler by the throat-pipe. **1660** *Albert Durer Revived* 4 A straight perpendicular line from the *Throat-pit down. **1672** SIR T. BROWNE *Let. Friend* §10 Some are so curious as to observe the depth of the throat-pit. **1871** DARWIN *Desc. Man* II. xii. II. 33 In the genus Sitana, the males alone are furnished with a large *throat-pouch. **1872** COUES *N. Amer. Birds* 18 Pelicans, cormorants, etc., that have a naked throat-pouch. **1903** *Med. Record* 7 Feb. 228 The various lymphatic structures in Waldeyer's so-called lymphatic *throat ring. **1843** CARLYLE *Past & Pr.* III. xii, Let me have elbow-room, *throat-room, and I will not fail! **1858** *Hilpert's Eng.-Germ. Dict.*, *Throat-root. **1884** MILLER *Plant-n.*, *Geum virginianum*, Throat-root, White Avens. **1684** tr. *Bonet's Merc. Compit.* II. 44 One..had his neck wonderfully swelled with the *Throat-Rupture. **1867** SMYTH *Sailor's Word-bk.*, **Throat-seizing*, in blocks, confines the hook and thimble in the strop home to the scores. **1886** CORBETT *Fall of Asgard* II. 9 There will be some merry *throat-slitting. **1661** LOVELL *Hist. Anim. & Min.* Introd., Amongst Birds..The *throat stopper is in none, yet they temper the motion so, that nothing may fall into the throat. **1877** KNIGHT *Dict. Mech.*, **Throat-strap*, the upper strap of a halter that encircles the horse's throat; also called jaw strap. *a* **1661** HOLYDAY *Juvenal* x. 191 Nero did..ne're contract With one *throat-swoln, gor-bellied, or crump-back'd. **1611** COTGR., *Sousgorge d'une bride*, the *throat-thong, or throat-band of a bridle. **1874** SCAMMON *Marine Mammals* 232 The cutting gear..consists of toggles, spades, boarding and leaning knives,..*throat-toggle, head axes, etc. **1839** URE *Dict. Arts* 997 The *throat-vents..are then left open. **1901** *Lancet* 2 Nov. 1203/1 The application of an antiseptic *throat-wash. **1875** *Zoologist* X. 4686 It [a bird] has but one medial *throat-wattle.

throat (θrəʊt), *v.* [f. THROAT *sb.*]

1. *trans.* To utter or articulate in or from one's throat; to speak in a guttural tone; ***to throat out***, to cry out or shout from the throat.

c **1611** CHAPMAN *Iliad* XIII. 135 So Hector hereto throated threats, to go to sea in blood. **1622** MABBE tr. *Aleman's Guzman d'Alf.* II. 113 Throating it out, wheresoever he comes,..'I am an Alguazil'. **1908** A. S. M. HUTCHINSON *Once aboard Lugger* v. iii. 304 'Barley water!' Mr. Marrapit throated. 'Barley water!' **1929** S. LESLIE *Anglo-Catholic* ix. 116 Music was being throated from a reed organ.

†**2. a.** To cut the throat of; to slaughter, slay. *Obs. rare.* (Cf. also THROATING-*knife*.)

1382 WYCLIF *2 Kings* x. 14 Whom when thei hadden taken alyve, thei throtyden [1388 strangliden, *Vulg.* jugulaverunt, LXX ἔσφαξαν] hem in the cystern, besyde the chaumbre.

†**b.** *Farming* (*local*). See quot. *Obs.*

1750 [implied in THROATING *vbl. sb.*]. **1763** *Museum Rust.* (ed. 2) I. 236 Mons. de L'Isle's workman cuts the wheat against the bending, or, as an Aylesbury-vale man would say, throats it.

3. *Building.* To furnish with a throat; to groove or channel. (Chiefly in *pa. pple.* and *vbl. sb.*)

1823 P. NICHOLSON *Pract. Build.* 311 [The fascia] is fluted or throated on its upper edge, to prevent the water from running over the ashlaring. **1876** *Encycl. Brit.* IV. 472/2 Sills are weathered and throated like the parts of a string course. **1881** YOUNG *Ev. Man his own Mechanic* §1299 A dash-board..may be made out of a solid piece sloped at the top..and 'throated' or channelled on the under surface with a deep groove. **1883** *Specif. Alnwick & Cornhill Railw.* 5 Ashlar Copings..no stone is to be less than 2 feet 6 inches in length, and the whole are to be weathered and throated.

throatal (ˈθrəʊtəl), *a.* [irreg. f. THROAT *sb.* + -AL[1].] Of or pertaining to the throat; guttural; cervical.

1905 *Sat. Rev.* 1 Apr. 415/2 The loudest..click..comes at the end of the liquid, throatal noise. **1908** *Westm. Gaz.* 1 Aug. 15/2 The throatal band that separates the white from the light blue of the breast and under-parts.

'throat-band.

1. *Saddlery.* = THROAT-LATCH.

1611 COTGR., *Sousbarbe*,..the throat-band of a bridle. **1794** W. FELTON *Carriages* (1801) II. 138 The Throat-Band [is] a narrow, short strap, with a buckle at each end. **1833** *Regul. Instr. Cavalry* I. 70 The throat-band must be..slack.

2. A band worn round the neck; also, a part of a garment encircling the neck; a neck-band.

1903 *Daily Chron.* 9 May 8/4 *Rebats*, to give the new throat bands with their short hanging fronts their correct French name. **1904** *Daily Chron.* 12 Mar. 8/4 The collars.. in others..are simply throat-bands elaborated into shoulder straps. **1907** *Blackw. Mag.* July 501 The grimy throat-band, originally white, of a common regimental shirt.

†**'throat-boll.** *Obs.* Forms: see THROAT *sb.* and BOWL *sb.*[1] [OE. *protbolla*, f. *prote*, THROAT + *bolla*: see BOWL *sb.*[1] and BOLL *sb.*[1] 5. Cf. OFris. *strotbolla* in same sense.] The protuberance in the front of the throat; the Adam's apple; hence, the larynx.

a **700** *Epinal Gloss.* (O.E.T.) 456 *Gurgulio*, throtbolla. *c* **725** *Corpus G.* 1000 & *a* **800** *Leiden G.* Ðrotbolla. *a* **901**

Laws K. Ælfred c. 51 ȝif monnes ðrotbolla bið þyrel, ȝebete mid xii scill. *c* **1000** ÆLFRIC *Gram.* ix. (Z.) 35 *Gurgulio*, ymel oððe ðrotbolla. *c* **1250** *Death* 173 in *O.E. Misc.* 178 þi þrotebolle þat þu mide sunge. *c* **1386** CHAUCER *Reeve's T.* 353 By the throte bolle he caughte Alayn..And on the nose he smoot hym with his fest. *c* **1450** *Two Cookery-bks.* 79 Take a Curlewe..; take awey the nether lippe and throte boll. **1529** RASTELL *Pastyme, Hist. Brit.* (1811) 292 One of them ..cut his throte bolle a sonder with a dagger. **1548–77** VICARY *Anat.* ii. (1888) 19 It is necessarie in some meane places to put a grystle, as in the throte bowel for the sounde. **1565** GOLDING *Ovid's Met.* III. (1593) 57 His throte-boll sweld with puffed veines. **1575** *Gamm. Gurton* III. iii. C iij b, Trounce her, pull out her throte boule. **1611** COTGR., *Gueneau*, the throtle, or throat-boll.

'throat-,cutter. Chiefly *Sc.* or *nonce-wd.* One who cuts throats; a cutthroat, an assassin.

1535 STEWART *Cron. Scot.* (Rolls) III. 18 Of throt-cutteris and all sic cursit cryme, And murderaris of leill men be the way. **1567** *Satir. Poems Reform.* vii. 66 Bludy bucheouris and throtcutters. *a* **1598** ROLLOCK *Wks.* (Wodrow Soc.) II. xv. 172 Two vagabonds, two throat-cutters. **1840** THACKERAY *Paris Sk. Bk.* Wks. 1900 V. 209 An executioner ..had come..to assist the professional throat-cutter.

So **'throat-,cutting** *vbl. sb.*, the cutting of the throat; also *fig.*, mutually destructive competition in trade; cf. *to cut one another's throats* s.v. THROAT *sb.* 3 d; *ppl. a.*, that cuts the throat.

1655 GURNALL *Chr. in Arm.* verse 14. I. iii. (1679) 7/2 He buys his Sleep dear, that pays his throat-cutting for it. **1840** GEN. P. THOMPSON *Exerc.* (1842) V. 23 Then come the murders, the throat-cuttings, the massacres of prisoners. **1859** *Habits Gd. Soc.* iii. 132 How difficult..has it been to abolish the stiff black hat and the throat-cutting collar. **1888** E. BELLAMY *Looking Backward* xxii. 323 Your contemporaries, with their mutual throat-cutting, knew very well what they were at. **1931** L. STEFFENS *Autobiogr.* II. III. xxxv. 609 It was not exactly a pool, but there had been a lot of throat-cutting in the trade; the competitive bidding had cut prices down till no man could make any profit.

throated ('θrəʊtɪd), *a.* [f. THROAT *sb.* or *v.* + -ED.] Having or furnished with a throat; having a throat of a specified kind (chiefly in combination), as ***deep-, dry-, large-, red-, white-throated.***

1530 PALSGR. 327/2 Throted, *gorgé.* **1601** ? MARSTON *Pasquil & Kath.* I. 76 Yon same drie throated huskes Will sucke you vp. **1746** FRANCIS tr. *Hor., Sat.* II. ii. 53 Give me, the Harpy-throated Glutton cries, In a large Dish a Mullet's mighty Size. **1850** *Beck's Florist* Dec. 292 One of the best of the white-throated kinds [of Petunias]. **1880** W. WATSON *Prince's Quest* (1892) 102 Sooth-tongued singers, throated like the bird.

b. *Building.* Having a throat or groove; fluted, channelled, grooved.

1847 SMEATON *Builder's Man.* 189 Bath proper sunk and throated sills.

'throater. *local.* A throating-knife: see THROATING *vbl. sb.* d; also, a man who uses this knife in cutting off the heads of fishes.

1846 *Knickerbocker* XXVII. 511 The 'throater', the 'header', the 'splitter' take stations at the speedily-erected table. **1891** *Cent. Dict.* cites from New Brunswick.

†**'throateral,** *a. Obs. nonce-wd.* [irreg. f. THROAT *sb.*, after *guttural.*] Guttural.

1662 J. WILSON *Cheats* III. iii, Guttural, that is to say, throteral.

'throatful. [f. THROAT *sb.* + -FUL.] As much as the throat can hold at once.

1920 D. H. LAWRENCE *Lost Girl* vii. 139 Geoffrey gulped beer in large throatfuls.

†**'throat-goll.** *Obs. rare.* [f. THROAT + ? *golle*, GULL *sb.* 4, throat, gullet.] The windpipe, or its upper part close to the epiglottis. (The word appears to have been somewhat vaguely used.)

14.. *Sir Beues* (C.) 2753 + 102 Sethen he went to the skulle [of the dragon] And hewyd asonder the throte golle [*v.r.* þrote bolle]. **14..** *Nom.* in Wr.-Wülcker 676/25 *Hoc epiglotum*, a th[r]otegole. *c* **1440** *Promp. Parv.* 493/1 Throte golle, *epiglotum, frumen.* **1530** PALSGR. 281/1 Throtegole or throtebole, *neu de la gorge, gosier.*

†**throat-hole,** occas. error for THROAT-BOLL.

'throatily, *adv.* [f. THROATY *a.* + -LY[2].] In a throaty manner; gutturally; hoarsely.

1893 *Scribner's Mag.* XIV. 61 A tame cornet tenored it throatily. **1899** B. CAPES *Lady of Darkness* xvii, Charlot sniggered throatily. **1901** *Blackw. Mag.* Dec. 820/1 The wind..ranged throatily round the coast.

throatiness ('θrəʊtɪnɪs). [f. as prec. + -NESS.] The condition of being throaty (in either sense).

1871 G. LAWRENCE *Anteros* xix, You might pick out..one or two clear cases of throatiness. **1883** G. STABLES *Our Friend the Dog* vii. 61 *Throatiness*, a term applied to loose skin about the throat, where none should exist, as in the Pointer. **1884** G. MOORE *Mummer's Wife* (1887) 163 In a few lessons I could get rid of that throatiness, and show her how to get a note or two from the chest. **1890** *Pall Mall G.* 25 Aug. 2/3 Influenza... The symptoms are always the same —rheumatism, throatiness, headache, and slight fever.

throating ('θrəʊtɪŋ), *vbl. sb.* [f. THROAT *v.* + -ING[1].] The action of the verb THROAT.

†**a.** *Farming* (*local*). (See quots.) *Obs.*

1750 W. ELLIS *Mod. Husb.* V. I. 68 (E.D.S.) When they mow beans against their bending, they [in the Vale of Aylesbury] call it throating. **1763** *Museum Rust.* (ed. 2) I. 236 It is only when they chance to have a thin crop, that they venture to mow them against their own bending (this they call throating).

b. *Building*, etc. The cutting of a 'throat' or channel; the undercutting of a projecting moulding in order to prevent rain water from trickling down the wall; *concr.* the channel or groove thus cut: = THROAT *sb.* 6 a (*d*).

1825 J. NICHOLSON *Operat. Mechanic* 543 In measuring strings, the weathering is denominated sunk work, and the grooving throatings. **1838** F. W. SIMMS *Public Wks. Gt. Brit.* 9 The coping shall [have] a throating of half an inch wide cut on its underside. *c* **1850** *Rudim. Navig.* (Weale) 160 *Wood-lock*, a piece of elm..in the throating or score of the pintle. **1898** *Speaker* 26 Feb. 264/1 Masses of greyish white —almost like a faint throating of snow.

c. *Shipbuilding.* The throat of a floor-timber.

1869 SIR E. J. REED *Shipbuild.* ii. 28 Keep its upper edge level with the throating of the floors.

d. *attrib.*: **throating-knife**, a knife used for cutting the throats of fish; **throating-line** = *cutting-down line* (CUTTING *vbl. sb.* 9 b); **throating-machine**, a machine for shaping the throats of wheel spokes (*Cent. Dict.*, *Suppl.* 1909).

1883 *Fisheries Exhib. Catal.* 197 Cod splitting, ripping and throating knives.

throat-latch, throat-lash, *sb. Saddlery.* [f. THROAT *sb.* + LATCH *sb.*[1] 1, LASH *sb.*[2] 1.] A strap passing under the horse's throat which helps to keep the bridle in position.

1794 W. FELTON *Carriages* (1801) II. 167 Bearing-reins hung to the throat-band by throat-latch dees. **1829** *Sporting Mag.* XXIV. 175, I never saw a horse driven in the throat-latch in Germany. **1890** 'R. BOLDREWOOD' *Col. Reformer* (1891) 106 He..held on to the bridle-rein with such tenacity that the throat-lash giving way, it was jerked over the horse's head, leaving the reins in the rider's hands.

transf. a **1825** FORBY *Voc. E. Anglia, Throat-latch*..2. The strings of a hat, cap, &c. fastened under the chin.

attrib. **1794** [above]. **1901** G. W. CABLE *Cavalier* xix, He had a retreating chin, a throat-latch beard and a roving eye.

Hence **throat-latch** *v. trans.*, to put a throat-latch upon.

1829 *Sporting Mag.* XXIV. 175, I throat-latched him, and never drove a better leader.

throatless ('θrəʊtlɪs), *a.* [f. THROAT *sb.* + -LESS.] Without a throat; having no throat.

1881 G. ALLEN *Evolutionist at Large* v. 49 A wasp whose head has been severed from its body and stuck upon a pin, will still greedily suck up honey with its throatless mouth. **1887** *Longm. Mag.* Sept. 539 Vast, featureless head, set throatless on a formless bust.

throatlet ('θrəʊtlɪt). [f. as prec. + -LET.] An article of ornament or protection for the throat; a woman's necklet; a small boa, usually of fur.

1865 LIVINGSTONE *Zambesi* v. 114 The Manjanga adorn their bodies [with] throatlets, bracelets and anklets of brass, copper, or iron. **1889** *Star* 29 Oct. 1/6 A throatlet of coral beads. **1896** *Echo* 15 Feb. 4/4 Capes, throatlets, and boas are the chief forms in which peltry seems to be worn.

throatwort ('θrəʊtwɜːt). [f. as prec. + WORT: see quot. 1597.] Name for the Nettle-leaved Bell-flower, *Campanula Trachelium*; also extended to other species, as *C. glomerata, latifolia*, and *Cervicaria*; also locally applied to the Foxglove, Figwort (*Scrophularia nodosa*), and American Button Snake-root (*Liatris spicata*).

1578 LYTE *Dodoens* II. xx. 170 This Throtewurte or Haskwurte..is..of three sortes,..the great and the small, and the creeping kinde. **1597** GERARDE *Herbal* II. cx. 363 The thirde sort of Canterburie Bels, called likewise Throtewoorte, of his vertue in curing the diseases of the throte. **1766** *Museum Rust.* VI. 446 Lesser Throatwort, or Canterbury Bells. **1813** SCOTT *Rokeby* III. viii, Where.. throatwort with its azure bell, And moss and thyme his cushion swell. *Note.* The Campanula latifolia, *Grand* [? error for *Giant*] *Throatwort*, or *Canterbury Bells*, grows in profusion upon the beautiful banks of the river Greta.

throaty ('θrəʊtɪ), *a.* [f. as prec. + -Y.]

1. Of vocal sounds, or of the voice: Produced or modified in the throat; guttural; hoarse.

c **1645** HOWELL *Lett.* (1650) II. lxxiii. 112 A rime of certain hard throaty words..accounted the difficultst in all the whole Castilian language. **1863** E. C. CLAYTON *Queens of Song* II. 108 In flexibility she was surpassed by few singers ..but for purity of tone and volume, her organ..was throaty. **1874** HULLAH *Speaking Voice* 12 Qualities to which we apply, somewhat vaguely, the epithets thick, thin, throaty, mouthy, and the like. **1876** GEO. ELIOT *Dan. Der.* xlvi, A wonderful mixture of the throaty and the nasal. **1906** *Times* 8 Nov. 11/3 Parts of her voice are very throaty in quality.

2. Of an animal: Having the skin about the throat too loose and pendulous; having a prominent throat or capacious swallow.

1778 *Reading Merc. & Oxf. Gaz.* 30 Nov., A little black Welch Bullock..with a white back, grizzle head and neck throaty. *a* **1843** SOUTHEY *Comm.-pl. Bk.* (1851) IV. 400/2 Some bulls of the middle-horned breed are reproached with being throaty, the skin too profuse and pendulous. **1897** *Outing* (U.S.) XXIX. 541/2 The Spanish pointer was huge of bone, coarse in head and muzzle, very throaty.

throb (θrɒb), *sb.* [f. THROB *v.*] An act of throbbing; a violent beat or pulsation of the heart or an artery.

1579 SPENSER *Sheph. Cal.* May 208 A thrilling throbbe from her hart did aryse. **1579** LYLY *Euphues* Wks. 1902 I. 264 As the throbbes and throwes in chyldbirth wrought hir payne. **1597** —— *Wom. in Moon* I. i. 171 What throbs are these that labour in my brest? **1612** tr. *Benvenuto's Passenger* II. i. §2. 361 Throbbes, yellings, teares. **1750** JOHNSON *Rambler* No. 76 ¶6 Another lenitive by which the throbs of the breast are assuaged. **1827** SCOTT *Surg. Dau.* vii, The feverish throb of his pulsation was diminished. **1852** MRS. STOWE *Uncle Tom's C.* xii, Not one throb of anguish, not one tear of the oppressed, is forgotten by the Man of Sorrows. **1889** M. GRAY *Reproach of Annesley* VI. ii, His heart gave a strong throb.

b. Applied to a (normal) pulsation.

1653 JER. TAYLOR *Serm. for Year* I. xvii. 231 Though it [the heart] strikes to one side by the prerogative of Nature, yet those throbs and constant motions are felt on the other side also. **1891** E. PEACOCK *N. Brendon* I. 230 The throb of the pulse in the temple.

c. *transf.* and *fig.*; cf. senses of THROB *v.* In first quot. used for a (formal) lamentation: cf. THRENE.

1626 JACKSON *Creed* VIII. xxiii. §5 The deepe straine of this particular threne or throb. **1836** W. IRVING *Astoria* I. 243 He..felt a throb of his old pioneer spirit, impelling him to ..join the adventurous band. **1868** J. H. BLUNT *Ref. Ch. Eng.* I. 333 We hear the dying throbs of that sad devotion. **1889** DOYLE *Micah Clarke* 245 There were half-a-dozen throbs of flame in the mist behind, and as many balls sung among our rigging. **1892** GUNTER *Miss Dividends* (1893) 184 Every throb of the locomotive..bears him away from Erma Travenion.

throb (θrɒb), *v.* Forms: 4 (*pr. pple.*) **þrobbant**, (6 frob), 6–7 **throbbe**, 6– **throb**. [The pr. pple. *throbbant* occurs in Piers Plowman, 1362; no other examples of the word are known till 1542, when *frob* occurs in a letter; *throbbe, throb* is known from 1553. Apparently echoic: no cognate word in Teutonic or Romanic.]

1. a. *intr.* Of the heart: To beat strongly, esp. as the result of emotion or excitement; to palpitate. Sometimes said of the pulse, bosom, temples, brain, or even of the blood in the vessels.

1362 [implied in THROBBING *ppl. a.*]. **1542** *St. Papers Hen. VIII*, IX. 124 My hart frobbed exceedingly. **1553** *Respublica* I. iii. 157 But een as against suche a thing my harte wyll throbbe. **1588** SHAKS. *Tit. A.* v. iii. 95 Your hearts will throb and weepe to hear him speake. **1596** SPENSER *F.Q.* IV. x. 53 Whome soone as I beheld, my hart gan throb. **1738** POPE *Epil. Sat.* i. 103 No cheek is known to blush, no heart to throb. **1741** RICHARDSON *Pamela* (1824) I. 120 O my exulting heart! how it throbs in my bosom. **1825** J. NEAL *Bro. Jonathan* III. 206 His temples throbbed—his head rang. **1848** THACKERAY *Van. Fair* xxx, His pulse was throbbing and his cheeks flushed. **1860** TYNDALL *Glac.* I. xi. 81 At each pause my heart throbbed audibly. **1865** SWINBURNE *Rococo* 55 Throbs through the heart of pleasure The purpler blood of pain.

b. To beat as the heart does normally; to pulsate. *rare.*

1653 [implied in THROB *sb.* b]. **1725** N. ROBINSON *Th. Physick* 27 The Hearts of several Animals..will throb and beat, some time after they have been exempted from the Body. **1831** SCOTT *Cast. Dang.* xx, Whose cause..the champions..were bound to avenge while the blood throbbed in their veins.

c. *transf.* Said of the emotion or the like which affects the heart. In quot. 1591 *trans. nonce-use* (cf. *weep* = bewail). Cf. PULSATE *v.* 1 b, PULSE *v.* 2 b.

1591 *Troub. Raigne K. John* x. 21 Deepe sorrow throbbeth misbefalne euents. **1799** HT. LEE *Canterb. T., Frenchm. T.* (ed. 2) I. 233 Fear still throbbed over her frame. **1819** BYRON *Juan* II. cxxxiv, Not even a vision of his former woes Throbb'd in accursed dreams. **1820** W. IRVING *Sketch Bk.* I. 176 The simple affections of human nature throbbing under the ermine. **1881** H. JAMES *Portr. Lady* xv, A feeling of freedom..which..occasionally throbbed into joyous excitement.

d. *transf.* Of a person, a body of people, etc.: To feel or exhibit emotion; to quiver.

1841–4 EMERSON *Ess., Love* Wks. (Bohn) I. 74 We..throb at the recollection of days when happiness was not happy enough. **1862** BURTON *Bk. Hunter* (1863) 8 The world throbs with the excitement of some wonderful criminal trial. **1863** KINGLAKE *Crimea* (1877) II. xi. 124 A vast empire was made to throb with the passions which rent the bosom of the one man Nicholas. **1878** R. W. DALE *Lect. Preach.* ix. 278, I like to have two or three hymns throbbing with emotion.

2. a. *gen.* To be moved or move rhythmically; to pulsate, vibrate, beat.

1847 EMERSON *Woodnotes* ii, And God said, 'Throb!' and there was motion, And the vast mass became vast ocean. **1865** HOLLAND *Plain T.* ii. 74 Her whole being throbbed and sparkled like the sea. **1870** MORRIS *Earthly Par.* III. IV. 15 The very air..Throbbed with sweet scent. **1889** DOYLE *Micah Clarke* 59 One great beacon throbbed upon the summit of Bulster. **1905** R. GARNETT *Shaks.* 106 The verdant level and the slow canal Shall bristle with our pikes, throb with our drums.

b. esp. said of a steamship with reference to the beat of the engine. Also *trans.* with *way* as obj.

1864 LOWELL *Fireside Trav.* 111 We embarked on the little steamer M., and were soon throbbing up the lake. **1873** BLACK *Pr. Thule* viii, Then the big steamer throbbed its way out of the harbour.

3. *trans.* To cause to throb or beat violently. *rare.*

1606 WARNER *Alb. Eng.* XV. xciv. (1612) 376, I know not why, but sure it throbs my heart of late. **1821** CLARE *Vill. Minstr.* II. 200 That intense, enthusiastic glow That throbs the bosom. **1911** KILPATRICK *N.T. Evangelism* 105 Samuel Rutherford..whose passionate devotion throbs his letters. **1939** T. S. ELIOT *Family Reunion* I. ii. 59 The cold spring now is the time For the ache in the moving root.. The slow flow throbbing the trunk.

throbber (ˈθrɒbə(r)). *rare.* [f. THROB *v.* + -ER[1].] A person or thing that throbs.

1890 G. MEREDITH *Let.* 10 Jan. (1970) II. 988 How glad is your poet that he secured his forgiveness before the Voice was.. sharpened to hush the Thousands, and whip or curb their hearts. Else—but this poor throbber would have broken. **1934** WEBSTER, *Throbber*,.. one who or that which throbs; esp., *Colloq.*, one whose emotions are easily moved. **1983** *Maledicta 1982* VI. 23 *Erection*,.. throbber.

throbbing (ˈθrɒbɪŋ), *vbl. sb.* [f. THROB *v.* + -ING[1].] The action of the verb THROB in various senses; an instance of this; pulsation, beating; vibration; rhythmic movement.

1676 WISEMAN *Chirurg. Treat.* VI. vi. 430 In the depending Orifice there was a throbbing of the Arteriall bloud. **1758** J. S. *Le Dran's Observ. Surg.* (1771) 152 He felt frequent Throbbings or Shootings in the Tumour. **1889** DOYLE *Micah Clarke* 234 On every side of us sounded the throbbing of the sea.

ˈ**throbbing**, *ppl. a.* [f. as prec. + -ING[2].] That throbs; beating, pulsating.

1362 LANGL. *P. Pl.* A. XII. 48, I.. þanked hure a þousand syþes with þrobbant hert. **1592** SHAKS. *Ven. & Ad.* 1186 My throbbing hart shall rock thee day and night. **1676** WISEMAN *Chirurg. Treat.* V. ii. 355 A throbbing pain in his Wound. **1746–7** HERVEY *Medit.* (1818) 152 When violent and barbarous blows.. fixed every thorn deep in his throbbing temples. **1876** T. HARDY *Ethelberta* (1890) 155 Ethelberta.. was brimming with compassion for the throbbing girl so nearly related to her. **1898** *Allbutt's Syst. Med.* V. 577 Slight periodic throbbing pains in the joints.

b. *transf.* and *fig.*

1633 G. HERBERT *Temple, Storm* ii, A throbbing conscience spurred by remorse Hath a strange force. **1746–7** HERVEY *Medit.* (1818) 24 Adapted to soothe the throbbing anguish of the mourners. **1847** EMERSON *Dæmonic Love*, The throbbing sea, the quaking earth. **1864** W. CORY *Lett. & Jrnls.* (1897) 140 The throbbing scarlet of the geraniums. **1890** 'R. BOLDREWOOD' *Col. Reformer* (1891) 154 A stately ocean steamer, with throbbing screw.., left a long line of smoke trailing behind her.

Hence ˈ**throbbingly** *adv.*, in a throbbing manner; with throbbing; with heart beating strongly.

a **1693** *Urquhart's Rabelais* III. xlviii. 389 Nor was the rapt of Polyxena more throbbingly resented. **1871** *Daily News* 14 Sept., The gunners on foot could not keep up with their pieces, and panted throbbingly after them. **1885** G. MEREDITH *Diana of the Crossways* II. xiii. 334 Letters, formally worded.. but throbbingly full.

throbless (ˈθrɒblɪs), *a.* [f. THROB *sb.* + -LESS.] Without a throb or throbs; that does not throb; without or destitute of feeling or emotion.

1748 RICHARDSON *Clarissa* (1811) VI. xiii. 67 Every heart quaking; mine, in a particular manner, sunk throbless. **1821** BYRON *Sardan.* v. i. 162 Let me.. fold that throbless heart To this which beats so bitterly. **1839** J. STERLING *Poems* 221 An hour in throbless quiet live.

throch, throcht, obs. Sc. ff. THROUCH, THROUGH, TROUGH.

throck (θrɒk). *dial.* [OE. *þroc*, of unknown origin.] In full *plough-throck*: The share-beam; = PLOUGHHEAD I.

a **1000** *Ags. Gloss.* in Wr.-Wülcker 219/6 *Dentale, s. est aratri pars prima in qua uomer inducitur quasi dens*, sule-reost, *uel* þroc. **1649** BLITHE *Eng. Improv. Impr.* xxviii. (1653) 190 For the Plough-head, some call them the Plough-throck, some the Plough-chip. **1688** R. HOLME *Armoury* III. 333/2 The Throck [of a Plow] is the piece of Timber on which the Suck is fixed. **1893** *S.E. Worc. Gloss.*, *Throck*, the lower part of a (wooden) plough. On the end of the throck the ploughshare is fixed.

throd, throdden, *pa. pple.*: see THRO *v.* Hence **throdden** *v.*, *north dial. intr.*, to grow, to thrive: see quots.

1641 BEST *Farm. Bks.* (Surtees) 5 Neyther will it [a lamb] throden (as the shepheardes say) till such time as the cowe milke bee all voyded. **1690** RAY *N.C. Words* 75 To *Throdden*; to grow, to thrive, to wax, to sturken. **1877** KATH. MACQUOID *Doris Barugh* i, T' stock throddens weel. **1894** *Northumb. Gloss.*, *Throdden*, to make grow, to thrive. Hence *throdden* and *throddy*, plump, fat, well thriven.

throe, †throw(e (θrəʊ), *sb.* Forms: α. 3 (?) **þrahe**, 4–5 **þraue, þrawe, thrawe**, 4–6 **thrau(e**, (4 traue), 4–5 (*Sc.* 6–) **thraw** (θrɔː, θrɑː). β. 3–4 **þrowe**, 4–7 **throwe**, (4 **throghe**), 6–8 **throw**. γ. 7– throe. [*Throe* is a late alteration (noted first in 1615) of the earlier *throwe*, *throw* (which survived as late as 1733). The origin and history of ME. *þrowe* (found *c* 1200), and its northern form *þraw(e, þraw, thrau* (known *c* 1300, and still in use in Sc.) is not quite clear.

The normal source of an Eng. *ōw*: Sc. *aw*, as in *blow*: *blaw*, *crow*: *craw*, *snow*: *snaw*, is an OE. *āw*; this would lead us to see in *þrow(e*: *þraw(e*, an early derivative from the verb *þrowen*: *þrawen*, OE. *þrāwan*, THROW *v.*[1], in its early sense 'to twist, rack, torture' (cf. THROW *v.*[1] I, quots. *c* 1000). Some suggest that the sb. represented OE. *þrawu*, 'painful infliction, affliction, plague, pang, evil' (Bosw.-Toller), which is perh. favoured by the instance *c* 1250 of *þrahes* riming with *lahes* 'laws' (if that belongs here). But *þrawu* would normally give in midland and southern Eng. not *throwe* but *thrawe* (cf. CLAW). On the other hand a derivation (also suggested) from OE. *þrówian*, THROW *v.*[2] 'to suffer', which would suit Eng. *throw*, would not explain the northern *thraw*. If then the word was orig. the OE. *þrawu*, we should have to suppose that this by 1200 (under the influence of *þrówian* to suffer) became *þrowe*, but remained in the north as *þrawe*, *thraw*, and eventually ran together with *thraw*, THROW *sb.*[2], from *thraw*, THROW *v.*[1]

The identity of *throe* with ME. *throwe*, makes its derivation from OE. *þrá*, ME. THRO, THRA *sb.* impossible. The change of *throw(e* to *throe* was app. merely quasi-phonetic; cf. *hoe*, *roe* (of fish) for earlier *howe*, *rowe*, also *bloe* as a 16th c. variant of *blow* sb., and on the other hand *slow-worm* for *slo-worm*, OE. *slá-wyrm*; *throe* would gain favour as making a distinction between this word and *throw* sb.[2] in its ordinary English use. In Scotland, on the other hand, where *thraw* vb. has kindred senses, *thraw* remains unchanged as the form of this sb., as in *deid-thraw* = death-throe.]

1. A violent spasm or pang, such as convulses the body, limbs, or face. Also, a spasm of feeling; a paroxysm; agony of mind; anguish.

a. In general sense.

α. *c* **1325** *Metr. Hom.* 36 Welthe to pride our hert draus, And wa geres us thol hard traues [*MS. C.* thrawes; *rime* draus]. ? *a* **1500** *Chester Plays* (E.E.T.S.) 438 Suffer I must many a hard Thraw. **1673** *Wedderburn's Vocab.* 19 (Jam.) *Tormen alvi*, a thraw in the bellie. **1793** BURNS *Blithe hae I been* ii, If she winna ease the thraws In my bosom swelling.

β. *c* **1374** CHAUCER *Troylus* v. 206 Troylus.. his sorwes þat he spared hadde He yaf an yssue large.. And in his þrowes frenetyk and madde He cursed loue. **1390** GOWER *Conf.* III. 273 And for thin ese.. Thi love throghes forto lisse. **1549** J. CHEKE in *Lett. Lit. Men* (Camden) 8 How honorable is it to fli from honors throws. **1597** GERARDE *Herbal* I. xxi. §2. 27 The throwes and gripings of the bellie. **1607** SHAKS. *Timon* v. i. 203 Their pangs of Loue, with other incident throwes That Natures fragile Vessell doth sustaine. **1719** DE FOE *Crusoe* (Hotten's repr.) 408 Frequent Throws and Pangs of Appetite, that nothing but the Tortures of Death can imitate.

γ. **1730–46** THOMSON *Autumn* 1322 His heart distends With gentle throes. **1787** BURNS *Let. to Earl of Glencairn*, I conjure your lordship, by the honest throe of gratitude. **1814** SCOTT *Ld. of Isles* II. i, But ask thou not.. If the loud laugh disguise convulsive throe. **1860** C. SANGSTER *Hesperus*, etc. 166 Tumultuous throes Of some vast grief. **1870** DISRAELI *Lothair* lvi, In the very throes of its fell despair.

spec. **b.** The pain and struggle of childbirth; *pl.* labour-pangs.

α. *c* **1250** *Comp. Mariæ* in Napier *Hist. Rood-t.* 78 Nou þu moostes, lauedi, lere Wmmone wo þat barnes bere, þa bitter and ta bale þrahes [*MS.* þrehes; *rime* lahes (laws)]. **13..** *K. Alis.* 606 Time is come the lady schal childe:.. The thrawes [*Bodl. MS.* þrowen] hire afongon.

β. *c* **1200** *Trin. Coll. Hom.* 181 Elch wimman.. þan hie beð mid childe bistonden.. nimeð hire stundmele so bittere þrowes. *Ibid.*, Ðat child on his burde þoleð ec bittere þrowe. *c* **1290** *S. Eng. Leg.* I. 472/354 Hire token ful strongue þrowes. **1390** GOWER *Conf.* III. 211 This hell [= hill] on his childinge lay, And whan the throwes on him come His noise.. Was ferfull. *c* **1440** *Promp. Parv.* 493/1 Throwe, womannys pronge. **1613** PURCHAS *Pilgrimage* VIII. xiv. 685 All the throwes.. of this hills monstrous trauells. **1690** C. NESSE *Hist. & Myst. O. & N. Test.* I. 52 The throws in birth be so torturing as no kind of torments can parallel. **1733** CHEYNE *Eng. Malady* II. x. §3 (1734) 220 The *Fœtus*, by its Motion or Pressure, raises those Throws and Convulsions in the Mother.

γ. **1615** CHAPMAN *Odyss.* XIX. 565 Moane for my daughters yet vnended throes. **1621** QUARLES *Esther* Div. Poems (1717) 131 By throes, God sends a joyful birth. **1667** MILTON *P.L.* II. 780 My womb.. Prodigious motion felt and rueful throes. **1715–20** POPE *Iliad* XVII. 6 Her new-fall'n young.. Fruit of her throes. **1742** YOUNG *Nt. Th.* I. 241 In this shape, or in that, has fate entail'd The mother's throes on all of woman born.

c. The agony of death; the death-struggle, death-throe (Sc. *deid-thraw*).

α. *a* **1300** *Cursor M.* 24317 (Cott.) Wit hard thraus [*Ed.* thrauis, *F.* þrawes, *G.* thraues] þat he throu, þai sagh þat he to ded drou. *Ibid.* 24726 (Edin.) Euir apon his þraues [*Gött.* passiun] þink. *Ibid.* 16762 + 6 (Cott.) For þe grete thraws of ded. *c* **1440** *Alphabet of Tales* 358 Hur husband lay in dead thrawis. **1549** *Compl. Scotl.* xiv. 121 Quhen darius vas in the agonya and deitht thrau. *a* **1823** G. BEATTIE *John o' Arnha'* (1826) 39 Some glowr'd an' thratch'd, in deadly thraws.

β. **13..** *K. Alis.* 720 (Bodl. MS.) In his deþ þrowe he was swowe. *c* **1330** *Asump. Virg.* 533 ȝif any.. walle on his last þrowe Schryue him. **1590** SPENSER *F.Q.* I. x. 41 O man! have mind of that last bitter throw. **1629** SIR W. MURE *True Crucifixe* 1581 Death's tormenting throws.

γ. **1814** SCOTT *Wav.* lxix, The throes of a mortal and painful disorder. **1833** HT. MARTINEAU *Tale of Tyne* vi. 113 The agony of.. outrage transcends the throes of dissolution.

2. *transf.* and *fig.* A violent convulsion or struggle preceding or accompanying the 'bringing forth' of something.

1698 CROWNE *Caligula* III. 18 For that poor chaff how will he thrash his brains, He is in throws before, but then he's eas'd. **1856** FROUDE *Hist. Eng.* (1858) II. ix. 373 When a nation is in the throes of revolution, wild spirits are abroad in the storm. **1860** TYNDALL *Glac.* I. viii. 59 A.. scene, suggesting throes of spasmodic energy. **1878** MISS J. J. YOUNG *Ceram. Art* (1879) 125 The author is represented seated at a table.. in the very throes of composition.

3. *attrib.* and *Comb.*

1835 STERLING in Carlyle *Life* II. ii. (1872) 101 The restless immaturity of our self-consciousness, and the promise of its long throe-pangs. **1839** BAILEY *Festus* xxxiv. (1852) 552 Awhile in dead throe-like suspense they stood. **1883** *Century Mag.* Oct. 819/1 The wild, throe-built, water-quarried rock gorges.

throe, †throw(e, *v. rare.* [f. prec. sb.]

†1. *trans.* To cause to suffer throes; to agonize as in childbirth; to torture. *Obs. rare.*

1610 SHAKS. *Temp.* II. i. 231 A birth.. Which throwes thee much to yeeld. **1683** KENNETT tr. *Erasm. on Folly* 51 How many.. pangs of a labouring mind ye are perpetually thrown and tortured with.

2. *intr.* To suffer throes; to agonize; to be convulsed, 'labour', struggle painfully.

a **1618** [see below]. **1880** L. WALLACE *Ben-Hur* (1887) 388 His memory began to throe and struggle.

Hence **throeing** *vbl. sb.*

a **1618** SYLVESTER *Honour's Fare-well* 105 Soul's sad Repenting, and Heart's heavy Throeing, Are surest Fruits that in the World are growing.

throe, obs. form of THRO *a.*, stubborn, etc.

ˌ**Throg'morton Street.** The name of the street in the City of London where the Stock Exchange is located, used allusively for the Stock Exchange or its members.

1900 A. CONAN DOYLE *Green Flag* 243 What could Worlington Dodds know at Dunsloe which was not known in Throgmorton Street? **1952** *Economist* 13 Sept. 658/2 If prosperity is to return to Throgmorton Street the Stock Exchange Council will have to attract more investors.

†throll. *Obs.* [app. related to THRILL *sb.*[1]] A nostril or breathing hole.

c **1430** *Bk. Hawkyng* in *Rel. Ant.* I. 301 But if it have hastely help it wol stop his nare throlles. **1555** *Douglas's Æneis* VII. x. 59 Ane horribill caue.. ane throll [*ed. Small* thyrll], or aynding stede, Of terribill Pluto.

†ˈthroly, *a. Obs. rare.* [app. f. THRO, THRA *sb.* (or ? *a.*) + -LY[1].] Vehement, persistent, painful.

c **1350** *Will. Palerne* 612 Al comes of a þroly þouȝt þat þirles min hert. *Ibid.* 910. *Ibid.* 3518 þe þroli þouȝt þat him meued.. sone he let ouer-slide.

†ˈthroly, ˈthraly, *adv. Obs.* Also 4 **þroliche**, throle. [f. THRO, THRA *a.* + -LY[2].] In a 'thro' manner; obstinately; angrily, furiously, fiercely, violently; eagerly, keenly.

13.. *Cursor M.* 196 (Cott.) Iuus iesu oft.. for his sermon thrali threte [so *F.*]. *Ibid.* 880 (C.) Mi fere, þat þou me gaf mi wijf to be; Ful thrali [so *F.*; *G.* stiffli] first sco bedde it me. **1340–70** *Alisaunder* 215 Hee thought on this thing þroliche in hert. *c* **1350** *Will. Palerne* 103 He.. þroliche þonked god mani þousand siþes. **1362** LANGL. *P. Pl.* A. IX. 107 þroly we eoden Disputyng on Dowel. ? *a* **1400** *Morte Arth.* 1150 þe theefe at þe dede thrawe so throly hyme thryngez, þat three rybbys in his syde he thrystez in sundere. *a* **1400–50** *Alexander* 707 (Dubl. MS.) Thik & thraly [*MS. Ashm.* þrathly] am I thrett & thole must I sone þe slauughter of my awne sonne. *c* **1400** *Destr. Troy* 1987 [It] Thonret full throly with a thicke haile. *Ibid.* 7040 Throly the þre men thronght hym aboute. *c* **1450** *St. Cuthbert* (Surtees) 5705 þe man thraly Forth on his way he ȝode. **1535** STEWART *Cron. Scot.* (Rolls) I. 407 So thralie than togidder that thai thrist, That speiris brak.

throm, obs. form of THRUM.

ˈ**thrombase.** *Physiol. Chem.* [mod. f. Gr. θρόμβ-ος clot, THROMBUS + *-ase*, after *diastase*.] A synonym of thrombin (on the assumption that that is an enzyme).

1908 BAYLISS *Nature of Enzymes* 73 According to Morawitz there exists in circulating blood a body 'thrombogen', which can be converted by a 'thrombokinase' present in all tissues into a precursor of the enzyme which acts upon fibrinogen to form fibrin. This precursor, or prothrombase, is changed into the active thrombase by calcium ions.

thrombin (ˈθrɒmbɪn). *Physiol. Chem.* [mod. f. as prec. + -IN.] The substance which by interaction with fibrinogen gives rise to fibrin, and is hence the immediate cause of the clotting of shed blood; fibrin-ferment.

1898 *E. A. Schäfer's Text-bk. Physiol.* I. 160 Fibrin-ferment (thrombin) or its precursor (prothrombin) producing the formation of fibrin from fibrinogen. **1900** E. H. STARLING *Elem. Hum. Physiol.* iii. (ed. 4) 78 The coagulation of the blood is due to the conversion of a soluble proteid present in the plasma—fibrinogen, into an insoluble proteid—fibrin, under the agency of a ferment, which is known as fibrin ferment or thrombin.

thrombo- (ˈθrɒmbəʊ), before a vowel **thromb-**, combining form of Gr. θρόμβο-ς THROMBUS, a formative in some pathological and chemical terms, as **thrombasˈthenia** (also **thrombo-**) [ad. G. *thrombasthenie* (E. Glanzmann 1918, in *Jahrb. f. Kinderheilkunde* LXXXVIII. 28), f. Gr. ἀσθένεια (see ASTHENIA)], a condition in which the number of platelets is normal but their clotting power is defective; so **thromb(o)asˈthenic** *a.*; **thromˈbectomy** *Surg.* [-ECTOMY], surgical removal of a thrombus from a blood vessel; ˌ**thromboangiˈitis obliterans** (-ændʒɪˈaɪtɪs) [L. *obliterans* OBLITERATING *ppl. a.*: see ANGIO-] = *Buerger's disease* s.v. BUERGER; ˈ**thrombo-arteˈritis**, arterial inflammation producing thrombosis; ˈ**thrombocyst** [mod.L. *thrombocystis* (Dunglison, 1857)], a cyst surrounding a clot of blood; **thrombo-cythæmia**, (U.S. **-hemia**) (-saɪˈhiːmɪə) [ad. G. *thrombozythämie* (E. Epstein 1929, in *Zeitschr. f. Stomatologie* XXVII. 377): see HÆMO-, HEMO-], thrombocytosis, esp. when it is a persistent or primary condition; ˌ**thrombocytoˈpenia** [ad. G. *thrombocytopenie* (H. Eppinger in L. Langstein et al. *Enzykl. der klin. Med.* (1920) v. 295): see -PENIA], a reduced number of platelets in the blood; hence ˌ**thrombocyto'penic** *a.*; **thrombocy'tosis** [-OSIS], a significantly increased number of platelets in the blood; **thrombo'embolism**, embolism of a blood vessel caused by the dislodgement of a thrombus from its site of origin; hence **thromboem'bolic** *a.*; **thrombo'embolus**, an embolus consisting of a thrombus which has become dislodged from its site; ˌ**thromboendarter(i)'ectomy** *Surg.* [f. END(O- + ARTER(Y *sb.* + -ECTOMY], an operation to remove a thrombus and part of the inner lining of an obstructed artery; '**thrombogen**, a hypothetical substance in the blood which converts fibrinogen into fibrin; the proenzyme of the fibrin-ferment; hence **thrombo'genic** *a.*, of or pertaining to thrombogen; producing coagulation; '**thrombokinase** (-kɪˌneɪs): see quot. s.v. THROMBASE; **thrombo'penia** [-PENIA] = *thrombocytopenia* above; hence **thrombo'penic** *a.*; **thrombophle'bitis**, phlebitis due to obstruction of the vein by a thrombus; **thrombo'plastic** *a. Med.*, causing or promoting the clotting of blood; **thrombo'plastin** *Med.* [-IN[1]], a natural thromboplastic substance; now *spec.* an enzyme converting prothrombin to thrombin during the early stages of blood coagulation; **thrombos'thenin** *Biochem.* [Gr. σθένος strength], a contractile protein or mixture of proteins in blood platelets; **throm'boxane** *Biochem.* [f. OX- + -ANE], any of several compounds formed from prostaglandin endoperoxides which, when released from blood platelets, induce platelet aggregation and constriction of arterial muscle.

1935 L. E. H. WHITBY *Disorders of Blood* xiv. 276 (*heading*) Hereditary hæmorrhagic *thrombasthenia. **1962** *Lancet* 22 Dec. 1316/2 This thromboasthenia is a familial hæmorrhagic disease in which the platelet-count is normal but the bleeding-time prolonged and clot retraction defective. **1974** PASSMORE & ROBSON *Compan. Med. Stud.* III. xxi. 45/1 Hereditary thrombasthenia or Glanzmann's disease is characterized by abnormal platelet aggregation and clot retraction. **1928** *Jrnl. Laboratory & Clin. Med.* XIII. 319 Chronic hereditary *thrombasthenic purpura.. still requires further study before it can be definitely said that the blood platelets are wholly responsible for the condition. **1979** *Nature* 6 Dec. 622/1 T-transferase activity was measured in lysates obtained from platelets isolated from a thrombasthenic and a Bernard-Soulier patient, respectively. **1910** *Lippincott's New Med. Dict.* 998/1 *Thrombectomy. **1945** *Urologic & Cutaneous Rev.* XL. 672/2 Thrombectomy is an extremely difficult and daring operation.. but.. in thrombosis of the renal vein prompt surgical intervention offers the only hope for a cure. **1972** D. A. K. BLACK *Renal Dis.* (ed. 3) vi. 165/1 Clinical improvement has been documented.. with thrombectomy. **1908** L. BUERGER in *Amer. Jrnl. Med. Sci.* CXXXVI. 567 (*heading*) *Thrombo-angiitis obliterans: a study of the vascular lesions leading to presenile spontaneous gangrene. *Ibid.* 580 Taking the true nature of the lesion into consideration, I would suggest that the names 'endarteritis obliterans' and 'arteriosclerotic gangrene' be discarded in this connection, and that we adopt the terms 'obliterating thrombo-angiitis' of the lower extremities when we wish to speak of the disease under discussion. **1914** [see BUERGER]. **1955** *Sci. News Let.* 11 May 377/2 The relation of cigarette smoking to thromboangiitis obliterans.. is well established. **1974** PASSMORE & ROBSON *Compan. Med. Stud.* III. xvii. 18/2 In thromboangiitis obliterans the upper limbs are more frequently affected. **1890** BILLINGS *Nat. Med. Dict.*, *Thromboarteritis. **1899** *Allbutt's Syst. Med.* VI. 205 An acute infective disease without anatomical lesions other than the thrombo-phlebitis, or thrombo-arteritis. **1860** MAYNE *Expos. Lex.* 1274/2 A cyst or membrane containing a clot of blood: a *thrombocyst. **1966, 1972** *Thrombocythæmia [see *thrombocytosis* below]. **1977** *Lancet* 9 Apr. 775/1 Thrombocythæmia predisposes patients to thrombosis. **1923** *Arch. Internal Med.* XXXII. 939 This constant diminution of the platelets without any known cause.. has given rise to the modern name of essential thrombopenia.. or better still, *thrombocytopenia. **1977** Thrombocytopenia [see *thrombocytosis* below]. **1925** *Jrnl. Amer. Med. Assoc.* 20 June 1888 (*caption*) Blood platelet variations following splenectomy in the *thrombocytopenic group of Banti's disease. **1978** *Detroit Free Press* 14 Apr. 4B/1 Andra had a rare blood disease called thrombocytopenic purpura, in which a deficiency of platelets causes bleeding. **1936** *Jrnl. Amer. Med. Assoc.* 21 Mar. 1005/2 (*heading*) Leukemia with *thrombocytosis. **1966** WRIGHT & SYMMERS *Systemic Path.* I. iv. 187/2 In disease, the number of circulating platelets may be greatly raised (thrombocytosis, or thrombocythaemia). **1972** W. J. WILLIAMS et al. *Hematology* lxxxiii. 704/1 Whereas the symptomatic rise in the platelet count termed thrombocytosis may be substantial, it is temporary and self-limited. In thrombocythemia the platelet counts are higher.. and persistently elevated: the condition is self-perpetuating and must be regarded as neoplastic. **1977** *Lancet* 9 Apr. 774/1 Thrombocytopenia caused by alcohol is reversible after alcohol withdrawal, and is followed by rebound thrombocytosis. **1940** *Acta Chir. Scand.* Suppl. LXI. 37 The first signs of the *thrombo-embolic disease itself.. can be venographically determined. **1981** *Brit. Med. Jrnl.* 7 Feb. 466/2 The best approach to the prophylaxis of thromboembolic disease is through low-dose heparin. **1907** *Jrnl. Amer. Med. Assoc.* 27 July 360/1 (*heading*) Postoperative *thrombo-embolism. **1941** *Archives Surg.* XLIII. 462 In heparin there is available an almost infallible prophylactic against thromboembolism. **1970** *Daily Tel.* 17 July 2/8 Investigations showed that the increased risk of thrombo-embolism declined rapidly after the patient stopped taking the pill. **1955** *Sci. News Let.* 17 Sept. 183/3 The primary reaction is the formation of plugs in arteries and veins. The plugs, or *thrombo-emboli as they are known technically, are made up of blood platelets stuck together. **1977** *Lancet* 29 Jan. 251/2 Fulton and Duckett report a significant correlation between high plasma-fibrogen levels.. and thromboemboli. **1948** *Index Medicus* XLIV. 1204/2 Aneurysmal development after dos Santos *thromboendarteriectomy. **1974** J. D. MAYNARD in R. M. Kirk et al. *Surgery* xi. 235/1 Thrombo-endarterectomy is successful in over 90 per cent of patients with disease above the inguinal ligaments. **1899** *Syd. Soc. Lex.*, **Thrombogen*, producing or giving rise to clots. *Ibid.*, **Thrombogenic enzyme*, an unorganised ferment having the power to cause clotting. **1908** Thrombogen, *Thrombokinase [see THROMBASE]. **1915** *Index Medicus* XIII. (Subject Index) 166/1 *Thrombopenia. **1922** *Nature* 20 May 666/1 The absence of the fat-soluble vitamin from the diet leads, in the rat,.. to a progressive diminution in the number of blood-platelets known as thrombopenia. **1981** *Cancer* XLVIII. 198/2 All staging systems isolate a high-risk group of patients defined by anemia and/or thrombopenia. **1934** *Lancet* 21 Apr. 845/1 This *thrombopenic hæmorrhagic diathesis occurs regularly when the bone-marrow with its megacaryocytes has been extensively damaged by proliferating lymphadenoid.. or neoplastic tissue. **1981** *Cancer* XLVIII. 202/1 The evidence was strong enough to justify putting anemic and thrombopenic patients aside. **1896** *Allbutt's Syst. Med.* I. 654 *Thrombo-phlebitis and localised abscesses are by no means uncommon. **1911** W. H. HOWELL in *Amer. Jrnl. Physiol.* XXIX. 189 They [*sc.* tissue extracts] furnish a substance, which may be designated as a *thromboplastic substance or thromboplastin. **1981** *Obstetrics & Gynecol.* LVII. 490/2 Acceleration of the rate of clotting of whole blood is due to the thromboplastic activity of amniotic fluid. **1911** *Thromboplastin [see *thromboplastic* adj. above]. **1979** R. HAWKEY *Side-Effect* xi. 86 We used a thromboplastin preparation... They're hardly likely to test for.. thromboplastins. **1961** BETTEX-GALLAND & LÜSCHER in *Biochim. & Biophysica Acta* XLIX. 537 We have named this protein '*thrombosthenin', firstly because of its role in thrombocyte function, and secondly because of its properties, which in many respects let it appear distinct from muscle actomyosin. **1974** *Encycl. Brit. Macropædia* II. 1107/2 There are about 250,000 platelets per cubic millimetre of blood... They.. contain.. a contractile protein (thrombosthenin) that allows platelets to extend and retract long footlike projections called pseudopodia. **1975** *Nature* 3 July 14/1 This new intermediate does not have a classical prostaglandin structure and has been named '*Thromboxane'.., because it is a very potent platelet aggregating agent. Since it is the first member of a new series of compounds and contains two double bonds it was further designated 'Thromboxane A_2': its metabolite.. becomes 'Thromboxane B_2.' **1979** *Ibid.* 6 Sept. 14/3 Because of their fish diet, Greenland Eskimos have high plasma levels of eicosapentenoic acid which is the precursor of the three series of endoperoxides—prostaglandins, thromboxane and prostacyclin.

thrombocyte ('θrɒmbəʊsaɪt). *Biol.* [ad. G. *thrombocyt* (M. C. Dekhuyzen 1892, in *Verh. d. Anat. Ges.* 94): see THROMBO- and -CYTE.]

a. A spindle-cell of the lower vertebrates, responsible for the clotting of blood.

1893 *Jrnl. R. Microsc. Soc.* 25 In analogy with Löwit's nomenclature he uses the ending 'blast' for young forms, and 'cyt' for those which are adult. He distinguishes.. thromboblasts and thrombocytes, as the 'spindles' of Eberth and Schimmelbusch may be called. **1910** *Jrnl. Morphol.* XXI. 273 The spindle cells or thrombocytes of certain amphibian blood have a cytoplasm which stains in the same way as does that of the megakaryocyte. **1979** *Nature* 1 Mar. 13/1 The rapid adhesion of platelets (or of their non-mammalian counterpart, the thrombocytes) to the vascular wall when the endothelial lining is breached has been a subject of interest since Wharton-Jones showed in 1851 that thrombocytes accumulated at points of local damage in blood vessels of the frog's foot.

b. A blood platelet.

1907 E. A. SCHÄFER *Essent. Histol.* (ed. 7) 35 These often seem to radiate from minute round colourless discoid particles less than one-third the diameter of a red corpuscle. .. These are the.. blood-platelets, or thrombocytes. **1938** W. MAGNER *Textbk. Hematol.* i. 1 The cellular elements of the blood are of three types: red corpuscles or erythrocytes, white corpuscles or leukocytes, and platelets or thrombocytes. **1977** J. RAYNOR *Anat. & Physiol.* x. 245 There are about 150,000-300,000 thrombocytes per cubic millimeter of blood.

thromboid ('θrɒmbɔɪd), *a. Path.* [f. Gr. θρόμβος clot of blood + -OID; cf. Gr. θρομβοειδής full of clots.] Resembling a thrombus.

1860 in MAYNE *Expos. Lex.* **1899** in *Syd. Soc. Lex.*

thrombolite ('θrɒmbəʊlaɪt). *Min.* Also **trombolite.** [ad. Ger. *thrombolith* (Breithaupt, 1838), f. Gr. θρόμβ-ος in sense 'curd', in allusion to its appearance + -LITE.] A mineral, found in amorphous masses, containing the oxides of copper and antimony; perh. a mixture.

1844-68 DANA *Min.* (ed. 5) 562 Thrombolite... Amorphous... Color emerald-, leek-, or dark green... Found with malachite in a fine-grained limestone at Retzbanya, Hungary. **1850** ANSTED *Elem. Geol., Min.* etc. §506 Trombolite and Pelocronite are varieties [of Phosphori-calcite].

thrombolytic (θrɒmbəʊ'lɪtɪk), *a.* and *sb. Med.* [f. THROMBO- + LYTIC *a.*] **A.** *adj.* Pertaining to or causing the dissolving and breaking down of a thrombus. **B.** *sb.* A thrombolytic agent.

1962 A. P. FLETCHER et al. in *Amer. Jrnl. Med.* XXXIII. 738/1 The adjective 'thrombolytic' will be used to designate biochemical moieties capable of inducing thrombolysis. **1965** *Zeitschr. f. d. Ges. Innere Med.* XX. 720/2 The thrombolytics really have enriched the palette of antithrombotics. **1971** *Times* 6 Aug. 4/1 Deaths among patients admitted to hospital with coronary thrombosis have been cut by a third in a trial of a compound, streptokinase. .. The thrombolytic treatment was assessed in 700 patients in eight hospital centres. **1974** R. M. KIRK in R. M. Kirk et al. *Surgery* ii. 14/1 The thrombus may be removed surgically; at present this is less expensive than giving thrombolytics.

thrombose (θrɒm'bəʊz), *v. Path.* [Back-formation from THROMBOSIS.] **a.** *trans.* To cause thrombosis in (a blood vessel). Cf. THROMBOSED *a.*

1910 *Practitioner* June 779 Acute endometritis... When sufficiently severe.. to thrombose the endometrial capillaries.

b. *intr.* To become occupied by a thrombus.

1938 *Arch. Path.* XXV. 486 When the hemorrhage occurs, into the deeper intimal layers, the capillaries adjacent to the point of rupture may thrombose. **1977** *Proc. R. Soc. Med.* LXX. 401/1 Small blood vessels thrombose but larger vessels appear to be undamaged.

Hence **throm'bosing** *ppl. a.*, undergoing or causing thrombosis.

1923 *Surg., Gynecol. & Obstetr.* XXXVI. 313/1 The thrombosing part can sometimes be palpated. **1965** *Revue Roumaine d'Inframicrobiol.* II. 71 Caudal thrombosing vasculopathies can be considered as manifestations of a latent pararickettsial infection.

thrombosed ('θrɒmbəʊzd), *a.* [f. implied vb. **thrombose* (f. THROMBOSIS) + -ED[1].] Affected with thrombosis.

1873 T. H. GREEN *Introd. Pathol.* (ed. 2) 327 These vessels communicate with the cavity of the thrombosed vessel. **1906** *Lancet* 27 Oct. 1142/1 The sinus was not thrombosed.

thrombosis (θrɒm'bəʊsɪs). [mod.L., a. Gr. θρόμβωσις a curdling, f. θρομβοῦσθαι to become curdled or clotted, f. θρόμβος THROMBUS: see -OSIS.] †A coagulation or curdling (*obs. rare*); *spec. Path.* a local coagulation of the blood in any part of the vascular system during life, the formation of a thrombus. Also *fig.* with reference to traffic congestion.

1706 PHILLIPS (ed. Kersey), *Thrombosis*, a congealing, or clotting together of any thing. **1866** A. FLINT *Princ. Med.* (1880) 28 The causes of thrombosis are, first, changes in the walls of the vessels, and, second, retardation of the circulation. **1891** *Lancet* 2 May 1003/2 In consequence of venous thrombosis in the right lower extremity. **1904** *Times* 20 Aug. 5/3 Lady H—— died.. from an attack of pulmonary thrombosis. **1959** *Ibid.* 27 Nov. 8/4 It was clear that the heart of London had traffic thrombosis, said Mr. Ernest Marples.. at a Press conference yesterday. **1975** *Times* 9 June 12/4 In the big cities expansion of car ownership has brought inevitable thrombosis.

thrombotic (θrɒm'bɒtɪk), *a.* [ad. Gr. type *θρομβωτικ-ός: see prec. and -OTIC.] Of, pertaining to, of the nature of, or caused by thrombosis.

1866 A. FLINT *Princ. Med.* (1880) 330 Portions of the granular or of the thrombotic deposits may be carried into the circulation as emboli. **1899** *Allbutt's Syst. Med.* VII. 224 The lesions were probably thrombotic.

‖**thrombus** ('θrɒmbəs). *Path.* [mod.L., a. Gr. θρόμβος lump, piece, clot of blood, curd of milk.] †**a.** A small tumour occasioned by the escape of blood from a vein into the adjacent cellular tissue, and its coagulation there. *Obs.* **b.** A clot which forms on the wall of a blood vessel or a chamber of the heart, often impeding or obstructing the flow.

milk thrombus, a tumour caused by accumulation of milk in the ducts during lactation (*Funk's Standard Dict.*, 1895).

1693 tr. *Blancard's Phys. Dict.* (ed. 2), *Thrombus*, the Coagulation of Blood or Milk into Clots or Clusters. **1706** PHILLIPS (ed. Kersey), *Thrombus*... Among Surgeons a small Swelling that arises after the Operation of Bloud-letting, when the Orifice is made too small. **1866** A. FLINT *Princ. Med.* (1880) 28 A coagulum formed during life in the heart or in the vessels is called a *thrombus*. **1873** RALFE *Phys. Chem.* 16 A thrombus blocks up a cerebral artery, and acute softening of the cerebral substance supplied by that artery is the result. **1901** OSLER *Princ. & Pract. Med.* i. 12 Inflammation of the arteries with thrombus formation has been frequently described in typhoid fever. **1961** R. D. BAKER *Essent. Path.* v. 82 There is danger of a portion of the thrombus breaking loose and passing as an embolus to the pulmonary artery and lungs. **1970** PASSMORE & ROBSON *Compan. Med. Stud.* II. xxvi. 3/1 In large vessels, the thrombus usually remains plastered as a plaque against the wall of the vessel, whereas in small arteries continuation of the process may lead to an occlusive thrombus which blocks completely the direct blood flow.

throme, thromm(e, obs. ff. THRUM *sb.*[2]

thron, þron, obs. contr. form of THEREON.

thronal ('θrəʊnəl), *a. rare.* [f. L. *thron-us* THRONE + -AL[1].] Of or pertaining to a throne; befitting or of the nature of a throne.

a **1711** KEN *Hymnotheo* Poet. Wks. 1721 III. 205 His Standard he erects of Thronal Light.

throne (θrəʊn), *sb.* Forms: α. 3-6 **trone**, (4 **tron, tronne**, 4-5 **troone**, 4-6 *Sc.* **trown, trowne**, 5 **troyne**, 5-6 *Sc.* **troune**, 6 *Sc.* **trune**). β. 3- **throne**, (4 **thron**, 6-7 **throan**). [a. OF. *trone* (12th c. in

Godef. *Compl.*), mod.F. *trône*, ad. L. *thron-us*, a. Gr. θρόνος an elevated seat.]

1. a. The seat of a potentate or dignitary; *esp.* the seat occupied by a sovereign on state occasions; formerly often an elaborate elevated structure, richly ornamented; now a more or less ornate chair, with a footstool, usually placed upon a dais and standing under a canopy.

α. *a* **1240** *Sawles Warde* in *Cott. Hom.* 259 Sitten in a trone se swiðe briht wid ȝimmes i-stirret. *c* **1290** *S. Eng. Leg.* I. 93/35 Þe Aumperour sat In is trone. *a* **1300** *Cursor M.* 9944 (Cott.) Wit-in þis tour.. Es sett a tron [*Gött.* trone]. *c* **1425** *Cast Persev.* 459 in *Macro Plays* 91 *Mundus.* Now I sytte in my semly sale; I trotte & tremle in my trew trone... Kyng, knyth & kayser, to me makyn mone. **1535** STEWART *Cron. Scot.* (Rolls) I. 94 Brutell beistis set vp in ane trune [*rime* mune]. *a* **1548** HALL *Chron., Hen. VI* 177 The trone royall, vnder the clothe of estate.

β. **1390** GOWER *Conf.* III. 167 Wher he was in his real Throne. *c* **1400** *Maundev.* (1839) xx. 217 The Emperoures throne fulle high, where he sytteth at the mete. **1570** LEVINS *Manip.* 168/10 A Throne, *thronus, ni.* **1591** DRAYTON *Harmonie of Ch.* (Percy Soc.) 20 See where Salomon is set In royal throan. **1611** BIBLE *Matt.* xix. 28 Ye also shal sit vpon twelue thrones, iudging the twelue tribes of Israel. **1732** LEDIARD *Sethos* II. VII. 32 A throne of red wood, rais'd by five steps. **1855** PUSEY *Doctr. Real Presence* Note S. 390 Make thy left hand as if a throne for thy right.

b. The seat occupied by a pope or bishop on ceremonial occasions.

c **1380** WYCLIF *Wks.* (1880) 457 Þe pope sittiþ in his troone & makiþ lordis to kisse his feet. *a* **1533** LD. BERNERS *Huon* lxii. 216 They founde the pope set in his trone. **1726** AYLIFFE *Parergon* 121 In those Times, the Bishops preach'd on the Steps of the Altar.., having not as yet assum'd to themselves the Pride and State of a Throne. **1845** M. PATTISON *Ess.* (1889) I. 15 No chair of dignified ease was a bishop's throne in the sixth century. **1910** *Kelly's Directory of Oxford*, The Cathedral... The bishop's throne..was erected as a memorial to the late Bishop Wilberforce.

c. A seat provided by portrait-painters for their sitters: see quot. 1859.

1838 DICKENS *Nich. Nick.* x, A very faded chair raised upon a very dusty throne in Miss La Creevy's room. **1859** GULLICK & TIMBS *Paint.* 199 The Throne is the name portrait painters give the chair provided for their 'sitters', from the circumstance of its being placed on a raised dais covered usually with red cloth.

d. *fig.* A lavatory bowl and pedestal or other supporting structure. *colloq.*

1922 JOYCE *Ulysses* 39 In a Greek watercloset he breathed his last... With beaded mitre and with crozier, stalled upon his throne. **1941** F. THOMPSON *Over to Candleford* vi. 95 The commode turned out to be a kind of throne with carpeted steps and a lid which opened. **1960** J. J. ROWLANDS *Spindrift* 52 Our plumber..revealed that the water level in the 'throne' works just like the old glass water barometer. **1981** S. RUSHDIE *Midnight's Children* I. 62 A wooden 'thunderbox'—a 'throne'—lay on one side, empty enamel pot rolling on coir matting.

2. a. As the seat of a deity, esp. of God or Christ.

the throne of grace or simply ***the throne***, the mercy-seat, the place where God is conceived as seated to answer prayer.

α. *a* **1240** *Ureisun* in *Cott. Hom.* 191 Þu ert hore blostme biuoren godes trone. *c* **1375** *Sc. Leg. Saints* xviii. (*Egipciane*) 794 Þu sittis with god in til his trowne. **1382** WYCLIF *Heb.* iv. 16 Therfore go we with trist to the trone of his grace. **1393** LANGL. *P. Pl.* C. II. 134 Þe trone þat trinite ynne sitteþ. **1398** TREVISA *Barth. De P.R.* I. (1495) 8 Cryste Iesus.. syttyng in his trone of iugement. **1508** FISHER *7 Penit. Ps.* vi. Wks. (1876) 9 Euery man & woman shall stande before the trone of almyghty god. **1526** TINDALE *Rev.* xiv. 5 They are with outen spott before the trone off God. **1559** *Mirr. Mag.* (1563) V iij, The trone of mighty Jove.

β. *c* **1290** *Beket* 2304 in *S. Eng. Leg.* I. 172 Bi-fore ore louerd sone..ase he sat in is throne. **1552** *Bk. Com. Prayer, Morn. Pr., Exhort.*, The throne of the heauenlie grace. **1662** GURNALL *Chr. in Arm.* verse 17. xiii. III. 101 It sends them to the Throne of Grace. *c* **1765** M. BRUCE *Hymn*, '*Where high* [etc.]' vi, With boldness, therefore, at the throne, Let us make all our sorrows known. **1849** W. K. TWEEDIE *Life J. MacDonald* 157 It was made a frequent errand to the throne. **1875** BP. BICKERSTETH *Hymn*, '*Peace, perfect peace*', Jesus we know, and He is on the throne.

b. Phr. ***the Great White Throne***, used of the throne of God with allusion to Revelation xx. 11. Also *fig.*

1850 BROWNING *Christmas-Eve & Easter-Day* 116 Is Judgment past for me alone?—And where had place the Great White Throne? **1873** C. M. YONGE *Pillars of House* III. xxxii. 212 It was his first mountain... He raised his hat with an instinct of reverence..then murmured, 'One seems nearer the Great White Throne!' **1922** E. E. CUMMINGS *Enormous Room* vii. 155 The Mecca of respectability, the Great White Throne of purity.

†**3.** In the phrase ***in* (*on*) *throne***: enthroned; esp. as said of God or Christ. *Obs.*

a **1225** *Ancr. R.* 40 Þi swete blisfule sune..sette þe ine trone. *a* **1340** HAMPOLE *Psalter* ix. 4 Þou sittis on trone þt demys rightwisnes. **1340** —— *Pr. Consc.* 5080 Hyde us Fra þe face of hym þat syttes in throne. *c* **1380** *Sir Ferumb.* 162, Y swere by cryst in trone. *c* **1440** *R. Gloucester's Chron.* (Rolls) App. XX. 446 To king he was iblessed at londone ywis & iset in trone [*v.r.* ine throne]. *c* **1500** *New Notbr. Mayd* 464 in Hazl. *E.P.P.* III. 19 Ye syttynge in throne. *a* **1600** MONTGOMERIE *Misc. Poems* xli. 44 With shyning bright shieldis [As] Titan in trone.

4. *fig.* A seat or position of dominion or supremacy; *spec.* in *Astrol.*: see quot. 1819.

a **1548** HALL *Chron., Hen. VI* 149 b, This Marques thus gotten vp, into fortunes trone. **1654** WHITLOCK *Zootomia* 361 The Pulpit a Throne of higher Authority..rewarding with Promises of far more elevating Hopes than any earthly one can. **1819** JAS. WILSON *Compl. Dict. Astrol.* s.v., Any part of a sign where a planet has two or more testimonies, *i.e.* essential dignities, is called its throne, chariot, or any other foolish name that comes to hand. **1855** BREWSTER *Newton* II. xiv. 23 [Leibnitz] had nearly placed himself on the throne which Newton was destined to ascend. **18..** B. TAYLOR *In the Meadows* Poems (1866) 299 The sun on his midday throne. **1892** HENLEY *Song of Sword*, etc. 45 We tracked the winds of the world to the steps of their very thrones.

5. *transf.* The position, office, or dignity of a sovereign; sovereign power or authority, dominion.

a **1300** *Cursor M.* 22122 In þe temple o salamon þan sal þat traitur sett his tron. **1387** TREVISA *Higden* (Rolls) III. 245 Artarxerses..saued his fader trone and his broþer lyf. **1474** CAXTON *Chesse* II. i. (1883) 20 Mysericorde and trouthe conserue and kepe the kynge in his trone. **1534** MORE *Comf. agst. Trib.* II. Wks. 1199/2, I will..set my trone on the sides of ye north. **1593** SHAKS. *3 Hen. VI*, II. i. 193 The next degree, is Englands Royall Throne. **1696** PHILLIPS (ed. 5) s.v., *Throne* also Synecdochycally is taken for Supream Command, or Sovereign Authority of those that sit upon the Throne. **1750** GRAY *Elegy* 67 To wade through slaughter to a throne. **1848** W. H. KELLY tr. *L. Blanc's Hist. Ten Y.* II. 84 Worthy..of occupying the first place in the state beneath the throne. **1849** HELPS *Friends in C.* II. i. (1854) I. 267 Mighty thrones and distant empires.

b. ***throne and altar***, the civil and ecclesiastical systems as established; cf. *Church and State* (CHURCH *sb.* 18); hence used *attrib.*

1822 *Edin. Rev.* XXXVII. 420 The poetical representation of the..Throne-and-Altar class. **1885** *Pall Mall G.* 12 Jan. 4/2 Two currents ran through the auditory. Gentlemen of high life and throne and altar journalists were hostile. Radical journalists..were brimful of sympathy. **1908** *Expositor* June 558 The guardian of the nation's throne and altar.

6. *transf.* Put for the occupant of the throne; the sovereign.

1762 GOLDSM. *Cit. W.* xlii, 'Here', cried he, addressing himself to the throne. **1818** LD. ALTHORP in *Parl. Deb.* 21 A time when they had to offer their condolence to the throne.

7. (With capital T.) *pl.* In mediæval angelology, The third of the nine orders of angels (see ORDER *sb.* 5).

13.. *Ipotis* 93 (Vern. MS.) in Horstm. *Altengl. Leg.* (1881) 342 Þe pridde [order] is cleped Trones. **1398** TREVISA *Barth. De P.R.* II. x. (1495) b vj/2 The thyrde Ordre [of angels] is the ordre of Thrones, and hath the name of the yefte of dome, for god syttyth in theym, and yeuyth his domes. **1584** R. SCOT *Discov. Witchcr.* xv. ii. (1886) 315 Twentie legions of divels, partlie of the order of vertues, & partlie of the order of thrones. **1667** MILTON *P.L.* v. 601 Thrones, Dominations, Princedoms, Vertues, Powers. *a* **1711** KEN *Hymnotheo* Poet. Wks. 1721 III. 201 Thrones, who God's Judgments hear, and then proclaim. *c* **1850** NEALE *Hymns East. Ch.* (1866) 134 Thrones, Principalities, Virtues, and Powers.

8. *attrib.* and *Comb.*, as ***throne adversary***, ***-bearer***, ***-chair***, ***-city***, ***gallery***, ***-power***, ***-rail***, ***-room***, ***-seat***, †***-sitter***, ***-step***; ***throne-capable***, ***-like***, ***-shattering***, ***-worthy*** adjs.; **throne-born** *a.*, born of a sovereign parentage; of royal birth; **throne-name**, a name given on ascending the throne; **Throne Speech** *Canad.* = *Speech from the Throne* s.v. SPEECH *sb.*[1] 8 d.

1651 *Serm. Coron. Chas. II at Scoon* in *Phenix* I. 266 A word of Encouragement against *Throne Adversaries. Your Enemies are the Enemies of the Lord's Throne. **1855** BAILEY *Mystic* etc., *Spir. Leg.* 131 Some crowned and sword-girt conqueror *Throne-born. **1851** SIR F. PALGRAVE *Norm. & Eng.* I. 547 There was only one clearly acknowledged legitimate heir or *throne-capable representative of Charlemagne. **1814** SIR R. WILSON *Diary* (1861) II. 344 Murat was seated as a Sultan—princes and dukes all standing behind his *throne-chair. **1906** *Westm. Gaz.* 6 June 1/3 The procession then proceeds to the *throne gallery. **1894** *Ibid.* 30 June 5/1 Two *thronelike chairs of larger growth stood in the centre. *c* **1875** *Queen's Printers' Bible-Aids* 139 The people make Shallum..King, he taking the *throne-name of Jehoahaz. **1864** SIR T. SEATON *From Cadet to Colonel* xvii. 361 The interior room is the King's *throne-room. **1889** *John Bull* 2 Mar. 149/2 The Queen.. entered the Throne-room shortly after three o'clock. **1941** W. FORTESCUE *Trampled Lilies* xxv. 247 Could I bear to walk through the kitchen to reach the only bath and throne-room? **1816** J. WILSON *City of Plague* 51 Lurid stars Prophetic of *throne-shattering wars. **1552** HULOET, *Trone sytter, or he that sytteth in maiestie, *altitronus*. **1955** *Toronto Daily Star* 2 Feb. 6/2 An experimental program for the treatment of drug addicts was announced in this year's *Throne speech at the opening of the British Columbia legislature. **1972** *Farm & Country* 19 Dec. 1/3 Informants ..say they will be 'very surprised' if the Throne Speech does not contain new provisions to help farmers transfer their properties to following generations.

throne (θrəʊn), *v.* [f. prec. sb.]

1. *trans.* To place on or as on a throne; esp. as symbolic of accession to sovereignty: = ENTHRONE.

1377 LANGL. *P. Pl.* B. I. 131 Þer treuthe is in Trinitee and troneth [A. I. 122 coroneþ; *v.r.* tronen] hem alle. **1387–8** T. USK *Test. Love* I. ii. (Skeat) l. 94, I lefte it for no tene, till he was troned in my blisse for his seruice. *a* **1400** *Pistill of Susan* 90 Turtils troned on trene. **1508** KENNEDIE *Flyting w. Dunbar* 400, I sall..with tresone trone the on the treis. **1549** LATIMER *2nd Serm. bef. Edw. VI* (Arb.) 58 Thus was Salomon throned, by the aduise and wyl of hys father. **1599** B. JONSON *Cynthia's Rev.* Induct., Why, throne your selfe in state on the stage. **1601** SHAKS. *Twel. N.* II. iv. 22 The seate Where loue is thron'd. **1624** F. WHITE *Repl. Fisher* 56 He trode vpon the necke of kings, throning and dethroning, crowning and decrowning them. **1673** MILTON *True Relig.* 10 The Pope..Thrones and Unthrones Kings. **1715–20** POPE *Iliad* VIII. 551 Th' eternal thunderer sat thron'd in gold. **1792** *Anecd. W. Pitt* III. xliii. 154 Mercy can do no harm, it will seat the King where he ought to be, throned on the hearts of his people. **1815** SCOTT *Guy M.* xi, Mrs. MacCandlish, throned in a comfortable easy chair..was regaling herself..with a cup of genuine tea. **1864** R. S. HAWKER *Quest Sangraal* 16 Foremost sad Lancelot, throned upon his Steed. **1866** CONINGTON *Virg. Æneid* VII. 686 To throne him in the seat of power. **1884** TENNYSON *Becket* I. iii. 70 That the King Would throne me in the great Archbishoprick.

2. *intr.* To be enthroned; to sit on or as on a throne; to sit in state. Often ***to throne it.***

1607 SHAKS. *Cor.* v. iv. 26 He wants nothing of a God but Eternity, and a Heauen to Throne in. **1848** *Blackw. Mag.* LXIII. 768 He throned it always like a tragedy king. **1903** LD. R. GOWER *Rec. & Remin.* 358 After seeing my Shakespeare [group statue] throning it in the centre of the Palais d' Industrie [Paris]. **1904** R. J. FARRER *Garden of Asia* 139 The abbot of imperial blood no longer thrones among the pines of Uyeno. **1905** *Westm. Gaz.* 20 Mar. 2/2 The sofa on which she had throned.

Hence '**throning** *vbl. sb.*, enthronement.

c **1400** MAUNDEV. (1839) xvi. 175 The dedicacioun of the chirche, & the thronynge [*Roxb.* tronyng] of the ydole.

throned (θrəʊnd, *poet.* 'θrəʊnɪd), *ppl. a.*

1. [f. THRONE *v.* + -ED[1].] Seated on or as on a throne; enthroned. Also in comb., as ***heaven-throned***.

c **1440** *York Myst.* xxvi. 86 Oure tempill is þe toure Of his troned sire. **1596** SHAKS. *Merch. V.* IV. i. 189 [Mercy] becomes The throned Monarch better then his Crowne. **1606** —— *Ant. & Cl.* I. iii. 28 Though you in swearing shake the Throaned Gods. **1621** G. SANDYS *Ovid's Met.* XI. (1632) 374 Ioue shunnes the bed Of Sea-thron'd Thetis. **1760–72** H. BROOKE *Fool of Qual.* (1809) IV. 14 Adam..had been constituted a throned lord and controller. **1839** BAILEY *Festus* xi. (1852) 136 Hear Thou, Heaven-throned! **1906** *Daily Chron.* 25 Sept. 3/4 In the song of the minor poet we often recognise the faint echo of a throned master.

2. [? f. THRONE *sb.*] (*a*) Having a throne; (*b*) Made like a throne.

1801 S. TURNER *Anglo-Sax.* III. iii. II. 59 A work which pretends to give to Denmark a throned existence [before Christ]. **1852** THACKERAY *Esmond* II. vi, The old Dean on his throned stall.

thronedom ('θrəʊndəm). *rare.* [f. THRONE *sb.* + -DOM.] The dominion of a throne; the position implied by a throne.

1820 J. H. WIFFEN *Aonian Hours* (ed. 2) 48 Of this frame Empires and thronedoms have been, and are made. **1859** SALA *Tw. round Clock* (1861) 165 The late Grand Duke of Tuscany..has been signally kicked off thronedom.

throneless ('θrəʊnlɪs), *a.* [f. as prec. + -LESS.] Without a throne; deposed from a throne.

1814 BYRON *Ode to Nap.* xiii, Thou throneless Homicide. **1846** W. E. AYTOUN *Lays Sc. Cavaliers* (1849) 213 Fitting for the throneless exile. **1897** TROTTER *Life J. Nicholson* x. (1908) 149 A throneless pensioner of the Indian Government.

thronelet ('θrəʊnlɪt). [f. as prec. + -LET.] A little or miniature throne.

1648 HERRICK *Hesper., Transfiguration*, When thou art set In thy refulgent thronelet.

†'**thronely**, *a. Obs. rare.* [f. as prec. + -LY[1].] Pertaining to the throne; applied to certain ranks of angels: see quots., and cf. THRONE *sb.* 7.

1486 *Bk. St. Albans, Her.* a iv, Ther be ix orderys of angelis, v. Jerarchie & iiij. Tronly. *Ibid.* a iv b, The iiij. Tronli be theys Principatus Trony Cherubyn and Seraphyn. **1586** FERNE *Blaz. Gentrie* 143 The cullors in this Coate, namely, white blew & guoles..are referred to the orders of Angels which be Thronely.

†'**throneship**. *Obs. rare*$^{-1}$. [-SHIP.] Occupancy or tenure of a throne; sovereignty; reign.

1599 NASHE *Lenten Stuffe* 10 That manner of prouostship or gouernment remained in full force and vertue all their fowre throneships, alias a hundred yeare.

†'**throness**, '**thraness**. *Obs. rare.* [f. THRO, THRA *a.* + -NESS.] The quality of being 'thro'; untowardness; obstinacy, reluctance.

13.. *Cursor M.* 26964 (Fairf.) Ne for na þranes [*altered in MS. to* mekenes, *C.* mekenes] þat mai be þe-seluin say bot soþ of þe. *Ibid.* 27608 (Cott.) O pride bicums thrones [*pr.* throues; *F.* þranes, *pr.* þraues; *Cott., G.* trauers] o thrett, Hething, threp, and athes grett.

throneward ('θrəʊnwəd), *adv.* [f. as prec. + -WARD.] Towards the throne.

1844 MRS. BROWNING *Dead Pan* xxvii, When His priestly blood dropped downward, And His kingly eyes looked throneward. **1886** LILLIAN B. FEARING *Sleeping World*, etc., My soul would gaze Throneward for God's dear blame or praise.

throng (θrɒŋ), *sb.* Also *Sc.* and *north. dial.* **thrang.** [ME. *þrang*, *þrong*, prob. shortened from OE. *ȝeþrang* throng, crowd, tumult, deriv. from verbal ablaut series *þring-*, *þrang-*, *þrung-*: see THRING *v.*: cf. MDu. *dranc(g-)*, Du. *drang*, MHG. *dranc* (earlier *gedranc*), Ger. *drang* throng, pressure, crowd; ON. *þrǫng* fem., throng, crowd. *Throng* sb., vb., and adj. appear about the 13–14th c., the adj. being the latest.]

I. 1. a. Oppression; distress, straits; trouble, woe, affliction; danger. Now *dial. rare.*

13.. *Cursor M.* 2585 Þai þat suld hald þam in þat thrang [*Trin.* þrong]. *Ibid.* 2622 'Fra mi lauedi', sco said, 'i gang,

For sco me halds fast in thrang' [*v.r.* ga..wa]. *Ibid.* 21867 Mikel on erth sal be þe thrang, þat sal be o men o-mang. **1375** BARBOUR *Bruce* VII. 251 His fayis hym haldis now in thrang. *c* **1470** HENRY *Wallace* v. 931 Thaim to reskew that was in fellone thrang. *c* **1470** HARDING *Chron.* XXI. v. (MS. Arch. Seld. B. 10. lf. 19 b), The maiden Castelle strong.. That on a Roche ful high stonte oute of throng. **1596** DALRYMPLE tr. *Leslie's Hist. Scot.* VII. (S.T.S.) II. 43 Now in sik thrang, that sche nathing culde find radie at hand, to halde the dur fast. **1855** *Woman's Devotion* I. 278 We'll hae o'er-much joy, to be thinking o' past thrangs.

†**b.** The pain of childbirth: usually *pl.*; = THROE *sb.* 1 b. *Obs.*

1545 RAYNOLD *Byrth Mankynde* Prol. D j, The laborynge woman hath bene greatly conforted, and alleuiatyd of her throngs and trauell. *Ibid.* 49 The parels, dangeours, and throngs, which chanse to women in theyr labor. *Ibid.* 85 Yf ..she feale greate thronge and payne.

II. 2. Pressing or crowding of people; an act of thronging or crowding; crowded condition.

1303 R. BRUNNE *Handl. Synne* 947 As þey stode, & made grete þrong. *c* **1440** *York Myst.* xxii. 2 Make rome by-lyve, and late me gang, Who makis here all þis þrang? **1556** *Aurelio & Isab.* (1608) P iv, Soddaineley all withe one thronge caste the poore Affranio to the grounde. **1600** J. PORY tr. *Leo's Africa* II. 88 The throng was so great at their entrance of the gates, that moe then fowerscore citizens were slaine therein. **1715** RAMSAY *Christ's Kirk Gr.* II. xv, He could get nae place.., For thrang that day. **1791** COWPER *Iliad* II. 63 Went the summons forth Into all quarters, and the throng began. **1870** FREEMAN *Norm. Conq.* (ed. 2) II. x. 502 Near to the great city, and yet removed from its immediate throng and turmoil.

3. *concr.* A crowded mass of persons actually (or in idea) assembled together; a crowd.

[**993** *Battle of Maldon* 299 He wæs on ȝeþrange hyra þreora bana.] *c* **1000** *Gloss.* in *Haupt's Zeitschr.* IX. 427/15 *Lixarum coetibus* (gl. *mercenariorum, qui aquam portant*), wæterberendra. *marg.* þran[gum]. *a* **1300** *Cursor M.* 13462 Iesus..bi-held þat folk..þat folud him til mikel thrang [*Trin.* þrong]. **13..** *E.E. Allit. P.* B. 754 ȝet for þretty in þrong I schal my þro steke. *c* **1470** HENRY *Wallace* IV. 247 Rudely fra him he reft it in that thrang. **1598** BARRET *Theor. Warres* IV. iv. 113 The people to passe foorth..not by thronges..but by litle and litle. **1665** MANLEY *Grotius' Low C. Warres* 199 The whole Throng of Ecclesiastical Persons were beyond the Inspection of the Magistrates. **1784** COWPER *Task* IV. 196 The pent-up breath of an unsavoury throng. **1832** W. IRVING *Alhambra* II. 153 To draw fashionable throngs to their saloons. **1840** DICKENS *Old C. Shop* xix, The streets were filled with throngs of people. **1912** 'SAKI' *Unbearable Bassington* x. 170 The Rutland Galleries were crowded..by a fashionable throng of art-patrons. **1955** S. WILSON *Man in Grey Flannel Suit* xxxiv. 256 He joined a throng of men pushing to get aboard the train. **1971** H. WOUK *Winds of War* iv. 53 Was Nazi Germany as strong as the ever-marching columns in the streets, and the throngs of uniforms in cafés, suggested? **1977** P. L. FERMOR *Time of Gifts* ii. 35 A throng of villagers had assembled round an enormous bonfire.

b. A great number of things crowded together, either actually or in idea; a multitude.

1549–62 STERNHOLD & H. *Ps.* lxxii. 16 The mighty mountaynes..Of corne shall beare such throng. **1602** MARSTON *Antonio's Rev.* II. iii, Throngs of thoughts crowde for their passage. *c* **1760** SMOLLETT *Ode to Sleep* 8 Attended by an airy throng Of gentle dreams. **1824** DIBDIN *Libr. Comp.* 205 A series, and almost throng, of Histories of England. **1980** D. ADAMS *Restaurant at End of Universe* xvi. 83 'The End of the Universe is very popular,' said Zaphod threading his way unsteadily through the throng of tables.

4. Pressure, or a pressing amount, *of* work or business. Now *dial.*

1642 CHAS. I *Message to both Ho.* 28 Apr. 4 We hope this Animadversion will be no breach of your Priviledges in this throng of Businesse, and Distemper of Affections. **1707** J. WODROW in *Life* (1828) 181 My throng of work that fell in on me stopped me. **1730** T. BOSTON *Fourfold St.* IV. iv, A great throng of business, but a great scarcity of faith and holiness. **1778** [W. MARSHALL] *Minutes Agric.* 6 Feb. an. 1776 *note*, The principal objection to a dog-day's-fallow is, that it falls amid the throng of hay time and harvest. **1896** CROCKETT *Grey Man* lii. 349 With all this throng of business on hand.

5. 'Intimacy' (Jam.), company; ***to keep throng***, to keep company, associate *with. Sc. dial.*

1768 ROSS *Helenore* 11 It sets them well into our thrang to spy. **1843** BETHUNE *Sc. Fireside Stor.* 78 He keepit thrang wi' Jenny M'Intosh his Landlady's daughter.

throng (θrɒŋ), *a.* (*adv.*) Now *Sc.* and *north. dial.* Also 4–5 **þ-**, **thrange**, 5–6, *Sc.* 6– **thrang.** [ME. *þrang*, *þrong*, from same root as prec. Cf. ON. *þrǫng-r*, narrow, close, crowded (Sw. *trång*, Da. *trang*), strait, narrow, close, tight.]

†**1.** In various early instances difficult to explain, all connected with THRING *v.* Among these may be distinguished the senses (*a*) Compressing; (*b*) Compressed, oppressed, distressed; (*c*) Pressing, earnest, eager. But in some cases the exact sense is uncertain; *thrange* may even be adverbial; cf. Ger. *gedrang(e* adv. and adj. *Obs.*

13.. *E.E. Allit. P.* A. 17 Þat dotz bot þrych my hert þrange, My breste in bale bot bolne & bele. *a* **1400–50** *Alexander* 4813 Neȝe throtild with þe thik aire & thrange in þare andes. *c* **1400** *Destr. Troy* 12235 And he þroly with þrong wil þreppit agayn. **14..** *Siege Jerus.* 2 A þrange þornen croune was þraste on his hed. [*a* **1535** *Frere & Boye* 254 in Hazl. *E.P.P.* III. 72 The frere amonge the thornes was thronge [? pa. pple. of THRING *v.*].]

2. Pressed or massed closely together as a crowd; crowded, thronged; †dense, close, thick (*obs.*).

c **1400** MAUNDEV. (Roxb.) xxvi. 124 When þai schall feight, þai hald þam so nere togyder, and so thrang þat, whare þer er xx[m] men, sum men wald suppose þer ware noȝt x[m]. *c* **1440** *Alphabet of Tales* 401 Nerehand all Rome was gadurd þedur, & þe peple was passand thrang. *c* **1500** *Lancelot* 3366 Thar was the batell dangerus and strong, Gret was the pres, bath perellus and throng. **1535** STEWART *Cron. Scot.* (Rolls) II. 379 Amang the Scottis, quhair tha war maist thrang, Or euir he wist wes closit thame amang. **1603** J. SAVILE *K. Jas.' Entertainm.* Introd. B ij b, The people were so throng. **1743** in Keble *Life Bp. Wilson* xxiv. (1863) 825 [The registry preserves the memorandum in the Curate's own hand of his having published this order in Rushen Church] in the presence of a throng congregation. **1770** *Lett. Jas. Murray, Loyalist* (1901) 134 As throng as three in a bed. **1896** PROUDLOCK *Borderland Muse* 269, I see the 'trouts' are 'rising' thrang.

3. Crowded with people, etc.; thronged; very fully attended or frequented.

1660 H. MORE *Myst. Godl.* I. ix. 28 What a[n]..unsutable representation is it of this throng Theatre in Heaven, made up of Saints and Angels? **1711** RAMSAY *On Maggy Johnstoun* ii, The barn and yard was aft sae thrang, We took the green. **1766** REID *Wks.* (1863) I. 46/2 We have had a thronger College this year than ever before. **1822** GALT *Provost* xxxiii, The street was as throng as on a market day. **1890** HALL CAINE *Bondman* I. x, [The hut] was all but as throng of people as it had been..on the day of 'Liza Killey's wedding. **1894** P. H. HUNTER *Jas. Inwick* i. (1900) 14 Oor Kirk keepit as thrang as afore.

4. Of times, seasons, places, etc.: Into which much is crowded; full of work; busy.

1568 *Satir. Poems Reform.* xlviii. 85 The merkit is thrang, and will not lest lang. **1615** BRATHWAIT *Strappado* (1878) 62 You Clients..that visit this throng Terme. **1715** *Wodrow Corr.* (1843) II. 75 The harvest is just at its throngest. **1764** *Museum Rust.* II. lxxvii. 265 The value of the time..in so throng a season as the summer, is very considerable. **1816** SCOTT *Old Mort.* iv, It will be hard for you to fill her place, especially on sic a thrang day as this. **1889** GRETTON *Memory's Harkb.* 111 It was wonderful to see..how way was made for him through the crowded streets at the afternoon throng hour. **1895** SNAITH *Mistr. D. Marvin* xlix, 'Tis a very throng time this week.

5. Of a person or persons: Closely engaged in work or business; pressed; fully employed, busy.

1623 SANDERSON *Serm., Job xxix. 14* §25 Great men..are as throng as ever in pulling down houses, and setting up hedges; in unpeopling towns and creating beggars. **1723** *Wodrow Corr.* (1843) III. 50, I have been so throng this day with my booksellers, that I was not in the Assembly. **1786** BURNS *Twa Dogs* 5 Twa dogs, that were na thrang at hame. **1804** TARRAS *Poems* 1 We see his sheep thrang nibblin on the height. **1863** MRS. GASKELL *Sylvia's L.* II. 8 When we're throng, I help Hester. **1896** BARRIE *Marg. Ogilvy* vi, 'I suppose you are terrible thrang', she says. 'Well, I am rather busy'.

6. Closely engaged together; intimately associated; 'thick'.

1790 D. MORISON *Poems* 136 (Jam.) Syne hame we scour'd fu' cheery and fu' thrang. **1865** G. MACDONALD *A. Forbes* 51 Him an' oor Willie's unco throng.

B. *adv.* Earnestly; busily.

c **1400** *Destr. Troy* 3094 And thus ho thought full thrange in hir thro hert, þat so semely a sight ho se neuer before. **1786** BURNS *Dream* ii, I see ye're complimented thrang By mony a lord an' lady. *a* **1810** TANNAHILL *Ambitious Mite* 10 Some brushing thrang their wings and noses.

throng (θrɒŋ), *v.* Also 4 (9 *dial.*) **thrang.** [ME. *þrange*, *þronge* wk. vb., in form a derivative from the stem of THRING *v.*, with which it agrees in sense. It may continue an unrecorded OE. **þrongian* = OHG. *drangôn*; or may be f. THRONG *sb.*: cf. *to crowd.* (A factitive from *thring* would have been in OE. **þreng(e)an*; cf. Ger. *drängen*, ON. *þrøngva* (Sw. *tränga*, Da. *trænge*, wk. vbs.).]

†**1.** *trans.* To press or compress violently; to squeeze, crush. *Obs.*

13.. *Cursor M.* 900 (Gött.) Þu sal waite womman to stang, And scho sal ȝeit þin hefde thrang. **1590** SPENSER *F.Q.* III. iv. 45 He [the Thames] raves With roring rage, and sore him selfe does throng. **1596** DANETT tr. *Comines* (1614) 223 *margin*, He was..thronged to death in the gate. **1601** HOLLAND *Pliny* (1634) I. 120 See into what great streights betweene both seas Asia is..as it were thronged. **1616** R. C. *Times' Whistle* v. 2141 This foolish prophesie, That, vnlesse throngd to death, thou ne're shalt die. **1825** BROCKETT *N.C. Words, Thrang*, to press, to thrust, to squeeze.

†**2.** *intr.* To push or force one's way, as through a crowd or against obstacles; to press. *Obs.*

? *a* **1400** *Morte Arth.* 3755 Thare they thronge in the thikke, and thristis to the erthe Of the thraeste mene thre hundrethe. *c* **1400** *Destr. Troy* 7040 Throly the þre men throng ht hym aboute. **1560** DAUS tr. *Sleidane's Comm.* 343 b, The people, which striue, who may first thronge in. **1582** STANYHURST *Æneis* I. (Arb.) 32 Hee throngs.. Through crowds of the pepil. **1593** SHAKS. *Lucr.* 1041 Her breath..thronging through her lips. **1603** KNOLLES *Hist. Turks* (1638) 90 The Enemy, thronging in as fast as he could. **1624** CAPT. SMITH *Virginia* III. ix. 80 Whereat they quickly thronged faster backe then before forward. *a* **1625** FLETCHER & MASSINGER *Laws of Candy* I. ii, Having taken breath, he throng'd before me, Renewed the fight.

3. a. *intr.* To assemble in a group or crowd; to collect in large numbers; to crowd; also, to go in a crowd.

15.. *Adam Bel* 79 in Hazl. *E.P.P.* II. 142 They rysed the towne..And came thronging to Wyllyames house. **1603** HOLLAND *Plutarch's Mor.* 410 The Greekes who thronged about his pavilion doores. **1647** COWLEY *Mistr., The Wish* v, Lest men..Should hither throng..And so make a City. **1710** PHILIPS *Pastorals* ii. 43 No more beneath thy Shade shall Shepherds throng. **1812** BYRON *Ch. Har.* II. lxvi, Childe Harold saw them..Thronging to war. **1832** W. IRVING *Alhambra* II. 277 The people thronged forth to see him with impatient joy. *a* **1839** PRAED *Poems* (1864) II. 164 We did meet in courtly hall, Where birth and beauty throng. **1969** M. PUZO *Godfather* II. xii. 163 The young beautiful girls thronged through the city like lemmings, lasting one year, some two. **1979** A. FRASER *King Charles II* I. ii. 25 This maddened mob was thronging round the palace of Whitehall.

fig. **1671** MILTON *Samson* 21 Restless thoughts, that like a deadly swarm Of Hornets..rush upon me thronging. **1803–6** WORDSW. *Intimations Immort.* iii, I hear the Echoes through the mountains throng. **1947** P. LARKIN *Girl in Winter* II. vi. 150 Besides—the impossibilities thronged upon her—she was sixteen, while Jane was twenty-five, middle-aged, and foreign, too. **1981** A. N. WILSON *Who was Oswald Fish?* xi. 121 A hundred half-memories of childhood thronged back: the smell of baking from the house next door —the Trenimans.

†**b.** *indirect pass.* (cf. 4). *Obs.*

1607 SHAKS. *Timon* IV. iii. 395 *Ape(mantus)*..Ile say th' hast Gold: Thou wilt be throng'd too shortly. *Tim.* Throng'd too? **1663** PEPYS *Diary* 13 June, To the Royall Theatre... Here we saw 'The Faithfull Sheepeardesse', a most simple thing, and yet much thronged after.

4. *trans.* To crowd round and press upon; to press upon as in a crowd, to jostle. Also *fig.*

1534 TINDALE *Mark* v. 24 Moche people folowed him, and thronged him. **1593** SHAKS. *Lucr.* 1417 Here one being throng'd bears back. **1692** BENTLEY *Boyle Lect.* 217 That particles so widely disseminated could ever throng and crowd one another into a close and compact texture. **1704** J. TRAPP *Abra-Mulé* I. ii. 299 Not so he look'd when throng'd with Multitudes Of the applauding Soldiers. **1850** TENNYSON *In Mem.* xxi. 15 When more and more the people throng The chairs and thrones of civil power.

5. To bring or drive into a crowd, or into one place; to collect closely, to crowd; to press or drive in a crowd (quot. 1615). Chiefly in *pa. pple.*

1578 BANISTER *Hist. Man* I. 7 Pericles..seemed..to throng and thunder out his wordes. *a* **1608** SIR F. VERE *Comm.* (1657) 6 The enemy coming..with ensigns displayed, very thick thronged together. **1615** HEYWOOD *Foure Prentises* I. Wks. 1874 II. 230 My Standerd..the sight whereof Will driue these stragglers in disordered rankes, And in a hurly burly throng them hence. **1652–62** HEYLIN *Cosmogr.* Introd. (1674) 8/2 Bochartus..hath thronged Joktan and his Sons into a little corner of Arabia Felix. **1677** SEDLEY *Ant. & Cl.* v. i, All she holds dear she has throng'd there but you, And now intreats that you will enter too. **1752** YOUNG *Brothers* II. i, Throngs the pride of ages in an hour. **1822** [see THRONGED 1].

6. a. To fill or occupy (a place, etc.) *with* a large number of things or persons, or quantity of something; to crowd, cram, stuff; to burden (quot. 1648).

1607 SHAKS. *Cor.* III. iii. 36 Throng [*Theobald's correction*; *folios* Through] our large temples with the shows of peace, And not our streets with war. **1634** MILTON *Comus* 713 Thronging the Seas with spawn innumerable. **1648** J. BEAUMONT *Psyche* III. xxv, If..I throng my Darling with this massy store, 'Twill to a Burden swell my Courtesy. **1704** *Elegy Author True born Eng.* xx, Nature to make amends for want of Sense, Has throng'd his Head with clear Impertinence. **1817** LADY MORGAN *France* (1818) I. 90 The rehearsals..occupied and thronged the streets of Paris for some days. **1842** TENNYSON *Locksley Hall* 36 Her whisper throng'd my pulses with the fullness of the Spring. **1874** PUSEY *Lent. Serm.* 268 To occupy and throng your thoughts with cares..of your own seeking.

b. Said of a multitude of persons or things: To occupy completely, fill, crowd (a place, etc.).

1819 SHELLEY *Prometh. Unb.* I. 2 All Spirits..who throng those bright and rolling worlds. **1853** C. BRONTE *Villette* xxxviii, Gay dresses, grand equipages, fine horses..throng the bright streets. **1860** TYNDALL *Glac.* II. i. 229 Insects which thronged the adjacent grass. **1873** 'OUIDA' *Pascarèl* I. viii, Great multitudes..thronged every square and street.

c. *pa. pple.* Occupied by a crowd or multitude of persons or things; crowded, crammed, filled (const. *with*, or *absol.*). See also THRONGED 2.

1594 DRAYTON *Idea* 649 With those the thronged Theaters that presse, I in the circuit for the Laurell strove. **1608** SHAKS. *Per.* II. i. 77 A man throng'd vp with cold, my Veines are chill. **1677** THORESBY *Diary* (1830) I. 4 The Glasshouse Lecture..was thronged. **1719** DE FOE *Crusoe* (1858) 338 We discovered the ship's boats..both thronged with people. **1772** BEDINGFIELD in *Lett. Lit. Men* (Camden) 405 The churches every where seemed well thronged. **1841** W. SPALDING *Italy & It. Isl.* I. iv. I. 149 The galleries of Italian palaces are still thronged with statues, as were the temples. **1894** HALL CAINE *Manxman* v. v, The streets were thronged.

d. *intr.* for *pass.* Now *dial.*

1757 EDWARDS *Orig. Sin* viii. (1837) 75 Multitudes that the Christian world throngs with. **1844** W. JAMIE *Muse* 112 (E.D.D.) The whisky tents began to throng.

throng(e, -en, obs. pa. t. and pple. of THRING *v.*

thronged (θrɒŋd, *poet.* 'θrɒŋɪd), *ppl. a.* [f. THRONG *v.* + -ED[1].]

1. Closely packed, as a multitude of people or things; crowded.

1652 BENLOWES *Theoph.* VII. iv, Those throng'd figures sum not Thee. **1713** ADDISON *Cato* II. i, The thick array Of his thronged legions. **1822** J. MACDONALD *Mem. J. Benson* 463 He addressed a thronged audience. **1860** PUSEY *Min. Proph.* 270 The mariners..ask Jonah thronged questions. **1908** MRS. E. WHARTON *Hermit & Wild Wom.* 41 The air shone with thronged candle-flames.

2. a. Of a place, etc.: Closely packed with people or things; crowded.

1594 [see THRONG *v.* 6 c]. **1613** W. BROWNE *Brit. Past.* II. v. 115 As vnder their [trees'] command the thronged Creeke Ran lessened vp. **1746–7** HERVEY *Medit.* (1818) 251 To slip away from the thronged city. **1831** SCOTT *Ct. Robt.* xxiii, A loud and varied murmur, resembling that of a thronged hive. **1889** GRETTON *Memory's Harkb.* 189 To me these thronged places are wearisome in the extreme.

b. Of time: Full of work or business; busily occupied; busy. Chiefly *dial.*

1791 ISABELLA WILSON in *Mem.* (1825) 36 We have had a thronged time with our harvest. **1832** *Yorkshire Dial.*, We had a very thronged day. **1943** *R.A.F. Jrnl.* Aug. 15 Members of the R.A.F. who in the midst of their thronged days find time to encourage and assist the Air Training Corps squadrons.

thronger ('θrɒŋə(r)). [f. THRONG *v.* + -ER^{1}.] One who throngs; see the verb.

1648 HEXHAM II, *Een dringer*, a Presser, a thronger, or a pusher. **1908** R. W. CHAMBERS *Firing Line* vii, The jewelled throngers of the horse-shows and motor-shows.

throngful ('θrɒŋfʊl), *a.* [f. THRONG *sb.* + -FUL.] Full of a throng or crowd; crowded.

1833 WHITTIER *Female Martyr* 44 Where The throngful street grew foul with death. **1866** —— *Snow-bound* 743 Dreaming in throngful city ways Of winter joys his boyhood knew.

thronging ('θrɒŋɪŋ), *vbl. sb.* [f. THRONG *v.* + -ING^{1}.] The action of the verb THRONG; pressing; crowding.

13.. *Cursor M.* 22683 (Cott.) Wit thranging sal þai samen threst. **1548** UDALL, etc. *Erasm. Par. Mark* v. 32 b, So was he payned with the throngyng of the people. **1581** MULCASTER *Positions* xxxix. (1887) 196 Why there is such thronging of all people that way. **1679** LUTTRELL *Brief Rel.* (1857) I. 7 Mr. Oates preached at Wood-street church .. and there was great thronging. **1724** P. WALKER *Peden* in *Biogr. Presbyt.* (1827) I. 153 Such a Thronging to the fearful Pit.

'thronging, *ppl. a.* [f. as prec. + -ING^{2}.] That throngs; crowding or crowded; assembling or assembled in large numbers; going in a crowd.

1582 STANYHURST *Æneis* II. (Arb.) 67 Theare weare the enymyes with thronging cluster asembled. **1600** HOLLAND *Livy* I. xiv. 11 All at once the enemies in thrunging manner sallied forth. **1697** POTTER *Antiq. Greece* I. viii. (1715) 41 Too weak to support the vast weight of thronging Multitudes. **1827** KEBLE *Chr. Y.*, *S. Matt.* v, Such brief rest As thronging cares afford. **1871** R. ELLIS *Catullus* lxiv. 33 Thronging hosts uncounted, a company joyous approaching.

Hence '**throngingly** *adv.*

1624 GEE *Hold Fast* 52 A glorious spectacle .. fit for vs to step out of our dores and throngingly to behold. **1731** BAILEY, *Throngingly*, crowdingly.

'throngly, *adv.* *Obs.* or *dial.* [f. THRONG *a.* + -LY^{2}.] Thickly, densely; busily.

1653 H. MORE *Conject. Cabbal.* ii. §7 The World of Life, which is everywhere nigh at hand, and does very throngly inequitate the moist and unctuous Aire. **1727** BAILEY vol. II, *Throngly* .. pressingly, crowdingly.

So '**throngness**, the state of being 'throng' or crowded; crowdedness.

1727 P. WALKER *Cameron* in *Biogr. Presbyt.* (1827) I. 276 When Prisons were more throng than ever, even in Dunnottar-Castle, where Eight-score and eight of us were driven into one Vault; and yet I never saw Throngness nor Irons marr any from writing.

† **thronize**, *v.* *Obs. rare.* Also 5 **tronyse**. [prob. aphetic for ENTHRONIZE: cf. also Gr. θρονίζεσθαι to be enthroned.] *trans.* To enthrone, to seat on a throne.

1494 FABYAN *Chron.* VII. 455 He was .. tronysed in the sayd moneth of May. **1559** *Act 2 Eliz.* in Bolton *Stat. Irel.* (1621) 283 Everie person and persons being hereafter conferred, invested, and consecrated, .. may from henceforth be thronized or installed. **1711** HICKES *Two Treat. Chr. Priesth.* (1847) II. 290 'To mount into his throne', or as we say to be thronized.

Hence † **throni'zation**, **tron-** [cf. ENTHRONIZATION], enthronement. *Obs. rare*$^{-1}$.

1526 R. WHYTFORD *Martiloge* 22 Feb. 21 At antioche the stallacion or tronizacyon of saynt Peter.

† **thro'nonical**, *a.* *nonce-wd.* [irreg. f. THRONE *sb.*, perh. after *canonical*.] Of or pertaining to the throne.

1591 HORSEY *Trav.* (Hakl. Soc.) 175 He [Ivan the Terrible] thonders owt his thrononicall threats to their ears.

† '**thrononize**, '**trononize**, *v.* *Obs. rare.* [irreg. f. as prec.: perh. after *canonize*; cf. also *intrononyzacion*, s.v. ENTHRONIZATION, quot. 1517.] *trans.* To enthrone.

c **1470** HARDING *Chron.* XVI. iii. (MS. Egerton 1992, lf. 14 b), Aftere his merites trononized [*so ed.* **1543**; *other MSS.* inthronized, intronozed, in thronyed] high in trone. **1509** HAWES *Joyf. Medit.* xxii, O God aboue, trononysed in heuen. **1533–4** *Act 25 Hen. VIII*, c. 20 §5 Every person .. chosen .. and consecrate to the dignitie or office of any Arche-bishop or Byshop .. shall .. be trononysed or installed as the case shall require.

throo, var. THRO, *Obs.*

throomb, obs. f. THRUM.

throp, thrope, obs. and dial. ff. THORP.

† **throplet.** *Obs. rare*$^{-1}$. [f. THROPPLE *sb.* + -ET^{1}.] The pharynx.

1720 W. GIBSON *Dict. Horses* i. (ed. 2) 10 The Jaws should be .. on the upper Part placed at a moderate Distance from each other, that the Head of the Pharynx or Throplet may easily fall between them.

thropple, thrapple ('θrɒp(ə)l, 'θrap(ə)l), *sb.* *Sc.* and *north. dial.* Forms: α. 4–6 **throppill**, 6 **-il, -el**, 6–8 **throple**, 7 **throp(p)ell**, 6– **thropple**. β. 8– *Sc. dial.* **thrapple**. [In use from 14th c. chiefly in the North. Origin obscure: its date is against its being an altered form of THROTTLE *sb.*

A conjecture that it is a descendant of OE. *þrotbolla*, THROAT-BOLL, does not fit phonology and local distribution.]

The throat; now *esp.* the windpipe or gullet. (More widely in use of a horse or other beast than of human beings.)

1375 BARBOUR *Bruce* VII. 584 [The king] hyt þe formast in þe hals, Till throppill and vassand [*v.r.* wesand] ȝeid in twa. **1533** BELLENDEN *Livy* I. x. (S.T.S.) I. 59 He straik this thrid brothir .. in þe throppil. **1562** TURNER *Herbal* II. 164 b, The violet .. swageth and softeneth the throple and the breste. **1562** —— *Baths* 8 b, The diseases of the longes and winde pipe or throppel. **1570** LEVINS *Manip.* 126/19 A Throppil, *ingulum*. **1607** MARKHAM *Caval.* III. (1617) 15 The throppell, or neather part of the necke [of a horse] which goes from the vnder chappes to the brest. **1690** *Lond. Gaz.* No. 2527/4 A Light grey Mare, .. one feather on each side her Thropple. **1755** JOHNSON, *Thrapple*, the windpipe of any animal. They still retain it in the Scottish dialect. *a* **1758** RAMSAY *Address of Thanks* xviii, Bring to the warld the luckless wean, And sneg its infant thrapple. **1815** SCOTT *Guy M.* i, Sorrow be in your thrapple then! **1825** BROCKETT *N.C. Words*, *Thropple*, the windpipe, the throat. 'A bull's thropple'. **1894** CROCKETT *Raiders* (ed. 3) 218 That dry yeukin' in my thrapple.

'**thropple**, '**thrapple**, *v.* *Sc.* and *north. dial.* [f. prec. sb.] *trans.* To throttle, strangle.

1570 LEVINS *Manip.* 170/16 To Thropple, *iugulare*. **1674** RAY *N.C. Words*, To *Thropple*, to Throttle or strangle. **1806** J. COCK *Simple Strains* (1810) II. 136 (E.D.D.) Some were maistly thrappl't Wi' grips that night. **1899** J. STRANG *Lass of Lennox* iii. 29 I could thrapple ye whaur ye staun'.

'**throppled**, '**thrappled**, *a.* [f. THROPPLE *sb.* + -ED^{2}.] Having a thropple (of a specified kind). Chiefly used of horses.

1607 MARKHAM *Caval.* III. (1617) 15 Cock-throppled [see COCK-THROPPLED]. **1614** —— *Cheap Husb.* (1623) 47 A full eye, open nostrill wide jawed, loose thropled, deepe neckt. **1725** *Bradley's Fam. Dict.* s.v. *Pursiness*, When the Horse is Cock-thropled, for that his Throple or Wind-pipe being so long, he is not able to draw it [breath] in and out with so much Ease and Pleasure as other Horses do that are loose thropled. **1834** Cock-thrappled [see COCK-THROPPLED].

throsche, throsh, obs. ff. THRASH, THRESH.

throst, -er, obs. forms of THROWST, -ER.

throstle ('θrɒs(ə)l). Forms: α. 1–3 **þrostle**, 4 **þrostel, -yl**, 4–5 **throstel(e**, 5 **-elle, -il, -yl(l**, 7 **throssel, throssle, (thrassel)**, 5– **throstle**. β. 4 **þrustel(e**, 4–8 **thrustle**, 5 **-ille, -yll(e**, 5–6 **thrustel(l**, 6 **-ele**, 7 **thrussel**. γ. 4 **þrestel, thristill**, (5 **thyrstylle**), 6 **threstyll, thrissell**, 8 **thrissel, thristle, thrystle**. [OE. *þrostle* or ? *þróstle*, wk. fem. For *þróstle*, cf. MLG. *drôsle* (Low Ger. dial. *dråssel*, *draussel*, *drausele*), app. pointing to an OTeut. **þramstala* (Kluge). For *þrostle*, cf. MHG. *drostel*, the root-form of which appears in ON. *þrǫstr* (Norw. *trost*, *trast*, Sw. *trast*, Da. *trost*):—OTeut. **þrastu*^{z}, commonly referred to Indo-Eur. **trozdu-s*, whence L. *turdus* (**trzdo-*), OPruss. *tresde*, and Lett. *strazds*, Lith. *strãzdas*, all meaning 'thrush'. Cf. also OSlav. *drozg*^{u} and Russ. *drozd*^{u}. (See Suolahti, *Deutsche Vogelnamen* 1909, 51–54.)

App. in origin distinct from THRUSH, though the derivative forms of the latter, *thruschel*, *thrusshill* in ME., *droschel*, *druschel* in Ger., come very near to *throstle*, *thrustle*, and MHG. *drostel*. The vocalization of ME. *thrustel*, *thristel*, *threstyl*, etc. seems also to have been influenced by that of *thrusche*, *thrysshe*, *threshe*, *thrishel*, etc.: see THRUSH^{1}.]

1. A thrush; *esp.* the song-thrush or mavis, *Turdus musicus*. Now only *literary* and *dial.*

In many ME. passages, esp. in alliterative verse, 'throstle' and 'thrush' are distinguished, and in several cases, e.g. quots. *c* 900, 1303, *c* 1440, and (?) 1601, *throstle* is applied to the blackbird. In quot. 1303, the original Fr. has in one MS. 'Le oysel est merle apelé, Neir est [*v.r.* Veu l'ay] en yuer & en esté'. Chaucer, also, in *Rom. Rose* 665 translates 'Melles [? merles] et mauvis', Thrustels, Terins, and Mauise.

c **725** *Corpus Gloss.* (O.E.T.) 2068 *Turdella*, ðrostle. *c* **900** WÆRFERTH tr. *Gregory's Dial.* 100 Sum swyþe sweart & lytel fuȝel, se is on folcisc þrostle ȝehaten. **956** *Charter of Eadwig* in Birch *Cart. Sax.* III. 141 Of þam lea on þrostlan wyl. *a* **1250** *Owl & Night.* 1659 Þaruore anan to hire cherde þrusche and þrostle and wudewale. **1303** R. BRUNNE *Handl. Synne* 7480 A fend of helle Yn a lykenes of a bryd. A 'þrostyl' ys þe name kyd. *c* **1350** *Will. Palerne* 820 Boþe þe þrusch & þe þrustele bi xxxti of boþe. **13..** *Minor Poems fr. Vernon MS.* xlvi. 181 Þe þrestel song ful schille. **1375** BARBOUR *Bruce* v. 4 Byrdis smale, As thristill and þe nychtingale. **1387** TREVISA *Higden* (Rolls) I. 237 Whan somer is hote þrostel syngeþ wiþ mery note. **1403** *Nottingham Rec.* II. 20, j. caige cum j. throstyll. *c* **1440** *Promp. Parv.* 493/1 Thrustylle, bryd (*P.* thrusshill or thrustyll), *merula*. *c* **1450** *Alphita* (Anecd. Oxon.) 188 *Turdus* auis est. g[allice] mauuys, an[glice] throstle. **1483** *Cath. Angl.* 386/2 A Throstelle, *mauiscus*. **1601** HOLLAND *Pliny* (1634) I. 293 Agrippina the Empresse .. had a Blackbird or a Throstle .. which could counterfeit mans speech. **1604** DRAYTON *Owle* 1259 The jocund Throstle, for his varying Note, Clad by the Eagle in a speckled Cote. **1661** WALTON *Angler* i. (ed. 3) 10 How doth the Black-bird and Thrassel .. bid welcome to the cheerful Spring! **1668** CHARLETON *Onomast.* 83 *Turdus*, .. the Thrush, Song-Thrush, Throssle, or Mavis. **1766** PENNANT *Zool.* (1768) I. 226 The throstle is the finest of our singing birds. **1798** WORDSW. *Tables Turned* iv, And hark! how blithe the throstle sings! **1841** BROWNING *Pippa Passes*, Oh, Lark, be day's apostle To mavis, merle and throstle.

2. A spinning-machine for cotton, wool, etc., a modification of that originally called a *water-frame*; differing from a *mule* in having a continuous action, the processes of drawing, twisting, and winding being carried on simultaneously.

As to the reason of the name see quot. 1877.

1825 J. NICHOLSON *Operat. Mechanic* 387 This construction of a water spinning-frame is called a throstle. **1835** URE *Philos. Manuf.* 110 Both systems of spinning, namely, the continuous or by throstles, and the discontinuous or by mules. **1876** J. WATTS *Brit. Manuf.* III. 138 The throstle, an extension and modification of the original spinning-frame, .. is employed in the spinning of yarn for warps. **1877** KNIGHT *Dict. Mech.* s.v., The throstle derived its name from the singing or humming which it occasioned.

3. *attrib.* and *Comb.* **a.** in sense 1, as ***throstle-throat***, ***-wing***; ***throstle-like*** adj.; **throstle-breast** (*Mining*): see quot.; **throstle-nest**, applied *attrib.* to a form of stag's horn (see quot. 1785). See also THROSTLE-COCK.

1747 HOOSON *Miner's Dict.*, **Throstlebrest*, a king of Ore or rather Knockings, mixt with a brown Tuft. **1902** F. CAMPBELL in *Temple Bar Mag.* CXXVI. 106 Mary's *throstle-like voice. **1785** BARKER in *Phil. Trans.* LXXV. 354 Horns .. which park-keepers in this part of the country call *throstle-nest horns, .. the upper part .. is branched out into a number of short antlers which form an hollow about large enough to contain a thrush's nest. **1898** *Westm. Gaz.* 5 Mar. 8/1 Antlers of the 'throstle nest' type. **17..** *Jolly Hind Squire* viii. in Child *Ballads* II. (1884) 429/2 The *thristle-throat is the next that sings Unto the nightingale. **1681** CHETHAM *Angler's Vade-m.* xxxiv. §14 (1689) 190 Feathers of .. Throstle-wing.

b. in sense 2, as ***throstle-frame*** (= 2), ***-piecer*** (PIECER 2), ***-spindle***, ***-spinner***, ***-spinning***, ***-yarn***.

1835 URE *Philos. Manuf.* 23 The water-twist, or throstle cotton mills. *Ibid.* 40 A throstle frame made in the best manner. *Ibid.* 71 The throstle twist, which has been so largely exported of late years. **1844** G. DODD *Textile Manuf.* i. 35 The roller principle, modified in a manner .. represented by the throstle machine, is that by which the strong and hard yarns are produced. **1862** *Illustr. Lond. News* XLI. 558/3 The Throstle Spinner .. has an assistant, called the Throstle Doffer, a little girl or boy. **1884** W. S. B. MCLAREN *Spinning* viii. (ed. 2) 150 There are four methods of spinning worsted, three of which come under the head of throstle frames... The fourth is the mule.

'**throstle-cock.** The male throstle or song-thrush; *dial.* the male missel-thrush.

c **1300** *Thrush & Night.* 121 in Hazl. *E.P.P.* I. 55 Threstelkok, thou hauest wrong. *c* **1386** CHAUCER *Sir Thopas* 58 (Harl.) The þrostilcok [*v.rr.* thrustel-, -il-] maad eek his lay. *c* **1430** LYDG. *Min. Poems* (Percy Soc.) 203 The thruschylcok nor the feldfare. **1530** PALSGR. 281/1 Thrustell cocke, *mauluis*. *a* **1600** MONTGOMERIE *Misc. Poems* xli. 5 The thissell-cok [*sic*] cryis On louers vha lyis. **1604** DRAYTON *Owle* 220 The warbling Throstle Cocke. **1825** JAMIESON, *Thrissel-cock*, the Missel-thrush or Shrite, Turdus viscivorus, Gesner; the *Throstle-cock* of the North of England. **1870** MORRIS *Earthly Par.* II. III. 169 A throstle-cock beside him broke Into the sweetest of his song.

[**throstling.** Probably in origin a misprint or other error for *throttling*. See quots.

1726 [? N. BAILEY] *Dict. Rust.* (ed. 3), *Throstling*, a Disease in Black Cattle, which proceeds from humours gathering under their throats, which so dangerously swell the Glands, that the Beast will be choak'd if not relieved. **1753** in CHAMBERS *Cycl. Suppl.* **1828–32** in WEBSTER; and in later Dictionaries; but not known to Veterinary Surgery.]

throte, throttene, obs. ff. THROAT, THIRTEEN.

throttle ('θrɒt(ə)l), *sb.* Forms: 6 **throtal, throttil**, 7 *dial.* **thrattle**, 8 **throtle**, 6– **throttle**. [Has the form of a dim. of *throte*, THROAT: cf. Ger. *drossel*, dim. of OHG. *drozza* throat. But the late appearance of the word (*c* 1550), its app. synonymy with the earlier THROPPLE (*c* 1375), and the earlier existence of THROTTLE *v.*, combine to make its actual history perplexing.

Sense 3, of 17th c., is evidently a noun of action from the vb., and might be treated as a distinct word.]

1. a. The throat. Now chiefly *dial.*

a **1547** SURREY *Æneid* IV. 361 Amid his throtal his voice likewise gan stick [L. *vox faucibus hæsit*, DOUGLAS the voce stak in his hals]. **1570** LEVINS *Manip.* 126/18 A Throttil, *guttus, uris, hoc*. A Throppil, *edem, iugulum*. *c* **1720** GIBSON *Farrier's Guide* I. iii. (1738) 28 This pipe is called the Trachea .. which Name it obtains from the Throtle to the Lungs. **1806–7** J. BERESFORD *Miseries Hum. Life* xx. 238 The neck of each bottle She thrusts down her throttle. **1823** F. COOPER *Pioneers* xxxiv, Under the grasp which the steward held on his throttle. **1871** B. TAYLOR *Faust* (1875) I. vi. 109 Now, here's a bottle, Wherefrom, sometimes, I wet my throttle.

b. The larynx. Now *rare.*

1615 CROOKE *Body of Man* 763 Because the actions of the Throttle or Larynx are perfourmed with voluntary motion, Nature hath giuen it muscles. **1646** SIR T. BROWNE *Pseud. Ep.* III. xxvii. 174 The windepipe..in this birde [bittern]..hath no Larinx or throttle to qualifie the sound. **1905** *Daily Chron.* 16 Mar. 3/4 He used to carry home to me..from his anatomy class..the throttles of all kinds of animals!—chickens, sheep and cows. You would imagine that these cartilaginous larynxes, red from the operating table, would have disgusted me.

c. *transf.* The throat or neck of a bottle.

a **1845** HOOD *Public Dinner* ii, Certain bottles Made long in the throttles.

2. (See quot.)

a **1864** GESNER *Coal, Petrol.*, etc. (1865) 79 The throttles..are small flues which distribute the heat around the still.

†**3.** The act of throttling or fact of being throttled; choking, suffocation. *Obs. rare*$^{-1}$.

1622 MABBE tr. *Aleman's Guzman d'Alf.* I. 24 They cramme their crawes like so many Capons in a Coope, till they can swallow no more, and so die of the throttle.

4. a. Short for *throttle-valve* (see 5); also a similar valve in a motor engine, and *transf.*, the throttle-control (of a motor vehicle, motor cycle, etc.).

1877 KNIGHT *Dict. Mech.*, *Throttle.* (*Steam.*) A name for the *Throttle-valve*. **1903** *Times* 30 Apr. 3/2 He had slowed down..the motor-cycle..and had almost closed the throttle. **1907** *Ibid.* 30 May 4/6 An experienced driver controlled the throttle and could pull up at once. **1908** *Ibid.* 6 Apr. 7/1 He was on watch in the engine-room and standing near the throttles. **1957** A. C. CLARKE *Deep Range* I. iv. 44 Franklin pressed down the throttle and felt the surge of power as the torpedo leaped forward. **1966** T. WISDOM *High-Performance Driving* viii. 74 You brake with the ball of your foot and blip the throttle with your heel or the side of your foot. **1983** *Listener* 28 July 13/1 Mine was no longer with a functioning throttle, gear change or front-brake on arrival.

b. Phrs.: ***to cut*** or ***chop the throttle***, to close the throttle in order to slow down or stop; ***(at) full, half, part***, etc., ***throttle***, (at) maximum, etc., power or speed (also *fig.*).

1936 *Motor Man.* (ed. 29) ii. 26 When the throttle is lying flat in the direction of the gas flow, the engine is running 'full bore', the term generally used for this being 'full throttle'. **1948** *N.Y. World-Telegram* 30 Dec. 11/8 The pilot, coming in, doesn't chop the throttle. The jet pilot 'turns down the wick'. **1958** [see CUT *v.* 21 f]. **1969** J. ARGENTI *Managem. Techniques* viii. 50 Once one has grasped the principle behind Cost-Benefit..one can use the technique at quarter throttle, so to speak. *Ibid.* 51 The results will be less impressive than when an expert uses it at full throttle. **1973** *Daily Tel.* 9 Jan. 1/5 The gunboat, believed to be the Odinn, avoided the ramming by sailing away at full throttle. **1977** J. F. FIXX *Compl. Bk. Running* iii. 42 Even in a race there's no need to run at full throttle if you don't want to.

5. *attrib.* and *Comb.*, as (in sense 1) ***throttle bone, -pipe***, (in sense 4) as ***throttle control***; **throttle damper**, an adjustable damper for a flue, etc. working like a throttle-valve; **throttle ice** (see quots.); **throttle jockey** *slang* (see quot. 1946), **throttle-lever**, a lever for opening or closing a throttle or throttle-valve; **throttleman**, one who controls the throttle(s) of an engine; **throttle-valve** (probably from the vb.), a valve for regulating the supply of steam, esp. to the cylinder of a steam-engine.

1681 GREW *Musæum* I. II. i. 11 The *Throttle Bone of a Male Aquiqui. **1910** *Westm. Gaz.* 10 Feb. 5/1 The *throttle control is well worth careful attention. **1884** KNIGHT *Dict. Mech.*, *Supp.* s.v., A *throttle damper, with arrow and quadrant, for regulating the passage of the flue and registering the same. **1942** *S.A.E. Jrnl.* Jan. 22/1 Ice which collects in the induction system was divided into three classes: impact ice, *throttle ice, and fuel evaporation ice... 'Throttle ice' is that which is formed at or near the throttle when the throttle is in a part-closed position due to the cooling effect of the increase in kinetic energy of the air in the restricted flow region. **1972** *Gloss. Aeronaut. & Astronaut. Terms* (*B.S.I.*) xv. 12 *Throttle ice*, ice formed in or near the engine throttle by the cooling due to isentropic expansion of the inspired air in the temperature range of 0°C to 5°C. **1946** *Amer. Speech* XXI. 310/2 **Throttle jockey*, a pilot. **1947** *Seafarers' Log* 25 Apr. 13/2 How could you crush a seamen's strike without captains and throttle-jockeys? **1864** WEBSTER, *Throttle-lever. **1882** SCUDDER *Noah Webster* vi. 184 He seems..to have his hand close to the throttle-lever without knowing it. **1904** *Everybody's Mag.* X. 663/1 When the officials came out and stood around the engine, there were *throttle-men on waiting locals. **1973** H. GRUPPE *Truxton Cipher* (1974) xiv. 140 The throttleman nervously wiped his sweating hands on a hank of oily cotton waste. **1982** *Fortune* 22 Mar. 172/2 The throttleman then has to reduce power because the boat's propellers are out of the water and meeting no resistance. **1632** BROME *Northern Lass* III. iii, I'le cut your *thrattle-pipe. **1824** R. STUART *Hist. Steam Engine* 129 A cock or valve, called the *throttle-valve or regulator, placed on the pipe conveying the steam from the boiler. **1877** KNIGHT *Dict. Mech.* 2564 Throttle-valve..in the Watt engine..a disk turning on an axis, and occupying in its transverse position the bore of the main steam-pipe..frequently an ordinary conical valve with a stem operated by a screw. **1899** F. T BULLEN *Log Sea-waif* 252 The grey-headed chief-engineer stood by the grunting machinery, his hand on the throttle-valve.

throttle ('θrɒt(ə)l), *v.* Forms: 5 **throtel**, 5–6 **throtil**, 5–7 **throtle**, 6–7 **thrattle, thratle**, 7 **thrattell**, 7 **throatle**, 6– **throttle**. [Late ME. *throtel, -il*, perh. f. THROAT + -LE *suffix*³.

App. not derived from THROTTLE *sb.*, which appears 150 years later. The Ger. *drosseln* (much later), now only in *erdrosseln*, is from *drossel* sb., so that *drosseln* and *to throttle* are not in their history parallel.]

1. a. *trans.* To stop the breath of by compressing the throat, to strangle; to kill in this way; *loosely*, to stop the breath of in any way, to choke, suffocate. The original meaning may have been 'to take or seize by the throat'. Also *refl.*

In some early quots. the meaning appears to be 'to kill by cutting or stabbing the throat' (rendering L. *jugulāre*).

a **1400–50** *Alexander* 4813 Þan come þai blesnand till a barme of a brent lawe, Neȝe throtild with þe thik aire & thrange in þare andes. *c* **1400** *Destr. Troy* 12752 Þan entrid this Engist,..And, with a thricche in the throte, throtlet the kyng. **1432–50** tr. *Higden* (Rolls) IV. 181 His felawes taken by Antonius,..caste in to prison, were throtelede [*strangulati*] in hit. *Ibid.* V. 321 Boecius..was throtelede [*eum jugulari fecit*] in the territory Mediolanense. **1564** HAWARD *Eutropius* IV. 44 This Aristonicus was thratled in prisone by the commandement of the Senate. **1582** N. T. (Rhem.) *Matt.* xviii. 28 He found one of his fellow-seruants..and..thratled him saying Repay that thou owest. **1602** ROWLANDS *Greene's Ghost* 15 One of them thratled him so sore by the wind-pipe, that he could make no noise, but sodainly sunke to the ground. **1609** HOLLAND *Amm. Marcell.* 349 Palladius..knit his necke in an halter, and so throtled himselfe, and died. **1693** DRYDEN *Persius' Sat.* III. 199 His Throat half throtled with corrupted Fleam. **1730** SWIFT *Misc.*, *True Eng. Dean* ix, Then throttle thy self with an Ell of strong Tape. **1816** SCOTT *Bl. Dwarf* vii, The dog..pulled down and throttled one of the hermit's she-goats. **1861** GEO. ELIOT *Silas M.* I. iii, 'Hold your tongue..', said Godfrey,..'else I'll throttle you'.

b. *transf.* To tie something tightly round the neck of; to compress by fastening something round.

1863 BRIERLEY *Waverlow* 228 The lower [portion of these figures] was..'throttled' in unyielding pantaloons. **1866** GEO. ELIOT *F. Holt* v, Let a man once throttle himself with a satin stock. **1869** BLACKMORE *Lorna D.* xxxv, I never had throttled a finger before, and it [the ring] looked very queer..upon my great..hand.

c. *intr.* or *absol.*

1837 CARLYLE *Fr. Rev.* III. III. iv, Party tugging and throttling with Party might have suppressed and smothered one another.

2. a. To check or break off (utterance) as if choking; †in qt. 1610, to utter in a choking voice.

1582 STANYHURST *Æneis* IV. (Arb.) 108 Her talck in the mydel, with this last parlye, she throtled. **1590** SHAKS. *Mids. N.* V. i. 97, I haue seene them shiuer and looke pale,..Throttle their practiz'd accent in their feares. **1610** TOFTE *Honours Acad.* I. 80 With a hollow voice, he thratled forth these few words. My dearest friends, let me intreat you [etc.].

b. *fig.* To stop forcibly the utterance of (a person or thing).

1641 MILTON *Animadv.* ii. Wks. 1851 III. 205 And thus you throttle your selfe with your owne Similies. **1647** TRAPP *Comm. Mark* iii. 2 It is a brave thing to throttle envy, to stop an evil mouth. **1838** EMERSON *Address, Cambr., Mass.* Wks. (Bohn) II. 196 The injury to faith throttles the preacher. **1901** *Scotsman* 7 Mar. 6/2 If it were given any quarter, it would throttle Parliament.

3. *intr.* To undergo suffocation; to choke.

1566 [implied in *throttling* ppl. a.]. *a* **1687** H. MORE in *Life R. Ward* (1710) 208 She dyed without any Fever,..drawing her Breath a while as one asleep, without throatling. **1828–32** WEBSTER, *Throttle*..2. To breathe hard, as when nearly suffocated. **1909** *Westm. Gaz.* 21 Aug. 3/1 The child throttled and died in my arms.

4. a. *trans.* To check or stop the flow of (a fluid in a tube, etc.) esp. by means of a valve, or by compression; to regulate the supply of steam or gas to (an engine) in this way. (Cf. *throttle-valve* in prec. sb. 5.) Also const. *down*.

1875 R. F. MARTIN tr. *Havrez' Winding Mach.* 75 It would be better to use the steam expansively, rather than to throttle it by means of the regulator. **1884** R. WILSON in *Pall Mall G.* 19 May 11/2 How..can the pressure be reduced from two inches or more to eight-tenths? By throttling the gas at the meter or at the burner. **1898** *Allbutt's Syst. Med.* V. 932 As the stenosis throttles the wave the increased velocity of the blood is counteracted by the rising pressure in the aorta. **1907** *Daily Chron.* 29 July 5/5 The [motor] bus started skidding. I throttled the engine and stuck to my seat as long as I could. **1914** HAMEL & TURNER *Flying* 134 Nearer and nearer we approach and now our pilot throttles down the engine.

b. *absol.* in phrs. ***to throttle back, down***, to close the throttle in order to slow down or stop.

1932 D. GARNETT *Rabbit in Air* III. 82 The altimeter was at 3000. I throttled back. *Ibid.* 91, I turned over the cement works, flew her level, and turned again by the river, throttled down and made my approach. **1953** C. A. LINDBERGH *Spirit of St. Louis* II. vi. 188 The air speed's still over 100 miles an hour... I throttle down to 1750. **1973** R. ROSENBLUM *Mushroom Cave* (1974) 101 The pilot throttled back to float the helicopter over a large network of paths. **1979** 'K. M. PEYTON' *Marion's Angels* viii. 130 He throttled down sharply for the turning to the church.

Hence **throttleable** ('θrɒt(ə)ləb(ə)l) *a.*; (of an engine) that can be controlled by means of a throttle; **throttled** ('θrɒt(ə)ld) *ppl. a.*, **'throttling** *vbl. sb.* and *ppl. a.*; also **'throttler**, one who or that which throttles: see also quot. 1895.

1960 *Aeroplane* XCVIII. 261/2 The Thiokol XLR-99 '*throttleable' rocket engine..has completed preliminary static tests and will shortly be installed in an X-15. **1969** *New Scientist* 1 May 243/2 The rotors could be fitted with small, throttleable rockets on their tips. **1818** SCOTT *Br. Lamm.* ix, The huntsman then withdrew the hounds from the *throttled stag. **1906** *Westm. Gaz.* 14 Nov. 9/2 The motor-car..has grown out of knowledge. Pneumatic tyres, multiple cylinders, a throttled engine, electric ignition,..are a few of the leading improvements. **1859** MAX MÜLLER *Sc. Lang.* ix. (1861) 367 All who have seen..the statue of Laokoon..may realise what those ancients felt..when they called sin *anhas*, or the *throttler. **1889** —— *Nat. Relig.* xv. 404 An enemy had been called a throttler. **1895** *Funk's Standard Dict.*, *Throttler*..2. A throttle-valve, or an engine having one. *a* **1687** *Throatling [see 3]. **1826** SCOTT *Jrnl.* 30 May, A sort of throttling sensation. **1863** GEO. ELIOT *Romola* xxii, [He] might easily check any rebellious movement by the threat of throttling. **1875** R. F. MARTIN tr. *Havrez' Winding Mach.* 79 The throttling of the steam at the regulator. **1566** STUDLEY tr. *Seneca, Agam.* E vij, The old mans *thratlyng throt I sawe (alas) I saw yborde With cruell Pirrhus blade [*senis in iugulo Telum Pyrrhi..tingui*]. **1700** DRYDEN *Pal. & Arc.* III. 406 The throttling quinsey 'tis my star appoints. **1830** SCOTT *Demonol.* i. 43 The broken cry of deer mangled by throttling dogs.

throu, obs. form of THROUGH.

†**throuch, through** (θrʌx). *Sc. Obs.* Also 6 **thrugh, throch, throuche**. [History and etymology unknown.

All the forms cited occur also as spellings of THROUGH *sb.*¹, but it is difficult to see any connexion with that word, unless it be that both are rectangular and flat.]

A sheet (of paper).

1502 *Acc. Ld. High Treas. Scot.* II. 343 For xxj thrugh of ymagery to be patrownis to the broudstar,..xxj s. **1546** *Ibid.* VIII. 450 For xij throuchis of Lumbart paper to be patronis for chargeouris of gunnis,..ij s. **1556–7** *Edinburgh Burgh Rec.* 9 Jan., To tak the inuentar of the habilite of all personis and the quantite of thair substance, and wryting the samyn, quhilk was xxviij throch of paper. **1572** *Satir. Poems Reform.* xxxiii. Ded. 5 To quhome can I this lytill throuch propyne, Bot vnto ane of excellent ingyne? *a* **1578** LINDESAY (Pitscottie) *Chron. Scot.* (S.T.S.) I. 407 The Cardinal held ane throch of paper to the king and causit him wreit his handwreit thairon. **1590** in *Acts of Sederunt* (1790) 18 That all letteris that conteinis mair nor ane throuche of paper, that everie battering, and end of the throuche, sall be subscrivit be him. **1618** *Rec. Elgin* (New Spald. Cl.) I. 237 For writin of half ane through of paper.

through (θrʌx, θrʌf, θrʊf), *sb.*¹ *Obs.* exc. *Sc.* and *north. dial.* Forms: 1 **thru(u)ch, throuch**, 1–3 **þruh**, (1 **þryh**), 4 **throuȝ, þrouhwe**, 4–5 **þrugh, þrouȝ**, 4–6 **throgh(e**, 4–6 (9 *Sc.*) **thrugh**, 5 **thrughe, throw(e, throh**, 6 **threwgh**, *Sc.* **throch, throwch, throuche, throcht, throucht**, 7 **throughe**, 6– **through**; 6– *Sc.* **throuch**, (9 **threuch, thruch, throoch**, *north. dial.* **thruff**). *β.* 4 **thoru**, 5 **thorow, thorw, thurwhe, thwrwe, thurgh**, 6 **thorgh, thorowgh**, 7 **thorough**. [OE. *þrúh*, a fem. cons. stem, oblique cases *þrýh*, cogn. with ON. *þró* fem. (pl. *prœr*) a receptacle hollowed out, a tube, chest, trough, whence *steinþró* stone-chest, stone-coffin; cf. also OHG. *drûha, truhâ* (MHG. *trûhe, truche*, Ger. *truhe*), which agrees in sense, but not in the initial consonant: see Kluge *Etymol. Wörterb.*]

†**1.** (Only in *OE.*) A trough, pipe, channel for water. [So ON. *þró* trough, watering trough.]

a **700** *Epinal Gloss.* (O.E.T.) 1000 *Tubo*, thruu[c]h [*Corpus* ðruh, *Erfurt* thruch]. *Ibid.* 232 *Caractis* [*cataractes*], uua[e]terthruch [*Corpus* uueterþruh, *Erfurt* uaeterthrouch]. *a* **900** *O.E. Martyrol.* 2 Sept., þa ȝesomnodon þa sticceo hi in þa þruh, þurh þa þe þæt wæter fleow; þa ne meahte þæt wæter flowan.

†**2.** A hollow receptacle for a dead body; orig. perh. a stone cist or coffin; hence a coffin generally, e.g. of wood; also a grave, tomb, sepulchre. *Obs.*

a **900** tr. *Bæda's Hist.* IV. xiv. [xi.] (1890) 296 þa wæs se lichoma sponne lengra þære þryh. *c* **1000** ÆLFRIC *Hom.* I. 216 Tweȝen ȝelyfede men..bebyriȝdon his lic ær æfene, on niwere ðryh. *Ibid.* II. 262 þa ȝeðafode Pilatus þæt hi..ða ðruh ȝe-innseȝelodon. *c* **1275** *Passion of our Lord* 511 in *O.E. Misc.* 51 Ioseph..hyne leyde in one þruh of stone. *a* **1300** *Cursor M.* 24637 (Edin.) Al til his þruh þai þrang. **13..** *Ibid.* 17288 + 13 (Cott.) Our lord opend not his throgh when he ros at morne. **13..** *Guy Warw.* (A.) 7306 + st. 296 þay tok a þrouȝ of marbel ston, & leyd his bodi þer-in anon. **13..** *Propr. Sanct.* 179 (Vernon MS.) in Herrig's *Archiv* LXXXI. 83 On domus-day, Al vre þrouhwes þen schul ouerþrowe. *c* **1400** *Laud Troy Bk.* 15570 Now he is ded & lith In throw [*rime* now]. *c* **1410** *Chron. Eng.* (Ritson) 747 Ant leggen in a throh of ston. **1483** *Cath. Angl.* 386/2 A Thrughe (*A.* Throghe), *mauseolum..cippus;..vbi* a grawe.

β. **13..** *Cursor M.* 17390 (Cott.) Þan þai badd be-for ham call þat gett [*v.r.* kepte] þe thoru þe knightes all. *c* **1400** *Trevisa's Higden* (Rolls) VII. 535 (MS. *β*) On caas ȝe mowe kepe my body..lay hit in a thorow [*MS. γ*, þrouȝ] of stoon and heleth hit with a lidde of lede. *a* **1450** Thurghis [see THRO *a.*¹ 1 b].

3. A large slab of stone, etc. laid upon a tomb; a flat grave-stone or grave-cover; also, a table gravestone resting on feet. (See THROUGH-STONE¹.)

a **1350** *St. Nicholas* 384 in Horstm. *Altengl. Leg.* (1881) 16 Enterd he was in toumbe of stone And a marble thrugh laid him opon. **1523** *Test. Ebor.* (Surtees) V. 174 To lay oppon my body & Alicie my wif a conveniente thrughe of stone. **1560** in *Edinb. Burgh Rec.* 62 To reparrall the kirk, to lay the throwchis thairof of new and sparge the samyn. **1593** *Rites of Durham* (Surtees 1903) 15 Two lyons..artificially wrought and sett forth all in brasse marueilously beautifyinge the said through of marble. **1606** [see THORTERSOME]. **1630** *Vestry Bks.* (Surtees) 185 Through the ignorance or negligence of the sexton or others,..the throughs and flaggs have been brooke, and once taken up never so well laid downe. *a* **1663** BP. BRAMHALL *Will*, I to be buried in the middle alley within the church of Alhallowes in Pontefracte under the greate blewe through at the end of the Maior and Aldresses stall. **1777** *Bothkennar Par. Reg.* 8

July, in *N. & Q.* 9th Ser. II. 237/1 John Simpson, tenant in Crofthead, hath 2 lairs with throughs in the churchyard of Bothkennar. **1804** Stagg *Misc. Poems* (1808) 4 Then great Job Bruff gat on a thruff. **1864** W. Chambers *Hist. Peebles.* 295 Throuchs or flat table-like stones.

through, *sb.*[2]: see THROUCH.

through (θruː), *sb.*[3] Also 8–9 *dial.* thruff (θrʌf). [f. THROUGH *adv.* or *adj.*, sometimes due to ellipsis of a sb.]

1. = THOROUGH *sb.* 2. *dial.*

1778 [W. Marshall] *Minutes Agric.* 10 June an. 1777, Mixes it with the sand and marl, which is thrown out in making their elaborate thruffs,—or sub-drains.

2. = THROUGH-STONE[2].

1805 [see THROUGH-STONE[2]]. **1828** *Craven Gloss.*, *Thruff*, a bond stone, or thorough stone. **1846** Brockett *N.C. Words* s.v. *Thruff-stone*, These walls being composed of fragments of all shapes and sizes, without mortar, the 'thruffs' are used as bond-stones and give great stability. **1892** J. T. Bent *Ruined Cities Mashonaland* iv. 97 Most of them [the stones] run back into the wall irregularly, acting in the same way as *throughs* in our dry-built walls.

3. A ladder-rung that goes through the sides. *local.*

1899 *N. & Q.* 9th Ser. III. 76/2 Ladders are often made with three or four flat bars, longer than the rounded ones, and projecting sufficiently on each side to admit a wooden peg... These are called flat rungs, sometimes 'throughs' (thrufs.).

through (θruː), *a.* [attrib. use of THROUGH *adv.*, primarily used with verbal sbs., nouns of action, agent-nouns, and the like, derived from vbs. qualified by the adv., or with ellipsis of a pple. of such a verb, as in *through* (going) *way*; afterwards in various extended or transferred uses.]

1. a. That passes, extends, or affords passage through something. (See also THROUGH *a.* 1; THROUGH- 2.)

spec. Of a bolt, rivet, etc.: Passing through the whole thickness of that in which it is fixed: see also *through-bolt* s.v. THROUGH- 2; in *Carpentry*, of a housing: running through the whole thickness of the member, not stopped. ***through bridge***: see quot. 1877. ***through lights***: see THOROUGH-LIGHT.

1523 [see *through-serewe, -spavin* in THROUGH- 2]. *a* **1578** [see THROUGH-PASSAGE]. **1596** Spenser *State Irel.* Wks. (Globe) 614/1 Was there not a through way then made by the swoord for the imposing of lawes uppon them? **1605** Bacon *Adv. Learn.* II. ii. §14 The opennesse and through passage of the world..were appointed to be in the same ages. **1865** *Once a Week* 10 June 679/1 Building houses back to back without any 'through' ventilation. **1877** Knight *Dict. Mech.*, *Through-bridge*, one in which the track rests on the lower stringer, in contradistinction to a *deck*-bridge. **1889** Welch *Text Bk. Naval Archit.* iv. 74 The rivets are of two kinds, through (or clenched) and tap. **1934** [see STOPPED *ppl. a.* 9]. **1979** A. B. Emary *Woodworking* iii. 18 (*caption*) Through housing.

b. That goes, extends, or conveys through the whole of a long distance or journey without interruption, or without change; as a ***through train, booking, carriage, passenger, line of railway, fare, ticket. through traffic***: (*a*) rail traffic continuing through to a further destination; (*b*) road traffic which passes through a particular town, etc., rather than stopping there.

1845 *Boston* (Mass.) *Transcript* 29 Nov. 3/2 Through tickets may be obtained for Montreal. **1846** *Boston* (Mass.) *Traveller* 2 July, Through trains from Boston. **1848** *Amer. Railroad Jrnl.* 29 July 482/1 A *through* passenger in the 9 and 4½ o'clock lines, pays more than $1.25, for each of those parts of the line. **1858** Hawthorne *Fr. & It. Note-Bks.* (1872) I. 1 Having taken through tickets to Paris by way of Folkestone and Boulogne. **1861** Jefferson Davis *Message to Confederate Congress Amer.* 18 Nov., The construction of this..line would give us a through route from North to South. **1861** *Sat. Rev.* 7 Sept. 236 The through traffic to Scotland has been carried on by eight independent Companies. **1869** *Bradshaw's Railway Man.* XXI. 43 Through-booking arrangements with the Scottish North Eastern. **1884** *Gt. West. Railw. Time Tables* July 10 The direct Through Trains between Aldgate and Richmond. **1890** *Daily News* 12 Nov. 7/2 Any railway to which there is through booking from Aldershot. **1891** S. J. Weyman *New Rector* I. iii. 28 Oh, dear, they are in a through carriage... I would rather go in another carriage and change. **1893** Earl Dunmore *Pamirs* I. 83 A few merchants carry on a through trade between India and Turkestan. **1905** *Sat. Rev.* 21 Oct. 522/2 What with the through travellers and the..traffic, there was no lack of variety. **1944** *Sun* (Baltimore) 16 Feb. 9/1 A mid-town express highway as a through-traffic route. **1961** Through-traffic [see ROUTE *v.*]. **1976** *Alyn & Deeside Observer* 10 Dec. 1/6 The new by-pass will provide an additional crossing of the River Dee that will enable much through traffic to avoid the city. **1978** O. S. Nock *Great Western* 110 In such conditions the through carriage was an inestimable boon.

c. Of an organ-stop: Extending through the whole compass of the keyboard.

1881 C. A. Edwards *Organs* 146 All the foundation.. stops of a really good organ should be through stops.

†**2.** Going through or affecting the whole of something: = THOROUGH *a.* 2. *Obs.*

through coal, or ***through and through coal***, coal as it comes from the pit, i.e. large and small mixed indiscriminately.

1542 Udall *Erasm. Apoph.* 80 That thei might..haue a through sight in it. **1581** Sidney *Apol. Poetrie* (Arb.) 49 From a through beholding the worthines of the subiect. **1607** Hieron *Wks.* I. 462 To speake of a true and through reformation. **1647** Clarendon *Hist. Reb.* III. §211 There was not a Grievance..to which there was not a through Remedy applied. **1696** Vanbrugh *Relapse* Epil. 22 You never saw a through republican a finish'd beau. **1710** Prideaux *Orig. Tithes* ii. 69 If on through search and examination they were approved of.

through, *v.* *Sc. rare.* ? *Obs.* [f. THROUGH *prep.* and *adv.*: cf. THOROUGH *v.*[1]]

1. *trans.* To carry through, put through, carry into effect. Hence 'throughing *vbl. sb.*

1638 R. Baillie *Lett. & Jrnls.* (1841) I. 74 His father's throughing of Perth articles. **1716** *Wodrow Corr.* (1843) II. 172, I am mistaken if this way they get their design throughed.

2. *intr.* To get through; to succeed. ***to make to through***, to make good, prove.

1786 Burns *Brigs of Ayr* 175 Faith ye've said enough, And muckle mair than ye can mak to through. **1863** Janet Hamilton *Poems & Ess.* 56 We've throught weel and thrivin this mony a year.

through (θruː), *prep.* and *adv.* From *c* 1700, abbreviated thro'; in 15–18th c., without ', thro. Forms: see below. [OE. *ðurh, þurh*, Northumb. *ðerh*, a Common WGer. prep. and adv.: cf. OFris. (from **thurch*) *thruch, truch* (WFris. *troch*, NFris. *truch, troch*); OS. *thurh, thuru*, **thurih* (MLG. *dorch, dörch, dor, dör*, LG. *dör, dôr*, MDu. *door, dōre, döre, deur, dor, dur*, Du. *door*); OHG. *duruh, durih, duri, dur* (MHG. *durch, dürch, dur, dür*, Ger. *durch*, dial. *dur, dör*). Not in Scandinavian; in Gothic with different ablaut grade *þairh* (= *þerh*); prob. cases of a sb., belonging to a pre-Teut. ablaut-series **terk-, tork-, trk-* to bore: cf. Goth. *þairkô* hole, and OHG. *durhil*, MHG. *dürchel, dürkel*, OE. **þyrhil, þyrel* bored, perforated: cf. THIRL *sb.* OE. *þurh* with full stress became *þuruh*, now THOROUGH, as *burh* has become *borough*, *furh furrow*, etc.; when unstressed and proclitic, *þurh* became *þŭr*, and with metathesis *þrŭh, þrŭ, throŭ, thrŏ*. The unstressed forms naturally prevailed in proclitic prepositional use, and the stressed in the adverb, and its derived adj. and sb. But with the restressing of the prep. *thrū* as *through* (θruː), this form has also become possible as an adverb, while on the other hand the stressed THOROUGH also survives as an archaic form of the preposition beside the normal *through*. *Thurf* is an early phonetic development of *þurh*, and *thruf* a more recent one of *þruh*, similar to (rʌf) for *rough*, *dwarf* from *dwergh*, (bɑːf) for *Bargh*, (brʊf) for *Burgh* (place-names), (ɪ'nʌf) for *enough*, (θɒf) for *though*, etc. The metathesis of *þruh* for *þurh* occurs already *c* 1300 in a s.w. text; but otherwise in ME. is usually northern. From Caxton onwards it was the standard English form.

See *Note* under THOROUGH *prep.* and *adv.*]

A. Illustration of Forms.

For disyllabic forms *þureh, þuruh, þurow*, etc.: see THOROUGH.

α. 1 **þurȝ** (**þerh**), 1–3 **þorh** (1 **þorch**), 1–4 **þurh**, 2–4 **þurch**, 3 *Orm.* **þurrh**, 3–4 **þurȝ**, **þorȝ**, **thurȝ**, 3–5 **þurgh**, 4 **þorgh**, **þorghe**, **þourh**, **þourȝ**, (**þour**), 4–5 **þourgh**, **thourgh**, **thurghe**, **thorgh**, 4–6 **thurgh**, 5 **thorȝ**, **þurȝe**, **þourȝe**, (**thour**), *Sc.* **thourch**. Also 3 **þurþ**, **þorþ**, 4 **þurth**, **þurȝth**, 5 **thourth**, (**dorth**); 4–5 **thurght**, **thorght**, 5 **þurght**.

(Final *þ, ð*, is frequently a scribal error for final *ȝ*, and *th* a copyist's error for *ch*; in Scotch *t* was often added to *-ch, -gh*, or *-th*.)

a **700** *Epinal Gloss.* (O.E.T.) 741 *Per seudoterum*, þorh ludgaet. *Ibid.* 757 *Per anticipationem*, þorch [*Erfurt* dorh] obst. *a* **800** Cynewulf *Elene* 289 þurh witȝena wordgeryno. *a* **900** þurh [see B. I. 7 b]. *c* **950** *Lindisf. Gosp.* Mark xv. 10 Ðerh æfist [*Rushw.* ðærh æfeste] ȝesaldon hine. *c* **1000** *Fates 12 Apostles* 13 (Gr.) þurȝ Nerones nearo-searwe. *c* **1000** *Ags. Gosp.* ibid., Ðurh andan hine sealdon. *a* **1175** *Cott. Hom.* 223 Ealle þing ȝeworhcte god þurch his worda. *a* **1200** *Moral Ode* 282 þe suneȝe þurð sihte. *c* **1200** þurrh [see B. I. 7]. **1297** R. Glouc. (Rolls) 681, & regnede þritti ȝer wel þor [*v.rr.* þoru, þurgh, thorugh, þrough] alle þinge. **13..** *Cursor M.* 11070 (Gött.) All þe cunthre thurght. *c* **1350** *Will. Palerne* 4219 þourh ȝour help. **13..** *Gaw. & Gr. Knt.* 310 þurȝ ryalmes so mony. **1377** Langl. *P. Pl.* B. I. 32 Thorw [*C.* Thorgh] wyn and þorw women þere was Loth acombred. **1393** *Ibid.* C. xxi. 399 So þat þorgh gyle was geten, þorwe grace is now y-wonne. *c* **1380** Wyclif *Serm.* Sel. Wks. I. 392 þourȝ Samarie and þe cuntre of Galile. *c* **1386** Chaucer *Frankl. T.* 137 Eterne god that thurgh [*v.rr.* thour, þurgh, þourgh, þoruhe] thy purueiance Ledest the world. *c* **1410** Thourh [see B. II. 5 b]. *c* **1425** *Seven Sag.* (P.) 522 Thourth the emperours commandement. *c* **1440** Thorgh [see B. I. 2]. *c* **1450** *Merlin* ii. 32 He hadde resceyved deth thourgh me. *c* **1460** *Launfal* 1031 The lady rod dorth Cardevyle. *c* **1460** Thourth; **1521** Thurgh [see B. II. 1; B. I. 1].

β. 3 **þruh**, 4 **þrouȝ**, 5 **þroughe**, **throwȝe**, **thruȝ**, **thrughe**, (**drogh**, **trogh**), 5–6 **thrugh**, **throughe**, 5–7 **throgh**, 6 **throwgh(e**, 5– **through** (8– *abbrev.* **thro'**); 4– **thru**, *Sc.* **thrw**, **threu**, **threw**, 4–7 (chiefly *Sc.*) **throu**, 4–8 (–9 *Sc.* or *dial.*) **throw**, 5 **þro**, 5– **thro**, 6 **throwe**, *Sc.* **throuw**; *Sc.* 4–6 **throuch**, 6 **thruch**, **thrwch**, **throwch**, 7 **throche**, 8 **throch**; 5 **throght**, (**troght**), 5–6 *Sc.* **throcht**, 6 **thruȝht**, *Sc.* **thrucht**, **throucht**.

thru: now used informally as a reformed spelling and abbreviation (chiefly) in *N. Amer.*

? *a* **1300** *Prayer to Virgin* 8 in *O.E. Misc.* (1872) 195 Bote þu þruh þin milde mod bringe me out of sunne. *Ibid.* 19. **13..** Thru, throu [see B. I. 1 b, 7 b]. *c* **1350** *Will. Palerne* 459 Mi wicked eyiȝen..lad myn hert þrouȝ loking þis langour to drye. **1375** Barbour *Bruce* I. 137 Throuch thar aller hale assent. *Ibid.* 533 Destroyit throw pwsoune. *c* **1375** *Sc. Leg. Saints* x. (*Mathou*) 52 Thrw sorcery & felone gyle. *Ibid.* xiii.[2] (*Marcus*) 49 Threw þe schewynge Of þe ewangele. *Ibid.* xxvi. (*Nycholas*) 806 Blyndyt threu gret cowatise. *c* **1400** *Sowdone Bab.* 2526 He..hade pardon Throgh prayere and specialle grace. *c* **1400** *Destr. Troy* 1129 Thrugh lemys of light. *Ibid.* 4977 þro mony long chaumburs. *c* **1425** *Eng. Conq. Irel.* 18 The gret peril that myght be-fall hym.. drogh the owt-comen folk þat was thus in-to the land I-com. *Ibid.* 26 Trogh al thynge. *Ibid.* 28 That thou ne hast y-done troght some grete lette. *c* **1470** Henry *Wallace* VIII. 709 Trocht falsheid, and thar subtilite. **1484** Caxton *Fables of Æsop* v. viii, The serpent..slewe the child through his venym. **1487–8** Throwȝe [see B. I. 4]. *c* **1489** Thrughe [see B. I. 1 h]. *a* **1500** *Cokwolds Daunce* 105 in Hazl. *E.P.P.* I. 43 Ffor that was thruȝht a chans. **1500–20** Dunbar *Poems* xlii. 81 Thrucht Skornes noss thai put a prik. —— Throucht [see B. I. 3]. **1508** —— *Gold. Targe* 28 Doun throu the ryce a ryuir ran. **1533** *Cal. Anc. Rec. Dublin* (1889) 396 Such merchunds..as cum throw Oxmantown. **1545–7** in *Archæologia* XXXIV. 41 Throwgh the weke. **1596** Throuch [see B. II. 4]. **1674** Brevint *Saul at Endor* 140 [He] may fall ..thro a broken bridge. *a* **1679** Hobbes *Rhet.* (1681) Pref., Throu the working of Belief. **1709** Prior *Despairing Shepherd* i, Wand'ring thro' the lonely Rocks. **1724** Ramsay *Vision* i, Throch feidom, our freedom Is blotit with this skore. *a* **1758** —— *Bonny Tweedside* i, I'll awa' to bonny Tweed side, And see my deary come throw. **1878** W. Whitman *Daybks. & Notebks.* (1978) I. 122 Sent piece 'Three Young Men's Deaths' $12 to Mr John Frazer, Tobacco Plant, Liverpool—thro Josiah Child. **1879**, etc. [see THOUGH *adv.* and *conj.* A. γ]. **1904** R. Garnett *Let.* in A. Mizener *Ford Madox Ford* (1971) ix. 96 If Conrad..paid £3 a week thro Pinker it would be a very considerable help. **1917** E. E. Cummings *Let.* c Nov. (1969) 40, I see the thing thru, alone. **1921** *Jrnl. Nat. Dental Assoc.* VIII. 609/1 As we look thru our daily papers and our magazines. **1971** *Black World* Mar. 57/1 When she wuz little and she had stuttered thru a sentence. **1977** *Hot Car* Oct. 11/1 Available for S types right thru to Mk 10s it retails for 26 notes.

γ. 3–4 **þurf**, 3–6 **thurf**, 8–9 (*dial.*) **thruff**.

c **1290** *St. Brendan* 149 in *S. Eng. Leg.* I. 223 þurf oure louerdes grace. *a* **1300** *Fragm. Pop. Sc.* (Wright) l. 11 Thurf dai & thurf niȝt. *a* **1500** *Childe of Bristowe* 520 in Hazl. *E.P.P.* I. 129 Thurf your good he is save. *a* **1800** Pegge *Suppl. Grose*, *Thruff and thruff*, i.e. through and through. *Derb.* **1864** Tennyson *North. Farmer, O. Style* xi, I.. runn'd plow thruff it an' all. **1888** Fenn *Dick o' Fens* 153 Go thruff yon reed-bed home.

B. Signification.

I. *prep.* The preposition expressing the relation of transition or direction within something from one limit of it to the other: primarily in reference to motion in space, hence in various derived senses.

1. a. From one end, side, or surface to the other or opposite end, side, or surface of (a body or a space) by passing within it; usually implying into, at one end, side, etc. and out of at the other.

(Expressing movement (or extension) either so as to penetrate the substance of a thing, or along a passage or opening already existing in it.) With various vbs. of motion forming prepositional phrases: cf. PASS *v.* 58 a, RUN *v.* 12–15, etc.

a **700** [see A. α]. *c* **950** *Lindisf. Gosp.* Matt. vii. 13 Inngeonges ðerh nearuo port. *c* **1000** *ibid.*, Gangað inn þurh þæt nearwe ȝeat. *c* **1400** *Destr. Troy* 4977 Led were þo lordes þro mony long chaumburs..þurgh mony gay Alys. **1446** *Registr. Aberdon.* (Maitl. Cl.) I. 245 A lonyng lyand þrow the mur betwix twa ald stane dykes. **1490** Caxton *Eneydos* xv. 60 Fyres..sodaynly sente throughe the cloudes in grete tempeste and murmure. **1521** Fisher *Wks.* (1876) 315 To condyth that people thurgh the deserte. **1557** N. T. (Genev.) *John* iv. 4 He must nedes go through [1526 Tindale thorowe] Samaria. **1605** Camden *Rem.* 193 An extreame cold winde passed throgh his sides. **1708** *Constit. Watermen's Co.* xl, If any person Row..through London-Bridge, on the Flood-Tide. **1758** Johnson *Idler* No. 15 ¶2 Sauntering about the Shop with her arms through her pocket-holes. **1848** Thackeray *Van. Fair* xxxii, George.. was lying..dead, with a bullet through his heart. *Mod.* There is a path through the wood.

b. Denoting transmission of light, or of sight, by an aperture or a transparent medium; also *fig.* (See also LOOK *v.* 20, SEE *v.* 24.)

13.. *Cursor M.* 11229 (Gött.) þe sune beme gas thru [*Cott.* thoru] þe glas. *c* **1386** Chaucer *Knt.'s T.* 217 Thurgh a wyndow..He cast his eye vpon Emelya. **1640** Nabbes *Bride* III. ii, A pigmie that cannot be discerned but through a multiplying glas. **1704** Pope *Disc. Past. Poetry* §5 Piety to the Gods should shine through the Poem. **1766** Goldsm. *Vic. W.* xvi, These instances of cunning, which she thought impenetrable, yet which everybody saw through. **1852** Dickens *Bleak Ho.* viii, Mrs. Pardiggle..had been regarding him through her spectacles.

(*b*) ***through-the-lens*** adj., used with reference to light measurement in which it is the light passing through the lens of the camera that is measured (the same light that would form the image).

1965 *Focal Encycl. Photogr.* (rev. ed.) I. 554/1 Through-the-lens exposure measurement has the advantage..that the meter cell receives light from exactly the same subject field as is taken in by the lens. **1977** J. Hedgecoe *Photographer's Handbk.* 14/3 Solid state through-the-lens metering, zoom lenses, motor-drive, are all part of an ever-widening 'system' built around the single lens reflex body. **1984** *What*

Video? Aug. 59/2 Fair picture, basic colour temperature controls, through-the-lens viewfinder.

c. In reference to a (more distant or fainter) sound heard simultaneously with another (nearer or louder) which does not 'drown' it or prevent it from reaching the ear.

1819 KEATS *Isabella* xxxvi, Languor there was in it, and tremulous shake,.. And through it moan'd a ghostly under-song. **1847** TENNYSON *Princess* IV. 554 Thy voice is heard thro' rolling drums.

d. In reference to the passages traversed by the breath in the production and modification of vocal sound, as ***to speak through the throat, the nose***, etc.

1588, 1741, 1850 [see NOSE *sb.* 3]. **1668** OWEN PRICE *Eng. Orthographie* 16 *Gh* soundes now like *h*, in *Almighty, although* [etc.]. *Note*, But the Ancients did, as the Welch, & Scots do still pronounce *gh*, thorow the throat.

e. With pl. (or collective) sb., expressing passage between or among things so as to penetrate the whole mass or body of them (without penetrating the individual things); through between. See also 2, and cf. THROUGH OTHER.

1535, 1684 [see THOROUGH B. I. 1 d]. **1709** PRIOR *Despairing Sheph.* i, Wand'ring thro' the lonely Rocks. **1712** ADDISON *Spect.* No. 327 ¶6 [Raphael's] Flight thro' the Choirs of Angels is finely imaged. **1852** R. S. SURTEES *Sponge's Sp. Tour* (1893) 85 He was small and wiry, with legs that a pig could run through. **1890** 'R. BOLDREWOOD' *Col. Reformer* (1891) 204 The slippery savage.. was bounding through the trees. *Mod.* Walking through the long grass.

f. In phr. *through* (one's) ***hands, through a machine***, etc., referring to something being handled, manufactured, subjected to some process, or dealt with in any way. (See also MILL *sb.*[1] 1 b.)

c **1320** *Sir Beues* (A.) 1035 Erst þow schelt pase þourȝ min hond. **1630** *R. Johnson's Kingd. & Commw.* 346 They are able in one day to make two hundred Harquibushes.. although there be no Harquebush that goeth through lesse than ten hands at the least. **1641** in Cochran-Patrick *Rec. Coinage Scotl.* (1876) I. Introd. 31 They would putt 1000 stane [of copper] throw the yrons in the yeire. **1709** BAGFORD in *MS. Rawl. Lett.* 21, lf. 8 All of them from yᵉ Bookes themselues which haue run throw my handes. **1815** SCOTT *Guy M.* xxxix, I had her through hands once, and could then make little of her. **1874** GREEN *Short Hist.* vii. §6. 408 Plot and approval alike passed through Walsingham's hands. *Mod.* It has passed through many hands since then.

g. In various directly figurative applications: e.g. (*a*) referring to the action upon the ears or nerves of a loud, shrill, harsh, or 'piercing' sound; (*b*) implying the overcoming of hindrance or obstruction (see also BREAK *v.* 56); (*c*) indicating connexion or transmission by an intermediate thing (or person) or a series of such, etc.

to pay through the nose: see NOSE *sb.* 11. ***through thick and thin***: see THICK AND THIN.

1543 [see THICK AND THIN A. 1]. **1581–1680** [see THOROUGH B. I. 1 f]. **1647** MAY *Hist. Parl.* II. vi. 127 Your Parliament, whose.. undiscouraged endeavours.. have passed thorow difficulties unheard of. **1766** GOLDSM. *Vic. W.* xxx, The circumstances of my unfortunate son broke through all efforts to dissemble. *a* **1784** JOHNSON in *Boswell* an. 1737 Knowledge of the world, fresh from life, not strained through books. **1849** MACAULAY *Hist. Eng.* v. I. 526 John Ayloffe, a lawyer connected by affinity with the Hydes, and through the Hydes, with James.

h. ***through and through***: repeatedly through; so as to penetrate both sides or surfaces of; right through, entirely through. Also *fig.* (Cf. II. 5.)

13.. [see THOROUGH B. I. 1 g]. *c* **1489** CAXTON *Sonnes of Aymon* xiv. 346 He shoved his swerde thrughe & thrughe his body. **1599** SHAKS. *Much Ado* v. i. 68 Thy slander hath gone through and through her heart. *a* **1716** SOUTH *Serm.* (1842) I. 321 His infinite, all-searching knowledge, which looks through and through the most secret of our thoughts. **1724** DE FOE *Mem. Cavalier* (1840) 227 He broke through and through them. **1745** P. THOMAS *Voy. S. Seas* 281 Our second Shot.. went thro' and thro' her upper Works. **1932** H. S. WALPOLE *Fortress* III. 562 The mist immediately surrounding him was.. so wetting that he was already soaked through and through his clothes.

i. After an auxiliary verb, with ellipsis of *go*. Cf. II. 6; THROUGH *v.* 2.

1567 MAPLET *Gr. Forest* 85 If a mans iourney lieth so, that he must nedes through the Forrest. **1606** SHAKS. *Tr. & Cr.* v. x. 26 You vile abhominable Tents,.. Ile through, and through you.

2. Of motion or direction within the limits of; along within; as in 1, 1 e, but not necessarily implying the traversing of the whole extent from end to end.

c **1050** *Byrhtferth's Handboc* in *Anglia* (1885) VIII. 298 þurh þæne yrnð seo sunne. *a* **1300** *Cursor M.* 23412 (Edin.) Al þat þe withstandand es Thurȝ sal [þou] þirle wit sweftnes. *c* **1440** *Pallad. on Husb.* VI. 36 A forgh iij footes deep thy londes thorgh. **1591** SHAKS. *Two Gent.* v. ii. 38 As he in pennance wander'd through the Forrest. **1667** MILTON *P.L.* II. 663 The Night-Hag.. riding through the Air. **1787** WINTER *Syst. Husb.* 82 Clouds, which being heavier than the air, of course fall thro' it. **1818** SHELLEY *Sonnet 'Lift not the painted veil'* 11 Through the unheeding many he did move, A splendour among shadows. **1819** KEATS *Eve St. Agnes* i, The hare limp'd trembling through the frozen grass. **1903** *Times* 14 Mar. 14/5 The Oxonians showed good form through choppy water.

3. a. Over or about the whole extent of, all over (a surface); so as to traverse or penetrate every part or district of; in or to all parts of (a region, or a body); throughout; everywhere in. (See also RUN *v.* 68 d.)

c **1000** *Ags. Gosp.* Luke xxiii. 5 He astyrað þis folc lærende þurh ealle iudeam. **13..** *Gaw. & Gr. Knt.* 243 Al stouned at his steuen.. þurȝ þe sale riche. *c* **1350** *Old Usages Winchester* in *Eng. Gilds* (1870) 359 Lat crye þe ban þorghe þe town þe þridde day by-fore þe selynge. *c* **1450** *Merlin* i. 10, I sought thourgh my chamber. **1500–20** DUNBAR *Poems* lxxiv. 14 Leif creuelte.. Or throucht the warld quyte losit is ȝour name. **1591** SHAKS. *1 Hen. VI*, III. iii. 13 We will make thee famous through the World. **1659** *Termes de la Ley* 146 b/2 That there should be but one scantling of weights and measures through all the Realm. **1727–46** THOMSON *Summer* 1168 And Thule bellows through her utmost isles. **1860** TYNDALL *Glac.* II. vii. 260 Minute particles diffused through the atmosphere.

b. Placed after the sb. *arch.*, *poet.*

a **1300** *Cursor M.* 11070 Noght allan ierusalem burgh, Bot elles al þe contre thurgh [*v.rr.* thurght, thorogh, þourȝe]. *Ibid.* 11824 þe fester thrild his bodi thurgh [*rime* scurf]. **1556** ROBINSON *More's Utop.* Shorte Meter (Arb.) 167 Platoes citie, Whose flame flieth the worlde throughe. *a* **1635, 1802** [see THOROUGH B. I. 3]. **1851** MRS. BROWNING *Casa Guidi Wind.* II. 266 A cry is up in England, which doth ring The hollow world through.

†**c.** Phr. ***through all thing*** [cf. F. *partout*]: in every point, in all respects, thoroughly. *Obs.*

c **1205** LAY. 10966 Ich sugge þe þurh alle þing, ich sloh Asclepidiot. *c* **1290** *Beket* 252 in *S. Eng. Leg.* I. 113 Euere he was chaste þoruȝ alle þing. **1297**, *c* **1380** [see THOROUGH B. I. 3 b]. *c* **1425** *Eng. Conq. Irel.* 26 A man full queynt, trow trogh al thynge, & stalwarth.

4. a. During the whole of (a period of time, or an action, etc., with reference to the time it occupies from beginning to end). See also GET *v.* 48 c.

a **1000** *Ags. Ps.* (Th.) lxxiii[i]. 21 [22] þurh ealne dæȝ [*tota die*]. *a* **1250** *Owl & Night.* 447 (Cott.) And ich so do þurȝ niȝt and dai. **1487–8** *Rec. St. Mary at Hill* 141 On euery sonday throwȝe þe yer. **1581** ALLEN *Apol.* 74 Al the Churches of Christ through al ages. **1593** SHAKS. *Lucr.* 718 Through the length of times he stands disgraced. **1667** MILTON *P.L.* x. 846 Thus Adam.. lamented.. Through the still Night. **1779** *Mirror* No. 37 ¶5 The same sanguine temperament of mind which.. has attended him through life. **1861** MRS. CARLYLE *Lett.* (1883) III. 81 A brass band plays all through our breakfast. **1896** T. F. TOUT *Edw. I*, iv. 80 All through his reign, the Lusignans helped him in Gascony.

b. Placed after a sb.; esp. preceded by *all*.

1535 [see THOROUGH B. I. 4]. **1864** MRS. GATTY *Parab. fr. Nat.* Ser. IV. 5 He was seldom seen without one [a flower] in his button-hole all the summer through. **1872** A. DE VERE *Leg. St. Patrick, Disbelief Milcho* 32 Fireless sits he, winter through. **1873** BLACK *Pr. Thule* iii, It will be like this all the night through.

5. a. From beginning to end of; in or along the whole length or course of (an action, an experience, a piece of work, etc.; also of a discourse, a book, etc.). See also GET *v.* 48, GO *v.* 63, PASS *v.* 58 b, RUN *v.* 68.

c **1449** [see THOROUGH B. I. 5]. **1578** TIMME *Caluine on Gen.* 326, I may not runne through vncertain speculations. **1766** GOLDSM. *Vic. W.* xiv, I had.. put my horse through all his paces. **1774** MITFORD *Ess. Harmony Lang.* 93, I can-not find any thing like [it].. thro the whole essay. **1831** MACAULAY *Let.* in Trevelyan *Life* (1876) I. iv. 233, I should have liked to have sat through so tremendous a storm. **1886** AD. SERGEANT *No Saint* I. vi. 105 An old land surveyor.. put him through a long catechism.

b. with emphasis on the intervening or intermediate stage or condition. (Leading on to 7.) Also used in sequences or lists, without necessarily denoting consecutive development.

1671 MILTON *P.R.* I. 5 Obedience fully tri'd Through all temptation. **1818** MOORE *Fudge Fam. Paris* vi. 103 They graduate Through job, red ribbon, and silk gown, To Chancellorship and Marquisate. **1837** DICKENS *Pickw.* lvii, Mr. Bob Sawyer, having previously passed through the Gazette, passed over to Bengal. **1870** W. MORRIS *Earthly Par.* III. *Story Rhodope* 20 The brown plain.. Changed year by year through green to hoary gold. **1881** STANLEY *Chr. Instit.* vii. (1882) 131 In the new crisis through which the world was to pass. **1938** M. K. RAWLINGS *Yearling* xi. 110 His wares included the necessities and scanty luxuries of the whole country-side, from plows, wagons, buggies and implements, through food staples to whiskey and hardware, dry goods and notions and medicines. **1962** *Listener* 26 July 130/2 Rents range from just over £3 a month for a small flat, through about £14 for a two-bedroom house, to £23 for the most elegant apartments. **1975** *Nature* 10 Apr. 501/2 Nine recognised glaze types, ranging in colour from pale blue, through green, to yellow, brown and red.

c. with emphasis laid upon the completion: To the end of. (Leading on to 6.)

1628 [see THOROUGH B. I. 5]. **1744** BERKELEY *Siris* §2 Seven children, who came all very well through the small-pox. **1824** *New Monthly Mag.* X. 19, I never could read through the Nouvelle Heloïse. **1843** MRS. CARLYLE *Lett.* (1883) I. 253, I seemed to be got pretty well through my sewing. *Mod.* When shall you get through your task? He has got through 'Smalls'.

d. *U.S.* Up to (a date, a number, a specified item, etc.) inclusively, up to the end of, up to and including, to, until; often correlative to *from*.

1798 T. HOLCROFT *Jrnl.* 4 Aug. in *Mem.* (1816) III. 31 Continued the opera through scene 9, Act 3. **1930** H. BROWN (*title*) Rabelais in English literature through Sterne. **1932** *Atlantic Monthly* May 538 Mr. Heffernan was mayor for four years, from 1927 through 1931. **1942** M. KRAITCHIK *Math. Recreations* vi. 130 Poisson calculated this probability, taking into account the cards dealt in the first hand. His result does not differ through the third decimal place. **1950** H. CRAIG *Hist. Eng. Lit.* 250 Spenser treats of England from the Reformation through the reign of Queen Elizabeth. **1967** *N.Y. Times* (Internat. ed.) 11 Feb. 1/6 At a background briefing early in November, the American command made available infiltration figures covering the year through Sept. 30 and a rough estimate for October. **1971** *Physics Bull.* Dec. 738/1 In the review copy pages 1469 through 1472 are already loose which does not say too much for the quality of the binding. **1977** *Time* 8 Aug. 19/3 We will continue to govern through the end of our term. **1981** L. DEIGHTON *XPD* xliii. 342 A.. notice stating that deliveries were only accepted between eight and eleven Monday through Friday.

6. Indicating a position or point ultimately reached. (Usually in predicate, after verb *to be*.) Cf. II. 3. **a.** *lit.* At a point beyond, or at the further end of. **b.** *fig.* Having reached the end of (a course of action, a book, etc.); having finished, completed, or done with. **c.** In reference to an examination, ***to be through*** is to have passed.

1791 JEFFERSON *Writ.* (1896) V. 330, I think I can be through them [a bundle of letters] by the end of the week. **1791** BURNS *Tam O'Shanter* 93 By this time he was cross the ford.. And thro' the whins, and by the cairn. **1801** tr. *Gabrielli's Myst. Husb.* II. 267 They stopped at an inn nearly through the town. **1804** SOUTHEY in *Life* (1850) II. 262, I am half through the poem. **1894** *Outing* (U.S.) XXIV. 428/2 You may as well tell him that you're through taking lessons. *Mod.* Is he through his examination?

7. a. Indicating medium, means, agency, or instrument: By means of; by the action of, by (*obs.* or *arch.*) Now *spec.* By the instrumentality of.

a **800** [see A. a]. *c* **950** *Lindisf. Gosp.* Luke xvii. 1 Wæ ðæm ðerh ðone hia cymes. *c* **1000** *Fates 12 Apostles* 63 (Gr.) We þæt ȝehyrdon þurh haliȝe bec. **1154** *O.E. Chron.* an. 1132 (Laud), þurh Godes milce & þurh þe biscop of Seresberi. *c* **1200** ORMIN 13254 3a þurrh fullubht, ȝa þurrh hannd-gang Att hadedd manness hande. **1258** *Proclam. Hen. III* 12 Oct., Henry thurȝ godes fultome king on Engleneloande. *c* **1305** *Pilate* 89 in *E.E.P.* (1862) 113 He huld him bitrayd þurf felonie. **1375** BARBOUR *Bruce* I. 137 Throuch þar aller hale assent, Messingeris till hym þai sent. **1475** *Bk. Noblesse* (Roxb.) 16 A grete navy.. ovyrcom throw myghty fyghtyng. **1579** W. WILKINSON *Confut. Familye of Loue* B iij, Abell was slayne.. through the handes of his brother Cain. **1763** J. BROWN *Poetry & Mus.* vii. 151 This Event happened.. thro' the Authority of the thirty Tyrants. **1793** BURKE *Corr.* (1844) IV. 153 The answer given to Monsieur Lesardier was through a young gentleman. **1849** MACAULAY *Hist. Eng.* vi. II. 123 [He] could not prevent the national sentiment from expressing itself through the pulpit and the press. **1883** SIR N. LINDLEY in *Law Rep. 11 Q. Bench Div.* 572 The.. Society.. seeks to do through him that which it cannot otherwise do. **1885** *Act 48 & 49 Vict.* c. 53 §15 Every notice .. sent through the post in a prepaid registered letter.

†**b.** Indicating the agent, after a passive verb: = BY *prep.* 33. *Obs.*

a **900** tr. *Bæda's Hist.* I. ix, Seo herȝung wæs þurh Alaricum.. ȝeworden. **971** *Blickl. Hom.* 9 Heofonrices duru .. sceal þonne þurh þe ontened beon. *c* **1000** *Ags. Gosp.* Matt. xxvi. 24 Wa þam menn þurh þone þe byþ mannes sunu be-læwed. **13..** *Cursor M.* 20909 (Cott.) In rome throu an þat hight neron.. Petre.. naild on þe rod he was. **1424** *Sc. Acts Jas. I* (1814) II. 5/1 Chargit be þe gret aithe throwe þe bischope. *c* **1425** *Eng. Conq. Irel.* 12 Vnnethes he was I-draw vp throgh his felowes, þat mych put har lyf in aduentur for to saw his lif. **1597** A. M. tr. *Guillemeau's Fr. Chirurg.* 43 b/1 The skinne beinge lift vp through some seruant, or through the Chyrurgiane with his Pinsers.

8. a. Indicating cause, reason, or motive: In consequence of, by reason of, on account of, owing to; from; for.

a **1000** *Cædmon's Gen.* 610 (Gr.) þa se forhatena spræc þurh feondscipe. *c* **1000** *Ags. Gosp.* Matt. xxvi. 31 þurh þæs hyrdes sleȝe byð seo heord todræfed. **1154** *O.E. Chron.* an. 1127 (Laud), þet wes eall ðurh þone kyng Heanri. *c* **1200** *Trin. Coll. Hom.* 191 þurch onde com deað in to þe worelde. *c* **1460** *Oseney Regr.* 3 þe paralytyke man.. heled of our lorde .. þroughe þe beleve off theyme þat bare hym. **1562** *Aberdeen Kirk Sess. Rec.* (Spald. Cl.) 9 Gryte thyft, committit throcht verray neid and necessite. **1671** MILTON *Samson* 369 If he through frailty err. **1697** DRYDEN *Virg. Georg.* II. 638 Thro' Wine they quarrell'd, and thro' Wine were slain. **1798** COLERIDGE *Anc. Mar.* II. xiii, Every tongue thro' utter drouth Was wither'd at the root. **1894** J. J. FOWLER *Adamnan* Introd. 56 The southern Picts.. embraced the truth through the preaching of St. Ninian.

†**b.** In oaths and adjurations: By, in the name of. (Cf. BY *prep.* 2.) *Obs.*

a **1000** *Cædmon's Satan* 694 Ic þe hate þurh þa hehstan miht, þæt ðu hellwarum hyht ne abeode. *c* **1000** ÆLFRIC *Gen.* xxii. 16 Ic sweriȝe þurh me sylfne, sæde se Ælmihtiȝa. *a* **1225** *Ancr. R.* 114 þurh þeo ilke neiles ich halse ou ancren, .. holdeð our honden wiðinnen ouwer þurles. *c* **1290** *Edmund Conf.* 307 in *S. Eng. Leg.* I. 440 'þurf oure louerdes passioun tel nou', he seide.

II. *adv.*

(For special combinations with verbs, as BREAK *through*, CARRY *through*, FALL *through*, GET *through*, GO *through*, PASS *through*, PULL *through*, PUT *through*, RUN *through*, etc., see the verbs.)

1. a. From end to end, side to side, or surface to surface (of a body or space) by passing or extending within; so as to penetrate: cf. I. 1.

a **1000** *Ags. Ps.* (Th.) lxxvii[i]. 15 [13] He sæ toslat, sealte yþa ȝefæstnade, and hi foran þurh. *a* **1225** *Ancr. R.* 272 Heo þurh stihten Isboset.. into þe schere. *c* **1400** *Destr. Troy* 6780 Mony shalke þurgh shot with þere sharpe gere. **14..** *Tundale's Vis.* 327 þo heyte of the fuyr dyd throw pas. *c* **1460** METHAM *Wks.* (E.E.T.S.) 91 Als strekyn thourth with oon lyne or with many lynes. *a* **1533** LD. BERNERS *Huon* lix. 205 Huon.. strake hym with his spere clene throwe. **1719**

WATTS *Hymns* II. lix. 2 Glory to God that walks the sky, And sends his blessing thro'. **1798** COLERIDGE *Anc. Mar.* I. xvii, The Ice did split with a Thunder-fit; The Helmsman steer'd us thro'! **1850** LEITCH tr. *C. O. Müller's Anc. Art* (ed. 2) §337 A..garment..drawn..over the right arm, or else through beneath it towards the left arm.

b. In reference to travel or conveyance: Along the whole distance; all the way; to the end of the journey; to the destination.

[*a* **1425** *Cursor M.* 11741 (Trin.) Of þritty dayes Iourney þro þou shal haue but a day to go [*earlier MSS.* lang.. gang].] **1617** J. BARGRAVE in *Buccleuch MSS.* (Hist. MSS. Comm.) I. 198 His packets sometimes fail when private letters go through. **1692** LUTTRELL *Brief Rel.* (1857) II. 376 He was accompanied part of the way by the queen..and Essex, who went thro'. **1732** POPE *Ess. Man* II. 274 Hope travels thro', nor quits us when we die. **1858** *Penny Cycl.* 2nd Suppl. 565/2 A man may now 'book through' from London to so many continental cities. **1858** HAWTHORNE *Fr. & It. Note-bks.* (1872) I. 3 The great bulk of our luggage had been registered through to Paris. *Mod.* The train goes through to Edinburgh.

c. In reference to size: As measured from side to side; in diameter.

a **1687** PETTY *Treat. Naval Philos.* I. iv. §5 A Mast above 30 inches through.

2. From beginning to end (of a time, course of action, life, trial, book, etc.); to the end or purposed accomplishment: cf. I. 4, 5.

a **1175** *Cott. Hom.* 237 He wes acende of þe clene mede þe efer þurh lefede mede. **1456** SIR G. HAYE *Law Arms* (S.T.S.) 85 Traistand in God, and in his gude rycht to bring him throuch. **1556** *N.C. Wills* (Surtees 1908) 239 Iff he helpe my executors through for the making of my accompte with the King. **1611** SHAKS. *Cymb.* v. v. 382 When shall I heare all through? **1790** BURKE *Fr. Rev.* 133 Who now reads Bolinbroke? Who ever read him through? **1865** SWINBURNE *Chastelard* I. i. (1894) 9 She must weep If she sing through. **1891** *Law Times* XCII. 18/2 Having heard the case through and seen the witnesses.

3. Predicatively, after the verb *to be*, indicating a position, point, or condition ultimately arrived at. **a.** *lit.* Having penetrated or traversed a body or space. **b.** More usually *fig.* Having completed or accomplished an action or process (*spec.* having passed an examination); completed, as an action, etc.; finished, at an end, 'done'; defeated, having no further prospects, no longer friends or associates, outmoded, 'done for'. ***to be through with***, to have finished or completed; to have done with, have no further dealings with; to be tired of, to have had enough of; also, to have arranged matters or come to an agreement with (a person) (now *dial.*): cf. quot. *a* 1500 s.v. THOROUGH *a.* 2.

1481–90 *Howard Househ. Bks.* (Roxb.) 480 My Lord is throughe with his servaunt Robert Worsley, for certayn men ..to be ready at all tymes at my Lordes wages. **1597** SHAKS. *2 Hen. IV*, I. ii. 45 If a man is through with them in honest Taking-up, then they must stand vpon Securitie. **1607** —— *Cor.* II. iii. 130, I am halfe through, The one part suffered, the other will I doe. **1840** R. H. DANA *Bef. Mast* xix. 57 We had just so much work to do, and when that was through, the time was our own. **1849** THACKERAY *Pendennis* I. xxi. 196 'This man has passed,' he thought, 'and I have failed!' ..'Good bye, Spavin,' said he. 'I'm very glad you are through.' **1866** *Belgravia* Nov. 76 The examiners..are now consulting together as to who is 'through' and who is 'plucked'. **1869** *Lonsdale Gloss.*, *To be through with any one*, to complete a bargain with him. **1887** *Scribner's Mag.* May 622/2 He..then..scrawled a dash underneath. 'There! I'm through!' he said. **1896** *Daily News* 18 July 3/1 [He] did not arrive till the speech was half through. **1897** J. L. ALLEN *Choir Invisible* ii. 22, I was through with the lessons. **1901** K. STEUART *By Allan Water* ii. 63 All knew that James Steuart was 'far through' [= near the end of his life]. **1902** W. N. HARBEN *Abner Daniel* vii. 55, 'I don't understand you.' 'Well, you will before I'm through with you.' *a* **1912** *Mod.* I saw the train enter the tunnel; it must be through now. **1930** J. B. PRIESTLEY *Angel Pavement* x. 508 'You're through then, eh?' 'All I can do to-night, Mr Smeeth. One or two things I've had to leave till tomorrow morning.' **1931** H. F. PRINGLE *Theodore Roosevelt* I. iii. 37 He..was through with breakfast by 8.30. **1934** G. B. SHAW *On Rocks* II. 271 We were born into good society; and we are through with it: we have no illusions about it, even if we are fit for nothing better. **1939** I. BAIRD *Waste Heritage* ii. 23 Now when we get down to the hall we're through, see? I don't want nothin' more to do with you, I don't even know your name. **1942** E. PAUL *Narrow St.* xxxi. 281 An outsider not familiar with French politics might have thought that Daladier was through. Not at all. He got himself elected by the Popular Front..in April, 1938. **1956** B. HOLIDAY *Lady sings Blues* (1973) xix. 154 It was only a few weeks before, people had been telling me I was through in the United States, that the public would never accept me. **1969** A. LURIE *Real People* 108, I hope you don't think anyone who doesn't paint soda-pop bottles and stripes is through artistically. **1970** *Wall St. Jrnl.* 30 Mar. 1/1 An executive with two dependent children earning the equivalent of $24,000 a year is left with $14,300 ..after the Board of the Inland Revenue is through.

c. Of a telephone call or caller: connected.

1929 *Telegr. & Teleph. Jrnl.* XVI. 47/2 'You are through' (which is the English way of saying 'here is your party'). **1932** D. L. SAYERS *Have his Carcase* iii. 33 The grocer announced that Harriet's call was through... 'Hullo!' she said. **1954** F. P. KEYES *Royal Box* i. 14 Won't you ever learn that when an English operator asks you if you're 'through', she doesn't mean have you *finished*, she means have you got your connection all right? **1977** *Rolling Stone* 30 June 80/3 Directly getting Honolulu information, I got a number for Wiley Hampson and presently was through to him at his home in Hawaii Kai.

4. Qualifying adjs. and pa. pples.: Through the whole extent, substance, or thickness; throughout; hence, entirely, completely, thoroughly. †**a.** Standing before a pple. or adj.; = THOROUGH *adv.* 4. *Obs.*

Formerly often hyphened to the following word; cf. THROUGH- *in comb.* 1.

a **1240** [see THOROUGH B. II. 4]. *c* **1440** *Anc. Cookery* in *Househ. Ord.* (1790) 459 When thai byn thurgh hot, take hom up with a skymmour. **1472** in Swayne *Sarum Churchw. Acc.* (1896) 2, j playne Chalice with his patent both through gilte. **1578** LYTE *Dodoens* v. lxxx. 651 The grapes be through ripe in September. **1594** NASHE *Unfort. Trav.* 31 To haue him stand in the raine till he was through wet. **1596** DALRYMPLE tr. *Leslie's Hist. Scot.* (S.T.S.) I. 32 In wintir quhen thay ar throuch fatt. **1631** HEYWOOD *2nd Pt. Maid of West* III. i, Through satiate with the pleasures of this night. **1639** FULLER *Holy War* III. xxvi. (1647) 156 Once through-hot long in cooling. **1665** MANLEY *Grotius' Low C. Warres* 762 Materials being now through dry by the heat of the weather. [**1692–1853**: see THOROUGH B. II. 4.] **1901** HAYDEN *Round Our Vill.* 154 (E.D.D.) Come in, you must be through wet.

b. Now regularly after the adj. or pple., and only in reference to physical condition, as ***wet through*** (see also WET).

a **1766** MRS. F. SHERIDAN *Sidney Bidulph* IV. 53 He had been wet quite through. **1821** CLARE *Vill. Minstr.* I. 165 Thy..trunk is nearly rotten through. *c* **1825** *Houlston Juv. Tracts, Forethought* 3 It is of no use to put up your umbrella when you are wet through. **1892** G. HAKE *Mem. 80 Years* lxiii. 259 The natives get hot-through in the..spring and summer months. *Mod.* This is a cold room; I am chilled through. It is barely warmed through.

5. ***through and through***: **a.** With repeated or complete penetration; through the whole thickness or substance; completely from beginning to end; right through, entirely through.

1470–85 [see THOROUGH B. II. 5]. **1611** SHAKS. *Wint. T.* IV. iv. 112 You'ld be so leane, that blasts of Ianuary Would blow you through and through. *c* **1643** LD. HERBERT *Autobiog.* (1824) 19 The English shot her [the Spanish ship] through and through so often that she run herself aground. **1709** *Lond. Gaz.* No. 4521/2 Having our Ship's Sides in a great many places shot through and through. **1894** SIR J. ASTLEY *Fifty Yrs. Life* I. 166 We were all wet through and through.

b. In all points or respects; thoroughly, wholly, entirely, out and out.

c **1410** *Chron. Eng.* (Ritson) 554 An holi wommon thourh ant thourh. **1531** in Hall *Chron., Hen. VIII* (1548) 197 We ..searched and examined through and through..bothe the bookes of holy scripture, and also the moste approued interpreters of the same. **1600** SHAKS. *A.Y.L.* II. vii. 59, I will through and through Cleanse the foule bodie of th' infected world. **1746** FRANCIS tr. *Hor., Sat.* I. ix. 134 One who knew My sweet Companion through and through. **1888** RHYS *Hibbert Lect.* 458 The Thorsteinn story..not corresponding through and through to any of the Celtic ones. **1894** ROOSEVELT in *Forum* (N.Y.) July 557 They must act as Americans, through and through, in spirit and hope and purpose.

c. ***through-and-through sawing***, ***sawn*** = *plain sawing* vbl. sb., *plain-sawn* ppl. adj. s.v. PLAIN *a.*[1] and *adv.* C. c. Also ***through-and-through method***.

1966 [see *plain-sawn* ppl. adj. s.v. PLAIN *a.*[1] and *adv.* C. c]. **1963** *Gloss. Terms Timber* (*B.S.I.*) 14 *Through-and-through sawing*, a method of converting..logs by parallel cuts in the general direction of the grain. **1979** A. B. EMARY *Woodworking* i. 9 Most of the timber at a merchant's will be from logs cut by the through and through method.

6. After an auxiliary vb., with ellipsis of *go*, *get*, *pass*, etc., in *lit.* or *fig.* senses (see above); thus functioning as a verb in the infinitive. (See also THROUGH *v.* 2.)

1423 JAS. I *Kingis Q.* lxiii, Bot, hert! quhere as the body may noght throu, Folow thy hevin! *c* **1470** HENRYSON *Mor. Fab.* x. (*Fox & Wolf*) xiii, This will not throw, but greit coist and expence. **1573**, **1670** [see THOROUGH B. II. 6]. **1644** NYE *Gunnery* (1670) 20 If you cannot sift it through the sieve, beat that again into powder which will not through. **1906** MARJ. BOWEN *Viper of Milan* xxi, We must pass, we must through this moment.

through, obs. form of THROW, TROUGH.

through-, in combination. (See THOROUGH-.)

1. a. Combinations of THROUGH *prep.* or *adv.* with verbs (pples., vbl. sbs.), or adjs. Chiefly *Obs.*

In OE. *through* qualifying a verb stood before it regularly in the infinitive and participles, and usually in the finite vb. in subordinate clauses. In such cases there was a tendency for it to be written in comb., as in mod. German *durchgehen*, *durchgehend*, *durchwachsen*. In some words this tendency became stronger in ME., and the combined form was used also in the finite verb. For these see the Main words below. The following illustrate the process, without any attempt to be exhaustive:

†**through-'carve (-kerf)** *v.*, *trans.* to cut through; hence **through-carved** *ppl. a.*, see quot.; †**through-'cast** *v.* [CAST *v.* 57], *trans.* to plaster throughout; **through-com'posed** *pa. pple.* and *ppl. a.* = DURCH-KOMPONIERT *a.*; †**through-'cut** *v.*, *trans.* to cut through, perforate by cutting; †**through-'drive** *v.*, *trans.* to drive a nail or spike through, to transfix; †**through-'ficche (thurghe-fyche)** *v.* [FICCHE *v.*], *trans.* to pierce through, transfix; †**'through-,formed** *ppl. a.*, thoroughly formed, full-grown; †**through-'galled** *pa. pple.* [GALL *v.*[1] 5], thoroughly harassed or disabled; †**through-handling**, management of details; carrying through; transaction; †**through-lanced** *pa. pple.*, pierced as with a lance, transfixed; †**through-look** *v.*, *trans.* to look through, examine thoroughly; †**through-nailed** *pa. pple.*, transfixed with nails; †**through-nim** *v.*, *trans.* to 'run through', transfix; *fig.* to penetrate; †**through-pierce (thorough-pierce)** *v.*, *trans.* to pierce through, transfix; hence ***through-***, ***thorough-piercing*** ppl. adj.; †**through-ride (thorough-ride)** *v.*, (*a*) *trans.* to ride through, make a raid through (cf. RIDE *v.* 2); (*b*) *intr.* to penetrate through (cf. RIDE *v.* 9); †**through-rive** *v.* (*pa. t.* **þurh-raf**) [RIVE *v.*], *trans.* to rive or tear through; †**through-run** (thurh-'ærn) *v.*, *trans.* to overrun; †**through-shed (þurȝsched)** *v.* (L. *perfundere*), *trans.* to suffuse; †**through-'shoot** (*pa. t.* **þurh-**, **þorȝschote**) *v.*, *trans.* to shoot through, pierce through; †**through-shove** *v.* (*pa. pple.* **þurgh-shove**), *trans.* to thrust through, transfix; †**through-'swim** *v.*, *trans.* to swim through; †**through-'thrilled** *pa. pple.*, pierced through; *fig.* thrilled through; †**through-'waxen** *pa. pple.* [*waxen*, pa. pple. of WAX *v.*], grown over; †**through-'won** *v.* [OE. *þurh-wunian*: see WON *v.*], *intr.* to abide, continue, or remain through; †**through-'wound** *v.*, *trans.* to wound through or deeply. See also THROUGH-BEARING, THROUGH-GO, etc. **b.** with adjectives: †**through-old** *a*, extremely old; antiquated; †**'through-wet** *a.*, wetted or wet through, saturated with moisture.

c **1330** *Arth. & Merl.* (Kölbing) 8141 Stel & yren his ax *þurchcarf Wher þurch mani starf. **1875** PARKER *Gloss. Archit.*, *Through Carved-work*,..in which the spaces between the ornamental parts are pierced entirely through. **1611** in Willis & Clark *Cambridge* (1886) II. 112 The whole passage to be *throughecast with lime and haire. **1884** F. NIECKS *Conc. Dict. Mus. Terms* 122 A durch-componiertes Lied, 'a *through-composed song', is a song of which each verse has a setting of its own. **1947** A. EINSTEIN *Music in Romantic Era* x. 117 In this prologue there is no longer any spoken dialogue; the scene is 'through-composed'. **1962** *Listener* 11 Jan. 105/2 The opera opens with a Prologue of the spirits..which is the only 'through-composed' portion. **1981** *Times Lit. Suppl.* 20 Feb. 203/2 The first 'Razumovsky' [Quartet]..abandoned the normal first-movement repeat, had the rarity of a through-composed scherzo (without trio or 'da capo'), and only repeated the exposition of the finale. *c* **1330** *Arth. & Merl.* 9286 Ich of hem on [o]þer hitt, Oþer heued ofsmot or bodi *þurch kitt. **1594** PLAT *Jewell-ho.* III. 34 How to graue any..deuise vpon an egge shel, & how to through-cut the same. *a* **1023** WULFSTAN *Hom.* iii. (Napier) 22 Him æȝðer *þurhdraf mid isenum næȝlum ȝe fet ȝe handa. *a* **1225** *Leg. Kath.* 1204 þurhdriuen upon þe rode. *Ibid.* 1943, & let þurhdriuen..þe spaken & te felien Mid irnene gadien. *c* **1340** HAMPOLE *Prose Tr.* 2 It has *thurghefychede my herte. **1664** H. MORE *Myst. Iniq.* Apol. 542 Who are so *through-formed Christians as cordially to believe all the Essential Parts of our Religion. **1594** KYD *Cornelia* v. 308 Scipio that saw his ships *through-galled, And by the foe fulfild with fire and blood. *a* **1586** SIDNEY *Arcadia* (1622) 177 (Skimming any thing that came before him) [He] was disciplined to leaue the *through-handling of all to his gentle wife. **1594** SPENSER *Amoretti* lvii, Seeing my hart *through-launced every where With thousand arrowes, which your eies have shot. *c* **1200** ORMIN Ded. 68, & te bitæche icc off þiss boc,..All to þurrhsekenn illc an ferrs, & to *þurrhlokenn offte. **1446** LYDG. *Two Nightingale P.* ii. 240 *Thurgh-nayled weren his holy handis tweyne. *c* **1205** LAY. 14711 Catiger þer com & mid his spere hine *þurh-nom. **1390** GOWER *Conf.* II. 249 Into wepinge Sche fell, as sche that was thurgh nome With love. **1639** FULLER *Holy War* II. xliv. (1647) 103 Then must he be a *through-old man. *Ibid.* v. xxix. 281 What credit there is to be given to that through-old if not doting prophecie. *c* **1330** *Arth. & Merl.* 7936, & wiþ gode hert & main fin þai *þurchperced þo Sarrazin. **1413** *Pilgr. Sowle* (Caxton) I. xiv. (1859) 11 Grete drede and heuynesse had thorughpercyd my herte. **1590** SPENSER *F.Q.* II. i. 38 Her tender hart was rent in twaine, Or thrild with point of thorough-piercing paine. **1609** HEYWOOD *Brit. Troy* XIV. xxv, Quite through-piercst the Greeke dropt down a corse. *c* **1205** LAY. 18082 He..smat hine i þere side þat þat spere *þurh-rade [*c* **1275** þorh-rod]. *c* **1330** R. BRUNNE *Chron. Wace* (Rolls) 14516 þat alle landes he wolde þorow ryde.. Cristen men to struye & quelle. *c* **1400** *Destr. Troy* 5008 Thy ..Rewme þurgh Riden, robbed þi goodis. *c* **1205** LAY. 23943 [He] smat i þere breoste þat þat spere *þurh raf [*c* **1275** þorh rof]. *Ibid.* 12129 þat lond heo *þurh arnden & herȝeden. *Ibid.* 16657 þat lond heo gunne þurh-ærnen & þa tunes fur-bernen. **1382** WYCLIF *Esther* xv. 8 She forsothe *thurȝshed [*Vulg.* perfusa] the chere with rose colour. **971** *Blickl. Hom.* 109 þonne he his byrnsweord ȝetyhþ & þas world ealle þurhslyhþ, & þa lichoman *þurh sceoteð. *c* **1330** R. BRUNNE *Chron. Wace* (Rolls) 4373 þer schaftes þorgh schoten body & schelde. *c* **1330** *Arth. & Merl.* 7959 þer was mani wombe *þurchschoue & mani heued cleued aboue. *c* **1420** *26 Pol. Poems* xvii. 189 His herte was wiþ a spere þurgh-shoue. **1615** CHAPMAN *Odyss.* VII. 384, I yet *through-swomme the waues, that your shore binds. *a* **1631** DONNE *Progr. Soule* xxvii, The net through-swome, she kept the liquid Path. **1605** SYLVESTER *Du Bartas* II. iii. I. *Vocation* 375 With our Swords and Lances..*Through-thrillèd (Villains) this shall be your last. **1608** *Ibid.* iv. IV. *Decay* 322 My heart's through-thrilled with your miseries. *c* **1205** LAY. 18338 Wes þe munt *þurh-wexen [*c* **1275** þorh-woxe] Mid ane wude feiren. **1583** T. WATSON *Centurie of Loue* xci, Then, hang your *throughwett garmentes on the wall. *c* **1000** *Ags. Gosp.* Matt. xxiv. 13 Witodlice seþe *þurhwunað oð ende, se byþ hal. *a* **1175** *Cott. Hom.* 227 þaða hire time com hi acennede and þurh-wunede meden. *c* **1205** LAY. 1384 An lond he ferde sechinde þer he mihte þurh-wunian Mid his wnfolke. *a* **1225** *Leg. Kath.* 662 þe wið godd hehfeder, & wið þen hali gast, þurhwunest in alre worlde world. *c* **1200** ORMIN 17443 þa neddress . . þeȝȝ tacnenn alle sinness, þatt stingenn & *þurrh-wundenn all þatt bodiȝ, & tatt sawle.

2. Combinations with sbs: (some could equally well be placed s.v. THROUGH *a.*)

'through-,arch *Archit.* (also *attrib.*), see quot.; **'through-ball** *Assoc. Football*, etc., a forward pass which goes through the other team's defensive formation; **'through-,blow**, a blowing or current of air passing through; **'through-,bolt** (**thorough-bolt**), a bolt passing through the objects fastened by it, and secured at each end; † **'through-,cold**, a penetrating or deep-seated cold or chill; **through deck**, a flight deck which runs the full length of a ship; **'through-deck 'cruiser**, a type of lightly-armed aircraft-carrier (see quots.); **'through-draught**: see *thorough-draught* s.v. THOROUGH- 2; **'through-fang** [FANG *sb.* 6 a] = *through-tang*; † **'through-,fast** [FAST *sb.*[1] 1], a fast all through a period, e.g. the fast of Lent; **'through-feed**, in centreless grinding, movement of the work-piece right through the space between the two wheels (cf. IN-FEED); also *attrib.*; **'throughflow**, the flowing of a fluid, air, etc., through something; also *attrib.*; **'through-joint**, a joint passing through the thickness of something; **'through-key** [KEY *sb.*[1] 9], a key or pin fitting into a hole which passes right through the parts to be fastened by it; † **'through-lock** (?): see quot.; **through-lounge** (stress variable): in a private house, a lounge that extends from the front to the back of the house; **'through-,mortise**, a mortise cut right through the timber; **'through-pass** = *through-ball* above; † **'through-,path**, a path or way through something; **'through-rod**, a rod passing or extending through or from end to end of some structure or piece of mechanism; † **through-serewe**, † **-spavin**, † **-splint**, names of diseases of the leg of the horse; see quots. and SEREWE, SPAVIN, SPLINT; also cf. THOROUGH-PIN; **'through-tang**, a method of hafting knives, forks, etc. by inserting the tang in a hole drilled right through the handle and riveting it at the end; **'through-valley** (see quot. 1972); **'through-work**, work extending through the thickness, or occupying the whole breadth of, some structure. See also THROUGH-STONE[2].

a **1878** SIR G. G. SCOTT *Lect. Archit.* I. vii. 283 The two systems may be distinguished as rere-arch windows and *through-arch windows—i.e., those in which the inner is distinct from the outer arch, and those in which the same arch runs through the wall, showing itself more or less similarly on its outer and inner faces. In thick walls and rich work there is often another order of through-arch within the tracery order, or rather the outer order re-appears within. **1969** *Punch* 12 Feb. 248/4, I wish I could recall the lingo —the *through-balls, high crosses, work-rates and searching diagonals. **1977** *Times* 28 Feb. 8/5 Another through ball and Souness was racing away to make a cross which Armstrong converted. **1908** *Times* 29 Dec. 4/5 No airing or '*through-blow' is possible in a . . flat where the openings are all on one side. **1837** *Civil Eng. & Arch. Jrnl.* I. 33/1 The outer and inner rows of piling . . are to be securely tied together, with two-inch wrought-iron *through bolts. **1864** *Daily Tel.* 19 Aug., The use of large-area solid plates [in ship-building], in combination with through bolts. **1874** KNIGHT *Dict. Mech.* s.v. *Bolt*, A *through-bolt* is one which goes through the pieces which are to be fastened together. Such are clinch-bolts, and bolts secured by nut and washer. **1601** HOLLAND *Pliny* (1634) II. 289 In drink, it dissolueth ventosities, riddeth away *through-colds, and namely the shiuerings . . in cold agues. **1969** *Times* 30 Oct. 2/7 Such an aircraft . . would be operated from a cruiser-type ship with a newly designed '*through-deck'. **1971** *Guardian* 22 Nov. 12/4 The Royal Navy is now considering the operation of Harriers from a new class of flat topped 19,000-ton ships euphemistically known as '*Through-deck cruisers'. **1980** A. PRESTON *Warships of World* 29/2 The troubled political background accounts for the ludicrous nomenclature applied to the class. First of all *Invincible* was a 'through-deck' cruiser to disguise the flight deck, then a command cruiser, and only now . . an aircraft carrier. *Ibid.* 221/2 *Through-deck cruiser*, cumbersome term concocted by the Royal Navy to obtain political and Treasury approval for a ship designed to operate helicopters and V/Stol aircraft. The 'through-deck' was a euphemism for a full-length flight deck. **1905** *Through-draught [see *thorough-draught* s.v. THOROUGH- 2]. **1976** B. LECOMBER *Dead Weight* vi. 73, I . . opened the pilots' side-windows in the pious hope of creating a through-draught of fresh air. **1851–4** TOMLINSON *Cycl. Arts* (1866) I. 487/2 A very good method is what is called *through-fang*, that is, to drill a hole completely through the handle, and to insert a . . prong projecting from the blade, riveting it at the opposite end. **1652** FULLER *Comm. Christ's Tempt.* ii. in *Sel. Rem.* (1891) II. 26 'He had fasted forty days and forty nights.' The words contain the *through-fast of Christ. **1937** COLVIN & STANLEY *Grinding Pract.* v. 73 There are two primary methods of grinding the work. One is the *through-feed method in which the work passes axially from one side of the machine to the other. **1963** JONES & SCHUBERT *Engin. Encycl.* 215 There are three general methods of centerless grinding which may be described as through-feed, in-feed, and end-feed methods. **1967** M. E. HALE *Biol. Lichens* vii. 96 Stemflow on trees . . has been shown to be enriched, relative to *throughflow, with potassium and calcium. **1974** *Country Life* 17 Jan. 103/1, 2 litre family saloon . . throughflow heating and ventilation. **1862** *Catal. Internat. Exhib.* II. x. 53 The *through-joints admit wet into the interior. **1548** *Acc. Ld. High Treas. Scot.* IX. 167 Thre gret *throuch lokes to the palice of Halyrudhous. **1962** JACKSON & MARSDEN *Educ. & Working Class* v. 157 The interview took place in the *through-lounge. **1976** *Evening Post* (Nottingham) 15 Dec. 15/5 (Advt.), Modern well situated detached house consisting of through lounge, fully fitted kitchen, [etc.]. **1937** F. N. S. CREEK *Association Football* iii. 58 Short passing should always consist of '*through' passes so that the ball is sent behind an opponent and never . . across his front. **1967** J. POTTER *Foul Play* (1968) ii. 29 If you're playing on the left wing I'll feed you with through-passes to the corner flag. **1976** *Denbighshire Free Press* 8 Dec. 24/7 Ian McCarter . . got to a splendid through pass from Wildermuth. **1632–5** CORBET *Sp. in aid St. Paul's* in Longman *Three Cathedrals* (1873) 60 Are we not beholding to it . . for a prayer or a *throwpath? **1523** FITZHERB. *Husb.* §96 Some horses haue a *throughe serewe on bothe sydes of the legge. *Ibid.* §106 Some horses haue *throughe spauen, and appereth bothe within and without. **1565** BLUNDEVIL *Horsemanship* IV. cxxvii. (1580) 58 Of the wet Spauen, or through Spauen. This is a soft swelling growing on both sides of the hough, and seemes to go cleane through the hough, and therefore may be called a through Spauen. **1607** TOPSELL *Four-f. Beasts* 401 A Splent is a sorance of the least moment, vnlesse it bee on the knee, or else a *through Splent, both which cannot bee cured. **1687** MIÉGE *Gt. Fr. Dict.* I, *Sur-os chevillé*, serew or through-splent. **1833** J. HOLLAND *Manuf. Metal* II. 14 Hafting table knives by the insertion of that portion of the blade which has been properly drawn out, quite through the handle . . is called *through-tang*. **1905** *Bull. Geol. Soc. Amer.* XVI. 233 In discussing this paper at the Geological Society meeting in Philadelphia, Professor Davis applied the very descriptive name of '*through valleys' to this condition of valleys connected across lowered divides. **1969** G. C. DICKINSON *Maps & Air Photographs* xiii. 208 A valley from one system may meet one from another system 'back-to-back' so that together they form a through valley with scarcely any feature separating the headwaters of the two systems. **1972** *Gloss. Geol.* (Amer. Geol. Inst.) 739/1 *Through valley*, a flat-floored depression or channel eroded across a divide by glacier ice or meltwater streams. **1686** PLOT *Staffordsh.* 384 He also cuts wreath'd pillars with the same Engine (that are not *through-work).

through-band: see *thorough-band* s.v. THOROUGH- 2.

'through-bear, *v. Sc.* [BEAR *v.*[1] II.] *trans.* To maintain, support. Hence **'through-bearing** *vbl. sb.* **a.** Support through (life), livelihood, maintenance. **b.** Supporting, upholding, maintaining (a cause).

1680 D. HACKSTON *Let.* 25 July in *Cloud Witnesses* (1871) 45 He will perfect His work in me and by me, either to a remarkable delivery, or through-bearing (*i.e.* upholding) me as He sees most for His own glory. **1730** T. BOSTON *Mem.* vii. (1899) 151 God would provide things necessary for our through-bearing. **1786** A. GIB *Sacr. Contempl.* 296 It secures all the outward through-bearing, preservation and protection, leading and guiding. **1813** CHALMERS *Let.* 12 Oct. in *Life* (1850) I. xii. 343 A day of mortification. Everything went against us by the through-bearing of the opposite party. **1857** A. WALLACE *Gloaming of Life* i. (1875) 3 She opened a small shop as the means of securing an honest throughbearing.

through-bred: see THOROUGHBRED.

through-cast to **-drive**: see THROUGH-.

through-draught: see *thorough-draught* s.v. THOROUGH- 2.

throughe, obs. f. THROW *v.*

througher ('θru:ə(r)). *Coal-mining.* [f. THROUGH *prep.* or *adv.* + -ER[1].] (See quots.)

1797 *Encycl. Brit.* (ed. 3) V. 101/1 The workings called *rooms* . . of the width of 12 feet; . . the workings called *throughers or thirlings*, 9 feet wide, wrought through at right angles from one room to another. **1883** GRESLEY *Gloss. Terms Coal Mining, Througher*, . . a thirl put through between two headings which are up-stoop.

through-fang to **-galled**: see THROUGH-.

through-fare, etc., see THOROUGHFARE, etc.

'through-gang, *sb. Sc. Obs.* or *rare.* [GANG *sb.* 4.] A way or road through; a passage; sometimes = thoroughfare.

1463 *Burgh Rec. Edinb.* (1869) I. 22 The througang is set to William Met for 8 s., on his own security. **1513** DOUGLAS *Æneis* II. viii. 80 Secrete throwgangs are schawin. **1587** *Reg. Privy Council Scot.* IV. 205 In the portche or throw-gang of the said West Kirk dure. **1862** G. HENDERSON *Matt. in Lowland Scotch* vi. 2 (E.D.D.) Dinna toot a trumpet afore thee, as the hypocrites do in the throwgangs.

b. *attrib.* or *adj.* Allowing passage through.

1523 *Acc. Ld. High Treas. Scot.* V. 220 For ane band to the throuchgang windo of the quenis chalmer. **1808** JAMIESON s.v., *A throwgang close* is an open passage, by which one may go from one street to another, as opposed to a blind alley.

So † **through-'gang** *v.*, *Sc. trans.* to go through, to traverse. **'through-ganging** (also **throwgaan'**) *a.*, that goes through any amount of work, active, energetic, thoroughgoing.

c **1000** *Ags. Ps.* (Th.) xc[i]. 6 Ne forhtast þu ðe on dæʒe flan on lyfte, þæt þu þuruh gangan garas on ðeostrum. *c* **1205** LAY. 1207 ȝif ich þat lond mai bi-ȝeten & mi folc hit þurh-gengen [*c* **1275** þorh-genge]. **1814** SCOTT *Wav.* xxxix, Ye . . should ken a horse's points; ye see that through-ganging thing that Balmawhapple's on. **1825** JAMIESON, *Through-ganging*, active, having a great deal of action; a term used by jockeys.

† **through-'gird**, *v. Obs.* [GIRD *v.*[2]] *trans.* To strike through, smite through, pierce with a cut or blow.

c **1386** CHAUCER *Knt.'s T.* 152 Thurgh girt with many a greuous blody wounde. *c* **1430** *Syr Gener.* (Roxb.) 5764 The king supposed . . Generides he had thurgh girt. **1513** DOUGLAS *Æneis* II. viii. [vii.] 118 Hypanis eik, and Dymas . . War by thair fallowis throw gird baith twa. **1573** TWYNE *Æneid* x. Ee iij, Then Pallas soone Sir Rhoeteus . . Through-girdes. *c* **1594** KYD *Sp. Trag.* IV. iv, Where hanging on a tree I found my sonne, Through girt with wounds.

† **through-'go**, *v. Obs.* [OE. *þurhgán*, pa. t. *þurhéode*, f. *þurh* adv. THROUGH + *gán* to GO (cf. OHG. *durhgân*).] *trans.* To go through, pass through, traverse.

c **1000** *Pop. Treat. Sci.* (1841) 9 Seo eorðe byð mid þam winterlicum cyle þurh-gan. *c* **1000** ÆLFRIC *Hom.* II. 502 Ic wille ðurhgan orsorh ðone here. *c* **1200** ORMIN 12860 þurrh þatt teȝȝ shollden all þurrh gan þiss middellærd to spellenn Off himm. *a* **1300** *E.E. Psalter* civ. [cv.] 18 Irne thurghyhode his saule ful grim. *a* **1400** *Isumbras* 522 That alle a syde of a cunntre he hase thurgh gane.

So **'throughgoing** *vbl. sb.*, passing through; a going through accounts, a taking to task; **'throughgoing** (*Sc.* **throwgaun**) *ppl. a.*, that goes or passes through; that goes through any amount of work, pushing, active, strenuous: cf. THOROUGHGOING.

1818 SCOTT *Rob Roy* xiv, The folk . . gae him sic an awfu' throughgaun about his rinnin' awa. **1820** *Blackw. Mag.* Dec. 265/1 A plump and jocose little woman; gleg, blithe, and throwgaun for her years. **1822** GALT *Provost* xxxiii, Those mighty masses of foreign commodities, the through-going of which left . . 'goud in goupins'. **1841** *Penny Cycl.* XIX. 254/2 In the Dublin and Kingstown railway an attempt was made to ensure increased solidity by introducing *throughgoing* stone blocks . . of granite, six feet long, . . stretched across the track. **1910** N. MUNRO in *Blackw. Mag.* Oct. 529/2 Maurice met her . . in a through-going close.

through-handling to **-look**: see THROUGH-.

† **through-light** ('θru:laɪt), *sb.* and *a. Obs.* **a.** *sb.*: see THOROUGH-LIGHT. **b.** *adj.* That lets light through; transparent. So **through-lighted**: see THOROUGH-LIGHTED.

1601 DONNE *Progr. Soul* Epist., If any coulors can deliver a minde so plaine and flatt and through-light as mine. **1612** —— *Funeral Elegy* 61 'Twas but a through-light scarfe, her mind t'enroule.

throughly ('θru:lɪ), *adv. arch.* [f. THROUGH *adv.* or *adj.* + -LY[2]. See also THOROUGHLY.]

1. Fully, completely, perfectly; = THOROUGHLY 2.

c **1440** *Generydes* 346, I prae yow . . That ye will . . teche hym throughely That att longith to hym to do. **1490** CAXTON *Eneydos* xxviii. 108 Lete vs loke to her wounde, and in her face, yf she is thrughly passed [gone, dead]. **1560** BIBLE (Genev.) *Ps.* li. 2 Wash me throughly from mine iniquitie. **1563** WINȜET *Four Scoir Thre Quest.* Wks. (S.T.S.) I. 68 Nocht throuchlie vnderstanding zour doctrine. **1596** SHAKS. *Merch. V.* IV. i. 173, I am enformed throughly of the cause. **1660** BOYLE *New Exp. Phys. Mech.* xi. 78 Throughly kindled Wood-coals. **1712** STEELE *Spect.* No. 264 ¶2 Throughly equipped from Head to Foot. *a* **1850** ROSSETTI *Dante & Circ.* I. (1874) 85 Mine inmost being then feels throughly quit Of anguish. **1885** DIXON *Hist. Ch. Eng.* III. 451 Hooper . . swept his unfortunate garner so throughly.

2. Through the whole thickness, substance, or extent; through, throughout, all through, quite through. *arch.*, *poet.*

1541 *Act 33 Hen. VIII*, c. 18 The kerseyes thereof made cannot be so certenly wroughte as the same . . myght kepe any true or just certentye of lenghe or breadeth throughlye. **1577** HARRISON *England* II. vi. (1877) I. 156 Barleie . . steeped in a cesterne . . vntill it be throughlie soked. **1603** OWEN *Pembrokeshire* (1892) 93 Being thus dried throwlie. **1634** SIR T. HERBERT *Trav.* 150 When tis throughly tosted . . they eat it. **1677** MOXON *Mech. Exerc.* i. 10 If it be not throughly welded at the first Heat. **1872** TENNYSON *Gareth & Lyn.* 1371 Then with a stronger buffet he clove the helm As throughly as the skull.

† **b.** Through, from beginning to end; for the whole length or time; all through. *Obs.*

1563 FOXE *A. & M.* 807 He was not throughly presente at the Byshoppes sermon. *c* **1590** MARLOWE *Faust.* vi. 189 Take this book; peruse it throughly. **1692** E. WALKER *Epictetus' Mor.* x, Thou hast but begun The glorious Race, nor hast it throughly run.

through-mortise to **-old**: see THROUGH-.

'through ,other, **'through-other**, *adv. phr.* and *adj.* Chiefly *Sc.* Also 6 throuch(e vther, 7 thorough other, 8–9 throw ither, throwither, thro'ither; throwther, throu'ther, 9 throuther; also 7 through others, 9 throughther, through-others. [f. THROUGH *prep.* + OTHER B. 8: i.e. 'through each other'. Cf. Ger. *durcheinander*.]

1. *adv. phr.* (Mingled) through each other or one another; promiscuously; indiscriminately; in disorder.

1596 DALRYMPLE tr. *Leslie's Hist. Scot.* x. (S.T.S.) II. 301 Captiues war numberit al throuch vther [L. *plus minus*] a thousand. **1632** LITHGOW *Trav.* III. 85 Figges, Orenges, Lemmons, . . growing all through other. **1637** MONRO *Exped.* I. 11 Having beene divers times Pell mel through others. **1637** RUTHERFORD *Lett.* (1862) I. 317 Hope and love, woven through other. *a* **1653** BINNING *Heart Humil.* xviii. Wks. (1735) 622/1 Sin and Judgment mixed in thorow other. **1768** ROSS *Helenore* II. 80 When she saw things had taken sick a cast, An' sae thro' ither warpl'd were. **1786** BURNS *Earnest Cry & Prayer* Postscr. iii, Till skelp—a shot—they're aff, a' throwther, To save their skin. **1818** SCOTT *Hrt. Midl.* xvi, They were a' speaking and gabbling through other.

2. a. In predicative use: Mingled or mixed up; in a medley; in confusion, in disorder. (In quot. 1630, Mixed up intimately.)

1630 RUTHERFORD *Lett.* (1862) I. 52 O sweet communion, when Christ and we are through other and are no longer two! **1855** RUSKIN *Let.* in Collingwood *Life* (ed. 5) 159 With all the pages through-other and backside foremost. **1865** *Church Times* 25 Nov., Everything..is opened and dragged out, shirts and books,..clothes and letters, all topsy-turvy, and (to use that most expressive Scotch adjective) 'through-other'. **1894** HALL CAINE *Manxman* v. i, A face..like a ghose's, and his hair all through-others. *a* **1889** G. M. HOPKINS *Poems* (1967) 97 For earth her being has unbound; her dapple is at an end, astray or aswarm, all throughther, in throngs.

b. *adj.* (in attrib. use). Confused, disorderly.

1720 *Wodrow Corr.* (1843) II. 492 About half an hour after I despatched mine to you,..my rude and through-other draught.

3. Of persons or their attributes (*pred.* or *attrib.*): Disorderly; wild, reckless; disordered.

1813 PICKEN *Poems* I. 62 (Jam.) Weel, tho' he was so sadly throu'ther, Since than he ne'er leuk'd o'er his shouther. **1853** *Whistle-Binkie* Ser. II. 10 He was idle and thro'ither, and drucken an' a'. **1863** J. BROWN *Horæ Subs.* (1882) 320 Leading a wild throughother life. **1880** *Jamieson's Dict.* s.v. *Through-ither*, Also used as an adj., implying rash, reckless, rattling; as, 'She's a wild, throwither lassie', *Clydes[dale]. Mod.* (*Sc.*, *Roxb.*) She was a very willing servant, but oh, so throwother! no sense o' order.

throughout (θruːˈaʊt), *prep.*, *adv.*, *adj.* ME. forms (more than 70) in **þurh, þuruh, þurgh, þurȝe, þurf, þoru, þorw, þoruȝ, þorȝ, þorȝe, þorou, þorow(e, thairgh, thurf, thorgh, thorow, thorough, thorrow, thru, thro, throw,** etc. with **út(e, out(e, owt(e,** etc.; also contr. 2 **þurut,** 5 **þrowte, throute,** 5–6 **thorowte, throwt,** etc. A prevalent form in 6–7 was **thorow-out; through-out** noted first in 6. Also (chiefly *N. Amer.*) **thruout, thru-out** (see *thru* s.v. THROUGH *prep.* and *adv.* A. *β*). [In OE. two words, *þurh* THROUGH, *út* OUT, later gradually combined or hyphened. Cf. Ger. *durchaus* (16th c. in Grimm).]

A. *prep.* † **1.** Through and out at the other side; completely or right through (a material body, or a place); sometimes simply = THROUGH *prep.* 1, 2. *Obs.* (or *arch.*).

c **1066** *O.E. Chron.* an. 1066 (MS. C.), He for þurhut Eoferwic. *c* **1205** LAY. 315 He..ihitte his aȝene fader þurh ut þere broste. *c* **1305** *St. Lucy* 151 in *E.E.P.* (1862) 105 Þo heo [St. Lucy] was þurfout þe þrote ismyte þe bet heo spac ynouȝ. **13..** *Cursor M.* 1036 (Cott.) Þis flummes four.. Thoru out all oþer contres rinnes. *c* **1380** *Sir Ferumb.* 4558 As liȝtliche as hit had ibeo wax, ran þe strok þanne of ys ax Chayne & tre þorȝoute. *c* **1400** MAUNDEV. (1839) v. 41 The Ryuere of Euphrate ran þorgh out the cytee. *c* **1420** *Anturs of Arth.* 315 (Thornton MS.) Me buse wende one my waye, thorowte this wode. *c* **1470** HENRY *Wallace* II. 56 Throuch oute the thikest of the pres he ȝeid. **1513** DOUGLAS *Æneis* VI. i. 121 The cald dreid..Thirland throwout hard banis. *c* **1614** MURE *Dido & Æneas* I. 153 Throughout the streets her hurling chariots roll. **1629** WADSWORTH *Pilgr.* iv. 35 [He] gaue vs two broad sides.., shooting..our ships through, and through out.

2. a. Through the whole of (a space, region, etc.); in or to every part of; everywhere in. (Cf. THROUGH *prep.* 3.)

† ***throughout all thing*** (quot. *c* 1380), in all points: = *through all thing* (THROUGH *prep.* 3 c).

c **1205** LAY. 29537 Þa iwende seint Austin vorð..þurh ut Englelond. **1297** R. GLOUC. (Rolls) 8589 Þoru out al þat lond it [the wind] dude sorwe inou. **1340** HAMPOLE *Pr. Consc.* 4359 Thurgh-out þe world, ferre and nere. *c* **1380** *Sir Ferumb.* 1500 Wel y-armed þorw-out al þyng euerechone þey ware. **1399** LANGL. *Rich. Redeles* II. 5 So ryff as þey ronne ȝoure rewme þoru-oute. *c* **1440** *R. Gloucester's Chron.* 6901 (MS. δ) Throute al þe londe sone þys word drou. **1558** WARDE tr. *Alexis' Secr.* (1568) 40 b, That great and vehement plague in the yere 1348 which crepte thorowe oute all the worlde. **1583** STUBBES *Anat. Abus.* II. (1882) 21 In euery parish through-out the Realme. **1599** CHAPMAN *Hum. Dayes Myrth* Plays 1873 I. 51 Yet hath the morning sprinckled throwt the clowdes, But halfe her tincture. **1674** BREVINT *Saul at Endor* 247 Thro-out all the Catholic Countries. **1783** HAILES *Antiq. Chr. Ch.* ii. 31 The Jews throughout the empire. **1883** GILMOUR *Mongols* xviii. 213 Throughout the length and breadth of the country. **1922** *Proc. IRE* X. 260 During the past winter an amateur spark station located at Cleveland, Ohio..was received nightly at Yonkers, New York..with sufficient intensity to enable the signals to be read thruout the room.

b. Through or during the whole of (a period of time or course of action); from beginning to end of. (Cf. THROUGH *prep.* 4, 5.)

c **1540** *Pilgr. T.* 195 in *Thynne's Animadv.* (1875) App. i. 82 And so thorow-out the hole story. **1591** SHAKS. *1 Hen. VI*, I. i. 42 Ne're throughout the yeere to Church thou go'st. **1641** MILTON *Church Govt.* I. i, There is not that thing in the world of more..urgent importance throughout the whole life of man, than is discipline. *a* **1672** WOOD *Life* 3 May an. 1661 (O.H.S.) I. 393 A. W...was present throut all the transactions. **1709** STEELE *Tatler* No. 78 ¶8 Hippocrates, who visited me throughout my whole Illness. **1799** NELSON in Nicolas *Disp.* (1845) III. 307 Throughout my command in the Levant seas. **1868** FREEMAN *Norm. Conq.* II. vii. 78 Harold and Swegen.., by their invasion of Denmark, gave him full occupation throughout the year.

† **3.** By means of, by the action of, by, from: = THROUGH *prep.* 7–8. *Obs. rare.*

a **1240** *Wohunge* in *Cott. Hom.* 271 Ich hit rewli fordide þurh-hut mine sunnes. **13..** *Cursor M.* 16317 (Cott.) Sai me nu qui þou ert als prisun tan, Thoruut þis biscop and his men? *c* **1400** *Rom. Rose* 3489 Thurghout my deming outerly, Than had he knowlege certeinly, That Love me ladde in sich a wyse.

B. *adv.*

† **1. a.** Right through, quite through, so as to penetrate completely. *Obs.*

c **1000** ÆLFRIC *Saints' Lives* xii. 55 Swa þæt þæt spere him eode þurh ut. *a* **1300** *Sarmun* xxxiv. in *E.E.P.* (1862) 5 Sei sinful man..well aȝt þi hert þroȝ ute cleue. *a* **1450** *Le Morte Arth.* 3115 Fele men lyeth..With bryght brondys throw-owte borne. **1470–85** MALORY *Arthur* XIX. vi. 781 One of the barres of yron kytte the braune of his handes thurgh out to the bone. *a* **1533** LD. BERNERS *Huon* lv. 186 The shelde was perced through out.

† **b.** Right through from beginning to end (of a time, an action, a book, etc.); to the end of a journey without stopping. *Obs.*

a **1400–50** *Alexander* 4737 Þus thre daies in þat thede thurgh-out þai lengid. **1656** D'CHESS NEWCASTLE *Nature's Pict.* C ij, I never read a Romancy Book throughout in all my life. **1660** F. BROOKE tr. *Le Blanc's Trav.* 24 The Merchants ..rest here in their journey to the Indies, whereas before they went throughout, without landing here.

2. a. Through the whole of a body, region, etc.; in or to every part, everywhere.

c **1175** *Lamb. Hom.* 27 Ane berninde glede þet hine al forbernað þurut to cole. *c* **1290** *St. Brendan* 476 in *S. Eng. Leg.* I. 232 Þoru-out swart and brenninde. *c* **1450** *Mirour Saluacioun* 1261 This virgine fulle of splendour and thorgh out lumynouse. **1544** *Test. Ebor.* (Surtees) VI. 210 A furde gowne lyned with foxe thorow-oute. **1607** SHAKS. *Timon* V. i. 212 Tell Athens, in the sequence of degree, From high to low throughout, that [etc.]. **1611** BIBLE *John* xix. 23 The coat was without seame, wouen from the top thorowout. *a* **1700** DRYDEN *Epit. on Sir P. Fairborne* 15 His youth and age..All of a piece throughout, and all divine. **1880** GEIKIE *Phys. Geog.* v. xxxi. 562 The plains of Central Europe..are clothed with a vegetation which has one common character throughout. **1968** *Globe & Mail* (Toronto) 17 Feb. 46/6 (Advt.), 6 room brick bungalow with 3 finished rooms in basement, new broadloom thruout. **1976–7** *Sea Spray* (N.Z.) Dec./Jan. 119/1 (Advt.), All kauri ply and timber used exclusively thru-out.

b. Through the whole of a time or course of action; at every moment or point; all through.

1766 FORDYCE *Serm. Yng. Wom.* (1767) II. ix. 56 Act on these Principles throughout. **1833** HT. MARTINEAU *Berkeley the Banker* I. ix, Do not treat me as if I had not been your friend and adviser throughout. **1866** J. MARTINEAU *Ess.* I. 206 Mr. Spencer treats the two cases as parallel through-out. **1885** *Manch. Exam.* 22 Sept. 5/6 To-day has been beautifully fine throughout.

† **3.** Completely, entirely, thoroughly. *Obs.*

c **1200** *Vices & Virt.* 73 Ȝif ðu wilt..bien ðurhut god mann. *a* **1250** *Owl & Night.* 877 Þeyh summe men beon þurhut gode & þurhut clene on heore mode. *c* **1300** *Beket* 262 If he hadde of his owe flesch thurfout seignurye. **1470–85** MALORY *Arthur* VII. xxiii. 250 Ther was no man.. sholde hele hym thorou oute of his wound.

† **C.** *adj. Obs.* **1.** Thorough, out-and-out.

1387–8 T. USK *Test. Love* II. v. (Skeat) l. 105 Often, when there is a throw out shrewe, he coineth al the gold,..to haue in his bandon. *Ibid.* vi. l. 69 All the bodily goods..comen oft to throw out shrewes. **1670** BROOKS *Wks.* (1867) VI. 115, I cannot charge such throughout saints..with that horrid profanation of the Sabbath.

2. That is so throughout; permanent. *rare.*

1701 BEVERLEY *Glory of Grace* 4 The uninterrupted, and throughout Efficiency of grace.

† **through'outly**, *adv. Obs.* Forms: see prec.; also 5 **throughtly.** [f. prec. + -LY².]

a. Completely, thoroughly: = prec. B. 3. **b.** In every part, all over: = prec. B. 2.

c **1200** ORMIN 5246 All Drihhtiness bodeword..Iss filledd þurrhutlike wel, Ȝiff þatt soþ lufe iss filledd. **13..** *E.E. Allit. P.* A. 858 We þurȝ-outly hauen cnawyng. *c* **1475** *Partenay* 3075 So huge a stroke..That quite clene the arme share off throughtly. **1552** in J. O. Payne *St. Paul's Cath. Edw. VI* (1893) 11 Not throughoutlye platedd with silver but to the myddes onlye. **1647** WARD *Simp. Cobler* (1843) 35 If this.. worke bee throughly and throughoutly dispatched.

through-paced: see THOROUGH-PACED.

'through-,passage. Also 6 thorow-. A passage through; a thoroughfare.

c **1566** [see THOROUGH *a.* 1]. *a* **1578** LINDESAY (Pitscottie) *Chron. Scot.* (S.T.S.) I. 333 Transses and throw passagis. **1615** CROOKE *Body of Man* 103 Albeit there be but one *ductus* or through-passage from the *pylorus* or mouth of the stomack. **1663** GERBIER *Counsel* 23 Free accesse to the double roomes, without making them through passage. **1684** S. G. *Anglorum Spec.* 483 Wind-again-Lane..in it there is no through-passage. **1886** WILLIS & CLARK *Cambridge* III. 187 The two large rooms..were thrown into one; the through-passage being placed at the east end.

through-pierce: see THROUGH- 1.

† **'throughpost.** *Obs.* Also 'thoroughpost. [f. THROUGH- + POST *sb.*² 1.] An express messenger riding post the whole way to his destination: see POST *sb.*² 1. ***to lay through posts***, to establish a line of posts at which fresh horses were supplied.

1558 *Act Privy Counc.* 29 Aug., The Quenes Majestie must..seke some new meanes to be served from tyme to tyme with a through poste. **1592** *Ibid.* 18 Apr., We have authorized this bearer Robert Gascoyns, postmaster for the court, to lay through postes betweene London and the court. **1603** in *Rep. Secr. Comm. Post Office* (1844) 39 Carriers or thorow-posts, riding in our affaires by speciall commission. **1609** *Ibid.*, Thorough Postes, through-posts [see POST *sb.*² 1]. **1696** in *Massachusetts Acts* (1895) VIII. 280 Such Master.. shall provide Horses and furniture to let to hire unto all through posts and persons rideing in post.

throughput (ˈθruːpʊt). [f. THROUGH-: cf. INPUT *sb.*, OUTPUT *sb.*] **1.** *Sc.* 'Energy, activity, capacity for or progress at work' (S.N.D.).

1808 JAMIESON *Etym. Dict. Sc. Lang.* I. s.v. *ithand*, He has nae great throw-pit, but he's very eident. **1845** *Chambers's Jrnl.* 28 June 412 They'd hang as long as I like at the plough-tail, but I want through-put; and so commend me to my own men and reasonable hours. **1923** G. WATSON *Roxburghshire Word-bk.* 309 *Throw-pit*, capacity for accomplishing work.

2. The amount of oil or other raw materials, etc., processed by an industrial plant; *transf.*, the amount or number of units passing through a system, the amount of data processed by a computer (over a stated time period). Also, processing, production, or handling capacity. Also *attrib.*

1915 J. WILSON *Lowland Scotch Lower Strathearn* 273/1 *Throo-put, n.* out-turn. **1922** *Daily Mail* 15 Nov. 3 Throughput of oil will necessarily be interfered with temporarily. **1930** *Daily Express* 22 May 15/2 The larger throughput was sufficient to..yield the handsome margin of £89 per ton of ore. **1945** H. D. SMYTH *Gen. Acct. Devel. Atomic Energy Mil. Purposes* xi. 113 By the middle of January 1942, a run had been made with a reasonable beam strength and an aggregate flow or through-put of appreciable amount which showed a much improved separation factor. **1950** *Engineering* 20 Jan. 69/1 Plant and machinery made ready to handle maximum throughputs. **1958** *Spectator* 1 Aug. 178/2 The Magheralin Creamery, N. Ireland, had a considerably higher throughput of milk. **1959** *Times Rev. Industry* Mar. 24/1 Coal throughput rates. **1961** B. FERGUSSON *Watery Maze* ii. 59 The drains..were unable to cope with the 'through-put', as industrialists say, of more than eighteen lavatories. **1962** *Economist* 20 Oct. 215/1 With Stonehenge and the Tower already showing maximum throughput. **1965** *New Scientist* 24 June 883 Time sharing (or multi-programming) is already well established as a means of increasing the throughput and utilization of a computer. **1967** *Listener* 31 Aug. 263/3 Russian economists now discover that pre-packaging..not only makes for better hygiene, but trebles a shop assistant's throughput. **1968** P. DICKINSON *Skin Deep* i. 6 Estate agents must be doing nicely down this way, with a constant through-put of moneyed youngsters moving in with one kid and moving out with three. **1969** J. ARGENTI *Managem. Techniques* 168 By re-siting the factory entrance gates at a cost of a few hundred pounds it was possible for one company to increase the throughput of customers' lorries by 50 per cent. **1970** D. KUT *Warm Air Heating* xx. 338 The grade of oil fuel best suited for a particular installation depends on the type of oil burner and on the hourly through-put of oil. **1972** *Daily Tel.* 11 May 2/4 Prince Philip said..that the criterion for a university was the quality and standard of its life and work, not the total through-put of students. **1974** *Information Handbk.* 1974–5 (Shell Internat. Petroleum Co.) 105 The graphs show that costs increase as throughputs exceed or fall below the 'optimum', that is the throughput at which the total unit cost reaches the lowest point. **1976** P. R. WHITE *Planning for Public Transport* iv. 76 An alternative means of maximizing station throughput is to build a station in which a single track carrying a one-way flow bifurcates to form a loop around an island platform. **1978** *Jrnl. R. Soc. Arts* CXXVI. 425/1 Increasing the throughput of vehicles on an existing highway.

through-ride to **-rod**: see THROUGH-.

through-ripe: see *thorough-ripe*, s.v. THOROUGH- 1.

† **through'seek**, *v. Obs.* Forms: see THROUGH *prep.* and SEEK *v.* [OE. *þurhsécan*, f. *þurh*, THROUGH *adv.* + *sécan* to SEEK: cf. OHG. *durh-suohhan*, Ger. *durchsuchen*.]

1. *trans.* To seek or search through; to search or examine thoroughly.

a **1050** *Liber Scintill.* 209 *Conquirens*, þurhsecende. *c* **1200** ORMIN 242 Her endenn twa Goddspelless þuss, & uss birrþ hemm þurrhsekenn. *a* **1225** *Leg. Kath.* 520 Þa he hefde al þet lond ouergan & þurhsoht. **1340** HAMPOLE *Pr. Consc.* 2440 When alle þi life sal be thurgh soght. **1489** SKELTON *Dethe Erle Northumbld.* 179 Whose pere is hard to fynd, Algife Englond and Fraunce were thorow saught.

2. To penetrate; to imbue or saturate thoroughly; in quot. *a* 1450, to pierce, run through with a weapon.

c **1200** *Trin. Coll. Hom.* 191 He..mid te shene attre þurh secheð al þe soule. *c* **1250** *Death* 54 in *O.E. Misc.* 170 And in euche lime Deþ us hafð þurh-soht. **1387–8** T. USK *Test. Love* I. i. (Skeat) l. 120 Purely mated with sorowe through sought. **1390** GOWER *Conf.* I. 106 His wit..is with pride so thurghsoght, That he alle othre set at noght. *a* **1450** *Le Morte Arth.* 2873 Thys qarell leve wyll I noght, Ne pees shall ther neuer be sayne Or thy sydes be throw sought.

through-shed: see THROUGH- 1.

† **'through-shine**, *a. Obs.* [In OE. *þurh-**scíne, -scýne, f. *scínan* to SHINE.] Through which light shines; transparent, translucent.

c **1000** ÆLFRIC *Voc.* in Wr.-Wülcker 148/7 *Specularis*, þurhscyne stan. *a* **1631** DONNE *To C'tess Bedford* 27 That wee May in your through-shine face our hart's thoughts see.

So † **through-'shine** *v.* [f. SHINE *v.*: cf. OHG. *durhskînan*, Ger. *durchscheinen*], *intr.* to shine through; hence † **'through-, 'thorough-,shining** *ppl. a.*, shining through, translucent, transparent.

1526 TINDALE *Rev.* xxi. 21 The strete of the cite was pure golde, as thorowe shynynge glasse. **1578** LYTE *Dodoens* I. xxxiv. 49 Rounde tender, through shining, and browne redde stalkes. **1603** FLORIO *Montaigne* I. xxv. (1632) 77 It ought to make her contentment to through-shine in all exteriour parts. **1634** PEACHAM *Gentl. Exerc.* I. xxvii. 95 Then buy the Goldsmiths red Ammell, which in any case let be very transparent and through-shining.

through-shoot, -shove: see THROUGH- I.

†**through-'sting,** *v. Obs.* [OE. *þurhstingan*, f. *stingan* to STING.] *trans.* To stab or pierce through.

c **1000** ÆLFRIC *Deut.* xv. 17 Nim þonne anne æl, & þurhsting his ear æt þines huses dura. *c* **1200** *Trin. Coll. Hom.* 207 þe honden and te fet weren mid irene nailen þurh stungen. *a* **1300** *Cursor M.* 17134 (Cott.) Brest, and hand, and fote thurghstungen [*v.r.* thorustongen]. *Ibid.* 24357 Wit spere þai stoked him wit wrang, þat ilk min hert it thoru-stang. *c* **1330** *Arth. & Merl.* (Kölbing) 6630 Wiþ hors fete þai riden hem on & þurch stongen mani on.

through-stitch: see THOROUGH-STITCH.

through-stone[1] ('θrʌxstəʊn, 'θrʌf-). Now only *Sc.* and *north. dial.* [f. THROUGH *sb.*[1] (q.v. for Forms) + STONE *sb.*] A horizontal grave-stone or slab over a tomb: = THROUGH *sb.*[1] 3.

13.. *Cursor M.* 16762 + 94 (Cott.) Throgh stones in sunder brast, And ded bodyes gon rise. *c* **1440** *Promp. Parv.* 493/2 Thurwhe stone, of a grave [*v.rr.* thwrwe ston, throwe or thorw ston, throwe or throwstone], *sarcofagus.* **1509** *Test. Ebor.* (Surtees) V. 5, I will have a thorgh ston of marbill to be laid uppon my grave. **1540** *N.C. Wills* (Surtees 1908) 167 Y[t] myne executoures shall bye a threwgh stone and laye upon my mother in Seynt Andrewes Church. **1593** *Rites of Durham* (Surtees 1903) 60 An other gentleman..was buryed in the said Garth..with a faire throwgh stone aboue hym. **1703** BP. W. NICOLSON *Misc. Acc.* (1877) 106 A couple of fair Freestone Monuments or Through-Stones. **1818** SCOTT *Br. Lamm.* xxiv, The muckle through-stane that stands on sax legs yonder. **1825** BROCKETT *N.C. Words*, *Thruff-stone.* **1848** *Edinb. Antiq. Mag.* Nov. 113 A group of beautiful 'throoch-stanes', *i.e.* the large flat stones on pillars. **1894** CROCKETT *Lilac Sunbonnet* 55 [He] set a big thruch stane ower his first wife.

through-stone[2] ('θruːstəʊn), **thorough-stone** ('θʌrəstəʊn). *Building.* [f. THROUGH *prep.* + STONE *sb.*] A stone placed so as to extend through the thickness of a wall; a bond-stone.

1805 DICKSON *Pract. Agric.* I. 112 Long stones should.. be selected for the purpose of being placed occasionally across the wall, in order to bind it well together. These are termed *throughs*, or *through stones.* **1825** J. NICHOLSON *Operat. Mechanic* 538 In each course of ashlar facing.. thorough-stones should occasionally be introduced. **1879** *Cassell's Techn. Educ.* II. 98 Thorough-stones or bond-stones. **1893** C. HODGES in *Reliquary* Jan. 9 The side walls ..are built of large stones, as wide as the walls are thick, *i.e.* they are all through stones.

through-swim, -tang, -thrilled: see THROUGH-.

throught, -ly: see THROUGHOUT, -LY.

'through-,toll. Also 7 thorough-. [See TOLL.] A toll or duty levied on persons, animals, or goods passing through certain places, esp. through a town or territory. Also, a toll which passes one through two or more turnpike gates.

1567-79 *Expos. Termes Law* s.v. *Tolle*, Through tolle, is where a Towne prescribes to haue tol for euery beast that goeth through their towne. **1610** HOLLAND *Camden's Brit.* (1637) 731 Bowes..where..the Earles of Richmond had.. a certaine custome called Thorough-toll. **1611** COTGR., *Droict de Chemage*, the passage-toll, or through-toll, thats taken at Sens. **1636** PRYNNE *Rem. agst. Shipmoney* 8 This Tax..layes a farre greater charge on the Subject then any new office, Murage, Toll-travers, or thorough-toll. **1892** *Daily News* 6 Apr. 5/4 The amount received at Newcastle for through toll in one year amounts..to nearly 7,000*l.*

through-touch: see *thorough-touch* s.v. THOROUGH- 2.

through-wax, -wort: see THOROUGHWAX, -WORT.

through-waxen to **-wound:** see THROUGH-.

throughway ('θruːweɪ). Also (*N. Amer.*) **thruway**, and with hyphen. [f. THROUGH- + WAY *sb.*[1]] **1.** *N. Amer.* An expressway; a large toll road.

1934 in WEBSTER. **1946** *Sun* (Baltimore) 25 Mar. 24/9 The proposal..for a throughway across a filled-in inner harbor. **1951** *Economist* 22 Sept. 685/3 Plans for a 'Thruway' from New York City..to Buffalo on Lake Erie, are well advanced. **1969** A. LURIE *Real People* 42 Down below the rose garden I can hear cars whirring past on the thruway. **1976** T. HEALD *Let Sleeping Dogs Die* ix. 176 The Dog Centre..was no more than three and a half hours' fast driving on the thru-way from Kennedy Airport.

2. *gen.* A way through; a means of passage through or between.

1935 C. DAY LEWIS *Time to Dance* 22 Speak up, speak up, you skyward man, Speak up and tell us true; To east or west —which is the best, The through-way of the two? **1977** 'E. CRISPIN' *Glimpses of Moon* xi. 233 The cradle jolts and jerks under their combined assault, but remains obstinately blocking the throughway.

throut(e: see THEREOUT, THROUGHOUT.

throve, past tense of THRIVE *v.*

†**throw,** *sb.*[1] *Obs.* Forms: α. 1 **þráȝ, þráh,** 3 **þraȝhe,** 4 **thrau(e,** 4-5 **þraw(e,** 4-6 **thraw;** 4 **trau, trawe,** (5 **drawe).** β. 3 **þroȝe,** 3-5 **þrowe,** 3-6 **throwe,** 5-6 **throw;** 5 **trowe.** γ. 5 **threwe.** [OE. *þráȝ, þráh* fem. a (point or space of) time, a season. Not found in the cognate langs.; if in OTeut., its form would naturally be **þraiȝā*, Goth. **þráiga.*]

1. The time at which anything happens; an occasion. ***many a throw,*** many a time, often.

Like *minute, instant,* often used in advb. phrases with preposition omitted, as ***that, this, any, the same throw.***

Beowulf 2884 Ferȝendra to lyt þrong ymbe þeoden þa hyne sio þraȝ becwom. *c* **888** K. ÆLFRED *Boeth.* xxxvii. §1 Onwæcnað sio wode þraȝ þære wrænnesse. **971** *Blickl. Hom.* 117 Nis þæt eower..þæt ȝe witan þa þraȝe & þa tide. *a* **1250** *Owl & Night.* 478 Blisse myd heom sume þrowe. *Ibid.* 1455, I singe myd heom one þrowe [*v.r.* þroȝe]. **1390** GOWER *Conf.* III. 36 This riche man the same throwe With soudein deth was overthrowe. **14..** HOCCLEVE *Compl. Virgin* 73 O thynke how many a throwe Thow in myn armes lay. *c* **1440** LOVELICH *Merlin* 9949 ȝoure Ryng to taken me jn this threwe, To ȝoure cosin le-ownces that j myhte it schewe. *c* **1460** *Towneley Myst.* xx. 380 Peter, thou shall thryse apon a thraw fforsake me, or the cok craw. **1513** DOUGLAS *Æneis* x. xiii. 53 The casting dart..Smate worthy Anthores the ilk thraw.

2. A space of time; a while; in later use always, a brief while, an instant, a moment.

a **1000** *Cædmon's Gen.* 1426 (Gr.) þær se halȝa bad sunu Lameches soðra ȝehata lange þraȝe. *a* **1000** *Juliana* 464 (Gr.) Is þeos þraȝ ful strong,..ic sceal þinga ȝehwylc þolian. *c* **1175** *Lamb. Hom.* 33 Nis nawiht þeos weorld; al heo aȝeð on ane alpi þraȝe. *c* **1200** ORMIN 3475 Wass mikell weȝȝe till þatt land..& forrþi wass hemm ned to don God þraȝhe to þatt weȝȝe. *c* **1205** LAY. 640 He tah hine aȝein ane þrowe. *a* **1300** *Cursor M.* 3281 (Cott.) Had he noght rested bot a thrau [*v.rr.* þraw, þrowe]. **1375** BARBOUR *Bruce* VII. 34 He..said eftir a litill thraw, þat he suld wenge in hy thar blude. *c* **1386** CHAUCER *Man of Law's T.* 855 Now lat vs stynte of Custance but a throwe [*v.r.* trowe]. **1423** JAS. I *Kingis Quair* xlv, Quhen I a lytill thrawe had maid my moon. *c* **1440** *Promp. Parv.* 493/1 Throwe, a lytyl wyle, *momentum.* *c* **1570** *Pride & Lowl.* (1841) 64 They were defaced in a throw. **1590** SPENSER *F.Q.* III. iv. 53 Downe himselfe he layd Upon the grassy ground to sleepe a throw.

b. ***be throwes,*** by turns, time about. *rare.*

1390 GOWER *Conf.* I. 55 After that cause and nede it ladde, Be throwes ech of hem it hadde.

throw (θrəʊ), *sb.*[2] Also 6-7 **throwe,** 6- *Sc.* **thraw.** [f. THROW *v.*[1]] The act expressed by THROW *v.*[1]; a twist; a cast.

I. A twist, a turn. * In Sc. form **thraw.**

1. An act of twisting or turning; the fact or condition of being twisted; a turn or twist round, or to one side, or out of the straight or regular line; a wrench, crook, warp; also the act of turning a key, or the like. Also *fig.* ***in a throw,*** crookedly, awry. *Sc.*

a **1585** POLWART *Flyting w. Montgomerie* 564 The bleared bucke..Hes right trim teeth, somewhat set in a thraw. **1632** LITHGOW *Trav.* x. 465 Each torture consisting of three winding throwes of euery pinne; which amounted to twenty one throwes. *a* **1653** BINNING *Serm.* (1845) 68 Man's fall from God hath made a wretched thraw and crook in the soul. **1785** BURNS *Halloween* xxii, She turns the key wi' cannie thraw. **1814** SCOTT *Wav.* xlviii, Deil be wi' me if I do not give your craig [neck] a thraw. **1902** *Westm. Gaz.* 15 May 10/2 When the beacon took a 'thrawe' and his workmen fled into the tower, then almost finished, he sat unmoved reading his Bible.

b. *fig.* A perverse twist of temper or humour; a fit of perversity or 'thrawnness'. *mod.Sc.*

1788 R. GALLOWAY *Poems* 93 (Jam.) Lasses were kiss'd.. Nor seem'd to tak it ill, Wi' thraw that day. **1814** J. TRAIN *Strains Mount. Muse* 113 (ibid.) Auld Lucky Nature..unto Miss Scotia, just out of a thraw, She gave a bleak wilderness, barren and raw. **1864** T. BRUCE in *Poets Ayrshire* (1910) 233 Agents an' corks, in ruthless thraw Sought out each scob an' tear.

c. Phrase. ***heads and thraws,*** *Sc.*: see quot. 1825.

1728 RAMSAY *To Robt. Yarde* 14 A laigh hut, where sax thegither Ly heads and thraws on craps of heather. **1765** *Museum Rust.* IV. cvi. 462 They lay root-ends and crop-ends together, or, as is commonly called, heads and thraws. **1819** SCOTT *Leg. Montrose* vi, The great barn would hold fifty more, if they would lie heads and thraws. **1825** JAMIESON, *Heads-and-thraws*, with the heads and feet, or heads and points, lying in opposite directions... *To play at heads and thraws*, to play at push-pin.

** In Eng. form **throw.**

2. *Mech.* The action or motion of a slide-valve, or of a crank, eccentric, or cam; also, the extent of this measured on a straight line passing through the centre of motion; the extent through which a switch or lever may be moved; also, a crank-arm; a crank.

1829 Three throw [see THREE III. 2]. **1864** in WEBSTER. **1874** KNIGHT *Dict. Mech.* s.v. *Crank*, A two-throw or three-throw crank-shaft is one having so many cranks set at different angles on the shaft. **1888** HASLUCK *Model Engin. Handybk.* (1900) 77 When the space between the bearings is limited, that part of the rod forming the crank throws, is made elliptical in section. **1904** LINEHAM *Text Bk. Mech. Engin.* 637 The eccentricity..must be measured from centre of eccentric sheave to centre of shaft. This amount we shall sometimes call the throw. **1975** *Gramophone* Sept. 533/3 These are toggle type switches,..and protrude quite appreciably from the facia. They therefore have quite a long throw. **1979** *SLR Camera* Jan. 41/2 The wind-on lever has a short throw of around 120 degrees.

b. *Electr.* (See quots.)

1890 E. ATKINSON tr. *Ganot's Elem. Treat. Physics* (ed. 13) x. ii. 794 When a current of very small duration is passed through a galvanometer, a momentary deflection or swing or throw of the needle will be produced. **1902** O'CONOR SLOANE *Electr. Dict.*, *Throw*, in a galvanometer, the instantaneous deflection of the needle when the contact or closing of the circuit is instantaneous, or when the discharge is completed before the needle begins to move. **1931** L. B. LOEB *Fund. Electr. & Magnetism* xxiii. 272 Even the first throw of the galvanometer has not the true value which it would have had in the absence of damping.

c. Deflection from the right line.

1858 MALLET in *Rep. Brit. Assoc.* I. 94 The obliquity of throw of each of the balls..from their respective cardinal and vertical planes.

3. A twist of some fibre (e.g. silk). *rare*[−1].

1873 BROWNING *Red Cott. Nt.-cap* IV. 857 That stalk whereto her hermitage She tacked by golden throw of silk.

4. A machine by which a rotary motion is given to an object while being shaped; a lathe, esp. one worked by hand: cf. *throw-lathe* in THROW- I.

1657 TOMLINSON *Renou's Disp.* 490 Boxes are..either made with a throwe, or composed of a thin broad chip. **1659** HOOLE *Comenius' Vis. World* (1777) 89 The turner sitting over the treddle, turneth with a throw. **1836-8** *Encycl. Metrop.* (1845) VIII. 454 The jigger, also called a throw, is larger than, yet much resembling a lapidary's wheel. **1879** HOLTZAPFFEL *Turning* IV. 29 The potter's lathe or 'throw'. .. The term throw, also applied to the clock throw.

II. 5. An act of throwing a missile, etc.; a forcible propulsion or delivery from or as from the hand or arm; a cast. Also *fig.* (As a fault in Cricket: see BOWL *v.*[1] 4 and cf. quots. 1901 here.)

to have a throw at (*fig.*), to attack, have an attempt at; to have a 'fling' at.

1530 PALSGR. 233/1 Hurle or throwe with a stone, *coup de pierre.* **1548** ELYOT *Dict.*, *Iactus*, a throwe, a hurle, a caste. **1590** SPENSER *F.Q.* II. v. 9 He hewd, and lasht, and foynd, and thundred blowes..Ne plate, ne male, could ward so mighty throwes. **1692** BENTLEY *Boyle Lect.* 157 It is so many million of millions odds to one against any single throw, that the assigned order will not be cast. **1698** COLLIER *Immor. Stage* iii. 101 The Old Batchelour has a Throw at the Dissenting Ministers. **1755** *Game at Cricket* 10 If in running a Notch, the Wicket is struck down by a Throw, it's out. **1884** *Mil. Engineering* (ed. 3) I. II. 45 Keep the shovellers back at least 10 feet from the edge of the excavation; otherwise they interfere with the throw of the diggers. **1895** CROCKETT *Men of Moss-Hags* l, We will hae a thraw at it, to see if we canna break through the Thieves' Hole. **1901** *Speaker* 5 Jan. 361/2 There is no satisfactory definition of a 'throw' [at Cricket]. What one man conscientiously regards as 'throwing', another..equally conscientiously passes as bowling. **1901** *Westm. Gaz.* 11 Jan. 5/2, I wonder what [he] would say if anyone told him he could not tell a throw from a fairly-bowled ball.

6. The distance to which anything may or is to be thrown: often qualified, as a ***stone's throw.***

1582 N. LICHEFIELD tr. *Castanheda's Conq. E. Ind.* I. lxvii. 138 The enimyes were come, within the throwe of a Dart. **1607** SHAKS. *Cor.* v. ii. 21 Like to a Bowle vpon a subtle ground I haue tumbled past the throw. **1704** SWIFT *Batt. Bks.* Misc. (1711) 252 The two Cavaliers had now approach'd within a Throw of a Lance. **1712** ARBUTHNOT *John Bull* I. ix, She stank so, that nobody durst come within a stone's throw of her. **1893** F. F. MOORE *I Forbid Banns* (1899) 16 The vessel steamed within a biscuit-throw of the southern cliffs.

7. *spec.* **a.** A cast at dice; the number cast. Also *fig.*

1577 STANYHURST *Descr. Irel.* in *Holinshed* I. 84/1 Fall how it will, this throwe is for an huddle. **1596** SHAKS. *Merch. V.* II. i. 33 The greater throw May turne by fortune from the weaker hand. **1611** SPEED *Hist. Gt. Brit.* IX. xx. §66 Freede from the awe of open challenges of the Crowne, and from throwes at his maine. *a* **1667** JER. TAYLOR *Serm. Ephes. v. 32-33* Wks. 1831 I. 319 They..cast a die..of the greatest interest in the world, next to the last throw for eternity. **1702** *Lond. Gaz.* No. 3839/4 The mark at Three Throws is to have him. **1710** PALMER *Proverbs* 368 A man's friends..on an ill throw don't care to go his halves. **1759** *Hist.* in *Ann. Reg.* 8/1 This able general, who never risques his fortune on a single throw, began to think of a retreat. **1850** ROBERTSON *Serm.* Ser. III. ii. (1872) 24 The gambler who improvidently stakes all upon a moment's throw. **1878** BOSW. SMITH *Carthage* 259 They had ventured their all, or nearly their all, on this one throw.

b. A cast of a net, a fishing-line, etc.; = CAST *sb.* 5, 5c. Also *fig.*

1548 UDALL, etc. *Erasm. Par. Acts* ii. 11 This was the firste caste and throwe of his nette. **1687** DRYDEN *Hind & P.* II. 20 With the self-same throw, To catch the quarry and the vermin too. **1851** NEWLAND *The Erne* 75 For the trout, the gillaroo, and the jenkin, the northern shore affords the best throws. **1867** F. FRANCIS *Angling* v. (1880) 159 When..he can manage this throw.

c. *Wrestling.* The throwing down of an opponent, which finishes a bout or round: cf. FALL *sb.*[1] 13, CAST *sb.* 11.

1819 *Sporting Mag.* IV. 236 The Irish trump again got the throw. **1861** PALEY *Æschylus* (ed. 2) *Choephoroe* 331 *note*, ἀτρίακτος, 'invincible,' from the three throws of a wrestler.

d. A felling of timber: cf. FALL *sb.*[1] 14; also, the direction in which a tree is caused to fall.

1879 JEFFERIES *Wild Life in S. Co.* 289 While all these throws of timber have successively taken place, no attempt has been made to fill up the gaps. **1880** —— *Gt. Estate* 173 The throw of oak that was going on in one part of the Chace.

8. *Geol.* and *Mining.* A dislocation in a vein or stratum, in which the part on one side of the fracture is displaced up or down; = FAULT *sb.* 9; also, the amount of vertical displacement so caused.

1796 OUTRAM in *Phil. Trans.* LXXXVI. 351 A fault, throw, or break of the strata, which was filled with shale. **1828** *Craven Gloss., Throw*,..a disrupture of the beds or strata. **1855** J. R. LEIFCHILD *Cornwall Mines* 86 The 'throw' or perpendicular distance between the corresponding strata on the opposites of a vein, varies from a few inches to thirty or forty, or even a hundred fathoms.

9. A decorative piece of fabric used as a casual covering for furniture, as a rug, counterpane, etc. Also, a shawl or stole. *N. Amer.* (chiefly *U.S.*).

1895 [see DRAPE *sb.*[1] c]. **1913** F. H. BURNETT *T. Tembarom* xl. 524 They..transformed the cot into a 'couch' by covering it with what Tracy's knew as a 'throw'. **1936** W. GREENE *Death in Deep South* II. 142 Her last summer's scarf made a throw over the pine table. **1952** E. FERBER *Giant* ii. 14 I'm only going to buy a little white mink cape throw. **1963** G. S. MAXWELL *Navajo Rugs* iii. 30 Continuing south we come to the city of Gallup, a center for the inexpensive rug known as a 'Throw'. **1980** M. MCMULLEN *My Cousin Death* (1981) xvii. 195 She..brought a plaid throw and tenderly tucked it in around him.

10. *colloq.* (orig. *U.S.*). A 'go' at anything; freq. in phr. —— *a throw*, preceded by a specified sum of money to denote 'so much a go' or 'so much apiece'.

1898 F. P. DUNNE *Mr. Dooley in Peace & War* 101 Smaller thin New York, but th' livin' was cheaper, with Mon'gahela rye at five a throw, put ye'er hand around th' glass. **1931** 'D. STIFF' *Milk & Honey Route* 177 Beer or wine at a jitney a throw. **1948** [see DOPE *sb.* 3 a]. **1958** B. MALAMUD *Magic Barrel* 30 A column..inviting contributions in the form of stories at five bucks the thousand-word throw. **1966** N. FREELING *Dresden Green* I. 38 Coffee-table books..at a hundred and forty francs the throw. **1975** *Author* Winter 153 The cost of research... The BBC Archives charge £2 a throw.

throw, *sb.*[3], earlier form of THROE *sb.*

throw (θrəʊ), *v.*[1] Pa. t. threw (θruː); pa. pple. thrown (θrəʊn). Forms: see below. [OE. *þráwan* (pa. t. *þréow*, pa. pple. *þráwen*) str. vb., to turn, twist; corresp. to OLG. **thrâjan*, MLG. *dreien*, LG. *draien*, *dreien*, MDu. *draeien*, Du. *draaien*, OHG. *drâen* (from **drájan*), MHG. *dræjen*, *dræn*, Ger. *drehen*, weak vb., to twist, twirl, turn; wanting in Gothic, where it would have been a reduplicated vb. **þráian*, like *wáian*; OTeut. root *þrǣ-*, pre-Teut. *trē-*, *ter-* to turn; in Gr. and L., to bore. In Eng. the orig. sense 'twist, turn' remained in the north, and in certain technical uses (see branch I); otherwise it passed in ME. into that of branch II, = OE. *weorpan*, perh. through an unrecorded sense 'throw by a turn or twist of the arm, or with a sling'. Cf. note to CAST *v.*]

A. Illustration of Forms.

1. *Present stem.* α. 1 **ðráw-an, 1–4 þraw-, 3–4 þrauw-, 3–7 thrawe, 5– *Sc.* thraw, (4 þrau-, 5–6 thrau, 9 *dial.* thraa, thrah, thra, tra(a)** (see *Eng. Dial. Dict.*).

c **1000** þrawan [see B. 1]. *a* **1300** Thrawe [see B. 8]. **1340** *Ayenb.* 17 God þrauþ doun prede. *c* **1450** *Two Cookery-bks.* 101 Thrawe it þorgh a streynour. *c* **1470** Thraw [see B. 1]. **1570** LEVINS *Manip.* 45/38 To Thrawe, cast, *iactare*, *mittere*. **1581** Thrau [see B. 3]. **1720** RAMSAY *Wealth* 141 I'll thraw my gab and gloom. **1787–1884** Thraw [see B. 5]. **1828** *Craven Gloss.*, *Thraa*, to throw; also to turn in a lathe.

β. **3–5 þrōw-en, 4–7 throwe, 6– throw (6–7 through, 7 throughe, thro', 9 *dial.* thro, trow).**

c **1250** *Long Life* 37 in *O.E. Misc.* 158 Weilawei, deþ þe schal adun þrowe. **1377** LANGL. *P. Pl.* B. XVI. 131, I shal ouertourne þis temple and adown throwe. **1387** þrow [see B. 37 a]. *a* **1400** þrowe [see B. 30]. **1552** HULOET, Throwe, *iacio*. **1580** Throw [see B. 15]. **1598** Through [see B. 14]. *c* **1614** SIR W. MURE *Dido & Æneas* II. 219, I, frome above, a tempest downe shall thro'. *c* **1620** Throughes [see B. 19].

2. *Past tense.* α. 1 **ðreow, 1–3 þreow, (3 þreuw), 3–4 þreou, þreu, þrew, -e, 4 þreuh, þruw, -e, threow, thrwe, 4–6 threwe, 5– threw, (5 threew, throwe, 7 thrue).**

c **1000** ÆLFRIC *Hom.* II. 510 He sona ðreow ðwyres. *c* **1205** LAY. 12321 þa cheorles up þreowen [*c* **1275** þreuwen]. *Ibid.* 807 þreou, aþreu [see B. 28]. *a* **1300** *K. Horn* 1162 Horn þreu [*v.r.* þrew] is ryng to grounde. **13..** *K. Alis.* 2427 Ded he threow him to grounde. **1362** LANGL. *P. Pl.* A. v. 201 He ..þreuh [*texts B., C.* þreu, þrew, threwe, throwe] to þe grounde. *c* **1374** Thrwe [see B. 43]. **1387** TREVISA *Higden* (Rolls) VI. 11 þe aungel..þrewe [*MS.* γ, þruw] þat cloop into þat fuyre. *a* **1400–50** Threw [see B. 46 a]. *c* **1422** Threew [see B. 48 a]. *c* **1449** PECOCK *Repr.* (Rolls) 260 Thou.. threwist doun hors and man. *c* **1470** HENRY *Wallace* v. 1020 Thom Haliday sone be the craig him threw. **1526** *Pilgr. Perf.* (W. de W. 1531) 304 The chyldren..toke vp stones & clay, & threwe them. **1618** Thrue [see B. 44 i].

β. (*dial.*) **7–9 throwed, 9 thrawed.**

1666 in Picton *L'pool Munic. Rec.* (1883) I. 315 þ[t]..hee throwed downe into the trench. **1820** Throwed [see B. 19]. **1871** Thrawed [see B. 2].

3. *Past pple.* α. 1–4 **þrawen (3 þrauwen, 4 y(þraw), 5–6 *Sc.* thrawen (5–7 -in, -ne), 6– *Sc.* thrawn, 9 *dial.* thraan.** See also THRAWN.

c **1205** þrauwen, **13..** þrawen [see B. 1]. *c* **1330** Y-þrawe [see B. 40 c]. **1483** Thrawen [see THROWN]. **1513** DOUGLAS *Æneis* v. v. 66 [The adder] In lowpis thrawin. **1591** Thrawne [see B. 4]. **1645** *Shetland Witch Trial* in Hibbert *Descr. Shetl. Isl.* (1822) 597 Scho..cam scouring hame.. having her head thrawin backward to her back. **1824** SCOTT *St. Ronan's* ix, He winna bide being thrawn.

β. **4–5 þrowen, (4 i-þrowen, 4–5 i-þrow(e), 4–7 (9 *dial.*) throwen, (4 throwyn, -un, 4–5 (y-)throwe, ytrowe, i-drow, 6 throwin), 6–7 throwne, 7– thrown, (6 trowne, 9 *dial.* threuwn.)**

c **1320** *Cast. Love* 739 Wiþ Cumpas I-þrowen and wiþ gin al I-do. **1382** WYCLIF *Acts* xxvii. 18 Vs throwun with greet tempest. **1387** TREVISA *Higden* (Rolls) III. 93 þe body..þat was so i-þrowe wiþ oute þe walles. *Ibid.* VII. 327 þe knyȝt þat hadde i-þrow hym downe. **1399** Throwe [see B. 8]. *c* **1400** *Laud Troy Bk.* 3867 Riche Troye..Schal be brent and doun ytrowe. *c* **1425** I-drow [see B. 40 c]. **1482** *Monk of Evesham* (Arb.) 74 They..were greuysly caste and throwe fro one place to anothir. **1535** COVERDALE *Lam.* i. 13 He hath ..throwne me wyde open. **1589** R. ROBINSON *Gold. Mirr.* (Chetham Soc.) Ep. to Rdr., Stones..thou would have throwen. **1647** Thrown [see B. 42 a].

γ. **8–9 (now *dial.*) throwed, 9 *north.* thrawed.**

1727–41 [see THROWED]. **1878** Throwed [see B. 20]. **1896** Thrawed [see B. 1].

B. Signification.

I. To twist, to turn, and derived uses.

***** *Sc.* in form **thraw**; ****** *technical*, in form **throw**.

*** 1.** *trans.* To twist, to wring; to turn to one side (also *fig.*); to twist about, twine, wreathe; to turn (a key or the like); in OE. to torture on the rack. Now *Sc.* and *north. dial.*

to thraw one's face, gab, mouth (*Sc.*), to pull a wry face, to contort the face, e.g. in pain, anger, or passion.

c **1000** ÆLFRIC *Hom.* II. 308 [He het] hine hon on heardre hengene..and mid hengene ðrawan to langere hwile. *c* **1000** —— *Saints' Lives* viii. 113 þa wearð se arleasa ȝehathyrt, and het hi on hencgene a-streccan and ðrawan swa swa wiððan wælhreowlice. *c* **1000** ÆLFRIC *Gram.* xxvi (Z.) 155 *Contorqueo*, ic samod þrawe. *c* **1205** LAY. 27359 Heȝe hare-marken..sixti þusende þrauwen mid winde. **13..** *Gaw. & Gr. Knt.* 194 þe tayl..þrawen wyth a þwong a þwarle knot alofte. *c* **1470** HENRY *Wallace* VII. 410 Than xx[ty] men he gert fast wetheis thraw,..Than festnyt thai with wetheis duris fast. **1536** BELLENDEN *Cosmogr.* xiv, Apperit than ane multitude of wormis thrawing thaim self out of sindry hollis and boris of this tre. **1583** *Calr. Scott. Pap.* VI. 356 [They] forcit thame..be towis thrawin about their heidis [to reveal the money]. **1689** BURNET *Tracts* I. 82 He threw it which way he pleased. **1728** RAMSAY *Fable, Fox & Rat* 26 He threw his gab, and girn'd. ? **17..** *Young Redin* xiv. in Child *Ballads* II. 146 Ye'll thraw my head aff my hause-bane, And throw me in the sea. **1816** SCOTT *Bl. Dwarf* ix, To thraw the keys, or draw the bolts, or open the grate. **1823** HOGG *Sheph. Cal.* i. (1829) I. 4 Ye're something ill for thrawing your mou' at Providence now and then. **18..** *Sc. Proverb*, Thraw the widdie [= withy] while it's green Between three and thirteen. **1881** W. WALKER in *Mod. Scot. Poets* III. 104 Hoo his een are starin: hoo he thraws his mouth. **1894** CROCKETT *Raiders* 144 I'll thraw your neck for that, Jerry. **1896** —— *Grey Man* i. 7 His countenance thrawed and drawn, his shrunk shanks twisted.

2. *intr.* To turn, twist, curl, twine, writhe; of a moored boat: to swing, sway. Chiefly *Sc.*

Quots. 1513, *a* 1650, appear to have the spec. meaning 'to writhe in death-throes'; they are closely connected with *thraw*, northern form of THROE *sb.*, and may perhaps be viewed as showing a Sc. form of THROE *v.* 2.

c **1000** *Gloss.* in *Haupt's Zeitschr.* IX. 435 *Crispantibus*, þrawendum *vel* cyrpsiendum, *marg.* cyrpsum loccum. *c* **1000** *Gloss.* in Wr.-Wülcker 527/2 *Rotante*, þrawende. *c* **1000** ÆLFRIC *Hom.* II. 510 Se lig..sona ðreow ðwyres wið þæs windes. *c* **1450** HOLLAND *Howlat* 823 Twa..fulis.. Callit him thryss thevisnek, to thrawe in a widdy. **1513** DOUGLAS *Æneis* XII. vi. 48 Down strowand eik vnder fut in the plane Diuers otheris ȝit thrawand and half slane. *a* **1650** *Sir Eger & Sir Gryme* 1611 in Laing *Early Metr. T.* (1826) 55 Gray-Steel unto his death thus thrawes; He walters, and the grass updrawes. *a* **1699** BONNELL in W. Hamilton *Life* II. (1703) 85 We stomach..Injuries that we think are done to us; we fling and throw under them. **1818** SCOTT *Br. Lamm.* xxiii, If the dead corpse binna straughted, it will girn and thraw. **1871** ROSSETTI *Stratton Water* xxxvii, The empty boat thrawed i' the wind, Against the postern tied. **1881** PALGRAVE *Visions Eng.* 248 The strong branches cry And start and thraw in that fierce furnance-flame.

3. a. *trans.* (*fig.*) To wrest, warp, or pervert the meaning or intention of; to do violence to, strain; also, to distort the pronunciation of. *Sc.*

1558 KENNEDY *Compend. Tract.* 6 Wrestand and thrawing the Scripture, contrare the godlie menynge of the samyn. **1581** HAMILTON in *Cath. Tractates* (S.T.S.) 77 The scripture, quhilk thaj thrau efter thair sensuall iugement. **1873** MURDOCH *Doric Lyre* 86 (E.D.D.) What though he thraw'd the law, a wee? **1877** G. MACDONALD *Mrq. Lossie* xxviii, They dinna thraw the words there jist the same gait they du at Portlossie.

b. To change detrimentally the colour of, to discolour or cause to fade: cf. CAST *v.* 24.

Mod. Sc. dial. The sun has quite thrown my silk gown.

†**4. a.** To obtain or extract by twisting or wringing; to wrench; chiefly *fig.* to extort. *Sc. Obs.*

1513 DOUGLAS *Æneis* XII. vi. 120 Owt of hys [an enemy's] rycht hand Richt austernly has he thrawin the brand. **1591** R. BRUCE *Serm.* R j b, When hee hath thrawne all these good turnes out of them. *a* **1598** ROLLOCK *Wks.* (1844) II. vi. 73 He throws another accusation out of the Jews.

†**b.** To force by torture or violence; to constrain. *Sc. Obs.*

1599 JAS. I *Βασιλ. Δωρον* (1682) 96 Beware of thrawing or constraining them thereto.

5. a. To cross, thwart, frustrate. Chiefly *Sc.*

1787 BURNS *When Guilford good*, etc. vi, Saint Stephen's boys, wi' jarring noise, They did his measures thraw. **1818** SCOTT *Rob Roy* xxvi, He's easy wi' a' body that will be easy wi' him; but if ye thraw him ye had better thraw the deevil. **1884** *Lays & Leg. N. Irel.* 11 If his Riv'rance released him he'd thraw him no more.

b. *intr.* To go counter, to act in opposition; to be at variance or awkward; to exhibit dislike or aversion; to quarrel or contend *with*. *Sc.*

a **1578** LINDESAY (Pitscottie) *Chron. Scot.* XXI. iv. (1728) 125 Bishop Forman had..caused the duke to thraw [*so* 3 *MSS.*; 2 *MSS.* stur(e)] with him till he gave certain Benefices to the Duke to give unto his friends. **1807** HOGG *Laird of Lairistan* xxiii, Jealous of the Stuart race, The English lords begin to thraw. **1824** MACTAGGART *Gallovid. Encycl.* (1876) 214 At nature ay to girn and thraw..Is sure a sin infernal. **1888** D. GRANT *Scotch Stories* 10 Thraw wi' him, an' he was just as stubborn an' rampageous as a wild ox.

**** 6.** *trans.* To form or fashion by means of a rotary or twisting motion. **a.** To turn (wood, etc.) in a lathe; to shape (round pottery) on a potter's lathe or 'throwing-wheel'. Now *techn.* or *dial.*

c **1440** *Promp. Parv.* 493/1 Throwyn, or turne vessel of a tre, *torno*. **1570** LEVINS *Manip.* 45/39 To Thraw or turne, *tornare*. **1604** *Shuttleworths' Acc.* (Chetham Soc.) 159 To the disshe-thrower, ix days throwing disshes and bassenes.. iij[s]. **1674** RAY *N.C. Words*, To *Throw*, to Turn as Turners doe. **1752** *Gentl. Mag.* Aug. 348 Rooms for throwing, turning, and stove drying the ware. **1755** JOHNSON s.v., Balls thrown in a lathe. **1839** URE *Dict. Arts*, etc. 1011 Throwing is performed upon a tool called the potter's lathe... The mass of dough to be thrown is weighed out or gauged by an experienced hand. **1900** *Daily News* 25 May 6/2 Further on a potter is 'throwing' pots on his wheel.

b. *Silk Manuf.* To prepare and twist (raw silk) into thread; *spec.* to form into thread by twisting two or more threads or 'singles' in the direction opposite to that of their component filaments.

1455 [implied in THROWSTER 1]. **1463–4** [implied in THROWN 2]. **1483** *Act 1 Rich. III*, c. 10 § 1 Calle sylk or coleyn silk throwen or wrought. **1670** BLOUNT *Law-Dict.*, *Silk-thrower*,..a Trade, or Mystery, that winds, twists, and spins, or throws silk, thereby fitting it for use. **1796** *Trans. Soc. Arts* XIV. 328, I became convinced that Bengal Silk could be thrown in this country. **1839** URE *Dict. Arts*, etc. 1105 The raw silk..requires to be regularly wound upon bobbins, doubled, twisted, and reeled in our silk-mills. These processes are called throwing silk, and their proprietors are called silk throwsters. **1877** KNIGHT *Dict. Mech.* s.v. *Thrown Singles*, Silk filaments are twisted to form *singles*. Several of these are combined and twisted together (doubling) forming *dumb singles*. A number of the latter are associated and twisted together (throwing), forming *thrown singles*. **1897** *Daily News* 9 Dec. 10/5 Silk is still 'thrown' at Derby.

c. To make by twisting: cf. THROW-CROOK.

1896 P. A. GRAHAM *Red Scaur* v. 78 We began to throw straw ropes for them.

†**7.** To form, fashion, dispose, arrange; = CAST *v.* 45. *Obs. rare.*

c **1320** *Cast. Love* 739 A Trone..Of whit Iuori..Wiþ Cumpas I-þrowen and wiþ gin al I-do. *Ibid.* 807 þe þreo baylys..þat wiþ þe cornels byth so feyre I-set, And throwen [*v.r.* I-cast] wiþ cumpas and walled abowte.

II. To project or propel through the air, and connected uses; to cast, fling, hurl, drive, shoot (away from the propelling agent).

8. a. *trans.* To project (anything) with a force of the nature of a jerk, from the hand or arm, so that it passes through the air or free space; to cast, hurl, fling; *spec.* to cast by a sudden jerk or straightening of the arm, esp. at the level of or over the shoulder (as distinguished from *bowl*, *pitch*, *toss*). Cf. CAST *v.* I.

Now the main sense of the word (= Fr. *jeter*, Ger. *werfen*, L. *jacĕre*, *jactāre*), which is contained or involved in all the later senses and applications; *throw* being the primary, most general, and most proper word for this action.

a **1300** *E.E. Psalter* cxxxix. [cxl.] 11 In fire sal tou thrawe þam swa. *a* **1300** *K. Horn* 1076 Horn hem ouer þe brigge. **1387** TREVISA *Higden* (Rolls) V. 9 Ignacius..was i-brouȝt to Rome, and i-þrowe to wylde bestes. **1399** LANGL. *Rich. Redeles* IV. 82 Ne had þei striked a strake..or þe blast come, þey had be throwe ouere þe borde backe-warde ichonne. *c* **1440** *Promp. Parv.* 493/1 Throwyn, or castyn, *jacto*. **1513** DOUGLAS *Æneis* XI. vi. 142 Ane lance towartis his aduersar thrawis he. **1530** PALSGR. 756/1, I threwe a potte at his head. **1567** *Satir. Poems Reform.* iii. 174 Jesabell, Quhome threw ane windo suirlie men did thraw. **1651** HOBBES *Leviath.* II. xxi. 108 When a man throweth his goods into the Sea for feare the ship should sink. **1724** DE FOE *Mem. Cavalier* I. 76 I'd throw it [money] all into the Elbe. **1818** SCOTT *Br. Lamm.* xxiv, He threw the fellow a dollar. *Ibid.* xxxiii, Throwing Craigengelt from him with such violence that he rolled down the steps. **1863** GEO. ELIOT *Romola* xx, There were practical jokes of all sorts, from throwing comfits to throwing stones. **1869** *Prov.* [see GLASS-HOUSE]. *Mod.* Throw me a rope.

b. *absol.* To hurl a missile, a weapon, etc.

13.. *Sir Beues* (A.) 3106 þow miȝt nouȝt sen ariȝt to þrowe. **1869** *Temple Bar Mag.* VI. 283 Parr threw 109 yards, the soldier only three yards less. **1889** DOYLE *M. Clarke* 34 The turnip on a stick at which we used to throw at the fairs.

†**c.** *trans.* To assail *with* missiles, to pelt. *Obs. rare*[−1].

13.. *K. Alis.* 4702 (Bodl. MS.) Men hem þrew wiþ drytt & dunge [*v.r.* to heom threowe drit and donge].

9. *refl.* To fling or cast oneself; to precipitate oneself; †of a river, to precipitate itself, fall *into* another river, a lake, etc. (*obs.*) Also *fig.*

13.. *Sir Beues* (A.) 2179 Beues in to þe sadel him þrew. **1387** TREVISA *Higden* (Rolls) III. 411 Alisaundre..þrewe hym self into a water þat renneþ þere. **1576** FLEMING *Panopl. Epist.* 310 Another throweth himselfe headlong from the topp of an house, and breaketh his necke. *c* **1630** RISDON *Surv. Devon* §220 (1810) 227 The river Thrushell..throws itself into Lyd. **1714** ADDISON *Spect.* No. 556 ¶6, I..threw myself into an Assembly of Ladies. **1794** MRS. RADCLIFFE

Myst. Udolpho xl, 'This is too—too much!' exclaimed Valancourt,..throwing himself into a chair. **1795** BURKE *Corr.* (1844) IV. 324 If you throw yourself into one of the early coaches, you would be here very quickly. **1843** LEVER *J. Hinton* xi, He threw himself upon his horse.

b. ***to throw oneself upon***: to attack with violence or vigour; to fall upon. (Cf. 28.)

1823 SCOTT *Quentin D.* iv, He threw himself upon the ragout, and the plate was presently vacant.

10. a. *trans.* To cast (dice) from the dice-box; to make (a cast) at dice; also *absol.* or *intr.* to cast or throw dice, to play at dice. Also *fig.*

† *to throw at all*: to stake or venture all one has (*obs.*).

1587 GREENE *Penelopes Web* Wks. (Grosart) V. 181 Least ..we set our rest on the hazard and so desperately throw at all. **1601** SHAKS. *All's Well* II. iii. 84, I had rather be in this choise, then throw Ames-ace for my life. **1605** —— *Lear* I. iv. 136 Set lesse then thou throwest. *a* **1667** JER. TAYLOR *Wks.* (1835) I. 533 (Cent.) That great day of expense, in which a man is to throw his last cast for an eternity of joys and sorrows. **1698** *Act 10 Will. III*, c. 23 §3 Every Person or Persons that..shall play throw or draw at any such Lottery ..shall forfeite for every such Offence the Sum of Twenty Pounds. **1720** *Lond. Gaz.* No. 5872/6 The Winning Horse to be thrown for at 40 Guineas by the Contributors. **1848** THACKERAY *Van. Fair* xxii, George had thrown the great cast. **1892** *Monthly Packet* May 558 If I should throw doublets, we will share the stakes.

b. To play (a card) out of one's hand; *esp.* to discard.

1748 [see *throw away*, 37 c]. **1879** 'CAVENDISH' *Card Ess.*, etc. 109 Throwing the ace of hearts to the last spade. **1891** *Harper's Mag.* Mar. 603/1 He can therefore safely throw his queen on the ace. **1891** *Field* 28 Nov. 842/3 We should throw four diamonds, and the seven of spades, but do not say it is the proper 'discard'.

c. To cast (a vote): = CAST *v.* 1 f.

1768 W. MUSGRAVE *Let.* 12 Feb. in *15th Rep. R. Comm. Hist. Manuscripts* App. VI. 241 *in Parl. Papers 1897* (C. 8551) LI. I. 1 But if they will be artful enough to throw their votes so as to choose one of your candidates, it is my opinion we ought to remain contented for the present. **1844** W. PHILLIPS in *Life of Garrison* (1889) III. iv. 99 No one can take office, or throw a vote for another to hold office. **1888** BRYCE *Amer. Commw.* I. v. 55 *note*, 37 additional presidential votes..all thrown for the Democratic candidate. **1890** *Spectator* 8 Mar., Their usual leaders do not know their thoughts, and until their votes are thrown, can form only guesses as to the way their sympathies are tending.

11. To hurl, project, shoot, as a missile engine does; also of a person using such an engine. Often *absol.* (esp. in reference to distance or direction).

1393 LANGL. *P. Pl.* C. XXI. 295 Sette mahon at þe mangonel and mulle-stones þrowep. *a* **1400–50** *Alexander* 2218 Thre thousand of thra men to thraw with engynes. **1726** LEONI *Alberti's Archit.* I. 69/1 This will baulk the aim of the military engines, and make them throw over the wall. **1880** *Daily Tel.* 23 Dec., Although throwing only a 7lb. projectile, they [guns] are [etc.]. **1890** CLARK RUSSELL *Ocean Trag.* II. xviii. 106 That gun 'll throw about three quarters of a mile. **1900** POLLOK & THOM *Sports Burma* vi. 212, I tried the weapon, and found that both barrels threw considerably to the left.

12. To put forth with a throwing action (a fishing net, line, or bait); to cast, make a cast with. Also *absol.*

1777 J. WOODFORDE *Diary* 8 May (1924) I. 203 Bill caught only one little Miney but he did not throw above four times. **1841** LANE *Arab. Nts.* I. ii. 101 And threw his net. **1889** CROMMELIN & BROWN *Violet Vyvian* II. ix. 154 Violet.. learnt to throw a fly. **1891** *Sat. Rev.* 20 June 734/1 Good anglers..can throw to a hairbreadth and not miss.

13. Of the sea or wind: †**a.** To toss or drive violently about; also, to drive, send, impel (*obs. rare*); **b.** *esp.* to drive or cast with violence (on rocks or a coast); to cast away, wreck.

1382 WYCLIF *Matt.* xiv. 24 Sothely the boot in the mydil see was throwen [L. *iactabatur*] with wawis. **1423** JAS. I *Kingis Q.* xvii, My feble bote full fast to stere and rowe,..the wynter nyght I wake, To wayte the wynd that furth-ward suld me throwe. **1659** D. PELL *Impr. Sea* Proœm. d ij b, They are thrown irrecoverably upon Rocks and Sands. **1879** MINTO *Defoe* ix. 142 [He] might have been thrown on a desert island. **1886** BURTON *Arab. Nts.* (abr. ed.) I. 126 A billow..threw me with a long cast on dry land.

14. a. To project (a ray, beam, light) *on, upon, over*, etc.; to emit (light); to project, cast (a shadow).

1598 B. JONSON *Ev. Man in Hum.* III. i, To through the least beame of regard upon such a [fellow]. **1600** FAIRFAX *Tasso* XVIII. xv, The morning's lusty queen, Begilding, with the radiant beams she threw, His helm. **1797** MRS. RADCLIFFE *Italian* vii, A nun, kneeling..beneath a lamp which threw its rays aslant her head. **1876** TAIT *Rec. Adv. Phys. Sc.* ix. (ed. 2) 213 Throwing the spectrum of light.. on the screen. **1893** *Harper's Mag.* Jan. 280/2 The great mound..threw a long shadow westward.

b. In *fig.* phrases, esp. ***to throw (a) light on***, to contribute to the elucidation of, to make clearer or plainer; ***to throw a lustre over***, to illuminate or render lustrous; also ***to throw a shadow, cloud, gloom, over***: see the sbs.

1598 [see prec. sense]. **1769** [see LUSTRE *sb.*[1] 4]. **1774** GOLDSM. *Nat. Hist.* (1776) V. 78 The testimony of a single witness..will throw more light on the subject than the reasonings of an hundred philosophers. **1825** MOORE *Sheridan* I. 510 It was in the power of the orator..to throw a lustre over the historian. **1825** T. HOOK *Sayings* Ser. II. *Passion & Princ.* ix. III. 153 Showers of rain..threw a gloom over the gaieties. **1875** JOWETT *Plato* (ed. 2) I. p. xviii, Ancient and modern philosophy throw a light upon one another. **1890** SIR A. KEKEWICH in *Law Times Rep.* LXIII. 684/1 The defendants' evidence does not throw much light on the question.

15. a. To direct (words, an utterance) *towards*, etc., esp. in hostility or contempt; to hurl, cast; to cause (sound, or *fig.* a gesture) to pass or travel; to waft (a kiss), to cast (a nod); to project (the voice); also, *spec.* as in ventriloquism. Cf. sense 44 c below.

1580 SIDNEY *Ps.* XXXI. ix, Those lips..Which..throw their words against the most vpright. **1600** SHAKS. *A. Y. L.* I. iii. 3 Not a word? *Ros.* Not one to throw at a dog. *a* **1748** WATTS (J.), There is no need to throw words of contempt on such a practice. **1822** SCOTT *Nigel* i, The poor youth had not a word to throw at a dog. **1831** —— *Cast. Dang.* ii, 'Never fear me, Augustine,' said the old man,..throwing a kiss towards the boy. **1844** MRS. BROWNING *Drama of Exile* Poems 1850 I. 75 The blessed nightingale which threw Its melancholy music after us. **1892** *Field* 19 Nov. 771/2 The hideous yells that were thrown at him. **1962** A. NISBETT *Technique Sound Studio* 263 In dead acoustics the ratio of direct to indirect sound cannot be varied, as indirect sound must be kept to a minimum. In this case it may help if an actor 'throws' his voice, simulating raising it to talk or shout from a distance. **1972** A. PRICE *Col. Butler's Wolf* xx. 222 He threw his voice past Ryleiev into the mist. **1976** *Listener* 23/30 Dec. 830/1, I can throw my voice. I could make a fortune as a medium.

b. ***to throw the tongue***: see TONGUE.

16. ***to throw one's eye*** or ***eyes, a glance, a look***: to turn or direct one's gaze, to look; *esp.* to look hastily, rapidly, or cursorily; to glance: = CAST *v.* 7.

1590 SPENSER *F.Q.* III. i. 16 Still as she fledd her eye she backward threw. **1779** *Mirror* No. 17. ¶1 To throw your eye sometimes upon the inferior ranks of life. **1800** *Char.* in *Asiat. Ann. Reg.* 45/1 The mother lifting up her eyes,.. instantly threw them to the ground. **1885** FITZPATRICK *T.N. Burke* II. 35 Happening to throw his eye over the address delivered..at Boston. **1892** *Longm. Mag.* Jan. 276 Mrs. Duffield..threw inquiring glances across the table.

17. a. To give, deliver (blows); also *absol.* or *intr.* to aim blows, strike. (Cf. to '*lay* about him'.) Now usu. in phr. ***to throw a punch***, to deliver a blow with the clenched fist; occas. with fist as obj.

c **1470** *Golagros & Gaw.* 709 Thai threw in that thrang Stalwart strakis and strang. **1590** SPENSER *F.Q.* III. ix. 16 Then drew he his bright sword, and gan about him throw. **1923** H. C. WITWER *Fighting Blood* xi. 348, I set myself, took careful aim and threw my right at his chin. **1950** J. DEMPSEY *Championship Fighting* xvi. 92 You're throwing perfect punches. **1976** J. LEWIS *Shadows of Death* iv. 54 Maybe the kid had a hammer in his glove; surely he couldn't have thrown a punch hard enough to hurt him like that one had. **1983** *Daily Tel.* 3 Feb. 3/3 Mr Oatway..threw punches at the second bandit.

†**b.** *trans.* ? To deliver a blow at; to strike.

c **1470** HENRY *Wallace* IV. 252 That staff he had, hewy and forgyt new, With it Wallace wpon the hede him threw, Quhill bayn and brayn all in to sondyr ȝeid.

18. a. To perform, execute (a somersault or a leap, in which the body is thrown with force); also ***to throw a fit***, to have a fit (*slang* (orig. *U.S.*)). Chiefly *fig.*

1826 *Examiner* 585/1 Throw a somerset, leap a stick, tumble through a hoop. **1889** BADEN-POWELL *Pigsticking* viii. 39 Mr. Kingscote threw about three back somersaults. *Ibid.* xiii. 99 Don't be surprised to find your horse unexpectedly 'throwing leps'. **1896** S. CRANE *Maggie* (rev. ed.) iii. 22 Deh ol' woman 'ill be trowin' fits. **1897** FLANDRAU *Harvard Episodes* 132, I don't suppose the creature thought I was throwing a fit like that just for exercise. **1926** *S.P.E. Tract* XXIV. 126 Father threw a fit when I came home drunk. **1930** *Observer* 4 May 15 Caesar throws his fit, off stage. **1954** KOESTLER *Invis. Writing* 172 One day this was discovered by Zsuzsa, who threw a fit. **1973** 'R. MACLEOD' *Burial in Portugal* v. 97 'Please, Jonathan. If I am late—.' 'The management will throw a fit,' he completed for her.

b. To give or hold (a party), esp. one of an informal or impromptu nature. *colloq.* (orig. *U.S.*).

1922 S. LEWIS *Babbitt* xxxix. 339 Saturday night, when they would..'throw a party'. **1937** *Even. News* 6 Mar. 11/5 Anona Winn threw a party a few nights ago at her flat in Maida Vale. **1960** *Sunday Express* 13 Mar. 12/7 She..threw a champagne and scampi party at a nearby pub. **1978** *Detroit Free Press* 5 Mar. B 2/2 When all else fails, throw a party.

c. ***to throw a wobbly***: see WOBBLY *sb.*[2]

III. Pregnant uses.

* = *throw down*; ** = *throw off*; *** = *throw out* or *up*.

* **19. a.** *trans.* To cause to fall to the ground; to cast down, knock down, prostrate, lay low; *spec.* in *Wrestling*, to bring (one's opponent) to the ground, also with double object, ***to throw one a fall***. Cf. *throw down*, 40.

13.. *K. Alis.* 2219 (Bodl. MS.) A riche kyng..smoot tholomewe þat he of his hors hym þrewe. Tholomeu on fote lep, And who hym þrewe he name gode kepe. **1530** PALSGR. 756/1 Wrestell nat with me, for I wyll throwe the on thy backe. *c* **1620** T. ROBINSON *Mary Magd.* 819 A newe delusion throughes Her pride as lowe as Phlegetonicke maine. **1820** *Sporting Mag.* VI. 177 Tom..throwed his opponent in masterly style. **1824** in *Examiner* 759/1 Cannon, grappling his man, threw him a tremendous fall. **1902** *Brit. Med. Jrnl.* No. 2154. 880 Three years ago [he] was thrown at football and hurt his knee.

b. *fig.* or in *fig.* context: To defeat in a contest; also, to be the cause of defeat to; to give or gain the verdict against in an action at law (*U.S.*): cf. CAST *v.* 14.

1850 TENNYSON *In Mem.* cix. 6 Seraphic intellect and force To seize and throw the doubts of man. **1887** in *Lisbon* (Dakota) *Star* 20 May 2/5, 'I am compelled to throw you in the cost', said a justice of the peace. **1888** *Poultry, Pigeons*, etc. 27 July 377 (Prize list) Third..a good black Red, but a little out of feather, which, no doubt, threw her. **1909** W. R. INGE *Faith* xi. (1910) 193 The sceptic cannot throw his opponent if his own feet are in the air.

c. To lose (a contest, race, etc.) deliberately or by corrupt prearrangement. *colloq.* (orig. *U.S.*).

1868 H. WOODRUFF *Trotting Horse Amer.* xxxi. 263 It was ..very unjust to charge Mr. Nodine with throwing the race. **1940** 'E. QUEEN' in *Blue Bk.* Oct. 27/1 'Brown threw the fight?' asked..a member of the Boxing Commission. **1951** *Manch. Guardian Weekly* 1 Mar. 15/1 Baseball games had been 'thrown' by bribed players. **1959** *News Chron.* 19 Aug. 6/3 He was accused of..fixing the World Series of 1919. This was the equivalent of arranging that one side in the Cup Final should throw the game. **1978** *Times* 9 Jan. 8/5 During the Chancellorship of Mr Roy Jenkins, Lord Allen had to 'throw' their occasional [tennis] matches for fear of puncturing the considerable vanity of his political master.

20. a. To cause forcibly (a tree or structure) to fall; to bring, knock, break, or cut down; to fell. In *Coal-mining*: see quot. 1881.

1568 GRAFTON *Chron.* II. 139 Some of them, they threwe to the grounde and consumed with fire. **1878** JEFFERIES *Gamekeeper at H.* i. 14 In the spring when the oak timber is throwed [*dial. speech*]. *Ibid.* iii. 52 The entire wood is thrown and renovated. **1881** RAYMOND *Mining Gloss.*, *Throwing*,..the operation of breaking out the spurns, so as to leave the hanging coal unsupported, except by its own cohesion. **1908** *Daily News* 25 Jan. 9 Some 40 telephone wires had to be temporarily cut, in order to enable the [chimney] shaft to be 'thrown'.

b. *spec.* ***to throw an ant-hill***: see quot. and cf. GELD *v.*[1] 3 d. *dial.*

1848 *Jrnl. R. Agric. Soc.* IX. I. 17 Ant-hills..are quickly checked by throwing, or gelding. *Ibid.* 25 [see GELD *v.*[1] 3 d].

** **21.** Of a horse, etc.: To cause (the rider) to fall off; to unseat, shake off; = *throw off*, 42 a; also in passive ***to be thrown*** (from a horse or vehicle).

1531 ELYOT *Gov.* II. xiii, The courser..will stere and plonge and endeuour hym selfe to throwe hym. **1623** MASSINGER *Bondman* II. ii, This morning, As I rode to take the air, the untutored jade Threw me, and kicked me. **1748** *Anson's Voy.* II. xii. 265 One of their horses fell down and threw his rider. **1890** J. PAYN *Burnt Million* II. xxx. 248 He was thrown from his horse in the steeplechase. **1893** *Field* 4 Mar. 335/3 Had the [bicycle-] rider been thrown or killed.

22. Of a snake, a bird, etc.: To cast (the skin); to moult (feathers). Of a horse: to cast or lose (a shoe).

1590 SHAKS. *Mids. N.* II. i. 255 There the snake throwes her enammel'd skinne. **1765** *Treat. Dom. Pigeons* 41 If your Pigeons..stop in their molting, so that they don't throw their feathers well. **1821** SCOTT *Kenilw.* ix, To shoe my horse,..you may see that he has thrown a forefoot shoe. **1841** J. T. HEWLETT *Parish Clerk* I. 168 The post-boy.. contrived to 'throw a shoe' [i.e. off his horse].

23. a. Of domestic animals: To produce as offspring; to give birth to, to drop. Also *absol.*, ***to throw true***, to produce offspring true to the parent type. (Cf. also *throw back*, 38 d.)

1845 *Jrnl. R. Agric. Soc.* V. II. 546 You cannot possibly tell what sort of foal your mare may throw. **1858** *Ibid.* XIX. I. 28 In a breeding sow for a dairy farm..we should have a disposition to throw large farrows and a good supply of milk. **1892** *Pall Mall G.* 16 June 2/3 Each of these [three varieties of the rabbit] has marked and unmistakable characteristics, and each of them, to use the naturalist's phrase, 'throws true'. **1903** *Times* 9 Jan. 5/2 In 1884 she threw a calf to a bison bull.

b. *gen.* To produce: see quots.

1891 *Morning Post* 25 Dec. 6/5 Indian or Ceylon teas.. throw a stronger liquor than the same amount of China tea would in double or treble the time. **1892** *Garden* 27 Aug. 194 Sown early and transplanted a good distance apart, the plants will throw immense heads of flowers.

*** **24.** Of a fountain or pump: To eject or project (water); to discharge; also *absol.* Of a locomotive steam-engine: ***to throw fire***, to discharge burning fuel from the funnel. Cf. *throw out, up*, senses 44, 48.

1644 EVELYN *Diary* 27 Feb., The fountain of Laocoon is in a large square pool, throwing the water neere 40 feet high. **1697** DRYDEN *Virg. Georg.* III. 374 (*orig.* 241) The Waters boil, and belching from below, Black Sands, as from a forceful Engine throw. **1806** O. GREGORY *Mech.* (1807) II. 175 A machine by which water is thrown upon fires. **1864** *Jrnl. R. Agric. Soc.* XXV. II. 293 The pumps..throw daily 60,000 to 70,000 gallons. **1893** *Field* 4 Mar. 332/3 Bad stoking may be..the cause of a locomotive 'throwing fire'.

25. A horse is said to *throw* his feet, when he lifts them well in moving, esp. over rough ground. Also *transf.* (*slang*): see quot. 1900. *U.S.*

1827 SCOTT *Chron. Canongate* ii, A famous piece of rough upland pasture, for rearing young colts, and teaching them to throw their feet. **1900** J. FLYNT *Tramping w. Tramps* IV. 397 *Throw the Feet*, to beg, 'hustle', or do anything that involves much action. **1907** [see *poke-out* s.v. POKE *sb.*[3] 1 b]. **1934** *Amer. Ballads & Folk Songs* 24 They had mooched the stem and threw their feet.

26. To form by throwing up with a spade or shovel; to cast up, raise (a mound, etc.); = *throw up*, 48 d. *rare.*

1843 MARRYAT *M. Violet* xlii, Nearly all the hills in this part of New York were thrown by human hands.

27. To vomit; cf. *throw up*, 48 b. *Sc.* and *dial.*

18.. WILSON *Tyneside Songs* (1890) 374 He retched an' he threw i' the hight oo his anguish. *Mod. Sc.* 'I no sooner get up but I begin to throw'.

IV. Intransitive senses related to II and III.

28. *intr.* To cast or fling oneself impetuously; to spring, start, leap, rush. *Obs.* exc. as in quots. 1812, 1891, and in sense 48j.

(Allied in sense to 9, but found earlier, and app. not derived from it.)

c **1205** LAY. 807 Of his horse he þreou [*c* **1275** aþreu]. *Ibid.* 12321 þa cheorles up þreowen [*c* **1275** vp þreuwen]. **1508** [see *throw out*, 44 o]. **1535** STEWART *Cron. Scot.* (Rolls) II. 192 Out of his wame ane meruelus multitude Of foule serpentis..thair threw. **1812** *Sporting Mag.* XXXIX. 186 Which she [the hare] was prevented doing by all the dogs throwing at her at the same time. **1891** ATKINSON *Moorland Par.* 83 The black dog, according to the expression used, 'threw at her'.

†**29.** *intr.* To fall with violence or force. *Obs.*

(Looks like an intrans. or passive of sense 19, but occurs earlier.)

1297 R. GLOUC. (Rolls) 6831 þe king bi an laddre to þe ssip clam an hey & þreu vp to doun in þe se. **1362** LANGL. *P. Pl.* A. v. 201 He þrompelde atte þrexwolde and þreuh [*v.rr.* fel, stey] to þe grounde.

V. Figurative and transferred senses.

30. a. *trans.* To cause to pass, go, or come into some place or position by some action likened to throwing; to put or place with haste, suddenness, or force; e.g. to put (a garment) *on* or *off* hurriedly, hastily, or carelessly.

(Many of these uses come very near the literal sense, and form a transition to the more fig. senses following.)

c **1384** CHAUCER *H. Fame* III. 235 And euery man Of hem ..Had on him throwen a vesture. *a* **1400** *Sir Beues* (E.) 3777 + 3 Euery knyȝt and hys squyer Fayre queyntyse on hem ganne þrowe For no man scholde hem knowe. **1655** STANLEY *Hist. Philos.* III. (1701) 101/1 He is now coming to Athens, being thrown out of his House by the People. **1711** *Spect.* No. 116 ¶6 The Hare immediately threw them [the hounds] above a Mile behind her. **1722** STEELE in *Addison's Drummer* Ded., He only spoke it, and I took all the Pains of throwing it upon Paper. **1786** J. HUNTER *Treat. Venereal Dis.* VI. iii. §2 (1810) 509 The quantity of mercury, to be thrown into the constitution..must be proportioned to the violence of the disease. **1799** *Med. Jrnl.* I. 424 No doubt but the father would have suffered equally with the son, had it [poison] not so soon been thrown off the stomach. **1806** COLERIDGE *Three Graves* xxxiii, Her arms Round Ellen's neck she threw. **1816** J. DALLAWAY *Stat. & Sculp.* 350 The paludamentum was a vestment..thrown over the cuirass and fastened over the shoulder with a golden clasp. **1843** R. J. GRAVES *Syst. Clin. Med.* vii. 84 *note*, I threw some common injection into the tibial arteries. **1859** *Musketry Instr.* 39 Throw the rifle smartly to the front of the right shoulder. **1891** A. GISSING *Moorland Idyll* II. iv. 102 To throw a hand to a drowning man.

b. In figurative uses of various phrases, as ***to throw the reins on, to throw a veil over***, etc.; ***to throw good money after bad***, to incur a further loss in trying to make good a previous one; ***to throw oneself*** or ***be thrown at*** (a man), of a woman, to put herself or be put designedly in the way of, so as to invite the attention of; ***to throw oneself into the arms of***, to become the wife or mistress of.

c **1611** CHAPMAN *Iliad* I. 214 Throw Reins on thy passions, and serve us. **1789** H. MORE *Lett.* (1925) 127 The women all threw themselves at his head. **1825** SCOTT *Talism.* iv, That modest pride which throws fetters even on love itself. **1831** —— *Ct. Robt.* xxxi, To be, without her own consent, thrown, as it were, at the head now of one suitor, now of another. **1833** J. H. NEWMAN *Arians* II. i. (1876) 147 However plausible may be the veil thus thrown over heterogeneous doctrines, the flimsy artifice is discomposed so soon as [etc.]. **1871** FREEMAN *Norm. Conq.* IV. xviii. 231 Their wives were throwing themselves into the arms of other men. *a* **1891** BESANT in J. M. Dixon *Idiom. Eng. Phr.* 336 As for the girls, Claire, they just throw themselves at a man.

c. With immaterial object (e.g. blame, influence, power, obstacles, etc.).

c **1620** T. ROBINSON *Mary Magd.* 301 So the bewitchinge oracle y[t] throughes, About the maidens fancy, strange Deludinge showes. **1697** DRYDEN *Virg. Georg.* IV. 325 Thro' Heav'n, and Earth, and Ocean's Depth he throws His Influence round. **1718** POPE *Iliad* XIII. 291 On Greece no blame be thrown. **1753** MISS COLLIER *Art Torment.* II. ii. (1811) 129 Throw a languidness into your countenance;.. appear so perfectly dejected and low-spirited, that [etc.]. **1856** *Jrnl. R. Agric. Soc.* XVII. II. 367 The carriage of materials is usually thrown upon the tenant. **1869** W. LONGMAN *Hist. Edw. III*, I. viii. 138 Philip threw every obstacle in the way of reconciliation. **1871** EARLE *Philol. Eng. T.* 133 They throw the accent often on the close of a word. **1890** TOUT *Hist. Eng. from 1689* 36 Skill in such arts gradually threw real power into the hands of a ring.

d. To put *into* as an addition; to add, incorporate; = *throw in*, 41 b.

1676 LISTER in *Ray's Corr.* (1848) 125, I would either put them [observations] out separately,..or throw them into Mr. Willughby's store. **1862** *Temple Bar Mag.* VI. 503 The saddle being thrown into the bargain. *a* **1904** A. ADAMS *Log Cowboy* vii. 85 Flood's attention once drawn to the brand, he ordered them thrown into our herd.

e. *colloq.* To engage (the clutch or gears) of a motor vehicle. Also *transf.* with the vehicle as obj. Usu. with *in, into.*

1904 A. B. F. YOUNG *Compl. Motorist* vii. 176 The mighty engine is fretting and heating itself with impatience, and the clutch is continually being thrown in and out. **1969** J. T. STORY *Dishonourable Member* ii. 16, I was forced to rev my engine and throw the gears into reverse. **1979** N. SLATER *Falcon* x. 177 He threw the cruising Alfa into third gear and powered away.

f. *trans.* = *throw down*, sense 40 d. Also *absol.*

1923 A. L. SIMON *Supply, Care & Sale of Wine* xvi. 111 If red wines be shipped and bottled too early, they will throw a heavy sediment in the bottle instead of lees in casks. **1930** FIELD & WEILL *Electro-Plating* iv. 64 With copper and zinc sulphate solutions..there is little tendency to 'throw'. **1956** S. M. TRITTON *Amateur Wine Making* iii. 89 The wine ..should not throw a deposit nor form bubbles round the perimeter of the liquid. **1970** *Daily Tel.* 7 July 13/1 Wines throw their deposit or sediment differently.

g. To operate (a switch), esp. by moving a lever. *colloq.* (orig. *U.S.*).

1930 E. B. WHITE *Let.* July (1976) 94 One of the men ran and threw the switch in the foundry, cutting off the current. **1940** 'N. SHUTE' *Landfall* 152 If it goes higher you must throw this switch. **1959** *Listener* 29 Jan. 211/1 If the trespasser's clothes are caught in moving machinery, is not the owner of the premises under a duty to throw the switch in order to stop the machine? **1978** *Times* 20 Nov. 2/3 More than 14,000 civil servants are engaged on government computer work. Those with the direct power to throw the switches..number 1,728.

31. *spec.* **a.** A person is said to be ***thrown into prison***, etc. when roughly or forcibly imprisoned.

1560 DAUS tr. *Sleidane's Comm.* 175 The Turke throweth his Ambassadoure in pryson. **1776** *Trial of Nundocomar* 73/1 When Maha Rajah was first thrown into confinement. **1849** MACAULAY *Hist. Eng.* v. I. 630 This impostor was thrown into prison for his fraud. **1892** GARDINER *Stud. Hist. Eng.* 285 Richard was carried to London and thrown into the Tower.

b. Troops, succour, supplies, or the like are said to be *thrown* into a besieged place, or a strategic position. Also *refl.*

1617 MORYSON *Itin.* II. 119 The Town had beene carried ..if Sir Francis Vere had not throwne himselfe into it with one thousand sixe hundred English. **1693** *Mem. Cnt. Teckely* II. 145 A great number of Gentry, who had thrown themselves into the place. **1736** LEDIARD *Life Marlborough* I. 157 The States..threw 12,000 Men into that Place. **1823** *Examiner* 95/2 Provisions had been thrown into Corinth previously to this incursion. **1836** ALISON *Hist. Europe* (1849–50) V. xxvii. §68. 58 He threw six thousand men across the principal arm into a wooded island. **1844** H. H. WILSON *Brit. India* III. ii. III. 57 A detachment was thrown forward to Ramoo. **1869** T. HUGHES *Alfred* ix. 108 He throws himself into a castle or fort called Cynwith.

c. A bridge or arch is said to be *thrown* from one side to another of, or *over*, a river, passage, or space. Also *fig.*

1751 J. BROWN *Shaftesb. Charac.* 74 This visionary arch which he hath..thrown over the depths of error. **1793** *Regal Rambler* 74 He proposes to throw a bridge over the Fleet-market. **1819** SCOTT *Ivanhoe* xlii. *note*, The skill to throw an arch,..or erect a stair. **1849** *Tait's Mag.* XVI. 16/1 A suspension bridge has been thrown over the river.

32. a. To cause to fall, pass, or come into or out of some condition or relation (or place or thing implying this); properly with the connotation of abruptness, suddenness, or force; to cast, force, drive, plunge, thrust. Usually with *prep.*

1560 BECON *Chr. Knt.* Wks. II. 148 Adam & Eua, whom after thou haddest deceaued through thy lyenge, thou threwest them hedlonge into synne and death. *a* **1652** J. SMITH *Sel. Disc.* IX. viii. (1859) 442 God hath never thrown the world from Himself. **1705** in Hearne *Collect.* 28 Sept. (O.H.S.) I. 49 They..threaten'd to..throw me out of my Chaplain's place. **1766** GOLDSM. *Vic. W.* xviii, The fatigues I had undergone threw me into a fever. **1809** MALKIN *Gil Blas* XII. vii. (Rtldg.) 432 Chance threw me across him, as he came out of a printing-house. **1815** SCOTT *Guy M.* xviii, I do not suspect his equanimity of being so easily thrown off its balance. **1821** *Examiner* 386/1, I cannot let the land be thrown out of cultivation. **1869** W. LONGMAN *Hist. Edw. III*, I. iv. 63 The Scots were thrown into confusion. **1893** *Nat. Observ.* 7 Oct. 527/1 Recruited by men thrown idle by the selfish policy.

b. To put deftly into a particular form or shape; to express in a specified form (in speech or writing); to convert or change *into* some other form; to turn or translate *into* another language.

1723 WATERLAND *2nd Vind. Christ's Div.* xxiii. Wks. 1823 III. 408, I have reason to complain of your..not throwing your disjointed materials into a more neat and regular order. **1740** J. CLARKE *Educ. Youth* (ed. 3) 177 A Master should be able to throw the Latin..into proper English. **1766** *Compl. Farmer* s.v. *Lucern*, A quarter of an acre; which we threw into fifty-four rows. **1789** MRS. PIOZZI *Journ. France*, etc. I. Pref. 6, I have not thrown my thoughts into the form of private letters. **1824** *Examiner* 362/1 Two dress boxes.. were thrown into one. **1892** H. R. MILL *Realm Nat.* xii. 233 The surface..is thrown into a sheet of ridges. **1893** TRAILL *Soc. Eng.* Introd. 30 Cædmon..throws Scripture into metrical paraphrase.

c. ***to throw open*** (***apart, asunder***): to set open (separate, break asunder) with a sudden or energetic impulse; hence *fig.* to make publicly accessible or available (also ***to throw open the gates of***). ***to throw open one's doors to***, to receive as a guest, to welcome.

1709–10 ADDISON *Tatler* No. 116 ¶1, I had ordered the Folding-Doors to be thrown open. *c* **1790** IMISON *Sch. Art* I. 72 The explosion of the gun-powder will throw asunder the roof. **1827** ROBERTS *Voy. Centr. Amer.* 235 The depositories were not thrown open. **1830** *Examiner* 408/2 The railway..will be thrown open..in August. **1844** A. B. WELBY *Poems* (1867) 46 As the blossom waits the breeze Before it throws the leaves apart. **1850** *Tait's Mag.* XVII. 85/2 Labouring to throw open the gates of commerce. **1885** MRS. C. PRAED *Affinities* vi, He..threw open the shutters. **1890** T. F. TOUT *Hist. Eng. from 1689* 192 A University Reform Act..threw open the endowments.

d. To disconcert or confuse (someone), to disturb, upset. Cf. sense 44 l. *colloq.* (orig. *U.S.*).

1844 E. B. BROWNING *Lett. to M. R. Mitford* (1983) II. 431 He appeared to me far more *thrown* by this last adversity than he ever was by the death of his Katy.

1941 B. SCHULBERG *What makes Sammy Run?* vi. 104 Don't let Julian's worries throw you. **1950** L. KAUFMAN *Jubel's Children* xxiii. 247, I knew my way around in a restaurant and a bill of fare. Sometimes, even those French dishes didn't throw me. **1961** C. WILLOCK *Death in Covert* ix. 172 Miche refused to be thrown. 'I rather like enthusiasms,' she said gallantly. **1964** MRS. L. B. JOHNSON *White House Diary* 16 June (1970) 169 Although I was a bit thrown by the mix-up over the two Mrs. Does, I felt this was one of those times that shows whether or not you've got poise and inner calm. **1978** *Browning Inst. Studies* VI. 72 One might almost suspect that Browning was trying to 'throw' his reader. **1981** P. DICKINSON *Seventh Raven* iv. 47 It'll throw those kids if they have to make the change at the last moment.

e. To break or render inoperable (something mechanical). *colloq.* (orig. and chiefly *U.S.*).

1954 *Amer. Speech* XXIX. 103 *Throw a clutch*,..to break a clutch, usually in speed-shifting. 'On the fourth run we threw a clutch, so that was the end.' **1976** *Billings* (Montana) *Gaz.* 1 July 4-E/1 A truck for Springfield, Va., threw its transmission near Towson. **1980** *Dirt Bike* Oct. 43/2 Suzuki teammate Barnett threw a chain while running fourth early in the race.

33. *refl.* ***to throw oneself on*** or ***upon***: to have urgent recourse to (some one) for succour, support, or protection; to commit oneself entirely to (his generosity, mercy, or the like). Also in *pass.* to be made or become dependent upon.

1650 JER. TAYLOR *Holy Living* iv. I. 235 In time of temptation be not busie to dispute, but..throw your self upon God. **1801** CHARLOTTE SMITH *Lett. Solit. Wand.* I. 87 To throw myself into the protection of my only parent. **1812** *Examiner* 24 Aug. 534/1 They are obliged to throw themselves on the parish for aid. **1830** *Ibid.* 550/1 Thrown upon their own resources. **1877** MISS YONGE *Cameos* Ser. III. ix. 80 His wife threw herself upon James's mercy. **1891** *Temple Bar Mag.* Apr. 489, I must throw myself upon Ida's indulgence.

34. a. ***to throw oneself into***: to engage in with zeal or earnestness.

1847 C. BRONTË *Jane Eyre* III. viii. 184 And try to restrain the disproportionate fervour with which you throw yourself into common-place home pleasures. **1868** in Q. Victoria *Life Highl.* Pref. 7 A mind..throwing itself..into the enjoyment of [etc.]. **1871** FREEMAN *Hist. Ess.* Ser. I. iv. 113 The faculty of throwing himself with a lively interest into times so alien to our own. **1881** GARDINER & MULLINGER *Stud. Eng. Hist.* I. v. 86 England threw herself..into a war of conquest against France. **1888** BURGON *Lives 12 Gd. Men* II. v. 46 He was..prepared to throw himself heart and soul into any project.

b. So ***to throw one's soul, heart, life, spirit, energy, efforts***, etc. *into* a thing or action.

1829 *Examiner* 373/2 She threw her whole soul into her voice. **1868** E. EDWARDS *Ralegh* I. iii. 43 He continued to throw all his energy into the distasteful duty. **1890** *Field* 8 Nov. 707/3 The Blackheath forwards threw great spirit into their play.

VI. In combination with adverbs.

35. throw about. a. *trans.* See simple senses and ABOUT.

1377 LANGL. *P. Pl.* B. xx. 163 This sleuthe..a slynge made, And threwe drede of dyspayre a dozein myle aboute. **1719** DE FOE *Crusoe* (1840) II. iii. 52 They..threw everything about in such a manner, that the poor men found ..some of their things a mile off. **1885** *Manch. Exam.* 6 May 5/1 A policeman had seen him throwing his arms about. **1942** *Tee Emm* (Air Ministry) II. 85 The operational fighter pilot..wants an aircraft..easily manœuvreable so that he can throw it about when necessary. **1959** *Motor* 11 Nov. 524/1 On the confined test ground it seemed easier to 'throw about' than the big B.M.W., but neither car could show its paces in the space available.

b. *Naut. absol.* or *intr.* To turn about at once; to go directly upon the other tack; to go about, put about. Also *fig.* Also ***to throw round.***

1591 SPENSER *M. Hubberd* 80, I..meane for better winde about to throwe. **1757** CAPT. RANDALL in *Naval Chron.* XIV. 98 They threw about, and stood for us again. **1894** *Times* 10 July 11/1 When the vessels next met the American was far enough ahead to throw about on the Britannia's weather bow. **1894** *Daily News* 24 July 8/4 Shortly afterwards Vigilant threw round, and stood in.

36. throw aside. a. *trans.* See simple senses and ASIDE.

1530 PALSGR. 281/1 Throwyng asyde, disordring, *debaux.* **1695** TELFAIR *New Confut. Sadd.* (1696) 10 His dog catcht a Fulmard by the way, which Andrew threw aside when he came into the House. **1841** LANE *Arab. Nts.* I. i. 44 When thou atest the date, and threwest aside the stone, it struck my son. *Ibid.* ii. 79 He threw aside the jar. **1857** MILLER *Elem. Chem.* (1862) III. 162 When masses of the husk of the grape ..are thrown aside, and allowed to ferment.

b. *spec.* To cast aside out of use, or as useless; *fig.* to discard, cease to use.

1827 CLARE *Sheph. Cal.* 59 The old beechen bowl..is thrown aside. **1857** MILLER *Elem. Chem.* (1862) III. 14 A little of the dried oxide of copper, which is thrown aside. **1880** FOWLER *Locke* viii. 128 He throws aside the technical phraseology of the schools.

37. throw away. †**a.** *trans.* To cast away from oneself; to reject; to refuse to admit or accept. *Obs.*

1382 WYCLIF *1 Sam.* xv. 23 Forthi..that thow hast throwen aweye the word of the Lord, the Lord hath throwen awey thee, that thow be not kyng. **1387** TREVISA *Higden*

(Rolls) VI. 12 þrow not awey þat þou hast to forhonde approved.

b. To cast away out of one's hands or possession as useless or unneeded.

1530 PALSGR. 756/2, I throwe awaye, as we do thynges that we care nat for.., *je deguerpis*,..*je desjecte*. *a* **1548** HALL *Chron., Edw. IV* 204b, The Lyncolnshyre men..threw away their coates, the lighter to runne away, and fled. *a* **1667** JER. TAYLOR (J.), He that will throw away a good book because not gilded, is more curious to please his eye than understanding. **1690** LOCKE *Hum. Und.* I. i. §5 They will.. throw away the Blessings their hands are fill'd with, because they are not big enough to grasp every thing. **1700** DRYDEN *Charac. Gd. Parson* 37 He melts, and throws his cumbrous cloak away. **1742** *Lond. & Country Brew.* I. (ed. 4) 64 A fresh Cask must be tapped..and the remaining Part of the other throw'd away. **1893** HODGES *Elem. Photogr.* (1907) 101 The used solution..is thrown away.

c. To spend or use without adequate return; to squander, waste; to bestow upon an unworthy object; also, to neglect to take advantage of (an opportunity, etc.); *spec.* at *Cards*, to play (a losing card) when one cannot follow suit, to discard; *spec.* in *Cricket*, to lose (a wicket) through careless play.

1653 JER. TAYLOR *Serm. for Year* I. xxii. 294 We are pleased to throw away our time. **1714** *Spect.* No. 624 ¶1 Advice..would be but thrown away upon them. **1748** HOYLE *Games Impr.* (1778) 56 Do not trump it, but throw away a losing Card, which makes room for your Partner's Suit. **1761** GRAY *Let. to Wharton* 9 May, I had rather Major G. throwed away his money than somebody else. **1798** WORDSW. *We are Seven* xvii, 'Twas throwing words away; for still The little Maid would have her will. **1861** *Temple Bar Mag.* II. 447 The Abbé's prayers will not be thrown away. **1898** K. S. RANJITSINHJI *With Stoddart's Team* (ed. 4) xii. 237 Many wickets were thrown away by the batsmen at critical periods by careless and hasty strokes. **1904** P. F. WARNER *How we recovered Ashes* ix. 185 Braund, Bosanquet, and Rhodes literally threw their wickets away. *a* **1912** *Mod.* Do not throw away your chance. **1977** *World of Cricket Monthly* June 42/3 Once in Lahore, Pakistan, he threw away his wicket so that Australia could win.

d. *refl.* ***to throw oneself away***: chiefly said of a woman in reference to marriage.

1680 OTWAY *Orphan* I. i, Where Dilatory Fortune plays the Jilt With the brave noble honest gallant man, To throw her self away on Fools and Knaves. **1891** E. PEACOCK *N. Brendon* I. 243 She had thrown herself away on one utterly unworthy of her.

e. *Theatr.* To deliver (lines) in a casual manner; to underemphasize or play down (usu. for increased dramatic effect). Also *absol.* and *transf.* Cf. THROW-AWAY B. 3.

1934 J. AGATE in *Sunday Times* 18 Nov. 4/1 The spectator becomes aware of a fixed determination on the actor's part to make as little as possible of anything that can be called the orthodox 'acting' of the part, to throw away—in the actor's sense—everything except the highest of its poetry and the most sensitive of its philosophy. **1957** *Times Lit. Suppl.* 11 Oct. 611/3 Mr Fleming can be exuberant; but he prefers, in the stage term, to 'throw away', something he does just as neatly and wittily as du Maurier used to do it in the theatre. **1959** *Times* 26 May 13/4 In this part he again covered up for his author by charmingly throwing away as many lines as possible. **1959** *Listener* 14 May 861/1 The acting was deliberately played down for microphone purposes... This no doubt necessary business of 'throwing it away' must involve some losses as well as some odd reading of parts.

38. throw back. a. *trans.* See simple senses and BACK *adv.*

a **1822** SHELLEY *A Juno* Wks. 1888 I. 410 The manner in which the act of throwing back one leg is expressed. **1831** SCOTT *Cast. Dang.* i, The reflection of the evening sun, sometimes thrown back from pool or stream. **1859** *Habits Gd. Soc.* iii. 148 The frock-coat should be ample and loose, and a tall well-built man may throw it back. **1890** GERARD *Sensitive Plant* (1891) III. III. xvi. 149 Each tall mirror threw back the image in the other.

b. To put back in time or condition; to delay, make late, throw behind; to retard or check in expected or desired progress; to reduce to a previous or lower condition.

1840 *Jrnl. R. Agric. Soc.* I. IV. 453, I..am not thrown back in getting the land sown. **1850** *Ibid.* XI. II. 419 Wet weather is what throws sheep back. **1858** *Ibid.* XIX. II. 294 The loss of that fortnight..throws an incoming tenant back a whole year. **1868** FREEMAN *Norm. Conq.* II. vii. 114 That.. parliamentary life which..the Norman Conquest threw back for many generations.

c. With *upon*: to compel to fall back upon, or recur to; cf. FALL *v.* 82.

1851 J. H. NEWMAN *Cath. in Eng.* Ded., The violence of our enemies has thrown us back upon ourselves and upon each other. **1892** *Chamb. Jrnl.* 4 June 355/2 If there is no comic boy,..we are thrown back upon Checkley.

d. *intr.* To revert to an ancestral type or character not present in recent generations; to exhibit atavism. *colloq.* Also *fig.* (Cf. 23.)

1879 'CAVENDISH' *Card Ess.*, etc. 63 'Throwing back' more nearly..to the parent games, Poker..is invented. **1887** A. LANG *Myth, Rit. & Relig.* I. 195 Another child may be said in the language of dogbreeders to have 'thrown back'. **1893** *Standard* 22 Apr. 4/3 In politics Lord Derby 'threw back' to the family creed of an earlier generation. **1899** *Allbutt's Syst. Med.* VIII. 279 She 'throws back' to her savage ancestors. **1911** GALSWORTHY *Patrician* II. i. 176 He and his ideas throw back to the Middle Ages.

e. *intr.* To go back in date *to*, to have a history reaching back *to*; to hark back, cast back.

1892 *Sat. Rev.* 28 May 635/1 His Metaphysic..begins with Kant, and only 'throws back' to Kant's forerunners. **1892** *Illustr. Sporting & Dram. News* 17 Sept. 39/2 An old hostelry that throws back nobody knows how many centuries..; throwing back three quarters of a century, a hundred men mustered here.

39. throw by. a. *trans.* To put aside with decision; to reject from present use; to discard.

1611 B. JONSON *Catiline* I. i, It can but shew Like one of Ivnoes..disguises..: and will..When things succeed, be throwne by, or let fall. **1674** FLAVEL *Husb. Spir.* ii. 27 My lazy heart throws by the shovel, and cryes, 'Dig I cannot!' **1770** *Hist.* in *Ann. Reg.* 39 Aly Bey..has thrown by the mask, and..boldly mounted the throne. **1825** J. NEAL *Bro. Jonathan* III. 187, I took another name. I threw by that of my father.

†**b.** To dismiss from consideration; to set aside.

1710 S. PALMER *Proverbs* 141 His best actions thrown by and lessen'd by false turns. **1710** HEARNE *Collect.* (O.H.S.) III. 36 They are very angry with him, and throw by what he has done as being against the Government.

40. throw down (†**adown**). **a.** *trans.* See simple senses and DOWN *adv.*

to throw down a horse, (of a rider) to cause or allow it to fall.

c **1250** *Long Life* 37 in *O.E. Misc.* 158 Weilawei deþ þe schal adun þrowe þer þu wenest heȝest to steo. *c* **1275** LAY. 12323 þe cheorles..þa king icnewen and hine adun þreuwe. **1387** TREVISA *Higden* (Rolls) VII. 349 A grym strook of liȝtnynge smoot þe cherche tour..and þrew [*v.r.* þruw] doun þe crucifex,..and þrew doun oure Lady ymage. *a* **1586** SIDNEY *Arcadia* III. (1598) 361 After her song with an affected modestie, she threw downe her eye. **1660** F. BROOKE tr. *Le Blanc's Trav.* 371 The Mountains..throw down divers Rivers. **1714** *Spect.* No. 558 ¶4 Another after a great deal of puffing, threw down his Luggage. **1787** 'G. GAMBADO' *Acad. Horsem.* (1809) 44 Take care never to throw your horse down, it is an unlucky trick.

b. Expressing a symbolic action; as ***to throw down one's arms***, to surrender; ***to throw down one's brief*** (of a barrister), to decline to go on with a case; so ***to throw down one's pipe***, etc.

to throw down the GAUNTLET or GLOVE: see these words.

1700 S. L. tr. *Fryke's Voy. E. Ind.* 58 Most of them threw down their arms. **1711** STEELE *Spect.* No. 49 ¶2 Mr. Beaver has thrown down his Pipe. **1833** DISRAELI *Cont. Flem.* I. i, I throw down the volume in disgust. **1855** MACAULAY *Hist. Eng.* xx. IV. 523 Williams threw down his brief.

c. To cause to fall, to overthrow, demolish (a building, etc.); also *fig.*

c **1330** *Arth. & Merl.* (Kölbing) 9306 Baners & castels adoun y-þrawe. **1340** *Ayenb.* 23 þe grete wynd, þet þrauþ doun þe greate tours. *c* **1425** *Eng. Conq. Irel.* 18 Thay lay all I-drow a-doune and I-cast to grond. **1528** *Sel. Cas. Star Chamb.* (Selden) II. 19 That the sayd J.M. shuld throwe downe and avoyde the sayde enclosures from the sayd comon grownde. **1530** PALSGR. 756/2, I throwe downe to the grounde, or distroye a thynge. **1645** EVELYN *Diary* 8 Feb., The ruines of a very stately Temple or Theatre..throwne downe by an earthquake. **1713** ADDISON *Cato* II. v. 67 Must one rash word..Throw down the merit of my better years? **1766** FORDYCE *Serm. Yng. Wom.* (1767) I. vii. 302 The admiration raised..is often..thrown down. **1838** THIRLWALL *Greece* III. 101 The Athenians..ordered the Potidæans to throw down the walls of their town on the side of the Peninsula of Pallene.

d. To deposit or cause to be deposited from solution; to precipitate.

1812 SIR H. DAVY *Chem. Philos.* 120 Earths, and oxides, are usually thrown down from their solutions in union with water. **1838** T. THOMSON *Chem. Org. Bodies* 188 Alcohol throws it down from its aqueous solution. **1864** *Jrnl. R. Agric. Soc.* XXV. II. 566 Water that contains much lime on boiling throws down a white deposit.

e. *Agric.* (*a*) To plough (land) so as to level it down; opposed to *gather up* (GATHER *v.* 16). (*b*) To convert (arable land) into pasture; to lay down *to* grass. (Cf. LAY *v.* 51 m.)

1844 STEPHENS *Bk. Farm* I. 477 The mode of ploughing exactly opposite to twice-gathering-up is that of cleaving or throwing down land. **1891** S. C. SCRIVENER *Our Fields & Cities* 143 It is capable of being applied..to almost any land, including that 'thrown down' to grass.

f. *fig.* To put down with force; to lower in rank or station; to degrade, humiliate; to deject in spirits; also, to destroy the effect of, bring to nought.

c **1450** tr. *De Imitatione* III. xxi. 89, I am sone þrowen doun with litel aduersite. **1567** *Satir. Poems Reform.* vi. 23 God wil haue the pride of man doune thrawin. **1610** HOLLAND *Camden's Brit.* (1637) 725 Lifting and throwing downe Princes at her pleasure. **1729** G. ADAMS tr. *Sophocl., Antig.* v. i. II. 65 Fortune raises up, and throws down, makes one fortunate, and another miserable.

g. *slang.* To overcome; to prove too much for; to floor, 'give a fall' to.

1891 *Harry Fludyer* 98 (Farmer), I think I shall floor mine ['exam.'], and Dick's sure to throw his examiners down.

h. *U.S. slang.* To discard, throw off.

Mod. U.S. 'Is she still engaged?' 'Why no, she threw her beau down.'

i. *Cricket.* To knock down (a wicket) with a throw-in from the field, with the intention of dismissing the batsman.

1860 *Baily's Mag.* Sept. 429 John Lillywhite..from long leg..threw down the wicket, and Mr. Davidson was thus run out. **1912** P. F. WARNER *England v. Australia* v. 44 Hobbs throwing down Kortlang's wicket from cover-point. **1962** E. W. SWANTON in Altham & Swanton *Hist. Cricket* (new ed.) II. xii. 244 All seemed over when Solomon from 25 yards range and square with the wicket on the leg-side threw down the stumps to run out Davidson.

41. throw in. a. *trans.* See simple senses and IN.

13.. *K. Horn* 1176 (Harl. MS.) þe ryng þat þou yn þrewe. **1679** M. RUSDEN *Further Discov. Bees* 91 Throwing in a few handsfull of peas. **1730** A. GORDON *Maffei's Amphith.* 303 The Window above that Stair throws the Light in. **1892** *Illustr. Lond. News* 21 May 634/3 He was thrown in with men who..had been intimately acquainted with the Zulu people. *Mod. Cookery Bk.* Throw in a bunch of sweet herbs.

b. To put in as a supplement or addition; to add, esp. to a bargain. Cf. 30 d.

1678 LADY CHAWORTH in *12th Rep. Hist. MSS. Comm.* App. v. 45 Lord Shrewsbury is like to marry Mr. Chiffens his daughter, who will be first and last made worth 40,000*l.* to him, and they talke as if the King should throw in a Dukedome. **1679** MRS. BEHN *Feign'd Curtizan* III. i, Cou'd you not..throw in a little Love and Constancy, to inch out that want of Honesty of yours? **1824** *Examiner* 471/2 Additional dialogue and incident should be..thrown in. **1892** *Black & White* 22 Oct. 476/1 [The] story turns..on murder and revenge, with a little love thrown in.

c. To introduce, insert, or interject in the course or process of something; *esp.* to interpose or contribute (a remark); to put in.

1704 NORRIS *Ideal World* II. xii. 509 A further reflection which it may be convenient to throw in to this explanatory account to make it more full and entire. **1739** tr. *Algarotti on 'Newton's Theory'* (1742) I. 7, I threw in, from Time to Time, little Digressions to vary the Conversation. **1821** CLARE *Vill. Minstr.* II. 85 The old dames..Throw in their hints of man's deluding ways. **1890** BARING-GOULD *Urith* xxxi, 'Not a grain', threw in Julian, hotly. **1891** *Harper's Mag.* Dec. 102/1, I wish to throw in a parenthesis.

d. In technical uses (often *absol.*). (*a*) *Fishing.* To make a cast (in quot. *fig.*). (*b*) *Hunting.* To start (hounds) upon the scent. (*c*) *Wrestling* and *Pugilism.* To toss one's hat into the ring as a challenge or acceptance; hence *fig.* to become a candidate, put in *for*. (*d*) *Football* and *Cricket.* Cf. *throw-in* sb. (THROW- 2).

1816 W. LAMBERT *Cricketer's Guide* (ed. 6) iii. 43 Long Stop. This man..should be one who is not afraid of the Ball, ..and who can throw in well. **1823** *Mirror* No. 14. I. 213/2 When you launch a good thing, which is only heard by the person next you, wait patiently for a pause, and throw in again. **1844** J. T. HEWLETT *Parsons & W.* liv, The hounds were thrown in. **1886** ELWORTHY *W. Somerset Word-bk.*, *Drow in*, to give or accept a challenge in a wrestling or cudgel-playing match. **1887** SHEARMAN *Athletics & Football* 348 [Association] The halves at the sides too must learn to throw in from touch, for this duty as a rule devolves upon them. **1889** H. VASSALL *Rugby Game* 27 There are endless ways of throwing in, and he must practise. **1892** *Field* 8 Oct. 553/3 [He] prefers the glory of winning the Cambridgeshire to throwing in for his chance of the £5000 to-morrow. **1938** *Times* 16 Apr. 8/1 Those 'girls' at the Oval..threw in from the boundary with an accuracy which would have done credit to a University side. **1976** J. SNOW *Cricket Rebel* 118 My back troubled me from the strain of bowling on the harder Australian wickets for four months and my right shoulder had 'gone' when it came to throwing the ball in.

e. ***to throw in one's lot with***: to enter into association with, so as to share the fortunes of (see LOT *sb.* 1 e); so with *fortune*, *interest*. Also *intr.* (chiefly *U.S.*), ***to throw in*** (***with***).

1867 [see LOT *sb.* 1 e]. **1870** ROGERS *Hist. Gleanings* Ser. II. 97 He would have thrown in his lot with the Hydes. **1889** MRS. C. CARR *Marg. Maliphant* III. xxx. 27 On which side do you suppose he would throw in his interest? **1890** *Eng. Illustr. Mag.* Dec. 173 He willingly threw in his fortune with theirs. **1923** *Century Mag.* Oct. 829/1 Lead me to them humans, and I'll throw in with them. **1954** W. FAULKNER *Fable* 359 When we threw in together that day..he didn't know how long he had been on the road. **1978** J. CARROLL *Mortal Friends* I. ii. 15 The important thing was that Jim Brady's best boy—a strong and not unwise lad—had thrown in for good with his own people. **1981** M. MOORCOCK *Byzantium Endures* xi. 262 We should have stayed with the peasants and not thrown in with Russians and Jews.

†**f.** *intr.* At the game of hazard: To throw a number the same as the main (MAIN *sb.*[3] 1: see note there) or which has a certain correspondence with it (see NICK *sb.*[1] 6); to win at hazard. *Obs.*

1880 *Encycl. Brit.* XI. 547/1 The player or 'caster' calls a 'main' (that is, any number from five to nine inclusive). He then throws with two dice. If he 'throws in', or 'nicks', he wins the sum played for from the banker or 'setter'... If the caster 'throws out' by throwing aces, or deuce ace (called crabs), he loses.

g. ***to throw in one's hand***: (*a*) to retire from a card game, esp. poker; (*b*) *fig.*, to give up a contest or struggle. *colloq.*

[**1904** R. F. FOSTER *Pract. Poker* 49 Players should be careful never to throw their hands into the deadwood until they have seen openers.] **1923** *Daily Mail* 3 July 8 Our plucky farmers are not 'throwing in their hands'. **1926** *Auction Bridge Mag.* July 119/1 People get so tired of throwing in hand after hand that they come in, regardless of their position... It needs great self-control to throw in hand after hand. **1938** G. MARCH-PHILLIPPS *Ace High* II. ii. 141 She turned it up and saw the six of Hearts... 'Bitched again!' Bobby said, and threw in his hand. **1957** *Economist* 5 Oct. 59/2 An international understanding outside Egypt is needed before the board can throw in its hand. **1962** D. FRANCIS *Dead Cert* ii. 20, I threw in my hand. I pushed the four chips across to him. **1973** J. ASHFORD *Double Run* ii. 9 Nina Ryan had thrown in her hand without bothering to buy cards. She wasn't really fond of poker. **1978** 'S. WOODS' *Exit Murderer* 145 Sykes looked at him for a long moment..and then suddenly threw in his hand. 'She knew,' he said positively.

42. throw off. a. *trans.* (*lit.* and *fig.*) See simple senses and OFF.

1447-8 J. SHILLINGFORD *Lett.* 2 Feb. (Camden) 36 How hit was procured and shortly throwen of. **1647** HAMMOND *Power of Keys* iii. 30 He had thus confidently thrown off these Epistles from being written by Ignatius. **1720** WATERLAND *Eight Serm.* 115, I was once inclinable to defer the Treating of it some time longer; thinking it most suitable

..to throw it off to the last part of what I intend upon this Subject. **1726** LEONI *Alberti's Archit.* I. 15/1 The Covering ..shou'd..incline of one side to throw off the Rain. **1747** FRANKLIN *Lett.* Wks. 1840 V. 182 To show that points will throw off as well as draw off the electrical fire. **1790** MRS. WHEELER *Westmld. Dial.* ii. 65 Bil Watson..flayd Galoway, et it set off a Gallop an thraad him off. **1823** J. BADCOCK *Dom. Amusem.* 52 A concave glass..will throw the objects off and reduce their size. **1892** *Sat. Rev.* 7 May 542/1 The pumps..were throwing off 7,000 gallons per minute.

b. To rid or free oneself by force from, to get rid of, shake off (a yoke, restraint, burden, etc.); to repudiate or reject the authority of; also, to cast off, disown (an associate).

1618 BOLTON *Florus* (1636) 131 The first who threw the yoake off, were the Macedonians. **1681** DRYDEN *Span. Friar* III. iii, 'Twould be better yet, Cou'd you provoke him to give you th' occasion, And then to throw him off. **1793** J. BOWLES *Real Ground Pres. War w. France* (ed. 5) 75 Throwing off every restraint of honour and principle. **1822** *Examiner* 229/2 The Spanish Colonies..have thrown off the yoke of the mother country. **1879** DOWDEN *Southey* iii. 64 Unless the disease were thrown off by regular exercise. **1899** *Allbutt's Syst. Med.* VIII. 156 An extraordinary power of throwing off fatigue.

c. To cast off, put off energetically (something put on or assumed, as a garment); to divest oneself of (a quality, character, habit, feeling, etc.); to lay aside quickly or decisively; to discard.

1681 DRYDEN *Span. Friar* IV. ii, Virtue must be thrown off; 'tis a coarse garment. **1697** J. LEWIS *Mem. Dk. Glocester* (1789) 8 To throw off childish toys, saying he was then a man. **1706** E. WARD *Wooden World Diss.* (1708) 41 He throws off his Gown and Hypocrisy together. **1872** C. E. MAURICE *S. Langton* i. 52 He throws off his chancellorship at once. **1885** *Manch. Exam.* 28 Sept. 5/3 If he should suddenly throw off his coat in a cold room. **1893** *Nat. Observ.* 7 Oct. 535/2 Monson threw off the pirate and appeared the king's officer.

d. To shake off or divert (a pursuer or competitor in a race); = *throw out*, 44 k; also, to throw off the scent.

1695 BLACKMORE *Pr. Arth.* I. 354 Reason..stops her pace, Is soon thrown off, and quits th' unequal Chase. **1891** *Blackw. Mag.* CXLIX. 468/1 He wasn't to be thrown off by a false scent. **1892** *Field* 2 Apr. 475/1 A check threw hounds off for a minute. **1893** *Ibid.* 11 Feb. 186/3 The leading hounds are very near him; he cannot throw them off.

e. *Hunting.* To free from the leashes, to start (hounds) in the chase; to let fly (a hawk, etc.). Now *esp. absol.* or *intr.*, of foxhunters or hounds: To begin hunting; hence *fig.* to make a beginning in anything; to begin.

1735 SOMERVILLE *Chase* II. 123 Where..the rank Mead Affords the wand'ring Hares a rich Repast; Throw off thy ready Pack. **1784** COWPER *Wks.* (1837) XV. 150 On Friday ..we attended an attempt to throw off a balloon at Mr. Throckmorton's. **1825** SCOTT *Betrothed* xxiii, Each holding a hawk on his wrist, and anxiously adjusting the mode in which they should throw them off. **1892** *Field* 7 May 664/2 They threw off the hounds, found an otter, and, after two hours, killed.

intr. **1789** *Loiterer* 14 Feb. 8 No sooner had the hounds thrown off than my horse grew..hot. *Ibid.* 11 Apr. 5, I have been assured by very experienced Hunters of Tufts, that they never threw off earlier than twelve. **1811** *Sporting Mag.* XXXVII. 88 They [hounds] throw off generally three times a week. **1818** COL. HAWKER *Diary* (1893) I. 162, I threw off in the great woods round Cold Henley. **1866** GLADSTONE in Morley *Life* (1903) II. v. ix. §5. 156, I had to throw off in my new capacity. **1892** *Field* 26 Nov. 808/1 Many packs would not have thrown off at all on such a morning.

f. To eject, emit, give off, esp. from the body or system; *esp.* to expel or discharge (waste or morbid products); *rarely*, to vomit.

1737 BRACKEN *Farriery Impr.* (1756) I. 235 These Creatures throw off a vast deal from their Lungs in Respiration. **1747** tr. *Astruc's Fevers* 105 A crisis, or critical depuration of the humours, whereby the peccant matter is thrown off:..just as we see in the small-pox, measles, &c. **1829** *Examiner* 267/2 When he found anything disagreeing with his stomach, he retired and threw it off. **1846** *Jrnl. R. Agric. Soc.* VII. II. 308 Plants decompose carbonic acid, and throw off oxygen. **1862** *Temple Bar Mag.* VI. 474 Dense volumes of smoke are thrown off. **1864** *Gd. Words* 102/1 They exude, or throw off from themselves, the spent materials which are excrementitious. **1891** *Harper's Mag.* Aug. 357/1 From all parts of the living body living gemmules are being thrown off.

g. To produce and send forth (as offspring or the like); esp. of a hive of bees: to send forth (a swarm). Cf. 23. Also = *throw out*, 44 d.

1828 *Examiner* 541/2 A swarm of bees thrown off from one of his scapes. **1842** J. AITON *Domest. Econ.* (1857) 268 The gray rabbit..generally throws off three, four, five, or six litters..by the first of June. **1862** *Temple Bar Mag.* IV. 548 A massive pillar..threw off rough branches of stone. **1892** *Gd. Words* Dec. 816/1 Its territory was small and it threw off many colonies.

h. To produce with speed and facility (a literary or artistic work or sketch); to execute in a ready and spontaneous manner.

1761 *Ramsay's Ever-green* I. 5 *note*, That this Way of throwing off a Verse easily was first introduced by him. **1823** J. BADCOCK *Dom. Amusem.* p. iv, The new articles..having been 'thrown off at a heat', stood particularly in want of re-revision. **1850** *Tait's Mag.* XVII. 115/2 Those exquisite works which..Chantrey so frequently threw off in marble. **1893** *Temple Bar Mag.* XCVIII. 518 Having thrown his compositions off at white heat.

i. *Printing.* To print off. (Often with mixture of the literal sense.)

1803 SCOTT *Let. to Ballantyne* 21 Apr., in *Lockhart*, I have to thank you for the accuracy with which the Minstrelsy is thrown off. Longman and Rees are delighted with the printing. **1873** SPENCER *Stud. Sociol.* vi. 126 Its own immense edition is thrown off in a few hours every morning.

j. To deduct from the total; to knock off.

1821 *Examiner* 385/2 An abatement of rent, Mr. S! Why ..last year I threw you off 200*l.* **1845** *P. Parley's Ann.* VI. 299 Perhaps, if you are a good girl, and pay regularly every week, I may throw you off something at the end of the year.

43. throw on. a. *trans.* See simple senses and ON. **b.** To put on (apparel) hastily or carelessly: the opposite of *throw off*, 42 c. **c.** To put (hounds) on the scent. †**d.** ? To win (a main) at hazard (*obs.*); cf. *throw in, throw out*, 41 f, and 44 m.

c **1374** CHAUCER *Compl. Mars* 99 He thrwe [*v. rr.* threw(e, throweth] on his helme of huge wyght. **1801** *Sporting Mag.* XVIII. 95 He once won 17,000*l.* at hazard, by throwing on, as it is called, fourteen successive mains. **1815** *Ibid.* XLV. 253 After the usual law, the hounds were thrown on. **1862** *Temple Bar Mag.* VI. 421 He throws on his colour at once, with a very evident freedom of pencil. **1873** J. RICHARDS *Wood-working Factories* 76 Watch persons trying to throw on a belt [upon a pulley]... The one will throw it on instantly.

44. throw out. (See also OUT-THROW.) **a.** *trans.* See simple senses and OUT; *spec.* of frost, etc.: to force (young plants) out of the ground.

1590 SPENSER *F.Q.* I. vi. 6 The pitteous mayden..Does throw out thrilling shriekes, and shrieking cryes. **1600** J. PORY tr. *Leo's Africa* II. 81 His theeues carcase is throwne out to be deuoured of dogs. **1706** E. WARD *Wooden World Diss.* (1708) 100 He..falls to throwing every Thing out at the Window. **1753** CHAMBERS *Cycl. Supp.* s.v. *Marygold*, The flowers of the common marygold..promote sweat, and are good to throw out the small-pox, or any other eruption. **1830** LYELL *Princ. Geol.* I. 406 [In an earthquake] Cones of sand, six or eight feet in height, were thrown out of the lands near the Runn [of Cutch]. **1840** *Jrnl. R. Agric. Soc.* I. III. 272 The wheat is usually only thrown out in severe frosts. **1847** *Ibid.* VIII. I. 66 The rolling and treading..prevent the plants being thrown out by alternate frosts and thaws. **1885** J. K. JEROME *On the Stage* 42 To make your voice 'carry', you have to throw it out, instead of letting it crawl out when you open your mouth.

b. To put out forcibly or suddenly from a place, office, or employment; to eject, expel, turn out.

1526 *Pilgr. Perf.* (W. de W. 1531) 18 Whome..god suffreth..vtterly to be throwen out from the kyngdome of glorye. **1710** HEARNE *Collect.* (O.H.S.) II. 348 Ld. Rialton ..will be thrown out the next Election. **1780** WARNER in Jesse *Selwyn & Contemp.* (1844) IV. 382, I suppose it is not possible to throw Barrow out. **1826** *Examiner* 387/2 General Palmer has been thrown out for Bath.

c. *transf.* and *fig.* To put forth vigorously from within; to emit, radiate (heat or light); to exude; to produce, be the source of; to send out, put forth (buds, shoots, etc.). Also, to project (the voice), esp. in singing. Cf. sense 15 a above.

1750 tr. *Leonardus' Mirr. Stones* 99 It grows warm, and throws out a heat. **1756** P. BROWNE *Jamaica* 236 Where-ever the trunk or larger branches of this tree are wounded, they throw out a thick resinous gum. **1792** H. NEWDIGATE *Let.* Feb. in A. E. Newdigate-Newdegate *Cheverels* (1898) ix. 123 Mortellari..is giving her an Artful Manner of throwing out her Voice to be heard in public. **1838** T. THOMSON *Chem. Org. Bodies* 995 Plants, when exposed to the light, absorb carbonic acid, decompose it, and throw out again the greatest part of the oxygen. **1845** *Jrnl. R. Agric. Soc.* VI. II. 580 Artichokes..throwing out stems from 7 to 10 feet in length. **1850** LYNCH *Theoph. Trin.* xii. 235 Truth and goodness throw out a vivifying electric agency. **1880** C. R. MARKHAM *Peruv. Bark* xviii. 210 The plants..had begun to bud and throw out young leaves.

d. To cause to project, protrude, stretch out, or extend; *spec.* in Bookbinding, see quot. 1880.

1849 THACKERAY *Pendennis* xxii, We'll throw a conservatory out, over the balcony. **1861** *Jrnl. R. Agric. Soc.* XXII. II. 352 Both ranges throw out spurs. **1880** ZAEHNSDORF *Bookbinding* 8 By mounting a map on a guard the size of the page it may be kept laid open on the table beside the book... This is technically called 'throwing out' a map. **1890** R. M. KETTLE *Old Hall* II. ii, The old trees.. throw out giant branches.

e. To bring into prominence or relief, to cause to 'stand out'.

1860 RUSKIN *Mod. Paint.* V. IX. viii. §4. 283 The tone of the whole is dark and gray, throwing out the figures in spots of light.

f. *Mil.* To send out (skirmishers, etc.) to a distance from the main body. Also in *fig.* context.

1834–47 J. S. MACAULAY *Field Fortif.* (1851) 265 The infantry will..throw out skirmishers, and..push on to support them. **1862** *Temple Bar Mag.* V. 373 Mamma throws out skirmishing parties among likely shops. **1863** LD. LYTTON *Ring Amasis* x, His senses, all on the alert, were throwing out scouts and outposts in every direction. **1893** FORBES-MITCHELL *Remin. Gt. Mutiny* 258 We bivouacked on the plain, strong piquets being thrown out.

g. To give utterance or expression to; now *esp.* to put forward tentatively, give (a hint or suggestion); also with obj. clause, to suggest.

1611 BEAUMONT & FL. *Maid's Trag.* IV. ii, I have thrown out words That would have fetch'd warm blood upon the cheeks Of guilty men. **1633** EARLE *Microcosm.* lxxviii. (Arb.) 103 Not a jest throwne out, but he will make it hitt him. *a* **1763** W. KING *Polit. & Lit. Anecd.* (1819) 246 Such an infamous appellation, that I scarce believe the most fiery sectarist among us..would dare to throw out. **1793** *Trial of Fyshe Palmer* 33 He at first threw out that till these were totally abolished we would contend with them. **1824** M. WILMOT *Let.* 26 May (1935) 214, I only throw out this idea to shew I am ready to act on it. **1869** A. W. WARD tr. *Curtius' Hist. Greece* II. III. ii. 392 Athens unhesitatingly accepted the challenge thrown out. **1891** *Cornh. Mag.* July 106 The hint of danger which Norbury threw out was the one thing needed.

h. To put forth visibly, display, exhibit; also †*refl.* to express oneself freely; to 'launch out'.

1710 POPE *Lett.* (1735) I. 116, I Resume my old Liberty of throwing out myself upon Paper to you. **1763** J. BROWN *Poetry & Mus.* v. 85 His warlike Genius threw itself out, in Subjects that were grand and terrible. **1798** JANE AUSTEN *Let.* 1 Dec. (1952) 34 He wants my mother to look yellow and to throw out a rash, but she will do neither. **1806** A. DUNCAN *Nelson* 32 The signal was thrown out for the..fleet to prepare for action. **1890** MRS. R. JOCELYN *M.F.H.'s Daugh.* xvii, Belton's horse also threw out signs of distress.

i. To dismiss from acceptance, use, or consideration; to reject; to leave out of a reckoning; in *Écarté*, to discard, 'throw away'.

1618 in Foster *Eng. Factories Ind.* (1906) 48 What I found grose I thrue out or cutt. **1660** MILTON *Free Commw.* Wks. (1847) 449/1 To us who have thrown it [monarchy] out, received back again, it cannot but prove pernicious. **1753** MISS COLLIER *Art Torment., Fable* 233 The letter L.. confined the competitors to the lion, the leopard, the lynx, and the lamb. The lamb, by almost general consent, was instantly thrown out, as knowing nothing of the subjects treated of. **1811** SIR WM. SCOTT *Dodson's Rep.* I. 31 Some circumstances stated on behalf of Captain Honeyman, which I may also throw out as immaterial. **1856** OLMSTED *Slave States* 241 They..made further clearings in the forest, and 'threw out', to use their own phrase, so much of the land as they had ruined. **1896** *Indianapolis Typogr. Jrnl.* 16 Nov. 407 When the contract expires, this newspaper will throw out its linotype machines.

j. Of a legislative assembly or a grand jury: To reject (a bill, etc.).

1707 *Vulpone* 2 This Proposal..occasion'd very great Debates..and was Scandalously Treated and thrown Out. **1732** HEARNE *Diary* 27 Sept., His petition..was thrown out of the house. **1817** *Parl. Deb. Ho. Lords*, The grand jury.. whose duty it was to find the bills had thrown them out. **1873** P. V. SMITH *Hist. Eng. Inst.* II. v. 175 The Ballot Bill ..was thrown out by the Lords.

k. *Sporting.* To put out of place or order by leaving behind in a chase or race; to distance, outpace.

1713 ADDISON *Cato* I. i, A Virtue that has cast me at a Distance, And thrown me out in the Pursuits of Honour. **1807** *Sporting Anecd.* 179 Jack was mounted on a hunter, which he assured me was never yet thrown out. **1823** SCOTT *Quentin D.* ix, I had been unluckily thrown out, and was riding fast, to be in my place. **1889** W. WESTALL *Birch Dene* III. xii. 202 More than once he threw them [his pursuers] out by a double.

l. To disturb (a person) from his self-possession, train of thought, normal or equable state of mind, or ordinary course of action (see OUT *adv.* 5); = *put out*, PUT *v.*[1] 47 f. Also *transf.*, of a plan, calculation, etc.

1824 H. DAVY *Diary* July (1836) II. v. 211 My *senza cura* servant, threw me out by not putting powder enough in my horn. **1844** J. H. NEWMAN *Lett.* (1891) II. 442 He was surprised and thrown out by finding I did not seem to be what he had fancied. **1891** *Murray's Mag.* Apr. 551 Seeing her there acting the part of a governess..threw him out. **1891** *Field* 28 Nov. 837/3 The visitors kicked off, but the heavy ground at first seemed to throw them out. **1892** A. W. PINERO *Magistrate* I. 24, I took five years from my total... It has thrown everything out. As I am now thirty-one, instead of thirty-six as I ought to be, it stands to reason that I couldn't have been married twenty years ago.

†**m.** *absol.* In the game of hazard, To make a losing cast (see note s.v. MAIN *sb.*[3] 1). *Obs.*

a **1680** BUTLER *Satyr Gaming* 80 Although he..crucify his Saviour worse Than those Jew-Troopers that threw out, When they were raffling for his Coat. **1765** EARL MARCH in Jesse *Selwyn & Contemp.* (1843) I. 308, I am very sorry to hear that you are still throwing out [*note*, at hazard] as well as me.

n. *Cricket.* Of a fieldsman: To put (the batsman) 'out' by throwing the ball so as to hit his wicket. So in *Baseball*, to put (a base-runner) 'out' by throwing the ball to a player on or near a base.

1871 HOPPE s.v. *Out*, '*Out*' wird der einzelne Schläger.. wenn ein andrer der *fielders* während des *crossing* den Ball gegen das *wicket* werfen kann (*he is thrown out*). **1892** *Field* 11 June 870/3 Mr. Jackson threw him out from cover-point, when the batsmen were attempting a short run.

o. *intr.* (for *refl.*) †To turn out, throng or press out (*obs.*); to move outwards from a centre; to strike out with hands or feet; to let oneself go; to push out (as a root). Cf. sense 9.

1508 DUNBAR *Flyting* 217 Off Edinburgh, the boyis as beis owt thrawis. **15..** *Peblis to the Play* v, Thai out threw Out of the townis untald. **1771** WOLLASTON in *Phil. Trans.* LXI. 561 The pendulum did not..throw-out so far by about 7' as it generally did. **1798** J. T. DUCKWORTH in *Naval Chron.* (1799) I. 78 The wind throwing out caused me to anchor. **1798** in *Spirit Pub. Jrnls.* (1799) II. 296 He threw out and kicked a good deal. **1809** MALKIN *Gil Blas* III. iv. ¶4 The fear of talking absurdly prevents you from throwing out at all. **1825** J. NICHOLSON *Operat. Mechanic* 518 The pallet A can throw out till it reach *a*,..B will throw out as far on the other side. **1855** *Jrnl. R. Agric. Soc.* XVI. I. 176 Such soils turn up as a fine mould..and the roots can throw out without impediment.

p. *intr.* or *absol.* Of a printing machine: To fail to register.

45. throw over. a. See simple senses and OVER.

1857 HUGHES *Tom Brown* II. viii, Jack Raggles is furious, and begins throwing over savagely to the further wicket.

b. To throw overboard (in *fig.* sense); to cast off (a lover, associate, or ally); to abandon; to cancel (an appointment) with someone, to put (someone) off.

1835 DICKENS *Let.* 5 Nov. (1965) I. 88, I will throw Bell's life over, altogether. **1836** T. HOOK *G. Gurney* II. 186, I was satisfied that Emma had thrown me over. **1874** STUBBS *Const. Hist.* I. vi. 163 *note*, Mr. Freeman..throws over the latter part of Palgrave's theory. **1890** T. F. TOUT *Hist. Eng. fr. 1689* 27 They threw over their allies. **1891** O. WILDE *Pict. Dorian Gray* iii. 62 'Are you disengaged Tuesday?' 'For you I would throw over anybody, Duchess.' **1903** G. B. SHAW *Man & Superman* I. 40 Tavy will kiss; and you will only turn the cheek. And you will throw him over if anybody better turns up. **1908** E. F. BENSON *Climber* x. 146 He had another engagement, and though I urged him not to throw it over when I heard that, he really insisted on coming.

throw round (*Naut.*): = *throw about*, 35 b.

46. throw to. †**a.** *trans.* To put quickly with something else which is already there. *Obs.*

a **1400–50** *Alexander* 2939 Anoþire boll was him broȝt, & bathe he deuoydid, And ȝit he threw to þe thrid, & thrast in þare-eftir.

b. To close (a door, etc.) with force.

1741 RICHARDSON *Pamela* (1824) I. xv. 26, I made shift to get into it [the chamber], and threw-to the door, and it locked after me. **1892** *Chamb. Jrnl.* 23 July 473/1 The slamming of one of the church doors, as if thrown-to by a draught.

47. throw together. a. *trans.* See simple senses and TOGETHER.

1717 BERKELEY *Let. to Pope* Wks. 1871 IV. 82 A wonderful variety of hills, vales, ragged rocks, fruitful plains, and barren mountains, all thrown together in a most romantic confusion. **1878** I. L. BIRD *Lady's Life Rocky Mountains* (1879) iii. 37, I threw a few things together and came here. **1967** E. SHORT *Embroidery & Fabric Collage* i. 18 A bundle of threads or fabrics accidentally thrown together may suggest an exciting scheme.

b. To put together hastily or roughly; to combine or collect without much care or finish. (Said in relation to literary work.)

1711 ADDISON *Spect.* No. 105 ¶3 On my retiring to my Lodgings, I could not forbear throwing together such Reflections as occurred to me upon that Subject. **1713** BERKELEY *Guard.* No. 88 ¶3, I shall throw together some passages relating to this subject. **1748** *Anson's Voy.* III. ii. 308, I shall..throw together the most interesting particulars ..in relation to..Tinian.

c. To bring (persons) casually into contact or association.

1818 SCOTT *Heart Midl.* I. viii. 226 The circumstances of their families threw the young people constantly together. **1831** *Society* I. 207 They were to meet as old friends, when they were next thrown together in London. **1889** FROUDE *Two Chiefs Dunboy* xxi. 313 They had been thrown together as children, but had rarely met since.

d. To prepare (a snack, meal, etc.) hastily or in an improvised manner.

1962 'E. FERRARS' *Busy Body* i. 13 If we haven't eaten she'll throw something together. **1980** P. G. WINSLOW *Counsellor Heart* iv. 64 She hadn't been listening much, throwing a quick supper together.

48. throw up. a. *trans.* See simple senses and UP. †*spec.* To throw open (a gate, etc.) (*obs.*).

to throw up the sponge, to give in, surrender: see SPONGE *sb.*, and cf. CHUCK *v.*[2] 2 b.

14.. *Sir Beues* (M.) 1655 + 20 Anon the gates he gan up throwe. *c* **1422** HOCCLEVE *Jereslaus' Wife* 364 Vp he threew an heuy syk. **1675** BROOKS *Gold. Key* Wks. 1867 V. 511 You may throw up your caps at them, and bid them do their worst. **1780** COXE *Russ. Disc.* 253 The chain of islands here laid down may..be considered as thrown up by some late volcanos. **1797** *Encycl. Brit.* (ed. 3) XVI. 492/2 When the cable is finished, to shorten it two fathoms more, which our workmen call *throwing the turn well up.* **1833** J. HOLLAND *Manuf. Metal* II. vii. 189 The fresh coals..will throw up.. a body of thick smoke. **1842** *Jrnl. R. Agric. Soc.* III. II. 171 Land..thrown up into very narrow ridges. **1850** *Ibid.* I. IV. 381 Milk..throws up less cream in glass than in wood. **1861** *Temple Bar Mag.* III. 221 She hastily threw up the window. **1893** *Argosy* Aug. 116 The seaweeds thrown up on his estate.

b. To discharge by vomiting; to vomit. Also *intr.* (now the usual use). Now chiefly *colloq.* or *slang.* Also (*slang*) *to throw up one's accounts*, in same sense (cf. CAST *v.* 83 b).

1732 ARBUTHNOT *Rules of Diet* iii, It is easy to judge of the Cause by the Substances which the Patient throws up. **1763** C. JOHNSTON *Reverie* I. 135 Before he can be on the guard, hitting him a plump in the bread-basket, that shall make him throw up his accounts. **1793** *Morning Chron.* 20 Feb. 3/1 In what odd ways we taste misfortune's cup—While France throws *down* the gauntlet—Pitt throws *up.* **1822–34** *Good's Study Med.* (ed. 4) II. 449 Blood from the stomach..thrown up by vomiting. **1887** V. MARTIN *Let.* in M. Collis *Somerville & Ross* (1968) iii. 44 To show that he was quite unembarrassed he began to play with the favourite pug, finally dancing it round on its hind legs. It immediately threw up and that I think ends the story. **1895** HERRON & BACON in A. Dundes *Mother Wit* (1973) 367/2 He made a tea which acted as an emetic and the patient threw up a variety of reptiles. **1934** T. N. WILDER *Heaven's my Destination* 6 He thought he was going to throw up. **1956** [see SHOWBUSINESS 1 b]. **1970** G. F. NEWMAN *Sir, You Bastard* i. 24 What if the scene was a man with the front wheel of a bus on his chest? Wasn't the calm, inspiring copper entitled to throw up? **1977** *New Yorker* 19 Sept. 49/3 I'm not sure anyone else even noticed, but it upset me so much I threw up. **1980** A. E. FISHER *Midnight Men* viii. 102 Ogy got drunk and threw up in the backyard.

c. To raise (the hands, eyes, etc.) quickly or suddenly; *spec.* in ***throw up your hands***, as a command to surrender: cf. *hands up* (HAND *sb.* 55).

1746 FRANCIS tr. *Hor., Sat.* II. vii. 54, I throw my Nose up to a savoury Steam. **1821** *Examiner* 524/1 Eternally throwing up their eyes to heaven. **1880** [see BAIL *v.*[3] 2]. **1887** I. R. *Lady's Ranche Life Montana* 37 He was suddenly aware of a horse galloping rapidly up behind him, and heard a shout: 'Throw up your hands!' **1890** FENN *Double Knot* III. i. 19 The woman threw up her hands and reeled. **1891** *Eng. Illustr. Mag.* No. 88. 306 Bail up, throw up your hands now, or I'll shoot every man jack of you.

d. To cast up (a heap or earthwork) with or as with the spade; to erect or construct hastily.

1586 DAY *Eng. Secretary* I. (1625) A iij, The gardner, who first throweth vp his earth on a rude heape. **1709** STEELE *Tatler* No. 6 ¶10 The Greeks threw up a great Intrenchment to secure their Navy. **1869** HUGHES *Alfred the Gt.* vi. 71 They..threw up earthworks, and entrenched themselves there. **1880** R. MACKENZIE *19th Cent.* III. ii. 287 Armed crowds began to appear, and barricades were thrown up.

e. To render prominent or distinct; to cause to 'stand out'; to make noticeable by contrast.

1882 MRS. OLIPHANT *Lit. Hist. Eng.* I. 288 A..background to throw up and bring into full relief the figure. **1885** MONKHOUSE in *Mag. Art* Sept. 474/2 The dado is darker.. and throws up the rest effectively. **1891** G. D. GALTON *La Fenton* vi, The black folds of her dress throwing up..the marble pallor of her face.

f. *Naut.* ***to throw*** (a ship) ***up in*** (***into, on***) ***the wind***, to turn the vessel into the wind till she points almost directly to windward; also *absol.* said of the navigator.

1769 FALCONER *Dict. Marine* (1789), *Donner vent devant*, to throw a ship up in the wind, or in stays. **1832** MARRYAT *N. Forster* xlvii, The Windsor Castle was thrown up on the wind. **1833** —— *P. Simple* xvi, We threw up in the wind.

g. To cease definitely to do, use, or practise; to give up participation in, or the exercise or use of; to relinquish, abandon, quit, give up; originally in the phrase ***to throw up the game*** or ***one's cards***, i.e. to place one's cards face upwards on the table on withdrawing from the game. Also *absol.*

1678 BUTLER *Hud.* III. III. 543 Bad Games are thrown up too soon, Until th' are never to be won. **1681** W. ROBERTSON *Phraseol. Gen.* (1693) 1225 To throw up his cards, *desistere a lusu.* *a* **1687** PETTY *Pol. Arith.* i. (1691) 33 To throw up their Husbandry, and make no use of their Lands, but for Grass [etc.]. **1731** *Gentl. Mag.* I. 539 The Evidence for the King being full and clear, the Defendant's Council threw up their Briefs. **1874** T. HARDY *Madding Crowd* xlvi, He.. threw up his cards and forswore his game for that time and always. **1889** *Repentance P. Wentworth* II. xii. 261 He decided to throw up his practice at the Bar. **1894** *Times* (weekly ed.) 19 Jan. 49/1 When he was 20 he threw up his employment.

h. ***to throw it up against, at, to one*** (*low colloq.*): to cast it in one's teeth, to upbraid one (with obj. cl.). Cf. *cast up* (CAST *v.* 83 i). Also without *it*, or with personal object: to hold (someone) up as an example, object of reproach, etc.

1815 R. FINDLEY *Let.* 6 Dec. in N. E. Eliason *Tarheel Talk* (1956) 300 Betsey..throwed up to me that I made a better bed for Sally then her little Betsey. **1870** 'MARK TWAIN' in *Galaxy* July 139/1 He [*sc.* Benjamin Franklin] would work all day and then sit up nights..so that all other boys might have to do that also or else have Benjamin Franklin thrown up to them. **1890** *Univ. Rev.* 15 Oct. 198 The children in the street throws it up against me I ain't got no father. **1957** R. LAWLER *Summer of Seventeenth Doll* I. i. 22 Every time he's away and we have a row, Emma throws him up at me like a dirty dish-cloth.

i. *intr.* Of hounds: To lift the head from the ground, the scent having been lost.

1832 *Q. Rev.* XLVII. 237 For heaven's sake, take care of my hounds in case they may throw up in the lane. **1856** 'STONEHENGE' *Brit. Rur. Sports* I. VI. v. 128/1 Whenever it happens, and the hounds begin to throw up, and really *cannot* hunt, it is better to take them away. **1893** *Field* 4 Feb. 170/2 Hounds suddenly threw up in a most unaccountable manner.

j. *intr. Falconry.* See quots. (Cf. 28.)

1881 *Graphic* 5 Nov. 470/3, I [a falcon] stopped my downward course..spread my wings, and 'threw up' towards the upper air. **1900** MICHELL *Art Hawking* 128 Instead of throwing up high, as they would if they had missed, they check their flight quickly, and..descend rapidly on the panting or dazed foe. **1901** FISHER *Remin. Falconer* 96 No hawk stooping from a very high pitch can readily clutch or grasp her prey. She rushes upwards (i.e. throws up) impelled by her momentum..turns over, and is on the grouse directly. *Ibid.* 113.

k. *trans.* To produce or provide. *colloq.*

1963 *Guardian* 23 Sept. 3/5 Their memories of this year's fortnight may last even longer than anything Uncle Ted can throw up from his family joke repertoire on Christmas Day. **1981** M. MOORCOCK *Byzantium Endures* xii. 287 Russia was throwing up better women than men at that time. All the worthwhile men had been killed.

VII. 49. In various proverbial, figurative, idiomatic, or colloquial phrases (beside those mentioned under the senses to which they belong), as *throw off one's* BALANCE, *over the* BAR, *the* BOOK *at*, COLD WATER *on*, *a* DAMP *on*, DIRT, *the* GAUNTLET, *off one's* GUARD, *the* HELVE *after the hatchet* (so the HANDLE *after the head*, *the* ROPE *after the bucket*), *the* HOUSE *out at* (*of*) *the windows*, *a* MONKEY-*wrench into the machinery*, OVERBOARD, *off the* SCENT, *into the* SHADE, *a* SPANNER *in the works*, *the* STOCKING (at a wedding), *down the* STREAM, *in one's* TEETH, *one's* WEIGHT *about*, *to the* WINDS, etc.; as to which see the sbs.

For the verb-stem in combination: see THROW- in Comb.

†**throw** (θrəʊ), *v.*[2] *Obs.* Forms: 1–2 **þrówian**, (2 **þrouwian**), 3 **þrowwenn** (*Orm.*), **þrowin**, **þruwen**, **ðhrow.** *Pa. t.* 1–3 **þrowode, -ede, -ude.** [OE. *þrówian* = OHG. *druoên* (Tatian *þruoên*), *drôên*, *trôên*, *trûên*:—OTeut. **þrôwjan*, f. **þrôw-*, ablaut-grade of **þraw-* in OE. *þrawu* painful pressure: see THREA *v.*]

1. *trans.* To suffer, bear, endure.

Beowulf 2606 ȝeseah his mondryhten under here-griman hat þrowian. *c* **888** K. ÆLFRED *Boeth.* xxxi. §1 Swa swa bearneacen wif acenð bearn & ðrowað micel earfoðu. **971** *Blickl. Hom.* 93 Feallaþ ofor us.., þæt we ne þurfon þysne eȝe leng þrowian. *c* **1000** ÆLFRIC *Gram.* xix. (Z.) 119 *Verbum* ys word..ȝetacniende oððe sum ðing to donne oððe sum ðing to þrowiȝenne. *a* **1175** *Cott. Hom.* 229 He wolde for hus deað þrowian.

2. *intr.* (or *absol.*). To suffer, undergo suffering or pain.

Beowulf 2595 Nearo ðrowode fyre befongen seðe ær folce weold. **971** *Blickl. Hom.* 65 He wolde þrowian for ealra manna hæle. *c* **1175** *Lamb. Hom.* 121 His ahȝenes þonkes he þrowede for us and binom ure sunnan. *c* **1200** *Trin. Coll. Hom.* 101 Ure helende þrowede on þe holi rode. *a* **1225** *Leg. Kath.* 1140 Hwi walde he þrowin as he dude, & þolien deð on rode?

Hence †**'throwing** *vbl. sb.*[2] [OE. *þrówung*], suffering; passion; *esp.* the Passion of Christ.

c **897** K. ÆLFRED *Gregory's Past. C.* xviii. 136 Ic eom eower efnðeowa & Cristes ðrowunge ȝewiota. *c* **1000** ÆLFRIC *Hom.* II. 506 On hwæs timan he ðrowunge under-hniȝe. *c* **1175** *Lamb. Hom.* 87 Nu is his þrowunge and his ariste ure ester tid. *c* **1200** *Trin. Coll. Hom.* 81 His holie þroweȝunge þe he wolde þolien. *c* **1200** ORMIN 15205 Inntill þrowwinnge & pine. *a* **1225** *Ancr. R.* 372 þuruh to stronge uondunges, soule þrowunge. *c* **1250** *Gen. & Ex.* 1317 Wið-uten long ðhrowing and fiȝt. *c* **1275** *Passion* 4 in *O.E. Misc.* 37 Cristes þruwinge þet he þolede her.

Here, apparently, belongs

†**'throwand**, *pr. pple.* and *ppl. a. Sc. Obs.*, suffering the throes of death, struggling in death-agony.

1375 BARBOUR *Bruce* xv. 230 About him slayne lay his menȝe..And he, redy to dey, throwand. **1513** DOUGLAS *Æneis* IV. xii. 60 Hir sistir An..Fast ruschis throw..the rout, And on the throwand [*morientem*]..Callis by name. *Ibid.* 102 Almychty Iuno..Hir maid Iris from the hevin hes send The throwand saull [*luctantem animam*] to lous. [Cf. *a* **1547** SURREY *Æneid* IV. 927 From heauen she sent the Goddesse Iris downe, The throwing sprite and jointed limmes to loose.]

(Since Barbour and Douglas here use *throwand* and not *thrawand*, we seem obliged to refer their word, in form at least, to this verb; although difficulty is caused by the lateness of the use, long after the last examples known in English. It is probable that Surrey, in imitating Douglas's rendering, used *throwing* in the sense of THROE *v.* 2, of which the Sc. form would be *thrawand*: cf. THROW *v.*[1], sense 2 *note.*)

throw: see THRO, THROE, THROUGH, TROW.

throw- in Comb. [THROW *sb.*[2] or stem of THROW *v.*[1], in comb. with sbs. or advbs., forming sbs. or adjs.]

1. In comb. with sbs. **a.** (from branch I of the sb. or vb.) **throw-crank**, a crank which converts rotary into reciprocating motion; **throw-disk** (*Cent. Dict., Suppl.*), **throw-lever**, a disk-crank or a lever having a specified or adjustable throw (sense 2); **throw-lathe**, a lathe driven by hand; **thraw-mouse** (*Sc. dial.*), the shrew-mouse: see quot.; **throw-wheel**, the driving-wheel of a throw or lathe. **b.** (from branch II of vb.) **throw-bait**, bait thrown to attract fish to a place; **throw cushion** *N. Amer.* = *scatter cushion* s.v. SCATTER *v.* 7 b; **throw-line**, a fishing-line thrown out by hand, a hand-line; **throw-net**, a fishing net cast out by hand; **throw pillow** = *throw cushion* above; **throw weight** (see quot. 1982[1]). See also THROW-CROOK, THROW-STICK. **c.** (sense 9 of THROW *sb.*[2]) ***throw rug***; ***throw-style***, ***type*** adjs. Cf. *throw cushion*, *pillow* above. *N. Amer.* (chiefly *U.S.*).

1867 URE *Dict. Arts*, etc. II. 783 A carrier, which is made to advance and recede alternately by means of a *throw-crank. **1970** *Toronto Daily Star* 24 Sept. 28/6 (Advt.), *Throw cushions, chests, dressers. **1877** KNIGHT *Dict. Mech.*, **Throw-lathe*, a small lathe which is driven by one hand, while the tool is managed by the other. **1904** *Brit. & Col. Printer* 10 Mar. 14/3 An intermediate adjustable or variable *throw lever. **1908** *Westm. Gaz.* 19 Sept. 10/2 One day when he was fishing off the rocks with *throw-lines. **1881** GREGOR *Folk-Lore N.-E. Scotl.* 127 The field mouse, called 'the *thraw mouse', running over the foot of a person, was supposed to produce paralysis in the foot. **1931** *Times Educ. Suppl.* 21 Mar. (Home & Classroom Suppl.) p. ii (*caption*), The photograph shows the different kinds of 'nets' used. On the left is the *throw-net. **1979** *Field* 9 May 975/4 For smaller fish the locals used circular throw-nets some eight feet in diameter. **1974** *Progress* (Easley, S. Carolina) 24 Apr. III. 5/2 (Advt.), Decorator *throw pillows. **1952** *Better Homes & Gardens* Feb. 173/1 How to vacuum your *throw rugs. **1978** R. LUDLUM *Holcroft Covenant* xi. 132 She leaned forward on the hassock, picking at an imaginary piece of lint on the throw rug beneath his feet. **1974** *Spartanburg* (S. Carolina) *Herald* 18 Apr. (Kmart Advts. Suppl.) 8 Tailored, *throw-style bedspread, elegantly puff-quilted to the floor. **1970** *Toronto Daily Star* 24 Sept. 37/4 (Advt.), Quilted *throw type bedspreads. **1969** *Sci. Amer.* Aug. 19/2 Parity

..is clearly not numerical equality in the number of warheads or in the number of megatons or in the total '*throw weight'. **1982** *Times* 10 May 22/1 The second stage would seek to achieve equal ceilings on ballistic missile 'throw weight' at less than current American levels. 'Throw weight' is the term used to describe the weight of the warheads which missiles can carry onto a target. **1982** H. KISSINGER *Years of Upheaval* vii. 264 The Soviets were ahead in numbers of land-based missiles and throwweight. **1884** F. J. BRITTEN *Watch & Clockm.* (1886) 304 *Throw*, a clockmakers' 'dead centre' lathe... A gut connects the large *throw wheel with a small pulley rotating freely on the lathe centre.

2. In comb. with adverbs, forming sbs. expressing the action of the corresponding verbal phrases (see THROW *v.*[1] VI.); as ***throw-in***, ***-up*** (an act of throwing in or up); **throw-down**, (*a*) a fall, as in wrestling; a come-down; a defeat (*slang*); (*b*) *Austral.* and *N.Z.*, a type of small firework, a squib; **throw-in**, (*a*) in Football, an act of throwing the ball into play again after it has crossed one of the touch-lines; (*b*) in Cricket, an act of throwing in the ball from the field to the wicket-keeper or bowler; (*c*) in Bridge, an end play in which the declarer throws the lead to an opponent who has to play into a tenace combination; (*d*) in Polo, the act of throwing the ball (by the umpire) between opposing ranks of players, each team being on its own side of the line of the throw, in order to (re)start the game; (*e*) in Baseball, a throw made by an outfielder to an infielder; **throw-on**, an act of throwing onwards or forwards; *spec.* in Rugby football: see quot.; **throw-out**, (*a*) an act of throwing out, or a thing thrown out; anything discarded or rejected; also *attrib.*; (*b*) in Cricket, the act of throwing out a batsman (see THROW *v.*[1] 44 n); (*c*) *Bookbinding* (see quot. 1976); (*d*) the mechanism by which the driven and driving plates of a clutch in a motor vehicle are separated; usu. *attrib.* See also THROW-BACK, -OFF, -OVER.

1896 E. TURNER *Little Larrikin* xxvi. 321 Lol was.. projecting jumping Jacks and *throwdowns on the floor, and keeping the cook..on the table. **1903** *Architect* 24 Apr. Suppl. 27/1 Any delay on the work is 'a throw-down for the boss'. **1948** D. W. BALLANTYNE *Cunninghams* xiv. 75 Kids were exploding throw-downs on the footpaths. **1864** *Baily's Mag.* July 173 What a recreation!—wherein..the hands, dropping for a while the pen.., can..deliver a '*throw-in' decisive of all argument. **1891** [see *goal-kick* s.v. GOAL *sb.* 6]. **1898** J. GOODALL *Assoc. Football* 61 The object of the Association was to make the throw-in from touch a superficial benefit. **1898** T. B. DRYBROUGH *Polo* xi. 245 Players should leave room for the ball to pass between them. In case of overlapping, the umpire may delay throwing-in or recall the throw, and he may recall a faulty throw-in. **1909** *Westm. Gaz.* 8 Feb. 12/2 This umpire seems..somewhat ignorant of the throw-in rule. **1935** [see EXIT *sb.* 2 b]. **1937** *Times* 12 July 5/2 Captain Robinson got away from the throw-in but broke his stick. **1940** *Sun* (Baltimore) 13 May 13 (*caption*) Dolph Camilli..slides safely into third..after a throw-in from outfielder Chuck Klein. **1952** *Ibid.* 2 Oct. 20/1 The Yankees might have had a big inning on the way since Martin had taken second on the throw-in. **1959** M. GILBERT *Blood & Judgement* x. 108 He settled down with *Reese on Play*, to study the tactics of the Throw-in. **1964** *Official Encycl. Bridge* 619/1 In a throw-in play, an opponent gains the lead, but it costs him a trick (or more) to do so. **1977** *Navy News* Sept. 38/4 (*caption*) All eyes on the ball at a throw-in during the Rundle Cup polo match between the Navy and Army at Tidworth. **1845** *Rules Footb. Rugby School* §4 *A Knock on*, as distinguished from *a *throw on*, consists in striking the ball on with the arm or hand. **1894** *Blackw. Mag.* Sept. 426/2 Catching these little fish by means of what are known locally as '*throw out' lines. **1901** *Law Rep.* 2 *K.B. Div.* 698 Small lots of timber called in the trade 'throw-outs'. **1907** *Daily Chron.* 9 Apr. 8/4 A patch of narcissus which nobody takes the trouble to gather. They are the 'throw-outs' from the fields. **1911** *Daily Graphic* 16 Jan. 20/3 'Witney Blanket Rugs': Manufacturers' Throw Outs. **1928** *Weekly Dispatch* 24 June 20/5 That 'throw-out' which has to be executed so quickly at cover-point. **1953** *Vocab. Bibliothec.* (Unesco) 190/1 Throw out (for maps, illus., etc.). **1966** *New Statesman* 18 Mar. 393/1 (Advt.), Illustrated and with 4 coloured throwout maps. **1969** *Catal. Austral., N.Z., & Pacific* (O.U.P., Melbourne) 16, 20 half-tone plates, 2 maps, end-paper map, 1 coloured throw out. **1970** K. BALL *Fiat 600, 600D Autobook* v. 46/2 (*caption*) Diagrammatic view of clutch throwout mechanism. **1976** *Gloss. Documentation Terms* (*B.S.I.*) 68 *Throw-out*, a leaf, usually bearing illustrative material, bound in at one edge and designed to fit the book when folded. **1979** P. WALLAGE *Restoration of Post-War Cars* 6 Clutch release bearing, throwout bearing. **1832** *Examiner* 508/1 He answered with a bold front and an important *throw up of his head.

throwable ('θrəʊəb(ə)l), *a.* [f. THROW *v.*[1] + -ABLE.] Capable of being thrown.

1888 LEES & CLUTTERBUCK *Ramble in Brit. Columbia* xxiii. 264 We had thrown every throwable article at him. **1966** J. DERRICK *Teaching English to Immigrants* iv. 172 If it is difficult to find throwable objects, balls can be used instead ..to represent them. **1977** G. V. HIGGINS *Dreamland* iii. 27, I reached for a throwable life preserver cushion.

throwand: see after THROW *v.*[2]

throw-away. [f. vbl. phr. *to throw away*: see THROW *v.*[1] 37.] **A.** *sb.* **1. a.** A printed sheet or work not intended for preservation after it has been read; also *attrib.* Now usu. with reference to ephemeral material distributed free of charge, as pamphlets, advertising leaflets, certain newspapers, etc.

1903 *Westm. Gaz.* 7 Oct. 12/2 Every now and then a little blue square of printed paper fluttered in the breeze. No one seemed to connect these little 'throw-aways' with the venerable figure on the front seat. **1905** *Daily Chron.* 20 Feb. 4/6 This present rag of a throwaway that you can get for a halfpenny. **1905** *Westm. Gaz.* 31 July 10/2 Lord Alverstone ..vigorously denounced the 'sixpenny throw-away rubbish'. **1922** JOYCE *Ulysses* 149 A sombre Y.M.C.A. young man..placed a throwaway in a hand of Mr Bloom. **1944** *Sun* (Baltimore) 1 June 16-0/3 The small throw-aways contain the latest authentic reports of the progress of the war. **1954** [see *junk mail* s.v. JUNK *sb.*[2] 5]. **1965** *Newsweek* 21 June 70/2 The advertisements in the two editions of the weekly shopper's throwaway. **1973** D. RAMSAY *Deadly Discretion* 102 Here's our throwaway. It's also the ad we run in the papers.

b. More generally, anything designed to be thrown away after use; *spec.* a disposable container. Cf. sense 2 a of the adj. below. *colloq.*

1953 *Sun* (Baltimore) 17 Feb. (B ed.) 30/7 The group of county delegates submitted a bill..which would ban the dispensing of alcoholic beverages in throw-aways. **1976** *Monitor* (McAllen, Texas) 29 Oct. 3A/3 Consumers could save millions of dollars a year in lower prices if soft drinks and beer were sold in returnable containers instead of throwaways.

2. An act of throwing away, or that which is thrown away, in various senses. Also *fig.*

1911 G. B. SHAW *Lett. to Granville Barker* (1956) 178 If the attempt proves a throw away, it is only a throw-away of the chance I promised him, not of the play. **1922** JOYCE *Ulysses* 223 A skiff, a crumpled throwaway..rode lightly down the Liffey. **1955** *N.Y. Times* 29 May VI. 15/1 Generally, the program opens with a line of girls in two or three minutes of fast-stepping, high-kicking precision dancing. This is a throwaway, designed to get late-comers settled into their seats before the real show starts. **1960** *Twentieth Cent.* Aug. 137 Each is a finely polished stylist: let no one be deceived by the easy, laconic throw-away of Ada Leverson. **1976** B. JACKSON *Flameout* vi. 115 It was a pity that the best question was a throwaway to the other reporters: they didn't deserve it. **1983** *Listener* 13 Oct. 21/1 Even in films they hiss 'What did he say?' at a throwaway of dialogue, thus ensuring that the next few minutes are lost to all around.

B. as *adj.* **1.** Of prices: so low as to represent virtually no return for the goods sold; 'give-away'.

1924 A. J. SMALL *Frozen Gold* xiii. 288 With a modicum of luck they might even be able to record every claim they had pegged—and then get rid of them at throw-away prices. **1967** *Spectator* 14 July 53/3 At throwaway prices everyone can afford the latest Camp, and there will be something new coming along next month. **1976** [see SATURATE *v.* 2 d].

2. a. Designating something designed to be thrown away after use; disposable.

1928 *Weekly Dispatch* 13 May 17 You can..clean your face at intervals with those throwaway hankies you buy from any chemist. **1945** *Forbes* (N.Y.) 15 Oct. 16/1 'Throw-away' towels will arrive soon. **1958** *Engineering* 7 Feb. 192/3 The butane comes from a throwaway cartridge. **1970** *Worship* Jan. 41 Already one hears of loose-leaf prayer books and throw-away hymn books. **1982** J. HANSEN *Gravedigger* iv. 33 Two plastic-handled throwaway razors.

b. Pertaining to or characterized by the use of disposable goods or those with a short life-span.

1969 *New Scientist* 25 Sept. 648/1 We will undoubtedly have a formidable litter problem in our 'throw away' world ..from..household equipment with built-in obsolescence. **1977** M. DRABBLE *Ice Age* II. 114 She thanked God that she lived in a consumer throw-away flush-away advertising society. **1980** *Jrnl. R. Soc. Arts* Mar. 188/1 At the same time the 'throw away' attitude developed in society.

3. Underemphatic or casual in style or technique; understated (usu. for increased effect). Cf. THROW *v.*[1] 37 e.

1955 *Time* 4 Apr. 77/2 It takes a certain nerve for a comedian to try a throwaway line. **1958** M. DICKENS *Man Overboard* vii. 102 He was more cunning than he seemed with that throw-away sixth-form voice. **1961** *John o' London's* 25 May 591/4, I remember his beautiful throw-away performance in *Mr. Deeds goes to Town*. **1969** *N.Y. Rev. Bks.* 30 Jan. 27/1 He will..carry us with him, a little breathless perhaps, and dizzy with his throw-away allusions and polyglot versatility. **1972** *Daily Tel.* 29 June 7/7 You can carry your enthusiasm..into casual slouchy nonchalance, and the outstanding collection of Stephen Adnitt had plenty of this throwaway chic. **1980** *Times Lit. Suppl.* 11 July 786/3 The style of the narrative is measured but evocative; a little throw-away, a little affected by the insidious influence of Peter Fleming.

'throw-back. [f. phr. *to throw back*: see THROW *v.*[1] 38.] An act of throwing back.

1. A backward movement or direction given. Also *attrib.* ***throw-back indicator***, see quot. 1902[2].

1901 *Blackw. Mag.* Aug. 192/1 Rob's head had a confident jerky throwback, like a gamecock's. **1902** *Daily Chron.* 19 Mar. 9/4 The Light Blues' throw-back of the bodies for the first catch is imposing. **1902** O'CONOR SLOANE *Stand. Electr. Dict.*, *Throw-back Indicator*, a drop annunciator, whose shutter or drop is electrically replaced.

2. An arrest or reverse in a course or progress; a check, set-back, relapse.

1856 H. R. REYNOLDS in *Life* v. (1898) 123 The little throw-back of my progress..was not such as to create any uneasiness. **1902** *Edin. Rev.* Oct. 286 The belief in popular principles held by most Englishmen before the great throw back of the French Revolution.

3. Reversion to an earlier ancestral type or character; an example of this. Chiefly *fig.* Also, a reversion to the technique or methods of an earlier period. Also applied to a person using such techniques.

1888 KIPLING *Plain Tales from Hills* 209 The queer, savage feeling..must be a 'throw back' to times when men and women were rather worse than they are now. **1889** *Athenæum* 14 Sept. 351/3 By a not unusual freak of heredity she is personally a 'throw-back' to an angel. **1894** *Temple Bar Mag.* Mar. 454 Our feeble throw-back to savagery. **1904** W. H. POLLOCK *Anim. that have Owned us* vii. 98 He must have been a freak or a 'throw back'. **1930** E. BLUNDEN in *Nation & Athenaeum* 6 Dec. 327/1 The Canterbury Poets were a throw-back to Cooke's little volumes. **1938** *Sun* (Baltimore) 19 July 8/3 His flight was harebrained and foolhardy... It was an unnecessary throwback to the romantic era of long-distance aviation. **1949** *Ibid.* 14 July 23/1 On the whole it was wartime baseball, a throwback to the hilarious 1945 World Series between the Tigers and the Cubs. **1976** *UCT Stud. in Eng.* (Univ. of Cape Town) Oct. 13 If..modern literature is distinctive in its claim on our moral attention, Stevens is distinctly un-modern, a transcendental throwback.

throwch, obs. Sc. f. THROUGH *sb.* and *prep.*

'throw-crook. *Sc.* & *n. dial.* **'thrawcrook.** [f. THROW *v.*[1] + CROOK *sb.*] A hooked implement for 'throwing' or twisting coarse rope from hay, straw, or hair.

a **1568** *Wowing of Jok & Jynny* 68 in *Bannatyne Poems* 389 Ane thrawcruk to twyne ane tedder. **1828** J. STRUTHERS *Hist. Scot.* II. 624 Ropes of hair twined upon the thraw-crook. **1829** BROCKETT *N.C. Gloss.* (ed. 2), *Thrawcrook*, an instrument acting on a swivel for twisting ropes. **1844** STEPHENS *Bk. Farm* III. 1092 The simplest instrument is the old-fashioned throw-crook.

throwe, obs. f. THROE, THROUGH, THROW.

throwed (θrəʊd), obs. or dial. (esp. *U.S.*) pa. t. and pa. pple. of THROW *v.*[1]; in quot. 1727–41 as *ppl. a.* = THROWN.

1727–41 CHAMBERS *Cycl.* s.v. *Silk, Throwed or twisted silks* are such, as, besides their spinning and winding, have received their milling or throwing..: properly,..throwed silks are those wherein the threads are pretty thick throwed, and are twisted several times. **1914** *Sat. Even. Post* 3 Oct. 20/3 This should ought to of gave me a record of 16 wins and 0 defeats because the only games I lost was throwed away behind me. **1930** [see HONKY-TONK 1]. **1949** [see GRAIN *v.*[1] 8]. **1968** E. J. GAINES in A. Chapman *New Black Voices* (1972) 91 He wiped his mouth and throwed his cup on his bunk.

thrower ('θrəʊə(r)). Also 5– *Sc.* and *north. dial.* **thrawer.** [f. THROW *v.*[1] + -ER[1].] One who throws, in various senses.

I. 1. One who fashions something by a rotary motion. †**a.** One who fashions wooden objects on a lathe; a turner. *Obs.*

1483 *Cath. Angl.* 385/1 A Thrawer, *tornator.* **1620** *Shuttleworths' Acc.* (Chetham Soc.) 243 P'd to the thrower for the chessotts making. **1688** R. HOLME *Armoury* III. 269/2 A Turners, or Throwers Tools.

b. One who shapes pottery on a potter's wheel or throw; a potter.

1604 [see THROW *v.*[1] 6 a]. **1744** *Indenture J. Wedgwood* in Eliza Meteyard *Life* (1865) I. 222 To Learn his Art Mistery Occupation or Imployment of Thrower and Handleing which he the said Thomas Wedgwood now useth. **1790** in *Guide Mus. Pract. Geol.* (1859) 98 About 90 painters..and about 200 throwers, turners, &c., were employed under one roof. **1881** *Guide Worcester Porcel. Wks.* (1906) 19 The man who works at the potter's wheel is called the thrower. **1894** SMILES *Wedgwood* iii. 22 The thrower is the person who sits in his shed, near the potter's wheel, and forms by hand from the moist clay as it revolves, the crock, the butter pot, the porringer or other such wares. **1903** *Daily Rec. & Mail* 1 July 4 The Potter's Wheel..is made of ash, and the thrower works upon it now in the same way as did the thrower thousands of years ago in Egypt.

c. One who twists filaments of silk into silk thread; a throwster.

1621 in Strype *Stow's Surv.* v. xiv. (1754) II. 321/1 To take Hearing and Consideration of the Petition of the Silk-throwers. **1662** *Act 14 Chas. II*, c. 15 §5 There is a necessity lying upon the Silke throwers to deliver to theire Winders or Doublers considerable quantities of silke which being of good value is..many times..deceitfully and falsly purloined..to the great damage and sometimes the utter undoing of the Thrower whoe employes the said persons.

†**2.** (In form **thrawer.**) One who twists, wrests, or perverts; a perverter of the sense. *Sc. rare*$^{-1}$.

1563 DAVIDSON *Confut. Kennedy* in *Wodrow Soc. Misc.* (1844) 229, I wald we war judgit, quhidder we be thrawers of the Scripturs.

II. 3. a. One who (or that which) casts, hurls, flings, or pitches: see the senses of THROW *v.*[1] II–V.

1519 HORMAN *Vulg.* 253 b, Come nat vpon that horsebacke: for he is a great throware. **1552** HULOET, Thrower of a stone with a hole therin for exercise, *discobolus.* **1579–80** NORTH *Plutarch* (1676) 173 Throwers with slings, Archers, and other light armed men. **1677** PLOT *Oxfordsh.* 10 If it be thrown in an oblique line, it returns not to the thrower but to another place. **1832** P. EGAN *Bk. Sports* 344/1 Mr. K—ngsc—e comes next... An excellent thrower—a hundred yards clear. **1850** 'BAT' *Cricket. Man.* 44 Long Leg must..be occupied by a good thrower. **1892** RIDER HAGGARD *Nada the Lily* 198 It is the bold thrower who oftenest wins. **1911** *Times* 3 Mar. 8/3 The thrower of the bomb was immediately arrested.

b. With various adverbs: cf. THROW *v.*[1] VI.

c **1450** tr. *De Imitatione* III. lx. 142 She is maistresse of troupe..þrower doun, dryuer awey of sorowe. **1611** SHAKS. *Wint. T.* III. iii. 29 Since Fate..Hath made thy person for the Thrower-out Of my poore babe. **1719** LONDON & WISE *Compl. Gard.* vi. 19 The Autumn Winds, those throwers down of Fruits. **1773** J. ALLEN *Serm. St. Mary's, Oxford* 26 We have no Ahaz, no thrower down nor changer of altars. **1860** GEN. P. THOMPSON *Audi Alt. P.* III. cxxiv. 78 It may be late, but they have not been the throwers away. **1963** N. STREATFEILD *Vicarage Family* vi. 75 Some of the members of his men's society..are coming by train as throwers-out. If there is a rumpus it will be all over almost before it begins.

throwing ('θrəʊɪŋ), *vbl. sb.*[1] [f. as prec. + -ING[1].] The action of THROW *v.*[1]

I. 1. (In form **thrawing.**) Twisting, wringing; turning or bending to one side; also *fig.* crossing, thwarting; quarrelling. *Sc.*

a **1585** MONTGOMERIE *Flyting* 376 They deemde, what death it sould die..'be throwing [*v.r.* thrawing] of the throate, Like a tyke ouer a tree'. **1785** BURNS *Halloween* xxiii, It chanc'd the stack..Was timmer-propt for thrawin'. **1816** SCOTT *Bl. Dwarf* viii, Speak him fair, Hobbie; the like o' him will no bear thrawing. **1897** *Daily Rec. & Mail* 17 Sept. 4 The present unsatisfactory condition of affairs is..due in great part to personal feeling and 'thrawing'.

2. a. The turning of objects from wood; the shaping of round pottery on a potter's wheel.

c **1440** *Promp. Parv.* 493/1 Throwynge, or turnynge of vesselle, *tornacio.* **1483** *Cath. Angl.* 385/1 A Thrawynge, *to[r]natura.* **1797** *Encycl. Brit.* (ed. 3) XVII. 811/1 (Stoneware) The mixture..is beat..and then is in order for throwing. **1832** G. R. PORTER *Porcelain & Gl.* 45 The operation of throwing consists in shaping such vessels as have a circular form, and is performed upon a machine called a potter's lathe. *a* **1882** SIR H. COLE *50 Yrs. Public Wk.* (1884) I. 105 Superintending the throwing, turning, modelling, and moulding of a tea service.

b. The twisting of raw silk into thread.

1621- [see SILK-THROWING]. **1662** *Act 14 Chas. II*, c. 15 §9 The said Corporation of Silk throwers shall not..make any Orders Ordinances or By-Lawes to sett any Rates or Prices whatsoever upon the Throwing of Silk. **1844** G. DODD *Textile Manuf.* vi. 192 The next process, called *throwing*, by which the two, three, five or a dozen threads are twisted firmly one round another. **1868** *Rep. U.S. Commissioner Agric.* 288 The twisting or 'throwing' process is done by passing the thread of raw silk from an upright bottom through the eye of a craned wire flyer, which rapidly spins with the top of the bobbin revolving above.

II. 3. Projecting, casting, flinging, hurling (*lit.* or *fig.*). ***throwing at cocks***: = COCK-THROWING.

13.. *Cursor M.* 22683 (Edin. MS.) þe stanis..Wit þrawing [*Cott.* thrauing, *Fairf.* casting, *Gött.* wid strenth] sal tai samin þrist, þat al to pecis sal tai brist. **13..** *K. Alis.* 1614 With launceynge and with rydyng With throwyng [*Bodley MS.* þraweynge], and with nymyng. **1375** BARBOUR *Bruce* XIII. 156 Thar wes..sic thrawing and sic thristing,..That it wes hyd-wiss for till her. *c* **1440** *Promp. Parv.* 493/1 Throwynge, or castynge, *jactura, jactus.* **1639** DRUMM. OF HAWTH. *Answ. to Objections* Wks. (1711) 214 By throwing of oat-meal in the people's eyes. *c* **1770** (*title*) A friendly admonition against throwing at Cocks and of Cockfighting. **1833** NYREN *Yng. Cricketer's Tutor* 90 Walker..began the system of throwing instead of bowling, now so much the fashion. At that time, it was esteemed foul play. **1897** *Daily News* 1 Nov. 5/2 The throwing nuisance, which has for years been the scandal of English cricket.

4. With adverbs, as ***throwing about, back, down, in, off, out, up***: see THROW *v.*[1] VI.

c **1440** *Promp. Parv.* 493/1 Throwynge downe, fro hey place.., *precipicium.* **1518** *Sel. Pl. Star Chamb.* (Selden) II. 131 Yf they had known the throwyng downe of the seyd iij gappes. **1653** H. MORE *Antid. Ath.* III. ix. §4 The watch-men of the Town..heard..the fallings and throwings of things about. **1772** WOLLASTON in *Phil. Trans.* LXIII. 68, I have set down the throwing-out of the pendulum,..on a scale behind it. **1785** M. GARTHSHORE in *Med. Commun.* II. 39 It terminated by the throwing off of sloughs. **1851** *Jrnl. R. Agric. Soc.* XII. I. 88 These straining efforts are sometimes so energetic as to cause 'throwing down' of the uterus. **1869** TOZER *Highl. Turkey* II. 331 Throwing back the head (ἀνανεύειν) is still..a negative answer.

III. 5. *attrib.* and *Comb.* **a.** for throwing pottery or silk: as ***throwing-clay, -house, -machine, -room***; **throwing-engine**, applied by Nicholson to the driving-wheel of a potter's wheel; **throwing-mill**, (*a*) a building in which silk-throwing is carried on; (*b*) a machine for twisting raw silk into thread; **throwing-table**, a descriptive name for a potter's wheel: see quot.; **throwing-wheel**, a potter's wheel; sometimes, as in quot. 1825, applied to the driving-wheel. **b.** for casting, hurling, etc.: as ***throwing arm*** (properly *ppl. a.*), ***-bat, -club, -hatchet, -knife, -net, -spear***; **throwing-balls**, the South American BOLAS; **throwing-board**, a spear-thrower, = THROWING-STICK a.; **throwing-iron**, a knife-like missile used by some African peoples. **c. throwing power**, the ability of an electrodepositing solution to produce an even coating on an irregularly shaped object.

a. 1686 PLOT *Staffordsh.* 122 All which they call *throwing clays, because they..will work on the wheel. **1825** J. NICHOLSON *Operat. Mechanic* 462 A strap is attached from the driven cone to the spindle of the *throwing-engine. **1733** P. LINDSAY *Interest Scotl.* 136 *Throwing Mills, after the Manner of that One at Darby. **1831** G. R. PORTER *Silk Manuf.* 201 Spinning or twisting the thread..wound upon the bobbins, is performed with the throwing mill. **1851** L. D. B. GORDON in *Art Jrnl. Illustr. Catal.* p. ii. **/2 The factories in which raw silk is spun into silk-thread for weaving are called throwing mills. **1881** *Guide Worcester Porcel. Wks.* 11 The *Throwing Room. **1877** KNIGHT *Dict. Mech.*, **Throwing-table*, a revolving, horizontal table on which earthen vessels are shaped by the potter. **1825** J. NICHOLSON *Operat. Mechanic* 461 The **throwing-wheel*, or, with greater propriety, the *throwing-engine*, consists of a large vertical wheel; having a winch or handle affixed to it, and a groove on the rim for the introduction of a cord [etc.].

b. 1972 J. MOSEDALE *Football* ii. 19 Thanks to his accurate *throwing arm, New Orleans was..one of the darkest cities in America. **1977** *World of Cricket Monthly* June 47/2 He had one of the strongest throwing arms ever seen in Australian cricket. **1891** *Cent. Dict.*, *Throwing-balls. **1845** C. H. SMITH in *Kitto's Cycl. Bibl. Lit.* s.v. *Arms*, Among these [instruments at first employed in the chase] were the club and the *throwing-bat. **1909** *Cent. Dict. Suppl.*, *Throwing-board. **1895** *Cornh. Mag.* Dec. 634 The soldiers ..had brought him down with *throwing-clubs. **1903** KIPLING in *Windsor Mag.* Sept. 370/1 Tegumai..was holding his stone *throwing-hatchet in one hand. **1898** tr. *Ratzel's Hist. Mankind* III. 71 The indispensable weapon was the *throwing-iron, of which many carried several specimens,..in sheaths of hide. *Ibid.* 72 *Throwing-knives are among the notable properties of the races of the Monbuttu type north of the Congo. **1902** L. LOAT in Boulenger *Zool. Egypt, Fishes Nile* Introd. (1907) 21 At Cairo..the commonest net of all is a circular *throwing-net, ..with an average circumference of about 50 feet and a half-inch mesh. **1900** A. B. LLOYD in *Daily News* 18 July 6/2 Each carried either bow and quiver of arrows, or short *throwing-spears.

c. 1922 *Trans. Amer. Electrochem. Soc.* XLI. 363 The object of this study was the development of a zinc plating bath of high 'throwing power'. **1932** *Metal Industry* XL. 501/2 He had to undertake the task of determining the throwing power of several selected plating baths. **1966** D. G. BRANDON *Mod. Techniques Metallogr.* 5 Electropolishing ..may even give a poor macropolish as a result of..poor throwing power in the electrolyte.

throwing, *vbl. sb.*[2], suffering: see THROW *v.*[2]

'**throwing-stick. a.** A short wooden implement by which a dart or spear is thrown, in order to give increased velocity to it: = SPEAR-THROWER, WOOMERA. **b.** A short club used as a missile; = THROW-STICK a.

1770 COOK *Voy. round World* III. viii. (1773) 641 An instrument which we called a throwing stick. This is a plain smooth piece of a hard reddish wood, very highly polished, about two inches broad, half an inch thick, and three feet long, with a small knob, or hook at one end, and a cross piece about three or four inches long at the other. **1802** G. BARRINGTON *Hist. N.S. Wales* i. 26 The throwing-stick is used in discharging the spear. **1865** LUBBOCK *Preh. Times* 403 For throwing the harpoon they use a short handle or throwing-stick, about two feet long. **1885** H. H. HAYTER *Carboona* 24 Warrk Warrk, having a dart on his throwing-stick ready adjusted, hurled it. **1901** *Athenæum* 11 May 599/2 The throwing-stick of the Moki [Pueblo Indians] is closely related to the Australian boomerang, but does not return to the thrower.

thrown (θrəʊn), *ppl. a.* [Pa. pple. of THROW *v.*[1], where see Forms. See also special Scotch senses under THRAWN.]

I. 1. a. Turned on a lathe, as woodwork. Now *dial.* **b.** Shaped on the potter's wheel. Cf. THROW *v.*[1] 6 a.

1483 *Cath. Angl.* 385/1 Thrawen (*A.* Thrawne), *tornalis.* **1495** *Nottingham Rec.* III. 40 Unam cathedram vocatam 'a throwen' cheyer'. **1535** COVERDALE *2 Chron.* iii. 5 He.. ouerlayed it with the best golde, and made palme trees and throwne worke theron. **1600** *Acc. Bk. W. Wray* in *Antiquary* XXXII. 279 A throwne chaire. **1853** URE *Dict. Arts* II. 455 When the 'thrown ware' is sufficiently dry, it is transferred to the hands of the 'turner'. **1883** *W. Yorks. Gloss.*, *Thrown*, turned in a lathe (as bed-posts, &c.).

2. a. Of silk: Twisted into thread.

thrown silk: silk thread consisting of two or more singles twisted together: = ORGANZINE. ***thrown singles***: silk thread consisting of a single strand of raw silk which has been cleaned, wound, and twisted: see quot. 1877 s.v. THROW *v.*[1] 6 b. Also (in trade) *absol.* as *sb.*

1463-4 *Rolls of Parlt.* V. 506/1 Wrought Silke, throwen Rybans and Laces. **1483** [see THROW *v.*[1] 6 b]. **1690** LUTTRELL *Brief Rel.* (1857) II. 45 An act for discouraging the importation of thrown silk. **1709** *Lond. Gaz.* No. 4523/4 Some Piemond Thrown Silk..saved out of an Italian Ship. **1719** W. WOOD *Surv. Trade* 87 Oil, Wine, Thrown and Raw-silk, Wrought Silks. **1812** J. SMYTH *Pract. of Customs* (1821) 214 Raw Silk has only one thread: the thrown Silk is distinguished from it by having two threads. **1844** G. DODD *Textile Manuf.* vi. 184 Thrown singles, is silk which has been wound, cleaned, and thrown. **1883** *Times* 16 May 11 In silk..Chinas have suffered from the reduced consumption of throwns. **1906** *Sat. Rev.* 13 Jan. 38/2 They buy their silk in the spun or thrown state.

†**b.** Twisted; in a state of torsion. *Obs.*

1674 N. FAIRFAX *Bulk & Selv. World* Contents, Open'd by the stirring of a watch, of thrown bodies, the springiness of an egge.

II. 3. Cast, pitched, hurled; unseated from a horse.

1833 HT. MARTINEAU *Berkeley the Banker* I. i. 18 The horse galloping away, and the thrown young lady lying on the ground. **1888** RUSKIN in *Mag. Art* Jan. 75/1 To put them together out of chance-thrown heaps.

4. With adverbs, as ***thrown-away, -back, -down, -on, -over, -together, -up***, expressing the completed action of the corresponding verbal phrases (see THROW *v.*[1] VI).

1778 'J. H. ST. JOHN DE CRÈVECŒUR' *Sk. 18th-Cent. Amer.* (1925) 323 Your neighbours won't thank you for this thrownaway humanity. **1890** W. JAMES *Princ. Psychol.* II. xxv. 484 The frowning brow, the thrown-back shoulders, and clenched fists of rage. **1891** C. ROBERTS *Adrift Amer.* 146 They sat..on the mound made of the thrown-up earth from the burrows. **1901** *Westm. Gaz.* 17 Oct. 2/2 The thrown-back front and sleeve both gave glimpses of their lining. **1903** *Ibid.* 8 Jan. 3/2 Some such thrown-on kind of wrap can be added for coming and going. *Ibid.* 4 June 5/2 One fire was caused by a thrown-down light. **1934** Thrown-together [see RED-HOT *a.* (and *sb.*) 4]. **1973** J. LEASOR *Host of Extras* v. 69 The beach was littered with..thrown-away cigarette packets.

throw-off. [f. the vbl. phrase *to throw off* (THROW *v.* 42).] **a.** *Fox-hunting.* The throwing-off of the hounds, the start of a hunt; by extension, of a race; hence, a start generally. **b.** A shaking off, getting rid of or free from. **c.** A mechanism by which some part of a machine is disconnected, or its action suspended. **d.** That which is thrown off; something produced or given off, an offshoot.

1843 *Ainsworth's Mag.* III. 144 The throw-off will be unusually great to-morrow. **1859** PALMERSTON in Lucas *Ld. Glenesk* (1910) 147 The throw-off is awkward, beginning with the insignificant word 'in'. **1864** WEBSTER, *Throw-off*, a start in a hunt or race. **1864** *Gd. Words* 104/2 These millions, these atoms of life—they are a free throw off from the Creative Beneficence. **1873** *Punch* 13 Sept. 107/1 Whither I had driven in order to see the throw-off. **1886** J. M. CAULFEILD *Seamanship Notes* 3 *Parts of the Capstan*,.. bar pins, throw off, spindle,..entablature. **1889** *Nature* 22 Aug. 393/1 No micro-seismic shock can ever take place otherwise than as a throw-off from some violent disturbance more or less remotely located. **1891** *Melbourne Punch* 4 June 377/2, I received an invitation to see the throw off of the Ballarat hounds in the afternoon.

'**throw-'over.** [f. the verbal phrase *to throw over* (THROW *v.* 45).] The act or result of throwing over, in various senses; also, *concr.*, a wrap to throw over the shoulders; a loose outer garment. **throw-over switch** *Electr. Engin.* (see quot. 1943).

1819 *Hermit in London* III. 212 They had practised what they technically termed a throw over. **1852** LEWIS *Lett.* (1870) 257 The complete and definitive throw over both of Protection and local burdens must loosen the hold of the Government upon the agricultural body. **1902** O'CONOR SLOANE *Stand. Electr. Dict.* App., *Throw-Over Switch*, a double throw knife switch designed to connect a three wire system in a building either to a three wire street main or to a single source on the two wire system. **1907** *Ladies' Field* 12 Jan. 3/2 White Foxaline long Stole or Throwover. **1909** *Westm. Gaz.* 3 Apr. 15/1 The nearest approach we have to the Marie Antoinette 'throw-over'—it cannot be called a tea gown..—is the Japanese kimono. *Ibid.* 16 Oct. 15/1 The drapery..has grown in its proportions till now it resembles a shawl, and nothing could be more convenient as a throw-over, either for day or evening purposes. **1919** *Wireless World* VII. 40/1 A simple differential indicator operated by a throw-over switch. **1943** *Gloss. Terms Electr. Engin.* (*B.S.I.*) 52 *Throw-over switch*, a switch for changing over from one set of connections to another set of connections.

† **throwst,** *v. Obs.* Also 7–8 **throst.** [irreg. back-formation from THROWSTER.] *trans.* To throw silk; = THROW *v.*[1] 6 b. So '**throwsting** *vbl. sb.*, silk-throwing; also attrib. ***throwsting-machine, -mill.***

1691 W. SEWEL *Dutch Dict.* s.v. *Reeden, Zy-Reeden*, to Throst silk. **1825** J. NICHOLSON *Operat. Mechanic* 396 A representation of the throwsting-mills. *Ibid.* 399 The bobbins being thus filled with double or triple threads, are carried back to the throwsting-machine, and are there spun or twisted together. **1844** G. DODD *Textile Manuf.* vi. 196 The processes of silk-throwing, or 'throwsting', may now be said to be finished.

throwster ('θrəʊstə(r)). Forms: 5 **throwestre, -er,** 6 **throwstar,** (7–8 **throster**), 7– **throwster.** [f. THROW *v.*[1] 6 b + -STER.]

1. One who twists silk fibres into raw silk or raw silk into thread, a silk-throwster; originally, a woman who did this, a SILK-WOMAN (the earliest term). †Also extended to a worsted-spinner (*obs.*).

1455 *Rolls of Parlt.* V. 325/1 The Silkewymmen and Throwestres of the Craftes and occupation of Silkewerk. **1530** PALSGR. 281/1 Throwstar, *deuideresse de soye.* **1620** MIDDLETON & ROWLEY *World Tost at Tennis* 95 Job a venerable silk-weaver, Jehu a throwster dwelling i' the Spitalfields. **1678** PHILLIPS (ed. 4), *Throster*, one that twisteth Silk or Thred. **1716** *Lond. Gaz.* No. 5401/4 A Worsted-Throwster by Trade. **1734** SWIFT *Compl. Deafness* 16 A woman's clack, if I have skill, Sounds somewhat like a throwster's mill. **1846** McCULLOCH *Acc. Brit. Empire* (1854) I. 713 The throwsters of the metropolis were formed into a fellowship in 1562, but they were not incorporated till 1629. **1880** CHARL. M. MASON *Forty Shires* 95 English throwsters did their work as well as those of Italy.

2. *Pottery.* = THROWER 1 b: see quot. (? error).

1894 H. SPEIGHT *Nidderdale* 384 *note*, Throwsters and drysters were potters' craftsmen; the throwster being the man who works the wheel, and..forms by the pressure of his hand the 'lining' for the dish or cup.

† **3.** A dice-thrower, a gamester. *Obs. rare.*

1832 J. WILSON *Noct. Ambr.* in *Blackw. Mag.* Sept. 388 A certain bold throwster had swept the pool.

'**throw-stick.** [f. THROW *v.*[1] + STICK *sb.*] **a.** A heavy, usually curved, piece of wood used as a missile; an ancient kind of boomerang. **b.** A stick with which a spear or dart is thrown: = THROWING-STICK a.

1837 WILKINSON *Mann. & Cust. Anc. Egypt.* viii. III. 38 The use of the throw-stick was very general. **1857** —— *Egypt. in Time Pharaohs* 80 Birds were felled with the throwstick, a weapon of hard wood,..slightly curved..like the boomerang. **1869** BOUTELL *Arms & Arm.* vi. (1874) 84 When the dart is discharged, the *wummera*, or throw-stick, ..remains in the warrior's hand. *c* **1875** H. B. TRISTRAM in *Queen's Printers' Bible-Aids* 57 In 1 Sam. xxvi. 20 allusion is made to chasing partridges on the hills with throw-sticks.

throwt(e, obs. contr. of THROUGHOUT.

throwther: see THROUGH-OTHER.

thru, thruch, thrucht, thruff, thrugh: see THROUCH, THROUGH *prep.* and *sb.*

thrub, obs. var. DRUB.

thrudde, thrulle, obs. ff. THIRD, THRILL *v.*[1]

†**thrum**, *sb.*[1] *Obs.* Forms: 1 **þrymm**, 1–2 **þrym**, 3–4 **þrum**, 4 **þrom**, 4–5 **throm**, **throme**, 5 **thrumme**. [app. OE. *þrymm* a host, a great body of people, a multitude (also strength, might, majesty, glory); cf. OS. *thrumme* in *mid heruthrummeon* 'with hostile power or strength'; cf. OS. *thrimman* to swell; also Flemish *drommen* in THRUM *v.*[1]]

1. A company or body of people (or animals); a band, troop, crowd; ***on a thrum***, in a body, in a crowd. Also, a bundle (of arrows, quot. *c* 1450). Also *attrib.* †**þrum-ferd** (FERD *sb.*[1] 3).

a **800** CYNEWULF *Christ* (Cod. Exon.) 1063 Se engla þrym. *c* **1000** ÆLFRIC *Saints' Lives* xxv. 841 Se hundredes ealdor.. com on ærne merȝen mid mycclum þrymme. *c* **1205** LAY. 1356 þer heo leof folc funden feower þrum ferden. *c* **1330** *Arth. & Merl.* 211 Whiles þou were in our þrome, No were we neuer ouercome. *a* **1350** *St. Andrew* 209 in Horstm. *Altengl. Leg.* (1881) 6 þe folk thrang efter al on a þrum. *c* **1400** *Laud Troy Bk.* 13236 Thei schal alle dye on a throme. *c* **1430** *Syr Gener.* (Roxb.) 2949 A hundred houndes on a throm He saw that were thider com. *c* **1450** *Ball. Death Robin Lyth* 48 (Ritson) Fowre and twenty goode arwys Trusyd in a thrumme.

2. Magnificence, splendour.

971 *Blickl. Hom.* 77 Emb þone þrym and þa fægernesse ðæs temples. *c* **1175** *12th Cent. Hom.* 130 þenne beoð þa welæn & þa glengæ aȝotene, & þe þrym tobrocen.

thrum (θrʌm), *sb.*[2] Forms: (1 **þrum**), 4–6 **throm(e**, 5 **thrum(e**, **thrwme**, 5–6 **thromm(e**, 5–7 **thrumm(e**, 6–7 **thrumbe**, (6 *Sc.* **throomb**), 6–9 **thrumb**, 6– **thrum**. [OE. *þrum* (in comb. in *tungeþrum* ligament of the tongue), ME. *thrum*, *throm*, = MDu. *drom*, Du. dial. *drom*, *drum* (in mod.Du. *dreum* m. 'thrum'), OHG., MHG. *drum* end-piece, remnant (in mod.G. *trumm* 'thrum', pl. *trümmer* remnants, ruins); cf. ON. *þrǫmr* edge, brim (Norw. *tröm*, *trumm*, *tram* edge, brim, Sw. dial. *tröm*, *trumm*, *trom* stump); formed, with various suffixes, from OTeut. ablaut-stem **þrum*-, **þram*-,:—Indo-Eur. **trmo*-; cf. L. *term-inus*, Gr. *τέρμ-α* end.

a **1000** *Lorica Gloss.* in *Sax. Leechd.* I. Pref. 70 *Sublinguæ*, tungeðrum [*Harl. MS.* ibid. 74 undertungeðrum].]

1. *Weaving.* Each of the ends of the warp-threads left unwoven and remaining attached to the loom when the web is cut off; usually in *pl.* (also *collect. sing.*) the row or fringe of such threads.

1429 *Rolls of Parlt.* IV. 360/2 The Weyvers..have taken ..in common usage,..what tyme yat yei have wroght a Clothe almost to ye end, to kitte away to yair singuler avauntage ye yerne yat leveth unwoven, and callen hit Thrommes [cf. Act 8 Hen. VI, c. 23 §1]. **14..** *Nom.* in Wr.-Wülcker 728/17 *Hoc licium*, a throm. **1449** *Maldon, Essex, Crt. Rolls* (Bundle 29, No. 3), Ricardus Vyce petit xxd. pro xx lb. de Thromes empt. **1590** SHAKS. *Mids. N.* v. i. 291 O Fates! come, come: Cut thred and thrum. **1591** R. BRUCE *Serm.* I j b, The Webster doth cut off the web from the throombs of his beam. **1611** BIBLE *Isa.* xxxviii. 12 He will cut mee off with pining sicknesse [*marg.* from the thrum]. **1649** ROBERTS *Clavis Bibl.* 447 A weavers web brought unto the thrum, and ready to be cut off. **1725** *Bradley's Fam. Dict.* s.v. *Wound*, If the Shot be quite thorough the Wound, then take a few Weavers Linnen Thrums..and dipping 'em first in Varnish, draw 'em through the Wound. **1847–78** HALLIWELL, *Thrum*, the extremity of a weaver's warp, often about nine inches long, which cannot be woven.

2. a. A short piece of waste thread or yarn (including the unwoven ends of the warp = 1); *pl.* or *collect. sing.* odds and ends of thread; also, a short or loose end of thread projecting from the surface of a woven fabric; a tuft, tassel, or fringe of threads at the edge of a piece of cloth, etc.

(In early quots. barely distinguishable from 1.)

1346 *Litt. Red Bk. Bristol* (1900) II. 5 Drap..estre fait de fil de lein appele thromes. **1439** *Deed* (Westm. Chapter Archives), Qui tunc dedit predicto Johanni Kirkeby capellum de thrummes fact[um] quod tunc temporis erat de noua coniectura. *c* **1440** *Promp. Parv.* 493/1 Thrvmm, of a clothe, *filamen*,..*villus*, *fractillus*. **1519** HORMAN *Vulg.* 167 b, The baudy thrummys of the carpettis toke me faste by the feete. **1530** PALSGR. 158 *Vng payne*, a thrumme of a hatte or suche lyke. **1541–2** *Act 33 Hen. VIII*, c. 18 §3 They.. shall..[not] make..any manner Kerseyes with flockis, thrummes or other deceivable thinge or thingis. **1555** W. WATREMAN *Fardle Facions* II. x. 215 Thei [Tartars] make.. litle pupettes of silke or of felte, or of thrumme. **1611** COTGR., *Pesles*, thrummes; or that which hangs at the end of a peece of cloth like fringe. *c* **1645** HOWELL *Lett.* (1650) III. 33 The wrong side of a Turky carpet, which useth to be full of thrums and knots, and nothing so even as the right side. **1675** V. ALSOP *Anti-Sozzo* 302 Tying both the Ends so handsomely together, that it may not Ravel out into Thrums. **1681** COLVIL *Whigs Supplic.* (1751) 4 Like pictures on the wrong side of Arras hangings, spoiled with thrumbs and threads. **1878** PATER *Child in House* Misc. Stud. (1895) 174 Childish treasures, glass beads, empty scent-bottles still sweet, thrum of coloured silks.

b. *Naut.* (*pl.*, also *collect. sing.*) Short pieces of coarse woollen or hempen yarn, used for mops, etc.: cf. THRUM *v.*[2] e, and THRUMMED[1] c.

1466 *Mann. & Househ. Exp.* (Roxb.) 346 Thrommes for pyche mapoltes. **1623** WHITBOURNE *Newfoundland* 75 Thrummes for Pitch mabs. **1848** [see THRUM *v.*[2] e]. **1867** SMYTH *Sailor's Word-bk.*, *Thrum*, any coarse woollen or hempen yarn. It is used for mops, &c., in the cabins.

c. *fig.*: *pl.* (or *collect. sing.*) Odds and ends, scraps.

1648–1833 Thread and thrum, Threads and thrums [see THREAD *sb.* 2 c]. *a* **1653** G. DANIEL *Idyll.* v. 180 Arguments For you to ravell; Thrumbs of Discontents: From the large Webbe of Care. **1872** MORLEY *Voltaire* III. (ed. 2) 147 It is this, which..makes life a whole instead of a parcel of thrums bound together by an accident.

†**3.** Short for *thrum cap* (see 7). *Obs. rare*$^{-1}$.

1719 D'URFEY *Pills* IV. 158 The Monmouth Cap, the Sailor's Thrumb. *Ibid.*, The Sea-man with his Thrumb.

†**4.** Applied to various structures in plants or animals resembling small threads, or a tuft of these. **a.** *pl.* The florets of the disk in a composite flower, or the stamens in a simple flower; also, *sing.* the disk, the central petals of a double flower, or the stamens collectively. *Obs.* (exc. in comb. ***thrum-eyed***: see 7).

1578 LYTE *Dodoens* II. xxxii. 189 Of Buphthalmos, or Oxe eye... The floure is of a fayre bright yellow colour, and large, with many small thrommes or yellow thredes in the middle, almost like to the floures of Marigoldes. **1657** W. COLES *Adam in Eden* ii. 4 Fair large red flours [of peony].. having..in the midst, yellow Threds or Thrums. **1668** WILKINS *Real Char.* II. iv. §4. 81 Consisting of..a circle of Leaves, and a Thrumm of short stamina, close set together. **1671** GREW *Anat. Plants* v. §17 The Florid Attire, is commonly known by the blind and rude Name of Thrums. **1694** WESTMACOTT *Script. Herb.* (1695) 99 The Water-Lillies..bearing a white flower, with yellow thrums in the middle. **1726** *Flower Gard. Displ.* (ed. 2) Introd., Thrums, Apices or Chives, when a great Number of them grow together in a Flower. **1812** *New Bot. Gard.* I. 33 The.. cutting winds in March will often cause them [double Anemones] to blow single, by destroying the thrum that is in the middle of the flower.

†**b.** A tuft, bundle, or fringe of any threadlike structures, as hairs on a leaf, fibres of a root, etc.

1578 LYTE *Dodoens* IV. lxvii. 529 Of Carline Thistel... Upon [the] stemme groweth a round flat head,..thromde like Ueluet, and round about that Ueluet throm, or Crowne, standeth a pale or inclosure, of..small white leaues, whiche is the flower. **1597** GERARDE *Herbal* I. xxxvi. §1. 51 A fringe or thrum downe the middle of the lower leaues. *Ibid.* II. xvii. §3. 200 The roote is nothing else but as it were a thrum or bundell of threedes. **1688** R. HOLME *Armoury* II. 61/2 Three [leaves]..each having a yellow freez, or thrum near the bottome.

†**c.** A bundle of minute blood-vessels, a plexus.

1615 CROOKE *Body of Man* 431 A thrumbe of crisped vessels called *Plexus Choroides*.., wherein the Animal spirits receiue their preparation.

5. *Brewing.* (See quots.) *dial.*

1828 *Craven Gloss.*, *Thrum*, a bundle of birch or twigs in a mash tub, to prevent the malt from escaping and through which the liquor percolates. **1877** *N.W. Linc. Gloss.*, *Thrum*, a small utensil of wicker-work affixed to the hole in a mash-tub in brewing, to hinder the malt from escaping when the wort is run off.

†**6.** Applied jocularly or contemptuously to a person (? one meanly or raggedly dressed). *Obs.*

1610 B. JONSON *Alch.* I. i, You were once..the good, Honest, plaine, liuery-three-pound-thrum; that kept Your masters worships house..For the vacations. **1705** ELSTOB in Hearne *Collect.* 30 Nov. (O.H.S.) I. 108 He eyes ye greasy Rout, Of gaping thrums, stand listning round about. **1727** SOMERVILLE *Canidia's Epithal.* 9 Each sprightly soph, each brawny thrum, Spent his first runnings here.

7. *attrib.* and *Comb.* **a.** *attrib.* Made or consisting of thrums or waste threads of yarn (or something resembling it), or having thrums inserted in or projecting from it (cf. THRUM *v.*[2], THRUMMED[1]): as ***thrum beard, bonnet, hat, mat, mop, night-cap***; pertaining to or dealing in thrums, as ***thrum shop***. **b.** *Comb.*: **thrum cap**, (*a*) a cap made of thrums; *transf.* a person wearing a thrum cap; (*b*) *Canad.* (*obs.* exc. in place-names), a small island with a conical shape suggestive of a thrum cap; hence †**thrum-capped** (-kæpt) *a.*, wearing a thrum cap; **thrum-chinned** (-tʃɪnd) *a.* (*jocular*), bearded; **thrum-eyed** (-aɪd) *a.*, applied by florists to the short-styled form of a flower (esp. of the genus *Primula*), which shows the boss of 'thrums' or anthers (cf. 4 a) at the top of the corolla-tube (opp. to PIN-EYED); so **thrum eye**; †**thrum-flower**, (of Petiver) *Astrocarpus Clusii*, a native of the western Mediterranean region; †**thrum-stone**, Grew's name for asbestos, as being a fibrous mineral. See also THRUMWORT.

1577 HANMER *Anc. Eccl. Hist.* (1619) 307 A long *thrum beard. **1827** SCOTT *Highl. Widow* i, Duncan with the *thrum bonnet, and the other lords of the..towers of Kilchurn. [**1439** Thrum cap: cf. quot. in 2.] **1624** MASSINGER *Renegado* I. iii, A witch with a *thrum cap, That sells ale underground. **1676** LADY FANSHAWE in *Mem.* Feb. an. 1650 (1829) 93, I.. desired him [the cabin-boy] to be so good as to give me his blue thrum cap he wore, and his tarred coat..and putting them on..I..stood upon the deck by my husband's side. **1690** DRYDEN *Don Sebast.* I. i, Hold, my dear Thrum-cap: I obey thee cheerfully. **1720** STRYPE *Stow's Surv.* (1754) I. I. xxvi. 196/1 (The Blue Coat Hospital) Their habit being now ..a round thrum Cap tied with a red band, yellow Stockings. **1832** T. BAILLIE *Acct. New Brunswick* 120 Opposite to this point an islet or thrum-cap..was once considered available for the purpose of drawing fish. **1903** G. S. WASSON *Cap'n Simeon's Store* xi. 248 They had.. taken to their boat and pulled for Thrumcap Island Light. **1966** T. H. RADDALL *Hangman's Beach* II. xiv. 217 'Why is this called the Thrum Cap?' 'Thrumb's a coarse kind of wool... Sailors used to wear knitted caps of red thrum... You notice the red bank of the knoll standing up like a thrum cap.' **1708** W. KING *Art Cookery* (1807) 73 Would our *thrum-capped ancestors find fault, For want of sugartongs, or spoons for salt? **1608** MIDDLETON *Trick to Catch Old One* IV. iii, [Widows] that will marry unfledged boys before comely *thrum-chinned gentlemen. **1888** *Pall Mall G.* 19 May 6/1 Auriculas..with their characters of grey or green edge, pin or *thrum eye, &c. **1861** DARWIN in *Jrnl. of Linnæan Soc., Botany* VI. 77 Florists who cultivate the Polyanthus and Auricula..call those which display the globular stigma at the mouth of the corolla 'pin-headed' or 'pin-eyed', and those which display the stamens *thrum-eyed. *c* **1711** PETIVER *Gazophyl.* VI. lii, Small Spanish Purple *Thrum-flower,..Grows a Span high on the stony Hills of Salamanca. **1543** *Acc. Ld. High Treas. Scot.* VIII. 180 Twa *thrum hattis of silk, price of the pece xiiij s. **1590** [TARLTON] *News Purgat.* (1844) 120 A thrumbe hat she had of red. **1770** COOK *Voy. round World* II. ix. (1773) 453 Ends ..hanging out..like the shag or *thrumb matts which [etc.]. **1883** *Man. Seamanship Boys' Training Ships* (Admiralty) (1886) 184 A thrum mat is made by cutting a certain number of yarns of equal length and reeving them through holes made in the mat, both ends to come through on one side. **1961** F. H. BURGESS *Dict. Sailing* 208 *Thrum mat*, a piece of canvas or other coarse material into which thrums are inserted, either roughly for chafing purposes and collision mats, or in decorative pattern with materials suitable for homes. **1753** HOGARTH *Anal. Beauty* vi. 74 The inelegant and inanimate figure of a *thrum mop or muff. **1768** STERNE *Sent. Journ.*, *The Husband*, He sits..in his *thrum night-cap. **1796** COLQUHOUN *Police Metropolis* p. viii, Petty Pilferers at Old Iron Shops,..Rag and *Thrum Shops. **1681** GREW *Musæum* III. I. v. 313 *Thrum-Stone, as I call it. *Amianthus Lapis & Asbestinus.*

thrum (θrʌm), *sb.*[3] [Echoic: cf. THRUM *v.*[3]] An echoic word representing various sounds, esp. the tones produced by 'thrumming' a guitar or similar instrument; also *dial.* the purring of a cat.

[*a* **1553** UDALL *Royster D.* II. i, Anon to our gitterne, thrumpledum, thrumpledum thrum.] **1798** LAWRENCE *Treat. Horses* II. i. 18 That..affectionate domestic the cat, ..its feet kneading in unison with the grateful thrum. **1814** *Sporting Mag.* XLIV. 128 The soft and melodious thrum evincing the happy state of his [a cat's] feelings. **1845** T. COOPER *Purgatory of Suicides* (1877) 110 Fear not Grimalkin! she doth sing 'three-thrum'. **1863** W. MILLER *Willie Winkie* ii, The cat's singing grey thrums To the sleeping hen. **1883** BERTHA THOMAS *George Sand* 119 The distant thrum of guitars. **1884** *Pall Mall G.* 4 July 4/1 The thrum-thrum, ting-ting, tum-a tum-tum of their banjoes filled the air.

†**thrum**, *v.*[1] *Obs. rare.* [? Related to THRUM *sb.*[1]: cf. Flemish '*drommen* = *dringhen*, premere, pressare, stipare, *drom*, *ghedrom*, pressura' (Kilian).]

1. *trans.* To compress, condense.

c **1205** LAY. 54 Feþeren he nom mid fingren & fiede on boc-felle..& þa þre boc þrumde to are [*i.e.* to one].

2. To press or crowd in; to cram.

1603 HARSNET *Pop. Impost.* 52 The Devills they had cast, did rebound back againe..which by this provision of Thrumming in Devills at the first might..have been avoided.

thrum, *v.*[2] Also 6 **throm**, 7–9 **thrumb**. See also THRUMMED[1]. [f. THRUM *sb.*[2]]

trans. To furnish or adorn with thrums or ends of thread (or something similar); to cover with thrums or small tufts, raise a pile upon (cloth); to make shaggy. Now *dial.*

c **1525** *Harl. MS.* 4217 art. 11 Hattes thrommyd with silke of diuerse collours. *a* **1562** CAVENDISH *Wolsey* (1893) 88 His hosyn, frome the kne upprward, was alltogether thrommed with sylke. **1598** FLORIO, *Irtare*, to thrum, to make rough, hairie or brislie. **1809** SOUTHEY in *Q. Rev.* II. 41 When the young king is first invested with the..red sash of royalty (which is made of net work, and thrummed with red and yellow feathers). **1887** *Suppl. to* JAMIESON, *Thrum*, to raise a tufted pile on knitted or woven woollen stuffs, to cover woollen cloth with small tufts like thrums.

†**b.** *transf.* and *fig.* To fringe or clothe. *Obs.*

1589 R. HARVEY *Pl. Perc.* 13 Leaue thrumming thy Pibault Iestes with Scripture, Iron and Clay will not be tempered togither. **1591** SYLVESTER *Du Bartas* I. vii. 27 A craggy Rocks steep-hanging boss (Thrumm'd half with Ivie, half with crisped Moss). **1630** DRAYTON *Muses' Elysium* iv. 82, I could wish..this bank were thickly thrumb'd with grass As soft as sleave or sarcenet ever was.

†**c.** To twist, curl, twine; also *intr.* To curl (as hair). *Obs.*

1598 FLORIO, *Cincinnare*, to curle, or thrum any haire. **1668** CULPEPPER & COLE *Barthol. Anat.* III. i. 128 So in Æthiopia by a peculiar thrumming of their hairs, they are defended from the heat.

†**d.** ***to thrum caps***: *lit.* to cover caps with thrums; a proverbial phrase expressing trifling, or waste of work and time. Also ***to thrum buttons***, and absol. *to thrum*. *Obs.*

1594 NASHE *Unfort. Trav.* 9 The King stood not long a thrumming of buttons there. **1602** *Narcissus* (1893) 160 Why stand wee heere, as it were cappes a thrumming? **1614**

J. Cooke *Greene's Tu Quoque* H ij b, I'de nere stand thrumming of Caps for the matter. **1626** Middleton *Women Beware Wom.* III. iii, I'll not stand all day thrumming, But quickly shoot my bolt. **1644** Quarles *Judgm. & Mercy* 18 Are we born to thrum caps, or pick straws?

e. *Naut.* To sew or fasten bunches of rope-yarn over (a mat or sail) so as to produce a shaggy surface, suitable to prevent chafing or stop a leak.

1711 [see THRUMMED^{1} c]. **1783** Capt. Inglefield *Narr. Loss Centaur* 16 All the officers, passengers and boys, who were not of the profession of seamen, had been employed thrumming a sail which was passed under the ship's bottom. **1820** Scoresby *Acc. Arctic Reg.* II. 448 *note*, By thrumbing the sail, that is, sewing long bunches of ropeyarn all over it. **1838** Poe *A. G. Pym* Wks. 1864 IV. 66 A sail was thrummed, and got under the bows. **1848** G. Biddlecombe *Art of Rigging* 36 *Thrumming*, interplacing, in a regular manner, through intervals of matting made by a fid, short pieces of thrums, or ropeyarn. **1867** Smyth *Sailor's Word-bk.* s.v., A vessel, when leaky, is thrummed by working some heavy spare sail, as the spritsail, into a thrummed mat, greasing and tarring it well, passing it under the bottom, and heaving all parts tight.

thrum, *v.*^{3} Also 7–9 **thrumb**. [Echoic: going with THRUM *sb.*^{3}]

1. a. *intr.* To play on a stringed instrument, as a guitar, harp, etc., by plucking the strings; to play on any stringed instrument in an idle, mechanical, or unskilful way; to strum.

1592 Greene *Disput.* 25 Neither had he any excellent quallities but thrumming on the gittron. **1669** Pepys *Diary* 12 Apr., After sitting a while, thrumming upon my viall, and singing. **1766** Goldsm. *Vic. W.* xvii, Sophy, love, take your guitar, and thrum in with the boy a little. **1822** W. Irving *Braceb. Hall* v, Sometimes he even thrums a little on the piano. **1872** Calverley *Fly Leaves* (1903) 72 Bang, twang, clatter and clang, Strum, thrum, upon fiddle and drum.

b. *trans.* To play (a stringed instrument, or a tune on it) idly, monotonously, or unskilfully; to strum upon; also, to pluck, twang (a string).

a **1625** [see *thrumming* below]. **1675** Covel in *Early Voy. Levant* (Hakl. Soc.) 215 A little pittifull instrument with three wire strings, which every fellow thrums ordinarily about the street. **1681** Dryden *Abs. & Achit.* 439 Th' old Harp on which he thrums his Lays. **1758** L. Temple *Sketches* (ed. 2) 28 The Productions of our present Italian Masters are thrummed over for a Season. **1782** [T. Vaughan] *Fashionable Follies* II. cci. 113 Thrumming his guittar under her window. **1841** Catlin *N. Amer. Ind.* I. xxii. 159 Bows were strung and thrummed to test their elasticity. **1866** Mrs. Stowe *Litt. Foxes* 117 They thrum a few tunes on the piano. **1873** 'Ouida' *Pascarèl* II. 15 The violin of Toccò thrummed a gay melody.

2. *intr.* To sound as an instrument or string when thrummed; to sound monotonously; to hum.

1763 *Poetry* in *Ann. Reg.* 245 With dead, dull, doleful, heavy hums..The sober hurdy-gurdy thrums. **1887** Gunter *Mr. Barnes* xxii. 159 And so with mandolins thrumming at their head they finally come up the avenue. **1900** *Westm. Gaz.* 9 Oct. 2/3 Looms are full of woollen webs, spinning-wheels are thrumming.

b. Of a cat: To purr. *dial.*

a **1810** Tannahill *Poems* (1846) 30 Auld baudrons sits, and croodling thrums. **1841** *P. Parley's Ann.* II. 324 She began to cock her tail,..and to purr and thrum as if all her sorrows were entirely forgotten.

3. a. *trans.* To recite or tell in a 'sing-song' or monotonous way; also, to hum over (a melody).

1710 Steele *Tatler* No. 173 ¶ 1 Horace and Virgil must be thrummed by a Boy as well before he goes to an Apprenticeship as to the University. **1807** W. Irving *Salmag.* XII. v. (1824) 216 Who the fair..vex, By thrumming for ever their weakness of sex. **1816** Scott *Antiq.* xxi, And then siccan stories as Sanders had..; and eh! as he wad thrum them ower and ower..ayont the ingle at e'en. *a* **1845** Hood *Compass* xxi, And as he walk'd to self he talked, Some ancient ditty thrumming, In under tone.

b. *intr.* To speak or read monotonously, to 'drone', mumble.

a **1774** Tucker *Lt. Nat.* (1834) II. 681 To despise every old woman that thrums over good books all day,..because she does not understand Latin. **1825** [see *thrumming* below]. **1829** Scott *Jrnl.* 26 Mar., Boswell..has thrummed upon this topic till it is threadbare. **1858** Bailey *Age* 152 Shall every ninny who can thrum on rhyme, Break all our ear-drums without tune or time?

4. To strike something with the fingers as if playing on a musical instrument; to drum upon (a table, etc.). **a.** *trans.*

c **1750** Shenstone *Colemira* 28 How I long..To view those rosy fingers strike the lyre! For late when bees to change their clime began How did I see 'em thrum the frying pan. **1848** Thackeray *Van. Fair* lxiii, She..dashing the pin through the card on to the table, sat thrumming it for a while.

b. *intr.* with *on* or *upon*.

1820 W. Irving *Sketch Bk.* I. 265 While I sat.. meditating..I was thrumming with the other hand upon the quarto. **1842** Tennyson *Will Waterproof* xx, I sit, my empty glass reversed, And thrumming on the table. **1865** G. Meredith *Rhoda Fleming* xv, The squire was thrumming on the back of his chair.

5. *slang.* (*trans.*) **a.** To beat (a person). ? *Obs.*

1604 Dekker *Honest Wh.* I. vii, Flat-cap,..y'are a flat foole, an Asse, a Gull, and I'le thrum you. **1676** Shadwell *Virtuoso* I. i, 'Sdeath! you sawcy Jades,..I'll thrum you. **1823** [see *thrumming* below].

b. In obscene sense: see quots. ? *Obs.*

1611 Florio, *Accencíre úna dónna*, to thrum a wench. **1762** Brydges *Burlesque Homer* (1797) I. 138 How they had thrum'd the maids of Troy.

Hence **thrummed** (θrʌmd) *ppl. a.*; **'thrumming** *vbl. sb.* and *ppl. a.*

a **1625** Fletcher *Woman's Prize* I. i, Your mistriss..must think This single thrumming of a fiddle..but even poor sport. **1681** Dryden *Span. Friar* I. ii, The thrumming of a guitar. **1697** Collier *Mor. Subj.* II. (1709) 19 As for Thrumming upon a Fiddle, he left it to such Finical Sparks as they were. **1823** Pyne *Wine & Walnuts* (1824) II. xv. 208 The ushers..begged a half holiday for the whole school,.. and thus they escaped a thrumming. **1825** Scott *Let.* 29 Nov., I am writing in the Court..little..enlivened by the thrumming of two very dull pleaders. **1840** Lady C. Bury *Hist. of Flirt* vii, Thrumming generally leads to whispering and love-making. **1876** Geo. Eliot *Dan. Der.* l, Little tinklings of mule-bells and whirrings of thrumbed strings. **1941** D. C. Peattie *Road of Naturalist* (1946) i. 9 Unleashed for the long stretch, the motor took up a loyal thrumming. **1969** *Daily Tel.* 14 Apr. 19/6 The arrival of a hovercraft.. brings a thrumming which rattles the window. **1977** *Islander* (Victoria, B.C.) 21 Aug. 10/1 Switch on, and the Yanmar diesel barked into life, warming up slowly to a soft thrumming.

† **'thrumble**, *v.*^{1} *Obs.* $rare^{-1}$. In 4–5 also **þrompel, thromle.** *intr.* In quot., To stumble.

1362 Langl. *P. Pl.* A. v. 201 He þrompelde [*v.rr.* stumblide, stumblid] atte þrexwolde and þreuh to þe grounde. **1393** *Ibid.* C. VII. 408 He thrumbled [*v.rr.* thromlide, trobled, stomblede, etc.] at þe þreshefold.

thrumble ('θrʌmb(ə)l), **thrimble** ('θrɪmb(ə)l), *v.*^{2} Chiefly, now only, *Sc.* and *north. dial.* Forms: α. 6– **thrumble**, (9 **thrummle**). β. 6 **thrimbil, thrymble, thrimle, thrymle, thrimmil,** 8 **thrimmle,** 9 **thrimal, thrimmel,** 7– **thrimble.** [app. a derivative of THRUM *v.*^{1} Cf. obs. Du. or Flem. '*drommel*, res simul compactæ et densæ; res compactiles' (Kilian); Du. *in een drommel verzamelen*, to crowd together.]

1. *trans.* To press, compress, squeeze; to crowd or heap together.

α. **1589** Bruce *Serm. Sacram.* iii. I v, Peter..sayis: Thou art thrumbled and thrusted be the multitude, and zit thou speeris quha hes twitched thee. **1600** Holland *Livy* XXVI. xxxix. 614 So thrumbled [L. *conglobati*] they were and thrust togither disorderly. **1603** —— *Plutarch's Mor.* 258 Wicked and leawd folke, who gather, thrumble, and heape up together all sorts of gaine.

β. **1513** Douglas *Æneis* III. ix. 67 Twa bodeis of our sort he [Polyphemus] tuke and raif; Intill his hiddius hand thaim thrimbillit and wrang. *Ibid.* V. xiii. 93 The fers Achil.. Chasand affrayit Troianis..The gret rowtis to the wallis thrymbland. **1596** Dalrymple tr. *Leslie's Hist. Scotl.* (S.T.S.) I. 49 Marr lyes on the costsyde neist, thrimmilit.. as it war intil a narrow boundes, in ane parte, bot in ane vthir parte..braider. **1836** M. Mackintosh *Cottager's Dau.* 78 The cruel boot, too, I hae hane Thrice thrimal'd on my leg.

b. *intr.* To make one's way by pushing or jostling; to push, jostle.

1500–20 [implied in *thrumbler* below]. *a* **1598** Rollock *Serm.* Wks. 1849 I. 493 She thrumbleth and thrusteth in at the gates of heaven. **1638** Adamson *Muse's Threnodie* i. (1774) 23 With kind embracements did we thurst and thrimble, (For in these days I was exceeding nimble). **1901** W. Morrison *Johnston of W.* vi. 37 Even with all their help they could scarce 'thrumble through'.

2. *trans.* To press or rub between the finger and thumb; to finger, handle.

1632 Sherwood, To thrumble, *frotter entre les doigts.* **1789** Davidson *Seasons* 36 Taylors, fain the gear to thrimmle Of coward coofs. **1828** *Craven Gloss., Thrimble*, to pull or draw out with reluctance, to press... 'He thrimbl'd out his sixpence wi' a deal to do'. **1906** J. Patterson *Wamphray* iv. 104 [Others] after 'thrimmling' the money in their fingers paid part of what they owed.

Hence † **'thrumbler**, in 6 **thrimlar**, *Sc. Obs.* $rare^{-1}$, one who thrumbles, or makes his way by pressing; a hustler; **'thrumbling** *vbl. sb.*

1500–20 Dunbar *Poems* lxiii. 47 Thrimlaris and thristaris, as thay war woid, Kokenis, and kennis na man of gude. **1649** Kenmure *Sp.* in *Sel. Biog.* (Wodrow Soc.) I. 398 The Kingdom of Heaven is not gotten but with much seeking, thrumbling and thrusting.

† **'thrumble**, *v.*^{3} *Obs.* $rare^{-1}$. [app. a derivative of THRUM *v.*^{3}] *intr.* = THRUM *v.*^{3} 1 a (in quot. *fig.*).

1685 Crowne *Sir C. Nice* II. 11 No, Madam, he's the General Guitarre o' the Town... *Vio.* Well, I have provided one shall thrumble on him.

thrummed (θrʌmd), *ppl. a.*^{1} Also 6 **thrombyed, throm(m)ed, thromde,** *Sc.* **thrumit,** 6–7 **thrumd, thrumbd, thrumb'd,** 6–9 **thrumbed,** 7–8 **thrum'd.** [f. THRUM *sb.*^{2} or *v.*^{2} + -ED.]

Covered or decked with thrums; having a nap or shaggy surface; also, fringed. *Obs.* or *dial.*

1535 *Bury Wills* (Camden) 126, I gyf and bequeth to Alys Mannyng,..iij s. iiij d. and on new thrombyed hate. **1546** *Aberdeen Regr.* (1844) I. 237 Ane blak thrumit hat. **1562** Bulleyn *Bulwark, Bk. Simples* 16 b, The flowers is like a Blewe or White thrummed hatte. **1578** in Feuillerat *Revels Q. Eliz.* (1908) 287 Hattes of crymson silk and sylver thrommed and wreythed bandes. **1602** *Inv.* in *Collect. Archæol.* (1863) II. 98 One thrummed blanquett xviij*d.* **1603** Knolles *Hist. Turks* (1621) 529 The common soldiors used thrumd caps. **1609–10** in Willis & Clark *Cambridge* (1886) III. 353 Item pro .12. thrummed quishions xliiij^{s}. **1615** Crooke *Body of Man* 94 So becomming a thrummed rugge to keepe warme the Membranous and vnbloody guts and stomacke vnder it. **1650** Fuller *Pisgah* IV. vi. 101 A fringe in Hebrew..represented the complication, or conjunction of Gods commandments among themselves,.. as the threads in those thrummed fringes were woven together. **1656** *Artif. Handsom.* 44 Many..by a thrumb'd stocking, a bumbast or bolstered garment,..endeavour to redeem themselves. **1665** Sir T. Herbert *Trav.* (1677) 223 Carpets of silks, silk and gold, and of course thrumd-wool.

† **b.** *transf.* and *fig.*; in quot. 1607 perh. used for 'thatched'. *Obs.*

1577 Kendall *Flowers Epigr.* 17 b, The sun, the starres, the thrunbed thrones with siluer perle and gold. **1578** Lyte *Dodoens* I. viii. 15 The sayde..knoppes do open and put forth a fayre purple, thromde, or veluet floure. **1607** Middleton *Michaelm. Term* I. ii, Wouldst thou..live in a poor thrummed house i' th' country?

c. *Naut.* Of a mat or sail: Having pieces of rope-yarn sewn upon or stuck through it so as to produce a dense shaggy surface: see quot. 1900.

1711 W. Sutherland *Shipbuild. Assist.* 162 *Paunch*, thrum'd Mats. **1798** Capt. Troubridge in *Naval Chron.* XXIII. 19 With thrummed sails [we] reduced the leak. **1835** Sir J. Ross *Narr. 2nd Voy.* liii. 686 The men had each a bed place with a canvas bottom, and a thrummed mat for a bed. **1900** F. T. Bullen in *Daily News* 7 Aug. 3/4 They must.. lay loosely spread the collision mat, a mass of rope and thrummed yarn, about fifteen feet square, four inches thick, and weighing about a quarter of a ton.

thrummed, *ppl. a.*^{2}: see THRUM *v.*^{3}

thrummer ('θrʌmə(r)). [f. THRUM *v.*^{3} + -ER^{1}.] One who thrums or strums on a stringed instrument; an idle or indifferent player.

1706 E. Ward *Hud. Rediv.* I. x. 8 A Welsh Thrummer's slaving Ass, That carr's his Harp from Place to Place. *a* **1810** Tannahill *Wand. Bard* Poems (1846) 108 No, thou old intruding thrummer, Thou canst have no lodging here. **1850** S. Dobell *Roman* vii, To the buttery-hatch, Ye strolling thrummers.

thrumming, *vbl. sb.* and *ppl. a.*: see THRUM *v.*^{3}

thrummy ('θrʌmɪ), *a.* Now *rare.* [f. THRUM *sb.*^{2} + -Y.] Consisting of, characterized by, or resembling thrums; covered with thrums; shaggy, downy, velvety. Formerly of flowers with conspicuous anthers, of fibrous roots, etc. (cf. THRUM *sb.*^{2} 4).

1597 Gerarde *Herbal* I. xi. § 2. 13 His roote is..made of many thrummie threds. **1598** Florio, *Velutoso*, soft, woolly, thrummie, full of silke or veluet. *c* **1600** Chalkhill *Thealma & Cl.* (1683) 102 In Furrs yclad, And on her Head a thrummy Cap she had. **1659** Torriano, *Filaccio*, course raw silk, thrummy yarn. **1697** J. Petiver in *Phil. Trans.* XIX. 680 At the top of each Branch stand small thrummy Flowers. **1703** Dampier *Voy.* III. I. 158 A Columella thick set with thrummy *apiculæ* which argue this Plant to belong to the Malvaceous kind. **1909** A. Reid *Kirriemuir* ii. 11 The weaver's dress was often very 'thrummy'.

thrump (θrʌmp). [Echoic.] The sound of a blow, heavy fall or beat, etc. Freq. redupl.

1871 *Daily News* 25 Jan., The heavy thrump, thrump of the mitrailleuse. **1886** *Century Mag.* Feb. 520/1 The banjo's thrump and strum. **1903** *Westm. Gaz.* 5 Oct. 2/1, I awoke with the music of marching men's feet in my ears—thrump, thrump, thrump, thrump.

† **thrums** (θrʌms). *Obs. slang.* Also quasi-*sing.* **thrum** (7 **thrumm**). [Repr. colloq. or dial. pronunc. of THRUP(P)ENCE.] = THREEPENCE.

1699 B. E. *New Dict. Canting Crew, Thrumms*, three-pence. **1846** *Swell's Night Guide* 78 There is a hanger on here who teaches the art of self defence—thrums (three pence) a lesson. **1865** *Leaves from Diary of Celebrated Burglar & Pickpocket* 108/2 His first putting-up place was at a low padding ken in St. Giles's, where he paid a 'thrum' per night for share of a 'doss'. **1880** W. H. Patterson *Gloss. Words Antrim & Down* 106 *Thrum*,..a threepence. A commission of three pence per stone of flax, paid by a flax-buyer to a person who brings the buyer and seller together in open market. **1933** *Bulletin* (Sydney) 23 Aug. 10/2, I haven't encountered a crook thrum yet.

thrumwort ('θrʌmwɜːt). [f. THRUM *sb.*^{2} + WORT.] A name for different plants having parts resembling thrums. **a.** The water-plantain, *Alisma Plantago* (or other species); also the allied star-fruit *Actinocarpus Damasonium.* **b.** 'Love-lies-bleeding', *Amarantus caudatus.*

1829 *Glover's Hist. Derby* I. 112 *Alisma ranunculoides*, lesser thrum wort... *Alisma lanceolata*, narrow-leaved thrum wort. **1866** *Treas. Bot.* 1147 Thrumwort, *Actinocarpus*; also *Amaranthus caudatus.* **1879** Prior *Names Brit. Plants, Thrum-wort*... The plant has its name from its long tassel-like panicles of red flowers, the florimer, *Amarantus caudatus.* **1886** Britten & Holland *Eng. Plant-n.*, Thrum-wort. (1) *Amaranthus caudatus*... (2) A book-name for *Actinocarpus Damasonium*... Thrum-wort, Great, *Alisma Plantago.*

thrung, thrunter: see THRING *v.*, THRINTER.

thrup(p)ence, thrup(p)enny ('θrʌpəns, 'θrʌpənɪ; 'θrʊ-). Repr. colloq. or dial. pronunc. of THREEPENCE, THREEPENNY *a.* (*sb.*).

1895 H. Nevinson *Neighbours of Ours* v. 142 They paid 'er fivepence for doin' each large flag... So she sublets to Ginger at thruppence a flag. **1962** *Spectator* 27 July 117 A letter with a thrupenny stamp.

thrus, thrusche: see THRUSH, THURSE.

† **thrusche**, *v.* *Sc. Obs.* [Etymology and meaning obscure; perhaps there are here two words.

In sense 2, possibly:—OE. **þyrscan* in *ȝe-*, *of-þyrscan*, 'to press, press down, repress'; but this does not suit sense 1, for which some suggest identity with FRUSH *v.*, with *th* for *f*; but this also seems to fail to give the sense 'cut or cleave'.]

1. *trans.* ? To cut asunder, cleave.

*c*1470 HENRY *Wallace* III. 190 The thrusande blaid his hals in sonder schayr. *Ibid.* XI. 252 His gud suerd.. His body in twa it thurschyt euirlikdeill. 1483 *Cath. Angl.* 387/2 To Thrusche. [No Latin.]

2. To thrust, press.

1600 *Sc. Acts Jas. VI* (1816) IV. 206/2 [He] pullit vp the brod of the windo Quhairvnto the said mr alexander had thrusschit his majesteis heid and schulderis. [Panton's *Dissert. Gowry Consp.* 1812, quotes the passage with *thrust.*]

thrush[1] (θrʌʃ). Forms: 1 **ðræsce, þrysce, þryssce, þrisce,** 3 **þrusche** (ü), **þruysse** (*for þrüshe*), 4 **þrusch,** 5-6 **thrusshe, thrushe** (5 **thryshe, thrusche, thrus,** 7 **thresh**); 6- **thrush.** [Two ablaut-forms in OE.: α. *þrýsce*, later *þryssce*, wk. fem.:—O. Teut. **þrûskjôn*. For the change of vowel in ME. *þrusche, thrush*, cf. *clutch, crutch, rush, thrutch*, with *u* (ʌ) from *y* (y); in 15th c., some dialects retained *þruysse* (=*þrüshe*) and *thryshe*, and *thrice-cock* (for *thrȳshe-cock*) is still a dialect-name of the missel-thrush. β. OE. had *a* 800 Anglian *þræsce* = WSax. **þréasce* = OHG. *drôsca*:—OTeut. **prauskôn*. Examples of this form are rare, and indeed not yet cited in ME., where it would be **presche*, **thresshe*; but *thresh* occurs in 17th c., and the derivative *thresher* is dialectal in Oxfordsh. and Berksh. Cf. also the U.S. *thrasher*. There are also the derivative forms *thrushel, thrishel, thrissel*, from the α type: see THRUSHEL.]

1. a. Historically, A name of two British and general European birds; (1) primarily, and without qualification, that also called *Throstle* and *Mavis*, distinctively *Song-thrush* (*Turdus musicus*); (2) the *Mistletoe thrush, Mistle-*, or *Missel-thrush* (*T. viscivorus*), a larger and less musical species. Thence extended (with qualifications) by ornithologists to other species of the genus *Turdus* (many of which, in vernacular language, have other names, and are not regarded as thrushes), or more widely, to all members of the family *Turdidæ*. By colonists, travellers, etc., transferred, with qualifications, to birds of other lands, allied to the European thrushes, or merely resembling these in general appearance or some feature; see b.

The song-thrush is locally known as THROSTLE and MAVIS, dialectally *thrushel, thrustle, thrusher, thrushfield, whistling thrush*; the missel-thrush, as *bull thrush, gawthrush, holm-t., horse-t., marble-t., Norman t., stone-t., wood-t., thrush-cock, throstle-cock, storm-cock*, etc. In OE. and ME., *thrush* and *throstle* are sometimes mentioned as distinct birds: see THROSTLE. Among the thrushes (*Turdi*) of ornithology, are the redwing, fieldfare, blackbird, ring-ouzel, of Great Britain, and the robin, veery, hermit-thrush, wood-thrush, and other species of North America.

α. *c*1000 *Voc.* in Wr.-Wülcker 260/30 *Trutius*, þrisce. *c*1000 *Voc.* ibid. 286/23 *Strutio*, þryssce. *a*1250 *Owl & Night.* 1659 þruysse [*MS. Cott.* þrusche] & þrostle & wode-wale. *c*1350 *Will. Palerne* 820 Briddes þat bliþeliche song, Boþe þe þrusch & þe þrustele. 1413 *Pilgr. Sowle* (Caxton) v. v. (1859) 76, I bethought me vppon the byrdes as thrusshes, and thrustels, and stares whiche I haue sene. 14.. *Voc.* in Wr.-Wülcker 595/20 *Mauiscus, anglice* a thryshe. 14.. *Nom.* ibid. 702/39 *Hic garulus*, a thrus. *c*1460 J. RUSSELL *Bk. Nurture* 438 Of quayle, sparow, larke, .. pygeoun, swalow, thrusche, osulle. 1530 PALSGR. 281/1 Thrusshe a byrde, *gryue*. 1596 SPENSER *F.Q.* VI. iv. 17 Abrode to wend, To take the ayre and heare the thrushes song. 1624 CAPT. SMITH *Virginia* II. 27 There are.. Thrushes and divers sorts of small Birds. 1668 CHARLETON *Onomast.* 83 *Turdus*,.. the Thrush, Song-Thrush, or Throssle, or Mavis. 1746 FRANCIS tr. *Horace, Epist.* I. xv. 51 A fat Thrush is most delightful Food, And a Swine's Paunch superlatively good. 1810 SCOTT *Lady of L.* III. ii, The blackbird and the speckled thrush Good-morrow gave from brake and bush.

β. *c*725 *Corpus Gloss.* (O.E.T.) 2063 *Truitius*, ðraesce. *c*1676 *Roxb. Ball.* (1886) VI. 305 'Oh!' says the squeaking little Thresh, 'My Sorrows now begin afresh'. [1904 *Eng. Dial. Dict.* s.v. *Thrusher*, Also in form *thresher* Oxf., Bucks. .. The song-thrush.]

b. With qualifying words (indicating native country, colour, food, habits, etc.) applied to various species of the genus *Turdus* or family *Turdidæ*; also popularly to numerous species of other families (starlings, warblers, shrikes, etc.) more or less resembling the true thrushes: as

babbling thrush: = *thrush-babbler* in 4. **Chinese thrush**, *Trochalopterum canorum*; † **golden thrush**: early name of the Golden Oriole. **harmonic thrush**, *Collyriocincla harmonica*, of Australia. **long-legged thrush**, any bird of Swainson's subfamily *Crateropodinæ*, also called *babblers*, formerly classed with the thrushes. **migratory thrush**, the American robin. **New York thrush**, an American Water-thrush, *Seiurus nævius*. **olive-backed thrush** = OLIVE-BACK. **Pacific thrush**, a Polynesian bird, *Lalage pacifica*. **red thrush, red-breasted thrush**, the American robin. **shining thrush**, a W. African glossy starling, *Lamprocolius splendidus*. **shrike-thrush**: see SHRIKE. **songster thrush**, *Calornis panayensis*, of the Philippines. **spectacle thrush**, *Garrulax perspicillatus*, of Southern China and Thailand. **varied thrush**, the Oregon robin, *Hesperocichla nævia*. **whidah thrush**, a W. African starling, *Pholidauges leucogaster*. **Wilson's thrush**, the VEERY of N. America. **wind-thrush**, local name of the REDWING. **wine thrush**, a S. African species, *Turdus olivaceus*. See also ANT-THRUSH, GROUND-THRUSH, HERMIT-THRUSH, ROCK-THRUSH, WATER-THRUSH, WOOD-THRUSH.

*a*1705 RAY *Syn. Avium & P.* (1713) 64 *Turdus viscivorus minor*.., the Mavis, Throstle, or Song-Thrush... *Turdus Iliacus*.., the Red-Wing, Swine Pipe or Wind-Thrush. 1731 MEDLEY *Kolben's Cape G. Hope* II. 160 The Wine-thrushes have their name from their loving of grape-stones. 1750 EDWARDS *Nat. Hist. Birds* III. 185 The Golden Thrush. Icterus... They are found in the Southern Parts of Europe all the Summer Season. 1754 CATESBY *Nat. Hist. Carolina* (ed. 2) I. 30 The red-leg'd Thrush, *Turdus viscivorus plumbeus*. *Ibid.* 31 The little Thrush (*Turdus minimus*). In shape and colour it agrees with the description of the European *Mavis*, or Song-Thrush, differing only in bigness. 1783 LATHAM *Gen. Synopsis Birds* II. I. 36 *Chinese Thrush*, less than a Redwing. *Ibid.* 61 *Spectacle Thrush*, a Trifle bigger than a Blackbird. *a*1792 S. HEARNE *Journ. Northern Ocean* x. (1795) 418 The Red-breasted Thrushes, commonly called in Hudson's Bay.. Red Birds. 1827 AUDUBON *Jrnls.* 2 May, The Red Thrush. 1843 *Ibid.* 27 May, This morning my ears were saluted by the delightful song of the Red Thrush. 1898 MORRIS *Austral Eng.*, *Thrush*, .. applied in Australia and New Zealand to four [*sic*] different genera of birds, viz.—(1) *Collyriocincla*, the Shrike-Thrushes... (2) *Geocincla*, the Ground-Thrushes. (3) *Oreocincla*, the Mountain-Thrush. (4) *Pachycephala*; called Thrushes, but more often Thickheads. (5) *Turnagra* (the New Zealand Thrushes).

†**2.** ***sea-thrush, thrush-fish***, names given (after L. *turdus*) to various species of wrasse (*Labrus*), of which *L. turdus* is common in the Mediterranean; *L. maculatus* the Ballan wrasse, and *L. mixtus* the striped wrasse, are found also on the British coasts.

1601 HOLLAND *Pliny* IX. xv. I. 244 Of Stone-fishes, such as live among rocks, the sea Thrush, the sea Merle, and the purple shell-fishes are not to be found. 1661 LOVELL *Hist. Anim. & Min.* 235 *Thrush-fish*... They are very difficultly concocted yet Pliny counteth them good. 1726 LEONI *Alberti's Archit.* I. 97/2 The Sea-thrush and Whiting feed best among the Rocks.

3. *fig.* A female singer. *U.S.*

1940 *Amer. Speech* XV. 205/1 *Thrush*, a songstress. 1966 *Crescendo* Oct. 31/2 She has established herself as one of the best female thrushes in this area. 1982 B. FANTONI *Stickman* iv. 38 The band's thrush and Moons argued so long over the tempo to play 'Lover Man' we ditched it.

4. *Comb.* as ***thrush-haunted, -like*** adjs.; **thrush-babbler** = BABBLER 4; **thrush-blackbird**, a name for the Rusty Grackle, *Scolecophagus ferrugineus* (*Cent. Dict.* 1891); **thrush-breast** *a.*, speckled like a thrush's breast; † **thrush-fish** = *sea-thrush* (sense 2 above); **thrush-nightingale**, a nightingale (*Daulias philomela*) with a slightly speckled breast, found in central and eastern Europe; **thrush-tit**, a book-name for birds of the genus *Cochoa* (or *Xanthogenys*), inhabiting the Himalayas, China, and Java (*Cent. Dict.* 1891).

1878 P. ROBINSON *In my Indian Gard.* II. 83 The feeble-winged *thrush-babblers were wrangling over worms. 1896 *Allbutt's Syst. Med.* I. 191 [The walls of the fatty heart] frequently present a 'tabby-cat' or '*thrush-breast' appearance. 1905 *Speaker* 9 Sept. 548 *Thrush-haunted woods and peaceful shades. 1842 *Penny Cycl.* XXIII. 173/1 The chief peculiarities of the grakles, viz. the strong *thrush-like bill [etc.]. 1872 COUES *N. Amer. Birds* 76 Aquatic thrush-like birds. 1840 *Penny Cycl.* XVI. 231/1 The *Thrush Nightingale.. inhabiting central Europe. 1904 *Westm. Gaz.* 30 Nov. 12/1 Known as the thrush nightingale, and in Germany as the 'Sprosser'.

thrush[2] (θrʌʃ). [Not known in either sense before the 17th c., though the phonology of the word, with *þ* and *sh*, indicates English origin, and points to an OE. **þrusc*. The only continental cognates appear to be, in sense 1, Sw. and ODa. *tørsk*, Da. *troske*, Sw. dial. *trosk*, which Falk and Torp refer to an ON. **þruskr*. See *Note* below.]

1. A disease, chiefly of infants, characterized by white vesicular specks on the inside of the mouth and throat, and on the lips and tongue, caused by a parasitic fungus (see *thrush-fungus* in 3); scientifically called *aphtha* or *parasitic stomatitis*. Also, an infection of any other part with the same fungus, esp. of a woman's vagina.

1665 PEPYS *Diary* 17 June, He hath a fever, a thrush and a hickup. 1712 *Pomet's Hist. Drugs* I. 47 A Gargle of it cures the Thrush. 1828 MRS. BRAY *Protestant* xvii. (1884) 180 The thrush, colic, and other disorders incidental to children. 1877 ROBERTS *Handbk. Med.* (ed. 3) I. 289 Thrush is frequently associated with typhoid fever. 1967 *Current Medicine & Drugs* Dec. 4/1 The occurrence of Thrush Bowel Infection after antibiotics is.. argued by the makers of Nystatin. 1970 PASSMORE & ROBSON *Compan. Med. Stud.* II. xviii. 19/2 Vaginal thrush is fairly commonly associated with pregnancy. 1977 *Spare Rib* Jan. 36/1 Thrush is very irritating and can make you extremely sore if it's allowed to continue.

2. In the horse, An inflammation of the lower surface of the frog of the hoof, accompanied with a fetid discharge. Cf. FRUSH *sb.*[2]

1753 J. BARTLET *Gentl. Farriery* (1754) 319 Of the Running Thrush. Bathe the thrush with this, wherever there appears a more than ordinary moisture, and lay over the ulcer a little tow dipped in the same. 1810 *Sporting Mag.* XXXVI. 154 It had a thrush, spavins and contracted knees. 1831 [YOUATT] *Horse* xvi. 307 Thrush is a discharge of offensive matter from the cleft of the frog. It is inflammation of the lower surface of the sensible frog.

3. *Comb.*: **thrush-fungus**, the parasitic fungus *Candida albicans*, which causes thrush (sense 1); **thrush-lichen, thrush-moss**, a species of lichen, *Peltigera aphthosa*, found on moist alpine rocks, and used in Sweden boiled in milk as a cure for thrush (sense 1); **thrush-paste**, an astringent paste for curing thrush in horses (sense 2).

1759 STILLINGFL. *Misc. Tracts* (1775) 217 The countrey people taught us the virtues of the thrush-moss for sore throats. 1858 SIMMONDS *Dict. Trade*, *Thrush Lichen*, the *Peltidea apthosa*. 1888 *Cassell's Encycl. Dict.*, Thrush-lichen... Thrush-paste. 1899 CAGNEY *Jaksch's Clin. Diagn.* iii. (ed. 4) 113 In a few cases, thrush-fungus and vegetations have been found in the nose.

[*Note*. Norw. has *frøsk, frosk* 'thrush', phonetically identical with *frosk* frog; cf. Norw. dial. *trausk* = *frausk*, 'frog', which seems to rest upon an old phonetic confusion of **þruskr* and *froskr*. Some would connect this with the fact that Gr. *βάτραχος* and L. *rāna, rānula*, 'frog', were also names of a disease in the mouth of cattle. The evidence of Eng. is however that **þrosc* = ON. **þruskr*, was the orig. word for the disease in sense 1. The connexion of sense 2 is not explained; can it be connected with Da. *trøske* rotten or decayed wood, 'rottenness in the bones'?]

thrush, variant of THURSE, goblin.

thrush, thrush-bush: see THRASH *sb.*[2]

thrush-a-thrush. *dial. rare.* Also **thrush.** Name of some boys' game.

1760-72 H. BROOKE *Fool of Qual.* (1809) I. 20 Leap-frog, and thrush-a-thrush. 1880 *Antrim & Down Gloss.*, Thrush.

thrushel (ˈθrʌʃəl). Now *dial.* Also 5 **thruschyl, thrusshill,** 9 **thrishell** (*Devon*). [A derivative of THRUSH *sb.*[1], prob. dim.; cf. OHG. *drôscala*, dim. of *drôsca*, MHG. *drôschele*, dial. *droschel, druschel, drouschel*. Dialectally these forms tend to fall together with variants of THROSTLE and Ger. *drossel*.] A name, now local, of the thrush or song-thrush.

*c*1430 LYDG., Thruschylcok [see THROSTLE-COCK]. 1499 *Promp. Parv.* (ed. Pynson), Thrusshill or thrustyll, *merula*. 1881 MISS JACKSON *Shropsh. Wordbk.* 441 *Thrushel*, same as *Throstle*: Bridgnorth. 1885 SWAINSON *Prov. Names Birds* 3 (Song Thrush) Thrusher (Berks and Bucks), Dirsh (Somerset), Thrushfield (Salop), Thrushel or Thrustle (Salop), Thirstle (Devon, Cornwall, Salop).

ˈthrushling. *nonce-wd.* [See -LING.] A young thrush.

1899 P. ROBINSON in *Contemp. Rev.* 347 Surely a thrushling sitting on a tennis lawn.

ˈthrushy, *a.* [f. THRUSH[2] 2 + -Y.] Pertaining to or affected with thrush (sense 2).

1831 [YOUATT] *Horse* xvi. 307 When the frog.. becomes.. diseased, the cleft.. penetrates even to the sensible horn within, and through this.. fissure the thrushy discharge proceeds. *Ibid.* 308 Turning out would be prejudicial rather than of benefit to thrushy feet.

thrust (θrʌst), *sb.* Also 6- *Sc.* and *north. dial.* **thrist.** [f. THRUST *v.*, in various senses.]

I. † **1.** An act of pressing or pressure (see sense 4 of the verb); chiefly *fig.* 'pinch', hardship. *Obs.*

In phr. ***heap and thrust***, app. used *attrib.* = heaped up and pressed down; cf. THRUTCH *sb.*, quot. 1678.

1513 DOUGLAS *Æneis* VI. ii. 33 Withdraw the from na perrellis, nor hard thrist. 1535 STEWART *Cron. Scot.* (Rolls) II. 548 Tak tent in tyme or ȝe be put in thrist. *a*1600 MONTGOMERIE *Misc. Poems* xxiv. 76 Sen thou art thrald, think thou mon thole a thrist. 1670 CAPT. J. SMITH *Eng. Improv. Reviv'd* 91, 16000 Bushels of Chaff or Hulls worth 3 pence the Bushel heap and thrust.

†**2.** Pressure or pushing of a crowd, jostling, crowding; a crowd, throng, 'press'. *Obs.*

1565 COOPER *Thesaurus* s.v. *Arceo*, *Arctum theatrum*.. wherin is great thronge or thrust. 1588 PARKE tr. *Mendoza's Hist. China* 295 They were verie faint with the great thrust and throng of the people. 1600 FAIRFAX *Tasso* XX. xvii, What can he do.. In that confusion, trouble, thrust and throng? 1615 CHAPMAN *Odyss.* III. 52 In thrust did all men draw About their entry. 1620 SHELTON *Quix.* (1746) IV. xx. 164 Two of them, bold Crack-ropes, came among the Thrust.

3. *Mech.*, etc. **a.** A pushing force exerted by one part of a structure, etc. upon another contiguous part: *spec.* (*a*) *Arch.*, etc. Such a force exerted laterally by an arch or other part of a building or structure against an abutment or support; (*b*) the driving force exerted by a paddle or propeller-shaft in a ship or aeroplane; (*c*) *Mining*: see quot. 1881; (*d*) *Geol.* a compressive strain in the earth's crust; (*e*) the propulsive force developed by a jet or rocket engine.

1708 J. C. *Compl. Collier* (1845) 30 [Lest it] bring a Thrust, or a general Crush in one of your Collieries. 1739 LABELYE *Short Acc. Piers Westm. Br.* 44 The lower an Arch is, in proportion to its Opening, the greater is the Thrust it exerts against its Piers. 1853 SIR H. DOUGLAS *Milit. Bridges* (ed. 3) 326 In.. truss-frame bridges.. there is no thrust or pressure against the abutments, as in arched bridges. 1869 SIR E. J. REED *Shipbuild.* i. 8 Intended to aid in distributing the thrust of the paddleshaft. 1870 *4th Ann. Rep. Aëronaut. Soc. 1869* 9 The thrust of aërial screw propellers. 1881 RAYMOND *Mining Gloss.*, *Thrust*, the breaking down or the slow descent of the roof of a gangway. Compare *Creep*. 1903 *Nature* 12 Feb. 359/1 Local thrusts and shear slips took place again, fragmenting the previous thrust-masses and igneous intrusions. 1909 *Westm. Gaz.* 18 Mar. 4/1 The result of revolving a screw in water or air is to project a current.. in a direction approximately parallel to the axis of the screw, and the reaction from this in the opposite direction to which the current is flowing is called the 'thrust', and the aim of every designer is to obtain the greatest possible thrust from any given dimensions of propeller when working at its designed speed. **1933** *Aircraft Engin.* Jan. 22/2 This series of tests were undertaken to determine how much the reaction thrust of a jet could be increased by the use of thrust augmentors. **1950** *Sci. News* XV. 72 Since news of Whittle's jet engine was released there has been a popular misconception that if there is no atmosphere for the exhaust gases to push against there will be no thrust. **1977** *R.A.F. Yearbk.* 31/1 Recovery..involves unstalling the wing and re-establishing lift rather than blasting the aircraft out with thrust. **1982** *Daily Tel.* 14 Jan. 16/5 The engine was a Russian-built Nene of higher thrust (6,000 lb) than the original models. **1983** D. STINTON *Design of Aeroplane* vii. 297 A propeller consists of a number of wing-like aerofoils designed to convert torque into thrust.

b. Short for *thrust-bearing*: see 8.

1875 BEDFORD *Sailor's Pocket Bk.* vi. (ed. 2) 211 Have every..part of the engines carefully oiled, especially cylinders, slide-valves, eccentrics, cranks, and thrust.

4. = *thrustings*, THRUSTING *vbl. sb.* 2.

1877 KNIGHT *Dict. Mech.*, *Thrust*,..the white whey which last leaves the curd in pressing.

II. 5. An act, or the action, of thrusting (in sense 1 of the vb.); a forcible push or pushing. Also *fig.*

1823 SCOTT *Quentin D.* xxii, 'Take away the carrion' (giving the bishop's corpse a thrust with his foot). **1860** TYNDALL *Glac.* I. iii. 26 The thrust of the descending glacier. **1866** J. MARTINEAU *Ess.* I. 151 A logical thrust of the ostrich-head into the sand.

6. a. An act of thrusting (in sense 5 of the vb.); a lunge or stab made with a weapon.

a **1586** SIDNEY *Arcadia* II. (1590) 153 b, Zelmane harkening to no more wordes, began with such wittie furie to pursue him with blowes and thrustes. **1592** SHAKS. *Rom. & Jul.* I. i. 120 While we were enterchanging thrusts and blowes. **1601** R. JOHNSON *Kingd. & Commw.* (1603) 203 Garments of cotten wooll so close and hard quilted that they woulde beare out the thrust of a lance or sword. **1687** A. LOVELL tr. *Thevenot's Trav.* I. 127 They were taught to bend the Bow, shoot exact, give a true thrust with a Launce. **1779**, **1828** [see PARRY *sb.* 1]. **1840** DICKENS *Barn. Rudge* xvii, I made a thrust at him. **1879** G. MEREDITH *Egoist* xliii, He depended entirely on his agility to elude the thrusts that assailed him.

b. *transf.* and *fig.*

1668 H. MORE *Div. Dial.* I. xi. 41 There is one thrust at your pure pretended Mechanism. **1852** MRS. H. B. STOWE *Uncle Tom's C.* xxii, The faithful old heart felt a sudden thrust. **1859** MEREDITH *R. Feverel* xlii, White thrusts of light were darted from the sky. **1872** MORLEY *Voltaire* i. 8 Those shrewd thrusts, that flashing scorn, that relentless fire,.. with which..Voltaire pushed on his work of 'crushing the Infamous'.

c. In phr. ***cut and thrust***: see CUT *sb.*[2] 2 c; ***thrust and parry*** (*lit.* and *fig.*).

1763–1875 [see CUT *sb.*[2] 2 c]. **1889** *Pall Mall G.* 18 Oct. 1/2 A rollicking candidate whose thrust-and-parry recalls the days of the hustings. **1894** A. BIRRELL *Men, Women & Bks.* (ed. 2) 209 Swaggering Bohemians, cut-and-thrust men. **1905** WARREN in Alderson *Asquith* ii. 20 In the rapid thrust and parry of passing repartee.

†d. A bout of thrusting; a contest or encounter with swords. *Obs.*

1602 EARL NORTHUMBLD. in Collins *Peerage* (1779) II. 413 They two should have a thruste together. **1816** SCOTT *Bl. Dwarf* xii, I should like well to have a thrust with him on the green turf.

e. The principal theme or gist (*of* remarks, an argument, etc.); a point, aim, or purpose. orig. and chiefly *U.S.*

1968 MRS. L. B. JOHNSON *White House Diary* 17 Apr. (1970) 667 He spoke well... His thrust was that we..'make open spaces and recreation facilities a part of the daily.. environment of people'. **1972** A. CHAPMAN *New Black Voices* 575 The Institute of the Black World in Atlanta... Its central thrust is towards the creation of an international center for Black Studies. **1973** *Globe & Mail* (Toronto) 1 Aug. 6/3 The thrust of your editorial..is premised on the discredited 'compact theory'. **1977** *Guardian Weekly* 28 Aug. 18/4 That was the thrust of the exclusive story in the New York Times on March 10. *Ibid.* 6 Nov. 16/1 The postwar thrust of U.S. policy..has been to enlist Thailand in an anti-Communist alliance. **1982** *Church Times* 15 Jan. 12/4 A major part of the thrust of my article was to dissuade others from proposing such a cutback.

7. *Geol.* = *thrust-fault* (sense 8 below.)

1888 *Q. Jrnl. Geol. Soc.* XLIV. 420 Outliers of the 'Fucoid-beds' and Serpulite-grit are found,..separated from each other by major thrusts. **1910** *Ibid.* LXVI. 593 Thrust is here employed in the sense of a fold-fault replacing the lower limb of an overturned anticline. Lag.. is employed in the sense of a fold-fault replacing the upper limb of an overturned anticline. **1926** *Ibid.* LXXXII. 315 The Creag-an-Lochan Thrust. [*Note*] Equivalent to the 'lag' of E. B. Bailey [*preceding quot.*]; but the term 'thrust' is preferred and used throughout this paper for all structures indicating differential resistance to folding forces at a comparatively early stage. **1934** B. & R. WILLIS *Geologic Structures* (ed. 3) vii. 153 The term 'thrust' too often connotes the idea of an overthrust, whereas the structure may be an underthrust. **1942** E. M. ANDERSON *Dynamics of Faulting* i. 1 Overthrusts, or more simply thrusts, are faults which are inclined, in theory, at well under 45° to the horizon, and in field experience it is found that they are sometimes nearly horizontal. **1942** [see OVERTHRUST *ppl. a.*]. **1971** C. R. TWIDALE *Structural Landforms* iv. 98 In a normal thrust the upper block rides over the lower..but in a lag thrust the lower block is thrust forward and upwards beneath the upper.

8. *Comb.* **thrust augmentor** *Aeronaut.*, a procedure or modification used with a jet engine to increase its thrust; so **thrust augmentation**; **†thrust-bearer**, **thrust-bearing**, a bearing designed to receive a thrust in machinery; *spec.* the bearing in which revolves the foremost length of propeller-shafting in a screw steamer, its function being to transmit the thrust of the shaft to the hull of the ship; **thrust-block**, a block supporting a thrust-bearing; the casting or frame carrying or containing the bearings on which the collars of the propeller-shaft press; **thrust-box**, a box-bearing which sustains the end-thrust of a shaft (*Cent. Dict.*); **thrust chamber** *Astronautics* (see quot.); **thrust-collar**, each of the series of collars on a propeller-shaft, through which the thrust of the shaft is transmitted to the thrust-block and thence to the hull of the ship; **thrust-fault** *Geol.*, a reversed fault: = OVERFAULT; in mod. use, a low-angle reverse fault; also, any low-angle fault; = sense 7 above; hence **thrust-faulted** *a.*, **-faulting** *vbl. sb.*; **thrust-hoe**: see HOE *sb.*[2] 1 b; **thrust-mass** *Geol.*, the displaced mass of rock in an overfault; **thrust-movement**, movement caused by a thrust (3 a *d*); **thrust-post**, a post so placed as to take the thrust from a load or force; **thrust reverser** *Aeronaut.*, a device for reversing the flow of gas from a jet engine so as to produce a retarding backward thrust; **thrust-ring**, a brass ring made in two halves fitted in between the collars on the thrust-shaft to transmit the horizontal thrust of the shaft to the thrust-block; **thrust screw**, a thrusting-screw (THRUSTING *vbl. sb.* 3); see also quot. 1888; **thrust-shaft**, a propeller-shaft; *spec.* that part of the shaft on which are the thrust-collars; **thrust spoiler** *Aeronaut.*, a device for deflecting the flow of gas from a jet engine so as to reduce the thrust quickly without reducing the engine power; **thrust vector**, a vector representing the direction (and magnitude) of the thrust produced by a jet engine, propeller, etc.; **thrust washer**, a washer (WASHER *sb.*[2]) against which a thrust-bearing rests. See also THRUST-PLANE.

1956 W. A. HEFLIN *U.S. Air Force Dict.* 534/2 *Thrust augmentation for jet engines is accomplished by after-burning, reheating, water injection, etc. **1967** N. E. BORDEN *Jet-Engine Fundamentals* 126 On some jet engines, it is advantageous to provide a means of thrust augmentation during take-off on warm or hot days. **1933** *Thrust augmentor [see sense 3 a (*e*) above]. **1947** *Jrnl. R. Aeronaut. Soc.* LI. 79/1 The pumping could be directly produced by a ducted fan, when again a thrust augmentor effect would result. **1869** SIR E. J. REED *Shipbuild.* xv. 287 In a Screw steam-ship it is necessary to make some arrangement by means of which the thrust of the propeller shaft shall be transmitted to the ship, and the injurious effects prevented which would result from the direct action of the thrust upon the machinery. For this purpose *thrust-bearers are fitted. **1858** *Mechanics' Mag.* 6 Mar. 230/2 (*heading*) *Thrust bearing for screw propeller. **1864** WEBSTER, *Thrust-bearing* (Screw-steamers). **1889** WHITHAM *Steam Engine Design* 264 Another form of thrust bearing often used consists of a single thrust collar, forged with the shaft. **1906** SENNETT & ORAM *Marine Steam Engine* 285 a, An ordinary plummer block should always be fitted close to the thrust bearing to take the weight of the shaft. **1893** *Pall Mall G.* 2 Jan. 5/2 The shaft in the *thrust-block is twenty-five inches in diameter, and of solid steel. **1906** SENNETT & ORAM *M.S. Eng.* 285 a, Thrust blocks are carried on strong plate bearers generally fixed to not less than three frames of the ship. **1918** *Blackw. Mag.* Mar. 291 Pretty drawings in colour of such things as *thrust-boxes and oil-pumps. **1962** F. I. ORDWAY et al. *Basic Astronautics* x. 413 The rocket *thrust chamber is a device into which propellants are injected and burned to form gases. The basic components of the thrust chamber are the injector, the combustion chamber, and the exhaust nozzle. **1889** *Thrust-collar [see *thrust-bearing*]. **1889** *Rep. Brit. Assoc. Adv. Sci. 1888* 659 He suggested a *thrust-fault through the Mendip axis carrying its upper portion northward. **1903** *Nature* 20 Aug. 375/1 The overfolding and repetition of strata by thrust-faults. **1915** C. SCHUCHERT in Pirsson & Schuchert *Text-bk. Geol.* I. xiv. 344 Reverse faults..having a gently inclined fault-surface are known as thrust-faults or simply thrusts. **1944** [see OVERTHRUST *sb.*]. **1972** J. G. DENNIS *Structural Geol.* xii. 271 Since thrust faults were originally considered a class of reverse faults, they should bring older rocks over younger. So many low-dip normal faults have been called thrusts, however, that we must include all low-dip faults in this class. **1980** *Sci. Amer.* Oct. 127/2 The thrust faults and folds indicate that the rocks were much compressed in the horizontal direction. *Ibid.*, The Valley and Ridge province is characterized by folded and *thrust-faulted strata of mostly unmetamorphosed sedimentary rocks formed between 600 million and 300 million years ago. **1912** *Q. Jrnl. Geol. Soc.* LXVIII. 59 The occurrence of these inliers is due to *thrust-faulting. **1936** *Geogr. Jrnl.* LXXXVII. 224 The Purari Plateau is characterized by..extensive uplifting with the accompanying development of block-faulting, probably more normal faulting than thrust-faulting. **1901** *Nature* 24 Jan. 294/2 Three higher tiers of *thrust-masses are present on the west of the Linth Valley. **1890** *Hardwicke's Sci. Gossip* XXVI. 238/1 An arch of Cambrian rocks.. repeatedly broken on the west side by *thrust-movements, causing newer beds to be driven over beds of various horizons, in some cases many thousands of feet apart in the succession. **1954** *Flight Handbk.* (ed. 5) xi. 164 (*caption*) A turbojet *thrust-reverser developed by the American Boeing company. The jet is deflected by a W-shaped pair of clamshell doors. **1976** B. JACKSON *Flame-out* (1977) x. 182 At his low altitude there was simply no way he could correct the thrust reverser before he hit the deck. **18..** WHITHAM *Const. Steam Engin.* 102 *Thrust-ring. **1906** SENNETT & ORAM *M.S. Eng.* 285 a, Another form of thrust block.. containing separate brass thrust rings fitted in the bearing to form the rubbing surfaces. **1858** SIMMONDS *Dict. Trade*, *Thrust-screw. **1888** *Lockwood's Dict. Terms Mech. Engin.* 374 *Thrust Screw*, a screw with or without the power of endlong adjustment, which takes the thrust of a revolving spindle. Examples of thrust screws occur at the top of the drill spindles of some drilling machines, and in the back centres of the headstocks of lathes. **1893** *Daily News* 6 Feb. 6/3 The Cunard steamer Umbria..will be placed in the graving dock..and refitted with new *thrust shaft. **1906** SENNETT & ORAM *M.S. Eng.* 285 a, These horseshoe collars fit between the collars on the thrust shaft. **1947** *Jrnl. R. Aeronaut. Soc.* LI. 679/2 The *thrust spoiler could be operated in one second. So that if a pilot came in with the thrust spoiled, failed to land, and wished to make another circuit, the full thrust was available in one second. **1962** *Flight Internat.* LXXXII. 395/1 In the pioneer SC.1 the lift units are arranged in two pairs both mounted on lateral trunnions to pivot some 25° fore and aft, in order to provide longitudinal thrust components to assist transition to and from wing-supported flight. This idea has now given way to a fixed installation with *thrust-vector control. **1975** *Offshore Engineer* Dec. 54/2 (Advt.), The whole unit, and thus the thrust vector, can be directed through 360°, which means that it has been possible to optimise the nozzle and propeller for one main flow direction. **1954** *Thrust washer [see SPACER 1 a]. **1962** [see *oil-retaining* s.v. OIL *sb.*[1] 6 b]. **1970** K. BALL *Fiat 600, 600D Autobook* ix. 106/2 If the line is out of centre, vary the number of shims beneath the thrust washer.

thrust (θrʌst), *v.* Pa. t. and pple. **thrust**. Forms: see below. [Early ME. (*c* 1200) *þrusten* (*ü*), *þrysten*, a. ON. *þrýsta* to thrust, press, compress, force (Norw. *tryste*, Aasen, to press, squeeze). ON. *þrýsta* (:—*prūstj-*) has been doubtfully referred to Indo-Eur. *trud-*, *trūd-*, in L. *trūdĕre* to thrust (Falk and Torp).]

A. Illustration of Forms.

1. *Inf.* and *Pres. stem.* α. 3 ***þrust-e** (ü), 3–6 **þrist-en**, 4 **þrist**, 4–6 **thrist**, 5 **thryste**.

c **1300** *Havelok* 1152, I shal hangen þe ful heye, Or y shal þristen vt þin eie. *c* **1330** þrist [see B. 3]. **1388** WYCLIF *Mark* iii. 9 Lest thei thristen hym. **1483** *Cath. Angl.* 386/1 To Thryste downe, *oppremere*. **1510–20** *Everyman* in Hazl. *Dodsley* I. 138 Go, thrist thee into the ground. **1596** DALRYMPLE tr. *Leslie's Hist. Scot.* VII. (S.T.S.) II. 43 Sche thristis in her tender arme into the hole of the bar.

β. 5 **þrust-e**, 6–7 **thruste** (7 **thurst**), 6– **thrust**.

c **1440** *Alphabet of Tales* 347 Yisterday he thristid down þe erth, and þis day þe erth þrustis hym down. **1530**, etc. Thrust [see B. 3, etc.]. **1560** DAUS tr. *Sleidane's Comm.* 216 b, He fortuned to thruste of a stone.

2. *Pa. tense.* α. 2–3 **þruste** (ü), 3–5 **þriste**, **þrist**, 4 **thryste**, 4–5 **thriste**.

[*c* **1175** *Lamb. Hom.* 131 He to-þruste þa stelene gate and to brec þa irene barren of helle.] *c* **1205** LAY. 30341 Æiðer þratte oðer swiðe and þruste mid worde. *c* **1250** ðrist, *c* **1290** þruste [see B. 1]. *c* **1374** þriste [see B. 6 b].

β. 5–6 **thruste** (5 **throste**, 6 **thurst**), 6– **thrust**.

c **1410** Thruste [see B. 5]. *c* **1470** HARDING *Chron.* XII. ii. (MS. Ashm. 34) lf. 12 b, This Gogmagog so throste [*v. rr.* thrast, -e] Coryneus. **1526**, **1535–** Thrust; **1560** Thruste [see B. 1, 1 c, etc.]. **1568** Thurst [see B. 6].

γ. 5 **thristid** (5–6 *Sc.* **-it**), 6 **thristed**; 7–8 **thrusted**.

c **1440** Thristid [see A. 1 β]. *c* **1475** Thristit [see B. 3]. **1560** ROLLAND *Crt. Venus* IV. 590 Swa in hir armis than scho him thristit. **1634** CANNE *Necess. Separ.* (1849) 194 He thrusted out Cain from the same. **1788** Thrusted [see B. 6 b].

3. *Pa. pple.* α. 4 **þryst**, 4–5 **thrist**, 5 **thriste**, **thryst**, **þirstyn**.

c **1330** R. BRUNNE *Chron. Wace* (Rolls) 8889 When þey ofte hadde put & þryst..ȝit stirede þey nought þe leste ston. **13..** Thrist [see B. 6 quot. *a* 1300]. **14..** *Gosp. Nicodemus* (A.) 1443 And in thraldame thrist hym þou has. **1435** MISYN *Fire of Love* I. v. 11 To god þai ȝelde no deuocion, for þe byrdyn of riches with þe whilk þai ar þirstyn to þe erth. **1483** *Cath. Angl.* 386/1 Thriste downe, *oppressus*. **1495** Thryst [see B. 6 b].

β. 4, 6– **thrust** (6 **thurst**); 4 *Sc.* **thrustyne**, **thrussine**.

c **1375** *Sc. Leg. Saints* xviii. (*Egipciane*) 581 Bot I, vnhappy, thrustyne sare, A fut mycht nocht get forthyr-mare. *Ibid.* xxxvii. (*Vincencius*) 285 He..wes..thrussine done. **1382** WYCLIF *Judg.* vi. 38 [Dew] thrust out of the fleese [Vulg. *expresso vellere*]. **1573–80**, **1577**, etc. Thrust [see B. 5, 1 b, etc.].

γ. 4–5 **þristed**, 4 *Sc.* **thristit**, 7–9 **thrusted**.

c **1375** *Sc. Leg. Saints* xl. (*Ninian*) 516 His stafe..has he.. in þe maste hoile..thristit ful faste. *c* **1425** tr. *Arderne's Treat. Fistula* 65 þat it may..be þristed out. **1665** Thrusted [see B. 1].

B. Signification.

I. 1. a. *trans.* To exert the force of impact upon or against (a body) so as to move it away; to push, shove, drive. Chiefly with adverb or advb. phr. (Now chiefly literary.)

[*c* **1175**: see A. 2 a.] *c* **1250** *Gen. & Ex.* 2110, vii. lene [ears of corn]..ðe ranc he hauen ðo ouer-cumen,..and, on a stund, ðe fette ðrist hem to ðo grund. *c* **1290** *S. Eng. Leg.* I. 328/188 Seint Clement..in grete wrath þe hire pulte a-wei and to þe grounde upriȝt þruste. *a* **1400–50** *Alexander* 1407 þai..Thristis ouir thikefald many threuyn bernes. **1526** TINDALE *Matt.* xxi. 39 They caught hym and thrust him out of the vyneyarde. **1587** TURBERV. *Trag. T.* (1837) 152 And up they thrust the same [door], And softly entred in. **1597** SHAKS. *2 Hen. IV*, II. iv. 202 Thrust him downe stayres. **1665** HOOKE *Microgr.* vi. 23 Another Ladle thrusted four or five inches under water. **1719** DE FOE *Crusoe* (1840) II. ix. 203, I caused the boat to be thrust in. **1860** TYNDALL *Glac.* I. xix. 135 The glacier is forcibly thrust..against the projecting base of the mountain.

b. *transf.* and *fig.* Applied to action of any kind having an effect analogous to that of physical pushing or moving. Often in phr. ***to thrust out***, to expel, eject.

c **1330** R. BRUNNE *Chron.* (1810) 217 Whan Sir Symon wist, þe dome ageyn þam gon, His felonie forth thrist. **1535** COVERDALE *Josh.* xxiv. 18 The Lorde thrust out before vs all the people of the Amorites. **1577** tr. *Bullinger's Decades* (1592) 161 Dionysius of Syracuse is reported for his tyranny to have been thrust beside his seate. **1598** SHAKS. *Merry W.* v. v. 156 Though wee would haue thrust vertue out of our hearts by the head and shoulders. **1610** HOLLAND *Camden's Brit.* (1637) 513 King Henry the Eighth thrust out the Monkes. **1655** JER. TAYLOR *Guide Devot.* (1719) 14 He only can preserve them in the same Being, and thrust them forward to a better. **1854** H. ROGERS *Ess.* (1860) II. 2 Thrusting aside all authority but that of Reason. **1855** MACAULAY *Hist. Eng.* xii. III. 222 They were now, without any trial, without any accusation, thrust out of their house.

c. *absol.* or *intr.* To push against something; to make a thrust. (*lit.* and *fig.*)

c **1205** [see A. 2 a]. c **1330** R. BRUNNE *Chron. Wace* (Rolls) 8886 Þey schouued, þey þriste, þey stode o strot. **1535** COVERDALE *Ps.* cxviii[i]. 13 They thrust at me, that I might fall. **1560** DAUS tr. *Sleidane's Comm.* 80 One of them with his staffe, thruste at the Image of a saincte, in so muche that it fell downe and brake. **1648** GAGE *West Ind.* 176 They still at the door thrusting.

†**2.** *intr.* To come *together* with force of impact; to strike together, collide. *Obs.*

13.. *Cursor M.* 22683 (Edin.) Al þe stanis þat er mad.. Wit þrawing sal tai samin þrist [*other MSS.* threst, þrest], þat al to pecis sal tai brist. **1500–20** DUNBAR *Poems* xxxv. 28 Thir terrible monsteris sall togidder thrist, And in the cludis gett the Antechrist.

3. a. *intr.* To push or force one's way, as through a crowd; to crowd *in*; to make one's way or advance as against obstacles; to press onwards or into a place, etc. Also *fig.*

c **1330** R. BRUNNE *Chron.* (1810) 277 Fleand fast þei þrist. c **1475** *Rauf Coilȝear* 694 He thristit in throw threttie all at anis. **1530** PALSGR. 757/1, I thrust in to a place thorowe a prease. **1611** SPEED *Hist. Gt. Brit.* IX. xvi. (1623) 854 It will be best abruptly to thrust into the narration. **1615** G. SANDYS *Trav.* 26 That night we came to Callipoly..and thrust into a little haven North of the towne. **1653** W. LAUSON in Arb. *Garner* I. 197 They thrust up little brooks to spawn. **1760** WESLEY *Jrnl.* 10 Aug., A person hugely daubed with gold thrust violently in. **1828** SCOTT *F.M. Perth* xii, She thrust in between them. **1865** KINGSLEY *Herew.* xvii, He thrust in with so earnest and sad a face that the servants let him pass.

†**b.** *trans.* To press upon or push against; to throng, to jostle. *Obs.*

c **1375** [see A. 3 β]. **1388** WYCLIF *Mark* v. 31 Thou seest the puple thristynge thee: and seist, Who touchide me? **1526** TINDALE *ibid.*, Thou seist the people thrustinge the on euery syde. **1589** BRUCE *Serm. Sacram.* iii. I v, Thou art thrumbled and thrusted be the multitude. **1642** [see THRUSTING *vbl. sb.* 1].

†**c.** To press (objects) into a confined space; also, to fill (a space) densely; to crowd, cram. *Obs.*

c **1380** [see THRUSTING *vbl. sb.* 1]. **1614** TOMKIS *Albumazar* I. iii, A Hall thrust full of bare-heads.

†**4.** *trans.* To press, compress, squeeze. *Obs.* (exc. in spec. reference to cheese-making: cf. THRUSTING *vbl. sb.* 2, *thrusting-screw, -tub*, ibid. 3).

1382 [see A. 3 β]. **1398** TREVISA *Barth. De P.R.* v. xxiv. (Bodl. MS.), With compressing and þrusting togederes þe wey of the breþe. c **1400** *Pety Job* 98 in *26 Pol. Poems* 124 To thryste me doune, and me accuse. c **1440** *Promp. Parv.* 491/2 Thrystyn, or pressyn, *premo, comprimo.* **1530** PALSGR. 757/1, I thrust togyther, *je compresse*... He hath thrust the appell so moche togyder that it is naugth. **1539** BIBLE (Great) *Judg.* vi. 38 He..thrust the flece togeather, and wronge the dewe therout. a **1550** *Freiris of Berwik* 168 in *Dunbar's Poems* (S.T.S.) 290 He thristit hir hand agane richt prevely. **1794** WEDGE *Agric. Chester* 52 Thrusting or hand-pressing the Cheese in the Vat [cf. THRUSTING *vbl. sb.* 2].

II. †**5. a.** To strike with a pushing action; to stab or pierce *with* a pointed instrument. *Obs.*

c **1410** *Chron. Eng.* (Ritson) 671 The thef braid out is knyf anon, Ant to the heorte the kyng thruste. **1526** *Pilgr. Perf.* (W. de W. 1531) 305 b, They..with a sharpe speare..thrust the..vnto thy blessed herte. **1573–80** BARET *Alv.* T 218 It is Thrust through with a needle,..*traiectatur acu.* **1593** SHAKS. *2 Hen. VI*, IV. vii. 10 He was thrust in the mouth with a Speare. c **1643** LD. HERBERT *Autobiog.* (1824) 91, I.. with my sword thrust him [a wild boar] twice or thrice without entering his skin. **1770** *Trial W. Spiggot*, etc. *Heref.* 3 That the said William Williams struck, thrusted, and stabbed him..with a certain sword.

b. *intr.* To make a thrust, stab, or lunge with a pointed weapon; *spec.* in *Fencing*. Also *fig.*

1596 SHAKS. *1 Hen. IV*, II. iv. 223 These foure..thrust at me; I..tooke all their seuen points in my target. c **1643** LD. HERBERT *Autobiog.* (1824) 64–5 To strike or thrust as he shall see occasion;..to strike or thrust high or low as his Enemy doth. **1700** DRYDEN *Ovid's Met.* XII. 642 He next his Fauchion try'd, in closer Fight;..He thrust; the blunted Point return'd again. **1826** SCOTT *Woodst.* xxxvii, His sword had no more power than had he thrusted with a tobacco-pipe. **1869** BOUTELL *Arms & Arm.* ii. (1874) 23 This formidable weapon served equally well to deliver blows.. and to thrust with the point. **1871** B. TAYLOR *Faust* (1875) I. xix. 172 Thrust home! **1878** BROWNING *La Saisiaz* 404 Fancy thrust and Reason parry!

6. a. *trans.* To cause (anything, esp. something grasped in the hand) to enter, pierce, or penetrate some thing or place by or as by pushing; to put, drive, or force into some place or position.

a **1300** *Cursor M.* 557 (Cott.) Als prient of seel in wax es thrist. c **1375** *Sc. Leg. Saints* xix. (*Cristofore*) 264 Thrist it [the staff] fast done in þe grownd. **1526** TINDALE *Rev.* xiv. 15 Thruste in thy sycle and rype. a **1550** *Freiris of Berwik* 134 in *Dunbar's Poems* (S.T.S.) 289 Scho..thristit on fatt caponis to the speit. **1568** GRAFTON *Chron.* II. 24 He.. sodenly thurst his speare into the kinges left eye. **1591** SHAKS. *1 Hen. VI*, III. ii. 23 By thrusting out a Torch from yonder Tower. **1647** WARD *Simp. Cobler* (title-p.), Coblers must thrust their awles up to the hefts. **1726** SWIFT *Gulliver* II. viii, I then fastened my handkerchief to a stick..and, thrusting it up the hole, waved it. **1832** HT. MARTINEAU *Ella of Gar.* i, A bunch of seabirds' feathers, which he thrust into Ella's hand. **1832** TENNYSON *Dream Fair Wom.* 259 You should have..thrust The dagger thro' her side.

b. To put forth, extend (a limb or member) into some place or in some direction; to put forth, throw out, or extend, as in the process of growth (a root, branch, or connected part) so as to project.

c **1374** CHAUCER *Troylus* III. 1525 (1574) With that his arm al sodeynly he þriste Vnder here nekke and at þe laste here keste. **1495** *Trevisa's Barth. De P.R.* VII. lii. (W. de W.), In the dropesye..yf ones fynger be thryst in to the flesshe it makyth an hole other a pytte. **1593** SHAKS. *Rich. II*, V. i. 29 The Lyon dying, thrusteth forth his Paw. **1596** [see A. 1 a]. **1610** HOLLAND *Camden's Brit.* 189 From S. Michaels mount Southward, immediatly there is thrust forth a bi-land or demi-Ile. **1748** SMOLLETT *Rod. Rand.* xlvi, I perceived him thrust his tongue in his cheek. **1788** *Lond. Mag.* 240 Each.. thrusted his head through a hole in the curtain. **1815** SCOTT *Guy M.* viii, Thrusting his hand in his pocket to find a half-crown. **1856** STANLEY *Sinai & Pal.* x. 353 Those hills are the western roots which Hermon thrusts out towards the sea. *Mod.* As a tree thrusts its roots deep into the soil and its branches high into the air.

c. *transf.* and *fig.* (See also 7.)

1588 SHAKS. *L.L.L.* v. ii. 398 Thrust thy sharpe wit quite through my ignorance. **1601** —— *Jul. C.* v. iii. 74 Thrusting this report Into his eares. **1770** LANGHORNE *Plutarch* (1879) I. 1/1 Geographers thrust into the extremities of their maps, those countries that are unknown to them. **1795** BURKE *Corr.* (1844) IV. 285, I shall say more..since you suffer me to thrust in my opinion. **1865** TYLOR *Early Hist. Man.* iii. 38 On the art of thrusting knowledge into the minds of such children.

III. 7. *fig.* To put (a person) forcibly *into* some condition or course of action (usually against his own will); *refl.* to put oneself rashly, 'plunge' (into danger, quot. 1639).

14.. [see A. 3 a]. **1639** in *Verney Memoirs* (1907) I. 186, I will not willfully thrust myself in danger. a **1649** DRUMM. OF HAWTH. *Prophecy* Wks. (1711) 179 To remedy our evils by the thrusting us into a civil war; and the medicine is worse than the disease. **1654** JER. TAYLOR *Real Pres.* iv. 75 Into the concession of this Bellarmine is thrust by the force of our argument. **1750** WHITEFIELD *Let. to Lady Huntingdon* 24 Mar., O that the Lord of the harvest would thrust out more labourers! **1879** FARRAR *St. Paul* (1883) 296 The very men who were now thrust into antagonism with his sentiments.

b. To put (something) improperly *into* some position; to insinuate (quot. 1574); esp. in phr. ***thrust in***, to introduce irrelevantly, interpolate.

1574 tr. *Marlorat's Apocalips* 5 Prouoke vs to impacience, or thruste any douting of Gods promise into vs. **1654** JER. TAYLOR *Real Pres.* Ep. Ded. A iv, It is..suspected, that.. the tale..was a long time after..thrust in by some Monk in a place to which it relates not. **1861** PALEY *Æschylus* (ed. 2) *Supplices* 267 *note*, The MSS. have ἔχονδ', in which δ' seems to have been thrust in for the sake of the metre.

8. a. To put (a person) forcibly *into* some position (against the will of others concerned); to intrude (some one) *upon* (a person or persons).

1559 in Strype *Ann. Ref.* (1709) I. App. viii. 23 Stephen Langhton, thrust into the archebisshopprycke of Canterbury by the pope. **1583** STUBBES *Anat. Abus.* II. (1882) 92 Why would you not haue pastors to be thrust vpon the churches, whether the churches will or not? **1848** W. H. KELLY tr. *L. Blanc's Hist. Ten Y.* II. 586 He..conjured his friends not to vote for a candidate who would be thrust upon them by the Centre.

b. *refl.* To intrude oneself *into* any position, condition, or circumstances, or *upon* another person; to push oneself forward.

1530 PALSGR. 757/1, I thruste my selfe in to a prease or amongest a company. **1613** SHAKS. *Hen. VIII*, II. ii. 65 How dare you thrust your selues Into my priuate Meditations? **1651** HOBBES *Leviath.* IV. xliv. 336 A stranger that thrusteth himself into the throne. **1797** MRS. RADCLIFFE *Italian* xvii, They would thrust themselves into my company. **1855** MACAULAY *Hist. Eng.* xviii. IV. 185 He ceased to insist on his right to thrust himself between the First Lord and the Chancellor of the Exchequer. **1867** AUG. J. E. WILSON *Vashti* xiv, I should not feel justified thrusting myself into her presence.

c. To put (something) forcibly (*into* the hands of a person); to press, force, or impose the acceptance of (*upon* some one).

1593 SHAKS. *Rich. II*, II. ii. 110 How..to order these affaires Thus disorderly thrust into my hands. **1601** —— *Twel. N.* II. v. 158 Some are born great, some atcheeue greatnesse, and some haue greatnesse thrust vppon em. **1865** TROLLOPE *Belton Est.* xxvii, She had no alternative but to assume the position which was thus thrust upon her.

IV. 9. *Comb.*, as **thrust stage** *Theatr.*, an open stage that projects into the auditorium so that the audience is seated around three sides.

1968 *Sat. Rev.* (U.S.) 1 June 22 The Fine Arts Theatre.. is a compact, multipurpose amphitheater seating 600, which can be utilized for conventional theatricals, as a thrust stage, or even—with the built-in pit—for musicals and intimate opera. **1969** *Guardian* 28 Oct. 7/3 Knighted actors argue the merits of a 'thrust' stage for the costly new Sheffield Theatre. **1977** *Times* 25 Aug. 15/4 Kate went to the University of Toronto where they had just built a superb thrust-stage theatre.

thrust, *ppl. a.* [See the vb.] With adverbs, as ***thrust-out*** adj. = OUT-THRUST *ppl. a.*

1872 R. W. BUCHANAN *St. Abe & his Seven Wives* 153 And with thrust-out jaw and set Teeth, the Yankee threatens yet. **1976** [see *snake-hipped* s.v. SNAKE *sb.* 11].

thrust(e, obs. forms of THIRST.

thrustel(l, -tille, -tle, obs. ff. THROSTLE.

thruster ('θrʌstə(r)). [f. THRUST *v.* + -ER[1].]

1. One who or that which thrusts: see the verb.

1597 A. M. tr. *Guillemeau's Fr. Chirurg.* b iv b/2 The expulser or thruster out (of teeth). **1612** J. DAVIES *Muse's Sacr.* (Grosart) 34/2, I was sore thrust at,.. But, thou o'er-threw'st my thrusters. **1794** *Hope's New Meth. Fencing* 221 After whatever Fashion the Thruster holds his Fleuret. **1825** *Chron.* in *Ann. Reg.* 4/2 The corves..were drawn to the shaft of the pit by several other men called hurriers, and a number of boys called thrusters [cf. THRUTCHER]. **1907** *Contemp. Rev.* Apr. 512 Brunetière was a keen thruster and never missed a parry.

2. a. *Hunting slang.* One who thrusts himself forward in the field, or rides too close to the hounds.

1886 *Field* 2 Jan. 3/1 His companion..chances to be a recognised thruster in the fullest sense of the term. **1892** *Ibid.* 9 Jan. 56/1 More than the average number of thrusters striving for a forward place. **1898** J. A. GIBBS *Cotswold Vill.* xiii. 305 That somewhat unpopular class of sportsmen, the 'thrusters' of the hunting field.

b. *fig.* One who pushes his way; an aggressive or go-ahead person. Also *spec.* with reference to driving.

1925 FRASER & GIBBONS *Soldier & Sailor Words & Phr.* 280 *Thruster, a*, an obnoxious, pushing person. A 'bounder'. **1927** *Observer* 6 Nov. 13/1 Those who described their more successful fellows as 'thrusters' and 'climbers'. **1927** *Morning Post* 28 Nov. 10/4 The 'road thruster', or the man with the 'passing' mania, is usually a nuisance. **1960** *Times* 7 June 13/7 The ordinary lorry or van driver..is often the worst thruster of all. **1964** C. WILLOCK *Enormous Zoo* ii. 21 Bere..was known as a thruster when it came to administration. **1974** R. HARRIS *Double Snare* xxvi. 197 Robert's car has fallen back, displaced by an Italian thruster's enormous red tourer. **1982** BARR & YORK *Official Sloane Ranger Handbk.* 106/1 She will not lend her support to any ambitious young thruster or leak the firm's secrets to a rival.

3. a. *Astronaut.* A small rocket engine on a spacecraft for providing the thrust needed to alter or correct its flight path or its attitude.

1962 J. GLENN in *Into Orbit* 146 This would include warming up the hydrogen peroxide thrusters so that they would go to work without delay when I activated the controls. **1965** *Newsweek* 13 Dec. 60 In past missions, excitement, the thump of the thruster rockets and a busy schedule all conspired to deprive the astronauts of sleep. **1969** *Guardian* 22 July 18/3 A 46-second firing of the reaction control thrusters altered Eagle's orbit. **1973** *Times* 28 Nov. 8/2 Small thrusters were fired yesterday which put the 570lb craft on course so that it will fly to within 81,000 miles of Jupiter on December 3. **1977** *Sci. Amer.* Feb. 61/1 The satellite is carefully tracked by ground stations, the propulsion vector needed to compensate for drift is computed and the appropriate thrusters are fired by radio command.

b. *Oil Industry.* Each of several jets or propellers on a drill ship or offshore rig, used for accurate manœuvring and maintenance of position.

1972 L. M. HARRIS *Introd. Deepwater Floating Drilling Operations* i. 3 Several vessels have been built, or are in the design and construction stage, that depend entirely upon thrusters, or powered units, to position the vessel dynamically. **1975** *Gen. Electric Investor* Winter 18/2 In the newest technique called 'dynamic positioning', gimbaled motors driving thruster propellers keep the rigs positioned over the drilling hole despite wind, waves and currents. **1983** *New Scientist* 2 June 627/2 When it is semi-submerged, a 'dynamic positioning' system, thrusters controlled by computers, keeps the ship within two metres of a programmed position in a force seven gale.

thrustful ('θrʌstfʊl), *a.* [f. THRUST *sb.* + -FUL.] Characterized by thrusting; energetic, pushful. Hence **'thrustfulness.**

1907 *Daily Chron.* 9 Sept. 9/3 Not an ideal centre forward, ..but he is all vigour and thrustfulness. **1909** *Ibid.* 16 Feb. 8/8 The half-backs neither tackle nor follow up keenly enough, and the forwards were not sufficiently thrustful or accurate. **1963** *Economist* 22 June 1236/1 A Butler government might be a force for..greater economic thrustfulness. **1978** *Church Times* 1 Sept. 1/4 Few men have a good word for the Curial cardinals... They are the automatic targets..of the frustrations of thrustful priests.

'thrusting, *vbl. sb.* [f. THRUST *v.* + -ING[1].]

1. The action of the verb THRUST (in various senses).

1375 BARBOUR *Bruce* XIII. 156 With sic thrawing and sic thristing That it wes hydwiss for till her. c **1380** WYCLIF *Wks.* (1880) 319 þristyng of ordris in oon cloystre or in oon hous. c **1440** *Alphabet of Tales* 297 His arm was als bla & als sare with þe thrustyng of Saynt Laurens as he had suffred it evyn on his body. **1552** HULOET, Thrustynge downe, *oppressio.* a **1584** MONTGOMERIE *Cherrie & Slae* 291 With wristing and thristing The faster still is scho. **1642** R. CARPENTER *Experience* III. iv. 17 That so many Angels may well stand together without much thrusting upon a needles point. **1794** *Hope's New Meth. Fencing* 224 Orderly and regular Parieing and Thrusting. **1859** GEO. ELIOT *A. Bede* ii, The thrusting out of his chin and stomach, and the twirling of his thumbs.

2. *concr.* in *pl.* ***thrustings*** = ***thrutchings***: see after THRUTCH *v.*, and cf. quot. s.v. THRUST *sb.* 4.

1794 WEDGE *Agric. Chester* 38 In the process of making whey butter,..the 'thrustings', or white whey, is set in 'cream mugs', to 'carve', and acidulate for churning. **1885** *Cheshire Gloss., Thrustings*, white whey, the same as *thrutchings*.

3. *attrib.* and *Comb.* Used in or worked by thrusting, as ***thrusting-bridge***, ***-pike***; **thrusting-screw**, a screw by which a press, esp. a cheese-press, is actuated and regulated; **thrusting-shaft**, a thrust-shaft (THRUST *sb.* 8); **thrusting-tub** (see quot.).

1761 STERNE *Tr. Shandy* III. xxv, He was determined.. to have one [bridge] of that particular construction which is made to draw back horizontally..; and to thrust forwards again..: but my father advising my uncle..to have nothing more to do with *thrusting bridges.., he changed his mind. **1856** GROTE *Greece* II. xciv. XII. 326 Arming them with the short Macedonian *thrusting-pike. **1794** WEDGE *Agric. Chester* 52 In many dairies, a lever is used to thrust or press the cheese... In other dairies, they use *thrusting screws. **1906** *Westm. Gaz.* 3 Oct. 8/1 The arm was caught in the *thrusting-shaft of my machine. **1846** *J. Baxter's Libr. Pract. Agric.* (ed. 4) I. 207 The '*thrusting-tub', in which the curd has now to be pressed, is round, and is perforated with holes at the sides and bottom for the whey to escape through.

'thrusting, *ppl. a.* [f. as prec. + -ING[2].] That thrusts: see the verb.

1898 *Allbutt's Syst. Med.* V. 981 The forcible heaving or thrusting movements of the ventricle. **1909** *Blackw. Mag.* Dec. 741/1 The bright thrusting blade of the sun seemed more endurable.

b. *Hunting slang.* That thrusts himself forward in the hunting-field: cf. THRUSTER 2.

1895 *Daily News* 22 Nov. 6/5 The difference between 'true sportsmen who "ride to hunt" and the thrusting steeplechasers who "hunt to ride"'. **1900** *Westm. Gaz.* 30 Nov. 4/3 There had been no need to request thrusting riders to 'Hold hard!'

'thrust-plane. *Geol.* The plane of dislocation in an overfault, along which the dislocated strata have been driven.

1884 GEIKIE in *Nature* 13 Nov. 30/1 The most extraordinary dislocations..are those to which..we have given the name of Thrust-Planes. They are, strictly, reversed faults, but with so low a hade that the rocks on their up-throw side have been, as it were, pushed horizontally forward. **1884** PEACH & HORNE *ibid.* 33/2 At length this intricate system of faults and folds culminates in a great dislocation which,..to distinguish it from the ordinary reversed faults, may be termed a Thrust-Plane. **1907** *Athenæum* 2 Nov. 554/3 The planes of disruption along which the masses travelled are known as thrust-planes.

thrutch (θrʌtʃ), *sb.* Now *dial.* Forms: 4 **þrich**, 5 **thricche, thrich**, 7- **thrutch**. [f. next.] An act of 'thrutching'; a thrust, push, press, squeeze; also, *concr.* a narrow gorge or ravine (*local*).

13.. *Gaw. & Gr. Knt.* 1713 Þer þre þro [hounds] at a þrich þrat hym [a fox] at ones. *c* **1400** *Destr. Troy* 12752 Þan entrid this Engist,..And, with a thricche in the throte, throtlet the kyng. *c* **1425** WYNTOUN *Cron.* v. iv. 606 [It] gert hym offt in thrichis [*v.rr.* thrystis, thryftis] thraw. **1678** RAY *Prov.* (ed. 2) 302 Maxfield measure, heap and thrutch [cf. THRUST *sb.* 1]. **1855** E. WAUGH *Lanc. Life* (1857) 33 The last sylvan stronghold of the fairies; where they would remain impregnable, haunting wild 'thrutches' and sylvan 'chapels', in lonely deeps of its cloughs and woods. **1881** WESTALL *Old Factory* xi. I. 150 Try what a good thrutch.. will do first.

thrutch (θrʌtʃ), *v.* Now *dial.* Forms: α. 1 **þryccan**, 4-5 **thricche, þrich(e.** β. 3 **þrucche**, 6, 8 **thruch**, 6- **thrutch**. *Pa. t.* and *pple.* 1 **þryhte, þryht**, 4 **þryȝt**, 4-5 **thricchet, thrucchit**; 5 **thright**. [OE. *þrycc(e)an* = OHG. *drucchen* (MHG., G. *drücken*) to press,:—WGerm. **þrukkjan*, nominal vb. f. **þrukki-*, whence OHG. *druck* (MHG. *druc*, G. *druck*) pressure.]

1. *trans.* To press, squeeze, crush; to crowd, throng; *fig.* to oppress.

c **888** K. ÆLFRED *Boeth.* iv, Sittað manfulle on heahsetlum, and haliȝe under heora fotum þrycað. **13..** *E.E. Allit. P.* A. 17 Þat dotz bot þrych my hert þrange. *Ibid.* B. 135 He fande..A þral þryȝt in þe þrong unþryuandely cloþed. *c* **1400** *Destr. Troy* 13461 Mony holes in the howses ..Ouer-growen with..thornes, Euyn thestur and thicke thricchet of wode. *c* **1440** *Anc. Cookery* §438 in *Househ. Ord.* (1790) 471 When hit is sothen, thricche oute the water. **1546** COVERDALE *Treat. Lord's Supp.* Transl. Pref. A iij, Thrutchyng vp into a corner yt parte whiche no place can conteyne. *c* **1746** J. COLLIER (Tim Bobbin) *View Lanc. Dial.* I Yet I'm war thrutcht, between two arran Rogues. **1888** *Sheffield Gloss., Thrutch*, to thrust, to squeeze.

b. *spec.* To press (cheese).

1688 R. HOLME *Armoury* III. viii. 335/1 Thruch them in the Cheese-Fate. **1818** WILBRAHAM *Cheshire Gloss.* 29 Squeezing or pressing the cheese is called thrutching it.

2. To thrust, push.

c **1205** LAY. 19483 He wænde mid his crucche us adun þrucche. **13..** *E.E. Allit.* P. A. 705 He..dyed Delfully þurȝ hondez þryȝt. **13..** *Gaw. & Gr. Knt.* 1443 For þre at þe fyrst þrast he þryȝt to þe erþe. *c* **1400** *Destr. Troy* 6732 He..wan to the knight, And xxx in the throng thrucchit to dethe. ? *a* **1500** *Chester Pl.* x. 406 When they their spears throughe him thright. **1885** *Cheshire Gloss.* s.v., I'st be thrutched off here.

3. *intr.* To push or press into a place; to jostle.

[*a* **1000** *Guthlac* (Exeter Bk.) 285 We þas wic maȝun fotum afyllan, folc in ðriceð meara þreatum and monfarum.] *c* **1837** in Stephens *Mem. R. Durnford* (1899) 75 'Thrutch him up' shouted some..malcontents at a..vestry meeting [at Middleton, Lancs.].. 'Thrutch away, gentlemen', replied the young Rector, jumping on to an oak chest. **1848** T. BLEZARD *Westmoreld. Songs* 35 (E.D.D.) At last we thrutch'd into th' Ship Inn.

Hence **'thrutching** *vbl. sb.* (in quot., squeezing, wringing); also *concr.* (in *pl.*): see quot. 1885. **'thrutcher**, *Lancash.*: see quot. 1901.

c **1400** *Destr. Troy* 1522 All his wongys were wete for weping of teres,..with thricching of hondys. *c* **1746** J. COLLIER (Tim Bobbin) *View Lanc. Dial.* Wks. (1862) 68, I stown a lyte Wetur-podditch, an some Thrutchings. **1885** *Cheshire Gloss., Thrutchings*, whey which is *thrutched* or squeezed out whilst the cheese is under pressure. **1901** F. E. TAYLOR *Folk-Sp. S. Lancs.* (E.D.D.), *Thrutcher*, specially applied to the pushers of a rush-cart, and to the boys who push the corves in a coal-pit.

thrutty, obs. f. THIRTY.

thruway, var. THROUGHWAY.

thrw, thrwch, obs. Sc. ff. THROUGH.

thrwenter, thrwnter, obs. ff. THRINTER.

thrwsse, var. THURSE, goblin.

thryd-e, thrydde, obs. ff. THIRD.

thrye, þrye, var. THRIE *Obs.*, thrice.

thryes(e, -ess, -is(s, thrys(e, thryss, obs. ff. THRICE.

†**'thry-,fallow**, *v. Obs.* [app. f. THRIE, THRYE, thrice + FALLOW *v.*, but perh. a later alteration of *three-fallow* (THREE III. 2) after *twy-*, TWIFALLOW.] *trans.* = TRIFALLOW.

1573 TUSSER *Husb.* (1878) 121 Thry fallow I pray thee, Least thistles bewray thee. **1641** *Terrier Plesheybury Manor, Essex* Sept. lf. 5 b, The tenaunt..to leave 10 acres of land sufficiently fallowed, twyfallowed, thryfallowed.

thryȝt, obs. pa. t. and pple. of THRUTCH *v.*

thryl, thryll(e, obs. ff. THRILL.

thrymsa: see THRIMSA.

thryn, var. THRINNE *Obs.*, three-fold.

thryng(e, obs. form of THRING *v.*

thrynne, þrynne, var. THEREINNE *Obs.*, THRINNE *Obs.*

thryssce, thryshe, obs. ff. THRUSH.

thryst(e, obs. ff. THIRST, THRUST.

thrystle, obs. f. THROSTLE.

thryttene, -tende, obs. ff. THIRTEEN, -TEENTH.

thryttethe, -ty, obs. ff. THIRTIETH, -TY.

thryve, obs. form of THRIVE, THRIVEN.

thuang, variant of obs. *thwang*, THONG.

thucholite ('θ(j)uːtʃəʊlaɪt). *Min.* Also **thucolite**. [f. Th, U, C, H, O, symbols of the constituent elements + -LITE.] A naturally occurring brittle, highly lustrous, black mixture or complex of carbon and hydrocarbons with uraninite.

1928 H. V. ELLSWORTH in *Amer. Mineralogist* XIII. 66 A remarkable carbon mineral, which will be described in another paper under the name of thucholite, is sometimes very intimately associated with both uraninite and samarskite. **1938** R. W. LAWSON tr. *Hevesy & Paneth's Man. Radioactivity* (ed. 2) v. 62 Fig. 22..shows the *L*-spectrum of the mineral thucolite. **1965** G. J. WILLIAMS *Econ. Geol. N.Z.* xiii. 207/2 'The radioactivity in the carbonaceous matter is due to myriads of minute uraninites, 1 to 5 microns in size, distributed at random or as strings of granules.' Mr Whittle identified this uraniferous mineral as thucolite. **1980** *Mineral. Abstr.* XXXI. 487/2 Assemblages of thucholite in sandstone, dolomite, and shale of Polish Zechstein rocks are described. The thucholite..forms disseminated spheroidal or irregular bodies.

thuck (θʌk). [Echoic.] The sound of a missile, as an arrow, bullet, etc., hitting a target.

1948 F. BLAKE *Johnny Christmas* I. 46 Knifings, head-blows muffled by sand, the *thuck* of arrows striking home. **1979** P. COSGRAVE *Three Colonels* 202 The whine of the rifle bullet and the *thuck* of its striking home.

thuck, dial. form of THILK *dem. pron.*

†**thucke.** *Obs. rare*[−1]. [Origin uncertain.

It answers in sense to Ger. *tücke* fem., mischievous trick, MHG. *tuck*, also *duck*, blow, knock, cunning stroke, knavery; and *duck*, if the original form, would answer to an Eng. **þuck*. Stratmann compares ON. *þykkr*, thwack, blow; OE. *tucian* to treat badly, harm, has also been compared; but that gave *tuke, tuc* in *Ancren R.*]

A malicious trick.

a **1225** *Ancr. R.* 326 He wule beon afered uorte don þe eft swuche þucke.

Thucydidean (ˌθjuːsɪdɪ'diːən), *a.* Also †**-æan, -ian.** [f. L. *Thūcȳdidēs* (Gr. Θουκυδίδης), name of a Greek historian of the fifth century B.C. + *-ean*; cf. *Thūcȳdidēus* adj. (Cicero).] Of, pertaining to, or characteristic of Thucydides or his work.

1752 *Phil. Trans. R. Soc.* XLVII. 385 The European plagues are much more violent than the eastern; those being really the Thucydidian, which sweep all away. **1826** K. H. DIGBY *Morus* 125 Having no character of solemn reserve or Thucydidean dignity of style to support. **1834** —— *Mores Cath.* v. vi. 183 The Thucydidæan expression. **1888** *Encycl. Brit.* XXIII. 326/2 The best clue to Thucydidean bibliography is in Engelmann's *Scriptores Graeci*. **1911** *19th Cent.* Apr. 697 He even heightens the pathos of the Thucydidean original. **1945** E. K. CHAMBERS *Eng. Lit. at Close of Middle Ages* iii. 130 It was not long before, in Thucydidean phrase, he had won his way to the mythical. **1977** *Trans. Philol. Soc. 1975* 128 The Hellenizing and specifically Thucydidean tradition of Sallust and Tacitus.

thud (θʌd), *sb.* Orig. *Sc.* Also 6 **thuid, thude.** [Appears *c* 1513 along with THUD *v.*[2], q.v.]

1. A blast of wind or tempest; a gust; a squall. (In later quots. including the notion of sound.) *Sc.*

1513 DOUGLAS *Æneis* I. i. 80 Aiax breist persit..Scho [Pallas] with a thuid [L. *turbine*] stikkit on ane scharp roike [= rock]. **1536** BELLENDEN *Cron. Scot.* (1821) II. 52 Quhen haistilie come sic ane thud of wind, that sail, mast, and taikillis wer blawin in the brim seis. **1606** tr. *Rollock's Lect. 1 Thess.* 121 (Jam.) All this worlde is full of tentations: the diuell blowes,..raising a storme: it is a stormie world, and all the thuds light on the sillie creature. **1724** RAMSAY *Vision* ii, The air grew ruch with bousteous thuds. **1825** JAMIESON s.v., 'The wind comes in thuds' when it comes in gusts; and especially when it strikes on any body that conveys the sound, as a door, &c. **1858** M. PORTEOUS *Souter Johnny* 30 Wud as tempest thud.

†**b.** A loud sound, as of a clap of thunder, or the discharge of a cannon. *Sc. Obs.*

1535 STEWART *Cron. Scot.* (Rolls) I. 384 Thair scheildis rave and all thair speiris brak, With sic ane thude evin lyke ane thunder crak. *a* **1586** in Pinkerton *Anc. Scot. Poems* (1786) 246 Hir voice sa rank..Most lyik the thundring thuds of canoun din. **1796** MACNEILL *Waes o' War* III. x, Loud the din o' streams fast fa'ing, Strak the ear wi' thundering thud.

2. A heavy blow; a thump with the fist. Also *fig.* a severe affliction, a 'blow'. *Sc.* and *n. dial.*

1787 W. TAYLOR *Scots Poems* 26 (E.D.D.) Wi' an etnach cud Than gae her Daddie sic a thud. **1790** MORISON *Poems* 151 (Jam.) He cocks his hand, and gi's his wife a thud. **1806** COCK *Simple Strains* (1810) 136 (ibid.) Lusty thuds were dealt about. **1847** EMILY BRONTË *Wuthering Heights* xix, 'Noa', said Joseph, giving a thud with his prop on the floor. **1876** D. GILMOUR *Paisley Weavers* ix. 91 Puir lass, it's a sair thud to thee.

3. A dull heavy sound without resonance, such as is produced when a heavy stone strikes the ground. (Orig. *north. dial.*)

1825 BROCKETT *N.C. Words, Thud*, the noise of a fall, a stroke causing a blunt and hollow sound. **1859** GEO. ELIOT *A. Bede* iv, Lisbeth heard the heavy 'thud' of a running foot-step on the turf. **1861** HUGHES *Tom Brown at Oxf.* x, The thud thud of the eight-oar. **1878** BESANT & RICE *Celia's Arb.* xi, The heavy thud of the steam-hammer. **1895** CLIVE HOLLAND *Jap. Wife* (ed. 11) 13 The sound of a mousmé pattering barefoot, her quick, short steps making a gentle thud, thud on the matting.

b. As interjection or adverb: With a thud.

1880 JEFFERIES *Gt. Estate* 197 We heard an apple fall.. thud on the sward. **1890** L. C. D'OYLE *Notches* 71 Bill shot again and the ball went 'thud!' into the bear.

†**thud**, *v.*[1] *Obs.* Forms: 1 **þyddan, þiddan**, 3 **þudde** (ü), 4 **thud.** *Pa. t.* 1 **þydde, þidde**, 3 **þudde.** *Pa. pple.* 3 **iþud.** [OE. *þyddan*, of uncertain origin. It would normally represent an OTeut. **þudjan*, from a stem **þud-*.]

1. *trans.* To strike or thrust with a weapon; to stab. Only in *OE.*

c **897** K. ÆLFRED *Gregory's Past. C.* xl. 294 Ða ðydde [L. *percussit*] Abner hiene mid hindewearde sceafte on ðæt smælðearme ðæt he wæs dead. *Ibid.* 296 Ðæt mon mid hindewearde sceafte ðone ðydde [L. *ferire est*] þe him oferfylȝe. *c* **1000** ÆLFRIC *Judg.* iii. 21 Þa abræd Aoth..his swurd..and hine hetelice þidde, swa þæt þa hiltan eodon in to þam innoðe.

2. To thrust, press, push (a thing *to* or *into* a place, etc.). Also *fig.*

c **1000** ÆLFRIC *Num.* xxii. 25 Se assa..þidde his hlafordes fot þearle to þam heȝe. *c* **1205** LAY. 1898 Geomagog..þudde [*c* 1275 þraste] Corineum frommard his breoste. *Ibid.* 9159 Moni hundred þusend þe iþud beoð to hellen. *a* **1225** *St. Marher.* 14 Ant þenne þudde ich in ham luueliche þohtes. **1400** in *Ancestor* July (1904) 19 And anon as i be ded thud me in the erthe.

3. *intr.* To press with force.

a **1225** *St. Marher.* 12 Þa þudde ha uppon þe þurs feste wið hire fot.

thud (θʌd), *v.*[2] Orig. *Sc.* [Occurs, with the corresp. sb., *c* 1513. Identity with the earlier THUD *v.*[1] is doubtful: formally it is quite possible; but there is a gap both of time and sense between the examples of the two. The present vb. and sb. may be purely echoic, imitating the sound which they express or imply; if historically connected with THUD *v.*[1], the vb. has changed its meaning under echoic influence, and a sb. of corresponding echoic meaning has arisen.]

1. *intr.* To come with a blast or gust, as the wind; sometimes including the notion of sound. *Sc.*

1513 DOUGLAS *Æneis* XII. vi. 136 As the blastis with thar bustuus sovn..cumis thuddand doun On the deip sey Egean. *a* **1584** MONTGOMERIE *Cherrie & Slae* 237 Throw cluddis so he thuddis so, And flew I wist not quhair. **1721** RAMSAY *Ode to Ph——* vi, Then upo' sight the hailstains thud. **1796** MACNEILL *Waes o' War* I. xii, Loud and sair the cauld winds thud.

b. *trans.* in causal sense: To drive in blasts. *Sc.*
1728 RAMSAY *Answer Ep. fr. Mr. Somerville* 59 Boreas nae mair thuds Hail, snaw, and sleet, frae blacken'd clouds.

2. *intr.* To produce a thud or dull heavy sound, as a falling or moving body by striking against something; to fall or impinge with a thud; also said of the body or surface struck.
1796, 1833 [see *thudding* below]. **1859** L. OLIPHANT *Earl Elgin's Mission to China* I. 127 Feeble rockets, barbed as arrows, thudded about and fizzed for a moment in the grass. **1862** SALA *Seven Sons* III. v. 120 The carriage came thudding by on the soft turf. **1885** TENNYSON *Balin & Balan* 316 He felt the hollow-beaten mosses thud And tremble. **1893** *Harper's Mag.* Jan. 247/1 They heard his feet thudding upon the stairs. **1908** H. WALES *Old Allegiance* xvii. 305 A bullet thudded into the wall above me.

b. *trans.* To strike (something) so as to produce a thud.
1899 J. LUMSDEN *Edin. Poems & Songs* 259 Blow all your trumps! thud all your drums!

Hence **'thudding** *vbl. sb.* and *ppl. a.* (whence **'thuddingly** *adv.*; also *fig.*); all from sense 2.
1796 A. WILSON in *Poems & Lit. Prose* (1876) II. 66 Cease, thou flighterin' thuddin' heart. **1833** M. SCOTT *Tom Cringle* i. (1859) 29 A puff of white smoak, then another, .. followed by thudding reports. **1901** LAWSON *Remin. Dollar Acad.* 87 A brilliant peroration accompanied by a thudding on the pulpit. **1904** MARIE CORELLI *God's Gd. Man* x, The quick gallop of hoofs echoed thuddingly on the velvety turf. **1976** *Daily Tel.* 16 Dec. 10/5 The man who shot her, incidentally, is called Lord Lichfield—just one of the names dropped thuddingly at every opportunity. **1979** *Ibid.* 18 July 16/3 'Human stories' .. even more thuddingly boring than the well-boiled cabbage-slabs of opinion.

thuder(e, thue, obs. ff. THITHER, THEW *sb.*[1]

†thuelle, obs. f. TEWEL, TUEL, chimney-pipe.
14.. *Pict. Voc.* in Wr.-Wülcker 777/13 *Hoc epicausterium*, a thuelle.

†thuet, erron. var. *tewet*, *tewit*, TEWHIT, lapwing.
In quot. applied to the HOOPOE.
1688 R. HOLME *Armoury* II. 254/2 Some call this Bird [Upupa] a Thuet. It is born by the name of Thuet.

thuff, þuff, obs. form of THOUGH.

†'thuften. *Obs.* [OE. *þyften*, *þeften* (erron. *-an*), representing an OTeut. **þuftinī*, doubtfully considered to be fem. of **ʒi)þuftô*, in OE. *ʒeþofta*, ON. *þópti* a bench-fellow (cf. THOFT); the suffix being -EN[2], as in OE. *þíwen* maidservant, *fyxen* VIXEN, etc.] A maidservant; a handmaid, female slave.
*a***1100** *Aldhelm Gloss.* I. 2349 (Napier *O.E. Gl.*) *Uernacula*, i. *ancilla* vel *serua*, þyftan. *Ibid.* 2716 *Uerna*, .i. *seruus*, þyften. *a***1100** in *Haupt's Zeitschr.* IX. 461/2 *Vernacula* (gl. *servula*, *ancilla*), þeftan. *a***1225** *Ancr. R.* 4 þeos riwle nis bute vorto serui þe oðer. þe oðer is ase lefdi: þeos is ase þuften. *c***1230** *Hali Meid.* 45 Mi lauerd biseh his þufftenes mekelac.

thug (θʌg, *prop.* thʌg), *sb.* Also 9 **thag, theg, t'hug.** [a. Hindī *ṭhag*, Mahr. *ṭhag*, *ṭhak* a cheat, swindler.] (With capital T.) One of an association of professional robbers and murderers in India, who strangled their victims; a p'hansigar. Also *attrib.*
Their methods were described already in Thevenot's *Voyages*, *c* 1665 (see Yule). They are mentioned under their more correct name of *p'hansigars* (*phanseegurs*), i.e. 'stranglers', by Forbes *Orient. Mem.* IV. 13 (1813), and as *Thugs*, *Thags*, or *Thegs* from 1810. Their suppression was rigidly prosecuted from 1831, and the system is now extinct.
1810 in *Hist. & Pract. Thugs* xxi. (1837) 329 It having come to the knowledge of Government, that several Sepoys .. have been robbed and murdered by a description of persons denominated 'Thugs', who infested the districts of the Dooab and other parts of the Upper Provinces. **1816** in *Asiat. Res.* XIII. 287 The term '*Theg*' is usually applied, in the western provinces, to persons who rob and murder travellers on the highways, either by poison, or the application of the cord or knife. **1839** M. TAYLOR *Confess. Thug* (1873) 2 You know not the high and stirring excitement of a Thug's occupation. **1897** *Daily News* 22 Sept. 6/4 When the Prince of Wales was in India, a Thug criminal showed him how victims were strangled.

b. *transf.* A cutthroat, ruffian, rough.
1839 CARLYLE *Chartism* i. 4 'Glasgow Thuggery', 'Glasgow Thugs'; it is a witty nickname. **1881** R. L. STEVENSON *Virginibus Puerisque* 164 Sometimes it [*sc.* death] leaps suddenly upon its victims, like a Thug. **1883** CABLE in *Century Mag.* June 230/1 A few 'thugs' terrorized the city with .. beating, stabbing, and shooting. **1889** *Boston* (Mass.) *Jrnl.* 24 Apr. 1/8 Thugs, plug-uglies, and 'flash sports'. **1895** J. BURNS in *Westm. Gaz.* 17 Jan. 2/1 They even engage 'knockers-out', who .. belabour and disable voters as they are entering the booths.. They are called 'election Thugs'. **1958** P. GIBBS *Curtains of Yesterday* xxvii. 216 'Isn't he a madman?' he asked. 'Isn't he raising an army of young thugs, his brutish young Brownshirts? Haven't they been fighting and brawling in Bavaria?' **1967** S. FAESSLER in *Atlantic Monthly* Apr. 103/2 The old man ducked for cover .., but not my father. Unarmed he stood up to the thugs, and was cracked over the head for it. **1982** *Daily Tel.* 7 Jan. 16/6 A plea .. that it [*sc.* corporal punishment] should be retained as the final deterrent for school 'thugs'.

Hence **thug** *v.*, *trans.* (*a*) to assassinate by thuggee; (*b*) *intr.* to be a thug (sense b). *U.S.*; **'Thugdom,** the domain of Thugs; **'Thuggess,** a female Thug; **'Thuggism,** the practice and principles of Thugs: = next.
1837 *Edin. Rev.* Jan. 369 If a single civilian or military man had been thugged, thuggee would have been abolished long ago. **1839** DE QUINCEY *Murder* ad fin., At length came the toast of the day—Thugdom in all its branches. **1856** FROUDE *Hist. Eng.* I. ii. 155 What teachers of Thuggism would appear to ourselves, the teachers of heresy actually appeared to Sir Thomas More. **1859** LANG *Wand. India* 100 The victim, another Thuggess, was supposed to be sleeping when the operation was performed. **1903** *Daily Chron.* 4 Dec. 5/2 Lord William Bentinck is .. known for his suppression of Thuggism, which made strangling a religious rite to the goddess Kali. **1937** *Sun* (Baltimore) 6 May 7/2 When I was thugging in Harlan county, .. Merle Middleton was the chief of the gang. **1965** W. SOYINKA *Road* 22 *Chief*: .. Are you .. one of the boys? *Samson*: I won't thug for you if that is what you mean.

thuggee (θʌ'giː). Also -ie. [a. Hindī *ṭhagī*, abstr. sb. f. *ṭhag* THUG.] The system of robbery and murder practised by the Thugs. Also *attrib.*
1837 *Edin. Rev.* Jan. 358 These .. people are known by the name of Thugs, and their profession is called Thuggee. **1858** J. S. MILL *Memo. of Improvements in Admin. of India during Last Thirty Years* 46 The work of the Thuggee Suppression Department was nearly completed. **1859** LANG *Wand. India* 98 The suppression of Thuggee in the British dominions. **1898** *Speaker* 26 Nov. 641/1 Colonel Sleeman .. had charge of the Thuggee inquiries. **1902** *Daily Chron.* 7 Aug. 3/5 Colonel Sir E. Bradford was appointed general superintendent of the operations for the suppression of 'thagi and dakaiti', as the India Office calls it.

thuggery ('θʌgərɪ). [f. THUG + -ERY.] = THUGGEE; also *transf.*
1839 [see THUG b]. **1849** E. B. EASTWICK *Dry Leaves* 58 The Amirs had no more power to prevent the robberies and murders .. than we have to extinguish the system of Thuggery or Dacoitism. **1865** *Reader* 26 Aug. 225/1 Ecclesiastical thuggery. **1930** E. D. SULLIVAN *Chicago Surrenders* xiv. 239 Thuggery .. has met no serious rebuff on any front. **1959** *Economist* 29 June 1154/2 The police are having an extremely difficult task combating thuggery. **1973** *Nation Rev.* (Melbourne) 31 Aug. III. 1445/2 Envoys confronted with unfamiliar thuggery can be as naive as Birmingham businessmen who have become top politicians.

thuggish ('θʌgɪʃ), *a.* [f. THUG *sb.* + -ISH[1].] Resembling a thug. Also *Comb.*, as ***thuggish-looking*** adj.
1953 W. BURROUGHS *Junkie* viii. 75, I .. got in conversation with a thuggish-looking young Italian. **1976** *Daily Tel.* 25 Oct. 2/4 Thuggish youths streaming from the rival demonstration. **1977** *N.Y. Rev. Bks.* 24 Nov. 41/1 The Nationalists .. had allowed some of their thuggish supporters to make [a mistake].

thught, þuȝt(e, þuhte, obs. pa. t. and pple. of THINK *v.*[1] and [2].

‖thugyi ('θədʒiː). Also 9 **thoogyee.** [Burmese.] The headman of a village.
1863 C. WILLIAMS *Jrnl.* 3 Feb. in *Through Burmah* (1868) 57 On the Thoogyee sending for some pieces, I found the characters to be Nagiri. **1887** *Rangoon Gaz. Weekly Budget* 7 Jan. 8/4 On 18th a thugyi successfully attacked dacoits and recovered dacoited cattle. **1934** 'G. ORWELL' *Burmese Days* xxv. 369 Old thugyis with their grey hair knotted behind their heads. **1957** *Encycl. Brit.* IV. 430/2 In the villages, the *thugyis* or headmen, chosen by the villagers and approved by the government, have limited magisterial powers and collect the revenue. **1980** J. SILVERSTEIN *Burmese Politics* ii. 26 The *thugyi* was directly responsible to the deputy commissioner.

thuid, obs. Sc. form of THUD.

‖thuja ('θjuːdʒə). [mod.L. (Linnæus): see THUYA.] The more common English form of the name of trees or shrubs of the botanical genus now called THUYA, q.v., also of the wood of *T. occidentalis*, and of drugs derived from it.
oil of thuja, an essential oil obtained by distilling the ends of the branches and the leaves of *T. occidentalis* with water.
1760 J. LEE *Introd. Bot.* (1788) 299 *Thuja*, Arbor Vitæ. **1865** VISCT. MILTON & CHEADLE *Northwest Passage by Land* 287 There were pines and thujas of every size. **1866** *Treas. Bot.*, *Thuja occidentalis* is the American Arbor Vitæ. **1868** *Rep. U.S. Commissioner Agric.* (1869) 186 After ascending some distance the mountain sides.., the wood .. consists particularly of a noble Thuja. **1884** Q. VICTORIA *More Leaves* 301 There are .. a wonderful old laurel and thuja which have spread to an immense size. **1884** *Mag. of Art* Mar. 179/2 The richly carved ceiling of thuja and cedar.

Hence names of chemical compounds obtained from the species *Thuja occidentalis* (all in *Cent. Dict.* spelt *thuy-*): **'thujene** = *thujone*; **'thujenin** or **thu'jigenin, thu'jetic** *acid*, **'thujetin, 'thujin, 'thujone**: see quots.; **thujaplicin** (-'plaɪsɪn) [L. *plic-ātus*, pa. pple. of *plicāre* to fold], any of three isomers of isopropyl-tropolone, $C_3H_7{\cdot}C_7H_5O_2$, that have fungicidal properties and occur in the conifer *Thuja plicata*.
1868 WATTS *Dict. Chem.* V. 789 *Thujetic acid*, $C_{28}H_{22}O_{13}$ .. is prepared: 1. by boiling thujetin with baryta-water [etc.] .. 2... by boiling thujin for some hours with baryta-water in an atmosphere of hydrogen. *Ibid.*, *Thujetin*, $C_{28}H_{28}O_{16}$... A compound obtained, together with crystallisable sugar, by heating thujin with dilute acids. *Ibid.* 790 *Thujigenin*, $C_{28}H_{24}O_{14}$... A compound occurring in .. the green parts of *Thuja occidentalis*, and produced, together with sugar, when thujin is heated with hydrochloric acid. *Ibid.*, *Thujin*, $C_{20}H_{22}O_{12}$... A crystallisable glucoside, occurring in the green parts of *Thuja occidentalis*... Thujin forms shining lemon-yellow crystals, appearing under the microscope as four-sided tables. *Ibid.* 791 *Thujone*, a volatile hydrocarbon, obtained by the action of iodine on oil of thuja. **1873** —— *Fownes' Chem.* 643 When heated .. with hydrochloric acid, [thujin] yields .. thujenin. **1894** MUIR & MORLEY *Watts' Dict. Chem.* IV. 714 Thujone, $C_{10}H_{18}O$, .. occurs, together with the terpene $C_{10}H_{16}$ .. in the essential oil of thuja. **1948** ERDTMAN & GRIPENBERG in *Nature* 8 May 719/2 The compound, m.p. 82°, is termed γ-thujaplicin because the isopropyl group occupies the γ-position in the cycloheptatrieneolone. **1964** *New Scientist* 4 June 613/1 The tropolones beta thujaplicin and gamma thujaplicin were highly toxic to the four test basidiomycetes. **1978** *Further Perspectives Org. Chem.* 29 He did visualize the formation of simpler natural tropolones—the thujaplicins—by ring expansion in some unknown way from a benzene ring and an attached carbon.

thuk, þuke, dial. variants of THILK.

thula ('θʊlə). [a. ON. *þula*.] A metrical list of names or poetic synonyms assembled in categories (orig. for oral recitation) to preserve traditional knowledge.
1936 K. MALONE *Widsith* 1 Three name-lists (and one fragment of such a list), to which I will refer by the technical term *thula*, taken from the Icelandic. **1937** —— in *Angl. Beibl.* XLVIII. 221 In an old thula-fragment quoted in the Icelandic *Hervararsaga* we are told that a certain Kiarr ruled the Valir. **1963** BROWN & FOOTE *Early Eng. & Norse Stud.* 113 It is undoubtedly because of these lists of names that the poem is called a þula. **1974** *Eng. Stud.* LV. 507 The first and third thulas are .. parallel in introducing kings uninterruptedly.

‖Thule ('θjuːliː). Forms: 1 Thila, 1, 4–5 Tyle, Tile, 7 Thyle, Tule, 6– Thule. [L. *Thūlē* (*Thȳle*) = Gr. Θούλη (Θύλη), proper name of unknown origin.]

1. a. The ancient Greek and Latin name (first found in Polybius's account of the voyage of Pytheas) for a land six days' sail north of Britain, which he supposed to be the most northerly region in the world.
(*Thule* has been variously conjectured to be the Shetland Islands (so app. in Pliny and Tacitus), Iceland, the northern point of Denmark, or some point on the coast of Norway.)
*c***888** K. ÆLFRED *Boeth.* xxix. §3 Oð ðæt iland þe we hatað Tyle. *c***893** —— *Oros.* I. i. §27 Be westannorðan Ibernia is þæt ytemeste land þæt man hæt Thila. *a***1000** *Boeth. Metr.* xvi. 15 An iglond .. þ is Tile haten. *c***1374** CHAUCER *Boeth.* III. met. v. (Camb. MS.), þe last Ile in þe see þat hyhte tyle [*v.r.* tile]. **1387** TREVISA *Higden* (Rolls) I. 325 Tyle is sixe dayes seillynge oute of Bretayne. **1598** SYLVESTER *Du Bartas* II. ii. IV. *Columnes* 230 From Africa to Thule's farthest Flood. **1613–16** W. BROWNE *Brit. Past.* I. v, Monster-breeding Nyle Or through the North to the unpeopled Thyle. **1665** SIR T. HERBERT *Trav.* (1677) 2 The fortunate Islands .. about which has been no small difference amongst Writers. Some placing them at the Azores .. but the Commentator upon Horace near the *Ultima Thule*. *a***1688** J. WALLACE (*title*) An Essay Concerning the Thule of the Ancients. **1730–46** THOMSON *Autumn* 864 Where the Northern Ocean .. Boils round the naked melancholy isles Of farthest Thule. **1847** MACAULAY in Trevelyan *Life* (1876) II. 190 Where more than Thule's winter barbs the breeze.

b. *transf.* As the type of the extreme limit of travel and discovery, chiefly (after Latin usage) in the phrase ***ultima Thule*** (farthest Thule); hence *fig.* the highest or uttermost point or degree attained or attainable, the acme, limit; the lowest limit, the nadir.
1771 SMOLLETT *Humph. Cl.* 3 Sept., I am now little short of the *Ultima Thule*, if this appellation properly belongs to the Orkneys or Hebrides. **1784–5** *Ann. Reg.* II. 12/1 An unknown coast, which he [Cook] named Sandwich Land, the *thule* of the Southern hemisphere. **1828** *Lights & Shades* II. 136 The caricature of a fop, the *ultima Thule* of extravagant frippery. **1878** *Times* 10 May (Stanf.), The expedition reached their Ultima Thule. **1954** M. LOWRY *Let.* 22 May (1967) 370 Before you write off that behaviour as being the ultima thule of ingratitude .. try to understand the effect your news .. had on me. **1976** L. DAVIDOFF et al. in Mitchell & Oakley *Rights & Wrongs of Women* iv. 157 The one who had 'fallen' out of the respectable society .. to the *ultima Thule* of prostitution.

2. *Archæol.* (with pronunc. (θuːl, θjuːl)). Used chiefly *attrib.* to designate a prehistoric Eskimo culture widely distributed from Alaska to Greenland *c* 500–1400 A.D. [From the name *Thule* (now Dundas), a settlement in N.W. Greenland.]
1927 T. MATHIASSEN *Archæol. of Central Eskimos* II. i. 2 We have .. found remnants of an older culture which, after a locality outside the Central Eskimo territory, in North Greenland, we have called the Thule culture. **1935** *Nature* 3 Aug. 188/1 He [*sc.* Mathiassen] regards the Thule culture as originating in Asia. **1956** G. FREEMAN tr. *Malaurie's Last Kings of Thule* I. vii. 87 The Thule Culture—neo-Eskimo—would be derived from an anterior continental culture—palaeo-Eskimo. **1962** *Times* 4 Aug. 7/7 Within recent historical times Greenland has known three Eskimo cultures. The most recent is that of the Thule people who moved across Canada from Alaska. **1972** *Country Life* 12 Oct. 880 About AD 1100 a second Eskimo culture, known to archaeologists as the Thule period because it was first identified at Thule in Greenland, spread eastward from Alaska. *Ibid.* 881 The Thule Eskimos lived in stone houses. **1974** *Encycl. Brit. Macropædia* I. 1130/2 The spread of Thule .. has been traced eastward from Alaska, arriving in Greenland about 1200... Later there was a resurge of Thule back toward the west, reaching all the way to Bering Strait. **1977** G. CLARK *World Prehist.* (ed. 3) IX. 411 The Neo-Eskimo bearers of the Thule culture, immediate forebears of the existing population.

Thulean ('θjuːlɪən), *a. Geol.* [f. THULE + -AN.] Of, pertaining to, or designating a region of

Tertiary volcanic activity including Iceland and parts of Britain and Greenland.

1925 *Glasgow Herald* 10 Nov. 11/5 Jan Mayen, he said, formed a part of the Thulean or Brito-Arctic petrographical province. **1938** A. K. WELLS *Outl. Hist. Geol.* xvii. 206 Evidently Britain lay on the fringe of a vast North Atlantic (or Thulean) volcanic province. **1976** P. FRANCIS *Volcanoes* vii. 219 The Giant's Causeway in Antrim, and Fingal's Cave on the island of Staffa both originated when the Thulean plateau was being formed.

† **thulge**, *v. Obs. rare.* [app. representing OE. (*ȝe*)*þyldȝian* to be patient, f. *ȝeþyldiȝ* patient; but this would normally give in ME. (*ȝe*)*þuld*(*i*)*en*.]

a. *intr.* To be patient, have patience, bear or put up *with*. **b.** *trans.* (only in OE.) To wait for.

[*c* **897** K. ÆLFRED *Gregory's Past. C.* xxxiii. 216 Ne mæȝ he ȝeðyldȝian ðæt he ðæt forhele. *a* **1000** *Ags. Ps.* (Spelm.) xxiv. 5 Ðe ic ȝeþyldȝode [Vulg. *te sustinui*] ealne dæȝ. *Ibid.* xci. 14 Wel þyldiȝende hi beoð [Vulg. *bene patientes erunt*].] **13..** *Gaw. & Gr. Knt.* 1859 Þenne he þulged with hir þrepe, & þoled hir to speke, & ho..bede hit hym swyþe.

thulia ('θju:lɪə). *Chem.* [mod.L., f. THULIUM after THORIA, YTTRIA, etc.] The sesquioxide of thulium, Tm_2O_3, a dense white powder.

1886 [see FRACTIONAL *a.* b]. **1924** J. W. MELLOR *Comprehensive Treat. Inorg. & Theoret. Chem.* V. xxxviii. 698 C. James has described processes for the extraction of thulia from ytterspar (Norwegian xenotime), euxenite, and a Norwegian columbate. **1968** C. A. HAMPEL *Encycl. Chem. Elements* 718/2 Should the demand arise, thulia, Tm_2O_3, could be isolated readily, as one of a number of individual rare earth by-products from the current (1967) commercial production of yttria by ion exchange, at a rate exceeding 1000 pounds per annum.

thulite ('θju:laɪt). *Min.* [ad. Ger. and Sw. *thulit*: named by Ekeberg, 1820, f. THULE: see -ITE[1].] A rose-red variety of ZOISITE.

1820 JAMESON *Syst. Min.* (ed. 3) I. 134 The rare blue variety [of the Pyramidal Garnet] is found..in Tellemark, in Norway, along with a hard peach-blossom coloured mineral named Thulite. **1888** RUTLEY *Rock-Forming Min.* 161 Thulite displays strong pleochroism.

thulium ('θju:lɪəm). *Chem.* [mod.L., coined in Fr. (P. T. Cleve 1879, in *Compt. Rend.* LXXXIX. 480), f. THULE + -IUM.] A rare metallic element of the lanthanide series that forms pale green salts in which it is trivalent. Atomic number 69; symbol Tm.

1879 P. T. CLEVE in *Chem. News* 12 Sept. 126/2 For the radical of the oxide placed between ytterbia and erbia..I propose the name of Thullium [*sic*], derived from Thulé, the ancient name of Scandinavia. **1923** U. R. EVANS *Metals & Metallic Compounds* II. 236 Thulium can be separated in a fairly pure state by oft-repeated recrystallization as bromate. **1924** [see HOLMIUM]. **1956** *Nature* 17 Mar. 494/2 Iridium-192 continues to be the source most commonly used in industry for gamma-radiography... Thulium-170 has only gained slightly in popularity. **1968** *Punch* 24 Apr. 604/3 Gold, silver and platinum are starting to look pretty square as well as pricey these days. More sophisticated speculators have already shifted into antimony and zinc: while an *avant garde* group is believed to have plunged heavily on thulium.

thulk(e, thulli(ch, (**þ-**): see THILK, THELLICH.

thuman, þ-: see THEOW *a.*, quot. 1297.

thumb (θʌm), *sb.* Forms: α. 1 th-, ð-, þuma, 3 þume, 3-4 þoume, 4-5 (6 *Sc.*) thoume, thowme, 4-6 thome, 5 thomme, 6 thom, 7-8 thum, 8-9 *Sc.* and *n. dial.* thoum, thoom. β. 3-4 þoumbe, 4 (6 *Sc.*) thoumbe, 4-5 þombe, 4-7 thombe, 5 þ-, thowmbe, 6-7 thumbe, 4- thumb. γ. 4-5 tumb, toumbe. [OE. *þúma* wk. masc. = OFris. *thûma*, *tûma*, *tumma*, WFris. *tumme*, *tomme*, Saterl. *tûme*, NFris. *tüm*, *tim*, OLG. **thûmo* (MLG. *dûme*, LG. *dûme*, *dûm*; MDu. *dûme*, Du. *duim*), OHG. *dûmo* (MHG. *dûme*, Ger. *daumen*); ON. wanting (deriv. *þumall* thumb of a glove); Norw. *tume*, *tumme*, *tome*, Sw. *tumme*, Da. *tomme* inch, *tommel*:—OTeut. **þûmon*-, pre-Teut. **tûmon*- the stout or thick (finger), f. root *tū*- to swell: cf. Zend *tûma* fat, Skr. *tūtumá* strong, *tumrá* fat, L. *tumēre* to swell. In ME. the excrescent *b* after *m* is found *c* 1290.]

1. a. The short thick inner digit of the human hand, opposable to the fingers, and distinguished from them by having only two phalanges; hence, *gen.*, the inner digit of a limb when opposable to and set apart from the other digits (as in the *Quadrumana* and opossums).

a **700** *Epinal Gloss.* 821 *Pollux*, thuma. *a* **901** *Laws K. Ælfred* c. 56 ȝif se ðuma bið ofaslæȝen, þam sceal xxx scill. to bote. *c* **1000** *Sax. Leechd.* III. 18 Swa greate swa ðin þuma. *a* **1225** *Ancr. R.* 18, & makieð on ower muþe mit te þume a creoiz. *c* **1290** *S. Eng. Leg.* I. 308/319 Strongue is þe þoumbe I-cleoped. *a* **1300** *Cursor M.* 21244 (Cott.) Men sais þat of his thumb [*G.* tumb, *F.* thowme, *T.* þombe] he smate, And þat was noght bot for to fle. *c* **1375** *Lay Folks Mass Bk.* (MS. B.) 158 Makes a cros vpon þo letter with his thoume. **13..** *Minor Poems fr. Vernon MS.* xxv. 296 Þi þhommes and þi ffyngres. *c* **1440** *Gesta Rom.* xxii. 72 (Harl. MS.) Tho anon he toke the thome of the dede man, and made him to seal hit [a charter] with a fals seal. *c* **1475** *Pict. Voc.* in Wr.-Wülcker 749/31 *Hic pollex*, a thumb. **1507** in Leadam *Sel. Cas. Star Chamber* (Seld.) I. 260 They hade maymed one William Thomson..& cutte of his right thom. **1596** SHAKS. *1 Hen. IV*, I. iii. 38 'Twixt his Finger and his Thumbe, he held A Pouncet-box. **1605** —— *Macb.* IV. i. 44 By the pricking of my Thumbes, Something wicked this way comes. **1662** *Reg. Privy Council Scotl.* Ser. III. I. 237 They..tortured the women by waking, hanging them up by the thombes, burning the soles of their feet at the fyre. **1662** STILLINGFL. *Orig. Sacr.* III. i. §16 The thumb, which may equally joyn with any of the fingers in taking hold of any thing. **1712** tr. *Pomet's Hist. Drugs* I. 152 A round Stalk, the Thickness of two Thumbs. **1833** *Penny Cycl.* I. 183/2 The hinder extremities [of the chimpanzee] are..marked by a thumb—a finger opposed to the other fingers. **1840** *Ibid.* XVI. 458/1 s.v. *Opossum*, The whole of this subfamily [*Didelphidæ*] have the inner toe of the hind foot converted into a thumb. **1869** HAZLITT *Eng. Prov.* 373 The richer the cobbler, the blacker his thumb. **1893** HODGES *Elem. Photogr.* (1907) 78 Held between the thumb and finger of the left hand.

fig. **1895** BARING-GOULD *Noémi* xxii, I must have more men. I dare not leave Domme [a fortress] without a thumb on it to hold it down.

† **b.** The corresponding digit of the foot; the great toe. *Obs.*

1432-50 tr. *Higden* (Rolls) II. 189 A thowmbe [L. *pollex*; TREVISA, greet too] in the ryȝhte foote of Pyrrhus kynge, the towchenge of whom ȝafe subsidy ageyne venom. **1535** COVERDALE *Judg.* i. 6 They cut of the thombes of his handes and fete. *a* **1643** J. SHUTE *Judgem. & M.* 38 Adonibezek cut off the thumbs both of the hands and feet of seventy kings.

c. In the lower animals generally: The inmost digit of the fore-foot; in a bird, the first digit of the wing, bearing the bastard-wing or alula; also the hind toe, inner hind toe, or hallux; in insects: see quot. 1826.

1607 TOPSELL *Four-f. Beasts* (1658) 424 The Nut-mouse, ..upon his forefeet..hath four claws or distinct toes, for he wanteth a thumb. **1797** *Encycl. Brit.* (ed. 3) XIV. 612/1 The fore-feet [of a seal] are like the human hand, the middle toe being the longest and the thumb short. **1826** KIRBY & SP. *Entomol.* III. 370 *Pollex* (the Thumb). A small accessory joint, attached to the *Ungula* of the *Manus* in *Mantis*. **1828** STARK *Elem. Nat. Hist.* I. 116 [Lemming] Fore-feet pentadactylous; nail of the thumb short and rounded. **1854** OWEN *Skel. & Teeth* in *Orr's Circ. Sc.* I. *Org. Nat.* 223 Those which are attached to the short outer digit,.. erroneously called the 'thumb', are the..bastard feathers. **1860** MAYNE *Expos. Lex.*, *Thumb*,..*Ornithol.*, applied to a small bone of the hand, or third portion of the anterior extremity..also to the shortest toe.., situated behind... *Zool.*, applied to the first finger of the anterior extremity, or fore-foot of certain of the *Reptilia*. **1872** COUES *N. Amer. Birds* 30 The forefinger hand-bone sticks out a little from the side of the principal one, and bears on its end one finger-bone..which is commonly, but wrongly, called the bird's 'thumb'. **1894** NEWTON *Dict. Birds* 737 *Pollex*, the thumb or first digit of the wing.

2. *transf.* The part of a glove or mitten which covers the thumb.

1888 in *Cassell's Encycl. Dict.*

3. A thing or part analogous to or in some way resembling a thumb; e.g. a projecting spur or stump of a woody plant, a tool, etc.; also (cf. *Tom Thumb*) a diminutive animal or object; see quots.

1745 tr. *Columella's Husb.* IV. ii, Having remarked the thumb of the former year [*superioris anni pollice*] one may leave one or two eyes from which it may germinate. **1778** [W. MARSHALL] *Minutes Agric.* 20 Sept. an. 1775, A corn-fork, without the thumb, is the best. **1854** *N. & Q.* 1st Ser. IX. 385/1 Three kinds..: the weasel, the stoat or stump, and the mousehunt or mousehunter, which is also called the thumb from its diminutive size. **1869** [Thumbs and fingers in *Colour-printing*: see FINGER *sb.* 11 b]. **1901** *Chronicle* 25 Oct. (E.D.D., Staffs.), 'Tot', a small mug, that held a quartern, sometimes also called a thumb. **1904** *Science* 20 May 803 (Cent. Suppl.) The extremely acute 'thumbs' and pinnacles which surmount the trap plateau of different parts of Greenland.

4. As a measure (also more fully, ***thumb's breadth***): The breadth of the thumb, taken as equal to an inch.

Formerly it was usual to allow a 'thumb' in addition to each yard (of cloth, etc.) measured; this is still the practice in the cloth trade.

[**1611** COTGR., *Poulcée*, an inch, or inch-measure; the breadth of a thumbe.] **1622** MALYNES *Anc. Law-Merch.* 52 A thumbe or Inch is 6 Graines or Barleycornes. **1634** SANDERSON *Serm. 1 Sam. xii.* 3 §29 False weights, false measures, false thumbs, false lights, false marks. **1711** *Act 10 Anne* c. 16 §4 One Table..with the Length of a Yard nailed or marked thereupon; to which shall be added one Inch more, which shall be used instead of that which is commonly called a Thumb's Breadth. **1812** J. SMYTH *Pract. of Customs* (1821) 126 (*Linen*) The practice of allowing what is termed a Thumb is now discontinued by the Board's order [8th May, 1806].

5. Phrases. **a.** ***thumb of gold, a golden thumb, miller's thumb***: in reference either to the alleged dishonesty of millers or to the lucrative character of their trade. † **b.** ***to bring*** (a person) ***above the thumb, to turn over the thumb***, to get or have under one's control; cf. 'to twist round one's finger'. *Obs.* **c.** ***one's fingers all thumbs*** (etc.): said of a person who is clumsy or wanting in dexterity. † **d.** ***to hit*** (†***cross***) ***one over*** (***of, on***) ***the thumbs***, to punish or reprove sharply, 'rap one's knuckles'. **e.** (*a*) ***to bite one's thumbs***, as an indication of anger or vexation; (*b*) ***to bite the thumb at***, as an insult: see BITE *v.* 16. † **f.** ***under*** (***the***) ***thumb***, secretly, confidentially. *Obs.* **g.** ***under the thumb of***, entirely at the disposal or direction of, completely subservient to. **h.** (*a*) In expressions referring to the use of the thumb by the spectators in the ancient amphitheatre, to indicate approbation or the opposite: see quot. 1880; (*b*) in mod. use (with significance the reverse of that in the ancient amphitheatre): ***thumbs down, up***, gestures made with the fingers closed and the thumb pointing vertically downwards (indicating disapproval or rejection) or upwards (as a sign of approval, acceptance, encouragement, etc.); also *attrib.* and *fig.*

a. *c* **1386-1876** [see MILLER[1] 1 b].

b. **1469** J. PASTON in *P. Lett.* II. 356 Thow thou can begyll the Dwk of Norffolk, and bryng hym abow the thombe as thow lyst, I let the wet thow shalt not do me so. **1577** NORTHBROOKE *Dicing* 48 The gaine gotten by this playe at Dice, where all is gotten with a trice ouer the thumbe. **1603** DEKKER *Wonderfull Yeare* F iv, Shee would haue tickled them, and turned them ouer the thumbs.

c. **1546** J. HEYWOOD *Prov.* (1562) G iij b, Whan he should get ought, eche fynger is a thumbe. **1870** *Echo* 16 Nov., Your uneducated man is all thumbs, as the phrase runs; and what education does for him is to supply him with clever fingers. **1872** *Routledge's Ev. Boy's Ann.* 155/2 Whose fingers were reported..to be 'all thumbs'.

d. **1522** SKELTON, Thwartyng ouer thom [see THWART *v.* 2]. *a* **1548** HALL *Chron., Hen. VII* 33 In the later ende of hys oracion, he a litle rebuked the lady Margaret and hyt her of [GRAFTON on] the thombes. **1553** T. WILSON *Rhet.* (1580) 3 The Philosopher..did hit a yong man ouer the Thumbes verie handsomely, for vsyng ouer old, and ouer straunge woordes. *Ibid.* 137, I haue knowen some so hitte of the thumbes, that thei could not tell..whether [etc.]. **1591** GREENE *Farew. to Follie* Wks. (Grosart) IX. 285 Peratio.. thought to crosse Benedetto ouer the thumbs. **1594** LODGE & GREENE *Looking Glasse* (Hunter. Cl.) 9 Well said Smith, that crost him ouer the thumbs.

e. **1573** *Satir. Poems Reform.* xlii. 266 The Clerk was like to byte his thowmis. **1592** SHAKS. *Rom. & Jul.* I. i. 49. [**1596** LODGE *Wits Misery* 23 Giuing me the Fico with his thombe in his mouth.] **1608** DEKKER *Dead Term* D iv b, What shouldering, what Justling, what Jeering, what byting of Thumbs to beget quarels. **1638** RANDOLPH *Muses Looking-Gl.* III. iii, Daggs, and Pistolls! To bite his thumb at me? **1670** G. H. *Hist. Cardinals* II. II. 158 The Spaniards were nettled, and bit their thumbs..in private. **1863** *Chambers' Bk. Days* 11 Mar. I. 358 It is very probable that..the act of biting the thumb was not so much a gesture of insulting contempt as a threat.

f. **1586** J. HOOKER *Hist. Irel.* in *Holinshed* II. 89/1 Diuerse other secret vnderminers, who wrought so cunninglie vnder the thumbe..as if Kildare had prospered,..their malice would not haue beene in manner suspected. **1596** DALRYMPLE tr. *Leslie's Hist. Scot.* II. (S.T.S.) I. 171 This consuetude..was, as we vse to speik, vndir thoume stil reteined. *a* **1693** *Urquhart's Rabelais* III. xxxvi. 299 Privily and under Thumb.

g. **1754** RICHARDSON *Grandison* IV. xxix. 181 She..is obliged to be silent. I have her under my thumb. **1809** MALKIN *Gil Blas* VII. xiii. ¶6 Authors..are under the thumb of booksellers and players. **1889** JESSOPP *Coming of Friars* ii. 65 The lord was a petty king, having his subjects very much under his thumb.

h. **1601** HOLLAND *Pliny* XXVIII. ii. 297 To bend or bow downe the thumbes when wee give assent unto a thing, or doe favour any person. **1693** DRYDEN *Juvenal's Sat.* iii. 68 Where..With Thumbs bent back, they popularly kill. **1880** LEWIS & SHORT s.v. *Pollex*, To close down the thumb (*premere*) was a sign of approbation; to extend it (*vertere, convertere*; *pollex infestus*) a sign of disapprobation. **1887** R. GARNETT *Life Carlyle* iv, They had unanimously turned their thumbs up. 'Sartor', the publisher acquainted him, 'excites universal disapprobation'. **1906** KIPLING *Puck of Pook's Hill* 180 We're finished men—thumbs down against both of us. **1907** R. Y. TYRRELL in *Academy* 9 Mar. 234/1 'Thumbs down' means 'spare him..': the signal for death was 'thumbs up'. **1917** A. G. EMPEY *Over Top* 311 *Thumbs up*, Tommy's expression which means 'everything is fine with me'. **1929** A. C. & C. EDINGTON *Studio Murder Myst.* iii. 26 The irrevocable 'thumbs down' on a lovely female actor, because certain shady pages in her past had been turned to the light. **1939** *War Illustr.* 4 Nov. p. iii/1 French peasants now return the 'thumbs up' gesture with which they are greeted by British troops on their way to the front. **1946** *Sunday Dispatch* 8 Sept. 1/2 He ran from his machine giving the thumbs-up sign. **1951** *Sport* 7-13 Jan. 16/3 The London team has been given the thumbs down sign by a meeting of 1st division promoters. **1951** S. SPENDER *World within World* v. 275 Our chief comedian was Buckfast... Everything about him suggested a 'thumbs up' attitude. **1954** R. SUTCLIFF *Eagle of Ninth* iii. 27 He laughed, and made the 'thumbs up' to his troops, calling 'Well done, lads!' **1961** *Guardian* 25 Mar. 6/7 The Chancellor of the Exchequer's thumbs-down to a National Theatre. **1967** *Technology Week* XX. 95/2 Giving a final 'thumbs up' on the rocket's readiness. **1971** *Sunday Times* (Johannesburg) 28 Mar. 5/1 She said the thumbs-down vote was not unanimous. **1976** *Scotsman* 25 Nov. 3/7 The market yesterday gave Sir Hugh the thumbs-up. The Fraser shares went up 3p to 58p on the report, which was apparently better than expected. **1979** R. FIENNES *Hell on Ice* i. 14 Both drivers gave a 'thumbs up'. **1982** *Daily Tel.* 5 Mar. 17/1 (*heading*) Baldwin statue gets thumbs down from Foot.

i. ***to get one's thumb out of*** (a person's) ***mouth***, to escape from, to get out of the clutches of. † ***the finger next one's thumb***, one's closest friend. So † ***to be finger and thumb***, to be on intimate terms. † ***a thumb under the girdle***: an expression denoting reserve or unsociableness. † ***to a cow's thumb***, exactly, perfectly, to a hair. ***there's my thumb*** (*Sc.*), in asseveration, in allusion to the practice of licking the thumb in sealing a bargain; see *thumb-licking* in 6. ***above one's thumb*** (*Sc.*), beyond one's reach or ability. ***to fash one's thumb*** (*Sc.*), to put oneself out, to worry or concern oneself. ***to clap, put***, or ***keep the thumb on*** (*Sc.*), to keep secret. ***to whistle on***

one's thumb (*Sc.*): cf. *to pipe in an ivy-leaf* (see IVY-LEAF). ***as easy as kiss my thumb. to have a green thumb***: see GREEN *a.* 1 k. ***to stick out like a sore thumb***: see SORE *a.* 9 f. See also RULE OF THUMB.

1481 CAXTON *Reynard* xx. (Arb.) 49, I shal by my wille neuer more come in the kynges daunger, I haue now goten my thombe out of his mouth. **1579** LYLY *Euphues* (Arb.) 68 In yat thou crauest my aide, assure thy selfe I will be the finger next thy thombe. **1607** WALKINGTON *Opt. Glass* 130 Wee count a melancholicke man.. the *aqua-fortis* of merry company, a thumb vnder the girdle. *a* **1613** OVERBURY *Charac., Old Man* (1614) E iij b, They call the thombe vnder the girdle grauitie. **1681** T. FLATMAN *Heraclitus Ridens* No. 40 (1713) II. 2 Let him alone, he'll trim their Whiskers and comb their Perukes for them to a Cow's thumb. **1722** RAMSAY *Three Bonnets* III. 104 There's my thumb That, while I breathe, I'se ne'er beguile ye. **1730–6** BAILEY (folio) s.v., They are Finger and Thumb, that is, they are so great together, there is no parting them. **1766** A. NICOL *Poems* 59 (E.D.D.) Your match is nane aboon your thumb. **1786** BURNS *Earnest Cry & Prayer* v, Speak out, an' never fash your thumb. **1818** SCOTT *Hrt. Midl.* xviii, We'll leave Mr. Sharpitlaw to whistle on his thumb. **1825** JAMIESON s.v., *To Clap or Put the Thoum on any thing*, to conceal it carefully, .. keep it secret. **1838** W. BELL *Dict. Law Scot.*, *Licking of Thumbs*, a symbolical mode of indicating that a bargain has been concluded. **1891** A. J. MUNBY *Vulgar Verses* 101, I lay it's as easy as kiss-my-thumb, For to have my way wi' her.

6. *attrib.* and *Comb.* **a.** Simple *attrib.*, as ***thumb-bone, -breadth, -joint, -knuckle, -unction***; **b.** in names of objects of comparatively diminutive size, as ***thumb-book, -brush, -wren***; **c.** in names of mechanical devices operated by the thumb, or of parts on which the thumb presses in grasping, etc., as ***thumb-catch, -cock, -ferule, -hole, -latch, -lever, -milling, -nut, -reel, -sneck, -switch, -wheel***; **d.** objective, instrumental, etc., as ***thumb-sucking, -twiddling*** (cf. TWIDDLE *v.*[1] 2 c); ***thumb-like, -made, -stained, -worn*** adjs. **e.** Special combs.: **thumb-ball**, the ball of the thumb (BALL *sb.*[1] 15); **thumb bird**, a local name for the Goldcrest; **thumb-bit, thumb-blue,** † **thumb-bolts** *sb. pl.*: see quots.; † **thumb-case**, a thumb-stall; **thumb-cleat** *Naut.*: see quot.; **thumb-finger**, the thumb; **thumb-fingered** *a.*, clumsy, not dexterous (cf. 5 c); **thumb-hand** *dial.*, the right hand; **thumb-index**, a reference-index consisting of grooves cut in the front edges of the leaves, or formerly of projecting tabs, or margins so cut as to show initial letters or titles, so that any division may be turned to by placing the thumb or finger on the proper initial, etc.; **thumb-kissing**, the kissing of the thumb with which the book is held instead of the book itself in taking an oath; **thumb-knot** = *overhand knot*: see OVERHAND *a.* 4; **thumb-lancet**, the usual form of lancet, having a broad two-edged blade; **thumb-licking** (*Sc.*), the licking and joining of thumbs by the parties concerned in token of the completion of a bargain; **thumb-lock**, (*a*) a kind of lock which is opened by pressing with the thumb; (*b*) *pl.* = THUMB-SCREW *sb.* 2; **thumb-loose** [LOOSE *sb.* 1] *Archery*, a method of releasing the bow-string with the thumb: cf. THUMB-RING c; † **thumb-measure**: see quot. and cf. 4; **thumb-mould**, a small mould usually having designs in intaglio, into which the clay is pressed with the thumb in making ornaments for the decoration of ware (*Cent. Dict.*, *Suppl.* 1909); **thumb-pad**, a pad covering the inner metacarpal bone in some batrachians (*Cent. Dict.*, 1891); **thumb paper** *U.S.*, a paper or card inserted in a book at the bottom of a page to protect it from thumb-marks; **thumb piano** *Mus.* = SANSA; **thumb pick** *Mus.*, a kind of plectrum; **thumb-pin** = *thumb-tack*; **thumb-piston** = PISTON *sb.* 2 b; **thumb position**, in violoncello playing, a position in which the thumb serves as a movable 'nut'; **thumb-pot**, (*a*) a flower-pot of the smallest size; (*b*) see quot. 1885; **thumb print**, the impression or mark of the inner surface of the top joint of the thumb, made with ink or otherwise upon a receptive surface; also *fig.*; **thumb-printing**, the use of 'thumbs and fingers' (see FINGER *sb.* 11 b) in the aquatint process; **thumb-read** *v.*, *trans.* to read cursorily; to turn the pages of (a book) with the thumb in glancing through it; **thumb-register** = *thumb-index*; **thumb-rule** = RULE OF THUMB; **thumb-stick**, a tall walking-stick with a forked thumb-rest at the top; **thumb-sucker**, (*a*) a child who habitually sucks his thumb; (*b*) *Journalists' slang* (see quots. 1974, 1980); **thumb-tack**, a tack with a broad head, which may be pushed in with the thumb; *N. Amer.* = *drawing-pin* s.v. DRAWING *vbl. sb.* 6 b; also as *v. trans.*; hence **thumb-tacked** *ppl. a.* See also THUMB-BAND, etc.

1821 *Blackw. Mag.* VIII. 430 Along his *thumb-ball, Will his pen-knife tries. **1885** SWAINSON *Provinc. Names Birds* 25 Goldcrest (*Regulus cristatus*)... Miller's thumb (Roxburgh). *Thumb bird (Hants). **1847–78** HALLIWELL, **Thumb-bit*, a piece of meat eaten on bread, so called from the thumb being placed on it. [Cf. THUMB-PIECE b.] **1858** SIMMONDS *Dict. Trade*, **Thumb-blue*, a name for small knobs of indigo used by washerwomen. **1711** C. LOCKYER *Acc. Trade India* iv. 95, I understand *Congas* [= cangue] to be *Thumbolts. *c* **1375** *Sc. Leg. Saints* xxxvi. (*Baptista*) 882 A-pon þe autere scho saw ly As a *thoume-bane propirly. **1715** M. DAVIES *Athen. Brit.* I. 77 A little *Thumb-Book, or Pamphlet, call'd, 'The Office of the Virgin Mary'. **1846** BROWNING *Let.* 20 July, You can't write 'so many lines a day' any more than you can paint a picture by *thumb-breadths. **1597** A. M. tr. *Guillemeau's Fr. Chirurg.* 39 b/2 As touching the thumbe and the fingers, we must haue a *thumbcase. **1844** STEPHENS *Bk. Farm* I. 139, 2 shutters.. to open on hinges, and fasten inside with a *thumb-catch. **1867** SMYTH *Sailor's Word-bk.*, **Thumb-cleat*, in shape resembling a thumb. **1886** R. C. LESLIE *Sea-painter's Log* vi. 137 Clumsy thumb-cleats, with more clothes-line twining about them. **1826** *Sporting Mag.* XVIII. 326 The cap and the *thumb-ferrel on the four-horse whips. **1855** J. DAVIES *Races of Lanc.* in *Trans. Philol. Soc.* 276 *note*, A word I have occasionally heard in my boyhood, though now obsolete, *thumb-finger. **1906** *Westm. Gaz.* 11 Aug. 16/1 The inner flight feathers grow first, leaving the thumb finger free until the feathers have grown long enough. **1903** *Med. Rec.* 28 Feb. 335 Iridectomy must be skilfully and delicately performed. No *thumb-fingered tyro need attempt it with hope of success. **1750** *Student* I. 332 The third house of your *thumb-hand in Blow-Bladder-Street. **1907** *N. & Q.* 10th Ser. VII. 467/1 This remarkable expression.. heard in the neighbourhood of Sheffield.. 'Ye mun go down there, and keep to t' thomb-hand side'. **1859** GULLICK & TIMBS *Paint.* 199 The '*thumb-hole' is, however, of recent introduction, and replaced projecting handles. **1902** *Daily Chron.* 24 Jan. 5/1, I was worrying about that palette of yours. Couldn't you have the thumb-hole in it padded? **1903** *Periodical* July 16 The *Oxford *Thumb-Index Bible* is the latest novelty. **1853** CARLETON *Traits*, etc. *Irish Peas.* (1860) II. 5 *Thumb-kissing is another feature in Paddy's adroitness. **1795** HUTTON *Math. Dict.* s.v. *Knot*, A **Thumb knot*.. the simplest of all. It is used.. by taylors &c. at the end of their thread. **1869** BLACKMORE *Lorna D.* ii, The Lord be with thee, Jan, and turn thy *thumb-knuckle inwards. **1903** *Med. Rec.* 30 May 853 At a time (1862) when the *thumb-lancet was hardly considered a necessity. **1761** *Essex Inst. Hist. Coll.* (1912) XLVIII. 96 Hinges, *thumb latches, hammers. **1801** NEMNICH *Waaren Lexicon* II. 686/2 *Thumb latches*, Thürklinken mit einem Drücker. **1844** STEPHENS *Bk. Farm* II. 167 The outer-door provided with a good thumb-latch, and lock and key. **1883** [see THUMB-PIECE a]. **1773** ERSKINE *Inst. Law Scot.* III. iii. §5. 447 Decrees are yet extant in our records.. sustaining sales upon summonses of *thumb-licking, upon this medium, That the parties had licked thumbs at finishing the bargain. **1895** S. S. BUCKMAN in *Pop. Sci. Monthly* Jan. 376 The big toe.. reveals its former *thumblike use. **1801** NEMNICH *Waaren Lexicon* II. 686/2 **Thumb locks*, Feder-Thürschlösser die mit einem Schlüssel ohne Bart, aufgedrückt werden. **1882** J. TAYLOR *Sc. Covenanters* 88 They carried with them.. iron fetters, and an instrument of torture called thumb-locks. **1844** STEPHENS *Bk. Farm* III. 979 It should be tied in bundles or sheaves with *thumb-made straw-ropes. **1611** COTGR. s.v. *Süant, A poulce süant*, by ynch, or *thumbe-measure; the breadth of a thumbe giuen betweene euerie yard in measuring. **1867** J. HOGG *Microsc.* I. iii. 204 The teeth answer the triple purposes of *thumb-milling, ratchet-stop, and graduation. **1794** *Thumb-nut [see THUMB-SCREW *sb.* 1]. **1965** LEE & KNOWLES *Animal Hormones* iii. 53 At sexual maturity in male frogs (for example *Rana temporaria*) there is hypertrophy of the muscles of the forearms and thickening of the *thumb-pads. **1843** B. R. HALL *New Purchase* I. xxx. 286 To have used.. any other than the *thumb-paper just named would have been considerably worse than ridiculous. **1888** E. EGGLESTON *Graysons* viii. 79 Fervid little love-notes.. were folded like the 'thumb-papers' that served to protect their books. **1942** F. WARNICK *Dial. Garrett County, Maryland* 15 *Thumb-paper*,.. a small piece of paper used to protect the pages. **1952** R. A. WATERMAN in *Proc. 29th Internat. Congress Americanists 1949* II. 212 Melodic instruments.. are utilized for their percussive value, as in the case of '*thumb pianos', [etc.]. **1974** *Encycl. Brit. Macropædia* I. 250/1 The *mbira* is also known as.. thumb piano, and by other regional names. The common term *sansa* is not correct; it is not found in Africa. **1969** *John Edwards Mem. Foundation Q.* V. 1. 13 Riley used a *thumb pick to achieve the heavy bass runs. **1973** Thumb pick [see PICK *sb.*[1] 5 c]. **1904** HARRISON & H. *Restoration Durh. Cath. Organ*, The *Thumb-Pistons will be of solid ivory. **1889** E. J. PAYNE in Grove *Dict. Mus.* IV. 300/2 (*Violoncello-playing*) At present.. the use of the *thumb positions is more restricted. **1851** *Beck's Florist* Dec. 267 As soon as they are sufficiently large to handle.. pot them singly in small *thumb-pots. **1885** M. COLLINS in *Eng. Illustr. Mag.* 687/2 [Roman pottery] Many are still called 'thumb-pots', the sides being indented with the potter's thumb. **1900** *Literature* 15 Dec. 486/2 The *thumb-print of Kangali Charan.. was compared with the magnified lines of the smudge. Identification was instant. **1906** *Daily Chron.* 2 May 7/5 To-day the photograph of his thumb prints was received from London. They exactly tally with Johnson's thumb-prints made here. **1967** G. STEINER *Lang. & Silence* 66 Rimbaud left his thumb-print on language, on the name and nature of the modern poet. **1979** *Time* 30 July 12 Caddell's thumb-prints also were on the energy speech that Carter delivered to the nation Sunday after returning to Washington. **1869** S. T. DAVENPORT in *Eng. Mech.* 31 Dec. 377/2 This was effected by small inking-rubbers, known as thumbs and fingers, and the printing was called *thumb-printing. **1825** SOUTHEY *Let. to H. Hill* 22 Mar., I had merely *thumb-read his book as a whole. **1844** J. T. HEWLETT *Parsons & W.* xi, A.. trolling-rod, and a large *thumb-reel. **1904** WORDSWORTH *Old Service-Bks.* 277 A kind of book-marker or *thumb-register, for finding the places in a book read in choir. **1906** *Westm. Gaz.* 2 July 2/2 The effect of this missionary work.. is not to be measured by any *thumb-rule. *a* **1825** FORBY *Voc. E. Anglia* s.v. *Snack*, A *thumb-snack, in which the latch is lifted by pressing the thumb on the broad end of a short lever which moves it. **1934** DYLAN THOMAS in *New Verse* XII. 11 The halves that pierce the pin's point in the air, And prick the *thumb-stained heaven through the thimble. **1945** *Sun* (Baltimore) 25 Oct. 4/3 Believing the *thumbstick to be mightier than the sword, the Boy Scouts are going to lend a hand in the formidable task of re-educating German youth. **1974** R. ADAMS *Shardik* xi. 79 Bel-ka-Trazet walked with the help of a long thumb-stick which Kelderek remembered to have seen him trimming the evening before. **1982** *Church Times* 2 Apr. (Advt. Feature) p. iv/4 Whether it is.. a military swagger cane, a stick you have whittled, a Shepherd's crook or a thumb stick from Scouting days. **1891** 'MARK TWAIN' tr. *Hoffman-Donner's Slovenly Peter* (1935, Ltd. Ed.) 25 Story of the *thumb-sucker. **1964** M. ARGYLE *Psychol. & Social Probl.* ix. 121 There is also some evidence that children who have little opportunity for sucking, either at the breast or at a dummy, are more likely to become thumb-suckers. **1974** S. ALSOP *Stay of Execution* I. 103 Walter Lippmann wrote the best straight think-pieces, or thumb-suckers as they are called in the trade, of any journalist of our time. **1980** *N.Y. Times Mag.* 11 May 12/4 Slurs like 'paper pusher' for bureaucrat, or 'thumbsucker' for columnist. **1858** GEO. ELIOT *Scenes Clerical Life* I. 36 Baby is given to the infantine peccadillo of *thumb-sucking. **1897** *Allbutt's Syst. Med.* II. 1039 Finger-nails must be kept short and clean, and thumb-sucking and nail-biting discouraged. **1884** I. M. RITTENHOUSE *Maud* (1939) 278 [He] coolly left me to put the *thumb-tacks in my picture by myself. **1908** *Daily Chron.* 27 Feb. 8/1 Fasten all securely to a flat surface.. with pins or thumb tacks. **1951** R. MAYER *Artist's Handbk. Materials & Techniques* v. 187 A much better way to preserve unstretched pictures.. is to *thumb-tack them face down to sheets of wallboard. **1975** *N.Y. Times* 14 Sept. x. 1/2 Thumbtacked to the bulletin board was a color snapshot. **1966** D. FRANCIS *Flying Finish* ii. 24 Round the walls hung framed charts.., a *thumb-tacked weather report. **1930** *Times* 26 Mar. 14/1 Conversation about the weather and sport.. often degenerates into dreary *thumb-twiddling. **1964** in M. McLuhan *Understanding Media* viii. 78 More aesthetic than thumb-twiddling, less expensive than smoking. **1826** SOUTHEY *Vind. Eccl. Angl.* 497 Among all my books there is no other which bears such marks of *thumb-unction. **1967** *Electronics* 6 Mar. 129/1 High and low limits can be set separately on the comparator by: Dialing *thumbwheel switches on the front panel during routine testing [etc.]. **1976** *Sci. Amer.* Jan. 130/3 There are even correcting thumbwheels for feeding in ambient air conditions in order to get standardized results on the digital display; they affect only the fourth digit and beyond. **1980** *Nature* 1 May p. xxii/2 A continuous rheostat thumbwheel control provides a full range of illumination. **1851** H. MELVILLE *Moby Dick* II. xi. 72 She will.. let her have some papers.. and *thumb-worn files. **1863** *Ecclesiologist* XXIV. 338 The thumb-worn binding.. would be enough to scare a fashionable Englishman. **1908** W. CHURCHILL *Mr. Crewe's Career* xvii, Certain thumb-worn schedules were referred to. **1844** *Zoologist* II. 511 Common wren, '*Thumb-wren', *Troglodytes europœus*.

thumb (θʌm), *v.* [f. THUMB *sb.*]

1. *trans.* To feel with or as with the thumb; to handle.

† *to thumb the belt of*, to be in subjection to. *Sc. Obs.*

1623, 1711 [see THUMBING *vbl. sb.*]. *a* **1758** RAMSAY *Addr. of Thanks* xxvii, They will be forc'd to thumb your belt At last, and a' knock under. **1765** E. THOMPSON *Meretriciad* (ed. 6) 30 None had the art To thumb the guineas. **1894** *Daily News* 17 Jan. 3/1 The ladies and children.. stroke his moist nose..; the men punch his ribs and thumb his brisket. **1898** F. WHITMORE in *Atlantic Monthly* Apr. 501/1 He thumbed an edge-tool like an artist.

2. To play (a wind instrument, an air) with or as with the thumbs; to perform or manipulate clumsily. Also *intr.* with *it*.

1593 G. HARVEY *New Lett. Notable Contents* C ij b, If the Princock must be playing vpon them, that can play vpon his warped sconce, as vpon a tabor, or a fiddle, let himselfe thanke himselfe, if he be kindly thummed. **1641** MILTON *Animadv.* ii. Wks. 1851 III. 209 If men should ever be thumming the drone of one plaine Song, it would bee a dull Opiat to the most wakefull attention. **1675** COTTON *Scoffer Scoft* 93 One winds a Horn.. Another thumbs it on a Tabor. **1755** JOHNSON, *Thumb*, to handle awkwardly.

3. a. To soil or wear (esp. a book) with the thumbs in using or handling; hence, to read much or often.

1644–7 CLEVELAND *Char. Lond. Diurn.* 1 The Emperick-Divines of the Assembly,.. thumbe it accordingly. **1673** [R. LEIGH] *Transp. Reh.* 43 Romances are thumb'd more than St. Thomas. *c* **1720** PRIOR *Female Phaeton* 9 Shall I thumb holy books, confin'd With Abigails, forsaken? **1849** MACAULAY *Hist. Eng.* iii. I. 391 Within a week after it had arrived it had been thumbed by twenty families. **1878** ARBER *Pref. to Caxton's Reynard* p. xii, These early editions were thumbed out of existence.

b. = *thumb-read* vb. s.v. THUMB *sb.* 6 e; freq. const. *through*. Also, to turn (pages) with or as with the thumb in glancing through a book, etc.

1930 D. HAMMETT *Maltese Falcon* xvi. 186 He took a battered memorandum-book from a vest-pocket, licked his thumb, thumbed pages, and held the book out open to Spade. **1934** WEBSTER, *thumb*.. *v.*,.. to run over the pages of, (a book, periodical, newspaper, pamphlet, or the like), as by turning them rapidly with the thumb. **1966** G. GREENE *Comedians* I. v. 140 He sat on the sofa and thumbed through *Paris-Match*. **1966** S. SMITH *Frog Prince* 37, I dare say he had thumbed a book about it. **1976** J. ARCHER *Not Penny More* v. 62 Stephen left his study for the Senior Common Room where he thumbed through the latest copy of *Who's Who* and found the noble lord.

4. a. To press, smooth, clean, spread, or smear with the thumb. **b.** To cover (the touchhole of a cannon) with the thumb; cf. THUMB-STALL d. (*Funk's Stand. Dict.*, 1895.)

1768 ROSS *Helenore* III. 112 Honest Jean.. thumb'd it [a cutty spoon] round and gae't unto the squire. **1856** J. BALLANTINE *Poems* 185 The tither cake, wi' butter thoom'd. **1899** B. CAPES *Lady of Darkness* iv. 220 A seed thumbed in too deep is often choked from sprouting. **1904** *Daily Chron.* 7 July 4/4 To thumb down the tobacco in his pipe.

c. *to thumb one's nose*: see NOSE *sb.* 8 f.

5. To seek or get (a ride or lift) in a passing vehicle by signalling with one's thumb the direction in which one hopes to travel (also *fig.*); to signal to (a driver or vehicle) with the thumb. Also *intr.*, to make *one's way* by thumbing lifts, to hitch-hike. orig. *U.S.*

1932 *Sun* (Baltimore) 4 Oct. 15/8 He was 'thumbed' into picking up two lads. **1933** *Ibid.* 26 Aug. 6/7 New England.. is filled with young men and young women who are continually thumbing their way from one camp to another. **1934** *Amer. Speech* IX. 111/1 Those not fortunate enough to possess a car of their own stand by the side of the road and attempt to thumb a ride. **1939** N. MONSARRAT *This is Schoolroom* xii. 250, I thumbed my way across England.. spending..four-and-sixpence and walking about thirty miles out of the hundred and fifty. **1944** H. NICOLSON *Diary* 1 May (1967) 369 Eventually an American lorry came along. We thumbed them. They stopped, and jumped off and with many jokes mended the tyre for us. **1952** J. CANNAN *Body in Beck* vii. 135 He had been thumbed for a lift by a desperate man. **1958** *Landfall* XII. 32 When a likely lift came by, Pat would..thumb it with a slow impressive sweep of his arm. **1958** *Oxford Mail* 15 Feb. 1/5 Photographed thumbing a lift near Wolverhampton are two..boys..who hitch-hiked to see the Wolves cup-tie with Darlington at Molineux. **1959** *News Chron.* 14 Aug. 7/5 The only Government-sponsored effort has been a plan to 'thumb a lift' in American rockets for British-made instruments. **1960** O. MANNING *Great Fortune* II. 146 He..had been 'thumbing' his way through Galicia when war broke out. **1975** D. NOBBS *Death of R. Perrin* 184 Reggie stood at the entrance to the lay-by and tried to thumb a lift. **1979** *Listener* 1 Mar. 314/2 Like many students..I had thumbed my way through France.

6. *intr.* To gesture with the thumb; *esp.* to signal with the thumb in the hope of getting a lift in a passing vehicle.

1935 G. STEIN *Let.* Dec. in R. L. White *S. Anderson/G. Stein* (1972) 99 Yesterday an American described thumbing on the roads. **1951** E. PAUL *Springtime in Paris* xvi. 309 Gilles thumbed over toward the Abbot. 'His Nibs should have given us the list in advance.' **1955** *Times* 18 Aug. 10/7, I thumbed for four hours without stopping a single vehicle. **1966** R. PRICE *Generous Man* (1967) ii. 142 He turned to Yancey.., thumbing to the house—'Is that all the house old Rooster can afford?' **1976** N. THORNBURG *Cutter & Bone* viii. 191 He was on the freeway entrance ramp, thumbing with his usual touch of calculated restraint.

†**'thumb-band.** *Obs.* A rope of hay or straw made by twisting the material round the thumb.

1639 T. DE GRAY *Compl. Horsem.* 85 Take of the hay.. making a thum-band thereof, rowle it about the leg. **1707** MORTIMER *Husb.* (1721) II. 78 Tie Thumb-bands of Hay or Straw round them. **1725** *Bradley's Fam. Dict.* s.v. *String Halt*, Wisp him with a soft Thumb-Band of Hay, from the Pastern to the Top of the Hoof.

'thumb-bottle. ? *dial.* A small flask, a phial.

1727 W. MATHER *Yng. Man's Comp.* 92 Put a Penny-worth of the Spirit of Vitriol in a Thumb Bottle. **1782** WOLCOTT (P. Pindar) *Odes R. Acad.* iii. 48 A walking thumb-bottle of aqua-fortis. **1830-3** CARLETON *Traits Irish Peas.* (1843) I. 44 If I don't cork you in a thumb-bottle for this, I'm not here.

thumbed (θʌmd), *a.* [f. THUMB *sb.* and *v.* + -ED.]

1. *adj.* Provided with or having thumbs (of a certain kind); chiefly in comb. as *black-thumbed*.

a **1529** SKELTON *E. Rumming* 41 A man would haue pytty To se how she is gumbed, Fyngered and thumbed. **1663** BUTLER *Hud.* I. II. 421 The Knight of Greece..With whom his black-thumb'd Ancestor Was Comerade.

2. *ppl. a.* Of a book or the like: Having the pages soiled or worn by the thumbs of readers; showing signs of much use. Often preceded by an adverb, as *little, much, well-thumbed*.

a **1800** S. PEGGE *Anecd. Eng. Lang.* (1803) 232 Our old thumbed friend, Littleton's dictionary tells us [etc.]. **1837** LOCKHART *Scott* xxv, He produced a well-thumbed copy. **1883** SYMONDS *Shaks. Predec.* vii. (1900) 197 They [plays] perished in thumbed MSS...before arriving at the honours of the press. **1886** STEVENSON *Kidnapped* xxiii, An old, thumbed, greasy pack of cards.

thumber ('θʌmə(r)). *N. Amer. colloq.* [f. THUMB *v.* 5, 6 + -ER[1].] One who 'thumbs' a lift, a hitch-hiker.

1935 *Even. Sun* (Baltimore) 8 Feb. 39/8 Chief of Police.. has turned 'thumbs down' on the 'thumbers'. **1973** *Daily Colonist* (Victoria, B.C.) 29 June 31/5 For the hitch-hiker, Canada's roads hold little but terror and horrors, say many thumbers from Toronto.

'thumb-flint. A simple kind of prehistoric flint implement; = SCRAPER 4 e.

1865 W. GREENWELL in *Archæol. Jrnl.* XXII. 101 Arrow-heads..and the so-called 'thumb-flints'. *Note.* The commonest type of the 'thumb-flint' is the round one..; an oval form is also frequent. **1896** SPURRELL *ibid.* LIII. 46 Thumb-flints, or slicking-knives. **1900** Thumbflint [see SCRAPER 4 e].

thumbful ('θʌmfʊl). [f. THUMB *sb.* + -FUL.] As much as a thumb can hold.

1930 E. POUND *XXX Cantos* xxii. 109 He..pulled out his snuff-box, And sniffed up a thumb-full. **1957** [see RIFFLE *v.* 3 b].

thumbikins, thumbkins ('θʌmɪkɪnz, 'θʌmkɪnz), *sb. pl. Sc.* Also 7 thumbe-, 7-8 thummi-, 7-9 **thumkins**, 8-9 **thumbikens**. [f. THUMB + *-i)kin* dim. suffix: cf. CUTIKIN.] = THUMB-SCREW 2.

1684 *Reg. Privy Council Scotl.* 23 July, Whereas..ther is now a new inventione and Ingyne called the thumbekins ..[the Lords] ordaine that when any persone shall be (by ther order) put to torture that the saids thumbekins or bootes or both be applyed to them. **1684** (Aug. 7) FOUNTAINHALL *Hist. Notices* (Bann. Cl.) 548 Spence..is again tortured, and his thumbs crushed with pilliwincks or thumbikins: It's a new invention..discovered by Generalls Dalzeell and Drummond, they having seene them used in Musco[vy]. **1690** in M. Napier *Visct. Dundee* (1860) II. 119 Nevil Pain..put to the torture of the thumbkins, and of the boot upon one leg before the thumbkins were taken off. **1715** CARSTAIRS *Let.* in Wodrow *Hist. Ch. Scot.* III. viii. (1722) II. 389 The King's Smith was called in [5 Sept. 1684], to bring in a new Instrument to torture by the Thumbkins, that had never been used before... And under this Torture I continued near an Hour and a Half. **1793** *Statist. Acc. Scot.* V. 583 *Greenock*, [He] has in his possession the identical thumbikins, with which the Principal [Carstairs] was severely tortured. **1818** SCOTT *Hrt. Midl.* x, Dread of bloody rope..pain of boots and thumkins.

thumbing ('θʌmɪŋ), *vbl. sb.* [f. THUMB *v.* + -ING[1].] The action of the verb THUMB, in various senses; *spec.* in dicing: see quot. 1711; also, the stretching of a fabric in order to produce a soft pliable finish; in quot. 1847 the keeping of a subordinate under one's thumb.

1623 FLETCHER & ROWLEY *Maid in Mill* v. ii, Miller, this is not for your thumming. **1711** PUCKLE *Club* 22 Gamesters have the top, the peep, eclipse, thumbing. [*Note.* Securing with the little finger a die on the outside of the box, Ditto with the thumb, when the person play'd with, sits on the right hand.] **1845** *Mech. Mag.* XLII. 14 It was a known practice to pull the cloth by hand, three or four persons being stationed on each side, for the purpose of 'thumbing' as it was termed. **1847-78** HALLIWELL, *Thumbing*, a Nottingham phrase, used to describe that species of intimidation practised by masters on their servants when the latter are compelled to vote as their employers please. **1889** JESSOPP *Coming of Friars* iii. 130 The perpetual thumbing and fingering would subject [books] to immense wear and tear.

thumble ('θʌmb(ə)l), *v.*[1] *dial.* [f. THUMB *sb.*: cf. *handle*.] *trans.* To touch with or as with the thumb; to handle clumsily; to fumble.

1623 *Wily Beguiled* C iv b, Stay quotha? To bee yauld and iauld at, and tumbled and thumbled [*ed.* 1606 tumbled and tumbled], and tost and turn'd as I am by an old Hagge. **1829** BROCKETT *N.C. Gloss.*, *Thrumble*, or *Thumble*, to handle awkwardly—to thumb.

†**'thumble,** *v.*[2] [? f. RUMBLE *v.*, influenced by THUNDER.] *intr.* To rumble as thunder.

a **1608** DEE *Relat. Spir.* I. (1659) 59 Now it thumbleth [so MS.] again very terribly, as though a whole town should fall down into a great Valley.

thumble, obs. form of THIMBLE.

thumbless ('θʌmlɪs), *a.* [See -LESS.] Having no thumb or thumbs; destitute or deprived of thumbs; *spec.* applied to the African *Colobus* and to the American Spider-monkeys (*Ateles*) in which the thumb is rudimentary or functionless.

1720 D'URFEY *Pills* VI. 351 And there'll be Bow-legg'd Bobby, And thumbless Kate's geud Man. **1859** OWEN *Classif. Mammalia* 48 The true Baboons..are African, as are the thumbless Monkeys (*Colobus*). **1870** J. ORTON *Andes & Amazons* xxi. (1876) 312 One genus, Ateles, 'the imperfect', is thumbless altogether. **1890** DOYLE *White Company* viii, Leaving the thumbless archer and his brood, the wayfarers struck through the scattered huts of Emery Down. **1906** *Westm. Gaz.* 24 Dec. 4/1 An African thumbless monkey is among the recent additions to the 'Zoo' menagerie.

b. *fig.* Clumsy; incompetent; cf. HANDLESS 2.

1648 HERRICK *Hesper.*, *Leprosie in Houses*, When to a house I come and see..The servants thumblesse.

thumble-toe. *north. dial.* In 5 thomble-, thomelle-, 9 *dial.* thummel-, -il-, etc. [a. ON. *þumal-tá* the great toe, f. *þumall* = OE. *þúma*, THUMB.] The great toe.

c **1440** *Alphabet of Tales* 13, I prikkid hur in hur thomble ta. *Ibid.* 14 Als sone as I prikkid in hur thomble ta sho wappid me in furris. **14..** *MS. Lincoln A. i. 17* lf. 301 (Halliw.) Thane blede one the fute..one the veyne that is bitwix the thomelle taa and the nexte. **1483** *Cath. Angl.* 384/1 A Thomelle too, *allux.* **1904** in *Eng. Dial. Dict.*, cited for Durh., Yorks., Lake Distr., etc.

thumbling ('θʌmlɪŋ). [f. THUMB *sb.* + -LING: cf. Ger. *däumling* in same sense.] A diminutive being; a dwarf, pigmy; a Tom Thumb or Hop-o'-my-thumb.

1867 *Contemp. Rev.* Oct. 50 Thumblings and Fingerlings whom the Pygmies have enslaved. **1879** M. D. CONWAY *Demonol.* I. II. vi. 163 The skill with which some little Jack or Thumbling overcomes his adversary. **1884** MARG. B. PEEKE in *Chicago Advance* 26 June, It was well for the little thumbling that he did not see the smile on his sister's and brother's faces.

'thumb-mark, *sb.* A mark made with the thumb, esp. on the page of a book in turning the leaves; also, such a mark made with the inked thumb for identification of a person. Also *attrib.*

1845 LONGF. *To Old Danish Song-bk.* iii, There are thumb-marks on thy margin, Made by hands that clasped thee rudely. **1866** G. MACDONALD *Ann. Q. Neighb.* xi, Thumb-marks I find very obnoxious. **1889** DOYLE *Micah Clarke* 185 It is impossible to get the thumb-marks of any two men to be alike. **1904** *Westm. Gaz.* 20 June 3/1 Thumb-mark impressions are to be taken—a precaution which in.. England..is only taken in the case of criminals.

b. *transf.* (See quot.)

1877 W. G. STABLES *Pract. Kennel Guide* iii. (ed. 3) 36 [Words used in the Fancy] *Thumb-mark*, an obliquely-shaped black mark crossing the foot of a well-bred Black-and-tan above the toes.

Hence **'thumb-mark** *v.*, *trans.* to make a thumb-mark upon; to mark with the thumb.

1891 J. L. KIPLING *Beast & Man in India* xviii. 400 St. Peter thumb-marked the haddock when he took from its gills the providential tribute money. **1909** KIPLING *Actions & Reactions* 114 Captain Parnall thumbmarks and passes it to Mr. Geary.

'thumb-nail.

1. The nail of the thumb. Often in allusive expressions; with quot. 1604 cf. SUPERNACULUM.

1604 DEKKER *1st Pt. Honest Wh.* I. v, *Cast.* Pledge him... *Flu.* So: I ha done you right on my thumb naile. **1648** HERRICK *Hesper.*, *To his Booke* (1869) 228 Be bold, my booke, nor be abasht, or feare The cutting thumb-naile, or the brow severe. **1727** SOMERVILLE *Sweet-scented Miser* 27 On his thumb-nail it might be wrote 'A penny sav'd's a penny got.' **1841-4** EMERSON *Ess.*, *Nat.* Wks. (Bohn) I. 228 The whole code..may be written on the thumbnail.

2. *transf.* A drawing or sketch of the size of the thumb-nail; hence *fig.* a brief word-picture. Chiefly *attrib.*, as *thumb-nail sketch*.

1852 E. E. HALE in *Sartain's Mag.* Jan. 39 (*heading*) The old and the new, face to face. A thumb-nail sketch. **1900** D. WOODSIDE *Life H. Calderwood* ix. 208 Small ink-sketches of the thumb-nail order. **1901** *Daily Chron.* 3 Jan. 4 (Cass. Suppl.) The truth of Dickens's vignettes and thumb-nails of humanity. **1909** *Westm. Gaz.* 4 Jan. 1/3 There are also 'thumb-nails' of some French figures, and..little pencil portraits of well-known faces. **1911** R. D. SAUNDERS *Col. Todhunter* 125 A full-length 'character-cartoon' of the Colonel surrounded by 'thumb-nail' impressions of his face and bodily pose. **1968** R. GITTINGS *John Keats* xi. 148 He wrote a brilliant thumb-nail sketch of Oxford.

3. *thumb-nail scraper* (Archæol.), a kind of microlith made for scraping.

1937 GARROD & BATE *Stone Age of Mt. Carmel* I. I. iii. 31 *Thumb-nail scraper*..a very well-made minute round scraper. **1977** G. CLARK *World Prehist.* (ed. 3) v. 226 Late Stone Age assemblages including..microliths and thumb-nail scrapers, which in this part of Africa [*sc.* Nigeria] were usually made of quartz.

thumb-piece ('θʌmpiːs). **a.** The part of a handle, etc., intended to receive the thumb; a part of a mechanism operated by pressure of the thumb.

1759 MOUNTAINE in *Phil. Trans.* LI. 290 A piece of the deal moulding..adjoining to the brass thumb-piece,..was splintered off. **1868** *Report Munitions of War* 63 The breech-block turns over and is secured in position, when closed, by a vertical bolt with a projecting thumb-piece at the side. **1883** ROMANES *Ment. Evol. Anim.* xx. 351 *note*, A cat which jumps at a thumb-latch, and while holding on to the curved handle beneath with one foreleg, depresses the thumb-piece with the other. **1894** *Proc. Soc. Antiq.* 22 Nov. 238 The lid [of a ewer]..has a thumb-piece.

b. (See quot.) *dial.*

1882 *W. Worc. Gloss.*, *Thumb-piece*, a piece of bread with cheese or meat, held between the thumb and finger. **1897** *Daily News* 5 Nov. 10/7 Eating his dinner, which consisted of a thumb piece of fat pork and bread.

c. A covering for the thumb, as the leathern pad worn by needle-grinders; the thumb of a glove or mitten (= THUMB *sb.* 2).

1891 in *Cent. Dict.* **1899** *Daily News* 15 July 7/4 The sleeves of this dress cover nearly half the hand, and can be made with thumb-pieces, like mittens.

'thumb-ring. **a.** A ring formerly worn on the thumb.

Often engraved with a seal, or inscribed with a posy.

1596 SHAKS. *1 Hen. IV*, II. iv. 365, I could haue crept into any Aldermans Thumbe-Ring. **1639** GLAPTHORNE *Wit in a Constable* IV. i. (1640) F ij, An Alderman..has no more Wit then the rest oth' bench: what lies in's thumbe-ring. **1714** *Spect.* No. 614 ¶8 The large Thumb Ring,..given her by her Husband, quickly recommends her to some wealthy Neighbour. **1754** J. SHEBBEARE *Matrimony* (1766) I. 4 She was..none of your meagre thin Things, which..might have been drawn through an Alderman's Thumb-Ring. **1877** *Smith & Wace's Dict. Chr. Biog.* I. 728/1 (*Cuthbert*) A plain massive thumb-ring, with a sapphire set in it. **1877** W. JONES *Finger-ring* 28 A thumb-ring of unusual magnitude and of costly material.

attrib. **1642** MILTON *Apol. Smect.* iii, Instead of well siz'd periods, he greets us with a quantity of thumring posies.

b. A ring for the thumb on the guard of a dagger or sword; also each of a pair of rings on the hilt of a dagger by means of which it may be fastened to a staff.

1891 in *Cent. Dict.*

c. *Archery.* (See quot. 1893.)

[**1727-41** CHAMBERS *Cycl.* s.v. *Larynx*, A ring which the Turks put on their thumb for the drawing of their bows.] **1893** *Smithsonian Rep.* 637 *Thumb ring*, a ring worn on the thumb in archery by those peoples that use the Mongolian release; called *sefin* by the Persians. **1907** PAYNE-GALLWEY *Projectile-Throwing Engines* II. 12, I can bend a strong bow much easier and draw it a great deal farther with the Turkish thumb-ring than I can with the ordinary European finger-grip.

'thumb-rope. Now *dial.* A rope made by twisting hay or straw on the thumb; cf. THUMB-BAND.

1601 HOLLAND *Pliny* (1634) I. 501 To lap and wrap them about with wreaths and thumb-ropes of straw. **1601** DEACON & WALKER *Spirits & Divels* 83 Matters that cleaue together like thombe-roppes of sand. **1679** V. ALSOP *Melius Inquir.* II. ii. 212 A Thumb-rope of Sand will make an excellent Cable for Fishers-Folly. **1733** TULL *Horse-Hoeing Husb.* xxi. 300 Winding Thumb-Ropes of Straw about the Iron Circles of the Wheels, and about the Spokes. **1805** FORSYTH *Beauties Scotl.* II. 448 When ready for stacking, they are bound with thumb-ropes, and put on the carts. **1894** *Northumbld. Gloss.*, *Thoom-rope*, a short straw-rope, extemporized by twisting it on the thumb of the right hand whilst the length required is drawn evenly through the left hand.

'thumb-screw, 'thumbscrew, *sb.* [f. THUMB *sb.* + SCREW *sb.*; cf. Ger. *daumschraube*.]

1. A screw with a flattened or winged head, adapted for being turned with the thumb and fingers; a butterfly screw; also a small clamp adjusted by such a screw.

1794 FELTON *Carriages* (1801) *Gloss.*, Thumb Nut or Screw. **1805** DICKSON *Pract. Agric.* I. Pl. xxiv, On the side of the tub is a thumb screw fixed to the lever underneath, which regulates the stones. **1888** *Lockwood's Dict. Mech. Engin.* s.v. *Screw Clamp*, Small screw clamps are sometimes called thumb screws. **1908** *Times* 22 Apr. 5/5 A thumb-screw securing the sashes had been removed.

2. An instrument of torture by which one or both thumbs were compressed; cf. THUMBIKINS; also called 'the screws' (SCREW *sb.*[1] 1 e).

[*a* **1715** BURNET *Own Time* xvi, Little screws of steel were made use of, that screwed the thumbs [etc.: see SCREW *sb.*[1] 1 e].] **1817** SCOTT *Old Mort.* xxxvi, An oaken table..on which lay thumb-screws, and an iron case, called the Scottish boot. **1832** G. DOWNES *Lett. Cont. Countries* I. 200 Such intellects as devised the rack and the thumb-screw. **1855** MACAULAY *Hist. Eng.* xiii. III. 290 The using of racks and thumbscrews for the purpose of forcing prisoners to accuse themselves. **1859** JEPHSON *Brittany* iii. 34 A grim functionary, whose countenance was suggestive of dungeons and thumb-screws.

'thumb-screw, 'thumbscrew, *v.* [f. THUMB *sb.* + SCREW *v.*, or f. prec.; evidenced earlier than the sb.] *trans.* To torture by screwing the thumbs; to torture with or as with thumb-screws. Hence **'thumb-screwing** *vbl. sb.* and *ppl. a.*

1771 E. LONG in Hone *Every-day Bk.* (1827) II. 199 He must..be *thumb-screwed*. **1792** *Gentl. Mag.* LXII. I. 260/2 Think what tortures we endur'd,..Whipp'd, chain'd, thumb-screw'd. **1835** *Tait's Mag.* II. 377 We tax, distrain, screw, thumb-screw, incarcerate. **1882** *Standard* 9 Sept. 5/5 His Highness admits that a case of thumb-screwing has come to his knowledge. **1892** *Pall Mall G.* 22 Dec. 2/2 We have little sympathy with the thriftless borrowers, but less with the thumbscrewing Shylock.

'thumb-stall. **a.** A shoemaker's or sailmaker's thimble (see quot. 1794).

1589 NASHE *Martin's Months Minde* Wks. (Grosart) I. 196 Farewell old shoes, thombe stall, and clouting lether. **1755** JOHNSON, *Thumstall*, a thimble. **1794** *Rigging & Seamanship* I. 90 *Thumb-stall*, a ferrule, made of iron, horn, or leather, with the edges turned up, to receive the thread in sewing. It is worn on the thumb to tighten the stitches. **1877** KNIGHT *Dict. Mech.*, *Thumb-stall*..2, a sailor's thimble used in sail-making.

b. A sheath worn on the thumb to protect it when injured.

1654 GAYTON *Pleas. Notes* III. v. 97 Gloves cut into thumb-stals. **1792** BURNS *Let. to Creech* 16 Apr. (in *W. Brown's Catal.* Aug. (1905) 64), As much mine as the thumb-stall I have just now drawn on my finger, which I unfortunately gashed in mending my pen. **1904** *Eng. Dial. Dict.* s.v. *Thumb* 2, *Thumb-cap*, a thumb-stall or covering for the thumb.

c. *Eccl.* = POUCER: see quots.

1849 ROCK *Ch. of Fathers* II. vi. 167 [The bishop's] thumb-stal was put upon the right hand thumb that had been dipped into the chrism. **1872** SHIPLEY *Gloss. Eccl. Terms*, *Pouser*, a thumbstall of silver or other precious metal, used formerly by bishops for anointing in confirmation.

d. *Mil.* In obsolete artillery: see quot.

1864 in WEBSTER. **1877** KNIGHT *Dict. Mech.*, *Thumb-stall* 1. (*Ordnance*), a stall of buckskin stuffed with hair, which a cannoneer wears on his thumb to cover the vent while the piece is being sponged and loaded.

thumby ('θʌmɪ), *sb. colloq.* Also **thummy, -ie.** [f. THUMB *sb.* + -Y, dim. suffix.] A little thumb; a kind of pet-name for the thumb.

1811 W. TENNANT *Anster Concert* in *Life* (1861) 26 He never fashed his thummie. **1859** LANG *Wand. India* 265 The little finger replied: 'Who told you so, Thummy, Thummy?' **1866** 'R. B. PAUL' *Let.* in *Mem.* xx. (1872) 353 Now thumby is beginning to make a grumble.

thumby ('θʌmɪ), *a. colloq.* [f. THUMB *sb.* + -Y[1].]

1. Soiled by thumb-marks.

1900 *Daily News* 11 Jan. 7/2 The report books look as prosaic as any ordinary account books, only very black and 'thumby'.

2. Clumsy, 'all thumbs'. Cf. THUMB *sb.* 5 c.

1909 R. A. WASON *Happy Hawkins* 103 One day we was kiddin' him about bein' so thumby. **1915** *Pearson's Mag.* XXXIX. 28 You have no idea how thumby your fingers are when fixing a bike under shrapnel fire. **1939** X. HERBERT *Capricornia* ix. 122 The box was set down, the stiff buckles of its mildewed straps tackled by a dozen thumby hands. **1974** P. WRIGHT *Lang. Brit. Industry* vi. 59 Their efficiency is affected when..they are known to be..awkward,.. numb-pawed, or thumby.

†thumerstone ('tu:məstəʊn). *Min. Obs.* [ad. Ger. *thumerstein* (Werner, 1788), f. Thum, in Saxony, where found.] A synonym of AXINITE. So **†thumite** ('tu:maɪt), in same sense.

1796 KIRWAN *Elem. Min.* (ed. 2) I. 273 *Thumerstone*,.. Glass Shorl. [*Ibid.* 274 It is found crystallized in Dauphiné.., and amorphous in Saxony, near Thum, whence Mr. Werner calls it Thumerstein. **1802** [see AXINITE].] **1868** DANA *Min.* 297 Axinite,..Thumerstein... Thumite.

†'thummart. *Sc. Obs.* Also 7 **thulmard,** 9 **thummert, thoumart.** A dialectal alteration of FOUMART, polecat: see TH (6).

1696 A. TELFAIR *True Relat.* 12 (Edinb. ed.) By the way his Dog Catched a Thulmard. **1785** BURNS *Twa Herds* vi, The thummart, wil'-cat, brock and tod, Weel kend his voice. **1850** J. D. BROWN *Ballads* (1856) 98 (E.D.D.) His cleidin was skins o' the thoumart and tod.

transf. **1822** GALT *Sir A. Wylie* x, There never was surely a droller like thummert o' a creature seen.

‖thummim ('θʌmɪm). [a. Heb. *tummīm*, also (after *w^e*, *b^e*, etc.) *thummīm*, pl. of *tōm*, completeness, integrity.] Used in the collocation ***Urim and Thummim***, rarely ***Thummim and Urim***: see URIM.

1539 BIBLE (Great) *Deut.* xxxiii. 8 Vnto Leui he sayde: Thumim & vrim [COVERD. Thy perfectnes and thy lighte] shalbe with the, & with euery one that is godly in the. **1616** BULLOKAR *Eng. Expos.*, *Thummim*, an Hebrew word signifying perfection. *Ibid.*, *Vrim*, an Hebrew word, which the high Priest of the Iewes wore with the word Thummim, in the plaits of the Rationall vpon his brest. **1623** COCKERAM, *Thummim*, perfection.

†'thumomancy. *Obs. rare*[−1]. [ad. Gr. type *θυμομαντεία, f. θυμόμαντις prophesying from one's own soul, f. θυμός soul, spirit: see -MANCY.] Divination by one's own soul: see quot., and cf. PSYCHOMANCY 1.

1651 HOBBES *Leviath.* I. xii. 56 Sometimes in their own hopes and feares, called Thumomancy, or Presage.

thump (θʌmp), *sb.* [Goes with THUMP *v.*]

1. a. 'A hard heavy dead dull blow with something blunt' (J.), as with a club or the fist; a heavy knock; also, the heavy sound of such a blow (not so dull as a *thud*). Also *fig.*

1552 HULOET, Bownce, noyse or thumpe, *bombus, crepitus*. **1563** B. GOOGE *Eglogs* iv. (Arb.) 43 Thou yat throwest the thunder thumps from Heauens hye, to Hell. *a* **1625** FLETCHER *Nice Valour* III. ii, Now your thump, A thing deriv'd first from your hemp-beaters, Takes a man's wind away, most spitefully. **1675** HOBBES *Odyss.* 262 Down with a thump he falls upon his face. **1716** ADDISON *Freeholder* No. 50 ¶4 Their Thumps and Bruises might turn to account,.. if they could beat each other into good Manners. **1784** COWPER *Task* I. 357 Thump after thump resounds the constant flail. **1834** DICKENS *Sk. Boz, Steam Excurs.*, The unfortunate little victim..receiving sundry thumps on the head from both his parents. **1886** A. WINCHELL *Walks Geol. Field* 85 Heavy thumps sometimes heard before and during the action, in geyser-holes.

†b. ***to cry thump***: to make a thumping sound; to thump. *Obs.*

1601 B. JONSON *Poetaster* III. iv, How can I hold my fist from crying thump? **1604** DEKKER *1st Pt. Honest Wh.* I. vii, Did you not heare something crie thump?

c. Repeated, expressing a series of thumps.

1850 BROWNING *Christmas-Eve* iv. 64 The thump-thump and shriek-shriek Of the train. **1885** FARGUS *Slings & Arrows* x. 193 The steady, monotonous thump, thump, thump of the engines. **1899** WERNER *Capt. of Locusts* 69 The thump-thump of the women's pestles pounding the maize in the grain-mortar.

d. *adverbially*: With a thump (also *fig.*).

1704 N. N. tr. *Boccalini's Advts. fr. Parnass.* I. 56 Here Tacitus..bid him leave off his fulsome Preambles, and fall thump to the Business of the Impeachment. **1840** THACKERAY *Catherine* i, Which..made his heart to go thump—thump! against his side.

2. *spec.* **a.** A knocking or pounding of machinery arising from slackness at a joint where there is reciprocal motion. **b.** *pl.* A beating of the chest in the horse due to spasmodic contractions of the diaphragm, analogous to the hiccup in man.

1903 *Rep. U.S. Dept. Agric.* (*On Dis. Horse* 140), Thumps or Spasm of the Diaphragm... Thumps is produced by causes similar to those that produce congestion of the lungs and dilatation or palpitation of the heart.

3. In Yorkshire (esp. Halifax): a local festival; a feast, wake, etc. **Thump Sunday**, the Sunday of the annual fair or festival week.

1884 *Folk-Lore Jrnl.* II. 25 Last Halifax Thump, a teetotaller..was punished, according to custom, by the company laying him face downwards and beating him on the back of the body with a heated fire-shovel. **1916** J. HARTLEY *Seets i' Yorks. & Lancs.* ii. 19 It'll be five year sin come Halifax thump Sunday. **1930** *Brit. Weekly* 4 Sept. 448/4 A correspondent sends us a description of 'Deanhead Thump Sunday', the..annual musical festival. **1976** H. WILSON *Governance of Britain* ii. 40 A prime minister must, and if he is a northerner usually does, understand the complex of Wakes Weeks and Feast Weeks, to say nothing of Longwood Thump.

thump (θʌmp), *v.* Also 6 **thomp,** 6–7 **thumpe.** [Only mod.Eng. (16th c.); of echoic formation. Parallel echoic formations are EFris. *dump* a knock, late Icel. *dumpa* to thump, Sw. dial. *dumpa* to make a noise, *dompa* to thump. The earliest evidence of the word-group in Eng. is in THUMPER 1. The following shows it as a mere imitation of a noise:

c **1550** BALE *K. Johan* (Camden) 53 Sedycyon *extra locum*. Alarum! Alarum! tro ro ro ro ro,..Thomp, thomp, thomp, downe, downe, downe, to go, to go, to go! *K. J.* What a noyse is thys..without the dore?]

1. a. *trans.* To strike or beat heavily, as with the fist, a club, or any blunt instrument, producing a dead, dull, somewhat hard sound; also, without reference to the sound produced, to hammer, pound, knock forcibly.

to thump a cushion, the pulpit, etc.: said of a preacher who uses violent gestures; cf. CUSHION-*thumper*.

c **1537** [implied in THUMPER 1]. **1548** ELYOT s.v. *Incurso*, *Pugnis aliquem incursare*, to renne on one to thumpe and beate hym with his fystes. **1565** COOPER *Thesaurus*, *Pertundo*, to beate with hammers: to thumpe, or knocke. **1582** STANYHURST *Æneis* I. (Arb.) 19 Thee pacient panting shee thumpt and launst wyth a fyrebolt. *a* **1635** CORBET *On Gt. Tom of Christ-Church* 1 Be dumbe ye infant Chimes, thumpe not your mettle. **1673** HICKERINGILL *Greg. F. Greyb.* 218 In thumping the pulpit..has frighted some from their seats. **1716** GAY *Trivia* I. 13 The sturdy Pavior thumps the ground. **1725** B. HIGGONS *Rem. Burnet* II. Hist. Wks. 1736 II. 79 He [Bp. Burnet] would..with greater Pleasure and Vehemence have thump'd a Cushion in that Congregation, we now call a Conventicle. **1746** *Exmoor Scolding* 6 Chell vump tha. **1803** G. COLMAN *John Bull* III. ii. 35 If he don't behave himself, I'll come in and thump him blue. **1807** CRABBE *Par. Reg.* I. 711 There was he pinch'd and pitied, thump'd and fed. **1848** THACKERAY *Vanity Fair* viii. 67 Don't you remember..how she was always thumping Louisa? **1907** *Q. Rev.* Apr. 393 It was left to the Navy League to thump the big drum. **1960** J. RAE *Custard Boys* II. xii. 145 If you interrupt me again, Felix, I'll bloody well thump you. **1978** D. DEVINE *Sunk without Trace* xxi. 194, I saw red. If I didn't get out, I would thump him.

b. With extension: To drive or force (*down*, *forward*, *off*, *out*, etc., or *into* some position or condition) by thumping. Also, with *out*: to produce (a tune, beat, etc.) by thumping.

1588 SHAKS. *Tit. A.* III. ii. 11 When my hart..Beats.., Then thus I thumpe it downe. **1596** SPENSER *F.Q.* VI. ii. 10 He with his speare,..Would thumpe her forward and inforce to goe. *c* **1611** CHAPMAN *Iliad* XVIII. 141 Thrice the feet the hands of Hector seized, And thrice th' Ajaces thumped him off. *a* **1677** BARROW *Serm.* Wks. 1716 II. 80 To think..a slow body may be thumpt and driven into passion..how can we..entertain such suppositions? **1821** CLARE *Vill. Minstr.* I. 4 Born to the flail and plough, To thump the corn out and to till the earth. **1929** T. WOLFE *Look Homeward, Angel* xxiii. 315 She..thumped out popular tunes on a battered piano. **1974** C. RYAN *Bridge Too Far* III. i. 134 The bass drummer..thumped out a symbolic beat in Morse code: three dots and a dash—V for victory.

c. Of the feet, etc.: To beat or strike (the ground, etc.) heavily and noisily; also of a body: to impinge upon with a thump; to strike violently.

1582 STANYHURST *Æneis* I. (Arb.) 21 Downe the pilot tumbleth..headlong. Thrise the grauel thumping. **1596** SPENSER *F.Q.* VI. x. 10 A shrill pipe he playing heard on hight, And many feete fast thumping th' hollow ground. **1902** ELIZ. L. BANKS *Newspaper Girl* 173 His tail would thump the floor most vigorously.

d. With that which beats, strikes, or knocks as object. ***to thump down***, to put or throw down with a thump.

1720 RAMSAY *Wealth* 72 While you may thump your Pows against the Wa'. **1821** CLARE *Vill. Minstr.* (1823) I. 9 And lumping knocks as one would thump a flail. **1852** HAWTHORNE *Blithedale Rom.* xvii, Baggage, which he thumped down upon the floors.

e. To express by thumps.

1928 *Manch. Guardian Weekly* 26 Oct. 335/3 His [*sc.* a dog's] tail..thumped a welcome.

2. *fig.* To 'beat' (in a fight), to drub, lick, thrash severely. *colloq.*

1594 SHAKS. *Rich. III*, V. iii. 334 These bastard Britaines, whom our Fathers Haue in their owne Land beaten, bobb'd, and thump'd. **1797–1802** G. COLMAN *Br. Grins*, etc., *Knt. & Friar* I. i, In our Fifth Harry's reign, when 'twas the fashion To thump the French..to excess. **1827** SCOTT *Jrnl.* 14 Nov., We have thumped the Turks very well.

3. a. *intr.* To strike or beat with force or violence, with an abrupt dull noise; to knock or bump with force. Also ***to thump it***.

1565 COOPER *Thesaurus* s.v. *Insulto*, *Insultare fores calcibus*, to thumpe or beate at the doore with heeles. *a* **1619** FLETCHER, etc. *Knt. Malta* III. i. *song*, Drums beat, Ensigns wave, and Cannons thump it. **1663** BUTLER *Hudibras* I. III. 520 Colon, chusing out a stone, Level'd so right, it thumpt upon His manly Paunch. **1691** E. TAYLOR *Behmen's Theos. Philos.* 340 That which melodiously ringeth in the Light, rumbleth and thumpeth in the dark. **1832** MARRYAT *N. Forster* xiii, I heard the boat thumping under the main channels. **1856** KANE *Arct. Expl.* I. vii. 72 The..floe-ice against which we were alternately sliding and thumping. **1883** *Pall Mall G.* 20 Dec. 3/2 No one thinks a drummer-boy a giant because he thumps away upon a big drum.

b. To walk with heavy sounding steps, to stump noisily; also, of a thing, to move with thumps or noisy jolts.

1604 T. M. *Black Bk.* in *Middleton's Wks.* (Bullen) VIII. 28, I thumped down stairs with my cowheel. **1825** T. HOOK *Sayings* Ser. II. *Passion & Princ.* xv. III. 378 Along..went the waggon, thumping and bumping up this hill and down that. **1894** MRS. DYAN *All in a Man's Keeping* 233 Long ropes..which thumped with wet swishes over the slippery decks. **1899** J. LUMSDEN *Edin. Poems & Songs* 77 He thumpeth down the stony street.

c. Of the heart, etc.: To beat violently or audibly; to throb forcibly.

1784 COWPER *Task* IV. 47 Who patient stands till his feet throb, And his head thumps. **1841** THACKERAY *2nd Fun. Napoleon* iii, Everybody's heart was thumping as hard as possible. **1879** BROWNING *Ned Bratts* 282 Hearts heaved, heads thumped. **1880** —— *Dram. Idyls* Ser. II. *Retio* 180 How my head throbs, how my heart thumps.

4. The verb-stem in combination with a sb.; as **'thump-cushion**, a preacher who thumps the cushion of the pulpit; in quot. *attrib.*

1827 G. DARLEY *Sylvia* 60 Grip him fast by his thump-cushion arm, lest he overdo the action.

† **'thumpatory**, *a.* *nonce-wd.* [f. prec. after words in *-atory*.] Characterized by thumping.

a **1693** *Urquhart's Rabelais* III. xx. 169 These thumpatory warnings.

thumper ('θʌmpə(r)). [f. THUMP *v.* + -ER[1].]

1. a. One who or that which thumps.

In quots. *c* 1537, *a* 1619, app. a cant name for some class of 'rogue', or for some coin. In quot. 1728, applied to the striking apparatus of a clock.

c **1537** *Thersites* in *Four Old Plays* (1848) 81 Tynckers, .. tryfullers, turners, and trumpers, Tempters, traytoures, trauaylers, and thumpers. *a* **1619** FLETCHER *Mad Lover* v. iv, *Chi.* (Takes out his purse, and shakes it.).. Here are thumpers, chequins, golden rogues. **1728** RAMSAY *To Starrat* 18 The thumper that tells hours upon the kirk. **1824** *New Monthly Mag.* XII. 344/2 The thumper on the great drum.

b. *Geol.* A device for creating artificial seismic waves in the earth.

1962 *Times* 18 Apr. 4/7 Another device is a hydroprod, more familiarly known as a 'thumper'... It transmits a powerful sound impulse which penetrates the sub-surface strata of the sea bed, the return echo recording the depths of the different layers of sea bed material. **1977** *Sci. Amer.* July 65/2 (Advt.), Seismic excitation—a shock wave from an explosive charge or a mechanical 'thumper'—is applied to the earth.

2. A thumping or heavy blow.

1682 T. FLATMAN *Heraclitus Ridens* No. 67 (1713) II. 163 I'll give you such a Thumper shall make your Shoulders ake.

3. Anything 'thumping' or strikingly big of its kind, *esp.* a 'thumping' lie; a 'whopper', 'whacker': cf. BOUNCER 3, 4. *colloq.*

1660 TATHAM *Charac. Rump* Dram. Wks. (1878) 287 You may call it the tail of the great dragon, and 'tis a thumper. **1677** W. HUGHES *Man of Sin* III. iii. 97 For Thumpers commend me to Abbot Bar, and St. Brendons Stories. **1711** SWIFT *Jrnl. to Stella* 8 Sept., You are apt to lie in your travels, though not so bad as Stella; she tells thumpers. **1804** J. COLLINS *Scripscrap.* 157 They gives me a Thumper of a Christmas Box. **1863** J. R. GREEN *Lett.* II. (1901) 125 His lies are such thumpers.

thumping ('θʌmpɪŋ), *vbl. sb.* [f. THUMP *v.* + -ING[1].] The action of the verb THUMP in various senses; an instance of this.

1577 NORTHBROOKE *Dicing* (1843) 171 They daunce with ..monstrous thumping of the feete. **1657** THORNLEY tr. *Longus' Daphnis & Chloe* 84 Leaping Dolphins, with the thumping of their tails, loosened the planks. **1722** in Boulton *Amusem. Old London* (1901) I. 29 She may expect a good thumping. **1862** B. TAYLOR *Poet's Jrnl.* II. *Autumnal Dreams*, The drowsy air is startled With the thumping of the flail. **1892** SYMONDS *M. Angelo* (1899) I. v. ii. 187 He was cast forth..with good round kicks and thumpings.

b. *attrib.*, as **thumping-board**, a loaded board placed across the keys of an organ just behind the part used by the fingers, to prevent an undue rising of the key when released by the finger.

1879 *Organ Voicing* i. 6 The *thumping-board* or *damper*, assists to keep the keys level. **1881** W. E. DICKSON *Organ-Build.* viii. 114 A heavy damper or 'thumping-board' should be laid across the key-board.

'thumping, *ppl. a.* [f. THUMP *v.* + -ING[2].]

1. That thumps, in various senses; beating; banging; throbbing.

1581 MULCASTER *Positions* xxvii. (1887) 107 The tumbling Cybistike, the thumping Pugillate, the buffeting Cestus. *a* **1597** PEELE *David & Bethsabe* III. ii, To scape the fury of their thumping beaks. **1859** *Habits Gd. Soc.* vi. 234 The loud, thumping style [of playing the piano] should be avoided. **1898** *Allbutt's Syst. Med.* V. 916 In slim, long-chested youths..a thumping or uncovered heart may well be mistaken for a hypertrophy.

2. *fig.* (*colloq.*) Of striking size, extent, or amount; exceptionally large or heavy; huge, 'whacking', 'whopping': cf. BOUNCING *ppl. a.*

1576 FLEMING *Panopl. Epist.* 402 He vseth great and thumping words. **1671** H. FOULIS *Hist. Rom. Treasons* (1681) 26 The thumping commendations of their Saints. **1719** D'URFEY *Pills* II. 48 Strong Wine, and thumping Glasses. *a* **1814** *He must be Married* III. i. in *New Brit. Theatre* IV. 268 A house-full of great, thumping, rosy-cheeked, boys and girls. **1826** W. E. ANDREWS *Crit. Rev. Fox's Bk. Mart.* II. 270 This is a thumping lie. **1855** THACKERAY *Newcomes* lv, Let us console that martyr..with thumping damages. **1865** SIR S. NORTHCOTE in *Daily News* 29 May 3 Producing sensational effects by the utterance of what I may call good, stout, thumping lies. **1902** C. G. HARPER *Holyhead Road* II. 94 The electors returned both himself and the other Conservative candidate by thumping majorities.

Hence **'thumpingly** *adv.* (*a*) *lit.*; (*b*) *colloq.*, very, exceedingly.

a **1693** *Urquhart's Rabelais* III. ix. 77 If I did not.. thumpingly bethwack her Gillets. **1923** *Chambers's Jrnl.* Apr. 211/1 [He] gripped my hand—Shook it thumpingly. **1948** *Manch. Guardian Weekly* 11 Nov. 3 There was a thumpingly false assumption made about the American farmer. **1977** *Times* 17 Feb. 8/5 A book of thumpingly high entertainment value. **1983** *N. & Q.* Feb. 85/2 Even the thumpingly main statement of the last couplet of Spenser's 'tradefull Merchants' sonnet can be regarded as a mere gesture.

'thump-up. *slang.* [f. THUMP *v.* + UP *adv.*[1]] = PUNCH-UP.

1967 H. W. SUTHERLAND *Magnie* vi. 80 There'd be a killing... But need it get as far as that?.. Just a thump up, maybe. **1978** *Maledicta 1977* I. 130 Teacher: 'What would you have if you had 10 apples, and the boy next to you took 6 apples from you?' Boy: 'A thump-up (fight), Miss.'

thumri ('thuːmriː, θ-). [a. Hindi *ṭhumrī*.] A light classical form of North Indian vocal or instrumental music; a piece in this form. Also *attrib.*, designating this style of music.

1834 N. A. WILLARD *Treat. on Mus. Hindoostan* 89 *Thoomree*. This is an impure dialect of the Vrujbhasha. The measure is lively, and so peculiar, that it is not mistaken by one who has heard a few songs of this class. **1914** A. H. F. STRANGWAYS *Music of Hindostan* vi. 165 'Hādi e illah' is a *Thumri* from Benares. **1964** AHMED ALI *Ocean of Night* II. v. 71 The poets were writing songs, sonnets, free verse, and no one cared for the *ghazal*, *thumri* or *mustezad*. **1972** P. HOLROYDE *Indian Music* iii. 97 Thumri style of singing evolved from the more austere forms of dhrupad and khayal. **1981** LD. HAREWOOD *Tongs & Bones* xvii. 257 The sarangi player..finished with a gentle and rather sentimental thumri.

‖ **Thunbergia** (tuːn'bɛəːrgɪə, θʌn'bɜːdʒɪə). *Bot.* [mod.L. (A. J. Retzius 1776, in *Handl. K. Physiografiska Sällsk. Lund* I. 163), f. the name of C. P. Thunberg, a Swedish botanist and traveller (1743–1822).] A genus of herbaceous (mostly climbing) plants, N.O. *Acanthaceæ*, natives of tropical and sub-tropical parts of Africa and Asia, of which many species are cultivated in greenhouses for the beauty of their various-coloured flowers. Also, a plant of this genus.

1797 H. ANDREWS *Botanist's Repository* I. 123 Twining Thunbergia... The Thunbergia, here figured, is a native of the East Indies. **1842** *Penny Cycl.* XXIV. 411/2 Retzius named a genus of plants in the natural order Acanthaceæ, in honour of him [C. P. Thunberg], *Thunbergia*. **1867** H. KINGSLEY *Silcote of Silcotes* I. xi. 110 Thunbergias, when clumsily gathered, are apt to come up by the root. **1893** MRS. C. PRAED *Outlaw & Lawmaker* II. 69 A trellis of Cape jasmine and thunbergia. **1898** J. D. REES in *19th Cent.* June 1017 The beautiful blue thunbergia. **1935** H. NICOLSON *Let.* 22 Feb. (1966) 198 On the wall..is a vast *Thunbergia* with blue morning-glory flowers. **1977** M. ALLAN *Darwin & his Flowers* xii. 215 The woody shoots of the wisteria move faster than those of the flexible Morning Glory and thunbergia.

thunche, variant of THINK *v.*[1] *Obs.*, to seem.

thunder ('θʌndə(r)), *sb.* Forms: α. 1 **þunor**, **-er**; 2–3 *dative* **þunre**, 3–5 **þonre**; 4 **thonir**, **-yr(e**, **-ure**, **thunure**, **thonner**, **-ere**, **-ir**, 4–5 **thoner**, **-or**, 5 **thonere**, **thonour**, **thouner**, **thownyr**, 6–9 *Sc.* and *north. dial.* **thunner**. β. 3 **ðhunder**, 3–4 **þondre**, 3–5 **þonder**, 3–6 **thundre**, 4 **þundir**, **thundir**, 4–5 **þunder**, **þondir**, **-ur**, 4–6 **thonder**, **thondre**, **thoundre** (6 **-ir**), 5 **þunre**, **thundyr**, **thwndur**, **thondour**, (**dondyr**), 5–6 **thondir**, *Sc.* **thwndyr**, 9 *s.w. dial.* **thinder**, 5– **thunder**. [OE. *þunor*, ME. *þoner*, etc. (later *þonder*, etc. with epenthetic *d*) = OFris. *thuner*, OS. *thuner*, (MDu., Du. *donder*), OHG. *donar* (MHG. *doner*, G. *donner*), ON. *þórr*, (:—**þonr-*: cf. Da. *torden*, Sw. *tordön* 'Thor's din'):—OTeut. **þonar-o*[z] f. Indo-Eur. ablaut series **ten*, *ton*, *tn* to stretch, resound, whence Skr. *tan* to sound, L. *tonāre* to thunder; cf. Skr. *stan* to sound, sigh, thunder, Gr. *στέν-ειν* to groan. (The *-on-* in ME. was the usual way of writing *-un-*, to avoid confusion.)]

1. a. The loud noise accompanying a flash of lightning (apparently following it, being heard after it at an interval depending on distance), due to the sudden violent disturbance of the air by the electric discharge; varying from a sharp report or crash to a prolonged roll or reverberation. Also, the unseen cause of the phenomenon, the meteorological condition or action (scientifically, the electric storm and discharge) from which the loud noise proceeds.

The popular use vaguely includes the phenomenon and its cause.

α. [*c* **725** *Corpus Gloss.* (O.E.T.) 1152 *Jovem*, þuner.] *a* **800** *Riddles* xlvii. 22 (Gr.) Stefne ðunures micles. *c* **950** *Lindisf. Gosp.* John xii. 29 Ðe here forðon ðio stod & ȝeherde cuoedun ðuner þætte auorden. *c* **1000** *Sax. Leechd.* III. 280 Swa hattra sumor, swa mara ðunor & liȝet on ȝeare. *c* **1175** *Lamb. Hom.* 43 Heore eþem scean swa deð þe leit a-monge þunre. *a* **1300** *Cursor M.* 22143 Thoner o-loft fal sal he gar. *c* **1325** *Gloss. W. de Bibbesw.* in Wright *Voc.* 160 *Tonere*, thonner. *a* **1340** HAMPOLE *Psalter* lxxvi[i]. 17 [18] þe voice of þi thunure in whele. *c* **1400** MAUNDEV. (Roxb.) xxxi. 140 We ware..striken doune to þe erthe with grete hidous blastez of wind and of thouner. **1483** *Cath. Angl.* 384/1 A Thonour, *tonitruus*. *Ibid.* 387/2 A Thownyr. **1500–20** DUNBAR *Poems* xxvii. 35 Ane rak of fartis lyk ony thunner. **1816** SCOTT *Old Mort.* xxxvii, Rather than ye suld ride on in the rain and thunner.

β. *c* **1250** Ðhunder [see b]. *c* **1290** *St. Brendan* 473 in *S. Eng. Leg.* I. 232 Gret betynge and noyse i-nouȝ, þondre ase þei it were. *c* **1384** CHAUCER *H. Fame* II. 100 The god of thonder Whiche that men callen Iupiter. *c* **1460** *Brut* 510 A gret tempest of thondre & lightenyng. *c* **1475** *Pict. Voc.* in Wr.-Wülcker 802/1 *Hic tonitrus*, thwndur. **1549** *Compl. Scot.* vi. 59 The thoundir is ane corrupt fume generit on the eird. **1595** SHAKS. *John* v. ii. 173 A drumme.. That shall.. mocke the deepe mouth'd Thunder. **1753** HOGARTH *Anal. Beauty* xii. 97 By the decreasing noise of thunder, we form the idea of its moving further from us. **1818** SCOTT *Br. Lamm.* viii. [ix.], The cloud..began now, by one or two distant peals, to announce the thunders with which it was fraught. **1858** STANLEY *Sinai & Pal.* ii. 124 The thunder, heard, not..in short and broken peals, but in one continuous roll. *Mod.* It is a sultry day; I think there must be thunder about. The farmer's wife says that the thunder turns the milk.

b. Regarded as the destructive agent producing the effects usually attributed to the lightning; (with *a* and *pl.*) a thunderstroke or 'thunderbolt'. Now only *poet.* or *rhet.* (exc. *fig.*).

c **893** K. ÆLFRED *Oros.* IV. ii. §1 þunor toslog heora hiehstan godes hus. *Ibid.* VI. xxix, Hiene ofslog an þunor. *c* **1250** *Gen. & Ex.* 1108 Oc siðen loth wente ut of hine, Brende it ðhunder, sanc it erðe-dine. **1390** GOWER *Conf.* I. 109 Fro the sky A firy thonder sodeinly He sende, and him to pouldre smot. *c* **1400** MAUNDEV. (Roxb.) ii. 7 þer schall na thunder ne na maner of tempest dere him. *c* **1460** *Towneley Myst.* iii. 346 Thise thoners and levyn downe gar fall..Castels and towres. **1593** SHAKS. *Rich. II*, I. iii. 81 Let thy blowes..Fall like amazing thunder on the Caske Of thy amaz'd pernicious enemy. **1686** tr. *Chardin's Trav. Persia* 209 The Thunder had thrown down a good part of it. **1707** *Curios. in Husb. & Gard.* 243 The Thunder fell upon her, and kill'd her outright. **1751** MACSPARRAN *Diary* (1899) 61 The Thunder struck Col. Northrup. **1769** COOK *Voy. round World* II. ii. (1773) 304 To acquaint them that we had weapons which, like thunder, would destroy them in a moment. **1820** SHELLEY *Vis. Sea* 61 Six the thunder has smitten, And they lie black as mummies.

c. (with *a* and *pl.*) A peal of thunder, a thunder-clap. Now only *poet.* or *rhet.*

c **1000** *Sax. Leechd.* III. 280 þa þuneras..on apocalipsin synd gastlice to understandenne. *a* **1300** *Cursor M.* 18124 þar come a mikel steuen, Als it a thoner war of heuen. **1382** WYCLIF *Rev.* x. 3 Whan he hadde cried, seuen thundres spaken her voices. **1601** HOLLAND *Pliny* II. xliii. 21 Thunders are nothing els but the blows and thumps given by the fires beating hard upon the clouds. *c* **1665** BAXTER in *Reliq.* 23 Apr. an. 1661 (1696) 303 As they were returning from Westminster-hall, there was very terrible Thunders, when none expected it. **1700** DRYDEN *Cymon & Iphigenia* 334 The thunders roll, the forky lightning flies. **1842** TENNYSON *Talking Oak* 279 Low thunders bring the mellow rain. **1855** —— *Maud* II. iv. 49 And a sullen thunder is roll'd.

d. (with *a* and *pl.*) A thunderstorm. *Obs.* exc. *dial.*

a **1300** *Cursor M.* 6019 Was a weder ful selcut snell, A thonor [*v.rr.* þondre, thoner, þondur] wit an haile sua kene. *c* **1400** MAUNDEV. (Roxb.) xiv. 65 In somer es þer grete thundres and leightens. *c* **1400** *Destr. Troy* 7619 A thondir with a thicke Rayn thrublit in þe skewes. **1470–85** MALORY *Arthur* VII. xxxi. 263 Thenne felle there a thonder and a rayne as heuen and erthe shold goo to gyder. **1623** BINGHAM *Xenophon* III. i. 42 It seemed to him, that in a thunder the bolt fell vpon his Fathers House. **1665** E. DIGGES in *Phil. Trans.* I. 26 Our Country of Virginia is very much subject to Thunders. **1892** HEWETT *Peas. Sp. Devon* 101, I zim arter thease mizzle us chell 'ave a thinder.

2. *transf.* Any loud deep rumbling or resounding noise. (Also with *a* and *pl.*)

1590 SHAKS. *Mids. N.* IV. i. 123, I was with Hercules and Cadmus once, When..they bayed the Beare With hounds of Sparta... I neuer heard So musicall a discord, such sweet thunder. **1595** —— *John* I. i. 26 The thunder of my Cannon shall be heard. **1611** BIBLE *Job* xxxix. 25 He smelleth the battaile afarre off, the thunder of the captaines, and the shouting. *a* **1674** CLARENDON *Hist. Reb.* XVI. §245 One continued thunder of Cannon. *c* **1800** H. K. WHITE *Poems* (1837) 143 Let the pealing organ play; And, while the harmonious thunders roll [etc.]. **1807–8** SYD. SMITH *Plymley's Lett.* vii. Wks. 1859 II. 162/2 Thunders of applause from the pit and the galleries. **1847** TENNYSON *Princ.* II. 452 The great organ..rolling thro' the court A long melodious thunder. **1887** BOWEN *Virg. Eclogue* v. 83 The thunder of surf on the shore.

3. *fig.* **a.** Threatening, terrifying, or strongly impressive utterance; awful denunciation, menace, censure, or invective, 'fulmination'; vehement or powerful eloquence. (*sing.* and *pl.*)

c **1380** WYCLIF *Wks.* (1880) 288 Drede we nouȝt þis þondir, for it turneþ aȝen & cursiþ þe welle þat it come fro. *c* **1540** NISBET *N.T. in Scot.* Prol. Romans (S.T.S.) III. 332 But the spret mon first cum,..and with the thwndyr of the lawe feare him. **1693** G. STEPNY in *Dryden's Juvenal* VIII. (1697) 197 Who felt the Thunder of the States Decree. **1712** ADDISON *Spect.* No. 407 ¶1 Pouring out the Thunder of his Rhetorick. **1781** GIBBON *Decl. & F.* xxi. (1869) I. 591 He directed the thunders of the church against heresy. **1852** MISS YONGE *Cameos* I. xxvii. 220 The barons..thought little of the thunders of the Pope. **1879** FARRAR *St. Paul* II. viii. (1883) 117 Something..made him [Stephen]..hurl in their faces the gathered thunder of his wrath and scorn.

b. In phrases denoting great force or energy (chiefly in versions or imitations of the Scriptures).

1535 COVERDALE *Job* xxvi. 14 Who can perceaue and vnderstonde y[e] thondre of his power? **1611** BIBLE *Job* xxxix. 19 Hast thou clothed his necke with thunder? **1754** GRAY *Poesy* 106 With necks in thunder cloath'd, and long resounding pace. **1796** ELIZA HAMILTON *Lett. Hindoo Rajah* (1811) I. 83 One of their ships of war, a huge edifice, whose sides were clothed with thunder. **1818, 1887** [see *thunder-maned*, *-shod* below].

c. ***struck with thunder*** = THUNDERSTRUCK 2 a. *rare*$^{-1}$.

1823 SCOTT *Quentin D.* xxiv, 'I am struck with thunder!' said Crèvecœur. 'Liege in insurrection!—..the Bishop murdered!'

d. Fig. phr. *to steal* (someone's) *thunder*: to use the ideas, policies, etc., devised by another person, political party, etc., for one's own advantage or to anticipate their use by the originator.

Derived from the utterance of John Dennis (1657–1734), 'Damn them!..they will not let my play run, but they steal my thunder,' on hearing the stage thunder produced by a method designed for his own play of *Appius & Virginia* being used for a performance of *Macbeth*. (Spence quoted in W. S. Walsh *Lit. Curios.* (1893) 1052; cf. Pope's note on *Dunciad* II. 223.)

1900 E. E. PEAKE *Darlingtons* iii. 23 You must all remember that papa had stolen my thunder. **1911** M. BEERBOHM *Zuleika Dobson* ix. 144 'Happy maid!' he murmured. Zuleika replied that he was stealing her thunder: hadn't she envied the girl at his lodgings? **1931** *Time & Tide* 12 Sept. 1049 Sir Oswald Mosley's exploit was to steal a little of the protectionist thunder temporarily abandoned by the Conservatives. **1937** 'G. ORWELL' *Road to Wigan Pier* xii. 222 It is important..to disregard the jealousy of the modern literary gent who hates science because science has stolen literature's thunder. **1973** A. BROINOWSKI *Take One Ambassador* ii. 19 He would have been watching the returns in the Senate elections I guess. This'll steal a bit of their thunder, that's for sure.

4. *slang* or *colloq.* Used vaguely in exclamations, imprecations, and expletive or intensive phrases.

1709–10 STEELE *Tatler* No. 137 ⁋3 Thunder, Furies, and Damnation! I'll cut your Ears off. **1826** *Massachusetts Spy* 23 Aug. (Th.), The bull roared like thunder! I split like lightning! **1834** C. A. DAVIS *Lett. J. Downing* xxxiii. 274 He turned..and giv me a look as black as thunder. **1841** H. GREELEY in R. W. Griswold *Passages from Corr.* (1898) 94 Why in thunder did you go off on Saturday without seeing me? **1842** S. LOVER *Handy Andy* xxv, 'Thunder and turf!' said the drunken giant. **1852** MRS. STOWE *Uncle Tom's Cabin* I. vii. 95 Go to thunder, gal! **1854** M. J. HOLMES *Tempest & Sunshine* xv. 204 Don't none on you tread on my corns for thunder's sake. **1867** H. J. DANIEL *Muse in Motley* 25 He'll screech like thoonder, iss he will. **1876** E. W. HEAP *Diary* 24 Nov. in *Publ. Amer. Dial. Soc.* (1969) LII. 55 Every paper around is giving the road Thunder. **1891** C. ROBERTS *Adrift Amer.* 66 Why in thunder, if you were hungry, did you not come and tell me? **1894** A. ROBERTSON *Nuggets*, etc. 79 Where in thunder did he get the money? **1916** G. B. SHAW *Pygmalion* v. 188 Of course they do. Then what in thunder are we quarrelling about? **1920** E. O'NEILL *Beyond Horizon* I. ii. 48 You kin go to thunder, Jim Mayo! **1927** —— *Marco Millions* II. i. 102 War is a waste of money which eats into the profits of life like thunder! **1940** W. FAULKNER *Hamlet* I. iii. 77 What in thunder are you fellows up to over at Varner's?

5. *attrib.* and *Comb.* **a.** *attrib.* Of, as of, pertaining to, or connected with thunder, as ***thunder-burst, -colour, -crackle, -crash, -fire, -gloom, -place, -psalm, -quake, -rain, -roll, -scar, -sky, -sound, -tent, -throne, -volley, -weather***; violent, destructive, or (esp.) loud as thunder, as ***thunder-blow, -bullet, -curse, -music, -shout, -voice, -yell.*** **b.** objective, etc., as ***thunder-thrower; thunder-breathing, -forging, -guiding, -ruling, -throning, -throwing, -wielding*** adjs.; ***thunder-delighting*** (delighting in thunder), ***-fearless, -free, -proof, -rejoicing*** adjs.; ***thunder-like*** adj. and adv. **c.** instrumental, as ***thunder-armed, -baffled, -charged, -cloven, -fraught, -girt, -heavy, -hid, -laden, -riven, -scarred, -scathed, -shod, -smitten, -splintered, -split, -splitten, -stormy, -teeming, -thwarted, -tipped*** adjs. **d.** parasynthetic and similative, as ***thunder-browed, -coloured, -footed, -maned, -tongued*** adjs.; ***thunder-purple, -red*** adjs.

1620 MIDDLETON & ROWLEY *World Tost at Tennis* 221 Imperial-crown'd, and *thunder-armèd Jove. **1819** SHELLEY *Prometh. Unb.* III. ii. 12 An eagle..his *thunder-baffled wings Entangled in the whirlwind. **1878** B. TAYLOR *Deukalion* I. iii. 28 We saw the *thunder-blows Given and taken. **1826** E. IRVING *Babylon* II. 380 Our *thunder-breathing ships. **1913** J. MASEFIELD *Daffodil Fields* 44 Full of wrath and *thunder-browed. **1605** *Tryall Chev.* I. ii. in Bullen *O. Pl.* (1884) III. 276 Lov'dst thou a towne, Ide teach thee how to woo her With words of *thunder-bullets wrapt in fire. **1882** *Imperial Dict.*, *Thunder-burst. *a* **1910** 'MARK TWAIN' *Autobiogr.* (1924) II. 176, I can remember those awful thunder-bursts and the white glare of the lightning yet. **1939** JOYCE *Finnegans Wake* 362 Thunderburst, ravishment, dissolution and providentiality. **1844** LEVER *Tom Burke* II. 162 A mass of heavy..clouds, dark and *thunder-charged. **1851** H. MELVILLE *Moby Dick* I. xxvii. 197 The barest..most *thunder-cloven old oak. **1873** G. M. HOPKINS *Jrnls. & Papers* (1959) 232 The others [*sc.* pigeons] are dull *thundercolour or black-grape-colour. **1907** R. BROOKE *Let.* Sept. (1968) 106 We have been sitting at an evil café sipping *thunder-coloured coffee from glasses. **1941** L. MACNEICE *Plant & Phantom* 20 *Thunder-crackle and the bounce of hail. **1826** K. DIGBY *Broadst. Hon.* (1846) II. *Tancredus* 5 The *thunder-crash broke over our heads. **1650** WELDON *Crt. Jas. I* (1817) 31 This dreadful *thunder-curse or imprecation. **1839** BAILEY *Festus* xix. (1852) 305 As an angel when He hears the thunder-curse of demon foe. **1848** BUCKLEY *Iliad* 15 *Thunder-delighting Jove. **1608** BEAUM. & FL. *Four Plays in One* Induct., Low at your sacred feet our poor muse lays Her, and her *thunder-fearless verdant bayes. **1855** BAILEY *Spir. Leg.* in *Mystic*, etc. 115 Rooted out..with threefold *thunder-fires. **1839** —— *Festus* xx. (1852) 343 The *thunder-footed coursers of the sun. **1779** R. POTTER tr. *Æschylus* (ed. 2) I. 106 The *thunder-forging Cyclopes. **1810** S. ROGERS *To old Oak* iv, Many a navy *thunder-fraught. **1841** BROWNING *Pippa Passes* II. 59 A Greek, in Athens,..Feasting, bay-filleted and *thunder-free. **1853** —— *Johannes Agric.* 14 Ere stars were *thundergirt. **1848** LYTTON *Harold* VIII. iv, Some *thunder-gloom of thine own destiny. **1868** ALEX. SMITH *Last Leaves* 154 He could watch the purple thunder-gloom gathering on the distant hills. **1874** GEO. ELIOT *Coll. Breakf. P.* 314 Rule Of *thunder-guiding powers. **1922** BLUNDEN *Bonadventure* xii. 68 After the storm, the air was *thunder-heavy all that day. *c* **1586** C'TESS PEMBROKE *Ps.* (1823) LXXXI. iii, *Thunder-hid I answer gave. **1865** tr. *Strauss's New Life Jesus* I. I. xliii. 373 The *thunder-laden Revelation. **1607** SHAKS. *Cor.* I. iv. 59 With thy grim lookes, and The *Thunder-like percussion of thy sounds. **1826** MRS. SHELLEY *Last Man* II. 73 A crash was heard. Thunderlike it reverberated through the sky. **1846** BROWNING *Let.* 7 Sept., How hot and thunder-like this oppressive air! **1818** MILMAN *Samor* 50 The *thunder-maned steed. **1850** TENNYSON *In Mem.* LXXXVII. ii, I..heard..*thunder-music, rolling, shake The prophets blazon'd on the panes. **1599** B. JONSON *Ev. Man out of Hum.* I. iii, Vnlesse his house and skin were *thunder-proofe. **1733** TULL *Horse-Hoeing Husb.* xiii. 149 The Giants found that even Mountains were not Thunder-Proof. **1822** SHELLEY *Chas. I*, iv. 58 Through palaces and temples thunderproof. **1821** —— *Epipsych.* 465 The wingèd storms, chaunting their *thunder-psalm To other lands. **1879** G. M. HOPKINS *Poems* (1967) 80 The *thunder-purple seabeach plumèd purple-of-thunder. **1940** J. BETJEMAN *Coll. Poems* (1958) 58 Not Satan's *thunder-quake Can cause the mighty walls of Heaven to shake. **1826** MRS. HEMANS *Forest Sanctuary* I. xiv, Sounds of thickening steps, like *thunder-rain That plashes on the roof. **1926** D. H. LAWRENCE *David* xi. 78 Till they drop in drops of blood, like thunder-rain, and the land is red. **1949** BLUNDEN *After Bombing* 15 And foam, pearl-pink and *thunder-red. **1848** BUCKLEY *Iliad* 45 In honour of *thunder-rejoicing Jove. **1831** CARLYLE *Sart. Res.* II. viii, The fire-baptised soul, long so scathed and *thunder-riven. **1844** MRS. BROWNING *Rhapsody Life's Progr.* v, Let the cloud meet the cloud in a grand *thunder-roll! **1749** G. WEST *Hymn of Cleanthes* 49 O great father, *thunder-ruling god! **1710** PHILIPS *Pastorals* 2 Yonder naked tree Which bears the *thunder-scar. **1842** SIR A. DE VERE *Song of Faith* 198 Cliffs..Wave-worn and *thunder-scarred. **1826** J. G. WHITTIER *Writings* (1888) IV. App. 303 Where the *thunder-scath'd peaks of Helvetia are frowning. **1846** PROWETT *Prom. Bound* 18 His brawny force All thunder-scathed and cindered. **1887** G. MEREDITH *Ballads & P.* 78 O for the time when *thunder-shod He champed the grain of the wrath of God. **1863** TYNDALL *Heat* vi. §210 The Earth..rang with the *thunder-shout of the liberated prisoner. **1818** SCOTT *Br. Lamm.* ix. [x.], The heavy and gloomy appearance of the *thunder-sky. **1825** J. NEAL *Bro. Jon.* III. 395 The..bare, *thunder-smitten tree. **1886** W. B. YEATS *Mosada* 7 The faint far *thunder-sound. **1810** SCOTT *Lady of L.* I. xi, A rocky pyramid, Shooting abruptly from the dell Its *thunder-splinter'd pinnacle. **1825** J. WILSON *Poems* II. 39 Like a *thunder-split oak-tree. **1818** SCOTT *Hrt. Midl.* xlv, The shattered and *thunder-splitten peaks of Arran. **1761** GLOVER *Medea* III. vi. 51 No *thunder-teeming cloud. **1818** KEATS *Endym.* III. 27 Ethereal things, that..Can..poise about in cloudy *thunder-tents. **1876** G. M. HOPKINS *Wreck of Deutschland* xxxiv, in *Poems* (1967) 62 Mid-numberèd he [*sc.* Christ] in three of the *thunder-throne! *a* **1918** W. OWEN *Poems* (1963) 135 That columnar, *thunder-throning cloud. **1614** SYLVESTER *Bethulia's Rescue* I. 315 Vassals of the *Thunder-Thrower. **1605** —— *Du Bartas* II. iii. IV. *Captaines* 920 God's *Thunder-throwing hand. **1855** BAILEY *Spir. Leg.* in *Mystic*, etc. 127 Black Babel's *thunder-thwarted pile. **1822** T. MITCHELL *Com. Aristoph.* II. 209 Speed With your tongues *thunder-tipt and tell Cleon our need. **1843** CARLYLE *Past & Pr.* I. v, It is Fact, speaking..in miraculous *thunder-voice. *a* **1847** ELIZA COOK *Song Seaweed* iii, The *thunder-volley shakes. **13..** *K. Alis.* 3729 (Bodl. MS.) Hij holdeþ hem alle togidre So flok of dere in *þonder wedre. **1900** SUTCLIFFE *Shameless Wayne* xxiv. 301 This thunner-weather that's coming up. **1816** WORDSW. *Feelings of French Royalist*, The *thunder-wielding hands Of Justice. **1887** BOWEN *Virg. Æneid* I. 298 Still yelling her *thunder-yells to the blast.

6. Special Combs.: **thunder-axe**, a popular name in Cornwall for a celt (cf. THUNDERBOLT 3 b); **thunder-ball**, (*a*) the electric phenomenon called a fire-ball or globe-lightning; (*b*) *poet.* a thunderbolt; (*c*) the common red poppy (*Papaver Rhœas*) (*dial.*); **thunder-beat** *v.*, *trans.* 'to beat with thundering strokes' (Davies); so **thunder-beaten** *pa. pple.*; **thunder-beating** *vbl. sb.*, beating down by thunder-storms; **thunder-bird**, (*a*) a species of Australian shrike or thickhead (*Pachycephala gutturalis*); (*b*) a mythical bird thought by some primitive tribes to cause thunder; **thunderboat** *U.S.*, an unlimited hydroplane; †**thunder bounce** (*humorously bombastic*), a loud sudden noise like thunder; **thunder-bowl**, a metal bowl used in a theatre to imitate thunder; **thunder-box** *slang*, a portable commode; by extension, any lavatory; **thunderbug** *dial.*, (*a*) *U.S.*, a horse-fly; (*b*) a midge; **thunder-carriage**, a name for the chariot of the god Thor in early Scandinavian art; †**thunder-clover** [OE. *þunor-clafre*], a plant, of doubtful identity; †**thunder-dart**, a thunderbolt (in art); so †'**thunder-,darter**, the wielder of thunderbolts, '**thunder-,darting** *ppl. a.*; **thunder-dint** (*arch.*), a thunder-stroke; **thunder-dirt**, name for a gelatinous fungus, *Ileodictyon cibarium*, eaten by the natives of New Zealand; **thunder-drop**, one of the large scattered drops of rain which fall at the beginning of a thunder-shower; **thunder-drum**, (*a*) a drum used in a theatre to imitate thunder; (*b*) a fabulous drum represented as the source of thunder; **thunder egg** *N. Amer.* and *Austral.*, a geode, esp. of chalcedony; **thunder-fish**, (*a*) a siluroid fish of African rivers, *Malapterurus electricus*, capable of inflicting electric shocks; (*b*) a European cyprinoid fish, *Misgurnus fossilis*, which burrows in mud, and comes to the surface before bad weather; also called *weather-fish*; **thunder-fit** (*nonce-wd.*), a shock or sound like thunder; **thunder-flash**: in military use, a harmless, very noisy, form of explosive; a firework imitating this; †**thunder-flone** *Obs.* [*flone*, FLANE, arrow], a thunderbolt or thunderstroke; lightning; **thunder-flower**, a local name for three different plants: (*a*) the common stitchwort, *Stellaria Holostea*; (*b*) the corn poppy, *Papaver Rhœas*; (*c*) the white campion, *Lychnis vespertina*; **thunder-fly**, a name for the insects of the genus *Thrips*; **thunder-god**, the god of thunder; a deity supposed to rule or control the thunder, as Jove in the Roman, or Thor in the Norse mythology; **thunder-hammer**, a popular name for a celt or other prehistoric implement (cf. *thunder-axe*); **thunder-head**, (*a*) a rounded mass of cumulus cloud seen near the horizon projecting above the general body of cloud, and portending a thunder-storm; hence **thunder-headed** *a.*, having, or of the nature of, a thunder-head; (*b*) *nonce-use*, a large head, as a whale's head; **thunder-house**, a small model of a house with electric conductors through which a discharge may be passed to illustrate the destructive effects of a thunderstroke; **thunder-master**, the master or lord of thunder, i.e. Jove; **thunder-mug** *slang* = CHAMBER-POT; †**thunder-pad** (*dial.*): see quot.; **thunder-peal**, a peal or resounding clap of thunder; so **thunder-pealed** *pa. pple.*, uttered loudly as by a thunder-peal; **thunder-pick**, a local name for a belemnite (cf. THUNDERBOLT 3 a); **thunder-plant**, a name for the house-leek, *Sempervivum tectorum*; **thunder-plump**, chiefly *Sc.*, a heavy and sudden thunder-shower [cf. PLUMP *sb.*[3] 3]; **thunder-pump** = next, (*a*); **thunder-pumper**, (*a*) the American bittern, also called *pump-thunder*; (*b*) the American fish *Haplodinotus grunniens*, also called *fresh-water drum*, *croaker*, or *sheepshead*: in both cases from the sounds which they emit; †**thunder-rod**, a lightning-rod or lightning-conductor (see LIGHTNING *sb.* 3 e); **thunder run** *Theatr.*, two wooden troughs down which iron balls were rolled to imitate thunder; **thunder-sheet** *Theatr.*, a piece of sheet metal shaken to imitate thunder; †**thunder-shot** *sb. Obs.*, thunderbolts collectively; lightning; †**thunder-shot** *pa. pple. Obs.*, struck by 'thunder' or lightning; **thunder-shower**, a shower of rain accompanied by thunder and lightning; now chiefly *U.S.*; **thunder-slain** *pa. pple.* (*obs.* or *dial.*), struck by 'thunder' or lightning; **thunder-smite** *v.*, *trans.* to smite as with thunder, to discomfit utterly; †**thunder-smith** *Obs.*, one who forges thunderbolts: applied to Vulcan, also *fig.*; **thunder-snake**, a name for snakes of the genus *Ophibolus* (also ***thunder-and-lightning snake***), and for the common little worm-snake, *Carphiophis amœna*, of the U.S.; perh. from their being forced out of their holes by a thunder-shower; **thunder stick**, a name said to have been given to a rifle or cannon by peoples who did not possess firearms; †**thunder-thump** *sb. Obs.*, ? a thunderbolt; †**thunder-thump** *v. Obs.*, *trans.* to thump or beat with thundering strokes; †**thunder-thumping** *ppl. a. Obs.*, (*a*) striking with thunder (*humorously bombastic*); (*b*) sounding like thunder when beaten, as a drum; also *fig.* of language, 'full of sound and fury'; **thunder-trunk** *Theatr.*, a trunk in which iron balls were rolled to imitate thunder; **thunder-tube** = FULGURITE 1, *lightning-tube* (LIGHTNING *sb.* 3 e); **thunder-worm**, 'an amphisbænoid lizard of Florida, *Rhineura floridana*: so called as forced out of its burrows by a thunder-shower' (*Cent. Dict.* 1891). See also THUNDER AND LIGHTNING, THUNDER-BLAST, etc.

1602 CAREW *Cornwall* 82 There are also taken vp in such works certaine little tooles heads of Brasse, which some terme *Thunder-axes. **1865** TYLOR *Early Hist. Man.* viii. 223 The country folk..still hold that the 'thunder-axes' they find, once fell from the sky. **1686** GOAD *Celest. Bodies* II. xiv. 351 The *Thunderball..entred the Church. **1819** SHELLEY *Prometh. Unb.* IV. 355 Caves cloven by the thunder-ball. **1889** W. B. YEATS *Wanderings of Oisin* II. 30 Trembling, on the flags we fall, Fearful of the thunder-ball. **1942** L. BENNETT *Jamaica Dial. Verses* 41 Wen..Him tun roun..Him se de sinting two yeye dem A roll like tunder-ball... It was a rollin' kealf. **1584** HUDSON *Du Bartas' Judith* v. 397 So he them *thunderbet wherso he went. **1669**

Worlidge *Syst. Agric.* (1681) 297 Shores..*Thunder-beaten with the Floods. **1560** Pilkington *Expos. Aggeus* (1562) 125 Corn..is subject to many daungers as ..*thunder-beating, layde with a raine. *a* **1827** Caley in *Trans. Linn. Soc.* XV. 239 This species is called *Thunder-bird by the colonists... The natives tell me, that, when it begins to thunder, this bird is very noisy. **1871** Tylor *Prim. Cult.* I. ix. 328 Among Caribs, Brazilians,..Basutos, we find legends of a flapping or flashing Thunder-bird. **1875** F. Parkman in *N. Amer. Rev.* CXX. 40 The thunder-bird is offended,..thunder-storms are occasioned by his anger. **1967** *Compton Yearbk.* 153/2 Through the previous 20 years, only three '*thunderboat' drivers had died in races. **1976** *Popular Mechanics* June 61/1 Officially, they are.. hydroplane racing boats... To their hundreds of thousands of fans, they are unlimited hydros, thunderboats, gold cuppers, or just unlimiteds—the fastest racing machines afloat. **1628** Ford *Lover's Mel.* I. i, When blustering Boreas tosseth up the deep, And thumps a *thunder bounce! **1939** Auden & Isherwood *Journey to War* vii. 182 We should wash the dishes and clean the *thunder-boxes. **1952** E. Waugh *Men at Arms* II. ii. 178 'If you *must* know, it's my thunderbox.'.. He..dragged out the treasure, a brass-bound, oak cube... On the inside of the lid was a plaque bearing the embossed title *Connolly's Chemical Closet.* **1955** N. Fitzgerald *House is Falling* xi. 188 When the plumber called for instructions, Hapleigh chose the ground floor for the new thunder-box. **1980** *Daily Tel.* 18 Oct. 18 Life in India was..coping with the indignities of the 'thunder box' (a portable earth commode) and searching sponges for stealthy scorpions. **1837** J. L. Williams *Territory of Florida* 71 Horse Fly.—..Of these there are five kinds.—1st. the large black, called *thunder bug, an inch long. **1875** W. D. Parish *Dict. Sussex Dial.* 66 Those thunder-bugs did kiddle [*sc.* tickle] me so. **1974** P. Haines *Tea at Gunter's* xx. 214 Outside the air was still heavy; there were thunderbugs everywhere... I felt them settle on my skin, my hair. **1882** Worsaae *Industr. Arts Denmark* 168 Another type of coarser work..represents Thor..on his *thunder-carriage. *c* **1000** *Sax. Leechd.* I. 374 ȝenim..*ðunorclafran blostman [etc.]. *c* **1265** *Voc. Names Plants* in Wr.-Wülcker 558/2 *Consolida media*, þundreclouere. **1569** Spenser *Vis. Bellay* iv. in *Theatre Worldlings*, *Thunder dartes for Jove. **1591** Sylvester *Du Bartas* I. i. 272 Th' immortall, mighty *Thunder-darter. **1606** Shaks. *Tr. & Cr.* II. iii. 11. **1601** B. Jonson *Poetaster* v. iii, You shall sweare By *thunder-darting Ioue, the King of gods. *c* **1374** Chaucer *Troylus* v. 1505 How cappaneus the proude With *thonder dynt was slayn. *c* **1440** *Jacob's Well* 100 He was smyten to deth, wyth leuenyng & wyth thunder-dynt. **1808** Scott *Marm.* I. xxiii, The Mount, where Israel heard the law, 'Mid thunder-dint, and flashing levin. **1883** R. Turner in *Gd. Words* Sept. 590/1 The gelatinous [fungus] which the New Zealand natives know as '*thunder-dirt'. **1832** Tennyson *Dream Fair Wom.* 122 As *thunder-drops fall on a sleeping sea. **1807–8** W. Irving *Salmag.* (1824) 270 The great *thunder-drum has been new braced. **1876** Blackie *Songs Relig. & Life* 175 When Jove beats loud his thunder-drum. **1967** *Stage* 2 Mar. 4/2 (Advt.), Thunder drums, bells, chimes, gongs and effects of every description. **1951** W. F. Heald *Scenic Guide to Oregon* 25 Agate- and opal-filled nodules called '*Thunder Eggs' can be found near Madras. **1962** E. Lucia *Klondike Kate* ix. 187 She never returned empty-handed, hauling back..petrified woods, agates.. thundereggs, [etc.]. **1973** *Sunday Mail Mag.* (Brisbane) 25 Feb. 14/5 The individual bays of the caravan park are marked off by 'thunder eggs' (round stones a foot and more in diameter, many of which contain fossilised fish). **1977** *Trailer Life* July 16/3 'Thunder eggs', the agate-colored nodules familiar to many rockhounds, are a variety of spherulite. **1882** Ogilvie (Annandale), **Thunder-fish*, a species of fish..found in the Nile, which, like the torpedo, can give an electric shock... The *Malapterurus electricus* of naturalists. **1886** *Nature* 25 Mar. 497/2 Additions to the Zool. Soc. Gardens..include..a Thunder Fish (*Misgurnus fossilis*) from Austria. **1798** Coleridge *Anc. Mar.* I. xvii, The ice did split with a *thunder-fit. **1943** C. C. Knights *What H.G. needs to know about Explosives* 10 The only 'fireworks' issued to the typical H.G. unit are crackers and *thunder-flashes used to give 'an air of verisimilitude to an otherwise bald and unconvincing' exercise. **1959** G. Adamson *Let.* 19 Mar. in J. Adamson *Born Free* (1960) 139, I went to visit Elsa... I let off three thunder flashes..and.. she suddenly appeared. **1977** 'E. Crispin' *Glimpses of Moon* xi. 210 And we did ought to have..used firecrackers and thunderflashes and horns and whistles. *c* **1380** Wyclif *Serm.* Sel. Wks. I. 186 Crist seiþ..þat he saiȝ Saþanas fallinge fro hevene, as þe *þunder floon falliþ fro þe cloude. *c* **1460** *Towneley Myst.* xii. 324 So bright as it shone, I wold haue trowed, veraly, it had bene thoner flone. **1853** G. Johnston *Bot. E. Bord.* 30 About Wooler it [the corn-poppy] was wont to be called *Thunder-flower or Lightnings, and children were afraid to pluck the flower, for if..the petals fell off..the gatherer became more liable to be struck with lightning. **1886** Britten & Holland *Eng. Plant-n.*, Thunder-flower. (1) *Stellaria Holostea*... (2) *Papaver Rhœas.—E.* Bord. Bot. E. Bord... (3) *Lychnis vespertina.—W. Cumb.* **1854** A. Adams et al. *Man. Nat. Hist.* 213 The tiny *Thunder-Flies which we often find during the summer in countless multitudes. **1840** Carlyle *Heroes* i. (1872) 33 Thor the *Thundergod changed into Jack the Giant-killer. **1907** *Q. Rev.* July 193 Kari, the thunder-god, who kills the wicked by lightning. **1851** H. Melville *Moby Dick* II. lxxiii. 59 Throw all these *thunder-heads overboard, and then you will float light and right. **1861** L. L. Noble *Icebergs* 138 An iceberg rises..after the figure of a thunderhead. **1879** J. Burroughs *Locusts & W. Honey* 94 A growing storm or thunder-head in the horizon. **1773** Henley in *Phil. Trans.* LXIV. 135 The apparatus known, to electricians, by the name of the *thunder-house. **1887** Gumming *Electricity treated Exper.* 147 An instructive experiment is that known as the Thunder House. **1611** Shaks. *Cymb.* v. iv. 30 No more thou *Thunder-Master shew thy spight on Mortall Flies. **1890** Barrère & Leland *Dict. Slang* II. 347/2 **Thunder-mug* (American low), a chamber utensil. **1942** D. Gilbert *Lost Chords* 6 His room furnishings were meager—a rag carpet,..a bowl and pitcher on a washstand whose closet concealed a chamber, or 'thunder mug'. **1966** 'L. Lane' *ABZ of Scouse* II. 108 *Thundermug*, a chamber-pot. **1700** *Phil. Trans.* XXII. 453 These animals [tadpoles] are known by the vulgar sort of people by the name of *Thunder-pads. **1804** J. Grahame *Sabbath* (1808) 15 *Thunder-peals compelled the men of blood To couch within their dens. **1860** Tyndall *Glac.* I. xi. 86 The breaking up of the weather was announced by a thunder-peal. **1878** Browning *La Saisiaz* 150 Truth is truth in each degree—*Thunder-pealed by God to Nature, whispered by my soul to me. **1801** *Med. Jrnl.* XXI. 85 A stone of the calcareous species,..called by the common people *thunder-pick. **1866** *Treas. Bot.* 1148 *Thunder plant, *Sempervivum tectorum.* **1821** Galt *Annals Parish* i. 22 It came on such a *thunder-plump, that there was not a single soul stayed in the kirk-yard to hear him. **1883** Mrs. Bishop in *Leisure Hour* 20/2 A heavy shower, like a 'thunder-plump', takes up a part of the afternoon. **1877** *Scribner's Monthly* July 285/2 The natives call these bitterns by the very appropriate if not euphonious name of '*thunder-pumper'. **1888** Goode *Amer. Fishes* 142 The name..'Thunder-pumper', also used for the bittern,..is heard along the Mississippi River. **1891** E. Roper *By Track & Trail* xxi. 312 The gurgle and the wheeze and the final explosion of a 'thunder-pumper' [bittern]. **1784** G. Adams *Ess. Electricity* ix. 154 When lightning strikes a tree..or a *thunder-rod, it is not because these objects are high..but because they communicate with..the surface of the ground. **1824** *Mechanic's Mag.* No. 57. 10 A good kitchen fire has more efficacy in preventing a house from being struck than a whole magazine of thunder-rods. **1944** *Archit. Rev.* XCV. 135/2 Archaic devices like the '*thunder run', the 'sloat' system of raising scenery, the 'drum and shaft' method of hanging it, still survive at Bristol. **1976** *Early Music* Oct. 401/1 The thunder simulated at the beginning and end of the Cave scene must be..baroque-artificial—for preference made by cannon-balls in a thunder run. **1913** 'V. D. Browne' *Secrets Scene Painting & Stage Effects* 66 Hung from flies. A *thunder Sheet. **1939** Joyce *Finnegans Wake* 503 Raindrum, windmachine, snowbox. But thundersheet? **1967** *Oxf. Compan. Theatre* (ed. 3) 947/2 The noise of thunder is usually produced off-stage by the shaking of a suspended iron sheet known as the Thunder Sheet. **1605** Sylvester *Du Bartas* II. iii. I. *Vocation* 1304 Heav'n flings down nought but flashing *Thundershot. **1626** T. H[awkins] *Caussin's Holy Crt.* 130 Some haue beene ..*thunder-shot in a bath. *a* **1699** Stillingfl. (J.), The conceit is long in delivering, and at last it comes like a *Thunder-shower, full of sulphur and darkness. **1766** Wesley *Jrnl.* 13 July, We were met..by a furious thunder-shower. **1856** E. B. Browning *Aurora Leigh* IV. 174 Softly, as the last repenting drops Of a thunder-shower. **1947** S. Bellow *Victim* i. 5 A thundershower began when he approached the outside door. **1980** *News & Observer* (Raleigh, N. Carolina) 28 Oct. 2/3 Clouds will prevail across much of North Carolina today, with some showers or thundershowers possible through Wednesday. *c* **1440** *York Myst.* xi. 320 So are they threst and *thondour slayne. **1732** P. Walker *Cargill* in *Biog. Presbyt.* (1827) II. 24 Frighted as if they were blasted or thunder-slain. **1875** Browning *Aristoph. Apol.* 1968 Hellas *thundersmote The Persian. **1592** G. Harvey *Four Lett.* iii. 37 That terrible *Thundersmith of termes. **1593** —— *Pierce's Super.* 190 Vulcan..the..thundersmith of..Iupiter. **1800** Lamb *Let. to Manning* 16 Oct., Whip-snakes, *thunder-snakes, pig-nose-snakes. **1863** T. W. Higginson *Army Life* (1870) 140 A thunder-snake, eight feet long. **1918** E. R. Burroughs *Tarzan & Jewels of Opar* (1919) xvii. 157 The ape folk fear the *thunder-sticks of the Tarmangani. **1947** I. L. Idriess *Isles of Despair* xxxiv. 229 A puff of smoke belched from the brig... They had expected resistance, but had hoped the vessel was too small to carry the 'big thunder sticks'. **1965** *Canad. Geogr. Jrnl.* Apr. 115/1 The white man came to shatter the silence of the wilderness with his thunder stick. **1563** B. Googe *Eglogs* iv. (Arb.) 43 O thou yat throwest the *thunder thumps From Heauens hye, to Hell. **1637** Bastwick *Litany* I. 11, I will soe *thunderthump Your Pautry Politans. *a* **1586** Sidney *Arcadia* (1598) 571 Now the *thunderthumping Ioue trans-fund his dotes into your excellent formositie. **1623** Lisle *Ælfric on O. & N. Test.* Ded. xii, The shriking trump, and thunder-thumping drum. **1679** V. Alsop *Mel. Inquirend.* II. iii. 250 They cannot cloath their thoughts in thunder-thumping Phraseology. **1767** D. Garrick *Peep Behind Curtain* I. 22 Ladies, you can't possibly have any thunder and lightning this morning; one of the planks of the *thunder-trunk started the other night. **1830** G. Colman *Random Rec.* I. vii. 229 For then did my Evil Genius enthrone himself upon a thunder-trunk, with a roll of play-bills in his hand.

thunder ('θʌndə(r)), *v.* Forms: see the sb.; also 3 **þondri**, 4 **thonyre**; 5 *pa. t.* **thunret**. [OE. *þunrian*, in 13th c. *þondren*, f. *þunor*, THUNDER *sb.*; cf. Du. *donderen*, LG. *dönnern*, OHG. *donarôn*, MHG. *donren*, MG. *dunren*, Ger. *donnern*; Norw. dial. *tora*; Sw. *dundra*, Da. *tordne*, *dundre* (from LG.).]

1. *intr.* **a.** Impersonally: ***it thunders***, thunder sounds, there is thunder.

c **888** K. Ælfred *Boeth.* xxxix. §3 Hit hwilum þunrað, hwilum na ne onginð. *c* **1000** *Ags. Gosp.* John xii. 29 Seo menio..þæt ȝehyrde sædon þæt hyt þunrode. *c* **1290** *S. Eng. Leg.* I. 198/37 þat weder..bi-gan to chaungie..hit bi-gan to þondri and hauli. *a* **1375** *Joseph Arim.* 235 Hit þester bi-gon and þonderde swiþe. *c* **1400** *Destr. Troy* 3691 Thunret full throly; thrappit the windes. **1526** Tindale *John* xii. 29 Then sayde the people that stode by and herde, it thoundreth. **1616** Surfl. & Markham *Country Farme* 25 If in Summer it lighten when it thundreth not. **1725** Watts *Logic* III. ii. §4 Thunder seldom comes without Lightning; but it thundered Yesterday; therefore probably it lightened also. **1890** Doyle *White Company* xv, I can well remember that in Navarre one day it thundered on the left out of a cloudless sky.

b. With subject (the or a deity, heaven, the clouds, the sky, etc.): To cause or give forth thunder; to sound with thunder.

a **1000** *Ags. Ps.* (Th.) xxvii[i]. 3 He is mæȝen-þrymmes God, and he þunrað ofer maneȝum wæterum. *a* **1300** *E.E. Psalter* xvi[i]. 14 [13] And laverd thonered fra heuen. *a* **1340** Hampole *Psalter, Cant.* 502 In heuyns he sall thonyre. **1535** Coverdale *Ps.* lxxvi[i]. 17 Yᵉ cloudes thondered, and thy arowes wente abrode. **1582** Stanyhurst *Æneis* I. (Arb.) 20 Thee skyes doo thunder. **1607** Shaks. *Cor.* III. i. 257 He would not flatter..Ioue, for 's power to Thunder. **1810** Southey *Thalaba* VII. xxii, Then darkness cover'd all, Earth shook, Heaven thunder'd.

c. *trans.* (with various objects): To deal *out* or inflict by thunder; to strike *down* by thunder; to utter in thunder. *arch. rare.*

1579 Gosson *Sch. Abuse* (Arb.) 47 Beeing the Sonnes of Iupiter, they..thunder out plagues to the proude in heart. **1608** Sylvester *Du Bartas* II. iv. IV. *Schisme* 1193 The Heav'nly Powrs, Who thunder-down the high-aspiring Towrs. *a* **1625** Jas. I *Ps. xxix.* in Farr *S.P. Jas. I* (1848) 4 God doth thunder his uoyce.

2. *transf.* **a.** *intr.* To make a loud resounding noise like thunder; to sound very loudly; to roar. Sometimes connoting violent movement: To rush or fall with great noise and commotion.

c **1374** Chaucer *Boeth.* II. met. iv. 31 (Camb. MS.) Al thowgh the wynde trowblynge the see thondre with ouer-throwynges. **1568** Grafton *Chron.* II. 1334 The great artillary began to thunder from either side. **1610** Holland *Camden's Brit.* (1637) 705 The Danes like a mighty storme thundring from out of the North-East. **1718** Pope *Iliad* II. 1017 His fiery coursers thunder o'er the plains. **1749** Fielding *Tom Jones* XIII. iv, A footman knocked, or rather thundered at the door. **1845** J. Coulter *Adv. Pacific* x. 124 A vast body of water passed down over a precipice about a hundred feet high, and thundered into the sea. **1855** Tennyson *Light Brigade* iii, Cannon in front of them Volley'd and thunder'd. **1860** Tyndall *Glac.* I. xxiv. 175 Avalanches thundered incessantly from the Aiguille Verte. **1934** J. B. Priestley *Eng. Journey* i. 4 The children of these fist-shakers now go thundering by in their own huge coaches and loll in velvet as they go. **1946** *R.A.F. Jrnl.* May 169 Lancasters..thundered through the night to pinpoint their objectives. **1951** 'J. Wyndham' *Day of Triffids* i. 9 The westbound buses thundered along trying to beat the lights. **1960** C. Day Lewis *Buried Day* ii. 38 We thundered down the steep hill into the centre of the town, the squawking hens bouncing up and down on the flat cart, straw and feathers flying.

b. *trans.* (with various objects): To deal or inflict, drive or impel, sound or give forth, strike, attack, or bombard, put *down* or overwhelm, etc. with a loud noise or other action like thunder.

1590 Spenser *F.Q.* I. vi. 43 They gan..To thunder blowes, and fiersly to assaile Each other. *Ibid.* III. x. 33 Forth the Boaster..begonne His stolen steed to thunder furiously. **1601** B. Jonson *Poetaster* IV. v, Thou anger'st vs,..we will thunder thee in peeces. **1638** Sir T. Herbert *Trav.* (ed. 2) 108 The English merchants ships thundred out his health by 200 great shot. **1687** Rycaut *Hist. Turks* II. 322 The Town would be thundred with greater violence. **1759** W. Wilkie *Epigon.* VI. 173 Learn to dread My vengeance thund'red on your wretched head. **1839** Bailey *Festus* xix. (1852) 304 Like to a foaming force, Which thunders down the echo it creates. **1894** Hall Caine *Manxman* IV. xii, He pounded it [a drum], boomed it, thundered it.

3. *fig.* **a.** *intr.* To speak in the way of vehement threatening or reproof; to utter terrible menace or denunciation; to 'fulminate'; to inveigh powerfully *against*; sometimes, to speak bombastically, or with powerful eloquence. Also simply, to speak in a very loud tone, shout loudly, vociferate.

a **1340** Hampole *Psalter* xvii. 15 Oure lord thonord, manaunsand pyne of hell til synful men. **1549** Coverdale, etc. *Erasm. Par. Tim.* 13 Thunder not at him with cruell wordes. **1575** Gascoigne *Making of Verse* in *Steele Gl.*, etc. (Arb.) 31 It is not inough..to thunder in Rym, Ram, Ruff, by letter (quoth my master Chaucer). **1617** Moryson *Itin.* I. 142 The Hoste so thundred among us like the bragging souldier. **1697** Dryden *Æneid* VI. 823 The queen of Furies ..thund'ring in their ears. **1722** De Foe *Plague* (1754) 33 The Ministers..thundered against these, and other wicked Practices. **1863** W. Phillips *Speeches* i. 9 James Otis thundered in this hall.

b. *trans.* To utter or publish in the way of terrible threatening, denunciation, or invective; also simply, to utter loudly, shout out, roar.

c **1380** Wyclif *Wks.* (1880) 287 Cursyngis purchased of þe pope and oþere felle sensuris þondured ouere til Englond. **1548** Udall, etc. *Erasm. Par. Matt.* xii. 74 Do not thunder sore threatenings. *c* **1590** Marlowe *Faust.* vi. 20 Fearful echoes thunder in mine ears, 'Faustus, thou art damned!' **1592** Greene *Groat's W. Wit* (1617) 27 The twelue labours of Hercules haue I terribly thundered on the Stage. **1604** Rowlands *Looke to it* 43 Thunder out Oathes, such as in Hell are bred. **1681** T. Flatman *Heraclitus Ridens* No. 31 (1713) I. 200 Adieu, ye Whigs, Poor Protestant Pigs, The Tories now will thunder us. *a* **1715** Burnet *Own Time* (1766) I. 274 Censures would have been thundered at Rome against all that should take any such test. **1839** Thackeray *Fatal Boots* Mar., He thundered out so much of his abuse of me,..that the boys roared with laughter. **1887** Bowen *Virg. Æneid* I. 747 Tyrians thunder applause.

c. To hurl or launch vehement threats or invectives against; to denounce violently; also, to drive or put *down* by denunciation. Now *rare* or *Obs.*

1677 W. Hughes *Man of Sin* II. vi. 103 S. Becket.. thunders from off the Earth, and down as low as Hell, vast numbers of Clerks, Bishops, and Nobles. **1694** Crowne *Married Beau* v. 62 Men thunder one another. *a* **1720** Sewel *Hist. Quakers* (1795) I. IV. 331 If he had..thundered down deceit.

'thunder and 'lightning.

1. For the literal use see THUNDER *sb.* 1.

2. *fig.* Denunciation, invective: cf. THUNDER *sb.* 3, *v.* 3.

1638 Chillingw. *Relig. Prot.* I. Ep. Ded. 4 They speak nothing but thunder and lightning to us. **1883** J. Parker *Tyne Ch.* 295 They assail with thunder and lightning the credulity..of official guides.

3. *transf.* †**a.** Applied to a cloth, app. of glaring colours, worn in 18th c., and perhaps later. **b.** *attrib.* (19th c.) Applied to articles of apparel of a 'loud' or 'flashy' style, or combining two strongly contrasted colours.

(Cf. **1815** NEMNICH *Britische Waaren Encycl.* s.v. *Thunder and Lightning* ..ein Borat oder wollenes Zeug von grellem Ansehen. **1891** FLÜGEL *Eng. Germ. Dict.*, *Thunder and Lightning*, eine Art Borat oder wollenes Zeug aus Schwarz und Gelb gemischt [*i.e.* mixed of black and yellow] (plattdeutsch *Klütjenstoff* oder *Wederschall* [*Widerschein*] Nemn.)) **1766** GOLDSM. *Vic. W.* xii, He had on a coat made of that cloth they call thunder and lightning. **1837** DICKENS *Pickw.* xxxii, He wore a black velvet waistcoat with thunder-and-lightning buttons. **1839** THACKERAY *Fatal Boots* Mar., I recollect my costume very well: a thunder-and-lightning coat, a white waistcoat.., a pair of knee-breeches. **1857** HUGHES *Tom Brown* II. v, A tall fellow, in thunder-and-lightning waistcoat. **1868** YATES *Rock Ahead* I. i, Gorgeous in..thunder-and-lightning neckties.

4. *slang* and *dial.* (See quots.)

1802 *Sporting Mag.* XX. 224 Thunder and lightning (i.e. gin and bitters). **1880** MISS BRADDON in *World* 3 Mar. 13 Treacle and clotted cream, alias thunder and lightning. **1904** *Eng. Dial. Dict.* s.v. *Thunder*, *Thunder-and-lightning*, (*a*) brandy-sauce when ignited; (*b*) bread spread over with cream and treacle.

5. ***thunder-and-lightning snake***: see *thunder-snake* s.v. THUNDER *sb.* 6.

6. *Angling.* A variety of artificial fly.

1910 *Encycl. Brit.* II. 26/1 In most fly-books great variety of patterns will be discoverable, while certain old standard favourites such as the Jock Scott, Durham Ranger, Silver Doctor, and Thunder and Lightning will be prominent. **1972** *Country Life* 23 Mar. 697/3 Three large salmon were clearly visible... I changed to a tiny low water Thunder and Lightning.

7. *attrib.* Melodramatic, startling, violent.

1892 'MARK TWAIN' *Amer. Claimant* ix. 71 Take What's-her-name, that plays those sensational thunder-and-lightning parts. **1981** J. WAINWRIGHT *All on Summer's Day* 12 Some thunder-and-lightning speed merchant on the opposing side bowled a yorker and chipped a bone in the batsman's ankle.

thunderation (θʌndəˈreɪʃən). *slang* (orig. and chiefly *U.S.*) [f. THUNDER *sb.* + -ATION.] Used as a vague expletive or intensive: cf. THUNDER *sb.* 4.

1836 *Crockett's Yaller Flower Almanac* 21, I don't know as I can say he was so all darned thunderation fat. **1887** *Century Mag.* Nov. 44/2 Everybody wants to know who in thunderation Rache will marry. **1901** *Munsey's Mag.* XXIV. 792/2 'I like you all to thunderation..', he said earnestly, dropping all reserve, 'but [etc.]'. **1939** JOYCE *Finnegans Wake* 245 Bing. Bong. Bangbong. Thunderation! **1949** *Sat. Even. Post* 9 July 86/2 Why in thunderation does he have to play such a hay-in-the-hair?

ˈthunder-ˌbearer. The bearer of thunder, or of thunderbolts, i.e. Jupiter. So **ˈthunder-ˌbearing** *a.*, that bears or carries thunder, laden with thunder; also *fig.*, bearing cannon.

1605 SHAKS. *Lear* II. iv. 230, I do not bid the Thunder-bearer shoote, Nor tell tales of thee to high-iudging Ioue. **1661** ROSS *Silius Italicus* XVII. 68 Thunder-bearing Birds, descending from The Gods Abodes. **1731** C. JOHNSON *Medæa* III. i, O Thunder-bearing Jove, most ancient Cause. **1754** M. MORGAN *Philoclea* II. iii. (Jod.), And thou, great thunder-bearer Jove, look down. **1823** BYRON *Island* II. x, The thunder-bearing strangers came, In vast canoes, begirt with bolts of flame.

ˈthunder-blast, *sb.* Chiefly *poet.* **a.** A peal or clap of thunder. **b.** A stroke of 'thunder'. Also *fig.*

13.. *Cursor M.* 18075 (Cott.) Þar come a steuen als thoner blast. *c* **1440** *Bone Flor.* 1643 Hys doghtur schulde be strekyn downe Wyth a thonder blaste. **1558** PHAER *Æneid* I. C j b, My son, that of the thunderblastes of hye Joue setst but light. **1839** BAILEY *Festus* xxiii. (1854) 414 Be still, ye thunderblasts and hills of fire! **1884** TENNYSON *Becket* III. iii, The Pope's last letters..threaten The immediate thunder-blast of interdict.

So **ˈthunder-ˌblasted** *a.*, blasted with 'thunder', struck by lightning.

1614 JACKSON *Creed* III. xvi. §5 God will not haue true faith thunderblasted in the tender blade. **1818** SCOTT *Br. Lamm.* xi, Our thunder-blasted dinner. *a* **1849** POE *To One in Paradise* 19 The thunder-blasted tree.

thunderbolt (ˈθʌndəbəʊlt), *sb.* Forms: see THUNDER *sb.* and BOLT *sb.*[1]; (9 *dial.* **dunderbolt**).

1. a. A supposed bolt or dart formerly (and still vulgarly) believed to be the destructive agent in a lightning-flash when it 'strikes' anything; a flash of lightning conceived as an intensely hot solid body moving rapidly through the air and impinging upon something: in mythology an attribute of Jove, Thor, or other deity. Cf. BOLT *sb.*[1] 2.

In later use often a vague rhetorical or poetic expression for a destructive lightning-flash or thunderstroke.

c **1440** *Alphabet of Tales* 49 Þis womman was burnyd to dede with a thondre-bolte. **1535** [see BOLT *sb.*[1] 2]. **1560** DAUS tr. *Sleidane's Comm.* 462 In the beginning of..Ianuary.. were horrible tempestes, thondering, and lightening, and thonderboltes. **1632** LITHGOW *Trav.* II. 69 Men should dread the thunder-bolt, when they see the lightning. **1710** W. KING *Heathen Gods & Heroes* x. (1722) 33 All the rest [of the Giants]..fell by the Thunderbolts of Jupiter. **1890** W. E. NORRIS *Misadventure* xvii, The intelligence..had fallen upon him like a thunderbolt from a clear sky.

b. An imaginary or conventional representation of the above as an emblem of a deity, a heraldic bearing, etc.

1727-41 CHAMBERS *Cycl.* s.v., On medals, the thunderbolt is sometimes found to accompany the emperors heads; as that of Augustus. **1823** P. NICHOLSON *Pract. Build.* 489 The head of Medusa, or the Furies, thunderbolts, and other symbols of horror. **1894** *Parker's Gloss. Her.* s.v., Azure, a sun between three thunderbolts, winged and shafted or.

2. *fig.* Something very destructive, terrible, or startling; *esp.* an awful denunciation, censure, or threat proceeding from a high authority; some sudden or unexpected, and hence startling event or piece of news, usually untoward.

1559 *Primer* in *Priv. Prayers* (1851) 91 To the thunderbolts of thy word put violence. **1591** SPENSER *Ruins of Rome* 150 To dart abroad the thunder bolts of warre. **1633** T. STAFFORD *Pac. Hib.* I. xv. (1821) 168 Terrified with the Priests Thunderbolts of Excommunication. **1787** MME. D'ARBLAY *Diary* 30 Jan., This information was a thunderbolt to her. **1860** READE *Cloister & H.* xxxviii, Awaking from the stupor into which this thunderbolt of tyranny had thrown him.

b. Applied to a person noted for violent or destructive action; one who acts with furious and resistless energy.

1593 HARVEY *Pierce's Super.* Wks. (Grosart) II. 48 Oratours..infinitely ouermatched by this hideous thunderbolt in humanity. **1599** HAYWARD *1st Pt. Hen. IV* 2 Prince Edward the thunderbolt of warre in his time. **1708** MRS. CENTLIVRE *Busie Body* III. iii, I have done you a piece of Service; I told the old Thunderbolt, that the Gentleman that was gone in, was [etc.]. **1742** R. BLAIR *Grave* 123 Where are the mighty thunderbolts of war? The Roman Cæsars? **1847** EMERSON *Repr. Men, Napoleon* Wks. (Bohn) I. 372 A thunderbolt in the attack, he was found invulnerable in his entrenchments.

c. In *Sport*, a fast hard-struck shot or stroke.

1959 *Times* 29 May 4/7 [Lawn Tennis] Maloney, with his 'thunderbolts' made no mistake in the next for the match. **1977** *Times* 7 Feb. 7/2 Heighway, at full steam, lashed a thunderbolt past Latchford from the edge of the box.

3. Locally applied to various stones, fossils, or mineral concretions, formerly or vulgarly supposed to be thunderbolts (sense 1): **a.** a belemnite or other fossil cephalopod; **b.** a flint celt or similar prehistoric implement; **c.** a mass or nodule of iron pyrites occurring in chalk.

1618 LATHAM *2nd Bk. Falconry* (1633) 160 Take a thunder-bolt, the which is found most commonly in the fields, in some channell or watercourse,..put it into a hot fire and burne it well. **1634-5** BRERETON *Trav.* (Chetham Soc.) 41 The dart of a thunderbolt about the length and thickness of your little finger. **1712** STEELE *Spect.* No. 431 ¶3 Thunder-bolts, a certain long, round bluish Stone, which I found among the Gravel in our Garden. **1814** SCOTT *Diary* 8 Aug., in *Lockhart*, The most superb collection of the stone axes..called celts. The Zetlanders call them thunderbolts, and keep them in their houses as a receipt against thunder. **1826** POLWHELE *Trad. & Recoll.* ix. II. 607 For 'the reumatis'..I knew an old woman who used to boil a celt (vulgarly a dunderbolt or thunderbolt) for some hours, and then dispense her water to the diseased. **1862** *Athenæum* 30 Aug. 280 Go..into any of the more productive chalk-pits.., and the workmen will offer you fragmentary 'thunderbolts' (belemnites) and nautili.

d. Erroneously or by confusion applied to a meteoric stone or meteorite.

1802 [see THUNDER-STONE 2]. **1830** HERSCHEL *Stud. Nat. Phil.* 120 These circumstances..long caused them to be confounded with an effect of lightning, and called thunderbolts. **1884** A. LANG *Custom & Myth* i. 10 Village wisdom determines that the wedge-shaped piece of metal is a 'thunderbolt'. **1949** 'J. NELSON' *Backwoods Teacher* vi. 57 We spoke of lightning and 'thunderbolts'. Of these latter, Fritz Baily said his uncle used to 'gather them up—and we still get lots kickin' 'round the barn.'.. He promised to bring me one. (Next morning he did—a meteorite the size of his fist.)

4. Applied (chiefly locally) to various plants: **a.** the corn poppy (= *thunder-flower* (*b*), THUNDER *sb.* 6); **b.** the bladder campion; **c.** the white campion; **d.** a species of iris, *Iris Xiphium*.

1847-78 HALLIWELL, *Thunder-bolt.* (1) The corn poppy. *West.* **1886** BRITTEN & HOLLAND *Eng. Plant-n.*, Thunder Bolts. (1) *Lychnis vespertina.* Rutl. (2) *Papaver Rhœas*... (3) *Silene inflata.* Kent.., where the children snap the calyxes, which explode with a slight report. **1898** *Westm. Gaz.* 28 June 3/1 That strangely beautiful Spanish iris the Thunderbolt, a large flower of browns and yellows and greyish purples.

5. *attrib.* **thunderbolt attack, raid,** a short-lived but heavy air-raid; **thunderbolt beetle,** a species of beetle, *Arhopalus fulminans*, with dark wing-cases crossed by zigzag grey lines; **thunderbolt-stone**: see quot., and cf. THUNDERBOLT 3.

1871 TYLOR *Prim. Cult.* xvi. II. 238 They [Sioux Indians] consider the lightning entering the ground to scatter there in all directions thunderbolt-stones, which are flints, etc. **1943** *Hutchinson's Pictorial Hist. War* 25 Nov. 1942–16 Feb. 1943 240/1 At night Lancasters and Halifaxes carry out a large-scale 'thunderbolt' raid on Duesseldorf, dropping several hundred tons of bombs in a 20-minutes attack. **1944** H. HAWTON *Night Bombing* v. 66 There is no necessary connection between concentrated and precision bombing, but it would be quite wrong to think that the 'thunderbolt attack', as it is sometimes called, lacks exactness. The Renault factory was almost completely demolished in an attack of short duration.

Hence **ˈthunderbolt** *v.*, *trans.* (*a*) to strike with or as with a thunderbolt; to astonish, amaze, or terrify; (*b*) to hurl or dart like a thunderbolt; **ˈthunderbolted** *ppl. a.*, struck by a thunderbolt; charged with thunderbolts.

a **1586** SIDNEY *Arcadia* III. (1622) 304 Sorrow not being able so quickly to thunderbolt her heart thorough her senses. **1593** G. HARVEY *Pierce's Super.* **iv b, He brandisheth the whurlewinde..And thunderbolteth fo-confounding shott. **1623** J. WODROEPHE *Marrow Fr. Tongue* 487/2 A culpable and indebted Man is alwayes thunder-bolted. **1819** W. TENNANT *Papistry Storm'd* (1827) 31 It beat the thunder-boltit leven. **1881** in Elworthy *W. Somerset Word-bk.* s.v., He (the tower) was thunderbolted about of a sixty year agone.

ˈthunder-clap. [f. THUNDER *sb.* + CLAP *sb.*[1]]

a. A clap or loud crash of thunder; formerly also, a thunderstroke. Often allusively used: cf. c.

c **1386** CHAUCER *Pars. T.* ¶100 The Eyr..shal be ful of thonder clappes and lightnynges. *c* **1489** CAXTON *Blanchardyn* liv. 218 Since it hath pleased..God to terrifie with his thunderclaps our feeble hearts. **1598** HAKLUYT *Voy.* I. 60 He was afterward slaine by a thunderclap. **1686** tr. *Chardin's Trav. Persia* 45 This Answer was like a Thunderclap. **1758** BORLASE *Nat. Hist. Cornw.* 15 The Thunder-claps were within a few minutes of one another. **1861** SALA *Dutch Pict.* xi. 161 The massacre of Scio burst upon us like a thunder-clap. **1864** C. KNIGHT *Passages Work. Life* I. i. 17 The loudest thunder-clap..would produce such a concussion of the air.

b. *transf.* of other loud noises.

1610 R. NICCOLS *Winter Nt.'s Vis.*, *K. Arthur* xxx, The thunder claps of clashing armes. **1711** ADDISON *Spect.* 40 ¶6 With what Thunder-claps of Applause he leaves the Stage. **1924** R. CAMPBELL *Flaming Terrapin* iv. 65 And steepled cities stun the hollow sky With thunderclaps of bells as they go by.

c. *fig.* A sudden startling or terrifying occurrence, act, utterance, or piece of news. (Cf. THUNDERBOLT 2.)

1610 HOLLAND *Camden's Brit.* (1637) 243 Untill that fatal thunder-clap [the Dissolution] overthrew all the Monasteries of England. **1665** SIR T. HERBERT *Trav.* (1677) 331 A thunderclap was heard..anathematizing Elharu-Esed. **1852** JERDAN *Autobiog.* II. v. 49 A thunder-clap burst open and astonished Europe; Buonaparte had escaped from Elba. **1886** G. ALLEN *Maimie's Sake* xxvii, It was as great a thunder-clap to me as to you.

ˈthunder-cloud. A storm-cloud charged with electricity, that sends forth thunder and lightning.

1697 DAMPIER *Voy.* I. iv. 79 These Tornadoe's commonly come against the wind.., as our Thunder-Clouds are often observed to do. **1794** MRS. RADCLIFFE *Myst. Udolpho* l, The thunder-clouds, being dispersed, had left the sky perfectly serene. **1860** PUSEY *Min. Proph.* 155 God's judgments rolled round like a thunder-cloud. **1871** tr. *Schellen's Spectr. Anal.* §7. 21 When the electric spark flashes from the thunder-cloud to the earth.

b. *fig.* Something threatening or dreadful figured as a cloud.

1783 COWPER *Valediction* 76 To scenes where competition, envy, strife, Beget no thunder-clouds to trouble life. **1898** *N. & Q.* 9th Ser. II. 138/2 The black thunder-cloud of Spain overshadowed half the heavens.

ˈthunder-crack. *arch.* or *dial.* = THUNDER-CLAP. **a.** *lit.*

c **1440** *Jacob's Well* 203 Þe feend, wyth a thunder-crakke, smote doun Þe cherche to Þe grounde. **1560** PILKINGTON *Expos. Aggeus* (1562) 180 The cloudes burstes, & the thunder-cracke comes. **1622** S. WARD *Life of Faith in Death* (1627) 79 Like fooles that feare the thunder cracke, and not the Bolt. *a* **1834** R. SURTEES *Poems* in Taylor *Life* 317 The sky looks..black, And so we get a thunder-crack.

†**b.** *transf. Obs.*

1595 B. BARNES *Spir. Sonn.* xxxiii, Thrice puissant generall..Whose voyce itselfe is dreadfull thunder-cracke.

†**c.** *fig. Obs.*

1577 VAUTROUILLIER *Luther on Ep. Gal.* 25 The Pope.. rappeth out his thundercrackes and cursings against the miserable and terrified in conscience. **1624** MIDDLETON *Game at Chess* II. ii. 179 Those thunder-cracks of pride, Ushering a storm of malice. **1646** P. BULKELEY *Gospel Covt.* I. 68 Had they not heard those thundercrackes?

†**ˈThunderday, ˈThundurday.** *Obs.* A rare synonym of THURSDAY, q.v.

c **1460** *Oseney Reg.* 138 Þe Þundurday [orig. L. *die Iovis*] nexte after the ffest of Þe Birth of owr lorde In the ȝere of the Reyne of Kynge Henry the v.

thundered (ˈθʌndəd), *ppl. a.* [f. THUNDER *v.* or *sb.* + -ED.] **a.** Dealt or inflicted as by thunder. †**b.** Struck by 'thunder' or lightning (*obs.*). **c.** Uttered or sounded with a noise like thunder. **d.** Affected by thunder; turned sour (as milk) by atmospheric electricity.

1600 FAIRFAX *Tasso* XX. ciii, So falles a thundred towre. **1819** SHELLEY *Masque Anarchy* xc, Like Oppression's thundered doom. **1823** BYRON *Juan* XI. xxix, Thunder'd knockers broke the..spell. **1877** BLACKIE *Wise Men* 326 Some, Like thundered milk, have turned the sweet to sour.

thunderer (ˈθʌndərə(r)). [f. THUNDER *v.* + -ER[1].] One who or that which thunders.

1. a. He who thunders or causes thunder: applied to God, or to a deity, as Jupiter or Thor.

c **1374** CHAUCER *Boeth.* IV. met. vi. 111 (Camb. MS.) The lawes of the heye thonderere, Þat is to seyn of god. **1552** HULOET, Thundrer, *altitonans, tis*, a name that the panyms gaue to God. **1611** SHAKS. *Cymb.* v. iv. 95 *Iupiter*... How dare you Ghostes Accuse the Thunderer? **1791** COWPER *Iliad* I. 492 Once the Gods..Conspired to bind the

Thund'rer. 1870 BRYANT *Iliad* I. I. 23 Make my suit to Jupiter The Thunderer.

b. A person employed at a dramatic representation to imitate thunder by some mechanical means.

1711 ADDISON *Spect.* No. 235 ¶2 Others will have it to be the Play-house Thunderer. 1807–8 W. IRVING *Salmag.* (1824) 270 It will be a further gratification to the patriotic audience to know that the present thunderer is a fellow-countryman.

2. *fig.* A resistless warrior; a powerful declaimer or orator, an utterer of violent invective, or the like; *spec.* as a sobriquet of the London *Times* newspaper.

1586 T. B. *La Primaud. Fr. Acad.* (1589) 615 Who will not wish to have the surname of Aristides the just.. rather than as many use to be called Conquerors, Besiegers, Thunderers? 1784 COWPER *Task* II. 221 To shake thy senate, and from heights sublime Of patriot eloquence to flash down fire Upon thy foes, was never meant my task: But I can feel thy fortunes.. with as true a heart As any thund'rer there. 1830 *Morning Herald* 15 Feb. 3/1 Any person or persons.. may receive further particulars.. by application.. at the office of *The Thunderer*, Printing House-square. 1840 CARLYLE *Let.* 13 June in *C. & Lond. Libr.* (1907) 58 Six and sixpence—for a *Times* advertisement, which the Thunderer dunned me for to-day! 1882 PEBODY *Eng. Journalism* xv. 114 It was the writing of Edward Sterling that gave the *Times* the name of the 'Thunderer'. 1884 W. M. DICKSON in *Harper's Mag.* June 64/1 He reappeared in the arena, again the thunderer of the scene.

3. Something that makes a noise like thunder; *spec.* a toy made of a flat thin piece of wood or an ox-rib with a string attached at one end, which makes a roaring noise when whirled round; a 'bull-roarer'.

1860 TYNDALL *Glac.* II. xxv. 364 A new [shaft] is hollowed out, in which.. the cataract plays the thunderer. 1908 [MISS E. FOWLER] *Between Trent & Ancholme* 81 'Thunderers', a bricklayer's thin lath, etc.

thunderful ('θʌndəfʊl), *a. rare.* [f. THUNDER *sb.* + -FUL.] Full of or charged with thunder; *loosely*, thundering, sounding like thunder.

1898 G. MEREDITH *Day of Daughter of Hades* ix, Legions of thunderful horse. 1910 *Westm. Gaz.* (weekly ed.) 30 Apr. 6/3 As clouds that are thunderful.

'thunder-gust. Chiefly *U.S.* A strong gust of wind accompanying a thunder-storm.

1748 FRANKLIN *Lett.* Wks. 1840 V. 220 Hence thunder-gusts after heats, and cool air after gusts. 1817 SHELLEY *Revolt of Islam* IV. xx, Like a thunder gust Caught by some forest. 1824 W. IRVING *T. Trav.* (1849) 389 A terrible black thundergust was coming up. 1876 BANCROFT *Hist. U.S.* IV. xxxvii. 122 During a violent thunder-gust and rain, Ulloa landed, with civil officers, three Capuchin monks, and eighty soldiers.

thundering ('θʌndərɪŋ), *vbl. sb.* [f. THUNDER *v.* + -ING[1].] The action of the verb THUNDER.

1. *lit.* (see THUNDER *v.* 1); also in *pl.*: = THUNDER *sb.* 1, 1 c (now *rare* or *arch.*).

*a*1100 *O.E. Chron.* an. 1086 [*miswr.* 1085], Swa stor þunring & lægt wes, swa þæt hit acwealde maniȝe men. 1297 R. GLOUC. (Rolls) 7763 Tempestes þer come þondringe & liȝtinge ek þat slou men ilome. 1398 TREVISA *Barth. De P.R.* XI. i. (1495) 381 Ayre strongly meuyd makyth wyndes lyghtnynge and thondrynge drawe togyder. 1526 TINDALE *Rev.* xix. 6 As the voyce off many waters, and as the voyce off stronge thondrynges [so 1539 (Great), 1560 (Genev.), 1611; 1881 *R.V.* thunders]. 1555 EDEN *Decades* 90 Soo many thunderinges, lyghtnynge, and tempestes wherwith they are soo often troubeled. 1727 [DORRINGTON] *Philip Quarll* (1816) 80 Great thundering and lightning. 1884 TAIT *Mind in Matter* (1892) 200 At the bidding of Moses, thunderings, lightnings, and hail, by divine command, exhibited [etc.].

2. *transf.* Loud resounding noise (see THUNDER *v.* 2): = THUNDER *sb.* 2.

1560 DAUS tr. *Sleidane's Comm.* 414 b, Than.. was the city [Metz].. beaten with shot,.. the noise and Thondering thereof was hard.. iiii Dutche miles beyond the Rhine. 1633 P. FLETCHER *Purple Isl.* XI. iii, Raise my soft strain to high thundering. 1822 BYRON *Werner* V. i. 113 The thundering Of far artillery. 1866 DICKENS *Lett.* (1880) II. 254 The thundering of applause.. was quite staggering.

b. Infliction of heavy and resounding strokes.

1592 WYRLEY *Armorie, Ld. Chandos* i, Whom sound he hits with staggring steps doth reel, They knew it sure that his sad thundring feel.

3. *fig.* Vehement threatening, invective, or the like (see THUNDER *v.* 3): = THUNDER *sb.* 3.

1564 KNOX *Bk. Com. Order* (1840) 158 Lawful excommunication (for the thunderings of that Roman antichrist are but vanity and wind). 1597 J. PAYNE *Royal Exch.* 42 What thundringe soever the scripture sownds agaynst yt. 1607 HIERON *Wks.* I. 183 The thundring out of the threatnings and terror of the law. 1893 E. L. WAKEMAN in *Columbus* (Ohio) *Dispatch* 11 May, By direst sacerdotal thunderings.

4. *attrib.* and *Comb.*, as **thundering-machine**, an apparatus for imitating thunder in a theatre.

1826 *Museum Crit.* II. 214 [The Greeks] had.. a βροντεῖον, or artificial thundering machine, consisting of a vessel filled with stones, which was rolled along a sheet of copper.

'thundering, *ppl. a.* (*adv.*) [f. as prec. + -ING[2].] That thunders, in various senses.

1. a. *lit.* Causing or sending forth thunder; †of or characterized by thunder, thundery (*obs.*).

1530 PALSGR. 281/1 Thundring, *altitonant*. 1573 TUSSER *Husb., Author's Belief* vii, That sendeth thundring claps, like terrours out of hell. 1621 in Foster *Eng. Factories Ind.* (1906) 242 We came to anchor.., and in a flat calme began to make thundering weather. 1751 J. BARTRAM *Observ. Trav. Pennsylv.*, etc. 56 A rainy thundering warm day. 1856 MASSON *Ess.* vi. 179 [He] resumed his place in the public eye as the thundering Jove of the Opposition.

b. *Thundering Legion*: see quots.

1650 BAXTER *Saints' R.* II. vi. §6 (1651) 264 Hence the Christian soldiers in their Army were called, the Thundering Legion. 1727–41 CHAMBERS *Cycl.*, *Thundering Legion, Legio Fulminans*, was a legion in the Roman army, consisting of Christian soldiers, who in the expedition of the emperor Marcus Aurelius against the Sarmatæ, Quadi, and Marcomanni, saved the whole army, then ready to perish of thirst, by procuring, with their prayers, a very plentiful shower thereon; and, at the same time, a furious hail, mixed with lightening and thunderbolts, on the enemy..: though some say, that the legion those Christians were of, was called the *thundering legion* before. 1831–3 E. BURTON *Eccl. Hist.* xix. (1845) 413. 1835 *Penny Cycl.* III. 105/1 Some unlucky legendist, not knowing that the 12th or Thundering Legion, which was engaged in this affair, had its name before it happened, took occasion to call it a Christian Legion, and to attribute the miraculous storm to the efficacy of its prayers.

2. *transf.* Making a noise like thunder, sounding very loudly; of sound, As loud as thunder.

† *thundering gold*, see note s.v. FULMINATING *ppl. a.*[1]

1576 GASCOIGNE *Spoyle of Antwerpe* B ij, The Castle had all this while, played at the Towne and trenches, with thundring shot. 1687 DRYDEN *Ode St. Cecilia's Day* iii, The double, double, double beat Of the thundring Drum. 1694 SALMON *Bate's Dispens.* (1713) 317/1 *Aurum Fulminans*: Lightning or Thundering Gold. *c*1764 GRAY *Owen* 23 There the thund'ring strokes begin. 1845 J. COULTER *Adv. Pacific* iii. 25 A long, deep, regular sea, with a fine thundering crest on the top of the wave. 1871 L. STEPHEN *Playgr. Eur.* xii. (1894) 283 The thundering fall of the Handeck becomes [in winter] a gentle thread of pure water.

3. *fig.* in reference to terrible invective, threatening, etc., or to powerful eloquence; sometimes to bombastic or inflated language.

1543 GRAFTON *Contn. of Harding* 463 The duke of Burgoyne.. wrote sharpe letters of thretenyng.. whose fyrye and thundryng wordes [etc.]. 1576 FLEMING *Panopl. Epist.* 357 To resist the.. outragious rule of thundering Tyraunts. *a*1674 CLARENDON *Hist. Reb.* XIII. §15 Thundering Letters came from the Parliament, with great menaces what they would do. 1727 POPE *Shaks. Wks.* Pref. I. 5 The most pompous Rhymes, and thundering Versification. *a*1797 WILKES in J. Almon *Mem.* (1805) V. 35, I hear of a thundering memorial against this country from Spain. 1883 J. PARKER *Apost. Life* II. 16 The thundering eloquence.

4. a. Very energetic or forcible, violent; hence as a mere intensive: Very great or big, excessive, immense, 'tremendous', 'terrific'. *colloq.* or *slang.*

1618 T. ADAMS *Love's Copy* Wks. 1862 II. 420 He goes a thundering pace, that you would not think it possible to overtake him. 1632 LITHGOW *Trav.* x. 476 They all three left mee in a thundering rage. 1681 OTWAY *Soldier's Fort.* I. i, I warrant him a thundering Rogue. *a*1704 T. BROWN *Aristænetus' Epist.* I. Wks. 1720 I. 249, I was drawing a thundring Fish out of the Water, so very large, that it made my Rod crack again. 1851 BORROW *Lavengro* xcix, What a thundering old fool you are! 1900 BARRIE *Tommy & Grizel* v, Such a thundering lie.

b. as *adv.* Excessively, immensely, 'tremendously'. *colloq.* or *slang.*

1809 *Salmagundi* 7 Mar. 95 He.. prefers.. telling his story among cronies of his own gender.. and thundering long stories they are. 1839 *Havana* (N.Y.) *Republican* 25 Dec. (Th.), He is thundering shy of me. 1852 DICKENS *Bleak Ho.* xxi, I was a thundering bad son. 1887 BLACK *Sabina Zembra* 228 Don't you think that a thundering good licking would knock the laziness out of him? 1890 'R. BOLDREWOOD' *Col. Reformer* (1891) 261 A thundering soft thing it is, in a general way.

Hence **'thunderingly** *adv.*, in a thundering manner; with a noise as of thunder; *fig.* violently, powerfully; with fierce denunciation; excessively (*slang* or *colloq.*).

1680 *Honest Hodge & Ralph* 19 To take the Charge off from the Pope,.. the more thunderingly to Clap it upon the Phanatick. 1759 H. WALPOLE *Let. to Mann* 10 May, It is well if he concludes this [campaign] as thunderingly as he did the last. 1885 C. GIBBON *Hard Knot* II. xxxiii. 229 It's thunderingly annoying.

†thunder-layt, -leit. *Obs.* Also -leite, -leyt(e. [f. THUNDER + *leyt, lait*, etc., in OE. *leȝet* (see LAIT *sb.*[1]) lightning.] See THUNDERLIGHT.

thunderless ('θʌndəlɪs), *a.* [f. THUNDER *sb.* + -LESS.] Unaccompanied by thunder (or noise like thunder).

1855 G. MEREDITH *Shav. Shagpat* (1856) 371 Flashes of thunderless lightnings. 1880 TENNYSON *Voy. Maeldune* iii, The long waterfalls Pour'd in a thunderless plunge to the base of the mountain walls.

'thunderlight. *arch.* [Alteration of the earlier *thunder-layt, -leit* (see above) by substitution of *light* for *leit*. The earlier form occurs in some of the Chaucer MSS.] Light of thunder, lightning.

*c*1374 CHAUCER *Boeth.* I. met. iv. 7 (MS. Camb. I i. 3. 21) Ne the wey of thonderlyht [*Add. MS.* þonder lyȝt; *MS. Camb.* I i. I. 38 thonder leit; *ed.* 1532 thonder leyte] þat is wont to smyten heye towres, ne shal not moeue þat man. *c*1386 —— *Pars. T.* ¶765 (Camb. MS.) After that he brente .v. ceteis with thundyr liȝth [*v.rr.* liȝt, lyht, lyght, lighte, *Ellesm.* leyt, *Harl.* layt].

1815 L. HUNT *Feast of Poets*, etc. 149 What shall move his placid might? Not the headlong thunderlight. 1834 LD. HOUGHTON *Mem. Many Scenes* (1844) 59 Under such a sky —Thus grave, thus streaked with thunderlight.

thunderous ('θʌndərəs), *a.* Also 6 **thunderus**, 7–9 **thundrous.** [f. THUNDER *sb.* + -OUS.]

1. Full of or charged with thunder; of or pertaining to thunder; thundery.

1582 STANYHURST *Æneis* I. (Arb.) 25 O God most puisaunt, whose mighty auctoritye.. mankind skeareth with thunderus humbling. 1667 MILTON *P.L.* x. 702 Notus and Afer black with thundrous Clouds. 1726 POPE *Odyss.* XIX. 513 Nor winter's boreal blast, nor thund'rous show'r, Nor solar ray, cou'd pierce the shady bow'r. 1876 BLACK *Madcap V.* xiv, The lurid and sultry evening had died down into a gloomy and thunderous darkness. 1904 M. HEWLETT *Queen's Quair* III. x. 484 The 10th of June had been a thunderous day.

2. Resembling thunder in its loudness.

1606 SYLVESTER *Du Bartas* II. iv. I. *Trophies* 370 Rushing with thundrous roar. 1820 KEATS *Hyperion* II. 8 Thunderous waterfalls and torrents hoarse. 1875 H. JAMES *R. Hudson* vii. 239 In a voice almost thunderous,.. he repeated, 'Sit down!' 1876 GEO. ELIOT *Dan. Der.* vi, Herr Klesmer.. at the piano, struck a thunderous chord. 1892 *Times* 10 June 9/1 Which [motion] was carried amid thunderous applause.

3. *fig.* Suggestive of thunder; of threatening aspect, or charged with latent energy, like a thunder-cloud; violent, destructive, or terrifying like thunder.

1844 MRS. BROWNING *Vis. Poets* xcix, Here, Homer, with the broad suspense Of thunderous brows. 1873 SYMONDS *Grk. Poets* vii. 218 Her [Medea's] fiery eyes and thundrous silence. 1874 BLACKIE *Self-Cult.* 57 The first Napoleon, in his thunderous career over our western world.

Hence **'thunderously** *adv.*, in a thunderous manner, with a noise like thunder, very loudly; with threatening aspect as if presaging thunder; **'thunderousness**, thunderous quality.

1842 L. HUNT *Palfrey* I. 184 Shaking him and his saddle right thunderously. 1886 MRS. PHELPS *Burglars in Paradise* vii, Some one knocked thunderously at the back door. 1903 A. SMELLIE *Men of the Covt.* vii. (1904) 103 The skies hung still more thunderously over Presbyterian Scotland. 1904 *Westm. Gaz.* 17 Mar. 2/1 The great organ-voice of many waters sounding in mellowed thunderousness.

thunder-stone ('θʌndəstəʊn).

1. = THUNDERBOLT 1. *arch.*

1598 MARSTON *Pigmal.* IV, Enuie, let Pines of Ida rest alone, For they will growe spight of thy thunder stone. 1601 SHAKS. *Jul. C.* I. iii. 49, I.. Haue bar'd my Bosome to the Thunder-stone. 1678 DRYDEN & LEE *Œdipus* IV. i, You merciless powers, Hoard up your thunder-stones. 1819 SHELLEY *Prometh. Unb.* IV. 341 Sceptred curse.. sending A solid cloud to rain hot thunderstones. 1888 LOWELL *Heartsease & Rue* 70 Splintered with thunder-stone.

2. Applied to various stones, fossils, etc. formerly identified with 'thunderbolts', as celts, belemnites, masses of pyrites, meteorites: = THUNDERBOLT 3.

1681 GREW *Musæum* III. I. i. 258 Thunder-Stone or hard Button-Stone. *Brontias.* So called, for that people think they fall sometimes with Thunder. 1703 MAUNDRELL *Journ. Jerus.* (1721) 52 Each tube had a small cavity in its Center, from which its parts were projected in form of rays, to the circumference, after the manner of the Stones vulgarly call'd Thunder-stones. *c*1710 CELIA FIENNES *Diary* (1888) 218 Ye oare as its just dug Lookes like ye thunderstone. 1778 *Encycl. Brit.* (ed. 2) II. 1090/1 *Belemnites*, vulgarly called thunder-bolts or thunder-stones. 1796 MORSE *Amer. Geog.* II. 16 Norway produces.. amethysts, agates, thunder-stones, and eagle-stones. 1802 HOWARD in *Phil. Trans.* XCII. 169 Because explosion and report have generally accompanied the descent of [meteorolites], the name of thunderbolt, or thunderstone, has ignorantly attached itself to them. 1907 *Q. Rev.* July 176 The 'thunderstones' were of human workmanship.

3. *poet.* Applied to a (? stone) cannon-ball.

1821 SHELLEY *Hellas* 370 The.. allies Fled from the glance of our artillery Almost before the thunderstone alit.

'thunder-storm. A storm of thunder and lightning, usually accompanied with heavy rain.

1652 BP. HALL *Invis. World* I. vi, A fearful thunder-storm arose. 1794 MRS. RADCLIFFE *Myst. Udolpho* xxxi, Along the open glen,.. less dangerous than the woods in a thunder-storm. 1839 DARWIN *Voy. Nat.* iii. (1852) 62 In the year 1793 one of the most destructive thunder-storms perhaps on record happened at Buenos Ayres. 1865 'L. CARROLL' *Alice in Wonderland* ix, There stood the Queen.. frowning like a thunderstorm.

transf. 1877 M. PRIOR in *Daily News* 1 Oct. 6/3 No troops could.. live in such a thunderstorm of leaden hail.

Hence **thunder-stormy** *a.*

1930 J. DOS PASSOS *42nd Parallel* II. 149 Hot thunderstormy Washington summers. *a*1974 R. CROSSMAN *Diaries* (1975) I. 197 A fairly restful Easter weekend of mixed, blowy, brilliant, shiny, thunder-stormy weather.

thunderstricken ('θʌndə,strɪk(ə)n), *a.* [f. THUNDER + STRICKEN.]

1. *lit.* = THUNDERSTRUCK 1.

1652 GAULE *Magastrom.* 310 Upon the Statue of Augustus there was inscribed Caesar. Now, it being thunderstriken,.. the letter C was thereby blotted out. 1818 BYRON *Ch. Har.* IV. lxxxviii, Thou the thunder-stricken nurse of Rome! She-wolf! 1845 G. MURRAY *Islaford* 37 A thunder-stricken corse was found.

2. *fig.* = THUNDERSTRUCK 2.

*a*1586 SIDNEY *Arcadia* III. (1590) 291 b, She.. stood as it were thunder-striken with amazement. 1780 MRS. THRALE *Let. to Johnson* 10 June, Mr. Thrale seems thunderstricken, he don't mind anything. 1890 L. C. D'OYLE *Notches* 135 When Mrs. Low hastily lighted the lamp.. and saw nothing, she was thunderstricken.

thunderstrike ('θʌndəstraɪk), *v.* Pa. t. and pple. thunderstruck (see also prec. and THUNDERSTRUCK). [prob. a back-formation from *thunderstricken*, that being taken as a pa. pple.]

1. *trans.* (*lit.*) To strike with 'thunder' or lightning (cf. THUNDER *sb.* 1 b). ? *Obs.*

1613 HEYWOOD *Brazen Age* IV. Wks. 1874 III. 232 My father [Jove]..startles vp to thunder-strike the lad [Phaeton]. **1666** T. NEALE in *Phil. Trans.* I. 247 The Account..by the learned Dr. Charleton, concerning the boy that was Thunder-struck near Nantwich in Cheshire. **1710** W. KING *Heathen Gods & Heroes* liv. (1722) 186 Charybdis ..was Thunder-struck by Jupiter, and transformed into a Sea-Monster. *a* **1711** KEN *Christophil* Poet. Wks. 1721 I. 442 Angels..Expected when Almighty Ire Shou'd Thunder-strike our guilty Sire. **1902** GREENOUGH & KITTREDGE *Words* 309 'Astonish' is literally 'to thunderstrike', and was once common in the physical sense of 'stun'.

2. *fig.* To strike as with 'thunder'. **a.** To strike with amazement, astonish greatly. *Obs.* exc. as in ***thunderstricken***, ***thunderstruck***.

1613- [see THUNDERSTRUCK 2 a]. **1721** G. ROUSSILLON tr. *Vertot's Rev. Portugal* 104 This message thunder-struck the Duke. **1789** M. NUBER *Let.* in *Ld. Auckland's Corr.* (1861) II. 324 This revolution thunder-strikes the keenest man. **1807** SOUTHEY *Espriella's Lett.* III. 183 The news.. thunderstruck all present.

b. To inflict severe or terrible vengeance, reproof, or the like, upon. In quot. 1818 in physical sense, to batter severely.

1638 SIR T. HERBERT *Trav.* (ed. 2) 71 He had..thunder struck him, with a storme of mighty words. **1650** TRAPP *Comm. Exod.* xix. 16 To terrifie and thunder-strike offenders. **1699** CIBBER *Xerxes* v, To Thunder-strike thy Soul. **1818** BYRON *Ch. Har.* IV. clxxxi, The armaments which thunderstrike the walls.

thunderstroke ('θʌndəstrəʊk). A stroke of 'thunder' (cf. THUNDER *sb.* 1 b); the impact of a lightning-flash.

c **1600** CHALKHILL *Thealma & Cl.* (1683) 5 The lofty Cedar, and the knotty Oak, Are subject more unto the thunder-stroak, Than the low shrubs. **1610** SHAKS. *Temp.* II. i. 204 They fell together..as by a Thunder-stroke. **1844** MRS. BROWNING *Dead Pan* vii, At the rushing thunderstroke would No sob tremble through the tree?

b. *transf.* and *fig.*

1587 GOLDING *De Mornay* xxvi. (1592) 397 The others cutting words which are the thunderstrooks doubled. **1780** BENTHAM *Princ. Legisl.* xiii. §4 During the first assault of passion as under a thunder-stroke the sentiments of virtue may yield for a moment. **1808** SCOTT *Marm.* II. i, When all the loud artillery spoke, With lightning-flash, and thunder-stroke. **1880** TREVELYAN *Early Hist. C. J. Fox* vi. (1910) 243 The thunder-stroke of such a confession..could not be parried.

thunderstruck ('θʌndəstrʌk), *ppl. a.* Also 7 **-stroken, -strucken.** (Usually in participial const., as predicate; less commonly in attrib. const., before the sb. For the purely ppl. use with auxiliary, see THUNDERSTRIKE.) [Orig. a later equivalent of *thunderstricken*.]

1. *lit.* Struck by lightning: cf. THUNDER *sb.* 1 b. Now *rare* or *Obs.*

1638 SIR T. HERBERT *Trav.* (ed. 2) 19 Falling downe as thunder-struck. **1676** *Phil. Trans.* XI. 648 Those Thunder-strucken ones [compasses] did never..recover their right positions. **1720** T. BOSTON *Fourf. St.* II. ii. (1784) 104 When a person is thunder-struck, oft-times there is not a wound to be seen in the skin. **1775** ADAIR *Amer. Ind.* 86 Esteeming thunder-struck individuals under the displeasure of heaven.

2. *fig.* **a.** Struck with sudden amazement, terror, or the like; greatly amazed, astonished, terrified, or confounded.

1613 W. BROWNE *Brit. Past.* I. i, The Thunder-stroken Swaine lean'd to a tree, As void of sense as weeping Niobe. **1687** BOYLE *Martyrd. Theodora* v, Thunder-struck with this unexpected answer. **1711** ADDISON *Spect.* No. 60 ¶4 The Lover was thunder-struck with his Misfortune. **1775** SHERIDAN *Duenna* I. iii, I'm astonished! I'm thunder struck! here's treachery and conspiracy with a vengeance! **1855** MACAULAY *Hist. Eng.* xx. IV. 402 Luxemburg was thunder-struck. He expostulated boldly and earnestly.

b. in reference to ecclesiastical censure, etc.: cf. THUNDER *sb.* 3 a, THUNDERBOLT 2. *rare.*

1649 BP. HALL *Cases Consc.* III. v. (1654) 202 How many famous Churches have beene..thunder-struck with direfull censures of Excommunication. **1680** H. MORE *Apocal. Apoc.* 132 Gregory the seventh, when he had excommunicated the Emperour Henry the fourth, said, he was *fulmine afflatus* thunder-struck by him.

thundery ('θʌndərɪ), *a.* Also 6-8 **thundry.** [f. THUNDER *sb.* + -Y.]

1. Of or pertaining to thunder; characterized by or betokening thunder.

1598 SYLVESTER *Du Bartas* II. ii. IV. *Columnes* 779 When (angry)..he throws down thundry storms. **1682** in Birch *Hist. Roy. Soc.* (1757) IV. 146 In thundry weather he [Mr. Hooke] supposed..hot sulphureous steams to issue out of the earth, which caused the sultriness that preceded. **1774** WHITE in *Phil. Trans.* LXV. 267 This bird [the Swift] is never so much alive as in sultry, thundry weather. **1894** *Daily News* 4 July 5/4 The sky..covered with heavy clouds of a very thundery type.

†**2.** Making a noise like thunder: = THUNDEROUS 2. *Obs.*

1605 SYLVESTER *Du Bartas* II. iv. IV. *Decay* 648 As a Cannon's thundry roaring Ball.

3. *fig.* Threatening an explosion of anger or passion; gloomy, frowning.

1824 MISS FERRIER *Inher.* xliv, Mr. R.'s brow looked rather thundery. **1845** CARLYLE *Cromwell's Lett. & Sp.* (1871) V. 40 *note*, That thundery countenance of yours. **1867** S. WILBERFORCE *Ess.* (1874) II. 85 A thundery state of the political and social atmosphere.

thung (θʌŋ), *sb.* ? *dial.* [Echoic: cf. THUNGE; also Lancash. dial. '*thwang*, a great blow' (*Tim Bobbin* 1746).] A dull heavy sound, as of a blow with the fist, but with some resonance. So **thung** *v.*, *intr.* to make such a sound.

1890 HALL CAINE *Bondman* x, The thud and thung of twenty hard fists on the table. **1894** —— *Manxman* V. iv, Nancy went back to her kneading... Nancy looked up at her thumping and thunging. *Ibid.* VI. xii, He went roaring down the stairs, but came thunging up again in a moment.

thung, thunk, dial. forms of THONG.

thunge (θʌndʒ), *sb. dial.* [Echoic.] 'A loud, hollow sound'; 'a heavy blow or fall producing such a sound'. So **thunge** *v.* (*Eng. Dial. Dict.*).

1849 'T. TREDDLEHOYLE' *Bairnsla Ann.* Feb. (E.D.D.), Sho wor startald wi a thunge at t' chaimber door. **1863** J. H. BURROW *Advent. Alfan* 350 He lay down..and listened to the thunges of the battering-ram. **1881** MISS JACKSON *Shropsh. Word-bk.*, *Thunge*..(2) *sb.* a thump; a heavy fall. 'I come down sich a thunge'. **1887** *S. Cheshire Gloss.*, *Thunge*, *s.* (1) a loud, hollow sound... It is the word always used to imitate the sound of a gun.

thunk (θʌŋk), *sb.*[1] Joc. var. THINK *sb.*

1922 JOYCE *Ulysses* 503 Have a good old thunk.

thunk (θʌŋk), *sb.*[2] (*int.* or *adv.*) [Onomatopœic.] A sound of an impact, either dull or plangent. Also *int.* or as *adv.*

1952 B. HARWIN *Home is Upriver* xviii. 178 He heard the dull thunk of wood against wood and felt the planking jar over his head. **1958** 'W. HENRY' *Seven Men at Mimbres Springs* vi. 70 Presently the sodden 'thunk!' of an ax blade caving in barrel staves echoed wetly. **1968** W. GARNER *Deep, Deep Freeze* ix. 109 The door said *thunk* in a well-bred whisper. **1970** M. CHISHOLM *McAllister says No* x. 93 The bullet tore through the canvas of the cover and went *thunk* into a barrel. **1971** A. ROSS *Huddersfield Job* 57, I heard the triple *thunk* of the undercarriage locks. **1979** *Herald* (Melbourne) 23 Apr. 2 The familiar 'thunk, zing, ding' of a pinball machine.

thunk (θʌŋk), *v.* [f. THUNK *sb.*[2]] *intr.* To make a thunk; to fall or land with a thunk.

a **1963** S. PLATH *Johnny Panic & Bible of Dreams* (1977) I. 133 With shovels and picks they crawled through the attic trapdoor and soon great masses of snow were thunking from the roof into the yard. **1972** *Daily Tel.* (Colour Suppl.) 14 Jan. 21/4 A quoit which thunks into the clay just to the left of the hob, leaning towards it, bevel downwards, is called a pot. **1976** *New Yorker* 3 May 44/3 Last night, I slept nine hours, rain thunking on the tent.

thunk (θʌŋk), dial. and joc. pa. t. and pa. pple. of THINK *v.*[2] Cf. THUNK *sb.*[1]

1876 C. C. ROBINSON *Dial. Mid-Yorks.* p. xlii, Think ..(Thuongk) The last form is less employed participially than in the past, in which tense it is of constant occurrence. **1887** *Lantern* (New Orleans) 15 Oct. 3/2 Who'd a thunk it? **1908** N. DUNCAN *Every Man for Himself* ii. 60 Leastwise, he *thunk* so, admittin' 'twas open t' argument. **1939** JOYCE *Finnegans Wake* 504, I then tuk my taken-place lying down, I thunk I told you. **1967** T. SAVAGE *Power of Dog* xiii. 240 Phil had most excellent use of the hides after all. Who'd a thunk it!

thunner, thunure, Sc. and obs. ff. THUNDER.

thunny, variant of TUNNY, fish.

†'**thunwang, -wange.** *Obs.* Forms: 1 **þun-,** 4 **thone-,** 5 **thun-, (thwn-, tun-), thon-, (thoun-);** 1-5 **-wong(e, -wang(e.** [OE. *þunwange*, *-wǫnge* (later also *-wang*), *þunwęnge*, f. *þun-* (:—OTeut. **þunnu-*: see THIN) + *wang*, *-e* cheek, jaw; lit. 'thin cheek'. Cf. OHG. *dunwangi*, *-węngi* (MHG. *tunewęnge*, LG. *dunninge*, *dünninge*, *dünnege*, *dunje* (Brem. Wbch.); also local G. *dünne*, *dünnung* temple, flank), ON. *þunnvangi*, *-vengi* (Sw. *tinning*, Da. *tinding*).] The temple (of the head).

a **1000** *Gloss.* in Wr.-Wülcker 228/7 *Dolor timporum*, þunwonga sar. *c* **1000** *Ælfric's Voc.* ibid. 156/17 *Timpus*, þunwang. *c* **1000** ÆLFRIC *Judg.* iv. 21 ȝelæhte seo wifman an þæra teldsticcena and..ȝesloh þa mid anum bytle bufan his þunwengan. *c* **1325** *Gloss. W. de Bibbesw.* in Wright *Voc.* 146 *Les temples*, thonewonges. *c* **1350** *Nom. Gall.-Angl.* 22 *Iowe temples et iernoun*, Cheke þonewonges and here-liste. *a* **1450** *Stockh. Med. MS.* ii. 76 in *Anglia* XVIII. 295 A playster of betonye..Is good on þe thonwongys for to leye. *c* **1450** *Mirour Saluacioun* 3265 Wham thorgh the thonwonges with a naile at last perced Jael. **1483** *Cath. Angl.* 387/2 A Thunwange (*A.* Thwnwynge), *tempus*.

thuong, thuortour, obs. ff. THONG, THORTER.

thur, þur, obs. f. THEIR; dial. var. THIR.

†**thural** ('θjʊərəl), *a. Obs. rare.* [ad. (rare) L. *tūrāl-is*, f. *tūs* (*thūs*), *tūr-* incense: see -AL[1].] Of, pertaining to, or of the nature of incense.

1624 DARCIE *Birth of Heresies* xvi. 66 In this little Thurall Coffer lay the Odors which the Priest tooke. **1714** *Solomon's Song* in R. Steele *Poet. Misc.* 242 Ripe thural Fruits their Frankincense exhale.

thurbarow, -barrowe, corrupt ff. THIRDBOROUGH.

Thurberesque (ˌθɜːbə'rɛsk), *a.* [-ESQUE.] Of or pertaining to the American cartoonist and writer James *Thurber* (1894-1961), the characters in his work, or his style of writing or drawing.

1954 *Encounter* June 88/1 The essentially sexual (we might almost say Thurberesque) nature of true comedy, its concern with the war of men and women. **1958** *Times Lit. Suppl.* 31 Oct. 626/4 A very amusing Thurberesque anecdote by Miss Rebecca West about meeting Pirandello, without knowing it, on a wild night out in New York in the 1920s. **1972** *Listener* 6 Apr. 458/1 A Thurberesque doodle. **1980** *Washington Star* 23 Oct. D6 Nabokov is in it as kind of a Thurberesque stage manager character.

thurd, obs. form of THIRD.

†**thure.** *Obs. rare.* [ad. L. *tūs*, *thūs* (stem *t(h)ūr-*) incense: see THUS *sb.*: perh. immediately repr. L. *thūra* pl.] Incense, frankincense.

c **1425** tr. *Arderne's Treat. Fistula* 63 Mirre, thure, mastike, ladanum. *Ibid.* 66 Bole armoniac, sang dracon, thure, aloe, vitriol combust. *c* **1440** *Pallad. on Husb.* XI. 412 A vnce of mascul thure, Wel smellynge.

thurf, þurf, obs. forms of THROUGH.

†**thurfe,** *a. Obs. rare*$^{-1}$. [In Ormin *þurrfe*, app. a. ON. *þurfe*, *-a* wanting, in need, f. stem *þurf-* of THARF *v.*] Needed, needful, wanting.

c **1200** ORMIN 9628 Lare inoh Off all þatt hemm wass þurrfe.

thurfte, þurfte, pa. t. of THARF *v. Obs.*, to need.

thurgh, þurȝ, þurgh, etc., obs. ff. THROUGH.

thurible ('θjʊərɪb(ə)l), *sb.* Forms: 5 **turrible, thoryble,** 7- **thurible,** (9 **thuribule**). [ad. L. *tūribulum*, *thūribulum* censer, f. *tūs*, *thūs*, *thūr-* incense: see THUS *sb.* So OF. *thurible* (Godef.).]

A vessel in which incense is burnt in religious ceremonies; a censer.

Now usually a metal vase with pierced cover, containing combustible material to burn the gums used as incense, which is swung in the hand (or suspended) by chains.

c **1440** *Promp. Parv.* 506/2 Turrible (or thoryble), *idem quod* sencere. **1660** JER. TAYLOR *Duct. Dubit.* II. ii. rule vi. §10 Upon the shekel of the Sanctuary was impress'd the image of Aarons rod and a pot of Manna, or thurible. *a* **1668** LASSELS *Voy. Italy* (1698) II. 239 They shewed us..the great Candlesticks and Thurible of beaten gold. **1805** SOUTHEY *Madoc in W.* xiii, Sweet incense from the waving thuribule Rose like a mist. **1877** J. D. CHAMBERS *Div. Worship* 262 Burning Incense from pendant Thuribles.

β. Also in L. form **thuribulum** (θjʊ'rɪbjʊləm).

1706 PHILLIPS (ed. Kersey), *Thuribulum*, a Censer or Smoaking-Pot, to burn Incence in. **1851** D. WILSON *Preh. Ann.* II. III. ii. 73 The thuribulum is very carefully executed.

b. *Comb.* **thurible-boat** = BOAT *sb.* 2 b.

1853 DALE tr. *Baldeschi's Cerem.* 159 They..deposit the thurible-boat and vase of holy water in the proper place.

Hence †'**thurible** *v.*, to cense.

c **1440** *Promp. Parv.* 506/2 Turryblon, or sencyn, *thurifico*.

thuribuler (θjʊ'rɪbjʊlə(r)). Also 9 **'thuribler.** [ad. med.L. *thūribulārius* (1312 in Du Cange), f. *thūribul-um* THURIBLE + *-ārius*, -ER[2] 2. So F. *thuribulier* (16th c. in Godef.).] An acolyte who carries the thurible; = next.

1504 in *Ripon Ch. Acts* (Surtees) 295 The vicars, dekenez, thuribulers, and the choristers. **1546** *Yorks. Chantry Surv.* (Surtees) 530 In the saide collegiate churche bee..ij thuribulers. **1877** J. D. CHAMBERS *Div. Worship* 111 When the Antiphon..is finished the Thuribler should retire. **1891** *Athenæum* 24 Oct. 544/1 The usual complement of..priests, deacons and subdeacons, choristers, thuribulers, and clerks.

thurifer ('θjʊərɪfə(r)). [a. mod.L. *thūrifer* 'incense-bearer', sb. use of *thūrifer* adj., f. *thūs*, *thūr-* incense (see THUS *sb.*) + *-fer* bearing. Med.L. had *thūriferārius* (Du Cange).] One who carries burning incense in religious ceremonies; = prec.

1853 ROCK *Ch. of Fathers* III. II. xi. 80 In this procession walked..thurifers with their smoking censers. **1853** DALE tr. *Baldeschi's Ceremonial* 62 At the proper time the Thurifer should prepare fire in some convenient place. **1871** C. B. PEARSON *Sarum Sequences* Pref. 6 A procession..consisting ..of the deacon.., preceded by a thurifer, candle-bearer, and cross-bearer, and the subdeacon.

thuriferous (θjʊə'rɪfərəs), *a.* [f. L. *thūrifer* incense-bearing (see prec.) + -OUS: see -FEROUS.] That produces frankincense.

1656 BLOUNT *Glossogr.*, *Thuriferous*, that beareth or brings forth frankincense. **1727-41** CHAMBERS *Cycl.* s.v. *Frankincense*, These thuriferous, or incense-bearing trees. **1863** J. G. MURPHY *Comm. Gen.* x. 29 A thuriferous range of hills.

†**thu'rific,** *a. Obs. rare*$^{-1}$. [f. L. *thūs*, *thūr-* incense + *-ficus* making.] = prec. So †**thu'rificate** *v. Obs.*, *trans.* = THURIFY 2.

1657 TOMLINSON *Renou's Disp.* Pref., Inhabiting the Thurifick Groves of Rerum Natura. **1623** COCKERAM, *Thurificate*, to perfume.

thurification (ˌθjʊərɪfɪˈkeɪʃən). [n. of action f. eccl. L. *thūrificāre* to THURIFY: see -FICATION. Cf. obs. F. *thurificacion* (15–16th c. in Godef.).] The action of thurifying; the burning or offering of, or perfuming with incense.

1496 *Dives & Paup.* (W. de W.) I. xv. 46/2 Thuryfycacyon & encensyng was by olde tyme an hyghe dyvyne worshypp. *a* **1529** SKELTON *Ph. Sparowe* 522 With armatycke gummes .. The way of thurifycation To make a fumigation. **1649** BP. HALL *Cases Consc.* III. iii. (1654) 185 Some semblance of an Idolatrous thurification. **1755** AMORY *Mem.* (1766) II. 193 The papal rites of..bowing the body, thurifications, deosculations. **1872** SHIPLEY *Gloss. Eccl. Terms* s.v. *Absolutiones* 5 Prayers, thurifications, and aspersions round the bodies of the dead.

thurify (ˈθjʊərɪfaɪ), *v.* [a. F. *thurifi-er* (15–16th c. in Godef.), ad. eccl. L. *thūrificāre*, f. *thūs*, *thūr-* incense + *-ficāre*: see THUS *sb.* and -FY.]

† **1.** *intr.* To burn or offer incense; = CENSE *v.*^{1} 2. *Obs. rare.*

c **1440** CAPGRAVE *St. Kath.* v. 350 If ȝe wil consent And thuryfye to Iubiter. *Ibid.* 534 Thanne shul ye now.. Thuryfie on-to that mageste Of grete appollo. **1460** —— *Chron.* (Rolls) 76 He [Pope Marcellus] wold not obey Maximiane, and thurifie.

2. *trans.* To perfume with incense; to burn incense before; to offer incense to; = CENSE *v.*^{1} 1. Also *transf.* (quot. 1599).

1570 FOXE *A. & M.* (ed. 2) 663/2 By thurifyeng or censing the aultars. **1599** NASHE *Lenten Stuffe* 65 This herring..was sensed and thurified in the smoake. **1737** G. SMITH *Cur. Relat.* I. iii. 417 The while the Corps remains in the House, the Priest comes every Day to thurify it. **1851** MADDEN *Shrines & Sepulchres* I. 313 Several Priests..came next to thurify the body.

Hence ˈ**thurifying** *vbl. sb.*

a **1618** SYLVESTER *Tobacco Battered* 183 The..smoak of Thurifying Of Images.

thurindale, obs. dial. f. THIRDENDEAL.

thuringer (ˈθjʊərɪŋə(r)). Also **thüringer**. [ad. G. *thüringer*, lit. = next.] Summer sausage.

1933 *Sausage Man. & Text Bk.* (Oppenheimer Casing Co.) 70 (*heading*) Thueringer (fresh Summer sausage) 120 lbs. regular beef trimmings, 40 lbs. beef heart, 60 lbs. chuck, 80 lbs. regular pork trimmings, [etc.]. **1938** *Packer's Encycl.* III. vii. 123 Hang thuringer on clean sticks and place in cooler. **1965** [see *summer sausage* s.v. SUMMER *sb.*^{1} 6 a]. **1978** *Chicago* June 241/2 The restaurant serves a variety of sandwiches..thuringer, and delicious homemade soups.

Thuringian (θjʊˈrɪndʒɪən), *a.* and *sb.* [f. the name *Thuringia* (see below) + -AN.] **A.** *adj.* Of or pertaining to (the inhabitants of) Thuringia, a region of central Germany, in mediæval times a principality. **B.** *sb.* A native or inhabitant of Thuringia.

1607 E. TOPSELL *Foure-footed Beasts* 293 The Thuringean horsses are neighbors to Hessis. **1618** SELDEN *Hist. Tithes* vi. 90 As in the examples which wee anon have of the Turingians, and those of Holtz. **1812** C. BUTLER *Hist. Revolutions of Empire of Germany* App. 35 The electorate was successively enjoyed by Frederick the warlike, and Frederick the wise, of the *Thuringian* branch of the Wittikindian stem. **1839** J. F. STANFORD *Jrnl.* 21 Sept. in *Rambles & Researches in Thuringian Saxony* (1842) 2 Old Palace of Friedenstein..commanding the finest view of the Thuringian Forest. **1839** —— *Let.* Aug. in *Ibid.* 158 In physical development the Thuringians..are..fine powerful men. **1881** C. C. HARRISON *Woman's Handiwork* III. 232 Small plates for tea or dessert, in Thuringian ware, imitating old Dresden. **1974** P. GORE-BOOTH *With Great Truth & Respect* 41 The Münchs had living with them..a brother of Frau Münch's, a general who..spoke such total Thuringian dialect that I never learned to understand a word he said. **1975** F. HEER *Charlemagne & his World* ix. 121 Hessians and Franconians were divisions of the Austrasian sub-kingdom. .. The Thuringians were a distinct group, but fairly well assimilated into France.

thuringite (θjʊˈrɪndʒaɪt, -ˈrɪŋgaɪt). *Min.* [ad. Ger. *Thuringit* (Breithaupt, 1832), f. Thuringia, in Central Germany, where found + -ITE^1.] A hydrous silicate of aluminium and iron, occurring as an aggregation of minute dark-green scales.

1844 DANA *Min.* (1868) 508 Thuringite is from Reichmannsdorf.

thurl, -ing, var. THIRL *sb.*^{1} and *v.*^{1}, THIRLING.

thurlepole, -polle, var. THIRLEPOLL, a whale.

† ˈ**thurlhead.** *Obs. rare*$^{-1}$. Alteration of *thurlepolle*, THIRLEPOLL, with *head* for *poll*.

1610 HOLLAND *Camden's Brit.* II. 184 There came to land a mighty multitude of great sea fishes, to wit, Thurlhedis.

thurow, obs. form of THOROUGH.

thurrock (ˈθʌrək). *Obs.* exc. *dial.* Forms: 1 **þurruc**, 4–5 **thurrok(e, thorrok(e**, 5 **thorrocke**, 8 **thorruck**, 9 *dial.* **thurrock, -uck**. [In sense 1, OE. *þurruc* 'cumba', small ship (?), bottom of a ship, bilge = Du. *durk* bilge (cf. *durck*, *dorck* 'sentina' in Kilian), of unknown etymology. It is doubtful whether senses 2 and 3 belong to the same word.]

1. The bilge of a ship. Also *fig.*

c **1050** *Suppl. Ælfric's Voc.* in Wr.-Wülcker 181/35 *Cumba, uel caupolus*, þurruc. *c* **1386** CHAUCER *Pars. T.* ¶ 363 The smale dropes of water that entren thurgh a litel creuace in to the thurrok [*v.r.* thorrok] and in the botme of the shipe. *Ibid.* ¶ 715 Ydelnesse is the thurrok [*v.r.* thorroke] of alle wikked and vileyns thoghtes. *c* **1440** *Promp. Parv.* 493/2 Thurrok, of a schyppe, *sentina*. **1450–1530** *Myrr. our Ladye* 109 A place in the bottome of a shyppe wherein ys gatheryd all the fylthe that cometh in to the shyppe... And that place stynketh ryghte fowle and yt ys called in some contre of thys londe a thorrocke. **1855** *Norfolk Words* in *Trans. Philol. Soc.* 37 *Thurruck*, the lower flooring of the stern of a boat. **1866** in NALL *Gt. Yarmouth & Lowestoft* 672. **1904** in *Eng. Dial. Dict.*

2. *dial.* A heap, *spec.* of muck or dirt.

1708 KERSEY, *Thorruck* (O.), a Heap. **1721** in BAILEY. **1881** *Leicester Gloss.*, *Thurrock*, a heap: chiefly applied to dirt or 'muck'.

3. *dial.* A covered drain. Cf. THOROUGH *sb.* 2.

1847–78 HALLIWELL, *Thurruck*, a drain. *Kent.* **1887** *Kentish Gloss.*, *Thurrock*, a wooden drain under a gate; a small passage or wooden tunnel through a bank.

thurrondell: see THIRDENDEAL.

thurrow: see THOROUGH *sb.* 3.

Thursday (ˈθɜːzdeɪ, -dɪ). Forms: α. 1 **Đunresdæȝ, þunres dæi, þur(r)es-, þursdæȝ**, 2 **ðursdai**, (3 **Thurday**), 3–4 **þures-**, 4 (**thrusdai**), 4–7 **Thursdaye**, 5 **Thurys-**, 6 (**thursdae**), **Thurss-, Thurse-**; 3– **Thursday**. β. 3–4 **þores-**, 3–5 **þ-, thoris-, Thorsday**, 4 **þorus-, Thoursday**; *Sc.* 6 **Thuirs-**, 7 **Thuris-**. γ. *Sc.* 6 **Furis-**, 6–9 **Fuirs-**, 8 **Fursday**. [The α forms represent OE. *þunresdæȝ*, 'day of Thunor or Thor', perh. in some cases affected by ON. The β forms are mainly from ON. *þórsdagr*, the long *ó* of which would give ME. *ō* and *ou* (uː), and mod.Sc. *ui* (øː). The γ Sc. forms show the interchange of *th* and *f*, referred to under TH (6). So Sw., Da. *Tors-dag*, MDu., Du. *Donderdag*, OHG. *Donares-tac*, MHG. *Donrestac*, Ger. *Donnerstag*, orig. rendering late L. *dies Jovis*, It. *Giovedì*, F. *Jeudi*. Cf. THUNDERDAY.]

1. The fifth day of the week.

α, β. [*c* **1000** ÆLFRIC *Hom.* II. 242 On ðam fiftan dæȝe ðe ȝe Đunres hatað. *c* **1000** *Sax. Leechd.* II. 346 Gang on þunres æfen þonne sunne on retle sie.] *c* **1000** *Ags. Gosp.* John v. 30 Đys sceal on þurs-dæȝ on þære oðre lencten wucan. *Ibid.* vii. 40 rubric, Đys god-spel sceal on þures dæȝ on þære fiftan wucan innen lenctene. *c* **1205** LAY. 13929 þa þunre heo ȝiuen þunres dæi [*c* **1275** þorisdai]. **1297** R. GLOUC. (Rolls) 11210 þe verste þorsdai in lente. **1377** LANGL. *P. Pl.* B. XVI. 140 þe þorsday [*v. rr.* thoresday, þorusday, þursday] byfore þere he made his maundee. **1426–7** *Rec. St. Mary at Hill* 65 þe thorisday in þe Whitson weke. **1591** H. SMITH *Lord's Supper* ii. (1611) 91 A schollers thursday, which he loves better then all the daies in the weeke, only because it is his play-day. **1637–50** Row *Hist. Kirk* (Wodrow Soc.) 515 To come in to Aberdeen on Thurisday thereafter. **1774** tr. *Helvetius' Child of Nat.* I. 235 Thursday next, I shall send for the answer. **1899** MRS. H. FRASER in *Book Lover* Apr. 3/1, I think I was born under the star of long journeys, a 'Thursday bairn that has far to go'.

γ. **1566** *Sc. Acts Jas. V*, *1540*, 141 b, Sonday, monounday, and furisday. **1569** *Reg. Privy Council Scot.* I. 673 Upoun fuirsday nix to cum. **1596** in *Analecta Scotica* II. 13 Ther ansuer..suld haue bein giuen in the last Furisday. **1791** A. WILSON *Laurel Disputed* Poet. Wks. (1846) 124 On this same Fursday night. **1861** RAMSAY *Remin.* Ser. II. 99 Mrs. So-and-so's funeral would be on Fuirsday. **1905** [Still used in some parts of Scotland: see Wright *Eng. Dial. Gram.* 648].

2. With defining words.

Bounds Thursday, Ascension Day, on which parish boundaries are traced (see BEAT *v.*^{1} 41). ***Carnival Thursday***, Thursday before Quinquagesima (see note s.v. CARNIVAL 1). ***Great***, also ***Great and Holy Thursday*** (in the Greek Church), ***Green Thursday***, the Thursday before Good Friday, Maundy Thursday. See also 3, and MAUNDY THURSDAY, SHEER THURSDAY.

1601–2 in *Archpriest Controv.* (Camden) II. 41 They.. arrived there upon madd thursday, otherwise called Carnivall thursday: wch is the thursday imediately before Shrove sonday.

3. Holy Thursday, a name that has been applied to various Thursdays.

a. Thursday in Rogation Week, Ascension Day. Also † ***Hallow Thursday***.

[*a* **901** *Laws Ælfred* c. 5 §5 Se ðe stalað on Sunnanniht, oððe on Gêhhol, oððe on Eastron, oððe on þone halȝan þunresdæȝ.] *c* **1290** *S. Eng. Leg.* I. 363/48 Men fastez..a-seint Marcus dai..And þreo dawes a-ȝein halewe-þoresday. *c* **1430** *Deuelis Perlament* 459 in *Hymns Virg.* 55 Oure lord,.. In erþe he was..Til hooly þursday comen were þat he stiȝ to heuene. *c* **1489** CAXTON *Sonnes of Aymon* ii. 59 The feste of Penthecoste after the holy thursdaye. **1530** PALSGR. 232/1 Holythursday, *le jour de lassention*. **1685** in *Verney Mem.* 28 May (1899) IV. 348 The House [of Commons] sitts not this day being Holy Thursday. **1869** *Chambers' Bk. Days* 5 May I. 595/1 Our..landlady at Matlock reminded us that on the following day, being Holy Thursday, or Ascension Day, there would take place the..ancient..custom of dressing the wells of Tissington with flowers. **1891** [see b].

b. The Thursday immediately preceding Easter; Maundy Thursday, Sheer Thursday.

In OE. and in Caxton prob. not a specific name; in 17th c. and later quots., after continental usage.

[*c* **1000** ÆLFRIC *Saints' Lives* xxiii. B. 621 To þam halȝan þurres-dæȝe ær þam drihten-lican easter-dæȝe. **1483** CAXTON *G. de la Tour* cxxiii, Vpon the Holy Thursday in the Passion weke.] **1645** EVELYN *Diary* 11 Apr., On Holy Thursday the Pope said masse. **1867** LADY HERBERT *Cradle L.* iii. 109 On Holy Thursday, the day of the institution of the Holy Eucharist. **1885** *Cath. Dict.* 404/2 Mediæval writers connect the procession with the Blessed Sacrament on Holy Thursday with our Lord's journey to the Mount of Olives after the Last Supper. **1891** *Ch. Q. Rev.* Jan. 449 *note*, By Holy Thursday an Englishman has hitherto always understood one day in the year, that is, Ascension Day... Some have nowadays..begun to use the term Holy Thursday as a name for the Thursday before Easter, which in old English is called Sherethursday or Maundy Thursday. This..is a mere borrowing from the Romance tongues, and is a cause of much confusion.

† **c.** The Thursday after Trinity Sunday; Corpus Christi day. *Obs.* (? error.)

1789 ANBUREY *Trav. Amer.* (1791) I. 184 Holy Thursday, which they term *La Fête Dieu*.

thurse (θɜːs). *Obs.* exc. *Hist.* Forms: 1 **þyrs**, 3 **þurs(e**, 4 **thirs**, 5 **thursse, thyrce, thirse, thrus(se, thrusche, thrwsse, trusse**, (6 **thrust**, 7–9 **thrush**, in HOBTHRUSH), 7– **thurse**. [OE. *þyrs* = OHG. *duris*, *turs*, str. m. (MHG. *dürse*, *türse*, *turse*, wk. m.), OS. *thuris* the rune þ; ON. *þurs* :—**þursa*^{z}:—OTeut. **þuriso*^{z}. Cf. Finnish *tursa-s* sea-monster, from ON.]

A giant of heathen mythology; in mediæval times, often, the devil, a demon; later, a goblin or hobgoblin of rustic superstition.

Beowulf 426 Ond nu wið Gren-del sceal wið þam aglæcan ana ȝe-hegan ðing wið þyrse. *c* **725** *Corpus Gloss.* (O.E.T.) 1457 *Orcus*, ðyrs, heldiobul. *a* **1225** *Leg. Kath.* 1880 Com þe þurs Maxence, þe wed wulf, þe heaðene hund aȝein to his kineburh. *a* **1225** *Juliana* 42 (R. MS.) Beelzebub þe alde þurs of helle. **1382** WYCLIF *Isa.* xxxiv. 15 Ther shal lyn lamya [*Gloss.*, that is, a thirs, or a beste hauende the bodi lic a womman and horse feet]. ? *a* **1400** *Morte Arth.* 1100 Thykke theese as a thursse,..Greesse growene as a galte, fulle grylych he lukez! *c* **1440** *Promp. Parv.* 491/2 Thyrce, wykkyd spyryte (*K.* thirse, goste, *S.*, *A.* tyrce). **1468** *Medulla Gram.* (Promp. Parv.) *Dusius, i. demon*, a thrusse, þe powke. *c* **1700** [see b]. [**1886** CORBETT *Fall of Asgard* (1889) I. 59 Never would land-wight, be he troll, thusse, vœtte, or dwarf, harm you.]

b. *Comb.* **thurse-hole, thurse-house**: see quot. *c* 1700; **thurse-louse**, a wood-louse (see also *thrush-louse* and *thurstlaas* in Eng. Dial. Dict.).

c **1450** *St. Cuthbert* (Surtees) 2180 A place with oute his cell, Now calde þe thrus house. **1658** J. ROWLAND *Moufet's Theat. Ins.* 1048 The English from the form call them Sowes... They are called also *Thurslows*..from a spirit that was not hurtful, to whom our Ancestors superstitiously imputed the sending of them to us. *c* **1700** BP. KENNETT *Lansd. MS. 1033*, lf. 396 A Thurse, an Apparition, a Goblin. *Lanc.*.. A Thurs-house or Thurse-hole, a hollow vault in a rock or stony hill... These were lookd on as enchanted holes.

thurst, -e, obs. ff. THIRST, dial. var. THRUST.

thurst, -e, thurt(e(þ-), pa. t. of THARF *v. Obs.*

Thurstone (ˈθɜːstən). *Psychol.* The name of the American psychologist, Louis Leon *Thurstone* (1887–1955), used *attrib.* to denote tests or methods devised by him, esp. for the measurement of mental abilities and attitudes, for factor analysis, and the study of personality.

1935 R. R. WILLOUGHBY in C. Murchison *Handbk. Soc. Psychol.* xii. 502 Perhaps the most definite evidence is that secured..with personality inventories of the Thurstone type. **1954** A. ANASTASI *Psychol. Testing* ix. 229 Another abbreviated adaptation..is to be found in the Thurstone Test of Mental Alertness. *Ibid.* xx. 538 The resulting inventory is known as the Thurstone Temperament Schedule. **1958** M. ARGYLE *Relig. Behaviour* viii. 97 A group of eighty-three delinquent girls scored higher on Thurstone scales measuring attitudes towards Sunday observance. **1972** *Jrnl. Soc. Psychol.* Dec. 243 Attitude toward reclaimed water for noningestive, close-contact use was assessed by a Thurstone-type scale.

thurtene, -teyn, obs. ff. THIRTEEN.

thurte ouer, variant of THWART-OVER *Obs.*

thurty, obs. form of THIRTY.

‖ **thus** (θʌs, θuːs), *sb.* [Late L. *thūs*, *thūr-*, cl. L. *tūs*, *tūr-*, generally held to be f. Gr. *θύος, -εος* sacrifice, offering, incense; cf. *θύ-ειν* to sacrifice.]

1. Frankincense. **a.** Olibanum. **b.** Resin obtained from the spruce-fir, and from various species of pine. ***American thus***, the resin of the Long-leaved Pine, *Pinus palustris*, and the Frankincense or Loblolly Pine, *P. Tæda*, both of the southern U.S.

[*a* **1387** *Sinon. Barthol.* (Anecd. Oxon.) 42 *Thus album, i. olibanum*, franke ensens.] **1398** TREVISA *Barth. De P.R.* (Bodl. MS.) lf. 232 b/2 *Thus* is þe name of a tre & of þe gomme þat woseþ and comeþ oute þerof. *Ibid.* 233/1 Thus is beste þat is white faste and sounde and euelong. **1706** PHILLIPS (ed. Kersey), *Thus* or *Tus*, Frankincense, Incense. **1712** tr. *Pomet's Hist. Drugs* I. 201 Thus, or Frankincense, is a Kind of white or yellowish Rosin. **1842** BRANDE *Dict. Sc.*, etc., *Thus*, the resin of the spruce fir. The term frankincense is also applied to it. **1880** C. R. MARKHAM *Peruv. Bark* xvi. 185 A milk-white fragrant resin, of a nature analogous to gum thus or gum elemi.

† **2.** By early writers, taken also as name of the tree yielding olibanum or frankincense. *Obs.*

1398 TREVISA *Barth. De P.R.* (Bodl. MS.) lf. 232 b/2 Thus is a tre of Arabia..And therof comeþ Iuse wiþ good smelle & is white as almaundes. *Ibid.* [see sense 1].

thus (ðʌs), *adv.* Now chiefly *literary* or *formal.* Forms: α. 1–3 **ðus**, 1–5 **þus**, 3 **þuss** (*Orm.*), **ð-, þusse**, 3–4 **þos**, 4 **þous**, *Sc.* **thws**, 6 *Sc.* **thuss**, 4–

thus. *β.* 3 (*Orm.*) tuss, 3–4 tus, 5 tas; (also 1, 4 dus). [= OS. *thus*, MDu., Du. *dus*, app. f. the demonstrative stem of THAT or THIS, but the pre-Teut. history is obscure. OHG. and MHG. have *sus*, MDu., Du. *zus*, which appear to belong to the stem of *so*. Cf. also THIS *adv.*]

1. In this way, like this. **a.** In the way just indicated. †*and thus far forth*, and so forth, 'and the like' (*obs. rare*⁻¹). (In quot. *c* 1430 pleonastically before *such*.)

c **725** *Corpus Gloss.* 26 *Sicini* [*siccine*], ac ðus. *c* **888** K. ÆLFRED *Boeth.* xvi. §4 Ða se Wisdom ða þis [spell] ðus areaht hæfde. **971** *Blickl. Hom.* 7 Hu mæȝ þis þus ȝeweorþan? *c* **1000** *Ags. Gosp.* Luke xxiv. 46 Ðus is awriten & þus ȝebyrede crist þolian. *c* **1200** ORMIN 235–7, & tuss ȝho seȝȝde inn hire þohht..þuss hafeþþ Drihhtin don wiþþ me. **1340** *Ayenb.* 52 þos he lyest al his time, and þe niȝt: and þane day. *Ibid.* 71 þous geþ al oure lyf. **1375** BARBOUR *Bruce* II. 508 Thws in the hyllis levyt he. *c* **1430** *Life St. Kath.* (1884) 45 By þus suche tormentes þou schalt somtyme se me wyth sayntes in blis. **1530** PALSGR. 720/1 You ought to be a shamed to skowlde thus as you do. **1606** HOLLAND *Sueton.* 103 Victualling houses, tavernes and thus farre foorth. **1689** HICKERINGILL *Wks.* (1716) II. 39 Thus the Hogen-Dutchman got Money. **1796** H. HUNTER tr. *St.-Pierre's Stud. Nat.* (1799) I. 459 It is thus that our general maxims become the sources of error. **1840** LARDNER *Geom.* 98 The base and altitude of the parallelogram thus formed. **1847** C. BRONTË *J. Eyre* iv, When thus gentle, Bessie seemed to me the best, prettiest, kindest being in the world. **1908** [MISS E. FOWLER] *Betw. Trent & Ancholme* 249 And thus the music goes on.

b. In the following manner; as follows; in these words.

c **888** K. ÆLFRED *Boeth.* xvi. §4 Ða ong[an he] eft ȝiddian & þus cwæð. *a* **900** *O.E. Martyrol.* 23 Apr. 60 Ond he sanctus Georgius him to dryhtne ȝebæd ond þus cwæd: 'Hælende Crist'. *c* **975** *Rushw. Gosp.* Matt. i. 18 Kristes soþlice kennisse þus wæs. *c* **1200** *Vices & Virt.* 3 Godes awene muðe, ðe ðus seið: 'Vade prius [etc.]'. *a* **1300** *XV Signs bef. Judgm.* 33 in *E.E.P.* (1862) 8 þe first tokning sal be þusse..þe sterris..sal adun..be cast. *c* **1330** R. BRUNNE *Chron.* (1810) 61 On þe Wissonday..Com bode to þe kyng, & þus gan þei seie, þat [etc.]. **1418** S. THOMAS in *E.E. Wills* (1883) 38 Knowe alle men þat I..make þus my testament. **1500–20** DUNBAR *Poems* xxv. 28 The dergy [dirige] begynis thuss. **1697** DRYDEN *Æneid* II. 2 From his lofty couch he thus began. **1766** GOLDSM. *Vic. W.* x, After tea..she began thus. **1837** LOCKHART *Scott* xliv, On the 13th [of May 1819] he wrote thus to Captain Ferguson.

c. In the manner now being indicated or exemplified.

c **1440** *York Myst.* vii. 6 Here vn-to you þus am I sente. **1535** COVERDALE *Jer.* li. 64 When thou hast redde out the boke, bynde a stone to it, and cast it in the myddest of Euphrates, and saye: Euen thus shal Babilon syncke. **1596** SHAKS. *Merch. V.* II. ii. 203 While grace is saying hood mine eyes Thus with my hat. **1605** —— *Macb.* II. i. 49 It is the bloody Businesse, which informes Thus to mine Eyes. **1727** W. MATHER *Yng. Man's Comp.* 36 A Period or full Stop, thus mark't (.). **1812** J. WILSON *Isle of Palms* II. 423 But why thus gleams Fitz-Owen's eye? **1850** TENNYSON *In Mem.* xcviii. 1 Risest thou thus, dim dawn?

d. Ellipt. for *thus says, said* (referring either to a preceding or subsequent speech). *poet.* or *arch.*

1568 GRAFTON *Chron.* II. 632 Thus much Hall. **1667** MILTON *P.L.* XII. 79 To whom thus Michael: Justly thou abhorr'st [etc.]. **1757** W. WILKIE *Epigon.* VI. 164 Cassandra thus; and thus the Paphian maid: Your gen'rous love [etc.]. **1847** TENNYSON *Princess* 160 'And yet, to speak the truth, I rate your chance Almost at naked nothing'. Thus the king; And I [etc.].

e. *thus and thus*, expressing minuteness or detail in the description given.

13.. *Cursor M.* 26203 (Fairf.) þus & þus do þi penaunce [*Cott.* For þus, and þus, þou do penance]. **1413** *Pilgr. Sowle* (Caxton) I. xxi. (1859) 21 Suche day and tyme he dyde thus and thus. **1535** COVERDALE *1 Kings* xiv. 5 Speake thou therfore vnto her thus & thus. **1605** SHAKS. *Lear* I. ii. 114 The wisedome of Nature can reason it thus, and thus, yet Nature finds [etc.]. **1662** STILLINGFL. *Orig. Sacr.* III. ii. §5 One of the same kind with our selves, thus and thus formed. **1892** KIPLING & BALESTIER *Naulahka* xviii. 211 Now we are come to our Kingdom, And the State is thus and thus. **1909** H. G. WELLS *Tono-Bungay* II. iv. 200 Nobody, no book, ever came and said to me, thus and thus is the world made and so and so is necessary. *Ibid.* 225 Thus and thus it was the Will in things had its way with me. **1942** R. CHANDLER *Let.* 15 Mar. (1981) 20 The reader expects thus and thus of Chandler because he did it before.

f. Preceded by redundant *as*. (Cf. AS *conj.* 34.)

1426 LYDG. *De Guil.'s Pilgr.* 4195, I mene as thus: conceyveth al [etc.]. **1430–40** —— *Bochas* (Bodl. MS.) If. 144, I meane as thus, I ha no fresshe licour. *Ibid.* 150/2, I meane as thus, yeff ther be sette a lawe. *c* **1450** —— *Secrees* 757, I mene as thus by a dyvisioun Toward hym sylff kepe his Estat Royal. **1847** C. BRONTË *J. Eyre* xxxvii, When I have clasped her once more to my heart, as I do now; and kissed her, as thus. **1865** J. T. WHITE in *Reader* No. 139. 234/1 The article next proceeds as thus.

g. *thus and so* = SO-AND-SO *a.*, *adv.* 2. *dial.* and *U.S.*

1824 W. CARR *Craven Dial.* i. 6 Hees lang been vara indifferent, and hees now nobbud thus an seea. **1901** F. E. TAYLOR *Folk-Speech S. Lancashire* s.v. *Thus an'-so*, 'Heawsto bin gerrin' on?' 'Well, nobbo thus an' so.' **1904** *N.Y. Even. Post* 23 Apr., The statement that matters will result thus and so 'if the crops turn out all right'. **1924** R. M. OGDEN tr. *Koffka's Growth of Mind* iii. 100 The present situation appears..not as one that is constituted thus-and-so. **1932** *Atlantic Monthly* Apr. 407/1 We know why we stand thus and so in the sample of conflicting faiths.

2. In accordance with this; accordingly, and so; consequently; therefore.

c **1200** ORMIN Pref. 81, & tuss iss Crist Amminadab þurrh gastliȝ witt ȝehatenn, Forr þatt he toc o rode daeþ Wiþþ all hiss fulle wille. *c* **1315** *Shoreham* vii. 859 And þos þat chyld to nyȝt y-bore, þaȝ hyt deyde, hyt were for-lore ȝef crystnynge nere. *c* **1407** H. SCOGAN *Moral Balade* 97 (MS. Ashm.) By avncetrye þus may yee no-thing clayme. **1591** SHAKS. *Two Gent.* III. i. 17 Thus (for my duties sake) I rather chose To crosse my friend..Then [etc.]. **1796** H. HUNTER tr. *St.-Pierre's Stud. Nat.* (1799) II. 34 Thus, for example, the signs of tempest off the Cape of Good-Hope far exceed those on our coasts. **1857** BUCKLE *Civiliz.* I. i. 19 Thus we have man modifying nature, and nature modifying man. **1892** STEVENSON *Across the Plains* 144 In this path he must thus have preceded..all contemporary roundeleers.

3. Qualifying an adj. or adv.: To this extent, number, or degree; as..as this; so; esp. *thus far*, to this point (often used to indicate the end of a quotation); *thus much*, so much, as much as this. In quot. 1393 correlative to *as* = as..as (*obs.*).

Beowulf 336 Ne seah ic elþeodiȝe þus maniȝe men modiȝlicran. *a* **700** *Epinal Gloss.* (O.E.T.) 1037 *Tantisper*, þus suiþae. *c* **725** *Corpus Gloss.* 1982 Ðus suiðe. *a* **800** *Erfurt Gloss.* 1037 Dus suidae. *c* **1000** ÆLFRIC *Hom.* I. 316 Seȝe me, beceapode ȝe ðus micel landes? *c* **1205** LAY. 29625 Woldest þu þus sone faren aȝein to Rome? *a* **1250** *Owl & Night.* 758 For ic kan craft & ic kan lyste & þarfore ic am þus þriste. *c* **1369** CHAUCER *Dethe Blaunche* 904 But thus moche dar I sayn. **1393** LANGL. *P. Pl.* C. IV. 181 Hue is assoilid þus [*v.r.* as] sone as hure self lykeþ. *a* **1451** FORTESCUE *Wks.* (1869) 550 Thus longe ys the cooste of Englonde on the oon syde of hym by see. **1531** *Dial. on Laws Eng.* II. xlv. Q iij b, There shall not be layde vpon a ded persone but..thus many tapers or candels. **1578** BANISTER *Hist. Man* I. 22, I write thus much for the excuse of Vesalius, because he is so apertly reproved. **1596** SHAKS. *Tam. Shr.* I. ii. 104 Therefore let me be thus bold with you. **1599** —— *Hen. V*, Epil., Thus farre ..Our bending Author hath pursu'd the Story. **1681** DRYDEN *Abs. & Achit.* 803 Thus far 'tis duty: but here fix the mark. **1746** FRANCIS *Hor., Epist.* I. xvii. 55 Then you confess, That who succeeds, thus difficult his Part, Gives the best Proof of Courage. **1823** SOUTHEY *Hist. Penins. War* I. xii. 617 The happy issue, thus far, of their civil administration. **1884** W. C. SMITH *Kildrostan* 53 Yet you can speak thus calmly of unsaying All we have said. **1888** FREEMAN in Stephens *Life* (1895) II. 374 The legend..has thus much of foundation.

Hence † **thus** *v.* (*nonce-use*) *intr.*, to do thus.

1605 SYLVESTER *Du Bartas* II. iii. IV. *Captaines* 212 Six dayes together had the Hebrews thus't About the Town, seven times the Seventh they must.

thusand, -sund, (θ-), obs. ff. THOUSAND.

Thuscane, obs. form of TUSCAN.

† **'thus-gate,** *adv. Obs.* or *Sc. arch.* [f. THUS *adv.* + GATE *sb.*²] In this way; thus.

a **1300** *Cursor M.* 13192 (Cott.) þus-gat was sant Iohan slan. *c* **1300** *Havelok* 2419 Sule ye þus-gate fro me fle? *c* **1330** R. BRUNNE *Chron. Wace* (Rolls) 14351 (Petyt MS.) And whan þe ton þus gate was ded On þat oþer bataille he bed. *c* **1475** *Rauf Coilȝear* 169 ȝit was I neuer in my lyfe thus gait leird. *a* **1550** *Freiris of Berwik* 578 in *Dunbar's Poems* (S.T.S.) 304 He said, 'ȝone Freir hes maid me thus gait say'. **1819** W. TENNANT *Papistry Storm'd* (1827) 148 But what befel him thus-gate daddit, In the neist sang ye'll find it addit.

† **'thus-gates,** *adv. Obs.* [f. prec. + *-s* of adverbial genitive.] = prec.

c **1375** *Cursor M.* 1242 (Fairf.) Til seth his sone, þus gates he spake. *c* **1400** *Destr. Troy* 4500 þus gatis to the gome þen the god saide. *c* **1450** in *Pol. Rel. & L. Poems* 108 If I my saule þusgates wil fede. **1513** DOUGLAS *Æneis* II. xii. (xi.) 17 Anchises..Lift..hands to hevin, and thus gatis said.

'thusly, *adv. colloq.* [f. THUS + -LY².] = THUS.

1865 *Harper's Mag.* Dec. 133/2 It happened, as J. Billings would say, 'thusly'. **1876** [see DINGUS]. **1889** *Boston* (Mass.) *Jrnl.* 17 Jan. 2/3 On his way home George mused thusly. **1893** LADY BURTON *Life Sir R.F. Burton* II. 3 Stories never lose anything in the recital, and consequently this one grew thusly.

thusness ('ðʌsnɪs). *colloq.* [f. THUS + -NESS.] The condition of being thus. Chiefly *humorous.*

1883 in W. Hamilton *Parodies* (1886) III. 159 Expound me this thusness I pray. **1888** F. HUME *Mme. Midas* I. xv, Why all this thusness? **1888** *Daily News* 27 Dec. 3/4 Why this 'thusness'? as our Transatlantic humourists would say. **1891** *Nature* 12 Mar. 435/1 Force produces motion, but what determines it and gives it its thusness?

thussocke, obs. form of TUSSOCK.

thuswise ('ðʌswaɪz), *adv.* [f. THUS + -WISE.] In this manner; = THUS. Cf. THISWISE.

13.. *Cursor M.* 11971 (Gött.) 'Sun', scho said, 'wirk noght þus wise' [*Cott., Tr.* þis wise; *Fairf.* suche wise]. **1509** BARCLAY *Shyp of Folys* (1570) 238 Howe longe shall ye mankinde thus wise oppres? **1526** TINDALE *Phil.* iii. 15 As many as be perfect be thus wyse minded. **1594** CAREW *Huarte's Exam. Wits* (1616) 172 This child, whom we goe thus-wise examining. **1843** E. JONES *Sens. & Event Poems* (1879) 8 Long ere the worms had fretted through The clay that thuswise spake. **1849** M. ARNOLD *In Utrumque Paratus* ii, O waking on a world which thuswise springs. **1887** MORRIS *Odyss.* XI. 504, I spake unto him and thuswise answered again.

So † **thus ways** *adv. phr. Obs. rare*⁻¹.

1616 J. HAIG in J. Russell *Haigs* vi. (1881) 139, I was no scholar to sustain ane argument against him, but thus ways leaves him.

thute, þuten, var. THEOTEN *v. Obs.*, to howl.

thutie, obs. form of TUTTY.

thutter ('θʌtə(r)), *v.* [Echoic; cf. *twitter, stutter*; also OE. *þoterian* to howl, wail.] *intr.* To make the sputtering or shaking sound suggested by the word. Hence **'thuttering** *ppl. a.*

1897 KIPLING *Captains Courageous* (ed. Tauchn.) 12 Blowing through a big conch-shell, he must needs stand up ..and send a grinding, thuttering shriek through the fog. **1904** —— *Traffics & Discov.* 370 The old mill shook and the heavy stones thuttered on the grist. **1905** J. C. LINCOLN *Partners of Tide* vii. 139 There boomed out of the dark a thuttering, shaking roar, that swelled to a shriek and died away—the voice of the great steam foghorn.

‖**Thuya** ('θ(j)uːjə). *Bot.* [An irregular repr. of Gr. θυία, more correctly θύα, name of an African tree (*Thuja articulata* Linn., now *Callitris quadrivalvis*), the source of the THYINE wood (Gr. ξύλον θύϊνον) of Rev. xviii. 12. See also THUJA.

Theophrastus *H. Pl.* 5. 3. 7 has θύον and θύα, rendered by Pliny *N.H.* 13. 16. 30 '*thyon*, ab aliis *thya*'. Med. Gr. MSS. and early printed edd. gave the Gr. as θύιον, θυία, which Theodorus Gaza *tr. Theophrastus* 1483, Latinized as *tyium, thuia*. Camerarius, 1577, has *thya* from Pliny and *thuia* after Gaza; he applies the name to the American *Arbor Vitæ, Thuya occidentalis*. Bauhin, 1671, has the barbarous form *Thuya* for *Thuia* or *Thuja*. Tournefort used *Thya* from Pliny, which was also preferred by Linnæus *Philos. Bot.* (1750) 175 '*Thya*, male *Thuja* et *Thuya*'. L. had himself used *Thuja* (var. of *Thuia*) in 1737, and reverted to it in his definitive *Sp. Pl.* 1753; and this was generally followed by British botanists and horticulturists, and is still in popular English use. But French botanists continued to use Bauhin's *Thuya* (Littré has '*Thuia* ou *Thuya*'), and this has been followed by Bentham and Hooker, and adopted at Kew as the generic name. (Sir W. T. Thiselton-Dyer.) The only defensible form etymologically is of course *Thya*.]

Name of a genus of coniferous trees, consisting of about ten species, of which the North American *T. occidentalis* and the Chinese *T. orientalis* are commonly cultivated under the name Arbor Vitæ. (The tree so called by the ancients is now known as *Callitris*.) Also *attrib.*, as *thuya-wood*.

[**1483** GAZA tr. *Theophr. H. Pl.* F iiij, Tyium quod thuia ab aliis appellatur. **1671** BAUHIN *Pinax* 488 Thuya Theophrasti. *Arbor Vitæ*, Bellonio; *Thuia sive Thya, vulgo.* Cam[erarius]. **1706** PHILLIPS (ed. Kersey), *Thya*, a kind of wild Cypress-Tree, whose Wood is very sweet and lasting; the Life-Tree.] **1707** MORTIMER *Husb.* (1721) II. 60 *Thuya*, or *Arbor vitæ*, grows of Layers or Slips to a tall straight goodly Tree. **1770** J. R. FORSTER tr. *Kalm's Trav. N. Amer.* (1772) II. 315 All the posts which are driven into the ground are made of Thuya wood. **1836** H. MURRAY, etc. *Hist. & Descr. Acc. China* I. i. 19 Richly clothed with trees, particularly the tallow, the camphor, the thuya or arbor vitæ. **1903** F. EDEN *Garden in Venice* iii. 17 A tiny square of garden, closed in with an unshapely hedge of thuya and euonymus.

thuyene ('θjuːjiːn), etc. *Chem.*: see THUJENE.

thwa, obs. erron. Sc. form of TWO.

thwack (θwæk), *sb.* [f. the verb.] A vigorous stroke with a stick or the like; a whack. Also as *int.*

1587 T. HUGHES, etc. *Misfort. Arthur* IV. ii, Boystrous bangs with thumping thwacks fall thicke. **1654** GAYTON *Pleas. Notes* III. ii. 76 A company of lusty shoulder-thumpers, who discharg'd the mutuall thwacks so stoutly, that they made a noise, as if they were beating of hemp. **1663** BUTLER *Hud.* I. II. 795 But Talgol first with hardy Thwack Twice bruis'd his head, and twice his back. **1704** SWIFT *T. Tub* xi. (1709) 131 Noble Captain, lend a reasonable Thwack..with that cane of yours. **1832** W. IRVING *Alhambra* (1851) 250 Bestowing a hearty thwack with a cudgel on the flanks of his donkey. **1859** G. MEREDITH *R. Feverel* xxiii, Sounding a thwack on his knee. **1908** L. M. MONTGOMERY *Anne of Green Gables* xv. 156 And then—Thwack! Anne had brought her slate down on Gilbert's head. **1976** *National Observer* (U.S.) 14 Aug. 6/3 Thwack! Boston's Jim Rice sends the first pitch sailing over the left-field wall.

thwack (θwæk), *v.* Also 6–7 **thwacke, thwak,** 6, 8 *dial.* **twack.** [app. echoic, from the sound of beating vigorously: see sense 1.

But it may have been altered from the earlier THACK *v.*², orig. to pat, to clap, but in 1480 used of showering blows, the initial *thw-* expressing more forcible effort than *th-*; the sense 'clap' might also pass easily into sense 3 here, which does not easily arise out of 1.]

1. *trans.* To beat or strike vigorously, as with a stick; to bang, thrash, whack.

a **1530** HEYWOOD *Johan & Tyb* (Brandl) 31, I shall bete her and thwak her. *a* **1535** MORE in Wordsw. *Eccl. Biog.* (1818) II. 123 Now I will speake but three words, and I durst jeopard a wager that none here [on the Continent] shall pronounce it after me: 'Thwarts [? *error for* Thwaites] thwackt him with a thwitle'. **1560** INGELEND *Disob. Child* G ij, Beynge full often with the staffe thwacked. *a* **1626** MIDDLETON *Mayor of Queenb.* v. i, Take all my cushions down and thwack them soundly. **1712** ARBUTHNOT *John Bull* IV. vii, To snatch the cudgel..that he might thwack Lewis with it. **1881** BESANT & RICE *Chapl. of Fleet* I. iv, To see two sturdy fellows thwack and belabour each other with quarter-staff, single-stick, or fists.

absol. **1573** TUSSER *Husb.* (1878) 43 Flailes lustily thwack, least plough seede lack.

b. *fig.* To 'beat' in a contest, to defeat severely.

1607 SHAKS. *Cor.* IV. v. 189 Here's he that was wont to thwacke our Generall, Caius Martius. **1821** SCOTT *Kenilw.* ii, What adventurous knight ever thought of the lady's terror, when he went to thwack giant, dragon, or magician,

..for her deliverance? **1869** BLACKMORE *Lorna D.* ii, If we count three before the come of thee, thwacked thou art.

c. *intr.* To fall with a thwack or sharp knock.

a **1851** MOIR *Winter Wild* vii, To the quaking sheet below, Down thwacks he, with a thud like thunder!

2. *trans.* To drive or force by or as by thwacking or beating; to knock (*down, in, out,* etc.). Also *fig.*

1566 DRANT *Wail. Hierim.* K iv, To thwacke downe walles, to even them with the flore. **1611** SHAKS. *Wint. T.* I. ii. 37 Wee'l thwack him hence with Distaffes. **1743** *Lond. & Country Brew.* II. (ed. 2) 126 Beating or Thwacking the Yeast into working Ale or Beer. **1906** *Outlook* 22 Sept. 374/1 If Busby's rhythmic rod thwacked Latin metre into the head of more than one poet.

3. a. To clap; to clap *together,* to pack or crowd together (things or persons); to clap *down.*

1589 FLEMING *Virg. Georg.* II. 24 The bushie thornie fields, Where many grauell stones be thwackt. **1610** BP. HALL *Apol. Brownists* 14 [He] thwacks fourteene Scriptures into the margent. **1641** MILTON *Animadv.* ii. Wks. 1851 III. 208 Who would have thought a man could have thwackt together so many incongruous similitudes? **1674** N. FAIRFAX *Bulk & Selv.* 151 The shruff, moss and hair, that the nest was thwackt together of. **1687** A. LOVELL tr. *Thevenot's Trav.* I. 25 Many of them being thwackt together into one Room, they are not a little straitned. **1760** [see THWACKING *vbl. sb.*]. **1902** *Daily Chron.* 17 Feb. 7/5 [Prisoner in Police Court], I don't care what you say; thwack me down three months' [hard labour] in the book, quick.

†**b.** *intr.* (for *refl.*) To crowd (*to* a place). *rare.*

1652 BROME *City Wit* II. ii, All the wise wenches i' the Town will thwack to such Sanctuaries, when the times are troublesome.

†**c.** *trans.* To pack or crowd (a thing or place). Const. *with* something. *Obs.*

Much used in this sense from *c* 1585 to 1700.

1582 STANYHURST *Æneis* III. (Arb.) 85 Weau'd wurcks thwackt with honor. **1588** A. MUNDAY in Farr *S.P. Eliz.* (1845) I. 229 He that had his barnes so thwakt, And bade his soul take rest. **1607** J. CARPENTER *Plaine Mans Plough* 15 The field was thwacked with thornes, tares, and noysome weeds. **1667** WATERHOUSE *Fire Lond.* 103 Its Streets were.. thwack'd with Carts, pester'd with Porters. **1698** FRYER *Acc. E. India & P.* 58 We could discern the River to be thwacked with small Craft.

†**d.** *intr.* (for *passive*). To be packed or filled full.

1650 HOWELL *Giraffi's Rev. Naples* I. 114 The Church.. was as full as it could thwack in thick multitudes.

4. The verb-stem in combination with a sb.: **thwack-coat** *a.*, that thwacks the coat; **thwack-stave**, a quarter-staff, a cudgel.

1593 G. HARVEY *Pierce's Super.* Wks. (Grosart) II. 126 To be sold at the signe of the Crabbtree Cudgell in Thwackcoate Lane. **1857** SIR F. PALGRAVE *Norm. & Eng.* II. 504 Every bodily exercise,..the footrace or the gallop, single-stick or thwackstave, spear or sword.

Hence **thwacked** (θwækt), *ppl. a.* (*a*) beaten; †(*b*) packed, crowded (*obs.*).

a **1670** HACKET *Serm. Incarnation* vii. Wks. (1675) 64 Let two or three be gathered together in his name..; but if you will multiply those two or three to hundreds..of souls, O then his desire is upon..those thwackt congregations.

thwacker (ˈθwækə(r)). *rare.* [f. prec. + -ER[1].]

1. One who or that which thwacks; a beater; *spec.* an implement for beating half-dried pantiles into shape on the thwacking-frame.

1867 URE *Dict. Arts,* etc. III. 902 When half-dry the tiles are taken out one by one, placed on the thwacking frame, and beaten with the thwacker to produce the required shape. **1877** KNIGHT *Dict. Mech., Thwacking-frame,* the tool by which the upper side [of half-dried pantiles] is beaten has the shape of the segment of a cylinder, and is called the thwacker. **1879** G. MEREDITH *Egoist* Prelude, Like cudgels of carpet-thwackers expelling dust.

†**2.** A thumper, a whacker; in quot., a 'thumping' lie. *Obs. rare*$^{-1}$.

1674 N. FAIRFAX *Bulk & Selv.* 108 It would follow, that our leasting were greater than somewhat else, or greater than it self; Which would be a thwacker.

thwacking (ˈθwækɪŋ), *vbl. sb.* [f. THWACK *v.* + -ING[1].] The action of the verb THWACK in various senses. Also *attrib.*: **thwacking-frame**, a stand on which pantiles are beaten into shape; **thwacking-horse, -stool**, a bench on which the thwacking-frame is placed; **thwacking-knife**, a knife for trimming the edges of pantiles.

1736 AINSWORTH *Lat. Dict.* 1, A thwacking, *verberatio, fustuarium, fustigatio.* **1760** MAIR *Tyro's Dict.* (1820) 372 *Stipatio,*..a cramming or thwacking of things together. **1820** W. IRVING *Sketch Bk.* II. 107 We heard a distant thwacking sound,..the rolling pin, struck upon the dresser by the cook. **1867** Thwacking frame [see THWACKER 1]. **1895** ZANGWILL *Master* III. ix, The thwacking of the dancers' feet in the barn.

thwacking (ˈθwækɪŋ), *ppl. a.* [f. THWACK *v.* + -ING[2].] That thwacks; that is a thwacker; big, strong, forcible; thumping, whacking.

1567 DRANT *Horace, De Arte Poet.* A iij, Put out no puffes, nor thwackyng words, words of to large assyce. **1620** MIDDLETON *Chaste Maid* v. iii, *Sec. Serv.* A bonfire, Sir? *Sir Oliver.* A thwacking one, I charge you. **1671** H. FOULIS *Hist. Rom. Treas.* (1681) 42 After all these thwacking Arguments. **1682** H. MORE *Annot. Glanvill's Lux O.* 191 In vertue of which thwacking expressions he has fancied himself able to play at Scholastick or Philosophick Quarter-Staff. **1890** *Daily News* 17 Dec. 5/7 Then..came a thwacking blow from Dr. Tanner's blackthorn.

Hence ˈ**thwackingly** *adv.*

1660 H. MORE *Myst. Godl.* VI. xvii. 270 In riveting the Godhead into his own person so thwackingly and substantially, as that he may give the World to understand that he was as much God as that Christ that died at Jerusalem.

thwait(e (θweɪt). *dial.* Also 7 **twaite.** [a. ON. *þveit, þveiti* a piece of land, a paddock, lit. a cutting, cut-piece, f. **þvíta* = OE. *þwitan* to cut, cut off, THWITE.] A piece of ground; *esp.* a piece of ground cleared from forest or reclaimed from waste. Now *rare* or *Obs.* as a separate word. (Hence the surname *Thwaites.*)

Entering into numerous place-names, esp. in Cumbria, and N. Lancashire, as *Applethwaite, Crosthwaite, Dowthwaite, Ormthwaite, Seathwaite,* etc..

1628 COKE *On Litt.* 4 b, *Twaite* signifieth a wood grubbed up and turned to arable. **1670** in BLOUNT *Law Dict.* s.v. **1777** NICOLSON & BURN *Hist. Westmld. & Cumbld.* II. 14 Several parts and parcels,..differing in form and quality of soil, or otherwise inclosed by the inhabitants from the barren waste of the fells, such parts and parcels are..called thwaits. **1825** BROCKETT *N.C. Words, Thwaite,* a level pasture field. **1832** J. BREE *St. Herbert's Isle* 125 A thwaite was a portion of ground cleared of wood for residence or cultivation.

thwang, thwang(u)e, obs. ff. THONG.

†**thwarl,** *a. Obs. rare*$^{-1}$. ? Twisted; ? tight.

13.. *Gaw. & Gr. Knt.* 194 Syþen þrawen wyth a þwong a þwarle knot alofte.

thwart (θwɔːt), *sb.*[1] Now *rare.* [f. THWART *v.*] An act or instance of thwarting; a check, hindrance, obstruction, frustration.

1611 COTGR. s.v. *Vent, Batu de mauvais vent,* crost by a contrarie, or malignant thwart. **1632** ROWLEY *New Wonder* I. 11 Full oft, and many have I heard complaine Of discontents, thwarts, and adversities. **1661** GLANVILL *Van. Dogm.* 81 Any considerable thwart in the Motion. **1742** H. WALPOLE *Lett. to Mann* (1834) I. 104 The number of blows and thwarts which the French have received. **1782** MISS BURNEY *Cecilia* II. iii, A certain discourteous person..in thwart of your fair inclinations, keepeth and detaineth your irradiant frame in hostile thraldom. **1902** *Blackw. Mag.* Apr. 547/1, I distrust that man—He's a thwart—a moral thwart.

thwart (θwɔːt), *sb.*[2] [app. a sb. use (which came in after 1725) of THWART *adv.* and *adj.*, having reference to the position of the rowing benches or seats *athwart* or across the boat. Whether its use was partly due to similarity of sound to *thaught, thawt,* or *thought,* previously applied to the same thing, is uncertain. Our latest contemporary instance of '*thaught* or *thought*' is of 1721, of *thoat* 1697, of *thout* 1725, while our first of '*thaughts* or *thwarts*' is of 1736, so that the appellations were continuous in use, as if the one had passed into the other. But, for the full determination of the relations between *thoft, thought* or *thaught,* and *thwart,* fuller evidence between 1500 and 1700 is needed. Cf. THOFT, THOUGHT[2].] A seat across a boat, on which the rower sits; a rower's bench.

[**1721** BAILEY, *Thoughts,* the Rowers Seats in a Boat.] **1736** —— (folio), *Thaughts,* v. *Thwarts. Ibid., Thwarts,* (a Sea Term) the boards or benches laid a-cross boats and gallies, upon which the rowers sit. **1770** COOK *Voy. round World* II. x. (1773) 462 A considerable number of thwarts were laid from gunwale to gunwale. **1776** *Falconer's Dict. Marine, Thwart,* the seat or bench of a boat whereon the rowers sit to manage the oars. **1897** F. T. BULLEN *Cruise Cachalot* 41 We drew each man his oar across the boat and lashed it firmly down with a piece of line spliced to each thwart.

thwart (θwɔːt), *adv., prep.,* and *adj.* Forms: 3 **þuert, ðwert,** (*Orm.*) **þwerrt,** 4 **thwert,** 5 **þwerte, twhert, thuart,** 5–7 **twart, thwarte, twhart,** 6–7 **thwarth, thawart(e, (qwarte, whart),** 7 **twarte,** 9 *dial.* **thort, thurt, thirt, thert,** 5– **thwart.** [Early ME. (*c* 1200) *þwert,* a. ON. *þvert* (Norw. *tvert, tvært,* Sw. *tvert, tvärt,* Da. *tvært*) adv., across, athwart, orig. neuter of the ON. adj. *þver-r* (Norw. *tver, tvær,* Sw. *tver, tvär,* Da. *tvær*), transverse, cross. Cf. OHG. *twer,* MHG. *twer, quer,* Ger. *quer,* and (with adv. gen. *-s*), OFris. *þweres, dwers,* Satl. *twars,* WFris. *dwerz, dwers,* EFris. *dwars, dwas,* MLG., MD. *dwers, dwars,* LG., Du. *dwars,* athwart, crossly, peevishly; ON. *þvers* = *þvert.* ON. *þver* was shortened from **þverh* = OE. *þwerh, þweorh* (genitive *þweores,* in comb. *þweor-*) crooked, cross, perverse = OHG. *dwerh, dwerah, twerh,* MHG. *dwerch, twerch,* Ger. *zwerch-* (in composition), Goth. *þwairhs* cross, angry,:—OTeut. **þwerh-* :—**þwerhw-*:—Indo-Eur. **twerkw-*, whence L. *torquēre* to twist, Skr. *tarkú* spindle. In Eng. the adv. is known *c* 1200, first in the combinations *þwert út* (THWERT-OUT) and *þwert-over* (THWART-OVER), later (*c* 1300) *over-þwert* (OVERTHWART). It was used as an adj., with a vb. *þwerten,* both *fig., c* 1250, and as a prep. bef. 1300. In all these *thwert* became *thwart* in the 15th c. *Thwart* sb. is found in the 17th c.

The ME. material is scanty, and the sense development is not illustrated fully by the extant quotations. The senses are therefore here arranged in what appears to be the logical order.]

A. *adv.*

†**1.** Across or transversely to the length, direction, or course of anything; from side to side; crosswise, transversely; = ATHWART A. 1. *Obs.*

a **1350** *St. Thomas* 85 in Horstm. *Altengl. Leg.* (1881) 21 A grete blak dog..Thwert in his mouth þe hand he broght. **1483** CAXTON *Gold. Leg.* 402/2 A man on hors backe which bare a longe tree thwarte and wold entre in to the temple, and he myght not by cause the tree laye thwarte. **1597** A. M. tr. *Guillemeau's Fr. Chirurg.* 24 b/1 An apertione accordinge to the length of that parte, and not thwart or crosseover. **1624** CAPT. SMITH *Virginia* III. 79 A great tree (that lay thwart as a barricado). **1664** EVELYN *Sylva* (1776) 405 Till you can lay them thwart, that the top of one may rest on the root or stub of the other.

†**b.** *fig.* Across the course of, so as to obstruct or oppose; adversely; = ATHWART A. 3. *Obs.*

a **1628** PRESTON *New Covt.* (1634) 146 There are many things in the Creature that are crosse to us, that fall thwart upon us. **1642** R. CARPENTER *Experience* II. xi. 214 A work that lyes thwart, and strives against the current of your naturall inclination.

2. From one side to the other of anything (with motion implied); across. *arch.*

1511 GUYLFORD *Pilgr.* (Camden) 6 We trauersed out of that ryuer into an other lytell ryuer, whiche brought us thawarte ayen into Latyze. **1880** WEBB *Goethe's Faust* I. i. 31 Up, down and thwart, without repose, To lead my scholars by the nose.

†**3.** *thwart of.* **a.** *Naut.* Opposite to, over against (a place on the coast); = OFF B. II. 6 b.

1556 W. TOWRSON in Hakluyt *Voy.* (1589) 98 We were thwart of Porto Sancto. **1670** NARBOROUGH *Jrnl.* in *Acc. Sev. Late Voy.* I. (1694) 16 Being thwart of the Shoals of Brazil.

†**b.** Transversely to, across the direction of. *Obs.*

1667 MILTON *P.L.* x. 703 With adverse blast up-turns them from the South Notus and Afer black with thundrous Clouds..; thwart of these as fierce Forth rush the Levant and the Ponent Windes Eurus and Zephir.

B. *prep.*

1. From side to side of, across: **a.** of position or direction; = ATHWART B. 1 b. *arch.* or *poet.*

1470–85 MALORY *Arthur* v. viii. 173 Lucyus smote Arthur thwart the vysage. **1585** T. WASHINGTON tr. *Nicholay's Voy.* II. x. 44 Our patrone..was..caste thwart the nose of our gallie. **1680** *Lond. Gaz.* No. 1550/4 [He] hath a Scar thwart the back of one of his Hands. **1741** in *Descr. Thames* (1758) 87 No Person..shall..bend any Net, by Anchors or otherwise, thwart the Channel, and so as to draw another Net into it. **1870** MORRIS *Earthly Par.* II. III. 192 A pink-tinged cloud spread thwart the shore.

b. of motion: = ATHWART B. 1 a. *arch.* or *poet.*

1583 STOCKER *Civ. Warres Lowe C.* III. 91 Came three messengers thwart the fieldes in at the wood gate. **1598** STOW *Surv.* iii. (1603) 14 Which ran..through that streete, thwart Grastreete, and downe Lumbard streete. **1738** GRAY *Tasso* 7 Thwart the road a River roll'd its flood tempestuous. **1813** T. BUSBY *Lucretius* II. 131 When shines the God of Day, And thwart the darkened chamber darts his ray. **1898** T. HARDY *Wessex Poems* 2 Thwart my wistful way did a damsel saunter.

2. Across the course or direction of; = ATHWART B. 3. ***thwart the hawse*** (†*halse*), across the stem of a ship. Chiefly *Naut.*

1495 *Trevisa's Barth. De P.R.* v. vi. (W. de W.) g v/1 Two holowe synewes whiche ben callyd Optici..come eyther thwart other, and ben Ioyned in a poynte. **1620** in Foster *Eng. Factories Ind.* (1906) 220 Intending with her to laie the Portingall admirall thwart the halse and soe to burne both together. **1622** R. HAWKINS *Voy. S. Sea* (1847) 85 For foure leagues into the sea (thwart it), lye banks of sand. **1737** BRACKEN *Farriery Impr.* (1756) I. 54 Fibres that cross and go thwart one another.

†**3.** Across the course of, so as to obstruct; = ATHWART B. 5. *Obs.*

1641 MILTON *Reform.* I. Wks. 1851 III. 31 Crosse-jingling periods which..come thwart a setl'd devotion worse then the din of bells and rattles.

C. *adj.*

1. Lying, extending, or passing across; transverse, cross; in quots. 1483, 1712, *perh.* oblique. †***thwart circle***, the zodiac (*obs.*). See also THWART-SAW.

1404 [implied in THWART-SAW]. **1483** CAXTON *Gold. Leg.* 121 b/1 It was made lyke a crosse thwart of whyche the two endes were fyxed in therthe. And that hys membres shold theron be broken. **1551** RECORDE *Cast. Knowl.* (1556) 30 The Zodiak (whiche many doo call the Thwarte circle). **1658** J. ROWLAND *Moufet's Theat. Ins.* 971 The last part is whitish, chequered with right and thwart fibres. **1712** J. JAMES tr. *Le Blond's Gardening* 41 The Diagonal or Thwart-walk. **1836** W. IRVING *Astoria* (1849) 86 They have thwart pieces from side to side about three inches thick. **1873** PROCTOR *Expanse Heav.* 282 The determination of the actual rate of any star's thwart motion.

2. *fig.* **a.** Of persons or their attributes: Disposed to resist, oppose, or obstruct; cross-grained; perverse, froward, obstinate, stubborn, awkward.

c **1250** *Gen. & Ex.* 3099 Ðo pharaun saȝ is lond al fre, His herte ðo wurð ðwert and hard. **1602** *2nd Pt. Return fr. Parnass.* III. iv, This old Sir Raderick it shall be thy taske to cudgell with thy thick thwart termes. **1605** BACON *Adv. Learn.* I. ii. §8 Ignorance makes them [the minds of men] churlish, thwart, and mutinous. **1656** BAXTER *Reformed Pastor* 234, I would not have any to be thwart and contentious with those that govern them. **1819** SHELLEY *Prometh. Unb.* II. ii. 90 Noontide would come, And thwart

Silenus find his goats undrawn. **1892** STEVENSON *Across the Plains* 238 The crass public or the thwart reviewer.

b. Of things: Adverse, unfavourable, untoward, unpropitious; esp. applied (with mixture of literal sense) to a wind or current: cross.

1610 HEALEY *St. Aug. Citie of God* 129 These thwart effects fell out even then when things were said to be carried ..so justly. **1621** LADY M. WROTH *Urania* 472 Not only neere it in blood, but allyed in thwart fortune. *a* **1660** *Contemp. Hist. Irel.* (Ir. Archæol. Soc.) II. 36 This secret and thwarte dealinge is worse then open and publicke violence. *Ibid.* III. 42 A demonstration of theire reciprocall thwarte dealinge. **1865** SWINBURNE *Atalanta* 184 A thwart sea-wind full of rain and foam. **1889** SKRINE *Mem. E. Thring* 235 In spite of these thwart currents, Thring built up his large school.

†**3.** Opposed, contrary (*to*); in quot. 1614, opposed in sense, antithetical, contrasted. *Obs.*

a **1601** ? MARSTON *Pasquil & Kath.* I. 304 Why should you runne an Idle counter-course Thwart to the path of fashion? **1614** T. ADAMS *Fatal Banquet* iv. Wks. 1861 I. 216 A pair of cross and thwart sentences, handled rather by collation than relation, whose conjunction is disjunctive. **1615** JACKSON *Creed* IV. II. vi. §5 A meaning as ridiculous, as thwart and contradictory to his purpose as the devil himself could have devised. **1624** BP. MOUNTAGU *Gagg* Pref. 23 To be thwart unto, and against the maine of the business negotiated.

thwart (θwɔːt), *v.* [f. prec. adv.]

I. 1. *trans.* To pass or extend across from side to side of; to traverse, cross; also, to cross the direction of, to run at an angle to. *Obs.* or *arch.*

1413 *Pilgr. Sowle* (Caxton) V. i. (1859) 70 A Cercle embelyfyng somwhat, and thwartyng the thycknes of the spyere. **1530** PALSGR. 757/2, I thwarte the waye, I go over the waye to stoppe one, *je trenche le chemyn.* **1608** SHAKS. *Per.* IV. iv. 10 Pericles Is now againe thwarting thy wayward seas. **1627** CAPT. SMITH *Seaman's Gram.* ix. 39 You set your sailes so sharp as you can to lie close by a wind, thwarting it a league or two,..first on the one boord then on the other. **1653** R. SANDERS *Physiogn.* 50 If the Hepatique line be thwarted by other small lines. **1769** FALCONER *Dict. Marine* N iij, The current thwarts the course of a ship. **1805–6** CARY *Dante's Inf.* xxv. 72 The lizard seems A flash of lightning, if he thwart the road. **1863** P. S. WORSLEY *Poems & Transl.* 10 That white reach Thwarting the blue serene, a belt of fire.

b. *intr.* To pass or extend across, to cross. *Obs.* or *arch.*

a **1552** LELAND *Itin.* (1744) VII. 53 The Towne of Cokermuth stondeth on the Ryver of Coker, the which thwartheth over the Town. **1598** STOW *Surv.* xli. (1603) 436 A close cart, bayled ouer and couered with blacke, hauing a plaine white Crosse thwarting. **1609** HEYWOOD *Brit. Troy* XIV. xciii, Through the mid-throng the nearest way he thwarted. **1627** HAKEWILL *Apol.* Pref. 10 It led them some other way, thwarting, and upon the by, not directly. **1856** T. AIRD *Poet. Wks.* 189 They scream, they mix, they thwart, they eddy round.

†**c.** *trans.* To cross the path of; to meet; to fall in with, come across. *Obs.*

1601 CHESTER *Love's Mart., K. Arth.* xx, Merlin..Who by great fortunes chance sir Vlfius thwarted, As he went by in beggers base aray. **1674** N. FAIRFAX *Bulk & Selv.* 146 Motions to be checkt..without the least hit or stop from other bodies that thwart them. **1812** CARY *Dante's Par.* IV. 89 Another question thwarts thee.

†**d.** *Naut.* Of a ship, etc.: To get athwart so as to be foul of. Also *intr. Obs.*

1809 *Naval Chron.* XXIV. 23 The boat having thwarted against the moorings. **1810** *Ibid.* XXIII. 97 The frigate now ..thwarted the Lord Keith's hawse. **1813** *Gen. Hist.* in *Ann. Reg.* 107/1 The Amelia twice fell on board the enemy in attempting to thwart his hawse.

†**2.** To lay (a thing) athwart or across; to place crosswise; to set or put (things) across each other.

thwart over thumb (quot. 1522) app. = *to cross* (one) *over the thumbs*: see THUMB *sb.* 5 d.

1522 SKELTON *Why not to Court* 197 Thus thwartyng ouer thom, He ruleth all the roste. **1588** SPENSER *Virgil's Gnat* 514 The noble sonne of Telamon..thwarting his huge shield, Them battell bad. **1602** CAREW *Cornwall* I. 25 b, Their bils were thwarted crossewise at the end, and with these they would cut an Apple in two at one snap. *Ibid.* 26 b, The inhabitants make use of divers his Creekes, for gristemilles, by thwarting a bancke from side to side. **1623** MARKHAM *Cheap Husb.* I. ii. (1631) 14 Carry your rod..in your right hand, the point either directly upright, or thwarted towards your left shoulder. **1632** LITHGOW *Trav.* VII. 309 They make..the signe of the Crosse.., thwarting their two foremost fingers.

3. To cross *with* a line, streak, band, etc. (Only in pa. pple.) *Obs.* or *arch.*

1610 GUILLIM *Heraldry* III. xiv. (1660) 162 The blacke line on the ridge of all Asses backes, thwarted with the like over both the Shoulders. **1615** G. SANDYS *Trav.* I. 63 Turbants are made like great globes of callico too, and thwarted with roules of the same. **1658** J. ROWLAND *Moufet's Theat. Ins.* 942 The body all over of a yellow colour, except where it is thwarted with cross streaks or lines. **1861** *Temple Bar Mag.* II. 256, I saw Vesuvius.. thwarted by a golden cloud.

b. To cross-plough; also, to cut crosswise.

1847 *Jrnl. R. Agric. Soc.* VIII. II. 318 The burnt earth is then spread on the land and thwarted in (that is, ploughed across the direction in which the land is ploughed when laid up in stetches for sowing). **1871** COUCH *Hist. Polperro* vi. 117 Land broken for wheat is thwarted in the Spring. **1888** ELWORTHY *W. Somerset Word-bk.* s.v. *Thurt,* Why, 'tis a wo'th vive shillings to thurt thick there butt. **1898** RIDER HAGGARD in *Longm. Mag.* Nov. 38 All my three ploughs were at work 'thwarting'—that is crossploughing—rootland on the Nunnery Farm.

4. To obstruct (a road, course, or passage) with something placed across; to block. *Obs.* exc. *fig.*

c **1630** RISDON *Surv. Devon* §65 (1810) 63 The rebellious commons..thwarted the ways with great trees. *Ibid.* §269. 278 [A stream] whose course is thwarted with a damm, which we call a wear. **1725** POPE *Odyss.* x. 72 What Dæmon cou'dst thou meet To thwart thy passage and repel thy fleet? **1760–72** H. BROOKE *Fool of Qual.* (1809) IV. 58 They met with a six-barred gate that directly thwarted their passage. **1807** CRABBE *Par. Reg.* II. 72 They sometimes speed, but often thwart our course. **1856** KANE *Arct. Expl.* II. v. 60 If no misadventure thwarted his progress.

II. 5. To act or operate in opposition to; to run counter to, to go against; to oppose, hinder. Also *absol.* Now *rare.*

c **1250** *Gen. & Ex.* 1324 Quat-so god bad, ðwerted he it neuer a del. *c* **1430**, **1530** [implied in THWARTING *vbl. sb.* 2 and *ppl. a.* 2]. **1600** HOLLAND *Livy* XXXV. xxxii. 907 Such as might..not sticke to speake their minds franckly, yea, & thwart the king his embassadour. **1671** BP. PARKER *Def. Eccl. Pol.* iii. §15. 298 To what purpose does he so briskly taunt me for thwarting my own Principles. **1676** W. ALLEN *Address Nonconf.* 130 The danger of Schism, and the evil of thwarting publick Laws. **1783** JUSTAMOND tr. *Raynal's Hist. Indies* VII. 379 They had unfortunately been so much thwarted by the winds as to prevent their landing before summer. **1802** PALEY *Nat. Theol.* xxvi. (1819) 436 General laws, however well set and constituted, often thwart and cross one another. **1811** L. M. HAWKINS *C'tess & Gertr.* II. 370 The countess was not always disposed to thwart and vex: a little flattery would soothe her.

b. *intr.* To speak or act in contradiction or opposition; to be adverse or at variance, to conflict. Const. *with.* Now *rare* or *Obs.*

1519 HORMAN *Vulg.* 59 b, I wyll nat multyplie wordes or thwarte with the. **1601** ? MARSTON *Pasquil & Kath.* II. 185 Is't possible that sisters should so thwart In natiue humours? **1656** *Burton's Diary* (1828) I. 15 This clause thwarts with his Highness's ordinances. **1737** BRACKEN *Farriery Impr.* (1757) II. 272 It would thwart with my intended Brevity. **1862** F. HALL *Hindu Philos. Syst.* 42 They also accept..the Smritis, the Puránas, &c., the work of Rishis, when those books do not thwart with the Veda.

6. *trans.* To oppose successfully; to prevent (a person, etc.) from accomplishing a purpose; to prevent the accomplishment of (a purpose); to foil, frustrate, balk, defeat. (The chief current sense.)

1581 MULCASTER *Positions* iv. (1887) 17 He may either proceede at his owne libertie, if nothing withstand him, or may not proceede, if he be thwarted by circunstance. **1641** EARL MONM. tr. *Biondi's Civil Warres* v. 166 The Earle seeing himselfe twharted, resolved to fight. **1697** J. LEWIS *Mem. Dk. Glocester* (1789) 34 From being sometimes a little thwarted, and thro' dissatisfaction, she grew sick. **1718** *Free-thinker* No. 65 ¶6 Perpetual Obstacles..thwarted his Designs. **1803** DK. WELLINGTON in Gurw. *Desp.* (1837) II. 352 Thus are all our best plans thwarted. **1849** MACAULAY *Hist. Eng.* iv. I. 429 The party which had long thwarted him had been beaten down. **1871** FREEMAN *Norm. Conq.* IV. xvii. 15 But all these good intentions were thwarted by the inherent vice of his position.

'thwarted, *ppl. a.* [f. THWART *v.* + -ED[1].]

†**1.** Placed across; crossed. *Obs. rare*$^{-1}$.

1655 FULLER *Ch. Hist.* III. iii. §11 All Knights-Templers make such saltire cross with their thwarted leggs upon their monuments.

2. Obstructed; frustrated, balked, defeated.

1828 CARLYLE *Misc., Burns* (1872) II. 13 Ever-thwarted, ever renewed endeavours. **1837** SIR W. HAMILTON *Metaph.* xlv. (1870) II. 504 A thwarted, and therefore a painful energy of thought. **1879** DIXON *Windsor* II. xx. 208 Harry.. understood the misery of a thwarted suit.

Hence **'thwartedly** *adv.*

1870 RUSKIN *Lect. Art* vii. (1875) 179 An atmosphere through which a burning sun shines thwartedly.

thwarteous ('θwɔːtjəs), *a.* [App. a ghost-word due to misreading *thwarteouer* in Clarendon's *Hist. Reb.* (1849) I. §174.] Perverse, contrary.

1890 R. BRIDGES *Chr. Capt.* v. 2319 Satan did persuade our thwarteous king To make a godless bargain. **1903** A. SMELLIE *Men of Covt.* i. (1904) 6 If he touched these treasures, he would find her humour 'thwarteous', indeed.

thwarter ('θwɔːtə(r)). [f. THWART *v.* + -ER[1].] One who or that which thwarts.

†**1.** One who traverses or goes across. *Obs. rare*$^{-1}$.

a **1693** *Urquhart's Rabelais* III. xlix. 394 Xenomanes the great Traveller, and Thwarter of dangerous ways.

2. One who or that which obstructs the path or action of another; an opponent, adversary, obstructor, frustrater.

1633 T. ADAMS *Exp. 2 Peter* i. 2 O happy soul, that can make his thwarters that cross him, become his porters to carry him to the place of his rest. **1687** WOOD *Life* 16 Aug. (O.H.S.) III. 224 Dr. Fell..would never suffer him to beare that office because a thwarter of him in severall public matters. **1738** tr. *Guazzo's Art Conversation* 71 Those whom I call Contentious and Thwarters are, for the most Part, gross, thick-headed Fellows. **1869** HUGHES *Alfred Gt.* xii. 141 The thwarters of the King's will repented.

thwarter-ill, variant of THORTER-ILL.

†**'thwarterous,** *a. Obs. nonce-wd.* [irreg. f. THWART: see -OUS, and cf. *boisterous.*] Tortuous, twisted, gnarled.

1625 J. WODROEPHE *Marrow Fr. Tongue* 336 The yellow wood so thwarterous [Fr. *torteux*], beares Fruit so precious.

thwarting ('θwɔːtɪŋ), *vbl. sb.* [f. THWART *v.* + -ING[1].] The action of the verb THWART.

†**1.** Going athwart, crossing. *Obs. rare*$^{-1}$.

c **1440** *Gesta Rom.* xlvi. 193 (Harl. MS.) By the Ringe we muste vndirstonde feithe, for that owithe to be Rounde like a Ringe, and with oute eny twartynge.

b. Cross-ploughing.

1847 *Jrnl. R. Agric. Soc.* VIII. II. 318 After the first thwarting of the fallow (cross-ploughing),..the clods are worked..into about the size of a hen's egg.

2. Opposition; hindrance, impediment; defeating, frustration.

c **1430** *Pilgr. Lyf Manhode* IV. lii. (1869) 200 þe arguynge, ne þe thuartinge is no thing worth ayens us, ne ayens deth neither. **1581** MULCASTER *Positions* xxviii. (1887) 109 A number of lettes and thwartings which art did prescribe. **1609** DOULAND *Ornith. Microl.* 79 A Discord..is the hard and rough thwarting of two sounds not mingled with themselues. **1653** R. SANDERS *Physiogn.* 53 Great thwartings and misfortunes by the means of women. **1825** SCOTT *Jrnl.* 23 Dec., Those thwartings are what men in public life do not like to endure.

thwarting ('θwɔːtɪŋ), *ppl. a.* [f. THWART *v.* + -ING[2].] That thwarts, in various senses.

1. Lying or passing crosswise; crossing, traversing, transverse; of the eyes: crossed, squinting. *Obs.* or *arch.*

c **1430** *Pilgr. Lyf Manhode* IV. iv. (1869) 176 With purblynde eyen and thwartinge may not be hool lookinge. **1625** K. LONG tr. *Barclay's Argenis* I. i. 3, I fled thorow the bushes, where the thwarting bowes loosened the knots of my hayre. **1632** LITHGOW *Trav.* (1906) 278 Slaine and hung up on two standing and a thwarting tree. **1653** R. SANDERS *Physiogn.* 48 If it [middle line of the palm] be right, continued, and without thwarting lines.

2. Conflicting, opposing, obstructing; perverse; frustrating, baffling; adverse, untoward.

1530 PALSGR. 306/2 Brablyng thwartyng or quarellyng, *noyseux. Ibid.* 327/2 Twhartynge or contraryeng, *captieux.* **1593** SHAKS. *3 Hen. VI,* IV. vi. 22 That the people of this blessed Land May not be punisht with my thwarting starres. **1658** *Whole Duty of Man* iv. §3 To entangle themselves by taking one oath cross and thwarting to another. **1718** *Free-thinker* No. 61 ¶9 A Thwarting, Cavilling Temper only promotes Contention. **1804** J. GRAHAME *Sabbath* (1839) 23/1 The thwarting surge Dash'd, boiling, on the labouring bark. **1878** J. R. SEELEY *Stein* II. 4 The very moment when the thwarting power..visibly intervenes.

Hence **'thwartingly** *adv.,* transversely; perversely; adversely.

1579 TOMSON *Calvin's Serm. Tim.* 359/1 Fetch no windelesses, nor goe anye by-wayes and as it were thwartingly. **1618** T. ADAMS *Chr. Walk* Wks. 1862 II. 407 The over-precise are so thwartingly cross to the superstitious..that they will scarce do a good work, because a heretic doth it. **1715** tr. *Pancirollus' Rerum Mem.* II. xiii. 359 These Films ..laid one upon another, some in a direct, and others thwartingly and in a transverse Position.

thwartle ('θwɔːt(ə)l), *v. Obs.* exc. *dial.* [dim. or freq. of THWART *v.*: see -LE 3.] *intr.* To speak or act in contradiction.

1647 TRAPP *Comm. Rom.* ii. 8 That wrangle and thwartle against clearest truths. **1847–78** HALLIWELL, *Thurtle,* to cross in discourse; to contradict. *Somerset. Whartle,* to cross; to tease. *Norf.*

†**'thwart,long,** *adv. Obs. rare*$^{-1}$. [f. THWART *adv.* + -LONG.] Crosswise, transversely.

1600 F. WALKER *Sp. Mandeville* 8 Some [children at birth] come forth thwartlong and some with their body double.

'thwartly, *adv.* Now *rare.* [f. THWART *a.* + -LY[2].] In a thwart manner.

1. Transversely, crosswise, obliquely. Also *fig.*

1541 R. COPLAND *Guydon's Quest. Chirurg.* Div b, The seconde bone of the heade in the hyndre parte..is enclosed by a commyssure thwartly in maner of a greke lettre called Lampda. **1654** Z. COKE *Logick* 181 Indirect Solution, is when we answer indirectly, and thwartly to the Syllogism proposed.

2. In the way of opposition or contrariety; perversely; 'crossly'.

1554 W. KETHE in Goodman *How Superior Powers,* etc. (1558) 235 Sith man then in iudgeinge, so thwartly is bente To satisfie fansie, and not true intente. **1581** RICH *Farewell* (Shaks. Soc.) 172 She answerd hym thawartly. *a* **1646** J. GREGORY *Terrestr. Globe* Posthuma (1650) 266 Som few Spanish Geographers..reckon the Longitudes quite contrarie, from East to West, but which was thwartly in it self, and, in the proof, inconsiderably don. **1914** HARDY *Satires of Circumstance* 192 Then grinned the Ancient Briton from the tumulus treed with pine: 'So, hearts are thwartly smitted In these days as in mine!'

†**'thwartness.** Now *rare.* [f. as prec. + -NESS.] The condition or quality of being thwart, in various senses; transverseness; opposition, contrariety; perversity.

1548–77 VICARY *Anat.* ii. (1888) 20 The third [property is] in thwartnes, in whom the vertue that holdeth hath might. **1614** SIR R. DUDLEY in *Fortesc. Papers* (Camden) 11 *note,* The thawartnes [*sic*]..of late the parlement useth towardes him. **1649** BP. HALL *Cases Consc.* IV. ii. (1654) 303 Some unkinde usages, or thwartness of disposition. *a* **1907** F. THOMPSON *Works* (1913) III. 66 It is full of thwartness and eating and drinking, and selffulness.

'thwart-,over, *prep., adv., adj. Obs.* exc. *dial.* Also 3 **þwert-**, 5 **twarte-, thurte-, thawrt-,** *dial.* 8 **thurt-**, 9 **thirtover.** See also THORTER. [Originally, and in A and B usually, two words:

THWART *adv.* and OVER *prep.* or *adv.* Cf. OVERTHWART.]

† **A.** *prep.* Athwart over; across one side to the other of. (Also in quot. *c* 1450 *in thurte* (= *a-thwart*) *over*.) *Obs.*

a **1225** *St. Marher.* 10 Ant [heo] droh þa endelong hire, ant þwertouer þrefter, þe derewurðe taken of þe deore rode. **1387** TREVISA *Higden* (Rolls) II. 45 The secounde chief kynges hiȝe weye hatte Watlynge strete, and streccheþ þwart ouer Fosse [orig. *per transversum prioris viæ*] out of þe souþ est in to þe norþ west. *c* **1400** *Lanfranc's Cirurg.* 143 (Add. MS.) Aftirwarde he [a band] schal be turnyde twarte offere þe forehed, þat..þe nose declyne to neiþere syde. *c* **1450** *Godstow Reg.* 374 The which lieth in the feld that is I-called Brademore, and strecchith hit-self in thurte ouer the feld in length toward the southe and towarde the northe. *Ibid.* 502 All ther tenementes..in the subarbis of Oxenforde toward the northe, fro the fore-named diche thurte ouer bewmounte vnto horsemonger-strete.

† **B.** *adv.* Crosswise; across. *Obs.*

1398 TREVISA *Barth. De P.R.* XVIII. xi. (Bodl. MS.), þe spiþer..strecheþ vpward wiþ wonder crafte fro þe neþer side to þe ouer and drawiþ and bringeþ ofte aȝen his þrede þwarte ouer fro pointe to pointe. *c* **1430** *Pilgr. Lyf Manhode* IV. iv. 176 Bakward she ran, and thwart ouer. **1502** ARNOLDE *Chron.* (1811) 141 The worlde is..viii M myle thwarte ouer and iiij M myle to the midel.

C. *adj.* † **a.** Crossing, lying athwart, cross. *Obs.* **b.** That thwarts or obstructs; obstructive; cross, contrary, perverse, self-willed. Now *dial.*

a **1225** *Ancr. R.* 82 Attri speche is eresie & þwertouer leasunge. **1387** TREVISA *Higden* (Rolls) II. 149 Þe souþ-syde of Scotlonde þat streccheth from þe þwart ouer wal of Romayn werk to þe Scottische see. *Ibid.* VII. 35 Al aboute þe feeldes and þwart over weies. **1422** tr. *Secreta Secret., Priv. Priv.* 188 An harde and a thawrtouer worde raysyth Stryfe and wodnesse. **1630** J. TAYLOR (Water P.) *Pr. Charles* Wks. III. 102/1 For fifteene long dayes and nights, the thwartouer and crosse North and Easterly Winde blew vs nothing but [etc.]. **1647** CLARENDON *Hist. Reb.* I. § 174 That thwartover humour was enough discovered to rule in the breasts of many. **1790** GROSE *Prov. Gloss.* (ed. 2) s.v. *Thurt*, A thurt-over fellow; a cross-grained or ill-tempered fellow. Berksh. **1891** HARDY *Tess* (1900) 107/2, I have been living on in a thirtover, lackaday way, and have not seen what it may lead to! **1894** MAXWELL GRAY *Innocent Impostor* 173 Things is thirtover when anybody's in a hurry.

'thwart-saw. Now *dial.* Forms: see THWART. A saw for sawing timber across; a cross-cut saw.

1404 *Durham Acc. Rolls* (Surtees) 396, iij sawes irined ex officio, et iij twhertsawes, ij handsawes. **1465** *Finchale Invent.* (Surtees) p. ccxcix, In primis,..j twortsaw, j twybyll, j hak, j pyk. **1567** *Wills & Inv. N.C.* (Surtees) I. 268 A whippt sawe, ij hand sawes, a twart sawe. **1577** *Ibid.* 414 In the Ireon Seller. Eighte qwarte sawes xvj[s].—thre whope sawes xx[s]. **1590** *Inv.* in *Midl. Co. Hist. Coll.* II. 31 Item iij wimbles a handsawe one whartsawe. **1611–12** *Knaresborough Wills* (Surtees) II. 34 My thwartsaw. **1888** ELWORTHY *W. Somerset Word-bk.*, *Thurt saw*,..cross-cut saw... 'Plase to tich up (sharpen) the thurt saw'.

thwart-ship, thwartship ('θwɔːt-ʃɪp), *a.* and *adv.* *Naut.* [f. THWART *prep.* + SHIP *sb.*]

A. *adj.* Placed or fixed across the ship's length. *thwartship tiller*, a tiller fixed at right angles to the rudder.

1829 H. L. MAW *Jrnl. Passage fr. Pacific to Atlantic* 314 Resting on small thwartship timbers. *c* **1850** *Rudim. Navig.* (Weale) 123 The 'thwartship pieces which frame the hatch-ways. **1897** *Outing* (U.S.) XXX. 228/1 The crew..manœuvers the craft by means of a five-foot thwartship tiller.

B. *adv.* ('θwɔːt-ˌʃɪp). From side to side of the ship; across the length of the ship.

1882 NARES *Seamanship* (ed. 6) 242 The correctors..are bar magnets in..holes, thwartship,..within the binnacle. **1895** *Outing* (U.S.) XXVI. 481/2 The modern canoeist puts it [ballast] in his own weight, on the end of the plank extended thwart-ship to windward.

thwart-ships ('θwɔːt-ʃɪps), *adv.* *Naut.* [f. as prec. + *-s* of adverbial genitive.] = prec. B.

a **1625** *Nomenclator Navalis* (Harl. MS. 2301) s.v., Anie thing that is done or lies acrosse y[e] Shipp from one side to thother wee saie that it lies thwart ships. **1718** STEELE *Fish Pool* 175 The depth of the arch of the deck thwart-ships is 4 inches.

thwartways ('θwɔːtweɪz), *adv.* *rare.* Also 7 thwartway. [f. THWART *a.* + -WAYS.] = next, A.

1665 HOOKE *Microgr.* xxii. 139 There were not more seem'd to lie horizontally then perpendicularly and thwartway. **1893** KIPLING *Many Invent.* 11 He lashed the canes together criss-cross and thwartways.

thwartwise ('θwɔːtwaɪz), *adv.* and *a.* [f. THWART *a.* + -WISE.]

A. *adv.* Crosswise, transversely.

1589 P. IVE *Fortif.* 16 Lay a trauers of trees in the bottome..laying them thwart wise in the work. **1661** LOVELL *Hist. Anim. & Min.* 191 Crab, *Cancer*, they goe thwartwise. **1894** CROCKETT *Mad Sir Uchtred* v, The troop passed thwart-wise over the mountain steep. **1899** —— *Black Douglas* (1900) 468 Margaret..rode thwartwise to intercept her.

B. *adj.* Situated or extending transversely; cross, transverse.

1890 CLERKE *Syst. Stars* 309 The directly measurable, thwartwise part of its motion. **1891** *Dublin Rev.* Jan. 157 Compounded..of thwartwise and end-on speed.

† **thwerl**, *v.* *Obs.* *rare*$^{-1}$. Origin and meaning obscure. (Some identify it with TWIRL or WHIRL.)

c **1489** CAXTON *Sonnes of Aymon* i. 32 Reynawde..thwerled his swerde by grete fyersnesse.

† **thwert-nay**: see under next.

† **thwert-out**, *adv.* *Obs.* In 3 þuertut, (*Orm.*) þwerrt ut. [f. *thwert*, THWART *adv.* + OE. *út* OUT.] Thoroughly, completely, utterly, absolutely: = THROUGHOUT B. 3.

c **1200** ORMIN 194 To ȝarrkenn her onnȝæness Crist All þwerrt ut haliȝ leode. *Ibid.* 313–316 Forr þatt all iss þwerrt ut soþ, & all þwerrt ut to trowwenn þatt standdeþþ o þe Goddspellboc þatt þwerrt ut nohht ne leȝheþþ. *c* **1200** *Trin. Coll. Hom.* 123 Þat mannisse þe ne understant ne bisecheð god, is þuertut forlore soule and lichame.

Hence † **thwert-ut nay**, *Early Eng. Law*, a complete or absolute 'Nay', a downright 'No'; a flat denial by the defendant of the plaintiff's charge.

1277 in Jeaffreson *Index to Leicester MSS.* 74–5 Si le defendant taunt tost cum la parole ly fust issue de la buche ne deist *thwertutnay*, il fut tenu cum non defendu, e ceo apelerent *swareles*. *Ibid.*, Ke le defendaunt ne poeit a la pleinte le pleintif autre chose respundre for tut granter ou tut dire *thwertutnay*. **1895** POLLOCK & MAITLAND *Hist. Eng. Law* II. 606 A defendant was treated as undefended unless, before he said anything else, he met the plaintiff's tale with a *thwertutnay*, that is a downright No. *Ibid. Note*, The idea of a *thwertutnay* is preserved in our *traverse*.

Originally, † **thwert-nay**, † **thwert-nik**. [f. *thwert*, THWART *adv.* or *a.*: see NICH and NICK *v.*[1], and cf. ON. *setja þvert nei* to deny flatly.] *lit.* A traversing or directly contradicting 'Nay' or 'Nik'; also the right or liberty to give such a direct denial.

(Under the influence of *Thwert-ut*, this became *Thwert-ut nay*.)

1218 *Earl Randal's Charter to Cheshire* (D. of Lanc. Misc. Bks. 12 lf. 25), Per twertnik se defendere poterit. **12..** *Leges Quat. Burgorum* c. 31 in *Acts Parl. Scot.* (1844) I. 338 Et est retinendum quod in placitis burgorum utitur Twertnay in defensionibus defendendo wrang and unlawe. [*15th c. transl.*, And it is to wyt þat in borow mutis þar is hantyd and oysyt thuertnay in defendande wrang and unlawe.] **1275** *Close Roll 3 Edw. I*, m. 5 Excepta..libertate quam dictus Robertus habuit in terris et tenementis suis in comitatu Cestrie que vocatur Thwertnik. **1296** *Chancery Inq. p. mort.* Edw. I, 79 (8) Quamdam libertatem que vocatur twertnyc. —— *Exchequer Inq. p. mort.* 5 (4) Libertatem que vocatur twertnyk.

thweten, obs. pa. pple. of THWITE.

† **thwick-thwack.** *Obs.* [Redupl. f. THWACK.] The repetition or exchange of thwacks.

1575 R. B. *Appius & Virg.* B ij b, With thwicke thwack, with thump thump, With bobbing and bum. **1582** STANYHURST *Conceits* in *Æneis*, etc. (Arb.) 138 With peale meale ramping, with thwick thwack sturdelye thundring. **1611** COTGR. s.v. *Torche*, *Torche lorgue*, words, like our thwicke thwacke, expressing a liberall and free dole of blowes. **1670** RAY *Prov.* 53 When a couple are newly married, the first moneth is honey-moon or smick smack: the second is, hither and thither: the third is, thwick thwack. **1783** AINSWORTH *Lat. Dict.* (Morell) I. s.v. *Thwack*, To lay on thwick, thwack, *ictus geminare*.

thwite (θwaɪt), *v.* *Obs.* exc. *dial.* Forms: 1 þwitan, þweoton; 4–7 thwyte, (7– *dial.*) thwite, (4–5 twhyte, 5 twyte, 6 thwight, 9 *dial.* tweet, twet, toight). *Pa. pple.* 4–5 thwyten, 6 thwytten, thweten, 6–7 thwitten; 5–7 thwyted, 6–7 thwitted, 5– thwited. See also WHITE *v.* [OE. *þwítan* (**þwát, þwiten*) to cut, cut off; not recorded elsewhere; but ON. had derivatives in *þveita* small axe, *þvita* a kind of axe, *þveit*, *þveiti* cut-off piece, parcel of land, THWAIT(E. In mod.Sc. and north. dial. the word has become *quhyte*, *hwite*, WHITE, in Aberdeen *fite*. See also THWITTLE, WHITTLE.]

trans. To cut down, whittle, pare, shave; to shape by paring; to cut away. Also *fig.* Phrase, *to thwite a mill-post* (etc.) *to a pudding-prick*.

a **900** tr. *Bæda's Hist.* III. xiv. [xvii.] (1890) 204 ꝥe[a] eac swylce of þære ilcan styðe sponas þweoton & sceafþan nomon [*v.r.* ðæt ȝeþwit naman]. *c* **1000** *Sax. Leechd.* II. 292 ȝenim þone neowran wyrttruman delf up, þwit niȝon sponas on ða winstran hand. ? *a* **1366** CHAUCER *Rom. Rose* 933 That other bowe..was peynted wel and thwyten [*MS.* twythen, *Thynne* thwitten]. *c* **1384** —— *H. Fame* III. 848 Somme [twigs] weren white Whiche as men to these cages thwite [*v.rr.* thwyte, twhyte] Or maken of these panyers. *a* **1500** in Arnolde *Chron.* (1811) 170 The ende of the graff that was vpward next the firmament must be thweten lyke the neder of a comon graffe. **1529** MORE *Dyaloge* III. Wks. 236/2 Here was a gret post wel thwyted to a pudding pricke. **1575** *Brieff Disc. Troub. Franckford* (1846) 157 It nippeth and thwitethe awaie a great deale off that liberalitie, which might come to us. *a* **1601** SIR T. FANSHAWE *Pract. Exch.* (1658) 112 The Cutter of the Tallyes..provideth a..hasell for the Tallies..and doth somewhat thwite every stick thereof into four square sides. **1674** RAY *N.C. Words*, To *Thwite*, to whittle, cut, make white by cutting. **1897** *Shetland News* 24 July (E.D.D.), A placid roadman 'tweetin' the grass in the ditches with a scythe.

b. *intr.* To whittle. Now *dial.*

c **1475** *Babees Bk.* I. 179 Kutte nouhte youre mete eke as it were Felde men..They ne rekke..how vngoodly they on theyre mete twyte. **1863** *Lanc. Fents, New Shirt* 5 After 'thwiting' at the topmost bar of the gate till he had made it look almost like a new one. **1870** E. WAUGH *Winter Fire* iii. 24 Let these lads thwite at it [beef] a bit.

Hence **'thwiting** *vbl. sb.*; *thwiting-knife*, ? a paring or scraping knife used by bowyers.

1393 LANGL. *P. Pl.* C. IX. 199 In þresshynge, in þecchyng, in thwytynge of pynnes. *c* **1440** *Promp. Parv.* 493/1 Thwytynge, or telwynge, *sectulatus*, *abscidula*, *abscindula*. **1659** HOWELL *Vocab.* li, A thwitting knife, nocksaws, a rasp, a riper, a share, a baldock, &c., *gli stromenti dell arciero* [the tools of the bowyer].

thwittle ('θwɪt(ə)l), *sb.* Now *dial.* Forms: 4–5 þw-, thwitel, thwytel, 5 -elle, *Sc.* thewtill, quhittil, 6 thwitle, 7 thwittel, 7– thwittle: see also WHITTLE. [f. THWITE *v.* + -EL, -LE.] A knife, a whittle.

[*c* **1325** *Gloss. W. de Bibbesw.* in Wright *Voc.* 168 *Coteus*, thiwilet (? *for* thwitel).] *c* **1386** CHAUCER *Reeve's T.* 13 A Sheffeld thwitel [*v.r.* thwytel] baar he in his hose. *c* **1470** HENRY *Wallace* I. 218 A Scottis thewtill [*ed.* **1570** quhittil] wndyr thi belt to ber. **1664** COTTON *Scarron.* 37 They rise and wipe their greasy thwittles. **1796** PEGGE *Derbicisms* (E.D.S.), With a Lancashire thwittle I thwited a flail-swipple. **1881** *Antiquary* Feb. 87 A bill-hook has been substituted for the thwittle.

thwittle ('θwɪt(ə)l), *v.* Now *dial.* [freq. and dim. of THWITE *v.*: see -LE 3.] *trans.* To pare down or away, to whittle (also *intr.*): = THWITE *v.*

1593 G. HARVEY *Pierce's Super.* Wks. (Grosart) II. 244 He hath thwittled the milpost of his huge conceit to a pudding-pricke. **1874** E. WAUGH *Jannock* ii. 12 He'll not like to dine off o' what we'n bin thwittlin' at.

thwndur, -yr, obs. forms of THUNDER.

thy (ðaɪ), *poss. adj.* Forms: 2–5 þi (ti), 4 þy (ty), 4–6 thi, (6 yi), 4– thy. [Early ME. *þī*, reduced form of *þīn*, THINE, used in ME. bef. consonants exc. *h*, but occurring before vowels in 15th c., and ultimately universal in prose use as the possessive adj. preceding its sb., = Ger. *dein*, *deine*, F. *ton*, *ta*, *tes*.]

Of or belonging to thee, that thou hast.

For restriction of use see note to THOU *pers. pron.* I.

a **1175** *Cott. Hom.* 225 Þe..and ti wif, and þine þreo sunes. *c* **1175** *Pater Noster* in *Lamb. Hom.* 57 Þi nome beo iblecced. *Ibid.* 59 Cume þi riche. *a* **1225** *Ancr. R.* 98 Þi stefne is me swete, & ti hwite schene. **13..** in *Rel. Ant.* I. 145 Wer es ty sire, wer es ty dame? **13..** *E.E. Allit. P.* B. 330 Enter þis ark with þyn aþel barnez & þy wedded wyf. **1388** WYCLIF *Ruth* i. 16 Thi puple is my puple, and thi God is my God. *c* **1450** *Bk. Curtasye* 71 in *Babees Bk.* 301 Let not þi spone stond in þy dysche. **1502** ATKYNSON tr. *De Imitatione* I. xx. 169 Lyft vp thy iyen to heuen. **1513** DOUGLAS *Æneis* IV. iv. 42 Apon thi top, mont Cynthus, walkis he. **1552** LYNDESAY *Monarche* 4131 Perfytlie prent in yi remembrance Off this Inconstante warld the variance. **1552** HULOET, Thy owne selfe, *te ipsum*, *temet*. **1667** MILTON *P.L.* V. 153 These are thy glorious works, Parent of good. **1852** MRS. STOWE *Uncle Tom's C.* xiii, [The Quaker Settlement] 'Where's thy baby, Ruth?' said Rachel... 'Thy Mary caught him as I came in.' **1859** TENNYSON *Enid* 347 Turn, Fortune, turn thy wheel and lower the proud.

† **thy**, *adv.* *Obs.* Forms: 1–2 þy, 2–3 þi. [OE. *ðý*, *þý*, instrumental case of demonst. and relative pron. *se*, *séo*, *þæt*: see THAT, and cf. THE *adv.*]

1. a. *orig.* By means or by reason of that, because of that, therefore. **b.** In relative sense: For the reason that, because.

c **897** K. ÆLFRED *Gregory's Past. C.* xxviii. 192 Ðy him is micel ðearf, ðonne he tela lærð, ðæt he eac tela do. *c* **1000** *Sax. Leechd.* II. 86 Smire mid huniȝ, þæt þy þe raþor sio hryfing of fealle. *c* **1175** *Lamb. Hom.* 93 Þi bileafden heo heore timbrunge. *c* **1200** *Trin. Coll. Hom.* 205 Wilfulshipe and lichamliche lustes and li ere lahtres, þi ne mai no man gode folȝen. *a* **1250** *Owl & Night.* 860 Ich rede þi þat men beo ware. *c* **1275** *Woman of Samaria* 39 in *O.E. Misc.* 85 Ich wot..þat þu me hauest soþ iseyd..þi of one þinge sey me iredynesse.

c. Hence in *for thy*, for that reason, therefore: see FOR-THY; also in OE. *mid þý*, with that, seeing that, since, when, while; *to þý*, to that end or purpose, therefore.

2. Preceding an adj. or adv. in the comparative degree: see THE *adv.*

thy, obs. f. THIGH.

Thyad: see THYIAD.

thyck, obs. f. THICK.

thyder, -ur, etc., obs. ff. THITHER.

thye, obs. f. THEE *v.*[1], THIGH.

thyef (þ-), thyefthe (þ-), obs. ff. THIEF, THEFT.

Thyestean (θaɪɛˈstiːən, θaɪˈɛstiːən), *a.* Also 7 -æan, 9 -ian. [f. L. *Thyestēus*, ad. Gr. *Θυέστειος* (f. *Θυέστης*, prop. name) + -AN.] Of or belonging to Thyestes, in ancient Greek legend brother of Atreus, who at a banquet made him eat of the flesh of his own two sons; hence used allusively.

1667 MILTON *P.L.* X. 688 The Sun, as from Thyestean Banquet, turn'd His course intended. **1667** J. OWEN *Plea Indulgence & Lib. Consc.* 7 Thiæstæan Banquets, promiscuous Lusts, and Incests. **1723** R. MILLAR *Hist. Propag. Chr.* II. v. 73 There is an infamous report that we are guilty of Thyestean feasts, that is feeding on murdered infants. **1746** FRANCIS tr. *Horace, Art of Poetry* 129 Nor will the direful Thyestean Feast In comic Phrase and Language be debas'd. *c* **1850** LOWELL *Fable for Critics* (ed. 2) Prelim. Note, I am not queasy-stomached, but such a Thyestean Banquet as that was quite out of the question. **1882** FARRAR *Early Days Chr.* I. iv. I. 65 Did not popular rumour charge them with nocturnal orgies and Thyestæan feasts?

thyf(e, obs. form of THIEF.

thyfe-thorn, variant of THEVE-THORN *Obs.*

thyft, -ly, obs. forms of THEFT, -LY.

thyg(g, thygh(e, thyh(e, thyght, obs. ff. THIG, THIGH, THIGHT, THIGHED.

Thyiad (ˈθaɪæd), **Thyad** (ˈθaɪæd). *Gr. Antiq.* [a. Gr. θυιάς, stem θυιαδ- (pl. -άδες) a frenzied woman; properly adj. fem. from verbal root θυι-, Æolic form of θυ- to rush, rage.] A Bacchante.

[**1710** W. KING *Heathen Gods & Heroes* xxvii. (1722) 134 The Women who accompany'd him [Bacchus] as his Priestesses, were call'd *Mænades*, from their Madness; *Thyades*, from their Impetuousness and Fury. **1835** T. MITCHELL *Acharn. of Aristoph.* 221 *note*, The older females figured as Thyades or Bacchantes.] **1846** H. G. ROBINSON *Odes of Horace* II. xix, The Thyads ever wantoning. **1871** R. ELLIS *Catullus* lxiv. 390 Often on high Parnassus a roving Liber in hurried Frenzy the Thyiads drave.

thyine (ˈθaɪɪn), *a.* Also 4 **tyyn, tyne, thyn,** 4–6 **thyne,** 6 **thynne, (thynen),** 7 **thine.** [ad. L. *thȳinus*, ad. Gr. θύϊνος of the tree θύα, *thya*, or THUYA. Formerly sometimes miswritten *tyme, thyme*, from reading *in* as *m*.] Epithet of a tree, and its wood, mentioned in Rev. xviii. 12; supposed to be the African coniferous tree *Callitris quadrivalvis*, which yields gum sandarac.

The Vulgate has *ligna thyina* also in 1 Kings x. 11–12, where the Greek is different, and the version of 1611, following the Heb., has *almug trees*.

1382 WYCLIF *1 Kings* x. 11 The nauee of Yram,..brouȝte to of Oofer manye tyyn trees [**1388** trees of tyme, Vulg. *ligna thyina*, LXX. ξύλα πελεκητά hewn trees, Heb. *almuggim*, COVERD. costly tymber, 1611 almug trees]. **1382** —— *Rev.* xviii. 12 The marchaundises of gold, and siluer, and precious stoon,..and ech tre thyine [*erron.* thyme, *Vulg.* et omne lignum thyinum, *Gr.* καὶ πᾶν ξύλον θύϊνον]. [**1398** TREVISA *Barth. De P.R.* XVII. clxv. (Bodl. MS.), Thina beþ certeyne treene moste precious.] **1526** TINDALE *Rev.* xviii. 12 Off pearle, and raynes, and purple, and scarlett, and all thyne wodde [so *Geneva & Rhem.*; COVERD. Thynen wod, *Great* thynne wodde, 1611 Thine wood, *mod. edd.* thyine wood]. *a* **1571** JEWEL *On 2 Thess.* ii. 1, 2 All manner of thyine wood. **1763** C. SMART *Song to David* lx, The wealthy crops of whit'ning rice 'Mongst thyine woods and groves of spice.

Thyisday, obs. Sc. form of TUESDAY.

thyke, þyke, obs. form of THILK.

† **thykston(e.** *Obs. rare.* [f. *thik*, var. of THEEK *v.* to roof + STONE *sb.*] Roofing flags; = *thackstone*: see THACK *sb.* 4.

1486–7 *Durham Acc. Rolls* (Surtees) 158 Pro adquisicione vj futhrez del thykston, ij s.

thylacine (ˈθaɪləsaɪn). [a. F. *thylacine*, in mod.L. *Thȳlacinus* (Temminck *Monogr. de Mammalogie*, 1827, I. 55), f. Gr. θύλακ-ος pouch + (app.) L. suffix *-inus*, -INE[1]. (But some think that Temminck meant to include in the name Gr. κύων, κυνός dog, and that it is short for *thȳlaco-cynus 'pouched dog', which is improbable. It had been previously described by Harris as *Didelphys cynocephalus*.)] The native Tasmanian 'wolf' or 'zebra-wolf', *Thylacinus cynocephalus*, the largest of existing carnivorous marsupials (now very scarce or extinct).

1838 OWEN in *Proc. Geol. Soc.* III. 19 In the number of the grinders the Phascolothere resembles the Opossum and Thylacine. **1841** G. R. WATERHOUSE *Marsupialia* 127 The *Thylacinus* inhabits Van Diemen's Land where it is called the Tiger, Hyæna. **1846** OWEN *Brit. Fossil Mammals* 67. **1891** *Daily News* 5 May 5/5 The Zoological Society have just acquired a pair of thylacines—a somewhat rare, carnivorous marsupial, from Tasmania. **1901** *Pall Mall G.* 27 May 5/3 The thylacine is confined to Tasmania, although its fossil remains have been found in New South Wales.

thylacothere (ˈθaɪləkəʊθɪə(r)). *Palæont.* [ad. mod.L. *Thȳlacotherium*, f. Gr. θύλακο-ς pouch + θηρίον beast.] An extinct mammal of the genus *Thylacotherium*, also called *Amphitherium* (see AMPHITHERE), variously supposed to have been a marsupial or an insectivorous placental. Hence **thylacoˈtherian** *a.*

1838 OWEN in *Proc. Geol. Soc.* III. 17 Objections against the mammiferous nature of the Thylacotherian jaws. *Ibid.* III. 19 In the position of the dental foramen, the Phascolothere, like the Thylacothere, differs from all zoophagous marsupials. **1850** BRODERIP *Note-bk. Naturalist* viii. (1852) 165 There cannot have been any very wide zoological interval between the forms of the thylacine and of the thylacothere.

thylakoid (ˈθaɪləkɔɪd). *Bot.* [a. G. *thylakoid* (W. Menke 1961, in *Zeitschr. f. Naturforsch.* B. XVI. 335/1), f. Gr. θυλακοειδ-ής pouch-like, f. θύλακ-ος pouch: see -OID.] Each of the flattened, fluid-filled, membranous sacs inside a chloroplast in which photochemical reactions take place.

1962 *Ann. Rev. Plant Physiol.* XIII. 35 These are designated discs by Gibbs, flattened vesicles by Mühlethaler, and thylakoids by Menke. **1967** [see GRANUM]. **1974** R. Y. STANIER in Carlile & Skehel *Evolution in Microbial World* 231 The enclosing thylakoid membrane provides an external constraint to prevent disaggregation.

thylk(e, obs. form of THILK.

thyll(e, obs. f. THILL[1], TILL *prep.* and *conj.*

thylose, -osis: see TYLOSE, -OSIS.

thymacetin (θaɪˈmæsɪtɪn). *Pharm.* A trade name of acetaminothymol, a colourless crystalline compound, used as a hypnotic.

1892 *Pharmaceutical Jrnl.* 27 Feb. 692 Thymacetin.. bears the same relation to thymol as phenacetin to phenol.

‖**Thymallus** (θaɪˈmæləs). [mod.L., a. Gr. θύμαλλος name of an unknown fish: see quot. 1706.] The genus of fishes containing the graylings; = GRAYLING 1 a.

[**1706** PHILLIPS (ed. Kersey), *Thymallus*, a Fish of the Trout-kind, that smells like the Herb Thyme.] **1797** *Encycl. Brit.* (ed. 3) XVI. 616/2 The thymallus, or grayling, haunts clear and rapid streams. **1921** *Chambers's Jrnl.* Jan. 114/2 We have fished that river again, and succeeded in capturing good baskets of thymallus.

thymate, *Chem.*: see THYMIC *a.*[1] 2.

thymbel(l, -bil(l, -byl(l, obs. ff. THIMBLE.

thyme (taɪm), *sb.* Forms: α. 4–8 **tyme,** 6–8 **time.** β. 5– **thyme** (5–7 **thime**). [a. F. *thym* (13th c. in Godef. *Compl.*), ad. L. *thymum*, in late med.L. often *timum, -us*, a. Gr. θύμον (θύμος), f. θύειν to burn sacrifice.]

1. a. A plant of the genus *Thymus*, N.O. *Labiatæ*, comprising shrubby herbs with fragrant aromatic leaves, found chiefly in the Mediterranean region; esp. *T. vulgaris* (Garden Thyme), a native of Spain and Italy, cultivated as a pot-herb, and *T. Serpyllum* (Wild Thyme), occurring on dry banks and pastures in Britain and throughout Europe. (See also b.)

α. *c* **1420** *Liber Cocorum* (1862) 53 Saveray, mynt and tyme. *c* **1440** *Promp. Parv.* 494/1 Tyme, flowre, *timus*... Tyme, herbe, *tima*. **1526** *Pilgr. Perf.* (W. de W. 1531) 65 Wo be to you pharisees, whiche tytheth myntes, rewe, tyme, & suche other small herbes. **1563** HYLL *Art Garden.* (1593) 80 The Garden Time is a plant right profitable. **1590** SHAKS. *Mids. N.* II. i. 249, I know a banke where the wilde time blowes. **1653** WALTON *Angler* ii. 57 Bruise..a little Time, or some other sweet herb. **1713** *Phil. Trans.* XXVIII. 193 Lemon Tyme.

β. **1398** TREVISA *Barth. De P.R.* XVII. lix. (Bodl. MS.) lf. 203 b/2 Epithimum is þe floure of thyme. *c* **1425** *Voc.* in Wr.-Wülcker 644/6 Nomina Herbarum..*Hic caulus*, uwle (?) or thyme. **1562** TURNER *Herbal* II. 155 b, Thyme hath the poure to driue furth fleme. **1637** MILTON *Lycidas* 40 Desert Caves, With wilde Thyme and the Gadding Vine o'regrown. **1657** S. PURCHAS *Pol. Flying-Ins.* I. xv. 94 Thyme, which onely yeeldeth Nectar. **1855** KINGSLEY *Heroes, Theseus* I. 199 The hills are sweet with thyme and basil.

b. With qualifying words, denoting various species or varieties: as **creeping thyme, mother of thyme, running t.** = *wild t.* (see 1); **garden thyme** (see 1); **lemon thyme,** † **musk thyme,** a cultivated variety of *T. Serpyllum*, having a scent like that of lemons (often called *T. citriodorus*); **savory thyme**, *T. virginicus* (see SAVORY 3). Also applied to plants of other genera, chiefly aromatic labiates, as BASIL *thyme*, CAT-*thyme*, HORSE-*thyme*; also **water-thyme**, a name of *Elodea canadensis* (*Anacharis Alsinastrum*).

1579 LANGHAM *Gard. Health* (1633) 636 Thyme: Running Thyme prouoketh the termes and vrine. **1597** GERARDE *Herbal* II. clxiv. §6. 457 Called..in English wilde Time, Puliall Mountaine,..running Time, creeping Time, Mother of Time. *Ibid.* clxv. 459 Our English women call it Muske Time. **1676** BEAL in *Phil. Trans.* XI. 587 The Thymes, denominated from Mastic, Lemon, Musk, Yellow and White Thyme. **1713** [see 1 a].

2. *oil of thyme*: a fragrant volatile oil obtained from the common thyme, used as an antiseptic.

1753 CHAMBERS *Cycl. Supp.* s.v. *Oil*, Mr. Geoffroy made a multitude of experiments on the oil of thyme. **1857** [see THYMENE 1]. **1876** HARLEY *Royle's Mat. Med.* 407 An odour resembling oil of thyme. *Ibid.* 474 [see THYMOL].

3. *attrib.* and *Comb.*, as **thyme-blossom, -leaf, -root; thyme-capt, -fed, -flavoured, -grown** adjs.; **thyme-camphor** = THYMOL; **thyme fish**, a name for the grayling, its smell being held to resemble that of thyme (whence the generic name *Thymallus*); **thyme-leaved** (-liːvd) *a.*, having leaves resembling those of thyme (rendering mod.L. *serpyllifolius* in specific names); **thyme-oil**, oil of thyme: see 2; † **thyme wart (wert)**, used by Holland to render L. *thymion*, Gr. θύμιον a kind of wart (= THYMUS 2).

1821 CLARE *Vill. Minstr.* (1823) I. 119 This *thyme-capt hill beneath one's feet. **1900** ELLIS *Rom. Rose* I. 19/545 Her breath was sweet as breeze *thyme-fed. **1756–7** tr. *Keysler's Trav.* (1760) I. 62 Very fine trouts, *thyme fish, and others. **1789** PILKINGTON *View Derby.* I. viii. 395 *Arenaria serpyllifolia*, *Thyme-leaved Sandwort. **1859** D. BUNCE *Trav. Dr. Leichhardt* iv. 27 *Decaspora disticha* and *Thymifolia*, the first two-leaved, and the latter the thyme-leaved *Decaspora*. **1972** Y. LOVELOCK *Veg. Bk.* III. 336 Small or thyme-leaved mint..is only found in Tasmania. **1868** WATTS *Dict. Chem.* V. 791 On continuing the distillation of the *thyme-oil, there passes over..a mixture of thymene (and cymene) with about ⅓ pt. of thymol. **1601** HOLLAND *Pliny* XXXII. x. 448 For the *thyme werts particularly, they vse them [Cackerell heads] raw.

Hence **thyme** *v.*, *trans.* to cover or scent with thyme; **thymed** (taɪmd) *a.*, covered with thyme.

1628 FELTHAM *Resolves* II. [I.] xii. 32 Nor does the sedulous Bee thyme all her thighes from one Flowres single vertues. **1885** *St. James' Gaz.* 17 Aug. 6/2 Upon its thymed banks.

thymectomy (θaɪˈmɛktəmɪ). *Surg.* [f. as THYMUS + Gr. -εκτομια, from ἐκτομή a cutting out.] Excision of the thymus gland. Hence **thyˈmectomize** *v.*, *trans.* to remove the thymus gland from.

1905 GOULD *Dict. Med. Terms* Suppl., Thymectomy. **1909** DORLAND *Med. Dict.* (ed. 5), Thymectomize, Thymectomy. **1963** *Lancet* 5 Jan. 43/1 In the adult animal, thymectomy is associated with little or no significant depression of the immune response. **1970** *Nature* 26 Sept. 1353/1 This preliminary observation on the long term persistence of T cells has been extended by thymectomizing CBA/Lac mice. **1974** R. M. KIRK et al. *Surgery* ii. 33 Neonatal thymectomy suppresses the immune response in experimental animals. **1976** *Ann. Rev. Microbiol.* XXX. 584 Some adjuvants fail to work in thymectomized mice treated with antilymphocyte (anti-T) serum.

thymelæaceous (ˌθɪmɪliːˈeɪʃəs), *a.* *Bot.* Also **thymelaceous.** [f. mod.L. *Thymelæaceæ* (or *Thymelāceæ*), f. specific name (*Daphne*) *Thymelæa*, ad. Gr. θυμελαία, f. θύμ-ον THYME + ἐλαία olive-tree: see -ACEOUS.] Belonging to the N.O. *Thymelæaceæ* or *Thymelaceæ*.

1837 *Penny Cycl.* VIII. 307/2 *Daphne*, a genus of thymelaceous plants. **1848** SMART *Suppl. to Walker*, *Thymelea*,..which gives the name thymelaceous to a natural order.

‖**thymele** (ˈθɪmɪliː). *Gr. Antiq.* [a. Gr. θυμέλη altar, f. θύειν to sacrifice.] The altar of Dionysus in the centre of the orchestra in an ancient Greek theatre.

1753 CHAMBERS *Cycl. Supp.*, *Thymele*, in the antient theatre, a kind of pulpit, where the singers called *thymelici* performed. **1827** *Buckham's Theat. Grks.* (ed. 2) 216. **1835** *Penny Cycl.* III. 298/1 Some large blocks..in front of the stage..supposed by Dr. Hunt to be the ruins of the Thymele. **1842** *Smith's Dict. Grk. & Rom. Antiq.* s.v. *Theatrum*, In the centre of the circle of the orchestra was the θυμέλη, that is, the altar of Dionysus... The chorus generally arranged itself..between the thymele and the stage. **1889** HAIGH *Attic Theat.* iii. §6. 132. **1907** H. TRENCH *New Poems* 24 The sacred oils On the fragrant thin-flamed thymele.

Hence **thyˈmelic,** † **thyˈmelical** *adjs. rare* [Gr. θυμελικός], of or pertaining to the thymele, scenic, theatric.

1656 BLOUNT *Glossogr.*, *Thymelical* (*thymelicus*), belonging to players in interludes and open dance. **1849** DONALDSON *Theat. Greeks* I. vii. (ed. 6) 152 There was another entrance to the thymelic platform.

thymelle, obs. form of THIMBLE.

thymene (ˈθaɪmiːn). *Chem.* [f. THYME + -ENE.]

1. A clear oily hydrocarbon, $C_{10}H_{16}$, of the terpene group, contained in the oil of thyme.

1857 MILLER *Elem. Chem.* III. 446 *Oil of Thyme*..consists of an oxidized portion, *thymole*, and of a hydrocarbon, *thymene*. The latter constitutes the more volatile portion of the oil. **1868** WATTS *Dict. Chem.* V. 792 Thymene is a colourless oil, having an agreeable odour of thyme. **1900** GILDEMEISTER & HOFFMANN *Volatile Oils* 625.

2. Commercially applied to a product of the oil of ajowan, used as a soap perfume.

1900 GILDEMEISTER & HOFFMANN *Volatile Oils* 558 The remaining part of the oil [of Ajowan], about one half, consists of hydrocarbons, which are sold in commerce under the name of thymene..a mixture of cymene and a terpene boiling at 172°.

‖**thymiˈama.** *Obs.* [a. Gr. θυμίαμα, f. θυμιᾶν to burn incense. In *thymyame* (Lydgate) a. OF. *thymiame, timiame* incense, perfume (12–14th c. in Godef.).] Incense.

[**1430–40** LYDG. *Bochas* VII. ix. (MS. Bodl. 263 lf. 361/1), Silk Synamome, franc ensens withal For sacrefise, the purpurate vesture W[t] Thymyame, the riche pectoral Which ordeyned wern,..For the Solempne place of places alle Sancta sanctorum.] **1697** tr. *Rodriguez' Chr. Perfect.* v. i. I. 269 The smell of well compos'd Thymiama is very delicious. **1706** PHILLIPS (ed. Kersey), *Thymiama*, Incense, Perfume; a Sweet-Gum.

thymiatechny (θaɪmɪəˈtɛknɪ). [f. Gr. θυμιᾶν (see prec.) + -τεχνία from τέχνη art, craft.] The art of employing perfumes in medicine.

1833–46 in DUNGLISON. Hence in later Dicts.

‖**thymiaterion** (ˌθaɪmɪəˈtɪərɪɒn). Pl. **-ia.** [a. Gr. θυμιατήριον, f. θυμιᾶν to burn incense.] A censer, as used by the ancient Greeks, or in the Greek Church.

1850 LEITCH tr. *C. O. Müller's Anc. Art* §406 (ed. 2) 547 Nike making libation..; another such, a thymiaterion in the other hand. **1857** BIRCH *Anc. Pottery* (1858) II. 93 The thymiateria or tall censers.

thymic (ˈθaɪmɪk), *a.*[1] [f. Gr. θύμος (ῠ) THYMUS + -IC.]

1. *Anat.* and *Path.* Of, pertaining to, or connected with the thymus gland.

1656 BLOUNT *Glossogr.* s.v. *Vein*, *Thymick veine*.., the first branch of the subclavicular, goes to the fag peece or kernel, which is under the kannel bone. **1831** R. KNOX *Cloquet's Anat.* 633 The arteries of the pericardium.. arise from the thymic, phrenic, bronchial, and œsophageal arteries. **1849–52** *Todd's Cycl. Anat.* IV. 1102/1 'Thymic asthma' may occur with an unnaturally small thymus. **1899** *Allbutt's Syst. Med.* VI. 90 Spasm of the glottis — the so-called 'thymic asthma'.

2. *Physiol. Chem.* In ***thymic acid***, $C_{16}H_{25}N_3P_2O_{12}$, a colourless acid obtained from the thymus gland. Its salts are **thymates** (ˈθaɪmeɪts).

1894 *Jrnl. Chem. Soc.* LXVI. I. 156 [see THYMINE]. **1896** *Ibid.* LXX. I. 658 Nucleic acid is decomposed by hydrolysis into thymic acid, adenine, guanine, and cytosine... *Barium thymate*, $C_{16}H_{23}N_3P_2O_{12}Ba$,.. dissolves readily in water, and, when anhydrous, is excessively hygroscopic... Thymic acid differs from the parent nucleic acid by its ready solubility in water. **1898** *Schäfer's Text Bk. Physiol.* I. 67.

thymic (θaɪ-, ˈtaɪmɪk), *a.*[2] *Chem.* [f. Gr. θύμον THYME + -IC.] Of, pertaining to, or derived from thyme; in ***thymic acid***, a synonym of *thymylic acid* or THYMOL. Hence **thyˈmicic** *a.*, derived from or containing thymol; = THYMOTIC.

1868 WATTS *Dict. Chem.* V. 792 Thymicic acid, synon. with thymotic acid. **1890** BILLINGS *Nat. Med. Dict.*, *Thymic acid*, thymol.

thymidine (ˈθaɪmɪdiːn). *Biochem.* [f. THYM(INE + -IDINE.] A pyrimidine nucleoside, $C_5H_9O_3 \cdot C_5H_4N_2O_2$, in which the base is thymine and the sugar deoxyribose, and which is obtained by the partial hydrolysis of DNA.

1912 *Jrnl. Biol. Chem.* XII. 414 Barium salts of a hexo-cytidine diphosphoric acid and a hexo-thymidine diphosphoric acid were obtained. **1931** LEVENE & BASS *Nucleic Acids* 335/1 (Index), Thymidine. *See* Thymine desoxyribonucleoside. **1963** *New Scientist* 21 Mar. 616/2 Before a cell can divide, it has to duplicate its own normal complement of DNA and this it synthesises from many different starting products, one of the most important being thymidine. **1978** *Bull. Amer. Acad. Arts & Sci.* Feb. 17 If, during the culturing process which forms an essential feature of the preparation of cells for examination of their karyotype, tritiated thymidine (a radioactive precursor of DNA) is added, the resultant metaphase chromosomes become radioactively labeled to a degree that is a function of their recent activity in synthesizing DNA.

thymidylic (θaɪmɪˈdɪlɪk), *a. Biochem.* [f. prec. + -YL + -IC.] ***thymidylic acid***: any phosphoric acid ester of thymidine, $C_5H_8O_2(PH_2O_4) \cdot C_5H_4N_2O_2$, one or other of which is one of the four nucleotides present in most DNA.

1951 *Jrnl Bacteriol.* LXI. 41 Samples of thymidylic acid, desoxyadenylic acid.. and desoxyguanylic acid.. were made available. **1968** A. WHITE et al. *Princ. Biochem.* (ed. 4) ix. 186 Deoxyguanylic, thymidylic, and deoxycytidylic acids esterified at positions 3′ and 5′ are also found in hydrolysates of DNA. **1972** *Sci. Amer.* Dec. 85/1 Until well into the 1930's DNA was generally thought to be merely a tetranucleotide composed of one unit each of adenylic, guanylic, thymidylic and cytidylic acids.

Hence **thyˈmidylate**, the anion derived from thymidylic acid by the loss of a hydrogen atom from the phosphate group.

1959 FLAKS & COHEN in *Jrnl. Biol. Chem.* CCXXXIV. 2981/1 We are designating the latter catalytic activity.. as 'thymidylate synthetase'. **1974** J. W. DRAKE in Carlile & Skehel *Evolution in Microbial World* 51 The *td* gene encodes the viral thymidylate synthetase.

thymine (ˈθaɪmɪn). Also **thymin**. [f. THYM(IC *a.*[1] + -INE[5].]

1. *Chem.* A colourless crystalline alloxur base, $C_5H_6N_2O_2$, obtained by the action of dilute sulphuric acid on thymic acid (THYMIC *a.*[1] 2).

1894 *Jrnl. Chem. Soc.* LXVI. I. 156 Thymic acid.. on heating with sulphuric acid.., *thymin*.. is formed. This substance has neither basic nor acidic properties; it.. is deposited from water in quadratic and hexagonal crystals. **1898** *Schäfer's Text Bk. Physiol.* I. 66. **1900** *Jrnl. Chem. Soc.* LXXVIII. I. 319 Thymin was originally described by Kossel as one of the decomposition products of the nucleic acid of the thymus gland. It has since been obtained from nucleic acid from other sources. **1903** *Amer. Chem. Jrnl.* XXIX. 481 On boiling this mercapto derivative with hydrochloric acid we obtained thymine. **1954** *New Biol.* XVI. 15 In desoxyribose nucleic acid the purine is either adenine or guanine, the pyrimidine either cytosine or thymine. **1976** *Sci. Amer.* Jan. 64/3 The DNA molecule consists of two long chains of nucleotides wound in a double helix... Each nucleotide consists of a deoxyribose sugar, a phosphate group and one of four nitrogenous bases: adenine, guanine, thymine or cytosine.

2. *Biochem.* = THYMOPOIETIN.

1968 G. GOLDSTEIN in *Lancet* 20 July 122/1 'Thymin'.. seems an appropriate name for this substance, which not only is present in normal thymus but also appears to be secreted normally and to have an effect in physiological concentrations on neuromuscular transmission. **1974** [see THYMOPOIETIN].

Hence **thymìnic** (θaɪˈmɪnɪk), *a. Chem.* in ***thyminic acid***, a synonym of *thymic acid* (THYMIC *a.*[1] 2).

1898 MANDEL tr. *Hammarsten's Physiol. Chem.* 100 From adenylic acid and.. other nucleic acids Kossel and Neumann have prepared an acid called by them *thyminic acid*.

thymle, obs. form of THIMBLE.

thymo-, combining form from Gr. θύμο-ν THYME, used in some chemical terms: **ˈthymoform** *Pharm.*, a yellowish antiseptic powder prepared from formaldehyde and thymol; **ˈthymoïl, thyˈmoïlol**, Lallemand's names for *thymoquinone* and *hydrothymoquinone*; thence **thymoˈïlamide, thyˈmoïlate, thymoˈïlic** *a.*; **ˌthymoquiˈnone**, $C_{10}H_{12}O_2$, a product of the oxidation of thymol, obtained in reddish-yellow 4-sided shining crystalline laminæ, having an aromatic odour.

1899 COBLENTZ *Newer Remedies* (ed. 3) 134 *Thymoform. **1857** MILLER *Elem. Chem., Org.* III. vii. §1. 447 According to Lallemand, when thymole is treated with oxidizing agents such as chromic acid,.. it yields a substance termed *thymoile [*ed.* **1862** *thymoïl*]. *Ibid.*, If treated with sulphurous acid or other reducing agents, it [thymole] combines with hydrogen and yields *thymoilole [*ed.* **1862** thymoïlol] $[C_{10}H_{14}O_2]$, the homologue of hydrokinone. **1868** WATTS *Dict. Chem.* V. 793 From these relations, thymoïl may be regarded as homologous with quinone, *thymoïlol with colourless hydroquinone. **1871** *Jrnl. Chem. Soc.* XXIV. 351 This body [Lallemand's thymoïlol] is hydrothymoquinone... Hydrothymoquinone is easily converted into *thymoquinone by ferric chloride, nitric acid, etc.

thymocyte (ˈθaɪməʊsaɪt). *Histology.* [f. THYM(US + -O + -CYTE.] A lymphocyte-like cell derived from the thymus gland; a T-lymphocyte.

1929 E. S. SCHAFER *Essent. Histol.* (ed. 12) xxii. 265 Besides lymphocyte-like cells (thymocytes) it [*sc.* the thymus] contains peculiar granular cells. **1976** *Nature* 13 May 139/1 Differentiation of T cells is generally depicted as involving transformation of prethymic cells to immunoincompetent thymocytes, which themselves are precursors of functionally mature, immunocompetent T cells.

thymol (ˈθaɪmɒl). *Chem.* [f. Gr. θύμον THYME + -OL.] The phenol of cymene, $C_{10}H_{13}.OH$, obtained from oil of thyme, also from the volatile oil of horse-mint, crystallizing in transparent rhomboidal plates; a powerful antiseptic.

1857 MILLER *Elem. Chem.* III. 446 Thymole [*ed.* **1862** thymol], $C_{20}H_{14}O_2$, is isomeric with cuminic alcohol; it.. constitutes about one-half of the essence of thyme. **1876** HARLEY *Royle's Mat. Med.* 474 Oil of Thyme.. consists of a fluid portion, separable into cymene.., and thymene.., and of a solid crystalline body called thymol.., which has a very pungent taste, and the aroma of the crude oil. **1911** *Contemp. Rev.* Feb. 231 The destruction of the parasite in its intermediary host [man] by quinine or thymol.

b. *attrib.* and *Comb.*

1883 *Athenæum* 10 Mar. 316/2 When thymolsulphonic acid is treated with nitric acid, paranitrothymol is formed. **1884** *Health Exhib. Catal.* 62/1 'Thymol-Cresol' Disinfecting Powder. **1899** CAGNEY *Jaksch's Clin. Diagn.* vii. (ed. 4) 344 Thymol appears in the urine as thymol sulphuric, thymol glycuronic.. acids. **1911** DORLAND *Med. Dict.* (ed. 6) s.v. *Thymol*, *Thymol-camphor*, a compound of thymol and camphor. *Ibid.*, *Thymol-gauze*, gauze impregnated with a 1 per cent. solution of thymol. *Ibid.*, Thymol-inhalation, -solution [etc.].

Hence **ˈthymolate**, a compound of thymol, in which the hydrogen of the OH group is replaced by a metal; **thyˈmolic** *a.*, of or pertaining to thymol, chiefly in compounds, as *sulpho-thymolic acid*, $C_{10}H_{14}SO_4$; **ˈthymolize** *v.*, *trans.* to treat (a solution) with thymol (as a preservative); **thyˈmoloform** = *thymoform*.

1880 *Athenæum* 27 Nov. 713/1 The authors.. have thus prepared aluminic methylate,.. cresylate, and thymolate. **1900** HELEN BALDWIN in *Jrnl. Exper. Med* 1 Oct. 30 The urine should be thymolized.. to prevent fermentation. **1911** DORLAND *Med. Dict.* (ed. 6), *Thymoloform*, a yellowish powder, a product of formaldehyd and thymol.

thymoleptic (θaɪməʊˈlɛptɪk), *a.* (*sb.*) *Pharm.* [f. Gr. θυμός soul, spirit + λῆψις seizing: see -IC.] (Of or pertaining to) a psychic energizer (see PSYCHIC *a.* (*sb.*) 1 a).

1959 *New Scientist* 31 Dec. 1351/2 So novel are these [psychotherapeutic] drugs that even the scientific terms used to describe their action—ataractic, thymoleptic—have been coined within the past few years. *Ibid.* 1353/1 The psychotherapeutic drugs fall at present into two classes:.. the major tranquillizers.. and those that relieve psychotic depression—the psychic energizers or thymoleptics. **1967** W. L. L. REES *Short Textbk. Psychiatry* xxxii. 281 The tricyclic (thymoleptic) group of anti-depressants are quite dissimilar in chemical structure to the monoamine oxidase inhibitors. **1971** H. B. MURPHREE in J. R. DiPalma *Drill's Pharmacol. in Med.* (ed. 4) xxiii. 437/2 A term used in Europe, thymoleptic.. has not gained currency in North America.

thymoma (ˈθaɪməʊmə). *Path.* [ad. G. *thymome* (F. Grandhomme *Ueber Tumoren des Vorderen Mediastinums* (1900) 43): see THYMUS, -OMA.] A rare, usually benign tumour arising from tissue of the thymus gland and often associated with myasthenia gravis.

1919 J. EWING *Neoplastic Dis.* xlvi. 894 Lymphosarcoma or thymoma is the most frequent form of thymus tumor. **1961** R. D. BAKER *Essent. Path.* xviii. 510 Thymomas may at times be lymphomas, and be associated with myasthenia gravis. **1974** J. D. MAYNARD in R. M. Kirk et al. *Surgery* x. 219 Thymoma is a soft lobulated tumour situated in the thymus or close to it.

thymo-nucleic (ˌθaɪməʊnjuːˈkliːɪk), *a. Physiol. Chem.* [f. Gr. θύμο-ς THYMUS + NUCLEIC.] Of or pertaining to the nuclein of the thymus gland; in ***thymo-nucleic acid***, either of two or more nucleic acids, which can be isolated from the cells of the thymus; now identified with DNA.

1904 *Jrnl. Chem. Soc.* LXXXVI. I. 127 (*heading*) Oxidation of thymonucleic acid with calcium permanganate. **1911** DORLAND *Med. Dict.* (ed. 6), *Thymonucleic acid*, any one of a series of acids which split up into thymin, esp. the compound $C_{25}H_{36}N_9O_{20}P_3$. **1942** *Nature* 17 Jan. 66/1 To these fibres.. are attached desoxyribose-, or thymo-, nucleic acid which is responsible for the specific aldehyde reaction given by the chromosomes in Feulgen's test. **1951** *New Biol.* X. 48 Phosphorus-32 uptake is found to be intimately related to the process of synthesis of thymonucleic acid.

thymopathy[1] (θaɪˈmɒpəθɪ). *rare*$^{-0}$. [f. Gr. θυμό-ς soul, spirit + -PATHY.] Any mental disease.

[**1857** DUNGLISON *Med. Lex.*, *Thymopathia, psychopathia*, ..a disease of the mind.] **1860** MAYNE *Expos. Lex.*, Thymopathy. Hence in later Dicts.

thyˈmopathy[2]. *rare*$^{-0}$. [f. Gr. θύμ-ος THYMUS + -PATHY.] A disease of the thymus gland.

1909 *Cent. Dict. Supp.* **1911** DORLAND *Med. Dict.* (ed. 6).

thymopoietin (ˌθaɪməʊpɔɪˈɛtɪn). *Biochem.* [f. THYM(US + -O + Gr. ποιητικ-ός (see POIETIC *a.*) + -IN[1].] A polypeptide hormone secreted by the thymus which stimulates the development of thymocytes.

1974 BASCH & GOLDSTEIN in *Proc. Nat. Acad. Sci.* LXXI. 1477/2 It has been brought to our attention that our term thymin for this polypeptide hormone is being confused with the base thymine... We therefore intend to change our terminology in the future and use the term thymopoietin. **1980** H. N. EISEN *Immunology* (ed. 2) xviii. 416/2 Thymopoietin, a small protein (49 amino acid residues), has been sequenced and synthesized. It causes pre-T cells.. to become somewhat sensitive to mitogens, but not to become immunologically competent.

thymoˈprivous, *a. Path.* [f. as THYMOPATHY[2] + L. *prīvāre* to deprive.] (See quot.)

1911 DORLAND *Med. Dict.* (ed. 6), *Thymoprivous*, pertaining to or caused by removal of the thymus.

thymosin (ˈθaɪməsɪn). *Biochem.* [f. Gr. θύμος THYMUS + -IN[1].] An extract of the thymus gland which has a stimulating effect on the immune system (see quots.).

1966 A. L. GOLDSTEIN et al. in *Proc. Nat. Acad. Sci.* LVI. 1010 We wish to report the preparation.. from calf thymic tissue of a product which stimulates incorporation of H^3-thymidine into mesenteric lymph node cells. The lymphocytopoietic factor, which we term thymosin, is active .. *in vivo*, as well as.. *in vitro*. **1980** H. N. EISEN *Immunology* (ed. 2) xviii. 416/2 Thymosin, a mixture of many active low-molecular-weight polypeptides.., probably comes closer than many others to behaving like a natural hormone... It restores immune function to neonatally thymectomized mice.

thymotic (θaɪˈmɒtɪk), *a. Chem.* [Arbitrarily f. Gr. θύμο-ν THYME, or THYMOL + -IC.] Of, pertaining to, or derived from thymol. ***thymotic acid***, $C_{11}H_{14}O_3$, a white, loosely coherent, crystalline solid, having a silky lustre, prepared from thymol. Also ***thymotic alcohol***, $C_{11}H_{16}O_2$; ***thymotic aldehyde***, $C_{11}H_{14}O_2$. Hence **ˈthymotate**, a salt of thymotic acid; **ˈthymotide**, $C_{11}H_{12}O_2$.

1868 WATTS *Dict. Chem.* V. 796 Thymotic acid heated with caustic baryta is resolved into thymol and carbonic anhydride... The thymotates of the alkali-metals are soluble in water. **1873** —— *Fownes' Chem.* (ed. 11) 824 Thymotic and Thymol-carbonic Acids are produced by the action of sodium and carbon-dioxide on thymol.

thymous (ˈθaɪməs), *a. rare*$^{-0}$. [ad. L. *thymōs-us* (Pliny), f. *thymum* THYME: see -OUS.] Abounding in or having the character of thyme; thymy.

1656 BLOUNT *Glossogr.*, *Thymous* (*thymosus*), full of thime, an herb so called. **1860** MAYNE *Expos. Lex.*, *Thymodes*, having or full of, or belonging to, thyme; smelling like thyme: thymous.

‖**thymus** (ˈθaɪməs). Pl. **thymi** (ˈθaɪmaɪ). [mod.L., a. Gr. θύμος (θῡ-) a warty excrescence; also the thymus gland (Galen).]

1. a. *Anat.* A glandular body of obscure function (one of the so-called 'ductless glands') situated near the base of the neck in vertebrate animals; in man usually disappearing after the period of childhood.

In the calf and lamb called by butchers *sweetbread*, or more precisely *neck* or *throat sweetbread*, for distinction from the pancreas or *stomach sweetbread*.

1693 tr. *Blancard's Phys. Dict.* (ed. 2), *Thymus*, a Glandule in the Throat, which separates watry Humour, called Lympha from the Blood, and empties it by the Lymphatick Vessels. **1704** J. HARRIS *Lex. Techn.* I, *Thymus*, is a conglobate Glandule in the Throat, growing to the upper part of the Mediastinum, and seated between the Divisions of the Subclavian Veins and Arteries. **1713** CHESELDEN *Anat.* III. xi. (1726) 232 Just within the Thorax is seated another [gland] called Thymus. **1868** OWEN *Vertebr. Anim.* xxxii. III. 567 The thymus in Monotremes lies between the episternum and the beginnings of the vessels from the aortic arch. **1881** MIVART *Cat* 237 The thymus..is of very large size during immaturity. **1888** ROLLESTON & JACKSON *Anim. Life* 350 The thymus atrophies in the higher *Vertebrata* as a rule. **1899** *Allbutt's Syst. Med.* VI. 89 Several instances of enlarged thymus have been reported of late years. **1904** *Brit. Med. Jrnl.* 10 Sept. 603 It is possible..that a similar extract prepared from human thymi would have a depressor action.

b. Now usually ***thymus gland*** (rarely ***body***).

1776 M. FALCONER (*title*) An Account of the Structure and Offices..of the Thymus Glands. **1797** M. BAILLIE *Morb. Anat.* (1807) 111 The thymus gland is subject to few diseases, and is only of temporary existence. **1847** YOUATT *Horse* xi. 231 It is 'the thymus gland', or, in vulgar language, the sweet-bread. **1862** MILLER *Elem. Chem.* III. 722 Hypoxanthine has also been found in the thyroid or thymus glands. **1899** *Allbutt's Syst. Med.* VI. 73 Abscesses beginning in the thymus body.

c. ***thymus nucleic acid*** = *thymonucleic acid* s.v. THYMONUCLEIC *a.* Now *Hist.*

1904 *Jrnl. Chem. Soc.* LXXXVI. I. 837 (*heading*) Thymus nucleic acid. **1938** [see DEOXYRIBONUCLEIC ACID].

†**2.** *Path.* A rugose wart resembling a bud of thyme. *Obs.*

1693 tr. *Blancard's Phys. Dict.* (ed. 2), *Thymus*,..also a fleshy Tumor that hangs upon the Body like a Wart, of a colour like the Flower of Time. **1811** in HOOPER *Med. Dict.*

3. *Comb.*, as ***thymus-dependent***, ***-derived***, ***-independent*** adjs.

1963 *Jrnl. Nat. Cancer Inst.* XXXI. 1466 In the thymectomized newborn mouse..re-establishment of immunologic competence..is also known to be thymus-dependent. **1977** *Proc. R. Soc. Med.* LXX. 524/2 This change may be responsible for the diminished response to thymus-dependent antigens that is seen in subjects with chronic liver disease. **1970** *New Scientist* 7 May 271/2 The thymus-derived T cells apparently move through the body more actively than the B cells. **1974** *Ciba Symposium* XX. 114 They suggest that, by one means or another, trypanosome infections break the control link between thymus-dependent lymphocytes (T cells) and thymus-independent lymphocytes (B cells).

thymy ('taɪmɪ), *a.* [f. THYME + -Y.]

1. Abounding in or overgrown with thyme.

1727 GAY *Fables* I. xxii. 11 Whene'er a thymy bank he [a goat] found, He roll'd upon the fragrant ground. **1827–35** WILLIS *Flor. Gray* 3 Upon Hymettus, and the thymy isles. **1860** TENNYSON *Sea Dreams* 38 Lingering about the thymy promontories.

2. Pertaining to or of the nature of thyme; *esp.* having the scent of thyme.

1747 P. FRANCIS tr. *Horace, Ep.* I. iii. 26 The thymy Fragrance of the Spring. **1874** J. BROWN *Lett.* (1907) 228 The thymy breath and free air of the braes and hills. **1880** MISS BROUGHTON *Sec. Th.* III. x, The thymy sweetness of the fell breeze.

thymyl ('θaɪmɪl). *Chem.* [f. Gr. θύμ-ον THYME + -YL.] The radical $C_{10}H_{13}$ of thymol and its derivatives; also used *attrib.* and in *comb.*, as ***thymyl hydride***, $C_{10}H_{13}.H$, ***thymyl sulphuric*** (acid), ***thymyl phosphate***, ***silicate***, ***sulphate***. Hence **'thymylamine**, $C_{10}H_{13}NH_2$; **thy'mylic** *a.*, in ***thymylic acid***, ***alcohol***, ***hydrate***, obs. synonyms of THYMOL.

1868 WATTS *Dict. Chem.* V. 797 Thymyl. *Ibid.* 793 Thymylic hydrate [etc.].

thyn(e, obs. ff. THIN, THINE, THYINE.

†**thyne** (ðaɪn), *adv. Sc.* and *north. dial. Obs.* Forms: 4 **þien**, **þein**, **þine**, 4–6 **thine**, 4–7 **thyne**, 5 **þeine**, **þeyn**, 5–6 **thyn**, 6 **thin**. [App. reduced from THETHEN; cf. *hyne*, *syne*, *whyne*.] = THENCE. (Also prec. by *fra*, *from*.)

c **1330** R. BRUNNE *Chron.* (1810) 190 Þe templers ilk a dele failed & þien fled. **13..** *Cursor M.* 6676 (Gött.) If he to min auter fly, Men sal him þein [*Cott.* þeþen] draw to die. *c* **1375** *Sc. Leg. Saints* ii. (*Paulus*) 419 Fra þine þire banis men has tane. *c* **1400** MAUNDEV. (Roxb.) iv. 12 Fra þeine men wendes to þe ile of Cophos. *c* **1440** *Alphabet of Tales* 179 He..had hur thyne owr a grete watir in-to a noder contreth. *c* **1450** *St. Cuthbert* (Surtees) 4271 As a pilgryme pure..Forth fra þeyn he fore. **1513** DOUGLAS *Æneis* III. x. 83 And fra thyne The fertile grownd of Helory passit syne. **1589** *Reg. Mag. Sig. Scot.* 573/1 Beginnand..at the fute of the Skitterane burne ..and fra thin streikand and ascendand up the said burne. *a* **1600** MONTGOMERIE *Misc. Poems* xlviii. 237 We weyd from thyn, and wald no langer byde. **1609** *Sc. Acts Jas. VI* (1816) IV. 443 Fra thyne doun Irving burne to ask.

Hence †**thyne-'forth** (**-furth**) *adv.* = THENCEFORTH; †**thyne-'forward** *adv.* = THENCE-FORWARD. Usually preceded by *from* (*fra*).

c **1375** *Sc. Leg. Saints* xxxviii. (*Adrian*) 272 Fra *þine furth sal þu nocht me se. *c* **1440** *Alphabet of Tales* 51 And fro thyne furth, evur after..he had more devocion vnto Saynt Andrew þan he had befor. *c* **1440** *Reg. Aberd.* (Maitland) I. 248 Þe burn of Nessoke, swa þat theyn furth is þe meris betwix þe bischape and þe Lord of Marr. *a* **1572** KNOX *Hist. Ref.* Wks. 1846 I. 378 The said Congregatioun..shall in no wayis from thynefurth use ony force or violence, in casting down of kirkis. *c* **1400** MAUNDEV. (Roxb.) xxiv. 110 Þai schuld fra *þeine forward hald þam payd of þat he wald giffe þam.

thynn(e, (θ-), obs. ff. THEN, THIN, THYINE.

thyratron ('θaɪrətrɒn). *Electronics.* [f. Gr. θύρα door + -TRON.] A thermionic valve utilizing an arc discharge in mercury vapour or low-pressure gas and having a heated cathode and at least one grid.

1929 *General Electr. Rev.* Apr. 213/1 The thyratron is an electrically controlled arc rectifier. **1948** *Jrnl. R. Aeronaut. Soc.* LII. 216/1 An automatic speed control has been provided in which the voltage from a tachometer generator driven by the fan shaft is composed with a pre-set standard voltage, and the difference amplified by thyratrons is fed back to an auxiliary field in the generator. **1981** [see THYRISTOR].

thyrce, **thyrd(e**, obs. ff. THURSE, THIRD.

thyreal ('θaɪəriːəl). *Ichth.* [f. Gr. θύρε-ός shield: see THYRO-.] = HYPOBRANCHIAL b.

18.. STARKS *Synonymy Fish Skel.* 518 (Cent. Supp.).

thyreo-, combining element repr. Gr. θυρεο- in θυρεο-ειδής THYROID, used esp. in forming names of chemical and pharmaceutical substances derived from the thyroid gland; see THYRO-.

‖**thyridium** (θaɪ'rɪdɪəm). *Entom.* Pl. **-ia.** [f. Gr. type *θυρίδιον, dim. of θυρίς, θυριδ- window, opening.] A whitish spot on the fore-wing of Trichoptera, marking a break in the cubital vein; also applied to similar spots occurring on the wing veins of some other insects.

1861 HAGEN *Synopsis Neuropt. N. Amer.* 259 Thyridium and first subapical areole with a whitish spot.

thyristor (θaɪ'rɪstə(r)). *Electronics.* [f. THYR(ATRON + TRANS)ISTOR.] A three-terminal semiconductor rectifier made up of four layers, *p-n-p-n*, so that when the fourth is positive with respect to the first, a voltage pulse applied to the third layer initiates a flow of current through the device which continues as long as it is greater than some minimum value.

1958 MUELLER & HILIBRAND in *IRE Trans. Electron Devices* V. 2/2 Because of its thyratron-like properties, the device has been named a Thyristor. **1965** *New Scientist* 19 Aug. 446/2 Its transmission system eliminates the commutator by employing thyristors (silicon-controlled rectifiers) as inverters under electronic control. **1981** J. SEYMOUR *Electronic Devices & Components* iv. 185 Industrial process control, the control of electrical machines and high voltage d.c. transmission are among the many areas in which thyristors are applied. They have superseded the thyratron..in all but the highest voltage applications.

thyrke, variant of THERK *Obs.*, dark.

thyrl(e, **thyrlepole**: see THIRL, THIRLEPOLL.

thyro- ('θaɪərəʊ), also (more correctly but less commonly) **thyreo-** ('θaɪriːəʊ), used as combining form of THYROID, in reference to the thyroid cartilage or the thyroid gland.

1. In reference to the thyroid cartilage.

thyro-arytenoid (-ærɪ'tiːnɔɪd) *a.* (rarely **thyreo-**), pertaining to or connecting the thyroid and arytenoid cartilages of the larynx; *t. ligaments* or *folds*, the vocal cords; *t. muscles*, a pair of muscles which relax the vocal cords; also as sb. = *t. muscle*. **thyrochon'drotomy**, surgical incision of the thyroid cartilage. **thyro-'cricoid** *a.*, pertaining to or connecting the thyroid and cricoid cartilages; also as *sb.* = *thyro-cricoid muscle*. **thyro-cri'cotomy**: see quot. **thyro-epiglottic** (-ɛpɪ'glɒtɪk) *a.* (also **thyreo-**), connecting the thyroid cartilage and the epiglottis; so **thyro-epiglottidean** (-ɛpɪglɒ'tɪdiːən) *a.* **thyro-hyal** (-'haɪəl) *a.* = next; usually as *sb.*, applied to the greater cornu of the hyoid bone in mammals, or to each of the long horns of the same bone in birds. **thyro-hyoid** (-'haɪɔɪd) *a.*, pertaining to or connecting the thyroid cartilage and the hyoid bone; *sb.* = thyro-hyoid muscle; so ˌ**thyro-hy'oidean** *a.* **thyro'palatine** *a.* (also **thyreo-**), connecting the thyroid cartilage and the palate: applied to part of the palato-pharyngeus muscle. **thyropharyngean** (-fə'rɪndʒiːən) *a.* (also **thyreo-**), connecting the thyroid cartilage and the pharynx (see quot.). **thy'rotomy** (also **thyreo-**) [Gr. τομή cutting], incision or division of the thyroid cartilage.

[**1693** tr. *Blancard's Phys. Dict.* (ed. 2), **Thyroarytænoides*, a pair of Muscles that proceed from the Cartilage called *Scutiformis*, and extending themselves forward to the Sides of the *Arytænoides*..serve to close the opening of the Larynx]. **1855** BAIN *Senses & Int.* II. iv. §32 (1864) 314 The..vocal cords..are two bands..attached in front to..the depression between the wings of the thyroid cartilage, and behind to the arytenoid cartilages; from this connexion they are called thyro-arytenoid ligaments. **1899** *Allbutt's Syst. Med.* VI. 818 The laryngeal muscles chiefly involved have been the internal thyro-arytenoids. **1911** DORLAND *Med. Dict.* (ed. 6), *Thyrochondrotomy. **1901** BENHAM in *Proc. Zool. Soc. Lond.* 2 Apr. 286 This longitudinal muscle is topographically a '*thyro-cricoid'. **1899** *Syd. Soc. Lex.*, **Thyro-cricotomy*, tracheotomy performed through the crico-thyroid membrane alone. **1857** DUNGLISON *Med. Lex.*, **Thyreo-epiglottic*... Sabatier and Santorini have given this name to the outer portion of the thyro-arytenoid muscle; because it passes from the thyroid cartilage to the anterior part of the epiglottis. **1890** BILLINGS *Nat. Med. Dict.*, Thyro-epiglottic ligament... Thyro-epiglottic muscle. **1901** BENHAM in *Proc. Zool. Soc. Lond.* 2 Apr. 286 The *thyro-epiglottidean muscle..is also a conspicuous constituent in the ventral region of the larynx. **1854** OWEN *Skel. & Teeth* in *Orr's Circ. Sc.* I. *Org. Nat.* 209 The basihyal has..coalesced with the *thyrohyals to form a broad cartilaginous plate. **1881** MIVART *Cat* 134 The thyrohyal muscle. **1831** R. KNOX *Cloquet's Anat.* 82 The digastric and *thyro-hyoid muscles. **1872** COHEN *Dis. Throat* 134 The *thyreo-palatine portion of the muscle. **1899** *Syd. Soc. Lex.*, Thyro-palatine. [**1857** DUNGLISON *Med. Lex.*, *Thyro-pharyngeus, Thyreo-pharyngeus.] **1860** MAYNE *Expos. Lex.*, *Thyreopharyngeus*,..applied to the middle portion of the constrictor pharyngis inferior muscle: *thyreopharyngean. **1880** M. MACKENZIE *Dis. Throat & Nose* I. 331 *Thyrotomy should never be undertaken until removal by the endolaryngeal method has been first attempted. **1890** BILLINGS *Nat. Med. Dict.*, *Thyreotomy*... *Thyrotomy*, section of the thyroid cartilage. **1899** *Syd. Soc. Lex.*, *Thyreotomy*, division of the thyroid cartilage for exploratory purposes.

2. In reference to the thyroid gland. (Often **thyreo-**.)

thyro-anti'toxin, an antitoxin developed in thyroid poisoning; trade-name of a thyroid preparation used as a therapeutic. ˌ**thyrocalcitonin** (-kælsɪ'təʊnɪn) [*calcitonin* f. L. *calx*, *calc(i)-* lime + TON(IC *a.* and *sb.* + -IN[1]], a polypeptide hormone secreted by the thyroid gland which reduces the levels of calcium in the blood; also called *calcitonin*. **'thyrocele**, a tumour of the thyroid gland; goitre. **thyro'colloid**, the colloid matter of the thyroid gland. **thyro'genic**, **thy'rogenous** *adjs.*: see quot. 1909. **thyro-**, **thyreo'globulin**, the essential albuminous principle of the thyroid gland, an iodized principle, which forms, together with another albuminous substance belonging to the nucleo-proteins, the colloid substance of the gland. **thyro'glossal** *a.*, in *t. duct*, a duct of the embryo extending from the thyroid to the base of the tongue. **thyro-'iodine**, a substance containing iodine, obtained by decomposition of thyroglobulin, which has been thought to be the active principle of the gland: now more usually called *iodo'thyrin*. **thyro'lingual** *a.* = *thyroglossal*. **thyro'lytic** *a.*, destructive of thyroid tissue. ˌ**thyropara-thyroi'dectomy**, excision of both the thyroid and the parathyroids; so ˌ**thyroparathyroi-'dectomize** *v. trans.*, **-'dectomized** *ppl. a.* †**thyro'proteid**, **thyro'protein**, the specific protein of the thyroid gland. **thyro'therapy**, treatment of disease by a preparation of the thyroid glands of sheep. **thyro'toxic** *a.*, **thyro'toxin**: see quots. 1909, 1911. **'thyrotoxiˌcosis**, a disorder in which there is an excessive amount of thyroid hormones in the blood. **thyro'trop(h)ic** *a.* (also †**thyreo-**) [-TROPHIC, -TROPIC], applied to a hormone secreted by the pituitary which regulates the activity of the thyroid gland; hence **thyro'trop(h)in**, thyrotropic hormone; ***thyrotrop(h)in-releasing factor***, ***hormone***, a hormone secreted by the hypothalamus which stimulates the release of thyrotropin from the pituitary.

1895 *Pall Mall G.* 16 Dec. 1/3 Dr. Fränkel, of Vienna,..has named it provisionally *thyreo-antitoxin. [He] states..that it will be possible to administer it clinically without the risk of ptomaine poisoning. **1899** *Allbutt's Syst. Med.* VIII. 57 Fränkel has succeeded in separating a basic product from the thyroid (thyreo-antitoxin). **1909** DORLAND *Med. Dict.* (ed. 5), Thyro-antitoxin. **1963** P. F. HIRSCH et al. in *Endocrinology* LXXIII. 252/2 Whether or not the thyroid hypocalcemic agent that we have demonstrated is the same as..calcitonin..it is of considerable pharmacological interest. As a tentative name for the substance we propose '*thyrocalcitonin'. **1974** D. & M. WEBSTER *Compar. Vertebr. Morphol.* xiii. 311 The parafollicular cells of the thyroid gland produce quite a different hormone, called calcitonin or thyrocalcitonin. **1886** *Buck's Handbk. Med. Sc.* III. 350/1 Goitre..*Thyreocele (P. Frank). **1909** DORLAND *Med. Dict.* (ed. 5), Thyrocele, *Thyrocolloid. **1887** *Buck's Handbk. Med. Sc.* V. 143 *Thyrogenic. **1909** DORLAND *Med. Dict.* (ed. 5), **Thyrogenous*,..originating in the thyroid gland. **1908** *Allbutt's Syst. Med.* IV. I. 325 Other bodies..have been separated from the gland,..among these may be mentioned Oswald's iodine-free *thyreo-globulin. **1911** MANDEL tr. *Hammarsten's Text-bk. Physiol. Chem.* (ed. 6) 356 It seems proven that the specifically active substance is ..a protein substance: Notkin's *thyreoproteid*, Oswald's *thyreoglobulin*. **1909** DORLAND *Med. Dict.* (ed. 5), *Thyroglossal duct. **1896** *Daily News* 30 Apr. 8/7 Professor Baumann and Dr. Roos..find that the active principle [of the thyroid gland] is a substance named '*Thyro-iodin'. **1897** *Allbutt's Syst. Med.* IV. 469 [see THYROID B. 2]. **1903** CUSHING *Text-bk. Pharmacology* 715 Iodothyrin was at first named *thyroiodin*, but this was liable to be confused with thyreoidin, a term used to indicate the simple extract of the gland. **1896** *Allbutt's Syst. Med.* I. 206 The *thyro-lingual duct. **1889** *Buck's Handbk. Med. Sc.*, App. 539 *Thyrolytic. **1956** *Nature* 21 Jan. 138/1 Six animals were adrenalectomized..: the remaining six were *thyroparathyroidectomized. **1932** *Amer. Jrnl. Physiol.* C. 262 (*heading*) Heterotopic bone formation in *thyroparathyroidectomized dogs. **1976** H. CAMPION et al. in B.E.C. Nordin *Calcium, Phosphate & Mineral Metabolism* xii. 466 Thyroparathyroidectomized (TPTX) rats had their serum phosphate levels manipulated by dietary means. **1920** *Nature* 9 Dec. 488/2 The effect of thyroid-feeding and of *thyroparathyroidectomy upon the pituitrin content of the posterior lobe of the pituitary. **1956** *Ibid.* 21 Jan. 138/1 The effect of thyro-parathyroidectomy on the blood changes induced by injected cortisone..has been studied. **1899** *Allbutt's Syst. Med.* VIII. 57 Notkin isolated a substance from the thyroid (*thyreo-protein). **1911** DORLAND *Med. Dict.* (ed. 6) s.v., It is probably one of the functions of the thyroid to produce a ferment which neutralizes the toxic effect of an accumulation of thyroprotein in the body. **1907** *Med. Record* 5 Oct. 584 He regretted that *thyrotherapy had been neglected in the treatment of skin diseases. **1904** *Nature* 18 Feb. 375 *Thyrotoxic. **1909** *Cent. Dict., Supp.*, Thyreotoxic. **1909** DORLAND *Med. Dict.* (ed. 5), *Thyrotoxic*,..marked by toxic activity of the thyroid gland. **1911** STEDMAN *Med. Dict.* 887/1 **Thyrotoxicosis*, exophthalmic goiter. **1912** *Jrnl. Amer. Med. Assoc.* 3 Aug. 328/1 A patient 23 years of age having an adenoma has a definite fixed chance of developing thyrotoxicosis during her thirty-seventh year. **1977** *Lancet* 27 Aug. 438/2 Simpson hypothesised an autoimmune basis for myasthenia gravis on account of its association with disorders thought to have an autoimmune ætiology—such as ..thyrotoxicosis. **1911** DORLAND *Med. Dict.* (ed. 6), **Thyrotoxin*, a cytotoxin specific for thyroid tissue. **1930** CREW & WIESNER in *Brit. Med. Jrnl.* 26 Apr. 777/1 (*heading*) On the existence of a fourth hormone, *thyreotropic in nature, of the anterior pituitary. **1957** *New Biol.* XXIII. 117 The pituitary gland exerts some control over the thyroid gland, as it secretes a 'thyrotropic' hormone. **1965** LEE & KNOWLES *Animal Hormones* ii. 21 Adrenocorticotrophic hormone..and thyrotrophic hormone..are also secreted by the adenohypophysis. **1944** *Hackh's Chem. Dict.* (ed. 3) 856/2 *Thyrotrophin. **1952** *New Biol.* XIII. 65 Activity of the thyroid is maintained by the stimulus of a hormone, thyrotropin. **1959** [see *TRF* s.v. T 6]. **1968** [see *TRH* s.v. T 6]. **1976** *Nature* 8 Apr. 480/2 The α subunit of HCG..is nearly identical to the α subunits of thyroid-stimulating hormone (thyrotropin)..and luteinising hormone. **1980** *Brit. Med. Jrnl.* 29 Mar. 895/1 Two patients..had impaired responses of serum thyroid stimulating hormone to thyrotrophin releasing hormone.

thyroid ('θaɪərɔɪd), *a.* (*sb.*) Also 9 **thyreoid** (in Dicts.). [Etymologically *thyreoid*, ad. Gr. *θυρεοειδής* shield-shaped (in Galen *χόνδρος θυρεοειδής* thyroid cartilage), f. *θυρεό-ς* oblong shield + *-ειδής*: see -OID. Cf. obs. F. *thyroide* (Paré, 16th c.), mod.F. *thyréoïde*.]

A. *adj.* Having the form of a shield, shield-shaped: applied to various natural structures (and hence *transf.* to others connected with them).

1. *Anat.* **a.** ***thyroid cartilage***: the largest of the cartilages of the larynx, consisting of two broad quadrilateral plates united in front at an angle, forming the projection in front of the throat known (in men) as 'Adam's apple'; within the angle are attached the vocal cords.

[**1693** tr. *Blancard's Phys. Dict.* (ed. 2), *Thyroides*, the Cartilage, called Scutiformis, of the Larynx.] **1726-41** MONRO *Anat.* (ed. 3) 163 Into this Concavity the Thyroid Cartilage is received. **1808** BARCLAY *Muscular Motions* 498 The larynx is partly composed of five cartilages, which are the cricoid, thyroid, the two arytænoid, and the epiglottis. **1854** BUSHNAN in *Orr's Circ. Sc.* I. *Org. Nat.* 121 The thyroid cartilage is wrapped round the essential parts of the larynx. **1857** DUNGLISON *Med. Lex.*, Thyroid, Thyreoid.

b. ***thyroid gland*** (also called ***thyroid body***): one of the so-called 'ductless glands', a very vascular body adjacent to the larynx and upper part of the trachea in vertebrates.

[**1693** tr. *Blancard's Phys. Dict.* (ed. 2), *Thyroideæ Glandulæ*, two, of a viscous..Substance,..situate about the lower seat of the Larynx]. **1726-41** MONRO *Anat.* (ed. 3) 163 The lymphatic Vessel..is..sent from the thyroid Gland. **1727-41** CHAMBERS *Cycl.* s.v. *Thymus*, Mr. Cheselden observes, that where the thymus in men is very small, the thyroid glands increase proportionably. **1830** R. KNOX *Béclard's Anat.* 240 Formless fibro-cartilages occur in some compound tumours of the thyroid body. **1872** HUXLEY *Phys.* v. 126 The thyroid gland..is that organ which when enlarged by disease gives rise to 'Derbyshire neck' or 'goitre'. **1899** L. HILL *Man. Hum. Physiol.* xxvi. 301 If a cretin be fed on thyroid glands taken from sheep his condition is improved... It is clear then that the thyroid gland produces a material necessary for the growth of the body.

c. Applied to various structures connected with the thyroid cartilage or gland, as the ***thyroid arteries***, ***nerves***, ***veins***, etc. ***thyroid axis***, a branch of the subclavian artery, distributed to the thyroid gland and adjacent parts. (See also B. 2 b.)

1831 R. KNOX *Cloquet's Anat.* 746 Right Inferior Thyroid Vein..similar to the left, with which it constitutes the thyroid venous plexus. **1840** E. WILSON *Anat. Vade M.* (1842) 271 The Superior Thyroid Artery curves downwards to the thyroid gland to which it is distributed. **1878** T. BRYANT *Pract. Surg.* I. 104 Thyroid cysts may be tapped in the same way as the cervical. **1881** MIVART *Cat* 209 The second branch given off from the subclavian..is the thyroid axis.

d. ***thyroid foramen***, ***membrane***: names for the obturator foramen and membrane of the hip-bone (see OBTURATOR 1), from their shield-like shape.

1890 BILLINGS *Nat. Med. Dict.*, *T[hyroid] foramen*, obturator foramen.

2. *Zool.* Applied to a shield-shaped colour-marking, or *transf.* to a bird having such a marking, as the thyroid woodpecker, *Sphyropicus thyroideus*.

1891 in *Cent. Dict.*

3. *Bot.* 'Shield-like, peltiform'.

1900 in B. D. JACKSON *Gloss. Bot. Terms* 270/2.

B. as *sb.* **1.** Short for *thyroid cartilage*.

1840 E. WILSON *Anat. Vade M.* (1842) 492 The Thyroid is the largest cartilage of the larynx. **1854** OWEN *Skel. & Teeth* in *Orr's Circ. Sc.* I. *Org. Nat.* 210 Extending beyond and sustaining the thyroid and other parts of the larynx. **1868** —— *Vertebr. Anim.* xxxiii. III. 603 Castration arrests that prominent growth of the thyroid, &c., which accompanies the elongation of the cords.

2. a. Short for *thyroid gland*; also for *thyroid extract* or *product* (see b).

1849-52 *Todd's Cycl. Anat.* IV. 1102/2 The normal weight of the thyroid is about one ounce. **1897** *Allbutt's Syst. Med.* IV. 469 The sheep's thyroid is relatively rich in thyro-iodine. *Ibid.* 476 In cases of..myxœdema the results of treatment by thyroid justify a strong expectation of cure. **1897** *Trans. Amer. Pediatric Soc.* IX. 65 In cretinism we are certain that the prolonged use of thyroids is followed by distinct changes in the blood.

b. *attrib.* **thyroid-stimulating** *a.* = *thyrotrop(h)ic* adj. s.v. THYRO-.

1895 *Pall Mall G.* 16 Dec. 1/3 The use of thyroid extract as a remedy for certain diseases..is looked upon as one of the most brilliant of recent medical discoveries. **1899** *Allbutt's Syst. Med.* VIII. 68 Thyroid treatment of cases of tetany. *Ibid.* 673 The horny growth fell off, while the patient was under thyroid feeding. **1941** *Trans. Amer. Assoc. Study Goiter* 159 Attempts have been made to demonstrate the thyroid stimulating hormone in the urine of patients with thyroid disease. **1974** D. & M. WEBSTER *Compar. Vertebr. Morphol.* xiii. 307 The thyroid-stimulating hormone, TSH, is produced by basophilic cells [within the pituitary].

Hence **thy'roidal**, **thy'roideal**, **thy'roidean** *adjs.*, pertaining to the thyroid cartilage or gland; **thyroi'dectomize** *v.*, *trans.* to subject to thyroidectomy; **thyroi'dectomized** *ppl. a.*, deprived of the thyroid; **thyroi'dectomy** [Gr. *ἐκτομή* a cutting out], excision of the thyroid gland; **thy'roidic** *a.* and *sb.*, (designating) a person with a disordered thyroid gland; **thy'roidin**, trade-name of a whitish powdered extract of the thyroid gland of the sheep, used as an alterative and an anti-fat; **'thyroidism**, a morbid state consequent on administration of thyroid extract; thyroid poisoning; **thyroi'ditis**, inflammation of the thyroid gland; **thyroidi'zation**, treatment with a preparation of the thyroid (Dorland); **'thyroidless** *a.*, having no thyroid gland; **thyroi'dotomy** [Gr. *τομή* cutting], incision of the thyroid gland.

1860 MAYNE *Expos. Lex.*, *Thyroideus*,..*thyroidal: *thyroidean. **1872** COHEN *Dis. Throat* 51 The anterior portions of the vocal cords attached to the thyroidal junction. **1827** ABERNETHY *Surg. Wks.* II. 127 The superior *thyroideal, lingual, and facial branches of the external carotid. **1854** JONES & SIEVEKING *Pathol. Anat.* (1874) 122 Ligature of the thyroideal arteries has caused considerable diminution of a goitrous tumour. **1932** J. S. HUXLEY *Probl. Relative Growth* VI. iv. 183 Groups of these [albino rats] were *thyroidectomized. **1974** *Nature* 5 Apr. 525/1 All rats were ovariectomised and thyroidectomised on day 1 of the experiment. **1899** *Allbutt's Syst. Med.* VIII. 57 The administration of thyroid in some form to *thyroidectomised animals or man. **1946** *Nature* 19 Oct. 557/2 Another series of experiments was carried out with thyroidectomized mice. **1889** *Buck's Handbk. Med. Sc.* VIII. 545/2 Until the middle of the eighteenth century no true *thyroidectomy..had been performed. **1891** *Lancet* 18 Apr. 907/1 M. Reverdin..has performed thyroidectomy in this disease in fourteen cases. **1897** *Allbutt's Syst. Med.* III. 314 Thyroid grafts prolong life after complete thyroidectomy. **1922** G. B. SHAW in S. & B. Webb *English Local Govt.* VI. p. lxiii, By all means let the endocrinists go on dividing abnormal people, in prison and out, into hyper and sub pituitaries and *thyroidics and adrenals. **1965** M. BRADBURY *Stepping Westward* i. 31 This was James Walker, a stout, slightly thyroidic, very shambling person. **1896** *Pharmaceutical Jrnl.* 5 Sept. 215 *Thyreoidin, the active principle of thyroid. **1897** *Allbutt's Syst. Med.* III. 315 A non-proteid substance containing a considerable percentage of iodine—the so-called thyroidin. **1897** *Ibid.* II. 78 In most of them the symptoms of *thyroidism were produced. **1889** *Buck's Handbk. Med. Sc.* VII. 96/1 Inflammation of the thyroid gland (*thyroiditis..) is most commonly..the.. result of remedial measures employed in the treatment of goitre. **1908** *Thyroidless [see *anti-thyroid* s.v. ANTI-[1] 3 b]. **1946** *Nature* 26 Oct. 590/1 During the third month, mortality was as high as 75 per cent in thyroidless animals, 60 per cent in the controls, and only 15 per cent of the hyperthyroid animals. **1890** BILLINGS *Nat. Med. Dict.*, *Thyroidotomy.

thyrolingual to **-toxin**: see THYRO- 1, 2.

thyronine ('θaɪərəniːn). *Chem.* [f. THYRO- + *-n-* + -INE[5].] The amino-acid $HOC_6H_4OC_6H_4CH_2CH(NH_2)COOH$, of which thyroxine can be regarded as a formal derivative (see quots.).

1928 C. R. HARINGTON in *Biochem. Jrnl.* XXII. 1430 In order to lessen the clumsiness of the systematic nomenclature of thyroxine derivatives it is proposed to call the amino-acid, desiodothyroxine, 'thyronine'..so that thyroxine would be '3:5:3':5'-tetraiodothyronine'. **1970** R. W. MCGILVERY *Biochemistry* xxiii. 562 (*caption*) The active thyroid hormone, thyroxine, is in a formal sense the tetraiodo derivative of an amino acid called thyronine.

thyroxine (θaɪə'rɒksiːn). *Biochem.* Also **-in**. [f. THYR(O- + OX(Y- + IN(DOLE *sb.*, after the original (erroneous) description of its chemical composition: see quot. 1918.] A hormone secreted by the thyroid gland which increases the metabolic rate and regulates growth and development in animals; tetraiodothyronine, $HO{\cdot}C_6H_2I_2{\cdot}O{\cdot}C_6H_2I_2{\cdot}CH_2CH(NH_2)COOH$.

1918 E. C. KENDALL in *Endocrinology* II. 90 It appeared desirable to emphasize the presence of the oxy-indol nucleus and it appeared equally desirable not to emphasize the presence of iodin. The substance was therefore named 'Thyro-oxy-indol', which has been shortened to 'thyroxin' for every-day reference to the substance. **1926** C. R. HARINGTON in *Biochem. Jrnl.* XX. 294 It is impossible to accept the formula proposed by Kendall, and..the constitution of thyroxine must be regarded as not proven. **1969** *Daily Tel.* 19 Dec. 11/7 Thyroxine, given to thyroid-deficient babies and adults, saves them from cretinism and myxoedema. **1979** ARMS & CAMP *Biology* xxx. 501 If the tail is removed from a tadpole and placed in a bath containing thyroxin, the white blood cells in the tail will digest it.

thyrse (θɜːs). Also 7 **thirse**. [a. Fr. *thyrse* (*a* 1502 in Hatz.-Darm.), ad. L. *thyrsus*, a. Gr. *θύρσος* stalk or stem of a plant; the Bacchic staff: see THYRSUS.]

1. *Gr.* and *Rom. Antiq.* = THYRSUS 1.

1603 HOLLAND *Plutarch's Mor.* IV. 712 There is a Thyrse or Javelot with tabours to be seene expresly printed aloft. **1710** W. KING *Heathen Gods* xxvii. (1722) 134 Their [the followers of Bacchus] Cloathing [was] only the Skins of Beasts, with Thyrses in their Hands. **1845** LONGF. *Drinking Song* iv, Fair Bacchantes, Bearing cymbals, flutes, and thyrses.

2. †**a.** A stem or shoot of a plant (= Gr. *θύρσος*, L. *thyrsus*). *Obs.* **b.** *Bot.* = THYRSUS 2.

1658 PHILLIPS, *Thyrse*, a stalk or stem of any herb. **1744** J. WILSON *Synopsis Brit. Plants, Bot. Dict.* 14 *Thyrsus*, a Thyrse, differs from a spike, in having flowers or fruit set more thinly on it. **1846** DANA *Zooph.* v. §91 (1848) 93 The thyrse of lilac blossoms. **1848** LINDLEY *Introd. Bot.* (ed. 4) I. 324 The Thyrse is an inflorescence at first centripetal, afterwards centrifugal. **1861** [see THYRSUS 2].

3. An ancient vessel resembling a pine-cone.

1876 R. M. SMITH *Persian Art* 12 From their.. resemblance..to pine cones they have been called thyrses, and are supposed to have been used for holding mercury.

4. *Comb.* as ***thyrse-bearing*** adj.; **thyrse-flower**, Lindley's name for the genus *Thyrsacanthus*.

1866 *Treas. Bot.* 1150 Thyrseflower, *Thyrsacanthus*. **1869** SWINBURNE *Ess. & Stud.* (1875) 207 No Bacchus..comes Here, nor mænads thyrse-bearing.

thyrsi- ('θɜːsɪ), combining form of THYRSUS, used in a few botanical terms. **thyrsiferous** (-'ɪfərəs) *a.* [-FEROUS], bearing thyrsi or contracted panicles. **thyrsi'florous** *a.* [L. *flōs*, *flōr-* flower], having the flowers in thyrsi. **'thyrsiform** *a.*, having the form of a thyrsus, thyrsoid.

1895 *Funk's Stand. Dict.*, Thyrsiferous. **1860** MAYNE *Expos. Lex.*, Thyrsiflorous. **1866** *Treas. Bot.* 1150 *Thyrse* (adj. *Thyrsiform*). **1880** GRAY *Struct. Bot.* (ed. 6) I. 159 A thyrsus or thyrsiform inflorescence.

thyrsill, obs. Sc. var. of *thrissill*, THISTLE.

thyrsoid ('θɜːsɔɪd), *a. Bot.* [f. THYRS-US + -OID: cf. Gr. *θυρσοειδής* thyrsus-like (Dioscorides).] Of the form of, or resembling, a thyrsus or contracted panicle. So **thyr'soidal** *a.*

1830 LINDLEY *Nat. Syst. Bot.* 61 Flowers terminal, usually thyrsoid. **1864** WEBSTER, *Thyrsoid*, *Thyrsoidal*. **1870** HOOKER *Stud. Flora* 238 Privet..Flowers in terminal thyrsoid cymes.

thyrst(e, -ylle, obs. ff. THIRST, THROSTLE.

‖**thyrsula** ('θɜːsjʊlə). *Bot.* [mod.L. dim. of THYRSUS.] (See quot. 1900.)

1832 LINDLEY *Introd. Bot.* I. ii. 112 Link terms this inflorescence a *thyrsula*. **1900** B. D. JACKSON *Gloss. Bot. Terms* 271/1 *Thyrsula*, the little cyme which is borne by most Labiates in the axil of the leaves.

‖**thyrsus** ('θɜːsəs). Pl. **thyrsi** ('θɜːsaɪ). [L., a. Gr. *θύρσος*: see THYRSE.]

1. *Gr.* and *Rom. Antiq.* A staff or spear tipped with an ornament like a pine-cone, and sometimes wreathed with ivy or vine branches; borne by Dionysus (Bacchus) and his votaries.

1591 L. LLOYD *Tripl. Triumphes* B iij b, Your Bacchus daunce is done,..Your sacred Thyrsus's wonne. *a* **1661** HOLYDAY *Juvenal* (1673) 110/2 The Thyrsus was a dart or javelin wrapt-about with ivy. **1734** tr. *Rollin's Anc. Hist.* (1827) I. 41 [They] carried a thyrsus in their hands, a kind of pike with ivy leaves twisted round it. **1856** MRS. BROWNING *Aur. Leigh* II. 52 Ivy..as good to grow on graves As twist about a thyrsus.

2. *Bot.*, etc. A form of inflorescence: † (*a*) a lax spike, as in some orchids (*obs.*); (*b*) a contracted kind of panicle, esp. one in which the primary branching is centripetal (racemose) and the secondary centrifugal (cymose), as in lilac and horse-chestnut.

1704 J. HARRIS *Lex. Techn.* I, *Thyrsus*, is a Word used by the Botanists, for the upright, and tapering Stalk: And 'tis often used for *Spica*, which is an Ear, or Blade of Corn. **1744** [see THYRSE 2]. **1760** J. LEE *Introd. Bot.* III. iv. (1765) 173 (tr.

Linnæus) A *Thyrsus*, is a Panicle contracted into an ovate Form. **1861** BENTLEY *Man. Bot.* (1870) 195 The Thyrsus or Thyrse is a kind of panicle in which the pedicels are generally very short. **1864** LOWELL *Fireside Trav.* 108 Hop-vines..hung their clustering thyrsi over the open windows.

3. *Comb.*, as ***thyrsus-bearer***, ***-staff***.

1844 L. SCHMITZ in *Smith's Dict. Grk. & Rom. Biog.* I. 1048/2 Bacchantic women,..carrying in their hands thyrsus-staffs. **1853** TRENCH *Proverbs* vi. 134 The thyrsus-bearers are many, but the bacchants few.

thyrtene, **thyrty**, etc.: see THIRTEEN, etc.

thysanopter (θɪsə'nɒptə(r)). *Entom.* [ad. mod.L. *Thysanoptera* (Haliday, 1836), f. Gr. *θύσανο-ς* tassel, fringe + *πτερόν* wing.] An insect of the order *Thysanoptera*, comprising *Thrips* and allied genera, characterized by long fringes on the wings. So **thysa'nopteran** *a.* = *thysanopterous*; *sb.* = *thysanopter*; **thysa'nopterous** *a.*, belonging to the order *Thysanoptera*.

[**1858** BAIRD *Cycl. Nat. Sci.* 549/1 *Thysanoptera*..an order of insects, lately separated from the order Hemiptera, to contain those insects formerly known as the genus *Thrips*.] **1864** WEBSTER, Thysanopter. **1891** *Cent. Dict.*, Thysanopteran, Thysanopterous.

thysanuran (θɪsə'n(j)ʊərən), *a.* and *sb.* *Entom.* [f. mod.L. *Thysanūra* Cuvier (f. Gr. *θύσαν-ος* tassel, fringe + *οὐρά* tail) + -AN.] **a.** *adj.* Belonging to the *Thysanura*, a wingless order of insects, comprising springtails, bristletails, etc., having filamentous appendages at the posterior end of the body. **b.** *sb.* An insect of this order. So **thysa'nurian** *a.*, **thysa'nurid** *a.* and *sb.* = *thysanuran*; **thysa'nuriform**, **thysanuri'morphous** *adjs.*, having the form of, or resembling, the *Thysanura*; **thysa'nurous** *a.*, belonging to or having the characters of the *Thysanura*.

1835 KIRBY *Hab. & Inst. Anim.* II. xiv. 20 The *Thysanuran, or Sugar-louse tribe. *Ibid.* xx. 314 The Thysanurans are remarkable for their anal appendages. **1842** BRANDE *Dict. Sc.*, etc., *Thysanurans*, *Thysanura*,..in which the abdomen is terminated by filaments, or by a forked tail adapted for leaping. **1891** J. H. COMSTOCK in *Cent. Dict.*, *Thysanurian. **1900** *Nature* 13 Dec. 161/2 The occurrence of *Proiapyx stylifer*, a primitive *thysanurid insect, in Liberia and Argentina. **1826** KIRBY & SP. *Entomol.* III. xxx. 166 Larvæ that approach to a true *Thysanuriform type. **1906** J. W. FOLSOM *Entomol.* iii. 162 Two types of larvæ are recognized by Brauer, Packard and other authorities: *thysanuriform* and *eruciform*. **1860** MAYNE *Expos. Lex.* 1277/2 An Order..which have particular organs of motion on the sides of the extremity of the tail, like fringes: *thysanurous. **1910** *Daily News* 30 May 4/2 A 'silver fish',..*Lepisma domestica*, a thysanurous insect occurring in houses and damaging books, wall-papers, etc. Some of its other common names are bristle-tail, fish-tail, shiner, and silvertail.

thyself (ðaɪ'sɛlf), *pron.* Forms: 1 **þe sylf**, 1–4 **þe self**, 3–4 **þi self**, **sulf**, **silf**, 4 **þi selue**, **zelue**, **self(e** (**þei-self**), 4–5 **thiselfe**, 5 (**thiselph**), **þy self(e**, **selffe**, 5–7 **thy self**, **thy selfe**, 6 **thyselfe**, (9 *dial.* **theeself**), 5– **thyself**. *β.* (*orig. oblique cases*) 1 **þe sylfne**, **sylfum**, 3–4 **þe selven**, 4–5 **þi seluen**, 5 **the seluen**, **-in**, **-un**, 6 *Sc.* **thy seluyn**, **selfin**. [In OE. *þé* 'thee' followed by the adj. *self*; the latter either in concord with *þé* (dat. *þé selfum*, acc. *þe*(*c*) *selfne*), or, in the constr. *þú þé self*, in concord with *þú* (*þé* being dative or instrumental): see SELF 4, and cf. MYSELF. From 13th c., *þi*, *þy*, *thy*, poss. adj., took the place of the pers. pron. *thee*; *self* being treated as a sb.]

As to restriction of use see note to THOU; cf. YOURSELF.

I. Emphatic uses: = Very thou, very thee.

1. Accompanying the subject-pronoun *thou* (or, after a verb in the imperative, without *thou*).

In mod. Eng., in *thou thyself*, *thyself* is grammatically in apposition to *thou*.

a **800** CYNEWULF *Crist* 114 Þæt þu þa beorhtan us sunnan onsende, ond þe sylf cyme. *a* **800** *Cædmon's Gen.* 608 Þu meaht nu þe self ʒeseon. *a* **1300** *Cursor M.* 4604 (Cott.) Lok þi seluen wit resun [*G.* þi selue, *F.* þi-self]. *Ibid.* 5429 Heit me truli þat þou þe seluen [*G.* þu þi selue, *F.* þou þi-self] Sal me wit mine foreldres deluen. **1340–70** *Alex. & Dind.* 511, Y haue sent þe my sonde as þou þei-self bade. *c* **1420** *Sir Amadace* (Camden) xlix, As thou thi seluun hase. **1535** COVERDALE *1 Kings* xx. 40 It is thine owne iudgment, thou hast geuen it thyselfe. **1597** SHAKS. *2 Hen. IV*, IV. v. 111 Then get thee gone, and digge my graue thy selfe. **1611** BIBLE *Luke* vi. 42 When thou thy selfe beholdest not the beame that is in thine owne eye. **1759** JOHNSON *Rasselas* xii, Thou art thyself weary of the valley. **1864** R. F. LITTLEDALE *Hymn*, '*O Fire of God, the Comforter*' ad fin., All praise to Thee..Who art Thyself all praise.

2. By ellipsis of *thou*, used as simple subject (with verb usually in 2nd person; occasionally in 3rd, *self* being treated as a sb.).

a **1300** *Cursor M.* 9568 (Cott.) 'Fader', sco said, 'þi doghter am i, Als þi-self wat witerli'. *c* **1375** *Ibid.* 876 (Trin.) Þi seluen is to wite I wis. *c* **1400** *Destr. Troy* 11982 Þat thyselfe shuld haue socourd. *c* **1475** *Songs & Carols* xxxii. 23 Man, I am thy frend ay; Thy self art thy foo. **1515** BARCLAY *Egloges* iv. (1570) C iv/2, Why is not thy selfe contented with thy part? **1611** BIBLE *1 Kings* xx. 40 So shall thy iudgement bee, thy selfe hast discided it. **16..** DRYDEN (J.), These goods thyself can on thyself bestow. **1742** WESLEY *Hymn*, '*Come, O thou traveller unknown*' ii, Thyself hast called me by my name. **1866** J. B. ROSE tr. *Ovid's Met.* 83 The phantom thou behold'st thyself hath made.

b. Used as predicate, or after *as* or *than*.

1535 COVERDALE *Ps.* xlix. [l.] 21 Thou..thinkest me to be euen soch one as thy self. **1590** SHAKS. *Com. Err.* III. ii. 76 Thou art Dromio, thou art my man, thou art thy selfe. **1593** —— *Merry W.* III. iv. 3 Thou must be thy selfe. **1611** BIBLE *2 Chron.* xxi. 13 Thou..hast slaine thy brethren..which were better then thy selfe. **1667** MILTON *P.L.* IV. 468 What there thou seest fair Creature is thy self. **1880** G. MACDONALD *Diary Old Soul* Aug. 8, It is thyself, and neither this nor that,..told, taught, or dreamed of thee.

3. Used instead of *thee* as object of a verb or preposition.

a **1400–50** *Alexander* 328 Noȝt as a prophet ne a prest I prays sall þi selfe. *c* **1400** *Destr. Troy* 7920, I am euyn fayn Of þe sight of þi Self. **1610** SHAKS. *Temp.* I. ii. 68 He, whom next thy selfe Of all the world I lou'd. **1671** MILTON *Samson* 789 If severely thou exact not More strength from me, then in thy self was found. **1857** G. B. BUBIER *Hymn*, My God, I love Thee for Thyself.

II. Reflexive uses.

4. As direct or indirect object of a verb, or in dependence on a preposition. (Orig. only emphatic refl.; later in general use, taking the place of *thee* reflexive, which is more decidedly archaic: see THEE *pron.* 2.)

c **975** *Rushw. Gosp.* Matt. xix. 19 Lufiʒe þa nehstum ðinum swa þæc seolfne [*Lindisf.* ðec seolfne; *Ags. Gosp.* þe sylfne]. *a* **1225** *Ancr. R.* 276 Þenc hwat tu hauest of þi sulf. **13..** *Cursor M.* 12804 (Cott.) O þe-self [*other texts* þi-self] quat wil þou sai? **1362** LANGL. *P. Pl.* A. I. 131 For to loue þi louerd leuere þen þi-seluen. **1382** WYCLIF *John* i. 22 What seist thou of thi silf? **1490** CAXTON *Eneydos* xvi. 64 Wylt enhabyte thiselfe in a strange contrey? **1535** COVERDALE *Isa.* lxiii. 14 To make thy self a glorious name. **1616** R. C. *Times' Whistle* III. 1120 Learn Solons saying, 'Mortall know thy selfe'. **1741** RICHARDSON *Pamela* II. 227 Well, Child,..how dost find thyself? **1819** SHELLEY *Cenci* IV. iv. 40 Be faithful to thyself. **1825** J. NEAL *Bro. Jonathan* II. 158 Take and read it for theeself. **1841** LANE *Arab. Nts.* I. 92 Thou assertest thyself to be the son of the King. **1847** TENNYSON *Princess* VII. 343 Yield thyself up.

† **thysi'astery.** *Obs.* *rare*$^{-1}$. [ad. Gr. *θυσιαστήριον* (LXX. and N.T.), f. *θυσιάζειν* to sacrifice, f. *θυσία* a sacrifice.] An altar.

1657 REEVE *God's Plea* 349 The Altar of Haliæus defended all that fled to it, and so would such a Thysiastery raised up in your City.

thystel, **-tell(e**, **-tle**, **-tylle**, obs. ff. THISTLE.

† **thyvel**, **thuvel**. *Obs.* Forms: 1 **þyfel**, **-þel**, 3 **þuuel**. [OE. *þȳfel* (or ? *þýfel*: see Note below), early ME. *þuvel*(*ü*).] A bush, a thicket.

a **1000** *Ags. Gloss.* in Wr.-Wülcker 244/20, 22 *Frutectum*, *i. arborum densitas*, *uel ramus*, þyfel. *Frutex*, *frutecta*, þyfel. *c* **1000** *Lambeth Ps.* lxxix. 11 His þyþelas *vel* twygu, *arbusta eius*. *c* **1000** ÆLFRIC *Gram.*, *Nom. Arb.* (Z.) 312 *Frutex*, þyfel. *c* **1000** —— *Voc.* in Wr.-Wülcker 139/24 *Spina*, *uel sentrix*, þyfel. *c* **1000** *Sax. Leechd.* I. 98 ʒenim þysse wyrte þe we leon fot nemdon fif ðyfelas butan wyrt-truman. *a* **1250** *Owl & Night.* 278 Vor þi ich am loþ smale vowele [*v.r.* foȝ(e)le] þat fleoþ bi grunde & bi þuuele.

[*Note.* The length of the stem-vowel in OE. is disputed; the dictionaries generally have *þýfel*, viewing it as a derivative of *þúf*, tuft of leaves; Sievers thinks that the *y* was certainly short. Whether *þyfel* or *þývel*, the form agrees remarkably with that of THIVEL a pot-stick; but no connexion of sense has been found, and there is a gap both of time and place between the Dorsetshire *þuvel* of 1250 and the Yorkshire *thyvelle* of 1483.]

thyxtill, **-yll**, **thyzle**, variants of THIXEL.

‖ **ti** (tiː). Also ti-ti. [Native Polynesian: cf. KI.]

a. Native name of several trees of the genus *Cordyline* (formerly included in *Dracæna*), N.O. *Liliaceæ*, with edible roots; in Polynesia, *C. terminalis*; in New Zealand, *C. australis* and *C. indivisa*; known also as *cabbage-palm*, CABBAGE-TREE, *club palm*, and *palm-lily* (PALM *sb.*[1] 1 c, 7).

1832 G. BENNETT in *London Med. Gaz.* 22 Sept. 795/2 *Dracæna indivisa*. *Ti* of the natives. This species of Dracæna ..attains an elevation of ten or twelve feet,..The leaves form an excellent food as sea stock for cattle, &c. **1839** DARWIN *Voy. Nat.* xviii. (1873) 410 A liliaceous plant called Ti. **1845** E. J. WAKEFIELD *Adv. N. Zealand* I. iii. 58 In these natural shrubberies..a kind of cabbage-tree, called ti by the natives, flourishes. **1896** *Contemp. Rev.* Aug. 240 The *ti* and the *apé* are taken out well cooked. The *apé* prevents the *ti* from getting too dry in the oven.

b. *attrib.*, as ***ti-leaf***, ***-palm***, ***-plant***, ***-root***, etc.; **ti-oven**, an oven for cooking ti-roots. Cf. TI-TREE, TEA-TREE 2.

1840 LUNDIE *Mission. Life Samoa* xiv. (1846) 89 Many women having no dress but the ti leaves round the waist. **1851** V. LUSH *Jrnl.* 25 Sept. (1971) 86 Planted 14 Ti-palms in various parts of my grounds. **1866** LADY BARKER *Station Life N. Zealand* viii. (1870) 52 Ti-ti palms are dotted here and there. **1882** T. H. POTTS *Out in Open* 297 (Morris) The tough, fibrous leaves of the ti-palm. **1896** *Contemp. Rev.* Aug. 240 The *ti*-ovens are frequently thirty feet in diameter.

ti: see TE[1], TI.

Tiahuanaco (ˌtiːəwə'nɑːkəʊ). *Hist.* The name of a ruined ceremonial site south of Lake Titicaca in Bolivia, used *attrib.* and as *adj.* with reference to a pre-Incan culture, esp. notable for its stonemasonry and distinctive pottery, which flourished in South America in the first millennium A.D. Hence **ˌTiahua'nacoid** *a.* [-OID].

1892 C. R. MARKHAM *Hist. Peru* i. 19 The work of the builders of the Tiahuanaco period is met with in other parts of Peru. **1926** *Brief Guide to Peruvian Textiles* (Victoria & Albert Museum, Dept. Textiles) 6 The culture of the highlands has been termed 'Tiahuanaco' after the place.. where stands the ruined archway. **1957** *Encycl. Brit.* II. 259 V/2 Nazca ceramics and textiles and Tiahuanaco stone carving. *Ibid.*, Concomitant with this change is the Peruvian-wide diffusion of an art style referred to as 'Tiahuanacoid'. **1973** D. MENZEL in D. R. Gross *Peoples & Cultures Native S. Amer.* I. ii. 20 The Inca-period vogue of antiquarianism which revives post-Tiahuanacoid styles first appears at a time just preceding the Inca conquest of the area. **1976** *Times* 16 Nov. 19/2 The Tiahuanaco culture.. flourished from about AD 130 to 1170.

tial ('taɪəl). *Obs.* exc. *dial.* Forms: 1–2 **tiʒel**, **tiʒl**, 4 **tiel**, 6–7 **tiall**, **tyall** (9 **tyal**), 7– **tial**. [OE. **tyʒel*, *tiʒel* = OHG. *zugil* (G. *zügel*), Du. *teugel*, ON. *tygell* (Da. *töile*):—OTeut. **tug-iloz*, f. **tug*, weak grade of **teuh*, **tauh*: see TEE *v.*[1] + *-ilo-*, -EL[1]. In later form taken as f. TIE *v.*, and assimilated to *denial*, *trial*.]

1. A rope used to pull, draw, or tow anything; a strap, thong, rein (quot. 1387).

c **1000** ÆLFRIC *Gram. & Gloss.* (Z.) 314 *Tractorium*, tiʒel. *a* **1100** *Ags. Voc.* in Wr.-Wülcker 327/33 *Tractorium*, tiʒl. **1387** TREVISA *Higden* (Rolls) IV. 77 Þe plowȝmen radde þat some of hem schulde wende home..and fecche þe reynes oþer þe tiels [*redirent pro loris*].

2. That with which something is tied; a rope, cord, string, or thread. Now *north. dial.* (see *Eng. Dial. Dict.*).

1549 LATIMER *6th Serm. bef. Edw. VI* (Arb.) 172 The greate belles clapper was fallen doune, the tyall was broken, so that the Byshop coulde not be runge into the toune. **1575** BANISTER *Chyrurg.* I. (1585) 90 The tiall or band must bee of such a matter, as will not easily putrifie; as threed of silke. **1600** SURFLET *Countrie Farme* I. xxviii. 178 He..shall carrie him [the colt] backe againe vnto his stable..and put him in his ordinary tiall or headstall. **1808** JAMIESON, *Tyal*, any thing used for tying a latchet.

† **b.** *fig.* A bond, lien, tie, obligation. *Obs.*

1621 FLETCHER *Wild Goose Chase* II. i, Nor to contract with such [a woman] can be a Tial. **1623** T. SCOT *Highw. God* 21 Religion then being the band or tyall whereby wee are fastned. **1653** GATAKER *Vind. Annot. Jer.* 153 No regard had..of relations and tials natural, civil or sacred.

Tia Maria ('tiːə mə'riːə). Also **tia maria**. [Sp., lit. 'Aunt Mary'.] The proprietary name of a coffee-flavoured liqueur based on rum, made originally in the West Indies. Also, a drink or glassful of this.

1948 *Trade Marks Jrnl.* 29 Sept. 794/2 *Tia-Maria*... Liqueurs (alcoholic). **1951** E. DAVID *French Country Cooking* 190 A tablespoon of rum liqueur such as Courantin or Tia Maria. **1954** *Official Gaz.* (U.S. Patent Office) 31 Aug. 968 Tia Maria. For liqueurs. **1957** J. FRAME *Owls do Cry* 127 Tim has said something about drinks, a liqueur, benedictine, or tia maria. **1967** C. DRUMMOND *Death at Furlong Post* vi. 80 'Justifies a taxi back..,' said Hart eventually, after a Tia Maria. **1981** 'D. KAVANAGH' *Fiddle City* vii. 133 Soft, package-tour airports where bandits swirl through the green channel in a bustle of tired perms and duty-free Tia Maria.

tiang (tiː'æŋ). [Dinka.] A small dark brown antelope belonging to a race of the korrigum, *Damaliscus lunatus*, found in the Sudan and neighbouring parts of Ethiopia.

1894 SCLATER & THOMAS *Bk. Antelopes* I. 63 The Tiang, as the well-known German traveller and naturalist Theodor von Heuglin proposed to call this Antelope, after its native name, is a representative form of the Korrigum in the upper valley of the Nile. **1920** *Blackw. Mag.* Nov. 668/2 Herds of hartebeeste and tiang. **1969** *Times* 30 Jan. (Ethiopia Suppl.) p. iii/3 The south-west corner of Ethiopia is an area inhabited by Sudanese lowland fauna, including..tiang.

‖ **tiao** ('tjɑːəʊ, tjaʊ). Also **tiaou**. [Chinese.] A string of Chinese 'cash' (perforated copper coins).

Nominally the *tiao* contained 1000 cash; but the actual number of coins varied from 1000 downwards, according to the custom of the locality.

1883 S. W. WILLIAMS *Middle Kingd.* (enlarged ed.) II. xvi. 86 (Banks and Paper Money) Their [the notes'] face value ranges from one to a hundred *tiao*, or strings of cash, but their worth depends on the exchange between silver and cash. **1886** *Rep. of Sec. Treas.* (U.S.) 390 (Cent. D.) Twenty miles from Peking the big cash are no longer in circulation. Small cash are used, [a nominal] 1000 [at Tientsin, really 500] of which make a *tiao*, and 3000 to 3500 of which are equal to a tael of silver. **1908** MORSE *Trade Chinese Emp.* v. 130 Cash are strung on strings, in rolls of 100, of which 10 go to the string or *tiao*, or *ch'uan*, formerly called *kuan*. **1910** *Blackw. Mag.* Dec. 763/2, I paid a tiaou for this; but I don't begrudge the money.

tiar ('taɪə(r)), *sb.* Chiefly *poet.* Also 6 **tyar(e**, 7–9 **tiare**, (7 **theare**). [Anglicized f. TIARA, prob. after F. *tiare* (14th c. in Godef. *Compl.*).]

1. = TIARA *sb.* 1. (In quot. 1513 *attrib.*)

1513 DOUGLAS *Æneis* VII. v. 126 The gret king Priame.. His ceptre als, and eik his tyar [*ed.* **1553** tyare] hat, Hallowit quhayrwyth at sacrifice he sat. **1614** SELDEN *Titles Hon.* 24 The King of Bulgarie..had also his Crown of Gold, his Tiar of Silk, and Red Shoes. **1725** POPE *Odyss.* x. 651 A tiar wreath'd her head with many a fold. **1818** MILMAN *Samor* 226 When the Median's brow the massy tiar Let fall.

2. = TIARA *sb.* 2.

1616 SHELDON *Miracles Antichr.* 165 His triple Tiare and Crowne. **1624** DARCIE *Birth of Heresies* xii. 51 The Myter or Theare, and some other decorations. **1841** *Fraser's Mag.* XXIV. 26 His triple tiare Is flung at his feet.

3. = TIARA *sb.* 4. Also *fig.* (In early instances perh. confused with TIRE *sb.*[1])

1660 JER. TAYLOR *Duct. Dubit.* II. iii. rule ix. §29 The spirit of humility and wisedome..ought to be the investiture of a Christians heart and the tiar of his head. **1667** MILTON *P.L.* III. 625 Of beaming sunnie Raies, a golden tiar Circl'd his [an angel's] head. **1802** in *Spirit Pub. Jrnls.* VI. 204 Head-dress a tiar of diamonds on purple velvet. **1819** KEATS *Lamia* 58 Sprinkled with stars, like Ariadne's tiar. **1886** W. ALEXANDER *St. Augustine's Holiday*, etc. 191 With sackcloth cast above the tiar of gold.

Hence **'tiar** *v.*, **'tiared** (-əd) *ppl. a.* = TIARA *v.*, TIARAED.

1824 *New Monthly Mag.* X. 334 Where the tiar'd Pharaohs sleep. **1882** J. WALKER *Jaunt to Auld Reekie* 172 Red-hatting thy cardinals and tiaring thy popes.

tiara (tiːˈɑːrə, taɪˈɛərə), *sb.* Also 6–7 **tyara.** [a. L. *tiāra*, a. Gr. τιάρα, τιάρας, Ionic τιήρης, of unknown origin. So It. *tiara* the papal crown.]

1. The raised head-dress or high peaked cap worn by the Persians and some other eastern peoples, varying in shape according to the rank of the wearer; a kind of turban.

1555 W. WATREMAN *Fardle of Facions* II. v. 148 The rounde cappe, whiche thei cal Tiara..passed from them [Medes] to the Persians. **1696** PHILLIPS (ed. 5), *Tiara*, a high sharp pointed Cap, worn by Sovereign Princes, and those of the Blood Royal, among the Persians. **1734** tr. *Rollin's Anc. Hist.* (1827) II. 378 The Persians wore no helmets, but only their common caps, which they called tiaras. **1847** GROTE *Greece* II. xxxiii. IV. 300 The upright tiara, the privileged head-dress of the Persian kings.

2. A high ovate-cylindrical or dome-shaped diadem worn by the pope, surmounted by the orb and cross of sovereignty, and encircled with three crowns symbolic of triple dignity, and usually richly wrought with jewels; often called ***the triple tiara*** or *triple crown.* Hence *transf.* the position or dignity of pope, the papacy. Also *fig.*

[**1616**: see TIAR 2.] **1645** EVELYN *Diary* 18 Jan., There were divers of the Pope's pantofles..also his tyara, or triple crown. **1700** ASTRY tr. *Saavedra-Faxardo* II. 316 This Tiara, or Triple-Crown, is the Touch-stone on which other Crowns are tried. **1845** S. AUSTIN *Ranke's Hist. Ref.* III. v. II. 173 When Pope Clement VII came to the tiara, he revoked all grants of this nature. **1860** HAWTHORNE *Marb. Faun* xxxiv, A figure of a pope, arrayed in his pontifical robes, and crowned with the tiara.

b. *Her.* A bearing supposed to represent the Pope's tiara; also called *triple crown.*

1780 EDMONDSON *Heraldry* II. Gloss., *Tiara*, or *Triple Crown*, with clouds in base issuing rays, being part of the arms of the Drapers' Company. **1894** *Parker's Gloss. Her.*, *Tiara*, the pope's triple crown occurs in the arms of one Company.

3. The head-dress of the Jewish High Priest.

1868 MARRIOTT *Vest. Chr.* 80 The Tiara..was at once a covering and an ornament to the head of the High Priest. **1877** C. GEIKIE *Christ* lviii. (1879) 709 Was not the tiara worn by a fierce Sadducee? **1890** P. H. HUNTER *After the Exile* xiii. 250 The tiara might be worn with safety, while the crown was impossible.

4. An ornamental frontal, coronet, or headband.

In modern use, a richly jewelled ornament worn by ladies in the hair, above the forehead.

[**1660**, **1667**: see TIAR 3.] **1718** PRIOR *Pleasure* 507 A bright tiara, round her forehead tied. **1761** H. WALPOLE *Let. to H. S. Conway* 9 Sept., Her tiara of diamonds was very pretty. **1895** RIDER HAGGARD *Heart of World* xxi, On her head was set a tiara of perfect pearls.

b. *fig.* (Cf. *crown, diadem.*)

1818 BYRON *Ch. Har.* IV. ii, She [Venice] looks a sea Cybele..with her tiara of proud towers. **1862** GOULBURN *Pers. Relig.* I. iv. (1873) 35 The tiara of the rainbow. **1880** JAS. LEGGE *Mem. J. Legge* iv. 45 Truth and love are the double tiara that should rest on his brow.

5. *Zool.* A mitre-shell, or a genus of mitre-shells.

1835 SWAINSON *Elem. Mod. Conchol.* 14 Tiara. *Sw.* Mouth narrowed at the base; with an internal upper groove. **1840** —— *Treat. Malacology* I. iv. 112 The real type of the *Mitrinæ* is our genus *Tiara*, and not that of *Mitra*, as formerly supposed. **1842** *Penny Cycl.* XXIV. 420/2 *Tiara*, ..Swainson's name for a genus of 'Mitrinæ'..which are termed 'Mitres' by collectors.

6. *attrib.* and *Comb.*, as ***tiara-crowned, -like, -shaped*** adjs.; **tiara night**, a night on which tiaras (sense 4) are worn at the opera.

1792 R. CUMBERLAND *Calvary* (1803) II. 123 Round his brows A cypress wreath tiara-like he wore. **1868** J. A. WYLIE *Road to Rome* v. 45 Popery—from its tiara-crowned chief to its sandal-shod friars. **1897** *Westm. Gaz.* 3 June 2/1 The guns sat each in its own little tiara-shaped entrenchment. **1900** *Daily Express* 28 June 1/1 The Opera-house presented a brilliant spectacle last night, the ladies in the audience.. having made it a 'tiara' night in expectation of the Khedive's presence.

Hence **ti'ara** *v.*, *trans.* to adorn with or as with a tiara; **ti'araed, -ra'd,** (-əd) *ppl. a.*, adorned with a tiara.

1822 MILMAN *Martyr of Antioch* 128 The high tiara'd Magian. **1837** *New Monthly Mag.* LI. 312 A pyramid of pilauf literally crowns, or rather tiaras the feast. **1840** CARLYLE *Heroes* iii. (1872) 79 All the Tiaraed and Diademed of the world.

‖**tiare** (tiːˈɑːreɪ). Also **tiara, tiaré, tiari.** [a. Fr. *tiare* tiara.] In Tahiti, one of several species of *Gardenia* bearing fragrant white flowers. Also *attrib.*

[*a* **1771** S. PARKINSON *Jrnl. Voy. S. Seas* (1773) 37 Plants of Use for Food, Medicine, &c., in Otaheite..E teea-ree Gardenia-florida.] **1888** W. HILLEBRAND *Flora Hawaiian Islands* 171 Cultivated species: *G[ardenia] Tahitensis*—Tiara [etc.]. **1891** D. HORT *Tahiti* ii. 25 The houses are.. surrounded by umbrageous trees, and..gardenias—called there *tiari.* **1914** R. BROOKE in *New Numbers* Aug. 110 With the starred *tiare's* white..Mamua, your lovelier head! **1919** W. S. MAUGHAM *Moon & Sixpence* xlix. 214 Tiaré..the white, scented flower which..will always draw you back to Tahiti in the end. **1931** A. WAUGH *Most Women* iv. 71 On her face was a look of serene contentment, and behind her left ear was the white tiare flower. **1960** H. E. BATES *Aspidistra in Babylon* 222 She was wearing in her hair not the big customary hibiscus flower but a little cluster of *tiare*, not more than six or seven blooms of small wax-white stars. **1980** *Daily Tel.* 26 Jan. 16 The local *tiaré* flower..is similar to a tiny gardenia.

tiarella (tɪəˈrɛlə). [mod.L. (Linnæus *Dissertatio Botanica qua Nova Plantarum Genera* (1751) 29), f. L. *tiara* turban + dim. suffix *-ella.*] A small perennial herb of the genus of this name, belonging to the family Saxifragaceæ, native to North America and Asia, and bearing basal, lobed leaves and clusters of small white or reddish flowers. Also *attrib.* Cf. *foam flower* s.v. FOAM *sb.* 5 b.

1759 P. MILLER *Gardener's Dict.* (ed. 7) s.v. Tiarella. Tiarella with Heart-shaped leaves. This is the Mitella Americana. **1871** *Scribner's Monthly* II. 470 Tiarella leaves just tipped with claret colour. **1887** *Harper's Mag.* July 303/1 The tiarella sent up feathery spikes of white. **1944** T. C. MANSFIELD *Border in Colour* 224 Tiarellas..are, fortunately, indifferent as to soil. **1976** J. BERRISFORD *Backyards & Tiny Gardens* vi. 47 Solomon's seal, epimediums and tiarella will also do well in shady places.

Tib (tɪb), *sb.* Also 6 **tyb,** 7 **tybb, tibb(e.** [Perh. the same as *Tib*, a shortened hypocoristic form of the female name *Isabel*; now rather rude or slighting (exc. playfully); also with dim. *-y* or *-ie*, *Tibbie*, a common female name in the north.

But in quot. *a* 1553 *Tib* is used as short for *Tibet.* A *St. Tibba* is mentioned in O.E. Chron. an. 963 (Laud MS.).]

†**1.** Formerly, a typical name for a woman of the lower classes, as in ***Tib and Tom*** (cf. *Jack and Gill*). Also, A girl or lass, a sweetheart, a mistress; *dyslogistically*, a young woman of low or loose character, a strumpet. *Obs.*

1533 J. HEYWOOD (*title*) A Mery Play betwene Johan Johan the husbande, Tyb his wyfe, and syr Johan the preest. *a* **1553** UDALL *Royster D.* I. iii. (Arb.) 19 (*Stage direct.*) Tibet Talk apace, sowyng. *Ibid.* II. iii. 36 Who shall then know our Tib Talke apace trow ye? **1582** STANYHURST *Æneis* IV. (Arb.) 102 A coy tyb, as vagabund in this my segnorye wandring. **1589** R. ROBINSON *Golden Mirr.* (Chetham Soc.) 54 The brauest tipling tib, that is within the towne. **1618** HORNBY *Sco. Dronk.* (1859) 19 Where tinkers and their tibs doe oft repaire. **1681** ROBERTSON *Phraseol. Gen.* (1693) 1226 A Tib, *mulier sordida.* **1689** *Descr. Summer in Poor Robin* C v, When Tib and Tom upon a Holy-day, Make fair assault on such good things as they. *a* **1700** B. E. *Dict. Cant. Crew*, *Tib*, a young lass.

2. Name for the ace of trumps in the game of gleek. *Obs.* exc. *Hist.*

1655 J. COTGRAVE *Wits Interpr.* (1662) 364 The Ace is called Tib, the Knave Tom, and the four of Trumps Tidie. *a* **1658** CLEVELAND *Hermaphrodite* 64 That Gamester needs must overcome, That can play both with Tib and Tom. **1688** R. HOLME *Armoury* III. xvi. (Roxb.) 71/2 The Ace is 15 in hand and 18 in play, which is called Tib. **1822** SCOTT *Nigel* xvi, Tib, which went for fifteen.

†**3.** ***Tib of the buttery*** (also simply *Tib*): a goose. *Obs. slang.*

1622 FLETCHER *Beggar's Bush* v. i, Mergery-praters, Rogers, And Tibs o' th' Buttery. **1641** BROME *Jovial Crew* II. Wks. 1873 III. 388 Here's G[r]unter and Bleater, with Tib of the Buttry, and Margery Prater, all drest without suttry. *a* **1700** B. E. *Dict. Cant. Crew*, *Tib of the Buttery*, a Goose. **1725** *New Cant. Dict.* Song xviii, On Redshanks, and Tibs thou shalt ev'ry Day dine.

†**4.** [? Another word.] Name of a kind of vehicle. *Obs. rare.*

1793 MAR. J. HOLROYD in *Girlhood of M.J.H.* (1896) 243 Papa says he will have a Pole put to the Tib, that it may be drawn by the two horses, like a Curricle. **1794** *Ibid.* 27 June 289 The Aunts go out in the Tib, which just suits them.

5. *Comb.* **Tib-cat**, *dial.*, also ***Tibby-cat***, a female cat (cf. TOM-CAT); **Tib's Eve**, *dial.*: see quots.; ***on Tib's Eve***, never.

1828 *Craven Gloss.*, *Tib-cat*, a female cat, a Tabitha. **1785** GROSE *Dict. Vulg. T.* s.v., *Saint Tibb's evening, the evening of the last day, or day of judgement; he will pay you on St. Tibb's eve (*Irish*). **1870** BREWER *Dict. Phr. & Fable*, *St. Tib's Eve*, never. **1893** in *N. & Q.* 8th Ser. IV. 507, etc. **1893** *Newcastle Weekly Chron.* Suppl. 23 Dec. 3 There is no such saint in the calendar as St. Tib. [But see note in Etymol.] Similar expressions to 'Tib's Eve' are 'At Latter Lammas', and 'When two Sundays meet', the time in each case being never. **1902** *N. & Q.* 9th Ser. IX. 109/1 'Yes.. it will be on Tib's Eve, neither before nor after Christmas', expressing thus his incredulity as to the event ever coming off.

tib (tɪb), *v.* *School slang.* [Origin unascertained.] *intr.* To slip out; to escape unobserved from school or house; to break bounds. Also **'tibble** *v.*, in same sense.

1840 J. T. HEWLETT *P. Priggins* iii, A trick acquired from tibbling-out down the lane, i.e. Charterhouse Lane, to the Red Cow. **1855** THACKERAY *Newcomes* ii, Tibbing out and receiving the penalty therefor. *Ibid.* lxxix, I used what they call to tib out and run down to a public-house.

‖**tibbin** (ˈtɪbɪn). Also **tibben, tibn.** [Arab. *tibn.*] Hay or chopped straw.

1900 A. CONAN DOYLE *Green Flag* 271 Each camel provided with his own little heap of tibbin laid in the centre of the tablecloth. **1909** T. E. LAWRENCE *Let.* 29 Aug. (1938) 77 A bed for the night in a threshing floor, on a pile of tibn, chopped straw. **1923** *Blackw. Mag.* Nov. 692/2 Their sister-craft in the Ægean..filling up with stores for the Army—tibben (or Egyptian hay), barley, firewood, eggs,..and pigs. **1958** L. DURRELL *Balthazar* iv. 73 Rivercraft moved about their task of loading *tibbin* (corn).

† **tiber-, tyber-stone.** *Obs.* [f. L. *Tibur*, a town of ancient Italy: cf. L. *lapis Tīburtīnus.*] A calcareous stone quarried at Tibur, now Tivoli; travertine: cf. TIBURTINE.

1726 LEONI *Alberti's Archit.* I. 58/2 One fourth part of Tyber-Stone, beat to powder.

Tiberian (taɪˈbɪərɪən), *a.* [ad. L. *Tiberiānus*, f. *Tiberius* (see def.) + *-ānus*, -AN.] Of or pertaining to (*a*) Tiberius, emperor of Rome 14–37 A.D. (also *fig.*), (*b*) the town of Tiberias in Galilee, where the Masoreth or Masora was formed.

1601 HOLLAND *Pliny* (1634) I. 439 The Tyberian peares beare the name of Tiberius the Emperor, for that of all others he loued that fruit best. **1659** OWEN *Integr. Hebrew & Grk. Text* Wks. 1853 XVI. 392 The points and accents were invented by the Tiberian Masoretes. **1742** YOUNG *Nt. Th.* v. 815 Tiberian arts his purposes wrap up In deep dissimulation's darkest night. **1837** R. WILSON *Pleas. Piety* v. 115, I see Him seated on a hill Near the Tiberian lake.

Tibert (ˈtɪbət, ˈtaɪbət). *arch.* Also 5 **Tybert.** [a. Flem. and Du. *Tybert, Tibeert*, OFr. *Tibert.*] The name of the cat in the apologue of Reynard the Fox; thence, used as a quasi-proper name for any cat, and (as a common noun), a cat. (By Shakespeare identified with *Tibalt*:—OF. *Thibauld, Thibaut*, Eng. *Theobald*, vulgo *Tibbald.*)

1481 CAXTON *Reynard* iii. (Arb.) 6 Wyth this so cam Tybert the catte..and sprang in emonge them. [**1592** SHAKS. *Rom. & Jul.* II. iv. 18 Is he a man to encounter Tybalt? *B.* Why what is Tibalt? *M.* More then Prince of Cats. *Ibid.* III. i. 78 Tybalt, you Rat-catcher, will you walke? *Tib.* What woulds thou haue with me? *Mer.* Good King of Cats, nothing but one of your nine liues.] **1616** B. JONSON *Epigr.* ad fin., *The Voyage itself* 135 Cats there lay divers had been flea'd and roasted... But 'mongst these Tiberts, who do you think there was? **1672** DRYDEN *Assignation* I. i, His violin..squeaks so lewdly, that Sir Tibert in the gutter mistakes him for his mistress. **1872** M. COLLINS *Pr. Clarice* II. iv. 61 He'd have killed that tibert, Tybalt, as willingly as he'd have killed a cat.

tiberune, obs. form of TIBURON.

Tibet (tɪˈbɛt). Also † **Thibet.** Name of a country in central Asia; used *attrib.* of wool obtained thence, or of cloth or garments made from this or in imitation of it; applied (usually *thibet*) to (*a*) a heavy stuff made wholly or partly of goats' hair; (*b*) a fine stuff used for women's dresses. *absol.* Tibet cloth, or a gown or shawl made of it. **Tibet dog, mastiff** = *Tibetan mastiff* s.v. TIBETAN *a.* 2.

1827 SCOTT *Surg. Dau.* Concl., 'How could you..collect all these hard words about India?'.. 'Like the imitative operatives of Paisley, I have composed my shawl by incorporating into the woof a little Thibet wool, which.. Colonel Mackerris..had the goodness to supply me with'. **1845** W. YOUATT *Dog* ii. 18 The colour of the Thibet dog is of a deep black slightly clouded on the sides... He has the broad short truncated muzzle of the mastiff. **1857** PARKHILL *Hist. Paisley* xiii. 97 Shawls of all kinds..such as thibet and cashmere shawls. *Ibid.* 98 Edinburgh had thibet in the manufacture. **1858** SIMMONDS *Dict. Trade*, *Thibet-cloth*, a camlet or fabric made of coarse goats'-hair. **1884** G. STABLES *Our Friend the Dog* xxv. 245 He was called a Thibet Mastiff. **1894** J. MACINTOSH *Ayrshire Nights' Entertainm.* vii. 129 A small production of thibets, coarse woollens, and muslins. **1900** MARY E. WILKINS *Parson Lord* 196 Her black thibet gown. *Ibid.* 197, I don't care about this old thibet.

Tibetan (tɪˈbɛtən), *sb.* and *a.* Also †**Thibetan.**

A. *sb.* A native or inhabitant of Tibet; also, the language of Tibet, a member of the Tibeto-Burmese sub-family of the Sino-Tibetan language group.

1822 tr. *Malte-Brun's Universal Geogr.* I. 571 The stock or family of the languages of Eastern Asia..differs entirely from that of the Indo-Germanic languages. It comprehends the *Thibetan*, the *Chinese*, the *Burman*, [etc.]. **1842** *Penny Cycl.* XXIV. 429/1 The Tibetans belong to the Mongol race. **1891** W. W. ROCKHILL *Land of Lamas* 97 It was with him..that I commenced studying Tibetan. **1962** L. DAVIDSON *Rose of Tibet* ii. 48 Caravan teamsters strolled everywhere; but..he noticed no Tibetans. **1979** A. HENNING tr. *Myrdal's Silk Road* (1980) ix. 71 Large steles.. inscribed in Han, Manchu, Oirat, and Tibetan.

B. *adj.* **1.** Of or pertaining to Tibet, its inhabitants, or their language.

1828 *Asiatick Res.* XVI. 410, I have added a few words from the Tibetan vocabularies of the *Asia Polyglotta.* **1888** *Encycl. Brit.* XXIII. 343/1 The centres for *Tibetan* trade. *Ibid.* 843/2 The Tibetan race is not thoroughly homogeneous. **1942** M. CABLE *Gobi Desert* 32 Flowing beards made from the soft white tail of the Tibetan yak. **1960** [see BHUTANESE *sb.* and *a.*]. **1974** *China Reconstructs* July 35/3 It used to be thought that the Tibetan plateau had no coal... For generations the Tibetan serfs used butter lamps and pine knots for lighting.

2. Special collocations: **Tibetan cherry**, a white-flowered cherry tree, *Prunus serrula*, native to western China; **Tibetan mastiff**, a large black-and-tan dog with a thick coat and drop ears, belonging to the breed of this name; **Tibetan spaniel**, a small white, brown, or black dog with a silky coat of medium length, belonging to the breed of this name; **Tibetan terrier**, a grey, black, cream, or particoloured terrier with a thick, shaggy coat, belonging to the breed of this name.

1948 C. INGRAM *Ornamental Cherries* II. 138 In cultivation the Tibetan Cherry tends to lose its squat, compact habit of growth. **1982** *Times* 20 Nov. (Saturday Suppl.) 3/3 A tree which likes to be stroked is the Tibetan cherry... The bark has probably the richest shade of all the coloured-bark trees —a striking mahogany is discovered when the outer bark peels away. **1852** T. SMITH *Narr. Five Years' Residence at Nepaul* II. 295 Young Porcupine. Tibetan Mastiff. Common Hare of central region. **1905** P. LANDON *Lhasa* I. xi. 403 The so-called Tibetan mastiff.. is a great shaggy creature, with a very massive head. **1976** T. HEALD *Let Sleeping Dogs Die* ix. 186 A more than generous helping of Tibetan mastiff, so fierce a dog that Aristotle thought it half tiger. **1930** *Observer* 9 Feb. 13/2 The foreign classes.. will contain such rarities as Lhasa terriers, Thibetan spaniels, [etc.]. **1970** *Times* 5 Feb. (Pedigree Dog Suppl.) p. ii/2 Recently there was a market tip for Tibetan spaniels, golden-coated, lion-like dogs of pleasing temperament. **1905** P. LANDON *Lhasa* I. xi. 387 The typical Tibetan terrier, a long-coated little fellow with a sharp nose, prick ears, and.. black from muzzle to tail. **1976** T. HEALD *Let Sleeping Dogs Die* i. 12 The latest is a Tibetan terrier in Tokyo.

Tibetian (tɪ'bɛtɪən, -iːʃən), *sb.* and *a.* Now *rare.* Also †**Thibetian.** [f. TIBET + -IAN.] = TIBETAN *sb.* and *a.*

1747 *Astley's New Gen. Coll. Voyages* IV. II. iv. 451/2 The Mogul's Empire; called by the Tibetians, Anonkek, or Anonjen. **1790** *Asiatick Res.* II. 32 We know, that rolls of Tibetian writing have been brought even from the borders of the Caspian. **1841** G. BORROW *Zincali* II. III. 108 Many of the principal languages of Asia are.. of the great Tartar family, at the head of which there is good reason for placing the Chinese and the Tibetian. **1889** J. J. REIN *Industries Japan* IV. iii. 517 Thibetian cats. **1973** *Times* 12 Apr. 8/6 [The Chogyal's] American wife.. is also said to be a devotee of Tibetian culture.

Tibeto- (tɪ'bɛtəʊ, -'biː-), combining form of TIBET, = 'pertaining to Tibet and ——', as **Tibeto-'Burman**: see below as main entry; **Tibeto-Bur'mese** *sb.* and *a.* = TIBETO-BURMAN; **Tibeto-Chi'nese** *a.* = *Sino-Tibetan* adj. s.v. SINO- 2; also as *sb.*; **Tibeto-Hima'layan** *a.* and *sb.*, (*a*) *adj.*, pertaining to Tibet and the Himalayas; (*b*) *sb.*, a branch of the Tibeto-Burmese sub-family of the Sino-Tibetan language group.

1954 PEI & GAYNOR *Dict. Linguistics* 217 Tibeto-Burmese (Tibeto-Burman). **1974** M. PEISSEL *Great Himalayan Passage* xv. 230 Tibetan is the root of the Tibeto-Burmese languages. **1910** *Encycl. Brit.* XIV. 384/1 Of the Tibeto-Chinese family, the Tibeto-Burman sub-family.. is spoken from Tibet to Burma. **1960** C. WINICK *Dict. Anthropol.* 537/2 *Tibeto-Chinese*, a language family that is both agglutinative.. and isolating... It has two sub-families: Tibeto-Burmese and Siamese-Chinese. **1961** L. F. BROSNAHAN *Sounds of Language* viii. 179 The Tibeto-Chinese languages.. have neither palatalisation nor simple accentuation. **1875** *Encycl. Brit.* II. 684/1 Tibeto-Himalayan mountains. **1939** Tibeto-Himalayan [see TIBETO-BURMAN *a.* and *sb.*].

Tibeto-'Burman, *a.* and *sb.* [f. TIBETO- + BURMAN *a.* and *sb.*] **A.** *adj.* Pertaining to Tibet and Burma; *spec.* designating or belonging to a group of languages spoken in Asia, belonging to the Sino-Tibetan family, or the peoples speaking any of these languages. **B.** *sb.* The Tibeto-Burman group of languages.

1878 R. N. CUST *Sk. Mod. Lang. E. Indies* 4 The great Tibeto-Burman sea. *Ibid.* 93 The Bhramu speak a purely Tibeto-Burman language. **1880** *Encycl. Brit.* XII. 777/2 The early peoples of India belonged to three great stocks, known as the Tibeto-Burman, the Kolarian, and the Dravidian. **1895** E. W. HOPKINS *Relig. India* (1896) xviii. 525 The native wild tribes of India (excluding the extreme Northern Tibeto-Burman group) fall into two great classes. **1939** L. H. GRAY *Foundations of Lang.* 389 *Tibeto-Burman* is divided into *Tibeto-Himalayan*, consisting of Tibetan..; and of Himalayan, [etc.]. **1976** W. H. CANAWAY *Willow-Pattern War* xv. 156 Thupten's own language was some impenetrable offshoot of Tibeto-Burman. **1982** *Whitaker's Almanack 1983* 803/2 The indigenous inhabitants who entered Burma from the north and east are of similar racial types and speak languages of the Tibeto-Burman, Mon-Khmer and Thai groups.

Tibetology (tɪbɛ'tɒlədʒɪ). [f. TIBET + -OLOGY.] The study of Tibetan culture. Also **Tibe'tologist**, one who specializes or is expert in this branch of study.

1964 *Bull. Tibetology* I. 5 Tibetology, that is, study of culture or cultures expressed through the medium of Po Key (Bod Sked = Tibetan language), is not confined to the geographical boundaries of Tibet. *Ibid.* 6 The very first difficulty which a Tibetologist faces is that of non-availability of literary data. **1974** M. PEISSEL *Great Himalayan Passage* iv. 84 Professor Tucci, the noted Italian Tibetologist, wrote of Nepal. **1982** *Bodl. Libr. Record* X. 371 The modern discipline of Tibetology.

‖**tibia** ('tɪbɪə). Pl. **-æ** (-iː). [L. *tībia* shin-bone, a pipe or flute.]

1. *Anat.* and *Zool.* The inner and usually larger of the two bones (*tibia* and *fibula*) of the lower leg, from the knee to the ankle; the shin-bone.

In birds the tibia is fused with some of the bones of the tarsus, forming that more strictly called TIBIOTARSUS.

1726–41 MONRO *Anat.* (ed. 3) 282 The superior Extremity of the Tibia is large. **1791** W. BARTRAM *Carolina* 505 A kind of flute, made of.. the tibia of the deer's leg. **1845** TODD & BOWMAN *Phys. Anat.* I. 100 The tibia is convex forwards and outwards. **1872** MIVART *Elem. Anat.* 183 The tibia, or shin-bone, is.. an elongated bone, more so than any other.. except the femur.

b. Applied also to the corresponding part of the leg itself; now esp. to the tibiotarsus of birds.

[**1693** tr. *Blancard's Phys. Dict.* (ed. 2), *Tibia*, the Leg, the part betwixt the Knee and the Ancle. So **1704** J. HARRIS *Lex. Techn.* I.] **1826** STEPHENS in Shaw *Gen. Zool.* XIII. 214 These birds differ.. in having.. the tibiæ divested of feathers. **1869** GILLMORE tr. *Figuier's Rept. & Birds* iv. 339 Woodcocks differ from Snipes in having.. the tibiæ feathered at the joint.

c. *Entom.* The fourth of the five joints of the leg of an insect, that between the femur and the tarsus.

1815 KIRBY & SP. *Entomol.* (1828) I. xv. 488 A pincer formed by the posterior metatarsus and tibia. **1868** DUNCAN tr. *Figuier's Insect W.* Introd. 8 When about to jump they bring the tibia into contact with the thigh. **1888** ROLLESTON & JACKSON *Anim. Life* 499 The thoracic limbs [in *Insecta*] consist typically of a coxa, trochanter, femur, tibia, and tarsus... The tibia is often armed with spines or calcaria.

2. *Antiq.* An ancient (single or double) flute or flageolet.

1705 ADDISON *Italy* 322 The same Variety of Strings may be observ'd on their Harps, and of Stops on their Tibiæ. **1834** LYTTON *Pompeii* I. ii, I paid a visit to Pliny; he was sitting in his summer-house writing while an unfortunate slave played on the tibia.

tibiad ('tɪbɪæd), *adv. Anat.* [f. TIBIA + *-ad*: see DEXTRAD.] Towards the tibial aspect.

1803 BARCLAY *New Anat. Nomencl.* 166 In the sacral extremities, Tibiad will signify towards the tibial aspect. **1808** —— *Muscular Motions* 306 They allow the femur to roll tibiad or inward, but not fibulad or outward.

tibial ('tɪbɪəl), *a.* (*sb.*) [ad. L. *tībiālis* pertaining to the shin-bone: see TIBIA and -AL[1].]

1. *Anat.* and *Zool.* Of or pertaining to the tibia. Also as *sb.*, *ellipt.* for *tibial artery, muscle*, etc.

1599 A. M. tr. *Gabelhouer's Bk. Physicke* 342/2 If it be a tibialle Fracture, he must continuallye lye on his Backe. **1786** J. PEARSON in *Med. Commun.* II. 99 The course of the anterior tibial artery. **1847** JOHNSTON in *Proc. Berw. Nat. Club* II. 231 The tibial joints.. are furnished with long hairs. **1898** J. HUTCHINSON in *Arch. Surg.* IX. No. 36. 338 The anterior and posterior tibials [*sc.* arteries]. **1899** *Allbutt's Syst. Med.* VI. 668 The nerve and its continuation supply the posterior tibial [*sc.* muscle].

2. Of or pertaining to a tibia or ancient flute.

1656 BLOUNT *Glossogr.*, *Tibial*, of, or belonging to pipes; meet to make pipes of. **1658** PHILLIPS, *Tibial*, belonging to a Pipe or Flute.

‖**tibicen** (tɪ'baɪsɪn). *Antiq.* [L. *tībīcen* a flute-player, f. *tībia* flute + *can-ĕre* to sing, also to play on an instrument.] A flute-player.

1776 BURNEY *Hist. Mus.* (1789) I. x. 173 When the Lacedaemonians went to battle a Tibicen played soft and soothing music to temper their courage.

tibicinate (tɪ'bɪsɪneɪt), *v.* *rare*⁻⁰. [f. L. *tībīcināt-*, ppl. stem of *tībīcin-āre* to play on the flute: see prec. and -ATE[3].] *intr.* To play on the tibia or flute. So **tibici'nation** (*rare*⁻⁰); **ti'bicinist** (*rare*) = prec.

1656 BLOUNT *Glossogr.*, *Tibicinate* (*tibicino*), to sing or pipe. [Hence in later Dicts.] **1658** PHILLIPS, *Tibicination*, a playing on a Pipe. **1776** J. HAWKINS *Hist. Music* I. p. xlvi, A scene in an ancient comedy, in which a tibicinist is delineated standing on the stage. **1846** RIMBAULT in *North's Mem. Music* 37 *note*, An engraving from a manuscript.. in which a tibicinist is delineated.. blowing on the *tibia pares*, or two equal flutes.

tibio- (tɪbɪəʊ), used as combining form of TIBIA, in anatomical terms in the sense 'pertaining to the tibia and (some other part)', as ***tibio-femoral, -fibular, -metatarsal, -peroneal, -popliteal***, etc., adjs.; **tibio'tarsal** *a.*, of or pertaining to the tibia and the tarsus; pertaining to the tibiotarsus; **tibio'tarsus**, *Ornith.*, the tibia of a bird's leg with the condyles formed by its fusion with the proximal bones of the tarsus.

1835–6 *Todd's Cycl. Anat.* I. 152/1 The inferior *tibio-fibular articulation. **1870** ROLLESTON *Anim. Life* 14 The *tibiometatarsal joint. **1803** BARCLAY *New Anat. Nomencl.* 174 In describing the direction of the superficial femoral artery,.. at first it is rotulo-tibial, then *tibio-popliteal. **1835–6** *Todd's Cycl. Anat.* I. 151/2 The anterior *tibio-tarsal ligament arises from this margin. **1872** COUES *N. Amer. Birds* 69 The leg is almost always feathered to or beyond the tibio-tarsal joint. **1883** MARTIN & MOALE *Vertebr. Dissect.* II. 124 The *tibio-tarsus.. consists not only of the tibia, but of the proximal bone of the tarsus, which becomes fused with it at an early period.

Tiborne, Tiburn(e, obs. forms of TYBURN.

tiburon (tɪbuː'rəʊn). Also 6–7 **tiberune, tuberon.** [a. F. *tiburon* (Joubert *Hist. Poiss.* 1558), *tibéron, tiburin* (Littré), Sp. *tiburon* (*tiburónes péces*, in Minsheu) = It. *tiburino* (Florio), Pg. *tubarão.* Origin uncertain; prob. taken into Sp. or Pg. from some W. Indian or E. Indian lang.] A name given by 16–17th c. navigators to one or more large species of shark; applied specifically to the bonnet-headed shark, *Reniceps tiburo*; now, on the Mexican Pacific coast, to *Carcharinus fronto.*

1555 EDEN *Decades* 201 The Tiburon.. is a very great fysshe and very quicke and swifte in the water, and a cruell deuourer... The sayde Tuberon [etc.]. **1565** SIR J. HAWKINS *2nd Voy. W. Ind.* (Hakl. Soc.) 22 Many sharks or Tuberons.. came about the ships [Sierra Leone]. [**1579** T. STEVENS *Let. fr. Goa* in Hakluyt *Voy.* (1589) 161 There waited on our ship [in the Atlantic within the Tropics] fishes as long as a man, which they cal Tuberones. **1598** W. PHILLIP *Linschoten* I. xlviii. (Hakl. Soc.) II. 12 There is in the rivers, and also in the Sea along the coast of India great store of fishes, which the Portingalls call Tubaron or Hayen.] **1622** R. HAWKINS *Voy. S. Sea* 68 The shark, or tiberune, is a fish like unto those which wee call dogge-fishes, but that he is farre greater. **1796** MORSE *Amer. Geog.* I. 728 Fish common to both oceans.. sword fish, saw fish, tiburones, manitis.

Tiburtine ('taɪbɜːtaɪn), *a.* [ad. L. *Tīburtīn-us*, f. *Tiburs, Tiburt-em*, adj., of Tibur.] Of or pertaining to the region or district of Tibur (now Tivoli) in ancient Latium. ***Tiburtine stone*** = TRAVERTINE: cf. TIBER-STONE.

c **1440** *Pallad. on Husb.* I. 372 Stone tiburtyne, or floody columbyne, Or spongy rede, lete brenne, or marble stone, For bylding better is the harder myne. **1644** EVELYN *Diary* 14 Nov., It is built of Tiburtine stone. **1840** *Civil Eng. & Arch. Jrnl.* III. 132/2 A bilingual inscription.. sculptured on both sides of a Tiburtine stone.

tic (tɪk). [a. F. *tic*, first known as the name of an equine affection: *ticq, tiquet* 'a disease which on a sudden stopping a horse's breath, makes him to stop, and stand still' (Cotgr. 1611). Origin uncertain; Diez compares It. *ticchio* whim, freak, caprice. See also TICK *sb.*[5]]

1. A disease or affection characterized by spasmodic twitching of certain muscles, esp. of the face; nearly always short for *tic douloureux*: see 2.

1822–34 *Good's Study Med.* (ed. 4) III. 219 The word *tic* is commonly supposed to be an onomatopy, or a sound expressive of the action it imports. **1849** CLARIDGE *Cold Water-cure* 106 A person.. suffering from Tic in his legs. **1860** DICKENS *Lett.* 5 June, Smith.. has been dreadfully ill with tic. **1873** STEVENSON *Lett.* (1901) I. 62, I do not expect any tic to-night. **1899** *Allbutt's Syst. Med.* VII. 868 Both in this country and in America, the term 'tic' has been applied to.. facial spasm ('tic non-douloureux'), or to facial neuralgia ('tic douloureux'). *Ibid.* VIII. 40 A phenomenon in the symptomatology of simple tic (habit-spasm).

‖**2.** ***tic douloureux*** (dulurø) [F., = painful twitching], severe facial neuralgia with twitching of the facial muscles.

(Often misspelt by English writers *dolo-, dolou-, douleu-*, and often mispronounced (dɒləruː), etc.)

1800 *Med. Jrnl.* III. 575 The *Dolor Faciei*, or, as the French call it, *Tic Douloreux*, is a disorder which has, in general, frustrated all attempts of the medical art. **1800** HOME in *Phil. Trans.* XCI. 20 The *Tic douleureux* is a remarkable instance. **1822** GOOD *Study Med.* I. 55 The maddening pain of *neuralgia faciei*, or tic douloureux. **1824** LAMB *Lett.*, *To B. Barton* (1838) II. 162, I hope.. thy *tick doleru*, or, however you spell it, is vanished. **1861** LYTTON *Str. Story* I. 58 A poor old gentleman, tormented by *tic-doloreux*. **1878** T. BRYANT *Pract. Surg.* I. 289 The disease known as 'tic-douloureux' is an affection of the fifth nerve and its branches, but any nerve in the body is liable to suffer.

3. A whim: = TICK *sb.*[5] 2.

1896 *Daily News* 30 Sept. 6/3 It is mere 'tic' or habit. **1927** F. M. FORD *Let.* 28 Mar. (1935) 172, I have such a tic against writing letters that I cannot do it. **1960** *Twentieth Cent.* Apr. 361 This is an irritating tic of the British Left, this substitution of moral gestures for practical policies. **1978** C. P. SNOW *Realists* vi. 176 He had the tic, common to many writers, of insisting that the table be kept pernicketily tidy.

tic, variant of TIG.

‖**tical** (*in Thailand* tɪ'kɑːl, *in Burma* 'tɪk(ə)l). Also 8 **tecul(l, tecal(l, teecall,** 9 **tickal, tycal, takel, tackal(l.** [Representing, through Pg. *tical*, the Indian *ṭaṅkā*, also *ṭakā*: see TANGA[1]. Carried in 16th c. to Siam (Thailand) by the Portuguese; later to Burma. (See Sir R. C. Temple in *Indian Antiquary* XXVIII. 235, 253.)] A term long in use by foreign traders in Siam (Thailand) and more recently in Burma, applied to a silver coin and its weight, representing roughly the Indian rupee (orig. the same as the *ṭaṅkā*), which has varied in value according to time and place, and in weight from more than to less than half an ounce Troy. (Sir R. C. Temple.) Also *attrib.*

In Siam, according to Crawfurd, a weight = 225½ grs. (according to Simmonds = 236 grs.); also a silver coin of this weight, the value of which fell with that of silver. In Burma, a weight = 255·6 grains, the quasi-standard weight of current (uncoined) silver, said to be equivalent in value to about 1¼ rupee.

1662 J. DAVIES tr. *Mandelslo's Trav.* 130 The money of this Country [Siam] is very good..; there are of it three sorts; *Ticals, Mases,* and *Foangs.* **1727** A. HAMILTON *New Acc. E. Ind.* II. xlvii. 164 Some were of pure Gold, others of Tecul Silver, which has no Alloy in it. **1800** *Misc. Tracts* in *Asiatic Ann. Reg.* 317/2 The cost of sinking a new well is 2000 tecals flowered silver of the country, or 2500 sicca rupees. **1840** MALCOM *Trav.* 41/1 They sometimes have a gold fuang, equal to eight ticals. The tical, assayed at the mint of Calcutta, yielded about one rupee three and a half annas, equal to 2s. 6d. sterling. **1858** T. DALTON in *Merc. Marine Mag.* V. 337 Last year the same rice sold for 19 ticals (equal to 60 cents each tical, or 2s. 6d. sterling). **1902** *Daily Chron.* 1 Dec. 5/7 A dispatch from Bangkok..says:—'The Siamese Government has issued a decree fixing the gold standard on the basis of seventeen ticals to the pound'. **1907** *Motor Boat* 19 Sept. 179/1 American two-stroke motors.. used to arrive in batches valued at 1,200 ticals each (1 tical = 1s. 5⅜d.).

ticarcillin (tɪkɑ'sɪlɪn). *Pharm.* [f. *ti-* (of unknown origin) + CAR(BOXY- + *-cillin*, after PENICILLIN.] A semisynthetic penicillin antibiotic, (6R)-6-[2-carboxy-2-(3-thienyl)-acetamido]penicillanic acid, usu. administered as the disodium salt, $C_{15}H_{14}N_2Na_2O_6S_2$.

1972 in *Approved Names* (Brit. Pharmacopœia Comm.) Suppl. v. 4. **1974** *Jrnl. Clin. Pharmacol.* XIV. 172/1 Ticarcillin..is a new semisynthetic penicillin, with a wide spectrum of activity against gram-positive and gram-negative bacteria. **1980** *Brit. Med. Jrnl.* 24 May 1240/2 Bacteriological monitoring of seriously ill patients may be rewarding if combined with early and energetic use of suitable antibiotics such as tobramycin, plus ticarcillin.., when septicaemia is clinically suspected.

‖**ticca** ('tɪkə, 'tiːkɑː). *East Indian.* Also **teeka, tikka.** [ad. Hindī *ṭhīkā* or *ṭhīkah* hire, fare, fixed price (Yule).] *attrib.* Engaged on contract, hired; esp. in *ticca gharry*, hired carriage.

1827 *Bengal Regulations* 27 June (Y.), A Rule, Ordinance and Regulation..for regulating the number and fare of Teeka Palankeens, and Teeka Bearers in the Town of Calcutta. **1878** *Life in Mofussil* II. 94 (Y.) We got into a 'ticca gharry', 'hired trap'. **1888** KIPLING *Soldiers Three* (1889) 10 That *tikka*..has been *owin'* an' *fere-owin'* all over the bloomin' *maidan.* **1895** MRS. B. M. CROKER *Village Tales* (1896) 48 You..can, no doubt, retire and set up a ticca gharry, or a shop. **1903** *Blackw. Mag.* Dec. 817 Engaged in a..wrangle with a Ticca carriage-driver. **1911** R. E. VERNEDE *An Ignorant in India* i. 5 He had collected enough porters to get it into a tikka ghari. **1928** *Blackw. Mag.* Apr. 498/1 Tikka-gharris, bullock-carts, hand-trucks, and coolies combined to raise..an excruciating din. **1978** 'M. M. KAYE' *Far Pavilions* ix. 151 The drivers of phaetons and *tikka-gharis*, tongas and *ekkas.*

†**ticchen.** *Obs.* [OE. *ticcen* = OHG. *zicchîn*:—WTeut. **tikk-în-*, dim. from the stem which also gave OHG. *ziga*, Ger. *ziege* goat. The modern Eng. form would have been *titchen.*] A kid, a young goat.

c **950** *Lindisf. Gosp.* Matt. xxv. 32 Sua hiorde to-sceadas scipo from ticȝenum [*c* **975** *Rushw. G.* ticnum; *c* **1000** *Ags. G.* tyccenum; *c* **1160** *Hatt.* ticchenan]. *c* **1000** ÆLFRIC *Gen.* xxvii. 9 Bring me twa þa betstan tyccenu. *Ibid.* 16 Heo.. befeold his handa mid þæra tyccena fellum. *a* **1225** *Ancr. R.* 100 þeos fif wittes he cleopeð ticchenes; for..of a ticchen, þet haueð swete vleschs, kumeð a stinkinde got.

tice (taɪs), *sb.* [f. TICE *v.*] **a.** An act of enticing, an enticement; *spec.* a stroke at croquet, or 'ball' (bowled) at cricket (see quots. 1843, 1901, etc.), which tempts or entices the opponent to take aim.

1843 'WYKEHAMIST' *Pract. Hints Cricket* 15 The 'Tice', which may be described as a short pitched full-pitch..is one of the most destructive Balls that can be bowled. **1869** L. M. ALCOTT *Little Women* II. ix. 128 The phrases, 'caught off a tice', 'stumped off his ground',..were as intelligible to her as Sanscrit. **1874** J. D. HEATH *Croquet-Player* 55 It is admissible to give a double shot as a 'tice', so as to tempt him to shoot where his missing would give you the dead ball. **1888** STEEL & LYTTELTON *Cricket* (Badm.) iii. 132 In the first over he [the bowler] should try a 'yorker'. This ball, called in days gone by a 'tice', an abbreviation of 'entice', is certainly one of the most deadly balls that can be bowled. **1900** A. LILLIE *Croquet up to Date* 41 The length of the tice should depend on the trueness of the ground. **1901** *N. & Q.* 9th Ser. VIII. 284/2 It might meet the requirements of present-day definition..if one classed a 'tice' as a lob, or to be more precise, an underhand yorker.

b. *Comb.* **tice-basket,** a decoy basket.

1884 *19th Cent.* Feb. 245 Fish..falling freely to the native net and tice-basket.

tice (taɪs), *v. Obs.* exc. *dial.* Forms: 3–7 **tyce,** 4–6 **tise,** 4–7 **tyse,** 5–6 *Sc.* **tyss,** (6 *Sc.* **tist, tyst, tyist(e, tyisce),** 5–7 (9 *dial.*) **tice,** 7 (9 *dial.*) **'tice.** [Aphetic form of *atise*, ATTICE or ENTICE, but found earlier than either of these, and perhaps taken immediately from OF. *a-tiser*, dropping the prefix.] *trans.* To entice; to induce or attract by the offer of pleasure or advantage. Also *absol.*

c **1275** *Moral Ode* (Jesus MS.) 266 þe þat were gaderares of þisse worldes ayhte And duden þat þe loþe gost heom tycede [*v.rr.* hechte to, tihte] and tahte. **1303** R. BRUNNE *Handl. Synne* 2152 To tyse a chylde swyche synne to do. *c* **1449** PECOCK *Repr.* v. xii. 548 Which schulde rather lette fro glorie than tice into glorie. **1533** BELLENDEN *Livy* I. xviii. (S.T.S.) I. 103 He tyistit þe ȝoung men of his ciete to his purpois. **1593** NASHE *Christ's T.* 48 b, If one tice a Prentise to robbe his Maister, it is Felony. *a* **1835** MRS. HEMANS *Let.* in Chorley *Mem.* (1837) I. 299 An old gardener of ours used to say of me..that Miss Felicia 'ticed him to do whatever she pleased'. **1859** GEO. ELIOT *A. Bede* xxxix, He's been false to me, and 'ticed her away.

Hence **'ticing** *vbl. sb.* and *ppl. a.*

a **1400** *Hampole's Psalter* liii. 4 þat þai take me noȝt in þaire wickidnes & liþere eggynge [*v.r.* tisynge]. **1456** SIR G. HAYE *Law Arms* (S.T.S.) 31 For na mede na othir tyssing. **1568** in H. Fleming *Mary Q. of Scots* (1897) 512 Be persuasioun and tyisting. **1582** T. WATSON *Centurie of Loue* lxxii. (Arb.) 108 My Loue, Whose tising face is of more liuely hewe. **1646** H. P. *Medit. Seige* 69 What a ticeing bayt is golden hope!

†**ticement.** *Obs.* Aphetic f. ENTICEMENT.

1303 R. BRUNNE *Handl. Synne* 12016 3yf þou wylt.. withstonde hys [the devil's] tycement. *c* **1400** *Brut* 182 Lewelyn, Prince of Walys, þrouȝ ticement of Dauid his broþer,..þouȝt disherite Kyng Edward.

ticer ('taɪsə(r)). [f. TICE *v.* + -ER[1].] An enticer.

a **1529** SKELTON *Mann. World* 143 So many carders, Revelers and dicers, And so many yl ticers, Sawe I never. **1869** E. FARMER *Scrap Bk.* (ed. 6) 27 All the lame and the old, With a few (just as ticers') are sent to be sold.

tich (tɪtʃ). *slang.* Also **Tich, titch.** The stage name Little *Tich* of the dwarfish music-hall comedian Harry Relph (1868–1928), who was given the nickname as a child because of a resemblance to the Tichborne claimant (see below), used as a name for any small person. Cf. TITCHY *a.*

Arthur Orton (1834–98), the Tichborne claimant, claimed in 1866 to be Roger Charles Tichborne (1829–54), the heir to an English baronetcy, who was lost at sea. Orton was finally discredited and imprisoned in 1874.

1934 W. POLLOCK *Cream of Cricket* xi. 66 'Tich' Freeman would toss up his slows with that maddening lure to come and commit cricket suicide which so many misguided batsmen cannot resist. **1959** I. & P. OPIE *Lore & Lang. Schoolch.* ix. 169 A chap who has got duck's disease is most often labelled 'Tich' in a friendly manner, or 'squirt'. **1960** D. ABSE in J. C. Trewin *Plays of Year 1960–61* XXIII. 147, I vowed to work harder. To make more money. For you and the titch. **1962** *Daily Mail* 7 Mar. 12/5 (*caption*) This will prove we're not 'tiches' in space communications.

tichorhine ('taɪkəʊraɪn), *a. Palæont.* Also **-orrhine, -orine.** [ad. mod.L. *tichorrhinus*, f. Gr. τεῖχο-ς wall + ῥίς (ῥῑν-) nose.] Having an ossified nasal septum; the English form of the specific name of the Woolly Rhinoceros.

1851 D. WILSON *Preh. Ann.* (1863) I. ii. 42 Man was contemporary with the tichorine rhinoceros. **1854** *Zoologist* XII. 4375 Entire carcases of the extinct mammoth and tichorhine rhinoceros have been handed down in Arctic Siberia. **1860** OWEN *Palæontology* 366 The discovery of the carcase of the tichorrine rhinoceros in frozen soil.

ticht (Sc.), obs. pa. pple. of TIE *v.*; var. TIGHT *v.*[2]; Sc. f. TIGHT.

tichy, obs. form of TETCHY.

Ticinese (tɪtʃɪ'niːz), *sb.* and *a.* Pl. Ticinese, ‖-esi. [a. It. *Ticinese*: see -ESE.] **A.** *sb. collect.* The natives or inhabitants of Ticino, an Italian-speaking canton in southern Switzerland. **B.** *adj.* Of or pertaining to Ticino or its inhabitants.

1961 'W. HAGGARD' *Arena* x. 84 Walter didn't much care for Ticinesi, but it was certain they weren't Swiss-Germans. **1964** *Language* XL. 287 The article gives a detailed description of Ticinese customs. **1974** *Sat. Rev. World* (U.S.) 19 Oct. 43/2 The Ticinese can manage most of the other tongues in current employ in Switzerland. **1978** [see SCHWEIZERDEUTSCH, SCHWYZERTÜTSCH].

tick (tɪk), *sb.*[1] Forms: (1 ticia), 5 **teke;** 4–7 **tyke,** 6 **tycke,** 6–7 **tike, ticke,** 7 **tique,** 7– **tick.** [*Ticia* (assumed to be an error for **tiica* = *tīca*, or **ticca*) appears once, in the Erfurt Gloss. *a* 800, after which the word is known only in 15th c. as *teke*, from 14th to 17th c. as *tȳke*, and from 16th c. as *tycke, tick. Teke* agrees with MD., MLG. *tēke*, Du. *teek*, also with the LG. forms *teke, täke. Tȳke, tīke* agree with suggested OE. **tīca*, with LG. *tieke, tiek*, whence Du. *tiek*, and mod.EFris. *tike, tîk*, applied to beetles generally (Dornkaat-Koolman). Thence also prob. F. *tique* (1464 in Godef.). The later *tycke, tick* may be shortened from *teke*: cf. *rick, sick, wick.* If = OE. **ticca* with OTeut. *cc*, it would correspond to Ger. *zecke* (whence It. *zecca*):—**tikkon* m. or **tikkôn* f.; if = **tīca*, to MHG. *zeche.* The various forms imply WGer. **tīka-*, **tika-*, **tikka-*. Ulterior etymology uncertain: see Kluge and Franck; also Falk and Torp s.v. *Tæge.*]

1. a. The common name for several kinds of mites or acarids, esp. of the genus *Ixōdes* or family *Ixōdidæ*, which infest the hair or fur of various animals, as dogs, cattle, etc., and attach themselves to the skin as temporary parasites; also for the similarly parasitic dipterous insects of the families *Hippoboscidæ* (bird-ticks, horse-ticks, sheep-ticks) and *Nycteribiidæ* (bat-ticks).

a **800** *Erfurt Gloss.* (O.E.T.) 1130 *Ricinus*, ticia *sax.* **1300–25** *Song agst. Retainers* 20 in *Pol. Songs* (Camden) 238 To shome he huem shadde, To fles ant to fleye, To tyke ant to tadde. *c* **1440** *Jacob's Well* xxi. 146 A waterleche or a tyke hath neuere ynow, tyl it brestyth. **14..** *Voc.* in Wr.-Wülcker 565/47 *Ascarida*, a Teke. **1523** FITZHERB. *Husb.* §135 There is ieopardy both for calues, foles and coltes, for tyckes, or for beynge lousye. **1575** TURBERV. *Venerie* 229 A receipt to kill fleas, lice, tykes, and other vermin on dogs. **1603** HOLLAND *Plutarch's Mor.* 393 The foxe in Æsops fables would not suffer the urchin to take off the tiques that were setled upon her bodie. **1658** ROWLAND *Moufet's Theat. Ins.* 934 The Tick or Sheep-fly. **1688** R. HOLME *Armoury* II. 198/2 The Tike is another kind of Louse,..a Companion for Dogs, Sheep, and Cattle. **1748** *Anson's Voy.* III. ii. 314 An insect called a tick, which, though principally attached to the cattle, would yet frequently fasten upon our limbs and bodies. **1839** DARWIN *Voy. Nat.* i. (1879) 10 A tick which must have come here as a parasite on the birds. **1882** *Garden* 14 Jan. 20/1 The horses..were covered with large blue ticks.

b. Applied in contempt or insult to a person. Freq. as *little tick. colloq.*

1631 A. WILSON *Swisser* II. i, Yee nigling Ticks you. **1909** WODEHOUSE *Mike* xl. 231 Can't you see that..we've got a chance of getting a jolly good bit of our own back against those Downing's ticks? **1928** J. VAN DRUTEN *Young Woodley* i. 17 Milner: 'Cope, your presence is urgently desired... Scrimshanking, the little tic.' **1952** E. O'NEILL *Moon for Misbegotten* I. 17 Everyone says you're a wicked old tick, as crooked as a corkscrew. **1973** R. FULFORD in D. Pryce-Jones *Evelyn Waugh & his World* ii. 17 How often in those early days did I hear those ominous words 'that awful little tick Waugh'.

c. Phr. *as full* (or *tight*) *as a tick*: full to repletion, esp. with alcoholic drink.

1678 J. RAY *Coll. Eng. Proverbs* (ed. 2) 284 As full as a pipers bag; as a tick. **1822** *Yankee Phrases* in *New Jersey Alm. 1823* (Elizabethtown, N.J.) 31 Though of love I'm as full as a tick. **1911** L. STONE *Jonah* 226 'Ard luck, to grudge a man a pint, with 'is own missis inside there gittin' as full as a tick. **1933** M. LOWRY *Ultramarine* iv. 177 He was tight as a tick so couldn't tell the difference. **1952** E. O'NEILL *Moon for Misbegotten* IV. 168 'You must have seen how blotto I was.'..'I did. You were as full as a tick.' **1981** A. PRICE *Soldier no More* v. 59 He was drunk as a lord..tight as a tick.

2. Short for *tick-bean*: see 3.

1765 *Treat. Dom. Pigeons* 28 Horse-beans are the next food... There is a sort which they call French ticks, which are good food. **1850–2** MORTON *Cycl. Agric.* (1855) I. 200/2 There are several other varieties of the Tick bean in cultivation, known locally [as] Harrow Tick, Flat Tick, Essex Tick, and French Tick.

3. *attrib.* and *Comb.*, as *tick genus, plague*; *tick-infested* adj.; **tick-bean,** a small-seeded variety of the common bean, *Vicia Faba*, so called from the resemblance of the seed to a dog-tick; **tick-bird,** a bird which feeds on the ticks that infest large quadrupeds, as the African genus *Buphaga* (rhinoceros-bird) and the S. American and W. Indian *Crotophaga ani*; **tick-borne** *a.*, transmitted by ticks; *tick-borne fever*, a mild, transient, rickettsial, febrile disease of sheep, cattle, and goats; **tick-eater** = *tick-bird*; **tick fever,** a fever (in men or cattle) caused by the bites of ticks; **tick-fly,** any of the dipterous insects called ticks (see 1); **tick paralysis,** paralysis caused by neurotoxin in the saliva of certain biting ticks; **tick pyæmia,** a type of blood-poisoning in sheep, esp. lambs, caused by *Staphylococcus aureus* and leading to lameness or death; **tick-seed,** name for various plants having seeds resembling ticks, as †the castor-oil plant, *Ricinus communis* (obs.), and the genera *Coreopsis* and *Corispermum*; also = *tick-trefoil*; **tick-seeded** *a.*, having seeds resembling ticks; **tick-spider,** name for a jumping spider; †**tick spot,** a marking as if bitten by a tick: cf. TICKED *a.*; **tick-trefoil,** a plant of the genus *Desmodium*, so named from the joints of the pods adhering like ticks to the fur of animals; **tick typhus** = *Rocky Mountain fever* s.v. ROCKY *a.*[1] 1 c; **tick-weed,** †(*a*) the castor-oil plant (see *tick-seed* above); (*b*) the American pennyroyal, *Hedeoma pulegioides.*

1744 W. ELLIS *Mod. Husbandman* Feb. ii. 17 Chilturn Farmers can get a full Crop of Horse or *Tick-beans. **1763** *Museum Rust.* (ed. 2) I. 187 The methods followed..in sowing horse beans, or tick-beans, as we sometimes call them. **1805** *Trans. Soc. Arts* XXIII. 36 One stalk of the tick bean had 70 pods. **1969** *Oxf. Bk. Food Plants* 40/1 Prehistoric specimens are all small-seeded forms—even smaller than the 'Horse bean' or 'Tick bean' varieties grown as food for livestock in modern times. **1850** T. E. POOLE *Life, Scenery, & Customs in Sierra Leone & Gambia* II. xiv. 220 Perched upon these animals [*sc.* cattle], which did not seem in the least to mind them, were a species of birds called '*Tick-birds', from the circumstances of their feeding upon certain insects of that name, which they find in great numbers on these beasts. **1863** W. C. BALDWIN *Afr. Hunting* ix. 389, I was much amused by watching the tick birds trying to alarm an old white rhinoceros, that we were approaching from under the wind. **1871** KINGSLEY *At Last* v, The black 'tick birds' (Crotophaga Ani), a little larger than our English blackbird. **1896** BADEN-POWELL *Matabele Campaign* xviii. 133 Colenbrander..they have called the 'tick-bird'—a bird which in this country always accompanies a bull, to relieve him of superfluous ticks. **1921** *Indian Med. Gaz.* LVI. 368/1 It [*sc.* Brill's disease] has no epidemiological relationship whatever with the Rocky Mountain fever which is *tick-borne. **1932** W. S. GORDON et al. in *Jrnl. Compar. Path. & Therapeutics* XLV. 122 A disease characterised by a low mortality, with an incubation period of about four days, followed by a sharp rise in temperature and a period of fever. .. We have .. shown .. that this reaction is a '*tick-borne fever'. *Ibid.* 301 This condition we have .. named 'tick-borne fever'. **1970** W. H. PARKER *Health & Dis. in Farm Animals* xviii. 241 In areas of late lambing, abortions in ewes are sometimes attributable to tick-borne fever. **1973** J. J. MCKELVEY *Man Against Tsetse* i. 42 Dutton died at Kasongo in February 1905 of tick-borne relapsing fever. **1903** *Daily Chron.* 11 June 3/3 The gulls, .. like the small *tick eaters which live on African game, delighted in warning their friends of our approach. **1901** *Lancet* 23 Nov. 1432/1 *Tick fever is widely distributed throughout the world... It is communicated to cattle by insects known as 'ticks'. **1658** ROWLAND *Moufet's Theat. Ins.* 949 Those things that kill and drive away the *Tyke-flies called *Ricini*, for the most part kill and drive away the Dog-flies. **1889** *Cent. Dict.* s.v. *Hippobosca*, *H. equina* is a winged tick-fly of the horse. **1822–34** *Good's Study Med.* (ed. 4) I. 263 Linnæus .. laboured .. to prove, that dysentery is the effect of a .. larva .. belonging to the acarus or *tick genus. **1932** C. FULLER *Louis Trigardt's Trek* 128 Our small stock were so *tick-infested that we despaired of saving them. **1960** *Times* 1 Oct. 7/7 Tick-infested hinterland. **1914** P. MANSON *Trop. Dis.* (ed. 5) xvii. 307 (*heading*) *Tick paralysis. **1962** GORDON & LAVOIPIERRE *Entomol. for Students of Med.* xliii. 260 In Australia, North America, South Africa and South Eastern Europe several species of ticks .. produce a type of ascending motor paralysis known as 'tick paralysis'. **1896** *Daily News* 23 Nov. 8/5 The *tick-plague in Queensland .. is not so terrible a scourge as the South African rinderpest. **1946** *Nature* 27 July 132/2 The sheep tick, *Ixodes ricinus*, is involved in the transmission of .. *tick-pyæmia. **1970** W. H. PARKER *Health & Dis. in Farm Animals* xviii. 241 Tick pyaemia is caused by the ubiquitous bacterium *Staphylococcus*. **1562** TURNER *Herbal* II. 116 Ricinus is called .. in English palma Christi, or *ticke sede... The sede .. when the huske is of .. looketh very lyke a dogge louse which is called a tyke. **1760** J. LEE *Introd. Bot.* App. 329 Tickseed, *Corispermum*. **1860** WORCESTER, *Tickseed sunflower*, a smooth-branched herb, having golden-yellow, showy rays; *Coreopsis trichosperma*. *Gray*. **1786** ABERCROMBIE *Arrangem.* in *Gard. Assist.* 54/2 *Coreopsis*, *tick-seeded sunflower. **1721** BRADLEY *Philos. Acc. Wks. Nat.* 135 The Jumper or *Tick Spider. **1704** *Lond. Gaz.* No. 4079/4 A .. Greyhound .. with some white *Tick Spots. **1853** THOREAU *Jrnl.* 31 July in *Writings* (1906) XI. 350 *Desmodium nudifloram*, naked-flowered *tick trefoil, some already with loments round-angled. **1857** GRAY *First Less. Bot.* (1866) 127 A one-celled ovary sometimes becomes several-celled .. by the formation of false partitions, .. as in the jointed pod of the Sea-Rocket and the Tick-Trefoil. **1921** *Indian Med. Gaz.* LVI. 370/2 (*heading*) Possible human origin of *tick typhus. **1981** D. R. BELL *Lect. Notes Trop. Med.* vii. 68 American tick typhus caused by *R[ickettsia] rickettsi* occurs in Colombia and Brazil. **1563** HYLL *Art Garden.* (1593) 32 The hearbe named *Tick-weed, otherwise in Latin *Palma Christi*. **1884** MILLER *Plant-n.*, Tick-weed, *Hedeoma pulegioides*.

tick (tɪk), *sb.*² Forms: α. 5 **tikke, tykk(e**, 6 **tycke**, 6–7 **ticke**, 6– **tick**; β. 5–6 **teke**, 7 **teike**; γ. (chiefly *Sc.*) 5– **tyke**, 6 **tyik**, 6– **tike** (taɪk). [Known from 15th c., in the forms *tikke*, *tēke*, *tȳke*; the second corresp. to MLG. and MDu. *têke* (mod.EFris. *têk*, Doornkaat-Koolman), cognate with OHG. *ziahha*, *ziecha*, MHG., Ger. *zieche* bed-tick, pillow-case; the third to MDu. *tîke*, *tijcke*, Du. *tijk*. These forms point to an earlier WGer. **tēka*, and later **tīka*, both a. L. *tēca*, *thēca*, a. Gr. θήκη case, whence also F. *teie*, *taie*, obs. Eng. TAY, TEY. The short vowel in *tykke*, *tikke*, *ticke*, *tick*, is prob. as in *rick*, *sick*, *wick*.]

a. The case or cover containing feathers, flocks, or the like, forming a mattress or pillow; also, from 16th c., applied to the strong hard linen or cotton material used for making such cases.

α. **1466** *Mann. & Househ. Exp.* (Roxb.) 362 For iij. tykkes [*pr.* tylkes] and bolsteres to the same fore federbeddes. **1480** *Wardr. Acc. Edw. IV* (1830) 118 To Lisbet Ketiller for a grete tikke xxxij s. **1530** PALSGR. 281/1 Ticke for a fetherbed, *coite de lit*. **1569** *Wills & Inv. N.C.* (Surtees) I. 311 One fether bed, the tycke therof I dyd by. **1586** *Rates of Custome* E viij b, Ticks called Brussel ticks, the Tick xiij.s. iiij.d. **1636** *Althorp MS.* in Simpkinson *Washingtons* (1860) App. p. lxxvii, For 2 feather bed ticks for Alexander. **1743** *Phil. Trans.* XLII. 367 Those Ticks and Pillow-biers covering the Matresses and Pillows. **1812** W. TENNANT *Anster F.* II. xxviii, Dunfermline, too, so fam'd checks and ticks. **1842** S. LOVER *Handy Andy* vi, The deep pocket of blue striped tick which hung at her side. **1853** *Heal & Son Catal.*: *Bedsteads* 3 Best Grey Goose .. in Fine Linen Ticks. **1908** L. M. MONTGOMERY *Anne of Green Gables* iv. 49 She made her bed less successfully, for she had never learned the art of wrestling with a feather tick. **1951** *People* 3 June 6/8 (Advt.), Pillow ticks black white striped. **1980** J. C. OATES *Bellefleur* (1981) IV. 329 A plain four-poster with white ruffled skirts, a cornhusk tick and feather bed on top.

β. **1494** FABYAN *Chron.* VII. 414 And of federbeddes [they] rypped the tekys. **1570** LEVINS *Manip.* 54/25 Ye Teke of a bed, *teca culcitaria*. *c* **1615** in Walcott *William of Wykeham* (1852) 167, 3 yeards of teike for a boulster.

γ. **1495** in Pitcairn *Crim. Trials* I. 20*, iij le tykis de feddirbeddis. **1502** *Acc. Ld. High Treas. Scot.* II. 295 For tua tikis of feddir beddis to hir. **1534** *Inv. Wardr. Kath. Arragon* in *Camden Misc.* (1855) 31 A paliotte of Brusells tyke filled with bastardedowne. **1545** *Rates of Custome* C vij, Tikes for beddes the dossen xxxvj.s. Tikes the pece iij.s. **1573–80** BARET *Alv.* T 241 The tike of a bed: a featherbed. **1580** *Aberdeen Regr.* (1848) II. 36 Auchtene codvarris witht sextene tyikis. **1618** SIR R. BOYLE in *Lismore Papers* (1886) I. 191, I bought 2 fetherbed tykes. **1806** FORSYTH *Beauties Scotl.* III. 146 The children sleep in beds .. with tikes filled with straw.

b. 'Used for the bed or bolster itself: as, "That's the tyke or tyken o' the bed: a guid feather tyke or tyken [= tyking]"' (*Suppl. to Jamieson*, 1887).

More distinctively *tyke o' bed*, or *tyke-a-bed*.

tick (tɪk), *sb.*³ Forms: 5 **tek, tekk**, 6–7 **ticke**, 7 **tyck**, 6– **tick**. [Not known *a* 1440, the vb. (TICK *v.*¹) appearing a century later. Parallels to sb. and vb. appear in Du. *tik* a pat, touch, tick, *tikken* to pat, tick, LG. *tikk* a touch, also a moment, instant, with *ticken* or *tikken* vb., Norw. *tikke* to touch lightly, also MHG. *zic* 'a light touch or push', and *zicken* vb. These may indicate a common OTeut. source, or they may be of later onomatopœic formation, the expression in 'vocal gesture' of the act or sound in question.]

1. a. A light but distinct touch; a light quick stroke; a pat, a tap. *Obs.* exc. *dial.*

c **1440** *Promp. Parv.* 487/2 Tek, or lytylle towche (*K.* tekk or lytyl strock), *tactulus*. **1580** SIDNEY *Let.* 18 Oct. in Collins *Lett.* (1746) I. 285 When you play at Weapons .. play out your Play lustilie, for indeed Tickes and Daliances are nothing in earnest. **1621** S. WARD *Life of Faith* 84 The least ticke befalls the not, without the ouer-ruling eye and hand .. of a wise God. **1625** LISLE *Du Bartas, Noe* 13 He makes us only afraid With fingers tyck. **1674** N. FAIRFAX *Bulk & Selv.* 96 If the forestroke give us but a little tick, the backstroke will be sure to give him a knocker. *a* **1825** FORBY *Voc. E. Anglia, Tick*, a very gentle touch, by way of hint, or as a token of endearment.

b. A children's game in which the object is to overtake and touch; = TIG *sb.* 2.

1622 DRAYTON *Poly-olb.* xxx. 144 The Mountaine Nymphs .. doe giue each other chase, At Hood-winke, Barley-breake, at Tick, or Prison-base. **1884** BLACK *Jud. Shaks.* iii, The children playing tick round the grave-stones.

2. a. A quick light dry sound, distinct but not loud, as that caused by the sudden impact of a small hard body upon a hard surface; *esp.* the sound produced by the alternate check and release of the train in the escapement of a watch or clock; also the similar sound made by the death-watch beetle.

Also (repeated) adverbially or interjectionally, as an imitation of this sound: see also TICK-TICK.

1680 AUBREY *Lives* (1898) I. 28 He [Thomas Allen] happened to leave his watch in the chamber windowe... The maydes .. hearing a thing in a case cry Tick, Tick, Tick, presently concluded that that was his Devill. **1702** RAY *Rem.* (1780) 324 The leisurely and constant Tick of the Death-Watch. **1861** *Walsall Free Press* 7 Dec., By a simple arrangement of ticks and intervals .. the clerk was enabled to copy the [telegraphic] messages with the utmost rapidity. **1871** TYNDALL *Fragm. Sc.* (1879) I. xxii. 496 Ellicott set one clock going by the ticks of another. **1910** *Nation* 8 Jan. 604/2 With just a 'tick' of his [a robin's] alarm note.

b. A beat of the heart or of the pulse.

1823 BYRON *Juan* X. xxxix, Her physician .. found the tick Of his fierce pulse betoken a condition Which augured of the dead. **1855** BROWNING *An Epistle* 194 Something, a word, a tick o' the blood within Admonishes.

3. a. A small dot or dash (often formed by two small strokes at an acute angle), made with a pen or pencil, to draw attention to something or to mark a name, figure, etc., in a list as having been noted or checked. In quot. 1860 used in plural for inverted commas.

1844 *Fraser's Mag.* XXX. 88/1 Neat pencil ticks indicated favourite passages. **1860** MRS. CARLYLE *Lett.* (1883) III. 48 To .. interlard his own note with single words or whole lines of yours 'in ticks'. **1863** *Reader* 28 Nov. 638 A tick at the beginning and end of it .. shows of what extent the passage is to be. **1865** DICKENS *Mut. Fr.* III. i, Those lots that I'd mark with my pencil—there's a tick there, and a tick there. **1898** SIR E. HAMILTON in *Daily News* 8 Nov. 6/1 Whether the copy was entered in a large letter-book, or made on a separate sheet, depended on his having made one 'tick' or two 'ticks' at the bottom of the first page.

b. A small spot or speck of colour on the skin or coat of an animal.

1873 D. MACLAGAN in *Mod. Scot. Poets* (1881) III. 181 The ticks upon his gawsy side Show him a new-rin saumon.

c. A ticked item on a list, esp. a list of birds to be observed. Also *Comb.*, as ***tick-hunter***, ***-hunting***.

1975 W. CONDRY *Pathway to Wild* vi. 93 R. S. Thomas .. saw it [*sc.* foreign travel] as an opportunity of adding to his life-list of birds. 'Tick-hunting' is what bird-watchers call it. You carry a card with a list of all the birds on it and you .. tick them off as you spot them. *Ibid.* 94 We saw a signpost on our right, 'La Route des Lacs', and what tick-hunter short of waterbirds could resist a lakeside road? **1981** *Birds* Autumn 60/3 Their [*sc.* the *Country Life* team's] ticks .. included glossy ibis, spoonbill, Savi's warbler, [etc.].

4. *transf.* (from 2). The time between two ticks of the clock; a moment, second, instant. *colloq.* ***on*** or ***to the tick***, exactly at the appointed time, punctually; cf. *on the dot* s.v. DOT *sb.*¹ 4 d.

1879 BROWNING *Ned Bratts* 193 Waste no tick of moment more. **1902** [see COMMUTER]. **1904** JEROME *Tommy & Co.* (ed. Tauchn.) 236 It's all right. Can explain in two ticks. **1907** PHYLLIS DARE *Fr. School to Stage* v, At eight o'clock to the tick, the day's regular lesson's began. **1909** HORNUNG *Mr. Justice Raffles* i. 6, I should have been spotted in a tick by a spy. **1913** A. BENNETT *Regent* ix. 262 If you don't clear out on the tick I'll chuck this cup and saucer down into the stalls. **1927** *Daily Express* 6 July 3/5, I am always here on the tick myself, and I do not see why jurors should not do the same. **1963** T. PARKER *Unknown Citizen* i. 38 Won't be a tick, don't go away. **1972** J. WILSON *Hide & Seek* i. 18 Just wait till I get these grotty old school things off, Mary. I won't be a tick. **1973** P. WHITE *Eye of Storm* ii. 83 Shan't be a couple of ticks, love. **1983** E. REVELEY *In Good Faith* vi. 104 Just wait a tick while I tell George where we'll be, and then we can go down together.

tick, *sb.*⁴ *colloq.* or *slang*. [app. abbreviation of TICKET *sb.*¹ 7 in the phrase *on the ticket*. Chronology forbids derivation from TICK *v.*¹ 3 or *sb.*³ 3, which has sometimes been conjectured.]

1. Phrases. ***on*** or ***upon*** (†***the***) ***tick***, on credit, on trust (cf. *on ticket*, TICKET *sb.*¹ 7); ***to go on tick*** (also ***go tick***), ***run on***, ***upon*** (†***in***) ***tick***, to buy on credit, run into debt.

1642 *Brit. Mus. Add. MS.* 37999 lf. 66 They would haue .. run on tick with Piggin for inke and songs, rather than haue lost the show of your presence. **1668** DRYDEN *Evening's Love* III. i, Play on tick, and lose the Indies, I'll discharge it all tomorrow. **1672** WYCHERLEY *Love in Wood* III. i, A poor wretch that goes on tick for the paper he writes his lampoons on! **1849** THACKERAY *Pendennis* ii, When he had no funds he went on tick. **1861** HUGHES *Tom Brown at Oxf.* i, 'Going tick' for everything which could by possibility be booked. **1892** STEVENSON *Across the Plains* ii. 100 This villainous habit of living upon tick.

2. Hence, Credit; trust; reputation of solvency and probity.

1668 SEDLEY *Mulb. Gard.* II. ii, I confess my Tick is not good, and I never desire to Game for more than I have about me. **1718** RAMSAY *Christ's Kirk Gr.* III. xiv, Wasted was baith cash and tick. **1788** *Trifler* No. 2. 26 If you can cure him, Dr. Bolus, you shall have the best cheese in my shop, and tick for another. **1894** BLACKMORE *Perlycross* 105 Giving tick unlimited, or even remission of all charges.

3. A debit account; a score, account, reckoning.

1681 PRIDEAUX *Lett.* 21 May (Camden) 83 The Marmayd Tavern is lately broke, and we Christ Church men bear ye blame of it, our ticks, as ye noise of ye town will have it, amounteing to 1500l. **1712** ARBUTHNOT *John Bull* III. vii, Paying ready Money, that the Maids might not run a Tick at the Market. **1755** *Connoisseur* No. 92 He .. had a long tick at the tavern. **1840** J. T. HEWLETT *P. Priggins* xiv, Oh, never mind paying; I've got a tick here. **1862** THACKERAY *Philip* xxxviii, There are some of my college ticks ain't paid now. .. Tailors' ticks, livery-stable ticks.

tick (tɪk), *sb.*⁵ [ad. F. *tic* in same senses: cf. TIC (which retains the Fr. spelling).]

1. The vice or morbid habit in horses called crib-biting or cribbing. Cf. TICK *v.*³

1720 W. GIBSON *Diet. Horses* v. (1731) 83 There is another Vice which some Horses are addicted to .. called the *Tick*.

2. A whim, a fancy; a peculiar habit or notion, an idiosyncrasy.

1900 'SARAH GRAND' *Babs* ix, She's got some tick in her head about being firm with me.

tick, *sb.*⁶ [Echoic.] A local name of the whinchat.

1848 *Zoologist* VI. 2137 The whinchat has the nickname 'utick', or, more simply is sometimes merely a 'tick' from its well-known note.

tick (tɪk), *v.*¹ [f. TICK *sb.*³: cf. Du. *tikken* to pat, tick, Norw. *tikke* to touch lightly.]

1. a. *intr.* To touch or tap a thing or person lightly; *esp.* to bestow light touches or pats by way of caressing; to dally; *esp.* in phr. ***tick and toy***; *fig.* to trifle. *Obs.* exc. *dial.*

1546 J. HEYWOOD *Prov.* (1867) 44 Their tickyng might haue tought Any yonge couple their loue tickes to haue wrought. **1550** LATIMER *Last Serm. bef. Edw. VI* 108 Stand not ticking and toying at the braunches .. but strike at the roote. **1682** BUNYAN *Holy War* xii. 268 His sons began to play his pranks, and to be ticking and toying with the daughters of their lord. **1684** —— *Adv. Sufferers* Wks. (ed. Offor) II. 738 Though they may but tick and toy with thee at first, their sword may reach thy heart-blood at last. *a* **1825** FORBY *Voc. E. Anglia, Tick*, *v.* to toy. Indeed the two are often used together; .. two fond sweethearts are sometimes seen 'ticking and toying'.

†**b.** *trans.* ***to tick up***: to lift smartly, whip up.

1586 WARNER *Alb. Eng.* II. xi, Then ticks he vp her tucked Frocke, nor did Calysto blush.

c. *trans.* = TIG *v.* 2.

1913 A. G. CATON *Romance of Wirral* viii. 69 One out of the one township would tick one out of the other. Then a chase over the country began between these two. **1969** I. & P. OPIE *Children's Games* ii. 64 In the west midlands they 'tick' him, and he is then said to have been 'took', 'tuck', or sometimes 'tucked'. **1981** T. THOMPSON *Edwardian Childhoods* iii. 83 We used to play .. tick... You had to .. tick your neighbour.

2. a. *intr.* Of a clock, watch, etc.: To make the light quick sound described under TICK *sb.*³ 2.

1721, 1746–7 [see TICKING *ppl. a.*¹, *vbl. sb.*¹ 2]. **1775** ASH, *Tick*, to make a small quick noise like that of a watch. **1806** J. TRAIN *Poet. Reveries* 94 (Jam.) When she heard the Dead-watch tick. **1812** H. & J. SMITH *Rej. Addr.*, *Playhouse Mus.*, I heard a trowel tick against a brick. **1820** W. IRVING *Sketch Bk.* I. 249 An old fashioned clock ticked in one corner. **1864** THACKERAY *D. Duval* iv, The watch is ticking on the table before me as I write.

b. *trans.* with various complements: To wear ***away*** or ***out***, bring to an end, in ticking; to throw ***off*** or deliver by ticking (as a telegraph).

c **1870** W. FREELAND in *Whistlebinkie* (1890) II. 322 You [a wagtail] wag and tick the ages out Quicker still and quicker.

1880 Miss Broughton *Sec. Th.* II. iv, More days pass;.. none bringing..much change in..Gillian's life. The clocks tick it monotonously away. **1892** *Leisure Hour* Apr. 411/2 Each slow moment as it ticked itself away was a blow to hope. **1902** *Strand Mag.* Jan. 71/1 The young woman laughed at the answer as it was ticked off to her. **1906** *Daily News* 20 Apr. 6 A telegraphist..ticking out tidings of the affair from its scene.

c. *transf.* (*intr.*) To beat, pulse, throb.

1868 Browning *Ring & Bk.* I. 37 When hearts beat hard, And brains, high-blooded, ticked two centuries since.

d. *intr.* with *over*. Of an internal combustion engine: to run or work with the propeller or gears disengaged, or at a low rate of revolutions; to idle. Also *transf.* and *fig.*, to function (merely); to work or operate continuously, esp. at a low capacity. Chiefly in *pres. pple.*

1916 H. Barber *Aeroplane Speaks* 50 The engine is awake again and slowly ticking over. **1934** *Humorist* 28 July 38/2 How shall I know when the influence is ticking over? **1950** *Sport* 7–11 Apr. 22/4 It is the money in the pocket of the man-in-the-street which keeps sport, the cinemas and the B.B.C. ticking over. **1952** A. Bevan *In Place of Fear* iv. 70 Old out-of-date steel plants were kept ticking over by means of bank overdrafts. **1953** C. A. Lindbergh *Spirit of St. Louis* I. i. 9, I..pull back my throttle until the propellor is just ticking over. **1960** 'M. Cronin' *Begin with Gun* vii. 81 Just the way you said, chief. All ticking over nicely. **1977** F. Webb *Go for Out* v. 97 The car engine fired. He let it tick-over for a moment, then switched it off.

e. *intr.* Of a taximeter (cab): to make a ticking sound while recording the fare due for a period of hire, esp. while waiting; also quasi-*trans.* with complement. With *up*, to record an increasing fare.

1926 W. S. Maugham *Constant Wife* III. 208, I don't want to hurry you, but the taxi is just ticking its head off. **1930** E. P. Oppenheim *Million Pound Deposit* xi. 104 'Got a car?' she enquired. 'No, a taxi, ticking up like blazes.' **1938** E. Bowen *Death of Heart* III. vi. 438 A taxi ticked outside. **1940** Dylan Thomas *Portrait of Artist as Young Dog* 155 The taxi was ticking away, and that worried Beatrice and Betti, and at last the sisters and the cousin and Mary drove together to the church. **1954** T. Rattigan *Sleeping Prince* I. i. 44 *Mary.* The taxi isn't ticking up, is it? *Regent.* No. They will tell us when it arrives. **1966** A. L. Coburn *Autobiogr.* vi. 72 He.. whisked away in the cab which he had kept ticking at the door. **1979** J. Grimond *Memoirs* vi. 93 The General was alarmed to find a taxi waiting, the clock on it ticking up from £15.8.6 to £15.8.9.

f. *intr. fig.* To work, function, operate; ***what makes*** (someone) ***tick***, what motivates (a person). *colloq.*

1931 E. F. Benson *Mapp & Lucia* i. 26, I want to get roused up again and shaken and made to tick. **1947** Auden *Age of Anxiety* (1948) I. 13 They watch others with a covert but passionate curiosity. What makes them tick? **1957** *Listener* 3 Oct. 541/1 Television could show the minds ticking; no need here for those stage directions. **1964** Mrs. L. B. Johnson *White House Diary* 6 Jan. (1970) 31 Then came the big event of the day—the White House staff reception... We would be meeting..everybody who makes the house tick. **1971** A. Price *Alamut Ambush* xii. 151, I still don't quite know what makes Razzak tick. You were going to find out about him. **1980** *Nature* 24 Apr. 695/2 The first step to correct this source of insecurity and fear is to learn what makes it 'tick'.

g. *intr.* with *by* or *away*: (of time, events, etc.) to pass, come to an end. Cf. sense 2 b.

1937 C. Odets *Golden Boy* 42 You don't know what it means to sit around here and watch the months go ticking by! **1974** *Publishers Weekly* 30 Sept. 15 (Advt.), Their father, his own life ticking away after a freak accident, must prepare his children for the grueling battle ahead. **1981** G. Boycott *In Fast Lane* xii. 92 A statement was expected by the hour but each hour ticked away without any news.

3. a. *trans.* To mark (a name, an item in a list, etc.) with a tick; to mark *off* with a tick, as noted, passed, or done with. Also *fig.*; *colloq.* to identify.

1854 Dickens *Hard Times* I. xiv. 108 He was not sure that if he had been required..to tick her off into columns in a parliamentary return, he would have quite known how to divide her. **1861** —— *Gt. Expect.* xxxiv, I compared each with the bill, and ticked it off. **1871** L. Stephen *Playgr. Eur.* (1894) xiii. 323 One more task ticked off from their memorandum book. **1874** Green *Short Hist.* vi. §6. 335 Fragments of his [Thos. Cromwell's] papers still show us with what a business-like brevity he ticked off human lives. **1893** G. Allen *Scallywag* I. 17 Ticking him off on her list. *a* **1912** *Mod.* I ticked him off as soon as I set eyes on him. **1932** A. Huxley *Let.* 1 Oct. (1969) 363 All that stupid unreal rhetoric of fascism... It's beautifully ticked off, in its earlier and different manifestation, by Tolstoy. **1966** N. Mailer *Cannibals & Christians* (1967) I. 38 Could you tick off just a few of the major issues you think will be in the campaign against the Democrats?

b. To mark with small ticks or spots of colour. (But cf. ticked *a.*, ticking *vbl. sb.*[1] 3.)

1910 *19th Cent.* May 915 The white ticked here and there with black.

c. To reprimand or scold. Cf. *to tell off* s.v. tell *v.* 23 d. *colloq.* (orig. *Mil. slang*).

1915 W. Owen *Let.* 2 Nov. (1967) 365 He has been 'ticked-off' four or five times for it; but is not yet shot at dawn. **1936** [see essence *sb.* 8]. **1957** *Listener* 29 Aug. 297/1 'Ticked off' by one of the boys for leaving his car unlocked and complete with ignition key. **1978** K. Amis *Jake's Thing* xvii. 182 He'd ticked Ed off without being told to.

d. To annoy, anger; to dispirit. Cf. ticked *ppl. a.* c. *U.S. slang.*

1975 *Washington Post* 19 Feb. c 12/7 We got hit somethin' fierce. It really ticked me off! We lost everything! **1979** R. L. Simon *Peking Duck* xvi. 117 Shit, it ticks me off I spent all the money on this tour and look what happens.

tick (tɪk), *v.*[2] *colloq.* or *slang.* [f. tick *sb.*[4]]

1. a. *intr.* To 'go on tick' (see tick *sb.*[4] 1); to deal with a tradesman, etc. on credit, to take credit; to run into debt, leave one's debts unpaid.

1648 Winyard *Midsummer-Moon* 6 He must tick with Charon, and have his Epitaph writ in chalk. *a* **1683** Oldham *Poet. Wks.* (1686) 90 Who thither flock to Ghostly Confessor, To clear old debts, and tick with Heaven for more. **1742** Fielding *Miss Lucy in Town* Wks. 1882 X. 310, I gave that sum to my wife..to buy her clothes. I'll take it from her again, and let her tick with the tradesmen.

b. *trans.* To leave (an amount) owing to be entered to one's debit. Also const. *up*.

1674 S. Vincent *Y. Gallant's Acad.* 80 He..tick[s] his reckoning, that he may keep half a Crown in his Pocket. **1712** Mrs. Centlivre *Perplexed Lovers* I. i, The Devil a bottle can I tick because he has forsworn the tavern. *c* **1926** 'Mixer' *Transport Workers' Song Bk.* 42 You've never 'ticked' a penny Whilst you worked. **1947** M. Morris in 'B. James' *Austral. Short Stories* (1963) 355 Best be off soon. No use ticking things up. **1966** 'J. Hackston' *Father clears Out* 114 Going on the slate and ticking up a few rounds of drinks.

2. a. *intr.* To give credit; to supply goods, professional aid, etc. on credit.

1712 Arbuthnot *John Bull* III. viii, The money went to the lawyers; counsel won't tick, Sir. **1721** Amherst *Terræ Fil.* No. 46 (1754) 247 Smarts in Oxford..who cannot afford to be thus fine any longer than their mercers, taylors, shoemakers,..will tick with them. **1840** J. T. Hewlett *P. Priggins* xiii, Sykes is your man—ticks for ever, and never duns.

b. *trans.* To give (a person) credit.

1842 Apperley ('Nimrod') *Life Sportsman* v, He never refused me a tandem, and he ticked me for a terrier at once.

†**tick**, *v.*[3] *Obs. rare.* [f. tick *sb.*[5]] *intr.* Of a horse: To practise crib-biting; = crib *v.* 9.

1720 W. Gibson *Diet. Horses* v. (1731) 84 While they do this, they give a Belch through their throat, which is that which we call *Ticking*. Some Horses Tick upon the Trench, and some..upon any post or rail they can come at..because it is sometimes communicated by example, a Ticker ought therefore to stand by himself.

tick, variant of teak.

tick-a-tick. [f. same source as tick *v.*[1] or *sb.*[3]] An imitation of the sound of a clock or watch; ticking; in quot. 1805, throbbing of the pulse. So **tick-a-tack.** (Cf. tick-tack *sb.*, tick-tick.)

1805 in *Spirit Pub. Jrnls.* IX. 243 Munro shall count of pulse his tick-a-tick. **1883** D. R. Sellars in *Mod. Scot. Poets* VI. 157 Tick-a-tick, tick-a-tick, My old clock's voice I hear. **1898** Doyle in *Speaker* 5 Mar. 298/1 The clock goes tick-a-tack.

ticked (tɪkt), *a.* [f. tick *sb.*[1] + -ed[2]: see quot. 1688, and cf. *flea-bitten*; in mod. use associated with tick *sb.*[3] 3 b.] Of a dog: Having small markings or spots as if bitten by ticks: cf. *tick spot* (tick *sb.*[1] 3); hence of birds, etc.: spotted, dotted.

1688 R. Holme *Armoury* III. 185/2 Ticked, when a Dog is spotted with black on white, or with white spots on black, and the like of the fallow and white, which proceeds from the biteing of Ticks. **1828** Miss Mitford *Village* Ser. III. Introd. 6 The puppy..is fawn-coloured with a dash of white, and promises to be ticked. Are you sportswoman sufficient to know that *ticked* means covered all over with white spots about the size of a pea? **1873** *Spectator* 22 Feb. 239/2 Canaries,..the evenly marked Yellows and Buffs, the 'ticked' or unevenly marked Yellows and Buffs. **1897** *Outing* (U.S.) XXIX. 367/2 Dora [a dog] was so closely ticked that when in a brush-heap checkered black and white, it was almost impossible to see her. **1902** *Fur & Feather* 19 Sept. 207/2 Cats... Female..smooth grey ticked.

ticked (tɪkt), *ppl. a.* [f. tick *sb.*[3] or *v.*[1] + -ed.]

a. Formed or represented by a series of ticks: as 'a ticked line'.

1833 Richardson *Merc. Mar. Arch.* 22 A ticked line through all these spots will form the cant frame. *c* **1850** *Rudim. Navig.* (Weale) 93 A batten..will form the ticked curve A D B.

b. Marked or marked *off* with a tick.

1863 Therry *Australia* (title-p.), A supplementary chapter on Transportation and the Ticked-off System.

c. ***ticked off***: angry, annoyed, 'fed up'. Cf. tick *v.*[1] 3 d. *U.S. slang.*

1959 *Amer. Speech* XXXIV. 156 When one is angry, he's *ticked* or *teed off*. **1972** 'T. Coe' *Don't lie to Me* (1974) v. 54 Now you can see why Grazko is so ticked off. **1977** C. McFadden *Serial* (1978) xxxiii. 72/1 Joan was beginning to get ticked off.

†'**tickel.** *Obs. rare.* [dim. (?) of tick *sb.*[1]: see -el[2].] = tick *sb.*[1] 1.

1577 B. Googe *Heresbach's Husb.* (1586) 143 If they [sheep] be lowsie, or full of tickels, they vse to beate the rootes of Maple, and seething them in water, and opening the wooll with their fingers, they powre the licour. **1741** *Compl. Fam.-Piece* III. 492 To destroy Ticks or Tickels in Sheep.

tickel, -ell, obs. forms of tackle, tickle.

ticken ('tɪk(ə)n). [A dialectal form of ticking *sb.*, the ending app. sometimes associated with -en[4], as in *hempen, woollen*, etc.] = ticking *sb.*, tick *sb.*[2] Also *attrib.*

1701 *Lond. Gaz.* No. 3739/4 Striped Ticken Breeches. **1707** E. Chamberlayne *Pres. St. Eng.* I. iii. (ed. 22) 20 The chief Manufactures are Woollen Cloaths, Cottons, and Ticken. **1769** *De Foe's Tour Gt. Brit.* I. 93 Part of a Street of Booths was taken up with Upholsters Ware; such as Tickens, Sackens,..Rugs, Quilts, &c. **1843** Borrow *Bible in Spain* xi. 78 A long loose tunic or slop, seemingly of coarse ticken.

†'**ticker**[1]. *Obs. rare.* [f. tick *v.*[3] + -er[1].] A cribbing horse, a crib-biter.

1720 [see tick *v.*[3]]. **1796** Lawrence *Treat. Horses* iv. 218 The crib-biter, formerly called a ticker... These horses will stand biting at the rack, or manger, or even at a post, throwing themselves backward, and sucking in the air with greediness.

'**ticker**[2]. *slang.* ? *Obs.* [? f. tick *v.*[2] + -er[1].] ? One who obtains goods 'on tick' and never pays for them; a fraudulent debtor.

1753 (*title*) The Thief-Catcher..Containing an ample Discovery of the..Frauds now practised by Highwaymen, Tickers, Gypsies, Horse-stealers [etc.].

ticker[3] ('tɪkə(r)). [f. tick *v.*[1] + -er[1].]

1. Something that ticks. **a.** The pendulum or escapement of a clock or watch; also (*slang*) a watch (rarely, as in quot. 1910, a clock).

1821 P. Egan *Boxiana* III. 622 To nail the ticker..or to mill the cly. **1828** [Moir] *Mansie Wauch* xxv. (1849) 204 Went to and fro like the ticker of a clock. **1829** Maginn in *Mem. Vidocq* IV. App. 261 Then his ticker I set a-going, With his onions, chain, and key. **1838** Dickens *O. Twist* xviii, If you don't take fogles and tickers..some other cove will. **1888** Rider Haggard *Col. Quaritch* xxviii, I've sold all my jewels down to my ticker. **1910** *Contemp. Rev.* July 36 Secreting a copy of Keats behind the ticker.

b. A telegraphic recording instrument, a tape-machine; a stock-indicator.

1883 F. M. Crawford *Dr. Claudius* (1892) 173 A couple of wheels that unwound..long strips of white paper.. covered with unintelligible signs. 'That is the ticker', said Barker; and he explained how every variation in the market was instantly transmitted to every place of business..in New York. *Ibid.* 174 'It [the ticker] is the pulse of New York', said Barker... 'It tells us everything. Nobody can live here without a ticker'. **1889** *Pall Mall G.* 22 Jan. 7/2 In New York..news agency 'tickers', messenger calls, private as well as public telephones, burglar and fire alarms,..are to be found in all well appointed offices. **1896** *Proc. N. Eng. Hist. Genealog. Soc.* 158 With Edison in 1870 he [F. L. Pope] invented the one-wire printing telegraph or 'ticker'. **1902** *Munsey's Mag.* XXVI. 542/2 Stock and general news tickers..reporting bad news.

c. *slang* (orig. *U.S.*). The heart; also *U.S.* and *Austral.*, courage, spirit, 'guts'. Cf. heart *sb.* 11.

1930 J. Tait *Big House* 7 Because the heart is a 'ticker'. **1935** D. Runyon *Money from Home* 87, I never see a guy with more ticker than Shamus. **1950** *Chambers's Jrnl.* Mar. 149/1 Then I leapt to my feet, and the sight that met my eyes made the old ticker miss more beats than it had done when Martin clamped his gun on the back of my neck. **1979** *Sunday Sun* (Brisbane) 4 Nov. 54/1 The lady has ticker... She didn't opt for the soft life. **1980** J. Cartwright *Horse of Darius* viii. 106 Put something at the bottom about your heart. Say, 'The ticker seems to be a little dodgy at the moment.'

2. Someone who ticks off items in a list, etc.; *spec.* = twitcher 4.

1980 *Guardian* 25 June 12/5 'Twitchers' or 'tickers'—the serious ornithologists' somewhat disparaging term for those bird watchers whose main interest in their hobby is adding new species to their lists. **1982** *Birds* Spring 70/2 Bird tickers contribute little to the well being of the environment and often do little but disturb it.

3. Special Comb.: **ticker tape**, the paper strip on which telegraphic messages are recorded in a tape-machine; this or similar paper material thrown from windows as a form of greeting for a celebrity; also *attrib.*

1902 H. L. Wilson *Spenders* 407 For two days he clung to the ticker tape as to a life line. **1957** *Listener* 10 Oct. 556/1 A traditional ticker-tape reception is to be accorded. **1972** D. E. Westlake *Cops & Robbers* (1973) x. 135 The Wall Street ticker-tape parade is a tradition. **1976** H. Wilson *Governance of Britain* iii. 51 On the afternoon of the second day, the ticker-tape carried a story that President Truman had said that General MacArthur, supreme commander in Korea, had the authority to use the nuclear weapon there, without reference to the President. **1980** L. St. Clair *Obsessions* ii. 48 Tomorrow's ticker-tape welcome to Commander Richard E. Byrd.

ticket ('tɪkɪt), *sb.*[1] Also 6 *Sc.* tikket, -ett, tek-, ticet, tikk-, tykkatt, tik-, tek-, tecat, 6–7 *Sc.* tiket, 6–8 tickett, 7 tik-, tyckett, tiquet, *Sc.* tickket. [In 16th c. (1528) *tiket*, aphetic form of **etiket*, a. obs. F. *etiquet* 'a little note, breuiate, bill, or ticket; especially such a one, as is stucke vp on the gate of a Court, signifying the seisure &c of an inheritance by order of iustice'; or the parallel F. *étiquette* 'a ticket fastened within the mouth of a Lawyers booke bag, and containing the titles of the bookes, [etc.]; any inscription, superscription, title, note, or marke set on th'outside of a thing..; also, a token, billet, or ticket, deliuered for the benefit, or aduantage of him that receiues it' (Cotgr.):—OF. *estiquet(te* (1387 in Hatz.-Darm.), f. *estiquer*, to stick, fix, from Teutonic; ad. OLG. *stek-an* = OHG. *stehhan*, Ger. *stechen* to stick, fix. The primary sense was 'a little note or notice affixed to anything, a label', whence extended as in Cotgrave, and in the senses below. It is notable that our earliest instances are Irish and Scotch; but English examples in some senses appear *c* 1600. See also ETIQUETTE, repr. a later sense of the Fr. word.]

1. a. A short written notice or document; a memorandum, a note, a billet. †***in ticket***, in writing (*Sc.*). *Obs.* exc. as in b, c.

This general sense is present in nearly all those that follow, which differ mainly in respect of the purpose or use to which the written statement or note is put.

1528 in *10th Rep. Hist. MSS. Comm.* App. v. 403 The Bailiefe shall not priese no flesh..unlesse he can get a tiket or bill of the merchanndes hand with the boucher to whom he had sold the same. **1589** *Reg. Privy Council Scot.* IV. 395 To present thair desiris in tikkatt to the Lordis compositouris. *c* **1600** JAS. VI in *3rd Rep. Hist. MSS. Comm.* 396/2 Sicc soumis as the Duike of Lenox hes in tickket. **1622** MALYNES *Anc. Law-Merch.* 411 The Bankers..haue a meeting, and by certaine tickets in writing euerie man doth deliuer his opinion, what the price of Exchange ought to be. **1627** USSHER *Lett.* (1686) 374 The Bishop of Derry hath left with me his Ticket, wherein he undertakes to pay 50£ unto any one of the Captains to whom your Lordship shall appoint. **1638** BAKER tr. *Balzac's Lett.* (vol. II.) 157 If your ticket had overtaken me at Orleans, I had certainly returned to Paris. **1661** PEPYS *Diary* 12 Apr., While I am now writing, comes one with a tickett to invite me to Captain Robert Blake's buriall. **1755** in *Hist. Rev. Pennsylvania* (1759), Every one votes as he pleases, the election being by written tickets, folded up and put in a box. **1760** HOOPER in *Priv. Lett. Ld. Malmesbury* (1870) I. 82 A page delivered him a ticket, importing that something had happened to the (late) King.

b. *spec.* A written tender for ore, made by the smelter. Cf. TICKETING *vbl. sb.* 2. *local.*

1778 PRYCE *Min. Cornub.* 287 The highest bidder or ticket should be the purchaser. *a* **1856** PARIS in Jago *Cornw. Gloss.* (1882) 291 Those [agents] of various Companies..produce a sealed ticket of the price they will give for ore; and he whose ticket is highest, takes the ore. **1870** J. PERCY *Metall. Lead* 496 Each Mine sends samples of its ore to the Smelters in various localities, along with a notice to the effect that tenders or tickets will be received up to a certain day, on which they will be opened and the highest offer accepted.

c. *Stock Exch.*: see quot. 1882–93.

1882–93 BITHELL *Counting-Ho. Dict.* s.v. *Ticket Day*, The day for the passing of tickets between brokers and jobbers, by means of which they learn the amount of stocks and shares they have respectively to deliver or receive on the day following. **1912** *Stock Exchange Ticket*, All rights in respect of this ticket are hereby claimed. *Ibid.*, If this Ticket be divided, insert Number and name of party dividing it, or New Ticket will not be paid for.

2. a. A written notice for public information; formerly, a notice posted in a public place; a placard; now *esp.* a slip of cardboard, metal, paper, etc., attached to an object, and bearing its name, description, price, or the like; a label, show-card.

(This may have been the original sense.)

1567 *Reg. Privy Council Scot.* I. 504 At the occasioun of sum tikkettis affixt on the Tolbuyth dur of Edinburgh, be his lettre sent to hir Majestie, [he] had desyrit James Erll Bothwell, and certane specifiit in the saidis tikkettis, to be apprehendit. *a* **1661** FULLER *Worthies, Buckingham.* (1662) I. 137 Giving notice of the time to his Auditours in a ticket on the School-dores. **1691-** [implied in TICKET *v.* 1]. **1766** in *Westm. Gaz.* 22 Apr. (1910) 2/3 The seats in the House of Commons were begun to be taken for the members by pinning down a ticket with their names in such seats as they chose, which were reserved for them till prayers began. **1804** *Aston's Manch. Guide* 162 A ticket is affixed to each patient's bed, mentioning his name, and that of his physician or surgeon; the time of admission, and the diet ordered for him. **1848** THACKERAY *Van. Fair* xl, The ticket in the window which announced 'Apartments to Let'. **1851** MANTELL *Petrifact.* iv. §1. 365 The same coloured margin as that on the ticket 'Quartz', surrounds every specimen of quartz in that Case.

b. An official documentary notification of an offence, esp. in connection with traffic regulations. Cf. *parking ticket* s.v. PARKING *vbl. sb.* 3 b. orig. *U.S.*

1930 *Outlook* 12 Feb. 249/1 He wrote the young professor a ticket for speeding. **1935** J. O'HARA *Appointment in Samarra* vii. 201 It was two blocks from the hotel, and he might get a ticket for parking, but if he couldn't get the ticket fixed it was worth the two-dollar fine to have things straightened out with Harry. **1956** S. BELLOW *Seize the Day* (1957) ii. 46 Some fool puts advertising leaflets under your windshield wiper and you have heart failure a block away because you think you've got a ticket. **1964** M. BANTON *Policeman in Community* iii. 62 A driver who made an illegal turn against a red light was 'given a ticket' (i.e. a citation was issued against him). **1981** C. DEXTER *Dead of Jericho* xxxii. 176 Cheque for £6, being the penalty fixed for the traffic offence detailed on the ticket.

c. ***big*** (or ***large***) ***ticket item***, something expensive. Cf. *price ticket* s.v. PRICE *sb.* 14. *N. Amer. colloq.*

1970 *Globe & Mail* (Toronto) 25 Sept. B2/2 Buying plans for big ticket items are up since the previous survey in May and June. **1972** *Mod. Law Rev.* XXXV. 20 Legal aid does not seem to have made much difference, except with regard to large ticket items in middle class communities. **1975** *Washington Post* 28 Jan. A19/3 His proposed tax rebate obviously is designed to stimulate consumption of what is known in this week's argot as 'big ticket items' like cars.

3. (More fully ***visiting ticket***.) A visiting-card. Now *Obs.* or *dial.*; also *Anglo-Ind.*

1673 [R. LEIGH] *Transp. Reh.* 142, I shall only therefore leave a ticket for his assignes. **1773** LADY MARY COKE *Jrnl.* 30 Nov., Sir Horatio Mann..has desired me to leave a ticket with the *Grande Maitresse* to-morrow. **1778** MRS. THRALE *Let. to Johnson* 11 Nov., Your visiting ticket has been left very completely in Wales. Was it the fashion to leave cards in Prior's time? **1782** MISS BURNEY *Cecilia* I. iii, Why, a ticket is only a visiting card, with a name upon it; but we all call them tickets now. **1862** THACKERAY *Philip* xiii, Poor dear Mrs. Jones..still calls on the ladies of your family and slips her husband's ticket upon the hall table. **1900** C. LEE *Cynthia* ii. 20 Mr. Gibbs come in just now..and left his ticket over the chimley.

†**4. a.** A writing in which something is certified or authorized; a certificate or voucher; a warrant, licence, permit. Also *fig.*

1529 *Aberdeen Regr.* (1844) I. 126 Conforme to the saidis maisteris of warkis tikatis. **1553** *Exch. Rolls Scotl.* XVIII. 377 Pas this rentell to the lard of Rawelloun..and kep this our tecat for your varrand. *a* **1592** GREENE *Jas. IV*, III. ii, I am the king's purveyor..Here's my ticket, deny it if thou darest. **1615** *Nottingham Rec.* (1889) IV. 334 The Schoole Wardens shall not hencefurth pay or doo any reparacions vpon the howse..without a tyckett for the same vnder Maister Maior's hand. **1641** EVELYN *Diary* 28 Aug., He..then deliver'd me a ticket by virtue whereof I was made excise-free. **1675** V. ALSOP *Anti-sozzo* 554 Paul would have past for a Righteous person upon his producing the Ticket of a blameless Conversation.

b. = CERTIFICATE *sb.* 3 b. *slang. spec.* an airman's or seaman's certificate of qualification.

c **1900** CUTCLIFFE HYNE *Master of Fortune* i. (Cent. Suppl.), I'm Captain of the whole of this show now,..and I intend to be respected as such, and hold a full captain's ticket. **1907** M. ROBERTS *Flying Cloud* 7 Seventeen years before he got his 'ticket', his second greaser's, second mate's ticket, he served in the foc'sle before the mast. **1910** *Flight* 26 Nov. 970/1 He did rolling practice in the morning, straight flights before luncheon, circuits in the afternoon, and qualified for his 'ticket' before dark. **1947** M. LOWRY *Under Volcano* iv. 111 If all goes well I'll be sailing from Vera Cruz in about a week. As quartermaster, you knew I had an A.B.'s ticket, didn't you? **1977** 'E. CRISPIN' *Glimpses of Moon* xiii. 268 George..had eventually got his Mate's ticket.

†**c.** A certificate given to children at Sunday school recording their progress in religious instruction, esp. their readiness for confirmation. *Obs.*

1838 J. ROMILLY *Diary* 18 July (1967) 153 George went.. to St Mary's vestry to be exam^d by Mr Carus:—he only asked him..'the meaning of "Sacrament"', & gave him his ticket. **1879** C. M. YONGE *Burnt Out* i. 11 Mother! mother! where's my ticket bag? Oh! my tickets! my tickets and my Bible and all my prize books!

5. a. A slip, usually of paper or cardboard, bearing the evidence of the holder's title to some service or privilege, to which it admits him; as a ***theatre-ticket***, ***railway*** or ***tramway ticket***, ***insurance-ticket***, ***lottery-ticket***, ***lecture-ticket***, ***platform-ticket***, ***communion-ticket***, ***member's ticket***, ***luncheon-ticket***, ***soup-ticket***, etc. ***meal ticket***: see MEAL *sb.*[2] 4.

1673 *Galston Sess. Rec.* in Edgar *Old Ch. Life Scot.* (1885) 173 *note*, Several hunders of tickets ar distribute. **1682** LUTTRELL *Brief Rel.* (1857) I. 179 The parties were invited by tickets, of which any man might have one for a guiney, it being the price thereof. **1697–8, 1710** [see LOTTERY 5, 1]. **1710** HEARNE *Collect.* (O.H.S.) III. 40 The Tickett of a 1000 lib^s per annum for 32 Years. **1741** WESLEY *Wks.* (1872) I. 301 To those who were sufficiently recommended tickets were given. *a* **1845** HOOD *Double Knock* 11 Sure he has brought me tickets for the play. **1878** F. S. WILLIAMS *Midl. Railw.* 626 The printing of tickets is effected by an ingeniously constructed machine. **1898** FLOR. MONTGOMERY *Tony* 17 You have got your ticket quite safe, haven't you? **1906** *Macm. Mag.* June 625 Subscribers may obtain from the Society supplies of food-tickets, each representing twopennyworth of food. *Mod.* Admission only by ticket.

b. *fig.*

1713 STEELE *Englishman* No. 21. 135 Your Approbation is the Ticket by which they gain Admittance into your Paper. **1784** COWPER *Task* III. 98 Well dressed, well bred, Well equipaged, is ticket good enough, To pass us readily through every door. **1852** THACKERAY *Esmond* II. xi, Within a month after this day, Mr. Addison's ticket had come up a prodigious prize in the lottery of life. **1864** *Soc. Sc. Rev.* I. 409 Men who have robbed employers, or in some other way sullied their fair fame (in cab language 'lost the ticket') but who have not been..prosecuted, easily become cabmen.

c. ***to have tickets on*** (a person or thing), to have a strong liking for; esp. ***to have tickets on oneself*** and varr., to be vain, to be conceited. *Austral. slang.*

1908 W. H. KOEBEL *Anchorage* viii. 140, I don't know whether she's got any tickets on me. **1938** 'R. HYDE' *Nor Years Condemn* ix. 179 You must have tickets on her, Starkie. **1941** K. TENNANT *Battlers* 20 'Arr,' the busker said disgustedly, 'you've got tickets all over yourself.' **1951** CUSACK & JAMES *Come in Spinner* iv. 32 If people have got any tickets on themselves, Blue don't get nowhere with them. **1970** J. HIBBERD *Plays* 227 You're the bastard that's always been smug and had tickets on himself.

d. ***to write one's own ticket***: to be able to stipulate one's own conditions, to be in an advantageous position. *colloq.*

1928 WODEHOUSE *Money for Nothing* v. 94 'But Oil's the stuff, and if you want to part with any of that Silver River of yours, Tom,' he said, 'pass it across this desk and write your own ticket.' **1961** C. COCKBURN *View from West* vii. 75 A prelate in the Archbishop's position can..write his own ticket as to what is in the mind of God. **1981** A. PRICE *Soldier no More* xvii. 246 He could make his own terms, and write his own ticket.

e. A (counterfeit) pass or passport. *slang.*

1969 R. AIRTH *Snatch!* ii. 23 A small but select stock of tickets—Ziggy sold only the best, no London-issued Lithuanians for him. **1973** G. M. FRASER *Flashman at Charge* 164 Russia—where everyone has to show his damned ticket every few miles.

f. A piece of paper impregnated with lysergic acid diethylamide (see quot. 1969). *slang* (chiefly *Austral.*).

1969 *Pix* 19 Apr. 11/1 It [*sc.* LSD] is sold usually in absorbent paper in a portion of 120 micrograms known as a ticket. When you take a ticket you are on a trip.

6. a. A pay-warrant; *esp.* a discharge warrant in which the amount of pay due to a soldier or sailor is certified. Also, any certificate of discharge from service, prison, etc.; freq. in phr. ***to work one's ticket***, to obtain (by scheming) one's discharge.

1596 SPENSER *State Irel.* Wks. (Globe) 657/2 There should be a pay-master appoynted, of speciall trust, which should paye everye man according to his captaynes tickett, and the accompte of the clarke of his bande. **1665** PEPYS *Diary* 5 Dec., Mr. Stevens, who is..paying of seamen of their tickets at Deptford. **1836** MARRYAT *Midsh. Easy* xl, Gascoigne, having received his discharge-ticket, went on board of the Rebiera. **1849** MACAULAY *Hist. Eng.* iii. I. 299 The sailors were paid with so little punctuality that they were glad to find some usurer who would purchase their tickets at forty per cent discount. **1858** SIMMONDS *Dict. Trade*, *Ticket, Seaman's*, a register ticket given to seamen from the General Register and Record office of Seamen. **1869** *Temple Bar* XXV. 217 'Coiners'..as a rule returned to their profession as soon as they got their 'ticket'. Prison is.. a great punishment to such men. **1899** H. WYNDHAM *Queen's Service* xxxiii. 231 It is a comparatively easy matter for a discontented man to 'work his ticket'. **1952** M. ALLINGHAM *Tiger in Smoke* iv. 77 He..attempted to work his ticket to one of these new-style open prisons. **1970** W. SMITH *Gold Mine* xxiv. 56 My boss boy has worked his ticket... Can you see that I get a good man to replace him?

b. Short for TICKET OF LEAVE.

1843 in *Occasional Papers Univ. Sydney Lang. Res. Centre* (1981) No. 19. 61, I have this day given the prisoner named in the margin a pass to proceed to Bathurst as he wished to have his Ticket issued for that District. **1904** A. GRIFFITHS *50 Years Public Service* xii. 169 Blue dress men of exemplary conduct, who were within a year of release on ticket. *Ibid.* xxiii. 354 Then he is on ticket now, and wanted for failing to report himself, no doubt.

†**7. a.** An acknowledgement of indebtedness, an IOU; a promise to pay; a note or memorandum of money or goods received on credit; a debit account, a score; hence phr. ***on, upon (the) ticket***, on credit, on trust. Cf. *on tick* (TICK *sb.*[4] 1).

Prob. the 'ticket' was orig. the 'note of hand' of the borrower, but it might easily be transferred to the statement of the same rendered by the creditor, and thus to 'a tradesman's bill', as suggested by Nares.

c **1600** DAY *Begg. Bednall Gr.* I. i, Your poor Vitler, Sir, where your Lordships men went o' th' ticket. **1632** J. HAYWARD tr. *Biondi's Eromena* 25 The Admirall lost some monies..and then playing on ticket, lost twenty thousand crownes. *a* **1634** RANDOLPH *Hey for Honesty* II. vi, I am resolved to build no more Sconces, but to pay my old tickets. **1643** DAVENANT *Unfort. Lovers* v. i, Let 'em not deal on the Ticket. You know ready Mony makes the Pot boil. **1656** HEYLIN *Surv. France* 147 He that hath..his gold ready shall have a sooner dispatch, then the best Scholar upon ticket.

b. = ***pawn-ticket*** s.v. PAWN *sb.*[2] 4.

1835 DICKENS *Sk. Boz* (1836) 1st Ser. II. 152 You leave your ticket here till you're sober, and send your wife for them two planes. **1863** E. BARLEE in N. Longmate *Hungry Mills* (1978) viii. 112 [He] coomed straight home, made up the fire and burnt every blessed ticket. **1899** KIPLING *Stalky & Co.* 45 Why, last month you and Beetle sold mine [*sc.* a watch]! 'Never got a sniff of any ticket.

8. In politics (orig. U.S.), The list of candidates for election nominated or put forward by a party or faction. Also, the subject or theme of an election campaign; the principles of a political party as presented for an election.

general ticket, a list of candidates put forward for a state or other large political division, equal in number to the entire representation to which the division is entitled, but not chosen to represent each local subdivision. ***mixed, scratch, split, straight ticket***: see quot. 1859.

1711 ISAAC NORRIS in *Penn-Logan Corr.* (1872) II. 438 Chester [Pennsylvania] carried their ticket entire. **1764** (Nov. 3) in *Life* etc. *J. Reed* (1847) I. 36 The Dutch Calvinists and the Presbyterians..to a man assisted the new ticket. **1766** SARAH FRANKLIN *Lett. to B. Franklin* (1859) 191 The old ticket forever! We have it by 34 votes! **1789** *Maryland Jrnl.* 2 Jan. (Thornton *Amer. Gloss.*), The Federal Ticket recommends Mr. Daniel Carroll for the Sixth District; and the opposite Ticket..Mr. Abraham Faw. **1859** BARTLETT *Dict. Amer.* s.v., According to circumstances a man is said to vote the *straight ticket*, i.e. the ticket containing the 'regular nomination' of his party without change; a *scratch ticket*, a ticket from which the names of one or more of the candidates are erased; a *split ticket*, a ticket representing different divisions of his party; or a *mixed ticket*, a ticket in which the nominations of different parties are blended into one. **1861** BLAIR in *Century Mag.* (1889) Sept. 687/2 Chase, who never voted a Democratic ticket in his life. **1863** *Clare Jrnl.* 18 May 2/4 We venture to tell Mr Vereker and Captain Knox that they need not..attempt to go into Parliament on the Conservative 'ticket'. **1888** BRYCE *Amer. Commw.* I. v. 54 Each party runs its list or 'ticket' of thirty presidential electors for that State. **1899** G. B. SHAW *Let.* 30 Dec. (1972) II. 127 Suppose we do run a ticket, how is it to be done? The [Fabian] Society would not vote a ticket except as between two rival tails to the Exec. **1927** A. HUXLEY *Let.* 24 Mar. (1969) 286 How are you going to make a strong working government from a body of people elected on a great variety of different tickets? **1962** *Listener* 22 Mar. 505/2 Lloyd George had actually fought the election of 1929 on the ticket 'We can conquer unemployment'. **1968** *Globe & Mail* (Toronto) 3 Feb. 3/8 Mr. Woodcock..is running on a youth ticket. **1974** *Argus* (Cape Town) 2 Aug. 8/7 In 1966, the then Mayor..had to contest an election... He won by topping the poll on a ticket of two. **1977** *Grimsby Even. Tel.* 14 May 7/4, I did not ask Mr. Muggeridge for permission to put his name on the 'ticket'. **1979** H. KISSINGER *White House Years* ii. 24 Dwight Eisenhower had been elected on the Republican ticket, but he owed little to the Republican Party.

9. *slang.* **a.** The correct thing; what is wanted, expected, or fashionable; esp. in phr. ***that's the ticket.***

Perh. from 8; or, as some have suggested, from the winning ticket in a lottery.

1838 HALIBURTON *Clockm.* Ser. II. xxi. 323 They ought to be hanged, sir, (that's the ticket, and he'd whop the leader). **1843** E. FITZGERALD *Lett.* (1889) I. 117, I fancy that moderately high hills (like these) are the ticket. **1847** *Ibid.* 179 This [idealizing of portraits] is all wrong. Truth is the ticket. **1854** THACKERAY *Newcomes* vii, Somehow she's not—she's not the ticket. **1866** *Routledge's Ev. Boy's Ann.* 411 That's the ticket! That's the winning game.

b. The program or plan of action; that which is to be done; the thing on hand.

1842 MARRYAT *Perc. Keene* xiii, 'Well', said Bob Cross, 'what's the ticket, youngster—are you to go abroad with me?' **1861** C. J. ANDERSSON *Okavango* x. 127 [The lion] suddenly squatted, evidently intending to spring upon me. 'Nay, old fellow', I muttered to myself, 'if that's the ticket, I will be even with you'.

10. *attrib.* and *Comb.* **a.** simple attrib., as ***ticket-box, -pocket, -punch, stub, -system, -tax***; **b.** 'having to do with the selling, etc. of tickets', as ***ticket agency, -agent, booth, -clerk, counter, -guard, hall, machine, -man, -money, -office, -official, -room, wagon, wicket, window***; **c.** 'to which admission is obtained by ticket', as ***ticket-gathering, -meeting***; **d.** obj. and objective genitive, as ***ticket-buyer, -clipper, -collector, -dispenser, -examiner, -holder, punch, -receiver, -seller, -snipper, -writer; ticket-clipping, -collecting, -issuing, -punching, -snatching, -writing.***

1923 *Variety* 1 Nov. 14/3 The ticket agencies took the attraction on the basis of an eight week buy. **1975** R. HOBAN *Turtle Diary* li. 206 A lady from the ticket agency where Miss Neap had worked. **1861** *Richmond* (Va.) *Examiner* 6 Dec. 3/3 Mr. John M. Parker, for several years the efficient General Freight and Ticket Agent of the Richmond and Petersburg railroad. **1976** SCOTT & KOSKI *Walk-In* (1977) I. iii. 20 The ticket agent was..the wrong side of middle age. **1926** E. HEMINGWAY *Sun also Rises* II. xvii. 196 The ticket-booths out in the square. **1981** P. FOX *Satan's Messenger* II. xiv. 108 A ticket booth where he paid 20p to proceed. **1878** F. S. WILLIAMS *Midl. Railw.* 628 The walls of the booking office are provided with ticket-boxes or tubes. **1884** *Law Times* 23 Aug. 301/1 He presented a ticket at the barrier.. saying to the ticket-clipper, 'I want the train for Canonbury'. **1889** KIPLING *From Sea to Sea* (1899) I. xx. 397 The crush of a ticket-collecting. **1897** *Daily News* 6 July 7/3 The minutes consumed in the stoppage for ticket-collecting. **1850** F. B. HEAD in E. R. Pike *Human Doc. Victorian Golden Age* 97 The ticket collector at Camden station. **1977** R. BARNARD *Blood Brotherhood* ii. 18 The Bishop..bestowed his ticket on the ticket-collector. **1862** *Railway Traveller's Handy Bk.* 68 An elderly lady presents herself at the ticket counter. **1962** A. LURIE *Love & Friendship* xv. 293 Will..leaning on the ticket counter below the boarded window. **1977** G. SCOTT *Hot Pursuit* iii. 34 When I got to the airport I..walked over to the ticket counter for my airline. **1976** P. CAVE *High Flying Birds* ii. 17 He turned the handle on his little ticket dispenser and delivered my receipt. **1943** K. TENNANT *Ride on Stranger* v. 48 He dived under the seat as they drew in at a station. The ranks drew together and out-stared the ticket-examiner. **1971** *Sunday Times* (Johannesburg) 28 Mar. 1/4 Mr. Manaka reported this to the ticket examiner. **1969** *Listener* 6 Mar. 295/3 The miners set about the job of unearthing a new ticket hall, designed to become the busiest in London. **1978** H. R. F. KEATING *Long Walk to Wimbledon* x. 165 She made her way..to the station entrance... There were yet more people inside the old ticket hall. **1859** J. ROBERT-HOUDIN *Memoirs* I. viii. 154 Suppose the ticket-holder declined, he was not admitted, and when matters came to that pass, people always paid. **1979** D. HURD *End to Promises* i. 15 To avert violence these rallies were to be for ticket-holders only. **1908** *Westm. Gaz.* 9 May 2/3 In full view of that stern and uncompromising ticket-inspector. **1952** *Evening News* (Port of Spain, Trinidad) 11 Jan. 2/1 Recently 'Tim', a ticket-issuing machine, was introduced to save time and money. **1964** A. WYKES *Gambling* x. 237 Mechanical ticket-issuing machines. **1963** *Times* 24 May (Suppl.) p. vii/4 Another relic of postwar contempt for the passenger is the refusal to install at Underground stations that have automatic ticket machines a single machine that will enable the passenger without small change to obtain it so that he can operate the ticket machine. **1979** *Listener* 18 Oct. 520/1 Ten-pence pieces have to be hoarded for..the ticket machine at St James's Park tube station. **1889** *Spectator* 9 Nov. 634/1 A quasi-public or ticket meeting. **1827** L. T. REDE *Road to Stage* 56, I remember Miss S——, at Drury, from neglecting this precaution, having to pay one hundred and ninety-eight pounds, out of her ticket money alone, to her co-partner in the benefit. **1902** 'MARK TWAIN' in *Harper's Weekly* 6 Dec. 4/2 The man could not get back the ticket-money. **1890** *Daily News* 22 Sept. 2/6 Wire-plyers and pincers, ticket-nippers, wrenches, spanners, &c. **1667** PEPYS *Diary* 4 Jan. (1974) VIII. 4 My lord Brouncker went away after dinner to the Ticket Office. **1835** J. H. INGRAHAM *South-West* I. 221 A noisy crowd was gathering around the ticket-office. **1980** J. O'FAOLAIN *No Country for Young Men* iii. 56 'No point travelling First', the man at the Euston ticket office had advised. **1897** *Pall Mall Mag.* July 384 He put the coin carefully in the ticket-pocket of his overcoat. **1934** L. A. G. STRONG *Corporal Tune* 80 He..then felt in the ticket pocket. **1978** F. MACLEAN *Take Nine Spies* vii. 266 Kim Philby..was..carrying a Soviet Secret Service Cipher in the ticket pocket of his trousers. **1866** *Outing* 7 Feb. 588/1 Conductor..H. is unlocking his little corner cupboard and taking therefrom his punch (I mean ticket-punch, of course). **1978** E. MALPASS *Wind brings up Rain* iv. 39 The girl sat down, fiddling with her ticket punch. **1893** GUNTER *Miss Dividends* 30 The ticket puncher looks astonished for a moment, and then..cries, 'Next!' **1895** *Westm. Gaz.* 10 Oct. 3/1 After the exhausting and exciting struggle in the ticket-room comes the preparation for the settling or pay day. **1844** J. COWELL *Thirty Years passed among Players* iv. 65 John Blake I appointed secretary of the treasury and principal ticket-seller. **1929** 'E. QUEEN' *Roman Hat Mystery* I. iii. 46 You'll be looking for ticket-stubs... Anything resembling half a ticket. **1979** 'M. HEBDEN' *Death set to Music* v. 50 'But I was in Paris!' 'We have only your word and two ticket stubs to confirm that.' **1824** T. CHALMERS in *Mem.* (1851) III. iii. 37 The ticket system operates admirably. **1848–9** CALHOUN *Const. U.S.* Wks. 1863 I. 370 The general ticket system; which has become..the universal mode of appointing electors to choose the President and Vice-President. **1872** O. W. HOLMES *Poet Breakf.-t.* vi, Toll-men and ticket-takers. **1895** *McClure's Mag.* June 55/1 The band-wagons and the chariots, the calliope, the chimes, the oil-tank, the sprinklers, the ticket-wagon..have arrived. **1946** E. O'NEILL *Iceman Cometh* I. 60 Thinking of the old ticket wagon brings those days back. **1892** KIPLING & BALESTIER *Naulahka* v. 49 Tarvin..stepped out through the ticket wicket into Rajputana. **1964** M. LAURENCE *Stone Angel* v. 124 The ticket wicket's straight ahead. You can't miss it. **1865** *Harper's Mag.* May 816/1 [He] asked me to await his return while he crowded to the ticket-window and procured tickets for both. **1979** P. THEROUX *Old Patagonian Express* xiii. 201 Ticket windows were only opened a few hours before the train was to go. **1858** SIMMONDS *Dict. Trade, Ticket-writer*, one who writes or paints showy placards and legible tickets for goods in shop windows. **1922** JOYCE *Ulysses* 471 Export bottlers, fellmongers, ticket-writers, heraldic seal engravers. **1962** E. GODFREY *Retail Selling & Organization* vii. 57 A ticket-writing department, where price tickets for displays and sales placards are written or printed. **1979** *Arizona Daily Star* 8 Apr. D1/1 Tucson travel agents and the University of Arizona are at loggerheads over the proposed creation of a taxpayer-financed ticket-writing service that would handle at least some of the $2 million the school expects to spend on air travel this year.

11. Special Combs.: **ticket barrier**, the point at a railway station beyond which one cannot proceed without a ticket; **ticket benefit**, an entertainment for which special tickets are sold, the proceeds being for the benefit of a particular person or object; **ticket broker** (*U.S.*), a dealer in unexpired or return railway tickets: = *ticket-scalper*; **ticket chopper** (*U.S.*), (*a*) a machine which mutilates used railway tickets deposited in it by passengers; also, a similar device used in cinemas; (*b*) the employee in charge of this machine; **ticket-day**: see quot. 1858; **ticket fine**, a fine imposed on a motorist for violation of traffic regulations by the issuing of a ticket (sense 2 b) rather than by prosecution in court; **ticket-holder**, (*a*) one who holds a ticket of admission, etc.; (*b*) a clip or other device for holding or attaching a ticket or label; †**ticket-jobber**, a jobber of lottery-tickets; **ticket-man**, (*a*) a ticket-holder; *spec.* a seaman who held a certificate exempting him from impressment (now *Hist.*); (*b*) a railway employee who collects or punches tickets; †**ticket-monger**, one who trafficked in the pay-warrants of seamen, giving ready money with a large deduction, and then presenting them for payment; **ticket-night**, a benefit performance: see quot. 1812; **ticket-scalper** (*U.S. slang*), = SCALPER^{2} 2 a, c; so **ticket-scalping**; **ticket-shop**, a shop displaying ticketed goods in the window; **ticket-splitting** *vbl. sb.* and *ppl. a. U.S.*, the practice of voting for candidates of different political parties in the same election; hence **ticket-splitter; ticket tout**, one who obtains tickets for sporting, theatrical, or other events and attempts to resell them at more than the published price. See also TICKET-PORTER.

1939 AUDEN in *New Writing* Spring 2 Crowds round the *ticket barrier. **1981** J. B. HILTON *Surrender Value* iii. 29 The man who stood beyond the ticket barrier, scanning the boat-train. **1898** *Daily News* 30 July 2/4 The London Trades Council has arranged for a *ticket benefit..in aid of the Welsh Miners' Relief Fund. **1902** FARMER & HENLEY *Slang Dict.* s.v. *Scalp, Ticket-scalper*, a *ticket-broker. **1898** C. B. DAVIS *Borderland of Society* 90 She took up with *ticket-chopper on the elevated road. **1905** *Daily Chron.* 8 Mar. 5/4 One hundred students from Columbia University ..volunteered their services to the company as guards and ticket-choppers. **1915** J. B. RATHBUN *Motion Picture Making* 119 To prevent the tickets from being used a second time a 'ticket chopper' may be used that mutilates the ticket in such a way that it is impossible to present it without detection. **1932** Ticket-chopper [see *movie house*]. **1858** SIMMONDS *Dict. Trade*, **Ticket-day*, the day before the settling or pay-day on the Stock Exchange, when the names of bona-fide purchasers are rendered in by one stockbroker to another. **1901** *Westm. Gaz.* 12 Dec. 11/1 The business of ticket-days..is entirely clerical, consisting chiefly..of the passing of buyers' names to sellers of stock or shares. **1959** *Daily Tel.* 18 Dec. 1 (*heading*) *Ticket-fine system for drivers opposed. **1979** T. SKYRME *Changing Image of Magistracy* vii. 80 Further relief came in 1960 with the introduction of 'ticket fines' for illegal parking and some other minor offences. **1877** KNIGHT *Dict. Mech.*, **Ticket-holder*, a device to hold a railway ticket in the hat or to the lappel of the coat; or a tag to a bale or package. **1737** *Gentl. Mag.* VII. 368/1 The Subscriptions being filled, whatever Reflections may be made, they can be of no Prejudice to the Lottery, but only affect the *Ticket-Jobbers. **1803** NELSON in Nicolas *Disp.* (1845) V. 46 This ship is navigated to Portsmouth by *Ticket-men (men who are protected from the impress by some cause or other). **1893** GUNTER *Miss Dividends* 37 Miss Travenion is conducted..past the ticket man at the gate, and on board the train. **1904** *Westm. Gaz.* 5 Feb. 10/1 Admission is by tickets, available for six nights, and..'ticket men' get the first chance of entrance. **1668** PEPYS *Diary* 5 Mar., To answer only one question, touching our paying tickets to *ticket-mongers. **1812** H. & J. SMITH *Rej. Addr.* xv, Some forth on *ticket-nights from tradesmen break, To mar the actor they design to make. [*Note.*] Ticket-nights are those whereon the inferior actors club for a benefit: each distributes as many tickets of admission as he is able among his friends. **1875** W. N. BRYANT *Railroad Guide* 12 It would prevent the deception daily practiced upon this class by *ticket scalpers. **1889** FARMER *Dict. Amer., Ticket scalper*, a speculator in unused railway tickets. **1935** *Time* 26 Aug. 27/1 Comedian Joe Brown..is locked out of his dressing room by mistake on his opening night and is compelled to pay $20 to a ticket scalper to get into the theatre in time for his entrance cue. **1892** *Pall Mall G.* 1 Nov. 2/1 (Farmer) **Ticket-scalping*..has reference to the transferability or otherwise of tickets rather than to their date of expiry. **1851** MAYHEW *Lond. Labour* I. 380/2 A thoroughfare full of *ticket-shops. **1972** DE VRIES & TARRANCE *Ticket-Splitter* i. 22 We will examine the way the *ticket splitter makes up his mind about politics and government. **1980** *Washington Star* 10 Oct. A-6 The area also has been very strong for Republican Gov. William Milliken, a moderate who has been elected three times by ticket splitters. **1957** *Amer. Pol. Sci. Rev.* LI. 308 (*heading*) Other motives and *ticket splitting. **1972** *Times* 13 Oct. 9/3 Mr Nixon..is obviously complacent at the prospect of ticket-splitting, under which Democrats are being invited to salve their consciences by voting for their local party candidates while giving their presidential vote to Mr Nixon. **1976** *National Observer* (U.S.) 22 May 5/1 This is the damndest crossover, ticket-splitting state in the nation. **1950** *Sport* 24–30 Mar. 20/4 A final word about the *ticket touts. **1982** *Times* 17 Mar. 11/2 *Cats*..is still giving the ticket touts an excellent living.

ticket ('tɪkɪt), *sb.*^{2} *dial.* [app. f. TICK *sb.*^{3} + -ET^{1}.] A minute quantity or part.

1634 *Reg. Privy Council Scotl.* V. 414 Seatoun threatned the notar, avowing to take a ticket aff his haffet if he gave out any instrument in this mater. **1731** FIELDING *Lottery* iii, I have not got it as yet—but, upon my shoul, I was within a ticket of it. **1904** in *Eng. Dial. Dict.* s.v., (Somerset) A donkey load would be called 'just a little ticket'.

ticket ('tɪkɪt), *v.* [f. TICKET *sb.*^{1}]

1. a. *trans.* To attach a ticket to; to mark with a ticket indicating the value, contents, description, origin, destination, or the like; to distinguish by means of a ticket; to label. Chiefly in *pa. pple.*

1611 [see *ticketed* below]. **1691** *Lond. Gaz.* No. 2624/4 There being one of the said Bags missing, Ticketed 68l. 3s. 6d. **1719** LONDON & WISE *Compl. Gard.* 107 Plant these Trees in Baskets, well tickketted, or..set down carefully in our Book. **1770** *Chron.* in *Ann. Reg.* 135/2 The post-boy.. was robbed..of the mail..containing two bags, ticketed Newcastle, and Newcastle and York. **1810** *Sporting Mag.* XXXVI. 128 Pictures which are sold during the exhibition will be ticketed as such. **1839** DARWIN *Voy. Nat.* xvii. (1852) 395 Of those [specimens] which were ticketed with their locality, not one was common to any two of the Islands.

b. *fig.* To describe or mark as by a ticket; to designate, characterize, set down (*as* so and so): = LABEL *v.* b.

1654 WHITLOCK *Zootomia* 435, I make no doubt but confident forwardnesse, and undertakings, would Ticket men passable..that could scarce tell which end of their Bibles to hold uppermost. **1713** BENTLEY *Rem. Disc. Free-think.* §40. II. 16 A few glittering Prizes..among an infinity of Blanks, drew troops of Adventurers; who, if the whole Fund had been equally ticketed, would never have come in. **1856** T. A. TROLLOPE *Girlh. Cath. de Medici* i. 10 We find certain characters ticketed from age to age in history as monsters of atrocity. **1884** *Chr. Commw.* 14 Feb. 424/2 There is a present fashion of ticketing all outspoken religion as sham talk.

2. To furnish with a ticket; to issue a railway or other travelling ticket to; to 'book'; also *absol.*, to issue tickets. *U.S.*

1842 LONGF. in *Life* (1891) I. 415 To borrow the expression of a fellow-traveller, we were 'ticketed through to the depot'. **1852** *Boston* (Mass.) *Traveller* 24 Dec. 3/2 Passengers ticketed through from New York to Cincinnati. **1882** *Kansas City Jrnl.* 19 Feb. Advt., We ticket directly to every place of importance.

3. *intr.* To make a tender *for* tin or copper ore by means of a 'ticket' or written tender: see TICKET *sb.*^{1} 1 b, TICKETING *vbl. sb.* 2. *local.*

1778 PRYCE *Min. Cornub.* 287 Three hundred tons of Ore belonging to the same Mine were to be ticketed for on a day appointed.

4. *trans.* To attach a parking ticket, etc. to (a vehicle); to serve with a ticket for a traffic or other offence. *U.S.*

1955 V. NABOKOV *Lolita* (1959) I. xxiii. 97, I should explain that the prompt appearance of the patrolmen..was due to their having been ticketing the illegally parked cars in a cross lane two blocks down the grade. **1966** *Cavalier Daily* (Charlottesville, Va.) 8 Feb. 2/1 If you don't park next to the curb, you're still liable to be ticketed. **1976** *Billings* (Montana) *Gaz.* 30 June 1-B/3 Two dog owners who were ticketed by animal wardens because their animals were allegedly involved in a wading pool melee are planning to fight back. **1979** R. BALLANTINE *Richard's Bicycle Bk.* (rev. ed.) I. vii. 122 Cyclists have been ticketed for causing an obstruction by riding too far to the right.

Hence '**ticketed** *ppl. a.*, marked with or bearing a ticket or tickets.

1611 COTGR., *Tiqueté*, ticketted, or appointed by ticket. **1827** SCOTT *Chron. Canongate* vi, A hackney coach.. that obscure vehicle, which was not permitted to degrade with its ticketed presence the dignity of Baliol's Lodging. **1828** DOBIE *Mem. W. Wilson of Crummock* (1896) 100 On the ball night she was my ticketed companion. **1836–9** DICKENS *Sk. Boz, Hor. Sparkins*, A dirty-looking ticketed linen-draper's shop, with goods of all kinds, and labels of all sorts and sizes, in the window.

ticketer (ˈtɪkɪtə(r)). [f. TICKET *sb.*[1] or *v.* + -ER[1].] One who tickets; one who has a ticket.

1778 PRYCE *Min. Cornub.* 288 One of the ticketers present produced his ticket before all the company, whose offer was nine pounds seventeen shillings per ton [cf. TICKETING 2]. **1865** G. MEREDITH *Rhoda Fleming* xii, I paid, and you're a ticketer... These chaps get tickets given 'm.

ticketing (ˈtɪkɪtɪŋ), *vbl. sb.* [f. TICKET *v.* + -ING[1].] The action of TICKET *v.*

1. a. Marking with or as with a ticket; labelling.

1844 G. DODD *Textile Manuf.* vii. 228 After a process of rolling, pressing, ticketing, &c., the article is finished. **1866** DK. ARGYLL *Reign Law* i. (ed. 4) 4 The mere ticketing and orderly assortment of external facts.

b. The buying and selling of (airline) tickets. Freq. *attrib.*

1962 *Flight International* LXXXII. 382/2 If after expiry of a 'ticketing time limit' a provisional reservation is cancelled by a passenger, his booking deposit.. must be forfeited. **1972** *Accountant* 28 Sept. 386/2 An International airline employing very many highly-qualified people—engineers, cabin-crew, pilots, ticketing and reservation clerks. **1977** 'O. JACKS' *Autumn Heroes* iii. 48 'Get the ticketing under way. Sixty-two.'..'Can you get me sixty-two air tickets?' **1983** *Jetaway* (Air New Zealand) Sept.–Oct. 26 (*caption*) Artist's impression of the completed 'ticketing street' in the West Terminal at Los Angeles International Airport.

2. Bidding by a 'ticket' or written tender; with *pl.* a sale of ore at which the bids are made in this way. *local.*

1778 PRYCE *Min. Cornub.* 288 The present mode of ticketing for Copper Ores. **1854** C. S. EDSALL (*title*) Copper Ore Tables,..with the method of conducting the Ticketings. **1912** *Financial Times* 30 Apr., Redruth Tin Ticketing.

3. *attrib.* (chiefly in sense 2).

1778 PRYCE *Min. Cornub.* 288 On this ticketing day a dinner almost equal to a city feast is provided at the expence of the Mines. *Ibid.*, A duplicate of a ticketing paper. **1839** DE LA BECHE *Rep. Geol. Cornwall*, etc. xv. 541 The copper-ore sales, or ticketing-days, as they are termed. **1905** HOLMAN-HUNT *Pre-Raphaelitism* I. 9 Securing from the 'ticketing room' a print of Britannia.

ticketless (ˈtɪkɪtlɪs), *a.* [f. TICKET *sb.*[1] + -LESS.] Having no ticket; without a ticket of admission, a railway ticket, etc.

1868 *Daily News* 6 July, Regulations which kept the ticketless public at a distance. **1946** F. WYLIE *Let.* 31 Aug. in Mansergh & Moon *Transfer of Power* (1979) VIII. 369 Simultaneously a regular campaign of ticketless travel on the railways will be started. **1979** P. NIHALANI et al. *Indian & Brit. English* I. 179, 2500 cases of ticketless travel and unbooked luggage were reported last month by the railway authorities.

ticket of leave. a. A ticket or document giving leave or permission; an order, a permit (*rare*). In specific use, a licence to be at large after the expiration of part of the sentence, formerly granted to convicts in the Australian colonies; after 1840, the usual colloquial name for an 'order of licence' giving a convict his liberty under certain restrictions before his sentence has expired, the proportion remitted being dependent on his conduct and industry. Now *Hist.*

1732 *Acc. Workhouses* 17 That no person presume to go out of the street door without a Ticket of Leave, to return in good order. **1801** *Hist. Rec. New S. Wales* (1896) IV. 300 All prisoners whose terms of transportation is [*sic*] not expired and are off the stores, or those with settlers, are to attend at the Secretary's office at Sydney.. to receive their tickets of leave. **1828** P. CUNNINGHAM *N.S. Wales* (ed. 3) II. 293 Whether in depriving an individual of a ticket of leave, or sentencing him to a penal gang, the periods should be always limited. **1843** *Act 6 & 7 Vict.* c. 7 (*title*) An Act to amend the Law affecting transported Convicts with respect to Pardons and Tickets of Leave. *Ibid.*, Permission to such Felons.. to employ themselves for their own Benefit (which Permissions are usually called and known by the Name of Tickets of Leave). **1876** *Yale Rev.* XXV. 769 Those [slaves] who went visiting, came for a 'ticket of leave'.. stating in a line or two the name of the person, and where he was going. **1895** *Times* 16 Jan. 14/5 A long list of former convictions, beginning in 1852, was proved against the prisoner... He was now on 'ticket-of-leave'. **1917** 'CONTACT' *Airman's Outings* v. 111 On the last occasion when I was let loose from the front on ticket-of-leave, I added twenty-four hours to my Blighty period. **1918** [see COUPON 4].

b. *attrib.* or *Comb.* (hyphened), as ***ticket-of-leave holder, man, woman.***

1807 *Hist. Rec. New S. Wales* (1898) VI. 292 A considerable injury to the colony had crept in: that of ticket-of leave [hyphenation *sic*] men—men that were taken off the stores, and permitted to work for themselves. **1837** J. D. LANG *N.S. Wales* I. 411 The overseer, on well-regulated farms, is generally a ticket-of-leave man or emancipated convict. *Ibid.* II. 19 A ticket-of-leave holder.. is confined to a particular district, and is liable to lose his ticket for various petty misdemeanours. **1862** *Lond. Rev.* 30 Aug. 178 A great proportion of these crimes were committed by 'Ticket-of-leave Men'. **1871** *Daily News* 25 July, In one of the.. most fashionable districts of London many hundreds of domestic servants are ticket-of-leave women.

Hence **ˌticket-of-ˈleaver**, a ticket-of-leave man; **ˌticket-of-ˈleavism** (*nonce-wd.*), the system or operation of tickets of leave.

1852 MUNDY *Our Antipodes* v. (1855) 107 The overseer.. may be a hireling convict—emancipist, expirer, or ticket-of-leaver. **1857** *Tait's Mag.* XXIV. 41 The atmosphere itself was redolent of ticket-of-leaveism. **1858** R. S. SURTEES *Ask Mamma* xlv, The oft-disappointed ticket-of-leaver was again installed in a butler's pantry.

ˈticket-ˌporter.

1. A member of a body of porters in the City of London who were licensed by the Corporation; orig. called *street-porters*, and distinct from the TACKLE-HOUSE *porters* of the twelve great Merchant Companies; in later times the two classes of porters were united in the *Society of the Tackle-house and Ticket Porters*. Now *Hist.*

1646 [see TACKLE-HOUSE b] The Ticket-Porters, otherwise called the Street-Porters of this City. **1770** *New Guide London* 257 Ticket-porters are all freemen, and their business is to load and ship off goods exported or imported. Also to house merchants' goods, metals, &c. **1800** COLQUHOUN *Comm. Thames* 328 The Ticket-Porters are persons appointed by the City of London... They give Security in 100*l.* for Fidelity, and have their Names and Numbers on a Metal Badge. **1833** (Dec. 12) *Rep. Court Com. Council* (London) *on Porters* 4 The Ticket Porters.. are entitled to the work or labour of unshipping, landing, carrying, loading, and housing all goods, wares and merchandize imported into the port of London from the several places mentioned in the Act of Common Council, 27th March, 1798, and also of shipping all goods, wares, and merchandize; and they are likewise entitled, by custom and usage, to perform the work at the public markets of this City. *Ibid.*, We were.. attended.. by the Rulers and Registers of the Society of Tackle-house and Ticket Porters. **1848** DICKENS *Dombey* xiii, The ticket-porter.. always ran officiously before to open Mr. Dombey's office-door.

2. A (railway) porter who collects tickets.

1852 *Aquatic Notes, Camb.* 80 A rush of men takes place from every carriage, and past the ticket-porter.

tickety-boo (ˌtɪkətɪˈbuː), *a. colloq.* Also **tickety-boo, tiggity-boo**, etc. [Etym. obscure: perh. f. Hindi *ṭhīk hai* all right; cf. also TICKET *sb.*[1] 9.] In order, correct, satisfactory.

1939 N. STREATFEILD *Luke* 186 Things ought to have shaped right... Couldn't have looked more tickety-boo. **1947** *Amer. N. & Q.* Sept. 94/1 Lord Mountbatten, now Governor General of India, is credited in the *New York Times Magazine* (June 22, 1947, p. 45) with 'giving currency' to the phrase 'tickety-boo' (or 'tiggerty-boo'). This Royal Navy term for 'okay' is derived from the Hindustani. **1954** 'G. CARR' *Death under Snowdon* xi. 143 'All tiggity-boo.' 'Tiggity——? Never mind, Sergeant. Go on.' 'Everything's jake, sir.' **1957** J. BRAINE *Room at Top* xxi. 179 Everything was tickety-boo again. **1960** D. FEARON *Murder-on-Thames* xviii. 168 'I never killed Mr. Evans either'. 'Then that's all ticketty-boo.' **1977** *Listener* 7 Apr. 450/3 Attempting vainly to get everything tickety-boo for the Big Day. **1981** S. RUSHDIE *Midnight's Children* I. 97 Everything's in fine fettle, don't you agree? Tickety-boo, we used to say.

tick-hole. [? f. TICK *sb.*[3] + HOLE *sb.*] A cavity in nodular stone, usually lined with a crystalline incrustation.

1829 *Glover's Hist. Derby* I. 92 At the lime-quarries, Milltown, Ashover, cavities or tick-holes are frequent in the .. limestone rock,.. lined with.. quartz crystals. **1881** in RAYMOND *Mining Gloss.*

tickil, obs. form of TICKLE *a.* and *v.*

ticking (ˈtɪkɪŋ), *sb.* Forms: α. 7 *Sc.* tyking, 7–8 tiking; β. 7–8 tickin, 7– ticking. See also TICKEN. [f. TICK *sb.*[2] + -ING[1].] The material of which bed-ticks are made: see TICK *sb.*[2]

α. **1649** *Caldwell Pap.* (Maitl. Cl.) I. 102 For ane new sheitt of tyking to ye lard's horss 1. 16. 0. **1674** JEAKE *Arith.* (1696) 65 In 1 Hundred of Tiking and Twill of Scotland, 120 Ells. **1726** SWIFT *Gulliver* IV. x, I had beaten hemp,.. and made of it a sort of tiking: This I filled with.. feathers.

β. *a* **1661** FULLER *Worthies, Lancs.* (1662) II. 106 It will be the safest way to wrap them all together in some Manchester-Tickin. **1815** J. SMITH *Panorama Sc. & Art* II. 735 Oil-paintings are generally executed on canvass... A kind of ticking has lately been much used. **1883** *Blackw. Mag.* Aug. 192 She wore over her gown of ticking a great apron of grey stuff.

b. Rarely applied to the tick or cover itself.

1683 TRYON *Way to Health* 595 You may have Flock-Beds, with Canvas-Tickings. **1833** MARRYAT *P. Simple* xxi, He.. put it.. away in the ticking of his bed.

c. *attrib.* Of the nature of or made of ticking.

1676 COVEL in *Early Voy. Levant* (Hakl. Soc.) 164 A bed .. of twilt or ticking sattin. **1682** WHELER *Journ. Greece* I. 16 Course Ticking-Cloth, well quilted with Wool. **1721** MRS. CENTLIVRE *Artifice* III, The dirtiest Trollup.. must have her Top-knot and Tickin-shoes. **1756** C. LUCAS *Ess. Waters* I. 229 A sliding seat, with a thin ticking bottom.

ticking (ˈtɪkɪŋ), *vbl. sb.*[1] [f. TICK *v.*[1] + -ING[1].]

1. Touching lightly or wantonly; dallying: see TICK *v.*[1] 1. *Obs.* exc. *dial.*

1546 J. HEYWOOD *Prov.* (1867) 58 Leaue lewde tickyng. **1611** COTGR., *Amourettes*, wanton loue-toyes, ticking, ticklings, daliances.

2. a. The beating sound of a clock or watch, or any similar sound: see TICK *v.*[1] 2, TICK *sb.*[3] 2.

1746–7 HERVEY *Medit.* (1767) II. 23 The Ticking of my Watch is distinctly heard. **1827** F. COOPER *Prairie* i, The ticking of gun-locks was heard. **1848** DICKENS *Dombey* xliii, She could.. count the ticking of the clock.

b. *transf.* A telegraphic message: cf. TICKER[3] b.

1888 M. ARNOLD in *19th Cent.* Apr. 490, I opened a Boston newspaper and came upon a column headed 'Tickings'. By tickings we are to understand news conveyed through the tickings of the telegraph.

3. Small spots or points of colour forming the marking of an animal.

This use may have arisen from TICKED *a.* by association with TICK *sb.*[3] 3, 3 b and TICK *v.*[1] 3.

1885 *Bazaar* 30 Mar. 1269/2 Belgian hare buck, good in colour and ticking. **1886** *Field* 20 Mar. 340/2 Interspersed with a profusion of longer black hairs, giving the appearance known as 'ticking'.

4. ***ticking-off***, a scolding or reprimand: see TICK *v.*[1] 3 c. Cf. *telling-off* s.v. TELLING *vbl. sb.* 2 c.

1950 J. CANNAN *Murder Included* ii. 16 Iona's a little beast, but she knows how to take a ticking off—she's learned that at St. Olaf's. **1960** *News Chron.* 23 July 5/5 The machine shop inspector.. expects a 'ticking-off' when he goes back to work. **1977** E. AMBLER *Send no More Roses* ii. 36, I gave him a ticking-off. Not that he cared. Too clever by half.

5. ***ticking-over***: the idling of an engine; also *transf.* See TICK *v.*[1] 2 d.

1972 J. WAINWRIGHT *Requiem for Loser* i. 9 Originally the talk.. had been meant as the first of a quartet of 'stop gap' lectures.., a ticking-over of the association's activities until the end of the holiday season. **1973** —— *Pride of Pigs* 88 The youth.. revved the engine, then quietened it down to the soft ticking-over.

ˈticking, *vbl. sb.*[2] *colloq.* or *slang.* [f. TICK *v.*[2] + -ING[1].] The action of TICK *v.*[2]; the taking of goods on 'tick' or credit.

1748 WARTON *Oxford Ale* 49 Hail, Ticking! surest guardian of distress! Beneath thy shelter pennyless I quaff The cheerful cup.

ˈticking, *ppl. a.*[1] [f. TICK *v.*[1] + -ING[2].]

1. That ticks, as a clock, etc.; making or characterized by a succession of ticks.

1566 in Peacock *Eng. Ch. Furniture* (1866) 116 A hammes hudde [= amice hood] and tickynge belle. **1721** BRADLEY *Philos. Acc. Wks. Nat.* 154 That ticking Noise, which is commonly called a Death-Watch.

2. ***ticking-over***: (merely) working or functioning; unproductive. See TICK *v.*[1] 2 d.

1960 *Guardian* 31 Dec. 6/3 It seemed to be rather a ticking-over year so far as new buildings.. were concerned. **1963** *Times* 13 June 8/6 As long as we have a 'ticking over' laity who are still living in the Victorian era and don't want to be shaken out of their complacency, so long will the ministry remain a reflection of the body of laity from which they came. **1974** 'J. ROSS' *Burning of Billy Toober* xvi. 149 Waiting like a ticking-over computer to be programmed.

3. Special collocation: **ticking bomb** = *time bomb* s.v. TIME *sb.* 59 a.

1960 WODEHOUSE *Jeeves in Offing* i. 13 But while equipped with eyes like twin stars.. B. Wickham had also the disposition and general outlook on life of a ticking bomb. **1980** G. M. FRASER *Mr American* II. xvii. 322 Mr Asquith.. would find himself out of office, and the ticking bomb of Ireland could be hastily passed to his successor.

ˈticking, *ppl. a.*[2] *colloq.* or *slang.* [f. TICK *v.*[2] + -ING[2].] That 'ticks' or 'goes on tick'; that gives 'tick' or credit; dealing on credit, running into debt.

1673 WYCHERLEY *Gentl. Dancing-Master* Prol., Ready to engage Against the flouting, ticking gentry who Citizen, player, poet, would undo.

ticklace, var. TICKLE-ACE.

tickle (ˈtɪk(ə)l), *sb.*[1] [Generally held to be derived from TICKLE *a.* or *v.*, and so to go with TICKLE *sb.*[2] (see quot. 1908); but some would identify it with Eng. dial. *stickle* 'a rapid shallow place in a river'. In Nova Scotia also *tittle.*] A name given on the coasts of Newfoundland and Labrador to a narrow difficult strait or passage.

1770 *Chart S.E. Part Newfoundland*, [A locality at the head of St. Mary's Bay marked] Tickles. **1792** G. CARTWRIGHT *Jrnl. Labrador* Gloss., *Tickle*, a passage between the continent and an island, or between two islands, when it is of no great width. **1837** *New Sailing Direct. Newf.* (ed. 3) 25 *note*, The word *Tickle* is a local name, in common use at Newfoundland, and signifies a passage between islands or rocks. **1861** L. L. NOBLE *Icebergs* 277 No sooner were we clear of the 'tickle', or narrows, than 'Iceberg ahead!'—'Ice on the lee bow!' was cried by the man forward. **1868** *Admiralty Chart* No. 225 (Labrador), Indian Tickle. **1871** *Ibid.* No. 291 (Newf.), Change Island Tickles... Stag Harbour Tickle. **1881** *Standard* 15 July 4/8 In many of the 'tickles', 'guts', 'runs', 'sounds',.. and inlets there are still to be found tiny villages which date from those old Acadian times. **1905** *Daily Chron.* 28 Apr. 3/3 See him clinging to the bowsprit, conning the vessel through tortuous 'tickles'. **1908** ABP. HOWLEY in *Newfoundld. Quarterly* Mar. 2 The Tickle... It has always been supposed that this name is a plain English word, implying a passage of some danger, so that it is a 'ticklish' matter to get safe through.

tickle (ˈtɪk(ə)l), *sb.*[2] [f. TICKLE *v.*]

1. An act of tickling, in various senses of the vb.; a touch that tickles; a tickling sensation; a tickled or pleasantly excited feeling.

1801 in *Spirit Pub. Jrnls.* IX. 376, I want you to give those dogs yonder a tickle, *en passant*. **1872** BLACKMORE *Maid of Sker* v, I gave her [a child] a little tickle; and verily she began to laugh. **1880** MRS. WHITNEY *Odd or Even* ix, And vibrant with an inward tickle. **1907** *Daily Chron.* 9 Dec. 4/7 The dinner was a tickle of the palate. *Mod.* (*Yorksh. saying*) To have 'tickles in the feet', said of one given to wandering, who will not settle to any useful work.

2. *Criminals' slang.* A successful deal or crime. Cf. TICKLE *v.* 6 e.

1938 F. D. SHARPE *Sharpe of Flying Squad* 333 *Tickle*, a successful deal. **1955** D. WEBB *Deadline for Crime* i. 13 If there is a good tickle, say for as much as £10,000, which is as much as anyone got from any job, it soon goes to the birds, ..the bookmakers, the hangers-on. **1960** [see GRAFT *v.*[4]]. **1979** 'P. O'CONNOR' *Into Strong City* I. xiv. 48 Keeps me going till the big tickle comes along.

tickle ('tɪk(ə)l), *a.* (*adv.*) Forms: see the verb; also 4–5 **tikil, -ul, tekil,** 5 **tekyl, -el, tykell,** 6 **tyckyll,** 6–7 **tickell,** 8 *dial.* **tikkle.** [Goes with TICKLE *v.*: the use of the vb.-stem as adj. is unusual; but cf. KITTLE *a.* beside KITTLE *v.*]

†**1.** (Sense uncertain: ? Threatening or in danger to fall. Cf. 6.) *Obs.*

c **1325** *Body & Soul* in *Map's Poems* (Camden) 346 þou hauest y-liued to longe, wo wruth the so suykel!.. Pynen harde ant stronge to þe bueþ nou ful tykel.

†**2.** Pleasantly stirred or excited. (Cf. TICKLE *v.* 1.) *Obs.*

c **1330** R. BRUNNE *Chron. Wace* (Rolls) 13413 When y byþenke on ȝoure godnesse.. Ffor þat ioye myn herte ys tykel.

†**3.** Easily moved to feeling or action; easily affected in any way; not firm or steadfast; loose; also, susceptible to tickling, easily tickled or tingled. *tickle credit*, ready or facile trust or belief; credulity. *Obs.*

1377 LANGL. *P. Pl.* B. (Crowley) v. 166 They are ticle of her tonges, & muste al secretes tel. *c* **1530** H. RHODES *Bk. Nurture* 695 Some men be tickle of tongue, and play the blabs by kynde. **1533** T. HEYWOOD *Play of Love* Cj, The paps so small And rounde with all The wast not myckyll But it was tyckyll. **1553** T. WILSON *Rhet.* (1580) 3 Euen these auncient Preachers must now and then plaie the fooles in the pulpit, to serue the tickle eares of their fletyng audience. **1563** *Mirr. Mag.*, *Hastings* xlii, Of tyckle credyte ne had ben the mischiefe. *Ibid.* lxxvii, Flye tickle credyte, shonne alyke distrust.

†**b.** With reference to incontinency. *Obs.*

1362 LANGL. *P. Pl.* A. III. 126 Heo is Tikel of hire Tayl, Talewys of hire tonge, As Comuyn as þe Cart-wei to knaues and to alle. *c* **1475** *Songs & Carols 15th C.* (Warton Cl.) 27 Under the tayl they ben ful tekyl. **1604** W. TERILO *Fr. Bacon's Proph.* 228 in Hazl. *E.P.P.* IV. 276 Wickednes was loath'd so much, That no man lov'd the tickle tuch.

†**4.** Having the quality of tickling, tickly. *Obs.* (Quots. *c* 1440, 1570 perh. belong here.)

[*c* **1440** *Promp. Parv.* 493/2 Tykel, *titillosus.* **1570** LEVINS *Manip.* 129/14 Tickil, *titillenus, -na.*] **1593** B. BARNES *Parthenophil, Madrigal* xvi, Soft things whose touch is tickle to the mind, Give no like touch, all joys in one to wrap.

5. Not to be depended upon; uncertain (in fact, action, duration, etc.); unreliable; changeable, inconstant, capricious, fickle, 'kittle'. Now *dial.*

13.. *E.E. Allit. P.* B. 655 May þou traw for tykel þat þou tonne moȝtez. *c* **1386** CHAUCER *Miller's T.* 242 This world is now ful tikel [*v.rr.* tekyl, -el, tikil, tykell] sikerly. **1537** *St. Papers Hen. VIII*, I. 531, I assure your Lordeship the people be very tykell. **1566** PAINTER *Pal. Pleas.* I. 58 Holde fast thy fortune, for she is tickle and can not be holden against her will. **1670** COTTON *Espernon* III. XII. 368 His sons ..were best acquainted with his tickle & impatient humour. **1737** J. BROADHEAD in *N. & Q.* (1895) 8th Ser. VII. 405/1 A pretty deal of Rain in some places westward, Mad[e] Harvest rather Tickle. **1795** *Chester Chron.* 27 Mar. (E.D.D.), So tikkle as times ar. **1888** DOUGHTY *Arabia Deserta* II. 158 He must learn the English tongue.. who can foresee the years to come, this world is so tickle.

6. In unstable equilibrium, easily upset or overthrown, insecure, tottering, crazy; also, easily set in motion or action; nicely poised; delicate, sensitive. Now *dial.* † *tickle of the sear*: see SEAR *sb.*[1] 1 b.

1515 in Foxe *A. & M.* (1583) 809/2 A stoole, which stoole stood vpon a bolster of a bed, so tickle, that any manne or beaste might not touch it so litle, but it was ready to fall. **1555** *Act 2 & 3 Phil. & Mary* c. 16 §2 Boates.. so shallowe & tickle that therby greate perill & danger of drowning hathe many tymes ensued. **1583–1602** [see SEAR *sb.*[1] 1 b]. **1612** CHAPMAN *Widowes T.* Plays 1873 III. 29, I haue set her hart vpon as tickle a pin as the needle of a Diall. **1883** *W. Yorks. Gloss.* s.v., A mouse-trap should be set *tickle*, i.e. easy to go off. **1904** in *Eng. Dial. Dict.* s.v., (Lancs.) That wall's very tickle, you'll have it deawn if yo'r not very careful.

b. *transf.* Of a place, condition, etc.: Insecure; precarious, slippery; risky, dangerous. *Obs.* or *arch.*

1579 SPENSER *Sheph. Cal.* July 14 In humble dales is footing fast, The trode is not so tickle. **1589** *Mar-Martine* 5 Thilke way & trood whilke thou dost swade, is steepe & also tickle. **1643** BAKER *Chron., Hen. VII* 148 These words.. seemed to expresse a tickle hold of Loyalty. **1665** BRATHWAIT *Comment 2 Tales* 129 Conventicles are Tickle places for Holy Sisters. **1681** COTTON *Wond. Peak* (ed. 4) 43 Footing.. still more tickle, and unsafe. **1834** SIR H. TAYLOR *2nd Pt. Artevelde* III. iii, I oft before have clomb to tickle places, But this will be the last of all my climbing. **1868** BROWNING *Ring & Bk.* IV. 51 The grey innocuous grub, of yore, Had hatched a hornet, tickle to the touch.

7. = TICKLISH *a.* 5. Now *dial.*

1569 STOCKER tr. *Diod. Sic.* I. xix. 28 The matter stoode upon this tickle and dangerous point. **1581** PETTIE *Guazzo's Civ. Conv.* II. (1586) 71 b, The trueth is a thing so tickle, that a man may incurre reprehension, not onely by disguising it in some part coulourably, but euen by very reporting of it simply. **1586** FERNE *Blaz. Gentrie* II. 3 So tickle and nyce be the precepts of those writers, that to swarue but one haire from their prescribed rules, hath fordone all thy former worke. **1595** GOODWINE *Blanchardyn* liv. 223 Seeing the tickle state of his fathers kingdome. *a* **1618** RALEIGH *Soul's Errand* viii. Tell wit how much it wrangles In tickle points of niceness. **1681** W. ROBERTSON *Phraseol. Gen.* (1693) 385 A very tickle point or controversie. **1868** E. WAUGH *Sneck-Bant* iv. (E.D.D.), Hoo's nobbut in a tickle state o' health. **1884** *Chester Gloss.* s.v., Au've getten raythe a tickle job here. **1887** BARING-GOULD *Red Spider* ii, The money-spinner is a tickle (touchy) beast, and may take offence at a godless word.

b. Delicate in the feelings or senses; fastidious, dainty, squeamish; easily upset or disordered. Now *dial.*

c **1456** PECOCK *Bk. Faith* (1909) 212 Whi schulde ȝe thanne be so tikil and squaymose? **1762** T. BRYDGES *Burlesque Homer* (1797) II. 96 Juno, whose nose was mighty tickle, Soon smelt their most unsavoury pickle. **1855** *Shevvild Chap's Ann.* 23 (E.D.D.) Thah's a varry tickle stomach. **1901** F. E. TAYLOR *Folk Speech S. Lanc.* (ibid.), He's very tickle abeawt what he ates an' sups.

c. Difficult to deal with.

1570 LEVINS *Manip.* 121/46 Tickle, *impatiens, intactilis.* **1582** STANYHURST *Æneis* Ded. (Arb.) 7 Virgil.. and Ouid.. are so tickle in soom places, as they rather craue a construction than a translation. **1887** BARING-GOULD *Gaverocks* xxx, There is a tickle (difficult) bit where I cannot plant a foot.

d. Of an animal: Easily scared; shy, wild. *dial.*

[**1737** *Gentl. Mag.* VII. 114/2 But if I shoot Not out of hand, The bird, which doth So tickle stand, May chance to fly away.] **1877** E. LEIGH *Chesh. Gloss.* 212 *Tickle* is also applied to game, particularly hares, when wild and ready to move. 'The snow or frost makes the hares very tickle'. **1877** *N.W. Linc. Gloss.* s.v., Fish, when they bite very shyly, are said to be 'strange an' tickle'. **1879** T. WARDEN *Crossford* I. 22 The birds were excessively tickle, and persistently got up out of shot.

†**8.** quasi-*adv.* (in senses 6 and 7): In a tickle or ticklish manner; insecurely, precariously. *Obs.*

1606 DANIEL *Funeral Poem* Poems (1717) 313 And this Important Piece.. did then so tickle stand, As that no Jointure of the Government But shook. **1692** R. L'ESTRANGE *Josephus, Wars Jews* IV. i. (1733) 689 The Houses stand so thick and tickle upon the Steep of the Hill ..as if they were ready to drop into the Precipice. **1699** J. WOODWARD in *Phil. Trans.* XXI. 224 Corpuscles.. absolutely Spherical, must stand so very tickle and nicely upon each other, as to be susceptible of every impression.

9. *Comb.* **a.** in sense 'easily moved or set in motion', as † **tickle-footed** (of a hawk), having an insecure grasp or clutch; † **tickle-headed**, light-minded, easily influenced; † **tickle-heeled**, having nimble or active heels; † **tickle-tongued**, loose of tongue, talkative, garrulous. See also TICKLE-TAIL. **b. tickle-plough** (*dial.*): see quot. 1875.

a **1616** BEAUM. & FL. *Scornf. Lady* v. iv, Lady I would not undertake ye, were you again a haggard, for the best cast of four ladys i' th' kingdom: you were ever *tickle-footed, and would not truss round. **1583** GOLDING *Calvin on Deut.* lxxiv. 455 In al ages men haue bin *tickleheaded:.. euery man would needs be casting of some peece or collup of his own making, to the things that God had commaunded. **1737** BRACKEN *Farriery Impr.* (1757) II. 35 A Horse may.. shew abundance of Life and Action, while under a *tickle heel'd Jockey-Boy. **1875** *Sussex Gloss.*, **Tickle-plough*, a plough with wooden beam and handles. **1884** *W. Sussex Gaz.* 25 Sept., Dead stock:.. three one-horse dung carts, tickle ploughs.. and small harrows. **1577** STANYHURST *Descr. Irel.* Ep. Ded., His historie.. being.. somewhat *tickle toonged, ..it twitled more tales out of schoole [etc.].

tickle ('tɪk(ə)l), *v.* Forms: 4 **tikelle,** 4–5 **tikl(en, tykel,** 4–6 **tikel,** 4–7 **ticle,** 5 **tykele, tykle, tykyl(l,** 5–6 **tyckel,** 6 **tikell, tykell, tickil, tykil, tyckle, tycle,** 6–7 **tickel,** 6– **tickle.** [Not recorded in OE., which however had *tinclian* to tickle. Known first after 1300 in form *tikelle*, side by side with the adj. *tykel, tikel*: origin and history doubtful. Falk and Torp take it as a freq. deriv. of TICK *v.*[1] to touch lightly, pat. It has also been inferred to be a metathetic form of KITTLE *v.*[1], parallel to Alemannic dial. *zicklen*, beside Ger. *kitzeln* to tickle. See Note below.]

I. Intransitive senses.

†**1. a.** To be affected or excited by a pleasantly tingling or thrilling sensation; to be stirred or moved with a thrill of pleasure: said of the heart, lungs, blood, 'spirits', etc., also of the person. *Obs.*

c **1330** R. BRUNNE *Chron.* (1810) 113 þe folk ferly mykelle ageyn him [Stephen] þei ros, & Dauid herte gan tikelle, þat him wex fele fos. **1577–87** HOLINSHED *Chron.* (1808) IV. 378 How the spirits and livelie bloud tickle in our arteries and small veines, in beholding you the light of this realme. **1589** *Pasquil's Ret.* 16, I needed no Minstrill to make me merrie, my hart tickled of it selfe. **1591** SPENSER *Muiopotmos* 394 Who.. with secrete ioy.. Did tickle inwardly in euerie vaine. **1624** HEYWOOD *Captives* II. i, I'l.. sett my mind downe in so quaint a strayne Shall make her laugh and tickle. *a* **1625** FLETCHER *Nice Valour* v. i, Oh, how my lungs do tickle! ha, ha, ha! **1647** H. MORE *Poems* 172 This pretty sport doth make my heart to tickle With laughter.

†**b.** Said of the feeling or its cause. *Obs. rare.*

1579 TOMSON *Calvin's Serm. Tim.* 14/2 For so much as.. this curiositie tickleth in many braines.

2. To tingle; to itch; also *fig.* to have an uneasy or impatient desire (usually *to do* something); to be eager. Now *rare.*

This sense was prob. in literal use much earlier, though quots. have not been found.

1542 UDALL *Erasm. Apoph.* 344 The fyngers of the Athenians ticleed to aid and succour Harpalus. **1557** N. T. (Genev.) *Acts* xvii. 19 *note*, People whose eares euer tickled to heare newes. **1591** SAVILE *Tacitus' Hist.* IV. xliii. 202 The Senatour's fingers euen tickled against him. **1906** N. MUNRO in *Blackw. Mag.* Dec. 802/2, I fairly tickle to take a walk along. *Mod.* My foot tickles.

II. Transitive senses (= L. *titillāre*).

3. Said of a thing, or impersonally with *it*: To excite agreeably (a person, his heart, ears, palate, etc.); to give pleasure or amusement to; to please, gratify. ***to tickle to death***: cf. DEATH *sb.* 12 b. Also in colloq. phr. ***to tickle pink***, to delight; to overcome with pleasure or amusement. Cf. sense 5.

c **1386** CHAUCER *Wife's Prol.* 471 It tikleth [*v.rr.* tikeleth, tykelith, ticleþ] me aboute myn herte roote. **1406** HOCCLEVE *Misrule* 204 So tikelid me þat nyce reuerence þat it me made larger of despense. **1495** *Trevisa's Barth. De P.R.* XVIII. i. (W. de W.) Yj/1 By gendrynge hete tyklyth and pryckyth: that falleth moost in spryngynge tyme whan the vertue of ye hete of heuen begynnyþ to haue maystry of bodyes of beestys. **1597** J. PAYNE *Royal Exch.* 7 More for desire of imitation, then of anie intent to tyckle hym with adulation. **1607** HIERON *Wks.* I. 166 Well might they.. haue their eares ticled with some pleasing noise. **1734** tr. *Rollin's Anc. Hist.* (1827) I. II. 210 Eating in Egypt was designed not to tickle the palate but to satisfy the cravings of nature. **1834** C. A. DAVIS *Lett. J. Downing* xv. 188 It has tickled me eny most to death. **1859** HAWTHORNE *Fr. & It. Note-Bks.* II. 233 Something.. that thrilled and tickled my heart with a feeling partly sensuous and partly spiritual. **1863** GEO. ELIOT *Romola* xxv, Elements that.. tickled gossiping curiosity, and fascinated timorous superstition. **1907** *St. Nicholas* May 607/1 I'm tickled to death to find some one with what they call human emotions. **1922** 'G. EMERY' in A. H. Quinn *Contemporary Amer. Plays* 238 He'll be tickled pink. **1939** W. FORTESCUE *There's Rosemary* xlvi. 268 Knowing the great artist, he had hopes that my rather cheeky suggestion might 'tickle him to death'. **1948** F. A. IREMONGER *William Temple* xxiv. 416 An American delegate who sat opposite Temple at the table—'Archbishop, you tickle me pink!' **1950** WODEHOUSE *Nothing Serious* 29 Your view, then, is that he is tickled pink to be freed from his obligations? **1976** *Scottish Daily Express* 23 Dec. 8/7 We are tickled pink that we were able to come home to do the concert at Liverpool Philharmonic Hall. **1977** E. LEONARD *Unknown Man No. 89* xvi. 141 'I'm tickled to death I'm talking to you,' Mr. Perez said.. smiling into the telephone.

4. a. To touch or stroke lightly with or as with the finger-tips, a straw, a feather, a hair, or the like; to tease, annoy, or irritate lightly, so as to cause a peculiar uneasy sensation. Also said of the thing. Also *absol.*

c **1450** *Voc.* in Wr.-Wülcker 571/23 *Catello*, to mewe or to tykele. [Cf. F. *chatouiller*, OF. *catouller* to tickle.] *c* **1532** DU WES *Introd. Fr.* in Palsgr. 940 To tickel, *catouller.* **1566** BLUNDEVIL *Horsemanship* IV. lxviii. (1580) 28 b, By eating a feather, or by eating dustie or sharp bearded strawe, and such like things: which tickling his throte causeth him to cough. **1590** SHAKS. *Mids. N.* IV. i. 28 If my haire do but tickle me, I must scratch. **1596** —— *1 Hen. IV*, II. iv. 340 To tickle our Noses with Spear-grasse, to make them bleed. **1704** NORRIS *Ideal World* II. iii. 239 Who ever thought of anything like pleasure in a feather that tickles his hand? **1710** J. CLARKE *Rohault's Nat. Phil.* (1729) I. 174 None of them will be able to prick the Tongue agreeably, but they will only tickle it in a disagreeable manner. **1837** DICKENS *Pickw.* xxxvi, First, something tickles your right knee, and then the same sensation irritates your left.

b. To touch, or poke (a person) lightly in a sensitive part so as to excite spasmodic laughter. Also *absol.*

1530 PALSGR. 349 He tykeleth my sydes, *il me catoille les costes. Ibid.* 758/1 And you tykell me thus I muste nedes laughe, *si vous me gattouillez.. il mest force de rire.* **1589** PUTTENHAM *Eng. Poesie* III. xxii. (Arb.) 266 Her Maiestie laughed as she had bene tickled. **1596** SHAKS. *Merch. V.* III. i. 68 If you tickle vs, doe we not laugh? **1675** WYCHERLEY *Country Wife* IV. iii, I am trying if Mr. Horner were ticklish .. I love to torment the confounded toad; let you and I tickle him. **1872** DARWIN *Emotions* xiii. 310 We can cause laughing by tickling the skin.

c. Applied to a method of catching trout or other fish: see quot. 1884 s.v. TICKLING *vbl. sb.* 3 c. Often in allusive use.

1601 SHAKS. *Twel. N.* II. v. 26 Heere comes the Trowt, that must be caught with tickling. **1706–7** FARQUHAR *Beaux Strat.* III. ii, He.. tickles the trout, and so whips it into his basket. **1745** POCOCKE *Descr. East* II. II. v. viii. 252 Men go into the water, tickle them on the belly, and so get them ashoar. **1823** SCOTT *Quentin D.* xxx, He spoke of fishing—I have sent him home a trout properly tickled! **1883** G. C. DAVIES *Norfolk Broads* xxiii. (1884) 177 The mode of tickling tench which at one time was common enough on some of the Broads.

5. *fig.* To excite amusement in; to divert; often in the phrase *to tickle the fancy.* Also *absol.*

a **1688** VILLIERS (Dk. Buckhm.) *Chances* Prol., There are Fools that tickle with their Face, Your gay Fool tickles with his Dress and Motions. **1771** SMOLLETT *Humph. Cl.* 26 June, The young squire, tickled by this ironical observation, exclaimed, '*O che burla!*' *a* **1774** TUCKER *Lt. Nat.* (1834) II. 129 Whose play had a quality of striking the joyous perception, or, as we vulgarly say, tickling the fancy. **1837** LOCKHART *Scott.* an. 1816 *note*, Such.. was the story that went the round of the newspapers at the time, and highly tickled Scott's fancy. **1858** DORAN *Crt. Fools* 10 Poor as the joke was, it.. tickled the fancy of the Tirynthians. **1871** BLACKIE *Four Phases* i. 69 Brilliant oratorical displays to tickle and amuse. **1885** *Manch. Exam.* 16 May 6/1 Lord Hartington's slow, quiet, dry answer, 'No, sir', somewhat tickled the House.

b. To puzzle: cf. Sc. *to kittle. Sc. dial.*

1865 TESTER *Poems* 47 (E.D.D.) I've got ye out, but it tickles my brain How the deuce I'm to pitch ye in again.

6. a. To touch (a stringed instrument, etc.) lightly as in tickling a person; to stir (a fire, etc.) slightly; to play or operate (the keys of a keyboard instrument or machine); esp. in phr. ***to tickle the ivories*** (IVORY 5 d). *colloq.*

1589 NASHE *Anat. Absurd.* Epist., To tickle a Cittern, or have a sweete stroke on the Lute. **1592** SHAKS. *Rom. & Jul.* I. iv. 36 Let wantons light of heart Tickle the sencelesse rushes with their heeles. **1740** SOMERVILLE *Hobbinol* I. 143 Hark from aloft his tortur'd Cat-gut squeals, He tickles ev'ry String. **1770** *Acc. Bks.* in *Ann. Reg.* 243/2 One of them began to tickle his guittar. **1796** PEGGE *Derbicisms* (E.D.S.), Tickle the fire. **18..** in *Daily Chron.* 10 Dec. (1902) 9/1 A country whose soil, it has been well said, only requires to be tickled with a hoe to laugh with a harvest. **1926** H. CRANE *Let.* 5 Dec. (1965) 278 Tickling the typewriter keys is a stiff proposition. **1930** S. SASSOON *Mem. Infantry Officer* VIII. ii. 194 He now told us that he had discovered a place where we could 'buy some bubbly and tickle the ivories'. **1940** M. SADLEIR *Fanny by Gaslight* II. 371 Chunks.. shouted to the pianist to tickle the ivories. **1980** *Times* 1 Oct. 12/6 The 24-year-old virtuoso who tickles the very keys once played by Reginald Dixon.

b. *ironically.* To beat, chastise.

1592 WARNER *Alb. Eng.* VIII. xliii. (1612) 207 Whose Knightes, in 2 Richards dayes, so tickeld France and Spaine. **1601** SHAKS. *Twel. N.* v. i. 198 If he had not beene in drinke, hee would haue tickel'd you other gates then he did. **1681** T. FLATMAN *Heraclitus Ridens* No. 35 (1713) I. 225 Our gracious Queen Elizabeth tickled their Tobies for them, for their Reformation. **1698** J. CRULL *Muscovy* 175 They soundly tickle his Back, in the same Manner as we beat the Dust out of Cloaths. **1800** C. K. SHARPE *Corr.* (1888) I. 94 These little rogues.. should be well tickled with the birch. **1861** *Sat. Rev.* XII. 199 Hogarth tickles the poor bardling with his pencil.

c. To touch *up*, trick *up*; to improve or decorate with light touches.

1833 C. MATHEWS *Let.* 11 Oct. in A. Mathews *Mem. Charles Mathews* (1839) IV. x. 208 If you do not tickle up my matter for me after I have put it down, I will not contrive my 'Life'. **1845** THACKERAY *Crit. Rev.* Wks. 1886 XXIII. 238 The picture is.. tickled up with a Chinese minuteness. **1852** —— *Let.* in *Esmond* (1900) p. xxxiii, Dolls—painted and tickled up in the most charming way.

d. (See quot. 1967.)

1919 C. P. THOMPSON *Cocktails* 257 We had got out to his cycle, and he bent to tickle the carburettor. **1967** D. M. DESOUTTER *Your Bk. of Engines & Turbines* viii. 33 Often the float chamber has a little plunger on top, and by pushing it you can sink the float a little and allow petrol to run through into the carburettor. People call this 'tickling the carburettor'.

e. *Criminals' slang.* To rob or burgle. Esp. in phr. ***to tickle the peter***, to rob the till or cash box; also in extended use. Chiefly *Austral.* and *N.Z.* Cf. TICKLE *sb.*[2] 2.

1945, etc. [see PETER *sb.*[1] 6 b]. **1950** *Austral. Police Jrnl.* Apr. 119 *Tickle the peter*, to embezzle or steal funds, usually by the servant of an employer. **1973** *Courier-Mail* (Brisbane) 14 Mar. 14/9 Senator Georges.. was accused in State Parliament last night of having 'tickled the peter' when he was 18. **1976** F. GREENLAND *Misericordia Drop* I. vi. 44 Get a Portuguese villain to tickle the place.

f. *Cricket.* Of a batsman: to deflect (a delivery) with a light stroke or glance. (In quots., with bowler as obj.)

1963 *Times* 5 Mar. 4/1 Dowling, who.. is probably New Zealand's finest batsman.. today tickled Trueman round the corner. **1977** *Sunday Times* 3 July 28/6 At last, however, Brearley tickled Doshi away behind the wicket for three.

†**7. a.** To excite, affect, move; also, to vex, irritate, provoke. *Obs.*

1547–64 BAULDWIN *Mor. Philos.* (Palfr.) 116 Some men there be, whom bodily lust tickleth not at all. *a* **1548** HALL *Chron., Edw. IV* 204 These newes sodaynly brought to the kynge did not a littell vexe & tykil hym. **1593** SHAKS. *2 Hen. VI*, I. iii. 153 Shee's tickled now, her Fume needs no spurres. **1693** DRYDEN *Persius' Sat.* I. 28, I cannot rule my Spleen; My Scorn Rebels, and tickles me within. **1698** FRYER *Acc. E. India & P.* 316 What once tickled the Spleen of a Philosopher, might here hourly give him the Diversion.

†**b.** To arouse by or as by tickling; to stir up, incite, provoke; to prompt or impel *to do* something.

1532 MORE *Confut. Tindale* Wks. 551/1 Y[e] pronity & mocions in the fleshe.. whereby we be ticled towarde great actuall deadely sinnes. **1581** MARBECK *Bk. of Notes* 603 When our flesh tickeleth vs to speake, we must resist it. *a* **1592** GREENE *Alphonsus* III. Wks. (Rtldg.) 237/1 What foolish toy hath tickled you to this?

c. With *up*: To stir up, arouse by tickling, excite to action.

1567 DRANT *Horace, Epist.* xiii. E iv, Such geare, As will embaite our Cesars eye, and tickle vp his eare. **1583** BABINGTON *Commandm.* vii. (1637) 67 These things.. tickle us up.. to the breach of this Commandement. **1642** [SIR J. SPELMAN] *View Observ. H. M. Late Answ.* 38 They so tickle up the crasie minds of the multitude. **1674** N. FAIRFAX *Bulk & Selv.* 127 If such a spring as this is, may be tickled and rous'd up again. **1898** *Daily News* 25 Nov. 2/2 Why don't you tickle up Sandys with those spurs?

d. To get or move (a thing) *into* or *out of* some place, position, or state, by action likened to tickling.

1677 GILPIN *Demonol.* (1867) 389 He endeavours.. to tickle Him into a humour of affecting the glory and admiration which [etc.]. **1688** R. HOLME *Armoury* III. 315/1 When the Butcher is to Blood them and tickle them out of their Lives. **1702** *Eng. Theophrast.* Pref. 2 Others.. have endeavoured to tickle men out of their Follies. **1704** F. FULLER *Med. Gymn.* (1711) 88 This is to Cheat People with the *Bellaria* of Physick, and Tickle Men into the Grave. **1725** BYROM *Let. to R. L.* ix, The cunning old Pug.. took Puss's two Foots, And so out o' th' Embers he tickl'd his Nuts. **1904** *Westm. Gaz.* 28 Dec. 2/2 He slipped from the chair, tickled his toes into his slippers, and threw his shoulders back.

†**8.** ***to tickle it***: (?) to bring to an agreeable end; to ensure a satisfactory result. *Obs.*

1599 B. JONSON *Cynthia's Rev.* IV. v, I am sorry the reuels are crost. I should ha' tickled it soone. **1672** DRYDEN *Assignation* III. i, Now, I think I have tickled it; this discovery has reinstated me into the Empire of my wit again. **1761** STERNE *Tr. Shandy* III. xx, Bless us!—what noble work we should make!—how should I tickle it off!

9. In various figurative phrases and expressions, mostly with reference to the pleasing effects of tickling. ***to tickle in the palm***, to gratify with a 'tip'.

1694 MOTTEUX *Rabelais* v. xiii. (1737) 54 We tickled the Men in the Palm. **1706** E. WARD *Wooden World Diss.* (1708) 31 The Ale-Wives tickle him in the Gills with the Title of Captain. **1742** YOUNG *Nt. Th.* VIII. 755 'Tis pride, or emptiness, applies the straw That tickles little minds to mirth effuse. **1807–8** W. IRVING *Salmag.* (1824) 224 This straw tickled the noses of all our dignitaries wonderfully. **1843** CARLYLE *Past & Pr.* II. viii, Tickle me, Toby, and I'll tickle thee! **1874** *Siliad* IV. 110 But, tickled by a shilling in his palm, [he] Walked on discreetly blind. **1901** *Scotsman* 4 Mar. 10/5 An officer.. when he gets on a palace-car, he can tickle the porter just as much as he desires at the expense of the Government pocket-book.

10. In combination with a sb.; as †**tickle-brain**, potent liquor; hence *transf.* one who supplies it; **tickle-grass**, name given in U.S. to various grasses, as the hair-grass, *Agrostis scabra*, the old-witch grass, *Panicum capillare* (*Cent. Dict.*); **tickle-moth**, **tickle-pitcher** (*slang*): see quots.; **tickle-text** (*slang*), a parson; **tickle-toby** [cf. quot. 1681 in 6 b, also Motteux *Rabelais* IV. xiii], a birch, rod, switch; also, the use of this; **tickle-weed**, swamp hellebore, *Veratrum viride*. See also TICKLE-TAIL.

1596 SHAKS. *1 Hen. IV*, II. iv. 438 Peace good Pint-pot, peace, good *Tickle-braine. **1639** DAVENPORT *New Tricke* III. i, A Cup of Nipsitate, briske and neate; The Drawers call it Tickle-Braine. **1833** *Veg. Subst. Materials of Manuf.* ix. 162 A species of grass growing spontaneously in that part of the United States [Connecticut], and popularly known by the name of *tickle-moth. *a* **1700** B. E. *Dict. Cant. Crew*, **Tickle-pitcher*, a Toss-pot, or Pot-companion. **1725** in *New Cant. Dict.* **1785** GROSE *Dict. Vulg. T.*, *Tickle pitcher*, a thirsty fellow, a sot. *Ibid.*, **Tickle text*, a parson. **1830** BENTHAM *Corr.* Wks. 1843 XI. 37 A touch, every now and then, of the *tickle-Toby, which I keep in pickle for you. **1842** THACKERAY (*title*) Miss Tickletoby's Lectures. **1909** *Daily Chron.* 24 July 3/2 Miss Aurora, who, to the peril of her neck, practises tickle-toby on Brother Gustavus's bare soles. **1762** MILLS *Syst. Pract. Husb.* I. 156 Swamp hellebore (known in different places by the several names of skunk-cabbage, *tickle-weed, bear-root).

Hence **tickled** ('tɪk(ə)ld) *ppl. a.*

a **1586** SIDNEY *Arcadia* III. (1605) 343 A smiling countenance,.. mixt betweene a tickled mirth, and a forced pittie. **1647** H. MORE *Song Soul* II. App. lxvi, His silvered sound would touch our tickled ear. **1880** G. MEREDITH *Tragic Com.* (1881) 11 They encouraged her with the tickled wonder which bids the bold advance yet farther into bogland. **1896** *Blackw. Mag.* May 769 No corn or tickled up seed could get them [wild-fowl] up the pipes.

[*Note.* Derivation from TICK *v.*[1], in sense 'to touch lightly', would, both in form and sense, suit the later use of *tickle*, but is not favoured by the chronology (since *tick* is not known so early as *tickle*), nor by the fact that the earliest recorded sense includes no notion of light touching or of the action of any external agent, but merely expresses a bodily sensation. These considerations partly also affect the theory of metathesis from *kittle*, inasmuch as the latter, exc. in the vbl. sb. *kitelung* (*a* 1100), *kitlyng*, has not been found before 1440, and is from the first trans., = L. *titillare* to tickle (some one). But in ON., *kitla*, like *hungra*, *þyrsta*, etc., was an impersonal vb. of primary sensation: *mig kitlar* 'it kittles me', like *mig hungrar* 'it hungers me'. Traces of this appear also with 'tickle': see 'it tikleth me' in sense 3. It was natural for an impers. vb. to develop both intrans. and trans. constructions: cf. the senses of IRK *v.*, and the modern *it grieves me* with *I grieve* and *you grieve me*. It seems possible that ONorse *kitla* was adopted at an early date in some parts of England as *kit(e)l-en*, *kittel-*, and in others, under the influence of *tick*, as *tikl-*, *tikel-*, and that the latter became the general Eng. form, while the more original *kitl-*, *kittle*, was used farther north, and was thus later in literary record. Neither form appears in *Cursor Mundi*.]

†**tickle**, (?) dial. form of TITTLE *v.*[1], to whisper.

1575 *Gammer Gurton* II. ii, Sig. B iiij, But Tib hath tykled in Gammers eare that you shoulde steal the cock.

tickle-ace ('tɪk(ə)leɪs). *Newfoundland* and *Labrador.* Also **ticklace**, **tickle-ass**, **tickle-else**, etc. [perh. imit. of the bird's cry.] The kittiwake.

1819 in H. J. Paddock *Languages in Newfoundland & Labrador* (1977) 16 Titlass-Gotheyet. **1889** J. P. HOWLEY in G. M. Story et al. *Dict. Newfoundland Eng.* (1982) 565/2 They were chiefly Murres, Turres, Pigeons and Tick-laces. **1909** P. W. BROWNE *Where Fishers Go* 207 The Kittiwake.. is known to fishermen as 'Tickelelse ("Ticklers'). **1932** J. BARBOUR *Forty-Eight Days Adrift* 53 The only thing alive, to be seen, was a tickalass, and we tried with poles to kill it, to eat. **1951** PETERS & BURLEIGH *Birds of Newfoundland* 235 Atlantic Black-legged Kittiwake... Local names: Tickle-lace, Tickle-ace, Tickle-ass. **1966** A. R. SCAMMELL *My Newfoundland* 36 Jim Parsons was out shooting tickle-aces yesterday. **1974** F. MOWAT *Boat who wouldn't Float* xviii. 219 She [*sc.* a boat] lay lightly on the harbour looking as pretty as a tickle-ass. **1975** T. RUSSELL *Chron. Uncle Mose* 23 There'd been a few ticklaces around that morning.., and being as how I liked ticklace soup as well as the next man, I wished I'd had my breech-loader and a few cartridges.

†'**ticklely, tickly**, *adv. Obs. rare.* Also 7 tickely, tickly. [f. TICKLE *a.* + -LY[2].] In an insecure or unstable manner; ticklishly.

1601 SIR W. CORNWALLIS *Disc. Seneca* (1631) 10 It is meet they should stand thus ticklely. *a* **1628** F. GREVIL *Alaham* II. ii, So tickely unworthinesse doth stand. **1674** N. FAIRFAX *Bulk & Selv.* 68 A Coach may be so tickly set upon the surface of the earth, as to give it self a trundling, one way or other.

Ticklenburgs ('tɪklənbɜːgz). Also 7 Ticklenburs, Ticklingburs. [For *Tecklenburg*, from a town and county of this name in Westphalia, noted for its manufactures of linen.] A kind of coarse linen cloth; see quots.

1696 J. F. *Merchant's Ware-ho.* 39 Ticklenburs is.. a coarse Linnen, and generally very uneven,.. the right Ticklingburs are almost as strong again as the Ozenbricks [Osnaburgs]... There is not many Cloths sold in England that hath so great Consumption as this. **1812** J. SMYTH *Pract. of Customs* (1821) 133 Linen: Ticklenburgs are known by that word being stamped on the Cloth. **1858** SIMMONDS *Dict. Trade*, *Ticklenburghs*, a coarse mixed linen fabric made for the West India market.

†'**tickleness.** *Obs.* [f. TICKLE *a.* + -NESS.] The quality or state of being tickle; insecurity, instability; critical situation, precariousness; inconstancy; uncertainty.

c **1390** CHAUCER *Truth* 3 Suffise þin owen þing þei it be smal For horde haþe hate & Clymbyng tykelnesse [*v.rr.* tekil-, tikul-]. **1549** in Tytler *Eng. under Edw. VI*, etc. (1839) I. 232 Weighing as well the state of the things above, as also the tickleness of the country. *a* **1625** in Gutch *Coll. Cur.* I. 182, I found such tickleness in the performance of such charges, that.. my prayers will be full of fear. **1674** N. FAIRFAX *Bulk & Selv.* 137 According to the tickleness of its lodging in the *machina mundi.*

tickler ('tɪklə(r)). [f. TICKLE *v.* + -ER[1].] One who or that which tickles, in various senses.

1. a. One who tickles by touching or stroking lightly.

1715 tr. *C'tess D'Aunoy's Wks.* 452 One of those ticklers of Cat-guts that march before the Milk-women upon May-day. **1736** CHESTERF. *Fog's Jrnl.* No. 377 ¶5, If, by chance, there be some few unhappy enough not to find ticklers, or some ticklers clumsy enough not find business, they comfort themselves at least with self-titillation.

b. A pianist. Cf. TICKLE *v.* 6 a. *slang.*

[**1948** *N.Y. Age* 9 Oct. 2/7 The Round Mr. Fletcher Butler, the distinguished Chicago piano tickler.] **1962** *Down Beat* 16 Aug. 26/3 He had a magnificent attack.. combined with the gaiety and shy humor that one looks for in a true 'tickler'. **1975** J. MCCLURE *Snake* vi. 86 Me? I'm the tickler. Pianist. Y'know.

2. Something that tickles or is used for tickling.

a. A thing (or person) difficult to deal with or understand; a teaser; a puzzler (*colloq.*). **b.** A feather brush used to tickle the face of passers, as a diversion at fairs and carnivals. **c.** A birch or rod used in castigation; also, a single-stick. **d.** An instrument used by frame-work knitters for slipping the loops off one needle of the stocking-frame on to another in narrowing or shaping the fabric. **e.** An instrument for extracting bungs from casks. **f.** An implement for stirring a fire, a poker. **g.** In a motor engine, a device by which a small quantity of petrol is pumped into the carburettor to facilitate the starting of the engine. **h.** A small measure (about half a pint) of spirits (*U.S. colloq.*). **i.** A small knife or pistol carried on the person (*U.S. colloq.*). **j.** A memorandum book, or a series of dated cards on which to enter engagements (*U.S.*). Also *transf.*, anything intended to serve as a reminder. **k.** A stern or severe letter. Cf. TICKLE *v.* 6 b. *rare.* **l.** An inductance coil in the anode circuit of a valve, giving positive feedback through another coil in the grid circuit. **m.** A hand-rolled cigarette or the tobacco from which it is made. *Naut. slang.*

a–j. 1680 COTTON *Compl. Gamester* (ed. 2) 4 The Knave and Rascal will violate his trust for profit, and lend him.. a Tickler shall do his business. **1765** E. THOMPSON *Meretriciad* (ed. 6) 27 The tickler you must use, And as you flog the Vet'rans, flog the Muse. **1808** J. BALLANTYNE *Let.* in Smiles *Mem. J. Murray* (1891) I. v. 108 A review, termed by Mr. Jeffrey a tickler, is to appear. **1825** JAMIESON, *Tickler*, anything puzzling. **1825** *Sporting Mag.* XV. 349 John now practised often with the 'ticklers'; nor was it long before he attained the reputation of a noted hand at single stick. **1839** *Civil Eng. & Arch. Jrnl.* II. 118/1 A new and important manufacture.. in the hosiery trade, in making lace caps from the stocking-frame, by the aid of the jack tickler machine. **1839** *Harry Franco* I. 74 (Thornton *Amer. Gloss.*), I don't see that I have got your name down in my tickler. **1840** HALIBURTON *Clockm.* Ser. III. xi. 155, I.. have half a mind to give you a tickler in the ribs. **1844** DICKENS *Mart. Chuz.* xxxiii, A sword-stick, which he called his 'Tickler'; and a great knife, which.. he called 'Ripper'. **1848** BARTLETT *Dict. Amer.*, *Tickler*, a common name among merchants and bankers for a book in which a register of notes or debts is kept for reference. **1861** DICKENS *Gt. Expect.* ii, Tickler was a wax-ended piece of cane, worn smooth by collision with my tickled frame. **1875** *Sussex Gloss.*, *Tickler*, an iron pin used by brewers to take a bung out of a cask. **1881** MISS JACKSON *Shropsh. Word-bk.*, *Tickler*, a slender steel rod.. used for stirring the fire. **1889** *Harper's Mag.* Aug. 388/2 Whiskey.. was not usually bought by the drink, but by the tickler.. a bottle.. holding a half-pint. **1891** T. ANDERTON *Lett. fr. Country Ho.* 237 They poke out the gleeds at the bottom with the tickler, and put them at the top with the tongs. **1892** *Labour Commission* Gloss., *Ticklers*, four small points firmly fixed into a piece of wood which are pressed upon the eyes of the needles and remove the stitches in the hosiery industry. This is the operation of *fashioning.* **1904** *Sat. Rev.* 18 June 784/1 Patriots, who with whisky, rattles, ticklers, Union Jacks and patriotic melody.. celebrated the relief [of Mafeking]. **1905** CALKINS & HOLDEN *Art Mod. Advertising* 351 A tickler is any small piece of printed matter sent out to keep open a prospective sale on the part of the inquirer. **1906** *Daily Chron.* 14 Nov. 9/3 The carburettor can be flooded without lifting the bonnet, by operating a 'tickler' situated outside the bonnet. **1970** *New Yorker* 3 Oct. 34/3 The new lineup of teams can be easily remembered with the aid of a handy mental 'tickler'.

k. **1846** LD. PALMERSTON *Let.* 27 Sept. in H. L. E. Bulwer *Life Palmerston* (1874) III. viii. 299 Do not mention it to anyone; but the Queen has written the King of the French a tickler in answer to a letter he sent her. **1902** G. W. E. RUSSELL *Onlooker's Notebook* xiv. 102 An Illustrious Personage wrote to the Dean [of Windsor] suggesting that, as Mr. Gladstone was engaged in violent attacks upon the Government, it might be better if his visits to the Deanery were discontinued. 'Whereupon,' said the stout old Dean ..'I wrote her a tickler'.

l. **1922** [see REACTION 3 e]. **1931** MOYER & WOSTREL *Radio Handbk.* VII. 335 A tickler.. usually more than makes up for this decrease in detection coefficient by increasing the strength of the impressed radio signal. **1948** [see RADIO *sb.* 2 a].

m. **1929** F. BOWEN *Sea Slang* 141 *Ticklers*,.. is also a name for cigarettes made from the monthly issue of naval tobacco. **1964** J. HALE *Grudge Fight* I. ii. 29 Brooks rolls and lights a tickler. **1977** G. MELLY *Rum, Bum & Concertina* iv. 54 'Tickler' is naval slang for duty-free tobacco.

3. A large American longicorn beetle, *Monohammus titillator*, with very long antennæ. *U.S.*

1841–52 T. W. HARRIS *Insects Injur. Veget.* ii. (1862) 105 The largest Capricorn-beetle,.. found in New England, is.. the tickler, so named probably on account of the habit which it has.. of gently touching now and then the surface on which it walks with the tips of its long antennæ.

4. *attrib.* and *Comb.*, as (sense 2 j) ***tickler card, file, system, telegram***; **tickler coil** = sense 2 l above.

1931 *New Yorker* 10 Oct. 21/1 He ran the tickler cards in their credit department. **1940** *Chambers's Techn. Dict.* 850/2 *Tickler coil*.., an inductance coil included in the anode circuit of a thermionic valve and magnetically coupled to the grid circuit to obtain reaction. **1975** R. L. SHRADER *Electronic Communication* (ed. 3) xviii. 433/1 To increase the sensitivity and selectivity of the grid-leak detector, a plate-circuit tickler coil can be used. **1939** C. MORLEY *Kitty Foyle* (1940) xix. 174 You might remind me of that sometimes. Put it in the tickler file. **1972** D. BAGLEY *Enemy* xiii. 105 Authority had lost interest in him and he would exist only in a tickler file to remind someone to give an annual check. **1962** 'A. A. FAIR' *Stop at Red Light* iii. 56 Real estate, subdivisions.. figuring interest, keeping a tickler system for time payments. **1938** *Sun* (Baltimore) 21 June 6/7 One father.. remembered last year to send admonitioning letters to each member of his family and follow them up with 'tickler' telegrams.

ticklesome ('tɪk(ə)lsəm), *a.* [f. TICKLE *v.* + -SOME.]

1. That tends to tickle; difficult, critical, delicate, precarious, ticklish. Now *dial.*

1585 PARSONS *Chr. Exerc.* II. v. 343 Miserable is that man which placeth the ankor of his eternall wealth.. vpon so ticklesome a point as this is. **1604** —— *3rd Pt. Three Convers. Eng.* 314 Hauinge moued such a matter.. in so dangerous and ticklesome a tyme. **1898** MACMANUS *Bend of Road* 200 Yis, marriage is a ticklesome subject.

2. ? Easily tickled; tickly; ticklish; suitable or fitted for tickling or laughter.

1844 HOOD *Let. to May Elliot* Apr., Wks. 1873 X. 404, I mean to come in my most ticklesome waistcoat, and to laugh till I grow fat. **1898** MACDONAGH *Irish Life & Char.* xvii. 313 The man's so ticklesome that sorra a tailor in the counthry can.. take his measure.

'tickle-tail. [f. TICKLE *a.* or *v.* + TAIL *sb.*]

1. A loose or wanton woman; cf. TICKLE *a.* 3 b. Now *dial.*

c **1430** LYDG. *Min. Poems* (Percy Soc.) 31 Canst thou no better come to holynesse, Than lese thiself al for a tikeltaylle? **1869** J. P. MORRIS *Lancs. Gloss.* (E.D.D.).

2. That which (or one who) tickles the 'tail'; see quots.

1785 GROSE *Dict. Vulg. T.*, *Tickle tail*, a rod, or schoolmaster. **1828** *Craven Gloss.*, *Tickle-tail*, a rod.

3. A game: = THREAD-NEEDLE 1. *dial.*

1821 *Blackw. Mag.* Aug. 36/2 Another game played by a number of children with a hold of one another, or tickle-tails, as it is technically called in Scotland, is, *Through the Needle-e'e.*

tickling ('tɪklɪŋ), *vbl. sb.* [f. TICKLE *v.* + -ING[1].] The action or condition denoted by the verb TICKLE.

1. An uneasy sensation as of the teasing of some sensitive part of the skin or mucous membrane; slight nervous irritation akin to itching.

1398 TREVISA *Barth. De P.R.* v. xxviii. (Bodl. MS.) lf. 16/1 Þe whiche wormes litel & litel wroteþ and eteþ þe skyn & makeþ tikeling and icching. *c* **1425** tr. *Arderne's Treat. Fistula* 61 When-someuer þe pacient feleþ tyklyng or ychyng or prykkyng in þe lure. **1626** BACON *Sylva* §766 All tickling is a light motion of the spirits, which the thinness of the skin, and suddenness and rareness of the touch do further. **1843** R. J. GRAVES *Syst. Clin. Med.* xx. 242 A sensation of tickling in the mucous membrane of the trachea. **1898** J. HUTCHINSON in *Arch. Surg.* IX. No. 36. 341 He had some tickling in his throat.

2. *fig.* A tingling or 'itching' to do something; uneasy desire, craving, hankering.

1553 *Short Catech.* in *Liturgies*, etc. (Parker Soc.) 521 Our will is commonly by tickling of affections and stirring of lusts, drawn to do those things that God is displeased with. **1558** KNOX *First Blast* (Arb.) 24 Women haue in them selues a tickling and studie of vaine glorie. **1683** BURNET tr. *More's Utopia* (1685) 101 These Things may create some Tickling in the Senses. **1874** GEO. ELIOT *Coll. Breakf. P.* 628 Whose brain.. Has feeble ticklings of a vanity.

3. a. A repeated light touching, stroking, or poking, such as to cause laughter; a state of being tickled; *fig.* pleasing excitation, gratification; also, excitement of the risible faculty, amusement.

1423 JAS. I *Kingis Q.* xxi, With the tiklyng of his hete and light, The tender flouris opnyt thame and sprad. *c* **1440** *Promp. Parv.* 493/2 Tykyllynge, *titillacio.* **1548** UDALL *Erasm. Par.* Pref. 3 The pleasaunt ticleyng or clawyng of adulacion. **1603** HOLLAND *Plutarch's Mor.* 311 They who naturally are enclined and disposed to laughter, are to avoid and decline the ticklings and soft handling in those parts of the body that are most smooth, sleicke and tender. **1662** PLAYFORD *Skill Mus.* I. xi. (1674) 39 A certain tickling of the ears of those who do not well understand what it is to sing Passionately. **1728** YOUNG *Love Fame* II. (1757) 94 Tickling is unsafe, If still 'tis painful while it makes us laugh. **1872** DARWIN *Emotions* viii. 201 This so-called tickling of the mind is curiously analogous with that of the body.

†**b.** Used as a term of endearment. *Obs. rare.*

1605 B. JONSON *Volpone* III. v, Thou art mine honor, Mosca, and my pride, My ioy, my tickling, my delight!

c. *spec.* The taking of trout and other fish by the method described in quot. 1884.

a **1616** BEAUM. & FL. *Scornf. Lady* III. ii, Leave off your tickling of young heirs like trouts. **1826** SCOTT *Woodst.* vii, Every fisher loves best the trouts that are of his own tickling. **1884** JEFFERIES *Red Deer* ix. 174 Groping for trout (or tickling)—is tracing it to the stone it lies under, then rubbing it gently beneath, which causes the fish to gradually move backwards into the hand, till the fingers suddenly close in the gills.

4. *attrib.*, as **tickling-house**, (*satirical slang*) a place of preaching: cf. *tickle-text* (TICKLE *v.* 10); **tickling stick** *joc.*, a feather duster or similar device used as a comedian's prop.

1681 T. FLATMAN *Heraclitus Ridens* No. 29 (1713) I. 192 A Boy that has but.. carried his Mistress's Bible to the Tickling-house. **1969** *Listener* 6 Mar. 299/2 Beneath your tickling stick and candy floss came Heath and Wilson and Woodcock. **1980** *Times Lit. Suppl.* 24 Oct. 1198/5 Hints of the tickling-stick [in a performance of *Peer Gynt*] vulgarized the first meeting with Solveig. **1983** *Sun* 8 June 4/4 Ken Dodd painted his famous tickling stick blue yesterday for a Liverpool walkabout in support of Mrs Thatcher.

'tickling, *ppl. a.* [f. as prec. + -ING[2].] That tickles, in various senses of the verb; exciting pleasantly, gratifying, alluring; amusing, diverting; delicate, tingling, itching; ticklish.

1558 PHAER *Æneid* I. Biij b, In her brest the tykling ioye her hart to myrth enclynes. **1595** SHAKS. *John* II. i. 573 That smooth-fac'd Gentleman, tickling commoditie. **1607** TOPSELL *Four-f. Beasts* (1658) 475 The tickling or itching humor, lying betwixt the skin and the flesh, causeth the poor Sheep either to bite the place with his teeth,.. or to rub it upon a tree or wall. **1675** CROWNE *Country Wit* I. i, Fie upon this tickling rheum! **1681** (*title*) Some Observations upon the Tickling Querie, viz. Whether the admitting of a Popish Successor be the best way to Preserve the Protestant Religion [etc.]. **1761** PULTENEY in *Phil. Trans.* LII. 346 A little tickling cough which had remained with him. **1863** GEO. ELIOT *Romola* ix, Such vague memories hang about the mind like cobwebs, with tickling importunity. **1887** RUSKIN *Præterita* II. 30 One evening.. a short tickling cough surprised me.

Hence **'ticklingly** *adv.*, so as to tickle.

1898 J. A. STEUART *Minister of State* I. iv, He smacked his lips and laughed again;.. the recollections of his aunt's choler [were] ticklingly comical.

ticklish ('tɪklɪʃ), *a.* [f. TICKLE *a.* or *v.* + -ISH[1].]

1. Easily tickled; sensitive to tickling.

1598 FLORIO, *Solético*, ticklish. **1615** CROOKE *Body of Man* 72 Some part of the skin is.. thin, as in the sides and soales of the feete, which is the reason that there men are ticklish. **1685** BOYLE *Effects of Mot.* v. 53 A ticklish man, by having the pulp of one's finger passed gently along the sole of his foot,.. has divers muscles and other parts of his body and face put into.. unusual motions. **1833** MARRYAT *P. Simple* xix, As for not standing the charge of bayonets, it was not because they were less brave, but the fact was, that they were most excessively ticklish. **1899** *Allbutt's Syst. Med.* VIII. 128 A peculiar mental affection, locally known as Latah (a word signifying nervous or ticklish).

†**b.** Sensitive, easily affected; of a horse: Sensitive to touch; tender. *Obs.*

1681 *Lond. Gaz.* No. 1589/4 She drags her hinder feet,.. cuts a little behind, she is very ticklish on her Crest. **1684** R. WALLER *Nat. Exper.* 6 After this manner may be had a very ticklish Thermometer. **1716** *Lond. Gaz.* No. 5415/4 [A mare] with a Malender on her near Fore Leg, and very ticklish to be touch'd on that Place.

2. Unstably balanced or poised; easily unbalanced or upset; unsteady; of a boat: easily capsized.

1601 HOLLAND *Pliny* (1634) II. 584 The follie of the blind & bold people of Rome went beyond al; who trusted such a ticklish frame, & durst sit there, in a seat so moueable. **1639** FULLER *Holy War* III. v. (1840) 123 So ticklish are the scales of victory, a very mote will turn them. **1687** A. LOVELL tr. *Thevenot's Trav.* I. 27 Little slight Boats or Wherries, and so tick'lish that by leaning more to one side than another, it is an easie matter to overset them. **1784** COWPER *Task* III. 550 The ticklish balance of suspense. **1861** DU CHAILLU *Equat. Afr.* xiv. 234 They are ticklish craft.

b. Of game: Difficult to approach; shy: = TICKLE *a.* 6 c.

1826 COL. HAWKER *Diary* (1893) I. 290 He got four wigeon, but found the birds very ticklish. **1829** *Ibid.* 359 Birds all scattered and ticklish.

3. *fig.* Easily upset in temper; apt to be offended, sensitive, touchy.

1581 MULCASTER *Positions* xxxvii. (1887) 152 Such parentes as be tikelish, and such scholers as be shifting, removing from maisters and renouncing of obedience. **1634** T. JOHNSON *Parey's Wks.* 1173 There is not any man so ticklish, which taketh not in good part what I have said. **1794** GOUV. MORRIS in Sparks *Life & Writ.* (1832) II. 426 Men are very ticklish in such revolutions as the present. **1821** BYRON *Let. to Moore* 16 Nov., You are ticklish on such points.

4. Unstable, unsteady, unsettled, uncertain, fickle.

1606 in Gardiner *Hist. Eng.* I. 408 *note*, Considering.. how ticklish their disposition is towards the State. *a* **1661** FULLER *Worthies* (1840) III. 265 But foreign friendship is ticklish, temporary, and lasteth no longer than it is advantaged with mutual interest. **1693** SOUTH *Serm.* 99 Uncertain ticklish and variable. **1770–4** A. HUNTER *Georg. Ess.* (1803) III. 514 Resisting the effects of bad weather in ticklish hay seasons. **1847** LD. PALMERSTON *Let.* 5 Feb. in Bulwer *Life* (1874) III. 337 A throne whose stability rests on the point of the bayonet has a very ticklish and uncertain basis.

5. Liable to end in disaster unless treated with great care; needing cautious handling or action; delicate, critical, precarious, risky, hazardous.

1591 SAVILE *Tacitus' Hist.* I. lxxxv. 48 To beare a man's selfe euenly in so nice and ticklish a case. **1600** HOLLAND *Livy* III. lxv. 133 So ticklish and dangerous a thing it is to keepe a meane in maintenance of libertie. **1666** W. BOGHURST *Loimographia* (1894) 81 This is a very ticklish disease, and the least error committed turnes a man out of dores. **1674** N. FAIRFAX *Bulk & Selv.* To Rdr., 'Tis a more ticklish thing to pen a Preface, than 'tis to write a Book. **1711** SWIFT *Lett.* (1767) III. 195 'Tis a plaguy ticklish piece of work, and a man hazards losing both sides. **1775** J. JEKYLL *Corr.* 30 May, Her rash, which perhaps was a critical symptom in her ticklish constitution. **1809** MALKIN *Gil Blas* XII. i. (Rtldg.) 423 A very ticklish predicament. **1899** F. T. BULLEN *Log Sea-waif* 27 This is a ticklish evolution to perform successfully in a crowded anchorage.

6. quasi-*adv.* Ticklishly; in a ticklish or easily moved state; unsteadily; delicately. Now *rare.*

1661 R. BAILLIE in *Lauderdale Papers* (Camden) I. 95, I think you stand tiklish. **1771** LUCKOMBE *Hist. Print.* 318 The upper sides of these Ribs must.. be somewhat arching ..then the Cramp-Irons run more easily and ticklish over them. **1775** T. HUTCHINSON *Diary* 24 Oct., Mr. Gibbon.. says the Minister who proposed them stands ticklish.

7. *Comb.*, as ***ticklish-tempered.***

1897 MARY KINGSLEY *W. Africa* 651 Ticklish-tempered native gentlemen.

ticklishly ('tɪklɪʃlɪ), *adv.* [f. prec. + -LY[2].] In a ticklish position or fashion; insecurely, critically, delicately.

1640 E. DACRES tr. *Machiavelli's Prince* 147 The forraine matters stand but ticklishly. **1762** KAMES *Elem. Crit.* xxiv. (1774) II. 478 A bare uniform cylinder.. without a base, appears too ticklishly placed to stand firm. **1794** WASHINGTON *Let. to T. Lear* 14 Dec., It is to be lamented however, that in plain matters—a little ticklishly circumstanced—such hazards.. should be unnecessarily encountered. **1846** D. JERROLD *Chron. Clovernook* Wks. 1864 IV. 424 Paste-board huts, so loosely, so ticklishly put together, that every wind that blows scares the tenants.

ticklishness ('tɪklɪʃnɪs). [f. as prec. + -NESS.] The quality of being ticklish: see the adj.

1583 GOLDING *Calvin on Deut.* lxxxii. 503 Besides y[t] ticklishnes which we haue alreadie of nature it pricketh vs forewarde to say why should not such a thing be good. **1598** FLORIO, *Gattorigole*, ticklings, ticklishness. **1607** MARKHAM *Caval.* v. (1617) 24 His vncomelinesse onely proceedes from ticklishnesse, or delight which he takes in the friction. *a* **1631** DONNE *Lett.* (1651) 355 You know the ticklishnesse of London-Pulpits. **1647** CLARENDON *Hist. Reb.* v. §116 Such was the ticklishness of the King's condition, that.. it was not thought Counsellable at that time.. to commit them to Prison. **1739** CHEYNE *Regimen* 200 (L.) We know by the ticklishness of the soles [of the feet] what a multitude of fine nervous fibres terminate in them. **1790** PALEY *Horæ Paul.* vi. (1849) 389 The difficulty and ticklishness of the times in which we live. **1905** *Longm. Mag.* Feb. 360 The mare.. was in high spirits, which demonstrated themselves by an affectation of extreme ticklishness, when a fly alighted on her shining flank.

tickly ('tɪklɪ), *a.* [f. TICKLE *a.* + -Y.] Ticklish; = KITTLY.

1530 PALSGR. 327/2 Tyckely, that can nat abyde tyckelynge. **1661** FELTHAM *Resolves* II. xxxv. 252 Nor did they, like ticklie Italians, pet at this and put another in his room. **1825** JAMIESON, *Tickly*, puzzling, difficult. **1897** FLANDRAU *Harvard Episodes* 223, I was laughing so that my wrists were all sort of tickly on the inside.

b. tickly-'benders, thin ice which bends under one's weight; = KITTLY-BENDERS.

1853 KANE *Grinnell Exp.* xxii. (1856) 179 The young ice glazing it over, so as to form a viscid sea of sludge and tickly-benders.

tickly: see TICKLELY *adv. Obs.*

'Tickney. *Obs.* or *dial.* [From *Ticknal*, name of a place near Derby where this earthenware was made.] Epithet of a coarse kind of earthenware (*Tickney ware*); hence, made of this ware (also *fig.*).

1680 V. ALSOP *Mischief of Impos.* viii. 78 Are Churchmen more afraid their Tickney Rules and China-Canons should be preserved than broken? **1688** R. HOLME *Armoury* III. 113/1 Potters [are] sellers of Earthen or Tickney Ware. *Ibid.* xiv. (Roxb.) 7/1 A drinking Jugg or a Tickney Jugge. [**1870** CHAFFERS *Porcelain* (ed. 3) 592 There was a Pottery at Ticknal near Derby as early as the 16th century, which produced articles of a coarse hard body, of a dull brown colour, sometimes decorated with yellow slip.] **1881** MISS

JACKSON *Shropsh. Word-bk.*, *Tickney*, *Tickney-ware*, *obsols.*, common, coarse earthenware.

'tick-off. *slang.* [f. vbl. phr. *to tick off*: see TICK *v.*[1] 3.] Fortune-telling; a fortune-teller. ***to work the tick-off***, to practise fortune-telling.

1934 P. ALLINGHAM *Cheapjack* ii. 18 Several show-people were in the bar. 'You're working the tick-off, aren't you?' said one of them. *Ibid.*, I discovered that 'tick-off' was the fair-ground slang for fortune-teller. **1966** *Punch* 3 Aug. 193/1 No palmists, tick-offs, character readers, mock auctions, pick-a-straw.

'tick-over. [f. vbl. phr. *to tick over*: see TICK *v.*[1] 2 d.] **1.** The running of an internal combustion engine while out of gear or at a low rate of revolutions. Cf. *ticking over* s.v. TICKING *vbl. sb.*[1] 5.

1931 *Flight* 2 Oct. 990/2 All engines were tested on a hangar with a propeller fitted before going away, for opening and for tick-over. **1960** *Times* 27 Sept. 5/3 The tick-over is inevitably 'lumpy' and uneven. **1981** P. O'DONNELL *Xanadu Talisman* iii. 60 The tick-over became a roar as a motor was revved.

2. *attrib.*, as ***tick-over speed***.

1965 [see IDLE *v.* 4 a]. **1978** *Country Life* 10 Aug. 393/1 A Mercedez-Benz dieselcar.. at tickover speeds.. almost runs on pure air.

tick-seed: see TICK *sb.*[1] 3.

tick-tack ('tɪk,tæk), *sb.* Also 6 *Sc.* **tik tak**, 7 **tic-tack**, **tick(e)-tacke**, 7–9 **tic-tac**. [Echoic: so Du., Norw. *tiktak*, Sw., Da., Ger. *tick-tack*, F. *tic-tac*. In sense 2 an adaptation or kind of translation of F. *trictrac*, a similar echoic word: see TRIC-TRAC.]

1. a. An imitation of a reduplicated or alternating ticking sound, esp. that made by a clock (see TICK *sb.*[3] 2); also that of the firing of small artillery. (Used as *adv.* or *interj.*, and hence as *sb.* to denote the sound.)

1549 *Compl. Scot.* vi. 42 Than the smal artailȝe cryit, tik tak, tik tak, tik tak, tik tak. **17..** in *Ritson's Gamm. Gurton's Garl.* (1783) 53 Here a nail, there a nail, Tick, tack, too. **1840** *P. Parley's Ann.* 54, I am quite tired of your [a clock's] tick tack. **1858** O. W. HOLMES *Aut. Breakf.-t.* viii, Our brains are seventy-year clocks... Tic-tac! tic-tac! go the wheels of thought. **1909** *Daily Chron.* 12 June 5/1 A Gatling gun.. played upon the infantry..; one heard the 'tick-tack', 'tick-tack' of the spitting fire.

b. In auscultation, The sound of the heart-beat. (Usually in Fr. form *tic-tac.*)

1853 MARKHAM *Skoda's Auscult.* 175 The normal sounds of the heart are generally indicated by the expression 'tic-tac'... This tic-tac I call the sounds (*Töne*) of the heart... By murmurs (*Geräusche*) I understand the abnormal sounds ..blowing, sawing, rasping, etc. *Ibid.* 207, I have occasionally heard two sounds.. in the place of the proper second sound: thus, instead of the ordinary 'tic-tac', a 'tic-tac-tac'. **1860** J. M. CARNOCHAN *Operat. Surg.* 136 (Cent. Dict.) The normal tick-tack of the heart beat with healthy precision.

c. Chiefly *N. Amer.* A contrivance, such as a button on a piece of thread, spun to make a clattering sound against a window or door as a practical joke, esp. at Hallowe'en.

1884 I. M. RITTENHOUSE *Jrnl.* in *Maud* (1939) 288, I formed plan after plan to frighten them. Finally a 'tick-tack' was decided on. **1947** *Sun* (Baltimore) 7 Oct. 16/3 The Park has decided to have an old-time Hallowe'en, with the old boys puttin' tick-tacks on windows.

d. *transf.*

1927 D. H. LAWRENCE *Mornings in Mexico* 63 Seeing the white monkeys for ever mechanically bossing, with their incessant tick-tack of work. **1934** S. BECKETT *More Pricks than Kicks* 133 'God' he exclaimed, executing a kind of passionate tick-tack through his pockets.

†**2.** An old variety of backgammon, played on a board with holes along the edge, in which pegs were placed for scoring. Also *fig. Obs.* (Also called TRIC-TRAC, in F. *trictrac.*)

1558 FORREST *Grysilde Sec.* I. xi. (Roxb.) 28 To pastyme at Tables, Tick-tacke or Gleeke. **1598** B. JONSON *Ev. Man in Hum.* III. iii. *c* **1618** MORYSON *Itin.* IV. IV. vi. (1903) 396 They play much at Tables, Commonly Tick Tack and lurch, but never at Irish. **1740** tr. *De Mouhy's Fort. Country-Maid* (1741) II. 188 Sometimes we plaid at Tick-tack.

3. = TICK-TACKER.

1918 G. FRANKAU *One of Them* xxi. 159 Silent the tic-tac's tell-tale Semaphore: On thousand tracks, unridden,.. Hay waves.

4. *attrib.* †**a.** Belonging, or addicted, to the game of tick-tack (*obs.*). **b.** *slang.* Applied to a system of 'telegraphy' or signalling used by bookmakers at race-meetings, and hence to the men who practise this (cf. TICKER[3] b).

1583 BABINGTON *Commandm.* ii. (1590) 104 If hee bee a drunken ale-stake, a ticktack tauerner. **1665** in *Boston* (Mass.) *Transcript* 17 Sept. (1910) II. 8/1 Two tick tack tables. *Ibid.*, A tick tack board with the pieces. **1899** *Daily News* 15 Mar. 5/5 Another class who are persecuted most absurdly, as it seems to me, are the 'tick tack' men. **1905** *Daily Chron.* 1 Feb. 3/6 A prisoner puzzled the Kingston Bench by describing himself as 'a racecourse telegraphist'. .. A detective explained that the man practised what is known as 'tick-tack telegraphy'—signalling by means of the arms to outside bookmakers.

Hence **tick-tacker**, one who practises tick-tack telegraphy; **tick-tacking** *ppl. a.*, making an alternating ticking sound.

1842 *Father Oswald* xii. 117 The death-watch.. is a little tick-tacking noise. *a* **1847** ELIZA COOK *Old Mill-stream* xxi, Thy pouring cascade, and the tic-tac-ing mill. **1912** *Daily News* 28 Mar. 4 Bookies, tipsters, tick-tackers, runners, welshers, backers, and all the great army who go racing.

tick-tack, *v.* Also **tic tac**, **tic-tac**. [f. the sb.]

1. *intr.* = TICK-TOCK *v.*

1842, *a* **1847** [implied at TICK-TACKING *ppl. a.*]. **1859** MRS. STOWE *Minister's Wooing* ii. 17 The solemn old clock that tick-tacked in the corner.

2. *intr.* and *trans.* To produce a whirring, clattering sound by spinning a tick-tack (sense 1 c) against a window, etc., as a practical joke. *dial.* and *N. Amer.*

1901 F. E. TAYLOR *Folk-Speech S. Lancs.* s.v. *Tick-tackin'*, a boys' practical joke. See Window-tackin'. **1970** J. H. GRAY *Boy from Winnipeg* 188 We got tired of the project and abandoned it in favour of ringing doorbells and tick-tacking windows.

3. *trans.* and *intr.* To signal (information) by means of tick-tack telegraphy.

1907 *Favourite* 30 Nov. 9/3 Kilbeg was 'tick-tacked' out at 4 to 1 by the private clerk of one particular firm. **1908** *Tatler* 3 June 247 The above system of signalling, which is known as tick-tacking, may be seen on any racecourse. **1927** *Observer* 27 Mar. 18/6 A man in the body of the hall was detected tictacing to Labour supporters and guiding the uproar. **1937** L. MANN *Murder in Sydney* xxv. 273, I also noticed Leon Caspar ticktacking to the girl in response to which the girl challenged two of those called on the panel. **1972** *Guardian* 11 Aug. 8/6 The policeman tic-taced to the judge what the punishment should be.

tick-tack-toe. [TICK-TACK *sb.*; cf. *tip-tap-toe* s.v. TIP-TAP, *tit-tat-toe* s.v. TIT *sb.*[2]] **a.** A children's game played on a slate, consisting in trying with the eyes shut to bring the pencil down on one of the numbers of a set, the number hit being scored.

1884 *Mag. of Art* Feb. 135/2 He saw those children playing tic-tac-toe. **1899** CROCKETT *Anna Mark* xii, Playing at quoits, tops, marbles, tic-tac-toe, jacks, knuckle-bones.

b. *U.S.* = *noughts and crosses* (see NOUGHT *sb.* 7 c; OUGHT *sb.*[3]); also the cross-shaped frame in which this game is played; also *fig.*

1960 S. PLATH in *Sewanee Review* LXVIII. 604 The jacket is patterned with brown squares the size of cigarette packs, each square boldly outlined in black. You could play tick-tack-toe on it. **1975** *Nat. Geographic* Apr. 500 (*caption*) Tick-tack-toe of a new apartment complex rises amid mud-and-wattle houses in Zanzibar town. **1976** N. THORNBURG *Cutter & Bone* xi. 266 A tick-tack-toe form filled with zeros. **1978** G. VIDAL *Kalki* i. 8 Just past the tall sick palms at the edge of the pool, the exhaust of a half-dozen jets was making a kind of tick-tack-toe in the dusty brown sky over Los Angeles. **1980** *Dædalus* Spring 46 A computer designed only to issue the company's pay-checks might stalemate me perpetually in tic-tac-toe.

tick-tick ('tɪk,tɪk). [Echoic.] An imitation of the ticking of a clock or watch, or a similar sound; hence a child's name for a clock or watch.

1774 FOOTE *Cozeners* III. Wks. 1799 II. 190 Marianne, who opened the window? *Mar.* Little massa, to shew me de tick-tick. *a* **1849** J. C. MANGAN *20 Gold. Y. Ago* viii, Tick-tick, tick-tick!—Not a sound save Time's. **1864** GLAISHER in *Circ. Sc.* (*c* 1865) I. 1209/2 We heard.. the tick-tick of a threshing machine. **1894** H. DRUMMOND *Ascent Man* 214 The child who says.. tick-tick for watch, or puff-puff for train, is an authority on the origin of human speech.

So **tick-tick** *v.*; hence **tick-ticking** *vbl. sb.*

1755 *B. Bright's New Jrnl.* 6 If.. his Mistress.. is absent, the Clock tick-ticks very slow. **1897** *Daily News* 17 May 3/3 The tick-ticking of the [telegraph] machines.

tick-tock ('tɪk,tɒk), *sb.* Also **tic-toc**. [Echoic.] An imitation of the ticking of a clock, esp. the slow ticking of a large clock; also of the sound of a double knock, or of resounding footsteps.

1848 THACKERAY *Van. Fair* xxiii, They were both so silent that the tick-tock of the.. clock on the mantelpiece became quite rudely audible. **1878** BROWNING *Poets Croisic* cxxvii, Bold tic-toc Announces there's a giant at the door. **1906** R. WHITEING *Ring in New* 197 The tic-toc of the high heels was insistent in the passages.

tick-tock ('tɪk'tɒk), *v.* [f. the sb.] *intr.* Of a clock, etc.: to make a rhythmic alternating ticking sound. Hence **tick-tocking** *vbl. sb.*

1921 H. S. WALPOLE *Young Enchanted* III. iii. 274 The gaudy clock.. now tick-tocked along in amiable approval of them both. *a* **1947** F. THOMPSON *Country Calendar* (1979) 201 The loud tick-tocking of the clock in the hall. **1950** G. BARKER *Dead Seagull* ii. 89, I heard the murmur in the distance and then the rumbled tick-tocking and then the appalling cacophony all around as the approaching train swept up and past us. **1962** L. DEIGHTON *Ipcress File* ix. 55 The clock tick-tocked on, adding a second or so to its seventy years of tick.

tick-trefoil, tick-weed: see TICK *sb.*[1] 3.

tickwood, obs. var. *teakwood* (TEAK).

1794 *Trans. Soc. Arts* XII. 314 Tickwood plant or Iattee.

ticky ('tɪkɪ), *sb.* Also **tiki, tickie, tikkie, tickey.** [Origin uncertain: see Note.] The colloquial name in South Africa for a threepenny piece.

[*a* 1860 Remembered in colloquial use at Cape Town.] **1877** J. A. CHALMERS *Tiyo Soga* xxii. 471 Those poured an unusually large quantity of tickies into the plates at the doors. **1895** *Westm. Gaz.* 6 Mar. 8/1 The coin of smallest value in the Transvaal is the 'tickie', or threepenny-bit. **1903** *Ibid.* 25 July 2/1 In purchasing-power the 'tickey' [of Johannesburg] is certainly not more than equal to the penny of London. In many cases its value is less than a halfpenny.

'*Note.* Residents of Cape Colony, whose memory goes back to *c* 1850, state that they have known 'ticky' all their lives. The prevalent notion is that the word was first used by the Caffres or other native labourers; it is at present in Sesuto (the Basuto lang.), *teke* ('teːke). But it is believed to have been a native imitation of some Dutch or Eng. word; e.g. of Cape Dutch *stukje* 'little piece, little bit', pronounced (stykɪ), and imitated by the natives as (*tüki, tiki*); according to others, of Eng. *ticket*, it being explained that on an occasion when a large body of natives were employed on a public work, they were, for want of small silver coin, paid with tickets for 3d., which were taken in payment by the provision stores, and redeemed at that rate by the authorities. Other statements or conjectures (e.g. that *tikki* was an attempt to say 'little') have been offered in the *Cape Times*, etc., April to June 1912, but nothing in the form of evidence has been adduced.'—N.E.D.

ticky ('tɪkɪ), *a.* [f. TICK *sb.*[1] + -Y.] Full of or infested by ticks.

1831 *Blackw. Mag.* XXX. 270 He [a turkey] becomes.. craven and crest-fallen, emaciated and ticky.

ticky-tacky ('tɪkɪ,tækɪ), *sb.* and *a.* orig. *U.S.* [Prob. redupl. f. TACKY *sb.* and *a.*[1]]

A. *sb.* Inferior or cheap material, esp. that used in uniform suburban building.

1962 M. REYNOLDS *Little Boxes* (1964) (*song*) 3 And they're all made out of ticky tacky, And they all look just the same. **1973** *Newsweek* 30 July 71 The real point is, will.. Watchung Pharmaceutical get those 250 unspoiled acres around Howard's tree farm which have been zoned for a park, there to produce more poppable pills and sprinkle company ticky-tacky over the landscape? **1978** M. BUTTERWORTH *X marks Spot* iii. 26 A large and gloomy Victorian pub, heavily overlaid with up-to-date ticky-tacky.

B. *adj.* Made of ticky-tacky; cheap, in poor taste.

1969 *Sat. Rev.* (U.S.) 10 May 19/1 Men who desecrate the landscape with hundreds of ticky-tacky houses and.. call themselves developers. **1970** O. NORTON *Dead on Prediction* iii. 46 The house was one of those ticky-tacky semi-bungalows, which are given a false air of expensiveness. **1977** *Jrnl. R. Soc. Arts* CXXV. 119/1 Critics of the private sector complain of ticky tacky little boxes spread all over the country.

ticle, obs. form of TICKLE.

‖**tic-polonga** (tɪkpəʊ'lɒŋgə). *Zool.* [According to *Madras Manual of Administration* III. 154, ad. Sinhalese *tit-polongā*, f. *tita*, in comb. *tit-*, speck, freckle, spot, mark + *polongā* viper. The form with *tic-* is app. due to substituting *tik* 'spot, freckle, mark, spot on tiger-deer', for *tit-*.] A venomous snake of India and Sri Lanka: the chain viper or necklace-snake, *Daboia Russellii*.

[**1681** R. KNOX *Hist. Ceylon* 29 There is another venomous Snake called *Polonga*, the most venomous of all.] **1825** MRS. HEBER in *H.'s Narr. Journ.* (1828) II. xxvii. 258 The Cobra de Capello is the most common, but its bite is not so certainly fatal as that of the Tic Polonga. **1834** CAUNTER *Orient. Ann.* vii. 80 A large dog, belonging to a Cingalese who accompanied us, was bitten by a snake, the ticpolonga. **1910** *Times* 13 Sept. 7/4 Three of the most deadly snakes known in India—the cobra, the tic-polonga or Russell's viper, and the banded krait.

tic-tac, tic-toc: see TICK-TACK *sb.*, TICK-TOCK *sb.*

tid (tɪd), *sb.*[1] *Sc.* [? unexplained var. of TIDE *sb.*]

1. A fit or favourable time or season; an opportunity, occasion.

1721 RAMSAY *Elegy Patie Birnie* xiii. **1728** —— *Fables, Fox & Rat* 40 He took the tid when Lowry was away. **1801** MACNEILL *Poet Wks.* (1844) 54 To catch the tids o' life is sage, Some joys to save.

2. *spec.* The proper season for some agricultural operation, as harrowing or sowing; hence, suitable condition of the soil for cultivation or cropping.

1799 J. ROBERTSON *Agric. Perth* 147 If it were not for fear of losing the proper opportunity (the *Tid* of sowing, as it is vulgarly called), the longer the wheat-seed is delayed.. the better. **1825** JAMIESON, *Tid*.. 2. The condition which any soil is in for the purpose of agriculture; as, 'The ground's no in tid'. *c* **1830** in Stephens *Bk. Farm* (1844) I. 537 A tid (or proper condition of the ground for harrowing) cannot be taken advantage of on the drained furrow until the other is dry. **1842** J. AITON *Domest. Econ.* (1857) 79 The 'tids' of seed-time, hay-time, and harvest, are in a great measure lost. **1863** MORTON *Cycl. Agric.* Gloss. (E.D.S.).

3. A humour, mood, or fancy to do something.

a **1774** FERGUSSON *Farmer's Ingle* Poems (1845) 38 Tak tent, case Crummy tak her wonted tids, And ca' the laiglen's treasure [i.e. the new milk] on the ground. **1825** JAMIESON s.v., *To tak the tid*, to be seized with a perverse or ungovernable humour. **1890** J. SERVICE *Thir Notandums* viii. 48 I'm no i' the tidd the noo.

tid, *sb.*[2] ? *local.* [app. an alteration of TIT *sb.*[3], in sense girl, young woman.] A girl or woman.

1888 BARRIE *When a Man's Single* i, Nanny was a terrible tid for cleanness. **1891** —— *Little Minister* xv, You're the bonniest tid I ever saw oot o' an almanack.

†**tid**, *a. Obs.* A word app. deduced by Bailey from *tid-bit*, but also in independent dialect use. From Bailey in Johnson, whence in later dicts.: also in nonce-use from *tid-bit*: see quots.

1727 BAILEY vol. II, *Tid*, nice, delicate, as a *Tid-Bit*. **1755** JOHNSON, *Tid*, adj. (tydder, Saxon), tender; soft; nice

.. *Titbi't* (properly *tidbit*; *tid*, tender, and *bit*), nice bit; nice food. [See note below.]
1730 *Panegyric on Swift* 13 While Dunces of the coarsest Clay.. Devour the Church's tiddest Bits, That only should be shar'd by Wits. **1799** E. Du Bois *Piece Family Biog.* I. 70 She is too tid a bit for us lubbers aboard the world.
[*Note.* The OE. word meant by J. is *tidre, tyddre* 'weak, fragile, easily broken; frail in health, infirm'; it could not give *tid* 'tender, soft, nice'. The latter does not appear as general Eng. before Bailey. But the *Eng. Dial. Dict.* has from Midl. counties *Tid, tidd* = 'fond, attached, careful (of), solicitous (about); (of a child) tender, nice, fanciful; (of a man) cunningly reserved'. J. D. Robertson's *Gloucester Glossary* (1890) has *Tid*, 'playful, frolicsome', and cites from John Smyth's Berkeley MSS. *c* 1640 (ed. 1885, III. 25) 'Tyd, i.e. wanton. Hee is very tyd, i.e. very wanton. A tyd bit, i.e. a speciall morsell reserved to eat at last'. These evidence the limited dial. use of an adj. *tid, tidd*, or *tyd*; though the senses given do not very closely agree with that deduced by Bailey from *tid-bit*.]

tid, *v. Sc.* [f. TID *sb.*[1]] *trans.* To choose the right time for; to time: esp. with reference to land or crops: cf. TID *sb.*[1] 2.
1808 Jamieson, *Tid*, v.a., to time, to choose the proper season. *The aitseed has been weill tiddit*, the proper season for sowing oats has been taken. **1883** J. Martin *Remin. Old Haddington* 317 He judiciously 'tidded' the land and manured highly so as to produce heavy crops.

tid, obs. var. *tit*, TITE *adv.*; obs. pa. t. and pple. of TIDE *v.*[1], TITHE *v.*[1]

tidal ('taɪdəl), *a.* [f. TIDE *sb.* II. + -AL[1].]
1. a. Of, pertaining to, or affected by tides; ebbing and flowing periodically.
tidal alarm, an audible signal, as a bell or whistle attached to a buoy, operated by the movement of the tides (*Cassell's Encycl. Dict.* 1888); **tidal crack** = TIDE-*crack* (*Cent. Dict.* 1891); **tidal friction**, frictional resistance to the motion of the tide-wave, tending to retard the earth's rotation; **tidal motor**, a mechanical motor deriving its power from the movement of tidal waters; **tidal river**, a river which is affected by the tides for some distance from its mouth; **tidal valve**, a valve in a sluice, which opens to the pressure of land water and closes under the influence of the incoming tide; **tidal wave**, see b.
1807 Vancouver *Agric. Devon* (1813) 300 Had the lots below.. the new Custom House.. in Dublin, been left open to the tidal waters, the waters of the Liffy would have preserved a deep channel for their discharge. **1830** Lyell *Princ. Geol.* I. 359 Suppose that.. the Mediterranean should form a gulf of the great ocean, and that the tidal current should encroach on the shores of Campania. **1853** Herschel *Pop. Lect. Sc.* i. §57 (1873) 45 The tidal action of the sun and moon on.. the earth's crust. **1878** Huxley *Physiogr.* i. 2 Up to Teddington.. the Thames is a tidal river. **1880** Haughton *Phys. Geog.* i. 9 When the length of the day shall have become equal to the length of the year, tidal friction will cease. **1884** F. J. Britten *Watch & Clockm.* 256 Tidal Clock.. designed.. for showing the time of high and low water, the state of the tides at any time of the day. **1911** *Encycl. Brit.* XXVI. 945/1 Tidal friction then diminishes planetary rotation, increases the satellite's distance, and diminishes the orbital angular velocity.
b. *tidal wave*: (*a*) the high water wave caused by the movement of the tide: = *tide-wave* (TIDE *sb.* 16 b); *erron.* (but now in common use) an exceptionally large ocean wave caused by an earthquake or other local commotion.
1830 Lyell *Princ. Geol.* I. 293 On mathematical principles, the rise of the tidal wave above the mean level of a particular sea must be greater than the fall below it. **1878** Huxley *Physiogr.* 2 The tidal wave occupies about two hours in coming up from the Nore to London. *Ibid.* 188 The terrible devastation wrought by the great tidal wave, which followed the earthquake at Lima. **1899** *Daily News* 13 June 8/2 The tidal wave sweeps round the earth twice in the twenty-four hours; the great wave produced by an earthquake, erroneously described sometimes as a 'tidal wave', has nothing tidal about it, and it is called by scientific men 'a free wave'.
(*b*) *fig.* A great progressive movement or manifestation of feeling, opinion, or the like.
1870 'Mark Twain' *Lett. to Publishers* (1967) 45 'We'll have somebody standing ready to launch a book right on our big tidal wave and swim it into a success. **1875** —— *Sketches New & Old* 213 A great tidal wave of grief swept over us all. **1884** *Boston* (Mass.) *Traveller* Aug., Van Buren was a candidate again in 1840, but the 'log-cabin and hard cider' tidal wave was sweeping over the country. **1888** Bryce *Amer. Commw.* III. iv. lxxx. 62 Now and then.. there comes a rush of feeling so sudden and tremendous, that the name of Tidal Wave has been invented to describe it. **1895** Scully *Kafir Stories* 50 The repression which he had to exercise.. caused tidal waves of passion to roll back on his soul, fraught with destruction to himself and to others.
(*c*) *Phys.* The main or primary height of flow in a beat of the pulse.
1896 *Allbutt's Syst. Med.* I. 314 Sphygmographic tracings show a lowering in the height of the tidal and dicrotic wave.
2. *transf.* and *fig.* That 'ebbs and flows'; periodic, intermittent; alternating, varying.
tidal air (*Phys.*), the air passing in and out of the lungs at each ordinary respiration; **tidal breathing** (*Path.*), respiration in which there are pauses alternating with shorter periods of respiratory activity; periodic respiration.
1872 Huxley *Phys.* iv. 92 In ordinary breathing 20 to 30 inches of what is conveniently called Tidal air pass in and out. **1876** Geo. Eliot *Dan. Der.* iv. xxix, This mood of youthful, elated desperation had a tidal recurrence. **1896** *Daily News* 4 May 3/3 Clerkenwell has.. become mixed in population and in its political opinions tidal. **1897** *Allbutt's Syst. Med.* IV. 646 Amongst.. the results of derangements of the pulmonary circulation must be placed the occurrence of 'periodic', 'tidal', or Cheyne-Stokes breathing.

b. *spec.* Of (esp. rush-hour) road traffic, its flow, or a road carrying it: that uses the same lane(s) for travel in opposite directions, depending on time and conditions.
1954 *Highway Engin. Terms (B.S.I.)* 55 *Tidal traffic*, traffic on a two-way road proceeding predominantly in one direction or the other according to time or recurrent circumstances. **1955** *Times* 25 Oct. 9 The reversible lane on tidal highways. **1960** *News Chron.* 26 Feb. 5/1 Tidal-flow traffic was introduced on Chelsea Bridge last year. **1960** *Guardian* 7 June 1/2 The 'tidal flow scheme'.. has already been tried out in London. **1969** *Soviet Weekly* 13 Sept. 2 All the flyovers, underpasses, tidal flows and one-way streets the authorities organized only eased the problem without curing it.
3. a. Dependent upon or regulated by the state of the tide or time of high water.
tidal basin, harbour, a basin or harbour which is accessible or navigable only at high tide; **tidal boat, steamer**, a vessel the sailings of which depend on the time of the tide; **tidal train**, a train running in connexion with a tidal steamer.
1855 Dickens in *Househ. Words* 29 Sept. 194/1 The South Eastern Company.. with their tidal trains and splendid steam-packets. **1858** Simmonds *Dict. Trade, Tidal basin*, a dock that is filled upon the rising of the tide. **1859** Lewin *Invas. Brit.* 27 Boulogne is a tidal harbour,.. it can only be entered or quitted at high water. **1859** Reeve *Brittany* ii. 12 The tidal hours of departure of the steam-packet. **1866** W. Collins *Armadale* II. 240 The tidal train.. was speeding nearer and nearer to Paris. **1888** Gunter *Mr. Potter* x, The tidal boat'll be 'ere in twenty minutes.
b. Elliptical for *tidal boat* or *train*.
1866 Dickens in *All Year Round* Christmas No. 18/1 A return pass by South-Eastern Tidal, to go right through.. to Marseilles. **1883** L. Oliphant *Altiora Peto* I. 202 He found himself just in time to take the tidal.
Hence **'tidally** *adv.*, in a tidal manner; by or in respect of the tides.
1879 G. H. Darwin in *Phil. Trans.* CLXXI. 713 On the Secular Changes in the Elements of the Orbit of a Satellite revolving about a Tidally Distorted Planet. **1880** *Ibid.* CLXXII. 513 In considering the effects of tidal friction the theory has been throughout adopted that the tidally-disturbed body is homogeneous and viscous.

tidance, tidand: see TIDING.

tid-bit, an earlier form of TIT-BIT.

†**tidder,** *v.*[1] *Obs.* Forms: 1 tíedran, týdran, týddr(i)an, 3 tuderen, (*Orm.*) tiddrenn. [OE. *týdran*, related to *tud(d)or* TUDDER, progeny, offspring.] **a.** *intr.* To be productive or prolific. **b.** *trans.* To produce (offspring), to engender.
a **1000** *Cædmon's Gen.* 1507 (Gr.) Tymað nu & tiedrað. *c* **1200** *Trin. Coll. Hom.* 177 þenne men michel tuderið.. and here tuder swiðe wexeð. *c* **1200** Ormin 18307 þa þe33re time wass all gan To tiddrenn & to tæmenn. *c* **1250** *Gen. & Ex.* 630 Of hem ben tudered maniȝon.

[† **'tidder,** *v.*[2] *Obs. rare*⁻⁰.
1755 Johnson, *Tidder*, v.a. (from *Tid*), to use tenderly; to fondle. (But there is app. some error here: no trace of such a vb. has been found elsewhere: cf. TID *a.*)]

tiddivate, dial. variant of TITIVATE *v.*

tiddle ('tɪd(ə)l), *v. Obs.* exc. *dial.* or *slang.* Also 7–9 tittle. [In sense 1 perh. connected with TID *a.* The two senses may be distinct words.]
1. *trans.* To fondle or indulge to excess; to pet, pamper; to tend carefully, nurse, cherish.
1560 *Nice Wanton* in Hazl. *Dodsley* II. 173 My parents did tiddle me: they were to blame. **1653** *Verney Memoirs* (1894) III. 203 To midwife it out, and to tittle it up and to bring it with you in your coach. **1730–6** Bailey (folio), *To Tiddle*, to indulge, or fondle, to make much of. **1755** Johnson, *Tiddle*, v.a. (from *Tid*), to use tenderly; to fondle. **1839** [Sir G. C. Lewis] *Herefordsh. Gloss.* (E.D.D.). **1881** Miss Jackson *Shropsh. Word-bk.*, *Tiddle*, to nurse and nurture tenderly. **1893** *S.E. Worc. Gloss.* s.v., You may tiddle a monkey 'till 'e befouls your trenchud.
2. a. *intr.* To potter, trifle, 'fiddle'; to fidget, fuss.
1747 Richardson *Clarissa* (1811) I. xlii. 322 To leave the family pictures.. to you, because you could tiddle about them, and.. wipe and clean them with your dainty hands! **1839** Holloway *Dict. Prov.* s.v., 'Tiddling about' is being busy about trifles. **1904** *Eng. Dial. Dict.* s.v. *Tittle*, (Cumbld.) I could par' [pare] the fut with a buttress while another is tittlin' over it with a draw-knife.
b. To move potteringly.
1881 W. D. Howells *Modern Instance* (1882) I. x. 173 Mr. Macallister, a slight little straight man.. tiddled farcically forward on his toes. **1970** *Times* 6 July 6/8 You can't just tiddle up to the town hall to see the man.
Hence **'tiddling** *ppl. a.*, that 'tiddles'; overindulgent; **'tiddlingly** *adv.*, indulgently.
1580 Lupton *Sivqila* 37 The most of our youth.. are so tydlingly, fondly, wantonly, and idlely brought up, that it is a griefe to the godlye.

tiddle, dial. form of TITTLE *v.* to tickle.

tiddled ('tɪd(ə)ld), *a. slang.* [f. TIDDLY *sb.* + -ED[2].] Drunk, tipsy; = TIDDLY *a.*[1]
1956 G. Durrell *My Family & Other Animals* xii. 163 'I've got the most splitting headache.' 'I'm not surprised; you were as tiddled as an owl last night.'

'tiddler[1]. [? Related to TITTLEBAT and *tiddly* 'little'.] Nursery name for a stickleback. Also applied to other small fish, as a minnow. Hence, a child; any small person or thing. So **'tiddling** *vbl. sb.*, fishing for 'tiddlers'.
1885 B. E. Martin in *Harper's Mag.* May 866/1 Them's tiddlers, they is. **1903** *Blackw. Mag.* Aug. 203/2, I used to come and catch tiddlers in it when I was a kid. **1908** *Daily Chron.* 3 Aug. 7/3 Within reach of that most delightful tiddling water in St. James's Park. **1911** *Daily News* 26 July 4 The long row of boys.. in St. James's Park fishing for tiddlers with sticks and bent pins. **1927** R. Lehmann *Dusty Answer* iv. 294, I remember you hated lightning when you were a tiddler. **1937** G. Frankau *More of Us* vi. 69 When father's under par, Mother suggests a tiddler at the bar. **1966** F. Shaw et al. *Lern yerself Scouse* 33 *Tiddler*, silver threepenny piece. **1971** *Daily Mail* 18 Feb. 5/6 They will scrap the ½p coin—the 'tiddler'—when they change to decimals. **1976** *Courier-Mail* (Brisbane) 26 Aug. 9/6 Pastime anglers would not be allowed to keep 'tiddlers'. **1980** E. Blishen *Nest of Teachers* I. viii. 43 A couple of days with Class 1A and.. he will know a deuce of a lot.. about the little tiddlers.

tiddler[2]. *slang.* [f. *tiddle*, by-form of TITTLE *v.* to tickle.] A feather or feather-brush for tickling; a 'teaser' or 'tormenter'; a tickler.
1900 *Daily Chron.* 21 May 5 (Cass. Supp.) In Cheapside .. you were titillated by 'penny tiddlers'. Anything, from a peacock's feather downwards, which is a foot long and tickles, is a 'tiddler'. *a* **1904** E. Smith *MS. Coll. Warwicksh. Wds.* s.v. (E.D.D.), At 'mops' and fairs in the Midlands the favourite tiddler.. drawn rapidly down the back,.. made a noise resembling that of the extinct 'rattle' of the policeman. Now the tiddler has degenerated into any light weapon of offence, which drawn across the face or neck, irritates the skin.

'tiddler[3]. *U.S. colloq.* [f. TIDDL(YWINK + -ER[1].] A tiddlywinks player.
1958 *N.Y. Times* 9 May 28 An Oxford University tiddler ..says there's a 100-year-old controversy over proper spelling of the sport. **1962** *Boston Globe* 14 Oct. 81 The Crimson tiddlers winked their way to a 23 to 12 victory over a green Purple team.

tiddly ('tɪdlɪ), *sb.* and *a.*[1] *slang.* Also 9 **titley**, 9– **tiddley.** [Origin uncertain: cf. TIDDLYWINK 1.]
A. *sb.* Drink; an alcoholic drink, esp. a 'short'.
1859 Hotten *Dict. Slang* 109 *Titley*, drink. **1864** *Ibid.* 258 *Titley*, drink, generally applied to intoxicating beverages. **1895** *Punch* 18 May 230/2 It took two 'ot tiddleys to warm 'er. *Ibid.* 12 Oct. 180/1 A helderly humorous gent, on the tiddley. **1923** E. P. Oppenheim *Inevitable Millionaires* xxiv. 259 Just a tiddley to drink success to the club. **1930** E. V. Lucas *Down Sky* 222 It wasn't oysters that she really wanted, but.. tiddly.
B. *adj.* Drunk, tipsy.
1905 *To-day* XLVI. 182/2 If ever you was tiddly in crossing the old 'un [*sc.* a bridge], it was as easy as anything to fall into that blarsted river. **1909** *Chambers's Jrnl.* 17 Apr. 316/1 Mind you don't get tiddley and blow the gaff. **1930** W. S. Maugham *Cakes & Ale* xxiii. 232, I don't say he ever got tiddly, but he used to like to sit in the bar and talk. **1958** B. Nichols *Sweet & Twenties* xvi. 208 No more wine, George, thank you. I shall be quite tiddly. **1979** 'J. Scott' *Angels in your Beer* xxv. 254 Yvonne giggled. 'I do believe I'm tiddly,' she said.

tiddly ('tɪdlɪ), *a.*[2] *colloq.* Also 9 **tidly; tiddley.** [var. TIDDY *a.*] Very little, tiny. Freq. in phr. *tiddly bit.*
1868 Trollope *He knew he was Right* (1869) I. xxiii. 183 The smallest little 'tiddly' things do so often turn up trumps. **1885** E. C. Sharland *Ways & Means in Devonshire Village* 42 I'd only got but a tiddly bit o' that mutton left. **1888** B. Lowsley *Gloss. Berks. Words* s.v. *Tidly*, I had un in my arms when a was a tidly little chap. **1937** *John o' London's Weekly* 5 Feb. 762/2 When there was a bad harvest he hung the little tiddley sheaves o' corn on his garden railing to let God Almighty know how badly he'd been treated! **1950** Wodehouse *Nothing Serious* 106 A mere tiddly seaside competition. **1956** 'N. Shute' *Beyond Black Stump* viii. 237 If I have one will you have just a little tiddly bit, in your coke? **1978** J. Goodman *Last Sentence* iii. 114 The whole bally case for the prosecution is built on tiddly bits of non-evidence.

tiddly ('tɪdlɪ), *a.*[3] *slang* (orig. and chiefly *Naut.*). Also **tiddley.** [perh. f. TIDY *a.*] **1.** Smart, shipshape, spruce.
1925 Fraser & Gibbons *Soldier & Sailor Words* 281 *Tiddly*, smartly dressed... Also applied to a ship of smart appearance. **1942** G. Hackforth-Jones *One-One-One* i. 7 Like all sailors he took great pleasure in keeping his surroundings what he described as 'tiddley'. **1960** 'N. Shute' *Trustee from Toolroom* ii. 25 We'll have to get everything all tiddley.' **1973** R. Dougall *In & out of Box* 119 The aim was to achieve as pale a blue on the collar as possible—this was considered 'tiddley', which in Naval parlance means smart or *comme il faut*. It was also tiddley to have smart horizontal creases in the bell-bottom trousers like a concertina.
2. Special collocation: **tiddly suit**, one's best suit of clothes.
1943 'Taffrail' *White Ensigns* 33 'Tiddley' suits with light jumpers and bell-bottomed trousers cut far wider than the regulation permitted. **1951** C. Causley *Farewell, Aggie Weston* 9 Farewell, Aggie Weston, the barracks at Guz, Hang my tiddley suit on the door.

tiddly-om-pom-pom (tɪdlɪ'ɒm'pɒm'pɒm). [Imit.: cf. POM-POM 2.] Representing the sound or regular beat of brass-band or similar music. Also **tiddly-pom** *a.*, with a simple beat or tune, trite.
1909 J. A. Glover-Kind *I do like to be beside the Seaside* (1970) (*song*) 4 The brass bands play tiddely-om-pom-pom. **1937** *Scrutiny* VI. 333 The tiddly-pom guitar accompaniment. **1958** *Times* 30 Dec. 7/4 The brass band

certainly plays tiddly-om-pom-pom with any amount of spirit at Association football matches. **1973** T. HEALD *Unbecoming Habits* iii. 76 The piano had a tiddly pom, tin pan alley, sort of complacency.

tiddlypush (stress variable). *colloq.* A meaningless word substituted for the name of a person or thing which the speaker has forgotten, does not know, or is unwilling to mention. Cf. THINGUMMY.

1923 J. MANCHON *Le Slang* 342 And tidderly push, et patati et patata. **1934** S. BECKETT *More Pricks than Kicks* 168 He wore a belt Whenever he felt A pain in his tiddly-push. **1939** WODEHOUSE *Uncle Fred in Springtime* ii. 27 It simply says 'The marriage arranged between George Tiddlypush and Amelia Stick-in-the-mud will not take place.' **1962** *Guardian* 17 July 16/4 Mr Randolph Churchill..said..he had shown that if he wanted to 'get rid of anyone—from Lord Salisbury down to Mr Tiddlypush—he does so'.

tiddlywink ('tɪdlɪwɪŋk), *sb.* Also tidley-, tiddley-, tiddle-a-wink, (sense 2 b, orig.) Tiddledy-Winks. [In sense 1 perh. connected with slang *tiddly* a drink, drunk; in 3 perh. with *tiddly* dial. or baby-talk for 'little'.]

1. a. An unlicensed public-house or pawnshop; a small beershop; also *kiddlywink*. *slang.*

1844 J. T. HEWLETT *Parsons & W.* xxxiv, Which does more to demoralise..the lower classes than a Tom and Jerry, tidley-wink, or gin-shop. **1887** BEATTY-KINGSTON *Music & Mann.* II. 15 All the tiny tiddlywinks and spacious beer-gardens filled to overflowing.

b. *Rhyming slang.* A drink.

1880 [see *pig's ear* s.v. PIG *sb.*[1] 16 c]. **1960** J. FRANKLYN *Dict. Rhyming Slang* 129/1 *Tiddly wink*..is applied more frequently to 'shorts'..than to beer.

2. a. A game played with dominoes. **b.** *pl.* A game in which small counters are caused to spring from the table into a bell-like or cylindrical receptacle, by pressing upon their edges with larger counters. Also *attrib.* Also used *fig.* of a useless or frivolous activity; *esp.* in phr. *to play tiddlywinks*, to waste time on trivia.

1857 'DUCANGE ANGLICUS' *Vulgar Tongue* 43 At *knock'emsdown* and tiddlywink, To be a sharp you must not shrink. **1870** HARDY & WARE *Mod. Hoyle* 104 (*Dominoes*) Tiddle-a-wink game... In this game..he who plays out first cries Tiddle-a-wink, having won. **1870** *Routledge's Ev. Boy's Ann.* Nov. 672 The marked difference between Tidley-wink and other games of dominoes. **1889** *Trade Marks Jrnl.* 15 May 476 Tiddledy-Winks... Toys or games. Joseph Assheton Fincher. **1890** *Amer. Stationer* 18 Sept. 691 In 'Tiddledy Wink Tennis' E. I. Horsman..has brought out a very pretty and lively parlor game. **1892** E. LYTTON *Let.* 24 Apr. in E. Lutyens *Blessed Girl* (1953) vii. 97 We all played the most exciting game that ever was invented, called Tiddleywinks. It consists in flipping counters in a bowl. **1895** *Montgomery Ward Catal.* Spring & Summer 236/2 Tiddledy Winks may be played by any number... Each player is provided with four to six counters ..and one larger one..to press to the edge of the smaller one and..cause it to jump into the cup..in the centre of the table. **1898** *Westm. Gaz.* 4 Jan. 2/1 Cards, tiddley-winks, and ludo are played. **1906** *19th Cent.* Mar. 509 The Empress suggested the game of tiddlywinks for the Emperor's amusement. **1919** *Collier's* 8 Feb. 7 There's trouble down there and I've been playing tiddledy-winks on Broadway! **1947** *Economist* 18 Oct. 626/1 The storm was long predicted ..yet when its first icy gust blew in the windows of the Cabinet room.., it found the Ministers playing tiddleywinks. **1964** *New Yorker* 4 Apr. 147 Others seem to take little interest in the organized activities, describing them as 'make-work' or 'tiddlywinks'. **1975** *Way to Play* 135/1 Tiddlywinks golf sets, with tiddlywinks, greens, obstacles, and holes, are produced by various toy manufacturers. **1980** *Disarmament Times* 6 Oct. 4/4 This is not a game of diplomatic tiddleywinks. It is, rather, the game of human survival.

c. Any of the counters used in the game of tiddlywinks (sense 2 b); hence, a similar counter used in other games.

1891 J. K. BANGS *Tiddledywinks Tales* 35 Jimmieboy thought a great deal of his Tiddledewinks and had been playing with them nearly all that day. **1939** J. STEINBECK *Grapes of Wrath* iii. 22 His front wheel struck the edge of the shell, flipped the turtle like a tiddly-wink,..and rolled it off the highway. **1949** 'G. ORWELL' *Nineteen Eighty-Four* III. 296 Soon he was wildly excited and shouting with laughter as the tiddleywinks climbed hopefully up the ladders and then came slithering down the snakes again. **1977** B. JEWELL *Sports & Games* 109 The object was to flip the tiddlywink into one of the window openings and so ring the bell.

3. *pl.* Knick-knacks of victuals. *slang.*

1893 J. A. BARRY *S. Brown's Bunyip*, etc. 34 A drop o' good stuff, now, to wash these 'ere tiddlewinks down with.

Hence (*slang*) **'tiddlywink** *v. intr.*, (*a*) to flip like a counter in tiddlywinks; (*b*) to play tiddlywinks; **tiddly'winker**, (*a*) a cheat, a trifler; (*b*) a tiddlywinks player; **tiddly'winking** *sb.* and *a.*, (*a*) trifling, pottering; (*b*) the activity of playing tiddlywinks; **tiddly'winky** *a. dial.*, tiny, insignificant.

1869 *Routledge's Ev. Boy's Ann.* 589 Performed some 'tiddly-winking' work, that is he had shifted a few spadesful of earth. **1888** 'R. BOLDREWOOD' *Squatter's Dream* vii, I wonder what old Morgan would say to all this here tiddley-winkin', with steam-engine, and wire-fences. **1893** J. A. BARRY *S. Brown's Bunyip*, etc. 143 It was a fair an' square game... There wasn't no tiddleywinkin' in the thing. *Ibid.* 145 They're nothin' but a lot o' tiddleywinkers up there. **1901** 'ZACK' *Tales Dunstable Weir* 23 Over against Martin's cottage there was a tiddliwinkie bit o' a wood. **1958** *Sports Illustrated* 7 Apr. M5 Each tiddlywinker plays with two large and four medium-size winks. **1965** *Northeastern Reporter* 2nd Ser. CCVI. 847/2 We have raised a lot of manhole covers, and you never walk across them to see if they are going to tiddlywink. **1971** *Ottawa Citizen* 6 Feb. (Canad. Mag.) 24 He loves the game so much that in 1967 he played in a 67-hour tiddlywinking marathon. **1975** *Milwaukee Jrnl.* 25 May IV. 2/2 Dean, a high school mathematics teacher, is certainly Britain's top Tiddlywinker. **1977** P. DICKSON *Mature Person's Guide* 162 The general consensus in tiddlywinking circles is that all of this might change if the game was given a new name. **1980** *Milwaukee Sentinel* 11 Feb. 1. 6/4 (*heading*) Fame opens the eyes of those who tiddlywink.

tiddy ('tɪdɪ), *sb.* [Origin unknown: perh. = TEDDY.] In the game of gleek, the four of trumps.

1655 [see TIB *sb.* 2]. **1680** COTTON *Compl. Gamester* vi. (ed. 2) 65 (*Gleek*) The turned up Card is the Dealers; and if it be Tiddy turn'd up is four apiece from each to the Dealer. The Ace is called Tib, the Knave Tom, the four of Trumps Tiddy. **1688** R. HOLME *Armoury* III. xvi. (Roxb.) 73/2. **1822** SCOTT *Nigel* xvi, I gained the cards, and lo you! it pleases his lordship to say that we played without tiddy.

tiddy ('tɪdɪ), *a. dial.* or *nursery.* [Origin obscure. (The spelling *tidy* in quot. 1781 is not recorded elsewhere and may be an error.)] Small, very small, tiny. Also (*redupl.*) **tiddy iddy** *a.*

1781 J. HUTTON *Tour to Caves* (ed. 2) 98 *Tidy*, small. **1869** W. S. GILBERT *Bab Ballads* x. 171 A tiddy iddy daughter, and a tiddy iddy son! **1896** KIPLING *Seven Seas* 191, I got me a tiddy live 'eathen... Doll in a teacup she were. **1907** *Daily News* 4 Feb. 2/5 It was only a 'tiddy' pup. **1958** M. KELLY *Christmas Egg* III. 99 Do you know this Richborough?.. There's a tiddy railway, power cables, and the castle. **1960** 'N. SHUTE' *Trustee from Toolroom* vi. 133, I filled out the buttocks a tiddy bit on this one.

tide (taɪd), *sb.* Forms: 1 tíd (tiid), týd, 2–5 tid, 2–7 tyd, 3–7 tyde, (5 tyyde, tiid), 3– tide. [OE. *tíd* = OS. *tîd* (MLG., LG. *tît*, Du. *tijd*), OHG. *zît* (*zîd*), MHG. *zît* (Ger. *zeit*), ON. *tíð* (Sw., Da. *tid*):—OTeut. **tî-d-iz*, referred by some to a root **tî-* to extend (whence also TIME). See also note under branch II.]

I. Time.

†**1.** A portion, extent, or space of time; an age, a season, a time, a while: = TIME *sb.* 1–3. *Obs.* (or ? *dial.*)

a **700** *Beowulf* 147 Wæs seo hwil micel, xii wintra tid torn ȝeþolode. *a* **900** tr. *Bæda's Hist.* v. xiii. [xii.] (1890) 432 þa ic sume tid fram ðe ȝewat. *c* **950** *Lindisf. Gosp.* Mark ix. 21 Huu miceles *vel* longes tides. **971** *Blickl. Hom.* 125 Uncuþ bið æghwylcum anum men his lifes tid. *c* **1000** *Ags. Gosp.* Mark ix. 21 Hu lang tid is syððan him þis ȝebyrede? *c* **1000** ÆLFRIC *Hom.* I. 312 Þreo tida sind on ðysre worulde: an is seo ðe wæs butan æ;..seo ðridde is nu æfter Cristes to-cyme. [Cf. *c* **1175** *Lamb. Hom.* 89.] *a* **1300** *Cursor M.* 391 (Cott.) Bath ware made sun and mon,.. In takening o tides to stand, Dais and yeirs. *c* **1400** *Destr. Troy* 1974 And þou tary in þis towne, or any tide lenge. *c* **1412** HOCCLEVE *De Reg. Princ.* 847, I mote..suffre storm after þe mery tyde. *c* **1450** *Cov. Myst.* v. (Shaks. Soc.) 50, I come aȝen withinne a tyde. *a* **1529** SKELTON *Poems agst. Garnesche* iv. 162 Stop a tyd, and be welle ware. **1590** SPENSER *F.Q.* I. ii. 29 There they alight.. and rest their weary limbs a tide. **1603** *Philotus* lxxvii, Prouyde Ane Pages claithis in the meine tyde. **1791** J. LEARMONT *Poems* 331 (E.D.D.), I wiss that tide had been a lang lang year. **1871** WADDELL *Ps.* xxxi. 15 My tides are a' i' yer han'.

†**2.** *spec.* = HOUR 1. *Obs.*

a **900** *O.E. Chron.* an. 879, Þy ilcan ȝeare aþiestrode sio sunne ane tid dæȝes. *a* **900** *O.E. Martyrol.* 30 June 110 Þonne se monoð byð ȝeendod þe we nemnað se ærra lyða, þonne byð seo niht six tyda lang ond se dæȝ eahtatyne tyda lang. *c* **1000** ÆLFRIC *Hom.* II. 388 An wæcce hæfd þreo tida; feower wæccan ȝefyllað twelf tida. *c* **1050** *Byrhtferth's Handboc* in *Anglia* (1885) VIII. 298 Ðæt ȝer byð ȝesett on þrim hund daȝum & fif & syxtiȝum daȝum & syx tidum. *a* **1200** *Moral Ode* 137 (Lamb. MS.) Hefde he bon þer enne dei oðer twa bare tide nolde he for al middenerd þe þerdde þer abiden. *c* **1290** *S. Eng. Leg.* I. 408/223 Huy stoden and bi-heolden sein Iohan longue, þe tidene and more. *a* **1300** *Cursor M.* 14193 (Cott.) Ten tides [*F.* oures] han þe dai and tua. *c* **1430** R. *Gloucester's Chron.* (Rolls) App. BB. 3 Þe foure & twenti tydes [*v.r.* houres] in day & in þe nyȝt..he dyȝte folwel & riȝt Mid þreo grete kandlen To berne eite tides [*v.r.* houres].

3. a. A point in the duration of the day, month, or year, of human life, or of other natural (or, later, artificial) period; in reference to an action or repetition = occasion: = TIME *sb.* 13, 14. *arch.* or *poet.*

c **897** K. ÆLFRED *Gregory's Past. C.* xvii. 120 Ðonne cymð his hlaford..on ða tiid ðæt he hiene ær nat. *Ibid.* xlvii. 356 A worpen mon bið a unnyt..& on ælce tid saweð wrohte. **971** *Blickl. Hom.* 21 Þæt leoht on nanre tide ne ablinneþ. *c* **1205** LAY. 14924 Hit ilomp an are tide heo nom hire to ræde. *a* **1300** *Cursor M.* 5733 (Cott.) Þe flok he fedd opon a tid, Bi a wildrin wod side. *c* **1385** CHAUCER *L.G.W.* 783 (*Thisbe*) Ffor to mete in on place at on tyde. *a* **1400** *Pistill of Susan* 149 Such toret and teone takeþ me þis tyde. *a* **1425** *Cursor M.* 5874 (Trin.) To stonde lete ȝe hem not bide As ȝe han done mony a tyde. *a* **1529** SKELTON *El. Rummyng* 155 Such a lewde sorte To Elynour resorte From tyde to tyde. *c* **1586** C'TESS PEMBROKE *Ps.* (1823) CXLIV. v, My closett where I wont to hide In troublous tyde. *a* **1605** POLWART *Flyting w. Montgomerie* 470 At that tyd [ane after midnight] was na time for trumpers to tarie. **1635** R. JOHNSON *Hist. Tom a Lincolne* (1828) 106 Which ship had beene seven yeares upon the sea..and before this tyde could never see land. **1805** WORDSW. *Elegiac Verses on J. Wordsw.* vi, But we will see it—joyful tide! Some day..The mountain will we cross. **1868** MORRIS *Earthly Par., Man born to be King* 1272 He, who, from ill death Saved me that tide.

b. A suitable, favourable, or proper time or occasion; opportune, fit, or due time; season; opportunity: = TIME *sb.* 16. *arch.* Cf. TID *sb.*[1]

c **888** K. ÆLFRED *Boeth.* xxix. §2 Se ðe his ær tide ne tiolað, þonne bið his on tid untilad. *c* **897** —— *Gregory's Past. C.* xxxviii. 274 Hwilum sie spræce tiid, hwilum swiȝȝean. *c* **950** *Lindisf. G.* Matt. xxiv. 45 Þætte he sella him mett in tid. *c* **1060** *Charter of Eadweard* in Kemble *Cod. Dipl.* IV. 212 Alle þingen ða ðar upaspringeð, inne tyd and ut of tid. *c* **1330** R. BRUNNE *Chron.* (1810) 164 Bi Cipres side Isaac to aspie, If he toke any tide out of lond to flie. *c* **1430** *Brut* 439 Whanne tyde of passage come, thei toke the see, and passid ouyr. **1590** SPENSER *F.Q.* III. ix. 32 Then Paridell,..glad of so fitte tide Him to commend to her, thus spake. **1657** M. LAWRENCE *Use & Pract. Faith* 147 The foolish virgins lost their tide: the wise had much ado to gain it. **1887** MORRIS *Odyssey* IX. 131 For the land is nothing evil, but would bear all things in tide.

†**c.** Appointed or fixed time: = TIME *sb.* 15. *Obs.*

a **900** tr. *Bæda's Hist.* III. xiv. [xix.] (1890) 210 Waciað ȝe, forðon þe ȝe ne weoton ne ðone dæȝ ne ða tide. *Ibid.* IV. iii. 262 Þa cwom his tid, þæt he scolde of middanȝearde to Drihtne feran. *c* **950** *Lindisf. Gosp.* John ii. 4, & cueð to him se hælend..ne ðaȝet *vel* cuom tid min. *a* **1300** *Cursor M.* 21511 (Cott.) Þe Iuu him spedd til-ward his tide, Ouer term durst he noght bide. *a* **1436** *Domesday Ipswich* v. in *Blk. Bk. Admiralty* (Rolls) II. 31 Att tide and hour and tyme, that is to wetyn with ynne the xv. day..that he plete to his aduersarye.

†**4. a.** Any definite time in the course of the day; as EVENTIDE, MORROW-TIDE, NOON-TIDE, q.v.; *spec.* the point at which any hour is completed; as 'at the tenth tide of the day'; = HOUR 3. *Obs.*

a **700** *Beowulf* 484 [see MORN-TIDE]. *a* **900** tr. *Bæda's Hist.* III. xix. [xxvii.] (1890) 240 Ymb þa teoȝðan tid dæȝes. **1056–66** *Inscr. on Dial Kirkdale Ch., Yorks.*, Þis is dæȝes sol merca æt ilcum tide. *c* **1160** *Hatton Gosp.* John i. 39 Hyt wæs þa seo teoðe tyd. *a* **1300** *Cursor M.* 19810 (Edin.) Apon a dai at tide of none, An angel come and stode him bi. *c* **1391** CHAUCER *Astrol.* II. §15 Thanne wol the point of thi label sit[t]en in the bordure, vp-on the verrey tid of the day. **1493** *Festivall* (W. de W. 1515) 7 He hyred people to labour by all the tydes of the day. **1903** *Westm. Gaz.* 10 June 2/3, I go to you at gloaming-tide.

b. A more or less definite point or season in the course of the year, of life, etc., usually defined by a prefixed word; as ***April-tide***, ***June-tide***; ***New-Year's tide***, ***summer's tide***, ***winter's tide***, etc.; also AUTUMN-TIDE, SPRING-TIDE, SUMMER-TIDE, WINTER-TIDE, etc. q.v.: = TIME *sb.* 13 b. *arch.* or *poet.*

a **900** tr. *Bæda's Hist.* IV. xxix. [xxviii.] (1890) 366 Þa ne com ðær næniȝ grownes up ne wæstm, ne furðum brordes oð sumeres tid. *c* **1000** ÆLFRIC *Hom.* I. 444 Swa swa on lengctenlicere tide, rosena blostman and lilian hi ymtrymedon. *c* **1122** *O.E. Chron.* an. 1006, In þære midde wintres tide. **1541** *Rutland MSS.* (1905) IV. 312 For bryngyng a bore at Newe Yere tide, ij s. iiij d. **1556–1840** New-year's tide [see NEW-YEAR 3 b]. **1870** MORRIS *Earthly Par.* I. I. 307 When April-tide was melting into May. **1872** TENNYSON *Last Tourn.* 241 High over all the yellowing Autumn-tide. **1900** *Westm. Gaz.* 3 July 2/3 The green woods under the Junetide skies Slope and gleam to the Solent strand. **1902** *Ibid.* 20 Mar. 9/1 The profits at Coronation-tide are expected to be heavy.

†**5.** Each of the seven canonical hours; also, the services recited at these; = HOUR 5. *Obs.*

c **1000** ÆLFRIC *Colloq.* in Wr.-Wülcker 90/6 Ic sincge ælce dæȝ seofon tida. *c* **1000** —— *Saints' Lives* xxxiii. 344 Nu wille ic þæt þu..singe þær þine tida. **1028–60** *Laws Northumbr. Priests* §36 ȝif preost on ȝesetne timan tida ne ringe oððe tida ne singe, ȝebete þæt. *c* **1200** *Trin. Coll. Hom.* 215 Þane hit time beð to done þe tiden. *a* **1225** *Ancr. R.* 22 Et þreo tiden siggeð Credo mit te Pater Noster, biuoren Uhtsong & efter Prime, & efter Cumpelie. *Ibid.* 44 Toward te preostes tiden herkneð se wel ȝe muwen. **1297** R. GLOUC. (Rolls) 7605 Vor him ne ssolde no day abide þat he ne hurde masse & matines & euesong & ech tide. **13..** *Minor Poems fr. Vernon MS.* xxxvii. 767 Atome þou maiȝt ful wel abyde Til he haue seid þe laste tyde. *c* **1400** [see HOUR 5]. **1557** in *10th Rep. Hist. MSS. Comm.* App. v. 386 The said Wardayn ..shall dayly saye or singe..in the quere the tydes or houres, as tercio, sexto and nono.

6. a. An anniversary or festival of the church: chiefly in the names of holy seasons or saints' days, e.g. ***St. Andrew's tide***, †***Saint Botulf's tide***. See also ALLHALLOWTIDE, CHRISTTIDE, EASTERTIDE, LAMMAS-TIDE, SHROVETIDE, WHITSUNTIDE, HIGH-TIDE, HOLY TIDE, etc.

a **900** *O.E. Chron.* an. 759, Her Bregowine wæs to ercebisč ȝehadod to Sc̃e Michaeles tide. *a* **900** *O.E. Martyrol.* 18 May 84 On þone eahtateoȝðan dæȝ þæs monðes bið sancte Johannes tid. *c* **1050** *Byrhtferth's Handboc* in *Anglia* (1885) VIII. 300 Fram easter tide þæt he eft cume. *c* **1200** *Trin. Coll. Hom.* 3 To dai is cumen ðe holie tid þat me clepeð aduent. *c* **1200** ORMIN 8895 Att þe Passkemessedaȝȝ..þe boc hemm tahhte To frellsenn þær þat heȝhe tid. **1297** R. GLOUC. (Rolls) 10877 Sir edward ibore was A seint botulfes tid. *c* **1400** *Brut* cxxxix. 146 Þe sege endurede fro Michelmasse vnto Seynt Andrewus tyde. *a* **1568** ASCHAM *Scholem.* I. (Arb.) 36 In a fair garden about S. Iames tyde. **1595** SHAKS. *John* III. i. 86 What hath this day deseru'd.. That it in golden letters should be set Among the high tides in the Kalendar? **1611, 1615** Michaels-tide, Michael-tide [see MICHAEL 2]. **1817–18** COBBETT *Resid. U.S.* (1822) 121 The country people, in England, go, to this day,..by the tides; and,..in some cases, by the moveable tides. My gardener..very reluctantly obeyed me..in sowing green Kale..because Whitsuntide was not come, and that, he said, was the proper season. **1839** J. H. NEWMAN *Par. Serm.* IV. xxiii. 385 Feast-day and fast-day, holy tide and other tide. **1903** E. K. CHAMBERS *Mediæv. Stage* I. i. 16 Holy week, and similar solemn tides. **1957** *Oxf. Dict. Chr. Ch.* 49/2 In the

Anglican Communion, St. Andrewstide is widely observed by intercessions for foreign missions. **1975** *Church Times* 15 Aug. 2/3 Last week—St Laurence-tide—all the churches supported a flower festival in the chapel. **1976** *Ibid.* 15 Oct. 5/1 It has become the custom at St. Luke's-tide for the Church to pray for doctors.

b. *dial.* A village 'feast' or fair (taking place on the festival of the patron saint of the parish).

1824 [see *tide-time* in 15a]. **1828** *Craven Gloss.*, *Tide*, a feast; as Bingley tide. **1863** MRS. TOOGOOD *Yorks. Dial.* (MS.), Boistall-tide will be next week. **1865** R. HUNT *Pop. Rom. W. Eng.* Ser. I. (1871) 62 The strongest beer, which was intended to have been kept for a tide. **1884** *Let. to Editor*, The Annual General Holiday at Bingley, Yorks., is still called 'Bingley Tide'.

II. Tide of the sea.

[This sense corresponds exactly to MLG. *getîde* neut., *tîde tie*, neut. and fem., LG. *tīde*, MDu. *ghetîde* neut., early mod.Du. *tijde*, Du. *tij* neut., 'tide of the sea', a particular application of MLG. *getîde*, 'fixed time, time of prayer, proper time, opportunity, space of time'. OE. had no form corresp. to *getîde* (using for 'tide' (of the sea) *flód* or *flód and ebba*); and *tíd* or *tide* in this sense is not known before 1340; it may have been then introduced from or used after the MLG. word; but as ME. *tide* had neither the difference of form nor of gender seen in *de tît* and *dat tîde*, actual formal evidence of the borrowing is wanting. There may have been a transference of sense in Eng. itself, as well as in LG. The following two early examples appear to mean 'the *time* of high water', rather than the flood tide itself, or the phenomenon of the tides:

1340 HAMPOLE *Pr. Consc.* 1215 For þe se, aftir þe tydes certayn, Ebbes and flowes, and falles agayn. *c* **1386** CHAUCER *Man of Law's T.* 1036 Fro day to nyght it changeth as the tyde.]

7. a. The flowing or swelling of the sea, or its alternate rising and falling, twice in each lunar day, due to the attraction of the moon and, in a less degree, of the sun; the alternate inflow and outflow produced by this on a coast, the flood and ebb.

c **1435** *Torr. Portugal* 1430, I Rede, we take down sayle & Rowe, While we haue this tyde. **1530** PALSGR. 281/1 Tyde of the see, *flet, flote.* **1563** GOLDING *Cæsar* III. (1565) 72 There was no comming to theym on foote, by reason of the rysyng of the tydes. **1590** SHAKS. *Com. Err.* IV. i. 46 Both winde and tide stayes for this Gentleman. **1593** —— *Lucr.* 1667 As through an Arch the violent roaring tide outruns the eye. **1599** —— *Hen. V*, II. iii. 14 Iust betweene Twelue and One, eu'n at the turning o' th' Tyde. **1698** KEILL *Exam. Th. Earth* (1734) 161 It is certain, that a Comet, when it passed by the Earth, would raise a very strong and prodigious Tide in the Seas that were then on the Surface. **1816** PLAYFAIR *Nat. Phil.* II. 326 The alternate rise and fall of the surface of the sea twice in the course of a lunar day, or of 24^{h} 50^{m} 48^{sec} of mean solar time, is the phenomenon known by the name of the Tides. **1831** FR. A. KEMBLE *Let.* in *Rec. Girlhood* II. viii. 237 The tide had not yet come in.

b. In phrases (chiefly technical), as **cross tide**, a tide running across the direction of another; **high tide**, (*a*) = HIGH WATER; (*b*) = SPRING TIDE; **low tide** = LOW WATER; **leeward**, **neap**, **windward tide**: see the defining words; also FLOOD-TIDE, SPRING TIDE, HALF-TIDE. Also in fig. uses.

1627 CAPT. SMITH *Seaman's Gram.* x. 47 You say as well tide of ebbe, as tide of flood, or a windward Tide when the Tide runnes against the wind, as a Lee-warde Tide, .. when the wind and the Tide goeth both one way. **1675** TEMPLE *Let. to Sir J. Williamson* Wks. 1731 II. 336, I chose this Conveyance by the Captain of the Yacht, as both surer and speedier too, if not hindred by cross Tides in the River. **1745** P. THOMAS *Jrnl. Anson's Voy.* 120 There having been two or three high Tides before we had finished, we found [etc.]. **1867** SMYTH *Sailor's Word-bk.*, *Cross-tide*, the varying directions of the flow amongst shoals that are under water. **1875** BEDFORD *Sailor's Pocket Bk.* v. (ed. 2) 172 In the English Channel .. it is ebb tide in the harbours, while the eastern, or flood stream .. is still running up, forming what is known to Pilots as 'Tide and half Tide'.

fig. **1579** W. WILKINSON *Confut. Familye of Love* 57b, When .. his high tyde of vpright fredome [shall] become to a falling water. *a* **1700** B. E. *Dict. Cant. Crew*, *High Tide*, when the Pocket is full of Money. *Ibid.*, *Low Tide*, when there's no Money in a Man's Pocket. **1856** EMERSON *Eng. Traits*, *Relig.* Wks. (Bohn) II. 98 Plenitudes of Divine Presence, by which high tides are caused in the human spirit.

c. *transf.* A recurrent flow, alternate rise and fall or increase and decrease, other than of the sea. ***acid tide***, a temporary increase of acidity of the urine while fasting; ***alkaline tide***, a corresponding decrease of acidity during digestion.

1604 E. G[RIMSTONE] *D'Acosta's Hist. Indies* II. xiii. 113 The return of the same windes, which otherwise they call the tide or winde of the sea. **1610** HOLLAND *Camden's Brit.* (1637) 558 A wonderfull Well .. which ordinarily ebbeth and floweth foure times in the space of one houre or thereabout, keeping his just Tides. **1786–7** BONNYCASTLE *Astron.* viii. 138 The aerial tides must be much more considerable than those of the ocean. **1822–34** *Good's Study Med.* (ed. 4) I. 676 There are two tides or fluxes [of fever] within the twenty-four hours, the one occurs in the morning, the other in the evening. *Ibid.* IV. 304 A fresh tide of water will not unfrequently accumulate, and the head become as much distended as before. **1856** BRYANT *Earth* 14 Swayed by the sweeping of the tides of air. **1897** *Allbutt's Syst. Med.* IV. 293 This increased excretion is most marked during the alkaline tide.

8. The space of time between two successive points of high water, or between low water and high water, in the sea; also, that portion of this time during which the height of the water ('state of the tide') allows of work being done, as in ***tide's work***: see quot. 1867. So, in *Mining*, a period of twelve hours (*Cassell's Encycl. Dict.* 1888).

1495 *Act 11 Hen. VII*, c. 22 §1 A Calker laboring by the tyde, for as longe tyme as he may labour above the Water and beneth the Water, shall not excede for his Wages for every tyde iiijd. **1534** *Acc. Ld. High Treas. Scot.* VI. 234 Payit .. to xv men to cast the space of xv tydis about the schip, viijd. the man for ilk tyde. **1724** DE FOE *Mem. Cavalier* (1840) 281 [They] might .. come by sea in two tides. **1758** J. BLAKE *Plan Mar. Syst.* 63 A ship going into dock for a tide or two to clean. **1793** SMEATON *Edystone L.* §175 We .. landed, and got a tide's work of four hours. **1803** R. PERING in *Naval Chron.* XV. 154 (Royal Naval Yards) The extra [work] was divided into nights and tides:—a night consisted of five hours, and a tide of an hour and an half. **1867** SMYTH *Sailor's Word-bk.*, *Tide's work*, the amount of progress a ship has made during a favourable tide. Also, a period of necessary labour on a ship during the ebbing and slack water of a tide.

9. *fig.* Applied to that which is like the tide of the sea in some way; as in ebbing or flowing, rising or falling, or 'turning' at a certain time.

1390 GOWER *Conf.* II. 61 Betre is to wayte upon the tyde Than rowe ayein the stremes stronge. *c* **1430** *Hymns Virg.* 69/368 Þe tyde [of life] is ebbid, & no more wole flowe. **1508** DUNBAR *Flyting* 188 Oft beswakkit with ane ourhie tyd. **1593** [see TURN *v.* 20]. **1601** SHAKS. *Jul. C.* IV. iii. 218 There is a Tide in the affayres of men, Which taken at the Flood, leades on to Fortune. **1777** PRIESTLEY *Matt. & Spir.* (1782) I. Pref. 10 The tide of popular prejudice may rise still higher. **1781** C. WESLEY *Protestant Association* in *Poet. Wks.* (1870) VIII. 464 His faithful troops from every side Are brought to turn the rapid tide. **1843** LYTTON *Last of Barons* I. I. vii. 117 This speech turned the tide. **1849** MACAULAY *Hist. Eng.* vi. II. 54 From that moment the tide of battle turned. **1900** *Daily News* 7 Dec. 8/5 The dramatic tide has its ebb and flow like other tides. **1915** MRS. BELLOC LOWNDES *Let.* 10 Mar. (1971) 57 There is an invasion scare but I don't believe in that... I do think the tide has now turned. **1935** E. WAUGH *Edmund Campion* i. 24 That generation was inured to change; sooner or later the tide would turn in their favour again. **1941** P. CARR *English are like That* i. 18 He must have patience—patience .. in the face of misrepresentation, patience to wait for the turn of the tide. **1982** *Church Times* 5 Feb. 8/3 After that [donation] who will be surprised to hear that the tide shows signs of turning at St. Christopher's? **1982** D. FRASER *Alanbrooke* iv. 79 In the autumn of 1918 the tide finally turned.

10. *spec.* = FLOOD-TIDE. Also *fig.*

1570 LEVINS *Manip.* 116/47 Ye Tyde, *accessus maris.* **1606** SHAKS. *Tr. & Cr.* V. i. 90, I haue important businesse The tide whereof is now. **1610** HOLLAND *Camden's Brit.* (1637) 633 The River at every tide riseth to a great heigth. **1652** NEEDHAM tr. *Selden's Mare Cl.* 249 By an exquisite observation of the Tides and Ebbings of the Sea they were wont to reckon their months and years. **1826** DISRAELI *Viv. Grey* III. i, There is that at work in England which, taken at the tide, may lead on to fortune [cf. quot. 1601 in 9]. **1893** STEVENSON *Catriona* iii. 27 It seemed the devil was in it, if I was to die in that tide of my fortunes.

11. a. *transf.* A body of flowing water or other liquid; a stream, a current. *poet.* and *rhet.*

[**15..** *Sir A. Barton* xxxix. in *Surtees Misc.* (1888) 75 Betwexte Trent tid and Tyne.] **1585** T. WASHINGTON tr. *Nicholay's Voy.* II. xii. 47b, The fishes being carried by the violence of the floud, and tyde of the Euxine Sea into Propontide. **1728–46** THOMSON *Spring* 563 Stands each attractive plant, and sucks and swells The juicy tide. **1738** WESLEY *Ps.* CXXXVII. i, Fast by the Babylonish Tide (The Tide our Sorrows made o'erflow). **1757** GRAY *Bard* 144 Deep in the roaring tide he plung'd. **1855** MRS. GATTY *Parab. fr. Nat.* Ser. I. (1869) 39 She used to sing to the tide of the river as it swept along. **1872** TENNYSON *Last Tourn.* 685 Feel this arm of mine—the tide within .. Pulsing full man.

b. *transf.* and *fig.*

1601 SHAKS. *Jul. C.* III. i. 257 Thou art the Ruines of the Noblest man That euer liued in the Tide of Times. **1697** DRYDEN *Virg. Georg.* II. 644 A lofty Gate .. T' admit the Tydes of early Visitants. **1781** COWPER *Retirement* 453 The tide of life .. May run in cities with a brisker force. **1830** SADLER *Law Popul.* I. 430 A tide of emigration has set in from the Old World to the New.

12. The water of the sea; the sea (esp. when the tide is flowing). *poet.*

[**1595** SHAKS. *John* II. i. 74 A brauer choyse of dauntlesse spirits .. Did neuer flote vpon the swelling tide.] **1791** COWPER *Odyss.* XX. 74 Whelm me deep in Ocean's restless tide! **1821** BYRON *Two Foscari* I. i, Bounding o'er yon blue tide. *a* **1847** ELIZA COOK *Rover's Song* 1 I'm afloat, I'm afloat on the fierce rolling tide, The ocean's my home and my bark is my bride.

III. Phrases.

†**13. a.** ***tide and*** (*or*) ***time*** (also ***time and tide***: see TIME *sb.* 31): an alliterative reduplication, in which the two words were more or less synonyms, or = time and (or) season. *Obs.*

a **1225** *St. Marher.* 18 And te tide and te time þat tu iboren were, schal beon iblescet. *c* **1425** *Cast. Persev.* 2456 in *Macro Plays* 150 Þer is no dysese nor debate, .. tyde nor tyme, erly nor late, but þat Couetyse is þe grounde. *c* **1475** *Rauf Coilȝear* 48, I leid my life in this land with mekle vnrufe, Baith tyde and tyme in all my trauale. **1583** STOCKER *Civ. Warres Lowe C.* I. 26b, At al tide and tymes whensoeuer they shall be commaunded. **1609** *Mulb. Trees* in *Harl. Misc.* (Malh.) III. 75 If dancers keep not tide and time in their measures.

†**b.** ***the tide abides for, tarrieth*** (***for***) ***no man, stays no man, tide nor time tarrieth no man***: now superseded by *time and tide wait for no man*: see TIME *sb.* 31. Here *tide* originally meant 'time', but from the 16th c. has usually meant the tide of the sea. Cf. TIME *and tide*, in both senses. *Obs.*

1430–40 LYDG. *Bochas* III. xi. (MS. Bodl. 263) 178/2 The tid abit nat for no maner man. **1546** J. HEYWOOD *Prov.* (1867) 6 The sure sea man seeth, the tide tarieth no man. *a* **1553** UDALL *Royster D.* I. ii. (Arb.) 13 Farewell all my good friendes, the tyme away dothe waste, And the tide they say, tarieth for no man. **1579** [see TARRY *v.* 5]. **1592** GREENE *Disput.* 22 Tyde nor time tarrieth no man. *a* **1625** FLETCHER *Woman's Prize* IV. v, The tide stays no man.

14. (***in***) ***double tides***, ? as if taking advantage of both the tides in one day; esp. ***to work double tides***, to work as hard as possible; so ***to roar, spin***, etc. ***double tides***. Cf. sense 8.

1788 MME. D'ARBLAY *Diary* July, I was most content to work double tides for the pleasure of his company. **1805** *Naval Chron.* XIII. 243 The .. Caulkers worked extra double tides in gangs. **1832** *Examiner* 745/2 The artisans work double tides, that is, they perform two days' labour in one. **1852** MISS YONGE *Cameos* (1877) II. vii. 95 There is not a spinster in Brittany who will not spin double tides until my purchase-money be raised. **1889** RIDER HAGGARD *Allan's Wife*, etc. 300 The wounded lioness was now roaring double tides.

IV. Combinations.

15. In senses belonging to I, as **tide-beef**, *dial.* beef provided for a 'tide' or feast; **tide-serving**, time-serving; **tide-time** (see 6b); † **tide-wise** *adv.*, at times, now and then.

1896 *Yorksh. Weekly Post* 29 Feb. (E.D.D.), He'd made up his mind they s'ould hae some reight *tide-beef. **1818** SCOTT *Br. Lamm.* xxv, The office shall just cost him as much time-serving and *tide-serving, as if [etc.]. **1824** MISS MITFORD *Village* Ser. I. (1863) 201 At *tide-times he loiters in the chimney-corner at the Rose. **1898** T. HARDY *Wessex Poems* 203 To eyes that had seen her in tide-times of weal. **1611** FLORIO, *Interpollatamente*, at certaine seasons, not continually, *tide-wise.

16. In senses belonging to II. **a.** (*a*) simple attrib. 'of the tide, tidal', as ***tide-bar*** (BAR *sb.*[1] 15), ***-channel, -edge, -flow, -flux, -lead*** (LEAD *sb.*[2] 3b), ***-level, -limit, -line, -mud, -print, -race*** (RACE *sb.*[1] 6), ***-reach, run, rush, -stream, -turn, -wash***; (*b*) 'dependent on or regulated by the state of the tide, tidal', as ***tide-coach, harbour***; 'filled, overflowed, or covered by the tide', as ***tide-hole, -flat, -land, -marsh, -pool, -rock***; in names of instruments for measuring the tides, or the like, as ***tide-ball, -dial, -gauge, -meter, -predictor, -staff***; (*c*) objective and obj. genitive, as ***tide-master, -turner***; ***tide-generating, -predicting, -producing, -taking*** adjs. and sbs.; (*d*) instrumental, etc., as ***tide-beat, -beset, -borne, -bound, -carved, -caught, -covered, -driven, -flooded, -free, -hoisted, -like*** (also adv.), ***-locked, -looped, -ribbed, -tongued, -tossed, -traced, -trapped, -washed, -worn*** adjs.

1867 SMYTH *Sailor's Word-bk.*, **Tide-ball*, a ball hoisted to denote when the depth of water permits vessels to enter a bar-harbour, or to take the bar outside. **1898** J. BUCHAN in *To Day* 5 Nov. 7/2 The river the noo is no three feet deep a' ower, wi' sands and the shift o' the *tide-bar. **1807** J. BARLOW *Columbiad* VII. 272 Two British forts the growing siege outflank, Rake its wide works and awe the *tide-beat bank. **1957** R. CAMPBELL *Coll. Poems* II. 99 The swirl, the spray, the nimbus, and the wave Of *tide-borne lust and beauty. **1910** *Q. Rev.* July 88 *Tide-bound at midnight in a small boat off .. Deathhole Creek. **1897** *Tide-carved [see PEDIMENT[1] 1b]. **1976** *National Observer* (U.S.) 4 Sept. 7/3 We clambered down to tide-carved caverns. **1856** KANE *Arct. Expl.* II. xiv. 142 The outside *tide-channel .. was now full of squeezed ice. **1748** SMOLLETT *Rod. Rand.* xxiv, He took a place in the *tide-coach for Rochester. **1756** J. FERGUSON *Astron.* §409. 262 The *Tide Dial... A moving elliptical Plate, painted blue, to represent the rising of the Tides, under, and opposite to, the Moon. **1931** W. FAULKNER *Sanctuary* xxiii. 221 A world left stark and dying above the *tide-edge of the fluid in which it lived. **1859** C. KINGSLEY *Glaucus* (ed. 4) 146 The *tide-flats below are still unfinished, dry land in the process of creation. **1929** W. FAULKNER *Sound & Fury* 211, I saw the last light supine and tranquil upon tideflats. *a* **1644** QUARLES *Sol. Recant.* Sol. viii. 82 As *tide-forsaken Rocks along the Main. **1861** J. BROWN *Lett.* (1907) 142 Glengariff is not *tide-free. **1840** *Civil Eng. & Arch. Jrnl.* III. 342/1 A description of a new *Tide Gauge. **1860** MAURY *Phys. Geog. Sea* (Low) i. §14 The tide-gauges showed that several well-marked .. waves had arrived off the coast. **1863** TYNDALL *Heat* iv. §122 (1870) 106 The *tide generating forces of the sun and moon. **1793** SMEATON *Edystone L.* §92 The false idea .. of its being a *tide harbour, with a Bar at its mouth. **1936** DYLAN THOMAS *Twenty-Five Poems* 41 The winder of the clockwise scene .. threw on that *tide-hoisted screen Love's image. **1856** KANE *Arct. Expl.* I. xx. 260 Our *tide-hole freezes every night alongside. *Ibid.* I. xxvi. 337 The *tide-leads .. one year ago had afforded a precarious passage to the vessel. **1865** MRS. L. L. CLARKE *Seaweeds* vi. 113 If the sea-marks change, and *tide-level varies. **1878** HUXLEY *Physiogr.* 180 The Ordnance Survey has fixed its datum line, or standard from which all heights are measured, as the mean tide-level at Liverpool. **1848** MRS. GASKELL *M. Barton* Pref., With ever-returning *tide-like flood. **1854** H. MILLER *Sch. & Schm.* iv. (1860) 40 We found the waves chafing among the rocks just where the *tide-line had rested 12 hours before. **1939** DYLAN THOMAS *Map of Love* 4 Or like the *tide-looped breastknot reefed again. *Ibid.*, The silent tide Lapping the still canals, the dry *tide-master Ribbed between desert and water storm. **1849** DICKENS *Dav. Copp.* xlvi, This low girl whom he picked out of the *tide-mud. **1853** *Zoologist* II. 4055 Almost every *tide-pool and hollow that retains the sea-water. **1898** *Academy* 5 Nov. 194/1 Lord Kelvin's *tide-predicting machine. **1891** *Cent. Dict.*, *Tide-predictor. **1898** *Academy* 5 Nov. 194/1 No more marvellous instrument has ever been invented than the mechanical tide-predictor devised by Lord Kelvin. **1939** DYLAN THOMAS *Map of Love* 9 Moonfall and sailing emperor, pale as their *tide-print. **1883** *Harper's Mag.* Aug. 375/1 These numerous *tide-races often make the St. Lawrence a rough passage for small craft. **1842** Faber *Styrian Lake*, etc. 43 Thus do idle poets stand Lonely on the *tide-ribbed sand. **1844** W. H. Maxwell *Sports & Adv. Scotl.* xiii. (1855) 118 The *tide-runs are traceable upon the surface of the ocean. **1857** R. Tomes *Amer. in Japan* v. 128 An officer and two men were also stationed on land, near where a *tide-staff had been planted, and were prepared to make observations. **1795** *Essex Inst. Hist. Coll.* (1918) LIV. 101 To compensate for any supposed inconveniences that may attend a *tide stream. **1875** Bedford *Sailor's Pocket Bk.* v. (ed. 2) 146 In describing tide-streams in the offing, caution must be observed in not confusing the 'flood' and 'ebb' streams. **1934** Dylan Thomas *New Verse* xii. 11 Among the rabble Of *tide-tongued heads and bladders in the deep. **1889** P. H. Emerson *Eng. Idylls* 42 *Tide-tossed trees..rise upon the face of the waters. **1936** Dylan Thomas *Twenty-Five Poems* 44 Cartoon of slashes on the *tide-traced crater. **1922** D. H. Lawrence *Fantasia of Unconscious* xv. 272 The moon is the *tide-turner. **1882** J. Geikie in *Nature* XXVI. 44 Tracts now within *tide-wash. **1832** Lyell *Princ. Geol.* II. 181 Almost every *tide-washed rock is carpeted with fuci and studded with corallines, actiniæ, and mollusca. **1858** N. J. Gannon *O'Donoghue* ii. 28 The spray That crowns the *tide-worn rock.

b. Special combinations: **tide-board**, a board placed to prevent buildings being flooded at high tides; **tide-crack**, in polar regions, an ice-crack near the shore caused by the rise and fall of the tide, which breaks the floating from the shore ice; **tide-current**, the current caused in a tidal channel by the rise or fall of the tide (Ogilvie, 1882); **tide-day** (see quot.); †**tide-duty**, import or export duty levied at a port; **tide-flap**, a tidal valve opening outwardly at the mouth of a drain or small tidal stream; **tide-house**, a (public) house adjacent to a tidal stream; **tide-land(s)** *N. Amer.*, land(s) covered by the tide; ***tide-land spruce*** = *Sitka spruce* s.v. Sitka; **tide-lock**, a double lock between tidal water and a canal or the like; a guard-lock; **tide-maker**, that which causes the tides; also, a vessel which is compelled to take advantage of the tide; **tide-plate**, a dial on which the state of the tide is indicated; **tide-register**, a record of tide-movements; also, an apparatus that registers tide-movements; **tide-river**, a tidal river; **tide-rode** *a.*, *Naut.* (for *tide-ridden*), swung by the tide, as a ship at anchor; opposed to *wind-rode*; **tide-runner**, a fish which moves with the tide (*U.S.*); **tide-time**, the time at which the tide serves at any place; **tide-wave**, the undulation which passes over the surface of the ocean, and causes high or low tide as its highest or lowest point reaches any place; also *fig.*; **tide-weather** (see quot.); **tide-wheel**, a water-wheel turned by the flowing and ebbing of the tide through a narrow channel; **tide-work**, work which can be carried on only during hours when the tide is low, or that is paid for by the tide (cf. 8); also, part of the mechanism of a tide-gauge. See also tide-boat to tideway.

1904 *Westm. Gaz.* 31 Dec. 7/2 Thousands of tons of water poured over the *tide boards and protecting walls of various warehouses, flooding the wharves and warehouses. **1856** Kane *Arct. Expl.* II. xiii. 131 He has risen by the side of an ice-berg..or through a *tide-crack. **1833** Herschel *Astron.* xi. 337 The *tide-day (i.e. the interval between two successive arrivals at the same place of the same vertex of the tide-wave. **1769** Falconer *Dict. Marine* (1789), *Compost*, a *tide-duty, or revenue, arising from shipping. **1843** *Civil Eng. & Arch. Jrnl.* VI. 426/1 At the end of the main sewer was placed a cast-iron frame, upon which were hung three *tide-flaps with brass facings. **1764** *Low Life* 100 The Landlords of *Tide-Houses, both up and down the River Thames, looking out sharp for Boats. **1787** W. H. Siebert *Loyalists in E. Florida, 1851–94* (1929) II. 239, 200 acres of rich *tide land well dam'd. **1891** *Cent. Dict.*, Tide-land. **1895** *Home Missionary* (N.Y.) Sept. 292 Deep alluvial valleys of great fertility, tide-lands similar to those of Holland. **1975** *N.Y. Times* 25 Feb. 16/3 Gas resources did not become a controversial issue until the mid-nineteenthirties when oil companies began drilling wells in the tidelands. **1884** C. S. Sargent *Rep. Forests N. Amer.* 206 *Tide-Land Spruce... A large tree of great economic value. **1969** R. C. Hosie *Native Trees Canada* (ed. 7) 68 Sitka Spruce. Tideland Spruce... Produces a long, branch-free, cylindrical trunk. **1808** B. H. Latrobe *Let.* 16 Mar. in *Niles' Reg.* (1818) XV. 54/2 It would be necessary to place the *tide lock as far out as possible. **1838** *Civil Eng. & Arch. Jrnl.* I. 148/2 The method by which the main or framing piles of the coffer-dam for the tide-lock..were fixed to the rock. **1875** [see *guard-lock* (guard *sb.* 18)]. **1903** *Westm. Gaz.* 6 Jan. 4/2 The moon is not only a *tide-maker in the marine sense. Its tangential 'pull' affects the earth's atmosphere. **1910** *Chamb. Jrnl.* Jan. 10/2 His hard overworked apprenticeship to the sea in coasting-schooners, in undermanned, under-engined 'tide-makers'. **1756** J. Ferguson *Astron.* §409. 263 The Elliptical or *Tide Plate, with the Moon fixt to it, is upon the Axis of the Wheel. **1825** J. Nicholson *Operat. Mechanic* 496 An error of three-quarters of an hour in each lunation will place the tide-plate H, three hours wrong in the space of about four months. **1856** Kane *Arct. Expl.* I. xi. 117 Our *tide-register was on board the vessel. **1739** Labelye *Short Acc. Piers Westm. Br.* 80 So wide a *Tide-River as the Thames. **1823** Crabb *Technol Dict.*, **Tide-road* (*Mar.*), the situation of a vessel which, being at anchor when the wind and tide are opposed to each other, has her head towards the current. **1882** Nares *Seamanship* (ed. 6) 197 When not tide rode, pick the lee anchor up. **1877** Hallock *Sportsman's Gaz.* 244 These big fellows [weak fish] are designated as *tide-runners. **1840** *Civil Eng. & Arch. Jrnl.* III. 182/1 *Tide-time for vessels of 12-feet draft, is denoted by 2 black balls being kept upon its flag-staff until 12-feet ceases upon the straight course. **1833** Herschel *Astron.* xi. 339 The *tide-wave rushing up a narrow channel, is suddenly raised to an extraordinary height. **1861** T. R. Birks *Bible & Mod. Th.* Introd. 5 The tidewave of sceptical thought, which threatens..to bury the old landmarks of Christian faith. **1740** Lynn in *Phil. Trans.* XLI. 689 When the Mercury has been a good while high,..there has fallen mistling Rain; especially about the New and Full Moon, with an Easterly Breeze, which the Borderers on the Coast of Lincolnshire and Norfolk call *Tide-weather, and may be occasioned by the Vapours arising from the Tides, which then cover a vast Wash of Sands in their Neighbourhood. **1864** Webster, **Tide-wheel*. **1888** Goode *Amer. Fishes* 205 A circular basin, ..aerated by a powerful fountain of sea water, forced up by a tide-wheel. **1739** Labelye *Short Acc. Piers Westm. Br.* 33 The Remainder being only common *Tide-work, has nothing worth relating. **1825** J. Nicholson *Operat. Mechanic* 493 The wheel-work and tide-work of this clock are represented by fig. 498. **1852** Wiggins *Embanking* 122 Some allowance is to be made for tide-work and night-work, for bad weather on the coast, loss of materials.

tide (taɪd), *v.*[1] Forms: 1 *tídan*, 3–5 *tiden* (3–4 *tyd*, 4 *tid*, 4–5 *tyden*, 4–7 *tyde*, 5 *tydyn*), 3– *tide*; *pres. t. 3rd sing.* (for *tideth*) 3–4 *tit*, *tyt*, *tyd*, 4 *tid*, 5 *tite*, *tytte*. *Pa. t.* 1–4 *tidde*, 4 *tydde*, *tyd* (6 *Sc.*), 4–5 *tid* (5 *tyde*, *tide*), 8– *tided*. *Pa. pple.* 3–4 *tid* (4–5 *tyd(d*, *tidde*, 5 *tide*, 6 *tydde*), 7– *tided*. [OE. *tídan* (oftener *ȝetídan*: see i-tide) to happen, come about, f. *tíd*, tide *sb.* Perfect tenses usually formed with *be*: cf. come *v.*]

1. *intr.* To happen, befall: = betide *v.* 1. Often impersonal. *arch.*

a **1131** *O.E. Chron.* an. 1123 Þa tidde hit on an Wodnes dei ..Þet se king rad in his der fald. **1297** R. Glouc. (Rolls) 8649 He..nolde no leng abide Þat he nolde to is game, tide wat so bitide. **13..** *Cursor M.* 27412 (Cott.) For nakin case Þat mai tide. **1375** Barbour *Bruce* i. 127 Ȝe traistyt in lawte, ..And wyst nocht quhat suld eftir tyd. ? *a* **1400** *Morte Arth.* 3655 Of theire termys they talke, how Þay ware tydd. **14..** *Sir Beues* (MS. M) 663 Tyde what wyll be-tyde The tone of vs shall dede abyde. *c* **1440** *Promp. Parv.* 493/2 Tydyn, *idem quod* happyn. *c* **1460** *Towneley Myst.* vi. 81 May tyde he wille oure giftis take. **1513** Douglas *Æneis* vi. v. 98 How tyde that cais; declair me, I pray the. **1680** A. Haig in J. Russell *Haigs* xi. (1881) 309 Com what will com, tyde what may tyde, A Haig shall be Laird of Bemersyde. **1808** Scott *Marm.* iii. xxii, Soothly I swear, that, tide what tide, The demon shall a buffet bide. **1875** Jas. Grant *One of the 600* ii, You..shall find that, tide what may, you are not forgotten.

†**b.** const. with *dative*: = betide *v.* 1 b. *Obs.*

c **1000** *Inst. Polity* c. 10 in Thorpe *Ags. Laws* II. 316 Þæt heora ȝewitan beon on æȝhwylcne timan, weald hwæt heom tide. *c* **1200** *Trin. Coll. Hom.* 29 Witte wel hwat Þu hauest, walte hwat Þe tide. **13..** *Guy Warw.* (A.) 4977 Al his lond him tit for-go. **1377** Langl. *P. Pl.* B. xi. 5 (MS. Rawl.) A merueillous meteles me tydde to dreme. *c* **1384** Chaucer *H. Fame* i. 255 Euery caas That hym was tyd vpon the see. *c* **1430** *R. Gloucester's Chron.* (Rolls) App. G. 213 Þi lyf Þe tydeÞ luse. *c* **1590** Greene *Fr. Bacon* xiii. 14 Some deadly act shall 'tide me ere I sleep.

†**2.** To fall as a lot or portion. (Const. *dative*.)

955 in Birch *Cart. Sax.* III. 75 ȝif Þan biscop[e] hwæt tide. *a* **1272** *Luue Ron* 20 in *O.E. Misc.* 93 Her he haueÞ seorewen ryue, Ne tyt him neuer Ro ne Rest. *c* **1300** *St. Margarete* 308 Bote Þu do Þis dede Ne tyt Þe no part wiÞ me. *c* **1305** *St. Swithin* 48 in *E.E.P.* (1862) 44 He so doÞ his dede mid bobance, him ne tyt non oÞer mede. *c* **1325** *Poem Times Edw. II* 236 in *Pol. Songs* (Camden) 334 He doth the wif sethe a chapoun and piece beof, Ne tit the gode man noht therof. *c* **1386** Chaucer *Reeve's T.* 255 This lange nyght ther tydes me na reste.

†**3.** To fare; to get on (well or ill). *Obs. rare*[−1].

c **1400** *Destr. Troy* 1202 The Troiens were tyde, & tid Þere Þe bettur.

¶**4.** *trans.* To meet with, experience (good or evil fortune). *Obs.*

This appears to be an erroneous use, originating with copyists who misunderstood the construction.

a **1400** *R. Brunne's Chron. Wace* (Rolls) 5495 (Petyt MS.) For chances Þat haf ben tyd [*Lamb. MS.* ffor swylke chaunces Þat han bytid]. *a* **1400** *Sir Beues* 1844 Go, or Þe tit [*v.r.* Þou tytyst] an euel diner. *c* **1472** *Chaucer's Compl. Mars* 202 (MS. Arch. Seld. B. 24) In mony a cas thay tiden oft tyme sorowe [*Fairfax and 2 other MSS.* hem tydeth, *ed. Jul. Notary* hem tyden].

tide (taɪd), *v.*[2] [f. tide *sb.* II.]

1. *trans.* **a.** To carry, as the tide does. Chiefly *fig.*

1640 Quarles *Enchirid.* iii. 48 Man's Will is the Streame that Tydes them [our actions] up and downe. **1693** Dryden *Persius' Sat.* vi. (1697) 494 The Relicks of the Wrack..are tided back By the wild Waves, and rudely thrown ashore. **1824** Lady Granville *Lett.* June, A flow of animal spirits and good humour..tided off anything approaching to bore. **1884** *Daily News* 30 Oct. 7/3 So long will each flood continue to tide up the river varying proportions of sewage or other offensive matter.

b. †To carry through (an undertaking) (*obs.*); to enable (a person) to surmount (a difficulty, etc.) as on a swelling tide.

1626 B. Jonson *Staple of N.* iv. iv, I will tyde this affayre for you; giue it freight and passage. *c* **1860** in Holman-Hunt *Pre-Raphaelitism* (1905) II. 196 We should like to tide him over his low-water difficulties. **1869** Goulburn *Purs. Holiness* viii. 73 As an exuberant mounting flood shall tide us over the difficulties of our career. **1870** J. Bruce *Life of Gideon* vi. 109 We are to be tided over all our doubts and difficulties by what I would call a swelling flood of evidences or proofs.

2. *intr.* (and with *it*). To flow or surge, as the tide; to flow to and fro; sometimes = 'flow' as opposed to 'ebb'. Also *fig.*

1593–1654 [see tiding *vbl. sb.* 1]. **1659** W. Brough *Schism* 555 When popular favour blows from us, and secular power tydes it against us and storms us. **1661** Webster & Rowley *Thracian Wonder* v, The seas, Whose equal valour neither ebbs nor tides. **1833** T. Hook *Parson's Dau.* ii. xii, The muddy stream of domestic correspondence [*i.e.* between the servants] which 'tided' between Binford and Severnstoke. **1843** E. Jones *Sens. & Event* Poems 3 The sounding crowd That far beneath him tides.

3. *trans.* To make to flow as a tide or stream.

1861 Dickens *Gt. Expect.* xix, Tiding it [a roll of cloth] out in a flowing manner over the counter.

4. *intr.* To float or drift on the tide; *spec. Naut.*, to navigate a ship by taking advantage of favouring tides, and anchoring when the tide turns; usually with adv. of direction. Often ***to tide it.***

1627 Capt. Smith *Seaman's Gram.* x. 47 To Tide ouer to a place, is to goe ouer with the Tide of ebbe or flood, and stop the contrary by anchoring till the next Tide. **1691** Luttrell *Brief Rel.* (1857) II. 244 Our fleet..are now sailed out, and are now tiding it down with the wind directly against them. **1716** Lady M. W. Montagu *Let. to C'tess of Mar* 3 Aug., We..set out in a calm, and he pretended there was nothing so easy as to tide it over [from Gravesend to Holland]. **1836** Marryat *Olla Podr* xxvi, We tided and warped how we could. **1893** H. M. Doughty *Wherry in Wendish L.* 71 We could in the morning tide it up further with the flood. **1896** A. Austin *Eng. Darling* iv. ii, Hither there tided The loose-limbed Briton.

b. *fig.* To pass or be carried as on the tide; to drift.

1835 Mrq. Londonderry in Dk. Buckhm. *Crt. Will. IV* (1861) II. vii. 186 These questions would certainly tide on till next year. **1842** Manning *Serm.* (1848) I. 86 He will most surely tide onward..down the broad current of eternal death.

c. quasi-*trans.* ***to tide one's way***: to make one's way by using the tides; also *fig.*

1833 Southey *Lett.* (1856) IV. 332 Ministers are now endeavouring to tide their way through the session. **1854** H. Miller *Sch. & Schm.* (1858) 361 We tided our slow way north.

5. *intr. fig.* ***to tide over***: to get over or surmount (a difficulty, time of stress, etc.) as if by rising on the flowing tide, or by taking advantage of a favourable tide. With *indirect passive.* Also †***to tide it out*** (obs.).

a **1659** Osborn *Ess.* ii. Wks. (1673) 558 Christianity..is prescribed by her Institutes to Tide it out, although the Stream of its Inconveniencies runs never so strong against the Nature of Man. **1821** Earl of Dudley *Lett.* 21 Apr., I wish we may be able to tide over this difficulty. **1865** Seeley *Ecce Homo* iv. (ed. 8) 36 The transgressor has but to tide over a few years. **1884** *Manch. Exam.* 12 May 4/7 We..believe that for the moment the difficulty is tided over.

tide, obs. pa. pple. of tie *v.*; obs. var. tite *adv.*

tide-boat. A boat or small vessel which travels with or by means of the tide.

1576 *The tyde taryeth no man* in Collier *Illustr. E.E. Pop. Lit.* (1863) 77 He dyed in a great madnesse, And went with the tyde boat straight into Hell. **1611** Cotgr., *L'Anguille*, the name of the tyde-boat which passes betweene Blaye, and Bourdeaux. **1710** *Brit. Apollo* III. No. 25. 3/2, I lately in Tide-Boat to Gravesend did steer. **1840** Dickens *Barn. Rudge* li, He may get to the Tower Stairs, and away by the Gravesend tide-boat.

tided ('taɪdɪd), *ppl. a.* [f. tide *sb.* + -ed[2].]

a. Having tides, tidal. **b.** Seasoned, as in ***well-tided***, well-timed, seasonable (*dial.*).

a. 1852 Whittier *Questions Life* 28 The tided oceans ebb and flow. **1858** —— *Swan Song* iii, Broad meadows reached out seaward the tided creeks between.

b. 1801 *Farmer's Mag.* Apr. 225 The operations of husbandry..have been carried forward..in that well-tided order and condition, as to induce us to form the most hopeful prognostication.

tideful ('taɪdfʊl), *a.* [f. tide *sb.* 3 b, 7 + -ful.]

†**1.** Seasonable, opportune, right, fit, convenient, expedient. *Obs.*

a **1300** *E.E. Psalter* xxxi. 7 [xxxii. 6] For Þat sal bid to Þe with blisse Al halegh in tideful time [Wyclif nedful time]. *a* **1340** Hampole *Psalter* cxliv. 16 [cxlv. 15] Þou gifis Þe mete of Þaim in tydefull tyme. **1382** Wyclif *Jas.* v. 7 An erthe tilyer abijdith precious fruyt of the erthe, paciently suffringe, til he receyue tymeful [*v.r.* tideful] and lateful.

2. Having a full tide; filled with the tide.

1622 Drayton *Poly-olb.* xix. 3 Stem vp his tyde-full streame, vpon that side to rise. *Ibid.* xxvi. 248 The lustie Salmon..stemming my tydefull Streame. **1887** *Blackw. Mag.* Oct. 539 Up fair Bristol's tideful channel.

Hence †**'tidefully** *adv.*, opportunely; †**'tidefulness**, a fit or expedient season; time of need.

a **1340** Hampole *Psalter* ix. 9 Helpere in tydfulnesses in tribulacioun. *Ibid.* 22 [x. 1] Þou dispises in tydfulnesis in tribulacyon [L. *despicis in oportunitatibus in tribulacione*]. *Ibid.*, Nedfully [*v.r.* tidfully] Þou suffris vs to be angird and tribled.

†**tide-gate**[1]. *Obs.* [f. tide *sb.* 7 + gate *sb.*[2]] = tideway.

1557 W. Towrson in Hakluyt *Voy.* (1589) 113 Like vnto a streame or tyde gate. **1599** Nashe *Lenten Stuffe* 8 Now.. graueld vp, and the streame or tyde gate turned another way. **1678** Phillips (ed. 4), *Tidegate*, in Navigation is where the Tide runs strongest. **1704** J. Harris *Lex. Techn.* I. s.v. *Tide*,

When the Tide runs very strong, they call it a Tide Gate. **1711** SIBBALD *Descr. Shetland* 3 The Rousts and high tide-gates of the Sea about the Promontories and the Isles. **1867** SMYTH *Sailor's Word-bk.*

tide-gate². [f. as prec. + GATE *sb.*¹] A gate through which the water passes into a dock or the like at flood-time, and by which it is retained during the ebb.

1755 JOHNSON, *Tidegate*, a gate through which the tide passes into a bason. **1838** *Civil Eng. & Arch. Jrnl.* I. 410/2 As the embankments rise, the tide-gates will be arranged so as to regulate the quantity of water inside the bays. **1858** SIMMONDS *Dict. Trade, Tide-gate*, the entrance gate of a dock.

tideless ('taɪdlɪs), *a.* [f. TIDE *sb.* + -LESS.] Having no tide; unaffected by tides; not washed or covered by a tide. Also *fig.*

1779 SHERIDAN *Critic* II. ii, Can the quick current of a patriot heart Thus..freeze in tideless inactivity? **1816** BYRON *Siege of Cor.* xvi, There shrinks no ebb in that tideless sea. **1865** *Pall Mall G.* 29 Sept. 11/1 In proximity.. to some tideless and stinking port. **1886** *Manch. Exam.* 12 Mar. 5/3 The waters of the tideless Mediterranean.

b. *Comb.* **'tideless-ˌblooded** *a.*, whose blood is unstirred by passion or emotion.

1785 BURNS *To Jas. Smith* xxvi, Douce folk, that live by rule, Grave, tideless-blooded, calm and cool. **1806** MAR. EDGEWORTH *Leonora* i, Is it possible that Olivia can envy these tideless-blooded souls their happiness?

Hence **'tidelessness**, tideless state or condition.

1901 *Westm. Gaz.* 7 Oct. 3/1 What I particularly like about this Mediterranean sea is its beautiful tidelessness.

tideling, obs. form of TIDLING, pet.

†**'tidely**, *adv. Obs.* [f. TIDE *sb.* 8 + -LY².] At each tide; each time the tide serves.

1482 in C. Welch *Tower Bridge* (1894) 89 Layers of wylchons, and other fysshers, lieing almost dayly and tydely at the said stadelynges.

tidely, obs. f. TIDILY; var. TITELY *Obs.*

tideman: see TIDESMAN.

'tide-mark. The mark left or reached by the tide at high or (rarely) low water; by extension, the mark left by a river flood. Also, a post or the like set up to mark the rise and fall of, or the point reached by the tide. Also *fig.*; *spec.* a line of dirt left on a surface, esp. at the limit to which water has reached (cf. HIGH-WATER MARK c).

1799 *Scotl. Described* (ed. 2) 16 Shells have been discovered..at a considerable distance above the highest tide-mark. **1861** DICKENS *Gt. Expect.* liv, Red landmarks and tidemarks stuck out of the mud. **1861** J. R. GREENE *Man. Anim. Kingd.* II. *Cœlent.* 232 Many..*Actinidæ*, it is well known, are numerous between tide-marks, the common Sea-anemone tending to encroach upon the line of high water. **1865** GEO. ELIOT *Ess.* (1884) 203 A particular class of facts..in their relation to certain grand tide-marks of opinion. **1907** *Daily Chron.* 27 Dec. 4/4 You may still trace the tidemark of the flood by tufts of dried grass and driftwood sticking in the branches above your head. **1907** N. MUNRO *Daft Days* xxii. 190 With a smut on your nose and tide-marks on your eyebrows. **1928** *Daily Express* 20 Dec. 5/3 Your fur collar leaves a horrid tide-mark after it has been worn for a time. **1934** A. HUXLEY *Beyond Mexique Bay* 197 A tide-mark of grit..running round the bath. **1957** J. M. MACKINTOSH in 'C. H. Rolph' *Human Sum* ix. 177 The succession of tide-marks round the necks of my young patients. **1973** C. EGLETON *Seven Days to Killing* ii. 27 She ..casually lit a cigarette; pink lipstick formed a tide-mark around the filter tip. **1976** T. HEALD *Let Sleeping Dogs Die* i. 21 From the hooks..she took three cups, chipped..and with tidemarks of tea clearly visible an inch below the rim. **1977** A. CARTER *Passion of New Eve* ix. 113 Dead peonies in enormous glass jars streaked with tide marks where the water had evaporated long ago.

†**'tidement**. *Obs. rare*⁻¹. [f. TIDE *sb.* + -MENT.] Time, tide, season.

1560 ROLLAND *Crt. Venus* I. 26 Quhilk..That tydement crauis be his operatioun.

'tide-mill. [f. TIDE *sb.* 7 + MILL *sb.*¹]

1. A mill driven by the flux and reflux of the tide acting on a water-wheel.

1640 *Essex Inst. Hist. Coll.* (1863) V. 169/2 Captane Traske hath leave to sett up a tyde myll upon the North River. **1755** *Mass. Prov. Acts* (1878) III. 810 Tide-mills that have or shall be set up on across the mouth of rivers. **1796** W. H. MARSHALL *W. England* II. 63 A low bank, thrown up across these marshlands,..gives effect to a tide mill, situated near one end of it. **1825** J. NICHOLSON *Operat. Mechanic* 94 Tide-mills,..are such as employ for their first mover the flowing and ebbing tide, either in the sea or a river. **1870** E. L. GARBETT in *Eng. Mech.* 11 Mar. 624/3 Corn has been ground by tide-mills.

2. 'A mill for clearing lands from tide-water' (Webster, 1828).

tidend(e, tider(r, obs. ff. TIDING, THITHER.

'tide-rip. [f. TIDE *sb.* 7 + RIP *sb.*⁵ I.]

1. A commotion of the sea caused by opposing currents, or by a rapid current passing over an uneven bottom.

1830 N. S. WHEATON *Jrnl.* 518 We are now on George's Bank, and surrounded with tide-rips, having precisely the appearance of those at the mouth of a river. **1860** MAURY *Phys. Geog. Sea* §752 Tide-rips present their most imposing aspect in the equatorial regions. **1875** R. F. BURTON *Gorilla L.* (1876) I. 2 When the current, setting to the north-west, meets a strong sea-breeze from the west, there is a criss-cross, a tide-rip.

2. A tidal wave or current.

1903 *Blackw. Mag.* Mar. 380/1 It was known as Fort Comosun or 'Rush of Waters' after the tide-rip that races up the Victoria arm. **1904** *Westm. Gaz.* 4 Feb. 5/2 A tidal wave —a 'tide rip', as the sailors call it, because they can see it approaching like a ripple on a smooth sea—is a disturbance on the surface of the ocean depending entirely on the influence of the moon.

tidesman ('taɪdzmən). Also 8–9 **tideman**.

†**1.** = TIDE-WAITER 1. *Obs.*

1667 *Lond. Gaz.* No. 194/4 Discovered by some of the Customehouse Tydes-men upon the Watch. **1773** EARL CARLISLE in *Selwyn & Contemp.* (1844) III. 46 Thank Charles for the Tideman's place. **1809** R. LANGFORD *Introd. Trade* 135 Tides men or tide waiters, officers appointed to inspect the loading and unloading ships to prevent contraband transactions.

2. One whose work depends on the tide.

1882 OGILVIE, *Tides-man*, one who is employed only during certain states of the tide. **1894** C. WELCH *Tower Bridge* 51 Twenty-one tidemen working at the ram.

'tide-surˌveyor. A customs official who supervised the tide-waiters. So **'tide-super-ˌvisor**.

1684 E. CHAMBERLAYNE *Pres. St. Eng.* II. (ed. 15) 243 Stephen Chuseman, Tide Supervisor of all the Tide Surveyors on the River of Thames. **1725** *Lond. Gaz.* No. 6390/7 John Etheridge, Gent... Tide Surveyor of His Majesty's Customs. **1806** in J. Smyth *Pract. of Customs* (1821) 145 The articles to be guarded from and to the Ships, and an account to be taken of them by the Tide-waiters, under the special superintendence of the Tide-surveyors. **1892** *Pall Mall G.* 24 Mar. 6/3 For many years tide surveyor and harbour-master at Pakhoi.

†**'tides-way**. *Obs.* [f. *tide's*, poss. of TIDE *sb.*] The way of the tide; = TIDEWAY.

1627 CAPT. SMITH *Seaman's Gram.* i. 1 You may hale in a ship..out of the tides way. **1793** SMEATON *Edystone L.* §157 A vessel lies..at moorings, though in a Tide's-way.

'tide-table. [f. TIDE *sb.* 7, 8 + TABLE *sb.* 10.] A table, or tabular list, showing the time of high water at a place or places on each day during the year or other period.

1594 J. DAVIS (*title*) The Seaman's Secrets,..wherein is taught the three kindes of Sayling,..also an Horizontall Tyde Table. **1710** *Brit. Apollo* III. No. 85. 2/1 Mr. Flamstead's Tide-Table..will shew him the Time of High-Water. **1840** *Encycl. Brit.* (ed. 7) XXI. 284/1 Tolerably accurate tide-tables have long been published annually for London, and still better for Liverpool.

'tide-ˌwaiter.

1. A customs officer who awaited the arrival of ships (formerly coming in with the tide), and boarded them to prevent evasion of the custom-house regulations. Now *Hist.*

1699 FARQUHAR *Constant Couple* I. i, These tidewaiters and surveyors plague us more with the French wines, than the war did with the French privateers. **1754** RICHARDSON *Grandison* (1781) I. xxxv. 247 That I shall get employment on the Keys, or as a tide-waiter extraordinary. **1821** J. SMYTH *Pract. of Customs* 3 Upon the receipt of the Warrants, the Landing-waiter is to give an order to the Tide-waiter on board the Ship, without which no Goods can be permitted to be unladen. **1876** SMILES *Sc. Natur.* xiii. 267 He was willing to be a police officer, a tidewaiter, or anything that would bring in a proper maintenance.

2. *fig.* One who waits for a favourable season.

1841 MIALL in *Nonconf.* I. 249 The tide-waiters and time-servers of reform are evidently at a discount. **1901** *Daily News* 15 Feb. 6/5 Political tidewaiters, whose loyalty..may ultimately be reconciled with high salaried posts.

Hence **'tide-ˌwaitership**, the office of a tide-waiter.

1855 THACKERAY *Newcomes* xi, He would ask the minister for a tide-waitership for him. **1866** LOWELL *Presid. on Stump* Prose Wks. 1890 V. 265 His own chance of reëlection, or that of some fourth cousin to a tidewaitership.

'tide-ˌwater. Also tidewater.

1. Water brought by the flood-tide.

1799 LD. HAWKE in R. Brown *Agric. Surv. W. Riding* xii. §6. 164 The tide water that has been previously admitted by the flood gate opens the clough again, and discharges itself. **1836** *Hull & Selby Railw. Act* 108 Conveying the tide-water from the river Ouse. **1911** QUILLER-COUCH *Shining Ferry* vii. 75 A mort o' tide-water have runned up an' down since you spoke they words.

2. *U.S.* Water affected by the ordinary ebb and flow of the tide; tidal water.

1772 *Va. Statutes at Large* (1821) VIII. 564 The extension of the navigation of James river..will be greatly promoted by cutting a canal..from the Westham to the tide water. **1832** J. F. WATSON *Hist. Tales N.Y.* 38 [Hudson City] is deemed at the head of tide water and ship navigation. **1876** BANCROFT *Hist. U.S.* V. ix. 424 The scanty naval stores..had to be transported from tide-water to the lake.

b. *attrib.* Designating or pertaining to regions situated on tide-water or affected by tides, *esp.* (also with capital initial) eastern Virginia. Also *ellipt.*, a tide-water region, esp. that of eastern Virginia.

1832 J. P. KENNEDY *Swallow Barn* I. xviii. 179 The tide-water country of Virginia. **1835** *Southern Lit. Messenger* I. 662 The tranquil and affectionate hearths of tide-water Virginia. **1868** *Rep. U.S. Commissioner Agric.* (1869) 389 Throughout the tide-water district, the whole country is believed to be underlaid by deposits of fossil shells. **1884** *Century Mag.* Apr. 825/2 Mr. Jones..[has] one of those thin, mournful faces common to tide-water Maryland. **1936** W. FAULKNER *Absalom, Absalom!* vii. 222 He didn't listen to the vague and cloudy tales of Tidewater splendor that penetrated even his mountains. **1943** *Sun* (Baltimore) 14 June 10/1 A comprehensive program to increase the annual harvest of the oyster industry has been submitted to conservation authorities in the various tidewater States. **1944** L. MUMFORD *Condition of Man* vi. 216 The stately tide-water mansions of Virginia. **1949** B. A. BOTKIN *Treas. S. Folklore* I. ii. 32 Within his state the Southerner thinks in terms of Eastern Shore or Tobacco Country, Tidewater or Valley, [etc.]. **1976** *Amer. Speech 1974* XLIX. 45 The Delmarva area..comprises southern Delaware, portions of the eastern shore of Maryland, and the peninsula and islands of tidewater Virginia. **1979** D. ANTHONY *Long Hard Cure* xxi. 166 A hardnosed captain of industry who wanted a pretty mannequin from tidewater aristocracy. **1980** *Amer. Speech* LV. 285 It is common in the Virginia piedmont and tidewater.

c. *attrib.* Designating bodies of water affected by tides.

1835 J. MARTIN *Descr. Virginia* 40 A tide water river, or more correctly a bay, the Chowan. **1888** GOODE *Amer. Fishes* 3 A deep hole in the bed of a tide-water creek. **1939** *WPA Guide to Florida* (1984) II. 177 Daytona Beach..is a city with a triple waterfront, one on the Atlantic Ocean and one on each side of a tidewater lagoon.

'tideway. A channel in which a tidal current runs; also the tidal part of a river; *transf.* a strong current running in such a channel; = TIDE-GATE¹.

[1627–1793: see TIDES-WAY.] **1798** *Hull Advertiser* 4 Aug. 2/4 A gunboat..being very manageable in a strong tideway. **1810** J. T. in *Risdon's Surv. Devon* p. xxxii, It..serves to convey shipping from the Tideway. **1856** KANE *Arct. Expl.* I. xxvii. 359 A moment's check would plunge the whole concern into the rapid tide-way. **1875** BEDFORD *Sailor's Pocket Bk.* v. (ed. 2) 153 Sounding in a tide-way it may be necessary to anchor the boat.

fig. **1821–30** LD. COCKBURN *Mem.* iii. (1874) 149 His shop, in the very tideway of all our business, made it the natural resort of..all sorts of literary idlers. **1880** G. MEREDITH *Tragic Com.* (1881) 60 A lead that..would roll him on a good tideway strong in his own passion and his lady's up against the last defences. **1883** *Century Mag.* Oct. 823/1 Henry VIII.'s palace has not been forever a barber's shop, or the Strand a tide-way of shop-keeping.

tidied ('taɪdɪd), *ppl. a.* [f. TIDY *v.* + -ED¹.] That has been made tidy; esp. with *up*.

1922 E. O'NEILL *Hairy Ape* v. 49 A general atmosphere of clean, well-tidied, wide street. **1959** *Daily Tel.* 28 July 5/3 (*heading*) Russians get 'tidied-up' version of Nixon clash.

tidier ('taɪdɪə(r)). [f. TIDY *v.* + -ER¹.] One who makes (something) tidy. Also **tidier-up**, (*colloq.*) **tidier-upper**.

1923 *Public Opinion* 15 June 565/3 He became a champion tidier from that moment on. **1961** J. WILSON *Reason & Morals* i. 8 The philosopher seems to be not so much a universal aunt as a sort of universal tidier-up. **1963** *Times Lit. Suppl.* 25 Oct. 849/3 Among scientists there are collectors, classifiers, and compulsive tidiers up. **1976** CULROSS & ROBB *Leaving Home* iv. 32 Nancy was the neat sort..and..an habitual tidier-upper.

†**'tidife, -ive**. *Obs. rare.* Also 4 tydif(e, tydyf, tideue, ti-, tydyue. [Origin and sense obscure: cf. also TYDIE, and TIDIVE = TIDY *a.*] Name of some small bird. (Swainson, after Skinner, suggests the Blue titmouse.)

c **1385** CHAUCER *L.G.W.* 154 And thoo [birds] that hadde doon vnkyndenesse As dooth the tydif [*v.rr.* tydyf, tydife] for new fangelness Besoghte mercy..And sworen on the blosmes to be trewe. *c* **1386** —— *Sqr.'s T.* 640 Alle thise false fowles As beth thise tidyues [*v.rr.* tydyues, tydifs, tideues] tercelettes and Owles. **1671** SKINNER *Etymolog.*, *Voc. Antiq.*, *Tidefes*..avis genus, nescio an illa avis quam nos Titmouse vocamus.

tidily ('taɪdɪlɪ), *adv.* Also 4–6 **tidely**. [f. TIDY *a.* + -LY².] In a tidy manner; †betimes, seasonably, duly (*obs.*); suitably, in an orderly manner, skilfully, neatly, etc.: see TIDY.

1340–70 *Alisaunder* 194 þe fairest feete þat euer freke kende, With ton [= toes] tidily wrought. *c* **1350** *Will. Palerne* 4454 Alphouns..buskes in to þe baþ..& fond it treuli a-tired & tidily warme. *Ibid.* 5482 He..tok to him tidely trewe cunsayl euere. *c* **1400** *Destr. Troy* 6839 þen the Troiens, with tene, tidely þai faght. **1557–8** LD. WENTWORTH in Hardwicke *St. Papers* (1778) I. 112, I will do what I can tidily to signify unto your Majesty our State. **1593** G. HARVEY *New Let.* Wks. (Grosart) I. 259 You haue lately..very tidely playde the Bees part. **1771** MRS. HAYWOOD *A New Present* 252 To dress herself tidily and quickly. **1832** R. & J. LANDER *Exped. Niger* I. iii. 112 The inhabitants are..very tidily clad in cotton dresses. **1870** MRS. RIDDELL *Austin Friars* i, The plates are all ranged tidily away.

tidiness ('taɪdɪnɪs). [f. as prec. + -NESS.] The quality or condition of being tidy (in various senses: see the adj.); †seasonableness; orderliness, neatness.

1567 MAPLET *Gr. Forest* 9 b, For lacke of their naturall.. growth and tidinesse in ripening. **1800** AMELIA OPIE *Let.* in *Life* v. (1854) 74 He has gotten a fit of tidyness on him. **1860** BOYD *Recreat. Country Parson* vi. 200 Tidiness is a great source of cheerfulness. **1879** SALA in *Daily Tel.* 9 June, One row of houses..admirable in their neatness, tidiness, cheerfulness, and commodiousness.

tiding ('taɪdɪŋ); pl. **tidings** ('taɪdɪŋz), *sb.* Forms: see sense 2 below. [Late OE. *tídung* f., early ME. *tiding*, as if f. OE. *tíd-an* vb. to happen, befall + -ING[1]; but prob. ad. ON. *tíðendi*, *-indi* neut. pl., 'events, occurrences, the reports of these, news, tidings', f. *tíðr* adj. happening, occurring + *-endi*, *-indi*, nominal suffix (see Vigfusson *Icel. Dict.* xxxiii/1); thence MSw. *tidhende* event, occurrence, news, Sw. *tidender* m. pl., Norw. and Da. *tidende* n. sing. tidings. In form, late OE. *tídung* (obl. cases **tídunge* (*-a*), pl. nom. *-a* (*-e*), gen. *-a*, dat. *-um*) might well be a deriv. of *tíd-an*, TIDE *v.*[1]; but the fact that, beside it, early ME. had also *tiðende*, *-inde*, *tīthend*, clearly from Norse, also *tiðing*(*e*, with Norse stem and Eng. suffix, and *tīdende*, *-inde*, with Eng. stem and Norse suffix, together with the fact that the word is unknown to OE. before the late 11th or early 12th c., and is recorded first in the transferred sense 'tidings', makes it probable that the whole group in Eng. was adopted from ON., in the north in the Norse form, in the south anglicized, in intervening districts with various mixtures of the two forms. It is noticeable that the English or fully anglicized form is that which happens to occur earliest in an extant writing, and also that which survives in mod.Eng., though the Norse type (with Eng. pl. *-s*) *tithand*(*e*)*s*, *tithans*, came down to 15th c. in north. Eng. and to 16–17th c. in Sc.

In ON. *tíðindi* is only plural; so Sw. *tidender*; in Norw. and Da. *tidende* is sing.; in early ME. *tiðende* was sing. or pl., with a tendency to make the sing. *tiðend*; the anglicized *tidung*, *-ing*, normally had the pl. **tidunga*, *tidinge*; but, as in other fem. sbs., the *-e* of the oblique cases of the sing. was often taken by the nom. A single instance of pl. *tiðenden* occurs in the later text of Layamon; but from *c* 1275 the plurals became *tidinges* and *tithand*(*e*)*s*. The existing form *tidings* is usually construed as pl., but sometimes as sing.: cf. *news*. Ger. *zeitung*, MHG. *zîtunge* (1321 in Niederrheinisch) = MLG. *tidinge* (1458 in Bremen Doc.), Du. *tijding*, which agree in form with Eng. *tiding*, are of later appearance, and by some held to be due to Scandinavian influence (Kluge).]

1. Something that happens; an event, incident, occurrence. *Obs.* or *arch.*

(This is the etymologically earlier sense; though not exemplified in Eng. quite so early as sense 2, it was no doubt current in the Danelaw district from the first. In the two late quots. a literalism of translation.)

c **1205** LAY. 7543 þa isæh Cesar tiðend þat him wes sær [*c* **1275** tidinge þat was sor]. *c* **1386** CHAUCER *Man of Law's T.* 628 How that this blisful tidyng [*Petw. MS.* tydyngges] is bifalle. **1502** *Ord. Crysten Men* (W. de W. 1506) v. vi. 411 In the delytes of paradyse is neuer founde ony varyacyon, alwayes in loue without tydynges. **1861** DASENT *Story of Burnt Njal* I. 107 It must be told what tidings [Icel. *hvat tíðenda*] happened at home. **1864** —— *Jest & Earnest* (1873) II. 192 The tokens that are left of those tidings which happened there.

†**b.** Custom, usage. *Obs. rare.*

(Cf. ON. *tíðr* customary, habitual, that happens, *tíðska* custom, usage, fashion.)

c **1205** LAY. 396 After þen heðene tidende [*c* 1275 lawe] þe wes in þan lande. *Ibid.* 2052 [see TIR]. *Ibid.* 14325 Hit beoð tiðende [*c* 1275 þe wone] Inne Sæxe-londe..þat [etc.].

2. The announcement of an event or occurrence; a piece of news (now *obs.* or *arch.*); usually in *pl. tidings*, reports, news, intelligence, information.

α. (1) *Sing.* 1–2 **tídung**, 3–4 **tidinge**, (3 **tidding**), 3–6 **tydinge**, 3–7 **tyding**, 4–5 **tid-**, **tydyng**(**e**, (5 **tytynge**), 2– **tiding**.

1069–1125 *O.E. Chron.* an. 995 (MS. F.), Ða wearþ se cing swyþe bliðe þissere tidunge. *c* **1250** *Gen. & Ex.* 2907 Moyses told hem ðis tidding. *c* **1275** LAY. 1376 þe tiding com to Corineum, þat [etc.]. *Ibid.* 22323 þe tyding com to þan kinge. **13..** *Cursor M.* 5114 (Gött.) þis tyding his soru slake. *c* **1385** CHAUCER *L.G.W.* 1424 (*Hypsipyle & Medea*) Theere was swich tydyng [*v.rr.* tidynge, tiding] oueral & swich loos. **1390** GOWER *Conf.* II. 238 This tyding Of Jason. *a* **1400** *R. Gloucester's Chron.* (Rolls) 7979 (MS. B) þer of com to normandie þe tydynge attelaste. *Ibid.* 9178 (MS. B) Tytynge him com þat [etc.]. *c* **1485** *Digby Myst.* (1882) III. 1087 To me þis is a Ioyfull tydyng. **1620** I. V. tr. *P. du Moulin's Serm.* 4 It is a blessed tyding of which Jesus Christ not only is the subject and substance, but also the bearer and proclaimer. **1879** L. SHEPHERD tr. *Guéranger's Liturg. Year* I. vi. 68 At such a tiding as this, what else can I, than cry out, ..Lord! I am not worthy.

(2) *Plural.* 1 ***tídunga**(**-e**), 2–3 **tid-**, **tydinge**, **tidynge**, 3–4 **tiding**; 3–6 **tid-**, **tydinges**, **-ynges**, 4–6 **-ingis**, **-yngys**, **-yngges**, 5 **tidenggez**, 5–8 **tydings**, 6 **tid-**, **tydyngs**, *Sc.* **-engs**, 6– **tidings**.

c **1200** *Vices & Virt.* 17 Ic scal iheren reuliche tidinge. *c* **1205** LAY. 3601 þe swein..seide þas tidinge [*c* **1275** þeos tiding]. *c* **1275** *Ibid.* 1038 þeos tidinge him were loþe. *Ibid.* 8582 þe tidinges him were lefue. *Ibid.* 24427 Many tidynge Mid Arthur þan kinge. *c* **1350** *Will. Palerne* 4877 þe murþe ..mad for þo tiding whan þei told were. **13..** *Cursor M.* 7798 (Gött.) I cum, to telle þe tydinges lele. **1486** *Plumpton Corr.* (Camden) 54 Sir, as for tydings, here is but few. **1535** COVERDALE *Jonah* iii. 6 The tydinges came vnto yᵉ kinge of Niniue. **1671** MILTON *P.R.* II. 62 Her Son,..left at Jordan, tydings of him none. **1782** COWPER *Gilpin* xlii, What news? what news? your tidings tell. **1852** MISS YONGE *Cameos* I. ii. 13 Further tidings were anxiously awaited. **1869** FREEMAN *Norm. Conq.* (1875) III. xiii. 260 Perplexed for a moment by the suddenness of the tidings.

β. (1) *Sing.* 3 **tiðinge**, (3 **tiþingue**), 4 **teþinge**, 4–5 **tiþ-**, **tyþ-**, **tyth-**, **tith-**, **-ing**, **-yng**(**e**, (6 **teytheyng**).

c **1290** *S. Eng. Leg.* I. 6/190 He seide þat one tiþingue to him fram is fader he brouȝte. *c* **1305** *St. Lucy* 155 in *E.E.P.* (1862) 105 A ioyful teþinge ic ȝou telle. *c* **1330** R. BRUNNE *Chron.* (1810) 14 þat Brittrik was dede him com tiþing. **1375** BARBOUR *Bruce* II. 454 He wes blyþ off þat tithing. **1483** *Cath. Angl.* 389/1 To telle Tythynge, *rumificare*. **1596** *King & Barker* 62 in Hazl. *E.P.P.* I. 7, Y know now teytheyng, the thanner seyde.

(2) *Pl.* 2–3 **tiðinge**; 3–5 **tiþ-**, **tithinges**, 4 **tethinges**, 4–6 **tyþ-**, **tyth-**, **tith-**, **-inges**, **-ynges**, **-yngus**, **-ingis**, **-ingys**, 5 **tithyngs**, **tythings**, **tithings**.

c **1175** *Lamb. Hom.* 93 Ða iwearð þer muchel eie..on alle þam þat þeos tiðinge iherdon. *c* **1200** *Trin. Coll. Hom.* 31 Gode tiðinge and murie to heren. *c* **1290** *Beket* 1493 in *S. Eng. Leg.* I. 149 þo þeos tiþinges to þe kingue..cam. *c* **1300** *Ibid.* 695 (Percy S.) 34 Tethinges to the kinge come. *c* **1380** WYCLIF *Serm.* Sel. Wks. I. 198 Good tiþingis of þe kyngdom of hevene. *c* **1400** MAUNDEV. (Roxb.) xxv. 119 When any tythings er herd in þe cuntree. *c* **1440** *Partonope* 2697 Sone after haue they tithings. **1530** RASTELL *Bk. Purgat.* Prol., What tythinges or news. **1567** *Gude & Godlie B.* (S.T.S.) 49 To zow thir tythingis trew I bring.

γ. (1) *Sing.* 3 **tiþennde** (*Orm.*), **tiðende**, **-end**, **-ind**, 4–5 **tythand**(**e**, 4–6 **tiþ-**, **tithand**(**e**, (4 **tyȝ-**, **tiȝand**), 5 **tiþond**(**e**, (9 **tithand**).

c **1200** ORMIN Ded. 158 Goddspell onn Ennglissh nemmnedd iss..god tiþennde. *c* **1205** LAY. 1376 þa tiðind [*c* 1275 tiding] com to Corineum þat [etc.]. *Ibid.* 7543 þa isæh Cesar tiðend [*c* 1275 tidinge] þat him wes sære. *a* **1300** *Cursor M.* 12785 þai sent þair messageres..To bring fra iohn certan tiþand [*Fairf.* tiþande, *Trin.* tiþond]. *c* **1430** *Syr Tryam.* 156 They..tolde the kynge hur tythande. **1513** DOUGLAS *Æneis* II. vii. [vi.] 50 How now, Panthus, quhat tithand do ȝe bryng? **1819** W. TENNANT *Papistry Storm'd* (1827) 69 He'd got some tithand from the coast.

(2) *Pl.* 3 **tiðende**; **-en**; 4 **tiþandus**, (**tyȝandes**, **tiþans**), 4–5 **tythandis**, 4–6 **tiþandis**, **-es**, **tythands**, 5 **tythandes**, **-andys**, **-ondys**, **tithands**, **-anndez**, **-aundes**, 6 **-indes**, *Sc.* **tythance**.

c **1205** LAY. 1038 þæs tiðende [*c* 1275 þeos tidinge] him weren læðe. *Ibid.* 13996 Heo sæiden to þan kinge neowe tiðenden. *a* **1352** MINOT *Poems* iii. 58 þe galay men.. thanked God of þir tiþandes. **13..** *Cursor M.* 15912 (Cott.) For tiþans þat war tald. *Ibid.* 10312 (Gött.) þis angel.. Brogh him tyȝandes sua gode. *Ibid.* 3322 (Fairf.) þe maydyn ranne hame tiþandus to tel. *c* **1440** *York Myst.* xxiii. 60 Som new tythandys. *c* **1450** *St. Cuthbert* (Surtees) 7802 þe tithands went to many towns. **1533** GAU *Richt Vay* (S.T.S.) 105/32 This promis is the vangel or ioiful tithandis. **1560** ROLLAND *Seven Sag.* 115 Of ȝour tythance I am richt wonder glaid. *a* **1584** *Satir. Poems Reform.* xx. 26 At me thay speir Quhat tythands in this land?

δ. (1) *Sing.* 3 **tidende**, **tidind**, 4 **tydand**, **-ant**, 4–5 **tydande**, 5 **tydond**, **tydynde**.

c **1205** LAY. 17466 þat tidende com to þan kinge. *c* **1275** *Ibid.* 9936 Come þe tidind [*c* 1205 þa tiðende] to Maurus þan kinge. *c* **1330** R. BRUNNE *Chron. Wace* (Rolls) 5005 Men tolde þe kyng tydant, þat Romayns were aryue on land. *Ibid.* 15936 Til hym cam ful smert tydande [*rime* on lande]. **13..** *Cursor M.* 10417 (Gött.) Quen þat scho herd þis tydand [*Cott.* tiþand, *Laud* tydond, *Trin.* tiþonde]. *c* **1400** *Laud Troy Bk.* 15242 To telle him of her tydande. *c* **1460** *Launfal* 838 Everych man therfore was wo That wyste of that tydynde.

(2) *Pl.* 3 **tidinde**, **-ende**; 5 **tid-**, **tydandes**, **-is**, **-annes**, **tytandis**, 6 *Sc.* **tydinnis**, **tydance**.

c **1205** LAY. 3332 For ȝef ferrene kinges Hiherde þa tidinde. *Ibid.* 5139 Selcuðe tidende. **1451** CAPGRAVE *St. Gilbert* 72 þe grete fere þat he hadde þat he schuld her no euel tytandis of hem. *Ibid.* 115 The archbischop..saide he was glad of þese tydannes. **1513** DOUGLAS *Æneis* XI. xvii. 65 All the maist cruell tydinnis fillis his eris. *a* **1585** MONTGOMERIE *Flyting* 72 Wee will heir tydance..of thy pow.

ε. *Sing.* and *pl.* 3 **þyþingue**, 4 **thiþand**, (**thyȝandez**), 5 **thythyng**, **-es**, **thiþynges**, 6 **-thingis**.

c **1290** *St. Lucy* 157 in *S. Eng. Leg.* I. 105 Ane Ioyeful þyþingue ich eou telle. **13..** *Cursor M.* 10994 (Cott.) To þam he moght tell na thiþand [*v.rr.* tiþand, tiþond, tydond]. ?*a* **1400** *Morte Arth.* 1567, I ȝif the for thy thyȝandez Tolouse þe riche. *c* **1400** *R. Gloucester's Chron.* (Rolls) 4251 Hom com tydinge [*MS. β.* thiþynges]. *c* **1425** *Seven Sag.* (P.) 1538 When he herde thys thythyng. *c* **1500** *Lancelot* 2279 Whar that al thithingis goith and cumyth son.

b. plural const. as singular.

c **1375** *Cursor M.* 15912 (Fairf.) Tiþinges þat was talde. **1595** SHAKS. *John* IV. ii. 115 The tydings comes, that they are all arriu'd. **1619** W. SCLATER *Exp. 1 Thess.* (1638) 214 When tidings is brought us of Brethrens faultings. **1643** TRAPP *Comm. Gen.* xxxv. 22 Jacob's great amazement at this sad tidings. **1839** CARLYLE *Chartism* (1842) 48 The tidings was world-old, or older.

†**c.** *fig.* Indications, traces. *Obs. rare.*

a **1440** *Sir Eglam.* 367 Where the bore had wonte to bee; Tydyngys of hym sone he fonde, Slayne men on every honde.

3. *Comb.*, as *tidings-bearer*, *-bringer*, *-bringing*, *-maker*.

c **1440** *Promp. Parv.* 493/2 Tydyngys berare, *rumigerulus*. **1483** CAXTON *Cato* g vj b, Thou arte a lyar and a tydynges maker. **1526** TINDALE *Acts* xvii. 18 He semeth to be a tydynges brynger off new devyls [COVERD. goddes]. **1535** COVERDALE *1 Sam.* iv. 17 Then answered the tydinge bringer, & sayde: Israel is fled before the Philistynes. **1552** HULOET, Tidynges carier, *renuncius*, *ij*. **1632** SHERWOOD, A Tidings bringing, *nunciation*.

Hence ˈ**tidingless** *a.*, without tidings.

1822 *Blackw. Mag.* XI. 398 As tidingless returning as before. **1870** MORRIS *Earthly Par.* III. 430 Tidingless a while day passed by day.

ˈ**tiding**, *vbl. sb.* [f. TIDE *v.*[2], or TIDE *sb.* + -ING[1].]

†**1.** The flowing or rising of the tide; also *fig.*

1593 B. BARNES *Parthenophil* Sonn. xli, More than blessed was I, if one tiding Of female favour set mine heart afloat! **1639** G. DANIEL *Ecclus.* xii. 16 The gust of Sin, may Stir a Surly tiding, In Seas pacifique. **1654** WHITLOCK *Zootomia* Pref. a v, Would you know (saith he) my manner of writing? it is a kind of voluntary Tiding of, not Pumping for; Notions flowing, not forced. **1675** E. WILSON *Spadacrene Dunelm.* 21 No more of the River comes back again by tiding than what the Sea forc'd up at the time of its tiding.

b. *attrib.* **tiding time**: in quot. *fig.*

1693 PASCHALL in *Phil. Trans.* XVII. 816 The Fits generally lasted all the Tiding time, and then went off in gentle kindly Sweats in the Ebbs.

2. A sailing or drifting with the tide.

1681 T. DUSELEY in *Trans. Kilkenny Archæol. Soc.* Ser. II. IV. 320 They very easily putt to sea.., a very small matter of tideing (if any) serves turne. **1711** W. SUTHERLAND *Shipbuild. Assist.* 164 Stream Anchor; which stops the Ship in tiding up a River. **1774** PENNANT *Tour Scot. in 1772* 241 After tiding for three hours anchor in the Sound. **1817** KEATINGE *Trav.* II. 143 Some little advantage in point of position..with convenience of tiding up inland.

ˈ**tiding**, *ppl. a.* [f. TIDE *v.*[2] + -ING[2].] That ebbs and flows; tidal.

1622 DRAYTON *Poly-olb.* xxx. 88 There is a Tyding-well, That daily ebbs and flowes. **1654** WHITLOCK *Zootomia* 372 If we fling our Bread upon the Waters, we chuse not Currents that run all one way (and that from us), but tyding waters. **17..** PHILIPS (J.), Wading within the Ouse, he dealt his blows, And sent them, rolling, to the tiding Humber. **1839** STONEHOUSE *Axholme* p. xiv, The Isle of Axholme.. admirably situated on the banks of a tiding river.

tidingman, U.S. var. TITHINGMAN[1] c.

†ˈ**tidive**, *a. Obs. rare*[−1]. [Alteration of TIDY *a.*, after adjs. in -IVE; perh. by association with HASTIVE, HASTY, *tardife*, TARDY, etc.] Timely, opportune: = TIDY *a.* 1.

?**17..** *Lord Barnett*, etc. xv. in Child *Ballads* III. (1885) 257/1 Being in the tidive hour.

tidliche, **tidlike**, **tidly**, var. TITELY *Obs.*

tidling (ˈtɪdlɪŋ). *Obs.* exc. *dial.* Also 6 **tideling** (**-ynge**), 9 *dial.* **tiddling**. [? deriv. of TIDDLE *v.* 1 or TID *a.*: see -LING[1].] A pampered or spoilt child; a darling, pet; a young, delicate, or puny child or animal, needing special care; a weakling, 'dilling'.

1520 WHITINTON *Vulg.* 37 b, These cokeneis and tidelynges wantonly brought vp. *a* **1553** *Nice Wanton* in Hazl. *Dodsley* II. 164 She for their sake, Being her tender tidlings, will me beat. [Cf. *ibid.* 173 [referring to the same persons] My parents did tiddle me: they were to blame; *ibid.* 174 Yet were we tiddled, and you beaten now and then.] *c* **1580** JEFFERIE *Bugbears* III. i. in *Archiv Stud. Neu. Spr.* (1897), The gray beard daunceth, and fareth as he weare dame venus tideling. **1657** TRAPP *Comm. Ps.* iii. Introd., Absalom his Son, his Darling, his Tidling, his one Eye. **1904** *Eng. Dial. Dict.* s.v. *Tiddle*, *Tiddling*, (*a*) a young animal, esp. a lamb, brought up by hand; a delicate child needing care; (*b*) the smallest pig in a litter.

tidology (taɪˈdɒlədʒɪ). *rare.* [irreg. f. TIDE *sb.* + -(O)LOGY.] The study or science that treats of the tides. Hence **tidoˈlogical** *a.*, of or pertaining to tidology.

1834 WHEWELL in Todhunter *Acc. Writ.* (1876) II. 194 Do not omit to mention what the Liverpool people..have done for Tidology. **1840** —— *Philos. Induct. Sci.* (1847) II. 509, I have ventured to employ the term *Tidology*, having been much engaged in tidological researches. **1843** MILL *Logic* VI. iii. §1 No one doubts that Tidology (as Dr. Whewell proposes to call it) is really a science.

tidy (ˈtaɪdɪ), *a.* (*sb.*, *adv.*) Forms: 3–5 **tidi**, 4–5 **tide**, 4–7, 9 *Sc.* **tydy**, 5 **tyde**, (**tithy**), 6 **tidie**, **tydye**, 6–8 **tydie**, 7 *Sc.* **tyddie**, (9 *dial.* **teydey**), 4, 7– **tidy**. [ME. f. *tíd* time, TIDE + -Y. Cf. OHG., MHG. *zîtig* (Ger. *zeitig*), Du. *tijdig*, Sw., Da. *tidig* timely.]

A. *adj.* †**1. a.** Timely, seasonable, opportune; in season.

c **1350** *Will. Palerne* 1339 Gret merþe..meliors þan made for þe tidy tidinges. *Ibid.* 1710 Til she say tidi time hire prey for to take. *c* **1475** *Partenay* 5722 Of nouel thinges..Nothing I fynd at no tydy stounde. **1594** CAREW *Tasso* (1881) 66 Nor place serues fit, nor season tidie growes. **1660** F. BROOKE tr. *Le Blanc's Trav.* 270 Hearing of this tydie accident, he was cautious to appear. **1721** RAMSAY *Horace to Virg.* 5 King Æol, grant a tydie tirl.

†**b.** *tidy cow*, a cow giving milk. *Sc. Obs.*

1493 *Act. Dom. Conc.* (1839) 300 þe mylk of thre tithy ky. **1533** in *Munim. Burgh Irvine* (1890) I. 39 Ane tydy kow. **1670** in *Proc. Soc. Ant. Scot.* (1896) XXX. 20 Too tydie kay & four yeell [i.e. dry] kay. **1678** *Ibid.*, Two tyddie key and a two yeir old kow.

2. In good condition, or of good appearance; fair, well-favoured, comely, bonny; fat, plump, healthy. In quot. 1340–70, showy, gorgeous. Now *dial.*

c **1250** *Gen. & Ex.* 2105, .vii. eares wexen fette of coren, On an busk ranc and wel tidi. **1340–70** *Alex. & Dind.* 599 We..no tidi atir in templus araie. **1393** LANGL. *P. Pl.* C. XIII. 187 Seedes þat been sowen and mowe suffre wyntres, Aren tydyour and tower. **1513** DOUGLAS *Æneis* III. iv. 23 Flockis and hirdis of oxin and of fee, Fat and tydye. **1573** TUSSER *Husb.* (1878) 131 If weather be faire, and tidie thy graine, Make speedily carrege, for feare of a raine. **1597** SHAKS. *2 Hen. IV*, II. iv. 250 Thou whorson little tydie Bartholmew Bore-pigge. **1607** TOPSELL *Four-f. Beasts* (1658) 518 When a Sow is very fat she hath alway but little milk, and therefore is not apt to make any good tidy Pigs. **1714** GAY *Sheph. Week, Friday* 76 Before my Eyes will trip the tidy Lass. **1803** R. ANDERSON *Cumbld. Ball.* 56 Bonny, teydey, blithe was she. **1808** JAMIESON, *A tydy bairn*, a child that is plump and thriving. **1881** GRANT WHITE *Eng. Without & Within* xvi. 387 Among them [the lower middle class] a tidy girl means a pretty girl, and particularly a girl with a good figure.

3. As an indefinite epithet of admiration or commendation. †**a.** Good, excellent, satisfactory, useful; of good character or ability; worthy, brave; able, skilful. (Also ironically.) *Obs.*

c **1350** *Will. Palerne* 2496 Forto telle what tidde of þat tide werwolf. *Ibid.* 5384 Al þat touched þer to a tidi erldome, To þe kowherd & his wif þe king ȝaf þat time. **1393** LANGL. *P. Pl.* C. XXII. 441 Trauaileþ..for a tretour al-so sore As for a trewe tydy man. *c* **1400** *Destr. Troy* 1035 Soudiours..Of the tidiest of Tessaile, tore men of strenght. **1567** DRANT *Horace, Ep.* II. ii. Hj, A seruaunte at his masters beck tydie, prompte, preste and fyne. **1613** BEAUM. & FL. *Coxcomb.* II. i, Thou art the tidiest wittol..I think above ground. *a* **1625** FLETCHER *Woman's Prize* IV. ii, What a hap had I, And what a tydie fortune, when my fate Flung me upon this bear-whelp?

b. Now in lighter use: Fairly satisfactory, 'pretty good', 'fair' (in quality); decent, of a good sort; nice. (*colloq.*)

1844 DICKENS *Lett.* (ed. 2) I 116 Which I thought for a coastguardman was rather a tidy question. **1851** MAYHEW *Lond. Labour* I. 133 Parsons and doctors are often 'tidy customers'. **1865** DICKENS *Mut. Fr.* III. i, A tidy shot that, I flatter myself. **1899** E. PHILLPOTTS *Human Boy* iii. 82, I hope he did [succeed], for he was a tidy chap, though queer.

c. Considerable (in amount or degree); 'pretty big'. ***a tidy penny*** = 'a pretty penny' (PRETTY *a.* 5). (*colloq.*)

1838 DICKENS *Nich. Nick.* xxxii, You came along at a tidy pace. **1851** MAYHEW *Lond. Labour* I. 352 If it is just after quarter-day, she generally gets a tidy tip. **1854** *Househ. Words* IX. 69/1, I have a tidy penny in the funds. **1881** BLACKMORE *Christowell* ii, A horse who had been to Exeter and back with a tidy load. **1893** LADY BURTON *Sir. R. F. Burton* II. 252 A very large garden..wherein one could take a very tidy walk. **1903** SIR M. G. GERARD *Leaves fr. Diaries* ix. 324 They do swear a tidy bit.

4. (The chief current use.) **a.** Of persons: Orderly in habits, or in personal appearance; disposed to keep things (or one's person or dress) neat and in order.

1706 PHILLIPS (ed. Kersey), *Tidy*, handy, neat, clean, as A tidy Servant. *a* **1800** PEGGE *Suppl. Grose, Tidy*, neat. North. **1818** SCOTT *Hrt. Midl.* xxxiii, If thou knowest of any tidy lass like thysell, that wanted a place, and could bring a good character. **1831** D. E. WILLIAMS *Life & Corr. Sir T. Lawrence* II. 72 [The child] folds up her things like a tidy lady's maid. **1849** LYTTON *Caxtons* 13 My dear mother was the tidiest woman in the world.

b. Of things, esp. of a house, room, receptacle, etc.: Neatly arranged; with nothing in disorder or out of place; orderly, neat, trim.

1828 WEBSTER s.v., The children are tidy; their dress is tidy... The apartments are well furnished and tidy. **1840** DICKENS *Barn. Rudge* iv, There was not a neater, more scrupulously tidy, or more punctiliously ordered house in Clerkenwell. **1859** *Habits Gd. Soc.* viii. 271 Some underbred ladies..put tidy their work-boxes, making you feel that you are secondary. **1880** JEFFERIES *Gt. Estate* 201 He objected to cut and trim them [shrubs, etc.]. 'For', said he, 'God made nothing tidy'.

5. *Comb.*, as ***tidy-mindedness***; ***tidy-looking***, ***-minded***, ***-sized*** (in sense 3) adjs.; **tidy-betty**, an ash-pan (*dial.*); **tidy bin**, a bin into which things may be discarded or tidied away, a waste-bin.

1884 *Health Exhib. Catal.* 71/2 Front Damper acting as a 'Tidy Betty' with Cinder-sifter. **1900** *Leeds Mercury* 9 May, He struck her on the head with a 'tidy-betty', and then kicked her with his clogs. **1972** *House & Garden* Dec. 84/3 Colourful bathroom accessories, including shelf units, tidy bins, mirrors. **1978** *People's Friend* 13 May 3/3 Lifting some toffee papers and preparing to transfer them to the tidy bin, she spotted the torn photograph. **1825** J. NEAL *Bro. Jonathan* I. 19 He was a small, meagre,..tidy-looking somebody. **1900** J. K. JEROME *3 Men on Bummel* vii. 156 Fit for a tidy-minded lover of German nature. **1951** *Essays & Studies* IV. 21 Too much tidy-mindedness and love of classification. **1975** J. P. MORGAN *House of Lords & Labour Govt.* vi. 163 Even if administrative tidy-mindedness..was the motive behind the Seats Bill.., its consequences would still transcend any administrative convenience. **1922** JOYCE *Ulysses* 628, I want to see everyone..having a comfortable tidysized income. **1945** W. DE LA MARE *Scarecrow* 128 'Lor bless me,' said Alice. 'The questions he asks!'.. 'And that's a tidy-sized one too!' said Alice, smiling at him again.

B. *sb.* **1.** A name for various articles intended to keep persons or things tidy or neat. **a.** A pinafore or overall. *dial.*

a **1825** FORBY *Voc. E. Anglia, Tidy*, a light outer covering worn by children, to keep their clothes from dirt and grease.

b. An ornamental loose covering for the back of a chair or the like, usually of fancy work; an antimacassar.

1850 *Knickerb. Mag.* XXXVI. 255 (Thornton *Amer. Gloss.*) One cane-seated rocking-chair, the back of which is covered with an unapproachable netting of spotless white, called a 'tidy'. **1861** J. PYCROFT *Agony Point* (1862) 126 After a few magic passes—the placing of a screen, the arrangement of a tidy or the folds of a curtain,..—a room..becomes..instinct with life, and grace, and comfort. **1882** MRS. L. C. LILLIE *Prudence* 61 Is that a tidy? Yes... They call them antimacassars and sofa-backs here.

c. A bag or other receptacle in which to keep scraps, odds and ends, etc.; a work-bag; a toilet-tidy.

1828 *Craven Gloss., Tidy*, a work bag, &c. **1863** W. B. JERROLD *Signals Distress* 207 It was in the days when..every scrap of cotton or linen found its way into the 'tidy'.

2. An act of making tidy; a period of time devoted to tidying. Freq. with *-up*.

1909 E. NESBIT *Daphne in Fitzroy St.* ix. 122 The dreadful neatness that follows a 'good tidy-up'. **1915** KIPLING *Diversity of Creatures* (1917) 428 We'll pull up the blinds and we'll have a general tidy. **1949** N. STREATFEILD *Painted Garden* xiii. 140 Rachel was going on to tell Jane to give her hair a tidy. **1970** C. WHITMAN *Death out of Focus* ix. 141, I bustled around..giving my flat a rough tidy-up. **1971** H. WILSON *Labour Govt.* xxxvi. 756, I went for a quick wash and tidy-up. **1980** 'T. HINDE' *Daymate* I. vi. 53 [She] is coming to give his house its Saturday morning tidy.

C. *adv.* Tidily; pretty well; nicely, finely; also *ironical*. *dial.* or *vulgar*.

1824 in *Spirit Pub. Jrnls.* (1825) 347 They've served me pretty tidy going along,..punching at me with their shilaleaghs as they would at a woolsack. **1851** MAYHEW *Lond. Labour* I. 355 Them as could patter tidy did the best. **1904** *Eng. Dial. Dict.* s.v., That there oak's coming out quite tidy.

Hence **'tidyism** (*nonce-wd.*), a principle or practice of extreme tidiness.

1856 MISS YONGE *Daisy Chain.* I. ix, His funny little old bachelor tidyisms.

'tidy, *v.* Chiefly *colloq.* [f. TIDY *a.*] *trans.* To make tidy or orderly; to put in order; to arrange neatly; *refl.* to put one's hair, dress, etc. in order; to make oneself neat. Often with ***up***.

1821 MISS MITFORD in L'Estrange *Life* (1870) II. 127, I mean to..have it whitened and tidied up this summer. **1847** C. BRONTË *J. Eyre* iv, Bessie..employed me as a sort of under nursery maid, to tidy the room, dust the chairs, &c. **1868** F. E. PAGET *Lucretia* 106 When the cook went up stairs, after tea, to tidy herself. **1897** MARY KINGSLEY *W. Africa* 73, My notes for a day will contain facts relating to the krawkraw, price of onions,..genealogies,..law cases,..&c., &c. And the undertaking of tidying these things up is no small one. **1898** G. B. SHAW *Plays* II. *Candida* 131 The large table has been cleared and tidied.

b. To stow *away* or clear *up* for the sake of tidiness.

1867 [see *tidying* below]. **1884** *Nonconformist* 1 May, It was left on the hall table..and had been 'tidied up' by one of those..housemaids who are the bane of every busy man. **1906** *Westm. Gaz.* 5 July 2/1 If anything is broken or tidied away beyond recall.

Hence **'tidying** *vbl. sb.* and *ppl. a.*; also with *-up*.

1867 H. LATHAM *Black & White* 90 After such a war..there is no small amount of sweeping up, and tidying away, ..to be done. **1884** *Blackw. Mag.* Dec. 734/2 Comte de Rivaulx! echoed Madame, pausing in her tidying. **1899** *Westm. Gaz.* 7 Jan. 3/2 Lovers of nature..view with horror the onslaughts of these tidying gentlemen. **1959** N. MARSH *False Scent* (1960) iv. 102 When they arrived..the tidying-up process had considerably advanced. **1964** M. MCLUHAN *Understanding Media* II. xx. 197 This immense tidying-up of our inner lives..has had its obvious parallels in our attempts to rearrange our homes and gardens. **1975** S. BRETT *Cast, in Order of Disappearance* vi. 47 He'd..even done a token tidying-up of his room.

tie (taɪ), *sb.* Forms: α. 1 **téaȝ, téȝ, tǽȝ,** 3 **teȝ, teiȝ,** 5 **tey,** 6 *Sc.* (*pl.*) **teis,** (5, 9 *dial.* **tee**). β. 5–9 **tye,** 7 **ty,** (*pl.* **tigges, tighes**), 6– **tie.** [OE. *teáh, téaȝ* fem., Anglian *tǽȝ*, later *téȝ* = ON. *taug* fem., rope:—OTeut. **tauȝ-ā, -o* str. fem., f. second grade of the verb-stem *teuh-*: *tauh-*: *tuh*: see TEE *v.*[1] The β-forms are assimilated to, or formed from, TIE *v.*]

1. That with which anything is tied; a cord, band, or the like, used for fastening something; a knot, noose, or ligature; a natural formation of this kind, a ligament (quot. 1659); *esp.* an ornamental knot or bow of ribbon, etc.

α. *a* **800** CYNEWULF *Crist* 733 He..cyning inne ȝebond..fyrnum teaȝum. *a* **1000** *Gloss.* in Wr.-Wülcker 210/36 *Collarium*, sweorclaþ, *uel* teȝ, *uel* sal. *c* **1205** LAY. 20998 Heo wolden..teien heom to-gadere mid guldene teȝen. *c* **1290** *S. Eng. Leg.* I. 308/301 A teiȝ doggue þat is in strongue teiȝe. **1537** *Acc. Ld. High Treas. Scot.* VI. 335 Thre elnis canves to lyne the teis of the mulatis. **1825** BROCKETT *N.C. Words, Tee*, or *Tie*, a hair-rope with which to shackle cows in milking.

β. **1601–2** *Shuttleworths' Acc.* (Chetham Soc.) 141, ij tigges for the maydes to mylke the kyne with, ij[d]. **1602** *Ibid.* 142 To a power man for vj tighes for the kyne, iiij[d]. **1615** CROOKE *Body of Man* 406 Intercept an arterie with a tye, and the part below the tye..will not beate. **1659** MACALLO *Can. Physick* 54 The tyes and ligaments of the brain. **1817** J. BRADBURY *Trav. Amer.* 60 The horse..broke his tie, and galloped off. **1837** DICKENS *Pickw.* xlix, Great formal wigs, with a tie behind. **1857** HUGHES *Tom Brown* I. iii, Putting impossible buttons and ties in the middle of his back.

2. *Naut.* **a.** A rope or chain by which a yard is suspended. See quot. 1841.

α. **1465** *Mann. & Househ. Exp.* (Roxb.) 200 For ij. teyis [for the ship] weyinge vij. stone,..xiij.s. ix.d. **1496** *Acc. Ld. High Treas. Scot.* I. 300 Making of a bonat and the lek [leech] to it, with smal takil and a tee. **1511** *Ibid.* IV. 300 Item..for hed towis to the gret schip..tua cordalis, x trosis, iij teis. **1513** DOUGLAS *Æneis* V. xiv. 6 Than all sammyn,..Did heis thar saill, and trossit doun ther teis.

β. **1485–6** *Naval Accts. Hen. VII* (1896) 13 An hauser for a tye weying Dlb. *Ibid.* 36 Halfe tyes short..ij. Bowe Sesynges. **1611** COTGR., *Estails*... tyes; the strings or ropes of sayles. **1627** CAPT. SMITH *Seaman's Gram.* v. 21 The Ties are the ropes by which the yards doe hang, and doe carry up the yards when wee straine the Halyards. **1762–9** FALCONER *Shipwr.* II. 318 While some above the yard o'erhaul the tye. **1829** MARRYAT *F. Mildmay* iv, I..regained my perch by the topsail-tie. **1841** R. H. DANA *Seaman's Man., Tye*, a rope connected with a yard, to the other end of which a tackle is attached for hoisting.

b. A mooring-bridle.

1867 SMYTH *Sailor's Word-bk., Ties*, an old name for mooring bridles. **1883** *Fisheries Exhib. Catal.* 24 White Manilla Boat Tie.

3. A knot of hair; a pigtail; also short for TIE-WIG. ? *Obs.*

1728 YOUNG *Love Fame* II. 225 The well-swoln tyes an equal homage claim. **1742** RICHARDSON *Pamela* IV. 64 So I think, cries the other; and tosses his Tye behind him, with an Air..of Contempt. **1760** FOOTE *Minor* II. Wks. 1799 I. 259 Some recommended a tye, others a bag: one mention'd a bob. **1817** SHELLEY *Rev. Islam* VI. xxxiii, Cythna's glowing arms, and the thick ties Of her soft hair.

4. a. A neck-tie, a cravat, a bow-tie. In mod. use the tie or neck-tie is usu. distinguished from the cravat.

1761 CHURCHILL *Rosciad* Poems 1763 I. 5 Thrice he twirl'd his Tye—thrice strok'd his band. **1860** TRISTRAM *Gt. Sahara* xx. 344 Seated in white gloves and ties at the soirée of Madame R——. **1862** 'SHIRLEY' *Nugæ Crit.* i. 6 Here..That badge of servitude, the white tie, is unloosed. **1895** 'F. ANSTEY' *Lyre & Lancet* I. 7 He'll come down to dinner in a flannel shirt and no tie. **1897** LD. TENNYSON *Mem. Tennyson* II. 222 Adorned by his accustomed blue tie.

b. A lady's ornamental necklet or scarf.

1860 C. M. YONGE *Hopes & Fears* I. II. iii. 204 Ladies affected coats and waistcoats..both cousins..wearing..black ties round the neck. **1895** *Montgomery Ward Catal.* Spring & Summer 79/2 White Hemstitch Lawn Ties, embroidered ends. (Size $4\frac{1}{4} \times 44$ inch.) **1919** *Queen* 4 Oct. 5 A..Mink Tie beautifully worked in three strands. **1930** *Daily Tel.* 8 Apr. 9/5 Wherever fashionable women may meet this Easter most assuredly will you mark the popularity of the Fur Tie. **1973** *Country Life* 22 Nov. (Suppl.) 721 Important auction sale... Mink & Astrakhan fur coats and ties.

5. A kind of low shoe fastened with a tie or lace.

1826 MRS. MCNEILL *Let.* in *Mem. Sir J. McNeill* vi. (1910), Two pair black satin slippers,..two pair neat walking ties. **1904** *Westm. Gaz.* 15 Apr. 10/2 What we call Oxford Ties, which is a brogue shoe, is a favourite form..for walking purposes.

6. a. *gen.* Something that connects or unites two or more things in some way; a link. (See also 8.)

1711 J. GREENWOOD *Eng. Gram.* 152 Called the subjunctive mood because it is added to the first sentence by some Cople or Tye. **1830** HERSCHEL *Stud. Nat. Phil.* II. vii. (1851) 193 Solid substance[s] retained by a force or united by a tie. **1857** MILLER *Elem. Chem.* (1862) III. 52 The tie between the two typical groups being..the dibasic radicle (C_2O_2).

b. *Mus.* A curved line placed over or under two notes on the same degree, to indicate that the sound is to be sustained (not repeated): = BIND *sb.* 1 c: cf. LIGATURE *sb.* 4.

Also placed over or under two or more notes to be performed *legato*, or to be sung to one syllable; in this case now called a *slur* (SLUR *sb.*[3] 4).

1656 M. LOCKE *Little Consort, Treble* Pref., In printing of Tyes, Holds, Slurrs. **1662** PLAYFORD *Skill Mus.* I. xi. (1674) 35 A Tye is of two uses, first, when the Time is broken..in the middle of the Note, it is usual to Tye two Minims, or a Minim and a Crotchet together. The second sort of Tye is, when two or more Notes are to be sung to one Syllable, or two Notes or more are to be plaid with once drawing the bow on the Viol. **1686** *New Method to Learn to Sing* 54 A Tye thus ⌒, over two or more Notes, signifying that they must be sung to one Syllable, or struck with one motion of the Bow upon an Instrument. **1848** [see SLUR *sb.*[3] 4].

c. The locking together of dog and bitch during copulation.

1951 E. F. DAGLISH *Dog Breeder's Man.* xi. 102 Penetration by the dog is usually followed by the 'tie'..usually considered evidence of a successful union. **1969** M. ROSLIN-WILLIAMS *Dual-Purpose Labrador* iv. 52 When the mating is effective and normal, the 'tie' will be so strong that the dog can be turned carefully round.

7. a. *Arch.*, etc. A beam or rod used to 'tie' or bind together two parts of a building or other structure by counteracting a tensile strain which tends to draw them apart.

1793 W. H. MARSHALL *W. England* (1796) II. 340 The ties, in this case, are large oak floor-beams. **1855** *Act 18 & 19 Vict.* c. 122 Sched. i, The height of every topmost story shall be measured from the level of its floor up to the underside of the tie of the roof. **1861** SMILES *Engineers* II. 183 The eight ribs were firmly connected together by braces and ties. **1869** SIR E. J. REED *Shipbuild.* i. 8 Some of the longitudinal ties of this ship were broken at the bulkheads.

b. *U.S.* A (transverse) railway sleeper.

(The transverse or 'cross' sleepers serve as ties to keep the rails from spreading under the lateral strain of the wheels.)

1857 *U.S. Patent Office Rep.* II. 116 The tie and pedestals cast in one piece, the chairs so constructed as to fit in or on said pedestals. **1869** *Daily News* 7 Oct., Fires..fed by piles of old sleepers, or ties as they are called here. **1881** *Times* 9 Sept., Heaps of 'ties' (the sleepers of the old world) piled up by the side of the road. **1891** *Railroad Gaz.* (U.S.), The requirements for ties comprise the largest consumption of wood in this country.

8. *fig.* Something that ties or binds in a figurative or abstract sense. **a.** Something that makes fast or secures; a security; something figured as a band or knot with which things are tied. *rare.*

a **1555** LATIMER in Foxe *A. & M.* (1563) 1313/1 They haue charitie in such sure tie that they cannot lose it. **1605** SHAKS. *Macb.* III. i. 17 Let your Highnesse Command vpon me, to the which my duties Are with a most indissoluble tye For euer knit. **1670** COTTON *Espernon* III. x. 531 He had concluded the Marriage.., a match that was to be the main tye of this Accommodation. **1810** SCOTT *Lady of L.* II. ix, Confusedly bound in memory's ties.

b. Something that restrains or obliges; a restraint, constraint; †something that enables one to restrain another, a hold *upon* a person (*obs.*); an obligation, a bond (of duty or the like).

1596 DRAYTON *Leg.* iii. 80 Which soone upon Him got so sure a Tye, As no misfortune e'r could it remove. **1621** ELSING *Debates Ho. Lords* (Camden) 45 The agents complained that they wanted a ty uppon the sylkemen. The bonde was advysed by others. **1641** LD. J. DIGBY *Sp. in Ho. Com.* 21 Apr. 6, I was..under tye of Secrecy. **1754** SHERLOCK *Disc.* (1759) I. xiii. 359 Bound..by..the Ties of Moral Duty. **1768** *Woman of Honor* III. 59 Love..flies with disdain from everything that has an air of tie, or constraint. **1835** J. H. NEWMAN *Par. Serm.* (1837) I. xv. 229 They do not like the tie of religion.

c. Something that connects or unites; a bond of union; a uniting principle; a link, connexion: usually with implication of mutual obligation (cf. b), in reference to social relations or the like.

a **1625** FLETCHER *Bloody Brother* IV. i, Mercy becomes a prince, and guards him best; Awe and affrights are never ties of love. **1629** CARLIELL *Deserv. Favourite* 82 To procure her bondage; For such she did account all ties of marriage Made by the parents without the childs consent. **1733** P. SHAW tr. *Bacon's De Sap. Vet.* III. ii. Expl., Philos. Wks. I. 591 The Bonds of Affinity, which are the Links and Ties of Nature. **1781** GIBBON *Decl. & F.* (1869) III. I. 149 We are bound to each other by the ties of honour and interest. **1874** GREEN *Short Hist.* i. §1. 1 The ties of a common blood, and a common speech. **1875** WHITNEY *Life Lang.* 271 There is no necessary tie between race and language.

d. Obligation of constant attendance; restraint of freedom.

1868 J. C. ATKINSON *Gloss. Cleveland Dial.* 534 T' au'd lady's a gret age. She'll be a desper't *tie* on em. *a* **1912** *Mod.* She finds the children a great tie on her. The place is easy, but you wouldn't like the tie. **1928** A. HUXLEY *Point Counter Point* xix. 343 Free, without ties, unpossessed by any possessions, free to do as one will, to go at a moment's notice wherever the fancy may suggest—it is good. **1960** R. COLLIER *House called Memory* iii. 45 We'd love to do an evening show sometimes but the children are *such* a tie.

e. *Logic.* Something that unites the elements of a linguistic construct, e.g. the verb 'to be'.

1918 W. E. JOHNSON in *Mind* XXVII. 14 In order to understand the verbal juxtaposition of substantive and adjective, we must recognise a latent element of form in this construct... This element of form constitutes what I shall call the characterising tie. **1921** —— *Logic* I. i. 10 The general term 'tie' is used to denote what..is involved in understanding the specific form of unity that gives significance to the construct. **1923** C. D. BROAD *Sci. Thought* ii. 75 Take first a very simple characterising judgment, lie '3 is a prime.'.. We might say that the first judgment is about the number 3 and the characteristic of primeness, and asserts that they are connected by the characterising tie. **1959** P. F. STRAWSON *Individuals* v. 168 To the characterizing tie between Socrates and the universal, *dying*, there corresponds the attributive tie between Socrates and the particular, his death.

¶ ***to ride in tie***: perversion of *to ride and tie* (see RIDE *v.* 22), *tie* being app. taken in sense 'connexion'.

1870 G. T. CURTIS *Life D. Webster* I. 37 As Mr Webster once humorously expressed their frequent interchange of study and labour for their joint support, as they had but one horse between them, they 'rode in tie'. **1908** *Academy* 8 Feb. 434/2 He rode all the way in tie with his black slave.

9. a. The fact or method of tying; the condition of being tied, bound, or united. (In quot. 1865 ? a bargain settled, a sale.)

1718 *Free-thinker* No. 66 ¶7, I understand the decent Tye of a Cravat. **1793** SMEATON *Edystone L.* §82 The tye was as good at the bottom as at the top. **1865** *Daily Tel.* 22 Aug. 6/5 The market expenses..are little enough: 2d a head toll, and 1½d 'a tie', as the phrase is—3½d, that is, per beast sold in the market.

b. *Mining.* = TEE *sb.*[1] 3.

1747 HOOSON *Miner's Dict.* O iij, He that comes first to the Pee, will take it, be he the older or younger, and he will make the other a way out if possible he can, otherwise if he cannot then it is called a Tye. **1851** [see TEE *sb.*[1] 3].

c. In silk hand-loom weaving: The tying together of a combination of heddle-strings, so as to move a series of warp-strings together.

1831 G. R. PORTER *Silk Manuf.* 297 Every variation in the order of succession of the harness used in weaving or in the weavers' language, every different tie, produces a different pattern.

d. In plastering: = KEY *sb.*[1] 10c.

1873 E. SPON *Workshop Receipts* Ser. I. 121/2 After the coat is laid on, it is scored in diagonal directions with a scratcher..to give it a key or tie for the coat that is to follow it.

10. a. Equality between two or more competitors or the sides in a match or contest; a match in which this occurs, a drawn match; a dead heat. Hence, ***to play off, shoot off***, etc. ***a tie***, to resolve or determine a tie, by playing another match.

1680 [see TIE *v.* 7]. **1736** in Waghorn *Cricket Scores* (1899) 16 A great single-wicket match..the country men got but 6, which made it a tie. **1837** T. HOOK *Jack Brag* iii, To see the ties shot off of the great pigeon match. **1844** DISRAELI *Coningsby* VIII. iii, The Government count on the seat, though with the new Registration 'tis nearly a tie. **1881** T. HARDY *Laodicean* II. vi, We are bracketed—it's a tie. The judges say there is no choice between the designs.

Hence, **b.** A deciding match played after a draw; also, a match played between the victors in previous matches or heats. (See also ***cup-tie*** s.v. CUP *sb.* 13c.)

1895 *Westm. Gaz.* 24 Sept., The..boys prefer the cup ties to the Church Catechism. **1904** *Ibid.* 22 Apr. 12/1 There is something impressive even to the unathletic man in these annual Cup-tie figures. **1905** *Daily Chron.* 17 Apr. 3/7 Probably the Cup-'tie' has been evolved from the phrase 'shooting off' or 'playing off a tie' after two competitors have 'tied'. The match between those who stand on a level gradually gets regarded as itself the 'tie'.

tie (taɪ), *v.* Inflected **tied, tying.** Forms: see below. [In the *a*-forms, OE. *tīᵹan*, for OWS. **tīeᵹan*:—**tēaᵹ-jan* to bind, f. *tēaᵹ* rope: see TIE *sb.*: cf. ON. *teygja* to draw. The ME. *β*-forms are commonly held to represent a non-WSax. (Mercian) form **tēᵹan* (for **tīeᵹan*); but cf. ME. *ēi* and *ī* forms under EYE, HIGH.]

A. Illustration of Forms.

1. *Pres. stem. a.* 1 **tíᵹ-an,** 3–4 **tiȝ-en,** 4 **tyȝe, tyen,** 4–9 **tye,** 6–7 **ty;** 4– **tie.** *Pr. pple.* **tying.**

c **1000** Tiᵹan [see B. 1]. *c* **1000** ÆLFRIC *Gram.* xliv. (Z.) 258 Hu þes dæl tigð þa word togædere. *c* **1275** LAY. 20997 And tiȝe heom to-gædere. **1377** LANGL. *P. Pl.* B. I. 96 And taken transgressores and tyen hem faste. *Ibid.* III. 139 And tieth hym faste. **1563** GOLDING *Cæsar* v. (1565) 138 He aduised him to tie the letter to the thong of a Iaueling, & so to throw it into his camp. **1570** *Satir. Poems Reform.* xxii. 92 To ty on tre. **1618** RALEGH in *Four C. Eng. Lett.* (1880) 38 Tyenge them back to backe. **1729** G. ADAMS tr. *Sophocl., Antig.* II. iv. II. 32 If Fear did not tye their Tongues.

β. 3 **teȝ-en,** 3–4 **teiȝ-en, tei-e(n,** 4–6 **teye, teie,** 5 **tey-yn, tey, tegh,** 6–7 **taye,** 7 **tay,** 9 *dial.* **tee.**

c **1205** LAY. 20997 And teien heom to-gadere. *c* **1250** *Hymn Virg.* 59 in *Trin. Coll. Hom.* 257 Herre teȝen he him nolde. *c* **1330** R. BRUNNE *Chron. Wace* (Rolls) 11187 Many fair palfray & stede..to wype, & to mangers teye. **1362** LANGL. *P. Pl.* A. I. 94 And teiȝen hem faste. **1387** TREVISA *Higden* (Rolls) IV. 79 Reynes..to teie wiþ oþer oxen. *c* **1440** *Promp. Parv.* 487/2 Teyyn wythe bondys. *c* **1440** *Gesta Rom.* xxiii. 81 (Harl. MS.) Tey him to Tailles of hors. **1533** MORE *Answ. Poysoned Bk.* Wks. 1041/2 Sampson tayeng the Foxes together. **1664** EARL OF TYRCONNEL *Let. to Lauderdale* 14 Nov. (in *Daniell's Catal.* July (1904) 37/2) That wee should taye them all bellye to bellye and throwe them in the sea.

2. *Pa. t. a.* [1 ***tiᵹede,** 3–4 ***tiȝede,** ***tyȝede**], 5–8 **tyed,** (5–6 **-it,** 6 **tight),** 6–7 **ty'd,** 7– **tied.**

c **1400, 1513** Tyed [see B 1, 1 b]. *c* **1470** *Golagros & Gaw.* 61 His hors he tyit to ane tre. **1596** SPENSER *F.Q.* VI. xii. 34 Thereunto a great long chaine he tight. **1604** E. G[RIMSTONE] *D'Acosta Hist. Indies* VI. xiv. 461 The bridges .. which they tied to the bankes. **1686** tr. *Chardin's Trav. Persia* 141 Forces, that ty'd his Hands. **1720** OZELL *Vertot's Rom. Rep.* I. v. 296 Grief..tyed his Tongue.

β. 3 **teide,** 5 **teyde, teghit, tayed.**

c **1290** *S. Eng. Leg.* I. 29/91 Huy..teiden ane rop a boute is necke. *c* **1400** *Destr. Troy* 3523 The kyng..teghit her in yernes. *c* **1400** *Three Kings Cologne* 26 Byside þat ox Ioseph teyde his asse. **1470–85** MALORY *Arthur* I. iii. 41 Sir Arthur ..tayed his hors to the style.

3. *Pa. pple. a.* 1 **ᵹe-tiᵹ(ᵹ)ed,** 3–4 **i-tiȝed,** 4 **ityȝed, tyȝed,** 5 *Sc.* **tichit, ticht;** 4–9 **tyed,** 6 **tiede,** 6–7 **tyde, tide,** 7–8 **ty'd,** 4– **tied.**

c **1000** ÆLFRIC *Hom.* II. 62 An ramm..ᵹetiᵹed be ðam hornum. *c* **1000** *Ags. Gosp.* Matt. xxi. 2, & þonne sona finde ᵹyt ane assene ᵹe-tiᵹᵹede [*c* **1160** *Hatton Gosp.* ᵹe-teiᵹᵹede [*v.r.* ᵹeteᵹᵹede]]. *c* **1275** I-tiȝed, *c* **1320** I-tyȝed [see B. 1]. **13** .. Tyȝed [see B. 4]. **1382** WYCLIF *Mark* xi. 2 A colt tyed [**1388** tied]. *c* **1450** HOLLAND *Howlat* 405 With tuscheis of trast silk tichit to the tre. *c* **1475** *Rauf Coilȝear* 457 Ane Tyger ticht to ane tre. **1590** SPENSER *F.Q.* I. vi. 21 In sacred bonds of wedlock tyde. **1608, 1688** Tyed [see B. 5]. **1699** J. LOWTHORP *Exper.* in *Misc. Cur.* (1708) II. 198 There was a Bladder ty'd below each Joint..and when it was fill'd with Water it was ty'd above it. **1718** Ty'd, **1816** Tyed [see B. 1].

β. 2 **ᵹe-teᵹᵹed, -teiᵹᵹed,** 3 **i-teied, -et, iteid,** 3–4 **teid,** 4 **yteyd, teiȝed, teied, teyde,** 4–6 **teyed,** 5 **teyghte,** 6 **teyd, tay(e)d,** 9 *dial.* **teed.**

c **1160** ᵹete[i]ᵹᵹed [see a]. *c* **1200** *Trin. Coll. Hom.* 181 Iteied [see B. 5]. *Ibid.* 217 þat me ne sholde none man bitechen bute he were teid to menden chirche. *c* **1230** *Hali Meid.* 27 Him..þat is..to eni eorðliche þing iteiet. *a* **1250** *Owl & Night.* 776 An hors..i-teid at mulne dure. *c* **1350** *Will. Palerne* 3226 þe sturnest stede in hire stabul teiȝed. *Ibid.* 3232 Teied in þe stabul. *c* **1386** Yteyd, **1387** I-teyed [see B. 1 b]. **1387** TREVISA *Higden* (Rolls) IV. 77 þe reynes þat þe oxen schulde be teyde by. **1390** Teid [see B. 5 c]. *c* **1400** *Laud Troy Bk.* 518 Eche a man on londe than gos,.. And lefft here schip teyghte fast. **1489** CAXTON *Faytes of A.* I. xvii. 49 Wel teyed with ropys. **1547** BOORDE *Introd. Knowl.* xiii. (1870) 156 Than am I tonge tayd. **1556** *Chron. Gr. Friars* (Camden) 98 Browte thorrow Cheppesyde teyd in ropes xxiiij[ti] tayd to-getheres as herrytykes. **1828** *Craven Gloss.*, Teed, tied.

B. Signification. I. The simple verb.

1. a. *trans.* To bind, fasten, make fast (one thing to another, or two or more things together) with a cord, rope, band, or the like, drawn together and knotted; to confine (a person or animal) by fastening to something.

c **1000** ÆLFRIC *Hom.* I. 432 Ualerianus..het tiᵹan [Ypolitus] be ðam fotum to unᵹetemedra horsa swuran. *c* **1205** LAY. 25972 Twælf swine iteied [*c* **1275** itiȝed] to-somme. *a* **1225** *Ancr. R.* 254 Sansumes foxes..weren bi þe teiles iteied ueste. *c* **1320** *Cast. Love* 1130 As fisch..þat whon þe worm he swoleweþ..He is bi þe hok i-tiȝed [*v.r.* i-tyȝed] fast. *c* **1400** *Laud Troy Bk.* 2733 Anker thei caste, And tyed here schippis in that porte And ȝede to londe. *c* **1440** *Pallad. on Husb.* IV. 752 [772] Stakes..To teye hem to. **1590** SPENSER *F.Q.* I. v. 6 Their shining shieldes about their wrestes they tye. **1638** JUNIUS *Paint. Ancients* 154 A great dogge tyed in a chaine. **1718** POPE *Iliad* II. 55 Th' embroider'd sandals on his feet were ty'd. **1816** SINGER *Hist. Cards* I. 52 Such bells were also tyed to Hawks.

b. To draw together the parts of (a single thing) with a knotted cord or the like; to fasten (a part of dress, etc.) in this way, esp. with strings already attached to it (as a bonnet, a shoe); also, to draw together (a cord or the like) into a knot, esp. for the purpose of fastening something.

c **1386** CHAUCER *Prol.* 457 Hir hosen were of fyn scarlett reed, Ful streite yteyd. **1387** TREVISA *Higden* (Rolls) V. 369 Hire hosen tilled to the hamme, i-teyed wiþ layners al aboute. **1513** MORE in Hall *Chron., Rich. III* (1548) 27b, After which tyme, the prince neuer tyed his pointes. **1592** SHAKS. *Rom. & Jul.* III. i. 31 Did'st thou not fall out..with another, for tying his new shooes with old Riband? **1662** J. DAVIES tr. *Mandelslo's Trav.* 80 They tye their Garments about with a Girdle. **1716** ADDISON *Drummer* III. i, He'll tye a wig. **1819** SHELLEY *Cenci* V. iv. 159 Tie My girdle for me. *Mod.* You must tie the string tighter, or the parcel will come undone.

c. *Surg.* To bind and constrict (an artery or vein) with a ligature, so as to prevent the flow of blood through it.

1597 [see TIED *ppl. a.* 1]. **1804** ABERNETHY *Surg. Obs.* 195 To tie the more superficial arteries. **1843** R. J. GRAVES *Syst. Clin. Med.* xi. 123 The effects produced by tying the carotid and vertebral arteries.

d. To make or form by tying (a knot, etc.).

1647 COWLEY *Mistr., The Tree* v, Go tye the dismal Knot (why shouldst thou live?). **1808** SCOTT *Marm.* I. Introd. 48 The garlands you delight to tie. **1838** THIRLWALL *Greece* II. xiv. 200 He tied sixty knots in a leathern thong. **1867** F. FRANCIS *Angling* x. (1880) 340 One of the most difficult things in tying flies.

e. ***tie neck and heels***: see NECK *sb.*[1] 7. ***ride and tie***: see RIDE *v.* 22.

f. *intr.* for *pass.*

1842 *Amer. Pioneer* I. 274 A pair of buckskin leggins,.. made to fit the leg and tie in at the ankle with the moccasins. **1924** A. D. SEDGWICK *Little French Girl* II. iii. 114 Straightly falling dress,..tying at the breast with tassels and at the waist with a loosely knotted sash.

2. In figurative phrases. ***to tie the hands of***: to deprive of freedom of action. ***to tie the knot***: to effect a union between two persons or things; *esp.* to perform the ceremony of marriage. †***to tie with St. Mary's knot***: to hamstring (*obs.*). ***to tie to the stake***, *fig.* to put into a position from which there is no escape. ***to tie*** a person's ***tongue***: to prevent (him) from speaking, to compel to be silent (see also TONGUE-TIED). ***tied to*** a woman's ***apron-strings***: see APRON-STRING. ***tie that bull outside*** or ***to another ashcan*** (*U.S. slang*): I do not believe you; 'tell me another'. ***to tie a can to*** (or ***on***) (*slang*): to reject or dismiss (a person); to stop (an activity). ***to tie one on*** [cf. *to tie a bun on* s.v. BUN *sb.*[5]] *slang* (chiefly *U.S.*): to get drunk.

1559 *Bk. Com. Prayer, Prayers Sev. Occasions*, Tyed and bounde with the chayne of our synnes. **1576** GASCOIGNE *Compl. Philomene* lxx. (Arb.) 99 Hir swelling sobbes, Did tie hir tong from talke. **1579** LYLY *Euphues* (Arb.) 52 Euphues being thus tyed to the stake by their importunate intreatie, began as followeth. ? *a* **1600** *Dick o' the Cow* in Child *Ballads* (1861) VI. 72 He has tied them a' wi' St. Mary's knot, A' these horses but barely three. **1605** SHAKS. *Lear* III. vii. 54, I am tyed to' th' Stake, And I must stand the Course. **1642** FULLER *Holy & Prof. St.* V. v. 375 When God intends a Nation shall be beaten, he ties their hands behind them. **1717** PRIOR *Alma* I. 332 So to the priest their case they tell: He ties the knot. **1781** COWPER *Friendship* 62 A fretful temper will divide The closest knot that may be tied. **1828** [see KNOT *sb.*[1] 11 b]. **1866** CRUMP *Banking* ix. 214 It seems very unjust to tie the hands of the directors in so important a particular. **1889** *The County* viii, One would have thought that very shame would have tied her tongue. **1921** J. DOS PASSOS *Three Soldiers* IV. i. 212 'Fellers, the war's over!'.. 'Tie that bull outside,' came from every side of the ward. **1922** H. CRANE *Let.* 10 Dec. (1965) 108 Life is meagre with me. I am unsatisfied and left always begging for beauty. I am tied to the stake—a little more wastefully burnt every day of my life. **1926** WODEHOUSE *Heart of Goof* viii. 265 What caused the definite rift was Jane's refusal to tie a can to Rodney Spelvin. **1928** C. SANDBURG *Good Morning, America* 16 They got a fat nerve to try to tie a can on you. **1932** J. T. FARRELL *Young Lonigan* ii. 60 Three-Star told Vinc to tie his bull to another ash can. **1933** E. O'NEILL *Ah, Wilderness!* I. 27 Aw say, you fresh kid, tie that bull outside! **1942** WODEHOUSE *Money in Bank* (1946) xix. 163 Tie a can to the funny stuff, see? If I want to laugh, I'll read the comic strip. **1951** *Western Folklore* X. 82 The Act of Drinking:.. to swill one down; to tie one on. **1959** *Listener* 4 June 971/1 That was what lost Mr. Acheson votes when he was tied to the Senatorial stake. **1962** J. ONSLOW *Bowler-Hatted Cowboy* xix. 186 You used to tie one on with the boys. **1972** WODEHOUSE *Pearls, Girls, & Monty Bodkin* v. 65 I'm warning you to kiss her goodbye and tie a can to her. Never marry anyone who makes conditions. **1982** A. MATHER *Impetuous Masquerade* vii. 107 He had..tied one on, if you know what I mean.

3. a. To fasten together, connect, join (material things) in any way; *spec.* in *Arch.* to connect and make fast by a rod or beam (cf. TIE *sb.* 7), or by other means (cf. BOND *sb.*[1] 13 a). Also with *into*, = *to tie in to* (see sense 11 a below).

1585 T. WASHINGTON tr. *Nicholay's Voy.* II. xviii. 51 [A] smal habitation,..made of..glasse, ioyned & tyed together with roddes of Tin. **1632** LITHGOW *Trav.* II. 67 Peloponnesus..is tied to the continent by an Istmus. **1851** RUSKIN *Stones Ven.* (1874) I. xv. 161 Every arch or gable not tied at its base by beams or bars, exercises a lateral pressure upon the walls which sustain it. *a* **1912** [see sense 3 e below]. **1969** D. ACHESON *Present at Creation* xliv. 402 The white telephone tied into the White House switchboard was used sparingly by considerate associates. **1974** *Sci. Amer.* Oct.

113/1 We began work at the complex by establishing over the target area a submerged grid of 10-meter squares that was tied into the Greek ordnance survey grid ashore.

b. To check or hinder the free movement or working of: see quots.

1597 A. M. tr. *Guillemeau's Fr. Chirurg.* 10/1 *Spasmus*.. with shakinge and quiveringe, with the tonge tiede, and with irremoveable eyes. **1602** CAREW *Cornwall* 11 The.. Axes and Wedges.. (not seldome) are so tied by the teeth, as a good workman shall hardly be able to hew three foote, in the space of so many weekes. **1879** JEFFERIES *Wild Life S.C.* 192 When sawing, the wood operated on often 'ties' the saw, as it is called, that is, pinches it—which makes it hard to work. **18..** *Dogs Gt. Brit. & Amer.* 45 (Cent.) There is a want of liberty in the play of the whole shoulder, because the elbow rubs against the ribs... This is called being tied at the elbow.

c. *Mus.* To connect (notes) by a tie or ligature: see TIE *sb.* 6b, LIGATURE *sb.* 4.

1597 [see LIGATURE 4]. **1662** PLAYFORD *Skill Mus.* I. viii. (1674) 28 Four or more Quavers are Tyed together by a long Stroke on the top of their Tails. *Ibid.* [see TIE *sb.* 6b].

d. *U.S.* To furnish (a railway line) with 'ties' or sleepers (cf. TIE *sb.* 7b).

1883 *W. Chester, Pa. Local News* II. No. 234. 1 Forty miles of road.. had to be.. graded, tied, rails laid.

e. To fasten or fix otherwise (e.g. †with nails).

1500–20 DUNBAR *Poems* lxxii. 69 Syne tyit him on with greit irne takkis, And him all nakit on the tre Thai raisit on loft. *a* **1912** *Mod.* The brick facing of the wall is tied into the concrete backing by headers at frequent intervals.

f. *intr.* and *trans.* Of a dog or bitch: to remain linked (with) for a period during copulation.

1910 J. S. TURNER *Kennel Encycl.* III. 919 Occasionally a dog does not tie in the normal fashion... A dog that regularly ties is preferable. **1934** F. W. COUSENS *Dogs & their Managem.* v. 83 When the stud dog is unable to 'tie' a bitch, he is unable to remain sufficiently long in position to impregnate the bitch properly. **1952** C. L. B. HUBBARD *Pembrokeshire Corgi Handbk.* v. 60 Not all breeds tie. **1968** J. F. GORDON *Pet Library's Beagle Guide* x. 149 Once the pair have tied, they can be steadied, and.. left to complete their task.

4. *fig.* To join closely or firmly; to connect, attach, unite, knit, bind by other than material ties; *esp.* to unite in marriage (now *dial.*).

c **1000** [see A. 1*a*]. *c* **1200** *Trin. Coll. Hom.* 183 Hie [the soul].. to þe licame.. seið.. Aweilewei þu fule hold þat ich auere was to þe iteied. **13..** *E.E. Allit. P.* B. 702 When two true togeder had tyȝed hem seluen. **1571** CAMPION *Hist. Irel.* II. vii. (1633) 100 Richard.. exceedingly tyed unto him the hearts of the noblemen. **1586** DAY *Eng. Secretary* I. (1625) 10 Eloquution is annexed vnto the stile, which.. is also tyed to the argument. **1684** *Contempl. St. Man* I. ii. (1699) 21 The greatest felicity of the World, was tyed to the greatest Mishap. **1715** DE FOE *Fam. Instruct.* (1841) II. I. i. 16 How could you think of tying yourself to such a family? **1814** WORDSW. *White Doe* VII. 314 At length, thus.. faintly tied To earth, she.. died. **1890** *Spectator* 24 May 714/1 If Washington could tie gold and silver together in the ratio of sixteen, so could the rest of the world. **1899** J. LUMSDEN *Edin. Poems & Songs* 287 Ma man was kill'd.. Before that we'd been foure days tied.

b. *intr.* for *refl.* To attach oneself (*to*). Also, *to tie to*: to fix one's confidence in, trust to, hold on to for support. *U.S. colloq.*

1879 TOURGEE *Fool's Err.* x. 43 He won't du tu tie ter. **1884** A. A. PUTNAM *Ten Y. Police Judge* xxiii. 200 The propensities of the thief strikingly tie somehow to the training begotten of ardent spirit. **1892** W. W. FENN *Bible in Theol.* 17 Those who, as they say, 'want something to tie to'.

5. a. *trans.* To bind, oblige, restrain, constrain *to* (also *from*) some course of action, etc.; to limit, confine, restrict. ***to be tied to*** (or ***for***) ***time***: to be bound or limited to a certain time for doing something. (See also phrases in 2.)

c **1200** *Trin. Coll. Hom.* 181 Ilch man of his wise noteð his swinhc swilch se he is to iteied. Clerc on his wise. Cniht on his wise... And ilches craftes þeau swo he beð to iteied. **1387–8** T. USK *Test. Love* III. ii. (Skeat) I. 144 If it wer nat in mannes own liberte of fre wil to do good or bad but to the one teied by bonde of goddes preordinaunce. *c* **1412** HOCCLEVE *De Reg. Princ.* 1474 God for-beede þou þe haddist tyed þer-to, but if þin herte myght han plyed For to obserue it wel. **1577** HANMER *Anc. Eccl. Hist.* (1619) 359, I will.. tie myself.. onto the truth of the historie. **1608** SHAKS. *Per.* II. v. 8 She hath so strictly Tyed her to her Chamber. **1688** R. HOLME *Armoury* III. 184/1 The White Friers.. were tyed to Fasting, Silence, and Canonical hours. **1713** BERKELEY *Guard.* No. 39 ¶12, I must tie this gentleman close to the argument. **1860** MRS. CARLYLE *Lett.* (1883) III. 38 Unfortunately I am tied to time. I must be back in London. **1901** *Daily Tel.* 22 Mar. 9/5 The British being to a certain extent tied in South Africa.

b. To bind, oblige; usually in *pass.* to be bound or obliged (*to do* something). Now only *dial.*

1596 SHAKS. *Tam. Shr.* I. i. 217, I am tyed to be obedient, For so your father charg'd me at our parting. **1608** WILLET *Hexapla Exod.* 498 The borrower.. is tied to make it good. **1625** BURGES *Pers. Tithes* 66 It was their purpose to tie his conscience the more to doe iustly herein. **1722** DE FOE *Plague* (1756) 108 Nor were they tied to carry the Dead to their respective Parishes. **1798** *Trans. Soc. Arts* XVI. 134 Why should the grower tie himself to plant an equal number of different sorts? **1892** M. C. F. MORRIS *Yorks. Folk-Talk* 259 We do not reckon *obliged* in the sense of forced as part of our vocabulary; instead we make use of *tied*.

†**c.** To bring into bondage; to enthrall. *Obs.*

1390 GOWER *Conf.* II. 129 It is impropreliche seid, For good hath him and halt him teid, That he.. is unto his good a thral. *a* **1425** *Cursor M.* 23307 (Trin.) Þei euer tyed were In þis lif for synnes sere. **1426** LYDG. *De Guil. Pilgr.* 17513, I teye my sylff.. And bynde me to my rychesse. **1594** KYD *Cornelia* I. 68 What helps it that thou ty'dst The former World to thee in vassalage? **1613** SHAKS. *Hen. VIII*, IV. ii. 36 One that by suggestion Ty'de all the Kingdome.

d. To bind by favour or service rendered: usually in *pass.*: = OBLIGE *v.* 6, 7.

1576 FLEMING *Panopl. Epist.* 123, I am so streigtly tyed to his courtesie. **1595** tr. *Blanchardine* Ded. A ij, Whose deserts haue tyed me during life the vassaile of.. their commaunds. **1611** SHAKS. *Cymb.* I. vi. 23 He is one of the Noblest note, to whose kindnesses I am most infinitely tied. **1864** BURTON *Scot. Abr.* II. ii. 137 We are also tied in duty to our comrades that were with us in danger.

e. To restrict (a dealer or firm) to a particular source for articles sold; only in *pa. pple.*, usually applied to a public house so restricted as to liquor. Hence *transf.* as in quot. 1899. See also TIED 2b.

1817 [see 10b]. **1853** *Rep. Sel. Committee Public Houses, Min. Evid.* 118, I am the owner of a free house, tied to nobody. **1884** *Lincoln*, etc. *Mercury* 22 Feb., The Masons' Arms Hotel... Tied for beer only. **1894** *Westm. Gaz.* 9 Apr. 2/3 The system of 'tied' trade.. is not confined to the drink trade... A retail draper was 'tied' to a wholesale house—i.e. ..he was under contract to buy all his goods from the wholesale draper in question. **1899** *Daily News* 7 Dec. 4/1 The farmers dictate the terms of tenancy. The cottages are 'tied'.

f. To impose conditions on (foreign aid), esp. by restricting its use *to* purchases from the source country. Cf. TIED *ppl. a.* 2c.

1965 *McGraw-Hill Dict. Mod. Econ.* 515 A considerable part of U.S. foreign aid has been tied. **1965** *New Statesman* 18 June 945/3 This strain [on the balance of payments] can be reduced by 'tying' aid—insisting that it be spent on British exports. **1976** *New Internationalist* Jan. 7/2 Virtually all aid from the USSR is tied to the purchase of Russian goods or expertise. **1980** *North-South* (Rep. Independent Comm. Internat. Devel. Issues) xii. 198 When they tie aid to their own sources the donor countries greatly limit choices and discourage local initiatives.

6. (*fig.* from 1b or d.) To make sure, confirm, ratify; to 'knit', 'cement'. ? *Obs.*

1613 SHAKS. *Hen. VIII*, III. ii. 250 That Seale.. the King ..gaue me.. and.. Ti'de it by Letters Patents. **1697** DRYDEN *Æneid* XII. 316 When thus in Public view the peace was ty'd With solemn Vows.

7. a. *intr.* To be equal (*with*) in a contest, etc.

1680 COTTON *Compl. Gamester* xv. (ed. 2) 93 If each win a trick and the third tyed, neither win, because it is trick and tye. **1870** *Routledge's Ev. Boy's Ann.* Oct. 600 The cricketers tied when they were so equally matched that neither won. **1882** *Standard* 31 Aug. 6/4 Captain Burridge.. scored 117, and tied with Mr. Meyler. **1902** LD. ROSEBERY in *Daily Chron.* 13 Oct. 7/1 We have not received intellectual faculties equal to Mr. Gladstone's, and we cannot hope to tie with him in their exercise.

b. *pass.* in same sense.

1868 *U.S. Newspaper*, The two political parties in Councils were tied on joint ballot.

†**c.** In the House of Commons: = PAIR *v.*[1] 4.

1829 O'CONNELL in *Corr.* May (1888) I. 188 To tie with a Government member.

d. *trans.* To be equal with (a competitor); to make the same score as. Now chiefly *N. Amer.*

1888 ELWORTHY *W. Somerset Word-bk.* s.v., My dog tied yours, so they must run again. **1966** *N.Y. Times* (Internat. ed.) 22 Apr. 12/5 Real Madrid tied Internazionale of Milan, 1–1, last night. **1968** *Globe & Mail* (Toronto) 17 Feb. 39 If Canada ties Russians, Swedes beat Czechs—Russia wins gold on goal spread, Canada takes silver. **1977** *Arab Times* 13 Dec. 9/1 The American Embassy is currently in second place and needs a victory to tie Dresser and force a play-off for the League Championship.

e. *N. Amer.* To match or equal (an existing record or score); colloq. phrases ***can you tie that?***, ***tie that!***, expressions of surprise or amazement. Cf. BEAT *v.*[1] 10h.

1918 *Collier's* 11 May 46/3 The French won't even admit he's dead yet—they call this joint the Invalides, which is only concedin' that he's *sick*! Can you tie that? **1930** *Sat. Even. Post* 28 June 162 'Can you beat that?' he muttered. 'Can you even tie it?' **1932** W. FAULKNER *Light in August* viii. 172 Well, say. Can you tie that. **1946** *Sat. Even. Post* 30 Mar. 46/2 Mr. Carter got hold of Billy Rose and offered him $1000 a day for 100 days if he would come to Fort Worth and put on a show that not only couldn't be beat but couldn't be tied. **1948** WODEHOUSE *Uncle Dynamite* vi. 83 Tie that for a disaster, Uncle Fred. **1968** *Globe & Mail* (Toronto) 15 Jan. 21/3 Willie Turner, a young sprinter who has yet to reach his peak, tied a world indoor standard Saturday. **1974** *State* (Columbia, S. Carolina) 3 Mar. 6-D/1 Cincinnati tied a school record by hitting 16 of 17 free throws. **1978** *Detroit Free Press* 5 Mar. C2/1 Connors, a 25-year-old lefthander from Belleville, Ill., quickly served a love game to tie the score.

8. *Hunting. intr.* Of a hound: To linger upon the scent instead of following it swiftly; to loiter, lag.

1781 P. BECKFORD *Hunting* xv. 188 They learn to tye upon the scent; an unpardonable fault in a fox-hound. *Ibid.* 190 If they [the hounds] tie upon the scent, and come hunting after, hang them up immediately..: there is no getting such conceited devils on. **1826** [see TYING *ppl. a.*].

9. *intr.* ***tie into***: to 'buckle to'. *U.S. colloq.* Also, to get to work vigorously on; to tuck into (food). *U.S.*

1904 S. E. WHITE *Forest* xii. 159 The day following we tied into it again. **1912** R. A. WASON *Friar Tuck* xiv. 99 They girded up their loins, an' tied into him a little harder. **1948** 'J. EVANS' *Halo for Satan* ix. 130 She put her head back and tied into her drink with the easy grace of a practiced drinker. **1965** M. BRADBURY *Stepping Westward* v. 238 I'm going to take a peanut-butter sandwich.. but I want to see these important men tie into something really good.

II. With adverbs.

10. tie down. a. *lit.* To fasten down or confine by tying: see sense 1 and DOWN *adv.*

1699 GARTH *Dispens.* I. 11 More had He spoke but sudden Vapours rise, And with their silken Cords tye down his Eyes. **1728** POPE *Dunc.* I. 37 Bards, like Proteus long in vain tied down, Escape in Monsters, and amaze the town. **1823** J. BADCOCK *Dom. Amusem.* 196 Strain it off, and keep it tied down with bladder. **1827** D. JOHNSON *Ind. Field Sports* 52 The dogs were accustomed to be tied down separately every night.

b. *fig.* To confine stringently (*to* some thing or action): cf. sense 5, and DOWN *adv.* 17.

1692 LOCKE *Educ.* §142 Being forced and tied down to their Books in an Age at enmity with all such restraint. **1720** DE FOE *Capt. Singleton* v. (1840) 90 We did not tie ourselves down when to march and when to halt. **1778** *Eng. Gazetteer* (ed. 2) s.v. *Rochester*, For the maintenance of its bridge, certain lands are tied down by parliament. **1817** *1st Rep. Committee Police Metrop.* 11 The.. practice.. for brewers to tie their tenants down to the purchase of specific articles from individuals named by them. **1884** W. C. SMITH *Kildrostan* 87 O you dull fellows, Tied down to facts, you lose the half of life.

11. tie in. a. *trans.* To connect or join *to* an existing structure or network.

1793 W. H. MARSHALL *W. England* (1796) II. 340 Firm purchases.. for the purpose of tying in the front wall. **1914** *Dialect Notes* IV. 164 *Tie in*, in surveying, to join or connect up. 'We'll run over to the monument and *tie in* this survey.' **1943** J. S. HUXLEY *TVA* xi. 95 The framing to the exit.. neatly ties in the air exhaust trough at the bottom of the walls. **1975** *North Sea Background Notes* (Brit. Petroleum Co.) 30 It is not impossible that a branch line from another nearby oilfield may be tied in to the Forties line in the future. **1978** *Lancashire Life* July 37/3 Instead of being tied-in to the building next-door this 19th century addition was simply slapped-up alongside it.

b. *intr.* To accord or be consonant (*with*); to be connected or associated (*with*).

1938 S. CHASE *Tyranny of Words* viii. 91 This ties in with Korzybski's central idea of knowledge as structural. **1954** 'A. GARVE' *Riddle of Samson* x. 97 There's another thing that ties in rather neatly, too. **1959** H. NIELSEN *Fifth Caller* xiv. 216 A stranger? That didn't tie in with the words Dr. Whitehall was quoted as having used in greeting. **1967** *Sci. Amer.* Sept. 276 The problem ties in with the discussion of Pascal's triangle. **1972** D. LODGE *20th Cent. Lit. Crit.* 174 Jung's theory of the Collective Unconscious tied in neatly with the anthropological study of primitive myth and ritual, initiated.. by Sir James Frazer in *The Golden Bough*.

c. *trans.* To associate or connect (*with*).

1958 'A. BRIDGE' *Portuguese Escape* ix. 146 How can they have tied the Monsignor in with the Duke's house? **1959** *Listener* 26 Feb. 364/1 Nowadays, more emphasis is placed on teaching foreign languages phonetically and on trying to tie lessons in with exchange visits of pupils abroad. **1972** 'T. COE' *Don't lie to Me* (1974) xi. 102 The detectives on the case think the two things are tied in. The killing and the acid. **1972** J. L. DILLARD *Black English* iv. 140 Pidgin has been tied in historically with a lot of regrettable racial and economic policies. **1982** R. LEIGH *Girl with Bright Head* xix. 131 'Just tell me what Mrs Storm wanted with you.' 'Not unless you can tie her in with the murder.'

12. tie off. a. *trans.* To close (a tubular vessel) by tying something round it. Also *transf.*

1903 J. J. MCGRATH *Surg. Anat. & Operative Surg.* I. 13 In resecting portions of the alimentary canal the mesentery or omentum that carries the blood-supply to the parts must be tied off. **1973** 'D. HALLIDAY' *Dolly & Starry Bird* ii. 27 You must have Digham tied off... I won't have you become preggy.

b. *trans.* To secure or make fast (a rope or line); also *fig.* Also *absol.*

1928 *Amer. Speech* IV. 69 [Stage-hand language.] The lines pass.. down to a fly-floor,.. where they are tied-off, or belayed. **1933** P. GODFREY *Back-Stage* vii. 88 Stage-hands are shouting strangely cryptic phrases to people overhead... 'Up on yer long—dead it—tie off at that—mark yer new set.' **1952** R. BISSELL *Monongahela* xix. 217 While the deckhand is tying off you jump down out of the brain box and knock the face wires loose. **1973** J. THOMSON *Death Cap* x. 143, I like all the ends tied off and *Finis* written on the file. **1974** H. MACINNES *Climb to Lost World* xi. 193, I.. asked him to tie-off the bottom end of Joe's rope.

13. tie up. a. *trans.* To fasten (a thing) with a cord or band tied round it, so as to prevent its moving or falling loose, or to secure it from being lost or injured; to bind up, wrap up. Also *intr.* for *pass.*

1530 PALSGR. 758/1, I tye up my heare, as a woman dothe, *je me atourne*. **1608** SHAKS. *Per.* III. ii. 41 Or Tie my treasure vp in silken Bagges. **1706** E. WARD *Wooden World Diss.* (1708) 70 His Bob Wig ty'd up behind like a Horse-tail. **1833** HT. MARTINEAU *Manch. Strike* ii. 19 He tore my arm one day,.. father got an apothecary to tie it up. **1838** DICKENS *Nich. Nick.* xxii, They had tied up the luggage. **1865** 'L. CARROLL' *Alice's Adv. Wonderland* xi. 172 A large canvass bag, which tied up at the mouth with strings.

b. To tie (a person or animal) to some fixed object or in some confined space, so as to prevent from escaping; to fasten up.

c **1560** [see c]. **1579** W. WILKINSON *Confut. Familye of Love* Ep. Ded. *iij, The bloudy bandoges of the Romish Sinagogue be tyed vp. **1611** SHAKS. *Cymb.* IV. i. 24 My Horse is tyed vp safe. **1719** DE FOE *Crusoe* (1840) I. iii. 53 A malefactor.. is tied up. **1883** GILMOUR *Mongols* xxiii. 285 He had stolen the horse, and tied it up in the mountains.

c. *fig.* To bind, restrain, or confine strictly; to restrict closely; to hinder from acting freely; to oblige to act in a particular way. (Cf. 5.) Also ***to tie up one's hands, one's tongue***: cf. phrases in 2. Also (chiefly *pass.*; orig. *U.S.*) to hold up; to keep busy or occupied.

[*c* **1435** *Torr. Portugal* 2658 Sith he did make vp-tyed Chirchus and abbeys wyde, For hym and his to praye.] *c* **1560** GRINDAL in Foxe *A. & M.* (1583) 1390/2 He hath deserued more gentlenesse at your hande, then to be tied vp so shorte. **1592** SHAKS. *Rom. & Jul.* IV. v. 32 Death that hath tane her hence.. Ties vp my tongue, and will not let me speake. **1658–9** *Burton's Diary* (1828) IV. 226, I would have you not to tie up your hands from consideration of either. **1768** COL. CHURCHILL in Jesse *Selwyn & Contemp.* (1843) II. 289 Being tied up by my father's will from assisting my younger children during my life. **1879** STAINER *Music of Bible* 173 It is not tied up in a strait-jacket like a modern chant. **1887** C. B. GEORGE *40 Years on Rail* vii. 140, I ran into a snow-storm that tied us up until we were six days making the run. **1907** *Springfield* (Mass.) *Weekly Republican* 10 Oct. 16 Traffic west of Springfield was tied up until about midnight. **1935** D. L. SAYERS *Gaudy Night* xiv. 295, I meant to come round yesterday evening, but I got tied up with people. **1941** B. SCHULBERG *What makes Sammy Run?* iii. 53 He was tied up in a story conference. **1959** W. D. PEREIRA *North Flight* ii. 29 Sir Arthur's terribly tied up at the moment and regrets he cannot speak to you. **1973** *New Yorker* 24 Feb. 36/1 The *World Almanac and Book of Facts* is a small buoy indeed but one that, whenever we stop to read it, ties us up for several hours. **1978** *Nature* 21 Sept. p. xii/2 The computer or scope is tied up only a fraction of a second while the exposure is made. **1980** D. LODGE *How far can you Go?* iv. 125 She sent her apologies, but she's tied up organizing some bazaar.

d. To moor (a ship or boat); also *absol.*, or (usually) *intr.* for *pass.* said of the vessel.

1853 KANE *Grinnell Exp.* xvi. (1856) 122 The ice was closing in every direction; and our master.. had no alternative but to tie up and await events. **1886** E. ARNOLD *India Revisited* iii. 33 At night every steamer 'ties up'. **1893** ELIZ. B. CUSTER *Tenting* 34 The great cable was used to tie us up to the bank.

e. *fig.* (from a): To invest or place (money or property) in such a way as to prevent it from being spent or alienated.

1822 J. W. CROKER in *C. Papers* 21 June, He has tied up his real estates as tight as he could. **1841** THACKERAY *Gt. Hoggarty Diamond* xiii, She is close of her money;.. she has tied up every shilling of it, and only allows me half-a-crown a-week for pocket-money. *a* **1859** MACAULAY *Hist. Eng.* xxiii. (1861) V. 34 To pass a prospective statute tying up in strict entail the little which still remained of the Crown property. **1870** MISS BRIDGMAN *Rob. Lynne* II. v. 111 Her money.. had been tied up all tight for her benefit.

f. *slang.* To give up, desist from, quit (a practice or course of action); also *absol.*

1760 FOOTE *Minor* I. Wks. 1799 I. 241, I have a great mind to tie up, and ruin the rascals. **1903** FARMER & HENLEY *Slang Dict.* s.v., *To tie up* = to forswear: e.g., *to tie up prigging* = to lead an honest life.

g. *slang.* To vanquish or disable in a contest; to finish; to 'knock out'.

1818 [implied in TIE-UP *sb.* 5]. **1903** FARMER & HENLEY *Slang Dict.* s.v., *To tie up*.. = to knock out (pugilists'); *tied-up* = (1) finished, settled. **1909** *Westm. Gaz.* 31 July 16/1 Inclined to lay odds that he and Barnes or Rhodes would have 'tied up' the Australian batsmen.

h. To join in marriage: cf. 4 (also *tie the knot* in 2). *colloq.* or *slang.*

1894 ASTLEY *Fifty Years Life* I. 158 A comelier couple parson has seldom.. tied up.

i. *to tie* (a person) ***up in(to) knots*** (or ***a knot***): see KNOT *sb.*[1] 10 a.

j. *intr.* To associate or unite oneself or one's interests *with* (or *to*). Also *trans.*, to associate (one thing) *with* another. orig. *U.S.* Cf. TIE-UP *sb.* 7 b.

1888 *Texas Siftings* 3 Mar. 3/1 He's all O.K. There is no subterfuge about him... He is a man who will do to tie up to. **1903** *N.Y. Even. Post* 5 Dec. 1 It becomes his first interest to make business for that yard. He can best do this by tying up with the other navy yard representatives on the committee. **1904** *Indianapolis News* 21 June 6 The assurance that Captain New is to have a good post may be the reason that so many fellows want to tie up to him. **1925** *Round Table* June 593 It is clearly to South Africa's interest to tie up definitely either with sterling.. or with gold. **1928** *Daily Express* 13 June 3/4 Registered readers.. have.. 'tied up' with the newspaper which.. offers the best.. insurance benefits. **1943** [see GENERATION 2 b]. **1958** *Times Lit. Suppl.* 19 Sept. 526/2 [He] does not rest solely on his spade but takes every opportunity of tying up archaeological discoveries with references obtainable from written authorities.

k. To bring to a satisfactory conclusion.

1954 'R. CROMPTON' *William & Moon Rocket* i. 25 Taking that lorry's number and giving a description of where the shed was on the Minster road. Tied things up a treat, that did. **1959** *Listener* 12 Feb. 305/1 When the play ends.. one is left intentionally with the feeling that not everything has been tied up. **1973** A. BROINOWSKI *Take One Ambassador* vii. 90 The trade mark of the few in the know. That ties it all up. **1980** S. BRETT *Dead Side of Mike* xiii. 147 It all fits in... It just ties up the whole package.

l. *intr.* = sense 11 b above.

1959 M. GILBERT *Blood & Judgement* xiii. 138 'That would make him.. in his late fifties now.' 'Which ties up all right with our man.' **1968** *Listener* 20 June 799/2 This may well tie up with the fact that he was an intensely religious person who believed in people going to hell and being saved. **1974** J. AIKEN *Midnight is Place* iv. 130 'He had had two men sent to jail for protesting.' 'Yes, that seems to tie oop with what we had heard.'

tie: see TYE *sb.*[1] and [2], and *v.*

tie- in combination. [f. TIE *sb.*[1] or *vb.*]

1. Attributive or objective combinations of TIE *sb.* in various senses: ***tie fabric***; **tie-block** *Naut.*, the block on the yard through which the tie passes (see TIE *sb.* 2 a); **tie-break, -breaker**, a means of deciding a winner out of two or more contestants who have tied; also *fig.*; so **tie-breaking** *ppl. a.* and *vbl. sb.*; **tie-clasp, clip**, a small ornamental clasp for securing the ends of a tie to one's shirt; **tie-maker**, a maker of ties (in quots., in senses 4 and 7 of the sb.); **tie-pin**, a pin, usually ornamental, worn in a man's neck-tie; **tie press**, an instrument for pressing ties; **tie rack**, a rack on which to hang neckties; **tie-shooting**, the shooting off of a tie (TIE *sb.* 10) in rifle practice; so **tie-shoot, -shot**; **tie silk**, a strong silk fabric used esp. for ties and clothing; cf. FOULARD 1; **tie tack**, a two-part ornamental fastener for a necktie, one part of which is worn under the shirt to receive the point of the part worn on the tie.

1745 P. THOMAS *Jrnl. Anson's Voy.* 145 We reev'd.. a new Strap to the Fore-top-sail *Tye-block. *c* **1860** H. STUART *Seaman's Catech.* 76 There are two iron straps round the yard for the tye blocks to shackle to. **1970** *Times* 5 Mar. 13 In principle, the *tie-break is an undesirable expedient, but there is a case for it in indoor tournaments confined to one court. **1974** *Observer* 1 Sept. 18/6 In the tie break Miss Mappin led 4–1. **1979** *Daily Tel.* 10 Dec. 19/1 Nigel.. failed in a tie-break to win the British Chess championship in August. **1961** WEBSTER, *Tie-breaker. **1970** *New Yorker* 10 Oct. 179/1 There are several species of tie-breakers, but the one that Bill Talbert, the tournament director, selected.. was the ninepoint sudden-death variety. **1971** *Computers & Humanities* VI. 68 The identifiers will be indexed and will serve as ultimate tie-breakers in all sorting operations. **1979** G. HAMMOND *Dead Game* xiv. 188 At the end of the quiz, honours were even.. and the chairman asked for a tie-breaker from the audience. **1982** *Daily Tel.* 21 Sept. 16/4 [Rifle-shooting.] Belither.. beat Paul Kent.. by a single point on a tiebreaker. **1970** *Times* 1 Oct. 10/6 Okker, of the Netherlands, had to battle through two *tie-breaking sets to beat El Shafei.. 7–6, 7–6. **1971** *Jrnl. Gen. Psychol.* LXXXV. 265 The stratification procedure entails a large number of random assignments and tie-breakings. **1978** R. NIXON *Memoirs* 85 His only important functions were to cast occasional tie-breaking votes in the Senate. **1955** W. GADDIS *Recognitions* II. i. 285 They.. fastened monogrammed *tie-clasps the more firmly. **1971** 'D. SHANNON' *Murder with Love* (1972) ix. 153 His dapper tailoring, gold cuff links and tie-clasp. **1898–9** *T. Eaton & Co. Catal.* Fall & Winter 16/1 *Tie clips... For holding the tie in place on shirt or blouse fronts, 2 for 5c. **1913** [see INNOVATION 6]. **1976** 'R. BOYLE' *Cry Rape* xii. 62 It wasn't an elegant tie-clip. Not the kind with a diamond or emerald in it. **1931** *Fairchild's Fabrics Buyers' Guide* I. 143 (*heading*) *Tie and muffler fabrics. **1977** *Man-Made Textiles in India* XX. 92/3 The attributes which make a tie fabric satisfactory in use are similar to those in a dress fabric. **1901** *Daily Chron.* 25 July 6/6 The girl.. is a *tie-maker. **1904** *Longm. Mag.* Aug. 306 Any moderately good tie-maker can turn out thirty ties a day in good timber. **1780** *Traveller's Guide*, A silver *tie-pin, three silver studs. **1899** *Daily News* 22 June 7/3 His stand-up collar and his tie-pin. **1926–7** *Army & Navy Stores Catal.* 757/3 '*Watts*' **tie press*.. $9\frac{1}{2}$ in. by $3\frac{1}{2}$ in. *a* **1974** T. R. DENNIS in J. Burnett *Useful Toil* (1974) III. 354 A very cheap watch from my parents.. a tie-press from a friend. **1916** *Daily Colonist* (Victoria, B.C.) 1 July 9/3 (Advt.), Pipe Racks, *Tie Racks and Collar Bags, regular to 75c. **1974** L. DEIGHTON *Spy Story* ii. 22 Rummaging through the wardrobe I.. noticed the tie rack had been moved. **1909** *Daily Chron.* 23 July 7/2 He tied for the 'Daily Telegraph' Cup and finished second in the *tie shoot. **1902** *Ibid.* 23 July 6/3 The *tie-shooting for the first Coronation Prize. **1887** *Daily News* 18 July 2/1 Many men might beat him in the *tie shots. **1920** M. S. WOOLMAN *Clothing* iv. 53 Ribbons, velvets, *tie silks ..and knitting silks are made of this fiber. **1934** *Vogue* 30 May 96 (*caption*) Jenny makes a tailored suit of checked tie silk. **1961** *Guardian* 30 Mar. 9/4 Charming and practical Tie-silk shirtwaisters. **1961** WEBSTER, *Tie tack. **1962** 'D. SHANNON' *Extra Kill* xi. 171 He'd always wear a tie clasp, or one of those new tie tacks. **1970** *New Yorker* 10 Jan. 56/3 (Advt.), Peace Tie Tac. **1980** *Outdoor Life* (U.S.) (Northeast ed.) Oct. 154/3 (Advt.), Detective profession. Easy home study; free tie tack or lapel pin.

2. Combinations of TIE *v.* with adverbs: **tie-back**, a contrivance for tying something back, esp. in a woman's dress; also, a device for holding a drawn curtain back from the window; **tie-down**, the state (of an aircraft, etc.) of being tied down or otherwise kept on the ground; also, a device to or with which something may be tied down; freq. *attrib.*; **tie-on** *a.*, that is fastened on by tying. See also TIE-IN, TIE-OFF, TIE-UP.

1880 *World* 29 Sept. 15 The days of 'tie-backs', either in the dressing of ladies or artificial flies, were not yet. **1891** *Daily News* 27 July 2/1 Even Lady Harberton could scarcely disapprove of the gored skirt with no tie-backs. **1927** *Ladies' Home Jrnl.* Dec. 35/3 Flat festoons of green used for tie-backs on the curtains. **1961** *Times* 14 Jan. 9/7 Brass tie-backs in various shapes for holding the drawn but voluminous folds of the mid-Victorian drawing room curtains became a period 'must'. **1982** BARR & YORK *Official Sloane Ranger Handbk.* 148/1 Sloane windows need curtains with a capital C: with pelmets, twiddly bits, bands, tassels, tie-backs, edging. **1952** *Sun* (Baltimore) 4 Aug. 1/5 $1 tiedown fees for [flying] saucers less than 1,000 feet in diameter. **1955** *Ibid.* 11 Feb. 2/4 Exhaustive 'tie-down' ground tests are scheduled for the XV-3.. before actual flight tests begin. **1956** W. A. HEFLIN *U.S. Air Force Dict.* 525/1 *Tie-down*, a ring, hook, stake, or the like to which something is secured; a tie-down fitting. **1969** *Jane's Freight Containers 1968–69* 418/1 Forklift entries and tie-down inserts are provided. **1971** *Flying* Apr. 13/1 Big tie-down areas for smaller airplanes. **1974** *Union* (S. Carolina) *Daily Times* 22 Apr. 7/7 (Advt.), Mobile homes anchored: Storm tie-downs to guard you against wind damage. **1978** F. MULLALLY *Deadly Payoff* xii. 171 He let the loosened end of the tie-down rope fall to the ground and kicked the chocks away from the front wheels. **1982** *Chicago Sun-Times* 31 Oct. 8 Another 30 residences.. have planes with tie-downs instead of hangars. **1910** *Times* 4 July 6/5 Tie-on labels should not be used. **1949** Tie-on [see OCCLUDER]. **1967** E. SHORT *Embroidery & Fabric Collage* iii. 80 Tie-on cushions for dining chairs. **1971** 'D. HALLIDAY' *Dolly & Doctor Bird* xii. 161 My skin became brown.. between my tie-on tops and my hipsters.

3. Combinations with sbs., in which the first element may be either TIE *sb.* or *v.*: **'tie-bar**, a bar which ties or acts as a tie, in a building or other structure; **'tie-beam**, a horizontal beam which acts as a tie: see *esp.* quot. 1823; **tie belt**, a belt which is fastened by tying; hence **tie-belted** *a.*; **tie-bolt** *sb.*, a bolt which ties together the component parts of a structure; hence **tie-bolt** *v.*, *trans.* to fasten with tie-bolts; **tie-cord**, a cord used for tying something; **tie-dye** *sb.* = *tie-and-dye*, sense 4 below; freq. *attrib.*; also as *v. trans.*, to dye by this process; also *absol.*; hence **tie-dyed** *ppl. a.*, **-dying** *vbl. sb.*; **tie game**, a game in which the result is a tie; **tie-knot**, a knot with which something is tied; **tie-match**, a subsequent match played to decide a tie; **tie-neck**, a collar attached at the back of the neck but left loose in front so that the ends can be tied; hence **tie-necked** *a.*; **'tie-,periwig** = TIE-WIG; **tie-plate**, (*a*) *Naut.* a narrow iron plate placed longitudinally or diagonally to space and strengthen deck-beams; (*b*) a plate to receive the pull of a tie-rod, and distribute the pressure on a supporting beam or wall; (*c*) a protecting metal plate laid between a sleeper and the rail; **tie-post**, a post to which a horse, etc. may be tied; **tie rail** orig. *U.S.*, a rail or railing to which horses may be hitched; **tie-rib**, a rib forming a tie in some structure (in quot. *fig.*); **tie rod**, (*a*) a long tie-bolt or iron rod which acts as a tie in a building or other structure; (*b*) a track rod, or one of the rods of which it is composed, in the steering gear of a motor vehicle; **tie-rope**, a rope for tying something; in quot. *c* 1525, ? = TIE *sb.* 2; **tie-stay**, a stay acting as a tie, used to support some part of a building; **tie-strap**, a strap for tying up a horse or other animal; **tie-string**, a string for tying something, e.g. a bonnet or other part of costume; **tie-teeth** *W. Indian colloq.*, any sticky foodstuff which is difficult to chew; **tie-tie**, one of several cords fastened to a hammock and serving to tie it up in a roll (*Cent. Dict.* 1891); a pidgin English name for any string; **tie-vote**, a vote resulting in a tie, the numbers on each side being equal: see TIE *sb.* 10; **tie-wall**, a wall having the function of tying together the parts of a structure; esp. 'a transverse wall in the hollow spandril of an arch, at right angles to the spandril-wall' (Knight). See also TIE-DOG, TIE-WIG.

1861 FAIRBAIRN *Iron* 91 The reverberatory furnace.. consists externally of an oblong casing of iron plates, firmly bound together by iron *tie-bars. **1823** P. NICHOLSON *Pract. Build.* 125 A *tie-beam is a piece of timber, connecting the feet of the principal rafters, in order to prevent them from spreading. **1851** SIR F. PALGRAVE *Norm. & Eng.* I. 436 The open roof and tyebeams of a Roman Basilica. **1853** SIR H. DOUGLAS *Milit. Bridges* (ed. 3) 308 Considered as a tie-beam its longitudinal strength depends upon the key. **1964** *McCall's Sewing* xii. 227/1 A *tie belt, without stiffening, becomes a string in no time. **1977** *Daily Mirror* 16 Mar. 16/2 (Advt.), The tie-belt style is 12–18. **1976** *Woman's Weekly* 6 Nov. 4/2 Tunic top is hip-length, *tie-belted and tie-necked. **1838** *Civil Eng. & Arch. Jrnl.* I. 126/1 Placing the *tie-bolts diagonally, instead of horizontally. **1874** THEARLE *Naval Archit.* 59 Grooved and tongued together at their edges, and nailed to the cants, being also *tie-bolted where necessary. **1907** C. C. BROWN *China in Leg. & Story* xvii. 240 A queue, scarce big enough to carry its black *tie-cord. **1904** G. WATT *Indian Art at Delhi* VII. xxxi. 255 From Chamba State has been received.. a most remarkable.. cotton fabric woven in alternate bands of cotton and gold thread, the cotton being *tie-dyed so as to show large wavy formations. **1926** *Daily Colonist* (Victoria, B.C.) 22 July 8/7 (Advt.), Marvelous tie-dye patterns, glorious color-blendings are amazingly simple to make. **1951** A. N. GULATI *Patolu of Gujarat* 18 The first essential step, therefore, is to tie-dye both warp and weft in conformity with the proposed design in the fabric. **1956** J. IRWIN in *Textiles & Ornaments India* 29 The so-called *ikat*-technique is another kind of tie-dye. **1970** *Time* 20 Apr. 72 The stars fussed with their see-through dresses, tie-dyes and black ties and then paraded up a red-carpeted walkway. **1971** *New Yorker* 4 Sept. 61 What the boys who tie-dye and the grandmothers who rug-hook are doing is, in effect, as mechanical as anything done by a machine. **1975** *Advocate-News* (Barbados) 28 June 1/7 Organza flowers, soft toys, tie-dye and other craft work will be displayed by the YWCA craft group. **1977** *Guardian* 10 Jan. 8/1 The pallid youth in the tie-die shirt with a sewn-on picture of Marx. **1904** G. WATT *Indian Art at Delhi* VII. xxxi. 257 The beauty of these warp and weft *tie-dyed textiles. **1978** J. UPDIKE *Coup* (1979) vi. 236 Their countrymen wearing cowboy hats, blue jeans, tie-dyed T-shirts. **1904** G. WATT *Indian Art at Delhi* VII. xxxi. 252 The once famous Bandana handkerchiefs may be given as the best known example of *tie-dyeing. **1939** G. CLARK *Archæol. & Society* iii. 63 The tunics of the notables, which were.. coloured by the tie-dying method. **1970** *Time* 26 Jan. 40 The art is almost as old as India—where it is called *bandhnu*. It is as new as the boutiques that blossom along Sunset Strip and Madison Avenue—where it is called tie-dying. **1742** in H. T. Waghorn *Dawn of Cricket* (1906) 12 That played the *tie game the beginning of the season. **1832** P. EGAN *Bk. of Sports* xxii. 347/2 In the first innings Woking gained 71 runs, Shiere then went in and got 71. Second innings, Woking 71; ditto, Shiere 71; it was consequently a *tye*-game, under circumstances unprecedented in the annals of cricket-playing. **1928** *Collier's* 29 Dec. 17/4 A tie game in football is certainly more thrilling..than a one-sided game. **1960** *Washington Post* 18 Oct. A18/1 It was Eddie Erdelatz, the Navy football coach, who once described a tie game as an unsatisfactory experience that permitted no enthusiasm. 'A tie game is like kissing your sister,' he said. **1800** COLERIDGE *Wallenst.* I. iii. 64 The *tie-knot here Is off—this hair must not hang so dishevelled. **1864** *Daily Tel.* 26 Oct., Third Kent (Lee) v. Eighth Kent (Sydenham).—These two corps fired for a *tie match. **1898** *Westm. Gaz.* 26 Feb. 3/3 In case of ties..the prizes are to be divided, except the first prize, which must be determined by a tie match of four games. **1968** J. IRONSIDE *Fashion Alphabet* 54 *Tie neck. **1983** *Daily Tel.* 28 Feb. 24/5 The Queen's outfit was a navy-and-white jacket and dress with..a tie neck. **1973** *Country Life* 22 Feb. 490/3 A *tie-necked silk shirt. **1977** *Harpers & Queen* Sept. 44/1 A tie-necked champagne blouse in washable crepe. **1727** GAY *Begg. Op.* I. iii, Three *tye-perriwigs and a piece of broad cloth. **1771** SMOLLETT *Humph. Cl.* II. 23 June, An old Scotch lawyer, in a tie-periwig. **1874** THEARLE *Naval Archit.* 119 The deck fastenings are not so efficient in iron as in wood beams, and hence both stringer and *tie-plates are of service in opposing the first tendency of the deck to elongate. **1861** *Harper's Mag.* Feb. 424/2 He alighted,.. throwing the reins over a *tie-post. **1884** *Ibid.* Jan. 328/2 Throwing the reins over a tie-post. **1920** C. E. MULFORD *Johnny Nelson* 238 He'll never forget my kickin' him off'n th' *tie-rail. **1970** *Sunday Mail Mag.* (Brisbane) 9 Aug. 14/2 The stranger dismounted and hitched his horse to the tierails in front of the pub. **1896** KIPLING *Seven Seas, Deep Sea Cables* ii, Here on the *tie-ribs of earth Words..flicker and flutter and beat. **1839** *Civil Eng. & Arch. Jrnl.* II. 191/2 Four iron *tye-rods with washers placed transversely through the arch. **1910** J. GUNN *Practical Design Motor Cars* ix. 230 The rod which transmits the motion of the steering gear to the front wheels should be connected at the front end ..to the tie-rod. **1922** JOYCE *Ulysses* 698 Water closet.. provided with opaque singlepane oblong window, tipup seat, bracket lamp, brass tierod brace. **1966** *McGraw-Hill Encycl. Sci. & Technol.* XIII. 640/1 In pressure piping, large forces are produced between connected parts. The pipes or parts are constrained by tie rods. **1976** *Jrnl.* (Newcastle) 26 Nov. (Advt.), Viva, 1969, white, taxed 11 months,..new balls and tie rods. *c* **1525** in *Archæologia* XLVII. 332, ij. roopes, called *tye ropes, for the *Henry Grace Dieu*. **1886** T. HARDY *Mayor of Casterbr.* iii, The pens for sheep, the tie-ropes for horses. **1892** *Daily News* 20 Feb. 3/4 The Repair of Canterbury Cathedral... A series of *tiestays are being inserted. **1877** KNIGHT *Dict. Mech.*, *Tie-strap. **1901** *Munsey's Mag.* XXV. 737/2 An attendant snapped a tie strap into his halter and led him back to barn or paddock. **1897** *Outing* (U.S.) XXX. 379/1 A rubber blanket..with *tie-strings at the four corners, can be made into a first-rate shelter by tying two corners to poles driven into the ground, and the other corners to pegs. *c* **1915** in Cassidy & Le Page *Dict. Jamaican Eng.* (1967) 444 *Tie-teeth. **1953** *Caribbean Q.* III. I. 9 *Tie-teeth* (candy, sweets, or other very sticky food). **1975** E. L. ORTIZ *Caribbean Cookery* (1977) 266 If it is overcooked the mango paste turns into what Jamaicans graphically call tie-teeth. **1774** E. LONG *Hist. Jamaica* II. 427 The Negroes seem very fond of reduplications..as..*tie-tie, lilly-lilly, fum-fum.* **1827** *Hamel, Obeah Man* II. 257 Stretching what they called a *tie-tie* of tent-ropes, hempen cordage, mahoe bark, and bush ropes, all spliced together, to form..a guide for those who could be induced to cross the bridge. **1883** MOLONEY *W. African Fisheries* 17 (Fish. Exhib. Publ.) The..occupants.. standing erect, or perched on seats—cross sticks, secured by tie-tie on gunwale of canoe. **1931** *Discovery* May 153/1 The whole of the frame-work [of a Nigerian house] is secured with what is known in pidgin English as *tie-tie* which is fibre from certain plants. **1958** C. ACHEBE *Things fall Apart* I. vii. 47 There were little holes..in the upper levels of the wall, and through these Okonkwo passed the rope, or *tie-tie*, to the boys and they passed it round the wooden stays and then back to him; and in this way the cover was strengthened on the wall. **1894** *Daily News* 6 Oct. 6/5 A proposal only lost ..by a *tie-vote.

4. Phrasal Comb.: **tie-and-dye**, a technique for producing a mottled appearance in dyed cloth by folding it and tying it before it is put in the dye bath; a garment or piece of cloth so dyed; freq. *attrib.* and unhyphened.

1886 *Jrnl. Indian Art* I. 117 The wonderfully constructed patterns of Patolo weaving with 'tie and die [*sic*]' warp and woof..testify..to the skill achieved by Indian dyers and weavers. **1928** *Daily Express* 21 May 5/2 The 'tie and dye' process—an old craft which gives a charming hazed effect. **1937** M. COVARRUBIAS *Island of Bali* I. vii. 196 The Balinese often decorate pieces of silk by the tie-and-dye process. **1976** *Billings* (Montana) *Gaz.* 7 July 9-B/7 Demonstrations in the hotel courtyard will include..silver casting, tie and dye, silk screening and oil painting.

tied (taɪd), *ppl. a.* Also 7 tide, tyed. [f. TIE *v.* + -ED[1].]

1. a. Bound or fastened with a cord or the like; joined, connected (as letters in printing, quot. 1891): see TIE *v.* B. 1-3. Also TONGUE-TIED.

1591 SHAKS. *Two Gent.* II. iii. 41 *Panth.* What's the vnkindest tide? *Lau.* Why, he that's tide here, Crab my dog. **1597** A. M. tr. *Guillemeau's Fr. Chirurg.* 38 b/2 The tyed Vayne might chaunce to vntye. **1614** GORGES *Lucan* VI. 253 He stonisht was.., His tyed tong no sound could blunder. **1758** J. S. *Le Dran's Observ. Surg.* (1771) 220, I dressed it with tied Dossils. **1864** BOWEN *Logic* xi. 365 The nervous fluid will not travel along a tied nerve. **1891** W. MORRIS in Mackail *Life* (1899) II. 252 We have no contractions, few tied letters. **1904** BUDGE *3rd & 4th Egypt. Rooms Brit. Mus.* 110 Oxen with tied feet.

b. ***tied note***: see quots. and TIE *sb.* 6 b, *v.* 3 c.

1716 (*title*) The Dancing-Master... Sixteenth Edition... The whole Work Revised and done on the New-Ty'd-Note. **1801** BUSBY *Dict. of Music, Tied-Notes*, notes, the tails of which are joined together by cross lines, as in united quavers, semiquavers, &c., or over the heads of which a curve is drawn to denote that they are to be slurred.

2. *fig.* United, joined; restrained, confined, etc.: see TIE *v.* B. 4, 5.

1876 T. HARDY *Ethelberta* (1890) 140 That's why married men advise others to marry. Were all the world tied up, the pleasantly tied ones would be equivalent to those at present free. **1907** *Daily Chron.* 22 Mar. 7/1 The sight of the Progressives banded together emphasized the fact of their being the tied party of the Chamber of Mines.

b. *spec.* Of an inn or public house: Of which the tenant is bound to take his liquor from a particular brewing firm (which usually owns the house), hence *transf.* of a labourer's cottage: of which the tenant is astricted to work on the farm.

1887 *Pall Mall G.* 23 July 16/1 Local breweries have almost entirely depended upon tied houses for the sale of their products. **1890** *Guardian* 17 Sept. 1434/2 The question of renewing licences to 'tied houses' has been considered at some of the licensing sessions. **1899** *Daily News* 7 Dec. 4/1 The labourers hate the 'tied cottage' system. **1901** *Ibid.* 16 Feb. 5/3 Certain brewers are in the habit of turning unsuccessful houses into tied-house clubs.

c. Of an international loan, etc.: given subject to conditions as to its use (see TIE *v.* 5 f).

1958 C. N. HENNING *Internat. Finance* IV. xxi. 441/1 The so-called 'tied loan' principle. **1961** *Ann. Reg. 1960* 470 The issue of tied grants and credits was the subject of some dispute at international meetings. **1965** *McGraw-Hill Dict. Mod. Econ.* 515 The advantages of tied loans are that they stimulate employment and income in the creditor nation and do not affect the balance of payments of that country adversely. **1976** *New Internationalist* Jan. 5 For the Third World, 'tied' aid generally means having to pay between 20% and 50% more for goods than the competitive world market level.

d. Of a retail garage: of which the tenant is bound to receive fuel from a particular supplier.

1957 *Economist* 7 Dec. 885/1 About a third of these 'tied garages' have been signed up for periods of five years or less; the other two-thirds, which sell over half the petrol sold through dealers, are tied to their suppliers for longer periods of up to 20 years. **1965** [see SOLUS *a.* 3 b].

3. a. ***tied up***, in *lit.* and *fig.* senses: see TIE *v.* B. 13.

1603 SHAKS. *Meas. for M.* I. iii. 32 It rested in your Grace To vnloose this tyde-vp Iustice. **1693** W. BOWLES in *Dryden's Juvenal* v. 13 And with a Matt, and Crutch, and ty'd up Leg, More honestly and honourably Beg. **1711-12** SWIFT *Jrnl. to Stella* 6 Jan., It was not proper to go to Court without a long wig, and his was a tied-up one. **1822** SAVAGE *Hints Decorative Print.* 46 Four or five octavo pages of tied up letter. **1876** [see 2].

b. ***tied-back***: held back by tying.

1895 M. BEERBOHM in *Yellow Book* IV. 280 The women wore jerseys and tied-back skirts. **1979** A. BUCK *Dress in Eighteenth-Century England* 32/1 (*caption*) The tied-back hair in a bag.

tied (taɪd), *a.* [f. TIE *sb.* + -ED[2].] Wearing a tie.

1911 G. K. CHESTERTON *Innocence of Father Brown* iv. 105 The red-tied youth. **1976** SCOTT & KOSKI *Walk-In* (1977) ii. 17 One clean-shaven, suited and tied, scrubbed Asian.

†**tie-dog.** *Obs.* Forms: see TIE and DOG. [See TIE- 3.] A dog kept tied or chained up, either to guard a house, or because fierce; = BANDOG. (In last quot. *fig.*)

c **1290** *S. Eng. Leg.* I. 308/301 þe deuel..ne may no man ..taken a-ȝein is wille, Nonmore þane a teiȝ dogge þat is in strongue teiȝe. *c* **1380** WYCLIF *Wks.* (1880) 252 þouȝ þei bynden hem not to o synguler place as a tey dogge. **1430-40** LYDG. *Bochas* III. i. (MS. Bodl. 263) 151/1 Cruel Orchus, the teidogge infernall Shal reende thi skyn..fro thi bonys. **1542** UDALL *Erasm. Apoph.* 127 b, Ther are tye dogges or mastifes for keepyng of houses. **1601** CHETTLE & MUNDAY *Death Earl of Huntington* II. i. E iij, I knowe the villaine.., But as a ty-dogge I will muzzle him. *c* **1700** MATHER in *Harper's Mag.* July (1883) 222/1 The Ty-dogs of the Pit are abroad among us.

†**tiego** ('taɪgəʊ). *Obs.* Colloq. or vulgar abbreviation of VERTIGO.

1634 MASSINGER *Very Woman* IV. iii, I am shrewdly troubled with a tiego Here in my head, madam, often with this tiego, It takes me very often.

tie-in ('taɪɪn). orig. and chiefly *U.S.* [f. vbl. phr. *to tie in*: see TIE *v.* 11.] **1. a.** A connection or association *with*; a link-up.

1934 in WEBSTER. **1941** W. KOZLENKO *100 Non-Royalty Radio Plays* 535/2 That's the tie in. He killed Tom and after that decided to really cripple the Dominion team so that we wouldn't have a chance at winning. **1949** M. MEAD *Male & Female* vii. 152 The tie-in with birth can be close. **1965** *Listener* 10 June 875/1 The London studio tie-in with the pictures from America was also very successful, with John Tidmarsh getting lucid technical comments out of Geoffrey Pardoe at each stage of the operation. **1972** 'T. COE' *Don't lie to Me* (1974) vii. 66, I didn't know the museum had a tie-in with City College. **1973** *Black Panther* 21 July 2/3 Could you say something about the tie-in of David Hilliard's case with Watergate?

b. Used *attrib.* with reference to sales that are made conditional upon the purchase of some additional item or items from the same supplier.

1943 *Amer. N. & Q.* July 54/2 The phrase 'tie-in sales' (referring to those whereby tradesmen are obliged to buy unwanted stock in order to get even a small amount of a scarce item) appears to have established itself..about the first week of June (1943). **1946** *Sun* (Baltimore) 8 Feb. 12/6 This [liquor] industry can put an immediate stop to tie-in selling. **1980** *Times* 13 Sept. 18/7 It was information from an individual 'mole', working temporarily in a discount store, that first alerted the National Consumer Council to..'tie-in sales' (a stipulation that a buyer must purchase part or all of his requirements of a second (tied) product from the supplier of a first (tying) product).

c. An association between two publicity campaigns in the form of a theme common to both, or an advertisement that appears in two different media.

1949 *Newsweek* 28 Nov. 70/1 By next May, Paramount expects to have spent $1,000,000 calling attention to the show by way of..tie-ins with fashion designers and department stores who will make and sell women's clothes influenced by the 'Minoan period' costumes [in a film about Samson and Delilah]. **1959** I. ROSS *Image Merchants* ix. 149 Ryland [of NBC] also spends a good deal of time working up promotional tie-ins with manufacturers, department stores ..and publications. It is a major coup when a national magazine can be persuaded to incorporate a TV plug in its own vast promotional outlay. **1962** *Economist* 10 Feb. 521/1 'Calories Don't Count' has been offered to the public as a promotional tie-in to encourage the purchase of safflower oil.

d. A book, film, or the like published to take advantage of the appearance of the same work in another medium.

1962 *Publishers' Weekly* 23 Apr. 43/1 Students show an interest in books which have been made into successful movies. Watch for these tie-ins. **1976** *Ibid.* 29 Mar. 42/1 The paper edition of Ibsen's 'Hedda Gabler and Other Plays' even has a movie tie-in cover with a still from the recent Glenda Jackson film. **1981** *Times Lit. Suppl.* 17 Apr. 425/2 The 1970s was the decade of the 'tie-in'—the almost simultaneous film of the novel, novel of the film, TV series of the novel.

2. (The making of) a connection between two pipelines or sections of pipeline. Freq. *attrib.*

1975 *North Sea Background Notes* (Brit. Petroleum Co.) 32 The line was welded, trenched and buried as quickly as possible, with only tie-in ends being left temporarily exposed. **1975** *Offshore Engineer* Nov. 18/2 The towing method..could be developed for installing a pipeline across the Norwegian trench in section, with tie-ins between them. **1976** *Ibid.* July 5/3 The 406mm line from SPAR to Brent B is being completed by Serra-Comex tie-in barge *Sandokan*. **1977** *Ibid.* Apr. 9/2 Three wells have been completed on the field and await tie-in when the production decision is made.

tiel, tield, variant of TIAL *Obs.*, TELD *Obs.*

tieless ('taɪlɪs), *a.* [f. TIE *sb.* + -LESS.] Without a tie; wearing no neck-tie.

1903 W. CHURCHILL *Crisis* II. ii, Every gentleman.. collarless, coatless, tieless and vestless. **1907** *Westm. Gaz.* 21 Mar. 2/1 His head was bare, and he was tieless.

'tie-line. [f. TIE- + LINE *sb.*[2]] **1.** *Surveying.* A line measured on the ground after the principal lines of a triangulated survey have been measured, with the object of checking the accuracy of the work.

1877 RANKINE *Man. Civ. Engin.* 24 The accuracy of the measurements in every important triangle should be checked by measuring a 'tie-line', from one of its angles to a known point in the opposite side.

2. *Teleph.* A line connecting two private branch exchanges. Also *transf.*

1923 T. E. HERBERT *Telephony* xvii. 437 Should an answering plug be inserted into a jack of the tie line, and the corresponding calling plug be placed into an exchange jack, [etc.]. **1955** E. F. RUSSELL *Somewhere a Voice* (1965) 107 Man is born of Earth and needs a tieline to Earth. **1969** J. MARTIN *Telecommunications & Computer* v. 91 Many companies have a leased system of telecommunications lines with switching facilities. To telephone a person in a distant company location, an employee must first obtain the appropriate tie line to that person's private branch exchange. **1978** *Broadcast* 29 May 9/2 Dring got a phone call out [of Zaire] via the BBC's New York office on tie line to the TV Centre just three minutes before the nine o'clock bulletin went out.

3. A line in a phase diagram joining two points that each represent the composition of two phases in equilibrium with one another.

1924 A. E. HILL in H. S. Taylor *Treat. Physical Chem.* I. ix. 400 No solution therefore can exist having composition indicated by points within the area *A-B-C-B'-A'*, but such compositions can lead only to two conjugate solutions of composition lying upon the curves at the intersections with the isothermal tie-lines. **1935** *Amer. Jrnl. Sci.* CCXXIX. 174 All liquids *a-b* are in equilibrium with olivine, each with an olivine of different composition as indicated by the tie-lines. **1961** *Geol. Mag.* XCVIII. 336 (*caption*) Tie-lines joining co-existing, chemically analysed pyroxenes from igneous rocks. **1979** *Nature* 3 May 53/2 (*caption*) Miscibility gap between carbonate and silicate melts... Conjugate liquids at 0·7 kbar and 7·6 kbar are joined by tie-lines.

4. A pipeline or transmission line connecting two distribution systems or two parts of a single system.

1949 *Sun* (Baltimore) 5 July 10/4 With the completion of a 48-inch tie-line..the city Bureau of Water Supply believes it could supply 4,000,000 gallons daily. **1962** *Newnes Conc. Encycl. Electr. Engin.* 348/1 If two machines [*sc.* a.c. generators] are to be coupled together by a tie-line perhaps 50 or 60 miles in length, there may be an appreciable impedance presented to the flow of the synchronizing current. **1974** *Sci. Amer.* Nov. 40/3 Its objective is to maintain the frequency within an area served by several generating stations and to maintain the sum of all active tie-line power exchanges between the area and its neighbors.

tiemannite ('tiːmənaɪt). *Min.* [ad. Ger. *Tiemannit*, named by Neumann, 1855, from the discoverer, Tiemann: see -ITE[1] 2 b.] Native selenide of mercury, occurring in dark grey masses or granules with a metallic lustre.

1868 DANA *Min.* 56.

‖**t'ien** (tiɛn). Also 7 tayn, 8 tyen, 8- tien. [Chinese *tiān*.] In Chinese thought: Heaven; the Deity.

1613 PURCHAS *Pilgrimage* IV. xvi. 373 All being a rude and vnformed Chaos, *Tayn* (say they) framed and setled the Heaven and Earth. **1710** *Memoires for Rome concerning State Christian Relig. China* iii. 71 He would not retract, nor acknowledge that *Tien*, that is to say, the visible Heavens was the God of the Christians. **1747** *Astley's New Gen. Coll. Voy.* IV. I. v. 202/1 It appears..that this *Tyen*, or first Being, is the Creator of all Things. **1788** tr. *Grosier's Gen. Descr. China* II. VI. i. 186 Between the *Tien* and man there is a relation. **1878** *Jrnl. North-China Branch R. Asiatic Soc.* XII. 122 Even in the time of Confucius the change from the personality of T'ien-tsze to the abstract idea of the modern T'ien does not seem to have been complete. **1904** *Athenæum* 17 Sept. 373/2 The Chinese Emperor is not regarded as other than the regent of the empire appointed by *t'ien* or heaven. **1940** E. POUND *Cantos* liv. 39 The rites of *Tien*, that is Heaven Were ploughing and the raising of silk worms. **1958** W. WILLETTS *Chinese Art* I. ii. 92 After the Chou displaced the Shang-Yin, they apparently came to equate the old Shang Ti with their own chief deity T'ien.

tien, obs. f. TINE *v.*

tiend, obs. f. TEIND, TIND.

tienda (tɪ'ɛndə). orig. and chiefly *U.S.* [a. Sp., = tent, awning, shop: see TENT *sb.*[1]] In the south-western U.S.: a shop or stall, esp. a draper's or general store.

1844 G. W. KENDALL *Santa Fé Exped.* II. ii. 38 Standing in front of a small tienda, or store. **1870** J. C. DUVAL *Adv. Big-Foot Wallace* xxxviii. 235, I searched in vain every shop and 'tienda' in the city for even a pair of No. 11's, though 12's fit me best. **1912** C. F. SAUNDERS *Indians of Terraced Houses* 71 Our proximity to the pueblo was indicated by our meeting Indians..on their way to the trader's *tienda* beneath the shady cottonwoods at Algodones. **1927** *Blackw. Mag.* Nov. 658/2 Its *tienda* with long counter, handsome shelves, and fabulous profits. **1948** F. BLAKE *Johnny Christmas* I. 10 Across the plaza, too, in the sprawling Martinez tienda, were articles that would trade or sell high in northeastern Texas.

‖**tiens** (tjɛ̃), *int.* [Fr., imp. sing. of *tenir* to hold.] An expression of surprise.

1932 G. HEYER *Devil's Cub* xi. 169 '*Tiens!*' said the Duchess with polite interest. 'My son is then a house-breaker.' **1958** L. DURRELL *Mountolive* viii. 179 *Tiens!* I forgot. Here is the thousand I promised you. **1975** A. CHRISTIE *Curtain* xiii. 133 Did he take it by accident or intention. *Tiens*, his fingerprints are not on the bottle.

‖**tienta** ('tjenta). [Sp., lit. 'probe'.] In Spain, an occasion at which young bulls in the field are tested for spirit as prospective stud and fighting bulls.

1909 J. VILLIERS-WARDELL *Spain of Spanish* vi. 110 It is necessary for the *ganadero*—an owner of cattle—to test his young bulls while they are still running wild... This testing of the young bulls is called a *tienta*. **1932** E. HEMINGWAY *Death in Afternoon* xii. 124 The strain of fighting blood.. can only be kept pure by conscientious testing in the tientas. **1957** R. CAMPBELL *Portugal* 109 His name..is given him along with his branded number and noted down on the day of the *tienta*. **1967** MCCORMICK & MASCAREÑAS *Compl. Aficionado* ii. 55 Memory of the *tienta* stirs and fires him to a prompt charge, his weariness forgotten.

tienthe, obs. f. TENTH.

‖**tiento** ('tjento). *Mus.* [Sp., lit. 'touch, feel'.] In sixteenth- and seventeenth-cent. Spanish music: a contrapuntal piece resembling a *ricercar*, orig. for strings and, later, organ.

1905 C. F. A. WILLIAMS *Story of Organ Music* xi. 163 The compositions of Cabezon's collection consist of nine practice pieces,..short preludes called Versos or Versillos, ..[and] longer preludes called Tientos. **1947** A. EINSTEIN *Music in Romantic Era* xvii. 294 The 'schools' of the ricercar, whether called fugue as in Germany, *tiento* as in Spain, or fancy as in England, were different; but the spirit and form were the same. **1976** D. MUNROW *Instruments Middle Ages & Renaissance* ix. 74/4 The solo *tiento* for harp or organ by Alonso Mudarra, published in his *Tres Libros* (1546). **1980** *Early Music* Apr. 248/1 Some polyphonic works of the period in the tradition of the *tiento* offer most remarkable variety within their stylistic limitations.

Tientsin (tjɛn'(t)sɪn, tɪn'(t)sɪn). The name of a city and port on the East coast of north China, used *attrib.* and *absol.* to designate carpets made or shipped from there.

1904, 1913 [see PEKING 1 b]. **1922** KENDRICK & TATTERSALL *Hand-Woven Carpets* I. I. vi. 66 Many carpets find their way to Tientsin for export, and on that account the term 'Tientsin Carpet' has come into use. **1980** D. CREED *Scarab* II. xiv. 132 Deep-piled Tientsin carpets covered the tiled floor.

tie-off ('taɪɒf, -ɔ:-). [TIE- 2.] **1.** *Show-jumping.* = JUMP-OFF 3.

1958 *Listener* 2 Oct. 536/3 We could see the tie-off for the Grand Prix between the Italian and German champions.

2. *Mountaineering.* (See quot. 1968.)

1968 P. CREW *Encyclopædic Dict. Mountaineering* 117/2 *Tie-off*, a method of reducing the leverage on a piton which has not been fully inserted, by tying a short loop of rope to the piton blade, close against the rock face. **1971** C. BONINGTON *Annapurna South Face* 247 We used huge quantities of tape for everything from tie-offs on pitons to belts for trousers. **1974** H. MACINNES *Climb to Lost World* x. 162 It took him most of the day to put a couple of bolts in, with some weird tie-off pegging to do.

Tiepolesque (tɪ,ɛpəʊ'lɛsk), *a.* [f. *Tiepolo* (see below) + -ESQUE.] Characteristic of or resembling the work of Giovanni Battista Tiepolo (1696–1770), or of his son Domenico (1727–1804), Italian painters famous esp. for (ceiling) frescos. Often used somewhat *loosely*.

1895 G. B. SHAW *Our Theatres in Nineties* (1932) I. 159 Goddesses in a Tiepolesque ceiling. **1934** *Burlington Mag.* Feb. 91/1 The purely Tiepolesque conception of the war-horse. **1958** *Times* 17 Oct. 17/6 The dash of Murillo in 'The Guerilla taking leave of his Confessor', or the much less happy Tiepolesque pose of the figure straining at the wheel of the gun in 'The Defence of Saragossa'. **1974** *Times Lit. Suppl.* 20 Dec. 1449/5 Her inability to understand Visconti's Tiepolesque conception of *Iphigénie en Tauride* is significant: she wanted to look Greek, primeval and savage whereas Visconti wished upon her the bejewelled artificiality of a Venetian fresco.

tier (tɪə(r)), *sb.*[1] Also 6-9 tire, 6-8 tyre, (6 teare, 7 tere, 7-8 teer, 8 tear). [Orig. *tire*, a. F. *tire*, in OF. (*c* 1210 in Godef.) 'suite, sequence, range, rank, order': cf. *tire à tire* in succession, one after another, f. *tirer* to draw, elongate. The phonetic history of the forms *teare, tere, teer*, is obscure. Pl. after a numeral sometimes *tier*.]

1. a. A row, rank, range, course; usually one of a series of rows placed one above another, or at least rising each above the preceding one; e.g. tiers of galleries, shelves, boxes in a theatre, or seats on a sloping floor; also of banks of oars in ancient ships or boats; see also b, c.

1569 STOCKER tr. *Diod. Sic.* III. viii. 114/2 Ten gallies of fiue tier of ores. *a* **1625** FLETCHER *Bloody Brother* II. ii, I have ballast for their bellies, if they eat a gods name, Let them have ten tire of teeth a piece, I care not. **1627** CAPT. SMITH *Seaman's Gram.* vii. 33 Caske..stowed tier aboue tier. **1686** J. DUNTON *Lett. New-Eng.* (1867) 35 He has three Tere of Teeth in his Chaps. **1730** A. GORDON *Maffei's Amphith.* 203 The..Stones..which form'd the first Tyre or Belt thereof. **1743** *Lond. & Country Brew.* III. (ed. 2) 182 The Worts now run swiftly into a single Teer of Backs. **1787** M. CUTLER in *Life*, etc. (1888) I. 311 There are two tiers of galleries, and the [meeting-] house was very full. **1796** MORSE *Amer. Geog.* II. 358 It consists of three bridges, or tires of arches one above another. **1844** LD. HOUGHTON *Palm Leaves* I Above the towers of tripple tire. **1867** SMYTH *Sailor's Word-bk.* 346 A round of grape-shot consists of three tiers of cast-iron balls, generally three in a tier. **1873** SYMONDS *Grk. Poets* ix. 280 The new theatre in Athens contained 30,000 spectators seated in semicircular tiers scooped out of the rock.

b. A row of guns or gun-ports in a man-of-war or (as in quot. 1573) in a fort.

1573 in *Calr. Scott. Pap.* IV. 475 Davyes towre..a courten with vj cannons..in loopes of stone..behynd the same standes another teare of ordina[nce] lyke xvj foote clym above the other. **1632** LITHGOW *Trav.* II. 54 [A] man of war..carrying two tyre of Ordonance. *a* **1647** PETTE in *Archæologia* XII. 283 The..distance of the lower tire of ports from the water. **1722** DE FOE *Col. Jack* (1840) 322 A good tier of guns kept the rest at a distance. **1813** BYRON *Corsair* III. xv, She bears her down majestically near, Speed on her prow, and terror in her tier.

c. A rank of pipes in an organ controlled by one stop (see RANK *sb.*[1] 1, quots. 1811, 1881).

1828-32 in WEBSTER. **1880** E. J. HOPKINS in Grove *Dict. Mus.* II. 580/2 Although the number of pipes to each key thus continued to be added to, no means was devised for silencing or selecting any of the several ranks or tiers.

d. *transf.* and *fig.* Rank, grade; stratum.

1590 SPENSER *F.Q.* I. iv. 35 Such one was Wrath, the last of this ungodly tire. **1646** CRASHAW *Sosp. d' Her.* xxxviii, A gen'ral hiss, from the whole tire of snakes. **1710** PALMER *Proverbs* 201 This is a sin of quality for the most part, tho' the lower tier of people are often tainted with it. **1882** W. B. WEEDEN *Soc. Law Labor* 66 The base Fuidirs composed the lower tier of society.

e. A range or line *of* contiguous lots, townships, counties, or states. *U.S.*

1693 in *Connecticut Hist. Soc. Coll.* (1912) XIV. 212 One lyeing in the Same Teere of lotts abutting on a Highway. **1720** in *New Eng. Hist. & Gen. Reg.* (1875) XXIX. 288 Eastward of the first tear of lots. **1722** *Conn. Col. Rec.* (1872) VI. 311 The northermost tier of the three tier of lots lying next to Midletown. **1824** in S. C. Cox *Recoll. Early Settlem. Wabash Valley* (1860) iii. 18 The land is sold in tiers of townships. **1856** *Spirit of Times* 18 Oct. 113/1 The great varying hare..is no longer to be found in our state,..until we reach the northern tier of counties, on the Canada line. **1949** *Ward County* (North Dakota) *Independent* 21 July 1/3 Each of the big wheat states in the tier from Texas up through North Dakota appears to be coming up with a crop just under that state's all-time record.

f. A mountainous scarp; a mountain. *Tasmania.*

1850 T. ARNOLD *Let.* 29 Sept. (1966) 55 The next day.. we all walked up a 'tier' ('Tasmanian for hill) near the house. **1902** *Encycl. Brit.* XXXIII. 185/2 The marginal crests of this mountain table-land, together with its upper surface,.. are known locally as 'Tiers'. **1965** *Austral. Encycl.* VIII. 425/2 Along the north-western coast [of Tasmania] there is a strip of rich, undulating land, climbing steadily to the base of steep escarpments called 'tiers'.

g. Each of a number of successively overlapping ruffles or flounces on a garment.

1934 in WEBSTER. **1938** F. P. WALKUP *Dressing Part* xv. 354 Tiers of ruffles, side pleats, and diagonal layers were introduced, for variety. **1978** *Detroit Free Press* 5 Mar. D12/1 Tiers will fall from little squared yokes, freely.

2. *Naut.* **a.** A row of ships moored or anchored at a particular place; hence, an anchorage or mooring-place where ships lie in rows or columns.

1732 *Lond. Mag.* I. 152 All the Ships Crews in the Teer gathered together. **1771** *Ann. Reg.* 148 A Dutch vessel.. broke from her mooring, ran foul of a tier of ships. **1774** *Hull Dock Act* 33 No more than three ships..shall lie in the same tier, within the said haven. **1865** DICKENS *Mut. Fr.* I. i, The tiers of shipping lay on either hand. **1907** *Law Rep., Probate* 61 A steamship..which was lying at Greenwich tier.

b. (See quot. 1882.)

1797 *Encycl. Brit.* (ed. 3) X. 644/2 He [the mate] is to have a diligent attention to the cables, seeing that they are well coiled and kept clean when laid in the tier. **1800** COLQUHOUN *Comm. Thames* iii. 94 Tea..stowed in the cable tier of a China Ship. **1825** [see TIERER[1]]. **1833, 1860** [see *cable-tier* s.v. CABLE *sb.* 7]. **1882** NARES *Seamanship* (ed. 6) 95 The tiers are large racks, and stow the stream cable, hawsers for the kedge, etc., anchor gear, runners and tackles,..clothes-lines, etc.

3. *attrib.* and *Comb.*: **tier-board**, a board belonging to a cable or rope tier: see 2 b; **tier-ranger**, a (Thames) river thief; **tier-saw**: see quot. 1877; **tier-shot**: see quot. 1867; **tiersman** *Tasmanian colloq.* (see quot.); cf. sense 1 f above.

1887 MATHER *Nor'ard of Dogger* (1889) 81 They spread some o' the trawl-warp *tier-boards along the thwarts, an' a rug on the top of 'em for me to lie on. **1858** DICKENS *Down with Tide* Repr. Pieces (1899) 198 *Tier-rangers, who silently dropped alongside the tiers of shipping in the Pool, by night. *Ibid.* 200 We took no Tier-rangers..nor other evil-disposed person or persons. **1862** MAYHEW *Lond. Labour* IV. 370/2 Tier-rangers or river pirates. **1877** KNIGHT *Dict. Mech.*, **Tier-saw*, one for cutting curved faces to bricks for arches and round pillars. **1828** J. M. SPEARMAN *Brit. Gunner* (ed. 2) 35 *Tier Shot.—At 50 rounds per gun. **1867** SMYTH *Sailor's Word-bk.*, *Tier-shot*, that kind of grape-shot which is secured in tiers by parallel iron discs. **1941** BAKER *Dict. Austral. Slang* 76 '*Tiersman': one who lives in the mountains. Tasmanian slang.

tier ('taɪə(r)), *sb.*[2] Also tyer. [f. TIE *v.* + -ER[1].]

1. One who ties; *spec.* a person employed to tie something. Also ***tier up***.

1633 P. FLETCHER *Poet. Misc.* 57 Hymen, the tier of hearts already tied. **1648** HEXHAM II, *Een Hechter*, a Fixer, a Fastner, or a Tyer to. **1848** *Jrnl. R. Agric. Soc.* IX. II. 554 The tiers can take the best to tie to the poles. **1876** PLUMMER tr. *Döllinger's Hippol. & Callistus* iii. 153 The Church..is the tyer of the marriage bond. **1895** *Daily Tel.* 18 Sept. 4/2 He begins life at the sandpaper works, as a tier up of bundles, at three and sixpence a week.

2. One who ties with another in a match or competition.

1810 *Sporting Mag.* XXXV. 97 The tyers to play with one another in the order they become tyers.

3. Something that ties or is used for tying; a band; *spec.* one for tying a sail; *pl.* = TIE-UP 4.

1844 *Jrnl. R. Agric. Soc.* V. I. 36 The beans are cut..and tied with strong tyers or straw bands. **1860** G. S. NARES *Naval Cadet's Guide* 81 The sail is then secured to the yard with tyers. **1873** 'VANDERDECKEN' *Yachts & Yachting* 265 Let the gaskets, or as they are sometimes called, the tyers, which confine the mainsail in its furl, be taken off. **1882** NARES *Seamanship* (ed. 6) 130 The sail is secured to the yard with tyers. **1895** *Sotheby's Catal.* 25 Apr. 52 (Kelmscott Press) Morris,..'The Defence of Guenevere', ornamental title and initial letters, vellum, silk tyers, uncut. **1939** A. RANSOME *Secret Water* iii. 44 In a minute or two, he had bundled the sail along the boom and put a couple of tiers to hold it there. **1947** —— *Great Northern?* viii. 101 The next few minutes were full of the regular drill of getting under way. Tyers were cast off the sails.

4. *U.S.* A pinafore or apron covering the whole front of the dress. (Also spelt *tire, tyre*, and referred by some to TIRE *sb.*[1] q.v.)

1846 WORCESTER, *Tier*, one that ties; a child's apron, tidy. See TIRE. **1864** WEBSTER, *Tier*, a child's apron without sleeves, and covering the upper part of the body, [1890] and tied with tape or cord. **1865** MRS. WHITNEY *Gayworthys* I. 106 She took care of Say; put on her long-sleeved tyers when she sent her out to play. **1889** L. LARCOM *A New Engld. Girlhood* 22 We sometimes smirched our clean aprons (high-necked and long-sleeved ones, known as tiers). **1902** *Dialect Notes* (U.S.) II. 254 (*Let. to G. Hempl*) Even among the older people [in New Engl.], 'cricket' has mostly given place to 'footstool', and 'tier' to 'apron'.

tier (tɪə(r)), *v.*[1] [f. TIER *sb.*[1]] *trans.* To arrange or pile in tiers.

1888-9 *N. York Produce Exch. Rep.* 301 (Cent.) Lightermen shall not..be required to tier or pile their freight on the docks.

tier, *v.*[2], erron. spelling of TEER.

1837 J. MATLEY in *Civil Eng. & Arch. Jrnl.* I. 54/2 Machinery for the operation of Tiering used in printing Cotton, Linen, &c. **1909** *Dundee Advert.* 25 Dec. 7 He commenced work..as a tier boy to a calico block printer.

tier, obs. form of TEAR *sb.*[1], TIRE.

tierce (tɪəs), *sb.* Forms: α. 4-8 terse, 6 teyrse, teers, 6-7 tearce, 7 tearse, teirce, teirse, ters, 5-9 terce: see also TERCE. β. 5 tyerce, tyrse, 5-6 tyerse, 6 tyers, tiersse, tiers, tirce, 6-7 tierse, 4- tierce. [a. OF. *terce, tierce*, fem. of *terz, tierz* (Roland, 11th c.), later *ters, tiers*, mod.F. *tiers*, fem. *tierce*:—L. *tertium*, fem. *tertiam* third.]

†**1. a.** A third part: = THIRD *sb.* 1. *Obs.*

1491 *Aberdeen Regr.* (1844) I. 326 Twa tercis beand defalkyt of þe sade some. **1555** EDEN *Decades* 351 Two smaule Ilandes standyng in the xxii degrees and a terce. **1624** CAPT. SMITH *Virginia* 16 We came to Hatorask in 36. degrees and a terse. **1651** DAVENANT *Gondibert* I. v. lvi,

Four-hundred leaders..And twice the tierce of these consists of those [etc.].

†**b.** = THIRD *sb.* 7. *Obs. rare*⁻¹.

c **1420** LYDG. *Thebes* I. 39 The heauenly mansions Clerely searched, by smale fraccions, First by secondes, terces, and eke quartes.

¶**c.** Abbreviated title of the treatise *Super Tertium Sententiarum* of Alexander Hales. *Obs.*

1502 *Ord. Crysten Men* (W. de W. 1506) IV. xxi. 240 It is sacrylege, after mayster Alexander de halis in his tyers.

2. *Eccl.* **a.** The third hour of the canonical day, ending at 9 a.m.; also, the period from 9 a.m. till noon. (Cf. PRIME *sb.*¹ 1.) *Obs.* exc. *Hist.*

c **1375** *Sc. Leg. Saints* xi. (*Symon & Iudas*) 197 To-morne, or it terse be,..sal cum to þe Messyngeris. *c* **1450** *Mirour Saluacioun* 3644 It was bot tierce of the daye ouer ayrly than for drynking. **1483** CAXTON *Gold. Leg.* 84/2 He..prayd fro tyerce vnto none. **1661** MORGAN *Sph. Gentry* IV. iii. 37 Upon St. George's Even, at the hour of Tierce. **1706** tr. *Dupin's Eccl. Hist. 16th C.* II. v. 43 The second [part of the 12 hours] which lasted till Noon, was called Tierce, because it began at the Third Hour of the day. **1844** LINGARD *Anglo-Sax. Ch.* (1858) I. vii. 272 *note*, The third of these hours was called undern or terce.

b. (Now usually spelt **terce**.) The office said at this hour.

c **1380** WYCLIF *Wks.* (1880) 41 Late lewid freris seie..for prime, tierce, vndren & noon, for eche of hem seuene pater nostris. **1526** *Pilgr. Perf.* (W. de W. 1531) 164b, The chirche..in..the..houres canonicall entendeth to.. worshyp at vij tymes in the daye, that is to saye, in matyns, pryme, tierce, sext, none, euensonge & complyn. **1753** CHALLONER *Cath. Chr. Instr.* 212 Terce, Sext, and None, begin with Pater, Ave, &c. and consist each of them of a proper Hymn, and six Divisions of the 118th Psalm. **1853** DALE tr. *Baldeschi's Ceremonial* 101 The vesting of the Bishop for Terce. **1897** E. BISHOP in *Prymer* (E.E.T.S.) *Introd.* 38 The day hours, prime and terce, and sext and none, said in every secular church.

3. *Sc. Law.* See TERCE.

1754 [see *tercer* s.v. TERCE, quot. *c* 1575].

4. An old measure of capacity equivalent to one third of a pipe (usually 42 gallons old wine measure, but varying for different commodities: cf. PIPE *sb.*² 2); also a cask or vessel holding this quantity, usually of wine, but also of various kinds of provisions or other goods (e.g. beef, pork, salmon, coffee, honey, sugar, tallow, tobacco); also such a cask with its contents.

1531 *Charterparty* in R. G. Marsden *Sel. Pl. Crt. Admir.* 36 Accounttyng..ij pipes for a ton iiij hoggeshedds for a ton and vj tercys for a ton. **1531–2** *Act 23 Hen. VIII*, c. 7 §5 The butte, tonne, pype..teers, barrell or rondlett. **1538** ELYOT Addit., *Hemicadia*, vesselles callyd a tierce, halfe a hoggesheed. **1588** *Wills & Inv. N.C.* (Surtees) II. 180, ix tearces of honeye, at 16*l.* per tonne, 24*l.* **1707** *Lond. Gaz.* No. 4337/4 On Wednesday..will be exposed to Sale..about 400 Hogsheads and 10 Tierces of..French Claret. **1800** COLQUHOUN *Comm. Thames* iii. 136 Beef and Pork.. contained in..Tierces and Barrels. **1825** *Gentl. Mag.* XCV. I. 216 [Coffee berries] closely packed in tierces for exportation. **1886** *Pall Mall G.* 19 June 6/1 The tobacco.. comes from abroad..in hogsheads..in what are called tierces (a smaller wooden barrel), and in bales.

†**5.** A band or company of soldiers (cf. TERCIO).

1577–87 HOLINSHED *Chron.* III. 1227/1 Foure hundred harquebusiers Spaniards, of the tierse of Sardigna. **1668** *Lond. Gaz.* No. 237/3 The Leavies of a Terse of Italian Infantry.

6. One of the positions in fencing; the third of the eight parries in sword-play, or the corresponding thrust: see quots. Also *fig.* (usually in conjunction with *carte* or *quarte*). Cf. CARTE², QUART *sb.*³ 1.

1692 SIR W. HOPE *Fencing-Master* (ed. 2) 4 When a Man holdeth the Nails of his Sword Hand quite downwards, he is said to hold his hand in Terce. **1707–1878** [see CARTE²]. **1779** SHERIDAN *Critic* III. i, O cursed parry!—that last thrust in tierce Was fatal. **1809, 1889** [see QUART *sb.*³ 1]. **1876** TENNYSON *Q. Mary* V. v, To reign is restless fence, Tierce, quart and trickery.

7. In piquet and other card games, a sequence of three cards in any suit.

tierce major, the highest three cards of a suit; ***tierce minor***, the lowest three, i.e. seven, eight, and nine; ***tierce to a king, queen***, etc., a tierce of which the king, queen, etc., is the highest. Cf. QUART³ 2, QUINT³ 1 b.

1659 *Shuffling, Cutting, & Dealing* 3, I have got a good Tearse. **1688** R. HOLME *Armoury* III. xvi. (Roxb.) 73/2 A Tierce Major, is the sequence of Queen, King and Ace in Picket, and of Knave, Queene and King in other games. **1765** STERNE *Tr. Shandy* VII. ix, That, Sir, is a terce to a nine in your favour. **1860** *Bohn's Hand-bk. Games* I. 14 Many good players, in playing tierce majors, begin with the king and queen. **1904** M. HEWLETT *Queen's Quair* I. xi. 146 I've a terce to my Queen, mistress.

8. *Mus.* **a.** The interval of a third (major or minor); the note at this interval above a given note. Now *rare* or *Obs.* **b.** The note two octaves and a major third (= a major 17th) above a fundamental note; hence, a mutation stop in an organ giving tones at this interval above the normal pitch.

tierce of Picardy (usu. in Fr. form ‖*tierce de Picardie*), a major third used instead of a minor in the final chord of a piece in a minor key.

1696 PHILLIPS (ed. 5), *Tierce*,..in Musick, a Concord. **1704** J. HARRIS *Lex. Techn.* I. s.v., If the Terms be as 5 to 4, 'tis called, a Tierce Major, or a Diton; but if the Terms are as 6 to 5, then 'tis called, a Tierce Minor, or Demi-Diton. **1776** BURNEY *Hist. Mus.* I. 138 The two stops of an organ, called the fifteenth and tierce. **1801** BUSBY *Dict. Mus.*, Tierce of Picardy. **1849** J. A. HAMILTON *Celebr. Dict.* 117 *Tierce de Picardie* (French), a term applied to the concluding chord of a piece of music in a minor key, when its third is made major by an accidental sharp or natural. **1879** tr. *Du Moncel's Telephone* 43 Vibrations..in the relation of a tierce major, that is in the relation of four to five. **1889** GROVE *Dict. Mus.* IV. 114/2 The Third, thus made major by an accidental sharp or natural, is called the 'tierce de Picardie'. **1940** *Scrutiny* IX. 128 Beneath the suspended F sharp of the concluding tierce de picardie, trombones, violas, and horns emphatically sing. **1959** D. COOKE *Language of Music* ii. 57 For centuries, pieces in a minor key had to have a 'happy ending'—a final major chord (the 'tierce de Picardie') or a bare fifth. **1978** *New Universities Q.* XXXII. 288 The final cadence achieves, and deserves, the bliss of a tierce de Picardie.

9. *Her.* **a.** A charge composed of three triangles, usually all of different tinctures, arranged in fesse, also in bend. **b.** The division of a shield by lines into three equal parts: see TIERCÉ, quot. 1883.

[*c* **1828** BERRY *Encycl. Her.* I. Gloss., *Tierces*, or *Tierches*, ..used by French heralds to express three figures which only take up the space of a fesse, but which are sometimes placed in bend.] **1847** WEBSTER, *Tierce*..a field divided into three parts. **1894** *Parker's Gloss. Her.*, *Tierce* (fr.), a charge occurring in some French arms, consisting of three triangles arranged generally in fesse. There may be two tierces in the same shield.

10. *attrib.* or as *adj.* in special collocations: **tierce guard, parade**: see sense 6; **tierce point**, *Arch.* [F. *tiers-point*], the vertex of an equilateral triangle, or of a pointed arch; **tierce rime** = TERZA-RIMA; **tierce-song**, the office of terce (= sense 2 b); cf. *undern-song*.

1692 SIR W. HOPE *Fencing-Master* (ed. 2) 116 The *Terce Guard, with the point higher than the Hilt. *Ibid.* 22 The *Terce Parade, or the Parade without the Sword, because you put by the thrust upon that side which is without your Sword. **1727–41** CHAMBERS *Cycl.*, *Third Point*, or **Tierce-point*... Arches or vaults of the *third point*, called by the Italians *di terzo acuto*, are those consisting of two arches of a circle, meeting in an angle a-top. **1842–76** GWILT *Encycl. Archit.* Gloss., *Tierce Point.* **1877** TOMLINSON (*title*) A Vision of Hell: The Inferno of Dante translated into English *Tierce Rhyme. **1852** ROCK *Ch. of Fathers* III. x. 473 St. Bede died a little after undern-time, or *tierce-song hour.

Hence **tierce** *v.* (in phr. *carte* or ***quart and tierce***: cf. QUART *v.*¹), *intr.* to parry or thrust in tierce (in quot. 1833 *transf.*); in quot. 1765 *trans.* ? to fence with (or ? as a vague threat).

1765 FOOTE *Commissary* III. (1782) 65 John, fetch me the foils; I'll carte and tierce you, you scoundrel. **1833** *New Monthly Mag.* XXXVIII. 343 He quarts and tierces for twenty minutes, slips, drops, and rolls.

‖**tiercé** (tjɛrse, 'tɪəseɪ), *a.* and *sb.* [F. *tiercé, -ée*, f. *tiercer* to divide into three parts (13th c. in Godef.).]

A. *adj. Her.* Said of a field divided *en tiercé*, i.e. into three equal parts all of different tinctures: cf. prec. 9. Also anglicized as **tierced** (tɪəst).

1725 COATS *Dict. Her.*, *Tiercé*,..a French Term importing that the Shield is divided into three equal Parts, when those Parts are of as many different Colours or Metals. **1864** BOUTELL *Her. Hist. & Pop.* xxxii. (ed. 3) 471. **1883** *Chambers's Encycl.* s.v., A shield may be tiercé in pale, in fess, in bend, in bend sinister, or in pall; all which, with other arrangements in tierce, are common in French heraldry.

B. *sb.* Also **tierce**. **a.** A method of betting in which the first three horses in a race have to be named in the correct order. **b.** A French horse-race at which this method prevails. **c.** *fig.*

1964 A. WYKES *Gambling* viii. 195 The French have developed a special way of betting... It is called 'Tiercé' and involves the selection of three horses to finish first, second, and third in specified races held on Sundays and holidays. **1966** *Economist* 24 Dec. 1336/4 The French happily bet vast sums on the *tierce*. **1974** *Times Lit. Suppl.* 6 Sept. 941/4 She had achieved a far more considerable success, having managed both to break up her sister Eliza's marriage..and, better still, indirectly to cause the death of her infant niece. .. This was not a *tiercé*, but it was a considerable double triumph. **1981** *Times* 30 June 6/5 Frenchmen had to do without the 'Tiercé'..yesterday. *Ibid.* 6/6 It was the third time since..May, 1968 that the Tiercé fixtures had not taken place.

tiercel, tiercelet: see TERCEL, TERCELET.

tierceron ('tɪəsərɒn). *Arch.* [a. F. *tierceron* (1518 in Godef. *Compl.*), f. *tiers*, *tierce* third + suffix *-on* (see -OON), with intercalated *-er-*: see Godef. §63. 1.] A subordinate arch springing from the point of intersection of two main arches of a vault.

1842–76 *Gwilt's Encycl. Archit.*, *Index*, Tierceron, in vaulting. **1890** C. H. MOORE *Goth. Archit.* i. 18 *note*, The additional ribs, *liernes*, *tiercerons*, etc., which appear in the later forms of vaulting,..are mere surface ribs having no real function. **1905** BOND *Goth. Archit.* 74 Intermediate ribs, or tiercerons, were added in Lincoln nave.

tierceroon, tiercet, var. TERCEROON, TERCET.

tiered (tɪəd), *a.* [f. TIER *sb.*¹ + -ED².] Having, or arranged in, tiers; formerly chiefly in parasynthetic comb., as ***high-tiered, three-tiered, triple-tiered***.

1807 J. BARLOW *Columb.* VII. 495 Flames, triple tier'd, and tides of smoke, arise. **1877** BLACKIE *Wise Men* 75 High-tiered, palatial dwellings. **1899** MACKAIL *W. Morris* II. 52 The passage of the shuttle through a double- or triple-tiered warp. **1909** *Daily Chron.* 16 Sept. 7/2 The tiered seats of the big 'demonstration' kitchen. **1930** *Antiquity* IV. 422 He regards the tomb of Cyrus as a reproduction in stone of such a tiered temple. **1939** M. B. PICKEN *Lang. of Fashion* 155/1 Tiered skirt. **1951** *Good Housek. Home Encycl.* 276/1 The tiered steamers have..three separate pans which fit on top of each other over a base pan. **1952** C. P. BLACKER *Eugenics* 294 Certain professions—the Church, the law, the fighting Services—have a hierarchical structure, and success can be gauged by the level attained by an individual in such a tiered system. **1955** V. CRONIN *Wise Man from West* 92 Among the limitless paddy-fields and tiered hills. **1971** *Daily Tel.* 28 July 11 The skirt tiered all the way down. **1978** *Morecambe Guardian* 14 Mar. 16/3 She was attended by her sister..who wore a pale blue chiffon tiered dress.

tierer¹ ('tɪərə(r)). [f. TIER *sb.*¹ or *v.*¹ + -ER¹.]

a. *Naut.* One who stows the cable in the tier: see TIER *sb.*¹ 2 b. **b.** One who arranges anything in tiers.

1825 H. B. GASCOIGNE *Nav. Fame* 48 Hard work the Tierers in the Tier below, The sturdy Cable in true coils to Stow. **1891** *Cent. Dict.*, Tierer.

'**tierer**², var. or erron. f. *teerer*: see under TEER *v.*

1836 in *Statist. Acc. Scotl.* (1845) VIII. 384 Block-printers, journeymen 16, apprentices 44, Tierers, one to each printer.

So **tiering**, = TEERING.

1904 *Eng. Dial. Dict.*, *Tiering*, the cieling or rendering of a roof; the plastering under slates.

tiering ('tɪərɪŋ), *a. rare.* [f. TIER *sb.*¹ (or ? TIER *v.*¹ taken in sense 'to form tiers') + -ING².] Forming or rising in tiers.

1892 KIPLING *Barrack-r. Ballads* 132 The skipper looked at the tiering guns and the bulwarks tall and cold. **1896** —— *Seven Seas* 137 You'll see her tiering canvas in sheeted silver spread.

tiering ('tɪərɪŋ), *vbl. sb.* [f. TIER *sb.*¹ + -ING¹.] Arrangement in tiers; the formation of tiers.

1969 T. E. B. HOWARTH *Culture, Anarchy & Public Schools* v. 78 Local authorities are required under circular 10/65 to plan a complete system of comprehensive education for their areas either by the erection of all-through comprehensive schools or by various devices of amalgamation or tiering ('middle schools', sixth form colleges and so on). **1971** *Daily Tel.* 28 July 11 Cardin has run amok..with the tucking and tiering attachments on his sewing machine. **1978** *Detroit Free Press* 5 Mar. D12/1 Tiering [of dresses] is a continuation of the peasant theme that has been with us for what seems like a long, long time. **1980** *Amer. Film* Oct. 25/1 Viewers are willing to pay generously..for more programming. There is a term for this program proliferation: 'tiering'. When a cable system adds another channel of programs for an extra fee, there is a new tier of service to offer subscribers.

tierme, obs. form of TERM.

‖**tierras** ('tjerras), *sb. pl. Mining. U.S.* [Sp. *tierras* earths, pl. of *tierra* earth:—L. *terra*.] Pulverulent ore, *spec.* of quicksilver, mingled with sand and earthy matter; in Mexico, inferior pulverulent ores generally. Also *attrib.*, as ***tierras-furnace, -ore***.

1874 RAYMOND *Statist. Mines & Mining* 397 In 1865, the amount of ore worked was 15,974 tons. Of which the Tierras amounted to 1,955 tons... Tierras yielded (estimated) 3 per cent., or 1,533 flasks. **1877** *Ibid.* 9 Number of tons tierras-ore roasted. *Ibid.* 17 A new tierras-furnace will take its place. **1881** —— *Mining Gloss.*, *Tierras*,..fine dirt impregnated with quicksilver ore, which must be made into adobes before roasting.

tiers, -e, tierselet, obs. f. TIERCE, TERCELET.

‖**tiers état** (tjɛrz eta). [Fr., = third estate: see TIERCE and ESTATE.] A third estate or class; *esp.* the third estate, the body of commons or their representatives in the French National Assembly before the Revolution; whence sometimes applied to the corresponding body in other countries: see ESTATE *sb.* 6.

1783 J. ADAMS *Diary* 27 Feb., There are..thirty classes in the *Tiers Etat.* **1794** J. GIFFORD *Reign Louis XVI* 260 The three orders united confirmed all those important decrees that had been made by the *Tiers Etat.* **1799** *Monthly Rev.* XXX. 548 Montesquieu mistakes in affirming that the natives of the country [Russia] are all either lords or slaves, and that there was no *tiers-état.* **1837** CARLYLE *Fr. Rev.* I. IV. i, Necker..emits, if any proclamation or regulation, one favouring the Tiers Etat.

‖**tiers monde** (tjɛr mɔ̃d). Also **Tiers Monde**. [Fr.: see THIRD WORLD.] = THIRD WORLD.

1963 *Listener* 28 Feb. 386/1 The book exemplifies the need for utter empiricism in our approach to the *tiers monde*. **1964** *Financial Times* 11 Feb. 7/6 France is strongly placed to make a success of her championship of the 'Tiers Monde'. **1966** *Listener* 18 Aug. 229/1 What has commonly come to be called the *tiers monde*, the uncommitted nations, Africa and Asia, have a position in the world.

tiestie, dial. var. TEISTIE, the black guillemot.

tieth, obs. form of TITHE.

Tietze ('tiːtsə). *Path.* [The name of A. *Tietze* (1864–1927), Polish surgeon, who described the condition in 1921 (*Berlin. klin. Wochenschr.* LVIII. 829).] ***Tietze's disease, syndrome***: a condition in which there is painful swelling of one or more costal cartilages without evident cause.

1932 *Index Medicus* XII. 1146/2 Tietze's disease; dystrophy of costal cartilage. **1942** *Brit. Med. Jrnl.* 19 Sept. 352/1 Among the many manifestations of subnutrition recently seen by us have been two cases of swelling of the costal cartilages, associated with weakness and lethargy, which conform to the description of Tietze's disease. **1945** *Canad. Med. Assoc. Jrnl.* LIII. 572/2 It is not suggested that these rib changes are necessarily due to Tietze's syndrome. **1977** *Daily Colonist* (Victoria, B.C.) 20 July 2/1 Tietze's disease can be mistaken for angina.

tie-up ('taɪʌp), *sb.* (*a.*) [f. *tie up*: TIE *v.* 11.]

I. Something tied up, or used for tying up.

†**1.** = TIE-WIG. *Obs.*

1714 C. JOHNSON *Country Lasses* II. i, The last tye-up I sold you was as light and bright as silver.. with a fine flowing large open curl.

2. a. A ribbon with which some part of a child's dress is tied or fastened up.

1896 *Blackw. Mag.* Oct. 520/2 The little ones.. rejoice in clean 'bishops' and 'tie-ups' of various hues. **1909** *Daily Chron.* 18 Nov. 7/1 Brief drawing-room appearances in a nurse's arms with robes and tie-ups—blue for a boy, pink for a girl.

b. A (makeshift) garter.

1970 R. HILL *Clubbable Woman* i. 5 One stocking was down. His tie-up hung loose round his ankle. **1976** E. DUNPHY *Only a Game?* v. 139 Laying the shirts out before the game, making sure the lads have chewing gum, tie-ups, tea at half-time.

3. a. An animal tied up as a bait for a beast of prey.

1895 MRS. B. M. CROKER *Village Tales* (1896) 27 Where's the chap with the buffalo—where is our tie-up? *Ibid.*, It will be an awful sell if there is no tie-up, and the tiger happens to go by.

b. A building or stall in which cattle are tied up for the night. orig. and chiefly *U.S.*

1851 J. S. SPRINGER *Forest Life* 82 At the further end of the 'tie-up' he thinks he hears a little clattering noise. **1883** *Rep. Maine Board Agric. 1882* 49 Those who have not the convenience for a barn cellar can save the manure very well by a tight floor in the tie-up. **1930** W. FAULKNER *As I lay Dying* 117 The cows were still in the tie-up. **1952** E. CALDWELL *Lamp for Nightfall* iii. 32 They constructed a chicken house.. and installed six tie-ups in the dairy barn. **1960** *Farmer & Stockbreeder* 2 Feb. 17/1 The property.. includes a farmhouse, two cottages and farm buildings in good condition with tie-up accommodation for 80 cows.

4. *Bookbinding. pl.* Tapes or ribbons attached to a portfolio, book-cover, etc., as a fastening.

1896 *D. Reeves' Catal.* Sept. 11/1 Parchment, with silk tie-ups. **1902** *Ibid.* Jan. 10/2, 4 sheets and a plan of London, 1572,.. in portfolio with tie ups, 21s.

II. Act of tying up, or state of being tied up.

5. *slang.* **a.** A finish, conclusion, 'wind-up'. **b.** *Pugilism.* A knock-out blow, a 'finisher': cf. TIE *v.* 11 g.

1818 *Sporting Mag.* II. 211 He knobbed his adversary well, and floored him by a smart tye-up at the fourth buttonhole. **1829** *Ibid.* XXIV. 99 By way of a tie up to the concern.. the Ladies' Purse of 50£ for the beaten horses was offered.

6. A stoppage of work or business, esp. on account of a lock-out or strike; a stoppage of transport, a traffic hold-up. orig. and chiefly *U.S.*

1889 *Sci. Amer.* 19 Jan. 32/3 In the event of a 'tie-up', or strike. **1894** *Times* 14 July 7/1 [The Great Northern Pacific Railroad] could not.. afford to face a tie-up. **1903** *Westm. Gaz.* 30 June 11/3 No such 'tie-up' has ever before been known in the American cotton industry. **1904** *N.Y. Tribune* 29 Oct. 1 An accident to one of the motor cars caused a tie-up of the southbound trains. **1923** C. R. COOPER *Under Big Top* xi. 227 Add to all this the handicaps of weather, of railroad tie-ups [etc.]. **1943** *Coast to Coast 1942* 181 Old McAlister had made a reference to some trouble on the Brisbane waterfront that threatened a temporary tie-up in the shipping of produce. **1962** E. SNOW *Other Side of River* (1963) xxiv. 183, I myself saw new motors and parts piled up unprotected in the weather and damaged or ruined because of transport tie-ups or lack of storage facilities. **1977** *Time* 18 July 14/2 Tie-ups extending for 30 miles are almost normal.

7. a. A condition of being 'tied up'; entanglement.

1906 *Statesman* (Calcutta) 30 Sept. 3/7 She had no desire, she said, to 'get into any more domestic tie ups'.

b. A connection or association. Cf. TIE *v.* 11 j.

1927 *Daily Express* 7 Mar. 11/5 There is a tie-up, too, over this firm with the gramophone records. Every record of the 'Happiness Boys' is an advertisement for Happiness Chocolates. **1938** F. SCOTT FITZGERALD *Let.* 18 Apr. (1964) 28, I had made the mental tie-up that work equals something unpleasant. **1945** E. DALY *House without Door* xi. 118 It's quite an interesting tie-up.... The Locke case and the Gregson murder case. **1960** *Guardian* 27 Sept. 8/4 The Labour Party.. has.. an out-of-date tie-up with the trades unions. *a***1963** L. MACNEICE *Astrol.* (1964) vii. 220 The modern astrological tendency.. to seek tie-ups between astrology and psychological knowledge. **1974** S. GULLIVER *Vulcan Bulletins* 32 'How the hell did he get in with the Libyans in the first place?' I asked. 'Old school tie-ups,' said Selby.

c. A telecommunication link or network. *U.S.*

1927 *Sci. Amer.* July 37/2, 27 stations.. were connected to the battery of microphones in front of the Capitol. This record tie-up of transmitters was surpassed.. when President Coolidge addressed a joint session of Congress.. through a network of 42 broadcasters. **1939** *Sun* (Baltimore) 24 Aug. 3/5 (*heading*) Western Union speeds deliveries with tieup. **1940** *Nature* 20 July 91/2 It is reported from Pittsburgh, Pa., that the Bell Telephone Co. has applied for a permit to install transmitters and receivers on what is called a 'tie-up' with existing telephone facilities.

III. **8.** as *adj.* Constructed by tying up.

1881 *Cheq. Career* 43 Thirty whares [houses] with their usual tie-up fences around them formed the outside Pah.

tiew, variant of TEW *Obs.*

'tie-wig. Also **tye-wig.** [Cf. TIE- 3.] A wig having the hair gathered together behind and tied with a knot of ribbon.

1713 GAY *Guard.* No. 149 ¶ 17 The smart tye-wig with the black ribbon. **1816** SCOTT *Antiq.* iii, In tie-wigs and laced coats. **1852** THACKERAY *Esmond* III. v, The gentleman-usher's horror when the Prince of Savoy was introduced to her Majesty in a tie-wig, no man out of a full-bottomed periwig ever having kissed the Royal hand before.

attrib. **1887** BROWNING *Parleyings, B. de Mandeville* iv, Addison's tye-wig preachment.

Hence **'tie-wigged** (-wɪgd) *a.*, wearing a tie-wig.

1763 *Brit. Mag.* IV. 605 The powder'd tye-wigged sons of soot Trip to the shovel with a shoeless foot.

†**tiff**, *sb.*[1] *Obs. rare*$^{-1}$. [f. TIFF *v.*[1]] Manner of dressing or arranging, get-up; the way in which the hair, wig, etc., is dressed.

1703 *The Levellers* in *Harl. Misc.* (1745) V. 419/2 Did you mark the beau Tiff of his Wig, what a deal of Pains he took to toss it back?

tiff (tɪf), *sb.*[2] *colloq.* or *slang.* ? *Obs.* Also 9 *Sc.* **tift.** [Origin obscure; perh. onomatopœic; cf. TIFF *v.*[2], TIFT *v.*[2]]

1. Liquor, *esp.* poor, weak, or 'small' liquor, 'tipple'.

*a***1635** CORBET *Poems, On J. Dawson*, So let your channels flow with single tiff, For John I hope is crown'd. **1661** A. BROME *Answ. Univ. Friend* Poems 165 Your next is money, which I promise, Full fifty pounds alas the summe is, That too shall quickly follow, if It can be rais'd from Strong or Tiffe. **1703** J. PHILIPS *Splendid Shilling* 15 With scanty offals and small acid tiff (Wretched repast!). **1736** AINSWORTH *Lat. Dict.* II, *Vappa*,.. palled wine that hath lost its strength, dead drink, poor tiff. **1823** SCOTT *Quentin D.* Introd., Drinking acid tiff, as above mentioned.

2. A sip or little drink of punch or other diluted liquor. Cf. WHIFF.

1727 BAILEY vol. II, *Tiff*, a small Quantity of potable Liquor, as a Tiff of Punch, etc. **1752** FIELDING *Amelia* VIII. x, What say you to.. a tiff of punch by way of whet? **1804** STAGG *Misc. Poems* (1807) 3 (E.D.D.) Monnie a tift o' yell. **1815** SCOTT *Guy M.* xi, Sipping his tiff of brandy punch with great solemnity. **1819** *Sporting Mag.* IV. 272 The gentleman can't take a tiff of beer in a morning. **1820** *Blackw. Mag.* VIII. 98 We shall take a tiff of Campbell and Somerville's best black strap.

tiff (tɪf), *sb.*[3] *colloq.* [Origin obscure; prob. onomatopœic, from the sound of a slight puff of air or gas.]

1. A slight outburst or fit of temper, pettishness, or ill-humour. Now *rare* or merged in 2.

1727 BAILEY vol. II, *Tiff*,.. also a small Fit of Anger, etc. **1729** MRS. DELANY in *Life & Corr.* (1861) I. 230 That common compassion (says he in a tiff) would give me but little satisfaction. **1739** 'R. BULL' tr. *Dedekindus' Grobianus* 102 Returning homewards in a furious Tiff. *a***1825** FORBY *Voc. E. Anglia*, *Tiff*, a pet; slight anger. 'She was in a tiff'. **1871** CARLYLE in *Mrs. C.'s Lett.* (1883) II. 164 Abrupt Captain Anthony being in some tiff of his own.

2. A slight or petty quarrel; a temporary ill-humoured disagreement; a 'breeze'; sometimes applied to a more serious quarrel.

1754 RICHARDSON *Grandison* (1781) IV. xxxviii. 268 My Lord and I have had another little *Tiff*, shall I call it? it came not up to a quarrel. **1755** KIDGELL *Card* II. 150 Your dear Letter fell into Mamma's Hands, and.. Madam thought herself entitled to open it.—So, my Dear, we had a violent Tiff upon it. **1868** LOUISA M. ALCOTT *Little Women* ix, More friendly than ever after their small tiff. **1888** BRYCE *Amer. Commw.* I. xi. 145 'Little tiffs' are frequent when the senatorial majority is in opposition to the executive.

3. A short outburst (of laughter, etc.). *rare.*

1858 CARLYLE *Fredk. Gt.* VII. i. II. 149 Wilhelmina.. answered.. him with tiffs of laughter, in a prettily fleering manner.

†**tiff**, *v.*[1] *Obs.* [a. OF. *tifer*, *tiffer* to adorn (12th c. in Godef.), mod.F. *attifer*: see ATIFFE.]

1. *trans.* To attire, dress, deck out, trick out, 'tittivate' (one's person, hair, etc.). (In 18th c. like F. *attifer*, usually familiar.)

*a***1225** [see TIFFING *vbl. sb.*]. **1303** R. BRUNNE *Handl. Synne* 3201 3yf þou tyfyst þe ouer proudly. **13..** *K. Alis.* 4109 Theo maydenes lokyn in the glas, For to tyffen [*Laud MS.* atyffen] heore fas. *c***1350** *Will. Palerne* 3183 Knew þow nou3t.. þat i was tiffed in a-tir when i wend fro þe. **1382** [see TIFFLE 1]. **1729** MRS. DELANY in *Life & Corr.* (1861) I. 225, I am sorry your ladies should tiff anything but their hair. **1768** TUCKER *Lt. Nat.* (1834) I. 40 Her desire of tiffing out her mistress in a killing attire.

b. *absol.* or *intr.*

1700 CONGREVE *Way of World* II. iv, Poor Mincing tift and tift all the morning. **1741** MRS. MONTAGU *Lett.* (1906) I. 65 While Deb is tiffing and tiffing till my hair is so pure and so crisp.

2. *trans.* **a.** To put in order, arrange. **b.** To prepare, make, construct.

13.. *Gaw. & Gr. Knt.* 1129, & þay busken vp bilyue, blonkkez to sadel, Tyffen her takles, trussen her males. *a***1400–50** *Alexander* 4465 Sum [idols] ere tiffid all of tree, and sum of tyn pured.

3. *intr.* To be idly employed, be busy about trifles.

*c***1440** *Promp. Parv.* 493/2 Tyffyn, werke ydylly, *idem quod* tymeryn.

Hence † **tiffed** *ppl. a.*, tricked out, adorned (in quot. *fig.*): see also TIFT *ppl. a.*

1303 R. BRUNNE *Handl. Synne* 11763 Yn tyfed [*v.r.* tyffede] wurdys þat slyked are, Semeþ þy synnes þat þey no3t were.

tiff, *v.*[2] *colloq.* or *slang.* ? *Obs.* [f. TIFF *sb.*[2] Cf. TIFT *v.*[2]] *trans.* To drink; *esp.* to drink slowly or in small portions, to sip.

1769 *Trinculo's Trip* 25, I was tiffing a stout cann of flip. **1809–11** COMBE *Syntax* v. 140 He tiff'd his punch, and went to rest.

tiff, *v.*[3] [f. TIFF *sb.*[3]] *intr.* To be in a tiff or pet; to have a tiff, or petty quarrel.

1727 BAILEY vol. II, To *Tiff*, to be angry, peevish, fretful, or displeased at. **1859** F. FRANCIS *Newton Dogvane* (1888) 59 The Captain was late, and Miss Bowers tiffed.

tiff, *v.*[4] *Anglo-Ind.* [app. abbreviation of or back-formation from *tiff-ing*, TIFFIN.] *intr.* = TIFFIN *v.*, to lunch.

1803 ELPHINSTONE in Colebrooke *Life* (1884) I. v. 116 We were interrupted by a summons to tiff. at Floyer's. After tiffin Close said he should be glad to go. **1816** 'QUIZ' *Grand Master* VIII. 230 The huntsman now inform'd them all, They were to *tiff* at Bobb'ry Hall. **1825** T. HOOK *Sayings* Ser. II. *Passion & Princ.* iii, 'I'm afraid you won't like our tiffin, Walford'... 'I have tiffed', said Walford. **1859** LANG *Wand. India* 16, I will tiff with you to-day at half-past two.

tiffany[1] ('tɪfənɪ). Also 7 **tiffanie, -enay, -eney, -inie, -iny, tifine, tifnie, tiphany,** 7–9 **tiffeny,** 9 **tiffney.** [a. OF. *tifinie* (*c* 1200), *tiphanie* (with 40 variants in Godefroy, s.v. *Tifaigne*):—L. *theophania*, THEOPHANY, applied to the Epiphany (see Du Cange). Sense 2 appears to be English only, and to have arisen about 1600; it is usually taken to be short for 'Epiphany silk' or 'muslin'; but as to the reason of the name no evidence has been found. (Perhaps it was a fanciful name, with allusion to the sense 'manifestation': see quots. 1601, 1645 in 2.)]

†**1.** The festival of the Epiphany or Twelfth Day (Jan. 6). *Obs.* (Scarcely an English use.)

[**1292** BRITTON II. xxi. §2 Del comencement del Advent jekes as utaves de la Tiphanie [*v.rr.* Tiphayne, Epiphanie; *tr.* from the beginning of Advent until the Octaves of the Epiphany]. **1323** in Tate *Househ. Ord. Edw. II* 62 *margin*, Le jour de la Tyffayne.] *a***1633** AUSTIN *Medit.* (1635) 56 This is Twelfe day... But more anciently and most properly it was called the Epiphany... Our great grand Fathers.. as the Legend sayes called it the Tiffany.. we must know it signifies Apparition or Manifestation from above.

2. A kind of thin transparent silk; also a transparent gauze muslin, cobweb lawn: see also quots. 1882.

1601 HOLLAND *Pliny* XI. xxii. I. 323 The invention of that fine silke, Tiffanie, Sarcenet, and Cypres, which instead of apparell to cover and hide, shew women naked through them. **1611** COTGR., *Gaze*,.. also (the sleight stuffe) Tiffanie. *a***1625** FLETCHER *Noble Gent.* I. i, Let her haue Veluets, Tiffinies, Jewels, Pearls. **1645** EVELYN *Diary* June, [Venetian ladies], their sleeves.., shewing their naked armes, thro' false sleeves of tiffany. **1671** SKINNER *Etymol.*, *Tiffeny*, Sericum tenuissimum & mollissimum. **1682** WHELER *Journ. Greece* I. 64 Silken Vail, as thin as Tiphany. **1685** *Lond. Gaz.* No. 2001/4, 33 Yards of Black Tiffeney for Mourning Scarves. **1718** LADY M. W. MONTAGU *Let. to C'tess Mar* 10 Mar., The table-cloth and napkins.. were all tiffany, embroidered with silk and gold. **1788** MRS. SHERWOOD in *Life* (1847) v. 63 A shepherdess's hat, of pale blue silver tiffany. **1796** MRS. GLASSE *Cookery* xxi. 325 Good clear isinglass.. tied up in a piece of thin tiffany. **1882** BECK *Draper's Dict.*, *Tiffany*.. a kind of transparent gauze stiffened with gum, still produced for employment in the production of artificial flowers. **1882** CAULFEILD & SAWARD *Dict. Needlework*, *Tiffany*, a thin description of semi-transparent silk textile, resembling gauze. *Ibid.*, *Tiffeny*, a description of muslin, of open make,.. employed for Needle Embroidery.

b. An article made of tiffany, as a head-dress, a garment, a sieve, etc.

1606 WARNER *Alb. Eng.* XVI. ci. (1612) 400 Fannes, Tifnies, Maskes, Bongraces. *c***1620** T. ROBINSON *Mary Magd.* I. 423 A tiffany shee wore about her head, Hanginge submissely to her shoulders white. **1788** W. MARSHALL *Yorksh.* Gloss., *Tiffany*, a fine gauze sieve, for separating fine flour. **1882** J. LUCAS *Stud. Nidderdale* 15 Flour.. separated from the bran by being worked through a hair-sieve tiffany, or temse.

c. *fig.*

*a***1624** BP. M. SMITH *Serm.* (1632) 132 Put on the silke of honesty, the tiffiny (as it were) of sanctimony, and the purple of chastity. **1650** B. *Discolliminium* 36 As a wel-wrought piece of tiffany or sophistry, but not as a sound Logicall or Theologicall Webbe. **1651** BIGGS *New Disp.* ¶ 250 From the Tiffany and thinner dresse of a vapour. **1829** T. HOOK *Bank to Barnes* 86 The trumpery tiffany of drawing-room tittle-tattle.

d. *attrib.* or as *adj.* Made of or resembling tiffany; *fig.* 'transparent', flimsy. **e.** *Comb.* as *tiffany-trader.*

1608 DEKKER *2nd Pt. Honest Wh.* II. i. Wks. 1873 II. 119 As arrant a whore as euer stiffned tiffany neckcloathes in water-starch. **1626** *Faithf. Friends* I. ii, This tiffany-trader wants customers. **1658** R. FRANCK *North. Mem.* (1821) 48 It's a tiffany plot; any man with half an eye may easily see through it. **1664** H. POWER *Exp. Philos.* I. 30 Another pair of filmy Tiffany long wings, like those of Flyes. **1699** EVELYN *Acetaria* (1729) 174 Stamp it as small as to pass thro' a fine Tiffany Sieve. **1703** MRS. CENTLIVRE *Beau's Duel* II. ii, Whose tiffany natures are so easily impos'd upon. **1823** LAMB *Elia* Ser. II. *New-Y.'s coming of age*, Twelfth Day.. came in a tiffany suit, white and gold.

Tiffany[2] ('tɪfənɪ). The name of Charles L. *Tiffany* (1812–1902), goldsmith and founder of a fashionable New York firm of jewellers *Tiffany and Co.*, and of his son Louis C. *Tiffany* (1848–1933), Art Nouveau decorator noted for his iridescent glassware, used: **a.** *attrib.* (sometimes with small initial) to designate objects made or designed by either of these (but esp. the son) or imitating his style, esp. as ***Tiffany glass, lamp.*** **b.** Allusively to denote organizations, etc., considered equal to Tiffany and Co. in high-quality craftsmanship or exclusiveness. Also *Comb.*, as ***Tiffany-style, -type*** adjs.

1895 *Montgomery Ward Catal.* Spring & Summer 153/1, 1K Diamond. Tiffany Setting. **1907** KIPLING *Let.* 10 Dec. (1983) 56 A slippery slidy red leather box—like a huge Tiffany jewel case. **1930** E. WAUGH *Labels* vii. 175 Gaudi alone was able to use it [*sc.* a mosaic of broken china and pebbles embedded in cement] with precision.. and make of it the craft which, in New York, is reverently known as 'Tiffany bathroom'. **1936** J. DOS PASSOS *Big Money* 307 Gladys kept.. tiffanyglass bowls full of freezias. [**1964** M. J. SIMON *New York This Way* iii. 31 Tiffany & Co., celebrated American jewellers whose name often is used colloquially to signify highest quality of product or service in any field.] **1969** A. LURIE *Real People* 89 The Tiffany lanterns [had been] lit beside the front door. **1971** P. A. WHITNEY *Listen for Whisperer* v. 95, I switched on the Tiffany lamp. **1973** *Synagogue Light* Sept. 4/2 By maintaining a small, specialized firm, we have been able to attain a consistently high calibre level of financial performance... It is the quality we are noted for, a Tiffany type organization. **1977** *Lancashire Life* Mar. 56/3 (*caption*) His policy is to supplement 'the world's finest exhibition' of Tiffany glass with a monthly change of exhibitions. **1977** *Texas Highways* Dec. 33/1 Tiffany-style lampshades. **1978** M. PUZO *Fools Die* xiii. 144, I had become the Tiffany's of bribe takers, with rich, trusting customers. **1979** *United States 1980/81* (Penguin Travel Guides) 425 This one.. has Tiffany lamps, antique tables, and a very friendly atmosphere. **1980** 'E. MCBAIN' *Ghosts* iv. 75 The Tiffany-style lamp on the end table.

† **'tiffety-'taffety**, *a. nonce-wd.* Reduplicated form of *taffety* adj. = TAFFETA B. 2 (cf. quot. 1621 there); perh. also associated with TIFF *v.*[1]

1595 *Maroccus Ext.* 13 Tush, she that I talke of can entertaine you with a duzen of tiffite taffetie girles in a morning.

tiffin ('tɪfɪn), *sb. Anglo-Ind.* Also 9 **tiffing**. [Appears to have originated in the Eng. colloq. or slang *tiffing*, vbl. sb. from TIFF *v.*[2] to take a little drink or sip (cf. quot. 1785), which has been specialized in Anglo-Indian use.

1785 GROSE *Dict. Vulg. Tongue, Tiffing*, eating, or drinking out of meal time. **1867** WEDGWOOD *Dict. Eng. Etymol., Tiffin*, now naturalised among Anglo-Indians in the sense of luncheon, is the North country *tiffing* (properly sipping).]

a. In India and neighbouring eastern countries, A light midday meal; luncheon.

1800 WARD in *Carey's Life* vi. (1885) 137 Krishna came to eat tiffin (what in England is called luncheon) with us. **1803** [see TIFF *v.*[4]]. **1810** T. WILLIAMSON *E. Ind. Vade M.* I. 352 The [Mahommedan] ladies, like ours, indulge in tiffings (slight repasts). *c* **1816** MRS. SHERWOOD *Stories on Ch. Catech.* xvi. 141 She gave them a good tiffing about one o'clock. **1831** TRELAWNY *Adv. Younger Son* II. 115 When the gong sounds one, you will find tiffin in the hall. **1896** 'H. S. MERRIMAN' *Flotsam* xx, I'll call for you after tiffin. **1906** *Peking & Tientsin Times* 9 May 1/2 Those wishing to have tiffins at the forthcoming spring meeting will please apply at the secretary's office. Price $2.00 per tiffin.

b. *attrib.*, as ***tiffin-bell, -table, -time.*** **tiffin-carrier**, a tiered container for transporting meals.

1811 MRS. SHERWOOD *Henry & Bearer* 31 The tiffin time was very stupid to the little boy. **1852** *Life in Bombay* 34 The preparation of the tiffin table. **1890** CLARK RUSSELL *Shipmate Louise* vi, The tiffin-bell rang. **1960** R. P. JHABVALA *Householder* i. 13 He always brought his breakfast with him in a tin tiffin-carrier.

Hence **'tiffin** *v.*, (*a*) *intr.* to take tiffin, to lunch; cf. TIFF *v.*[4]; (*b*) *trans.* to provide with tiffin.

1866 MISS BRADDON *Lady's Mile* xi, I'd tiffin them if they were my visitors. **1880** P. GILLMORE *On Duty* 51 Here I tiffined. **1903** LD. R. GOWER *Rec. & Remin.* 388 We tiffined at a tea-house in the village.

tiffing ('tɪfɪŋ), *vbl. sb.* [f. TIFF *v.*[1] + -ING[1].] The action of TIFF *v.*[1]; decking or tricking out, personal adornment.

a **1225** *Ancr. R.* 420 (MS. C.) Wrihen ha schal hire scheome, as sunfule Eue dohter;.. & naut drah þ wriheles to tiffung & te prude. **1303** R. BRUNNE *Handl. Synne* 3243 Moche she loued feyre tyfyng On here hede. **1635** CRANLEY *Amanda* 33 Thus with thy tiffing, trimming, and thy mending, Thou spend'st whole houres together without ending. **1741** MRS. DELANY in *Life & Corr.* (1861) II. 168 Now for curling, tiffing, etc. Our Duchess will be almost as fine as the Nabob's lady.

'tiffish, *a. colloq. rare*—[0]. [f. TIFF *sb.*[3] + -ISH[1].] Given to tiffs, ready to take offence; pettish, peevish.

1855 in CLARKE. **1864** in WEBSTER.

tiffle ('tɪf(ə)l), *v.*[1] *Obs.* exc. *dial.* Forms: 4 **tifle**, 5 **tiffel, tyffle**, 6 **tyf(f)ell**, 9 **tiffle**. [Dim. or freq. of TIFF *v.*[1]]

† **1.** *trans.* To dress up, adorn, deck or trick out (in a trifling or time-wasting way). *Obs.*

1388 WYCLIF *Ecclus.* xxxii. 15 In the our of risyng, tifle [1382 tyff] thee not. *Margin*, That is, make thee no tariyng in araiyng, ether tiflyng of heeris, as wymmen doon.

2. *intr.* To busy oneself idly, 'fiddle', trifle; to potter about. Now *dial.*

c **1440** *Promp. Parv.* 493/2 Tyfflynge, or vnprofytabylle werkynge (*S.,A.,P.* tyffynge). **1530** PALSGR. 758/1, I tyfell with my fyngers, or busye my selfe longe aboute a thyng.., *je tiffe.* You have spente two houres to tyffell about this thyng. *a* **1825** FORBY *Voc. E. Anglia, Tiffle*, to be mightily busy about little or nothing.

Hence **'tiffler**, one who 'tiffles'; in quot. app. one who dresses up; in mod. dial. a trifler, idler.

c **1400** *Plowman's T.* 195 But Antichrist they serven clene, Attyred all in tyrannye;.. Tiffelers attyred in trecherye.

tiffle, tifle ('tɪf(ə)l), *v.*[2] Chiefly *dial.* [app. onomatopœic.] *trans.* To disorder, disarrange, entangle, ravel; ***tiffle out***, to ravel out.

1811 WILLAN *Words W. Riding* in *Archæol.* (1814) XVII. 161 *Tifle*, v. to entangle, to mix and knot threads together. **1815** *Monthly Mag.* 1 Mar. 125/1 *Essex Dialect, Tiffle*, to disarrange. **1825** BROCKETT *N.C. Words, Tifle, tyfell*, to entangle,.. to ruffle. **1880** *Plain Hints Needlework* 121 Tifflings.. is used in some parts to describe the ravellings or threads. 'To tiffle out', to ravel out or unweave.

tiffoon, obs. form of TYPHOON.

† **ti'ffure.** *Obs. rare*—[1]. [a. OF. *tifeure* a head-dress (*a* 1200 in Godef.), f. *tifer*, TIFF *v.*[1]: see -URE.] Dressing up, adornment.

1303 R. BRUNNE *Handl. Synne* 3290, Y suffre þys mysauenture For on my heuede ouer feyre tyfure.

tiffy ('tɪfɪ), *sb. Naut. slang.* [Contraction of ARTIFICER.] An engine-room artificer.

1899 F. T. BULLEN *Way Navy* 34 My life-long admiration for the blue-jacket proper will be shared by his brothers in arms, the stoker and engine-room artificer ('tiffy' as we call him). **1904** KIPLING *Traffics & Disc.* 57 Those dirty engine-room objects which we call 'tiffies'.

tiffy ('tɪfɪ), *a.* [f. TIFF *sb.*[3] + -Y.] Given to tiffs; in a tiff; pettish, ill-humoured; faddy.

1810 *Splendid Follies* II. 126 The old lady felt quite tiffy, and mumbled her roll in silence. **1883** *Bread-Winners* (1884) 27 She's too tiffy for poor folks like us.

tifle ('taɪf(ə)l), *v.* Chiefly *dial.* Also 8–9 **tyfle**. [Origin unascertained.] *intr.* Of a horse: To get a strain in the back: chiefly in **tifled** *ppl. a.*

1703 THORESBY *Let. to Ray* s.v. (E.D.S.), A tifled horse, when broken above the loins. **1708** J. C. *Compl. Collier* (1845) 33 Least a Horse or two Tyfle, or be out of Order by a Fall. **1828** *Craven Gloss., Tifled*, sprained in the back. **1863** MRS. TOOGOOD *Yorksh. Dial.* (MS.), The horse will never do any more work; he is tyfled in the back.

tift (tɪft), *sb.*[1] *Sc.* and *north. dial.* [History obscure; ? related to TIFT *ppl. a.* and TIFT *v.*[1]] Condition, order; condition of mind, mood, humour.

1717 RAMSAY *Elegy on Lucky Wood* vii, Beef, dry fish, or cheese, Which kept our.. health in tift. **1722** WODROW *Hist. Ch. Scot.* II. III. iv. §4. 140 The King's Horse being in good Tift. **1725** RAMSAY *Gentle Sheph.* I. i, I'm in tift to hear you play and sing. **1824** MACTAGGART *Gallovid. Encycl.* 449 A poet's muse is in tift when she sings well; corn also is in tift when it is dry, viz., in tift to lead. **1904** in *Eng. Dial. Dict.* cited Cumberld., to Cheshire, and n.-w. Derbysh.

tift, *sb.*[2] *Sc.* and *dial.* [app. var. of TIFF *sb.*[3]]

1. A slight fit of ill-humour or offendedness; a petty quarrel or disagreement: = TIFF *sb.*[3] 1, 2.

1751 SMOLLETT *Per. Pic.* (1779) IV. xc. 83 It [his intimacy] was now chequered with occasional tifts. **1761** MRS. F. SHERIDAN *Sidney Bidulph* III. 42 She supposed he married in a tifft, upon my refusal of him. **1808** ELEANOR SLEATH *Bristol Heiress* III. 81 My wife and I have often a bit of a tift. **1887** P. MCNEILL *Blawearie* 61 The last time we met—Bob and I—we had a 'tift', ye ken what that is.

2. A puff, breath, or slight blast (of wind).

a **1765** *Ld. Thomas*, etc. xvii. in Child *Ballads* III. (1885) 183/1 Four and twanty siller bells Wer a' tyed till his mane, And yae tift o the norland wind, They tinkled ane by ane.

† **tift**, *ppl. a. Sc. Obs.* [Goes with TIFT *v.*[1]] Prepared, ready; set in order; provided, furnished.

13.. *Cursor M.* 1761 (Cott.) Quen al was tift [*v.rr.* wroȝt, don] was þar na bide, þe stormes ras on ilka side. *Ibid.* 5089 Mas your gere al redi tift, Your seckes sal i fil o gift. *Ibid.* 24807 Wit trissor son his scipp was tift. *c* **1375** *Sc. Leg. Saints* xviii. (*Egipciane*) 870, I cane fond To þat flume.., And wesche in yͤ bath handis & face; Syne come agane, & with schryfte And contryt hart mad me tyfte.

tift, *v.*[1] *Obs.* exc. *dial.* [Origin uncertain; in quots. *c* 1425, 1600 it appears to be a var. of TIFF *v.*[1]; but in the rest it may be a different word: cf. TIFT *sb.*[1], TIFT *ppl. a.*] *trans.* To prepare, make ready, put in order; to dress.

13.. *Cursor M.* 19425 (Cott.) Steuen tifted him al bun [*so Gött.; Fairf. & Tr.* made him redi bun], And þan bigan a gret sarmun. *c* **1425** *St. Mary of Oignies* I. i. in *Anglia* VIII. 135/34 Tressynge and tifting of here [= hair]. **1600** ABP. ABBOT *Exp. Jonah* 591 Beholding a woman most curiously trimmed, and exquisitely tiffted up. **1641** BEST *Farm. Bks.* (Surtees) 32 There are many thinges belonge to tiftinge of hay; as spreadinge,.. turninge, rakinge, and cockinge. *Ibid.* 33 If it [hay] bee eyther wette or greene when yow cocke it, yow are not to lette it stande above three dayes afore yow throwe it out againe and gette it well tifted [*pr.* tifled] in. *Ibid.* 61 For tiftinge of a newe hive. **1790** MORISON *Poems* 25 (Jam.) The fidler tifted ilka string. **1876** *Whitby Gloss.* s.v., 'Tifted up', cleansed and put into order.

tift, *v.*[2] *Sc.* and *dial.* [var. of TIFF *v.*[2]] *trans.* To drink, quaff; = TIFF *v.*[2] (also *intr.*).

1722 W. HAMILTON *Wallace* III. i. 18 They.. tifted canty wine. **1819** W. TENNANT *Papistry Storm'd* (1827) 101 The siller stoups, on heigh upliftit, Were tootit in a whip, and tiftit. **1833** M. SCOTT *Tom Cringle* x. (1859) 203 The Captain was stowing his cargo with great zeal and tifting away at the fluids as became an honest sailor.

tift, *v.*[3] *Obs.* or *dial.* [f. TIFT *sb.*[2]] *intr.* To have a tiff; = TIFF *v.*[3]

1777 SHERIDAN *Sch. Scand.* I. ii, We tifted a little going to church, and fairly quarrelled before the bells had done ringing.

tig (tɪg), *sb.*[1] Also 9 **tigg, tic.** [f. TIG *v.*]

1. A touch: usually a light but significant touch, a tap or pat, = TICK *sb.*[3] 1; rarely applied to one that hurts. *Sc.* and *north. dial.*

1721 KELLY *Sc. Prov.* 243 Many Masters, quoth the Poddock to the Harrow, when every Tin[e] gave her a Tig. **1822** GALT *Sir A. Wylie* I. v. 36 It's bairnly to mak sic a wark for a bit tig on the haffet. **1825** BROCKETT *N.C. Words, Tig*, a slight touch; as a mode of salutation. **1897** LD. E. HAMILTON *Outlaws* ii. 21 Just a tig of the cheek, Gavin... There's nothing in that to shame an honest man, surely?

2. A children's game, in which one of the players—usually designated *tig* or *it*—pursues the others until he overtakes and touches or 'tigs' one, who in his turn becomes 'tig': the same as TAG *sb.*[2]

Cf. TICK *sb.*[3] 1 b, and Sanders *Wörterb.* (1865) *Der Zeck*, ein Spiel der Kinder, wobei eins dem Andern einen Schlag giebt.

1816 S. M. TAIT in *Remin. Lady Wake* v. (1909) 62 If it is wet, we play at tigg up and down the stairs. **1854** WARTER *Last of Old Squires* ii. 15 The sons.. would have a start with the fleetest youths of the hamlet at prisoner's-base, or the old fashion'd game of tic. **1885** H. O. FORBES *Nat. Wand. E. Archip.* 68 With varieties of chevy, tig, and blind-man's buff. **1894** MRS. H. WARD *Marcella* I. 12 The mad games of 'tig' which she led.. in the top playground.

3. *colloq.* (orig. *Sc.*). A fit of bad temper.

1773 R. FERGUSSON in *Weekly Mag.* XXII. 209/1 What tig then takes the fates, that they can thole, Thrawart to fix me i' this weary hole? **1895** R. FORD *Tayside Songs* 71 She left me in a tig. **1934** N. MARSH *A Man lay Dead* xii. 206 'You shall have every opportunity,' soothed Alleyn. 'What a tig you are in, to be sure!' **1943** —— *Colour Scheme* xii. 217, I must say.. that I can't see why you're getting into such a tig over it. **1962** *Punch* 24 Oct. 587/1 The spectacle of a man in a tig, even of two men in a tig, is not as a rule wholly entertaining.

tig, *sb.*[2] variant of TYG, a drinking-cup.

tig (tɪg), *v.* [History obscure. It may be, as some think, a variant or alteration of TICK *v.*[1], or a parallel formation. Cf. the parallelism of MHG. and Ger. *zecken* to pat, and *der zeck* the game of tig (TIG *sb.*[1] 2).]

1. *intr.* To give light or playfully rough touches; esp. *fig.* to trifle, dally *with*; † *to tig and tar = to tick and toy*: see TICK *v.*[1] 1. *Sc.* and *north. dial.*

c **1470** HENRYSON *Mor. Fab.* v. (*Parl. Beasts*) i. [The fox] That luifit weill with pultrie to tig and tar. **1634** RUTHERFORD *Lett.* (1862) I. 140 He may get up and lend them a blow who are tigging and playing with Christ and His spouse. **1815** G. BEATTIE *John o' Arnha'* (1826) 41 It was nae joke To tig wi' fiends that vomit smoke. **1825** JAMIESON s.v., Young people are said to be tigging, when sporting with gentle touches, or patting each other.

b. *fig.* To interfere, meddle, have to do *with*. *Sc.*

1599 JAS. I *Βασιλ. Δωρον* (1603) 29 As for the matter of forefaltures,.. it is not good tigging with these things. **1813** W. BEATTIE *Fruits Time Parings* (1871) 30 They that tig wi you Will soon hae cause to claw. **1873** W. ALEXANDER *Johnny Gibb* xix, Nedder you nor Mr. Sleekaboot made yer plack a bawbee by tiggin wi' her.

2. *trans.* To touch in the game of tig (TIG *sb.*[1] 2). Also *absol.* (see also b).

1821 *Blackw. Mag.* Aug. 38 To join the merry ring at.. Tig me if you can. **1828** *Craven Gloss., Tig*, to touch lightly;.. to have the last touch when leaving school. **1866** A. W. BUCHAN *Song of Rest* II. 29 Some tig and run, some ride upon the wall. **1893** E. L. WAKEMAN in *Columbus* (Ohio) *Dispatch* 19 Oct., The chief point in this game [French Tig] is always to tig on a portion of the body difficult to hold whilst tigging another.

b. *intr. fig.* To 'pluck' or 'dig' *at*, as if playing tig; to annoy one by petty provocations. *dial.*

1802 R. ANDERSON *Cumberld. Ball.* 54 Now, tiggin at me suin and late, They're cleekin but the yellow bait. **1844** *Songs of Nursery* in *Whistlebinkie* (1890) II. 153 Father, settle Sandy! He's cryin names to me. He's aye tig, tigging, And winna let me be.

3. *intr. transf.* To run from place to place, as if chased. *dial.*

1834 LOVER *Leg. & Stor. Irel.* Ser. II. 297 He run undher a stool, and kept tiggin' about from one place to th' other. **1882** J. WALKER *Jaunt to Auld Reckie* 13 Like cattle tiggin' frae the clegs and flees Awa they scamper.

‖**tige** (tiʒ). [F. *tige* stalk:—L. *tībia* shank, pipe.] The shaft of a column; also *transf.*, in a fire-arm or cartridge, see quot. 1877; in *Bot.*, see quot. 1900. **tige-arm**, a fire-arm fitted with a tige (*Cent. Dict.* 1891).

1664 EVELYN tr. *Freart's Archit.* 126 That round and long Cylinder diversly named by Authors, Scapus, Vivo, Tige, Shaft, Fust, Trunke. **1710** J. HARRIS *Lex. Techn.* II, *Tige*, in Architecture, is the Shaft of a Column from the Astragal to the Capital. **1727–41** CHAMBERS *Cycl.*, *Tige*, in architecture, a French term for the shaft or fust of a column, comprehended between the astragal and the capital. **1877** KNIGHT *Dict. Mech.*, *Tige*... a stem or stalk. A pin at the base of the breech in the Thouvenin system of fire-arms, for expanding the base of the ball; an anvil or support for the cap or primer in a central-fire cartridge. **1900** B. D. JACKSON *Gloss. Bot. Terms* 271/1 *Tige*,.. stem.

‖**tigelle** (tiːˈʒɛl). *Bot.* Also **tigel**, and in L. form **tigella** (tɪˈdʒɛlə), (*erron.* tiˈgellum, tiˈgellus). [F. *tigelle* caulicle, radicle, dim. of *tige*.

(*Tibia, tige, tigelle* are fem., hence the correct Latin form is *tigella*.)]

The embryonic axis or primitive stem, which bears the cotyledons; the caulicle or radicle. Sometimes applied to the plumule, which is properly the growing top of the tigelle. Hence **tigellate** (ˈtɪdʒəleɪt) *a.*, having a tigelle; **tigellule** (tɪˈdʒɛljʊl), see quot. 1860; whence **tiˈgellular** *a.*, pertaining to or of the nature of a tigellule.

1860 MAYNE *Expos. Lex.*, *Tigella*, term for that part of the vegetable embryo which unites the radicle to the cotyledon. *Ibid.*, *Tigellatus*, applied to the *plumula* when supplied with a visible *tigella*, as in the *Faba*: tigellate. *Ibid.*, Tigellular. *Ibid.*, *Tigellula*, term by Turpin for the short and sterile filaments which are one of the two elementary organs of the mass of the truffle: a tigellule. **1866** *Treas. Bot.*, *Tigellate*, having a short stalk, as the plumule of a bean. **1900** B. D. JACKSON *Gloss. Bot. Terms* 271/1 *Tigelle, Tigella*,.. a miniature or initial stem, used for (*a*) caulicle or hypocotyl, (*b*) plumule.

tiger (ˈtaɪgə(r)), *sb.* Forms: 1 (*pl.*) tigras, (-es); 4–7 tygre, 4–8 tigre, 5 tigir, -yr, tygyr, -ur, 5–9 tyger, 6 tygir, *Sc.* tegir, tegre, 6–7 tigar, 7 tygar, 7– tiger. [ME. a. OF. *tigre* (*c* 1150 in Godef. *Compl.*), ad. L. *tigrem*, nom. *tigris*, whence also rare OE. pl. *tigras, -es*; Ger., Da., Sw. *tiger*, Du. *tijger*, Sp., Pg., It. *tigre*. L. *tigris* was a. Gr. τίγρις, a foreign word, evidently oriental, introduced when the beast became known.

(Some have conjectured connexion with Zend *tighri* arrow, *tighra* sharp, pointed, in reference to the celerity of its spring; but no application of either word, or any derivative, to the tiger is known in Zend.)]

1. A large carnivorous feline quadruped, *Felis tigris*, one of the two largest living felines, a cat-like maneless animal, in colour tawny yellow with blackish transverse stripes and white belly; widely distributed in Asia, and proverbial for its ferocity and cunning.

Bengal tiger, royal tiger (†***tiger royal***), the tiger of Bengal, where it attains its typical development.

a **1000** *De rebus in Oriente* in Cockayne *Narrat.* 38 Ymb þa stowe beoð..fore hundum tigras & leopardos þ hi fedað. *c* **1000** ÆLFRIC *Hom.* II. 492 Twa hreðe deor, þe sind tigres ᵹehatene, þær urnon. **13..** *K. Alis.* 5227 (Bodl. MS.) Lyouns, Olyfaunz, Tygres, and dragouns, Vnces grete, and leopardes. *c* **1386** CHAUCER *Sqr.'s T.* 411 Ther nys Tygre [*v.r.* tigre], ne noon so crueel beest..That nolde han wept. **1484** CAXTON *Fables of Auian* xiii, Whan he sawe passe the tygre before the busshe, he shote at hym an arowe. **1581** PETTIE *Guazzo's Civ. Conv.* III. (1586) 124 So monstrous a creature..that it was doubtfull whether she were a woman or a tigar. **1605** SHAKS. *Macb.* III. iv. 101. **1698** FRYER *Acc. E. India & P.* IV. v. 176 A Youth killed a Tigre-Royal... It was a Tigre of the Biggest and Noblest Kind. **1777** ROBERTSON *Hist. Amer.* I. IV. 260 America gives birth to no creature that equals the lion or tyger in strength and ferocity. **1847** EMERSON *Repr. Men, Napoleon* Wks. (Bohn) I. 369 A man of stone and iron..with the speed and spring of a tiger in action. **1882** F. M. CRAWFORD *Mr. Isaacs* x, Crashing through the jungle after tiger with varying success.

2. a. Applied to other animals of the same genus, as in America to the Jaguar, *Felis onca*, and the Puma or Cougar, *F. concolor* (rare); and esp. in South Africa to the Leopard or Panther, *F. pardus*.

1604 E. G[RIMSTONE] *D'Acosta's Hist. Indies* III. xv. 166 Vpon the sea shoare the Caymant with his taile gaue great blowes vnto the Tygre. **1698** FRYER *Acc. E. India & P.* IV. v. 177 The lesser sort of Tigres spotted like a Leopard. **1708** tr. F. Leguat in R. Raven-Hart *Cape of Good Hope 1652–1702* (1971) II. 431 The Company gives twenty Crowns to anyone that kills a Lion, and ten to him that kills a Tigre. **1748** *Anson's Voy.* II. xii. 267 There were great numbers of tygers in the woods [Pacific coast, Mexico].. they are by no means so fierce as the Asiatic or African tyger. **1785** G. FORSTER tr. *Sparrman's Voy.* (1786) II. 252 The animals which I and the colonists in this part of Africa call tygers,..represented in..M. de Buffon's work, under the denomination of panthers and leopards. **1832** MACGILLIVRAY tr. *Humboldt's Trav.* xvi. (1836) 215 When the tigers approached the edge of the forest, a dog which the travellers had began to howl. **1894** E. EGGLESTON in *Century Mag.* Apr. 849 The panther was long called a 'tyger' in the Carolinas. **1907** P. FITZPATRICK *Jock of Bushveld* (1909) 252 Tigers—as they are almost invariably called, but properly, leopards—were plentiful enough.

b. esp. with qualifications.

†***American t.***, †***Mexican t.***, the jaguar; ***black t.***, a dark variety of (*a*) the jaguar, (*b*) the leopard; ***clouded t.***, ***marbled t.***, ***tortoiseshell t.***, species of TIGER-CAT; †***poltroon t.***, †***red t.***, earlier names for the puma; †***spotted t.***; (*a*) the leopard, (*b*) the cheetah (also †***tiger of chase***).

1774 GOLDSM. *Nat. Hist.* II. xiv. 332 The tyger of Bengal has been seen to measure twelve feet in length,..whereas the American tyger seldom exceeds three. *Ibid.* III. vii. 244 An animal of America, which is usually called the Red Tiger, but Mr. Buffon calls it the Cougar. **1784–5** *Ann. Reg.* II. 20 His tygers of chase likewise pay him a visit... These are the spotted tygers. **1790** BEWICK *Hist. Quad.* (1824) 220 It [the Cougar] is sometimes called the Poltron tiger. **1825** WEDDELL *Voy. S. Pole* 210 The American tiger, called by the Spaniards jaguar, is often seen on the coast. **1826** HONE *Every-Day Bk.* I. 1176 Panther, or spotted tiger of Buenos Ayres. **1827** ROBERTS *Voy. Centr. Amer.* 95 A species of black tiger will also watch the turtle. **1842** *Penny Cycl.* XXIV. 440/2 The Black Tiger, *Felis melas*,..is considered as only a dark variety of the Leopard. *Ibid.* 441/1 The Mexican Tiger of Pennant is said to be a representation of *F. macroura*. **1863** BATES *Nat. Amazon* xi. (1864) 352 The black-tiger appears to be more abundant than the spotted form of jaguar in the neighbourhood of Ega. **1879** E. P. WRIGHT *Anim. Life* 84 The Clouded Tiger (*Felis macrocelis*) seems to be of a less mischievous disposition than many of the other cats. **1896** *List Anim. Zool. Soc.* 56 *Felis nebulosa*, Clouded Tiger. *Hab.* Assam.

c. Applied to other than feline beasts.

(*a*) ***Tasmanian*** or ***native tiger***: names given to the THYLACINE, the striped wolf or zebra-wolf of Tasmania. (*b*) ***sabre-toothed tiger***: see SABRE *sb.* 4 b.

1829 H. WIDOWSON *Present State Van Dieman's Land* xviii. 179 The hyena, or as it is sometimes called, the tiger, is about the size of a large terrier; it frequents the wilds of Tasmania. **1832** ROSS *Hobart Town Almanack* 85 (Morris) During our stay a native tiger or hyena bounded from its lair beneath the rocks. **1879** E. P. WRIGHT *Anim. Life* 217 The Tiger, or Striped Wolf of the colonists (*Thylacinus cynocephalus*), inhabits Tasmania. **1892** A. SUTHERLAND *Elem. Geog. Brit. Colonies* xiii. 273 The 'Tasmanian Tiger' is of the size of a shepherd's dog, a gaunt yellow creature, with black stripes round the upper part of its body.

†**d.** Applied (in L. form) to fabulous creatures, beasts or birds: see quots. *Obs.*

1481 CAXTON *Myrr.* II. vi. 73 In ynde ben ther other bestes grete and fyrs whiche ben of blew colowr, and haue clere spottes on the body,..and ben named Tygris. *c* **1511** *1st Eng. Bk. Amer.* (Arb.) p. xxxii/2 Byrdes the whyche ben called Tygris, and they be so stronge that they wyll bere or cary in theyr neste a man syttyng vpon an horse all armyd fro the hede to ye fote.

3. The figure or representation of a tiger; *esp.* one used as a badge or crest; hence, popularly applied to an organization or society having this badge; also, a member of such a society.

spec. (***Tammany Tiger***), the Tammany organization (*U.S.*).

c **1475** *Rauf Coilȝear* 457 He bair grauit in Gold and Gowlis in grene, Ane Tyger ticht to ane tre, ane takin of tene. **1725** COATS *Dict. Her.* s.v., The Heads of Tigers are also born in Arms either Couped or Eraz'd. **1871** *Harper's Weekly* 25 Nov. 1099/2 The tiger, symbol of the Americus Club, is used in a manner to produce the effect of a telling retort. **1874** *Chamb. Jrnl.* 801 (Farmer) The 17th [foot].. the Bengal Tigers, from their badge—a tiger. **1894** *Parker's Gloss. Her.* s.v., This beast, as drawn by ancient painters, is now often called the heraldic tiger, as distiguished from the natural. **1901** *Scotsman* 7 Nov. 4/3 New York..cannot be worse governed in the future than it has been under the rule of the Tammany Tiger. **1910** *Westm. Gaz.* 14 Mar. 14/2 (*Hockey*) The cup-holders were defeated by the Leicestershire Regiment (the Tigers) by 2–1.

4. *transf.* and *fig.* Applied to one who or that which in some way resembles or suggests a tiger.

a. A person of fierce, cruel, rapacious, or blood-thirsty disposition; also sometimes, a person of very great activity, strength, or courage. Also *spec.*, a native of the Fens (in full, ***fen tiger***). *colloq.*

1500–20 DUNBAR *Poems* xxxviii. 11 The auld kene tegir, with his teith on char, Quhilk in a wait hes lyne for ws so lang. **1581** *Satir. Poems Reform.* xliv. 175 Thou hes Blasphemit our prophet, Preist, and heid; O filthie tegre Babylonical! **1585** *Thanksgiving* in *Liturg. Serv.* (1847) 585 To save her [Queen Elizabeth] from the jaws of the cruel Tigers that then sought to suck her blood. **1649** ROBERTS *Clavis Bibl.* 510 Antiochus Epiphanes that cruellest Tyger and Persecutor of the Church. **1806** FESSENDEN *Democr.* I. 77 *note*, The blood-thirsty tygers of the French revolution. **1893** BARING-GOULD *Cheap Jack Z.* I. 149, I who have lived in the Fens and among the tigers all my days. **1963** 'C. MARCHANT' *Fen Tiger* ii. 40 The term 'fen tiger'... Andrew explained it was the name given to a type of fen man, now almost extinct but not quite, for here and there a descendant of the type of man who had lived deep in the trackless, treacherous fenland, and who fought against the land being drained with cunning, craftiness, and even murder, was still to be found. **1971** *Country Life* 28 Oct. 1128/3 A scattered crowd of rough 'Fen Tigers' in corduroy trousers. **1981** S. MARSHALL *Everyman's Bk. Eng. Folk Tales* 13, I was..not accorded the welcome I would have expected to be given to a fen-tiger returning home from choice.

b. Any animal of savage or vicious temper or of great rapacity.

1859 *Art of Taming Horses* i. 23 The boasting Mr. ——.. was beaten pale and trembling out of the circus by that equine tiger. **1884** 'R. BOLDREWOOD' *Melbourne Mem.* xxi. 153 Many of the others [horses] were 'regular tigers', requiring any horseman who essayed to ride them habitually to be young, valiant, in hard training. **1885** LADY BRASSEY *The Trades* 211 The right time of the moon for the 'tigers of the sea' [sharks] to be about. **1894** *Outing* (U.S.) Feb. 393/1, I saw one of these sea-tigers [small sharks] glide towards it, and then a sudden splashing struggle began.

c. The tigerish spirit or disposition. Cf. DEVIL *sb.* 6 a.

1825 T. HOOK *Sayings* Ser. II. *Passion & Princ.* ix. III. 139 The incalculable quantity of nonsense which the admiring fools talked, had nearly roused the tiger. **1877** TENNYSON *Harold* I. i, I trust the kingly touch that cures the evil May serve to charm the tiger out of him.

d. *colloq.* (chiefly *Austral.* and *N.Z.*). One who has an insatiable appetite *for* something. Cf. GLUTTON *sb.*

1896 *Bulletin* (Sydney) 24 Oct. (Red Page), His father thought a lot of Henry; he used to call him a tiger for work. **1927** R. LEHMANN *Dusty Answer* II. 98 Martin..was still.. a tiger for raw vegetables. *Ibid.* IV. 259 You're a tiger for conversation, aren't you? **1935** W. HATFIELD *Black Waterlily* 15 'Tiger for work, aren't you?' he smiled. 'A good fault, of course, if you don't carry it to extremes.' **1972** P. NEWTON *Sheep Thief* xx. 170 Don't tell me you're up to your capers again... You're a tiger for punishment.

e. A sportsman or climber of outstanding skill and confidence. Cf. RABBIT *sb.*[1] 2 a. *colloq.*

1929 E. BOWEN *Joining Charles* 166 They may be tigers at ping-pong. **1935** D. PILLEY *Climbing Days* ii. 27 Wet ground, where most climbers—bar the latest 'tigers'—find that they slip. **1941** R. R. MARETT *Jerseyman at Oxford* ix. 138, I was never really worth more than bare scratch, and clean outside the 'tiger' class [in golf]. **1957** CLARK & PYATT *Mountaineering in Britain* x. 178 'Tiger' is the word used to describe the climber whose abilities are outstandingly in advance of his generation. **1974** *Times* 23 Feb. 13/3 There is a third [golf] course strictly for tigers; rabbits should try the excellent par three to seawards of the big course. **1979** *Country Life* 24 May 1674/2 Odon has less of a reputation as a tiger on difficult climbs than his father.

†**5.** A speckled hemipterous insect of the family *Tingitidæ*, which infests the leaves of pear and other trees. Cf. *tiger-babb* in 14. [F. *tigre*, *punaise tigre*.] *Obs.*

1706 LONDON & WISE *Retir'd Gard.* I. I. xiv. 68 Pear-trees planted in an Espalier, have upon trial been found so subject to Tigers, which creates a sort of Sickness in the Trees. **1719** LONDON & WISE *Compl. Gard.* VII. x. 181 Another incurable Distemper is Tigers, which stick to the back of the Leaves of Wall-Pear-Trees, and dry them up, by sucking all the green Matter that was in them. **1725** *Bradley's Fam. Dict.* s.v. *Diseases of Trees*, Tigers attack only Wall Pear-trees, and never Dwarfs.

6. a. A smartly-liveried boy acting as groom or footman; formerly often provided with standing-room on a small platform behind the carriage, and a strap to hold on by; less strictly, an outdoor boy-servant. *obs. slang.*

c **1817** [see quot. 1880]. **1825** HOOK *Sayings* Ser. II. *Man of Many Fr.* I. 247 'Ah!' said Arden, 'seven hundred pounds a-year, and a tiger!' **1827** LYTTON *Pelham* xliv, I sent my cab boy (*vulgo* Tiger) to inquire [etc.]. **1836–7** DICKENS *Sk. Boz, Gt. Winglebury Duel*, Leaving his tiger and cab behind him. **1842** W. IRVING in *Life & Lett.* (1886) III. 218 The young gentlemen have made a page, or tiger, of a nephew of Lorenzo. **1855** THACKERAY *Newcomes* xxv, He is the valet or tiger, more or less impudent and acute. **1880** W. H. HUSK in Grove *Dict. Mus.* II. 111/2 Lee, Alexander [1802–1851]... When a boy he entered the service of Lord Barrymore as 'tiger', being the first of the class of servants known by that name.

b. *Naut. slang.* A captain's personal steward.

1929 F. C. BOWEN *Sea Slang* 141 *Tiger, the*, the steward who acts as personal servant to the captain of a liner. **1936** E. T. BRITTEN *Million Ocean Miles* iii. 30 Croughan is my 'Tiger', as the Captain's steward is called at sea. **1961** 'R. GORDON' *Doctor on Toast* x. 87 In the old days, you could have swapped the Captain's tiger for the butler in any stately home in the kingdom, and no one would have been the wiser. **1982** *Times* 11 May 6/6 Captain Jackson's 'tiger'—the merchant navy equivalent of a batman..was married after the weekend.

†**7. a.** A vulgarly or obtrusively overdressed person; also a sponger, hanger-on, parasite; a roué, rake, swell-mobsman. *slang. Obs.*

1827 SCOTT *Jrnl.* (1890) I. 367 Our young men..have one capital name for a fellow that *outrés* and outroars the fashion. .. They hold him a vulgarian and call him a tiger. **1837** T. HOOK *Jack Brag* i, Every well dressed woman..whom he happened to see with the tigers in whose set he mingled. **1849** THACKERAY *Pendennis* xix, 'A man may have a very good coat-of-arms, and be a tiger', the Major said.., 'that man is a tiger, mark my word—a low man'.

b. (See quot.) *slang.*

1899 *Westm. Gaz.* 29 Aug. 8/1 The convict wears a dull yellow cap... The thick rough jacket and trousers are of the same yellowish hue... A favourite form of insubordination is to tear to pieces these yellow suits, the punishment for which is that the 'tiger' appears in the quarry next day arrayed in board-like black canvas.

8. *U.S. slang.* A shriek or howl (often the word 'tiger') terminating a prolonged and enthusiastic cheer; a prolongation, finishing touch, final burst.

1845 *Florence de Lacey* 28/1 Nine cheers for old Tip—one, two, three, four, five, six, seven, eight, nine, and a tiger. **1856** *Knickerb. Mag.* XLVIII. 258 (Thornton) Terrific cheers and a tiger. **1859** BARTLETT *Dict. Amer.* (ed. 2) s.v., In 1826 the [Boston Light] Infantry visited New York.., and while there the Tigers at a public festival awoke the echoes ..by giving the genuine howl... Gradually it became adopted on all festive and joyous occasions, and now 'three cheers and a tiger' are the inseparable demonstrations of approbation in that city [New York]. **1869** R. F. BURTON *Highl. Brazil* I. 239 When the ceremony ends, the scamp of the party..proposes three cheers and a tiger for Mr. Gordon. **1880** *Daily Tel.* 8 Oct., 'Three cheers' in properly hearty unison, without the hysterical American supplement of 'tigers'. **1892** *Sat. Rev.* 31 Dec. 759/1 The new festival..

introduced as a sort of 'tiger' to these three days of cheer. **1904** *N. China Herald* 27 May 1119/1 All the guests rising and singing.., giving three times three cheers, followed by a vigorous 'Tiger'.

9. a. The game of faro. ***to buck*** or ***fight the tiger***, at faro or roulette, to play against the bank; also, less strictly, to gamble, play cards. *U.S. slang.*

1851 *Adv. Simon Suggs* iv. (Thornton *Amer. Gloss.*) (heading) Simon starts forth to fight the Tiger. **1852** *Knickerb. Mag.* XL. 317 (ibid.) Such is 'the tiger', as the faro-table is called at the Springs: why, I never could learn. **1863** *Rocky Mountain News* 29 Jan. (ibid.), Bucking the tiger, which we wouldn't advise any one to do. **1888** *Daily Inter-Ocean* (Chicago) 14 Feb. (Farmer *Amer.*), More than one unsuspecting wife will have her eyes opened to the fact that the wicked tiger, and not legitimate business has been detaining her husband out so late at night.

b. A hand at poker: see quots.

1889 Guerndale *Poker Bk.* 23 *Tiger.* This hand is, fortunately, very seldom played. It consists of the lowest possible combination of five cards; these are two, three, four, five, and seven. **1909** *Cent. Dict. Supp.*, *Tiger*, in poker, a hand which is seven high and deuce low, without a pair, sequence, or flush.

c. ***blind tiger***, an establishment at which intoxicating drinks are surreptitiously sold (*U.S.*).

1892 *Evening Echo* 30 June 1/7 The proprietor of a 'blind tiger' (an illicit drinking place) in Lancaster, a..town of Kentucky, has been fined in 577 cases.

10. As a name for various implements: see quots.

1864 Webster, *Tiger*,..a pneumatic box or pan used in sugar-refining. **1877** Knight *Dict. Mech.*, *Tiger* (Sugar), a tank having a perforated bottom, through which the molasses escapes. **1881** Raymond *Mining Gloss.*, *Tiger*. See *Nipping-fork*. A tool for supporting a column of bore-rods while raising or lowering them.

11. Short for *tiger-moth*, *-shark*, *-snake*, *-wolf*, etc.

1797 *Encycl. Brit.* (ed. 3) XVII. 714/1 *Squalus*, Shark... 5. *Tigrinus*, or tigre, is about 15 feet long; the body is..black, interspersed with white stripes and spots, irregularly and transversely. **1819** G. Samouelle *Entomol. Comp.* 418 *Arctia Caja.* The Garden Tygey. **1870** *Eng. Mech.* 21 Jan. 449/3 One of the handsomest moths belonging to..the 'Tigers', is that called the wood tiger (*Chelonia plantaginis*). **1895** *Westm. Gaz.* 14 Sept. 2/3 The traveller in the bush often comes across two 'tigers' pegging away at each other for dear life... Sometimes snakes in captivity are trained to fight, and an owner will occasionally be found to 'back his "tiger" to fight any snake of his inches in New South Wales'. **1895** *Chamb. Jrnl.* XII. 645/1 The sharks..are at certain seasons a serious drawback, the tiger more especially. **1901** *Scribner's Mag.* XXIX. 455/1 Going out into the garden,.. stopping beside the tigers [tiger-lilies] and peonies.

12. a. In proverbial phrases: ***to ride a tiger*** and varr. [after the Chinese proverb 'He who rides a tiger is afraid to dismount' (W. Scarborough *Coll. Chinese Proverbs* (1875) xvi. 388)]: to take on a responsibility or embark on a course of action which subsequently cannot safely be abandoned; ***to have a tiger by the tail*** and varr.: to catch a Tartar (see Tartar *sb.*[2] 4).

1902 A. R. Colquhoun *Mastery of Pacific* xvi. 388 These colonies are..for her [*sc.* France] the tiger which she has mounted (to use the Chinese phrase), and which she can neither manage nor get rid of. **1940** *Daily Progress* (Charlottesville, Va.) 27 Nov. 1/7, I believe that Hitler is riding a tiger in trying to keep all Europe under control by sheer force. **1969** *Guardian* 7 July 9/5 All African politics to-day is concerned with the art of riding this terrible tiger [*sc.* tribalism]. **1972** 'E. Lathen' *Murder without Icing* (1973) iii. 30 Convulsions..could be expected... The Sloan Guaranty Trust..might well have a tiger by the tail. **1979** P. Driscoll *Pangolin* xii. 101 You're taking on an organization with.. reserves you know nothing about. How do you know you won't be catching a tiger by the tail? **1981** W. H. Hallahan *Trade* iii. 79 It was done. They were all riding the tiger now.

b. ***to put a tiger in one's tank*** [after an Esso Petroleum Co. advertising campaign of 1965]: to invest one with energy or 'go'; also in similar allusive phrases.

1965 *Guardian* 31 May 4/7 Esso's tiger has pounced on to the national consciousness within two months. The phrase 'Put a tiger in your tank' has become part of everyday conversation. **1967** *Listener* 22 June 835/2 Westin and Friedman are young men with ideas of their own... They are the tigers in the Ford [Foundation] tank. **1973** P. Geddes *Ottawa Allegation* iii. 32 Lorimount..began pouring tea... The movements were brisk and purposeful. No safety belts worn here, they said, there's a tiger in the tank. **1981** *N.Z. Tablet* 10 June 10/4 Young girls must be made to realise that boys of the same age have a 'tiger in their tank' as far as sexual desire goes.

c. ***paper tiger***: see paper *sb.* 12.

13. *attrib.* and *Comb.* **a.** simple attrib., as ***tiger cage***, ***country***, ***-cub***, ***-drive***, ***-hunt***, ***-jungle***, ***-pit*** (pit *sb.*[1] 5), ***-skin***, ***-spring***, ***-stripe***, ***trap***; objective and obj. genitive, as ***tiger-hunting***, ***-shooting*** sb. and adj., ***-slayer***.

1763 J. Bell *Trav. from St. Petersburg* xi. 162 There appeared two troops of Tartars, clothed in coats of tiger-skins. **1800** *Misc. Tr.* in *Asiat. Ann. Reg.* 343/1 Jackets, turbans, and handkerchiefs, marked with the *bubberee*, or tyger stripe... The tyger stripe was the royal mark, and was peculiar to Tippoo and his family. **1815** Scott *Guy M.* xxv, He had..ridden a-tiger-hunting upon an elephant with the Nabob of Arcot. **1848** tr. *Hoffmeister's Trav. Ceylon*, etc. vii. 244 We remained for several days, on account of a tiger-hunt. **1859** Lang *Wand. India* 358 He had enough of tiger-shooting in that one tiger. **1865** Sir T. Seaton *Fr. Cadet to Colonel* II. 26 There was no tiger-jungle within thirty miles of the spot. **1886** Kipling *Departm. Ditties*, etc. (1899) 56 A pet tiger-cub in wreaths of rhubarb leaves, symbolical of India under medical treatment. **1895** *Daily News* 27 Nov. 6/3 At Shrovetide, 1509,..Princess Mary, afterwards Queen, wore a black mask as an Ethiopian queen, and a little jacket of tigerskin. **1906** *Macm. Mag.* Aug. 778 The spears showed that a tiger-drive was contemplated, for across each, some eighteen inches below the point, a little piece of wood was lashed on at right angles to the shaft. **1931** E. A. Robertson *Four Frightened People* v. 178 This was tiger country, she knew, but she had never yet seen one of those animals. **1934** M. Mitchell *Warning to Wantons* x. 324 They were like two big game-hunters whose elaborate tiger-trap has netted..a domestic cat! **1936** T. S. Eliot *Coll. Poems 1909–35* 153 The tiger in the tiger-pit Is not more irritable than I. **1970** *Daily Progress* (Charlottesville, Va.) 8 July 5A/3 Harkin said more than 200 men, crammed three to five in 86 5-by-8-foot tiger pits in one building, were unable to stand because they had been there so long. **1970** *Guardian* 8 July 1 (*caption*) Political prisoners peering up out of a 'tiger cage' in Con Son prison in South Vietnam. **1978** 'M. M. Kaye' *Far Pavilions* xxv. 369 Biju Ram would only have had to wait until they were in tiger country—preferably..where there was known to be a man-eater. **1980** N. Freeling *Castang's City* viii. 47 She was extremely sharp. One kept falling..into tiger traps full of pointed bamboo stakes. One got little out of her. **1982** *Times* 28 Sept. 3/4 (*caption*) An apprentice animal trainer, in the tiger cage with six Bengal tigers.

b. (*a*) passing into *adj.* 'tiger-like, tigerish', as ***tiger despair***, ***fury***, ***joy***, ***spasm***, ***thirst***; (*b*) 'distinguished by or marked with the figure of a tiger (or tiger's head)', as ***tiger gun***, ***soldier***.

1800 *Chron.* in *Asiat. Ann. Reg.* 150/1 Tippoo's Tiger grenadiers..are met by a party of the 73d regt. *Ibid.*, A severe conflict is maintained with the leader of the Tiger men by a serjeant of the Highlanders. **1827–39** De Quincey *Murder* Wks. 1862 IV. 64 The impression of his natural tiger character. **1842** *Penny Cycl.* XXIV. 440/1 The tiger soldiers of Hyder Ali and Tippoo Saib were among the choicest of their troops. **1845** Stocqueler *Handbk. Brit. India* (1854) 288 The arsenal, the gate of which is flanked by two of Tippoo's brass tiger guns, the muzzle representing the open mouth of that animal. **1856** Mrs. H. O'B. Conant *Eng. Bible* xix. (1881) 144 To foster..that tiger thirst for blood. **1885** Tennyson *Anc. Sage* in *Tiresias*, etc. 61 The tiger spasms tear his chest. **1910** *Westm. Gaz.* 22 Mar. 5/2 The ideal Othello, played with a perfect mastery of all the modes of expressing tiger fury and tiger despair.

c. parasynthetic, instrumental, similative, etc., as ***tiger-footed***, ***-hearted***, ***-looking***, ***-marked***, ***-passioned***, ***-proof***, ***-striped*** adjs. See also tiger-like.

1597 Beard *Theatre God's Judgem.* (1612) 220 The poore old man thus cruelly handled..departed comfortlesse from his Tygre-minded sonne. **1607** Shaks. *Cor.* iii. i. 312 This Tiger-footed-rage..will (too late) Tye Leaden pounds too's heeles. **1616** R. Niccols *Overbury's Vision* in *Harl. Misc.* (Malh.) III. 350 Such monsters were my tyger-hearted foes. **1752** Sir J. Hill *Hist. Anim.* 153 The tyger-spotted Porcellana. **1796** Charlotte Smith *Marchmont* I. 205 This tiger-looking man..was..an Attorney. **1820** Keats *Hyperion* ii. 68 Now tiger-passion'd, lion-thoughted, wroth. **1835** J. Duncan *Beetles* (Nat. Libr.) 92 The tiger-marked boa, his tail fixed to the trunk of a tree,..lies in ambush on the bank. **1892** *Daily News* 7 June 5/4 Lofty and tiger-proof night shelters for travellers. **1896** *Ibid.* 13 July 7/2 Pansies, bronzed, tiger-striped, and deep purple.

14. a. Special combs.; chiefly names of animals and plants with tiger-like markings: † **tiger-babb** [? bob *sb.*[1] 9], a parasite infesting the pear tree: = sense 5; **tiger barb**, any of several brightly coloured freshwater fishes of the genus *Barbus*, esp. *B. tetrazona*; **tiger-beetle**, any species of the family *Cicindelidæ*, characterized by variegated colouring, activity, and voracity; **tiger-bird**, (*a*) a South American scansorial barbet: = thick-head 2 b; (*b*) = *tiger-bittern*; **tiger-bittern**, a South American bittern of the genus *Tigrosoma*, with striped plumage; **tiger-chop**, a species of fig-marigold, *Mesembryanthemum tigrinum*, the toothed leaf of which suggests a 'chop' or jaw: cf. *cat-chop* (cat *sb.*[1] 18); **tiger-civet**, a name for the linsang: see quot.; **tiger-cowrie**, a white cowrie, *Cypræa tigris*, with brown spots; **tiger-dog**, a dog resembling a tiger (cf. sense 2); *spec.* the striped carriage-dog; **tiger-eye** = *tiger's-eye*: see b; **tiger-finch**, a name of the Amadavat, *Estrilda amandava*; **tiger-fish**, a large fresh-water fish of South-east Africa; **tiger-flower**, any plant or species of *Tigridia*, a genus of tropical American bulbous plants bearing large purple, yellow, or white spotted flowers; esp. *T. Pavonia* (also *Peacock* or *Mexican tiger-flower*, *tiger-iris*, *flower of Tigris*) with brilliant orange blooms; **tiger-foot** = *tiger's-foot* (see b); **tiger-frog**, the leopard-frog or shad-frog (*Rana halecina* or *virescens*) of N. America; **tiger-grass (palm)**, a dwarf fan-palm, *Nannorhops* (*Chamærops*) *Ritchieana*, of Western India and Persia; **tiger-hound**: see quot., and cf. *tiger-dog*; **tiger-hunter**, one who hunts the tiger; also, a gambler (*U.S. slang*: cf. sense 9 a); **tiger-iris**, see *tiger-flower*; **tiger-lily**, a tall garden lily, *Lilium tigrinum*, with bell-like orange flowers marked with black or purplish spots; also called ***tiger-spotted lily***; **tiger maple** *N. Amer.*, a kind of maple-wood with strongly contrasting light and dark lines in the grain; **Tiger Milk**, a name given to Yugoslavian dessert wine made from over-ripe grapes; **tiger-mosquito**, any striped or banded mosquito of the genus *Stegomyia*; **tiger-moth**, a moth of the family *Arctiidæ*, esp. the British species *Arctia caja*, a large scarlet and brown moth spotted and streaked with white; **tiger-mouth** (also *tiger's-mouth*), a local name for the Snapdragon, Foxglove, and various species of Toad-flax; **tiger-nut**, the edible rhizome of *Cyperus esculentus*, used locally as food, also eaten locally as a sweetmeat by children, and also medicinally; the rush-nut; **tiger-owl**, the tawny or brown owl; **tiger-party**, a tiger-shooting party; **tiger prawn** *Austral.*, a large prawn marked with dark bands, *Penæus esculentus*; **tiger-python**, the Indian python; **tiger salamander**, a name for the large western salamander, *Ambystoma tigrinum* (*Cent. Dict. Supp.* 1909); **tiger-shark**, a name for various voracious sharks, as *Galeocerdo maculatus* of warm seas, *Stegostoma tigrinum* of the Indian Ocean; in New Zealand, the Porbeagle, *Lamna cornubica*; **tiger-shell** = *tiger-cowrie*; **tiger-snake**, (*a*) a venomous Australian snake, of the elapid genus *Notechis*, esp. *N. scutatus*; in Tasmania also called *carpet-snake*; (*b*) a slightly venomous southern African colubrid snake of the genus *Telescopus*, esp. *T. semiannulatus*; **tiger-spider**, a large American burrowing spider, *Lycosa tigrina*, the legs of which are ringed with grey and black; † **tiger-stone**: see quot.; **tiger-stripe(d)** = tiger-cat d; **tiger suit**, a striped combat uniform worn as camouflage in jungle warfare; **tiger-swallowtail**, a large North American butterfly, having yellow wings striped with black; the turnus; † **tiger-table**: see quot.; **tiger-ware**, sixteenth- or seventeenth-century German stoneware with a mottled brown glaze, or English stoneware made in imitation of this; **tiger-wolf**, (*a*) the Spotted Hyena (*Hyæna crocuta*); (*b*) = sense 2 c(*a*) (Ogilvie, 1882); **tiger-wood**, a streaked black and brown cabinet-maker's wood: = itaka-wood; also, a variety of citron-wood. See also tiger-cat.

1693 Evelyn *De la Quint. Compl. Gard.* I. 81 The Persecution of the *Tyger-babbs [Fr. *tigres*] keeps the Pears too far off from the Assistance of Wall-trees. **1951** R. Dutta *Right Way to keep Pet Fish* xviii. 155/2 *Tiger barbs. **1962** *Listener* 22 Nov. 852/2, I brought home a tiger barb, round and flat with bold orange and black stripes. **1976** *Norwich Mercury* 19 Nov. 4/8 (Advt.), This week's Fish Centre offers: Neons..Silvertips..Tiger-barbs. **1826** Kirby & Sp. *Entomol.* III. xxx. 152 That beautiful *tiger-beetle, the *Cicindela campestris* L., not uncommon on warm sunny banks. **1835** J. Duncan *Beetles* (Nat. Libr.) 115 The majority are variegated with spots and streaks of yellow. Their rapacity and agile movements have procured for them the name of Tiger-beetles. **1869** A. R. Wallace *Malay Archip.* I. 409 One beautiful group of insects, the tiger-beetles. **1817** Waterton *Wand. S. Amer.* ii. (1825) 136 The small *Tiger-bird... The throat, and part of the head, are a bright red; the breast and belly have black spots on a yellow ground. **1879** J. G. Wood *Explan. Index* ibid. (1882) 474 The Tiger-Bird utters its cry in the early morning and late in the evening. **1785** Latham *Gen. Synopsis* V. 63 *Tiger Bittern..the plumage deep rufous, marked with black, like the skin of a tiger..inhabits Cayenne, Surinam, and other parts of South America. **1894** Lydekker *Royal Nat. Hist.* I. 456 On account of their striking and handsome coloration, the name of *tiger-civets has been suggested for these animals [the Linsangs]. **1839** J. Pye Smith *Script. & Geol.* 408 A well-known species is on almost every mantel-piece, the *tiger-cowry. **1682** Creech *Lucretius* (1683) 90 The *Tyger-dog will flie pursuing Deer. **1883** R. Groom *Gt. Dane* 8 The name Tiger Dog, as used in Germany, was applied to those specimens with patches and spots of black upon a white ground. **1891** *Cent. Dict.*, *Tiger-eye. **1896** Chester *Dict. Names Min.*, *Tiger-eye*, a popular name for a siliceous pseudomorph after crocidolite, in allusion to its yellow-brown colour and chatoyant lustre. **1900** *Feathered World* 28 Sept. 399 The common Avadavat is the *Tiger-finch... Brown and reddish copper, spotted with white. **1893** Selous *Trav. S.E. Africa* 303 Burnett.. caught a fine *tiger-fish. **1894** *Sat. Rev.* 24 Nov. 563/1 In fly-fishing..the chief quarry, the 'tiger-fish', ran to 8½ lbs., and afforded nearly as good sport as salmon. **1797** *Encycl. Brit.* (ed. 3) XI. 671/2 A beautiful flower called the *tyger-flower, with three red pointed petals, the middle part mixed with white and yellow. **1845–50** Mrs. Lincoln *Lect. Bot.* 175 The Mexican tiger-flower, genus Tigridia, is a splendid plant of this order [*Iridaceæ*]. **1888** *Nicholson's Dict. Gard.*, *Tigridia*, Mexican Tiger Flower; Tiger Iris. This genus includes about seven species of..bulbous plants, from Mexico, Central America, Peru, and Chili... *T. pavonia*.. Flower of Tigris; Peacock Tiger Flower. **1836** Smart, **Tiger-foot* (a plant). **1884** Miller *Plant-n.*, Palm, *Tiger-grass, *Chamærops Ritchieana*. **1891** *Cent. Dict.*, *Tiger-grass*, a dwarf fan-palm, *Nannorhops Ritchieana*, of western India, extending into Persia. **1880** Lewis & Short, *Tigris* ii. 2, The name of the spotted *tiger-hound of Actæon. **1896** Lillard *Poker Stories* iii. 87 The unsophisticated young *tiger hunter had something on his mind. **1824** Miss Mitford *Village* Ser. i. (1863) 40 Those fierce and warlike flowers the *tiger-lilies. [**1952** J. Downs *Amer. Furnit.* p. xxxii,[In] Queen Anne maple furniture..the curly figure is produced by fibers which develop spirally, without any known reason, giving a tiger-stripe pattern much prized by collectors.] **1961** Webster, *Tiger maple. **1967** *Canad. Antiques Collector* Apr. 4/1 (Advt.), Canadian Tiger maple desk,..circa 1830. **1978** *Times* 13 Mar. 20/4 Another American Chippendale piece was a tiger maple desk and bookcase. **1961** *Guardian* 21 Nov. 16/5 Yugoslavia is now exporting..'*Tiger Milk',..an excellent dessert wine. **1977** T. Heald *Just Desserts* vii. 172 Not just claret..but.. Tigermilk (or Ranina Radgona Spatlese). **1835** Marryat *Olla Podr.* v, No one can have an idea how hard the *tiger-musquito can bite. **1816** Kirby & Sp. *Entomol.* xxi. (1818) II. 226 The caterpillar of the great *tiger-moth (*Bombyx Caja*, F.). **1864–5** Wood *Homes without H.* xiv. (1868) 286 The well known Tiger Moth whose scarlet, white, and brown robes are so familiar. **1886** Britten & Holland *Eng. Plant-n.*, **Tiger*, or *Tiger's Mouth*. **1887** Moloney *Forestry W. Afr.* 72 The *tiger nut, the tuber of the *Cyperus esculentus*, is well known in West Africa. **1927** W. E. Collinson *Contemp. Eng.* 18 Bull's eyes.., acid drops, fondants..are still in demand, though the popularity of monkey-nuts and tigernuts has somewhat waned. **1957** J. Kirkup *Only Child* ix. 122 We knew..the illicit joy of spending our Sunday school collection money on 'tiger-nuts' and coconut ice. **1972** *Country Life* 30 Nov. 1481/3 The sort of boy who would..find such delight in munching tiger nuts. **1864** Trevelyan *Compet. Wallah* (1866) 133 An account of our *tiger-party in Nepaul. **1893** J. D. Ogilby *Edible Fishes & Crustaceans N.S.W.* 203 This is the '*Tiger Prawn' of the Sydney fishermen. **1952** W. J. Dakin *Austral. Seashores* xv. 176 The tiger-prawn is a large northern species that..has dark vertical bands on its body. **1978** O. White *Silent Reach* vi. 72 It could be arranged..for a marine biologist..to complete his thesis on the breeding habits of..the tiger prawn. **1926** J. K. Strecker in J. F. Dobie *Rainbow in Morning* (1965) 63 In the plains region of Western Texas, the large *tiger salamander is a common animal. **1966** R. C. Stebbins *Field Guide Western Reptiles & Amphibians* 33 Tiger salamander... A large stocky salamander with small eyes. **1784–5** *Ann. Reg.* 241 The squalus or true *tyger shark,..well known to our seamen in the West Indies. **1898** Morris *Austral Eng.* s.v. *Shark*, Tiger Shark (N.S.W.), *Galeocerdo rayneri*... New Zealand. .. Tiger Shark, *Scymnus spinosus* (Maori name, *Mako*). **1753** Chambers *Cycl. Supp.*, **Tiger-shell*, the English name of the red voluta, with large white spots. **1869** *Tiger-snake [see *brown-banded snake* s.v. brown *a.* 7]. **1874** Beveridge *Loot Life* 50 [He] eyed me as a tiger snake The bull-frog or the fieldmouse eyes. **1890** *Science Gossip* XXVI. 37/2 The tiger-snake reaches the length of eight, or occasionally even ten feet. **1907** *Westm. Gaz.* 25 Sept. 12/1 The venom of the tiger-snake is fourteen times more deadly than that of the black snake. **1910** F. W. Fitzsimons *Snakes S. Afr.* iii. 54 Tiger Snake... Average length 2 feet to 2 feet 6 inches. **1941** K. Tennant *Battlers* xviii. 193 The driver of the car..very efficiently despatched a large tiger snake. **1947** J. Stevenson-Hamilton *Wild Life S. Afr.* xxxvi. 330 The tiger snake..is a yellowish snake spotted with brown. **1966** *Southerly* XXVI. 109 A fisherman had been bitten by a tigersnake there and had died. **1974** *Stand. Encycl. S. Afr.* X. 504/1 Tiger-snake..is conspicuously marked throughout its length with alternate black and yellow to reddish brown cross-bands. **1829** *Glover's Hist. Derby* I. 94 Fluor with barytes, commonly called *tiger-stone, being opaque, and full of dirty brown spots. **1977** *Time* 31 Oct. 49/1 His tabby—a *tiger-stripe he calls Dr. Carleton P. Forbes—has amassed $3,000 worth of 'cat toys' by filching checks from Steve's mailbox. **1981** P. Mallory *Killing Matter* ii. 23 The cat..was a big grey tiger-stripe. **1965** F. Manolson *C is for Cat* 187 A striped cat (even if it's the result of the mating of a *Tiger striped with a Tabby striped) is either one or the other. **1970** A. Marin *Rise with Wind* xx. 241 The soldier was dressed in a *tiger suit. **1977** M. Herr *Dispatches* (1978) 5 [He] took his pills by the fistful, downs from the left pocket of his tiger suit and ups from the right. **1601** Holland *Pliny* (1634) I. 395 The wood curleth in and out along the graine, and therefore such bee named Tigrinæ (*i.* *Tigre-tables). **1874** C. Schreiber *Jrnl.* (1911) I. 325 A grand old cruche of *Tiger Ware, with Royal Arms of England, and date 1604. **1928** *Daily Express* 5 June 4 There are few [objects] which exercise a stronger fascination over collectors than old stone wine jugs known as tiger-ware. High prices—up to £1,500—have been paid for these 'stone pottes garnished with sylver'. **1983** *Country Life* 1 Dec. (Suppl.) 85/1 A rare Elizabeth I Norwich Tigerware jug. **1731** Medley *Kolben's Cape G. Hope* II. 108 The Lion, Tiger, and Leopard are bitter enemies to the *Tiger-Wolf. **1838** *Penny Cycl.* XII. 369/1 The Spotted Hyæna, or Tiger-Wolf of the [South African] colonists. **1858** Simmonds *Dict. Trade*, **Tiger-wood*, a valuable wood for cabinet making,.. obtained in Guiana. **1866** [see itaka-wood].

b. Combs. with *tiger's*: **tiger's-claw**, (*a*) a weapon for secret attack used by the Mahrattas, consisting of short sharp curved steel blades fixed to a plate or strap which is secured to the palm of the hand; (*b*) in *Mech.* a boring or rifling rod in which the cutting tool is automatically sheathed as it enters the bore and expands on the cutting stroke; **tiger's-eye**, popular name for (*a*) a yellowish brown quartz wth brilliant lustre, used as a gem (also called *tiger-eye*): see crocidolite; (*b*) a crystalline pottery glaze, with auriferous reflections (*U.S.*); **tiger's-foot**, a convolvulaceous plant, *Ipomœa Pes-tigridis*, common in India, with hairy palmate leaves; **tiger's horn, tiger's tooth**, old names for species of *Strombus* or wing-shell; **tiger's milk**, (*a*) an acrid white juice of *Excœcaria Agallocha*, a small euphorbiaceous East Indian tree; (*b*) gin (*slang*); (*c*) = *Tiger Milk*, sense 14 a above; **tiger's mouth** = *tiger-mouth* (see 14 a).

1891 *Cent. Dict.*, *Tiger's claw, *Tiger's-eye. **1896** Chester *Dict. Names Min.*, *Tiger's eye*, same as tiger-eye. **1893** E. A. Barber *Pottery & Porcelain U.S.* xiii. 290 The highest achievements in glazing are the so-called tiger's-eye and gold-stone, which glisten in the light with a beautiful auriferous sheen. **1828–32** Webster, *Tiger's-foot (citing Lee). **1713** Petiver *Aquat. Anim. Amboinæ* Tab. iv, *Strombus*..Brown *Tygers Horn. **1850** R. G. Cumming *Hunter's Life S. Afr.* (1902) 9/1 A fountain of *tiger's milk had started in the stern of the waggon. **1959** W. James *Word-bk. Wine* 155 *Ranina*, the 'Tiger's Milk' wine of Radgona, in Yugoslavia, a sweet and strong dessert wine made from late-gathered grapes. **1965** O. A. Mendelsohn *Dict. Drink & Drinking* 277 *Ranina*, Yugoslavian (Radgona) dessert wine. Syn. 'Tiger's Milk'. **1886** *Tiger's Mouth [see *tiger-mouth* in 14]. **1713** Petiver *Aquat. Anim. Amboinæ* Tab. v, *Strombus*..Thick *Tygers-tooth.

Hence (*nonce-wds.*) †**tige'rantic** *a.* [? after *elephantic*] = tigerish 1; **tige'rette**, a diminutive she-tiger, a 'cat'; **'tigerling**, a young or diminutive tiger; **tige'rocious** *a.* [*nonce-wd.* after *ferocious*], = tigerish 1.

a **1704** T. Brown *Lett. fr. Dead* Wks. 1720 II. 216 In what Sheeps-head Ordinary have you chew'd away the meridian Altitude of your Tygerantick Stomach? **1858** Mrs. Gore *Heckington* xxxi, Miss Corbet, on whom the tamed tigerling [a small boy] was now lavishing his endearments. **1874** F. W. Newman in Davies *Heterodox Lond.* II. 311 He is dietetically, neither swinish nor tigerocious. **1906** *Daily Chron.* 23 Aug. 5/7 Amongst the tigeresses who devour, and the tigerettes who scheme, you will not find a woman who can claim to have passed through a public school and university training.

tiger ('taɪgə(r)), *v.* [f. the sb.] **1.** To act, behave, or walk to and fro, like a tiger. *nonce-wd.*

1898 Ménie M. Dowie *Crook of Bough* 52 He finished his cigar by tigering on the platform, his hands behind him, his head turning from side to side.

2. *trans.* To mark like a tiger with lines or streaks of contrasting colour.

1930 R. Campbell *Adamastor* 50 Striped with the fiery colours of the sky, Tigered with war-paint..The green waves charged the sunrise. **1934** —— *Broken Record* iii. 74 She [*sc.* a dog] was tigered with wounds from head to tail. **1960** T. Hughes *Lupercal* 56 Pike, three inches long, perfect Pike in all parts, green tigering the gold.

Hence **'tigered** *ppl. a.*, striped or broken into stripes; **'tigering** *vbl. sb.*, a striated condition (see quot. 1961).

1961 R. D. Baker *Essent. Path.* xiv. 344 The yellowness of the heart muscle may be diffuse or concentrated in narrow stripes forming a peculiar and distinctive pattern especially along the papillary muscles and the inside of the ventricles. .. This striated appearance has suggested the descriptive designation of 'tigering' or 'thrush breast'. **1969** *Burpee Catal.* 50/2 *Calceolaria*... Many [flowers] are attractively tigered, blotched, spotted and laced in most unique patterns. **1980** J. O'Faolain *No Country for Young Men* ix. 197 Tigered light which fell slantwise through a Venetian blind.

'tiger-,cat. **a.** A name for any of the feline beasts of moderate or small size which resemble the tiger in their markings or otherwise; including the Margay, Ocelot, Serval, etc. (In Zool. Society's *List* applied to two species: see quot. 1896.) Also *fig.*

1699 Dampier *Voy.* II. ii. 62 The Beasts of Prey that are bred in this Country are Tigre-Cats, and..Lions. The Tigre-Cat is about the bigness of a Bull-Dog. **1774** Goldsm. *Nat. Hist.* III. vii. 255 Descending to animals..still smaller, we find the Catamountain, which is the Ocelot of Mr. Buffon, or the Tiger Cat of most of those who exhibit it as a show. **1785** G. Forster tr. *Sparrman's Voy. Cape G.H.* (1786) II. 80 An opportunity of seeing an amorous combat between two tiger-cats. **1842** *Penny Cycl.* XXIV. 440/2 Tiger-Cats. Under this title may be classed all those lesser striped and spotted Asiatic, African, and American Cats which do not come under the well-understood denominations of Tigers, Leopards, and Panthers. **1863** M. Braddon *Aurora Floyd* II. v. 112, I should get nothing—but my revenge upon a tiger-cat. **1871** Kingsley *At Last* xi, No jaguar or tiger-cat..would care to meddle with anything so exquisitely nasty. **1896** *List Anim. Zool. Soc.* 58 *Felis planiceps*.., Rusty Tiger Cat. *Hab.* Malacca... *Felis chrysothrix*.., Red Tiger Cat. *Hab.* Gold Coast, West Africa. **1907** *Daily Chron.* 19 Feb. 7/4 The dusky African tiger cat, a new animal about the size of a leopard. **1959** *Times* 7 Jan. 13/5 Whether as a tiger-cat, a hard-headed business woman..her command of the character was superb. **1979** P. Alexander *Show me a Hero* xx. 208 If she's a trained resistance girl she'll be a tiger-cat.

b. In Australasia applied to two carnivorous marsupials, *Dasyurus viverrinus* and *D. maculatus*.

1832 J. Bischoff *Van Diemen's Land* ii. 52 The skins of the..opossum, tiger-cat, and platypus..are exported. **1852** R. C. Gunn *Papers & Proc. Roy. Soc. Van Diemen's L.* II. 11 (Morris) *Dasyurus maculatus*..the Spotted Martin... 'Tiger Cat' of the Colonists of Tasmania,..distinguished from *D. viverrinus*, the 'Native Cat' of the Colonists, by its superior size.

c. Applied to a hybrid between the domestic cat and the wild cat (*F. catus*) (*Cent. Dict.* 1891).

d. = *tabby cat* s.v. tabby *a.* 2, esp. a tabby cat with vertical stripes in its markings.

1903 F. Simpson *Bk. of Cat* xix. 216/1 The term 'tiger cat' is, I believe, often used in America, and it well describes the true type of a brown tabby. **1915** *Century Mag.* Sept. 673/2 She has..a nice purry tiger cat asleep on a braided rug. **1939** I. M. Mellen *Pract. Cat Bk.* i. 4 The striped tabby or tiger cat..is the most ancient type of cat known to science. **1969** R. Lowell *Notebk. 1967–68* 52 A first tiger cat stationed on the record-player spies on a second.

tigerhood ('taɪgəhʊd). [f. tiger + -hood.] The state or condition of being a tiger (in any sense); in quot. 1846, the post of boy-groom (see tiger 6).

1846 Mrs. Gore *Eng. Char.* (1852) 118 Advantages attached to the tigerhood of his establishment. **1871** Blackie *Four Phases* i. 34 The true humanity of man as distinguished from tigerhood and spiderhood. **1885** Hornaday *2 Yrs. in Jungle* xiv. 159 A splendid specimen every way, just in the prime of tiger-hood.

tigerine, variant of tigrine.

tigerish ('taɪgərɪʃ), *a.* Also 6–7 **tygrish**, 6, 9 **tigrish**. [f. tiger *sb.* + -ish[1].]

1. Like, or like that of, a tiger; *esp.* of the nature or having the qualities of the tiger; cruel, bloodthirsty, fierce, relentless.

1573 L. Lloyd *Marrow of Hist.* (1653) 265 Her cruel and Tigrish heart. *a* **1586** Sidney *Arcadia* (1622) 467 Were thy eyes so stonie, thy breast so tygrish? **1604** Earl Stirling *Aurora* xci, And with my ashes glut thy Tygrish heart. **1846** *Blackw. Mag.* LIX. 406 [Their] craving for possession is treacherous and tigerish. **1887** Miss E. Money *Lit. Dutch Maid.* (1888) 95 A wild-cat skin with handsome tigerish stripes. **1909** *Daily Chron.* 18 Feb. 7/4 There are many predatory and tigerish plants, of which the sundew is a notable example.

b. Loud, flashy: cf. tiger *sb.* 7.

1831 [see 3]. **1836** *New Monthly Mag.* XLVIII. 458 Whatever deviates from the unique standard of gentlemen's dressing is tigerish. **1853** Lytton *My Novel* vi. xx, Nothing could be more vagrant,..and, to use a slang word, *tigrish*, than his whole air.

2. Abounding in or infested with tigers.

1819 *Sporting Mag.* IV. 175 They had crossed again Firoze's canal, which appeared very tigerish. **1851** *Fraser's Mag.* XLIV. 19 Through the thickest and most tigerish section of the jungle.

3. *Comb.*, as ***tigerish-looking***.

1831 *Society* I. 48 A tigerish looking man planted himself where he could very rudely stare at Miss Delamere.

Hence **'tigerishly** *adv.*, **'tigerishness**.

1869 *Daily News* 12 June, A well-known plunger, whose attendant tiger is a miracle of tigerishness. **1879** J. Todhunter *Alcestis* 125 This sudden flood of fearful rapture, which Tugs my heart tigerishly.

tigerism ('taɪgərɪz(ə)m). [f. tiger *sb.* + -ism.]

1. The qualities or characteristics of a 'tiger' (tiger *sb.* 7); vulgar ostentation or affectation; pretentiousness, 'side', 'swagger'. ? *Obs.*

1836 *New Monthly Mag.* XLVIII. 455 We have the neologismal appellatives, 'tiger', and 'tigerism',—words of great intensity and signification, without which it would be impossible to get on for 'one calendar day' in genteel society. **1863** R. H. Gronow *Remin.* II. 144 All his imitators fell between the Scylla and Charybdis of tigerism and charlatanism. **1868** Lever *Bramleighs* I. x. 137 His lordship now placed his hat on his head, slightly on one side. It was the 'tigerism' of a past period.

2. The condition and functions of a 'tiger' or juvenile groom (tiger *sb.* 6).

1846 Mrs. Gore *Eng. Char.* (1852) 117 The nature and attributes of tigerism, however, as set forth by the gallant captain, were far from unsatisfactory.

tigerkin ('taɪgəkɪn). [f. as prec. + -kin.] A diminutive tiger; a tiger-cub; also, a cat.

1849 Lytton *Caxtons* xiv. ii, It is only from the attic that you can appreciate the picturesque which belongs to our domesticated tigerkin! **1867** *Lond. Rev.* 26 Jan. 116/2 The tigerkin whose claws are not grown and whose habits are.. playful.

'tiger-like, *adj.* and *adv.* [f. as prec. + -like.]

A. *adj.* Like, or like that of, a tiger; tigerish.

1577–87 Holinshed *Chron.* I. 126/1 Which is more than tigerlike crueltie. **1828** Sewell *Oxf. Prize Ess.* 40 Tyger-like thirst for blood. **1905** *Westm. Gaz.* 28 Jan. 4/2 In colour and markings the wild cat is very tiger-like.

B. *adv.* In a tigerish manner.

1576 Gascoigne *Philomene* cxxxi. (Arb.) 107 (Tygrelike) she toke The little boy. **1587** Turberv. *Trag. T.* (1837) 67 The tyrants mother Calvia, tygreleeke, Procurde her plagues. **1850** R. G. Cumming *Hunter's Life S. Afr.* (1902) 142/2 My eye fixed tiger-like upon him.

tigerly ('taɪgəlɪ), *a. rare.* [f. as prec. + -ly[1].] Tiger-like, tigerish.

1633 D. Dyke in Spurgeon *Treas. Dav.* Ps. xciv. 12 Tigerly and tyrannical persecutors. **1648** *King's Gracious Messages for Peace* 39 They are not ashamed..to appropriate unto him their own Tigerly dispositions. **1855** *Chamb. Jrnl.* IV. 289 You might mollify the heart of the most tigerly disposed of the human race.

So †**'tigerness** *Obs.*, tigerishness, ferocity.

1535 Stewart *Cron. Scot.* (Rolls) I. 91 He changit syne.. To tigirnes and greit tiranitie.

†**'tigerous**, *a. Obs. rare.* Also 6 tigrous. [f. as prec. + -ous.] = tigerish. Hence †**'tigerously** *adv. Obs. rare*$^{-1}$.

1532 W. Walter tr. *Guistard & Sisimond* (1597) B ij, Yet thought her not soe tigrous and cruell. **1698** [R. Fergusson] *View Eccles.* 117 He hath Tygerously fallen upon the Dead and Endeavoured to Blacken their Memory.

tigery ('taɪgərɪ), *a. rare*$^{-1}$. [f. as prec. + -y.] Tigerish, tiger-like.

1859 *All Year Round* No. 36. 218 The Tchirgee..is of a choleric and rather tigery nature.

tigger ('tɪgə(r)). [f. tig *v.*[1] + -er[1].] One who 'tigs' or touches; the pursuer in the game of 'tig'.

1893 E. L. Wakeman in *Columbus* (Ohio) *Dispatch* 19 Oct., This impedes the tigger's running.

tiggy ('tɪgɪ). [Perh. rel. to dial. *tig* little pig (*Eng. Dial. Dict.*)] = hedgehog 1.

[**1905** B. Potter *Tale Mrs. Tiggy-winkle* 85 Mrs. Tiggy-winkle was nothing but a Hedgehog!] **1938** T. H. White

Sword in Stone xxi. 303 Us be'nt no common tiggy Mëaster, for to be munched and mumbled.

tigh, tighe, tiȝe, obs. forms of TYE, TIE *sb.*

tigh-hee, tighie, obs. forms of TEE-HEE *int.*

† **tight, tyht**, *sb.*[1] *Obs.* Forms: 1–4 **tyht** (1 **tiht**), 3 **tuht** (ü). [OE. *tyht* m. (with change of gender) = OS. *tuht* (MLG., MDu., LG., Du. *tucht*), OHG., MHG. *zuht* (G. *zucht*), Goth. **tauhts* in *ustauhts* completion:—OTeut. **tuhti*[z] fem., f. **tuh*, weak grade of verb-stem **teuh* (see TEE *v.*[1], and -T *suffix*[3] a).]

1. The action of drawing, draught; going, marching, march, course, way. Only OE.

a **800** CYNEWULF *Elene* 53 Werod wæs on tyhte. *a* **850** *Phœnix* 525 Fyr bið on tihte, æleð uncyste.

2. Bringing up, rearing, training, education; (good) breeding; behaviour.

c **888** K. ÆLFRED *Boeth.* viii, Ic ðe ȝeongne..me to bearne ȝenom, & to minum tyhtum ȝetyde... þu me wære..leof ..ær þon þe ðu cuðe minne tyht & mine þeawas. *a* **1240** *Sawles Warde* in *Cott. Hom.* 247 For þat is þeaw in euch stude ant tuht forte halden. *c* **1330** R. BRUNNE *Chron. Wace* (Rolls) 9307 What for laughynge & oþer tyhtes, What for presentes & oþer delites [*v.r.* sightes], þe Erl perceyued..þe kyng [Uther] louede his wyf Igerne.

tight, *sb.*[2]: see TIGHT *a.* 13; also TIGHTS.

tight (taɪt), *a.* (*adv.*) Forms: 5–6 **tyght**, 6– *Sc.* **ticht, tycht**, 5– **tight** (also *erron.* 7–8 **tite, tyte**). [App. an altered form of THIGHT, with which in its early literal senses it was synonymous. *Tonne-tight* and *tonne-thight* occur together in *Rolls of Parlt.* 1379: see sense 14. The change from *thight* to *tight* was perh. due to the influence of native words from the **teuh*, **tauh*-, **tuh*- verbal system: see TEE *v.*[1], and cf. TAUT *a.*, TIGHT *v.*[1], and *ticht* pa. pple. of TIE *v.*]

A. *adj.* † **1. a.** Dense, as a wood or thicket; = THIGHT 1; superseded by *thick* (THICK *a.* 4) *Obs. rare*[−1].

c **1435** *Torr. Portugal* 589 Hys squyer Rod all nyght In a wod, that wase full tyght.

† **b.** Close or compact in texture or consistency, as a solid body or substance; dense, solid; = THIGHT 3. *Obs. rare.*

1513 DOUGLAS *Æneis* IX. ii. 64 The wyld wolf..Abowt the bowght, plet all of wandis tyght, Bayis and gyrnis. **1677** GREW *Anat. Fruits* v. §18 The Outer Part..is softer and more succulent; the Inner a tite and strong Membrane. *a* **1728** [implied in TIGHTNESS 1]. **1797** *Encycl. Brit.* (ed. 3) XVII. 424/1 Construct a block of as tight wood as possible.

2. Of such close texture or construction as to be impervious to a fluid, etc. **a.** as the second element in combinations, as ***water-, wind-, air-, gas-, oil-, light-tight***, the first element denoting that which the vessel keeps in or out.

1507 *Rec. St. Mary at Hill* 23 Yat they..y[e] said tenement ..shall kepe, repaire and mayntene, wynd tyght, water tyght. **1760** [see AIR-TIGHT]. **1831** Gas-tight [see GAS *sb.*[1] 6]. **1896** *Pop. Sci. Jrnl.* L. 267 The human mind is not built in thought-tight compartments. **1905** *Westm. Gaz.* 11 Mar. 14/2 Untoned prints should be kept under close pressure in a light-tight and air-tight box.

b. as simple word.

(See also *tight barrel, cask, cooper*, etc. in C. 3.)

[**1501**: see THIGHT 4.] **1661** [see d]. **1669** BOYLE *Contn. New Exp.* I. xxxvii, The Nose of a pair of Bellows that are Tite enough is well stopt. **1749** BERKELEY *Word to Wise* Wks. III. 443 A tight house, warm apparel, and wholesome food. **1856** OLMSTED *Slave States* 2, I have faith that there is a tight roof above the very much cracked ceiling. **1857** MILLER *Elem. Chem.* (1862) III. 144 A portion of bread was enclosed in a tight case, to prevent loss of water by evaporation.

c. *esp.* Of a ship: Water-tight; well caulked and pitched; not leaky. Cf. THIGHT 4.

1568 *Satir. Poems Reform.* xlvi. 4 Quhat pylett takis my schip in chairge, Mon hald hir clynlie, trym, and ticht. **1596** SHAKS. *Tam. Shr.* II. i. 381 Two Galliasses And twelue tite Gallies. **1615** BP. HALL *Contempl.*, *O.T.* XI. iii, As some tight vessel that holds out against wind and water, so did Ruth against all the powers of a mother's persuasions. **1704** J. HARRIS *Lex. Techn.* I, *Tite*, the Seamen say a Ship is Tight, or Tite, when she is so staunch as to let in but very little Water. **1747** *Gentl. Mag.* 170 The pitch being put in very hot will..make the ship as tight as a bottle. *a* **1826** A. CUNNINGHAM *Wet Sheet & Flowing Sea* ii, The good ship tight and free.

d. *transf.* and *fig.* leading to 3. Uncommunicative; secret; *spec. Oil Industry*, applied to a well about which little information is released.

1661 FELTHAM *Resolves* II. xxix. 240 They are not tyte enough to trust with a secret. **1730** in J. Copywell *Shrubs Parnassus* (1760) 130 Old Chaucer and Drayton I found in good plight, And Shakespear and Spencer appear pretty tight. **17..** C. DIBDIN *Song, The Island* i, O, 'tis a snug little island! A right little, tight little island! **1809** MALKIN *Gil Blas* VII. i. ⁋5 He is a tight vessel, well armed and manned. **1817** COBBETT *Wks.* VI. 31 A Sinecure, which you have secured for your Son,..who is (if all remains tight) to enjoy it for his life after your death. **1865** DICKENS *Mut. Fr.* I. viii, Mr. Boffin's notions of a tight will. **1949** *Amer. Speech* XXIV. 34 If information about the *venture* is withheld from the public, then it becomes a *tight well*. **1966** *Natural Resources Jrnl.* (Univ. New Mexico) VI. 55 If the draining well is what is commonly known in the industry as a 'tight hole', the information concerning its performance is probably more closely guarded than most national defense secrets. **1976** M. MACHLIN *Pipeline* ii. 32 'Who knows about this [*sc.* an oil-strike]?' 'Nobody but me and a couple of guys here on the platform know for sure... Communication is lousy here, but rumour travels faster than radio waves.' 'Okay. Shut it off..and see if you can keep it as tight a hole as possible.' **1977** B. FREEMANTLE *Charlie Muffin* v. 59 The British..[have] gone completely silent... The British Embassy is tighter than the Kremlin itself.

3. *fig.* of a person, expressing somewhat indefinite commendation: Competent, capable, able, skilful; alert, smart; lively, vigorous, stout; also in ironical use: cf. FINE *a.* 12 c. *Obs.* exc. *dial.*

1598 [implied in TIGHTLY 1]. **1606** SHAKS. *Ant. & Cl.* IV. iv. 16 Thou fumblest Eros, and my Queenes a Squire More tight at this then thou. **1653** R. BAILLIE *Dissuas. Vind.* (1655) Pref., That reverent, famous, most able, and tight writer. **1735** BRACKEN *Burdon's Pocket Farrier* 81 *note*, The less Physick the better, provided your Judgment's tite. **1822** SCOTT *Pirate* xl, He..swore..that if he had a thousand daughters, so tight a lad, and so true a friend, should have the choice of them. *a* **1825** FORBY *Voc. E. Anglia*, *Tight*,.. prompt; active; alert. 'A tight fellow!' **1829** MARRYAT *F. Mildmay* ii, I'll pay you off for this, my tight fellow. **1851** HAWTHORNE *Ho. Sev. Gables* xiii, It will take a tighter workman than I am to keep the spirits out of the seven gables. **1891** WRENCH *Winchester Word-bk.*, *Tight*, fast, hard. A tight bowler, etc.

4. a. Neat in appearance; neatly and carefully dressed; trim, tidy, smart; also, Of a neat compact build, well-made, shapely. *arch.* or *dial.* Cf. TAUT *a.* 2 b.

1697 DAMPIER *Voy. round World* (1699) 11 They wear good Cloaths, and take delight to go neat and tight. **1706–7** FARQUHAR *Beaux Strat.* I. i, But you look so bright, And are dress'd so tight. **1712** ARBUTHNOT *John Bull* III. ii, Though the girl was a tight clever wench, as any was. **1721** RAMSAY *Bessy Bell*, etc. iii, She blooming, tight, and tall is. **1821** SCOTT *Kenilw.* iii, There thou stand'st in thy velvet waistcoat, as tight a girl as England's sun shines on. *c* **1830** MRS. SHERWOOD *Houlston Tracts* III. No. 81. 2, I was tight and smart in my own person; so that, as the neighbours used to say, every thing looked well upon me. **1886** M. K. MACMILLAN *Dagonet the Jester* 8 The tightest and cleanliest lads in the village.

b. Of things: Neatly arranged or constructed; tidy, neat, snug, compact. Now *dial.*

1720 RAMSAY *Edinburgh's Salut.* v, Than I, nor Paris, nor Madrid, Nor Rome, I trow's mair able To busk you up a better bed, Or trim a tighter table. **1725** T. THOMAS in *Portland Papers* VI. (Hist. MSS. Comm.) 126 Improved grounds..with tight, low, new farm houses. *c* **1813** MRS. SHERWOOD *Stories Ch. Catech.* xvi. 139 Sarah was contented with the coarsest gown..if it were but clean and tight. **1831** J. OGILVIE in *Aberdeen Mag.* Dec. 638 His wordy wife.. Hauds a' thing tight about the house.

5. Firmly fixed or bound in its place; strongly attached or secured; not easily moved; also *fig.* faithful, steadfast, constant.

1513 DOUGLAS *Æneis* III. viii. 52 Our fallowis fangis in thair salis tycht [*Vela legunt socii*]. **1687** A. LOVELL tr. *Thevenot's Trav.* I. 23 To gird it about with great bars of Iron to keep it tight, and hinder it from falling. **1690** C. NESSE *O. & N. Test.* I. 153 His faith..kept him all along tight, steady and constant. **1715** DESAGULIERS *Fires Impr.* 129 You may fix it without any trouble, and be sure that it is tight. **1902** MABEL BARNES-GRUNDY *Thames Camp* 202, I pulled and strained, but it was as tight as wax.

b. On terms of close friendship, intimate. Cf. THICK *a.* (*sb.*) 10. *U.S. slang.*

1956 B. HOLIDAY *Lady sings Blues* (1973) ii. 23 Blue..had me busted... He and Bub were real tight with the cops. **1971** *Current Slang* (Univ. S. Dakota) VI. 10 *Tight*, very much in love; very friendly. 'John and Mary were really tight for awhile but they seem to have drifted apart.' **1977** *Rolling Stone* 5 May 55/1, I was very tight with him for a long time.

6. a. Drawn or stretched so as to be tense; not loose or slack: said of a rope, etc., or of a surface; = TAUT *a.* 1, 2.

1576 FLEMING *Panopl. Epist.* 256 (Like vnto a bowe) sometimes bent very tight, and sometimes againe made slack for the nones. **1589** PEELE *Tale Troy* 256 Away they flye, their tackling teft [*ed.* 1604 toft] and tight. **1703** DAMPIER *Voy.* III. 19 When the Rope is hal'd tight. **1800** COLERIDGE *Christabel* II. 49 That (so it seem'd) her girded vests Grew tight beneath her heaving breasts. **1846** BRITTAN tr. *Malgaigne's Man. Oper. Surg.* 39 The knots ought to be tight enough to hold in apposition the edges of the wound; but not so tight as to cut the skin when the inflammation comes on, and the parts swell. **1857** HUGHES *Tom Brown* I. iv, Tom has eaten..and imbibed coffee, till his little skin is as tight as a drum. **1885** *Law Rep.* 15 *Q.B. Div.* 360 The belt ..was passed over the drums..and drawn tight.

b. *fig.* Strict, stringent; severe.

1872 BAGEHOT *Physics & Pol.* (1876) 37 The efficacy of the tight early polity and the strict early law. **1884** STORRS *Div. Orig. Chr.* v. 152 The larger moral power won by woman, by degrees made the tightest legal restrictions loose and elastic. **1887** *Poor Nellie* (1888) 294 Every boy wants a good tight hand over him.

c. Of an organization or group: strict, disciplined, well co-ordinated; *spec.* of a pop group or an individual member of it.

1968 L. DEIGHTON *Only when I Larf* vi. 80, I ran a tight unit, and if that meant repeating my lecture every week, then I'd do that. **1971** *Melody Maker* 9 Oct. 21/3 Keef can be proud of his [jazz-rock] band... It's well rehearsed, tight and above all fun. **1977** *Ibid.* 26 Mar. 46/6 (Advt.), Wanted. Good tight drummer for funky group. **1980** MOTSON & ROWLINSON *European Cup 1955–80* ix. 190 This tight triumvirate, Smith in the boardroom, Robinson at the administrative helm, and Paisley on the training ground, headed an Anfield staff which worked as efficiently..as the team.

7. Drunk; tipsy. Cf. SCREWED *ppl. a.* 6. *slang.*

1830 [implied at TIGHTISH *a.* 3]. **1840** in *Amer. Speech* (1951) XXVI. 184 After supper I got tight, sick with oysters, and slept. **1853** *Household Words* 24 Sept. 75/2 For the one word drunk, besides the authorised synonyms tipsy, inebriated, intoxicated, I find of unauthorised or slang equivalents..thirty-two, viz.: in liquor,..half-seas-over, far-gone, tight [etc.]. **1860** LEVER *One of Them* II. 151 (Flügel) He was very 'tight', as we call it..far gone in liquor, I mean. **1868** —— *Bramleighs* xxiv. II. 46 'No, sir, not a bit tipsy', said Harding, interpreting his glance; 'not even what Mr. Cutbill calls "tight"!' **1882** SALA *Amer. Revis.* (1885) 269 By the time they reached their hotel [they] were quite 'tight'.

8. a. Of a garment, etc.: Fitting closely, tight-fitting; often = *too tight*, closely fitting because not large enough. ***a tight fit***, a garment, etc. which fits tightly; hence *transf.* (*colloq.*).

1779 COOK *Voy. Pacific* VI. vii. (1784) III. 377 A pair of tight trowsers, or long breeches, of leather. **1831** *Examiner* 11/2 It's rather a tight fit. **1840** DICKENS *Barn. Rudge* vi, A very particular gentleman with exceedingly tight boots on. **1867** TROLLOPE *Chron. Barset* xxxv, A wedding-ring growing always tighter as I grow fatter and older. **1872** *Punch* 15 June 250/2 A tight uniform is so bad a thing for the soldier.

b. Of ground: allowing (vehicles) little room for manœuvre. Of a turn, curve, etc.: having a short radius.

1937 *Sun* (Baltimore) 20 Apr. 4/2 He expressed a hope the airport work would be completed as rapidly as possible, pointing out that Logan Field was 'rather tight' for large transports. **1947** A. C. DOUGLAS *Gliding & Advanced Soaring* i. 24 He based this opinion on the belief..that they [*sc.* contemporary airplanes] could not be turned in tight circles like the birds. **1958** *Times* 19 Feb. 5/4 She [*sc.* an aircraft] started to turn to starboard, and it seemed clear that the turn became tighter and tighter. **1969** *Times* 23 May 1/3 The L.M. was due to spend about an hour in a tight orbit approaching within eight nautical miles of the surface. **1979** *Beautiful Brit. Columbia* Fall 19/1 The highway narrows down to one lane which clings in tight curves around a sheer mountainside.

c. Applied to persons: tough, hard, unyielding; also, aggressive, 'stroppy'. *U.S. dial.* or *slang.*

1928 R. FISHER *Walls of Jericho* 306 *Tight*, tough; redoubtable; hard. **1950** PATTERSON & CONRAD *Scottsboro Boy* I. iii. 30 'You'll get it [*sc.* a bath] Saturday,' he said. Saturday came and he put me off... I got tight with him. 'I got to have a bath!' *Ibid.* 31, I was a tight guy who would not show people tears, but I felt the water behind my lids. *Ibid.* II. vii. 129 There were guys there [*sc.* in a prison], they made reputations for themselves as tight guys and killers just from defending themselves against the insane. **1960** L. BUCKLEY *Hiporama of Classics* 16 He was a hard, tight, tough Cat.

9. Difficult to deal with or manage; hard, severe, 'tough', 'stiff'; esp. in phr. ***a tight place, corner, squeeze***, etc., a position of difficulty. *colloq.*

1764 FOOTE *Mayor of G.* II. Wks. 1799 I. 180 Is Lady Barbara's work pretty tight? **1772** NUGENT tr. *Hist. Fr. Gerund* I. 10 This question of yours is a tight one. **1852** TOWNSHEND (of Ohio) in *House Repr.* 23 June (Thornton), I felt myself in a tight spot. **1855** HALIBURTON *Nat. & Hum. Nat.* xvi. II. 121 It's a tight squeeze sometimes to scrouge between a lie and a truth in business. **1864** *Daily Tel.* 26 Sept., When they find they are getting into a tight place—to borrow an Americanism—[they] gather up their gold, and run off. **1889** GRETTON *Memory's Harkb.* 80 We were subjected to a very tight examination; for the prize was one of considerable value. **1891** *Daily News* 14 Nov. 2/3 [It] would suffice to drive the Bears of Russian stock into a tight corner.

10. *colloq.* or *tech.* **a.** Said of a contest in which the combatants are evenly matched; close; so of a bargain: with little margin of profit. *orig. U.S.*

1828 WEBSTER s.v., A tight bargain. **1848** BARTLETT *Dict. Amer.*, *Tight match*, a close or even match, as of two persons wrestling or running together. **1903** *Westm. Gaz.* 1 Sept. 3/1 The tighter the match the better he plays.

b. Of a person: Unwilling to part with money, close-fisted; **c.** *Finance*, Of money: Difficult to obtain except on high terms; also *transf.* of the money-market when money is scarce. Of a person: in financial straits, hard up (*dial.* or *slang*).

1805 LEWIS & CLARK *Orig. Jrnls. Lewis & Clark Exped.* (1904) III. 278 They are tite Deelers, value Blu and white beeds very highly, and sell their roots also highly. **1828** WEBSTER s.v., A man tight in his dealings. **1846–7** MRS. WHITCHER *Widow Bedott Papers* 30 (Bartlett) The Deacon was as tight as the skin on his back; begrudged folk their victuals when they came to his house. **1846** *Daily News* 21 Jan. 4/6 In Paris money is 'tight' also, and discounts difficult. **1859** HOTTEN *Dict. Slang* 109 *Tight*,..hard up, short of cash. **1864** J. S. LE FANU *Uncle Silas* II. xvi. 247 It is a hard case, Miss, a lad o' spirit should be kept so tight. I havn't a shilling. **1866** CRUMP *Banking* vii. 152 A tight money market will force sales, and make purchasers.. reluctant to buy. **1868** LEVER *Bramleighs* xvi. I. 219 Money was 'tight' being the text of all he said. **1892** 'T. COBBLEIGH' *Gentleman Upcott's Daughter* ix. 173 Any man might find himself tight—temporarily.

d. *Journalism.* (See quot. 1970.) Hence also of (a day of) restricted newspaper space.

1927 *Amer. Speech* II. 241/2 If advertising crowds out news, the paper is said to be 'tight'; if advertising is scant, the paper is 'wide open'. **1927** *New Republic* 12 Oct. 202/1 Possibly space was 'tight' that day, and the newspapers didn't have room for this minor angle of the story. **1928** *Amer. Speech* IV. 135 The 'desk' must know whether 'room' is 'tight', 'fair', 'good' or 'wide open'. If news is 'heavy' on a 'tight day' and is permitted to 'run' in length practically as written, 'oversets'..may result. **1970** R. K. KENT *Lang. Journalism* 133 *Tight.* 1. designating a newspaper that has little room for news because there is a great deal of advertising: opposite of *open*. 2. designating a newspaper on a day when there are a great many newsworthy events to record, and hardly enough space to cover them all.

11. a. Closely packed (cf. TIGHTEN *v.* 1 b). Of a group or formation: having the individual members positioned close together. Freq. in *Sport*; also *transf.* (esp. in *Cricket*), that allows the opposition little chance to score, etc.: ***tight bowling, fielding***, etc.

1856 KANE *Arct. Expl.* I. xxiv. 313 For thirty-five miles south the straits are absolutely tight [i.e. with ice]. **1942** *R.A.F. Jrnl.* 13 June 22 They lived in dread of our fighters, and normally kept a tight formation. **1961** F. C. AVIS *Sportsman's Gloss.* 138/2 *Tight field*, the fieldsmen when drawn closely round the wicket, so preventing the easy scoring of runs. **1961** *Times* 12 May 4/1 Surrey's bid for quick runs.. was foiled by tight bowling. **1965** *Daily Express* 13 Aug. 15/5 *Tight position*, an area of the field in which there are a large number of players, both attacking and defending. **1968** I. URE *Ure's Truly* xvii. 116 Let's have expressions such as 'a steady defence' rather than a side being described as 'tight at the back'. **1976** *Milton Keynes Express* 11 June 41/5 Farnham Royal found it difficult to score against the tight Wolverton bowling. **1977** *Arab Times* 13 Dec. 9/6 Tight fielding by the Airlines prevented easy scoring and the FSC batsmen had to rely on quick singles and doubles.

b. Of language: Terse, concise, condensed. Also in general, of literary, artistic, or intellectual work: kept within strict limits; pared to essentials; disciplined, taut, not loose or diffuse.

1870 SWINBURNE *Ess. & Stud.* (1875) 85 The highest form of ballad.. must condense the large loose fluency of romantic tale-telling into tight and intense brevity. **1958** C. A. LARSON *Who: Sixty Yrs. Amer. Eminence* 75 Quaint little items and details were often inserted in these early biographical sketches which would scarcely survive the tight editing of a modern Marquis editor. **1962** [see PILOT *sb.* 1 f]. **1979** *Sci. Amer.* Aug. 24/1 The author.. seeks the answer in this small book of tight argument.

c. *Art slang.* Lacking freedom or breadth of treatment; cramped.

1891 SPIELMAN in *Contemp. Rev.* July 60 It [Tenniel's art in 1850] is certainly 'tighter': it is younger. **1902** *Encycl. Brit.* XXVII. 252/1 In his first style [Corot] painted traditionally and 'tight'—that is to say, with minute exactness, clear outlines, and with absolute definition of objects throughout. **1905** *Q. Rev.* July 234 His style, if a little what artists call 'tight', has the rare gift of being entirely lucid in the expression of subtleties.

d. Of the edge of a saw: Compressed by hammering (*Cent. Dict.* 1891).

e. Of a schedule or timetable: packed with engagements, leaving little free time. Also applied to a space of time which is limited or restricted.

1959 J. POPE-HENNESSY *Queen Mary* III. ii. 386 Princess May concentrated on seeing as many of the wonders and beauties of the spacious old Imperial city as she could crowd into four days and a tight social schedule. **1968** P. G. HOLLOWELL *Lorry Driver* ii. 31 The older drivers are constantly aware that schedules are getting tighter. **1971** J. SANGSTER *Your Friendly Neighbourhood Death Pedlar* vii. 187 It was unlikely that anything would happen that night, and the following morning was going to be awfully tight for time. **1972** M. CRICHTON *Terminal Man* I. v. 42 'I can't see her to-day,' Morris said, 'and to-morrow is tight.' **1976** *New Yorker* 1 Mar. 30/3 'How about seven at O'Hoolihan's?' I'm going there with Pat and Betsy.' 'Seven's a little tight.' **1981** P. HARCOURT *Turn of Traitors* ix. 82 Time's going to be tight, so take my car.

12. *Billiards. slang.* (*a*) Said of balls when they are in contact: 'fast', 'frozen'. (*b*) Of pockets: Having a small opening compared with the diameter of the balls.

1909 in *Cent. Dict. Supp.*

13. The adjective used absolutely. (See also TIGHTS.) **a.** *Rugby Football* = SCRIMMAGE *sb.* 4.

1904 *Westm. Gaz.* 19 Nov. 15/1 The forwards are strong and hard workers in the tight, but in the loose are slow and cumbersome... Both in the tight and loose they must remember to watch and follow the ball. **1905** *Daily Chron.* 1 Nov. 9/5 They have shown little dash in the open and no skill in the tight. **1939** *Daily Tel.* 18 Dec. 11/1 They were better served by their forwards in the tight. **1979** *Times* 12 Dec. 9/1 They outscrummaged their opponents in the tight.

b. An awkward situation, predicament, 'tight corner' (TIGHT *a.* 9). Usu. in phr. ***in a tight***; occas. const. *for*. *U.S. dial.* or *colloq.*

1896 in *Dialect Notes* (1916) IV. 348 *Tight*, n. (From *tight place*.) A difficult or precarious position. **1902** W. N. HARBEN *Abner Daniel* xxi. 182 It would tempt five men out of ten if they were inclined to go wrong, and were in a tight. **1930** W. FAULKNER *As I lay Dying* 29, I tell him again I will help him out if he gets into a tight, with her sick and all. **1938** M. K. RAWLINGS *Yearling* xv. 177 Jody's in a tight for a name for the new Baxter. **1950** PATTERSON & CONRAD *Scottsboro Boy* II. xi. 175 'You scared that man almost to death.' 'I was in a tight jam then, Warden. I was trying to get out of a tight.' **1979** G. SWARTHOUT *Skeletons* 18 Pat Garrett.. had said of him in public: 'I would rather have Wood with me in a tight than any man I know.'

†**14.** Formerly (14th–17th c.) appended to *ton, pipe, hogshead, dolium*, as measures of capacity, originally and especially stating the number of tons burden (*i.e.* the tonnage) of a ship; also as an equivalent weight of stones, gravel, salt, etc. See also TON, TONNAGE, TUN.

[**1894** C. N. ROBINSON *Brit. Fleet* 217 The unit of ship measurement, both in England and on the continent, at the time [of Henry VII], was, as heretofore, the tun cask of wine, and the stated tons or tuns burthen of a ship meant the number of tuns or butts of wine she could carry. Warships' tonnage was estimated by roughly comparing their bulk with merchant-ships of known carrying capacity.]

1379 *Rolls of Parlt.* III. 63/2 Pur prendre de chescun nief & craier, de quele portage q'il soit, qe passe par la mier dedeinz le dite Admiralte alant & retournant, par le voiage de chescun tonne-tight vj d... Item, de prendre de chescun vesseau pessoner, qe pessent sur la mier du dit Admiralte entour Harang, de quele portage q'il soit, en un simaigne de chescun tonne-tight, VI d... en troiz simaignes de chescun tonne-thight, VI d. **1410** in *Proc. Privy Council* (1834) I. 327 La somme des gages & regardz des gens darmes archers conestables & marins deinz especifiez, ovesque le tonnetyght samontent par un q^art.. viij^ml ccxlj. li. xviij. s. vjd. **1427–9** *Rolls of Parlt.* IV. 365/1 To have Lettres Patentz.. for to take and resceyve of every Vessell ladon of .. C tonnetite VIII d, and of every Vessell of lesse tite IIII d. *Ibid* [French version], P[re]ndre & avoir de chacun Nief del portage de.. C tonelx.. VIII d., & de chacun autre Vessell de meyndre portage.. IIII d. **1428–9** *Rec. St. Mary at Hill* 70 For a tonne tyght of northerin ston for þe new chirche porche.. vijs viijd. *a* **1483** *Liber Niger* in *Househ. Ord.* (1790) 74 The kinge hathe it intytled by his prerogative to have of every shippe from xx dol' tyght before the mast & behynd to have ii dol' wyne; and soe of every shippe tyll he come to the tyght of ccc dol'; then the kinge hath before and behynd of every such shippe iiii dol' wyne. **1495** *Naval Accts. Hen. VII* (1896) 154 Payed.. for ccccl xviij ton tyght of.. Stones vij*li.* xvj*s.* As for c iiij^xx vj ton tyght of gravell xxiiij*s.* vj*d.* **1497** *Ibid.* 186 For the hyre of hys bote conteynyng vij Tonne Tight. *Ibid.* 228 A pipe Tyghte yron price xl*s.* &.. for a hoggeshed Tyghte yron price—xx*s.* *a* **1500** in Arnolde *Chron.* (1811) 127 A crane sufficient and able to take vp from the water of the Thamis the weight of a tonne tight. **1504** *Sel. Cas. Crt. Star Chamber* (Selden) 212 Of & for eny ton or ton tyght of marchaundis conteigned in the same vessellesvj d. **1603** OWEN *Pembrokeshire* (1892) 139 In bargayninge by the toone yt requireth that yt be expressed what nomber of barrells the toonne shalbe of, ffor of late yeares.. toonne tight, wh^ch comonly is vsed in bargaynes of freight, differreth from the toonne by measure both of corne and salte.

B. *adv.* (The adj. used adverbially.)

1. Soundly, roundly; = TIGHTLY 1. Now chiefly in colloq. phr. (***good night***) ***sleep tight***, a conventional (rhyming) formula used when parting for the night or at bedtime. Also in slang phr. ***blow me tight***: see BLOW *v.*[1] 29.

1790 J. FISHER *Poems* 61, I charg'd them tight, An' gart them pay o' lawing clink, Mair than was right. **1898** *Elizabeth & German Garden* 29 She had been so tight asleep. **1933** E. O'NEILL *Ah, Wilderness!* III. ii. 101 Good night, Son. Sleep tight. **1957** [see NIGHTY-NIGHT *int.*]. **1960** D. LESSING *In Pursuit of English* iii. 99 When we left him, she patted his shoulder with triumphant patronage, and said: 'Sleep tight. And keep your dreams clean.' **1976** 'R. BOYLE' *Cry Rape* xxi. 94 Goodnight, Anne. Sleep tight.

2. a. Firmly, closely, securely; so as not to allow any movement: = TIGHTLY 3.

1680 MOXON *Mech. Exerc.* xii. 208 You may without more ado screw up your Work tight. **1768** TUCKER *Lt. Nat.* (1834) I. 194 The prospect of getting a livelihood holds them tight to their work. **1838** DICKENS *Nich. Nick.* liii, Holding tight on with both hands. **1878** T. L. CUYLER *Pointed Papers* 206 The tighter I clung the safer I felt.

b. ***to sit tight***, †to apply oneself closely *to* (*obs.*); to maintain one's position firmly in reference to something; also, to sit close, to remain under cover. *colloq.*

1738 *Lond. Mag.* 131 Andromache and all the great Ladies 3000 Years ago, sat very tight to their Stitching. **1890** G. B. SHAW in *Star* 27 Nov. 2/7 I, therefore, again urge Mr Parnell to 'sit tight'. **1897** VIOLET HUNT *Unkist, Unkind* xiv, 'Sit tight!' she exclaimed, pinching my arm violently. She always talks slang when she is excited. **1898** *Daily News* 10 Feb. 3/2 No money is forthcoming, and banks sit tight. **1909** *Athenæum* 20 Mar. 345/3 Is not 'Sit tight' the watchword of constitutionalism?

3. With close constriction or pressure; closely, tensely; = TIGHTLY 2.

1818 SCOTT *Rob Roy* xxxii, A horse-girth buckled tight behind him. **1853** LANDOR *Imag. Conv., Hare & L.* Wks. 1891 IV. 423 He whose dress sits tight upon him.

4. ***as tight as*** ——: as quickly or rapidly as ——. Cf. TITE *adv. U.S. dial.*

1833 S. SMITH *Life & Writings J. Downing* lix. 200 The President shook hands with all his might an hour or two until he couldn't hardly stand it... I.. stood behind him and reached my arm round under his, and shook for him for about a half an hour as tight as I could spring. **1867** W. L. GOSS *Soldier's Story of his Captivity* 185 Captain Sherman ..was making for Macon as 'tight as he can come'. **1884** 'MARK TWAIN' *Huck. Finn* xix. 180 A couple of men were tearen up the path as tight as they could foot it.

5. Close *up to, after*, or *on*. *dial.* or *colloq.*

1886 F. T. ELWORTHY *W. Somerset Word-bk.* 756 The bitch was tight arter'n. **1901** *Century Mag.* May 123/1 They was tight up t'me all the way. **1919** J. C. SNAITH *Love Lane* xxx. 160 He lived to be tight on ninety.

C. Combinations.

1. Adjectival, as ***tight-belted*** (having a tight belt), ***-bodied, -booted, -hosed, -limbed, -skinned, -skirted, -sleeved, -waisted*** adjs; cf. TIGHT-LIPPED *a.* (Sometimes not clearly distinguishable from next.)

1767 S. PATERSON *Another Trav.* I. 315 Their habit is entirely white.. and being tight-bodied, gives them the appearance of a company of millers in their holiday-cloaths. **1836** T. HOOK *G. Gurney* v, Perhaps a tight-skinned sailor walking his way to town from Portsmouth. **1859** G. MEREDITH *R. Feverel* ii, The boy was.. not so tight-limbed and well-set. **1896** HOWELLS *Impressions & Exp.* 73 She wore a tight-skirted black walking-dress. **1896** EDITH THOMPSON in *Monthly Packet* Christmas No. 80 Tight-booted and tight-belted in correct Continental military style.

2. Adverbial, as ***tight-bound*** (= tightly bound), ***-closed, -draped, -drawn, -fitting, -looking, -made, -packed, -pressed, -rooted, -shut, -stretched*** adjs.; ***tight-reining*** sb.; ***tight-clasp, -tie*** verbs. See also TIGHT-LACED, etc.

1801 MAR. EDGEWORTH *Angelina* ii, She was hospitably received by a tight-looking woman. **1819** KEATS *Ode Melancholy* i, Go not to Lethe, neither twist Wolf's bane, tight-rooted, for its poisonous wine. **1832** *Scoreby Farm Rep.* 8 in *Libr. Usef. Knowl., Husb.* III, A large and tight-bound sheaf will require to stand two days longer than a small one. **1844** DICKENS *Mart. Chuz.* v, I did not think you were half such a tight-made fellow! **1846** E. A. POE in *Godey's Lady's Bk.* Nov. 216/1 He had on a tight-fitting parti-striped dress. **1860** READE *Cloister & H.* (1861) I. 20 Clad in a pair of tight-fitting buckskin hose. **1865** DICKENS *Mut. Fr.* IV. vii, With the palms of his hands tight-clasping his hot temples. **1879** BROWNING *Ivan Ivanovitch* 166 I'll.. tight-tie you with the strings Here of my heart! **1884** YATES *Recoll.* ii. (Tauchn.) 80 After tight-reining and regular hours. **1896** A. PALMER in *Academy* 25 Jan. 80/3 It is strange how the tight-stretched tambourine can be called *molle*. **1905** *Daily Chron.* 21 Oct. 5/2 Strong men stood with tight-drawn lips. **1918** G. FRANKAU *One of Them* xxix. 223 Tight-packed as, face to tail and tail to face, Bristle in Watson's tins the silvery 'Skippers'. **1950** PARTRIDGE *Slang To-day & Yesterday* (ed. 3) III. iii. 257 The ten-page, tight-packed chapter entitled 'War Words' in Collinson's Contemporary English.

3. Special combs.: **tight back** *Bookbinding*, a book cover which is stuck directly on to the spine; cf. *fast back, fastback*, s.v. FAST *a.* 11; **tight barrel** or **cask**, a barrel for liquids; also called *wet barrel* or *cask*; cf. SLACK *a.* 10; so **tight cooper** (see quot.); **tight-corking** (*Angling*), a method of float-fishing in which the line (with the float or cork) is kept taut between the point of the rod and the plummet at the bottom; **tight end** *N. Amer. Football*, an offensive end (END *sb.* 3 g) who lines up close to the tackle; the position occupied by this player; **tight-fisted** *a.*, parsimonious, close-fisted; hence **tight-fistedness**; **tight head** *Rugby Football*, (the position of) the prop forward supporting the hooker on the opposite side of the scrum from the loose head; ***to win a tight head*** = ***to win the ball against the head*** (see HEAD *sb.* 26 c); **tight-jeff**: see JEFF; **tight junction** *Cytology*, a specialized connection of two adjacent animal cell membranes such that the space usually lying between them is absent; **tight-lock** *dial.* (see quot.); **tight shop**, a cooperage where *tight work* is done; **tight work** (see quot.).

1913 *Funk's Stand. Dict.* II. 2518/1 **Tight back* (Bookbinding), a back that clings to the signatures or to the paster attached to them: distinguished from *loose back* or *spring back*. **1929** A. J. VAUGHAN *Mod. Bookbinding* I. 2 (*caption*) A limp paper book bound with a tight back. Effect of a tight back binding upon stiff paper. **1957** E. A. CLOUGH *Bookbinding for Librarians* vi. 60 Because the tight back bends with the spine of the book, there is a tendency for the tooling on the spine to crack. **1884** KNIGHT *Dict. Mech.* Suppl., *Slack Barrel*, one for flour, sugar, cement, fruit, and what not, of a dry character. In contradistinction to *tight barrel. **1759** ELLIS in *Phil. Trans.* LI. 209 This was put into a *tight cask. **1877** *Encycl. Brit.* VI. 338 Tight or wet and dry or slack cask manufacture. **1889** *Cent. Dict.* s.v. *Cooper, Wet* or **tight cooper*, a cooper who makes casks for liquids. **1867** F. FRANCIS *Angling* i. (1880) 59 **Tight-corking* is using a heavyish float well shotted and plumbed some two feet two deep. **1963** HUFF & SMITH *Defensive Football* vi. 72 When playing the *tight end head to head, the linebacker must be aware [etc.]. **1972** J. MOSEDALE *Football* ii. 29 With Fears spread out on one side and Shaw in close, the 'three end offense' was born. Today the positions are called split end, tight end and flanker. **1978** J. IRVING *World according to Garp* viii. 162 A standout tight end for the Philadelphia Eagles. **1844** DICKENS *Christmas Carol* i, He was a *tight-fisted hand at the grindstone. **1975** *Church Times* 25 Apr. 2/3 Let it be seen.. that we have asked the very necessary questions about the liberality or *tight-fistedness of the [European] Community's policy on trade with the under-developed countries. **1959** *N.Z. Listener* 28 Aug. 7 You can't afford to give *tight heads in your own 25 when you've got fast backs like that against you. **1960** V. JENKINS *Lions down Under* xiii. 170 Dawson won six tight-heads to three in the scrums. **1969** *Advanced Coaching* (Rugby Football Union) 73 On the tight head it may still be preferable to hook with the nearside foot, *but* with the body facing the *loose* head side so as to hook the ball with the *inside*.. part of the foot. **1978** *Rugby World* Apr. 17/1 There seems nothing to stop Graham Price reigning for many years to come as the world's outstanding tight-head prop. **1961** *Jrnl. Exper. Med.* CXIV. 706 The normal slits as well as the *tight junctions have structural features reminiscent of usual epithelial desmosomes. **1982** *Nature* 1 Apr. 464/1 Our evidence, which is based on direct rapid freezing of newly formed tight junctions between rat prostate epithelial cells, indicates that individual tight junction strands are pairs of inverted cylindrical micelles sandwiched between linear fusions of the external membrane leaflets of adjacent cells. *a* **1825** FORBY *Voc. E. Anglia*, **Tight-lock*, any species of coarse sedge growing in marsh ditches. So called, from its being used to bind the sheaves of beans or oats, growing very luxuriantly on such land. **1892** *Labour Commission Gloss.*, **Tight Shops*, workshops in which tight work is performed. *Ibid.* s.v. *Work*, *Tight work is a term used in the coopering industry to denote the making of casks or any vessels to hold water or liquids.

† **tight**, *v.*[1] *Obs.* Forms: 1 tyhtan, tihtan, 3 tuhten (ü), tuihten, tihhtenn (*Orm.*), 4 tyȝt. *Pa. t.* 1 tyhte,

1–3 tihte, 2–3 tuhte (ü), 4 tyȝt, tyht, 4–5 tiȝt, tight. *Pa. pple.* 1 ȝetiht, 2–3 ituht, 4 itiȝt, y-tyght, tyght, tyȝt, tiȝt, tight, *Sc.* tycht. [OE. *tyhtan* = OHG. *zuhten* (*zuhtôn*), MHG. *zühten* (G. *züchten* to breed, train):—OTeut. **tuht-jan*, denominative verb f. **tuht-*: see TIGHT *sb.*[1]]

1. *trans.* To draw, pull; = TEE *v.*[1] 1; to stretch.

a **1000** in *Anglia* XIII. 421/806 Oferbrædels..onbutan ȝetiht, *uelamen..in gyro tensum.* *a* **1240** *Ureisun* in *Cott. Hom.* 203 Þi sune was ituht on rode. **13..** *Sir Beues* (A.) 3215 Þanne was be-fore his bed itiȝt..A couertine on raile tre, For noman scholde on bed ise. **13..** *Gaw. & Gr. Knt.* 568 Fyrst a tule tapit, tyȝt ouer þe flet..þe styf mon steppez þeron. *Ibid.* 858 Tapytez tyȝt to þe woȝe, of tuly and tars, And vnder fete, on þe flet, of folȝande sute. *c* **1375** *Sc. Leg. Saints* xl. (*Ninian*) 1331 Quhene it [his curtain] vpe ves tycht, þane wist he he [had] tynt þe sycht.

2. *fig.* To draw, attract, entice, allure (*to* some action, or *to do* something); = TEE *v.*[1] 2.

c **1000** ÆLFRIC *Hom.* I. 174 On ðreo wisan bið deofles costnung: þæt is on tihtinge, on lustfullunge, on ȝeðafunge. Deofol tiht us to yfele, ac we sceolon hit onscunian. **11..** *Departing Soul's Addr. Body* 423 Þe [deofel] tuhte his hearpe ant tuhte þe to him. *Ibid.* 437 Ac efre he tuhte þe. *c* **1175** *Lamb. Hom.* 121 Þe deofel heom tuhte to þan werke. *c* **1200** ORMIN 7048 Tihhtenn & turrnenn hæþenn follc..To lefenn uppo Criste.

3. To train, discipline; = TEE *v.*[1] 3; to chastise.

a **1000** *Ags. Ps.* (Th.) xciii[i]. 12 Þe þu hine..ȝetyhtest [*quem tu erudieris*]. *a* **1225** *Ancr. R.* 184 Hwon he haueð inouh ibeaten his child, & haueð ituht hit wel. *Ibid.* 268 Tu ne schuldest nout tuhten, ne chasten þi meiden uor hire gult. *a* **1240** *Sawles Warde* in *Cott. Hom.* 267 Ah efter þat wit wule þat is husebonde tuhten ant teachen þat wit ga euer biuore.

4. *refl.* and *intr.* To betake oneself; to go, proceed, advance; = TEE *v.*[1] 6 a, b.

c **1205** LAY. 810 His horn he vastliche bleu. Iherden hit Troynisce & tuhten [*c* 1275 toȝe] to þon Gricken. *Ibid.* 27321 Ure drihten heo bi-læueð And to Mahune heo tuhteð. *a* **1300** *Cursor M.* 3157 Quen he þe sted sagh þar he tight, þe child he dide o þe ass light. *Ibid.* 20506, I sal far þar mi sun has tight. **13..** *K. Alis.* 7164 (Bodl. MS.) Þat neiȝ þe kyng hij ben ytiȝth. *c* **1330** R. BRUNNE *Chron.* (1810) 93 To hunte þer he had tight in his new forest. **13..** *E.E. Allit. P.* A. 717 Do way, let chylder vnto me tyȝt. *a* **1400–50** *Alexander* 2304 To þe temple he tight tithanndez to herken. *c* **1400** *Destr. Troy* 1358 All tight to þe tempull of þere tore goddes, For drede of the dethe.

Hence †ˈ**tighting** *vbl. sb.*, persuading, enticement.

c **1000** [see 2]. *a* **1175** *Cott. Hom.* 229 Þurh diofles tihtinge beswicen. *c* **1200** *Trin. Coll. Hom.* 29 Þat is þe defles tuihting and mislore.

†**tight**, *v.*[2] *Obs.* Forms: 4 tyȝt; *pa. t.* 4 tiȝte, tyȝte, tyȝt, tight, 5 tiȝt, tyght; *pa. pple.* 4 y-tiȝt, tiht, tyȝt, tyȝte (thit, tithte), 4–5 tiȝt, tight(e, 5 tiȝte, *Sc.* ticht. [Etymology obscure: see Note below.]

1. *trans.* To appoint, ordain, set, fix (a time, etc.); to devise, contrive; to prepare, get ready. Cf. DIGHT *v.* 2, 11, 14.

a **1300** *Cursor M.* 24344 (Edin.) To ten al tiht [*v.r.* tight] vs was þat tim Quen we na hel moht se on him. *Ibid.* 18323 (Cott.) Þat þou thoru prophet tald and tight Nu es it fulfilled be-for vr sight. *Ibid.* 11050 (Gött.) [Gabriel says to Zacharias] All þat þe is tight [*v.r.* hight] sal be-tyde. *c* **1330** R. BRUNNE *Chron. Wace* (Rolls) 5488 Atte water Hamon doun lyght, Intil a bot Hamon had tyght. **13..** *E.E. Allit. P.* A. 502 Of tyme of ȝere þe terme watz tyȝt. *Ibid.* B. 1153 Ȝif ȝe wolde tyȝt me a tom telle hit I wolde. *a* **1425** *Cursor M.* 4124 (Trin.) Þe foly þat his breþeren tiȝt. *c* **1470** *Golagros & Gaw.* 744 The renkis of the Round Tabill, That has traistly thame tight to governe that gait.

2. With *inf.* or *absol.* (rarely *refl.*): To fix it in one's mind; to determine, intend, purpose; to set oneself *to do* something.

a **1300** *Cursor M.* 1301 (Cott.) Wen þat drightim had him tight To send him þe oile þat he him hight. *c* **1300** *Havelok* 2990 Hwou the swikes haueden tiht [*MS.* thit] Reuen hem that was here riht [*MS.* rith]. **13..** *Sir Beues* (A.) 838 A stiward was wiþ king Ermin, þat hadde tiȝt to sle þat swin. **13..** *Gaw. & Gr. Knt.* 2483 Mony a-venture..þat I ne tyȝt, at þis tyme, in tale to remene. *c* **1380** *Sir Ferumb.* 729 To slen him had he tiȝte. *a* **1400** *Octouian* 1476 To brewe the Crystene mennys banys Hy hadden tyght. *c* **1475** *Songs, Carols*, etc. 85/64 Alone to be, she hath her tight. ?*a* **1500** *Chester Pl.* xi. 165 Therfore a songe, as I haue tighte,..I will shewe here in thy sighte.

3. To set, set firmly, fix, set up (an edifice), pitch (a tent). Cf. DIGHT *v.* 5, 8.

1382 WYCLIF *Judg.* xx. 33 So alle the sones of Yrael..tiȝten shiltron in the place that is clepid Baalthamar. *c* **1394** *P. Pl. Crede* 168 Wiþ tabernacles y-tiȝt to toten all abouten. *a* **1400–50** *Alexander* 1373 (Ashm.) Quen he had tiȝt vp þis tram and þis tild rerid. *c* **1420** *Anturs of Arth.* 355 Þe tasses were of topas, þat were þere to tiȝte [*v.r.* tyghte]. *c* **1440** *Bone Flor.* 377 They tyght ther pavylons in a stede. *c* **1470** *Golagros & Gaw.* 526 Ane hie toure, that tight wes full trest.

b. ? To set down in writing, to state. Cf. DIGHT *v.* 6.

13.. *E.E. Allit. P.* A. 1052 Þe hyȝe trone..With alle þe apparaylmente vmbe pyȝte, As Iohan þe apostel in termez tyȝte.

c. To set or deck *with* jewels. Cf. DIGHT *v.* 10.

c **1475** *Rauf Coilȝear* 473 Bricht braissaris of steill..Ticht ouir with Thopas, and trew lufe atanis.

[*Note.* No word answering to ME. *tihtan* appears in OE. or in the cognate langs., and its origin is a puzzle. Sense 1 corresponds closely to that of OE. *stihtan*, ME. STIGHT, 'to dispose, arrange, regulate, direct, rule'; senses 1 and 3 b correspond also to various senses of OE. *dihtan*, DIGHT *v.* Formal connexion with the latter seems impossible; derivation from the former by loss of *s*, if not impossible in such constructions as *is (s)tight*, *was (s)tight*, cannot be assumed without some direct evidence.]

tight (taɪt), *v.*[3] Also *Sc.* 6 teicht, 7 ticht. [f. TIGHT *a.*] *trans.* To make tight, in various senses.

†**a.** To make (a vessel) water-tight. *Obs.* †**b.** To stretch, tighten, brace; to draw tight, compress. *Obs.* **c.** (also *refl.*) To put in order, make tidy or neat. *dial.* Hence ˈ**tighted** *ppl. a.*

1532 *Acc. Ld. High Treas. Scot.* VI. 156 For boyingis and teichtein of the xij barrellis of aill forsaidis. **1581** MULCASTER *Positions* xvii. (1887) 76 Wrastling..tightes the sinews. **1587** J. MELVILL *Diary* (Wodrow Soc.) 255 His lessone was a tichted upe abregment of all he haid tetched the yeir bypast. **1611** COTGR., *Goudronner*..to pitch, trimme, or tight a ship. **1661** *Sc. Acts Chas. II* (1820) VII. 230/2 The said barrells to be well tichted and double girthed before the transporting thairof. **1775** S. J. PRATT *Liberal Opin.* lxxxvi. (1783) III. 138 Mr. Benjamin..had so spruced and tighted himself up, that he really looked quite interesting. **1895** *Gloss. E. Anglia* s.v., 3. = Tidy. 'Tight yourself up'.

tight, tiȝt, obs. ff. TITE; pseudo-arch. pa. t. TIE.

ˈ**tight-ass**, *sb.* (and *a.*) *slang* (orig. and chiefly *U.S.*). Also **tight-arse**. [Back-formation from next.] An inhibited or strait-laced person; occas. a stingy person, a skinflint. Freq. *attrib.* passing into *adj.* = next; occas. applied (*lit.*) to clothes: fitting tightly around the buttocks.

1969 P. ROTH *Portnoy's Complaint* 79 A really constrained and tight-ass human being. **1970** J. G. VERMANDEL *Dine with Devil* iii. 11 A well-muscled, virile-looking type with a neat little beard, who favors tight-ass pants and rather beautiful, flowing shirts. **1972** 'E. MCBAIN' *Sadie when she Died* x. 105 'Don't be such a tight-ass,' the girl said. 'I'm thirsty as hell here.' **1972** *Southerly* XXXII. 103 Jenny was very friendly but very tightarse inhibited headinnaness. **1981** M. GORDON *Company of Women* II. iv. 190 My three o'clock class was an incredible bummer. Bunch of tight asses. Tight-ass kids. **1982** J. SHERWOOD *Shot in Arm* x. 96 As though any policeman in his senses would pocket cash..with a virgin-faced tight-arse like Verney looking on.

ˈ**tight-assed**, *a. slang.* Also **tight-arsed**. [f. TIGHT *a.* + ASS, vulg. and dial. spelling of ARSE *sb.* + -ED[2]: see prec.] **a.** Of a woman: (see quot. 1903). **b.** Unwilling to relax or enjoy oneself, full of inhibitions or constraints; occas. stingy, mean.

1903 FARMER & HENLEY *Slang* VII. 126/1 *Tight-arsed*, chaste; close-legged. **1961** PARTRIDGE *Dict. Slang* 885/2 *Tight-arsed*, stingy. **1967** J. ORTON *Diary* 28 July in J. Lahr *Prick up your Ears* (1978) 16, I hate this tight-assed civilization. **1974** D. SEARS *Lark in Clear Air* iv. 50 Rough quarterings of pine that even the tight-assed mill owners considered too lean to..ship to Toronto. **1976** *Listener* 15 July 54/4 Me and Gambaccini would like tight-assed British radio to relax a bit. **1981** T. HEALD *Murder at Moose Jaw* ix. 112 I'd sooner have an entertaining shit than a tight-arsed saint.

tighten (ˈtaɪt(ə)n), *v.* [f. TIGHT *a.* + -EN[5].]

1. a. *trans.* To draw tight or tighter; to make taut or tense, to draw close; hence, to fix tightly, to make strict or rigid; to secure. Also *fig.*

1727 BAILEY vol. II, To *Tighten*, to make straight, as a Line, Cord, etc., also to dress after a tight Manner. **1755** JOHNSON, To *Tighten*, to straiten, make close. **1774** GOLDSM. *Nat. Hist.* VII. 257 The spider only wants to have one end of the line fast, in order to secure and tighten the other. **1810** SCOTT *Lady of L.* I. vi, What reins were tightened in despair. **1846** BRITTAN tr. *Malgaigne's Man. Oper. Surg.* 39 The stitches should not be tightened until all the threads are in; and the rule is, that those of the middle, or angles, should be first tightened. **1859** *Handbk. Turning* 59 If it cuts too deep, tighten the screws a little more. **1896** LADY A. KERR *Life Seb. Valfré* 232 We find him..revising and tightening-up the rules of a community.

intr. for *pass.* **1973** *Daily Tel.* 9 Feb. 2/8 Yellow line no-waiting regulations are to tighten up in London.

b. To press closely together; to pack; to compress. Also *fig.*

1845 FAIRBAIRN *Typol. Script.* (1657) I. I. ii. 49 A type so tightened and compressed as to admit of nothing but what pertained to the tabernacle worship. **1853** KANE *Grinnell Exp.* xvi. (1856) 123 A gradually increasing breeze from the E.S.E...had tightened the floes.

c. *absol.* = TIGHT-LACE *v. colloq.*

1896 *Daily News* 29 Oct. 9/5 A fellow servant..used to ask why 'she didn't tighten a little more'.

2. *intr.* To grow tight or tense; to be stretched tight or drawn close. Freq. const. *up*. Also *fig.*

1846 LANDOR *Imag. Conv., Emp. China & Tsing-Ti* Wks. 1853 II. 118/1 My skin seemed too small for them, it tightened so. **1868** ROGERS *Pol. Econ.* xi. (1876) 150 As the market tightens..the rate of discount rises. **1871** L. STEPHEN *Playgr. Eur.* vii. (1894) 158 The rope once or twice tightened unpleasantly. **1897** *Allbutt's Syst. Med.* II. 788 The radial artery is felt to tighten day by day. **1933** P. GODFREY *Back-Stage* vi. 86 As the day of the dress rehearsal draws near the acting tightens up. **1947** *Milwaukee Jrnl.* 25 Apr. 2 His stomach tightened up on him. **1959** *Listener* 2 July 24/3 We should alter the tax laws to tighten up on tax-dodging.

†**3.** *refl.* To make oneself 'tight' or tidy; cf. TIGHT *a.* 4. *Obs. rare.*

1786 MRS. A. M. BENNETT *Juvenile Indiscr.* II. 113 Her daughter was run up to tighten herself, fit, as she said, to walk with them.

Hence ˈ**tightening** *vbl. sb.* and *ppl. a.*

1846 J. NICHOLSON *Operat. Mechanic* 34 Placing the tightening roller in the position represented by the dotted lines. *Ibid.* 806 Two of the bracing chains, with their tightening shackle. **1836** W. IRVING *Astoria* I. 139 The tightening of the padding and the pressing of the head to the board is gradual. **1877** KNIGHT *Dict. Mech.*, *Tightening pulley*, one which rests against the band in order to tighten it. **1902** *Words Eyewitness* 135 Men..who would have met untold sorrow with but a tightening of the lips.

tightened (ˈtaɪt(ə)nd), *ppl. a.* [f. prec. + -ED[1].] Made or become tight; drawn tight or close; tense, stretched; firm, rigid; constricted.

1760 FAWKES tr. *Anacreon, Ode* lix. 7 With tighten'd Rein, I'll urge thee round the dusty Plain. **1810** SCOTT *Lady of L.* II. xxxvi, Malcolm did..bind..His ample plaid in tightened fold. **1833** COLERIDGE *Table-t.* 10 Aug., Like a sigh heaved up from the tightened chest of a sick man. **1880** G. MEREDITH *Tragic Com.* (1881) 291 The tightened grasp of her hand confessed her understanding of the thing she pressed to hear repeated. **1899** *Allbutt's Syst. Med.* VI. 48 The pulse may be but little changed [in angina], yet it is sometimes tightened.

tightener (ˈtaɪt(ə)nə(r)). [f. TIGHTEN *v.* + -ER[1].] One who or that which tightens.

1829 *Nat. Philos., Prelim. Treat.* 32 (U.K.S.), [In lizards] the two toes or tightners, by which the skin of the foot is pinned down. **1851** MAYHEW *Lond. Labour* I. 66 What is elegantly termed a tightner, that is to say, a most plentiful repast. **1890** *Illustr. Lond. News* 6 Sept. 298/3 A minstrel..a tightener of the strong sinews of warlike hearts! **1891** *Wheeling* 25 Feb. 402 Wrenches, spoke tighteners, and padlocks and chain; bearings, hubs, and pedals. **1895** *Standard* 21 Nov. 5/2 There is no such tightener of the purse strings as want of confidence.

†ˈ**tighter.** *Obs. rare.* [f. TIGHT *v.*[3] + -ER[1].]

1. One who makes tight the seams of ships; a caulker.

1611 COTGR., *Goildronneur*, a pitcher, trimmer, or tighter of ships. **1653** URQUHART *Rabelais* II. xxx, Julius Cæsar and Pompey were boatwrights and tighters of ships.

2. 'A ribband or string by which women straiten their clothes' (J.).

tightish (ˈtaɪtɪʃ), *a.* [f. TIGHT *a.* + -ISH[1].]

1. a. Rather tight or close-fitting.

1775 S. J. PRATT *Liberal Opin.* xcvi. (1783) III. 202 Are they [the clothes] not a little tightish? **1848** CURZON *Visits Monast.* I. v. 58 It comes up high upon the neck, and has tightish sleeves. **1893** QUILLER-COUCH *Delectable Duchy* 223 In a tightish uniform.

b. as *adv.* Somewhat tightly.

1767 J. FERGUSON *Lect., Suppl.* 31 The top goes on tightish, but must be made to turn round on the cylinder.

2. Somewhat difficult to accomplish, attain to, etc.; rather 'stiff' or difficult.

1786 MRS. A. M. BENNETT *Juvenile Indiscretions* III. 207 Amounted to a pretty tightish sum. **1801** tr. *Gabrielli's Myst. Husb.* II. 96 They have had a tightish day's work. **1832** WILSON in *Blackw. Mag.* XXXI. 859 'Tis a tightish swim across. **1890** 'BOLDREWOOD' *Col. Reformer* (1891) 418, I had a tightish ride to get over before I caught the mail.

3. Somewhat drunk. Cf. TIGHT *a.* 7. *colloq.*

1830 H. LEE *Mem. of Manager* I. iii. 110 'I think they be getting on pretty tightish!' 'What do you mean, getting drunk?'

ˈ**tight-ˌlaced** (-leɪst), *a.* That is laced tightly; having the laces drawn tight; wearing stays tightly laced; constricted or compressed by tight-lacing.

1741 [see b]. **1828** *Lights & Shades* II. 132 The tight-laced spark of fashion, with his hat on one side. **1860** W. G. CLARK in *Vac. Tour.* 43 We saw..the belles of the island,..with..tight-laced black bodices. **1871** *Figure Training* 106 May I add a little practical information..on the health of tight-laced ladies? **1905** H. D. ROLLESTON *Dis. Liver* 11 Tight-laced livers are often associated with dyspepsia.

b. *fig.* Strict in the observance of rules or usages of morality or propriety. (Usually dyslogistic.)

1741 RICHARDSON *Pamela* I. Introd. 26 He made a too tight-laced Objection, where he quarrels with the spann'd Waist of Pamela. **1831** T. L. PEACOCK *Crotchet Castle* vi, Even in these tight-laced days, the obscurity of a learned language allows a little pleasantry. **1844** ALB. SMITH *Adv. Mr. Ledbury* liv. (1886) 164 Etiquette is not over tight-laced upon the mountains. **1881** LARWOOD *Lond. Parks* xiv. 282 This somewhat tight-laced gentleman was greatly shocked.

ˈ**tight-ˈlacing**, *vbl. sb.* The action or process of lacing tightly; *spec.* the practice of wearing tightly-laced stays in order to reduce or preserve the form of the waist.

1834 *Tait's Mag.* I. 101/2 The demon of tight-lacing is still in existence. **1871** *Figure Training* 47 My two daughters..can bear me out in my favourable opinion of tight-lacing, and their good health speaks volumes in its praise. **1897** *Allbutt's Syst. Med.* IV. 343 Cruveilhier long ago pointed out the influence of tight lacing as a cause of displacement [of the kidney].

Hence ˈ**tight-ˈlace** *v.* (back-formation) *trans.*, to lace tightly, to compress (the waist) by wearing tightly-laced stays; also *refl.* and *absol.*; so ˈ**tight-lace** *attrib. phr.*, affected by tight-lacing; ˈ**tight-ˈlacer**, one who practises tight-lacing.

1859 *Habits of Gd. Society* 172 It is often difficult to convince the practised tight-lacer; for vanity is generally obstinate. **1880** tr. *Ziemssen's Cycl. Med.* IX. 40 In slight grades of the so-called 'tight-lace liver' only a shallow transverse furrow is observable. **1897** *Allbutt's Syst. Med.* IV. 343 The tight-lace line on the liver is on the same level as the upper pole of the kidney. **1898** *Daily News* 19 Jan. 9/2 She told me that she tight-laced herself to present a good figure in the shop. **1907** *Daily Chron.* 14 Sept. 5/7 The majority of tight lacers develop thick unshapely legs sooner or later.

'tight-,lipped, *a.* [f. TIGHT *a.* + LIPPED *ppl. a.*] Having the lips firmly closed, esp. as a sign of determined suppression of emotion; also *transf.* and *fig.* Also, determinedly reticent or uncommunicative.

1876 Miss Braddon *J. Haggard's Dau.* II. 47 How would that tight-waisted, tight-lipped damsel get on with a lovely young wife. **1918** H. G. Wells *Joan & Peter* iii. 62 Her pride was white and tight-lipped. **1936** P. Fleming *News from Tartary* v. ii. 194 This, I know, is my cue for tight-lipped heroics. **1952** [see INSTALMENT[2] 3]. **1958** *Observer* 15 June 15/2 Joan Mitchell's rather beautiful painting 'Hudson River Day Line' (which has a sensitive, tight-lipped, almost Slade School quality). **1970** J. Sangster *Touchfeather, Too* ii. 32 The Russians, notoriously tight-lipped normally, had been approached through tortuous channels. **1979** A. Price *Tomorrow's Ghost* iii. 37 She smiled her careful tight-lipped smile. **1981** D. Hopkinson *Edward Penrose Arnold* iv. 40 Here is that melancholy resignation which Matthew Arnold so often..conveys... But his finest poetry..is stoically tight-lipped. **1983** *Times* 2 Apr. 10/2 All parties are keeping tight-lipped. A spokesman for DTR issued a firm 'no comment'.

tightly ('taɪtlɪ), *adv.* [f. TIGHT *a.* + -LY[2].] In a tight manner.

1. Soundly, properly, well; effectively; stoutly, vigorously. Cf. TIGHT *a.* 3. Now *dial.*

1598 Shaks. *Merry W.* I. iii. 88 Hold Sirha, beare you these Letters tightly. *Ibid.* II. iii. 67 He will Clapper-claw thee tightly. **1598** B. Jonson *Ev. Man in Hum.* II. ii, He shall heare on't, and that tightly too. *a* **1625** Fletcher, etc. *Fair Maid Inn* II. ii, When we have cozen'd 'em most tightly, thou shalt steal away the innkeeper's daughter. *a* **1700** B. E. *Dict. Cant. Crew* s.v. *Sock*, I'll Drub ye tightly. **1700** S. L. tr. *Fryke's Voy. E. Ind.* 193 Our eight Boats..pursued them so tightly, that..by Noon our Boats were all got within a quarter of a League of 'em. *a* **1713** Ellwood *Autobiog.* 163 He stood up titely to them. **1786** Burns *Inventory* 41 An' ay on Sundays duly nightly, I on the questions [= catechism] tairge them tightly. *a* **1825** Forby *Voc. E. Anglia*, *Tightly*,.. promptly; actively; alertly.

2. With constriction, tension, or compression; closely, tensely; strictly; not loosely. Also *fig.*

1758 Rutty *Spir. Diary* (ed. 2) 104 A busy week; yet kept to all meetings tightly. **1776** *Trial of Nundocomar* 60/1 A paper, wrapped in a wax cloth..bound tightly down with a string. **1816** Scott *Let.* 22 Nov., I have settled Walter tightly to his Greek and Latin. **1859** *Habits of Gd. Society* iii. 145 Anything which binds any part of the body tightly impedes the circulation. **1879** Stevenson *Trav. Cevennes* (1886) 34, I was tightly cross-examined about my journey. **1883** *Harper's Mag.* Nov. 904/2 The contests were..more tightly fought out than by the trotting equines.

3. Firmly, securely.

1866 Mrs. Gaskell *Wives & Dau.* xlviii, Trying to take one of his hands; but he kept them tightly in his pockets. **1898** Flo. Montgomery *Tony* 13 Their hands clasped tightly.

4. Neatly, tidily, smartly.

1825–9 Mrs. Sherwood *Lady of Manor* II. xv. 297 It does me good to see you going about..so tightly dressed in your neat little cap and blue apron.

5. In comb. with ppl. adj. (used attrib.), as ***tightly-clenched, -corsetted, -reined, -wrapped***, etc.

1825 T. Hook *Sayings* Ser. II. *Passion & Princ.* xii. III. 292 The tightly-strained white kid gloves. **1866** Howells *Venet. Life* xi. 154 Her tightly-corsetted waist. **1888** 'J. S. Winter' *Bootle's Childr.* iii, Between her tightly-clenched teeth.

tightly, tiȝtli, erroneous spellings of TITELY.

tightness ('taɪtnɪs). [f. TIGHT *a.* + -NESS.] The quality or condition of being tight.

1. Closeness of texture; denseness, solidity (*obs.*); compactness of structure, impermeability. Also *fig.*

a **1728** Woodward (J.), The bones are inflexible, which arises from the greatness of the number of corpuscles that compose them, and the firmness and tightness of their union. **1759** Ellis in *Phil. Trans.* LI. 207 The tightness of the cask would secure them from the salt water. **1865** Dickens *Mut. Fr.* I. viii, Make me as compact a little will as can be reconciled with tightness.

2. a. The condition of being drawn tight, stretched, or strained; tenseness, tautness.

1780 *New Newgate Cal.* V. 152 Placing a fife within the cord so as to twist it to a proper tightness. **1793** Beddoes *Scurvy* 63 It was not occasioned by any tightness of dress. **1869** Spurgeon *Treas. David* Ps. iii. 2 Harp-strings..need to be screwed up again to their proper tightness. **1885** *Manchester Exam.* 7 Oct. 5/2 The very tightness with which the screw is being applied renders the probability of a breakdown of the machinery more probable.

b. *transf.* Constriction felt (as in breathing); hardness (of the pulse). Cf. TIGHTENED.

1785 J. Pearson in *Med. Commun.* II. 68 A sense of tightness across the chest. **1898** *Allbutt's Syst. Med.* V. 37 Nothing will relieve the tightness of the chest and the hardness of the cough..better than antimony. **1899** *Ibid.* VI. 49 Diminution in size and increase in tightness of the pulse.

3. The condition of being tipsy. *slang.*

1861 E. Cowell *Diary* 1 Jan. in *Cowells in Amer.* (1934) 234, I congratulated him on his remaining free from 'tightness' after so many calls. **1864** *Daily Tel.* 4 Oct., At the first blush, the Americans strike a foreigner as being an exceedingly drunken people... You cannot fail to observe an immense amount of 'tightness' during your walks abroad.

4. *Comm.* Scarcity of money in the market.

1847 *Punch* XIII. 77/1 There is a tightness at present in the Omnibus Market. **1858** R. S. Surtees *Ask Mamma* lxvii, In consequence of the tightness of the money-market, an early settlement would be agreeable. **1901** *Scotsman* 7 Mar. 6/2 The tightness of money is again beginning adversely to affect gilt-edged stocks.

5. As an artistic quality: (*a*) crampedness, lack of freedom, constraint; (*b*) sense of control, rigorousness.

1933 *Burlington Mag.* Jan. 22/1 The effort to achieve a difficult and unfamiliar piece of modelling gives the penwork a certain tightness. **1959** *Listener* 26 Mar. 542/1 Lack of balance between voice and accompaniment, acoustic 'tightness', restricted and uneven frequency-range. **1973** *Art Internat.* Mar. 73/2 Erlebacher's tightness makes her poetic allegories more like kitsch.

tight rope, 'tight-rope, *sb.* Now freq. as one word. **1.** A tightly stretched rope, wire, or wire cable, on which rope-dancers and acrobats perform feats of equilibristic skill. Also *fig.* (Contrasted with SLACK-ROPE.)

1801 Strutt *Sports & Past.* III. iv. (1810) 188 Tumbling and jumping through a hoop..and dancing upon the tight-rope. **1861** Thackeray *Four Georges* iv. (1876) 105 A charming young Prince who danced deliciously on the tight-rope. **1934** *Essays & Stud.* XIX. 123 He moves with complete security on the tight-rope of serio-comic wit. **1959** *Daily Tel.* 30 Nov. 1 For 35 minutes the Deputy Leader balanced himself on a verbal tightrope which purported to bridge the awesome gap within the party. **1979** *Sci. Amer.* Nov. 126/3 The nocturnal *S. laevistriatus* beetles are on an energy tightrope.

2. *Comb.*, as ***tight-rope dancer, dancing, walk, walker, -walking*** vbl. sb. and ppl. adj.

1824 *Advt.* (Theatre-Royal, Worcester) in *Henry Bristow Ltd. Catal.* (1973) No. 205, The celebrated Mr. Wilson, the tight rope dancer. **1890** *Spectator* 22 Nov. 729/2 An interview with a tight-rope dancer. **1800** W. Dyott *Diary* July (1907) I. 138 Besides rural sports in the gardens, such as gipsies guying, lofty tumbling and tight-rope dancing. **1890** Tight-rope-dancing [see *billiard-playing* s.v. BILLIARDS 2]. **1952** R. Knox *Hidden Stream* vi. 55 We, in this tight-rope-walk business of trying to live our lives..want more than a metaphysical conviction that God exists. **1869** *Atlantic Monthly* July 83/2 This tight-rope walker was one of the most exemplary domestic little bodies imaginable. **1910** *Encycl. Brit.* IV. 77/1 *Blondin* (1824–1897), French tight-rope walker and acrobat. **1979** R. Jaffe *Class Reunion* (1980) II. xi. 287 When he was drunk he had a slow and precise quality, like a tightrope walker. **1982** C. Castle *Folies Bergère* i. 24 Tightrope walkers, magicians and sleight-of-hand artists..attracted Parisians and tourists. **1958** *Spectator* 30 May 675/1 Admiral Auboyneau, who had been doing some tightrope-walking of his own in the previous weeks, finally came out for the rebels. **1981** *Times Lit. Suppl.* 3 Apr. 368/2 Ours is the age of heartless efficiency and tight-rope-walking virtuosity in music.

Hence **'tight-rope** *v., intr.* to perform on the tight-rope; *trans.* to walk along as if on a tight-rope.

1858 A. Mayhew *Paved with Gold* II. vii, A small.. garden, intersected with gravel paths not broader than deal boards, which entailed balancing on those who tight-roped its walks. **1908** *Daily Chron.* 1 Feb. 5/6 He has tumbled and tight-roped, slept under hedges, and accepted presents from reigning potentates.

tights (taɪts), *sb. pl.* [Elliptical use of TIGHT *a.*]

a. Tight-fitting breeches, worn by men in the 18th and early 19th centuries, and still forming part of court-dress.

1827 M. Wilmot *Let.* 24 May (1935) 260 His [*sc.* a jockey's] shirt-collar was open, so were the knees of his 'tights'. **1833** Marryat *P. Simple* xxxi, The frill of his shirt, extending from his collar to the waistband of his nankeen tights, which were finished off at his knees with huge bunches of riband. **1857** Dickens *Lett.* (1880) II. 26 A pair of common nankeen tights, to button below the calf. **1889** W. S. Gilbert *Foggerty's Fairy* I, If tights and trunks came in again.

b. Garments of thin elastic material, fitting tight to the skin, worn by dancers, acrobats, and others to facilitate their movements or display the form; skin-tights. Sometimes covering the whole body, but usually the legs only.

1836–7 Dickens *Sk. Boz, Mrs. Joseph Porter* (1870) 300 None of the performers could walk in their tights, or move their arms in their jackets. **1845** Alb. Smith *Fort. Scatterg. Fam.* xlii. (1887) 140 Gentlemen in flesh tights jumped over strips of cloth, coming down on the horse again. **1897** *Times* 4 Oct. 8/1 [She] would be well advised to abandon her tights and resume the garb of her sex.

c. A woman's or girl's one-piece stretchable garment covering the legs and body up to the waist, worn in place of stockings; formerly, an undergarment taking the place of knickers and stockings.

1897 *Sears, Roebuck Catal.* 241/2 Ladies' summer drawers and tights..Ladies' fine jersey ribbed fast black open summer tights,..knee length. **1908** *Ibid.* 962 Wool and fleece lined underwear for children..Union suits, tights and sleeping garments. **1929** R. S. & H. M. Lynd *Middletown* xii. 159 Today flannel underwear is almost as obsolete as the long black equestrian tights, high-necked, long-sleeved nightgowns for women, and the heavily-lined trousers of the working men of a generation ago. **1965** P. O'Donnell *Modesty Blaise* ix. 105 Modesty wore..a full black skirt, with black stretch tights. **1967, 1970** [see *panty-hose* s.v. PANTIES 3]. **1977** C. McCullough *Thorn Birds* xviii. 469 A five-guinea pair of tights.

tightwad ('taɪtwɒd), *sb.* (and *a.*). *slang* (orig. and chiefly *U.S.*). Also **tight-wad.** [f. TIGHT *a.* + WAD *sb.*[1] 2 b.] A miserly person; one who keeps his wad of paper money tightly rolled. Also *attrib.* and (*rarely*) as *adj.* Also *fig.*

[**1900** Ade *More Fables* 30 Henry was undoubtedly the Tightest Wad in the Township.] **1906** S. Ford *Shorty McCabe* ii. 32 Keep these, and found a home for Incurable Tight-Wads. *a* **1911** D. G. Phillips *Susan Lenox* (1917) I. xv. 255 You've forgotten what a lot of tightwads and petty swindlers they are. **1914** *Wells Fargo Messenger* III. 9 (*caption*) Tight-wad Tim. **1934** *Punch* 26 Dec. 715/3 'A spendthrift', countered Chloe, 'makes a much more satisfactory husband than a tight-wad.' **1945** S. Lewis *Cass Timberlane* xviii. 107 Hey, don't be so tightwad with that hootch. *Ibid.* xxxii. 228 The man said to his wife, 'Our friend here has made a pretty good joke?' She said, 'Come on now—don't be a tightwad—what's his pretty good joke?' **1959** 'A. Gilbert' *Death takes Wife* xv. 188 He may be a bit of a tightwad. **1971** *Sunday Express* (Johannesburg) 28 Mar. (Comic Suppl.) 1/2 Blondie, I have a great idea to get a raise out of old tight-wad Mr. Dithers. **1976** *National Observer* (U.S.) 26 June 10/2 When hard times hit..salesmen put the blame for their dwindling commissions on everybody else: the manufacturers, tightwad consumers [etc.]. **1977** *Sunday Tel.* (Colour Suppl.) 31 July 19/4 Bleeding tightwad! You'd think with all that cash he'd take a taxi.

tiglic ('tɪglɪk), *a. Chem.* [f. mod.L. *Tigl-ium*, specific name of the croton oil plant, *Croton Tiglium* (Linn.), of the Coromandel coast in India, the seeds of which were known in 17th cent. pharmacy as *grana tiglia* and *grana tilli*; according to Wittstein, 1856, f. Gr. τῖλος liquid fæces, as in diarrhœa, from their purgative quality. If so, the spelling *tiglia* or *tiglii* for *tilia*, *tilli* prob. arose in Italy.] Contained in or derived from croton oil; ***tiglic acid***, $C_5H_8O_2$ (Watts) = $CH_3.CH:C(CH_3).CO.OH$, a colourless crystalline compound, crystallizing in triclinic plates or rods, obtained from croton and other oils; stereo-isomeric with angelic acid. Also called *methyl-crotonic acid.* So **'tiglate**, a salt of this acid; **'tigline** (see quot. 1900); **ti'glinic** *a.*, tiglic.

1875 Watts *Dict. Chem.* VII. 395 (*Croton oil, acids obtained from*) Geuther and Fröhlich designate this acid provisionally as tiglic acid, and point out that it is, perhaps, identical with Frankland and Duppa's methyl-crotonic acid. .. Barium tiglate, $(C_5H_7O_2)_2Ba + 10\ H_2O$. **1876** Harley *Royle's Mat. Med.* 440 It is composed of the ordinary fatty acids, and volatile, acetic, butyric, and valerianic, tiglinic acid. **1900** B. D. Jackson *Gloss. Bot. Terms*, *Tigline*, the acrid principle in the seeds of *Croton Tiglium*, Linn.

||**tignon** ('tiːjɒn). [Louisiana Fr., f. F. *tigne*, dial. var. of standard F. *teigne* moth.] A handkerchief worn as a turban head-dress by Creole women.

1884 *Daily Inter-Ocean* (Chicago) 2 July 1/5 [The women's heads were] adorned with the traditional head handkerchief of the tignon. **1935** M. Morphy *Recipes of All Nations* 664 The old Creole women..with their brightly coloured bandana *tignons* or head-dress. **1961** M. G. Eberhart *Cup, Blade or Gun* i. 3 A..Negro woman, in a dark dress and snowy white apron and *tignon.* **1979** —— *Bayou Road* xix. 187 Liss's tightly wrapped tignon, her dark face.

tigon ('taɪgən). Also **tiglon, tigron.** [f. TIG(ER *sb.* + LI)ON *sb.*, etc.: cf. LIGER.] The offspring of a tiger and a lioness.

1927 G. Jennison *Nat. Hist. Animals* 57 It should be noted particularly that the markings of the Tigon are not stripes, but rhomboids, almost like the markings on the Clouded Leopard. **1932** *Times Educ. Suppl.* 16 Jan. p. iv/2 The male parent of the 'tigon' was a tiger, the female an Indian lioness. **1938** *Times* 28 May 7/7 The name liger is given to the offspring of a male lion and tigress, the opposite cross being called a tigron. **1947** *Partisan Rev.* XIV. 395 Mr. Gielgud's gravity, his sensitive, melancholy profile, here becomes exquisitely comic—he looks like a tiglon with a heart. **1964** *Sunday Mail Mag.* (Brisbane) 8 Nov. 4/6 For many years the London Zoo possessed a magnificent 'Tigon'—a tiger-lion hybrid. **1972** *Times* 15 Feb. 6/5 A 'tigon' has been born in a Calcutta zoo from cross-breeding a tiger with a lioness. **1976** *Observer* (Colour Suppl.) 5 Sept. 42/1 (*caption*) This animal, one of the world's rarest cats, is a tiglon, a cross between a tiger and a lion. **1981** M. Duffy *Gor Saga* v. 214 'Can you combine the sexual elements from two different species?' 'Like tigers and lions making tigrons you mean?'

Tigray (tɪ'graɪ). Also †**Teegray.** An alternative name for TIGRINYA.

a **1860** W. C. Plowden *Trav. Abyssinia* (1868) i. 10 They call their language Teegray. **1939** [see TIGRINYA]. **1954** Pei & Gaynor *Dict. Linguistics* 217 *Tigray*, an alternative name for *Tigriña.*

Tigre (tɪ'greɪ), *sb.* and *a.* Also **Tigré.** [Native name.] **A.** *sb.* A Semitic language spoken in northern Ethiopia and adjoining parts of Sudan (distinguished from TIGRINYA, spoken in Tigre itself). **B.** *adj.* Of or pertaining to the province of Tigre in northern Ethiopia. Cf. TIGREAN *sb.* (*a.*).

1878 *Encycl. Brit.* VIII. 612/2 There are at least two modern languages which have sprung from the ancient Geez, distinguished in modern philology by the conventional names of Tigriña and Tigré. **1908** [see TIGRINYA]. **1933** L. Bloomfield *Language* iv. 66 Ethiopian. .. The present-day languages of this group are Tigre, Tigriña, and Amharic. **1972** *Bk. Thousand Tongues* (rev. ed.) 429/1 Tigré is spoken by about 175,000 Muslims living in northern Eritrea and spreading into Sudan. **1978** *Observer* 29 Jan. 10/7 Tigre nationalism: The Tigre people, who inhabit Northern Ethiopia want to redress the balance of power lost with the defeat of the ancient kingdom of Gondar towards the end of the last century.

Tigrean (tɪˈgreɪən, -ˈiːən), *sb.* (*a.*). Also †Tigrian. [f. *Tigre* (see prec.) + -AN; cf. -IAN.] A native of the Tigre province in northern Ethiopia. Also *attrib.* or as *adj.* Cf. TIGRE *a.*

1842 ISENBERG & KRAPF *Jrnl.* 22 Apr. (1843) 500, I must confess that I had conceived a more favourable idea of the hospitality of the Tigrians. **1901** [see STEW *v.*[2] 2 c]. **1960** E. ULLENDORFF *Ethiopians* iii. 37 A greater measure of non-Semitic ingredients in the Amharic language may accurately reflect a lesser degree of ethnic Semitization among the Amharas than is the case with the Tigreans. **1977** *Daily Tel.* 4 May 1/6 The secessionist Eritreans and Tigreans in the North. **1980** *Observer* 21 Sept. 7/5 Guerrillas of the Tigrean People's Liberation Front.

tigress (ˈtaɪgrɪs). (Also 9 tigeress.) [f. TIGER + -ESS, after F. *tigresse.*]

1. A female tiger.

1611 COTGR., *Tigresse*, a Tigresse, a she Tiger. **1624** MASSINGER *Renegado* III. v, If Christians have mothers, sure they share in The tigress' fierceness. **1647** R. STAPYLTON *Juvenal* xv. 278 The Indian tigresses firme peace enjoy. **1891** E. PEACOCK *N. Brendon* II. 117 She turned on him like a tigress at bay.

2. *fig.* A fierce, cruel, or tiger-like woman: cf. TIGER *sb.* 4.

1700 MOTTEUX *Quix.* I. IV. iv. II. 400, I never will give any body reason to call me Tigress and Lioness. **1706** PHILLIPS (ed. Kersey), *Tigress*,..a ranting Woman, a cruel Mistress. **1871** M. COLLINS *Marq. & Merch.* I. iii. 121 The proper subjugation of the young heiress and tigress.

†**b.** A vulgarly or obtrusively overdressed woman: cf. TIGER 7. *Obs.*

1836 *New Monthly Mag.* XLVIII. 460 Tigresses, too, shone in a near approach to nudity, in Greek draperies and a Brutus' wig.

3. *attrib.* and *Comb.*, as ***tigress-heart***, ***-like*** adj.

1844 LOUISA S. COSTELLO *Béarn & Pyrenees* II. 341 Adieu, tigress-heart! Shepherdess without affection. **1910** *Q. Rev.* Jan. 13 Started in tigress-like revenge by a lady of quality.

‖**Tigridia** (taɪˈgrɪdɪə). *Bot.* [mod.L., named by Ker 1805, f. Gr. τιγριδ-, variant stem of τίγρις TIGER + -IA[2]; so called from the spotted flowers.] Name of a genus of bulbous plants, N.O. *Iridaceæ*, known as *Tiger-iris* or *Tiger-flower*, esp. *T. Pavonia*, the Peacock Tiger-flower, a native of Mexico, Central America, and tropical S. America.

1866 in *Treas. Bot.* **1888** *Pall Mall G.* 10 Nov., I feel bound to say a word in praise of the orchid-like tigridia, a bulbous plant of about a foot in height, and whose blossoms, like those of the cistus, never last longer than a day.

tigrine (ˈtaɪgraɪn), *a.* (Also tigerine.) [ad. L. *tigrīn-us* (Pliny) marked like a tiger: see -INE[1].] Of, pertaining to, or resembling a tiger, esp. in marking or colouring; in specific names of animals translating L. *tigrinus*.

1656 BLOUNT *Glossogr.*, *Tigrine*, of or like the swift beast called a Tigre. **1800** SHAW *Gen. Zool.* I. 408 Tigerine weesel ..of the size of a Cat, and of mild manners. The body..with a black stripe from head to tail, and spotted on the sides with brown. **1803** *Ibid.* IV. 556 Tigrine Holocentrus..native of the Indian seas. **1842** *Penny Cycl.* XXIV. 440/1 Two soldiers..habited and shielded so as to exhibit a tigerine aspect. **1861** G. MEREDITH *Evan Harrington* xl, With tigrine claw thou manglest my speech. **1908** *Times* 8 June 6/3 Carpet, diamond and tigrine snakes.

Tigrinya (tɪˈgriːnjə). Also Tigriña, Tigrine. [Native name.] A Semitic language spoken in the Tigre province of Ethiopia. Cf. TIGRAY.

1878 [see TIGRE]. **1908** T. G. TUCKER *Introd. Nat. Hist. Lang.* 172 Along with Amharic (of South-West Abyssinia) go the contaminated dialects Tigre (of the north), Tigrine (of the centre), and Harari (of Harai, east of Gallaland). **1939** L. H. GRAY *Foundations of Lang.* 364 Ethiopic..still serves as a learned language, though its true linguistic successor is Tigriña or Tigray, which is written by few except officials of the Italian colony of Eritrea. **1955** F. R. PALMER in E. P. Hamp et al. *Readings in Linguistics II* (1966) 341 The paradigms that may be set up for the nominals in Tigrinya..consist of two members. **1976** D. TOPOLSKI *Muzungu* iii. 35 She smacked my hand sharply and said something loudly in Tigrinya.

tigrish, tigrous: see TIGERISH, TIGEROUS.

tigroid (ˈtaɪgrɔɪd), *a.* [f. Gr. τιγροειδής like a tiger: see -OID.] Resembling a tiger or tiger's skin; marked like a tiger. ***tigroid body*** (*Path.*): see quots. Also *absol.* as *sb.*

1901 *Buck's Handbk. Med. Sc.* II. 338 The tigroid in the cell bodies of the nuclei of origin of the motor cerebral nerves. *Ibid.*, A part of the dendrite where tigroid bodies disappear. **1904** TITCHENER tr. *Wundt's Physiol. Psychol.* I. 41 When highly magnified, most nerve-cells show..a fibrillated structure; clusters of granules are set..between the meshes of this fibrillar network... The granular deposits are named, from their discoverer, the corpuscles of Nissl; they are also known as tigroid bodies, or as chromophilous substance. **1909** *Cent. Dict. Suppl.* s.v. *Granule*, *Nissl granules*, small, deeply staining bodies found by Nissl in the cytoplasm of nerve-cells... Also called *Nissl's bodies* and *tigroid*.

Hence **tigrolysis** (taɪˈgrɒlɪsɪs) [Gr. λύσις dissolution], the breaking down of the tigroid substance in the nerve-cell; **tigrolytic** (-əʊˈlɪtɪk) *a.*, of or pertaining to tigrolysis.

1903 *Buck's Handbk. Med. Sc.* VI. 264 This disintegration ..of the tigroid has been variously designated... Kohnstamm gives it the name *tigrolysis*,..which I prefer. *Ibid.*, Cells still tigrolytic may be observed.

tiˈgrology. *nonce-wd.* [See -O)LOGY.] The branch of zoology which treats of tigers.

1822-56 DE QUINCEY *Confess.* Wks. V. 70 The indignation arose naturally against my three tormentors (guardian, Archididascalus, and the professor of tigrology).

tigron, var. TIGON.

tig-tag (ˈtɪgˈtæg), *v.* *Sc.* [Reduplicated formation, suggesting the continuous alternation of the game of TIG or TAG.] **a.** *intr.* To continue in reciprocal action; to bicker; to haggle in bargaining. **b.** *trans.* To drive to and fro, to keep (a person) running to and fro. Hence **tig-tagging** *vbl. sb.*

1643 BAILLIE *Lett., to W. Spang* 7 Dec., The King came ..with purpose to break up Waller's quarters,..but.. Waller is recruited, from Kent, with horse and foot, and minds to stand to it. They may tig tag on this way this twelve month. **1825** JAMIESON, *Tig-taggin*, the act of hagglin; as, We had an awfu' tig-taggin about it, before we coud mak our bargain. **1844** W. CROSS *Disruption* xxxv. (1846) 383 They've..been tig-tagit for years, waiting on this Bill and the ither Bill.

Tigurine (ˈtɪgjʊraɪn), *a.* and *sb.* [ad. L. *Tigurīn-us* in *Tigurīnus pāgus* (Cæsar), a district of ancient Helvetia, generally identified with Zürich (*Turicum*).] **a.** *adj.* Of or pertaining to Zürich (cf. *Consensus Tigurinus*, the Zürich Consensus of 1549); hence = ZWINGLIAN. **b.** *sb.* A Zwinglian.

a **1651** CALDERWOOD *Hist. Kirk* (1843) II. 331 The interpretatioun of the Confessioun of the Tigurine kirk made by Mr Robert Pont. **1674** HICKMAN *Quinquart. Hist.* (ed. 2) 59 Blessed is the man who hath not gone in the counsel of the Sacramentarians, nor stood in the way of the Zuinglians, nor sate in the seat of the Tigurines. **1675** V. ALSOP *Anti-sozzo* 273 Those low-spirited, phlegmatic Tigurine doctors, who trade all in..unwieldy systems of Divinity. **1697** POTTER *Antiq. Greece* I. i. (1715) 3 Cf. the Tigurine Version with that of Geneva. **1788** G. CAMPBELL *Four Gospels* (1807) I. 143 This has been followed by the Tigurine translator.

tigurye, obs. variant of TUGURY.

ti-he, -hee, obs. ff. TEE-HEE *int.*

tiht, obs. f. TIGHT, TITE *adv.*

‖**tika** (ˈtika). Also tikka. [Hindi *ṭikā*, *ṭikkā*: cf. TILAK.] Among Hindus, a mark on the forehead indicating caste, status, sectarian affiliation, etc., or worn simply as an ornament. Also *attrib.*, as ***tika mark***, etc.

1884 in J. STORMONTH *Dict. Eng. Lang.* 1053/2. **1960** Z. EGLAR *Punjabi Village in Pakistan* xi. 114 A *ṭika* is a gold ornament worn on the forehead. **1963** S. S. IKRAMULLAH *Purdah to Parliament* xvi. 137 The use of *tikka* (a red spot on the forehead, originally a caste-mark among Hindus but now used more or less for its decorative effect). **1965** P. ROBINSON *Pakistani Agent* iii. 46 On her forehead was the red *tika* dot of marriage. **1973** *Australian Women's Weekly* 27 June 75/4 This colorful tika adds to the Indian woman's adornment. **1979** P. MATTHIESSEN *Snow Leopard* i. 22 The vermilion tikka dot on the women's foreheads. **1980** *Old Lady* June 76/3 We were invited to witness the *tika* ceremony... Granny..had given the first *tika* mark to her eldest son, Naina Singh.

tikal, var. TICAL.

tikat, obs. f. TICKET.

†**tike, tyke**[1]. *Obs. rare*[−1]. [Generally taken as = TYKE, dog, sense 2; but perh. ad. Welsh *taeog* (taiog), in OWelsh *taiawc* villain, churl, Cornish *tioc* or *tiac* husbandman, farmer, ploughman, rustic:—OCeltic **tegācos*, deriv. of **teg-os*, Welsh *ty* a house: cf. for the sense COTTAR, med.L. *cotarius*, from *cota*; VILLEIN, med.L. *villanus*, from *villa*.] One of a class of persons subject to tallage (cf. TALLAGEABILITY, quot. 1888); a churl, villein.

1377 LANGL. *P. Pl.* B. XIX. 37 The iuwes, þat were gentil men, ihesu þei dispised, Bothe his lore & his lawe; now ar þei lowe cherlis. As wyde as þe worlde is, wonyeth þere none But vnder tribut & taillage as tykes & cherles [**1393** C. XXII. 37 tikes and cheorles].

[*Note.* On this word see A. L. Mayhew in *Guardian* 10 Nov. 1909. *Taeog* was in Welsh a technical term (*Anct. Welsh Laws* 216, 266), and may have been known west of the Severn in English counties on the Welsh Border. *Tike* = 'dog', appears later, and then only in the north.]

tike[2], var. TYKE, a low-bred dog.

tike, tikel, -ell(e, -il, tiket, tikkat, -et, obs. forms of TICK, TICKLE, TICKET.

tiki (ˈtiki). Also 8 tigi. Pl. tiki, tikis. [a. Eastern Polynesian *tiki* image; cf. HEI-TIKI.] A large wooden image of Tiki, the creator and first created being of the Maoris and Polynesians, or of an ancestor; also, a small, usu. greenstone, image of the same, worn as a charm or ornament. Also *attrib.*

1777 D. SAMWELL *Jrnl.* 24 Feb. in Cook *Jrnls.* (1967) III. II. 1001 They [*sc.* the Maoris] had brought many Articles of Trade such as Ahoos, green Images called Tigis, Stone Adzes &c. **1840** J. S. POLACK *Manners & Customs New Zealanders* II. xxi. 178 Around the neck, similar kinds of ornaments are worn, but the principal favourite is the *Tiki*. **1889** HOCKEN *Catal. N.Z. Exhib.* 81 (Morris), Wooden Tikis, some of immense size, usually represented the ancestors. **1921** *Outward Bound* June 46/2 The beautiful and valuable greenstone from which the Maoris fashion all their..tikis. **1955** W. J. PHILLIPPS *Maori Carving Illustrated* 12 The body is U shaped, humanised below after the manner of a Maori tiki. **1963** *Times* 26 Feb. 8/5 Gas-flared tiki torches. **1974** T. HEYERDAHL *Fatu-Hiva* iii. 123 Some large wooden images, *tiki*, barred the entrances. **1975** *Times* 17 Mar. 1/6 (Advt.), By the flickering light of a Tiki lamp, you'll delight in sampling exotic dishes. **1977** *Chicago Tribune* 2 Oct. IV. 13/2 Papeete, the main town of Tahiti, generally isn't considered much of a shopping port, but it can bring surprises. Carved wooden, bone, and shell tikis and other jewelry; [etc.].

tikka (ˈtɪkə). [a. Hindi *ṭikka*.] In Indian and Pakistani cookery, (a dish of) small pieces of meat or vegetable marinaded in spices and cooked on a skewer. Freq. with qualifying word indicating the type of meat, etc. used. Also *attrib.*

1955 *Times* 28 May 5/1 Enormous dishes of *tikka kabab* —pieces of lamb deliciously roasted on skewers. **1960** *Dawn* 17 Apr. 12/5 President Nasser relished 'kabab' and 'tikka' dishes. **1961** *Guardian* 16 Feb. 12/4 You will hear all the gossip..over chicken tikka at Farooq's. **1980** J. PASSMORE *Indian Cookery* 110 A whole, smallish bird will take a maximum of 30 minutes, while smaller 'Tikkas' (pieces) only a few minutes. **1982** L. CODY *Bad Company* xxx. 200 She set out to find a chicken tikka and some live music.

tikka, var. TICCA, TIKA.

Tikopian (tɪˈkəʊpɪən), *sb.* and *a.* Also 9 Tucopean. [f. *Tikopia* (see below) + -AN.] **A.** *sb.* A native or inhabitant of Tikopia, one of the Solomon Islands. **B.** *adj.* Of or pertaining to Tikopia.

1832 A. EARLE *Narr. Res. N.Z.* 207 Savages are not much affected by music; but these two Tucopeans were excited to a most extraordinary degree. **1874** C. M. YONGE *Life J. C. Patteson* II. xii. 456 Three Tikopian giants had made a visit at Mota. **1951** W. J. GOODE *Relig. among Primitives* 234 The Tikopian emphasis is clearly on the culture-hero.

‖**til**[1] (tɪl). *East Ind.* Also teel, teal. [a. Hindi *til*:—Skr. *tilá*.] The Indian name of the plant *Sesamum indicum*; chiefly attrib. or in comb., as ***til seed***; **til oil, til-seed oil**, the oil obtained by bruising the seeds. ***black til*** = RAMTIL, *Guizotia oleifera* (formerly called *Verbesina sativa*).

1840 *Penny Cycl.* XVI. 417/1 India, whence..sesamum or til seed is..largely imported, as well as from Egypt. **1845** STOCQUELER *Handbk. Brit. India* (1854) 514 It is..inferior ..to the oil of til (*sesamum*). **1849** BALFOUR *Man. Bot.* §951 Teel seeds, the produce of *Sesamum orientale*, supply a bland oil. *c* **1865** LETHEBY in *Circ. Sc.* I. 101/2 Sessama, gingilie, or teal oil. *a* **1875** *Table Customs-Duties British India* (Yule), Oils, Jinjili or Til. **1905** *Statesman* 23 Aug. 5/4 The Sesamum (Til or Jinjili) crop of the season.

‖**til**[2]. [Native name in Madeira: perh. a local use of Pg. *til*, TEIL or linden.] A lauraceous tree, *Oreodaphne fetens*, of the Canary Islands and Madeira; also its wood, which has a fetid smell. Chiefly *attrib.*, as ***til-tree***, ***til-wood***.

1858 HOGG *Veg. Kingd.* 623 *Til-wood*, produced by *G[œppertia] fœtens*, a native of the Canaries, has a most disagreeable odour. **1884** MILLER *Plant-n.*, *Oreodaphne* (*Laurus*) *fœtens*, Fetid Laurel, or Til-tree. **1885** LADY BRASSEY *The Trades* 30 The black Til..or native laurel.

'til (tɪl). Var. of TILL *prep.*, *conj.* or short for UNTIL *prep.* and *conj.*

1939 P. G. PERRIN *Index to Eng.* 606 Till, *until*, (*'til*), these three words are not distinguishable in meaning. Since *'til* in speech sounds the same as *till* and looks slightly odd on paper, it may well be abandoned. **1956** H. KURNITZ *Invasion of Privacy* iii. 27 You sit on your tail 'til they come up with another story. **1978** M. DUFFY *House-spy* v. 126, I shall have to tell the P.M. but not 'til I'm sure.

til, obs. form of TEIL, TILE, TILL.

tilak (ˈtɪlæk). Also tilaka, tilka. [a. Hindi *tilak*, Skr. *tilaka*, f. Skr. *tíla* sesamum.] = TIKA.

1879 E. ARNOLD *Light of Asia* II. 72 Slender hands and feet new-stained With crimson, and the tilka-spots stamped bright. **1895** *Funk's Stand. Dict.*, Tilak. **1961** *Spectator* 3 Mar. 281 The traditional welcome with music and *tilak* (a red mark placed in blessing on the honoured guest's forehead). **1969** 'R. FARRE' *Beckoning Land* xiii. 151 On his forehead was a tilak mark showing that he was a follower of Shiva. **1974** *Encycl. Brit. Micropædia* IX. 1009/1 Among Śaivas (followers of Lord Śiva), the *tilaka* usually takes the form of three horizontal parallel lines across the forehead, with or without a red dot.

tilapia (tɪˈleɪpɪə). [mod.L. (A. Smith: see quot. 1849), perh. f. Gr. τίλων, a fish name used by Aristotle + ἄπιος distant.] A freshwater fish of the genus of this name, belonging to the family Cichlidæ, native to Africa but introduced elsewhere as a food fish or an aquarium species.

1849 A. SMITH *Illustr. Zool. S. Afr.*: *Pisces* 5 The *fossæ* or caverns connected with the gills are very indistinct, yet such traces of them exist as appears to warrant our regarding *Tilapia* as a fish of an aberrant form. **1901** *Trans. Zool. Soc.* XV. 18 In these *Tilapiæ*..the function of protecting the eggs devolves on the male sex. **1932** *Discovery* Feb. 43 (*caption*) The photograph shows a cat-fish with a *Tilapia* from its stomach. **1954** V. BARTLETT *Rep. from Malaya* iii. 56 A fish imported from Egypt, the tilapia,..hatches its eggs in its mouth and provides a refuge there for its young in moments of danger. **1965** A. J. MCCLANE *Standard Fishing Encycl.* 947/2 Tilapias have been experimentally bred in the southern United States (Alabama and Florida) where they have been stocked and caught in public waters. **1971** *Daily Tel.* 13 May 13/5 Families [in Uganda] are widely encouraged to cultivate their own stocks of tilapia, a fat, flat-bodied fish common throughout Africa.

tilasite ('tiːləsaɪt). *Min.* [ad. Sw. *tilasit* (H. Sjögren 1895, in *Geol. Föreningens i Stockholm Förhandlingar* XVII. 291), f. the name of D. *Tilas* (1712–72), Swedish mining engineer: see -ITE[1].] A fluor-arsenate of calcium and magnesium, $CaMg(AsO_4)F$, that is isostructural with sphene and occurs as translucent monoclinic crystals that are colourless, green, or greyish.

1897 *Jrnl. Chem. Soc.* LXXII. II. 325 Tilasite or fluor-adelite from Långban... Irregular grains of this new mineral are found with hausmannite, berzeliite and calcite in a grey limestone. **1968** [see ISOKITE]. **1979** *Mineral. Abstr.* XXX. 293/1 Tilasite crystals < 2·5 mm across have been found with friedelite and baryte at the Sterling Hill mine, Ogdensburg, Sussex County, New Jersey.

tilbury ('tɪlbərɪ). [f. proper name *Tilbury*, in sense 1 that of the inventor, in sense 2 of the place: see quot. 1796.]

1. A light open two-wheeled carriage, fashionable in the first half of the 19th c.

1814 *Sporting Mag.* XLIII. 240 Fifteen tilburies, drawn by fine blood horses. **1842** DICKENS *Amer. Notes* vi. (1850) 55/2 Gigs, phaetons, large-wheeled tilburies, and private carriages. **1863** 'OUIDA' *Held in Bondage* (1870) 44 We stood waiting for his tilbury.

†**2.** A sixpenny piece; sixpence. *slang. Obs.*

1796 GROSE *Dict. Vulg. T.* (ed. 3), *Tilbury*, sixpence; so called from its formerly being the fare for crossing over from Gravesend to Tilbury fort. **1805** in *Brathwait's Barnabees Jrnl.* (1818) Introd. 43 *note*, As if a man..should say 'Arriving at Tilbury-fort, I gave a beggar a Tilbury (sixpence) for the name's sake'. **1812** J. H. VAUX *Flash Dict.*, *Tilbury*, a sixpence.

Hence **'tilbury'd** *a.*, of driving gloves, having the finger-palms strengthened with leather to resist the friction of the reins.

1901 *Trade Catalogue*, Knitted tilbury'd gloves.

†**tild.** *Obs.* Forms: 4 tyle, 5 tyll, tilde, tylde, 5–6 tyld. [In 14–15th c. *tyle, tyll*, app. a. OF. *tille* a piece or portion: cf. *une tille de son bacon* (12th c.), *tille de lart* (14th c. in Godef.).] Each of the four cuts or portions into which a quarter of beef may be divided.

1342–3 *Durh. Acc. Rolls* (Surtees) I. 38 In j quart. carn. Bou' recent. et ij tyles et j carcos. porc. **1417** *Ibid.* 55 In v Carcass. j qart. et j tyld Carn. bov. *c* **1420** *Ibid.* 56 In iiij carcas ij tyll bov. sals. **1514–15** *Earl Northumberland's Househ. Bk.* (1770) 135 There shal be strikkyn of every Carcass of Beef lxiiij Stroks, whiche is..after iiij Tilde in every Quarter and after iiij Stroks in every Tylde.

tild, -e, var. TELD *sb.* and *v. Obs.*; obs. f. TILE.

‖**tilde** ('tɪldeɪ). [Sp. *tilde*, a popular metathetic form of the type **tidlo* for *tit(u)lo*, ad. L. *titulus* TITLE. Diez cites as a parallel instance *cabildo*, L. *capitulum*.] **1. a.** The diacritic mark ˜ placed in Spanish above the letter *n* to indicate the *mouillé* or palatalized sound (ɲ), as in *señor* (seɲor). Also, the mark placed in Portuguese above the letters *a* and *o* to indicate nasalization. Used similarly in systems of phonetic transcription.

Orig. the *mouillé* sound was written *nn*, as in the parallel *ll*; the *tilde* is an abbreviated form of the second *n*.

1864 in WEBSTER. **1889** *Pall Mall G.* 21 Jan., It is not considered [by the authoress] of any importance if the word señor remains without its tilde. **1915** G. NOËL-ARMFIELD *General Phonetics* xvi. 88 The phonetic symbol for nasalised vowels is [˜] (the Spanish *tilde*) placed over the vowel symbol. **1958** J. L. TAYLOR *Portuguese-Eng. Dict.* (1959) p. x/2 If a word bears a tilde..stress the syllable so marked. **1974** *Encycl. Brit. Micropædia* VIII. 147/2 Typical of the Portuguese sound system is the use of nasal vowels, indicated in the orthography by *m* or *n* following the vowel ..or by the use of a tilde..over the vowel.

b. *Palæography* and *Early Printing*. The diacritic mark ˜ placed above a letter to indicate contraction of a following *n* or *m*.

1959 *N. & Q.* Feb. 77/2 From c. 1560 the tilde was used in printed English dramatic texts only over the vowels *a*, *e*, *o*, and *u*. **1975** J. BUTCHER *Copy-Editing* xi. 205 Superscript letters and tildes (nunnation marks) in contractions are normalized to modern usage unless there are good reasons to the contrary.

2. Used as a symbol in *Math.* and *Logic*, chiefly to indicate negation.

1958 *New Scientist* 10 July 364/2 If A is a matrix it is usual to denote the transpose of A by A' or A*, and the trace of A by tr A. However, the author plays the part of 'the odd man out' by placing a tilde (˜) over A to denote the transpose of A. **1971** [see HOOK *sb.*[1] 10 d]. **1979** D. R. HOFSTADTER *Gödel, Escher, Bach* viii. 212 With the tilde in front, the whole statement is denied. **1982** *S. Afr. Jrnl. Philos.* I. 117/1 The standard interpretation of the propositional calculus identifies the tilde with the English word *not*.

tile (taɪl), *sb.*[1] Forms: α. 1 tiȝule, 1–2 tiȝele, 3 tiȝel, 4 teȝele, tijl, 4–5 tiel, 4–6 tyel, 4–9 tyle, 5 til, tyl, tille, tyell, tyil, tyȝl(l, tele, 5–6 teylle, tylle, 4–tile. β. *Sc.* and *north. dial.* 5–6 tild, tyld(e. [OE. *tiȝule, tiȝele*:—WGer. *tegala*, ad. L. *tēgula* a tile, f. *teg-ĕre* to cover. So OHG. *ziagal* (MHG., G. *ziegel*), Du. *tegel, tichel*, ON. *tigl* (Sw. *tegel*, Da. *tegl*).]

1. A thin slab of burnt clay, shaped according to the purpose for which it is required; usually unglazed and flat or curved for covering the roofs of buildings, flat for lining ovens, etc.; flat, usually glazed and sometimes encaustically ornamented when used to pave floors, or line walls, fire-places, etc.; semi-cylindrical or tunnel-shaped when used for purposes of drainage. Now freq. made of concrete.

a. originally and generally as used for roofing purposes; hence also applied to similar coverings of metal, marble, †wood 'shingles', etc.

a **725** *Corpus Gloss.* 1992 (O.E.T.) *Tegula*, tiȝule. *c* **825** *Vesp. Ps.* xxi. 16 [xxii. 15] Adruȝade swe swe tiȝule [L. *testa*] meȝen min. *c* **1000** *Sax. Leechd.* II. 156 ȝebærn under tiȝelan to ahsan. *a* **1300** *Cursor M.* 18930 þe fire es god to strengh þe tile. **1340** *Ayenb.* 167 Tribulacion makeþ pacience ase þet uer makeþ þe teȝele hard. *c* **1400** *Brut* ccxlii. 352 A large hous of tymbir..couered with tylez ouyr. *c* **1425** *Voc.* in Wr.-Wülcker 667/22 *Hec tegula*, teylle. **1552** HULOET, Tyles of woode called shyngles. **1555** EDEN *Decades* 150 Their houses..are couered eyther with tyles, slates, reades, or stalkes of certeyne herbes. **1613** PURCHAS *Pilgrimage* (1614) 467 The house wherein his Pagode.. standeth, is couered with Tiles of siluer. **1617** MORYSON *Itin.* I. 64 The building is very faire, of free stone.., but covered with tiles of wood for the most part. **1678** CUDWORTH *Intell. Syst.* I. iv. 460 He uncovered another Temple.., and taking off the Marble-Tyles thereof, sent them into Spain to adorn his new erected Temple withal. **1746–7** HERVEY *Medit.* (1818) 27 Even a single tile, dropping from the roof, may be as fatal as the fall of the whole structure. **1840** R. H. DANA *Bef. Mast* xiii. 30 The better houses..have red tiles upon the roofs. **1850** LEITCH tr. *C. O. Müller's Anc. Art* §53 Byzes of Naxos invented the art of cutting marble tiles about the 50th Olympiad. **1857** BIRCH *Anc. Pottery* (1858) I. 162 Tiles were extensively used in Greece for roofing.

†**b.** As used in building generally, and including thicker slabs of the shape and quality of bricks: cf. TILE-STONE 1. *Obs.*

(Cf. the corresponding use of G. *ziegel*. The word *brick* first appears in E. in the 15th c.)

c **893** K. ÆLFRED *Oros.* II. iv. §7 [Se weall] is ȝeworht of tiȝelan & of eorðtyrewan. [*c* **1250–1387**: see 2.] *c* **1385** CHAUCER *L.G.W.* 709, & wallis make Ful hye of harde tilis wel I-bake. **1481** CAXTON *Myrr.* III. xi. 158 They made other [pillar]..of tyles all hole wythoute ony Ioyntures.

c. (*a*) As used for paving floors, lining walls, fireplaces, etc.

c **1386** CHAUCER *Sompn. T.* 397 Ne of our pauement Nys nat a tyl yet with-Inne oure wones. [*c* **1394, 1426–7**: see 2.] **1611** COTGR., *Quarreau*,..a square tile, or bricke, fit to paue with. **1688** R. HOLME *Armoury* III. 343/2 Roman Tiles.. found in Vaults and Cellars in Chester. **1715** LEONI *Palladio's Archit.* (1742) I. 27 The Floors may be made..of square Tyles. **1727–41** CHAMBERS *Cycl.*, *Flemish or Dutch Tyles* are of two kinds, antient and modern.—The antient were used for chimney foot-paces... The modern Flemish tyles are commonly used plastered up in the jaumbs of chimneys, instead of chimney-corner-stones. **1735** BERKELEY *Querist* §117 Whether tiles and plaster may not supply the place of Norway fir for flooring. **1844** DICKENS *Christmas Carol* i, The fireplace..paved..with quaint Dutch tiles. **1888** MISS BRADDON *Fatal Three* I. v, The walls were lined with Minton tiles.

(*b*) *transf.* Regularly-shaped pieces (often squares) of floor- or wall-covering made of some other material, as ***carpet*** (***cork***, etc.) ***tile***.

1960 *Mrs. Beeton's Cookery & Househ. Managem.* 44 (*heading*) Cork tiles. **1975** *N.Y. Times* 6 Apr. II. 40/4 Carpet tiles are installed by starting at the center of the room. **1976** *Evening Post* (Nottingham) 15 Dec. 20/1 (Advt.), Super savings on all branded Axminsters, Wiltons, Foambacks, Cords and Carpet tiles. **1982** *Habitat Catal.* 1982/83 140 Wipe clean natural cork tiles, pre-sealed with polyurethane varnish for protection.

d. As used for draining land, roads, buildings, etc., or for other purposes. These are either hollow tubes or semicircular and open.

1830, 1844 [see *tile-draining*, *-machine* in 6]. **1869** BOUTELL *Arms & Arm.* iv. (1874) 60 One of these shields is an elongated and convex oblong, somewhat resembling a hollowed water-course tile. **1870** EMERSON *Soc. & Solit.* vi. 122 See what the farmer accomplishes by a cartload of tiles: he alters the climate by letting off water. **1875** W. MCILWRAITH *Guide Wigtownshire* 118 The spring..has been diverted into tiles, and forms a spout-well. **1883** *Fisheries Exhib. Catal.* 297 Tiles prepared for collecting Spat... Knives for detaching the young oysters from the chalked tile.

e. *Metallurgy*. A small flat piece of baked earth or earthenware used to cover vessels in which metals are fused.

1741 CRAMER *Art Assaying Metals* 67 In Fusions, it is often necessary to cover the Vessels with Tiles... These are made of the same Matter as the melting Pots and Crucibles. **1753** CHAMBERS *Cycl. Supp.*, *Tile*, or *Tyle*, in assaying, a small flat piece of dried earth, used to cover vessels in which metals are in fusion... The Tile sits close upon the vessel. **1877** KNIGHT *Dict. Mech.*, *Tile*..2. (*Brass-founding*.) The cover of a brass furnace. Now made of iron, but formerly a flat tile... 3. (*Metallurgy*.) A clay cover for a melting-pot.

f. The name given to a small flat plate of copper: cf. *tile copper* in 6.

1868 JOYNSON *Metals* 96 The copper..is cast into 'ingots', 'tiles', or 'wire bars'.

g. ***to have a tile loose*** (and similar expressions derived from roofing tiles): to be slightly crazy, or not quite right in the head. *slang.*

1846 W. H. MAXWELL *Brian o' Linn* xvii. (1848) II. 212 'There is not a tile off your upper story', as they say in the north. **1870** G. MACDONALD *Back of North Wind* xix, He's not right in the head, you know. A tile loose. **1877** BESANT & RICE *Harp & Cr.* iv, Is he cracked? Has my cousin dropped a tile?

h. ***on the tiles***: [after the nocturnal activities of cats] on a spree, on a debauch. *slang.*

1887 H. BAUMANN *Londinismen* 125/2 *On the tiles*, auf dem Nachtbummel. *c* **1906** GALSWORTHY *Silver Box* (1910) 7 Been on the tiles and brought 'ome some of yer cat's fur. **1948** 'J. TEY' *Franchise Affair* xi. 119 I'd say she was what is known as 'out on the tiles', sir. A very cool customer she was. **1977** C. MCCULLOUGH *Thorn Birds* xviii. 458 They all went out on the tiles... It was some night.

2. a. The material of which tiles or bricks consist, burnt clay (cf. BRICK *sb.*[1] 1); tiles (or †bricks) collectively (in early use const. as pl.). † ***oil of tile*** = brick-oil (BRICK *sb.*[1] 10). *Obs.*

α. *c* **1250** *Gen. & Ex.* 2552 Ðo sette sundri hem to waken His tiȝel and lim, and walles maken. *a* **1300** *Cursor M.* 1533 (Cott.) Tua pilers þai mad, o tile þe tan, þe toþer it was o merbul stan. **1387** TREVISA *Higden* (Rolls) IV. 297, I fonde a citee of brend tyle, and now I leve a citee of marbil. *c* **1394** *P. Pl. Crede* 194 Þat cloister..was..y-paued wiþ peynt til, iche poynte after oþer. **1426–7** *Rec. St. Mary at Hill* 64 Payd for xj[xx] pavyng tyle. **1566** in J. Morris *Troubles Cath. Forefathers* (1877) 336 All the residue of tile, timber, and stuff. **1632** LITHGOW *Trav.* IV. 139 The couertures being erected..after the Italian fashion with gutterd tyle. **1634** J. B[ATE] *Myst. Nat.* 64 Take of oyle of Tile one pound. **1707** MORTIMER *Husb.* (1721) I. 142 To do them with Dutch Tile, such as they set Chimneys with. **1842** DICKENS *Amer. Notes* xi. (1850) 112/1 Cincinnati is a beautiful city..with..its well-paved roads, and foot-ways of bright tile.

β. *c* **1425** WYNTOUN *Cron.* I. v. 235 He gert twa pilleris sone be maid: Off tild or plaister wes the tane, The toþer wes of merbill stane. *c* **1450** *Maitl. Club Misc.* III. 205 A litill basyn of payntit tild for the hee alter. **1552** LYNDESAY *Monarche* 1702 All fell to warke, boith man and chylde, Sum holkit claye, sum brynt the tylde. **1553–4** *Burgh Rec. Edinb.* (1871) II. 346 Item, to Maister Johne Prestoun for ane hundreith tylde..xv[s].

†**b.** The covering of a roof, roofing. *Obs. rare.*

1611 CORYAT *Crudities* 362 The tyle of most of their houses is made of pieces of wood.

3. *slang.* A hat. Cf. TILED *ppl. a.* 1 c.

1813 M. EDGEWORTH *Let.* 1 May (1971) 33 A number of *Fellows* and scholars with black tiles on their heads. **1823** in *Spirit Pub. Jrnls.* 55 The prompter's boy threw up his tile. **1825** *Sporting Mag.* XVI. 59 The Suffolk Champion took off his tile, and made a silent appeal. **1837** DICKENS *Pickw.* xii, Afore the brim went it was a wery handsome tile. **1873** O. W. HOLMES *Centenn. Dinner Boston Pier* 22 The square-toed boys in the three-cornered tiles.

4. a. Applied to an ancient Greek game: see quot.

1837 B. D. WALSH *Aristoph.*, *Knights* II. iv. 212 *note*, 'The game of tiles' was played [thus].—A tile is provided,..black on one side, and white on the other. The players are separated into two..parties, the blacks and the whites. A child tosses up the tile in the air,..if it falls with the black side uppermost, the blacks run after the whites [etc.].

b. A thin flat piece used in a game, esp. in mah-jong or Scrabble.

1923 [see MAH JONG *v.*]. **1973** *Times* 17 Nov. 2 A mah-jong set with ivory tiles. **1976** 'M. ALBRAND' *Taste of Terror* ix. 56 The original..was..printed in red block letters. They seemed to think that tiles from a scrabble set had been used.

5. Short for TILE-FISH.

1893 *Worthington's Mag.* (Hartford, Conn.) I. 150 The Tile should be obtainable in numbers equal to the cod..its flesh is more delicate and has a better flavor.

6. *attrib.* and *Comb.*, as ***tile-hat***, ***tile pavement***, ***paving***, ***roof***, ***roofing***, ***sole***, ***-top***; ***tile-layer***, ***-moulder***, ***-scraper***; ***tile-clad***, ***-covered***, ***-floored***, ***-hatted***, ***-like***, ***-lined***, ***-paved***, ***-roofed***, ***-topped*** adjs.; **tile-and-a-half tile**, a tile one and a half times the width of the tiles used with it; **tile-burner**, one who burns or bakes clay into tiles, a tile-maker; **tile-clay**, a kind of clay adapted for making tiles; **tile copper**, impure copper or 'bottoms' (BOTTOM *sb.* 8 b) made in flat rectangular plates or 'tiles'; **tile creasing**: see CREASING *vbl. sb.*[2] 2; **tile-drain** *sb.*, a drain constructed of tiles; so **tile-drain** *v. trans.*, to drain (a field, etc.) by means of tiles; **tile-drainage**, drainage constructed of tiles; **tile-draining** *vbl. sb.*; **tile-earth** = *tile-clay*; **tile-field**, a piece of ground where tiles are made: cf. *brick-field*; **tile game**, a game played with flat pieces; **tile-hanging**, tiling fixed vertically to an outside wall, for its weather-resisting and decorative properties; hence **tile-hung** *a.*; **tile-laths**, laths supporting the tiles of a roof; **tile-machine**, a machine for making tiles, esp. drain-tiles; † **tile-oast** = TILE-KILN; **tile-ore**, an earthy variety of cuprite or copper ore, usually of a reddish colour; **tile-oven** = TILE-KILN; **tile-pipe**, a hollow cylindrical tile for drainage; **tile-**

pit, a pit in which clay for tiles is dug; **tile-red** *a.* and *sb.*, (of) a red colour like that of tiles; **tile-root**, name for the South African genus *Geissorhiza* of iridaceous plants, from the overlapping scales on the rhizome, the remains of the bases of the leaves; **tile-seed**, name for the Australian genus *Geissois* of saxifragaceous trees, from the flattened seeds; † **tile-stricker**, a workman who formed the clay into a brick or tile; **tile-tea**, an inferior kind of brick-tea: see quots.; † **tile-theeker**, one who covers roofs with tiles, a tiler; **tile-ways** *adv.*, in the manner or form of a tile or tiles; **tile-work**, work consisting of tiles; formerly including brick-work, and pottery in general; **tile-works**, a place in which tiles are made; **tile-wright** [repr. OE. *tiȝel wyrhta*], a maker of tiles; **tile-yard**, a yard or enclosure where tiles are made. See also TILE-FISH, -KILN, etc.

1940 *Chambers's Techn. Dict.* 850/2 *Tile-and-a-half tile.., a purpose-made tile of extra width, used to form the bond at a laced valley. **1563-6** in *Archæologia* XXXVI. 303 To the *tyle burner. **1830** *Cumb. Farm Rep.* 62 in *Lib. U.K., Husb.* III, The engagement with the Staffordshire tile burner. **1849** CLOUGH *Amours de Voyage* III. 233 Looking down on the *tile-clad streets. **1707** MORTIMER *Husb.* (1721) I. 78 A sort of yellow *Tile-Clay. **1825** J. NICHOLSON *Operat. Mechanic* 714 The copper should be tough cake, and not *tile. **1870** ROSKELL in *Eng. Mech.* 18 Feb. 547/3 They are then separated..and worked up to make an inferior quality of copper, known in the trade as 'tile copper'. **1854** H. MILLER *Sch. & Schm.* (1858) 316 Dingy, low-roofed, *tile-covered hovels. **1591** PERCIVAL *Sp. Dict.*, *Tejo*, a *tile couering. **1866** MRS. GASKELL *Wives & Daughters* II. i. 4 He had taken the lead among the neighbouring landowners, when he first began *tile-drainage. **1971** *Power Farming* Mar. 36/4 First-time sub-soiling over an existing satisfactory tile drainage system. **1844** STEPHENS *Bk. Farm* I. 585 The Marquis of Tweeddale..has..*tile-drained extensively. **1830** *Cumb. Farm Rep.* 67 in *Lib. Usef. Kn., Husb.* III, The system of *tile-draining is..begun in Ayrshire. **1828** WEBSTER, **Tile-earth*, a species of strong clayey earth; stiff and stubborn land. **1882** OGILVIE s.v. *Tile-field*, The palace of the Tuileries is thus named from standing on what was once a *tile-field. **1849** DICKENS *Dav. Copp.* x, The *tile-floored kitchen. **1950** E. CULBERTSON *Culbertson's Hoyle* p. xiii, *Tile Games: Mah Jongg.. Dominoes. **1974** *Encycl. Brit. Macropædia* II. 1149/2 Board and tile games are games played with a number of pieces on a specially constructed or marked board or with marked pieces (tiles) on a tabletop or other flat surface. **1932** *Times Lit. Suppl.* 7 July 494/3 Suffolk, Essex and Norfolk, counties remarkable for their brick-work, *tile-hanging and weather-boarding. **1977** M. GIROUARD *Sweetness & Light* viii. 202 Stucco was replaced by red brick and tile-hanging. **1937** PARTRIDGE *Dict. Slang* 886/1 *Tile*,..extant as **tile-hat*, esp. in Glasgow. **1976** C. BERMANT *Coming Home* I. iii. 40 The topper, or a tile-hat as it was known in Scotland..was virtually the badge of office of the Rabbi. **1924** *Glasgow Herald* 24 Dec. 6 There is something as Christmas-like as snow in the sight of a *tile-hatted gentleman purchasing a sausage-balloon. **1948** J. BETJEMAN *Coll. Poems* (1958) 140 Gabled lodges, *tile-hung churches, catch the lights of our Lagonda. **1977** FEDDEN & JOEKES *National Trust Guide* (ed. 2) v. 375 Filled with brick nogging and tile-hung. **1844** STEPHENS *Bk. Farm* I. 188 A tile roof requires *tile-lath, 1½ inch square, and 11 inches apart. **1851** RICHARDSON *Geol.* (1885) 448 Ancient reptiles..; their..covering consisted of long, narrow, wedge-shaped, *tile-like, horny scales. **1895** *Jrnl. Roy. Inst. Brit. Archit.* 14 Mar. 348 The *tile-lined walls of the Alhambra. **1844** STEPHENS *Bk. Farm* I. 581 The ..*tile-machine..makes tiles at the rate of 10,000 tiles a day. **1591** PERCIVAL *Sp. Dict.*, *Tejar*, a *tile ost. **1823** URE *Dict. Chem.* (ed. 2), **Tile ore*, a sub-species of octohedral red copper ore. **1535** COVERDALE *2 Sam.* xii. 31 He broughte them forth..and burned them in *tyle ouens. **1891** in *Cent. Dict.* **1715** LEONI *Palladio's Archit.* (1742) I. 27 Square *Tyle-Pavements are more agreeable to the Eye. *c* **1440** *Pallad. on Husb.* I. 431 And yote on hit *tyl pauyng playn and stronge. **1849** *Ecclesiologist* IX. 356 Cylindrical *tile-pipes. **1656** HEYLIN *Surv. France* 120 Many lime-kils and *Tile-pits. **1805-17** R. JAMESON *Char. Min.* (ed. 3) 71 *Tile-red is hyacinth-red, mixed with greyish-white... Examples, Porcelain-jasper and zeolite. **1600** HOLLAND *Livy* XXXVI. xxxvii. 939 Two tame oxen climed up a ladder in the street Carinæ, to the *tyle-roofe of a certaine house. **1962** E. SNOW *Other Side of River* (1963) xxxi. 239 On the Sungari River at Harbin I saw a *tile-roofed structure really elaborate enough to be called a palace. **1977** H. FAST *Immigrants* II. 86 Seven thousand dollars for the tile-roofed, tile-floored house..was a tremendous bargain. **1844** STEPHENS *Bk. Farm* I. 199 In *tile-roofing, tiles are made on purpose to hold a pane of glass. **1829** LOUDON *Encycl. Plants* (1836) 40 *Geissorhiza*, *Tile-Root. **1884** MILLER *Plant-n.*, *Tile-seed. **1844** STEPHENS *Bk. Farm* I. 530 The bricks..could form either a smooth inclined sole like *tile-soles, or a series of steps. **1585** *Canterbury Marr. Licences* 22 May (MS.), *Tyle-stricker. **1858** SIMMONDS *Dict. Trade*, **Tile-tea*, a kind of flat brick tea, of much solidity, made in China,..sold to the Armenians and Tartars, who distribute it to the Caucasian provinces and Eastern Siberia... It is..stewed with milk, butter, salt, and herbs, constituting rather an article of food than a..beverage. **1882** OGILVIE, *Tile-tea*, a kind of inferior tea prepared by stewing refuse leaves with milk, butter, salt, and herbs, and solidifying the mixture by pressing it into moulds. *c* **1440** *York Myst.* xiv. *(heading)* The *tille thekers. **1907** *Yesterday's Shopping* (1969) 129/1 Bamboo *tile top table..12/4. **1931** 'G. TREVOR' *Murder at School* xiii. 253 A sort of lounge, fitted up with *tile-topped tables and deep armchairs. **1979** J. LEASOR *Love & Land Beyond* iii. 52 He sat down at a tile-topped table. **1789** MRS. PIOZZI *Journ. France* II. 272 The roofs are all wood cut *tile-ways. **1535** COVERDALE *Isa.* ix. 10 The *tyle worcke is fallen downe, but we will buylde it with harder stones. **1865** ELIZA METEYARD *Jos. Wedgwood* I. 42 The..term of tilework embraced every article manufactured by the Saxon, and later by the Norman Potter. **1882** OGILVIE, *Tile-work* [? **Tile-works*], a place where tiles are made; a tilery. **1891** *Cent. Dict.*, Tile-works. **1906** A. B. TODD *Autobiog.* vii. 70, I went to labour at the Lanfine tile-works. *c* **1000** *Ags. Gosp.* Matt. xxvii. 10, & hiȝ sealdon þæt on *tiȝelwyrhtena æcyr. **1865** ELIZA METEYARD *Jos. Wedgwood* I. 93 Every worker in its clays became a tile-wright, whether he moulded tiles, or formed the homely pipkin or porringer, the slab-like dish, or ale-vat for the hall. **1832** *Scoreby Farm Rep.* 24 in *Lib. U.K., Husb.* III. The price..at the *tile-yards is from thirty-five to forty-two shillings per thousand. **1848** DICKENS *Dombey* vi, Some very uncomfortable places, such as brick-fields and tile yards.

† **tile**, *sb.*[2] *Obs. rare*⁻¹. [ME., ? absol. use of OE. *til* adj. serviceable, competent, good, excellent.] ? Gain, profit; wealth, possessions, goods.

c **1250** *Gen. & Ex.* 1519 An hundred so mikel wex his tile, So may god friðe ðor he wile.

tile (taɪl), *v.* Also 4- **tyle.** [f. TILE *sb.*[1]; in sense 2, back-formation from TILER 2.]

1. *trans.* To cover with tiles; to overlay (a floor or roof) or line (a wall, fire-place, etc.) with tiles; in quot. 1812, to roof.

c **1375** *Sc. Leg. Saints* xl. (*Ninian*) 930 þar-of eftire, in schort quhile, He gert his quere rycht wele tyle. **1467** in *Eng. Gilds* (1870) 386 That the owners..tyle the thacched houses. **1591** in *Gentl. Mag.* (1779) XLIX. 81 Many offices new builded..all which were tyled. **1605** in Willis & Clark *Cambridge* (1886) II. 494 Thomas Yates to Slate and Tyle ye Kytchen. **1704** N. N. tr. *Boccalini's Advts. fr. Parnass.* III. 272 My Spanish Palace, which I might easily have Tiled with Massie Gold or Silver. **1812** BIGLAND *Beauties Eng. & Wales* XVI. 629 Open hay barns, tiled with slate. **1829** D. CONWAY *Norway* 152 Assisting to tile a house. **1901** *Westm. Gaz.* 10 Jan. 7/3 The tunnels are to be tiled-up.

b. *transf.* and *fig.* To cover as with tiles; to cover *over*, cover *up*: *spec.* of overlapping leaves, scales, etc. (= IMBRICATE *v.* 2). †In quot. 1641-2, to place (a thing) upon another so as to cover it.

1512 *Acc. Ld. High Treas. Scot.* IV. 298 To tile the kingis oratour in the Margret schip, xxxv elnis Kendillye. **1641-2** J. SHUTE *Sarah & Hagar* (1649) 62 God..hath heaped up blessings upon us; yea, tyled one favour upon another. **1719** LONDON & WISE *Compl. Gard.* IX. 322 By tyling up, or wrapping about, or Earthing up, or otherwise covering them. **1776** WITHERING *Brit. Plants* (1796) III. 783 Sphagnum... Leaves..concave, soft, tiling the branches. **1884** W. K. PARKER *Mammalian Desct.* iv. (1885) 95 The Pangolin is tiled over with patches of cemented hair.

2. *Freemasonry.* (Usually **tyle.**) To protect (a lodge or meeting) from interruption and intrusion, so as to keep its proceedings secret, by placing a TILER before the door. Also *transf.* to bind (a person) to secrecy; to keep (any meeting or proceeding) strictly secret.

1762 *Key to Free-Masonry* (1776) 4 *Master to the Junior Deacon.* What is the chief Care of a Mason? *Ans.* To see that the Lodge is tyled. **1768** T. WILSON *Master-Mason* (ed. 2) 26 The master asked his brother warden, if he was a mason, if the lodge was tiled from whence he came. **1846** THACKERAY *Bk. Snobs* xxv, Come, come, Snob my boy, we are all tiled, you know. **1859** SALA *Tw. round Clock* (1861) 308 The doors of those mysterious meeting-places are 'tiled' as securely as Freemasons' lodges. **1896** *Law Times* CII. 123/2 A Parliament chamber [at the Inns of Court] is close tiled, except for purposes of discipline affecting character.

tile, obs. form of TEIL, lime-tree, TILL *v.*

tiled (taɪld), *ppl. a.* [f. TILE *v.* + -ED[1].]

1. Covered, roofed, lined, or laid with tiles.

c **1450** *Godstow Reg.* 495 Bitwene the tyled house of Isabell ..and the ovyn of the same Isabell. **1546** J. HEYWOOD *Prov.* (1867) 58 A tyeld house. **1609** *Ev. Woman in Hum.* IV. ii, He that has not a tilde house must bee glad of a thatch house. **1849** DICKENS *Dav. Copp.* xxi, She was in the tiled kitchen. **1881** 'RITA' *Lady Coquette* iii, A bright wood fire burns in the old tiled fireplace.

b. *Nat. Hist.* Covered with or composed of overlapping leaves, scales, or the like (also said of the leaves, etc.); imbricated. ? *Obs.*

1750-1 MRS. DELANY *Life & Corr.* (1862) III. 27 A present..of a tiled cockle, that weighs above a hundred weight. **1776** WITHERING *Brit. Plants* (1796) I. 139 Scirpus. .. Spike tiled on every side, the florets separated by Scales. *Ibid.* 364 The tiled leaves at the extremity of the plant. **1805** PRISCILLA WAKEFIELD *Domestic Recr.* (1806) I. 12 The third order have four tiled or feathered wings.

c. *slang.* Hatted.

1792 *Misc. Ess.* in *Ann. Reg.* 153/2 Nor were living heads only new tiled in this taste. The statues of their favorite poets were crowned with a red cap.

2. Locally applied to fish dried in the sun (? upon tiles).

1808 SCOTT *Autobiog.* in Lockhart, Dined at Prestonpans on tiled haddocks very sumptuously. **1830** —— *Diary* 27 June, [At Cockenzie] we had a tiled whiting, a dish unknown elsewhere.

3. *Freemasonry.* See TILE *v.* 2.

tile-fish. [Suggested by the termination of the generic name *Lopholatilus*, and by the brilliant colouring resembling ornamental tiles.] Name for the fish *Lopholatilus chamæleonticeps*, found in abundance in 1879 off the coast of New England, and valued as food; supposed to be extinct from the early part of 1882 till 1892, after which year its numbers again increased.

1881 TANNER in *Rep. U.S. Comm. Fish & Fisheries* (1884) 34 One of the tile-fish taken in the morning was boiled for dinner and served with egg sauce. **1884** GOODE *Fisheries of U.S.* I. 360 The Tile-fish..a form discovered on a hitherto unexplored ground, eighty miles southeast of Noman's Land, Massachusetts, in [May] 1879... Captain Kirby of Gloucester, who was the first to obtain specimens of this fish, caught in a few hours several hundred. **1893** *Worthington's Mag.* (Hartford, Conn.) I. 150 The Tile Fish, with its back of pale violet hue and greenish-yellow spots, is one of the most brilliantly colored fishes in the world. **1902** JORDAN & EVERMANN *Amer. Food Fishes* 504 The famous tilefish, whose discovery only a few years ago, and sudden disappearance a few months later, has interested commercial fisherman and scientists as well... It was not until 1892 that they were found again.

'**tile-kiln.** Also 6-7 **-kil(l.** A kiln in which tiles are baked.

1531 *Lett. & Pap. Hen. VIII*, V. 180 A longe cart caryng of tylys from the tyle kyll at Newname Brige unto the Kinges storehouse within the towne of Calais. **1675** COVEL in *Early Voy. Levant* (Hakl. Soc.) 185 There is also just by this town a tile kill. **1830** *Cumb. Farm Rep.* 62 in *Lib. Usef. Knowl., Husb.* III, A proper tile-kiln, shed, etc., were erected.

tilekum, tilicum, varr. TILLICUM.

'**tile-maker.** A maker of tiles; a workman employed in making tiles.

1415 *Ordo pagin. ludi Corp. Cr.* in *York Myst.* Introd. p. xxv, Tielmakers, Milners. **1548** *Nottingham Rec.* IV. 4 Robertus Walesby, tylemaker. **1562** [see TILER 1]. **1688** LUTTRELL *Brief Rel.* (1857) I. 453 The princes nurse is..a tilemaker's wife. **1724** *Lond. Gaz.* No. 6251/3 Every Brickmaker and Tylemaker. **1837** PRICHARD *Phys. Hist. Man.* (ed. 3) II. 135 A caste of potters and tile-makers.

So '**tile-making.**

1437 *Coventry Leet-bk.* 188 That the meire with hys Councell haue the oversight off Tyle-makyng. **1844** STEPHENS *Bk. Farm* I. 581 Clay of excellent quality for tile-making.

† '**tileman.** *Obs.* = TILE-MAKER.

1479-81 *Rec. St. Mary at Hill* 105 Payd to Knyghte, Tyleman, for ij ml tyle, x s viij d. **1609** *MS. Acc. St. John's Hosp., Canterb.*, Payd vnto the tyll mane for a thousand and a haulfe of tylles.

tile-pin. A 'pin' (PIN *sb.*[1] 1) or peg of hard wood used to fasten the tiles to the laths of a roof.

1338 in Dugdale *Monasticon* (1846) II. 585/2 In latthenayles..*jd.* Item in latthes, j d... Item in tyelpynnes, ob. **1422-3** *Abingdon Rolls* (Camden) 97 In tyȝlpynnes emptis viij d. **1426-7** *Rec. St. Mary at Hill* 65 A buschel tyle pynnes viij d. **1563-4** in Swayne *Sarum Churchw. Acc.* (1896) 109 A peck of tylepyns—3d. **1679** MOXON *Mech. Exerc.* viii. 145 Tile-pins of Oak. **1825** J. NICHOLSON *Operat. Mechanic* 550 A square of plain tiling will require a bundle of laths,..two bushels of lime, one bushel of sand, and a peck of tile-pins.

tiler ('taɪlə(r)). Also 3 **tyelere**, 5 **tylare, tyller, tiller, tiellere, teyller, teler**, 6 **tyloure, tylar, teiler**, 7 **tylere**, 5-9 **tyler.** [f. TILE *sb.*[1] and *v.* + -ER[1].]

1. One who covers the roofs of buildings with tiles, a tile-layer, also formerly, a tile-maker.

? *a* **1300** *Deed* in *Shropsh. Arch. Soc. Trans.* (1878) I. 368 De domo mea..que est inter domum Willi le galeys et domum Martini le Tyelere. **1415** *Ordo pagin. ludi Corp. Cr.* in *York Myst.* Introd. p. xxi, Tylers. **1467** in *Eng. Gilds* (1870) 374 That euery tyler marke his tyle. **1483** *Cath. Angl.* 379/1 A Teler,..*tegulator.* **1562** *Act 5 Eliz.* c. 4 §30 Tharte or Occupation of a..Bricklayer. Tyler, Slater, Healyer, Tilemaker. **1663** GERBIER *Counsel* 51 The Tiler, who often removes ten Tiles to lay two new ones. **1735** BERKELEY *Querist* §399 Whether..tilers, plumbers, and glaziers would not find employment if..building prevailed? **1824** LANDOR *Imag. Conv.* xii. Wks. 1846 I. 49 Like tilers, in mending one hole, they make another.

2. *Freemasonry.* (Usually **tyler.**) The doorkeeper who keeps the uninitiated from intruding upon the secrecy of the lodge or meeting.

c **1742** in Hone *Every-day Bk.* (1827) II. 525 Two Tylers, or Guarders..are to guard the Lodge, with a drawn Sword, from all Cowens and Eves-droppers. **1762** *Key to Free-Masonry* (1776) 39 As soon as you come to the Door of the Lodge, you will find the Tyler on the Outside, with a drawn Sword in his Hand, and a white Apron on. **1888** [see TILING 1 b].

† **3.** (See quot.) *slang. Obs.*

1659 *Caterpillers of Nation Anat.*, Tilers, or Cloyers, equivalent to shoplifters.

4. A tile-kiln.

1877 in KNIGHT *Dict. Mech.*

5. A cat that frequents the tiles or roofs.

1905 VIOLET HUNT *Autobiog. Cat* ix. 108 A nice tiler and mouser would be more appropriate.

† **6.** ? A pimple. *Obs. rare*⁻¹.

1660 HOWELL *Parly of Beasts* 25 [The Ass says] Our very Urine is found to be good against Tilers or Morphews in Ladies faces.

tilery ('taɪlərɪ). [f. TILE, TILER: see -ERY.] A place where tiles are made; a tile-field or -kiln.

1846 J. BAXTER *Libr. Pract. Agric.* I. 237 From the tilery to his farm. **1856** *Farmer's Mag.* Jan. 75 In cases where estates extensively require draining, tileries and kilns should be erected. **1871** RUSKIN *Fors Clav.* vi. 11 The first rough potter's fields, tileries, as they called them, or Tuileries.

† '**tile-sherd.** *Obs.* or *dial.* [f. TILE *sb.*[1] + SHERD, SHARD; cf. *potsherd.*] A broken piece or fragment of tile.

1527 *Luton Trin. Guild* (1906) 190 For careeg' of a loode of tyle sherdis to vndre pyn wtall. **1533** *MS. Rawl. D.* 776 lf. 147 b, A loode of Tyle sherdes ffor the levelyng vppe of the vnderpynnyng of the said wharffe. **1616** CHAMPNEY *Voc. Bps.* To Rdr., Little children that build Castles of Tileshards. **1777** HOWARD *Prisons Eng.* (1780) 369 Some prisoners were employed in beating or pounding tile-sherds for the bricklayers. *a* **1825** FORBY *Voc. E. Anglia, Tile-sherd,* ..a fragment of a tile, as potsherd of a pot.

tilestone (ˈtaɪlstəʊn). Forms: see TILE and STONE. [OE. *tiȝelstán,* f. *tiȝele,* TILE *sb.*^{1} + *stán,* STONE *sb.* Cf. MHG. *ziegelstein.*]

†**1.** A brick or tile; the material of bricks or tiles: = TILE *sb.*^{1} 1, 2. *Obs.*

a **1100** *Gloss.* in *Eng. Studien* XI. 66 *Hec imbrex,* tiȝel-stan. **1382** WYCLIF *Gen.* xi. 3 Cometh, & make we tile [**1388** tiel] stoons, and sethe we hem with fier. **1388** —— *Isa.* ix. 10 Tijl stoonys fellen doun, but we schulen bilde with square stoonys. **1432–50** tr *Higden* (Rolls) II. 233 Oon ston was of marbole,..that other was of tyleston. *c* **1425** tr. *Arderne's Treat. Fistula* 82 Tak a tile stone or a scarþe of a potte, and putte it in þe middez of brynnyng colez. **1573** L. LLOYD *Marrow of Hist.* (1653) 21 Pyrrhus..was killed by a..woman with a Tile stone. **1600** NASHE *Summer's Last Will* in Hazl. *Dodsley* VIII. 25 For fear of wearing out my lord's tile-stones with your hobnails. **1681** CHETHAM *Angler's Vade-m.* iv. §20 Dry them on a Fire-Shovel or Tilestone or in an Oven.

2. *Geol.* Any laminated flagstone, splitting into layers thicker than *slate,* suitable for roofing-tiles; *spec.* a group of sandstones forming the transition beds between the Silurian and Devonian systems.

1668 CHARLETON *Onomast.* 242 *Saxum Fissile*..Slate or Tyle-stone. **1719** STRACHEY in *Phil. Trans.* XXX. 971 At Stanton they have..an Iron-Gritt or grey Tile-Stone, which is a Fore-runner of the Coal-Clives. **1778** *Eng. Gazetteer* (ed. 2), Norton under Hambden-Hill, Som...has large quarries of free-stone,..as well as of tile-stone, &c. **1842** SEDGWICK in Hudson *Guide Lakes* (1843) 213 Three groups—the lowest characterized by red flagstone (or 'tilestone'). **1876** A. H. GREEN *Phys. Geol.* ii. §7 If the layers are thin enough for roofing purposes the rock is called a Tilestone.

†**tiˈlette.** *Obs. rare*$^{-1}$. [f. TILE *sb.*^{1} + -ETTE.] A small or minute tile.

c **1440** *Pallad. on Husb.* VI. 195 Brode and thynne Tilette [L. *tesellas*] or tabulette of marbul stoon.

†**tilˈfoir,** *conj. Sc. Obs.* [f. *til-* = TO- prefix + *foir,* FORE *adv.* and *prep.*] = TOFORE, BEFORE.

15.. *Aberd. Reg.* (Jam.), A yeir tilfoir he deceissit.

†**tilˈgiddire,** *adv. Sc. Obs.* [for TOGETHER, with *til-* = TO-.] Together.

c **1375** *Sc. Leg. Saints* xl. (*Ninian*) 420 To god þe fadir be lowinge,..To god þe sone ay honoure be,..Til haly gaste als,..& til þame til-giddire richt.

tiliaceous (tɪlɪˈeɪʃəs), *a. Bot.* [f. L. *tiliāce-us* (f. *tilia* lime-tree) + -OUS: see -ACEOUS.] Belonging to the Natural Order *Tiliaceæ,* typified by the genus *Tilia,* the lime or linden tree.

1891 in *Cent. Dict. Mod.* Jute is obtained from species of the tiliaceous genus *Corchorus.*

†**tilie.** *Obs.* Also 2 teolie, 4 tilye. [OE. *tilia,* agent-n. f. *tilian* to TILL.] One who tills or cultivates the soil; a husbandman; = TILLER *sb.*^{1}

c **1000** *Ags. Gosp.* Matt. xxi. 38 þa ða tylian [*c* **1160** *Hatt. G.* tylien] þone sunu ȝesawun, þa cwædon hiȝ [etc.]. *c* **1175** *Lamb. Hom.* 133 Alse þe wise teolie þenne he wule sawe nimeð ȝeme of twam þingen, an is hweðer þet lond beo bicumelic to þe sede. *c* **1200** *Trin. Coll. Hom.* 155 On tilie ferde ut and sew. *a* **1225** *Ancr. R.* 416 þeos riche ancren þet beoð eorðe tilien, oðer habbeð rentes i-sette. *c* **1325** *Chron. Eng.* 93 (Ritson) Muche folk..That were erthe tilyes gode.

tilie, obs. form of TEIL, lime-tree, TILL *v.*^{1}

tilier, obs. form of TILLER *sb.*^{1}

tiling (ˈtaɪlɪŋ), *vbl. sb.* [f. TILE *v.* and *sb.*^{1} + -ING^1.]

1. a. The action of the verb TILE; the covering (of a roof, etc.) with or as with tiles.

c **1440** *Promp. Parv.* 494/1 Tylynge, of howsys, *tegulacio.* **1591** PERCIVAL *Sp. Dict., Albañeria,* tiling, Tilers art, Masons craft. **1624** CAPT. SMITH *Virginia* VI. 209 Free-stone for building, Slate for tyling. **1726** LEONI *Alberti's Archit.* I. 57/1 Another..convenient way of Tiling.

b. *Freemasonry.* (Usually tyling.) The proper guarding of a lodge.

1888 *Pall Mall G.* 31 Oct. 7/2 Brother W—— E——, Acting Past Master..deliberately broke the tyling of the lodge, and placed the tyler inside along with the ladies.

2. a. *concr.* Work consisting of tiles; the tiles forming the covering of a roof, floor, etc., collectively.

1526 TINDALE *Luke* v. 19 They went vp..and lett hym doune thorowe the tylynge. **1634** SIR T. HERBERT *Trav.* 61 Churches..their outside tyling, pargetted with azure stones. **1694** tr. *Marten's Voy. Spitzbergen* in *Acc. Sev. Late Voy.* II. 135 The Head of the Whale..goeth down sloaping like unto the tyling of an House. **1725** *Bradley's Fam. Dict.* s.v. *Building,* Tiling is measured by ten Foot Square... Three Bushels of Lime will do a Square of Tiling. **1883** MRS. BISHOP *Sk. Malay Pen.* ii, in *Leisure Hour* 21/2 Dutch tiling and Dutch..conceits of all kinds abound.

b. = *tile-draining* vbl. sb. s.v. TILE *sb.*^{1} 6.

1943 J. W. DAY *Farming Adventure* xii. 138 The land was drained by tiling and moling, given three ploughings, and by the end of July sown with wheat. **1960** *Times* 5 July (Agric. Suppl.) p. v/3 More tiling has been undertaken.

3. *attrib.*

1703 MOXON *Mech. Exerc.* 248 A Tyling Trowel, to take up the Morter and lay it on the Tiles. **1765** *Museum Rust.* IV. 80 Tiling lath, 2s. 10d. per bunch. **1907** *Westm. Gaz.* 1 Oct. 7/3 Two shillingsworth of cement and sand would be..required for a yard of tiling-work.

tilka, var. TILAK.

till (tɪl), *sb.*^{1} Forms: 5–6 tylle, 6 tille, 6–7 tyll, 7 til, 6– till. [Origin obscure.]

†**1.** A small box, casket, or closed compartment, contained within or forming part of a larger box, chest, or cabinet; sometimes one that could be lifted out, sometimes a drawer in a cabinet or chest of drawers; used for keeping valuables, documents, etc., more safely. *Obs.* except as in 2.

1452 in *Munimenta Academica* (Rolls) II. 653 Prout patet in scriptis indenturis positis in 'le tylle' in studio meo Oxoniæ. **1530** PALSGR. 281/1 Tyll in a chest, *chettron.* **1534** *Inv. Wardr. Kath. Arragon* in *Camden Misc.* (1855) 40 One cofar..having foure tilles therin, the fore fronte of every of them gilte. **1547–53** SIR R. SADLER *List* in *30th Rep. Dep. Kpr. Publ. Rec.* (1869) 224 Bagges of Bokes, Lettres, and other Writenges remayneng in the study at Westminster, and in several tilles within the same. **1549** in Palgrave *Anc. Kal. & Inv. Excheq.* (1836) III. 417 Which lettres patentes do lye in the nethermost tyll under the tyll wheron is written in text hand Acquietauncies. **1561** in Nichols *Progr. Q. Eliz.* (1823) I. 118 By Anthony Anthony a corbonett fall [full] of tylls. **1591** PERCIVAL *Sp. Dict., Caxon de arca,* the till of a chest, *loculus.* **1633** G. HERBERT *Temple, Confess.* i, Within my heart I made Closets; and in them many a chest;..In those chests, boxes; in each box, a till. **1651** DAVENANT *Gondibert* III. I. liv, A spacious cabinet, with all things fraught.., she by degrees Lifts every till, does every drawer draw. **1664** PEPYS *Diary* 8 Jan., Going to his secret till in his desk, wherein the key of his cash-chest lay. **1719** DE FOE *Crusoe* I. 229 When I came to the Till in the Chests, I found there three great Bags of Pieces of Eight. **1737** [S. BERINGTON] *G. de Lucca's Mem.* (1738) 13 Two little Cabinets..full of intricate Drawers or Tills.

2. Now *spec.* A drawer, money-box, or similar receptacle under and behind the counter of a shop or bank, in which cash for daily transactions is temporarily kept.

1698 *Lond. Gaz.* No. 3363/4 Lost out of Mr. Wray's Shop in Little-Britain, a Til. **1801** MAR. EDGEWORTH *Contrast* v, James swept some loose money off the counter into the till. **1866** CRUMP *Banking* i. 31 All the money..excepting what must be kept in the 'till' for immediate use. **1908** *Times* 22 Apr. 5/5 Officers..suspected they had contemplated robbing the tills.

fig. **1886** *Harper's Mag.* Jan. 242 There is generally a race to see who shall first tap nature's till [i.e. strike oil].

3. *Printing.* Each of the spaces or cells between the ribbed projections of the platen of a hand printing-press, in which the pressman keeps various small requisites.

1888 JACOBI *Printers' Vocab.* 141 *Tills,* the cell-like divisions in the top side of the platen of a hand printing press.

4. *attrib.* and *Comb.* (from 2), as *till-lock, -money, -robber, -robbing*; **till-alarm**, a device by which a bell is automatically rung when the till is opened; **till-box** = sense 1; **till-roll**, a roll of paper recording an account of the transactions made at the till to which it is attached; **till-tapping**, pilfering from a till; so **till-tapper**.

1692 *Lond. Gaz.* No. 2756/4 Stolen..a Till-box with some Money in it. **1737** *Salmon's Country Builder's Estimator* (ed. 2) 110 Cabinet Locks, Till Locks, and Scrutoire Locks. **1862** *Catal. Internat. Exh., Brit.* II. No. 5152 Ticket, receipt, and till protector. **1877** KNIGHT *Dict. Mech., Till-alarm.* **1891** *Daily News* 3 Feb. 2/4 Part of their reserves..being necessary 'till-money' for daily transactions in small change. **1893** *Columbus* (Ohio) *Disp.* 14 Nov., For some time the firm has been a loser by persistent till-tapping... The camera lens closed automatically with the photographs of the till tappers. **1895** SNAITH *D. Marvin* xxvii, Pete declared it [the money stolen] was a month's till money. **1972** *Times* 18 Oct. 4/4 The butcher..examined his till roll, and there was no record of anyone having paid that amount.

till, *sb.*^{2} Orig. and chiefly *Sc.* [Origin unascertained: cf. THILL^2 in similar sense.]

1. A term applied to a stiff clay, more or less impervious to water, usually occurring in unstratified deposits, and forming an ungenial subsoil. Originally a term of agriculture in Scotland.

1765 A. DICKSON *Treat. Agric.* II. (ed. 2) 222 They [plowmen] are so inattentive, as to leave good soil in some places, and turn up till in others. **1799** J. ROBERTSON *Agric. Perth* 19 On the declivities of almost all the hills a strong stiff till abounds. *Ibid.* 477 Like all the land on the south aspect of the Seedlaws being a red till, capable of high cultivation and in most places approaching to the nature of loam. **1805** FORSYTH *Beauties Scotl.* II. 66 *Till,*..is in universal use among farmers,..implying very various mixtures of mineral substances placed under the fertile mould... In general,..a hard clay of any sort, which in a very slight degree admits the passage of water, and is impenetrable by the roots of plants. **1816** SCOTT *Antiq.* iv, Placing paving-stones beneath the tree when first planted..a barrier between his roots and the unkindly till. *Ibid.* xxiii, We're down to the till now,..and the ne'er a coffin or ony thing else is here.

fig. **1831** BREWSTER *Nat. Magic* xi. (1833) 287 It may lie long unproductive in the ungenial till of human knowledge.

b. In the majority of cases this clay belongs to the Glacial or Drift period, and in geological use 'till' has the specific sense 'boulder clay'.

1842 DARWIN in *Life & Lett.* (1887) I. 300 A contribution to the Geological Society, on the boulders and 'till'of South America. **1851** *Jrnl. R. Agric. Soc.* XII. I. 281 This clay..rests upon 'till', or boulder clay. **1863** LYELL *Antiq. Man* xii. (ed. 3) 218 Erratics of Scandinavian origin occur chiefly in the lower portions of the till. **1863** A. C. RAMSAY *Phys. Geog.* xxiv. (1878) 384 Much of the Lower Boulder-clay is known as 'Till' in Scotland.

2. Hard or soft shale; app. = THILL^2. *dial.*

1672 SINCLAIR *Misc. Observ. Hydrost.* 260 (Jam.) All metals, as stone and tilles (which are seems of black stone, and participat much of the nature of coal), ly one above another, and keep a regular course. **1831** W. PATRICK *Plants Lanark* Pref. 18 The stratum itself lies on a bed of till above the main coal.

3. *Comb.* **till-stone**, a fissile shale, in coalmines, etc.

c **1830** *Glouc. Farm Rep.* 4 in *Lib. Usef. Kn., Husb.* III, A thin wet clay, of a most adhesive nature, covering the thin fissile till-stone.

†**till,** *sb.*^{3} *Obs.* or *dial.* Abbrev. of LENTIL, *quasi* 'Lent-till': see quot. 1640. (Chiefly in *pl.*)

1388 WYCLIF *Ezek.* iv. 9 Take..wheete, and barli, and beenys, and tillis [1382 lent]. **1398** TREVISA *Barth. De P.R.* XVII. xcvi. (Bodl. MS.), Malice off Tille is temprid ȝif þe skynne is ido aweye & þe piþ sode in fresche water. **14..** *Voc.* in Wr.-Wülcker 594/5 *Lupinus,* Tylles. **1607** *Schol. Disc. agst. Antichr.* I. ii. 95 What maketh the fitches, tylles, tares..which are mingled with the wheate? **1640** PARKINSON *Theatr. Bot.* 1068 Wee in English [call it] Lentills, but the country people in Hampshire, and other countries..call it Tills, leaving out the Lent, as thinking that word agreeth not with the matter. **1669** WORLIDGE *Syst. Agric.* (1681) 42 The least of all Pulses is the Lentil, in some places called Tills. **1760** J. LEE *Introd. Bot.* App. 330 Tills, *Ervum.*

till, *sb.*^{4} *Printing.* [Cf. MHG., Ger. *tülle* (LG. *dulle,* Du. *dille*) a socket in which something is fixed, or through which a rod or spindle passes.] In the early forms of hand printing-presses, a horizontal cross-piece extending between and fixed to the two main uprights, through which passes the hose or sleeve, and the shank of the spindle; also called *shelf.*

1611 COTGR., *Planche,*..the Till of a Printers Presse, or the shelfe that compasseth the Hose. **1683** MOXON *Mech. Exerc., Printing* x. ¶6 The Till is a Board about one Inch thick... In its middle it hath a round Hole..for the Shank of the Spindle to pass through. **1771** LUCKOMBE *Hist. Print.* 366 It may..be botched up by putting scabbord between the Hose and the square holes of the Till. **1841** SAVAGE *Dict. Printing* 796 *Till* or *Shelf,* a mahogany shelf that clasps the hose and causes it and the spindle to come down perpendicularly without any play.

till, *sb.*^{5} *Obs.* or *dial.* [f. TILL *v.*^{1}]

1. An act of tilling or ploughing land: see TILL *v.*^{1} 4.

1647 *Husbandman's Plea agst. Tithes* 36 Item for plowing of the fallow for Wheat at 3 tilles at 5s. the Acre, for every of the three times plowing 60 li. **1760** BROWN *Compl. Farmer* II. 32 In Oxfordshire..they give their sour land a till, according to the..condition of their lands.

b. *concr.* (See quots.)

1794–1806 *Rep. Agric., Lanc.* 27 (E.D.S.) *Till,* a compost of earth and lime, mixed. **1828** *Craven Gloss., Till, Tillage,* manure, compost.

2. ? Labour, toil: cf. TILL *v.*^{1} 1.

? *a* **1800** *Dame Oliphant* xii. in Child *Ballads* (1886) IV. 409/1 Willie he gaed hame again, To his hard task and till.

†**till,** *sb.*^{6} *Obs. rare*$^{-1}$. [f. TILL *v.*^{3}] Allurement, enticement.

1596 COLSE *Penelope* (1880) 179, I feare me he hath caught some doue, And keepes her tame, with tills of loue.

till (tɪl), *v.*^{1} Forms: α. 1–2 tilian (1 til(i)ȝan), 2–5 tilie(n, 3 tiliȝen, tillien, 3–5 tylye, 3–6 tile, tyle, 3–7 tille, 4 tilye, tylie, tilly, 4–6 tylle, 4–7 til, 6 tyll, 6– till. β. 1 tiol-, teolian, 2 teolien, 2–3 teliȝen, 4 telie(n, tell, teile, 4–5 (*Sc.* 6) tele, 5 telle, 6–7 *Sc.* teil, teill, 8–9 *dial.* teel. γ. 1–2 tylian, 3–4 tulie(n (ü), 4 tulye (ü). [OE. *tilian* to strive, acquire = OFris. *tilia* to get, cultivate, OS. *tilian* to obtain (MDu., Du. *telen* to breed, raise, cultivate, cause, etc.), OHG. *zilôn, zilên* to strive (G. *zielen* to aim, strive):—OTeut. **tilô-jan,* **tilêjan,* denom. f. **tilom*: see TILL *prep.* By breaking of *i* before *l,* *tilian* became *tiolian, teolian,* later *tele*: cf. PILL *v.*^{1}, PEEL *v.*^{1} (Sievers *Ags. Gram.* ed. 3, §105, 3, §107 Anm. 4, §416, 14a.).]

I. To labour, work for or at, cultivate.

†**1.** *intr.* To strive, exert oneself, labour, work.

α. *c* **897** K. ÆLFRED *Gregory's Past. C.* xix. 147 He sceal tilian ðæt he liciȝe. *c* **1000** ÆLFRIC *Saints' Lives* xxviii. 168 To þisum swicolum life we swincað and tiliaþ and to þam towerdan life we tiliað hwonlice. *c* **1175** *Lamb. Hom.* 19 Nu sculle we..tilian to þere saule bihofðe. *c* **1200** *Trin. Coll. Hom.* 37 Sume men..tiliȝet[h] michel to oðre mannæs bihofþe. *a* **1225** *Ancr. R.* 404 Ure Louerd..tiled efter hore luue.

β, γ. **971** *Blickl. Hom.* 219 Se deada man cwic eft..& teolode to arisenne. *c* **1000** ÆLFRIC *Hom.* I. 412 Oxa teolað his hlaforde. *Ibid.* II. 76 þa tyliað..Gode, þa ðe ne secað heora aȝen ȝestreon ðurh ȝytsunge. *c* **1175** *Lamb. Hom.* 133 þenne heo fundieð to teoliende efter istreone. *c* **1200** *Trin. Coll. Hom.* 155 þanne hie wilen tulien after strene.

†**2.** *trans.* To labour after, seek after, provide; to get by effort, to obtain, acquire, or earn by labour; also (later) *simply,* to get, obtain. In OE. and Early ME. const. with genitive, later with acc. *Obs.*

a **900** *Ags. Psalter* (Th.) xlviii. 7 Full neah ælc mann þæs tiolað..hu he on ecnesse swincan mæȝe. *c* **1000** Ælfric *Hom.* II. 552 Se asolcena ðeowa, þe nolde tilian nan ðing his hlaforde. *c* **1016** *O.E. Chron.* an. 1016 (Laud), Hi..heom metes tilodon. *a* **1175** *Cott. Hom.* 223 þu scealt mid ærfeðnesse þe metes tylian. *c* **1220** *Bestiary* 80 in *O.E. Misc.* 3 Ne maiȝ he [the eagle] tilen him non fode. **1297** R. Glouc. (Rolls) 974 Hii..swonke & tylede hor liflode. *c* **1330** R. Brunne *Chron.* (1810) 220 His luf to tak & tille. **1377** Langl. *P. Pl.* B. xiv. 67 Many wyntres men lyueden and no mete ne tulyeden [*v.rr.* teleden, tiliden, tilieden, tylied; C. xvi. 271 no mete telden]. *c* **1380** Wyclif *Wks.* (1880) 300 Pore men..þat hauen greet neede..to þyng þat freris tillen of hem. *c* **1425** *Cast. Persev.* 2538 in *Macro Pl.* 153 A-forn mele, men mete schul tyle [*rimes* skyl, wyl, hyle]. *c* **1440** *York Myst.* vi. 59 Adam!..tille with-alle þi meete and drynke for euer-more.

†**3.** To take care of or attend to medically; to treat (a patient, or a disease). Const. as in 2. Only *OE.*

a **850** *Laws Ecgbert, Poenit.* iv. c. 20 Wifman..ȝif heo tilað hire cilde med æniȝum wiccecræfte. *c* **897** K. Ælfred *Gregory's Past. C.* lxii. 457 Hwæðres..ðara yfela is betere ær to tilianne? *a* **1000** *Life St. Guthlac* xxii. (Goodw.) 96 His læces hine mid sealfum lange teolodon. *c* **1000** *Sax. Leechd.* II. 60 þonan se micla ȝeoxa cume, oþþe hu hit mon tilian scule.

4. *trans.* To bestow labour and attention, such as ploughing, harrowing, manuring, etc., upon (land) so as to fit it for raising crops; to cultivate.

α. *c* **1205** Lay. 2618 þat lond heo lette tilien [*c* **1275** tilie]. *a* **1300** *Cursor M.* 23851 (Edinb.) Il worþe it es to til [*v.rr.* tile, tille, *Gött.* tell] þe fild, þat noht ogain þe sed mai yeld. *c* **1400** Maundev. (Roxb.) xxxii. 147 þe folk nowþer tillez ne sawez na land. *c* **1449** Pecock *Repr.* iii. i. (Rolls) 275 Feeldis ..which thei hem silf tilien. **1535** Coverdale *Gen.* ii. 5 Nether was there eny man to tylle the earth. **1625** Carpenter *Geog. Delin.* ii. i, He began..to till and manure the soyle with all heedfull industrie. **1765** Hutchinson *Hist. Mass.* I. 207 Light land being easily tilled. **1835** Thirlwall *Greece* I. ix. 342 The prisoners were forced to till the enemy's land.

β. *c* **1200** *Vices & Virtues* 75 And land teliȝen and weriȝen. **13..** Tell [see quot. *a* 1300 in α]. *c* **1400** Maundev. (Roxb.) xxii. 103 Men of oure stature, þe whilk telez þe land. *c* **1450** *Godstow Reg.* 33 In londes I-telyd and not I-telyd. **1536** in *Reg. Mag. Sig. Scot.* 1538. 394 Licence..to ryfe, outbreke and teill yeirlie 1000 acris of thair commounlandis. **1569** *Reg. Privy Council Scot.* I. 653 Na Scottisman dwelland in Scotland sall tak or teill ony ground in England. **1882** Jago *Cornw. Gloss.*, *Teel*, to plant or sow.

b. *spec.* To plough (land).

1377 Langl. *P. Pl.* B. xix. 256 My plowman Piers shal ben.., And for to tulye [*v.r.* tilie] treuthe a teme shal he haue. **1513** Douglas *Æneis* vi. xiv. 96 Quhair thow thi riggis telis for to saw. **1535** Coverdale *1 Sam.* xiv. 14 Halue an aker of londe, which a pare of oxen maye tyll in one daye. **1652** Needham tr. *Selden's Mare Cl.* 260 An Hide..is so much Land as a Man can till with one Plow for a year. **1863** Fawcett *Pol. Econ.* i. iv. (1876) 42 The same ploughs till the land for many successive crops.

c. *absol.*

1100-21 *O.E. Chron.* an. 1097, On unȝewederan þa man oððe tilian sceolde oððe eft tilða ȝegaderian. **1340-70** *Alex. & Dind.* 854 Whan ȝe mow take no tol to tilien on erþe. *a* **1400-50** *Alexander* 4581 How suld ȝe tellel withouten toles? **1596** Dalrymple tr. *Leslie's Hist. Scot.* v. (S.T.S.) I. 293 This Haii..was behaldeng in the neist feild how the pluche teilet. **1652** Bp. Hall *Invis. World* i. viii, They then must purvey for their own food, and either till, or famish. **1850** Mrs. Jameson *Leg. Monast. Ord.* (1863) 125 They drained, they tilled, they planted.

†**5.** *trans.* To raise, rear (a crop); to tend and cultivate (a plant) so as to promote growth. *Obs.*

c **1250** *Gen. & Ex.* 1278 Abraham..tillede corn and sette treen. **1387** Trevisa *Higden* (Rolls) II. 309 To ere and sowe and haue corne i-teled. *c* **1400** Maundev. (1839) v. 50 Men maken all weys þat bawme to ben tyled of the cristen men. **1483** Caxton *Gold. Leg.* 391 b/1 Of hym that tylyeth the vyne.

6. *fig.* To cultivate (something figured as land or as a crop, e.g. the mind, a 'field' of knowledge, a virtue, etc.).

1393 Langl. *P. Pl.* C. i. 87 Bisshopes..Ben chargid with holy churche charyte to tulie, þat is, leel loue..a-mong lered and lewed. **1535** Coverdale *Ezek.* xxxvi. 9 Vnto you will I turne me, that ye maye be tylled and sowen. **1642** Gauden *Three Serm.* 132 Hee becomes tild and polished for the best society. *a* **1764** Lloyd *Author's Apol.* Wks. 1774 I. 6 And tills their minds with proper care. **1889** Roscoe in *Nature* 10 Oct. 579/1 His most important researches have entered upon fields hitherto tilled, with but scanty success, by the biologist.

II. To prepare, set, or spread in readiness.

7. *trans.* To spread (a net), set (a trap or snare). Also, to set in any position. Now *s.w. dial.* Cf. teld *v.* 4. Also *absol.*

a **1225** *Ancr. R.* 334 (MS. Nero) þer me sit mid þe greahundes forte kepen þe hearde, oðer tillen [*v.rr. Vern.* tilleþ, *Corpus, Cleop., Caius* tildeð, *Titus* tildes] þe nettes aȝean ham. **1587** Turberv. *Trag. T.* 33 The wilie witted boy That tiles his trappe to take the subtile foxe. **1613** W. Browne *Sheph. Pipe* ii. (1614) D j b, Nor knowes a trappe nor snare to till. *c* **1750** Mrs. Palmer *Devon. Dial.* (1837) 2 Took a bard out of the springal that little maester had a-teel'd. **1799** in Southey *Comm.-pl. Bk.* (1851) IV. 523 [By Newton Bushel we saw a board] Man Traps and Spring Guns are tilled in this Garden. **1880** Carnegie *Trapping* 5 It is ten chances to one that the rabbit will go over or to the place at which you did not (as it is called in the West) 'till' your gin. *Ibid.* 36 In..trapping rooks..there is no difficulty in telling what part of the field to 'till' in. **1882** Jago *Cornw. Gloss.*, *Teel*, to set or 'teel a trap'. **1890** *Gloucestersh. Gloss.*, *Tile* or *Teel*..to tile a trap, to set a trap; to tile a gate, to set it open. **1895** Quiller-Couch *Wand. Heath* 80 He and his mates went out and tilled the trammel.

†**8.** To pitch (a tent): = teld *v.* 1; to set (a sail). *Obs.*

1362 Langl. *P. Pl.* A. ii. 44 Ten þousend of Tentes I-tilled [*v.rr.* I-teldyde, teldit, teled] be-sydes. **1628** Digby *Voy. Medit.* (Camden) 11 We had not men enough to till our sailes untill the other shippes were gone past our discerning.

III. †**9.** *Comb.* of verb-stem. **till-land** (teleland), tilled land, land under cultivation; so **till-ridge** (teill ryge). *Sc. Obs.*

1437 *Registr. Aberdon.* (Maitland) I. 247 Merkand northwest our a moss to þe nerrast teleland of Ardgrane. **1549** *Aberdeen Regr.* (Spald. Cl.) I. 274 That na maner of takismen..ryif out..ony landis..without thair teill ryge of auld.

†**till**, *v.*[2] *Obs.* Forms: 3-4 tille; also *3rd sing. pres.* 3 **tilþ, tylþ**; *pa. t.* 3 **tylde**, 3-4 **tilde**, 5 **tilt**. [OE. **tillan*, in comb. *ȝetillan* to touch, reach, attain, *atillan* to touch; cf. Goth. *gatilôn* to attain, obtain.] *intr.* To reach, extend (to a specified point or distance; in quot. 1393, to a specified length).

[*a* **1000** *Blickl. Glosses* (E.E.T.S.) 262/2 Weras bloda & facenfulle na healfe ȝetillað.] *c* **1290** *St. Brendan* 616 in *S. Eng. Leg.* 236 His her tilde doun to is fet, of berde and of heued. **1297** R. Glouc. 174 Fram douere in to chestre tilleþ watelinge stret. **1387** Trevisa *Higden* (Rolls) II. 107 The kyngdom of Deyra tillede and streiȝte from þe ryuer of Humber anon to þe ryuere of Tyne. **1393** Langl. *P. Pl.* C. vii. 220 Ich putte hem in pressours..Tyl ten ȝerdes oþer twelue tilled [A. v. 128 tolden; B. v. 214 tolled] out þrettyne.

b. *trans.* (*a*) To stretch to, attain to, reach, touch. (*b*) To stretch (a thing) out.

[*c* **961** Æthelwold *Rule St. Benet* vii. (Schröer) 23 ȝif we þone hrof þære healican eaðmodnesse ȝetillan willað.] *c* **1400** *Destr. Troy* 914 As he tilt out his tung with his tethe grym.

†**till**, *v.*[3] *Obs.* [Forms: 1 **tyllan**, *pa. t.* **tylde**], 3 **tulle(n (ü)**, *pa. t.* **tulde**, 4-5 **tille, tylle**, 5 **tyll**, 4-7 **till** (4 **til**, 6-7 *pa. t.* and *pple.* **tild**): see also toll *v.*[1] [OE. **tyllan* (in comb. *fortyllan* to draw away, seduce), early ME. *tullen* (*ü*), ME. *tylle, tille, till.* Ulterior history obscure.]

1. *trans.* To draw, attract, persuade; to entice, allure, coax; to win over.

a **1225** *Ancr. R.* 320 Mi liht onswere, oðer mine liht lates, tulde him erest upon me. *Ibid.* 414 Ne tulle ȝe to þe ȝete none unkuðe harloz. *a* **1300** *Cursor M.* 12175 (Cott.) To þe scole him for to till [*v.r.* tille]. *a* **1340** Hampole *Psalter* xxiv. 2 þof þai waite nyght and daye with ill suggestions to till me til syn. **13..** *Minor Poems fr. Vernon MS.* xxix. ii. 38 On of þe Iewes Malicious Tilled þe child in to his hous. *c* **1375** *Sc. Leg. Saints* xxx. (*Theodera*) 159 For eth is a man to til To do it þat is his wil. **1471** Ripley *Comp. Alch.* v. xliii. in Ashm. (1652) 158 Lest wyth theyr flatteryng they so the tyll That thou agre unto ther wyll. **1581** A. Hall *Iliad* iv. 71 He tild them for to trye And proue with him the combate. **1600** Holland *Livy* xxi. xi. 399 By tilling them on, and alluring them with hope of great rewards. **1609** C. Butler *Fem. Mon.* ii. (1623) D iv, The sunne rising doth oftimes till them forth. **1666** M. M. *Solomon's Prescript.* 83 Devils.. labouring to..till thee on.

b. *absol.*

13.. *Cursor M.* 27307 (Cott.) He sal him til a-mendes drau,..wit wordes soft and mild, Als moder tilland dos hir child. *a* **1591** H. Smith *Wks.* (1866-7) I. 299 As though his eyes would draw his heart, as the bait tilleth on the hook.

2. To draw (physically).

a **1400-50** *Alexander* 5479 þai [sirens] droȝe þam doun into þe depe & drowned þaim..Or els þai tillid þaim to þe trees.

b. *intr.* ? To proceed, go. (Cf. 'draw near'.)

1297 R. Glouc. (Rolls) 2492 Sire graunte me þanne, quaþ hengist, ȝif it is þi wille As moche place as mid a þuong ich may aboute tille. *c* **1330** R. Brunne *Chron.* (1810) 128 To gile no to fraude wild he neuer tille. [But this may be 1.]

till (tɪl), *v.*[4] [mod. f. till *sb.*[1]] *trans.* To put (money) into a till.

1841 J. T. Hewlett *Parish Clerk* III. 68 Having tilled the fourpence three farthings. **1891** Goschen in *Standard* 9 July 2/3 Coins..which have been tilled for many years, thereby not being exposed to any friction.

till (tɪl), *prep.*, *conj.*, *adv.* Forms: 1, 3-7 **til**, 4-5 **tille, tylle**, 4-6 **tyl, tyll**; 3 (*Orm.*), 4- **till** (in 18th c. often printed '*till* as if short for until). Also 4 **tel**, 4-5 **tell**, 5 **telle**; 5 (9 *dial.*) **tul**, 6 (8 *dial.*) **tull**; 5 **thyll(e**. [ONorthumb. *til*, a. ON. *til* prep. with genitive (e.g. *til Islands*, to Iceland, *til dauða-dags* to the day of death); mod. Icel., Færo., Norw., Da. *til*, Sw. *till*; also OFris. *til* prep. with dative. Prob. originally a sb. **til* = OE. *till* fixed point, station, OHG., MHG. *zil*, Ger. *ziel* neut. end, limit, point aimed at, goal, late MLG. *tel*, *til* aim, (fixed) point of time; cf. ON. *aldrtili* end of life, death; hence the const. with genitive: prop. 'with the limit or goal of (the place or time named)'. In ON. it filled the place of the WGer. prep. *tô*, *ti*, *te*, Ger. *zu*, *zi*, *ze*, OE. *tó*, to. Characteristically northern in reference to place or purpose (though in ME. occasionally midl. or south.); in reference to time, general Eng. from *c* 1300, though now often superseded by the compound until. To the same root belong OE. *til* adj. 'to the purpose, serviceable, good', and OE. *tilian*, *-tillan*, till *v.*[1], *v.*[2]]

A. *prep.* **I.** Local and dative. Now only *n. dial.* and *Sc.*, where normally used instead of *to* before a vowel or *h*.

1. = to *prep.* **a.** In the ordinary local sense of *to*.

a **800** *Inscription, Ruthwell Cross, Dumfries* in *O.E.T.* 126 Hweþræ þer fusæ fearran kwomu æþþilæ til anum. *c* **1200** Ormin Ded. 170 He..stah þa siþþenn upp till heffne. *a* **1300** *Cursor M.* 10832 (Cott.) Ar he his wijf til hus wald bring. *c* **1330** R. Brunne *Chron.* (1810) 3 þe fled out of Wales away tille Ireland. *c* **1380** Wyclif *Sel. Wks.* III. 445 Suche gone prively til helle. *c* **1386** Chaucer *Knt.'s T.* 2106 They goon Hoom til Atthenes. *c* **1460** *Towneley Myst.* xv. 113 Tyll egyp weynd shall we. **1489** Caxton *Faytes of A.* ii. xiii. 114 He dyde goo from one place tyl another. **1582-8** *Life James VI* (1804) 256 The Earle of Atholl sent aduertisement heirof till Argyll. *a* **1618** J. Davies *Eglogues* Poems (1772) 114 Whan we wenden till another place. **1807** J. Stagg *Poems* 36 As king Solomon hath said, The place I'll not turn tilt [= to it]. **1816** Scott *Antiq.* ix, Rab..bang'd out o' bed, and till some of his readiest claes.

b. As far as; so as to reach. Cf. also C. 3.

1375 Barbour *Bruce* x. 682 Swerdis..War till the hyltis all bludy. *c* **1400** Maundev. (1839) ix. 107 The forpartie of the heed til vnder the chyn is at Rome. **1483** Caxton *Gold. Leg.* 80/2 Nabugodonosor..sente vnto all Regyons aboute ..tyl the mountes of ethyope. **1535** Coverdale *Judg.* xx. 43 They..folowed vpon them..and trode them downe tyll afore Gibea. **1561** Hollybush *Hom. Apoth.* 38 That it maye reache..from the nauell tyll the priuy membres. **1828** Buchan *Ballads* I. 2 He read it till an end.

2. In senses of *to* derived from the local.

a. where the object is not a point in space. Now *Sc.*

c **1200** Ormin Ded. 18 þu þohhtesst tatt itt mihhte wel Till mikell frame turrnenn. *a* **1340** Hampole *Psalter* xxiv. 2 Ill suggestions to till me til syn. *c* **1400** Maundev. (Roxb.) Pref. 2 What lufe he had til his sugets. *Ibid.* iv. 12 Changed..fra a faire damysell til a dragoun. **1509** Bp. Fisher *Funeral Serm. C'tess Richmond* Wks. (E.E.T.S.) i. 294 She restrayned her appetyte tyl one mele & tyl one fysshe on the day. **1513** Douglas *Æneis* vi. Prol. 64 Till vertu thaim to brod. **1582-8** *Life Jas. VI.* (1804) 260 He was putt till extreme tortor. **1655** Fuller *Ch. Hist.* iv. iii. §40 He was.. restored till his liberty and archbishoprick. **1826** J. Wilson *Noct. Ambr.* Wks. (1855) I. 125, I venerate the adherence till't. **1858** Ramsay *Remin.* v. (1870) 104 'They're what we must all come till'.

†**b.** Conformably to, in accordance with, after. *Obs. rare.*

1340 Hampole *Pr. Consc.* 90 Ilk man..God made til his awen lyknesse. *c* **1400** Maundev. (Roxb.) Pref. 2 How dere he boght man þat he had made til his awen liknes. *c* **1489** Caxton *Blanchardyn* xix. 59 He was not armed tyl his plesure.

†**c.** To or for the purpose of, in order to be; to become, as. *Obs.*

a **1352** Minot *Poems* xi. 40 þat he may at his ending haue heuin till his mede. *a* **1450** *Le Morte Arth.* 637 The feyrest lady..Tille his lemman chosen hath he. *c* **1489** Caxton *Blanchardyn* xxv. 93, I wolde haue gyuen you tyl his wyff.

3. Expressing the indirect object or dative relation. After verbs of giving, telling, comparing, hearkening, pertaining, addition, affecting action; adjs. and sbs. of likeness, agreeableness, belonging, relationship, etc. Now *n. dial.* and *Sc.*

c **950** *Lindisf. Gosp.* Matt. xxvi. 31 Ða cueð til him ðe hælend. *c* **1200** Ormin 803 He seȝȝde þuss till himm. **13..** *Cursor M.* 13632 (Cott. & Fairf.) Hald þe til [*Gött. & Trin.* to] him. **1340** Hampole *Pr. Consc.* 1833 Of twa [reasons] byfore I spake, Now wil I other twa til þam take. **1357** *Lay Folks Catech.* 29 (MS. T.) Of the lawe and þe lare þat langes till halikirke. *Ibid.* 89 Iesu crist..Is sothefastly god euen til [= equal to] his fadir. **1375** Barbour *Bruce* i. 565 þe Endentur till him gaf he. *Ibid.* xiii. 511 Till hym neir syb wes he. *c* **1400** Maundev. (Roxb.) Pref. 2 Knawen openly til all men. *Ibid.* iii. 9 þai schuld be obedient til him. *c* **1460** *Towneley Myst.* xviii. 239 Whi dos thou tyll vs thus? **1521** Fisher *Serm. agst. Luther* i. Wks. (E.E.T.S.) i. 317 How that shadowe & this thynge agreeth..one tyll another. **1724** Ramsay *Tea-t. Misc.* (1733) I. 21 Wad ye compare ye'r sell to me, A Docken till a tansie. **1790** Mrs. Wheeler *Westmld. Dial.* (1821) 59 He hes dun tull em oa [= all] alike. **1815** Scott *Guy M.* xv, The death of the grey mare..was naething till't. **1818** —— *Hrt. Midl.* xviii, 'Hear till her', said Madge.

†**4.** In prec. senses, often placed after its object, for metrical reasons. *Obs.*

a **1300** *Cursor M.* 3712 (Cott.) And sithen his sun he cald him till. *c* **1350** *Will. Palerne* 2350, I wold wend hem tille wiþ-oute ani stint. *c* **1380** *Sir Ferumb.* 5264 þus he spak him tille. *c* **1420** *Chron. Vilod.* 1412 Alle his askyng þey grauntede hym tylle. *a* **1562** G. Cavendish *Poems* (1825) II. 19, I espied certeyn persons comyng me tyll.

II. Of time.

5. a. Onward to (a specified time); up to the time of (an event); during the whole time before; until. (Denoting continuance up to a particular time, and usually implying cessation or change at that time: cf. B. 1.)

c **1330** R. Brunne *Chron. Wace* (Rolls) 27 Fro Eneas till Brutus tyme. *c* **1375** *Cursor M.* 498 (Fairf.) Sa þai sal tille [*Cott., Gött.* to] domes day. *a* **1400** *Sir Perc.* 25 Fro thethyne tille his lyves ende. *a* **1548** Hall *Chron., Edw. IV* 232 b, He kepte all these thinges secret, tyll his retorne. **1588**, **1827** [see morn 2 b]. **1591** Shaks. *1 Hen. VI*, i. ii. 127 Fight till the last gaspe. **1611** Bible *Exod.* xvi. 19 Let no man leaue of it till the morning. **1632** Le Grys tr. *Velleius Paterc.* Ded. 7 From the foundation of the city till the ruine of the Macedonian kingdome. **1824** Scott *St. Ronan's* xxxviii, She doubted if the woman would live till morning.

b. After a negative, denoting the continuance of the negative condition up to the time indicated (and implying its cessation then); thus nearly equivalent to *before*. Cf. B. 1 b.

1590 SHAKS. *Com. Err.* II. ii. 164, I neuer saw her till this time. **1649** HEYLIN *Relat. & Observ.* II. 155 To give no account for it till Doomes-day in the afternoone. **1671** LADY MARY BERTIE in *12th Rep. Hist. MSS. Comm.* App. v. 22 The grand ballett is not to be danced till Shrove-Munday. **1719** DE FOE *Crusoe* (1790) I. 28 [He] begged of me not to go on shore till day. **1861** M. PATTISON *Ess.* (1889) I. 41 It was not till the fourteenth century that their guild rose into wealth and importance. **1887** MRS. OLIPHANT *Makers Venice* II. ii. 177 The news..did not reach him till long after the event.

c. Followed by an adverb (or adv. phr.) of time. Cf. NOW 13, THEN 7.

c **1380** WYCLIF *Last Age Church* 30 Fro Crist til now, þrittene hundrid ȝeer and sixe and fyfty. *a* **1518** SKELTON *Magnyf.* 319 Fare you well tyll sone. **1535** COVERDALE *Prov.* xxix. 11 A foole poureth out his sprete alltogether, but a wyse man kepeth it in till afterwarde. **1598** SHAKS. *Merry W.* v. i. 28, I knew not what 'twas to be beaten, till lately. **1667** MILTON *P.L.* II. 744, I know thee not, nor ever saw till now Sight more detestable. **1746** FRANCIS tr. *Horace, Epist.* I. vii. 107 Till then farewel. **1844** KINGLAKE *Eothen* viii, It was not till after midnight that my visit..came to an end. *Mod.* I stayed till after ten o'clock.

d. = TO *prep.* 6 b, in stating the time of day. *U.S.*

1949 [see QUARTER *sb.* 8 c]. **1962** M. & G. GORDON *Journey with Stranger* (1963) iv. 36 'Ten till,' he said... 'I'll go in first.'

III. = *To* with the infinitive. Now only *Sc.*

6. a. as prep. introducing the infinitive of purpose.

Not in Norse. Closely akin to 2 c; *þare sorrow til amese* = to or with the aim of, or for the purpose of, amesing their sorrow, to the mitigation of their sorrow.

13.. *Cursor M.* 5330 (Cott.) He praid þe god men þat þar wer To lith a quil his word til her. *c* **1375** *Sc. Leg. Saints* xxi. (*Clement*) 519 Thane, þare gret sorow til ames, Petyre þame tald how It was Hapnyt. *c* **1425** WYNTOUN *Cron* IX. xxv. 2838 Tyll ete ore drink, syng ore dance. **1513** DOUGLAS *Æneis* VIII. vii. 31 Sen Nereus douchtir, Thetis, mycht.. Induce the till enarme hir son Achill. **1535** STEWART *Cron. Scot.* (Rolls) III. 323 For till reskew Thair libertie.. Beseikand him to tak auctoritie In that mater and afald ay till be. **1599** A. HUME *Epist. to G. Moncrieff* 164 Till execute their office man be hyred.

b. as sign of the simple infinitive; esp. after *for*.

Now chiefly used before a vowel or *h*.

c **1375** *Cursor M.* 12989 (Fairf.) For tille [*v.r.* to] be myne vnderloute. **1375** BARBOUR *Bruce* I. 98 Trawayllyt for to wyn senyhory, And throw hus mycht till occupy Landis. **1424** *Coldstream Chartul.* (1879) 42 Be it mad kend..me Jon of Swynton..till haue fulli grantit to ye priores [etc.]. *c* **1485** *Digby Myst.* (1882) IV. 1252 Now aught I sore till irke! **1513** DOUGLAS *Æneis* VI. xv. 10 For til excers the art of geometrye. **1816** SCOTT *Antiq.* xxv, An ye had wussed till hae been present. *c* **1880** LYTTLE *Paddy McQuillan* 85 (E.D.D.) Get Mickey Mooney till gie me a lift wi' them.

B. *conj.* (orig. the prep. governing the demonstrative pron. *that*, in apposition with the following clause.) Cf. UNTIL, similarly used.

(From the earliest ME. times both *till that* (see THAT *conj.* 1 c) and the simple *till* occur; supplanting OE. *óþ þæt*, early ME. *oþat, a þat* (see O *prep.*[2], A *prep.*[3]), also OE. *óþ þe* and the simple *óþ*. *Till that* represented ON. *til þess* (MSw. *til þes* (*at*), *til þet*, Sw. *til dess at*.)

1. a. To the time that; up to (the point) when; until. (Denoting the continuance of the action or state expressed by the principal clause up to the time expressed by the dependent clause, and usually implying that at that time such action or state ceases and a different or opposite one begins.)

Formerly often (and still *arch.*) with dependent clause in subjunctive when expressing supposition, contingency, or expectation (in ME. sometimes even when expressing fact); so also in subordinate senses below.

1154 *O.E. Chron.* (Laud MS.) an. 1137, Þar he nam þe biscop..& ..hise neues & dide ælle in prisun til hi iafen up here castles. *c* **1200** ORMIN 126 Swa þeȝȝ leddenn heore lif Till þatt teȝȝ wærenn alde. *Ibid.* 9147 Fra þatt he wass full litell Till þatt he waxenn wass. *a* **1225** *Leg. Kath.* 720 Þeos meiden..abad baldeliche aðet me [*v.r.* til þet men] come & fatte hire. *c* **1320** *Cast. Love* 44 To wonen and welden to such ende, Til þat he scholde to heuene wende. **13..** *Cursor M.* 8421 (Gött.) Þu sett him to fostering, Tille he be lerid himself to lede. **1420–30** *Prymer* (E.E.T.S.) 64 Alle þe daies in whiche y trauele now, y abide til my chaungyng come. **1526** TINDALE *Luke* xv. 8 What woman..doth not..seke diligently, till she finde it? **1560** INGELEND *Disob. Child* (Percy Soc.) 22, I thought it surely a whole hundred yere, Tyll in this place I sawe you here. **1588** SHAKS. *L.L.L.* I. ii. 131 Forbeare till this company be past. **1610** —— *Temp.* I. ii. 465, I will resist such entertainment, till Mine enemy ha's more pow'r. **1611** BIBLE *Dan.* ii. 34 Thou sawest till that a stone was cut out without hands. **1625** MASSINGER *New Way* III. iii, She..sits on thorns, till she be private with him. **1707** E. CHAMBERLAYNE *Pres. St. Eng.* II. xv. (ed. 22) 194 They.. forfeited their Places if they did marry, till by Act of Parliament..they were allowed to take Wives. **1796** *Hist. Ned Evans* II. 213, I shall count the hours till I return. **1833** HT. MARTINEAU *Three Ages* iii. 89 To be left at the Blue Lion till called for. **1850** TENNYSON *In Mem.* xiii. 8 Silence, till I be silent too.

b. With negative (expressed or implied) in the principal clause, and the dependent clause with *till* denoting the continuance of the negative condition up to the specified time, and usually (as in 1) implying its cessation or reversal (i.e. the commencement of the opposite or positive condition) at that time.

Here *before* can be substituted for *till*, but is not strictly synonymous with it, since in that case the negative qualifies the whole statement including the dependent clause. This may also be the case with *till*, e.g. 'You need not wait till I come back' (sense 1); cf. 'You must not go till I come back' (1 b). Hence some sentences of this form are ambiguous; but usually the context or circumstances make it clear which is meant.

c **1220** *Bestiary* 19 Ne stireð he nout of slepe Til ðe sunne haueð sinen ðries him abuten. **13..** *Seuyn Sag.* (W.) 1276 For thef of steling wil nowt blinne Til he honge bi the chinne. *c* **1386** CHAUCER *Prol.* 21 Til we be roten, can we nat be rype. **1463** *Bury Wills* (Camden) 27 This mony not to be delyuerid..tyl the messe of Requiem be endyd. **1526** TINDALE *John* xiii. 38 The cocke shall nott crowe, till thou have [1611 hast] denyed me thryse. **1648** HERRICK *Hesper.*, *Glorie*, Seldome comes Glorie till a man be dead. **1676** LISTER in *Ray's Corr.* (1848) 125, I shall resolve upon nothing till I see you. **1766** GOLDSM. *Vic. W.* xviii, Man little knows what calamaties are beyond his patience to bear, till he tries them. **1780** *Mirror* No. 104 ¶8 At length we set out..but not till repeated instructions were given [etc.]. *a* **1814** *Spaniards* IV. i. in *New Brit. Theatre* III. 239 Nor will the flaming sword of war..Be sheath'd again till that the Moorish pride Be humbled. **1832** HT. MARTINEAU *Demerara* i. 15 We shall never prosper..till the system is wholly changed. **1864** LEVER *Men & Women*, etc. Ser. I. 91 'Never imagine', said a wise prelate, 'that you will root Popery out of England till you destroy Oxford'.

c. Formerly, and still dial. and in U.S., used after a negative principal clause, where *before* (or *when*) is now substituted in Standard English.

c **1420** ? LYDG. *Assembly of Gods* 1130 No man cowde hym let tyll he came there. **1559** *Mirr. Mag., Edw. IV* iii, I could not be ware tyl I was begiled. **1632** LITHGOW *Trav.* v. 231 Scarcely were wee well aduanced in our way, till wee were beset with more then three hundred Arabs. **1725** DE FOE *Voy. round World* (1840) 79, I had not been many hours on board, till I was surprised with the firing of three muskets. **1756** MRS. CALDERWOOD in *Coltness Collect.* (Maitl. Cl.) 186, I was not long set till Margaret came to see me.

d. Depending on a principal clause containing an expression of long duration of time or delay before the act or state expressed by the dependent clause begins or takes effect. Now *dial.*

c **1330** *Assump. Virg.* (B.M. MS.) 121 Alle him þenkeþ swiþe longe Til þou comest hem amonge. **1450** MARG. PASTON in *P. Lett.* I. 178, I thynk ryth longe tyll I haue some god tydyngys fro yow. *c* **1530** LD. BERNERS *Arth. Lyt. Bryt.* 445, I shal think tyll that season be come as long or longer than ye shal do. *a* **1533** —— *Gold. Bk. M. Aurel.* R iv b, The mayden that tarieth long tyll she be maried. **1590** MARLOWE *Edw. II*, II. i. 82 Come, leade the way, I long till I am there. **1602** SHAKS. *Ham.* IV. vii. 182 But long it could not be, Till that her garments..Pul'd the poore wretch..To muddy death. **1640** tr. *Verdere's Rom. of Rom.* III. iv. 13 He.. thought it long till hee was in the Citie. **1825** CARLYLE *Schiller* III. (1845) 189 It was not long till..he set about turning this new knowledge to account. **1866** HOWELLS *Venet. Life* (1880) 122 So at first she seemed, and it was long till we doubted her perfection.

e. Indicating the ultimate result or outcome of a continued action expressed by the principal clause: So long or so far that; so that at length.

c **1220** *Bestiary* 65 Ðer-ouer he fleȝeð, and up he teð, Til ðat he ðe heuene seð. *a* **1300** *Cursor M.* 10991 (Cott.) Quen þai had beden til þai war irk. **1377** LANGL. *P. Pl.* B. II. 96 And þanne to sitten and soupen til slepe hem assaille. *c* **1430** *Chev. Assigne* 96 He wente þorow a foreste..Thylle he come to a watur. **1508** DUNBAR *Gold. Targe* 239 Thay fyrit gunnis ..Till that the reke raise to the firmament. **1610** SHAKS. *Temp.* I. i. 8 Blow till thou burst thy winde. **1766** GOLDSM. *Vic. W.* xii, He..stands out and higgles, and..tires them till he gets a bargain. **1895** MRS. H. WARD *Bessie Costrell* ii. 31 Bessie ran till she was out of breath.

†f. After *so long*, *so far*, etc., indicating ultimate result. *Obs.* (Now expressed by *that*, or by *till* with omission of *so long*, etc. as in e.) (Cf. MSw. *swa lange til þes*; Ger. *so lang bis*.)

c **1386** CHAUCER *Sompn. T.* 58 So longe he wente hous by hous, til he Cam til an hous ther he was wont to be Refresshed. **1470–85** MALORY *Arthur* XVII. xxiii. 724 He rode so fast tyl he came to Camelot. **1590** SPENSER *F.Q.* II. ii. 12 So long they traveiled..Till that at last they to a Castle came. **1593** SHAKS. *2 Hen. VI*, III. i. 362 [He] fought so long, till that his thighes with Darts Were almost like a sharpe-quill'd Porpentine. **1599** A. M. tr. *Gabelhouer's Bk. Physicke* 44/1 Vse it as long till it return noe more. **1643** TRAPP *Comm. Gen.* xxxii. 26 The importunate widow teacheth us, to press God so far, till we put him to the blush. *a* **1738** J. SKINNER *Christmas Ba'ing* xiii. Poems (1809) 45 Leitch.. gae 'im sic a kick, Till they a' thought him slain. [**1800** COLERIDGE *Piccolom.* IV. v, And till we are indemnified, so long Stays Prague in pledge.]

g. Indicating purpose: in order that (one) may, (*loosely*) 'and let me'. *Sc.* and *Ir.*

1881 A. MACKIE *Scotticisms* 18 Give me a match till I light the gas. **1904** W. B. YEATS *Pot of Broth* 78 Give me some vessel, till I give this sky-woman a taste of it. **1931** A. J. CRONIN *Hatter's Castle* III. iv. 525 Come till I give ye a grand, big hug. *a* **1966** 'M. NA GOPALEEN' *Best of Myles* (1977) 57 Will yez all come in here..till I show yez me new picture.

†2. During the time that; so long as; while.

c **1330** R. BRUNNE *Chron.* (1810) 18 His childre he wild auance tille he o lyue were. *c* **1375** *Sc. Leg. Saints* Prol. 82 Til saule & body togydir ves. *Ibid.* 107 Til þat he ves vith þaim in lyfe. **1558** BP. WATSON *Sev. Sacram.* xvi. 102 Let vs ..make haste to amende our lyues tyll we haue tyme. **1604** T. WRIGHT *Passions* (1620) 14 To prosecute pleasures.. enjoy the roses til they flourish.

†C. *adv.* = TO *adv. Obs. rare.*

1. In conjunction with *fra* (= fro): see FRO *adv.*, and cf. TO AND FRO.

a **1300** *Cursor M.* 11937 Þat water moght rin fra and till, Vte of þe flum al atte will. **13..** *Evang. Nicod.* 195 in Herrig's *Archiv* LIII. 395 Sir Pilates wife..Till hir lord þus gan say Deme noght Ihesu tyll ne fra. *c* **1386** CHAUCER *Reeve's T.* 119 How that the hopur wagges til and fra.

2. = *to* prep. (see A. 1) with ellipsis of sb.

c **1330** R. BRUNNE *Chron.* (1810) 107 Þe gode erle of Aniowe, of Mald herd he say Fulle richely to trowe tille tok his way. *c* **1375** *Cursor M.* 14523 (Fairf.), & þer-to gode couenande þai hiȝt, & iche an tille þaire trauþis pliȝt.

3. Used to qualify *to*, *into*, *unto*. In Wyclif rendering L. *usque* (*ad*, *in*), even, as far as, on (to).

1382 WYCLIF *Acts* xxiii. 1, I with al good conscience haue lyued bifore God, til into [*Vulg.* usque in] this dai. *Ibid.* xxviii. 24 Fro the moru til to euentijde. **1388** —— *Jer.* li 9 The doom therof cam til to [*Vulg.* usque ad, 1382 vnto] heuenes. *c* **1435** *Torr. Portugal* 992 That thys fynd hym yeld A-non to me tylle [*rime* wylle]. **14..** in *Hist. Coll. Citizen London* (Camden) 90 The sayde Adam was mayre tylle unto the xxj day of Marche. **1577** KNEWSTUB *Confut.* (1579) 70 b, Euen so remember the suffering of Christ..til vnto his comming.

tillable ('tɪləb(ə)l), *a.* [f. TILL *v.*[1] + -ABLE.] Capable of being tilled or cultivated; usually, capable of being ploughed, arable.

1573 NORTHBROOKE *Poore Mans Gard.* To Rdr., The Earth then remained to man as a thing tillable. **1610** W. FOLKINGHAM *Art of Survey* I. x. 26 Wee found it scarce tillable with a strong Teeme of Oxen. **1784** TWAMLEY *Dairying* 22 The greater number of Dairys are on Tillable or Arable Farms. **1810** G. CHALMERS *Caledonia* II. II. vii. 135 The most common divisions of tillable lands were carucates, or plough lands, and bovates, or oxgangs. **1893** J. W. HOFF *200 Miles on Delaware River* 125 The cultivated and tillable soil..in this region is formed from decayed rock.

tillage ('tɪlɪdʒ). Also 6 **tilladge**, 6–7 **tyllage**, 7 **tilage**, **tilledge**. [f. TILL *v.*[1] + -AGE.]

1. a. The act, operation, or art of tilling or cultivating land so as to fit it for raising crops; cultivation, agriculture, husbandry.

1538 STARKEY *England* I. iii. 96 Me semyth ther ys a grete faute in tyllage of the ground. **1616** SURFL. & MARKH. *Country Farme* 555 Barley asketh the greatest tillage of all graines. **1707** MORTIMER *Husb.* (1721) I. 137 Pease and Beans belong to Garden-Tillage, as well as that of the Field. **1712** J. JAMES tr. *Le Blond's Gardening* 166 There is no Danger in giving the Trees a good Tillage, that is to say, in breaking up the Ground pretty deep. **1735** BERKELEY *Querist* §85 If all the land were tilled that is fit for tillage. **1833** HT. MARTINEAU *Briery Creek* iii, The farmer makes his land yield double by good tillage.

b. The state or condition of being tilled or cultivated. ***in tillage***, in or under cultivation.

1488–9 *Act 4 Hen. VII*, c. 19, xx. acres of lond..lyeng in tillage or husbondrie. **1523** FITZHERB. *Surv.* 2 It is at the lordes pleasure wheder they shall lye to pasture or to tyllage. **1523** —— *Husb.* §123 As moche land kept in tyllage. **1669** WORLIDGE *Syst. Agric.* (1681) 37 There is much waste Land,..although for the most part..it may be reduced into Tillage, and become very fruitful. **1787** WINTER *Syst. Husb.* 33 When land has been long in tillage. **1897** G. ALLEN *Type-writer Girl* iii, They have bought ten acres of wild land..; they are getting it into tillage.

c. *fig.* The culture of the mind or spirit.

1555 EDEN *Decades* (Arb.) 64 If I shal perceaue the fruites of this my tyllage to be delectable. **1586** T. B. *La Primaud. Fr. Acad.* I. (1594) 47 The true medicine and tillage of the soule whereby all vertue is taught us. **1683** TRYON *Way to Health* 472 We do also esteem that Country most miserable, that doth neglect the proper Tillage, and Education of Children. **1878** T. L. CUYLER *Pointed Papers* 185 He needs the tillage of prayer and Bible-study.

d. *fig.* Sexual intercourse (with a woman). *poet.*

c **1600** SHAKES. *Sonnets* (1609) sig. B1[v], For where is she so faire whose vn-eard wombe Disdaines the tillage of thy husbandry? **1918** E. POUND *Pavannes & Divisions* 41 Some men will live as prudes in their own village And make the tour abroad for their wild tillage.

2. *concr.* Tilled or ploughed land; land under crops as distinct from pasturage; the crops growing on tilled land.

1543 *Act 35 Hen. VIII*, c. 17 §3 Noe persons..shall converte or torne into pasture or tillage anye suche Coppies. **1632** LITHGOW *Trav.* v. 191 It is also beautified with all the ornaments of nature, as Herbage, Tillage, Pastorage, Fructiferous Trees. **1649** *Alcoran* 228 Will ye forsake eternall riches..to put your trust in your gardens, your fountains, your tillages, your dates, and fruits? **1681** WORLIDGE *Syst. Agric.* viii. §3 (ed. 3) 159 Of Beans, Pease, Melons, Cucumbers, Asparagus, Cabbage, and several other sorts of Garden-Tillage..An Acre of ground will yield far more of Tillage than of Corn. *c* **1710** CELIA FIENNES *Diary* (1888) 108 Lands..with all sorts of Herbage and tillage. **1894** LD. WOLSELEY *Life Marlborough* I. 334 The fence..which divided the tillage from the moorland.

fig. **1582** BENTLEY *Mon. Matrones* 70, I praie God all men ..may haue grace to become meete tillage for the fruits of the Gospell. **1611** BIBLE *1 Cor.* iii. 9 Ye are Gods husbandry [*marg.* tillage], ye are Gods building.

3. *attrib.* and *Comb.*

1542 in J. H. Glover *Kingsthorpiana* (1883) 73, xxx acres of tyllage land. **1583** *Exec. for Treason* (1675) 5 These.. Jesuits..have as Tillage-men, laboured..to perswade the people. **1585** T. WASHINGTON tr. *Nicholay's Voy.* II. x. 43 b, Gardens.., tillage grounds and pastures. **1712** J. MORTON *Nat. Hist. Northampt.* 7 Tillage-land or Fielden. **1834** *Brit. Husb.* I. 40 Tillage Farms are the most profitable to the community.

Hence '**tillaged** (-ɪdʒd) *a.*, brought under tillage.

1854 *Jrnl. R. Agric. Soc.* XV. I. 24 The servitude of day labour upon the newly tillaged Fens.

‖**Tillandsia** (tɪ'lændzɪə). *Bot.* [mod.L. (Linnæus), named after Elias Tillands, a Swedish botanist.] A large genus of herbaceous plants of the pine-apple family (*Bromeliaceæ*), found in tropical and subtropical America and the West Indies, chiefly epiphytic on trees.

T. usneoides, also called *long-beard*, *long-moss*, *hanging moss*, or *Florida moss*, forms long pendent grey tufts, the fibres of which are used for stuffing mattesses, etc.; other species, as *T. utriculata*, have the leaves dilated at the base so as to form a reservoir for water; many others are cultivated for ornament.

1759 B. STILLINGFL. tr. *Biber's Econ. Nat.* in *Misc. Tracts* (1762) 76 The tillandsia, which..grows on the tops of trees in the desarts of America, has its leaves turned at the base into the shape of a pitcher..; in these the rain is collected, and preserved for thirsty men, birds, and beasts. **1860** GOSSE *Rom. Nat. Hist.* 61 The tillandsias nestle at the ramification of the smaller branches,..where they often grow to an immense size. **1863** RUSSELL *Diary North & South* I. 220 The overlacing arms and intertwined branches of the tillandsia or Spanish moss, a weeping, drooping, plumaceous parasite, which..clings to the tree everlastingly. **1896** *Daily News* 16 Mar. 6/5 A number of species of the so-called air plants—Tillandsias—exhibited.

tilled (tɪld), *ppl. a.* [f. TILL *v.*[1] + -ED[1].] Of land: see TILL *v.*[1] 4.

1546 *Reg. Mag. Sig. Scot.* 10 Exceptis terris aratis vulgariter telitland. **1577–95** *Descr. Isles Scotl.* in Skene *Celtic Scotl.* III. App. 435 The teillit earth. **1733** TULL *Horse-Hoeing Husb.* i. 8 When Roots are in a Till'd Soil. *a* **1859** MACAULAY *Hist. Eng.* xxiii. (1861) V. 95 In that thickly peopled and carefully tilled region.

tiller ('tɪlə(r)), *sb.*[1] Now *literary* or *arch.* Forms: 3–4 tiliere, 4 teoliare, telier, tylier, tileer, 4–5 tilier, tylyer, tilyer, 5 tylyar, telar, tillour, tylere, tyllare, 5–6 tyllar, 6 tyller, *Sc.* telare, 5– tiller. [ME. *tiliere*, taking the place of OE. *tilia* (TILIE), f. *tilian*, TILL *v.*[1] + *-ere*, -ER[1]; subseq. spelt conformably to the verb.] One who tills the soil, or cultivates any crop or plant; a husbandman, cultivator; a farmer or farm labourer. See also EARTH-TILLER, *land-tiller* (LAND *sb.*[1] 10 b).

c **1250** *Gen. & Ex.* 1482 Esau wilde man huntere, And Iacob tame man tiliere. *c* **1300** *Life Jesus* (Horstm.) 589 Ich am, he seide, a riȝt soth vine, and mi fader teoliare is. **1377** LANGL. *P. Pl.* B. XIII. 239 For alle trewe trauaillours and tilieres of þe erthe. *c* **1400** *Plowman's T.* 453 What knoweth a tillour at the plow The popes name? *c* **1412** HOCCLEVE *De Reg. Princ.* 4418 The Tylere [*v.r.* tilyer] with his pore cote and land. **1530** PALSGR. 187 *Uigneron*, a tyller of vygnes. **1661** J. CHILDREY *Brit. Baconica* 11 The tiller can commonly take but two crops of wheat. **1767** A. YOUNG *Farmer's Lett. People* 74 The little farmer is always considered as the chief tiller of his land. **1849** MACAULAY *Hist. Eng.* iii. I. 418 The remuneration of workmen employed in manufactures has always been higher than that of the tillers of the soil.

'**tiller**, *sb.*[2] Forms: (4 AF. teiler), 5 telor, tiler, 6 tyller, -our, 6–7 tillar, 6– tiller. [a. OF. *telier* (*a* 1200 in Godef.), *tellier*, in sense 1; orig. a weaver's beam (*telier des tisserands*, Godef.), med.L. *tēlārium*, f. L. *tēla* web: see -ARY[1].]

†**1. a.** *Archery*, etc. In a cross-bow: The wooden beam which is grooved for reception of the arrow, or drilled for the bolt or quarrel; the stock. *Obs.*

[**1353** *Mag. Rot. 27 Edw. III* in *Archæol. Jrnl.* (1862) XIX. 72 In..xl. lignis vocatis cost' pro balistis inde faciendis, xl. lignis pro telar' balistarum..cxx. clavis vocatis somernailes pro telar'. **1361** *Indenture 35 Edw. III* ibid. (1854) XI. 385, xxiiij. arc pur arblastes de corn saunz teilers.] **1412–20** LYDG. *Chron. Troy* IV. 1370 He..hent a bowe þat passingly was stronge, And with an arwe to his tiler longe. **14..** *Voc.* in Wr.-Wülcker 615/44 *Tenorcula*, a telor of an arblast. *c* **1532** DU WES *Introd. Fr.* in *Palsgr.* 914 Tyller of a crosbowe, *cormier.* **1544** in *Lett. & Pap. Hen. VIII* (1905) XIX. II. 405 Oon tyllour, oon paire of chekes, and oon bender,..oon crossbowe case and oon dosen di of crossbowe stringes. **1609** HOLLAND *Amm. Marcell.* 221 An expert..workeman..cunningly bestoweth in the hollow passage of the beame or tiller [of a balista] a shaft of wood. **1611** COTGR., *Arbrier*, the Tillar of a Crosse-bow. *a* **1618** SYLVESTER *Woodman's Bear* xliv, Eyes that arme Love's Arches tillar.

†**b.** A stock or shaft fixed to a long-bow to admit of its being used as a cross-bow, for greater convenience or precision of aim. *Obs.*

1590 BARWICK *Briefe Disc.* 11 Whether a Cros-bowe, or a Long-bowe in a Tyller, shoot more certainly. **1611** BEAUM. & FL. *Philaster* II. ii, Use exercise, and keep a Sparrow-hawk, you can shoot in a Tiller.

†**c.** *transf.* A bow fitted with a tiller. *Obs.*

1572 J. JONES *Bathes Buckstone* 12 Rather wyth longe Bowe, than wyth Tyller, Stone bowe or Crosse bowe. **1598** FLORIO, *Balista*,..a crosse bow, a stock-bow or tillar. **1616** SURFL. & MARKH. *Country Farme* 508 Neither is the crosse-bow so daungerous, whether it be the tiller, or the bullet. **1688** R. HOLME *Armoury* III. xvi. (Roxb.) 77/1 The Tiller hath the Bow of wood either Ash or Yew whose string is held vp (when..drawne) by a wooden Nutt as it is called, and a handle to let it off.

d. (See quot. 1801.)

1545 [app. presupposed in TILLERING *vbl. sb.*[1]]. **1801** T. ROBERTS *Eng. Bowman* 295 *Tiller*, an instrument made of a straight piece of wood, with a notch at the end, and notches on the upper side; in which a bow is placed and drawn, to try how it bends.

†**e.** A stock or shaft in the earliest forms of hand-gun or cannon. *Obs.*

[**1353** *Mag. Rot. 27 Edw. III* in *Archæol. Jrnl.* (1862) XIX. 74 Pro..portagio x. gunn' cum telar'. **1885** DILLON *Fairholt's Costume* II. Gloss., *Telar*, the stock of a hand gun (with above reference).]

2. *Naut.* A horizontal bar or beam attached to the rudder-head, acting as a lever by means of which the rudder is moved in the act of steering.

(Not in Fr., where the tiller is 'barre du gouvernail'.)

a **1625** *Nomenclator Navalis* s.v. (Harl. MS. 2301), The Helme and Tiller is all one..only the word Tiller is properlie used for that which we steere the Bote by. **1627** CAPT. SMITH *Seaman's Gram.* ii. 12 The Tiller is a strong peece of wood made fast to the Rudder..whereby the Rudder is so turned to and fro as the Helmesman pleaseth. **1704** J. HARRIS *Lex. Techn.* I, *Tiller*, the very same with the Helm of a Ship: It is most properly used in a Boat where that which would be the Helm in a Ship, is called the Tiller. **1743** BULKELEY & CUMMINS *Voy. S. Seas* 17 The Ship struck a second Time, which broke the Head of the Tiller. **1836** MARRYAT *Midsh. Easy* xix, Easy wrested the tiller from Gascoigne's hand. **1875** HELPS *Soc. Press.* vi. 76 You are either..a slave at the oar, or a serf at the tiller. **1905** A. C. BENSON *Upton Lett.* (1906) 39 Not fit..to take the tiller.

b. Also *loosely*, the steering-gear of a rowing-boat; cf. *tiller-line*, *-rope* in 4.

3. In various technical uses: see quots.

1630 J. TAYLOR (Water P.) *A Thiefe* Wks. II. 119/2 As once a Windmill (out of breath) lack'd winde A fellow brought foure bushels then to grinde, And hearing neither noyse of knap or tiller, Laid downe his corne, and went to seeke the miller. **1789** BRAND *Hist. Newcastle* I. 687 *note*, A piece of wood, called a tiller, is..applied to one wheel, and pressed thereon. *a* **1825** FORBY *Voc. E. Anglia*, *Tiller*, the handle of a spade. **1877** KNIGHT *Dict. Mech.*, *Tiller*. 1. A transverse handle at the upper end of a pit saw. **1881** RAYMOND *Mining Gloss.*, *Tiller*. See *Brace-head.*

4. *attrib.* and *Comb.*: †**tiller-bow** = sense 1 c; **tiller-chain**, a chain answering the same purpose as a tiller-rope; on steamships, used in conjunction with steel-wire to connect the rudder with the steam steering-gear; **tiller-head**, the extremity of the tiller to which are secured the two ends of the tiller-rope or -chain; **tiller-lines**, two lines or ropes fastened each to one arm of the tiller-yoke in a boat; also called *yoke-lines*, *yoke-*, *tiller-ropes*; **tillerman** *U.S.*, a fireman who controls the rear portion of a fire-engine; **tiller-post**, the upper part of the rudder-stock; **tiller-rope**, (*a*) the rope (now usually a chain) connecting the tiller-head with the drum or barrel of a ship's steering-gear; (*b*) a rope leading from the tiller-head to each side of the deck, to assist in steering in rough weather; (*c*) *pl.* = *tiller-lines*; **tiller soup**, the minatory wielding of a tiller by the coxswain to encourage his boat's crew; **tiller-steerage**, **-steering**, the arrangement for steering a motor-car by means of a lever (as distinct from wheel-steerage); **tiller-wheel**, a wheel by which a rudder is actuated, a steering-wheel; **tiller-yoke**, a yoke fixed on the rudder-head of a boat and serving as a tiller.

1583 W. M. *Remembr.* in Roberts *Eng. Bowman* (1801) 261 Every one bearing a *tiller-bow or cross-bow, and broad arrows. **1590** BARWICK *Disc. Weapons* 11 He..then can either loose Long-bowe, Tiller-bowe, or Cros-bowe. **1591** PERCIVAL *Span. Dict.*, *Zebretana*, a tiller bowe, *balistæ genus.* **1841** R. H. DANA *Seaman's Man.* Dict. s.v. *Tiller-ropes*, Ropes leading from the *tiller-head round the barrel of the wheel. **1905** *Westm. Gaz.* 3 Jan. 4/2 With one hand on the *tiller-lever he can perform all the functions of driver and steersman at once. **1889** J. K. JEROME *Three Men in Boat* 76 Harris at the sculls and I at the *tiller-lines. **1968** L. LOKOS *House Divided* vii. 226 A hook and ladder truck went to answer the alarm without the *tillerman aboard to control the rear portion. **1890** *Daily News* 9 Jan. 6/3 Her *tiller post had been carried away, and other damage done to the stern. **1745** P. THOMAS *Jrnl. Anson's Voy.* 148 Our old *Tiller-Rope being much worn, we unreev'd it, and reev'd a new one. **1872** BLACK *Adv. Phaeton* v, Bell pulled the white tiller-ropes over her shoulder. **1929** F. C. BOWEN *Sea Slang* 141 **Tiller soup*, the man-handling with the tiller by threat of which a coxswain encourages his boat's crew. **1947** *Sea Breezes* III. 151 We boys got a few gentle taps with the boat's tiller, too. We called it 'tiller soup'.

'**tiller**, *sb.*[3] Now *dial.* Forms: 1 (see etymol.); 7– **tiller**, 8–9 **tillar**, **tellar**, **teller**; 9 *dial.* **tellow**, **tillow**, **telly**. [App. repr. OE. *telȝor*, *tealȝor* str. m., also *telȝra* wk. m. (see sense 1), extended forms of *telȝa* wk. masc., 'branch, bough, twig' = ON. *tjalga* fem., MLG., LG., Du. *telg*, MDu. *telch*, *telg-*, m. and n., MHG. *zelch*, *zelge*, *zilge* m.:—OTeut. **telgo(n)*, *telgôn-* twig, branch, sprout. Not found in Eng. between 1100 and 1660; the phonetic history is obscure. The dial. *tellow*, *tillow* may repr. OE. *telȝa*.]

†**1.** (In OE.) A plant, a shoot, a twig; *esp.* a shoot or sucker from the root. *Obs.*

a **1000** *Blickl. Glosses* (E.E.T.S.) 261/2 Tealȝras, *propagines.* *c* **1000** ÆLFRIC *Gen.* ii. 5 And ælcne telȝor on eorðan ær ðam þe he uppasprunge on eorðan. *a* **1050** *Herbarium* in *Sax. Leechd.* I. 276 Ðeos wyrt. of anum wyrttruman maneȝa telȝran asendeþ. *Ibid.*, Hypericon..Of anum stelan maneȝa telȝran weaxaþ. *Ibid.* 324 Heo eal..wið þa eorðan hyre telȝran tobrædeþ. *a* **1050** *Medicina de Quadrup.* ibid. 332 Do on anne telȝran [þæs morbeames] ðe sy adune ȝecyrred.

2. A young tree, a sapling; *esp.* a stock-shoot, rising from the stock or stool of a felled tree.

1664 EVELYN *Sylva* III. iv. §29 (*Charcoal*) This [ladder] they usually make of a curved Tiller fit to apply to the convex shape of the heap. **1706** PHILLIPS (ed. Kersey), *Tillar* (in Husbandry), a small Tree left to grow till it be fellable. **1712** J. JAMES tr. *Le Biond's Gardening* 50 They are obliged to leave sixteen Tillers on an Acre. **1768** TUCKER *Lt. Nat.* (1834) I. 322 First shoots up a tender twig, which then becomes a sapling, a waiver, a tellar, and at last a perfect oak laden with acorns. **1794** W. PEARCE *Agric. Berks* 55 [They] permit their labourers, during the winter months, to take up the old roots, from which no heir or teller is rising. **1832** *Planting* 92 in *Libr. Usef. Knowl.*, *Husb.* III, Tiller or Tellar, a shoot selected..from those produced by a coppice stool to stand for a timber-tree. **1875** *Sussex Gloss.*, *Teller*, *Tillow*.., a young oak tree. **1878** *N. & Q.* 5th Ser. X. 223 The lessee covenants not to cut down tellows and stemners.

3. One of the lateral shoots from the base of the stalk of corn or grass or other herbaceous plant.

1733 TULL *Horse-Hoeing Husb.* xi. 132 The same Plant that when poor sends out but Two or Three Tillers, would if well nourish'd..send up a Multitude of Tillers, as is seen in Ho'd Wheat and Sown Wheat. **1759** tr. *Duhamel's Husb.* I. xiii. (1762) 70 New stalks, or, as some call it, tillers. **1764** *Museum Rust.* III. XII. 46 If the season is lost to encrease the number of tillers, we may enlarge the ears. **1811** W. LESLIE *Agric. Surv. Moray* Gloss., *Tiller*, the rising blade of growing corn shooting out several stems from one seed. [Cf. **1828** *Craven Gloss.*, *Telly*, a single stalk of grass or corn.]

†**tiller**, *sb.*[4] *Obs. rare*[−1]. [app. f. TILL *sb.*[1] + -ER[1], ? after *drawer.*] = TILL *sb.*[1] 1.

1693 DRYDEN *Juvenal* vi. 383 Search her Cabinet, and thou shal find Each Tiller there with Love-Epistles lin'd.

tiller ('tɪlə(r)), *v.*[1] Also 7 **tillar**, 9 **tillow**. [f. TILLER *sb.*[3]] *intr.* Of corn or other plants: To produce 'tillers' or side shoots from the root or base of the stem; also said of the shoots thus arising. Also with *out*, *forth.*

1677 PLOT *Oxfordsh.* 245 The Seed in the rich [Land] does tillar, i.e. sprout into several blades and spread on the ground. **1733** TULL *Horse-Hoeing Husb.* xix. 270 More Stalks would have Tillered out. **1743** MAXWELL *Sel. Trans. Soc. Improv. Agric. Scot.* 24 Clover-plants, when they have room to grow, tiller or stool, and employ more Ground than those of Corn. **1805** R. W. DICKSON *Pract. Agric.* I. 463 Oats do not tiller so much as other grains. **1813** VANCOUVER *Surv. Hampshire* 196 The more that the crown of this plant is..divided, the greater disposition it has to stool and tillow forth in additional stems and succours. **1868** *Rep. U.S. Commissioner Agric.* (1869) 406 It [wheat] tillered astonishingly, as many as fifty heads growing from one kernel.

b. *trans.* To throw *out* (stalks, etc.) by tillering.

1787 WINTER *Syst. Husb.* 207 The roots of the drilled [wheat] tillered out from ten or twelve to upwards of thirty stalks on each root.

Hence '**tillered** *ppl. a.*, having several shoots or stems springing from one root; '**tillering** *vbl. sb.* and *ppl. a.*

1733 TULL *Horse-Hoeing Husb.* vii. 72 These Tillered Ho'd Stalks, if they were planted sparsim all over the Interval, it might seem well cover'd. **1764** *Museum Rust.* III. XII. 46 There is a particular season for its tillering, or spreading; another for its upright growth. **1833** *Ridgemont Farm Rep.* 137 in *Libr. Usef. Knowl.*, *Husb.* III, By a rapid and early vegetation of the wheat, the tillering branches of the young plant are apt to exhaust themselves. **1885** W. K. PARKER *Mammalian Descent* vi. 158 The multiplied (or tillered) stems of a wheat-plant.

†**tiller**, *v.*[2]: see TILLERING *vbl. sb.*[1]

tiller, dial. form of THILLER.

†**tillerate**, *v. Obs. rare*[−1]. = TILLER *v.*[1]

1759 tr. *Duhamel's Husb.* III. i. (1762) 299 The roots which stood thin in the rows, tillerated out from ten or twelve.

†'**tillering**, *vbl. sb.*[1] *Obs. rare.* [Implies a verb *tiller*, from TILLER *sb.*[2] 1 d: see -ING[1].] The putting of a bow upon a tiller (TILLER *sb.*[2] 1 d) in order to stretch or bend it.

1545 ASCHAM *Toxoph.* II. (Arb.) 114, I woulde desyre all bowyers to season theyr staues well, to woorke them and synke them well, to giue them heetes conuenient, and tylleringes plentye. *Ibid.* 115, I suppose that nether yͤ bowe can be to goœd and chefe woode, nor yet to well seasoned or truly made, wyth hetynges and tilleringes. **1801** T. ROBERTS *Eng. Bowman* 295 *Tillering*, trying a bow by the tiller. Altering a bow by scraping it.

tillering, *vbl. sb.*[2]: see after TILLER *v.*[1]

tillerless ('tɪləlɪs), *a.* [f. TILLER *sb.*[2] + -LESS.] Without or lacking a tiller.

1870 *Routledge's Ev. Boy's Ann.* Feb. 86 The rudder was tillerless.

tillet[1] ('tɪlɪt), **tillot** ('tɪlət). Forms: 5 **tyllete**, tillette, 6 **tyllet**, 7 **tillett**, -it, 6– **tillet**, 9 -ot. [app. ad. OF. *tellette* (14th c. in Godef. *Compl.*), collateral form of *teilete*, *toilete* a wrapper of cloth: see TOILET.]

1. A kind of coarse cloth, used for wrapping up textile fabrics and (formerly) garments; also for making awnings.

1466 *Mann. & Household Exp.* (Roxb.) 211 Paid to Iohn Felaw for xij. yerdes of tyllete for the spynas. **1530** PALSGR. 281/1 Tyllet to wrap clothe in, *toyllette.* **1590** *Inv. Sir T.*

Ramsey in *Archæologia* XL. 327 A scarlet cloke faced wth gray with the tillet. **1637** *Specif. S. Mason's Patent* No. 106 The sole dying of buckromes and tillits. **1837** WHITTOCK, etc. *Bk. Trades* (1842) 246 The tillet, or little cloth, for encasing glazed stuffs intended for a foreign market, was the first approach towards pattern floor-cloth painting. **1904** *Times* 5 Sept. 1/2 Mr. Justice Farwell.. restrained.. the said Defendants.. from wrapping up any goods.. in lining papers and tillots supplied by the Plaintiffs.

b. A bag made of thin glazed muslin, used as a covering for dress-goods.

1871 in MCELRATH *Dict. Commerce* (Funk).

†**2.** A tilt or awning. *Obs.*

1497 *Naval Acc. Hen. VII* (1896) 110 Cartes with tillettes for shott with all apparelle.

Hence ˈ**tilloting**, in *tilloting cloth*, a cloth used as a wrapper, esp. for textile fabrics.

1884 *Specif. Tiller's Patent* No. 2357 Improvements in tillotting cloths.

†**tillet**[2]. *Obs.* Also 7 tylet. [a. OF. *tillet, teillet* (14–15th c. in Godef.), dim. of *til, teil*; see TEIL and -ET[1].] A lime or linden-tree.

1601 HOLLAND *Pliny* (1634) II. 7 The thin barks of the Linden or Tillet tree. *Ibid.* 185. **1686** tr. *Chardin's Trav. Persia* 370 Groves of Poplers and Tylets, which they plant to serve 'em for building their Houses.

‖**tilleul.** [F. *tilleul* (tijœl) linden-tree:—L. **tiliolus*, dim. of **tilius* = *tilia* linden.]

1. A lime or linden-tree.

1530 PALSGR 281/1 Tylleull, a kynde of frute [error for *tree*], *tilleul*. **1825–9** MRS. SHERWOOD *Lady of Manor* II. xiv. 180 The gardens of orange trees; the avenues of tilleul; the groves of myrtle.

2. *attrib.* **a.** Name of a shade of colour: a pale yellowish green like that of the leaves of the lime-tree.

1884 *Cassell's Fam. Mag.* May 371/2 A light tilleul ground, just the tint of lettuce, shot with white. **1909** *Daily Chron.* 26 June 4/5 Lady St. Germans.. becomingly dressed in tilleul voile.

b. *tilleul tea*, an infusion of lime-tree flowers, used as a remedy for headache, etc.

1908 *Daily Chron.* 14 Nov. 4/4 Ordinary tea [has been replaced] by the bitter-tasted tilleul variety, which was first on show at an hotel in Paris.

tilleyite (ˈtɪlɪaɪt). *Min.* [f. the name of C. E. *Tilley* (1894–1973), Australian-born English petrologist + -ITE[1].] A silicate and carbonate of calcium, $Ca_5Si_2O_7(CO_3)_2$, found as white monoclinic crystals.

1933 LARSEN & DUNHAM in *Amer. Mineralogist* XVIII. 469 An examination of blocks of the material from the Wet Weather quarry.. has revealed the presence of a new lime silicate-carbonate mineral, with distinctive optical and chemical properties. For the new mineral the name tilleyite is proposed in honor of Professor C. E. Tilley of Cambridge University.., in recognition of the contributions he has made to the study of metamorphism. **1977** *Mineral. Abstr.* XXVIII. 71/1 At Kushiro, Tojo-cho, Hiroshima Prefecture, various rare skarn minerals occur in the contact zone between dioritic rock and limestone. These include.. tilleyite.

Tilley lamp (ˈtɪlɪ læmp). Also (*erron.*) **Tilly lamp**, and with small initial. [f. the name of the manufacturing company.] The proprietary name of a type of portable oil or paraffin lamp in which air pressure is used to supply the burner with fuel. Also *ellipt.* as *Tilley*.

1932 R. F. FORTUNE *Sorcerers of Dobu* iv. 181 My great shadow cast.. by my Tilley lamp. **1948** *Trade Marks Jrnl.* 17 Mar. 201/2 *Tilley*... Lighting and heating lamps employing liquid fuel. The Tilley Lamp Company Limited, .. Brent Works, Brent Street, Hendon, London, N.W.4; manufacturers. **1953** G. M. DURRELL *Overloaded Ark* vi. 115, I left the Tilly lamp in the middle of the swaying hypnotised circle. **1960** A. WESKER *I'm talking about Jerusalem* I. 23 Light the tilly lamp for me. **1966** *Guardian* 22 Dec. 5 Get that 'Tilley' goin', Gary. **1981** J. B. HILTON *Surrender Value* v. 42 Men filed out with Tilley-lamps, wicker baskets and rod-bags.

†**till-hew**, *v. Obs. rare.* [f. *till-* for TO- *prefix*[2] + HEW *v.*] *trans.* To hew or cut to pieces.

1375 BARBOUR *Bruce* II. 381 He all till-hewyt þat he our-tuk. *Ibid.* xx. 367 So fast till-hewyn wes all his face.

tilli, in *tilli berries*: see TILLY *sb.*[1]

tillicum (ˈtɪlɪkəm). *N.W. Amer.* Chiefly in *pl.* Also **tilicum, tilekum.** [a. Chinook Jargon *tilikum* people, ad. Chinook *tilxam*, f. *t-* pl. prefix + *ilxam* village.] **1.** A member of one's own tribe or people; also *pl.*, the people, common people.

1847 J. PALMER *Jrnl. Trav. Rocky Mts.* 105 A long time ago the Great Spirit became angry with them, set the mountain on fire, destroyed their towns, turned the *tiye* (chief) and *tilicums* (people) into stone, and cast them in the ocean outside of Cape Lookout. **1859** *Brit. Colonist* (Victoria, B.C.) 30 Apr. 2/2 Four Haidah Indians.. came to the house of Mr. Oxner, Colquitz Farm, and after agreeing to work for him, one left, when the rest said they preferred to go with tilekum. **1922** E. P. JOHNSON *Legends of Vancouver* 35, I saw her graceful, high-bowed canoe heading for the beach that is the favourite landing-place of the 'tillicums' from the Mission.

2. A friend.

1869 *Mainland Guardian* (New Westminster, B.C.) 9 Oct. 3/2 The rescue from the courthouse at Kootenay, by his tillicums, of the Indian taken there by the Prices when caught in the act of robbing their sluices. **1906** *Daily Colonist* (Victoria, B.C.) 5 Jan. 2/4 Mr. French expects to resume his citizenship of Princeton after about four years' absence, his present hurried trip precluding a visit with many old tillicums here about. **1969** *Islander* (Victoria, B.C.) 30 Nov. 3/2 Thiepval was in Hakodate when we were there and during our stay in that port we had all become good tillicums.

tilling (ˈtɪlɪŋ), *vbl. sb.* [f. TILL *v.*[1] + -ING[1].] The action of TILL *v.*[1]; work done upon land for raising crops; cultivation, tillage.

a **1225** *Ancr. R.* 296 þe winȝeardes.. þet mot muche tilunge to uorte beren windberien. **1377** LANGL. *P. Pl.* B. XIV. 63 Fourty wynter folke lyued with-outen tulyinge. **1387** TREVISA *Higden* (Rolls) II. 281 Konnynge of telienge [*v. rr.* tellynge, tillyng] of feeldes þey cleped Cereres. **1475** *Bk. Noblesse* (Roxb.) 70 In tilieng, ering, and labourage of his londis to bere corne and fruit. *a* **1610** HEALEY *Theophrastus* (1636) 12 The well tilling and husbanding of the ground. **1678** SIR G. MACKENZIE *Crim. Laws Scot.* I. xix. §9 (1699) 101 The stealers of Pleugh-graith.. in the time of Teiling.. are to be punished to the death. **1710** *Lond. Gaz.* No. 4703/2 A Bill.. for encouraging the Tilling of Land with Bullocks. **1817** W. SELWYN *Law Nisi Prius* (ed. 4) II. 1206 Whether the land is of such a nature as to require an extraordinary expence in manuring or tilling.

fig. **1483** CAXTON *Gold. Leg.* 271 b/1 Lyke a tylyer of Ihesu cryst he prouffyted in spyrytuel tylyeng. **1640** H. WOODWARD (*title*) A Childes Patrimony laid out upon the good culture or tilling over his whole man.

†**b.** *concr.* The produce of tilling; a crop: = TILLAGE 2 b. *Obs. rare.*

1680 J. GOODYEAR in *Hereford Dioc. Reg.* 4 Oct., Wanting ropes in the time of Harvest to carry in his tilling with.

c. *attrib.*, as **tilling land**, land fit for tilling, arable land.

1387 TREVISA *Higden* (Rolls) II. 89 But now wodes beþ i-hewe adoun and newe telynge lond i-made. **1488** *Cal. Anc. Rec. Dublin* (1889) 494 Parte of the tyllyng land.

ˈ**tilling**, *ppl. a.* [f. TILL *v.*[1] + -ING[2].] That tills or cultivates land.

c **1380** WYCLIF *Serm.* Sel. Wks. I. 319 þe first was an heerde, and þe toþer a tiliyng man. **1906** *Daily Chron.* 15 Sept. 3/1 Nor spurn my muse because it sings.. Of tilling men who plough and reap.

tillite (ˈtɪlaɪt). *Geol.* [ad. G. *tillit* (A. Pencke 1906, in *Geogr. Zeitschr.* XII. 608): see TILL *sb.*[2], -ITE[1].] A sedimentary rock composed of glacial till compacted into hard rock.

1907 E. BLACKWELDER in B. Willis et al. *Res. in China* (Carnegie Inst. Publ. No. 54) I. I. xii. 267 (*heading*) Basal quartzite and glacial tillite. [*Note*] Tillite, a term recently proposed for consolidated till. **1944** A. HOLMES *Princ. Physical Geol.* xxi. 500 Tillites of the same age have been found in the north of Angola, in the eastern Congo, in Uganda, and in Madagascar. **1977** A. HALLAM *Planet Earth* 87 (*caption*) Striations on smaller rock bodies may be used to identify those as tillites (glacial till converted to rock) rather than tilloids, which are superficially similar.

†ˈ**tillman.** *Obs.* [f. TILL *v.*[1] + MAN *sb.*] A man employed in tillage; a farmer, husbandman; a ploughman, peasant; a tiller of the soil.

940 *Grant of land in Wilts.* in Birch *Cart. Sax.* II. 483 Lang weges þæt ofer tilmannes dene. **13..** *Cursor M.* 4696 (Cott.) Tilmen oueral þe land a-boute.. þair sede had saun. *c* **1375** *Sc. Leg. Saints* xl. (*Ninian*) 201, & he þane, as gud tele-man, To wirk in goddis ȝard begane. *c* **1440** *Jacob's Well* 237 Summe feendys komyn as tylmen wyth here hors & carte. **1573** TUSSER *Husb.* (1878) 34 Good shepheard, good tilman, good Jack and good Gil, Makes husband and huswife their cofers to fil. **1620** T. GRANGER *Div. Logike* 56 The till-man plowing in the field, findeth a treasure.

tillocrat (ˈtɪləʊkræt). *nonce-wd.* [f. TILL *v.*[1] 4 + -(O)CRAT.] A ruling member of an agricultural class.

1858 BAILEY *Age* 5 Farmers, bankers, millocrats, Officials, manufacturers, merchants, tillocrats.

tillodont (ˈtɪləʊdɒnt). *Palæont.* [f. mod.L. *Tillodontia*, f. Gr. τίλλ-ειν to pluck + ὀδούς, ὀδοντ- tooth.] A member of the *Tillodontia*, a group of extinct mammals apparently combining the characters of ungulates, rodents, and carnivora, whose remains are found in the Eocene of N. America.

[**1875** *Amer. Jrnl. Sci.* Ser. III. IX. 221 At the last meeting of the Connecticut Academy, Feb. 17th, Professor O. C. Marsh made a communication on a new order of Eocene Mammals, for which he proposed the name Tillodontia. **1876** MARSH *ibid.* XI. 249.] **1889** NICHOLSON & LYDEKKER *Palæont.* II. 1408 The characters presented by the Tillodonts harmonise with the view that both the Ungulates and Rodents have been derived from a primitive Carnivorous stock.

tilloid (ˈtɪlɔɪd). *Geol.* [f. TILL *sb.*[2] + -OID.] A sedimentary rock which is similar in appearance to a tillite but is not known to be of glacial origin; a sedimentary rock composed of non-glacial deposits.

1931 E. BLACKWELDER in *Bull. Geol. Soc. Amer.* XLII. 903 For these reasons the scarcity of striated stones in the McGee tilloid* need not be given undue weight. [*Note*] *Meaning a till-like deposit of doubtful origin. **1957** F. J. PETTIJOHN *Sedimentary Rocks* (ed. 2) vi. 265 The non-glacial conglomeratic mudstones or tilloids vary from a chaotic unassorted assemblage of coarse materials set in a mudstone matrix to a mudstone with sparsely distributed cobbles. **1966** *Earth-Sci. Rev.* II. 251 When there is any doubt about the origin of a till-like deposit, we encourage the use of tilloid, as a non-genetic term. **1977** [see TILLITE].

tillot: see TILLET[1].

tillow, var. TILLER *sb.*[3], *v.*

†ˈ**tillsman.** *Obs.* In 6 *Sc.* telisman, 6–7 tilsman. Alteration of TILLMAN, with inserted *s*, after *huntsman, spokesman, steersman*, etc.

1561–2 in Keith *Hist. Ch. Scot.* (1734) I. App. 179 All and sindrie Parochinaris, Takkismen, Telismen, Fewaris, Rentalaris, Possessouris. **1589** NASHE *Anat. Absurd.* 30 Theyr father was a Tilsman attendant. **1645** WARD *Serm. bef. Ho. Com.* 26 *Mar.* 31 Like a piece of ground that hath beene stirred by the Plough, and the tils-man doth not follow on to give it more earths in due season.

tillward: see TILWARD.

tilly (ˈtɪlɪ), *sb.*[1] Also 8 tilli, tyle. [app. a. F. *tilli*, ad. med.L. *tiglium*, in It. *tiglia*: cf. TIGLIC.] In *tilly-seed*, the seed of a species of *Croton* (formerly called *C. Pavana*, now identified with *C. Tiglium*), which yields Croton oil.

1712 tr. *Pomet's Hist. Drugs* I. 144 The smooth Fruit call'd in the Shops, Tyle Seed, or Tilli-Berries [orig. *Ricinus arbre à fruit lisse, nommé grain de Tilli*]. **1858** SIMMONDS *Dict. Trade*, *Tilly-seed*, a small tree, the *Croton Pavana* of Hamilton,.. the seeds of which have the same properties as those of the *Croton Tiglium*.

tilly (ˈtɪlɪ), *sb.*[2] [f. Ir. *tuilleadh* an additional quantity, a supplement.] In Ireland and places of Irish settlement, an additional article or amount unpaid for by the purchaser, as a gift from the vendor.

1922 JOYCE *Ulysses* 15 She poured again a measureful and a tilly. **1958** M. & P. COLUM *Our Friend James Joyce* II. ii. 120 As the price of the little volume [*sc. Pomes Penyeach*] was a shilling, one expected to find twelve poems in it, one for each penny. Actually there were thirteen, the additional one being named 'Tilly'. In this Joyce was being obscurely local: the extra half-cup of milk that the milkman left in the Dublin householder's jug in the morning was a 'tilly'—something unpaid for. **1975** *Canadian Antiques Collector* Mar.–Apr. 22/2 [In Newfoundland] we have still in common use such Anglo-Irish terms as:.. tilly (a small amount over and above what is purchased).

tilly (ˈtɪlɪ), *a.* [f. TILL *sb.*[2] + -Y.] Abounding in, or of the nature of, till or tenacious clay.

1799 J. ROBERTSON *Agric. Perth* 14 Houses composed of this mortar or tilly clay. **1812** SIR J. SINCLAIR *Syst. Husb. Scot.* I. 227 Stiff stubborn tilly land. **1844** STEPHENS *Bk. Farm* I. 169 Clay, and tilly clay even more than the unctuous, retains a great deal of water.

Tilly, tilly: see TILLEY LAMP.

tilly-vally, *int. Obs.* or *arch.* Also 6 **tully valy**, 7 **tillie vallie**, 7, 9 **tilly-fally**, 9 **tilley-valley**. [Origin unknown.] An exclamation of impatience: Nonsense! fiddlesticks!

a **1529** SKELTON *Manerly Marg. Mylk & Ale* 5 Tully valy, strawe, let be, I say! **1597** SHAKS. *2 Hen. IV*, II. v. 90 Tilly-fally (Sir Iohn) neuer tell me, your ancient Swaggerer comes not in my doores. **1601** —— *Twel. N.* II. iii. 83 Am not I consanguinious? Am I not of her blood? tilly vally. *c* **1630** *Life Sir T. More* iv. 127 Tillie vallie, tillie vallie: will you sitt and make goslings in the ashes? **1816** SCOTT *Antiq.* vi, Tilley-valley, Mr. Lovel—which, by the way, one commentator derives from *tittivillitium*, and another from *talley-ho*—but tilley-valley, I say, a truce with your politeness. **1864** *St. James' Mag.* 334 Tilly-fally, man!—But go on with your evidence, brother Burt.

‖ˈ**tilma.** [Mexican Sp., ad. Nahuatl *tilmatli*, in comb. *tilma-*.] A kind of simple cloak or blanket secured with a knot, worn by the Indians of Mexico.

1851 MAYNE REID *Scalp Hunt.* x, We see mangas and tilmas, and men wearing the sandal as in Eastern lands. *Ibid.* xx, There were pueblos clad in their ungraceful tilmas. **1895** *Daily News* 6 Nov. 3/5 The shrine of our Lady of Guadaloupe had its origin in an alleged apparition of the Madonna to an Indian, Juan Diego, in the early days of the Conquest [9 Dec. 1531]... A picture of the Virgin is said to have appeared on the coarse tilma or cloak of the Indian.

tilorone (ˈtɪlərəʊn). *Biochem.* [f. *tilor-*, of unkn. origin + -ONE.] An aromatic amine which induces the production of interferon and acts as an anti-viral agent.

1970 *Science* 18 Sept. 1213/1 Tilorone hydrochloride, the orange, water-soluble dihydrochloride salt of 2,7-bis[2-(diethylamino)ethoxy]fluoren-9-one, is a broad spectrum, orally active antiviral agent. **1978** *Nature* 29 June 760/1 Tilorone, statolon and Newcastle disease virus (NDV), all potent inducers of interferon in mice, induced a marked increase in spleen cell cytotoxicity.

tilsent, early perversion of TINSEL *sb.*[3]

Tilsit (ˈtɪlsɪt). Also **Tilsiter, tilsit(er).** [The name of a town in East Prussia (now Sovetsk, U.S.S.R.); *Tilsiter* f. Ger. (= of Tilsit).] In full *Tilsit cheese*. A semi-hard cheese orig. made at Tilsit.

1936 *N.Y. Herald-Tribune* 8 Aug. 12/7 First on his list is tilsit, a sharp cheese from Denmark. **1950** J. G. DAVIS *Dict. Dairying* 130 *Tilsit cheese*,.. an East Prussian hard-pressed cheese made from cow's whole milk. **1961** WEBSTER, Tilsiter. **1965** *Harrods Food News* May, Tilsiter (German —per lb. 6/6). **1971** J. AIKEN *Nightly Deadshade* iv. 46 They go at once to the larder and eat two pounds of Tilsit cheese.

tilt (tɪlt), *sb.*[1] Also 5 **telt(e**, 5–7 **tylt**, 6 **tylte**, 7 **tillte**. [Collateral form of ME. *tild*, TELD *sb.*, perh. influenced by *tent*.]

1. A covering of coarse cloth, in early quots. of hair-cloth; an awning; a booth, tent, or tabernacle.

c **1440** *Promp. Parv.* 488/1 Telte, or tente, *tentorium.* **1547** *Privy Council Acts* (1890) II. 133 Tyltes of heare to couver the powder. **1556** TOWRSON in Hakluyt *Voy.* (1589) 110 On shoare, wee made a Tilt with our Oares and saile. **1633** T. ADAMS *Exp. 2 Peter* i. 13 The apostle compares his life to a tabernacle; a little shed or tilt, wherin the immortal soul dwells. **1688** R. HOLME *Armoury* IV. xii. (Roxb.) 504/1 The coffin had ouer it a tilt or stately frame of wood couered with black. **1771** SMOLLETT *Humph. Cl.* 1 July, Machines.. fitted with tilts, that project from the seaward ends of them,.. to screen the bathers from the view.

2. *spec.* An awning over a boat.

1611 MIDDLETON & DEKKER *Roaring Girl* IV. ii, A boat, with a tilt over it. **1716** GAY *Trivia* I. 164 The rowing Crew To tempt a Fare, cloath all their Tilts in blue. **1887** BESANT *The World went* ii, A broad canvas tilt or awning rigged up from stem to stern.

3. An awning or cover for a cart, wagon, or motor vehicle, usually of canvas or tarpaulin.

1620 SHELTON *Quix.* (1746) III. xi. 69 The Waggon's Self was opened, without Tilt or Boughs. *a* **1656** USSHER *Ann.* vi. (1658) 228 They covered the Cart with a base dirty tilt made of skins. **1753** *Scots Mag.* Nov. 541/1 The tilt or some other conspicuous place of his waggon. **1834** PRINGLE *Afr. Sk.* ii. 141 Each wagon is provided with a raised canvas tilt to protect the traveller from sun and rain. **1893** SELOUS *Trav. S.E. Africa* 24 My waggon.. on the hinder part of which stood a tilt or tent where I slept. **1976** *Milton Keynes Express* 16 July 31/3 (Advt.), 1975 Mini Pick-up, green, one owner, fitted tilt. **1977** 'D. RUTHERFORD' *Return Load* iv. 77 One of his employees was fastening the blue canvas cover to the hooks on the side of one of the big, steel-framed tilts that were in such great demand for Continental journeys.

4. In Labrador and Newfoundland: A fisherman's or wood-cutter's hut; also, a lean-to shelter.

1612 in G. M. Story et al. *Dict. Newfoundland Eng.* (1982) 567/2 They had made a tilte with a sayle, that they got from some Christian. **1819** L. A. ANSPACH *Hist. Island of Newfoundland* 468 They call *tilts* temporary log houses, which they erect in the woods to pursue there their winter occupations. **1895** R. G. TABER in *Outing* (U.S.) XXVII. 20/1 A score of shoresmen's 'tilts'—rude turf-covered huts, some little cleaner than the Esquimaux' habitations. **1906** *Toilers of Deep* June 150/2 (*Labrador*) A few wooden 'tilts' nestled at the edge of the river... The 'tilts' are all very much alike—the general 'living-room',.. and the beds in curtained-off recesses. The little colony.. come from their homes at Cape Charles only for the winter's trapping and wood-cutting.

5. *attrib.* and *Comb.*, as ***tilt-maker***, ***-weaver***, ***-window***; ***tilt-like*** adj.; also **tilt-bonnet**, a woman's or girl's bonnet in the form of a wagon-tilt, made by bending a piece of pasteboard into a half-cylinder, and covering it with linen or calico, a drawing-string holding it in shape, the material being extended to cover the crown and form a curtain (T. Hardy): cf. *coal-scuttle bonnet*; **tilt-cloth**, = senses 1–3; †**tilt-hair**, ? hair-cloth for tilts; **tilt-roof**, 'a round-topped roof, shaped like a tilt or wagon-cover' (Knight *Dict. Mech.* 1877); †**tilt-sail**, ? a sail made of coarse cloth; **tilt-wherry**, a wherry having a tilt, a TILT-BOAT.

1874 T. HARDY *Far fr. Madding Crowd* xxv, The women .. wore *tilt bonnets covered with nankeen. **1611** in *10th Rep. Hist. MSS. Comm.* App. IV. 432 For a *tylt cloth, 2*s.* 6*d.* **1790** LUCKOMBE *Eng. Gazetteer* III, *Witney, Oxf*... Tilt-cloths for bargemen are likewise made here. *c* **1440** *Promp. Parv.* 488/1 *Telte hayyr (*H.*, *A.*, *P.* telt, hayre), *gauda.* **1562** in Rogers *Agric. & Prices* III. 576/1 Tilt hair. 35½ bolts @ 1/4, 94 pieces @ 11/-. **1834** H. MILLER *Scenes & Leg.* xiii. (1857) 203 The grey ruins, and the mossy, *tilt-like hillocks. **1847** ADDISON *Contracts* II. vii. §2 (1883) 921 The defendant ordered the plaintiff to make him a waggon, and .. employed.. a *tiltmaker to put on a tilt. **1620** SHELTON *Quix.* (1746) IV. xxii. 178 The General made all the Gallies strike their *Tilt-sails. **1579** *Transcr. Faversham Parish Regr.* (MS.), Erosamas Smalwodd, a tylte-weuer. **1573** in Feuillerat *Revels Q. Eliz.* (1908) 219, ii *Tylt whirreyes that caryed the Masking geare & Children. **1799** *Hull Advertiser* 3 Aug. 4/1 She.. thrust it out at one of the *tilt-windows.

tilt (tɪlt), *sb.*[2] Also 6 **tylt(e**, 6–7 **tilte**. [In branch I from TILT *v.*[1] 1; in br. II fr. TILT *v.*[1] II.]

I. 1. a. A combat or encounter (for exercise or sport) between two armed men on horseback, with lances or similar weapons, the aim of each being to throw his opponent from the saddle; = JOUST *sb.* 1; also, the exercise of riding with a lance, or the like, at a mark, as the quintain.

1511 in Ellis *Orig. Lett.* Ser. II. I. 181 Thise iiij Knightes shall present themself.. in harneys for the Tylte. **1553** T. WILSON *Rhet.* (1580) 13, I maie commende hym for plaiyng at weapons, for runnyng vppon a greate horse, for chargyng his staffe at the Tilt. **1656** EARL MONM. tr. *Boccalini's Advts. fr. Parnass.* I. lvii. (1674) 74 [To] spend a hundred thousand Crowns in Tilt and Turney. **1745** SIR C. WILLIAMS in H. Walpole *Mem. Geo. II* (1847) II. App. 396 Low pleasures, such as operas, plays, masquerades, tilts, and tournaments. **1859** TENNYSON *Enid* 52 Forgetful of the tilt and tournament.

b. *transf.* and *fig.* An encounter, combat, contest; a debate, public dispute or discussion. In 17–18th c. often applied to a duel.

1567 TURBERV. *Epit. Dame Elyz. Arhundle* 3 Who ran hir race in vertues tylt aright, And neuer had at Fortunes hand the foyle. *a* **1670** HACKET *Abp. Williams* II. (1692) 21 He would not fly the tilt nor start from any colour of accusation. **1693** *Humours Town* 27 A modish Tilt upon a foolish hot-headed Punctilio. **1709** STEELE *Tatler* No. 39 ¶16 We.. generally conducted our Dispute and Tilt according to the last that had happen'd between Persons of Reputation. **1882** F. M. CRAWFORD *Mr. Isaacs* ii, I trust that our collision in the flesh has had no worse results than our tilts in print. **1906** *Spectator* 3 Feb. 173/2 She enjoys the tilt of rather rough speech.

c. A thrust of a weapon, as at a tilt. Now only *fig.*

1716 ADDISON *Freeholder* No. 10 ¶5 His Majesty.. entertain'd him with the Slaughter of two or three of his Liege Subjects, whom he very dexterously put to Death with the Tilt of his Lance. **1754** RICHARDSON *Grandison* (1781) I. xiv. 82 Miss Barnevelt took a tilt in heroics. **1863** COWDEN CLARKE *Shaks. Char.* viii. 200 She has a tilt at him, jeering, joking, mystifying, obfuscating him.

2. A place for holding tilts or justs; a tilting ground or yard; the lists.

a **1510** *Justes May & June* 1507. 68 in Hazl. *E.P.P.* II. 116 Two seruauntes of this lady of delyte Sholde bemounted armed and redy dyght At atyltes ende. **1530** PALSGR. 183 *Vnes lices*, a tylte to lerne to juste at. *a* **1548** HALL *Chron.*, *Hen. VIII* 45 b, The kyng.. rode about the Tylt. **1564** HAWARD *Eutropius* VII. 75 He fynyshed sondry pieces of work at Rome among which was.. the Tilt [L. *forum transitorium*], a place for men to run in. **1586** WARNER *Alb. Eng.* II. ix. (1589) 35 In beaten Pathes, ore boorded Tylthes [? Tyltes] to breake their staffe-like Reeds.

3. Phr. (from 1 or 2). **a.** ***to run at (the) tilt***: to ride in a tilt or just.

1548 ELYOT *Dict.*, *Decurrere in armis*, to renne at the tylte in harneys. **1590** MARLOWE *Edw. II*, v. v, When for her sake I ran at tilt in France, And there unhors'd the Duke of Cleremont. **1611** COTGR., *Courir la lance*, to tilt, or, to run at tilt. **1636** P. RANDALL in *Ann. Dubrensia* (1877) 19 As they at Tilt, so wee at Quintain runne. **1649** JER. TAYLOR *Gt. Exemp.* III. Disc. xx. 143 Henry II was killed running at Tilt.

b. So ***to run a tilt*** (see also A-TILT 2, A *prep.*[1]); also *fig.* Also rarely ***to run tilt.***

1591 SHAKS. *1 Hen. VI*, III. ii. 51 Break a Launce, and runne a-Tilt at Death. **1674** N. FAIRFAX *Bulk & Selv.* 145 If you make two such bodies.. to run a tilt upon such a line of odd leastings. **1762–71** H. WALPOLE *Vertue's Anecd. Paint.* (1786) I. 158 The next.. exhibits two knights running a tilt on the foreground. **1831** CARLYLE in Froude *Life* (1882) II. viii. 170 With her.. I was provoked.., so pert was she, to run tilt, and I fear transfix her. **1871** MISS MULOCK *Fair France* i. 3 Like Don Quixote with his windmill.. it is running a tilt against perfectly imaginary foes. **1891** *Temple Bar Mag.* Sept. 102 He runs tilt against the hypocrisies of social life.

c. ***full tilt*** (advb. phr.): at full speed and with direct thrust; with utmost adverse force or impetus.

? *a* **1600** *Hist. Tom Thumb* II. 45 in Hazl. *E.P.P.* II. 213 The cook was running on full tilt, When Tom fell from the air. **1679** *Hist. Jetzer* 24 Drawing out his knife, [he] made at her Ladyship full tilt. **1861** *Temple Bar Mag.* IV. 83 Managers of schools should run full tilt at the whole scheme. **1889** GRETTON *Memory's Harkb.* 145 The Earl rode full tilt at him as though he would have unhorsed him.

II. 4. a. The act of tilting, or fact or condition of being tilted (TILT *v.*[1] 4); a sudden or abrupt divergence from the normal vertical or horizontal position; inclination upward or downward.

[Implied in quots. 1562, 1658, 1706 in b.]

1837 BABBAGE *Bridgew. Treat.* App. 246 The variation of pressure, and the infirmity of supports broken by weights or softened by heat, to produce tilts. **1859** *All Year Round* No. 29. 67 The twinkle of his eye, and the saucy tilt of his ragged cap, spoke volumes. **1872** *Routledge's Ev. Boy's Ann.* Apr. 262/1 Until one tilt, stronger than the others, upset the lamp. **1906** *Daily News* 5 Mar. 6 Leaning against the wall.. with his stool at a perilous tilt.

b. ***on*** or ***upon the tilt***: in a tilted position, like a cask or vessel raised on one end or side when nearly empty: = A-TILT 1. Also *fig.*

1562 J. HEYWOOD *Prov. & Epigr.* (1867) 194 Till tubbe stande a tilte. **1658** T. GOODWIN *Fair Prospect* Ep. Ded., When her natural strength, and Abilities began to run low, and on Tilt, as it were; Her Spiritual affections seemed as if but fresh broached. **1706** BAYNARD in Sir J. Floyer *Hot & Cold Bath.* II. 419 When (low drawn) Time's upon the Tilt, Few Sands and Minutes left to run. **1712** *Spect.* No. 292 ¶4 Liberality.. performed with such Chearfulness.. that may shew Good-nature and Benevolence overflowed, and do not, as in some Men, run upon the Tilt, and taste of the Sediments of a grutching uncommunicative Disposition.

c. *Geol.* An abrupt upheaval of strata to a considerable angle from the horizontal. **d.** *gen.* A slope, or sloping portion, of the surface of the ground.

1859 PAGE *Geol. Terms*, *Tilted up*, applied to strata that are suddenly or abruptly thrown up at a high angle of inclination. *Tilts* of this nature are usually accompanied by fractures and crushings of the strata. **1903** G. A. SMITH in *Expositor* Jan. 7 This tilt towards Olivet does not exhaust the eastern bent and disposition of the city. **1910** *Daily News* 27 Aug. 4 As we crossed a tilt of the torn heath I saw suddenly between myself and the moon a black shapeless pile.

e. *Television* and *Cinematogr.* (See quot. 1959.)

1959 HALAS & MANVELL *Technique Film Animation* 342 *Tilt*, the upward or downward pivoting movement of the camera across the screen. **1963** D. BOTTING in A. Smith *Throw out Two Hands* App. I. 266 A Miller tripod with a fully fluid head.. giving smooth, controlled pans and tilts even with extreme long-focus lenses.

f. *fig.* An inclination; a bias.

1975 *N.Y. Times Bk. Rev.* 11 May 14 The contribution to the American language of other cultures has long been acknowledged.. but it is unscholarly to insist on a 'tilt' toward minority contribution to satisfy resentment over past neglect. **1978** *Time* 18 Dec. 40 The pro-Soviet tilt of the new rulers in Kabul, the Afghan capital, is already stirring some recriminations in Washington.

†**5.** The liquor, or sediment, obtained by tilting a vessel; dregs, lees. *Obs.*

a **1603** T. CARTWRIGHT *Confut. Rhem. N.T.* (1618) 449 The tilt and lees of traditions, dregges of custome, and poyson of Popish decrees.

6. A contrivance used in North America in fishing through a hole in the ice, in which a stick or cross-piece is tilted up when the fish takes the hook.

1891 in *Cent. Dict.*

b. On a pinball table or machine, a device that stops the game if the table or machine is jarred or lifted (see quot. 1976[2]). Also *fig.* and *attrib.*, as ***tilt mechanism***, etc.

The tilt mechanism was invented by H. Williams in 1933, and was first used on a 'Signal' machine manufactured by Bally Co. in 1934. Early illustrations of this use are not easy to trace.

[**1934** *Billboard* (Cincinnati) 17 Nov. 67 (Advt.), Anti-tilt.] **1953** *Business Week* 19 Dec. 55/2 Tilt, says Court... A federal court handed down a ruling that would put a pinball machine in the same category as a slot machine if a player gets a cash payoff. **1972** G. L. MORRISEY *Appraisal & Devel. through Objectives & Results* v. 62 We should bear in mind that a performance expectation or standard is a red flag. It says, 'Whoa! Stop! Tilt! Something's wrong!' **1976** H. MCKEOWN *Pinball Portfolio* viii. 156/2 If a table is moved too much during a game in an effort to alter the course of the ball, a tilt mechanism cancels either the whole game or the ball in play. *Ibid.*, When the game is tilted all the lights go out and the word *tilt* is illuminated in the backflash glass. **1983** *Times* 30 Dec. 22/7 The pinball machine flashes 'tilt'.

c. ***to (light up and) say 'tilt'***, to register by one's look or reaction that something is wrong. *colloq.*

1953, **1972** [see sense 6 b above]. **1974** L. DEIGHTON *Spy Story* xvi. 173 Anything concerning submarines made Dawlish light up and say tilt. **1980** G. HAMMOND *Reward Game* xi. 157 'No, we've already been offered forty by Frank Hutch—' 'That should make him light up and say "Tilt",' Keith said with satisfaction. **1984** L. DEIGHTON *Mexico Set* viii. 113 'It's nothing to do with virtue and evil... It's a game of chance.' 'Is there nothing that lights up and says 'tilt' when you cheat?'

7. In Newfoundland, A pier on which fishermen unload and dress their fish.

1891 in *Cent. Dict.*

8. Short for TILT-HAMMER.

1831 J. HOLLAND *Manuf. Metal* I. 241 The annexed figure is the plan of a tilt. **1858** GREENER *Gunnery* 167 [By] welding and forging by the heavy hammer, reducing by a tilt and rolling down to the smallest description of rod, a most excellent, tenacious, and dense body of iron is thus obtained. **1896** *Daily News* 27 Jan. 8/5 The activity at the forges, rolling mills, and tilts where large quantities.. are prepared.

III. 9. The stilt or long-legged plover of North America. (Cf. TILT-UP A. 2.)

1831 A. WILSON & BONAPARTE *Amer. Ornith.* III. 77 The name by which this bird is known on the seacoast is the stilt or tilt, or long-shanks. **1859** BARTLETT *Dict. Amer.*, *Lawyer.* 1. (*Himantopus nigricollis.*) The black-necked Stilt.. known also by the names of Tilt and Longshanks.

IV. 10. *attrib.* and *Comb.*, as ***tilt-day***, ***-horse***; **tilt cab**, a cab of a lorry, etc., which can tilt forwards; **tilt-cart**, a cart of which the body can be tilted so as to empty out the contents; **tilt-forge**, a forge in which a tilt-hammer is used; **tilt guard**: see under TILT-YARD; **tilt house** = *tilt-mill* (*b*); **tiltmeter** *Geol.*, an instrument for measuring changes in the steepness of a slope; **tilt-mill**, (*a*) the machinery for working a tilt-hammer; (*b*) a building in which a tilt-hammer is worked; **tilt-rod**, a curved rod projecting from the rear of a tricycle so as to catch the ground in the event of the machine being tilted backward; **tilt-staff**, a staff used instead of a lance in tilting; **tilt-top** *a.*, having a top that tilts; **tilt-wheel**, (*a*) a little wheel at the end of the tilt-rod of a tricycle; (*b*) *U.S.*, a steering wheel that tilts; **tilt-wing** *a.* and *sb.*, (designating) an aircraft with wings that tilt. See also TILT-HAMMER, TILT-YARD.

1963 *Lebende Sprachen* VIII. 166/1 *Tilt cab. **1977** *Horse & Hound* 10 June 42/1 (Advt.), Container 21ft Williams with Luton for tilt cab, metal framed and in sound order. **1834** J. B. BUCKSTONE *Wreck Ashore* II. iii. 40, I ha' just brought him home from the Physickiners in a *tilt cart. **1844** STEPHENS *Bk. Farm* II. 660 If they are tilt or coup-carts, he elevates the front a few inches. **1605** CAMDEN *Rem.* 174 At the next *Tilte-day following. **1836** *Blackw. Mag.* XXXIX. 339 We passed some *usines*, *tilt-forges, where the makers of nails [etc.] use the power to tilt hammers of small water wheels placed on one of the.. streams. **1894** *Times* 28 May 6/1 The 2nd Life Guards, furnishing the *tilt guard, sent a squadron of about 50 of all ranks. **1909** *Daily Chron.* 20 Feb. 5/3 What we call the Horse Guards, which was then called the Tilt Yard (where the guard, I think, is still called the Tilt guard). **1562** J. HEYWOOD *Prov. & Epigr.* (1867) 178 A *Tilt horse, *alias* a beere horse to bee, Which wouldst thou bee? **1864** STRAUSS, etc. *Eng. Workshops* 90 Two hammer or *tilt houses. **1937** *Nature* 10 Apr. 616/1 In both the Tango and Ito districts, *tiltmeters.. were erected. **1980** *New Scientist* 26 June 388/2 Everything that is happening to Mount St Helens is a 'classroom' experience for geologists and scientists scrambling to gather as much data as they can with seismic recording instruments, tiltmeters, and water level gauges. 1825 J. Nicholson *Operat. Mechanic* 337 The *tilt-mills employed in the manufacture of steel. 1912 J. T. Fowler *Let. to Editor*, Modern tricycles cannot be tilted backward, and so do not require *tilt-rods. 1650 W. Saunderson *Aulicus Coquin.* 69 He medled not with the *Tilt-staff. 1940 I. Crump *Our Airliners* vii. 138 For this disassembling operation, the engine is bolted on a portable *tilttop table. 1973 *Canadian Antiques Collector* Jan.–Feb. 12/1 A birch tilt-top candlestand with an oval top. 1886 *Cycl. Tour. C. Gaz.* IV. 144 *Tilt wheels loose are very noisy. 1974 *State* (Columbia, S. Carolina) 15 Feb. 19-B/7 (Advt.), Power steering, power brakes, tilt wheel, vinyl roof, rally wheels. 1953 W. A. Shrader *Fifty Years of Flight* 124/2 Spratt Aircraft Co...test-flies another in a series of *tilt-wing flying boats designed by George Spratt. 1963 *Times* 2 Dec. 9/7 Two prototypes of a twin-engined 'tilt-wing' short and vertical take-off and landing transport aircraft. 1970 *New Scientist* 23 Apr. 173/1 Several tilt-wings have flown satisfactorily.

† **tilt**, *sb.*[3] *slang. Obs.* In 7 tylt. A cant name for some species of rogue.

1620 Dekker *Dreame* (1860) 38 Base heapes tumbled together,..high-way-standers, Foists, nips, and tylts, prinadoes, bawdes, pimpes, panders.

tilt (tɪlt), *v.*[1] Also 4 tylte, 7 tylt. *Pa. t.* and *pple.* tilted; also 4 *pa. t.* tult, *pa. pple.* tylt, 5 *pa. t.* and *pple.* tilt. [In I, ME. *tylten*, repr. an OE. **tyltan* for **tieltan*:—**talt-jan*, f. OE. *tealt* unsteady, shaky, tealt (whence OE. *tealtian*:—**talt-ôjan* to be unsteady). Cf. Norw. *tylten* adj. inclined to fall over, unsteady, Sw. *tulta* to totter. Branch II is from I; but br. III is from tilt *sb.*[2] 1 (deriv. of 1 here); br. IV from tilt-hammer: these are thus, strictly, separate vbs. of secondary origin.]

I. † **1.** *trans.* To cause to fall; to thrust, push, throw down or over; to overthrow, overturn, upset. *Obs.* (exc. as in 4 c, 6 b).

13.. *E.E. Allit. P.* B. 832 þe trestes tylt to þe woȝe & þe table boþe. *Ibid.* 1213 Ouer-tok hem, as tyd, tult hem of sadeles. *a* 1400–50 *Alexander* 1303 Sone þe top of þe toure he tiltis in-to þe watir. 1577–87 Holinshed *Chron.* III. 1063/1 He..said to his wife; Mistrys Alice what milke haue you giuen me here? Wheerewithall she tilted it ouer with her hand, saieng, I weene nothing can please you.

† **2.** *intr.* To fall over, tumble; be overthrown.

13.. *E.E. Allit. P.* C. 252 With-outen towche of any tothe he [Jonah] tult in his [the whale's] þrote. *Ibid.* 361 Truly þis ilk toun schal tylte to grounde. *a* 1375 *Joseph Arim.* 4 Feole temples þer-inne tulten to þe eorþe, For heore false ymages þat þei on leeueden. ? *a* 1400 *Morte Arth.* 1144 Untenderly fro þe toppe thai tiltin to-gederz.

3. *intr.* To move unsteadily up and down; *esp.* of waves or a ship at sea, to pitch.

1590 Shaks. *Com. Err.* iv. ii. 6 (Fols. 2 & 3) What obseruation mad'st thou in this case Of [*Fol.*[1] Oh,] his hearts Meteors tilting in his face? 1594 Marlowe *Dido* i. i, Phrygian ships..so wrack'd and welter'd by the waves, As every tide tilts 'twixt their oaken sides. 1667 Milton *P.L.* xi. 747 The floating Vessel..with beaked prow Rode tilting o're the Waves. 1725 Pope *Odyss.* xiv. 289 And tilting o'er the bay the vessels ride. 1822–56 De Quincey *Confess.* (1862) 238 To and fro, up and down, did I tilt upon those mountainous seas. 1826 A. A. Watts *Death Pompey* v, A bark comes tilting through the spray. 1878 Mrs. Stowe *Poganuc P.* xxviii. 238 The..tree..where the bobolink was tilting up and down.

II. 4. a. *trans.* To cause to lean abruptly from the vertical or incline abruptly from the horizontal; to slope, slant; *to tilt up*, to raise one end or side above the other, to tip up. Also *fig.*

In *Geol.* used in *passive* of strata inclined abruptly upwards from their horizontal position: cf. tilt *sb.*[2] 4 c.

1594 Plat *Jewell-ho.* iii. 59 It is also very good to tilt your beere, when the Vessel is little more then halfe drawn off, for so you shall draw your beere good euen to the latter end. 1607 Middleton *Michaelm. Term* iv. iv, Give her more air; tilt up her head. 1807 Herschel in *Phil. Trans.* XCVII. 199 By gently lifting up or tilting the lens. 1833 Lyell *Princ. Geol.* III. 340 Sedimentary beds tilted up, and more or less contorted on the flanks of the mountains. 1868 Joynson *Metals* 19 Where the waggons are tilted and their contents shot out. 1908 *Blackw. Mag.* Sept. 319/2 His helmet tilted well to the rear to screen his neck. 1976 *Globe & Mail* (Toronto) 12 Nov. 1/3 The UN [*sc.* Union Nationale] will have taken seats from the Liberals and acted as spoiler in many other ridings, tilting the victory toward the Parti Quebecois. 1979 *N.Y. Post* 8 Aug. 2/5 Yesterday Israeli Foreign Minister Moshe Dayan charged that the U.S. was tilting its policy toward the PLO to appease Saudi Arabia and insure a steady flow of oil at reasonable prices.

b. *intr.* To move into a slanted position or direction; to incline, slope, slant, heel over, tip *up*. Also *fig.*

1626 Bacon *Sylva* §155 Keeping it even, that it may not tilt on either side. 1683 Moxon *Mech. Exerc., Printing* xxii. ¶2 Letting the hither side of the Board rest upon the hither Ledge of the Rincing-Trough; that the Form may tilt downwards. 1795 Herschel in *Phil. Trans.* LXXXV. 408 The tube..by its great weight..will..tilt backwards. 1861 Smiles *Engineers* II. 274 He accidentally set his foot upon a loose plank, which tilted up, and he fell into the water. 1909 *Daily Chron.* 24 Feb. 1/5 South Africa also tilts to the east in summer and to the west in winter. This is probably traceable to the seasonal rainfall. 1967 *Globe & Mail* (Toronto) 10 Nov. 2/9 During the India-Pakistan war, President Nixon ordered assistance to one side... Press reports at the time said Mr. Nixon wanted to 'tilt' in favour of Pakistan. 1978 *Guardian Weekly* 22 Jan. 17/3 Officials tend to tilt toward secrecy from a parochial view of their responsibilities.

c. *trans.* To pour or empty out (the contents of a vessel), or cause them to flow to one side, by tilting the vessel.

a 1613 [see tilted *ppl. a.*[2] 2]. 1865 Lewes in *Fortn. Rev.* II. 702 To tumble out their sentences as they would tilt stones from a cart. 1865 Dickens *Mut. Fr.* i. xii, He poured the wine into his mouth, tilted it into his right cheek. 1883 *Hardwich's Photogr. Chem.* xiii. (ed. Taylor) 281 Tilt the developing fluid backwards and forwards upon the film for about thirty seconds. 1899 *Daily News* 20 Nov. 7/5 They object to being tilted out of a truck like potatoes out of a sack.

d. *Television* and *Cinematogr.* To move (a camera) in a vertical plane.

1915 A. Lockett in B. E. Jones *Cinematograph Bk.* iv. 26 Tilting the camera causes convergence of upright lines.

III. [f. tilt *sb.*[2] 1.]

5. a. *intr.* To engage in a tilt or just; to just or joust.

1595 T. Edwardes *L'Envoy to Cephalus & Procris* vii, Although he differs much from men Tilting under Frieries. 1611 Cotgr., *Courir la lance*, to tilt, or, to run at tilt. 1622 in *Crt. & Times Jas. I* (1848) II. 305 He ran at the ring, and tilted with the Lord Montjoy. 1697 Collier *Ess. Mor. Subj.* i. (1709) 131 'Tis not yet the Fashion for Women of Quality to Tilt. 1859 Tennyson *Enid* 480 But in this tournament can no man tilt, Except the lady he loves best be there.

† **b.** *transf.* See quots. *Obs.*

a 1700 B. E. *Dict. Cant. Crew*, *To tilt*, to fight with a Rapier. 1706 Phillips (ed. Kersey), To *Tilt*, to run at Tilts, to fence or thrust with Swords or Foils.

c. *transf.* and *fig.* To engage in a contest; to combat, encounter, contend (*with*); to strike or thrust *at* with a weapon, to charge or impinge *against*.

1588 Shaks. *L.L.L.* v. ii. 483 Loe, he is tilting straight. 1589 Greene *Menaphon* (Arb.) 74 Her eyes were like the fierie torches tilting against the Moone. 1592 Shaks. *Rom. & Jul.* iii. i. 163 He Tilts With Peircing steele at bold Mercutio's breast. 1613–16 W. Browne *Brit. Past.* ii. i, Against whose naked brest The surges tilted. *a* 1661 Fuller *Worthies, Lond.* (1662) ii. 193 With which Horn he tilteth at his prey. 1733 Pope *Hor. Sat.* ii. i. 70 Satire's my weapon, but I'm too discreet To run a muck, and tilt at all I meet. 1809 Pinkney *Trav. France* 25, I resolved..never to tilt with a French lady in compliment. 1908 [Miss E. Fowler] *Betw. Trent & Ancholme* 12 Coifi struck down the idol..tilting at it with his spear.

d. To 'charge' into a place or on some one; to run *against*, rush or burst *in*, *through*, etc.

1831 T. L. Peacock *Crotchet Castle* xviii, He..seized a long lance, threw open the gates, and tilted out on the rabble. 1854 H. Miller *Sch. & Schm.* ii. (1857) 21 Not at all sure that I might not tilt against old John in the dark. 1873 Howells *Chance Acquaint.* iv, Tilting along through the crowd with a half-staggering run.

6. *trans.* (loose uses): **a.** To poise (the lance) for a thrust.

1708 J. Philips *Cyder* ii. 603 Sons against Fathers tilt the fatal Lance. *c* 1870 B. Harte *Twenty Years* Poems (1886) 36 The apple-blooms shook on the hill; And the mullein-stalks tilted each lance.

b. To tilt at; to rush at, charge; to drive or thrust by tilting.

1796 Morse *Amer. Geog.* II. 465 Shooting at a mark or tilting it with darts. 1822 W. Irving *Braceb. Hall* xxiv, Never so happy as when they can tilt a gentleman logician out of his saddle. 1893 *Cornh. Mag.* June 597 The woodcock often disport themselves,..tilting one another with ruffled plumage.

c. To drive or thrust with violence.

1582 Stanyhurst *Æneis* i. (Arb.) 29 A tempest..Oure ships to Libye land with rough extremitye tilted. 1697 Collier *Ess. Mor. Subj.* i. (1709) 115 If it was the Custom to Tilt your Head against a Post.

IV. [f. tilt-hammer.] **7.** *trans.* To forge or work with a tilt-hammer.

1825 J. Nicholson *Operat. Mechanic* 770 It is cast into ingots, which by gentle heating and careful hammering, are tilted into bars. 1831 J. Holland *Manuf. Metal* I. 241 All steel, whether cast or skear, which is to be used for the best articles, should be tilted to the strength required. 1889 *Q. Rev.* July 137 When 'piled' and 'tilted'; that is..cut up into short lengths, laid in bundles, reheated, welded, and consolidated into a solid mass under the tilt hammer.

tilt (tɪlt), *v.*[2] [f. tilt *sb.*[1]] *trans.* To cover with a tilt or awning. (Chiefly in *pa. pple.*)

1499 [implied in tilting *vbl. sb.*[2]]. 1587 M. Grove *Pelops & Hipp.* Poems (1878) 22 Omaus king doth stay Ere this time long in closet tilte To heare what we can say. 1588 Parke tr. *Mendoza's Hist. China* 295 A great barke..very well tilted and dressed. 1625 *Gonsalvio's Sp. Inquis.* 64 To row vpon the riuer in Barges tilted with purple and silke. 1818 W. Taylor in *Monthly Rev.* LXXXVII. 479 Felt, with which they tilted their waggons. 1839 *Sat. Mag.* Supp., June 253/2 The cart is tilted with canes and straw neatly wattled.

tilt, pa. t. of till *v.*[2] *Obs.*; obs. f. tilth.

tiltable ('tɪltəb(ə)l), *a.* [f. tilt *v.*[1] + -able.] Able to be tilted.

1934 in Webster. 1955 *Sci. Amer.* Mar. 42/3 Their tiltable antenna has four such units, each 320 feet long and 40 feet wide. 1979 *Observer* (Colour Suppl.) 22 Apr. 94 (Advt.), The steering column is tiltable.

'tilt-boat. [f. tilt *sb.*[1] (or short for *tilted*) + boat *sb.*] A large rowing boat having a tilt or awning, formerly used on the Thames, esp. as a passenger boat between London and Gravesend.

1463 *Mann. & Househ. Exp.* (Roxb.) 251 For a tylt bote to London..iiij.d. 1576 in Feuillerat *Revels Q. Eliz.* (1908) 268 For the Cariadge of stuff to Hampton Court..by Tilt bote. 1615 G. Sandys *Trav.* 17 A vessel..like in proportion to a Graves-end tilt-boate. 1737 *Act 10 Geo. II*, c. 31 §8 It shall not be lawful for any Person..who shall..navigate any Tilt-boat..to receive..or carry..at one and the same Time, any more than thirty-seven Passengers. 1764 *Low Life* (ed. 3) 3 Waiting..to go in the Tilt-Boat to Gravesend. 1859 Sala *Tw. round Clock* (1861) 11 Now..we go to Gravesend by the steamer, instead of the tilt-boat.

tilte, obs. pa. pple. of tilt *v.*[2]

tilted ('tɪltɪd), *ppl. a.*[1] [f. tilt *sb.*[1] or *v.*[2] + -ed.] Having, or covered with, a tilt or awning.

c 1440 *Promp. Parv.* 488/1 Teltyd, *gaudatus* (A. *caudatus*). 1562 Bulleyn *Bulwark, Sicke Men* 67 b, To be rowed up and doune, in a tilted Boat or Barge. *a* 1656 Ussher *Ann.* vi. (1658) 230 He was in his poor tilted cart. 1819 H. Busk *Vestriad* iii. 557 Wheel off, like Tartars in their tilted towns. 1844 Dickens *Mart. Chuz.* xlii, Faces full of consternation in the tilted waggons that came tearing past.

'tilted, *ppl. a.*[2] [f. tilt *v.*[1] + -ed[1].]

1. Poised or thrust, as a weapon in tilting; (*loosely*) fought or engaged in, as a tilt or tournament.

1776 Mickle tr. *Camoens' Lusiad* viii. 330 At just and tournay with the tilted lance Victors they rode. 1803 Visct. Strangford *Camoens' Lusiad* vi. xlii, Their own compatriots..Who erst the tilted fight 'gainst England's Twelve maintain'd. 1861 Lytton & Fane *Tannhäuser* 23 And from that hour, in court, And chase, and tilted tourney, many a month,..Men miss'd Tannhäuser.

2. Abruptly inclined or sloped from the erect or the horizontal position. In quot. *a* 1613, obtained or emptied out by tilting the vessel.

a 1613 Overbury *Characters, Whore* (1615) E ij, Her body is the tilted Lees of pleasure. 1892 *Pall Mall G.* 4 June 1/3 The steep northern escarpment, the tilted strata of which..suggest..the denudation of the Weald. 1906 *Daily News* 3 July 6 The question of speed..is..of the greatest importance where a train runs round what I may call a tilted curve.

tilter ('tɪltə(r)), *sb.*[1] [f. tilt *v.*[1] + -er[1].]

1. One who tilts or justs; a combatant in a tilt; also *fig.*

1611 Florio, *Fólla*..a course in the field where many horsemen or tilters, after they haue runne single one to one, they runne pell mell altogether. 1612 Webster *White Devil* iii. i, None are judges at tilting, but those that have bene old tilters. 1749 Smollett *Gil Blas* v. i. (1782) II. 148, I was shocked at the inequality of the combat, and, as I am naturally a tilter, flew to the assistance of the old man. 1827 Scott *Tales Grandfather* Ser. i. xxiii. (1828) II. 216 The best tilter with the spear received from the King a lance with a head of pure gold. 1898 J. Hollingshead *Gaiety Chron.* i. 37, I was always a tilter at windmills.

† **b.** A rapier or sword. *slang. Obs.*

1688 Shadwell *Sqr. Alsatia* ii. Wks. 1720 IV. 47 Let me see your Porker; here's a Porker! here's a Tilter! 1691 *Islington-Wells* 7 A young spruce City Fop,..With a Long-Wig and Tilter on. 1713 Steele *Guard.* No. 143 ¶5 To..reduce their tilters to a more reputable, as well as a more portable size.

2. One who or that which tilts, inclines, or slopes (something) up or down; *spec.* (*a*) an apparatus for tilting a cask so as to empty it without stirring up the dregs; (*b*) a workman who tilts or empties out the coal into trucks at the pit's mouth.

1630 *Maldon, Essex, Documents* Bundle 217 No. 22 In the butterye, i beer stalle and i tilter, 8*d.* 1892 J. Lumsden *Sheeph. & Trotters* 213 The neatest tilter and emptier of a brandy and water glass I ever saw. 1896 *Daily News* 1 May 2/1 The only persons in the vicinity of the pit mouth were the banksmen, blacksmiths, and tilters.

3. One who works with a tilt-hammer.

1829 E. Elliott *Vill. Patriarch* i. i, Loud thumps the forge; bright burns the cottage fire, From which the tilter's lad is loth to go. 1831 J. Holland *Manuf. Metal* I. 242 During the operation of hammering,..the tilter sits on a seat reaching nearly to the ground.

'tilter, *sb.*[2] *dial.* [prob. rustic pronunciation of tilture: cf. *pictur*, *picter* for *picture*.] Proper condition; order: perh. *orig.* of cultivated land, and afterwards of things generally.

1674 N. Fairfax *Bulk & Selv.* 75 The single shove or heave of the spring..puts the Watch thus fadg'd together and in tilter into motions round, right on,..forwards, backwards, upwards, downwards, and otherwayes. *a* 1880 *Kentish Dial.*, This thurruck is out o' tilter all the way along. 1887 *Kent Gloss.* s.v., He's left that farm purty much out o' tilter, I can tell ye.

'tilter, *v. dial.* [app. freq. of tilt *v.*[1], sense 3; cf. OE. *tealtrian* to be unsteady, shake, totter, extended form of *tealtian* (tilt *v.*[1]): see -er[5].

Cf. *a* 800 Cynewulf *Christ* 371 Hu we tealtriȝað tydran mode. *a* 1000 *Haupt's Glosses* 529 Tealtrian, *vacillare, titubare.*]

intr. To sway up and down.

1845 S. Judd *Margaret* i. xiv, A bobolink clung tiltering to the breezy tip of a white birch. 1895 Kate D. Wiggin *Vill. Watch-Tower* 36 Butterflies..perch on the..stalks and tilter up and down in the sunshine.

tilth (tɪlθ), *sb.* Forms: 1 tilð, tilðe, 1–5 tilþe, (3 *erron.* tilæhðe, tylehþe), 4 tulthe (ü), *Sc.* tiltht, 4–6 (8–9) tilthe, 4–7 tylth, (5 telþe, telth(e), 5–6 tylthe, (7–9 tilt), 4– tilth. [OE. *tilþ* str. fem., *tilþe* wk.

fem., f. OE. *til-ian*, TILL *v.*[1] + -TH *suffix*[1]; cf. OFris. *tilath* cultivation.]

† **1.** Labour, work, or effort directed to useful or profitable ends. *rihtlic tilð*, honest labour. (OE.)

a **1023** WULFSTAN *Hom.* x. (Napier) 72 Se ðe wære scaðjende, weorðe se tiliȝende on rihtlicre tilðe.

2. *esp.* Labour or work in the cultivation of the soil; tillage, agricultural work, husbandry. (In full in OE. *eorþtilþ.*)

c **1000** [see EARTH-TILTH]. *a* **1100** *Gerefa* in *Anglia* (1886) IX. 259 Se scadwis ȝerefa sceal witan ælcre tilðan timan ðe to tune belimpð. *a* **1200** *Moral Ode* 57 Vre swinc and ure tilþe is ofte iwoned to swinden. *a* **1300** *Cursor M.* 3504 He delt als wit tilth o corn. *c* **1375** *Sc. Leg. Saints* xxix. (*Placidas*) 450 Telemen left þe tiltht . . & folouyt hym. *a* **1380** *Poems fr. Vernon MS.* l. 269 ȝif þou wolt knowe þe tilþe of eorþe, þat þe fayle corn none, Go and red virgiles bok. **14..** *Tretyce* in *W. of Henley's Husb.* (1890) 44 Comaunde your bayle straytly to kepe þis maner off gydynge in telthe. **1573** TUSSER *Husb.* iv. (1878) 13 Tilth wele done, in season due. **1660** SHARROCK *Vegetables* 98 After four years tilth, lay down your land. **1799** J. ROBERTSON *Agric. Perth* 12 Clay . . when dried by a long tract of weather, without rain . . becomes so hard . . as to lose the benefit of any tilth formerly given it by frequent ploughings. **1870** FREEMAN *Norm. Conq.* (ed. 2) I. App. 709 To betake himself to the tilth of the ground.

b. *fig.* The cultivation of knowledge, morality, religion, the mind, etc.

a **1225** *Ancr. R.* 78 'Cultus justiciæ silencium': þe tilðe of rihtwisnesse, þet is silence. **1550** BALE *Apol.* Pref. 11 In the ydell slouthfulnesse of the churche whan the profytable tylthe of Christe was not regarded. **1810** CRABBE *Borough* xxi. 260 Numbers there were defiled by mire and filth Whom he recovered by his goodly tilth. **1847** DE QUINCEY *Schlosser's Lit. Hist.* Wks. 1862 VII. 75 What a tilth of intellectual lava must [Burke] have interfused amongst the refuse and scoria of such mouldering party rubbish.

c. (with *pl.*) An act of tilling; a ploughing, harrowing, or other agricultural operation.

1565 COOPER *Thesaurus* s.v. *Nouo*, *Agrum nouare*, to vse the seconde tilth: to till the seconde time. **1649** BLITHE *Eng. Improv. Impr.* (1652) 103 The nature of the Land [will not be] changed with fewer Tilths. **1707** MORTIMER *Husb.* (1721) I. 76 They give their sowre Land a tilt. **1844** *Jrnl. R. Agric. Soc.* V. I. 5 The tilths being given at intervals of about one month.

d. The condition of being under cultivation or tillage; hence, (good or bad) condition (of land under tillage).

1488-9 *Act 4 Hen. VII*, c. 19 Leyeng to pasture londes which custumeably have ben used in tilthe. **1552** HULOET, Brynge lande in due trempe, or tilthe, with dygging, and labour. **1674** N. FAIRFAX *Bulk & Selv.* 132 The ground that was to be sown that year in as good tilt as in the other. **1805** R. W. DICKSON *Pract. Agric.* I. 538 It is . . necessary that the soil should be reduced to a considerable degree of fineness, or what by writers on husbandry is termed tilth. **1825** JAMIESON, *Tilt, tilth*, plight, condition, good or bad . . ; 'The land's in sae bad a tilth, that we canna saw'. **1884** *Times* 20 June 4 Working ground into a clean tilth.

† **3.** *transf.* The result or produce of tillage; crop, harvest. Also *fig. Obs.*

a **1100** *Gerefa* in *Anglia* (1886) IX. 261 Fela tilða ham gæderian. *a* **1300** *Cursor M.* 1068 Vr louerd loked noght par-till . . O þe tilth þat he wit delt. **1377** LANGL. *P. Pl.* B. xix. 430 God . . *Qui pluit super iustos & iniustos* . . And sent þe sonne to saue a cursed mannes tilthe [C. xxii. 434 tulthe, *v. rr.* tilþe, telþe], As bryȝte as to þe best man & to þe beste woman. **1390** GOWER *Conf.* II. 190 So that the tilthe is nyh forlorn, Which Crist sew ferst his oghne hond. **1612** DRAYTON *Poly-olb.* xiii. 342 That cruell Bore . . Whose tusks turn'd vp our Tilths. **1781** COWPER *Hope* 46 Banks clothed with flowers . . The yellow tilth, green meads.

4. Land under cultivation, as distinguished from pasture, forest, or waste land; tilled or arable land; a piece of tilled land, a ploughed field.

c **1375** *Sc. Leg. Saints* xxix. (*Placidas*) 326 Towne & tilth al mad wast. *c* **1460** *Oseney Reg.* 133 Whereof xij. acris of londe lien in the North felde at Radawelle, that is to say, in þe telth þe which is i-called Brerefurlonge. *Ibid.* 134 Vppon Ramme dune, iij. telthis, þe which conteynen xij. acris. *a* **1577** GASCOIGNE *Wks.*, *Hearbes, Weedes*, etc. (1587) 149 As men can clense the worthless weedes from fruitfull fallowed tilth. **1616** SURFL. & MARKH. *Country Farme* 20 Lead forth your dung, compasse, or manure to your tilth or fallow field. **1851** WORDSW. *Prelude* x. 7, I paused, and cast Upon his rich domains, vineyard and tilth, Green meadow-ground, and many-coloured woods . . a farewell look. **1881** *Gd. Words* XXII. 44/1 A 'summer tilt' is, or was, a field which was let alone for a season. Now-a-days people want crops off every acre, every year.

b. The prepared surface soil; the crumb, or depth of soil dug or cultivated.

1743 *Lond. & Country Brew.* iv. (ed. 2) 252 Where Turneps have been eaten off, the Barley . . is . . not esteemed so good, as that from off a pure Tilth. **1846** J. BAXTER *Libr. Pract. Agric.* (ed. 4) I. 372 The surface or tilth should be made as fine and level as possible. **1881** WHITEHEAD *Hops* 45 The ground is kept stirred till the first week in July, by which time there should be a good tilth, or crumb, at least a foot deep.

5. *attrib.* and *Comb.*, as *tilth-ground*, *-land*, *-man*.

1638 MARKHAM *Farew. Husb.* (ed. 4) Pref., The third or fourth part of al arable ground is lost in the fallow or tilth ground. **1657** J. WATTS *Dipper Sprinkled* 92 It is called Tilth-land and a Wheat-field. **1657** REEVE *God's Plea* 235 A lamentable tilth-man, which doth plow and sow for others, and hath not . . any crop of his own.

tilth, *v. Obs.* or *rare.* [f. prec. sb.] *trans.* To till, cultivate. Hence **'tilthed** *ppl. a.*; † **'tilthing** *vbl. sb.*, tillage; also † **'tilther**, a tiller, cultivator.

1495 *Trevisa's Barth. De P.R.* xvii. cxiv. (W. de W.) S j/2 The wyld cole growyth wythout tylthyng [*Bodl. MS.* teleinge]. *Ibid.* clxxx, The erthe tylthers [*Bodl. MS.* tiliers] & kepers of vynes. **1496** *Dives & Paup.* (W. de W.) I. xxii. 58/1 They . . gyue them to tylthe the londe. **1866** J. B. ROSE tr. *Ovid's Met.* (1899) 113, I cast the viperous teeth in tilthèd ground. *Ibid.* 202 The husbandman beholds the unharnessed bull Fall in the tilthèd furrow.

'tilt-hammer. [f. TILT *sb.*[2] or *v.*[1]] A heavy hammer used in forging, fixed on a pivot and acted upon by a cam-wheel or an eccentric, which alternately tilts it up and allows it to drop.

1773 *Gentl. Mag.* Oct. 513/2 Any plating forge to work with a tilt-hammer. **1825** J. NICHOLSON *Operat. Mechanic* 345 The tilt-hammer used . . weighs about 100 pounds, and makes 130 strokes per minute. **1881** RAYMOND *Mining Gloss.*, *Tilt-hammer*, a hammer for shingling or forging iron, arranged as a lever of the first or third order, and 'tilted' or 'tripped' by means of a cam or cog-gearing, and allowed to fall upon the billet, bloom, or bar. **1894** *Harper's Mag.* Jan. 422 Before James Nasmyth's great invention of the steam hammer, trip or tilt and helve hammers had been the forging tools.

tilting ('tɪltɪŋ), *vbl. sb.*[1] [f. TILT *v.*[1] + -ING[1].]

1. a. The action of TILT *v.*[1] in sense 5; charging on horseback with a lance against an opponent, or a mark; justing.

1610 HOLLAND *Camden's Brit.* (1637) 250 Having unhappily slaine his onely sonne while he trained him at Tilting. **1617** MORYSON *Itin.* I. 190 On the right hand as you come in . . is a place for Tylting, called Tournelles. **1730** A. GORDON *Maffei's Amphith.* 250 The Armour People put on at tilting with Lances. **1893** KATE SANBORN *Truthf. Woman in S. California* 172 The tournament is exciting, where skilful riders try tilting at rings, trying to take as many rings as possible on lance while galloping by.

b. With *a* and *pl.* A tilt, a just. Now *rare* or *Obs.*

c **1618** MORYSON *Itin.* iv. v. i. (1903) 465 They haue Tiltings, Runnings with lances against a Post Armed like a man at all peeces. **1621** SIR W. ALEXANDER in *Sidney's Arcadia* III. (1629) 337 At a Tilting in Iberia . . I ranne in a Pastorall shew against the Corinthian Knights. **1761** HUME *Hist. Eng.* II. xxxi. 197 At a tilting at Greenwich.

c. *transf.* and *fig.*

1668 HOWE *Bless. Righteous* (1825) 175 A perpetual hostility, a very tilting at his cross. **1752** FIELDING *Amelia* v. ix, His Brother and the Lieutenant were gone out with a Design of Tilting. **1878** STEVENSON *Edinburgh* (1889) 2 Perpetual tilting against squalls.

2. a. The action of TILT *v.*[1] in sense 4; inclination from the vertical or horizontal; sloping, slanting.

1658 OSBORN *Adv. Son* (1673) 70 Though a Vessel may yield the more for tilting or stirring. **1835-6** *Todd's Cycl. Anat.* I. 655/2 This tilting forwards of the apex gives the heart a pulsation against the ribs. **1850** DANA *Geol.* iii. 238 There are no tiltings—no anticlinal and synclinal valleys. **1878** ABNEY *Photogr.* (1881) 245 Tilting should be cautiously and sparingly used.

† **b.** *concr.* (*pl.*) The dregs of the liquor in a cask, collected by tilting it. *Obs.*

1611 COTGR., *Bessieres*, the tiltings, dregs, or bottomes of low-running wine, &c.

c. *Television* and *Cinematogr.* Movement of a camera in a vertical plane.

1938 G. H. SEWELL *Amateur Film-Making* ix. 80 Movement [of the camera] in the up and down direction is known as 'tilting'.

3. Working with a tilt-hammer.

1839 URE *Dict. Arts* 1173 Condensed . . by the operation of tilting, under a powerful hammer driven by machinery. **1864** STRAUSS, etc. *Engl. Workshops* 88 The blistered steel is prepared for tilting.

4. *attrib.* and *Comb.* (mostly in sense 1), as ***tilting armour***, ***bout***, ***encounter***, ***field***, †***furniture***, ***ground***, ***horse***, ***match***, ***sport***; **tilting bucket conveyor**, a means of transporting coal or other substances, constructed of two endless chains between which on trunnions are slung buckets, the contents of which are tilted or tipped at any given spot by a tippling device; **tilting coffer**, a chest carved with representations of tournaments; **tilting-fillet**, a wedge-shaped slip of wood placed under the front edge of the first or lowest course of slates in a roof, to give to that course the same inclination as in the courses above; **tilting gauntlet**, a form of gauntlet used in tilting, having a hook with which it could be fastened so as to secure the lance in the grasp of the hand; **tilting-helm, -helmet**, a large heavy helmet worn over the ordinary one in tilting, completely covering the head and face, with slits for breathing and vision; **tilting-lance**, a form of lance used in tilting, often ornamental, with a large guard or vamplate, and a blunt point or a coronal; **tilting-mill** = *tilt-mill* (see TILT *sb.*[2] 10); **tilting-shield**, a shield used in tilting, so constructed as to cause the opponent's lance to glance off sideways; **tilting spear** = *tilting-lance*; **tilting-staff**, a staff used instead of a lance in tilting; **tilting-target** = *tilting-shield*; **tilting-yard** = TILT-YARD.

1819 SCOTT *Let. to D. Terry* 18 Apr., in *Lockhart*, I see Mr. Bullock . . advertises his museum for sale. I wonder if a good set of real *tilting armour could be got cheap there. **1827** —— *Chron. Canongate* vi, A suit of tilting armour of bright steel, inlaid with silver. **1754** RICHARDSON *Grandison* (1810) I. ii. 5 We had . . a *tilting-bout . . but are sworn friends now. **1911** *Encycl. Brit.* VII. 56 The gravity or *tilting bucket conveyor can be used as a combined elevator and conveyor. *Ibid.* VI. 107 There is a whole class of chests known as '*tilting coffers'. **1599** MARSTON *Sco. Villanie* I. ii, To wage *Tilting incounters. **1859** TENNYSON *Guinevere* 329 In open battle or the *tilting-field. **1823** P. NICHOLSON *Pract. Build.* 399 The slater . . nails down these *tilting fillets. **1833** LOUDON *Encycl. Archit.* §83 Tilting fillets are used to give a slight inclination to the verge or border-slates, where they butt against brick-work. **1667** MILTON *P.L.* IX. 34 *Tilting Furniture, emblazon'd Shields, . . Caparisons and Steeds. **1850** MARSDEN *Early Purit.* (1853) 77 Cartwright, if dissatisfied, should have . . challenged other hearers than his pupils, and upon some other *tilting-ground than the fenced enclosures of a university. **1880** *Academy* 20 Nov. 371/3 A very fine *tilting helm with the wooden crest of Sir John Gostwick, Master of the Horse to Henry VIII. **1846** FAIRHOLT *Costume in Eng.* 119 [The figure] represents [Sir Geoffrey Loutterell] . . receiving from the ladies of his family his *tilting-helmet, shield, and *pavon*. **1623** in *Crt. & Times Jas. I* (1848) II. 385 He hath . . sent for his arms and *tilting horses. **1863** THORNBURY *True as Steel* III. 318 This iron hand of mine can handle a *tilting lance better than a pen. **1854** MILMAN *Lat. Chr.* VIII. v. III. 359 Abélard became the most powerful combatant in the intellectual *tilting matches of the schools. **1835** URE *Philos. Manuf.* 61 These are . . the foundations of kindred works, such as . . *tilting-mills. **1602** MARSTON *Ant. & Mel.* I. Wks. 1856 I. 13 He is made like a *tilting staffe. **1606** DRUMM. OF HAWTH. *Let. fr. Greenwich* Wks. (1711) 232 His lodging . . was in the house of the *tilting yard, where the king bore him company at supper. **1617** MORYSON *Itin.* I. 10 The same Court serves for a Tilting-yard.

'tilting, *vbl. sb.*[2] [f. TILT *v.*[2] or *sb.*[1] + -ING[1]: cf. *carpeting*.] The action of covering with a tilt or awning; *concr.* a tilt, or material for tilts.

1499 *Promp. Parv.* 488/1 (Pynson) Teltinge, *gaudacio*. **1720** DE FOE *Capt. Singleton* vi, Our mats . . are our beds to lay under us, and our tilting to cover us. **1862** *Catal. Internat. Exhib.*, *Brit.* II. No. 4014 Witney blankets, tiltings, yarns.

'tilting, *ppl. a.* [f. TILT *v.*[1] + -ING[2].] That tilts, in various senses.

1. Moving unsteadily, rising and falling, swaying up and down. (See also 3.)

1605 SYLVESTER *Du Bartas* II. iii. I. 123 Sea's foaming Course, whose ever-Tilting Tide (Ebbing or flowing) is confin'd to Season. *c* **1630** in Risdon *Surv. Devon* §225 (1810) 239 Her tilting tides near unto Appledore Have clean swept Hubba's trophy off the shore. **1841** CATLIN *N. Amer. Ind.* (1844) I. vi. 40 He approached . . with a slow and tilting step.

2. Justing: encountering in, or as in, a tilt.

1679 CROWNE *Ambitious Statesm.* III, I have seen . . their tilting lips meet close, and grapple.

3. Causing something to tilt or slant; also, that is or can be tilted.

1807 HERSCHEL in *Phil. Trans.* XCVII. 190 A tilting motion, given to the lens . . will move the two sets of rings from side to side. **1907** *Daily Chron.* 14 May 6/3 The cost of tilting standards and electroliers was shown to be excessive.

til-tree: see TIL[2].

tilt-up, *sb.* and *a.* [Uses of phr. *to tilt up*: see TILT *v.*[1]] **A.** *sb.* Something that tilts up.

1. *Fishing.* = TILT *sb.*[2] 6. *U.S.*

1891 in *Cent. Dict.*

2. The American sandpiper. *U.S.*

1848 [see TEETER *sb.* 2].

B. *adj.* That tilts up; = TIP-UP B.

1891 *Daily News* 13 Nov. 2/1 St. James's Hall will be . . reseated, the balcony being supplied with 'tilt up' stalls.

† **'tilture.** *Obs. rare.* [irreg. f. TILL *v.*[1], app. after *culture*, etc.: see also TILTER *sb.*[2]] Tilth, tillage, agriculture.

1573 TUSSER *Husb.* (1878) 92 Good tilth brings seedes, euill tilture, weedes. **1577** B. GOOGE *Heresbach's Husb.* I. (1586) 16 b, Let me here your opinion of the Feeld, and the tilture thereof.

tilt-yard ('tɪltjɑːd). Also tylt-. [f. TILT *sb.*[2] + YARD.] A yard or enclosed space for tilts and tournaments; a (permanent) tilting-ground.

Tilt Yard guard, the name of the guard mounted on the site of the tilt-yard of the old Royal Palace of Whitehall. Also called later *tilt guard* (see TILT *sb.*[2] 10). Discontinued 15th Nov. 1898.

1528 FOX in Pocock *Rec. Ref.* I. 141 Who at that time . . lay in the gallery in the Tiltyard. **1711** STEELE *Spect.* No. 109 ¶3 He was the last Man that won a Prize in the Tilt-Yard. **1825** SCOTT *Talism.* vi, A fine figure on horseback, and can bear him well in the tilt-yard.

1735 *Regimental Hist. Coldstream Guards* 29 Oct. (MS.), The Officers to mount all guards in their regimentals and gaiters during his Majesty's residence in town, and the serjeants to mount in their regimentals, the Tylt Yard guard as well as the King's.

† **'tilward**, *prep. Obs. rare.* Also 4 tillwar(d. [f. TILL *prep.* + -WARD.] In the direction of, toward. (In first quot. = TO.)

a **1300** *Cursor M.* 938 (Cott.) 'Loo', he said of adam, 'hu Lik es made tilward us nu, Bath þe god and il knauand'. *Ibid.* 15187 'Gas til-ward [*Gött.* till-ward] þe tun', he said. *Ibid.* 17636 (Gött.) Vp tillwar heuen his heued he bedd.

til-wood: see TIL[2].

†'**tily**, *a.* *Obs. rare*$^{-1}$. [f. TILE *sb.*[1] + -Y.] Consisting of 'tiles' or bricks.
1382 WYCLIF *Jer.* xliii. 9 In the caue, that is vnder the tily wal [1388 wal of tiil stoon: Vulg. *muro latericio*].

tilye, tilyer, obs. ff. TILIE *sb.*, TILL *v.*[1], TILLER *sb.*[1]

†**tim**[1], *Obs.* A term of personal abuse.
1610 B. JONSON *Alch.* IV. vii, Then you are an Otter, and a Shad, a Whit, A very Tim. **1673** *S'too him Bayes* 73.

TIM[2] (tɪm). Also Tim, etc. Repr. pronunc. of *TIM* (the first three letters of TIME *sb.*), the dialling code formerly used to obtain the telephone service giving the correct time in words; hence, this telephone service itself.
1936 [see *talking clock* s.v. TALKING *ppl. a.* 2]. **1939** *Times* 23 Mar. 13/5 Public appreciation of the service was shown by the 18,000,000 or so calls a year that were made on 'Tim'. **1951** W. DE LA MARE *Winged Chariot* 7 Though every minute of your life's your own,..you ring up TIM; consult the telephone. **1978** E. ST. JOHNSTON *One Policeman's Story* ii. 41 Always receptive to innovations and new ideas, he [*sc.* Sir Donald Banks] introduced TIM, 999, Greetings Telegrams and the neo-Georgian style of post office buildings.

timaliine, variant of TIMELIINE.

Tima(n)nee, var. TEMNE.

‖**timar** (ti'mɑr). *Hist.* Also 7 -arr. [Persian (and Turkish) *tīmār* attendance, watching.]
a. Formerly, in the feudal system of Turkey, a fief held by military service: see quots.
1601 R. JOHNSON *Kingd. & Commw.* (1603) 51 It is the custome of Ottoman princes to sieze vpon al the land which they take from their enimies, and assigning a small parcell.. to the auncient Lordes, they deuide the resydue into Timars, to euery gallant seruitor a portion; but vpon condition, to find so and so many seruiceable horse for the war. **1632** LITHGOW *Trav.* IV. 166 These Timars or grounds, entertaine..two hundreth and fifty thousand horses. **1681** NEVILE *Plato Rediv.* 87 Planting above sixty thousand Souldiers upon Lands in Lombardy; That is, erecting so many *Beneficia*, or Timarr's. **1819** T. HOPE *Anastasius* (1820) II. xiii. 303 The Spahees, or horse soldiers, on the contrary, often only holding their Zeameth or Timar from some grandee as the wages of domestic service. **1877** J. BAKER *Turkey in Europe* 157 A Timar contained from three to five hundred acres of land. **1974** *Encycl. Brit. Macropædia* XIII. 776/2 The newly conquered lands were assigned to their commanders in the form of *timars*.
¶**b.** *erron.* One holding a timar: = TIMARIOT.
1598 DALLINGTON *Meth. Trav.* K iij b, They are bound to serue the Great Turke with horse and in person in his warres. These are called his Timars. **1638** SIR T. HERBERT *Trav.* 232 The Timarrs or Turqmars are more despicable [i.e. than the ranks and degrees before mentioned].

timarau, variant of TAMARAU.

timarchy ('taɪmɑːkɪ). *rare.* [ad. Gr. τῑμαρχία, f. τῑμή honour + -αρχία government.]
= TIMOCRACY.
c **1643** *Maximes Unfolded* 4 That they all be present.., his Majestie as the heire of the Kingdome, his Peeres by their Birth, and the Commons by the peoples Election. The first sheweth a Monarchie, the second an Aristocracie, and the third a Timarchie. *Ibid.* 5 *Timarchy*, or *Plutarchy*, is when great men of meanes, wanting the honour of Peeres,..have the dignity of Gravity and discretion to make them reputed, and to be well esteemed amongst the people. *Ibid.* 28 When the best in wealth and estates governe the poore, it is called Plutarchie, the Empire of riches, or Timocracie, the command of honour, which is also named Timarchie. **1852** [see TIMOCRACY 2].

timariot (tɪ'mɑːrɪət). *Hist.* Also 7 ty-, -ott, *erron.* timorat. [a. F. *timariot*, ad. It. *timariotto* (Florio, 1598), f. Persian *tīmār* TIMAR + -OT[2].] The holder of a TIMAR. Also *attrib.*
1601 R. JOHNSON *Kingd. & Commw.* (1603) 52 They can no sooner stirre, but as so many falcons these Timorats are presently on their neckes. **1629** MASSINGER *Picture* I. i, Who knows but some party Of his Timariots..May fall upon us? **1690** TEMPLE *Ess.* II. *Heroic Virt.* 120 The Division of all Lands in conquered Countries into Timariots or Soldiers Shares. **1813** BYRON *Br. Abydos* I. vii, First of the bold Timariot bands. **1913** A. H. LYBYER *Government of Ottoman Empire* 101 The *Zaims* and Timariotes..were a class of country gentlemen. **1981** A. TOYNBEE *Greeks & their Heritage* 183 Ottoman Muslim timariots.

timbal, tymbal ('tɪmbəl). Also timbul. [= mod.F. *timbale* (1646 in Hatz.-Darm.), It. *timballo*, Sp. *timbal*, Pg. *timbal*, *timbale*, substituted for, and app. altered from, earlier F. *attabale* (Cotgr. 1611), It. *taballo* (Florio 1611), Sp. *atabal*, Pg. *attabale*, see ATABAL. It is not clear in which lang. or under what influence the change was made (perh. in It., which had already dropped initial *a*): cf. the F. alteration of *tabour* to *tambour*. The spelling *tymbal* was app. due to the influence of *cymbal*.]
1. A kettledrum. Now *Hist.* or *arch.*
1680 *Lond. Gaz.* No. 1484/1 The Trumpets and Timbals led the way. *c* **1709** PRIOR *Charity* 15 A tymbal's sound were better than my voice. **1713** *Lond. Gaz.* No. 5106/2 Two hundred of their People [Turks] riding..with Timbals and Chalumeaux. **1788** GIBBON *Decl. & F.* l. (1846) V. 15 A chorus of women, striking their tymbals, and displaying the pomp of their nuptials. **1813** *Arabian Nts.* III. 345 [They] danced and skipped about him to the sound of the tymbals.
2. = TIMBALE 1.
1929 J. G. MYERS *Insect Singers* vi. 77 The essential elements of the [sound-producing] apparatus are the tymbals and the tymbal-muscles. **1969** R. F. CHAPMAN *Insects* xxviii. 585 In the dorso-lateral region of the first segment of *Platypleura* (Cicadidae) there is on each side an area of very thin cuticle supported by a thick cuticular rim. .. This area of cuticle forms the tymbal.
So †'**tymbalon** (arbitrary form of prec.).
1817 MOORE *Lalla R.*, *Veiled Proph.*, With gong and tymbalon's tremendous chime.

‖**timbale** (tɛ̃bal). [F.: see prec.]
1. *Entom.* A membrane (resembling a drum-head) in certain insects, as the cicada, by means of which a shrill chirping sound is produced.
1854 BUSHNAN in *Circ. Sc.* (*c* 1865) I. 295/1 [In the cicada] the muscles..act upon the *timbales*, stretching them out or bringing them into their natural state, whereby the sounds are produced. **1867** MARSHALL *Physiol.*, *Hum. & Comp.* I. 271 The noises in certain species [of insects] are dependent upon the rapid movements of folded membranes, called the *timbales*,..moved by..special..muscular fibres.
2. *Cookery.* A dish made of finely minced meat, fish, or other ingredients, cooked in a crust of paste or in a mould: so called from its shape.
1824 BYRON *Don Juan* xv. lxvi. 38 Then there was God knows what 'à l'Allemande',..'timballe', and 'Salpicon'. **1866** MRS. GASKELL *Wives & Daughters* I. xv. 178 Mr. Gibson had to satisfy his healthy English appetite on badly-made omelettes, rissoles, vol-au-vents, croquets, and timbales. **1880** 'OUIDA' *Moths* I. 25 Eating her last morsel of a truffled timbale. **1899** *Westm. Gaz.* 16 Sept. 1/3 'If I could only have a little sweetbread timbale', she said longingly. **1908** *Daily Chron.* 10 Apr. 7/5 Chicken Timbales with Sauce.
3. *Comb.* **timbale-iron**, a cooking utensil with a bulging head used to form a cup-shaped crust.
1895 in *Funk's Stand. Dict.*

timbales (tɪm'bɑːlɪz), *pl.* [a. F. *timbales*, pl. of *timbale* (or a. Sp., Pg., pl. of *timbal*): see TIMBAL, TYMBAL.] Two single-headed drums played as a pair with drumsticks (a percussion instrument of Caribbean or African origin). Also *attrib.*
1928 [see MARACA]. **1955** [see CONGA 2]. **1966** *Crescendo* Dec. 27/1 L/A bands heavily feature bongoes, timbales and conga drums. **1974** *Nation* (Barbados) 3 Mar. 5/1 The BRC were doing a calypso and cut for drummer 'Boo' and stand-in timbales player L.O.D. to go into a lengthy drumming session.

timber ('tɪmbə(r)), *sb.*[1] Forms: α. 1- timber; 4-5 -bir, 4-7 -bre, 5 -bur (7 -berr), 3-7 tymber, 4-6 -bre, 5 -byr, -bir(e, 5-6 -bur, (tembre). β. *Sc.* and *north. dial.* 4-5 tymyr(e, 5 tymmir, -yr(e, (temir, -yr), 5-9 tymmer, 6 tymer, -ir, (temmer), 8-9 timmer. [OE. *timber* = OFris. *timber*, OS. *timbar* (Du. dial. *timmer*), OHG. *zimbar* (MHG. *zimber*, G. *zimmer* room), ON. *timbr* timber (Sw. *timmer*, Da. *tømmer*), Goth. **timr* (cf. *timr-jan* to build, *timr-ja* builder, etc.):—OTeut. **tim-ram*:—**tem-rom*:—Indo-Eur. **dem-rom*, f. ablaut series **dem*: **dom*: **dm*, to build: cf. Gr. δέμ-ειν to build, δόμ-ος, L. *dom-us* house.]
†**1. a.** A building, structure, edifice, house. Also *fig.* *Obs.* (? only OE.)
a **750** *Cædmon's Gen.* 135 Þa seo tid ȝewat ofer timber [*MS.* tiber] sceacan middanȝeardes. *c* **825** *Vesp. Psalter* ci. 8 Swe swe spearwa se anga in timbre [*unicus in aedificio*]. *Ibid.* cxxviii. 6 Sien swe swe heȝ timbra [*faenum aedificiorum*]. *a* **900** tr. *Bæda's Hist.* III. xiv. [xvii.] (1890) 204 Þa næȝlas ..þe heo mid þæm to þæm timbre [*ædificio*] ȝefæstnad wæs. *Ibid.* IV. iii. (1890) 262 Þæt..þa lifiȝendan stanas þære cirican of eorðlicum seþlum to þæm heofonlican timbre ȝebær. *c* **950** *Lindisf. Gosp.* Mark xiii. 1 ȝesih hulco stanas & huliȝ timber [*Ags. Gosp.* hwylce ȝetimbrunga, *Vulg.* quales structuræ]. *c* **1000** *Sax. Leechd.* II. 198 Sio [liver] is blodes timber, & blodes hus & fostor. *c* **1330** R. BRUNNE *Chron. Wace* (Rolls) 3692 Þey logged hem, & tymber teld [*Petyt MS.* timbred teld = constructed tents (which is prob. the correct reading)].
†**b.** The process of building. *Obs.* (only OE.)
c **1000** *Sax. Leechd.* III. 178 On .vi. nihtne monan..he is ..god circan on to timbrane and eac scipes timber on to anginnanne.
†**2.** Building material generally; material for the construction of houses, ships, etc., or (in extended sense) of any manufactured article; the matter or substance of which anything is built up or composed; matter, material, stuff. *Obs.* Cf. BELLY-TIMBER, *flesh-timber* (FLESH *sb.* 13).
In early use including 3; in later use prob. fig. from it.
a **900** tr. *Bæda's Hist.* III. xvi. [xxii.] (1890) 224 Þætte ne meahten godo beon, þa ðe monna hondum ȝeworhte wæron of eorðlicum timbre, oðþe of treom, oðþe of stanum. *a* **1000** *Laws Ecgbert, Poenit.* in Thorpe *Ags. Laws* Addit. 16 II. 234 Ne sceal cyrcean timber [L. *ligna ecclesiæ*] to æniȝum oðrum weorce. *a* **1300** *Cursor M.* 333-4 (Cott.) Þis wright..Fra al oþer, sundri and sere, For þai most oþer timber take, Bot he þis self can timber make. **1607-12** BACON *Ess.*, *Goodness* (Arb.) 206 Such disposicions are..the fittest tymber to make great Pollitiques of. **1840** M. F. SHEPHERD in *Life of Adam Clarke* viii. 261 There is much sound timber in these sermons.
3. *spec.* Wood used for the building of houses, ships, etc., or for the use of the carpenter, joiner, or other artisan; wood in general as a material; esp. after it has been suitably trimmed and squared into logs, or further adapted to constructive uses.
(A restricted use of sense 2, and in early quots. often not distinguishable from it.)
a **1100** *Gerefa* in *Anglia* (1886) IX. 261 On wintra erian and in miclum ȝefyrstum timber cleofan. *c* **1200** *Vices & Virtues* 27 And ðe wrihte his timber to keruen after ðare mone. *c* **1205** LAY. 22929 Timber me lete biwinnen and þat beord bi-ginnen. *a* **1300** *Cursor M.* 1724 Now wat sir noe quat wark to do And hent timber þat fel þar-to. **1398** TREVISA *Barth. De P.R.* XIV. ii. (Tollem. MS.), Ararat is þe hyȝest hill of Armenia;..and ȝit to þis day þe tymber of þe schip is sene in þe mounteyne. **1466** *Burgh Rec. Edinb.* (1869) I. 23 Mak the ruiffes of guid tymmer and theik thame with sclaitt. **1562** TURNER *Herbal* II. 29 Y^e tymmer of ye larche tre..is very..profitable for bildyng. *a* **1674** MILTON *Hist. Mosc.* i. Wks. 1851 VIII. 472 Thir Boats of Timber without any Iron in them. **1712** W. ROGERS *Voy.* 338 Vessels ..chiefly imploy'd in carrying Timber, Salt,..and other Commodities. **1830** LINDLEY *Nat. Syst. Bot.* 84 The timber of the Beam Tree (*Pyrus Aria*) is invaluable for axletrees. **1832** *Planting* 92 in *Lib. Usef. Kn.*, *Husb.* III, When the wood of a stem or branch of any species of plant attains to the dimensions of 24 inches in circumference, or upwards of eight inches in diameter, it is termed timber.
b. Wood as a substance, or as the material of small utensils or parts of them. Now *dial.*
1530 RASTELL *Bk. Purgatory* II. xii, A cup of tymber or metal. *a* **1631** DRAYTON *Robin Hood & Merry Men* 31 Their arrows finely paired, for timber and for feather. **1663** WOOD *Life* 30 Nov. (O.H.S.) I. 503 For setting up a strip of timber on my window, 6*d.* **1688** R. HOLME *Armoury* II. 84/2 The Wood, or Timberr, is between the Sap and Heart. **1793** T. SCOTT *Poems* 364 (E.D.D.) A breast o' timmer an' a heart o' stane. **1834** SMART *Rhymes* 135 (ibid.) Her wheels were made o' timmer.
4. a. Applied to the wood of growing trees capable of being used for structural purposes; hence collectively to the trees themselves: ***standing timber***, trees, woods. Rarely in *pl.* ***tall timber***: see TALL *a.* 7 e.
c **893** K. ÆLFRED *Oros.* IV. vi. §2 Æfter siexteȝum daȝa þæs þe ðæt timber [L. *arbores*] acorfen wæs. **1426** LYDG. *De Guil. Pilgr.* 11808 A kanker..the werm..That ffreteth the herte off a tre, And..Doth to tymber gret damage. **1566** in *Reg. Mag. Sig. Scot.* 1584. 209/1 Habere lie wattillis et lie fallin tymmer de silva de Cleue. **1634** WOOD *New Eng. Prosp.* (1865) 16 The Timber of the Countrey growes straight, and tall. **1718** *Free-thinker* No. 59 ¶11 A naked Ground, blest only with a small Group of Timber. **1787** G. WHITE *Selborne* viii. (1789) 22 A rough estimate of the value of the timbers..growing at that time in the district of The Holt. **1841** W. ROBINSON *Assam* 41 Another large and elegant timber indigenous to the forests of Assam, is the Cedrela Toona. **1880** C. R. MARKHAM *Peruv. Bark* 158 We continued our journey..through a forest of grand timber.
b. *spec.* in *English Law*, Trees growing upon land, and forming part of the freehold inheritance: embracing generally the oak, ash, and elm, of the age of twenty years or more; in particular districts, by local custom, including other trees, with various limitations as to age.
As to the legal bearing of this, see quots. 1766, 1818.
1766 BLACKSTONE *Comm.* II. xviii. §6. 281 Timber also is part of the inheritance. Such are oak, ash, and elm in all places: and in some particular countries, by local custom, where other trees are generally used for building, they are thereupon considered as timber; and to cut down such trees, or top them, or do any other act whereby the timber may decay, is waste. **1818** CRUISE *Digest* (ed. 2) I. 131 By the custom of some countries, certain trees, not usually considered as timber, are deemed to be such, being there used for building... And all the Justices at Serjeants' Inn were of opinion that in the county of York birch trees were timber, and belonged to the inheritance; therefore they could not be taken by the tenant for life. **1891** *Daily News* 19 Jan. 5/4 By the custom of the county of Buckingham beech trees are timber.
c. *int.* The warning call of the feller when a tree is about to fall.
1912 J. SANDILANDS *Western Canad. Dict.* (ed. 2) 47 *Timber-r-r!* the long-drawn melodious warning call of the sawyers in a lumber camp when a tree is about to fall. **1935** 'L. FORD' *Burn Forever* 56 There was a stentorian shout: '*Timber!!*' **1968** *Islander* (Victoria, B.C.) 15 Dec. 2/1 The sharp ring of Father's axe echoed in the icy air, and we cried 'timber' as our tree fell.
5. *transf.* Applied to any object familiar to the speaker, composed wholly or chiefly of wood, as †a spear-shaft; †a bowl; a ship; the stocks (*slang*); wooden gates and fences (*Hunting slang*); a wicket (*Cricket slang*); an arrow (*rare*); ***small timber***, lucifer matches (*street slang*).
c **1400** *Rowland & O.* 455 Theyre Ioynynge was so harde that tyde That theyre timbir in sondire gan ryde. *c* **1435** *Torr. Portugal* 2349, I pray, that thou woldist my son lere, Hys Tymber ffor to assay. *c* **1450** *Merlin* 117 [They] mette to-geder on the sheldis, so that the horse ne myght not passe ferther till the tymbres were broken. **1725** RAMSAY *Gentle Sheph.* III. ii, Come, turn the timmer to laird Patie's health. **1791** 'G. GAMBADO' *Ann. Horsem.* vi. (1809) 90 The leaps large and frequent, and a great deal of timber to get over. **1840** [see SCREW *sb.*[1] 11 c]. **1851-4** D. JERROLD *Men of Char.*, *Chr. Snub* i, The squire..gives me over to the beadle, who claps me here in the timber. **1857** LAWRENCE *Guy Livingstone* iii. 17 They..would grind over..the March Gibbon double timber as..undauntedly as over the accommodating Bullingdon hurdles. **1871** R. ELLIS *Catullus* iv. 3 Nor yet a timber o'er the waves alertly flew. **1876** in Bettesworth *Walkers of Southgate* (1900) 332 Appleby.. dislodged Webbe's timbers by his second ball in the first over. *c* **1879** G. M. HOPKINS *Poems* (1967) 180 Yet Arthur is

a Bowman: his three-heeled timber'll hit The bald and bóld blinking gold when áll's dóne.

b. *spec.* A wooden leg: cf. *timber-toe* in 10; hence *transf.* a leg. *slang.*

1807 RUICKBIE *Wayside Cottager* 9 (E.D.D.). **1821** CLARE *Vill. Minstr.* I. 35 Boys, miss my pegs.. and hit my legs, My timbers well can stand your gentle taps. **1862** WHYTE MELVILLE *Ins. Bar* (ed. 12) I. 230 [The hounds] have a strong family likeness in the depth of their girth.. and the quality of the timber on which they stand.

6. A single beam or piece of wood forming or capable of forming part of any structure. Also collectively in *pl.* **a.** *gen.*

c **1555** HARPSFIELD *Divorce Hen. VIII* (Camden) 288 The treasure that was made of the timbers, bells, and leads, and the ornaments of the church. **1623** GOUGE *Serm. Extent God's Provid.* §15 The massy timber [a summer] shivered in two, as suddenly as the other knapped asunder. **1793** SMEATON *Edystone L.* §85 To fasten the outside Timbers. **1859** W. S. COLEMAN *Woodlands* (1866) 11 The original timbers after this immense lapse of time are still sound internally. **1893** *Labour Comm. Gloss., Pair of Timber*, two timbers placed against the sides of the tunnels in a mine at acute angles with the bottom. They support not only these sides but also another timber, which upholds the roof.

b. *pl. spec. Naut.* The pieces of wood composing the ribs, bends, or frames of a ship's hull: see FRAME *sb.* 11 d, quot. 1769.

Often preceded by a qualifying word, as *cant-*, *compass-*, *cross-*, *filling-*, *floor-*, *futtock-*, *head-*, *knee-*, *knuckle-*, *rising-*, *side-*, *square-*, *stern-*, *top-timbers*: see these words.

1748 *Anson's Voy.* II. iv. 158 Her spirkiting and timbers were very rotten. **1782** COWPER *Royal George* 29 Her timbers yet are sound. **1809** A. HENRY *Trav.* 185 We dragged our barges over the neck of land, but not without straining their timbers. **1857** COLQUHOUN *Comp. Oarsman's Guide* 29 All the ribs underneath these [floor-boards] are called floor timbers, the rest simply timbers. **1885** SIR J. C. MATHEW in *Law Times Rep.* LII. 265/1 Her timbers, no doubt, held together, but she was no longer a ship.

fig. **1751** SMOLLETT *Per. Pic.* xxxvii, My timbers are now a little crazy, d'ye see; and God knows if I shall keep afloat till such time as I see thee again. **1850** B. TAYLOR *Eldorado* xiii. (1862) 132, I, whose timbers were somewhat strained, laboured after him.

c. *Naut. slang*, in exclamations, as ***my timbers! shiver my timbers!*** (see SHIVER *v.*).

1789 DIBDIN *Song, Poor Jack* ii, My timbers! what lingo he'd coil and belay.

7. *fig.* Bodily structure, frame, build. In later use, the 'stuff' of which a person is made; personal quality or character; preceded by a qualifying word: suitable quality or character for the specified office, etc. Cf. MATERIAL *sb.* 7. Chiefly *U.S.*

1612 PAULE *Life Abp. Whitgift* §138. 93 For his small timber, he was of a good quicke strength, straight and well shaped. **1611** BEAUM. & FL. *Knt. Burn. Pest.* II. ii, The twelve Companies of London cannot match him, timber for timber. **1670** MILTON *Hist. Eng.* VI. Wks. 1851 V. 261 Canute.. doubting to adventure his body of small Timber, against a man of Iron sides. **1822** LAMB *Elia* Ser. I. *Some old Actors*, He was not altogether of that timber out of which cathedral seats and sounding-boards are hewed. **1892** *Chicago Tribune* 4 Apr. 4/5 Senator Cullom of Illinois is better Presidential timber than was generally supposed. **1906** *Munsey's Mag.* Jan. 411 His wish to be courteous to men of Cardinal Rampolla's timber. **1914** *Emporia Gaz.* 13 Jan. 2/1 He is everlastingly.. N.G. as gubernatorial timber. **1954** *Sat. Even. Post* 6 Nov. 64/4 CIA recruits many employees from our colleges and universities through a process beginning even before individual students realize that they are being singled out as possible CIA timber. **1967** R. S. CHURCHILL *Winston S. Churchill* II. vi. 193 His parliamentary stature had grown and he had proved that he was of Cabinet timber. **1975** *Times Lit. Suppl.* 13 June 661/2 My contention that he [*sc.* J. F. Kennedy] was potential Presidential timber.

8. *attrib.* or *adj.* Made or consisting of wood; wooden. (See also 9, 10.)

1529 RASTELL *Pastyme* (1811) 291 The said duke, protectour.. toke the lorde Hastynges.. and.. caused his hede to be smytten of upon a tymber log within the Towre. **1535** COVERDALE *Isa.* xxii. 8 Then was sene the sege of the tymbre house. **1560** DAUS tr. *Sleidane's Comm.* 323 b, The Spaniardes with theyr ordenaunce beate doune a timber walle. **1565** COOPER *Thesaurus* s.v. *Cassandra*, The treason of the tymber horse at the siege of Troye. **1663** GERBIER *Counsel* 23 The making of Timber partitions. **1700** R. SINCLAIR in *Leisure Hour* (1883) 205/2 Timber cups and dishes. **1799** J. ROBERTSON *Agric. Perth* 92 A timber mallet wrought by the hand was all they had.. to break the clods. **1890** SERVICE *Notandums* viii. 48 The leg will be stiff for mony a day to come, and like a timmer ane for vera thrawnness.

b. *Sc. dial.* Unmusical; having no musical ear; dull, 'wooden'; unimpressionable.

1815 SCOTT *Guy M.* iii, He was a good deal diverted with the harsh timber tones which issued from him. **1874** OUTRAM *Annuity* ix. in *Mod. Sc. Poets* (1881) II. 218 The timmer limmer daurs the knife To settle her annuity. **1875** JAS. GRANT *One of the 600* vi. 46, I regretted my own timbre tones. But I must confess to being enchanted while Louisa sang. **1893** STEVENSON *Catriona* vii. 75 You have the finest timber face. **1901** *Blackw. Mag.* July 58/1 If I were not, so far as music goes, as timber as the table there.

9. *Comb.* **a.** attrib. (often two words, as in 8), 'of or for timber', as ***timber-ash***, ***-bar***, ***-beam***, ***-broker***, ***-butt*** (BUTT *sb.*^{3}), ***-claim***, ***colour***, ***-crib*** (CRIB *sb.* 14), ***-culture***, ***elm***, ***-factor***, ***forest***, ***growth***, ***harvest***, †***-haw*** (HAW *sb.*^{1}), ***-house***, ***jinker*** (Austral.) (JINKER^{2}), ***-land***, ***-log***, ***management***, ***-market***, ***-mell*** (MELL *sb.*^{1}), ***-merchant***, ***-mill***, ***-monger***, ***-nail***, ***-oak***, ***-patch***, ***-plank***, ***-post***, ***preservation***, ***production***, ***-raft***, ***-shade***, ***-ship***, ***-sled***, ***-slide***, ***-trade***, ***truck***, ***value***, ***-wain***, ***-wright***. **b.** obj. and obj. gen., as ***timber-borer***, ***-cutter***, ***-devourer***, ***-feller***, ***-floater***, ***-harvester***, ***-worker***; ***timber-boring***, ***-carrying***, ***-cutting***, ***-devouring***, ***-eating***, ***-floating***, ***-harvesting***, ***-producing*** sbs. and adjs. **c.** instrumental and parasynthetic, as ***timber-built***, ***-ceilinged***, ***-covered***, †***-heeled***, ***-laden***, ***-lined***, ***-propt***, ***-skeletoned***, ***-strewn*** adjs.; also ***timber-like*** adj.

1707 *Timber Ash [see *timber oak*]. **1685** BOYLE *Effects of Mot.* v. 44 In the striking of a *timber-beam at one end, the motion.. may become sensible at the other. **1815** KIRBY & SP. *Entomol.* viii. (1818) I. 235 The most extensive family.. of *timber-borers are the capricorn beetles. **1817** *Ibid.* xxi. (1818) II. 235 A little *timber-boring beetle. **1703** T. S. *Art's Improv.* 23 An Observation of an Experienced *Timber Broker. **1825–9** MRS. SHERWOOD *Lady of Manor* xii, An old *timber-built cottage. **1608** T. COCKS *Diary* (1901) 32 Payde.. for bringinge home my two *tymber butts. **1903** LD. R. GOWER *Rec. & Remin.* 226 A handsome *timber-ceiling'd hall. **1857** *Lawrence* (Kansas) *Republican* 4 June, *Timber claims.. may be purchased on better terms than in any place of equal distance from Lawrence. **1890** L. C. D'OYLE *Notches* 124 He took up a 'homestead' and a 'timber-claim' with the.. intention of raising cattle and a family. **1663** GERBIER *Counsel* (1664) 84 Frames.. gilded, the ground a *Timber colour. **1895** *Outing* (U.S.) XXVII. 44/2 Enclosed between three great peaks—one *timber-covered to its top. **1888** LIGHTHALL *Yng Seigneur* 11 A *timber-crib which was going to run a rapid. **1887** *Daily News* 3 Nov. 5/4 Buying under the homestead and *timber-culture laws. **1775** ROMANS *Florida* App. 30 Fires.. occasioned by the hunters and *timber-cutters, who burn the woods to clear them of under-wood. **1826** KIRBY & SP. *Entomol.* III. xxxiv. 430 In the stag-beetle, and some other *timber-devourers. *Ibid.* xxx. 146 A small *timber-devouring beetle. **1815** *Ibid.* viii. (1818) I. 237 *Timber-eating beetles. **1731** *Gentl. Mag.* Nov. 502/2 James Jelly.. *Timber-Factor and Wharfinger. *c* **1611** CHAPMAN *Iliad* XI. 79 When in hill-environ'd vales the *timber-feller takes A sharp set stomach to his meat. **1922** E. M. FORSTER *Life to Come* (1972) 74 There was a tolerable road, made by the timber-fellers. **1854** HOOKER *Himal. Jrnls.* I. xvii. 398 The shelter of *timber-floaters. **1887** MOLONEY *Forestry W. Afr.* 205 The Gambia *timber-floating industry. **1968** *Ceiba* XIV. 29 (*heading*) Forecasting *timber growth by the point center extension modification of the Bitterlich system. **1969** *U.S. Forest Service Resource Bull.* No. PNW30 (*title*) 1968 Washington *timber harvest. **1965** *Canad. Geogr. Jrnl.* Sept. 86/2 The.. economic arguments of *timber-harvesters. *Ibid.* 86/1 It may also be that top park administrators.. apply the terminology and techniques of *timber harvesting to areas in which the primary use is recreational. **1442, 1457** *Tembre haw, tymbre hawes [see HAW *sb.*^{1}]. **1640–1** *Kirkcudbr. War-Comm. Min. Bk.* (1855) 149 Women's schoes, *tymber heilled, of the best sort. **1535** *Tymbre house [see 8]. **1723** MANDEVILLE *Fab. Bees* (1725) I. 419 If.. Ships should always have fine Weather,.. Ships would last as long as Timber-Houses. **1871** KINGSLEY *At Last* xii, A roomy timber house, beautifully thatched with palm. **1916** J. B. COOPER *Coo-oo-ee* i. 1 Along the tracks heavy *timber-jinkers groaned on their way to the Ironbark Sawmill. **1977** *Weekly Times* (Melbourne) 19 Jan. 57/2 (Advt.), Quality trucks at lowest prices.. also semi trailers, semi tippers, low-loaders, timber jinkers, tippers. **1654** *Suffolk Deeds* (Boston, Mass.) (1883) II. 55 Howses fence or gardens, *Tymber Lands broaken & vnbroaken. **1804** P. GASS *Jrnl.* 26 Aug. (1807) ii. 31 We.. passed some timber land on the south side. **1981** *Bull. Yale Univ. School Forestry* No. 92. 15 Ownership of timberlands by the forest products industry.. grew by almost 10 million acres in the past twenty-five years. **1842** *Penny Cycl.* XXIV. 191/1 The right to timber and *timber-like trees belongs to the landlord. **1856** W. WHITMAN *Leaves of Grass* (ed. 2) xii. 225 You *timber-lined sides! You distant ships. **1897** P. WARUNG *Tales Old Regime* 95 The walls of the shaft were.. timber-lined. **1529** *Tymber log [see 8]. **1583** GOLDING *Calvin on Deut.* viii. 44 That there is no more zeal in vs than in a timberlogge. **1681** DRYDEN *Spanish Fryar* III. i. 32 What are become of those two Timber-loggs that he us'd to wear for Leggs? **1969** *U.S. Forest Service Research Paper* No. so 40. 1 (*title*) 29 years of selection *timber management on the Crossett Experimental Forest. **1477** in *Charters, &c. Edinb.* (1871) 141 The wod and *tymmer merket. **1981** *Bull. Yale Univ. School Forestry* No. 92. 39 This model could be implemented empirically on a data set for which information on both the land and timber markets were available. **1721** RAMSAY *Horace to Virgil* 41 Hercules, wi's *timber-mell, Plays rap upo' the yates of hell. **1679–88** *Secr. Serv. Money Chas. II & Jas. II* (Camden) 206 John Martyr, *timber merchant. **1771** SMOLLETT *Humph. Cl.* 11 June, He lived some time as a clerk to a timber-merchant. **1946** A. R. M. LOWER *Colony to Nation* 209 The timber merchants.. bought square timber and deals.. to ship them to England. **1908** *Chambers's Jrnl.* Nov. 702/2 Tasmania prides itself on its.. giant *timber-mills. **1275** *Memoranda, K.R.* 2 & 3 Edw. I, 11 b (P.R.O.), Recognicio Iohannis le *Tymbermongere. **1552** HULOET, *Tymber nayle, *impago*. **1707** MORTIMER *Husb.* (1721) II. 106 In the above Scheme, the first Column is the Names of the Fields,.. the third the number of *Timber Oaks, the fourth the Timber Ash, the fifth the Timber Elms. **1886** EBBUTT *Emigr. Life Kansas* 96 We could not.. get down to our *timber patch. **1609** BIBLE (Douay) *Gen.* vi. 14 Make thee an arke of *timber planke. **1622** CALLIS *Stat. Sewers* (1647) 213 Piles and *Timberposts are set in the waters. **1966** *Encycl. N.Z.* I. 724/1 As building authorities have rightly been unwilling to accept this non-durable sap-timber, a sizable *timber preservation industry has grown up. **1887** MOLONEY *Forestry W. Afr.* 3 The approximate extent of *timber-producing forests. **1968** *Wisconsin Agric. Exper. Sta. Research Bull.* No. 272. 1 (*heading*) Mycorrhizae: their role in tree nutrition and *timber production. **1785** BURNS *Halloween* xxiii, It chanc'd the stack he faddom't thrice, Was *timmer-propt for thrawin'. **1818** F. HALL *Trav. Canada & U.S.* xiii. 118 The frequent sail, or heavy *timber-raft, 'floating many a rood'. **1853** SIR H. DOUGLAS *Milit. Bridges* 236 The large timber-rafts which descend the St. Lawrence. **1626** BACON *Sylva* §936 Plaine Champaignes.. Or else *Timber-Shades, as in Forrests. **1704** *Lond. Gaz.* No. 4005/2 Her Majesty's Ship the Shoreham, having under her Convoy 4 *Timber Ships. **1852** MUNDY *Our Antipodes* (1857) 198 The snow affords a road.. where the *timber-sled, with its ponderous log, runs glibly down to the creek. **1836** *Bytown* (Ottawa) *Gaz.* 21 July 2/5 This improvement with many others (amongst the rest a *timber slide at the Chats) the country owes to.. George Buchannan. **1884** S. E. DAWSON *Handbk. Canada* 287 The timber-slides, by which the lumber from the upper river passes down.. into the navigable water below. **1732** in *Calendar of State Papers Colonial Series, Amer. & W. Indies 1732* (1939) XXXIX. 243 Abundance of saw-mills are erecting for the *timber trade. **1855** A. MORRIS *Canada* iv. 64 A new branch of the timber trade has been established during the present year. **1859** D. BUNCE *Travels with Dr. Leichhardt* iii. 23 These pipes.. afforded excellent substitutes for bridges, wherever it was necessary for a road to be made for the *timber-trucks. **1976** M. BIRMINGHAM *Heat of Sun* vi. 75 The timber trucks —great articulated monsters each carrying thirty-odd tons of timber, usually in the form of three huge logs. **1917** *Chambers's Jrnl.* Jan. 9/2 What bearing has the presence, or the increase, of woodpeckers upon the problem of *timber-values? **1981** *Bull. Yale Univ. School Forestry* No. 92. 33 Some timber values must be foregone to obtain additional nontimber values. **1832** HT. MARTINEAU *Homes Abroad* iv. 59 The creaking *timber-wain. **1848** BUCKLEY *Iliad* 239 Some pine which *timber-workers have cut down. *c* **1450** *Cov. Myst.* xv. 6, I.. am a pore *tymbre wryht [*MS.* wryth], born of the blood of Davyd.

10. Special combs.: **timber beast** *N. Amer.*, a logger; **timber-beetle**, any beetle which, in the larval or the perfect state, is destructive to timber; **timber berth** *Canad.*, a tract of forested land the bounds of which have been established by the government, which leases or sells the rights to fell and remove timber; **timber-brick**, a brick-shaped block of wood, inserted in brickwork; **timber-capricorn**, a kind of timber-beetle (CAPRICORN 3); **timber carriage** = *timber-cart*; **timber-cart**, *spec.* a high-wheeled cart for carrying heavy timber, which is slung under the axles; **timber-chain**, an iron chain used in hauling timber; **timber cruise** *N. Amer.* = CRUISE *sb.* 2; **timber-cruiser** *N. Amer.* [CRUISER 3], a timber prospector; hence **timber cruising**; **timber-dog**, a short wrought iron rod with both ends turned down and sharpened, for driving into and holding together timbers in tunneling or the timbering of trenches; **timber-doodle**, (*a*) *U.S. local*, the American woodcock, *Philohela minor* (*Cent. Dict.* 1891); (*b*) *slang*, spirituous liquor; **timber drive** *N. Amer.*, an organized floating of loose timber down a waterway; a quantity of timber so floated; **timber due** *Canad.*, a tax paid to the government on each tree taken out of a timber berth; **timber-fall**, a mass of fallen trees; **timber-frame**, †(*a*) timber for use in frames (FRAME *sb.* 10); (*b*) see quot. 1877; (*c*) *attrib.* = *timber-framed* adj.; **timber-framed** *a.*, having a frame of timber, framed in wood; **timber-framing**, the construction of buildings having frames of timber; **timber-getter** *Austral.*, a lumberman or logger; **timber-grouse**, *U.S.*, any species of grouse frequenting woodlands; **timber-head**, (*a*) *Naut.*, the head or end of any timber; *spec.* such an end rising above the deck and serving as a bollard: see KEVEL *sb.*^{2}, quot. *c* 1860; (*b*) *slang* (*rare*) = BLOCKHEAD 2; **timber-headed** *a.*, wooden-headed, dense or obtuse in intellect; **timber-hitch** *sb.*, a knot used in attaching a rope to a log or spar for hoisting or towing it: see quot. 1815; hence **timber-hitch** *v., trans.* to make fast with a timber-hitch; **timberjack** *N. Amer.*, a lumberman or logger; **timber jam** = LOG-JAM 1; **timber-jumper** (*Hunting slang*), a horse good at jumping over gates and fences; **timber-leader**, *Coal Mining* (see quot.); **timber licence** *Canad.*, a licence to cut timber on a timber berth on payment of dues to the government; **timber-limit**: (*a*) *Canad.*, see quot. 1876; (*b*) any tract of forested land suitable for lumbering; (*c*) = TIMBERLINE; **timber-lode**, in *Feudal Law*, a service by which a tenant was bound to carry wood felled in the forests to the lord's house (cf. BORD-LODE); **timber-mare**, a kind of wooden horse on which offending soldiers and others were made to ride as a punishment; **timber-pond**, a recess in a dock or harbour where timber may be floated; **timber rattler**, **rattlesnake**, a venomous snake, *Crotalus horridus horridus*, found in the northeastern United States and marked with dark bands or blotches; **timber-road**, a road laid with timber for wheels to run upon, an early form of railroad; **timber-rot**, (*a*) rotting of wood caused by various hymenomycetous fungi; (*b*) *New Eng.*, a hot-house disease of cucumbers (*Funk's Stand. Dict.*); **timber-**

scribe [SCRIBE *sb.*[2]]: see quots.; **timber-sow**, a wood-louse or sow-bug, *Oniscus*; †**timber-stairs** (*slang*), the pillory; †**timber-taster**, a dockyard official formerly employed in testing the measurement, soundness, and quality of timber; **timber-toe** (*slang*), a wooden leg; hence **timber-toe, -toes**, a wooden-legged man; so **timber-toed** *a.*; **timber-topper** = *timber-jumper*; so **timber-topping**; **timber-tower**, a wooden tower on wheels formerly used in sieges; **timber-tug**: see quot. *a* 1800; †**timber-turner**, humorously used for a player at bowls; **timber-wolf**, *N. Amer.*, the grey wolf, *Canis lupus occidentalis*, as distinct from the prairie-wolf; **timber-worm**, a 'worm' or larva injurious to timber. See also TIMBERMAN, -TREE, etc.

1919 *Camp Worker* 26 Apr. 5/2 A large number of our city folk imagine that a '*timber beast' has just about as much need for brain as a Canadian soldier in Siberia has for refrigeration machinery. **1975** J. GORES *Hammett* (1976) xiii. 93 They thought he was a timber beast out of Seattle. **1841–52** T. W. HARRIS *Insects injur. Veget.* (1862) 58 The first was obtained by beating the limbs of some forest-tree. It may be called *Lymexylon sericeum*, the silky *timber-beetle. **1837** *Times* (Halifax, Nova Scotia) 17 Jan. 22/1 The selling of Crown lands by auction—and the disposal of the *timber berths. **1957** *Camsell Arrow* (Edmonton, Alberta) Christmas 68/3 The mission bought a sawmill and set it up on a timber berth just north of the Sunchild reserve buildings. **1802** BINGLEY *Anim. Biog.* (1813) III. 138 The *Timber Capricorn. Both in its perfect and in its larva state ..feeds principally on fir timber, which has been felled. **1747** E. PUREFOY *Let.* 12 May in *Purefoy Lett.* (1931) i. 41 This day I ordered the *Timber Carriage to be set up by Simon Hobcroft the Carpenter. **1901** 'L. MALET' *Hist. Sir R. Calmady* II. iii. 110 A miller's tented waggon,..a timber-carriage, and a couple of spring-carts. **1884** KNIGHT *Dict. Mech., Suppl.*, **Timber Cart*... The timber, after the cart is driven over it, is raised to the axle by crank-gearing and tackle. **1707** MORTIMER *Husb.* (1721) I. 308 The quickest way of pulling them [shrubs and bushes] up, is to inclose in a *Timber-Chain as many of them as you can, and to clap to them a Team of Horses. **1933** E. MERRICK *True North* 319 The people in Mud Lake remember the lumbermen by.. their *timber cruises. **1949** *Boston Globe* 17 July (Fiction Mag.) 8/1 Hard years in mine and timber cruise had given Flood a certain steadiness and maturity. **1956** T. RADDALL *Wings of Night* (1957) iii. 33 Someone offered me a job on a timber cruise up in the north Ontario bush. **1894** *Century Mag.* Mar. 671/2 The *timber-cruiser is a hero... The location of a choice tract of timber is a secret to be guarded with his life. **1981** *Publ. Amer. Dial. Soc.* LXVII. 5 In 1890 the area was inhabited only by a few transient timber cruisers and mineral prospectors. **1933** *Meccano Mag.* Mar. 195/1 Another activity confined largely to the Eastern Lines is '*timber cruising', which consists of the surveying and mapping out of various forest areas. **1956** T. RADDALL *Wings of Night* (1957) xviii. 143 Winter was a good time for timber cruising. A pair of snow-shoes would carry you anywhere. **1842** DICKENS *Amer. Notes* I. iii. 141 Mint Julep, Sherry-cobbler, *Timber Doodle, and other rare drinks. **1856** *Spirit of Times* 25 Oct. 129/1 While we have been dosing timberdoodles with infinitesimal blue pills, they shall have..been doctoring bruins. **1873** *Punch* 17 May 201/2 Any description of beverage possessing the properties of American 'timberdoodle'. **1979** *Globe & Mail* (Toronto) 24 Oct. 41/1 Any hunter who has ever overheated his shotgun barrel trying to down the elusive timberdoodle knows..of the erratic flight of the woodcock. *a* **1861** T. WINTHROP *Life in Open Air* (1863) 23 The head-driver of a *timber-drive leads a disorderly army. **1920** *Blackw. Mag.* Nov. 616/1, I caught sight..of a second log, followed by a third and yet others in an apparently endless procession. I had never encountered a timber drive before. **1957** B. HUTCHISON *Canada* 101 He had heard only vague rumors of the old timber drives in the days of Peter Emberley. **1883** J. FRASER *Shanty Life Backwoods of Canada* 87 How easily this could be balanced in the treasury accounts by the smallest additional fraction upon *timber dues. **1936** A. R. M. LOWER *Settlement & Forest Frontier in Eastern Canada* 77 To Crown timber dues was added 'timber licence', 'timber-limit', or 'timber-berth' arrangement. **1897** MARY KINGSLEY *W. Africa* 289 We climbed up one hill,..went through our athletic sports over sundry *timber falls, and struck down into the ravine. **1703** T. N. *City & C. Purchaser* 237, 7*s.* which indeed is the common price for sawing a good large siz'd *Timber-frame..per Load. **1877** KNIGHT *Dict. Mech.*, *Timber-frame*, a *gang-saw*; the name by which it is known in England. **1967** *Times Rev. Industry* Apr. 32/2 Timber-frame houses are composed of lightweight sections and therefore are easy to erect. **1843** *Civil Eng. & Arch. Jrnl.* VI. 179/2 Along a whole range of lofty *timber-framed roofs. **1904** *Essex Rev.* XIII. 215 The house is timber-framed in oak, standing on plinth of brick and septaria. **1967** *Times Rev. Industry* Apr. 32/2 *Timber-framing has completely overcome the postwar 'pre-fab' image of industrialized building. **1912** *Contemp. Rev.* Aug. 248 The professional *timber-getter is a Southern miscreant. **1970** M. KELLY *Spinifex* vi. 103 The word's Timber Getter, not lumberjack. **1891** *Cent. Dict.*, *Timber-grouse. **1894** *Outing* (U.S.) XXIV. 305/1 We..had great fun with the timber-grouse and the sage-hens. **1794** *Rigging & Seamanship* II. 287 The head-rail and *timber-head, on the fore side of the cathead. **1840** R. H. DANA *Bef. Mast* x, We went aft and manned the slip-rope which came through the stern port with a turn round the timber-heads. **1849** H. MELVILLE *Redburn* 37 You timber-head..take this bucket here, and go up the rigging. **1666** W. BOGHURST *Loimographia* 74 Such *timber-headed fellows that they could make noe accurate observations. **1815** BURNEY *Falconer's Dict. Marine* s.v. *Hitch*, *Timber Hitch..is made by taking the end of a rope round the spar, or timber head, leading it under and over the standing part, and passing several turns round its own part. *c* **1860** H. STUART *Seaman's Catech.* 2 What is a timber hitch used for? For bending to a spar, to haul it along, sending it aloft, &c. **1893** F. M. CRAWFORD *Childr. King* II. xii. 214 He slipped the line under the bags of ballast, and made a timber-hitch with the end, hauling it well taut. **1882** NARES *Seamanship* (ed. 6) 87 The standing part is *timber-hitched round the yard. **1916** A. BRIDLE *Sons of Canada* 5 He was a *timberjack in the hardwood bush of western Ontario. **1953** D. CUSHMAN *Timberjack* 127 You boys hired out to be timberjacks. **1888** LEES & CLUTTERBUCK *B.C. 1887* 186 On one of the huge *timber jams which so often occurred we passed close to a wolverene. **1910** J. LONDON *Lost Face* 133 Crossing a timber jam on the frozen bed of the Teelee, the sled suffered a wrenching capsize. **1937** KIPLING *Something of Myself* iv. 101 The removal of the key-log in a timber-jam starts the whole pile. **1832** *Q. Rev.* XLVII. 237 'Now for the *timber-jumper,' cries Osbaldeston, pleased to find himself upon Clasher. **1847** THACKERAY *Contrib. to Punch* Wks. 1902 VI. 498, I never put my leg over such a timber-jumper in my life. **1891** *Labour Commission Gloss.*, **Timber-leader*,..a person whose duty is to ensure the sufficiency of props, planks, brattice, and crown trees, supplied to each hewer in northern coal mines. **1921** *Daily Colonist* (Victoria, B.C.) 16 Mar. 5/2 It was a wide open invitation to the speculator to buy up large numbers of *timber licences in arrears. **1966** *Canad. Forest Industries* Nov. 55/1 Amendments made to the Forest Act in 1965 now permit: Application of the cost of timber sales to the timber licence as a whole, or to cutting permits issued pursuant to the licence. **1854** T. C. KEEFER *Ottawa* 56 No *timber limits are without water—for it is by water alone that the timber can reach its market. **1876** *Encycl. Brit.* IV. 774/1 The Governments of the different provinces [Canada] grant licences..to cut timber over vast tracts of land, under the name of 'timber limits'. **1890** *Grip* (Toronto) 8 Feb. 83/2 A Journal..is..agitated lest, by disputing our timber-limits.., the Ontario Government shall bring the province to direct taxation. **1898** W. T. JENNINGS *Rep. Routes to Yukon* 9 The whole valley and slopes to the timber limit are clothed with cotton-wood, spruce and alder trees. **1914** H. BINDLOSS *Intriguers* 108 We want to get as far north as the timber limit. **1960** *Ottawa Citizen* 18 June 38/5 A Blackfoot Indian band in 1892 surrendered a timber limit in Alberta. *c* **1400** WILL. THORNE *Chron.* an. 1364, Pro schippeshere, *timberlode & bordlode, vel cariare extra waldam per mare. *a* **1670** SPALDING *Hist. Troub. Scotl.* (1850) I. 290 He causit big wp..ane *tymber meir, quhairvpone runnaget knaves and runaway soldiouris sould ryde. **1755** JOHNSON, *Horse*,..a wooden machine which soldiers ride by way of punishment. It is sometimes called a timber-mare. **1840** *Evid. Hull Docks Comm.* 9 The *timber-pond to which I allude is at this spot. **1936** E. G. BARNARD *Rider of Cherokee Strip* 51 Some called it the *timber rattler or the black diamond rattler. **1974** A. DILLARD *Pilgrim at Tinker Creek* xiii. 223 The only other poisonous snake around here is the timber rattler. **1950** *Chicago Tribune* 16 Mar. II. 12/2 With him to the zoo went five *timber rattlesnakes. **1982** J. S. BORTHWICK *Case of Hook-Billed Kites* (1983) xlviii. 171 He swept from the timber rattlesnake..to the western diamondback. **1803** *Naval Chron.* IX. 279 Four low wheels,..to run..upon a rail-way or *timber-road. **1858** SIMMONDS *Dict. Trade*, **Timber-scribe*, a metal tool or pointed instrument for marking logs and casks. **1877** KNIGHT *Dict. Mech.*, *Timber-scribe*, a scoring-tool for timber; a race-knife. **1626** BACON *Sylva* §692 Creatures bred of Putrefaction;..as Earth-Wormes, *Timber-Sowes, Snails. *c* **1750** in Herd *Songs* (1776) II. 181 Up stairs, down stairs, *Timber stairs fears me. **1803** T. NETHERTON in *Naval Chron.* XV. 220 The *timber tasters..have been paid at the same rate..as the labourers. **1806** *3rd Report Revising Commission*, The several Measurers, Timber Tasters, Converters, and Plug Keepers [etc.], are to be called Single-stationed-men. **1785** GROSE *Dict. Vulg. T.*, **Timber toe*, a man with a wooden leg. *a* **1845** HOOD *Forget-me-nots* iv, Why did he plant his timber toe on my toe. *a* **1814** *Sailor's Ret.* II. iii. in *New Brit. Theatre* II. 343 The old *timber-toed pensioners. **1883** *Standard* 12 Feb. 2/6 The champion *timber-topper of the day. **1904** *Daily Chron.* 26 Feb. 9/3 An animal who is to be condemned to the drudgery of *timber-topping. **1614** SYLVESTER *Bethulia's Rescue* III. 111 Here, th' Enginer begins his Ram to rear;..Brings here his Fly-Bridge, there his batt'ring Crow: Besides high *Timber-Towers, on rowling Feet Mov'd and remov'd. *a* **1800** PEGGE *Suppl. Grose*, **Timber-tug* (Kent), the carriage of a waggon for conveying timber, with a long perch, which may be adapted to any length, or shortened. **1977** N. FREELING *Gadget* III. 142 Sturdy horses could haul carts, timber-tugs, sleds in winter. **1599** PORTER *Angry Wom. Abingd.* (Percy Soc.) 20 Com Swonds, where be these *timber turners, these trowle-the-bowles, these greenemen, these ——? **1860** *Nor' Wester* (Red River Settlement) 28 Feb. 4/2 We also saw a large *timber wolf (not a wolf made of wood, but a gentleman who inhabits prairies and wooded country). **1891** *Century Dict.*, Timber-wolf. **1904** *Westm. Gaz.* 28 Apr. 12/1 Last year the female timber-wolf in the Zoological Gardens produced eight cubs. **1936, 1964** [see *grey wolf* s.v. GREY, GRAY *a.* 8 b]. **1980** *Beautiful Brit. Columbia* Spring 19 In the warehouse, red and silver fox furs hang beside the sleek pelts of lynx, timber wolf and beaver. **1530** PALSGR. 281/1 *Tymbre worme. **1599** T. M[OUFET] *Silkwormes* 23 Before thou wast, were Timber-worms in price? **1658** ROWLAND tr. *Moufet's Theat. Ins.* 1083 The Philosopher saith that *Kis* is a little Creature bred in wood, like Worms bred in Corn; the English call them Timber-worms, because they are seldome in any wood but that which is cut, and prepared for building. **1668** CHARLETON *Onomast.* 55 *Cossi*, Timber-worms.

timber ('tɪmbə(r)), *sb.*[2] Forms: α. 4–6 **tymbre**, 5, 9 **timbre**, 6–7 **tymber**, 6– **timber**. β. *Sc.* 5 **tymmyr, tymire**, 5–6 **tymir**, 6 **tymyr**. [In OF. *timbre* (1350 in Godef.), med.L. *timbrium, timbria* (1207 Rouen, in Du Cange, also 1314 Upsala); MLG. *timber* (13th c.), *timmer*, LG. *timmer*; MHG. *zimber* (13th c.), Ger. *zimmer*; Norse *timbr* (app. 13th c. in Vigf.), Sw. *timmer*, Da. *simmer* (from Ger.). Supposed to be ultimately a special use of TIMBER *sb.*[1], which prob. arose in the fur trade in Low German, whence it spread into other langs. The immediate source of ME. *timbre* appears to have been French. For the reason of the name cf. quot. 1597, and see TAVELIN. But some suppose a sense 'heap, pile': see Schade, and Falk & Torp; others suspect that it was an eastern word.]

A definite quantity of furs, a package containing 40 skins (i.e. half-skins, 20 pair) of ermine, sable, marten, and the like. (After a numeral usually *timber*, less commmonly *timbers*.)

a **1150** *Assisa Regis David. R. Scott.* in *Acta Parl. Scot.* I. 667 De custuma tymbriarum. De tymbria uulpium cirogrillorum Martinorum Murelegorum Sabinorum Beueriorum uel similium. De vnaquaque timbria ad exitum. iiij. d. [*15th. c. transl.*, Of a tymmyr of skynnis of toddis quhytredijs mertrikis cattis beueris sable ferrettis or swylk vthyr; of ilk tymmyr at the outpassing iiij d.]. *c* **1290** FLETA II. xii. §8 Lunda autem pellium continet triginta duo timbria. **1390–1** *Earl Derby's Exp.* (Camden) 92 Pro j furrura de grys..de vj tymbre, et de ij tymbre de meniuer, xij nobles. *Ibid.* 93 Pro ij furruris de grys,..quolibet de xij tymbre. **1473–4** *Acc. Ld. High Treas. Scot.* I. 31, iiij tymire of grece to purfell that govne,..the tymire contenand iij dosane iiij bestis. **1480** *Wardr. Acc. Edw. IV* (1830) 133, xxxij tymbres off ermyns. **1503** *Acc. Ld. High Treas. Scot.* II. 201 For xij tymir of gray grece to lyne the samyn, ilk tymir contenand xl bestis. **1566** A. EDWARDS in Hakluyt *Voy.* (1886) III. 392, I have further received two timbers of Sables. **1577** HARRISON *England* II. v. (1877) II. 122 The prince hath fiue yardes of cloth for his gowne and whood.. beside fiue timber of the finest mineuer. [*margin*] A timber conteineth fortie skins. **1597** SKENE *De Verb. Sign.*, *Timbria Pellium*..ane Timmer of skinnes: That is, swa monie as is inclused within twa broddes of Timmer, quhilk commounlie conteinis fourtie skinnes: In the quhilk manner, merchandes vsis to bring hame Martrick, Sable, and vther coastlie skinnes and Furringes. **1707** E. CHAMBERLAYNE *Pres. St. Eng.* III. ii. 256 Of Furrs, Fitches, Grays, Jennets, Martins, Mincks, Sables, 40 Skins is a Timber; other Skins five Score to the Hundred. **1714** *Fr. Bk. Rates* 41 Ermine per Timber of 20 Couple. **1858** SIMMONDS *Dict. Trade* s.v., In some skins, however, the timbre counts to 120. **1901** *Westm. Gaz.* 27 Nov. 8/2 Ten years ago..ermine..cost 28s. to 30s. per timber of forty skins. The price for a timber to-day..is 176s.

timber ('tɪmbə(r)), *v.* Forms: see TIMBER *sb.*[1] [OE. *timbran* and *timbrian* = OS. *timbrian* (MDu., Du. *timmeren*), OHG. *zimberen, zimbarôn* (MHG. *zimber(e)n*, Ger. *zimmern*), ON. *timbra* (Sw. *timbra*, Da. *tömmre*), Goth. and OTeut. *timr-jan*, f. **tim-r-* TIMBER *sb.*[1]]

1. *trans.* To build, construct, make (as a house, ship, etc.); *spec.* (in later use) to build or construct of wood. *Obs.* or *arch.*

a **750** *Cædmon's Gen.* 1692 Weall stænenne up forð timbran. *a* **900** tr. *Bæda's Eccl. Hist.* III. xvii. [xxiii.] (1890) 232 Neowan stowe mynster to timbrenne oð þe cirican. *c* **1000** *Ags. Gosp.* Matt. xvi. 18 Ofer þisne stan ic timbriȝe mine cyricean. *c* **1200** ORMIN 13368 To timmbrenn himm an haliȝ hus. *c* **1350** *Will. Palerne* 2015 Sche chold sone be bischet..In a ful tristy tour timbred for þe nones. *a* **1400–50** *Alexander* 2110 (MS. Dubl.) Þar fand he tembret on þe topp & tyldit vp a cyte. **1565–73** COOPER *Thesaurus* s.v. *Contabulo*, *Contabulare murum turribus*..to make towers, to tymber plankes euen with the walles. **1857** SIR F. PALGRAVE *Norm. & Eng.* II. 128 Here had Guillaume timbered and thatched a rustic habitation.

b. *absol.*; *spec.* of a bird, to build (*scil.* its nest).

c **897** K. ÆLFRED *Gregory's Past. C.* lviii. 445 On ðæm botle, ðær ðær we timbran willen. *a* **1100** *Gerefa* in *Anglia* (1886) IX. 261 Me mæiȝ on sumera..tymbrian, wudian, weodian, faldian. *a* **1300** *Cursor M.* 8763 (Cott.) Quils he was timberand to þis thing. **1377** LANGL. *P. Pl.* B. XI. 352 Moche merueilled me..who tauȝte hem [birds] on trees to tymbre so heighe. **1692** R. L'ESTRANGE *Fables* lxxii. 71 There was a Bargain struck up betwixt an Eagle and a Fox. The One Took-up in a Thicket of Brushwood, and the Other Timber'd upon a Tree hard by. **1706** PHILLIPS (ed. Kersey), To *Timber* (in *Falconry*), to nestle, to make a Nest; as Birds of Prey do.

†**c.** with advb. extension: To build *up*. *Obs.*

1555 W. WATREMAN *Fardle Facions* II. vii. 156 They timbre vp drie stickes together.

†**2.** *fig.* To construct, frame, effect, do, form, cause, bring about, bring into existence or operation (any action, condition, etc.). *Obs.*

c **897** K. ÆLFRED *Gregory's Past. C.* xxxiii. 215 Ða godan weorc ðe he..timbrede. *a* **1000** *Ags. Ps.* (Th.) cxxviii[i]. 2 [3] Ofer minum bæce bitere ongunnon þa firenfullan facen timbrian. *c* **1205** LAY. 6620 Hit wes vmbe fif winter..seoððen he þas seorȝe him seolfen hæfde itimbred. *a* **1225** *Ancr. R.* 124 Þeos hond..haueð itimbred me þe bliscen of heouene. ? *a* **1400** *Morte Arth.* 3742 That traytoure..That this tresone has tymbyrde to my trewe lorde. *c* **1450** *Bone Flor.* 560 That hath tymberde all my teene. **1646** SIR T. BROWNE *Pseud. Ep.* I. v. 14 Heads that were never timber'd for it.

†**3.** To make up or add fuel to (a fire). *Obs.*

1486 *Bk. St. Albans* F vij b, A ffyre Tymbered. **1513** *Bk. Kerving* in *Babees Bk.* (1868) 265 Tymbre that fyre. **1530** PALSGR. 758/2, I tymber a fyre, *je accoustre*, or *je mets a poynt*. **1688** R. HOLME *Armoury* III. 85/1 Timber the Fire, is to mend the Fire, make it burn better, by putting more Fuel or Wood or Coles to it.

4. To furnish with timber. (See also TIMBERED *ppl. a.*) †**a.** To supply or arm with spears: cf. TIMBER *sb.*[1] 5. *Obs.*

a **1578** LINDESAY (Pitscottie) *Chron. Scot.* (S.T.S.) II. 98 The earle of Angus was weill temmert witht so money sharp speiris and lang.

b. To put in or apply timber to support the roof of a mine or working, the sides of a shaft or a trench, the roof and sides of a tunnel, etc.

1702 SAVERY *Miners Friend* 6 The more Shafts or Pits are sunk, the more Wood-work will be necessarily imployed in Timbering them. **1725** T. THOMAS in *Portland Papers* (Hist. MSS. Comm.) VI. 106 The lining of it [the pit shaft] with wood in order to hinder it from falling in, is timbering of it. **1844** SIMMS *Pract. Tunnelling* xii. 121 The leaving the lower part of the excavation without being timbered was not general throughout the tunnel. **1872** R. B. SMYTH *Mining Statist.* 62 The new shaft..has been sunk, timbered, and centred to a depth of 260 feet. **1904** *Times* 28 Jan. 10/4 The gang had to timber up the roof.

c. To cover or frame with timber or wood.

1850 HAWTHORNE *Scarlet L.* i. (1883) 67 A wooden edifice, the door of which was heavily timbered with oak. **1904** *Westm. Gaz.* 26 Aug. 3/1 If you have the floor of the butt timbered or stoned.

5. *intr.* Of a tree: To form timber. ? *Obs.*

1610 [implied in TIMBERING *vbl. sb.* and *ppl. a.*].

†**6.** *trans.* ***timber out***, to divide (timber) into beams, planks, etc., suited for building. Also *fig.*

1628 *MS. Acc. St. John's Hosp., Canterb.*, To appoynte the tymber to be brought home and to be tymbered out for diuerse vses. **1637** *Ibid.*, Payed for timberinge out of our woode j s. **1662** HIBBERT *Body Div.* I. 69 Many men engage in undertakings, for which their heads were never squared or timbred out.

timber, obs. form of TIMBRE.

timbered ('tɪmbəd), *ppl. a.* [f. TIMBER *sb.*[1] and *v.* + -ED.]

1. Constructed of timber; built or made of wood, wooden.

c **1412** HOCCLEVE *De Reg. Princ.* 5338 Castels doun bette, and tymbred houses brent. **1552** HULOET, Tymbred, *materiatus*,..*materior*,..to worke in tymber. **1632** LITHGOW *Trav.* VIII. 351 A great thicket of wood, where their timberd Cabine stood. **1699** DAMPIER *Voy.* II. I. ix. 172 About a hundred yards from the Fort..there is a low timbered House. **1848** LYTTON *Harold* I. iv, They entered London, a rude, dark city, built mainly of timbered houses. **1905** A. C. BENSON *Upton Lett.* (1906) 139 A little ancient church, with a timbered spire.

2. a. Of a thing (concrete or abstract): Having a structure (of a specified kind); constructed, framed, built, made. (In parasynthetic comb., or qualified by an adv.)

1570 FOXE *A. & M.* (ed. 2) 1333/1 Loe here the mighty reasons, the stronge tymbered argumentes. **1602** SHAKS. *Ham.* IV. vii. 22 My Arrowes Too slightly timbred for so loud a Winde, Would haue reuerted to my Bow againe. **1697** COLLIER *Ess. Mor. Subj.* II. (1709) 80 Let them be as Sleek and well Timber'd as those Atoms Epicurus made his Soul of. **1771** SMOLLETT *Humph. Cl.* 28 Sept., Lord Oxmington was well known to have his brain very ill timbered.

b. Of a person or animal: Having (such and such) a bodily structure or constitution; framed, built. (Usually in parasynthetic comb.)

1581 MULCASTER *Positions* xxxvii. (1887) 144 Your childe is weake tymbred, let scholing alone. **1622** FLETCHER & MASSINGER *Spanish Curate* II. i, A fine straite timber'd man and a brave soldier. **1769** *Stratford Jubilee* II. i, I'm as well timbered about the legs and face, as one can meet. **1861** *Times* 27 Sept., Cart-horses, young, and well-timbered, and quick walkers.

3. Furnished with growing trees; wooded.

1701 *Lond. Gaz.* No. 3724/4 Piggott's Farm.., being well Timbred. **1754** FIELDING *Fathers* II. i, That estate..of yours in Hampshire is a very ill-timbered estate. **1854** BARTLETT *Mex. Boundary* I. ix. 234 So rich a timbered country. **1887** MOLONEY *Forestry W. Afr.* 6 About one half of the timbered land in the island belongs to the Government.

'timberer. [f. TIMBER *sb.*[1] + -ER[1].]

1. = TIMBERMAN 3.

1891 in *Cent. Dict.*

2. A ship engaged in the timber trade.

1849 CUPPLES *Green Hand* ix. (1856) 81 'I'd say she's—not a cruiser, Captain Williamson—no, nor a Greenock Indyman—nor a—' 'Oh!' said Finch, 'some African timberer or other'.

timbering ('tɪmbərɪŋ), *vbl. sb.* [f. TIMBER *v.* + -ING[1].]

1. The action of the verb TIMBER, in various senses.

c **1175** *Lamb. Hom.* 93 þi bileafden heo heore timbrunge. *a* **1225** *Ancr. R.* 124 Al is to his biheue, & timbrunge touward his blisse. **1591** PERCIVAL *Sp. Dict.*, *Maderamiento*, timbering, *contignatio*. **1610** FOLKINGHAM *Art of Survey* I. iii. 6 The boaling, spreading, arming, timbring and tapering of Trees. **1844** SIMMS (*title*) Practical Tunnelling..the setting out of the works; Shaft sinking,..Timbering [etc.]. **1893** *Labour Commission Gloss.*, *Timbering*, propping up the roof or sides of a mine by means of planks and cogs, &c.

2. *concr.* Building material (esp. of wood); timber-work; *spec.* in *Mining*, the timber used to support the sides of a shaft or the roof of a working.

1486 *Bk. St. Albans, Hawking* a ij, We shall say that hawkys doon draw when they bere tymbering to their nestes. **1791** NEWTE *Tour Eng. & Scot.* 241 Oak..fit for agricultural utensils, and timbering for the roofs of houses. **1844** SIMMS *Pract. Tunnelling* xii. 121 The whole of the timbering of the top of the new length is..complete down to the first sill. **1867** MUSGRAVE *Nooks O. France* II. i. 6 A lofty domicile..exhibiting laths, timbering and slatework.

'timbering, *ppl. a.* [f. as prec. + -ING[2].] That timbers; constructing, building; of a tree, producing timber.

1610 FOLKINGHAM *Art of Survey* I. iii. 6 The high timbring Oake dilating mightie armes in large extent. **1648** EARL OF WESTMORELAND *Otia Sacra* (1879) 155 Thou maist as well make wonder less, By fancying of two Timbering Phœnixes At the same time.

timberless ('tɪmbəlɪs), *a.* [f. TIMBER *sb.*[1] + -LESS.] Without timber; devoid of forest-trees.

1859 R. F. BURTON in *Jrnl. Geog. Soc.* XXIX. 140 Tracts of dense bush and timberless woods. **1870** *Daily News* 15 Feb., Those prairie States..are mostly timberless States.

'timberline. Chiefly *N. Amer.* Also **timber line, timber-line.** [TIMBER *sb.*[1]] **1.** On a mountain, the line or level above which no trees grow. Freq. with omission of *the*. Also *attrib.*

1867 *Harper's Mag.* June 17/2 A high mountain ridge divided into innumerable peaks, all of which tower above the timber-line. **1874** COUES *Birds N.-W.* 272 The flowers growing far above timber-line of Mount Lincoln. **1904** *Bull. Geol. Soc. Amer.* XIV. 557 On the mountains of central Idaho, the cold timberline is sharply drawn at an elevation of about 10,000 feet, while the dry timberline, equally well defined, has an elevation of about 7,000 feet. **1936** *Scrutiny* IV. 443 Timber-line settlers. **1961** R. M. PATTERSON *Buffalo Head* ii. 40 'The timberline country I would learn to call it in the years to come. **1966** *Encycl. N.Z.* I. 730/1 Upper timber-line belts are largely composed of broadleaf shrubs. **1980** *Outdoor Life* (U.S.) (Northeast ed.) Oct. 100/2 Hunters working from 8,000-feet to timberline.

2. In the northern hemisphere, the line north of which no trees grow.

1896 C. WHITNEY *On Snow-Shoes to Barren Grounds* 287 How well I remember that birch-tree! And how delighted I was, for I knew by that sign the timber-line was very close. **1934** P. H. GODSELL *Arctic Trader* 288 We had a warm camp that night, as we were still within the timber line. **1977** A. HALLAM *Planet Earth* 88 In practice we find that the zone of continuous permafrost is limited to those areas where the mean annual temperature is −15°C..and this also roughly coincides with the timber-line, the northernmost point where trees exist.

timberling ('tɪmbəlɪŋ). [f. TIMBER *sb.*[1] + -LING.] A young timber-tree; a sapling.

1787 W. MARSHALL *Norfolk* I. 99 The timbers, pollards, and timberlings should first be inspected. **1796** —— *W. England* I. 83 The ancient law..requires that a certain number of Timberlings should be left standing. *Ibid.* II. 156 Train up the young stands, or timberlings, so as to give them length of stem.

timberman ('tɪmbəmən). [f. TIMBER *sb.*[1] + MAN *sb.*[1]]

1. †**a.** A man who supplies or deals in timber. *Obs.*

1429 *Rec. St. Mary at Hill* 70 Payd to more tymberman for tymbre for gretynges hous. **1625** BACON *Ess.*, *Riches* (Arb.) 235 A Great Sheepe-Master, A Great Timber Man. **1656** [? J. SERGEANT] tr. *T. White's Peripat. Inst.* 420 Trees are thrown by Timber-men into the Water.

b. A man employed in handling timber.

1890 GORDON *Foundry* vi. (*heading*), Among the timbermen. *Ibid.* 114 We turn into Canada Dock, and are at once among the timbermen. **1891** *Labour Commission Gloss.*, *Timbermen*, men who discharge timber cargoes from ships, and stock timber on shore and upon raft on water.

c. *Canad.* An owner or manager of a company engaged in lumbering.

1889 W. H. WITHROW *Our Own Country—Canada* 527 The trees, where the timbermen have not culled out the finest, are most picturesque. **1963** F. W. LINDSAY *B.C. Outlaws* 7 Among them is..a prominent timberman who recently became interested in timber limits at Quatsino.

†**2.** One who makes things of timber; a carpenter. [So Du. *timmerman*, G. *zimmermann.*] *Sc. Obs.*

1466 *Sc. Acts Jas. III* (1814) II. 87 þe master of þe schip sal fynd sufficiand stermane, tymmerman, & schipmen conuenient for þe schip. **1496** *Acc. Ld. High Treas. Scot.* I. 282 To Hermyn, tymmyr man, Duchman, for v^e and xij rachteris. **1502** *Ibid.* II. 281 To fee tymirmen to pas to the wod with the said wricht. **1534** *Ibid.* VI. 234 To Thomas Corry, thre tymmermen,..to pas to calfet the Kingis schip. **1643** in Cramond *Ann. Banff* (1891) I. 90 Any wright or other timberman burger or inhabitant.

3. A man employed in timbering the shafts or roofs of a mine, the sides of a trench, or any other excavation.

1849–50 WEALE *Dict. Terms*, *Timber-man*, in mining, the man employed in placing supports of timber in the mine. **1877** FOSTER & GALLOWAY tr. *Callon's Lect. Mining* I. 231 The timberman who sets up the props has usually no special tool except his axe. **1881** *Echo* 14 Jan. 1/6 A timberman..had seen..one of the men give a light to the manager, both having their lamps open.

4. A species of timber-beetle.

1894 *B'ham Weekly Post* 14 Apr. 4/7 That curious and interesting beetle the Timberman (*Astinomus ædilis*).

timbersome, variant of TIMORSOME.

timber-tree. A tree yielding timber or wood fit for building or construction.

c **1505** *Plumpton Corr.* (Camden) 198 Tha will bey none without they have tymmer tres. **1558–9** *Act. 1 Eliz.* c. 15 Any Tymber Tree or Tymber Trees of Oke, Beeche, or Ashe. **1601** R. JOHNSON *Kingd. & Commw.* (1603) 15 The noblemen doe make great profit by selling great quantities.. for firewood, but greater by sales of timber trees; for..the greatest part of their buildings consist of timber. **1726** SWIFT *Gulliver* I. viii, Cutting down some of the largest timber trees for oars and masts. **1766** *Act 6 Geo. III*, c. 48 All Oak, Beech, Chestnut, Walnut, Ash, Elm, Cedar, Fir, Asp, Lime, Sycamore, and Birch Trees, shall be deemed and taken to be Timber Trees within the true Meaning..of this Act. **1865** *Chambers' Encycl.* s.v. *Poplar*, The cottonwood of North America is valued as a timber-tree.

timber-wood. Now *rare.* Wood suitable for structural purposes; = TIMBER *sb.*[1] 3.

c **1483** CAXTON *Dialogues* 40 Alle the tymbre woode, *tous les boys charpentifs*. **1579** E. K. *Gloss* in *Spenser's Sheph. Cal.* Feb. 146 *Trees of state*, taller trees fitte for timber wood. **1602** FULBECKE *2nd Pt. Parall.* 52 He shal not meddle with great timber-woode without the assent of his lessor... But the cutting of dead wood is not waste. **1653** H. MORE *Antid. Ath.* II. iii. (1712) 47 (*heading*) The designed Usefulness of Quarries of Stone, Timber-Wood, Metals, and Minerals. **1899** *Westm. Gaz.* 15 Feb. 7/3 There have..been many substitutes proposed..for breakwaters... Well-knit timber-wood, filled in with stones, does very well.

timber-work.

1. Work executed in timber; the wooden part of any structure.

1390 GOWER *Conf.* II. 200 A wilde fyr..They caste among the timberwerk. *c* **1470** HENRY *Wallace* VIII. 617 The temir werk thai brynt wp all in playn. **1574–5** *Reg. Privy Council Scot.* II. 432 Amendiment of the ruif and tymmer werk of thair..parroche kirk. **1703** T. N. *City & C. Purchaser* 215 Window-frames..Friezes, and Cornishes, and all other Timber-works that are expos'd to the Weather. **1864** A. MCKAY *Hist. Kilmarnock* (1880) 255 The inner roof [is composed] of open, oak-varnished timber-work.

fig. **1594** T. B. *La Primaud. Fr. Acad.* II. *Seneca*, The bones as it were the frame and timberworke of mans body.

2. *pl.* An establishment where timber is prepared or worked up.

1875 W. MCILWRAITH *Guide Wigtownshire* 94 Here are extensive timber-works.

timbery ('tɪmbərɪ), *a. rare.* [f. TIMBER *sb.*[1] + -Y.] Abounding in or characterized by timber.

1859 SALA *Tw. round Clock* (1861) 354 The bleak, timbery city of Copenhagen.

timber-yard. An open yard or place where timber is stacked or stored.

In cricket slang applied to the place in which the wickets are pitched. Hence ***a row in his t.***, in reference to the wickets being struck with force by the ball.

1482–3 *Acc. Exch. K.R.* Bundle 496 No. 25 (P.R.O.) Pro cariagio..de diversis locis..usque dictum castrum, le tymber-yard. **1545** *Act 37 Hen. VIII*, c. 12 §10 Any Mansion-house with a Shop..Timber-yard, Teinter-yard, or Garden belonging to the same. **1768** EARL CARLISLE in Jesse *Selwyn & Contemp.* (1843) II. 272 Why did you not set his timber-yard a-fire? **1853** 'C. BEDE' *Verdant Green* I. xi, The wicket-keeper..informed him 'there was a row in his timber-yard'. **1869** *Routledge's Ev. Boy's Ann.* 638 After a desperate lunge he was startled with a 'row in his timber yard'.

†**'timbester.** *Obs.* [app. for *timberster* or *timbrester*, f. TIMBRE *v.*[1] + -STER: cf. TIMBRER.] A female performer on the timbrel.

?*a* **1366** CHAUCER *Rom. Rose* 769 Ther was many a timbestere [F. *tymberresses*]... The timbres up ful sotilly They caste, and henten [hem] ful ofte Upon a finger faire and softe. **1721** BAILEY, *Timbestores* [later edd. *-ters*], Players on Timbrels. **1843** LYTTON *Last Bar.* I. ii, A young maiden was struggling..to extricate herself from a troop of timbrel girls, or *tymbesteres*.

timbo (ti:m'bəʊ). Also **timbó**. [a. Tupi.] **1.** Any of various South American woody vines cultivated as a source of fish poison and the insecticide rotenone, esp. those of the genus *Lonchocarpus* (family Leguminosæ); also, the poison itself.

1725 H. SLOANE *Voy. to Islands of Madera,..Jamaica* II. 40 Timbo, a sort of With, intoxicates Fishes. **1930** *Jrnl. Econ. Entomol.* XXIII. 868 Rotenone also occurs in 'cube' roots (*Lonchocarpus nicou*) and in timbo, haiari, and other members of the genus Lonchocarpus. **1949** *Thorpe's Dict. Appl. Chem.* (ed. 4) IX. 306/2 South American sources of rotenone..have been developed recently, chiefly the cubé of Peru, and the timbo of Brazil. **1971** *Nat. Geographic* Sept. 435 Like most Brazilian Indians, they usually fish with the sap of a vine called timbo.

2. A South American timber tree of the genus *Enterolobium* (family Leguminosæ) from which a soft red wood is obtained and used for making furniture.

1924 RECORD & MELL *Timbers Trop. Amer.* 205 'Timbó' is well known to the trade in Argentina..in the form of squared logs and because of its softness and ease of working is used as a cheap substitute for cedar. **1969** T. H. EVERETT *Living Trees of World* 196/2 *Enterolobium*. Ten New World species comprise this genus. The best known are the timbó ..(*E. contortisiliquum*) and the guanacaste or elephant's ear (*E. cyclocarpum*).

† **timbre** ('tɪmbə(r)), *sb.*[1] *Obs.* Also 4–5 **tymbre, tymber** (5 **-yr(e, -ere**), 5–6 *Sc.* **tymmer** (8 **timber**). [a. OF. *timbre* (12th c. in Hatz.-Darm.) :—**timbne*:—late pop.L. **timbano*, for L. *tympanum*, a. Gr. τύμπανον timbrel, kettledrum. In OF. *timbre* was used in 13th c., and in ME. by Wyclif, to render L. *tympanum* in Ps. 150. This and the next two words all represent senses of the same French word, but having been taken into Eng. at different dates, and without the intervening links by which the senses were connected in French, are here treated as distinct words.] = TIMBREL *sb.*[1]

[*a* **1300** *French Ps.* in *Lib. Psalm. Versio Gallica* (F. Michel, Oxford 1860) App., Ps. cl. 4 Loés-l'en timbre en concorde (*Vulg.* Laudate eum in tympano et choro).]

13.. *K. Alis.* 191 Orgles, tymbres [*Laud MS.* chymbes], al maner gleo, Was dryuen ageyn that lady freo. **13..** *E.E.*

Allit. P. B. 1414 Tymbres & tabornes, tulket among. ? *a* **1366** [see TIMBESTER]. **1382** WYCLIF *Isa.* v. 12 Harpe, and syngende instrument, and tymbre, and trumpe [1388 Harpe and giterne, and tympan, and pipe]. **1390** GOWER *Conf.* III. 63 Ther was ful many a tymber bete And many a maide carolende. *c* **1440** *Promp. Parv.* 494/1 Tymbyr, lytyl tabowre, *timpanillum.* **1525** LD. BERNERS tr. *Froiss.* II. clxxi. [clxvii.] 499 They sowned tymbres and tabours, accordynge to their vsage. *c* **1560** A. SCOTT *Poems, Of May* 12 In May gois gallandis bring in symmer, And trymly occupyis thair tymmer With 'Hunts vp', every morning plaid.

b. *attrib.* in ***timbre weights***, app. = timbrels or tambourines as formerly used in May-day merry-makings.

A *weight* (Sc. *wecht*) is a vessel like a sieve without holes, formed by stretching a skin across a hoop of a few inches depth. In shape it resembles a tambourine, which may therefore be called, as Jamieson points out, a *timbre* or *timbrel weight*. *Wychtis* appears to be erroneous for *wechtis* or *weights*, and *waits* to embody a false etymology.

c **1560** A. SCOTT *Poems, Of May* 9 And now in May to madynnis fawis [*i.e.* falls] With tymmer wechtis to trip in ringis. **1593** in *14th Rep. Hist. MSS. Comm.* App. III. 41 Dischairgeing [*i.e.* forbidding] also pasche playis, tymmer wychtis, banefyris and ringing of baisingis [basins]. [**1756** *Gentl. Mag.* Feb. 73/2 After having completed this circuit, they again enter the town [Alnwick] sword in hand, and are generally met by women dressed up with ribbons, bells, and garlands of gum-flowers, who welcome them with dancing and singing, and are called timber-waits. [*Note*] Perhaps a corruption of *timbrel-waits*, players on timbrels, *waits* being an old word for those who play on musical Instruments in the streets.]

timbre, tymber ('tɪmbə(r)), *sb.*[2] *Obs.* exc. *Hist.* Also 4–6 **tymbre,** (4 *Sc.* **tymmer**), 5–7 **timber.** [a. F. *timbre* (14th c.), the same word as in prec., which in OF. was transferred to a kind of bell, esp. a hemispherical clock- or table-bell, and thence to a skull-cap of metal, a helmet, and in Heraldry to the crest over the shield in a coat of arms. (Thence also to a crest impressed or stamped upon a legal or official document, a stamp, whence to a postage-stamp: see TIMBRO-.)]

The crest of a helmet; hence, the crest or exterior additions placed over the shield in heraldic arms: see quot. 1894.

1375 BARBOUR *Bruce* XIX. 396 Twa novelreis that day [1327–8] thai saw, That forrouth in scotland had beyn nane. Tymbrys [*v. rr.* Tymbres, Tymmeris] for helmys wes the tane, That thame thoucht than of gret bewte, And alsua wounder for to se. **1478** in W. G. D. Fletcher *Shropsh. Grants of Arms* (1909) 12 A shild of azure and pourpll parted in pale, a cross engrayled gold or bythwen foure rosses silver, and to his tymbre a gauntelet sillver sette in a wrethe gold and azure. **1513** DOUGLAS *Æneis* X. v. 136 (ed. 1555) The creist or schynand tymber, that was set Aboue Eneas helme and top on hicht. **1572** BOSSEWELL *Armorie* II. 88 b, The Tymbre, a palme of an hande dexter, d'Ermyne, sette on a Wreath Or, and Sable, manteled Azure. **1586** [see ACHIEVEMENT 3]. **1894** *Parker's Gloss. Her., Timbre*, this French term..comprises the exterior ornaments of the escutcheon, that is (1) the helmet, (2) the mantelling, (3) the crest. By some, however, it is held to include (4) the escroll, (5) the wreath, (6) the motto, (7) the supporters, as well as (8) the cap of dignity and crown.

timbre (tɛ̃br, 'tæmbə(r)), *sb.*[3] [a. mod.F. *timbre*: see TIMBRE *sb.*[1] and [2]. From the sense 'bell', 'small bell' (see TIMBRE *sb.*[2]) arose that of 'sound of a bell', 'sonorous quality of any instrument or of a voice', and finally that of 'character or quality of sound' (= Ger. *klangfarbe*), in which the word has passed into English use, retaining its French pronunciation.]

The character or quality of a musical or vocal sound (distinct from its pitch and intensity) depending upon the particular voice or instrument producing it, and distinguishing it from sounds proceeding from other sources; caused by the proportion in which the fundamental tone is combined with the harmonics or overtones (= Ger. *klangfarbe*).

In first quot. only a nonce-use of the Fr. word.

1849 C. BRONTË *Shirley* x, Your voice..has another 'timbre' than that hard, deep organ of Miss Mann's. **1853** MARKHAM *Skoda's Auscult.* 53 The voices of individuals, and the sounds of musical instruments, differ, not only in strength, clearness, and pitch, but (and particularly) in that quality also for which there is no common distinctive expression, but which is known as the tone, the character, or timbre of the voice. The timbre of the thoracic, always differs from the timbre of the oral, voice... A strong thoracic voice partakes of the timbre of the speaking-trumpet. **1876** tr. *Blaserna's Sound* viii. 147 There are scarcely any two individuals who have exactly the same timbre of voice. **1890** 'R. BOLDREWOOD' *Col. Reformer* (1891) 184 [His] voice..being mild and small of timbre.

† **timbre,** *v.*[1] *Obs.* [f. TIMBRE *sb.*[1]: cf. F. *timbrer.*] *intr.* To play on the timbrel. Hence † '**timbring** *vbl. sb.*

c **1400** *Song Roland* 54 Blowinge off bugles.., Trymlinge of tabers And tymbring soft. **1530** PALSGR. 758/1, I tymber, I playe on an instrument or a tymber, *je timbre.* The maydens of London were wonte to tymber more than they do nowe.

'**timbre,** *v.*[2] [f. TIMBRE *sb.*[2]] *trans.* To furnish or adorn with a crest; to surmount as a crest. Hence '**timbred** *ppl. a.*, crested; '**timbring** *vbl. sb.*

1513 DOUGLAS *Æneis* XII. ii. 100 Eik his tymbret helm wyth crestis two. **1606** SYLVESTER *Du Bartas* II. iv. III. *Magnificence* 1034 Loe, the Cock..A purple Plume timbers his stately Crest. **1610** GUILLIM *Heraldry* VI. v. 264 In some Countries,..it is not permitted to persons inferior to the degree of a Knight, to Timber their Armes, that is to say, to adorne them with Helme, Mantle, Crest, &c. *Ibid.* 267 Rodolph Duke of Lorraigne..was the first that bare his Armes Tymbered. **1688** R. HOLME *Armoury* IV. vi. (Roxb.) 320/1 Concerning the coate and Tymbreing in the seale thereof. **1894** WOODWARD *Eccles. Heraldry* 255 The others [helmets] were timbred with the Crest of the See of Mainz.

timbre, obs. form of TIMBER.

timbred (tɛ̃brəd, 'tæmbəd), *a.* [f. TIMBRE *sb.*[3] + -ED[2].] Having a timbre of a specified kind.

1942 C. HIMES *Black on Black* (1973) 183 His voice, timbred with a quality of raw intensity, encompassed them both. **1969** 'E. LATHEN' *When in Greece* xvii. 182 Her splendidly timbred voice.

timbrel ('tɪmbrəl), *sb.*[1] Now chiefly *biblical.* Also 6 **tumbrel(le, timbril, -elle, tymbrel(le,** *Sc.* **timberall,** 6–7 **tym-, timbrell,** 7 **timbrill.** [app. a dim. of the earlier TIMBRE *sb.*[1] in same sense: see -EL[2]. So far as appears, it was an Eng. formation; but Sp. has a somewhat parallel dim. form in *tamboril* tabor, tabret, from *tambor* drum (cf. F. *tambourin*). More's spelling appears to be due to confusion with the earlier word TUMBREL *sb.*, which was also sometimes written *timbrel.*]

A musical instrument of percussion; a tambourine or the like that could be held up in the hand.

Chiefly used (to render Heb. *tōph*) in versions of the Bible from Coverdale onward, or in allusions to the biblical use, and in reference to Oriental instruments thought to be the same or similar. Cf. the earlier TIMBRE *sb.*[1]

1500–20 DUNBAR *Poems* lxxvii. 45 Syne come thair four and twentie madinis ȝing,..Playand on timberallis, and syngand rycht sweitlie. **1534** MORE *Comf. agst. Trib.* III. Wks. 1261/2 If the Turke stode euen here with all his whole army about him, &..fel al at once in a shoute, with trumpets, tabrets, & tumbrels al blowen vp at once. **1535** COVERDALE *Exod.* xv. 20 Miriam the prophetisse..toke a tymbrell in hir hande, and all the women folowed out after her with timbrels in a daunse. **1553** EDEN *Treat. Newe Ind.* (Arb.) 14 A great noyse of cimbals, drumslades, timbrelles, shames, pipes, flutes,..and diuerse other musical instrumentes. **1662** J. DAVIES tr. *Olearius' Voy. Ambass.* 277 The Indian Timbrels are two foot long, but broader in the middle than at the Extremities, much after the fashion of our Barrels. [app. = tom-toms.] **1768** BEATTIE *Minstr.* I. xxxv, With merriment, and song, and timbrels clear. *c* **1850** *Arab. Nts.* (Rtldg.) 165 A little hunchbacked fellow came..and began playing on a timbrel, which he accompanied with his voice.

b. ? A figure of a timbrel. (Cf. *bells*, etc.)

a **1548** HALL *Chron., Hen. VIII* 7 Of their hosen..the nether partes were of Scarlet, poudred with tymbrelles of fyne golde.

c. *attrib.* and *Comb.*

1552 HULOET, Tymbrell player, *tympanista,.. tympanistria.* **1757** DYER *Fleece* II. Poems (1761) 102 O'er all the timbrel-sounding squares and streets. **1843** LYTTON *Last Bar.* I. ii, The timbrel-girl sprang into the crowd and vanished.

† **timbrel,** *sb.*[2] *Sc. Obs. rare.* In 5 **tymeral,** 6 **tymbrall, -ell, -ill.** [f. TIMBRE *sb.*[2] + -EL[2].] The crest of a helmet; = TIMBRE *sb.*[2]

c **1450** HOLLAND *Howlat* 613 Four helmes full fair, And in thar tymeralis tryid trewly thai bere The plesand Povne.. provde to repair. **1513** DOUGLAS *Æneis* II. viii. [vii.] 88 The portratour of armes was mysknaw, All war bot Grekis tymbrallis at thai saw.

'**timbrel,** *v.* [f. TIMBREL *sb.*[1]] *intr.* To play upon a timbrel; *trans.* to accompany with a timbrel or similar instrument. Hence '**timbrelled** (-brəld) *ppl. a.*, accompanied by the playing of timbrels; also '**timbreller**, a performer on the timbrel.

1629 MILTON *Hymn Nativity* xxiv, In vain with Timbrel'd Anthems dark The sable-stoléd Sorcerers bear his worshipt Ark. **1785** S. ROGERS *Ode Superstit.* 68 A timbrelled anthem swells the gale. **1833** BOWLES *St. John in Patmos* II. 165 There the timbrelled hymn Rings to Osiris. **18..** L. HUNT *Death & Ruffians* 14 To let their timbrellers and tumblers in. **1854** S. DOBELL *Balder* xxiv. 152 A country song..Fit to be timbrelled to the tambourine.

timbrel(l, obs. form of TUMBREL.

† **timbrer.** *Obs. rare.* In 5 **tymberer, tymbrer.** [f. TIMBRE *v.*[1] + -ER[1].] A timbrel-player.

c **1425** *St. Eliz. of Spalbeck* in *Anglia* VIII. 109/29 þis newe tymbrer settiþ her flesche for an harpe, and hir chekys for a tymber. *c* **1425** *St. Mary of Oignies* II. v. ibid. 166/22 She, þat ȝonge tymberer, hadde strecchyd hir body, and dryed hit as by-twix two trees of þe crosse.

† **timbro-,** combining form repr. Fr. *timbre* (*-poste*) postage-stamp [see TIMBRE *sb.*[2]], used for a short period to form terms relating to stamp-collecting; now superseded by PHILATELY and related words. **tim'brology** [-LOGY] = *timbrophily*; **timbro'mania** [F. *timbromanie*], a craze or mania for collecting stamps; hence **timbro'maniac, tim'bromanist; tim'brophily** [F. *timbrophilie*, Gr. φιλία love, friendship], stamp-collecting; = PHILATELY; hence **timbro'philic** *a.*, **tim'brophilist.**

1864 LEWINS *Her Majesty's Mails* 265 It only remains to refer for a moment to the timbromanie or stamp mania. **1865** *Routledge's Ev. Boy's Ann.* 722 We hold timbromania to be just as sensible a pursuit as a taste for numismatics... The timbromaniac..studies history. **1867** *Philatelist* I. 2 Timbromania was its first designation. Timbrophily and Timbrology next had a short reign as a technical term, till Philately..has proved to be the right word. *Ibid.* 203 Timbrophilists would be a respectably large array. **1880** *Bric-a-Brac* Oct. 2 A proof of the great profits made by timbromanists. **1891** *Cornh. Mag.* July 36 Which he will dispose of to Western timbromaniacs.

timbrous (tɛ̃brəs, 'tæmbrəs), *a.* [f. TIMBRE *sb.*[3] + -OUS.] Sonorous, resonant.

1929 W. FAULKNER *Sartoris* IV. 283 The other one bayed her single timbrous note. **1973** T. WICKER *Facing Lions* 67 The low, timbrous voice was as hesitant and its words as rambling and loosely collected as those of the farmers who preceded him.

Timbuctoo (ˌtɪmbʌk'tuː). The name of a town (now officially spelt *Timbuktu*) on the edge of the Sahara in West Africa, used as the type of the most distant place imaginable.

1863 L. DUFF-GORDON *Lett. from Egypt* (1969) 104 It is growing dreadfully Cockney here [*sc.* Cairo]. I must go to Timbuctoo. **1935** A. CHRISTIE *Death in Clouds* xiv. 148 'She's sorry—' '—but she may be going to Timbuctoo' finished Norman. **1974** V. CANNING *Painted Tent* ix. 182 Trevor Green wished Smiler in Timbuctoo, but since that couldn't be arranged, he just wished him ill. **1981** *Times* 19 Feb. 2/4 Electors promising to follow their 'Shirl' [*sc.* Shirley Williams] to Timbuctoo if she should choose to go there.

Hence ˌ**Timbuc'toot** *a.* (fanciful *nonce-wd.*), of or pertaining to Timbuctoo, foreign, outlandish.

1930 D. H. LAWRENCE *Nettles* 16 And the world it didn't give a hoot If his blood was British or Timbuctoot.

timburine, obs. variant of TAMBOURINE.

time (taɪm), *sb.* Forms: 1–2 **tíma, týma,** 2–8 **tyme,** 4 **tim, teme, teyme,** 4–6 **tym,** 6 **taym,** 2– **time.** [OE. *tíma* = ON. *tími*, wk. masc., time, fit or proper time, (first, etc.) time, good time, prosperity (Da. *time*, Sw. *timme* an hour), :—OTeut. **tî-mon-*, app. f. a root *tî-* to stretch, extend (see TIDE *sb.*) + abstr. suffix *-mon, -man* (see Kluge *Stammbildungslehre* §154).]

I. = A space or extent of time.

1. a. A limited stretch or space of continued existence, as the interval between two successive events or acts, or the period through which an action, condition, or state continues; a finite portion of 'time' (in its infinite sense: see 24), as ***a long time, a short time, some time, for a time.***

in no time, in less than no time (colloq.), immediately, very quickly or soon. ***absolute time***: see quot. 1842.

c **893** K. ÆLFRED *Oros.* IV. v. §5 Ymbe ðone timan þe þiss wæs. *c* **1000** ÆLFRIC *Hom.* I. 60 Hit wæs ȝewunelic on ðam timan. *a* **1225** *Leg. Kath.* 437 He heold on..long time of þe dei. *c* **1330** R. BRUNNE *Chron. Wace* (Rolls) 4190 [Caesar] tok his leue.. To wende fro þem for longe teymes. **1377** LANGL. *P. Pl.* B. XVIII. 63 And tolde whi þat tempest so longe tyme dured. *c* **1386** CHAUCER *Clerk's T.* 386 Nat longe tyme after that this Grisild Was wedded, she a doghter hath ybore. *c* **1440** *Promp. Parv.* 494/1 Tyme, *idem quod* tyyde (*P.* tyme, whyle, *tempus*). **1572** FORREST *Theophilus* 263 in *Anglia* VII, By so longe tyme as his busshoppe dyd lyue. **1610** SHAKS. *Temp.* III. ii. 93 After a little time Ile beate him too. **1662** GERBIER *Princ.* 28 No New Building could stand any time without Proppings. **1662** STILLINGFL. *Orig. Sacr.* III. iv. §5 The highest mountains in the World..may be ascended in three dayes time. **1670** SIR S. CROW in *12th Rep. Hist. MSS. Comm.* App. v. 15 [Hangings] that—for a time—will look better to the eye. **1711** ADDISON *Spect.* No. 37 ¶1 It was some time before the Lady came to me. **1762** KAMES *Elem. Crit.* (1833) 479 A child perceives an interval, and that interval it learns to call time. **1794** MRS. RADCLIFFE *Myst. Udolpho* xxv, Annette..was absent a considerable time. **1832** In no time [see NO *a.* 3 b]. **1843** BORROW *Bible in Spain* xxix. (1901) 417 Follow me..and I will lead you to Finisterre in no time. **1849** MACAULAY *Hist. Eng.* iii. I. 291 The time occupied..was not to exceed fourteen days in one year. **1875** JOWETT *Plato* (ed. 2) I. 195 In less than no time you shall hear. **1842** BRANDE *Dict. Sci.*, etc. s.v., Absolute Time is time considered in itself without reference to that portion of duration to which it belongs, however noted or marked. **1868** DK. ARGYLL in *Mem.* (1906) II. xlvi. 540 Have we any link connecting time-relative with time-absolute?

b. † (*a*) The space of an hour (for OE. *tíd*, TIDE *sb.* 2). *Obs. rare.* (*b*) A space of time, generally understood to mean a year. (A literalism of biblical translation.)

(*a*) *c* **1320** *Cast. Love* 1403 Riht in to helle he eode, Fourti tymen [*v.r.* tymes] þer he wes [*orig.* Quarante ures i demora] Er þat he vp risen ches.

(*b*) **1382** WYCLIF *Dan.* iv. 13 [16] The herte of wijlde beest be ȝouen to it, and seuen tymes be chaungid vpon hym. *Ibid.* xii. 7. **1382** —— *Rev.* xii. 14 She is fed bi tyme, and tymes, and the half of tyme [*v.r.* half a tyme]. **1535** COVERDALE ibid., She is noryszhed for a tyme, two tymes, and halffe a tyme. [So in later versions.] **1827** G. S. FABER *Sacr. Calend. Prophecy* (1844) I. 27 Of such numbers, the three times and a half, the 42 months, and the 1260 days, are mutually equivalent.

2. A particular period indicated or characterized in some way. † ***that time*** (obs.),

at, for the time, for (the) time being (†***during***), during the period under consideration.

c **1000** ÆLFRIC *Hom.* II. 340 Hit is awriten be ðam yfelum timan. *a* **1023** WULFSTAN *Hom.* ii. (Napier) 19 Æfter þisum fæce ȝewurðan sceall swa eȝeslic tima, swa æfre ær næs. *Ibid.* xiii. 81 Wa ðam wifum, þe þonne tymað and on þam earmlican timan heora cild fedað. **1154** *O.E. Chron.* an. 1137 (Laud MS.), On al þis yuele time heold Martin abbot his abbotrice. **1377** LANGL. *P. Pl.* B. x. 72 Sithen þe pestilence tyme. **1474** CAXTON *Chesse* II. iv. (1883) 53 As the Knyghtes shold kepe yͤ peple in tyme of peas. **1486** *Rec. St. Mary at Hill* 2 That the forsaid tenementes & Rent.. shall hoolly remayn to the parisshens.. for the tyme beyng for euer. *Ibid.* 15 The Mayre or Wardeyn of the Citee of london for the tyme beyng. **1542** UDALL *Erasm. Apoph.* 75 b, He had the best right & title for the tyme duryng, to the shadoe of the Asse. **1680** BUTLER *Rem.* (1759) I. 114 To pass his Times of Recreation In choice and noble Conversation. *a* **1774** TUCKER *Lt. Nat.* (1834) II. 645 Though the time for them be over, yet time itself is not exhausted. ? *a* **1864** (*attributed to Pres. Lincoln*), You can fool all the people some of the time, and some of the people all the time, but you cannot fool all the people all the time. **1875** JOWETT *Plato* (ed. 2) IV. 233 All times of mental progress are times of confusion. **1883** 'MARK TWAIN' *Life on Mississippi* xliii. 440 It's human nature—human nature in grief. It don't reason, you see. 'Time being, it don't care a dam. **1913** *Granta* 22 Feb. 225/1 When listening to a singer of such extraordinary natural gifts as Madame Melba, one loses the faculty of criticism for the time being. **1948** V. MASSEY *On being Canadian* xi. 176 It is perhaps natural that there should be a period of pause; that we should not for the time-being be 'on the march'. **1977** J. CROSBY *Company of Friends* xx. 127 The pilot's one of ours—for the time being.

3. a. A period in the existence or history of the world; an age, an era. In later use more indefinite, esp. in *pl.*

c **1000** ÆLFRIC *Hom.* II. 190 þry timan sind on þyssere worulde: Ante legem, Sub lege, Sub gratia... Se tima is 'ær æ' ȝecweden, þe wæs fram Adam buton æ oð Moysen. *c* **1200** *Trin. Coll. Hom.* 3 [Advent] bitocneð þre time. On þe was bi-fore þe olde laȝe, þe oðer was on þe holde laȝe, and þe þridde was on þe newe laȝe. **1297** R. GLOUC. (Rolls) 192 Fram þe biginning of þe world to þe time þat now is Seuene ages þer habbeþ ibe as seue times iwis. þe verste age & time was fram our ferste fader adam To noe. **1483** CAXTON *Chron.* (colophon), Here ende the Croniclis if englonde with the frute of timis. **1560** DAUS tr. *Sleidane's Comm.* 471 Tully calleth an history the witnes of tymes, and light of veritie. **1638** WILKINS *New World* xiv. (1707) 125 Rondoletius, to whose Diligence these later Times are much beholden. **1686** W. HOPKINS tr. *Ratramnus* Dissert. iii. (1688) 59 The Southern Parts of France, where the Albigenses and Waldenses.. have abounded in all Times ever since. **1734** tr. *Rollin's Anc. Hist.* (1827) I. 120 Lay aside the prejudice of birth, nations and times. **1861** M. PATTISON *Ess.* (1889) I. 39 With Northern Germany our connexion was, from the earliest times, most intimate. **1884** W. C. SMITH *Kildrostan* 86 It is a folly, man, A superstition of these modern times.

b. ***time(s past, past time(s; old, olden,*** or ***ancient time(s***, etc.

a **1067** in Kemble *Cod. Dipl.* IV. 202 Swa he on ældum timum ȝelæȝd wæs. **1340** HAMPOLE *Pr. Consc.* 796 He loves men þat in ald tyme has bene. **14..** *Voc.* in Wr.-Wülcker 564/26 *Antiquitus*, yn olde tyme. *c* **1470** HENRY *Wallace* I. 6 It has beyne seyne in thir tymys bywent. **1474** CAXTON *Chesse* III. ii. (1883) 88 In tyme passid the philosophres dyde the same. **1549** *Compl. Scot.* xi. 88 Thai sal intend veir contrar ȝour maister.. as there forbears did in alld tymis. **1605** [see OLDEN *a.* 1]. **1610** HOLLAND *Camden's Brit.* (1637) 259 A towne in ancient time of great fame. *Ibid.*, It was fortified in times past with a castle. **1611** COTGR. s.v. *Argent*, In good old times when men were loath to publish their owne goodnesse. **1784** COWPER *Task* VI. 715 Encomium in old time was poet's work. **1845** M. PATTISON *Ess.* (1889) I. 11 The memory of the great and the saintly of ancient time.

c. ***time(s to come***, (†***time coming***), ***times to be*** (arch.), future time; *esp.* future ages, the future.

c **1340** HAMPOLE *Prose Tr.* i. 4 þay sall joye nowe.. and in tym to come. **1376** in *Eng. Gilds* (1870) 53 Hopyng in tyme comyng to haue ben encresyd. *c* **1440** *Alphabet of Tales* 107 þe paynys þat er ordand.. for syn in tyme to com. **1578** *Reg. Privy Council Scot.* III. 36 That na pensionis of victuall be gevin in tyme cuming furth of the said superplus. **1891** LD. COLERIDGE in *Law Times Rep.* LXV. 581/1 It may become necessary to decide this point in time to come; it is not now.

d. ***the time*** (***the times***): the age now or then present. Cf. ***the day, the hour, the moment.***

[**1588** SHAKS. *L.L.L.* v. ii. 791 Rated them.. As bumbast and as lining to the time.] **1596** —— *Merch. V.* II. ix. 48 How much honor Pickt from the chaffe and ruine of the times, To be new varnisht. ? **1640** *New Serm. of Newest Fashion* (1877) 45 Hee is the onelie man of the time, hee is the onelie able man. *a* **1704** T. BROWN *Two Oxf. Scholars* Wks. 1730 I. 3 Cannot I.. sigh for the Iniquities of the Times? **1850** TENNYSON *In Mem.* cvi. 18 Ring out the want, the care, the sin, The faithless coldness of the times. **1869** FREEMAN *Norm. Conq.* III. xi. 55 An act which ran counter to the religious feelings of the time.

e. (***there's***) ***a good time coming.***

1817 SCOTT *Rob Roy* III. v. 149 'There's a guid time coming.' 'No time like the time present, Mr Campbell.' **1846** C. MACKAY *Voices from Crowd* (1851) 9 There's a good time coming, boys, A good time coming: We may not live to see the day. **1873** TROLLOPE *Lady Anna* (1874) I. iii. 35 She did not believe in the good time coming as did her mother.

4. With possessive or *of*: The period contemporary with the life, occupancy, or activity of some one; (his) age, era, or generation. Often *pl.* = DAY *sb.* 14.

962-3 *Laws Edgar* Suppl. B. *Leges sæculares* c. 2, On minum timan, swa.. on mines fæder. **1154** *O.E. Chron.* an. 1135 (Laud MS.), On þis kinges time wes al unfrið & yfel. *c* **1200** ORMIN 14429 Fra þatt tatt Adam shapenn wass Anan till Nowess time. *a* **1300** *Cursor M.* 10 Non in his tim was like. *c* **1380** WYCLIF *Serm.* Sel. Wks. I. 27 Phariseis.. weren religiouse in Cristis tyme. **1484** CAXTON *Fables of Poge* v, Poge of Florence recyteth how in his tyme one named Hugh prynce of the medycyns sawe a catte whiche had two hedes. **1552** *Bk. Com. Prayer, Ordin.* Pref., From the Apostles tyme there hathe bene these ordres of Ministers. **1625** BACON *Ess., Riches* (Arb.) 235 A Nobleman.. that had the greatest Audits, of any Man in my Time. **1712** STEELE *Spect.* No. 497 ¶2 In the time of Don Sebastian of Portugal. **1814** WORDSW. *White Doe* I. 42 In great Eliza's golden time. **1832** TENNYSON *Dream Fair Women* ii, The spacious times of great Elizabeth. **1865** DICKENS *Mut. Fr.* I. i, In these times of ours.

5. a. A period considered with reference to its prevailing conditions; the general state of affairs at a particular period. Chiefly *pl.*

Often in colloq. phrases, as ***as times go*** (= as things go in these times); ***behind the times*** (= behind the modes or methods of these times); ***to move with the times***: see MOVE *v.* 19 c.

1484 CAXTON *Fables of Æsop* II. viii, Men say comynly that after that the tyme goth, so must folke go. **1602** SHAKS. *Ham.* I. v. 188 The time is out of ioynt. **1712** STEELE *Spect.* No. 298 ¶3 Persons, of tolerable Figure too as Times go. **1757** FRANKLIN *Ess.* Wks. 1840 II. 96 We may make these times better, if we bestir ourselves. **1837** J. H. NEWMAN *Par. Serm.* (ed. 2) III. xii. 178 When times grew cold and unbelieving. **1846** DICKENS *Dombey & Son* (1848) ix. 87 I'm old-fashioned, and behind the time. **1881** FROUDE *Short Stud.* IV. II. i. 163 How times had changed in the last forty years. *a* **1912** *Mod.* We live in perilous times. **1921** E. O'NEILL *Diff'rent* II, in *Emperor Jones* 244 You needn't think we're *all* so behind the times.. here just because you've been to France and all over. **1937** 'G. ORWELL' *Road to Wigan Pier* viii. 163 Here I shall be accused of being behind the times, for I was a child before and during the war and it may be claimed that children nowadays are brought up with more enlightened notions.

b. *pl.* Used as the name of a newspaper. Also used *attrib.* to designate typefaces designed for *The Times.*

1788 (*title*) The Times. **1801** G. ROSE *Diaries* (1860) I. 439, I found here the *Times* of Saturday. **1829** (*title*) South Wales Times. **1854** HAWTHORNE *Eng. Note-Bks.* (1883) I. 477 Every Englishman runs to 'The Times' with his little grievance. *a* **1912** *Mod.* There is an obituary notice in the Oxford Times. **1932** S. MORISON in *Monotype Recorder* XXXI. 12 (*heading*) The Times New Roman. *Ibid.* 13/1 A set of drawings was completed some two years ago, and the first size of what is now '*The Times* New Roman' was cut in 9 point at the Monotype Works, Redhill, in April, 1931. **1963** *Times* 4 June 8/4 *Time*, the weekly news magazine, appears this week with a changed type face—Times Roman instead of the former old style. **1972** *Times* 9 Oct. 1/4 After 40 years *The Times* today appears in a new body type, Times-Europa. This has been designed for *The Times* to suit changing printing methods and largely replaces Times Roman.

c. ***big time***: see BIG *a.* B. 2. See also SMALL TIME, SMALL-TIME *sb.* and *a.* (*phr.*).

6. A period considered with reference to one's personal experience; hence, an experience of a specified nature lasting some time; esp. in (***to have***) ***a*** (***good, bad,*** etc.) ***time*** (***of it***); ***to make a time***, i.e. a demonstration, fuss (*U.S. colloq.*).

to have a good time (= a time of enjoyment) was common in Eng. from *c* 1520 to *c* 1688; it was app. retained in America, whence readopted in Britain in 19th c. (See also GOOD *a.* 10 d.) So ***to have the time of one's life***, i.e. the best one has ever had; ***to have one more time*** (*U.S. colloq.*), to have a very good time; ***a good, etc., time was had by all.*** Also, (without specification, depending on context) a good or bad experience lasting some time; *N. Amer.* a social occasion, a party.

a **1529** SKELTON *Bk. 3 Foles* Wks. 1843 I. 200 For to haue good tyme and to lyue meryly. **1647** TRAPP *Comm. Ep.* 59 They would have a fine time of it. *Ibid.* 199 Those poor.. souls.. have an ill time of it. **1666** PEPYS *Diary* 7 Mar., I went and had as good a time as heart could wish. **1673** *S'too him Bayes* 26 It seems his servants had a good time on't. **1709** MRS. MANLEY *Secret Mem.* (1736) I. 97 Berintha.. thought she should have a melancholy Time of it. **1836** MRS. STOWE in *Life* (1889) 81, I wish I were a man in your place—if I wouldn't have a grand time! **1856** OLMSTED *Slave States* 82, I was having a very good time with her, when her father came in and told her she was 'troubling the gentleman'. **1860** H. J. HAWLEY in *Wisconsin Mag. Hist.* (1936) Mar. 323, I had a time biding them good by. **1878** in G. M. Story et al. *Dict. Newfoundland Eng.* (1982) 568/2 But.. while on a visit to Bett's Cove [he] got on a time and 'let the cat out of the bag'. **1882** I. M. RITTENHOUSE *Maud* (1939) 149 I've had a 'time' with Mr. Blauvelt. **1883** A. PINKERTON *Spy of Rebellion* xxi. 328 While there I met some of the boys, and we had a little 'time'. **1886** P. S. ROBINSON *Valley Teet. Trees* iii, We'll have a high old time together. **1887** [see LIFE *sb.* 8 a]. **1888** *Boston Jrnl.* 31 July 2/5 She doesn't weep at the parting or make any time over it. **1898** E. N. WESTCOTT *David Harum* 14 Mis' Perkins don't hev much of a time herself. **1901** *N. Amer. Rev.* Feb. 228 No other troops made such a time about water as the Americans. **1902** ELIZ. L. BANKS *Newspaper Girl* i, Think of that when you are tempted to have a good time instead of studying hard. **1913** H. KEPHART *Our Southern Highlanders* xiii. 286 'We had one more *time*' means a rousing good time. **1921** R. HICHENS *Spirit of Time* 186 Arab chieftains.. having the time of their lives in the redecorated hotels. **1921** E. O'NEILL *Diff'rent* II, in *Emperor Jones* 251, I told her to cut the rough work and behave—and a nice time was had by all. **1933** GREENLEAF & MANSFIELD *Ballads & Sea Songs Newfoundland* p. xxii, To raise money for the schoolhouse and the church, the Sally's Cove people held a 'toime' on Orangemen's Day, which took the form of an all-day fair and was held in the school-house. **1949** F. MACLEAN *Eastern Approaches* III. ix. 406 After that we mixed a delicious drink in the bath tub, and a good time, as the saying goes, was had by all. **1956** B. HOLIDAY *Lady sings Blues* (1973) ii. 18 So I.. decided I'd get off the train in New York, take the subway to Harlem, have myself a time. **1963** L. DIACK *Labrador Nurse* IV. xxxiii. 155 A 'Time' was an evening Social, with Sale of Work, supper and dance, and all the food served at the 'Time' was supplied and cooked and served by those same women. **1964** *Amer. Folk Music Occasional* I. 15 Ah yes, they used to have some times... That was in the old days. **1967** *Boston Sunday Herald* 7 May VI. 8/8 The state stages such exciting and colorful events as the annual Clam, Broiler, Potato, .. and Blueberry Festivals.., not to mention .. scores of other 'times'. **1969** in Halpert & Story *Christmas Mumming in Newfoundland* 82 A 'time' is any function given in the school, or local Orangemen's Lodge: a card party, a dance, or a dance combined with a 'soup supper'. **1976** 'W. TREVOR' *Children of Dynmouth* i. 13 He hoped.. that Lavinia wasn't having a time with the twins, cooped inside on a damp afternoon.

7. Period of duration; prescribed or allotted term. **a.** Period of existence or action; period of one's life, life-time.

c **1000** ÆLFRIC *Hom.* I. 4 His tima ne bið na langsum; forþan þe Godes grama hine fordeð. *c* **1200** *Vices & Virt.* 39 Behoueþ to charite on alle ðines liues time. *c* **1400** *Brut* cxxxv. 142 þo seisede Kyng Henry al Normandye into his hand, & helde hit al his lifes tyme. **1535** COVERDALE *Ps.* cii[i]. 15 That a man in his tyme is but as is grasse. **1549** *Compl. Scot.* i. 21 Of this sort euere thyng hes ane tyme. **1577** in *Exch. Rolls Scotl.* (1899) XX. 373 In the resyngnatioun, to hymself [and] his wyf, for their tym. **1600** SHAKS. *A.Y.L.* II. vii. 142 One man in his time playes many parts. **1657** THORNLEY tr. *Longus' Daphnis & Chloe* 55, I am older then Saturn, and the whole time of this Universe. **1833** CARLYLE *Ess., Cagliostro* ii, The foul sluggard's comfort: 'It will last my time.'—It will last thy time, thy worthless sham of an existence.

b. *spec.* (*a*) The period of gestation. (*b*) The menstrual period; *transf.* menstruation. (*c*) (One's) term of apprenticeship. (*d*) The duration of a term of imprisonment; usually in phrase ***to do time*** (slang). (*e*) An unexpired period of compulsory service (*U.S.*). (*f*) The prescribed duration of the interval between two rounds in boxing, or of a round or game in athletics, football, etc., or the moment at which this begins or ends; also *ellipt.* as the signal to begin or end a bout, as in ***to call time.*** (*g*) The periodic time of a heavenly body: see PERIODIC *a.* 1. (*h*) The prescribed duration of opening-hours at a public house; the moment at which this ends; also *ellipt.* as the signal for closing-time.

(*a*) *c* **1000** ÆLFRIC *Hom.* I. 30 Hire tima wæs ȝefylled, ðæt heo cennan sceolde. **1577** B. GOOGE *Heresbach's Husb.* III. (1586) 127 A cowe and a quene haue both one time. **1809** MALKIN *Gil Blas* XI. i. (Rtldg.) 392 Beatrice's time was up first: she was safely delivered of a daughter. **1965** P. WRIGHTSON *Thirteen paint Portrait* I. 59 Marion looks rather ghastly. Poor girl, she is nearly at the end of her 'time'.

(*b*) **1564-78** BULLEYN *Dial. agst. Pest.* (1888) 41 Certaine people maie not bleede, as women whiche haue their times aboundauntlie. **1704** *Collect. Voy.* (Churchill) III. 582/1 Women, who shall not be subject to the monthly times. **1889** [see MONTHLY *a.* 1 b].

(*c*) *c* **1645** HOWELL *Lett.* (1650) I. 227 To be both of one trade, because when they are out of their time they may join stocks together. **1718** *Free-thinker* No. 21 ¶1 The.. Indiscretion of Apprentices Marrying Servant-Wenches, before their Time is expired. **1808** BYRON *Eng. Bards* 63 A man must serve his time to every trade, Save censure—critics all are ready made.

(*d*) **1837** DICKENS *O. Twist* (1838) I. xviii. 306 His 'time' was only out an hour before. **1865** [see DO *v.* 11 i]. **1888** 'R. BOLDREWOOD' *Robbery under Arms* xli, People can't be expected to associate with men that have 'done time'. **1904** GRIFFITHS *50 Years Publ. Service* xiii. 185 He did his 'time' without protest.

(*e*) **1769** *Boston Gaz.* (U.S.) 20 Nov. (Thornton *Amer. Gloss.*), To be sold for five Years, The Time of a hearty young Man, who is a good Sailor. **1843** *Missouri Reporter* (U.S.) 28 Jan. (ibid.), I have for sale a very likely yellow woman, about 24 years of age... She has between five and six years to serve. The balance of her time will be sold very low.

(*f*) **1812** *Sporting Mag.* XXXIX. 102 George was the first to call 'time'. **1821** EGAN *Boxiana* (1829) III. 571 When time was called, the men were to be immediately brought up to the scratch. **1829** P. EGAN *Boxiana* 2nd Ser. II. 519 The Gas was *defeated*, nay, *hit* out of time.. to the great loss and chagrin of his friends. **1832** MARRYAT *N. Forster* xlvii, It's a finisher—can't come to time. **1833** *Sporting Mag.* Aug. 354/2 On time being called, Pilch went in again. **1840** DICKENS *Barn. Rudge* xxii, In prize-fighting phraseology, [he] always came up to time with a cheerful countenance. **1857** HUGHES *Tom Brown* i, Three whiffs of which would knock any one else out of time [see KNOCK *v.* 14 d]. **1892** J. HIGSON *Hist. Salford Football Club* 52 A fight began, and the game was brought to an abrupt termination about five minutes before 'Time'. **1926** [see END *sb.* 22 f]. **1976** *Sunday Mail* (Glasgow) 28 Nov. 44/6 Scorers were Martin, in the first half, and Johnston just before time.

(*h*) **1912** G. FRANKAU *One of Us* xi. 104 Lingered a remnant; querulous to these, one spake unceasing: 'Gentlemen! Time, Please!!' **1922** T. S. ELIOT *Waste Land* ii. 23 Hurry up please its time. **1932** L. GOLDING *Magnolia St.* I. iii. 47 Collecting empty glasses and shouting, 'Time, gentlemen, please!' **1953** J. MORTIMER *Like Men Betrayed* v. 87 It's not very comfortable in our pub... They're always shouting 'time' and turning the lights on and off. **1979** 'C. BRAND' *Rose in Darkness* ii. 20 Soon he must turn her out.. five minutes to Time. **1984** *Daily Tel.* 4 Jan. 15/7 A car crashed into the Mermaid public house.. and ended up in the bar just as the landlord.. was calling time.

8. a. The length of time sufficient, necessary, or desired for some purpose; also, time available for employment; leisure or spare time.

c **1220** *Bestiary* 256 Ðus ȝe tileð ðar wiles ȝe time haueð. *c* **1470** HENRY *Wallace* VIII. 502 No teyme we haiff off segyng now to bid. **1585** T. WASHINGTON tr. *Nicholay's Voy.* I. xv. 16 b, There was yet time inough to pleasure them. **1689** *Tryal Bps.* 34 These Gentlemen have had time enough to have prepared Precedents. **1723** *Pres. St. Russia* II. 325 In case the Russian Troops should get time of rallying. **1743** BULKELEY & CUMMINS *Voy. S. Seas* 88 He must have Time to consider of it. **1796** MME. D'ARBLAY *Camilla* II. 23 Pray take your own time. I am not in any haste. **1865** RUSKIN *Sesame* ii. §62, I could multiply witness upon witness..if I had time.

b. The (shortest) period in which a given course of action is completed.

1842 *Congress. Globe* 2 Mar. App. 188/2 A single horse in a sulky would..be able to make..even better time, with the letter mail alone. **1894** *Times* 19 Nov. 7/3 Various new tandem times were made by the winners. **1899** F. V. KIRBY *Sport E.C. Africa* v. 61 One of them [the boys] came in sight, making excellent time towards the nearest tree, with the wounded cow in close pursuit. **1908** *Daily Chron.* 15 Jan. 7/5 The times..did not compare with those established by the amateurs the day before. Still some wonderful times were put up.

c. ***pressed for time***, short of time, in a hurry.

1817 [see PRESS *v.*[1] 6 e]. **1833** T. HOOK *Parson's Dau.* iii. ii, Being pressed greatly for time, in order to get back to London. **1942** W. FAULKNER *Go down, Moses* 274 Not impatient but just pressed for time.

d. ***it takes*** (a person) ***all his time***, it presents great difficulties to, it requires great effort from. *colloq.*

1900 R. GUTHRIE *Kitty Fagan* 208 We've a ticklish job on hand, an I'm boond to say, it's taken us all our time. **1905** in *Eng. Dialect Dict.* VI. 151/2 It'll tak him all his time to mak that theäre public paay it waay. **1941** E. CARR *Klee Wyck* 89 It took Jimmie all his time in the shallows to keep us in the channel.

e. Imp. phr. ***give*** (a person) ***time***, be patient with (another), in expectation of some future change of attitude, competence, etc.

1902 [see SMILE *v.* 8 b]. **1940** W. FAULKNER *Hamlet* I. iii. 60 He'll pick it up though... Just give him time. **1962** J. F. POWERS *Morte d' Urban* vii. 151, I don't say the present population wants it, but give 'em time.

f. With a quantifier: ***to have no*** (***a lot of***, etc.) ***time for***, to have no, etc., respect or admiration for. *colloq.*

1911 E. M. CLOWES *On Wallaby* vi. 166 The merely fictitious value of age they [*sc.* Australian youth] 'have no time for'. **1922** C. WILSON *Rambles in Bookland* 3, I never had much time, to use an effective colloquialism, for the list of 'the best hundred books'. **1938** N. MARSH *Artists in Crime* xi. 156 The only one they seemed to have much time for was the Honourable Basil Pilgrim. **1952** A. GRIMBLE *Pattern of Islands* ix. 177 He never had much time for pen-pushers, as he called them. **1966** J. CLEARY *High Commissioner* xi. 247, I don't think he'd harm her... I think he had a lot of time for my wife. **1979** M. ALLEN *Spence at Blue Bazaar* xix. 121 'Yes, I've got a lot of time for Lester,' the Vicar continued. .. 'He'll always lend a hand at a fête or whatever.'

g. Time available for a certain purpose, *spec.* for an advertising broadcast.

1930 *Daily Express* 6 Sept. 4/6 To the big advertiser the broadcasting stations came with an offer to 'sell time' to pay the cost of broadcasting programmes. **1935** S. LEWIS *It can't happen Here* iv. 42 Father Charles Coughlin, of Detroit.. first thought out the device of freeing himself from any censorship of his political sermons..by 'buying his own time on the air'. **1967** *Boston Sunday Herald* 26 Mar. I. 11/1 CBS-TV explained..that its policy 'prohibits..the sale of time for the expression of views on current issues other than in connection with elections'. **1970** *Daily Tel.* (Colour Suppl.) 18 Sept. 30 The world's 1300 or so professional astronomers who obtain 'time' on the big telescopes all have different programmes in different parts of the sky. **1977** *Zigzag* June 10/3 A friend of mine who was an engineer rang up to see if I had any songs I wanted to cut, because he could get me some time.

h. ***to take*** (***one's***) ***time***: see TAKE *v.* 28 a; ***lost time***: see LOST *ppl. a.* 3.

9. *spec.* **a.** The amount of time worked under a specific contract; hence, in workmen's speech, pay equivalent to the period worked; also an account or certificate showing the days, hours, etc. worked, and wages due: usually called ***back time***.

1795 NELSON in Nicolas *Disp.* (1845) II. 116 This time as Mid is absolutely necessary as a part of the long six years. You had better get out his Time from the Navy Office. **1887** *Courier-Journal* (Louisville, Kentucky) 12 Jan. 6/3 All that remained for the brakemen and switchmen to do was to go to the office..and call for what is known in railroad parlance as their 'time'. **1902** S. E. WHITE *Blazed Trail* viii. 56 So Pat and Henrys were not discharged—were not instructed to 'get their time'. **1908** *Somerset Mag.* Apr. 564 Tim added 'And I'd like my time'. Time, in the cattle idiom, meant back pay up to date. *a* **1912** *Mod.* If you can't move a bit quicker, I'll send you to get your back time. **1926** J. BLACK *You can't Win* xx. 317 He threw down his shovel, walked over to the boss, and demanded his 'time'. I heard the foreman say: 'All right, you're no good anyway. I was going to fire you to-night.' **1935** A. J. CRONIN *Stars look Down* III. xiv. 608 It broke his heart to give these fifty their time, to send them to join the six hundred men from the Neptune already on the dole.

b. ***time and a half*** and varr., one and a half (or one and a quarter, etc.) times the usual rate of pay.

1888 *Times* 29 Sept. 6/6 The men asked to be paid [for overtime] at the rate of time and a half, but the Masters refused a greater rate than time and a quarter. **1921** *Daily Colonist* (Victoria, B.C.) 16 Mar. 3/4 The extra payment was due to the time and a half allowance for overtime. **1931** *Economist* 14 Mar. 552/2 Extra pay for night duty is to be reduced from 'time and a quarter' to 'time and an eighth', and for duty on Sunday, Christmas Day and Good Friday from 'time and a half' to 'time and a third'. **1970** *Daily Tel.* 9 Jan. 9 The claim..is for payment of time-and-a-quarter for the first six hours' overtime, time-and-a-half for the next six, and double time payments thereafter. **1976** *Ibid.* 12 Nov. 2/1 They want holiday pay, at present single time, increased to time and a third. **1978** M. KENYON *Deep Pocket* ii. 28 Tell the men I'm paying time and a half for every forty yards dug by the weekend.

10. *Anc. Prosody.* A unit or group of units in metrical measurement. Also *transf.* in *Mus.*

A ***single***, ***primary***, or ***least time*** is the duration of utterance of a short syllable; = MORA[1] 3; a ***double*** or ***compound time*** is composed of two or more single times.

[*c* **1050** *Byrhtferth's Handboc* in *Anglia* VIII. 314 Ðæt riht meter vers sceal habban feower and twentiȝ timan. *Ibid.*, Dactilus stent on anum langum timan and twam sceortum and spondeus stent of feowrum langum.] **1589** PUTTENHAM *Eng. Poesie* II. xii. (Arb.) 132 A new inuention of feete and times. **1686** *New Method to Learn to Sing* 50 In this Example, you have two Staves of Lines; in the upper are Semibreves, each of which is a Time, and fill up a Bar. **1727–41** CHAMBERS *Cycl.* s.v., Some call each half of the measure in common time, a time. **1749** J. MASON *Numbers in Poet. Comp.* 8 The Measure of single Time is the Space in which we commonly pronounce any of the Liquids or Consonants, preceded by a Vowel, e.g. *an*, *of*, *it*, *in*. **1832** *Encycl. Amer.* XI. 591 The short syllable..is considered as the original unit for the measure of time in the rhythm, and is called a *time*, or *mora*.

11. *Mil.* The rate of marching, calculated on the number of paces taken per minute. ***slow time***: see the adj.; see also DOUBLE TIME, QUICK TIME. ***to mark time***: see MARK *v.* 10 b.

1802–1876 [see QUICK TIME]. **1853** STOCQUELER *Milit. Encycl.* s.v. *Pace*, In quick time, 108 paces, or 270 feet, are taken in a minute; and in slow time, seventy-five paces, or 187 feet. In double time, 150 paces of thirty-six inches, making 450 [feet] in a minute. **1859** *Field Exerc. Infantry* 21 The time having been given on a drum, on the word March, the squad will move off.

12. *Music.* **a.** †The duration of the breve in relation to the semibreve; cf. MOOD *sb.*[2] 3 a, PROLATION 2 (*obs.*); hence, the rhythm or measure of a piece of music, now marked by division of the music into bars, and usually denoted by a fraction expressing the number of aliquot parts of a semibreve in each bar (***time-signature***, see 60 a). ***to beat time***: see BEAT *v.*[1] 32. ***in time***, ***out of time***, in or out of correct rhythm. †***perfect***, ***imperfect time***: see PERFECT *a.* 10, IMPERFECT *a.* 7.

1531 ELYOT *Gov.* I. xxi, The associatinge of man and woman in daunsing, they bothe obseruinge one nombre and tyme in their meuynges. **1609** C. BUTLER *Fem. Mon.* v. (1623) Kiij, Now and then she beginneth in duple time some two or three Semibriefes. **1706** A. BEDFORD *Temple Mus.* iii. 62 'Tis..in the same Time and Tune. **1710** ADDISON *Tatler* No. 153 ¶14 To play out of Time. **1854** HELMORE *Pract. Lect. Church Music* 6 It is sometimes said.. that in Plain Song 'there is no time'. **1884** ROCKSTRO in Grove *Dict. Mus.* IV. 117/2 In modern Music, the word Time is applied to rhythmic combinations of all kinds, mostly indicated by fractions, ($\frac{3}{8}$ etc.) referring to the aliquot parts of a Semibreve—the norm by which the duration of all other notes is and always has been regulated. **1893** STEVENSON *Catriona* i. 4 A..brisk tramp of feet in time and clash of steel.

b. The rate at which a piece is performed; the tempo; hence, the characteristic tempo, rhythm, form, and style of a particular class of compositions (usually in combination, as ***dance-time***, ***march-time***, ***waltz-time***).

[**1446** LYDG. *Two Nightingale Poems* i. 80 But, doun descendyng, she said in hasti tyme: 'My lyfe be kynde endure shall nor longe'. **1602** MIDDLETON *Blurt* III. i. Ej, To keep quick time unto the owl.] **1887** BARING-GOULD *Gaverocks* xiii, Little feet beat the dance time on the..floor. **1903** *Critic* XLIII. 361/1 Rag-time music, which interprets that divine art only for vulgar heels and toes. *Mod.* A movement in slow time.

c. The time-value or duration of a note. (Not in technical use.)

1727–41 CHAMBERS *Cycl.* s.v., Where the time or duration of the notes is equal, the differences of tune alone are capable to entertain us. **1776** BURNEY *Hist. Mus.* (1789) I. vi. 63 The most common application of this term [Rhythm] has been to express the Time or duration of many sounds heard in succession.

II. = Time when: a point of time; a space of time treated without reference to its duration.

The 'point' may be an instant (as the time when a star crosses the meridian), or it may have some duration (as the time for sowing), but the question of its length is not considered, only the question *when* it occurs (i.e. *where it is situated* in the period), and its distinctive qualification.

13. a. A point in the course of time or of a period: = TIDE *sb.* 3; spec. in early ME., the hour of the day; = OE. *tid*: see TIDE *sb.* 4. In mod.Eng. ***what is the time?*** i.e. the hour and minute as shown by the clock. ***what time***, ***at what time***, = when, (at) the time that: see WHAT.

c **1200** ORMIN 12745 Þatt time..Wass rihht swa summ itt off þatt daȝȝ þe tende time wære. *a* **1225** *St. Marher.* 8 As þah hit were þe seoueðe time of þe dei. *c* **1391** CHAUCER *Astrol.* II. §3 To knowe..euery tyme of the nyht by the sterres fixe. **1823** J. BADCOCK *Dom. Amusem.* 162 By the light you shall catch a few words in the book, or the time on the watch. **1834** *Nat. Philos.* III. *Astron.* i. 35/1 (Usef. Knowl. Soc.) The difference between the actual time of the sun's being on the meridian and the beginning of the mean solar day. **1908** R. BAGOT *A. Cuthbert* viii, Find out what time the marchesa intends to breakfast.

b. A point or fixed part of the year, a season, as in ***time of year***; in comb. in ***spring-time***, ***summer-time***, ***autumn-time***, ***winter-time***; also ***term-time***, ***vacation-time***, ***holiday-time***, etc.; also, of a day, as ***time of day***, ***time of night***, ***day-time***, ***night-time***, ***morning-time***, ***evening-time***; also ***dinner-time***, ***bed-time***, etc.; also, a point in the moon's age.

c **1000** ÆLFRIC *Num* xiii. 21 Hit wæs ða se tima ðæt winberian ripodon. *c* **1050** *Byrhtferth's Handboc* in *Anglia* VIII. 312 Feower timan beoþ... Uer ys lengten tima,..se oðer tima hatte æstas..Se þridda tima ys autumnus on lyden ȝecweden. *c* **1175** *Lamb. Hom.* 119 Vre drihtnes halie passiun..is nu icumen in,..þe ure drihten þolede for us on þisse timan. **1398** TREVISA *Barth. De P.R.* IX. iii. (Bodl. MS.), Þe ȝere of þe sonne..conteyneþ foure tymes, winter, springingtyme, somer, and harueste. *c* **1400** tr. *Secreta Secret., Gov. Lordsh.* 74 Heruest bygynnes..and lastys lxxxviij dayes... In þis tyme ys also þe day and þe nyght euyne. *a* **1529** SKELTON *On Tyme* 23 The rotys tak theyr sap in tyme of vere. **1566** BLUNDEVIL *Horsemanship* IV. xxxii. (1580) 16 The horse that hath this disease, is blind at certaine times of the Moone. **1825** T. HOOK *Sayings* Ser. II. *Passion & Princ.* ix. III. 153 Fleeting showers of rain, unseasonable at the time of year.

†**c.** A season or part of the year considered with reference to the weather experienced; weather (of some kind). *Obs. rare.* (Cf. F. *temps* in similar sense.)

c **1400** tr. *Secreta Secret., Gov. Lordsh.* 93 Þe right of hym þat reygnyth ys more profitable to subgitz þan plente of good tyme. **1422** *Ibid.*, *Priv. Priv.* 220 The colerike by kynde.. sholde haue a stomake good y-nowe, namely in colde tyme.

d. *Stock Exch.* The account.

1901 W. G. CORDINGLEY *Dict. Stock Exch. Terms* 89 Time Bargains refer to those speculative transactions which are made for settlement on the next Account. They are made 'for time', and are 'Bought for the Account' or 'Sold for the Account'. **1928** *Daily Mail* 13 Aug. 18/2 Dealing for 'new time',..the new Stock Exchange account.

14. A point in duration marking or marked by some event or condition; a point of time at which something happens, an occasion. †***on a time***, on one occasion, once. ***at no time***, on no occasion.

c **893** K. ÆLFRED *Oros.* IV. v. §5 Ymbe ðone timan þe þiss wæs. *c* **1000** ÆLFRIC *Hom.* I. 78 Herodes..ȝeornlice hi befran to hwilces timan se steorra him ærst æteowode. *a* **1050** *O.E. Chron.* an. 1009 (Laud MS.) On þisum ilcan timan oððe litle ær þet [etc.]. *c* **1205** LAY. 2582 Seoððen him a time com mid teonen he wes i-funden. *c* **1275** *Ibid.*, Suþþe him com a time þat he to wode wende. *a* **1225** *Leg. Kath.* 2 Constantin & Maxence weren, on ane time..hehest in Rome. **13..** *Gaw. & Gr. Knt.* 2243 At þis tyme twelmonyth þou toke þat þe falled. *c* **1386** CHAUCER *Frankl. T.* 830 Aurelius..Curseth the tyme þat euere he was born. **1470–85** MALORY *Arthur* II. i. 75 Soo it befelle on a tyme whanne kyng Arthur was at London. **1538** STARKEY *Let.* in *England* p. lxxiii, Long and much at sundry tymis. **1590** SIR J. SMYTH *Disc. Weapons* 36 From that time forward he would hold the Bowe to be the onelie weapon of the world. **1766** GOLDSM. *Vic. W.* xii, By this time the unfortunate Moses was undeceived. **1837** J. H. NEWMAN *Par. Serm.* (ed. 3) I. vii. 99 Surely man is at all times the same being. **1845** M. PATTISON *Ess.* (1889) I. 27 This..trick escaped detection at the time. **1873** BLACK *Pr. Thule* xxv, It will be nearly two by the time you get down.

15. a. The appointed, due, or proper time.

c **897** K. ÆLFRED *Gregory's Past. C.* lxiii. 459 Nu us is tima ðæt we onwæcnen of slæpe. *c* **1000** ÆLFRIC *Colloq.* in Wr.-Wülcker 102/1 Hwænne wylle ȝe syngan?.. þonne hyt tima byþ [*Quando tempus erit*]. **1154** *O.E. Chron.* an. 1011, Mann nolde him to timan [*MS. C.* atiman] gafol bedan. *c* **1175** *Lamb. Hom.* 103 Þeo deð þet mon et er timan and drinceð. **13..** *Cursor M.* 11814 (Cott.) Nu neghes tim to tak his lai. *c* **1400** *26 Pol. Poems* xxv. 539 Tyme ys that men now for me pray, For *Parce michi, domine!* *c* **1412** HOCCLEVE *De Reg. Princ.* 1274 Sires, it is tyme þat we hennes hye. *c* **1489** CAXTON *Blanchardyn* xxiii. 74 It was tyme to go to bed. *a* **1586** SIDNEY *Ps.* XII. i, Lord, helpe, it is hyghe tyme for me to call. **1741–2** GRAY *Agrippina* 158 'Tis time to go, the sun is high advanc'd. **1809** MALKIN *Gil Blas* VIII. i, My business consisted in..dunning the farmers, and keeping them to time in their payments. **1872** *Routledge's Ev. Boy's Ann.* 349/1 See that you are up to time.

b. Qualified by poss. pron., as ***his***, ***her***, ***its***; often ellipt. for ***time of death***, ***of childbirth***, etc.; ***before*** (***his***, etc.) ***time***, prematurely.

c **1000** *Ags. Gosp.* Matt. xxvi. 18 Min tima is ȝe-hende. —— John v. 4 Drihtenes engel com to his timan [*Hatton* to hys tyme] on þone mere & þæt wæter wæs astyred. **1388** WYCLIF *Prov.* xxv. 11 A goldun pomel in beddis of siluer is he, that spekith a word in his [= its] time. *c* **1440** *Aiphab. Tales* 11 Sho wex grete & drew nere hur tyme. **1560** DAUS tr. *Sleidane's Comm.* 451 b, Yᵉ Quene..was with childe, and nere her time. **1689** HICKERINGILL *Ceremony-monger* 126 A young Lady..Excommunicated for breaking her Leg or coming before her time. **1700** DRYDEN *Sigism. & Guiscard.* 26 In the prime Of youth, her lord expired before his time. **1799** WORDSW. *Lucy Gray* viii, The storm came on before its time. **1841** THACKERAY *Gt. Hoggarty Diamond* xii, in *Miscellanies* (1857) IV. 428 My poor wife, then very near her time, insisted upon accompanying me. **1853** C. BRONTE *Villette* 180 'Ten minutes behind his time', said she. **1890** *Field* 31 May 799/3 The Banksia roses..are bent on coming out before their time. **1931** H. S. WALPOLE *Judith Paris* III. 582 Judith was very near her time, and, in consideration.. that this was her first child, it had been wiser of her perhaps not to have come. **1980** R. BUTLER *Blood-Red Sun at Noon* (1981) I. i. 19 She..became pregnant... What she called 'her time' approached.

16. A or the favourable, convenient, or fitting point of time for doing something; the right moment or occasion; opportunity. (Often with ***his***, ***her***, etc.)

c **897** K. ÆLFRED *Gregory's Past. C.* xxxiii. 220 Se wisa hilt his spræce & bitt timan. **1297** R. GLOUC. (Rolls) 7633 Huld hem euere in Scotland, & poer to hem nome, To worri vpe king willam, wanne god time come. **1382** WYCLIF *Eccles.* iii.

4 Time of weping, and time of laȝhing [**1388** Tyme to wepe, and tyme to leiȝe]. *c* **1386** Chaucer *Melib.* ¶.14 Whan she saugh hir tyme, she seyde hym in this wise: 'Allas! my lord'. *a* **1533** Ld. Berners *Huon* lxvii. 230 When he sawe his tyme, he cryed his worde & token. **1590** Nashe *Pasquil's Apol.* i. Wks. (Grosart) I. 233 There is a time for speech, and a time for silence. *c* **1610** Bodley in *Reliq.* (1703) 108 A Clock and a Bell will be needful for the Library..: but every thing must have his time. **1709** Steele *Tatler* No. 36 ¶4 When Stocks are lowest, it is the Time to buy. *a* **1722** Fountainhall *Decis.* (1759) I. 9 They must wait their tour, since the devil bides his time. *c* **1810** W. Hickey *Mem.* (1960) xix. 309 Now's your time, Hickey. That beast Mordaunt was called away..so that you will have a couple of days' enjoyment together. **1849** Macaulay *Hist. Eng.* iv. I. 512 An adversary of no common prowess was watching his time. *Mod.* Now's your time!

17. a. Any one of the occasions on which something is done or happens; each occasion of a recurring action. Often qualified by a numeral. (= OE. *sīð*: see sithe *sb.*[1] 4–5.) With a price: (so much) ***a time***, on each occasion, (*colloq.*) for each item.

For †***one time***, †***two times*** have been substituted *once*, *twice*. ***at a time***, at one time, at once, simultaneously.

c **1300** *St. Julian* 108 (Ashm. MS.) Let me go at þis one tyme. I ne schal neuereft derie þe. *c* **1380** Wyclif *Sel. Wks.* III. 350 How þat men shulde snybbe þer breþeren bi þre tymes. *c* **1400** *Destr. Troy* 8272 The next tym þou noyes me, þou neghis to þe fer. **1454** *Rolls of Parlt.* V. 241/1 At too tymes hath be made requestes to the seid Lieutenaunt. **1526** *Pilgr. Perf.* (W. de W. 1531) 300 b, How he wolde deny the thre tymes that nyght. **1560** Daus tr. *Sleidane's Comm.* 441 b, The third way..hath bene diuers times assaied. **1611** Bible *John* xxi. 16 He saith to him againe the second time, Simon Sonne of Ionas, louest thou me? **1660** R. Ellsworth in *Extr. S. P. rel. Friends* ii. (1911) 122 Heere they..haue their Meeteings at all Seasons..sometymes about 1000 or 1200 att a tyme. **1712** Steele *Spect.* No. 422 ¶1 An utter Aversion to speaking to more than one Man at a time. **1718** R. Grosvenor in C. T. Gatty *Mary Davies* (1921) II. 205 One that is grown pretty rich by his attendance upon Patients in Garrets at Half-a-Crown a time. **1829** Landor *Imag. Conv.*, *Villèle & Corbière* I. 123 He did it fifty times, at the very least. **1876** Trevelyan *Macaulay* II. ix. 125 The publishers..are still pouring forth reprints by many thousands at a time. **1976** *West Lancs. Evening Gaz.* 13 Dec. 7/5 Buying..cashmere scarves at £15 a time.

b. *Agric.* (See quots.) *dial.*

1813 R. Kerr *Agric. Surv. Berw.* 198 The completest harrowing is called a double double time; in which the harrow goes four times successively over the same range. **1857** *N. & Q.* 2nd Ser. IV. 80/1 'A time'..in some parts of Scotland is the act of once furrowing between two ploughings. **1894** *Northumbld. Gloss.*, *Time*, the journey once across a field in agriculture. *Time-aboot*, a double journey in field work, extending from heedrig to heedrig and back again.

c. ***every time***: see every *a.* 1 e.

18. ***many a time***, †***many time***, ***many times***, also ***times and often***, ***times without number***, ***many a time and oft*** (***often***), ***many's the time***, on many occasions, in many instances; often, frequently. Also elliptically ***times*** (also sometimes, at times).

c **1250** *Kent. Serm.* in *O.E. Misc.* 30 Ure lord god almichti ..habbeþ mani-time maked of watere wyn gostliche. **1375** Barbour *Bruce* i. 336 That may mony tyme awaill. *c* **1400** *Rom. Rose* 6974, I am gladly executour And many tymes a procuratour. **1535** Coverdale *Ps.* lxxvii. 38 Many a tyme turned he his wrath awaye. **1560** Ingelend *Disob. Child* D ij b, Many a tyme and oft, I am fayne To playe the Priest, Clarke, and all. **1590** Sir J. Smyth *Disc. Weapons* Ded. 6 Which I haue heard manie, and manie times publikelie reported by manie valiant Gentlemen. **1622** R. Hawkins *Voy. S. Sea* (Hakl. Soc.) 115 Which..many time is cause of dissention. **1701** De Foe *True-born Eng.* ii. 312 Englishmen have done it many a time. **1760–72** H. Brooke *Fool of Qual.* (1809) IV. 51 Many a time and oft..you carried me in your arms. **1808** Eleanor Sleath *Bristol Heiress* III. 94 The fine handsome young officer, who has been here times and often. **18..** G. Meredith *Juggling Jerry* ii, We've travelled times to this old common. **1892** *Law Times* XCII. 147/1 Times without number the courts in bankruptcy have been called upon to decide the question. **1899** Trine *In Tune with Infinite* (1903) 186 Those who take great pride in speaking of their own practicality are many times the least practical. **1920** E. O'Neill *Beyond Horizon* ii. i. 67 Many's the time I've said to her [etc.]. **1936** Wodehouse *Laughing Gas* xxiii. 247 You have many a time and oft referred to her as a piece of cheese. **1938** M. K. Rawlings *Yearling* xvii. 213 Seems to me, times, hit ain't done nothin' to you but sharpen your tongue. **1956** A. Wilson *Anglo-Saxon Attitudes* i. iii. 48 Many's the time Sir Beerbohm Tree's stood outside the theatre. **1968** C. Aird *Henrietta Who?* xiv. 130 Times, it's a bit quiet at Holly Tree. **1980** P. G. Winslow *Counsellor Heart* iii. 52 There's one that likes a joke. Times I've had her in fits. **1982** S. Johnson *Of Wilful Intent* i. 13 'And you say this has all been reported before?' the sergeant asked him. 'Times,' came the despondent reply.

19. a. Preceded by a cardinal numeral and followed by a number or expression of quantity: used to express the multiplication of the number, etc. Also *attrib.* with *table* or *ellipt.*, designating the multiplication table of the preceding cardinal number. Cf. *times table*, sense 60 below.

c **1380** Wyclif *Sel. Wks.* II. 309 As foure tymes sixe maken þis noumbre. *c* **1425** *Crafte Nombrynge* 2 Ten tymes twene is twenty. *Ibid.* 4 If it stonde in the secunde place of þe rewle, he betokens ten tymes hym selfe, as þis figure 2 here. *c* **1440** *Jacob's Well* 45 Thre tymes ten is thretty. **1726** Swift *Gulliver* ii. iii, An animal of ten times my strength. **1798** Coleridge *Anc. Mar.* iii. xvi, Four times fifty living men. **1868** G. Duff *Pol. Surv.* 48 His territories in Asia.. are more than twenty-one times the size of Scotland. **1906** Kipling *Puck of Pook's Hill* 38, I don't know my Nine Times—not to say it dodging. **1973** J. Wainwright *Touch of Malice* 124 A long-suffering father explaining the two-times-table to his dull-witted son. **1976** D. Storey *Saville* xi. 133, I want you to recite the two times, the three times, right through to your twelve times. **1982** *Sunday Tel.* 2 May 11/1 (*heading*) Know your 6-times table.

b. Also followed by an adj. or adv. in the comparative degree, or in the positive by *as* (formerly *so*) with an adj. or adv., expressing comparison.

1551 Crowley *Pleas. & Pain* 229 This might you reade, and ten tymes more In the Bible. *c* **1567** Stow in *Surv.* (1908) I. p. li, Fabyan..was a very nowghty cronycle, and Copin..was x. tymes worse. **1583** Stubbes *Anat. Abus.* ii. (1882) 45 They shall pay tenne times so much as it is worth. **1644** Nye *Gunnery* i. 5 Which composition I will call 6--1--1, meaning six times so much Peter [nitre], as one time Sulpher, and one time Cole. **1712** Addison *Spect.* No. 415 ¶8 A Gothick Cathedral tho' it be five times larger than the other. **1876** Gladstone *Glean.* (1879) II. 289 Men who had ten or twenty times less to remember. *Mod.* We have five times as many as we can use.

†**20.** *Gram.* = tense *sb.* 2. *Obs.*

1530 Palsgr. Introd. 32 In these syxe modes be dyvers tymes. *Ibid.* 84 Tenses or tymes they have in every of these modes. *c* **1620** A. Hume *Brit. Tongue* (1865) 31 Tyme is an affection of the verb noating the differences of tyme, and is either present, past, or to cum.

21. *Fencing.* See quots., and cf. *time-attack*, *time-thrust* in 60.

1727–41 Chambers *Cycl.* s.v., Time in fencing.—There are three kinds of time; that of the sword, that of the foot, and that of the whole body. All the times that are perceived out of their measure, are only to be considered as appeals, or feints, to deceive and amuse the enemy. **1753** *Ibid.*, *Supp.* s.v. *Binding*, Binding is a method of pursuit more safe and certain..than taking of time. **1809** Roland *Fencing* vii. §1 To take the time, is making your thrust by a judicious discernment on the motion of your adversary.

22. *Manège.* (= F. *temps.*) Applied to each completed motion or action.

1753 Chambers *Cycl. Supp.* s.v., Time, in the manege, is sometimes taken for the motion of a horse, that observes measure and justness in performing a manege. In the manege of a step and a leap, the horse makes by turns a corvet between two caprioles; and in that case the corvet is one Time that prepares the horse for the caprioles. *Ibid.*, A good horseman disposes his horse for the effects of the heel, by beginning with one Time of the legs, and never runs precipitately upon his Times.

23. *pl.* Originally (in sense 15), The fixed hours of the day at which an omnibus started from its various stations; hence, the established business enterprise of running an omnibus on a given route at such times, and the 'good-will' thus created by the owners of public service vehicles over particular routes, as a recognized vendible asset.

1863 E. Yates *Business of Pleasure* (1865) I. 40 They [the London General Omnibus Company] possessed themselves of the 'times' of all the important routes in London and the suburbs. These 'times' are, in fact, the good will of the roads, and were considered so valuable, that in some cases as much as from £200 to £250 were given for the 'times' of one omnibus. **1906** *Westm. Gaz.* 15 May 2/3 Emphasis [is] laid in one of the various motor-'bus prospectuses, just now.. upon the value of the 'times' owned by each member of the associated companies. *Ibid.*, The 'times', which are a special privilege, religiously guarded by the omnibus fraternity,.. were also made over as a part of the bargain.

III. In generalized sense.

24. Indefinite continuous duration regarded as that in which the sequence of events takes place.

a. Attempts to define or explain.

1398 Trevisa *Barth. De P.R.* ix. ii. (Bodl. MS.), Tyme is mesure of chaungeable þinges, as Aristotel seith. **1597** Hooker *Eccl. Pol.* v. lxix. §2 Now as Nature bringeth forth Time with Motion, so wee by Motion haue learned how to diuide Time, and by the smaller parts of Time, both to measure the greater, and to know how long all things else indure. *Ibid.*, Some haue defined time to be the measure of the motion of heauen. **1690** Locke *Hum. Und.* ii. xiv. §17 This Consideration of Duration, as set out by certain Periods, and marked by certain Measures or Epochs, is that, I think, which most properly we call Time. **1854** Calderwood *Philos. Infinite* v. 88 Add event to event, still Time is recognised as stretching forth, and still there is room for more. **1862** Spencer *First Princ.* ii. iii. §47 (1875) 163 The abstract of all sequence is Time.

b. Examples of this use of the word. ***time will tell*** (and varr.); ***borrowed time***: see borrowed *ppl. a.* 1; ***the*** (***very***) ***nick of time***: see nick *sb.*[1] 9.

1480 *Robt. Devyll* 121 in Hazl. *E.P.P.* I. 224 The tyme drewe so, that nyne monethes was past. **1539** R. Taverner tr. *Erasm. Prov.* f. 37 *Tempus omnia reuelat.* Tyme discloseth all thynges. *Ibid.* f. 38 There is no dyspleasure so great, no hatred so impotent, no sorowe so immoderate, but tyme asswageth it. **1616** T. Draxe *Bibliotheca Scholastica* 205/2 Time reuealeth all things. **1638** Junius *Paint. Ancients* 29 In processe of time. **1651** Hobbes *Leviath.* ii. xxx. 176 Time, and Industry, produce every day new Knowledge. **1743** Blair *Grave* 479 Think we, or think we not, Time hurries on With a resistless, unremitting Stream. **1748** B. Franklin *Adv. Yng. Tradesman* Wks. 1799 II. 34 Remember that time is money. **1771** C. Stuart *Let.* 15 Apr. in *Publ. Miss. Hist. Soc.* (1925) V. 50 Time only will shew how far those Informations have been well founded. **1794** Mrs. Radcliffe *Myst. Udolpho* xxx, The few gray locks which time had spared on his temples. **1821** Byron *Cain* iii. i, The mind then hath capacity of time, And measures it by that which it beholds, Pleasing or painful. **1863** C. Reade *Hard Cash* I. v. 164/2 She shall speak as distinctly to music as you do in conversation. *Sampson*... Time will show, madam. **1908** *Programme of Modernism* 169 We have cast the seed in the furrow, Time will do the rest. **1913** E. H. Porter *Pollyanna* xxiii. 234 The doctor had looked very grave..and had said that time alone could tell. **1957** A. Huxley *Lett.* (1969) 839 It may turn out, of course, that the experts are right and that their play is better... Time will show. **1971** D. Eden *Afternoon Walk* vii. 94 Time will tell, Mrs. Simpson. **1980** J. Gardner *Garden of Weapons* iii. xi. 332 'Big Herbie gone over, has he?' Fincher said that time would tell. **1983** *Sunday Tel.* 20 Feb. 16/4 Whether this general mania for physical purification extends also to schoolgirls we are not told. Time alone will tell.

c. ***it's*** (***only***, etc.) ***a question*** (or ***matter***) ***of time***: said of an event that is thought certain to happen sooner or later.

1867 E. A. Freeman *Hist. Norman Conquest of England* I. iv. 251 The definitive alliance of Rouen and Paris fixed the extinction..of the royalty of Laôn. It was a question of time. **1928** E. O'Neill *Strange Interlude* iii. 94 I'm making good, all right..since I got married— and it's only a question of time. **1960** S. Barstow *Kind of Loving* ii. viii. 273 It's just a question of time now, apparently. Making all the arrangements and all that. **1960** D. Storey *This Sporting Life* ii. v. 236 Mrs. Hammond was in a coma. It seemed only a matter of time before she died. **1963** 'J. le Carré' *Spy who came in from Cold* viii. 81 It was only a matter of time before it packed up. **1982** *N.Y. Times* 30 Sept. c 18/4 It's only a matter of time before something terrible happens.

d. ***to kill time***: see kill *v.* 5; ***time hangs heav***(***il***)***y***: see hang *v.* 15 b; ***to redeem the time***: see redeem *v.* 8.

25. Personified as an aged man, bald, but having a forelock, and carrying a scythe and an hour-glass. Also called ***Father Time***. ***to take Time by the forelock*** (†***by the top***), to seize one's opportunity, to act promptly: see also forelock *sb.*[2] 2.

1509 Hawes *Past. Pleas.* xliv. (1555) C iv, Sodainly came Time in breuiacion Whose similitude, I shall anone expresse Aged he was, with a bearde doubtles Of swalowes feaders. **1590** Shaks. *Com. Err.* ii. ii. 71 The plaine bald pate of Father time himselfe. **1606** —— *Tr. & Cr.* iii. iii. 145 Time hath, my Lord, a wallet at his backe, Wherein he puts almes for obliuion. **1594** [see forelock *sb.*[2] 2]. [**1711** Addison *Spect.* No. 63 ¶4 Equipped (like the figure of Time) with an Hour-glass in one Hand, and a Scythe in the other.] **1820** W. Irving *Sketch Bk.* II. 24 Time is ever silently turning over his pages. **18..** Marsden *What is Time?* 32, I ask'd old Father Time himself at last; But in a moment he flew swiftly past!

26. In restricted sense, Duration conceived as beginning and ending with the present life or material universe; finite duration as distinct from eternity.

1388 Wyclif *Rev.* x. 6 And the aungel..lifte vp his hond ..and swoor bi hym that lyueth in to worldis of worldis.. that time schal no more be [**1526** Tindale, that there shulde be no lenger tyme; **1557** *Geneva*, that tyme should be no more; **1611**, that there should be time no longer]. **1573** Tusser *Husb.* (1878) 65 For time is it selfe but a time for a time, Forgotten ful soone, as the tune of a chime. **1635** Swan *Spec. M.* i. §3 (1643) 15 All time compared with eternitie is but short time, yea indeed as no time. **1650** Crashaw *Death Herrys* 36 Weak time shall be pour'd out Into eternity. **1745** *Scotch Transl. & Paraphr.* xxxv. ix, He lov'd us from the first of Time, And loves us to the last. *a* **1758** Ramsay *Some of Contents of Evergreen* xi, A monument..Quhilk sall endure quhyle tymis telled out be days. **1803** Heber *Palestine*, His voice amid the thunder's roar, His dreadful voice, that time should be no more. **1827** Pollok *Course T.* x, Time gone, the righteous saved, the wicked damned, And God's eternal government approved. **1836** H. Rogers *J. Howe* i. (1863) 8 Time, with him, derived all its importance from a reference to eternity. *Mod.* Entirely occupied with things of time and sense.

27. a. A system of measuring or reckoning the passage of time. ***standard time***, a standard system of reckoning time adopted throughout a country or region, now based on the time zone in which it is situated; cf. *zone time* s.v. zone *sb.* 9 a. With preceding place-name or possessive pronoun, the time as reckoned at the place referred to (normally differing from one's own). Cf. *Greenwich time* s.v. Greenwich, summer time 2, railway time.

1706 Phillips (ed. Kersey) s.v., Relative, Apparent, or Vulgar Time, is the sensible and outward Measure of any Duration or Continuance estimated by Motion; and this is commonly us'd instead of true Time. **1727–41** Chambers *Cycl.* s.v., Astronomical time, is that taken purely from the motion of the heavenly bodies, without any other regard. Cvil time, is the former time accommodated to civil uses. **1764** Maskelyne in *Phil. Trans.* LIV. 344 There are three different kinds of time used by astronomers, sidereal time, apparent solar time, and mean solar time. **1834** *Nat. Philos.* III. *Math. Geog.* v. 16/1 (Useful Knowl. Soc.) A common sun-dial shows the hour of apparent time. Time-keepers or chronometers, common watches and clocks, are made to show the hour of mean time. **1840** *Minutes Board of G.W.R.* in *Railway Gaz.* (1935) 30 Aug. (G.W.R. Suppl.) 7/2 Outside clock to be provided for each station so as to be seen by passing trains, in order to ensure punctuality. London time to be adopted at all stations. **1841** *G.W.R. Timetable* in *Ibid.*, London time is about 4 min. earlier than Reading time. **1847** H. Booth *Uniformity of Time* 4 The managers [of the Post Office]..are quite aware of the advantages of one uniform system of time..; accordingly all their movements are regulated by 'London Time'. **1847** *Minutes Railway Clearing House Committee* 22 Sept. in *Vistas in Astron.* (1976) XX. 221 That it be recommended to each company to adopt Greenwich Time as soon as the Post Office permits them to do so. **1847**, etc. [see railway time]. **1861** [see Greenwich]. **1863** Dickens in *All Year Round* 2 May 232/1 They don't keep 'London time' on a French railway. **1879** S. Fleming *Papers on Time-Reckoning* 13 On a journey from Paris to Vienna..the standard time employed by the railways changes frequently. **1883** *N.Y. Times* 19 Nov. 5/2 Standard time clocks were set to correspond to the new signals. **1893** [see GREENWICH]. **1917** *Whitaker's Almanack* 90/1 Since the year 1883 the system of Standard Time by Zones has been gradually accepted, and now the majority of the countries of the world use as Standard Time the time of some meridian which differs from that of Greenwich by a multiple of 15°. **1924** J. C. W. REITH in *Radio Times* 4 Jan. 42/3 We broadcast standard time. **1935** *Cook's Continental Time Table* Mar. 102 Moscow time is two hours later than that of Greenwich. **1941** *Ann. Reg. 1940* 126 A state of war existed..as from 9 a.m. (Eastern standard time). **1948** A. N. KEITH *Three came Home* xviii. 295 He telephones me from Australia... We speak at twelve midnight, my time. **1958** 'N. SHUTE' *Rainbow & Rose* vi. 229, I would hand over to him at two in the morning, Honolulu time. **1974** *Encycl. Brit. Macropædia* XVIII. 415/1 All clocks in the United States were kept one hour ahead of standard time for the interval February 9, 1942–September 30, 1945... Since then, the time in a large part of Europe has been kept one hour ahead of standard zone time without any change during the summer. **1979** P. HILL *Washermen* xxxiv. 81 [He] arrives at Kai Tak Airport, Hong Kong, 3 p.m. tomorrow afternoon our time.

b. *Phrenol.* (See quot.)

1860 MAYNE *Expos. Lex.*, *Time*,..*Phrenol.*, a Faculty.. giving the power of judging of time, and of intervals in general.

IV. Phrases. (See also sense 18.)

* With another sb.

28. time of day. a. The hour or exact time as shown by the clock; hence, a point or stage in any course or period (somewhat *colloq.*).

1596 SHAKS. *1 Hen. IV*, I. ii. 1 Now Hal, what time of day is it Lad? **1634** FORD *P. Warbeck* III. i, How runs the time of day? Past ten, my lord. **1699** COLLIER *Answ. Stages Survey'd* (1730) 382 The Favour of a Prince was not.. unreputable at that Time of Day. **1771** SMOLLETT *Humph. Cl.* 17 Apr., I will not begin at this time of day to distress my tenants, because they..cannot make regular payments. **1862** GEN. P. THOMPSON in *Bradford Advertiser* 15 Mar. 6/1 No man at this time of day pretends to maintain, that [etc.]. **1870** JAS. NICHOLSON *Idylls* 25 A watch... At least 'twad ha'e tald him the time o' the day.

b. In salutations, as †*good, fair time of day* (obs.); also, *to give one*, or *pass, the time of day* (now *dial.* and *colloq.*), to greet, salute, exchange salutations: see also PASS *v.* 52 c. *not to give* (a person) *the time of day* (colloq.), not to help or cooperate with (a person) at all, to be surly or mean towards.

1594 SHAKS. *Rich. III*, I. iii. 18 Good time of day vnto your Royall Grace. **1599** —— *Hen. V*, v. ii. 3 To our Sister Health and faire time of day. **1608** —— *Pericles* IV. iii. 35. **1611** COTGR., *Saluër*, to salute, greet,..giue the time of the day vnto. **1707** J. STEVENS tr. *Quevedo's Com. Wks.* (1709) 300 It shall be always allow'd to give the Time of the Day, but no New-Years-Gifts. **1851** MAYHEW *Lond. Labour* (1861) II. 489/2 The police..they're very friendly, they'll pass the time of day with me. **1864** *Let. to Editor*, In Radnorshire a clergyman told me the other day that 'there was not one in the parish who would not give him the time of day'. He meant, say 'How do' or 'a fine day, Sir'. **1951** N. MAILER *Advts. for Myself* (1961) 146 You don't even give me the time of day. You're the coldest man I've ever known. **1979** A. MALING *Koberg Link* (1980) xxiii. 123 You've come to the wrong place. Paul Carmichael won't give me the time of day. **1982** A. PRICE *Old 'Vengeful'* vii. 112 Lippy wouldn't have given Danny the time of day on a wet Sunday afternoon, not if he'd have come to him on bended knees.

c. *colloq.* or *slang.* The prevailing aspect of affairs; the state of the case; (to know) 'what's what'; also, the right way of doing anything; the latest dodge or 'wrinkle'; cf. *to know what o'clock it is* (CLOCK *sb.*[1] 3 d).

1667 POOLE *Dial. betw. Protest. & Papist* (1735) 144 No, Friend, it is not that time of Day. **1682** BUNYAN *Holy War* 11 If that be done, I know, quickly what time of day 'twill be with us. **1837** DICKENS *Pickw.* xxxix, Steady, Sir, steady! That's the time o' day! **1840** —— *Barn. Rudge* xxxviii, Hurrah for the Protestant religion! That's the time of day. **1897** 'OUIDA' *Massarenes* xxvii, 'She knows the time o' day', said the other.

29. time of life, the age of a person, *esp.* middle age, the menopause.

1764 GRAY *Candidate* 10 At our time of life 'twould be silly, my dear. **1838** MRS. GASKELL *Let.* 17 Aug. (1966) 25 We agreed..that when people are come to *yr time of life*, there is no use having long engagements. **1971** 'E. FERRARS' *Stranger & Afraid* vi. 100 Whatever's wrong with a woman over forty, it seems to me, people say it's her Time of Life. **1981** J. MANN *Funeral Sites* xxii. 132 Aidan has already threatened me with psychiatrists. He says it is 'my time of life'.

30. time of memory: see quot. 1848. **time out of mind** (also, †*out of memory*), from a time or during a period beyond human memory; so *time*, † *times* (also *for, from time*) *immemorial*.

Also †*without* or †*out of t. of mind*, †*within time of mind*, †*before t. of mind had*, †*during t. of no mind*; †*from t. whereof is no mind*, or *whereof the memory of man is not (to) the contrary*; †*during, from, out of, of t. that no (man's) mind is the contrary*. See also MIND *sb.*[1] 2 f.

1407 *Waterf. Arch.* in *10th Rep. Hist. MSS. Comm.* App. v. 329 The nonpaying..during time of noo mynde. **1425** *Rolls of Parlt.* IV. 267/2 Beyng Erles, of tyme yat no mynde is ye contrarie. **1480** *Coventry Leet Bk.* 460 Ther haue ben Chirchewardens..tyme out of mynde electyff yerely. **1504** *Sel. Cas. Crt. Star Chamber* (Selden) I. 211 Which all weyes withoute tyme of mynde hath be made. **1511** *Waterf. Arch.* in *10th Rep. Hist. MSS. Comm.* App. v. 325 Noo such custum here..oute of tyme of mynde. **1515** *Sel. Cas. Star Chamb.* (Selden) II. 93 Bying and sellyng frely within tyme of mynd. **1516** *Ibid.* 107 Liberties..vsed the tyme wherof mannys mynde is not to the contrarie. **1523** FITZHERB. *Surv.* 7 Except it haue ben vsed tyme out of mynde. **1527** *Sel. Cas. Star Chamber* (Selden) II. 16 So hath been oute of tyme of mynd. **1553** in Leadam *Court Requests* (Selden) 196 Whether it grewe first..before tyme of mynde had. **1602** [see IMMEMORIAL]. **1622** CALLIS *Stat. Sewers* (1647) 89 He and his Predecessors had used time out of memory to repair such a Bridge, which was in decay. **1759** GOLDSM. *Bee* No. 1. ¶11 This deformity..it had been the custom, time immemorial, to look upon as the greatest ornament of the human visage. **1760** *Impostors Detected* III. x. II. 103 The beavers having been in possession of it [the island] for time immemorial. **1765** BLACKSTONE *Comm.* I. viii. 281 The king's ordinary revenue is such, as has either subsisted time out of mind in the crown; or else has been granted by parliament. **1831–2** *Act 2 & 3 Will. IV*, c. 71 §1 Time Immemorial, or Time whereof the Memory of Man runneth not to the contrary. **1848** WHARTON *Law Lex.* s.v. *Memory*, By Statute Westminster the First, 3 Edw. I., A.D. 1276, the time of memory was limited to the reign of Richard 1st, July 6th, 1189. **1887** T. A. TROLLOPE *What I remember* II. iii. 37 An ancient..goblet, which has belonged to the Musgraves time out of mind.

31. time and tide, an alliterative reduplication, in various senses of *time*; now only or mainly in proverbial phrases, as *time and tide wait (stay) for no man*, etc., superseding the earlier *tide (tide nor time) tarrieth no man*, etc. (see TIDE *sb.* 13 b).

*a*1300 *Cursor M.* 778 He wat wel wat tim or tide þat ȝee hade eten o þis tre. *c*1550 R. BIESTON *Bayte Fortune* B j, And founden wast thou fyrst in euyll time and tyde. **1581** MARBECK *Bk. of Notes* 804 For their penaunce, according to the number, manner, time and tide giuen them by their ghostly father. **1602** MARSTON *Antonio's Rev.* II. iv, The divell in his good time and tide forsake thee. **1639** J. CLARKE *Paræmiologia Anglo-Latina* 233 Time and tide tary on no man. **1796** 'A. BARTON' *Disappointment* II. iv. 50 Let's step into the state-room, you know the old saying, 'Time and tide waits for no one'. **1935** J. MASEFIELD *Box of Delights* i. 21 Time and Tide and Buttered eggs wait for no man. **1979** 'C. AIRD' *Some die Eloquent* x. 112 Time and tide and newspapers wait for no man. **1983** *Out of Town* Dec. 19/2 Only two years ago it [*sc.* The National Trust] completed a major repair to the tiny and beautiful Mullion Harbour on the Lizard Peninsula. Time and tide wait for no man.

32. time after time, on many occasions, repeatedly.

1631 GOUGE *God's Arrows* iii. §6. 192 The like hath been verified time after time. **1881** JOWETT *Thucyd.* I. 42 Time after time we have warned you.

** With a following adv.

33. time about, alternately, in turns. (Formerly with *their*.) Chiefly *Sc.* or *northern*.

1537 *Registr. Aberdon.* (Maitland) I. 413 Sex of þe foirsaid viccaris þair tyme about ilk Satirdaye..sall syng þe foirsaid anteme. *a*1670 SPALDING *Troubles Chas. I* (1850) I. 131 Becaus..diuerss of his freindis sould cum..thair tyme about, and attend his lordschipis seruice. **1756** MRS. CALDERWOOD in *Coltness Collect.* (Maitl.) 272 That a protestant emperor should be chosen time about with a popish. **1816** SCOTT *Antiq.* xxv, Time about's fair play. **1828** *Craven Gloss.* s.v., *Times about*, in turns, in rotation. **1859** G. WILSON *Gateway Knowl.* (ed. 3) 39 Two paviours, driving in stones, bring down their mallets time about.

34. a. time (also **times**) **and again, time and time again**, with frequent recurrence; repeatedly, very often.

1864 D. G. MITCHELL *Seven Stor.* 49 Time and again I looked over the way. **1870** [see AGAIN *adv.* 4 b]. **1878** MRS. H. WOOD *Pomeroy Abb.* I. 85 Times and again she had wondered..who the recreant truant could be. **1887** J. HARTLEY *Halifax Orig. Illuminated Clock Almanack* 48 He's browt us in a bit o' dinner time an' time again. **1897** HALL CAINE *Christian* IV. xiv, Time and again I thought John's love of you was near to madness. **1957** E. WAUGH *Ordeal of Gilbert Pinfold* i. 2 He would dearly have liked to revise it, envying painters, who are allowed to return to the same theme time and time again. **1977** *It* May 29/2 Time and time again we have been told of the desperate need to coordinate squatting activities.

b. *times and often*; *times without number*; *many a time and oft*: see 18.

35. time back, at some past time. *Obs.* or *dial.*

1834 LANDOR *Exam. Shaks.* Wks. 1846 II. 298/1 The girl's mother, sir, was housemaid and sempstress in your own family, time back. **1887** *S. Chesh. Gloss.*, *Time ago*.., *Time back*.., some time ago.

36. time enough, soon enough, in time, sufficiently early.

1377 LANGL. *P. Pl.* B. XI. 35 A man may stoupe tymes [C. XII. 197 tyme] ynow whan he shal tyne þe croune. **1470–85** MALORY *Arthur* VII. xi. 228 Thou shalt see hym tyme ynough. **1583** STOCKER *Civ. Warres Lowe C.* III. 117 b. **1669** R. MONTAGU in *Buccleuch MSS.* (Hist. MSS. Comm.) I. 458 That I may prepare time enough to fit my equipage for the journey. **1726** SWIFT *Stella's Birthday* 7 To-morrow will be time enough To hear such mortifying stuff. **1864** MRS. GATTY *Parables fr. Nat.* Ser. IV. 27 Time enough to go into the depths when you have used up what is so much easier got at.

37. time off, a break from one's occupation, absence from work, school, service, etc. (cf. OFF *adv.* 4 d); also, remission of part of a prison sentence.

1930 H. CRANE *Let.* 30 Sept. (1965) 356 I'm taking 'time off' to answer in the hope that you'll write me more news. **1951** 'J. TEY' *Daughter of Time* i. 9 Benny would get time off for good behaviour. **1954** *Spectator* 10 Dec. 736/2 Theorists who indulge the undemocratic vice of taking time off to think. **1977** *Whitaker's Almanack 1978* 580/2 The *Financial Times* was not published because of a dispute between management and N.G.A. compositors over time-off.

38. time out, time-out, timeout (orig. and chiefly *U.S.*). **a.** (Usu. as one word.) In various games: a deduction of playing time for a stoppage; a (usu. brief) break in play called by a coach, referee, or player.

1896 CAMP & DELAND *Football* vi. 61 *Time out*, time taken out by the referee when play is not actually in progress. **1930** *Sun* (Baltimore) 26 Dec. 11/7 The game..takes up about two and a quarter hours, when one allows for the intermission between halves and the innumerable 'times out'. **1946** [see DOLLY VARDEN]. **1972** J. MOSEDALE *Football* v. 61 We'd just stopped them on our one-yard line and called time-out. **1979** *Arizona Daily Star* 5 Aug. C 1/2 Clark's directive created a difference of opinion during a Tucson timeout in the opening game. **1981** *Times* 11 Nov. 8/8 Experts said Korchnoi might postpone the fifteenth game, which is due on Thursday. Each man has used up two of the three timeouts allowed each player under the championship rules.

b. A break from one's occupation.

1939 I. BAIRD *Waste Heritage* vi. 76 An' I took time out to tell you why we got to have those rules. **1962** J. D. MACDONALD *Girl, Gold Watch, & Everything* ix. 115 Everybody in such a damn hurry, sugar, it's good for them to take a little time out. **1978** *Chicago* June 131/2 Sandwiching Sunday-morning Mass between an appearance on *Meet the Press* and a press conference back at the Ramada Inn was the only time-out Schtafly took in Houston.

*** With a governing preposition.

39. about time, approximately the right time; usu. *iron.*, long past the right time; (also with *too*) this should have happened much earlier, this is long overdue.

1920 E. O'NEILL *Beyond Horizon* II. i. 67 It's about time you put a stop to his nonsense. **1931** [see CURVE *sb.* 2]. **1940** W. FAULKNER *Hamlet* IV. i. 285, I reckon it's about time to get dinner started. **1952** M. R. RINEHART *Swimming Pool* xxvii. 240 'It's about time,' he said, pushing aside the junket Jennie had served him. **1977** A. CLARKE *Letter from Dead* ix. 103 'Now you're talking,' said Jill, 'and about time too.'

40. against time, in competition with the passage of time; so as to finish one's task before the expiry of a certain period.

1835 DICKENS *Sk. Boz* (1836) 1st Ser. II. 178 The kennels seem to be doing matches against time. **1854**, **1868** [see AGAINST *prep.* 12 d]. **1872** *Punch* 10 Feb. 57/2 No member shall speak against time or his own convictions. **1883** SWINBURNE in *Encycl. Brit.* XV. 556/2 A man who..was often..compelled to write against time for his living. **1887** RUSKIN *Præterita* II. 171 [To] walk against time up a regular slope of eight feet in the hundred is the most trying footwork I know. **1933** D. L. SAYERS *Hangman's Holiday* 37 It must have been put in the wrong way round... You know, sir, we often have to work against time, and I suppose—but it's very careless. **1935** 'E. QUEEN' *Adventures* 86 What would you gentlemen expect a thief, working against time, to do under these circumstances? **1975** *Economist* 1 Feb. 16 Sheikh Mujib's 'second revolution' last weekend was his personal answer to this race against time. **1982** *Washington Post* 11 Nov. D 11 Whether it realizes it or not, the government of Japan is in a race against time.

41. at time(s, etc. **a.** *at times*, †*at (a) time* (obs. rare), at one time and another, at various times, occasionally. Also *at times and again*.

1529 MORE *Dyaloge* III. Wks. 245/1 Our sauiour at tyme taught his apostles a part. **1604** SHAKS. *Oth.* II. iii. 319 You, or any man liuing, may be drunke at a time, man. **1611** BIBLE *Judg.* xiii. 25 The Spirit of the Lord beganne to mooue him at times. **1779** *Mirror* No. 39 ¶9, I believe most men have, at times, wished to be..possessed of the power of moulding the world to their fancy. **1864** *Reader* 634/3 Some blacks, at times and again, hovering over a few coals. **1884** W. C. SMITH *Kildrostan* 46, I blame myself at times.

b. *(at) one time with (and) another*, during various detached periods; on various occasions.

1612 R. FENTON *Usury* 37 If they could with their owne free stocke raise the like gaine one time with another. **1845** COIT *Puritanism* 252 Winthrop..was governor, at one time with another, eleven years. **1884** MRS. OLIPHANT *Sir Tom* II. vi. 84 He had seen a good deal of her one time and another in his life.

c. *at the same time*, during the same period, at the same moment, not before or after. (Formerly without *at*.) Also used in introducing a reservation, explanation, or contrast, = 'while saying this, nevertheless, however, yet, still'.

1526 TINDALE *Matt.* xviii. 1 The same tyme the disciples cam vnto Iesus, saying [etc.]. —— *Acts* xix. 23 The same tyme there arose no litell a do aboute that waye. **1563** PILKINGTON *Burn. Paules Ch.* D ij b, Tertulian who lyued at the same time of this Pope. **1705** STEELE *Tender Husb.* Ded., At the same time I hope I make the Town no ill Compliment ..in acknowledging that it has so far rais'd my Opinion [etc.]. **1749** WEST tr. *Pindar, Nem. Ode* xi. Argt., Lest he should be too much puffed up with these Praises, he reminds him at the same Time of his Mortality. **1780** *Mirror* No. 100 ¶4 In two of Shakespeare's tragedies are introduced, at the same time, instances of counterfeit madness, and of real distraction. **1891** 'J. S. WINTER' *Lumley* xv, Give them my best wishes. At the same time I must say I do not envy the girl.

42. between times, in the intervals between other actions; at intervals, between-whiles.

[**1580**, *a*1641 Between-time *sb.*: see BETWEEN B. 4.] **1902** ELIZ. L. BANKS *Newspaper Girl* 159 She served me faithfully till the very last, packing her humble belongings in between times.

†**43. by time, by times. a.** *by time*: in good time, early; = BETIME *adv.* *Obs.*

*c*1250, *a*1300 [see BETIME *adv.* 1, 2]. **1340–70** *Alex. & Dind.* 368 We ne sain but soþ & sesen by time. *c*1425 *Cast. Persev.* 413 in *Macro Plays* 89 3a, on þi sowle þou schalt þynke al be tyme. **1565** W. ALLEN in Fulke *Confut. Purg.* (1577) 142 Therfore deare brethern let vs turne and amende by time.

†**b.** ***by times***: (*a*) in good time, early; = BETIMES *adv.*; (*b*) at various times; from time to time; at times, now and then. *Obs.*

c **1314**, *c* **1380** [see BETIMES *adv.* 1, 3]. *c* **1460** FORTESCUE *Abs. & Lim. Mon.* xi. (1885) 135 The kynge..hade be tymes, sithen he reigned vpon vs, livelod..nerehand to the value of þe vth parte off is Reaume. **1530** TINDALE *Answ. More* Wks. (1572) 251/1 Let therfore M. More and his company awake be tymes ere euer their sinne be ripe. **1657** *North's Plutarch* (1676) 960 He slept in the day, and by times in the night. **1743** in Egan *Boxiana* (1830) I. 49 Gentlemen are therefore desired to come by times. **1825** KNAPP & BALDW. *Newgate Cal.* IV. 177/1 The prisoner and I were on good terms by times. **1825** SCOTT *Betrothed* xi, His nephew ..was despatched by times every morning.

†**c.** ***by a time***, at times, occasionally. *Obs.*

1721 KELLY *Prov.* 26 A Horse with four Feet may snapper, by a time.

†**44. for time**, for the time being. *Obs.*

1464 *Rolls of Parlt.* V. 510/2 Any persone or persones for tyme dwellyng..within the same Chapell. **1483** *Ibid.* VI. 257/1 The Goodes and Chattells of the seid Provost and Fellawes for tyme founden upon the seid Lande.

45. from time to time. a. At more or less regular intervals; now and again, occasionally; in quot. 1382, †at stated times, at definite intervals (*obs.*); in quot. *c* 1412 with ellipsis of *from*.

1382 WYCLIF *Ezek.* iv. 11 Fro tyme vn to tyme [1388 fro tyme til to tyme] thou shalt drynke it. *c* **1412** HOCCLEVE *De Reg. Princ.* 4189 Tyme to tyme he ȝaf hem Of his goode. **1423** *Acts Privy Council* III. 88 Ye desire to be acertained fro tyme to tyme of oure prosperite and welfare. **1651** HOBBES *Leviathan* III. xl. 255 From thence proceeded from time to time the civill troubles..of the Nation. **1891** *Law Rep., Weekly Notes* 136/1 The passage..was used only from time to time, and not continuously.

†**b.** Denoting succession of periods without intervals: Continuously, constantly, at all times.

1553 T. WILSON *Rhet.* 14 Heaven is theirs, saieth David, that doe justly from tyme to tyme. **1586** T. B. *La Primaud. Fr. Acad.* (1589) 519 Therefore nothing was more esteemed from time to time among the auncients, than the institution of youth, which Plato calleth Discipline.

46. in time, †**in times. a.** ***in time.*** (*a*) In the course of time, sooner or later. (*b*) Soon or early enough, not too late. †(*c*) At a suitable time; seasonably; opposed to *out of time*, 49 a (*a*). *Obs. rare.* (*d*) *Mus.* In the correct rhythm: see 12 a.

(*a*) *c* **1450** tr. *De Imitatione* III. xxxv. 103 Consolacion shal come to þe in tyme. **1594** WILLOBIE *Avisa* xlvii, I thinke in tyme she may be wonne. **1656** EARL MONM. tr. *Boccalini's Advts. fr. Parnass.* I. xxiii. (1674) 24 Potent men..would certainly in time work their revenge. **1818** SCOTT *Hrt. Midl.* xvi, The inner turnkey's office to begin wi', and the captainship in time.

(*b*) **1467–8** *Rolls of Parlt.* V. 623/1 Yf it were used in tyme. **1605** SHAKS. *Macb.* II. iii. 6 Come in time, haue Napkins enow about you. **1742** *Observ. Methodists* 4 It will be too late to remedy it if not attended to in Time. **1834** *Picture of Liverpool* 73 Letters put into any of the Receiving Houses before twelve o'clock will be in time for the early mails. **1912** *Eng. Hist. Rev.* Jan. 44 Mansel soon returned..in time to assume the custody of the seal in September 1238.

(*c*) **1377** LANGL. *P. Pl.* B. IX. 184 Whan ȝe haue wyued, bewar and worcheth in tyme. **1583** STUBBES *Anat. Abus.* II. (1882) 78 The worde of God is to be preached night and day, in time, and out of time, in season and out of season.

†**b.** ***in times.*** (*a*) At various times, on several different occasions. (*b*) ***in times..in times***, sometimes..sometimes; at one time..at another.

1422 tr. *Secreta Secret., Priv. Priv.* 181 He that is a gouernoure in tymes he shall Spare, and in tymes vengeaunse take. **1612** *MS. Acc. St. John's Hosp., Canterb.*, Payd vnto Thomas Williames in times in consederation of a challing of sartayn tythe wood.

c. ***in good time.*** (*a*) After the lapse of a suitable interval; in due course or process of time; at a proper time, when it seems good. (*b*) Soon or early; quickly. †(*c*) At the right or a seasonable moment; luckily. *Obs.* †(*d*) As an expression of ironical acquiescence, incredulity, amazement, or the like: To be sure!, indeed!, very well! (Cf. Fr. *à la bonne heure.*) *Obs.*

(*a*) *c* **1440** LOVELICH *Merlin* 9985 Forth on his message he gan to gon, and dyde his message al in good tyme. **1622** in *Crt. & Times Jas. I* (1848) II. 343 But God, in his good time, will amend all that is amiss. **1777** SHERIDAN *Sch. Scand.* IV. i, I shall be rich and splenetic, all in good time. **1822** SCOTT *Pirate* ix, 'The devil take him!' said Mordaunt, in impatient surprise. 'A' in gude time', replied the jagger. **1883** GILMOUR *Mongols* xvii. 206 Every true-hearted follower shall, in good time, arrive at the desired goal.

(*b*) **1585** T. WASHINGTON tr. *Nicholay's Voy.* II. xxii. 60 [They] come home againe in good time without the knowledge..of their husbands. **1872** *Punch* 19 Oct. 158/1 My aunt wants to be back in good time.

(*c*) **1586** A. DAY *Eng. Secretary* II. (1625) 62 If it please you then to returne by him those parcels.., they will come now in very good time. **1590** SHAKS. *Com. Err.* II. ii. 65 Learne to iest in good time, there's a time for all things. **1639** S. DU VERGER tr. *Camus' Admir. Events* 7 This came in good time to keepe this poore family from necessity.

(*d*) **1610** SHAKS. *Temp.* II. i. 95 Sowing the kernels of it [an island]..bring forth more Islands... Why in good time. **1650** FULLER *Pisgah* II. vi. 149 There..even at this day, are shewed the ruines of those three tabernacles built according to Peters desire. In very good time no doubt! **1789** MRS. PIOZZI *Journ. France* II. 50 Bonducci..calls him emulous of Milton, in good time! *Ibid.* 369 Making fat the objects of his partial tenderness with their best treasures—in good time!

d. ***what*** (***why***, etc.) ***in time..***, 'what (etc.) in the world..' or 'on earth..'. *U.S. colloq.*

1849 J. T. FIELDS *Let.* 28 Feb. in R. W. Griswold *Passages from Corr.* (1898) 250 Why in Time don't you come our way and see the boys? **1883** *Harper's Mag.* Jan. 212/1 He wondered what In time made 'em keep the cars so hot. **1904** J. C. LINCOLN *Cap'n Eri* vii. 125 What in time did you tell the Doctor that she was a relation of mine for?

47. not before (*dial.* **afore**) **time,** not soon enough, almost too late, long overdue.

1905 in *Eng. Dialect Dict.* VI. 15/1 Ah see they're beginnin' ti mend rooad, an nat afoor time. **1955** 'N. SHUTE' *Requiem for Wren* v. 144 She got her clothes brush from her quarters and gave him a grooming with it, not before time. **1967** *Listener* 26 Oct. 553/3 The Minister..is right: 'the licensed victualler must now recognise that he has to provide a different kind of social life in his pub.' It is not before time. **1972** *Observer* 16 July 13/6 It all points to a wind of change blowing in the direction of the Ordinary shares..: and not before time either. **1974** *New Statesman* 29 Nov. 766/1 It's ..goodbye to cheap sugar—and perhaps not before time so far as the developing countries are concerned.

48. on time. a. Punctually; also *pred.* punctual. Formerly chiefly *U.S. colloq.* See also 53. Also (with hyphen) *attrib.* (see ON-[1] 4 b).

1821 R. CADELL *Let.* 28 Nov. in *Times Lit. Suppl.* (1933) 7 Sept. 592/2 In order to effect this *and on time* we have resolved [etc.]. **1878** MRS. STOWE *Poganuc P.* xxiii. 209 His wife had always been on time, and on duty. **1890, 1892** [see ON *prep.* 6 d]. **1893** *Scribner's Mag.* June 781/2 My endeavors to get the family out of the house and into our pew on time. **1904** *Daily Chron.* 5 Feb. 3/4 An Americanism here and there out of place (as..when the native dwarf, Cerberus..speaks of his mistress as being 'on time' in her return from a trance). **1965** *Economist* 13 Feb. 675/1 Exact scheduling..and perfect coordination to assure on-time completion of the project. **1967** R. J. SERLING *President's Plane is Missing* (1968) i. 13 As my airline friends would say, I prefer on-time departures.

†**b.** ***on a time***: see 14. *Obs.*

c. On credit. *N. Amer.*

1840 *Spirit of Times* 15 Aug. 277/1 *On time*, the prices would at once be enhanced. **1873** W. MATHEWS *Getting on in World* xix. 316 We need not expect that the practice of selling goods on time will ever be abandoned. **1925** *Sat. Even. Post* 10 Oct. 133/1 It's like peddling lots on time, instead of selling and developing acreage. **1972** J. M. MINIFIE *Homesteader* vi. 44 Everything was bought 'on time', hardly any transactions involved cash. **1979** R. L. SIMON *Peking Duck* xx. 144 On the table with Harvey's Sony tape recorder was a Nikon FT... I wondered if he had bought it all on time.

49. out of time. a. *adv. phr.* †(*a*) At an inappropriate time; unseasonably. *Obs.* (*b*) After the prescribed period has elapsed; too late. See also 7 b (*f*). (*c*) *Mus.* See 12 a.

(*a*) **1393** LANGL. *P. Pl.* C. XI. 291 Ȝe þat han wyues, beþ war worcheþ nat out of tyme. *c* **1420** *Avow. Arth.* xxiii, I, Kay, that thou knawes, That owte of tyme bostus and blawus. **1579** LYLY *Euphues* (Arb.) 100 Doth not Tryacle as well poyson as helpe, if it be taken out of time? **1583** [see 45 a (*c*)]. **1780** WARNER in Jesse *Selwyn & Contemp.* (1844) IV. 325, I went like a thing born out of time, and had the door almost shut in my face.

(*b*) **1884** GRAHAM HASTINGS in *Law Times Rep.* L. 175/1 On that view of the case also they are out of time, as they took no steps in the matter until Oct. 1883. **1886** *Law Times* LXXX. 241/2 Counsel for the respondent took a preliminary objection that the appeal was out of time.

b. *adj. phr.* Unseasonable: see OUT-OF-TIME.

c. ***out of one's time***, in an era unsympathetic to one's attitudes, aspirations, etc.; at the wrong season.

1950 'D. DIVINE' *King of Fassarai* xvi. 125 Kellie was born out of his time. Last piece of history he could have flourished in was the Alaska rushes. **1958** B. BEHAN *Borstal Boy* III. 334 It was a little undersized goat born out of its time, and it was so small now that it wouldn't be any bigger than a lamb at Christmas when we put on the play. **1973** R. LEWIS *Of Singular Purpose* vi. 130 'Major Cornelius Van Rijk.' He laughed shortly. 'A man out of his time.' **1976** L. HENDERSON *Major Enquiry* xii. 78 You know, Mildred, you were born out of your time, you really belong to the naughty nineties.

50. over time, gradually, during a period of (past or future) time.

1966 *Rep. Comm. Inquiry Univ. Oxf.* II. 46 The proportion from independent schools has fallen over time. **1973** *New Society* 1 Nov. 258/3 Like the Foot-Steel proposals, these would be introduced over time.

51. to time. †**a.** For all time, for ever. *Obs.*

c **1200** *Trin. Coll. Hom.* 183 For þine gulte ishal nu to pine, rotie mote þu to time. **1607** SHAKS. *Cor.* v. iii. 127, I..that brought you forth this boy To keepe your name liuing to time.

†**b.** *conj. phr.* To the time that, until such time as, till. Also ***into, unto, till time.*** *Obs.*

a **1352** MINOT *Poems* (1887) iv. 6 In þat land..Ordanis he still for to dwell, To time he think to fight. *c* **1449** PECOCK *Repr.* II. xvi. (Rolls) 246 Thei [images] wolden not at alle tymes ȝeue answeris..into tyme thei weren myche preied. *c* **1470** HENRY *Wallace* III. 432, I sall do nocht till tyme I tak my leyff. *c* **1500** *Melusine* 170, I shal neuer departe fro this land vnto tyme I be al dyscomfyted, or þat I haue put them to flyght. **1506** GUYLFORDE *Pilgr.* (Camden) 18 A lytell cave, where they shytte him in, to tyme the Jewes had.. determynyd what they wolde do with hym.

c. Within certain limits of time; so as to complete something by the end of a certain period.

1874 ETHEL DE FONBLANQUE *Life A. Fonblanque* 40 A growing dislike to the act of 'writing to time'.

52. with time, with the lapse of time, in the course of time; = *in time* (46 a (*a*)).

1578–9 *Reg. Privy Council Scot.* III. 82 Your Hienes sal have pruif with tyme of my following thair trew..service to your Grace. **1650** EARL MONM. tr. *Senault's Man bec. Guilty* 104 When with time he is grown greater. *Ibid.* 272 Ambition increasing with time. *Mod.* With time it will come all right.

†**53. without time,** outside of or independent of time; for ever; eternal(ly). *Obs.*

a **1400** *Prymer* 6 Holi modir of god..þat we..moun stie up to þe seete of endeles blis, þere þou dwellist wiþ þi sone wiþ-outen tyme. **1509** HAWES *Past. Pleas.* xliv. (Percy Soc.) 215 Withouten tyme is no erthly thynge, Nature, fortune, or yet dame Sapyence. **1587** GOLDING *De Mornay* vi. 79 This Minde is without time and onely everlasting.

†**54.** In commercial phraseology, ***at, for, on time***, at the rate which may be current on the day appointed for settling; cf. TIME-BARGAIN. *Obs.*

1651 MARIUS *Adv. Conc. Bills Exch.* 74 Goods sold one part for ready Mony, the rest at Time. **1727** SWIFT *What passed in London* Wks. 1755 III. I. 188 There were many who called themselves Christians, who offered to buy for time. **1766** W. GORDON *Gen. Counting-h.* 10 Debited..to the persons of whom they are bought, if on time.

**** With a verb.

55. (**the**) **time was** (**hath been, shall be**), inversion of *there was* (etc.) *a time* (*when*).

1509 BARCLAY *Shyp of Folys* (1874) I. 35 The tyme hath ben, nat longe before our dayes Whan [etc.]. **1549** COVERDALE, etc. *Erasm. Par. Gal.* v. 18 The tyme was, when it was nedefull. **1611** BIBLE *Transl. Pref.* 5 The same Hierome elsewhere affirmeth, that he, the time was, had set forth the Translation of the Seuenty for his countrymen of Dalmatia. **1791** COWPER *Iliad* I. 300 Time shall be, when Achilles shall be miss'd. **1874** MICKLETHWAITE *Mod. Par. Churches* 251 Time was when we had a national style.

56. to keep time. a. *Mus.* To mark the rhythm by movements of the hand or baton; to beat time; also, of a performer, to adhere to the correct rhythm and rate of the music, to keep pace *with* a measure or another performer, etc. Also *fig.*

1599 B. JONSON *Cynthia's Rev.* I. i, Slow, slow, fresh fount, keep time with my salt tears. **1662** PLAYFORD *Skill Mus.* I. ix. (1674) 29 In keeping time your hand goes down at one half, and up at the next. **1687** LOVELL tr. *Thevenot's Trav.* II. 85 They beat this Stuff with one hand two and two over against one another,..keeping time to this tune. **1817** BYRON *Beppo* lxiii, I can't well break it, But must keep time and tune like public singers. **1821** SCOTT *Kenilw.* xviii, Thy reward shall be princely, if thou keep'st time and touch, and exceedest not the due proportion.

b. Of a timepiece: To register the passage of time correctly.

1899 P. N. HASLUCK *Clock Jobber's Handbk.* 61 The clock is ready..with every probability of going and keeping time for two or three years.

57. ***to make time*** (***with***): see MAKE *v.*[1] 66.

V. Ellipt.

58. as *conj.* At or by the time that; as soon as; when. *U.S. dial.* and *colloq.*

1919 E. O'NEILL *Moon of Caribbees* 6 It *was* in New Guinea, time I was shipwrecked there. **1938** M. K. RAWLINGS *Yearling* iv. 30 You'll likely not be so merry, time the day be done. *Ibid.* ix. 78 You git on to the sink-hole, son, and I'll foller time I've skinned out your 'coon hide. **1950** R. MOORE *Candlemas Bay* 13 Time Joel Walls had his net, one night he caught seven hogsids.

VI. Combinations.

59. a. Simple *attrib.* (*a*) 'Of or pertaining to time', as ***time-basis, -behaviour, -consciousness, -co-ordinate, -cycle, -depth, -dimension, -direction, -displacement, -division, -drop, -evolution, -factor, -flow, -foot, -gap, -guide, -horizon, -integral*** (INTEGRAL B. 4 a), ***-interval, -mark, -measure, -ocean, -order, -pattern, -period, -perspective, -plane, -process, -ratio, -reference, -relation, -rhythm, -schedule, -scheme, -sense, -sequence, -shift, -slip, -span, -sphere, -stream, -succession, -unit, -variation, -word***; also, 'of time as distinct from eternity', as ***time-pattern, -state, -vesture, -world***; (*b*) 'relating to, based upon, or indicating the amount of time occupied in some work or process', as ***time-allowance, -board, -budget, -chart, -log*** (LOG *sb.*[1] 8), ***-march, -prize, -race, -record, -ticket***; (*c*) in names of instruments, machines, or appliances used as time-signals or timed to operate at a given moment, as ***time-alarm*** (ALARM *sb.* 7), ***-bomb*** (also *fig.* and *attrib.*), ***-fuse, -glass*** (cf. HOUR-GLASS), ***-gun, -measure, -taper***.

1877 KNIGHT *Dict. Mech.*, **Time-alarm*, an audible notice at the expiration of a set time. *a* **1974** R. CROSSMAN *Diaries* (1975) I. 259 A mere day and a half was a crazy *time-allocation if only because the eight new clauses and fifty amendments..would take all the time available. **1883** D. KEMP in *Fortn. Rev.* 1 Sept. 324 The yachts..were sailed in classes without *time-allowance. **1849** J. A. CARLYLE tr. *Dante's Inferno* p. xxxi, The whole *time-basis of his mighty song has become dim and cold. **1955** FRIEDMAN & WEISSKOPF in W. Pauli *Niels Bohr* 153 We can then examine the *time behaviour of the outgoing parts of the wave packet as they pass a given radius. **1977** *Jrnl. R. Soc. Arts* CXXV. 765/2 Other types of lasers..can be controlled in either frequency or time-behaviour with the limits set only by the Uncertainty Principle. **1890** W. J. GORDON *Foundry* 34 As the men come in past the time-office they take their piece or *time-boards from the rack, where each is placed against its proper number. **1895** *Times* 7 Jan. 3/3 In the case of one large yard the men have come out on strike against the introduction of the 'timeboard' system. **1893** *Daily Tel.* 9 Nov. 5/7 The engine of destruction was not a *time bomb. **1939** DYLAN THOMAS *Map of Love* 21 Strike in the time-bomb town. **1941** B. SCHULBERG *What makes Sammy Run?* vi. 128 Sammy Glick is a time bomb in my brain and it's going to go off. **1966** N. NICOLSON *Diaries & Lett. H. Nicolson* 275 Harold Nicolson had long been aware that a constitutional time-bomb was ticking beneath the throne. **1981** 'M. UNDERWOOD' *Double Jeopardy* xxiii. 181 His official diary could become a time bomb. **1948** *Time-budget [see PARTICIPANT *sb.* 1]. **1976** P. R. WHITE *Planning for Public Transport* ii. 46 Within a fixed time-budget, as work trips become longer, less time is available for shopping and recreational trips on weekdays. **1934** *Burlington Mag.* Jan. 50/1 The author establishes his *time-chart, proving conclusively that the wide early influence..has no foundation in fact. **1958** *Times Lit. Suppl.* 17 Jan. 33/2 Mr Sullivan..gives a much more orderly unfolding of the time-chart of discovery because he sticks to a straightforward chronology. **1890** W. JAMES *Princ. Psychol.* I. xv. 632 Th. Waitz is guilty of similar question-begging when he explains our *time-consciousness. **1963** H. LINDENBERGER *On Wordsworth's 'Prelude'* vi. 199 The dissolution of the traditional literary genres and the increasing eccentricity of structure..have proved coincidental with..the development of time-consciousness among writers. *a* **1942** B. MALINOWSKI *Sci. Theory of Culture* (1944) iii. 20 In order ..to make an historical process..significant in terms of explanation or analysis, it is..necessary to prove that we are, along the *time coördinate, linking up phenomena that are strictly comparable. **1903** A. W. PATTERSON *Schumann* 7 That the mind should work in a regular *time-cycle, passing from one phase of sentiment to another with almost mechanical exactness. **1968** *Brit. Med. Bull.* XXIV. 197/2 All disease, whether it be physical or emotional, appears to have its time-cycles. **1957** P. WORSLEY *Trumpet shall Sound* 266 There is *time-depth to all social action. **1978** *Archivum Linguisticum* IX. 76 The ultimate sources of the verbal root *es- can never be definitively known because of the huge time-depth involved here. **1877** E. CAIRD *Philos. Kant* II. x. 415 The schematism of the categories, the translation of them into *time-determinations is no mere idle play of the imagination. **1937** *Mind* XLVI. 162 It is rather unfortunate that philosophers..should have paid little attention to the problem suggested by Minkowski's imaginary *time-dimensions. **1982** M. DUKE *Flashpoint* vii. 46 Shmuel let his mind slip into a new time-dimension. The near future looked good. **1890** W. JAMES *Princ. Psychol.* I. ix. 283 With each prolongation of the scheme in the *time-direction, the summit of the curve of section would come further towards the end of the sentence. **1937** *Mind* XLVI. 177 We may agree..to regard as the time-direction that in which the number of beats registered by the clock is increasing. **1890** W. JAMES *Princ. Psychol.* I. xi. 411 The cases he [*sc.* Wundt] describes are really cases of anachronistic perception, of subjective *time-displacement, to use his own term. **1901** Time-displacement [see ATTENTIONAL *a.*]. **1888** J. PRESTWICH *Geol.* II. 3 The great *time-divisions are of almost universal application. *a* **1711** KEN *Preparatives* Poet. Wks. 1721 IV. 39 Minutes..On these *Time-drops eternal Joys depend. **1937** R. A. WILSON *Birth of Language* II. ii. 79 To one..who tries to work out a concrete philosophical view of the world..on the basis of a *time-evolution of all its forms from matter to man, the mechanistic hypothesis appears..to obscure the real problem of the beginnings of life. **1911** *Aeronaut. Jrnl.* XV. 66 This switch has a '*time-factor' approximating to that of the motor. **1976** M. & G. GORDON *Ordeal* (1977) xxix. 198 He worked fast, conscious of the time factor. **1936** J. KANTOR *Objective Psychol. Gram.* xvii. 240 Grammarians mean by time the abstract points in a field-spread or an equally abstract *time-flow. **1956** E. L. MASCALL *Christian Theol. & Natural Sci.* iv. 134 This continuous activity of God is not to be thought of as if it were the insertion of the creatures into a time-flow which existed antecedently to them. **1883** *Time-foot [see *rhythm-foot* s.v. RHYTHM *sb.* 9 a]. **1862** *Catal. Internat. Exhib.* II. xi. 23 A fuse..placed and used like the ordinary simple *time fuse. **1890** W. JAMES *Princ. Psychol.* I. ix. 237 Interruptions, *time-gaps during which the consciousness went out altogether to come into existence again at a later moment. **1978** *Early Music Gaz.* Oct. 15/2 Leonhardt emphasises the large time-gap between the two books of the so-called '48'. **1804–6** SYD. SMITH *Mor. Philos.* (1850) 122 If you were to say that man was like a *time-glass,—that both must run out, and both render up their dust. **1875** *Zoologist* X. 4587 He wished it to be a *time-guide to the appearance of butterflies and moths. **1878** STEVENSON *Edinburgh* 133 The *time-gun by which people set their watches. **1965** H. I. ANSOFF *Corporate Strategy* iii. 40 To make this concept meaningful, we need the idea of the **time horizon* of a firm —the period over which the firm seeks to optimize its resource conversion efficiency. **1983** *Listener* 8 Dec. 23/3 The time-horizon over which policy is formulated would become markedly biased towards the short-term. **1873** J. C. MAXWELL *Electr. & Magn.* II. 186 The *time-integral of a force is called the Impulse of the force. **1885** TAIT *Rec. Adv. Phys. Sc.* (ed. 3) 359 Momentum is the Time-Integral of Force because force is the rate of change of Momentum. **1871** *Cornh. Mag.* July 58 The imagination is wholly unable either to conceive the duration of the *time-intervals.. occupied by these wonderful processes. **1975** *Language for Life* (Dept. Educ. & Sci.) xxv. 503 We had to ask whether the width of the time intervals had forced the pattern of responses and rendered suspect our method of calculating average times. **1868** *Time-log [see LOG *sb.*[1] 8]. **1891** *Labour Commission* Gloss., *Time-Log*, the printed statement of times allowed for making garments in the tailoring trade, agreed upon between employers and employed. **1896** *Daily News* 22 Dec. 6/6 Captain M——..was thrown from his horse yesterday near Fleet during a *time march. **1901** *Spectator* 20 July 93/2 The continually recurring *time-marks of winter and summer. **1726** LEONI *Alberti's Archit.* Pref. 3 Vehicles, Mills, *Time-measures, and other such minute things. **1911** W. JAMES *Some Probl. Philos.* xi. 179 Mr. Bertrand Russell..treats the Achilles-puzzle as if the difficulty lay only in seeing how the paths traversed by the two runners..should have the same time-measure if they be not themselves of the same length. **1943** *Mind* LII. 61 From no sort of correlation between space-measures and time-measures can the obliteration of the ontological distinction between space and time be validly inferred. **1864** LOWELL *Fireside Trav.* 125 The old *time-ocean throws upon its shores just such rounded and polished results of the eternal turmoil. **1890** W. JAMES *Princ. Psychol.* I. iii. 88 The whole succession is so rapid that perception seems to be retrospective, and the *time-order of events to be read off in memory rather than known at the moment. **1960** *Colston Research Soc. Symposium* XII. 90 These paranormal cognitive powers, it seems, are indifferent in some degree to a physical time order, which of course raises frightful difficulties. **1946** R. BLESH *Shining Trumpets* ii. 42 The.. sequential *time-patterns of human or divine speech. **1968** D. L. CLARKE *Analytical Archaeol.* vi. 254 The time pattern regularities..in the trajectories and traditions of many quite different cultures. **1894** *Jrnl. Inst. Electrical Engineers* XXIII. III. 295 It was due to synchronism between the changes of load *on the engines* and the *time-period of the governor. **1953** *Scottish Jrnl. Theol.* VI. 162 We believe that patterns and expanding purposes have been established through such time-periods. **1965** *Canad. Jrnl. Linguistics* Spring 125 Seven languages..died out during the twenty-three year period ending in 1964... In this same time-period Coos was reduced to a single informant. **1890** W. JAMES *Princ. Psychol.* I. xv. 639 In hashish-intoxication there is a curious increase in the apparent *time-perspective. **1907** *Gentl. Mag.* July 80 The Australian child is deficient not so much in imagination as in what may be called time-perspective. **1969** BENNISON & WRIGHT *Geol. Hist. Brit. Isles* ii. 26 Lines indicating contemporaneity, so-called '*time-planes', are normally presented diagrammatically as horizontal. **1977** G. CLARK *World Prehist.* (ed. 3) I. 24 Among the factors that caused peoples living on the same time-plane to retain or discard old forms while adopting new ones were..variations in the environment to which they had to adapt. **1897** *Outing* (U.S.) Aug. 494/1 In 1890 Murphy was on scratch, and won the *time-prize. **1887** A. SETH *Hegelianism* v. 170 The *time-process of the finite world is ..the reality with which we are immediately acquainted. **1938** E. BEVAN *Symbolism & Belief* iv. 114 The time-process goes on throughout a universe of which our planet is, spatially, only an infinitesimal part. **1852** BATEMAN *Aquatic Notes* an. 1844, P. M—— [won the sculls] after a good '*time-race' with R——. **1964** W. S. ALLEN in D. Abercombie et al. *Daniel Jones* 3 Whereas in modern verse the rhythms are marked by 'stress', the classical rhythms were expressed solely in terms of *time-ratios. **1965** *Wireless World* July 336/2 The same idea of time-ratio control can be used in regulated power supplies. **1887** E. MOORE (*title*) The *Time-References in the Divina Commedia, and their Bearing on the Assumed Date and Duration of the Vision. **1877** E. CAIRD *Philos. Kant* II. xi. 445 So far as sensations are represented as objects, they must be represented as events in time, and thus..considered as the real subjects of *time-relations like any other events. **1924** R. M. OGDEN tr. *Koffka's Growth of Mind* iii. 118 When a pianist..articulates a series of muscular innervations..fixed time-relations are determined in the series of sound-waves. **1962** D. NICHOLS *Echinoderms* v. 71 There is no clear-cut evidence as to the origin of the echinoids. Time-relations do not allow their derivation from the Ophiocistioidea of the Silurian. *c* **1873–4** *Time-rhythm [see BEAT *sb.*[1] 5]. **1934** J. J. HOGAN *Outl. Eng. Philol.* iv. 29 Quantity or time-rhythm, consisting of the alternation of longer and shorter, not of stronger and weaker beats, is the rhythm of music. **1904** *Daily Chron.* 31 Dec. 6/7 The reconstruction of an old [line], when the working moments must be snatched in the gaps of the *time-schedule, and the greater part of the work must be carried out during a period of four hours at dead of night. **1904** *Mind* Oct. 468 The distribution of terms in our inner *time-scheme and space-scheme must be an exact copy of the distribution in real time and space of the real terms. **1978** *N. & Q.* Feb. 55/1 Given Sterne's complicated time-scheme..such inconsistencies are surprisingly rare. **1890** W. JAMES *Princ. Psychol.* I. xv. 611 The units of duration..which the *time-sense is able to take in at a single stroke, are groups of a few seconds. **1899** *Syd. Soc. Lex.*, *Time sense*, the perception of the lapse of time. **1890** W. JAMES *Princ. Psychol.* II. xxviii. 671 The principle [of causality] expresses a demand for *some* deeper sort of inward connection between phenomena than their merely habitual *time-sequence seems to us to be. **1974** G. JENKINS *Bridge of Magpies* viii. 135 What the time sequence of events was in regard to the two killings I'd never know. **1933** F. M. FORD *Let.* 24 Aug. (1965) 222 To them, on account of the '*time-shift'..they [*sc.* novels] must be quite incomprehensible. **1958** *Times Lit. Suppl.* 18 July 414/2 This device, moreover, involves Mr. Young in irritating time-shifts and flash-backs and rather strained symbolism. **1978** CADOGAN & CRAIG *Women & Children First* xi. 268 The technical problems involved in the time-shift structure have simply failed to interest the author. **1983** *Listener* 24 Nov. 37/2 The whole business of recording broadcasts and watching them later is known to the trade as 'time-shift'. **1952** P. WENTWORTH *Brading Collection* xii. 72 It brought a horrid feeling that there had been a kind of *time-slip— that they had been caught back again, she and Charles, to where they were three years ago. **1974** *Bookseller* 10 Aug. 999/2 (Advt.), Four children, a disused railway line, a time-slip to an Edwardian scene—this enchanting fantasy [etc.]. **1981** V. GLENDINNING *Edith Sitwell* xv. 195 Old Beau Nash, in her *Bath*, sees the past float by... This conceit, or technique of the time slip was not unique. **1933** A. N. WHITEHEAD *Adventures of Ideas* vi. 98 The recent shortening of the *time-span between notable changes in social customs is very obvious, if we examine history. **1979** A. STORR *Art of Psychotherapy* ii. 11 Attention is difficult to sustain without a break beyond a time-span of forty-five to fifty minutes. **1928** H. POUTSMA *Gram. Late Mod. Eng.* (ed. 2) I. I. i. 43 *Should*, as a modal verb, is a preterite conditional, used irrespective of the *time-sphere of the predication. **1957** R. W. ZANDVOORT *Handbk. Eng. Gram.* iv. 61 The perfect tense usually denotes an action that falls within the time-sphere of the present. **1937** R. A. WILSON *Birth of Lang.* II. i. 69 In his emergence to consciousness man rose above the *time-stream of sense. **1978** P. G. WINSLOW *Coppergold* 125 At some point a man begins to feel out of place in the time stream. **1890** W. JAMES *Princ. Psychol.* II. xx. 147 There enters thus an element of *time-succession into our perception of ourselves which transforms the latter from an act of intuition to one of construction. **1922** A. S. EDDINGTON *Theory of Relativity* 18 It [*sc.* the relativity theory] fully recognizes that the chain of events in such a time-succession is a series of an entirely distinctive character from the succession of points along a line in space. **1810** SOUTHEY *Kehama* VIII. vii, Lo! the *time-taper's flame ascending slow. **1903** R. WALLACE *Life* iii. 52 This view of the 'Sabbath' as a sacrifice or *time-tax paid to the Deity. **1900** H. LAWSON *Over Shiprails* 123 The door opened. Arvie..took his *time-ticket, and hurried in. **1925** J. JOLY *Surface-Hist. Earth* v. 79 Our *time-units have become millions of years. **1968** R. A. LYTTLETON *Mysteries Solar Syst.* iv. 133 The time-unit of the abscissa is 50,000 years. **1881** MAXWELL *Electr. & Magn.* II. 223 The third term..depends on the *time-variation of the magnetic field. **1831** CARLYLE *Sart. Res.* III. viii, Nature, which is the *Time-vesture of God, and reveals Him to the wise, hides Him from the foolish. **1933** W. A. RUSSELL *Devel. Art of Lang.* viii. 57 The thought of an action is intimately associated with the thought of time; so much so that some grammarians have called the verb the **Time-word*. **1973** *Archivum Linguisticum* IV. 5 The distinction between /bin/ and /dɔŋ/ is clear when we consider..the time words with which they collocate. **1843** CARLYLE *Past & Pr.* II. vi, This *Time-world..plays and flickers in the grand still mirror of Eternity.

b. Objective and obj. gen., as ***time-beater***, ***-giver***, ***-measurer***, ***-observer***, ***-pleaser***, ***-saver***, ***-setter*** (1340), ***-spender***, ***-waster*** (1661), etc.; ***time-allocation***, ***-beguiling*** (1592), ***-bettering***, ***-breaking***, ***-consuming***, ***-deluding***, ***-devouring***, ***-economizing***, ***-measuring***, ***-noting***, ***-reckoning***, ***-saving***, ***-setting*** (1340), ***-spending*** (1509), ***-wasting***, etc., adjs. and sbs.; **c.** instrumental, as ***time-authorized*** (*a* 1628), ***-battered***, ***-bent***, ***-bewasted*** (1593), ***-blackened***, ***-blanched***, ***-blurred***, ***-born***, ***-bound***, ***-cleft***, ***-conditioned***, ***-constrained***, ***-controlled***, ***-discoloured***, ***-dulled***, ***-eaten***, ***-gnawn***, ***-hallowed***, ***-limited***, ***-mellowed***, ***-obsessed*** (also *absol.*), ***-rent***, ***-ridden***, ***-rusty***, ***-sanctioned***, ***-shaken***, ***-shrouded***, ***-stained***, ***-taught***, ***-tested***, ***-tormented***, ***-tried***, ***-wasted***, ***-wearied***, ***-white***, ***-withered***, etc., adjs.; **d.** in various relations with pples. and adjs., as ***time-based***, ***-centred***, ***-conscious***, ***-dead***, ***-dependent***, ***-enduring*** (†***-during***), ***-faced***, ***-independent***, ***-kept***, ***-lasting***, ***-lost***, ***-marked***, ***-old***, ***-pressed***, ***-proof***, ***-served***, ***-varying*** adjs.

1951 PARSONS & SHILS *Toward General Theory of Action* II. iii. 143 A compulsive fixation on *time-allocation is a familiar phenomenon. *a* **1628** F. GREVIL *Sidney* xv. (1652) 199 Those *time-authorized assemblies. **1976** P. R. WHITE *Planning for Public Transport* vi. 123 The classification of *time-based, mileage-based and peak-vehicle-based costs.. was adopted. **1729** SAVAGE *Wanderer* v. 44 *Time-batter'd Tow'rs frown awful in Decay. **1881** *Athenæum* 5 Mar. 342/3 To feel at once the important difference between a conductor and a *time-beater. **1592** SHAKS. *Ven. & Ad.* 24 A sommers day..wasted in such *time-beguiling sport. **1863** *Pilgr. over Prairies* II. 302 The grey and *timebent grandsire. *c* **1600** SHAKS. *Sonn.* lxxxii, Some fresher stampe of the *time bettering dayes. **1593** —— *Rich. II*, I. iii. 221 My oyle-dride Lampe, and *time-bewasted light. **1806** SURR *Winter in Lond.* I. 178 *Time-blanched locks. **1916** A. HUXLEY *Burning Wheel* 24 Some lover of an older day Has carved in *time-blurred lettering One word only:—'Alas'. **1628** GAULE *Pract. The. Panegyr.* 59 He *time-borne Sonne, got from eternitie. **1647** FULLER *Good Th. in Worse T.* (1841) 132 When we are *time-bound, place-bound, or person-bound. **1924** R. GRAVES *Mock Beggar Hall* 79 Neither eternal nor time-bound, Not certain, nor in change. **1978** *Dædalus* Summer 168 Our ideas about childhood..are very much time-bound and culture-bound. **1601** SIR W. CORNWALLIS *Ess.* II. xxxvi. (1631) 109 After comes the torture of the *time-breaking wheele. **1964** I. L. HOROWITZ *New Sociol.* i. 25 We can draw..upon the information available from the historian and the journalist to forge a *time-centered sociology. **1977** P. JOHNSON *Enemies of Society* iii. 33 Against this background of a time-centred religion, there were also solid economic reasons why the fulcrum of progress would shift northwards across the Alps. **1800** HURDIS *Fav. Village* 182 The *time-cleft arch Of ancient chantry. **1951** R. A. KNOX *Stimuli* i. 3 We force our *time-conditioned minds, once a year, into an artificial mood of expectancy. **1934** A. HUXLEY *Beyond Mexique Bay* 218 What causes a people..to become as acutely *time-conscious as the priestly mathematicians of the Maya Old Empire? **1962** J. GLENN in *Into Orbit* 43 All of us wear very exact watches... As you can see, we are extremely time-conscious during a mission. **1967** A. BATTERSBY *Network Analysis* (ed. 2) ix. 146 If we simply say that the project must be completed as quickly as possible, we have what is called a '*time constrained' network. **1979** *Jrnl. R. Soc. Arts* Dec. 9/1 Colleges will be asked..to specify the learning objectives which they wish to assess by time-constrained examination. **1890** *Proc. Soc. for Psychical Research* Dec. 654, I dropped my inquiries..for a period of about two years,..being over-freighted with *time-consuming duties. **1978** R. MITCHISON *Life in Scotland* viii. 161 There were a great many strenuous, unpleasant and time-consuming tasks to be done in any house. **1954** *Gloss. Highway Engin. Terms* (*B.S.I.*) 58 **Time controlled traffic signals*, signals in which the aspects are displayed for fixed periods which are determined by manual or time-clock adjustment of the controller. **1960** *Farmer & Stockbreeder* 23 Feb. 100/2 Light for time-controlled poultry-house lighting. **1971** P. C. SYLVESTER-BRADLEY in I. G. Gass et al. *Understanding Earth* ix. 124/1 Evolution is a time-controlled process. **1923** L. HUGHES in *Crisis* (N.Y.) Feb. 174/2 When Susanna Jones wears red, A queen from some *time-dead Egyptian night Walks once again. *a* **1617** HIERON *Wks.* (1620) I. 10 Idle loyterers..or *time-deluding triflers. **1955** O. KLEIN in W. Pauli *Niels Bohr* 113 We need a *time-dependent operator. **1974** J. W. DRAKE in Carlile & Skehel *Evolution in Microbial World* 53 When *E. coli* is maintained in the chemostat, mutant accumulation is generation-dependent when growth is limited by glucose, but becomes time-dependent when growth is limited by amino acids. **1742** MRS. DELANY in *Life & Corr.* (1861) II. 198 Accustomed to the many hurries and *time-devouring accidents of this huge place. **1836** H. COLERIDGE *North. Worthies* Introd. (1852) 17 To..run his eye along the *time-discoloured pages. **1922** JOYCE *Ulysses*

238 Stephen Dedalus watched..the lapidary's fingers prove a *timedulled chain. **1548** UDALL, etc. *Erasm. Par. John* xi. 80 Not..that it is an uncouth or a *time duryng thyng to me. **1831** POE *City in Sea* i, *Time-eaten towers that tremble not. **1839** BAILEY *Festus* xi. (1852) 142 Now go I forth again.. Upon my *time-enduring pilgrimage. **1936** DYLAN THOMAS *Twenty-five Poems* 38 Now Jack my fathers let the *time-faced crook..Sneak down the stallion grave. **1613** DANIEL *Coll. Hist. Eng.* (1626) 33 The King..was no *time-giuer vnto growing dangers. **1863** HAWTHORNE *Our Old Home* (1879) 162 A gray, *time-gnawn, ponderous, shadowy structure. **1749** W. COLLINS in R. Dodsley *Collection of Poems* IV. 65 Where..some *time-hallow'd pile, Or up-land fallows grey Reflect it's last cool gleam. **1959** J. L. AUSTIN *Sense & Sensibilia* (1962) vi. 61 His wholesale acceptance of the traditional, time-hallowed, and disastrous manner of expounding them [*sc.* arguments]. **1974** DAWA NORBU *Red Star over Tibet* i. 30 The nomads were given a time-hallowed concoction. **1953** *Physical Rev.* XCI. 740/1 Initial and final currents that are *time-independent with respect to different reference systems. **1970** G. K. WOODGATE *Elem. Atomic Struct.* ii. 14 The value of *E'* has to be found from eq. (2.22)..which is a time-independent eigenvalue equation. **1934** T. S. ELIOT *Rock* i. 7, I journeyed to London, to the *timekept City. **1674** N. FAIRFAX *Bulk & Selv.* 40 This *time-lasting World, and every while-being thing in it. **1947** PARTRIDGE *Usage & Abusage* 51/1 Turn those sentences into *to be* equivalents: 'To receive wounds is no fun'; 'To become a casualty is no fun'; 'To be wounded is no fun': crisp, clear-cut, single-action, *time-limited connotations. **1977** *Jrnl. R. Soc. Arts* CXXV. 462/2 The price he pays for that time-limited monopoly is to give up any other advantages which the usual rights of exclusive ownership..might otherwise confer on him. **1930** L. HUGHES in *Crisis* (N.Y.) July 235/1 Subdued and *time lost are the drums. **1888** E. CLODD *Story Creation* xi. 217 The rude..chant of the savage, *time-marked by yell and tamtam. **1864** HAWTHORNE *S. Felton* (1883) 265 The *time-measurer of one whose mortal life he had cut off. **1904** *Edin. Rev.* Jan. 200 The pendulum was..assigned its function as a time-measurer. **1890** W. JAMES *Princ. Psychol.* I. xiv. 557 The *time-measuring psychologists of recent days have tried their hand at this problem. **1959** *Publ. Mod. Lang. Assoc. Amer.* LXXIV. 589/2 Music—or at least music with bar-lines—is precisely a time-measuring notation; it divides the time into equal intervals. **1974** tr. *Wertheim's Evolution & Revolution* 363 The relatively rapid and consistent process of evolution—slow as it was in terms of time-measuring as applied by mankind. **1615** BRATHWAIT *Strappado* (1878) 109 My *Time-noting lines ayme not at thee. **1647** TRAPP *Comm. Luke* xiv. 7 Ministers, though they may not be time-servers, yet they must be *time-observers. **1945** AUDEN *Coll. Poetry* 12 These only feared another kind of Death To which the *time-obsessed are all condemned. **1951** S. SPENDER *World within World* 137 No wonder that the literature of this period is time-obsessed, time-tormented, as though beaten with rods of restless days. **1861** J. R. LOWELL *Washers of Shroud* in *Poems* (1912) 476 The *time-old web of the implacable Three. **1922** D. H. LAWRENCE *England, my England* 8 The wide, black, time-old chimney. **1601** SHAKS. *Twel. N.* II. iii. 160 The diu'll a Puritane that hee is, or any thing constantly but a *time-pleaser. **1607** —— *Cor.* III. i. 45 Time-pleasers. **1886** HARDY *Mayor of Casterbridge* I. ix. 110 The bow-windows protruded like bastions, necessitating a pleasing *chassez-déchassez* movement to the *time-pressed pedestrian at every few yards. **1920** A. S. EDDINGTON *Space, Time & Gravit.* ii. 31 Observers with different motions use different space- and *time-reckoning. **1964** L. MACNEICE *Astrol.* iv. 112 The skies were observed..for the old time-reckoning reasons. **1806** J. GRAHAME *Birds Scot.* 74 In some vacant niche, Or *time-rent crevice. **1936** T. S. ELIOT *Burnt Norton* in *Coll. Poems 1909–35* 188 A flicker Over the strained *time-ridden faces. **1639** FULLER *Holy War* v. xxix. 279 How would a Herald sweat with scouring over these *time-rustie titles. **1838** J. S. MILL in *London & Westm. Rev.* Aug. 469 The inconsistencies and absurdities of *time-sanctioned opinions and institutions. **1873** HAMERTON *Intell. Life* IV. i. (1876) 135 The best *time-savers. **1891** A. JAMES *Diary* 24 June (1965) 216 A restricted nature, not admirable or generous in its impulses, but highly practical and *time saving. **1960** *Farmer & Stockbreeder* 15 Mar. 140/2 The light tractor with all the features for time-saving. **1977** *Listener* 10 Nov. 607/2 The amounts that air travellers would be willing to pay for the time-savings that it [*sc.* Concorde] made possible. **1982** R. LUDLUM *Parsifal Mosaic* xiv. 215 It's basically an economic, time-saving decision. **1900** *Daily Express* 13 June 5/2 All the men..at the bureaus for *time-served soldiers. **1960** *Times* 18 Feb. 3/3 Only time-served engineers..will be considered. **1979** *Navy News* Feb. 9/1 To say that every seaman is a good seaman by virtue of being a time-served man would be very much open to question. **1340** *Ayenb.* 36 þe *time-zettere ontrewe... Vor hire *time-zettinge hi destrueþ and makeþ beggeres þe kny3tes. **1949** DYLAN THOMAS in *Botteghe Oscure* IV. 399, I who hear..the notes on this *time-shaken Stone. **1794** COLERIDGE *Monody Death Chatterton* ad fin., Sweet Harper of *time-shrouded Minstrelsy. **1670** G. H. *Hist. Cardinals* I. I. 12 Those impertinent *time-spenders, the Priests. **1509** HAWES *Past. Pleas.* xliv. (Percy Soc.) 215 Eyther hell or heaven, wythout lesynge, Alway he getteth in his *tyme spendynge. **1835** W. C. BRYANT in *N.Y. Mirror* 19 Sept. 92/1 How the *time-stained walls That earthquakes shook not from their poise, appear To shiver. **1904** W. S. KENNEDY *Walt Whitman's Diary in Canada* p. v, The transcribing of these out-door notes from the worn and time-stained fragments of paper. **1799** CAMPBELL *Pleas. Hope* II. 224 The *time-taught spirit, pensive not severe. **1930** *Times Lit. Suppl.* 10 July 566/3 The kind of faith which cheerfully believes things about the East which *time-tested experience has proved to be untrue. **1977** *Daily Express* 29 Jan. 7/1, I will defend..the right of the ingenious and time-tested Mr. [Peter] Hall to spend my taxes any way his fancy takes him. **1947** AUDEN *Age of Anxiety* v. 125 Transpose our plight like a poignant theme Into twenty tongues, *time-tormented But His People still. **1951** Time-tormented [see *time-obsessed* adj. above]. **1870** RUSKIN *Lect. Art* i. (1875) 28 Faithful servant of *time-tried principles. **1962** W. B. THOMPSON *Introd. Plasma Physics* vii. 151 A particle going past a point target at a distance *l* produces a *time-varying field at the target. **1981** *Word 1980* XXXI. 172 The time-varying spectral pattern of the processed stimuli differed radically from that of the natural speech. **1814** SCOTT *Ld. of Isles* I. Introd. iv, Through fields *time-wasted, on sad inquest bound. **1661** BAXTER *Last Work Believer* Wks. (1846) 253 She was a stranger to pastimes, and no companion for *time-wasters. **1930** J. BAILEY *Let.* 5 Apr. (1935) 311 All these new inventions are time wasters for people like you and me. **1980** M. DRABBLE *Middle Ground* 118 Sally was a moaner and a timewaster. **1845** GEO. ELIOT *Let.* c 16 Apr. (1954) I. 187, I am..full of hope that..I shall be able to ward off these *time-wasting visitations. **1853** C. M. YONGE *Heir of Redclyffe* I. xv. 258 Abstaining from the time-wasting that might have tempted him if he had had plenty of money to spend. **1976** S. R. SIMPSON *Land Law & Registration* viii. 144 Sporadic survey is expensive and time-wasting. **1981** 'J. ROSS' *Dark Blue & Dangerous* x. 58 The time-wasting had gone on long enough. **1741–2** GRAY *Agrippina* 139 The slacken'd sinews of *time-wearied age. *c* **1611** CHAPMAN *Iliad* VIII. 454 To warn the youth, yet short of war, and *time-white fathers.

60. a. Special combs.: **time-and-motion**, used *attrib.* to designate a study, person, etc., concerned with the measurement of the efficiency of an industrial or other operation; **time-attack** (*Fencing*) = *time-thrust*; **time-average** *Physics* and *Math.*, an average evaluated over a period of time; hence **time-averaged** *a.*; **time-barred** *a.*, disqualified or invalid by reasons of arriving or being presented after the expiry of a statutory time-limit; **time-bill**, (*a*) a time-table of trains, etc.; (*b*) a record kept by the guard of a train of the time it leaves each station; **time-book**, (*a*) a book in which an entry is made of the time worked by employees; (*b*) a chronicle (cf. Ger. *zeitbuch*); (*c*) = *time-bill* (*a*); **time-candle** (see quot.); **time capsule**, a container used to store for posterity a selection of objects thought to be representative of life at a particular time; also *fig.*; **time-card**, (*a*) a card on which a record is kept of time worked; (*b*) a card time-table; **time-catch**, in a photographic camera, a catch which retains the shutter for a fixed time; **time-catcher**, in *Fencing*, one who 'takes the time': see 21; **time-change**, (*a*) change that takes place with the passage of time; (*b*) the difference in standard time between widely separated localities, as experienced by travellers; **time-charter** (see quot. 1891); *v. trans.*, to hire (a vessel) under a time-charter agreement; **time check**, (*a*) *Canad.*, a chit from a foreman stating the number of hours for which a man is due to be paid; (*b*) the act of ascertaining or stating the exact time; **time-clause** *Gram.*, an adverbial clause of time, a temporal clause; **time clock**, (*a*) a clock with a mechanism for recording the time on time-cards pressed into it; (*b*) a clock which can be set to switch an appliance on or off at specified times; **time-constant** *Electr.* the time taken by an exponentially varying quantity to change by a factor $1 - 1/e$ (approximately 0.6321), regarded as a parameter of the system in which the variation occurs; more widely, a time taken as representative of the speed of response of a system; **time-course** *Naut.*, (*a*) a ship's run, as in a fog, calculated by the vessel's speed, the time occupied, and the direction; (*b*) the period of time in which something happens, the length of time taken; **time-curve** (see quot.); **time-delay** = *time-lag*; used chiefly *attrib.* of a mechanism, system, etc., into the operation of which a time-lag has been deliberately introduced; **time deposit** (orig. *U.S.*), a sum placed in a bank at interest and not to be drawn before a set maturity date; **time derivative** *Physics* and *Math.*, a derivative of a variable with respect to time; **time-detector**, a clock (stationary at a point) or watch (carried by the watchman) having additional mechanism, operated by the watchman, to show the times at which he was at certain points of his round (Knight *Dict. Mech.* 1877): cf. TELL-TALE 2 g; also called *time-watch*; **time difference**, (*a*) the difference between the lengths of time taken by different operations or processes; (*b*) the difference in standard time between widely separated localities; **time differential**, (*a*) = *time difference* (b) above; (*b*) the difference in the length of time taken by a process in different places or at different stages; **time dilatation** or **dilation** *Physics*, the apparent slowing down of the passage of time in a frame of reference moving relative to the observer, a relativistic effect analogous to the increase in mass and the Lorentz contraction of length; **time-disc**, an instrument used in conjuction with the kymograph for investigating the time-sense; **time-distance**, used *attrib.* of the relation (*esp.* as expressed in graphs) between time and distance; **time division** *Telecommunication*, allocation of transmission time to each of a number of signals in quick rotation, so that all can be transmitted over the same channel if the sampling rate is sufficiently high; usu. *attrib.*; **time-element**, (*a*) time conceived as the natural element of temporal beings; (*b*) time as a factor to be taken into consideration; **time-expired** *a.*, (*a*) whose term of engagement has expired; also of convicts: whose term of sentence has expired; (*b*) of perishable goods: of which the term of safe storage (before sale or use) has expired; **time-exposure** *Photogr.*, exposure for a regulated time, as distinguished from instantaneous exposure; so **time-exposed** *a.*; † **time-fellow**, a contemporary; **time-frame**, a limited and established period of time during which an event, etc., took place or is planned to take place; a schedule; **time-globe**, a terrestrial globe rotated once in twenty-four hours by a clock-movement, and encircled at the equator by a stationary graduated zone, showing the local time at any meridian; **time-lag**, the length of time separating two correlated physical phenomena; **time lapse**, lapse of time; *spec.* (usu. with hyphen) *attrib.*, designating or pertaining to a technique of taking a sequence of photographs at set intervals to record changes that take place slowly over time; **time-line**, (*a*) *pl.* a certificate of apprenticeship (see LINE *sb.*^{2} 23 f); (*b*) an undulating line indicating small fractions of a second, by which the time or rate of some process may be measured; (*c*) a schedule, a deadline; **time-lock**, a lock with clockwork attachment which prevents its being unlocked until a set time; **time machine**, an imaginary machine capable of transporting a person backwards or forwards in time; **time-marker**, (*a*) an automatic device in a cab, etc., which registers the time it is in use, with the fare payable; (*b*) *Electr.* (see quot. 1902); **time-notice**, a notice given a definite time before; **time-of-flight** *a. Physics*, designating techniques and apparatus that depend on the time taken by particles to traverse a set distance, e.g. in the separation of ions according to their mass; **time-payment**, (*a*) payment by instalments; (*b*) payment on the basis of time worked; **time pencil**, a type of delayed-action firing-switch or detonator for setting off explosive devices; **time-policy** (see quot. 1848); **time-rate**, (*a*) rate in time; (*b*) rate of payment on the basis of time worked; **time-recorder**, an apparatus which records the time of an act or event; **time-release** *a.* = *slow-release* adj. (b) s.v. SLOW *a.* 16 d; **time-resolved** *a. Chem.* and *Physics*, produced by or pertaining to a spectroscopic technique in which the spectrum is obtained at known times after excitation; **time reversal** *Physics*, a transformation in which the passage of time (and so all velocities) is imagined to be reversed; ***time reversal invariance***, invariance of laws of nature under this transformation, so that all processes allowed by them are also allowable when all motions in them are reversed; so **time-reverse** *v. trans.*, to subject to time reversal; **time-reversed** *a.*; **time-sampling**, the collection of data or observation of events at given times or intervals or within given periods of time; **time-scale**, (the relative length of) the period of time in which a sequence of events takes place, the successive stages of a process, operation, etc.; a representation or exposition of the stages of such a sequence, etc.; **time-series**, (*a*) the sequence of events which constitutes or is measured by time; (*b*) a series of values of some quantity obtained at successive times (often with equal intervals between them); ***time-series analysis***, the statistical analysis of such series; **time-sheet**, a time-table (on a sheet); the paper on which are entered the names of workers and the hours worked by them; **time-shutter**, in the photographic camera, a shutter for time-exposures; **time-sight** *Naut.*, an observation of the altitude of the sun or a star for the purpose of ascertaining the time and, hence, the longitude (*Cent. Dict.*); **time-signal**, (*a*) a visible or audible signal made at an observatory, etc., to announce the exact time, e.g. the fall of a time-ball, or firing of a time-gun; (*b*) a signal transmitted to indicate the exact time of day, *esp.* that broadcast by the BBC at certain hours; **time-signature** *Mus.*, a sign placed at the beginning of a piece of music, or where the time changes, to show the measure or rhythm; rhythmical signature; **time slice**, (*a*) a short period in the continuum of time; (*b*) *Computers*, each of the short intervals of time during which a computer or its central processor deals uninterruptedly with one user or program, before switching to another; so **time-slicing** *vbl. sb.*, the division of processor running time into a succession of short intervals that are allocated in turn to different users or programs; **time slot**, (*a*) a portion of time allocated to a purpose or person, *esp.* to an individual broadcast programme; (*b*) *Computers*, = *time slice* (b) above; **times table**, a multiplication table; cf. sense 19 above; **time-stamp**, a mechanical device for stamping letters, tickets, etc., with the date and time of receipt; hence as *v. trans.*; **time-stamped** *ppl. a.*; **time step**, an even-timed basic tap-dancing step; **time study**, a time-and-motion study; the close observation of an industrial or other process with a view to time-saving alterations in procedure; also *attrib.*; **time switch**, a switch that acts automatically at a set time; **time-taker**, † (*a*) = TIME-SERVER 1; (*b*) one who takes a note of the time occupied in any work or course; **time-taking** *a.*, that takes time, leisurely, slow; **time term**, a term of an equation in which time is the main variable; **time-thrust** (*Fencing*), an offensive-defensive counter-stroke made within the time of the adversary's movement of attack, and preventing its completion; **time train** = *going train* s.v. TRAIN *sb.*[1] 15; **time travel** = *time-travelling* vbl. sb. below; also (hyphened) as *v. intr.*, **time-traveller**, one who practises time-travelling; **time-travelling** *vbl. sb.*, the imagined activity of travelling into the past or future, hypothetical movement through time; also *fig.* and as *ppl. a.* (also = 'extending through time'); **time trial**, a test of individual speed over a set distance, a race in which competitors are separately timed; **time-value** *Mus.*, the relative duration of a note; **time wage** (see quot. 1892); **time-waiter**, one who awaits a favourable turn of events; cf. TIDE-WAITER 2; **time warp** *Science fiction*, a distortion of space-time that is conceived as causing or enabling a person to remain stationary in time or to travel backwards or forwards in time; also (with hyphen) as *v. trans.*, to transport in a time warp; **time-watch** = *time-detector*; **timewise** *adv.*, with regard to time; **time-work**, work which is paid for on the basis of the time occupied; distinguished from *piece-work*; so **time-worker**; **time-zone**, any one of the twenty-four divisions of the surface of the globe (each bounded by two meridian lines), within each of which the standard time adopted is the mean solar time of the meridian distant from Greenwich a number of complete hours (strictly, an improper designation, for the regions so bounded are not *zones* in the orig. sense). See also TIME-BALL, -BARGAIN, -WORN, etc.

1932 C. REYNOLDS *Production Planning* ix. 87 (*heading*) *Time and motion studies. **1959** *Listener* 5 Nov. 762/2 That sinister figure, the man with the stop-watch, the time-and-motion expert, disliked by union men the world over. **1966** *Punch* 20 July 127/1 Time-and-motion study techniques, applied to American office workers, enable employers to reorganise office procedures and streamline routine chores. **1973** M. WOODHOUSE *Blue Bone* vi. 61 We have decided to divide the job according to the best work-study, time-and-motion principles. **1980** *Daily Tel.* 11 Sept. 29 (Advt.), Knowledge of..time and motion studies is very advantageous. **1889** DUNN *Fencing* 62 '*Time' attacks, whereby, having anticipated in what line your opponent's attack will be delivered, you intercept his blade as he gives in his attack. **1875** *Encycl. Brit.* III. 39/1 In a material system in a state of stationary motion the *time-average of the kinetic energy is equal to the time-average of the virial. **1914** *Phil. Mag.* XXVIII. 826 The ratios have been calculated using the time-average values. **1965** PHILLIPS & WILLIAMS *Inorg. Chem.* I. i. 11 Time-average potential and kinetic energies. **1946** *Time-averaged [see *space-averaged* adj. s.v. SPACE *sb.*[1] 20]. **1957** *Financial Times* 23 Mar. 4/3, I would appreciate advice..whether such a claim is now *time-barred or not. **1971** *E. Afr. Standard* (Nairobi) 10 Apr. 1/3 The fourth car in the Datsun 240Z team..was time-barred at Korogwe. **1978** *Observer* 4 June 16/6 Employees must make their claim..within six months of ceasing work. Failure to do this results in employees being 'time-barred'. **1847** (July 1) *East. Counties & E. Union Railways* (*Railw. Mag.* Jan. 1910. 46) *Time bills of a prior date are not correct. **1858** SIMMONDS *Dict. Trade*, *Time-bill*, a time-table of the arrivals and departures of trains, omnibuses, steamers, &c. **1878** F. S. WILLIAMS *Midl. Railw.* 658 To ascertain the precise moment that the train clears certain stations, that he [the guard] may..chronicle the same in his time-bill. **1898** *Daily News* 19 Oct. 3/2 She looked down the timebill for a place a long way off, and seeing Blackpool and the distance it was off took a ticket for there. **1854** H. MILLER *Sch. & Schm.* xiii. (1858) 271, I still retained the *time-book in my master's behalf. **1867** tr. *Ewald's Hist. Israel* 92 Like a true time-book (or chronicle) terminated with the description of the most recent great deeds. **1877** KNIGHT *Dict. Mech.*, **Time-candle*, one in which the size and quality of the material and the wick are so regulated that a certain length will burn in a given time. **1938** *N.Y. Times* 19 Aug. 21 A record of the world of the present era..will be buried on the site of the World's Fair in the hope that it will give to historians 5,000 years hence a picture of the middle twentieth century... The record will be contained in a '*time capsule', a specially devised container of metallic alloy of high corrosion resistance. **1947** CAMPBELL & ROBINSON *Skeleton Key to 'Finnegans Wake'* 8 The *Wake*..is a huge time-capsule, a complete and permanent record of our age. **1965** *Christian Century* 27 Oct. 1313/1 With the cooperation of a hospital physician, the hospital administrator, a funeral director and a local commercial firm which happened to be building 'time capsules' or cryogenic (low temperature) storage units.. preparations were made for this pioneering effort. **1973** *Art Internat.* Mar. 56/1 This image of Venice, as a waterlogged time capsule, is very much the creation of outsiders. **1982** *Daily Tel.* 6 July 12/4 George Howard, the BBC chairman, is..asking around for corporation 'artefacts' to be sealed into an age-proof time capsule, so future generations may be able to discover the wonder of our broadcasting services. **1891** *Cent. Dict.*, **Time-card*. **1898** *Engineering Mag.* XVI. 41 Each workman perforates a five-minute time-card for each job on which he is employed, simply piercing the card at the five-minute points most nearly representing his times of beginning and ending. **1890** *Anthony's Photogr. Bull.* III. 383 The *time catch is on the other side, and by means of two slots and pins, is arranged so that it cannot fall backwards or forwards when not in use. **1753** CHAMBERS *Cycl. Supp.* s.v. *Binding*, The great objection made by some people, particularly those *time-catchers, against the frequent use of binding, is [etc.]. **1937** BLUNDEN *Elegy* 31 To haunt and cling To this one ground, whatever closed Of strange power, or *time-change. **1941** *Mind* L. 182 A person as a 'self' exhibits beside its individuality and its identity in time-change the peculiar character of self-assertion through vicissitudes. **1969** N. DENNY tr. *Veraldi's Spies of Good Intent* xi. 177 I'm suffering from the time-change. With me it's three in the morning. **1976** 'M. DELVING' *China Expert* i. 9 I'd been in Honolulu two days before, and when I got back to New York I'd forgotten about the time change. I lost eight hours. **1891** *Labour Commission* Gloss., **Time-charter*, an agreement under which the owner hires his vessel for a stipulated monthly payment, generally in advance, in which case the charterer loads and discharges the vessel. **1963** *Times* 10 June 21/5 The companion for our new ship will be time-chartered..until we decide about building another. **1974** *Information Handbk.* *1974–5* (Shell Internat. Petroleum Co.) 100 Ships time-chartered by Shell companies total 235 of 20·6 million dwt. **1911** *Daily Colonist* (Victoria, B.C.) 26 Apr. 2/4 He cashed a *time check after working a short time on a log drive. **1937** *Printer's Ink Monthly* May 45/1 *Time check*, synchronizing the time pieces of all concerned in a broadcast. **1968** M. WOODHOUSE *Rock Baby* xv. 149, I..got a time-check to correct my watch. **1887** C. B. GEORGE *40 Yrs. on Rail* 56 [He] pulled a wire leading to a *time-clock. **1930** *Engineering* 1 Aug. 130/1 Special terms for night service has encouraged the use of heat-storage ovens... In France, on weekdays, the luncheon interval lasts two hours, and that gives a pause in the factory power consumption which, with the aid of time-clocks, allows of a valuable heat storage period. **1943** Time-clock [see PUNCH *v.*[1] 3 d]. **1961** *Listener* 19 Oct. 629/3 Running costs also tend to be higher but a judicious use of time clocks can keep these in check. **1976** *Billings* (Montana) *Gaz.* 4 July 6-c/4, I am not the nine-to-five cat—couldn't punch a time clock if my life depended on it. **1869** LD. RAYLEIGH in *Phil. Mag.* XXXVIII. 4 There is for every conducting circuit a certain *time-constant which determines the rapidity of the rise or fall of currents, and which is proportional to the self-induction and conductivity of the circuit. Thus, to use Maxwell's notation,..the time-constant is $L/R = \tau$. **1892** O. LODGE *Lightning Conductors* xxvi. 297 A column shows the time taken for the current amplitude to decay to one-millionth of its initial value, *i.e.*, 14 times what is ordinarily called the 'time constant'. **1895** *Funk's Stand. Dict.*, Time-constant. **1902** SLOANE *Stand. Electr. Dict.*, *Time Constant*. (*a*) If..we divide the inductance in henries by the resistance in ohms, the ratio gives the time-constant of the circuit, or it expresses the time which it will take for the current to reach 0·63 of its final value. (*b*) In a static condenser the time required for the charge to fall to one 2·7183th part of its original value. **1943** *Electronic Engin.* XV. 346 The amplifier ..is a standard three-stage..circuit. The time constant of the stages is 6 seconds. **1962** A. NISBETT *Technique Sound Studio* v. 94 The PPM is a special type of voltmeter... It has a rapid rise characteristic (the BBC version has a time constant of 2·5 milliseconds; this gives 80% of full deflection in 4 milliseconds). **1977** *Nature* 1 Sept. 11/1 The radiative time constant is the time taken for a mass of air to warm up or cool by radiating in the infrared portion of the spectrum. **1971** *Jrnl. Gen. Psychol.* Jan. 38 The *time course for recovery from these effects was found to be slower for the subfusional stimulation effect than the suprafusional stimulation effect. **1977** J. L. HARPER *Population Biol. Plants* 678 The way in which the time course of the risk of death is related to the time course of producing offspring. **1909** *Cent. Dict. Suppl.*, **Time-curve*, a curve so plotted that one of its coördinates represents time, or periods of time. **1959** H. BARNES *Oceanography & Marine Biol.* 183 Instead of using a bottom release to start the camera, a *time-delay mechanism, set for the depth to which it is intended to work, is used. **1963** *Times* 15 Feb. 7/6 The levels from which different frequencies are reflected are thus obtained from the time-delay between outgoing pulse and received echo. **1978** *Tucson Mag.* Dec. 30/1 A digital time-delay system.. that brings 'concert hall sound' into the living room. By delaying the impulse coming out of the back speakers..by something under one one-thousandth of a second, this tiny wonder simulates the spatial quality of sound present in large auditoriums. **1851** C. CIST *Sk. Cincinnati in 1851* 90 Their policy of taking **time* deposits and allowing eight and ten per cent interest..[has] attracted public attention. **1930** J. M. KEYNES *Treatise on Money* II. xxiii. 7 In the United States the law requires that the amounts of Time Deposits and Demand Deposits respectively shall be separately published. **1982** *Bank of England Q. Bull.* Dec. 519/1 Sight deposits grew by 28% and time deposits by 30%. **1956** *Nature* 11 Feb. 267/1 The passage of electrolytic current through the first coil induces its *time-derivative in the second one. **1909** E. B. TITCHENER *Text-Bk. Psychol.* I. 134 In ordinary life, these *time-differences escape notice, so that we may regard two tastes as occurring together when really they occur in succession. **1953** [see CAPITALIZE *v.* 1 c]. **1981** 'W. HAGGARD' *Money Men* iii. 38 Seven-thirty from Schiphol and an hour for the flight. Time difference at the moment one hour. **1968** J. SANGSTER *Touchfeather* xi. 112 With the *time differential on my side, I was back in Los Angeles by three-thirty p.m. local time. **1974** tr. *Wertheim's Evolution & Revolution* i. 33 The differential in space-time between more or less parallel processes in the past..might ..imply time differentials in future developments. **1980** L. ST. CLAIR *Obsessions* xvii. 291 Due to the time differential between New York and Paris, which he had left at sundown, he arrived at La Guardia shortly after 10 P.M. **1973** *Time dilatation [see RELATIVITY 2]. **1934** R. C. TOLMAN *Relativity, Thermodynamics & Cosmology* ii. 24 This *time dilation and the conclusions as to the setting of clocks..are to be regarded except for experimental difficulties as an entirely verifiable mutual property of systems of clocks in relative motion. **1968** *Guardian* 28 Dec. 9 After two years the spacecraft's velocity would be such for 'time dilation' to have an effect. In other words time would be slowing down on board the craft and, to those on board, a single lifetime would be longer than for those on earth. **1981** *Sci. Amer.* Feb. 108/1 The relativistic effect of time dilation prolongs the life of pions and kaons that are particularly energetic. **1901** E. B. TITCHENER *Exper. Psychol.* I. x. 338 The most useful appliance for investigation is, probably, Meumann's 'time-sense' apparatus, consisting of Baltzar kymograph, *time-disc, set of contacts, and sound-hammers. **1936** *Time-distance [see P III 3]. **1965** *Math. in Biol. & Med.* (Med. Res. Council) v. 230 The question whether short distances are correlated with short times is represented by the third degree of freedom, the interaction of the table, and for this reason this component can be referred to as a space-time, or time-distance, interaction. **1905** *Time-division [see SKIDDAVIAN *a.*]. **1938** *Proc. IRE* XXVI. 56 Many proposals have been offered for multiplexing. These divide naturally into two major categories: (1) frequency division and (2) time division. *Ibid.* 57 The major disadvantage of time-division multiplex..is that provision must always be made to insure accurate timing of the channel assignments. **1947** [see QUANTIZATION b]. **1975** D. G. FINK *Electronics Engineers' Handbk.* XXII. 35 In time-division multiplexing message information from many channels is sampled briefly in time sequence. **1831** CARLYLE *Sart. Res.* III. viii, Pierce through the *Time-element, glance into the Eternal. **1936** J. M. KEYNES *Gen. Theory Employment* xxii. 317 The explanation of the *time-element* in the trade cycle. **1979** D. ANTHONY *Long Hard Cure* ix. 77 The time element fits... You heard the shot about nine forty-five. That gave him half an hour. **1885** SIR H. GREEN in *Pall Mall G.* 14 Feb. 2/1 *Time-expired soldiers in India will not, as a rule, re-enter the ranks. **1931** *Times Lit. Suppl.* 21 May 402/4 The kindly Egyptian prince who..helped time-expired convicts to find honest employment. **1972** *Times* 17 Oct. 14/7 Return of time-expired stock like sausages and yoghurt. **1973** [see HOT-HOUSE, HOTHOUSE *sb.* 3 b]. **1974** *Ciba Symposium* XX. 253 Those of us who have used 'time-expired' human blood from blood banks in culture media have frequently found that some batches are highly toxic to trypanosomes. **1889** *Anthony's Photogr. Bull.* II. 79 To level your camera when taking *time-exposed pictures and hence get straight lines. **1893** J. A. HODGES *Elem. Photogr.* (1907) 18 A tripod stand will be required..when '*time' exposures are given. **1899** A. B. LLOYD in *Daily News* 9 Jan. 2/3, I couldn't give a time exposure, as the pigmies would not stand still. **1577** HARRISON *England* I. xviii. (1880) 131 My *Synchroni* or *time fellows can reape at this present great commoditie in a little roome. **1638** CHILLINGW. *Relig. Prot.* I. vi. §23. 340 The disinterested time-fellowes or immediate Successors of Liberius. **1964** *Sunday Times* 5 July 14/4 All three considerations argue for abandoning the artificial *time-frame which the Johnson Administration has now set. **1969** *Ottawa Commons Debates* 24 July 11573/1 In a timeframe of less than seven decades in length,..man has ceased to remain earthbound. **1976** 'R. B. DOMINIC' *Murder out of Commission* xx. 179 Somebody had..shot him. The time frame was pretty well established: between twelve o'clock, when he had phoned the desk, the twelve fifteen, when Ben and Tony arrived. **1980** D. BLOODWORTH *Trapdoor* xii. 71 It's right outside our brief, and our time-frame would not allow it. **1983** *Listener* 16 June 37/2 The time-frame is one intense, meandering weekend. **1862** *Cat. Internat. Exhib., Brit.* II. No. 5516 *Time globe, planetary clock. **1892** O. J. LODGE *Lightning Conductors* vii. 48 Lord Rayleigh..thinks these induced peripheral currents competent to explain magnetic *time-lag in every case. **1939** *John o' London's* 7 Apr. 46/2 There is often a necessary time-lag between discovery and application. **1979** *Bull. Amer. Acad. Arts & Sci.* Mar. 40 Even if it were granted that a given intervention would..produce a given result..there would inevitably be time lags..which would diminish the efficacy of the remedy. **1937** *Mind* XLVI. 169 The duration which will be indicated as a '*time-lapse' in the standard clock which S carries. **1937** *Discovery* June 192/1 Experimenters in time-lapse photography and nature photography in general. **1956** *Kenyon Rev.* XVIII. 418 The time-lapse between any two primary stresses tends to be the same irrespective of the number of syllables and the junctures between them. **1957** [see HIGH-SPEED *a.*]. **1957** *New Scientist* 19 Sept. 14/1 The study of living cells by time-lapse cinematography... Special ciné-cameras are used to take microphotographs..at the rate of about eight photographs per minute. **1974** *Sci. Amer.* Apr. 123/2 In that industrial valley, the time-lapse photographs show, exposure from A.D. 1702 up to 1908 induced only light damage. **1983** *Listener* 3 Nov. 35/3 Time-lapse, slow-motion, stop frame, microscopic, infra-red and underwater techniques are part of the stock-in-trade of the TV wildlife producer. **1890** W. JAMES *Princ. Psychol.* I. iii. 86 Another electric pen..traces alongside the former line a '*time-line' of which each undulation or link stands for a certain fraction of a second. **1895** *Daily News* 5 Dec. 2/2 The masters, it is admitted, would be acting quite within their powers if they refuse to grant the apprentices their time lines. **1898** *Allbutt's Syst. Med.* V. 814 No pulse is regular, as a time line at the foot of a sphygmographic tracing will prove. **1967** *Sci. Year* 51 The *time line* (sequence of the mission) and trajectory of the specific mission are analyzed. **1976** *New Yorker* 30 Aug. 59 They were well behind the timeline, for the ground had allotted only ten minutes to move from one experiment to the next. **1871** *Rep. Comm. Patents 1869* (U.S.) II. 224/2 **Time-Lock*... The combination of the shaft [etc.]. **1877** KNIGHT *Dict. Mech.*, *Time-lock*, a lock having clock-work attached which..

prevents the bolt being withdrawn when locked, until a certain interval of time has elapsed. **1908** *Daily Chron.* 10 June 7/1 The time-lock on the door of a bank's vaults makes it impossible for the bank's officers themselves to enter the strong room after closing-time. **1895** H. G. WELLS (*title*) The *time machine. **1944** C. DAY LEWIS *Poetry for You* ii. 12 *How Poetry Began.* To find this out, we'll have to jump into a Time Machine, put its gear-lever into reverse, and race backwards through many thousands of years into prehistoric time. **1960** *Guardian* 7 Oct. 16/4 Nigel and Wendy arrive by time-machine in the Garden of Eden. **1978** I. WATSON in C. Priest *Anticipations* 22 The assumption that a time machine should proceed to its destination *instanter* instead of at a snail's pace. **1898** *Westm. Gaz.* 11 Mar. 7/2 Five hundred cabs provided with the *time and fare marker were put on the stands. **1902** SLOANE *Stand. Electr. Dict.* Suppl., *Time-marker*, a light flexible stylus actuated by an electro-magnet in circuit with an electro-magnetic tuning-fork. It is used for recording tuning fork vibrations on a chronograph drum. **1902** *Westm. Gaz.* 7 Feb. 2/2 The Bill .. provides for a *time-notice of seven years to the holders of licences to sell liquor for consumption on the premises. **1908** *Ibid.* 23 Mar. 2/3 The Government proposal.. gives a fourteen years' time-notice for licences which until 1904 were granted for one year only. **1945** H. D. SMYTH *Gen. Acct. Devel. Atomic Energy Mil. Purposes* xii. 131 One elegant scheme for studying the effects of neutrons of a single, arbitrarily-selected velocity is the '*time of flight' method. **1948** S. A. GOUDSMIT in *Physical Rev.* LXXIV. 622/2 (*heading*) A time-of-flight mass spectrometer. **1969** EGELSTAFF & POOLE *Exper. Neutron Thermalisation* iv. 74 Measuring the velocity of the scattered neutrons by the time-of-flight technique. **1975** *McGraw-Hill Yearbk. Sci. & Technol.* 189/2 Both types exceed a mass resolution $M/\Delta M$ of 1000,.. and in addition the time-of-flight version is completely free of artifacts. **1898** *Daily News* 5 Dec. 6/6 This *time payment system is far too much bother for me, and I look on it as undignified for our trade. **1927** *Ladies' Home Jrnl.* Dec. 45/2 Chrysler dealers are in a position to extend the convenience of time-payments. **1955** *Times* 25 Aug. 6/6 The Government had been greatly concerned at the rapid expansion of time payment and hire purchase and its effects upon the economy. **1955** J. THOMAS *No Banners* xix. 171 Two sticks of plastic, a primer bound with a length of instantaneous fuse, and a ten-minute *time pencil. **1977** J. HUTCHISON *That Drug Danger* xi. 88/1 Having pressed the time pencil which set off the explosive a quarter of an hour or one or two hours later. **1848** ARNOULD *Mar. Insur.* I. v. (1866) I. 219 A *time policy is one in which the limits of the risk are designated only by certain fixed periods of time. **1895** KENNEDY in *Law Times Rep.* LXXII. 861/1 The policy is a time policy for six months from the 9th Jan. 1894 to the 8th July 1894. **1882** MINCHIN *Unipl. Kinemat.* 60 The *time-rate of description of area round the fixed centre is constant in all positions of the moving point. **1902** ELIZ. L. BANKS *Newspaper Girl* 263 We always pay the expenses and time rates when you go off on a job like that. **1898** *Engin. Mag.* XVI. 41 Workmen use a mechanical *time-recorder requiring the vibration of a lever on entering and leaving the shop. **1977** H. J. EYSENCK *You & Neurosis* iv. 135 They were told that this was a peripheral-acting *time-release muscle-relaxant known to be effective. **1980** *Holistic Health News* Sept./Oct. 2/1 This treatment is called 'Magnetroph' and was developed by Dr. Ernest Pescetti, renowned as 'the father of the time-release principle'. **1956** *Nature* 4 Feb. 222 (*caption*) Optical arrangement for spectrochemical analyses with *time-resolved spectra. **1977** *Ibid.* 17 Feb. 659/2 (*heading*) Time-resolved resonance Raman spectroscopy of bacteriorhodopsin. [**1922** I. FISHER *Making of Index Numbers* iv. 64 The *time reversal test... The index number reckoned forward should be the reciprocal of that reckoned backward.] **1955** *Proc. Glasgow Conf. Nucl. & Meson Physics 1954* VIII. 341 The superselection rule on the parity of spinor-particle number is derived from a consideration which does not depend on double time-reversal. **1958** *Physical Rev.* CX. 783/2 We see that at least one prediction of time reversal invariance is very well fulfilled. **1979** *Sci. Amer.* June 116/3 The discovery of an electric dipole moment of the neutron would reveal a violation of the physical principle known as time-reversal symmetry. **1971** *Ibid.* Dec. 97/1 *Time-reverse all motions and the three will return at the same instant to the starting point. **1962** M. A. PRESTON *Physics of Nucleus* xvi. 475 The wave function of a *time-reversed state is obtained by taking the complex conjugate of the wave function of the original state and reversing all spin directions. **1981** T. D. LEE *Particle Physics & Introd. Field Theory* xiii. 283 If the T-invariant classical system consists of a large number of particles, although the time-reversed sequence is always possible, it is in general improbable. **1960** J. B. CARROLL in *Encycl. Educ. Research* (ed. 3) 746/1 Careful *time-sampling and situation-sampling designs seem to be in order if one wants purely normative or 'typical' data. **1973** *Jrnl. Genetic Psychol.* Sept. 99 Time sampling has been demonstrated to be an effective observational technique. **1979** J. JAFFE et al. in Aaronson & Rieber *Psycholinguistic Research* 404 Assume the two states are digitized as 'one' or 'two' by discrete time sampling at intervals that must be shorter than the expected minimum time the system spends in any state. **1890** W. JAMES *Princ. Psychol.* I. ix. 283 We make a solid wooden frame with the sentence written on its front, and the *time-scale on one of its sides. **1923** N. SHAW *Air & its Ways* v. 46 The time-scale of the operations which tend to cause deviation is so large that the course of the operations escapes observation. **1934** *Discovery* Aug. 227/1 The constructing of a geological and meteorological time-scale for the Southern Hemisphere. **1958** F. E. ZEUNER *Dating Past* 5 All these studies aiming at the establishment of absolute time-scales for the past are comprised by the term *Geochronology*. **1972** *Country Life* 23 Mar. 672/2 The timescale of planning is a long one. **1979** *Jrnl. R. Soc. Arts* CXXVII. 409/1 We must also bear in mind the timescale involved in exploitation of oil and gas discoveries. **1892** J. ROYCE *Spirit Mod. Philos.* 431 This transcending of a *time-series.. is in fact what one might call the soul of the natural order. **1919** *Rev. Econ. Statistics* Apr. 123/2, *x* and *y* represent the deviations of the items of two time series from their respective linear secular trends. **1928** *Jrnl. Amer. Statistical Assoc.* XXIII. 407 The inferential possibilities of time series analysis are contingent upon segregating from the specific historical the repeatable, recurrent element. **1978** *Nature* 19 Oct. 630/2 The resulting time series is then smoothed by using a 13-month running mean average to remove seasonal variations. **1979** *Daily Tel.* 6 July 16 He has confirmed his original time series analysis with a more recent cross-sectional study. **1979** J. HICKS *Causality in Economics* v. 64 There are two kinds of time-series, with different kinds of time reference. In one of them each item relates to a point of time, in the other to a period. **1893** *Westm. Gaz.* 7 July 5/1 An elegantly printed *time-sheet had been laid on the table for the use of the Duke and Princess. **1907** *Daily Chron.* 3 May 9/2 A light folding quarter-plate camera, with good lens, *time and instantaneous shutter. **1853** *Rep. Brit. Assoc. Adv. Sci. 1852* II. 131 On the 5th of August 1852, the first *time-signal passed; .. the clock at Greenwich.. originates the signals. **1862** *Monthly Notices R. Astron. Soc.* XXII. 119 At any time, day or night, when the wire is not wanted for ordinary work, London can receive time-signals from Liverpool every minute. **1877** KNIGHT *Dict. Mech.* s.v., The electro-magnetic telegraph has been used for operating time-signals..; thus, the Greenwich time is indicated at Liverpool.. by the dropping of a ball. **1923** [see NEWS *sb.* (*pl.*) 5 c]. **1972** P. LIVELY *Driftway* v. 59 Through the atmospherics there came the time-signal, and then a man reading the news. **1875** STAINER & BARRETT *Dict. Mus. Terms* s.v. *Signature*, There are two kinds of signature, the *time signature and the key-signature... It would be more proper to call the time-signature the measure sign, as it shows the contents of a bar, but not the pace at which the music should be performed. **1965** *Language* XLI. 193 To the comparativists of the 1870's.. a 'synchronic' view could be nothing more than taking a relatively thin *time-slice and doing the best one can with it. **1973** MURRILL & SMITH *Introd. Computer Sci.* i. 31 A user receives the processor's undivided attention for one time slice but then receives no attention over the next three time slices. **1981** *Kilobaud Microcomputing* June 35/2 At the end of the current user's time slice, he is put on hold by the scheduler, and the next user gets to run his program. **1967** J. MARTIN *Design of Real-Time Computer Systems* 628/2 (Index), *Time-slicing. **1978** W. S. DAVIES *Information Processing Systems* xv. 328 The whole purpose of the time-slicing approach.. is to prevent any single user from dominating the system at the expense of everyone else. **1962** *Time slot [see *programme planning* s.v. PROGRAM, PROGRAMME *sb.* 4]. **1967** J. MARTIN *Design of Real-Time Computer Systems* ix. 130 When the time-slot.. for one user ends, it may be necessary to bring in a completely new set of data and programs for the next user. **1979** *Arizona Daily Star* 5 Aug. I. 7/5 It.. will be interesting to learn what the viewer response is to a program concept of this dimension when aired at an odd afternoon time slot. **1980** PUŽMAN & POŘIZEK *Communication Control in Computer Networks* iii. 168 Time division multiplexing means that a certain time slot is to be assigned for a station for the time during which it can exchange data with another station. **1982** 'W. R. DUNCAN' *Queen's Messenger* vi. 49 People were units to be fitted into Sir John's available time slots. **1960** N. HILLIARD *Maori Girl* I. ii. 14 Netta was supposed to learn her words and the older ones their *times-tables. **1983** *Cotswold Life* Nov. 19/1 Here the infants practised wobbly letters, began to chant the Times Tables, and spilt paint water all over the floor. **1984** *Reader's Digest* Jan. 81/2 Children.. slipping from ignorance to knowledge .., until one day finally they know their times tables. **1892** *Work* IV. 75/3 The *time-stamp is altered every minute. **1963** L. MEYNELL *Virgin Luck* viii. 181 Each slip is time-stamped as it comes from the telephonist who takes the bet. **1973** *Times* 6 Dec. 9/8 Waiter's [*sic*] checks are time-stamped on receipt... This way, the clerk knows exactly when each item was ordered. **1962** *Times* 16 Apr. 11/3 The 'limpet' meter for issuing *time-stamped tickets. **1929** *Time-step [see STOOGE *sb.* 1]. **1956** B. HOLIDAY *Lady sings Blues* (1973) iii. 32, I knew exactly two steps, the time step and the crossover. **1975** Time step [see PULL-BACK 1 d]. **1911** F. W. TAYLOR *Princ. Scientific Managem.* 75 A careful *time study of men working under these conditions will disclose facts which are ludicrous as well as pitiable. **1928** *Britain's Industrial Future* (Liberal Industr. Inquiry) III. xvi. 194 There should be means of revising rates.. in consultation, with all the facts and time-study figures on the table. **1944** *Jrnl. R. Aeronaut. Soc.* XLVIII. 257 Mr. Westbrook asked whether time study was used sufficiently to convince shop superintendents of the amount of labour necessary for any job. **1970** T. LUPTON *Managem. & Social Sci.* (ed. 2) i. 14 The organization as a whole, or at least those members of it with whom they have close contact, the supervisor, the time study man, and so on. **1979** J. HARVEY *Plate Shop* iii. 15 He was the best plater in the shop, and the Time Study would never believe he was working as fast as he could; and it was true, he always did work slow when studied, out of loyalty to his mates. **1902** *Specifications of Patents* (U.S. Patent Office) 14 Oct. 1560/1, I, William B. Coulter,.. have invented certain new and useful Improvements in *Time-Switches for Electric Lights. **1963** *Listener* 3 Jan. 47/1 Portable time-switches vary in elaborateness and price. *a* **1977** *Harrison Mayer Ltd. Catal.* 64/2 A time switch can be installed on any kiln. **1630–56** GORDON *Hist. Earld. Sutherld.* (1813) 325 That *tyme-takers wold be now easalie decerned from true freinds. **1867** LIVINGSTONE in Blaikie *Life* xix. (1910) 323 His time-taker had no conscience and could not be trusted. **1838** DICKENS *Nich. Nick.* i, Mr. Nickleby.. was a slow and *time-taking speaker. **1920** A. S. EDDINGTON *Space, Time & Gravit.* vi. 103 Leaving aside now the *time-term as sufficiently discussed, we consider the space-terms alone. **1974** *Nature* 15 Mar. 204/1 If.. the true P_n velocity is 8·0 km s^{-1}, then the average time terms are slightly reduced and the resulting crustal thickness estimates are about 5–10% lower. **1809** ROLAND *Fencing* 81 To leave his body exposed to receive, in the interim of his motion, a *time thrust. **1834** *Encycl. Brit.* (ed. 7) IX. 503 Time thrusts are so called because the success of these movements depends entirely upon their being executed at the exact moment of time employed by the adversary in planning or in executing his attack.. *Ibid., Passim.* **1889** *Fencing* (Badm. Libr.) 91 The time-thrust is an attack made with opposition on a complicated attack, and intended to intercept the line where such an attack is meant to finish. **1965** E. TUNIS *Colonial Craftsmen* vi. 146 Both the *time train and the striking train of a Terry clock are driven by weights wound up by a key. **1977** *Lancashire Life* Jan. 39/2 One of the chief technical advances in the making of watches.. was the improved design of the escapement, the device which secures uniformity in the rate of movement of the time-train. **1953** A. C. CLARKE *Prelude to Space* xxvi. 137 That lurid magazine.. that goes in for hyperspace *time-travel. **1969** *Punch* 1 Jan. 35/2 This intelligent and ingenious story.. has a fascinating climax where people from both sides time-travel back to see the Passion and Crucifixion. **1975** G. EWART *Be my Guest!* I. 23 Belief in Time Travel and supernatural facilities. **1930** *Wonder Stories* Nov. 489 We have purposely allowed our *time travellers to become known to the people of the eras that they visit, for in this way the great drama of the story becomes apparent. **1934** C. LAMBERT *Music Ho!* II. 69 The most successful time traveller of our days was undoubtedly Serge Diaghileff. **1972** M. CRICHTON *Terminal Man* III. i. 106 Slowly.. he seemed to emerge like a time-traveler advancing through the years. **1871** SWINBURNE *Songs before Sunrise* 171 Mother of man's *time-travelling generations,.. The temples and the towers of time thou breakest. **1895** H. G. WELLS *Time Machine* iv. 28, I am afraid I cannot convey the peculiar sensations of time travelling. They are excessively unpleasant. **1934** C. LAMBERT *Music Ho!* II. ii. 73 By his adoption or even invention of the particular type of present-day pastiche that can conveniently be described as time travelling Diaghileff immediately established a position of mastery again. **1961** *Guardian* 16 June 9/5 This musical time-travelling is presumably deliberate. **1981** CRAIG & CADOGAN *Lady Investigates* viii. 152 In children's fiction in general.. magic and time-travelling were acceptable forms of the supernatural; ghosts were not. **1954** *Amer. Speech* XXIX. 103 **Time trial*,.. a competitive event.. in which cars are separately timed for top speed over set distances. **1976** *Scottish Daily Express* 24 Dec. 13/6 Ten days ago an unknown sprinter ran an impressive time-trial against local man Jim Smith. **1977** *Wandsworth Borough News* 16 Sept. 10/4 The Wandsworth and District Cycling Club Open 10 miles' Time-trial.. resulted in a win for Eddie Adkins.. in the fine time of 22 mins, 4 secs. **1887** MOORE & AVELING tr. *Marx's Capital* II. VI. xx. 553 The converted form under which the daily, weekly, &c., value of labour-power presents itself, is hence that of *time-wages, therefore day-wages, &c. **1892** D. F. SCHLOSS *Methods Industrial Remuneration* i. 11 The two leading forms of Industrial Remuneration under the wage-system are time-wages and piece-wages... The employee engaged on time-wage sells to his employer the labour which he shall perform within a given period, irrespective of the amount of labour performed within that period. **1859** SALA *Tw. Round Clock* (1861) 175 You never see these ghostly *time-waiters anywhere but on 'Change, and out of 'Change hours. **1899** *Globe* 30 June, During the debate Mr. Courtney call'd himself first a Liberal Unionist and then a Time-waiter. **1954** W. M. MILLER in *Fantastic* Jan.–Feb. 34/1 They showed me a dozen pictures of moppets with LTR-guns, moppets in *time-warp suits, moppets wearing Captain Chronos costumes, [etc.]. **1954** *Sociological Rev.* Dec. 242 Instead of the 'dream' to move us out of lived time, it [*sc.* science and fantasy fiction] uses some machine to 'move across the "time-warp"', 'to cut across the 4th dimension'. **1971** *Guardian* 17 June 10/5 The time warp effect was.. intensified by having David Frost—essentially an early sixties figure. **1974** *Times* 22 Aug. 6 He pauses in his narrative and time-warps it back to South Staffs. **1976** N. THORNBURG *Cutter & Bone* i. 13 A sensation that always made him feel as if he had been time-warped back into wet diapers. **1983** *Listener* 3 Nov. 32/3 Molly Kean's images are of psychic rather than physical decay, of families able to live beyond their means because they are trapped in a peculiar time-warp. **1953** *Sun* (Baltimore) 27 Aug. 21/3 Of course, we [*sc.* railroads] can't meet the planes *time-wise. **1981** J. D. MACDONALD *Free Fall in Crimson* xx. 229 'How far are you from a pay phone, timewise?' 'Ten minutes.' **1829** BENTHAM *Justice & Cod. Petit., More Abr. Petit. Justice* 3 He is paid according to the time during which he is occupied.. in doing the work: this is called.. *time work. **1910** *Edinb. Rev.* Jan. 12 The advantages which piecework has over timework are more completely secured. **1917** W. S. CHURCHILL in M. Gilbert *Winston S. Churchill* (1975) IV. iv. 63 These advances arose out of an intention to remedy the contrast between the wages of skilled *time workers in certain munitions industries which had grown up during the war. **1971** *Daily Tel.* 15 Sept. 7/1 Representatives of nearly 3,000 'timeworkers' at the Austin-Morris car body plant.. have said that [their] pay offers.. are not acceptable. **1892** E. NOEL *Internat. Time* 4 The country [*sc.* United States of America].. is divided into *time-zones, each stretching over fifteen degrees of longitude, and differing one hour in time from the zone on either side of it. **1906** *Outlook* 9 June 774/1 To move the Observatory.. would involve the adoption of a new starting-point for the meridians of longitude and for the time-zones into which the world is divided. **1929** [see DIACHRONOUS *a.* 1]. **1976** M. MACHLIN *Pipeline* lv. 553 Due to the time zone differences, they would have plenty of time to make the six o'clock news coast to coast. **1982** *Daily Tel.* 24 Apr. 9/1 They conclude.. that rapid travel through time zones precipitates psychiatric illness in people already predisposed to it.

b. Comb. with *time's*: **time's arrow**, the temporal asymmetry whereby many macroscopic phenomena do not occur in reverse even though such an event would not conflict with the laws of nature.

1928 A. S. EDDINGTON *Nature of Physical World* iv. 69, I shall use the phrase 'time's arrow' to express this one-way property of time which has no analogue in space. **1937** *Nature* 27 Feb. 356/2 Eddington's statement.. that the second law of thermodynamics holds 'the supreme position among the laws of nature'. His reason is that this law alone reveals 'time's arrow'. **1972** S. WEINBERG *Gravitation & Cosmol.* xv. 597 It is the expansion of the universe that, by providing a heat sink, sets the direction of time's arrow in thermodynamic processes.

time (taɪm), *v.* Pa. t. and pple. **timed** (taɪmd). [f. TIME *sb.*: cf. OE. *ȝetimian* to happen, befall. In sense 1, app. substituted for TIDE *v.*[1], when *time* sb. was superseding *tide*.]

I. † **1.** *intr.* To befall, to happen; = TIDE *v.*[1] 1. *Impers.* or with subject *it.* (Perf. with *be.*)

c **1205** LAY. 27978 þa wes hit itimed [*c* **1275** ifunde] þere þat Merlin saide while. *c* **1230** *Hali Meid.* 35 Ofte hit timeð þat tat leoueste bearn.. sorheð & sweameð meast his eldren on ende. *c* **1250** *Gen. & Ex.* 3820 Do we us alle in godes red, Vs sal timen ðe betre sped. *c* **1350** *Will. Palerne* 5433 þe same sey i be þe, so me wel time. ? *a* **1400** *Morte Arth.* 3150 In-to Tuskane he tournez, whene thus wele tymede.

†**b.** *intr.* To fare (well or ill); *spec.* to fare well, prosper. *Obs.*

c **1250** *Gen. & Ex.* 1023 Bi ðan sal sarra selðe timen Ðat ȝe [= she] sal of a sune trimen. *Ibid.* 3392 Amalech fleȝ, and israel Hadde heȝere hond, and timede wel. *Ibid.* 4024 Ðis folc..Is vnder god timed wel. *c* **1460** *Towneley Myst.* ii. 26 God gif you ill to tyme!

II. 2. *trans.* To appoint or arrange the time of (an action or event); to choose the moment or occasion for. Usually (in context), to do (a thing) at the right time; 'to adapt to the time.' (J.).

13.. *Gaw. & Gr. Knt.* 2241 Þou hatz tymed þi trauayl as true mon schulde. *c* **1440** *Promp. Parv.* 490/1 Tymyn, or make in tyme (and) in seson, *temporo.* **1625** BACON *Ess., Of Delays* (Arb.) 525 There is surely no greater Wisedome, then well to time the Beginnings, and Onsets of Things. *c* **1708** BEVERIDGE *Thes. Theol.* (1710) II. 329 To teach us to submit to His wisdom..in timing all things. **1786** MME. D'ARBLAY *Diary* 6 Oct., This visit was not so timed as to compose me. **1802** MAR. EDGEWORTH *Moral T., Forester* iii, Pray let me go to sleep..and time your explanations a little better. **1821** SCOTT *Kenilw.* xvi, 'Why, how now, Bowyer', said Elizabeth, 'thy courtesy seems strangely timed!' **1865** KINGSLEY *Herew.* v, They had timed their journey by the tides. **1884** COURTHOPE *Addison* v. 113 Nothing could have been better timed than the appearance of the *Spectator.*

b. To arrange the time of arrival of (a train, a ship, etc.); hence, to regulate the rate of travelling of; also, to calculate or judge the moment of impact of (a ball or moving body).

1861 *Times* 22 Aug., The Royal train was timed to reach Leamington at 1.17 p.m. **1866** *Routledge's Ev. Boy's Ann.* 356 Educating, so to speak, his eye to time the ball correctly. **1880** NEWTON *Serm. Boys & Girls* (1881) 167 Not timing himself right..he met him just in the road. **1889** ACWORTH *Railw. Eng.* 198 The best train each way..is timed at over 45 miles an hour. *Ibid.* 202 The Great Northern..timed their trains to Doncaster..in 6 minutes less. **1890** *Punch* 12 July 15 Special trains, timed to take at least half-an-hour longer. **1893** [see TIMING *vbl. sb.* 2].

c. To adjust (a clock, etc.) to keep accurate time.

1825 J. NICHOLSON *Operat. Mech.* 504 The easy Timing of Watches by the Vibrations of the Pendulum. **1884** F. J. BRITTEN *Watch & Clockm.* 264 [A] Timing Box [is] a brass box for the reception of an uncased watch movement while it is being timed. *Mod.* Your watch is finished, but has not been exactly timed yet.

3. To mark the rhythm or measure of, as in music; to sing or play (an air or instrument) in (good or bad) time. Also *fig.*

c **1500** in Grose, etc. *Antiq. Rep.* (1809) IV. 408 Yet *rationalis lingua expellit* instrumentis all, Wel tymede and tewnede. **1602** MARSTON *Ant. & Mel.* v, If that thou canst not give, goe hang thy selfe: Ile time thee dead, or verse thee to the rope. **1607** SHAKS. *Cor.* II. ii. 114 He was a thing of Blood, whose euery motion Was tim'd with dying Cryes. *a* **1711** [see TIMING *vbl. sb.* 2]. **1837** LOCKHART *Scott* Mar. an. 1815, He then..joined with a stentorian voice in the cheering, which the Prince himself timed.

b. To set the time of; to cause to coincide in time with something (const. *to*).

1655 H. VAUGHAN *Silex Scint., Isaac's Marr.* 67 Others were tym'd and train'd up to 't. *a* **1719** ADDISON tr. *Ovid* III. *Mariners Transf. Dolphins* 52 Old Epopeus..Who over-look'd the oars, and tim'd the stroke. **1725** POPE *Odyss.* VII. 419 How fleet our sail, When justly tim'd with equal sweep they row. **1805** SOUTHEY *Madoc in W.* xvii, Hark! 'tis the mariners with voice attuned Timing their toil! **1808** SCOTT *Marm.* I. ii, Timing his footsteps to a march, The warder kept his guard. **1871** TYNDALL *Fragm. Sc.* (1879) I. vi. 197 Timing the pull to the lurching of the ship.

c. *intr.* To keep time *to*; to sound or move in unison or harmony *with.*

1850 WHITTIER *Elliott* iv, Timing to their stormy sounds, His stormy lays are sung. **1855** TENNYSON *Maud* I. xviii. 8 Beat, happy stars, timing with things below, Beat with my heart more blest than heart can tell. *a* **1892** WHITMAN *Out of Cradle* 8 The savage old mother, incessantly crying, To the boy's soul's questions sullenly timing.

†**4.** *trans.* To 'give' or tell the time to (any one). *Obs. rare.*

1583 MELBANCKE *Philotimus* C ij, The fyre to warme thee, the scortching of the sunne: thy clocke to time thee, the scritching of ye owle.

5. To fix the duration of; to assign the metrical quantity of (a syllable) or the duration of (a note); also, to regulate the operation or action of (a mechanism, etc.) as to duration (see also 7).

1589 PUTTENHAM *Eng. Poesie* II. xii[i]. (Arb.) 131 It could not possible be by vs perfourmed, because their sillables came to be timed some of them long, some of them short. **1597** [see TIMING *vbl. sb.* 2]. **1835** *Fraser's Mag.* XII. 416 Lamarck has defined nature to be motion, and law, and space, and time, without reference to a being moving or moved, legislating or legislated upon, and timing or spacing, or being timed and spaced. **1885** *Manch. Exam.* 12 Jan. 5/2 The clockwork apparatus, timed to run for two hours. **1893** J. A. HODGES *Elem. Photogr.* (1907) 58 If we have correctly timed our exposure.

†**b.** *to time it out*, to procrastinate, delay, spin out the time. *Obs.*

1613 DANIEL *Coll. Hist. Eng.* 81 They timed it out all that Spring, and a great part of the next Sommer. *a* **1649** DRUMM. OF HAWTH. *Hist. Jas. II*, Wks. (1711) 32 Others advised him..to time it out a while: in this lingring war a truce might be agreed upon.

6. To ascertain or note the time at which (something) is done or happens; to note the time occupied by or the duration of (an action, etc.).

1670 MILTON *Hist. Eng.* IV. Wks. (1847) 527/2 So different they often are one from another, both in timing and in naming. **1692** NORRIS *Curs. Refl.* 19 The Question will be concerning the Timing of it, whether any of these Impressions be Original Characters or no. **1723-4** DK. WHARTON *True Briton* No. 71 II. 602 The Timing of the subsequent Piece obliges us to insert the following Letter. **1859** LANG *Wand. India* 393 Slowly as he read, it was over in twelve minutes, for I timed him. **1878** BROWNING *La Saisiaz* 193 We who, darkling, timed the day's birth. **1896** *Daily News* 13 Jan. 8/2 Another letter..timed 9 p.m. states that during the night of the 8th and 9th inst. the Shoans made an attack by surprise. **1907** *Academy* 14 Sept. 885/2 He does not believe in what he cannot see, or time, or measure, or weigh.

7. *Mech.* To adjust the parts of (a mechanism) so that a succession of movements or operations takes place at the required intervals and in the desired sequence; to arrange the time of (an operation) in a mechanical cycle or series.

1895 in *Funk's Stand. Dict.* **1898** *Engineering Mag.* XVI. 108/1 When..a timing valve is used, instead of permitting the ignition to be timed by the compression.

8. *Fencing.* = *to take the time* (TIME *sb.* 21, quot. 1809).

1809 ROLAND *Fencing* 109 The too frequent practice of timing their adversary, because they will render their modes of play..very disagreeable to each other. **1889** DUNN *Fencing* 83 There is always a large element of risk in timing.

9. *to time out*: to parcel out or apportion (a space of time). Cf. *to space out.*

1902 *Fortn. Rev.* June 1036 When a man is always timing out his day, and dovetailing together the duties which compose his daily life.

time, obs. form of THYME.

'time-ball. A ball moving on a vertical rod or pole, placed in some prominent elevated position, for the purpose of indicating mean time, which it does by dropping at a certain moment each day from the top to the bottom of the rod, usually by the closing of an electric circuit.

The time thus indicated is usually 1 p.m., in U.S. noon.

1858 SIMMONDS *Dict. Trade, Time-ball*, a ball, moved by electricity, which is dropped from the summit of a pole to indicate the true meridional or mid-day time. **1878** LOCKYER *Stargazing* 279 This [wire] is used for dropping the time-ball at Deal. **1884** BRITTEN *Watch & Clockm.* 263 The time ball at Greenwich Observatory is of very thin copper.

'time-,bargain. A contract for the sale or purchase of goods or stock at a stipulated price on a certain future day; in Stock Exchange parlance, a transaction in which one accepts the liability to profit or lose by the amount of the difference between the prices of the stock involved on the day of dealing and on the settling-day.

1775 MORTIMER *Ev. Man his Own Broker* 63 *note*, Time-bargains, which have no foundation in real property. **1844** HARVEY *Rep. Sel. Comm. on Gaming* Q. 869 A time-bargain is in the nature of a bet upon what will be the price of stocks on a given day. **1882** BITHELL *Counting-ho. Dict.* (1893) s.v., Time bargains originated in the practice of closing the bank for six weeks in each quarter for the preparation of the dividends. As no transfer could be made during that period, it became a practice to buy and sell for the opening. **1888** J. S. NICHOLSON in *Encycl. Brit.* XXIII. 89/1 A curious example of legal evasion [of taxes on the transfer of stocks and shares] is furnished by time-bargains; and the imposition of the tax directly on the contracts of sale, instead of as at present on the actual transfer, has been strongly urged.

time base. *Electronics.* [f. TIME *sb.* + BASE *sb.*[1]]

a. A line on a cathode-ray tube display representing the time axis, usu. horizontally. **b.** A signal for uniformly and repeatedly deflecting the electron beam so as to produce such a line, usu. consisting of a saw-tooth waveform. **c.** Also ***time-base generator.*** A circuit for generating such a signal; a sweep generator.

1925 *Proc. Physical Soc.* XXXVII. 167 Circular and elliptical time-bases were not nearly so useful as a linear and unidirectional base obtainable from a special type of triode oscillator circuit. **1933** R. A. W. WATT et al. *Applications Cathode Ray Oscillograph* ii. 44 The general nature of the e.m.f. desirable as a linear time-base for use with a cathode-ray oscillograph. **1942** *Electronic Engin.* XV. 102/2 An outstanding case where stroboscopic viewing is a necessity is in conjunction with a spiral timebase. *Ibid.* 664 The mechanism of the time-base circuit. **1959** DAVIES & PALMER *Radio Studies of Universe* iii. 43 As the speed of radio waves is 3×10^5 km/s, the horizontal trace of the tube, called the time base, can be calibrated in range directly. **1960** *Practical Wireless* XXXVI. 408/2 A lead from the timebase is brought out to the front panel of the oscilloscope. **1962** SIMPSON & RICHARDS *Physical Princ. Junction Transistors* xiii. 309 This form of operational amplifier..has been used extensively as a time-base generator. **1977** *Broadcast* 7 Feb. 5 (Advt.), VPR-1 systems, with..timebase correction..for installation in studio.

timed (taɪmd), *ppl. a.* [f. TIME *v.* (and *sb.*) + -ED.] †**a.** Matured by time, seasoned. *Obs. rare*$^{-1}$. **b.** Done, made, or occurring at a (proper or improper) time; †done at the right time, well-timed, timely (*obs.*). **c.** Of music or verse: Written in measure. **d.** Fixed or regulated as to time.

Also, as second element in a compound, as ***ill-timed, well-timed, even-timed; two-, three-, four-timed.***

1628 FELTHAM *Resolves* II. [I.] xliv. 130 There is a flowing noblenesse, that some men be graced with, which farre out-shines the notions of a timed Student. *a* **1760** HOGARTH in Cunningham *Brit. Paint.* (1829) I. 167 The stagnation rendered it necessary that I should do some timed thing to recover my lost time and stop a gap in my income. **1888** *Bookseller* 5 Sept. 920 Two-timed metre is identified with the octave or root, three-timed metre with the fifth, and four-timed metre—the last of the uncompounded metres, and including the other two—is identified with the third. **1896** R. G. MOULTON *Lit. Stud. Bible* iv. 117 The oratorio combines recitative with timed music. **1898** G. MEREDITH *Odes Fr. Hist.* 83 A timed artillery speaks full-mouthed. **1901** R. ELLIS tr. *Aetna* 4 These..kilns the Cyclops used, when bending..to their even-timed strokes, they shook the dreadful thunder-bolt with the beat of their ponderous hammers.

Time-ese, Timese (taɪm'iːz), *sb.* and *a.* [-ESE.] (Characteristic of) the prose style of *Time* magazine.

1958 C. LOGUE in *Times Lit. Suppl.* 15 Aug. p. xxiii/1 They can model their syntax on the new 'international-English' style—a compound of Hemingway and *Time*-ese. **1967** *Time* 17 Mar. 7 The humor of a *Playboy* cartoon is often more sophisticated than the cleverness of Timese. **1973** *N.Y. Times Mag.* 8 July 4/2 Mr. Kanfer's prose: part showbiz, part Time-ese, and all posturing absurdity. **1977** *Globe & Mail* (Toronto) 15 Mar. 6/3 Elaine Dewar's review ..is..bad book reviewing with a Timese style.

timeful ('taɪmfʊl), *a.* Now *rare.* [f. TIME *sb.* + -FUL.]

1. Seasonable, due; = TIMELY *a.* 2.

a **1300** *E.E. Psalter* cxliv. [cxlv.] 16 þou giues þar mete in time ful tide. **1614** RALEIGH *Hist. World* I. vi. §9 (1634) 83 Interrupting..all offer of timefull returne towards God. **1825** CARLYLE *Schiller* II. 92 The timeful change of Christendom;..The universal Spring that shall make young The countenance o' th' Earth.

†**2.** Early in season; = TIMELY *a.* 1. *Obs.*

1382 WYCLIF *Jas.* v. 7 Paciently suffringe, til he receyue tymeful and lateful [1388 *adds* fruyt; *Vulg.* temporaneum et serotinum; TINDALE the yerly and the latter rayne]. **1388** —— *Jer.* v. 24 Oure Lord God, that ȝiueth to vs reyn tymeful, and lateful in his tyme.

†**3.** Occurring in or consisting of time; temporal, durational. *Obs.*

a **1400** HYLTON *Scala Perf.* II. xxiv. (W. de W. 1494), The nyghte as a tymefull space bytwix dayes two.

Hence **'timefully** *adv.*, with timely action.

1837 CARLYLE *Fr. Rev.* I. III. iii, Warned by friend Talleyrand..he timefully flits over the marches. **1845** —— *Cromwell* (1871) I. 105 The Five Members, timefully warned, were gone into the City.

'time-,honoured, *a.* Honoured or made honourable by length of time; revered or respected on account of long existence or old establishment.

1593 SHAKS. *Rich. II*, I. i. 1 Old Iohn of Gaunt, time-honoured Lancaster. **1751** MASON *Elfrida* Poems (1774) 90 That old minstrelsy, which breath'd Through each time-honour'd grove of British oak. **1831** WILLIS *Poem Brown University* 57 They have grown time-honoured on their shrines. **1887** SIR R. H. ROBERTS *In the Shires* ix. 141 A time-honoured custom had prevailed for years.

timeist ('taɪmɪst). Now *Obs.* or *rare.* [f. TIME *sb.* + -IST.] = TIME-KEEPER, TIMEKEEPER 3.

1830 W. T. PARKE *Musical Mem.* II. 320 This habit [of playing in concert] made him a good timeist. *a* **1837** E. C. KNIGHT *Autobiogr.* (1861) I. i. 7 The dancing-master was.. graceful without affection, a good time-ist, and..a good domestic character.

'time-,keeper, timekeeper.

1. a. An instrument for registering the passage of time; a timepiece; formerly, a specially constructed timepiece for scientific use, a chronometer.

1686 MOLYNEUX *Scioth. Telesc.* Title-p., For Regulating and Adjusting Curious Pendulum-Watches and other Time-Keepers. **1764** *Chron.* in *Ann. Reg.* 99/2 Mr. Harrison's new invented time-keeper. **1776** COOK *Voy. Pacific Ocean* I. i. (1784) I. 4 The Board, likewise, put into our possession the same watch, or time-keeper, which I had carried out in my last voyage, and had performed its part so well. **1878** HUXLEY *Physiogr.* 7 True noon does not always coincide with 12 o'clock as indicated by an ordinary timekeeper.

transf. **1868** LOCKYER *Guillemin's Heavens* (ed. 3) 6 According to the happy expression of Humboldt, they make of the Universe an eternal timekeeper.

b. Applied to an almanac. *nonce-use.*

1778 MISS BURNEY *Evelina* lxxviii, It would make me quite melancholy to have such a time-keeper in my pocket.

2. One who notes, measures, or records time; *spec.* **a.** one who is employed in keeping account of workmen's hours of labour; **b.** one who beats time in music; **c.** one who marks the time occupied by a race, the rounds in a pugilistic encounter, etc.

1795 SOUTHEY *Lett. fr. Spain* (1808) I. 294 The time-keeper..then turned up an hour-glass. **1829** P. EGAN *Boxiana* 2nd Ser. II. 128 *Maurice*..repeated the signal for fighting. *Randall* was the time-keeper. **1851** MAYHEW *Lond. Labour* I. 356/1, I went to a firm..at Beckenham, near Croydon, as working time-keeper, or foreman. **1879** 'E. GARRETT' *House by Works* II. 185 A post as timekeeper at some great engineering works. **1896** [see CORNER *sb.*[1] 13 d].

1903 *Daily Chron.* 28 Nov. 5/2 The Duke of Wellington called [Sir Thomas McDougall] Brisbane the 'timekeeper of the Army'. **1950** *Sport* 7–11 Apr. 7/1 Did the timekeeper and second.. want to catch the early train home?

3. With qualifying word: A person or thing that keeps (good or bad) time.

1899 P. W. HASLUCK *Clock Jobber's Handbk.* 2 Being very cheap..and fair time-keepers, American clocks are exceedingly popular. *Mod.* He is a good executant, but a bad time-keeper.

Hence **'time,keepership**, the position or office of a time-keeper. So **'time-,keeping** *sb.*, the keeping of time; *adj.* that keeps time (in various senses of the phrase: see TIME *sb.* 56.)

1816 HERVÉ *Beauties Paris* I. 211 No swing of the shoulders from side to side with graceless timekeeping. **1825** J. NICHOLSON *Operat. Mech.* 522 This degree of time-keeping cannot reasonably be expected from any other clock. **1887** *Pall Mall G.* 16 Sept. 11/1 The need existed for a timekeeping watch at a low price. **1891** *Wheeling* 25 Feb. 414/3 The Timekeepership of the London Centre. **1895** *Daily News* 20 Apr. 2/1 The right of the employer to make reasonable regulations for time-keeping.

'time-,killer. One who or that which 'kills' time (see KILL *v.* 5): said of a person, an amusement, etc. So **'time-killing** *sb.* and *a.*

1751 RICHARDSON in *Johnson's Rambler* No. 97 ¶24 Another seasonable relief to those modern time-killers. **1825** *Blackw. Mag.* XVII. 28 Much resorted to by.. antiquity hunters, view-hunters, Time-killers. **1882** W. CORY *Lett. & Jrnls.* (1897) 484 Hard up for time-killing occupation. **1895** *Outing* (U.S.) XXVI. 427/2 Reading it with the idle interest of a time-killer.

timeless ('taɪmlɪs), *a.* (*adv.*) [-LESS.]

1. a. That is out of its proper time; untimely; unseasonable, ill-timed; *esp.* occurring or done prematurely. Chiefly *poet.*, now *arch.* or *Obs.*

c **1560** *Trag. Rich. II* (1870) 96 Wert thou aliue to see How Ile reuenge thy tymless tragedye On all ther heads. **1590** MARLOWE *2nd Pt. Tamburl.* v. iii. ad fin., Let earth and heaven his timeless death deplore. *c* **1611** CHAPMAN *Iliad* VI. 349 Wretched man! So timeless is thy spite That 'tis not honest. **1621** LADY M. WROTH *Urania* 40 A timelesse, and vnseasonable birth. **1751** FALCONER *To Pr. of Wales* 78 Well mayst thou mourn thy patriot's timeless end! **1850** DOBELL *Roman* iii, Cease these timeless babblings.

b. as *adv.* = TIMELESSLY a.

1586 KYD *Answ. Tychborne's Lament.* iii. Wks. (1901) 341 Thy glorie and thy glasse are timeles runne. **1631** CHAPMAN *Cæsar & Pompey* II. iv. 152 And 'tis their repaire That timelesse darken thus the gloomy ayre. **1876** SWINBURNE *Erechtheus* 256 To slay thee timeless with my proper tongue.

2. a. Not subject to time; not affected by the lapse of time; existing or operating without reference to duration; eternal. Chiefly *poet.* and *rhet.*, esp. in phr. *timeless moment.*

a **1628** F. GREVIL *Hum. Learn.* xcvi, Curious mystery Of timelesse time. **1678** CUDWORTH *Intell. Syst.* I. v. §21. 781 The reason why we cannot frame a Conception of such a timeless Eternity. **1742** YOUNG *Nt. Th.* ii. 222 When worlds ..headlong rush To timeless night, and chaos, whence they rose. **1819** *Blackw. Mag.* V. 323 There timeless, spaceless, dwells the Eternal One. **1871** R. ELLIS *Catullus* ci. 10 Yea, take, brother, a long Ave, a timeless adieu. **1942** T. S. ELIOT *Little Gidding* i. 9 Here, the intersection of the timeless moment Is England and nowhere. Never and always. *Ibid.* v. 15 History is a pattern Of timeless moments. **1957** L. MACNEICE *Visitations* 22 A timeless moment where the nether blue meets the upper blue. **1981** J. BRABAZON *Dorothy L. Sayers* xix. 238 The timeless moment after death, when choices made while living are seen in the light of eternal reality.

b. *absolutely.* Cf. ETERNAL B.

1825 COLERIDGE *Aids Refl.* (1848) I. 22 All the truths, acts, and duties, that have an especial reference to the timeless, the permanent, the eternal. **1892** TENNYSON *Akbar's Dream, Hymn* ii, Kneel adoring Him the Timeless in the flame that measures Time!

3. †**a.** Of no duration; brief, short-lived. *Obs. rare*$^{-1}$. **b.** Destitute or ignorant of musical time. **c.** Having reference to no particular time.

1657 COKAINE *Obstinate Lady* Poems (1669) 339 Thy timeless inexperience doth deceive thee. **1821** BYRON *Juan* IV. lxxxvii, An ignorant, noteless, timeless, tuneless fellow. **1837** G. PHILLIPS *Syriac Gram.* 112 The participle is timeless; i.e. it has no time of its own; but partakes of every time with which it may be connected.

timelessly ('taɪmlɪslɪ), *adv.* [f. prec. + -LY².] In a timeless manner. **a.** Unseasonably, out of due time. *arch.* or *Obs.* **b.** Without reference to time, independently of the passage of time.

1625 MILTON *Death Fair Infant* i, Soft silken Primrose fading timelesslie. *c* **1750** SHENSTONE *Ruin'd Abbey* 73 The cruel meed Of virtuous ardour timelessly display'd. **1824** *Blackw. Mag.* XVI. 580 Destined to be severed timelessly and know no fruitage. **1833** J. H. NEWMAN *Arians* II. v. (1876) 210 Brought into existence 'timelessly', independent of that succession of second causes.

So **'timelessness**, the quality of being timeless.

1872 *Spectator* 7 Sept. 1138 Even nature almost witnesses to the timelessness of the Divine Being. **1894** SWETE *Apost. Creed* iii. 33 Because Tertullian has not grasped the timelessness of the mutual relations of the Divine Life.

‖**Timelia** (taɪ'miːlɪə). *Ornith.* [Altered by Sundevall (1872) from Horsfield's name *Timalia* (1820), said to be from an E. Ind. name.] A genus of East Indian oscine birds, the type of which is *T. pileata*, a small bird found from Nepāl to Cochin China and Java. Hence **ti'melian** *a.*; ‖**ti'meliidæ** *pl.*, a provisional family or group of passerine birds, which have been supposed to be related to *Timelia*; **timeliine** (taɪ'miːlɪaɪn) *a.*, allied, or assumed to be allied, to *Timelia.*

1896 NEWTON *Dict. Birds* 963 The *Troglodytidæ* (Wren) ..were referred to the **Timeliidæ*, whereas if their union were necessary, the *Timelias should have been referred to the Wrens. *Ibid., note*, A solution of the *Timelian difficulty will indeed be a great feat. **1874** *Ibis* Jan. 89 (Cass. Supp.) Description of a new *Timaliine bird from West Africa. **1881** R. B. SHARPE *Catal. Birds Brit. Mus.* VI. 301 Birds which are true Wrens and others which are truly Timeliine. **1898** *Field* 12 Apr. 518 The concave Timeliine shape of the wing..is reckoned of little worth.

'time-like, *a. Physics.* [f. TIME *sb.* + -LIKE.] Being or related to an interval between two points in space-time that lie inside one another's light cones (so that a signal or an observer can pass from one to another).

1914 [see *four-vector* s.v. FOUR C. 2]. **1920** [see SPACE-LIKE *a.*]. **1955** O. KLEIN in W. Pauli *Niels Bohr* 112 We divide the *k*-states into those belonging to time-like *k*-vectors..and those belonging to space-like *k*-vectors.., a division which is relativistically invariant. **1959** [see NULL *a.* 4 d]. **1978** PASACHOFF & KUTNER *University Astron.* xxvii. 694 The world lines of light divide space-time into spacelike and timelike regions.

†**'timelily,** *adv. Obs. rare.* [f. TIMELY *a.* + -LY².] = TIMELY *adv.*

1608 H. CLAPHAM *Errour Left Hand* 85 God giue the truth to preuaile timelily with me and all his people.

'time-,limit. A limit in time, or to the duration of some action or condition; e.g. a limit to the length of speeches in parliament, etc.; also, a limit to the duration of a licence or privilege.

1880 PLUMPTRE in *Dict. Chr. Biog.* II. 192/2 He [Origen] taught the perpetual freedom of the will, and therefore set no time limits to the capacity for restoration. **1891** KIPLING *Light that Failed* x. 199 'What is my time-limit, avoiding all strain and worry?' 'Perhaps one year.' **1894** *Westm. Gaz.* 3 Jan. 1/2 The stronger.. the case appears for..time-limit by Standing Orders. **1899** *Ibid.* 6 Feb. 2/2 Should this be effected, there will be a time-limit granted of from three to five years before any public-house is closed.

timeliness ('taɪmlɪnɪs). [f. TIMELY *a.* + -NESS.] The quality of being timely. †**a.** Early development or maturity. *Obs. rare.* **b.** Seasonableness, suitableness to the time.

1599 SANDYS *Europæ Spec.* (1632) 81 Difficulties..kindle ..the generous spirits, and adde that to their diligence which was wanting in their timelinesse. **1612–13** C. BROOKE *Elegy* Poems (1872) 180 His timelinesse did so preuent his date, That ere the floure was look't for came the fruit. **1860** EMERSON *Cond. Life* iii. (1861) 53 The art of getting rich consists not in industry, much less in saving, but in a better order, in timeliness, in being at the right spot. **1868** RUSKIN *Arrows of Chace* (1880) II. 195 All measures of reformation are effective in exact proportion to their timeliness.

†**'timeling.** *Obs.* [f. TIME *sb.* + -LING¹.] A time-server.

1563 BECON *Humble Supplic.* Wks. III. 21 Mynisters, whiche are faynteharted, and..but tymelynges, seruing rather the tyme (as the manner of the worldlynges is). **1631** WILSON *Sweiser* II. i. 158 What sayes my Lip-Ladds? My little Time-lings?

timely ('taɪmlɪ), *a.* Forms: 2–3 timelich, 4 timlich, tymeli, 5 -lie, 5–6 -ly, 6–7 -lye, timelie, 6– timely. [f. TIME *sb.* + -LY¹: cf. ON. *timalig-r* temporal. (Not recorded in OE., and rare in ME.; it may have arisen later than the adv. under its influence.)]

1. Occurring or appearing in good time; early; †of a plant, fruit, etc., bearing or ripening early. Now *rare* or *Obs.* (exc. as blending with 2).

1382 WYCLIF *Jer.* v. 24 Oure God, that ȝyueth to vs tymeli rein. **1530** PALSGR. 327/2 Tymely, *temprif.* **1563** HYLL *Art Gard.* (1593) 86 To haue timely Roses. **1585** ABP. SANDYS *Serm.* xv. (Parker Soc.) 301 The timeliest fruit often cometh to least proof. **1598** GRENEWEY *Tacitus. Ann.* II. ii. (1622) 34 Short summers, and timely winters. **1612** T. TAYLOR *Comm. Titus* ii. 6 (1619) 405 It filled Paul with ioy to remember Timothies timely faith. *a* **1715** BURNET *Own Time* (1766) II. 8 If a timely stop were not put to the progress.

2. Occurring, done, or made at a fitting or suitable time; seasonable, opportune, well-timed.

c **1200** *Trin. Coll. Hom.* 13 [He] nutteð timeliche metes, and ȝemeð his muðes meðe. *a* **1541** WYATT *Compl. Love to Reason* 59 Though my timely death hath been so slow. **1580** SIDNEY *Ps.* I. ii, Lyke a freshly planted tree,..Whose braunches faile not timelie fruite to nourish. **1605** SHAKS. *Macb.* III. iii. 7 Now spurres the lated Traueller apace, To gayne the timely Inne. **1738** WESLEY *Psalms* XVIII. iv, He.. sent the timely Rescue down. **1782** COWPER *Gilpin* xliii, Now Gilpin had a pleasant wit, And loved a timely joke. **1890** *Spectator* 31 May 763/2 With the general drift of his essay we heartily agree, and think it both wise and timely.

†**3.** Of or in time, as opposed to eternity; temporal, earthly. *Obs. rare.*

1340 *Ayenb.* 209 We habbeþ niede..of gostliche guodes and of timliche guodes. *c* **1400** *Lay Folks Mass Bk.* App. III. 123 Þat he absteyne hym from alle þingis tymely þat myȝtte fylen his soule. *a* **1615** DONNE *Ess.* (1651) 30 Saying that after John's eternal Beginning, and before Moses's timely beginning, Christ had his beginning.

†**4. a.** Of time or duration; pertaining to the time of day. **b.** Keeping time or measure. *Obs.*

1590 SPENSER *F.Q.* I. iv. 4 A Diall told the timely howres. *Ibid.* v. 3 And many Bardes, that to the trembling chord, Can tune their timely voices cunningly.

timely ('taɪmlɪ), *adv.* Forms: 1 tímlíce, 2–3 timliche, 3 timeliche, -lyche, 4 tymliche, 4–6 tymely (5 tymli, -ly 6 *Sc.* tymlie), 4– timely. [Late OE. *tímlíce*, f. *tíma* TIME + -LY²: possibly suggested by ON. *tímaliga* adv. timely, early.]

1. Early, betimes; in good time; soon, quickly. Now *arch.* or *poet.*

c **1000** ÆLFRIC *De Vet. et de Nov. Test.* ad init., Ic þe ne ȝetiðode ealles swa timlice, ær þam þe þu mid weorcum þæs ȝewilnodost æt me. *c* **1205** LAY. 31369 Penda..seide þat he wolde sahtnesse wurche and timliche him speken wið. *a* **1225** *Leg. Kath.* 2117 Ȝef þu þe timluker [*maturius*] do þe i þe ȝeinturn. *a* **1225** *Juliana* 9 Ase timliche as he hefde iherd þis. *a* **1375** *Joseph Arim.* 415 Þe kyng..Comaundes hem to meeten him tymely on þe morwen. **1390** GOWER *Conf.* II. 107 As tymliche as I may, Fulofte whanne it is brod day. **1455** *Paston Lett.* I. 338, I had lever ye were at London a weke the rather and tymelyer then a weke to late. **1578** LYTE *Dodoens* III. i. 314 The Aristolochias do flowre..timelier in hoate Countries. **1596** DALRYMPLE tr. *Leslie's Hist. Scot.* (S.T.S.) I. 26 Gif in a schip, tymlie in the morning ȝe passe by the craig. **1602** CAREW *Cornwall* 4 b, The Spring visiteth not these quarters so timely, as the Eastern parts. **1680** O. HEYWOOD *Diaries*, etc. (1881) II. 299 Came home pretty timely of the day. **1716** S. SEWALL *Diary* 5 Oct., Got up so timely, that the Comissions were read by 11. *mane.* **1827** KEBLE *Chr. Y., Morning* v, Oh! timely happy, timely wise, Hearts that with rising morn arise!

2. †Soon enough, in time, not too late (*obs.*); hence, In due season, at the right or a fortunate time; seasonably; opportunely as regards time.

c **1175** *Lamb. Hom.* 25 Ȝet ic mei longe libben and alle mine sunne timliche ibeten. **1552** HULOET, Tymely or in dew season, as nother to tymely nor to late. **1621** FLETCHER *Isl. Princess* v. ii, A virtuous point of gratitude, Timely, and nobly taken. **1678** WANLEY *Wonders Lit. World* v. ii. §8. 469/1 Ruffinus..sought to betray him to the Goths, but was timely discovered to his ruine. **1715** LEONI *Palladio's Archit.* (1742) I. 1 All requisite materials timely provided. **1828** D'ISRAELI *Chas. I*, II. x. 247 Buckingham had timely perished to be saved from the reproach of one more political crime. **1842** ARNOLD *Hist. Rome* II. 208 The attempt of L. Fulvius to surprise Rome..was timely baffled.

3. Usually hyphened to an adj. or pple. when used attributively.

1593 SHAKS. *2 Hen. VI*, III. ii. 161 Oft haue I seene a timely-parted Ghost, Of ashy semblance. **1651** JER. TAYLOR *Holy Dying* v. §5 (1727) 221 Our timely-repented and often forsaken habits of sin. *Mod.* Your timely-offered help.

†**timen**, variant of TAMIN *Obs.*, stamin.

1756 MRS. CALDERWOOD *Jrnl.* (1884) 334 Window-curtains of English stuff..about the substance of a timen or crape.

timenoguy ('tɪmɪnɒgɪ). *Naut.* Also timm(e)y-nog(gy). [app. f. F. *timon* TIMON² + GUY *sb.*¹] (See quots. 1794–1867) In extended sense, a gadget.

1794 *Rigging & Seamanship* I. 178 *Timenoguy*, a Rope fastened at one end to the fore-shrouds, and nailed at the other end to the anchor-stock, on the bow, to prevent the fore-sheet from entangling. **1841** DANA *Seaman's Man.*, *Timenoguy*, a rope carried taut between different parts of the vessel, to prevent the sheet or tack of a course from getting foul, in working ship. **1867** SMYTH *Sailor's Word-bk.*, *Timenoguy*, formerly [*as in Dana*; *but adds*] specially from the fore-rigging to the anchor-stock, to prevent the fouling of the fore-sheet. *Ibid.*, *Timonogy*, this term properly belongs to steering, and is derived from *timon*, the tiller, and the twiddling-lines, which worked in olden times on a guage in front of the poop.., by which the position of the helm was easily read even from the forecastle. **1880** W. BOTTRELL *Traditions W. Cornwall* 3rd Ser. 198/2 *Timmy-noggy*, a notched square piece of wood, used to support the lower end of the Vargord. **1886** [see GADGET]. **1925** FRASER & GIBBONS *Soldier & Sailor Words* 282 *Timmynoggy*,..a name given to various strop and toggle gadgets on board ship... A device more or less makeshift, to enable something to be done more expeditiously than would be possible in the ordinary way. **1963** R. M. NANCE *Gloss. Cornish Sea-Words* 160 *Timmy-noggy*,..may be a nautical substitute word like 'thingum-a-bob'. **1976** *Oxf. Compan. Ships & Sea* 870/2 *Timenoguy*,.. more recently it was a rope made fast in the mizen rigging with a thimble in the end through which passed the hauling part of the mainbrace.

timeous, timous ('taɪməs), *a.* (*adv.*) Chiefly *Sc.* Forms: 5 tymys, 6 tymouse, -ouis, -ose, tymmos, 6–7 tymous, -eous, 7– timeous, timous. [f. TIME *sb.* + -OUS; perh. after *wrongous, righteous.* Occasionally pronounced ('taɪmiːəs) or ('tɪmjəs), from the spelling: cf. *righteous.*]

1. Early (in the morning, or in the season); sufficiently early; done betimes: = TIMELY *a.* 1.

c **1470** [implied in TIMEOUSLY]. *c* **1520** NISBET *N.T. in Scots* Jas. v. 7 Pacientlie suffring, till he resaue tymouse and laatsum fruit. **1564** *Reg. Privy Council Scot.* I. 292 Upoun lauchfull and tymous warning. *a* **1578** LINDESAY (Pitscottie) *Chron. Scot.* XXI. xvii. (S.T.S.) I. 324 Sayand..that thai sould haue goode huntting on the morne and bad him be tymmos. **1637–50** ROW *Hist. Kirk* (Wodrow Soc.) 319 It cannot be a lawfull Assemblie when there is not lawfull and tymous intimation and premonition made. **1687** *Royal Proclam.* 12 Feb., in *Lond. Gaz.* No. 2221/5 We do hereby Command, Our Lyon King at Arms,..to make timeous Proclamation thereof at the Mercat-Cross of Edinburgh. **1825** JAMIESON s.v., See that ye keep timeous hours, i.e. that ye be not too late. **1910** *Highland Railw. Time-table* July,

Stops to take up for East of Aviemore [Inverness] on timeous notice being given to the Station Master.

b. as *adv.* Early, betimes. Now *dial.*

a **1578** LINDESAY (Pitscottie) *Chron. Scot.* XXII. xxiv. (S.T.S.) II. 135 Tymose in the morning he departit of the toun. **1679** J. RUSSELL in Kirkton *Hist. Ch. Scot.*, etc. (1817) App. 430 Timous in the morning they went to their prayers. **1892** *Ballymena Obs.* (E.D.D.), A'll be up gye an' timus in the mornin'.

2. Coming in due time; suitable or proper in respect of time; well-timed, seasonable, opportune; = TIMELY *a.* 2.

a **1626** BACON (J.), By a wise and timous inquisition, the peccant humours and humourists may be discovered, purged, or cut off. **1656** J. FERGUSSON *On Colossians* 136 Those fruits were timeous, and constant. **1729** WODROW *Corr.* (1843) III. 451, I fear his writings do a world of mischief, without a timeous antidote. **1849** AYTOUN *Lays. Scot. Cav.* (ed. 2) 96 His retreat was timeous, for General Mackay..had despatched a strong force..to make him prisoner. **1884** *Athenæum* 1 Mar. 271/1 The book [R. McCormick's 'Voyages'] is timeous.

3. a. Temporal; of finite time: = TIMELY *a.* 3. **b.** Keeping time, moving in time or measure. *nonce-uses.*

1855 BAILEY *Spir. Leg.* in *Mystic*, etc. 103 Duration, timeous and æterne, and space. **1884** D. GRANT *Lays & Leg. North* 112 Never yet to mortal measures Raise and fell sic timous feet.

timeously ('taɪməslɪ), *adv.* [f. prec. + -LY[2].] In a timeous manner; †at an early hour or season, in good time (*obs.*); hence, early or soon enough, in time; at the right or a fitting time; seasonably, opportunely.

c **1470** HENRY *Wallace* VIII. 1180 To souppar went, and tymysly thai slepe. **1473** *Rental Bk. Cupar-Angus* (1879) I. 188 A chalder of quhet als arly and tymsly sawn as it ma be. **1571–5** *Diurnal of Occurr.* (1833) 259 Certane..horsmen, and fyftie hagbutaris past furth tymouslie in the mornyng. **1637–50** ROW *Hist. Kirk* (Wodrow Soc.) 319 If one presbyterie was not warnit tymeouslie, all the rest conveening cannot justlie make any conclusion whilk may binde that presbyterie. **1708** *Roy. Proclam.* (Scotl.) in *Lond. Gaz.* No. 4456/2 We Ordain Our Solicitor timeously to dispatch Copies of the above Proclamation. **1758** WASHINGTON *Let.* Writ. 1889 II. 34 Differences..which, if not properly, and timously attended to may be productive of the most serious consequences. **1820** SCOTT *Monast.* ix, That fitting preparation may be timeously made. **1824** SYD. SMITH *Amer.* Wks. 1859 II. 52/1 The existence of slavery,.. if not timously corrected, will one day entail (and ought to entail) a bloody servile war upon the Americans. **1901** *Scotsman* 13 Mar. 11/3 Undue detention of two vessels occasioned by the defenders failing timeously to deliver coals for loading.

'timepiece. [PIECE 17.] An instrument for measuring and registering the passage of time; in a general sense, any kind of chronometer, including clocks and watches; *spec.*: see quot. 1884.

1765 (*title*) Minutes of the Proceedings of the Commissioners, concerning Mr. Harrison's Time Pieces. **1784** COWPER *Task* II. (*title*) The Time-piece. **1823** *Mechanic's Mag.* No. 17. 269 What kind of time piece is best adapted for the pocket. **1876** G. CHAMBERS *Astron.* 733 An ordinary good parlour time piece..will meet all the requirements of the amateur. **1884** F. J. BRITTEN *Watch & Clockm.* 264 Any timekeeper above the size of a watch which does not strike at the hours is called a timepiece.

timer ('taɪmə(r)). [f. TIME *v.* and *sb.* + -ER[1].]

†**1.** One who is skilled in time or measure; a musician. *Obs. rare*[−1].

c **1500** in Grose, etc. *Antiq. Rep.* (1809) IV. 407 How may a mysmovede tymere judge a trew instrument?

2. One who appoints or fixes the time for an action, event, etc.

1841 LOWELL *Ode* II. 3 [The Poet] fits his singing, like a cunning timer, To all men's prides and fancies as they pass.

3. a. A watch or clock, with reference to its time-keeping qualities; a (good or bad) time-keeper. **b.** One who times clocks, etc., i.e. who keeps them to exact time. **c.** One who marks the time in athletics, etc.; = TIME-KEEPER 2 c.

1884 *Graphic* 20 Sept. 303/2 Guaranteed good Timers. **1884** F. J. BRITTEN *Watch & Clockm.* 14 The want of constancy in the force of the balance spring..is one of the chief difficulties of the timer. **1890** *Century Mag.* June 205/2 The English are partial to a single watch in the hands of an experienced timer, but to make a record in this country requires the presence of three timers or measurers. **1891** *Cycling* 21 Feb. 82, I am aware that timers of professional events in the Midlands use the old-fashioned type.

d. An instrument for automatically timing a process or activating a device at a set time or set times; a time-switch; ***egg-timer***: see EGG *sb.* 7; ***oven timer***: see OVEN *sb.* 4.

1908 *Sears, Roebuck Catal.* 266/1 Stem wind, jeweled horse timer. This timer is operated from the crown by merely pressing down the..mechanism. **1939** C. MORLEY *Kitty Foyle* i. 9 They worked right round the clock..making some kind of timers for shells. **1953** R. CHANDLER *Long Good-Bye* ii. 25, I stirred the coffee and covered it. I set my timer for three minutes... The bell of the timer went just as I got back. **1961** *Which?* Dec. 335/1 Two..were clockwork dial timers, similar to kitchen timers, which have to be wound up by rotating the dial. **1972** *Jrnl. Social Psychol.* Dec. 225 The timer was preset so that the signals for all shock options were of three seconds duration, with a 15-second intertrial interval. **1977** *New Yorker* 27 June 89/1 Attached to the timer of the bomb was a note. **1982** *Listener* 15 July 34/3 These timers are perfectly adequate for some domestic tasks, like..switching lights on and off in a house to fool..burglars.

4. As the second element in combinations, as FULL-TIMER, HALF-TIMER, OLD-TIMER, TWO-TIMER; **fast timer**, one who or that which completes a race, etc. in fast time.

1891 *Daily News* 28 Dec. 3/5 The fastest timers ran in the deciding round. **1903** *Motor. Ann.* 163 In the mile race the fastest timers in the different classes were [etc.].

†**ti'merity.** *Obs.* Also 7 *erron.* **temerity**. [f. *timerous*, TIMOROUS, app. on mistaken analogy of *temerity* from *temerous* 'rash'; it may also sometimes have been a corruption of *timidity*.

As *timerous* and *temerous* ran together in use, so *temerity* was sometimes put for *timerity*, as n. of quality from *timerous*, TIMOROUS, as well as from *temerous* 'rash'.]

Fear, timidness, timidity.

1582 MUNDAY *Disc. E. Campion* F viij, The great timeritie and unstable opinion of his conscience..would not suffer him to utter it. **1601** CHESTER *Love's Mart.* (1878) 8 Nature was struck with pale temeritie, To see the God of thunders lightning eyes. **1618** LATHAM *2nd Bk. Falconry* (1633) 2 Without much timeritie or fearfulnesse. *a* **1660** *Contemp. Hist. Irel.* (Ir. Archæol. Soc.) I. 248 Such was the timeritie and cowardize and feare of all men there.

timerity, obs. form of TEMERITY.

timerosity, timerous, obs. ff. TIMOROSITY, TIMOROUS, q.v.

'time-ˌserver. [agent-n. from the phrase '*to serve the time*' (cited 1560): see SERVE *v.*[1] 11.]

1. One who adapts his conduct to the time or season; usually, one who on grounds of self-interest shapes his conduct in conformity to the views that are in favour at the time; a temporizer, a 'trimmer'.

(By Fuller used in a neutral or good sense.)

1584 G. BABINGTON *Frailty & Faith* (1596) 49 Will then a dissembling time-seruer not be vncased? **1638** SIR T. HERBERT *Trav.* (ed. 2) 136 This brave man is a Georgian by discent, a Mussulman by profession, a Time-server for preferment. *a* **1680** BUTLER *Rem.* (1759) II. 219 A Time-server wears his Religion, Reason, and Understanding always in the Mode. **1770** LANGHORNE *Plutarch* (1879) II. 904/2 He was never a timeserver either in word or action. **1849** MACAULAY *Hist. Eng.* ii. I. 188 The Puritan..deserted by all the timeservers who, in his prosperity, had claimed brother-hood with him. **1898** L. STEPHEN *Stud. Biog.* I. v. 148 Every autobiography is interesting, even when it unveils a mere time-server and hypocrite.

1642 FULLER *Holy & Prof. State* III. xix. 202 He is a good time-server, that complys his manners to the several ages of this life; pleasant in youth, without wantonness; grave in old age, without frowardness... He is a good time-server, that finds out the fittest opportunity for every action.

†**2.** One who serves only for a time, and afterwards deserts or 'falls away'. *Obs. rare.*

Apparently with reference to the parable of the sower, Matt. xiii. 21, Mark iv. 17, Luke viii. 13.

a **1575** BP. PILKINGTON *Expos. Neh.* iv. 15 (1585) 65 Such be those time-seruers which the Gospel speaketh of, that for a time make a shew in seruing the Lord, but in the tyme of triall they fall away.

'time-ˌservice. [See prec. and SERVICE.]

1. = TIME-SERVING *vbl. sb.*

1883 SYMONDS *Shaks. Predec.* v. (1900) 150 This freedom from time-service..give[s] a dignity to Heywood's character.

2. The work done by an observatory staff in daily furnishing the correct time to the community.

1890 *Smithsonian Rep.* 160 Observations of nebulæ and physical observations of Jupiter and Saturn; time service. **1899** *Athenæum* 29 July 161/3 The time-service has also occupied part of the energy of the observatory.

'time-ˌserving, *vbl. sb.* [See TIME-SERVER, and SERVE *v.*[1] 11.] The action or conduct of a time-server; 'trimming'.

1621 BURTON *Anat. Mel.* II. III. vi. 419 Let them goe on, get wealth,..by impudence, and time-seruing, let them.. crosse me on every side. **1642** FULLER *Holy & Prof. St.* III. xix. 202 There be foure kinds of Time-serving: first out of Christian discretion, which is commendable; second, out of humane infirmity, which is more pardonable; third and fourth, out of ignorance, or affection, both which are damnable. **1712** ADDISON *Spect.* No. 445 ¶6, I have been accused by these despicable Wretches of Trimming, Time-serving. **1894** MRS. OLIPHANT *Hist. Sk. Q. Anne* vi. 315 It was all devotion, not time-serving as the vulgar thought.

'time-ˌserving, *ppl. a.* [f. as prec. with -ING[2].]

†**1.** Serving the time or season; serviceable, seasonable. *Obs. rare*[−1].

1627 PERROT *Tithes* 70 His ships..full richly stowed with all manner of choice and time-serving commodities.

2. Characterized by interested compliance; 'trimming', temporizing.

1630 PRYNNE *Anti-Armin.* 77 Not by some one or two ambitious, time-seruing, nouellizing Diuines. **1638** SIR T. HERBERT *Trav.* (ed. 2) 99 His owne two sonnes..brought also to Mahobet by tyme-serving Madoffer-chan to abide his mercy. **1809** MALKIN *Gil Blas* XII. iii. (Rtldg.) 428 The school of time-serving morality. **1860–70** STUBBS *Lect. Europ. Hist.* I. viii. (1904) 100 The leading man..was a time-serving rogue.

Hence **'time-ˌservingness.**

a **1734** NORTH *Lives* (1826) I. 2, [I] ascribe it chiefly to ignorance, although I think time-servingness and malice hath the greatest share. **1812** SHELLEY in Hogg *Life* (1858) II. 196 The address..so barefaced a piece of time-servingness. **1890** *Lippincott's Mag.* May 763 The cowardice and the time servingness.

'time-sharing, *vbl. sb.* [f. TIME *sb.* + SHARING *vbl. sb.*[2]] **1.** *Computers.* The automatic sharing of (central) processor time so that a computer can serve two or more users or devices concurrently, switching between them rapidly and automatically so that each user has the impression of continuous exclusive use. Also *attrib.*

1953 *Digital & Analog Computers* (Amer. Soc. Mech. Engineers) 41 'Time-sharing' can be relatively simple. Nearly all the machines have convenient features for changing the problems easily. **1958** *Computer Jrnl.* Apr. 4/1 If time-sharing is being employed it can be arranged that the control unit proceeds to another branch of the program which is not held up in the same way. **1960** *Information Processing* 336 Time sharing, in the sense of causing the main computer to interrupt its program to perform the arithmetic and control operations required by external or peripheral equipment, has been used on a limited scale for a long time. This paper explores the possibility of applying time sharing to a large fast computer on a very extensive scale. **1964** *Discovery* Oct. 56/2 The advent of time-sharing machines. **1965** *Math. in Biol. & Med.* (Med. Res. Council) 295 Without time-sharing, the 'on-line' use of a fast modern machine would be unthinkably costly. **1969** *New Scientist* 2 Jan. 16/1 With a time-sharing system, the user can now call the system over the ordinary GPO network using an adapted telephone. **1980** P. WAY *Icarus* iii. 20 'Where is this computer?' 'Texas... You dial a telephone number. Ring it up. Bounces off a satellite. It's called time-sharing.'

2. The ownership or right to use of a property (esp. as a holiday home) for a fixed limited time each year. Also *attrib.* orig. *U.S.*

1976 *Time* 30 Aug. 67 In exchange for guaranteed occupancy over an extended period time-sharing resorts offer low prices, [etc.]. **1977** *Detroit Free Press* 11 Dec. 17-C/1 Time-sharing..is proving to be a popular concept for vacations. **1980** *Country Life* 27 Nov. 2038/3 The concept of time-sharing (that is, buying an annual choice of weeks in a holiday home instead of buying the home outright).

Hence **'time-share** *sb.*, (*a*) = TIME-SHARING *vbl. sb.* 2 (freq. *attrib.*); (*b*) a share in a property under a time-sharing scheme; **'time-share** *v. trans.*, to use concurrently with others on a time-sharing basis; **'time-shared** *ppl. a.*; **'time-sharer** *sb.*, a participant in a time-sharing scheme.

1954 *Jrnl. Assoc. Computing Machinery* I. 136/1 It seems reasonable to investigate the possibility of time-sharing one or more integrators in such circuits. **1962** *Spring Joint Computer Conf.* 307/1 By having these programs time share areas of memory, the program may be executed. **1973** *Lebende Sprachen* XVIII. 72/2 Subsequent data processing can then be carried out with a small and cheap dedicated computer, by a time-shared processor or off-line on a large computer. **1977** *Sci. Amer.* Sept. 135 (*caption*) One head can serve for both reading and writing on a time-shared basis. *Ibid.* 177/1 At a terminal an operator is connected to the computer and time-shares the computer with other operators. **1978** *Detroit Free Press* 2 Apr. 6F/1 The Minnesota resort is among more than 150 time share facilities in 26 states. **1980** R. REJNIS *Her Home* 73 A time-share can be very inexpensive..compared to hotel costs. **1980** *Times* 13 Oct. 24/4 (Advt.), Time-share ownership of luxury 8-berth yacht in Mediterranean. **1981** *Times* 31 Jan. 17/5 An organization..which offers an exchange service with other timesharers elsewhere. **1981** *Sunday Express Mag.* 14 June 33/2 It is important for the public to be aware that time-share is a property-based purchase.

†**'timesome**, *a.* *Obs. rare.* [f. TIME *sb.* + -SOME.] Of, pertaining to, existing in, or subject to time as opposed to eternity; of finite duration; temporal. Hence †**'timesomeness**.

1674 N. FAIRFAX *Bulk & Selv.* 33 Everlastingness is no more All at Once, as a Now of Time is,..than it is it self Timesom. *Ibid.* 154 God..may as well be brought down to the timesomness of that which is bounded, as that which is every way bounded, may be lifted up to the alwayness of him who is unbounded. *Ibid.* 181 When we say, the body is dying or timesom, the soul deathless or endless, we do not mean the body should thereby lose its bodyhood, but only its suchness.

time-'space, *sb.* and *adj. phr.* [f. TIME *sb.* + SPACE *sb.*[1]] **A.** *sb.* = SPACE-TIME *sb.*

1916 [see METRIC *a.*[1] 2]. **1942** E. WAUGH *Put out More Flags* i. 86 Metaphysical war, war in time-space, war eternal ..all war is nonsense. **1978** *Church Times* 15 Dec. 6/5 Using the discoveries of Einstein concerning the nature of time-space, Professor Macquarrie sketches in a theory of both individual and cosmic hope which depends upon the idea that God occupies every point in space-time.

B. *adj. phr.* = SPACE-TIME *adj. phr.*

1951 N. M. GUNN *Well at World's End* xxviii. 264 Giving and receiving are aspects of the same thing; as time and space are aspects of the one time-space continuum, according to the latest mode of scientific utterance. **1961** G. CLARK *World Prehistory* 4 It is important to avoid European or other regional bias, yet it would be pointless to try and achieve a kind of time-space parity for its own sake. **1968** D. L. CLARKE *Analytical Archaeol.* viii. 327 Strongly localized and smaller time-space entities..by contrast suggest culture group transforms in time depth. **1977** *Brit. Med. Bull.* XXVII. 20/1 One of the most interesting features has been the recognition in some areas of time-space clusters.

'time-,spirit. [transl. of Ger. *Zeitgeist.*] The spirit of the time, the genius of the age.

1831 CARLYLE *Sart. Res.* II. ix, To me, in this our life.. which is an internecine warfare with the Time-spirit, other warfare seems questionable. **1873** M. ARNOLD *Lit. & Dogma* (1876) p. xxi, To say that the Church-dogmas of his time..on which the Time-Spirit had not then turned his light, were false developments. **1880** T. HODGKIN *Italy & Inv.* III. ix. II. 547 One is disposed to look the present Time-Spirit boldly in the face and ask why it..must be infallible and eternal.

'time,table, time-table, *sb.* A tabular list or schedule of the times at which successive things are to be done or happen, or of the times occupied in the parts of some process.

spec. **a.** A printed table or book of tables showing the times of arrival and departure of railway trains at and from the stations; also a similar table of times of arrival and departure of passenger boats or other public conveyances. **b.** A chart used in railway traffic offices, showing by means of cross lines, in one direction representing hours and minutes and in the other miles, the position of the various trains at any given moment (*Cassell's Encycl. Dict.* 1888). **c.** A time-sheet on which a record is kept of the time worked by each employee. **d.** A table showing how the time of a school or other educational institution, for any day, or for a week, is allotted to the various classes and subjects. **e.** *Mus.* A table of notes showing their relative time-value.

1820 *Edin. Monthly Rev.* Jan. 15 One of the most striking epochs in music, as we conceive, was that of the invention of the time-table. **1838** OSBORNE *Guide to Grand Junction or Birm'ham, Liverpool & Manch. Rail.*, On and after Wednesday May 23rd... Time Table shewing the Hours [etc.]. **1838** *Cornish's Grand Junction* [etc.] *Railway Companion*, ed. 3, Time Table, shewing the hour of each Train [etc.] after 18th June 1838. **1839** *(title)* Bradshaw's Railway Time Tables..10th Mo. 19th. **1844** J. ALLEN *Rept. Schools S. Distr.* in *Min. Comm. of Council on Education* II. 91 For the morning's work, I have sometimes suggested the following time-table. **1844** F. C. COOK *Rept. Schools E. Distr.* ibid. 178 The time-table should contain an exact account [etc.]. **1856** F. E. PAGET *Owlet Owlst.* 194 The time-table of that man's life was a curiosity in its way. **1858** SIMMONDS *Dict. Trade, Time-table*, a register of the time of high-water, and of the departure of steam boats, railway trains, etc.; a check upon the period of labour of workmen. **1861** M. ARNOLD *Pop. Educ. France* 98 The present time-table..of the lay public schools of Paris. **1862** MISS BRADDON *Lady Audley* xxviii, He walked straight back to the hotel, where he called for a time-table. An express for London left Wildernsea at a quarter-past one. **18..** HULLAH in Stainer & Barrett *Dict. Mus. Terms* (1875) s.v. *Nomenclature*, The Germans call these notes..the *whole note*, the *half note*, the *quarter note*, and so on. These appellations..form of themselves a time-table. **1889** W. S. ROCKSTRO in Grove *Dict. Mus.* s.v., The earliest known indication of a Time Table is to be found in the well-known work on *Cantus mensurabilis*, written by Franco of Cologne about the middle of the 11th century... The modern Time Table, denoting the proportionate value of all these notes, is too well known in our schoolrooms to need a word of description here. **1889** G. FINDLAY *Eng. Railway* 8 It was not until after some time..that the time-table became a recognised institution. **1907** *Westm. Gaz.* 7 May 2/2 This is the first time that a time-table has been arranged in advance for a whole [parliamentary] Bill, but it seems to us that the procedure was justified.

2. ***timetable motion*** = *guillotine motion* s.v. GUILLOTINE 4 a.

1976 S. LLOYD *Mr Speaker, Sir* iii. 76 Peyton protested about the timetable motion, and asked why aid to Norton-Villiers had suddenly become so urgent. **1977** *Whitaker's Almanack 1978* 349/2 A third timetable motion to limit debate on Lords' amendments to the Bills..was carried by 312–296.

'time,table, time-table, *v.* [f. the sb.] *trans.* To schedule, to plan or arrange according to a time-table, to include in a time-table.

1917 'CONTACT' *Airman's Outings* v. 111 The leave train at Arrière was time-tabled for midnight. **1939** G. GREENE *Confidential Agent* I. i. 29 'My employers..wouldn't understand the delay.' They would have time-tabled his movements. **1970** *Times* 20 Oct. 4 Next year the school will admit 15 musically talented children who will be separately timetabled to give full scope for their abilities. **1974** *Times* 3 June 7/5 Headmistresses..were adamant that non-examinable, creative subjects must be time-tabled in girls' schools.

Hence **'time,tabled** *ppl. a.*; **'time,tabling** *vbl. sb.*

1960 *Farmer & Stockbreeder* 22 Mar. 47/1 Apart from complex timetabling, his work included liaison with police ..and dovetailing turn-rounds. **1963** *Times* 24 May p. xii/5 Regular timetabled lorry services between the depots and Acton. **1969** *Guardian* 24 Oct. 9/2 Some will protest that the division of school time into 40-minute periods is essential for time-tabling. **1975** *Language for Life* (Dept. Educ. & Sci.) xxv. 403, 93 per cent of classes..were taught English as a separately time-tabled subject. **1977** *Modern Railways* Dec. 481/3 The obsolete layout at Liverpool Street is a major timetabling handicap particularly in that there has to be a comfortable margin at Platform 9 between the 00.30 Norwich departures and the 00.39 arrivals. **1978** P. BAILEY *Leisure & Class in Victorian England* vii. 167 Cutting down ad libs and encores..helped ensure the predictable time-tabling of acts. **1982** *Daily Tel.* 12 Feb. 2/5 While many timetabled [rail] services will be axed, staff shortages mean there will be few cuts in services operated.

timeward ('taɪmwəd), *a.*, *adv.* [f. TIME *sb.* + -WARD.] Towards what belongs to time; temporal.

1883 H. DRUMMOND *Nat. Law in Spir. W.* v. (1884) 158 The mind of the flesh,..by its very nature, limited capacity, and time-ward tendency, is..Death.

'time-worn, *a.* Worn by process of time; impaired by age.

1729 SAVAGE *Wanderer* v. 3 By time-worn Steps a steep Ascent we gain. **1813** W. S. WALKER *Poems* 152 On the green margin of the quiet flood,..a time-worn exile stood. **1901** BIRRELL *Misc.* iii. (1902) 82 An ancient, time-worn ritual, which gives dim expression to ghostly ideas.

timid ('tɪmɪd), *a.* [ad. L. *timid-us*, f. *tim-ēre* to fear. Cf. F. *timide* (*a* 1528 in Godef. *Compl.*).] Subject to fear; easily frightened; wanting boldness or courage; fearful, timorous. Rarely const. *of* (cf. TIMOROUS 1 a). Also *fig.*

1549 *Compl. Scot.* Ep. Ded. 6, I vas lang stupefact ande timide, for falt of ane peremptoir conclusione. **1697** BENTLEY *Phal.* 14 Another sort of Proofs, that will affect the most slow Judgments, and assure the most timid or incredulous. **1730–46** THOMSON *Autumn* 401 Poor is the triumph o'er the timid hare. **1764** *Museum Rust.* II. 270 Lucern..in its infant state..is very tender, and timid of frost. **1841** ELPHINSTONE *Hist. Ind.* II. 545 The troops became more timid than ever. **1865** DICKENS *Mut. Fr.* IV. xii, Bella was so timid of him.

b. Characterized by or indicating fear.

1741–2 GRAY *Agrippina* 87 Carry to him thy timid counsels. **1812** WILSON *Isle of Palms* III. 168 With a timid smile. **1873** BLACK *Pr. Thule* vi, She has given him some timid encouragement.

timidity (tɪ'mɪdɪtɪ). [ad. L. *timiditās*, f. *timid-us* TIMID: see -ITY. Cf. F. *timidité* (*a* 1429).] The quality of being timid; fearfulness.

1598 FLORIO, *Timidita*, timiditie, feare, dread [etc.]. **1603** HOLLAND *Plutarch* 285 This proceedeth from..extreame folly and timiditie of heart. **1658** SIR T. BROWNE *Pseud. Ep.* III. xvii. (ed. 4) 182 [The hare] figured..pusillanimity and timidity from its temper. **1762** SYMMER in Ellis *Orig. Lett.* Ser. II. IV. 450 Lord Weymouth..spoke with grace and dignity, though with the timidity of a young man. **1849** MACAULAY *Hist. Eng.* vii. II. 244 Burnet was well aware of his danger: but timidity was not among his faults.

timidly ('tɪmɪdlɪ), *adv.* [f. TIMID *a.* + -LY[2].] In a timid manner; shrinkingly, apprehensively.

1767 S. PATERSON *Another Trav.* I. 375 To the timidly-superstitious..they would seem a company of necromancers. **1843** BETHUNE *Sc. Fireside Stor.* 137 The lady..glanced timidly at me to ascertain if I observed her. **1885** *L'pool Daily Post* 11 Apr. 4/9 One traveller timidly attempts the fraudulent experiment.

'timidness. *rare.* [-NESS.] = TIMIDITY.

1828–32 in WEBSTER. **1889** STEVENSON *Master of B.* ii, He looked up..with a kind of timidness.

† **'timidous,** *a. Obs. rare.* [f. L. *timid-us* TIMID + -OUS.] = TIMID.

1663 BUTLER *Hud.* I. III. 396 Fortune th' audacious doth *juvare*, But lets the timidous miscarry. *a* **1734** NORTH *Lives* (1826) I. 371 His lordship knew him to be..a timidous man. *Ibid.* 421 His timidous manner of creating and judging.. points, some on one side, and some on another.

timing ('taɪmɪŋ), *vbl. sb.* [f. TIME *v.* + -ING[1].] The action of TIME *v.* in various senses.

†**1.** Happening, occurrence, hap; (good or ill) fortune; an event, occurrence, case. *Obs.*

c **1250** *Gen. & Ex.* 31 Almiȝtin louerd, heȝest kinge ðu giue me seli timinge. *Ibid.* 1194 Swilc timing was hire bi-tid. *Ibid.* 2644 Bissop Eliopoleos Saȝ ðis timing, & up he ros. *c* **1310** *K. Horn* 164 Crist him ȝeue god tymyng. *c* **1400** *Brut* clxviii. 191 Thus staterand Scottes,..Erly in a mornyng in an euel tyming went ȝe fro Dunbarr.

2. a. The fixing, ascertaining, noting, or recording of time: see TIME *v.*; in *Cricket*, see quot. 1893.

1597 MORLEY *Introd. Mus.* 9 *Phi.* What is the timing of a note? *Ma.* It is a certayne space or length, wherein a note may be holden in singing. **1656** *Eirenicon* 20 Let thy charity advance To give them timeing of an Ordinance. **1658–9** in *Burton's Diary* (1828) III. 154 There is no exception against the petition, but against the timing of it. **1693** J. EDWARDS *Author. O. & N. Test.* 357 Josephus is often faulty as to the timing of things. *a* **1711** KEN *Psyche* Poet. Wks. 1721 IV. 278 The Voice, the Lute, the Passion sweet and strong, The Timing, the adapting of the Song. **1863** *Boys' Jrnl.* I. 264/1 He..showed us all the power and velocity resulting from hitting the balls at the right time. He called this the art of *timing*. **1889** ACWORTH *Railways Eng.* 202 The acceleration over the ordinary timing of the 2 p.m. was no more than 4 minutes. **1893** W. L. MURDOCH *Cricket* 29 Timing is the working in perfect unison of the hands, arms, legs and all the necessary muscles which are subservient to the eye. **1908** *Daily News* 7 Dec. 9 This, considering the heavy state of the roads, was excellent timing.

b. *attrib.* and *Comb.*, as ***timing box, nut, screw, valve, -wheel.***

1884 F. J. BRITTEN *Watch & Clockm.* 264 Timing Box [see TIME *v.* 2 c]. *Ibid.* 265 [The] Timing Screws [are] four screws or nuts placed at equal distances round the rim of a watch compensation balance,..used for getting the watch to mean time. *Ibid.*, In a marine chronometer there are two timing nuts. **1898** Timing valve [see TIME *v.* 7]. **1907** *Westm. Gaz.* 21 Nov. 4/2 All the timing-wheels are made of fibre and brass, and are contained in an oil-tight aluminium case in front of the engine [of a motor-car].

3. In an internal-combustion engine, the times when the valves open and close, and the time of the ignition spark, in relation to the movement of the piston in the cylinder. Freq. *attrib.*, as ***timing diagram***; **timing chain**, the chain that drives the camshaft of an engine from the crankshaft, part of the timing gear; **timing gear**, the mechanism by which the valves of an internal-combustion engine are made to open and close at the right moment; **timing mark**, each of the marks on an engine that are used as guides when assembling the timing gear or altering the valve timing.

1915 V. W. PAGÉ *Automobile Repairing made Easy* iii. 304 In these diagrams the timing used is: Inlet opens at 8 degrees past the upper center; [etc.] *Ibid.* 306 Two typical valve timing diagrams, one for a four cyclinder engine having a flywheel diameter of 15⅝ inches, the other of a six cylinder engine are given. **1929** —— *Ford Model A Car* vii. 270 *(caption)* Diagram showing timing marks on crankshaft and camshaft timing gears of Ford model A engines. **1935** F. J. CAMM *Practical Motorist's Encycl.* 319/1 Timing chain. **1970** K. BALL *Fiat 600 D Autobook* i. 20/1 Replace and secure timing gear gasket, cover and crankshaft oilseal. *Ibid.*, Install camshaft, crankshaft sprockets with timing chain so that timing marks are adjacent. **1977** *Hot Car* Oct. 81/1 When setting the timing on a Mini engine with a stroboscopic light, it is often difficult to see the timing marks. **1977** 'J. FRASER' *Hearts Ease* ix. 107 That lorry.. needed the tappets adjusting. And I don't think the timing was right.

Timini, Timmanah, Timni, obs. varr. TEMNE *sb.* and *a.*

† **'timish,** *a. Obs. rare.* [f. TIME *sb.* + -ISH[1].] **a.** Of the nature of time; temporal, temporary. **b.** Belonging to the time; in the style of the times, modish, fashionable. Hence †**'timishness.**

1674 N. FAIRFAX *Bulk & Selv.* 20 The reality of time being grafted in its timeishness, not in its boundlesness; so that every little share of time must have a little of this little reality, and every little must make a mickle. **1676** *Life Muggleton* in *Harl. Misc.* I. 612 A timish gentleman, accoutered with sword and peruke, hearing the noise this man caused.., had a great desire to discourse with him.

timist ('taɪmɪst). Also 8–9 timeist. [-IST.]

†**1.** One who follows or complies with the humour of the time; a time-server. *Obs.*

a **1613** OVERBURY *Charac., Timist* Wks. (1856) 56 A Timist is a noune adjective of the present tense. He hath no more of a conscience then feare, and his religion is not his but the princes. **1620** BRATHWAIT *Five Senses* iii. 33 The dissembling appearances of all obseruing Timists. **1658** J. JONES *Ovid's Ibis* 162 So Timists and Hypocrites change their opinion.

†**2.** A timepiece, clock. *Obs. nonce-use.*

1711 E. WARD *Vulgus Brit.* v. 61 To bring the poor condemn'd Machine To th' flaming Pile, and cast therein The costly Timist.

3. One who keeps correct time in music.

1765 GOLDSM. *Ess.* Misc. Wks. 1837 I. 203 Neither the one or the other are, by any means, perfect timists. **1774** J. COLLIER, etc. *Mus. Trav.* (1775) 8 She introduced me to Mr. Dilettanti, a most illustrious timeist. **1866** ENGEL *Nat. Mus.* ix. 339 The Chinese are known to be excellent timists, and they have several marks for indicating how the time is to be beaten.

4. One who confines his outlook to time, i.e. to the present life. *rare.*

1801 R. CECIL *Mem. J. Bacon* Wks. 1881 I. 203 Let the whole world be divided into two great sects, viz. Timists and Eternalists.

5. A chronologer. *rare.*

1897 S. J. HUMPHREY in *Chicago Advance* 23 Sept. 422/1 The next day (Tuesday, Apr. 25, A.D. 60, for so the timists calculate) they [Paul and his companions] came to Rhodes.

6. One of a sect of Adventists. *U.S.*

1884 *Independent Almanac* 18 Only a small company [of Adventists], called 'Timists', now venture to fix a definite time for the advent.

7. *Cricket.* One who 'times' (well or badly).

1893 W. L. MURDOCH *Cricket* 30, I think Lord F—— B—— must have had all the attributes of a good timist..for ..it is written of him..that he had a greater variety of hits than anyone else and they were all along the ground.

timit ('tɪmɪt). [Native name in Galibi.] A species of palm, *Manicaria saccifera*, var. *Plukenetii*, a native of Trinidad, and of the tidal swamps of the Amazon. Also *attrib.*

1858 CRUGER *Outl. Flora Trinidad* 5 The timit (Manicaria) grows in light sandy soils. **1871** KINGSLEY *At Last* xi, Rows of posts, probably of palm-stems thatched over..with the leaves of the Timit palm. *Ibid.* xii, Each Negro..carried a Timit-leaf, and hooked it on to his head when a gush of rain came down.

timmele, obs. Sc. form of THIMBLE.

† **timmen,** variant of TAMIN *Obs.*, stamin.

1824 MISS FERRIER *Inher.* lxxi, Broadcloth and timmen.

timmer, obs. and dial. form of TIMBER.

timmersome, variant of TIMORSOME.

timmy whisky: see TIMWHISKY.

timocracy (taɪ'mɒkrəsɪ). Also 6 -cratie. [a. OF. *tymocracie* (Oresme 14th c.), mod.F. *timocratie*, ad. med.L. *tīmocratia* (in 13th c. transl. Aristotle), a. Gr. *τιμοκρατία*, used by Plato and by Aristotle in two distinct senses, f. *τιμή* (*a*) honour, (*b*) value or valuation + *-κρατία*: see -CRACY. The Aristotelian, the later sense in Greek, was the first to appear in Eng. literature.]

1. In the Aristotelian sense: A polity with a property qualification for the ruling class.

1586 T. B. *La Primaud. Fr. Acad.* (1589) 548 The third kind of a good and right common-wealth is of a Greeke word called *Timocratie*, which we may cal the power of meane or indifferent wealth. **1594** *Mirr. Policy* (1599) D iij, Between the two kinds of a depraved Commonweale, to wit, Oligarchie and Democratie, this Commonweale Timocratie is founded. *a* **1647** SIR R. FILMER *Observ. Aristotle's Pol.* (1652) 6 Of all the right kindes of Government Monarchy was the best, and a Timocratie the worst. **1818** T. TAYLOR *Aristotle's Rhet.*, etc. II. 311 The polities indeed are, a kingdom, an aristocracy, and the third is derived from the distribution of honours through the medium of wealth, which as it seems may be appropriately called a timocracy. **1835** THIRLWALL *Greece* I. x. 408 The scale of the timocracy was gradually lowered, until it was wholly abolished. **1847** GROTE *Greece* II. xi. III. 159 Such were the divisions in the political scale established by Solon, called by Aristotle a Timocracy, in which the rights, honours, functions and liabilities of the citizens were measured out according to the assessed property of each.

2. In the Platonic sense: A polity (like that of Sparta) in which love of honour is said to be the dominant motive with the rulers.

1656 STANLEY *Hist. Philos.* v. (1701) 195 Of a Common-wealth he asserteth five kinds, the first, *Aristocracy*, when the best Rule; the second, *Timocracy*, when the Ambitious; the third, *Democracy*, when the People; the fourth, *Olygarchy*, when a few; the last, *Tyranny*, which is the worst of all. **1845** MAURICE *Mor. & Met. Philos.* in *Encycl. Metrop.* II. 620/1 The fraternal type of equality will be preserved in all friendships under a timocracy. **1852** DAVIES & VAUGHAN tr. *Plato's Rep.* (1858) 307 We will begin on the present occasion by examining the ambitious constitution—(I do not know of any other name in use; we must call it Timocracy or Timarchy). **1871** MORLEY *Crit. Misc.* Ser. I. 333 A timocracy in which the energetic ambitious and military type will become dominant.

timocratic (taɪməʊˈkrætɪk), *a.* [ad. med.L. *tīmocratic-us*, a. Gr. τῑμοκρατικ-ός, f. τῑμοκρατία: see prec. and -IC. So F. *timocratique*.] Of, belonging to, or characterized by a timocracy.

a. In the Aristotelian sense: see prec. 1.

1847 GROTE *Greece* II. xxxi. IV. 168 The timocratic classification of Solon..continued to subsist. **1869** A. W. WARD tr. *Curtius' Hist. Greece* II. II. iv. 89 These were the timocratic constitutions, which arrange the citizens in divisions, and determine the measure of their rights according to the standard of property. **1875** POSTE *Gaius* I. (ed. 2) 32 The Comitia Centuriata was a timocratic assembly, or one in which the ascendency belonged to wealth.

b. In the Platonic sense: see prec. 2.

1852 DAVIES & VAUGHAN tr. *Plato's Rep.* (1858) 312 Such we find to be the character of the timocratic young man, who resembles the timocratic state. **1905** *Contemp. Rev.* Apr. 556 The timocratic man who seeks honour may easily degenerate to the mere money lover.

timoˈcratical, *a.* [f. as prec. + -AL¹: see -ICAL.] = prec.

a. *a* **1647** SIR R. FILMER *Observ. Aristotle's Pol.* (1652) 6 It may very properly be called a timocratical Government, where Magistrates are chosen by their wealth. **1844** THIRLWALL *Greece* VIII. lxi. 85 A timocratical restriction on the exercise of the franchise.

b. **1822** T. MITCHELL *Aristoph.* II. 13 In..Plato's Republic..the author traces out the origin of four different sorts of government (viz. the timocratical or Lacedæmonian [etc.]). **1875** JOWETT *Plato* (ed. 2) III. 99 Beginning with the timocracy, let us go on to the timocratical man.

timolol (ˈtɪmələl). *Pharm.* [f. *tim-* (of unknown origin) + *-olol*, after PROPRANOLOL.] A β-adrenergic blocking agent used in the treatment of hypertension; (−)-1-*tert*-butyl-amino-3-(4-morpholino-1, 2, 5-thiadiazol-3-yloxy)-propan-2-ol, $C_{13}H_{24}N_4O_3S$.

1973 *Arch. Internat. de Pharmacodyn. et de Thérapie* CCV. 92 As a β-adrenergic blocking agent, timolol was found to be more potent than propranolol. **1976** *Nature* 22 July 307/2 Neither phentolamine..nor timolol, a specific blocker of beta-receptors..had any effect.

Timon¹ (ˈtaɪmən). [Gr. Τίμων, personal name.] The name of a noted misanthrope of Athens, the hero of Shakspere's play of the same name; hence, one like Timon, a misanthrope.

1588 SHAKS. *L.L.L.* IV. iii. 170 And Critticke Tymon laugh at idle toyes. **1711** SHAFTESB. *Charac.* (1737) II. 197 You discover'd so much aversion, as wou'd make one believe you a compleat Timon, or man-hater. **1819** LADY MORGAN *Autobiog.* (1859) 281 She had grown into a sort of female Timon—not of Athens—bitter, and always going over old, past scenes. **1886** *Pall Mall G.* 15 June 6/1 Both Mr. Ruskin and Mr. Froude have long been known as highly cultivated disciples of the latter-day Timon of Cheyne-row.

Hence **Tiˈmonian** *a.*, of, pertaining to, or like Timon; **ˈTimonism**, misanthropy; **ˈTimonist**, a misanthrope; **ˈTimonize** *v. intr.*, to play the Timon or misanthrope.

1770 LANGHORNE *Plutarch* (1851) II. 997/1 He left his *Timonian retreat. **1886** *Pall Mall G.* 15 June 6/1 No new Timon arose, for *Timonism had been found out to be a fraud. **1590** GREENE *Mourn. Garm.* (1616) 2 Yet was he not ..such a *Timonist, but hee would familiarly conuerse with his friends. **1602** DEKKER *Satirom.* L iij, I did it to retyre me from the world; And turne my Muse into a Timonist. **1713** *Gentl. Instr.* II. viii. (ed. 5) 180, I should be tempted to *Timonize, and clap a Satyr upon our whole Species.

†**timon**², **temon.** *Obs. rare.* [a. F. *timon*, *temon* pole, staff, handle of rudder, helm:—L. *tēmōn-em* beam, pole.] The rudder of a ship.

[**1392–3** *Earl Derby's Expedition* (Camd.) 225 Item pro reparacione j tymon per le scriuen.] **1506** GUYLFORDE *Pylgr.* (Camd.) 76 Tournynge with suche vyolence yᵗ with the jumpe and stroke of yᵉ falle of yᵉ galye to the rok, the sterne called the temon sterte and flewe frome the hokes.

timoneer (taɪməˈnɪə(r)). *rare.* [a. F. *timonier* (12th c. in Godef. *Compl.*), It. *timoniere*, f. *timon* helm: see prec. and -EER¹.] A helmsman, steersman.

1762–9 FALCONER *Shipwr.* II. 178 The helm the attentive timoneer applies. *Ibid.* III. 67, 115 [etc.]. **1806** G. PINCKARD *Notes W. Ind.* I. 183 The timoneer left the helm; and the ship remained immoveable upon the water. **1883** G. C. DAVIES *Norfolk Broads* xxv. (1884) 188 Her timoneer sitting ..with the tiller in one hand and the sheet in the other.

timor¹ (ˈtɪmə(r)). *rare.* [a. L. *timor* fear.] Fear.

1599 A. M. tr. *Gabelhouer's Bk. Physicke* 102/2 For Asthmasye, or shortnes of breath, and timor of the consumptione. **1850** P. CROOK *War of Hads* 43 In slothful timor.

Timor² (ˈtiːmɔː(r)). The name of an Indonesian island off the north-west coast of Australia, part of which was before 1976 a Portuguese colony, used *attrib.* in **Timor pony**, a small, stocky horse belonging to a variety first found there. Also *absol.*

[**1841** G. GREY *Jrnls. Two Exped. N.-W. & W. Austral.* I. iv. 68 The vessel could then proceed..to the Island of Timor, to procure the requisite number of ponies for our expedition.] **1895** A. B. PATERSON *Man from Snowy River* (1896) 4 He was something like a racehorse under-sized, With a touch of Timor pony. **1928** 'BRENT OF BIN BIN' *Up Country* xv. 253 He rode a yellow bay with a dash of Timor, hardy and sure-footed as a goat. **1933** *Bulletin* (Sydney) 27 Sept. 21/2 Those Timor ponies..date back to 1840. **1965** *Austral. Encycl.* IV. 552/1 The Timor pony possesses remarkable hardiness and stamina.

timorat, erron. variant of TIMARIOT. *Obs.*

†**timorate**, *a. Obs. rare*⁻⁰. [ad. late L. *timorāt-us* (Vulg.) full of the fear of God, f. *timor* fear: see -ATE². Cf. F. *timoré* (Cotgr.), It. *timorato* (Florio, 1611).] Devout, full of reverence.

1570 LEVINS *Manip.* 41/24 Timorate, *timoratus*.

Timorese (tiːmɔːˈriːz), *sb.* and *a.* [f. *Timor* (see TIMOR²) + -ESE.] **A.** *sb.* (A member of) the indigenous people of Timor, of Indonesian-Malay stock. **B.** *adj.* Of, pertaining to, or characteristic of Timor or its inhabitants.

1869 A. R. WALLACE *Malay Archipelago* I. xiii. 290 The native Timorese predominate. **1875** [see PAPUAN *a.* 1]. **1964** M. DICKSON *World Elsewhere* iii. 122 The standard of the game was mainly due to the exemplary keenness..of the Timorese and Dusan opponents. **1979** *Times* 28 Dec. 16/2 Left-wing Timorese students..began to return to the island. *Ibid.*, Not a few Timorese are in somewhat uneasy cooperation with the Indonesians.

†**ˈtimorist.** *Obs. rare.* Also **tymor-**. Derivation and sense doubtful: the context appears to require 'Timist, time-server'.

c **1620** FELTHAM *Resolves* xx. 60 What would the world think of me, that could thus in one, be hot, and cold? should I not be censured as a Timorist? [*ed.* **1647** Tymorist.]

†**timoˈrosity.** *Obs.* Forms: (5 **tymorysite**), 6 **timerosity, -itie, tymer-,** (**temer-**), **timorositie,** 6–7 **timorosity.** [f. as TIMOROUS + -ITY; cf. obs. It. *timorosità* (Florio).] Timorousness, timidity.

1490 CAXTON *Eneydos* iv. 20 For tymorysite..his tonge.. clyued to the palate of his mouuth. **1531** ELYOT *Gov.* I. xxi, Audacitie with timerositie maketh Magnanimitie. *Ibid.* III. viii, The surplusage is called Audacitie, the lacke Timorositie or feare. **1538** *St. Papers Hen. VIII*, III. 12 In the end, temerositie putt apart, I have determinid playnly to expres to your Lordship suche thinges..as restith in my knowledg. **1547–64** BAULDWIN *Mor. Philos.* (Palfr.) 151 In men we note audacitie, but commonly in women timerosity. **1647** *Sp. Ho. Com.* 23 June 1 The timorosity of Offending, the volubility of Scandal.

timorous (ˈtɪmərəs), *a.* Forms: α. 5–6 **tymerous(e,** (5 **tumerous**), 6–8 **timerous,** (6 **-ouse**). (β. 6 **temerous.**) γ. 5–6 **timorouse,** 6 **tymorous,** 6–8 **timourous,** (6 **-ouse,** 7 **timrous,** 7–8 **tim'rous**), 6– **timorous.** [= OF. *temeros*, *-ous* (14th c. in Godef.), later *timoureus*, *timoreux*, OSp., Pg. *temeroso*, It. *timoroso*, med.L. *timōrōsus* (11th c. in Du Cange, and prob. in late L.), f. L. *timōr-em* fear.

The existence of the forms *timerous*, *temerous* brought this word into formal confusion with TEMEROUS rash; whence *temerity*, properly n. of quality from TEMEROUS, was also used as deriv. of *timorous* in sense 'timidity': see TIMERITY.]

1. Full of or affected by fear (either for the time or habitually); fearful. **a.** Feeling fear; frightened, apprehensive, afraid. (Sometimes const. *of*, or with inf. or clause.) Now *rare*.

c **1450** *Mankind* 805 in *Macro Plays* 30 He ys so tymerouse; me semyth hys vytall spryt doth expyre. *c* **1530** *Crt. Love* 1 With timerous [*ed.* **1561** temerous] herte, and trembling hand of drede. *c* **1555** HARPSFIELD *Divorce Hen. VIII* (Camd.) 185 The King's doings..may seem..to have proceeded from a tymerous fearful conscience to offend God. **1613** W. BROWNE *Brit. Past.* II. v, Timerous of death. *a* **1631** DONNE *Holy Sonnets* xii. 10 You have not sinned nor need be timourous. **1707** *Reflex. upon Ridicule* 11. 269 Our Friends are for the most part timerous. **1750** JOHNSON *Rambler* No. 75 ⁋15 He is now more timorous lest his freedom should be thought rudeness. **1840** DICKENS *Barn. Rudge* lxxii, He..was rather timorous of venturing on Joe.

b. Subject to fear; of a fearing disposition; easily frightened; timid. †In early use sometimes in good sense: Modest, reverential.

1474 CAXTON *Chesse* II. ii. (1883) 32 A Quene ought to be well manerd & amonge alle she ought to be tumerous and shamefast. *Ibid.* III. ii, Maysters and marroners on the see.. yf they be tumerous and ferdful they shold make aferde them that ben in theyr shippis. **1502** ATKYNSON tr. *De Imitatione* II. x. 189 The grace wherby we may be made humble & tymerous to God. **1534** MORE *Comf. agst. Trib.* II. Wks. 1182/1 Thys faute of pusillanimitye and tymorous mynde. *a* **1557** MRS. M. BASSET tr. *More's Treat. Passion* ibid. 1358/1 O temerous & weake sely shepe, thynke yt sufficient for thee, onely to walke after me, which am thy shepehearde. **1600** HOLLAND *Livy* II. lv. 81 Their own timerous conceits & imaginations. **1774** GOLDSM. *Nat. Hist.* (1776) IV. 3 Animals of the hare kind..are inoffensive and timorous. **1855** MACAULAY *Hist. Eng.* xvi. III. 636 Conjunctures such as have often inspired timorous and delicate women with heroic courage.

c. Indicating or proceeding from fear; characterized by timidity. Also *fig.*

1581 J. BELL *Haddon's Answ. Osor.* 477 b, Tymerous feare of men hath straightened it. **1603** H. CROSSE *Vertues Commw.* (1878) 139 The linke of wofull wretchednes maketh his death timerous and fearfull by his leaud life. **1652** CRASHAW *Carmen Deo Nostro* Wks. (1904) 254 The timerous light of stares. **1701** C. WOLLEY *Jrnl. New York* (1860) 60 There is the timorous objection: the Ship may founder by springing a Leak. **1781** GIBBON *Decl. & F.* xxvi. (1869) II. 48, I shall proceed with doubtful and timorous steps. **1838** PRESCOTT *Ferd. & Is.* (1846) I. iii. 151 His troops murmured at this timorous policy.

†**2.** Causing fear or dread; dreadful, terrible. *Obs.*

1455 *Rolls of Parlt.* V. 281/1 In as rigorous and timorouse manere as the Chirche wol suffre it. **1513** BRADSHAW *St. Werburge* II. 766 They set theyr ordinaunce agaynst the towne..timorous for to se. **1608** R. JOHNSON *Seven Champions* 45, I grant thee..by the law of arms to choose thy death, els hadst thou suffered a timorous torment. **1632** LITHGOW *Trav.* VI. 262 Wee came to the most scurrile and timorous Discent of the whole passage.

3. *dial.* (See quots.)

1691 RAY *N.C. Words*, *Timorous*, by the Vulgar is here used for furious or passionate. **1828** *Craven Gloss.*, *Timorous*, difficult to please, fretful; also, nice, particular in dress.

timorously (ˈtɪmərəslɪ), *adv.* [f. prec. + -LY².] In a timorous manner; timidly.

1548 UDALL, etc. *Erasm. Par. John* xxi. 117 He aunswereth sincerely..but timerously and very lowlye withal. **1560** DAUS tr. *Sleidane's Comm.* 273 b, Rendryng so lightly and timourously. **1655** STANLEY *Hist. Philos.* III. (1701) 99/1 Timerously shunning all publick Affairs. **1697** JOS. WOODWARD *Relig. Soc. London* I. (1701) 13 You will stand idly or timorously, when the Goliahs of darkness come forth and blaspheme the living God. **1835** LYTTON *Rienzi* I. iii, 'Hush', said a third, timorously looking round. **1885** *Manchester Exam.* 3 June 5/4 Reflections..timorously emphasised by a letter.

timorousness (ˈtɪmərəsnɪs). [f. as prec. + -NESS.] The quality or state of being timorous; fearfulness, timidity.

1494 FABYAN *Chron.* VI. clxxv. 172 Gosselyne and Conrade..complaynynge theym vnto her of the vnstablenesse of her lorde and tymerousnesse. **1533** ELYOT *Cast. Helthe* (1541) 75 b, In case that either for age or for timourousenesse a man wyll not be lette bloude. **1624** DONNE *Serm.* ii. (1640) 15 Gideon, in a modest timorousnesse askes a signe. **1681** R. KNOX *Ceylon* 168 Whom we perceiving to be free from timerousness at the sight of us. **1748** HARTLEY *Observ. Man* I. iv. 454 The Ridicule cast upon Timorousness by Boys and Men. **1876** BANCROFT *Hist. U.S.* I. viii. 228 Afflicted..with..an overpowering timorousness of nature.

timorsome (ˈtɪməsəm), *a.* Now *dial.* Also 7–9 **timer-**, **timour-**, *erron.* **timber-**, (8 **timbor-**, 8–9 **timmor-**). [app. f. *timor-ous*, *timer-ous*, with substitution of *-some* suffix for *-ous*; cf. *burthen-ous*, *burthen-some*, *quarrel-ous*, *quarrel-some*, and esp. *humorous*, *humoursome* (but *humour* was in common English use, which *timor* was not).]

1. Subject to or characterized by fear; timorous, timid.

1599–1600 G. RUGGLE *Club Law* I. iv, Impossible for a man to be a..Headsman..that is timbersome or afraid. **1602** SEGAR *Hon. Mil. & Civ.* I. xxx. 39 The second was impotent of his feet, and the third timersome. *a* **1652** BROME *Covent Gard.* v. i, I never saw a man so timoursome. **1749** FIELDING *Tom Jones* VIII. viii, He is a timborsome Man every Body knows. **1818** SCOTT *Let. to D. Terry* 30 Apr., in *Lockhart*, Last night..the very same noise occurred. Mrs. S., as you know, is rather *timbersome*, so up got I, with Beardie's broadsword under my arm... But nothing was out of order. **1840** MARRYAT *Poor Jack* xxii, A mighty timorsome sort of young chap he appeared for to be. **1897** BARING-GOULD *Bladys* xxvi, I'm forced, when feeling timorsome of nights, to bolt my door.

2. Inspiring fear, fearful, dreadful; = TIMOROUS 2. *rare*.

1894 BLACKMORE *Perlycross* 191 It looks..so..strange and ungodly, and—and so timoursome.

timothy (ˈtɪməθɪ). [A Christian name, ad. L. *Timotheus*, Gr. Τιμόθεος (= 'honouring God').]

1. Short for TIMOTHY GRASS.

1747 B. FRANKLIN *Let.* Wks. 1887 II. 77 You made some mistake when you intended to favor me with some of the new valuable grass seed..for what you gave me..proves mere timothy. **1840** J. BUEL *Farmer's Comp.* 225 *Timothy*, better known in the east as *herds-grass*, and in Europe as meadow cat's-tail..is the general forage grass of the northern States. **1887** *Daily News* 18 Oct. 3/8 Timothy is scarce both in America and Germany, whence our supplies are mainly derived, and is likely to be dear.

b. *attrib.*, as ***timothy field, hay, seed, sod.***

1772 *Pennsylvania Gaz.* 16 Apr. 4/3 (Advt.), Timothy and blue grass hay to be sold. **1784** *Pennsylvania Gaz.* 17 Mar. 3/2 Timothy seed. **1868** *Rep. U.S. Commissioner Agric.* (1869) 420 A timothy sod plowed late in spring. **1884** ROE *Nat. Ser. Story* viii, The mowing machine would be used in the timothy fields. **1902** *Encycl. Brit.* XXVI. 535/2 Clover seed 60 lb.; timothy seed 48 lb. **1911** *Daily Colonist* (Victoria, B.C.) 25 Apr. 6/1 (Advt.), *Horses.* Try some of our Washington Timothy Hay—big load just in.

2. 'A brew or jorum of liquor' (*Sc. slang*; *E.D.D.*).

1855 STRANG *Glasgow & its Clubs* (1856) 338 Rum filled the crystal timothies. **1890** J. SERVICE *Thir Notandums* xii. 87 Drink fair, pree and pree aboot, wi' that timothy o' toddy that you've been hirpling aboot to mak.

timothy grass. [See quots. 1765, 1894.] A name (originally American) for Meadow Cat's-tail Grass, *Phleum pratense*, a native British grass, introduced into cultivation under this name in the North American colonies in the eighteenth century.

a **1736** J. ELIOT *Ess. Field Husb.* (1760) 57 Herd-Grass (known in Pennsylvania by the name of Timothy-Grass)... It is said that Herd-Grass was first found in a swamp in Piscataqua by one Herd, who propagated the same. **1747** FRANKLIN *Let.* Wks. 1887 II. 83 A bushel of clean chaff of timothy or Salem grass will yield five quarts of seed. **1750** W. ELLIS *Mod. Husbandm.*, St. Timothy Grass. **1763** *Museum Rust.* (ed. 2) I. 233 Timothy grass..delights in a..moist soil, and has a running root like couch grass. **1765** *Nat. Hist.* in *Ann. Reg.* 143/2 Another artificial grass called Timothy-grass..because it was brought from New York to Carolina by one Timothy Hanson [according to the Century Dict., about 1720]. **1809** KENDALL *Trav.* I. xxiii. 228 Timothy, here called *English* grass, is the grass cultivated. **1894** *Times* 23 Apr. 12/3 Although *Phleum pratense*, long known as meadow catstail, is a native British grass, its cultivation as an agricultural plant was originated last century by Timothy Hanson, an American, after whom the grass got called timothy grass.

timous: see TIMEOUS.

†timp, -e. *Obs. rare*⁻¹. [App. shortened from L. *tympanum*, TYMPAN.] A tambourine.

c **1205** LAY. 7003 Ne cuðe na mon swa muchel of song, Of harpe & of salteriun,..Of timpe & of lire. [*Timpe* is prob. dative case.]

timp, var. of TYMP.

timpan(e, -phan, timpanie, obs. ff. TYMPAN, TYMPANY.

timpani (ˈtɪmpənɪ), *sb. pl.* Also **tympani.** [a. It., pl. of *timpano* kettledrum (also used), f. L. *tympanum* drum: cf. TYMPANUM, TYMPANY 3.] **a.** The kettledrums. **b.** Timpani-players, timpanists.

[**1557**: see TYMPANY 3.] **1740** J. GRASSINEAU *Mus. Dict.* 283 *Timpano.* See *Tympanum.* **1876** STAINER & BARRETT *Dict. Mus. Terms*, Tympani. *Ibid.* 435/1 Timpani, (*It.*) kettle-drums. **1906** [see TYMPANIST]. **1917** *Lit. Digest* 25 Aug. 28/2 The thirty-seconds scored for the tympani in some of the modern Russian music. **1927** *Melody Maker* May 483/1 There has been much controversy concerning the practical use of tympani in the dance band, and many dance drummers have, owing to the infrequency of tympani passages in dance arrangements, regarded them as instruments unnecessary for dance work altogether. **1947** A. EINSTEIN *Mus. in Romantic Era* ii. 14 One of them, that in G minor, renounces trumpets and timpani. **1962** N. DEL MAR *R. Strauss* v. 161 It takes the form of a powerful pedal-point reinforced by regular strokes on the timpani. **1965** G. McINNES *Road to Gundagai* xi. 200 The man with the bass drum and tympani was responsible for the heavy artillery. **1970** J. BLADES *Percussion Instruments* xii. 270 The soft pulsation of the C timpano. **1977** *Listener* 27 Jan. 128/3 BBC Northern Orchestra..requires: Timpani and Percussion... Salary £3,876 per annum.

Hence **ˈtimpanist**, one who plays the kettle-drums.

1939 J. HARRISON *Brahms & his Four Symphonies* vi. 79 The Timpanist reiterates those challenging Cs. **1948** *Penguin Music Mag.* June 40 The timpanist's job is extremely responsible. **1978** *Washington Post* 28 Mar. c2/3 The kid snuck down to the front and got a wink from the timpanist in the orchestra.

timps (tɪmps), *sb. pl.* Colloq. abbrev. of prec.

1934 S. R. NELSON *All about Jazz* ii. 50 There were drummers who could already read and play timps, etc. **1948** *Penguin Music Mag.* June 40 He himself was a 'timps' player as well as conductor. **1978** R. DONINGTON in J. M. Thomson *Future of Early Music in Britain* 15 The baroque orchestra..should have a basic need for..trumpets and timps as required.

timse, var. TEMSE, a sieve.

Timurid (ˈtɪmjʊrɪd), *a.* and *sb.* [f. the personal name *Timur* (see below) + patronymic suff. *-id.*] **A.** *adj.* Descended from Timur Lenk (see TAMERLANE, TAMBURLAINE); of or pertaining to the Turkic dynasty which ruled in Central Asia after the death of Timur in 1405 until 1506. **B.** *sb.* A descendant of Timur Lenk; a member of the Timurid dynasty.

1889 G. N. CURZON *Russia in Central Asia* vii. 216 The *Koktash*, or coronation-stone, of the Timurid sovereigns. **1908** C. ELIOT *Turkey in Europe* (ed. 2) iii. 87 Shah Shaitan ..and his descendants struggled with the Timurids for the supreme power in Transoxiana. **1934** A. TOYNBEE *Study of Hist.* I. II. 369 The Timurid Empire had held together..for half a century longer. **1947** AUDEN *Age of Anxiety* v. 110 The Timurids and Torguts. **1958** O. CAROE *Pathans* x. 138 His claim to the Delhi throne was based on his Timurid ancestry. **1975** [see SAFAVID *a.* and *sb.*].

†timˈwhisky. *Obs.* Also 8–9 **-whiskey**, (8 **timmy whisky, -whiskee**). [A compound of WHISKY, a light one-horse carriage: first element uncertain.] A kind of high light carriage, seated for one or two, drawn by a single horse or by two horses driven 'tandem'; a gig; a whisky.

1764 T. BRYDGES *Homer Travest.* (1797) II. 324 In spite of him these younkers frisky Went out and hir'd a timmy whisky. **1768** H. WALPOLE *Let. to Conway* 9 Aug., The apprentices that flirt to Epsom in a Tim-whisky. **1769** BURKE *Corr.* (1844) I. 182 Lord Chatham passed by my door on Friday morning, in a jimwhiskee [*error for* tim-] drawn by two horses, one before the other. **1769** CHESTERF. *Lett. to Godson* 15 Aug., Many of our young nobility push for it [fame] by driving a Chaise and four, or a Tim Whiskey. **1813** SOUTHEY in *Q. Rev.* X. 126. **1824** SCOTT *St. Ronan's* xiv, That almost forgotten accommodation, a whiskey, or, according to some authorities, a tim-whiskey. **1837** SOUTHEY *Doctor* Interch. xiv. IV. 43 The difference between a Baptist and an Anabaptist, which Sir John Danvers said, is much the same as that between a Whiskey and a Tim whiskey, that is to say no difference at all.

tin (tɪn), *sb.* Forms: 1–3 **tin**, 3–7 **tyn**, 4–6 **tynne**, 5 **tyne**, 5–7 **tynn**, (6 **teene**, *Sc.* **twne**, **tun**), 6–7 **tinne**, 7 **tinn**, 7– **tin**. [OE. *tin* neut. = MLG., MDu. *tin(n, tēn* (LG., EFris., Du. *tin*), OHG., MHG. *zin* (G. *zinn*), ON. *tin* (Da. *tin*, Sw. *tenn*):—OTeut. **tin-o*ᵐ; not known outside Teutonic. Ir. *tinne* is from Eng.

The 16th c. Sc. forms *twne, tun* are difficult to account for.]

1. a. One of the well-known metals, nearly approaching silver in whiteness and lustre, highly malleable and taking a high polish; used in the manufacture of articles of block tin, in the formation of alloys, as bronze, pewter, etc., and, on account of its resistance to oxidation, for making tin-plate and lining culinary and other iron vessels.

Tin is rarely if ever found native, but occurs in two ores, the dioxide, SnO_2, called *tin-stone* or *cassiterite*, and, less commonly, in tin-pyrites or sulphide of tin, SnS_2. Chemically it is a dyad metallic element, symbol Sn (*stannum*), atomic weight (O = 16) 119 (*Internat. Committee* in *Jrnl. Chem. Soc.* Sept. 1912, 1832); sp. gr. about 7·3. In Alchemy represented by the same sign (♃) as the planet Jupiter.

c **897** K. ÆLFRED *Gregory's Past. C.* xxxvii. 266 Ðis Israhela folc is ʒeworden nu me to sindrum & to are & to tine & to iserne & to leade inne on minum ofne. *c* **1200** *Trin. Coll. Hom.* 163 Ðe caliz [in church is] of tin and hire [the priest's concubine's] nap of mazere and ring of golde. **1297** R. GLOUC. (Rolls) 144 Metal, as led and tyn. **1382** WYCLIF *Num.* xxxi. 22 Brasse, and yren, and tynne. *a* **1450** *Voc.* in Wr.-Wülcker 613/20 *Stannum*, tyn. *Ibid.* 653/14 *Hoc stagnum*, tyne. **1544** PHAER *Regim. Lyfe* (1560) C iv, Kepe them in a boxe of tinne. **1548** *Aberdeen Regr.* (1844) I. 259, vij platis of twne,..item, iij quartis of twne. **1561** *Ibid.* 336 Ane charger of tun, ane plait of tun, ane dische of tun. **1559** *Will R. Hoope* (Somerset Ho.), Beades of Teene. **1610** HOLLAND *Camden's Brit.* (1637) 184 Rich and plenteous mines of tinne. **1796** KIRWAN *Elem. Min.* (ed. 2) II. 195 The colour of Tin is greyish white... Fracture hackly, crackles.. when bent. **1815** J. SMITH *Panorama Sci. & Art* II. 388 Equal parts of tin and bismuth form a brittle alloy. **1863** LYELL *Antiq. Man* ii. 10 Bronze is an alloy of about nine parts of copper and one of tin.

b. With defining attribute, as

bar-tin = *block tin*; **black tin**, tin ore (the dioxide, SnO_2) prepared for smelting; **block tin**, tin of second quality cast into blocks; solid tin as distinct from tin plate; a receptacle made from this; **grain tin**, a very pure tin obtained by fusing stream tin in a blast furnace supplied with charcoal, and breaking it into small pieces; **phosphor tin**, an artificial compound of tin and phosphorus; **stream tin**, tin ore washed from the sand or gravel in which it occurs; **white tin**, refined metallic tin.

1870 YEATS *Nat. Hist. Comm.* 361 Stream ores produce the grain tin,..and the others the *bar or block tin. **1873** WATTS *Fownes' Chem.* 443 Two varieties of commercial tin are known, called grain- and bar-tin. **1610** HOLLAND *Camden's Brit.* (1637) 185 *Black tin..is tinne ore broken and washed. **1865** E. BURRITT *Walk Land's End* 320 The mine produces about 430 tons of black tin annually. **1668** CHARLETON *Onomast.* 295 Mundick, and *Block Tin. **1688** LUTTRELL *Brief Rel.* (1857) I. 455 There is a new patent passing empow'ring commissioners for the making of new tinn farthings of block tinn. **1836** DICKENS in *Bell's Life in London* 17 Jan. 1/1 The little block-tin temple sacred to 'baked 'taturs'. **1842** *Penny Cycl.* XXIV. 472/2 After refining, the tin is cast into blocks of about three cwt. each. .. Tin thus prepared is sold as *block tin.* **1852** DICKENS *Bleak Ho.* (1853) xxvi. 259 He could play 'em a tune on any sort of pot you please, so as it was iron or block tin. **1879** M. E. BRADDON *Vixen* I. xiii. 255 The silver kettle..was conducting itself as spitfireishly as any blackened block-tin on a kitchen hob. **1910** G. B. SHAW *Let.* 21 Mar. (1972) II. 915 You inherited from your father a sense of the importance of block-tin piping. **1796** KIRWAN *Elem. Min.* (ed. 2) II. 201 *Grain Tin approaches to the silvery white. Common block Tin is bluer. **1877** KNIGHT *Dict. Mech.* 2575/1 Grain-tin is prepared by plunging blocks of tin into a bath of molten tin, and when they have assumed a brittle crystaling texture, they are broken with a hammer; or, after being heated nearly to the fusing-point, they are allowed to fall from a considerable hight; they are thus broken up into elongated grains. **1884** *Ibid.* Suppl., **Phosphor Tin*... Useful in making phosphor bronze. **1796** KIRWAN *Elem. Min.* (ed. 2) II. 201 In Cornwall the best Tin Ores are those that are washed down the hills by torrents, and thence called *Stream Tin Ores. **1842** BRANDE *Dict. Sc.*, etc., s.v. *Tin*, Stream tin,..from it the purest metal is obtained. **1674** RAY *Words, Prepar. Tin* 124 Two pound of black tin..yields a pound of *White or more. **1706** *Lond. Gaz.* No. 4241/2 A new Invention of Smelting..of Black Tin-Ore into White Tin.

2. a. A vessel made of tin, or more usually of tinned iron; *spec.* a vessel in which meat, fish, fruit, etc., is hermetically sealed for preservation (= CAN *sb.*[1] 3); locally, a small cylindrical drinking vessel or mug with a handle.

1795 S. MARTIN *New Experienced Eng.-Housekeeper* v. 73 Butter the tins, and bake them in a pretty quick oven. **1821** CLARE *Vill. Minstr.* II. 73 With shining tin to keep his dinner warm Swung at his back. **1851** MAYHEW *Lond. Labour* I. 354 The sellers of tins, who carry them under their arms, or in any way on a round,..are known as hand sellers. **1853** KANE *Grinnell Exp.* xxx. (1856) 258 Now we had to quarry out the blocks [of ice]..and then melt it in tins for our daily drink. **1861** MRS. BEETON *Bk. Househ. Managem.* 100 Many cooks use the tinned turtle..preserved in hermetically-sealed canisters... The cost of a tin..is about £2. **1898** *British Printer* XI. 218 A couple of opened ink tins. **1900** H. G. GRAHAM *Soc. Life Scot. in 18th C.* IV. ii. (1901) 135 They partook of a tin of ale. **1901** *Westm. Gaz.* 29 Nov. 8/2 An action..that concerns 200,000 tins of strawberry jam for the troops in South Africa. The manufacturers are proceeding against the tin-makers, as the tins leaked. *Mod.* To open a tin of sardines. (*Scotl.*) Each child brought a tin and received her tinful of milk.

b. Tin-plate as the material of such vessels.

1879 MRS. A. E. JAMES *Ind. Househ. Managem.* 85 A tin writing case is much more useful..for in tin nothing will mildew as it is liable to do in leather. **1886** RUSKIN *Præterita* I. 283 Meat of their own herds, untainted by American tin.

c. Cricket colloq. ***the tins***, rectangular metal pieces each with a single white number painted on a black ground, set on the score-board or 'telegraph' to show the score, etc., during a match. Phr. ***on the tins***, on the score-board.

1903 D. L. A. JEPHSON in H. G. Hutchinson *Cricket* iv. 97 Poor old Surrey in the soup again!.. The mouldy eight runs on the tins were only hoisted there by a mighty effort. **1944** E. BLUNDEN *Cricket Country* i. 19 The call from the pavilion ..sent the tins hustling up on the score-board.

d. *Squash Rackets.* A strip of metal or other material fitted along the bottom of the front wall of the court, which resounds when struck by the ball, showing it to have dropped out of play. With *the.*

[**1926** C. ARNOLD *Game of Squash Rackets* i. 1 On the front wall is fixed the playboard or tell tale. This consists of a piece of boarding backed with tin extending to a height of 19 inches from the ground. A ball striking this surface would not count, hence the name and the tin backing which sends forth a metallic clang when struck.] **1933** *Times* 18 Nov. 5/7 Time after time he got his opponent out of position and then, in too great a hurry to finish off the rally, put the ball on to the tin. **1960** *Times* 29 Nov. 17/4 Gordon..cast away his chances into the tin. **1973** M. RUSSELL *Double Hit* xxv. 187 The boy aimed a stroke which missed. The fourth he returned into the tin.

3. *slang.* **a.** Money, cash. Cf. BRASS *sb.* 3 b.

Said to have been first applied to the small silver coins of the 18th c., which before their recall in 1817 were often worn quite smooth without trace of any device, so as to resemble pieces of tin. See quot. for *tin-like* in 4 c.

1836 SMITH *Individual, Thieves' Chaunt* 5 (Farmer) Because she lately nimm'd some tin, They have sent her to lodge at the King's Head Inn. **1840** DICKENS *Old C. Shop* ii, How much better would it be..to hand over a reasonable amount of tin. **1854** MARION HARLAND *Alone* xxiv, She married a rich old man for his 'tin'.

b. ***the Tins***: a nickname of the Household Cavalry (from their cuirasses).

1918 G. FRANKAU *Poet. Works* (1923) 181 Why ride the Tins in full review-array? 'Tis Hazeline Tredither's wedding-day! **1947** *Times* 16 Sept. 5/4 The Household Cavalry are the 'Tins', in allusion to their cuirasses; the shrapnel helmet of our day is a 'tinhat'. **1982** BARR & YORK *Official Sloane Ranger Handbk.* 90/1 Household Cavalry (the Tins: the Life Guards, and the Blues & Royals).

c. The badge or shield of a policeman. *U.S.*

1949 PARTRIDGE *Dict. Underworld* 725/2 *Tin*,..as 'a sheriff's badge', it is American s[lang]. **1956** 'E. MCBAIN' *Cop Hater* (1958) xiii. 109 They reached for the leather cases to which their shields were pinned... They pinned the tin to their collars. **1975** 'S. MARLOWE' *Cawthorn Jrnls.* (1976) II. xix. 170 Mason Reed flashed the tin. 'Police officer. March right out of here.'

4. *attrib.* and *Comb.* **a.** *attrib.* or as *adj.* Made or consisting of tin (or of tin-plate), as ***tin bar, basin, box, bucket, button, farthing, filings, flagon, metal, -nail, roof, saucepan, -solder, spoon, thread, trunk, -ware, whistle***; of, pertaining or relating to, producing, or concerned with tin, as ***tin-amalgam, -dip, -farm, -float*** (FLOAT *sb.* 19), ***-furnace, -grain, -kiln, -law, -lode, -merchant, -mine, ore, -pit,***

-shop, *trade*, *vein*; put up or preserved in tins, tinned, as *tin junk*, *milk*.

1839 URE *Dict. Arts* 593 The glass..with its interior coating of *tin-amalgam. **1487** *Cely Papers* (Camden) 157 A *tyn basson w[t] oder geyr. **1723** J. NOTT *Cook's & Confectioner's Dict.* sig. I i 8, You may boil it [*sc.* spinach] in a *Tin-box, which shuts so close, that no Liquor can get in. **1858** SIMMONDS *Dict. Trade*, *Tin-box*, *Tin-case*, a strong iron box tinned and japanned, for holding papers, dress articles, etc. **1642** in J. Lister *Autobiog.* (1842) 78 Michael Woodhead was shot upon his *tin-buttons. **1775** ASH, **Tin-canister*, a canister made of tin. **1839** URE *Dict. Arts* 1253 (*Tin-plate*) The final *tin-dip is useful to remove the marks of the brush. **1758** BORLASE *Cornwall* 190 The *tin-farm of Cornwall at this time amounted to..one hundred marks per annum. **1688** *Tinn farthings [see *block tin* in sense 1 b]. **1822–34** *Good's Study Med.* (ed. 4) I. 288 The anthelmintic virtues of *tin-filings. **1589** *Exch. Rolls Scotl.* XXII. 73 Aucht *tin flauconis contenand ane point the pece. **1681** GREW *Musæum* III. II. ii. 328 A Slag, remaining in the bottom of the *Tin-Floate. **1695** WOODWARD *Nat. Hist. Earth* IV. (1723) 213 *Tin-Grains, and other Ores of Metalls. **1710** J. HARRIS *Lex. Techn.* II, **Tin-kiln*, is used for the Burning of the Mundick from the Tin-ore. **1611** SPEED *Theat. Gt. Brit.* xi. (1614) 21/1 This Earle made certain *tinne-laws which with liberties and priviledges were confirmed by Earle Edmund his sonne. **1839** DE LA BECHE *Rep. Geol. Cornwall*, etc. x. 301 Wheal Friendship lode differs but a few degrees from east and west, as is also the case with Wheal Jewel *tin-lode on the north of it. **1708** *Lond. Gaz.* No. 4461/4 Richard Balhatchett,..Tinner, or *Tinn-Merchant. **1882** *Three in Norway* v. 35 When we have only *tin milk. **1610** HOLLAND *Camden's Brit.* 185 The incursions of the Mores had stopped up the *tinne mines of Spaine. **1839** URE *Dict. Arts* 1241 The tin-mines of the Malay peninsula. **1381–2** *Durham Acc. Rolls* (Surtees) 389 In CCC *Tinnail et vernys empt. pro ostio parliamenti in claustro. **1610** *Tinne ore [see *black tin* in 1 b]. **1766** WESLEY *Jrnl.* 12 Sept., My horse was just stepping into a *tin-pit. **1912** E. LUTYENS *Let.* May in M. Lutyens *Edwin Lutyens* (1980) vii. 105 It is..very English!—to have a capital as Simla is entirely of *tin roofs. **1982** M. DUKE *Flashpoint* x. 69 Untidy shanties with tin roofs. **1834** *Tait's Mag.* I. 181/2, I have known a blacksmith..unaware of the fact that what are called '*tin saucepans' are made of tinned plate iron. **1851** H. MAYHEW *London Labour* I. 336/1 The street-sellers of that order are supplied at the '*tin-shops'. **1979** *United States 1980/81* (Penguin Travel Guides) 546 The bakery, tin shop and garden house look..as if they were still open for business. **1603** HOLLAND *Plutarch's Mor.* 189 Like as *tin-soder doth knit and rejoyne a crackt peece of brasse. **1669** STURMY *Mariner's Mag., Penalties & Forfeit.* 2 *Tin and Leaden Spoons. **1674** tr. *Scheffer's Lapland* 105 Adorned with needle work of *tin-thred upon diverse colour'd cloth. **1839** DE LA BECHE *Rep. Geol. Cornwall*, etc. xv. 525 The chief emporium of the *tin trade was Bruges. **1922** E. H. YOUNG *Bridge Dividing* II. i. 79 Henrietta went to her room to unpack the brown *tin trunk which contained all her possessions. **1981** R. GRAYSON *Death of Abbé Didier* xiv. 125 He could see in the bedroom two large tin trunks. **1610** HOLLAND *Camden's Brit.* 185 The *tynne veines in Germanie..were not as yet knowen. **1812** 'H. BULL-US' *Diverting Hist. John Bull & Brother Jonathan* xiii. 91 These people are also very ingenious in making *tin ware, brooms, cider-brandy, wooden bowls, and tallow candles. **1860** PIESSE *Lab. Chem. Wonders* 36 It is this substance which constitutes our famous tin-ware. **1825** J. NEAL *Bro. Jonathan* I. 90 As if he were sounding a charge with..a *tin-whistle.

b. *fig.* in reference to tin as a base metal, esp. in comparison with silver: Mean, petty, worthless, counterfeit. (Cf. COPPER *sb.*[1] 9 c.) Freq. in phr. (*little*) *tin god*. Also *tin Jesus* (only in the work of G. B. Shaw).

1886 KIPLING *Departm. Ditties* (1899) 24 The Little Tin Gods harried their little tin souls. **1902** *Daily Chron.* 10 July 3/3 Those funny little tin revolutions affected by the South American States. **1905** H. A. VACHELL *Hill* ix. 187, I hope he's not going to make a sort of tin parson of you. **1909** *Our German Cousins* xv. 89 In Prussia alone there are 492 Landräte—a sort of district commissioner—all Government officials or directly in touch with the central government, and all little tin gods in their own district. **1917** S. LEWIS *Job* xiii. 193 If they'd work like sixty they might get to be little tin gods on wheels like himself? **1928** R. CAMPBELL *Wayzgoose* ii. 55 Of Tin Gods you may oft have heard or read But this one was entirely made of lead. **1930** G. B. SHAW *What I really wrote about War* xii. 368 The victorious Chauvinists..derided him [*sc.* Woodrow Wilson] as 'a tin Jesus'. **1951** E. COXHEAD *One Green Bottle* v. 115 We economists are going to be the little tin gods of this generation. **1978** 'M. M. KAYE' *Far Pavilions* VI. xxxvi. 534 With luck the 'Tin Gods' who had banished him to Gujerat ..would leave him alone.

c. objective and obj. genitive, as ***tin-beater***, ***-maker***, ***-melter***, ***-miner***, ***-pedler***, ***smelter***, ***-stamper***, etc.; ***tin-bearing***, ***-dressing***, ***-getting***, ***-mining***, ***-smelting***, ***-stamping***, etc., sbs. and adjs.; instrumental, as ***tin-poisoning***, ***-roofing***; ***tin-lined***, ***-mailed***, ***-roofed*** adjs.; parasynthetic, as ***tin-bottomed***, ***-coloured***, ***-handled***, ***-tabled*** adjs.; similative, as ***tin-white*** adj. and sb.; also ***tin-like*** adj. and adv.

1899 *Daily News* 30 Nov. 2/1 (Prospectus) Two immense deposits of *tin-bearing drift. **1848** W. H. KELLY tr. *L. Blanc's Hist. Ten Y.* II. 272 François Foucret, *tin-beater, ..living in Vaise. **1872** CALVERLEY *Fly-leaves* (1903) 73 Hit a *tinbottom'd tray Hard with the fireshovel, hammer away! *c* **1515** *Cocke Lorelles B.* 10 Balancers, *tynne casters, and skryueners. **1606** SYLVESTER *Du Bartas* II. iv. II. *Magnificence* 926 On his back he wears *Tin-colour'd Tissue. **1896** *Daily News* 17 Nov. 3/5 He was given a *tin-handled knife. **1846** MRS. GORE *Eng. Char.* 6 Many persons ..remember the villanous old coinage of George III. [properly Queen Anne to Geo. II, still current under Geo. III, but gradually withdrawn after 1817], the *tin-like sixpences, which added a word to the slang dictionary, and the button-like shillings, of which the image and superscription might have been Cæsar's. **1868** *Rep. U.S. Commissioner Agric.* (1869) 192 Heated by circulated air.. ascending in *tin-lined flues. **1879** MRS. A. E. JAMES *Ind. Househ. Managem.* 21 Articles..should be securely packed in tin boxes, or else in boxes tin-lined. **1887** RUSKIN *Præterita* II. 401 The delicately *tin-mailed and glittering spires of the village church. **1592** CHETTLE *Kinde-harts Dr.* (1841) 26 The receipte which the *tinne-melters wife ministred. **1899** R. MUNRO *Prehist. Scot.* i. 6 Diodorus Siculus makes mention of the *tin-miners. **1812** J. K. PAULDING *Beauties Bro. Bull-Us* 53 Feather-merchants, rag-men, *tin-pedlars, and horse-jockies. **1841** EMERSON *Ess.* Ser. I. iv. (1876) 112 He hears and feels what you say of the seraphim, and of the tin-pedler. **1904** *Westm. Gaz.* 20 Sept. 3/2 These could not have saved him from *tin-poisoning or a touch of ophthalmia. **1882** J. G. WHITTIER in *Atlantic Monthly* Feb. 145 Its *tin-roofed chapel stood Half hid in the dwarf spruce wood. *c* **1886** KIPLING *Railway Folk* 59 Walk into a huge, brick-built, tin-roofed stable. **1885** *List of Subscribers, Classified* (United Telephone Co.) (ed. 6) 211 *Tin Smelters... Redruth Tin Smelting Co. **1977** *Whitaker's Almanack 1978* 757 Some of the country's more important industrial installations include..a tin smelter. **1885** *List of Subscribers, Classified* (United Telephone Co.) (ed. 6) 151 Anglo-American *Tin Stamping Co., Limited. **1839** URE *Dict. Arts* 1253 Paid for brushing and *tin-washing 225 plates. **1800** HENRY *Epit. Chem.* (1808) 252 The colour of this metal [tellurium] is *tin-white, verging to lead-grey. **1855** J. R. LEIFCHILD *Cornwall Mines* 39 Good specimens of tin-white cobalt.

d. Applied disparagingly to buildings (esp. Nonconformist churches) made partly of corrugated iron: ***tin chapel***, ***tabernacle*** (cf. TABERNACLE *sb.* 6 b), etc. Also, ***tin town***.

1884 *Lichfield Diocesan Mag.* Jan. 11/2 It was decided to build 'a little bit of a tin tabernacle'. **1886** MARQUESS OF BUTE *Let.* 17 Apr. in D. H. Blair *John Patrick 3rd Marquess of Bute* (1921) ix. 154 The persistent wish of my Lord of Argyll to have what he calls an 'opening' of the tin temple in August. **1897** E. EDWARDS *Journey through S. Afr.* viii. 48 It would not be out of place to refer to Kimberley as a 'tin town'. **1919** A. T. BASSETT *S. Barnabas' Oxford* iv. 36 This was before the 'tin' church at Cowley S. John existed. **1929** J. B. PRIESTLEY *Good Companions* I. vi. 242 That's the Station Refreshment Rooms, a tin place, just opposite. **1934** DYLAN THOMAS *Let.* Oct. (1966) 143 We made a tour of the pubs..drinking to the..destruction of the Tin Bethels. **1937** *New Statesman* 13 Nov. 802/2 The several designs of late-Victorian tin-chapel in the slums of a northern industrial town. **1962** 'J. LE CARRÉ' *Murder of Quality* x. 108 That parson man from the tin tabernacle. **1979** 'P. O'CONNOR' *Into Strong City* II. xxix. 103 *Being born again* had become no longer a derisive tin chapel slogan but a phrase to describe what was happening to me.

5. Special Combs.: **tin-arsed** *a. Austral.* and *N.Z. slang*, very lucky; **tin-back** *Austral. slang*, a very lucky man; **tin-bath** (BATH *sb.*[1] 18), the mass of melted tin in a tin-furnace; **tin bill**: see quot.; †**tin-blain**, a blain or inflammatory swelling of the tongue in horses; †**tin-boat**, a pontoon or the like made of tin (or some alloy of tin): cf. PONTOON *sb.*[1] 1, quots. 1710 and 1811; **tin-bound** *sb.* = BOUND *sb.*[1] 3 c; hence **tin-bound** *v. trans.*, to mark out the boundaries of (a piece of ground) for tin-mining; whence **tin-bounder**, **-bounding**; **tin can**, (*a*) (see sense 2 a above); (*b*) *slang* (chiefly *U.S.*), a warship, esp. a destroyer (often, one of an older design); also applied to a submarine; **tin-canning** *N.Z.*, a greeting or serenading on a special occasion by beating tin cans; hence **tin-can** *v. trans.* (cf. TIN-KETTLE *v.*); **tin-clad** *a.*, covered with tin; *sb.* [after *iron-clad*], a lightly amoured boat; **tin disease** = *tin pest* below; **tin ear**, (*a*) *slang* = *cauliflower ear* s.v. CAULIFLOWER 2; (*b*) *colloq.* (usu. with indefinite art.), tone-deafness, aural insensitivity, esp. in phr. ***to have a tin ear***; also *fig.*; hence **tin-eared** *a.*; **tin-enamel**, white tin-glaze decorated in enamel colours; hence **tin-enamelled** *a.*; **tin-field**, a tract of country yielding tin; **tin fish**: see FISH *sb.*[1] 1 h; **tin-floor**, (*a*) a floor made of tin; (*b*) a horizontal course or stratum of tin ore: see FLOOR *sb.* 12; **tin-frame**: see quot.; **tin-glaze**, a glaze for fine pottery, having an oxide of tin as a basis; hence **tin-glazed** *a.*; **tin-gravel**, gravel containing tin ore, which is obtained by streaming; **tin-ground** = *tin-field*; **tin-hammer**, a hammer with a heavy tin head, used to drive home tightly fitting bolts, etc.; **tin hare** *slang* (chiefly *Austral.*) = *electric hare* s.v. ELECTRIC *a.* 2 b; also fig. (in quot. 1941 a nickname for a train); **tin helmet** = TIN HAT 1 a; hence **tin-helmeted** *a.*; **tin-house**, (*a*) a house constructed of tin; (*b*) a building where tin is worked; **tin-liquor**, a solution of tin in strong acid mixed with common salt, used as a mordant in dyeing; **Tin Lizzie**: see LIZZIE 2; **tin-loaf**, a loaf baked in a tin, a pan-loaf; **tin-mordant**, a mordant consisting of a solution of tin in acid, as *tin-liquor*; **tin-mouth**, a sun-fish found in the Mississippi, the crappie; **tin-opener**, an instrument for opening soldered tins; **tin pest**, the crumbling of pure tin that occurs at low temperatures as the ordinary white allotrope changes to grey tin; cf. *grey modification* s.v. GREY, GRAY *a.* 8 c; **tin printing** (see quot. 1957); **tin-pulp**, the precipitate from a solution of tin chloride and yellow prussiate of potash, used for dyeing; **tin-putty**, putty-powder; **tin-pyrites**, a sulphide of tin: see PYRITES; **tin-rock**, a variety of rock pigeon; **tin-salt**, the crystalline hydrated chloride of tin, $SnCl_2 2H_2O$, obtained by dissolving tin in hot hydrochloric acid; also, with *pl.*, any salt of tin; **tin-saw**, 'a saw used by bricklayers for cutting kerfs in bricks' (Knight *Dict. Mech.* 1877); **tin-scrap**, the waste tin-plate in the manufacture of tin-ware; **tin-silver**, imitation silver made of tin; **tin-spar** (see quot. 1796); **tin-spirits** = *tin-liquor*; **tin-stuff**, a miner's name for tin ore; **tin-vat**, a vessel in which tin-liquor is kept; **tin wash**, stream tin (see 1 b); **tin-washing** = TIN-STREAMING; *pl.* works where tin-streaming is done; **tin wedding** orig. *U.S.*, the tenth anniversary of a wedding (cf. WEDDING *vbl. sb.* 2 b); **tin-witts**: see quots.; **tinwoman**, a woman who sells tin (cf. TINMAN); **tin-work**, often *pl.* **-works**, a place where tin is worked or manufactured; so **tin-worker**, **-working**; **tin-worm**, the 'worm' or spiral tube of a still, made of tin. See also TINFOIL, -GLASS, -KETTLE, -POT, -TACK, etc.

1937 PARTRIDGE *Dict. Slang* 888/1 *Tinny*, adj... Occ. *tin-arsed. **1971** R. F. BRISSENDEN *Winter Matins* 25 This tin-arsed character Hasn't been there six months before he starts To fidget, gets to grizzling in his beer. **1897** W. T. GOODGE *Hits! Skits! & Jingles!* (1899) 150 And a '*tin-back' is a party Who's remarkable for luck. **1839** URE *Dict. Arts* 1249 (*Tin-Refining*) Into the *tin-bath, billets of green wood are plunged. **1778** PRYCE *Min. Cornub.* v. iv. 291 The manner of agreeing for or buying the Tin Ore..being to give *Tin bills or promissory notes to the owners thereof. *Ibid.* 292 This makes what they call the Tin bill trade so noted in this county. **1614** MARKHAM *Cheap Husb.* I. vi. (1668) 74 For the Blain on the tongue, of some called the *Tin-blain, it is a blister which groweth at the roots of the tongue. **1677** *Lond. Gaz.* No. 1199/3 Some of the biggest Cannon out of the Magazine at Delft, and the *Tin Boats from the Hague. **1692** *Siege Lymerick* 4 This day there came into our Camp Twenty Nine Tin-Boats. **1865** *Standard* 11 July, The Beam mine had been worked by *tin bounders under the custom of Cornwall. *Ibid.*, Up to 1858 the mine had been worked under the custom of *tin bounding. **1883** POLLOCK *Land Laws* ii. (1887) 50 In Cornwall..called 'tin-bounding', from the setting out of the working by bounds which is the adventurer's first step towards establishing his claim. **1770** G. WASHINGTON *Diary* 18 Nov. (1925) I. 442 I was to pay 6 Dollars and give them a Quart *Tinn Can. **1858** SIMMONDS *Dict. Trade*, *Tin-can*, a metal vessel for holding liquids. **1877** KNIGHT *Dict. Mech.*, *Tin Can*, the ordinary name for the cans of tinned iron now so widely used. **1937** *Sun* (Baltimore) 20 Apr. 15/3 Of the forty-seven destroyers out with the United States fleet..thirty-nine are the 'tin cans' of the World War days. **1957** J. FRAME *Owls do Cry* II. xix. 84 We tin-canned them and threw rice at them. **1959** *N.Z. Listener* 10 July 5/3 With us were the first warships I had seen in the heavy seas, and some of the American tin cans they gave us under Lease Lend. **1974** H. GRUPPE *Truxton Cipher* iii. 31 He had noticed the Admiral's wince at Pozo's use of the archaic phrase 'tin cans' to denote destroyers. **1981** G. MARKSTEIN *Ultimate Issue* 27 'Boy, you must have been cramped in that sub.'.. 'Plenty of space. You'd be surprised how roomy those tin cans are.' **1926** A. F. WEBB *Miss Peters' Special* vii. 62 A promoter of most of the *tin-canning parties when anyone got married. **1953** M. SCOTT *Breakfast at Six* (1960) ii. 19 The chaps are coming up tonight. Tin-canning. The usual thing. Thought I'd better warn you. **1873** HOWELLS *Chance Acquaintance* ii, The slender *tin-clad spire of its church. **1887** *Sci. Amer.* 23 Apr. 263/3 He converted..seven transports into what were called 'tinclads', or musket-proof gunboats. **1908** H. C. COOPER tr. *Holleman's Text-bk. Inorg. Chem.* (ed. 3) 275 It [*sc.* white tin] turns very slowly into gray tin, falling to powder, probably because of the increase in volume (this phenomenon is called the '*tin-disease'). **1965** PHILLIPS & WILLIAMS *Inorg. Chem.* I. vii. 246 In cold countries the disintegration of organ pipes and other tin objects has..been observed, and the phenomenon was known as tin disease. **1923** *Dialect Notes* V. 239 **Tin ear on, to put a*, v. phr. To strike or beat, especially, about the head. **1935** *Peabody Bull.* (Baltimore) Dec. 42/2 A player has a 'tin ear' when his intonation is poor and his playing is mechanical. **1958** *Times Lit. Suppl.* 24 Jan. 39/2 He gives the, possibly false, impression, that he has a 'tin ear', as his countrymen put it, for many of the popular art-forms he discusses. **1962** YOUNG & WILLMOTT *Family & Kinship in E. London* (rev. ed.) I. vi. 101 A man with skill as a boxer, and a 'tin ear' (cauliflower ear) to prove it, had.. prestige. **1975** *Times* 17 Apr. 14/4 Manson had a tin ear but ..the Beach Boys recorded at least one of his songs. **1981** L. DEIGHTON *XPD* xviii. 159 'Do you play the piano?'.. 'My wife insisted I get it for Billy, but that kid's got a tin ear.' **1975** *New Yorker* 28 Apr. 130/1 Who but a *tin-eared organ fancier.. can bear to listen to elaborate contrapuntal textures sounded in consecutive fifths? **1900** F. LITCHFIELD *Pottery & Porcelain* ii. 14 Stanniferous or *tin-enamel. **1964** H. HODGES *Artifacts* ii. 51 Today the terms faience, majolica and tin-enamel glaze are all variously applied to mean wares with a red body covered with a tin-opacified lead glaze which has been coloured with over-glaze designs. **1981** 'J. GASH' *Vatican Rip* x. 86 Forged nineteenth-century tin-enamel porcelain maiolicas. **1933** *Burlington Mag.* July 16/1 The *tin-enamelled ware, façon de Pise, especially for the shelves of pharmacies and still-rooms. **1974** *Country Life* 5 Dec. 1728/1 Faience is tin-enamelled earthenware, not porcelain. **1898** *Daily News* 26 Apr. 9/4 The tin wash and tailings of the leading tin sluicing mines of the Ringarooma *Tinfield. **1907** *Daily Chron.* 28 Sept. 5/4 Prospectors in the Government tin-fields at Waterberg. **1707** MORTIMER *Husb.* (1721) I. 185 On this *Tin-floor or Bed may the Hops be turned..with less expence of Fuel. **1839** URE *Dict. Arts* 1241 The stanniferous small veins,..interposed between certain rocks, . . are commonly called tin-floors. **1881** RAYMOND *Mining Gloss.*, **Tin-frame*, Corn[wall], a sleeping-table used in dressing tin-ore slimes, and discharged by turning it upon an axis . . and then dashing water over it. **1897** C. F. BINNS *Ceramic Technol.* ii. 17 These wares were uniformly coated with opaque *tin glazes. **1975** *Times* 18 Feb. 13/1 Tin glaze earthenware chalice. **1904** *Daily Chron.* 7 July 8/4 The *tin-glazed ware of Delft, and the salt-glazed stoneware of Germany. **1874** J. H. COLLINS *Metal Mining* 55 The deposit of *tin gravel at the mouth of the Carnon Valley. **1839** DE LA BECHE *Rep. Geol. Cornwall*, etc. xiii. 401 To fill up the space once occupied by the *tin-ground. **1934** WEBSTER, *Tin hare. **1941** K. TENNANT *Battlers* 159 The 'Tin Hare's' whistle was heard in the distance. **1969** *Northern Territory News* (Darwin) *Focus '69* 109/1 Many top notch tin hare chasers tried at open coursing are 'left for dead' by very ordinary live hare chasers. **1934** WEBSTER, *Tin helmet. **1942** E. WAUGH *Put out More Flags* i. 40 A man in a tin helmet shouted . ., 'Take cover, there.' **1980** 'T. HINDE' *Sir Henry & Sons* i. 10 He mounted a tin helmet on the top of a rifle. **1939** 'N. BLAKE' *Smiler with Knife* xi. 156 The black-faced miners, *tin-helmeted. **1983** C. DEXTER *Riddle of Third Mile* i. 10 The tin-helmeted head spattered with blood. **1798** H. M. WILLIAMS *Tour in Switzer.* I. x. 133 This admirable mimick-creation of silver torrents, mossy forests, *tin-houses and glass lakes. **1904** *Daily News* 19 Nov. 12 The mills and tin house were stopped for nearly an hour. **1858** SIMMONDS *Dict. Trade*, *Tin-liquor. *Ibid.* s.v. *Loaf*, The cottage loaf; *tin loaves. **1839** URE *Dict. Arts* 1252 *Tin mordants, for dyeing scarlet. **1878** C. HALLOCK *Sportsman's Gaz.* 378 Sand Perch, or Bachelor Perch; called also '*Tin-Mouth'. **1888** GOODE *Amer. Fishes* 71 *Pomoxys annularis* . . has other names of local application as 'Tin Mouth', 'Bridge Perch'. **1895** *Daily News* 21 June 3/7 Duggan and Farrell struck at her with a *tin opener. **1902** H. C. COOPER tr. *Holleman's Text-bk. Inorg. Chem.* 261 It [*sc.* white tin] turns very slowly into gray tin, falling to powder (this phenomenon is called the *tin-pest). **1933** *Jrnl. R. Aeronaut. Soc.* XXXVII. 540 This change does not proceed with disintegrating effects until considerably lower temperatures, when the 'Tin-Pest', experienced in organ-pipes, during cold winters on the Continent, occurs. **1960** E. S. HEDGES *Tin & its Alloys* i. 2 There seems to be a paucity of very ancient objects made entirely of tin—a lack which is sometimes laid at the door of the disintegration of tin through 'tin pest'. **1887** *Amer. Lithographer & Printer* 2 Apr. 192/3 Could you give me something practical on *tin printing? **1957** *Encycl. Brit.* XIV. 214/1 Tin Printing, which was introduced about 1875, is the application of the lithographic process to the decoration of metal plate. A substantial percentage of can-label work formerly done by the paper lithographer has in recent years gone to the tin lithographers. . . Sheets of prepared tin . . are fed into the press and are then oven dried at high temperature, this procedure being repeated for each additional colour. **1968** *Gloss. Terms Offset Lithogr. Printing* (*B.S.I.*) 33 *Tin printing machine*, (deprecated) a machine for printing on sheet metal. **1874** W. CROOKES *Dyeing & Calico-Print.* II. i. 166 The so-called prussiate of tin, or *tin-pulp, is chiefly used as an ingredient in printing steam-blues on cotton. **1839** URE *Dict. Arts* 801 The last polish is given [to marble] with *tin-putty. **1796** KIRWAN *Elem. Min.* (ed. 2) II. 75 *Tin Pyrites. **1839** URE *Dict. Arts* 1241 There are only two ores of tin; the peroxide, or tin-stone, and tin pyrites. **1892** GREENER *Breech-Loader* 237 The greater portion of the pigeons used for trap shooting are brought over from that port [Antwerp], and sold here as *Tin Rocks. **1849** D. CAMPBELL *Inorg. Chem.* 229 Boiling with phosphorous acid or *tin salt. **1681** GREW *Musæum* III. I. v. 307 A Yellow *Tin-Spar from Ireland. **1796** KIRWAN *Elem. Min.* (ed. 2) II. 198 The yellowish grey [tin stone] is often called Tinspar. **1877** O'NEILL in *Encycl. Brit.* VII. 574/2 The solution of tin used by dyers . . commonly called '*tin spirits'. **1778** W. PRYCE *Min. Cornub.* 67 The Tinners or Miners . . give it the name of *Tin-stuff. **1865–72** WATTS *Dict. Chem.* III. 252 In the *tin-vat, commonly used for calico-printing, the indigo is reduced by a solution of stannous oxide in caustic potash or soda. **1898** *Tin wash [see *tin-field* above]. **1869** A. R. WALLACE *Malay Archip.* I. 43 Extensive *tin-washings, employing over a thousand Chinese. **1863** *Harper's Mag.* Nov. 856/2 Mr Jones's people made him a *tin-wedding visit on the tenth anniversary of his marriage. **1981** *N.Y. Times* 19 July II. 25/4 A tin wedding bouquet and a brooch of jewelled flowers sit side by side. **1853** URE *Dict. Arts* II. 858 '*Tin witts': the ore obtained from the stamp floors. **1881** RAYMOND *Mining Gloss.*, *Tin-witts*, Corn[wall], the product of the first dressing of tin-ores, containing, besides tinstone, other heavy minerals (wolfram and metallic sulphides). **1884** M. E. WILKINS in *Harper's Mag.* June 29/2 Her customers . . had grown used to the novelty of a *tinwoman, instead of a tinman. **1475** *Rolls of Parlt.* VI. 134/2 A *Tyn werk within the said Counte of Cornewaill, called the Myne of the Cleker. **1610** HOLLAND *Camden's Brit.* 184 Of these Mines or tinne-workes, there be two kinds. **1839** DE LA BECHE *Rep. Geol. Cornwall*, etc. xiii. 408 An epoch corresponding with that to which the Cornish stream tin-works belong. **1610** HOLLAND *Camden's Brit.* 185 Hee delivered rules and precepts to these *Tinne-workers. **1827** G. HIGGINS *Celtic Druids* Pref. 51 Before this *tin-working nation dived into the bowels of the earth. **1800** tr. *Lagrange's Chem.* II. 53 The *tin-worms of stills.

tin (tɪn), *v.* Forms: see prec. [f. prec. sb. Cf. Du., LG. *-tinnen*, Ger. *-zinnen*.]

1. *trans.* To cover with a thin deposit of tin; to coat or plate with tin.

1398 TREVISA *Barth. De P.R.* XVI. xxxvii. (Tollem. MS.), Brasen vessel ben sone reed and rousti . . and haue an yuel sauoure and smel, but þey be tynned. *c* **1440** *Promp. Parv.* 494/1 Tynnyn wythe tynne, *stanno*. **1599** A. M. tr. *Gabelhouer's Bk. Physicke* 54/1 Take a copper basen which is not tinned. **1601** HOLLAND *Pliny* (1634) II. 517 A deuise to tin pots, pans, and other pieces of brasse . . with white lead or tinglasse. **1747** MRS. GLASSE *Cookery* v. 68 Take great Care the Pots or Sauce-pans . . be well tinned, for fear of giving the Broths or Soops any brassy Taste. **1816** P. CLEAVELAND *Min.* 525 Tin-plate . . consists of iron, whose surface is tinned to prevent oxidation. **1832** BABBAGE *Econ. Manuf.* xix. (ed. 3) 182 The man who pickles and tins the pins.

2. In soldering iron, brass, etc., To perform the preliminary process of heating the surfaces and covering them with a thin coating of the solder.

1873 E. SPON *Workshop Receipts* Ser. I. (1888) 366/1 First clean the iron and brass well and then tin them before placing them together for soldering. . . The articles can be tinned by rubbing while hot with rosin; then rubbing them over with solder.

3. To put up or seal (provisions) in a tin for preservation; to can. (In quot. 1887 *intr.* for *pass.*)

1887 *Cassell's Mag.* Feb. 148 Some fish 'tin' well, others do not. **1890** *Daily News* 16 Apr. 6/2 The method of tinning milk for use of troops.

tin, obs. form of *þin*, THINE (after a dental).

tin, var. TIND *v. Obs.*, to kindle; var. TINE *sb.*[2] *Obs.*, loss.

tinacle, obs. form of TUNICLE.

‖**tinaja** (ti'naxa). Formerly Anglicized, as 6 **'tinage, 'tynage**, 7 **'tynaxe**; also in Sp. forms 6 **ti'naio** (i.e. *tinajo*), 7 **ti'naxa**. [a. Sp. *tinaja*, †*tinaxa* = It. *tinaccio*, augmentatives of *tina* and *tino*, L. *tīna* wine-vessel.]

1. In Spain: a large earthenware jar used to hold wine, oil, olives, or salted fish or meat; in parts of Spanish America, such a jar used for storing water.

1574 HELLOWES *Gueuara's Fam. Ep.* (1584) 241 His souldiers . . haue drunke out a whole tinage of wine. **1582** N. LICHEFIELD tr. *Castanheda's Conq. E. Ind.* I. xlix. 106 Sixe great Tynages of fine Earth, which they doe call Porcelanas. **1598** W. PHILLIP *Linschoten* I. vi. 16/2 The water that they drinke . . they keepe in great pots (as the Tinaios in Spaine). **1622** R. HAWKINS *Voy. S. Sea* xii. 25 The Inhabitants doe reserue water . . in their Cisterns and Tynaxes. **1676** LADY FANSHAWE *Mem.* (1830) 195 That admirable wine is kept in great tinajas, which are pots holding about 500 gallons each. **1845** FORD *Handbk. Spain* I. 231/1 At Coria are made the enormous earthenware jars in which oil and olives are kept: these tinajas are the precise amphoræ of the ancients. **1885** *Encycl. Brit.* XIX. 629/1 The earliest kinds now existing of Spanish pottery without either enamel or glaze are chiefly large wine-jars, 'tinajas', about 3 or 4 feet high, of graceful amphora-like shape, stamped with simple patterns in relief. **1924** GORGAS & HENDRICK *William Crawford Gorgas* v. 179 An assault on the water barrels, cisterns, tinajas, and dish pans of the cities of Colon and Panama involved greater difficulties. **1949** *Jrnl. N.Y. Bot. Garden* Mar. 59 The women look like animated tea cozies . . loaded down . . with *tinajas* (jars) or rolls of mats made of reeds. **1971** L. BOGER *Dict. World Pott. & Porc.* 343/1 Tinajas were produced in all parts of Moslem Spain with . . little variety in design.

2. *South-west U.S.* A rock hollow where water is retained; hence, any temporary or intermittent pool.

1835 T. COULTER *Notes on Upper California* 65 The only water to be had is found . . in excavations called Tinajas, made by the Indians. **1857** A. SCHOTT *Obs. on Country along Mexican Boundary* 69 Permanent water is found under a cleft of igneous rocks, and does not properly deserve the name of a spring, but is rather a tinaja supplied by water trickling through the rocks from water-holes above. **1896** *Science* 3 Apr. 494/1 Knowledge of the few widely separated tinajas and springs was bought at the price of many lives. **1958** 'W. HENRY' *Seven Men at Mimbres Springs* v. 55 The wells were pothole water tanks, rock *tinajas*.

‖**tinamou** ('tɪnəmuː). [a. F. *tinamou* (Barrère 1741, Buffon 1771), a. *tinamu*, native name in Galibi.] A bird of the genus *Tinamus* (Latham 1790) or family *Tinamidæ*, dromæognathous birds, according to Huxley forming the bond of union between the *Carinatæ* and *Ratitæ*. The species have an external resemblance to partridges or quails, the place of which they fill on the pampas.

1783 LATHAM *Synopsis Birds* II. 724 Genus LII. Tinamou. No. 1. Great T[inamou]. . . *Tinamou de Cayenne*. . . This is found in the woods of several parts of South America, particularly of Cayenne and Guiana. **1842** *Penny Cycl.* XXIV. 476/2. **1884** G. ALLEN in *Longm. Mag.* Jan. 293 All other modern birds . . are linked . . to the still earlier toothed ancestral types, by the South American tinamous. **1889** P. L. SCLATER *Argentine Ornith.* II. 207 The Tinamous constitute one of the most singular and characteristic types of the Neotropical avifauna. **1895** F. W. HEADLEY *Struct. & Life Birds* xiii. 343 The Spotted Tinnamou, or common Partridge of the Pampas. **1896** NEWTON *Dict. Birds* 964 In 1830 Wagler . . placed the Tinamous in the same Order as the Ostrich and its allies. **1902** *Q. Rev.* Oct. 427 Another some-what less distinguished game-bird . . is the *tinamu*.

tin-bath to **-bounding:** see TIN *sb.* 5.

tincal ('tɪŋkəl), **tincar** ('tɪŋkə(r)). Forms: α. 7 **tyncall**, 8–9 **tinkal**, 7– **tincal**; β. 7–8 **tinkar**, 8– **tincar**. [In form *tincal*, a. Malay *tingkal*:—Skr. *ṭankaṇa*; in Pers., Arab., Urdū *tankār*, *tinkār*, whence the β-forms and ALTINCAR.] Crude borax, found in lake-deposits in Tibet, Persia, and other Asiatic countries.

α. **1635** in Foster *Crt. Min. E. Ind. Co.* (1907) 99 Tyncall [to Mr. Allen]. **1678** *Phil. Trans.* XII. 1050 If any Dross or filth be in the Melting-Pot, they throw in some Tincal, which gathers the dross together. **1762** tr. *Busching's Syst. Geog.* I. 44 Borax. . . Its species are a bluish kind called Tinkal, and the proper borax, which is a purified Tinkal and appears white. **1811** A. T. THOMSON *Lond. Disp.* II. (1818) 371 The borax is dug in large masses from the edges and shallows of the lake. . . In this state it is named tincal, and is brought home packed in chests, in masses of adhering crystals, of a grey yellowish, or greenish white colour. **1873** WATTS *Fownes' Chem.* (ed. 11) 341 It is imported in a crude state from the East Indies under the name of tincal.

β. **1678** PHILLIPS (ed. 4), *Tinkar*, a Chymical word for *Borax*. **1706** *Ibid.* (ed. Kersey), *Tincar* (Arab.), a sort of Nitre, or Salt-peter . . dug out of the Earth. **1756** P. BROWNE *Jamaica* 38, 6° Borax. I. Tinkal or Tinkar.

tincalconite (tɪn'kælkənaɪt). *Min.* [f. TINCAL + Gr. κον-ία powder + -ITE[1].] A hydrated basic borate of sodium, $Na_2B_4O_5(OH)_4.3H_2O$, occurring as a fine white powder with rhombohedral symmetry and formed by the dehydration of borax.

[**1878** C. U. SHEPARD in *Bull. Soc. Franç. de Minéral.* I. 144 Tincalconite (Shepard). Borax pulvérulent et efflorescent, de Californie.] **1892** E. S. DANA *Dana's Syst. Min.* (ed. 6) 887 Tincalconite. **1930** *Prof. Papers U.S. Geol. Survey* No. 158. 164/2 Tincalconite can readily be made by boiling a solution of borax until crystallization ensues. **1977** *Mineral. Abstr.* XXVIII. 280/2 Tincalconite and meyerhofferite are thought to be metastable, and unsuccessful attempts to bring about their dehydration to kernite and colemanite are reported.

tincel, obs. form of TINSEL *sb.*[3]

tinchel ('tɪŋxəl, 'tɪŋkl). *Sc.* Forms: 6 **tinchill, tynchal, teinchell**, 6–7 **tinchell**, 6, 9 **tainchel(l**, 7 **tinckhell**, 8–9 **tinkell**, 9 **tinckell, tinkal, tinchal, tinchel**. [ad. Gael. *timchioll* ('tʃimxəl) circuit, compass, round (as prep. = 'around, about').] In Scotland, A wide circle of hunters driving together a number of deer by gradually closing in upon them. Also *attrib.*

1549 D. MONRO *Descr. West. Isles* § 15 All the Deire of the west pairt of that forrest will be callit [= driven] be tainchels to that narrow entres, and the next day callit west againe be tainchels through the said narrow entres, & infinit Deire slaine ther. *Ibid.* § 100 The Deire will be callit upwart ay be the Teinchell. *a* **1578** LINDESAY (Pitscottie) *Chron. Scot.* (S.T.S.) I. 56 Ilk ane lyand wait for wther as they had ben settand tinchellis for the murther of wyld beistes. **1618** J. TAYLOR (Water P.) *Pennyles Pilgr.* Wks. (1630) 136/1 Those foresaid Scouts which are called the Tinckhell, doe bring downe the Deere. **1814** SCOTT *Wav.* xxiv, These active assistants spread through the country far and near, forming a circle, technically called the *tinchel*, which, gradually closing, drove the deer in herds together towards the glen where the Chiefs and principal sportsmen lay in wait for them. **1820** HOGG *Tales & Sk.*, *Bridal Polmod* xiii, The tinkell was raised at two in the morning. *Ibid.* xvi, Tinckell. **1834** MUDIE *Brit. Birds* (1841) I. 283 He [dipper] gives chase, with all the confidence of one who drives deer into a tinchal, or ducks into a decoy. **1868** *Nat. Encycl.* I. 238 Hunting, which sport they carry on like the Scottish 'tinkal'. **1904** *Blackw. Mag.* June 757/2 A *tainchel* or hunting drive was to meet at Figinthas.

tinck(e, tinckle: see TINK *v.*, TINKLE.

tin-clad: see TIN *sb.* 5.

tincle, obs. form of TINKLE, TINSEL *sb.*[3]

tinct (tɪŋkt), *sb.* Now only *poet.* [ad. L. *tinct-us* a dyeing, f. *tingĕre* to dye, stain.]

1. Colour, hue, tint; colouring matter, dye: = TINCTURE *sb.* 1, 2.

1602 SHAKS. *Ham.* III. iv. 91 There I see such blacke and grained spots, As will not leave their tinct. **1611** —— *Cymb.* II. ii. 23 White and Azure lac'd With Blew of Heauens owne tinct. **1706** PHILLIPS (ed. Kersey), *Tinct*, or *Teint* (Lat.), a Colouring. **1748** THOMSON *Cast. Indol.* I. xliv, Raising a world of gayer tinct and grace. *a* **1855** MISS MITFORD *Poems*, *A Portrait*, Such brilliant white, such rosy tinct, The apple blossom shows. **1861** WYNTER *Soc. Bees* 500 The difference of colour is entirely owing to the tinct of the fluid which fills the hollow tube in each hair. **1884** BROWNING *Ferishtah*, *Bean-Stripe* 347 There's no single tinct Would satisfy the eye's desire to taste The secret of the diamond.

b. *fig.* A touch, trace, tinge (*of* something): = TINCTURE *sb.* 4.

1752 FOOTE *Taste* I. Wks. 1799 I. 8 If I do now and then add some tincts of antiquity to my pictures. **1794** MRS. PIOZZI *Synon.* II. 195 That lovely season of life gives to every thing a tinct of its own greenness.

†**2.** *Alch.* A transmuting elixir; = TINCTURE *sb.* 6. *Obs.*

1471 RIPLEY *Comp. Alch.* XII. i. in Ashm. *Theat. Chem. Brit.* (1652) 184 And Tynct in Projeccyon all Fyers to abyde. **1601** SHAKS. *All's Well* v. iii. 102 Platus himselfe, That knowes the tinct and multiplying med'cine. **1606** —— *Ant. & Cl.* I. v. 37 Yet comming from him, that great Med'cine hath With his Tinct gilded thee.

tinct, *ppl. a. poet.* [ad. L. *tinct-us*, pa. pple. of *tingĕre*: see prec.] Coloured, tinted; dyed, tinged; imbued. Const. as *pa. pple.*

1579 SPENSER *Sheph. Cal.* Nov. 107 The blew in black, the greene in gray is tinct. **1615** BRATHWAIT *Strappado*, etc. (1878) 284 Her sanguine colour tinct with Lyons iawes. **1819** KEATS *Eve St. Agnes* xxx, Lucent syrops, tinct with cinnamon. **1839** BAILEY *Festus* xxxi. (1852) 530 In robes Of seagreen hue, engirdled with a zone All variously tinct.

†**tinct**, *v. Obs.* Also 6 **tinkt**. [f. L. *tinct-*, ppl. stem of *tingĕre* to dye, colour. First used in pa. pple. *tincted*: cf. TINCT *ppl. a.*]

1. *trans.* To colour; to dye; to tinge, tint.

1594 PLAT *Jewell-ho.* II. 22 Water deepelie died, or tincted with . . colour of the hearbe. **1596** DRAYTON *Leg.* ii. 541 My delicious Cheeke Tinkted with Crimson. **1626** B. JONSON

Masque, Fort. Isles, I will but touch your Temples, .. and tinct the Tip, the very Tip of your Nose. *a* **1648** DIGBY *Chym. Secr.* II. (1682) 174 It will Tinct itself as red as blood. **1650** ASHMOLE *Chym. Collect.* 127 A Dry earthy Body tincts not unlesse it be tincted. **1686** GOAD *Celest. Bodies* II. xiii. 337 In dry Seasons the Solar Halo's are sometimes tincted with red.

2. *transf.* and *fig.* To imbue or impregnate with some substance or quality, esp. in a slight degree; to tinge, tincture, taint. **a.** with a physical substance or quality: = TINCTURE *v.* 2 a.

a **1626** BACON *New Atl.* (1650) 27 Artificiall Wells and Fountaines, made in Imitation of the Naturall Sources and Bathes; As tincted upon Vitrioll, Sulphur, Steele, Brasse, Lead, Nitre, and other Mineralls. **1626** —— *Sylva* §882 So the strainer itself is tincted with salt. **1638** RAWLEY tr. *Bacon's Life & Death* (1650) 48 That towards the Morning, there be used some Anointing, or Shirt tincted with Oyle. **1644** DIGBY *Nat. Bodies* xxiv. (1658) 280 Although the heart should be tincted from its first origine with an undue virtue from some part.

b. with a mental or moral quality, or with knowledge, etc.: = TINCTURE *v.* 2 b.

1599 B. JONSON *Ev. Man out of Hum.* Ded., To take it in your hands, perhaps may make some bencher, tincted with humanity, read and not repent him. **1666** SANCROFT *Lex Ignea* 23 Conjectures .. so tincted and debaucht with private prejudice. *a* **1734** NORTH *Exam.* I. iii. §15 (1740) 132 To suppose his Reader .. tincted beforehand with what was ordinarily understood by the Plot.

3. *Alch.* To subject to a transmuting elixir: see TINCTURE *sb.* 6.

1599 [see *tincting* below]. **1601** DOLMAN *La Primaud. Fr. Acad.* (1618) III. 844 Iron too much concocted and highly tincted, is easily changed into brasse. **1610** B. JONSON *Alch.* II. iii, I meane to tinct *C* [a retort] in sand-heat to-morrow, And giue him imbibition. **1655** *Fulke's Meteors, Observ.* 163 Cyprus Copper is made of Brasse and Iron .., and high tincted is easily changed into Brass, and rechanged .. into Copper.

Hence **'tincted** *ppl. a.*, **'tincting** *vbl. sb.*

1599 THYNNE *Animadv.* (1875) 33 Fermentacione ys a peculier terme of Alchemye .. whiche is before tinctinge, or gyvinge tincture or cooler. **1626** BACON *Sylva* §960 Tincted Lanthorns, or Tincted Skreens of Glasse Coloured into Green, Blew, Carnation &c. **1672** BOYLE in *Phil. Trans.* VII. 5110, I applied a seal'd Weather glass, furnished with tincted spirit of wine.

tinction ('tɪŋkʃən). [ad. late L. *tinctiōn-em* a dipping; baptism administered by non-Catholics (Cyprian *a* 258, Ep. 71/1 and 75/8), n. of action f. *tingĕre* to dip, dye.]

†**1.** Dipping (in baptism); cf. TINCTURE *sb.* 8. *Obs.*

1657 J. WATTS *Dipper Sprinkled* 33, I yeild tinction or dipping, and immersion to be one and the same likewise in this matter. *Ibid.*, Both perfusion and tinction are called baptism.

2. The action of imbuing with colour; colouring, tinging, tinting.

1888 BILLINGS in *Amer. Nat.* Feb. 118 These micro-organisms .. color more diffusely with the same degree of exposure to the tinction.

tinctorial (tɪŋk'tɔərɪəl), *a.* [f. L. *tinctōri-us* (Pliny) (f. *tinctōr-em* dyer) + -AL[1].] Of, pertaining to, or used in dyeing; yielding or using dye or colouring matter.

1655 HOW *Let. to Sir T. Browne* 20 Sept., in *B.'s Wks.* (Bohn) III. 517 After wee have thus circumscribed the plant wee shall adde our experiments; .. hortensiall, .. medicinall, .. tinctoriall. **1811** W. TAYLOR in *Monthly Mag.* 1 Oct. 258/2 Plants, oleaginous, tinctorial, textile, medical, and culinary. **1837** *Penny Cycl.* IX. 227/1 Tinctorial colours are either simple or compound. **1887** *Pall Mall G.* 5 Sept. 7/2 Mr. C. O'Neill .. discoursed on the change of fashion in colour, in a paper on 'The extent to which calico printing and the tinctorial arts are affected by the introduction of modern colours'.

Hence **tinc'torially** *adv.*

1895 *Sci. Progress* II. 418 In 'acid' solutions the staining principle is the acid although the dye may be a chemically neutral salt; tinctorially it reacts as a free acid. **1898** *Allbutt's Syst. Med.* V. 412 The stain acts tinctorially as a free acid.

tinc'torious, *a. rare.* [f. as TINCTORIAL *a.* + -OUS.] = TINCTORIAL.

1786 ABERCROMBIE *Arr.* in *Gard. Assist.* 66 Tinctorious yellow Virginian. **1909** in B. D. JACKSON *Gloss. Bot. Terms.*

tinctumutant (ˌtɪŋktju:'mju:tənt). *Zool. rare*$^{-1}$. [f. L. *tinctu-s* (see TINCT *sb.*) + *mūtānt-em* changing.] An animal that changes colour. So **ˌtinctumu'tation**, change of colour.

1895 J. WEIR in *Pop. Sci. Monthly* Jan. 388 The chameleon is the best known of all the tinctumutants. *Ibid.*, Physiological changes that take place in the act of tinctumutation.

tincturation (tɪŋktjʊə'reɪʃən). [f. TINCTURE *v.* + -ATION: cf. med.L. *tinctūrātio* dyeing.] The preparation of a tincture of some substance.

1860 *Ure's Dict. Arts* III. 427 Tincturation. Musk, .. ambergris, .. vanilla, civet, and a few other odorous substances, yield their odours to spirit by tincturation, that is, by putting the fragrant material into the spirit and allowing it to remain .. till the alcohol has extracted all the scent.

tincture ('tɪŋktjʊə(r), -tʃə(r)), *sb.* [ad. L. *tinctūra* a dyeing, tinging, f. *tinct-*, ppl. stem of *tingĕre* to dye: see -URE.]

†**1.** A colouring matter, dye, pigment; *spec.* a dye used as a cosmetic. *Obs.*

c **1400** *Lanfranc's Cirurg.* 180 If a man desiriþ for to haue blac heeris .., þanne make þis tincture. **1606** WARNER *Alb. Eng.* XVI. ci. 401 Tinctures, Tiers, Maske, Fardingale, and Fan. **1613** PURCHAS *Pilgrimage* (1614) 646 Some of them .. rubbed his skin, to see whether his whitenesse were naturall, .. perceiuing it to be no tincture, they were out of measure astonished. **1692** DRYDEN *Juvenal* Ded. (1697) 36 When the Wooll has taken the whole Tincture, and drunk in as much of the Dye as it can receive. **1717** LADY M. W. MONTAGU *Let. to C'tess Mar* 1 Apr., The Greeks and Turks have a custom of putting round their eyes .. a black tincture, that .. adds very much to the blackness of them. **1825** J. NICHOLSON *Operat. Mechanic* 730 Extract, by infusion, the tincture of the colouring substances.

2. a. Hue, colour: esp. as communicated (naturally or artificially) by a colouring matter or dye, or by something that stains; a tinge, tint. Now *rare.*

1477 NORTON *Ord. Alch.* Proem in Ashm. *Theat. Chem. Brit.* (1652) 7 All such Men as give Tincture to Glasse. **1555** EDEN *Decades* 328 Certeyne waters .. do .. shewe .. dyuers tinctures of mynerall substaunce. **1594** PLAT *Jewell-ho.* II. 11 If you may not giue a tincture to your creame before you chearne it. **1602** MARSTON *Ant. & Mel.* III. Wks. 1856 I. 30 The shuddering morne that flakes, With silver tincture, the east vierge of heaven. **1713** ADDISON *Cato* I. iv, 'Tis not .. The tincture of a skin, that I admire. **1800** HELENA WELLS *Constantia Neville* (ed. 2) I. 254 The heat of the mask had given to her complexion such a tincture of red. **1822–34** *Good's Study Med.* (ed. 4) IV. 374 The matter has a bloody tincture and a bilious smell.

b. *Her.* Inclusive term for the metals, colours, and furs used in coats of arms, etc.

1610 GUILLIM *Heraldry* I. ii. (1611) 7 Tincture is a variable hew of Armes and is common as well to differences of Armes as to the Armes themselues. **1725** COATS *Dict. Her.*, *Tincture*, is no other than the Hue or Colour of any thing in Coat-Armour, and under this Denomination may be also included the two Metals Or and Argent .. because they are often represented by Yellow and White, and they themselves bear those Colours. **1842** BRANDE *Dict. Sc.*, etc., *Tinctures*, in Heraldry are of three descriptions: metals, colours, and furs. The former are or, argent; the second gules, azure, sable, vert, purpure, sanguine, and tenny. The chief furs are ermine and vair; but there are several varieties of both, distinguished by different names. **1864** BOUTELL *Her. Hist. & Pop.* iv. 20 The representation of the Tinctures by means of dots and lines was not in use .. before .. the accession of the Stuarts. **1891** *Scott. N. & Q.* Apr. 210/2 At the foot of the stone there is cut the armorial coat .. carved so as to show the tinctures, viz., Sable, a fess between three mascles, two and one, or.

†**3. a.** The action of dyeing, staining, or colouring.

1601 HOLLAND *Pliny* (1634) II. 619 This stone [Chrysoprase] is very apt to be counterfeited, and especially by tincture. **1650** BULWER *Anthropomet.* ii. 58 This Tincture of Hair is most shameful and detestable in men. **1681** tr. *Willis' Rem. Med. Wks.* Vocab., *Tincture*, a dying or colouring.

†**b.** *fig.* A stain, blemish. *Obs.*

a **1640** J. BALL *Answ. to Canne* ii. (1642) 9 Our service was picked and culled out of the masse booke .. so it might, and yet be free from all fault and tincture. *a* **1658** CLEVELAND *Poems*, etc. (1677) 149 To offend against so Gracious a Patron, would add a Tincture to our Disobedience.

†**4.** *fig.* An imparted quality likened to a colour or dye; a specious or 'colourable' appearance; a quality or character with which anything is imbued, esp. a derived quality; a tinge. *Obs.*

1590 NASHE *Pasquil's Apol.* I. D ij, They that abused thys place, .. had a little more tincture from hence to lay uppon theyr opinion, than Penrie can haue. **1640** HARVEY *Synagogue* (1647) 7 Hypocrisie in Church is Alchymie, That casts a golden tincture upon brasse. **1652** L. S. *People's Liberty* vii. 13 His speech .. having a tincture from his guilty conscience. **1711** STEELE *Spect.* No. 144 ¶7 A goodness mixed with Fear, gives a Tincture to all her Behaviour. **1757** BURKE *Abridgm. Eng. Hist.* II. i, The Saxon language received little or no tincture from the Welsh. **1806** SURR *Winter in Lond.* I. 242, I attributed this tincture of mind in a great degree to his peculiar destiny.

†**5. a.** A physical quality (other than colour) communicated to something; *esp.* a taste or flavour, a taint. *Obs.*

1610 HOLLAND *Camden's Brit.* I. 306 Whether it bee by the nature, or tincture and temper thereof. **1625** N. CARPENTER *Geog. Del.* II. v. (1635) 77 They receiue their tincture of saltnesse from some salt minerals of the Earth. **1697** BP. PATRICK *Comm. Exod.* xiii. 6 Anything .. that might give a Tincture of Acidity to the Bread. **1727** *Bradley's Fam. Dict.* s.v. *Distilling*, The Waters .. smell of Smoke, and had a Tincture of Adustion.

b. A slight infusion (*of* some element or quality; a tinge, a shade, a flavour, a trace; a smattering (*of* knowledge, etc.).

1612 SELDEN *Illustr. Drayton's Poly-olb.* xi. 184 They had lived here C.L. yeers by the common account without tincture of true religion. **1697** BURGHOPE *Disc. Relig. Assemb.* 107 This irreligious custom .. has a tincture of atheism in it. **1711** STEELE *Spect.* No. 38 ¶5 This, perhaps, cannot be called Affectation; but it has some Tincture of it. **1775** TYRWHITT *Chaucer* IV. 26 We may fairly conclude, that the English language must have imbibed a strong tincture of the French, long before the age of Chaucer. **1858** CARLYLE *Fredk. Gt.* I. iv. (1872) I. 31 Ernst August has some tincture of soldiership at this time.

†**6.** *Alchemy.* **a.** A supposed spiritual principle or immaterial substance whose character or quality may be infused into material things, which are then said to be tinctured; the quintessence, spirit, or soul of a thing. ***universal tincture***, the Elixir. *Obs.*

1599 T. M[OUFET] *Silkwormes* 68 A Quintessence? nay wel it may be call'd A deathlesse tincture, sent vs from the skies Whose colour stands, whose glosse is ne'er appall'd. **1649** J. E[LLISTONE] tr. *Behmen's Epist.* Pref. 10 This .. conduces to the attainment of the Universall Tincture and Signature; whereby the different secret qualities, and vertues, that are hid in all visible and corporeall things .. may be drawne forth and applyed to their right naturall use. *Ibid.* iii. §34 Operation of the philosopher's stone or universal tincture from me. **1693** tr. *Blancard's Phys. Dict.* (ed. 2), *Tinctura*, a Tincture, or *Elixir*, the Extraction of the Colour, Quality, and Strength of any thing.

†**b.** An active principle, of a physical nature, emanating or derivable from any body or substance; a liquid or volatile principle. *Obs.*

1602 T. FITZHERB. *Apol.* 48 If by chaunce her Maiestie had layed her hand vpon the poysoned pomel of the Sadle in the moneth of Iuly when the pores and veynes are open she might haue byn poysoned or receaue maligne vapors or tinctures. **1671** GREW *Anat. Plants* ii. §23 The purest part [of the Sap] .. recedes, with its due Tinctures, from the said Cortical Body, to all the parts of the Lignous. *Ibid.* vi. §4 Precipitation is made by the mixture and reaction of the Tinctures of the Lignous and Cortical Bodies upon each other. *a* **1677** HALE *Prim. Orig. Man.* II. xii. 241 The Fertility of their Soil by the Inundation of Nilus, which at its recess leaves so fruitful a Tincture, that thereby and by the heat of the Sun, Animals have their visible production. *Ibid.* III. iv. 267 The .. Dew exhaled from some sorts of Herbs or Weeds, .. carries with it the Seminal Tincture of the Herb.

7. *Chem.* and *Pharm.* †**a.** In early chemistry, and in derived uses: The (supposed) essential principle of any substance obtained in solution. Also, the extraction of this essential principle. *Obs.*

tincture of gold, POTABLE gold, aurum potabile. ***tincture of the moon*** (i.e. of silver, Luna): see quot. 1706.

1610 B. JONSON *Alch.* II. iii, Infuse vinegar, To draw his volatile substance and his tincture. **1626** —— *Fort. Isles* Wks. (Rtldg.) 649/1 This little gallipot Of tincture, high rose tincture. **1651** FRENCH *Distill.* vi. 179 A way by which the tincture of gold which is the soule thereof, .. may be .. extracted. **1669** WORLIDGE *Syst. Agric.* (1681) 39 Many of our best Mechanicks being too much addicted to the tincture of this Grain [barley]. **1675** E. WILSON *Spadacrene Dunelm.* Pref. 12 As to the discovery of Metalline tinctures in waters. **1696** PHILLIPS (ed. 5), *Tincture* .. In Chymistry, the Extraction of the Colour, Quality and Strength of any thing. **1706** *Ibid.* (ed. Kersey), *Tincture of the Moon*, is a Dissolution of some of the more rarify'd parts of Silver, made in Spirit of Wine, and whetted by Alkali-Salts. **1707** MORTIMER *Husb.* (1721) I. 355 'Tis not unlikely that Grain may afford its Tincture, and that excellent Beer and Ale may be made thereof without Malting.

b. *Mod. Pharmacy.* A solution, usually in a menstruum of alcohol, of some principle used in medicine, chiefly vegetable, as tincture of opium (laudanum), but sometimes animal, as tincture of cantharides, or mineral, as tincture of ferric chloride.

More particularly called an ***alcoholic tincture***. But the menstruum may also be sulphuric ether or spirit of ammonia (both mainly alcohol), which give ***ethereal*** and ***ammoniated tinctures*** respectively; when wine is used they are called *medicated wines*. A tincture is *simple* when it is a solution of one substance only, *compound* when of two or more substances.

a **1648** DIGBY *Chym. Secr.* (1682) 172 An excellent Spirit of Wine, fit to draw Tinctures. **1704** J. HARRIS *Lex. Techn.* I, *Tincture*, in Chymistry, is a Dissolution of the more fine, and volatile Parts of a mixt Body in Spirit of Wine, or some such proper Menstruum. **1712** tr. *Pomet's Hist. Drugs* I. 184 A Tincture is likewise extracted with Spirit of Wine Tartariz'd. **1789** BUCHAN *Dom. Med.* (1790) 695 Aromatic Tincture. Infuse two ounces of Jamaica pepper in two pints of brandy, without heat, for a few days; then strain off the tincture. **1800** tr. *Lagrange's Chem.* II. 327 Alcohol dissolves resins and resinous gums: these solutions are called Tinctures, Elixirs, Quintessences, &c. **1813** J. THOMSON *Lect. Inflam.* 83 The results were the same when tincture of opium was employed. **1842** BRANDE *Dict. Sc.* etc., s.v., The term tincture is sometimes applied to alcoholic solutions of resins, of which tincture of myrrh, of assafœtida, &c. furnish instances. **1871** GARROD *Mat. Med.* (ed. 3) 162 Tincture of Aconite. (Aconite root, in coarse powder, two ounces and a half; rectified spirit, twenty fluid ounces. Prepared by maceration and percolation.)

c. An alcoholic drink, a 'snifter'. *colloq.*

1914 JOYCE *Dubliners* 115 Weathers made them all have just one little tincture at his expense. **1980** INGRAMS & WELLS *Dear Bill* 36 Rough diamond, especially after a tincture or two.

†**8.** Affectedly used for 'baptism'. Cf. late L. use of *tingĕre* (to dip) for 'baptize', and TINCTION 1.

1612 SELDEN *Illustr. Drayton's Poly-olb.* iv. 73 Honoured in holy tincture of Christianity with the name of Robert. *Ibid.* ix. 146 Cadwallader .. received of P. P. Sergius, with holy tincture, the name of Peter.

'tincture, *v.* [f. prec. sb.]

1. *trans.* To impart a tincture or dye to; to dye; to colour, tinge, imbue. (Chiefly in pa. pple.)

1616 [see *tincturing* below]. **1634** SIR T. HERBERT *Trav.* 147 Cheekes tinctured with Vermillion. **1664** H. MORE *Myst. Iniq.* 310 The River that will run tinctured with bloud three hundred years hence. **1715** tr. *Pancirollus' Rerum Mem.* I. I. i. 2 This Juice .. which Wooll and Purple-Silk .. were tinctur'd with. **1814** WORDSW. *Excursion* VII. 188 Homespun wool But tinctured daintily with florid hues. **1822–34** *Good's Study Med.* (ed. 4) I. 325 One of the latest fluids that becomes tinctured is the milk in icteric wet-nurses. **1828** MOORE *'Tis sweet to think* ii, It will tincture Love's plume with a different hue.

2. *transf.* and *fig.* To imbue or impregnate with a quality; to communicate some quality to; to affect, tinge, taint. (Chiefly in pa. pple., const. *with*.) †**a.** with a physical quality, as smell or taste. *Obs.*

1668 H. MORE *Div. Dial.* v. xxxviii. (1713) 515 Innocuous Whirl-winds of sincere Air, tinctured only with a cool refreshing smell. **1671** GREW *Anat. Plants* ii. §23 The remainder..is in part carried off into the Cortical Body back again, the Sap whereof it now tinctures into good Aliment. **1678** R. BARCLAY *Apol. Quakers* VII. xii. 237 Water may be capable to be tinctured with uncleanness. **1820** MAIR *Tyro's Dict.* (ed. 10), *Aluminosus*,..tinctured with, smelling or tasting of alum.

b. with a mental or moral quality or character; with reference to knowledge (*pass.* with *with*), to have a smattering of. (In early use often with allusion to alchemy: cf. prec. 6.)

1636 HEYWOOD *Love's Mistr.* Prol., So pure a mind, As if tinctur'd from Heaven. **1651** WITTIE tr. *Primrose's Pop. Err.* I. xiii. 47 He professed himselfe to be a Physician (although he was but lightly tinctured with the knowledge of Physick). **1662** SPARROW tr. *Behme's Rem. Wks.*, *Apol. conc. Perfect.* 147, I must be Tinctured or else I cannot be Transmuted; If Christ do not Tincture me with his Bloud, then my Holy Paradise-Life remaineth faded. **1718** *Free-thinker* No. 7 ¶2 His Conversation was tinctured through-out with the Ancient Mythology. **1878** SPURGEON *Treas. Dav.* Ps. cxv. 1 The prayer is evidently tinctured with a consciousness of unworthiness.

c. *intr.* for *pass.* To take or have a tinge *of* something. *rare*$^{-1}$.

1787 'G. GAMBADO' *Acad. Horsemen* (1809) 15 It [a portrait] is like, but a likeness that tinctures of the prejudice of friendship.

†**3.** To deposit (one metal *upon* another). *rare*.

1670 *Specif. Pr. Rupert's Patent* 2 A new Invencion or Art of Tincturing Copper vpon Iron. **1679** *Essex Papers* (Camden) I. 235 Of tincturing of Copper upon Iron as to him or them shall seem meet.

Hence **'tincturing** *vbl. sb.*

1616 T. TUKE (*title*) A Treatise against Painting and Tincturing of Men and Women. **1656** *Artif. Handsom.* 110 Hangings, pictures, carvings, guildings, and tincturings. **1679** [see 3 above]. **1902** W. M. ALEXANDER *Demonic Possession in N.T.* iii. 65 [They] may contain a tincturing of medical lore.

tinctured ('tɪŋktjʊəd), *ppl. a.* [f. TINCTURE *v.* (or *sb.*) + -ED.] Imbued with a tincture or colour; having a tincture (esp. of a specified kind); dyed, coloured, stained, tinged.

1626 CAPT. SMITH *Virginia* I. 17 Very rocky, and much tinctured stone like Minerall. **1737** M. GREEN *Spleen* 737 And fancy's telescope applies With tinctur'd glass to cheat his eyes. **1782** ELIZ. N. BLOWER *Geo. Bateman* II. 155 The blood-tinctured weapon. **1908** *Daily Chron.* 17 Aug. 4/7 Zinc and other metallically tinctured ointments.

tincy, variant of TINSEY.

tind (tɪnd), *v. Obs.* exc. *dial.* Forms: α. (1 tendan), 2–3 tenden, 3–5 tende, 4 (*3rd pers. sing.*) tent; *pa. t.* 3–5 tende, 4 tendede; *pa. pple.* 2–4 itend, 2 itent, itende, 3–5 tende, 4 ytend, 4–5 tend. β. 4 teende, 6–7 (9 *dial.*) teend; *pa. pple.* 4 teendid. γ. 3 tiende, 5 tynd, 6 tinde, 6–7 tynde, 5– tind; *pa. pple.* 6 tynded, 6–7 tinded. δ. 6 tīnde, 6–7 ? tynde, 6–9 tīnd. ε. 5 tynne, 6–7 tinne, 7–9 tin; *pa. t.* and *pple.* 7 tinn'd. ζ. 5–6 tyne, 7 tine; *pa. t.* 6 tynde, tind; *pa. pple.* 5 tyned, 6 tynde, tind, 6–7 tined. η. 5–6 teyne, *pa. pple.* y-, iteyned. θ. 7, 9 teen, *pa. t.* and *pple.* teened. [ME. had *tend-e(n* from 1175 to 1425; also, in Wyclif and down to 17th c., with lengthened vowel, *teende(n*, in some mod. dialects *teend* (tiːnd). From *c* 1400 onward also *tind* and *tīnd* (see γ, δ forms). Later with loss of final *d* from both forms (perh. arising out of shortened pa. pple. *tind, tīnd, teend*, taken as = *tin-d, tīne-d, teen-d*, hence inf. *tin, tīne, teen*; but reduction of *-nd* to *-n* is found in many other words). In mod. dial. surviving from Scotl. to Cornwall as (tɪnd, taɪnd, tɪn, taɪn, tiːn): see quots. and *Eng. Dial. Dict.* Early ME. *tenden* corresponded to an OE. **tęndan* (in comp. *ontęndan, atęndan, fortęndan*, to set fire to, kindle, and in vbl. sb. *tęnding*, Napier *Contrib. to OE. Lexic.*), corresp. to Goth. *tandjan*, Da. *tænde*, Sw. *tända*; causal of **tindan* str. vb. (ablaut series *tind-, tand-, tund-*), to be on fire, burn, glow, represented by MHG. *zinden* str. vb., in same sense. The history of early ME. *tiende, tinde*, now *tind, tīnd* (taɪnd), is more difficult: as no other example is known of OE. and ME. *-end* becoming later *-ind*, much less *-īnd*, it is probable that we have here a parallel formation, representing an OE. **tyndan* (from the weak ablaut grade *tund-*), cognate with OHG. *zunten* (from **zuntjan*:—**tundjan*), MHG. and Ger. *zünden* to set on fire, kindle, and OE. *tynder* TINDER. In that case, *tend* (*teend, teen, teyne*) and *tind* (*tynd, tīnd, tin, tīne, tyne*) are two distinct but parallel and synonymous formations from the same root verb.]

1. *trans.* To set fire to, ignite, light, kindle (a fire, lamp, torch, flame, etc.).

α. [*a* **901** *Laws K. Ælfred* Prol. c. 27 Gif fyr sie ontended ryt to bærnanne. *a* **1000** tr. *Bæda's De Temporibus* in *Sax. Leechd.* III. 242 Đonne he [moon] of hyre [sun] ontend byþ. *a* **1050** *O.E. Chron.* an. 994 (MS. C) Eac hi mid fyre on tendon woldan. *c* **1100** *Charms* in *Sax. Leechd.* III. 286 Ontend þreo candela.] *c* **1175** *Lamb. Hom.* 81 He wule aquikien and al þe brond tenden. **1340–70** *Alex. & Dind.* 233 Of a torche þat is tend, tak an en-sample. **1377** LANGL. *P. Pl.* B. XVIII. 238 Þo þat weren in heuene token *stella comata*, And tendeden hir [C. XXI. 250 tenden hit] as a torche. **1387** TREVISA *Higden* (Rolls) II. 17 I-tend in þe fire hit feseþ awey serpentes. *c* **1400** *Laud Troy Bk.* 17978 The Troyens..tende hire fir more than ten sithe, But it ȝede out. *c* **1425** *Seven Sag.* (P.) 2183 He tende hys torche at a cole.

β. **1382** WYCLIF *Isa.* l. 11 Lo! ȝee alle teendende vp [1388 kyndlynge] fyr. —— *Ecclus.* viii. 13 Teende thou not colis of synneres..lest thou be tend with the flaume of the fyr of the synnes of hem. **1388** —— *Matt.* v. 15 Ne men teendith not [1382 Nether men tendyn] a lanterne, and puttith it vndur a busschel. **1598** SYLVESTER *Du Bartas* II. i. IV. *Handy-crafts* 707 Teend again Truth's near-extinguisht Taper. **1605** *Ibid.* iii. II. *Fathers* 306 Thou whetst a sword, and thou dost teend a brand. **1648** HERRICK *Hesper.*, *Candlem. Day* ii, Kindle the Christmas brand..Part must be kept wherewith to teend The Christmas log next yeare.

γ. *a* **1400–50** *Alexander* 4179 It tinds on tend lowe trappour of stede, And many costious costis consumes in-to askis. **1589** R. HARVEY *Pl. Perc.* 20, I see no more Candles tinded then wont to be. **1622** MABBE tr. *Aleman's Guzman d'Alf.* II. 19 Those coales, that were already throughly tinded. *a* **1663** SANDERSON *Serm.* (1689) 56 As one candle tindeth a thousand. **1706** PHILLIPS (ed. Kersey), To *Tind*, to light; as *To tind a Candle*. **1904** *Eng. Dial. Dict.*, *Tind*, to light, kindle. [Generally diffused, Scotl. to Heref., Northamp., Bedford, Berks, Cornwall.] **1910** *Old man at Gorsley, Glo'ster*, Get up and tind (tīnd) the fire.

δ. *c* **1548** UDALL, etc. *Erasm. Par. John* v. 40 Only a burnyng candell tynded at our fyre. **1558** PHAER *Æneid* III. G ij, Altars vp againe we make and fiers on them we tinde [*rime* blind]. [**1590** SPENSER *F.Q.* II. viii. 11 Stryful Atin in their stubborne mind Coles of contention and whot vengeaunce tind. **1594** CAREW *Tasso* I. (1881) 27 For if one feare to crueltie him tinde [*rime* finde], Another greater doubt bridles no lesse.] ? **1623** in *10th Rep. Hist. MSS. Comm.* App. IV. 433 Paied for sixe faggottes to tynde the coales, 4*d*. **1834** *Tait's Mag.* I. 341/2 For him it [the heavenly torch] beams not,—can but tind [*rime* blind], And lands and cities turn to dust.

ε. **1497** *Croscombe Churchw. Acc.* (Som. Rec. Soc.) 27 Paid to W. Toyt for tynnyng of the lyght. **1562** PHAER *Æneid* VIII. B b ij b, Her couchyd harth she steeres and sturging sparkes of fire doth tinne. **1638** FARLEY *Emblems* v. B vj, That learned dogge, at noone-tyde tinn'd his light. **1655** H. VAUGHAN *Silex Scint.* II. *Cockcrow.* (1858) 142 It seems their candle, howe'er done, Was tinn'd and lighted at the sunne. **1674** RAY *S. & E.C. Words*, To *Tine* or *tin* a Candle, to light it. *Mod. Bedford & Northampt. Dial.*, I get up at six, tin the fire, and then sweep the room up.

ζ. [**1471** RIPLEY *Comp. Alch.* XI. ii. in Ashm. *Theat. Chem. Brit.* (1652) 181 For yt ys Fyer whych tyned wyll never dye.] *c* **1511** (see *Tinding*), Tynyng. **1591** SPENSER *Virg. Gnat* 394 Whose bridale torches foule Erynnis tynde [*rime* unkinde]. *Ibid.* 504 Flames, weapons, wounds, in Greeks fleete to have tynde [*rime* minde]. **1594** T. B. *La Primaud. Fr. Acad.* II. 514 With the same fire wherewith that was first tined. **1612** *Pasquil's Night-Cap* (1877) 26 Though others tine their candles at my light. **1667** MILTON *P.L.* x. 1075 As late the Clouds Justling or pusht with Winds rude in thir shock, Tine the slant Lightning. **1700** DRYDEN *Iliad* I. 635 The priest..was seen to tine The cloven wood, and pour the ruddy wine.

η. **1482** CAXTON *Trevisa's Higden* I. xxiv. 30 b, Whan it was ones yteyned [*ed.* **1527** Iteyned] and sette a fyre.

θ. **1847–78** HALLIWELL, *Teen*, to light a candle. Var. dial. **1864** E. CAPERN *Devon. Provinc.*, 'Teen the candle' is often used for light the candle. **1895** QUILLER-COUCH *Wandering Heath* 85 She struck flint over touchwood and teened a fire.

2. *intr.* To catch fire, kindle, become ignited, begin to burn.

c **1290** *St. Michael* 523 in *S. Eng. Leg.* I. 314 And ȝwane it comez a-mong þe fuyre, sone it bi-gynnez fortO tiende [*Harl. MS.* 2277 sone hit gynneþ tende: *rime* ende]. **1382** WYCLIF *Ecclus.* xvi. 7 Wrathe shal waxe ful out tend [1388 yre schal brenne]. *c* **1400** *Brut* xcvi. 94 Þe fire biganne to tende and brenne al þe toune. **1648** HERRICK *Hesper.*, *To Maids*, Wash your hands, or else the fire Will not teend to your desire.

3. *fig.* *trans.* To inflame, excite, arouse, inspire.

c **1175** *Lamb. Hom.* 81 For hwat he scal his sunne uorsaken and bileuen and bon itent of þen hali gast. *Ibid.*, Ho weren itende of þan halie gast. *a* **1225** *Leg. Kath.* 156 Swa itend of wraððe þat wod ha walde wurðen. *a* **1240** *Lofsong* in *Cott. Hom.* 215 Tend mine heorte. **1382** WYCLIF *Prov.* xxviii. 4 Who kepen, shul ben tend [1388 kyndlid] vp aȝen hym. *c* **1450** MYRC *Festial* 60 Yn token he was yn hyr wombe þat schuld aftyr tynd mony mannys charite. **1590**, **1594** [see 1 δ]. **1622** MABBE tr. *Aleman's Guzman d'Alf.* I. 234 He was some-what too touchy, and would..quickly be tinded. **1682** DRYDEN *Duke of Guise* I. i, Shop-consciences,..Preach'd up, and ready tined for a rebellion.

b. *intr.* To become inflamed or excited.

1297 R. GLOUC. (Rolls) 4416 In is wod rage he wende Vor to awreke is vncle deþ, as fur is [= fire his] herte tende.

Hence **'tinded (tende)** *ppl. a.*, **'tinding** *vbl. sb.* and *ppl. a.*

a **900** WÆRFERTH *Dial. Gregory* (1900) 101 (MS. H.) He..hine sylfne nacodne awearp..on þæra netela tendingum. **1297** R. GLOUC. (Rolls) 11022 Þo nome tende taperes þe bissops in hor hond. **1382** WYCLIF *Num.* xi. 3 He clepide the name of that place Tendynge [1388 Brennyng, *Vulg.* incensio] for thi that the fier of the Lord was tende [1388 kyndlid, *Vulg.* incensus fuisset] aȝens hem. **1497** Tynnyng [see 1 ε]. *c* **1511** in Swayne *Sarum Churchw. Acc.* (1896) 61 To Ros for tynyng of the rode light xij d. **1591** SYLVESTER *Du Bartas* I. ii. 654 Incessantly th'apt tinding fume is tost Till it inflame. **1662** HIBBERT *Body Div.* I. 30 The Romans divided their night into ten parts,..2 Prima fax, candle-tinning.

tind, obs. form of TINE *sb.*[1], prong.

‖**tindal**[1] ('tɪndəl). *E. Ind.* [ad. Malayālam *taṇḍal*, Telugu *taṇḍelu*, also Hindūstānī *taṇḍēl*, chief or head man of a body of men.]

1. A native petty officer of lascars, on board ship, or in the ordnance department; also the foreman of a gang of labourers on public works (Yule); a boatswain; a foreman.

1698 FRYER *Acc. E. India & P.* 107 The Captain is called *Nucquedah*, the Boatswain *Tindal*. **1778** R. ORME *Hist. Milit. Trans.* II. IX. 339 One Tindal, or corporal of the Lascars. **1800** WELLINGTON in Gurw. *Desp.* (1844) I. 93 A detachment of gun lascars, consisting of 1 tindal and 20 lascars. **1803** R. PERCIVAL in *Naval Chron.* X. 26 Each of the boats carries..a *tindal*, or chief boat-man, who acts as pilot. **1848** tr. *Hoffmeister's Trav. Ceylon*, etc. x. 343 The '*Tindal*', or superintendent of the coolies, was dismissed. **1849** E. B. EASTWICK *Dry Leaves* 23 Our Tindal jumped out on the bank, on which was not four feet water.

2. A personal attendant: see quots.

1859 LANG *Wand. India* 36 Almost every one who visits the Hills keeps a servant called a *tindal*. His duty is to look after the men who carry your janpan, to go errands, to keep up the fire. *Ibid.* 40 My tindal aroused me at eleven, and informed me that a young man wished to see me.

†**tindal**[2]. *Obs.* See quots.

1859 SALA *Tw. round Clock* 22 [At Billingsgate] Sprats are sold on board the ships by the bushel. A 'tindal' is a thousand bushels of sprats. **1863** SIMMONDS *Dict. Trade* Suppl., *Tindal*, a thousand bushels of sprats.

tinder ('tɪndə(r)), *sb.* Forms: α. 1 tyndre, tyndir, 1–7 tynder, 5 -yr, 3– tinder (7 -ar). β. 3–7 (9 *dial.*) tunder, 4 tonder, tondre, 4–5 tundyr, 5 *Sc.* toundire. γ. 3–4, 6 tendre, 5 tendern, tendere. [OE. *tynder* ? m., and *tyndre* wk. fem. (?:—**tundrio-*, **tundriôn-*), from OTeut. **tund-* weak grade of **tind-* to kindle: see TIND *v.* Cognate forms (varying in suffix and gender) are MLG., LG. *tunder*, Du. *tonder*, ON. *tundr* (Sw. *tunder*, Da. *tønder*), OHG. *zuntara* fem. (MHG. *zunder* m. and n., Ger. *zunder* m.). ME. and mod.Eng. *tinder* regularly represent OE. *tynder*; ME. *tunder* (*toundir, tonder*), also mod. dial. (Linc.), may be from ON. *tundr*. The 13–16th c. forms *tendere, -dre, -der* (implied for 13th c. in TINDER *v.*), were prob. assimilated to the α-type of TIND *v.*]

a. Any dry inflammable substance that readily takes fire from a spark and burns or smoulders; esp. that prepared from partially charred linen and from species of *Polyporus* or corkwood fungus (AGARIC 1), formerly in common use to catch the spark struck from a flint with a steel, as the means of kindling a fire or 'striking' a light. ***German tinder***: see AMADOU.

α. *a* **700** *Epinal Gloss.* (O.E.T.) 562 *Isca*, tyndirin [*a* **800** *Erfurt* tyndrin]. *Ibid.* 685 *Naphtha, genus fomenti, id est* tyndir. *a* **800** *Leiden Gloss.* 179 *Isica*, tyndri. *c* **1000** ÆLFRIC *Gloss.* in Wr.-Wülcker 149/30 *Fomes*, ȝeswælud spon, *uel* tynder. *a* **1050** *Liber Scintill.* 210 Na elleshwar ȝewilnunge tyndran onæleþ. *c* **1205** LAY. 29267 Þa..he..lette þe curneles ut draȝen & tinder nom And lette i þan scalen don. **1398** TREVISA *Barth. De P.R.* x. viii. (1495) 379 Of a lytill sperkyll in an hepe of towe or of tyndyr cometh sodaynly a grete fyre. **1582** STANYHURST *Æneis* I. (Arb.) 23 In spunck or tinder thee quick fyre he kindly receaued. **1610** B. JONSON *Alch.* I. i. **1664** EVELYN *Sylva* (1679) 27 Nor may we..omit to mention the..fungus's to make Tinder. **1682** N. O. *Boileau's Lutrin* III. 57 The spark in Tinder cherisht, toucht with Match In Sulphur dip't, kindles with quick dispatch The Torch. **1773** COOK *Voy. round World* I. vii. (1777) I. 113 In one there was the stone they strike fire with, and tinder made of bark. **1812** SIR H. DAVY *Chem. Philos.* 90 A machine for setting fire to tinder of the agaric by the compression of air has been for some time in use. **1837** HOWITT *Rur. Life* II. iii. (1862) 115 He strikes a light with his tinder, for lucifers he never saw. **1867** BAKER *Nile Tribut.* xv. (1872) 263 The grass was as inflammable as tinder. **1879** *Cassell's Techn. Educ.* VIII. 114/2 The internal spongy portion of several species of Polyporus, soaked in a solution of nitre, forms tinder.

β. *c* **1220** *Bestiary* 535 Of ston mid stel in ðe tunder Wel to brennen one ðis wunder. **1303** R. BRUNNE *Handl. Synne* 7925 Hyt fareþ wyþ hem as fyre and tundyr [*rime* wundyr]. *c* **1375** *Sc. Leg. Saints* xlix. (*Tecla*) 72 Wod dry as toundire. **1377** LANGL. *P. Pl.* B. XVII. 245 Bot þow haue towe to take it with tondre [*v.r.* tunder; **1393** C. XX. 211 tonder, tendere] or broches. **1483** *Cath. Angl.* 396/1 Tundyr, *Incentinum*,..*receptaculum ignis, ignicippium*. **1530** PALSGR. 283/2 Tunder to lyght a matche, *fusil*. **1562** TURNER *Herbal* II. 29 b, Agarik ..where of som make tunder bothe in England and Germany. **1612** *Sc. Bk. Rates* in *Halyburton's Ledger* (1867) 291 Boxes called fyre or tunder boxes the grosse iiii li.

γ. *c* **1380** WYCLIF *Sel. Wks.* III. 102 Þanne maist þou wiþ tendre gete fuyre of þat ston. **1393** Tendere [see quot. 1377 in β]. *c* **1400** *R. Gloucester's Chron.* App. S. 7 (MS. δ) Þo let he nime tendern [*other MSS.* tynder, tunder]. **1541** R. COPLAND *Guydon's Quest. Chirurg.* M j, They be made of softe tendre, as of seare olde lynen cloth.

†**b.** *transf.* Fire; a spark; a tinder-box; phr. *to strike* (*on*) *a tinder*. *Obs.*

1570 LEVINS *Manip.* 77/10 Tynder, *incendium*. **1604** SHAKS. *Oth.* I. i. 141 Strike on the Tinder, hoa: Giue me a Taper. **1607** DEKKER & WEBSTER *Northw. Hoe* III. Wks. 1873 III. 44 Ile goe strike a Tinder. *c* **1626** *Dick of Devon.* I.

ii. in Bullen *O. Pl.* (1883) II. 12 So from a tinder at the first kindled Grew this heartburning twixt these two great Nations.

c. *fig.*

c **888** K. ÆLFRED *Boeth.* v. §3 We habbað nu giet þone mæstan dæl þære tyndran þinre hæle. *a* **1050** *Liber Scintill.* lxxvii. (1889) 206 Tyndre [*fomentum*] and ceap godes cynnes lærestre mæʒenes deð on criste wunian symle. **1595** *Polimanteia* (1881) 61 They haue strook fire into the tinder of my soft heart. **1643** BAKER *Chron., Hen. II* 73 Finding his hot spirit to be fit tinder for such fire. **1794** WOLCOTT (P. Pindar) *Pindariana* Wks. 1812 IV. 212 Nothing to gild thy solitary tinder Save the rude flint and steel of Peter Pindar.

d. *attrib.* and *Comb.*, as ***tinder-lighter, -pouch, -purse***; ***tinder-cloaked, -dry, -like*** adjs.; **tinder-fungus**, a fungus from which tinder is made, as **tinder-polypore**, *Polyporus fomentarius*; **tinder-ore, tinder-water**, see quots.

1647 CLEVELAND *Char. Diurn. Maker* Wks. (1677) 101 It is like over-reach of Language, when every Thin, *Tinder-cloak'd Quack must be called a Doctor. **1891** KIPLING *Light that Failed* ii. 33 The *tinder-dry clumps of scrub. **1896** CROCKETT *Cleg Kelly* vi, He crossed the marshy end of Duddingstone Loch. It was tinder-dry with the drought. **1895** *Funk's Standard Dict.*, **Tinder-fungus*, a large leathery fungus..growing on trees; the amadou of commerce. **1915** V. ASQUITH *Let.* 16 Nov. in M. Gilbert *Winston S. Churchill* (1972) III. Compan. II. 1272 Is there anything you *haven't* got for the Front? Compass? Luminous wristwatch? Muffler? *Tinderlighter? **1977** 'J. GASH' *Judas Pair* ii. 25 Flintlocks..the standard tinder-lighter of history. **1607** SHAKS. *Cor.* II. i. 55 Said to be..hasty and *Tinder-like vppon to triuiall motion. **1887** RIDER HAGGARD *Jess* xxviii, The tinderlike roof burst into a broad sheet of flame. **1868** DANA *Min.* 91 Zundererz, or Bergzunderz (= *Tinder Ore) of G. Lehmann.., which is soft like tinder and dark dirty red in color,..proves to be jamesonite or feather ore mixed with red silver and arsenopyrite. **1883** R. TURNER in *Gd. Words* Sept. 591/1 The common *tinder-polypore has..been found in the lake-dwelling at Lochlee. **1883** *Fisheries Exhib. Catal.* 236 *Tinder-pouch..used by Hungarian fishermen. **1662** J. BARGRAVE *Pope Alex. VII* (1867) 122 We had..*tynder purses.., with flint, steel, and match, to lighten our torches and candles when they went out. **1748** SMOLLETT *Rod. Rand.* xlvi, *Tinder-water!.. Water extracted from tinder. .. An universal specific for all distempers.

Hence **'tindered** *a.*, burnt to tinder; **'tinderish, 'tinderous** *adjs.*, of the nature of tinder, tinder-like; **'tinderly** *adv.*, like tinder, in a tinder-like degree.

1809 T. COWDELL *Poet. Jrnl.* 40 in *Nova Scotia Minstr.* (1811) 47 Her tinder'd garments in my hand. **1825** T. HOOK *Sayings* Ser. II. *Passion & Princ.* xiv. III. 343 Harriet was tinderly tender. **1837** A. LANGTON *Jrnl.* 8 July in *Gentlewoman in Upper Canada* (1950) 15 From her gingham never having been washed I suppose it was more tinderish than my sister's and mine. **1870** *Daily News* 18 July, The furze is dry and tinderous. **1889** CLARK RUSSELL *Marooned* (1890) 213 So damp and tinderous too was the timber. **1890** —— *Ocean Trag.* xii, A sound as of the pressure of a light foot upon tinderish brushwood.

† **tinder, tender,** *v. Obs. rare*$^{-1}$. [ME. *tendren*, f. *tendre*, y-form of TINDER *sb.*] *intr.* To become inflamed, glow, burn.

c **1230** *Hali Meid.* 31 Ti neb ute-wið tendreð ut of tene.

'tinder-box. A box in which tinder was kept (also usually the flint and steel with which the spark was struck, and sometimes the brimstone matches with which the flame was raised).

1530 PALSGR. 283/2 Tunder boxe, *boytte de fusil.* **1580** HAKLUYT *Voy.* (1599) I. 442 Tinder boxes with Steele, Flint, & Matches and Tinder. **1612** [see TINDER β]. **1697** COLLIER *Ess.* II. (1703) 84 One would think we might..with a good flint and steel strike consciousness into a Tinder-box. **1759** DUMARESQUE in *Phil. Trans.* LI. 485 They make use of a wooden machine (instead of a tinder-box), to light fire with. **1836** MARRYAT *Japhet* xlvii, I..found a tinderbox. I struck a light. *c* **1840–5** (*Tunder-box* in use in N. Lincolnsh.). **1893** LELAND *Mem.* I. 47 The use of the tinderbox and brim-stone was universal.

b. *fig.* A thing or person likened to a tinder-box, esp. as being very 'inflammable' or a source of heated strife.

1598 SHAKS. *Merry W.* I. iii. 27, I am glad I am so acquit of this Tinderbox. **1608** SYLVESTER *Du Bartas* II. iv. v. *Decay* 12 Huff-pufft Ambition, tinderbox of warre, Downfall of Angels, Adam's murderer. **1839** J. MACDONALD in Tweedie *Life* iv. (1849) 335 The tinder-box of mortality within me may at any moment take fire. **1897** *Current Hist.* (Buffalo, N.Y.) VII. 313 One of the chief danger-points in Europe, a veritable tinder-box.

c. *attrib.* and *Comb.*

a **1704** T. BROWN *Lett. to Gentl. & Ladies* Wks. 1709 III. II. 107 A Couple of Tinderbox-cryers. **1856** KANE *Arct. Expl.* I. xxix. 379 He struck them together after the true tinder-box fashion.

† **'tindern,** *a. Obs. rare* [f. TINDER *sb.* + *-n*, -EN^4: cf. *leathern, silvern.*] In ***tindern iron***: ? a steel used in striking the flint to light tinder.

1586 FERNE *Blaz. Gentrie* 172 Betweene four tindern irons, or fusils argent. **1688** R. HOLME *Armoury* III. 289/2 Tindern Irons, or Clothiers Bench Hooks.

tindery ('tɪndərɪ), *a.* [f. TINDER *sb.* + -Y.] Of the nature of or resembling tinder, tinder-like; also *fig.* easily inflamed, 'inflammable', passionate.

1754 RICHARDSON *Grandison* (1781) IV. xviii. 146 What woman would have herself supposed capable of such a tindery fit? **1795** MME. D'ARBLAY *Lett.* 15 June, I love nobody for nothing; I am not so tindery! **1814** —— *Wanderer* I. 100 You were in such a tindery fit as to be kindled by that dowdy. **1886** MISS BRADDON *One Thing Needful* v, Sheets of tindery paper.

tindle ('tɪnd(ə)l). *dial.* [app. a deriv. of TIND *v.* to kindle; akin to TANDLE and TENDLE, or a var. of the latter.] In *pl.*, A name given locally to small fires lighted out of doors at the beginning of May and November. (Cf. TANDLE.)

See fuller quot. in E.D.D., and references to N. & Q. and Glossaries there given.

1784 *Gentl. Mag.* Nov. 836/2 At..Findern, in Derbyshire,..the boys and girls..in the evening of the second of November..light up a number of small fires amongst the furze..and call them..*Tindles.* **1872** C. HARDWICK *Traditions Lancs.* 30 In Derbyshire these fires [on 1st May] were called Tindles, and were kindled at the close of the last century.

'tindling, misreading of *tuidling*, TWEDDLING = TWILLING.

1565 *Aberdeen Regr.* (Jam.), Ane new sark of tindling.

tine (taɪn), *sb.*^{1} Forms: α. 1, 3–6 tind, 4–6 tynde, 5 tyynde, 6 (9 *dial.*) tynd. β. (5 tene), 5–9 tyne, 6– tine. [OE. *tind* = MHG. *zint* sharp point, ON. *tindr* tine (Sw. *tinne*, Da. dial. *tind* tooth of a rake):—OTeut. **tind-i*^{z}. (To the same root prob. belongs OHG. *zinna* merlon of a wall:—OTeut. **tindjôn-*.) OE. *tind* became in ME. *tīnd*, as in *bind*, etc.; whence, by loss of *d*, *tine*, as in TIND *v.* Cf. WFris. *tine*, tooth of fork, etc.]

1. Each of a series of projecting sharp points on some weapon or implement, as a harrow, fork, eel-spear, etc.; a prong, spike, tooth.

α. *a* **700** *Epinal Gloss.* (O.E.T.) 873 *Rostris*, foraeuuallum, *uel* tindum. *c* **725** *Corpus Gloss.* (ibid.) 1753 *Rostri*, tindas. ? *a* **1400** *Erasmus* (Bedf. MS. lf. 280) in Horstm. *Altengl. Leg.* (1878) 202 Castyng hym oftyn on þe tyndes of an harow. *c* **1400** *Laud Troy Bk.* 15724 Thei..Sclow hem thikkere with her arwes Than tyndes of tre stondis In harwes. *c* **1440** *Promp. Parv.* 494/1 Tyynde, prekyl (*K.* tynde, pryke), *carnica.* **1668** R. B. *Adagia Scot.* 37 Many maisters, quoth the Poddock to the Harrow, when every tind took her a knock.

β. **1554** *Lydgate's Bochas* IX. vi. 200 b/2 The fiery tines of his brennyng arow. **1591** GREENE *Art Conny Catch.* II. (1592) 25 A long hooke..that hath at the end a crooke, with three tynes turned contrary. **1642** FULLER *Holy & Prof. St.* III. xxi. 211 That fork needing strong tines wherewith one must thrust away nature. **1644** [WALSINGHAM] *Effigies True Fortitude* 12 An old man..with his Pitchforke ran at Captaine Smith, and twice stroke the tynes thereof against his breast. **1649** BLITHE *Eng. Improv. Impr.* xvi. (1653) 104 Two or three sorts of Harrows, each Harrow having his Teeth or tines thicker than other. **1721** [see TIG *sb.*^{1} 1]. *a* **1734** NORTH *Lives* (1826) II. 201 A fork with five tines. **1789** *Trans. Soc. Arts* I. 100 A harrow composed of coulters instead of tines. **1828** *Craven Gloss.*, *Tine*, the prong of a fork ..; also the tooth of a harrow. **1968** J. ARNOLD *Shell Bk. Country Crafts* 92 The larger, called a drag rake, carrying about thirty tines compared with fifteen for the garden rake. **1978** *Cornish Guardian* 27 Apr. 10/4 (Advt.), 60in rotavator with new tines. **1979** P. THEROUX *Old Patagonian Express* (1980) xiv. 289 The man jerked the tines of his fork into a slab of ham.

2. a. Each of the pointed branches of a deer's horn.

α. [*a* **1000** *Sal. & Sat.* (Kemble) 150 Anra ʒehwylc deor hæbbe synderlice xii hornas irene, and anra ʒehwylc horn hæbbe xii tindas irene, and anra ʒehwylc tind hæbbe synderlice xii ordas.] *c* **1375** *Sc. Leg. Saints* xxix. (*Placidas*) 105 A gret hart..he saw betwen his tyndis brycht A verray croice schenand lycht. *c* **1430** *Syr Tryam.* 1085 The herte stroke hym wyth hys tyndys. **1513** DOUGLAS *Æneis* VII. ix. 18 This hart..With large heid and tyndis fwrnest fayr. **1593** *Rites of Durham* (1903) 24 Dyd cast backe his handes betwixt ye Tyndes of ye said harte to stay him selfe.

β. **1495** *Trevisa's Barth. De P.R.* XVIII. xxx. 792 The aege of hartys is knowe by auntlers and tynes of his hornes, for euery yere it encreacith bi a tyne vnto vii yere. **1616** SURFL. & MARKH. *Country Farme* 684 You may likewise iudge of their age by the tynes of their hornes. **1825** SCOTT *Talism.* xxiv, A stag of ten tynes. **1877** *Encycl. Brit.* VII. 23 The antlers of the Stag are rounded, and bear three 'tines' or branches, and a crown consisting of three or more points... The antlers during the second year consist of a simple unbranched stem, to which a tine or branch is added in each successive year, until the normal development is attained.

† **b.** A small branch or twig of a tree; the stalk of a fruit. *Obs. rare.*

13.. *E.E. Allit. P.* A. 78 As bornyst syluer þe lef onslydez, Þat þike con trylle on vcha tynde [*rime* schynde]. **13..** *Minor Poems fr. Vernon MS.* lii. 82 His hed nou leoneþ on þornes tynde. *c* **1440** *Pallad. on Husb.* IV. 395 Pomes take, The tenes with, to stonde in cannes saue.

c. *transf.* Each of two branches of a stream.

1875 R. F. BURTON *Gorilla L.* (1876) II. 73 We reached a shallow fork, one tine of which..comes from the Congo Grande.

† **3.** A rung or step of a ladder. *Obs. rare.*

a **1225** *Ancr. R.* 354 Scheome and pine, ase Seint Bernard seið, beoð þe two leddre stalen..and bitweonen þeos stalen beoð þe tindes ivestned of alle gode þeawes, bi hwuche me climbeð to þe blisse of heouene.

4. [f. TINE *v.*^{3}] An act of harrowing.

1778 [W. MARSHALL] *Minutes Agric.* 12 Dec. an. 1776, Our first tine was with fine harrows, which broke the crum, without tearing-up the sod. **1825** JAMIESON s.v., *A double tynd*, or *teind*, is harrowing the same piece of ground twice at the same yoking. **1854** *Jrnl. R. Agric. Soc.* XV. II. 403 Some sow it after the barley, and give it a tine with the harrows.

† **5.** *attrib.* and *Comb.*: **tine-knife**, see quot.; **tine nail** (*tynd nale*), a large sharp-pointed nail, a spike. *Obs.*

1555–6 *Burgh Rec. Edinb.* (1871) II. 322 For xix^{xx} of grait tynd nalis to the greit yat of the tolbuith. **1888** *Sheffield Gloss.*, *Tine-knife*, a knife whose haft is made from a tine of a stag's antler.

† **tine,** *sb.*^{2} *Obs. rare*$^{-1}$. In 4 tin. [f. TINE *v.*^{2}] Loss.

c **1320** *Sir Tristr.* 3006 In wining and in tin Trewe to ben ay, In ioie and in pin, In al þing, to say.

† **tine,** *sb.*^{3} *Obs.* Also tyne. [a. F. *tine* large vessel, tub (*c* 1230 in Godef.), Sp., It. *tina*:—L. *tina* wine-jar.] A vessel for brewing; a tub, vat.

[**1310** *Letter-Bk. D. Lond.* lf. 99 b, Item bona capta.. super Aliciam relictam Walteri le Cuuer .j. Cumelina et .j. Tyna, precium vj d.] **1337** *Ibid. F.* lf. 20 Hoi'es bracinas tenentes..qui mittunt... Braciatores suos cum vasis suis vocatis Tynes ad dictum Conductum. **1388–9** *Abingdon Rolls* (Camden) 57, ij vates et j tyne. *a* **1400** CHAUCER *Balade to Rosemounde* 9 For thogh I wepe of teres ful a tyne [cf. *Fr.* Le jor i ot plore de larmes pleine tine (see Skeat's *Chaucer* I. 549).]

tine, *sb.*^{4} *Obs.* exc. *dial.* Also tyne. [Etymology uncertain: see Note below.] A wild vetch or tare; a name for certain leguminous plants growing as weeds in corn, etc., and climbing by their tendrils, esp. the strangle-tare, *Vicia hirsuta*; also locally *V. Cracca*, and *Lathyrus tuberosus*.

c **1540** J. HEYWOOD in J. Redford *Mor. Play Wit & Sc.* (Shaks. Soc.) 79 This vice I lyken to a weede That husbondmen have named tyne, The whych in corne doth roote or brede. **1567** GOLDING *Ovid's Met.* v. (1593) 120 The tines and bryars did overgrow the wheate. **1573** TUSSER *Husb.* (1878) 109 The titters or tine makes hop to pine. **1707** MORTIMER *Husb.* (1721) I. 128 The Docks, Tyne, Tares, Mayweed, &c. pull up by hand. **1726** *Dict. Rust.* (ed. 3), *Chalkly-Lands*..naturally produce May-weed, Poppeys, Tine, &c. **1733** W. ELLIS *Chiltern & Vale Farm.* 300 Wild Thetch, Tyne, or Bind-weed, is an ugly Companion amongst the Corn.

b. Also called ***tine-grass, tine-tare*** (***tintare, tyntare***), ***tine-weed***.

c **1450** *Alphita* (Anecd. Oxon.) 186 *Trifolium acutum, an.* wildetare *uel* tintare. *Ibid.* 189 *Viciola, angl.* tintara. **1577** B. GOOGE *Heresbach's Husb.* I. (1586) 35 It groweth halfe a yarde hie, leaued like Tyntare. **1621** G. SANDYS *Ovid's Met.* v. (1626) 101 Tintare [*pr.* kintare], and Darnell [L. *lolium tribulique*] tire The fetter'd Wheat; and weeds that through it spire. **1733** W. ELLIS *Chiltern & Vale Farm.* 302 Cliver or chickweed..twists about the Wheat, like the Tyne-weed. **1744–50** —— *Mod. Husbandm.* I. I. 143 The Tyne-grass and the Lady-finger grass are the two best sorts of Natural Meadow Grasses. **1861** MISS PRATT *Flower. Pl.* II. 134 *Vicia hirsuta* (Hairy Tare)..the Tine Tare as it is called in some counties. *c* **1878** *Oxford Bible-Helps* 217 *Lentiles*,..a species of vetch, resembling the tine-tare, grown on poorer soils.

[*Note.* As *tintare, tine-tare*, appears to occur nearly a century earlier than the simple form *tine*, it was possibly the original name, its first element being one of the other TINE words. If originally applied to *Vicia hirsuta*, the sense 'small or diminutive tare' (f. TINE *a.*) would be appropriate enough. But perhaps derivation from TINE *v.*^{2}, or TINE *sb.*^{1} or ^{2}, in reference to the injury or trouble which it causes, is more likely. Cf. the name *strangle-tare*.]

† **tine,** *sb.*^{5} *Obs.* Also 6 tyne. (Only in and after Spenser.) [By-form of TEEN *sb.*^{1} in various senses. Perh. from Norse: cf. Norw. dial. *týne* injury: cf. TINE *v.*^{2} 2.] Affliction, trouble, sorrow.

1590 SPENSER *F.Q.* I. ix. 15 To seek her out with labor and long tyne. **1591** —— *Teares Muses* 3 Those piteous plaints and sorrowfull sad tine [*rime* nine]. **1600** TOURNEUR *Trans. Met.* To his Booke, The more the world doth seeke to work their tine. **1610** FLETCHER *Faithf. Sheph.* I. iii, And far more heavy be thy grief and tine.

† **tine,** *a.* and *sb.*^{6} *Obs.* Also 5 tyn, 5–7 tyne. [Appears as *adj.* and *sb.* about or soon after 1400; origin unknown: see Note below, and TINY *a.*]

A. *adj.* Very small, diminutive: = TINY *a.*

App. always preceded by *little*: cf. Sc. *little wee* (*bairn*). *a* **1400–50** *Alexander* 507 Scho had layd in his lape a litill tyne egg. ? *c* **1450** *Song* ii. in *Two Cov. Corpus Chr. Plays* (E.E.T.S.) 32 Lully, lulla, thow littell tine child, By by, lully lullay, thow littell tyne child. *c* **1460** *Towneley Myst.* xii. 467 Hayll, lytyll tyn mop, rewarder of mede!.. Hayll, lytyll mylk sop! hayll, dauid sede! **1597** SHAKS. *2 Hen. IV*, v. i. 29 A ioynt of Mutton, and any pretty little tine Kick-shawes. *Ibid.* v. iii. 60 Welcome my little tyne theefe. **1605** —— *Lear* III. ii. 74 He that has and a little-tyne wit.

B. *sb.* or quasi-*sb.* A very little space, time, or amount; a very little; 'a bit'.

App. always prec. by *little*: cf. similar Sc. use of *wee*: BARBOUR *Bruce* VII. 182 The kyng than wynkit a little wee. *c* **1420** (?) LYDG. *Assembly of Gods* 1063 He was constreynyd..A lytyll tyne abak to make a bew retret. *Ibid.* 1283 A lyttyll tyne hys ey castyng hym besyde. **1523** SKELTON *Garl. Laurel* 505 Sir, I pray you a lytyll tyne stande backe. **1546** J. HEYWOOD *Prov.* I. xi. Wks. (1562) D ij, For when prouander prickt them a little tyne. **1556** —— *Spider & F.* lx. Cc iv b, But stey a litle tine [*rime* fine].

[*Note.* In the absence of evidence, the etymology of *tine*, its accidence, and its relation to TINY, have received a good deal of discussion: see Wedgwood *Dict. Eng. Etym.* (1872) 684, Skeat *Notes on Eng. Etymol.* 300, E. Weekley in *Trans. Philol. Soc.* 1909. Prof. Skeat inclines to take *tine* as a later shortening of **tiné*, afterwards *tiny*, and **tiné* as a sb., possibly a. OF. *tinée* 'tubful'. But though it is possible that *tine* was orig. a sb., in sense 'bit', the evidence is that it was always a monosyllable. Prof. Weekley suggests the possibility of *tine, tiné, tiny* being aphetic for OF. *un tantin* or *tantinet* 'a little time or quantity', related to L. *tantillus* 'so small, so little'. This would suit the sense, but evidence connecting the forms has not been found (cf. TINY *a.*).]

tine, tyne (taɪn), *v.*[1] *Obs.* exc. *dial.* Forms: see below. [O.E. *týnan* = OFris. *tîna*, OLG., MLG., LG. *tûnen*, EFris. *tûnen, tünen*, MDu. *tûnen*, Du. *tuinen*, OHG. *zûnen* (MHG. *ziunen*, G. *zäunen*):—OTeut. **tûn-jan*, f. **tûno-* enclosure: see TOWN. From OE. *týn-an*, ME. had three dialect types, α. southern, *tün-, tuin-*; β. midl. and north. *tyn-, tin-, tine*; γ. Kentish *tēn, teen-*.]

A. Illustration of Forms.

α. *Present.* 1 týnan, 3 tunen (ü), 5 tuyne, tuynde. *Pa. t.* 1 týnde, 3 tunde. *Pa. pple.* 1 ȝetýned, 4–5 ytund.

688–95 *Laws of Ine* c. 42 Gif..hæbben sume ȝetyned hiora dæl, sume næbben. *a* **900** tr. *Bæda's Hist.* IV. iii. (1890) 268 Þonne tynde he his bec. *c* **950** *Lindisf. Gosp.* Matt. xxiii. 13 ȝie tyndon ric heofna. *a* **1000** in *Anglia* IX. 261 Me mæiȝ ..on sumera..tynan. *c* **1200** *Trin. Coll. Hom.* 43 Ne þat þe deuel me swelȝe, ne þat þe pit tune ouer me his muð. *Ibid.* 181 Hie tuneð to hire fif ȝaten, and penneð wel faste. *c* **1205** LAY. 15320 Þa ȝæten heo tunden uaste. *c* **1400** *Trevisa's Higden* (Rolls) VI. 229 Þe ȝates..were i-schette [*MSS.* β. tynde, γ. ytund]. *a* **1450** MYRC *Par. Priest* 63 Tuynde þyn ye þat thow ne se The cursede worldes vanyte.

β. *Present.* 3 tinen, 4–5 tynen, tynde, 5 tyn-yn, 5–6, 9 *dial.* tyne, 7–9 *dial.* tine. *Pa. t.* 4 tyned, 5 tynd. *Pa. pple.* 3 tined, 5 tynde, tynyd, tyndyd, 9 tined.

c **1200** *Trin. Coll. Hom.* 43 Þe pit tineð his muð ouer þe man, þe lið on fule synnen. *Ibid.* 101 Þe ȝiate of paradis, þe þurh Eue gilte wið hem was er tined. **1382** Tyndynge [see B. 1]. *c* **1400** Tynde [see α]. *a* **1400–50** *Alexander* 2193 Þen tened þe Thebees folke & tynd to þe ȝatis. *c* **1440** *Promp. Parv.* 494/1 Tynyn, or make a tynynge, *sepio.* *c* **1460** *Pol. Rel. & L. Poems* 167 Aȝen þee wole y my ȝatis tyne. **1585** JAS. I *Ess. Poesie* (Arb.) 56 And efter that made Argus for to tyne..all his windois. **1674** RAY *N.C. Words*, To Tine, to shut, fence. *Tine* the door; shut the door. **1825** BROCKETT *N.C. Words, Tine*, to shut, to inclose. **1874** Tined [see B. 1].

γ. *Present.* 4 tende, 6 tene, 7 teene, 7–9 *dial.* teen. *Pa. t.* 4–5 tende. *Pa. pple.* 4 i-tend, 5 yteynd, 7 *dial.* teened.

1387 TREVISA *Higden* (Rolls) IV. 443 Ȝif eny dore were i-tend [γ. ytund]. *Ibid.* 453 To tende [see B. 1]. *c* **1420** *Chron. Vilod.* 3725 Bot þe durus of þat chapelle weron þo y-teynde. **1626** in *Archæol. Cant.* (1902) XXV. 40 Peter Denham hath lately teened and fenced up a common foot-way. **1674** RAY *N.C. Words* 49 To enclose, fence, hedge, or teen. *c* **1700** KENNETT *MS. Lansd. 1033* lf. 389 To *Teen* (Lanc. to *Tine*), to hedge or to enclose a field, in Kent. **1887** *Kentish Gloss., Teener, Tener*, a man who teens or keeps in order a raddle-fence.

B. Signification.

1. *trans.* To close, shut (a door, gate, or window; a house, one's mouth, eyes, etc.). Also with *to* adv. (cf. SHUT *to*), and *absol.*

a **900** [see A. α]. *c* **950** *Lindisf. Gosp.* Luke xiii. 25, & tyneð þæt duro. *a* **1225** *Ancr. R.* 62 An ancre nule nout tunen hire eiðurles aȝein deað of helle & of soule. **1382** WYCLIF *Gen.* xix. 6 Loth gon oute to hem..and tyndynge to the dore, seith. **1387** TREVISA *Higden* (Rolls) IV. 453 Þe Est ȝate of þe temple..was so hevy of sound bras þat twenty men were besy i-now for to tende [*MSS.* α.tynde, β.tyne, γ.tuynde] it. *a* **1450** MYRC *Par. Priest* 490 To tuynen and open at heyre byddynge. **1523** FITZHERB. *Husb.* §141 Yf ony gate..go not lyghtly to open and tyne. **1561** *Child-Marriages* 114 That she did se hym tyne the windowes, and put to the dore with his fote. **1674** [see A. β]. **1874** T. HARDY *Far fr. Madding Crowd* xv, Cainy and I haven't tined our eyes to-night.

2. a. To enclose or shut (a thing) up *in* something.

13.. *E.E. Allit. P.* B. 498 Tyl þay had typyng fro þe tolke þat tyned hem þer-inne [*i.e.* in the ark]. **1888** A. S. WILSON *Lyric Hopeless Love* XXVIII. 92 Come, choral voices,..And in my soul the sweetness tine Which harps of Eden wear.

b. To enclose with a hedge or fence; to fence, to hedge in.

688–95 [see A. α]. *c* **1440** *Promp. Parv.* 494/1 Tynyd, or hedgydde (*P.* tyndyd), *septus.* **1570–6** LAMBARDE *Peramb. Kent* (1826) 376 Their [the Saxons'] woorde (Tynan) to tyne, or inclose with a hedge. **1598** STOW *Surv.* xlix. (1603) 547 To inclose or tyne. **1604** in *Eng. Gilds* (1870) 437 That they leaue to tine and keep so that his neighbor be harmelesse by the cattel. **1864** W. BARNES in *Macm. Mag.* Oct. 477 An' there wer my orcha'd a-tined Wi' a hedge on a steep-zided bank. **1892** BROOKE *Hist. E. Eng. Lit.* ix. 202 The place was tyned or girded with a fence of rods.

c. To make or repair (a hedge or fence).

1522 *MS. Acc. St. John's Hosp., Canterb.*, Paied for tenying of a hedge. **1630** *Ibid.*, For two bundles of bushes to teene our orchard hedges viij d. **1887** *Kentish Gloss., Teen*, to make a hedge with raddles [= green sticks].

†**3.** *fig.* To confine, restrain *to* something. *Obs.*

c **1430** *Hymns Virg.* 25 To þat loue y schal me so faste tyne, Þat y in herte it euermore holde.

tine, tyne (taɪn), *v.*[2] Chiefly (now only) *north. dial.* and *Sc.* Pa. t. and pple. tint (tɪnt). Forms: 3– tine; also 4 tin, 4–6 tyn, 4–9 tyne, (5 teyn, 6 tyen). *Pa. t.* 4 tinte, 4–6 tynt(e, 4– tint; also 5 tynit, 6 (Spenser) tyned, 8 tined. *Pa. pple.* 4 itint, y-tint, y-tent, 5 ytynt; 4–6 tinte, tynt, 5 tynte, tynde, 4– tint. [a. ON. *týna* (:—**tiunjan*), Norw., older Da. and Sw. dial. *tӯne*, to destroy, lose, to perish, deriv. of *tjón* loss, damage (cogn. with OE. *téon* injury, etc.: see TEEN *sb.*[1], *v.*[1]).]

1. *trans.* To lose; to suffer deprivation of; to cease to have or enjoy.

a **1300** *Cursor M.* 5518 (Cott.) Þan has þair will our wiþer-win, And we ma sua our landes tin [*v.rr.* tine, tyne]. *c* **1300** *Havelok* 2023 That he ne tinte no catel. **13..** *Sir Beues* (A.) 4386 Treitour! now is þe lif itint. *c* **1320** *Sir Tristr.* 1911 Þou hast y tent þi pride. *c* **1330** R. BRUNNE *Chron.* (1810) 15 He is now in poynt his regne forto tyne. *a* **1340** HAMPOLE *Psalter* lxi. 10 It is a harmefull winninge to win cattell & tine rightowsnes. **1377** LANGL. *P. Pl.* B. XVIII. 140 Þat was tynt þorw tre, tree shal it wynne. *a* **1400** *Octouian* 1147 Tho both hys armes were y-tent. *c* **1400** *Destr. Troy* 12467 Trees, thurgh tempestes, tynde hade þere leues. *c* **1460** *Towneley Myst.* i. 160 Oure Ioye is tynt. **1549** *Compl. Scot.* x. 83 There can no thing be tynt, bot quhen he that tynis ane thing ..knauis nocht quhair it is. **1575** CHURCHYARD *Chippes* (1817) 184 Our greedy mind gaines gold and tyens good name. **1596** DALRYMPLE tr. *Leslie's Hist. Scot.* (S.T.S.) I. 51 The Salmonte..tynes in smal watiris,..the gret fatnes, that they fand in the braid Sey. **1606** WARNER *Alb. Eng.* XIV. lxxxvii. (1612) 358 Both their Kings in following fight did brauely tyne their liues. **1721** RAMSAY *Prospect of Plenty* 162 To stow them..In barrels tight, that shall nae liquor tine. **1752** J. LOUTHIAN *Form of Process* (ed. 2) 31 The Repledger ..tined his Court for Year and Day. **1790** BURNS *Tam o' Shanter* 188 Tam tint his reason a' thegither. **1865** G. MACDONALD *A. Forbes* 51, I dinna think the Lord 'll tyne the grip o' his father's son. **1886** STEVENSON *Kidnapped* xix, James must have tint his wits.

b. To fail to gain, attain, or win: = LOSE *v.* 7, 8; *absol.* to lose the battle, be defeated: = LOSE *v.* 8 b.

c **1250** *Gen. & Ex.* 3518 For if ðu it ȝernes and ȝisse, ðu tines vn-ended blisce. **1340** HAMPOLE *Pr. Consc.* 2054 Þus sal þai dyghe and heven blis tyne And be putted til endeles pyne. *a* **1400** *Relig. Pieces fr. Thornton MS.* 38 Þou tynes þe mede of þi seruyce. **1549** *Compl. Scot.* ix. 80 He tint threttyne battellis. *c* **1560** A. SCOTT *Poems* (S.T.S.) ii. 48 To se quha tynt or wan The feild. **1681** COLVIL *Whigs Supplic.* (1751) 25 Whether he gain the day or tine, He never misseth to kill nine. **1721** RAMSAY *Prospect of Plenty* 50 She grasps the shadow, but the substance tines. *a* **1810** TANNAHILL *Poems* (1846) 101 I'm fear'd that I may tyne The love that ye hae promised me.

c. To spend in vain or to no purpose, to waste: = LOSE *v.* 6.

c **1330** R. BRUNNE *Chron.* (1810) 43 Kyng Suane gaf assaut,..Mykelle folk he les, & tynt his trauaile. **1393** LANGL. *P. Pl.* C. XV. 8 Ich haue..counsailede þe..No tyme to tyne. **1563** DAVIDSON *Confut. Kennedy* in *Wodrow Soc. Misc.* (1844) 216 Thay doctours tynt thare tyme. **1631** A. CRAIG *Pilgr. & Heremite* 9 My true travell shall bee tint. **1827** SCOTT *Two Drovers* Introd., If they had burned the rudas queen for a witch, I am thinking, may be, they would not have tyned their coals.

†**d.** To cause the loss of: = LOSE *v.* 9 a. *Obs.*

c **1470** HENRYSON *Mor. Fab.* x. (*Fox & Wolf*) vi, This tarying will tyne the all thy thank. **1588** A. KING tr. *Canisius' Catech.* 223 Receauing trew and Christian iustice..in stead of that whilk Adam by his inobedience tint to him and vs.

e. *absol.* or *intr.* To suffer loss: = Lose *v.* 4.

1340 HAMPOLE *Pr. Consc.* 1457 Now haf we ioy, now haf we pyn, Now we wyn, now we tyn. *c* **1400** *Destr. Troy* 1208 Þe Troiens..tynte of þere folkes. *c* **1470** HENRY *Wallace* VI. 460 Bot thow be war, thow tynys off thi chaffair. **1862** HISLOP *Prov. Scot.* 27 A tale never tines in the telling.

†**f.** *trans.* To incur (a penalty): cf. LOSE *v.* 3 g.

1426 *Reg. Mag. Sig. Scot.* 11/1 Wnder the payn off perel that efter folowys, and al that yhe may teyn enent ws. **1478** *Rental Bk. Cupar-Angus* (1879) I. 212 At al thir pwntis forsad be treuly kepit ondyr al peynis tha ma tyne of law.

g. To let slip from one's remembrance, to forget: = LOSE *v.* 5 d.

1513 DOUGLAS *Æneis* IX. v. 76, I hecht forsuith that deid sall nevyr be tynt. **1837** R. NICOLL *Poems* (1843) 123 Thae auld-warld fancies may heart winna tyne. *Ibid.* 188 Your father's dying counsels from Your bosoms never tine.

h. To leave far behind, as in a race; to outstrip entirely; to get far ahead of: = LOSE *v.* 5 c. *dial.*

1871 W. ALEXANDER *Johnny Gibb* vii, Oor 'Liza an' you ees't to be heid-y-peers, but ye're tynin her a'thegither.

II. †**2.** To ruin, destroy, bring to nought: = LOSE *v.* 2. (Cf. L. *perdĕre* to destroy, and to lose.)

a **1300** *Cursor M.* 2911 Sua tin [*v.r.* tyne] þai þam witouten end þat wil noght þam in time mend. *Ibid.* 4774 For þof he proue his freind wit pine, þar-for wil he noght him tine. **13..** *E.E. Allit. P.* B. 907 We schal tyne þis toun & trayþely disstrye. *c* **1400** *Apol. Loll.* 43 If God schal tyne alle þoo þat spek lesyng. *c* **1520** NISBET *N. Test. in Scots* Mark xii. 9 He sal cum and he sal tyne the teelars [WYCLIF tilieris], and geue the wyneyarde to vtheris. **1589** R. BRUCE *Serm.* (Wodrow Soc.) 110 He has power only to save and tine.

3. *intr.* To be lost, ruined, or destroyed; to perish: = LOSE *v.* 1.

13.. *Sir Beues* (A.) 652 Tiding com to king Ermyn, þat Beues hadde mad his men tyn. **13..** *Cursor M.* 13511 (Cott.) Quen þai had eten, þat drightin Bad þam late na crummes tin. *c* **1475** *Rauf Coilȝear* 58 Baith myself and my hors is reddy for to tyne. **1570** *Satir. Poems Reform.* xii. 97 For want of ane I wald nocht all suld tyne. *c* **1575** *Balfour's Practicks, Ship Laws* (1754) 623 Gif ony ship tine be storm of wether. **1792** BURNS *Gallant Weaver* ii, I was fear'd my heart would tine, And I gied it to the weaver. *a* **1810** TANNAHILL *Poems* (1846) 97 I'll tend thee..Wi' love that ne'er shall tyne.

tine, *v.*[3] [f. TINE *sb.*[1]]

1. *trans.* To furnish with tines or prongs: see also TINED.

a **1518** SKELTON *Magnyf.* 728 My tonge is with Fauell forked and tyned. **1760** [see TINING *vbl. sb.*[3]].

2. To scratch or work with tines; to harrow.

1766 [see TINING *vbl. sb.*[3]]. **1854** *Jrnl. R. Agric. Soc.* XV. II. 405 Two drills are tined at a time.

tine, variant of TIND *v. Obs.*, to kindle.

tine, obs. form of THINE (after a dental).

‖**tinea** ('tɪniːə). [L. *tinea* a gnawing worm, a moth, bookworm.]

1. *Path.* Technical name of the disease RINGWORM.

1398 TREVISA *Barth. De P.R.* VII. iii. (Bodl. MS.) Þe heed is ofte dissesed with an yuel þatt children haue ofte..and we clepith þat yuel Tinea a moþþe, for it freeteþ and gnawith þe oure parties of þe skynne of þe heed as a moþþe freteþ cloop. *c* **1400** *Lanfranc's Cirurgie* 181 Cirurgians..clepid tineam þere þat þere is corrupcioun in þe skyn wiþ harde crustis & quytture. **1693** tr. *Blancard's Phys. Dict.* (ed. 2) s.v., If running Sores in the Head..continue long..they grow into Tineas, crusty stinking Ulcers of the Head, which gnaw and consume its Skin. **1804** ABERNETHY *Surg. Obs.* 169 A circle of small sores, like what takes place in tinea. **1862** H. MACMILLAN in *Macm. Mag.* Oct. 466 Yeast..granules may be made to induce the ordinary parasitic skin diseases—a few germs rubbed into the head..producing..tinea.

2. (With capital initial.) *Entom.* Name given by Haworth to a genus of small moths (*Microlepidoptera*), the larvæ of which are very destructive to cloth, feathers, soft paper, decaying wood, stuffed birds, etc., examples of which are the common clothes-moths, *T. tapetzella*, and *T. pellionella*, and the very destructive pest in museums of natural history, *T. destructor*. In earlier times the word was applied to other destructive insects and worms.

1658 ROWLAND *Moufet's Theat. Ins.* 1100 Pliny saith that Tineæ do destroy the seeds of Figs... Niphus cals that little Scorpion which eats books Tineas, whereof I spake in the history of Scorpions. **1706** PHILLIPS (ed. Kersey), *Tinea*,.. the Moth, an Insect that eats Clothes. *Mod.* The genus Tinea contains about 100 species, of which 15 were recorded as British in Rennie's *Conspectus* 1832.

Hence **'tinean, 'tineid** *a.*, of or belonging to the genus *Tinea* or family *Tineidæ*; *sb.* a member of this genus or family.

1842 T. W. HARRIS *Insects Injurious to Vegetation* 361 The Tineans..have four short and slender feelers. **1888** *Insect Life* I. 191 These insects..are cloth-feeding Tineids. **1890** *Ibid.* II. 330 The Tineid Leaf-miner..affects the younger leaves only. **1891** *Cent. Dict.*, Tinean, Tineid. **1924** J. A. THOMSON *Science Old & New* x. 55 There is a very interesting Tineid caterpillar, found in the tree-nest of one of the Termites. **1964** EDWARDS & HEATH *Princ. Agric. Entom.* xiii. 285 Corn moth..is one of the most common Tineid moths which attacks grain.

tined (taɪnd), *a.* Also 5–6 tynyd, 6 tinded, 7 tyned. [f. TINE *sb.*[1] (or *v.*[3]) + -ED.] Furnished with or having tines. **a.** Of a fork, rake, harrow, or other implement. Chiefly in comb., as ***long-tined, three-tined***, etc.

c **1440** *Promp. Parv.* 494/1 Tynyd, wythe a tyne. **1523** FITZHERB. *Husb.* §15 They be lyke sloted and tinded. **1577** HARRISON *England* III. viii. (1878) II. 53 The heads of saffron are raised in Iulie, either with plough, raising, or tined hooke. **1611** SPEED *Hist. Gt. Brit.* VI. v. 58 In his hand for a Scepter, a Mace three-tined, as Neptune or God of the Sea. **1698** G. THOMAS *Pensilvania* 8 Their Ground is harrowed with Wooden Tyned Harrows. **1886** R. E. G. COLE *Gloss. S.-W. Lincs.* 154 He was charged with stealing a steel-tined fork. **1971** *Farmers Weekly* 19 Mar. 84 There was plenty to interest traditionalists, particularly among tined implements.

b. Of a deer's horns. In quot. 1530 *Her.* having the tines of a specified tincture.

c **1410** *Master of Game* (MS. Digby 182) xxiv, An hert þat bereth an hye heede þat is wyde and hye ytyneded with longe beemes. **1530** in *Ancestor* XI. (1904) 182 A hertes hede silver tynyd gold. **1878** S. LANIER *Rev. Hamish* 1 A ten-tined buck in the bracken lay. **1902** *Times* 13 Nov. 13/6 A goodly proportion of strongly tined heads.

[**tineman**, a spurious word; being a misreading in Harrison of the word *túnman* in a MS. *c* 1570 of *Cnut's Forest Laws* (*c* 1185), whence app. in Manwood and in Spelman 1664, and thence in later writers, and taken to repr. L. *minūtus homo* (as if f. TINE adj. 'very small' + *man*). (The actual OE. *túnman* is found in an 11th c. Vocab. (Wr.-Wülcker 332/22), rendering L. *villanus* villein.)

c **1185** *Cnut's Constit. de Foresta* §4, Camb. MS. *c* 1570 (Liebermann 621) Sub horum iterum quolibet sint duo minutorum hominum, quos tunman [or ? timman] Angli dicunt; hii nocturnam curam et ueneris et uiridis, tum seruilia opera subibunt. So **1577** HARRISON *England* II. xix. (1877) I. 315 [*the same, with* Tineman *and* hi]. **1592** *transl.* in Manwood *Brefe Collect. Lawes of Forest*, Againe, vnder euery one of these meane men, let there be two of the least men of account of the Forest (which Englishmen do call 'Tyne-men'): these persons shall vndertake the seruile labour, and also the night charge of Vert and Venison. **1598** MANWOOD *Laws Forest* (1615) 2 (quoting prec. Latin) *margin*, Tineman. These are they that now are called Foresters or Keepers. **1670** BLOUNT *Law Dict.*, *Tineman* or *Tienman*, was of old a Petty Officer in the Forest, who had the Nocturnal care of Vert and Venison, and other servile employments. **1906** DOYLE *Sir Nigel* x, The tineman and verderers have not forgotten me yet.]

tiner ('taɪnə(r)). *Sc. Obs.* or *arch.* In 6 tyner, -ar. [f. TINE *v.*[2] + -ER[1].] A loser.

1540 *Sc. Acts Jas. V* (1814) II. 375 It is statute..þat þe tynar of þe cause pay the wynnaris expensis. **1560** ROLLAND *Seven Sages* 81 O subtell schrew,..Tyner of treuth, with toung Intoxicat. **1596** DALRYMPLE tr. *Leslie's Hist. Scot.* v.

lxxx. (S.T.S.) I. 292 Victor and Vanquist, tyner and Winner war baith present.

tinet: see TINNET.

tine-tare, tine-weed: see TINE *sb.*[4]

tinewald, var. TYNWALD.

† **'tine-worm.** *Obs. rare.* Also 8 tin-. An unidentified 'worm', said to be injurious to sheep; ? = TAINT-WORM.

1587 MASCALL *Govt. Cattle* (1596) 15 Against the swelling in a beast by eating of a Tyne-worme. *Ibid.* 250 The tine worme is a small red worme with many legs, much like a hog lowse, and they will creepe in grasse: if sheepe or other cattell do eate one, they will swell and within a day die, if he be not remedied. **1704** *Dict. Rust.*, Tinworm.

tin-field, -floor, etc.: see TIN *sb.* 5.

tinfoil ('tɪnfɔɪl), *sb.* Forms: see TIN *sb.* and FOIL *sb.*[1]; also 6 tynfule. [f. TIN *sb.* + FOIL *sb.*[1]] Tin hammered or rolled into a thin sheet; also, a sheet of the same rubbed with quicksilver, used for backing mirrors and precious stones; a similar sheet of an alloy of tin and lead, or of aluminium, used as a wrapping esp. for protection from moisture or air.

1467–8 *Durham Acc. Rolls* (Surtees) 92 Pro le Tynfole empt. pro ornacione et pictura del Soteltez erga festum Natal. Domini, xj d. **1477–9** *Acc. Exch. K. R.* Bundle 496 No. 18 (P.R.O.) Pro..Tynnefoile, Canvas [etc.]. **1481–3** *Ibid.* No. 26, vij dos' Tynfoill. **1525–6** *Durham Acc. Rolls* (Surtees) 108 Pro preparacione le borehede et tynfule. **1586** *Rates of Customes* E viij b, Tin foile the groce iiij.s. **1681** GREW *Musæum* III. II. iii. 335 With this the Tin-Foile is made to stick close to the backsides of Looking-Glasses. **1762** FRANKLIN *Lett.*, etc. Wks. 1840 V. 408 It is what they call tinfoil, or leaf-tin, being tin milled between rollers. **1825** J. NICHOLSON *Operat. Mechanic* 715 The tin-foils are only used in the case of colourless stones. **1839** URE *Dict. Arts* 1251 Tin-foil coated with quicksilver makes the reflecting surface of glass mirrors. **1876** HARLEY *Royle's Mat. Med.* 256 Tin-foil, so largely used by druggists to wrap up medicines and form capsules for bottles, is an alloy of tin, and contains from 25 to 75 per cent. of lead.

attrib. **1849** NOAD *Electricity* (ed. 3) 146 By a tin-foil communication, a connection is made. **1862** *Catal. Internat. Exhib., Brit.*, II. No. 5142 Plain, fancy, and tinfoil papers.

'tinfoil, *v.* [f. prec. sb.] *trans.* To cover or coat with tinfoil. Hence **'tinfoiled** (-fɔɪld) *ppl. a.*, esp. *fig.*

1598 B. JONSON *Ev. Man in Hum.* I. ii, This man! so graced, guilded, or to use a more fit metaphor..so tinfoild by nature. **1621** BURTON *Anat. Mel.* II. iii. III. 399 T'is *bracteata fælicitas*, as Seneca termes it, tin-foyl'd happines if it be happines at all. *a* **1658** CLEVELAND *Hecatomb* 9 My Text defeats your Art, ties Nature's tongue, Scorns all her Tinfoyl'd Metaphors of Pelf. **1887** *Sci. Amer.* 1 Oct. 215/3 The glass..after being tinfoiled, is..pushed across the table containing the mercury.

tinful ('tɪnfʊl). [f. TIN + -FUL.] As much as a tin will contain.

1896 A. MORRISON *Child of the Jago* 169 Tobacco pillaged from a tin-full his father had brought.

ting (tɪŋ), *sb.*[1] [f. TING *v.*: cf. DING *sb.*[2]] **a.** The sound emitted by a small bell, or other resonant body, as a thin glass vessel, as the result of a single stroke; a thinner or sharper sound than that expressed by TANG. Also *advb.*, or without grammatical construction, esp. when repeated.

1602 MIDDLETON *Blurt* IV. ii, Midnight's bell goes ting, ting, ting. **1611** COTGR., *Tinton*,..the ting of a bell. **1677** WALLIS in *Phil. Trans.* XII. 842 A thin..Venice-glass, cracked with the..sound of a Trompet..sounding an Unison or a Consonant note to that of the Tone or Ting of the Glass. **1859** CORNWALLIS *Panorama New World* I. 178 The liquid ting—ting—ting of the bell-bird. **1895** ZANGWILL *The Master* II. ix, His own turn came, announced by the sharp ting of a hand-bell. **1898** G. W. E. RUSSELL *Coll. & Recoll.* xxxiv. 473 The shrill ting-ting of the division-bell. **1906** *Daily Chron.* 14 Feb. 6/7 'Ting' went the bell.

b. *ting-a-ling* (*ling*), *ting-a-ring*, *tingating* (*rare.*), the sound of the continued ringing of a small bell, or the like. Also *advb.* Cf. *tink-a-tink* s.v. TINK *int.* and *sb.*

1833 MRS. MARCET *Seasons* II. *Spring* iv. 54 The great dinner-bell went ting a ring a ring a ring. **1862** C. C. ROBINSON *Leeds Gloss.* 436 'Ting-elin, all in'... 'Its ommast ting-elin now'. **1879** MACDONALD *Sir Gibbie* xix, I hae naething till acquaint yer honour wi', sir, but the ting-a-ling o'tongues. **1906** *Westm. Gaz.* 20 Jan. 5/1 Ting-a-ling. Telephone again. 'Who's there?' **1922** JOYCE *Ulysses* 734 And he so quiet and mild with his tingating zither. **1932** T. S. ELIOT *Sweeney Agonistes* 12 *Telephone*: Ting a ling ling. Ting a ling ling.

‖ **t'ing** (tɪŋ), *sb.*[2] Also ting. [Chinese *tíng.*] In China: a small open pavilion, esp. in which one may rest or enjoy the landscape.

1853 *North-China Herald* 7 May 159/2 Another accommodation for travellers, called *ting*, are of more frequent occurrence. **1947** *Archit. Rev.* CII. 12/2 An island in a lake will have its t'ing, a bridge spanning the water is crowned by a t'ing, and a t'ing will invariably mark any particularly charming viewpoint. **1958** W. WILLETTS *Chinese Art* II. viii. 701 A small Chinese open pavilion (*t'ing*) of traditional form at Fuchow in Fukien, dating from the nineteenth century.

Ting (dɪŋ, tɪŋ), *sb.*[3] Also **Ding. a.** The name of a county in Hebei province, China, used *attrib.* to designate a type of white porcelain first made there during the Tang dynasty and perfected during the Song dynasty. **b. Ting-yao**, the name of a kiln in this county, used *attrib.* and *absol.* to denote the porcelain made there.

1904 E. DILLON *Porcelain* v. 67 In the Ting yao of the Sung dynasty..we have the oldest type of an important class of porcelain. **1915** R. L. HOBSON *Chinese Pott. & Porc.* I. iv. 51 Many of the white Ting wares are thin enough to be translucent. **1933** *Burlington Mag.* June 265/1 The standard Ting ware was white..porcelain, which was either perfectly plain or decorated with free-hand carved designs. **1953** B. GRAY *Early Chinese Pott. & Porc.* v. 31 To return to the Ting wares. The most characteristic Ting shape is a conical bowl on a small foot. **1958** W. WILLETTS *Chinese Art* II. vi. 446 North is Ting Chou and the district where Ting wares are supposed to have originated. **1971** L. A. BOGER *Dict. World Pott. & Porc.* 343/2 As a rule the Ting bowls had a raw edge, as though placed in the furnace in an inverted position. **1972** *Times* 30 May 11/2 (Advt.), A carved ting yao plate. **1980** *Catal. Fine Chinese Ceramics* (Sotheby, Hong Kong) 32 A small Ding (Ting) Ware bowl with curved sides, freely carved with a lotus blossom in the interior.

‖ **ting** (dɪŋ, tɪŋ), *sb.*[4] [Chinese *dǐng.*] An ancient Chinese vessel, usu. bronze, having two looped handles and three or four legs (see quots.).

1904 S. W. BUSHELL *Chinese Art* I. iv. 80 The word *ting* is occasionally rendered 'tripod', but this is hardly applicable to a second not uncommon form which has a rectangular body of oblong section supported by four legs. **1958** W. WILLETTS *Chinese Art* I. iii. 138 The Han dictionary *Erh ya* defines the *ting* as a *li* with solid legs. **1959** G. SAVAGE *Antique Collector's Handbk.* 40 The *ting* is a bowl of hemispherical shape with three legs and two upstanding handles. **1973** *Genius of China* 12/1 In 219 BC the Ch'in emperor tried to recover from a river the nine *ting* tripods on which the power of the Chou king over his feudal subordinates was said to depend.

ting (tɪŋ), *v.* [Echoic. Cf. PING; also obs. Du. *tinghe, tanghen* 'tintinare'.]

1. *trans.* To cause (a small bell or the like) to emit a ringing note; in quot. 1607, to try (a coin) by ringing in order to test its genuineness.

1495 *Trevisa's Barth. De P.R.* XVIII. xii. (W. de W.), Wyth betynge of basynes, tyngynge & tynkynge of tymbres they [bees] ben comforted & callyd to the hyues. **1552** *Berks. Ch. Goods* (1879) 39 A bell used to be tynged before dede corses. **1607** R. C[AREW] tr. *Estienne's World of Wonders* 131 They sticke not to ting and peize the money. **1611** COTGR., *Tintiner*, to ting, or toll, a bell. *a* **1825** FORBY *Voc. E. Anglia*, *Ting*, to ring a small bell.

b. *to ting bees*, to make a ringing sound, as with a key and shovel, when bees swarm, to induce them to settle: cf. quot. 1495 in 1; also TANG *v.*[2] 4, RING *v.*[2] 10 b.

1609 C. BUTLER *Fem. Mon.* i. (1623) 3 Tinging of swarmes to make them come downe. *a* **1825** FORBY *Voc. E. Anglia* s.v., 'To *ting* bees', is to collect them together, when they swarm, by the ancient music of the warming-pan and the key of the kitchen-door.

c. To announce (a person) by 'ringing in' (see RING *v.*[2] 7 c). *rare.*

1880 HARDY *Trumpet-Major* II. xxiii. 157 'There, they be tinging in the passon!' exclaimed David,..as the bells changed from chiming all three together to a quick beating of one.

2. *intr.* Of a bell, a metal or glass vessel, or the like: To emit a high-pitched ringing note when struck, to ring.

1562 PHAER *Æneid.* IX. D d j, His helmet tincgling tings. **1607** ROWLANDS *Diog. Lanth.* 21 If we but heare a Bell to ting..Into a hole we straite may skippe. **1653** URQUHART *Rabelais* I. v, Bowls [began] to ting, glasses to ring. **1840** [see TINGING *vbl. sb.*].

b. *trans.* To announce (an hour) by tinging; to ring or strike (the hour). Also *ting out.*

1888 F. W. ROBINSON *Youngest Miss Green* III. 78 The clock..then tinged out 'One'.

3. *intr.* To make a ringing sound *with* a bell, etc. Also *to ting it.*

1605 ARMIN *Foole upon F.* (1880) 8 They tinged with a knife at the bottome of a glasse. **1613** PURCHAS *Pilgrimage* (1614) 492 Often tinging with a little Bell of Siluer. *a* **1693** *Urquhart's Rabelais* III. Prol. 6 There did he..ting it, ring it, tingle it, towl it. **1872** T. HARDY *Under Greenwood Tree* V. i. II. 186 So he jist stopped to ting to 'em [bees] and shake 'em.

ting: see THING *sb.*[2]

ting-a-ling, ting-a-ring: see TING *sb.*[1] b.

tinge (tɪndʒ), *sb.*[1] [f. TINGE *v.*]

1. A slight shade of colouring, *esp.* one modifying a tint or colour.

1752 J. HILL *Hist. Anim.* 411 But with more of the reddish tinge. **1796** KIRWAN *Elem. Min.* (ed. 2) II. 290 This blue tinge has sometimes occasioned it to be taken for Cobalt. **1815** J. SMITH *Panorama Sc. & Art* II. 540 In purifying the silks which are to remain white, a tinge is given by the addition of a small quantity of different colouring matters. **1907** *Edin. Rev.* Oct. 510 The blue, instead of being converted into buff, had a tinge of red in it.

b. *transf.* A minute quantity of colouring matter or dye.

1770 DUNN in *Phil. Trans.* LX. 71 Dying away like a drop of tinge thrown into water. **1825** J. NICHOLSON *Operat. Mechanic* 716 These colours may be had..from a tinge wholly dissolved in spirit of wine.

2. *fig.* A modifying infusion or intermixture; a slight admixture of some qualifying property or characteristic; a touch or flavour of some quality.

1797 SCOTT *Let. to Miss C. Rutherford* Oct., in *Lockhart*, A very slight tinge in her pronunciation is all which marks the foreigner. **1800** HT. LEE *Canterb. T.* (ed. 2) III. 121 [It] had given that slight, and almost imperceptible tinge to her manners. **1840** *C. O. Müller's Hist. Lit. Greece* XV. §7 The language [of Pindar's Odes] is epic, with a slight Doric tinge. **1849** MACAULAY *Hist. Eng.* viii. II. 275 His political opinions had a tinge of Whiggism.

3. *Trade.* (See quot.)

1850 *Chamb. Jrnl.* XIV. 217/1 A trader [draper] who has too much window stock upon his hands at the approach of spring tinges his winter goods, after which they rapidly decrease in amount. The tinge is a cabalistic sign appended to the private mark, by which all the shopmen know that a premium is attached to the sale of the article bearing it.

tinge, *sb.*[2] ? *dial.* (See quot.)

1812 SIR J. SINCLAIR *Syst. Husb. Scot.* I. 119 If given raw, to horses especially, they are one great cause of the tinge or gripes.

tinge (tɪndʒ), *v.* Also 6–7 ting. [ad. L. *ting-ĕre* to dye, colour.]

1. *trans.* To impart a trace or slight shade of some colour to; to tint; to modify the tint or colour of (const. *with*). Also *absol.*

1477 RIPLEY *Comp. Alch.* XI. vi. in Ashm. *Theat. Chem. Brit.* (1652) 182 Saffron when yt ys pulveryzate, Tyngyth much more of Lycour. **1577** HARRISON *England* III. viii. (1878) II. 55 As their saffron is not so fine as that of Cambridge shire and about Walden, so it will not cake, ting, nor hold colour withall. **1577** HOLINSHED *Chron., Descr. Scot.* vii. 9/2 Theyr fleshe moreouer is redde as it were tynged with Saffron. **1658** A. FOX *Würtz' Surg.* III. xvi. 265 Which will tinge the Aquavitæ to a redness. **1725** *Bradley's Fam. Dict.* s.v. *Oak*, A way of tinging Oak..so as it will resemble coarse Ebony. **1769** N. NICHOLLS *Corr. w. Gray* (1843) 99 Just when Autumn had begun to tinge the woods with a thousand beautiful varieties of colour. **1863** MARY HOWITT *F. Bremer's Greece* II. xvi. 138 The summit of Parnassus was tinged with the red light of morning.

b. *transf.* To impart a slight taste or smell to; to affect slightly by admixture.

1690 C. NESSE *O. & N. Test.* I. 236 Fragrant flowers and fruits, the sweet odours whereof had likely ting'd those goodly garments. **1707** MORTIMER *Husb.* (1721) II. 353 Liquors tinged with the spirituous Flavour of other Fruits. *c* **1826** *Lond. Encycl.* s.v. *Barometer*, Common water, tinged with a sixth part of aqua regia. **1863** MRS. OLIPHANT *Salem Chapel* xiii, The sweet atmosphere was tinged with the perfumy breath which always surrounded her.

2. *intr.* To become modified in colour; to take a (specified or implied) tinge.

1662 R. MATHEW *Unl. Alch.* §107. 174 Put on more Vinegar..till thou seest that it will ting no more. **1756** C. LUCAS *Ess. Waters* I. 15 The solution..upon the addition of new spirit of salt, tinges a kind of orange color. **1821** CLARE *Vill. Minstr.* I. 93 He [the oak] tinges slow with sickly hue.

3. *fig.* To affect in mind or feeling by intermixture, infusion, or association; to qualify, modify, or slightly vary the tone of.

1674 N. FAIRFAX *Bulk & Selv.* 47 Our souls are indeed so far ting'd with body. **1681** WOOD *Life* 14 Mar. (O.H.S.) II. 526 Fame tells us that he is tinged with presbyterian leven. **1702** C. MATHER *Magn. Chr.* III. I. iii. (1852) 303 His exact education..tinged him with an aversation to vice. **1784** COWPER *Task* IV. 553 The town has ting'd the country. **1856** EMERSON *Eng. Traits, Lit.* Wks. (Bohn) II. 106 The influence of Plato tinges the British genius. **1884** JENNINGS *Croker Papers* I. vi. 182 This grief tinged the whole of Mr. Croker's subsequent life.

† **4.** *trans. Alchemy.* To change by the action of a tincture: cf. TINCTURE *v.* 2 b, TINCT *v.* 3. *Obs.*

1650 FRENCH *Distill.* (1651) Ded. A iv b, As men bring lead to Philosophers to be tinged into gold. **1660** tr. *Paracelsus' Archidoxis* I. v. 75 So likewise doth this Tincture tinge the Hydropical..Body into a sound State.

5. *Trade.* To mark with a tinge (TINGE *sb.*[1] 3).

1850 [see TINGE *sb.*[1] 3].

Hence **tinged** (tɪndʒd) *ppl. a.*

1658 A. FOX *Würtz' Surg.* III. xvi. 265 This ting'd Aquavitæ is to be extracted per Balneum. **1774** M. MACKENZIE *Maritime Surv.* 110 With a smoked or tinged Glass before your Eye. **1867** DEUTSCH *Rem.* (1874) 23 To be dependent on the possibly tinged version of an interpreter.

tingeing: see TINGING *ppl. a.*[2]

tingent ('tɪndʒənt), *a.* Now *rare* or *Obs.* [ad. L. *tingent-em*, pres. pple. of *ting-ĕre* to colour, TINGE.] That tinges or colours, colouring, dyeing.

1650 ASHMOLE *Chym. Collect.* 118 Those two Bodies are shining, in which are tingent splendid Raies. **1667** SPRAT *Hist. R. Soc.* 304 In some Colours and Stuffs the Tingent Liquor must be boyling. **1727–41** CHAMBERS *Cycl.* s.v. *Dying*, Some tingent liquors are fitted for use by long keeping. **1813** E. BANCROFT *Dyeing*, etc. I. 166 *note*, The tingent matter was in union with too great a proportion of the other constituents of the plant.

† **tinger**[1] ('tɪŋə(r)). *Obs. rare.* [app. from a vb. **ting*, OE. **tengan* = ON. *tengja* to make fast, fasten, tie together.] A workman employed in raising and making fast the body of a cart after it has been emptied by tipping.

1587 FLEMING *Contn. Holinshed* III. 1544/2 There were also eight tingers, whose speciall office was to lift vp the courts [= carts] immediatelie after they were vnloden, and to make fast their tackle... There attended also..men called vntingers, to loose and vndoo the tackle..before the vnloding. *Ibid.* 1545/1 The driuer neuer staied, but went foorth for a new lode: the tinger runneth after and pulleth vp the court, and fasteneth the tackle.

tinger[2] ('tɪndʒə(r)). [f. TINGE *v.* + -ER[1].] One who or that which tinges.

1814 W. TAYLOR in *Monthly Mag.* XXXVII. 146 Girdle of the summer rain, Tinger of the dews of air. **1864** in WEBSTER.

'tingible, *a. rare.* [ad. L. type **tingibilis*, f. *tingĕre* to TINGE: see -IBLE.] Capable of being tinged or coloured.

1656 BLOUNT *Glossogr.*, *Tingible*, (*tingibilis*), that may be stained, dipped or died. **1901** *Jrnl. Exper. Med.* 29 Nov. 58 The adjacent tingible substances in the nucleus.

tinging ('tɪŋɪŋ), *vbl. sb.* [f. TING *v.* + -ING[1].] The action of the verb TING; ringing.

1495 [see TING *v.* 1]. **1528** PAYNEL *Salerne's Regim.* Y iij, Whiche..causeth tyngynge or ryngynge in the eare. **1562** TURNER *Baths* A ij b, The wyndenes or synging or tynging of the eares. **1611** COTGR., *Tintement*, a tinging, ringing, tingling. **1840** *P. Parley's Ann.* I. 54 It goes click clack, tick tack,..ting, ting, ting, ting, and stops between its tinging almost as if it were out of breath.

tinging ('tɪŋɪŋ), *ppl. a.*[1] [f. TING *v.* + -ING[2].] That tings; ringing, as metal; that emits a ringing sound, as the ***tinging frog***.

1609 HOLLAND *Amm. Marcell.* XXIV. iv. 250 Neither the tinging sound [L. *tinnitus*] of the yron tooles digging hard by could bee heard. **1611** COTGR., *Charivaris de poelles*, the carting of an infamous person, graced with the harmonie of tinging kettles, and frying-pan Musicke. **1802** SHAW *Gen. Zool.* III. I. 135 Tinging Frog... Smaller than the European Tree Frog. Native of South America.

tinging, tingeing ('tɪndʒɪŋ), *ppl. a.*[2] [f. TINGE *v.* + -ING[2]. The distinctive spelling *tingeing*, on the analogy of *singeing*, appears in Webster 1864, *Cent. Dict.*, Funk's *Standard Dict.*] That tinges or colours slightly.

1663 BOYLE *Usef. Exp. Nat. Philos.* I. i. 14 My curiosity leading me to abstract the Menstruum from the tinging Powder. **1758** J. KENNEDY *Curios. Wilton House* (1786) p. xiv, Places, where no tinging or fouling Substances touched them. **1838** T. THOMSON *Chem. Org. Bodies* 400 A Florentine, named Federigo, discovered..the tinging properties of this lichen.

tin-glass. Now *rare.* [f. TIN *sb.* + GLASS.]

1. An old name for BISMUTH.

a **1558** *Off. Augm., Misc. Bk.* XLI. No. 194 (P.R.O.) Vaynes and Mynes..of..Antimonia and tyne glas and Sonddrye markasites. **1577** HARRISON *England* III. xi. (1878) II. 72 It [pewter] consisteth of a composition, which hath thirtie pounds of kettle brasse to a thousand pounds of tin, whervnto they ad three or foure pounds of tinglasse. **1682** HARTMAN *Preserv. & Restorer Health* 342 The preparation of Magistery of Bistmuth or Tinglass. **1704** J. HARRIS *Lex. Techn.* I, *Bismuth*, or *Tin Glass*, by the Ancients was thought to be a natural Marcasite or Mineral. **1815** J. SMITH *Panorama Sc. & Art* II. 397 Bismuth is known among artisans by the name of tinglass.

†**2.** Tin. *Obs. rare.*

1601 HOLLAND *Pliny* XXXIV. xvi. II. 517 This white lead or tinglasse [*plumbum album*: see LEAD *sb.*[1] 1 b] hath been of long time in estimation, even since the warre of Troy, as witnesseth the Poet Homer, who calleth it Cassiteron. *Ibid.* xvii, A devise to tin pots, pans, and other peeces of brass.. with white lead or tinglasse.

tin-glaze, -glazed: see TIN *sb.* 5.

tingle ('tɪŋg(ə)l), *sb.*[1] *techn.* Also 4–5 **tyngyl, -il,** 6 **tyngle.** [Cognate with MHG. *zingel* 'little tack, little hook' (Lexer), of which the LG. form would be *tingel*. App. f. the same verbal stem *ting-*, *teng-* as in TINGER[1] + instrumental suffix *-el*: see -LE *suffix* 1. The original sense was thus 'that which fastens', a name susceptible of many applications.]

1. A very small kind of nail; the smallest size of tack. Usually **tingle nail** (also **tingle sprig**).

[**1288** *Bosham Acc.* (Sussex) in Rogers *Agric. & Pr.* I. 472/4 Tingle 750 @ /1½.] **1377–8** *Durham Acc. Rolls* (Surtees) 587 In D.C. tyngylnaile empt. pro fenestr. in granario, xij d. [**1415** *York Acc.* in Rogers *Agric. & Pr.* III. 447/4 Tingle nail 4 m 3 c @ 1/-.] **1449–50** *Durham Acc. Rolls* (Surtees) 239 CC[ma] del Tyngilnaill. **1582** *Wills & Inv. N.C.* (Surtees) II. 67, vj hondert hetche naills 3/-, xv hondert latt brods 6/-, xij hondreth tyngle naills 5/-. **1831** J. HOLLAND *Manuf. Metal* I. 194 The smallest tingle nails of about a quarter of an inch. **1886** G. R. SIMS in *Daily News* 4 Dec. 5/6 The smallest [nails], which he calls 'tingles', he can buy a farthing's worth of. **1892** *Labour Commission* Gloss., *Tingles*, also called tacks.

2. a. A strip of metal bent into an **S** shape, forming a clip to support heavy panes of glass on roofs; also, a strip of lead turned up at one end, used in replacing slates; also, a strip of lead bent in the middle, of which the lower half is nailed to the board, while the upper half forms a core on which the edges of two contiguous sheets of lead are folded together, to form a close joint.

1884 *Spon's Mechanic's own Bk.* (1886) 627 Tingle for fixing Ridge. **1887** *Notes Building Constr.* (Rivingtons) 420 When [the roof panes] are large and heavy, any tendency for them to slip down is prevented by hanging the tail of each on to the head of the pane below by means of a zinc or copper tingle. *Ibid.* (1901) 218 The ends of two adjacent sheets are turned up against one another..; the two are then bent over together to form a roll... Between the ends of the two sheets so treated is a 'clip' or 'tingle'..a narrow strip of lead, of which about 2 inches is nailed to the boards.

b. A sheet of metal, usu. copper, used for making temporary repairs on a small wooden boat when it has been holed.

1909 in WEBSTER. **1932** F. B. COOKE *Cruising Chats* xxv. 228 The best material for a tingle is a piece of thin sheet lead. **1961** B. FERGUSSON *Watery Maze* ix. 222 Plans should never be regarded as immutable. If they leak when first floated, it is no good patching them up until they are all tingles and no hull: scrap and start again. **1969** *Beaver* Spring 30/2 It has been suggested that these pieces [of sheet copper] may be nothing more than a tingle or patch on a ship's boat.

3. *Bricklaying.* A small loop of string attached at intervals to a bricklayer's line, to keep it horizontal and prevent sag. The *tingles* (Sc. *latchets*) are supported on bricks laid at intervals along the course, and kept in place by laying another brick upon each. (In some handbooks the name *tingle* is erroneously given to the supporting bricks.)

1886 COL. SEDDON *Builder's Work* 43 To prevent sagging, if the line be long, it must be carefully propped at intervals ..by..tingles.

'tingle, *sb.*[2] [f. TINGLE *v.* Cf. WFlem. *tingel* nettle.] An act, instance, or condition of tingling. **a.** A tingling or tinkling sound. Also advb. or without construction, as imitation of the sound. **b.** A tingling sensation in the ears, or in some other part of the body; the tingling action of cold, etc.

a **1700** in *O.H.S. Collect.* IV. 183 Tingle, tingle, tingle Says the little bell att 9 To call the beerers home. **1841** HOOD *Tale Trumpet* xxxviii, That like the bell With muffins to sell, Her ear was kept in a constant tingle! **1848** LOWELL *Fable for Critics* 1557 A Leyden-jar always full-charged, from which flit The electrical tingles of hit after hit. **1879** BEERBOHM *Patagonia* iv. 49 The wind was just cold enough to give that exciting tingle to the blood which influences one's spirits like a subtile wine. **1906** *Daily Chron.* 8 Mar. 6/4 A tingle of regret runs through me that I have lost my good manners. **1908** *Blackw. Mag.* Oct. 682/2 One feels the tingle of the morning air.

tingle, *sb.*[3] [Abbrev. of *whelk-tingle* s.v. WHELK[1] d.] Any of several marine molluscs, esp. the rough tingle, *Ocenebra erinacea*, the smooth tingle, *Nucella lapillus*, or the American tingle, *Urosalpinx cinerea*, all of which bore holes in the shells of oysters and other molluscs.

1930 *Essex Naturalist* XXII. 299 In the autumn of 1928 samples of living tingles dredged in the River Blackwater were forwarded to me. **1959** *Times* 25 Aug. 5/6 The investigation was designed to control the tingles. **1974** P. R. WALNE *Culture of Bivalve Molluscs* vi. 125 The introduction of the American slipper limpet..and the American tingle.. on to the south-east coast of England..are well-documented examples.

tingle ('tɪŋg(ə)l), *v.* Also 4–5 **tyngle,** 6 **tingil, tincgle.** [app. in origin a modification of TINKLE *v.*[1] (in both branches), for which it is substituted in some MSS. of the second Wycliffite version: cf. *crinkle, cringle*. It has the form of a frequentative of TING *v.* and *sb.*[1], and has prob. in later use (in branch II) been associated with that group, but is found earlier.]

I. 1. *intr.* Said of the ears: To be affected with a ringing or thrilling sensation at the hearing of anything. Cf. RING *v.*[2] 5.

Perh. the original notion was 'to ring or resound in response to a loud noise'; but it was very early applied to the result of hearing something mentally shocking or painful, without any reference to sound.

1388 WYCLIF *2 Kings* xxi. 12 Yuelis..that who euer herith, bothe hise eeris tyngle [1382 tynclyn; 1388 *v.r.* tyncle or ringe]. **1581** MULCASTER *Positions* x. (1887) 57 To much shrilnesse straynes the head [of the speaker], causeth the temples pante,..the eyes to swell, the eares to tingle. **1598** HAKLUYT *Voy.* I. 585, Least I cause good and learned mens eares to tingle at his leud and vnseemely rimes. **1623** GOUGE *Serm. Extent God's Provid.* §11 A judgement which would make a mans eare to tingle again. **1715** ATTERBURY *Serm.* (1734) I. v. 133 Imprecations, which the Ears of sober Heathens would tingle at. **1847** L. HUNT *Jar Honey* x. (1848) 141 His ears tingled, his head turned giddy. **1850** MERIVALE *Rom. Emp.* (1865) I. ix. 355 Senators and knights retuned to Rome, their ears tingling with his compliments.

b. Said also of the cheeks under the influence of shame, indignation, or the like.

(Here there is no notion of sound, but only of the sensation caused by the rush of blood to the cheeks.)

1555 in Strype *Eccl. Mem.* (1721) III. App. I. 163 So that thy swoln cheeks shal even tingle at the hearing. **1779** MME. D'ARBLAY *Diary* 3 Nov., Miss Burney, do not your cheeks tingle? **1828** D'ISRAELI *Chas. I*, I. v. 129 This would have made an English Protestant's cheek tingle with indignation.

2. Of other parts of the body: To be thrilled by a peculiar stinging or smarting sensation, physical or emotional; to smart, thrill, vibrate; also *fig.* of inanimate things, companies or bodies of persons, etc.

1398 TREVISA *Barth. De P.R.* VII. lxvii. (Bodl. MS.), A tokene of venym..ȝif he..dreueleþ and þe lippes..smarten and tinglen. *c* **1530** LD. BERNERS *Arth. Lyt. Bryt.* lvii. (1814) 214 The stroke lyght on a grete rocke soo rudely, that his handes tynger [? tyngel] so sore therwith. **1664** PEPYS *Diary* 3 Sept., My blood tingles and itches..all over my body. **1742** POPE *Dunc.* IV. 147 The pale Boy-Senator yet tingling stands, And holds his breeches close with both his hands. **1848** THACKERAY *Van. Fair* xxxiii, Wounds tingle most when they are about to heal. **1853** KANE *Grinnell Exp.* xxxi. (1856) 273 Your lungs tingle pleasantly as you draw [the cold air] in. **1878** T. L. CUYLER *Pointed Papers* 124 His conscience begins to tingle. **1884** *Times* 13 Feb. 11/4 All England tingles with the pain of the blow. **1898** W. WATSON *Ode in May* i, And Earth, unto her leaflet tips, Tingles with the Spring.

b. Predicated of that which causes the sensation: To thrill, vibrate; to pass with a thrill.

1819 SHELLEY *Prometh. Unb.* I. i. 133 It tingles through the frame As lightning tingles, hovering ere it strike. **1848** THACKERAY *Van. Fair* xvi, Every note..tingled through his huge frame. **1865** KINGSLEY *Herew.* vii, Hereward..felt the lust of battle tingling in him from head to heel. **1875** LOWELL *Under Old Elm* I. i. 4 The boy feels deeper meanings thrill his ear, That tingling through his pulse life-long shall run.

3. *trans.* To cause to tingle; to affect with a thrilling, smarting, or stinging sensation (physical or mental); to sting, excite, stimulate. (Cf. L. *auriculas tinnīre* to tingle or tickle the ears; also WFlem. *tingelen* to sting as a nettle, or like the cold.)

1572 MASCALL *Plant. & Graff.* (1592) 49 Small spotts.. which will..tingle & trouble you like Nettles. **1607** DEKKER & WEBSTER *Hist. Sir T. Wyatt* Wks. 1873 III. 106 That picture should haue power to tingle Loue In Royall brests. **1860** EMERSON *Cond. Life, Fate* Wks. (Bohn) II. 310 The cold, inconsiderate of persons, tingles your blood. **1875** LOWELL *Fight Concord Bridge* iii, That I might praise her in rhyme Would tingle your eyelids to tears. **1892** MRS. OLIPHANT *Marr. Elinor* III. xxxvii. 63 It tingled her to her very fingers' ends.

b. *absol.* or *intr.*

1872 BEECHER *Lect. Preach.* ix. 178 Don't whip with a switch that has the leaves on if you want to tingle. **1883** E. INGERSOLL in *Harper's Mag.* Jan. 199 Pepper-woods, whose leave..tingle upon the tongue like curry.

II. 4. *intr.* To make a continued light ringing sound: nearly = TINKLE *v.*[1] 2. Now *rare* or *spec.* as in quots. 1771, 1906.

1398 TREVISA *Barth. De P.R.* XVIII. xii. (Bodl. MS.), Wiþ betinge of bacyns, trillinge and tingelinge þei [bees] beþ icomforted and icleped to þe huyues. *c* **1450** *Wyclif's Bible, 1 Cor.* xiii. 1 (MS. Arundel 104), Y am maad as bras sownynge, or a cymbal tinglinge [*other MSS.* tynkynge, *once* tynclynge]. *a* **1535** SIR T. MORE in Grose, etc. *Antiq. Rep.* (1809) IV. 654 Clerck he was in Wellis, Where tingle a great many belles. *a* **1652** BROME *Queen's Exch.* II. ii, The great Bells of our Town, they tingle they tangle. **1771** N. NICHOLLS *Corr. w. Gray* (1843) 144 Little bells of different tones perpetually tingling for the elevation of the host. **1806–7** J. BERESFORD *Miseries Hum. Life* (1826) x. lx, A little shrill bell..that..keeps tingling. **1820** MAIR *Tyro's Dict.* (ed. 10) 385 *Tinnio*,..to tinkle or tingle. **1906** 'BARONESS ORCZY' *Son of People* xvi, When the little bell had ceased to tingle, few heads dared as yet to look towards the altar.

5. *trans.* To cause (a bell) to ring lightly; to ring (a bell, a chime, etc.). Now *rare*.

1649 G. DANIEL *Trinarch., Rich. II* ccxlvi, Hee..tingles out A Chime. **1775** S. J. PRATT *Liberal Opin.* ciii. (1783) III. 234 He..gave the usual signal..by tingling a bell. **1812** H. & J. SMITH *Rej. Addr., Macbeth* i, I'd thank her to tingle her bell. **1843** J. BALLANTINE *Gaberlunzie's Wallet* v. 122 We might as weel get the town-crier and gaur him tingle his bell.

b. *to tingle bees*: to charm or influence bees by a tingling or metallic sound: cf. TING *v.* 1 b.

1649 G. DANIEL *Trinarch., Hen. IV* cccxxviii, As you may tingle Bees Hee charmes the gaddings of opinion.

tingler ('tɪŋglə(r)). [f. prec. + -ER[1].] Something that causes tingling, as a blow; a 'stinger'.

1829 P. EGAN *Boxiana* 2nd Ser. II. 703 Johnson fell from a tingler on the left lug. **1831** WILSON in *Blackw. Mag.* Feb. 411/1 But the flogging..is far from being equal to his deserts. So he must get some more—one other stripe—but a tingler. *a* **1836** G. COLMAN in W. Irving *Goldsmith* xxxiv. (1849) 291 Which amiable act I returned with a very smart slap in the face; it must have been a tingler.

'tingle-'tangle[1]. [Reduplication of TINGLE.] A confused tinkling or ringing, as of a number of bells. (In quot. 1653 *attrib.*) Also *fig.* a disturbance, to-do, fuss.

1653 URQUHART *Rabelais* I. xl, With a tingle tangle jangling of bells they trouble..all their neighbours. **1670** AUBREY *Introd. Nat. Hist. N. Wilts.* in *Misc.* (1714) 35 The tingle tangle of their Convent Bells,..like the College Bells at Oxford. **1880** SPURGEON *Serm.* XXVI. 527 There is a great tingle-tangle over nothing.

'tingle-'tangle[2]. Also **tingel-tangel.** [ad. G. *tingeltangel* (with orig. reference to Berlin café chantant music); cf. TINGLE-TANGLE[1].] A cheap or disreputable music-hall or night-club, esp. in Germany; cabaret.

1911 *Mariner's Mirror* I. 190/1 Those sing-song houses of ill repute, which in German and Scandinavian ports are called 'tingle-tangles'. **1939** ADELER & WEST *Remember Fred Karno?* 71 The music halls in Glasgow in those days were pretty rough houses. There was one called The White Bait, where the artistes were all girls, as in the Continental Tingel-Tangels. **1948** [see PECK HORN]. **1972** *Sat. Rev.* (U.S.) 25 Mar. 68/2 Cabaret in Germany never managed to be counted as a major or serious artistic venture... People came to refer to cabaret by a term whose unimportance needs no translation: *Tingel-tangel*.

tingling ('tɪŋglɪŋ), *vbl. sb.* [f. TINGLE *v.* + -ING[1].] The action or condition expressed by the verb TINGLE, in its various senses.

I. 1. The ringing of the ears; a thrilling or unpleasant tickling of the ear.

1398 TREVISA *Barth. De P.R.* XVII. xii. (Bodl. MS.), Warmod istamped with boles lyuoure & ido into þe eres destruyeþ ringinge and tingelinge þat is þerein. **1607** TOPSELL *Four-f. Beasts* (1658) 93 For the tingling of the ears, take with this gall the Oyl of Roses. **1611** BP. HALL *Impresse of God* I. Wks. (1624) 442 Ten times..is the same word dually used; for Cymbals; and the Verbe of this root [*tsalal*, to tinkle, tingle, vibrate, quiver] is the same, whereby God would expresse the tingling of the eares.

2. A thrilling, stinging, or smarting sensation; an emotion likened to this, a thrill.

1398 TREVISA *Barth. De P.R.* VII. lvi. (Bodl. MS.), Tyngling and fleting in þe riggebone and aboute þe schuldres. **1584** R. SCOT *Discov. Witchcr.* XI. xiii. (1886) 162 The tingling in the finger, the elbowe, the toe. **1597** SHAKS. *2 Hen. IV*, I. ii. 129. **1653** W. G. *Bacon's Hist. Winds*, etc. 222 Also sharp and violent cold produceth a kinde of tingling, like unto burning. **1658** A. FOX *Würtz' Surg.* III. xxiii. 293 When that member felt a tickling or tingling, it was a sign of healing. **1769** PRIESTLEY in *Phil. Trans.* LIX. 62 The explosion..gave it [my hand] a violent jar, the effect of which remained, in a kind of tingling. **1843** LEVER *J. Hinton* xxxiii, Feeling a kind of tingling of shame. **1847** EMERSON *Repr. Men, Uses Gt. Men* Wks. (Bohn) I. 279 We cannot read Plutarch without a tingling of the blood. **1899** *Allbutt's Syst. Med.* VI. 705 Numbness and tingling in the fingers and toes.

II. 3. A continued light ringing sound of a small bell or the like; nearly = TINKLING *vbl. sb.* 2.

1398 [see TINGLE *v.* 4]. *a* **1533** FRITH *Disput. Purgat.* (1829) 134 St. Dominic's box (which hath such power, that as soon as the tingling is heard in the box, so soon the soul is free in heaven). **1653** GATAKER *Vind. Annot. Jer.* 53 They were wont..to keep a whooping and halowing,..and blowing of horns, and tingling of bels. **1817** LADY MORGAN *France* I. (1818) I. 92 We were awakened..by the noise of hammering, and the tingling of bells. *a* **1828** H. NEELE *Lit. Rem.* (1829) 219 And distant tinglings mingled with the lay.

'tingling, *ppl. a.* [f. as prec. + -ING².] That tingles: see the verb, in its various senses.

1. Thrilling; stinging, smarting (as with cold); quivering, vibrating.

1716 GAY *Trivia* II. 336 The harness'd Chairman.. Swings, around his Waste, his tingling Hands. **1735** SOMERVILLE *Chase* I. 361 Quick Pleasures sting Their tingling Nerves. **1751** CAMBRIDGE *Scribleriad* V. 20 The Scratching-stick with which the Seer subdued The tingling tumults of his boiling blood. **1842** TENNYSON *Morte d'Arth.* 199 A cry that shiver'd to the tingling stars. **1863** GEO. ELIOT *Romola* xxxvi, She felt a tingling shame at the words of ignominy she had cast at Tito.

2. Ringing lightly, as a small bell; tinkling; jingling.

c **1450** [see TINGLE *v.* 4]. **1581** SIDNEY *Apol. Poetrie* (Arb.) 63 A confused masse of words, with a tingling sound of ryme. **1651** *Burton's Anat. Mel.* II. ii. VI. iii. 300 Bees..when they hear any tingling [*earlier edd.* tinkling] sound, will tarry behinde. **1700** ASTRY tr. *Saavedra-Faxardo* I. 73 Their tingling shrill sound is like a Voice.

Hence **'tinglingly** *adv.*, (*a*) in a way that makes some part of the body tingle; (*b*) quiveringly, tremulously; ticklishly, delicately.

1889 *Temple Bar Mag.* Nov. 397 Lest..the sanctity of the Sabbath [should] be impressed tinglingly on me. **1905** *Westm. Gaz.* 13 Apr. 10/1 He [Shaks.'s Rich. II] is so nicely balanced, so tinglingly poised.

'tinglish, *a.* [f. TINGLE *sb.*² or *v.* + -ISH¹.] Characterized by tingling; quivering.

1855 BROWNING *Old Pict. in Flor.* xxix, For them the panels may thrill, The tempera grow alive and tinglish.

tingly ('tɪŋglɪ), *a.* [f. TINGLE *sb.*² or *v.* + -Y.] Characterized by tingling.

1898 J. HUTCHINSON in *Arch. Surg.* IX. No. 36. 332 His finger-tips became numb and tingly, as if frostbitten. **1945** B. MACDONALD *Egg & I* (1946) 185 There was already beginning to be a tingly feel of autumn in the air. **1975** R. H. RIMMER *Premar Experiments* (1976) iii. 219 Arguing with Bren is like standing under a cool needle shower spray. He forces you into an alive, tingly state.

tin-gravel, -ground: see TIN *sb.* 5.

ting-tang ('tɪŋ,tæŋ), *sb.* Also **ting-tong.** [Echoic.] A succession of two ringing sounds, differing in tone or force.

1. The alternating sound made by the ringing of a small bell; hence *transf.* a small bell, esp. the sanctus bell. In quot. 1680 *advb.*

1680 V. ALSOP *Mischief of Impos.* Ep. Ded., That [bell] which..goes Ting tang, ting tang, before the Hoste, when carried to the sick. *a* **1800** PEGGE *Suppl. Grose, Ting-Tang*, called in the South The Saint's-bell. **1808–18** JAMIESON, *Ting-tang*, sound of a bell. *a* **1825** FORBY *Voc. E. Anglia, Ting-tang*, a small and shrill bell, to summon the family to dinner, the congregation to prayers, &c. **1848** NOAKE *Rambler Worc.* I. 308 There is a peal of six bells, besides a 'ting tang'. **1881** MISS JACKSON *Shropsh. Word-bk., Ting-tang*, a peal of two bells; a term derived from the sound—the lighter bell being *ting*, the heavier *tang*.

b. Jingling repetition of sounds, rime.

1686 F. SPENCE tr. *St. Euremont's Misc.* Pref., Blank-verse ..without the necessity of cursing Arabique customs or Moorish innovations, which forced a man to spoil a good thought by tagging it with Ting-tong.

2. *attrib.*, as ***ting-tang bell***; **ting-tang clock,** see quot. 1884.

1777 in Picton *L'pool Munic. Rec.* (1886) II. 278 A small or Ting Tang bell. **1862** *Catal. Internat. Exhib., Brit.* II. No. 3302, Ting tong carriage clock. **1875** J. W. BENSON *Time & Time-tellers* (1902) 99 St. Paul's Cathedral Clock..may be described as a ting-tang quarter on the rack principle. **1884** F. J. BRITTEN *Watch & Clockm.* 265 Ting Tang Clock..[is] a clock that sounds the half hours or quarters on two bells only.

Hence **ting-tang** *v. dial.* [cf. WFris. *tingetangen*].

1881 MISS JACKSON *Shropsh. Word-bk., Ting-tang*, to ring into church with two bells. **1888** W. RAYMOND *Misterton's Mistake* viii, As if Wycherney volk had nothing..to do but to listen to hear the parish bell ting-tangey.

tinguaite ('tɪŋgwəaɪt). *Petrogr.* [ad. G. *tinguait* (H. Rosenbusch *Mikrosk. Physiogr. der massigen Gesteine* (ed. 2, 1887) II. 628), f. Serra de *Tinguá*, name of a spur of the Serra do Mar, W. of Rio de Janeiro: see -ITE¹.] A hypabyssal rock similar to phonolite and nepheline-syenite, composed essentially of alkali feldspar, nepheline, and ægirine (acmite), the last occurring usu. as acicular crystals and conferring a greenish colour.

1893 *Mineral. Mag.* X. 173 More markedly porphyritic types are a rock with porphyritic elæolite, an 'elæolite tinguaite' with porphyritic orthoclase. **1965** G. J. WILLIAMS *Econ. Geol. N.Z.* xi. 167/2 Among these rocks is a tinguaite consisting of a network of aegirine crystals with phenocrysts of anorthoclase in a groundmass of anorthoclase, cancrinite and nepheline. **1978** S. R. NOCKOLDS in S. R. Nockolds et al. *Petrol. for Students* xv. 173 Some tinguaites have small amounts of a sodalite mineral, of analcite.., or of cancrinite. More rarely, one or other of these becomes an important constituent.

tin-hammer, etc.: see TIN *sb.* 5.

tin hat. *slang.* **1. a.** A metal hat or helmet; *spec.* a steel helmet worn for protection against shrapnel. Chiefly *Mil.*

1903 A. M. BINSTEAD *Pitcher in Paradise* viii. 194 A Tommy in a tin hat as I squared with a couple o'blow. **1917** W. E. MOLESWORTH *Let.* Mar. in A. J. L. Scott *Sixty Squadron R.A.F.* (1920) iii. 38 We managed to collect some tin hats, bombs,..and a few other odds and ends. **1923** *Sci. Amer.* Nov. 360/2 The trench hat, 'the old tin hat', is coming into quite extensive use as a means of head protection against small falls of rock in mines. **1932** G. CAMPBELL *Number Thirteen* vii. 107, I happened to be dressed in a rather extraordinary rig, consisting of a tin hat, a naval monkey-jacket, grey flannel trousers, and puttees. **1940** *War Illustr.* 5 Jan. 563 'Tin Hats' for the Heads of Britain's Defenders. **1961** JOSWICK & KEATING *Combat Cameraman* xiv. 124 An upside-down tin hat lay nearby. **1976** 'A. HALL' *Kobra Manifesto* vi. 86 We haven't got a single tin hat in the place... Not even a blinking first aid kit!

†**b.** A general officer. Cf. *brass-hat* s.v. BRASS *sb.* 7. *Mil. Obs.*

1919 *Athenæum* 18 July 632/2 May I add one or two more army slang terms? 'Tin hat' or 'brass hat' for general officer.

2. Used predicatively, usu. in *pl.*: drunk.

1909 J. R. WARE *Passing Eng.* 246/2 *Tin hat* (Anglo-Port Said), drunk—two tin hats very drunk—three, incapable, and to be carried on board. **1916** 'TAFFRAIL' *Pincher Martin* ii. 24 'No, sir, not drunk, only a bit shaky like,' I sez, though I knowed orl the time I'd bin properly tin 'ats. **1919** W. LANG *Sea-Lawyer's Log* 69 If you do come off tin 'ats (i.e. inebriated), go quietly below to the Mess Deck.

3. Phr. ***to put the tin hat on*** (*it, things*, etc.): to bring something to a (usu. unwelcome) close or climax. Cf. *to put the lid on* s.v. LID *sb.* 1 e.

1919 *Athenæum* 8 Aug. 727/2 The shrapnel helmet was invariably a 'tin hat', and 'to put the tin hat on it' is..'to ki-bosh it'. **1927** 'SAPPER' *Saving Clause* i. 22 This second exhibition of cowardice had put the tin-hat on. **1933** WODEHOUSE *Mulliner Nights* vii. 225 It was the limit, he felt, the extreme edge. It put the tin hat on things. **1943** 'C. DICKSON' *She died a Lady* xx. 177 Next..came the point that put the tin hat on it. **1977** J. M. JOHNSON in Douglas & Johnson *Existential Sociol.* viii. 244 He reflected that, at the time, he thought his efforts had 'put the tin hat on it'.

Hence **tin-hatted** *a.*, wearing a metal helmet or helmets.

1926 *British Worker* 10 May 2/3 At the Iron Bridge, at Canning Town, I met a half company of soldiers, tin-hatted, and with rifles and packs, marching into the docks. **1940** HARRISSON & MADGE *War begins at Home* iii. 46 A tin-hatted policeman began to push the crowd back. **1978** E. MALPASS *Wind brings up Rain* xxvi. 232 A tin-hatted Air Raid Warden.

tinhorn ('tɪnhɔːn), *a.* and *sb. slang* (orig. and chiefly *U.S.*) Also **tin-horn.** [f. TIN *sb.* + HORN *sb.*; cf. quot. 1931, sense A 1 below.]

A. *adj.* **1.** ***tinhorn gambler***: a cheap gambler, esp. one who acts showily.

1885 *Weekly New Mexican Rev.* 26 Feb. 4/2 We have been greatly annoyed of late by a lot of tin horn gamblers and prostitutes. **1912** *Maclean's Mag.* Mar. 478/1 He says he aint no piker, and he is a game loser, and nobody can walk around his collar, and he begins to put on airs like a tin horn gambler. **1931** G. F. WILLISON *Here they dug Gold* 216 Chuck-a-luck operators shake their dice in a 'small churn-like affair of metal'—hence the expression, 'tinhorn gambler', for the game is rather looked down upon as one for 'chubbers' and chuck-a-luck gamblers are never admitted within the aristocratic circle of faro-dealers. **1958** P. BERTON *Klondike Fever* 6 A circus parade of camp-followers crowded in upon them, saloon-keepers,..tinhorn gamblers and three-card monte men. **1963** *Punch* 17 July 102/2 A Western..with..tinhorn gamblers, fisticuffs, guns and so on.

2. Inferior, contemptible; pretentious, flashy. Cf. TIN-POT 4.

1886 *San Juan* (Colorado) *Prospector* 4 Sept. 3/7 The Silverton vigilantes have notified the tin-horn element to meander. **1903** A. ADAMS *Log of Cowboy* xii. 80 A tin horn lawyer. **1935** E. POUND *Let.* 25 Sept. (1971) 276 All American Communists are, as far as I can discover, absolute boneheads, tinhorn repeaters. **1959** R. STOUT *Crime & Again* vii. 104 'You tin-horn Casanova,' she said... 'Hinting to me that you had her, and I knew all the time you didn't.' **1977** C. WESTON *Rouse Demon* xxiii. 111 This godforsaken tinhorn paradise.

3. ***tinhorn sport***: a contemptible person.

1906 S. FORD *Shorty McCabe* ii. 34 He wasn't no Johnnie, and he wasn't no tinhorn sport. **1925** S. LEWIS *Arrowsmith* v. 47 I'm a——I'm a——Martin, I'm a tin-horn sport! **1958** 'W. HENRY' *Seven Men at Mimbres Springs* x. 120 The stage roads of this whole plateau are littered with the bones of tinhorn sports who didn't have the brains to fort up before morning. **1975** R. DAVIES *World of Wonders* (1977) I. vi. 57 Swifty Dealer, the village tin-horn sport.

B. *sb.* A poor or contemptible person, esp. one who is pretentious or flashy; *spec.* one who gambles for low stakes.

1887 F. FRANCIS *Saddle & Moccasin* 225 The tin-horns were there in a body, with a few stacks of chips, playing light. **1908** S. E. WHITE *Riverman* vi. 55 You ain't a tin-horn yourself? **1922** S. LEWIS *Babbitt* ii. 22 I'll bet I make a whole lot more money than some of those tin-horns that spend all they got on dress-suits. **1949** *Penguin New Writing* XXXVI. 91 A guy got off at the next stop and came back for the change. A tin-horn. **1962** E. LUCIA *Klondike Kate* iii. 65 Conditions produced the greatest opportunity for the tinhorns in the history of nineteenth-century gold strikes. **1977** D. ANTHONY *Stud Game* xix. 118 Tony Hunter called me... 'Greetings, Tinhorn,' he said.

tinily ('taɪnɪlɪ), *adv.* [f. TINY *a.* + -LY².] In a tiny degree; minutely, diminutively.

1862 *Temple Bar Mag.* IV. 552 Hands so tinily, delicately lovely. **1897** F. THOMPSON *To Snow-flake* 18 So purely, so palely, Tinily, surely, Mightily, frailly, Insculped and embossed.

tininess ('taɪnɪnɪs). Also 7 **tinyness.** [f. as prec. + -NESS.] The quality of being tiny; extreme smallness; minuteness.

1674 N. FAIRFAX *Bulk & Selv.* 21 'Tis such a kind of some-whatkin, as truckles beneath the very tinyness of an half nothing. **1830** J. G. STRUTT *Sylva Brit.* 7 When we consider the tininess of its origin. **1891** *Pall Mall G.* 2 Feb. 6/1 His pictures owe much of their fame to their tininess.

'tining, *vbl. sb.*¹ *Obs.* exc. *dial.* [f. TINE *v.*¹ + -ING¹.] **a.** The action of TINE *v.*¹; enclosing, fencing, hedging; making or repairing of a hedge. **b.** *concr.* A hedge or fence, *esp.* a new one made from dead thorns. **c.** *attrib.*, as **tining-gloves,** gloves worn in repairing hedges, hedging-gloves.

c **1440** *Promp. Parv.* 494/2 Tynynge, drye hedge, *sepes.* **1522** *MS. Acc. St. John's Hosp., Canterb.*, Paied for tenyng of a hedge. **1546** in Boys *Sandwich* (1792) 80 Paid for tenyng and mendyng of gapps 10d. **1616** T. ADAMS *End of Thorns* Wks. 1862 II. 486 Men commonly deal with their sins as hedgers do when they go to plash thorn bushes; they put on tining gloves, that the thorns may not prick them. **1813** T. DAVIS *Agric. Wilts* Gloss., *Tining*, a new enclosure made with a dead hedge. **1894** ATKINSON *Old Whitby* 53 He must do the 'tyning' or fencing-in with stoup or stake, and wattle or brush.

tining, *vbl. sb.*² Now only *Sc.* and *north. dial.* [f. TINE *v.*² + -ING¹.] The action of losing, loss; †destruction. ***between the tining and the winning***: said of being in a critical position, which may issue either in ruin or in success.

a **1300** *Cursor M.* 18261 (Cott.) Ha! sathan..all þat þu wan ..thoru þe tinning of paradis, Nu has þou tint on oþer wis. *c* **1375** *Sc. Leg. Saints* v. (*Johannes*) 212 Sa gret besynes He has for to get riches, And besy thocht of þe kepynge, And gret dut of þe tynynge. *c* **1400** *Destr. Troy* 7611 For the tene, þat hom tyde, & tynyng of pepull. *c* **1520** NISBET *N. Test. in Scots* (S.T.S.) III. 283 (Ecclus. l. 4) The gret preest..that delyuirit thame fra tynyng. **1720** RAMSAY *Rise & Fall of Stocks* 146 A' the country is repining, And ilka ane complains of tining. **1825** SCOTT *Diary* 28 Dec., in *Lockhart*, At present he is between the tyning and the winning.

tining ('taɪnɪŋ), *vbl. sb.*³ [f. TINE *v.*³ (or *sb.*¹) + -ING¹.] **a.** The action of TINE *v.*³; harrowing. **b.** *concr.* (*pl.*) The tines or teeth of a harrow, etc. collectively.

1760 WASHINGTON *Writ.* (1889) II. 163 A new harrow made of smaller and closer tinings. **1766** *Compl. Farmer* s.v. *Tine*, The common phrase, of giving two or three tinings, signifies to draw the harrows twice or thrice over the same spot of ground.

tink (tɪŋk), *int.* and *sb.*¹ [Echoic.] A representation of the abrupt sound made by striking resonant metal with something hard and light: cf. CHINK, CLINK; often reduplicated in imitation of the repetition of such a sound, also with such variations as ***tink-tank, tink-a-tink***, etc. Hence as *sb.* a single sound of this kind; also *fig.* in reference to rime or verse (cf. *jingle*). † ***to cry tink***, to make such a sound, to tinkle (*obs.*).

1609 B. JONSON *Sil. Wom.* II. iii, How it [the poem] chimes, and cries tinke i' the close, diuinely! **1840** DICKENS *Barn. Rudge* xli, There issued forth a tinkling sound..Tink, tink, tink—clear as a silver bell. *a* **1847** ELIZA COOK *Rory O'More* vii, Mars chiming in with his rude tink-a-ting..He had turned into cymbals the sword and the shield. **1890** J. H. STIRLING *Gifford Lect.* xii. 239 It was in the heroic ten-syllabled tink-a-tink, and read like Pope's Homer. **1901** *Blackw. Mag.* Aug. 251 The metallic clang-clank, tink-tank of chisel and hammer and stone saw.

tink (tɪŋk), *sb.*[2] Chiefly *Sc.* Colloq. abbrev. of TINKER *sb.* 1 b; hence, a foul-mouthed, brawling, or disreputable person.

1857 J. STEWART *Sketches Sc. Character* 74 Nae swearing tink', nor beggar body That tak's a glass. **1894** J. B. SALMOND *B. Bowden* (1922) iv. 36 To sleep on the Common amon' the tinks. **1914** R. B. CUNNINGHAME GRAHAM *Sc. Stories* 19 Ca' ye yon man a gentleman? I just ca' him naething better than a tink. **1939** J. M. CAIE *'Twixt Hills & Sea* 58 There's kindly, honest, eident fowk There's kyaards an' tinks forbye. **1968** A. MACLEOD *Dam* i. 15 How disgusting it was to..back up a drunken tink like Sorley. **1980** D. K. CAMERON *Willie Gavin* viii. 73 A fear that had driven her..in the hope that she might spot..another human soul (a tink on the road, some shepherd walking the hill fields).

tink (tɪŋk), *v.*[1] Forms: 4–6 **tynke**, 6 **tyncke**, 6–7 **tinck, tinke**, 7 **tincke**, 7 **tink**. [Echoic; cf. EFris. *tinken*.]

1. *intr.* To emit a metallic sound with very short resonance, e.g. as is done by a cracked bell, but sometimes used as = TINKLE; to chink, clink. In quot. 1655 of rime (cf. *jingle*). ? *Obs.*

Prov. ***as the fool thinketh, the bell tinketh***: i.e. to the fool the bell seems to say what he wants it to say; referring to a superstitious notion that the tinkling of a bell sometimes gives an oracular monition or answer. Cf. SOUTHEY *Doctor* xxxii. 1, the legend of Dick Whittington, etc.

1382 WYCLIF *1 Cor.* xiii. 1, I am maad as bras sownnynge, or a symbal tynkynge. *c* **1540** J. HEYWOOD *Four P.P.* B ij, Syr after dryngking, while the shot is tinkynge, Som heades be swiming, but mine wilbe sinking. **1627** J. CARTER *Plain Expos.* 34 Other folkes must thinke as his bels tinke. **1655** FULLER *Ch. Hist.* II. 167 If the verses do but chime and tinck in the close, it is enough to the purpose.

b. *trans.* To utter or express by emitting such a sound (with allusion to the proverb: see 1). ? *Obs.*

1624 BP. MOUNTAGU *Gagg* 283 Even as the Bell tinketh whatsoever the foole thinketh.

2. *intr.* Of a person: To make such a sound by striking upon metal or other resonant substance. **b.** ***tink out*** (*trans.*): to express or give out in this way. ? *Obs.*

1533 MORE *Debell. Salem* Wks. 955/1 That the tinkar would haue tinked out of his pannes bottome a reason that woulde at the leaste wise ring a little better then this. **1609** ARMIN *Maids of More-Cl.* C iij b, Toures tincks vpon his pan drinking. **1658** ROWLAND *Moufet's Theat. Ins.* 894 According as he that tinks on the brazen kettle, pleaseth, so they slack or quicken their flying.

3. *trans.* To cause (something) to emit an abrupt metallic sound; sometimes = to tinkle (a bell, etc.). Now *rare*.

1495 [see TING *v.* 1]. **1532** *Henryson's Test. Cres.* 144 (ed. Thynne) Cupyde the kynge tynkyng [*ed. Charteris* (1593) ringand] a syluer bel. *c* **1537** *Thersytes* in *Four O. Pl.* (1848) 80 Mercolfe monyles..Tyncke wyll the tables thoughe he there not tary. **1968** B. HINES *Kestrel for Knave* 168 The glass shone. He tinked it with his nails, tapped it with a knuckle, then rapped it with his knuckles.

Hence **'tinking** *vbl. sb.* and *ppl. a.*

1382 [see sense 1]. **1530** PALSGR. 281/2 Tynkynge, the sowndyng of metalls, whan they be strycken togyder, *tintyn.* **1610** BOYS *Expos. Dom. Epist. & Gosp.* Wks. (1622) 205 Wee were but as a sounding brasse, or as a tincking cymball.

tink, *v.*[2] ? *Obs.* Also 5 **tynky.** [Goes with TINKER *sb.*, of which, if its history could be traced farther back, it may be the source; but it may also be a back-formation from *tinker*.] *trans.* To mend, solder, rivet (rarely, to make) pots and pans, as a tinker. Hence **'tinking** *vbl. sb.*

14.. *Voc.* in Wr.-Wülcker 576/39 *Crusto*, to tynky. *Crustator*, a tynkere. *c* **1500** *World & Child* (1905) 179 Art thou any craftsman? Yea sir, I can bind a sieve and tink a pan. **1565** HARDING in Jewel *Def. Apol.* (1611) 525 Tinkers and Tapsters..what should they doe there [at the General Council]? For there is no tinking, nor tipling. **1825** JAMIESON, *To Tink, v.a.*, to rivet, as including the idea of the noise made in the act of rivetting; a Gipsy word, Roxb.

[*Note.* L. *crusto* meant 'to cover with a rind, shell, crust, embossing, plaster-work'. It is not easy to apply this to a tinker's work, unless perh. in the sense of 'to cover with a plate or patch', or ? 'with tin' or 'with solder'. Identity of 'tink' = *crustare*, with TINK *v.*[1] seems unthinkable.]

tink (tɪŋk), *v.*[3] Repr. dial. or foreign pronunc. of THINK *v.*[2]

1767 'A. BARTON' *Disappointment* I. ii. 53, I put too much confidence in dose I tought my friends, and dey deceib'd me. **1801** T. TENNEY *Female Quixotism* II. xi. 117 How cou'd I tink, ma'am, it was John, in massa chamber? **1821** J. F. COOPER *Spy* II. xii. 186 'I don't tink he look a bit like me,' said Caesar. **1916** E. O'NEILL *Bound East for Cardiff* in *Provincetown Plays* 1st Ser. 7 Yust tink of it! **1933** M. LOWRY *Ultramarine* i. 20, I tink you are very much English all the same. **1944** in H. Wentworth *Amer. Dial. Dict.* 637 'I never t'ought it would happen... I have to keep t'inkin' about de dough I'm gettin',' mumbled Bill in his best Brooklynese. **1973** *Nation* (Barbados) 25 Nov. 1/1 Yuh tink it easy?

tinkal, -ar: see TINCAL, TINCHEL.

tinkar's (also **tinker's**) **root** or **weed.** See quots. (Also called *fever-root* and *fever-wort.*)

1760 J. LEE *Introd. Bot.* (1788) 333/2 Doctor Tinker's Weed, *Triosteum.* **1882** OGILVIE, *Tinkar's-root.* (From Dr. Tinkar, who first brought the root into notice.) A North American shrub (*Triosteum perfoliatum*), N.O. *Caprifoliaceæ*, whose root is an emetic and mild cathartic.

tinker ('tɪŋkə(r)), *sb.* Forms: (3 **tynekere**), 4 **tinkere**, 4–5 **tynkere, -are**, 4–7 **tynker**, 5 **tenker**, 6 **tinkar, tyncar, tinkard(e, tynkard**, 6–7 **tincker**, 6– **tinker.** [Origin uncertain; goes with TINK *v.*[2], either as source or derivative.

Often taken as agent-noun from TINK *v.*[1], in reference to the noise made in hammering metal: cf. *Promp. Parv. c* 1440, and Johnson 'because in their work they make a tinkling noise'. This explanation is not in itself very plausible, and its support by the Sc. form *tinkler*, as an assumed parallel derivative of *tinkle*, is overthrown by the fact that *tinkle* vb. was app. not in Sc. use. Moreover Sc. *tinkler* and Eng. *tynkere* appear as trade names or surnames in 1175 and 1265 respectively, and in many instances before 1300, long before any trace of *tink* or *tinkle* has been found.]

1. a. A craftsman (usually itinerant) who mends pots, kettles, and other metal household utensils.

The low repute in which these, esp. the itinerant sort, were held in former times is shown by the expressions *to swear like a tinker, a tinker's curse* or *damn, as drunk* or *as quarrelsome as a tinker*, etc., and the use of 'tinker' as synonymous with 'vagrant', 'gipsy' (see b).

c **1265** in *6th Rep. Hist. MSS. Comm.* 578/2 (Corporation of Wallingford) [The lowest assessment is that of] Editha le Tynekere [at 2 pence]. **1362** LANGL. *P. Pl.* A. v. 160 Tomkyn þe Tinkere [**1393** C. VII. 364 tynkere] and tweyne of his knaues. **1377** *Ibid.* B. Prol. 220 Taillours and tynkeres & tolleres in marketes. **14..** [see TINK *v.*[2]]. *c* **1440** *Promp. Parv.* 494/2 Tynkare,..*tintinarius*; *et capit nomen a sono artis, ut tintinabulum, sus, et multa alia, per onomotopeiam.* *c* **1510** BARCLAY *Mirr. Gd. Manners* (1570) C ij, What should a hardie knight be felowe to a knaue, Or with a trifling tinkarde a clarke companion. **1566** *Eng. Ch. Furniture* (Peacock) 33 One crysmatorie sold to a tincker. **1573–80** BARET *Alv.* T 265 A Tincker, or tinkeler, *sarctor aerarius.* **1590** SHAKS. *Mids. N.* I. ii. 63. **1597** *Shuttleworths' Acc.* (Chetham Soc.) 108 The tynkard for mendynge of mylkinge vessells vij[d]. **1608** DEKKER *2nd Pt. Honest Wh.* Wks. 1873 II. 149 He..swore like a dozen of drunken Tinkers. **1611** COTGR., *Il iure comme vn Abbé* [etc.], [he swears] like a Tinker, say we. **1674** *Warrant for Arrest* (*Westm. Gaz.* 16 Mar. 1904, 5/1), One John Bunnyon of yor said Towne Tynker hath divers times within one Month last past.. preached or teached at a Conventicle Meeteing or assembly under color or pretence of exercise of Religion. **1717** PRIOR *Alma* III. 577 And, for the metal, The coin may mend a tinker's kettle. **1832** BABBAGE *Econ. Manuf.* i. 10 Worn-out saucepans and tin ware..beyond the reach of the tinker's art. **1854** MACAULAY *Biog.*, *Bunyan* (1867) 27 The tinkers then formed a hereditary caste.

b. In Scotland and north of Ireland, the ordinary name for a gipsy: see TINKLER[1]. Also, applied to itinerant beggars, traders, and performers generally; †a vagabond, tramp, or reputed thief (*obs.*).

The chief ostensible business of travelling gipsies in Scotland used to be the sale or mending of pots, pans, kettles, and metal-ware generally; hence *tinkers*, or rather *tinklers*, was their ordinary designation.

1561 AWDELAY *Frat. Vacab.* (1869) 5 A Tinkard leaueth his bag a sweating at the Alehouse..and..goeth abrode a begging. **1597** *Act 39 Eliz.* c. 4 §2 All Juglers Tynkers Pedlers and Petty Chapmen wandring abroade. **1609** ARMIN *Maids of More-Cl.* C iv, *Lady.* Is this the tinker you talke on? *Hum.* I madame of Twitnam, I haue seene him licke out burning fire brands with's tongue, drinke two pense from the bottome of a full pottle of ale [etc.]. **1801** STRUTT *Sports & Past.* III. v. §29 Another itinerant, who seems in some degree to have rivalled the lower classes of the jugglers, was the tinker. **1806** *Gazetteer Scotl.* (ed. 2) 615/2 Yetholm... This town has been long inhabited by tinkers or gypsies. **1896** KATH. TYNAN in *Westm. Gaz.* 14 Nov. 1/3 The 'tinkers' are the gipsies of the Irish country-side... Tinkering is their ostensible trade, but they are supposed not to be particular about *meum* and *tuum.* They are a wild lawless set, and 'tinker' has come to be an abusive term in Ireland from its association with them.

c. A clumsy or inefficient mender; a botcher; also *fig.* In U.S. also applied to a 'jack-of-all-trades' (*Cent. Dict.*).

1644–7 [implied in *tinkerwise* below]. *a* **1704** T. BROWN *Praise Pov.* Wks. 1730 I. 89 To cure one hole, like a true tinker, he here makes two. **1905** *Westm. Gaz.* 13 Oct. 3/1 Not so, however, the new Secretary of State proved himself, but a 'tinker' like the rest.

d. ***not to care, be worth,*** (etc.), ***a tinker's curse, cuss,*** or ***damn,*** (ellipt.) ***a tinker's,*** an intensification of the earlier 'not to care, or be worth, a curse or damn' (see CURSE *sb.* 2 ¶, DAMN *sb.* 2), with reference to the reputed addiction of tinkers to profane swearing: see 1. Cf. also quot. 1884, in which 'not to care a straw' is similarly intensified. (An ingenious but baseless conjecture suggesting another origin appears in quot. 1877.)

[**1824** MACTAGGART *Sir Balderdash* v. in *Gallovid. Encycl.* s.v. *Balderdash*, A tinkler's curse she did na care What she did think or say.] **1839** THOREAU *Jrnl.* 25 Apr. in *Writings* (1906) VII. 78 'Tis true they are not worth a 'tinker's damn'. **1865** [see CUSS *sb.* 1]. [**1877** KNIGHT *Dict. Mech.*, *Tinker's-dam*, a wall of dough raised around a place which a plumber desires to flood with a coat of solder. The material can be but once used; being consequently thrown away as worthless, it has passed into a proverb, usually involving the wrong spelling of the otherwise innocent word 'dam'.] **1884** *St. James' Gaz.* 24 Apr. 12/1, I don't care two tinkers' straws if you do. **1891** KIPLING *Light that Failed* vii. 137 The real world doesn't care a tinker's—doesn't care a bit. *a* **1894** STEVENSON *St. Ives* xxv, I care not a Tinker's Damn for his ascension. **1907** *Westm. Gaz.* 28 Oct. 2/3 'A tinker's curse', as used in the two new plays 'Irene Wycherley' and 'The Barrier'. *Ibid.*, The suggestion that the phrase really refers to a 'tinker's dam'..does credit to the speculative person who earliest associated it with the familiar old saying. **1947** [see HOOT *sb.*[2]]. **1973** *Jewish Chron.* 2 Feb. 19/3 It doesn't matter a tinker's cuss whether you amend the constitution to call the chairman president. **1983** J. SYMONS *Name of Annabel Lee* II. viii. 139, I don't give a tinker's, if you'll forgive the old fashioned way of putting it, who killed Ira Wolfdale.

e. A rascal, a persistently naughty child. As a term of mild contempt, usu. familiarly or playfully. Cf. BEGGAR *sb.* 6.

1925 R. REES *Lake of Enchantment* 50 I'll soon settle the young tinker if he's up to them tricks. **1953** K. TENNANT *Joyful Condemned* xiv. 124 She's a little tinker... Even *you* couldn't do anything with her. **1960** J. STROUD *Shorn Lamb* xxiii. 247 I'm not so sure about Clement, he's a bit of a tinker at the moment. **1971** G. SIMS *Deadhand* II. viii. 141 Did the boys scare you? I expect they did. The tinkers!

2. [f. TINKER *v.*] An act or bout of tinkering; a stroke of tinker's work; *fig.* a bungling or unskilful attempt at mending something.

1857 HUGHES *Tom Brown* I. i, They must..spend their time and money in having a tinker at it.

3. Local name for various fishes, birds, etc. **a.** The skate. **b.** The stickleback. **c.** *U.S.* A small or young mackerel; also, the chub-mackerel (*Cent. Dict.*). **d.** 'The silversides, a fish' (*ibid.*). **e.** The razor-billed auk. *Newfoundland* and *Labrador.* **f.** The guillemot: = TINKERSHERE. **g.** 'A kind of seal. *Newfoundland*' (*Cent. Dict.*).

1771 G. CARTWRIGHT *Jrnl.* 1 June (1792) I. 128 They killed a duck and a tinker. **1836** YARRELL *Brit. Fishes* II. 421 The Skate. Blue Skate, and Grey Skate, Scotland. Tinker, Lyme Regis. **1856** E. NEWMAN in *Zoologist* XIV. 5125 We have in the ditches round London myriads of a very minute fresh-water fish, known to every boy..by the name of 'tinker'. *Ibid.*, The Tinker or 9-spined Stickleback (*Gasterosteus lævis*). **1856** ATWOOD in Goode *Fisheries* (1884) 298 The tinkers, two years old... The mackerel..are denominated as follows: Large ones, second size, tinkers, and blinks. **1861** COUES in *Proc. Acad. Nat. Sci. Philad.* 251 It [the razor-billed auk] is known..to all fishermen and eggers..by the singular name of 'Tinker'. **1886** *Sci. Amer.* 5 June 352/3 Young mackerel or 'tinkers'. **1896** NEWTON *Dict. Birds, Tinker*, or *Tinkershire*, one of the many names of the Guillemot.

4. *Ordnance.* Name for a small mortar fixed on the end of a staff, and fired by a trigger and lanyard. *U.S.*

1877 in KNIGHT *Dict. Mech.*

5. *attrib.* and *Comb.*, as ***tinker-like*** adj. and adv., ***-preacher, -tool***; **tinker-bird**, any of several African birds having a call like repetitive hammering, esp. a barbet of the genus *Pogoniulus*; **tinker mackerel** = sense 3 c; **Tinkertoy** orig. and chiefly *U.S.*, the proprietary name of a type of child's construction set; a toy made of this; also *fig.*

a **1884** T. AYRES in R. B. Sharpe *Layard's Birds S. Afr.* (1884) 175 The note of this curious little bird so much resembles the tapping of a hammer on an anvil (having that peculiar metallic ring) that it is called in Natal the *tinker bird. **1960** G. DURRELL *Zoo in my Luggage* 12 A tinker-bird was giving its monotonous cry, toink..toink..toink.., like someone beating forever on a tiny anvil. **1705** HICKERINGILL *Priest-cr.* II. viii. 90 Lest we make *Tinker-like Work, like that of the Presbyterian-Directory, mend one hole, and make two. **1753** T. CIBBER *Let. to Warburton* 53 This unmerciful Editor, who, Tinker-like, makes many Holes for one he mends. **1888** GOODE *Amer. Fishes* 179 A considerable school of these fish..were taken in company with the *Tinker Mackerel. **1900** *Westm. Gaz.* 26 May 8/1 Bedford ..so intimately associated with the *tinker-preacher's life and work. **1857** BORROW *Romany Rye* xix. 118 *Tinker-tools. **1914** *Official Gaz.* (U.S. Patent Office) 3 Feb. 283/2 Charles H. Pajeau, Chicago, Ill. Filed June 27, 1913. **Tinkertoy.* Particular description of goods.—Games, Toys, and Children's Building-Blocks. Claims use since June 12, 1913. **1915** *Trade Marks Jrnl.* 22 Dec. 1279 *Tinkertoy...* Toys. Charles Hamilton Pajeau, McCormick Building, 332, South Michigan Avenue, Chicago, County of Cook, State of Illinois, United States of America; manufacturers. **1918** *Sears, Roebuck Catal.* Fall 829/1 Tinker Toy is the Wonder Builder. **1938** *Harper's Mag.* Dec. 72 At the Tinkertoy factory in Evanston, Illinois, I was shown a Japanese imitation of the construction sets faithful even to the trademark drawing and two typographical errors in the instruction sheet. **1972** *Newsweek* 19 June 23/3 McGovern will go into the campaign against Nixon with those Tinkertoy proposals of his.

Hence **'tinkerdom**, a realm or domain of tinkers; the condition or practice of a tinker; **'tinkerwise** *adv.*, in the manner of a tinker; **'tinkery**, the business of a tinker (in quot. *attrib.*).

1630 *Tinker of Turvey* 12 A budget fastened with a thong, ..wherein are All his tooles and tinkery ware. **1644–7** CLEVELAND *Char. Lond. Diurn.* 8 What did this Parliament ever go about to reforme, but Tinkerwise, in mending one hole they made three? **1834** CARLYLE *Let.* 27 June, in *Life* (1882) II. 439 His [Hunt's] house excels all you have ever read of—a poetical Tinkerdom, without parallel even in literature. *Ibid.* 440 Yet the noble Hunt receives you in his Tinkerdom in the spirit of a king. **1887** *Scott. Leader* 27 Oct. 7 Cis-pontine prejudices fed by poultry-larceny and tinkerdom.

tinker ('tɪŋkə(r)), *v.* [f. prec. sb.]

In all senses usually depreciative.

1. a. *intr.* To work as a tinker; to mend metal utensils (and hence *gen.* any material objects), esp. in a clumsy, bungling, or imperfect way.

1592–1857 [see TINKERING *vbl. sb.* and *ppl. a.*].

b. *fig.* To work at something (immaterial) clumsily or imperfectly, esp. in the way of attempted repair or improvement; also more vaguely, to occupy oneself about something in a trifling or aimless way; to trifle, potter. Const. *at*, *with*.

1658 GURNALL *Chr. in Arm.* verse 14. xiii. (1669) 53/1 He that will be tinkering with his own heart, and not seek out to Heaven for help, will in the end where he mends one hole, he'll make two worse. **1856** KANE *Arct. Expl.* II. xiii. 134 When in-doors and at rest, tinkering over their ivory harness-rings. **1880** MCCARTHY *Own Times* IV. lviii. 258 The public were tired of government which merely tinkered at legislation. **1894** JESSOPP *Random Roaming* Pref. 5 A work of art does not admit of being tinkered at indefinitely. **1903** G. B. SHAW *Man & Superman* 193 Parliaments and synods may tinker as much as they please with their codes and creeds. **1936** *Discovery* Sept. 273/2 When the harbour is reached he will be at liberty to tinker with it [*sc.* a boat] to his heart's content. **1955** *Times* 2 May 13/7 Nobody is prepared to tinker with a social structure that has withstood every kind of outside pressure. **1977** J. L. HOULDEN *Patterns of Faith* iii. 39 Matthew often 'tinkers' with Mark's work as he received it.

2. *trans.* To mend as a tinker; to repair or put into shape in an imperfect or makeshift way; to patch *up*. **a.** material objects; also, human beings (in reference to medical or surgical treatment).

1769 J. WEDGWOOD *Let.* 23 Feb. (1965) 71, I have settled a plan.. to Tinker all the black Vases that are crooked. **1814** JEFFERSON *Writ.* (1830) IV. 240 However we may tinker them [our machines] up for a while, all will at length surcease motion. **1835** F. B. HEAD in Smiles *Mem. J. Murray* (1891) II. xxxi. 362 The waters will tinker you up in a most extraordinary manner. **1851** MAYHEW *Lond. Labour* I. 325/1 If the old article were of good quality, it was polished and tinkered up for sale in the Saturday evening street-markets, and often 'went off well'. **1885** S. O. JEWETT in *Harper's Mag.* Jan. 209/2 She tinkered the rickety bee-hives. **1892** C. T. DENT *Mountaineer.* ii. 68 An axe that does not come out right at first can rarely be tinkered into a good one by alterations.

b. *fig.* (immaterial things).

1753 [see TINKERING *vbl. sb.*]. **1768** H. WALPOLE *Hist. Doubts* Pref. 6 Chronology and astronomy are forced to tinker up and reconcile, as well as they can, those uncertainties [of ancient history]. **1768** —— *Let. to Gray* 18 Feb., I am criticised for the expression *tinker up* in the preface... I think such a low expression, placed to ridicule an absurd instance of wise folly, very forcible. **1866** BRIGHT *Sp. Reform* 20 Nov. (1876) 388 The Tory party refused even to have it tinkered. **1879** MCCARTHY *Own Times* II. xxv. 257 Little plans of adjustment were tinkered up and tried. **1887** LOWELL *Democr.* 38 Men are prone to be tinkering the work of their own hands.

c. *Pugilistic slang.* To batter, maul.

1826 *Sporting Mag.* XVIII. 253 Tom completely tinkered his antagonist's upper-crust.

Hence **'tinkered** (-kəd) *ppl. a.*; also **'tinkerer**, one who tinkers or works at mending something in a clumsy or ineffective way.

1862 LYTTON *Str. Story* xx, I clamped and soldered dogma to dogma in the links of my *tinkered logic. **1867** FROUDE *Short Stud.* I. 40 The reconciliation.. is no tinkered-up truce, or convenient Interim. **1906** *Athenæum* 28 Apr. 505/3 He reprints Hayley's tinkered version.. instead of the *editio princeps* in John Duncombe's 'Works of Horace in English Verse'. **1894** W. H. HOTCHKISS in *Review of Rev.* June 683/1 An examination of the checks on the charter *tinkerer in other constitutions.

tinkering ('tɪŋkərɪŋ), *vbl. sb.* [f. TINKER *v.* + -ING[1].] The work of a tinker; the action of TINKER *v.* (in *lit.* and *fig.* senses).

1592 R. D. *Hypnerotomachia* 48 b, What a stately porche ..with his stone of Phenicea with all the tinkering and pullishing about it. **1753** H. WALPOLE *Lett.* (1846) II. 478, I left the tinkering of the bill. **1857** BORROW *Romany Rye* (1905) II. App. v. 328 He [the Gipsy] took to tinkering and smithery, because no better employments were at his command. **1885** *Athenæum* 14 Feb. 221 A very good [picture].. free from any after-meddling and tinkering.

attrib. **1813** *Examiner* 1 Feb. 72/1 The terrible tinkering work there must be. **1841** HOOD *Tale of Trumpet* xxxviii, Or Trudge and his ass at a tinkering job.

'tinkering, *ppl. a.* [f. as prec. + -ING[2].] That tinkers (in *lit.* and *fig.* senses): see the vb.

1598 MARSTON *Sco. Villanie* (1599) 167 Fidlers, scriueners, pedlers, tynkering knaues. **1818** BYRON *Juan* Ded. xiv, A tinkering slave-maker, who mends old chains. **1880** E. WHITE *Cert. Relig.* 44 A purblind tinkering criticism.

tinkerly ('tɪŋkəlɪ), *a.* ? *Obs.* [f. TINKER *sb.* + -LY[1].] Having the character of a tinker or of tinker's work; clumsy, bungling, unskilful; of poor quality; mean, low, disreputable. (*Depreciative.*)

1586 W. WEBBE *Eng. Poetrie* (Arb.) 31, I meane this tynkerly verse which we call ryme. **1592** LYLY *Midas* IV. i, Thou art Pan and all, all Pan and tinkerly. **1593** G. HARVEY *Pierce's Super.* 183 Shewe me any halfe page without piperly phrases, and tinkerly composition. **1647** TRAPP *Comm. Eph.* iv. 25 A base tinkerly sin, as Plutarch calleth it, shamefull and hatefull. **1681** HICKERINGILL *Sin Man-Catching* Postscr., The wary Hollanders.. suffer no Tinkerly Pleading, of mending one hole, and making too.

tinkerman, error for TRINKERMAN, q.v.

tinkershere, -shire ('tɪŋkəʃɪə(r)). Also (? erron.) -shue. [f. TINKER *sb.* (cf. 3 f): the second element is obscure.] A local name for the common guillemot; also for the black guillemot.

1799 R. PULTENEY *Catal. Birds*, etc. *Dorset* (1813) 17 *Colymbus Troile*... The Foolish Guillemot Diver; called here The Tinkershire. **1802** G. MONTAGU *Ornith. Dict.* Q ij b, Guillemot, Foolish... Provincial. Sea-hen. Scout... Willock. Tinkershire. **1831** RENNIE *Montagu's Ornith. Dict.*, Tinker's-hue. **1864** ATKINSON *Provinc. Names Birds*, Tinkershue, Black Guillemot, *Uria grylle*. **1885** SWAINSON *Provinc. Names Birds* 218 Common Guillemot... Tinkershire, or Tinkershue. From its black head and back. **1889** H. SAUNDERS *Man. Brit. Birds* 684 By fishermen it is known as 'Scout', 'Marrot' or 'Tinkershere'.

tin-kettle, *sb.* A kettle of tinned iron.

Often *fig.* with allusion to its being fastened to a dog's tail to tease and frighten it, or to the noise made by beating it.

1775 R. CHANDLER *Trav. Asia M.* viii. (1825) I. 28 [Our cook's] tin kettle boiling over a fire in the open air. **1831** CARLYLE *Sart. Res.* II. iii, A Conquering Hero, to whom Fate.. has malignantly appended a tin-kettle of Ambition, to chase him on. **1864** TREVELYAN *Compet. Wallah* (1866) 172 A new Montgomery.. to whose tail fastidious middle life may attach the tin kettle of hostile criticism. **1895** MRS. CROKER *Village Tales* (1896) 42 Battered old tin kettle as it was, that despised piano had cost one hundred pounds!

Hence **tin-kettle** *v.*, *trans.* to serenade roughly or opprobriously, also to cause (swarming bees) to settle, by beating a tin-kettle; whence **tin-kettling** *vbl. sb.*; also **tin-kettly** *a.*, like a tin-kettle.

1875 A. J. ELLIS tr. *Helmholtz' Sensations Tone* 119 Their quality of sound is.. unmusical, bad, and tin-kettly. **1881** A. BATHGATE *Waitaruna* xvii. 234, I was wakened by the din caused by a lot of the diggers tin-kettling the newly-married pair. **1892** B. BOAKE *Where Dead Men Lie* (1897) 103 What cheering and tin-kettling Had they after at the 'settling'. **1898** *N. & Q.* 9th Ser. I. 116/2 An inn-keeper was reported to have beaten his wife,.. so [his neighbours] 'tin-kettled' him right royally. **1900** H. LAWSON *On Track* 5 The diggers ..gave them a real good tinkettling in the old-fashioned style. *Ibid.* 20 We'd tin-kettle 'em [bees],.. and.. they'd settle on a branch.

tinkle ('tɪŋk(ə)l), *sb.* [f. TINKLE *v.*[1] (sense 2).]

a. The act or action of tinkling; a sharp light ringing sound, such as that made by a small bell, or by pieces of metal, glass, or the like, struck together, etc.

1804 J. GRAHAME *Sabbath*, etc. (1808) 66 Its runnel by degrees Diminishing, the murmur turns a tinkle. **1825** SCOTT *Betrothed* ix, The shrill tinkle of a harp. **1847** EMERSON *Merlin* i, No jingling serenader's art, Nor tinkle of piano strings. **1871** R. ELLIS *Catullus* lxiv. 262 Now with a cymbal slim would a sharp shrill tinkle awaken. **1877–8** HENLEY in *Ballades*, etc. (Canterb. Poets) 77 Of ice and glass the tinkle, Pellucid, silver-shrill.

b. *fig.* in reference to speech or verse. Cf. TINKLE *v.*[1] 2 c, 3 b.

1725 P. WALKER *Life A. Peden* To Rdr. (1827) 17 None of their Addresses have had the Tinkle or Sound of the Declarations and Faithful Warnings of the General Assemblies of this Church. **1776** MICKLE tr. *Camoens' Lusiad* Introd. 141 *note*, There are a race of Critics.. who would strip poetry of all her ornaments,.. who would leave her nothing but the neatness, the cadence, and the tinkle of verse. **1789** BELSHAM *Ess.* I. xii. 226 What Dryden calls the tinkle in the close of the couplet. **1795** MASON *Ch. Mus.* ii. 114 The tinkle of the words is all that strikes the ears.

c. Reduplicated, expressing repetition of such sounds; also as *adv.*

1682 *Bells of Oxford* in *Wit & Drollery* 302 Tincle, tincle, goes the little Bell, To call the Students home. **1879** JEFFERIES *Wild Life in S. Co.* 260 There comes the tinkle-tinkle of a bell. **1888** DOUGHTY *Arabia Deserta* I. 149 They make, as the daughters of Jerusalem, a tinkle-tinkle as they go.

d. *colloq.* A telephone call. Usu. in phr. *to give* (someone) *a tinkle*. Cf. RING *sb.*[2] 3 c.

1938 F. D. SHARPE *Sharpe of Flying Squad* xxiii. 241 As soon as we find 'em I'll give you a tinkle on the blower. **1939** N. MONSARRAT *This is Schoolroom* ix. 207 Shall I give you a tinkle later? **1949** S. GIBBONS *Matchmaker* 51 And then not another word for three weeks! Not even a tinkle to ask if my cold was better! **1959** 'D. BUCKINGHAM' *Wind Tunnel* xix. 153 Shall we give Robin a tinkle and tell him that you're home? **1960** H. E. BATES *Aspidistra in Babylon* 143 Give us a tinkle. **1980** B. BAINBRIDGE *Winter Garden* xii. 89 'Next time you're in London,' advised Ashburner, 'give me a tinkle and I'll take you to my Oxfam shop.'

e. *colloq.* An act of urination. Cf. TINKLE *v.* 6.

1965 J. R. HETHERINGTON *Selina's Aunt* 54 *Tinkle* (have a)..., No. 1. **1974** E. BRAWLEY *Rap* (1975) II. xiv. 239 And went over and had a tinkle. **1978** C. MACLEOD *Rest you Merry* (1979) vi. 57, I was making my tinkle.

tinkle ('tɪŋk(ə)l), *v.*[1] Forms: 4 tyncle(n, 4–6 tynkle, 5 -kel, -kyll, 6 -ckle, tinkel, 6–7 tincle, 6–8 tinckle, 6– tinkle. [*Tinkle* has the form of a frequentative of TINK *v.* (see -LE 3), which also suits the chronology. In some MSS. of the later Wyclif version, it takes the place of the earlier *tink*, as said of a cymbal; and it is frequent from 1450 of the sound of bells, etc.

In both Wyclif versions *tyncle* is also used of the 'ringing' and 'tingling' of the ears; but in some MSS. of the later version *tingle* is substituted. In the 16th c. *tinckle* is said even of the nose. Here it might be thought to represent OE. *tinclian* 'to tickle', L. *titillare*, if there were any trace of that vb. in ME. But it is to be remembered that L. *tinnīre*, which Wyclif rendered *tynke* and *tyncle*, was used of the ringing both of metals and of the ears, and even in the sense 'tingle'. In mod. use, *tinkle* may be said of the ears in the sense 'ring', implying sound objective or subjective, but the thrilling nervous sensation is expressed by *tingle*; 'my ears tingle', like 'my hands tingle': see TINGLE *v.* Cf. WFlem. *tinkelen*, to tingle (as the fingers with the cold), also said of the sound of a drop falling into water.]

I. 1. *intr.* Of the ears: To ring, to tingle: = TINGLE *v.* 1 (now *rare*). †Of the nose or other parts: = TINGLE *v.* 2, TICKLE *v.* 2 (*obs.*).

1382 WYCLIF *1 Sam.* iii. 11 Loo, Y doo a word in Yrael, the which who so euere herith, bothe his eeris shulen tynclen [1388 tyncle, rynge]. —— *Jer.* xix. 3 Eche that shal heren it, tyncle hys eres [1388 hise eeris tyngle]. **1581** MARBECK *Bk. of Notes* 589 Who so heareth of it his eares shall tinckle. ? *a* **1600** J. CONYBEARE *Lett. & Exerc.* (1905) 40 Nasturtium called cresses being eaten doth make the nose tinckle. **1700** DRYDEN *Theod. & Hon.* 94 His Ears tinckled, and his Colour fled. **1722** RAMSAY *Three Bonnets* III. 44, I ha'e a secret to impart.. will set baith your lugs a tinkling. **1871** R. ELLIS *Catullus* li. 11 With inward Sound the full ears tinkle.

II. 2. a. *intr.* To give forth a series of short light sharp ringing sounds. Said of bells, musical instruments, and other resonant objects (cf. TINKLE *sb.*).

a **1400–50** *Alexander* 1385 (Dubl. MS.) Now tynkyll vp taburnes þat all þe towne ringes. *c* **1440** *Wyclif's Bible*, *1 Cor.* xiii. 1, Y am maad as bras sownynge, or a cymbal tynclynge [1382 tynkynge, 1388 (MS. 1420) tynkynge, (MS. 1450) tinglinge]. **1526–1563** [see TINKLING *ppl. a.*[1]]. **1617** MORYSON *Itin.* I. 69 Wee could not sleepe for little bels tinckling all night. **1697** DRYDEN *Æneid* II. 745 [The javelin] faintly tinckl'd on the brasen Shield. **1724** RAMSAY *Tea-t. Misc.* Ded. iii, The spinnet tinkling with her voice. **1819** WIFFEN *Aonian Hours* (1820) 50 A sheepbell tinkles on the heath. **1831** POE *Bells* i, How they tinkle, tinkle, tinkle, In the icy air of night! **1873** T. W. HIGGINSON *Oldport Days* ix. 216 The dry snow tinkled beneath my feet.

fig. **1654** JER. TAYLOR *Real Pres.* xii. 281 The bell alwayes must tinkle as they are pleased to think. [Cf. TINK *v.*[1] 1.]

b. To flow or move with a tinkling sound.

1822 W. IRVING *Braceb. Hall* xvii, A small rill tinkled along close by. **1851** HAWTHORNE *Snow Image*, *My Kinsman* (1879) 248 The latch tinkled into its place. **1855** BROWNING *Love among Ruins* i, Our sheep Half-asleep Tinkle homeward through the twilight. **1859** KINGSLEY *Misc.* II. 288 A stream tinkling on from one rock-basin to another. **1871** HOWELLS *Wedd. Journ.* (1892) 29 The street-cars that slowly tinkled up and down.

c. *transf.* To rime or jingle.

1626, 1822 [see TINKLING *ppl. a.*[1] b]. **1684** DRYDEN *Ep. to Earl Roscomon* 14 A kind of hobbling prose, That limped along and tinkled in the close. **1711** E. FENTON *Ep. to Southerne* Poems (1717) 82.

3. a. *intr.* Of a person: To produce such a sound.

17.. *Bob Norice* ix. in Child *Ballads* IV. (1886) 267/2 But whan he came to Lord Barnet's castel He tinklet at the ring [cf. TIRL *v.*[3] 3 a]. **1809** MALKIN *Gil Blas* v. i. ¶29 Our host ..was tinkling on a cracked guitar. **1860** HAWTHORNE *Marb. Faun* x, The musicians scraped, tinkled, or blew.

b. *fig.* To utter empty sounds or senseless words, talk idly, prate.

1641 R. BAILLIE *Parallel Liturgy w. Mass-bk.*, etc. 54 All the question wee and they have long tinkled on for the worshipping of Saints. **1645** MILTON *Tetrach.* II. i. Wks. 1851 IV. 201 We are but crackt cimbals, we do but tinckle, we know nothing, we do nothing. **1646** R. BAILLIE *Let. to Henderson* 16 May, If that man now go to tinkle on bishops, and delinquents, and such foolish toys, it seems he is mad. **1781** COWPER *Conversat.* 892 The tide of speech.. No longer labours merely to produce The pomp of sound, or tinkle without use. **1871** [see TINKLING *ppl. a.*[1] b].

4. *trans.* **a.** To make known, call attention to, or express by tinkling (*lit.* or *fig.*).

1562 in Blomefield *Norfolk* (1806) IV. 355 *note*, A woman for whoredom to ryde on a cart.. and tynkled with a bason. **1861** *All Year Round* V. 13 Flattery in the fluent phrase that just Tinkled the tender moral o'er the dust Of greatness. **1862** SALA *Seven Sons* I. iv. 76 The multitude of clocks.. were tinkling out the hour of nine.

b. To affect, attract, or summon by tinkling. *to tinkle bees*: see TING *v.* 1 b.

1582 STANYHURST *Æneis* I. (Arb.) 29 Of Troy seat yf haplye the rumoure Youre ears hath tinckled. **1639** SALTMARSH *Policy* §130. 111 Bees are best tinckled together when they rise. **1832** J. WILSON *Noct. Ambr.* in *Blackw. Mag.* Feb. 264 The very kirk.. whose small bell tinkled the joyous school-boy to worship.

c. = TICKLE *v.* 3. *rare*.

1883 W. M. ADAMSON in *Evang. Union Worthies* 316 The flimsy sensational preacher, whose desire is to tinkle the ear, more than touch the conscience.

5. To cause (something) to tinkle or make a short light ringing sound; †to produce by tinkling.

1582 STANYHURST *Æneis* III. (Arb.) 74 Moonewise Coribants on brasse their od harmonye tinckling. *Ibid.* 80 Thee place she tinckled [*omnem Implevit clamore locum*]. **1617** MORYSON *Itin.* III. 209 Many drums were beaten and basons tinckled about them. **1798** JANE AUSTEN *Northang. Abb.* i, She was very fond of tinkling the keys of the old forlorn spinnet. **1834** SOUTHEY *Doctor* i, I finished my glass of punch, tinkled the spoon against its side. **1900** H. G. GRAHAM *Soc. Life Scot. in 18th C.* VII. i. (1901) 245 The 'bell pennies'—for tolling or tinkling the 'dead bell' before the coffin at funerals.

6. *intr.* To urinate. Cf. TINKLE *sb.* e. *colloq.*

1960 WENTWORTH & FLEXNER *Dict. Amer. Slang* 547/1 *Tinkle*.. *v.i.*, to urinate. Common usage by small children; humorously used by adults. **1972** *Sat. Rev.* (U.S.) 17 June 77/2 The handy man.. picked the wrong moment to urinate on the roses. 'He's been tinkling on the roses for twenty-five years.' **1976** 'E. MCBAIN' *Guns* (1977) vii. 198 I'm looking for the loo... I really have to tinkle.

Hence **tinkled** ('tɪŋk(ə)ld) *ppl. a.*, made to tinkle.

1821 CLARE *Vill. Minstr.* I. 160 The tinkled latch startled her.

† **tinkle,** *v.*[2] *Obs.* [Back-formation from TINKLER[1].] = TINKER *v.* 1. Hence **tinkling** *ppl. a.*

1599 MARSTON *Sco. Villanie* III. ix, I once did know a tinkling Pewterer. **1630** B. JONSON *New Inn* I. i, Who tinkles then, or personates Tom Tinker?

tinkler[1] ('tɪŋklə(r)). *Sc.* and *dial.* [app. f. TINKER, with different suffix: cf. *pedder, peddler, pedlar.*] A tinker, or worker in metal; in Scotland, north of England, and Ireland, usually a gipsy, or other itinerant mender of pots, pans, and metal-work.

c **1175** *Carta Willelmi Regis* in *Liber Ecclesie de Scon* (1843) 30 [Terra] que iacet inter terram serlon incisoris et terram Jacobi tinkler. **1484** *Nottingham Rec.* II. 346 Christoferus Tynkeler,..tynkeler. **1570** LEVINS *Manip.* 77/12 A Tinkler, [*sartor ærarius*]. **1572** *Satir. Poems Reform.* xxxii. 49 We Tinklaris, Tailȝeouris... We wait of nocht bot mekill cair and cummer. **1605** *N. Riding Rec.* (1884) I. 3 Joh. Jackson, tinkler. **1681** O. HEYWOOD *Diaries*, etc. (1881) II. 228 Her mother brought a panne to a tinkler's house. **1785** BURNS *Jolly Beggars* Air vi, My bonnie lass, I work in brass, A tinkler is my station. **1818** SCOTT *Hrt. Midl.* xlix, This fellow had been originally a tinkler, or 'caird', many of whom stroll about these districts. **1825** BROCKETT *N.C. Words* s.v., The celebrated Wull Allen was for many years the king of the tinklers in the North. **1847** C. BRONTË *J. Eyre* xviii, She looks such a tinkler. **1911** *19th Cent.* Sept. 546 These wandering cairds or 'tinklers' had four separate languages at their command.

attrib. **1786** BURNS *Twa Dogs* 18 Ev'n wi' a tinkler-gipsey's messan. **1787** —— '*When Guilford good*' v, An' Charlie Fox threw by his box, An' lows'd his tinkler jaw, man.

'**tinkler**[2]. [f. TINKLE *v.*[1] + -ER[1].] That which tinkles; *esp.* a descriptive name for a small bell, etc. (in *slang* = 'bell'); in quot. 1600, a name for some base coin.

1600 *Stirling Kirk Sess. Reg.* (Bann. Cl.) 133 Ane great part of the almus gevin to the Pure is fals cunȝie callit Tinklaris. **1767** ANNA SEWARD *Let.* in *Poet. Wks.* (1810) I. 195 A Spinnet.., the little tinkler is a wretched substitute for my dear harpsichord. **1787** WOLCOTT (P. Pindar) *Ode upon Ode* Wks. 1812 I. 419 Thus when the Oxford Bell, baptized Great Tom, Shakes all the city with his iron tongue, The little Tinklers might as well be dumb. **1838** DICKENS *O. Twist* xxv, 'Hark!' cried the Dodger at this moment, 'I heard the tinkler'. **1852** R. S. SURTEES *Sponge's Sp. Tour* iii, Giving the little tinkler of a bell a pull as he spoke. **1901** R. ANDERSON *Hist. Kilsyth* vii. 65 The old 'tinkler' which..had done service in the belfry of the disused church.

b. A person who tinkles; a rimester.

1731 A. HILL *Adv. Poets* xxii, But, ah! far short th' unsolid Tinklers rise; Nor soar, but flutter, in the Muse's Skies.

tinklerman, error for TRINKERMAN, q.v.

1840 THACKERAY *Catherine* xiv, The ferries..and..the pirates who infest the same—namely tinklermen, petermen, hebbermen, trawlermen. *Ibid.*, A combat..between the crews of a tinklerman's boat and the water-bailiff's.

'**tinkle-'tankle,** *sb.* (also *attrib.*). [Varied reduplication of TINKLE.] Tinkling with alternation of sound. So '**tinkle-'tankling** *vbl. sb.* and *ppl. a.*

a **1619** FLETCHER *Wit without M.* v. i, Here is such a tinkle-tanklings that we can ne're lie quiet. **1859** SALA *Tw. round Clock* (1861) 186 Plenty of good heavy choruses, tinkle-tankling instrumental music. **1882** J. WALKER *Jaunt to Auld Reekie* 205 Stringed guitars with tinkle-tankle tones. **1901** EL. G. HAYDEN *Trav. round Vill.* 125 A flute or violin whose quaint tinkle-tankle adds to the archaic character of the proceeding.

tinkling ('tɪŋklɪŋ), *vbl. sb.* [-ING[1].]

I. The action of TINKLE *v.*[1]

1. The (subjective) ringing of the ears. Now *rare.*

1495 *Trevisa's Barth. De P.R.* XVII. clv. (W. de W.) T vij/2 Senuey..dooth awaye tynkelynge [*Bodl. MS.* tingelinge] & ryngynge of the eere. **1544** PHAER *Regim. Lyfe* (1553) C vj, Deafenesse by wynde..in the eare,..causeth tyncklyng in the heade. **1635** BRATHWAIT *Arcad. Pr.* 104, I feele a perpetuall tinckling and swoning [? sowning] in mine eares. **1803** *Med. Jrnl.* IX. 145 Affected..with a difficulty of hearing, and a tinkling in the ears.

2. A succession of short light ringing sounds, as of a cymbal or a small bell; jingling. Also *fig.*

1549 COVERDALE, etc. *Erasm. Par. 1 Cor.* xiii. 35 A cymball, that with his vnprofitable tinklyng troubleth the eares. **1617** MORYSON *Itin.* III. 32 The Papists at the tinckling of a little Bell, lift up the consecrated Bread. **1651** DAVENANT *Gondibert* Pref. (1673) 9 Old Men..think it lyes in a kinde of tinkling of words. **1750** GRAY *Elegy* 8 Drowsy tinklings lull the distant folds. **1784** COWPER *Task* VI. 1021 Idle tinkling of a minstrel's lyre. **1800** *Hull Advertiser* 8 Nov. 3/3 Pretended half-guineas.., and nothing but the test of tinkling can lead to detection. **1881** BROADHOUSE *Mus. Acoustics* 197 That peculiar high inharmonious noise which we are accustomed to call 'tinkling'.

II. **3.** Short for *tinkling grackle*: see next, c.

tinkling ('tɪŋklɪŋ), *ppl. a.*[1] [f. TINKLE *v.*[1] + -ING[2].] That tinkles; making a short light ringing sound, or a succession of such; jingling.

c **1440** [see TINKLE *v.*[1] 2]. **1526** TINDALE *1 Cor.* xiii. 1, I were even as soundynge brasse, and as a tynklynge Cymball. **1563** WINȜET *Four Scoir Thre Quest.* vii. Wks. (S.T.S.) I. 75 Lyke soundand metell, or ane tincland cimbal. **1621** BURTON *Anat. Mel.* II. ii. VI. iii. 373 Bees..when they heare any tinkling [*ed.* 1651 tingling] sound, will tarry behind. **1663** COWLEY *Verses & Ess.*, *Complaint* vii, The tinckling strings of thy loose minstrelsie. **1717** POPE *Eloisa* 158 The grots that echo to the tinkling rills. **1829** SCOTT *Anne of G.* xiii, A long train of mules—a jolly tinkling team. **1877** MAR. M. GRANT *Sun-Maid* i, There came the tinkling musical echo of a bell.

b. *fig.* of speech (or a speaker), or verse.

1626 B. JONSON *Fort. Isles* Wks. (Rtldg.) 650/1 In Rhime! fine tinckling Rhime! and flowand Verse! **1692** WASHINGTON tr. *Milton's Def. Pop.* Pref., M.'s Wks. 1851 VII. 10 Them, I say, together with their tinkling Advocate, ..we shall e'en let whine on, till they cry their eyes out. **1822** HAZLITT *Table-t.* Ser. II. v. (1869) 120 Keep to your sounding generalities, your tinkling phrases. **1871** B. TAYLOR *Faust* (1875) I. i. 24 Beware, a tinkling fool to be!

c. ***tinkling grackle***, also simply *tinkling*: a bird, a species of grackle (*Quiscalus crassirostris*) found in Jamaica; so called from its note.

1847 GOSSE *Birds Jamaica* 217 Tinkling Grakle. *Ibid.* 219 Like the Ani, the Tinkling feeds on the parasites of cattle. **1890** *Blackw. Mag.* June 787 The tinkling may be seen feeding greedily in the pastures. **1896** NEWTON *Dict. Birds*, *Tinkling* or *Tin-tin*, the name in Jamaica for one of the American Grackles, *Quiscalus crassirostris.*

Hence '**tinklingly** *adv.*, in a tinkling way.

1894 CROCKETT *Mad Sir Uchtred* 25 As she spoke she laughed tinklingly.

tinkling, *ppl. a.*[2]: see TINKLE *v.*[2]

tinkly ('tɪŋklɪ), *a.* [f. TINKLE *v.*[1] or *sb.* + -Y.] Characterized by tinkling.

1892 KIPLING *Barrack-r. Ballads* 52 The tinkly temple-bells. **1894** *Outing* (U.S.) XXIV. 71/2 An ex-captain sits at the tinkly piano.

tink-tank: see TINK *int.* and *sb.*[1]

tinktinkie (tɪŋk'tɪŋkɪ). *S. Afr.* [Afrikaans.] = *tinker-bird* s.v. TINKER *sb.* 5.

1874 [see BUSHMAN, BUSHMAN 3]. **1908** F. C. SLATER *Sunburnt South* 186 The little mouse-coloured tinktinkie.. is a most mischievous little creature. **1956** A. G. MCRAE *Hill called Grazing* iii. 24 Big birds and small birds, from huge vultures..to the tiniest tink-tinkies piping their thin little reeds of song.

tinley, variant of TINDLE *sb. dial.*

1788 *Gentl. Mag.* July 602/2 It is a custom with the Papists in some parts of the kingdom, upon the eve of All Souls, to illuminate some of their grounds, by bearing round them straw..kindled into a blaze. The ceremony..is called a *Tinley*; and the account vulgarly given of it..is, that it is meant emblematically to signify the lighting of souls out of Purgatory. **1825** HONE *Every-day Bk.* I. 1414.

tin-liquor to **tin-mouth:** see TIN *sb.* 5.

tinman ('tɪnmən). [f. TIN *sb.* + MAN *sb.*]

1. A man who works in or with tin; a tinsmith; a dealer in tin-ware. In Cornwall, a man employed in dressing tin ore. Also *transf.* a ship engaged in the carriage of tin ore.

1611 COTGR., *Estamier*, a Tynner, Tynne-man; Pewterer. **1667** *Lond. Gaz.* No. 154/1 A New England Vessel of 16 Guns..was forced with some Tinmen and Colliers to put into St. Ives. **1704** PRIOR *Simile* 2 Didst thou never pop Thy head into a tin-man's shop? **1840** *Civil Eng. & Arch. Jrnl.* III. 284/2 The common soldering irons used by tin-men and plumbers. **1855** J. R. LEIFCHILD *Cornwall Mines* 228 'Tinmen are not copperers', as the Cornish miners say. **1887** *Contemp. Rev.* Sept. 398 Thirty or forty years ago, the tinman..was recognized as one of the leading and most skilful mechanics.

2. Comb. **tinman's solder**, a common low-melting solder composed of tin and lead in similar proportions, suitable for joining either of those metals; **tinmen's snips** = TINSNIPS.

1937 *Archit. Rev.* LXXXI. 272/1 Solders vary in their proportions, fine solder or 'tinman's' consisting of equal parts of lead and tin and 'wiping' solder two of lead to one of tin. **1976** *Pract. Householder* Nov. 46/1 With a soft flamed blow lamp..tin the tube end with tinmans solder. **1950** *N.Z. Jrnl. Agric.* June 563/2 Tinmen's snips are used by almost every beekeeper, as they are necessary for cutting sheet metal or wire gauze. **1974** G. STOKES *Jewelry Making* v. 76 A small pair of tinmen's snips for shaping sheet metal.

tinne, variant of TIND *v. Obs.*, to kindle.

tinned (tɪnd), *ppl. a.* [f. TIN *sb.* or *v.* + -ED.]

1. Coated or plated with tin.

c **1384** CHAUCER *H. Fame* III. 392 A pilere That was of tynned yren clere. **14..** *MS. Sloane* 2463 lf. 159 b, Boile hit eftesones in a tynned panne. **1533** *MS. Rawl. D.* 776 A payer of Jemewes for the same Dore..ffor Tynned naylles ffor the same Jemewes. **1691** *Patent Specif.* (1856) No. 282. 1 Iron plates tinned over comonly called tinned plates. **1831** M. RUSSELL *Egypt* x. (1853) 420 A small chafing dish of tinned copper. **1839** *Civil Eng. & Arch. Jrnl.* II. 361/2 Manufacturer of zinc and of tinned iron.

2. a. Preserved in air-tight tins; canned. ***tinned dog*** (*Austral. slang*), canned meat.

1861 MRS. BEETON *Bk. Househ. Managem.* 100 When live turtle is dear, many cooks use the tinned turtle. **1879** *Echo* 18 Oct. 1/5 The trade in tinned food is enormous, and is constantly on the increase. **1883** *Fisheries Exhib. Catal.* 371 Cooked and tinned Salmon. **1895** SUFFLING *Land of Broads* 19 Try a tinned pineapple. **1895** *Bulletin* (Sydney) 17 Aug. 27 We gave him some 'tinned dorg' and a drink. **1950** G. CASEY *City of Men* 326 We'll be living in a tent and eating tinned dog. It's no place for a woman.

b. ***tinned air***, air supplied by an artificial ventilation system (*Naut. slang*); also (chiefly *joc.*) air sealed in a tin for sale.

1913 *Rep. Brit. Assoc. Adv. Sci. 1912* 635 The fresh air driven in by fans through the metal conduits..is spoken of by the officers [in the battleship]..as 'tinned' or 'potted' air. **1929** F. BOWEN *Sea Slang* 142 *Tinned air*, artificial ventilation. **1962** *Daily Tel.* 12 Dec. 13/3, I shouldn't think even the American who bought Brooklyn Bridge would fall for tinned air as a serious buy.

c. Of music: = CANNED *ppl. a.* b. Cf. POTTED *ppl. a.* 3 b.

1924 J. REITH in *Radio Times* 23 May 1/3 The sound is metallic and unsatisfying, and..we do not like our music tinned. *a* **1976** A. CHRISTIE *Autobiogr.* (1977) IV. v. 196 There was..no 'tinned' music in those days: no broadcasting, no tape-recorders, no stereophonic gramophones.

3. Baked in a tin.

1890 STROUD *Judicial Dict.* 310 Tinned Loaves, made crusty all round..is not 'French or Fancy Bread'.

tinneis, obs. Sc. form of TENNIS.

† '**tinnen,** *a. Obs.* [OE. *tinen*, f. TIN *sb.* + -EN[4]. So WFlem. *tinnen.*] Made or consisting of tin.

c **1000** ÆLFRIC *Gram.* vi. (Z.) 15 *Stagnum*, tin, *stagneus*, tinen. *c* **1440** *Pallad. on Husb.* VI. 99 Other with tynnen tounges take her strynges. **1551-2** in Swayne *Sarum Churchw. Acc.* (1896) 278 For a tynnen Bottell to fetch Wyne in. **1631** BP. WEBBE *Quietn.* (1657) 82 A tinnen or earthen vessel. **1653** H. COGAN tr. *Pinto's Trav.* xxiv. 91 The women wore great tinnen Bracelets about..their arms.

tinner ('tɪnə(r)). [f. TIN *sb.* or *v.* + -ER[1].]

1. One who gets or digs tin ore; a tin-miner.

1512 *Act 4 Hen. VIII*, c. 8 All other tynners..dyggyng of tyn in the severall soyle of the said Richard. **1602** CAREW *Cornwall* 8 b, Where the finding of these affordeth a tempting likelihood, the Tynners goe to worke. **1670** PETTUS *Fodinæ Reg.* 12 The King for advancement of the Stannaries ..frees the Tinners from all pleas of the Natives touching the Court. **1743** WESLEY *Jrnl.* (1903) 147 Nine or ten miles east of St. Ives, where we found two or three hundred tinners. **1883** R. T. DYER in *Leisure Hour* Dec. 733/2 In Cornwall, the second Monday before Christmas is a festival kept by the tinners.

2. One who works in tin; a tin-plater, tinman, tinsmith.

1611 COTGR., *Estaingnier*, a Pewterer, a Tinner. *a* **1817** T. DWIGHT *Trav. New Eng.*, etc. (1821) II. 53 His trade was that of a tinner. **1890** *Anthony's Photogr. Bull.* III. 45 Have made for you at any tinner's, a tin pan about an inch larger all around than your toning tray.

3. One who tins meat, fruit, etc.; a canner.

1906 *Referee* 26 Aug. 9/2 Then down with the kickshaws that all taste alike, And the stock of cold storer and tinner.

4. Local name for the pied wagtail: see quot.

1880 *W. Cornwall Gloss.*, *Tinner*... 'A water wagtail'. Bottrell. **1904** *Athenæum* 4 June 274/3 The pied wagtail.. known [at Land's End] as the 'tinner', because it builds its nest in the mouth of old mine-shafts.

tinnery ('tɪnərɪ). [f. TINNER + -Y, or f. TIN + -ERY.] Tin-mining; *pl.* tin-mines or tin-works.

1769 *De Foe's Tour Gt. Brit.* I. 409 There is still a great Resemblance between the Scilly Islands and Cornwall, in their Culture, Plants, and other Produce, their Tinnery, Fishery, &c. *a* **1787** S. JENYNS *Wks.* (1790) II. 238 Miners from tinneries, and coal-pits.

'**tinnet.** *Obs.* exc. *dial.* Also 7 **tennett, tinet,** 8 *dial.* **teenet.** [repr. OE. type **týnet*, f. *týnan*, TINE *v.*[1] + *-et*, as in *thicket.*] Brushwood for making or repairing hedges or fences. Cf. TINSEL *sb.*[2]

[**1443** *Carta Ric. Moninton* (Blount), Et prædictus Firmarius habebit tinettum sufficiens extra boscum ipsius R. ad clausurandum terras & pasturas supradictas.] **1650** *Parl. Surv. Sussex* in *Sussex Archæol. Coll.* XXIII. 311 The Coppiehold[rs] of Duddleswell doe claime to have ffrith and tennett out of the said Parke for fencing their lands. **1691** *Blount's Law Dict.* (ed. 2), *Tinet* (*Tinettum*).., Trouse, Brushwood and Thorns to make and repair Hedges. **1701** *Cowell's Interpr.*, *Tinettum*, Trouse..is still in Kent called *Teenet.* **1753** CHAMBERS *Cycl. Supp.*, *Tinet*, *Tinettum.* **1904** *Eng. Dial. Dict.*, *Tinnet* [cited from Heref., Glouc., Suss.].

tinnicle, obs. form of TUNICLE.

† '**tinnient,** *a. Obs.* [ad. L. *tinnient-em*, pr. pple. of *tinnīre* to ring, tinkle.] Ringing, resonant.

1668 H. MORE *Div. Dial.* II. v. (1713) 100 A sportful passage of Nature, to try how tight and tinnient her new workmanship was. **1753** *Ess. on Action for Pulpit* 86 It will make every religious string, so to say, more intense and tinnient.

'**tinnified,** *ppl. a. rare.* [f. TIN or TINNY *a.* + -FY + -ED[1].] Made tinny or like tin; impregnated with tin; in quot. 1794 *depreciative.*

1794 *Manners France* 80 Has Horace or Ovid their fair ladies clad In the tinnify'd charm of cork rumps or a pad? **1855** J. R. LEIFCHILD *Cornwall Mines* 38 Stannified granite ..which the plain reader may call tinnified granite.

'**tinnikin.** *Sc. rare.* [f. TIN or TINNY *sb.* + -KIN: cf. *mannikin.*] A very small tin or mug.

1896 CROCKETT *Cleg Kelly* viii, He brought his mistress a drink in a little tinnikin.

† '**tinniment.** *Obs. rare*[−0]. [ad. L. *tinnīment-um* a ringing or tinkling ('tinnīmentum auribus', Plautus), f. *tinnīre* to ring, jingle.]

1656 BLOUNT *Glossogr.*, *Tinniment*, a ringing or tinckling, as metals do. **1658** PHILLIPS, *Timiment*, (lat.) a tingling, or sounding of metals.

'**tinniness.** [f. TINNY *a.*] Tinny quality.

1891 KIPLING *Life's Handicap* ii. 37 Tinned beef of surpassing tinniness.

tinning ('tɪnɪŋ), *vbl. sb.* [f. TIN *v.* or *sb.* + -ING[1].]

I. The action of the verb TIN.

1. Coating, lining, or plating with tin; working at tin-ware.

c **1440** *Promp. Parv.* 494/2 Tynnynge wythe tynne, *stannacio.* **1487–8** *Rec. St. Mary at Hill* 130 Paide to Westwode, smyth,..for tynnyng of the same boltes. **1537** *Acc. Ld. High Treas. Scot.* VI. 337 Item, for grathing and dichting and tynnyng of ten tua handit suerdis. **1611** COTGR., *Plombement*, a leading, or tinning. **1789** *Trans. Soc. Arts* I. 13 Tinning with pure Tin. **1800** tr. *Lagrange's Chem.* II. 107 The tinning of copper consists in applying a coating of tin to the surface of that metal. **1851** MAYHEW *Lond. Labour* (1864) I. 302/1 As you see, sir, I work at tinning. I put new bottoms into old tin tea-pots, and such like. **1873** E. SPON *Workshop Receipts* Ser. I. 9/1 When the article is prepared for tinning, it may be immersed in the tinning metal.

b. *concr.* A tin coating or lining.

1761 *Chron.* in *Ann. Reg.* 143/1 This accident was.. occasioned by using a copper sauce pan, from which the tinning was worn off. **1839** URE *Dict. Arts* s.v. *Alloy*, Tinning, gilding, and silvering may also be reckoned a species of alloys.

2. The putting up and sealing of meat, fish, fruit, etc., in tins for preservation; canning.

1903 *Daily Chron.* 13 Jan. 6/1 The tinning of sprats from Honfleur and other points.

II. 3. Tin-mining.

1855 J. R. LEIFCHILD *Cornwall Mines* 197 For a long period in the early history of tin-mining, the mines of Cornwall appear to have been in the hands of the Jews... When the Jews were hotly persecuted, those engaged in 'tinning' were particularly exempted.

III. 4. *attrib.*

1860 TOMLINSON *Arts & Manuf.* Ser. II. *Pins* 47 Then comes the whitening, or tinning process. **1868** JOYNSON *Metals* 104 The plates are now received one by one from the tinning bath. **1898** *Daily News* 11 Aug. 7/2 Tinning factories have more than they want. **1909** *Eng. Rev.* Mar. 621 [They] put them into patent tinning-pots.

tinnis, obs. form of TENNIS.

tinnitate ('tɪnɪteɪt), *v. nonce-wd.* [f. L. *tinnītāt-*, ppl. stem of *tinnītāre*, freq. of *tinnīre*: see next.] *intr.* To ring, give forth a ringing sound.

1866 J. B. ROSE tr. *Ovid's Fasti* IV. 231 And high and mighty Ida tinnitates To drown the infant's cries.

‖**tinnitus** (tɪ'naɪtəs). *Med.* [L. *tinnītus* (*u*-stem), f. *tinnīre* to ring, tinkle.] A sensation of ringing in the ears.

[**1693** tr. *Blancard's Phys. Dict.* (ed. 2), *Tinnitus Aurium*, a certain Buzzing or tingling in the Ears.] **1843** R. J. GRAVES *Syst. Clin. Med.* xiv. 170 On admission, he complained of headache, tinnitus aurium. **1879** *St. George's Hosp. Rep.* IX. 649 The development of constitutional symptoms, such as tinnitus and slight deafness.

tinny, tinnie ('tɪnɪ), *sb.* [f. TIN *sb.* + *-ie*, -Y, dim. suff.] **1.** *Sc.* A small tin mug, a child's tin.

1825 JAMIESON, *Tinnie*, the small jug or porringer..used by children. **1864** *Auld Ayr* 86 Let us have a tinny of grog. **1906** *Scott. Chron.* 6 July 482/2 They turned up..each with his or her 'tinnie' well in evidence.

2. *Austral. colloq.* A can of beer.

1974 *Telegraph* (Brisbane) 2 Mar. 6/5 In olden days audiences took the equivalent of a cut lunch and a few tinnies to the theatre and expected to be entertained for hour after hour. **1978** *Sydney Morning Herald* 20 Feb. 1 Next time you feel inclined to toss that scrap of paper or tinnie carelessly to the ground, give a thought. **1980** *Truck & Bus Transportation* Feb. 34/3 We doubt if the driver would have enough room on board to stow his lunch box or a couple of tinnies.

tinny ('tɪnɪ), *a.* [f. TIN *sb.* + -Y.]

1. Consisting of, abounding in, or yielding tin; formerly also, Of tin, made of tin.

1552 HULOET, Tynny or of tynne, *stanneus.* **1576** BAKER *Jewell of Health* 231 Let this be kept in a Sylver or Tynnie vessel. **1596** SPENSER *F.Q.* IV. xi. 31 Dart, nigh chockt with sands of tinny mines. **1612** DRAYTON *Poly-olb.* i. 157 Those armes of sea that thrust into the tinny strand. **1695** BLACKMORE *Pr. Arth.* VI. 419 Pale Tinny Oar, and Copper's brighter Vein. **1881** *Standard* 28 Oct. 1/2 The lode is six feet wide, and tinny throughout.

2. a. Like or resembling tin or that of tin; characteristic of tin; *esp.* of sounds; in *Painting*, hard, crude, metallic. Also applied dismissively to (a device which produces) sound of poor quality from which the lower frequencies are largely missing; cheaply contrived.

1877 HALLOCK *Sportsman's Gaz.* 379 Long tinny mouth [of a fish]. **1884** *Encycl. Brit.* XVII. 831/1 The tone tends towards a certain quality which may be described as 'tinny' or metallic. **1892** *Sat. Rev.* 21 May 597/2 We have accused Mr. Parsons of a hard tinny quality in colour and form. **1904** KATE D. WIGGIN *Affair at Inn* 177 She was sitting at the old tinny-sounding spinet. **1908** *Daily Chron.* 24 Oct. 3/1 How tinny look Claude's landscapes in the room at the National Gallery. **1926** *Encycl. Brit.* III. 281/2 When the low notes are dropped out, the result is 'tinny'—high-pitched, shrill, mechanical, lacking in body. **1933** A. HUXLEY *Lett.* (1969) 377 The particular nature of the device gives to the brevity something rather tinny, something (in an undesirable sense) artificial. **1980** G. LANCASTER *Seward's Folly* vi. 66 A tinny radio was playing pop music.

b. Tasting or smelling of tin; tinged with tin.

1873 'S. COOLIDGE' *What Katy did at School* ii. 30 The cans gave the oysters a curious taste,—tinny, or was it more like solder? **1906** *Blackw. Mag.* Aug. 213/1 One of the pans in the dairy smelt suspiciously 'tinny'.

3. *slang.* Having plenty of 'tin'; rich, wealthy.

1871 *Punch* 14 Oct. 160/2 There's heaps of tinny fellows who'll be awful glad to give.

4. *Austral.* and *N.Z. slang.* Lucky. †***on the tinny luck***: by a lucky chance. Cf. *tin-arsed* adj., *-back* s.v. TIN *sb.* 5.

1918 *Chrons. N.Z.E.F.* 7 June 205/1 Remarks are heard on the 'tinny' luck. **1919** W. H. DOWNING *Digger Dialects* 50 *Tinny*, lucky. **1947** I. DOUGLAS *Opportunity in Australia* 90 *Tinny*—lucky. **1951** D. W. BALLANTYNE in *Landfall* V. 168 And this one's yours, Edith. Hey, you're tinny, aren't you? **1959** G. SLATTER *Gun in Hand* xvii. 229 He'll score because some people are tinny and always win. **1978** O. WHITE *Silent Reach* xvii. 173 You'll have to be pretty tinny to pin down those blokes.

Hence **'tinnily** *adv.*, with a tinny sound.

1927 J. MASEFIELD *Midnight Folk* 298 He had no sooner wished, than invisible someones came silently, blocked up the approach to Otter's lair, tinnily reported, 'Entrance blocked securely', and disappeared. **1954** M. SHARP *Gipsy in Parlour* III. xiii. 133 A bell above my head rang tinnily. **1980** A. DESAI *Clear Light of Day* iv. 171 Teacups clinked on the saucers, tinnily.

tinoceratid (taɪnəʊ'sɛrətɪd), *a.* and *sb. Palæont.* [irreg. f. Gr. τείν-ειν to stretch, as if = stretching out + κέρας, κερατ- horn + -ID.] **a.** *adj.* Of, pertaining to, or having the characters of the *Tinoceras*, a very large fossil mammal. **b.** *sb.* A fossil of this genus (*Cent. Dict.* 1891). So **tino'ceratine** *a.*, **tino'ceratoid** *a.* and *sb.*

1889 NICHOLSON & LYDEKKER *Palæont.* lxi. II. 1389 The genus [*Uintatherium*] may be divided into a Dinoceratine and a Tinoceratine group. **1891** *Cent. Dict.*, Tinoceratid, *a.* **1895** *Funk's Stand. Dict.*, Tinoceratid, Tinoceratoid, *a.* and *sb.*

tin-opener to **tin ore**: see TIN *sb.* 4, 5.

tin pan. 1. A pan made of tin, also *attrib.* in reference to the noise made by beating such.

1806 *Austin Papers* (1924) I. 102, 1 doz. Tin pans. **1843** *Knickerbocker* XXII. 50 With discordant fife and old tin-pans for drums. **1854** EMERSON *Lett. & Soc. Aims, Poet. & Imag.* Wks. (Bohn) III. 169 What we once admired as poetry has..come to be a sound of tin pans.

2. A cheap, 'tinny' piano. Cf. TIN-PANNY *a. U.S. slang.*

1882 C. FARRAR *Amat. & Prof. Stage Life* viii. 156 It was now Linwood's turn, and with a wail, that sounded like 'Oh, if I only had a decent piano!' he went out and tackled the old 'tin-pan' again.

3. Special Comb. **Tin Pan Alley** *colloq.* (orig. *U.S.*), the world of the composers and publishers of popular music; also applied *loosely* to a district where song publishing houses abound, *spec.* (formerly) in New York in 28th Street and in London around Denmark Street (see DENMARK).

1908 *Hampton's Broadway Mag.* Oct. 456/2 Oh it's a world in itself, is Tin Pan Alley. It has its laughter and its tears. **1909** *Busy Man's Mag.* Jan. 48/1 Down Twenty-eighth Street, which is known as 'Tin Pan Alley', a dozen music publishing houses grind out new song 'hits' daily. **1926** WHITEMAN & MCBRIDE *Jazz* viii. 161 Like everybody else, I think of the Alley as a street. As a matter of fact, Tin Pan Alley exists now only as a tradition. **1934** [see *Denmark Street* s.v. DENMARK]. **1944** S. BELLOW *Dangling Man* 132, I guess she sees herself in Tin-Pan Alley, her face streaked with tears. **1950** BLESH & JANIS *They all played Ragtime* (1958) xi. 220 While Tin Pan Alley was squeezing ragtime dry, a few people made a lot of money and a great number of people made a little. **1979** P. O'CONNOR *Into Strong City* I. xvii. 61, I found Seven Dials... Then Denmark Street. O this is Tin Pan Alley it belongs in the pages of the Melody Maker.

Hence as *v. trans.*, to serenade in derision by beating tin pans; **tin-panny** *a. U.S.*, of a piano: tinny-sounding; cf. sense 2 above.

1885 *Daily News* 8 Jan. 6/6 The female portion of the community 'tin-panning' the rev. gentleman, a great uproar being caused by the beating of old trays, kettles, &c. **1904** J. C. LINCOLN *Cap'n Eri* ii. 30 On the platform of one [shop] a small crowd was gathered, and from the interior came shouts of laughter and the sound of a tin-panny piano. **1931** G. O. RUSSELL *Speech & Voice* III. xv. 158 The high partials become 'metallic' like the tin-panny piano.

tinpan, obs. (erron.) form of TYMPAN.

'tin-'plate. Sheet-iron or, in recent use, often sheet-steel, coated with tin; a plate of this.

1677 YARRANTON *Eng. Improv.* To Rdr., In order to the establishing of the like [trade] in England, to set the Poor on work, which was the Linen, Thread, Tape, and Tin-plates. **1758** REID tr. *Macquer's Chym.* I. 70 Tin-Plates are no other than thin plates of Iron tinned over. **1812** SIR H. DAVY *Chem. Philos.* 393 Tin plate is formed by dipping thin plates of iron into melted tin. **1839** URE *Dict. Arts*, etc. s.v., The formation of tin-plate, or white-iron.

b. *attrib.* and *Comb.*

1720 STRYPE *Stow's Surv.* (1754) II. v. xv. 323/1 The Company of Tin plate workers were incorporated by charter in the 22nd year of King Charles II. **1815** J. SMITH *Panorama Sc. & Art* II. 794 A japanned tin-plate tray is of less value than a paper one. **1860** PIESSE *Lab. Chem. Wonders* 37 England is the tin-plate manufacturer for the whole world. **1906** *Westm. Gaz.* 10 Jan. 2/1 The transformation at Welsh tinplate works has been very great.

So **'tin-'plated** *ppl. a.*, plated with tin; **'tin-'plater**, a workman who makes tin-plates.

1890 *Engineer* LXIX. 496 The [search-light] projector barrel is 16 in. diameter, rolled out of steel sheet tinplated and very strong. **1903** *Westm. Gaz.* 1 Sept. 5/1 The unions contend..that..the tin platers so treated have a claim for damages against the masters.

tin-pot ('tɪn'pɒt, 'tɪnpɒt).

1. (as two words) A pot made of tin or tin-plate.

1772 T. SIMPSON *Vermin-Killer* 21 A pound of arsenick.. put into a tin pot or kettle.

2. The pot of molten tin into which the sheet of iron is dipped in the manufacture of tin-plate.

1839 URE *Dict. Arts* 1253 The first rectangle in the range is the tin-pot. **1864** STRAUSS, etc. *Eng. Workshops* 78 The first pot, called the *tinman's-pan*... The second pot, called the *tin-pot.* **1880** FLOWER *Hist. Trade Tin* xiii. 170 From the palm-oil bath by means of tongs, the sheets are passed by the tinman..to the tin pot, which is full of molten tin, and here they remain to soak for a period of 20 minutes.

3. Short for *tin-pot bell*: see 4.

1895 MISS E. P. THOMPSON *Veil of Liberty* ix. 176 The.. church next door began to clink its miserable tin-pot—it had once had a good set of bells, but it had felt it prudent to give these to the nation.

4. *attrib.* Resembling or suggesting a tin pot in quality or sound; hence *contemptuously*, without solid worth, of inferior quality, shabby, poor, cheap.

1838 *Remarks G. F. Taylor's Factory Strike* 5 in *Pattie's Mod. Stage* II, Mr. Taylor, is a patriot in his little tin pot way. **1865** *Slang Dict.* s.v., 'He plays a tin-pot game', *i.e.*, a low or shabby one. *Billiards.* **1875** W. MORRIS in Mackail *Life* (1899) I. 309 Within sound of those tin-pot bells. **1891** KIPLING *Light that Failed* iii, To the tin-pot music of a Western waltz the naked Zanzibari girls danced furiously. **1897** *Daily News* 23 Mar. 6/7 Made a sacrifice to some miserable tin-pot politicians. **1907** *Ibid.* 4 Oct., Some tin-pot comic opera receives praise from the very same critics.

Hence **'tin-,potter** *Naut. slang*, see quot.; **'tin-'pottery**, tin pots or tin-ware collectively.

1867 SMYTH *Sailor's Word-bk.*, *Tin-potter*, a galley skulker, shamming Abraham. **1850** SCARGILL *Eng. Sketch-Bk.* 7 Dealing in grocery, drapery, and tin-pottery.

tin-pulp to **tin-scrap**: see TIN *sb.* 5.

tinsel ('tɪns(ə)l), *sb.*[1] Chiefly *north.* and (from c 1400 only) *Sc.* Also 3 tinsil, 4 -ill, -elle, 4–7 -ell, 5–7 -ale, -all, 6 -aill; 4 tynsil, -yll, 4–6 -al(l, 4–7 -ell, 5–7 -el, 6 -ele; 5 tensale, -elle. [ME. *tinsel*, *tynsel*, etc., prob. ad. ON. **týnsla*, f. *týna* (= ME. *tin-en*, *tyn-en*, TINE *v.*[2]) to lose, perish, destroy, with the Norse suffix *-sla* (as in *geymsla*, *rennsla*, etc.): cf. mod.Norw. *tynsla* destruction, damage, spilling.]

†**1.** The losing of something, or the sustaining of harm, damage, or detriment; loss. *Obs.*

a **1300** *Cursor M.* 916 (Cott.), I most couer þis tinsel [*T.* loos] are. *a* **1340** HAMPOLE *Psalter* cxxxvi. 1 Worldis men gretis bot nouȝt for tynsil of þair godes. *a* **1400** *R. Brunne's Chron. Wace* 2352 (Petyt MS.) Hure ouer-þoughte mykel more þe wraþthe of hure fader þe kyng..þan þe tynsell of oþer thyng. *c* **1400** *Laud Troy Bk.* 9936 What harme that day to the be-felle! Thow may telle of thi tenselle. *c* **1470** HENRY *Wallace* v. 387, I meyn fer mar the tynsell off my men. *c* **1520** M. NISBET *N. Test. in Scots, Acts* xxvii. 22, I counsale you to be of good counfort, for tynsele [WYCLIF, los; Gr. ἀποβολή] of na persoun of you salbe. **1556** LAUDER *Tractate* 382 In this Consistis, with-outtin faill, Boith the wynning and tinsaill. *a* **1600** MONTGOMERIE *Misc. Poems* xxxii. 67 Quhair tentles bairnis may to their tinsall tak The neiv with na thing, and the full refuse. **1728** RAMSAY *Twa Cut-purses* 33 Where'er your tinsel be, Ye canna lay the wyte on me. **1737** —— *Scots Prov.* xv. (1750) 42 He that's far frae his gear is near his tinsel.

†**2.** The condition of being 'lost' spiritually; perdition, damnation. *Obs.*

a **1300** *Cursor M.* 11946 (Cott.) Þou godds fede, Sun o tinsel and o ded! *a* **1300** *E.E. Psalter* lxxxvii[i]. 12 [11] Wher ani in thrughes sal telle þi milthnes, Ore in tinsel [L. *in perditione*] þi sothnes? *c* **1375** *Sc. Leg. Saints* ii. 828 Als he slew petir and paule, Till eke þe tynsale of his sawle.

3. *Sc. Law.* Forfeiture, deprivation; now only in some archaic phrases: see quot. 1838.

1424 *Sc. Acts Jas. I* (1814) II. 5/1 Vnder the payne of tynsal of all gold and siluer that beis fundyn. **1565–75** *Diurn. Occurr.* (Bann. Cl.) 80 Vnder the paynes of tynsall of lyif, landis and goodis. *c* **1575** *Balfour's Practicks* (1754) 17 Under the pane of ten pundis, and tinsell of his office. **1678** SIR G. MACKENZIE *Crim. Laws Scot.* I. xxx. §6 (1699) 155 Punished with tinsel of Life and Goods. **1838** W. BELL *Dict. Law Scot.*, *Tinsel of the Feu*, is an irritancy incident to every feu-right, by the failure to pay the feu-duty for two years whole and together... *Tinsel of Superiority*, is a remedy.. for unentered vassals whose superiors are themselves uninfeft, and therefore cannot effectually enter them.

†**tinsel**, *sb.*[2] *Obs.* [Known from late 15th c.; f. TINE *v.*[1], OE. *týn-an* to enclose, fence, hedge, with Norse suffix *-sl*, prob. taken over from north. dial. *gar-sell*, GARSIL (= ON. **gerðsl*), meaning the same thing.] Brushwood for hedging or fencing.

1486 *Nottingham Rec.* III. 254, ij. lodes of tynsell' from þe Copy. **1610** W. FOLKINGHAM *Art of Survey* I. vi. 13 For woods..how enterlaced, as Timber with Tinsell, Coppice, or vnderwood. **1620** in *N. & Q.* 1st Ser. (1851) III. 478 A few underwoods..of hasell, alders, withie and thornes.. which the tenants doe take and use for Tinsel as need requires. **1637** in *Chesh. Gloss.* (1885) s.v., To take sufficient trouse and tynsel..for the fencing in and repairing of the hedges. **1793–1813** *Rep. Agric., Derby* 45 (E.D.S.) Having stone provided in the quay, and tinsel crop for fencing.

tinsel ('tɪns(ə)l), *sb.*[3] and *a.* Forms: α. 6– tinsel; also 6 tynsel(le, -sil(l, -syll, tincel, tincle, tensell, 6–7 tyn-, tinsell, -sill, 7–8 -sil. β. 6 tylsent, tilsent. γ. 6 tynsyn, tensyn, -sen, tinsin, 7 tynsin. See also

TINSEY. [The etymology, though certain in its main fact, presents difficulties of detail, owing chiefly to the want of early OF. examples. Evidently *tincel*, *tinsel*, arose out of OF. *estincelle*, mod.F. *étincelle* 'a sparke or sparkle of fire, a flash', Cotgr. (:—pop.L. **stincilla* for *scintilla* spark), and OF. *estincelé*, mod.F. *étincelé* 'sparkled, sparked, also powdered or set with sparkles', pa. pple. of OF. *estinceler* 'to sparke, to sparkle as fire; to twinkle as a starre or Dyamond; to set thicke with sparkles' (:—pop.L. **stincillāre* for *scintillāre* to sparkle, glitter). In 14–15th c. Fr., the *s* of *es-* had long been mute, and the pronunciation was actually as in mod.Fr. *étincelle*, *-elé*; of this the initial *e* disappeared (app. in Anglo-F. or Eng.) by aphesis, giving *tincel(le*. Our earliest examples show the word used attrib. or as adj. in *tinselle satin*, app. representing a Fr. *satin étincelé* (with *-e* mute in Eng., as in some other words), or else the Eng. 'tinselled satin' (see TINSELLED) with *d* lost between *l* and *s*. Thence sense 2, *tinsel* alone = *tinsel satin*, *tinsel cloth*, etc. Sense 3, which is later, may represent the Fr. sb. *étincelle*. *Tilsent* and *tinsin*, early popular perversions, scarcely survived the 16th c.; they also were at first attrib. in *tylsent satin*, *tynsyn satten*.]

1. *adj.* passing into *sb.* used *attrib.* Of satin, etc.: Made to sparkle or glitter by the interweaving of gold or silver thread, by brocading with such thread, or by overlaying with a thin coating of gold or silver.

α. **1502** *Priv. Purse Exp. Eliz. of York* (1830) 9 Blake tynselle saten of the riche making. **1537** in *Reliquary* Jan. (1893) 37 A nother Tynsell Satten with a Crowne ouer the breste of the seid lorde Mounte Egles Armes. **1552** HULOET, Bawdkyn or Tynsel clothe.

β. **1510–12** *Wardr. Acc. 2–3 Hen. VIII* 52/2 (in *N. & Q.* 8th Ser. I. 129) Tylsent satin. **1547** in Kempe *Losely MSS.* (1836) 67 Twoo baces of clothe of golde reysed wth red sylke, tylsent satten. Twoo baces of clothe of golde, blewe tilsent crymsin and purple vellett in clocks.

γ. **1509–10** *Act 1 Hen. VIII*, c. 14 Clothe of Golde or cloth of Sylver or tynsyn Satten. **1530** PALSGR. 281/2 Tynsyn satten, *satyn broché*. **1531** *Rec. St. Mary at Hill* 41 Small schredes of tensyn satten. **1552** in Dillon *Calais & Pale* (1892) 97 One Vestimente of reed Tensen satten without albe. **1603** *Ceremonies Coronat. Jas. I* (1685) 11 The Dean.. arrayeth the King.. with the Tynsin Hose.

†**2.** A kind of cloth or tissue; tinselled cloth; a rich material of silk or wool interwoven with gold or silver thread (cf. BAUDEKIN); sometimes apparently, a thin net or gauze thus made, or ornamented with thin plates of metal; later, applied to a cheap imitation in which copper thread was used to obtain the sparkling effect. *Obs.*

α. **1526** in *Inv. Goods Dk. Richmond* in *Camden Misc.* (1855) 18 A Testour, panyd with clothe of golde, grene tynsell, and crymsen velwet. **1529** *N.C. Wills* (Surtees 1908) 93 My bedde of grene tynsill and white satteyne embrotherid with blue velvit. *a* **1548** HALL *Chron., Hen. VIII* 3 Richely appareled in Tissues, clothe of Golde, of Siluer, Tynsels and Veluettes Embroudered. **1552** *Inv. Ch. Surrey* (1869) 18 A sute of vestimentes of white tynsell. **1552** HULOET, Tynsell or bawdkyn cloth, *intertextus*. **1583** STUBBES *Anat. Abus.* I. (1879) 47 Euery place was hanged with cloth of gold, cloth of siluer, tinsell, arrace, tapestrie. **1599** B. JONSON *Cynthia's Rev.* v. ix, The fourth, in watchet tinsell, is the kind and truly benefique Evcolos. **1603** KNOLLES *Hist. Turks* (1621) 1203 The Embassador and 16 of his companie, received each of them a robe of tinsell. **1611** COTGR., *Brocatel*, tinsell; or thin cloth of gold, or siluer. **1639** MAYNE *City Match* Ep. Ded., Masquers, who spangle, and glitter for the time, but tis through a tinsell. *c* **1645** HOWELL *Lett.* (1650) III. 3 In that more subtill air of yours tinsell sometimes passes for tissue. **1656** BLOUNT *Glossogr.*, *Tincel*.. signifies with us a stuff or cloth made partly of silk, and partly of copper; so called, because it glisters or sparkles like stars or fire. Hence **1721** BAILEY, *Tinsel*, a glittering Stuff made of Silk and Copper. **1755** JOHNSON, *Tinsel*, a kind of shining cloth.

β. **1547** Tilsent [see 1 β]. *c* **1547** in H. Ainsworth *Constable Tower* I. v. (1861) I. 71 [The Earl of Surrey.. appeared in a doublet of black] tylsent [welted with cloth of silver].

γ. **1523** in *Archæologia* XXXVIII. 363 A sparver payned with cremesyn tynsyn, and blake velvet. *a* **1548** HALL *Chron., Hen. VIII* 75 b, Clothe of Golde, Clothe of Siluer, Veluettes, Tinsins, Sattins embroudered.

3. Very thin plates or sheets, spangles, strips, or threads, originally of gold or silver, later of copper, brass, or some gold- or silver-coloured alloy, used chiefly for ornament; now esp. for cheap and showy ornamentation, gaudy stage costumes, anglers' flies, and the like: see also quot. 1903.

1593 G. FLETCHER *Licia* (1876) 28 As twinckling starres, the tinsell of the night. **1596** NASHE *Saffron Walden* 49 As day-light [is] beyond candle-light, or tinsell or leafe-gold aboue arsedine. **1732** GRAY in *Phil. Trans.* XXXVII. 228 A Piece of Sheet-Brass, commonly called Tinsel. **1782** V. KNOX *Ess.* I. viii. 38 The character of a man of integrity and benevolence is far more desirable than that of a man of pleasure or of fashion. The one is like solid gold, the other like tinsel. **1809** MALKIN *Gil Blas* IV. viii. ¶6 Those who are behind the scenes are not to be dazzled by the tinsel of the property-man. **1839** G. BIRD *Nat. Phil.* 211 These gentlemen fixed one end of a cord covered with tinsel.. to the cap of an electrometer, and tying the other to an arrow, they projected it.. into the air. **1859** LANG *Wand. India* 66 Beside him his.. bride, dressed in garments of red silk, trimmed with yellow and gold tinsel. **1867** F. FRANCIS *Angling* x. (1880) 343 Silver tinsel and twist. **1903** *Electr. World & Engin.* 29 Aug. 341 (Cent. Suppl.) The stranded conductors are universally made of very fine copper or copper bronze wire, or what is technically called tinsel.

4. *fig.* Anything showy or attractive with little or no intrinsic worth; something that gives a deceptively fine or glittering appearance.

1660 JER. TAYLOR *Rule of Consc.* I. iv. rule x. §3 There is more gold now than before, but it is.. so hidden in heaps of tinsel, that when men are best pleased, now adays they are most commonly cozened. **1747** RICHARDSON *Clarissa* (1811) I. iii. 14 If Miss Clary were taken with his tinsel. **1751** JOHNSON *Rambler* No. 147 ¶7 That poverty of ideas which had been hitherto concealed under the tinsel of politeness. **1825** JEFFERSON *Autobiog.* Wks. 1859 I. 105 Chaste eloquence, disfigured by no gaudy tinsel of rhetoric or declamation. **1863** GEO. ELIOT *Romola* vi, An age worse than that of iron—the age of tinsel and gossamer.

5. *attrib.* and *Comb.*, as ***tinsel-foil***, ***-lace***, ***-maker***; ***tinsel-clad***, ***-covered***, ***-paned***, ***-slippered*** adjs.; similative, as ***tinsel-pink***, ***-violet***; **tinsel-embroidery**, see quot. 1882.

1575 *Lanc. Wills* (Chetham Soc.) II. 159 One dublite of crimsine satten and one tynsell paned. **1634** MILTON *Comus* 877 Thetis tinsel-slipper'd feet. **1840** HOOD *Up the Rhine* 207 Waxen tapers, Smartened with tinsel-foil and tinted papers. **1858** SIMMONDS *Dict. Trade*, *Tinsel lace-maker*, a maker of imitation gold or silver lace. **1882** CAULFEILD & SAWARD *Dict. Needlework* 495/1 *Tinsel Embroidery*. This is worked upon net, tulle, and thin muslin materials, and is an imitation of the Turkish Embroideries with gold thread upon crepe. **1897** *Daily News* 24 Feb. 5/2 Naked or tinsel-clad savages. **1906** *Daily Chron.* 27 Jan. 3/2 Description of a tinsel-maker in Delhi. **1920** E. SITWELL *Wooden Pegasus* 49 As I, a puppet tinsel-pink, Leap on my springs. **1956** D. BARNHAM *One Man's Window* vi. 67 The hills are tinsel-violet with distance, encrusted with the Valetta buildings and almost encircled by the blue waters of Grand Harbour.

6. a. *attrib.* passing into *adj.* †Glittering, splendid (*obs.*); chiefly in disparagement: Of deceptively brilliant or valuable appearance; showy with little real worth; cheaply gaudy, tawdry.

1595 *Polimanteia* (1881) 39 Then should not the muses in their tinsell habit be so basely handled. **1633** P. FLETCHER *Purple Isl.* VII. xxvi, Upon his arme a tinsell scarf he wore,.. spangled fair. **1635** QUARLES *Embl.* II. v, False world thou ly'st. Thy tinsill boosome seems a Mint Of new-coynd treasure. **1663** J. SPENCER *Prodigies* Pref., All the tinsil-miracles among the Papists most fatally wound Religion. **1667** MILTON *P.L.* IX. 36 Bases and tinsel trappings, gorgeous knights. **1680** BURNET *Rochester* (1692) 175 Neither their tinsel wit, nor superficial learning will hold them up then. *a* **1704** T. BROWN tr. *Æneas Sylvius* Wks. 1709 III. II. 63 A Good of no Value, a mere tinsel Bauble. **1733** BERKELEY *Th. Vision* §3 A certain way of writing, whether good or bad, tinsel or sterling, sense or nonsense. **1769** *Junius Lett.* xxi. (1770) 132 You assure me, that my logic is puerile and tinsel. **1783** BLAIR *Lect. Rhet.*, etc. xviii. I. 384 Nothing can be more contemptible than that tinsel splendor of Language, which some writers.. affect. **1844** KEBLE *Lyra Innoc.* IX. xiv. (1846) 299 The ears that hear its murmuring, crave No tinsel melodies of earth.

b. Special Comb.: **Tinseltown**, a nickname for Hollywood; also *transf.*, the supposedly glittering world of Hollywood cinema; the Hollywood 'myth'.

1975 *Bookseller* 16 Aug. 1305/1 The tinseltown stuff when Wodehouse won the applause of the theatre-going fans. **1984** *Times* 5 Mar. 8/7 When a filmmaker starts cherishing the natural roar of traffic on the soundtrack.. you know she believes in Tinseltown.

† **'tinsel**, *v.*¹ *Sc. Obs. rare.* [f. TINSEL *sb.*¹] *trans.* To subject to loss; to impoverish, to endamage; to punish by a fine, to mulct.

1475 *Aberdeen Regr.* (1844) I. 34 He is sa tensalit in gudis, that he is nocht of povar to pay certane dettis and soumes of money awing be him. **1609** SKENE *Reg. Maj.* 114 He that swa is essonzied may be tinselled and skaithed.

'tinsel, *v.*² [f. TINSEL *sb.*³]

1. *trans.* To make glittering with gold or silver (or imitations thereof) interwoven, brocaded, or laid on. Also *fig.* **b.** To embellish (pictures, letters, etc.) with gold leaf; 'to embellish (ceramic ware) with metallic effects' (*Cent. Dict. Suppl.* 1909). Hence **'tinselling** *vbl. sb.*

1594 NASHE *Unfort. Trav.* E iv, Hir daintie lims tinsill hir silke soft sheets, Hir rose-crownd cheekes eclipse my dazeled sight. **1611** COTGR., *Pourfiler d'or*, to purfle, tinsell, or ouercast with gold thread, &c. *Ibid.*, *Pourfileure*,.. purfling;.. baudkin-worke; tinselling. **1730–6** BAILEY (folio), *Tinselling*, a border of silver. **1851** MAYHEW *Lond. Labour, Answ. Corr.* xvii, I want to do something in the evening on my own account (tinselling pictures, for instance).

2. To give a speciously attractive or showy appearance to; to cover the defects of with or as with tinsel.

1748 WARBURTON *Alliance betw. Ch. & St.* I. v. (ed. 3) 83 The Gloom of Equivocation, which spreads itself thro' the formal Chapters of the one; and the Glare of puerile Declamation, that tinsels over the trite Essays of the other. **17..** —— *Unpubl. Papers* (1841) 449 False honour may thus tinsel over the gaudy slaves of an absolute master. *a* **1774** TUCKER *Lt. Nat.* (1834) II. 265 The hopes that tinsel the gay and busy hours of life.

tinselled ('tɪnsəld), *ppl. a.* Also 6–7 tinceld. [In sense 1, app. representing F. *étincelé*: see TINSEL *sb.*³; in sense 2, mostly f. TINSEL *v.*² + -ED¹.]

1. Made to sparkle or glitter with gold or silver thread, brocade, or embroidery. **b.** Embellished with gold or silver leaf.

1532–3 *Act 24 Hen. VIII*, c. 13 No Man, vnder the State of an Erle [shall].. weare.. any Clothe of Golde or Syluer, or tynseld Saten. **1545** *Rates of Customs* c iv b, Satten tynseld with gold the yarde XIII. s. IIII. d... Satten of bruges counterfete tynselde the yarde III. s. IIII. d. **1634** SIR T. HERBERT *Trav.* 146 Their out Garment or Vest.. of cloth of gold and Tinselled. **1653** URQUHART *Rabelais* I. lvi. 244 Figured sattin tinselled and overcast with golden threads. **1748** RICHARDSON *Clarissa* VI. 3 Tinselled hobby-horses, gilt gingerbread. **1853** KANE *Grinnell Exp.* v. (1856) 40 Some of these huts were garnished with little tinseled pictures. **1871** ROSSETTI *Last Confession* 387 Before some new Madonna gaily decked, Tinselled and gewgawed, a slight German toy, I saw her kneel.

2. *transf.* and *fig.*; in later use often depreciative or contemptuous (cf. b).

c **1620** *Convert Soule* in Farr *S.P. Jas. I* (1847) 89 Then dream of shadowes, make thy coate Of tinsel'd cobwebs. **1648** EARL OF WESTMORELAND *Otia Sacra* (1879) 6 As the Tincell'd Night gives way At th' opening o' th' true Golden Day. **1738** *Gentl. Mag.* VIII. 521/2 Observe the Gentleman in that gaudy slight French Dress, how he is tinsel'd and pouder'd over. **1741** RICHARDSON *Pamela* (1824) I. 180 Tinselled toy! said I (for he was laced all over). *a* **1774** TUCKER *Lt. Nat.* (1834) II. 126 Clouds.. whose tinselled edges glitter in the western sun.

b. *fig.* Having a flashy superficial splendour without intrinsic value.

1651 CLEVELAND *Poems* 4 His tinsil'd metaphors of pelf. **1820** HAZLITT *Lect. Dram. Lit.* 144 Beaumont and Fletcher .. laid the foundation of the artificial diction and tinselled pomp of the next generation.

tinselly ('tɪnsəlɪ), *a.* [f. TINSEL *sb.*³ + -Y.] Of the nature of, characterized by, or abounding in tinsel; hence, cheaply splendid or sparkling, gaudy without real worth, 'pinchbeck'.

1811 MISS MITFORD in L'Estrange *Life* (1870) I. v. 148 Sometimes pedantic, and sometimes tinselly, none of her works were ever simple.. or natural. **1836** *Backwoods of Canada* 289 These Indians appear less addicted to gay and tinselly ornaments. **1885** *Athenæum* 15 Aug. 205 None of that false ornamentation, that tinselly glitter.

So **'tinselly** *adv.* [-ly²], showily and cheaply. **1864** in WEBSTER; whence in later Dicts.

tinselry ('tɪnsəlrɪ). [f. TINSEL *sb.*³ + -RY.] Showy and tawdry material or ornamentation.

1830 S. WARREN *Diary Physic.* (1838) I. xiii. 258 The ghastly visage of Death, thus leering through the tinselry of passion,.. was a horrible mockery of the fooleries of life! **1869** S. BOWLES *New West* xxvii. 518 The poor tinselry of the worship.

tinsen, -sin, obs. corrupt forms of TINSEL *sb.*³

tinsey ('tɪnsɪ). Also 7 tincy, 8–9 tinsy. A popular corruption of TINSEL *sb.*³

1685 *Lond. Gaz.* No. 2001/4 A Groce of Gimp Lace mixt with Tincy. **1707** E. WARD *Hud. Rediv.* II. III. 10 Built for imaginary Princes To strut in Buskins and in Tinseys. **1771** SMOLLETT *Humph. Cl.* 15 May, I've shown him how little I minded his tinsy and his long tail. **1831** J. WILSON *Noct. Ambr.* Wks. 1856 III. 301 Ye think the peacock's harl and the tinsy hae slipped frae your jaws. **1889** STODDART *Angling Songs* 254 Awa' wi' yer tinsey sae braw!

b. *attrib.* or *adj.*; also in *Comb.*

1699 E. WARD *Lond. Spy* x. (1709) 237 The Quality of the Fair, strutting round their Balconies in their Tinsey Robes. **1704** F. FULLER *Med. Gymn.* (1718) 234 They clap a Saddle upon 'em, cover'd with a Sort of Tinsey Stuff. **1721** RAMSAY *Morning Interview* 162 His head reclin'd upon a tinsy roll. **1753** SMOLLETT *Ct. Fathom* (1784) 81/1 You come over like a walking atomy, with a rat's tail at your wig, and a tinsey jacket. **1828** *Blackw. Mag.* Sept. 298/1 [*Angling*] The yellow-bodied, tinsey-tailed, black-half-heckle.

tinsmith ('tɪnsmɪθ). [f. TIN + SMITH: cf. *goldsmith*, *silversmith*, etc.] A worker in tin; a maker of tin utensils; a whitesmith.

1858 SIMMONDS *Dict. Trade*, *Tinsmith*, a worker in tin. **1865** J. CAMERON *Malayan India* 61 These are.. blacksmiths, tinsmiths, gunsmiths. **1892** LE CARON *25 Years Secr. Service* (1893) 303 Burke called at a tinsmith's shop, and asked the smith to solder up a box for him.

Hence **'tin,smithing** *vbl. sb.* [see -ING¹], doing tinsmith's work; working in tin.

1897 *Westm. Gaz.* 15 Feb. 10/1 His occupation is that of a tinsmith in Leith, and one of his platform stories deals with the tinsmithing job that he was tackling when elected M.P. **1902** *Times* 14 July 12/5 The various industries.. included tinsmithing, carpentry, engineering.

tinsnips, *sb. pl.* Also **tin snips**. [f. TIN *sb.* + SNIP *sb.* 8 (*pl.*).] A pair of hand-held clippers used for cutting (sheet) metal. Cf. *tinmen's snips* s.v. TINMAN 2.

1944 *Living off Land* vii. 131 Materials required are: four sound kerosene tins, tin snips, soldering-iron and flux. **1947** J. CONROY *Midland Humor* 182 Ain't you got no tinsmiths in this town?.. Get a pair of tinsnips, extra large. **1964** C. WILLOCK *Enormous Zoo* v. 85 Our work.. consisted of cutting off lengths of heavy gauge wire with tin snips. **1976** *Conservation News* Sept./Oct. 24/1 As a parent I am very wary of allowing a child not considered competent at fixing an electric plug to be playing about with tin snips.

'tin-stone. The most commonly occurring form of tin ore; cassiterite, native tin dioxide (peroxide). Also *attrib.*

1602 CAREW *Cornwall* 86 They discouer these workes, by certaine Tynne-stones, lying on the face of the ground. **1671** *Phil. Trans.* VI. 2098 Most Tin-stones are porous, not unlike great bones almost throughly calcined. **1805–17** R. JAMESON *Char. Min.* (ed. 3) 210 Annular tinstone.. is a four sided prism, truncated on all the edges and angles. **1839** URE *Dict. Arts* 1241 There are only two ores of tin; the peroxide, or tin-stone, and tin pyrites. **1905** *Times* 11 Aug. 3/4 In the tinstone works of Malacca.

'tin-stream. Usually in *pl.* See quot. 1891, and cf. *stream tin* s.v. TIN *sb.* 1 b.

1855 J. R. LEIFCHILD *Cornwall Mines* 200 There is no regularity in these tin-streams, as they are of different breadths, though seldom less than a fathom. **1891** *Labour Commission* Gloss., A *tin streams* (not stream) deals either with alluvial deposits or with the refuse of the mines..and separates what is valuable..by washing processes.

So **'tin-,streamer**, one who obtains tin from a deposit of sand or gravel by washing; **'tin-,streaming**, the washing of tin from such a deposit.

1839 DE LA BECHE *Rep. Geol. Cornw.* etc. xiii. 405 Whole ground, as the tin-streamers term the stanniferous gravel and superincumbent beds which have not been previously disturbed by the old men. *Ibid.* xv. 545 Tin-streaming seems to have been conducted in Pryce's time much as it is at present. **1881** H. H. DRAKE in *Athenæum* 1 Oct. 432/3 Tin-streaming was a wealthy and influential industry, that enriched landlords, tenants, and 'bounders', who..set Acts at defiance. **1899** BARING-GOULD *Bk. of West* II. 83 This rubble has been turned over and over by tin-streamers.

tint (tɪnt), *sb.*[1] [app. altered from the earlier TINCT, which may already have been so pronounced; but It. *tinta* tint, hue, may have influenced the technical use in painting.]

1. a. A colour, hue, usually slight or delicate; a tinge; *esp.* one of the several lighter or deeper shades or varieties, or degrees of intensity, of the same colour: see quots. 1848–79 in sense 2.

1717 POPE *Epist. to Mr. Jervas* 5 Whether thy hand strike out some free design,..Or blend in beauteous tint the colour'd mass. **1754** GRAY *Pleasure* 42 Chastised by sabler tints of woe. **1798** WORDSW. *Thorn* v, Ah me! what lovely tints are there Of olive green and scarlet bright. **1834** MRS. SOMERVILLE *Connex. Phys. Sc.* xxxvi. 387 Exhibiting all the variety of tints that indicates the changes of combustion. **1838** T. THOMSON *Chem. Org. Bodies* 516 It is nearly colourless, having only a slight tint of yellow. **1878** DALE *Lect. Preach.* v. 128 Autumn tints of brown and gold.

b. *fig.* in various senses; *esp.* Quality, character, kind; a slight imparted or modifying character, a 'tinge' *of* something.

1760 STERNE *Serm.* xix, Each one lends it something of its own complexional tint and character. **1768** —— *Sent. Journ., Passport, Hotel at Paris*, Liberty!.. No tint of words can spot thy snowy mantle. **1817** BYRON *Manfred* III. ii, Our inborn spirits have a tint of thee. **1825** JEFFERSON *Autobiog.* Wks. 1859 I. 114 His virtue was of the purest tint. **1901** *Empire Rev.* I. 369 In New South Wales..free trade was the dominant tint [at the election].

c. *Hairdressing.* An artificial colouring, less permanent than a dye, applied to enhance the colour of the hair; an application of this.

1921 [see TINTER d]. **1957** *Encycl. Brit.* VI. 496A/2 The tint ..is only temporary and is not a dye in the true sense. **1979** 'M. HEBDEN' *Pel & Faceless Corpse* x. 109 What is it you wanted? Tint? Shampoo? Or a cut?

2. *spec.* **a.** *Painting*: see quots. ***middle tint***, ***prime tint***: see MIDDLE *a.* 6, PRIME *a.* 9 a.

1753 HOGARTH *Anal. Beauty* xiii. 179 Light and shades.. become, as it were, our materials, of which 'prime tints' are the principal. By these I mean the fixed and permanent colours of each object, as the green of trees, &c. **1784** J. BARRY in *Lect. Paint.* v. (1848) 183 The middle tint, or intermediate passage between the two masses of light and dark. **1848** WORNUM *ibid.* 211 *note*, Although there are but three primitive colours, painters have nine. These are yellow, red, blue,..orange, purple, green,..russet, olive, citrine... All other gradations of colour are mere tints of the above; dark or light, according as they are mixed with black or white, or according to the proportions in which they are compounded. Thus the variety of tints is infinite. **1859** GULLICK & TIMBS *Paint.* 8 *note*, Tints differ from each other in being simply lighter or darker, but hues differ in colour. *Ibid.*, In ordinary usage, however, by 'tints' we frequently mean colours generally, and the word is often substituted for 'hues'. **1879** POLE in *Nature* 6 Nov. 15/2 *note*, In technical language mixtures of a colour with white are called *tints*, with black, *shades*.

b. *Engraving.* The effect produced by a series of fine parallel lines more or less closely drawn so as to produce an even and uniform shading.

crossed tint, one produced by lines crossing at right angles. ***ruled tint***, one produced by a single series of parallel lines. ***safety tint***, that used on bills of exchange, cheques, etc., either as a ground of the whole surface, or specially on the parts which have to be completed in writing, as a security against alterations.

1880 *Print. Trades Jrnl.* xxxi. 6 Worked in black, and light tints, on a stone coloured paper.

3. *attrib.* and *Comb.*, as ***tint work***; **tint-block**, a block of wood or metal hatched with fine parallel lines suitable for printing tints; **tint-drawing**, drawing in diluted shades of various colours, or in one colour so that the gradations are produced by washes of pigment; **tint-tool**, an implement used for hatching or graving a tint-block.

1869 *Eng. Mech.* 10 Dec. 298/3 Tint-tools. **1873** E. SPON *Workshop Receipts* Ser. I. 147/1 The parallel lines forming an even and uniform tint, as in the representation of a clear sky, are obtained by what is called the tint-tool. **1884** *St. James' Gaz.* 24 Oct. 7/1 Mr. Linton..draws an emphatic distinction between wood-cutting..and wood-engraving, or white-line tint-work. **1897** *Daily News* 23 Apr. 6/5 He.. is seen to most advantage in tint works, such as the View over Romney Marsh.

tint, *sb.*[2] *dial.* [Origin uncertain: perh. two different words.

In sense 1 *tint* may be a variant of *tent* dial., lit. 'trial', f. L. *tentare* to try. It is also possible that *tint* in sense 2, quot. 1886, has the same origin (quasi 'not a taste, not a trace'); but it is very doubtful whether this origin can be assumed for quot. *a* 1225.]

1. ? A trial, taste, touch; a foretaste; a trace, indication (*of* anything). *Sc.*

1768 ROSS *Helenore* III. 122 Great search for her was made, baith far an' near, But tint nor tryal never cud appear. **1878** W. THOM in *Whistle Binkie* (1890) II. 44 The half-ta'en kiss.. Is, heaven kens, fu' sweet amen's, An' tints o' heaven here. **1887** *Suppl. to Jamieson, Tint*, proof, evidence, indication; forecast, foretaste; 'The beast's awa, and ye'll ne'er get tint or wittins o't'.

2. After negative: (Not) a bit, particle, atom.

[*a* **1225** *Leg. Kath.* 1254 þæt nefde hare nan tunge to tauelin a tint wið.] **1886** ROSA MULHOLLAND *Marcella Grace* xii, We haven't had a tint o' milk these three days.

tint (tɪnt), *ppl. a.* Now only *Sc.* and *north. dial.* [pa. pple. of TINE *v.*[2]] Lost.

a **1340** HAMPOLE *Psalter* xvii. 18 Bot if ȝe lefe ȝoure syn and doe penaunce ȝe be tynt men. *c* **1375** *Sc. Leg. Saints* iii. (*Andreas*) 438 How þe tynt sawlis of al men War brocht to þe restorynge Of þe croice. *c* **1500** KENNEDY *Passion of Christ* 214 Lord and King, Send fra þe hevin the tynt man to recure. *a* **1584** MONTGOMERIE *Cherrie & Slae* 816 Tint tyme we may not get again. **1725** RAMSAY *Gentle Sheph.* III. iii, But we're nae sooner fools to give consent, Than we our daffin, and tint power repent.

tint (tɪnt), *v.* [f. TINT *sb.*[1]] **a.** *trans.* To impart a tint to; to colour, esp. slightly or with delicate shades; to tinge. Also *absol.*

1791 MRS. RADCLIFFE *Rom. Forest* i, The sun at length tinted the eastern clouds and the tops of the highest hills. **1833** J. RENNIE *Alph. Angling* 22 Silken or hempen lines may be tinted by a decoction of oak bark. **1860** TYNDALL *Glac.* I. xvi. 106 The sun..still tinted the clouds with red and purple. **1873** BLACK *Pr. Thule* xxvii, The beautiful colours of August tinting the great masses of rock. **1893** *Westm. Gaz.* 28 Feb. 3/1, I can't call him a painter at all. A man of marvellous imagination, a surprising flow of lovely fancies —but a painter, no! He merely tints.

fig. **1799** ANNA SEWARD *Sonn.* i. Poet. Wks. 1810 III. 122 No more young Hope tints with her light and bloom The darkening scene. **1861** HOLLAND *Less. Life* v. 72 All truth is tinted by the medium through which it passes.

b. *techn.* (See quot.)

1857 YOUMANS *Handbk. Househ. Sc.* §161 By the addition of black the red is said to be shaded, by the addition of white it is tinted.

c. *intr.* for *pass.* To become tinted or coloured.

1892 *Pict. World* 7 May 32/3 The forced leaves..begin to tint in about three hours.

d. *trans. Hairdressing.* To colour (the hair) with a tint. See TINT *sb.*[1] 1 c.

1921 [implied at TINTER d]. **1966** J. S. COX *Illustr. Dict. Hairdressing* 149/2 *Tint*, to dye. The word tint, used for dye, is one of the many euphemisms employed in the hairdressing craft. **1977** A. MORICE *Scared to Death* xvii. 119 I'm going a bit grey... So I have it tinted three or four times a year.

Hence **'tintable** *a.* [-ABLE], capable of being tinted.

1974 *Spartanburg* (S. Carolina) *Herald* 18 Apr. (K mart Advts. Suppl.) 10 Washable latex acrylic is tintable to hundreds of colors! **1979** *Chatelaine* (Canada) Jan. 95/2 (Advt.), The bifocals with no lines. They're featherweight and tintable.

tint, obs. f. TENT *sb.*[4]; pa. t. of TINE *v.*[2]

'tin-'tack. **a.** A tack, or short light iron nail, coated with tin.

1839 DICKENS *Nicholas Nickleby* xxxv. 346 A..parcel of tin tacks and a very large hammer. **1840** —— *Old C. Shop* xxviii, Mrs. Jarley served out the tin tacks from a linen pocket. **1887** G. R. SIMS *Mary Jane's Mem.* vii. 91 He had trodden on a tin-tack on the carpet, point up.

b. Colloq. phr. ***to come*** (or ***get***) ***down to tin tacks*** = ***to come*** (or ***get***) ***down to brass tacks*** s.v. BRASS *sb.* 5 b. (Found only in the work of G. B. Shaw.)

1921 G. B. SHAW *Pen Portraits* (1932) 183 Keats..had he lived, would no doubt have come down from Hyperions and Endymions to tin tacks as a very full-blooded modern revolutionist. **1949** —— *Buoyant Billions* (1950) III. 45 Do let us get back to tin tacks. Is Clemmy going to marry him or is she not?

'tintage. *rare.* [f. TINT *sb.*[1] + -AGE.] Tints in the mass; tinting.

1859 R. F. BURTON *Centr. Afr.* in *Jrnl. Geog. Soc.* XXIX. 213 The sight wearies with the unvarying tintage—all shining green and vivid blue.

tintamarre (tɪntə'mɑː(r)). Now *rare.* Forms: 6 **tyntamar**, 7 **tintamare, -marr, tintimare, -marre, (tinamar)**, 7–8 **tintamar**, (9 **-mara, -merre, timtimar**), 7– **tintamarre**. [a. F. *tintamarre* (15th c.), of obscure origin: see suggestion in Littré.] A confused noise, uproar, clamour, racket, hubbub, clatter.

1567 FENTON *Trag. Disc.* 418, I leave you to judge what a tyntamar entred the head of therle. **1603** FLORIO *Montaigne* III. xiii. 644 Hee learnd and profited much by that hurly burly or tintimare. **1640** HOWELL *Dodona's Gr.* 64 He preservd Ampelona..without the least tintamarre or noise of commotion. **1705** VANBRUGH *Confed.* v. ii, But amongst all this tintamar, I don't hear a word of my hundred pounds. **1806–7** J. BERESFORD *Miseries Hum. Life, Post. Groans* xxiii, During its intolerable, indomitable, and interminable tintamara. **1834** H. GREVILLE *Diary* 21 Nov. (1883) 40 Such a *tintamarre* I never heard, but the audience were enthusiastic. **1901** *Academy* 28 Dec. 635/1 The just..praise he wishes to utter is forestalled by a tintimar of rash eulogy.

tintare, obs. f. *tine-tare*: see TINE *sb.*[4] b.

tint-block, -drawing, etc.: see TINT *sb.*[1] 3.

tinte, obs. form of TENT *sb.*[4] (wine).

tinted ('tɪntɪd), *ppl. a.* [f. TINT *v.*] **a.** Coloured, tinged or dyed (*lit.* or *fig.*); coloured in a manner specified by defining word in Comb. ***tinted drawing*** = tint-drawing: see TINT *sb.*[1] 3.

1756 *Crit. Rev.* II. 340 The French author is not much oblig'd..to his English translator. We meet with..*tinted* ideas, *propell'd*,..*devastated, bilious*, and many others of this kind. To what language these most properly belong the translator best knows, most certainly not to our own. **1816** SOUTHEY *Poet's Pilgr.* I. iv. 92 The autumnal-tinted groves. **1821** CRAIG *Lect. Drawing* i. 15 Mr. Sandby..denominated this manner tinted drawing. **1831** WILLIAMS *Life & Corr. Sir T. Lawrence* II. 351 *note*, The tinted drawings of Lawrence are calculated to give the finest feelings to the imagination. **1852** THACKERAY *Esmond* II. xi, A face..like a tinted statue. **1905** *Daily Chron.* 8 May 8/5 Talking of make-up reminds me of what we now call 'tinted' hair. **1905** *Westm. Gaz.* 1 July 14/1 Frowning heights the outline of which stood out dark and desolate against the orange-tinted sky. **1973** E. LEMARCHAND *Let or Hindrance* xiii. 160 A small brisk woman with auburn-tinted hair.

b. Coloured, as for reducing the strength of light, e.g. ***tinted glass***.

1905 *Proc. R. Soc.* LXXIV. 528 A similar experiment was tried on a sample of the purple-tinted glass. **1911** *Index Catal. Libr. Surg.-Genl.'s Office, U.S. Army* XVI. 222 (*heading*) Spectacles (tinted). **1978** *Morecambe Guardian* 14 Mar. 32/6 (Advt.), 1974 Ford Capri..black vinyl roof, tinted glass.

tintenaga, tintenagall, erron. var. TUTENAG.

tinter ('tɪntə(r)). [f. TINT *v.* + -ER[1].] **a.** One who or that which tints; now *esp.* an artist or painter skilful in tinting; *spec.* **b.** a tinted glass slide used with plain slides in a magic lantern; **c.** an instrument or machine for tinting or colouring paper or engraving tint-blocks; **d.** *Hairdressing.* One employed to tint hair. Cf. TINT *v.* d.

1823 BYRON *Juan* XIII. cxi, Good hours of fair cheeks are the fairest tinters. **1830** CUNNINGHAM *Brit. Painters* II. 181 He was a most splendid tinter, but no colourist. **1862** THORNBURY *Turner* I. 48 The tinters of backgrounds still survive. **1891** LEWIS WRIGHT *Optical Projection* viii. (1906) 122 Tinters may add very much to the pleasing effect of plain photographs, if used with suitable subjects. **1921** *Dict. Occup. Terms* (1927) §920 *Tinter*,..washes and applies tint or colour to human hair on the head or in the manufacture of wigs. **1966** J. S. COX *Illustr. Dict. Hairdressing* p. ix, Words denoting a person engaged in some aspect of the Hairdressing or Wigmaking crafts..*tinter*.

†**tinternel.** *Obs.* Also tyn-. [Origin unascertained. (Cf. F. *tinter* to ring).] ? Some form of instrumental music. Hence †**tinternelling** *a.*

1575 GASCOIGNE *Adv. F.I.* Wks. 210 Calling the musitions [he] caused them softly to sounde the Tynternall. *Ibid.* 218 His Mistres could not be quiet vntill she heard hym repeat the Tinternell which he had vsed ouer night. *Ibid.*, She demanded secretly and in sad earnest, who deuised this Tinternell. **1593** NASHE *Christ's T.* (1613) 69 The Virgins on their loud tinternelling Timbrils..should haue descanted on my praises. [**1847–78** HALLIWELL, *Tinternell*, the name of an old dance. (Hence in later Dicts. Authority for this statement is not given.)]

†**tint for tant.** *Obs.* Also tint for taunt. [A reduplicated phrase with antithetic modification of the first member: cf. *tit for tat.* Probably altered from *taunt for* (*pour*) *taunt* (TAUNT *sb.*[1] 1).] Retaliation, retort in kind.

1620 T. GRANGER *Div. Logike* 124 Regestion is commonly termed like for like, pin driuing out a pin, tint for taunt, &c. **1677** COLES *Eng.-Lat. Dict.* s.v. *Tint*, To give one tint for tant, *par pari referre.* **1710** (*title*) Tint for Taunt. The Manager Managed..in Remarks..upon a Sermon..in.. St. Paul Covent-Garden..by..R. L. Lloyd. **1828** *Craven Gloss.* s.v., 'Tint for tant', a requital, similar to *tit for tat.*

tinticite ('tɪntɪkaɪt). *Min.* [f. *Tintic* (see quot. 1946) + -ITE[1].] A hydrated basic ferric phosphate, $Fe_6(PO_4)_4(OH)_6.7H_2O$, found as whitish masses of submicroscopic crystals.

1946 B. STRINGHAM in *Amer. Mineralogist* XXXI. 395 A creamy white clay-like substance with unusual optical and chemical properties was found as a wall coating in a limestone cave near the Tintic Standard Mine in the Tintic Mining District, Utah. The chemical analysis and *x*-ray comparative data shows the mineral to be new and is here named tinticite. **1967** *Virginia Jrnl. Sci.* XVIII. 189/2 Secondary minerals, formed primarily by weathering processes, include aragonite..rozenite..and tinticite.

tintiness: see after TINTY *a.*

tinting ('tɪntɪŋ), *vbl. sb.* [f. TINT *v.* + -ING^{1}.] The action of TINT *v.*; the result of this; tint or tints; colouring. Also *attrib.*; **tinting-tool** = *tint-tool* (TINT *sb.*^{1} 3).

1853 KANE *Grinnell Exp.* ix. (1856) 64 The water and the sky..had a pearly or ash-colored tinting. **1856** E. CAPERN *Poems, Gentle Annie*, Scarce fifteen rosy years had left Their tintings on her cheek. **1879** ATCHERLEY *Boërland* 72 In colour it is very pleasing, the ground tinting being a cinnamon brown.

tintinnabulant (tɪntɪ'næbjʊlənt), *a.* [f. as next + -ANT^{1}.] Ringing or tinkling as a small bell; jingling. (This and the allied words all pedantic.)

1812 H. & J. SMITH *Rej. Addr.*, *Johnson's Ghost*, That ligneous barricado..decorated with frappant and tintinnabulant appendages. **1865** *Daily Tel.* 12 June, The tintinnabulant fancies of an Edgar Poe.

tintinnabular (tɪntɪ'næbjʊlə(r)), *a.* [f. L. *tintinnābul-um* bell + -AR.] = next.

1767 S. PATERSON *Another Trav.* I. 392 The vulgar tintinnabular art of pulling ropes. **1835** *Fraser's Mag.* XII. 97 He seems..to sympathise with the bell-ringer in his tintinnabular enthusiasm. **1856** 'C. BEDE' *Tales College Life* 57 He threw down the [morning paper], and immediately responded to the tintinnabular call.

tintinnabulary (tɪntɪ'næbjʊlərɪ), *a.* (*sb.*) [f. as prec. + -ARY^{1}. Cf. med.L. *tintinnābulārius* 'bell-man' (*Oxford Laudian Statutes*).] Of or pertaining to bells or bell-ringing; of the nature of a bell; characterized by bell-ringing.

1787 G. COLMAN *Prose Sev. Occas., Let. fr. Lexiphanes* Gloss., *Ding-dong*, Tintinabulary chimes, used metaphorically to signify dispatch and vehemence. **1839** *New Monthly Mag.* LVII. 131 That truly tintinnabulary peculiarity of the British nation, the 'half-hour bell'. **1886** T. FROST *Country Jrnlist.* 101 The boy who responded promptly to the tintinnabulary summons.

b. *sb.* A bell-ringer.

1825 *New Monthly Mag.* XIV. 494 Sacred, but at the same time thoughtless tintinnabularies.

tintinnabulate (tɪntɪ'næbjʊlət), *a. rare.* [ad. L. *tintinnābulāt-us* furnished with a bell or bells, f. *tintinnābulum* bell: see -ATE^{2} 2.] Bell-shaped.

1874 RUSKIN *Val D'Arno* i. §22 (1886) 13 How that tintinnabulate roof differs from the dome of the Pantheon.

So **tinti'nnabulate** *v.*, *intr.* to ring, tinkle.

1906 *Daily Chron.* 4 Sept. 4/4 For some days past..the ox-bells have clinked and tintinnabulated.

tintinnabulation (ˌtɪntɪnæbjʊ'leɪʃən). [n. of action f. L. *tintinnābulum* bell: see -ATION.] A ringing of a bell or bells, bell-ringing; the sound or music so produced.

1831 POE *Bells* i, Keeping time..To the tintinabulation that so musically swells From the bells. **1883** READE in *Harper's Mag.* Jan. 259/1 All this tintinnabulation.. gratified Vladimir's vanity.

tintinnabulatory (tɪntɪ'næbjʊlətərɪ), *a.* [f. as TINTINNABULATE *a.* + -ORY.]

= TINTINNABULARY.

1827 W. G. S. *Excurs. Vill. Curate* 129 Tapster of the tintinnabulatory *cerevisiarum, vulgo* ale-house. **1880** *Daily Tel.* 10 Dec. 5/3 A clause authorising the tintinnabulatory 'promulgation' of muffins.

tintinnabule. *humorous nonce-wd.* [ad. L. *tintinnābul-um.*] A bell.

1834 *Fraser's Mag.* IX. 711 The tintinnabule..brought to my hand the promised jug of bubbling water.

tinti'nnabulism. *nonce-wd.* [f. as prec. + -ISM.] The art or practice of bell-ringing. So **tinti'nnabulist**, a professional bell-ringer.

1826 *New Monthly Mag.* XVI. 474 An Armenian mass, with all its 'tintinabulism', and nasal singing, and 'incondite music'. **1830** *Fraser's Mag.* II. 450 An army of red-coated tintinnabulists are called for to remind the greasy citizens of the time.

tintinnabulous (tɪntɪ'næbjʊləs), *a.* [f. L. *tintinnābul-um*: see next and -OUS.] Characterized by or pertaining to bell-ringing.

1791–3 in *Spirit Pub. Jrnls.* (1799) I. 225 Tintinnabulous Intrepidity, or scenes of bell-ringing. **1822–56** DE QUINCEY *Confess.* (1862) 214, I, with many others who suffered from his tintinnabulous propensities. **1897** F. THOMPSON *Poems*, *New Year's Chimes*, Tintinnabulous, tuned to ring A multitudinous-single thing, Rung all in rhyme.

‖ **tintinnabulum** (tɪntɪ'næbjʊləm). Pl. **-a.** [L., a bell f. *tintinnā-re* to ring, clink, jingle + *-bulum*, suffix of instrument.] A small tinkling bell. Also *fig.* **b.** See quot. 1877.

[**1398** TREVISA *Barth. De P.R.* XIX. cxxviii. (1495) 935 Tintinabulum is the belle that is often hangyd abowte the neckes of houndes & fete of foules and byrdes.] **1597** *1st Pt. Return fr. Parnass.* V. i. 1465 Thoue whorsonn tintunabulum, thou that art the scorne of all good witts. **1782** COWPER *Table-t.* 529 Beating alternately, in measured time, The clockwork tintinnabulum of rhyme. **1877** KNIGHT *Dict. Mech.*, *Tintinnabulum*, a musical instrument of percussion, consisting of a number of bells suspended in a frame.

† **'tintinnate,** *v. Obs. rare*$^{-0}$. [f. ppl. stem of L. *tintinnāre* to ring: see -ATE^{3} 5.] *intr.* To ring, as a bell; to tinkle. Hence † **tinti'nnation** *Obs. rare*$^{-0}$, a ringing, a tinkling.

1623 COCKERAM, *Tintinate*, to ring like a bell. **1658** PHILLIPS, *Tintinnation*, a ringing like a bell.

tintinnid (tɪn'tɪnɪd). [a. mod.L. family name *Tintinnidæ*, f. generic name *Tintinnus* (F. von P. von Schrank *Fauna Boica* (1803) III. 302): see TINTINNABULUM and -ID^{3}.] A ciliated protozoan of the family Tintinnidæ or the order Tintinnina, often distinguished by a bell-shaped test. Also *attrib.*

1945 M. F. GLAESSNER *Princ. Micropalaeont.* ii. 12 The structural analogy between *Calpionella* and the chitinous tintinnid tests suggestive of taxonomic relations. **1953** SHROCK & TWENHOFEL *Princ. Invertebr. Paleontol.* (ed. 2) ii. 67 Fossil tintinnids have been found in Pleistocene peat bogs. **1970** *Nature* 25 July 381/1 Microzooplankton.. consisting mostly of copepod nauplii, with some veligers, polychaete larvae and tintinnids. **1979** *Jrnl. Protozool.* XXVI. 415/1 The process of lorica building by tintinnids is poorly understood.

tintist ('tɪntɪst). [f. TINT *sb.*^{1} + -IST 4.] One skilled in tinting, a tinter; one who prefers tinting to colouring.

1890 *Univ. Rev.* May 32 There are the camps of the colourists and the tintists.

tintless ('tɪntlɪs), *a.* [f. TINT *sb.*^{1} + -LESS.] Having no tint or tints; devoid of colour.

1789 E. DARWIN *Bot. Gard.* I. 491 The Adept..Shades with pellucid clouds the tintless field. **1813** T. BUSBY *Lucretius* I. II. 811 Tintless themselves, no colours seeds unfold. **1878** *Fraser's Mag.* XVIII. 767 The blue heaven, as we rise into it, is mere tintless air.

tinto ('tɪntəʊ), *sb.*^{1} [a. Sp. *tinto* tinted, deep-coloured, in *vino tinto* 'a blackish wine in Spaine' (Minsheu).] Tent wine; = TENT *sb.*^{4} Also the name of a French wine: see quot. 1833. In recent use, short for *vino tinto* s.v. VINO 1 a or [Pg.] *vinho tinto* s.v. VINHO (= red wine); a glass or drink of this.

1599 MINSHEU *Sp. Dict.*, *Dial.* 6 Which will you haue Sir, Sack or Tinto [Sp. *blanco o tinto*]? *Marg.*, Tinto is a wine in Spaine red and blackish. **1833** C. REDDING *Wines* (1851) 138 In the arrondissement of Montelimart [in France]..there is a vineyard..in the commune of Rochegude, and the wine produced there, called Tinto, sells for a hundred francs the hectolitre. **1858** SIMMONDS *Dict. Trade*, *Tinto*, a red Madeira wine, wanting the high aroma of the white sorts; and, when old, resembling tawny port. **1958** K. AMIS *I like it Here* x. 128 What about some wine? Will you have the *branco* or the *tinto*? **1978** M. WALKER *Infiltrator* iii. 35 We got to one of the Galician bars..and I ordered two *tintos*.

† **tinto** ('tɪntəʊ), *a.* and *sb.*^{2} *Obs.* [a. It. *tinto* dyed, tinted; a dye.] *adj.* Tinted; *sb.* a tint: see quots.

1686 AGLIONBY *Painting Illustr.* Explan. Terms, *Tinto*, is, when a thing is done only with one Colour, and that generally Black. **1739** ELIZ. CARTER *Algarotti on 'Newton's Theory'* (1742) I. 203 You will see Colours and half Tintos appear.

Tintometer (tɪn'tɒmɪtə(r)). [f. TINT *sb.*^{1} + -OMETER.] The proprietary name for an apparatus for the exact determination of colour: see quots., and cf. COLORIMETER.

1889 *Daily News* 9 May 5/7 Royal Society Soiree... Mr. J. W. Lovibond, of Salisbury, exhibited an instrument called the Tintometer, an invention which, by means of numberless slips of coloured glasses, measures colour blindness and differences of colour vision between the two eyes. **1893** J. W. LOVIBOND *Measurement of Light & Colour Sensations* 3 This work is a record of some investigations on light and colour carried out whilst the author was perfecting a colorimeter, which he terms 'The Tintometer'. **1895** *Westm. Gaz.* 11 Nov. 3/1 The inventor of a tintometer has told us recently that he can account for 60,000,000 shades of colour. **1898** *Allbutt's Syst. Med.* V. 433 With the tintometer..three sets of definitely graded glasses are provided. **1957** G. E. HUTCHINSON *Treat. Limnol.* I. vi. 416 Kalle (1938), in his studies of the color of the sea, has introduced a tintometer which permits the color to be expressed as a single equivalent wave length. **1966** *Trade Marks Jrnl.* 17 Aug. 1188/1 Tintometer. B856,033. Colorimeters. The Tintometer Limited... 1st November, 1963.

Hence **Tinto'metric** *a.*, of or pertaining to a tintometer; **Tin'tometry**, the use of a tintometer.

1901 *Buck's Handbk. Med. Sc.* II. 58 Dark Box for Estimating Percentage of Hæmoglobin by the Tintometric Method. **1909** *Cent. Dict. Suppl.*, Tintometry.

† **'tintregh.** *Obs.* Forms: 1 **tintreȝ, -a, tinterȝ,** 3 **tintreo, -he, tintreow.** [OE. *tintreȝ* str. neut., *tintreȝa* wk. masc. The second element is the same as in OE. *treȝa*, ON. *tregi* wk. masc., Goth. *trigo* wk. fem., grief, woe, affliction, OE. *treȝian*, ON. *trega*, OS. *tregan* to grieve, afflict. The first part is uncertain; Sievers, on metrical grounds, holds the vowel to be long, *tíntreȝa*.] Torment, torture.

c **893** K. ÆLFRED *Oros.* I. xii. §4 þonne he þara manna tintreȝo oferhierde. *c* **950** *Lindisf. Gosp.* Matt. x. 28 Ða sauel & lic-homa losiȝe *vel* fordoa in tinterȝo *vel* cursung. —— Luke xvi. 23 In helle ahof ða eȝo his miððy were in tinterȝum. *c* **1000** *Ags. Gosp.*, *ibid.*, þa he on þam tintreȝum wæs. *a* **1023** WULFSTAN *Hom.* xl. (Napier) 185 In þa ecan tintreȝu. *a* **1225** *Leg. Kath.* 41 Wið stronge tintreohen & licomliche pinen. *a* **1225** *Juliana* 18 For teone ne for tintreow þat ȝe mahen timbrin. *a* **1240** *Sawles Warde* in *Cott. Hom.* 261 Eorðliche tintreohen.

Hence † **'tintreghe** (in 2 **tintraȝen**) *v. trans.*, to torment, torture.

c **1175** *Lamb. Hom.* 13 Swa þet heo eow tintraȝed and heow iswenchet.

tint-tool: see TINT *sb.*^{1}

tinty ('tɪntɪ), *a.* [f. TINT *sb.*^{1} + -Y.] Full of tints; having the tints too prominent or inharmoniously combined. Hence **'tintiness.**

1883 *Athenæum* 2 June 705/2 The prevalence of tinty colouring, thinness of tone, and lack of solidity..is still observable among the members' works. **1886** *Ibid.* 18 Sept. 377 What painters call tintiness when they observe that the brilliancy of local tints severally affects their harmony and the tertiaries are weak.

tin-type ('tɪntaɪp). *Photogr.* Also **tintype.** [f. TIN *sb.* + TYPE.] **a.** A photograph taken as a positive on a thin tin plate: cf. FERROTYPE 2. Also *attrib.*

1864 E. W. PEARSON *Lett. from Port Royal* (1906) 243 You will probably in due course..see the tin-types of Rose and Demus. **1875** KNIGHT *Dict. Mech.* 1684/2 Ferrotypes, or tintypes, as they are sometimes called. **1889** *Anthony's Photogr. Bull.* II. 173 Having dallied with our very attractive art since the early days of tintypes. **1894** *Brit. Jrnl. Photogr.* XLI. 68 The tin-type man still continues to employ collodion.

b. Colloq. phr. (orig. *U.S.*) ***not on your tintype***, certainly not. Cf. *not on your Nelly* s.v. NELLY^{2}.

1900 ADE *Fables in Slang* 78 Oh, rats! Not on your Tintype. **1918** E. E. CUMMINGS *Let.* 11 Sept. (1969) 52 Not on your tintype; as Uncle George ecstatically would remark. **1934** C. STEAD *Seven Poor Men of Sydney* iii. 100 Does the Pope keep beggars, or the Vatican police hand out alms? Not on your tintype! But you do, Jo. **1963** P. H. JOHNSON *Night & Silence* xvii. 109 No,..she couldn't make a breakfast for three gentlemen... 'I got standards... Two gents, just about. Three, not on your tintype.' **1970** S. J. PERELMAN *Baby, It's Cold Inside* 118 Let's eschew all pious cant to the effect that it turned to ashes in my mouth. Not on your tintype—it was nectar.

Hence **'tin-typer**, a photographer who takes tin-types.

1892 STEVENSON & L. OSBOURNE *Wrecker* iii. 43 The trade of a tin-typer proved too narrow for the lad's ambition.

tin-vat to **tin-work:** see TIN *sb.* 5.

tin-worm: see TIN *sb.* 5 and TINE-WORM.

tiny ('taɪnɪ), *a.* (*sb.*) Compared **tinier, -iest.** Also 6 **tynie,** 7 **tyny, tiney, -ye,** 9 *dial.* **teeny.** [app. f. TINE *a.* and *sb.* + -Y (? after adjs. in -y).

But some would take *tiny* as a later spelling of **tiné*, assumed as the original form of *tine*: see Note to TINE *a.*]

A. *adj.* **a.** Very small, little, or slight; wee, minute.

(In early use usually, and still often, preceded by *little*.)

1598 TOFTE *Alba* (1880) 21 Yet still (me thinkes) mine Ayme, being not base, I should deserue some little tynie Grace. **1599** NASHE *Lenten Stuffe* 4 A patterne or tiny sample [*printed* tiny-sample] what my elaborate performance would bee in this case, had I a ful-sayld gale of prosperity to encourage mee. [**1656** BLOUNT *Glossogr.*, *Tiney* (a word used in Worcestershire and thereabouts, as a *little tiney*).] **1664** COTTON *Scarron.* 97 This Cupid was a little tyny, Cogging, Lying, Peevish Nynny. **1677** *Man of Sin* II. v. 93 In what part of the World are such Tiny Crustlings used For Bread? **1691** RAY *N.C. Words*, *Tiny*, puny, little: it is usually joyned with 'little' as an intensive: so they say, a little tiny thing. **1740–6** MRS. DELANY in *Life & Corr.* (1861) III. 31, I told you I was to have a tiny ball on Monday. **1812** J. WILSON *Isle of Palms* I. 63 The tiniest boat that ever sailed Upon an inland lake. **1858** LYTTON *What will he do* I. vi, On that knee she clasped her tiny hands. **1879** AGNES GIBERNE *Sun, Moon & Stars* II. i. (1880) 115 Examination with the microscope only shows tinier and yet tinier wonders of form and life. **1887** *Poor Nellie* (1888) 168 Adela had of late been one tiny bit exacting towards George.

b. ***tiny garment***, an article of clothing made for an expected baby.

1965 'E. QUEEN' *Fourth Side of Triangle* i. 12 Her 'needlework'..consisted of 'tiny garments', prepared for a lay sisterhood which aided 'unfortunate' young women. **1978** N. FREELING *Night Lords* i. 9 She..had managed to get herself pregnant..but there was no display of tiny garments.

c. ***tiny mind***: exc. when used self-deprecatingly, a term of abuse suggesting an absence of common sense. Chiefly in colloq. phr. ***out of one's tiny mind***, an emphatic form of *out of one's mind* s.v. MIND *sb.*^{1} 19 a.

1965 'W. HAGGARD' *Hard Sell* vi. 68 Why don't you use your tiny mind? **1970** K. BENTON *Sole Agent* vi. 71 We'd had a row... I was nearly out of my tiny mind. **1977** D. BEATY *Excellency* xix. 215 Everyone with the possible exception of H. E. was scared out of their tiny British minds.

B. as *sb.*

† **1.** A very small amount: = TINE *sb.*^{6} (perh. only a copyist's error for this.) *Obs. rare*$^{-1}$.

a **1650** *Lord of Learne* 272 in Furniv. *Percy Folio* I. 192 Thou hast striken the Lord of learne a litle tinye aboue the knee.

2. a. A tiny one, a very small child, an infant. Usu. in pl. ***tinies*** (cf. *grown-ups*).

1797 F. BURNEY *Jrnls. & Lett.* July (1973) III. 326 He.. hesitated before he could persuade himself to give at all to any bigger Children, if they came accompanied by tinies. **1863** 'HOLME LEE' *Annie Warleigh* II. 270 The little ones.. marshalled by the infant class mistress, and by Alice who was a clever manager amongst the very tinies. **1883** *Sword & Trowel* Jan. 37 Sure to please the growing tinies. **1883** G. MEREDITH *Love in Valley* xxii, When she was a tiny.

b. A nickname for a very large or tall man. Cf. TICH.

1931 *Literary Digest* 18 Apr. 40 A big fat guy will be called 'Babe' or 'Tiny'. **1976** *Burnham-on-Sea Gaz.* 20 Apr. 12/8 He is 6ft 7in tall and not unnaturally, is known as 'Tiny'.

tinyness, obs. form of TININESS.

tinzenite ('tɪnzənaɪt). *Min.* [ad. G. *tinzenit* (J. Jakob 1923, in *Schweiz. mineral. und petrogr. Mitteil.* III. 234), f. *Tinzen*, name of a mountain in Graubünden, Switzerland: see -ITE[1].] A basic silicate of calcium, manganese, aluminium, boron, and iron that occurs as triclinic yellow crystals and is now regarded as a member of the axinite group.

1924 *Chem. Abstr.* XVIII. 3337 Tinzenite: yellow; radial platy masses in quartz. **1968** *Amer. Mineralogist* LIII. 1409 The name 'tinzenite' must be used for those axinites with Ca $< 1{\cdot}5$ and Mn > Fe (but usually Mn ≫ Fe). At this stage it is impossible to say whether tinzenite is an independent mineralogical species or only a variety.

-tion, a compound suffix, representing, often through Fr. *-tion*, OF. *-cion*, ME. *-cio(u)n*, L. *-tio*, *-tiōn-em*, consisting of *-io*, *-ion-em* added to the *-t* of a L. participial stem, as in *rela-t-ion*, *comple-t-ion*, *frui-t-ion*, *muni-t-ion*, *protec-t-ion*, *deten-t-ion*, *op-t-ion*: see -ATION and -ION[1]. Rarer forms are *-sion*, *-xion*, as *suspen-s-ion*, *infle-x-ion*. The etymological meaning was primarily 'the state or condition of being (what the pa. pple. imports)', e.g. the condition of being *related*, *completed*, *protected*, *detained*, *suspended*, *inflected*, etc. But already in L. *-tio* was used for the action or process of *relating*, *completing*, *suspending*, etc., and also concretely or quasi-concretely, as in *dictio*, the condition of being said, the saying of something, a saying, a word; so *nātio* birth, a brood, a nation; *ōrātio* mode of speaking, an oration. In Eng. the most usual sense is that of a noun of action, equivalent to the native ending -ING[1], and having also the kindred uses mentioned under the suffix.

Tio Pepe ('tiːəʊ 'pɛpeɪ). [a. Sp., lit. 'Uncle Joe'; cf. TIA MARIA.] The proprietary name of a dry Spanish fino sherry. A glass or drink of this.

1886 *Trade Marks Jrnl.* 15 Sept. 953 *Tio Pepe*... Gonzalez, Byass, & Co.,.. London, E.C.; Wine and Spirit Merchants. **1907** *Yesterday's Shopping* (1969) 95/1 'Tio Pepe', very dry, delicate—per doz. botts...48/6. **1920** G. SAINTSBURY *Notes on Cellar-Bk.* ii. 18 Some of the finer kinds are really supernacular—the best 'Tio Pepe', for instance. **1943** G. GREENE *Ministry of Fear* II. i. 115 He.. took out a glass and a bottle of sherry... 'Tio Pepe,' Digby said. **1955** N. FITZGERALD *House is Falling* xi. 177 They had brought in a bottle of Tio Pepe to keep them company. **1968** *Official Gaz.* (U.S. Patent Office) 16 Apr. 141/2 Gonzalez Byass & Co. Limited.. *Tio Pepe*.. For Wines.. First use 1905. **1976** H. MACINNES *Agent in Place* xvii. 182 Tony ordered a Tio Pepe.

-tious, compound suffix, repr. L. *-t-iōsus*, consisting of *-iōsus*, -IOUS, appended to the *-t* of a L. participial stem. It thus serves to form adjectives belonging to sbs. in *-tion*, as in *ostentation*, *-tious*, *ambition*, *-tious*, *caution*, *-tious*, *contention*, *-tious*, *nutrition*, *-tious*, *superstition*, *-tious*; but its range is much narrower than that of *-tion*.

tip (tɪp), *sb.*[1] Forms: 5–6 **typpe, typ**, 6–7 **tippe**, 7 **tipp**; 6– **tip**. [In 15th c. *typ*, *typpe*, the former = MLG., MDu., LG., Du., EFris. *tip*, MHG. *zipf*, Da., Norw. *tip*, Sw. *tipp*, all = 'point, extreme end, very top'. Not known in OE., ON., OS., or OHG.; but perhaps cognate with *tip(p)en*, TIP *v.*[1], though the connexion of sense is not clear. The modern cognate langs. have in the same sense a derivative form:—**tippul*, MDu., Du., MLG., LG. *tippel*, MHG., Ger. *zipfel*.

(So far as is known, *tip* has no etymological connexion with *top*; but the proximity of form and relative quality of sound in the two words have caused *tip* to be felt as denoting a thinner or more delicate *top*; cf. *drip*, *drop*, *chip*, *chop*, also TIP-TOP.)]

1. a. The slender extremity or top of a thing; *esp.* the pointed or rounded end of anything long and slender; the top, summit, apex, very end.

(The earlier existence of the sb. is evidenced by the derivs. *tipping c* 1325, *tipped* or *tipt* and *tip-toe c* 1386.)

c **1440** *Promp. Parv.* 494/2 Typpe, or lappe [*MS. S.* typ or lap] of the ere, *pinnula*. *Ibid.*, Typ, of the nese. **1526** TINDALE *Luke* xvi. 24 Sende Lazarus that he maye depe the tippe off his fynger in water and cole my tonge. **1535** COVERDALE *1 Sam.* xxiv. 4 Dauid stode vp, & cut of the typpe of Sauls garment quyetly. **1568** C. WATSON *Polyb.* 68 This hill.. hauing a plain on ye very tippe, twelue miles in compasse. **1582** STANYHURST *Æneis* I. (Arb.) 21 In typs of billows soom ships wyth danger ar hanging. **1613–16** W. BROWNE *Brit. Past.* I. ii. 30 Where the Raine-bow in the Horizon Doth pitch her tips. **1634** SIR T. HERBERT *Trav.* 8 The Pole-star.. in the tip of the little Beares taile. **1753** FRANKLIN *Lett.*, etc. Wks. 1840 VI. 179 That spout.. was an inverted cone, with the tip or apex towards the sea. **1844** STEPHENS *Bk. Farm* II. 175 The tip of the horn is used by the makers of knife-handles. **1875** DARWIN *Insectiv. Pl.* xii. 280 Long narrow leaves gradually widening towards their tips. **1881** —— in *Life & Lett.* (1887) I. 98 How many and what admirably well adapted movements the tip of a root possesses.

†**b.** *fig.* Utmost point, extremity; highest point, apex, crown. *Obs.* (Cf. also TIPE *sb.*[1])

a **1225** *Ancr. R.* 338 On oðer half, moni mon abit to schriuen him uort þe nede tippe. [But this may be TIP *v.*[1] I.] **1567** HARMAN *Caveat* (1869) 20 Not one amongst twenty wyll discouer, eyther declare there scelorous secretes: yet with fayre flatteringe wordes, money, and good chere, I haue attained to the typ by such as the meanest of them hath wandred these xiii. yeares. **1581** RICH *Farewell* (Shaks. Soc.) 47 From the tippe and heeght of degnitie, you have not spared.. to become a subject of all mishaps. **1581** MULCASTER *Positions* xxxix. (1887) 220 The prince and soueraigne being the tippe of nobilitie. **1626** B. JONSON *Staple of N.* II. v, He is.. my Chiefe, the Point, Tip, Top, and Tuft of all our family.

†**c.** Old name for an anther, or summit of a stamen. Cf. APEX *sb.* 6 a. *Obs.*

1776 WITHERING *Brit. Plants* (1787) I. 133 *Polycarpon.* Allseed... Chives 3... Tips roundish. **1807** CRABBE *Par. Reg.* I. 619 Esteemed of old but tips and chives.

2. a. A small piece of metal, leather, etc., attached or fitted on to something so as to form a serviceable end; as the buckle of a girdle (*obs.*), a ferrule, the leather pad on the point of a billiard-cue, a protecting cap or plate for the toe of a shoe, etc.

c **1440** *Promp. Parv.* 494/2 Typpe, of a gyrdylle, *mordaculum*. **1545** *Rates of Customs* c viij, Typpes for hornes the C. IIII. d. **1570** LEVINS *Manip.* 140/16 Y[e] Tippe of a staffe, *ferretum*. **1801** SOUTHEY *Thalaba* VI. xvi, There hung a horn beside the gate,.. He took the ivory tip, And through the brazen-mouth he breath'd. **1840** H. MOZLEY *Let.* 11 Feb. in D. Mozley *Newman Family Lett.* (1962) III. 86 They danced very prettily, though he had 'tips'. **1873** BENNETT & CAVENDISH *Billiards* 9 About 1807 the leathern tip [of the cue] was invented. **1877** KNIGHT *Dict. Mech.*, *Tip*... 3. (*Shoemaking.*) A protecting cap at the toe end of a shoe. 4. The nozzle of a gas-burner. 5. A ferrule; as the tip of a bayonet scabbard. **1878** JEVONS *Prim. Pol. Econ.* 15 The metal iridium.. is wanted for making the tips of gold pens.

b. *Costume.* The end of a tail or fur, or of a feather, as used in trimming, etc.

1681 *Lond. Gaz.* No. 1649/8 A large Muff of Sable Tipps for a Woman. **1886** *Cassell's Encycl. Dict.*, *Tip*.. 3. *Millinery*: The end of a feather in trimming. **1904** *Daily News* 25 Mar. 7 Her hat was set at an alarming angle, and its nodding 'tips' followed her every movement.

c. *Angling.* The topmost joint of a fishing-rod.

1891 *Cent. Dict.* s.v., A tip made of split bamboo is called a quarter-section tip, and by English makers a rent and glued tip. **1895** *Outing* (U.S.) XXX. 431/1 Putting the bait tip on a ten-ounce split bamboo, I tied a spoon and a flight of swivels to the line.

d. *Hat-making.* The upper part of the crown of a hat; a stiff lining pasted in this part.

1864 WEBSTER, *Tip*,.. 5. The lining of the top of a hat;—so called among hatters. **1877** KNIGHT *Dict. Mech.*, *Tip*... A circular piece of scale or paste board pasted on the inside of a hat crown to stiffen it.

e. Used in *pl.* to denote the leaf-buds used in tea-making, preceded by an adj. or trade-name to designate a particular brand of tea.

1897 *Sears, Roebuck Catal.* 8/1 Golden tips. **1952** 'W. COOPER' *Struggles of Albert Woods* II. iv. 98 He said: 'I hope you'll like my tea.'.. 'What sort is it?'.. 'Ty-phoo tips.' **1978** *Listener* 16 Nov. 642/3 (*caption*) Come back to my pad, man, I've got some amazing PG tips.

f. Formerly, a band of (gold, etc.) paper round a cigarette at the end held by the lips; now, = FILTER *sb.* 3 c. Cf. *gold-tipped* adj. s.v. GOLD[1] 10 a.

1897 KIPLING *Captains Courageous* v. 107 Cigarettes with gold-leaf tips. **1981** *Times* 25 July 3/8 Filter cigarettes were ..assumed to be safer than those without tips.

3. A thin flat brush, made of camel's or squirrel's hair (originally the tip of a squirrel's tail) fixed between two pieces of cardboard glued together, used for laying gold-leaf, as in bookbinding; also, a piece of wood covered with flannel, similarly used.

1815 J. SMITH *Panorama Sc. & Art* II. 801 The instruments used in gilding are the following: A cushion... A knife... The tip, which consists of a squirrel's tail with the hairs cut short. It is used for taking up whole leaves of gold, and applying them to the surface to be gilt. **1837** WHITTOCK *Bk. Trades* (1842) 117 (Carver and Gilder) The brush with which the gold is applied to the work; this is called a tip, and is formed by putting a few fine hairs between two pieces of card. **1888** *Arts & Crafts Catal.* 85 Finally, the gold (gold leaf) is applied by a pad of cotton wool, or a flat thin brush called a 'tip'.

4. a. A light horse-shoe, covering only the front half of the hoof. **b.** = FOOTHOLD 2.

1831 J. HOLLAND *Manuf. Metal* I. 172 On turning horses out to grass, it is common to remove their heavy shoes, and furnish them with light ones, or tips as they are called. **1903** *U.S. Dept. of Agr., Spec. Rep. Dis. Horse* 404 A shoe, called a 'tip', is made by cutting off both branches at the center of the foot and drawing the ends down to an edge. The tapering of the branches should begin at the toe.

5. Phrases. **a.** ***from tip to toe***: from top to bottom (more usually ***from top to toe***: see TOP *sb.*). †**b.** ***in the tip of the mode***: in the height of fashion (cf. 1 b). †**c.** ***neither tip nor toe***: not a particle or trace, none at all. **d.** ***on*** (or ***at***) ***the tip of one's tongue***: on the point of being, or ready to be, spoken. So (rarely) ***at the tips of one's fingers***, ready to be performed or executed. **e.** ***arse over tip***: see ARSE *sb.* 1 b.

1610 HOLLAND *Camden's Brit.* I. 520 There is neither tippe nor toe remaining in it [Leicester] of the name Ratæ. **1709** *Brit. Apollo* II. No. 79. 2/2 She.. will always be in the Tip of the Mode. **1722** DE FOE *Moll Flanders* (1840) 184 She had arguments at the tip of her tongue. **1823** LOCKHART *Reg. Dalton* VIII. vii, Out with the word, man—it's on the tip. **1853** KANE *Grinnell Exp.* xxx. (1856) 263, I give in detail my dress... Here it is, from tip to toe. **1859** W. COLLINS *Q. of Hearts* i, All the modern accomplishments at the tips of her delicate fingers.

6. *attrib.* and *Comb.*, as ***tip-drip***, ***-eared*** adj., ***-end*** (also *fig.*: cf. 1 b); spec. in *Aeronaut.* with reference to the extremity of an aerofoil, as ***tip loss***, ***speed***, ***stall***, ***stalling***, ***tank***. **tip-foot**, a form of club-foot in which the heel is drawn up; **tip-paper**, a stiff kind of paper used for lining hat-crowns (cf. 2 d); **tip-stretcher**, an apparatus for stretching hat-crowns; **tip-touch** *v. trans.*, to touch with the tips of one's fingers; **tip-worm**, the larva of a gall-fly (*Cecidomyia vaccinii*) which infests the buds of the American cranberry (*Cent. Dict.*).

1895 MRS. PHELPS *Chapters fr. Life* vi. 116 How dainty was the *tip-drip of the icicles from the big elm-bough. **1880** *Mem. J. Legge* 258 Is man.. the derivative of tailed and *tip-eared progenitors? **1680** MOXON *Mech. Exerc.* x. 179 The *Tip-end of an Horn with its Tip downwards. **1803** FESSENDEN *Poet. Petition* 6 Discover'd worlds within the pale Of tip end of a tadpole's tail. **1885** *Century Mag.* XXIX. 190/2, I mean to flirt with him to the very tip end of my powers. **1857** DUNGLISON *Med. Lex.* s.v. *Kyllosis*, *Talipes equinus*,.. *Tip-foot. **1938** *Jrnl. R. Aeronaut. Soc.* XLII. 380 The engine r.p.m. can with advantage be increased until the tip speed of the airscrew approaches the speed of sound, at which speed there are serious *tip losses which reduce the thrust. Thin bladed metal airscrews show less tip loss due to high speed than the thicker sections. **1969** *Gloss. Aeronaut. & Astronaut. Terms* (*B.S.I.*) IV. 15 *Tip loss*, loss of lift at the tip of an aerofoil associated with the formation of tip vortices. **1877** KNIGHT *Dict. Mech.*, **Tip-paper*, a variety of paper of a rigid quality, made for lining the tips or insides of hat-crowns. **1911** R. M. PIERCE *Dict. Aviation* 231 **Tip speed*, the oscillatory speed of the tip of a reciprocating wing; the up-and-down velocity of a wing-tip in flapping flight. **1925** *Flight* 22 Oct. 686/2 (*caption*) The 'Autogiro'... Note how the high tip speed of the windmill beat our photographer. **1969** *Gloss. Aeronaut. & Astronaut. Terms* (*B.S.I.*) V. 20 *Tip speed*, the mean angular velocity of the rotor multiplied by the rotor radius. **1946** *Jrnl. Brit. Interplanetary Soc.* VI. 95 The phenomenon of *tip stall is brought about by spanwise drift in the boundary layer over a swept wing. **1937** *Jrnl. R. Aeronaut. Soc.* XLI. 205, I consider wing tip slots as the most efficient means known at present to prevent *tip stalling of highly tapered wings. **1877** KNIGHT *Dict. Mech.*, s.v., Eickemeyer's power *tip-stretcher is shown in Fig. 6470. **1952** *Wall St. Jrnl.* 15 Apr. 5 First conceived in 1938, *tiptanks became standard as auxiliary fuel containers for the early-day F-80 jet fighters. **1977** *R.A.F. Yearbk.* 11/1 Max range with tip tanks, 900 mls ..at 35,000 ft. **1922** JOYCE *Ulysses* 523 Must I *tiptouch it with my nails? **1956** H. GOLD *Man who was not with It* (1965) i. 6 Tricksie with her pretty little hand tip-touching the black-and-blue spot.

tip, *sb.*[2] Also 5 **tippe**. [app. f. TIP *v.*[1]] An act of tipping, a light but distinct impact, blow, stroke, or hit; a noiseless tap; a significant touch. †***tip for tap*** = tit for tat: see TIT *sb.*[2], and cf. *tap for tap* in quot. 1597 s.v. TAP *sb.*[2] I. ***foul tip*** (Baseball), a foul hit in which the ball is only grazed: cf. FOUL *a.* 14.

a **1466** CHAS. DK. ORLEANS *Poems* (Roxb.) 7 Strokis grete, not tippe nor tapp. **1575** GASCOIGNE *Adv. F. I.* Wks. II. 249 Much greater is the wrong that rewardeth euill for good, than that which requiteth [*pr.* requireth] tip for tap. **1577** tr. *Bullinger's Decades* (1592) 154 Not to bragge of any thing ouer arrogantly, not to answere tip for tap [L. *non responsare*]. **1608** WILLET *Hexapla Exod.* 488 He that abused his parents.., that gaue them but a tip, or a reuiling word. *a* **1825** FORBY *Voc. E. Anglia*, *Tip*,.. a smart but light blow. **1844** STEPHENS *Bk. Farm* II. 695 A smart tip of the whip will take the courage out of him. **1889** *Century Mag.* Oct. 837/1 Wont to wear a small piece of rubber in the mouth as a protection to the teeth from foul tips.

tip, *sb.*[3] [f. TIP *v.*[4] sense 2 (which occurs *c* 1700).]

a. A small present of money given to an inferior, esp. to a servant or employee of another for a service rendered or expected; a gratuity, a douceur: see TIP *v.*[4] 2. Also, a present of money given to a schoolboy by an older person.

1755 J. BAREBONES in *Connoisseur* No. 70. 417, I assure you I have laid out every farthing.. in tips to his servants. *c* **1810** W. HICKEY *Mem.* (1960) ii. 38, I secured a handsome tip, the Westminster phrase for a present of cash. **1812** J. H. VAUX *Flash Dict.* s.v., To *take the tip*, is to receive a bribe in any shape; and they say of a person who is known to be corruptible, that he will *stand the tip*. **1818** *Sporting Mag.* II. 165 A handsome tip was demanded at the gate. **1825** T. HOOK *Sayings* Ser. II. *Doubts & F.* i, Sir Harry was liberal in his 'tips', and consequently a great favourite of Phillips [the waiter]. **1855** THACKERAY *Newcomes* xvi, What money is better bestowed than that of a schoolboy's tip? **1877** BLACK *Green Past.* xxx, Two sovereigns was the least tip to be slipped into the hands of the custom-house officer. *Mod.* The porter will expect a tip.

b. *attrib.* and *Comb.*

1813 *Sporting Mag.* XLI. 106 The tip-money, or usual fee to the purchaser's coachman, upon the sale of horses. **1899**

MORROW *Bohem. Paris* 149 After the bill is paid, the tip-box is supposed to receive two sous for Marie and Augustine.

tip, *sb.*[4] *colloq.* or *slang.* [perh. from TIP *v.*[1], with the notion of tipping or lightly touching the arm or elbow of a person by way of a private hint, or from TIP *v.*[4] in the phrase *to tip* (any one) *a wink*.]

a. A piece of useful private or special information communicated by an expert; a friendly hint; *spec.* 'an advice concerning betting or a Stock-Exchange speculation intended to benefit the recipient' (Farmer *Slang*); also, a hint as to special points thought likely to come up in an examination; hence *transf.* a special device, 'wrinkle', 'dodge'.

The simple word was prob. in use before 1845.

1845 *Athenæum* Oct. 964/2 Xenophon's Expedition of Cyrus, Books i. ii. iii. Translated literally... Of such books as this ('tip-books' as school-boys call them,)..we doubt the value. **1865** *Daily Tel.* 4 Dec. 4/4 Dejected prophets who have never yet made a single lucky political 'tip'. **1867** F. FRANCIS *Angling* i. (1880) 44 A tip from a good man on the spot is most useful. **1868** *Morning Star* 10 Mar., The evil of cramming and of 'tips' will be increased by the new scheme, instead of being diminished. **1886** *Q. Rev.* July 175 To keep the Foreign Office promptly supplied with every commercial 'tip' that can be of use to British trade. **1888** ANNIE S. SWAN *Doris Cheyne* i, My father was a stockbroker, and he taught me all the tips he knew. **1899** T. M. ELLIS *Three Cat's-eye Rings* 21 Offering her good tips for sporting events. *Mod.* A successful crammer, clever at giving 'tips' for an examination.

b. ***the straight tip***: see quots.

1871 *Punch* 26 Aug. 78/2 Honest advice as to wagering will henceforth be known as the straight tip. **1873** *Slang Dict.* s.v., The 'straight tip' is the tip which comes direct from the owner or trainer of a horse. Of late years a 'straight tip' means a direct hint on any subject. **1879** MISS BRADDON *Clov. Foot* xxxviii, That's a kind of thing we never tell. We got the straight tip; that's all you need know. **1894** DOYLE *S. Holmes* 7 Let me have the straight tip and you won't be a loser.

c. *transf.* Something with respect to which a 'tip' is given; e.g. the probable winner in a race.

1873 BESANT & RICE *Little Girl* II. xxiii, He had on some ..occasions taken a long shot, backed a tip or a fancy. **1886** *St. Stephen's Rev.* 13 Mar. 11/2 Florin [racehorse], who was a great tip, performed most moderately.

d. ***to miss one's tip***: orig. in circus slang (see quot. 1897); hence, to fail in one's aim or object.

1847 *Punch* 9 Oct. 138/1 You attack him for making himself conspicuous at the sale of Shakspeare's house. You seem to think he has missed his tip. **1854** DICKENS *Hard T.* I. vi, Jupe [a circus clown] has missed his tip very often, lately... Was short in his leaps and bad in his tumbling... In a general way that's missing his tip. **1857** HUGHES *Tom Brown* I. iv, One..runs right at the leaders, as though he'd ketch 'em by the heads, only luck'ly for him he misses his tip, and comes over a heap o' stones first. **1887** W. WESTALL *Two Millions* xx. I. 175 One of those fellows who have missed their tip somehow, and come down in life. **1897** BARRÈRE & LELAND *Dict. Slang*, *To miss the tip*, (circus),..in exhibitions it has a special application to the performer not understanding or catching the tip or word which indicates that he must act.

e. *Comb.*, as ***tip-book***, ***-sheet*** (orig. *U.S.*), ***-slinger*** (*Austral. slang*).

1845 Tip book [see sense a above]. **1945** *Sun* (Baltimore) 21 Feb. 12 (*caption*) Tip sheet. **1955** *Sci. News Let.* 20 Aug. 126/3 Tip sheets may feature an electrocardiogram of the long-shot horse's heart before long. **1972** *Daily Tel.* 14 Nov. 18 A tip sheet on ways of fitting in smoothly in America has been handed to the 1,000 Asian refugees accepted by the United States. **1983** *Times* 11 Nov. 16/6 A and C Black.. enjoyed the day's most spectacular gain—up 58p to 321p on a tip-sheet comment. **1926** 'J. DOONE' *Timely Tips for New Australians* 24 *Tipslinger*, the slang term for race-course tipster. **1934** *Bulletin* (Sydney) 15 Aug. 49/1 By their conversation most of them were tipslingers or urgers.

tip, *sb.*[5] [f. TIP *v.*[2], esp. senses 1 b, 2, 3.]

I. *Skittles.* (Cf. TIP *v.*[2] 1 b.)

†**1.** The knocking over of a pin by another which falls or rolls against it, as distinct from knocking one down by the immediate impact of the bowl. In some forms of the game applied also to other modes of knocking down, distinct from bowling.

1673 [R. LEIGH] *Transp. Reh.* 54 Down they [nine-pins] all come at a tip and throw. **1694** S. JOHNSON *Notes Past. Let. Bp. Burnet* I. 39 That is a cleaverer Tip..than taking out the Middle Pin, and throwing down none of the rest. **1773** A. JONES (*title*) The Art of Playing at Skittles... Shewing Both the Old and the New Methods of forming General Goes and Tips. *Ibid.* 20 The greatest go that can be had is 40, or 20 at the bowl and the same at the tip; the least go must be 1.

(*b*) **1801** STRUTT *Sports & Past.* III. vii. §10 Dutch-pins. The player first stands at a certain distance from the frame, and throws his bowl at the pins..; afterwards he approaches the frame and makes his tipp by casting the bowl among the pins. **1819** *Pantologia* X. s.v. *Skittles*, The bowler must stand to take his tip with one foot upon the spot where the bowl stopped.

II. The act of tilting and derived uses.

2. An act of tipping up or tilting, or the fact of being tilted; inclination. (Cf. TIP *v.*[2] 2.)

1849 CUPPLES *Green Hand* viii. (1856) 72 Back again it [a shark] came..towards us, till it sank with a light tip, and a circle or two on the blue water. **1862** GROVE *Corr. Phys. Forces* (ed. 4) 138 The 'tip', or the raising of the weight, is performed by the electrical repulsion and attraction. *Mod.* Give the cask a slight tip.

3. A place or erection where wagons or trucks of coal, etc. are tipped and their contents discharged into the hold of a vessel, or into a cart, etc. **b.** A wagon or truck from which coal, etc. is tipped; short for *tip-cart*, *tip-car* (*Cent. Dict.*). (Cf. TIP *v.*[2] 3.)

1862 *Castlemaine* (Australia) *Daily News* 2 July, A young man..met with an accident whilst working the 'tip' at the railway embankment, behind Bruce's Foundry. **1885** SIR J. PEARSON in *Law Times Rep.* LII. 546/1 There is a spring.. close to the bottom of the tip as it at present stands. **1889** *Daily News* 19 July 2/8 There were seventeen fixed tips in the dock..for coal loading, and foundations had been laid for two more tips. **1891** *Labour Commission* Gloss., *Tip*, a lofty erection of wood and iron placed upon the quay wall at the side of the deck, and under which ships are placed to receive their cargoes of coal... *Tips*[1], screens or other arrangements upon which the mineral is upset from the tub or tram and conveyed into a waggon, cart, or boat. *Tips*[2], 'staiths' or other erections with shoots into which the coal is emptied from waggons and then shot or tipped into the hold of the vessel. **1904** A. GRIFFITHS *50 Years Public Service* xii. 169 Long rows of trucks..were hauled up by steam power and run on to the 'tips'.

4. a. The mound or mass of rubbish, etc. that is tipped. **b.** A place or receptacle into which earth or rubbish is tipped or shot; a dumping-ground.

1863 SIMMONDS *Dict. Trade*, *Tip*,..the rubbish thrown from a quarry. **1890** *Lancet* 14 June 1311/2 Near to the affected dwellings is the town 'tip' for refuse. **1901** *Daily News* 5 Jan. 6/5 From the temporary termination of the Goldsworth tip to the western side of Brookwood station the work is as yet one of preparation only. **1910** *Times* 18 Jan. 3/1 The defendant corporation had the use of the tip, and their carts were..crossing the field..to the tip.

5. *Comb.*: see TIP- *in comb.*

†**tip**, *sb.*[6] *slang. Obs.* [Perh. from TIP *v.*[2] sense 4 or 5; but possibly shortened from TIPPLE *sb.*] Intoxicating liquor; a draught of liquor. Also in comb. **tip-merry** *a.*, merry with liquor, slightly intoxicated.

1612 *Burford Reg.* in *Hist. MSS. Comm.*, *Var. Collect.* I. 85 [One man is described as unfit to keep an alehouse] because he will be tipmerrie himself. *a* **1700** B. E. *Dict. Cant. Crew* s.v. *Bub*, *Rum-bub*, c. very good Tip [in **1725** *New Cant. Dict.*, '*Tipple*']. *Ibid.* s.v., *A Tub of good Tip*, (for Tipple) a Cask of strong Drink. **1717** RAMSAY *Elegy on Lucky Wood* vi, (*Sc.*) She ne'er..kept dow'd tip within her waws. **1738** SWIFT *Pol. Conversat.* 144 *Miss* (with a Glass in her Hand). Hold your Tongue, Mr. Neverout, don't speak in my Tip.

tip, *v.*[1] Forms: 6 tippe, 7- tip. *Pa. t.* and *pple.* **tipped, tipt.** [ME. (?) and 16th c. *tippe* agrees in form and sense with Du., LG., mod.Ger. *tippen*, Sw. *tippa* to strike, poke or touch smartly or lightly; of obscure origin, but perhaps from the same Teut. root as TIP *sb.*[1], q.v. Of this TIP *sb.*[2] is app. a derivative. It is not certain that senses 2 and 3 belong to the same word; sense 2 might be directly from *tiptoe*; but cf. ON. *tifa-sk* 'to move the feet quickly, to trip', which Falk and Torp incline to refer to the same root.]

1. a. *trans.* To strike or hit smartly but lightly; to give a slight blow, knock, or touch to; to tap noiselessly.

[Quot. *a* 1225, in TIP *sb.*[1] 1 b, may perh. belong here with the sense 'until the need or necessity strikes or hits'.]

1567 GOLDING *Ovid's Met.* v. 57 b, One Cromis tipped of his head [v. Fab. i. 104 Huic Cromis..Decutit ense caput.]: his head cut off streight way Vpon the Altar fell. **1579** GOSSON *Apol. Sch. Abuse* (Arb.) 64 Libels, which are but clay, and rattle on mine armour, or tippe me on the shinnes. *a* **1607** J. RAYNOLDS *Proph. Haggai* x. (1649) 114 To keep them [their sheep] in by threatning them, and a little tipping them. **1708** *Reply to Bickerstaff Detected* in *Swift's Wks.* (1755) II. I. 166 A third rogue tips me by the elbow, and wonders, how I have the conscience [etc.]. **1840** THACKERAY *Bedford-Row Conspir.* ii, [He] felt himself suddenly tipped on the shoulder.

b. *Cricket.* To hit (a ball) lightly. Also *spec.*, to glance or touch with the edge of the bat.

1816 W. LAMBERT *Cricketer's Guide* (ed. 3) iii. 43 It is..to such [balls] as are just tipped with the edge of the Bat..that he [*sc.* long-stop] will have to attend. **1851** J. PYCROFT *Cricket Field* x. 185 Put in two batsmen..to tip and run. **1858** 'G. FORREST' *Playground* ix. 132 If you only tip the [fast] ball, it will go far enough without giving you the trouble of striking it.

(*b*) ***tip-and-run***, cricket in which the batsman must run for every hit; also *transf.* in *attrib.* use, esp. to designate short, sudden attacks in war.

1891 GRACE *Cricket* viii. 236 S. M. J. Woods and G. McGregor..almost played tip-and-run for a few overs. **1918** *Chambers's Jrnl.* June 477/2 Any dark night might see one of the enemy's favourite 'tip-and-run' dashes to sea. **1927** *Rep. Commissioner Police Metropolis 1926* 16 Stolen cars are used in..'tip and run' raids on jewellers' shops. **1942** *R.A.F. Jrnl.* 13 June 26 The Italians, with their half-hearted enthusiasm and their 'tip-and-run' type of bombing. **1946** J. W. DAY *Harvest Adventure* xvi. 273 At Mersea Island..we exposed the Committee's folly in placing a machinery dump within a hundred yards of the sea and tip-and-run raiders.

c. *U.S. Sport.* To hit (a ball, puck, etc.) into the net or goal with a light touch or push. Freq. const. *in*(*to*).

1958 G. F. PINHOLSTER *Encycl. Basketball* ix. 111 The player with the best position tries to tip in the goal as the other two players block for him. **1963** F. A. LINDEBORG *How to play and teach Basketball* vi. 131 The tip-in shot is used when a player has the opportunity to tip an offensive rebound up into the air again and into the basket... The shooter times his jump so that he is able to tip the ball with the fingers of his right hand. **1968** [see RAP *v.*[1] 2 a].

2. *intr.* To step lightly; to trip; to walk mincingly, or on tiptoe; also *fig.*

1819 *Blackw. Mag.* V. 401/2 The shortened notes more trip-somely tipped over than in the modern airs. **1881** L. B. WALFORD *Dick Netherby* v. 49 The sicht o' her..tippin' up to her chair..garred me lauch sae. **1890** *Harper's Mag.* Aug. 390/2 He stopped breathlessly, and then tipped on cautiously, keeping the encircling line of bushes between him and the carriage.

3. *Mus.* (See TIPPING *vbl. sb.*[3] b.)

4. 'To toss, as carded hair, so that it will fall in tufts' (*Funk's Stand. Dict.* 1895): see TIPPING *vbl. sb.*[3] c.

tip, *v.*[2] Forms: α. 4-7 **type**, 5-6, 9 *dial.* **tipe** (taɪp); *infl.* 5 **tipen**, 6 **typed.** β. 6- **tip**; *infl.* 7 **tippeth, tipt**, 7-8 **tip'd**, 7- **tipped**, 8 **tipp'd**; 7-9 **tipping.** [Origin and form-history obscure: known first in form *tȳpe* (14th c.), *tīpe*, in literary use as late as 1632 (sense 8), and still dialectal from Cumbria to Shropsh. and E. Anglia. *Tip* with short vowel appears in 1581 (sense 7).

The ME. verb may have been *tīpe*, *tipte*, *tipt* (cf. *keep*, *kept*, *kept*), and the short *i* of the past have been later taken over into the present (perh. under the influence of TIP *v.*[1], though not necessarily so).]

I. Transitive senses.

1. a. To overthrow, knock, or cast down, cause to fall or tumble; to overturn, upset; to throw down (off a support, out of a vehicle, etc.) by effort or accidentally.

α. **13..** *E.E. Allit. P.* C. 506, & if I..type doun 3onder toun when hit turned were. *a* **1400-50** *Alexander* 1303 (Dubl. MS.) Sone þe toppe of þe toure he typys [*Ashmole MS.* tiltis] in þe water. *Ibid.* 1418 Som..Typed torrettes doune, towres on hepes. **1530** PALSGR. 758/2, I type over, I over-throwe, or overwhelme, *je renuerse*. **1570** LEVINS *Manip.* 141/47 To Type a ball, *profligere*. **1862** C. C. ROBINSON *Leeds Gloss.* 442 Type that box off o' that cart. **1887** *South Chesh. Gloss.* s.v., Nai, sey as yo dunna tipe that can o'er wi' yur foot. **1904** in *Eng. Dial. Dict.* s.v.

β. [**1567** in TIP *v.*[1] 1 may possibly belong here.]

a **1680** BUTLER *Rem.*, *Panegyric on Sir J. Denham* 26 No China Cupboard rudely overthrown; Nor Lady tip'd, by being accosted, down. *a* **1715** BURNET *Own Time* an. 1677 (1823) II. 107 Here would be a precedent to tip down so many lords at a time. **1741** RICHARDSON *Pamela* (1824) I. 77 They..tipped me into the dam, crying, Lie there, parson, till tomorrow! **1791** 'G. GAMBADO' *Ann. Horsem.* ix. (1809) 106, I tipp'd my nag over a broken place in the wall. **1869** TOZER *Highl. Turkey* II. 268 [She] tipped the pot over. **1880** MARY FITZGIBBON *Trip to Manitoba* xii. 138 A wonder we were not tipped over the horse's back. **1894** *Outing* (U.S.) XXIV. 190/1 It would be far from the truth to state that a canoe cannot be upset. Under certain conditions it is easier tipped than a boat. **1909** *Nation* 6 Mar. 851/2 Caricatures of fat Jews tipped out of motor cars.

b. *Skittles.* †(*a*) In the older game, said of a pin: To knock down another by falling or rolling against it, as distinguished from the direct action of the bowl. *Obs.* (*b*) In some forms of the game, applied to other modes of knocking down a pin.

1679 A. LOVELL *Judic. Univ.* 237, I have carried four and tipped six Pins. **1773** A. JONES *Art Skittle Playing* 16 The next in height and value [to the king or middle pin] were the four corner pins..these were called Dukes, Lords, and Nobles... These four counted for three each when tipped by the King or his consequents, but if by the bowl or any other from it, either of their own height or lower, they only counted for two each. The remaining four were called Common,..and counted for two each when tipped by the King, but by any other only one each. **1884** *Sat. Rev.* 18 Oct. 494/2 The skill was to hit over the King, and make him 'tip' as many pins as possible over with him, as thus the greatest number of points was scored.

(*b*) **17..** *Rules & Instr. for playing at Skittles* (*Sat. Rev.* 18 Oct. 1884, 498/2), Care should be taken in Tipping not to jump into the Frame immediately after, as in this case he is not allowed any of the Pins he Tips. **1785** GROSE *Dict. Vulg. T.* s.v., Tipping, at these games, is slightly touching the tops of the pins with the bowl. **1801** STRUTT *Sports & Past.* III. vii. §9 In playing at skittles, there is a double exertion; one by bowling, and the other by tipping: the first is performed at a given distance, and the second standing close to the frame upon which the pins are placed, and throwing the ball through the midst of them. **1819** *Pantologia* X. s.v. *Skittles*, When the learner is to tip for four upon game, he should choose the eighth, seventh, sixth, and fourth pins.

2. a. To cause to assume a slanting or sloping position; to raise, push, or move into such a position; to incline, tilt. Often with *up*.

1624 HEYWOOD *Gunaik.* v. 233 Shee tipped up the table and flung down all that was upon it. **1840** R. H. DANA *Bef. Mast.* vii. 16 We hove in upon our chain, and..tipped our anchor, and stood out to sea. **1856** EMERSON *Eng. Traits*, *Voy. Eng.*, I waked..with the belief that some one was tipping up my berth. **1868** LOCKYER *Guillemin's Heavens* (ed. 3) 479 How much the south pole will be tipped up—how the axis will exactly lie. **1894** CROCKETT *Raiders* 55 May Mischief seemed to incline her ear, tipping it a little to the side to listen.

b. ***to tip the scales***: to tilt or depress the scale of a balance by excess of weight; to turn the scale; also *fig.* Similarly ***to tip the balance, the beam.***

1884 *Harper's Mag.* June 111/2 Single fish often tipping the scales at from five to seven pounds. **1893** *St. Louis Globe-Democrat* Oct., She tips the scales at 150 pounds. **1895** FUNK *Stand. Dict.*, To tip the beam. **1927** *Observer* 11 Dec. 13/3 The view which will tip the beam is that of a member who said [etc.]. **1956** *People* 13 May 8/8 In an effort to tip the balance, New Zealand began to take British shopgirls and hairdressers. **1972** *Times* 20 Oct. 8/7 This might be the beginning of a process where the balance might be 'tipped' from predominantly white to predominantly black.

c. ***to tip one's hand(s)*** (or ***mitt***): to disclose one's intentions inadvertently. *slang* (orig. and chiefly *U.S.*).

1917 G. ADE *Let.* 8 July (1973) 67 For a time in the play it should appear that the plans of the smooth citizen are working out perfectly. He becomes confident and over reaches himself, 'tips his hands', so to speak. **1930** *Sat. Even. Post* 28 June 162/2 They've tipped their mitt. That guy's probably got a rod under his coat. **1938** *New Republic* 26 Oct. 331/1 That would be tipping her mitt too much. **1966** M. WOODHOUSE *Tree Frog* xviii. 133 We couldn't very well oppose it without tipping our hand. **1979** *Economist* 17 Nov. 122/2 Mr Hunt will not tip his hand on the price at which he will buy more bullion.

d. *Bookbinding.* ***to tip in***, to attach a single leaf, often an illustration, to the neighbouring leaf of a book by a thin line of paste down its inner margin.

1926 S. UNWIN *Truth about Publishing* v. 131 Should an extra page..be needed, it may have to be separately printed and specially 'tipped' or 'pasted in' as a frontispiece often is. **1949** MELCHER & LARRICK *Printing & Promotion Handbk.* 289/2 The leaf to be tipped in is first given a narrow coating of paste along its inner edge. **1966** H. WILLIAMSON *Methods Bk. Design* (ed. 2) xix. 322 So far as placing the plates appropriately in the text is concerned, the best method is to tip them into the section. **1978** W. WHITE in W. Whitman *Daybks. & Notebks.* III. 724 Tipped in here is a clipping from a magazine, with a notation in the margin in WW's hand.

3. To empty out (a wagon, cart, truck, or the like, or its contents) by tilting it up; to dump.

1838 *Civil Eng. & Arch. Jrnl.* I. 354/1 On this stage the waggons are run, and the contents tipped with great rapidity. **1842** *Ibid.* V. 85/2 The sub-contractor..had..to keep the road in repair, and tip or turn the dirt. **1895** *Law Times Rep.* LXXIII. 157/1 The Holyhead breakwater..was constructed by tipping into the harbour some 6,000,000 tons of large stones. **1910** *Times* 18 Jan. 3/1 A piece of land which was used for the purpose of tipping rubbish.

†**4.** *fig.* (from 2). To render unsteady, make drunk, intoxicate. *slang. Obs.* (Cf. TIP *sb.*[6])

1605 [see TIP *v.*[3]]. **1633** MARMION *Antiquary* IV. i, Your master is almost tipt already. **1708** [see TIPPED *ppl. a.*[2]].

5. To drink off, 'toss off'. *slang* and *dial.*

a **1700** B. E. *Dict. Cant. Crew, Tip it all off*, Drink it all off at a Draught. *c* **1765** FLLOYD *Tartarian T.* (1785) 46/2 A large glassful, which I tipped off. **1784** R. BAGE *Barham Downs* II. 49 As good claret as ever was tip'd. **1850** P. CROOK *War of Hats* 47 Who tip sly drams, while feigning to cry 'Sweep'. **1878** *Cumberland Gloss.* s.v., Tipe 't up, man, we've plenty mair.

6. To dispose of or kill (a person). Also *fig.* Cf. sense 10 and *to bump off s.v.* BUMP *v.*[1] 1 c. *slang.*

1920 W. CAMP *Football without Coach* vii. 129 Time after time methods such as these have 'tipped off' keen football players and have spelled the failure of good plays. **1928** *Evening News* 18 Aug. 11/5 Jake's sort o' done me a good turn, getting himself tipped off.

II. Intransitive senses.

†**7.** To be overthrown, to fall. *Obs.* (exc. as in 8).

c **1400** *Death & Life* 194 in *Percy Folio* III. 64 Trees tremble for feare, and tipen to the ground. **1581** A. HALL *Iliad* VIII. 142 He thrild them through with deadly wounds, they down to ground do tip.

8. To fall by overbalancing; to be overturned or upset; to tumble or topple over.

α. **1530** PALSGR. 758/2 His carte typed over [*se renuersa*] agaynst a banke. **1632** SANDERSON *Serm.* 558 When they are ready, with catching at babies in the water, to type over. *a* **1825** FORBY *Voc. E. Anglia, Tipe*, to kick up or fall headlong, from being top-heavy. **1904** in *Eng. Dial. Dict.* s.v.

β. **1620** SANDERSON *Serm.* I. 161 Like a ship all sail and no ballast, that tippeth over with every blast. **1890** W. A. WALLACE *Only a Sister* 325 Over tips table, candle, and cloth and all.

9. To assume a slanting or sloping position; to incline, tilt; e.g. of a balance; now *esp.* of a cart, a plank, etc. (usu. with *up*), to tilt up at one end and down at the other so that anything supported by it is (or may be) thrown off or emptied out.

1666 BUNYAN *Grace Ab.* §175 Still my life hung in doubt before me, not knowing which way I should tip. **1807** VANCOUVER *Agric. Devon* (1813) 125 They are made to tip like tumbrils. **1849** ALB. SMITH *Pottleton Leg.* xxxi, His dog-cart..tipped back last year..and lifted the horse in the air. **1864** BOWEN *Logic* ix. (1870) 301 Perhaps I do not know how the table tips. **1885** *Law Times* LXXVIII. 391/2 As the cart was being unloaded, it unfortunately tipped up, and one of the heavy flagstones fell.

10. ***to tip off***, also simply ***to tip***, or ***tip (over) the perch***: to die. *slang* or *dial.*

β. *a* **1700** B. E. *Dict. Cant. Crew, To Tip off*, to Dye. **1727** GAY *Begg. Op.* III. i, If that great man should tip off, 'twould be an irreparable loss. **1735** SAVAGE *Progr. Divine* 294 She, with broken heart, Tips off—poor soul! **1737** [see PERCH *sb.*[2] 3 e]. **1808** BENTHAM *Mem. & Corr.* Wks. 1843 X. 444 What if you should happen to tip the perch before all the children are grown up?

α. **1828** *Craven Gloss., Tipe*, 'to tipe our', to fall down, to swoon. 'To tipe off', to die. **1904** in *Eng. Dial. Dict.*

tip, *v.*[3] Pa. t. and pple. **tipped, tipt** ('tɪpɪd, tɪpt). Forms: 5–6 **typpe**, 7– **tip**. *Pa. t.* 5 **typpud**, 5– **tipped**, 7– **tipt** (6 **typte**, 7 **tip'd**). [f. TIP *sb.*[1] But perhaps partly representing ON. *typpa* (Norw. *typpa*) to tip or top, and ON. *typptr* (Norw. *typpt*), tipped, topped.]

trans. To furnish with a tip; to put a tip on, or put something on at the tip (const. *with*); to form the tip of, or adorn at the tip.

1483 *Cath. Angl.* 389/1 To typpe, *cornutare*. **1530** PALSGR. 758/2, I typpe a staffe with yron, *je armoye*. **1605** CAMDEN *Rem.* (1637) 414 He that did tip stone iugges about the brimme, Met with a blacke pot, and that pot tip'd him. **1718** POPE *Iliad* VII. 501 Arose the golden chariot of the day, And tipp'd the mountains with a purple ray. **1728** —— *Dunc.* I. 142 [162] Quarto's, octavo's, shape the less'ning pyre; And last, a little Ajax tips the spire. **1821** CLARE *Vill. Minstr.* II. 37 The faint sun tipt the rising ground. **1866** ROGERS *Agric. & Prices* I. xix. 471 Steel..to tip the shares and ploughshoes. **1897** FLANDRAU *Harvard Episodes* 104 Two brilliant spots of pink tipped his high cheek-bones.

b. Most freq. in pa. pple. (See also TIPPED *ppl. a.*[1] 2.)

c **1386** CHAUCER *Sompn. T.* 32 His felawe hadde a staf tipped [*v.r.* typped] with horn. *c* **1400** *Laud Troy Bk.* 6968 A stalworth spere..With stelen hed that wel was tipped. **14..** *Tundale's Vis.* 870 His snowte was with irne typped. **1555** EDEN *Decades* 21 Arrowes typte with bones. **1610** HOLLAND *Camden's Brit.* (1637) 254 Their Hunters horne..tipt with silver. **1667** MILTON *P.L.* VI. 580 In his hand a Reed Stood waving, tipt with fire. **1776** WITHERING *Brit. Plants* (1796) II. 342 Flowers..white tipped with green. *Ibid.* III. 284 Scales..fringed, tipt and edged with black. **1821** JOANNA BAILLIE *Metr. Leg., Lady G. B.* 27 With ink-stain tipt. **1905** *United Free Ch. Mag.* Feb. 8 The first arrow was tipped with stone of the neolithic age, and the next..with electric telegraph wire, a theft from the twentieth century.

c. *fig.*

1577 NORTHBROOKE *Dicing* (1843) 17 Their venomous tongs (typped with the mettal of infamy and slander). **1607** BEAUMONT *Woman-Hater* IV. ii, Sir, enter when you please, and all good language tip your tongue. **1635** SIBBES *Soul's Confl.* ii. (1638) 18 Doth not Satan tippe the tongues of the enemies of religion now, to insult over the Church? **1735** WEST *Let.* in *Gray's Poems* (1775) 6 The very thought, you see, tips my pen with poetry. **1860** READE *Cloister & H.* lii, An intelligent smile tipped with pity.

tip, *v.*[4] [Orig. Rogues' Cant, of obscure origin. (Possibly related to TIP *v.*[1], through the notion of touching lightly, but this is very uncertain.)]

1. *trans.* (*Rogues' Cant*, and *slang*.) To give; to hand, pass; to let one have; to put on, present, or exhibit the character of: usually with dative of person. **a.** in various connexions and shades of meaning; sometimes little more than 'do'.

1610 ROWLANDS *Martin Mark-all* Eij, Tip me that Cheate, Giue me that thing. **1676** COLES *Dict.*, *Tip the cole to Adam Tiler*, give the (stoln) money to your (running) Comrade. *a* **1700** B. E. *Dict. Cant. Crew, Tip*, to give or lend. **1712** STEELE *Spect.* No. 324 ¶1 Some are celebrated for a happy Dexterity in tipping the Lion upon them; which is performed by squeezing the Nose flat to the Face, and boring out the Eyes with their Fingers. **1742** FIELDING *Jos. Andrews* II. xvii, You must not tip us the traveller; it won't go here. *a* **1743** LD. HERVEY *Mem. Geo. II*, I. 408 The King tipped Horace the 'puppy' once or twice. **1763** *Brit. Mag.* IV. 372 Frank, tip us a chaunt; which he did. **1779** MME. D'ARBLAY *Diary* 28 May, I think you should tip the doctor the same compliment. **1798** WOLCOTT (P. Pindar) *Tales of the Hoy* Wks. 1812 IV. 409 My Lord Carlisle can tip ye a hundred rhymes in half an hour. *a* **1825** LD. TAMWORTH *Let. to Parr* Parr's Wks. 1828 VII. 29 My wife has said she means to tip that excellent fellow a visit in the Autumn. **1842** MRS. GORE *Fascin.* 15 'Tip us your fist, old boy!' cried he. **1884** PAE *Eustace* 129 'Tip me your fin, my heart of oak', said Joe. **1904** HICHENS *Woman w. Fan* ix, You've only got to tip her a note of thanks.

b. With a coin or sum of money as obj. (Hence sense 2, in which the person, here the indirect or dative, becomes the direct obj.) Also with *up* and *absol.*

1610 ROWLANDS *Martin Mark-all* E iv, Tip a make ben Roome Coue, Giue a halfepeny good Gentlemen. **1673** R. HEAD *Canting Acad.* 13 Tip him no Cole, give him no Money. **1719** D'URFEY *Pills* VI. 143 You will tip me a Guinea. **1829** P. EGAN *Boxiana* 2nd Ser. II. 13, I shall expect, before we part, that you will tip up my half of the prize. **1851** MAYHEW *Lond. Labour* I. 325/2 If I could tip up the 5*s*. the day after I'd paid the last week's 1*s*., I must [etc.]. **1884** PAE *Eustace* 33 Come, tip me a shilling.

absol. **1848** THACKERAY *Van. Fair* xiii, I am quite out of cash until my father tips up. **1965** *Sunday Times* (Colour Suppl.) 7 Nov. 41/2 For t'first two year she tipped up, she give me her wage packet and I give her her spending money.

2. *colloq.* (orig. *slang*). **a.** To give a gratuity to; to bestow a small present of money upon (an inferior), esp. upon a servant or employee of another, nominally in return for a service rendered or in order to obtain an extra service; also upon a child or schoolboy. Const. *with.*

1706–7 FARQUHAR *Beaux Strat.* II. ii, Then I, Sir, tips me the Verger with half a Crown. **1733** SWIFT *Legion Club* 134 Tipping him with half a crown, Now, said I, we are alone. **1747** *Gentl. Mag.* Mar. 147/1 T'wou'd have paid The reck'ning clean, and tipp'd the maid. **1752** FIELDING *Amelia* XI. v, He advised his friend..to begin with tipping (as it is called) the great man's servant. *c* **1810** W. HICKEY *Mem.* (1960) x. 164 Joseph Polt..whom I had frequently called upon, and tipped at Eton School. **1848** THACKERAY *Contrib. to 'Punch'* Wks. 1886 XXIV. 189 You..used to tip me when I was a boy at school. **1883** J. H. INGRAM in *Harper's Mag.* July 231/2 He had..tipped him to the extent of a sixpence. **1939** G. B. SHAW *Geneva* II. 38, I havnt exchanged twenty words with the boy since I tipped him when he was going from Eton to Oxford.

b. *absol.* To give a gratuity or gratuities.

1727 GAY *Begg. Op.* III. i, Did he tip handsomely? **1825** C. M. WESTMACOTT *Eng. Spy* I. 322 He used to tip pretty freely. **1906** *Sat. Rev.* 22 Sept. 358/2 He always manages to secure attention... It is not because he tips: others tip, and get left.

3. a. Phrase. ***to tip the*** (or ***a***) ***wink***, to give a wink to a person as a private signal or warning. Also ***to tip a nod.***

1676 ETHEREDGE *Man of Mode* I. i, I only tip him the wink, he knows an Ale-house from a Hovel. **1698** VANBRUGH *Æsop* v. 71 Tip but the wink, he understands you. **1712** STEELE *Spect.* No. 498 ¶3 The coachmen began..to tip the wink upon each other. **1726** SWIFT *Dog & Thief* iii, The stock-jobber..tips you, the freeman, a wink. **1757** SMOLLETT *Reprisal* II. iii, I came as soon as you tipped me the wink. **1841** MARRYAT *Poacher* xxii, The lad tipped a wink to Joey. **1861** DICKENS *Gt. Expect.* xxv, I tipped him several more [nods], and he was in great spirits.

†**b.** To indicate privately by a wink or the like.

1749 FIELDING *Tom Jones* VIII. xii, I will tip you the proper person..as you do not know the town.

tip, *v.*[5] *colloq.* [from TIP *sb.*[4]]

1. *trans.* To give a 'tip' or piece of private information about; *esp.* to mention or indicate as a probable winner, a profitable speculation, etc.

1883 [see TIPPING *vbl. sb.*[5]]. **1889** E. DOWSON *Let.* 16 Nov. (1967) 117 Ye gods what of the Manchester Nov. I have been tipped (i) Lady Roseberry (ii) Goldseeker (iii) Phil—(by you). **1894** *Westm. Gaz.* 24 Feb. 7/2, I am inclined to 'tip' Aston Villa both to head the League and to win the Cup. **1897** *Ibid.* 6 July 9/2 Florio Rubattino..has been 'tipped' by some of the papers for this race. **1902** *Ibid.* 15 Jan. 11/1 At this time when South African shares are being 'tipped'. **1909** *Ibid.* 6 Sept. 10/1 A run up to 90, the price for which the shares are tipped, would be the easiest thing in the world.

2. To give a 'tip' to; to furnish (a person) with private information as to the chances of some event; to warn, alert, or inform (a person); to make known or give away (someone or something). Freq. const. *off*. *slang* (orig. *U.S.*).

1891 in *Cent. Dict.* **1893** L. W. MOORE *His Own Story* xxi. 292 This was 'tipped off' to me on Thursday, and also that the arrest of the whole party was to be made. *Ibid.* xxxiv. 445 When I saw he had 'tipped me off' to her, I said, 'Look at me, for I am the man he told you to identify.' **1895** *Funk's Standard Dict.* s.v., The jockey tipped the bookmaker. **1896** *Chicago Tribune* 28 June 4/2 The fact that the telegram to her had 'tipped off' the situation made Mrs. Jones particularly downhearted. **1899** S. CRANE *Monster* xix. 76, I told him to keep his trap shut... You know how he'll go all over town yapping about the thing. I thought I'd better tip you. **1932** E. WALLACE *When Gangs came to London* xv. 136 He was doing badly and was tipped off there was good money in England. **1950** *Harper's Mag.* Feb. 70/2 Marks that have been tipped off are those that have been pointed out by others. **1955** M. GILBERT *Sky High* xiii. 184 That one [crime] we got tipped off about and put out a dragnet. **1960** M. SPARK *Bachelors* x. 163 'Someone has tipped the police,' said Mike Garland. **1964** MCLUHAN *Understanding Media* (1967) II. xxxi. 359 There could be no more telling touch to tip us off to the character of TV. **1975** T. ALLBEURY *Special Collection* xiv. 96 Was there any mileage in tipping them off? Experience said that tippers-off always got their hands caught in the machinery. **1978** G. MCDONALD *Fletch's Fortune* xix. 130 Who tipped you?.. Who told you about the editorial, and the campaign?

3. *intr.* To furnish 'tips'; to carry on the business of a tipster.

1903 FARMER & HENLEY *Slang Dict.*, *Tip*... As *verb* = to impart exclusive information. **1909** *Westm. Gaz.* 8 Apr. 8/3 I'm a racing man, and I've tipped on all the principal racecourses in England.

tip, variant of TUP *sb.* 'a ram', and *v.*

tip-, the stem of TIP *v.*[2] (or TIP *sb.*[5]), in combination: esp. in names of vehicles constructed to tip or tilt (endwise or sideways) for the purpose of emptying out the contents at the end or side of the track, as ***tip-car***, ***-cart***, ***-sled***, ***-truck***, ***-van***, ***-wagon***; also **tip-head**, the top of the slope over which material or rubbish is tipped; **tip-horse**, the horse which runs out the wagons to the tip-head; **tip-road**, a road along which tip-cars or -wagons run to a tip-head. See also TIP-CAT, etc.

1891 *Cent. Dict.*, *Tip-car,..a gravel-car or coal-car pivoted on its truck, so that it can be upset to discharge its load at the side of the track; a dump-car. **1879** WEBSTER, Suppl., *Tip-cart. **1883** J. QUINCY *Figures of Past* (1884) 180 Springless tip-carts, very like those used..for the carting of gravel. **1888** H. E. SCUDDER in *Atlantic Monthly* Aug. 226/2 The idle muses are set at work. Pegasus is harnessed to a tip-cart. **1842** *Civil Eng. & Arch. Jrnl.* V. 85/2 The sub-contractor..had to..take up and relay the road at the gullet and *tip-head. *Ibid.* 336/1 The limitation of the quantity of earth-work capable of being executed in one day, occurs at the battery or tiphead. **1912** A. BENNETT *Matador of Five Towns* 207 The old horse-car..climbing hills with the aid of a *tip-horse and a boy perched on the back thereof. **1852** WIGGINS *Embanking* 65 The rapidity with which a bank could be built..would be limited by the number of *tip-roads. **1877** KNIGHT *Dict. Mech.*, *Tip-sled, a dumping-sled. The box is supported on trunnions and on a front post, to which it is connected by a hook. **1899** *Westm. Gaz.* 13 Nov. 9/1, 3 engines and 6 boilers, *tip trucks. **1901** *Daily Tel.* 14 Nov. 4/5 *Tip vans for the vestry. **1852** WIGGINS *Embanking* 61 The best way is thought to be by tram-roads and *tip-waggons. **1878** G. DENMAN in *Law Rep. 3 Com. Pleas Div.* 502, 100 tip-waggons at 18*l.* each.

tip-cat. [f. TIP *v.*^{2} + CAT *sb.*^{1}]

1. A short piece of wood tapering at both ends, used in the game described in 2: = CAT *sb.*^{1} 10 a.

1676 GREW *Disc. Salts Plants* ii. §6 The Crystals..were about the bigness of a Rice-Corn. In Figure almost like a Tip-Cat, which Boys play with. **1688** R. HOLME *Armoury* III. xvi. (Roxb.) 82/1 Striker or cat stick and tip cat. **1798** *Sporting Mag.* XII. 194 [He] nearly got his eye knocked out by a boy's tip cat. **1853** *Times* 12 Apr., Persons whose eyes have been hopelessly destroyed by blows from tip-cats.

2. A game in which the wooden cat or tip-cat (see 1) is struck or 'tipped' at one end with a stick so as to spring up, and then knocked to a distance by the same player: = CAT *sb.*^{1} 10 b.

1801 STRUTT *Sports & Past.* II. iii. §22 Tip-cat, or perhaps more properly the game of cat, is a rustic pastime well known in many parts of the kingdom. **1854** MACAULAY *Biog., Bunyan* (1860) 30 The..chief sins..were dancing, ringing the bells of the parish church, playing at tipcat. **1876** *World* VI. No. 106. 11 The game of tip-cat is also..in full swing. **1907** *Sat. Rev.* 30 Mar. 390/1 Playing tip-cat..requires a good deal of neatness and quickness to tip the cat smartly.

[**tip-cheese**, ? a mistake for prec.

1837 DICKENS *Pickw.* xxxiv, He forgets the long familiar cry of 'knuckle down', and at tip-cheese, or odd and even, his hand is out.]

†**tipe, type,** *sb.*^{1} *Obs.* [Origin and history obscure. Sense 2 seems to be synonymous with TIP *sb.*^{1} 1 b.]

1. A small cupola or dome.

1532 in Low *Hampton Court* (1885) I. xxvii. 347 Takyng downe of the iiij types upon the great White Tower, and casting and chasyng of the same iiij types. *a* **1548** HALL *Chron., Hen. VIII* 157 A porche with a tipe and crokettes gilt. **1577–87** HOLINSHED *Chron.* III. 932/1 To Leaden hall, where was a goodlie pageant with a type and a heauenlie roofe, and vnder the type was a roote of gold set on a little mounteine. **1607–8** in Willis and Clark *Cambridge* (1886) II. 493 Half ynch bord to cover y^e type of y^e Lover [= Louver]. **1613** CHAPMAN *Inns of Court* Plays 1873 III. 95 Aboue all, was a *Coupolo*, or Type. **1708** *New View Lond.* I. 98/2 A Marble Font, whose Tipe or Cover has the Enrichments of Cupids, Fruit Leaves.

2. *fig.* The summit, acme, or highest point (*of* honour, dignity, or other state). Cf. TIP *sb.*^{1} 1 b.

a **1548** HALL *Chron., Edw. IV* 199 How muche more ought a noble man to fume..when the high tipe of his honor is touched. **1579–80** NORTH *Plutarch* (1676) 917 Some of them..attained to the tipe of royal dignity. **1591** *Troub. Raigne K. John* II. (1611) 106 As if your highnes were now in the highest tipe of dignitie. **1603** KNOLLES *Hist. Turks* (1621) 506 You shall through your rashnesse..tumble downe headlong from the type of so great majestie.

tipe (taɪp), *sb.*^{2} *dial.* [f. *tipe*, variant and earlier form of TIP *v.*^{2}] A kind of trap for catching mice, rabbits, etc., in which a board balanced on a pivot is tipped or tilted by the weight of the animal passing over it. Also ***tipe-trap***. (See *Eng. Dial. Dict.*)

1788 W. MARSHALL *E. Yorks.* II. Gloss., *Tipe*, a trap or devise for catching rabbits. Also for taking mice, rats, or other vermin. The general principle is that of a balance [etc.]. **1828** *Craven Gloss.*, *Tipe*, a mouse trap, consisting of a board suspended over a vessel of water, and nicely balanced on a pivot. **1846** *J. Baxter's Libr. Pract. Agric.* (ed. 4) I. 335 The usual methods adopted in catching rabbits are by fold-nets, spring-nets, and tipes, a species of trap, being a pit or cistern covered with a floor, with a small trap-door, nicely balanced near the centre, into which the rabbits pass by a narrow passage.

tipe (taɪp), *v.* Obs. or dial. form of TIP *v.*^{2}

tipet, obs. f. TIPPET.

tip-foot: see TIP *sb.*^{1}

tiphany, obs. form of TIFFANY^1.

†**tiphe.** *Obs.* Also 6–7 typhe, 7 typh. [a. L. *tiphē* = Gr. τίφη 'acc. to Sprengel, Peter's-corn, one-grained wheat, *Triticum monococcum*, Linn.'] A species of wheat having the ripe ear laterally compressed, the spikelets in two very compact rows, each containing, as a rule, one grain. Also *attrib.*

1578 LYTE *Dodoens* IV. iv. 456 Of Typhewheate, called in Latine Triticum Romanorum. *Ibid.* 457 Typhe wheate or Bearded wheate. **1598** FLORIO, *Pane di tritello*, rie or typhe-bread. **1611** COTGR., *Meteil*,..typhe wheat, bearded wheat, flat wheat, Roman wheat. **1688** R. HOLME *Armoury* II. 56/1 Typh Wheat..is very like to our Rye..and doth make very black Bread. **1790** J. BRUCE *Trav. Source Nile* V. 79 (*Teff*) There is one [cereal] which he [Pliny] calls Tiphe, but says not whence it came.

tipi, var. TEPEE.

tip-in. [f. vbl. phr. *to tip in*: see TIP *v.*^{1} 1 c and *v.*^{2} 2 d.] **1.** *Bookbinding.* = PASTE-IN *sb.*

1949 MELCHER & LARRICK *Printing & Promotion Handbk.* 359/2 Illustrations on coated paper are often inserted as wraps or tip-ins. **1969** C. IRVING *Fake!* (1970) xii. 149 Large color reproductions in many fine art books and portfolios, so that they can be removed and individually framed by the buyer, are often only lightly glued to the center of the page. .. Such detachable reproductions [are] sometimes called tip-ins.

2. *U.S. Sport* (esp. *Basketball*). A score made by tipping a rebound into the basket or net.

1958 G. F. PINHOLSTER *Encycl. Basketball* ix. 110 Tipping a basketball into the basket is a spectacular feat of timing, coordination, and jumping ability... Several tip-ins in a game can mean the difference between victory and defeat. **1963** [see TIP *v.*^{1} 1 c]. **1969** [see LAY-UP 3]. **1980** *Washington Star* 17 Dec. E3 Theus..led all scorers with 23 points, including a tip-in with 1:51 [left] that put the Bulls in front.

tipioca, obs. f. TAPIOCA.

tip-it, tippit. Also *dial.* -et, -ut, tibbets. [From the phrase *tip it* = give or hand it out.] A game of chance, played by two parties of two or three a side; in one of the hands on one side a button or the like is hidden, and a player on the opposite side has to guess in which hand it is, touching the hand and saying *tip it.* (When played for money or drinks it is reckoned a form of gambling.)

1889 T. A. GUTHRIE *Pariah* IV. vi, A lively..pastime known as 'Tibbets', which consisted in passing a paperweight from hand to hand under a table-cover, and guessing at a given moment in whose hand it was concealed. **1897** *B'ham Daily Gaz.* 28 Aug. (E.D.D.), Playing tip it for drinks. **1902** *Westm. Gaz.* 8 May 7/3 The offence..was that a servant allowed some miners to play at the game of tippit for beer. **1908** *Daily Chron.* 5 Mar. 5/6 The skill of members at such games as tippit, darts, rings, and dominoes.

tipiti (tɪpɪˈtiː). [a. Tupi.] A strainer used by Amazonian Indians for expressing the poisonous juice of the cassava.

1860 MAYNE REID *Odd People* 52 A long elastic cylinder-shaped basket or net, of the bark of the 'jacitara' palm (*Desmoncus macrocanthus*). This is the tipiti. **1866** LINDLEY & MOORE *Treas. Bot.* I. 396/1 Indians use strips of the stem [of the Jacitara palm] for platting the tipitis or strainers used for squeezing out the poisonous juice of the mandioc root. **1952** G. SARTON *Hist. Sci.* I. i. 5 The South American tipiti is an elastic plaited cylinder of jacitara-palm bark which is used to express the juice of the cassava.

tiplage, tiple, etc., obs. ff. TIPPLAGE, TIPPLE.

tiple (ˈtiple). [a. Sp., lit. 'treble'.] Any of various high-pitched stringed instruments played in Spain and the Spanish-speaking parts of the Americas, each resembling a small guitar.

1942 N. MACDONALD *Orchid Hunters* xi. 125 He strummed lightly on the tiple, changed to one of the quick-tempoed, popular Colombian airs. **1964** S. MARCUSE *Mus. Instruments* 525/2 *Tiple*... 1. syn. of guitarillo..; 2. in Cuba a small bandurria with 5 pairs of strings. **1976** *New Yorker* 12 Apr. 111/1 He played the tiple (a stringed instrument between the guitar and the ukulele).

tipless (ˈtɪplɪs), *a.*^{1} [f. TIP *sb.*^{1} + -LESS.] Without a tip; that has lost its tip or point.

1904 E. F. BENSON *Challoners* vi, A bagatelle board with torn cloth and tipless cues.

ˈ**tipless,** *a.*^{2} [f. TIP *sb.*^{3} + -LESS.] Characterized by absence of 'tips' or gratuities.

1903 *Daily Chron.* 10 Feb. 5/1 Must tipless guard Look stern and hard With nought but thanks to gain? **1909** *Westm. Gaz.* 30 Aug. 5/4 This will be the first hotel in the world to adopt a tipless system.

tiplet (ˈtɪplɪt). [f. TIP *sb.*^{1} + -LET.] A small or minute tip or point.

1890 C. L. MORGAN *Anim. Life & Intell.* (1891) 106 The feathers composing their tiplets..are of so beautiful a colour that they beggar description. **1899** *Blackw. Mag.* Apr. 671/2 Pale heads of meadow-rue dusted with ruddy tiplets.

tipmost (ˈtɪpməʊst), *a.* *nonce-wd.* [f. TIP *sb.*^{1} after *topmost*.] Situated at the extreme tip. In quot. = 'very tip of the (lance)'.

1871 TENNYSON *Last Tourn.* 441 The Red Knight..Even to tipmost lance and topmost helm, In blood-red armour sallying.

ˈ**tip-off.** Also tip off, tipoff.

1. [f. vbl. phr. *to tip off*: see TIP *v.*^{5} 2.] **a.** Information, a 'tip', esp. about criminal activity; a hint or 'give-away'. *slang* (orig. *U.S.*).

1901 J. F. WILLARD *World of Graft* 164 'So much down now,' he said, 'and so much when the show's over. Otherwise it's a tip-off and pinch.' **1918** H. C. WITWER *From Baseball to Boches* IV. i. 142 Nobody knew we was comin' up to the front... The first real tip off was when they served out the identification tags. **1938** E. WAUGH *Scoop* II. xii. 138 Now *he* had something under his hat; a tip-off straight from headquarters, news of high international importance. **1945** *Richmond* (Va.) *Times-Dispatch* 23 May 8 One of the first tipoffs on this romance came when La Bacall followed 'The Leer' to New York some months ago. **1955** W. TUCKER *Wild Talent* xi. 151 Karen was driving the tip-off car. **1960** *Observer* 24 Jan. 5/2 There was a tip-off available about when it [*sc.* a bank] was going to be stacked up with cash. **1977** *Birds* Winter 15/2 There was a tip-off about the robbery and RSPB staff lay in wait near the nest.

b. A person supplying information, esp. in connection with criminal activity. *slang.*

1941 M. ALLINGHAM *Traitor's Purse* xiv. 163 The other little syndicate..must have a tip-off in the police somewhere. **1961** J. WELCOME *Beware of Midnight* xiii. 166, I don't know which of the servants here is a tip-off to the Secret Police, but one of them is. **1973** R. BUSBY *Pattern of Violence* vi. 90 They've got a good tip-off man on the inside.

2. [f. TIP *v.*^{1} 1 a, after *kick-off*, etc.] *Basketball.* A method of (re)starting play, in which two opposing players contest a jump-ball; an instance of this.

1924 [see *jump-ball, jump ball* s.v. JUMP-]. **1937** F. C. ALLEN *Better Basketball* 181 On the tip-off, a player should tap the ball up and over his opponent. **1977** *Evening Gaz.* (Middlesbrough) 11 Jan. 13/9 Loughborough are the visitors to Newton Aycliffe on Sunday for a 3 p.m. tip-off.

tippable (ˈtɪpəb(ə)l), *a.* [f. TIP *v.*^{2} and *v.*^{4} + -ABLE.] **1.** [TIP *v.*^{4}] Designating one who may be tipped, or who is open to tips or *douceurs*. Occas. *absol.* as *sb.*

1907 *Sat. Rev.* 21 Dec. 752/1 The great aim of the tippable is to squeeze. **1921** S. GRAHAM *Europe—Whither Bound?* 27 A tippable man was keeping a queue of all the rabble of the East.

2. [TIP *v.*^{2}] Of seats, etc.: that can be tilted or tipped up.

1936 *Times* 15 Oct. 8/4 The Austin Seven seems fresher than ever... In its latest form the front tippable seats have a longer range of adjustment.

tip-paper: see TIP *sb.*^{1} 6.

tipped, tipt (tɪpt), *ppl. a.*^{1} [f. TIP *sb.*^{1} or *v.*^{3} But perh. a. ON. *typptr* tipped, from *typpa* to tip.]

†**1.** (Meaning uncertain.)

Quot. *c* 1300 may belong to sense 2; but it looks rather like 'having the tips cut off, clipt'. Quot. 13.. is glossed by editor 'extreme', which seems improbable.

c **1300** [see TIPPET 1 a]. **13..** *E.E. Allit. P.* C. 77 He telles me pose traytoures arn typped schrewes.

2. Having a tip, pointed; furnished or adorned with a tip, or with something at the tip.

c **1386** CHAUCER *Nun's Pr. T.* 83 Tipped was his tayl, and bothe hise eeris With blak. *c* **1470** HENRYSON *Mor. Fab.* IX. (*Wolf & Fox*) vi, My tippit twa eiris, and my twa gray Ene. **1483** *Cath. Angl.* 389/1 Typped, *cornutatus.* **1888** *Berks. Gloss.*, *Tipped an' naailed.* Boots for field wear have the soles thus furnished.

†**3. tipped staff. a.** A staff tipped with metal: = TIPSTAFF 1. Also ***tipped mace, stick, wand.***

c **1386** CHAUCER *Sompn. T.* 29 With scrippe and tipped [*v.r.* typped] staf ytukked hye. **1485** *Rutland Papers* (Camden) 9 That the Marshall of England be well accompanyed with men having long tipped staves. **1574** *Reg. Privy Council Scot.* II. 365 Nane suld tak upoun hand to execute ony chargeis without his blason, blawing horne and tippet wand. **1598** MARSTON *Pygmal.* III. 148 Some spirit with a tippet Mace. **1617** MINSHEU *Voc. Hisp. Lat.*, *Verguéro*, a Vergier, one that carrieth a tipped stick before the Iustices..or the Deane.

†**b.** An officer bearing such a staff: = TIPSTAFF 2.

1494 FABYAN *Chron.* VII. 565 The Erle of Westmerlande, than newely made marshall, rode about the halle w^t many typped staues about hym. *c* **1500** *God Speed the Plough* 77 in *P. Pl. Crede*, etc. 71 Then commeth the tipped-staves for the Marshalse, And saye they haue prisoners mo than Inough. *a* **1548** HALL *Chron., Hen. VIII* 3 b, To Westminster hall..where by the Lord Marshall and his tipped staues, was made rome.

4. = *filter-tipped* adj. s.v. FILTER *sb.* 5. Also *absol.*, filter-tipped cigarettes.

1964 M. DRABBLE *Garrick Year* ii. 27 'I don't smoke tipped,' I said. *Ibid.* 28 He let me have the other Gauloise, and smoked the tipped cigarettes himself. **1972** *Guardian* 24 June 9/6 Have you got any cigarettes?.. Anything tipped. **1978** C. A. BERRY *Gentleman of Road* ix. 81 The gamut of grades of the cigarette-ends, ranging from..the complete cigarette left in a thrown-away packet..to the abhorred tipped variety and the trodden-out stub.

5. *Bookbinding.* Of a leaf, plate, etc.: inserted in a book by attaching to another leaf with a narrow strip of paste at the inner edge. Usu. with *in*. Cf. TIP *v.*^{2} 2 d; TIP-IN 1.

1912 A. J. PHILIP *Business of Bookbinding* 217/2 *Tipped-in*, when a leaf, illustration, map, etc., is pasted in without guarding it is said to be tipped in. **1952** J. CARTER *ABC for Book-Collectors* 175 *Tipped in*, lightly attached, by gum or paste, usually at the inner edge. **1960** J. BETJEMAN *Summoned by Bells* v. 47, I bought a book with tipped-in colour plates. **1966** H. WILLIAMSON *Methods Bk. Design* (ed. 2) xix. 322 Unless the tipping is very accurate.., the tipped plate will raise the text page to which it is attached when it is turned. **1977** W. MATHESON in *Q. Jrnl. Libr. Congr.* July 233/2 The collector's difficulties are further complicated by the fact that the tipped-in plates by Augustus Peck are sometimes lacking.

tipped, tipt, *ppl. a.*^{2} [f. TIP *v.*^{2} + -ED^1.] Inclined, tilted; overturned, upset; †drunken (*obs. slang*).

1708 T. WARD *Eng. Ref.* (1716) 174 In Songs Obscene and Tipt discourse. **1907** KATE D. WIGGIN *New Chron. Rebecca* iii, The good deacon sat..in his tipped-back chair.

tippee (tɪˈpiː). Also tipee.

1. [f. TIP *v.*^{4} 2 + -EE.] One who is 'tipped'; the receiver of a 'tip' or gratuity.

1897 *Daily News* 23 Sept. 5/1 The working of economic law frustrates the..intention of both tipper and tippee. **1907** LADY GROVE *Soc. Fetich* v, The system of 'tips' is..at times humiliating to both 'tipper' and 'tippee'.

2. [f. TIP *v.*^{5}] One who receives inside information about a company or business enterprise and uses it to trade profitably in stocks and shares. orig. and chiefly *U.S.*

1961 L. LOSS *Securities Regulation* (ed. 2) III. ix. 1451 To hold 'tippees' liable under Rule 10b-5 when they had no reason to suspect that their informant was an insider might result in an unreasonable entrapment of innocent persons. **1967** *Federal Suppl.* CCLVIII. 284/2 This is strong circumstantial evidence that Darke must have passed the word to one or more of his 'tippees' that drilling on the Kidd 55 segment was about to be resumed. **1973** *N.Y. Law Jrnl.* 23 July 5/5 New rules for tippors [*sic*] and tippees. **1978** *Times* 12 Oct. 29/1 What about so called 'tipees'—people who come by price sensitive information often because of a breakdown in security by a professional adviser or within the company? **1980** *U.S. Reports* CCCCXLV. 242 It [*sc.* the SEC] did not hesitate to extend *Cady, Roberts* to reach a 'tippee' of a Government insider.

tippence, -penny, Sc. ff. TWOPENCE, -PENNY.

tipper[1] ('tɪpə(r)). [f. TIP *v.*[2], [3], [4], [5] + -ER[1].] One who or that which tips, in various senses of the verbs. *spec.*

†**1.** in *Skittles*: see TIP *v.*[2] 1 b. *Obs.*

1819 *Pantologia* X. s.v. *Skittles*, If the tipper give a sweep round with his hand and bring down any pins by means of his hand or coat-sleeve, that is deemed unfair, and he must lose one pin.

2. a. A workman employed in tipping or emptying out coal-wagons, trucks, etc.

1861 *MacMillan's Mag.* Dec. 143/2, I got some work in Sussex, as a 'tipper'. **1872** *Daily News* 8 Oct. 3 Mr. Pickard contended that engine-men, bankers, tippers, blacksmiths, &c., ought not to be admitted, as their interests were no more identical with those of the miner than the shopkeepers who are the friends of the pitman. **1890** *Ibid.* 29 July 6/5 The s.s. Tasso..was placed under the tips yesterday afternoon; but when it was discovered that the seamen..were non-Union men, the tippers and trimmers refused to load, and left work in protest. **1891** *Labour Commission* Gloss., *Tippers* (1) Those who empty coal waggons or trucks by tipping up one end. (2) The men at the docks who tip the coal into the hold of a vessel by means of the hydraulic lifts..called 'tips'.

b. A device or apparatus for tipping or tilting; *spec.* for tipping and emptying coal-wagons.

1870 ATKINSON tr. *Ganot's Physics* ii. §69 a (ed. 4) 54 The top of this mass [of iron] is provided with a tipper which catches against the end of a bent lever. **1884** *Health Exhib. Catal.* 59/2 Shrewsbury Tipper Flushing Water Closet. **1901** *Scotsman* 15 Oct. 4/8 The coals..in hutches of 10 cwts. ..are..pushed on to the revolving power-driven tippers, which land the coal on to three distributing jiggers.

c. A wagon or truck constructed to tip earth, etc., sometimes distinguished according to its action as an ***end-tipper*** or a ***side-tipper***: cf. TIP- in comb. Freq. *attrib.*

1920 *Glasgow Herald* 18 Apr. 10 The farmer can get on with his work, and the waggon which, in preference to being a 'tipper' would have a moving lattice floor and a removable drum..would spread the manure direct on the fields. **1950** *Engineering* 3 Feb. 140/1 Specialised vehicles, such as tippers. **1955** *Times* 14 June 4/5 There had been a shortage of tipper vehicles for emergency purposes. **1977** *Jersey Even. Post* 26 July 25/7 (Advt.), Tipper lorry (high sided), immediately available for contract work, etc. **1979** *West Lancs. Even. Gaz.* 10 Sept. 12 (Advt.), Tipper driver required. **1983** *Truckin' Life* Aug. 70/3 I've watched some poor little tipper struggling up a 5 per cent grade in second gear with two or three tonnes of topsoil.

3. [TIP *v.*[3]] A person employed in fitting on tips to umbrellas or other articles.

Mod. Newsp. Advt., Umbrella tippers wanted, indoors.

4. [TIP *v.*[4]] One who gives a 'tip' or gratuity.

1877 CRAUF. TAIT *Let.* 1 Aug., in W. Benham *Cath. & C. Tait*, This is better both for the class of tippers and tipped than our system. **1894** *Daily News* 18 Dec. 5/3 There are no tippers so hardened and profuse as Anglo-Indian tippers. **1900** *N. & Q.* 9th Ser. V. 526/2 Thackeray, the unfailing tipper of schoolboys, slipped a sovereign into my hand.

5. [TIP *v.*[5]] One who gives 'tips' or private information; a tipster.

1891 in *Cent. Dict.*

ˈ**Tipper**[2]. [Named from one Thomas Tipper (d. 1785), who first brewed it.] A kind of ale brewed in Sussex.

[**1785** *Tipper's Tombstone* (Newhaven Churchyard), The best old stingo he both brewed and sold.] **1844** DICKENS *Mart. Chuz.* xix, A pint of the celebrated staggering ale or Real Old Brighton Tipper at supper.

tippet ('tɪpɪt), *sb.* Forms: 4-6 **tipet**, 4-7 **typet**, (4 **typeth**, 4-5 **tepet**), 5 **typett, -itte**; 5-6 **typ-**, 6 **tipp-, typpett(e**, 6-7 **typpet, tippit**, 7 **tipit**; 4- **tippet**; also *Sc.* 5 **tipat (tuppat)**, 5-6 **tipp-, typp-, typat, tepat, -e**. [Origin uncertain; some suggest identity with OE. *tæpped, tæppet*, **tęped* (pl. *tæppedu, tepedu*) carpet, hanging, etc. = OHG. *teppid, -ith, -it, tepid, -it*: both ad. L. *tapēte* (*-a, -um*) a carpet, tapestry hanging, bed-cover, table-cover. But there are great difficulties both of phonology and of sense. Others suggest a derivative of TIP *sb.*[1] See *Note* below.]

1. a. A long narrow slip of cloth or hanging part of dress, formerly worn, either attached to and forming part of the hood, head-dress, or sleeve, or loose, as a scarf or the like. *Obs.* exc. *Hist.*

c **1300** in *Langtoft's Chron.* in *Pol. Songs* (Camden) 303 For he haves ovirhipped, Hise tipet [*v.r.* typeth] is typed, Hise tabard es tome. [**1342** *Concilium Lond.* c. 2 Et caputiis cum tipettis miræ longitudinis.] *c* **1386** CHAUCER *Reeve's T.* 33 On haly dayes biforn hir [his wife] wolde hee [Symkyn] go With his typet y-bounde about his heed. **1401** *Pol. Poems* (Rolls) II. 69 What meenith thi tipet, Jakke, as longe as a stremer, that hangith longe bihinde, and kepith thee not hoot? **14..** *Beryn* 662 He wissh a-wey the blood, And bond the sorys to his hede with the typet of his hood. *c* **1440** *Promp. Parv.* 494/2 Typett, *liripipium* [a long band or scarf (Du Cange)]. **1463** *Bury Wills* (Camden) 41 My tepet of blak sarsenet. **1473-4** *Acc. Ld. High Treas. Scot.* I. 16, j½ elne of vellous for ij tuppatis to the King. *Ibid.* 17 A typpat to the King. **1502** *Ibid.* II. 197 For ane tepat and ane belt to the King. **1532-3** *Act 24 Hen. VIII*, c. 13 §2 It shalbe lefull to all..Doctors of the one Lawe or the other..to weare.. blacke saten, in their tippittes. *a* **1548** HALL *Chron., Hen. VIII* 7 Their heades rouled in pleasauntes and typpets lyke the Egipcians. *a* **1626** BACON *New Atl.* (1650) 6 His Turban was white with a small red Crosse on the Topp. He had also a Tippet of fine Linnen. **1688** R. HOLME *Armoury* III. 12/1 The Tippet [of a Hood] hangs from the hinder part of the Crown, and reacheth backwards to the ground. *Ibid.*, A French Hood..having the Flap or Tippet hanging down the wearers Back, may be termed a Mourning-hood. **1756** NUGENT *Gr. Tour, France* IV. 81 The students [of the Sorbonne]..are qualified for the degree of batchelors, and wear lambskins and tippets two years. **1834** PLANCHÉ *Brit. Costume* 128 From the sleeves of this cote..depended long slips of cloth,..which were called tippets.

b. A garment, usually of fur or wool, covering the shoulders, or the neck and shoulders; a cape or short cloak, often with hanging ends. Now worn chiefly by women and girls, or by men as a part of certain official costumes.

In many early quots. (omitted here), senses a and b are not distinguishable.

1481 CAXTON *Myrr.* III. xvi. 172 They be not alle clerkes that haue short typettis. **1554** Turner *Sel. Rec. Oxford* 219 [He] shall weare..a typpet of velvett as other Aldermen have accustomyd yn thoffyce of Mayraltie to do. **1684-5** WOOD *Life* 11 Feb. (O.H.S.) III. 128 The mayor with his scarlet, and stole or tippet over it. **1686** *Lond. Gaz.* No. 2115/4 Lost a Sable Tippet with scarlet and silver strings to it. **1709-10** ADDISON *Tatler* No. 116 ¶9 The Lynx shall cast its Skin at her Feet to make her a Tippet. **1848** DICKENS *Dombey* i, She had furry articles for winter wear, as tippets, boas, and muffs. **1880** MISS BRADDON *Just as I am* iii, She gave the village children smart hats and tippets for summer.

c. *Eccl.* A band of silk or other material worn round the neck, with the two ends pendent from the shoulders in front; = SCARF *sb.*[1] 2.

1530 PALSGR. 281/2 Typpet for a preest, *cornette*. *a* **1555** BRADFORD in Coverdale *Lett. Mart.* (1564) 441 If God's word had place..Priestes should be otherwise knowen then by their shauen crownes and typets. **1588** *Marprel. Epist.* (Arb.) 9 Your corner caps and tippets will do nothing in this poynt. **1604** *Const. & Canons Eccles.* §58 It shall be lawful for such Ministers as are not Graduates to wear upon their Surplices, instead of Hoods, some decent Tippet of black, so it be not silk. **1617** MINSHEU *Ductor*, *Tippet*, or habit which Vniuersitie men and Clergie men weare ouer their gownes L. *Epitogium*. **1678** PHILLIPS (ed. 4), *Tippet*, a certain long Scarf which Doctors of Divinity wear when they go abroad in their Gowns. *a* **1750** T. GORDON *Cordial for Low Spirits* (1751) II. 78, I cannot for my heart think, that a Piece of Lawn, or a red Tippet, can make men holier than their neighbours. **1870** DISARELI *Lothair* vi, He..wore..over his cassock a purple tippet. **1903** P. DEARMER *Parson's Handbk.* (new ed.) 128 There are many clergymen in Ireland..who can still remember the ecclesiastical scarf called a tippet... The Canons on the subject must be misunderstood when the modern foreign idea of a short cape [see 1 b] is read into the word tippet. **1903** *Church Times* 11 Dec. 784/2 A deacon is entitled, like any other clergyman, to wear the broad black tippet, or scarf, over his surplice.

d. Applied to a part of ancient or mediæval armour: = CAMAIL 1. *rare.*

c **1400** *Melayne* 960 The Bischoppe gart hym with a spere Appon his tepet lighte. **1845** C. H. SMITH in *Kitto's Cycl. Bibl. Lit.* I. 226/2 In Egypt..a more ancient national form was a kind of thorax, tippet,..or square, with an opening in it for the head, the four points covering the breast, back, and both upper arms. **1869** BOUTELL *Arms & Arm.* viii. (1874) 127 The *camail*..is the lower part of a mail coif, a hood, or a tippet of mail, which was fixed to the basinet, and hung gracefully over the shoulders, covering the upper part of the body-armour.

†**e.** Phr. ***to turn*** (***one's***) ***tippet***: to change one's course or behaviour completely; in bad sense, to act the turncoat or renegade. *Obs.*

1546 J. HEYWOOD *Prov.* (1867) 44 So turned they their typpets by way of exchaunge, From laughyng to lowryng. **1563** FOXE *A. & M.* 1049/2 He changed his typpette, and played the Apostata. *a* **1577** GASCOIGNE *Flowers* (1587) 18 Those trifling bookes from whose lewde lore my tippet here I turne. **1598-9** B. JONSON *Case is Altered* III. iii. You, to turn tippet! fie, fie! **1650** TRAPP *Comm. Exod.* xii. 38 Strangers, that took hold of the skirts of these Jews..but afterwards turned tippet.

†**2.** A jocular name for a hangman's rope: usually ***Tyburn tippet*** (also Sc. ***St. Johnston's tippet***: cf. RIBAND *sb.* 3 a). *Obs.*

?**1462** *Paston Lett.* II. 86 The seide Perys tyed by an halter... This is a presoner, ye may knowe by his tepet and steff. **1549** LATIMER *2nd Serm. bef. Edw. VI* (Arb.) 63 He should haue had a Tiburne tippet, a halpeny halter, and all suche proude prelates. *c* **1592** MARLOWE *Jew of Malta* IV. iv, When the hangman had put on his hempen tippet, he made such haste to his prayers. **1680** C. NESSE *Church Hist.* 143 The cart at Tyburn drives away when the tippet is fast about the necks of the condemned. **1814** SCOTT *Wav.* xxxix, As I hae dealt a' my life in halters, I think nae mickle o' putting my craig in peril of a St. Johnstone's tippet. **1823** —— *Quentin D.* vi, Were I to be hanged myself, no other should tie tippet about my craig.

3. An organ or formation in animals resembling or suggesting a tippet; in birds, dogs, etc. = RUFF *sb.*[2] 3; in insects = PATAGIUM c.

1815 [implied in *tippet cuckoo*, in 5]. **1826** KIRBY & SP. *Entomol.* III. xxxv. 539 The *tegulæ* that cover the base of the primary wings of insects of this Order..are what..I have called in the table *patagia*, or tippets. **18..** MRS. CAMERON *Little Dog Flora* 8 A very small dog..covered with long brown hair, with its tippet and feet quite white. **1866** DK. ARGYLL *Reign of Law* v. (1871) 236 A species of Lophorius with a tippet of emerald spangles. **1872** COUES *N. Amer. Birds* 18 Conspicuous among these are the ruffs, or tippets, of some birds.

4. *Angling.* **a.** A length of twisted hair or gut forming part of a fishing-line. *Sc.* **b.** Part of an artificial fly: see quot. 1867, and cf. 3.

1825 JAMIESON, *Tippet.* 1. One length of twisted hair or gut in a fishing-line. **1867** F. FRANCIS *Angling* x. (1880) 343 The wing is composed of a white ribbed snipe's feather, with longish tippets on either side. **1908** *Dundee Advertiser* 26 Oct. 8 We came upon a young fisherman 'makin' tippits', as he explained. The tippit is of horse-hair, woven in thin strands, knotted at either end.

5. *attrib.* and *Comb.*, as ***tippet armour*** (cf. 1 d), ***-box***; ***tippet-like*** adj.; † **tippet-captain, knight, man**, contemptuous nicknames for a priest or ecclesiatic (cf. 1 c); so † **tippet-scuffle** *nonce-wd.*, an ecclesiastical wrangle; **tippet cuckoo, grouse**, names for species of these birds having a 'tippet' or ruff (cf. 3); **tippet-grebe**, a species of grebe, of which the skin, with the feathers on, is used for tippets.

1845 C. H. SMITH in *Kitto's Cycl. Bibl. Lit.* I. 226/2 The late Roman legionaries..again wear the *tippet armour, like that of the Egyptians. **1694** *Lond. Gaz.* No. 2980/4 Left in a Hackney-Coach.., a Wainscot *Tippet-Box with 2 Tippets, one Sable,..the other black Ribbond. **1550** BALE *Apol.* 104 Thys *typpet captayne, in bringing fourth here S. Augustynes authoryte..is like to be pearced through wyth hys owne weapon. **1815** STEPHENS in *Shaw's Gen. Zool.* IX. I. 112 *Tippet Cuckow. **1776** PENNANT *Brit. Zool.* II. 418 *Tippet Grebe... The under side of them being drest with the feathers on, are made into muffs and tippets; each bird sells for about fourteen shillings. **1829** COL. HAWKER *Diary* (1893) I. 352, I knocked down a tippet grebe. **1550** BALE *Eng. Votaries* II. L iij, The order of portasse men, *tippet knyghtes, or new shauen Syr Ihons. **1839** *Penny Cycl.* XIII. 439/2 A small *tippet-like appendage..on each side..at the base of the wings. **1550** BALE *Eng. Votaries* II. L iij, The first order of *tippet men, or secular priests. **1641** MILTON *Reform.* II. Wks. 1851 III. 54 To make a Nationall Warre of a Surplice Brabble, a *Tippet-scuffle.

Hence ˈ**tippet** *v.*[1], *intr.* to wear a tippet; *trans.* to furnish or adorn with a tippet; † ˈ**tippeter**, a member of New College, Oxford, who wore a tippet: see quot. and context.

1563 BECON *Acts Christ & Antichr.* §22 Wks. III. 398 b, Antichrist hath his Chaplens knowen by docking & doucking,..by *tippeting and gowning. **1889** DOYLE *Micah Clarke* xvii. 155 Sweeping gowns of black silk trimmed and tippeted with costly furs. *a* **1677** in Rashdall & Rait *New College* vi. (1901) 156 We call it a Habit, such as New College *Tippiters alwaies wore above their gownes. **1901** *Ibid.*, Who constituted this class of tippeters we are unable to explain.

[*Note.* The normal and regular repr. of OE. *tæppet* down to 1600 was TAPET; and phonetic development of *i* out of *a* would be abnormal; the rare ME. *tepet* and Sc. *tepat* are prob. from *tipet*. The ordinary meaning of the OE. and ME. word, and of the OHG., was 'carpet', as in Latin, but in *Ælfric's Vocabulary*, *tæppet* occurs under the heading *Vestium Nomina*, as if a name of a garment. Yet the gloss '*Sipla* an healfhruh tæppet', seems to come from the same source as one in the 15th c. *Nominale*, under the heading *De Lectis et Ornamentis eorum*, 'Hec amphicapa est tapeta ex utraque parte villosa. Hec sipha idem est' (Wr.-W. 744/5), where the *sipha* or *tapeta* is evidently a bedcover; so that the Ælfric entry is prob. placed under the wrong heading. A change of meaning from 'carpet' or 'bedcover' to the senses above, is very improbable. Derivation of *tippet* from *tip* is favoured by the fact that Ger. *zipfel*, orig. diminutive of *zipf* 'tip', has the senses 'tip, point, end, lappet, tail', etc.]

tippet ('tɪpɪt), *v.*[2] [perh. alteration of TIPTOE *v.*] To move on tiptoe. Also *transf.* and *fig.* Hence ˈ**tippeting** *vbl. sb.*

1916 W. DE LA MARE *Songs of Childhood* (new ed.) 3 See they're tippeting at the door; Their wee feet in measure falling. **1932** E. BOWEN *To North* vii. 72 Then someone's wife opened a cold piano: she tinkled, she tippetted, she struck false chords and tried them again. **1934** —— *Cat Jumps* 84 Her affronted, muddled and rather tippeting manner. **1944** R. LEHMANN *Ballad & Source* 258 Their wives tippet about on the bank in high heels.

tippet, obs. form of TIPPED, TIPT.

ˈ**tipping**, *vbl. sb.*[1] Also tippen. [f. TIP *v.*[3] (or *sb.*[1]) + -ING[1].]

1. The action of furnishing or fitting with a tip.

1559 *Dunmow Churchw. MS.* lf. 44 Payed to John Hootte for typpinge of a spade. **1905** *Longm. Mag.* Feb. 355 There is no tipping of split sticks with sulphur to make matches.

2. *concr.* **a.** A piece fashioned or fitted on to form a tip, esp. of a different material or colour.

c **1325** *Gloss. W. de Bibbesw.* in Wright *Voc.* 150 De la ceynture le pendaunt, *gl.* the girdilis ende tipping. **1483** *Cath. Angl.* 389/1 A Typpynge of A boltt. **1647** H. MORE *Poems* 7 Crudled clouds, with silver tippings dight. **1785** *Phil. Trans.* LXXV. 399 Reckoning from the extremities of the bell-metal tippings.

b. = TIPPET *sb.* 4 a.

1881 W. GREGOR *Folk-Lore N.E. Scotl.* 52 Lines, hair for tippens, hooks. **1924** *Chambers's Jrnl.* Oct. 710/1 Many of the books have been torn from their tippings.

3. *Hort.* A method of grafting, also called *tonguing*: see quot.

1763 MILLS *Pract. Husb.* IV. 217 The third method [of whip-grafting], which is an improvement of the last, is properly named *tipping* or *tonguing*.

4. *Bookbinding.* (See quot. 1931.) Usu. with *in*. Cf. TIP *v.*[2] 2 d; TIP-IN 1.

1931 A. ESDAILE *Man. Bibliogr.* 183 *Tipping-in*; pasting the edge of a single leaf to the next leaf. **1963** W. CLOWES *Guide to Printing* i. 8 Sometimes..tipping-in might not give sufficient strength. **1966** [see TIPPED, TIPT *ppl. a.*[1] 5].

ˈtipping, *vbl. sb.*^{2} [f. TIP *v.*^{2} + -ING^{1}.] The action of TIP *v.*^{2} in various senses: *spec.*

1. Tilting, inclination, upsetting.

1853 DICKENS in *Househ. Words* 7 May 218/2 'Tippings' ..denotes the spiritual movements of the tables and chairs. **1863** HOLLAND *Lett. Joneses* vii. 105 Scraping of fiddles, and the tipping of tables. **1866** *Lond. Rev.* 25 Aug. 206/2 Whether this tipping of the mental balance was not a physical rather than a mental mishap. **1901** *Essex Weekly News* 8 Mar. 3/3 Owing to the frequent tipping of the tumbril.

2. *Skittles.*

1801 [see TIP *v.*^{2} 1 b(*b*)]. **1819** *Pantologia* X. s.v. *Skittles*, If in tipping the bowl is caught or stopped by one of the opposite party, who, in so doing, stops or impedes a live pin, the party who stops loses one from his own score.

3. a. The tilting up of a truck so as to discharge its contents; the emptying out of the contents of a truck, etc., by tilting; dumping.

1838 *Civil Eng. & Arch. Jrnl.* I. 354/1 A contrivance to facilitate the tipping of the earth-waggons. **1842** *Ibid.* V. 85/2 The price he paid for tipping was 13s. 6d. per hundred wagons. **1878** F. S. WILLIAMS *Midl. Railw.* 51 The Oakenshard cutting and embankment..required the quarrying and tipping of some 600,000 yards of rock.

b. *pl.* (*concr.*) Material tipped or emptied out from a quarry, etc. **c.** A railway embankment. *local.*

1884 *Chesh. Gloss.*, *Tipping*, a railway embankment formed by tipping wagons full of soil or stone. **1888** *Pall Mall G.* 3 Aug. 5/1 The quarries at Llanberis, whose tippings are gradually filling up the once beautiful Llyn Peris.

d. *attrib.*, as ***tipping machine***, ***platform***, ***wagon***: cf. TIP-.

1877 *Scotsman* 1 Sept. 4/7 Tipping machine. **1885** DUCANE *Punishm. & Prevent. Crime* 180 Removing the earth..by means of..tipping waggons. **1891** *Daily News* 6 Feb. 6/3, 200 clerks have intimated their readiness to do the tipping work till other arrangements have been made. **1901** *Feilden's Mag.* IV. 436/2 A 'tipping platform' for the storage of the refuse and for the feeding of the furnaces.

ˈtipping, *vbl. sb.*^{3} [f. TIP *v.*^{1} + -ING^{1}.] The action of TIP *v.*^{1}; in quot., in sense 2 of the vb.

1819 *Blackw. Mag.* V. 402/1 Leaving out compass, emphasis, shakes, holds, cadences, and tippings.

spec. **b.** *Mus.* The action of striking the tongue against the palate so as to produce a *staccato* effect in playing certain wind-instruments; also called TONGUING, q.v.

1898 STAINER & BARRETT *Dict. Mus. Terms, Tipping.* (Double tongueing.) *Ibid.*, *Double-tongueing*, a peculiar action..to ensure a brilliant and spirited articulation of staccato notes.

c. (See quot.)

1891 *Cent. Dict.*, *Tipping*^{2}, *n.*.. 2. In the preparation of curled hair, the operation of tossing the carded hair about with a stick so that it will fall in tufts, to be afterwards consolidated by rapid blows.

ˈtipping, *vbl. sb.*^{4} [f. TIP *v.*^{4} + -ING^{1}.] The action of TIP *v.*^{4}; the bestowing of gratuities: see TIP *v.*^{4} 2.

1761 R. LLOYD *To G. Colman* Poet. Wks. 1774 I. 113 And walking gravely thro' the croud, Which stood obsequiously, and bow'd To keep the fashion up of tipping, Dropt in each hand a golden pippin. **1869** in *Daily News* 24 July, A system of tipping had prevailed at Somerset-house and in the dockyards..which he would endeavour to uproot. **1893** G. E. MATHESON *About Holland* 30 A good deal of tipping..has to be done in Holland.

ˈtipping, *vbl. sb.*^{5} [f. TIP *v.*^{5} + -ING^{1}.] The giving of 'tips' or private information as to the chances of sporting events, etc. Also *attrib.*

1883 *Pall Mall G.* 24 Oct. 4/1 The 'glorious uncertainties' of turf 'tipping'.

ˈtipping, *ppl. a. dial.* and *slang.* [f. TIP *v.*^{3} + -ING^{2}, after *topping*: cf. *tip-top.*] First-rate, excellent, = TOPPING. (Cf. *ripping.*)

1887 *South Chesh. Gloss.* s.v., They bin tippin' cheers; they'n do well for go i' ahr parlour. **1903** FARMER & HENLEY *Slang Dict.*, *Tipping*..(schools'), first-rate; jolly. **1903** ROSA N. CAREY *Passage Perilous* (Tauchn.) 119 It is tipping, Chriss, and suits you down to the ground.

†**ˈtipplage.** *nonce-wd.* In 7 tiplage. [f. TIPPLE *v.*^{1} + -AGE.] Intoxicating drink generally, tipple.

1653 URQUHART *Rabelais* II. i. 3 The Vine, from whence we have that..liquor which they call the *piot* or *tiplage*.

tipple (ˈtɪp(ə)l), *sb.*^{1} *colloq.* or *slang.* [f. TIPPLE *v.*^{1}] Drink, liquor for drinking; *esp.* strong drink. Also *attrib.* (quot. 1617; or perh. there the verb-stem in combination).

1581 A. HALL *Iliad* IX. 165 Of pleasant wine their tipple in they take. **1617** in *Essex Rev.* (1907) XVI. 205, vj cushions, 3 tiple pottes, 8 spoones. **1655** tr. *Com. Hist. Francion* I. 8 Where hast thou got tipple to make thy selfe drunke this night? **1706** E. WARD *Wooden World Diss.* (1708) 47 To lay in a Cargo of fresh Peck and Tipple. *a* **1763** SHENSTONE *Ode Dr. Brettle* 3 Come let's be merry; stir the tipple. **1832** MARRYAT *N. Forster* xxxvi, Champagne is very pretty *tipple*. **1861** HUGHES *Tom Brown at Oxf.* xli, Ah! that's not bad tipple after such a ducking as we've had. **1893** FORBES-MITCHELL *Remin. Gt. Mutiny* 67 Something more potent than blue-ribbon tipple. **1893** SELOUS *Trav. S.E. Africa* 121 A cup of tea, the usual tipple of South African hunters and travellers.

ˈtipple, *sb.*^{2} *dial.* [? f. TIP *sb.*^{1}] A bundle of hay tied near the top so that it tapers to a point.

1799 *Trans. Soc. Arts* XVII. 226 A truss of Clover Hay, and a few tipples of Lucerne Hay. **1812** SIR J. SINCLAIR *Syst. Husb. Scot.* I. 401 It is proper to make the tipple as soon as the grass is mown, if dry.

ˈtipple, *sb.*^{3} *U.S. local.* [f. TIPPLE *v.*^{3}] = TIP *sb.*^{5} 3.

1886 *N. Amer. Rev.* Aug. 181 The law allows a check weighmaster on each tipple. **1894** *Current Hist.* (U.S.) IV. 138 The excited mob [near Bridgeville, Pa.] burned coal cars and coal tipples, and destroyed some mining machinery.

tipple (ˈtɪp(ə)l), *v.*^{1} Forms: 6– tipple. Also 6 typle, typple, typpel(l, typpil, 6–8 tiple, 7 tippel. [Known (in simple tenses) from 1544, in pres. pple. *tippling* (as *ppl. a.*), app. before 1500; in vbl. sb. *tippling* from 1531. But the agent-noun TIPPLER occurs as an established and app. legal term in 1396, and frequently in the 15th c.; so that either the verb must have existed before 1400, though not yet in evidence, or *tippler* must have originated otherwise, and *tipple* have arisen from it as a back-formation: cf. PEDLAR, PEDDLE *v.*

The ulterior history is uncertain; *tipple* or *tippler* cannot, from the date, be a freq. deriv. of TIP *v.*^{2} in any sense; nor is it easy to connect it with LG. and Du. *tippel* 'tip, extreme point' (TIP *sb.*^{1}). But according to Aasen, Norw. dial. *tipla* 'to drip slowly', which Falk and Torp derive from *tippa* to project, to drip, from *tip* 'point', has also the sense 'to drink in small quantities', 'tipple', evidently related to the Eng. word, though the mode of relationship is not clear. An ultimate connexion with TAP *sb.*^{1}, *v.*^{1} has also been thought possible, but connecting links are wanting.]

†**1. a.** *trans.* To sell (ale or other strong drink) by retail (see TIPPLER^{1} 1). **b.** *absol.* or *intr.* To carry on the trade of a 'tippler'; to draw and retail liquor, sell from the tap. *Obs.*

? *a* **1500** [see TIPPLING *ppl. a.* 1]. **1531** [see TIPPLING *vbl. sb.*^{1} 1]. **1544** *Coventry Leet Bk.* 771 That noon inhabitaunt of this Citie shall..brewe or tiple eny ale within this Citie to sell but onelie suche..persones as shal-be therunto appoynted. **1594** in J. Morris *Troub. Cath. Forefathers* (1877) 281 Dorothy Browne,..who by reason she is an obstinate recusant, was heretofore discharged in open sessions from brewing and tippling,..doth not give over the same, but continually since hath brewed and tippled. **1611** in *N. Riding Rec.* (1884) I. 215 John Pearson..for tunning of ale from Yorke with a lycence..and tipling and selling it in his house. **1662** J. DAVIES tr. *Olearius' Voy. Ambass.* 294 The Taverns where they Tiple, and sell all sorts of Provisions.

2. a. *intr.* To drink of intoxicating liquor: in earlier use, to drink freely or hard; to booze; now *esp.*, to indulge habitually to some excess in taking strong drink.

1560 DAUS tr. *Sleidane's Comm.* 265 b, In this conflict was hurt Albert Brunswick, the sonne of Duke Philip, going vnaduisedly after he had wel tippled. **1570** LEVINS *Manip.* 128/18 To Typpil, *potitare.* **1603** FLORIO *Montaigne* II. ii. 198 By making an Ambassador to tipple square..he wrested all his secrets out of him. **1661** PEPYS *Diary* 23 Apr., I wondered to see how the ladies did tipple. **1706** PHILLIPS (ed. Kersey), To *Tipple*, to drink hard. **1749** GRAY *Let. to Wharton* 25 Apr., We shall smoke, we shall tipple, we shall doze together. **1861** TULLOCH *Eng. Purit.* ii. 289 They taught school, and tippled on the week-days.

b. *trans.* To drink (intoxicating liquor), esp. to take (drink) constantly in small quantities.

1581 A. HALL *Iliad* II. 31 Tipling the plesaunt wine they downe to table sit. **1591** GREENE *Disc. Coosnage* Pref. (1592) 3 He..had tipled so much malmsey, that he had neuer a readie word in his mouth. **1681** W. ROBERTSON *Phraseol. Gen.* (1693) 1327 How the slut tipples off the wine. **1698** FRYER *Acc. E. India & P.* 93 Sack and Brandy out of the Bottle they will Tipple, till they are well warmed. **1749** FIELDING *Tom Jones* VII. xi, The beer, of which having tippled a very large quantity. **1849** CLOUGH *Dipsychus* II. ii. 168 We sit at our tables and tipple champagne.

c. *transf.* and *poetic.* To drink, sip. *intr.* and *trans.* Now *rare* or *Obs.*

1648 HERRICK *Hesper.*, *Captiv'd Bee* 4 It chanc't a bee did flie that way,..To tipple freely in a flower. **1649** LOVELACE *To Althea fr. Prison* ii, Fishes that tipple in the deep Know no such liberty. **1781** CRABBE *Library* 578 No more the midnight fairy tribe I view, All in the merry moonshine tippling dew.

d. *trans.* with *away*, †*up*: To spend, squander, lose, or get rid of by tippling.

a **1619** FLETCHER *Wit without M.* II. iv, That annuity You have tippled up in taverns. **1687** J. RENWICK in *Biogr. Presbyt.* (1827) II. 251 Ye must not be Lovers of Strong Drink, nor tipple away Time in Alehouses. **1824** W. IRVING *T. Trav.* II. x. 42, I took to the bottle, and tried to tipple away my cares.

†**3.** *trans.* To intoxicate, make drunk. See also TIPPLED *ppl. a.* below. *Obs.*

1566 PAINTER *Pal. Pleas.* (1890) II. 13 When they had well whitled and tippled themselues. **1625** PURCHAS *Pilgrims* IX. xix. §4. 1660 The most part eate Opium,..which tipples, intoxicates and duls them. **1648** GAGE *West Ind.* xix. (1655) 144 By thus cheating and tipling poor Indians.

†**4.** *advb. phr.* ***tipple square***: cf. 1603 in 2.

1605 ARMIN *Foole upon F.* (1880) 41 But he..got downe into the Seller, and fell to it tipple square.

5. *intr.* To rain heavily; to gush, to pour. Freq. const. *down.*

a **1930** D. H. LAWRENCE *Last Poems* (1932) 204 Now it is almost night, from the bronzey soft sky Jugfull after jugfull of pure white liquid fire, bright white Tipples over and spills down. **1968** J. PORTER *Dover goes to Pott* xiv. 177, I saw her from the office window. No hat, no coat, nothing... It was tippling down too, absolutely tippling. **1971** *Country Life* 27 May 1283/1 After getting out of bed on the wrong side because the day is overcast or rain is tippling down.

Hence †**ˈtippled** *ppl. a.*, intoxicated, drunk.

Orig. pa. pple. active, 'that has tippled'; cf. *well read*, *well spoken*, etc.

1564 J. RASTELL *Confut. Jewell's Serm.* 66 b, Whether God be..forgetfull, or well tipled. **1581** A. HALL *Iliad* I. 7 Thou tipled Knight, a snarring curre, to sight and shew thou art. **1611** COTGR., *Enyvré*..drunke..mellow, tipled. **1660** MRQ. OF DORCHESTER *Lett. to Ld. Roos* 2 A Tippl'd Fool, and a Bragging Coward. **1669** DRYDEN *Tyrannic Love* IV. i, Merry, merry, merry, we sail from the East, Half tippled at a rainbow feast.

ˈtipple, *v.*^{2} *dial.* [f. TIPPLE *sb.*^{2}] *trans.* To bind (hay) in tipples (see TIPPLE *sb.*^{2}). Also *absol.*

1799 *Trans. Soc. Arts* XVII. 228, I tippled upwards of eighty acres. *Ibid.* 230 A husbandman..who..tippled some clover for me. **1812** SIR J. SINCLAIR *Syst. Husb. Scot.* I. 402 In a moderate crop, one woman will tipple to one mower, and a woman will rake to two tipplers or two swathes.

ˈtipple, *v.*^{3} *dial.* [freq. from TIP *v.*^{2} Cf. *topple.*]

1. *intr.* To tumble or topple over.

1847–78 HALLIWELL, *Tipple*, to tumble; to turn over, as is done in tumbling. **1850** F. W. NEWMAN *Phases of Faith* iii. 98 To tipple over irrecoverably. **1866** HALLAM *Wadsley Jack* iv. (E.D.D.), I scream'd an tippled back into 't midden.

2. *trans.* To throw, pitch.

1887 HARTLEY *Clock Alm.* 11 in *Leeds Merc. Suppl.* 15 Apr. (1899), Others..started o' tipplin' th' furnitur aght.

tippler^{1} (ˈtɪplə(r)). Forms: 4–5 tipeler, 5 -ar, tippelar, -ilar, typuler, 5–8 tipler, 6 typpler, typlar, 6–7 -er, 6– tippler. [In form and in sense the agent-noun in -ER from TIPPLE *v.*^{1}, but actually known 150 years earlier than the vb., and prob. a century earlier than TIPPLING *ppl. a.*, so that the exact nature of the relationship of these words is uncertain: see TIPPLE *v.*^{1}]

†**1.** A retailer of ale and other intoxicating liquor; a tapster; a tavern-keeper. *Obs.*

1396 *Nottingham Rec.* I. 314 Johannes Jolivet et Johannes Smyth sunt communes tipelers, et vendunt infra domos suas cum discis et ciphis, contra Assisum. *c* **1420** *Durham Acc. Rolls* (Surtees) 359 Adam Sharp bras' tipelar, Alicia Mut tipelar, Joh'es Hunter tipelar. [So many instances 1424–5, etc.] **1478** *Nottingham Rec.* II. 298 Fines pro licentia merchandizandi Alicia Bult, tipler..iiij d. **1530** in W. H. Turner *Select. Rec. Oxford* (1880) 80 In-holders, and typlers w^{t}in the Towne of Oxford. **1552** HULOET, Typpler or vitayler, *stabularius.* **1564** in *Rep. Hist. MSS. Comm.*, *Var. Coll.* IV. 224 That the bruers or typlars shall not sell any bere or ale above the prices above set. **1642** *Ord. & Declar. Lords & Com. Lords Day* 6 That expresse charge be given to every keeper of any Taverne, Inne, Cooks shop, Tobacco-house, Ale-house, or any other Tipler or Victualler.

2. One who tipples; a habitual drinker of intoxicating liquor (implying more or less excess, but usually short of positive drunkenness).

1580 HOLLYBAND *Treas. Fr. Tong*, *Vn bon Biberon*, a bibber, a tippler. **1622** MASSINGER & DEKKER *Virg. Martyr* II. i, Bacchus,..grand patron of rob-pots, upsie-freesie tiplers, and super-naculum takers. **1738** *Gentl. Mag.* VIII. 527/1 Which might be apply'd to much higher People, than poor Ale-house Tiplers. **1829** LYTTON *Devereux* II. v, The women love not an early tippler. **1899** *Allbutt's Syst. Med.* VIII. 724 The moist palm of the habitual tippler is familiar to every one.

ˈtippler^{2}. *dial.* [f. TIPPLE *v.*^{2} + -ER^{1}.] One who binds up hay in tipples: see TIPPLE *sb.*^{2}

1812 [see TIPPLE *v.*^{2}].

ˈtippler^{3}. [f. TIPPLE *v.*^{3} + -ER^{1}.] One who or that which tips or turns over: *spec.*

1. A frame or cage into which a wagon, truck, or tub is run, and which is then revolved so as to invert the wagon and discharge its contents.

1831 J. HOLLAND *Manuf. Metal* I. 46 Instead of the old corve and water bucket, an iron box, mounted on wheels, and called a tippler, and somewhat resembling in shape a common coal skip is made to travel completely round. **1891** KIPLING *City Dreadf. Nt.* 83 The tub is run out into a 'tippler' and discharges itself into a coal-truck. **1911** *Encycl. Brit.* VI. 591 The tub..is run into a 'tippler', a cage turning about a horizontal axis, which discharges the load..and brings the tub back to the original position.

2. A variety of tumbler pigeon: see quot. 1879.

1847–78 HALLIWELL, *Tippler*, a tumbler; hence, when they talk of a tumbler pigeon, you hear them say, 'What a tippler he is!' **1879** L. WRIGHT *Pigeon Keeper* x. 128 [*Tipplers* throw only one such] backward somersault in the air at a time... *Tumblers* often make two, three, or more backward revolutions without stopping. **1885** *Bazaar* 30 Mar. 1265/1 Tipplers.—4 pairs of Macclesfield tipplers. Price 4/- per pair.

tippling (ˈtɪplɪŋ), *vbl. sb.*^{1} [In form and sense, the ordinary vbl. sb. in -ING^{1} from TIPPLE *v.*^{1}; as to date, etc., see the latter.] The action of TIPPLE *v.*^{1}

†**1.** The retailing of ale or other strong drink; the business of a 'tippler' (TIPPLER^{1} 1). *Obs.*

1531 in W. H. Turner *Select Rec. Oxford* (1880) 106 Persons that occupye any typpellyng or coblers crafte. **1579** *Ibid.* 400 To be discharged from keepinge of any tipplinge. **1550–1** in W. Hudson *Leet Jurisd. Norwich* (1892) 87 Amercyd for typplyng of ale and bere with unlawfull metts & measures. **1594** in J. Morris *Troub. Cath. Forefathers* (1877) 280 Also Dorothy Browne, widow who..was heretofore discharged in open sessions from brewing and tippling.

2. The drinking of intoxicating drink, esp. in small quantities and often; habitual indulgence in liquor (to some degree of excess, but usually not amounting to positive drunkenness).

1567 *Let.* in *A. Jenkinson's Voy. & Trav.* (Hakl. Soc.) II. 214 If this typling be not left we will sende no more wyne. **1665** NEEDHAM *Med. Medicinæ* 406 Perpetual Tiplings and large drinking Bouts. **1771** WESLEY *Wks.* (1872) VI. 152 Preventing tippling on the Lord's day, spending the time in alehouses. **1868** *Regul. & Ord. Army* ¶942 No tippling or gambling is to be allowed in any of the barrack rooms.

3. *attrib.* and *Comb.* (See also TIPPLING-HOUSE.)

Tippling Act, Act 24 Geo. II, c. 40.

1579–80 NORTH *Plutarch* (1595) 135 But in the ende.. this bribing wretch was forced for to hold a typling booth, most like a clowne or snuch. **1616** SYLVESTER *Tobacco Battered* 215 'Tis vented most in Taverns, Tippling-cots, To Ruffians, Roarers, Tipsie-Tostie-pots. **1621** BURTON *Anat. Mel.* Democr. to Rdr. (1628) 55 We liue wholly by Tippling-Innes and Ale-Houses. **1755** W. DUNCAN *Cicero's Sel. Orat.* xvi. (1816) 623 Under his roofs are.. tippling-shops instead of dining rooms. **1784** COWPER *Task* VI. 695 The rabble all alive From tipling-benches.. Swarm in the streets.

ˈtippling, *vbl. sb.*^{2} *dial.* [f. TIPPLE *v.*^{2} + -ING^{1}.] The binding of hay in tipples.

1770–4 A. HUNTER *Georg. Ess.* (1803) III. 194 The expense of tipling did not exceed five shillings a statute acre. **1812** SIR J. SINCLAIR *Syst. Husb. Scot.* I. 401 Tippling.. he considers.. to be not only a cheap, but a superior mode of making hay.

ˈtippling, *ppl. a.* [f. TIPPLE *v.*^{1} + -ING^{2}.] That tipples.

†**1.** That carries on the business of a 'tippler' (TIPPLER^{1} 1); that sells liquor by retail. *Obs.*

?*a* **1500** *Chester Pl., Harrow. Hell* (Shaks. Soc.) II. 82 With all tiplinge tapsters that are cuninge, Mysspendinge moche maulte, brewinge so theyne. **1552** HULOET, Typplyng wyfe, *stabularia mulier*.

2. That habitually indulges (to some excess) in strong drink; given to drinking.

1567 HARMAN *Caveat* 59 One of these tipling Tinckers.. robbed by the high way iiij Pallyards. **1693** J. EDWARDS *Author. O. & N. Test.* 210 Bacchus.. the poets tippling deity. **1818** SCOTT *Hrt. Midl.* xlviii, That tippling body, the Captain. **1872** J. TIMBS *Clubs & Club Life* I. 146 A merry company of tippling citizens and jocular change-brokers.

ˈtippling-house. *Obs.* exc. *Hist.* [f. TIPPLING *vbl. sb.*^{1} + HOUSE *sb.*] A house where intoxicating liquor is sold and drunk; an ale-house, a tavern.

1547 BOORDE *Introd. Knowl.* xxxi. (1870) 200 The best fare is in prestes houses, for they do kepe typlynge houses. **1551–2** *Act 5 & 6 Edw. VI*, c. 25 *Preamble*, Comen Ale-houses and other houses called Tiplinge houses. **1639** LAUD *Wks.* (1853) V. 239 Our university of Oxford had heretofore the government and correction of all manner of ale-house-keepers, ale-houses, and other tippling-houses. **1757** WASHINGTON *Let.* Writ. 1889 I. 502 Instances of the villainous Behavior of those Tippling-House-keepers. **1817** SCOTT *Let. to Morritt* 11 Aug., in *Lockhart*, There is a terrible evil in England to which we are strangers,—the number, to-wit, of tippling houses, where the labourer.. spends the overplus of his earnings. **1877** BURROUGHS *Taxation* 393 'To regulate and restrain tippling houses', confers no power to tax them.

tipply (ˈtɪplɪ), *a. colloq.* [f. TIPPLE *v.*^{3} + -Y.] Apt to 'tipple' or tip over; unsteady; = TIPPY *a.*^{2}

1906 *Westm. Gaz.* 11 June 8/2 A narrow river crowded.. with pleasure-craft—launches and 'party-boats', safe tubs and tipply canoes.

tippy (ˈtɪpɪ), *a.*^{1} (*sb.*) [f. TIP *sb.*^{1} + -Y.]

I. *colloq.* or *slang.* **1. a.** In the height of fashion; smart, fine, fashionable, 'swell', 'tip-top'. ? *Obs.*

1810 *Splendid Follies* I. 31 'My curricle has.. never yet carried a bear', 'Except its Master', thought Seraphina, as she gazed on this tippy-bob. **1825** JAMIESON, *Tippy*, adj., dressed in the highest fashion, modish. **1826** *Sporting Mag.* XVII. 177 With his hosen so tight, and his castor so white, and his caxon in tippy curl. **1847** *Blackw. Mag.* LXII. 47 His horse was the swiftest, his coat the tippiest, his cigar the longest. **1871** P. CARTWRIGHT *50 Years Presiding Elder* 216 It was not one of your tippy, fashionable, silver-slippered kind of conversions, but it was a backwoods conversion.

†**b.** *absol. the tippy*: the height of fashion; the 'swell' or fashionable thing. *Obs.*

1790 A. M. WOODFORDE *Let.* 3 Sept. in *Parson Woodforde Soc. Jrnl.* (1972) V. III. 55 Your Bonnets are quite the *Tippy*. **1794** *Sporting Mag.* III. 104 Being estimated.. as quite the Tippy. **1803** *Ibid.* XXI. 145 The two-shilling gallery is now quite the tippy for the boxes. **1804** CHARLOTTE SMITH *Conversations*, etc. I. 25 Germain says, I shall be quite the thing, the tippy. **1811** *Ora & Juliet* III. 133 Do you see that handsome young man there?.. he at the bottom,.. that's so dressed in the tippy.

†**c.** as *sb.* A dandy. *Obs.*

1798 *Monthly Mag. & Brit. Reg.* VI. 173/1 His dress.. will be, elegant; exhibiting no articles of apparel but such as are 'All the rage', he is 'Quite the tippy'. **1844** 'J. SLICK' *High Life N.Y.* II. 92 You wouldn't ketch one of our York tippies at that, let alone a ginuine Lord.

2. Highly ingenious or clever; neat, smart. [perh. associated with TIP *sb.*^{4}]

1863 M. DODS *Early Lett.* (1910) 344 A tippy little bit of criticism by Pressensé. **1906** *Daily Chron.* 11 Oct. 3/5 All we think of is the 'tippy' way in which he is got rid of.

II. 3. Of tea: Containing a large proportion of the 'tips' or leaf-buds of the shoot.

1892 WALSH *Tea* (Philad.) 87 The dried leaf [of Paklum] is also very black, fairly made and often 'tippy' in the hand. *Ibid.* 107 The leaf [of Neilgherry] is black, coarse, 'tippy' and unsightly in the hand. **1895** *Times* 21 Jan. 13/5 For the finest qualities: for handsome tippy teas, which are becoming scarce; and for good Darjeelings, the tendency is to higher quotations.

ˈtippy, *a.*^{2} *colloq.* [f. TIP *v.*^{2} + -Y.]

Characterized by tipping or tilting; unsteady. *U.S.*

1886 *Philadelphia Times* 16 Jan. (Cent.), The tippy sea. **1923** E. F. WYATT *Invisible Gods* III. i. 93 A tippy, wire-legged table.

tippy-toe (ˈtɪpɪtəʊ), *sb.* (*adv.*, *a.*). Also **tippi-toe.** [Alteration of TIPTOE, TIP-TOE *sb.* (*adv.*, *a.*): cf. -Y^{6}.] **A.** *sb. pl.* The tips of the toes. Usu. in phr. *on* (one's) *tippy-toes*. Occas. also as collect. *sing.*

1899 *Century Mag.* Nov. 47/2 The whole court now stood on its tippy-toes. **1965** *New Statesman* 3 Dec. 897/2 Illustrations.. show the dear little mite standing on tippy-toe to feed famished and deserted nestlings. **1980** *Dirt Bike* Oct. 68/1, I stood on tippi-toes to watch.

B. *adv.* Short for *on tippy-toes* (see sense A above).

1901 'ZACK' *Dunstable Weir* 216 The rocking stone stud tippy-toe above his girt shadder. **1975** R. HELMS *Tolkien's World* iv. 126 A rather vulgar sugar-iced concoction, with a doll tippy-toe on its pinnacle as the Fairy Queen.

C. *adj.* Standing or walking on tiptoe. Also *fig.*

1951 J. STEINBECK *Log from 'Sea of Cortez'* p. xli, Ed would be smiling and doing his tippy-toe mouse dance. **1968** *Courier-Mail* (Brisbane) 8 Nov. 1/5 He [*sc.* Richard Nixon] is not as cautious and tippy-toe as he appeared to many voters. **1980** S. T. HAYMON *Death & Pregnant Virgin* ix. 71 When Jack Ellers was excited he rose up on the balls of his feet... Now he came into the dreary room.. all tippy-toe.

ˈtippy-toe, *v.* Also **tippie-toe.** [f. prec.] *intr.* To go on tiptoe, to move lightly. Also *fig.* Cf. TIPTOE *v.* 2.

1901 'ZACK' *Dunstable Weir* 232, I tippy-toed back to the fire. **1942** C. MORLEY *Thorofare* xxxvi. 169, I tippy-toed down one side to join the Confed'racy while my old man was pretending to look up the other. **1974** *Globe & Mail* (Toronto) 29 Oct. 6/6 Did he tippy-toe across the press? **1980** *Daily Tel.* 2 Sept. 11/2 The roly-poly little girl who tippy-toed through Sandy Wilson's enchanting 'Big Best Shoes' number in 'Valmouth' all those years ago.

Hence **ˈtippy-toed** *ppl. a.* (in quot. as quasi-*adv.*).

1938 M. K. RAWLINGS *Yearling* iv. 31 A deer track'll prove the same. A deer or bear that's fat and heavy'll sink in that-a-way [at the heel]. A lettle ol' light doe or yearlin' 'll walk tippy-toed, and you'll not see more than the front of their hooves.

tipsify (ˈtɪpsɪfaɪ), *v.* [f. TIPSY + -FY.] *trans.* To make tipsy; to intoxicate (in quot. 1837 slightly or partially). Hence **tipsifiˈcation**, intoxication; **ˈtipsifiˌcator**, **ˈtipsifier**, one who tipsifies (in quots., one who gets drunk, a tippler or toper); **ˈtipsified** *ppl. a.*, made tipsy, (slightly) intoxicated. (All more or less *nonce-wds.*)

1830 *Fraser's Mag.* I. 740 In all matters of coenic revelry and tipsified jollification. **1837** CARLYLE *Misc.*, *Mirabeau* (1857) IV. 95 The man was but tipsified when he went; happily, when he returned, which was very late, he was drunk. **1848** THACKERAY *Bk. Snobs* xxiii, Poor Raff is tipsifying himself with spirits. **1864** SALA in *Daily Tel.* 27 July, The sharp New England mind.. has long since endorsed the locution 'as tight as a peep' to express an utter state of tipsification. **1873** LELAND *Egyptian Sketch-Bk.* 288 The last thing attended to by the tipsificators. **1873** MRS. WHITNEY *Other Girls* iv, Our first man was a tipsifier, and the last was a rogue. **1888** STEVENSON *Black Arrow* 169 A certain air of tipsified simplicity and good-fellowship.

tipsily (ˈtɪpsɪlɪ), *adv.* [f. as prec. + -LY^{2}.] In a tipsy manner; unsteadily as from intoxication.

1818 KEATS *Endym.* IV. 217 Near him rode Silenus on his ass, Pelted with flowers as he on did pass, Tipsily quaffing. **1824** in *Spirit Pub. Jrnls.* (1825) 203 Tom Moore to Lord Lansdown is tipsily speeching. **1864** LOWELL *Fireside Trav.* 89 Knocked down by a tipsily-driven sleigh.

tipsiness (ˈtɪpsɪnɪs). [f. as prec. + -NESS.] The state or condition of being tipsy; a partial degree of intoxication; also *fig.*

1598 FLORIO, *Ebbriachezza*, dronkennes, tipsines. **1681** H. MORE *Exp. Dan.* Pref. 7 Partly out of tipsiness, and partly out of consternation of mind. **1840** DICKENS *Barn. Rudge* iii, Firmly set upon his legs on that neutral ground which lies between the confines of perfect sobriety and slight tipsiness. **1855** GEO. ELIOT *Ess.* (1884) 290 No tipsiness can be more dead to all appeals than that which comes from fitful draughts of sleep on a railway journey by night.

tip-sled: see TIP- *vb. stem.*

tipstaff (ˈtɪpstɑːf, -æ-). Pl. **-staffs** (-stɑːfs, -æ-), or **-staves** (-steɪvz). [Contraction of *tipped* or *tipt staff*: see TIPPED *ppl. a.*^{1} 3.]

†**1.** A staff with a tip or cap of metal, carried as a badge by certain officials: see 2. *Obs.*

1541–2 *Act 33 Hen. VIII*, c. 12 §26 Anye of the Kinges.. officers, that.. shall strike any person.. withe anye staffe commonye called a Tipp staffe. **1579–80** NORTH *Plutarch* (1676) 219 Sergeants and other Officers holding Tipstaves in their hands. **1695** CONGREVE *Love for L.* I. iv, Two suspicious Fellows like lawful Pads, that would knock a Man down with Pocket Tipstaves.

†**b.** *pl.* Used for 'stilts'. *Obs. nonce-use.*

1582 STANYHURST *Craking Cutter* in *Æneis*, etc. (Arb.) 143 Linckt was in wedlock a loftye Thrasonical huf snuffe: In gate al on typstau's stalcking, in phisnomye daring.

2. An official carrying a tipped staff; *spec.* **a.** A sheriff's officer, bailiff, constable; **b.** An officer appointed to wait upon a court in session; a court crier or usher. *arch.*

1570 FOXE *A. & M.* (ed. 2) 1365/1 The knight Marshall with all hys tippe staues. **1600** HOLLAND *Livy* XLV. xxix. 1220 When they saw the tipstaves and huishers to keepe the doores and places of entrie. **1687** *Magd. Coll. & Jas. II* (O.H.S.) 148 Then their Lordships.. commissioned Atterbury the Tipstaff to fetch a Smith to force them open. **1710** J. HARRIS *Lex. Techn.* II, *Tip-staves*, are the Warden of the Fleets Officers attending the Queen's Courts with a Painted Staff, for taking into Custody such Persons [etc.]. **1831** CARLYLE *Sart. Res.* I. ix, Those ministering Sheriffs and Lord-Lieutenants and Hangmen and Tipstaves. **1882** SERJT. BALLANTINE *Exper.* xli. 387 They were tipstaves, prepared to take [him].. into custody. **1888** GOW *Comp. School Classics* 290 Order was maintained by tip-staffs, ῥαβδοῦχοι.

Hence **ˈtipˌstavery** (*nonce-wd.*), a body of tipstaffs.

1911 B. CAPES *Loaves & Fishes* 224 Cracking their inevitable chestnuts for the benefit of an obsequious tipstavery.

tipster (ˈtɪpstə(r)). [f. TIP *sb.*^{4} + -STER. (In sense 2 erron. f. TIP *sb.*^{3})]

1. a. A man who makes a business of furnishing 'tips' or confidential information as to the probable chances of an event on which betting depends, esp. in horse-racing. Also *attrib.*, as *tipster sheet* (U.S.). Cf. *tip-sheet* s.v. TIP *sb.*^{4} e.

1862 *Times* 31 Dec., Prophets, tipsters, and welshers—the parasites of the ring—are flourishing upon the infatuation or the ignorance of society. **1865** *Ibid.* 23 Sept., His Lordship asked the meaning of the word 'tipster'. Mr. Soper said it was one who prophesied, or pretended to tell the winners —who 'tipped' the word. **1897** *Daily News* 20 Oct. 3 To stop solicitations from tipsters and bookmakers to persons under the age of twenty-one. **1933** *Sun* (Baltimore) 17 July 1/2 Warning against the use of 'tipster sheets' and 'market service' by stock market and other investment patrons was issued today.

b. *transf.* One who furnishes 'tips' in general.

1884 *Manch. Exam.* 17 Nov. 5/2 If it is ever of great consequence to follow the rôle of the political tipster. **1900** *Westm. Gaz.* 11 May 9/1 No wonder the price of.. shares has given way... The fall is due entirely to the overthrow of the tipsters, who led us to expect so much, only to plunge us into the deepest disappointment.

2. One who systematically gives 'tips' or gratuities: see TIPPER^{1} 4.

1889 *Pall Mall G.* 18 Feb. 7/3 It is not uncommon for the 'tipster' to pay to the employé of the purchaser a fixed commission of so much per pound or ton on all goods purchased by the master. It then becomes the interest of the servant to make his master buy as much as possible of any article from the 'tipster'.

ˈtip-stock. [f. TIP *sb.*^{1} or *v.*^{2} + STOCK *sb.*] A form of gun-stock: see quots.

1891 *Cent. Dict.*, *Tip-stock*, the movable tip or fore end of a gunstock, situated under the barrel or barrels, especially when it is a separate piece, in front of the breech or trigger-guard. A hinged or detachable tip-stock is required for breech-loaders which break in the vertical plane. **1895** *Funk's Standard Dict.* s.v. *Tip^{1}*, *v.*, *Tip-stock*, a gun-stock arranged to hinge or tip, as for convenience in loading.

tip-stretcher: see TIP *sb.*^{1} 6.

tipsy (ˈtɪpsɪ), *a.* Also 6–8 **tipsie**, 7–9 **tipsey.** [app. f. TIP *v.*^{2} sense 8 (or ? 4, 5): cf. *tricksy*: see F. Hall *Mod. Eng.* 272.]

Affected with liquor so as to be unable to walk or stand steadily; partly intoxicated: often *euphemistic* for Intoxicated, inebriated, drunk.

1577 HANMER *Anc. Eccl. Hist.* (1663) 117 About ten of the clock, whenas they were somewhat tipsie, and well crammed with victuals. **1590** SHAKS. *Mids. N.* V. i. 48 The riot of the tipsie Bachanals. **1623** MIDDLETON *More Dissemblers* IV. i, He that's a gipsy may be drunk or tipsy. *a* **1668** DAVENANT *Play-house to Let* V. i, Sure Tony and you have drunk till y'are tipsey. *a* **1700** B. E. *Dict. Cant. Crew*, *Tipsy*, a'most Drunk. **1706** PHILLIPS (ed. Kersey), *Tipsy*, that is a little in Drink, fuddled. **1777** MME. D'ARBLAY *Early Diary* 7 Apr., She forced wine and water.. down her throat, till she was almost tipsey. **1889** STEVENSON *Master of B.* viii, I have seen them flee from him when he was tipsy, and stone him when he was drunk.

b. *transf.* Characterized or accompanied by intoxication; arising from or causing tipsiness.

1634 MILTON *Comus* 104 Tipsie dance, and Jollity. **1760** FAWKES tr. *Anacreon, Ode* xli. 24 Then let me, warm with Wine, advance, And revel in the Tipsy Dance. **1851** THACKERAY *Eng. Hum.*, *Swift* (1858) 32 He was not bred up in a tipsy guard-room.

c. *fig.* Affected as if by intoxicating liquor; unsteady as if from drink; inclined to tip or tilt.

1754 RICHARDSON *Grandison* VI. ix. 31 Lord G. could not keep his seat: He was tipsy poor man with his joy. **1852** H. ROGERS *Ess.* I. vii. 339 He was.. intellectually as tipsy as ever nitrous oxide could have made him. **1895** *Funk's Standard Dict.*, *Tipsy*.. 3. Bobbing and swaying; tipping about; also, liable to tip;.. as, a tipsy boat. **1905** *Daily News* 26 Aug. 6 They ['To Let' boards] lean into the street at all sorts of tipsy angles.

d. ***tipsy key***: a kind of watch-key invented by Bréguet: see quot.

1884 F. J. BRITTEN *Watch and Clockm.* 36 [A] Tipsy key [is] a watch key in which the upper and lower portions are connected by means of a ratchet clutch kept in gear by a spring, so that the upper part will turn the lower part in the proper direction for winding.

e. *Comb.* **'tipsy-'topsy** *a.* (*nonce-wd.*) [cf. *topsy-turvy*], upset or in disorder as if tipsy.

a **1845** HOOD *She is far fr. the Land* 59 Trunks tipsy-topsy, The ship in a dropsy.

Hence **'tipsy** *v., trans.* to make tipsy, tipsify.

1673 SHADWELL *Epsom Wells* I, Why, I..got a little tipsy'd, as they say, and forgot it. **1691** —— *Scowrers* v, I was tipsied last night. **1849** JAMES *Woodman* iv, A butt of it would not have tipsied a sucking lamb.

'tipsy-,cake. A cake saturated with wine or spirit, stuck with almonds, and served with custard.

1806 MISS MITFORD in L'Estrange *Friendships Mary R. Mitford* (1882) I. 10 We had..tipsey cake on one side, and grape tart on the other. **1845** J. C. ATKINSON in *Proc. Berw. Nat. Club* II. No. 13. 134 Red gypsum, externally set as full of..dog's-tooth crystals as a tipsy-cake with almonds. **1859** *Habits of Gd. Society* xiii. 338 As indispensable an element of the ball-supper as trifle, tipsy-cake, and mayonnaise.

tipsy-turvy, obs. var. TOPSY-TURVY.

tipt, pa. t. and pple. of TIP *v.*; now less used than TIPPED.

tip-tail. [f. TIP *sb.*[1] + TAIL *sb.*[1], after *tiptoe.*] The tip of the tail: only in phr. ***on*** or ***upon tip-tail.***

1836-48 B. D. WALSH *Aristoph., Acharnians* II. vi, You sat all the time upon tip-tail [Gr. ἐπ' ἄκρων πυγιδίων on the tips of their rumps]. **1876** MISS BRADDON *J. Haggard's Dau.* xxv, A curly serpent standing on tip tail between them. **1900** A. B. COOK in *Jrnl. Hellenic Stud.* XX. 2 Straightway struck by the crown you sat there on tip-tail.

tip-tap ('tɪptæp), *sb.* (*a.*), *v.* [f. TIP *sb.*[2] or *v.*[1] + TAP *sb.*[2] or *v.*[2]; or reduplication of TAP *sb.*[2] or *v.*[2], with alternation of vowel (cf. *zig-zag, pit-a-pat*).] **a.** A repeated tapping or light knocking of alternating character, or the sound made by it. **b.** *attrib.* or *adj.* That taps repeatedly. **c.** *vb.* To tap repeatedly or in alternation; hence **tip-'tapping** *ppl. a.* **d.** as *adv.* With a tapping sound. Also **tip-tap-toe** = TICK-TACK-TOE.

1604 MARSTON *Malcontent* III. v, Liues not more faith in a home thrusting tongue, Then in these fencing tip tap Courtiers? *a* **1847** ELIZA COOK *Winter is here* i, The old robin has come To remind us with tip-tapping bill. **1849** [DINSDALE] *Durham Gloss.* (E.D.D.), Tip-tap-toe. **1892** BARRETT *Essex Highways*, etc. 56 The tip-tap of the flail may yet be heard. **1905** *Westm. Gaz.* 29 Nov. 1/3 Many a time and oft have I sat in the sun and hearkened to the tip-tap, tip-tap of his tiny hammer. **1911** H. S. WALPOLE *Mr. Perrin & Mr. Traill* vi. 104 He came tip-tap across the floor to him.

'tip-,tilted, *a.* [f. TIP *sb.*[1] + TILTED *ppl. a.*[2]] Having the tip 'tilted', i.e. turned up. Hence **tip-'tilt** *v., trans.* to turn up at the tip.

1872 TENNYSON *Gareth* 576 And lightly was her slender nose Tip-tilted like the petal of a flower. **1877** MRS. FORRESTER *Mignon* II. 51 Mignon 'tiptilts' her nose. **1882** ANNIE EDWARDES *Ballroom Repent* I. 12 A Diana with..a tip-tilted nose. **1884** SIR C. W. WILSON in *Q. Statem. Palestine Explor. Fund* Jan. 48 The tip-tilted shoes are the ordinary sandals of the country.

tiptoe, tip-toe ('tɪptəʊ), *sb.* (*adv., a.*) Forms: *pl.* 4-5 tiptoon, 5 typtoon, -ton, -toos, tiptos, 6 typtoes, tippetoes, *Sc.* typtays, typtaes, 6- tiptoes, 7- tip-toes; *sing.* 5 typto, tiptoo, 6 tipto, typtoe, 6- tiptoe, 7- tip-toe. [f. TIP *sb.*[1] + TOE *sb.*, pl. in ME. *toon*, mod.E. *toes.*]

1. *pl.* The tips of the toes; almost always in phr. ***on*** or ***upon*** (one's) ***tiptoes***, denoting a posture (in standing or walking) with the heels raised so that the body is supported upon the tips or balls of the toes. (Now more usually *on tiptoe*: see 2.)

c **1386** CHAUCER *Nun's Pr. T.* 487 He moste wynke..And stonden on his tiptoon [*v.rr.* typton, typtoon, typtoos, tiptos] ther-with-al, And strecche forth his nekke long and smal. ? *c* **1400** LYDG. *Æsop's Fab.* i. 44 [The cock] On his typton disposyd for to syng. **1513** DOUGLAS *Æneis* IX. xii. 53 Standand on his typtays. **1573-80** BARET *Alv.* G 368 To go soft and faire on his tippetoes. **1591** SPENSER *M. Hubberd* 1009 Vpon his tiptoes nicely he vp went. **1642** FULLER *Holy & Prof. St.* III. ix. 171 He needs to stand on tiptoes that hopes to touch the moon. **1712** *Spect.* No. 460 ¶7 Gallantry strutting upon his Tip-toes. *a* **1845** HOOD *As it fell upon a Day* ii, And then upon her tiptoes jumping.

transf. **1848** TENNYSON in Ld. Tennyson *Mem.* (1897) I. xiii. 281 We arrived at the banks of the loch, and made acquaintance with the extremest tiptoes of the hills.

b. *fig.*: usually in reference to expectation or eagerness (formerly to pretension or haughtiness).

1579 TOMSON *Calvin's Serm. Tim.* 550/1 Because men stand willingly vppon their tiptoes, and thinke no man worthie to haue preheminence aboue his fellowes. **1639** FULLER *Holy War* II. ix. (1840) 60 All stood on the tiptoes of expectation. **1651** N. BACON *Disc. Govt. Eng.* II. xxvii. (1739) 125 The minds of men are at a gaze; their Affections and Passions are on their Tiptoes. **1682** N. O. *Boileau's Lutrin* I. 333 Their figg'ring Souls do now on Tiptoes stand.

2. *sing.* The tips of the toes collectively; almost always in phr. ***on*** or ***upon tiptoe*** (cf. 1).

c **1440** [see b]. **1525** W. SMITH *Wido Edyth* in *Laneham's Let.* (1871) p. xlv, Than Wa[l]ter stode on tipto, and gan him self avance. **1607** DAVIES *Summa Totalis* B ij b, But when we stand on Tip-toe, or a Ball, (Though sliding still) we finally must fall. **1760-72** H. BROOKE *Fool of Qual.* (1809) IV. 124 [He] entered my chamber on tip-toe. **1833** L. RITCHIE *Wand. by Loire* 164 Standing on tiptoe, [he] looked into one of the windows. **1861** HUGHES *Tom Brown at Oxf.* xxxii, He followed his cousin on tip-toe.

b. *transf.* and *fig.*: cf. 1 b. (Often ***the tiptoe.***)

c **1440** *Pallad. on Husb.* XI. 46 And right so on the typto [*v.r.* tiptoo] lete hem [vines] gey. **1602** MARSTON *Antonio's Rev.* IV. iii, Your eyes should sparkle joy, Your bosome rise on tiptoe at this news. **1642** MILTON *Apol. Smect.* iv. Wks. 1738 I. 118 What with putting his fancy to the tiptoe in this description of himself. **1799** NELSON in Nicolas *Disp.* (1845) III. 374 We are on the tip-toe of expectation. **1860-1** FLOR. NIGHTINGALE *Nursing* 38 Do not keep his expectation on the tip-toe.

c. ***a-tiptoe*** = on tiptoe: see A-TIPTOE.

B. *adv.* Short for *on* or *a-tiptoe*: see 2 above.

1592 SHAKS. *Rom. & Jul.* III. v. 10 Nights Candles are burnt out, and Iocond day Stands tipto on the mistie Mountaines tops. **1612** *Two Noble K.* I. ii. 57 To go tip-toe Before the streete be foule. **1821** CLARE *Vill. Minstr.* I. 186 Then tiptoe round the maidens bound, All sorrow lags behind. **1854** EMERSON *Soc. Aims* Wks. (Bohn) III. 182 It is not that they wish you to stand tiptoe, and pump your brains.

C. *adj.* Standing or walking, or characterized by standing or walking, on tiptoe.

1593 [see b]. **1744** H. BROOKE *Love & Van.* 120 Why, what unfashion'd stuff you tell us Of buckram dames and tiptoe fellows! **1781** COWPER *Expost.* 84 With tip-toe step Vice silently succeeds. **1801** MAR. EDGEWORTH *Gd. French Gov.* (1831) 146 Grace..made her tiptoe approaches. **1848** MRS. GASKELL *M. Barton* ii, He, with habitual tip-toe step, approached the poor frail body.

b. *transf.* and *fig.* in various senses: e.g. straining upwards, ambitious; eagerly expectant; tripping, dancing; silent, stealthy.

1593 NASHE *Christ's T.* Wks. (Grosart) IV. 122 Hath no chyld of Pryde so many Disciples as thys tiptoe Ambition. **1789** E. DARWIN *Bot. Gard.* I. 386 You..Bade his bold arm invade the lowering sky, And seize the tiptoe lightnings, ere they fly. **1818** KEATS *Endymion* I. 831 How tiptoe Night holds back her dark-grey hood. **1823** SCOTT *Peveril* iv, The Cavaliers..were filling the principal avenue to the Castle with tiptoe mirth and revelry. **1879** G. MEREDITH *Egoist* xii, Man or maid sleeping in the open air provokes your tip-toe curiosity.

D. *Comb.* of the *adv.*, as † ***tiptoe-nice*** (so nice or particular as to walk on tiptoe), †***-strouting, -tripping*** adjs.

1593 NASHE *Christ's T.* Wks. (Grosart) IV. 218 So typtoe-nyce in treading on the earth, as though they walkt vpon Snakes. **1600** S. NICHOLSON *Acolastus* (1876) 39 Their tipto-tripping pace bred double mazing. **1602** *2nd Pt. Return fr. Parnass.* III. iv. 1386 To honour me: For my high tiptoe strouting poesye.

'tiptoe, *v.* [f. prec.]

1. *intr.* To raise oneself or stand on tiptoe.

a **1661** HOLYDAY *Juvenal* vi. (1673) 101 Then a girle-pygmie shee's more dwarf..and tiptoes for a kisse and flout. **1851** J. H. NEWMAN *Cath. in Eng.* 243 They crowd up together,..tiptoeing and staring, and making strange faces. **1888** *Century Mag.* Nov. 90/1 The..girls..left their seats to tiptoe and look over each other's shoulders.

2. To go or walk on tiptoe; to step or trip lightly. Also ***to tiptoe it.***

1748 RICHARDSON *Clarissa* (1811) VI. xxv. 104 Mabell tiptoed it to her door. **1883** MRS. ROLLINS *New Eng. Bygones* 62, I tiptoe across the fragile floor and look out. **1897** HOWELLS *Landl. Lion's Head* 68 Ladies..lifting their skirts and tiptoeing through the dew.

Hence **'tiptoed** *ppl. a.*, (*a*) raised on tiptoe; also *fig.*, rising aloft; (*b*) performed on tiptoe; **'tiptoeing** *ppl. a.*, standing or going on tiptoe.

1632 LITHGOW *Trav.* x. 499 Meandring Forth from tip-toed Snadoun, the prospicuous mirrour for matchlesse Maiesty. **1682** D'URFEY *Butler's Ghost* 92 To please the tip-toed Girl of Ten. **1819** *Metropolis* III. 164 Eagle-eyed curiosity staring you in the face, tip-toed anxiety standing on either hand. *a* **1847** ELIZA COOK *Rory O'More* viii, His tip-toeing feet seemed inclined for a jig.

'tip-'top, *sb., a., adv. colloq.* Also **tiptop.** [f. TIP *sb.*[1] + TOP, or reduplicated form of the latter.]

A. *sb.* **1.** The very top; the highest point or part; the extreme summit.

1702 [see 2]. **1759** *Compl. Letter-writer* (ed. 6) 219 Upon the tip top of the monument. **1826** S. THOMAS in Hone *Every-day Bk.* II. 186 The tip-top of the plant. **1857** DICKENS *Let.* 15 Apr., On the tip-top of Gad's Hill, between this and Rochester,..I have a pretty little old-fashioned house. *a* **1887** in Frith *Autobiog.* II. ii. 37 You should paint him sitting on the tip-top of the mast of a big ship.

2. *fig.* **a.** Highest pitch or degree; extreme height; acme.

1702 S. PARKER tr. *Cicero's De Finibus* IV. 228 When a Wise Man is at the Tip-top of all Felicity, can he wish Things were better with him? **1747** WESLEY *Wks.* (1872) XII. 83 The tip-top of all inconsistencies. **1798** O'KEEFFE *Wild Oats* III. i, All on the tip-top of expectation. **1832** HAWTHORNE *Twice-told T.* (1851) I. x. 171, I cry aloud to all and sundry..at the very tiptop of my voice.

b. *sing.* and *pl.* People of the highest quality or rank (collectively); 'grandees', 'swells'. ? *Obs.*

1753 *School of Man* 125 To figure among high company.. this his marriage has done at once, and among the Tip Top. **1797** MRS. A. M. BENNETT *Beggar Girl* (1813) III. 278 The spark was kin to some of the tip-tops of his own kindred. **1849** THACKERAY *Pendennis* lx, We go here to the best houses, the tiptops, I tell you.

3. *Angling.* A line guide on a fishing-rod. *N. Amer.*

1961 *Washington Post* 5 Feb. c6/6 A tiptop for flyrod and casting rod. **1971** *Islander* (Victoria, B.C.) 5 Sept. 5/3 Many cases of broken lines can be traced to cracks or nicks on a fishing rod's guides or tiptop.

B. *adj.* Situated at the very top; very highest; almost always *fig.* of the highest quality or excellence; first-rate, prime, superlatively good; of persons, belonging to the highest rank or class.

1722 BYROM *Epil. Hurlothrumbo* Poems 1773 I. 215 Proud of your Smiles, he's mounted many a Story Above the tip-top Pinnacle of Glory. **1732** *Tricks of Town* 8, I have known a tip-top Physician sent for by an Express [etc.]. **1755** SMOLLETT *Quix.* I. II. iv. (1803) I. 93 He made carols for Christmas eve, and plays for the Lord's day;..and every body said, they were tip-top. **1825** *Sporting Mag.* XVI. 272 One hundred guineas, a tip-top price in those days. **1840** THACKERAY *Paris Sk.-bk.* ii, Quite select, and frequented by the tip-top nobility. **1857** HUGHES *Tom Brown* II. v, He is in tip-top training. **1880** DISRAELI *Endym.* xxi, Our friend Ferrars seems in tiptop company.

C. *adv.* In the highest degree, superlatively, extremely well.

1888 STOCKTON *Dusantes* III. 120 'That suits us tip-top, ma'am', said the coxswain.

D. *Comb.*: **tip-top-castle**, name of some boys' game; **tip-top-gallant** *a.* (*nonce-wd.*) [after *top-gallant*], of superlatively high rank or quality.

1834 KEIGHTLEY *Tales*, etc. i. 12 He was a capital player at *tip-top-castle. **1730** SWIFT *Vind. Ld. Carteret* Wks. 1841 II. 117/1, I do not find how his excellency can be justly censured for favouring none but..*tiptopgallantmen.

Hence **,tip-'topmost** *a. colloq.*, (*a*) highest; (*b*) best; **,tip'topness; tip-'topper,** a 'tip-top' person or thing; in quot. 1822, applied to a glass filled to the very top, a bumper; **tip-'topping** [TOPPING *ppl. a.*], **tip'toppish** (hence ***tip'toppishness***), **tip'topsome** *adjs.* = B.

1937 G. FRANKAU *More of Us* ii. 26 Clashed home the gates. Slow to *tip-topmost storey Groaned lift. **1960** *Guardian* 22 Apr. 8/5 All their tip-topmost British merchandise. **1891** *Boston Daily Globe* 24 Mar. 5/2 The very topmost *tiptopness of Harvard thought. **1822** *Blackw. Mag.* XI. 89 So I think it but proper to fill a *tip-topper Of Sherry to drink to the King. **1829** P. EGAN *Boxiana* 2nd Ser. II. 239 Some *tip-toppers* on the *Corinthian list* were witnessed getting over the ground as 'gaily as larks'. **1837** THACKERAY *Ravenswing* i, One of the first swells on town ma'am—a regular tip-topper. **1882** ANNIE EDWARDES *Ballroom Repent.* I. 243 Give me your operatic tip-toppers —Patti and Trebelli, or nothing. **1827** S. P. in Hone *Every-day Bk.* II. 54 This is mostly with the *tip-topping part [of people]. **1855** W. K. KELLY tr. *Cervantes' Exemp. Novels* 475 All she had told him of the merits, worth, beauty, modesty, and *tiptoppishness..of her mistress, he quite believed. **1819** *Blackw. Mag.* V. 717 In the *tiptopsomest degree.

‖**Tipula** ('tɪpjʊlə). *Entom.* Pl. **tipulæ** (-liː). [L. *tippula* (incorrectly *tipula*) a water-spider or water-bug; so used also by mediæval and early modern writers. The current use is due to Linnæus.] A genus of dipterous insects, typical of the family *Tipulidæ* or crane-flies, the common British species of which are familiarly known as *daddy-long-legs*.

[**1658** ROWLAND *Moufet's Theat. Ins.* 1023 We shall take Gaza's Tipulæ into our consideration among the Water-worms. **1706** PHILLIPS (ed. Kersey), *Tipula* (Lat.), a Water-spider with six Feet, that runs on the top of the Water without sinking. **1817** KIRBY & SP. *Entomol.* xxiii. (1818) II. 371 Linné, in his Lapland tour, noticed a black Tipula which ran over the water, and turned round like a Gyrinus.]

1752 J. HILL *Hist. Anim.* 36 The great Tipula. This is the largest and the most beautiful of the Tipula kind. **1774** GOLDSM. *Nat. Hist.* (1776) VIII. 152 The tipula is a harmless peaceful insect, that offers injury to nothing; the gnat is sanguinary and predaceous. **1831** *Brit. Farmer's Mag.* VI. 321 The grub of this tipula commits its ravages chiefly in the first crop.

Hence **tipularian** (-'ɛərɪən) *a.*, belonging or allied to the genus *Tipula* or family *Tibulidæ*; also as *sb.* (*sc.* insect); **tipulary** ('tɪpjʊlərɪ) *a.* = prec. adj.; **'tipulid, ti'pulidan,** *a.* belonging to the family *Tipulidæ*; *sb.* an insect of this family, a crane-fly; **tipu'lideous** *a.* = prec. adj.

1828 *Tipularian [see *tipulidan*]. **1832** MACGILLIVRAY tr. *Humboldt's Trav.* xviii. (1836) 248 On the streams..the *tipulary flies do not make their appearance. **1852** TH. ROSS *Humboldt's Trav.* II. xxiv. 438 Perhaps, also, the destruction of forests..will somewhat tend to diminish the torment of the tipulary insects. **1893** *Athenæum* 20 May 641/2 Dicranota, a Carnivorous *Tipulid Larva. **1951** C. N. COLYER *Flies Brit. Isles* xxv. 317 It will seem a far cry from the large, long-winged, long-legged Tipulids. **1976** *Nature* 22 Jan. 251/2 There is no evidence that hen grouse do eat tipulids during incubation. **1817** KIRBY & SP. *Entomol.* xxii. (1818) II. 277 The grub of a kind of gnat.., and also another, probably of the *Tipulidan [*ed.* 1828 Tipularian] tribe.., have each a fleshy leg on the underside of the first segment. **1826** *Ibid.* III. xxix. 79 The eggs of..gnats and other Tipulidans [are] set afloat upon, or submerged in, the water. **1840** WESTWOOD *Classif. Insects* II. 170 Checking the over-production of some of the minute *Tipulideous insects.

'tip-up, *sb.* and *a.* [f. phr. *tip up*: TIP *v.*[2]]

A. *sb.* Something that tips or tilts up.

1. A name for the American sandpiper.

1848 [see TEETER *sb.* 2].

2. A wagon with wheels set near together.

1887 LADY BRASSEY *Last Voy.* xiii. (1889) 299 Another conveyance, familiarly known as a 'Tip-up', its narrow wheels making it liable to upset except on good roads.

3. = TILT *sb.*² 6. (*N. Amer.*)

1850 S. F. COOPER *Rural Hours* 42 The boys call these contrivances 'tip-ups', from the bit of stick to which the line is attached, falling over when the fish bite. **1880** *Harper's Mag.* Mar. 517 With baited lines and tip-ups set, we waited. **1923** H. E. WILLIAMS *Spinning Wheels & Homespun* 247 Fishing through the ice... With the aid of what they call 'tip-upses' several lines can be used simultaneously. **1978** *Globe & Mail* (Toronto) 1 Feb. 34/1 Anglers using jigs were more successful than those waiting by a tipup.

4. A tip-up seat (see sense B).

1966 'A. HALL' *9th Directive* xxvi. 234 The other sat on the tip-up behind the front seat.

B. *adj.* Constructed to tip or tilt up, as a receptacle, for the purpose of emptying out its contents, or as a seat (in a theatre, etc.) when not occupied, so as to give room for passing. Esp. as ***tip-up seat***; also with reference to a method of opening, as ***tip-up door***.

1884 *Health Exhib. Catal.* 46/1 Lavatories, fitted complete with Tip-up Basins. **1887** *Times* 25 Aug. 4/5 Turn-tables, tip-up machines.. are provided at distances of 100 ft. apart along the quay. **1904** *Westm. Gaz.* 20 Jan. 10/1 The green upholstery of the comfortable 'tip-up' seats. **1905** *Ibid.* 18 Mar. 10/2 Industrial vehicles, which include.. lorries, tip-up wagons, carts, brewers' drays, and other wagons for heavy traction. **1936** N. STREATFEILD *Ballet Shoes* xiii. 203 Mr. French pulled down the tip-up seat next to him. **1959** *News Chron.* 7 July 6/5 A local vicar, whose garage had tip-up doors. **1973** J. DRUMMOND *Bang! Bang! You're Dead* xxxvii. 127 Garages with tip-up doors. **1980** *Oxf. Diocesan Mag.* May 8/1 They are halls with tip-up seats designed for secular entertainment.. as well as worship.

tiquet, obs. Sc. form of TICKET.

†**tir** (tiːr). *Obs.* Also 3 tyr. [OE. *tír* glory, honour, cognate with ON. *tírr* str. masc. glory, renown; related to OHG. *zêri*, *ziari*, MHG. *ziere* adj. costly, splendid, whence OHG. *ziarî* fem., MHG. *ziere*, Ger. *zier* splendour, beauty, adornment, Ger. *zierat* ornament.] Glory, honour, majesty. Hence †'**tirful** *a.*, mighty, glorious.

Beowulf 1654 Hwæt we þe þas sælac.. lustum brohton tires to tacne. *a* **1000** *Sal. & Sat.* 364 (Gr.) Ne bið hira tir ȝelic. *a* **1000** *Ags. Ps.* (Th.) lxxix. 14 Tires Wealdend. *c* **1205** LAY. 2051 Seoððen com oþer tir [*c* **1275** tyr] & neowe tidinde. *Ibid.* 4327 Here tir wes at-fallen. *Ibid.* 2893 Appollones temple þe wes þe tirfulle feond.

tirable ('taɪərəb(ə)l), *a. rare.* [f. TIRE *v.*¹ + -ABLE.] That may be (easily) tired.

1607 TOPSELL *Four-f. Beasts* (1658) 241 A sign of an unskilful Rider, or of a weak and tireable Horse.

†**tirable**, obs. form of TERRIBLE.

1562 BULLEYN *Bulwark, Bk. Simples* 37 Doth kepe the minde.. from tirable and fearefull dreames.

tirade (tɪ-, taɪ'reɪd), *sb.* [a. mod.F. *tirade* (16th c.) a draught, pull, shot; a long speech, declamation; passage of prose or verse, stanza, paragraph; ad. It. *tirata* a volley, etc., f. pa. pple. of *tirare* to draw, etc. (cf. TIRE *sb.*³): see -ADE.]

1. A volley of words; a long and vehement speech on some subject; a declamation; a protracted harangue, *esp.* of denunciation, abuse, or invective.

1801 MAR. EDGEWORTH *Angelina* iv, 'Another cup of tea..', said Miss Hodges, when she had finished her tirade. **1809** HAN. MORE *Cœlebs* II. 236 A fine high-sounding *tirade*, Charles, spoken *con amore*. **1818** COBBETT *Pol. Reg.* XXXIII. 115 Let him hear this debate, these tirades of infamous falsehoods. **1823** SCOTT *Quentin D.* xxiii, She listened with a melancholy smile to her guide's tirade in praise of liberty. **1858** DORAN *Crt. Fools* 27 Tirades of bombastic nonsense. **1874** GREEN *Short Hist.* vi. §4. 306 The King.. had.. to impose silence on the tirades which were delivered from the University pulpit. **1899** E. W. GOSSE *Donne* I. 131 The preface is a curious tirade.

2. *spec.* A passage or section of verse, of varying length, treating of a single theme or idea.

1806 SCOTT *Let.* Sept. (1932) I. 321 Tales they had heard in infancy with here & there a tirade really taken from an old poem. **1878** HUEFFER *Troubadours* 250 *note*, Tirades or paragraphs of varying lengths, bound together by the same rhyme. **1879** SAINTSBURY in *Encycl. Brit.* IX. 638/1 The lines [in the *chansons de gestes*] are arranged, not in couplets or in stanzas of equal length, but in *laisses* or *tirades*, consisting of any number of lines from half a dozen to some hundreds... Sometimes the tirade is completed by a shorter line. **1900** SANTAYANA *Poetry & Relig.* 257 Euphuism contributes not a little to the poetic effect of the tirades of Keats and Shelley. **1901** J. HALL *K. Horn* p. li, The poem extends to 5,250 alexandrines rhymed in tirades.

3. *Mus.* (See quot.)

1876 STAINER & BARRETT *Dict. Mus. Terms, Tirade*, the filling up of an interval between two notes with a run, in vocal or instrumental music.

Hence **ti'rade** *v.*, *intr.* to utter or write a tirade; to inveigh or declaim vehemently.

1871 R. B. VAUGHAN *St. Thomas Aquinas* II. 683 *note*, They tirade against the influence of dogma. **1905** *Westm. Gaz.* 16 Jan. 2/1 The papers tirade against England. **1907** J. F. FRASER in *Standard* 13 Mar., A Welsh member tiraded on what the Welsh Church Commission should not do.

‖**tirage** (tiraʒ). [Fr., action of drawing, bringing out, producing, printing, etc., f. *tirer* to draw, etc. (TIRE *v.*²): see -AGE.] A pulling or reprint of a book, from the same type or stereotype (distinguished from an *edition*): cf. IMPRESSION 3 c.

1873 *Rep. Brit. Assoc.* I. 144 The 1838 edition (or rather *tirage*) has the following notice of errata contained in it. **1888** *Encycl. Brit.* XXIII. 10/1 Babbage, 'Table of the Logarithms of the Natural Numbers from 1 to 108,000' (London, stereotyped in 1827; there are several tirages of later dates), is the best for ordinary use.

‖**tirailleur** (tirajœr). [Fr. (1740 in Dict. Acad.), f. *tirailler* to shoot in independent firing, f. *tirer* to draw, shoot (TIRE *v.*²).] One of a body of skirmishers employed in the wars of the French Revolution (1792); a skirmisher, a sharp-shooter; a soldier (usually of infantry) trained for independent action. Also *attrib.*

1796 *Campaigns* 1793–4 I. I. vii. 65 The tiralleurs and riflemen could easily.. discover and take aim at the Republicans. **1812** *Examiner* 14 Sept. 582/1 Woods, filled with tirailleurs. **1847** DE QUINCEY *Span. Nun* Wks. 1860 III. 44 Any Spanish tirailleur's bullet. **1898** *Daily News* 17 Oct. 3/7 A column consisting of tirailleurs and irregulars was dispatched to suppress a rising of the Boubourys.

tiralee ('tɪrəliː). Also 6 tireli, 7 tirlery. [Echoic. Cf. OF. *turelu* a comic or burlesque refrain, and see TIRRA-LIRRA.] **a.** The note of the lark; = TIRRA-LIRRA. **b.** A representation of a bugle note or cadence.

1596 FITZ-GEFFRAY *Sir F. Drake* (1881) 24 Even as the Larke.. Mounteth her basinetted head on high,.. Quav'ring full quaintlie forth her Tireli. ? *c* **1600** in *E.E. Lyrics* (1907) 255 Tirlery lorpin, the laverock sang. **1847** MARY HOWITT *Ballads* 130 And the bugles blew with a 'tira lee'! As they came by the way.

tiran, -ant, -anny, obs. ff. TYRANT, TYRANNY.

‖**tirasse** (tiras). [Fr., a draw-net, hence, a pedal-coupler, f. *tirasser*, augmentative or pejorative of *tirer* to draw (TIRE *v.*²).]

1. *Organ-building.* (See quot.)

1876 STAINER & BARRETT *Dict. Mus. Terms, Tirasse* (Fr.), the pedals of an organ which act on the keys or manuals.

2. A draw-net. Hence **ti'rassing** *vbl. sb.*, the netting of game with the draw-net.

1897 *Pall Mall Mag.* Dec. 514 The 'tirasse' or drag-net. *Ibid.* 515 In Louis XIV's time 'tirassing' pheasants and partridges was sport which the king and his ladies often witnessed.

tirdil, tirdle, obs. ff. TREDDLE, sheep's dung.

tire (taɪə(r)), *sb.*¹ Forms: 4 tyr, 5–9 tyre, 6 tier, 6–7 tyer, 6– tire. [Aphetic f. *atir*, ATTIRE *sb.*]

†**1.** Apparatus, equipment, accoutrement, outfit: = ATTIRE *sb.* 1. *Obs.*

13.. *Guy Warw.* (A.) 7306 + st. ccli, A swift ernand stede.. His tire it was ful gay. *c* **1330** *Amis & Amil.* 1245 That knight, With helm and plate and brini bright, His tire it was ful gay. *c* **1400** *R. Gloucester's Chron.* 1188 A þousend gode kniȝtes þerinne were adreint & al hor atir [*MSS.* α, β tyr, tire] & tresour was also aseint. **1608** SHAKS. *Per.* III. ii. 22, I much maruaile that your Lordship, Hauing rich tire about you, should at these early howers, Shake off the golden slumber of repose. **1622** F. MARKHAM *Bk. War* III. x. §5 Ordnance ready mounted with all their cooplements, Ornaments, Tires, and necessaries which belong vnto the same. **1705** J. PHILIPS *Blenheim* 78 Immediate Sieges, and the Tire of War Rowl in thy eager Mind.

2. Dress, apparel, raiment; = ATTIRE *sb.* 3. *arch.*

†*bonnet of tire* (*Sc. Obs.*), a cap of estate, cap of maintenance (see CAP *sb.*¹ 4 g).

13.. *Coer de L.* 332 In anothir tyre he hym dyght. **1340–70** *Alex. & Dind.* 883 þat.. ȝoure wiuus Ne gon in no gay tyr. *a* **1400** *Siege of Troy* 1190 in *Archiv neu. Spr.* LXXII. 37 His modir.. sende him into þeo lond of Parchy In a maydenes tyr [*v.r.* wede]. **1473–4** *Acc. Ld. High Treas. Scot.* I. 32 To covir hire bonatis of tyre. **1536** BELLENDEN *Boece's Cron. Scot.* XIII. viii. (1821) II. 327 This legat als presentit ane bonat of tire, maid in maner of diademe, of purpoure hew; to signify that he was defendar of the faith. *c* **1600** SHAKS. *Sonn.* liii. 8 You in Grecian tires are painted new. **1612** DRAYTON *Poly-olb.* xii. 517 Of all their stately tyres disrobed when they bee. **1719** D'URFEY *Pills* (1872) IV. 81 It is not your flaunting Tires, Are the cause of Men's Desires. **1850** BLACKIE *Æschylus* II. 96 Your tire rich-flaunting with barbaric pride Bespeaks you strangers.

†**b.** *transf.* and *fig.* 'Vesture', 'attire'. *Obs.*

1594 CAREW *Tasso* (1881) 96 Or she her shamefast and downe clyned eyes With tire and taint of honesty embowres. *a* **1600** M. COSOWARTH in Farr *S.P. Eliz.* (1845) II. 407 If thou disrobe me of th' earthe's tyre I weare. *a* **1660** HAMMOND *Serm.* Wks. 1684 IV. 572 Had not the second person of the Trinity.. come down in his tire and personation of flesh. **1695** WOODWARD *Nat. Hist. Earth* VI. (1723) 294 They [plants] display themselves, shewing their whole Tire of Leaves.

3. *spec.* A covering, dress, or ornament for a woman's head; a head-dress; = ATTIRE *sb.* 4; in some cases perh. confused with TIAR, tiara. Also *transf.* and *fig. arch.*

c **1425** *Cast. Persev.* 223 in *Macro Plays* 84 [Devil says] On Mankynde is my trost, in contre I-knowe, With my tyre & with my tayl, tytly to tene. **1481–90** *Howard Househ. Bks.* (Roxb.) 442 Item.. fur a peyer of tyres.. and a serclett for my Lady Barnes. *a* **1548** HALL *Chron., Hen. VIII* 7, vi. ladyes.. with marueylous ryche & straunge tiers on their heades. **1560** BIBLE (Genev.) *Isa.* iii. 18 In that day shal the Lord take away the ornament of the slippers, & the calles, & the rounde tyres. *Ibid.* 20 The tyres of the head, and the sloppes. **1590** SPENSER *F.Q.* I. x. 31 And on her head she wore a tyre of gold. **1610** *Histrio-m.* II. 117 *Post.* My maisters, what tire wears your lady on her head? *Bel.* Four squirrels tails tied in a true loves knot. **1630** DRAYTON *Muses Elizium* ii. 213 And for thy head Ile haue a Tyer Of netting. **1639** *Bury Wills* (Camden) 183 A mourning tire on their heads, such as gentlewomen weare at the time of ffuneralls. **1653** J. HALL *Paradoxes* 67 What Towers doe the Turkish Tires weare upon their womens heads? **1851** D. WILSON *Preh. Ann.* (1863) II. III. v. 148 The maiden coronet or tire for the hair. **1851** C. L. SMITH tr. *Tasso* I. xlvii, Her forehead lacked its tire. **1887** *Suppl. to Jamieson, Tire, Tyre*, a snood or narrow band for the hair, worn by females.

4. Ornamentation of various kinds: see quots. *dial.* or *local.*

1876 *Whitby Gloss., Tire*, the metallic embellishments of cabinet work. **1887** *Suppl. to Jamieson, Tire, tyre*.. an ornamental edging used by cabinet-makers and upholsterers; the metal edging of coffins, which is also called coffin-tyre.

5. A pinafore or apron to protect the dress; also (perh. better) written *tier*: see TIER *sb.*² 4. *U.S.*

1846 WORCESTER, *Tire*.. attire, a child's apron. See *Tier*. **1849** LOWELL *Biglow P.* Ser. I. Introd., The humble school-house.. Where well-drilled urchins, each behind his tire, Waited in ranks the wished command to fire. **1864** WEBSTER, *Tire*, a child's apron,.. a tier. **1867** O. W. HOLMES *Guard. Angel* iii, The child untied her little 'tire', got down from the table. **1883** ROLLINS *New Eng. Bygones* 136 This humble serving woman.. in her homespun tyre, filled with wild herbs and roots.

6. *attrib.* and *Comb.* (in sense 2; *Obs.* or *arch.*): **tire-glass**, a dressing-glass, toilet-glass; †**tire-house**, the wardrobe of a theatre; also = TIRING-HOUSE; **tire-maid** = TIRE-WOMAN; †**tire-maker**, a head-dress-maker; †**tire-man**, (*a*) a man in charge of the costumes at a theatre; (*b*) a man who assists at the toilet; a dresser or valet; also, a tailor; †**tire-pin**, a pin used in the toilet; **tire-room**, a dressing-room, tiring-room.

1844 MRS. BROWNING *Duchess May* xxxv, In her *tire-glass gazed she. *c* **1620** *Songs Lond. Prentices* (Percy Soc.) 96 To the *tire-howse broke they in, Which some began to plunder. **1871** ROSSETTI *Dante at Verona* xiv, *Tire-maids hidden among these Drew close their loosened bodices. **1611** RICH *Honest. Age* (Percy Soc.) 18 Shee holdeth on her way.. to the *Tyre makers shoppe. **1611** COTGR., *Perruquiere*, a Tyre-maker, or Attire-maker; a woman that makes Perri-wigs, or Attires. **1599** B. JONSON *Cynthia's Rev.* Induct., To have his presence in the tiring-house.. [to] curse the poor *tireman. **1711** SHAFTESB. *Charac.* (1737) I. 84 Neither the magistrate, nor the tire-men themselves, cou'd resolve, which of the various modes was the exact true-one. *a* **1450** *Knt. de la Tour* (1906) 63 The settinge of her *tyre pynnes and array. **1681** *Religio Clerici* 52 Strip it naked of its plain English, and send it to be drest in their *Tire-room. **1855** BROWNING *Bp. Blougram's Apol.* 70 Then going in the tire-room afterward, Because the play was done, to shift himself.

tire (taɪə(r)), *sb.*² Forms: 5, 7, 9 tyre, (8–9 tier), 7– tire. See also TYRE. [Probably the same word as prec., the *tire* being originally (sense 1) the 'attire', 'clothing', or 'accoutrement' of the wheel. From 15th to 17th c. spelt (like prec.) *tire* and *tyre* indifferently. Before 1700 *tyre* became generally obsolete, and *tire* remained as the regular form, as it still does in America; but in Great Britain *tyre* was revived in the nineteenth cent. as the popular term for the rubber rim of bicycle, tricycle, carriage, or motor-car wheels, and is sometimes used for the steel tires of locomotive wheels. During the twentieth cent. *tyre* became standard in the British Isles.]

†**1.** *collective sing.* The curved pieces of iron plate, called strakes or streaks, placed end to end or overlapping, with which cart and carriage wheels were formerly shod (now rarely used, and only for heavy agricultural vehicles, artillery carriages, etc.).

1485 in *Ripon Ch. Acts* (Surtees) 373, j tyre pro rota plaustri. **1601** HOLLAND *Pliny* XXXIV. xiv. (1634) II. 514 Yron.. such as will not serue one whit for stroke [= strake] and naile to bind cart-wheels withall, which tire indeed would be made of the other that is gentle and pliable. **1624** *Althorp MS.* in Simpkinson *Washingtons* (1860) App. p. lvii, For a new tire for a waine. **1662** *Act 14 Chas. II*, c. 6 §8 Any Waggon Wayne Cart or Carriage.. the Wheeles whereof are lesse in breadth then foure Inches in the Tyre. **1753** *Scots Mag.* Nov. 540/1 Unless the wheels and tire of such carriages were made broader. **1769** [see *tire-smith* in 3]. **1803** WELLINGTON in Gurw. *Desp.* (1837) I. 580, I wait only for some iron.. to put Tires on some new wheels which I have made. **1827** MEADEN *Patent Specif.* No. 5574, I do not claim.. binding them with concave iron tires in streaks or separate plates.

2. a. A rim of metal encompassing the wheel of a vehicle, consisting of a continuous circular hoop of iron or steel.

1782 NEWCOME *Patent Specif.* No. 1320 The main or outside rim or tire consists of one whole sound ring. **1787** BRODIE *Patent Specif.* No. 1599 The tier is then heated a black red and put on the wheel. **1827** MEADEN *Patent Specif.* No. 5574 My improvements on wheels for carriages consist in binding them with an iron hoop tire having its internal surface concave. **1831** YOUATT *Horse* 436 A strong circular frame of wood.. is bound together by a hoop, or several hoops of iron, called tires. **1843** *Penny Cycl.* XXVII. 317/2 The introduction of solid or hoop tires is an immense improvement. **1845** THOMSON *Patent Specif.* No. 10990, I claim..the application of elastic bearings round the tire of carriage wheels. **1858** O. W. HOLMES *Aut. Breakf.-t.* vi, You couldn't pry that out of a Boston man if you had the tire of all creation straightened out for a crowbar. **1860** PIESSE *Lab. Chem. Wonders* 122 The tires of wheels previously to their being fixed are made hot. **1862** *Fraser's Mag.* Nov. 634 Specimens of tires for locomotive engines..made with-out a weld. **1886** HALL CAINE *Son of Hagar* II. xi, The tires of the wheels were still crusted with unmelted snow.

[*Note.* Thomson's patent (quot. 1845 above) is known as the foundation of the pneumatic tire or tyre (2 b), and was largely cited in the great actions for infringement during the 'tyre boom'. T. did not actually use the expression 'elastic tire' or 'tyre', but spoke of an 'elastic band' around the (iron) tire. This 'band' was however exactly what is now termed a 'pneumatic tyre'—a distended inner tube with an outer cover or jacket. (H. V. Hopwood, Dep. Librarian, Patent Office Lib.)]

b. An endless cushion of rubber, solid, hollow, or tubular, fitted (usually in combination with an inner tube filled with compressed air: cf. PNEUMATIC 1 b) on the rim of a bicycle, tricycle, or motor-car; now also often upon the wheels of invalid and baby-carriages, and light horse vehicles. In this sense now commonly spelt *tyre* in Great Britain (see TYRE); *tire* is retained in America.

1877 KNIGHT *Dict. Mech.* III. 2579 At the same time Mr. Dunlop patented a tire of annealed cast-iron, grooved to receive an india-rubber band. Various other patents followed, embracing india-rubber as a material to be used in constructing tires. **1887** BURY & HILLIER *Cycling* 63 The iron tire was necessarily incompatible with the light iron wheel; rubber tires were introduced. **1905** [see *tire-cover* in 3]. **1910** *Encycl. Brit.* VII. 683/1 Rubber tires, in place of iron ones, appeared in 1868. **1911** WEBSTER, *Tire*...4. Commonly spelt *tyre* in British usage... The pneumatic tire for a bicycle or automobile serves primarily to reduce vibration or shock.

3. *attrib.* and *Comb.*, as ***tire-cover, -cutter, -maker, pressure, repair, -smith, track***; **tire-bender**, a machine in which tires are rolled to a uniform curve (Knight *Dict. Mech.* 1877); **tire-bolt**, a bolt used in securing the tire to the felloes (*Cassell's Encycl. Dict.* 1888); **tire-cement**, cement for fixing or repairing rubber tires; **tire chain**, a metal chain designed to be attached to the tyre of a motor vehicle to prevent skidding on snow or ice; **tire-drill**, a drill adapted to hold and perforate metal tires (Knight); **tire-heater**, a furnace for heating metal tires (*Ibid.*); **tire-iron**, one of the strakes forming the tire of a wheel (see sense 1); also (*N. Amer.*), a length of steel flattened at one end, used as a lever for removing tyres from wheel-rims; **tire-measurer**, a measure for ascertaining the length of the tire required by a wheel (Knight); **tire-press**, a hydraulic press in which the tires of railway wheels are forced on (*Ibid.*); **tire-roller**, a mill in which tires for railway wheels are rolled to develop the flanges, etc. (*Ibid.*); **tire-screw** = *tire-bolt* (*Cent. Dict. Suppl.*); **tire-setter**, a machine for forcing cart and carriage wheel tires into position and compressing them on the wheel (*Cent. Dict.*); **tire-shrinker**, a machine for compressing a heated tire lengthways to decrease the circumference (Knight); **tire-upsetting-machine** (see quot.). See also under TYRE.

1894 BOTTONE *Electr. Instr. Making* (ed. 6) 33 When quite dry and set firm, the surface..should be painted over with 'bicycle *tire cement'. **1917** *T. Eaton & Co. Catal.* Spring & Summer 282 Every car owner should carry a pair of *tire chains. **1980** 'E. MCBAIN' *Ghosts* ii. 20 Carella could hear the sounds of tire chains jangling. **1905** *Times* 1 Aug. 14/1 With tire and *tire-cover gone, ten miles away from a garage ..Crœsus..is in as lame a case as the man of modest means. **1897** *Outing* (U.S.) XXX. 213/1 These formidable *tire-cutters [clam-shells] lie along the coastal roads like dead leaves in a windrow. **1852** MUNDY *Our Antipodes* (1857) 32 Our carriages trundled on the nails of their new *tire-irons into Blackheath. **1952** R. ELLISON *Invisible Man* xxv. 426 You could hear that gun striking that ole shield like somebody dropping tire irons out a twelve-story window. **1976** *Globe & Mail* (Toronto) 16 Feb. 10/1 Two 19-year old brothers have been arrested after a man, his wife and son were assaulted with tire irons in a Towers Department Store parking lot. **1920** *T. Eaton & Co. Catal.* Spring & Summer 224 *Tire pressure gauge. Accurate and reliable for correct air pressure. **1895** *Montgomery Ward Catal.* Spring & Summer 556/3 Pneumatic *tire repair outfit. **1975** J. GRADY *Shadow of Condor* viii. 128 The man..stowed the tire-repair items..in the trunk. **1769** *Public Advertiser* 6 June 3/2 A Coachmaker's or *Tiresmith's Tool for..wrenching the Tire off wheels. **1947** E. S. GARDNER in *Amer. Mag.* Aug. 150/3 Mason, studying the *tire tracks, said, 'It was an automobile and a horse trailer.' **1973** T. PYNCHON *Gravity's Rainbow* I. 113 The Dutch resistance will then 'raid' this site, making a lot of commotion, faking in tire-tracks and detailing the litter of hasty departure. **1877** KNIGHT *Dict. Mech.*, **Tire-up-setting Machine*, a machine for shrinking tires without cutting.

† **tire**, *sb.*[3] *Obs.* Also 6–7 **tyre.** [ad. F. *tir* in sense 'shot, volley', verbal sb. from *tirer* to draw, to shoot (*Roland*, 11th c.) = Prov., Sp., Pg. *tirar*, It. *tirare*:—Common Romanic **tīrāre*: see TIRE *v.*[2]] The simultaneous discharge of a battery of ordnance; a volley or broadside. Also *transf.* of thunder.

(Collective pl., esp. after numeral, *tire*.)

1575 LD. GREY in *Comm. Serv. & Charges* (Camden) 20 They guave us vij or viij sutche terryble tyres of batterie as tooke cleane awaye from us the top of owre vammure. **1577–87** HOLINSHED *Chron.* (1807) IV. 213 Before that two tires of the artillerie had gone off, they within offered to parlee. **1593** PEELE *Ord. Garter* Wks. (Rtldg.) 586/1 Ordnance pealing in mine ears, As twenty thousand tire had play'd at sea. **1598** FLORIO, *Salua*..a volie or tire off ordinance. **1611** SPEED *Hist. Gt. Brit.* IX. xii. §92 Discharging sundry tire and peales of Thunder. **1667** MILTON *P.L.* VI. 605 In posture to displode thir second tire Of Thunder. **1687** DRYDEN *Hind & P.* III. 317 The foe discharges every tire around.

† **tire**, *sb.*[4] *Obs. rare.* In 6 **tyre.** [f. TIRE *v.*[2] 2.] A tough morsel given to a hawk: see TIRING *vbl. sb.*[2]

1589 GREENE *Menaphon* (Arb.) 67 For all she hath let you flie like a Hawke that hath lost hir tyre.

tire (taɪə(r)), *sb.*[5] *dial.* and *colloq.* [From TIRE *v.*[1]]

1. Tiredness, fatigue.

1859 F. E. PAGET *Curate of Cumberworth* 86 The settee which was adding discomfort to his tire. **1891** A. MATTHEWS *Poems & Songs* 60, I clean forgot my tire and pain. **1896** KIPLING *Seven Seas, M'Andrew's Hymn*, Sick, sick, wi' doubt an' tire. [**1904** in *Eng. Dial. Dict.* from Scotld. to Devon.]

2. pl. *tires*: see quot.

1855 DUNGLISON *Med. Lex.* (ed. 12), *Milk Sickness*, Sick stomach, Swamp sickness, Tires, Slows... A disease occasionally observed in..Alabama, Indiana, and Kentucky, which affects both man and cattle, but chiefly the latter... Owing to the tremors that characterize it in animals, it is called the Trembles. **1899** in *Syd. Soc. Lex.*

† **tire**, *sb.*[6] *Obs.* [? a. F. *tire*, from *tirer* to draw, pull: see TIRE *v.*[2]] In ribbon-weaving: A cord which pulls the high-lisses (LISSE *sb.*[2]) up.

1759 *Gentl. Mag.* 517 Description of a new invented machine for drawing the tire in a ribbon loom. *Ibid.*, The tumblers that draw the tire moving with their upper ends in the rake. *Ibid.*, A ribbon that requires tire may be work'd as a plain course, there being no loss of time required in the tire's draught. **1766** CROKER, etc. *Dict. Arts* s.v. *Ribband*, 4. The tires, or the riding cords, which run on the pullies, and pull up the high-lisses... 25. The tumblers, or pullies, to which the tires are tied, to clear the course of cords through the high lisses... 27. The tire-board.

† **tire, tyre**, *sb.*[7] Variant of TEAR *sb.*[3] b, the finest fibre of flax, etc.

1601 HOLLAND *Pliny* XXXVII. iii. II. 608 They will burne.. more cleare than weekes or matches made of the very tire and best of flax. **1790** *Churchw. Acc. W. Hoathly, Sussex* 27 Feb., Dame Steles wants some tyre—Allowed ½ dozen 7*d.* **1875** *Sussex Gloss.*, *Tire*, flax for spinning. (Probably obsolete, but frequently found in old parochial accounts.)

tire (taɪə(r)), *v.*[1] Forms: α. 1 **tiorian, teorian**, 2 **teorien**; 5 **tere.** β. 1 (late) (**ʒe**)**tyrian**; (2–3 (**a**)**tieren**); 5 **tyere**, *Sc.* **tyr**, 5–8 **tyre**, 6 **tyar**, *Sc.* **tyir**, 6–7 **tyer, tier**, 6– **tire.** [OE. *tíorian, téorian* (also with short *io, eo* (Sievers); in comb. *ʒetíorian, ʒetéorian*; with umlaut (late) *ʒetýrian*), also *a-téorian*, with umlaut *a-tíerian, a-térian*; also vbl. sb. *tiurung* 'lassitudo' (Gallée), and *ʒetéorung*. As this vb. does not appear in the cognate langs., it is difficult to determine its original form in OE., and the phonetic relations between the OE. and ME. forms, esp. the origin and history of the current form *tire* (†*tyre*), which appears first in Scottish writers in the 15th c.

Prof. Sievers thinks that the various OE. and ME. forms may be explained by the existence of an OE. **tíran* trans., beside *tíorian* (*tíorian*) intr., both formed from an OTeut. verbal root **terh-*; the sound-relations being similar to those between OE. *fíras* and *feorh, féores* (*feores*), from root **ferhw-*.]

I. *intr.* † **1.** To fail, cease (as a supply, etc.); to diminish, give out, come to an end. *Obs.*

c **725** *Corpus Gloss.* (O.E.T.) 668 *Desisse*, tiorade [*c* **1050** in Wr.-Wülcker 385/9 *Fort. Dunsætas* c. 4 *heading*, Be ðone ðe lad teorie. *a* **1000** *Ags. Ps.* (Th.) cxviii[i]. 82 Eaʒan me swylce eac teoredon. **11..** *Soul & Body* in Phillipps *Fragm. Ælfric's Gramm.* etc. (1838) 5 Him trukeþ his iwit, him teoreþ his miht. [*c* **1200** *Trin. Coll. Hom.* 29 Vnwreste þu best ȝef þu wreche ne secst..ȝief mihte þe ne atiereð.]

2. To become weak or exhausted from exertion; to have one's strength reduced or worn out by toil or labour; to become fatigued.

c **1000** *Sax. Leechd.* II. 16 Ʒif mon on langum weʒe teoriʒe. *c* **1470** HENRY *Wallace* IX. 1771 The Scottis hors mony began to tyr [*rime* fyr]. *c* **1470** *Golagros & Gaw.* 34 Tuglit and travalit thus trew men can [= did] tyre. *c* **1480** HENRYSON *Test. Cres.* (ed. 1593) 516 To beir his Scheild his Breist began to tyre. **1587** MASCALL *Govt. Cattle, Horses* (1627) 178 Lap it about his bit,..and then bridle him, and ride him, and he wil not lightly tyer. **1588** SHAKS. *L.L.L.* II. i. 120 Your wit's too hot, it speeds too fast, 'twill tire. **1593** —— *Rich. II*, II. i. 36. **1599** PORTER *Angry Woman Abingd.* (Percy Soc.) 41 A swift horse will tier, but he that trottes easilie will indure. **1611** SHAKS. *Wint. T.* IV. iii. 135 A merry heart goes all the day, Your sad tyres in a Mile-a. **1660** F. BROOKE tr. *Le Blanc's Trav.* 230 His horses so tiring, that the servants were fain to carry the baggage themselves. **1716** LADY M. W. MONTAGU *Lett.* 16 Aug., Our horses tired at Stamel, three hours from [Cologne]. **1845** J. COULTER *Adv. Pacific* xiii. 169 They tire—others supply their places.

3. To have one's appreciation, power of attention, or patience exhausted by excess; to become or be weary or sick *of*, to 'have enough' *of*.

1500–20 DUNBAR *Poems* lxvi. 94 Of this fals failȝeand warld I tyre. *a* **1578** LINDESAY (Pitscottie) *Chron. Scot.* XXI. xi. (S.T.S.) I. 307 The quenis grace tyrit of him and pairtit witht him. *a* **1584** MONTGOMERIE *Cherrie & Slae* 99 Quha wald haue tyrit to heir that tune. **1763** GOLDSM. *Misc. Wks.* (1837) II. 484 Unwearied himself, he supposed his readers could never tire. **1803** *Edwin* III. iv. 60 His tongue spoke of nothing but the field, and his ear tired with any other theme. **1819** SCOTT *Bl. Dwarf* xviii, Mareschal..tired of the country, went abroad, served three campaigns, came home. **1857** RUSKIN *Pol. Econ. Art* 54 You will never tire of looking at it. **1897** *Century Mag.* Feb. 623/2 [The squirrel] would grasp one of my fingers with his two paws, and lick it till he tired.

4. To become weary with waiting *for* something; to 'weary' or long *for*. *Sc.* ? *Obs.*

1801 BARBARA MAXWELL in G. Ewing *Mem. B. Ewing* (1829) 41, I really tire for your letters. **1827** ISAB. CAMPBELL in *Mem.* viii. (1829) 247, I tire much for this—I long to be completely conformed to the image of Jesus.

II. *trans.* **5.** To wear down or exhaust the strength of by exertion; to fatigue, weary (by either mental or physical exercise). Also *absol.*

a **1000** *Ags. Ps.* (Th.) cxli[i]. 3 Ʒif mine grame þenceað gast teorian. *a* **1400–50** *Alexander* 1009 All þe ȝeris of oure ȝouthe es ȝare syne passid And we for-traualid & terid [*Dubl. MS.* for-tyred]. *Ibid.* 1404 (Dubl. MS.) It wald tere ony tong hys tournays to reken. **1470–85** MALORY *Arthur* XV. v. 661 The whyte knyghtes helde them nyghe about syr launcelot for to tyere hym and wynde hym. **1500–20** DUNBAR *Poems* lxxix. 7 For rekkyning of my rentis and roumes, ȝe neid nocht for to tyre ȝour thowmes. **1530** PALSGR. 758/1, I tyer a horse, I make him that he can go no farther. **1588** SHAKS. *L.L.L.* IV. iii. 307 Motion and long during action tyres The sinnowy vigour of the trauailer. *c* **1590** MARLOWE *Faust.* I. i. 61 Here, Faustus, tire thy brains to gain a deity. **1621** T. WILLIAMSON tr. *Goulart's Wise Vieillard* 50 Not tyring himselfe, and spending his spirits with much labour and studie. **1698** FRYER *Acc. E. India & P.* 177 The Tigre is..not long Nimble, Three Leaps Tiring him. **1749** BERKELEY *Word to the Wise* Wks. III. 444 The same work tires, but different works relieve. **1845** J. COULTER *Adv. Pacific* ix. 111 Being well tired by my day's march, and excitement, I lay down.. and slept soundly until daylight. **1875** JOWETT *Plato* (ed. 2) III. 338 They would rather not tire themselves by thinking about possibilities.

6. To weary or exhaust the patience, interest, or appreciation of (a person, etc.) by long continuance, sameness, or want of interest; to satiate, make sick of something; to bore. Also *absol.*

1500–20 DUNBAR *Poems* xvi. 17 Sum is for gift sa lang requyrd Quhill that the crevar be so tyrd That, or the gift deliuerit be The thank is frustrat and expyrd. **1599** SHAKS. *Much Ado* I. i. 309 Thou wilt..tire the hearer with a booke of words. **1692** LOCKE *Toleration* ii. Wks. 1727 II. 288, I am tired to follow you so often round the same Circle. **1774** GOLDSM. *Nat. Hist.* (1776) VII. 104, I hope I have not tired your Lordship with my long tale. **1874** L. STEPHEN *Hours in Library* (1892) I. i. 39 He cannot tire us with details, for all the details of such a story are interesting.

b. *fig.* To exhaust (another's patience, bounty, efforts, etc.); to wear out, spend (time) (*obs.*).

1589 GREENE *Menaphon* (Arb.) 46 To trie our wittes, and tire our time. ? *c* **1600** *Distracted Emperor* in Bullen *O. Pl.* III. 169 My constant industry shall tyer the day And out-watche night. **1601** SIR W. CORNWALLIS *Ess.* II. li. (1631) 326 Hee hath tyred his purse before hee can overtake the fashion. **1613** BEAUM. & FL. *Coxcomb* I. i, To tire anothers bounty, And let mine owne grow lusty. **1665** SIR T. HERBERT *Trav.* (1677) 181 After he had tyred out a few more minutes with impatience. **1697** DRYDEN *Virg. Georg.* IV. 597 Till tiring all his Arts, he turns agen To his true Shape. **1788** SHERIDAN in *Sheridaniana* (1826) 101 Others tired the chairs in the parlours. **1902** GOSSE in *Daily Chron.* 13 Mar. 3/1 The great artist, who had seemed..to have tired his pen a little.

7. With extension. ***to tire out, tire to death***, to tire to utter exhaustion. *colloq.* ***to tire down***, to exhaust (a hunted animal) by persistent pursuit: cf. *to run down* (RUN *v.* 73 h).

1563–87 FOXE *A. & M.* (K.O.), Tire him out. **1632** SANDERSON *Serm.* 39 They would quickely tyre out them-selues without spurring. **1711** HEARNE *Collect.* (O.H.S.) III. 246 The King being then tired out by factious People. **1740** tr. *De Mouhy's Fort. Country-Maid* (1741) I. 206 He was tired to Death, altho' they used their Endeavours..to amuse him agreeably. **1766** H. WALPOLE in *Lett. C'tess Suffolk* (1824) II. 324, I am tired to death of the place. **1835** W. IRVING *Tour Prairies* xviii, A pack of..wolves..were in full chase of a buck, which they had nearly tired down. **1855** MACAULAY *Hist. Eng.* xvii. IV. 1 William, tired out by the voyage,..determined to land in an open boat.

Hence **'tiring** *vbl. sb.* and *ppl. a.*, wearying, fatiguing; **'tiringly** *adv.*, in a tiring manner, to a wearisome degree.

1588 SHAKS. *Tit. A.* V. ii. 24 Witnesse the tyring day, and heauie night. **1603** KNOLLES *Hist. Turks* (1638) 220 The politicke tyring of the strong forces of Bajazet, was the safe-gard of his own. *a* **1774** GOLDSM. tr. *Scarron's Com. Romance* (1775) I. 132 This accomplished courtier being tired with tiring of them. **1869** PR. ALICE *Mem.* 1 June (1884) 215 It is always so tiring to see things at Berlin. **1894** E. FAWCETT *New Nero* XX. 219 'It's a trifle tyrannical, is it not?' 'Yes; amusingly so.' 'Never tiringly so.'

tire (taɪə(r)), *v.*[2] *arch.* Also 4–7 **tyre**, 6–7 **tyer**, 7 **tier.** [a. F. *tire-r* = Prov., Sp., Pg. *tirar*, It. *tirare*:—Com. Romanic **tīrāre* to draw, etc., of uncertain origin. (Hatz.-Darm. rejects the derivation from Teut. *tairan*, OLG. *teren*, conjectured by Diez.)]

I. † **1.** *intr.* and *trans.* To draw, pull, tug. *Obs.*

a **1300** *Floriz & Bl.* 736 Floriz forþ his nekke bed And blauncheflur wiþ draȝe him ȝet. Blauncheflur bid forþ hire suere And floriz aȝen hire gan tire. **14..** *Beryn* 2565 Stillith ȝewe..for howe so evir yee tire, More þen my power yee owȝte nat desire. **1580** LYLY *Euphues* To Gentl. Schollers Oxf. (Arb.) 207 Sending me into the Countrie to nurse, where I tyred at a drie breast three yeares, and was at the last inforced to weane my selfe.

II. 2. *Falconry. intr.* Of a hawk: To pull or tear with the beak at a tough morsel given to it that it may exercise itself in this way; also, to tear flesh in feeding, as a hawk or other bird of prey. Const. *on*, *upon*. (So OF. *tirer*.) ? *arch.* or *Obs.*

c **1220** *Bestiary* 438 He billeð one ðe foxes fel.. and he tireð on his ket. *c* **1374** CHAUCER *Boeth.* III. met. xii. 84 (Camb. MS.) The fowl þat hihte voltor..is so fulfyld of his song þat it nil etin ne tyren no more. *c* **1450** *Bk. Hawkyng* in *Rel. Ant.* I. 296 Loke that thy hawke tire every other day while she is fleyng, for nothyng..woll clense a hawkes hedde as tyryng. **1486** *Bk. St. Albans* C viij, An hawke..tyrith vppon Rumppys, she fedith on all maner of flesh. **1558** PHAER *Æneid* VI. R ij, A gastly Gripe, that euermore his growing guttes outdrawes, And tiring tearith furth his euerduring liuer vaines. **1612** DAVIES *Why Ireland*, etc. (1787) 59 An eagle, with three eglets tiring on her breast, and the fourth picking at one of her eyes. **1737** OZELL *Rabelais* I. xli. I. 319 As the Falconers, before they feed their Hawks, do make them tire at a Hen's Leg, to purge their Brains of Phlegm.

b. *transf.* of persons. To feed greedily *upon*.

1598 DALLINGTON *Meth. Trav.* G ij, The Kitchin Doctor gaue his patient the necke and bones to tyre vpon, and kept the wings himselfe. **1599** NASHE *Lenten Stuffe* (1871) 58 The stall fed foreman..was grown as fat as an ox with tiring on the sirloins. *Ibid.* 86. *a* **1629** HINDE *J. Bruen* viii. (1641) 29 Rob wife and children of their meanes..and oftentimes tyre upon the carkasses.

† **c.** *fig.* To prey *upon*. *Obs.*

1581 T. HOWELL *Deuises* (1879) 208 Your loue the Grype that tyers vpon your harte. **1594** MARLOWE & NASHE *Dido* V. ii, The grief that tires upon thine inward soul. **1610** *Histrio-m.* V. 136 O, how this vulture (vile Ambition) Tyers on the heart of greatnesse. **1624** BP. HALL *True Peace-maker* Wks. 539 Is there any of you..whose heart is daily tyr'd upon by the vultur of his secret guiltinesse?

d. To exercise oneself *upon* (in thought or action).

1607 SHAKS. *Timon* III. vi. 4 Vpon that were my thoughts tyring when wee encountred. **1611** —— *Cymb.* III. iv. 96 When thou shalt be disedg'd by her That now thou tyrest on.

† **3.** *trans.* To tear at, tear, pluck. *Obs. rare.*

c **1374** CHAUCER *Troylus* I. 787 Whos stomak foughles tiren [*v.r.* tyren] euere mo.

† **b.** (*causal.*) To cause (a hawk) to 'tire'. In quot. *transf. Obs.*

1594 ? GREENE *Selimus* Wks. (Grosart) XIV. 217 Like a lion fierce, Tiring his stomacke on a flocke of lambes.

tire (taɪə(r)), *v.*³ Also 4–7 tyre, 6 tyer, tyere, tier. [Aphetic form of ATTIRE *v.*¹; but in sense 1 perh. a. F. *se tirer*.]

† **1.** *refl.* To put oneself in order *to do* something; to get ready; also, to get ready to go somewhere; to take one's way, go. Cf. ATTIRE *v.*¹ 1, 2; DRESS *v.* 6, 15. *Obs.*

c **1330** R. BRUNNE *Chron.* (1810) 274 To Dunbar þei þam drowe, þe sege þer to sette, þei tirede þam to kest smertly to þe assaute. *c* **1400** *Destr. Troy* 2778 We may tyre vs with truthe to tene hom agayne. *Ibid.* 3625 With a nauy full nobill, naite for þe werre, We shall tyre vs to Troy tomly to gedur.

2. *trans.* † **a.** To equip; to fit out with arms, accoutrements, etc.; to arm; = ATTIRE *v.*¹ 3 a.

c **1330** R. BRUNNE *Chron.* (1810) 151 His folk armed & tired, & ay redy to fight. *a* **1400–50** *Alexander* 3603 Thretty tulkis in ilk toure tired in platis. *c* **1400** *Laud Troy Bk.* 984 He toke his armure and tyred him swythe.

† **b.** To attire, clothe duly, dress, adorn; = ATTIRE *v.*¹ 3 b. *Obs.*

c **1350** *Will. Palerne* 263 A gret lord þat gayly is tyred. *Ibid.* 4478 To tire him in his wedes. *a* **1400** *Libeaus Desc.* (Kaluza) 891 In a robe of samite Anoon sche gan her tire. **1526** TINDALE *1 Pet.* iii. 5 After this manner in the olde tyme did the wholy wemen which trusted in god tyre them selves. **1589** GREENE *Menaphon* (Arb.) 76 But am not I a Gentleman, though tirde in a shepheardes skincote? **1602** MARSTON *Antonio's Rev.* V. iii, Slinke to my chamber then, and tyre thee. **1706** PHILLIPS (ed. Kersey), To *Tire*, to dress.

c. To dress (the hair or head), esp. with a tire or head-dress (TIRE *sb.*¹ 3); = ATTIRE *v.*¹ 3 c. *arch.*

1539 BIBLE (Great) *2 Kings* ix. 30 Iezabel..starched her face, and tired her heed, and looked out at a window. **1594** CAREW *Tasso* (1881) 74 With lockes of wrythed snakes some tire their pates. **1603** *Eng. Mourning Garment* in *Select. fr. Harl. Misc.* (1793) 208 She never could abide to gaze in a mirror, or looking-glass; no not to behold one, while her head was tyred and adorned. **1907** *Daily Chron.* 8 Aug. 4/4 With her flaxen hair tired in Greek fashion.

3. To plaster or decorate (a building). Now *dial.*

a **1400–50** *Alexander* 5644 Off tried topaces & trewe tyrid was þe wawes. *c* **1400** *Destr. Troy* 8751 This tabernacle tristy was tyrit on hegh. **1688** R. HOLME *Armoury* III. xiv. (Roxb.) 19/1 To mixt haire and Lyme together to make plaster, or straw and clay together for the tyreing of the inside of thatched houses. **1904** in *Eng. Dial. Dict.* s.v., (Somerset) I suppose you was all day yesterday tiring the church?

† **4.** *spec.* To prepare or dress (an egg) as food.

1486 *Bk. St. Albans* F vij b, An Egge Tyred. **1513** *Bk. of Keruynge* in *Babees Bk.* (1868) 265 Termes of a Keruer... Tyere that egge. **1530** PALSGR. 758/1, I tyer an egge... Let me se who can best tyer this egge. **1542** BOORDE *Dyetary* xii. (1870) 265 That they [eggs] be tyred with a lytell salte and suger. **1688** R. HOLME *Armoury* III. 78 Tire that Egg.

tire (taɪə(r)), *v.*⁴ [f. TIRE *sb.*²] *trans.* To furnish (a wheel or vehicle) with a tire or tires: see TIRED *ppl. a.*², TIRING *vbl. sb.*⁴ See also TYRE *v.*

1891 *Cent. Dict.*, *Tire*, to put a tire upon, as to tire a wheel or a wagon.

tire, obs. f. TEER *v.*, TIER *sb.*¹, TYRE.

'tireball. In 6 tyreboll, 9 tireballe. [a. F. *tireballe*, in same senses, f. *tire* draw, extract (TIRE *v.*²) + *balle* BALL.] **a.** An instrument for extracting the charge from a muzzle-loading firearm. **b.** A bullet-forceps. *Obs.* (exc. as French).

1591 *Garrard's Art Warre* 4 The carefull souldier may with his Tyreboll pull out hys bullet. [**1611** COTGR., *Tire-balle*, an Instrument wherewith Surgeons draw bullets out of the bodie.] **1857** DUNGLISON *Med. Lex.*, *Tire-balle*, forceps (bullet). **1877** KNIGHT *Dict. Mech.*, *Tireballe* (Surgical), the bullet-forceps.

† **'tire-brain.** *Obs. rare.* [f. TIRE *v.*¹ + BRAIN.] One who (or that which) tires the brain by constant thinking; a 'busy-brain'.

1589 WARNER *Alb. Eng.* V. xxv. (1597) 124 Not adding or abstracting as conceited Tire-braines will.

tired (taɪəd), *ppl. a.*¹ [f. TIRE *v.*¹ + -ED¹.]

1. Weakened or exhausted by exertion, etc.; fatigued, wearied; also, sick or weary *of*, impatient *with* (something); *slang*, habitually disinclined to exertion, incorrigibly lazy.

a. in the predicate. Also in slang phr. ***to make*** (someone) ***tired*** (orig. *U.S.*): to get on the nerves of, irritate.

a **1400–50** [see TIRE *v.*¹ 5]. *c* **1470** HENRY *Wallace* IV. 28 The hors was tyryt, and mycht no forthyr pas. **1523** FITZHERB. *Husb.* §15 The horses..wyll soone be tyred, and sore beate, that they may not drawe. *a* **1550** *Freiris of Berwik* 257 in *Dunbar's Poems* (S.T.S.) 294, I am verry tyrit, wett and cauld. **1562** TURNER *Herbal* II. 32 b, Medicines which refreshe them that are wery or tyrede. **1573** *Nottingham Rec.* IV. 150 A horse that wase leafte ther tyard. **1590** SHAKS. *Com. Err.* IV. iii. 24 The man, sir, that when gentlemen are tired giues them a sob, and rests them. **1704** F. FULLER *Med. Gymn.* (1711) 29 Thro' the greatness of the Perspiration they grow tyr'd. **1782** COWPER *Gilpin* xxxvii, 'The dinner waits, and we are tired:' said Gilpin— 'So am I!' **1852** MRS. CARLYLE *Lett.* (1883) II. 196, I am very tired; and the tireder I am, the less I sleep. *c* **1883** C. H. HOYT *Bunch of Keys* I, in *America's Lost Plays* (1941) IX. 13 That makes me tired! **1888** 'J. S. WINTER' *Bootle's Childr.* vii, I got tired out with him at last. **1897** *Westm. Gaz.* 15 Apr. 2/3 He 'lived nowhere, did nothing, and, in fact, he was born tired', was what he told the inspector when he was arrested, and it was a graphic summary of a worthless life. **1904** S. E. WHITE *Blazed Trail Stories* IV. 65 Such talk made Daly tired, and he said so. **1925** W. J. LOCKE *Great Pandolfo* xiii. 172 'Women like you,' said Myrtilla a trifle sourly, 'make me tired.' **1950** 'P. WOODRUFF' *Island of Chamba* viii. 124 They make me tired... Things are bound to get worse.

b. in attrib. use.

1508 DUNBAR *Tua Mariit Wemen* 176 Was neuer sugeorne wer set na on that snaill tyrit. **1581** A. HALL *Iliad* VIII. 138 Thy chare, thy driuer, and thy seate, a tiered countenaunce shew. **1672** MARVELL *Reh. Transp.* I. 129 The tyred Magistrates asked them, whether they had not Halters. **1746–7** HERVEY *Medit.* (1818) 211 The tired shepherd has imposed silence on his pipe. **1871** MRS. BROOKFIELD *Influence* II. 74 Nothing is more delicious than the atmosphere of a country house to a tired-out Londoner in the month of August.

c. ***tired Tim*** (or ***Timothy***), usu. associated with ***weary Willie***: the names of two tramps, characters in the comic magazine *Illustrated Chips*; hence both used as nicknames for tramps or other work-shy people. Also *attrib.*

1906 *Daily Chron.* 15 Feb. 3/5 Heroes of the Tired Timothy stamp. **1927** W. E. COLLINSON *Contemp. Eng.* 27 Comic papers..brought home to us the picturesque language of Weary Willy and Tired Tim (the genial tramps —whence these words are frequently used as appellatives for 'tramps' in general). **1930** H. HERD *Diagnosis of Mental Deficiency* 10 Mental defectives are the 'weary Willies and tired Tims' *par excellence*. **1932** W. S. CHURCHILL *Let.* 6 Feb. in Ld. Boothby *Recoll. Rebel* (1978) vi. 86 These two old tired Tims of the Commons have ceased to command my allegiance. **1972** J. PORTER *Meddler & her Murder* xii. 157 With Miss Jones in..her Tired-Tim-and-Weary-Willie mood, there was no temptation to linger.

d. ***the tired business man***: a cliché, often used with satirical allusion to the short working hours and pleasure-loving habits popularly ascribed to business men.

The phrase is said to have been used by Mark Twain in 1896.

1913 *Vanity Fair* Nov. 37/2 'I mean simply this, my dear,' replied the Tired Business Man. **1927** A. HUXLEY *Proper Studies* 186 From the fetish-worshipper to the metaphysician, from the tired business man to the mystic.. every type of human being can find in Catholicism the spiritual nourishment which he or she requires. **1940** I. BROWN in *Best One-Act Plays of 1939* 141 Oh, how I've longed to be a Tired Business Man once more—office at ten, out at twelve-thirty, back at three, sign the letters, off home! **1969** *Listener* 20 Mar. 399/1 We often use the cliché of the tired businessman to define the low response..that sustains leg-shows.

2. *transf.* and *fig.* Worked out, exhausted, used up; in quot. *a* 1548, exhausting. Also, of language, literature, etc.: hackneyed, trite.

a **1548** HALL *Chron.*, *Hen. V* 49 In a long fight and tyred battaile. **1748** RICHARDSON *Clarissa* VI. 64, I must here lay down my tired pen! **1766** *Museum Rust.* VI. 440 When the upper stratum is tired and foul, the owner may..turn down the worn-out soil. **1899** *Times* 16 June 4/1 The Paris, to use an expressive Americanism, was a tired ship. *Ibid.* 4/2 The fact that the Paris was a tired ship was one result of the continual striving for records and averages. **1951** *Chambers's Jrnl.* Sept. 521/1 The start of the paper was promising enough, for Greenwood collected a group of writers around him equal to deserving that tired word 'brilliant'. **1956** *Sat. Rev.* (U.S.) 30 June 34/1 It [*sc.* a book] is (to use a tired phrase) history made interesting. **1966** *Listener* 28 Apr. 630/3 *The Pipeline*..turned out to be as tired and cliché-ridden a spy story as any I have heard.

b. Of food, flowers, etc.: limp with long exposure, no longer fresh. Of clothes: crumpled, shapeless, or baggy with long wear.

1897 *Daily News* 28 July 8/4 The muslin gowns begin to look more than a little tired. **1909** *Daily Chron.* 3 May 4/7 Colour and shape remind one of a tired cabbage leaf. **1933** *N. & Q.* 26 Aug. 130/1 Today people speak of stale vegetables or fruits as 'tired'. **1934** E. BOWEN *Cat Jumps* 252 Tired dance dresses. **1947** H. NICOLSON *Diary* 9 May (1968) 97 The spring-garden has lost its early bloom... The primroses are looking a trifle tired. **1958** *Spectator* 15 Aug. 222/1 The last batch of eggs I got from the local grocer turned out to be very tired. **1963** *Times* 11 June 10/6 In the present heat, merchants are reluctant to pay high prices for 'tired' fish. **1974** A. LURIE *War between Tates* (1977) V. 117 He is ill-dressed in a tired grey turtleneck sweater and sagging work pants. **1977** G. MARTON *Alarum* 16 Chris read ..occasionally munching on a very tired cheese sandwich.

c. ***tired and emotional***: joc. euphem. for 'drunk'.

[**1967** *Private Eye* 29 Sept. 9/4 Mr Brown had been tired and overwrought on many occasions.] **1981** LYNN & JAY *Yes Minister* I. iii. 72 Another paper's headline was *Hacker tired and emotional after embassy reception.* **1982** *Financial Times* 21 May 12/4 Each lock is battery powered so that if the hotel has a power failure the tired and emotional guest can still make [= reach] his bed. **1986** *Daily Tel.* 10 Dec. 13/2 Sensing that Penrose's efforts might have left him tired and emotional, the four Eye men called at the Mirror building.

3. *Comb.*, as *tired-eyed*, *-faced*, *-looking*.

1841 L. HUNT *Seer* (1864) 85 Happy in their tired-heartiness to get to the first bit of holiday ground they can reach. **1895** CLIVE HOLLAND *Jap. Wife* 91 We leave the terrace, with its lingering crowds of tired-faced holiday-makers. **1905** *Daily Chron.* 30 Aug. 4/7 The tired-eyed conductor took her fare. **1907** *Westm. Gaz.* 3 Dec. 1/3 Vases of somewhat tired-looking pink chrysanthemums.

tired (taɪəd), *ppl. a.*² [f. TIRE *sb.*² or *v.*⁴ + -ED.] Fitted or furnished with a tire or tires; chiefly as the second element in a combination, as ***iron-tired***. See also TYRED.

1894 [see *pneumatic-tired* (PNEUMATIC *a.* 5)]. **1896** C. ALLEN *Papier Mâché* 118 With a weighty parade of iron-tired Juggernaut justice, they marched in state. **1912** J. MASEFIELD in *Eng. Rev.* Feb. 414 Four newly-tired cartwheels hung to cool.

tiredly ('taɪədlɪ), *adv.* [f. TIRED *ppl. a.*¹ + -LY².] In a tired manner; wearily.

1659 TORRIANO, *Alla-strácca*,..wearisomely, tiredly. **1891** MISS DOWIE *Girl in Karp.* xiii, How tiredly she nodded the white-fair, weary head! **1896** MRS. CAFFYN *Quaker Grandmother* 104 Her hands dropped tiredly into her lap.

tiredness ('taɪədnɪs). [f. as prec. + -NESS.] The state of being tired; weariness, fatigue.

1552 ABP. HAMILTON *Catech.* (1884) 175 Hungir and thryst, heit and cald,..tyritnes, service or bondage. **1627** W. SCLATER *Exp. 2 Thess.* (1629) 279 Tedious yrkesomenesse, or tirednesse in Gods service. **1644** VICARS *God in Mount* 143 The tyrednes of the Souldiers with their travell. **1804** tr. *W. Heberden's Comm.* lxx. (1806) 369 *note*, At the height of 13 or 1400 toises above the sea, a peculiar tiredness often comes upon those who are ascending. **1889** E. W. BENSON in A. C. Benson *Life* (1900) II. 277 The last fortnight has only driven the London tiredness more over the system.

‖ **tire-fond** (tirfɔ̃). *Surg.* [Fr., f. *tire* draw + *fond* lowest part.] (See quots.)

1857 DUNGLISON *Med. Lex.*, *Tire-fond*, a surgical instrument formerly used to elevate the piece of bone sawed off by the trephine. **1899** *Syd. Soc. Lex.*, *Tire-fond*, an instrument for penetrating a cavity or tissue, transfixing and with-drawing foreign bodies, usually made in the form of a gimlet.

‖ **tire'larigot**, *Obs.*, in *to drink a tirelarigot* = Fr. *boire à tire-larigot* to drink hard, drink like a fish: see Littré s.v. *larigot*.

1653 URQUHART *Rabelais* I. vii, To quiet the childe they gave him to drink a tirelarigot, that is, till his throat was like to crack with it.

tireless ('taɪəlɪs), *a.*¹ [f. TIRE *v.*¹ + -LESS.] Untiring, indefatigable. **a.** Of persons (or their attributes) or other agents.

1591 SYLVESTER *Du Bartas* I. iv. 597 To sing the swiftness of thy tyer-less Teem. **1827** WILLIS *Healing Daughter Jairus* 13 The same loved, tireless watcher. **1867** H. C. LEA *Sacerdot. Celibacy* 70 The tireless pen of St. Jerome was called into requisition. **1884** R. BRIDGES *Prometh. Firegiver* 195 Attending with tireless ears. **1887** G. HOOPER *Campaign Sedan* 280 Their soldiers..seemed to be tireless, for they never halted.

b. Of qualities, actions, etc.

a **1826** HEBER *Transl. Pindar* iv. 1 Oh! urging on the tireless speed Of Thunder's elemental steed. **1859** *Times* 31

Mar. 10/2 Nothing can give our men the tireless elasticity of these Mahrattas. **1889** *Ibid.* 10 Aug. 9/1 With that tireless persistency which they usually display.

tireless ('taɪəlɪs), *a.*[2] [f. TIRE *sb.*[2] + -LESS.] Of a wheel: Without a tire or tires.

1862 R. H. PATTERSON *Ess. Hist. & Art* 218 A rough ricketty conveyance, with wooden axletrees and tireless wheels.

'tirelessly, *adv.* [f. TIRELESS *a.*[1] + -LY[2].] In a tireless manner; without tiring; untiringly.

1867 AUGUSTA WILSON *Vashti* xxxi, Tirelessly the wife and hired nurse watched the progress of the dreadful disease. **1903** *Times* 25 Feb. 10/2 For 30 years he had been tirelessly active.

So **'tirelessness**, the quality or condition of being tireless; indefatigableness.

1887 J. C. FERNALD in *Voice* (N.Y.) 6 Jan. 3 The enthusiasm and energy and tirelessness of youth. **1898** *Daily News* 21 May 2/4 If there was a fault in his strategy it was his tirelessness.

† **tireling** ('taɪəlɪŋ), *sb.* (*a.*) *Obs.* [app. f. TIRE *v.*[1] + -LING: cf. *hireling, shaveling.*] A tired person or animal: in quots. *attrib.* or as *adj.*: cf. *hireling priest*, etc.

1590 SPENSER *F.Q.* III. i. 17 His tyreling iade he fiercely forth did push. **1596** *Ibid.* VI. vii. 40. **1599** BP. HALL *Sat.* IV. iii. 57 Whiles like a tireling jade he lags half-way. **1613** J. DENNYS *Secr. Angling* I. ix, Neither of Mare nor Gelding let it be; Nor of the tyreling Iade that beares the packe.

† **'tirement.** *Obs.* [f. TIRE *v.*[3] + -MENT, after OF. *atirement*; ATTIREMENT was later.] Attire; *pl.* articles of attire; garments, or ornaments as a whole.

a **1400-50** *Alexander* 4918 With cumly knottis & with koyntis & knopis of perle It ware to tere me to tell þe tirement to-gedire. **1553** BRENDE *Q. Curtius* III. 27 b, As their tirementes were moste precious, the more violently thei plucked them away. **1555** EDEN *Decades* 290 The whyte cappes or other tyrementes they weare on theyr heades.

‖ **tiremoelle** (tirmwal). *Obs.* [Fr., f. *tire* draw, extract + *moelle* marrow.] A marrow-spoon.

1669 R. MONTAGU in *Buccleuch MSS.* (Hist. MSS. Comm.) I. 448, 2 forks, 2 knives, a toothpick-box, and a tiremoelle.

tirer ('taɪərə(r)). *rare.* [f. TIRE *v.*[3] + -ER[1].] One who attires or dresses.

1862 MERIVALE *Rom. Emp.* (1865) V. xlv. 355 The tirers of her person.

† **'tiresol.** *Obs. rare*[−1]. [ad. obs. Sp. and Pg. *tirasol* (= *quitasol*, 'a kinde of hat vsed in China very broad, which the principall men carry ouer their heads, with a short poll or staffe, like a canopie, to keepe the..sunne from them' (Minsheu), f. Pg. *tira-r* to take away, remove, banish + *sol* sun.] A (Chinese) umbrella or parasol.

1613 PURCHAS *Pilgrimage* V. xvi. 452 Next to whom commeth the King with a Tiresol over his head, to keepe off the Sunne.

tiresome ('taɪəsəm), *a.* [f. TIRE *v.*[1] + -SOME; cf. *meddlesome, wearisome.*]

1. Having the property of tiring by continuance, sameness, or lack of interest; wearisome, tedious.

1500-20 DUNBAR *Poems* lxvi. 82, I wait [it] is for me provydit, Bot sa done tyrsum [*v.r.* tyresum] it is to byd it. **1603** DANIEL *Def. Ryme* in *Panegyr.*, etc. H vj, Those continuall cadences of couplets..are very tyresome, and vnpleasing. **1697** DRYDEN *Virg., Ess. Georgics* (1721) I. 203 The inculcating Precept upon Precept, will at length prove tiresome to the Reader. **1778** MISS BURNEY *Evelina* (1791) I. xii. 33 London soon grows tiresome. **1854** LEWIS *Lett.* (1870) 279 It is slow, tiresome work. **1875** JOWETT *Plato* (ed. 2) IV. 350 What a tiresome being is a man who is fond of talking.

b. *loosely.* Troublesome, disagreeable, unpleasant; irksome, annoying, vexatious. *colloq.*

1798 CHARLOTTE SMITH *Yng. Philos.* I. 11 The tiresome custom you have got of never being ready. **1836** *Backwoods of Canada* 237 The tiresome things fell to pieces directly they became dry. **1862** MRS. CARLYLE *Lett.* (1883) III. 99 At the top of the house he is safe enough from tiresome interruptions. **1898** FLOR. MONTGOMERY *Tony* 12 A tiresome fidgety schoolboy as a travelling companion.

† **2.** Causing physical fatigue; fatiguing, tiring. *Obs.* (Now merged in sense 1.)

1598 HAKLUYT *Voy.* I. 612 The way was all of dry deepe slyding sand.., and by that meanes so tiresome and painefull as might be. **1710** PHILIPS *Pastorals* ii. 16 The tiresome Burden doubles its Increase. **1725** SWIFT *Let. to Sheridan* 11 Sept., In an employment precarious and tiresome,..this new weight of party malice had struck you down. **1728** MORGAN *Algiers* I. iii. 40 He led his Enemies a tiresome Dance, often drawing them into Ambuscades.

Hence **'tiresomely** *adv.*

1847 C. BRONTE *J. Eyre* xxxiv, A tiresomely importunate instinct reminded me that vivacity (at least in me) was distasteful to him. **1902** *Times* 14 Mar. 7/5 Mr. Seddon [is] now regarded..as tiresomely insistent upon Imperial views.

'tiresomeness. [f. prec. + -NESS.]

† **1.** The condition of being tired; weariness. *Obs. rare.*

1646 TRAPP *Comm. John* i. 10 For thou hast created all things,..without help, tool, or tiresomeness. **1715** NELSON tr. *T. à Kempis' Chr. Exerc.* III. xvii. 146 Give me..good occupation..against the Tiresomness and Drowsiness of the Heart.

2. The quality of being tiresome; wearisomeness, tediousness.

1668 H. MORE *Div. Dial.* II. xxiii. (1713) 162 The tiresomeness of the Fight makes the Victory more pleasant and sensible. **1817** MAR. EDGEWORTH *On Bores* ¶ 11 Others are not endured long enough in society to come to the perfection of tiresomeness.

† **tiret**, obs. f. TERRET; in quot. in sense a.

1587 HOLINSHED *Chron.* III. 539/1 About his arme he wore an hounds collar set full of SS of gold, and the tirets likewise being of the same metall.

‖ **tiretaine** (tirtɛn). [Fr.; 1247 in Godef. *Compl.* (also ? *c* 1400 *tierteine*, 1449 *tirtaine* (1718, Littré), 1487 *tertaine*; 1581 *tritaine*): cf. TARTAN.] A cloth woven of wool mixed with linen or cotton, 'worne ordinarily by the French peasants' (Cotgr.); linsey-woolsey.

1863 SALA *Last Crusader* 213 'Many and many a time', writes the good Sire de Joinville,..'have I seen the good king..vestured in a coat of camlet, a surcoat of tiretaine without sleeves, a mantle above the black sandalette'. [**1866** ROGERS *Agric. & Prices* II. xxii. 579 We find kersey, tirretin [*c* 1284-5: cf. I. 536/3], murrey, burell, rosete, keynet, reynes, and taursmaurs.] **1901** tr. *V. Hugo's Notre-Dame* xxiii, The petticoat of tiretaine with red and blue stripes. **1910** *Sat. Westm. Gaz.* 15 Jan. 6/2 Plump dames in tiretaines.

‖ **tire-tête** (tirtɛt). *Obstetr.* [Fr., f. *tire-r* to draw + *tête* head.] (See quot. 1857.)

1754-64 SMELLIE *Midwif.* I. Introd. 56 He also invented a tire-tête, which cannot be used until the skull is opened with a knife. **1771** *Encycl. Brit.* III. 238/2 Let Leverot's tire-tête, with the three sides joined together, be introduced along the accoucheur's hand. **1857** DUNGLISON *Med. Lex.*, *Tire-tête*, a name given to different instruments used for extracting the head of the child when left in the uterus.

'tire-woman. Also 7-8 tyre-. [f. TIRE *sb.*[1] + WOMAN.] A woman who assists at a lady's toilet; a lady's maid (*arch.*); †also, a woman employed in the making or sale of women's clothing; a dressmaker, costumier (*obs.*).

1615 BRATHWAIT *Strappado* (1878) 126 T'was some tyre-woman he tooke them fro. *c* **1626** *Dick of Devon* III. iv. in Bullen *O. Pl.* (1883) II. 58 Have they forsaken the Divell and all his fashions? banishd their Taylors and Tyrewomen? **1667** PEPYS *Diary* 20 Feb., To Mrs. Grotier's, the Queen's tire-woman, for a pair of locks for my wife. **1709** STEELE *Tatler* No. 79 ¶ 1 Dressed with all the Art and Care that Mrs. Toilet the Tire-Woman could bestow on her. **1790** CATH. M. GRAHAM *Lett. Educ.* 108 Why should they not.. value themselves for this outside fashionableness of the taylor or tire woman, when their parents have so early instructed them to do it? **1847** MARRYAT *Childr. N. Forest* xxv, They will make very nice tire-women to some lady of quality. **1867** 'OUIDA' *C. Castlemaine* (1879) 7 To while time away by scolding her tire-woman.

tirful, *a.*: see TIR.

tiriac, obs. f. THERIAC.

tiring, *vbl. sb.*[1] and *ppl. a.*[1]: see after TIRE *v.*[1]

tiring ('taɪərɪŋ), *vbl. sb.*[2] ? *arch.* Also 5-7 tyr-. [f. TIRE *v.*[2] + -ING[1].] The action of TIRE *v.*[2]; the pulling or tearing of a hawk at a tough morsel given to it to exercise itself; *concr.* a piece of food given to a hawk for this purpose. Also *fig.*

c **1450** *Bk. Hawkyng* in *Rel. Ant.* I. 296 The swetteste tyryng that is to goshawke and sperhawke is a pigge is tayle. **1486** *Bk. St. Albans, Hawking* b viij b, She shall nether at the fedyng ner at the tyryng ne at the lightyng ne at the Rysyng hurtte hir selffe. **1575** TURBERV. *Falconrie* 146 Gyve hir tyring of a wing or a foote of the sayde pullet. **1891** HARTING *Gloss. Falconry, Tiring*,..any tough piece (as the leg of a fowl with little on) given to a hawk when in training to pull at, in order to prolong the meal, and exercise the muscles of the back and neck.

tiring ('taɪərɪŋ), *vbl. sb.*[3] Also 6-7 **tyring.** [f. TIRE *v.*[3] + -ING[1].] The action of TIRE *v.*[3]; attiring, dressing (*arch.*: see b); dressing the hair; †fitting out (*obs.*); also *concr.* attire, apparel, head-dress (*arch.*); †equipment, apparatus, garnishing (*obs.*); *spec.* see quot. 1869 (*dial.*).

1552 HULOET, Byrlet or tyrynge for women. **1558** in Feuillerat *Revels Q. Eliz.* (1908) 23 Sarcenet..imployed into..Shertes.., translated into lyninge pullinges oute tuftes tyringes and other garnisshinge. *Ibid.* 82 Sarsenettes ..spent in rowles and wrethes tuftinge tyringe of hedpeces and gyrdells. **1602** DEKKER *Satirom.* Wks. 1873 I. 186 Such delayes in rising, in fitting gownes, in tyring [etc.]. **1620** SHELTON *Quix.* (1746) IV. xxix. 228 In Hell they are working Tapistry Work, and there are made Tyrings and Net-works. **1656** *Artif. Handsom.* 67 Whose either haire, or complexion, or tiring is not natively their own. **1869** *Lonsdale Gloss., Tiring*, the plastering under slates. **1909** *Daily Chron.* 18 Mar. 3/1 He wears his learning as lightly as the tiring of the hair of Aphrodite, borne upon her swan in a Douris vase.

b. *attrib.* and *Comb.*, as ***tiring-chamber***, ***-closet***, ***-glass***, ***-man***, ***-place***; **tiring-woman**, a lady's maid. Also TIRING-HOUSE, -ROOM. *Obs.* or *arch.*

1645 EVELYN *Diary* 27 Feb., A cart, or *plaustrum*, where the scene or tiring-place is made of boughs in a rural manner. **1732** FIELDING *Mod. Husb.* IV. iv, I know several women of fashion I could not support for a tiring woman. **1825** SCOTT *Betrothed* xxii, The..intercession of the tiring-woman obtained admission for travelling merchants, or pedlars. **1844** MRS. BROWNING *Duchess May* lxxii, The smile upon her face, ere she left the tiring-glass Had not time enough to go. **1856** BOKER *Francesca da Rimini* I. i, I'll be Your tiring-man, for once. **1860** LD. LYTTON *Lucile* II. iv. 77 From the dark tiring-chamber behind, straight reissue With new masks the old mummers.

tiring ('taɪərɪŋ), *vbl. sb.*[4] [f. TIRE *sb.*[2] or *v.*[4] + -ING[1].] The fitting of a wheel with a tire; the condition or mode of being fitted with tires.

1831 HOLLAND *Manuf. in Metal* I. 157 The tiring, the breadth, and the inclination of the wheels.

'tiring-house. *Obs.* or *arch.* Also 6- tyring-. [f. TIRING *vbl. sb.*[3] + HOUSE.] A dressing-room; *esp.* the room or place in which the actors dressed for the stage; = TIRING-ROOM.

1590 SHAKS. *Mids. N.* III. i. 4 This greene plot shall be our stage, this hauthorne brake our tyring house. **1612** RALEIGH *Poems* (1870) xviii. 29 Our mothers' wombs the tiring-houses be, Where we are dressed for life's short comedy. **1620** MELTON *Astrolog.* 31 While Drummers make Thunder in the Tyring-house. **1639** FULLER *Holy War* IV. vii. (1840) 189 That actor who cometh off with the dislike of the spectators stealeth as invisibly as he may into the tiring-house. **1678** CUDWORTH *Intell. Syst.* I. v. 877 Dying, to the Rational or Humane Soul, is nothing but a withdrawing into the Tyring-house, and putting off the Cloathing of this terrestrial Body. **1908** *Q. Rev.* Apr. 453 He runs his lateral curtains back to the tyring-house wall.

tiring-irons ('taɪərɪŋ,aɪənz), *sb. pl.* Also 7-8 **tyring-, tarrying-,** 8 **tarring-.** [In its current form, f. *tiring*, pr. pple. of TIRE *v.*[1] + IRON; but *tarrying-iron* (also *tarriour*) appears to occur as early, and to have been the more prevalent in the 17th and 18th c. This belongs to TARRY *v.*, in its transitive sense 'to delay, retard, protract, prolong, hold in check' (if not to *tarry*, TARY *v.*).

The evidence does not decide whether *tiring* or *tarrying* was the original epithet, and as both are descriptive, they may have been independent.]

A popular name of the ***puzzling rings*** or ***ring-puzzle*** (esp. when made of iron, and of large size), in which a number of rings, usually seven or ten, are placed on an oblong closed wire loop or bow, each being also fastened to a wire within the bow, which passes through the next ring, and is loosely attached by its other end to a thin flat piece of metal or bone of nearly the same length as the loop. The puzzle is to take all the rings thus fettered off the loop or bow.

'This perplexing invention is of great antiquity, and was treated on by Cardan, the mathematician [1501-1576]' (*Boy's Own Book* (1828) 420, in which there is a figure and detailed explanation of the moves).

1601 DEACON & WALKER *Answ. to Darel* To Rdr. 4 The very frame itselfe of their whole proceeding resembleth fitlie a paire of tarriours, or tyring yrons. **1627** DRAYTON *Elegies, To W. Jeffreys* 100 A Tarrying-iron for fooles to labour at. **1661** BAXTER *Mor. Prognost.* I. xvi. 4 Like a Boy with a pair of Tarrying-Irons. *a* **1675** LIGHTFOOT *Serm. 2 Sam. xix. 29* Wks. 1684 II. 1246 They are not unriddleable riddles, and tyring-irons never to be untied. **1690** C. NESSE *O. & N. Test.* I. 277 He would lay his tarrying-irons upon him, and not permit him to go away. *a* **1763** SHENSTONE *Upon Riddles* i. in Dodsl. *Coll. Poems* (1782) V. 63 Have you not known a small machine Which brazen rings environ, In many a country chimney seen, Y-clep'd a tarring-iron? **1828** *Boy's own Bk.* 420 It may be purchased at most of the toy-shops, very lightly and elegantly made. It also exists in various parts of the country, forged in iron,..and aptly named 'The Tiring Irons'. **1879** LOUISA POTTER *Lanc. Mem.* 115 One was called 'tiring-irons', a set of iron rings and two iron bars fastened together.

tiring-room ('taɪərɪŋruːm). [f. TIRING *vbl. sb.*[3] + ROOM.] A dressing-room (*arch.*); *spec.* the dressing-room of a theatre. Also *transf.* and *fig.*

1623 I. M. *Pref. Verse* in *Shaks. Wks.*, From the Worlds-Stage, to the Graues-Tyring-roome. *a* **1639** WOTTON *De Morte* 2 in *Reliq.* (1651) 539 Mans life's a Tragedy. His mothers womb (From which he enters) is the tyring room. **16..** FLETCHER *Poems* 208 (Nares) The stars are all with-drawn from each glad sphear Within the tyring rooms of heaven. **1666** PEPYS *Diary* 19 Mar., But my business here was to see the inside of the stage and all the tiring-rooms and machines. **1749** SMOLLETT *Gil Bl.* XII. i. (1782) IV. 217 After the play I..found her in the tyring-room, talking to some gentlemen. **1848** DICKENS *Dombey* vi, Then converting the parlour, for the nonce, into a private tiring room, she dressed her.

tirl (tɜːl, *Sc.* tɛrl), *sb.*[1] Chiefly *Sc.* Also 5-8 tirle, 6 tirrill, 7 tirrle, turle. [app. related to TIRL *v.*[3]]

1. A round or turn at doing anything; a slight experience or trial of something; a touch, taste.

c **1660** J. GUTHRIE in *Union Mag.* Oct. (1902) 463 Many a man has touched the cross, and it has scalded him; and he has given it a tirl and letten it lie. **1697** CLELAND *Poems* 32 She was tyred with his speeches; She would far rather had a tirrle Of an Aquavitae barrel. **1715** RAMSAY *Christ's Kirk Gr.* II. vii, The young swankies on the green Took round a merry tirle. **1721** —— *Horace to Virg.* 5 King Æol, grant a tydie tirl. **1742** FORBES *Shop Bill* x. in *Ajax*, etc. (1755) 40, I hae..some for those that tak a tirle amo' the sheets.

2. A revolving piece of mechanism like a turnstile; a wheel of some kind. *dial.*

1691 W. B. *Hist. Roman Conclave* ii. 7 In several parts of the Wall of the Conclave, there are seven *Rote*, or Holes with

Turles in them, just as there are in Nunneries, wherein the Victuals are put in from without, and turned round to be Received within. **1793** *Statist. Acc. Scot.* V. 193–4 The tirl occupies the same situation under this mill, as the trundles in the inner part of an ordinary mill; and it performs the same office. The diameter of the tirl is always equal to that of the millstones. **1883** *W. Yorks. Gloss.*, *Tirl*, the wheel of a [wheel] barrow.

3. An act of twirling; a twirl, whirl. *dial.*

1790 D. MORISON *Poems* 6 (E.D.D.) The temper pin she gi'es a tirl, An' spins but slow.

†**4.** ? A whirled or circular pattern. *rare*$^{-1}$.

a **1584** MONTGOMERIE *Cherrie & Slae* 334 With dansing, and glansing, In tirlis [*v.r.* tirle] lik dornik champ.

†**5.** A name of some disease: editors suggest St. Vitus's dance. *Obs. rare.*

a **1585** MONTGOMERIE *Flyting* 321 The phtiseik, þe twithȝaik, þe tittis, and þe tirrillis [*v.r.* The tisicke, the toothaike, the tites and tirles].

6. *Comb.* †**tirl-bed**, a trundle- or truckle-bed on low wheels or castors.

1488 *Coventry MSS.* in *1st Rep. Hist. MSS. Comm.* 101/2, iii. staynding beddes iii. tirle beddes well bothomed.

tirl, *sb.*^{2} *Sc.* [f. TIRL *v.*^{3} II.] An act of tirling (see TIRL *v.*^{3} 3); *loosely*, a tap or tapping. Also as *int.*

1808 JAMIESON, *Tirl*,.. a sharp tap or stroke. **1818** *Blackw. Mag.* III. 531 The slight tirl on the lozen, or tap at the window. **1819** W. TENNANT *Papistry Storm'd* (1827) 19 Whan, hark! upon the gowden door, Tirl! comes a rap.

tirl, *sb.*^{3}, Sc. var. THRILL *sb.*^{3}, vibration, tremor.

1882 JAMIESON, *Tirl, Tirle*, a vibration, the act of vibrating. **1894** HALIBURTON *Furth in Field* IV. 183 A good woman.. with a pathetic 'tirl' in her tone.

tirl, *v.*^{1} *Sc.* Also 6 **tyrle**. [Origin uncertain: app. not connected with any sense of TRILL; but cf. THRILL *v.*^{1} 6.]

†**1.** *intr.* To pluck *at*; *esp.* to pluck at the strings of a harp, or the like, so as to cause them to sound. *Obs.*

c **1470** HENRYSON *Mor. Fab.* VII. (*Lion & Mouse*) xiv, Sum [of the mice] tirlit at the campis of his [the lion's] beird, Sum sparit not to claw him on the face. **1567** *Gude & Godlie B.* (S.T.S.) 93 Tak harpe in hand.. Tyrle on the ten stringit Instrument.

2. *trans.* To pluck (a tense string, etc.) so as to cause vibration.

1882 JAMIESON s.v., (Clydesdale) He tirled the strings. **1894** R. REID in *Poets Dumfries.* x. (1910) 305 That queer wild cry frae the gurly sky Can tirl my heart-strings still.

tirl, *v.*^{2} *Sc.* and *north. dial.* [Apparently related to TIRVE *v.*^{1} and TIRR *v.* in same senses; perh. orig. a freq. **tyrflian*: cf. *whirl* from *hwirfl-*.]

1. *trans.* To roll or turn back, pull or strip off (a garment or the clothes from a person, his back, etc.; the bed-clothes from a bed; the thatch or roof from a house, stack, etc.).

a **1500** *Priests Peblis* 993 Off his coate thay tirlit be the croun. **1810** *Cromek's Rem. Nithsdale Song* 33 The wind blaws loud and tirls our strae. **1819** W. TENNANT *Papistry Storm'd* (1827) 211 Nae thing was prosperin' there and thrivin', But tirlin' roofs and rafter-rivin'. **1826** L. PROUDLOCK *Poet. Wks., Cuddie & Crawing Hen* 43 Winds loud blew, wi' fury flew, And threat to tirl its riggin'. **1835** HOGG *Tales & Sk.* (1837) V. 275 He was tied to a tree, and his shirt tirled over his head. **1880** *Antrim & Down Gloss.* s.v. *Tirl, thirl*, The wun' thirled the thatch las' nicht. **1894** *Northumbld. Gloss.* s.v., To 'tirl the bed-claes', to strip off the bed-clothes.

2. To uncover by rolling back the covering; to strip (a person) naked; to unroof (a building): often ***tirl naked, tirl bare***.

1721 RAMSAY *Lucky Spence* x, Suppose then they should tirle ye bare, And gar ye fike, E'en learn to thole. **1785** BURNS *Addr. to Deil* iv, Whyles on the strong-wing'd tempest flyin, Tirlin the kirks. **1816** SCOTT *Old Mort.* xxiii, Our folk had tirled the dead dragoons as bare as bawbees. **1843** NICHOLSON *Hist. & Trad. Tales* 120 Wi' hideous yells she filled the air, And tirled Simon's cottage bare.

b. To uncover (the peat in a moss, the stone in a quarry, etc.) by removing the surface soil, overlying earth, clay, etc.; to lay bare (anything) by removing its covering.

1815 *Pennecuik's Wks.* 71 *note*, After removing the surface soil with the roots of the heath, or ling, growing on it (called the tirling of the moss). **1816** SCOTT *Antiq.* xxiii, 'If your honours are thinking of tirling the floor', said old Edie, '.. I would begin below that muckle stane'. *Mod. Sc.* About 1845 a new section of Denholm Hill Freestone Quarry was tirled.

tirl, *v.*^{3} Now chiefly *Sc.* and *north. dial.* Forms: 6 **tyrle**, (**turle**), 7 **tirle**, 8– **tirl**. [Metathetic form of TRILL *v.*^{1} Cf. EFris. *tirreln, tirlen* to turn about quickly.]

I. 1. *trans.* To turn; to cause to rotate or revolve; to twirl, spin, twiddle; to turn over (and over); to move by rolling; = TRILL *v.*^{1} 1. Also, to turn over rapidly (the leaves of a book).

1543 TRAHERON *Vigo's Chirurg.* IV. 137 He muste guyde and tyrle the sayd nedle toward the panicle called cornea, tyl he touche the myddes of the apple of the eye and a lytle more. **1582** T. WATSON *Centurie of Loue* lxii. Poems (Arb.) 98 Like Sisyphus I labour still To turle a rowling stoane against the hill. **1593** G. HARVEY *Pierce's Super.* Wks. (Grosart) II. 150 That rowling stone of Innouation was neuer so turled and tumbled, as since those busie limmes began to rowse, and besturre them. **1638** H. ADAMSON *Muse's Threnodie* v. (1774) 133 O how they bend their backs and fingers tirle! **1781** J. HUTTON *Tour to Caves* (ed. 2) Gloss. (E.D.S.), *Tirl, v.*, to turn over, as leaves in a book. **1825** BROCKETT *N.C. Words, Tirl*,.. to turn over the leaves of a book quickly. **1844** *Ayrshire Wreath* 155 We had a tough game at tirlin' the trencher. *a* **1869** C. SPENCE *Poems* (1898) 72 Soft wind sighing o'er the waste, Tirling the seared leaves. **1894** *Northumbld. Gloss.* s.v., 'Tirled heels up', suddenly overturned or turned inside out.

†**b.** ? To cause to move; to circulate; in phrase ***tirl on the berry***, ? pass round the wine. Cf. *troll the bowl. Obs.*

1519 *Interl. Four Elem.* B ij, Make rome, syrs, and let vs be mery, With huffa galand synge tyrll on the bery, And let the wyde worlde wynde. *c* **1537** *Thersytes* in *Four O. Plays* (1848) 79 And we shall make merye And synge tyrle on the berye. [*a* **1553** UDALL *Royster D.* II. iii. (Arb.) 36 Heigh derie derie, Trill on the berie.]

2. *intr.* To turn over; to rotate in moving or falling; to roll, whirl.

1824 MACTAGGART *Gallovid. Encycl.* s.v. *Cankert*, Afore she tirl'd owre [= died] my prayers war fervant. **1860** BLACKIE *Lyr. Poems, Jenny Geddes* vii, Stool after stool, like rattling hail, came tirling through the air. **1894** *Northumbld. Gloss.* s.v., Slates are said to 'come tirlin doon' when they are stripped off in a gale.

II. 3. *intr.* To make a rattling noise by turning or moving something rapidly to and fro or up and down. **a.** In the phr. ***to tirl at*** (†***upon***) ***the pin***, to make such a noise on some part of the gate or door, in order to gain admittance; also ***to tirl at the latch, at the sneck***.

An old phrase of ballad poetry, which in the 19th c. was taken up and used by Scott, and others after him. Now generally identified by antiquaries with the use of the appendage called the *risp and ring* (RISP *sb.*^{3} 2), formerly used for this purpose. (Cf. TINKLE *v.*^{1} 3, *Bob Norice* ix, 'When he came to Lord Barnet's castel He tinklet at the ring'.) But in this identification there are difficulties; a *risp* is not a 'pin', nor has it any resemblance to a 'pin', in any known sense of the word; the *pin* of a door was the latch or handle which was 'lifted' or 'turned' to open the door: see quots. under PIN *sb.*^{1} 1 b; whereas the 'risp' was a fixed appendage which could neither be lifted nor turned, having no connexion with the latch or door-handle. Hence it would seem that 'to tirl at the pin' was to make a noise by moving the latch up and down rapidly. It is possible that the 'risp and ring' was a later device, which came to be erroneously considered as the apparatus by which the 'tirling at the pin' was performed.

[*c* **1500** *Songs, Carols*, etc. 111 Hogyn cam to bowers dore, He tryld vpon þe pyn for love, Hum, ha, trill go bell.. Vp she rose & lett hym yn.] **15..** *Ld. Beichan* in *Ballads & Songs* (Percy Soc.) 90 When she came to Lord Beichan's gate, She tirled softly at the pin. ? **16..** in *Ramsay's Tea-t. Misc.* (1762) 324 Ay he tirled at the pin, But answer made she none. ? **17..** *Pr. Robt.* ix. in *Minstr. Scot. Bord.* (1869) 381 O he has run to Darlinton, And tirled at the pin. **1816** SCOTT *Antiq.* xl, There cam.. first Pride, then Malice, then Revenge, then False Witness; and Murder tirl'd at the door-pin, if he camna ben. **1833** M. SCOTT *Tom Cringle* xii. (1859) 270, I hear my next door neighbour Madam Adversity tirling at the door pin. **1843** NICHOLSON *Hist. & Trad. T., Brownie o' Blodnoch* 80 He tirled na lang, but he glided ben Wi' a dreary dreary hum. **1879** *Perthshire in Bygone Days* II. v. 300 My Nannie will smile in her sleep and awake When I tirl at the latch of my door. **1895** CROCKETT *Men of Moss-Hags* xiii, She tirled fretfully at the pin, the servant-maid opened, and we went within.

b. *trans.* in ***to tirl the sneck***. *Sc. rare.*

[Cf. the name, Jonnie Tirlsneck, of the beadle in Scott's *St. Ronan's Well.*]

a **1794** PICKERING '*Keen blaws the Wind*' in *Burns' Wks.* (1856) IV. 91 The Gaber-lunzie tirls my sneck And shivering tells his waefu' tale. **1892** J. LUMSDEN *Sheep-head & Trotters* 44 They.. tirl the neebors' snecks Like ouphes this nicht.

4. *intr.* Said of the sound of rain on a roof. *rare.*

1886 STEVENSON *Kidnapped* xxvi, When the wind gowls in the chimney and the rain tirls on the roof.

Hence **'tirling-pin**, the 'pin' or latch on which persons 'tirled' for admittance: see above, sense 3.

1875 JAS. GRANT *One of the 600* i, The old Scotch tirling-pin—to be found now nowhere save in Fife—in lieu of bells and knockers. **1878** *N. & Q.* 5th Ser. IX. 319, I have seen and tirled at an original tirling-pin on the chief entrance door of the vicarage house at Ovingham-on-Tyne. **1894** *Northumbld. Gloss.* s.v. *Tirl*, Doors were formerly provided with a long, notched, iron handle on which a loose iron ring was hung. Instead of rousing the house with a knock, the caller tirled the ring up and down the notches of the 'tirling pin', or handle. [But this was the *risp and ring*.]

tirl(e, tyrl(e, *v.*^{4} *Sc.* Var. of THIRL *v.*^{1}, ^{3}, THRILL *v.*^{1}

1825–82 JAMIESON, *Tirl, Tirle*,.. to quiver, vibrate, thrill. *a* **1870** THOMSON *Musings* (1881) 120 Tyrants will ne'er care a snuff for your word, Till ance they hear't tirl frae the point o' your sword.

tirleis, -lies, obs. Sc. forms of TRELLIS.

†**'tirler.** *Obs.* [f. TIRL *v.*^{3} + -ER^1.] One who tirls; ***tirler of square bones***, a thrower of dice, a dicer.

[Cf. *c* **1550** *Lusty Juventus* D iij, I wyll trill the bones while I haue one grote.] **1609** HOLLAND *Amm. Marcell.* XXVIII. iv. 340 Certaine.. who decline the name of *Aleatores*, *i.* Dice-players, and therefore are desirous to be called *Tesserarij*, *i.* Tirlers of square bones.

†**'tirlery**, *a.* (or ? *sb.*) *Obs.* Also **tyr-, -liry, -lary**. [? Related to TIRL *v.*^{3}] ? Whirling, flighty, trifling, trumpery: in a few obs. combs.: see quots., and cf. TERLERIE.

1546 BALE *Eng. Votaries* I. (1550) 24 b, Bertha the quene.. then beynge a Frenche woman caused kynge Ethelbert to admit them wyth al theyr tyrlery trashe. *c* **1560** *Dr. Doubble Ale* 437 in Hazl. *E.P.P.* III. 321 Farewell and adewe, With a whirlary whewe, And a tirlary typpe; Beware of the whyppe. **1638** FORD *Lady's Trial* III. i, The best.. prove themselves but flirts, and tirliry-pufkins [see PUFFKIN].

'tirlie, 'tirly, *sb.* and *a. Sc.* [f. TIRL *sb.*^{1}, *v.*^{3}]

A. *sb.* **1.** (See quot.)

1882 *Jamieson's Dict.*, *Tirlie, tirly*, sb. applied to a waving or ornamental line in scroll-work or carving; also, to the ornament itself.

2. A turnstile.

1824 MACTAGGART *Gallovid. Encycl.*, *Tirlies*, little circular stoppages in pathways which turn round.

B. *adj.* Full of twirls or whirls, as in **tirly-toy**, **'tirlie-'whirlie**, a whirled figure, ornament, or pattern; anything having this form; a whirligig; a musical twirl or turn of the voice: also *attrib.*

a **1807** SKINNER *Misc. Poet.* (1809) 183 What can ye be that cou'd employ Your pen in sic a *tirly-toy? **17..** *Dainty Davie* ii. in Herd *Coll.* (1776) II. 215 It was in and through the window broads, And a' the *tirlie wirlies o'd; The sweetest kiss that e'er I got. **1742** FORBES *Shop Bill* x. in *Ajax*, etc. (1755) 40, I hae to fit the little girl.. Wi' mony a bony tirly wirl about the queets [= ankles]. **1816** SCOTT *Antiq.* xxi, They hae contrived queer tirlie-wirlie holes, that gang out to the open air, and keep the stair as caller as a kail-blade. **1885** 'STRATHESK' *More Bits* xiv. (ed. 2) 274 Matthew Riddell.. sang with a great many 'tirlywirlies' and grace-notes the following curling song.

tirling, tirling-pin: see TIRL *v.*^{3}

tirlist, obs. Sc. form of TRELLISED.

Tir-na-nog ('tɪənænəʊg). *Irish Mythol.* Also **Tir-nan-og, Tir-n-an-oge**, etc. [a. Ir. *Tír na nÓg* land of the young.] A fabled land of perpetual youth, an Irish version of Elysium. Also *transf.*

1889 W. B. YEATS *Let.* 29 July (1954) 132 The Irish peasant's notion that Tir-n-an-oge (the Country of the Young) is made up of three phantom islands. **1898** E. C. BREWER *Reader's Handbk. Allusions* (new ed.) 590/2 The ancient inhabitants of Erin had.. the vague belief that there somewhere existed a land where people were always youthful.. and lived for ever. This country went by various names, as *Tir-na-nóg*, etc. **1906** P. E. MORE *Shelburne Ess.* 4th Ser. 245 It is the Tir-nan-og of the Celts, the country of the young. **1938** L. MACNEICE *I crossed Minch* II. x. 155 Don't talk to me about the Isles of Youth. These are the Isles of Senescence, of Inactivity... I do not want to sleep or dream of Tir n'an Og. **1955** *Bull. Atomic Sci.* Mar. 82/3 Without a better balance, the science-created *Tir na nog*, the legendary Irish land of youth on earth, must result in the rigid Malthusian principle which population experts sternly predicted. **1980** *London Mag.* Mar. 23 The old Irish myth of Tir nan-Og, the land of everlasting youthfulness.

tiro, tyro ('taɪərəʊ). Pl. **-oes, -os** (-əʊz). Forms: α. 7 **tyron, tyrone**, *pl.* 7–9 **tyrones** (-'əʊniːz). β. 7–9 **tyro**, 8–9 **tiro**, *pl.* 7–8 **tyro's**, 7– **tyros, tyroes**, 8– **tiroes**. [a. L. *tīro*, pl. *tīrōnēs* (in med.L. often spelt *tyro, tyrones*: so in Du Cange), a young soldier, a recruit, a beginner; It. *tirone*, Sp. *tiron*. Commonly spelt *tyro*, after med.L., down to the date of Cowper's *Tirocinium*, 1784, and still so spelt by the majority of writers; in the 17th c. *tyrone* was even written for It. *tirone*, and *tyrones* as plural after L. is found down to 1824. But a plural of English form *tyroes* (cf. *heroes, negroes*) is found in 1672, and *tyros* in 1690; Cowper has *tiroes*.]

A beginner or learner in anything; one who is learning or who has mastered the rudiments only of any branch of knowledge; a novice.

1611 CORYAT *Crudities* 63 Of those punies, those tyrones that are brought up under those threescore, there are no less then a thousand and five hundred. **1647** R. STAPYLTON *Juvenal* 109 Exercising and training like the tyrones or young souldiers in Camp Mart. **1656** BLOUNT *Glossogr.*, *Tyrone*.., a fresh water-souldier; a young beginner in any art or science, a novice. **1670** E. MAYNWARING *Physician's Repos.* 92 They do but qualify you as a Tyro. **1672** MANLEY *Cowell's Interpr.* Pref., The Students of the Law be no Tyroes in other Learning; or, at least, ought not to be. **1697** EVELYN *Numism.* vii. 252 For the Ease and Benefit of Tyros. **1699** GARTH *Dispens.* III. 31 There stands a Structure on a rising Hill, Where Tyro's take their Freedom out to kill. **1726** LEONI *Alberti's Archit.* III. 24/1 The Tyroes in the art of Painting. **1784** COWPER *Tiroc.* 220 The management of tiroes of eighteen Is difficult. **1797** *Monthly Mag.* III. 240/1 Dr. Travis.. was.. on entering into this province of theological polemics, a Tiro, compared with his antagonists. **1810** *Edin. Rev.* XV. 399 The tyro will not complain that it [the word] is obscure. **1824** SCOTT *Redgauntlet* let. xiii, A subject upon whilk all the *tyrones* have been trying their whittles. **1828** WHATELY in *Encycl. Metrop.* (1845) I. 282/1 It will.. be advisable for a tiro in composition to look over what he has written. **1851** RUSKIN *Mod. Paint.* (ed. 2) I. Pref. 36 The merest tyro in art knows that [etc.]. **1869** FARRAR *Fam. Speech* ii. (1873) 49 The youngest tiro is hardly surprised to learn that *lieu* and *coucher* both spring from one root. **1875** JOWETT *Plato* (ed. 2) IV. 13 It is difficult to acquit Plato.. of being a tyro in dialectics, when he overlooks such a distinction. **1880** SWINBURNE *Stud. Shaks.* 14 Easily recognisable by the veriest tiro in the school of Shakespeare.

attrib. *a* **1660** *Contemp. Hist. Irel.* (Ir. Archæol. Soc.) I. 162 Those tyron souldiers and novices in the arte militarie. **1860** PIESSE *Lab. Chem. Wonders* 142 A tyro-chemist in search of the philosopher's stone. **1903** H. G. HUTCHINSON in Watson *Eng. Sport* 272 Conveying some information to the tiro golfer. **1905** *Daily Chron.* 14 July 5/7 Rifle Clubs' Tyro Competition, open to teams of five tyro members.

tiro-: see also TYRO-.

‖**tirocinium** (taɪrəʊˈsɪnɪəm). Also (less correctly) tyro-. [L. *tīrōcinium* first military service or campaign, young troops, f. *tīro*, TIRO + *-cinium*, as in *latrōcinium* robbery, *vāticinium* prophecy.]

a. First experience of or training in anything; apprenticeship, pupilage, novitiate; hence, inexperience, rawness. b. *concr.* A band of novices or recruits.

1651 *Life Father Sarpi* (1676) 89 The *Tyrocinium* or the young Militia of state in the Commonwealth. **1654** GAYTON *Pleas. Notes* 37 It is the right discipline of Knight-Errantry, to be rudimented in losses at first, and to have the Tyrocinium somewhat tart. **1711** SHAFTESB. *Charac.* (1737) III. v. ii. 274 There the Tyrocinium of Genius's is annually display'd. **1784** COWPER (*title*) Tirocinium; or, A Review of Schools.

† **ti'rociny.** *Obs.* In 7 tyro-. [ad. L. *tīrōcinium*: see prec.] = prec.

1600 TOURNEUR *Transf. Metam., Ded. Sir C. Heydon* 14 Mæcenas, strengthen my Tyrocinie. **1646** G. BUCK *Rich. III*, I. 1 The Linage, Family, Birth, Education, and Tyrociny of King Richard the third. **1663** WATERHOUSE *Fortescutus Illustr.* 138 The King incorporated them into the Tyrociny of Nobility. **1670** W. SIMPSON *Hydrol. Ess.* 30 Your tyrociny in these abstruse studies plead your excuse.

tirodite (tɪˈrəʊdaɪt). *Min.* [f. *Tirodi*, name of a village in Madhya Pradesh, India + -ITE[1].] A monoclinic mineral, $Mn_2Mg_5Si_8O_{22}(OH)_2$, of the amphibole group which forms a series with dannemorite ($Mn_2Fe_5Si_8O_{22}(OH)_2$); also, any member of this series having more magnesium than iron.

1938 DUNN & ROY in *Rec. Geol. Survey India* LXXIII. 295 (*heading*) Tirodite, a manganese amphibole from Tirodi, Central Provinces. **1973** *Indian Jrnl. Earth Sci.* I. 38/2 The colour of tirodite is distinctive as opposed to the vivid colours shown by other manganese-bearing amphiboles occurring in the area.

† **ti'rology.** *Obs. nonce-wd.* [f. TIR-O + -OLOGY.] Properly, the science of tiroes; in quots. used for Elementary knowledge.

1560 BECON *Cast. Comfort* Wks. II. 106 Some of the papistes..where so euer they finde *Ignis*, take it for Purgatory streyghtwayes. O noble doctors of Tyrology, rather than of Theology. **1563** —— *Display. Popish Mass* ibid. III. 39 But where learned ye this tyrologye? For theologie is it not.

tiron, tirone, obs. forms of TIRO.

T-iron: see T 3.

Tironian (taɪˈrəʊnɪən), *a.* [ad. L. *Tīrōniān-us*, in *notæ Tīrōniānæ* Tironian notes.] Of or pertaining to Tiro, the freedman of Cicero: ***Tironian notes***, a system of shorthand in use in ancient Rome, said to have been invented or introduced by Tiro.

1828 *Edin. Rev.* Dec. 359 Manuscripts written entirely in the Tironian notes are not unfrequent in libraries of the date of the seventh century, as it is supposed. **1887** *Daily News* 6 Oct. 5/3 One of the earliest examples shown is a psalter in Tironian notes—the shorthand characters..invented by Marcus Tullius Tiro, the freedman of Cicero; it is in Latin —written early in the tenth century.

tironic, tyronic (taɪˈrɒnɪk), *a. nonce-wd.* [f. L. *tīrōn-*, stem of *tīro*, TIRO + -IC.] Of, pertaining to, or characteristic of a tiro; betraying inexperience; amateurish. So (*nonce-wds.*) **'ti-, 'tyronism**, inexperience; **'ti-, 'tyronist** = TIRO; **'ti-, 'tyronize** *v., intr.* to play the tiro, to be a beginner; hence **'ti-, 'tyronizing** *ppl. a.*

a **1660** *Contemp. Hist. Irel.* (Ir. Archæol. Soc.) I. 29 As ignorant of martiall discipline, as the most tyronizinge of them all. **1716** M. DAVIES *Athen. Brit.* III. 3 They..are fitter for Veterans and Criticks in Closets and Libraries, than for Tyronists and Trivialists in Schools. **1832** *Examiner* 660/1 The critic,..though modest and professing tyronism, is a good moderator. **1909** *Daily Chron.* 23 June 3/1 His handling of form and plot is occasionally tyronic, if one may be permitted a word that ought to exist.

† **tir'peil.** *Obs.* Forms: 4 tirpell, -peile, tyrpeyl, -payl, turpel, 5 -pell, -pele. [Metathetic form of OF. *trepeil* uproar, trouble (12th c. in Godef.); according to Diez from OF. *trepeiller* to run hither and thither, f. *treper* to hop, TRIP, of German origin: cf. MLG. *trippen* to tread; also mod.F. *trépigner* to stamp.] A broil, encounter, tumult.

c **1330** R. BRUNNE *Chron. Wace* (Rolls) 1665 Þe Troiens þat had ben yn turpel [*v.r.* tirpell], At midnight tok þey conseil. *Ibid.* 15422 Þey [Britons] gadered þem to consail How to venge þat tyrpayl. *c* **1330** —— *Chron.* (1810) 216 With-outen his conseile, or þe kynges wittyng, To maynten þer tirpeile he suore ageyn þe kyng. *c* **1400** *Laud Troy Bk.* 8841 But not-for-thi so it be-fell, That he was hurt at that turpell. *Ibid.* 18020 Foure hundrid of damyseles That lyued afftir that turpeles.

tirr (tɪr, tɜːr), *v. Sc.* and n. *dial.* Also 6–7 tyr, tyrr, 6–9 tir, 7 tirre, 9 terr. [app. a reduced form of TIRVE *v.*[1] in same sense (see quot. 1553 in 1 b), and cf. Sc. *ser'* for *serve*, *turris* for *turves*.]

1. *trans.* To strip or tear off (a covering, esp. the thatch, slates, or roofing of a house).

1571–5 *Diurnal Occurr.* (Bann. Cl.) 219 Ane commandement gevin..to tir and tak doun all the tymmer werk of all houssis in Leith Wynd and Sanctmarie Wynd. **1584** *Reg. Privy Council Scot.* III. 681 [He] tirrit and reft doun the faill and thak of his barnis. **1635** DICKSON *Pract. Wks.* (1845) I. 83 He shall tirr the visorne off your faces. **1670** R. LAW *Mem.* (1817) 33 It tirred the sclates off it. **1777** in Cramond *Ann. Banff* (1893) II. 97 There is no mending of the slating without tirring the sclates. **1795** A. WILSON *Spouter* 581 Mony a fierce storm had tirred the thack.

2. To strip (a person) naked; to uncover, unroof (a house, etc.). Also *fig.*

1553 *Douglas's Æneis* IX. viii. 78 In quhat land lyis thou manglit and schent, Thy fare body and membris tyrryt [*ed. Small* tyrvit] and rent? **1572–5** *Diurnal Occurr.* (Bann. Cl.) 307 The laird of Collingtonis hous in Forrestaris Wynd wes half tirrit. **1578–9** *Reg. Privy Council Scot.* III. 83 Als meikle to say 'Tyr the kirk and theik the queir'. **1590** *Reg. Privy Council Scot.* IV. 492 Eftir thay wer tirrit to thair sarkis. **1644** *Ibid.* VIII. 101 They causit thair officers and hangman tirre us mother naked. *a* **1670** SPALDING *Troub. Chas. I* (1850) I. 70 Quhilk the said James espying, fallis to shortlie and tirris the houss. *Ibid.* (1851) II. 407 Thir cruell Irishis, seing a man weill cled, wold first tyr him and saif the clothis onspoyllit, syne kill the man. **1763** in *Lauder & Lauderd.* (1902) 86 The west side of the Manse must be tirred and sclated anew. **1808** JAMIESON s.v., Tir one to the skin, i.e. strip him naked. **1894** P. H. HUNTER *J. Inwick* xi. (1900) 153 A man..that cares na wha be tirred gin he be theekit. **1901** *Dundee Advert.* 11 Feb. 6 In a minute or two the whole of the north side of the roof was completely tirred.

b. *intr.* (for *refl.*) To take off one's clothes; to strip, undress.

1787 W. TAYLOR *Scots Poems* 67 Hame I gaed..An' than I tirr'd, an' to my bed. **1825** JAMIESON, *Tirr*,..to undress, to pull off one's clothes. **1891** A. MATTHEWS *Poems & Songs* 52, I quickly tirr'd doon to the sark.

3. *trans.* To bare (land) of its surface covering; to pare off (the turf or surface soil) from land; to lay bare (the stone in a quarry) by removing the superincumbent soil and clay. With the thing laid bare, or the covering, as object. Also *absol.*

c **1567** *Survey Shilbottle* in *New County Hist. Northumbld.* (1899) V. 425 The ground also, by reason of castyng so great numbre of turves, [is] so tyrred and maide baire, that of a greate parte therof groweth no grasse. **1593** *Aberdeen Regr.* (1848) II. 85 The saidis Inchis ar sa flayne and tirrit, that..thair is na faill to be had thairin. **1808** JAMIESON, *Tirr*,..to pare off the sward by means of a spade..before casting peats. **1867** D. D. BLACK *Hist. Brechin* ii. 18 The earth was tirred from the garden on the top of the bank. **1899** MONTGOMERIE-FLEMING *Notes on Jamieson* 169 *Tirr*,..to remove the soil and sub-soil from above a bed of sand-stone in a quarry.

Hence **tirr** *sb.*, the soil or sub-soil removed from the bed of a quarry (Montgomerie-Fleming *Notes on Jamieson*, 1899); **'tirring** *vbl. sb.*, the stripping off of the incumbent soil, etc.

1794 *Statist. Acc. Scot.* XIII. 201 These quarries require very little tirring. **1902** *Daily Record & Mail* 11 Sept. 3 A couple of men had agreed to do some quarry tirring... The tirr suddenly collapsed and a man..was killed.

tirracke, -ick, -ook, Sc. dial. ff. TARROCK.

1792 *Statist. Acc. Scot.* V. 189 Redshanks, herons, tirricks. **1822** SCOTT *Pirate* x, The querulous cry of the tirracke and kittiewake. **1825** JAMIESON, Tirracke, Tirrook.

tirra-lirra (ˈtɪrəˈlɪrə). Also 7 teery-larry, -lerry, -leery, tyra-lyra. Cf. TIRALEE. [Echoic. Cf. OF. *turelu, tureluru*, 'a comic or burlesque refrain' (Godefroy), *turelure* a bagpipe, a refrain, F. *turlut* a titlark; and quot. 1889.] A representation of the note of the skylark, or of a similar sound uttered as an exclamation of delight or gaiety.

1611 SHAKS. *Wint. T.* IV. iii. 9 The Larke, that tirra-Lyra chaunts. **1613** W. BROWNE *Brit. Past.* I. v, The Larke.. With the shrill chanting of her teery-lerry. **1688** R. HOLME *Armoury* II. 310/2 The Lark singeth Tyra Lyra. **1832** TENNYSON *Lady of Shalott* III. iv, 'Tirra lirra', by the river Sang Sir Lancelot. **1889** GROVE *Dict. Mus.* IV. 805/1 *Ture-Lure*, or *Toure-Loure*, a very ancient lyrical burden or refrain, probably of Provencal origin. The old English form is 'tirra-lirra'.

Hence as *v. intr.*, to sing tirra-lirra; † **tirri'lirring** *ppl. a.*, that sings tirra-lirra; † **tiry-tiry-leerer**, a lark.

1659 TORRIANO, *Tirilirante lódola*, the Tiriliring lark. **1599** T. M[OUFET] *Silkwormes* 50 Let Tiry-tiry-leerers [*marg.* larkes] vpward flie. **1879** G. MEREDITH in *New Q. Mag.* July 83 Duchess Susan was distinguished coming across a broad, uncut meadow, tirra-lirraing beneath a lark.

tirran, -and, -ane, -ant, obs. Sc. ff. TYRANT.

tirret, tirrill, obs. ff. TERRET, -IT, TIRL *sb.*[1]

tirrit (ˈtɪrɪt). *rare.* [perh. illiterate for *terror* (Nares).] A fit of fear or temper; an 'upset', disturbance of one's equanimity.

1597 SHAKS. *2 Hen. IV*, II. iv. 220 Here's a goodly tumult: Ile forsweare keeping house, before Ile be in these tirrits, and frights. **1892** *Harper's Mag.* Feb. 405/2 My lady will have her tirrets.

tirri'vee, 'tirrivie. *Sc.* Also tiri-, tiry-, tirry-, tirrie-, tery-, turry-, tira-, tirravee, -vie. [Origin obscure: some suggest a corruption of TAILYEVEY.] A fit or display of ill temper or passion; an unchecked outburst.

1813 HOGG *Queen's Wake* 342 *note*, He suspected his spouse had taken some of her tirravies. **1814** SCOTT *Wav.* lxix, A very weel-meaning good-natured man..when he wasna in ane of his tirrivies. **1898** N. MUNRO in *Blackw. Mag.* Feb. 184/2 I'm willing to make some allowance for a lover's tirravee. **1910** W. FINLAY in *Poets Ayrshire* 273 When a party ends up in a wild tirivee.

tirrs, obs. Sc. form of TRUSS.

‖**tirshatha** (tɪrˈʃɑːθə). [Heb. *tirshāthā*, a. OPersian *tarsāta* 'his reverence', in LXX ἀθερσασθά (-αθά), Vulg. *athersatha* (i.e. *hat-tirshāthā*).] The title of an ancient Persian viceroy or prefect; applied in O.T. to Nehemiah.

1382 WYCLIF *Ezra* ii. 63 Athersatha [**1388** Attersatha]. —— *Neh.* viii. 9 Athirsata. **1535** COVERDALE *Ezra* ii. 63 Hathirsatha. **1611** *Ibid.*, The Tirshatha. **1890** HUNTER *After Exile* II. ix. 192 He stood forward with all the authority that belonged to him as Tirshatha. **1902** *Hastings' Dict. Bible* IV. 779 The Tirshatha appears to have been a royal commissioner..invested with the full powers of a satrap or viceroy, and employed on a special mission.

‖**Tirthankara** (tɪəˈθæŋkərə). Also **Tirthankar, tirthankara, Tirthanker.** [Skr., lit. 'maker of a ford', f. *tīrthá* ford, passage + *kará* maker.] In the Jain religion, one of the twenty-four founding prophets or Jinas, venerated as having successfully crossed the stream of time and having made a path for others to follow.

1835 J. WILSON *Let.* 13 Mar. in G. Smith *Life of John Wilson* (1878) vi. 205 In the inferior parts there are the images of all the twenty-four Tirthankars. **1881** *Encycl. Brit.* XIII. 543/2 The Jains count twenty-four such prophets, whom they call Jinas, or Tīrthankaras, that is, conquerors or leaders of schools of thought. **1901** KIPLING *Kim* vi. 159, I'd give a month's pay to hear how he explained it all at the Tirthankers' Temple at Benares. **1961** A. J. TOYNBEE *Between Oxus & Jumna* xii. 37 At Ludra..there is a Jain temple containing a hallowed image of the last Jain tirthankara but one. **1971** *Illustr. Weekly of India* 11 Apr. 8/1 (*caption*) Rishabha and Vardhamana are the most honoured among the twenty-four Tirthankaras.

† **tirve,** *v.*[1] *Obs.* Forms: 4–6 tirue, tyrue (= -ve), 4 turue (= -ve), (5 terve), 6 tirve, tyrff. [Not in OE.; known from 1300. Identical in meaning with TIRR *v.* (which seems to be a reduced form of the same word), and TIRL *v.*[2] App. distinct in sense from next; but, formally, **tyrfan* and **tierfan* might both be derived from different grades of a verbal ablaut series **terƀ-, tarƀ-, turƀ-*.

It has also been suggested to represent an OE. **tyrfan*, deriv. of *turf*, TURF, to have originally meant 'to strip the turf off the ground', and to have been extended to stripping the turf or thatch off roofs, the clothes off persons, and the hides off beasts. This is plausible, but is not favoured by the chronology of the senses.]

1. *trans.* To roll or pull back, or pluck *off* (the covering, clothes, skin, etc. from a person or animal); to strip off (clothes, armour; the thatch, slates, or roof of a house, stack, etc.).

c **1300** *Havelok* (1902) 603 [They] sone..funden, Als he [= they] tirueden of [= off] his serk On his rith shuldre a kyne merk. **13..** *E.E. Allit. P.* B. 630 He [Abraham] cached to his cobhous & a calf bryngez..bed tyrue of þe hyde. **13..** *Gaw. & Gr. Knt.* 1921 Syþen þay tan raynarde & tyruen of his cote. *a* **1400–50** *Alexander* 4114 Tuke out þe tuskis & þe tethe & teruen of þe skinnes. **1513** DOUGLAS *Æneis* V. v. 32 A habirgeoun..Quhilk he,..with his strang handis two, Tirvit and rent of bald Demoleo.

b. To strip (a person) of his clothes, etc., (an animal) of its skin, (a house) of its roof; to strip naked or bare; to unroof.

[*c* **1300** *Havelok* 918 Ful wel kan ich cleuen shides, Eles to-turuen of here hides.] *c* **1386** CHAUCER *Can. Yeom. Prol. & T.* 721 (Ellesm.) The deuel out of his skyn Hym terve [*other MSS.* torne, turne] I pray to god. **1500–20** DUNBAR *Poems* lxxii. 23 Of his claithis thai tirvit him bair. *Ibid.* 33 In tene, thai tirvit him agane, And till ane pillar thai him band. **1533** BELLENDEN *Livy* V. xi. (S.T.S.) II. 187 He gart tirve [*v.r.* tyrff] þis maister nakit of al his clothis. **1590–1** *Reg. Privy Council Scot.* IV. 587 The said Naper..and others..come and tirvit the said complenaris houssis, and tuke of the rigging and thak thairof.

† **tirve, terve,** *v.*[2] *Obs.* Forms: 5 tirue(-ve), tyrve, -we, 5–6 terue (-ve), (9 tirvie). [Known *c* 1330 in the comp. OVER-TERVE: app. representing an OE. **tierfan* = OLG. **tęrƀan*, OHG. *zęrben*,:—**zarƀjan*, refl. to turn, turn over or about: cf. OE. *tearflian* to roll over and over, wallow. If this is right, the better form is *terve*. (Texts of MSS. printed before 1900 have usually *n* for *u* (= *v*), the word being taken as a variant of *turn*.)]

1. *intr.* To turn; *esp.* to turn upside down, topple over, fall down; also *fig.* to turn *to* some course or action.

c **1400** *Destr. Troy* 430 Erthe dymmed by dene, ded men Roose, The gret tempull top terued to ground. *c* **1425** *Disp. Mary & Cross* xxxvii. in *Leg. Rood* 207 (MS. Roy.) Truyt and treget to helle schal terve. *c* **1440** *Psalmi Penitent.* (1894) 45 To trecherie schulde we noght terve [*rime* kerve]. **1567** GOLDING *Ovid's Met.* v. Ivb, Ioues ymage..made with crooked welked hornes that inward still doe terue [*rime* serue]. [**1819** W. TENNANT *Papistry Storm'd* (1827) 206 He made him tirvie down and tapple Head-foremost wi' a bang.]

2. *trans.* To turn; *esp.* to overturn, overthrow; also *fig.*

c **1400** *Destr. Troy* 1512 How his towne was taken and tiruyt to grounde. *Ibid.* 4763 The grete toures þai toke, tiruyt the pepull. *Ibid.* 10197 To take you with tene & tirue you to ground. *c* **1420** *Brut* 378 Our stakez made hem top ouyr terve, eche on oþer, þat þay lay on hepis. *c* **1422** HOCCLEVE *Min. Poems* xxiv. 573 Shee That had him terued with false deceitis.

b. To turn *to* some course or *to do* something.

c **1400** *Destr. Troy* 2943 Throgh whiche treason betydes, & teruys vmqwhile Bolde men to batell and biker with hond.

c. To turn over, up, or down (the edge or hem of a garment). (Cf. TARF, TURF *sb.*²)

1482 CAXTON *Contin. Higden's Polycron.* VIII. xiii, The yemanry hadde theyr hosen teruen [? terued] or bounden bynethe the knee hauynge longe jackys.

Hence †**tirving** *vbl. sb.*, turning; *concr.* a border turned back or up.

c **1400** *Promp. Parv.* 494/2 Tyrf, or tyrvynge [*v.r.* tyrwynge] vp on an hoode or sleue.

tirvis, obs. Sc. pl. of TURF *sb.*

†**tirwhit, tirwit**, obs. var. TEWHIT, lapwing.

1671 in SKINNER *Etymolog.* Hence **1706** in PHILLIPS, etc.

†**tiry** (ˈtaɪərɪ), *a. Obs.* [f. TIRE *v.*¹ + -Y.] Tired, weary. Hence †**ˈtiriness**, tiredness.

1611 CORYAT *Crudities* 37 My horse began to be so tiry that he would not stirre one foote out of the way. **1697** R. PEIRCE *Bath Mem.* I. ix. 192 Having a great share of this Tyrie Distemper. *Ibid.* II. iii. 295 [She] was not unsensible of her Tyryness and Dispiritedness.

'tis (tɪz). Also **'tes**. Abbreviation of *it is*, formerly common in prose, now *poet.*, *arch.*, *dial.*, or *colloq.*; see also IT A. γ.

c **1450** *Mankind* 821 in *Macro Plays* 30 Alas! tys pety yt schuld be þus. *a* **1566** R. EDWARDES *Damon & Pithias* (1744) 280 Tis a pestens queen. **1598-** [see IT A. γ]. **1896** I. T. THURSTON *Well Won* iv. 39 'Henderson, is that true?' demanded Gordon sternly... For once, Henderson absolutely looked ashamed of himself..as he said sulkily, 'Yes, 'tis.' **1922** JOYCE *Ulysses* 58 'Lovely weather, sir.' ''Tis all that.' **1922** E. O'NEILL *Anna Christie* III. 177 'Tis quare, rough talk, that—for a dacent girl the like of you! **1932** S. GIBBONS *Cold Comfort Farm* iv. 53 'Tes the cowshed! 'Tes our Feckless openin' the door fer me! **1977** P. HILL *Liars* (1978) xii. 154 'Tis your business if'n you want to waste your time.

tis, ME. assimilated form of THIS after dentals, etc.: see T 8.

tisan, tisane, var. PTISAN, barley-water.

tisane (tɪˈzæn). [Mod. re-adoption of Fr. *tisane*: see PTISAN, which it has largely supplanted.] A medicinal tea or infusion made from herbs.

1931 W. CATHER *Shadows on Rock* I. iv. 29 He kept them away from doctors,—gave them tisanes and herb-teas and poultices. **1941** W. FORTESCUE *Trampled Lilies* v. 52 A communicating room could be used as a kitchen..where hot chocolate, coffee, and *tisanes* could be prepared for the men. **1959** *News Chron.* 6 July 6/5 Old ladies..drink herb teas in France, where they are called tisanes. **1965** *Punch* 7 July p. xii/2 The health food shop with..lime flower tisanes and heather honey. **1981** M. GEE *Dying, in Other Words* xlix. 114 And the tea, the lime-flower *tisane* which was good for her chest and smelled citrous and fresh, singing to her when she drank it of blue summer skies over yellow-green lime trees.

tisar (tɪˈzɑː(r)). *Glass-manuf. rare.* [ad. F. *tisart* opening of a furnace, f. *tiser* to poke, stir, etc.: see TEASE *v.*²] The fireplace or furnace used to heat the annealing arch for plate-glass.

1839 URE *Dict. Arts* 587 The carquaise is heated by means of a fire-place of a square form called a *tisar*, which extends along its side.

tische, -ey, obs. Sc. ff. TISSUE.

tischera, var. TEZKERE.

tise, obs. f. TICE *v.*

Tiseday, obs. Sc. f. TUESDAY.

Tiselius (tɪˈseɪlɪəs, tɪˈz-). *Biochem.* [The name of A. W. K. *Tiselius* (1902–71), Swedish biochemist.] ***Tiselius*** (***electrophoresis***) ***apparatus***: an apparatus in which electrophoresis is carried out in free solution in a U-tube (see quot. 1964).

1939 *Jrnl. Franklin Inst.* CCXXVIII. 798 (*heading*) U-tube portion of the Tiselius electrophoresis apparatus. **1946** *Nature* 13 July 41/2 The Tiselius electrophoresis apparatus is now established as an essential part of the equipment of protein chemists... Its first appearance.., in 1937, was the result of a careful technical study. **1964** G. H. HAGGIS et al. *Introd. Molecular Biol.* ii. 23 In the Tiselius apparatus a potential is applied across a boundary between the solution containing the proteins and a protein-free buffer solution (moving boundary electrophoresis).

‖**Tisha b'Av** (ˈtiʃa bɔv). Also **Tisha be-Ab, Tisha Bov**, etc. [Heb. *tišʿāh bəʾāḇ.*] The ninth day of the month Av, on which both the First and the Second Temples are said to have been destroyed: observed by Jews as a day of mourning.

1938 *Vallentine's Jewish Encycl.* 2/1 The 9th of Ab (*Tisha be-Ab*..) is a fast day commemorating the destruction of the 1st and 2nd Temples. **1958** A. L. EISENBERG *Story Jewish Calendar* 19 Later on, the three months in which Hannukah, Purim, and the fast day of Tisha B'Av occur were also included. **1970** *New Yorker* 19 Sept. 32/2 My grandfather always fasted on Tisha b'Av and slept with his head on a stone. **1973** *Synagogue Light* Sept. 12/1 On Tish B'Av [*sic*], the traditional day of mourning, we take off our shoes. **1978** I. B. SINGER *Shosha* I. ii. 10 The day that Zelig and Bashele moved..was like Tisha Bov for me.

tisheldar, var. TAHSILDAR.

tishew, -oo, -ue, obs. ff. TISSUE.

‖**Tishri** (ˈtɪʃriː), **Tisri** (ˈtɪzriː). [ad. late Heb. *tishrī*, f. Aramaic *shᵉrā* to begin.] The Babylonian name of the first month of the Jewish civil year, or the seventh of the ecclesiastical, corresponding to parts of September and October: substituted after the captivity for the earlier name ETHANIM.

1833 [see ABIB]. **1877** C. GEIKIE *Christ* xlix. (1879) 578 The seventh month Tisri, part of our Sep. and Oct. **1904** *Daily Chron.* 9 Sept. 6/7 To-night marks the advent of Tishri, the most important month in the Jewish calendar. **1904** *Jewish Encycl.* VIII. 672 Tishri is characterized as the month of the birth of the Patriarchs.

tisick, tisical, (tiss-), obs. and dial. forms of PHTHISIC, -AL. Hence **tis(s)icking** *a.* = next; †**tisickness**, phthisic or asthmatic quality.

1533 ELYOT *Cast. Helthe* (1539) 82 Tisiknesse or shortnesse of breth. *a* **1825** FORBY *Voc. E. Anglia, Tissick*, ..a tickling faint cough; called also a 'tissicky cough'. **1888** DOUGHTY *Arabia Deserta* II. 521 The Sherif visited Beyrût some years ago..for the health of a tisical son. **1890** *Blackw. Mag.* CXLVIII. 463/2 Snipe hummed and bleated out a tissicking music. **1904** in *Eng. Dial. Dict.* s.v. *Tissick*, etc.

tisicky (ˈtɪzɪkɪ), *a.* Also **tissicky, tizzicky**. [dial. var. of PHTHISICKY *a.*] Wheezy, asthmatic; also *transf.*, delicate, squeamish.

a **1825** [see prec.]. **1905** E. PHILPOTTS *Secret Woman* II. x. 193 Once a labourer have gone in the back an' thighs, an' growed tisicky in the breathing parts—then [etc.]. **1924** *Western Daily Press* (Bristol) 18 Mar. 8/3 A person troubled with a slight but frequent and annoying cough is said to be Tissicky. **1961** 'K. NORWAY' *Waterfront Hospital* iii. 44 Men are more tissicky than women when it comes to telling people the worst. They're kinder by nature. **1969** J. CLARKE *Foxon's Hole* iii. 23, I can see you've a good appetite. None of Frances's tizzicky ways.

†**tisince**, obs. form of *ptisans*, pl. of PTISAN.

c **1623** LODGE *Poore Mans Talentt* (Hunter. Cl.) 9 The patient..must bee content to drink Tisince, balme water, or the Iuleb of roses.

'tisn't (ˈtɪzənt), dial. or colloq. shortening of *it isn't* (= it is not); see IT *pron.* A. γ; NOT *adv.* 2, 3. Cf. 'TIS.

1803 G. COLMAN *John Bull* IV. i. 42, I be but the guide, and 'tisn't for I to go first. **1888** KIPLING *Under Deodars* 93 Remember, Bobby, 't isn't the best drill..it's the man who knows how to handle men. **1924** M. KENNEDY *Constant Nymph* II. viii. 117 ''Tisn't yours,' cried Antonia... 'It ought to be mine.' **1972** P. CLEIFE *Slick & Dead* I. i. 14 Oh, come now—'tisn't always like that.

tisor, variant of TEASER², fireman.

Tisri: see TISHRI.

tissane, obs. var. PTISAN, barley-water, etc.

†**tissed**, *ppl. a. Obs.* [ad. F. *tissu*, pa. pple. of OF. *tistre*:—L. *texere* to weave (cf. TEXTILE): see -ED¹.] In phr. ***gold tissed***, ***cotton tissed***, modelled on F. *or tissu*, *coton tissu* (cf. *gold of tisshue*, quot. 1501 s.v. TISSUE *sb.* 1 a).

1585 T. WASHINGTON tr. *Nicholay's Voy.* I. xxi. 27 b, A gowne of cloth of gold tissed [*orig.* vne robbe de drap d'or figuré]. *Ibid.* II. xxii. 60 A fine & long smock of cotton tissed [*orig.* vne fine & longue chamisolle de cotton tissue].

tissey, obs. f. TIZZY¹.

tissick, etc.: see PHTHISIC, TISICK.

tisso, var. TEESOO.

†**tissu**, *ppl. a. Obs. rare*⁻¹. [a. F. *tissu*, pa. pple.: see TISSUE *sb.*] Woven. (Const. as *pa. pple.*)

1549 *Compl. Scot.* vii. 69 Ane syde mantil..the quhilk hed bene tissu ande vrocht be thre syndrye fassons of verkmenschips.

tissual (ˈtɪʃ(j)uːəl, ˈtɪsjuːəl), *a. rare*⁻¹. [irreg. f. next + -AL¹, after *virtual*, etc.] Of or pertaining to (living) tissue: see next, 5.

1837 P. KEITH *Bot. Lex.* 343 Plants..exhibiting.. indications of such tissual and organic susceptibilities as are proper to their rank in the scale of being.

tissue (ˈtɪʃ(j)uː, ˈtɪsjuː), *sb.* Forms: α. 4–5 **tyssu**, 4–6 **tissewe**, 5 **tyssew, -eu, -ywe**, (*pl.* **-eux**), 5–6 **tyssue**, 5–7 **tissu, tissew**, 6 **tyssewe, tysswe**, 5– **tissue**. β. 5–6 **tisshue, tisshewe**, *Sc.* **tusche, (tuscha)**, 5–8 **tishew**, 6 **tyshew, tysshewe, tyshiew, tushwe**, *Sc.* **tischey, -ay, tische, tysche**, 7 **tishue, tishoo**. [a. OF. *tissu* sb., applied to a kind of rich stuff (*c* 1200 in Godef. *Compl.*), from pa. pple. of obs. F. *tître*, OF. *tistre*:—**tissre*:—L. *tex-ĕre* to weave.]

1. a. A rich kind of cloth, often interwoven with gold or silver. *Obs.* exc. *Hist.*

? *a* **1366** CHAUCER *Rom. Rose* 1104 The barres were of gold ful fyne, Upon a tyssu of satyne. **1429** in Dugdale *Monast. Angl.* II. 222 Cum tribus capis choralibus de panno Tyssewys vulgariter nuncupato. **1501** in *Calr. Doc. rel. Scotl.* (1888) 336 A gown of tawny cloth of gold of tisshue. **1509** HAWES *Past. Pleas.* xvi. (Percy Soc.) 61 With cloth of tyssue in the rychest maner The walles were hanged. **1513** BRADSHAW *St. Werburge* I. 1647 Fresshely embrodred in ryche tysshewe and fyne. **1543** GRAFTON *Contn. Harding* 591 The quene..clothed in a riche mantell of tissue. **1562** in Feuillerat *Revels Q. Eliz.* (1908) 114 Cloth of Silver purple tysshiew. **1585** T. WASHINGTON tr. *Nicholay's Voy.* III. viii. 82 Girded with a large girdle of Tissue, or of silke and golde. **1648** CRASHAW *Delights Muses* Wks. (1904) 160 Something more than Taffata or Tissew can. *c* **1710** CELIA FIENNES *Diary* (1888) 4 Good bed Chambers and well furnished velvet damaske and tissue. **1785** G. A. BELLAMY *Apology* I. 130 A dress for me to play the character of Cl[e]opatra,..the ground of it was silver tissue.

b. Now applied to various rich or fine stuffs of delicate or gauzy texture.

1730 SWIFT *Lady's Dressing-room* Wks. 1755 IV. I. 113 Array'd in lace, brocades and tissues. **1769** *Public Advertiser* 2 June 1/3 Sale of Silks..Brocades, Tissues. **1821** JOANNA BAILLIE *Metr. Leg., Wallace* liv, Tissue of threaded gems is worn. **1910** *Westm. Gaz.* 12 Mar. 15/2 Tissues studded with jewels are lightly draped over satin.

†**2.** A band or girdle of rich stuff. *Obs.*

c **1374** CHAUCER *Troylus* II. 590 (639) His helm..That by a tissew heng his bak byhynde. *c* **1430** *Pilgr. Lyf Manhode* I. xciv. (1869) 51 The scrippe was of greene selk, and heeng bi a greene tissu. *c* **1440** *Partonope* 6726 That tyssew and bocle ..all to peses brak. *c* **1450** HOLLAND *Howlat* 405 Mony schene scheld With tuscheis of trast silk tichit to the tre. **1488** *Acta Dom. Conc.* (1839) 98/2 A tuscha of silk siluerit price v merkis. **1503** *Acc. Ld. High Treas. Scot.* II. 388, xj½ elne tisches to mend the bordoring of the Kingis sadill bordorit with tischeis. **1508** *Test. Ebor.* (Surtees) IV. 274 A gyrdill wᵗ a golde tushwe. **1513** DOUGLAS *Æneis* I. vii. 136 And quhair hir pap was for the speir cut away Of gold thairon was belt ane riche tischay. *Ibid.* XII. v. 133 Quhar as the wovin gyrdill or tysche Abufe his navill was beltit, as we se. **1603** HOLLAND *Plutarch's Mor.* 629 Venus..cast aside her daintie jewels..and threw away that tissue and lovely girdle of hers.

3. Any woven fabric or stuff. In quot. 1850 *transf.* weaving.

1565 COOPER *Thesaurus, Trilix*,..tissue made of three threads of diuers colours. **1757** GRAY *Bard* I. iii, They.. weave with bloody hands the tissue of thy line. [Cf. II. i, Weave the warp, and weave the woof The winding-sheet of Edward's race.] *a* **1765** SHENSTONE *Progr. Taste* I. 24 Constant wear..turns the tissue into tatters. **1850** GLADSTONE *Homer* II. ii. 129 In the arts of tissue and embroidery. **1879** LUBBOCK *Sci. Lect.* v. 155 Tissues of woven flax have been found in some of the Swiss lake-villages.

4. *fig.* Something likened to a woven fabric, as being produced by the intertwining of separate elements; an intricate mass or interwoven series, a 'fabric', 'network', 'web' (*of* things abstract, most usually of a bad kind, as absurdities, errors, falsehoods, etc.). Also, the structure or contexture of such a 'fabric'.

1711 ADDISON *Spect.* No. 62 ¶6 Those little occasional Poems..are nothing else but a Tissue of Epigrams. **1762** GOLDSM. *Cit. W.* xlii, The history of Europe,..a tissue of crimes, follies, and misfortunes. **1793** JEFFERSON *Writ.* (1859) IV. 89 The hasty amendments..had so broken the tissue of the paragraph, as to [etc.]. **1820** W. IRVING *Sketch Bk.* I. 104 The tissue of misrepresentations..woven round us. **1842** WHITTIER *Raphael* xvi, The tissue of the Life to be We weave with colors all our own. **1878** GLADSTONE *Prim. Homer* 107 He works it..into the tissue of the poems.

5. *Biol.* The substance, structure, or texture of which an animal or plant body, or any part or organ of it, is composed; *esp.* any one of the various structures, each consisting of an aggregation of similar cells or modifications of cells, which make up the organism. **a.** in animals.

The chief forms of tissue in the higher animals are the *epithelial* (incl. *glandular*), *connective* (incl. *cartilaginous* and *osseous*), *muscular*, and *nervous* tissues. (The term is sometimes extended to include the *blood* as a 'fluid tissue'.)

1831 CARLYLE *Sart. Res.* I. i, Every cellular, vascular, muscular Tissue. **1834** J. FORBES *Laennec's Dis. Chest* (ed. 4) 279 Chronic inflammation..of the pulmonary tissue. **1846** G. E. DAY tr. *Simon's Anim. Chem.* II. 40 Materials.. to supply the place of those that have been removed from the body in consequence of waste of tissue. **1857** BUCKLE *Civiliz.* I. xiv. 818 The tissues of the teeth are..analogous to those of other parts. **1861** HULME tr. *Moquin-Tandon* II. I. 41 The organic Tissues are three in number: 1st, cellular tissue; 2nd, muscular tissue; and 3rd, nervous tissue... Some writers admit other organic tissues. **1869** HUXLEY *Phys.* i. (ed. 3) 11 Every such constituent of the body, as epidermis, cartilage, or muscle, is called a 'tissue'. **1880** BASTIAN *Brain* 28 Nerve tissues are..divided into 'grey' and 'white' matter. **1889** MIVART *Truth* 149 The arteries, veins and heart are full of a fluid 'tissue'—the blood.

b. in plants.

The various forms of plant tissue may be generally reduced to two classes, typified by *parenchyma* and *prosenchyma*. In the higher plants there are three systems of tissues, the *epidermal*, *fundamental*, and *fibro-vascular*.

1837 [implied in TISSUAL]. **1845** LINDLEY *Sch. Bot.* x. (1858) 159 Tissue is called Woody Fibre when it is composed of slender tubes placed side by side. **1875** BENNETT & DYER *Sachs' Bot.* 68 Every aggregate of cells which obeys a common law of growth..may be termed a

Tissue. *Ibid.* 103 The relationship of the three systems of tissue may be observed .. in .. foliage-leaves.

c. *generally*; also *fig.*

1856 DOVE *Logic Chr. Faith* II. §2. 114 The new chart must clothe the world with its living tissues. **1858** LEWES *Sea-side Stud.* 400 Histology is the doctrine of the tissues; and tissues are the webs out of which the organism is fabricated. **1872** BAGEHOT *Physics & Pol.* 178 The germ might be foreign, but the tissue was native. **1878** BELL *Gegenbaur's Comp. Anat.* 16 Conversion of the cells into tissue.

6. a. Short for TISSUE-PAPER, q.v.

(The reference in the 18th-c. quots. was prob. to sizes of specially prepared tissue-paper (now spoken of as 'printing paper' and 'printing tissue'), on which designs were printed from copper plates for transference to pottery-ware. This was specially taxed.)

1780–1 *Act 21 Geo. III*, c. 24 §2 For every Bundle of Paper made in Great Britain for Printing, called Demy Tissue. For every Bundle of Paper called Crown Tissue. **1797** NEMNICH *Waaren-Lexicon* 30/1 Die Englischen Papiersorten... Crown, single, inferior, double, double inferior, and tissue;.. Demy single, inferior, plate, short, tissue, writing [etc.]. **1880** J. DUNBAR *Pract. Papermaker* 32 (*heading*) Lilac tissue, deep shade. **1937** E. J. LABARRE *Dict. Paper & Paper-Making Terms* 244/1 *Tissue* or tissue-papers are fine, thin, soft papers made of strong materials such as rag and hemp fibres... They are usually unsized, nearly transparent, chiefly used for wrapping and protective purposes. **1977** J. HEDGECOE *Photographer's Handbk.* 309 Carefully trim the print, with its attached tissue.

b. *Racing.* A sheet of paper showing the 'form' of the horses competing in a race (see also quot. 1866).

1866 *Daily Tel.* 24 Feb. 3/4 A 'tissue' is a slip of paper written for a telegraph company, showing results of betting transactions and accounts. **1914** JOYCE *Dubliners* 59 No one knew how he achieved the stern task of living, but his name was vaguely associated with racing tissues. **1972** G. F. NEWMAN *You Nice Bastard* ii. 83 Manso quickly got a bet on the fifth and sixth, and studied the tissue for the previous races.

c. A piece of soft absorbent paper used as a handkerchief, for drying or cleaning the skin, etc. Hence as *v. trans.*, to wipe with a tissue.

1929 *Punch* 10 Apr. p. xv. (Advt.), Two or three times every day you should massage the hands with Ponds' Cold Cream, removing the cream after a minute or so with a Ponds' Cleansing Tissue. **1938** [see COMPLEXION *sb.*]. **1958** M. DICKENS *Man Overboard* x. 162 Ben grabbed a make-up stick and scrawled it [*sc.* an address] on the side of a box of tissues. **1960** *Woman* 25 Apr. 2/1 Pond's Cold Cream .. goes on moisturising long after you tissue it off. **1976** M. & G. GORDON *Ordeal* (1977) 142 Sniffling, he asked Penny for a tissue. **1981** *Economist* 8 Aug. 79/1 The battle against the common cold may not be over... So do not throw away your tissues yet. **1983** *Harrods Mag.* Spring/Summer 72 Yellow Herbal Astringent is sprayed on .. then tissued dry.

d. A cigarette paper. *Austral.* and *N.Z. slang.*

1952 *Here & Now* (N.Z.) Jan. 32/2 Better go and see if the parole-jumper in Number 8 has got any tissues left. **1966** G. W. TURNER *Eng. Lang. Austral. & N.Z.* viii. 164 In Hobart the [expression] .. 'Got a tissue, mate?' [is commoner than elsewhere]. A *tissue* is a cigarette paper.

7. *Photogr.* Paper made in strips coated with a film of gelatine containing a pigment, used in carbon printing.

1873 E. SPON *Workshop Receipts* Ser. I. 267/1 This carbon tissue consists of a layer of gelatine containing the carbon or other permanent pigment spread on paper. **1878** ABNEY *Photogr.* xxiv. 165 Many improvements in the manufacture of the tissue have been made, and the different substances added to the gelatine are only partially known to the public. **1891** *Anthony's Photogr. Bull.* IV. 80 Tissue can be obtained from London and sensitized as required for use.

8. Collector's name for two species of moth, *Scotosia* (*Triphosa*) *dubitata* and *cervinata*.

1832 RENNIE *Butterfl. & Moths* 128 The Tissue (*T[riphosa] dubitata*, Stephens)... Wings .. brown, shining; first pair having a tinge of purple. *Ibid.*, The Scarce Tissue (*T. cervinata*, Stephens).

9. *attrib.* and *Comb.* **a.** *attrib.* Made or consisting of tissue (sense 1); in quot. *a* 1625, dressed in tissue.

1480 *Wardr. Acc. Edw. IV* in *Privy Purse Exp. Eliz. York*, etc. (1830) 149 A long gowne of grene velvet upon velvet tisshue cloth of gold. **1570** FOXE *A. & M.* (ed. 2) 2143/2 The Vicechauncellour hauing on a tyshew cope. *a* **1625** FLETCHER *Love's Cure* I. iii, Smooth City fools or tisseu Cavaliers. **1704** *Lond. Gaz.* No. 3981/4 A rich Silver Tishia Gown. **1708** *Brit. Apollo* No. 37 2/2 Tishew Sleves. **1796** MAR. J. HOLROYD in *Girlhood M. J. H.* (1896) 373 Milady wore .. a Gold Tissue .. Train.

b. *Comb.*, chiefly in sense 5, as ***tissue-building*** sb. and adj., ***-cell, -change, -death, -dwelling*** adj., ***-element, -form, -former, -forming*** adj., ***-growth, -like*** adj., ***-product, -specific*** adj., ***-specificity, -system, -transformation***; **tissue-bank** [BANK *sb.*[3] 7 f], a place where a supply of human or animal tissue for grafting is stored; **tissue culture**, a culture [CULTURE *sb.* 3 c] of cells derived from tissue; the practice of culturing such cells; **tissue fluid**, extracellular fluid which bathes the cells of most tissues, arriving via blood capillaries and being removed via the lymphatic vessels; **tissue-lymph**, lymph derived from the tissues (not directly from the blood); **tissue-secretion**: see quots. 1848, 1861; **tissue type** *Med.*, a class of tissues all of which are immunologically compatible with each other; **tissue-type** *v. trans.*, to determine the tissue type of; **tissue typing** *Med.*, the assessment of tissue in order to predict its immunological compatibility with other tissue, esp. prior to transplantation. See also TISSUE-PAPER.

1968 *Punch* 14 Feb. 239 Donald Pleasence plays the night attendant at a central *tissue-bank in Montreal... A stupid, illiterate man with inexplicable operatic aspirations, he thinks that if he can only get the right larynx he will be able to sing. **1971** *New Scientist* 8 Apr. 101/2 Tissue Banks where human and animal tissues could be readily obtained. **1886** A. WINCHELL *Walks Geol. Field* 308 The processes of digestion, .. assimilation, and *tissue-building. **1873** T. H. GREEN *Introd. Pathol.* (ed. 2) 88 The pulmonary pigment .. may be seen .. within the connective *tissue-cells. **1873** T. H. GREEN *Introd. Pathol.* (ed. 2) 24 The increased *tissue-change which accompanies acute febrile diseases. **1912** *Anat. Rec.* VI. 91 The character of the growth in *tissue cultures varies primarily with the kind of tissue used. **1926** J. S. HUXLEY *Ess. Pop. Sci.* 283 A fundamental experiment from which sprang the whole sub-science of tissue-culture. **1955** *Sci. News* XXXVI. 8 It is interesting to compare the events in regeneration with what happens in tissue culture. **1975** *Daily Tel.* 8 Sept. 8/4 At present, if a dog or other animal is sick or dies it takes several days to grow the virus in tissue culture to be sure rabies is to blame. **1896** *Allbutt's Syst. Med.* I. 213 It is quite possible that a trace of albumose might thus be formed after *tissue-death. **1964** M. HYNES *Med. Bacteriol.* (ed. 8) xxviii. 443 The *tissue-dwelling parasites which cause relapses [in malaria] are not affected. **1974** *Ciba Symposium* XX. 309 Few drugs have any significant action against its tissue-dwelling amastigotes. **1900** E. H. STARLING *Elem. Human Physiol.* (ed. 4) vii. 292 This absorption depends on the small proportion of proteid contained in the *tissue-fluid as compared with the blood-plasma. **1954** S. DUKE-ELDER *Parsons' Dis. Eye* (ed. 12) i. 4 It [*sc.* the cornea] has no blood vessels with the exception of minute arcades, about 1 mm. broad, at the limbus so that it is dependent for its nourishment upon the diffusion of tissue-fluid from the vessels at its periphery and materials from the aqueous humour. **1976** D. JENSEN *Princ. Physiol.* ix. 524/1 The interstitial (or tissue) fluid forms the actual internal environment of the body. **1875** BENNETT & DYER tr. *Sachs' Bot.* 78 In this manner arise in the higher plants .. systems of *tissue-forms, which may be designated simply as Systems of Tissue. **1872** HUXLEY *Phys.* vi. 139 Proteids are *tissue-formers. *c* **1890** A. MURDOCH *Yoshiwara Episode* 26 He .. wondered .. what the soft, flimsy, *tissue-like paper was. **1903** G. OLIVER in *Lancet* 3 Oct. 942/1 Physiologists are divided as to whether *tissue lymph is a pressure product .. or a secretion. **1866** ODLING *Anim. Chem.* 1 Recent advances in chemistry of *tissue-products. **1848** DANA *Zooph.* iv. 51 Secretions formed within the animal which are mostly calcareous .. may be called *tissue-secretions... These secretions take place from the tissues of the sides and the base of the polyp. **1861** GREENE *Man. Anim. Kingd.*, *Cœlent.* 153 The sclerobasic corallum is by Mr. Dana termed 'foot secretion'; the sclerodermic, 'tissue secretion'. **1962** *Sci. Survey* III. 224 This type of change may be associated with the changes in *tissue-specific antigens. **1932** J. S. HUXLEY *Probl. Relative Growth* vi. iv. 177 The *tissue-specificity is apparently the same .. in both sexes. **1967** *Science* 25 Aug. 942/1 The first two explanations should be tested more critically if applied to a single *tissue type. **1968** *Times* 7 Nov. 3/2 In a year or two it might be possible to store human hearts for a period of hours; this would enable donors and recipients to be tissue-typed on an international basis. **1969** *Private Eye* 6 June 3/2 Experts from Guys Hospital came to tissue type her to see if she was a 'suitable donor'. **1971** H. FESTENSTEIN et al. in R. Y. Calne *Clin. Organ Transplantation* vi. 158 It may be possible to tissue type potential recipients from several hospitals in one central laboratory. **1973** *Daily Tel.* 27 Feb. 2/7 Simon has a tissue type shared by only one in 50,000 of the population. **1965** *Israel Jrnl. Med. Sci.* I. 498/2 This seems .. a hopeful avenue toward the goal of *tissue typing. **1967** *Observer* 26 Nov. 1/5 Research on tissue-typing has reached the stage where tissues from different people can be matched (just as blood can be matched) so that grafts will 'take' without resort to drugs to suppress the immune mechanism. **1971** *New Scientist* 8 July 63/2 One or two of these cases, particularly when recipient and donor have been well 'matched' by tissue typing, have been spectacularly successful.

'tissue, *v.* Now *rare.* [f. TISSUE *sb.*] *trans.* To make into a tissue, to weave; *spec.* to weave with gold or silver threads, to work or form in tissue; to adorn or cover with tissue (cf. prec. 1 a).

1483 CAXTON *Gold. Leg.* 237/1 A whyte mantel In whiche there were litil ouches and crosses of gold tissued. **1491** —— *Vitas Patr.* (W. de W. 1495) II. 249/2 To tyssue the sayd roddes & palmes to make mattes. **1547** *Harl. MS. 1419 B*, lf. 535 b, Clothe of silver tissued withe flowres of golde and silver. **1562** in Feuillerat *Revels Q. Eliz.* (1908) 114 Gold tysshewed with silver. *a* **1626** BACON *New Atl.* (1650) 25 The Charriot was covered with cloth of Gold tissued upon Blew. *a* **1851** MOIR *Birth Flowers* vi, Her vesture seem'd as from the blooms Of all the circling seasons wove, .. And tissued with the woof of Love.

b. *fig.*

1637 WOTTON in *Reliq.* (1672) 104 To Countenance any Great action; and then .. to Tissue upon it some Pretence or other. **1800** MOORE *Anacreon* xlvi. 14 Cultured field, and winding stream, Are sweetly tissued by his beam. **1905** *Athenæum* 6 May 558/2 'Dream and Reality' is tissued from a series of such metaphors.

tissued ('tɪʃ(j)uːd, 'tɪsjuːd), *ppl. a.* [f. prec. vb. (or sb.) + -ED.]

1. Woven; *spec.* woven with gold or silver thread: see TISSUE *sb.* 1 a and *v.*

1584 in Feuillerat *Revels Q. Eliz.* (1908) 365 The pages sute of Oringe tawney tissued vellet. **1619** *Rutland MSS.* (1905) IV. 516, 19 yardes ½ of tissued grogram at 48s. the yard. **1790** COWPER *Mother's Picture* 75 Thy vesture's tissu'd flowers. **1879** FARRAR *St. Paul* (1883) 224 He entered the theatre .. in an entire robe of tissued silver.

fig. **1629** MILTON *Ode Nativity* 146 Mercy .. With radiant feet the tissued clouds down stearing. **1789** E. DARWIN *Bot. Gard.* (1791) II. 52 Long threads of silver light Dart on swift shuttles o'er the tissued night! **1790** MERRY *Laurel Lib.* 7 Where starry Night weaves thick her tissued rays.

2. Dressed or arrayed in 'tissue': see TISSUE *sb.* 1.

? **16..** WHARTON (Webster 1864), Crested knights and tissued dames.

'tissueless, *a.* [f. TISSUE *sb.* + -LESS.] Destitute of tissue (i.e., in quot., of flesh).

1864 BLACKMORE *Clara Vaughan* lxxxi, It rang among the skeletons, and rattled their tissueless joints.

'tissue-'paper. [See quot. 1880, which may be correct; but earlier authority is wanted.] A very thin soft gauze-like unsized paper, used for wrapping delicate articles, for covering engravings or other illustrations in books, as copying-paper, etc.

Various grades are distinguished, as *silver tissue*, specially prepared for wrapping silver ware; *copying tissue*, for copying letters, etc.; *printing tissue*: see TISSUE *sb.* 6.

1777 HENLY in *Phil. Trans.* LXVII. 114 A number of circular pieces of tissue-paper. **1815** J. SMITH *Panorama Sc. & Art* II. 161 The paper must be of that kind called tissue or silver paper. **1854** *Phemie Millar* 24 Encasing in tissue paper a set of ivory handled knives. **1865** LOWELL *Wks.* (1890) V. 285 Leaping through a hoop with nothing more substantial to resist than tissue-paper. **1880** BIRDWOOD *Ind. Arts* II. 75 The flimsy paper called tissue-paper was originally made to place between the tissue to prevent its fraying or tarnishing when folded.

tissuey ('tɪsjuːɪ, 'tɪʃ(j)uːɪ), *a.* [TISSUE *sb.* + -Y[1].] Having the quality or texture of tissue.

1867 G. MEREDITH *Vittoria* III. xlii. 196 Letting her .. crumble the black tissuey fragments to smut in her hands. **1965** P. WYLIE *They both were Naked* I. i. 4, I could see that overcast less than a hundred feet above .. its tissuey substance was rolling and boiling. **1974** J. HELLER *Something Happened* 210 The .. silken feel of the tissuey things between her legs the first time she let me touch her there.

tist, tiste: see TICE *v.*

'tisty-'tosty, *int.*, *sb.*, *a. dial.* Forms: 6– tisty-tosty, 6 tistitostie, 9 teesty-tosty. [In sense 1 perh. a mere ejaculation. In sense 3 it has been compared with †*tyte tust(e* or †*tussemose* a nosegay: see TUZZY-MUZZY; but current dialect use associates it rather with *toss*, and *tost*, *tossed*.]

†1. *int.* as an ejaculation of triumph or exultation.

1568 FULWEL *Like Will to Like* C iij, Hey tisty tosty an owle is a bird. *c* **1570** *Marr. Wit & Science* IV. iv. E j, Mother must I haue his Cote, now mother must [I]? Chal [= I shall] be a liuely lad, with hey tistye tosty.

†2. *sb.* A swaggering or blustering fellow (? one who uses the ejaculation). Also *attrib.* or *adj. Obs.*

1598 FLORIO, *Sbrauo*, a swash-buckler, a swaggrer, a hackster, a cutter, a tistitostie. *Ibid.*, *Squassa pennacchio*, .. a tisti-tostie-fellow, a swaggrer.

3. *sb.* A bunch of flowers, a nosegay (*obs.*); in *mod. dial.*, a cowslip-ball: also ***tisty-tosty ball.***

1825 JENNINGS *W. Country Gloss.*, *Teesty-tosty*, the blossoms of cowslips collected together, tied in a globular form, and used to toss to and fro for an amusement called *teesty-tosty*... Sometimes called simply a tosty. **1865** *Cornh. Mag.* July 41 'Blossom-ball' .. is evidently formed after the West-country 'cowslip-ball', the 'tisty-tosty ball' of Dorsetshire and Somersetshire, which children yearly make.

b. *attrib.* or *adj.* Round like a cowslip-ball; plump and comely.

1888 T. HARDY *Wessex Tales* (1889) 35 She's a rosy-cheeked, tisty-tosty little body enough.

tiswas ('tɪzwɒz). *slang.* Also **tis-was, tizz-wozz,** etc. [Perh. a fanciful enlargement of TIZZ, TIZ.] A state of nervous agitation or confusion; occas. a state of physical disorder or chaos.

1960 M. CECIL *Something in Common* xvii. 195 Gets you all of a tiswas, when he's up the wall. **1974** *Observer* 27 Oct. 5/5 A young man rang up in quite a 'tis-was. **1980** *Encounter* May 7 She doesn't clean, but circumvents the dirt. Chairs stand on tables—'All of a tizz-wozz.' Has that been spelt before?

tiswin (tɪs-, tɪz'wiːn). *U.S.* Also **tizwin.** [ad. Amer. Sp. *texguino.*] An intoxicating drink made from maize, wheat, or mesquite beans by the American Indians.

1877 *Rep. Indian Affairs* (U.S.) 162 Addicted .. to the use of intoxicating liquors, 'tiswin', which they manufacture from corn, and whiskey obtained from strangers. **1891** J. G. BOURKE in *Cent. Mag.* Mar. 655/1 The Apache intoxicant, 'tizwin' .. [is] beer, made from fermented corn. **1911** WEBSTER, Tiswin, tizwin.

tit (tɪt), *sb.*[1] *dial.* (chiefly *Sc.*) [? f. TIT *v.*[1]] A sharp or sudden pull; a tug, jerk, twitch.

1340 HAMPOLE *Pr. Consc.* 1915 Yf þat tre war tite pulled oute At a titte with al þe rotes oboute. **1581** *Satir. Poems Reform.* xliii. 75 Sa Fortoun mountit neuer man sa hie, .. Bot with ane tit sho turnis the quheill. **1827** KINLOCH *Ballad Bk.* 63 He gied the tow a clever tit That brocht her out at the lum. **1881** PAUL *Aberdeen.* 111 The craetur' gied a tit, an' afore I kent fat I was about, I was lyin' o' the braid o' my back.

tit, *sb.*[2] [Goes with TIT *v.*[2]]

1. In phr. **tit for tat** [app. a variation of *tip for tap*, known a century earlier: see TAP *sb.*[2], TIP *sb.*[2], and cf. prec. But perh. wholly or partly onomatopœic.] One blow or stroke in return for another; an equivalent given in return (usually in the way of injury, rarely of benefit); retaliation. Also used as rhyming slang for 'hat'. Cf. TITFER.

The whole phrase is used sometimes as a *sb.*, sometimes as *adj.* or *adv.*; also, elliptically or as *interj.*

1556 J. HEYWOOD *Spider & F.* xxxvii. 26 That is tit for tat in this altricacion. **1586** J. HOOKER *Hist. Irel.* in *Holinshed* II. 94/1 That they would not sticke to set his seruants at libertie, so he would redeliuer them the youth of the citie, which was nothing else in effect, but tit for tat. **1710** ADDISON *Tatler* No. 229 ⁋3, I was threatened to be answered Weekly Tit for Tat. **1809** J. QUINCY in *Life* 181, I shall..give..what politicians call a Rowland for their Oliver, and what the ladies term tit for tat. **1881** SAINTSBURY *Dryden* iv. 80 A fair literary tit-for-tat in return for the *Rehearsal*. **1891** *Daily News* 16 July 5/1 Fair Traders, Reciprocity men, or believers in the tit-for-tat plan of dealing with other nations. **1905** H. A. VACHELL *The Hill* viii, Tit for tat. If I do this for you, will you do something for me? **1925** FRASER & GIBBONS *Soldier & Sailor Words & Phrases* 285 *Tit for tat*, hat. (Rhyming slang). **1930**, **1937** [see TITFER].

2. A light stroke or tap; a slap: cf. TIP *sb.*[2]

1808 JAMIESON, *Tyte, tit*... 2. A slight stroke, a tap. **1891** *Hartland Gloss.* s.v., I'll gi'e 'ee a tit under the yur.

3. *Comb.*: **tit-tat**, an imitation of the sound of alternating taps or blows; **tit-tat-toe**, (*a*) the beginning of a formula used in 'picking' or fixing upon a person or thing, hence a children's game; (*b*) *dial.* or *U.S.* = *noughts and crosses* (see NOUGHT *sb.* 7 c); see also TICK-TACK-TOE, *tip-tap-toe* s.v. TIP-TAP.

In quot. *a* 1700 imitating the noise made in toddling. The precise nature of the activity referred to in quot. 1865 is uncertain and cannot be determined from the context.

a **1700** B. E. *Dict. Cant. Crew*, *Tit-tat*, the aiming of Children to go at first. **1855** ANNE MANNING *O. Chelsea Bun-house* xiii. 211, I played at Tit-tat-to with Joe, and posed him with hard riddles. **1865** TROLLOPE *Can you forgive Her?* II. xxi. 164 The signing-clerk's clerk..playing tit-tat-to by himself upon official blotting-paper. **1888** B. LOWSLEY *Gloss. Berks. Words & Phrases* 164 *Tit-tat-toe*, the first game taught to children when they can use a slate pencil, the words 'Tit-tat-toe, My first go', being said by the one who first makes three crosses, or noughts in a row. **1898** A. T. SLOSSON *Dumb Foxglove* 11 Checkers, and tit-tat-toe, and fox-and-geese, and set down games like those. **1909** *Daily Chron.* 22 July 7/1 Drawing to be diversified by noughts and crosses and 'tit tat toe'. **1961** *New Scientist* 9 Nov. 367 Noughts and Crosses (known in America as Tit-Tat-To). **1973** J. SCARNE *Encycl. Games* 583 Tit-tat-toe. This simple game, also called Noughts and Crosses in Great Britain, is played on diagrams consisting of intersecting parallel lines.

tit, *sb.*[3] Also 6 tyt, titte, 6–8 titt, 7 tytt. [app. of onomatopœic origin, as a term for a small animal or object; found also to some extent in Scandinavian and Icel.; cf. Norw. dial. *titta* little girl, *tîta* a little fish, trout, sprout, minute growth, little kernel, little ball or marble, Icel. *tittr* a little plug or pin, also, a titmouse (Norw. *tite*): see also TITLING, TITMOUSE, in which *tit* occurs much earlier than by itself.]

I. 1. a. A name for a horse small of kind, or not full grown; in later use often applied in depreciation or meiosis to any horse; a nag. Now *rare*.

1548 PATTEN *Exped. Scotl.* D j, He rode on a trottynge tyt well woorth a coople of shillynges. **1563** GOLDING *Cæsar* IV. (1565) 85 But such [beastes] as are bred among them though they be littel tittes & yll shapen, they make..to be very good of labor. **1598** FLORIO, *Bidetto*, a little horse, a nagge, a tit, a little doing horse. **1616** SURFL. & MARKH. *Country Farme* 538 If you will let them haue anie Tytt or meane Iade to goe before them, and lead the way. **1706** PHILLIPS (ed. Kersey), *Tits*, a Country-word, for small Cattel. **1726** *Dict. Rust.* (ed. 3), *Tit*, a little Horse, and some call a Horse of a middling Size a double Tit. **1797** *Sporting Mag.* IX. 338, I keep a curricle and a brace of tits. **1821** SCOTT *Kenilw.* xi, I have as good a tit as ever yeoman bestrode. **1894** ASTLEY *50 Years Life* II. 186 A very promising tit named Woodstock.

†**b.** *fig.* of a person, etc. See also 2. *Obs.*

1706–7 FARQUHAR *Beaux Strat.* I. i, As to our Hearts, I grant 'ye, they are as willing Tits as any within Twenty Degrees. *a* **1734** NORTH *Exam.* I. iii. §40 (1740) 145 As the willing Tits of the Party, and weaker Brethren.

2. a. A girl or young woman: often qualified as *little*: cf. *chit*; also applied indiscriminately to women of any age (? *dial.*). (*a*) Usually in depreciation or disapproval: esp. one of loose character, a hussy, a minx. (*b*) Sometimes in affection or admiration, or playful meiosis. (Common in 17th and 18th c.; now *low slang*.)

1599 MIDDLETON *Micro-Cynicon* Wks. (Bullen) VIII. 122 He hath his tit, and she likewise her gull; Gull he, trull she. **1606** *Sir G. Goosecappe* IV. ii. in Bullen *O. Pl.* III. 69 Hang am Tytts! ile pommell my selfe into am. **1606** *Choice, Chance*, etc. (1881) 66 His Dad a Tinker, and his Dam a Tit. **1693** *Humours Town* 11 My little Tit..loves the Town, as well as my self. **1787** BECKFORD *Italy* (1834) II. 363 A bevy of young tits dressed out in a fantastic, blowzy style..drew their chairs round us [at an assembly in Madrid]. **1837** T. CREEVEY *Papers*, etc. (1904) II. 324, I am sure from Lady Tavistock that she thinks the Queen a resolute little tit. **1886** FENN *Master Cerem.* vii, She's a pretty little tit. **1922** E. R. EDDISON *Worm Ouroboros* xxxi. 397 The Demons,..since they had a strong loathing for such ugly tits and stale old trots, would no doubt hang her up or disembowel her. **1932** S. O'FAOLAIN *Midsummer Night Madness* 62 I'm sorry for his two tits of sisters, though. **1969** H. E. BATES *Vanished World* ix. 87 'The old tit' doddered forth... I see her as a kind of..diminutive nun, untouched and unprotected.

†**b.** Rarely applied to a lad or young man. *Obs.*

1599 MASSINGER, etc. *Old Law* III. ii, Must young court tits Play tomboys' tricks with her, and he [her husband] live?

II. 3. A word used in comb. in the names of various small birds as TITLARK, TITLING, TITMOUSE, TOMTIT, q.v. Used alone, as a shortened form of TITMOUSE, applied to **a.** any bird of the genus *Parus*, and, more widely, any member of the family *Paridæ*; **b.** With qualification: some birds of other families as the ***bearded tit***: see TITMOUSE 2 b; ***hill-tit***: see HILL *sb.* 4 f.

1706 PHILLIPS (ed. Kersey), *Tit*, or *Titmouse*, a little Bird. **1802** Marsh Tit [MARSH 4 b]. **1831** Bearded Tit [see *reed-pheasant*, REED *sb.*[1] 14]. **1843** [see COAL-TIT]. **1845** Blue-tit [BLUE *a.* 12 a]. **1851** Bottle-tit [BOTTLE *sb.*[1] 5]. **1859** TENNYSON *Geraint & Enid* 275 Tits, wrens, and all wing'd nothings peck him dead! **1880** A. R. WALLACE *Isl. Life* ii. 20 These are all the European tits, but there are many others. **1906** *Westm. Gaz.* 14 Apr. 15/2 No longer do bands of tits drift through the woods or along the hedgerows... Strange ..that the long tailed tit, the only species of the group that builds its nest in a bush, should be the first to start.

c. *attrib.* and *Comb.*, as ***tit-like*** adj.; **tit-babbler**, one of several species of hill-tits, esp. *Trichostoma rostratum*; **tit-bell**, a bell-shaped container filled with seeds, fat, etc., and suspended out of doors to supply food to tits and other birds of similar habits; **tit-pipit**, a name of the TITLARK or meadow pipit, *Anthus pratensis*; **tit-warbler**, 'a bird of the subfamily *Parinæ*' (Swainson).

1893 NEWTON *Dict. Birds* 26 The..Babblers, often with a prefix such as Bush-Babbler, Shrike-Babbler, *Tit-Babbler, ..belong chiefly to the Ethiopian and Indian Regions. **1934** J. M. CROSTHWAITE in H. M. Batten *Our Garden Birds* 184 Mr. Mortimer Batten has..invented and developed many ingenious and artistic feeding devices... The *tit bell is filled with melted fat, which is allowed to set, after which the bell is hung. **1976** *Southern Even. Echo* (Southampton) 3 Nov. 12/3 Another useful device for feeding tits and woodpeckers is to make a 'tit bell'. **1907** *Westm. Gaz.* 15 Mar. 4/2 But all the rest are bustling about in their own restless, *tit-like manner. **1819** G. SAMOUELLE *Entomol. Compend.* 303 Inhabits the black grouse and *tit-pippit.

tit, *sb.*[4] *techn.* [Of uncertain and possibly diverse origin; in sense 1 perh. related to TIT *sb.*[1] or [2]; in sense 2 perh. = TEAT.]

1. *Nail-making.* A loose piece of steel used to jerk the finished nail out of the bore.

1902 BARING-GOULD *Nebo the Nailer* ii, Working in the bore is the 'tit' that..ejects the finished nail. **1912** *Let. to Editor*, The 'tit' is a small loose plain piece of steel which is placed in the 'bore' for the purpose of ejecting the nail from the bore after the nail is headed.

2. A small core of metal accidentally left by the shifting of the drill point in boring a hole.

1884 F. J. BRITTEN *Watch & Clockm.* 129 If the centre is missed a tit is formed which gives trouble.

tit, *sb.*[5] [? Infantile variant of KIT *sb.*[3]] Used as a call to a cat.

1828 *Craven Gloss.*, *Tit*, this, with its adjunct puss, is frequently used for calling a cat. **1837** DICKENS *Pickw.* xvi, 'It must have been the cat, Sarah', said the girl... 'Puss, puss, puss—tit, tit, tit'.

tit, *sb.*[6] [Var. of TEAT.]

1. a. Var. of TEAT. Now *Obs.* exc. *dial.* and in senses below.

b. *pl.* A woman's breasts. Also in *sing. slang* (orig. *U.S.*).

1928 in A. W. Read *Classical Amer. Graffiti* (1935) 80 A girl may sit & finger her tits and play with her cunt all day. **1947** C. WILLINGHAM *End as Man* 93 'Well,' said Munro. 'That girl ought to go to Hollywood.' 'She wouldn't make it out there,' blushed Wilson. 'No tits.' **1962** J. HELLER *Catch-22* xviii. 181 How do you expect anyone to believe you have a liver condition if you keep squeezing the nurses tits every time you get a chance. **1969** *Oz* May 40/2 Mary Anne Shelley, with the best tits off-off-Broadway. **1980** J. BARNES *Metroland* I. xi. 63 Tits? I asked myself in furtive panic. Well, you couldn't really see, not with that dress.

c. ***to get on one's tits*** or (occas.) ***tit***: to irritate intensely, get on the nerves of. *slang*.

1945 BAKER *Austral. Lang.* vi. 121 Someone or something disagreeable is said *to get on one's..tit*. **1966** 'L. LANE' *ABZ of Scouse* 40 *Gets on me tits*, annoys me very much. **1967** N. FREELING *Strike out where not Applicable* 114 Those women, who even wear a corset under riding breeches..they're the ones who get on my tits. **1973** P. WHITE *Eye of Storm* vii. 304 Much as she disliked men, Sister Manhood began to think women got on her tits as badly. **1977** J. WILSON *Making Hate* xiii. 153 This Sherlock Holmes act of yours gets right on my tits.

d. ***tits and ass*** or ***arse***: slang phr. used to denote crude sexuality. Similarly ***tits and bums***. Also *transf.*, a magazine containing photographs of nude women; also called ***tit mag(azine)***.

1972 R. A. WILSON *Playboy's Bk. Forbidden Words* 288 The late Lenny Bruce once suggested that 'Tits and Ass' would be the most accurate advertisement for most night-club acts. **1975** *New Society* 3 July 26/3 His lascivious sisters in the tit mags who part their legs and leer. **1975** *Wentworth & Flexner's Dict. Amer. Slang* Suppl. 750/1 *Tits and ass* [taboo] adj., of, being, or pertaining to commercial photographs of nude young women. **1976** N. THORNBURG *Cutter & Bone* i. 24 A tits-and-ass independent, you might call him. **1977** D. FRANCIS *Risk* xii. 150 On Wednesday, paragraphs in all the dailies... 'Fun Jock Twice Removed?' from a tits and bums. **1977** *Zigzag* Apr. 34/1 Not unless you look at some jerk-off magazine, a tit-and-ass magazine disguised as some junior hippy kind of thing. **1978** K. AMIS *Jake's Thing* (1979) v. 49 A keen buyer of tit-magazines. **1978** *Globe & Mail* (Toronto) 4 Nov. 13/2 Victor Matthews, chairman of Express Newspapers..put his people to work on plans for a new tabloid 'with plenty of tits and bums'. **1980** in S. Terkel *Amer. Dreams* 1 There are certain images that come to mind when people talk about beauty queens. It's mostly what's known as t and a, tits and arse. No talent. **1982** *Sunday Times* 2 Sept. 29/1 Ugly George, America's prime TV porn artist (who invites women to undress for his video camera), with his 'tit n' ass' cable channel.

e. ***arse over tit***: see ARSE *sb.* 1 b.

2. = TEAT 2; *spec.* a push-button, esp. one used to fire a gun or release a bomb. orig. *Forces' slang*.

1942 J. GLEED *Arise to Conquer* iv. 30 Pull the tit. [*Note*] This is the emergency control which, by driving the supercharger at its very maximum pace, gives the aeroplane considerable extra speed. **1943** 'T. DUDLEY-GORDON' *Coastal Command at War* xvii. 165 It was time to release the depth-charges... I pressed the tit and that was the last I saw of it [*sc.* the bomb] for a bit. **1972** A. PRICE *Colonel Butler's Wolf* xii. 135 They've built this mock-up in the Museum... You press the tit, and the lights go out. **1976** 'J. ROSS' *I know what it's like to Die* xxi. 136 He pressed the tit of the bell push and she opened the door.

tit, *sb.*[7] *slang*. [Of uncertain origin: perh. f. TIT *sb.*[6]; cf. TIT *sb.*[3], TWIT *sb.*[1] 2 b.] A foolish or ineffectual person, a nincompoop.

1947 *Landfall* (N.Z.) Dec. 290 Why didn't Lachlan go, the silly tit? **1965** M. FRAYN *Tin Men* (1966) xv. 69 'Who are all these people?' they shouted at one another. 'All which people?' 'All these tits in tweed sports jackets.' *Ibid.* 70 'Peculiar friends he has.' 'Tits, a lot of them.' **1968** *Listener* 19 Sept. 370/2, I don't think much of this little tit Hitler, do you, ducky? **1978** S. WILSON *Dealer's Move* vii. 122 We always took a gun, and it kept me quite alert, not wishing to make a tit of myself in front of the laird.

tit, *a.* *Obs.* exc. *dial.* Editors suggest, in quot. *c* 1400, 'Dear, loved'. In *mod. dial.* Fond: cf. TID *a.*, TIT-BIT.

c **1400** *Destr. Troy* 7106 Þen vnhappely hys hest he hastid to do, þat angart hym after angardly sore, Turnyt hym to tene & all the tit Rewme. **1854** MISS BAKER *Northampt. Gloss.* s.v., When a person is particularly attentive to, or indulgent to another, it is said, 'He is very tit of her'.

tit, *v.*[1] *dial.* (chiefly *Sc.*) Also 4–5 tyt, 4–6 titte; *pa. t.* 4 tite, (tyd), 4–5 tit, titt, tyt, 5 tyte, 7– titted (9 -et); *pa. pple.* 4 tytted, 5 tyt, tytt, 6–7 tit, 7– titted. [Etymology obscure: goes with TIT *sb.*[1]; see Note below.]

trans. To pull forcibly, to tug; to snatch. Also *intr.* to pull *at*.

13.. *Cursor M.* 15303 (Cott.) His fote ful tite he til him tite [*Gött.* titt], Him schamed it was well sene. *Ibid.* 15837 (Gött.) And als þai fra þe erd him titt [*Trin.* pulde] His bodi was all stund. **1375** BARBOUR *Bruce* v. 603 He tit the bow out of his hand. *c* **1470** HENRY *Wallace* VI. 143 Ane maid a scrip, and tyt at his lang suorde; 'Hald still thi hand', quod he, 'and spek thi word'. *c* **1470** HENRYSON *Mor. Fab.* IX. (*Wolf & Fox*) xxiv, The wecht thairof neir tit my tuskis out. **1873** J. OGG *Willie Waly*, etc. 115 Hoo angry he was when ye tittet his tails. **1896** BARRIE *Tommy* xxiv. 281 She realised that Miss Kitty was titting at her dress.

†**b.** To pull *up*, esp. in a halter; hence, to hang. *Obs.*

c **1375** *Sc. Leg. Saints* xl. (*Ninian*) 983 About his nek þai knyt a rape, & tit hym vpe, & lefit hyme þare. *c* **1470** HENRY *Wallace* VII. 212 Be he entrit, hys hed was in the swar; Tytt to the bauk, hangyt to ded rycht thar. **1500–20** DUNBAR *Poems* xvii. 28 Sum..nevir fra taking can hald thair hand, Quhill he be tit vp to ane tre. **1638** BRATHWAIT *Barnabees Jrnl.* III. (1818) 125 A piper being here committed, Guilty found, condemn'd and titted.

†**c.** To lay hold of forcibly, clutch, seize; ? to pull or drag about. *Obs.*

c **1425** WYNTOUN *Cron.* IV. vii. 1074 His stewart made on hym a schot And tyt [*v.r.* claucht] hym dourly be þe throte. *c* **1450** HOLLAND *Howlat* 837 The Golk..tit the Tuchet be the tope, ourtirvit his hed. *c* **1475** *Rauf Coilȝear* 123 He tyt the King be the nek. *Ibid.* 432 For to towsill me or tit me, thocht foull be my clais, Or I be dantit on sic wyse, my lyfe salbe lorne.

[*Note.* The sense agrees with that of TIGHT *v.*[1], sense 1, but regular Sc. forms of that appear in 14th c. as *ticht*, *tycht*, and the disappearance of the *ch* would be abnormal. It is unlikely that OE. *tyhtan*, *tihtan*, should have become **titte* in the language of the Danes in England, in accordance with the treatment of *ht* in ONorse itself.]

tit, *v.*[2] Now *dial.* [Goes with TIT *sb.*[2]: app. an onomatopœic match to TAT *v.*[1], the lighter vowel expressing lighter action and sound: cf. *tip* and *tap*, *pit-a-pat*, etc.]

1. *trans.* and *intr.* To strike or tap lightly, pat, tip.

(Quot. 1589 appears to be a parody of 'Come tit me, come tat me, Come throw a kiss at me', quoted of date 1607 under TAT *v.*[1] This seems to have been a couplet from an old song, current before 1589.)

1589 [? LYLY] *Pappe w. Hatchet* B j b, Elderton swore hee had rimes lying a steepe in ale, which shoulde marre all your reasons: there is an olde hacker that shall take order for to print them... The first begins, Come tit me, come tat me, come throw a halter at me. **1607** [see TAT *v.*[1]]. **1901** G. DOUGLAS *Ho. w. Green Shutters* v. 42 He's a brother o'—eh ..(tit-tit-titting on his brow)—oh, just a brother o' Dru'cken Will Goudie.

2. † *to tit one in the teeth*: to cast in one's teeth, upbraid one *with* (*obs.*); hence *to tit* (simply), to twit, upbraid; *intr.* to scoff or jeer *at*.

1622 MABBE tr. *Aleman's Guzman d'Alf.* I. 147 Or that it should be tit in my teeth, that I had beene at the Court, and not seene the King. *Ibid.* II. 133 They would vpbraid me therewith..; Titting and flouting at me. **1629** J. M. tr. *Fonseca's Devout Contempl.* 424 Notwithstanding all this Absalon titted him in the teeth, saying, Is this thy loue to thy friend? **1631** *Celestina* XII. 146 Doe not tit mee in the teeth with these thy idle memorialls of my Mother. **1891** *Hartland Gloss., Tit*..to twit or teaze. **1904** *Eng. Dial. Dict.* s.v., To tit a person about anything.

tit, obs. 3rd sing. pres. of TIDE *v.*[1]; var. TITE *adv.*

Titan[1] ('taɪtən). [a. L. *Tītan, -ānem*, name of the elder brother of Kronos, and ancestor of the Titans; also in poetry his grandson, the Sun-god = Hēlios; a. Gr. Τιτᾶν, in pl. Τιτᾶνες, the Titans, a race of gods expelled by Zeus out of heaven. So F., Sp. *Titan*, Pg. *Titão*, It. *Titano*, Du., Ger. *Titan*.]

1. Used (chiefly in poetry) as a name for the Sun-god, Sol, or for the sun personified.

1412-20 LYDG. *Chron. Troy* III. 5416 Þe dede cors to carien in-to toun Of worþi Hector, whan Titan went doun. **1501** DOUGLAS *Pal. Hon.* Prol. 33 The assiltrie and goldin chair of price Of Tytan, quhilk at morrow semis reid. **1606** SHAKS. *Tr. & Cr.* v. x. 25 Let Titan rise as early as he dare. **1638** SIR T. HERBERT *Trav.* (ed. 2) 2 The third of April at Titans first blush [*ed.* 1634 early in the morning] we got sight of Porto Santo. **1708** J. PHILIPS *Cyder* I. 10 Then wo to Mortals! Titan then exerts His Heat intense, and on our Vitals preys. **1911** SIR E. RIDLEY in *19th Cent.* May 870 Till flaming Titan nigh to either Pole Beheld thy empire.

2. a. *Gr. Mythol.* In *sing.* The ancestor of the Titans: see etymology above. In *pl.* a family of giants, the children of Uranus (Heaven) and Gæa (Earth), who contended for the sovereignty of heaven and were overthrown by Zeus.

1667 MILTON *P.L.* I. 510 Th' Ionian Gods..Titan Heav'ns first born With his enormous brood, and birthright seis'd By younger Saturn. **1727-41** CHAMBERS *Cycl.* s.v., This war lasted ten years; but at length the Titans were vanquished; Jupiter remained in peaceable possession of heaven, and the Titans were buried under huge mountains thrown on their heads. **1858** BUSHNELL *Serm. New Life* ii. (1869) 19 A race of Titans broken loose from order amd warring on God and each other. **1908** G. K. CHESTERTON *Orthodoxy* viii. (1909) 258 The Titans did not scale heaven; but they laid waste the world.

b. *transf.* and *allusively*, usually denoting a person (mountain, tree, etc.) of gigantic stature or strength, physical or intellectual, a 'giant'; sometimes, one who belongs to the race of 'giants' as distinct from the *Olympians* or 'gods'.

1828 SCOTT *F.M. Perth* xxvii, The clan of Titans seemed to be commanded by their appropriate chieftains—..Ben Lawers, and..Ben Mohr. **1829** —— *Anne of G.* vi, The sun was just about to kiss the top of the most gigantic of that race of Titans [the Swiss mountains]. **1838** EMERSON *Addr., Lit. Ethics* Wks. (Bohn) II. 205 Men looked..that nature.. should reimburse itself by a brood of Titans. **1870** SWINBURNE *Ess. & Stud.* (1875) 260 The ranks of great men are properly divisible, not into thinkers and workers, but into Titans and Olympians. **1903** J. STEWART *Dawn in Dark Cont.* i. 22 The weary Titan need not complain too much.

c. Applied descriptively to machines of great size and power; e.g. a dredger, crane, etc.

1876 *Daily News* 30 Oct. 6/4 A novel kind of dredger is in use, consisting of a centrifugal pump, called a 'Titan', which raises the sand together with a certain proportion of water, and discharges it in the barges. **1894** *Times* 29 Jan. 14/2 A titan steam crane will be mounted on deck for moving any of the heavy parts for examination or repair. **1911** *Encycl. Brit.* IV. 479 These sloping blocks are laid by powerful overhanging, block-setting cranes, called Titans, which travel along the completed portion of the break-water, and lay the blocks in advance.

3. *Astron.* Name of the largest of Saturn's satellites.

1868 LOCKYER *Guillemin's Heavens* (ed. 3) 252 The diameter of Titan, the largest satellite,..is..more than half the diameter of the Earth. **1878** NEWCOMB *Pop. Astron.* III. iv. 353 The smallest telescope will show Titan.

4. *attrib.* or as *adj.*; *transf.* Titanic, gigantic.

1697 DRYDEN *Æneid* VI. 782 The rivals of the Gods, the Titan race. **1851** MAYNE REID *Scalp Hunt.* i, As though.. hurled from the hands of Titan giants! **1858** N. J. GANNON *O'Donoghue*, etc., *Lines on Late War*, Such hands as theirs have more than Titan strength. **1860** TYNDALL *Glac.* I. xx. 139 The Titan obelisk of the Matterhorn. **1860** C. SANGSTER *Hesperus*, etc. 53 Titan strength and queenly beauty.

b. *attrib.* and *Comb.* (chiefly in sense 2), as *Titan-born, -like* adjs.; also (from 1) †**Titan beam**, a sunbeam.

a **1649** DRUMM. OF HAWTH. *Poems* Wks. (1711) 44 Whilst eagles stare on Titan beams. **1816** BYRON *Ch. Har.* III. cv, Their steep aim Was, Titan-like, on daring doubts to pile Thoughts which should call down thunder and the flame Of Heaven. **1839** BAILEY *Festus* xxvii. (1852) 467 Thoughts which were once my masters, now I hold In retributive bondage, Titanlike. **1847** EMERSON *Poems* (1857) 45 Titan-born, to hardy natures Cold is genial and dear. **1904** *Speaker* 28 May 206/2 The Trip-shake and Tumble-tread of Titan-footed Reels.

†'**titan**[2]. *Obs. rare.* [ad. F. *titane*, ad. mod.L. TITANIUM.] **a.** *Chem.* = TITANIUM. **b.** *Min.* = TITANITE. Also *attrib.*

1803 in *Trans. Roy. Irish Acad.* (1806) X. 17 Rutilite. Calcareo-siliceous titan ore of Kirwan. **1828** WEBSTER, *Titan, Titanium*, a metal of modern discovery. **1882** in OGILVIE (Annandale).

titanate ('taɪtəneɪt). *Chem.* [f. TITAN-IC *a.*[2] + -ATE[4].] A salt of titanic acid.

1839 URE *Dict. Arts* 1254 By calcination with nitre, it [titanium]..forms titanate of potassa. **1873** WATTS *Fownes' Chem.* (ed. 11) 429 The titanates have not been much studied.

Hence **tita'nation**: see quot.

1904 VAN HISE in *U.S. Geol. Surv., Monogr.* XLVII. 205 Titanation is the union of titanic acid with base, or the substitution of titanic acid for another combined acid, in either case producing titanates.

Titanesque (taɪtə'nɛsk), *a.* [f. TITAN[1] + -ESQUE.] Resembling or having the characteristics of the Titans; colossal, gigantic.

1882 FROUDE *Carlyle* xx. I. 383 His extraordinary metaphors and flashes of Titanesque humour. **1906** MARIE CORELLI *Treas. Heaven* xi, Titanesque human figures with threatening arms outstretched.

Titaness ('taɪtənɪs). [f. TITAN[1] + -ESS.] A female Titan; a giantess. Also *fig.*

1596 SPENSER *F.Q.* VII. vi. 4 So likewise did this Titanesse [Mutability] aspire Rule and dominion to her selfe to gaine. **1649** T. FORD *Ludus Fort.* 82 We can find no place free from the rule of this Titanesse. **1853** C. BRONTE *Villette* xli, Truth,..O Titaness amongst deities! **1862** B. TAYLOR *Home & Abr.* Ser. II. II. iv. 90 St. Helene..rises grandly above all the neighboring chains... This Titaness is robed in imperial hues. **1904** BRANDES *Main Curr. 19th C. Lit.* V. xii. 168 In that generation of heaven-storming Titans and Titanesses he appears a peculiarly earth-bound creature.

titania (taɪ'teɪnɪə). *Chem.* [f. TITAN(IUM + -IA[1], after YTTRIA, etc.] = *titanium dioxide* s.v. TITANIUM b.

1922 *Jrnl. Amer. Chem. Soc.* XLIV. 387 Titania was prepared by dissolving the oxide in hot conc. sulfuric acid, diluting with 10 volumes of water and precipitating as with alumina. **1971** *Materials & Technol.* II. v. 326 Titania and its compounds..are important for high-capacity condensers, and have considerably displaced the natural product mica.

Titanian (taɪ'teɪnɪən), *a.*[1] [f. L. *Tītāni-us* of or belonging to the Titans + -AN.] Of, pertaining to, or like the Titans; Titanic. Also (quot. 1614) of the sun-god; solar, sunlike.

1614 RALEIGH *Hist. World* I. (1634) 6 The Moone's bright Globe, and Stars Titanian. **1667** MILTON *P.L.* I. 198 As whom the Fables name of monstrous size, Titanian, or Earth-born. **1685** COTTON tr. *Montaigne* (1711) I. iv. 27 The Thracians..fall to shooting against Heaven with Titanian madness. **1776** J. BRYANT *Mythol.* III. 76 All these were of the Giant, or Titanian race. **1820** BYRON *Mar. Fat.* IV. i. 83 Titanian fabrics, Which point in Egypt's plains to times that have No other record.

ti'tanian, *a.*[2] *Chem.* [f. TITANI-UM + -AN.] †**a.** Of or pertaining to titanium. *Obs.* (Superseded by TITANIC *a.*[2])

1828 in WEBSTER. **1846** in WORCESTER (citing URE).

b. *Min.* [-IAN 2.] Of a mineral: having a (small) proportion of a constituent element replaced by titanium.

1930 *Amer. Mineralogist* XV. 572 Titanium—titanian. **1944** [see PLUMBIAN *a.*]. **1967** *Amer. Mineralogist* LII. 780 Zr also has been reported in amounts up to a few weight percent in titanian andradite (melanite).

Titanic (taɪ'tænɪk), *a.*[1] [ad. Gr. τιτανικ-ός, f. Τιτᾶν-ες the Titans: see -IC.]

†**1.** Of or pertaining to the sun. *Obs. rare*[−0].

1656 BLOUNT *Glossogr., Titanic*,..of or belonging to the Sun. **1658** in PHILLIPS.

2. Pertaining to, resembling, or characteristic of the Titans of mythology; gigantic, colossal; also, of the nature or character of the Titans.

1709 J. CLARKE tr. *Grotius' Chr. Relig.* v. ix. (1818) 226 *note*, Some wicked Daemons and (as I may call them) Titanic or Gigantic ones who were rebellious against the true God. **1818** BYRON *Ch. Har.* IV. xlvi, We pass The skeleton of her [Rome's] Titanic form. **1852** KELLY tr. *Cambrensis Eversus* III. 483 He has assailed heaven itself with titanic audacity. **1858** CARLYLE *Fredk. Gt.* I. i. (1872) I. 6 The figure of Napoleon was titanic.

ti'tanic, *a.*[2] [f. mod.L. TITANI-UM + -IC 1 b.] Of, pertaining to, or derived from titanium; in *Chem.* applied to compounds in which titanium has its higher valence, as ***titanic oxide*** (***t. acid***), a white tasteless powder, TiO_2. In *Min.*, ***titanic iron-ore*** = ILMENITE; ***titanic schorl*** = RUTILE.

1826 HENRY *Elem. Chem.* II. 701 Method of separating titanic acid from oxide of iron. **1839** URE *Dict. Arts* 682 All volcanic rocks contain a greater or less quantity of titanic iron-ore. **1842** BRANDE *Dict. Sc.*, etc. s.v. *Titanium*, The peroxide, or titanic acid, exists nearly pure in titanite, or rutilite. **1868** JOYNSON *Metals* 87 Bessemer metal containing phosphorus may be dephosphorised by employing titanic pig-iron, in repeated doses, to eliminate the phosphorus. **1894** BOWKER in *Harper's Mag.* Jan. 410 Ilmenite, or titanic iron $(FeTi)_2O_3$..is an ore in which one of the iron molecules of hematite is replaced by the metal titanium.

Titanic, *sb.* [f. TITANIC *a.*[1]] The name of a giant British liner which sank on its maiden voyage in 1912 after collision with an iceberg; used allusively or as a metaphor for a vast and supposedly indestructible organization fated to disaster. Also ***Titanic clause*** (see quot. 1915).

1915 *N.Y. World* 3 Aug. 5/4 When he executed his will on March 16, 1914, Joseph E. Greenfield inserted what is known as a 'Titanic' clause, which anticipated the possibility of the testator and his wife meeting death together in a catastrophe. **1975** S. LAUDER *Killing Time on Corvo* x. 91 It was some horrifying *Titanic* disaster. **1975** *Times* 3 Sept. 10/6 The implications of the final song, that England is a Titanic with a crew composed only of vagabonds and privileged yachtsmen. **1976** *Times* 13 May 1/3 The hapless President's campaign manager..sounded ..fatalistic... 'I'm not going to do anything to re-arrange the furniture on the deck of the Titanic,' he said. **1980** K. HAGENBACH *Fox Potential* vi. 57, I wanted to leave England. .. I did not intend to be aboard when that particular Titanic finally foundered in a sea of bureaucracy.

†**Titanical** (taɪ'tænɪkəl), *a.* *Obs. rare.* [f. as TITANIC *a.*[1] + -AL[1]: see -ICAL.] = TITANIC *a.*[1] 2.

1642 H. MORE *Song Soul* II. i. I. xxi, Rash labour, a Titanicall assay To pluck down wisdome from her radiant seat. **1678** CUDWORTH *Intell. Syst.* I. ii. §3. 61 A Gigantical and Titanical Attempt to dethrone the Deity.

Hence **Ti'tanically** *adv.*, in a titanic manner.

1816 T. TAYLOR *Pamphleteer* VIII. 57 She is bound in body Prometheically and Titanically. **1891** G. MEREDITH *One of our Conq.* vi, A more than Titanically audacious balloonist.

ti'tanico-, *Chem.*, combining form of TITANIC *a.*[2], esp. in names of double salts, resulting from the combination of a titanic with another salt. **titanico-hydric** *a.*: see quot. (now *hydrotitanic*).

1860 MAYNE *Expos. Lex., Titanico-hydricus*..applied by Berzelius to a titanic haloid salt..combined with the hydracid of the same halogenous body..: titanicohydric.

titaniferous (taɪtə'nɪfərəs), *a.* [f. TITAN-IUM + -I-FEROUS.] Containing or yielding titanium.

1828 in WEBSTER (citing CLEAVELAND). **1829** J. PHILLIPS *Geol. Yorks.* 105 Magnetic sand (oxydulated titaniferous iron). **1836-41** BRANDE *Chem.* (ed. 5) 872 Titaniferous Oxide of Iron, which is more abundant than rutilite, may be used as a source of titanium. **1883** *Encycl. Brit.* XVI. 426/1 Schorlomite (Ferrotitanite)... Perhaps a titaniferous garnet.

titanious (taɪ'teɪnɪəs), *a. rare.* [f. TITANI-UM + -OUS.] **a.** *Min.* Containing or combined with titanium. †**b.** *Chem.* Obs. f. TITANOUS.

1853 TH. ROSS *Humboldt's Trav.* III. xxix. 169 Rocks.. charged with oxidulated and titanious iron, are probably of similar origin.

Titanism ('taɪtənɪz(ə)m). [a. F. *titanisme* (? *a* 1825 in Littré): see -ISM.] The character of a Titan. **a.** Revolt against the order of the universe. **b.** Titanic force or power.

1851 H. MELVILLE *Moby Dick* II. xliv. 297 Where infantileness of ease undulates through a Titanism of power. **1867** M. ARNOLD *Celtic Lit.* Wks. 1903 V. 126 Titanism as we see it in Byron. **1887** *Athenæum* 29 Oct. 566 Their dignity of expression, their melancholy Titanism of feeling. **1900** *Q. Rev.* July 128 Echoes of Schopenhauer's Pessimism, of Nietzsche's Titanism. **1902** *Ibid.* Oct. 369 He has a good deal that is fanciful to say of the Celtic Titanism with its 'indomitable reaction against the despotism of fact'. **1904** G. S. HALL *Adolescence* xi. II. 123 The soul is filled with a Titanism that would achieve a *vita nuova* upon a higher plateau, where the music of humanity is no longer sad but triumphant.

titanite ('taɪtənaɪt). *Min.* [ad. Ger. *titanit* (Klaproth, 1795), f. TITAN-IUM + *-it*, -ITE[1]; named from its containing the metal titanium.]

1. A mineral composed chiefly of calcium titanosilicate, $CaO.TiO_2.SiO_2$; also called *sphene*.

Iron is present in varying amounts, sometimes also manganese and yttrium.

1858 DANA *Min.* (1868) 385 Titanite occurs in imbedded crystals in granite, gneiss, mica, schist, syenite [etc.]. **1879** RUTLEY *Stud. Rocks* x. 140 Sphene (titanite) crystallises in the monoclinic system.

†**2.** Erroneously applied by Kirwan to the mineral now called RUTILE, a form of titanium dioxide, which he took to be an element. *Obs.*

1796 KIRWAN *Elem. Min.* (ed. 2) II. 329. **1799** *Monthly Rev.* XXX. 349 Among the metals, are overlooked the Tellurite..and Titanite. **1812** SIR H. DAVY *Chem. Philos.* 430 Titanium is obtained from a mineral long known by the name of red schorl or titanite.

† **tita'nitic**, *a. Min. Obs. rare.* [f. prec. + -IC.] = TITANIC *a.*[2]

1796 KIRWAN *Elem. Min.* (ed. 2) II. 330 [Titanite] melted ..with 5 times it's weight of mild Tartarin... When dissolved in boiling water, it soon let fall a white substance. .. This I call Titanitic Calx. *Ibid.* 331 Titanitic Ores.

titanium (taɪ'teɪnɪəm). *Chem.* [f. Gr. Τιτᾶν-ες the Titans (see TITAN[1]) + -IUM. Named by Klaproth 1795, on the analogy of URANIUM previously named by him.

Cf. *Beitr. z. Chem. Kenntn. d. Mineralkörper* I. 244 Diesem zufolge will ich den Namen, wie bei dem Uranium geschehen, aus der Mythologie..entlehnen, und benenne also dieses neue Metallgeschlecht: *Titanium*.]

a. One of the rare metals, never found free in nature, but obtainable as an iron-grey powder with a metallic lustre. It belongs to the same group as zirconium, cerium, and thorium. Symbol Ti; atomic weight 48·1 (O = 16).

Discovered by Klaproth as a constituent of a mineral (now called Rutile) from Boinik in Hungary. The same metal had been previously discovered by M'Gregor in a mineral (now called Ilmenite) found in Manaccan in Cornwall, and had been named by him *Menakanet* (*Crell's Chem. Ann.* 1791, I. 119).

1796 PEARSON in *Phil. Trans.* LXXXVI. 426 *note*, A new metal, named Titanium, lately announced in the German Journals. **1800** tr. *Lagrange's Chem.* I. 393 The substance from which titanium is extracted is a red schorl, found chiefly in Hungary. **1812** SIR H. DAVY *Chem. Philos.* 430 The oxide of titanium was discovered by McGregor in 1781 in an ore found in the valley of Menachan in Cornwal, but metallic titanium was not produced till 1796 by Vanquelin and Hecht. **1868** JOYNSON *Metals* 28 A small quantity of titanium improves the quality of steel.

b. *attrib.* **titanium dioxide**, the oxide TiO_2, occurring naturally as the minerals rutile, anatase, and brookite, and used esp. as a white pigment and opacifying agent; **titanium green**, ferrocyanide of titanium, a green pigment precipitated by ferrocyanide of potassium from a solution of titanic chloride (Watts *Dict. Chem.* V. 849); **titanium oxide**, any oxide of titanium, esp. the dioxide; **titanium sand**, pulverulent titaniferous iron (Watts *Dict. Chem.* V. 849); **titanium sponge**, titanium in a porous form; **titanium white**, a white pigment consisting chiefly or wholly of titanium dioxide.

1877 *Jrnl. Chem. Soc.* I. 688 Sulphate of titanium dioxide, $TiS_2O_8 + 3H_2O$, is a yellow resinous mass. **1963** R. R. A. HIGHAM *Handbk. Papermaking* iv. 94 Titanium dioxide has the property of extreme chemical inertness, i.e., it is not affected by acids, alkalis, or the common solvents at standard temperature and pressure and is insoluble in water. **1982** *Sci. Amer.* Oct. 58 (Advt.), Titanium dioxide makes the plastic of your coffee cup opaque and the color of your telephone deep and bright. **1885** *Jrnl. Chem. Soc.* XLVIII. I. 640 The author describes the hydrated titanium oxide with phosphoric acid and various earths from the diamond diggings of Diamantina, in Brazil. **1955** *Sci. News Let.* 9 Apr. 233/1 A liquid at ordinary temperatures, titanium tetrachloride changes to smoky fumes of titanium oxide when air touches it. **1977** *Whitaker's Almanack 1978* 152/2 The M stars, like Betelgeuse, show very complex molecular spectra, chiefly of titanium oxide. **1950** *Metal Industry Handbk. & Directory* (ed. 39) I. 39/1 The resultant mixture of molten magnesium chloride, unused magnesium and titanium sponge is allowed to cool..and the product is bored out as chips. **1978** *Jrnl. R. Soc. Arts* CXXVI. 679/1 The extraction method normally used now is to chlorinate rutile (TiO_2), turning it into titanium tetrachloride ($TiCl_4$) liquid, which is then reduced with magnesium or sodium to produce titanium sponge which can subsequently be melted and cast into ingots. **1920** *Chem. Abstr.* XIV. 355 (*heading*) Titanium and titanium white. **1934** H. HILER *Notes on Technique of Painting* ii. 101 Titanium white is the oxide of a metal which until lately was considered as a curiosity in the laboratory.

titano-[1], a. Gr. τῑτāνο-, combining form of Τῑτάν, TITAN[1], in **tita'nolater**, an admirer of titanic attributes; so **tita'nolatry** [-LATRY]; **tita'nomachy** [-MACHY], the warfare of the Titans; **'titano,saur**, ‖**titano'saurus** [Gr. σαῦρος lizard], a gigantic fossil dinosaur from the chalk; ‖**Ti,tano-**, **,Titano'therium** [mod.L., f. Gr. θηρίον beast], also anglicized **'titano,there** [cf. F. *titanothère*], an extinct genus of ungulates from the Tertiary formation, resembling gigantic rhinoceroses; hence **titano'therian** *a.*, of or pertaining to the genus *Titanotherium*; **titano'therioid** *a.*, resembling or allied to this genus; also as *sb.*

1846 HARE *Mission Comf.* 601 Considered as a higher pitch of heroism by the *Titanolaters. **1867** *Hare's Guesses*, *Mem.* 47 A protest against what he called the *Titanolatry paraded in them. **1887** GLADSTONE in *Contemp. Rev.* June 760 The great myth of the *Titanomachy. **1892** *Pall Mall G.* 22 Mar. 7/1 In Colorado have been found great deposits of the bones of *titanosaurs, the biggest land animals that ever existed. They grew to be 65 ft. long and stood 40 ft. high when erect upon their hind legs. **1881** LUBBOCK in *Nature* 1 Sept. 406/2 Marsh has made known to us the *Titanosaurus, of the American (Colorado) Jurassic beds. **1862** DANA *Man. Geol.* 515 The *Titanothere..having some relations to the modern Tapir. *Ibid.* 532 White River or *Titanotherian beds. **1890** *Nature* 13 Feb. 347/1 These *Titanotherioids appear to have been most nearly allied to the Rhinoceroses among existing forms. **1865** PAGE *Handbk. Geol. Terms*, **Titanotherium*,..a large herbivorous mammal occurring in the Lower Miocene beds of the Missouri district.

titano-[2] (taɪtənəʊ), combining form of TITANIUM (and TITANITE), used in the names of chemical and mineral compounds, as ***titano-cyanide***, ***-ferrite***, ***-fluoride***, ***-silicate*** (= *silico-titanate*); **tita'naugite** *Min.* [ad. G. *titan-augit* (A. Knop *Der Kaiserstuhl im Breisgau* (1892) ii. 72)], a variety of augite containing titanium; **titan(o)'hæmatite** (also **-hem-**) *Min.*, a variety of hæmatite containing titanium dioxide in solid solution; **tita'nolivine**, 'a variety of olivine (chrysolite) containing titanic acid' (Chester); **,titanomag'hemite** [MAGHEMITE] *Min.*, a titanian variety of maghemite; **titano'magnetite** *Min.* [ad. G. *titanomagnetit* (P. Groth *Tabellarische Übersicht der Min.* (ed. 4, 1898) 79)], a variety of magnetite containing titanium; **titano'morphite**, 'an uncertain alteration product, near titanite' (Chester); † **tita'noxide**: see quot.

1933 *Zeitschr. für Kristallogr.* LXXXVI. 112 The *titanaugite in question forms a small patch or segregation within a sphene-rich, plagioclase-diopside-hornfels xenolith in the Haddo norite. **1963** W. A. DEER et al. *Rock-Forming Minerals* II. 109 Titanaugites are the typical pyroxenes of basic alkaline rocks, *e.g.* teschenite, essexite and nepheline dolerite. **1970** *Nature* 28 Nov. 850/2 The principal minerals in the rock are zoned plagioclase..; nepheline; and titanaugite, grading at the edges of the crystals into aegirine. **1938** A. B. EDWARDS in *Proc. Australasian Inst. Mining & Metallurgy* No. 110. 42 This 'white ilmenite' is quite distinct from ordinary hematite... The name '*titanhematite' is here suggested to indicate its difference from pure hematite. **1945** *N.Z. Jrnl. Sci. & Technol.* B. XXVI. 299 A range from pure titanomagnetite to pure titanhæmatite is..present in a small percentage of the iron-ore grains. **1971** I. G. GASS et al. *Understanding Earth* xvii. 255/1 Ultimately, in the highest state of oxidation.., the original titanomagnetite has been converted mainly to pseudobrookite (Fe_2TiO_5) and titanohaematite (Fe_2O_3) containing a little titanium. **1953** E. Z. BASTA *Mineral. Aspects of System FeO-Fe_2O_3-TiO_2* (Ph.D. Thesis, Univ. of Bristol) vi. 71 For those minerals with composition approaching (Fe, Ti)$_2O_3$ (e.g. the Bushveld maghemites) I propose the new name '*titano-maghemite'. **1971** *Nature* 5 Mar. 28/1 Under conditions of low temperature and high oxygen fugacity.. titanomagnetite tends to oxidize to an equilibrium mineral assemblage of rutile and haematite, with intermediate formation of titanomaghemite, ilmenite and iron-rich titanomagnetite. **1900** *Mineral. Mag.* XII. 393 *Titano-magnetite... Titaniferous magnetite. [(Fe, Ti)O_2]$_2$Fe. **1945** [see *titanohæmatite* above]. **1962** W. A. DEER et al. *Rock-Forming Minerals* V. 68 A considerable amount of Ti can enter the magnetite structure, there being a continuous relationship between magnetite and the ulvöspinel molecule, Fe_2TiO_4... The term titanomagnetite is best restricted to those specimens where the presence of an ulvöspinel phase can be demonstrated. **1971** I. G. GASS et al. *Understanding Earth* xvii. 255/1 The mineral which accounts for the magnetic properties of most rocks, and especially basalts, is titanomagnetite. **1880** *Nature* XXI. 425 Under the name of *Titanomorphite, A. von Lasaulx describes a new lime-titanite from the gneiss of the Eulengebirge. **1884** *Athenæum* 16 Aug. 212/3 Titanomorphite crystallizing in the oblique system. **1860** MAYNE *Expos. Lex.*, *Titanoxydum*,..term by Beudant for a combination of titanium with oxygen: a *titanoxide.

‖**'titanos.** *Alch. Obs. rare.* Also **-us.** [a. Gr. τίτανος gypsum, chalk, white earth.] = MAGNESIA 1.

c **1386** CHAUCER *Can. Yeom. Prol. & T.* 901 Take the stoon that Titanos men name. Which is that quod he? Magnasia is the same Seyde Plato. **1477** NORTON *Ord. Alch.* iii. (MS. Harl. 853 No. 4 (1589) lf. 40 b), Chawcer rehearseth how Titanos is the same In the Cannon his tale. **1584** R. SCOT *Discov. Witchcr.* XIV. ii. (1886) 295 The end.. is, to atteine unto the composition of the philosophers stone, called Alixer, and to the stone called Titanus.

titanous ('taɪtənəs), *a. Chem.* [f. TITAN-IUM + -OUS.] Containing titanium, spec. in its lower valence, as ***titanous oxide***, sesquioxide of titanium, Ti_2O_3; contrasted with TITANIC *a.*[2]

1866 ROSCOE *Elem. Chem.* 206 The oxides of titanium correspond to those of tin; viz. titanous and titanic oxides. **1868** WATTS *Dict. Chem.* V. 842 Titanous oxide dissolves in acids, forming violet solutions. **1873** —— *Fownes' Chem.* (ed. 11) 448 Titanous fluoride is obtained as a violet powder by igniting potassio-titanic fluoride in hydrogen gas.

‖**titar** ('tiːtɑː(r)). *E. Ind.* [Hindī, etc. *tītar*, *-ur.*] Native name of the Grey Francolin, or 'Grey Partridge' of India, *Francolinus ponticerianus.*

1895 in *Funk's Stand. Dict.* **1898** BLANFORD *Fauna Brit. India, Birds* IV. 139 The Grey Partridge, Titar, Ram-titar, Gora-titar.

tit-bit ('tɪt,bɪt), **tid-bit** ('tɪd,bɪt). [In 17th c., *tyd bit*, *tid-bit*, f. TID *a.* + BIT; later also *tit-bit*, perh. after compounds of TIT *sb.*[3]

tid-bit is now chiefly *N. Amer.*]

a. A small and delicate or appetizing piece of food; a toothsome morsel, delicacy, *bonne bouche.*

α. *c* **1640** J. SMYTH *Lives Berkeleys* (1885) III. 25 A tyd bit, i.e. a speciall morsell reserved to eat at last. **1701** COLLIER *M. Aurel.* (1726) 13 To be always loading the table, and eating of tid-bits. **1755** *Connoisseur* No. 87. (1774) III. 123 For fear any tid-bit should be snapped up before him, he snatches at it..greedily. **1834** L. RITCHIE *Wand. by Seine* 185 The sturgeons, the finest salmons, and other tid-bits of the fishery. **1895** *Outing* (U.S.) XXVI. 436/2 [The coon] locating many a tid-bit by means of his sharp nose and bright eyes. **1906** U. SINCLAIR *Jungle* xiv. 162 Things.. went into the sausages in comparison with which a poisoned rat was a tidbit. **1968** *Globe & Mail* (Toronto) 17 Feb. 28 An unusually good selection of hot and cold tid bits.

β. **1694** MOTTEUX *Rabelais* IV. xlvi, He promis'd double Pay..to any one that should bring him such a Tit-bit piping-hot. **1727** ARBUTHNOT *John Bull* Postscr. ix, How John pamper'd Esquire South with Tit-bits, till he grew wanton. **1861** J. PYCROFT *Agony Point* (1862) 363 To see.. such tarts and tit-bits. **1865** TROLLOPE *Belton Est.* xxv, No more tit-bits of hashed chicken specially picked out for her.

b. *fig.*; *spec.* a brief and isolated interesting item of news or information; hence in *pl.*, name of a periodical consisting of such items.

α. **1735** FIELDING *Eurydice* I. i, My farce is an Oglio of tid-bits. **1776** FOOTE *Capuchin* III. Wks. 1799 II. 401 A fine girl, as I live! too nice a tid-bit for an apprentice. **1883** C. READE in *Harper's Mag.* June 94/1 He furnished me..several tidbits that figure in my printed works. **1941** AUDEN *New Year Let.* I. 26 Add his small tid-bit to the rest. **1976** *Time* 27 Dec. 49/3 There were enough tidbits of good news last week to soothe the fears of some Ford Administration economists.

β. **1708** *Brit. Apollo* No. 40. 2/2 Many of them [women] are Tit Bits. *a* **1814** *Last Act* Prol. in *New Brit. Theatre* II. 361 A new tit bit fresh from some author's brain. **1887–9** T. A. TROLLOPE *What I remember* II. vi. 100 During the singing of the well-known tit-bits of any opera.

c. *attrib.*

1767 A. CAMPBELL *Lexiph.* (1774) 56 We expedited ambassadors with plenary powers to procure us buttered buns,..tart tit-bit tartlets. **1820** T. MITCHELL *Aristoph.* I. 167 Such dainty little schemes—such tit-bit thoughts. **1900** *Jrnl. Sch. Geog.* (U.S.) June 240 The danger..is that it should lead to the application of the tit-bits method to the teaching of geography.

Hence **tit-'bitical**, **'tit-,bitty** *adjs.* (*nonce-wds.*), of the nature of, consisting or full of tit-bits.

1887 GURNEY *Tertium Quid* II. 24 He is really the tit-bittiest of composers. **1890** *Speaker* 5 Apr. 369/1 Those journalistic abortions of the tit-bitical kind..now so common. **1899** J. G. MILLAIS *Life Sir J. E. Millais* I. iii. 81 Every tit-bitty paper..repeated the tale.

† **tit-bore.** *Sc. Obs.* Also teet-bo (Jam.). [First element perh. Sc. *teet* vb., to peep, sb. a peep, a glance; second perh. = *boh!* interj.: cf. *keek-bo* (KEEK *v.* 3).] The childish game of *bo-peep* or *peep-bo*. Also reduplicated, ***titbore tatbore*** (cf. *tit tat*).

16.. FORBES *Disc. Pervers Deceit* 4 (Jam.) What is this, but (as children in their sporting, childishly practise and more childishly speak) to play titbore tatbore with vs? **1825** JAMIESON s.v., In Aberdeenshire..the phrase *Titbo tatbo* is still used by some old people.

titch, dial. form of TOUCH.

titch, var. TICH.

titchie, **titchy**, obs. and dial. ff. TETCHY.

titchy ('tɪtʃɪ), *a. colloq.* [f. *titch*, var. of TICH + -Y[1].] Insignificantly small, diminutive, tiny.

1950 A. BUCKERIDGE *Jennings goes to School* vii. 139 Well, anyway,..there'll be a titchy hunk all round, so no one'll have any reason to grumble. **1958** *Spectator* 13 June 768/2 Towering six foot three inches over a titchy Laertes. **1967** J. PORTER *Chinks in Curtain* ii. 20 Titchy little automatics. **1978** *Lancashire Life* Sept. 96/1 'E 'olds a titchy rod an' line An' angles in a pond.

tite (taɪt), **tit** (tɪt), *adv.* (*a.*) *Obs.* exc. *dial.* Forms: α. 3– tite, 4–5 tyt, tytt(e, 4–8 tyte, 4–9 tit. β. 3–5 tid, tyd, 8 tide. γ. 4 tyȝt, tiȝt, tiht, 5 tyght(e. Compared *titter*, *tittest*: see TITTER *adv.* [From Scandinavian: cf. ON. *títt* adv., 'frequently, often', neuter of *tíðr* adj., 'frequent, eager', OSw. *tid* 'repeatedly, quickly' (Södervall II. 627), Norw. and Sw. dial. *tidt* 'quickly' (Aasen, Ross, Rietz), the development being 'repeatedly, at short intervals, quickly'. The γ-forms are app. erroneous spellings.] Quickly, soon. *Obs.* exc. as in c.

a **1225** [implied in TITELY]. *a* **1300** *E.E. Psalter* xxxvi. 2 Als wortes of grenes tite fal sal þai. *a* **1300** *Cursor M.* 18497 þai war transfigurd als tite [*Laud* tyȝt] Was neuer i-wis snau sa quite. *c* **1330** R. BRUNNE *Chron. Wace* (Rolls) 13235 Archers ..on þe Romayns smyten ful tit. *c* **1350** *Will. Palerne* 133 But truly tiȝt hadde þat quene take hire to rede. *c* **1400** *Destr. Troy* 7126 Full tid in hire tene turnys he þe qwell. *Ibid.* 8002 Ector toke hit full tyd. ? *c* **1410** *Sir Cleges* 291 Goo bake.. Full tyghte without teryyng! *c* **1450** *Mankind* 152 in *Macro Plays* 6 Felouse, go we hens tyght! **1575** *Gamm. Gurton* I. iv. A iv, That chal, gammer, swythe and tyte, and sone be here agayn. ? **16..** in Drake *Eboracum* I. vi. (1736) 192 The serjeants shall bring sufficient distress to the court, such as will most disease him and the tittest will gar him answer.

† **b.** *as, als, also tit, als tid*, etc.: as soon, as quickly, immediately. (Cf. F. *aussitôt*; also ON. *semtíðast* with all speed, at once, immediately.)

[*c* **1320–1450**: see ALSTITE, ASTITE.] **13..** *E.E. Allit. P.* B. 1213 Ouer-tok hem, as tyd, tult hem of sadeles. **1377** LANGL. *P. Pl.* B. XVI. 61, I shal telle þe as tite [*v.rr.* tyt, tyte, tid] what þis tree hatte. **14..** *Lybeaus Disc.* 784 Than seyde Lybeaus al so tyte [etc.]. **14..** *Tundale's Vis.* 686 And als tyte [*v.r.* tyd] was he all hale. *c* **1435** *Torr. Portugal* 690 To the grownd he felle ase tyght. *c* **1450** *Cov. Myst.* iii. (Shaks. Soc.) 38 Ha don, and answere me as tyght. *c* **1460** *Towneley Myst.* iii. 219 We shalle assay as tyte.

c. *as tite..as*, as soon..as, as readily, willingly, or well..as. *dial.*

1587 *Durham Depos.* (Surtees) 322, I may as tite be a ladye as thou a lord. **1876** *Whitby Gloss.* s.v., 'I had as tite go as stay'. **1878** *Cumberld. Gloss.*, 'I'd as tite dea't as nut'.

† **d.** as *adj.* Quick, swift. (*rare* and *doubtful.*)

c **1400** *Destr. Troy* 6738 Menelaus, And Thelamon the tore kyng with theire tite batels. **1535** STEWART *Cron. Scot.* (Rolls) II. 258 Tytest that tyme he wes of ony vther Agane Modred. *Ibid.* 305 Oswald, that tyme tytest of other. **1768** ROSS *Helenore* I. 32 Wi' weet an wind sae tyte into my teeth, That it was like to cut my very breath.

tite, obs. pres. 3rd sing. of TIDE *v.*[1]; obs. erron. f. TIGHT *a.*

titel, obs. form of TITLE, TITTLE.

'titely, 'titly, *adv.* *Obs.* or *dial.* Forms: α. 3 tidlike, 3–4 tidliche, 4 tidly, 5 tydely. β. 4 titli, titliche, 4–5 titly, tytely, 5 tytly, -lye, 5, 8 titely. γ. 4 tiȝtly, -li. [f. TITE, TIT *adv.* + -LY[2].] Quickly, speedily, smartly; soon. ***as titely*** (cf. F. *aussitôt*), immediately.

α. *a* **1225** *Juliana* 58 þe reue het.. swingen hit swiftliche abuten ant tidliche turnen. *c* **1250** *Gen. & Ex.* 3353 Tidlike hem was ðat water wane, Ðor he grucheden for ðrist hane. **1340–70** *Alisaunder* 974 It betid in a time tidly therafter. **1460** *Paston Lett.* I. 528, I trust to God to com tydely i now. *c* **1460** *Towneley Myst.* iii. 291 Tent hedir tydely, wife, and consider.

β. *c* **1320** *Sir Tristr.* 2518 His swerd he drouȝ titly. **1340–70** *Alisaunder* 7 Tend yee tytely to mee & take goode heede. *c* **1350** *Will. Palerne* 2528 Titliche schuld þei be take. *Ibid.* 2694 þei titly turned aȝen. *c* **1400** *Destr. Troy* 3006 These tythandes full titely told were to Parys. *a* **1400–50** *Alexander* 888 Heraudes.. Touchis titly [*Dubl. MS.* titely] þar tale. *c* **1425** *Cast. Persev.* 223 in *Macro Plays* 84 With my tyre & with my tayl, tytly to tene. *c* **1746** J. COLLIER (Tim Bobbin) *View Lanc. Dial.* Rdr., Wks. (1862) 37 Otto con tell th' tele, and seyth 'Rimes be rot, titely.

γ. *c* **1350** *Will. Palerne* 2476 Tiȝtli al here tene was turned in-to ioye. *Ibid.* 1706. *Ibid.* 285 Tiȝtly.

titengis, obs. form of TIDINGS.

titer, var. TITRE; obs. f. TITTER *v.*[2]

titfer ('tɪtfə(r)). *slang.* Also **titfa, titfor.** [Shortened from *tit for tat* used as rhyming slang: see TIT *sb.*[2] 1.] A hat.

1930 BROPHY & PARTRIDGE *Songs & Slang Brit. Soldier* 171 *Tit-for*, tit-for-tat, i.e. hat. **1937** N. GAY *Me & my Girl* I. i, in J. Franklyn *Dict. Rhyming Slang* (1960) 172 *Duchess*: I hope you enjoyed your drive. *Bill*: Not 'arf—but I nearly lost my titfa! *All*: Titfa? *Bill*: Me tit for tat. *All*: Tit for tat? *Bill*: My Hat! **1939** J. B. PRIESTLEY *Let People Sing* x. 257 I'll see Billy Fitt, with me titfer in me 'and. **1943** HUNT & PRINGLE *Service Slang* 67 *Tin titfor*, steel helmet. **1952** M. TRIPP *Faith is Windsock* x. 151 I've got a lucky scarf too, so's Jake. Dig always takes his titfer, and Arthur's got a brassiere. **1960** *Observer* 20 Mar. 10/3 Last week I told you about the time I popped my titfa. **1976** U. HOLDEN *String Horses* viii. 102 The old lady made a show... Lil Pratt forgot to fill her mouth... She'd not seen a titfer like that since the film of mountain people in the Dardanelles, made after World War one.

†tith, *a.*, *adv.* *Obs.* App. a dial. or colloquial variant of TIGHT *a.* or THIGHT *a.*

1618 FLETCHER *Loyal Subj.* III. iv, This [lass] is not so strongly built; but she's good mettle, Of a good stirring strain too: she goes tith, sir. **1619** —— *Mons. Thomas* II. ii, *Thom.* Then take a Widow, A good stanch wench, that's tith. *Ibid.* I. iii. [see TEW *sb.*[2] 1]. *a* **1625** —— *Woman's Prize* III. v, A ship—which.. With more continuall labour than a gally To make her tith, either she grows a tumbrel,.. or springs more leaks.

tith, obs. form of TITHE.

tithable ('taɪðəb(ə)l), *a.* (*sb.*) Also 5–8 **tythable**, 5–9 **titheable**, 6–8 **tytheable**. [f. TITHE *v.*[2] + -ABLE.]

1. Of produce: Subject to the payment of tithes.

c **1440** *Jacob's Well* 56 Of heyȝ, corn, wode, fruyte, wolle, chese,.. & of all manere thynges tythable. **1548** *Act 2 & 3 Edw. VI*, c. 13 §3 Any beastis or other cattell tytheable. **1619** SIR J. SEMPIL *Sacrilege Handled* App. 39 By Tradition from their Fathers, all things growing out of the earth, and fit for mans meat, are Titheable. **1632** *Star Chamb. Cases* (Camden) 100 Mines are not titheable by the lawe because they doe not *renovare*. **1737** *Gentl. Mag.* VII. 344 This Piece of Land is Tythe-free, That Piece is Tytheable. **1834** *Brit. Husb.* I. 77 The young of those, which are titheable, pay at the time of their being weaned.

2. Liable to pay tithes. *rare.*

1722 R. BEVERLEY *Virginia* IV. v. §18. 218 The Levies.. are a certain Rate or Proportion of Tobacco charged upon the Head of every tithable Person... They call all Negroes above sixteen Years of age tithable, be they male or female; and all white Men of the same Age. But Children and white Women are exempted from all Manner of Duties.

B. *absol.* as *sb.* One who or that which is subject to payment of tithes.

1680 *Virginia Stat.* (1823) II. 488 It is declared.. that such servants soe unsold ought not to be listed as tythables that yeare. **1775** A. BURNABY *Trav.* 12 There are a hundred and five thousand titheables, under which denomination are included all white males from sixteen to sixty. **1828** *Examiner* 210/1 From various tenants and titheables he [the archbishop] receives some 25,000*l.* a-year. **1893** *Nation* (N.Y.) 27 Apr. 309/2 The population of a Virginian county .. was probably considerably more than three times as great as its number of tithables.

tithal ('taɪðəl), *a.* *rare.* [f. TITHE *sb.*[1] + -AL[1]: cf. *tidal.*] Of or pertaining to tithes.

1882–3 *Schaff's Encycl. Relig. Knowl.* III. 2365 The principal tithal rules are as follows.

tithand(e, -ans, obs. forms of TIDING, -S.

tithe (taɪð), *a.*[1] and *sb.*[1] Forms: α. 1 **teoᵹoða**, etc. (see TENTH A. 1 α), 3 **tiȝeðe, tiȝðe**, 4 **tyþe**, 4–5 **tiþe**, (5–7 **tyth**, 6 **tieth (thiethe)**, 6–7 **tith**, 7 **tyethe**), 4– **tithe, tythe**. β. 1 **téoða**, etc. (see TENTH A. 1 β), 3 **tēoþe**, 3–4 **tēþe**, 5–6 **tethe**, (5 **theth(e**, 6 **teyth**). [Early ME. *tiȝeðe*, *tiȝðe*, ME. *tīþe*, *tȳþe* = OE. *teoᵹoþa*, *téoþa*, forms of the numeral TENTH, which as a sb. acquired a specialized sense, in which this form has been retained, while the adj. has become *tenth*. For the general sense- and form-history see TENTH A. 1 α, β, B. 1. Cf. also TEIND, the specialized northern form.]

A. *adj.* Tenth. **†a.** Of order: see TENTH A. 1 α. *Obs.* **b.** Of a division or part; in ME. esp. in ***tithe deal***. In modern use, since 16th c., app. taken anew from the sb., B. 3.

α. *c* **1250** *Gen. & Ex.* 895 Habram ȝaf him ðe tiȝðe del Of alle [h]is biȝete. *c* **1330** *Arth. & Merl.* (Kölbing) 5429 Erl Does sone.. þe .ix. was..; Grifles so was tiþe, Wiȝt he was & noble swiþe. *c* **1350** *Will. Palerne* 5346 Ne þe tiþedel of hire atir to telle þe riȝt. *c* **1375** Tyþe [see TENTH A. 3]. **1377** LANGL. *P. Pl.* B. xv. 480 Persounes and prestes.. þat han her wille here,.. þe tithe del þat trewemen biswynkyn. *c* **1440** *Jacob's Well* 24 Alle þo þat ȝeuyn þe tythe scheef to þe reperys for here hyre, in takyng vp here cost for þe repyng, & ȝeuyn þe xj. scheef for þe tythe.

β. **854–971** Teoða [see TENTH A. 3]. **1297**, **1387** Teþe [see TENTH A. 2].

1601 SHAKS. *All's Well* I. iii. 89 One good woman in ten Madam..: Weed finde no fault with the tithe woman. **1606** —— *Tr. & Cr.* II. ii. 19 Euery tythe soule 'mongst many thousand dismes, Hath bin as deere as Helen. *a* **1814** *He must be married* I. i. in *New Brit. Theatre* IV. 239 Why the veriest shrew.. cannot muster a tythe part of the vagaries which abound in my composition. **1872** *Westm. Rev.* July 90 We have not space to follow Dr. Newman through a tithe part of his illustrations.

B. *sb.* Absolute use of adj.: cf. TENTH B.

In OE. the ordinal *téoða*, pl. *téoðan*, was so used: see TENTH B. 1 b.

1. The tenth part of the annual produce of agriculture, etc., being a due or payment (orig. in kind) for the support of the priesthood, religious establishments, etc.; *spec.* applied to that ordained by the Mosaic law, and to that introduced in conformity therewith in England and other Christian lands. (The latter sense appears first in quots.) Also, in recent use, in certain religious denominations: a tenth part of an individual's income which is pledged to the church. (Cf. TITHE *v.*[2] 1 b, 2.)

a. in *sing.*

α. *c* **1200** *Trin. Coll. Hom.* 83 Hie giuen here tiȝeðe noht for to hauen heuene blisse, ac for to hauen here þe hereword of eorðliche richeise. *c* **1330** R. BRUNNE *Chron.* (1810) 19 He [Adelwolf] was first of Inglond, þat gaf God his tiþe. **1362** LANGL. *P. Pl.* A. VII. 85 For of my Corn and Catel heo Craueþ þe Tiþe. *a* **1425** *Cursor M.* 1067 (Trin.) For þis tiþe [*Laud* tythe] þat þei delt, Caym.. To his broþere ire bare. **1535** COVERDALE *Mal.* iii. 10 Brynge euery Tythe in to my barne. **1551–2** *Rec. St. Mary at Hill* 394 Iohn Crovcher oweth.. The Tyth of his hovs. **1611** BIBLE *Lev.* xxvii. 30 And all the tithe of the land.. is the Lords. **1621** BP. MOUNTAGU *Diatribæ* 185 It being vncertaine in it selfe, whether Abraham gaue or receiued Tithe. **1771** FRANKLIN *Autobiog.* Wks. 1840 I. 9 My father intending to devote me, as the tythe of his sons, to the church. **1831** *Lincoln Herald* 1 July 3/3 There were three heifers to be canted [sold by auction] for tithe. **1845** McCULLOCH *Taxation* II. iv. (1852) 180 It will be seen that half the cultivated land of Great Britain is unaffected by tithe. **1884** J. TAIT *Mind in Matter* (1892) 206 The last symptom of restiveness.. manifested by the Jews related to the tythe.

β. *c* **1450** *Godstow Reg.* 43 He grauntyd & gaf to the holy my[n]chons a-foreseyde tethe of hys too Millis of Sewekeworth [= Seacourt] in corne, money, & fysshes.

b. chiefly in *plural*, including the various amounts thus due or received.

α. *c* **1200** *Vices & Virt.* 139 Chierche-þinges, tiȝeþes, ne offrendes, ne almesses. *c* **1250** *Gen. & Ex.* 1628 Her ic sal offrendes here don And tiȝðes wel ȝelden her-up-on. *c* **1380** WYCLIF *Sel. Wks.* III. 313 We reden not where he took tyþes as we don. *c* **1386** CHAUCER *Prol.* 539 Hise tithes payde he ful faire and wel Bothe of his propre swynk and his catel. **1388** WYCLIF *Gen.* xiv. 20 And Abram ȝaf tithis of alle thingis to hym [1382 And he ȝaue hym dymes of alle thingis]. **1483** CAXTON *Cato* gjb, The tythes whyche they owen to God and the holy chyrche. **1547** in *Richmond Wills* (Surtees) 64, I give to the hye alter for oblited thiethes a newe altare clothe. **1651** R. CHILD in *Hartlib's Legacy* (1655) 23 The Tythes of wine in Glocestershire, was in divers Parishes considerably great. *a* **1660** *Contemp. Hist. Irel.* (Ir. Archæol. Soc.) II. 36 A donation of all the tyethes and other casualties. **1764** BURN *Poor Laws* 2 The whole tithes of the diocese were then paid to the bishop. **1850** KINGSLEY *Alt. Locke* xi, His own tithes here aren't more than thirty pounds. **1965** M. J. C. CALLEY *God's People* ix. 106 The 1960–1 income of a London congregation of the New Testament Church of God which claimed fifty-nine members in 1961 consisted of £900 from tithes and £200 from free-will offerings.

β. *a* **1100** Teoþan [see TENTH B. 1 b]. *c* **1440** *Eng. Conq. Irel.* 67 Euery crystyn man lawfully pay his thethis. *c* **1450** *Godstow Reg.* 46 Certen possessions, tethys, dewteys & othyr thynges. **1517** in *10th Rep. Hist. MSS. Comm.* App. v. 397 Every shippe.. shall paye half tethes to the Colladge of all suche fishe as they shall take.

c. Variously qualified:

agistment tithe, t. of agistment, see AGISTMENT 4; ***coarse t.*** = *great t.*; ***crying t.***, tithe of young live stock; ***great t.***, the chief predial tithes, as corn, hay, wood, and fruit; also called *large t.*; ***mixed t.***, see MIXED *ppl. a.* 11, and quots. there; ***parochial t.***, ? small or vicarial tithes; ***personal t.***, tithe of the produce of labour or occupation; ***petty t., privy t.*** = *small t.*; ***predial t.***, see PREDIAL *a.* 2 b, and quots. there; ***rectorial t.***, tithes pertaining to the rector of the parish, the great tithes; ***small t.***, such predial tithes as are not great tithes, together with the personal and mixed tithes; ***vicarial t.***, tithes pertaining to the vicar of the parish, the small tithes.

1464 [see PREDIAL *a.* 2 b]. **1530**, **1765** [see PRIVY *a.* 8]. **1531**, *a* **1634**, **1672** [see MIXED *ppl. a.* 11]. **1531** *Dial. on Laws Eng.* II. lv. (1638) 169 Some.. say there is no tith but it is either a prediall tith, or a personal tith. **1546** *Yorks. Chantry Surv.* (Surtees) 228 The sayd incumbent hathe.. all offeryngнes and pety tythes. **1589** *Shuttleworths' Acc.* (Chetham Soc.) 51 For the smale or pryve tythes of Hetton iij^{l} ij^{s} vj^{d} ob. **1710** PRIDEAUX *Orig. Tithes* ii. 106 Though it be the practice in setting out of Personal Tithes to separate the Charges from the Profits.. yet there was never any such thing in predial Tithes. **1718** in *Shropsh. Parish Doc.* (1903) 19 The Vicar hath also all small Tythes as Hemp, Flax, Geese, Eggs, Piggs, Fruit and the Like. **1793** BLACKSTONE *Comm.* (ed. 12) I. xi. 387 The tithes of many things.. are in some parishes rectorial, and in some vicarial tithes. **1813** T. N. PARKER in *Gentl. Mag.* May 449/2 Aftermath (or a second mowing of a meadow in the same year) yields a great tithe, as turnips sown on a stubble yield a small tithe. **1817** W. SELWYN *Law Nisi Prius* (ed. 4) II. 1197 The late vicar.. made certain compositions with his parishioners for the vicarial tithes, which were payable on the 29th September. **1861** MIALL *Title Deeds Ch. Eng.* (1862) 4 Parochial tithes constitute.. the provision for the pecuniary support of the Church of England. **1862** BURTON *Bk. Hunter* (1863) 294 The Bishop of Lichfield.. was Dean of Durham, and owner of the great tithes in the parish. **1889** LIPSCOMB in *Land Agent's Record* 6 Apr. 316 In parishes where the great or rectorial tithes remain devoted to the Church, we find a rector and a rectory.

2. In more general sense: Any levy, tax, or tribute of one tenth. ***Saladin tithe***: see *Saladine tax* (SALADINE *a.*).

1600 HOLLAND *Livy* v. xxv. 196 As for the collation and gathering of a smal donative, rather than a tithe, he [Camillus] said nothing of it. **1838** THIRLWALL *Greece* II. xi. 64 To defray the expense of these and his other undertakings, he [Pisistratus] laid a tithe on the produce of the land. **1871** DIXON *Tower* III. xiii. 129 The admirals took tithe on every ship and cargo seized at sea.

3. A tenth part (of anything); = TENTH B. 1; now chiefly hyperbolical: a very small part.

1494 FABYAN *Chron.* VI. ccix. 223 He slewe alway .ix. and saued the .x. and yet.. he eft agayne tythed agayne the sayd tythe, & slewe euery tenth knyght of theym. **1552** HULOET, Tythe or tenth part, *decima*. **1589** NASHE in *Greene's Menaphon* Pref. (Arb.) 11 No Colledge in the Towne was able to compare with the tythe of her Students. **1648** MILTON *Observ. Art Peace* Wks. 1851 IV. 576 These illiterate denouncers never parallel'd so much of any Age as would contribute to the tithe of a Century. **1772** WILKES *Corr.* (1805) IV. 107 A little parish church, with about a tythe of the people who frequent our chapel. **1836** SIR W. HAMILTON *Discuss.* (1852) 341 A tythe of the agitation. **1838** ARNOLD *Hist. Rome* I. 45 The tithe of the spoil was forty talents of silver. **1848** RICHTER *Levana* 45 From a woodcut some thousand impressions may easily be taken; but from a copperplate only a tithe of that number. **1872** BLACK *Adv. Phaeton* xix, I cannot tell you a tithe of what he said.

4. *attrib.* and *Comb.* **a.** Due or paid as tithe. See also TITHE-PIG.

c **1450** *Godstow Reg.* 318 Nicholas Iordan.. paid.. for the tythe hey, ijd. ob. **1455** *Rolls of Parlt.* V. 307/2 In recompense for the tithe veneson in the Forest of Wyndesore. **1555** W. TURNER *Spir. Physic* 50 b, Wyth muche shame, they come wyth tythe pygges by theyr tayles, wyth tythe egges, and tythe hemp and flaxe. **1609** *Mem. Ripon* (Surtees) III. 334 All the Tythe Grain, Hay, Wooll and Lamb. **1765** *Museum Rust.* III. li. 224 Let him by no means attempt to buy tythe barley, for that he is sure is mixed. **1808** TOLLER *Law of Tithes* v. (1816) 152 Tithe-ore is not due of common right, but by particular custom only.

b. Of or pertaining to tithes, as ***tithe-accounts, -audit, -bill, -bond, -campaign, -charge, -claim, -commission, -dinner, -map, -monger, -proprietor, -publican, -right, -system, -war***; objective, etc., as ***tithe-collector, -commutation, -farmer, -gatherer, -giving, -haling, -holder, -owner, -payer, -paying, -redemption, -stealer, -taker***; ***tithe-free*** adj. See also TITHE-BARN, -MAN, -PROCTOR.

1781 J. WOODFORDE *Diary* 6 Nov. (1924) I. 329 Being obliged to go to Lenewade Bridge to settle Dr. Bathurst's *Tithe accounts. *Ibid.* 4 Dec. 333, I asked them to dine with us.. this day being my *Tithe Audit. **1878** F. KILVERT *Jrnl.* 5 Feb. (1977) 302 Today was the Tithe audit and tithe dinner to the farmers, both held at the Vicarage. About 50 tithe payers came. **1736** *Gentl. Mag.* VI. 708 Debate concerning the Quakers *Tythe-Bill. **1666** *Ormonde MSS.* in *10th Rep. Hist. MSS. Comm.* App. v. 24 The said Henry kept *tyth bonds soe long by him that the debitors became insolvent. **1808** TOLLER *Law of Tithes* ix. (1816) 237 It also appeared by ancient *tithe-books of the parson. **1832** COBBETT *Weekly Reg.* 21 Apr. 134 Look at the *tithe-campaign preparing for Ireland; the tithe-war, indeed. **1845** McCULLOCH *Taxation* II. iv. (1852) 185 The limitation of the *tithe-charge. **1858** SIMMONDS *Dict. Trade*, **Tithe-collector*, a receiver of tithes. **Tithe-commissioner*,.. one of a board authorized to arrange propositions for commuting or compounding for tithes. **1859** J. W. ROSSE *Index of Dates*, *Tithe Commutation Bill (England), introduced, Feb. 9; passed, Aug. 13, 1836. **1878** *Tithe dinner [see *tithe-audit* above]. **1780** A. YOUNG *Tour Irel.* I. 217 These *tythe farmers are a bad set of people. **1720** *Lond. Gaz.* No. 5829/3 An Estate.., well wooded, and *Tythe-free. **1960** *Farmer & Stockbreeder* 29 Mar. 31/3 Gentleman's tithe-free residential farm. **1591** *Shuttleworths' Acc.* (Chetham Soc.) 66 Spente by the *tythe getherares, v^{d}. **1792** A. YOUNG *Trav. France* 433 When the state.. permits the cultivators to become the prey of a tythe-gatherer, or loads them with the support of the poor. *a* **1693** *Urquhart's Rabelais* III. xlviii. 386 The Edecimation and *Tith-haling of their Goods. **1785** PALEY *Mor. Philos.* VI. xi. 636 This commutation.. might.. secure to the *tithe-holder a complete and perpetual equivalent for his interest. **1895** *Law Jrnl. Rep., Queen's Bench* LXIV. 159/2 The late Master of the Rolls held that a *tithe-map was not evidence of boundaries between two adjoining owners. **1910** *Edin. Rev.* Jan. 119 The tithe-maps constructed on all sorts of scales. **1647**

Husbandm. Plea agst. Tithes 33 Calves, milk, lambe .. and all other things that the *Tithe-mongers will have to be titheable. **1805** DICKSON *Pract. Agric.* I. 468 The *tithe-owner refused three guineas per acre for the tithe of the barley. **1621** BP. MOUNTAGU *Diatribæ* 315 Appointed for the Rendez-vous of Tithe-takers, and *Tithe-payers. **1878** Tithe-payer [see *tithe-audit* above]. **1621** BP. MOUNTAGU *Diatribæ* 185 In the matter of *Tithe-paying vnto the Priests of the Gospell. **1863** FAWCETT *Pol. Econ.* IV. iv. (1876) 578 It is quite possible that *tithe-proprietors may be ultimately injured by this commutation. **1657** J. WATTS *Vind. Ch. Eng.* 157 Forced to pay the same unto *Tythe-publicanes and Tol-gatherers. **1549** CHALONER *Erasm. on Folly* P iij, How warlyke .. the good vicares can strive for theyr *tytheright. **1711** ADDISON *Spect.* No. 112 ¶7 The 'Squire has made all his Tenants Atheists and *Tithe-Stealers. **1890** *Boston* (Mass.) *Jrnl.* 1 Mar. 2/4 The French-Canadians are beginning to rebel against the *tithe system, which, in the interest of the Catholic Church, takes a large portion of the farmers' products. **1832** *Tithe-war [see *tithe-campaign* above]. **1979** V. BOGDANOR *Devolution* v. 123 The 'tithe war', under which tithes were withheld.

† **tithe**, *sb.*[2] *Obs.* [OE. **tizð* fem., contr. *tíð* (obl. case *tíðe*):—OTeut. **tigiþá*. Not known outside English.] A granting; a concession, boon. ***bene-tiðe, -tuðe***: see BENE b.

a **900** tr. *Bæda's Hist.* III. xii. [xiv.] (1890) 196 Moniȝ oðer uncymre hors .. þæt wit meahton þearfum to tiȝðe sellan. *c* **1000** ÆLFRIC *Hom.* I. 384 Fela wundra ȝelumpon .. ðurh ðæs Hælendes tiðe. *c* **1200** *Trin. Coll. Hom.* 201 þat he .. ȝife us bene tuðe.

† **tithe**, *a.*[2] *Obs.* [OE. *tiȝþa, tīþa, -e*, f. *tiȝð*, TITHE *sb.*[2]] To whom a concession or grant is made; successful in prayer or beseeching.

a **900** tr. *Bæda's Hist.* IV. xxx. [xxix.] (1890) 372 þæt he wæs from Dryhtne tiȝða þære bene, ðe he bæd. *c* **1000** *Ags. Gosp.* Matt. xxi. 22 Ealles þæs þe ȝe biddað ȝe beoð tiþa ȝyf ȝe ȝelyfað. *c* **1200** *Trin. Coll. Hom.* 27 We muȝen mid one worde þese þrie þing bidden and ben bene tiðe. *Ibid.* 119 þat þe fewe word þe we on ure bede seien be tuðe alle haleȝen.

† **tithe**, *v.*[1] *Obs.* Forms: 1 **tiȝþian, tyȝþian**, 1–2 **tíþian**, 2 **teiþian**, 2–3 **tiðen, tuþen** (ü), 3 **tythe**. Pa. t. and pple. (*north.*) 4 **tid(d, tyd(e**. [OE. *tiȝþian* (:—**tigiþójan*), f. *tiȝð*, TITHE *sb.*[2]] *trans.* To grant, concede, bestow.

c **893** K. ÆLFRED *Oros.* VI. xxxiv. §3 þa oferhoȝode he .. þæt he him tiȝþade. *a* **900** tr. *Bæda's Hist.* III. xv. [xxi.] (1890) 220 Ne hine mon on oðre wisan his bene tyȝþian wolde. *c* **1000** ÆLFRIC *Hom.* II. 108 Ic wæs nacod, nolde ȝe me wæda tiðian. *c* **1160** *Hatton Gosp.* Matt. xxi. 22 Eow beoð ȝe-teiþað [*v.r.* ȝetiðad]. *c* **1200** *Trin. Coll. Hom.* 135 God haueð herd þine bede, and tiðed te bene. *c* **1200** ORMIN 5365 Forr all þatt æfre ned uss iss All Godess Gast uss tiþeþþ. *a* **1225** *St. Marher.* 9 Nawt [ha] ne þohte þeron þ hire nu were ituðet hire bone. *a* **1240** *Lofsong* in *Cott. Hom.* 207 Leafdi .. tuðe me mine bone to þine eadi sune. **1297** R. GLOUC. (Rolls) 2474 Ac o þing icholde bidde þe ȝif þou me woldest tiþe. *a* **1300** *Cursor M.* 10966 (Cott.) Drightin has þe tid [*Gött.* tidd] þi bon. *c* **1375** *Sc. Leg. Saints* xxxiii. (*George*) 829 þat god his askine had hyme tyde for þaim þat hyme worchyp dyde.

Hence †'**tithing** *vbl. sb.*, thing granted, reward.

c **1275** *Fragm. Song* 7 in *O.E. Misc.* 101 þat .. he vs skere of þe tyþing þat sunfule schulle an-vnderfon.

tithe (taɪð), *v.*[2] Forms: α. 1 **tio-, teoȝoðian, teȝðeȝian, tæȝþiȝan, teiȝðian, teȝði(ȝ)an**, 4 **tiþe(n, tyþe(n**, 5 **tyth**, 6 **tieth**, 6–7 **tith**, 4– **tithe, tythe**. β. 1 **téoði(ȝ)an**, 3 **tēoþeȝen, tēþeȝen, theoþe**, 4 **teoþe**, 4–5 **tēþe, tethe(n**, 5 **teothe, teith(e, teythe**, 6 **teethe**. [OE. *teoȝoðian*, etc., f. *teoȝoða, téoða* tenth, TITHE *sb.*[1]] *gen.* To take the tenth of, to decimate.

1. a. *trans.* To grant or pay one tenth of (one's goods, earnings, etc.), esp. to the support of the church; to pay tithes on (one's goods, lands, etc.).

to tithe mint (and anise) and cummin (Matt. xxiii. 23), to be conspicuously scrupulous in minutiæ while neglecting important matters of duty.

c **897** K. ÆLFRED *Gregory's Past. C.* lvii. 439 ȝe tioȝoðiað eowre mintan & eowerne dile & eowerne kymen. *c* **950** *Lindisf. Gosp.* Luke xi. 42 ȝiæ teiȝðas meric & cumela & ælc wyrt. *c* **975** *Rushw. Gosp.* ibid., ȝe teȝðiȝas merece [etc.]. *c* **1000** *Ags. Gosp.* ibid., ȝe teoþiað. *c* **975** *Rushw. Gosp.* Matt. xxiii. 23 ȝe þe tæȝþiȝaþ [*Lindisf.* ȝeteȝðeȝes] mintæ & dile & cymen. *c* **1000** *Ags. Gosp.* ibid., ȝe þe teoðiað [*v.r.* teoðiȝað]. *c* **1000** ÆLFRIC *Hom.* II. 428 Ic teoðie ealle mine æhta. *a* **1225** *Ancr. R.* 28 Hwat se beo of oþer hwat vntreouliche iteoþeȝed. **1297** R. GLOUC. (Rolls) 5263 þe king þer after .. teþeȝede wel al is lond, as hii aȝte, wel ynou. **1303** R. BRUNNE *Handl. Synne* 898 Tyþeth weyl alle ȝoure þynges. **13..** *Min. Poems fr. Vernon MS.* xxxvii. 528 Hose wol not tiþe þat god him haþ I-lent, His lyf and his soule boþe schul be schent. *c* **1410** *Master of Game* (MS. Digby 182) xxxv, þan shulde þe mayster of þe game begynne at one rowe .. and tyth alle þe deere reght as þei ligge, rascayle and oþer, and delyuere it to þe procuratoures. **1562** *Child-Marr.* 138 The maner of tiething pigge and gose is, yf one have vijth, to pay one. **1570** LEVINS *Manip.* 89/42 To Teethe, *decimare*. *Ibid.* 152/5 To Tythe. *a* **1641** SPELMAN *Tythes* xvi. (1647) 81 Military spoil, and the prey gotten in war is also tithable, for Abraham tithed it to Melchisedek. **1778** *Eng. Gazetteer* (ed. 2) s.v. *Rye*, A peculiar way of tithing their marsh-lands, whereby they pay only 3d. per acre to the rector, while in pasture, but, if ploughed, 5s. **1782** PRIESTLEY *Corrupt. Chr.* II. x. 265 Ethelwolf tithed the kingdom of England. **1879** FARRAR *St. Paul* I. 63 Serio-comic questions as to whether in tithing the seed it was obligatory also to tithe the stalk. **1901** DAKYNS tr. *Xenophon's Anab.* v. iii. §9. 141 Here with the sacred money he [Xenophon] built an altar and a temple, and ever after, year by year, tithed the fruits of the land in their season and did sacrifice to the goddess.

b. With the tenth which is paid or delivered as the object: To pay or give as tithe. Also *gen.*, to pledge or contribute as a levy.

854 *Grant by Adulf* in Birch *Cart. Sax.* II. 79 He teoðode ȝynd eall his cyne rice ðone teoðan del ealra his landa. **1393** LANGL. *P. Pl.* C. XIV. 84 None tythes to tythen [*v.r.* tetheȝen]. *c* **1450** *Cov. Myst.* iii. (1841) 35, I tythe it [the lamb] to God of gret mercy. **1539** BIBLE (Great) *Deut.* xxvi. 12 When thou hast made an ende of tythinge all the tythes of thyne encrease. **1630** *R. Johnson's Kingd. & Commw.* 510 These slaves are either the sonnes of Christians, tithed in their childhoods, Captives taken in the warres, or Renegadoes. **1967** *Observer* 6 Aug. 4/5 A reply sent to a young member by the sect's letter-answering department was more precise: 'A person working for wages is to tithe one-tenth of the total amount of his wages before income tax, national health, or other deductions are removed.' **1976** *Billings* (Montana) *Gaz.* 20 June 6-c/1 Former Southern officers prospered and tithed up to 50 percent for Civil War II, which never came.

2. *intr.* To pay tithe; to pay the tenth, esp. to the church. Revived in recent use in connection with voluntary church giving. Cf. TITHE *sb.*[1] 1.

c **1200** *Trin. Coll. Hom.* 215 þe prest þe meneȝeð rihtliche teðien. *c* **1275** *Sinners Beware* 149 in *O.E. Misc.* 77 If he .. theoþe ryht vnder his honde, To heouene he cume myhte. **1362** LANGL. *P. Pl.* A. VIII. 65 Laborers .. þat treuliche .. tiþen. **1375** *Creation* 482 in Horstm. *Altengl. Leg.* (1878) 130 Kaym .. tyþede of þe worste þynge, And Abel of his beste. *c* **1450** MYRC *Par. Pr.* 349 They schule teythe welle & trewe. ? *a* **1500** *Chester Pl.* (E.E.T.S.) 439 To holy Church neuer Teithed I, for me thought that was lorne. **1530** PALSGR. 758/2 He must nedes go forwarde for he doth tythe well. **1606** S. GARDINER *Bk. Angling* 93 He was not displeased that the Pharisee .. should tythe rightly. **1942** *Esquire* Sept. 174/2 They went to the Six Hickories church—tithed—and behaved themselves. **1968** N. GIOVANNI in W. King *Black Short Story Anthol.* (1972) 23 He quit church after a couple of months, but he continued to tithe every month faithfully and never drank again.

3. a. *trans.* To impose the payment of a tenth upon (a person, etc.); to exact tithe from.

1382 WYCLIF *Heb.* vii. 9 Leeuy, that took tithis, is tithid. **1546** BALE *Eng. Votaries* I. (1560) 94 b, As he and his monkes wer able to geue no more mony they tithed them after this sorte. **1582** N. T. (Rhem.) *Heb.* vii. 9 Leui also, which receiued tithes, was tithed. **1647** TRAPP *Comm. Heb.* vii. 6 Melchisedech did not only take that which Abraham was pleased to give him, but he tithed him, saith the text, he took the tenths, as his due. **1843** MARRYAT *M. Violet* xlii. 348 The cost .. has been defrayed by tithing the whole Mormon Church. Those who reside at N... have been obliged to work every tenth day in quarrying stone.

b. To exact or collect one tenth from (goods or produce) by way of tithe; to take tithe of (goods).

1591 *Troub. Raigne K. John* (1611) 62 The Monks, the Priors, and holy cloystred Nunnes, Are all in health, .. Till I had tithde and tolde their holy hoords. **1641** BEST *Farm. Bks.* (Surtees) 24 When the parson or procter cometh to tythe his woolle. **1807–8** SYD. SMITH *Plymley's Lett.* Wks. 1859 II. 136/2 No man who talks such nonsense, shall ever tithe the product of the earth. **1817** W. SELWYN *Law Nisi Prius* (ed. 4) II. 1050 The subject matter was not in a proper state to be tithed, until it came into grass cocks.

c. *intr.* To levy tithe *upon* (in quot. *transf.*).

1822 T. L. PEACOCK *Maid Marian* vi. 210 Those who tithe and toll upon them for their spiritual and temporal benefit.

†**4. a.** *trans.* To take every tenth thing or person from (the whole number); to take one tenth of (the whole); to divide into tenths. *Obs.*

c **1000** ÆLFRIC *Hom.* I. 178 ȝif we teoðiað þas ȝearlican daȝas, þonne beoð þær six and ðritiȝ teoðing-daȝas. **1610** HOLLAND *Camden's Brit.* (1637) 705 Keeping alive .. two principall persons, that they might be tithed with the souldiers... Every tenth man of the Normans they chose out by lot, to be executed. **1632** MASSINGER & FIELD *Fatal Dowry* v. i, But tithe our gallants, .. and you will find, In every ten, one—peradventure two—That smell rank of the dancing-school or fiddle. *a* **1641** SPELMAN *Hist. Sacrilege* (1698) 67 Coming to a Desart of Sand, divers of them were constrained to tithe themselves, and eat the tenth Man.

†**b.** *spec.* To reduce (a multitude) to one tenth of its numbers by keeping only every tenth man alive.

The instances all relate to the sacking of Canterbury by the Danes in 1011, *tithe* rendering *decimare* used with this unusual meaning; Higden's words are 'Grex Christi decimatur, novem scilicet occisis et decimo reservato'.

1387 TREVISA *Higden* (Rolls) VII. 89 þe folk of Crist was tiþed, þat is to seie, nyne slayn and þe tenþe i-kepte. **1494** FABYAN *Chron.* VI. cxcix. 206 The monkes of Seynt Augustynes abbey they tythed, that is to meane, they slewe .ix. by cruell turment, and ye tenth they kepte alyue. **1577–87** HOLINSHED *Chron.* I. 170/2 They tithed the people after an inuerted order, slaieng all by nines through the whole multitude, and reserued the tenth. **1670** MILTON *Hist. Eng.* VI. Wks. 1851 V. 251 The multitude are tith'd, and every tenth only spar'd.

†**c.** To reduce the number of (a body of soldiers, etc.) by putting to death one in every ten; also *rhet.* to destroy a large proportion of; = DECIMATE *v.* 3, 4 b. *Obs.*

1597 BEARD *Theatre God's Judgem.* (1612) 292 Then tithing again the said tith, he slue euerie tenth knight, and that by cruell torment. **1609** HOLLAND *Amm. Marcell.* D iij b, The Thebane Legion .. was first tithed, that is, every tenth man thereof was executed. **1614** SYLVESTER *Bethulia's Rescue* III. 146 These proud rocks .. Which yer you scale undoubtedly will cost Ladders of Bodies; and even Tythe your Hoast. **1650** GENTILIS *Considerations* 185 Whole Armies have bin tithed, putting each tenth man to death, for faults which have bin committed in them.

†**d.** ***to tithe out***: to take out by lot every tenth (person or thing). *Obs.*

1608 WILLET *Hexapla Exod.* Ded. 1 Irefull Cambyses .. caused euery tenth man to be tithed out for foode. *Ibid.* 759 The Emperour would tithe them out, and put euerie tenth man .. to death. **1613** PURCHAS *Pilgrimage* v. iii. 391 Which Armie .. he [the Kyng] tythed out of his people, taking one onely of tenne.

†**e.** To form the tenth part of (anything). *Obs.*

1586 WARNER *Alb. Eng.* I. v. (1612) 18 Her sorrowes did not tith her ioy.

Hence '**tithing** *ppl. a.*

1965 M. J. C. CALLEY *God's People* ix. 111 Everybody [in the congregation] .. gives generously, probably more than the tenth required by tithing sects.

titheable: see TITHABLE.

tithe-barn. A barn for holding the parson's tithe-corn.

1546 *Yorks. Chantry Surv.* (Surtees) 14, j teyth barne and a garth lyeng in Clyfton. **1643** [ANGIER] *Lanc. Vall. Achor* 18 Four or five Priests .. and other great Papists, whom they had at hand in a tythe-Barn. **1852** MISS YONGE *Cameos* (1877) II. i. 7 The tenth [sheaf] was .. lodged in the rector's tithe-barn. *a* **1878** SIR G. G. SCOTT *Lect. Archit.* (1879) I. 21 The tithe barns of an English village are .. as admirable and as appropriate as the minster at Rheims.

tithed (taɪðd), *ppl. a.* [f. TITHE *v.*[2] + -ED[1].] Subject to, charged with, or liable for the payment of tithes; taken or paid by way of tithe.

1607 SHAKS. *Timon* v. iv. 31 By decimation and a tythed death .. take thou the destin'd tenth. **1845** MCCULLOCH *Taxation* II. ii, It is the common opinion that a farm tithe-free is better worth twenty shillings an acre than a tithed farm .. is worth thirteen shillings. **1882** W. CORY *Mod. Eng. Hist.* II. 410 A league of 'Right men', who bound themselves by oath not to pay a high price to clergymen for tithed chattels.

titheless ('taɪðlɪs), *a.* [f. TITHE *sb.*[1] + -LESS.] Without tithes, not in receipt of tithes.

1615 SYLVESTER *Job Triumphant* III. 555 Tithe-lesse, Taxe-lesse, Wage-lesse, Right-lesse. **1850** WHIPPLE *Ess. & Rev.* (ed. 3) I. 10 The Edinburgh Review .. was projected by two briefless barristers and a titheless parson.

†'**titheling.** *Obs. rare.* [f. TITHE *sb.*[1] + -LING.] Tenth part, tithe.

c **1320** *Cast. Love* 1180 Kuynde ne may for no þinge þolen her þe tiþelynge.

tithely, obs. form of TIGHTLY, TITELY.

'**tithe-man.** [f. TITHE *sb.*[1] + MAN *sb.*[1]]

†**1.** = TITHINGMAN[1] a. *Obs. rare.*

c **1450** *Godstow Reg.* 69 At þe lawdai .. william edrich, tetheman, & his felawis I-swore, presentid þat [etc.].

†**2.** *U.S.* = TITHINGMAN[1] c. *Obs. rare.*

1638–9 *Laws Maryland* in *Archives Md.* (1883) I. 54 The Lord of every Mannour .. Shall yearly .. nominate some Inhabitant of the Mannour .. to be tithman of that Mannour.

†**3.** One who pays tithes. *Obs. rare.*

1680 C. NESSE *Church Hist.* 186 By their Seventh-year Sabbath they [Israelites] acknowledged that their Land belonged to God, and that they were onely Gods tenants and tythe-men.

4. A collector of tithes; = TITHING-MAN[2]. Now *Hist.*

1747 HOOSON *Miner's Dict.* V iv, In my time I have known it taken every twentieth Dish in some Places by the Tyth-man; in others every tenth. **1772** T. SIMPSON *Vermin-Killer* 19 Crows are worse than tithe-men, as they take their tithes at three different times a year. *c* **1830** *Glouc. Farm Rep.* 22 in *Libr. Usef. Knowl., Husb.* III, Nothing can be more galling to an industrious man, than that .. the tithe-man should come and take the tenth of the fruits of his industry, capital and talent. **1898** J. A. GIBBS *Cotswold Vill.* 36 The titheman came with the parson's horses and took the stuff away to the barn.

tithend, -s, obs. forms of TIDING, -S.

'**tithe-pig.** A pig due or taken as tithe.

1555 [see TITHE *sb.*[1] 4 a]. **1562** *Child-Marr.* 138 He thinkes the tithe pigge withelden, was worth xx^{d},—for so they sell. **1592** SHAKS. *Rom. & Jul.* I. iv. 79 Somtime comes she with Tith pigs tale [tail], tickling a Parsons nose as a lies asleepe. **1602** *2nd Pt. Return fr. Parnass.* III. i. 1074 A parson that was neuer in the vniuersity, is a liuing creature that can eate a tithe pigge. **1663** BUTLER *Hud.* I. III. 1206 Where ev'ry Village is a See As well as Rome, and must maintain A Tithe-Pig Metropolitan. **1772** R. GRAVES *Spir. Quixote* (1820) II. 249 Then the rector, In sleek surcingle with good tithe-pig stuff'd. **1826** SCOTT *Woodst.* xvi, The parsons .. have lost their tithe-pigs.

'**tithe-ˌproctor.** An agent employed to collect a parson's tithes, or one who farmed the tithe; = PROCTOR[1] 2 c.

1780 A. YOUNG *Tour Irel.* I. 103 They begun with the tythe-proctors, (who are men that hire tythes of the rectors) and these proctors either screwed the cotters up to the utmost shilling, or re-let the tythes to such as did it. **1807**, **1898** [see PROCTOR[1] 2 c]. **1817** LADY MORGAN *France* I. (1818) I. 46 The frugal savings of laborious industry do not go to feed the rapacity of the tythe-proctor. **1879** MORLEY *Burke* ii. 24 A church which tried to spread Christianity by the brotherly agency of the tithe-proctor.

tither ('taɪðə(r)), *sb.*[1] [f. TITHE *v.*[2] + -ER[1].] One who tithes. **a.** One who pays tithes; usually with qualification, as ***false, small, true tither***. Now *rare*.

c **1386** CHAUCER *Friar's T.* 14 And smale tytheres [*v.r.* tithers] weren foule yshent. *c* **1400** *York Man.* (Surtees) 223 Ye shule pray specially for trew tythers and devout offerers. *c* **1440** *Jacob's Well* 44 Whann þe euyll tythere seeth or heryth þat þou trewely tythest to god, it greuyth him sore. **1573** TUSSER *Husb.* (1878) 25 Yet we doe see ill tithers ill thriuers most commonlie bee. **1705** STANHOPE *Paraphr.* III. 377 Such distinguishing Titles, as the Punctual Tither, the Constant Faster.

b. An exactor or receiver of tithes; also, a supporter of the system of ecclesiastical tithes.

1591 FLORIO *2nd Fruites* 83 You are..not onely Parson or tither, but absolute possessor of whatsoeuer I haue. **1653** MILTON *Hirelings* Wks. 1851 V. 376 Tithers themselves have contributed to thir own confutation, by confessing that the Church liv'd primitively on Alms. **1736** BAILEY (folio), *Tither*, a tithe-gatherer. **1884** J. PAYNE *Tales fr. Arabic* I. 273 A certain tither, who exceeded all his brethren in oppression of the people and foulness of dealing.

tither ('tɪðə(r)), *sb.*[2] [Of obscure origin; cf. Hampshire dial. *to be on tither-thorns* 'to be tremulously anxious' (*Eng. Dial. Dict.*) and DITHER *sb.*] A state of feverish excitement.

1960 V. JENKINS *Lions Down Under* vi. 91 His amazing side-stepping and running had the crowd in a tither. *a* **1974** R. CROSSMAN *Diaries* (1977) III. 640 He adored discussing the Health Service, he was all of a tither and quiver of excitement at having the Secretary of State there.

tither ('tɪðər), Sc. and dial. form of TOTHER.

Esp. in *the tither* = *thet other*, that other: see OTHER.

1479–81 *Rec. St. Mary at Hill* 98 And for the tithyr ij quarters euery quarter x s. **1786** BURNS *Twa Dogs* 23 The tither was a ploughman's collie. **1858** M. PORTEOUS *Souter Johnny* 32 On the tither haun.

tither, obs. form of TETHER *sb.*

tithinde, -s, tithing(e, -s, obs. ff. TIDING, -S.

tithing ('taɪðɪŋ), *sb.* Forms: α. 1 **téoþung, -ing,** 3 **(theoþinge), toðing(e, teuþing(e,** 3–4 **teþing, -yng, (thething),** 4 **tuþing, tueþyng, tethinge, teothinge.** β. 1 **teiȝðuncg, tiȝeðing,** 3–5 **tiþing,** 5–9 **tything,** 6– **tithing.** [OE. *téoðung*, Anglian *tiȝeðing*, f. *téoða*, *tiȝeþe* TITHE *sb.*[1] or *téoðian* TITHE *v.*[2]: see -ING[1], [3].]

1. One tenth given to the church; = TITHE *sb.*[1] 1.

α. **925–***c* **936** *Laws of Athelstan* I. Prol., Ic Æðelstan cyningc..eow bidde..þæt ȝe ærest of minum aȝenum gode aȝifan ða teoðunga. *c* **1000** ÆLFRIC *Hom.* I. 178 We sceolon ..of ures ȝeares teolunge Gode þa teoðunge syllan. *c* **1000** *Ags. Gosp.* Luke xviii. 12 Ic sylle teoþunga [*c* 1160 *Hatton Gosp.*, Ic ȝife teondunge]. *c* **1200** *Trin. Coll. Hom.* 215 Þu bitechest þe prest alle þine teðinge. *c* **1275** *Sayings of Bede* 137 in Horstm. *Alteng. Leg.* 141 If he may..stelen Cristes teuþinge [*v.r.* theoþinge]. *a* **1325** *MS. Rawl. B.* 520 lf. 38 Offrendes ore Tuþinges þat habbez ben iȝiuene ant vsed. **1387** TREVISA *Higden* (Rolls) VIII. 257 All teþynge [*MS. γ.* tueþyng] schulde be payde to þe moder chirche. **14..** *Childe of Bristowe* 364 in Hazl. *E.P.P.* I. 124 Tethynges and offrynges, sone, he sayd, for y them never truly payd.

β. *c* **950** *Lindisf. Gosp.* Luke xviii. 12 Teiȝðuncgas [*Rushw.* teȝðunge] ic sello allra ða ðe ic ah. *a* **1040** *Bidding Prayer* in *Eng. Hist. Rev.* (1912) Jan. 10 Mid lihte and mid tiȝeðinge. *c* **1200** *Trin. Coll. Hom.* 129 Þeh we gon to chirche and giuen rihte tiðinge. **1382** WYCLIF *Tobit* i. 7 He mynystrede alle tithing [1388 hise tithis]. *c* **1440** *Gesta Rom.* vi. 16 (Harl. MS.) Þey have not of hire owne to lyve with, but of tythingis. **1538** BALE *Thre Lawes* 1000 If we maye haue the tythynges And profytable offerynges. **1861** BERESF. HOPE *Eng. Cathedr. 19th C.* viii. 280, I plead..for a tithing of wealth and art and mechanical power offered at the altar of the Most High.

b. *spec.* A shock or stook of ten sheaves (orig. so set up for the convenience of the tithe-proctor): see quots. *dial.*

1764 *Museum Rust.* II. cvii. 362 Repeating the practice till there be thirty or forty tything brought together. **1794** T. DAVIS *Agric. Wilts.* 76 The general custom..is, to set up the sheafs in double rows, usually ten sheaves together, (provincially a tything) for the convenience of the tything-man. **1813** *Ibid.* Gloss., *Tithings*, ten sheaves of wheat set up together in a double row.

†**2.** A tenth part of anything. *Obs.*

1382 WYCLIF *Isa.* vi. 13 ȝit in it tithing. **1388** *Ibid.*, And ȝit tithing [*gloss* ether tenthe part] schal be ther ynne. *a* **1425** tr. *Higden* (Rolls) VII. App. 520 (MS. β) Hym thouȝt that the tethinge were to many ylefte; and teothed efte the teothinge. **1609** BIBLE (Douay) *Isa.* vi. 13 And yet there shal be tithing in it, and she shal be converted [1611 But yet in it shalbe a tenth, and it shall returne].

3. A company (originally) of ten householders in the system of FRANK-PLEDGE; now only as a rural division (originally regarded as one tenth of a hundred) to which this system gave its name.

c **930–40** *Laws of Athelstan* VI. c. 8 § 1 Þæt we us ȝegaderian ..þa hyndenmenn and þa þe ða teoþunge bewitan. **1297** R. GLOUC. (Rolls) 5402 He by vond..þat ech man wiþ oute gret lond In þe teþinge were ydo & þat ech man knewe oþer þat in teþinge were. *a* **1400** in *Eng. Gilds* (1870) 361 ȝef a foreyne empledy þe teþynge, þe teþynge ne haþ bote þre dayes to shewynge... Whanne þe teþynge empledeþ a foreyn, þe foreyn haþ his delay. **1432** [see TITHINGMAN[1]]. **1538** FITZHERB. *Just. Peas* 129 In Towne, Tithinge, Village, or Hamlet. **1570–6** LAMBARDE *Peramb. Kent* (1826) 18 Some were called..Tithings,..bicause there were in eche of them to the number of ten persons, whereof eche one was suretie and pledge for others good abearing. **1610** HOLLAND *Camden's Brit.* (1637) 158 Hee caused the Counties to be parted into Centuries, that is Hundreds, and Decimes, that is Tithings. **1646** W. HUGHES *Mirr. Justices* I. ii, These divisions in some places are called hundreds..and in some places Tythings or Wapentakes, according to the English. **1754** HUME *Hist. Eng.* (1761) I. ii. 49 The neighbouring householders were formed into one corporation, who, under the name of a tithing, decennary, or fribourg, were answerable for each other's conduct. **1839** KEIGHTLEY *Hist. Eng.* I. 81 The institution of tithings did not prevail all through England, perhaps not to the north of the Trent. **1874** STUBBS *Const. Hist.* I. 86 *note*, Tithings at present exist in Somersetshire and Wiltshire.

4. *attrib.* and *Comb.*, as *tithing-barn*, *-sheaf*, *table*. See also TITHINGMAN[1], -PENNY.

c **1540** *Old Ways* (1892) 45 The said Hayside had sowlde the said tythyng ootys. **1654** VILVAIN *Theol. Treat.* Supp. 238 Not a tithing part of Mankind can possibly find place to stand on a new Earth. **1666** *Lond. Gaz.* No. 66/2 A Bill for abolishing of Oblations and Mortuaries, and appointing a Tything Table throughout the Kingdom. **1865** KINGSLEY *Herew.* i, A palace..beside which King Edward's new Hall at Westminster would show but as a tything-barn. **1907** *Contemp. Rev.* June 796 The farmer was bound to cart his tithing-sheaves to the parson's barn.

tithing ('taɪðɪŋ), *vbl. sb.* [f. TITHE *v.*[2] + -ING[1].] The action of TITHE *v.*[2]

a. Payment of tithes. Cf. TITHE *v.*[2] 2.

c **1305** *St. Swithin* 40 in *E.E.P.* (1862) 44 Ech man wolde þurf þe lond his teoþing wel do. **1548** UDALL *Erasm. Par. Luke* xix. 149 Their colde & feble doctryne..concernyng the true tithyng of myntes & rue. **1573** TUSSER *Husb.* (1878) 25 Though some in their tithing be slack or too bold. **1682** BURNET *Rights Princes* i. 20 That the tything of Mint and Anise should not be left undone. **1929** R. S. & H. M. LYND *Middletown* xxii. 356 Traditionally every Christian 'returns a tenth of his substance to the Lord'. A few families in Middletown continue this practice of tithing, but..the great majority contribute far less than a tenth.

b. Exaction of tithes. Also *transf.*

1630 *R. Johnson's Kingd. & Commw.* 513 The tithing of Springals is made every third yeare. **1768** BLACKSTONE *Comm.* III. 89 If the defendant pleads any custom..or other matter whereby the right of tithing is called in question. **1791** BURKE *App. Whigs* Wks. VI. 289 Taxing and tything. **1843** MARRYAT *M. Violet* xxxix, He is receiving regular pay, derived from the tithing of this warlike people.

†**c.** The killing of every tenth; decimation; sometimes, the killing of all but the tenth. *Obs.*

1586 T. B. *La Primaud. Fr. Acad.* (1589) 716 The tithing of armies..when every tenth man throughout a whole hoste was by lot put to death. **1601** F. GODWIN *Bps. Eng.* 24 In that same terrible tithing of the Danes..all the monks were slaine, except onely fower.

d. *attrib.*, as *tithing port*, *-system*, *-time*, etc.

1548 *Act 2 & 3 Edw. VI*, c. 13 §2 As often as the saide predyall Tythes shalbe due, and at the tythinge tyme of the same. *a* **1786** COWPER *Yearly Distress* 8 But oh! it cuts him like a scythe, When tithing time draws near. **1850** GROTE *Greece* II. lxiii. (1862) V. 462 This place he..erected..into a regular tithing port for levying toll on all vessels coming out of the Euxine. **1853** ROCK *Ch. of Fathers* III. II. 65 These days [Lent] are the tithing-days of the year. **1904** F. W. MAITLAND *Let.* 19 May (1965) 305 We still want a little more light on the tithing system. **1978** *Daily Mirror* 12 Jan. 6/6 Much of their wealth comes from the use of the 'tithe-ing' system—members of the religion are required (like the Mormons) to donate one-tenth of their income to the funds.

tithingman[1] ('taɪðɪŋmæn). [f. TITHING *sb.* 3 + MAN *sb.*[1]] **a.** Anciently, The chief man of a TITHING (*sb.* 3), a headborough; in later use, a parish peace-officer, or petty constable (CONSTABLE 5 c). Now *Hist.*

946–*c* **961** *Laws of Edgar* c. 2 Cyðe hit man ðam hundredesmen, & he syððan ðam teoðingmannum. **1432** *Rolls of Parlt.* IV. 403/1 The Decennare and Decennes, oder wyse called Thethyngman and Thethyngs. **1441–2** *Act 20 Hen. VI*, c. 8 Chescun Conestable, Tythingman, ou chief plegge, de chescun ville ou hamell. **1581** LAMBARDE *Eiren.* I. iii. (1588) 15 For Borowhead, Borsholder, and Tithingman, be three seueral names of one self same thing, and doe signifie, The chiefe man of the free pledges within that Borow, or Tithing. **1626** BERNARD *Isle of Man* (1627) 34 There be foure sorts of Officers which may attach Felons by warrant, The Deputy-constable, the Tything-man, the Petty Constable, and the Head Constable. *c* **1640** J. SMYTH *Lives Berkeleys* (1883) II. 345 The Thirdburrow or Tithingman ought to come to Portbury Leete. **1724** *Lond. Gaz.* No. 6232/2 [They] were by his Mittimus put into the Custody of a Tithingman with a strong Guard. **1857** TOULMIN SMITH *Parish* 15. **1874** STUBBS *Const. Hist.* I. v. 90 *note*, The tithingman is of course an elective officer.

†**b.** A chief or ruler of ten: rendering L. *decānus*, *decurio*. *Obs.*

c **1000** ÆLFRIC *Exod.* xviii. 21 ȝesete of him þusendmen and hundrydmen and fifties men and teoðingmen. —— *Deut.* i. 15 And ic nam wise menn and sette hiȝ to.. teoðingmannum. **1608** WILLET *Hexapla Exod.* 275 A ruler of ten, or tithing man.

c. Also **tidingman.** In Maryland and New England: A former elective officer of a township, whose functions were derived from those of the English tithingman (sense a) in the 17th c.; in particular he was charged with the prevention of disorderly conduct; in New Eng., in later times, chiefly with enforcing the observance of the Sabbath and of order during divine service. Now *Hist.* See *Johns Hopkins Hist. Studies*, No. 1.

1638 *Laws of Maryland*, A Tything-man in each Manor, a Constable in each Hundred. **1677** *Laws of Massachusetts* 23 May, To prevent..Prophanation of the Sabbath.. Tithing man or men shall..have power in the absence of the Constable to apprehend all Sabbath-breakers. **1703** *Early Rec. Groton, Mass.* (1880) 123 For tiding men [for the year 1703] Joseph gilson Benjmen farnworth. [**1727–8** Last tithing-men chosen in Boston.] **1836** *Rev. Stat. Mass.* 180 At the annual meeting, every town shall choose..Tything-men, unless the towns shall vote that it is not expedient to choose the same. [Repealed in 1860.] **1895** A. B. HART in *Forum* (N.Y.) May 377 The interference with Sunday travel by the tithingmen of the Puritan Connecticut towns. **1878** MRS. STOWE *Poganuc People* vi. 63 They're goin' clean agin everything—Sunday laws and tiding man and all.

'tithing-man[2]. [f. TITHING *vbl. sb.*] A collector of tithes; a tithe-proctor.

1625 BURGES *Pers. Tithes* 60, I will produce Mr. Selden (none of the best Proctors for vs Tithing-men, but One with whom we poore Vicars are daily nosed). **1693** *Rector's Bk. Clayworth* (1910) 103 Tything men 3 entred yᵉ Fields. **1736** *Gentl. Mag.* VI. 705/2 He may often lose his whole Crop, in waiting for the Incumbent's Tything-man. **1807–8** SYD. SMITH *Plymley's Lett.* Wks. 1859 II. 145/2 Soften some of the most odious powers of the tything-man.

†**'tithing-penny.** *Obs.* [f. TITHING *sb.* 3 + PENNY, q.v. for Forms.] A customary duty formerly paid by manorial tenants to the lord, and also a payment by lords of manors at the hundred court.

1208 in *Calr. Charter Rolls* (1903) I. 29 Libera et quieta de ..wardpeny et averpeny et thethingpeny et hengwite. **1297** *Inq. Post Mortem* Edw. I 80 (6) (P.R.O.) De tethyng-peny ad visus de hockday et ad festum Sancti Martini xl.*s.* **1334** *Inq. P.M.* Edw. III 37 (22) (P.R.O.) Est ibidem [West Winterslow] quoddam feodum vocatum tethyngpeny viz ad festum Pasche et ad festum Sancti Michaelis xx.*s.* *a* **1600** *MS. Cott. Vitell. C.* 9 lf. 226 b, *Tythinge-pany*, hoc est quieti de tallagio decenæ sive Tythinge per consuetudinem. **1706** PHILLIPS (ed. Kersey), *Teding-*, *Tething-*, or *Tithing-Penny*, a Tax or Allowance formerly paid to the Sheriff, from every Tithing, towards the Charge of keeping Courts.

tithly, obs. form of TITELY *adv.*

tithond(e, obs. form of TIDING.

Tithonian (taɪ'θəʊnɪən), *a.* *Geol.* [ad. G. *tithonisch* (A. Oppel 1865, in *Zeitschr. der deutsch. geol. Ges.* XVII. 535), f. L. *Tīthōnus*, Gr. *Τιθωνός*: see -IAN.] Designating a stage of the European Upper Jurassic, thought to correspond to the Portlandian, or the Portlandian and part of the Kimmeridgian, in Britain; also *ellipt.*

1871 *Q. Jrnl. Geol. Soc.* XXVII. 208 The deposition of the Wealden strata..commenced before the close of the Oolitic period; it continued during the whole of the Tithonian. **1882** A. GEIKIE *Text-bk. Geol.* 800 At the top of the Alpine Jurassic series an important group of deposits occurs to which the name of Tithonian stage was given by Oppel. **1975** *Nature* 13 Mar. 108/1 Two different directions have been obtained from sediments in the lower and upper parts of the Morrison formation (Kimmeridgian-Tithonian respectively).

†**tithonic** (taɪθ-, tɪ'θɒnɪk), *a.* *Obs.* [Fancifully f. Gr. *Τιθων-ός*, spouse of Eos (Aurora) + -IC.] Pertaining to or characterized by 'tithonism'; = ACTINIC. Hence †**titho'nicity** *Obs.* = ACTINISM 2.

1842 (Dec.) DRAPER in *Philos. Mag.* XXI. 455 Such words as Tithonoscope, Tithonometer, Tithonography, Tithonic effect, Diatithonescence, are musical in an English ear. In this paper I shall therefore use the term Tithonicity and its derivatives. *Ibid.*, The proof of the physical independence of Tithonicity and Light. *Ibid.*, The existence of dark Tithonic rays, analogous to the rays of dark heat. *Ibid.* 457 To insulate a visible red and yellow ray that are without tithonic power, and an invisible tithonic ray beyond the violet. **1854** J. SCOFFERN in *Orr's Circ. Sc., Chem.* 93 The immediate mode of agency of the power—'actinism', 'tithonicity', 'energia', or whatever we may call it—is.. unknown. **1882** *Nature* XXV. 274 The works..from Draper's pen upon the chemical and physical properties of the ultra-violet, or as he styled them, *tithonic* rays.

†**'tithonism.** *Obs.* [f. as prec. + -ISM.] = TITHONICITY, ACTINISM 2. So †**'tithonize** *v.*, *trans.* to subject to actinic influence (hence †**tithoni'zation**, 'tithonic' or actinic action; **'tithonized** *ppl. a.*); †**ti'thonograph**, a photograph produced by the action of 'tithonic' rays on a sensitized surface (so **tithono'graphic** *a.*, **-'nographist**, **-'nography**); †**titho'nometer**, †**ti'thonotype**, see quots.

1854 J. SCOFFERN in *Orr's Circ. Sc., Chem.* 93 That peculiar associate of light which has been termed..actinism, *tithonism, and energia. **1844** (July) DRAPER in *Philos. Mag.* XXV. 7 The indigo ray forms the muriatic acid as well as produces the preliminary *tithonization. *Ibid.*, Before placing the tubes in the prismatic spectrum we *tithonize them in the daylight. *Ibid.* 2, I shall speak of chlorine which as been exposed to the beams of the sun, as **tithonized chlorine.* **1842** (Dec.) *Ibid.* XXI. 456 The comparison of different spectras and their corresponding *tithonographs. *Ibid.* 461 If the *tithonographic compound radiates whilst it is undergoing decomposition. **1878** LOCKYER *Spectr. Anal.* iii. §2. 82 Draper..in his 'tithonographic representation', had..not succeeded in registering the lines of the yellow, orange, and green parts of the spectrum. **1842** DRAPER in *Philos. Mag.* XXI. 456 A principle..which makes the spectra of different *tithonographists comparable. **1842** *Tithonometer [see TITHONIC]. **1843** (Dec.) DRAPER in *P.M.* XXIII. 401 Description of the Tithonometer, an instrument for measuring the Chemical Force of the Indigo-tithonic Rays. **1843** (May) *Ibid.* XXII. 366 As a name for these processes of copying the surface of a Daguerreotype, I would suggest the word **Tithonotype.*

tithy, var. TETHY *Obs.*; obs. f. TIDY.

†**tithymal.** *Herb. Obs.* Forms: α. 6–8 **tithi-, tithymal, -e,** 7 **tithymall, -e, tythimal, -l, tythymalle.** β. 5 **tytymal, titi-, titymalle,** 8 **titimale.**

[ad. L. *tithymal(l)us* spurge, *tithymalis* sea-spurge (Pliny), a. Gr. τιθύμαλος, τιθυμαλίς. Cf. F. *tithymale* (13th c. in Godef. *Compl.*).] An old name of the Spurge genus of plants.

c **1400** *Lanfranc's Cirurg.* 294 Take þe grete titimalle & þe smale, & boile hem in vinegre & in oile. *c* **1410** *Master of Game* (MS. Digby 182) xi, An erbe þe whiche is cleped tytymal, þe whiche poticaryes knoweth well. **1578** LYTE *Dodoens* III. xxix. 355 There are.. seuen sortes of Tithymal. **1601** CHESTER *Love's Martyr* (1878) 84 There Mugwort, Sena and Tithiemailes. *a* **1687** PETTY *Pol. Anat.* xiii, What is said of the herb Mackenbory is fabulous, only that 'tis a tythimal, which will purge furiously. **1712** tr. *Pomet's Hist. Drugs* I. 36 The Esula or Spurge is a kind of Tithymal.

titi[1] ('tiːtiː). [Native or local name, of various origin.]

1. In U.S., a name given to certain trees of N.O. *Cyrillaceæ*, as *Cliftonia monophylla*, Buckwheat tree, the ***black titi*** of Southern U.S., also to species of genus *Cyrilla*, esp. *C. racemiflora*, the Leatherwood of south-eastern U.S., distinguished as ***red*** or ***white titi***.

1860 CHAPMAN *Flora South. U.S.* 273. **1880** *Libr. Univ. Knowl.* (N.Y.) III. 147 Buckwheat Tree..an evergreen shrub in the gulf states... Its local name is *titi*. **1908** BRUTTON & SHAFER *N. Amer. Trees* 618.

2. A name of *Oxydendron arboreum*, N.O. *Ericaceæ*.

1903 SMALL *Flora S.E. United States* 890.

3. See TI.

titi[2] ('tiːtiː). Also **teetee.** [Native name in Tupi.] A small long-coated monkey of the genus *Callicebus*, native to the tropical forests of S. America.

1832 MACGILLIVRAY *Humboldt's Trav.* xvii. (1836) 230 The titi or Simia sciurea seems to have been a special favourite with Humboldt. **1879** E. P. WRIGHT *Anim. Life* 49 The Collared Teetee..is of a dark reddish-brown... It inhabits Brazil. **1883** *Athenæum* 28 Apr. 545 The Secretary ..called special attention..to an American teetee monkey of the genus *Callithrix*. **1896** *List Anim. Zool. Soc.* 40 Genus *Callithrix*... Moloch Teetee..Black-fronted Teetee.. Brown Teetee..Grey Teetee..Black-handed Teetee. **1927** *Ann. Mag. Nat. Hist.* 9th Ser. XIX. 509 (*title*) On the Titi Monkeys. *Ibid.*, The British Museum has received..some further specimens of..the Yellow-handed Titis. **1963** *Mammalia* XXVII. 3 Other names..have been applied to the titis of eastern Brazil. **1976** *Nature* 23 Sept. 321/1 Titi monkeys..remain paired throughout the year. **1978** *Ibid.* 18 May 193/2 Titis and siamangs carry the infant(s) for much of the day.

titi, ti-ti, variant of TEETEE.

Titian ('tɪʃ(ɪ)ən), *sb.* and *a.* [The name Titian, for Tiziano Vecellio, Venetian painter, died 1576.] **A.** *sb.* A picture by Titian; a person with Titian or bright auburn hair. **B.** *attrib.* or as *adj.* Painted by or in the style of Titian; also denoting a colour of the hair favoured by Titian in his pictures, described as a 'bright golden auburn', and more loosely used as an appreciative word for 'red'; freq. in *Comb.*, as ***Titian-haired*** (occas. with small initial).

As examples showing the distinctive colour are given 'Ariadne' and 'The Magdalene' in the National Gallery, London, 'Flora' in the Uffizi Palace, Florence, etc.

1824 BYRON *Juan* XVI. lvi, A special Titian, warranted original. **1841** M. E. LUCY *Diary* 10 Mar. (1983) 66 Lord Byron's favourite, Countess Guiccioli was there; she had.. reddish auburn hair..looking very much like a Titian Magdalene. **1892** S. WATERLOO *Man & Woman* xiii. 97 A setter, with Titian hair and big eyes, which slept on the clover beside him. **1896** J. ASHBY-STERRY *Tale Thames* xix. (1903) 111/1 Three maidens..all with Titian-tinted tresses. **1903** H. JAMES *Ambassadors* III. vii. 86 Standing with his fellow-visitor before one of the splendid Titians. **1904** *Dundee Advertiser* 27 June 8/1 Twenty years ago hair with a reddish tinge was called 'carrots'; now 'Titian-coloured' locks are reckoned a definite beauty. **1904** BENSON *Challoners* v, The girl..had Titian hair in golden glorious profusion. **1923** *Times* 3 May 14/6 (Advt.), Tecla pearls.. are equally becoming whether worn by blondes, brunettes or Titians. **1934** *Times Lit. Suppl.* 25 Oct. 732/2 His Titian-haired wife. **1959** W. BURROUGHS *Naked Lunch* 77 Titian-haired Venetian lads. **1982** 'D. SERAFIN' *Madrid Underground* 103 The tall, titian-haired girl.

Hence **Titi'anic** *a.*, of or belonging to Titian; **Titia'nesque** *a.* [see -ESQUE], in the style of Titian.

1842 TENNYSON *Gard. Dau.* 167 You cannot fail but work in hues to dim The *Titianic Flora. **1801** FUSELI in *Lect. Paint.* ii. (1848) 403 The *Titianesque colour of Hans Holbein. **1864** LOWELL *Fireside Trav.* 49 He said, 'Excuse me, sir', in a very Titianesque manner. **1895** TROTTER *Mrq. Dalhousie* iii. 76 A noble handsome Titianesque head.

titifill, -fyl, var. TITIVIL *Obs.*

titil, -ile, -ill, obs. forms of TITLE, TITTLE.

titillate ('tɪtɪleɪt), *v.* Also 8 titulate, titilate. [f. L. *titillāt-*, ppl. stem of *titillāre* to tickle.]

1. *trans.* To excite or stimulate as by tickling; *esp.* to excite agreeably, gratify (the sense of taste, smell, or touch, the imagination); = TICKLE *v.* 3.

1620 VENNER *Via Recta* vi. 92 It..exciteth the appetite, by corrugating the mouth of the stomacke, and titillating the pallate. **1706** MRS. CENTLIVRE *Love at Venture* I, The elegance of my Fabric has titulated the imagination of many a fine Lady. **1799** SOUTHEY *Snuff* 2 A delicate pinch! oh how it tingles up The titillated nose. **1829** MACAULAY *Misc. Writ.* (1860) I. 291 Not to titillate his palate but to keep up his character for hospitality. **1882** J. PARKER *Apost. Life* I. 74 Your fancy has been titillated.

2. To touch lightly; to irritate slightly; = TICKLE *v.* 4. Also *absol.*

1837 DICKENS *Pickw.* x, The landlady..proceeded to vinegar the forehead, beat the hands, titillate the nose,..of the spinster aunt. **1872** COHEN *Dis. Throat* 7 If the epiglottis be titillated with the tip of the tongue-depressor. **1879** O. W. HOLMES *Motley* xviii, The feathered end of his shaft titillates harmlessly enough.

titillating ('tɪtɪleɪtɪŋ), *ppl. a.* [f. prec. + -ING[2].] That titillates; pleasantly exciting, exhilarating, stimulating.

1712–14 POPE *Rape Lock* v. 84 The pungent grains of titilating dust. **1809–10** COLERIDGE *Friend* (1818) I. 27 A petty titillating sting, from affected point and wilful antithesis. **1902** MISS BROUGHTON in *Times* 11 Nov., An object that has nothing of the..abnormal or the titillating.

¶ **b.** Itching, tingling; craving, hankering.

1858 *Times* 20 Nov. 8/5 [He] sits down with a titillating palate to his plump dainties.

Hence **'titillatingly** *adv.*

1876 R. M. JEPHSON *He would be a Soldier* x, The chevaux-de-frise [moustache] wandered titillatingly about the wretched recruit's face. **1900** MISS BROUGHTON *Foes in Law* xxiii, A fashionable preacher, while he titillatingly lashes smart bonnets.

titillation (tɪtɪ'leɪʃən). Also 5 tytul-, 6 titil-, 7 tittul-, 7–8 titul-. [ad. L. *titillātiōn-em*, n. of action f. *titillāre* to TITILLATE. Cf. F. *titillation* (14th c. in Hatz.-Darm.).

The form with *-ul-* occurs in med.Lat. (11th c.: see Du Cange). The OF. also had this spelling (Godef. *Compl.*).]

1. Excitation or stimulation of the mind or senses; *esp.* pleasing excitement, gratification.

c **1425** *St. Mary of Oignies* II. ii. in *Anglia* VIII. 154/18 Wheþer she felte any titillacione of veynglorye of mennys preisynges. **1491** CAXTON *Vitas Patr.* (W. de W. 1495) I. xxxvi. 37/2 To resyste & wythstonde theyr tytulacyons and cauyllacyons as moche as we maye. **1598** MARSTON *Met. Pygmal., Auth. in Prayse of prec. Poem*, Crowne my head with Bayes, Which..wantonly displayes The Salaminian titilations. **1602** CAMPION *Art Eng. Poesie* ii. 5 The noble Grecians and Romaines..abandoning the childish titillation of riming. **1690** C. NESSE *O. & N. Test.* I. 45 Then arises an inward titillation or contemplative delight. **1762** KAMES *Elem. Crit.* (1763) I. vii. 356 A certain sort of titillation, which is expressed externally by mirthful laughter. **1876** T. HARDY *Ethelberta* II. 29 More or less pervaded by thrills and titillations from games of hazard.

2. A sensation of being tickled; a tingling, an itching.

1621 BURTON *Anat. Mel.* I. i. II. vi, The five senses, of touching, hearing, seeing, smelling, tasting, to which you may add Scaliger's sixth sense of titillation if you please. **1704** J. HARRIS *Lex. Techn.* I, *Titillation*, is that sensation we have in any Part of the Body when tickled. **1816** KIRBY & SP. *Entomol.* xvi. (1818) II. 14 *Thrips Physapus*, the fly that causes us in hot weather such intolerable titillation. **1822–34** *Good's Study Med.* (ed. 4) III. 212 The sense of itching, which may be defined a painful titillation local or general, relieved by rubbing. **1855** BAIN *Senses & Int.* II. iv. §19 (1864) 287 A titillation of the throat is sometimes perceptible.

3. The action of tickling, or touching lightly so as to tickle.

1623 MASSINGER *Bondman* I. ii, These bristles give the gentlest titillations. **1711** SHAFTESB. *Charac.* (1737) II. II. II. ii. 152 Laughter provok'd by Titillation, grows an excessive Pain. **1872** COHEN *Dis. Throat* 25 If it cannot be retracted by titillation or astrigent applications, the exuberant portion must be clipped off.

†**4.** *transf.* A means of titillating. *Obs. rare.*

1606 *Sir G. Goosecappe* II. i. in Bullen *O. Pl.* (1884) III. 40 Tis a pretty kinde of terme new come up in perfuming, which they call a Titillation. **1610** B. JONSON *Alch.* IV. iv, Your Spanish titillation in a gloue [is] The best perfume.

titillative ('tɪtɪleɪtɪv), *a. nonce-wd.* [f. TITILLATE *v.* + -IVE: see -ATIVE.] Tending to tickle, having the power of tickling.

1736 CHESTERF. in *Fog's Jrnl.* No. 377 One Publick Tickler of great Eminency,..whose Titillative Faculty must be allowed to be singly confined to the Ear.

titillator ('tɪtɪleɪtə(r)). [agent-n. in L. form from *titillāre* to tickle: see -OR 2 b.] One who or that which titillates; a tickler.

1823 *New Monthly Mag.* VII. 36 These Protean combinations are the stimulants of fancy, the titillators of the imagination. **1892** *Blackw. Mag.* Sept. 367 Our lives were made miserable by the titillator.

'titillatory, *a.* [f. as prec.: see -ORY[2].] Pertaining to or characterized by titillation.

1762 J. WILKES *N. Briton* No. 7 Doctor Ticklewrist thinks it more his duty..to acquaint the public, that his Titillatory Elixir is a sovereign remedy for the present epidemical distemper. **1862** *Macm. Mag.* Mar. 426 The titillatory powers of his [the fly's] six feet and extended sucker, would be together too much for the skins of reapers.

titimal(e, -malle, var. TITHYMAL *Obs.*

Titius ('tɪʃəs). *Astr.* [The name of J. D. *Titius* (1729–96), German astronomer, who published the law in 1766, six years before Bode.] ***Titius-Bode law***: = *Bode's law* s.v. LAW *sb.*[1] 17 c.

1954 H. ALFVÉN *Origin of Solar System* viii. 128 The so-called Titius-Bode's law gives an empirical formula for the distance of the planets from the sun. **1972** *Nature* 21 Apr. 374/2 The chief facts which have to be explained are..the peculiar regularities in the planetary and satellite spacings, summed up by the Titius-Bode law.

titivate, tittivate ('tɪtɪveɪt), *v. colloq.* Also tidi-, tiddi-. [In early examples *tidi-* or *tiddivate*, perh. from TIDY with a quasi-Latin ending, after *cultivate*.] **1. a.** *trans.* To make small alterations or additions to one's toilet, etc. so as to add to one's attractions; to make smart or spruce; to 'touch up' in the way of adornment, put the finishing touches to. Also with *off, up.*

1805 [implied in TITIVATION]. **1824** in *Spirit Pub. Jrnls.* (1825) 35 Decorated with his white flag in front, and tiddivated up to his elbows in a pair of unblemished.. Holland sleeves. **1827** *Sporting Mag.* XIX. 341 The shot manufacturers want titivating too. **1833** MARRYAT *P. Simple* xxxiv, You'd better make yourself scarce, Peter, while I tidivate myself off a little, according to the rules and regulations..when you are asked to dine with the skipper. **1843** HALIBURTON *Attaché* xxii, I'll arrive in time for dinner, I'll titivate myself up, and down to drawin'-room. **1852** R. S. SURTEES *Sponge's Sp. Tour* xxv, He..saw him titivating his hair and arranging his collar. **1885** MRS. B. M. CROKER *Proper Pride* ix, Helen was calmly titivating herself at the glass. **1893** COUCH *Delectable Duchy* 60 Come here, and let me tittivate you. **1897** *Daily News* 22 Dec. 8/3 It was drawn through the Fair..by eight oxen tidivated with ribbons and flowers.

b. *intr.* for *refl.*

1836–9 DICKENS *Sk. Boz, Charac.* vii, Regular as clock-work—breakfast at nine—dress and tittivate a little. **1859** THACKERAY *Virgin.* xlviii, Whilst you call in your black man, and titivate a bit.

¶ **2.** Used by confusion for TITILLATE *v.* 1.

1915 [see EROTICIZE *v.*]. **1933** DYLAN THOMAS *Let.* Sept. (1966) 23 Even now twelve heartfelt pages are titivating the senses of a Dead Letter superintendent. **1976** *Telegraph-Journal* (Saint John, New Brunswick) 27 Aug. 2/4 What would the exhibition be without the midway, with its sounds, sights and smells to titivate the senses?

Hence **'titivated, 'titt-** *ppl. a.*, **'titivating, 'titt-** *vbl. sb.* and *ppl. a.*; **titi-, titti'vation,** the action of titivating; **'titi-, 'tittivator,** one who titivates; ¶ = TITILLATOR; **'titivatory** *a.* ¶ = TITILLATORY *a.*

1805 *Sporting Mag.* XXV. 187 Affords infinite amusement during the ceremony of titivation. **1831** *Fraser's Mag.* IV. 462 One worthy with a titivated brown wig and a sprigged waistcoat. **1876** E. JENKINS *Blot on Queen's Head* 15 He had a fancy for titivation..and for splendour and display. **1889** W. S. GILBERT *Gondoliers* II, Spend an hour in tittivating. **1895** *Sat. Rev.* 1 June 726/2 People who never.. compare the scene-painter's titivated imitations with the.. originals. **1902** C. G. HARPER *Cambridge, Ely,* etc. 56 The furbishers and titivators of things ancient and worshipful. **1928** GALSWORTHY *Swan Song* I. iv. 29 The papers were like cocktails—titivators mostly of the appetite and the nerves. **1964** E. HUXLEY *Back Street New Worlds* ix. 95 Displaying a shapely but naked midriff, eyelids kohl-ed, hands henna'd, perfumed with eastern essences as titivating to the senses as they were no doubt unsettling to the aldermen. **1975** *Time Out* 24 Jan. 5/2 All the magazine lacks is a titivatory piece on 'what they do in bed'.

†**'titivil.** *Obs.* Forms: 5 Tyti-, Tyty-, Titi-, Tityuillus, -villus, 5–6 Tutiuillus, -villus, Tytyuyllus; 6 titiuil, -ille, -ylle, (Tom Titiuile), titti-, tytyuell(e, tittifill, tyttyfylle, titifyl, 7 -fill. Also 5 Tytyuylly, Tytiuilly. [ad. med.L. *Tuti-*, *Titivillus*, in OF. also *Tutiville*: of unknown origin. Connexion has been suggested with L. *tītivillitium* used once by Plautus, and inferred to mean 'a mere trifle, a bagatelle'.

But in some of the earliest continental instances of the name, it is written *Titinillus*, or *Tutinillus*, and in many it is impossible to say whether the middle consonant is *n* or *u* (*v*). At an early date English usage settled on *u* (later *v* and *f*). Titivillus was evidently in origin a creation of monastic wit, but in its English form the name passed from the Mystery Plays into popular speech as a term of the vernacular, still in use after 1600.]

1. Name for a devil said to collect fragments of words dropped, skipped, or mumbled in the recitation of divine service, and to carry them to hell, to be registered against the offender; hence, a name for a demon or devil in the mystery plays. Also found in France and Germany, 13–15th c.

What generally passes as the earliest mention of the name and function of Titinillus or Titiuillus, occurs in a Latin sermon (Wackernagel *Gesch. der Deut. Litt.* II. 466, note) conjecturally attributed to the Dominican Petrus de Palude, a native of Burgundy and student of Paris, who became Patriarch of Jerusalem, and died in 1342. A very similar and app. equally early account is printed in T. Wright's *Latin Stories* (Percy Soc. 1842), from a Brit. Mus. MS. (Arundel 506, lf. 46) of German origin, of first half of 14th c. Both these stories cite the verse, so often quoted by later writers, 'Fragmina psalmorum Titiuillus colligit horum', the former adding 'Quaque die mille vicibus sarcinat ille' (Every day he fills his bag a thousand times). Titiuillus is also mentioned, 1382–85, by Gower *Vox Clamantis* IV. 864; and in the 15th c., esp. *c* 1450, references become frequent. The earliest Eng. form is app. Lydgate's *Tytyuylly*, or ? *Tytyuyll*, *c* 1420 (sense 2).

c **1450** *Mankind* 468 in *Macro Plays* 18 *Titivillus* [enters, drest like a devil, and with a net in his hand]. Ego sum dominancium dominus, and my name ys Titivillus. *Ibid.* 869 Tytiuilly, þat goth invisibele, hynge hys nette before my eye. *c* **1460** *Lansd. MS. 763* lf. 60 b, Janglers cum japers, nappers, galpers, quoque drawers, Momlers [etc.] Fragmina verborum Tutivillus colligit horum. *c* **1460** *Towneley Myst.* xxx. 249 Mi name is tutiuillus, my horne is blawen;

Fragmina verborum tutiullus colligit horum, Belzabub algorum, belial belium doliorum. *c* **1475** *Donce MS. 104* lf. 112 b, Tutiuillus þa deuyl of hell He wryteþ har names soþe to tel. *c* **1475–1530** *Myrr. our Ladye* I. xx. 54, I am a poure dyuel, and my name ys Tytyuyllus... I muste eche day.. brynge my master a thousande pokes full of faylynges, and of neglygences in syllables and wordes.

2. Hence, a term of reprobation: A bad or vile character, scoundrel, knave, villain. **b.** *esp.* A tattling tell-tale, mischievous tale-bearer.

c **1420** ? LYDG. *Assembly of Gods* 694 What pepyll they were that came to that dysport... Ther were.. Tytyuyllys, tyrauntes, with turmentoures. **1508** KENNEDIE *Flyting w. Dunbar* 513 Cankrit Caym, tryit trowane, Tutiuillus. *c* **1537** *Thersytes* (1820) 67 All the courte of conscience in cockoldshyres, Tynckers and tabberers, typplers, tauerners: Tyttyfylles, tryfullers, turners and trumpers. **1546** J. HEYWOOD *Prov.* (1867) 19 There is no mo such titifyls in England's ground, To holde with the hare, and run with the hounde. *a* **1553** UDALL *Royster D.* I. i. (Arb.) 11 Somewhyles Watkin Waster maketh vs good cheere.. Sometime Tom Titiuile maketh vs a feast.

b. **1523** SKELTON *Garl. Laurel* 642 Theis titiuyllis with taumpinnis wer towchid and tappid. *a* **1529** —— *Col. Cloute* 418 Thus the people telles.. And talkys lyke tytyuelles, Howe ye brake the dedes wylles. *a* **1548** HALL *Chron., Hen. VI* 125 b, The deuill.. did apparell certain catchepoules, and Parasites, commonly called titiuils and tale tellers, to sowe discord and dissencion. *Ibid., Edw. IV* 220 Mistrustyng lest her counsayl should by some titiuille, bee published and opened to her aduersaries. **1561** AWDELAY *Frat. Vacab.* 15 This tittiuell knaue commonly maketh the worst of the best betwene hys Maister and his friende. **1611** COTGR., *Coquette*, a pratling, or proud gossip;.. a cocket, or tatling houswife; a titifill, a flebergebit.

†titiviller. *Obs. rare.* Also 6 *Sc.* tutivillar. [Extended form of prec.] = prec.

1500–20 DUNBAR *Poems* xiv. 67 (S.T.S.) 83 Sa mony rakkettis, sa mony ketche-pillaris, Sic ballis, sic nackettis, and sic tutivillaris. **1581** J. BELL *Haddon's Answ. Osor.* 8 Here our clamorous titiviller taketh occasion to scorne my to to foreward diligence. **1583** STUBBES *Anat. Abus.* K iv b, Such Titivillers, flattering Parasits and glosing Gnatoes.

titlark ('tɪtlɑːk). [f. TIT *sb.*³ + LARK *sb.*¹] A bird of the genus *Anthus* or some allied genus, resembling a lark; a pipit; *esp.* in England, the meadow pipit, *A. pratensis*, also called *tit-pipit*; in U.S., *A. ludovicianus* (American titlark).

1668 CHARLETON *Onomast.* 81 *Alauda Pratensis*, the Tit-Lark. **1676** GREW *Musæum, Anat. Stomach & Guts* viii. 37 The House-Sparrow, Linnet, Titlark, and many more. **1773** G. WHITE *Selborne* xxxix, Titlarks not only sing sweetly as they sit on trees, but also as they play and toy about on the wing. **1872** COUES *N. Amer. Birds* 90 Titlarks.. are terrestrial and more or less gregarious birds, migratory and insectivorous.

b. *slang.* (See quot.)

1799 in *Spirit Pub. Jrnls.* III. 352 Found the beaks and titlarks reading the papers. *Ibid.* 355 Glossary of fashionable or cant Phrases... *Titlarks*, spectators at Bow Street.

title ('taɪt(ə)l), *sb.* Forms: 1 titul; 4 tytel, -e, 4–5 titel, (5 -ell), tityll, 4–6 titil, -ill, (4 titille), 4–7 tytle, 5 titul, -lle, (tetle), 5–6 tytill, -e, 5–7 tytyl, -el(l, ty-, titile, (6 tetel), 8 titule, 4– title; also 6 tyttel, -yll. [ME. a. OF. *title* (12th c. in Godef. *Compl.*):—L. *titulus* superscription, title; in mod.F. *titre*. OE. *titul* was directly from L., as is the later by-form *titule*.

The *i* in OE. and early ME. was prob. short, after L.: see also TITTLE.]

1. †**a.** An inscription placed on or over an object, giving its name or describing it; a legend; sometimes, a placard hung up in a theatre giving the name of the piece, etc. *Obs.*

In earliest use repr. L. *titulus*, the inscription on the Cross.

c **950** *Lindisf. Gosp.* Mark xv. 26, & wæs titul (*vel* tacon *vel* merca) intinges his on awritten cynig iudea. *a* **1300** *Cursor M.* 16685 Abouen his hefd,.. A bord was festen plate, þar-on was þe titel [*Laud* tytle] writen, Thoru þe rede o sir pilate. **1382** WYCLIF *Mark* xv. 26 And the title of his cause was writun, Jhesus of Nazareth, kyng of Jewis. *a* **1400–50** *Alexander* 5071 Þis titill was of twa tongis tane out & grauen. **1535** COVERDALE *Isa.* xix. 19 An aulter.. with this title ther by: Vnto the Lorde. **1592** KYD *Sp. Trag.* IV. iii, Hang up the Title: Our scene is Rhodes. **1611** BIBLE *John* xix. 20 This title then read many of the Iewes:.. and it was written in Hebrewe, and Greeke, and Latine. **1645** EVELYN *Diary* 23 Jan., On the bases of one of whose columns is this odd title: Fl. Eugenius Asellus C.C. Præf. Urbis V.S.I. reparavit.

†**b.** An inscribed pillar, column, tombstone, or the like. (A literalism of transl.) *Obs. rare.*

1388 WYCLIF *Gen.* xxxv. 14 Iacob reiside a title [*gloss.* ether memorial] of stoonys [1382 a stonen signe of worship], in the place where ynne God spak to hym. *Ibid.* 20 Iacob bildide a title [*v.r.* memorial; 1382 a signe of preysing] on the sepulcre of hir. **1609** BIBLE (Douay) *ibid.*

c. A piece of written material introduced into a film or television programme to explain action or represent dialogue; a caption; cf. SUB-TITLE *sb.* 3. Also, a credit title (see CREDIT *sb.* 13 d).

1905 *Billboard* 21 Oct. 42 All our films come with red titles, and show our trade mark. **1909** *Moving Picture World* 10 July 57 We make film titles, 5 feet for 50 cents in any color desired. **1922** [see CREDIT *sb.* 13 d]. **1929** I. MONTAGU tr. *Pudovkin's On Film Technique* III. 45 *Scene I...* A passer-by, coming towards the waggon, pauses... The driver turns to him. Title: '*Is it far to Nakhabin?*' The pedestrian answers, pointing with his hand. **1958** *Punch* 27 Aug. 285/3, I shall remember [this film] as the first exception I have noticed to the rule that amusingly well-designed titles.. mean a good film. **1961** G. MILLERSON *Technique Television Production* xix. 358 Roll titles give us a continuous, unbroken stream of information. **1964** T. RATTIGAN *Heart to Heart* in *Coll. Plays* III. 498 Cut, sound. Start titles... Cue grams.

2. a. The descriptive heading of each section or subdivision of a book (now only in law-books); the formal heading of a legal document; hence, †a part or division of a book, or of a subject (*obs.*).

13.. *Cursor M.* 29530 (Cott.) Þir pointes of cursing haf i .. scortly samen laid, And þar-for sett in titles sere þat þou may lightloker þam here. **1387** TREVISA *Higden* (Rolls) I. 329 For to come to cleer and ful knowleche of þat lond, þese tyteles þat folweþ oponeþ þe way... *De situ Hiberniæ locali. .. De ejus quanto et quali* [etc.]. **1494** FABYAN *Chron.* IV. lxviii. 46 In the firste Chapitre of the .ix. tytle of his Werke called Summa Antonini. **1581** MULCASTER *Positions* xl. (1887) 228 The fifth title of the fifth booke, *De Magistris*. **1714** *Fr. Bk. of Rates* 412 His Majesty judged it proper to comprehend all the said Regulations and the Merchandizes therein expressed under one Title. **1781** GIBBON *Decl. & F.* xvii. II. 62 *note*, The first twenty-eight titles of the eleventh book of the Theodosian Code are filled with the circumstantial regulations on the important subject of tributes. **1847** WHARTON *Law Lex.*, *Title*, a general head, comprising particulars, as in a book.

†**b.** app. Subject, matter. *Obs.*

13.. *Propr. Sanct.* (Vernon MS.) in Herrig's *Archiv* LXXXI. 97/18 Whon Petur saih þat disciple Speke to Ihesu of þat title. *c* **1330** R. BRUNNE *Chron.* (1810) 8 Henry of Huntyngton testimons þis title. Þe kyngdom of Westsex, he sais, it was not litelle.

†**c.** *transf.* A document; a writing, a letter. *Obs.*

c **1330** [see 7 d]. *a* **1400–50** *Alexander* 1044 Þare tuke he tribute þat tyme þe titill recordis. *Ibid.* 3566 His tulkis of þis titill quen þai þe tenour herd, Þan ware þai sory of þa sawes.

3. a. The name of a book, a poem, or other (written) composition; an inscription at the beginning of a book, describing or indicating its subject, contents, or nature, and usually also giving the name of the author, compiler, or editor, the name of the publisher, and the place and date of publication; also = TITLE-PAGE. Also, the designation of a picture or statue.

a **1340** HAMPOLE *Psalter* cxix. 1 Þe tityll of þese fyfeten psalmys is sange of degres. *c* **1430** LYDG. *Min. Poems* (Percy Soc.) 163 Go litel bille withoute title or date. **1560** DAUS tr. *Sleidane's Comm.* 29 He bad that the titles of the Bokes should be read and shewed. **1651** HOBBES *Leviath.* III. xxxiii. 200 In titles of Books, the subject is marked, as often as the writer. **1737** BRACKEN *Farriery Impr.* (1757) II. 137 Bad Books, which are more beholden for their Sale to the Booksellers than to the Author, by reason the first had a better Knack at tossing up a Title. **1863** DICKENS *Lett.* (1880) II. 194, I have found a first-rate title for your book. **1891** C. CREIGHTON *Epidemics in Brit.* I. Pref. 5 The title and contents-table of this volume will show sufficiently its scope.

b. *Bookbinding.* The label or panel on the back of a book giving a brief title (*binder's title*).

1891 in *Cent. Dict.*

c. (*a*) Chiefly in *Publishing*, a book, a magazine, a newspaper; (*b*) a gramophone record.

1895 *Montgomery Ward Catal.* Spring & Summer 62/1 Burt's Library of the World's Best Books... This series comprises titles selected from the standard works of the world's literature. **1908** *Sears, Roebuck Catal.* 200 Columbia P Records. Your own selection of subjects, any of the titles shown on the list. **1935** A. C. BAUGH *Hist. Eng. Lang.* viii. 246 In England over 20,000 titles in English appeared by 1640, ranging all the way from mere pamphlets to massive folios. **1953** J. MORTIMER *Like Men Betrayed* v. 83 I'd never read any titles by Dickens, but we're thinking of bringing out a Victorian Omnibus so I read one. **1958** G. BOATFIELD in P. Gammond *Decca Bk. Jazz* xxiv. 313 A 1938 session with Pete Brown on alto and flamboyant trumpeter Charlie Shavers produced eight titles. **1977** *Times* 10 Sept. 2/5 The *Daily Express*.. Mr Matthews thought 'had lost its way'... Mr Matthews is.. fairly satisfied with Beaverbrook's other titles, the *Sunday Express* and *Evening Standard*. **1979** P. THEROUX *Old Patagonian Express* xix. 301, I.. introduced myself as the author of the three titles I had seen in the book-stores in Tucuman. **1982** *Times* 4 May 15/2 The latest casualty is the IPC romantic weekly for teenage girls, Love Affair... The title is no longer profitable.

4. A descriptive or distinctive appellation; a name, denomination, style.

c **1383** in *Eng. Hist. Rev.* Oct. (1911) 741 Clerkis moun haue temporal godis bi title of almese. **1523** LD. BERNERS *Froiss.* I. cxci. 227 Thus in euery parte was the realme of Fraunce warredde in the tytell of the kynge of Nauer. **1549** LATIMER *3rd Serm. bef. Edw. VI* (Arb.) 76 He was taken and naped in the head wyth the title of an heretique. **1560** DAUS tr. *Sleidane's Comm.* 61 b, Ye are farre vnworthy of the name of Christians. Whiche tytle.. you doe vsurpe to your selues. **1621** SIR G. CHAWORTH in Kempe *Losely MSS.* (1836) 444, I will.. beseech you to accept well of my service, under yᵉ titles of faythfull and obedyent. **1756** C. LUCAS *Ess. Waters* II. 59 Some [are] dignified with the venerable titule of physician. **1774** GOLDSM. *Nat. Hist.* (1862) II. VII. iii. 205 To believe this bird to be the same with that described by Wicquefort, under the title of the Alcatraz. **1840** A. JOLLY *Sunday Serv.* 114 This bears the title of Bethphany or the Manifestation in the house. **1861** PALEY *Æschylus* (ed. 2) *Agam.* 946 *note*, But the title Ζεὺς Τέλειος, the god of marriage .., was perhaps a distinct attribute.

5. a. An appellation attaching to an individual or family in virtue of rank, function, office, or attainment, or the possession of or association with certain lands, etc.; *esp.* an appellation of honour pertaining to a person of high rank; also *transf.* (*colloq.*) a person of title (quot. 1900).

1590 SPENSER *F.Q.* II. vii. 43 Every pillour decked was full deare With crownes, and Diademes, and titles vaine, Which mortall Princes wore. **1610** HOLLAND *Camden's Brit.* (1637) 570 From the death of this young Earle of Warwicke this title lay asleepe. **1613** SHAKS. *Hen. VIII*, III. i. 140, I dare not make my selfe so guiltie, To giue vp willingly that Noble Title Your Master wed me to. **1709** STEELE *Tatler* No. 73 ¶9 A gay young Gentleman, who has lately succeeded to a Title and an Estate. **1761** HUME *Hist. Eng.* xxvii. II. 132 Lord Herbert obtained the title of Earl of Worcester. **1837** LOCKHART *Scott* vii, Alexander Fraser Tytler, afterwards a Judge of the Court of Session by the title of Lord Woodhouselee. **1900** HOWELLS in *Scribner's Mag.* Sept. 375/2 He [Lowell] was sorry that he could not have me meet some titles who.. found pleasure in my books.

b. *Sport.* The championship or supremacy in a contest or competition; the game or contest in which this is decided.

1922 *Encycl. Brit.* XXXII. 566/1 J. J. McDermott won the [golf] open tournament both in 1911 and 1912. Travers defeated Anderson for the amateur title in 1913. **1930** *Amer. Speech* VI. 121 *Title*, championship: Al Brown Signed For Title Battle. **1939** *Encycl. Brit. Bk. of Year* 117/1 Joe Louis reigned as world heavyweight champion and defended his title three times. **1955** R. BANNISTER *First Four Minutes* vi. 59 To win the 100 and 200 metre titles in the World Student Games. **1971** *Rand Daily Mail* 4 Sept. 3/6 The visit of South African squash players to Hobart to compete in the Australian squash titles. **1973** P. EVANS *Bodyguard Man* iv. 33 He goes straight into the Fiorentina first team, in his first year helps to win the League title for his new club.

6. That which justifies or substantiates a claim; a ground of right; hence, an alleged or recognized right. Const. with *inf.*, or *to*, *in*, *of* the thing claimed.

a **1300** *Cursor M.* 20874 (Cott.) His nam es giuen til him o ded, And titel [*Trin.* titul] of his might o mede. **1377** LANGL. *P. Pl.* B. XVIII. 291 We haue no trewe title to hem for þorwgh tresoun were þei dampned. **1412–20** LYDG. *Chron. Troy* IV. 973 Oure comynge hider,.. Had no grounde founded on resoun Nor cause roted on no titel of riȝt. **1502** *Ord. Crysten Men* (W. de W. 1506) III. iii. 144 Vagabondes, .. the whiche haue no good tytle for to begge. **1625** BURGES *Pers. Tithes* 36 Hee.. would manifestly declare.. his iust Title to Bedlam. **1718** *Free-thinker* No 12 ¶7 He can have no farther Title to the Esteem of his Fellow-Subjects. **1822** SCOTT *Nigel* Introd. Epist., The.. evidence.. brought forward to prove Sir Philip Francis's title to the Letters of Junius, seemed at first irrefragable. **1827** —— *Surg. Dau.* i, All farther title of interference seemed now ended. **1868** GLADSTONE *Juv. Mundi* Pref. (1869) 11, I have not the same title to expect obedience.

7. *spec. Law.* **a.** Legal right to the possession of property (esp. real property); the evidence of such right; title-deeds.

[**1292** BRITTON II. xvi, Title de fraunc tenement pora hom aver en plusours maneres.] *c* **1420** LYDG. *Siege Thebes* 2005, I shal lette hym,.. That he shal not be title of no bond, Reioysse in Thebes half a foot of londe. *c* **1440** *York Myst.* xxxii. 347 What title has þou þer-to? is it þyne awne free? *c* **1460** FORTESCUE *Abs. & Lim. Mon.* ix. (1885) 130 Off mariages, purchasses, and oþer titles. **1481** *Cov. Leet Bk.* 490 The title to be examyned be ij persones there chosen afore þe lordez. **1552** HULOET, Tytle of the eldest chyld in enheritaunce, *primogenia*. **1583** *Exch. Rolls Scot.* XXI. 575 Andro Murray.. demittit and overgaif his heretable rycht and titill of the kyngis park.. in the kyngis majesties favouris. **1628** COKE *On Litt.* I. 345 b, Euery right is a title, but euery title is not such a right for which an action lieth. **1672** *Cowell's Interpr.*, *Title of Entry*, is, when one is seised of Land in Fee, makes a Feoffment thereof on condition, and the condition is broken; after which the Feoffor hath title to enter into the Land, and may do so at his pleasure. **1765** BLACKSTONE *Comm.* I. iii. 184 Yet while I assert an hereditary, I by no means intend a *jure divino* title to the throne. **1832** AUSTIN *Jurispr.* (1879) II. 1011 Properly speaking the Vendor's title merely consists of the fact by which his right was acquired. **1858** LD. ST. LEONARDS *Handybk. Prop. Law* v. 29 Where difficulties arise in making out a good title, you should not take possession of the estate until every obstacle is removed.

†**b.** *in title*, of a benefice: (Held) as one's proper cure; opposed to *in commendam* (see COMMENDAM). *Obs.*

1579 *Reg. Privy Council Scot.* III. 177 Upoun the vacance of ony prelacie the kirkis thairof salbe disponit to qualifiit ministeris in titill. **1658** BRAMHALL *Consecr. Bps.* viii. 186 It may be objected, that he held all these Bishopricks as a Commendatory, not in Title.

†**c.** An assertion of right; a claim. *Obs.*

1534 WHITINTON *Tullyes Offices* I. (1540) 17 It may be vnderstande that no warre is iust, except that which after iust tytle demaunded is done, or els it be denounced or proclaymed before. **1685** WOOD *Life* 12 Aug. (O.H.S.) III. 157 The King of England hath now an army.. raised upon defeat of Monmouth, under pretence to keep him in safety against false titles and fanaticks. **1701** SWIFT *Contests Nobles & Com.* Wks. 1755 II. I. 40 An eagerness after employments in the state was looked upon by wise men, as the worst title a man could set up.

†**d.** A title-deed. *Obs. rare.*

c **1330** R. BRUNNE *Chron.* (1810) 248 Þei brouht.. þe olde chartres and titles, þat wer in Abbays hand. **1579** TOMSON *Calvin's Serm. Tim.* 140/1 If that man should make a stewes of that house.. and shuld go and make away the titles and writings to depriue the maister of his house.

8. *Eccl.* A certificate of presentment to a benefice, or a guarantee of support, required (in ordinary cases) by the bishop from a candidate for ordination.

1377 LANGL. *P. Pl.* B. XI. 281–3 Þe title þat [ye] take ordres by telleth ȝe ben auaunced;.. For he þat toke ȝow ȝowre tytle shuld take ȝow ȝowre wages. **1530** *Knaresborough Wills* (Surtees) I. 26 He shall have his tytle and singynge geyr boughte at the coste of my sayd wyeffe. **1588** J. UDALL *Demonstr. Discipl.* (Arb.) 24 The ordination that is made without a title, let it be void. **1597** HOOKER *Eccl. Pol.* v. lxxx. §9 Euery man lawfully ordained must bring a Bow which hath two strings, a Title of present Right, and another to prouide for future possibilitie or chance. **1720** WHITE *Monit. Clergy Peterbo.* I. 16 If you retain any Curate, to whom you did not give a Title for Orders. **1845** STEPHEN *Comm. Laws Eng.* (1874) II. 661 By the canon law no person shall be admitted into holy orders without a title. **1860** J. GARDNER *Faiths World* s.v., If a bishop ordain any one without sufficient title, he must keep and maintain the person whom he so ordains with all things necessary until he can prefer him to some ecclesiastical living.

9. *Eccl.* Each of the principal or parish churches in Rome, the incumbents of which are cardinal priests; a cardinal church (CARDINAL *a.* 6).

In L. *titulus.* Bingham (*Antiq.* VII. i. 10) explains the name from the fact that the churches gave a 'title of cure or denomination' to the presbyters who were set over them. See *Catholic Dict.* s.v.

c **1460** *Oseney Reg.* 111 Guale, By the mercy of god, title of Seynte Marteyne preste cardinall, popis legat. **1597** HOOKER *Eccl. Pol.* v. lxxx. §9 The Fathers at the first named oratories and houses of prayer titles. **1642** JER. TAYLOR *Episc.* §43 [He] appointed twenty-five titles or parishes. **1706** tr. *Dupin's Eccl. Hist. 16th C.* II. v. 95 Formerly the Sacraments were administred only in these Titles (i.e. Churches so called) and those that presided in them were called Cardinals (if we believe Paurinius) because they were the chief and the principal of those that resided upon these Titles. **1833** WADDINGTON *Hist. Ch.* xxiii. 509 Even the Titles of the Cardinals, abandoned by those who derived their dignities from them, were left without roof, or gates, or walls. **1854** CDL. WISEMAN *Fabiola* (1855) 186 'He distributed the titles'; that is, he divided Rome into parishes, to the churches of which he gave the name of 'title'.

10. *Assaying*, etc. The expression in carats of the degree of purity of gold (= F. *titre*).

1873 E. SPON *Workshop Receipts* Ser. I. 364/1 Jewellers solder with gold of a lower title than the article to be soldered. **1879** F. VORS *Bibelots & Curios* 58 Carat..is only an imaginary weight; the whole mass is divided into twenty-four equal parts, and as many as there are of these that are of pure gold constitute the *title* of the alloy.

11. *attrib.* and *Comb.*, as ***title-leaf***, ***-plate***, ***-scroll***, ***-trouble***; ***title-mad*** adj.; obj. and obj. gen., as ***title-holder***, ***-hunter***, ***-hunting*** sb. and adj., ***-licenser***, ***-registration***, ***-search***, ***-searching***, ***-seeker***, ***-sifter***; **title-banner**, a banner on which a title is inscribed; **title catalogue** *Librarianship* (see quots.); **title entry** *Librarianship*, an entry for a book in a library catalogue made under the title (as opp. under the author); **title-essay**, an essay, usually the first in a volume, giving name to the whole collection; so **title-poem**, **title-story**; **title fight** *Boxing*, a match held to decide the championship; **title-holder**, (*a*) one who holds title-deeds; (*b*) *Sport*, the reigning champion in a particular field; **title insurance** *U.S.*, insurance protecting the owner or mortgagee of real estate against lawsuits arising from defective title; **title letter**, **type**, type of a size and kind used in printing titles; **title-music**, music played during the credits at the beginning of a film or television programme; **title-part**, **-rôle**, the part in a play, etc., from which the title of the piece is taken; **title-piece**, an essay, piece of music, etc., giving its name to the collection of which it forms part; **title-sheet**, the first sheet of a book, one page of which bears the title; **title song**, **-track**, the song or track giving its name to a long-playing record. See also TITLE-DEED, -PAGE.

1880 J. ROSS *Hist. Corea* x. 332 The bearer of the *Title-banner advances forward one step. **1876** C. A. CUTTER in *Public Libraries in U.S.A.* xxvii. 528 **Title-catalogue*, one in which the entries are arranged alphabetically according to some word of the title, especially the first, (a dictionary of titles). **1910** A. E. BOSTWICK *Amer. Public Library* 175 If they [*sc.* entries] are arranged alphabetically by the chief word in the title, it is a title catalogue. **1968** P. QUIGG *Theory of Cataloguing* vi. 63 The *author catalogue* is a catalogue with, in the main, authors' names... The entries will, however, usually include..for certain works..title entries. Added entries for significant titles are usually included..so that..the form of the catalogue should be designated as an *author/title catalogue.* **1875** C. A. CUTTER in *Nation* 4 Mar. 151/1 Especially impressed with the usefulness of *title-entries. **1935** *Library Q.* V. 459 He..had obtained permission to change entries in the university library catalog for publications of corporate bodies from title entry to entry under their names. **1969** P. S. DUNKIN *Cataloging U.S.A.* iii. 46 So much for author entry, title entry, and arbitrary entry and the heading which introduces each. **1902** *Daily Chron.* 7 Feb. 3/4 'Love's Cradle, and Other Papers'. The *title-essay deals with the age of the troubadours. **1951** *Sport* 7 Jan. 14 The forthcoming feather-weight *title fight between champion Ronnie Clayton and veteran Al Phillips. **1973** 'S. HARVESTER' *Corner of Playground* I. viii. 71 She went away, walking on her heels like a boxer after thirteen rounds of a title fight. **1904** *Daily News* 27 May 12 Scotland Yard..has got its eye on some of the bogus *title-holders. **1938** *Encycl. Brit. Bk. of Year* 113/1 Three of the title-holders, Louis (heavy), Lewis (light-heavy), and Armstrong (bantam), are negroes. **1978** H. COOPER *Great Heavyweights* 86 Willie Pastrano, the then world light-heavy titleholder and a boxer of beautiful science. **1797** MRS. M. ROBINSON *Walsingham* II. 203 She was a perpetual *title-hunter. **1893** GOLDW. SMITH *Ess. Quest. Day* 156 Anybody can guess what titles and *title-hunting in colonial society must beget. **1902** C. J. PIDGIN *Stephen Holton* 260 That was a mighty good idea of yours, Mr. Lethbridge—telling me to go to a *title insurance company. **1942** *Federal Reporter* (U.S.) CXXXII. 44 The contention of the appellant is that premiums paid for title insurance are earned when received. **1979** *Arizona Daily Star* 5 Aug. D2/4 The firm has been a division of First American Title for 20 years, offering title insurance and escrow services nationally. **1597** SHAKS. *2 Hen. IV*, I. i. 60 Yea, this mans brow, like to a *Title-leafe, Fore-tels the Nature of a Tragicke Volume. **1936** *Discovery* Dec. 384/2 The booksellers also displayed the title-leaves of new works as advertisements. **1771** LUCKOMBE *Hist. Print.* 225 To those..we will give the name of *Title Letters; considering that [they]..are used in Titles of Books. *Ibid.* 279 As for Four Lines Pica, and Five Lines Pica, they best become the name of Title Letters. **1673** [R. LEIGH] *Transp. Reh.* 26 The gentleman might be advanced to the office of *title-licenser. **1886** W. J. TUCKER *E. Europe* 237 The *title-mad and pocket-filled Jewesses. **1977** *Gramophone* Apr. 1555/3 The opening and closing are of great impact (like the *title-music for one of the more dramatic of those films). **1898** G. B. SHAW in *Sat. Review* 5 Feb. 171/2 Miss Irene Vanbrugh, in the *title part..vanquishes it easily and successfully. **1927** F. HARRIS *My Life* III. xix. 334 'Poil de Carotte', (Carrots!) I think it was, with Madame Nau in the title part. **1927** *New Republic* 12 Oct. 211/1 He has possibly scored some moderate hits: in 'Manhattan Mary', 'Broadway', 'The Five Step'.., a curiously constructed sob-song called 'Memories', and the *title-piece. **1936** in A. Huxley *Olive Tree* (dust-jacket), This is one of the best collections of essays that Mr. Huxley has ever made. The title-piece is a completely new departure in technique. **1968** ROBERTS & MOORE in D. H. Lawrence *Phoenix II* p. xii, 'The Gentleman from San Francisco' appeared as the title-piece of a collection of Bunin's stories. **1762–71** H. WALPOLE *Vertue's Anecd. Paint.* (1786) III. 107 The *title-plate to a history of Oxford designed by him, and engraved by White in 1674. **1893** *Dict. Nat. Biog.* XXXIII. 440 The *title-poem..is followed by smaller pieces. **1971** A. AXELROD et al. *Land Transfer & Finance* 693 Patton has been a strong proponent of *title registration. **1886** *Boston* (Mass.) *Globe* 15 Aug., A grand production of 'The Gladiator', with that talented young tragedian..in the heroic *title role. **1900** *Westm. Gaz.* 30 July 10/1 Mr. Chatterton revived the play [Byron's 'Manfred'] (in 1863) with Phelps in the title-rôle. **1864** TENNYSON *Aylmer's F.* 656 Heaps of living gold that daily grow, And *title-scrolls and gorgeous heraldries. **1965** *Amer. Bar Assoc. Jrnl.* LI. 1071/1 In the second step the contract is drawn up by the lawyer and he handles the closing, but the *title search is conducted by full-time, salaried employees of the title company. **1980** *Daily Tel.* 16 Jan. 23/3 They will ask you to complete a 'title search' on the new property to make sure that all deeds and papers are in order. **1899** G. B. SHAW *Let.* 1 Aug. (1972) II. 95 After much *title-searching, I have resolved to give that play..the ugly but arresting name 'Captain Brassbound's Conversion'. **1971** A. AXELROD et al. *Land Transfer & Finance* 499 This loss of title searching and examination illustrates the vulnerability of lawyers in private practice to competition from specialized high volume businesses and professions. **1771** LUCKOMBE *Hist. Print.* 392 The Signature of the *Title-sheet, viz. great A;..we put Little a to the first sheet after the Title sheet. **1615** J. STEPHENS *Ess. & Charac., Informer*, Let him be a *tytle-sifter and he will examine lands as if they had committed high treason. **1961** *New Musical Express* 6 Jan. 4/2 *Am I that easy to forget*..is the *title song of a soft-sung album by Debbie Reynolds. **1970** *Melody Maker* 21 Feb. 21/3 It's hard to believe that the same man who could write and play the extraordinary title track could also be responsible for 'Spirits' and 'Search'. **1887** *Lit. World* 23 July 229/2 The *title-story, 'Ivan Ilyitch,' alone could be pronounced repulsive. *a* **1619** FLETCHER *Wit without M.* I. i, How bravely now I live,..how free from *title-troubles!

title ('taɪt(ə)l), *v.* Forms: see prec. [f. TITLE *sb.*, or perh. a. OF. *titler* (now *titrer*), ad. L. *titulāre*; from the latter directly came the rarer form TITULE.]

I. †**1.** *trans.* To write, set down, or arrange under titles or headings; to make a list of; to set down in writing; to inscribe, record, chronicle. *Obs.*

1340 HAMPOLE *Pr. Consc.* 9535 Now haf I..Fulfilled þe seven partes of þis boke þat er titeld byfor, to have in mynde. *c* **1430** *Brut* 458 There were many iourneyes done in dyuers partyes of Fraunce and Normandy, which be not titled in this boke. **1459** *Test. Ebor.* (Surtees) II. 227 The chapell, in the which ar titled of olde tyme the Obitts of the auncetors. *c* **1552** THOMAS *Pilgrim* (1861) 44 Some of the selfsame commissioners found of their own wives titled among the rest.

2. To furnish with a title; to give a (specified) title to (a book or other literary composition); also, to inscribe the title on (a book or the like); to write the heading or headings to or in (a manuscript book or account). Cf. ENTITLE *v.* 1.

1387 TREVISA *Higden* (Rolls) III. 351 Helmand seeþ þat Plato usede to title his bookes by names of his maistres. **1387–8** T. USK *Test. Love* II. i. (Skeat) l. 99 This worke have I writte; and to thee, tytled of Loves name, I have it avowed in a maner of sacrifyse. **1570** T. WILSON tr. *Demosthenes* (title-p.) His fower Orations titled expressely & by name against king Philip of Macedonie. **1653** W. RAMESEY *Astrol. Restored* 37 They had but small reason to title that weak piece, *Judicial Astrology Judicially condemned.* **1721** WODROW *Corr.* (1843) II. 600, I wrote to Mr. M'Euen to pack up eight copies for you, and send to Borrowstounness, bound and titled. **1824** MISS FERRIER *Inher.* lvi, It was titled 'Correspondence with Colonel F. Delmour — Private, No. 1'. **1894** R. H. DAVIS *Eng. Cousins* 167 In the Order of the Day these questions now appear numbered and titled.

†**3.** To dedicate (by name); to assign, ascribe.

c **1386** CHAUCER *Pars. T.* ¶820 Thise ordred folk ben specially titled to god. **1390** GOWER *Conf.* II. 84 The gold is titled to the Sonne, The mone of Selver hath his part. **1399** *Rolls of Parlt.* III. 452/1 Reservyng evermore to Hymself that Dignite of his Grace and of his Mercy as it longes to his real Estate, and that no man title that to hym bot atte his owne will. **1584** PEELE *Arraignm. Paris* II. ii, And think queen Juno's name, To whom old shepherds title deeds of fame, Is mighty.

†**4. a.** To inscribe as a title. *Obs. rare.* **b.** To attach as a label. *Obs. rare*$^{-1}$. Cf. TITLE *sb.* 1.

a **1400–50** *Alexander* 5640 And þar was grauyn in þos gomes with grekin letteris, And titild in þe tried names of his twelfe princes. [**1588**: see TITULE *v.*] **1642** MILTON *Apol. Smect.* Wks. 1851 III. 251 By the intrapping autority of great names titl'd to false opinions.

†**5.** = ENTITLE *v.* 4. *Obs.*

13.. *Cursor M.* 22093 (Cott.) Sua sal þe feind him þis Chese him stede o birth iwise, þat best es titeld [*v.rr.* stiglid, stighlid, ordeyned] til his stall. **1633** G. HERBERT *Temple, Offering* ii, Yet one, if good, may title to a number; And single things grow fruitfull by deserts.

II. 6. To designate by a certain name, indicative of relationship, character, office, etc.; to speak of or describe as, term, style, name, call. Cf. ENTITLE *v.* 2.

1590 GREENE *Orl. Fur.* (1599) 30, I scorne to title her with daughters name. **1610** BP. HALL *Apol. Brownists* xxx, The presbyters chose one out of their number in euery citie whom they titled their bishop. *c* **1610** ROWLANDS *Terrible Battell* 43 One builds a house, and titles that his owne, Giues it his name, to keep his name in sound. **1667** MILTON *P.L.* XI. 622 That sober Race of Men, whose lives Religious titl'd them the Sons of God. *a* **1734** NORTH *Lives* (1826) I. 399 These his lordship had..titled..'Impudent Assertions'. **1827** POLLOK *Course T.* II. 19 That little orb..was made for man, And titled Earth. **1864** BRYCE *Holy Rom. Emp.* vi. (1890) 86 Their sovereign titled himself king of the Franks.

b. To endow or dignify with a title of rank; to speak of by a title of dignity.

1746 [see TITLED]. **1760–72** H. BROOKE *Fool of Qual.* (1809) IV. 154 He is titled below his merits; it was for an emperor that nature intended him. **1868** BROWNING *Ring & Bk.* I. 779 How title I the dead, alive once more? **1895** *Outing* (U.S.) XXVI. 362/2 When old Bajee Rao died the British Government refused to title 'Nana Sahib', and decided that the titular dignity had ceased.

titled ('taɪt(ə)ld), *ppl. a.* [f. prec. + -ED[1].] Having or furnished with a title, esp. a title of rank.

1746 FRANCIS tr. *Horace, Epist.* I. i. 82 Yet want a little of the Sum, that buys The titled Honour, and you ne'er shall rise Above the Croud. **1790** MME. D'ARBLAY *Diary* Aug., The titled part of the females were admitted to the Royal table. **1885** *Civilian* 3 Jan. 141/2 The authorities might conveniently adopt and issue some general form of titled Survey Book suitable for use in distillery stations. **1901** J. E. H. THOMSON *Rev. Mod. Crit.*, etc. 19 An untitled Psalm follows a titled one. **1909** *Blackw. Mag.* Jan. 25/2 A younger scion of a titled family.

title-deed ('taɪt(ə)ldiːd). A deed or document containing or constituting evidence of ownership. Also *fig.* (Most common in *pl.*)

a **1768** ERSKINE *Inst. Law Scot.* I. vii. §24 Tutors..ought carefully to preserve the title-deeds of the minor's estate. **1830** PRAED *Poems* (1865) I. 185 Your agent steals your title-deeds. **1855** MACAULAY *Hist. Eng.* III. 393 It was.. desirable that..this titledeed by which the King held his throne and the people their liberties, should be put into a strictly regular form. **1865** KINGSLEY *Herew.* ii, They..got to themselves lands by the title-deed of the sword. **1889** JESSOPP *Coming of Friars* v. 224 He lost all his title deeds, the evidences and charters whereby he held his little estate.

titleless ('taɪt(ə)llɪs), *a.* [f. TITLE *sb.* + -LESS.] Having no title, destitute of a title (in various senses of TITLE *sb.*); untitled.

c **1386** CHAUCER *Manciple's T.* 119 Right so bitwixe a titlelees tirant And an Outlawe or a theef errant The same I seye ther is no difference. **1607** SHAKS. *Cor.* v. i. 13 He was a kinde of Nothing, Titlelesse, Till he had forg'd him-selfe a name a'th'fire Of burning Rome. **1881** *Blackw. Mag.* May 619/1 The titleless condition of her father. **1888** *Vicary's Anat.* App. ii. 121 In the Cofferer's (titleless) Acount, $\frac{29}{?}$, 1 Oct. 1560 to 30 Sept. 1561, Vicary's Annuity is on the back of leaf 7 from end.

'title-page. The page at (or near) the beginning of a book which bears the title. Also *fig.*

a **1613** OVERBURY *Charac., Meere Scholer* Wks. (1856) 89 In a word, he is the index of a man, and the title-page of a scholler,..much in profession, nothing in practice. **1630** *R. Johnson's Kingd. & Commw.* A ij b, Our Title page acknowledges him to be that famous Botero, the Italian. **1651** JER. TAYLOR *Serm. for Year* II. v. 57 Repentance is a great volume of duty; and Godly sorrow is but the frontispiece or title page. **1703** J. TIPPER in *Lett. Lit. Men* (Camden) 307 Upon the Title-page is the Picture of the Queen in copper. **1742** YOUNG *Nt. Th.* VIII. 333 The world's all title-page, there's no contents. **1830** D'ISRAELI *Chas. I*, III. vii. 154 He had insisted..that his name should appear in the title-page.

titler ('taɪtlə(r)). Also 6–7 **tytler**, 7 **titeler**. [app. f. TITLE *sb.* + -ER[1].]

†**1.** One who claims or asserts a legal title. *Obs.*

1594 PARSONS *Confer. Success.* II. Pref. Q iv b, His meaning was..to lay down sincerly what..might iustly be alleaged in fauour or disfauour of euery tytler. **1599** DANIEL *Musophilus* xix, Leuell'd with th' earth, left to forgetfulnesse; Whilst titlers their pretended rights decide. **1613** DANIEL *Hist. Eng.* (1626) 169 John Comyn his cousen German being a Titeler himself. **1634** *Two Noble Kinsmen* v. iii. 83 The two bold Tytlers, at this instant are Hand to hand at it.

2. Trade name for a truncated cone of refined sugar.

1858 SIMMONDS *Dict. Trade, Titlers*, a description of refined sugar. **1859** *Times* 24 Oct. 9/4 Conical loaves of sugar called titlers. **1891** *Ibid.* 9 Oct. 9/3 Titlers, 18s. 9d.; crushed f.o.b., barrels, 20s.

titleship ('taɪt(ə)lʃɪp). *rare.* [f. TITLE *sb.* + -SHIP.] Possession of a title; right of ownership.

1780 S. J. PRATT *Emma Corbett* (ed. 4) I. 154 An impertinent old fellow..who presumes upon a sum of money and a paltry piece of titleship. **1876** G. MEREDITH *Beauch. Career* ii, The pretensions of the town to read things for themselves, documents, titleships, rights and the rest.

titling ('tɪtlɪŋ), *sb.* [f. TIT *sb.*[3] + -LING. Cf. Norw. dial. *titling* a small size of dried stockfish (Aasen), Icel. *titlingr* sparrow: see Biörkman *Indog. Forsch.* XXX. 269.]

†**1.** A small size of stockfish. *Obs.*

1386–7 *Letter Bk. H. Lond.* lf. 212 b, De qualibet centena de alio Stokfissh vocat' Croplyng et Titlyng. **1545** *Rates of Customs* c vj, Stokfish called cropling the last v. li... Stokfysshe called tytling the last l.s. **1660** *Act Chas. II*, c. 4 *Sched. Rates Inwards*, Stockfish *voc.* Cropling, Lubfish, Titling. **1818** SCOTT *Rob Roy* ii, 'Stockfish—Titling—Cropling—Lubfish. You should have noted that they are all, nevertheless, to be entered as titlings.—How many inches long is a titling?'.. 'Eighteen inches, sir'. **1858** SIMMONDS *Dict. Trade*, *Titling*, an old Customs name for stockfish.

2. Name for various small birds. **a.** The hedge-sparrow. (Now only *Sc.* and *north. dial.*) **b.** = TITLARK. **c.** (*rarely*) = TITMOUSE.

1549 *Compl. Scot.* vi. 39 The titlene follouit the goilk, ande gart hyr sing guk guk. **1552** ELYOT, *Curruca*.., a litle byrd, which hatcheth and bryngeth vp cuckow byrdes. It is supposed to be an hedge sparowe, or rather a titlyng. **1611** COTGR., *Argatile*, a kind of titling, or titmouse. **1655** MOUFET & BENNET *Health's Impr.* (1746) 191 The Cuckow ever lays her Egg in the Titling's Nest. **1802** G. MONTAGU *Ornith. Dict.*, Warbler, Hedge,..Provincial. Titling. Dunnock... Commonly called Hedge Sparrow. **1831** *Ibid.* 246 Hedge Chanter... Provincial..Dunnock, Dick-Dunnock, Titling. *Ibid.* 512 Titling. A name for the Meadow Pipit and Hedge Chaunter. **1808** JAMIESON s.v. *Titlene*, When two persons are so intimate that the one obsequiously follows the other, it is said, 'They are as grit as the gowk and the titlene'. **1829** E. ELLIOTT *Vill. Patriarch* IV. vii, Hark, how the titling whistles o'er the road! **1852** F. O. MORRIS *Brit. Birds* II. 166 Rock Pipit. Rock Lark. Sea Lark. Field Lark... Sea Titling. **1882** J. HARDY in *Proc. Berw. Nat. Club* IX. No. 3. 429 He had frequently.. watched young cuckoos while being fed by titlings (*Anthus pratensis*). **1885** SWAINSON *Provinc. Names Birds* 45 Meadow Pipit..also Titling, or Tit.

titling ('taɪt(ə)lɪŋ), *vbl. sb.* [f. TITLE *v.* + -ING[1].] The action of TITLE *v.* †**a.** A writing down under titles or heads; an abstract. *Obs.* **b.** The giving of a title; a naming.

1465 J. PASTON in *P. Lett.* II. 219 He must..see his billes of payment, and take therof a titelyng. **1523** FITZHERB. *Surv.* xix. 34 b, He must begyn at a certayne place..and there to make his tytelynge where he beginneth. **1894** H. GAMLIN *Romney* 148 The titling of the engraving came about this way.

c. The action of providing a film, television programme, or photograph with captions or titles (sense 1 c).

1913 *Moving Picture World* 4 Oct. 25 The perfect picture tells its story without any titles, but as there are very few perfect pictures good titling becomes a necessity. **1958** *Punch* 1 Jan. 80/2 This horrible cliché of TV drama presentation, known to the trade as delayed titling. **1966** *Ibid.* 22 June 922/1 We may have seen an unsuccessful copy [of the Yugoslavian film *Covek Nija Tica*], and certainly the titling wasn't very efficient. **1970** *Amateur Photographer* 11 Mar. 61/1 Positive in the camera comes into its own for titling.

titlist ('taɪtlɪst). *U.S. Sport.* [f. TITLE *sb.* + -IST.] A title-holder or champion.

1924 [see STRING *sb.* 12 c]. **1955** M. REIFER *Dict. New Words* 209/2 *Titlist*, one who has won a title, usually in a sport or game contest. **1973** *Internat. Herald Tribune* 15 June 15/2 Defending titlist Manuel Orantes of Spain joined other top seeds on the sidelines of the German tennis championships. **1976** *Billings* (Montana) *Gaz.* 11 July 7-G/1 Carner, the 1971 titlist, a winner three times on the LPGA tour this year.

titly, variant of TITELY *adv.*

titmal. *local.* A titmouse, esp. the blue titmouse (*Eng. Dial. Dict.*).

'titman. *local U.S.* [f. TIT *sb.*[3]] The smallest pig, etc. of a litter; hence, a man who is stunted physically or mentally; a dwarf, a 'croot'.

1849 THOREAU *Week on Concord, Friday* 401 We titmen are only able To catch the fragments from their table. **1854** —— *Walden, Reading* (1884) 117 We are a race of tit-men, and soar but little higher in our intellectual flights than the columns of the daily paper.

titmouse ('tɪtmaʊs). Pl. **titmice** (-maɪs). Forms: α. 4 **titemose**, 4–6 **titmose**, 5 **tyte-**, **tetmose**, **tytmase**, 6 **tytmus**. β. 6 **tytmouse**, (6–7 **tytti-**, **tittimous(e**, 7–9 **titty-**), 6– **titmouse**. [ME. *titmōse*, f. TIT *sb.*[3] 3 + MOSE *sb.* a titmouse. In the 16th c., when *mose* had long been obsolete as an independent word, and in *titmose* had become stressless (cf. the form *tytmus*), it was interpreted as *mouse*, with pl. *titmice*. The smallness and quick mouse-like movements of the common species probably aided the corruption. *Titty-mouse* was app. a childish or rustic adaptation.]

1. A bird of the genus *Parus* or family *Paridæ*, comprising small active birds, of which numerous species are distributed over the northern hemisphere, several being common in Britain: see 2. (Now commonly shortened to *tit*: see TIT *sb.*[3] 3.)

α. *c* **1325** *Gloss. W. de Bibbesw.* in Wright *Voc.* 165 (Fr.) *Musenge*, a titemose. *c* **1400** LYDG. *Flour Curtesye* 57 The sely wrenne, the titmose also. *c* **1425** *Voc.* in Wr.-Wülcker 640/28 *Nomina auium... Hic frondator*, tytmase. *c* **1440** *Promp. Parv.* 494/2 Tytemose, bryd, *frondator*. *c* **1475** *Pict. Voc.* in Wr.-Wülcker 762/32 *Hec agredula*, a tetmose. *c* **1537** *Thersytes* in *Four O. Pl.* (1848) 82 The tothe of the tytmus. **1570** LEVINS *Manip.* 149/3 Titmose.

β. **1530** PALSGR. 281/2 Tytmouse a byrde, *musangere*. **1573–80** BARET *Alv.* T 271 A Tittimous bird, *fringillago*. **1576** GASCOIGNE *Compl. Philomene* 26 Sometimes I wepe To see Tom Tyttimouse, so much set by. **1606** SYLVESTER *Du Bartas* II. iv. III. *Magnif.* 705 Finch, Linot, Tit-mouse, Wag-tail (Cock & Hen). **1655** MOUFET & BENNET *Health's Impr.* (1746) 191 Titmice are of divers Shapes with us in England. **1688** R. HOLME *Armoury* II. 243/1 The Bird Cole-Mouse..we in our Countrey call Tittimous or Mop. **1796** MORSE *Amer. Geog.* II. 259 A little species of titmouse. **1872** COUES *N. Amer. Birds* 80 The Titmice compose a natural and pretty well defined group.

2. With qualification, denoting various species of *Parus* or of the family *Paridæ*, as

black-cap or **black-headed titmouse**, any species having black feathers on the head, as the COAT-TIT (*Parus ater*), the American CHICKADEE (*P. atricapillus*), or the *marsh-titmouse*; **blue t.**, *P. cæruleus*, also called BLUECAP or NUN; **coal t.**, *P. ater* (see COAL-TIT); **crested t.**, *Parus* (*Lophophanes*) *cristatus*, or any species of the sub-genus *Lophophanes*; **fen t.** = *marsh t.*; **great t.**, *Parus major*, also called OX-EYE; **long-tailed t.**, *Acredula caudata*; **marsh t.**, *Parus palustris*; **penduline t.**, *Ægithalus pendulinus* (see PENDULINE 1).

1609 Great titmouse [see COALMOUSE]. **1611** COTGR., *Mesange à la longue queuë*, the long-tayled Titmouse. **1668** CHARLETON *Onomast.* 90 *Parus Cristatus*, the Crested, or Juniper Titmouse. *Ibid.*, *Parus Palustris*..the Black Cap, or Fen-Titmouse. **1674** RAY *Collect.*, *Eng. Birds* 87 The black-headed Titmouse: *Parus ater*. *Ibid.*, The Marsh Titmouse: *Parus palustris*. *Ibid.* 88 The blew Titmouse: *Parus cæruleus*. **1713** DERHAM *Phys.-Theol.* I. i. (1714) 5 *note*, I made.. Experiments in compressed air,..one with the Great Titmouse, the other with a Sparrow. **1774** G. WHITE *Selborne* xl, The titmouse, which early in February begins to make two quaint notes, like the whetting of a saw, is the marsh titmouse. *Ibid.* xli, The blue titmouse or nun is a great frequenter of houses, and a general devourer. *Ibid.*, The blue, marsh, and great titmice will, in very severe weather, carry away barley and oat straws from the sides of ricks. **1858** KINGSLEY *Misc.*, *Winter-gard.* I. 146 That flock of long-tailed titmice, which were twinging and pecking about the fir-cones.

b. bearded titmouse, a small bird (*Panurus biarmicus*), of doubtful affinity, frequenting reedbeds; also called *reed-pheasant*.

1848 [see *reed-pheasant*, REED *sb.*[1] 14]. **1896** NEWTON *Dict. Birds* 969 The so-called 'Bearded Titmouse',..has habits wholly unlike those of any of the foregoing, and certainly does not belong to the Family *Paridæ*.

3. *fig.* A small, petty, or insignificant person or thing. Also *attrib.*

1596 NASHE *Saffron-Walden* Wks. (Grosart) III. 197 Noddy Nash,..his Apostrophe Sonnet, and tynie titmouse Lenuoy, like a welt at the edge of a garment. **1623** MIDDLETON *More Dissemblers* III. i, You can keep a little tit-mouse page there. **1680** OTWAY *Caius Marius* v. xi, *Nurse.* Wake her? Poor Titmouse. **1691** WOOD *Ath. Oxon.* II. 446 In..Sept. 1658..the Titmouse Prince called Richard was inaugurated to the Protectorate.

Titoism ('tiːtəʊɪz(ə)m). [f. *Tito*, name adopted by Josip Broz (? 1892–1980) premier of Yugoslavia from 1945 + -ISM.] The ideas or policies associated with Marshal Tito; *spec.* a form of communism which concentrates on the national interest without reference to the Soviet Union.

1949 *Economist* 2 July 5/1 During the year which has followed the famous resolution of the Cominform expelling Jugoslavia from its membership, Titoism has become an international phenomenon. **1949** [see TITOIST *sb.* and *a.*]. **1958** F. W. NEAL (*title*) Titoism in action. **1962** [see MAOISM]. **1965** *Listener* 30 Sept. 480/1 Where communism cannot be avoided the best hope is to steer it towards affluence and Titoism. **1973** R. J. ALEXANDER *Latin Amer. Polit. Parties* xx. 397 Titoism was more attractive to some of the Latin American Socialist parties than to the Communists of the area. **1978** *Time* 3 July 7/2 Exactly 30 years after fiercely independent Yugoslavia was expelled from Joseph Stalin's Cominform for what became known as 'Titoism'.

Titoist ('tiːtəʊɪst), *sb.* and *a.* [f. as prec. + -IST.] **A.** *sb.* A follower or adherent of Titoism. **B.** *adj.* Of, pertaining to, or resembling Titoism.

1949 *Newsweek* 15 Aug. 9 Titoism has now infected the Communist Party in the Middle East, a split is developing between Stalinists and Titoists in Beirut. **1949** *N.Y. Times* 30 Oct. I. 17/1 The delegation denied any intention of starting a Titoist 'movement' in Italy. **1951** *Round Table* CLXIII. 247 (*heading*) The Titoist schism. **1954** KOESTLER *Invisible Writing* ii. 21 These [*sc.* communist cells] are living, pulsating units..susceptible to various diseases—to the Titoist virus, to bourgeois infection or Trotskyist cancer. *Ibid.* xiv. 155 Every Communist who had lived in the Soviet Union for some length of time, returned to his country as a Titoist at heart. **1961** *Listener* 9 Nov. 754/1 This aspect of Titoist reforms looms large in official literature. **1971** 'P. KAVANAGH' *Triumph of Evil* iii. 25 Dorn, a Croat, had spent the war years with Ante Pavelic, killing Serbs and Titoist partisans. **1977** *Time* 27 June 12/3 My son recently wrote to me that he is a liberal conservative. I replied, 'In Yugoslavia, that means a Titoist.'

Titoite ('tiːtəʊaɪt), *sb.* (and *a.*) [f. as prec. + -ITE[1].] = TITOIST *sb.* Also *attrib.* or as *adj.* Usu. with derog. implication.

1955 H. HODGKINSON *Doubletalk* 129 Soviet writers have not thought fit to elevate Tito's heresy to the rank of an 'ism'... He and his colleagues were..referred to abusively as Titoites. **1961** *Spectator* 9 June 829 He was..not even a Titoite or fellow-traveller. **1973** R. J. ALEXANDER *Latin Amer. Political Parties* xx. 396 (*heading*) The Titoite heresy. *Ibid.*, In the Communist-controlled countries of Eastern Europe, the Titoite dissidence had considerable support.

‖**titoki** (tiː'tɔki). [Native Maori name.] A New Zealand tree, *Alectryon excelsum*, N.O. *Sapindaceæ*, producing tough, crooked timber, and bearing panicles of reddish flowers, with leaves like those of the ash. Also called New Zealand Oak and New Zealand Ash. Also *attrib.*

1845 E. J. WAKEFIELD *Adv. in N.Z.* II. xii. 317 The berry of the titoki tree might also be turned to account. **1872** DOMETT *Ranolf* xvi. 253 The youth, with hands beneath his head, Against a great titoki's base.

titrate ('tɪtreɪt, 'taɪ-), *v. Chem.* [f. F. *titre-r* in same sense (f. *titre* title, qualification, fineness of alloyed gold or silver; in *Chem.*, proportioning of the fixed weight of a reagent which a given volume of a liquid contains in solution): see -ATE[3] 6.] *trans.* To ascertain the amount of a constituent in (a mixture, or (less usually) a compound) by volumetric analysis; i.e. by adding to a solution thereof of known proportion, a suitable reagent of known strength, until a point is reached at which reaction occurs or ceases.

1870 G. E. DAVIS in *Eng. Mech.* 4 Mar. 605/2 In titrating iron solutions, the ferrocyanide is not used. **1872** WATTS *Dict. Chem.* VI. 154 It is easy by means of the latter to titrate sulphuric, oxalic, or any other acid with perfect certainty. **1899** CAGNEY *Jaksch's Clin. Diagn.* i. (ed. 4) 4 Tauszk weighs the blood used, and titrates with tropæolin or litmus.

Hence **ti'tratable** *a.*, capable of being titrated; **'titrated** *ppl. a.* = F. *titré*: see quot.; also **'titrate** *a. rare*, titrated.

1863 *Intell. Observ.* III. 457 Titrated solutions are thus named from the French, and signify their having a definite strength, or power, so that the action of precipitation or otherwise exerted by a given quantity is readily capable of arithmetical expression, and thus indicates the quantity of the substance acted upon. **1881** *Nature* 6 Oct. 552/1 Determination of phosphoric acid by titrated liquors, by M. Perrot. **1885** *Athenæum* 11 July 54/1 Dr. R. Dubois's apparatus for applying anæsthetics composed of titrate mixtures of chloroform and air was described on June 22nd ..before the Academy of Sciences. **1919** *Jrnl. Physiol.* LIII. 189 Duplicate estimations were made..of titratable acidity and ammonia by the method of Folin. **1929** *Amer. Jrnl. Physiol.* LXXXVII. 538 During the experiments no marked change occurred in the titratable acid concentration of the urine. **1963** [see END-POINT 1]. **1973** *Nature* 14 Dec. 425/1 Calculation of the total titratable acid in the collected effluent.

titration (tɪ'treɪʃən). [n. of action f. prec.: see -ATION.] The action or process of titrating; volumetric analysis. Also *attrib.*

1864 WEBSTER, *Titration*, the process of analysis by means of standard solutions. **1868** WATTS *Dict. Chem.* V. 849 *Titration.* See *Analysis, volumetric* (I. 254 [dated 1863: word not used there]). **1872** *Ibid.* VI. 154 Titration of Compound Ethers. **1877** W. THOMSON *Voy. Challenger* I. i. 26 The amount of baryta neutralized is then ascertained by titration. **1899** CAGNEY *Jaksch's Clin. Diagn.* vii. (ed. 4) 377, 80 cc. of the titration fluid, i.e. sulpho-cyanide, was used. **1900** *Jrnl. Soc. Dyers* XXI. 4 The formation..as shewn by Bernthsen by titration, has now been proved by gravimetric analysis.

titrator (taɪ-, tɪ'treɪtə(r)). *Chem.* [f. TITRATE *v.* + -OR.] An apparatus for automatically performing a titration.

1948 *Analytical Chem.* XX. 288/1 The recorder switch should be set so that when the titrator stops finally the potential of the indicator electrode will coincide with the equivalence point potential of the particular titration. **1964** *Oceanogr. & Marine Biol.* II. 103 Many commercially produced titrators would doubtless prove suitable for routine work of moderate accuracy. **1979** *Nature* 25 Jan. p. xx/3 The range, consisting of Karl Fischer, endpoint, *ph* stat and recording titrators, all incorporate a unique photoelectric counting device.

‖**titre, titer** ('tiːtə(r), 'taɪtə(r)). [a. F. *titre*: see TITRATE.] **1.** The fineness of gold or silver; in *Chem.* the strength of a solution as determined by titration; in *Med.*, the concentration of an antibody, as measured by the extent to which it can be diluted before ceasing to give a positive reaction with antigen.

1839 URE *Dict. Arts* 858 The French rule for finding the par of a foreign gold coin,..is to multiply its weight by its standard or titre. **1868** *Chem. News* 13 Mar. 132/1 Provided the 'tinctorial' power, and consequently 'titre' of the ammonia standard be correctly ascertained in terms of the iodine solution, the former may be dispensed with. **1903** *Amer. Chem. Jrnl.* Mar. 188 The solution was kept cooled to 15°. One cc. was removed at intervals (5 cc. in all), and the 'immediate' titer was found to gradually decrease from its original value of 6·4 to 1·2 in about one-half hour, the total active oxygen content..remaining the same. **1918** [see PEPTIDASE]. **1947** *Ann. Rev. Microbiol.* I. 337 If soluble antigen has been released it may be detected in relatively high titer in the supernatant fluid. **1958** *Spectator* 19 Sept.

379/1 The shot I'm going to give you..ought to moderate the symptoms until you've developed a high anti-body titer of your own. **1979** *Jrnl. R. Soc. Arts* CXXVII. 421/1 As the anti-body titres waned they would go through a succession of mid-gestation abortions.

2. (See quots.)

1895 J. LEWKOWITSCH *Chem. Analysis Oils, Fats, Waxes* iv. 100 The temperature will continue to fall, but then it will rise suddenly..and reach a maximum, remaining thereat stationary for some little time before it falls again. This point is called the titer or solidifying point. **1951** KIRK & OTHMER *Encycl. Chem. Technol.* VI. 153 (*heading of table*) Fat or oil... Titer range, °C. **1972** *Materials & Technol.* V. viii. 193 Fats containing fatty acids with a titre above 40°C are known as tallows. (The titre of an oil is the highest temperature reached when the liberated water-insoluble fatty acids are crystallizing under controlled conditions. It is generally taken to be the solidification point of the fatty acids.)

ti-tree ('tiː,triː). The cabbage-tree of New Zealand, *Cordyline*: = TI.

(Also confused with TEA-TREE 2 and erroneously used as a name of species of *Melaleuca*.)

1864 R. ANDERSON *Hawaiian Islands* vii. 134 Then came gigantic ferns, and an extensive tract covered with the *ti* trees. **1881** MRS. C. PRAED *Policy & P.* I. 109 The tender shoots of the young ti-trees. **1890** W. COLENSO in *Trans. New Zeal. Inst.* XXIII. 486 (Morris) In these plains stand a number of cabbage-trees, the ti-trees of the Maori. **1912** J. H. MAIDEN (Dir. Bot. Gdns., Sydney) *Let.* 20 Aug., The name Ti-tree belongs to New Zealand *Cordyline*. For nearly 30 years I have endeavoured by precept and example to stamp out the name Ti-tree for Australian Tea-trees, but the error is full of vitality. **1981** M. GEE *Meg* xiii. 116 A ti-tree prop.

titrimetry (tɪ'trɪmɪtrɪ). *Chem.* [f. F. *titre*: see TITRATE *v.* and -METRY.] = TITRATION. So **titri'metric** *a.*, of or pertaining to titrimetry.

1891 M'GOWAN tr. *E. von Meyer's Hist. Chem.* vi. 365 The application of permanganate of potash to the estimation of iron by Margueritte in 1846, and, more particularly, Bunsen's process with equivalent solutions of iodine and sulphurous acid..are landmarks in the history of 'titrimetry', which soon after this began to rank alongside of gravimetric analysis. **1902** I. K. PHELPS in *Amer. Jrnl. Sc.* Dec. 440 The Titrimetric Estimation of Nitric Acid. **1904** *Ibid.* Mar. 201 A method for the titrimetric estimation of nitric acid or nitrates... It consisted, briefly, in the measurement of the amount of ferrous salt oxidized in the reduction of the nitric acid to nitric oxide by an excess of ferrous sulphate in the presence of hydrochloric acid.

tit-tat-toe: see TIT *sb.*² 3.

titte, obs. f. TIT.

titted, dial. form of TEATED *a.*, having teats.

†**tittee,** obs. var. TITI², a kind of monkey.

1756 P. BROWNE *Jamaica* 489 The Tittee. This creature is very small... The head is bare about the ears and eyes.

†'**titter,** *sb.*¹ *Obs. rare.* [Derivation unascertained.] Some kind of weed found in cornfields; perh. a wild vetch (strangle-tare, tine).

1573 TUSSER *Husb.* (1878) 109 The titters or tine Makes hop to pine. *Ibid.* 113 From wheat go and rake out the titters or tine, If eare be not foorth, it will rise againe fine.

titter ('tɪtə(r)), *sb.*² [f. TITTER *v.*¹] The act of tittering; a stifled laugh, a giggle.

1728 MORGAN *Algiers* II. v. 314, I do not think I ever can forget it: for it so often sets me on the Titter. **1777** MME. D'ARBLAY *Early Diary* 7 Apr., He kept a continual titter among the young ladies. **1874** BURNAND *My Time* xvii. 144 Irrespressible titters among those of the audience most remote from the stage.

b. *transf.* A sound as of tittering; a rustling.

1856 BRYANT *Gladness Nat.* iv, There's a titter of winds in that beechen-tree.

titter, *sb.*³ *slang.* [Of uncertain origin: cf. TIT *sb.*³, TIT *sb.*⁶] A young woman or girl.

1812 J. H. VAUX *Vocab. Flash Lang.* in *Mem.* (1964) 274 *Titter*, a young woman or girl. **1845** E. J. WAKEFIELD *Adventure in N.Z.* I. xi. 319 A chief was called [by whalers] a 'nob'; a slave, a 'doctor'; a woman, a 'heifer'; a girl, a 'titter'. **1882** *Sydney Slang Dict.* 6/2 Nark, to watch, to look after; 'Nark the *titter*', watch the girl. *a* **1890** in Barrère & Leland *Dict. Slang* (1890) II. 356/2 Only a glass of bitter! Only a sandwich mild! Only a stupid titter! Only she's not a child! **1953** *Landfall* (N.Z.) Sept. 179 Boys, she's a larky little titter.

titter ('tɪtə(r)), *v.*¹ [app. echoic: cf. Sw. dial. *tittra* to giggle (Rietz); but perh. related to TITTLE *v.*¹] *intr.* To laugh in a suppressed or covert way (often as a result of nervousness, or in affectation or ridicule); to giggle.

a **1619** FLETCHER *Wit without M.* IV. ii, I could so titter now and laugh. **1657** [see TITTERING *vbl. sb.*]. **1706** PHILLIPS (ed. Kersey), To *Titter*, to giggle, or laugh wantonly. **1748** SMOLLETT *Rod. Rand.* xix, She went away tittering. **1792** A. YOUNG *Trav. France* 117, I observed him several times playing off that small sort of wit, and flippant readiness to titter, which, I suppose, is a part of his character. **1838** DICKENS *Nich. Nick.* xxvii, Upon which Mrs. Nickleby tittered, and Sir Mulberry laughed, and Pyke and Pluck roared. **1864** KNIGHT *Passages Work. Life* I. v. 221 The young women tittered when the old clerk indulged in his established joke.

b. *trans.* To utter or say with suppressed laughter.

1787 *Minor* I. viii. 28 No, it shall never be tittered about as at the last races. **1838** DICKENS *Nich. Nick.* ix, 'Never mind me', tittered Miss Squeers.

Hence **titte'ration** *nonce-wd.*, tittering.

1754 RICHARDSON *Grandison* (1781) V. xliii. 276 The holding up of a straw will throw me into a *titteration*.

titter ('tɪtə(r)), *v.*² Now *dial.* Forms: 5–7 titer, 7 tyter, tytter, tetter, 8–9 titter. [ME. *titer*, implied in *titering*; = ON. *titra* to shake, shiver, OHG. *zittarôn* (G. *zittern*):—OTeut. **titrôjan*; not found outside Teutonic. Cf. TEETER.]

1. *intr.* To move unsteadily, as if about to fall; to totter, reel; to sway to and fro.

c **1374** [see *tittering* below]. *a* **1618** RALEIGH *Seat Govt.* (1651) 60 So would the other [*i.e.* Kings' Crowns] easily tytter were they not fastened on their heads, with the strong chains of Civil Justice and Martial Discipline. **1644** G. PLATTES in *Hartlib's Legacy* (1655) 198 Then the floor of the sellar will rise up, and tetter and swim like a bog-mere. **1798** FRERE & CANNING *Loves Triangles* I. 26 in *Anti-Jacobin* 16 Apr. (1852) 107 Fair sylphish forms.. Wave the gay wreath, and titter as they prance. **1904** *Eng. Dial. Dict.* s.v., (Worc.) Take care, the table titters.

2. *intr.* To see-saw. See also TITTER-TOTTER.

a **1825** FORBY *Voc. E. Anglia*, *Titter*, to ride on each end of a balanced plank. Otherwise '*titter-cum-totter*'. **1854** MISS BAKER *Northpt. Gl.*, *Titter*, to ride on a balanced plank.

Hence **'tittering** *vbl. sb.*², the action of tottering or swaying; unsteady movement; *fig.* hesitation, vacillation; *ppl. a.*² that totters or sways about.

c **1374** CHAUCER *Troylus* II. 1695 (1744) (Campsall MS.) In titeryng and pursuyte and delayes The folk deuyne at waggynge of a stre. **1661** K. W. *Conf. Charac.*, *Juryman Rustick* (1860) 37 Then he gallops a titering pace home. **1739** J. SPENCE *Let.* 23 Dec., in *Academy* 20 Feb. (1875) 191/3 So full of tittering and uncertainty in his carriage.

'titter, *adv.* Now only *north. dial.* Also 3 titer, 4 tyttar, 4–5 -er, 7–8 tider. [Comparative of TITE *adv.*, with shortened vowel; cf. *rather*, *latter*, *elder*, *utter*. Cf. ODa. *tidre* more quickly, sooner, compar. of *tit* (Kalkar IV. 338).]

More quickly; sooner, earlier.

a **1300** *Cursor M.* 22481 (Edin.) Titer sal tai rin on grund þan firslauht dos quen it es stund. **13..** *E.E. Allit. P.* C. 231 He [Jonah] watz no tytter out-tulde þat tempest ne sessed. *c* **1460** *Towneley Myst.* viii. 293 Go, say to hym we wyll not grefe, Bot thay shall neuer the tytter gang. **1674** RAY *N.C. Words* s.v. *Astite*, *Tide* in the North signifies soon, and *tider* or *titter* sooner. 'The tider..you come, the tider you'll go'. **1684** G. MERITON *Yorks. Dial.* 287 (E.D.S.) He had come titter..if he had knawn. **1874** WAUGH *Chimney Corner* (1879) 8 It brings 'em down, titter or latter,—as how strung they are.

b. More readily, more willingly, sooner, rather.

13.. *Cursor M.* 28120 (Cott.) And titter wald i lesyng make þan man my wesche vn-treu to take. **1375** BARBOUR *Bruce* II. 518 þai chesyt tyttar with þaim to ta Angyr and payn, na be þaim fra. *c* **1440** *Alphabet of Tales* 428 He grauntyd vnto þaim..at he wulde furste tytter take þe charge of þe empyre rather þan þe wurschup þeroff. **1724** in *Ramsay's Tea-t. Misc.* (1733) I. 63, I had titter die than live wi' him a year. **1807** R. ANDERSON *Cumberld. Ball.*, *Aul Hollow Tree* v, Far titter than wear them, She'd burn them or tear them. **1855** ROBINSON *Whitby Gloss.* s.v., 'I would titter go than stay'.

c. ellipt. ***the titter up***, the one that is up sooner or first of two. *north. dial.*

1787 GROSE *Provinc. Gloss.* s.v., *Tider up caw*, let him that is up first call the others. **1790** MRS. WHEELER *Westmld. Dial.* (1821) 112 We set dawn that titter up sud coe tudder up neisht mornin. **1876** *Whitby Gloss.* s.v., 'T' titter up t' sprunt mun ower [= hover] a bit': the first up the hill must wait awhile.

titter, dial. form of TETTER.

titterer¹ ('tɪtərə(r)). [f. TITTER *v.*¹ + -ER¹.] One who titters or laughs restraindedly; a giggler.

1828 *Craven Gloss.*, *Titterer*, a laugher. **1866** GEO. ELIOT *F. Holt* iv, He was too shortsighted to notice those who tittered at him—too absent from the world of small facts and petty impulses in which titterers live.

†**titterer**², obs. variant of TITTLER¹, a tatler.

1377 LANGL. *P. Pl.* B. xx. 297 And made pees porter to pynne þe ȝates Of alle taletellers and tyterers [*v.rr.* titeleris, tutelers; C. XXIII. 299 titereres, *v.r.* titeris] in ydel.

'tittering, *vbl. sb.*¹ [f. TITTER *v.*¹ + -ING¹.] The action of TITTER *v.*¹; giggling.

1657 THORNLEY tr. *Longus' Daphnis & Chloe* 129 The winking, nodding, laughing and tittering that was between them. **1759** DILWORTH *Pope* 124 This story..was the cause of so much tittering, wherever her ladyship went. **1833** D. MACMILLAN in Hughes *Mem.* iii. (1882) 50 The everlasting tittering and smirking is loathsome.

'tittering, *ppl. a.*¹ [f. as prec. + -ING².] That titters; giggling, laughing with suppressed mirth; characterized by such laughter.

1748 SMOLLETT *Rod. Rand.* lv, A whisper circulated at our expence..accompanied with many..tittering observations. **1802** MAR. EDGEWORTH *Moral T.* (1816) I. viii. 62 Young tittering ladies. **1879** SALA *Paris herself again* (1880) II. xxiii. 338 A group of tattling and tittering..sight-seers.

Hence **'titteringly** *adv.*

1831 *Examiner* 355/1 'The naughty man', as he will be titteringly styled. **1892** G. HAKE *Mem. 80 Years* xxvii. 86 They had to smile titteringly as well as to listen.

tittering, *vbl. sb.*² and *ppl. a.*²: see TITTER *v.*²

titter-totter ('tɪtə'tɒtə(r)), *sb.* (*adv.*) Now *dial.* Also 9 titter-a-tauter, titter-cum-totter, etc.: see *Eng. Dial. Dict.* [Reduplication from stem of TITTER *v.*² or TOTTER *v.*]

1. The pastime of see-saw. Also, a see-saw.

1530 PALSGR. 282/1 Tytter totter, a play for chyldre, *balenchoeres.* **1607** R. C[AREW] tr. *Estienne's World of Wonders* 266 He played with a little boy at titter-totter. **1611** in COTGR. s.v. *Hausse.* **1801** STRUTT *Sports & Past.* IV. i. §21 We may add another pastime well known with us by the younger part of the community, and called Titter-Totter. **1846** WORCESTER, Tetter-totter [erroneously referred to Strutt]. **1887** W. RYE *Norfolk Broads* xi. 95 We..tried quoits, and 'tittem-a-tauter', as the natives call the pastime of see-saw.

†**2.** One who totters or reels. *Obs.*

a **1700** B. E. *Dict. Cant. Crew*, *Titter-totter*, who is upon the Reel, at every jog, or Blast of Wind. **1785** GROSE *Dict. Vulg. Tongue*, *Titter tatter*, one reeling, and ready to fall at the least touch.

B. *adv.* In a tottering manner; unsteadily; also *fig.* hesitatingly, waveringly.

1725 BAILEY *Erasm. Colloq.* 35 Don't stand titter, totter, first standing upon one Foot and then upon another. **1762** CHURCHILL *Ghost* Poems 1767 II. 85 Having, as usual, said his pray'rs, Go titter, totter, to the stairs. **1828** *Craven Gloss.*, *Titter-totter*, in a wavering state, on the balance. **1889** *N.W. Linc. Gloss.* (ed. 2), *Titter-totter*, (1) in a state of unstable equilibrium; (2) in hesitation of mind, or wavering.

Hence **'titter-'totter,** etc. *v.*, *intr.* to see-saw.

a **1825** in FORBY *Voc. E. Anglia.* **1864** in WEBSTER. **1897** *Q. Rev.* Jan. 146 They titter-cum-totter. **1901** *Daily News* 12 Jan. 6/4 How few really know East Anglian dialect... What does 'tittymatauterin' mean?.. It simply means 'see-sawing'. **1907** *Black Cat* June 25 [He] called back to the figure teter-tottering with the bowing of the log it rode.

†**tittery** ('tɪtərɪ), *sb. slang. Obs.* Also 8 titery, (tityre). [app. f. TITTER *v.*² + -Y, lit. unsteady, unstable, tottering.] A slang name for gin.

1725 G. SMITH *Compl. Body Distilling* I. 49 Geneva hath more several and different names and titles, than any other liquor that is sold here: as double Geneva, royal Geneva, celestial Geneva, Tittery..and has gain'd..universal applause. **1730** BAILEY (folio), *Tityre* or *Tittery*, a Nickname given to the Liquor..called Geneva.., prob. because it makes the Drinkers merry, laugh, and titter. **1751** GORDON *Another Cordial* II. 14 A Shop where Titery, Quorum, or Gin (call it by what name you will) is sold.

tittery ('tɪtərɪ), *a.* [f. TITTER *v.*¹ or *sb.*² + -Y¹.] Of laughter, remarks, etc.: having a nervous, tittering quality.

1936 M. MITCHELL *Gone with Wind* xxxv. 591 The tittery cackling laugh which she always found so annoying. **1962** E. O'BRIEN *Lonely Girls* ii. 23 He would have seen me..saying foolish tittery things to amuse the others. **1983** *Financial Times* 15 Sept. 13 After a richly funny beginning the characters and story fracture into a series of fluttery, tittery vignettes.

tittie, variant of TITTY *sb.*¹ and *sb.*³

tittifill, tittivate, var. TITIVIL, TITIVATE.

tittish, dial. form of TETTISH, TEATISH.

1808 in JAMIESON.

tittle ('tɪt(ə)l), *sb.* Forms: 4 titil, -el, 5 ty-, tytylle, -tille, titelle, 5–9 title, 6 tittil, -yl, tytle, tyttle, 6– tittle. [ME. *titel*, *-il*, orig. the same word as TITLE, but with a special sense developed in late L. and Romanic (see below), and retaining the short *i* of L. *titulus*. The spelling *tittle* is found 1535; *title* is occasional after 1600.

For the mediæval and Romanic senses of L. *titulus* akin to Eng. *tittle*, cf. *a* **1286** BALBI *Catholicon*, 'Titulus etiam dicitur nota quæ causa brevitatis apponitur dictionibus'; also *a* **800** *Corpus Chr. L. & Ags. Gloss.* (Hessels 1890) E 242 Epigramma, titulum; 243 Epigramma, abreuiata scriptura; *a* **1200** NECKAM *De Utensilibus* (Wright *Vocab.* 1857, 117) Glosa enim per subbrevitatem et compendiosam per apices [*Fr. gloss* titles] scribi debet. Diez also cites Sp. *tilde*, Cat. *titlla*, Pg. *til*, 'little stroke, accent, esp. the mark over ñ', also Wallachian *titlĕ*, 'the circumflex', and Prov. *titule*, 'the dot over *i*', as representatives of the L. word in the modern Romanic langs. As *apex* was used by the Latin grammarians for the accent or mark over a long vowel, *titulus* and *apex* became to some extent synonymous; hence Wyclif's use of *titil*, *titel*, to render L. *apex*.]

1. A small stroke or point in writing or printing.

a. Orig. rendering L. *apex* 'point, tip', applied in classical L. to any minute point or part of a letter, also to the mark over a long vowel, as *á*, later also to a line indicating an abbreviation. More recently applied also to the Spanish *tilde* or circumflex over *ñ*, formerly to the cedilla under *ç*. By extension, any stroke or tick with a pen.

The literal notion of a point of a letter passed over to that of the smallest point of that which was written or prescribed. This took place already in late Heb. with the word *qōts*, lit. 'thorn, prick', represented in Greek by κεραία 'horn, projecting point', and in L. by *apex*, in Wyclif translated *titil*: see the quots.

1382 WYCLIF *Matt.* v. 18 Til heuen and erthe passe, oon i [*gloss* that is leste lettre], or titil [**1388** o lettir or o titel; *Vulg.* apex], shal nat passe fro the lawe, til alle thingis be don. —— *Luke* xvi. 17 Forsothe it is liȝter heuene and erthe to passe ouer, than o titil [TINDALE (1526), *Geneva*, 1611 title; TIND. (1534), *Great* tytle; COVERD. tittle (*Matt.* v. 18 tyttle),

Rheims tittle] falle fro the lawe. *c* **1440** *Promp. Parv.* 494/2 Tytylle, *titulus, apex.* **1483** *Cath. Angl.* 389/2 A Tytille (*A.* Tityile), *titulus, apex, epigrama.* **1570** LEVINS *Manip.* 124/15 A Tittil, *apex.* **1636** JACKSON *Creed* VIII. xxvii. §3 The words ..answered punctually and identically to every apex or title of S. Matthew's quotation or paraphrase. **1648** GAGE *West Ind.* 216 This letter ç, or c with a tittle under it, is pronounced like s. **1712** F. T. *Shorthand* 4, I in the beginning of a Word is express'd by a small Tittle or touch of the Pen. **1911** W. CAVEN in *Fundamentals* IV. 61 'Tittle', literally little horn or apex, designates the little lines or projections by which Hebrew letters, similar in other respects, differ from each other.

b. The dot over the letter *i*; a punctuation mark; a diacritic point over a letter; any one of the Hebrew and Arabic vowel-points and accents; also, a pip on dice.

1538 ELYOT, *Punctus, seu punctum*, a poynte or tytle. **1552** HULOET, Tytle or prycke in letters, *punctus.* **1556** WITHALS *Dict.* (1568) 64b/1 *Canicula*, is the litle blacke title in the dyse,..as sise, sinke, catre, trey. **1665** HOOKE *Microgr.* 121 The smallest black spot or tittle of Ink. **1666** TILLOTSON *Rule Faith* II. v. Wks. 1742 IV. 648 The transcribing..of such myriads of words, single letters and tittles or stops. **1676** MOXON *Print Lett.* 28 The Stem and Tittle of this j is made like i. **1783** MRS. DELANY in *Life & Corr.* Ser. II. (1862) III. 151 Y[e] person said, 'y[e] D[k] [of Marlborough] puts no tittles upon the i's'. 'O', says y[e] Prince [Eugene], 'it saves his Grace's ink'. **1785** TRUSLER *Mod. Times* III. 92 Only take care to put the tittles to your i's, and the crosses to your t's. **1888** DOUGHTY *Arabia Deserta* II. 43 [He knows] his jots and his titles (the vowel points in their skeleton writing), and he knows nothing else.

†**c.** A name for the (usually) three dots (.·˙), following the letters and contractions, in the alphabet on horn-books, where it is usually followed by *Est Amen*; so that ***tittle est Amen*** came to be used for 'the end or conclusion'. *Obs.*

(See cuts 166–168 in Tuer *Hist. Horn-book* II.)

a **1548** HALL *Chron., Rich. III* 35, I then..began to dispute with my selfe, little considerynge that thus my earnest was turned euen to a tittyl not so good as, estamen. **1594** NASHE *Terrors Night* Wks. (Grosart) III. 251 This is the Tittle est amen of it. **1596** —— *Saffron Walden* G iv b, A per se, con per se, tittle, est, Amen!..why he comes vppon thee (man) with a whole Horn-booke. **1602** *How a Man may chuse gd. Wife* III. i. E ij b, In processe of time I came to & [*printed* e] percee, and com perce, and tittle; and then I got to a, e, i, o, u. **1630** T. JOHNSON *New Bk. New Conceits* A v, In old time they vsed three prickes at the latter end of the Crosse row,..which they caused children to call tittle, tittle, tittle: signifying that as there were three pricks, and those three made but one stop, euen so there were three Persons, and yet but one God.

†**d.** A dot-like anther in a flower. *Obs. rare.*

1578 LYTE *Dodoens* II. xlv. 203 There hange also sixe smal thrommes, or short threds, with litle titles or pointed notes, like as in the Lillies.

2. *fig.* The smallest or a very small part of something; a minute amount. Often in phrase ***jot or tittle*** (from sense 1 a): see JOT *sb.*[1]

[Cf. **1382** in 1 a.] *c* **1400** *Apol. Loll.* 34 So is no man worþi to mak a letter or title of his to go by vnfillid. **1555** W. WATREMAN *Fardle Facions* App. 314, I neither wille penne any thyng other wise..ne adde..any title of myne owne. **1581** J. BELL *Haddon's Answ. Osor.* 41 Images crept into the Church by title and litle. **1610** G. FLETCHER *Christ's Vict.* I. xxxvi, Thy love? he hath no title to a tittle. **1730** T. BOSTON *Mem.* x. (ed. Morrison) 303 This makes me to account the better of these titles of the law, as divine. **1820** SCOTT *Let. to Ld. Montagu* 22 Feb., in *Lockhart*, I owe much more to his father's memory than ever I can pay a tittle of. **1884** F. TEMPLE *Relat. Relig. & Sc.* i. (1885) 9 Every tittle of the evidence is valued.

b. ***to a tittle***, with minute exactness, to the smallest particular, to a T.

1607 BEAUMONT *Woman Hater* III. iii, I'll quote him to a tittle. **1700** BP. PATRICK *Comm. Deut.* xxviii. 53 This was fulfilled to a tittle by Vespasian and his son Titus. **1805** FESSENDEN *Democr.* (1806) II. 81 That I might suit them to a tittle, Have stretch'd the truth—and lied a little. **1855** BROWNING *Fra Lippo Lippi* 26 He's Judas to a tittle, that man is!

Hence †**'tittled** *a. Obs. rare*, marked by tittles or vowel-points; having the Semitic vowel-points inserted, pointed: cf. POINT *v.*[1] 3 c.

1684 N. S. *Crit. Eng. Edit. Bible* iv. 28 There is none of them that make use of Tittl'd Vowels.

tittle ('tɪt(ə)l), *v.*[1] Now *dial.* or *colloq.* Forms: 4–7 **title**, 5 **tytyll**, 6 **tytle**, **tyttle**, 8– **tittle**. [Of obscure origin; hardly known before 1400; app. onomatopœic. In use somewhat earlier than TATTLE, but app. treated as a parallel form of that vb. with lighter vowel expressing lighter sound; cf. the reduplicated TITTLE-TATTLE. Its relation to the earlier TUTEL, TOTEL, in the same sense, is difficult to determine.] *intr.* and *trans.* To speak in a whisper or in a low voice, to whisper; also, to tell or utter by way of tattle or gossip; *esp.* †to whisper in the ear of, to tell (a person) confidentially (*obs.*): cf. TICKLE *v.*[2]

1399 [implied in TITTLER[1]]. *c* **1450** *Mankind* 550, in *Macro Plays* 21, I xall go to hys ere and tytyll þer in. **1525** LD. BERNERS *Froiss.* II. xxiv. 60 They tytled the prince euer in his eare, and entysed hym to haue made warre. *a* **1548** HALL *Chron., Hen. VII* 22 He caused diuerse to inculcate and put in her hed & tyttle in her eare, that the mariage made with Maximilian was of no strength. *c* **1610** SIR J. MELVIL *Mem.* Pref. (1735) 21, I should have..titled in the Queen's ear that her rebellious subjects should have been exemplarily punished. **1887** J. SERVICE *Dr. Duguid* xii. 77 They were a' tittlin' thegether and talkin' in this form.

Hence **'tittling** *vbl. sb.*[1] and *ppl. a.*

13.. *S. Eng. Leg.* (MS. Bodl. 779) in Herrig's *Archiv* LXXXII. 339/169 ȝif þis titlyng come al to þe emperour no man ne may don him non help. **1565–73** COOPER *Thesaurus* s.v. *Argutus*, *Meretrix arguta*, a harlot full of wordes: a titlyng harlot. **1596** DALRYMPLE tr. *Leslie's Hist. Scot.* II. (S.T.S.) I. 134 Ferleg..was steired vpe throuch titling of sum of the courteouris in his eires. **1785** BURNS *Holy Fair* ix, Here sits a raw o' tittlin jades.

tittle ('tɪt(ə)l), *v.*[2] *dial.* Also 9 **tiddle**. [perh. in origin a dial. var. of TICKLE *v.*; also locally confused with TIDDLE *v.* Cf. also L. *titillāre* to tickle; but influence of this is doubtful.] *trans.* and *intr.* = TICKLE *v.* in various senses. Hence **'tittling** *vbl. sb.*[2], tickling; †**'tittler (titler)**, one who or that which tickles, a tickler.

13.. *Gaw. & Gr. Knt.* 1726 Þer he [the fox] watz þreted, & ofte þef called, & ay þe titleres at his tayl, þat tary he ne myȝt. **1579** HAKE *Newes Powles Churchyard* vii. F viij b, The countrey maides that come from far, as straungers to the towne: Whome still the Trottes doe tittle so, that straight all shame layde downe, They yelde them selues as captiues queanes, vnto some whorish caue. *a* **1825** FORBY *Voc. E. Anglia, Tittle, v.* to tickle. **1866** J. G. NALL *Gt. Yarmouth & Lowestoft* 693 A girl says 'I 'ont be tiddled by you nor no one'. **1877** *N.W. Linc. Gloss., Tittling*, tickling. **1881** *Leicestersh. Gloss., Tittle*, v. a., var. pron. of 'tickle'. **1888** J. HARTLEY *Clock Alm.* 8 (E.D.D.) Her nose end's sewer to tittle like mad. **1900** *Daily News* 6 June 6/3 The..vendors of 'tiddlers' sold them quickly—for the 'tiddled' naturally wanted to 'tiddle' others in turn. [See also TIDDLER[2].]

tittle, var. TIDDLE *v.*, to fondle; to trifle.

tittlebat ('tɪt(ə)lbæt). Also **-back**. A variant of STICKLEBACK, of childish origin. Hence **tittle'batian** *a. nonce-wd.*, pertaining to tittlebats.

1820 KEATS & HUNT *K.'s Wks.* (1889) III. 34 They.. follow the fish into cool corners, and say millions of 'My eyes!' at 'tittle-bats'. **1837** DICKENS *Pickw.* i, There sat the man who had..agitated the scientific world with his Theory of Tittlebats. *Ibid.*, He had felt some pride when he presented his Tittlebatian Theory to the world. **1844** THACKERAY *Greenwich Whitebait* Misc. Ess. (1885) 430 A fresh dish of tittlebacks or gudgeons. **1869** H. S. LEIGH *Carols of Cockayne* 120 In this brook that flows lazily by I believe that one tittlebat dwells.

tittler[1] ('tɪtlə(r)). Now *dial.* Forms: 4–5 **titeler**, **tituler**, 5 **titler**, (*Sc.* **titlar**, **tittillar**); 9 *dial.* **tittler**. [f. TITTLE *v.*[1] + -ER[1].] One who 'tittles' or tattles; a whisperer, tell-tale, gossip.

1399 LANGL. *Rich. Redeles* IV. 57 Somme were tituleris and to þe kyng wente, And fformed him of foos þat good ffrendis weren. **14..** Titeleris [see quot. 1377 s.v. TITTERER[2]]. **1463** *Paston Lett.* II. 133 Prevy titlers and flaterers. *c* **1470** HENRYSON *Poems* (S.T.S.) III. 139 (*title*) Aganis haisty credence of titlaris. *Ibid.* 21 The tittillaris [*v.r.* tutelar] so in his eir [*MS.* heir] can [= gan] roun. **1904** *Eng. Dial. Dict.* (Warwicks.), *Tittler*, a babbler, a tell-tale.

tittler[2], a tickler: see TITTLE *v.*[2]

tittle-tattle ('tɪt(ə)l,tæt(ə)l), *sb.* Also 6 **tyttel tattyll**, 6–8 **title(-)tatle**, 7 **tittel tattel**. [A reduplicated compound of TATTLE *sb.*, expressing repeated and alternate action: cf. next.]

1. Talk, chatter, prattle; *esp.* empty or trifling talk about trivial matters, petty gossip.

(In quot. *a* 1529 perh. used advb.)

a **1529** SKELTON *Phyllyp Sparowe* 357, I played with him tyttel tattyll, And fed him with my spattyl, With his byll betwene my lippes. **1542** UDALL *Erasm. Apoph.* 226 Rhymerales..made muche tittle tattle nor would in no wyse lynne pratyng therof. **1573** G. HARVEY *Letter-bk.* (Camden) 106 'Tis but..fond womens title tatle. **1667** PEPYS *Diary* 28 June, After a great deal of tittle-tattle with this honest man, we to bed. **1768** TUCKER *Lt. Nat.* (1834) I. 176 To..be let into all the scandal and tittle tattle of the town. **1820** *Edin. Rev.* XXXIII. 309 The literary tittle-tattle of the age. **1893** LELAND *Mem.* I. 153 Inordinately given to knowing everything about everybody, and to 'tittle-tattle'.

b. with *a* and *pl.* An act or spell of petty talk; an item of small talk or gossip. Now *rare* or *Obs.*

1570 T. WILSON tr. *Demosth.* 47 Every man devising one tittletattle or other, as his owne vaine heade imagines. **1639** N. N. tr. *Du Bosq's Compl. Woman* II. 42, I see many..to give themselves to these tittle tattles of other folks matters. **1699** R. L'ESTRANGE *Erasm. Colloq.* (1711) 127 The Tittle-tattles of the Nuns.

†**2.** A habitual tattler, one given up to gossip; esp. a woman so addicted. *Obs.*

1580 HOLLYBAND *Treas. Fr. Tong, Languarde*, a tittle tattle, a chatting dame. **1611** COTGR., *Babillarde*, a title-tatle; a pratling gossip; a babling houswife; a chatting or chattering Minx. **1710** ADDISON *Tatler* No. 157 ¶3 Your Castanets or impertinent Tittle-Tattles, who have no other Variety in their Discourse but that of talking slower or faster.

3. *attrib.* or as *adj.* Characterized by or addicted to tattling; gossiping.

1719 *Freethinker* No. 150 ¶6 Would not an English-Man be provoked to hear the same Person cry up the Softness, the Politeness, the Copiousness of that Tittle-Tattle Language, and find Fault with the Roughness and Barrenness of his own. **1768** MME. D'ARBLAY *Early Diary* (1889) I. 14 Such a set of tittle-tattle, prittle-prattle visitants! Oh dear! **1780** —— *Diary* May, Bath is as tittle-tattle a town as Lynn. **1866** MRS. GASKELL *Wives & Dau.* xvi, In such a tittle-tattle place as Hollingford.

'tittle-'tattle, *v.* [A varied reduplication of TATTLE *v.*; cf. prec. and LG. *titel-tateln.*] *intr.* To chatter, prate, talk idly; to gossip.

1583 BABINGTON *Commandm.* ix. (1637) 92 Any woman, when she hath met with her gossip, to tittle tattle, to the slander of another. **1611** SHAKS. *Wint. T.* IV. iv. 248. **1691** SOUTHERNE *Sir A. Love* v. i, A good-natur'd, old merry fellow,..who can tittle-tattle and gossip in their families upon an ancient privilege. **1765** BICKERSTAFF *Accomplish'd Maid* I. ii, It does not become servants to be tittle tattling of their masters and mistresses affairs. **1848** THACKERAY *Let.* Oct., I should like to take another sheet and go on tittle-tattling, it drops off almost as fast as talking.

Hence **'tittle-'tattling** *vbl. sb.* and *ppl. a.*; **,tittle-'tattler**, one addicted to tittle-tattle, an idle talker, a gossip.

a **1586** SIDNEY *Arcadia* II. (Sommer) 163 You are ful of your tittle tattling of Cupid. **1600** W. WATSON *Decacordon* (1602) 37 But for anie other secret..they seldome or neuer impart it to these tittle tatlers. **1780** MME. D'ARBLAY *Diary* 6 Dec., His lady—tittle-tattling, monotonous, and tiresome. **1887** SMILES *Life & Labour* 343 It is better even to have a useless hobby than to be a tittle-tatler and a busybody.

tittup ('tɪtəp), *sb.*[1] Chiefly *dial.* Also 8–9 **tit-up**. [app. echoic, from the sound of the horse's feet.]

1. A horse's canter; a hand-gallop; also, a curvet.

1703 E. WARD *Lond. Spy* VI. (1706) 145 Citizens in Crowds..all upon the Tittup, as if he who Rid not a Gallop was to Forfeit his Horse. **1710** —— *Poet's Ramble* 6 With Whip and Spur, he might be beat-up, Into a Canterbury Tit-up. **1868** BROWNING *Ring & Bk.* IV. 322, I..Had held his bridle, walked his managed mule Without a tittup the procession through. **1882** *Lanc. Gloss., Titherup*, a hand-gallop. From the sound. Also called *tit-up*.

†**b.** *transf.* A cantering horse. *Obs.*

1805 in *Essex Herald* 9 Apr. (1901) 8/2 Dianas also of the Chase,..some in riding habit, mounted on titups, others.. in gigs. *c* **1875** [Remembered in use in Westmorland].

2. An impudent or forward woman or girl; a hussy, a minx. [Cf. TIT *sb.*[3] 2.] *dial.*

1762 D. GARRICK *Farmer's Return fr. Lond.* 9 Some Tittups I saw, and they maade me to stare! [**1901** F. E. TAYLOR *Folk-Speech S. Lanc.* (E.D.D.), *Titty-ups*, also ..*titty-haups*, a pert, forward girl.]

3. As *adv.* With a tittup; at a canter.

a **1764** R. LLOYD *Poet. Wks.* (1774) II. 82 Perhaps my muse..Which, slouching in the doggrel lay, Goes tittup all her easy way.

4. ***on the tittup*** (*dial.*), in a state of excitement; mentally upset.

1906 *Westm. Gaz.* 6 Oct. 2/2 He couldn't find it [the wedding ring]... Everything was at a standstill, and we was all on the titup.

†**tittup**, *sb.*[2] *Obs. rare*$^{-1}$. In 6 **titup(p.** [f. vbl. phr. *tit up*, pull up, TIT *v.*[1]] The trigger of a cross-bow.

1536 BELLENDEN *Boece's Cron. Scot.* XI. x. (1541) 163/2 Als sone as ony man maid him to throw this apill out of the hand of the image, the wrying of the samyn drew all the tituppis of the crosbowis [*ed.* 1585 quarrels of the crosse-bowes] vp at anis, & schot at hym y[t] threw ye apill. [*orig.* quam primum quispiam pomum manu tractando loco etiam paulum moueret: expeditæ ballistarum chordę, catapultas in tractantem ingenti vi emitterent.]

tittup ('tɪtəp), *v.* Also **titup**. [Goes with TITTUP *sb.*[1]] *intr.* To walk or go with an up-and-down movement; to walk in an affected manner; to mince or prance in one's gait; of a horse or other animal, to canter, gallop easily; also, to prance; hence of a rider, or one driving a vehicle; of a boat, to toss with abrupt jerky movements. Also *fig.*

1785 in *European Mag.* (1786) IX. 176 Then tittup'd along with a light mincing step, Little Yoffer Van-Sploom—a well known demi-rep. **1844** J. T. HEWLETT *Parsons & W.* xxxix, A hare that came tit-upping by me. **1852** R. S. SURTEES *Sponge's Sp. Tour* li, [He] saw the horsemen titt-up-ing across a grass field. **1862** THACKERAY *Philip* viii, A magnificent horse dancing and tittuping. **1878** STEVENSON *Inland Voy.* 234 The Abstract Bagman tittups past in his spring gig. **1881** E. WARREN *Laughing Eyes* (1890) 26 The little dingy [a boat] tituppped over the swell. **1904** A. GRIFFITHS *50 Yrs. Publ. Serv.* 71, I can see him now tittupping over the heather on his fat grey pony. **1910** E. M. FORSTER *Howard's End* xiv. 121 No one felt uneasy as he titupped along the pavements. **1968** B. HEALEY *Murder without Crime* vii. 126 Like benevolent Mr. Pickwick he tittuped along beside us. **1972** N. FREELING *Long Silence* I. 51 'We're not very happy about art,' Van der Valk tittupped on.

Hence **'tittuping** *vbl. sb.*

1833 *New Monthly Mag.* XXXVIII. 300 The appropriateness of the harmony itself sinks before the tittuping of an arpeggio bass. **1868** *Morn. Star* 30 Jan., For such poetic cantering, such tit-tupping of Pegasus in a rhythmic Rotten Row.

tittuping ('tɪtəpɪŋ), *ppl. a.* [f. prec. + -ING[2].] That tittups; bouncing, cantering, prancing; *transf.*, rollicking, lively; also, unsteady, rickety.

1796 *Campaigns* 1793–4 II. vii. 44 My pen glances off into tittupping strains. **1809** THEO. JONES *Hist. Breckn.* II. 542 The poem concludes in such galloping tittuping rhymes as almost compel the reader to forget the merits the author certainly possesses. **1824** SCOTT *St. Ronan's* xiii, The 'Dear me's' and 'O laa's' of the tittupping misses, and the oaths of the pantalooned or buckskinned beaux. **1895** MRS. B. M. CROKER *Village Tales* (1896) 76 They kept up a steady tittuping canter, raising a cloud of dust.

tittupy (ˈtɪtəpɪ), *a. colloq.* [f. TITTUP *sb.*[1] or *v.* + -Y.] Apt to tittup or tip up; unsteady, shaky.

1798 JANE AUSTEN *Northang. Abb.* ix, Did you ever see such a little tittuppy thing in your life? There is not a sound piece of iron about it. **1865** MISS A. MANNING *Selvaggio* 189 'Shall we have a little sail?' 'Hum—I think not... I think the Petrel a tituppy little thing'. **1881** *Leicestersh. Gloss.*, *Tittupy*, adj. unsteady; shaky; ricketty: often applied to furniture.

titty (ˈtɪtɪ), *sb.*[1] *Sc. colloq.* Also tittie. [perh. infantile pronunciation of *sissie*, sister; ? associated with TIT *sb.*[3]] A sister; a young woman or girl. Cf. KITTY[1].

tittie and billie, sister and brother (cf. BILLY[1] 3); hence ***to be tittie-billie***, to be closely associated as brother and sister, or as brothers or sisters.

1725 RAMSAY *Gentle Sheph.* III. ii, That clattern Madge, my titty. **1790** BURNS *Tam Glen* i, My heart is a-breaking, dear Tittie! Some counsel unto me come len'. **1818** SCOTT *Hrt. Midl.* v, 'Has she not a sister?' 'In troth has she—puir Jeanie Deans..; she was here greeting a wee while syne about her tittie'. **1825** JAMIESON s.v., Tam's a great thief, but Will's tittie-billie wi' him. **1896** J. LUMSDEN *Poems* 18 A band of billies And frisky titties.

ˈtitty, *sb.*[2] [dial. or infantile var. of KITTY[2].] A kitten, a cat; pussy.

1821 CLARE *Vill. Minstr.*, etc. (1823) I. 165 Now she wails o'er Titty's bones With anguish deep. **1828** *Craven Gloss.*, *Titty-pussy*, a cat. *c* **1880** *Northampt. Dial.*, Oh, mother, mother! titty is drinking the milk.

ˈtitty, *sb.*[3] Also **tetty, tittie. 1.** Formerly, a dial. and nursery dim. of TEAT, the breast, esp. the mother's breast. Now *colloq.* or *slang* and also as dim. of TIT *sb.*[6] (chiefly *pl.*): applied both to a nipple (sometimes of a boy) and to a woman's breast including the nipple; ***tough titty***: see TOUGH *a.* 6 d.

1746 *Exmoor Courtship* 376 (E.D.S.) Es wont ha' ma Tetties a grabbled zo. **1825** [see TEAT 1 a]. **1857** DUNGLISON *Med. Lex.*, *Titty, mamma*, nipple. [See *Eng. Dial. Dict.* s.v.] **1922** JOYCE *Ulysses* 738 Yes I think he made them a bit firmer sucking them like that so long he made me thirsty titties he calls them. **1940** C. MCCULLERS *Heart is Lonely Hunter* I. iii. 39 His little titties were like blue raisins on his chest. **1957** J. FRAME *Owls do Cry* vii. 33 She had pink bulges where Daphne had mere tittie dots. **1972** *Screw* 12 June 10/2 Man, those firm nice buttocks and titties filled that bikini to overflowing. **1976** M. MACHLIN *Pipeline* iv. 46 Man, that *is* cold. My titties feel like a pair of Pecos strawberries.

2. *Comb.*, as **titty-bag**, a sweetened object given to a baby to suck; **titty-bottle**, a baby's feeding bottle with teat.

1923 J. MANCHON *Le Slang* 314 *Titty-bag*, un suçon. **1976** A. HILL *Summer's End* x. 147 A titty-bag was a piece of rag with sugar poured inside, then the rag was tied up with string and the sugar-lump stuck into the blarting mouth. **1871** B. BRIERLEY *Cotters of Mossburn* iv. 46 He's suckin' th' sofy bowster i' th' bar an' doesno' know but it's a titty-bottle. **1920** D. H. LAWRENCE *Lost Girl* xi. 280 'Eh, tha can ta'e th' titty-bottle wi' thee,' said the labourer.

titty (ˈtɪtɪ), *a. dial.* and *colloq.* [f. TIT *sb.*[3] + -Y[1].] Diminutive, insignificant.

1884 *Rep. & Trans. Devonshire Assoc.* XVI. 118 A titty piece of cake. **1943** J. W. DAY *Farming Adventure* iii. 41 War Agricultural Committee officials, whom he described as 'titty little bits on motor-bikes—never got their feet wet yet'. **1967** K. GILES *Death & Mr. Prettyman* viii. 156 One of those titty little bikes with a one-horse engine. **1969** E. MCGIRR *Entry of Death* iii. 38 It was a sliver of card... 'This titty little bit of card could be anything.'

Hence in reduplicated form **titty-totty** *a.* (*sb.*) (*dial*).

1893 H. COZENS-HARDY *Broad Norfolk* 56 *Titty totty*, extremely tiny. **1943** J. W. DAY *Farming Adventure* v. 62 He hed a little owd titty-totty boy from Tollesbury as a hand —a furriner! **1970** *Morning Star* 28 Mar. 2/8 It is a titty-totty of a tree, a crab apple, a tree nonetheless.

tittymeg (ˈtɪtɪmɛg). *U.S.* Also 8 **titymagg**, 9 **tittameg, tickomeg; attikimek, attihawmeg.** [From Amer. Indian: in Odjibway *atika-meg*, Menominee *attaikummeeg*, Chippeway *adikumaig*: see quot. 1851.] A whitefish of Canadian and North American lakes, *Coregonus clupeiformis*.

1748 H. ELLIS *Hudson's Bay* 185 Called by the French, White Fish, but by the Indians and English, Titymagg. **1768** WALES in *Phil. Trans.* LX. 127 Fishermen up the river ..brought us down plenty of pyke, mathoy, and tittymeg: these two last being fish peculiar to this country [Churchill River, Hudson's Bay]. **1851** SIR J. RICHARDSON *Arctic Search Exped.* xiv. II. 51 'White-fish', to which the Chippeways..have given the figurative appellation of 'reindeer of the waters', *Adikumaig*. **1879** D'ANVERS tr. *J. Verne's Fur Country* (1890) 21 Countless legions of tittamegs. **1905** A. HAGGARD *Bond of Sympathy* 120 Even attikimek, the whitefish, this year can no longer be captured in nets.

tittyry: see TITYRE-TU.

titubancy (ˈtɪtjʊbənsɪ). *rare.* [ad. rare late L. *titubāntia*, f. *titubāre* to TITUBATE.] The condition of being titubant; unsteadiness, tipsiness.

(This and allied words all more or less affected.)

1800 COLERIDGE *Let. to W. Godwin* 3 Mar., Not that..I felt, after I quitted you, any unpleasantness or titubancy. **1829** T. L. PEACOCK *Misfort. Elphin* xi, That amiable state of semi-intoxication which..sets the tongue..tripping, in the double sense of nimbleness and titubancy.

titubant (ˈtɪtjʊbənt), *a. rare.* [ad. L. *titubānt-em*, pr. pple. of *titubāre* to TITUBATE.] Staggering, reeling, unsteady; *transf.* and *fig.* stammering; rollicking, tipsy; uncertain, hesitating, wavering.

1817 T. L. PEACOCK *Melincourt* v, Sir Oran's mode of progression being very vacillating, indirect, and titubant. **1836** *Fraser's Mag.* XIV. 204 Dryden's..frequently rollicking and titubant progress through the Æneid. **1875** *Anderida* II. iii. 52 His tongue was as titubant as his gait. **1880** F. HALL *Dr. Indoctus* 61 Not the titubant, perplexed, nerveless, and hide-bound English of half-educated, scruple-mongering, provincial pedantry.

Hence **ˈtitubantly** *adv.*, in a titubant manner, stammeringly.

1861 R. F. BURTON *City of Saints* v. 317 The discourse began slowly, word crept titubantly after word.

titubate (ˈtɪtjʊbeɪt), *v. rare.* [f. L. *tibubāt-*, ppl. stem of *titubāre* to stagger. (See note to TITUBANCY.)]

1. *intr.* To stagger, reel, totter, stumble; to rock, roll.

1575 LANEHAM *Let.* (1871) 24 His mare in hiz manage did a littl so titubate, that mooch a doo had hiz manhod to sit in his sadl, & too scape the foyl of a fall. **1715** tr. *Gregory's Astron.* I. (1726) I. 149 At least it [the Sun] ought to titubate or reel as it were, being sometimes attracted more this way, sometimes more that way, according as more Planets happen to come together on the same side. **1854** BADHAM *Halieut.* 530 As neither servants nor links were allowed, it was unpleasant to go titubating home in the dark. **1879** WEBSTER Suppl., *Titubate*, to rock, or roll, as a curved body on a plane.

2. *fig.* To stammer; to falter in speaking.

[Cf. Ovid. *A.A.* I. 598 titubat lingua.]

1623 COCKERAM, *Titubate*, to stammer in speaking. **1656** BLOUNT *Glossogr.*, *Titubate*,..by metaphor to stutter or stammer in speaking. **1820** L. HUNT *Indicator* No. 53 (1822) II. 6 His voice a little titubating with wine.

Hence **ˈtitubating** *ppl. a.*

1653 WATERHOUSE *Apol. Learn.* 29 But what became of this titubating..mountain of snow? **1899** *Allbutt's Syst. Med.* VII. 87 A titubating gait.

titubation (tɪtjʊˈbeɪʃən). *rare.* [ad. L. *titubātiōn-em*, n. of action f. *titubāre* to TITUBATE. So F. *titubation* (16th c. in Godef. *Compl.*).] The action of titubating; staggering, reeling, tottering; unsteadiness in gait or carriage, *spec.* in *Path.*; *fig.* faltering, suspense, perplexity, embarrassment; also, †stammering, stuttering (*obs.*).

1641 R. DEY *Two Looks over Lincolne* 32 Gentle Reader, to avoyd titubations, correct these errors with a pen. **1650** S. CLARKE *Eccl. Hist.*, *Lives Fathers* (1654) 590 He went on [with his Lecture] without the least..hesitation in his voice, or titubation of his tongue. **1710** W. HUME *Sacred Succession* 288 Stretches, or mutterings, or titubations of charity are not to be argued from. **1849** *Blackw. Mag.* LXVI. 106 To follow the titubations of Herr G——'s magic wand, which, in its uncertain route, would skip from Europe to Africa and back again. **1910** *Edin. Rev.* Apr. 442 The aimless and besotted titubations of a drunkard.

‖**titulado** (tituˈlado), *sb. Obs.* [Sp., pa. pple. of *titular* to title; = L. *titulātus*.]

1. A titled Spaniard or Portuguese; a man of title.

1609 TUVILL *Vade-mecum* (1629) 16 Such as be the puffe-past Tituladoe's of these our times. **1622** MABBE tr. *Aleman's Guzman d'Alf.* I. II. v. 138 Any Knight or Titulado. **1659** RUSHW. *Hist. Coll.* I. 77 Attended and served with Grandees and Tituladoes. **1751** *Affecting Narr. of Wager* 143 Accompanied by no less than a Brasilian Titulado.

2. A thing that has only a nominal existence.

1659 *Ant. Land-Mark betw. Prince & People* 15 Meer Tituladoes, Shaddows, or aiery Notions. **1679** V. ALSOP *Melius Inquir.* II. 310 Whilst they deck his Atchievements with Titulado's, useless and cumbersome Regalities,..for thus it has been ever the way of Church-men to sell shadows for substances.

Hence † **tituˈlado** *v. Obs.*, *trans.* to title, entitle; to decorate with a grandiose title.

1663 *Flagellum or O. Cromwell* (1672) 84 Cromwel was.. tituladoed with the Style of Lord Governor of Ireland.

titular (ˈtɪtjʊlə(r)), *a.* and *sb.* [ad. L. type **titulār-is*, f. *titul-us* TITLE: see -AR[1]. Cf. F. *titulaire* (16th c.).]

A. *adj.* **1. a.** That exists or is such only in title or name, as distinct from *real* or *actual*; holding or bearing a title without exercising the functions implied by it; nominal, so-styled. (Cf. NOMINAL *a.* 4.)

titular abbot, one holding the title of abbot from a monastery that no longer exists as a religious community; ***titular bishop***, in R.C. Ch., a bishop deriving his title from an ancient see lost to the control of the Roman pontificate: cf. quot. 1885.

1611 SPEED *Hist. Gt. Brit.* VI. xli. §2. 145 After hee had enioyed a Titular Soueraignty only eighty dayes. **1612** BREREWOOD *Lang. & Relig.* xvi. (1614) 133 Euer since then ..the Church of Rome, hath, and doth still create successiuely, imaginary or titular Patriarchs (without iurisdiction) of Constantinople, Antiochia, Ierusalem, and Alexandria. **1640** YORKE *Union Hon.* 22 Hee was invested tituler King of Sicile and Apulia. **1762–71** H. WALPOLE *Vertue's Anecd. Paint.* (1786) I. 58 Her mother the titular queen of Naples and Jerusalem. **1767** A. BUTLER *Short Acct. Life & Virtues of Mary of Holy Cross* p. xviii, He repeated this Charge..to his Coadjutor and Successor the Right Reverend Benjamin Petre, titular Bishop of Prusa. **1856** FROUDE *Hist. Eng.* (1858) II. viii. 247 Nothing remained of Strongbow's conquests save the shadow of a titular sovereignty. **1885** *Catholic Dict.* 797 His Holiness Leo XIII has..by a recent decision substituted the phrase 'Titular Bishop' for 'Bishop in Partibus Infidelium'. **1907** *Q. Rev.* Jan. 100 His titular successors never once visited their confiscated diocese. **1934** WEBSTER, Titular abbot. **1977** *Church Times* 1 July 14/2 Coventry. Benedictine anniversary... The Titular Abbot of Westminster will preach.

b. With limiting words, as *but*, *mere(ly*, *only*, expressing entire absence of the reality.

1591 G. FLETCHER *Russe Commw.* (Hakl. Soc.) 44 They are but men of a titular dignitie,.. of no power, authoritie, nor credit. **1681–6** J. SCOTT *Chr. Life* (1747) III. 36 To convince us that he is not a mere titular Deity. **1868** FREEMAN *Norm. Conq.* (1877) II. vii. 49 Recent events have abolished even the titular position of the city as the see of a Bishop.

2. Of, pertaining to, consisting of, or denoted by a title of dignity; also, having a title of rank, titled; bearing, or conferring, the appropriate title.

1611 SPEED *Theat. Gt. Brit.* (1614) Pref., Armes of the titular nobles. **1623** HEXAM *Tongue-Combat* 50 You finde them without traine, or pompe, or titular vanities. **1669** PENN (*title*) No Cross, no Crown; or several sober Reasons against Hat-Honour, Titular Respects, You to a Single Person, with the Apparel and Recreations of the Times. *a* **1704** T. BROWN *Praise Poverty* Wks. 1730 I. 97 A vain pride of birth and titular dignity. **1863** KINGLAKE *Crimea* (1876) I. vii. 103 So far as concerns official and titular rank [he] was one of the chief of the Czar's subjects.

3. Of or pertaining to a title or name; of the nature of or constituting a title (in various senses). ***titular character***, title-rôle.

1656 EARL MONM. tr. *Boccalini, Pol. Touchstone* (1674) 269 Upon such a titular occasion as this. **1659** PEARSON *Creed* (1839) 292 By the propriety of the punishment, and the titular inscription, we know what crime was then objected to the immaculate Lamb. **1771** LUCKOMBE *Hist. Print.* 390 They set the first line of a Titular Summary all in Capitals. **1889** *Daily News* 7 June 2/3 Madame Gargano in the titular character appeared to far better advantage than in 'Il Barbiere'.

4. From whom or which a title or name is taken; *spec.* noting the parish churches of Rome from which the titles of the cardinals are derived (see TITLE *sb.* 9); hence *transf.* of a cardinal.

1664 FULLER *Triana & Paduana* in *Wounded Consc.* etc. (1867) 185 As for Bondi, in a large oration he expressed his thankfulness before the company to his titular Saint. *a* **1668** LASSELS *Voy. Italy* (1670) II. 162 [The church of St. Lawrence] is one of the five Patriarchal Churches, and therefore not titular of any Cardinal. **1706** tr. *Dupin's Eccl. Hist. 16th C.* II. v. 93 There are five Patriarchal Churches in Rome, Twenty-eight Titular ones, and Eighteen Diaconal ones. **1745** BUTLER *Lives Saints* 11 May (1759) V. 199 He [St. Cataldus] is titular saint of the cathedral [Tarentum]. **1854** CDL. WISEMAN *Fabiola* (1855) 141 The cardinals, or titular priests, received instructions about the administration of sacraments..during the persecution.

B. *sb.* **1.** *Sc. Law.* In full ***titular of the teinds*** (***tithes***): a layman who became possessed of the title to the tithes of an ecclesiastical benefice at or after the Reformation; a lord of erection.

1613 EARL WIGTON *Let.* in Hunter *Biggar & Ho. Fleming* xxvi. (1862) 337 Purchessing the Titular's consent to the samin did stand me at no less rate than ten thousand poundis Scottis. **1630** *Reg. Mag. Sig. Scot.* 1634. 13/2 Johnne lord Halyruidhous, titular of the personage teyndis of the parochin. **1799** J. ROBERTSON *Agric. Perth* 398 Every land-holder may buy up the tiends affecting his estate at a specific price from the titular, who now holds them. **1838** W. BELL *Dict. Law Scot.* s.v. *Teinds*, At the Reformation, the King.. created the monasteries and priories into temporal lordships, the grantees to which were styled Lords of Erection, or Titulars of the Tithes. **1845** MCCULLOCH *Taxation* II. iv. (1852) 191 The tithes in possession of the titulars or lay impropriators were more rigorously exacted than they had ever been by the clergy. **1894** J. RUSSELL *Reminisc. Yarrow* ix. 219 The Deans of the Chapel Royal, under the Crown, are the titulars of the tiends.

2. a. One who holds a title to an office, benefice, or possession, irrespective of the functions, duties, or rights attaching to it; *spec.* a cleric who bears a title (TITLE *sb.* 8) whether he performs the duties or not; esp. short for *titular bishop*.

1620 BRENT tr. *Sarpi's Counc. Trent* VI. 560 The Titular of Philadelphia, though a Dutch-man, said, that to deny it.. was dangerous, and pernicious to grant it. **1682** T. FLATMAN *Heraclitus Ridens* No. 66 (1713) II. 159 The whiffling Titular of Nova Scotia pretends to say something against our Veracity. **1826** SOUTHEY *Vind. Eccl. Angl.* 204 The candid and urbane Titular says that the poet ought to be dragged down to the solid ground of authentic documents. **1885** *Pall Mall G.* 31 Dec. (Cassell), The small advocate who has become the titular of a portfolio.

b. *transf.* One who has a title or appellation of some kind.

1824 LANDOR *Imag. Conv.*, *Washington & Franklin* Wks. 1846 I. 125/1 Gaming is the vice of those nations..which unite the worst qualities of both conditions [barbarous and civilized]; as for example, the rags and lace of Naples, its lazzaroni and other titulars. **1846** *Ibid.*, *Emp. China & Tsing-Ti* II. 117/1 He employed a humbler observer, known ..by the more ordinary appellation of *Spy*, though the titular is never gazetted. **1828** P. CUNNINGHAM *N.S. Wales* (ed. 3) II. 115 If he inquires his way through Sydney of one of our titulars [a convict with a mark or badge], (even decorated with a C.B. appendage), he runs a risk of having his pocket picked.

3. One who bears a title of rank; a titled person.

1757 *Herald* No. 8 (1758) I. 126 No titular among them will accept..an employment beneath that of ambassador. **1829** LANDOR *Imag. Conv., Penn & Ld. Peterb.* Wks. 1846 I. 521/2 All titulars else must be produced by others; a knight by a knight, a peer by a king, while a gentleman is self-existent.

4. *R.C. Ch.* (See quot. 1885.)

1621 BP. MOUNTAGU *Diatribæ* 496 They now, and the Pagans then, did vse to bestow them vpon the Saint and deity Tutelar and titular of the place. **1885** *Cath. Dict., Patron and Titular of church, place, &c...* The titular is a wider term comprehending the persons of the Trinity, mysteries (*e.g.* Corpus Christi), and saints; the patron of a church can only be a saint or an angel... The feast of the principal titular or patron is a double of the first class with an octave.

titularity (tɪtjʊˈlærɪtɪ). *rare.* [f. prec. + -ITY.] The quality or state of being titular, or merely titular.

1646 SIR T. BROWNE *Pseud. Ep.* VII. xvi. 374 Julius Augustus and Tiberius with great humility or popularity refused the name of Imperator; but their Successors have challenged that title, and retaine the same even in its titularity. **1777** H. WALPOLE *Let. to Mann* 15 May, Your new Prince of Nassau is perfectly ridiculous—a real peer of England [Earl Cowper] to tumble down to a tinsel titularity.

titularly (ˈtɪtjʊləlɪ), *adv.* [f. as prec. + -LY[2].] In respect of title, name, or style; in or by title or name; *esp.* in name only, nominally.

1625 BP. MOUNTAGU *App. Cæsar* II. ii. 116 A Generall Councell; not titularly so, as the Conventicle of Trent; but plenarily true, generall, and lawfull. **1642** J. EATON *Honey-c. Free Justif.* 309 That we are not imaginarily counted, and titularly called righteous. **1700** ASTRY tr. *Saavedra-Faxardo* I. 20 What else..rendred the Emperour Charles really great, as well as titularly so? **1853** LANDOR *Imag. Conv.* Wks. 1876 VI. 566 England is titularly a kingdom. **1905** *Times, Lit. Supp.* 15 Dec. 440/2 Wilkes was court-martialled for wearing a captain's uniform while titularly only a lieutenant.

b. By way of hereditary title (of rank). *rare.*

1756 C. LUCAS *Ess. Waters* III. Ded., You greatly disdain to rely on honors titularly transmitted.

titulary (ˈtɪtjʊlərɪ), *a.* (*sb.*) Now *rare.* [f. L. *titul-us* TITLE + -ARY[1].]

1. = TITULAR *a.* 1, 1 b.

1606 G. W[OODCOCKE] *Lives Emperors* in *Hist. Ivstine* Ll ij, The first action that Adolphus count of Nassau titularie Emperor vndertooke. **1617** MORYSON *Itin.* II. 93 The titulary Earle of Desmond could never after draw 100 men together. **1797** EARL MALMESBURY *Diaries & Corr.* III. 386 The title of King of France..was merely titulary. **1882–3** *Schaff's Encycl. Relig. Knowl.* I. 157 Stephan Evadi Assemani..was titulary archbishop of Apamaea in Syria.

2. = TITULAR *a.* 2.

1603 H. CROSSE *Vertues Commw.* (1878) 21 What is all this worlds pompe, or titulary preferments, if not atchieued by Vertue? **1721** STRYPE *Eccl. Mem.* I. ii. 35 The King seemed to boast much of this titulary honour bestowed upon him so solemnly by the Pope and Cardinals. **1804** EUGENIA DE ACTON *Tale without Title* II. 129 If any man values a titulary distinction.

†**3.** = TITULAR *a.* 3. *Obs.*

a **1618** RALEIGH in Gutch *Coll. Cur.* I. 89 To embrace a vain and titulary conceit of land continuing a name, intimateth Paganism rather then Christianity. **1647** N. BACON *Disc. Govt. Eng.* I. xxxvii. (1739) 56 The trial by Battle..was in criminal matters with sharp Weapons; but in titulary matters with blunt Weapons.

†**4.** = TITULAR *a.* 4. *Obs.*

1664 FULLER *Triana* in *Wounded Consc.*, etc. (1867) 189 You..have abused your titulary Saint, by pretending his relics the immediate cause of your restored sight.

B. *sb.* **a.** One who holds a title to something; = TITULAR *sb.* 2. **b.** One who bears a title of rank; = TITULAR *sb.* 3.

1726 AYLIFFE *Parergon* 190 Persons..deputed for the Celebration of these Masses..were neither Titularies, nor perpetual Curates; but Persons entirely conductitious. **1792** *State Papers* in *Ann. Reg.* 257 False titularies destitute of all canonical appointment. **1824** LANDOR *Imag. Conv., Alfieri & Salomon* Wks. 1846 I. 188/2 Their..influence, and..character place them..above the titularies of our country, be the rank what it may.

titulate, -ation, obs. erron. ff. TITILLATE, etc.

titulation. [Cf. TITULE *v.*] = INTITULATION.

1868 M. PATTISON *Academ. Org.* vi. 238 Those who pass this examination might have any titulation which it might be thought expedient to give them.

titulature (ˈtɪtjʊlətjʊə(r)). *Anc. Hist.* [f. late L. *titulātum*, pa. pple. of *titulāre* to give title to: see -URE.] The set of titles borne by an official; the form of title by which an official is known.

1893 E. G. HARDY in *Classical Rev.* VII. 49/1 It is well known how carefully the proconsulare imperium was omitted in the imperial titulature. **1971** R. BROWNING *Justinian & Theodora* iii. 97 The memory of it [*sc.* the city Justiniana Prima] remained, and its name appeared in the titulature of certain Serbian archbishops down to 1718. **1973** J. BRISCOE *Commentary on Livy Books XXXI–XXXIII* 5 The titulature of the governors of the Spanish provinces is a more complex problem. L[ivy] describes them variously as praetors, propraetors and proconsuls.

titule, *sb.*, rare variant of TITLE *sb.*

titule (ˈtɪtjuːl), *v.* [f. L. *titul-āre* to title: cf. INTITULE.] Occasional variant of TITLE *v.*, esp. in pa. pple. or ppl. adj. **ˈtituled**.

In quot. 1569 app. To set down in writing: cf. TITLE *v.* 1.

1569 ABP. PARKER *Let. to Sir W. Cecil* 3 June (Lansd. MS. 11, lf. 128), Onys at the request of my L. of leycestre,..I tituled to hym my phantasie, from the w[ch] I do not moche disagre at this tyme. **1588** PARKE tr. *Mendoza's Hist. China* 277 He asked..what those letters did signifie that were tituled ouer his head. **1591** NASHE *Prognost.* Wks. (Grosart) II. 155 Diuers selfe conceited fooles..tituling themselues by the names of Martinistes. **1635** HEYWOOD *Hierarch.* VII. 463 This is tituled by the name of Principate. **1655** FULLER *Ch. Hist.* II. ii. §107 A great Council (for so it is tituled) was held at Becanceld by Withred, King of Kent. **1894** *Daily News* 16 June 6/1 The foreign favouritism which was tituled one of the most real and serious grievances of those times.

tituler, obs. f. TITTLER *sb.*[1]

‖**titulus** (ˈtɪtjʊləs). [L.: see TITLE *sb.*] An inscription on or over something; esp. the inscription on the Cross.

1918 *By an Unknown Disciple* xx. 238 He ordered the centurion to have it so inscribed on the Titulus. **1927** A. H. MCNEILE *Introd. N.T.* 10 There was a deep irony in the mockery by the soldiers, and in the *titulus* on the Cross. **1963** *N. & Q.* May 166/2 The best-known type [of 'illustrated' poem] is the inscription-poem used as a *titulus*, carved or painted on tombs or the walls of buildings.

titup: see TITTUP.

tit-warbler: see TIT *sb.*[3] 3 c.

†**tityre-tu** (ˈtɪtɪreɪˈtuː, -rɪtjuː). *Obs.* Also **Titire-Tu, Tytire tu, Tytere-tu, Tittery tu, tittyry.** [From L. *Tītyre tū*, the first words of Virgil's first eclogue, 'Tityre, tu patulæ recubans sub tegmine fagi', adopted as a designation.]

One of an association of well-to-do 'roughs' who infested London streets in the 17th c.

The name 'meant to imply that these blades were men of leisure and fortune, who "lay at ease under their patrimonial beech trees"' (Brewer *Reader's Handbk.*).

1623 J. CHAMBERLAIN *Let. to Sir D. Carleton* 6 Dec., in *Crt. & Times Jas. I* (1848) II. 438 There is a crew or knot of such people..who..have made an association, and taken certain oaths and orders devised among them selves;..having certain nicknames, as Tityre-tu, and such like, for their several fraternities. **1630** J. TAYLOR (Water P.) *Navy Land Ships* Wks. I. 77/2 Roaring boyes, and Rough-hewd Tittery tues. **1648** HERRICK *Hesper., New-Yeares Gift to Sir S. Steward*, No newes of navies burnt at seas; No noise of late spawn'd tittyries. **1693** SOUTHERNE *Maid's Last Prayer* II. ii, I remember your Dammee-Boyes, your Swashes, your Tuquoques and your Titire-Tues. **1849** MACAULAY *Hist. Eng.* iii. I. 361 *note*, It may be suspected that some of the Tityre Tus, like good cavaliers, broke Milton's windows shortly after the Restoration.

Tityrus (ˈtɪtɪrəs). *Myth.* [L. *Tītyrus*, name of a shepherd, a. Gr. *Τίτυρος*, said to be Doric for *σάτυρος* satyr.] A fictitious monster supposed to be bred between a sheep and a goat.

1610 GUILLIM *Heraldry* III. xxv. (1660) 255 Like as the Tytirus is ingendred between a Sheep and a Buck Goat, as Upton noteth. **1710** W. KING *Heathen Gods & Heroes* xxvii. (1722) 134 Several cruel Dæmons, Satyrs, Sileni and Tityri, us'd to accompany him [Bacchus] with Cymbals and huge Exclamations. [**1906** VINYCOMB *Fict. & Symb. Creatures in Art* 217 In Guillim's 'Display',..said to be a bigenerous beast, of unkindly procreation, engendered between a goat and a ram, like the Tityrus, the offspring of a sheep and goat, as noted by Upton.]

‖**ti-tzu** (ˈdiːdzə). *Mus.* Also **Ti tzu.** [Chinese *dízi.*] A type of Chinese bamboo flute (see quots.).

1874 *Jrnl. N. China Branch R. Asiatic Soc.* VIII. 109 The modern *Ti-tzu*..has seven holes besides the embouchure. **1917** *Encycl. Sinica* 389/1 The *Ti tzŭ* is a very popular flute, about 26 inches long, formerly with 11 finger-holes, one of which was covered with membrane, but now having 6 finger-holes and a 7th covered with membrane. **1954** *Grove's Dict. Mus.* (ed. 5) II. 235/2 *Ti* (to-day usually *ti-tzu*), a transverse flute, the common or popular flute of China... A bamboo tube..pierced with 8 holes (6 fingerholes, 1 blown across and 1 covered with a paper membrane). **1975** C. P. MACKERRAS *Chinese Theatre in Mod. Times* 16 The *K'un-ch'ü*..found most of its admirers among the gentry, officials and scholars. Its music was softer and more melodious than that of the popular drama and it was accompanied principally by the *ti-tzu*, or Chinese transverse flute.

Tiuchiu, var. TEOCHEW.

Tiv (tɪv), *a.* and *sb.* [Native name.] **A.** *adj.* Of, pertaining to, or designating a people of central Nigeria, who live on either side of the Benue River, or the language spoken by them. **B.** *sb.* **a.** A member of this people; also *collect.* **b.** The Bantu language of this people.

1939 R. M. EAST tr. B. Abiga (*title*) Abiga's story: the Tiv tribe as seen by one of its members. **1957** W. M. HAILEY *Afr. Survey* (rev. ed.) iii. 101 The languages of the Tiv group are largely used in mass literacy schemes in the Benue Province. **1960** *Guardian* 15 July 14/4 The important smaller peoples like the Tivs, Kanauris, Binis and Ibibias. **1962** *Listener* 25 Jan. 187/3 Artists and critics among the Tiv of Nigeria. **1973** T. KOCHMAN *Rappin' & Stylin' Out* 83 [Charles Keil] studied Tiv language, culture, music, and aesthetics, and Yoruba urban music. **1976** *Nigeria Herald* 21 May 2/2 News in Kanuri, Tiv and Yoruba. **1977** *Language* LIII. 290 Loanwords are not all lumped into one class (as they tend to be in Tiv). **1982** B. EMECHETA *Destination Biafra* i. 8 In Nigeria..there are smaller groups..surrounding each major tribe... Around the Hausas you have the Tivs, the Fulanis.

tiver (ˈtɪvə(r)), *sb. dial.* [mod., app. repr. OE. *téafor* (*téapor*), glossing 'minium' (red lead); in form = OHG. *zoubur*, Ger. *zauber*, ON. *taufr*, secret or magic writing, charm, talisman, sorcery: see Pauls *Grundrisz* (ed. 2) 251.] A red colouring matter: see quots. Hence **ˈtiver** *v. dial., trans.* to mark or colour with tiver.

[*c* **975** *Sax. Leechd.* II. 56 Do æȝes þ hwite to & meng swa þu dest teapor. *a* **1100** *Ags. Voc.* in Wr.-Wülcker 314/21 *Minium*, teafor. *a* **1200** *Ibid.* 541/11 *Minium*, teapor. **1200–1225** *Peri Didaxeon* in *Sax. Leechd.* III. 88 Eft nim ladsar þ teafur & galpani oþres healfes paniȝe whit.] **1792** *Gentl. Mag.* LXII. 521 Strayed sheep..tivered between the shoulders and across the loins. *a* **1825** FORBY *Voc. E. Anglia, Tiver*, a composition of which tar is the principal ingredient, to colour and preserve boards exposed to the air. **1863** MORTON *Cycl. Agric.* Gloss. (E.D.D.), *Teen* or *Tiver* (Suff.), red ochre for marking sheep. **1887** *Kentish Gloss.*, Tiver. **1895** *E. Anglia Gloss.* s.v., The sheep are tivered across the loins.

Tivoli (ˈtɪvəlɪ). [Said to be from *Tivoli*, a town near Rome.] A game resembling bagatelle, played on a sloping board or table set with upright pins and hoops, by which the ball shot from a side alley against the curved top of the table is deflected into numbered compartments at the other end.

tivy (ˈtɪvɪ), *int.* and *v. rare.* [See TANTIVY.]

a. *int.* = TANTIVY D. **b.** *vb.* = TANTIVY *v.* 1.

1669 DRYDEN *Tyrannic Love* IV. i, In the bright moonshine while winds whistle loud, Tivy, tivy, tivy, we mount and we fly. **1719** [see TANTIVY D]. **1842** *Tait's Mag.* IX. 528 Thence tivy'd they all, with speed of a sledge, And buried them deep in the hazel hedge.

Tiwesday, tiwill, obs. ff. TUESDAY, TEWEL.

†**tixell**, obs. form of THIXEL *dial.*

1542 *Richmond Wills* (Surtees) 35 Item a tixell and a chysell iiij*d*.

tixt, tixte, obs. forms of TEXT.

‖**tiza** (ˈtiːzə). *Min.* [a. Quichua (Peruvian) *t'isa* to card wool; from its fibrous appearance (Webster, 1911).] Ulexite or hayesine.

1865 PAGE *Handbk. Geol. Terms* (ed. 2), *Tiza*, the name by which borate of lime (*Hayesine*) is called in southern Peru, where it occurs on the dry plains or *salinas* in the neighbourhood of Iquique in white reniform masses. **1868** DANA *Min.* 599 Ulexite..occurs..in the province of Tarapaca (where it is called *tiza*).

tizanne, obs. var. PTISAN, barley-water, etc.

tizwin, var. TISWIN.

tizz, tiz (tɪz), shortened form of TIZZY[2].

1954 B. BOLAND *Return* II. iii, in *Plays of Year* IX. 326 *Peter*: Nothing matters. *Angela*: Practically nothing. All the things people get in such a tizz about—. **1958** 'N. BLAKE' *Penknife in my Heart* iv. 52 Miriam was as usual in a tiz. **1967** R. RENDELL *New Lease of Death* vi. 54 When Burden looked murderous, he added, 'Don't get in a tiz with me.' **1978** *Illustr. London News* Nov. 97/1 The people of Morecambe were thrown into a tizz by this idea of a barrage [across Morecambe Bay].

tizzick, obs. f. PHTHISIC.

tizz-wozz, var. TISWAS.

tizzy[1] (ˈtɪzɪ). *slang.* Also **tizzey, tissey.** [Origin obscure.] A sixpenny-piece. Also *Comb.*, as **tizzy-snatcher** *Naut. slang*, an assistant paymaster.

1804 J. COLLINS *Scripscrap.* 156 So I gets a Tizzy for to let them alone. **1809** in *Spirit Pub. Jrnls.* XIII. 119 That a tizzey be given out of the corporate funds in support of said Colonel Waddle. **1829** *Sporting Mag.* XXIV. 163 The..rustics, who had ventured their few tisseys and bobs upon their Squire's famous horse. **1835** HOOD *Dead Robbery* viii, Just show me, if you can, A doctor's—if you want to earn a tizzy! **1901** *Longm. Mag.* Oct. 571 A man reads, at a 'tizzy', what he had not read when priced at twelve times the humble tanner. **1914** 'BARTIMEUS' *Naval Occasions* xiii. 107 'Bloomin' tizzy-snatcher' he muttered slipping the coins into his trousers pocket. He referred to the A.P. (Assistant Paymaster, who had mulched him of sixpence). **1916** 'TAFFRAIL' *Pincher Martin* v. 74, I cursed them for a couple of tizzy-snatchers. **1946** J. IRVING *Royal Navalese* 176 *Tizzysnatcher*, a disillusioned Nor' Easter's name for the Paymaster. The derivation is the Cockney 'tizzy' meaning sixpence.

tizzy[2]. *colloq.* (orig. *U.S.*). [Of uncertain origin.] A state of nervous excitement, agitation or worry, a 'flap'; esp. in phr. ***in a tizzy***.

1935 *Amer. Speech* X. 192/1 The *tizzy* in which a huge wedding kept society columnists for weeks. **1938** *Ladies' Home Jrnl.* Oct. 14/2 Maybe it's better for the future of the race to live from daze to daze in a perpetual tizzy like Alix. **1952** A. WILSON *Hemlock & After* II. iii. 170 Politics and the sun together always put me into a mad tizzy. **1958** N. MARSH *Singing in Shrouds* (1959) v. 83 Gets in a tizzy over details. **1967** *Spectator* 10 Nov. 582/3 John Whiting's play..about the tizzies of English gentlefolk involved in the Napoleonic invasion scare. **1974** *Courier-Mail* (Brisbane) 14 Sept. 10/6

A small band of private fliers has had the RAAF base at Amberley in a tizzy. **1983** *Daily Tel.* 8 June 20/3 He hopes this mass production of original art may throw 'into a state of total tizzy' an art world where 'more and more money is being made by less and less people'.

tjaele (‖ˈʃɛːlə, ˈtʃeɪlə). *Geol.* Also **taele, tjäle.** [a. Sw. *tjäle* ice in frozen ground.] Frozen ground; also, permafrost. Freq. *attrib.*

1924 *Geogr. Jrnl.* LXIII. 210 The arrangement of materials can usually be traced right down to the tjaele. *Ibid.* 211 The tjaele ice was still very close to the surface. **1937** *Nature* 4 Sept. 410/1 The Third Glaciation is represented in the north-west by the Irish Sea Drifts,..and by taele-gravels and melt-water flood-gravels. **1939** *Geogr. Jrnl.* XCIV. 451 Near the edge of the snow the *tjäle* approaches the surface and underneath the snow the soil is completely frozen. **1960** B. W. Sparks *Geomorphol.* xiv. 314 Solifluxion gravels of various sorts have long been recognised and mapped in Great Britain, where they are known by a variety of names, e.g. head, coombe rock, taele gravel..warp and trail. **1970** R. J. Small *Study of Landforms* iv. 124 A climatic refrigeration, allied to the onset of periglacial conditions and the formation of permafrost or annual taele.., is capable of rendering permeable rocks impermeable.

‖**tjalk** (tjalk). [Du. and LG. *tjalk*, a kind of ship, a. WFris. *tsjalk* (tʃalk), according to Franck, perh. dim. of **tjal* for *kjal* = OE. *céol* KEEL.] A kind of Dutch ship or sailing boat.

1861 *Mitchell's Maritime Reg.* 1417/1 Eja, Dutch tjalk, Bronuma, from London for Amsterdam, was totally lost Nov. 1 at West Kapelle. **1889** *Blackwood's Mag.* Aug. 183 Half a dozen big tjalks laden with peat. **1907** *Outlook* 16 Mar. 341/2 The quiet ripple under the bows of tjalks—those large, useful, picturesque craft favoured by Dutch designers—sailing across the wide Friesland Meers.

Tjirbal, var. Dyirbal.

T-joint: see T 3.

tjurunga, var. churinga.

‖**tlachtli** (ˈtlætʃtliː). Also **tlaxtli.** [Nahuatl.] The ceremonial ball-game of the Aztecs; = pok-ta-pok. Also *attrib.*, as *tlachtli-court*, *-field*.

1875 H. H. Bancroft *Native Races Pacific States N. Amer.* II. viii. 297 The national game of the Nahuas was the *tlachtli*, which strongly resembled in many points our game of football. **1914** T. A. Joyce *Mexican Archaeol.* vi. 165 But the national game, tlaxtli, was closely connected with the worship of the gods, and the tlaxtli-courts..were generally associated with temples. **1959** *Times* 27 Apr. (Rubber Industry Suppl.) p. v/1 The sacramental Tlachtli played by Aztecs in the temple courts of Mexico. **1963** [see pok-ta-pok]. **1968** H. Helfritz *Mexican Cities of Gods* xv. 157 The playing area, or *tlachtli*-field,..is 199 ft. wide.

Tlapanec (ˈtlæpənɛk), *sb.* (and *a.*) Also **Tlapaneco, Tlappanec.** [ad. Sp. *tlapaneca*, *tlapaneco*, ad. Nahuatl (Aztec) *tlapanecatl*.]

a. An Indian people of south-west Guerrero, Mexico. **b.** The language of this people, formerly classified as Hokan but now regarded as Otomanguean. Also *attrib.* or as *adj.* Also in *Comb.*, as ***Subtiaba-Tlapanec*** (see Subtiaba).

1875 H. H. Bancroft *Native Races Pacific States N. Amer.* I. vi. 677 The Tlapanecs, Coviscas, Yopes, Yopis.., Chochos,..or Popolucas are one and the same people, who by different writers are described under one or other of these names. *Ibid.* III. x. 752 Several tongues, of which..I find nothing mentioned but the names;..further there are mentioned the Chatino, Tlapanec, and Popoluca. **1900** F. Starr *Notes Ethnography S. Mexico* 71 The name Chocho is said by Orozco to be applied to a language in Oaxaca, while to the same language in Puebla is given the name *popoloco*; it is also the *tlapaneco* of Guerrero..and the ancient *Yope*. **1911** Thomas & Swanton *Indian Languages Mexico & Central Amer.* 53 Sahagun..says the Tlapaneco language is precisely the same as those called Tenime, Pinome..in the singular Pinotl..This brings Tlapaneco into the same relation as that given by Orozco y Berra. *Ibid.* 54 The Tlapanec group is located by Orozco y Berra in Guerrero. **1925**, etc. [see Subtiaba]. **1940** J. A. Mason in *Maya & Their Neighbors* v. 61 According to Sapir..Subtiaba in Nicaragua differs hardly more than dialectically from Tlapanec in Guerrero. **1972** *Bk. Thousand Tongues* (Amer. Bible Soc.) (rev. ed.) 430/2 The Tlapaneco Indians..live in Guerrero, Mexico. Tlapaneco, spoken with numerous dialectal variations, is a Hokan language, related in Mexico to Seri and Chontal of Oaxaca. **1974** *Encycl. Brit. Macropædia* XI. 960/1 The Tlapanec complex was first correctly identified by Walter Lehmann..in 1920. *Ibid.*, He [*sc.* Sapir] believed Tlapanec to be Oto-Manguean.

Tlingit (ˈklɪŋkɪt, ˈklɪŋgɪt; also, incorrectly, tl-), *sb.* and *a.* Also **Thlinget, Thlinkeet, Tlinget, Tlinkit,** etc. [a. Tlingit *tłingít*, *'łingít* person, Tlingit.] **A.** *sb.* **a.** (A member of) an Indian people of the coasts and islands of south-eastern Alaska. **b.** The language spoken by this people.

1865 M. Macfie *Vancouver Island & British Columbia* xvi. 452 The 'Clingats', which name is applied to all the northern tribes, relate the following tradition. **1876** *Encycl. Brit.* V. 187/2 This [*sc.* exogamy] is illustrated in the case of the Thlinkeets, or Kolosches, who inhabit the coasts and islands from Mt. St Elias to the River Nass. **1901** G. W. James *Indian Basketry* 50 In Alaska the chief basket-makers are the Thlinkets and Haidas. **1908** *26th Ann. Rep. Bureau Amer. Ethnol.* 472 In Tlingit..*p* and *b* do not occur in words of native origin. *Ibid.* 407 The Tlingit..trace the origin of nearly all their clans..to the neighborhood of the mouth of the Skeena river. **1921** E. Sapir *Language* iv. 84 A good example of such a pitch language is Tlingit, spoken by the Indians of the southern coast of Alaska. **1951** R. Firth *Elem. Social Organiz.* iv. 145 The *potlach* of the Haida, Tlinkit and other Indians of the American North-West coast. **1965** *Canad. Jrnl. Linguistics* X. 97 To this Athapaskan-Eyak unit, Tlingit seems related definitely but remotely. **1970** *Language* XLVI. 401 Similar problems are presented by the so-called 'third modals' of Tlingit. **1978** *Amer. Poetry Rev.* Sept./Oct. 18/4 The Tlingit of Alaska prescribe the wearing of broad-brimmed hats.

B. *adj.* Of, pertaining to, or designating these Indians.

1881 [see Aleut]. **1908** *26th Ann. Rep. Bureau Amer. Ethnol.* 463 Each Tlingit shaman was guarded by a number of helpers and possessed a number of masks. *Ibid.* 472 The Tlingit language tends to shorten its vowels. **1932** D. Jenness *Indians of Canada* xxi. 331 Feasts and ceremonies occurred constantly in all the Tlinkit villages. **1963** *Times* 29 Apr. 5/5 A Thlinget Indian from Alaska. **1966** [see Chilkat]. **1976** *Times* 25 Sept. 12/8 The Tlingit screen.. was used as a partition in the house of Chief Shakes of the Tlingit tribe in Wrangell, Akaska.

‖**tmema** (ˈtmiːmə). Pl. **-ata.** [a. Gr. τμῆμα a part cut off, a section.] A segment, a section.

1891 in *Cent. Dict.* **1900** B. D. Jackson *Gloss. Bot. Terms*, *Tmema*.., a cell ruptured in setting free a Mossgemma (Correns).

‖**tmesis** (ˈtmiːsɪs). *Gram.* and *Rhet.* (Also 6 **timesis.**) [a. Gr. τμῆσις a cutting, from verbal ablaut series τεμ-, τομ-, τμ- to cut.] The separation of the elements of a compound word by the interposition of another word or words.

(Often a reversion to the earlier uncompounded structure.)

1586 Day *Eng. Secretary* ii. (1625) 83 *Timesis* or *Diacope*, a diuision of a word compound into two parts, as, What might be soeuer vnto a man pleasing,..for, whatsoeuer might be, etc. **1678** Phillips (ed. 4), *Tmesis*,..a figure of Prosody, wherein a compounded word is, as it were, cut asunder, and divided into two parts by some other word which is interposed, as *Septem Subjecta Trioni*, for *Subjecta Septemtrioni*. **1844** *Proc. Philol. Soc.* I. 265 Though the constituent parts of compound terms may be disjoined by tmesis, the elements of truly simple words never are. **1889** *Athenæum* 23 Mar. 373/1 Forgive the quaint tmesis of his opening line:—How bright the chit and chat!

†**ˈtmetic**, *a.* *Med. Obs. rare.* [ad. Gr. τμητικ-ός cutting, f. τμητός cut: cf. prec.] Cutting; loosening, resolving.

1661 Lovell *Hist. Anim. & Min.* 87 Antepilepticks, having a tmetick, or inciding faculty.

to, *a.* *Obs.* exc. *dial.* Forms: α. (*Sc.* and *n. dial.*) 4–6 **ta**, 5 **taa**, 5 (8–9 *Sc.*) **tae**, 9 **teae**; 9 *n. dial.* **tea, teea.** β. 4–7 **to**, 5 **too**, 7 **toe.** [ME. *tā*, *tō*, shortened form of *tān*, *tōn* tone *a.*, when standing before a sb. (orig. only before a consonant). For history see tone *a.*, and cf. *o*, *oo*, *a*, *ae*, shortened forms of one *a.*]

a. The collocation ***the ta***, ***the to***, properly ***that a***, ***that*** (***thet***) ***o***, 'the one', as opposed to *the tother* = *that other*, 'the other'.

α. *a* **1340** Hampole *Psalter* lvii. 4 The snake that festis the ta ere til the erth, and the tothere stoppis with hire taile. **1387** *Charters, &c. Edinb.* (1871) 35 Betwene worthy men and nobyl..on the ta half, and..masounys on the tothir half. *a* **1400–50** *Alexander* 3978 Þi semble o þe taa syde & myne on þe tothire. *c* **1440** *Alphabet of Tales* 181 Þer war a hate oven on þe ta side me, & þe shapp of hym on þat other partie. **1513** Douglas *Æneis* x. vii. 175 Pallas on the ta part ..Lawsus resistis on that vthir syde. **1721** Ramsay *Horace to Virgil* 10 Bring hame the tae haff o' my saul. **1826** J. Wilson *Noct. Ambr.* Wks. 1855 I. 128 Up with the tae side, down with the tither.

β. *c* **1330** R. Brunne *Chron.* (1810) 176 Þe to kyng & þe toþer assailed it so hard. **1423** *Rolls of Parlt.* IV. 256/2 That the too half be forfet to the..Kyng and the tother half to hym. *c* **1425** *Seven Sag.* (P.) 3270 That to [error for *that o* or *the to*] raven was ful holde. **1495** *Trevisa's Barth. De P.R.* xviii. ix. (W. de W.), He hath tweyne heedys, one in the to [*Bodl. MS.* þat one] ende and a nother in the tother ende. **1609** W. M. *Man in Moone* (1849) 18 Tradesmen treade on the to side of the way. **1642** Rogers *Naaman* 193 The Angell gave him a bunch on the to-side.

b. Used without *the* after a poss. pron. (or case), as in ***his to eye***, his one eye, the one of his eyes.

1513 Douglas *Æn.* iv. ix. 91 The quene..Hir ta fut bair.

†**c.** In phr. ***a to-side***, on one side. *Obs.*

In part of northern England where *the* regularly becomes *tĕ*, *tă*, *t'* (as *tă fells*, *t'measter*, *t'titter oop caw t'udder*, *t'aud lad*), *to*, *tone*, *tother* stand for *t'o*, *t'one*, *t'other*, i.e. *the o*, *the one*, *the other*; so in colloq. Eng. more widely, *t'one or t'other*, *t'other man*, *t'other day*; hence it is possible that *a-to-side* represents *on-th'o-side*; the northern ME. was *o þe taa side*, mod. Sc. *o*(*n*) *the tae side*.

1601 Holland *Pliny* viii. xxiv. 208 Turning his head a to-side. **1606** *Choice, Chance*, etc. (1881) 70 Lookes a toside, and swears at euery word. **1609** Holland *Amm. Marcell.* 389 Winding atoe side and going crosse. **1678** Bunyan *Pilgr.* i. 139 Then Christian stept a little a to-side to his Fellow Hopeful. **1684** *Ibid.* ii. 67 He called you a to-side.

†**to**, *v.* *Obs.* Also 5 **too**; *pa. t.* 4–5 **to**, *pa. pple.* 4–5 **ton**, 6 **tone.** The ME. apocopate northern forms *tā*, *tān* for take, *taken*, with the *ā* rounded in north midland speech, or transliterated by midland or southern writers to *tō*, *tōn*; in the pa. t. *to* was apocopated from the original *tóc*.

All the rimed examples of the pres. and pa. pple. rime with words having *ā* in northern dialect; in earlier instances the change of *a* to *o* was mostly scribal; but in late Sc. it was mostly the work of the author anglicizing his native *ā* to *ō* on the analogy of *sā*, *sō*, *bān*, *bōne*, etc.

13.. *Cursor M.* 16454 (Cott.) Quen þai þe fine gold for-soke, And to [*v.r.* toke] þam to þe lede. *c* **1320** *Sir Tristr.* 947 Þe truage was com to to [*rimes* so, þo, go] Moraunt, þe noble kniȝt. *Ibid.* 1484 His tong haþ he ton [*rime* nek bon] And schorn of bi þe rote. *Ibid.* 2112 Þen sall þis rewel eft furth be ton [*rime* gon]. *c* **1425** *Seven Sag.* (P.) 1432 To speke fayre he to hede. *c* **1440** *Bone Flor.* 887 And Awdegone hur cowncelde soo Oon of thes lordys for to too. **1500–20** Dunbar *Poems* xlvi. 102 That he..nocht in the feindis net be tone [*rime* allone].

to (tuː, tʊ, tə), *prep.*, *conj.*, *adv.* [OE. *tó*, in form = OFris., OS. *tô* (MDu., Du. *toe*, MLG., LG. *tô*, *to*), OHG. *zô*, *zuo*, *zua*, MHG. *zuo*, Ger. *zu*:—OTeut. **tô* adv.; beside which OTeut. had **ti*, OFris., OS. *ti*, *te* (Fris., MDu., Du., MLG., LG. *te*), OHG. *za*, *ze*, *zi* (MHG. *ze*) prep. OTeut. **tô* and **ti* (? *ta*) unite in a pre-Teut. *dŏ*, *de*, cognate with OSl. and OIr. *do*, Lith. *da-* prefix, Gr. -δε, L. *-do* suffix. Gothic used only the form *du*, and ON. substituted *til*, till. In prehistoric OE. the prep. was already levelled with the adv. in the form *to* (*tó*, *to*), as in Ger. both are now *zu*. But while *tó* adv., retaining its stress, came at last to be written *too* (tuː), the prep., being usually stressless, remained at *to* (tʊ, tə), and in dialectal specimens is now often written *ta*, *tae*, *teh*, *ti*, *tu* (meaning (ta), (te), (tə)), some of which forms are occasional also in earlier writing. (In some northern dialects (te) develops before a vowel into *tev*, *tiv*.)

Exceptional and dialectal forms. (Chiefly with inf., where also before a vowel it was formerly often reduced to *t* or *t'*, as in *tamend*, *t'enjoy*: see T'[1].)

a **1175** Tu [see A. 1]. *c* **1200** *Trin. Coll. Hom.* 5 Þat is te cumen a domes dai. *a* **1225** *St. Marher.* 19 He..demde hire te deaðe. **13..** *Cursor M.* 14913 (Gött.) For fast it draus te þe nede. *c* **1380** Wyclif *Sel. Wks.* III. 433 To [*v.r.* te] kepe Cristis religioun. *c* **1400** *Rom. Rose* 3156 That comest so slyghly for tespye. **1535** Stewart *Cron. Scot.* (Rolls) I. 541 Mony ratche ta ryn under the ryss. **1583** T. Washington tr. *Nicholay's Voy.* i. vi, The Ambassadour..returning too his Gallies. **1822** W. Tennant *Thane of Fife* i. 2 Euterpe, aidant come, t'adorn my song. **1894** 'Ian Maclaren' *Bonnie Brier Bush* v. (1895) 181 It only 'threatened tae be weet'. **1896** R. Reid in *N. York Scot. Amer.* Oct., Aff tae the muirs.]

A. *prep.* (in ordinary use, before a sb.)

The OE. prep. *tó* normally 'governed' or was followed by the dative case, sometimes, idiomatically, by the genitive or the instrumental (esp. in *tó þæs* and *to þý*), rarely by the accusative. In later Middle and in mod.Eng., *to* is followed by the ordinary 'objective' case, which in sbs. is formally identical with the nominative, and in pronouns is the dative-accusative, *me*, *him*, etc. In Middle and mod.Eng. *to* not only represents the OE. preposition, but also takes the place of the OE. inflected dative case. Even in OE. the simple dative was often reinforced by *tó*, or (what came to the same thing) was supplanted by *tó* and its case. This was very frequent in late OE., and (helped no doubt by the example of French, which had similarly substituted the construction with *à* (L. *ad*) for the L. dative) became universal in ME., the simple dative remaining only in pronouns and substantives as the indirect or remoter object, known by its position before the direct object (as in 'give me the book', 'tell John the news'). Both with pronouns and sbs., the prepositional construction may, and in some cases must, be used (e.g. 'give the book to me', 'tell it to John'). In OE. many verbs 'governed' or took a dative object; with the loss of the dative inflexion, this case could no longer be distinguished from the accusative, and such verbs are now treated as ordinary transitive vbs. governing the objective (e.g. sio heord folȝað ðæm wordum & ðæm ðeawum ðæs hirdes, 'the herd follows the words and the thews [customs] of the shepherd').

The senses and uses of *to* may be arranged in various ways, every way having its peculiar difficulties owing to cross-currents of history and usage. OE. and the West Germanic Languages had two prepositions with the sense of modern *to*, viz. *tó* and *óð*; the second of these always expressed motion reaching its object; it is therefore probable that *tó* had originally the sense of 'direction towards', without any implication of reaching; and in a truly historical account of the word, it would perh. be necessary to start with the two main divisions of 'toward' and 'actually to'. But even in the earliest written OE. this distinction had, so far as concerns *tó*, faded away, and in the various transferred and later senses it could not be successfully carried out. Even the later distinction between *to* as a preposition implying motion, and *to* representing the dative inflexion, can, from the falling together of these notions, only be partially exhibited. The arrangement here followed is thus largely tentative and practical, and not in every case historical.

I. Expressing a spatial or local relation.

1. Expressing motion directed towards and reaching: governing a sb. denoting the place, thing, or person approached and reached. The opposite of from. Also with adv. prefixed, as *away*, *down*, *out*, *up*, etc.

Sometimes preceding another preposition (of position): see quot. *c* 1300, and cf. from 15 b.

Beowulf (Z.) 2010 Ic ðær furðum cwom, to ðam hring-sele. *c* **893** K. Ælfred *Oros.* v. xi. §4 Mon lædde Aristobolus to Rome ȝebundenne. **1154** *O.E. Chron.* an. 1132 (Laud MS.) Ðis ȝear com Henri king to þis land. *a* **1175** *Cott. Hom.* 229 He com tu us. *c* **1300** *Cursor M.* 21792 (Edin.) Out of þe bridil he [þe nailis] lachte And to biscide þe croz þaim taȝte. *c* **1386** Chaucer *C.T. Prol.* 16 And specially from euery shires ende Of Engelond to Caunturbury they wende. *c* **1489** Caxton *Blanchardyn* liv. 211 The beautifull Queene was royally led to and from the Church. **1583** Stubbes *Anat. Abus.* ii. (1882) 27 When the poore man might turne out a cow, or two..to the commons. **1611** Bible *2 Kings* xv. 29 [He] caried them captiue to Assyria. **1802** Mar.

EDGEWORTH *Moral T.* (1816) I. i. 2 Forester was sent to Edinburgh. **1904** F. C. KITTON *Dickens Country* 63 Dickens returned to London. *Mod.* He has removed to near Rugby. Take this child to his mother's house. Come here to me.

b. In figurative expressions of motion; the following sb. denoting (*a*) a state or condition attained, or (*b*) a thing or person reached by some action figured as movement.

c **875** *O.E. Chron.* an. 871, þa feng Ælfred .. to Wesseaxna rice. *c* **897** K. ÆLFRED *Gregory's Past. C.* xiv. 300 Hie ðonne astigað to Godes anlicnesse. *c* **1175** *Lamb. Hom.* 27 Hit hine tið to þan bittre deðe. *c* **1200** ORMIN 11219 He biginneþþ .. Att Abraham, & reccneþþ a33 Dunnwarrd fra mann to manne. *c* **1449** PECOCK *Repr.* III. iv. (Rolls) 293 If thou wolte entre to lijf, kepe the comaundementis. **1555** J. PROCTOR *Hist. Wyat's Reb.* 64 Nowe to retourne to Wyat. **1625** LAUD *Wks.* (1847) I. 95 When he came to the crown. **1766** GOLDSM. *Vic. W.* xviii, To reclaim a lost child to virtue. **1855** MACAULAY *Hist. Eng.* xii. III. 216 The only debate of which any account has come down to us. **1905** M. HUME *Span. Infl. on Eng. Lit.* 97 To trace how the germ of the stories came to Spain. *Mod.* Do not let it run to seed.

c. Elliptical uses. (*a*) with ellipsis of *go* or other verb of motion, esp. in commands, or (*arch.*) after an auxiliary verb. (*b*) = Gone to; in going to, on the way to. (Chiefly *dial.*) (*c*) after a sb. implying or suggesting motion: = That goes, or takes one, or causes one to go, to.

(*a*) *c* **1425** *Cast. Persev.* 3038 in *Macro Plays* 167 þou muste to helle. **1539** BIBLE (Great) *1 Kings* xii. 16 To youre tentes, O Israel! **1633** G. HERBERT *Temple, Assurance* iv, I will to my Father. **1663** PEPYS *Diary* 19 Oct., She waked and gargled her mouth, and to sleep again. **1666** *Ibid.* 28 Apr., My wife to her father's, to carry him some ruling work. **1843** *Blackw. Mag.* LIV. 733 I'll to bed. **1884** BROWNING *Ferishtah, Eagle* 35 To Ispahan forthwith!
(*b*) **1451** MARG. PASTON in *P. Lett.* I. 221 The Lady Boys .. is to London to compleyn to the Kyng. *c* **1500** *Melusine* lix. 360 For now the sonne is to his rest. **1908** [MISS E. FOWLER] *Betw. Trent & Ancholme* 45 She wore, to church, a black cottage-bonnet.
(*c*) *a* **900** K. ÆLFRED *Solil.* Pref. (1902) 2 þæt ic maȝe rihtne weiȝ aredian to þam ecan hame. **971** *Blickl Hom.* 109, & him tæcean lifes weȝ & rihtne gang to heofonum. **1535** COVERDALE *Gen.* xvi. 7 By the well in the waye to Sur. **1673** [see ROAD *sb.* 4]. **1758** GOLDSM. *Mem. Protestant* (1895) II. 137 He had some Business to Nice. **1849** MACAULAY *Hist. Eng.* iii. I. 371 If he asked his way to St. James's. **1852** TENNYSON *Ode Dk. Wellington* 202 The path of duty was the way to glory. **1862** *Chambers's Encycl.* III. 321/1 The railway to C. was opened in 1856. **1874** KINGSLEY *Lett.* (1877) II. 426 We are promised free passes .. to California. *Mod.* The first train to London.

2. Expressing direction: In the direction of, towards.

c **890** tr. *Bæda's Hist.* I. vii. (1890) 38 His eaȝan ahof upp to heofonum. *c* **1000** *Ags. Ps.* (Th.) lxx[i]. 2 Ahyld me þin eare to [*Vulg.* inclina ad me aurem tuam]. **1388** WYCLIF *Ps.* xxiv. [xxv.] 15 Myn iȝen ben euere to the Lord. **1590** SPENSER *F.Q.* II. vii. 1 As pilot .. That to a stedfast starre his course hath bent. **1667** MILTON *P.L.* VI. 558 Vanguard, to Right and Left the Front unfould. **1697** DRYDEN *Virg. Georg.* III. 472 A Cote that opens to the South. **1802** MAR. EDGEWORTH *Moral T.* (1816) I. 232 Standing with his back to me. **1843** *Blackw. Mag.* LIV. 14 He pointed to a clump of trees.

b. After *look, smell* = mod. *at*; also † *behold to*, † *see to* = look at. *Obs.* or *dial.*

a **900** *Ags. Ps.* (Th.) xii. 3 Beseoh to me, Drihten, .. and ȝehyr me. *Ibid.* xxiv. 14 [xxv. 16] ȝeloca to me, Drihten, and ȝemiltsa me. **1375**– [see LOOK *v.* 21 a]. **1382** WYCLIF *Gen.* iv. 4 þe Lord bihelde to Abel and to his ȝiftis. **1393** LANGL. *P. Pl.* C. II. 55 The dupe dale and durke vnsemely to see to. *c* **1475** *Stans puer* 55 in *Q. Eliz. Acad.* (E.E.T.S.) 58 When þou spekys .. Be-hold to þi souereyn in þe face. **1586** B. YOUNG *Guazzo's Civ. Conv.* IV. 191 b, Manie, .. before they had dronke, would smell to their wine. **1611** BIBLE *Josh.* xxii. 10 A great altar to see to. **1852** HAWTHORNE *Blithedale Rom.* ix, A young girl's heart, which he held in his hand, and smelled to, like a rosebud.

c. In expressing the position of something lying in a specified direction. (Cf. ON *prep.* 4.)

c **890** tr. *Bæda's Hist.* I. ix. [xi.] (1890) 44 Eardædon Bryttas binnan þam dice to suðdæle. **1671** MILTON *P.R.* III. 273 Here thou behold'st Assyria, .. And .. to south the Persian bay. **1789** G. WHITE *Selborne* i, To the north-west, north and east of the village, is a range of fair enclosures. **1820** SCOTT *Monast.* iii, The extensive range of pasturage .. lay to the west. **1855** TENNYSON *Charge Light Brigade* iii, Cannon to right of them, Cannon to left of them. **1861** MRS. CARLYLE *Lett.* (1883) III. 79 The bedrooms to the back are much larger.

d. In figurative expressions of direction (inclination, tendency, etc.). Also *fig.* from c, in phr. *to the bad, to the good* (= on the wrong, or right, side of the account), *to the fore*; in *to the contrary* with both senses (2 and 2 c).

See BAD B. 1 b, GOOD C. 5 b, FORE *a.* 4.

c **1300** *Cursor M.* 19326 (Edin.) þai durste na uiolence þaim do For þe folc þaim heeldit to. *a* **1400** *Birth Jesus* 4 in Horstm. *Altengl. Leg.* (1875) 65 Icome he is .. to wham is al oure hope. **1512**– [see CONTRARY B. 1 b, c]. **1637**– [see FORE *a.* 4]. **1753** CHAMBERS *Cycl. Supp.* s.v. *Lime*, Oblong, with a tendency to a rhomboidal shape. **1815** SCOTT *Guy M.* xxxvi, He .. commanded Barnes to have an eye to the Dominie.

e. With a sb. or pron. (or sb. phrase) followed by *ward* or *wards* (now commonly written as a suffix, hyphened or joined to the preceding word); e.g. *to God-ward*: see -WARD, -WARDS, and cf. TOWARD. *arch.*

3. Indicating the limit of a movement or extension in space: As far as (to); = OE. *oð*.

Sometimes followed by another preposition (of position), as in quot. 1641: cf. FROM 15 b. Often correlative to *from*, indicating the remoter, or the second, of two limits: see FROM 2. See also *up to* s.v. UP.

971–1884 [see FROM 2]. *a* **1300** *Cursor M.* 2742 þe smike it reches to þe scki. **13..** *Sir Beues* (A.) 1538 Til þe her on is heued greu to his fet. *c* **1384** CHAUCER *H. Fame* III. 840 So grete a noyse, That .. Men myghte hyt han herd .. To Rome. *c* **1420** ? LYDG. *Assembly of Gods* 462, I smete hym to the hert. **1599** SHAKS. *Much Ado* II. i. 258 She would infect to the north starre. **1641** J. JACKSON *True Evang. T.* I. 62 If their candle had burned to within the Socket. **1843** *Fraser's Mag.* XXVIII. 652 Protestant to the backbone. **1873** TRISTRAM *Moab* i. 14 Wet to the skin. *Mod.* The thermometer has risen to above 32°.

b. After expressions of distance, indicating the remote limit (formerly also the near limit, at which the speaker is actually or in idea): = FROM 5 a, OF 4 b.

c **888** K. ÆLFRED *Boeth.* xxxv. §4 Hi woldon witan hu heah hit wære to ðæm heofone. *c* **893** —— *Oros.* I. i. §17 Hit mihte beon þreora mila brad to þæm more. **1551** *Reg. Privy Council Scot.* I. 115 Dwelland within four mylis to this burch. **1605** SHAKS. *Macb.* I. iii. 39 How farre is't call'd to Soris? *Mod.* It is eleven miles (from Oxford) to Witney.

4. Expressing simple position: At, in (a place, also *fig.* a condition, etc.). Cf. Ger. *zu Berlin, zu hause*. Now only *dial.* and *U.S. colloq.* Cf. HOME *sb.*[1] 14.

925–*c* **935** *Laws of Æthelstan* II. c. 14 §2 On Cantwarabyriȝ VII myneteras .. to Hrofeceastre III .. to Lundenbyriȝ VIII [etc.]. *c* **1175** *Lamb. Hom.* 27 Swa dreieð his erme saule in eche pine to helle grunde. **13..** *Guy Warw.* (A.) 384 þou art y-tauȝt to a liþer scole. *c* **1420** *Chron. Vilod.* 1696 þat his body to Schaftesbury were leyde. *c* **1500** *Melusine* lvii. 335, I haue herd say that there is to Mountferrat .. a deuoute & holy place. **1658** in Morris *Troub. Cath. Foref.* I. vi. (1872) 314 Sister Cornelia who had lain to bed about thirty years. **1795**, etc. [see HOME *sb.*[1] 14]. **1801** J. QUINCY in *Proc. Mass. Hist. Soc.* (1888) 2nd Ser. IV. 130 Mr. William Hammatt and Mr. Josiah Barker .. called and invited us to a party they had made for us to the East end of the Island. **1818** L. D. CLARK *Jrnl.* 10 Sept. in *Firelands Pioneer* (1920) XXI. 2321 Stayed to Canfields all night. **1835–40** HALIBURTON *Clockm.* (1862) 57, I guess, said he, they have enough of it to home. **1855** KINGSLEY *Westward Ho* xxvi, Lucy Passmore, the white witch to Welcombe. **1889** JEFFERIES *Field & Hedgerow* 272 In Somerset .. it is correct to say 'I bought this to Taunton'. **1901** *Harper's Mag.* CII. 672/1 You can get real handsome cups and saucers to Crosby's. **1977** *New Yorker* 15 Aug. 37/2 Suzanne said, 'What about Sunday? We could do something in the afternoon. Were you ever to the Botanic Gardens?'

b. *to work*: at work, working. *U.S. colloq.*

1776 *Proc. Mass. Hist. Soc.* (1886) 2nd. Ser. II. 304 [We] met some people to work on the High: way. **1827** S. S. ARNOLD *Proc. Vermont Hist. Soc.* (1940) VIII. 111 Her husband .. had died instantly in the barn, where he was to work. **1834** C. A. DAVIS *Lett. J. Downing* 116, I have been to work on it ever since we was at the Rip-Raps. **1858** *Rome* (N.Y.) *Sentinel* Sept., The boiler .. passed through the main building .. without injuring the workmen there, although men were to work on each side of where the boiler passed. **1949** *N.Y. Herald Tribune* 6 Dec. 1 Some 450,000 miners were back to work today. **1978** M. Z. LEWIN *Silent Salesman* xxvii. 146 He's to work... Don't rightly know what time he'll be back.

5. Expressing the relation of contact or the like.

a. Into (or in) contact with; on, against. Often expressing more than mere position, and so passing into transferred senses. See also ON TO.

c **890** tr. *Bæda's Hist.* IV. xxv. [xxiv.] (1890) 348 Ond his heafod onhylde to þam bolstre. **13..** *Guy Warw.* (A.) 4844 'Lordinges', he seyd, 'nimeþ þis bodi, & to þe grounde it lay wel softli'. *c* **1400** MAUNDEV. (Roxb.) iii. 9 [They] held to þaire noses spoungez moisted with water .., for þe aer þare was so drie. *a* **1533** LD. BERNERS *Huon* lxxxi. 250 Huon withdrewe .. & lened hym to a pyller. **1536** CROMWELL in Merriman *Life & Lett.* (1902) II. 90 A request .. the accomplishement wherof I haue .. moche to harte. **1599, 1626** [see FEEL *v.* 2 a]. *a* **1715** BURNET *Own Time* an. 1669 (1823) I. 469 He stood up to the wall. **1837** DICKENS *Pickw.* xxv, Applying plenty of yellow soap to the towel. **1893** D. HYDE *My Grief on Sea* vi, His breast to my bosom, His mouth to my mouth.

b. Expressing contiguity or close proximity: By, beside. Also *fig.* or with additional implication, as in *to one's face, teeth*, etc. = 'in presence and defiance of' (Schmidt *Shaks. Lex.*): cf. 25 b, and see FACE *sb.* 5 c, TOOTH *sb.*; *to hand*: see HAND *sb.* 34; *to stand to one's post, guns*, etc.: see STAND. *v.*

c **1000** ÆLFRIC *Saints' Lives* xxxi. 629 He sæt to þam casere. *c* **1400** *Rom. Rose* 6355 To Ioly folk I enhabite. *c* **1449** PECOCK *Repr.* III. i. (Rolls) 279 The suburbis .. ligging to the same citees. **1614** BP. J. KING *Vitis Palatina* 30 They that walke side to side, and cheeke to cheeke. **1752** J. LOUTHIAN *Form of Process* (ed. 2) 202 The Clerk bids the Keeper set the Prisoners .. to the Bar. **1855** MACAULAY *Hist. Eng.* xvii. IV. 59, I sit down to table; but I cannot eat.
1597 SHAKS. *2 Hen. IV*, III. i. 64 Euen to the eyes of Richard Gaue him defiance. **1602** —— *Ham.* IV. vii. 57, I shall liue and tell him to his teeth, Thus diddest thou. **1739** ELTON in Hanway *Trav.* (1762) I. I. iv. 12 We instantly stood to our arms. **1822** HAZLITT *Table-t.* II. ii. 25 He had taken his part boldly and stood to it manfully. **1843** *Blackw. Mag.* LIV. 219 They will find everything ready to their hands.

II. Expressing a relation in time.

6. Indicating a final limit in time, or the end of a period: Till, until; often correlative to *from*: see FROM 3. (Formerly sometimes preceding an adv. of time, e.g. *now, then*: cf. FROM 15 a, TILL *prep.* 5 b.) †Also *rarely* expressing an extent in time: For, during, till the end of (*obs.*); esp. in phr. *to term of life* (see TERM *sb.* 4 b).

c **1000** ÆLFRIC *Hom.* II. 356 He worhte his weorc to seofon nihtum. *c* **1175** *Lamb. Hom.* 87 Fram þan halie hester dei boð italde fifti daȝa to þisse deie. **1297** R. GLOUC. (Rolls) 190 Fram þe biginning of þe world to þe time þat now is. *c* **1375** *Sc. Leg. Saints* xviii. (*Egipciane*) 276 Scho saw hyme neuir to þan. *c* **1380** WYCLIF *Serm.* Sel. Wks. II. 37 To þe daie þat Noie wente into þe ship. *c* **1490** CAXTON *Rule St. Benet* lxx. 139 Children to the xv. yere of age shall stande euer vndir .. discipline. **1509** [see THEN 7]. **1582** L. KIRBY in Allen *Martyrd. Campion* (1908) 77 Yours to death, and after death. **1711** ADDISON *Spect.* No. 159 ¶4 From the Beginning of the World to its Consummation. **1799** WORDSW. *Lucy Gray* xv, Some maintain that to this day She is a living child. **1849** MACAULAY *Hist. Eng.* vi. II. 36 The parliament was prorogued to the tenth of February. **1855** DICKENS *Dorrit* v, The business hours .. were from ten to six.

b. (So long) before (a definite future time); *esp.* in stating the time of day: (so many minutes) before (an hour). Opposed to *past*.

c **1000** *Soul's Addr. to Body* 37 (Gr.) þæt hit wære xxx. þusend wintra to þinum deaðdæȝe. **1519** in *Fabric Rolls York Minster* (Surtees) 269 To ryng to matyns at evere daie, .. at halfe oure to v. **1596** SHAKS. *Merch. V.* v. i. 303 Or goe to bed, now being two houres to day. **1641** R. CARPENTER *Experience* I. Med. xiv. 102 It wil not be long to this time. **1833** T. HOOK *Parson's Dau.* I. iii, How long is it to dinner, sir? **1842** TENNYSON *Walking to the Mail* in *Poems* II. 47 *James.* The mail? At one o'clock. *John.* What is it now? *James.* A quarter to. **1843** *Blackw. Mag.* LIV. 733 It was exactly a quarter to four o'clock. **1852** R. S. SURTEES *Sponge's Sp. Tour* (1893) 35 'We shall be late. See, it's only ten to now' [i.e. 10 minutes to the hour], continued he, pointing to the timepiece above the fire. **1968** 'R. PETRIE' *MacLurg goes West* II. vii. 60 'I thought we might just catch you before dinner,' said Mrs. Robbins to them quickly. 'It's twelve minutes to.'

c. *from .. to*, with repeated sb. of time, denoting regular recurrence; as *from day to day, from time to time, from month to month.*

1014 WULFSTAN *Serm. ad Anglos* in *Hom.* (Napier) 156 (MS. E.) For folces synnan fram dæȝe to dæȝe. **1297–1712** [see DAY *sb.* 19]. *c* **1325–1895** [see FROM 3 b]. **1423–1891** [see TIME *sb.* 45 a].

7. At (a time), on (a day) (now *dial.*); † in, during (a time) (*obs. rare*). Cf. TODAY, TOMORROW, TONIGHT, TO-YEAR.

This use of *to* in *tódæȝ*, etc., has been explained as originating in sense 6, through phrases like *nu ȝyt to dæȝ* 'now still to this day', shortened to *to dæȝ*; but it is doubtful whether this covers the whole ground. The mod. s.w. use of *to* with expressions of time seems parallel to its use with place in 4.

c **890** tr. *Bæda's Hist.* I. ix. [xii.] (1890) 46 (MS. B.) Eorðweall .. þone mon nu ȝyt to dæȝe sceawian mæȝ. *Ibid.* I. ix. [xi.] 44 Ceastre & torras .. þa we to dæȝ sceawian maȝon. *c* **893** K. ÆLFRED *Oros.* II. iv. §5 Nu ȝiet todæȝe hit is on leoðum sungen. *c* **1000** *Ags. Gosp.* Luke xi. 5 Hwylc eower hæfð sumne freond, & gæþ to midre nihte to him [etc.]. *c* **1000** ÆLFRIC *Hom.* II. 194 Swa micel .. swa he to ðam dæȝe ȝeðicgan mihte. *c* **1300** *Beket* 769 Com to morwe to speche time. **13..** *Guy Warw.* (A.) 4595 þat to hir comen y schold To on day þat was y-sett. **1551** HOOPER *Injunctions* xix. Wks. (Parker Soc.) II. 136 In no parish .. shall the bells be rung to noon upon the Saturdays. **1886** ELWORTHY *W. Somerset Word-bk.* s.v., I'll be ready to dree o'clock.

b. Indicating the precise time at which something is to be done, or at which one is to arrive: At and not after (an appointed time), precisely or punctually at or on.

1722 DE FOE *Col. Jack* (1840) 230 The duke .. pressed earnestly to put it to a day, and come to a battle. *a* **1785** LD. SACKVILLE in *Eng. Hist. Rev.* Apr. (1910) 316, I shan't be to my time. **1849** MACAULAY *Hist. Eng.* iii. I. 287 Unable to pay their hearth money to the day. **1893** *Chamb. Jrnl.* 1 July 406/1 Ainsworth came to his time.

III. Expressing the relation of purpose, destination, result, effect, resulting condition or status.

8. Indicating aim, purpose, intention, or design: For; for the purpose of; with the view or end of; in order to. (Now often replaced by *for*.)

Beowulf (Z.) 3016 Nalles eorl weȝan maððum to ȝemyndum. *c* **893** K. ÆLFRED *Oros.* I. i. §15 Hiora hyd bið swiðe god to sciprapum. *c* **1000** ÆLFRIC *Hom.* I. 82 To ði he com þæt he wolde his heofenlice rice .. mannum forȝyfan. **1297** R. GLOUC. (Rolls) 10691 In gibet hii were anhonge as to more vilte [disgrace]. *c* **1380** WYCLIF *Sel. Wks.* III. 347 þei .. traveiliden more bisili to growyng and profiting of þe Chirche. *c* **1450** *Godstow Reg.* 365 I-strengthed with the seales of bothe chapiters to more suerte. **1585** J. B. tr. *Viret's School Beastes* A vj b, To the ende that the seedes whiche they hyde in the earth, shoulde not growe. **1683** MOXON *Mech. Exerc., Printing* x, He was bred up to Joynery. *a* **1715** BURNET *Own Time* an. 1661 (1823) I. 318 There were few books set out to sale. **1726** LEONI *Alberti's Archit.* Pref. 3 Waters .. employ'd to so many different and useful purposes. **1843** *Fraser's Mag.* XXVIII. 715 The captain .. came to our rescue. **1894** C. N. ROBINSON *Brit. Fleet* 50 The indispensable means to our end.

b. Combining the notions of 'purpose' and 'motion so as to reach' (1) or 'contiguity' (5 b).

c **897** K. ÆLFRED *Gregory's Past. C.* xliv. 328 Dryhten .. ðonne he cymð to ðæm dome. **1471**– [see GRASS *sb.* 5, 5 b]. *a* **1523** HAWES *His Epitaph*, Though the daye be never so long, At last the bells ringeth to evensong. *a* **1592** GREENE *Orpharion* Wks. (Grosart) XII. 69 They sate downe .. to dinner. **1648** GAGE *West. Ind.* 154 That solemn meeting of the people to Fairs and mirth. **1806** A. HUNTER *Culina* (ed. 3) 133 You sit down to writing at your bureau. **1838** TICKNOR in *Life*, etc. (1876) II. viii. 147 We were out .. to breakfast.

c. *spec.* Towards or for the making of; as a contributory element or constituent of.

c **1450** *St. Cuthbert* (Surtees) 807 Stikkes to a fyre þai gadird fast. *c* **1500** *Demaundes Joyous* in *Rel. Ant.* II. 74 Howe many strawes go to gose nest? R. None, for lacke of fete. **1579** *Ibid.* I. 255, 10 yerds yelow lace that went to my lether dublett. **1621** BURTON *Anat. Mel.* III. iv. I. iii. (1651) 667 To the roof of Apollo Didymeus Temple..a thousand okes did not suffice. **1890** *Harper's Mag.* May 961/2 Whole gardens of roses go to one drop of the attar.

d. Indicating the crop with which ground is planted. Chiefly *U.S.*

1799, etc. [see PLANT *v.* 6a]. **1833** S. SMITH *Life & Writings Major J. Downing* 22 [He]..planted the ground all over to corn, and potatoes. **1848** F. A. DURIVAGE *Stray Subjects* 21 Having laid down a few acres to oats. **1902** *Times* 21 July 13/6 Land..planted to walnuts. **1945** B. MACDONALD *Egg & I* (1946) I. iii. 45 The garden..was planted to peas, beets, beans, corn, Swiss chard, lettuce, cabbage, onions, turnips, celery, cucumbers, tomatoes and squash. **1980** *Daily Tel.* 17 Sept. 8/3 The area sown to winter barley was greatly increased.

9. Indicating destination, or an appointed or expected end or event. (After *ready, prepared*, etc., *for* is now substituted.)

c **1205** LAY. 13428 A he seide þat Bruttes Neoren noht to nuttes. **13..** *K. Alis.* 2451 (Bodl. MS.) Ten hundreþ weren to deþ ydiȝth. **1388** WYCLIF *Ps.* xxxvii[i]. 18[17], Y am redi to betyngis. *c* **1430** *Hymns Virg.* 99 To bie oure soulis to blis. *a* **1540** BARNES *Wks.* (1573) 342/2 Your stockes bee made to the fyer. **1697** DRYDEN *Virg. Georg.* IV. 463 Born to bitter Fate. **1865** KINGSLEY *Herew.* xxviii, He had..made up his mind to the event. **1887** BESANT *The World went* ii, He was ..sentenced to transportation.

10. Indicating result, effect, or consequence: So as to produce, cause, or result in.

For *to one's cost* or *charge* see COST *sb.*[2] 5d, CHARGE *sb.* 10.

c **893** K. ÆLFRED *Oros.* I. vii. §1 þæt wæs þæt forme, þæt hyra wæter wurdon to blode. *c* **1175** *Lamb. Hom.* 27 Mare hit him deð to herme þenne to gode. *c* **1380** WYCLIF *Sel. Wks.* II. 210 What caas þat fallip to him, it mut nedis falle to his betere [= betterment, advantage]. *c* **1425** WYNTOUN *Cron.* I. v. 206 He dang him with his bow to deid. **1563** *Homilies* II. *Inform. Offence H. Script.* II. (1850) 380 Though the rehearsal of the genealogies..be not to much edification. **1623** GOUGE *Serm. Extent God's Provid.* §13 Fire brake out to the destruction of many. **1802** MAR. EDGEWORTH *Moral T.* (1816) I. xi. 92 To his..astonishment. **1888** *Times* (weekly ed.) 6 Apr. 16/4 To light those buildings by electricity, to the total exclusion of gas. **1908** R. BAGOT *A. Cuthbert* xxviii, But now, to his despair, he felt that his patient herself was fighting against his skill.

†**b.** *to take* (etc.) *to the best* or *worst*: to put the best, or worst, construction upon; to make the best, or worst, of. *Obs.*

c **1440** *Jacob's Well* 286 Euyr-more þou demyst euyll & to þe werste. **1563** BALDWIN in *Mirr. Mag.* X viij b, The good take yll thynges to the best. **1569** J. ROGERS *Gl. Godly Loue* (1876) 183 With a loving patience to take all things to the best. **1629** N. CARPENTER *Achitophel* 43 More honour found Homer in expressing mens manners to the best, than Hegemon to the worst.

11. Indicating a state or condition resulting from some process: So as to become: = INTO 6a. Also *colloq.* (after the vb. *to be*, in *all to pieces* or the like): Reduced to the condition of, having become.

†*all to naught*: see ALL C. 12, NAUGHT *sb.* 1d.

c **893** K. ÆLFRED *Oros.* V. iv. §4 Ealle ða clifu..forburnan to ascan. *c* **1000** ÆLFRIC *Lev.* i. 6 And hyldon þa offrunga & ceorfon to sticcon. *c* **1175** *Lamb. Hom.* 143 He is þet makeð twa to an. *c* **1205** LAY. 9425 Al þa wunliche burh heo barnden to duste. *c* **1400** MAUNDEV. (Roxb.) v. 14 After a ȝere it turnez to whyte. **1470–85** MALORY *Arthur* IV. xvi. 140 Brente to coles. **1612** CAPT. SMITH *Map Virginia* 31 Tops of Deeres hornes boyled to a jelly. *a* **1720** VANBRUGH *Journ. to London* III. ad fin., The glasses [of the coach] are all to bits. **1802** MAR. EDGEWORTH *Moral T.* (1816) I. iv. 24 Forester.. took the flowers..and pulled them to pieces. **1870** *Eng. Mech.* 28 Jan. 477/1 Shaped to an accurate figure.

b. Indicating resulting position, status, or capacity: For, as, by way of, in the capacity of. *Obs.* or *arch.* exc. in certain phrases, as ***to take to wife, to call to witness***, etc.

c **890** tr. *Bæda's Hist.* III. xv. [xxi.] (1890) 222 Se wæs..his freond [and] hæfde his sweostor to wife. *c* **1000** *Ags. Gosp.* Luke iii. 8 We habbað us to fæder abraham. *c* **1000** ÆLFRIC *Gen.* xx. 12 Ic ȝenam hiȝ þa to wife. —— *Deut.* iv. 26 Ic hæbbe todæȝ to ȝewitnisse heofen and eorþan. *c* **1175** *Lamb. Hom.* 117 Ic þe ȝef to scawere mine folke israeles hirede. **13** .. *St. Ambrosius* 125 in Horstm. *Altengl. Leg.* (1878) 10/1 Ambrose..To vr bisschop we wol haue. *c* **1386** CHAUCER *Pars. T.* ¶271 He ne hadde no mete but herbes and water to his drynke. *c* **1460** FORTESCUE *Abs. & Lim. Mon.* x. (1885) 131 The qwene off Ffraunce hath but v. M[l] marke yerely to huyr douer. **1590** SPENSER *F.Q.* I. i. 28 So forward on his way (with God to frend) He passed forth. **1632** MILTON *Penseroso* 113 Who had Canace to wife? **1879** SWINBURNE *Stud. Shaks.* i. (1880) 28 The high-born poem which had Sackville to father and Sidney to sponsor.

12. Indicating that to which something tends or points. **a.** Indicating the object of inclination, desire, or need: For. Also (after *to drink*, etc.), As an expression of desire for (one's health, success, or the like): cf. 26b.

c **1200** [see LONGING *vbl. sb.*[1] 1]. *a* **1300** *Sarmun* li. in *E.E.P.* (1862) 6 To met no drink þer nis no nede. **1366** [see APPETITE *sb.* 3]. **1451** CAPGRAVE *Life St. Aug.* 4 þei herd sey þat her child had a grete corage to lernyng. **1605–** [see MIND *sb.*[1] 13d]. **1605–** [see DRINK *v.* 13b]. **1760** [W.R. CHETWOOD] *Voy. W. O. G. Vaughan* I. 38 You'll spoil her Stomach to her dinner. **1827** SCOTT *Highl. Widow* v, 'To your health, mother!' said Hamish. **1865** KINGSLEY *Herew.* xxxii, Instead of marrying Torfrida.., I have more mind to her niece.

b. Indicating the object of a right or claim.

c **1205** [see RIGHT *sb.*[1] 7]. **1377** LANGL. *P. Pl.* B. XVIII. 291 We haue no trewe title to hem. **1481–** [see PRETEND *v.* 13]. **1600** W. WATSON *Decacordon* (1602) 292 When men receiue the Gospell and are baptized..they receiue thereby an interest to the kingdome of heauen. **1602** [see HEIR *sb.* 2]. **1623** *Dial. Laws Eng.* xlvii. 149 If a man buy a horse in open market of him that in right had no propertie to him. **1752** [see CLAIM *sb.* 2]. **1879** M. J. GUEST *Lect. Hist. Eng.* xxv. 252 Thirteen..came forward as claimants to the crown. **1890** LD. ESHER in *Law Times Rep.* LXIII. 694/1 This lease..is a document of title to land.

IV. Followed by a word or phrase expressing a limit in extent, amount, or degree.

13. Indicating a limit or point attained in degree or amount, or in division or analysis, and thus expressing degree of completeness or exactitude: As far as; to the point of; down to (an ultimate element or item), as in phr. *to a hair* (HAIR *sb.* 8c), ***to the last man; to a man*** (including every man, without exception); within (a limit of variation or error), as ***to an inch, to a day***. (See also quots. s.v. DOWN *adv.* 14.)

c **1000** ÆLFRIC *Saints' Lives* xx. 42 Heo wel drohtnode to anum mæle fæstende. *a* **1300** *Cursor M.* 21527 Of he kest al to his serk. **1377** LANGL. *P. Pl.* B. v. 173 þei..do me faste frydayes to bred and to water. **1552** HULOET, To the vttermost peny, *ad assem.* **1606–** [see HAIR *sb.* 8c]. **1607–** [see TITTLE *sb.* 2b]. **1618** BOLTON *Florus* (1636) 149 They might have had the killing of all his Army to a man. **1670** MILTON *Hist. Eng.* II. Wks. (1847) 491/1 That he would root them out to the very name. **1766** GOLDSM. *Vic. W.* xi, Sir Tomkyn ..swore he was hers to the last drop of his blood. **1779** *Mirror* No. 34 ¶5 He was generally punctual to a minute. **1867** FROUDE *Short Stud., Erasm. & Luther* ii. 99 The bishops were hostile to a man. **1872** YEATS *Techn. Hist. Comm.* 349 Balances are made sensitive to the fraction of a grain.

b. Indicating the final point or second limit of a series, or of the extent of a variable quantity or quality; correl. to *from* (expressed or implied).

1699 [see FROM 2b]. **1725** DE FOE *Voy. round World* (1840) 111 Here they found eleven to thirteen fathom soft oozy sand. **1823** F. CLISSOLD *Ascent Mt. Blanc* 23 The western arc of the misty circle kindled, from a rosy to a deep reddening glow. **1866** LAWRENCE tr. *Cotta's Rocks Class.* (1878) 141 A granular to compact aggregate. **1891** J. LEYLAND *Peak Derbysh.* i. 15 Every style from early Norman to late perpendicular.

14. Indicating the full extent, degree, or amount: So as to reach, complete, or constitute. Chiefly in advb. phrases, as ***to a certainty, to a degree, to*** (***that***, etc.) ***extent, to a fault, to the full***, etc.: see also the sbs. See also *up to* s.v. UP.

c **1000** ÆLFRIC *Lev.* xxvi. 5 ȝe etaþ to fylle. *c* **1407** LYDG. *Reson & Sens.* 220 The beaute of hir face..so bryght, That the goddesse Proserpyne..To hir beaute ne myght appere. **1473** WARKW. *Chron.* (Camden) 15 Knyghtes, squyers, and comons to the nombre of xx. m[l]. **1596** DANETT tr. *Comines* (1614) 140 They should not be able to pay a ransome to the value of the spurs and bridle bits in his campe. **1628** GAULE *Pract. The. Panegyr.* 60 Done, Done to full, whatsoe're he came to doe. **1720** *Lond. Gaz.* No. 5814/2 Bank Bills..to the Value of three hundred and sixty Millions of Livres. **1829** SCOTT *Wav.* Introd., Gallant, courteous, and brave, even to chivalry. *Mod.* He was generous to a fault.

b. Combining the notion of 'extent' with 'result' (10): So far or so much as to cause.

[*c* **1000** *Ags. Gosp.* Matt. xxvi. 38 Unrot ys min sawl oþ deað.] *c* **1175** *Lamb. Hom.* 121 Crist..wes ibuhsum þan heuenliche federe to þa deðe. ?*a* **1500** *Wycket* (1828) 1 In greate suffirance of persecution euen to the death. **1625** MASSINGER *New Way* II. ii, Yet he to admiration still increases In wealth. **1749** FIELDING *Tom Jones* v. vi, She was in love with him to distraction. **1834** M. SCOTT *Cruise Midge* vi. (1863) 100 We were laughing at this to our heart's content. **1873** RALFE *Phys. Chem.* 108 The filtrate and washings are..evaporated..to dryness. **1890** *Harper's Mag.* Mar. 564/2 The schoolroom was hot to suffocation.

c. After a verb (or derived sb.) denoting limitation or the like, and before a sb. (or sb. phr.) expressing the amount, extent, space, etc. *to* which something is restricted.

1518 *Sel. Pl. Star Chamb.* (Selden) II. 128 Without that the seid Inhabitauntes..haue byn lymytted..to eny certen nowmber of Catell. **1649–** [see CONFINE *v.* 7b]. **1691–** [see CONFINEMENT 2]. **1697** VANBRUGH *Relapse* I. iii, Your honour's side-face is reduced to the tip of your nose. **1701** W. WOTTON *Hist. Rome, Marcus* vi. 106 Marcus..fix'd their Allowance to two Attic Talents a Man. **1885** *Law Times Rep.* LIII. 527/2 There is nothing on the face of this will to cut down the widow's absolute interest to a life estate.

V. Indicating addition, attachment, accompaniment, appurtenance, possession.

15. In addition to, besides, with. Now only indicating food taken in addition to a dish or meal, and in this use *dial.*

c **897** K. ÆLFRED *Gregory's Past. C.* xli. 303 Se læce, ðonne he bietre wyrta deð to hwelcum drence. *c* **1000** ÆLFRIC *Saints' Lives* xxviii. 19 Candidus and uitalis and fela oþre to him. **1387** TREVISA *Higden* (Rolls) III. 73 He putte [orig. *addidit*] Ianeuer and Feuerrer to þe bygynnynge of þe ȝere. **1495** *Coventry Leet Bk.* 567 ȝe shall haue drynk to your Cake. **1593** SHAKS. *Lucr.* 1589 Foretell new stormes to those alreadie spent. **1653** WALTON *Angler* viii. 171 Mix these together, and put to them either Sugar, or Honey. **1742** RICHARDSON *Pamela* III. 327 To the Charms of Person, [she] should have a humble, teachable Mind. **1792** W. COWPER *Let.* 30 Nov. in J. A. Roy *Cowper & his Poetry* (1914) viii. 166 It is impossible any longer to find a pound of butter or cream to our tea in all the country. **1876** RUSKIN *Fors Clav.* lxix. §12 (1906) III. 403 He can't have cream to his tea. **1916** 'TAFFRAIL' *Pincher Martin* vii. 107 My poor John was fond of a hegg to 'is tea. **1925** V. WOOLF *Let.* 20 Sept. (1977) III. 213, I am growing old, and want more mustard to my meat.

b. To the accompaniment of; as an accompaniment to; also indicating the tune to which words are set; ***to ride to hounds***: see HOUND *sb.*[1] 2.

1561 T. HOBY tr. *Castiglione's Courtyer* II. (1900) 118 Syngynge to the Lute..is more plesaunte. **1591** [see TUNE *sb.* 2a]. **1676** tr. *Guillatiere's Voy. Athens* 397 Dancing-Masters, who danced to Two or Three Base-Vials, or Instruments very like them. **1611, 1702** [see GO *v.* 17]. **1794** MRS. RADCLIFFE *Myst. Udolpho* l, Performing a sprightly dance,..to the sounds of a lute and tamborine. **1825** *Sporting Mag.* XV. 346 We formerly rode after hounds, now we ride to them. **1825** C. WATERTON *Wanderings S. Amer.* iv. 279 There is an old song, to the tune of La Belle Catharine. **1894** NEWTON *Dict. Birds* 693 The old-fashioned practice of shooting Partridges to dogs. **1906** BELLOC *Hills & Sea* 116 The two trumpets of the battery sounding the call which is known among French gunners as 'the eighty hunters', because the words to it are '*Quatre-vingt, quatre-vingt..chasseurs*'.

16. After words denoting attachment or adherence; hence, sometimes = Attached, fastened, or joined to. (*lit.* or *fig.*)

c **890** tr. *Bæda's Hist.* III. xiv. [xvii.] (1890) 204 þa næglas ..þe heo mid þæm to þæm timbre ȝefæstnad wæs. *c* **1050** *Byrhtferth's Handboc* in *Anglia* VIII. 324 Man..ða ræftras to ðære fyrste ȝefæstnaþ. **1297** R. GLOUC. (Rolls) 277 He wilnede mest of alle þing to him·eliance. **1382** WYCLIF *2 Kings* i. 8 A row3 man, and with an hery gyrdyl to the reenys. **1583** STUBBES *Anat. Abus.* II. (1882) 109 An old gowne girded to him with a thong. **1596** SHAKS. *Tam. Shr.* IV. i. 7 My very lippes might freeze to my teeth. **1780** COWPER *Progr. Err.* 285 As creeping ivy clings to wood or stone. **1800** ADDISON *Amer. Law Rep.* 1 The infant was found dead in the..river, with a stone to it. **1849** MACAULAY *Hist. Eng.* vi. II. 113 Sincerely attached to the Established Church. **1875** JOWETT *Plato* (ed. 2) I. 176 To that opinion I shall always adhere.

17. After *belong* and verbs of similar meaning (q.v.); also after *be* with the sense of *belong*; also after a sb., in the sense 'appertaining or belonging to': sometimes equivalent to 'of' or the possessive case of the sb.

c **893** K. ÆLFRED *Oros.* I. i. § 21 þæt Witland belimpeð to Estum. **972** *Charter* in Birch *Cart. Sax.* III. 589 Ðis sind þa land ȝemæra þæs londes þe lympð to Sture. **1451** *Rolls of Parlt.* V. 226/2 Godes..that were sumtyme to the seid William. *c* **1530** LD. BERNERS *Arth. Lyt. Bryt.* 299, I am doughter to a king. **1605** CAMDEN *Rem.* (1637) 281 Katherine, wife to Charles Brandon, Duke of Suffolke. **1719** DE FOE *Crusoe* (1840) I. i. 2 Lieutenant-colonel to an English regiment of foot. *Ibid.* 5 Clerk to an attorney.

b. Combining the notions of 'appurtenance' and 'addition' (15) and 'attachment' (16).

c **1420** *Chron. Vilod.* 3510 To delyuer hit to a golde-smyȝt, to make a shrene þat body to. **1538** *Acc. Ld. High Treas. Scot.* VI. 13 Gevin for four roundellis to speris, vj cronis. **1682** N. O. *Boileau's Lutrin* II. 126 This paltrey Jack Had scarce a Shooe to 's foot, a Rag to 's back. **1711** ADDISON *Spect.* No. 108 ¶2 Your Whip wanted a Lash to it. **1832** HT. MARTINEAU *Life in Wilds* iii, One little boy complained.. that there was no rim to his plate. **1840** R. H. DANA *Bef. Mast* xix. 53 Without clothing to his back, or shoes to his feet. **1847** HELPS *Friends in C.* I. v. 80 Both will and courage. Courage is the body to will. **1886** C. E. PASCOE *Lond. of To-day* xxx. (ed. 3) 269 The Hall now forms the vestibule to the Houses of Parliament.

c. In colloq. phrases with *there is* and a quantitative or pronominal expression: belonging as a quality, attribute, or capacity to (someone or something, freq. *it*); ***that is all there is to it***: it is that and nothing more; ***there's nothing to it***: see NOTHING *sb.* 10c. orig. *U.S.*

1880 'MARK TWAIN' *Tramp Abroad* ii. 36 There's more to a blue-jay than any other creature. **1883** —— *Life on Mississippi* xlv. 459 The steamboat shoved out up the creek. That was all there was 'to it'. **1895** KIPLING *Day's Work* (1898) 83 'That's all there is to it,' seethed the white water roaring through the scuppers. **1903** A. H. LEWIS *Boss* 14 Tell me what there is to this shindy. **1914** V. CASTLE *Mod. Dancing* 44 Simply *walk* as softly and smoothly as possible. .. This is the One Step, and this is all there is to it. **1936** L. C. DOUGLAS *White Banners* xvi. 343 He's a wonderful person, you know. There's a lot to him that doesn't show up on the surface. **1974** J. THOMSON *Long Revenge* iii. 40 He had the feeling that there was a great deal more to it [*sc.* a case] than he had so far discovered. **1976** *New Yorker* 26 Apr. 38/1, I thought she had a lot to her, a lot to offer.

VI. Expressing relation to a standard or to a stated term or point.

18. Expressing comparison: In comparison with, as compared with. Also † *as to* (obs.). (See also 21.)

c **1000** ÆLFRIC *Hom.* II. 13 Ðes is ure God, and nis nan oðer ȝeteald to him. **1470–85** MALORY *Arthur* I. xxii. 69 Your myghte is nothyng to myn. **1523** LD. BERNERS *Froiss.* I. cclxviii. 396 His enemyes were but a handfull of men, as to the nombre of his. **1546** J. HEYWOOD *Prov.* (1867) 46 There is no foole to the olde foole. **1602** SHAKS. *Ham.* I. ii. 140 So excellent a King, that was, to this, Hiperion to a Satyre. **1666** PEPYS *Diary* 21 Apr., It was so thick to its length. **1742** RICHARDSON *Pamela* III. 351 Now, by..good Physick,..pretty well, to what they had been. **1863** COWDEN CLARKE *Shaks. Char.* viii. 202 The men are noodles to her.

19. a. Connecting the names of two things (usu. numbers or quantities) compared or opposed to each other in respect of amount or value, as the odds in a wager or contest, the terms of a ratio, or the constituents of a compound: Against, as against.

1530 Palsgr. 712/1 Twenty to one he is ondone for ever. *a* **1548** Hall *Chron., Hen. V* 76 b, Their enemies.. wer foure to one. **1596** Shaks. *1 Hen. IV*, ii. iv. 592 O monstrous, but one halfe penny-worth of Bread to this intollerable deale of Sacke? **1628** Hobbes *Thucyd.* (1822) 127 There is no nation ..that are..able one nation to one to stand against the Scythians. *c* **1790** Imison *Sch. Art* i. 212 The visible part of an object will be to the lens, as the focal distance of the lens, to the distance of the eye. **1836** J. Romilly *Diary* 30 Nov. (1967) 109 The grace..was thrown out in the White hood house by 30 to 21; it past in the black by 23 to 20. **1846** *Penny Cycl.* Suppl. II. 432/1 The composition..consists of three-fourths of the putty..to one-fourth of calcined gypsum. **1885** *Manch. Exam.* 16 May 6/2 Mr. Gladstone's motion was carried by 337 to 38.

b. Connecting two expressions of number or quantity which correspond to each other, or of which one constitutes the amount or value of the other: In; making up. (*to the* = in every.)

c **1000**, **1297** [see c]. **1494** *Act 11 Hen. VII*, c. 4 That there be but only viii. Bushels rased and stricken to the Quarter of Corn. **1545** *Rates of Customs* c v, Twelue ounces to the pounde. **1593** Shaks. *2 Hen. VI*, iv. vii. 25 He..made vs pay ..one shilling to the pound. **1660** Jer. Taylor *Duct. Dubit.* iii. iv. xiii. §17 Three weeks of five days to the week. **1801** W. Huntington *Bank of Faith* Ded. 21 Thirteen to the dozen. **1891** S. C. Scrivener *Our Fields & Cities* 44 An open country..with solitary houses—a house to about five square miles.

†**c.** Introducing an expression denoting price or cost: For, at. *Obs.* (exc. as coinciding with b).

c **893** K. Ælfred *Oros.* iii. vii. §5 þæt hie þa æt nihstan hie selfe to nohte bemætan. *c* **1000** *Ags. Gosp.* Matt. x. 29 Hu ne becypað hiȝ tweȝen spearwan to peninge? **1297** R. Glouc. (Rolls) 8334 An ey [= egg] to tueie ssillinges..þo hii boȝte, & an hen vor viftene. **1483** in *Eng. Gilds* (1870) 337 Thath all Bakers of the said Cite..make butt ij. horse-lofys to a peny. **1656** H. Phillips *Purch. Patt.* (1676) 12 Profit, at least to the rate of eight in the hundred. **1862** Thackeray *Philip* ii. (1884) 110 Delicious little Havannahs, ten to the shilling.

20. Expressing agreement or adaptation: In accordance with, according to, after, by. (See also 21.)

c **897** K. Ælfred *Gregory's Past. C.* xxxvi. 249 Se ðe to Godes bisene ȝesceapen is. *a* **1300** *Cursor M.* 12946 Bidd þir stanes be bred to will. **1483** Caxton *G. de la Tour* k v, I pray yow that ye take ensample to them. **1664** Dryden *Rival Ladies* Ep. Ded., Ess. (Ker) I. 9 The greatest part of my design has already succeeded to my wish. **1754** Richardson *Grandison* (1781) I. xxxvi. 256 He dresses to the fashion. **1838** Macaulay *Ess., Sir W. Temple* (1897) 419 Temple is not a man to our taste. **1878** Morley *Diderot*, etc. I. v. iii. 203 As the neutral scribe writing to the dictation of an unseen authority.

b. Combining the senses 'according to' and 'to the extent of' (14): esp. in phr. ***to one's knowledge***, †***power*** (obs.), ***remembrance***, etc. (= as far as one knows, is able, remembers, etc.), now usually ***to the best of..***; ***to all appearance***; etc. (See also the sbs.)

to my knowledge, qualifying a positive statement = 'as I actually know'; qualifying a negative statement = 'as far as I know'.

1399 *Rolls of Parlt.* III. 452/1 If it were so taken and construed to the hegheste sentence and most rigorouste. *c* **1430** *Syr Gener.* (Roxb.) 1680, I shal help, to my power. **1512** *Act 4 Hen. VIII*, c. 20 *Preamble*, Strikyng with.. swordes..and oder wepons to the uttermost of their powers. *a* **1548** Hall *Chron., Hen. VII* 3 b, The lyke was neuer harde of, to any mannes remembraunce before that tyme. **1636** Massinger *Gt. Dk. Flor.* Ded., It is above my strength..to celebrate to the desert your noble inclination. **1749** Fielding *Tom Jones* iv. xiv, I will be sworn, to the best of my remembrance, I was in a passion. **1793** To all appearance [see appearance 8]. **1885** Sir H. Cotton in *Law Rep. 30 Chanc. Div.* 12 They were to all appearances distinct bills.

1542 N. Udall in *Lett. Lit. Men* (Camden) 3 To my knowlege I have not eftsons offended. **1828** Marly *Life Planter Jamaica* 78 To my own knowledge he often tries to dissuade. **1883** Sir W. B. Brett in *Law Rep. 11 Q.B. Div.* 512 The article was, to the knowledge of the defendant, supplied for the use of the wife. *Mod.* He has not been here to-day to my knowledge.

21. After words expressing comparison, proportion, correspondence, agreement or disagreement, and the like: see also these words themselves.

In some cases now replaced by or interchangeable with other prepositions, esp. *with*; after *worthy*, and words denoting precise proportion, as *double*, now replaced by *of*; after *different*, *from* is considered more correct. After *like* adj. and adv., *to* is now usually omitted. See these words.

c **1290** *Beket* 324 in *S. Eng. Leg.* I. 116 He nam..þan clerkene Robe, ase to is stat bi-cam. *a* **1300**- [see like *a.* 1 a]. **1382** Wyclif *Heb.* xi. 38 To which the world was not worthi. **1387** Trevisa *Higden* (Rolls) I. 45 þe proporcioun of þe roundenesse aboute of a cercle is to þe brede as is þe proporcioun of two and twenty to seuene. **1470-85** Malory *Arthur* v. viii. 175 Arthur.., to whome none erthely prynce may compare. **1550** Crowley *Way to Wealth* Sel. Wks. (E.E.T.S.) 133 The rentes be..some double, some triple, and some four fould to that they were. **1599** Shaks. *Much Ado* v. ii. 38, I can finde out no rime to Ladie but babie, an innocent rime. **1651** Wittie *Primrose's Pop. Err.* 432 Those things which are the same [= equal] to one third are the same among themselves. **1737** Whiston *Josephus' Antiq.* Dissert. i, This..testimony..exactly agrees to him under that character. **1823** F. Cooper *Pioneers* iii, Strangely contrasted to the chill aspect of the lake. **1849** Macaulay *Hist. Eng.* vi. II. 17 Lewis was not inferior to James in generosity and humanity, and was..far superior to James in all the abilities..of a statesman.

†**b.** After an adj. in the comparative degree: Than. Now *rare* or *Obs.* (Cf. *inferior to*, *superior to*, in prec. sense.)

c **1315** Shoreham *Poems* i. 590 Nys none of wymman beter ibore To seint Iohan þe baptyste. **14..** *MS. Harl. 2261* lf. 225 An oþer Decius, yonger to hym. **1569** J. Sanford tr. *Agrippa's Van. Artes* 69 There are..philosophers..herein no lesse ridiculouse to the poetes, which write [etc.]. **1771** T. Hull *Sir W. Harrington* (1797) IV. 108 The really good are so far less in number to the bad. **1895** P. White *King's Diary* 96 A more formal repast, fashioned on a smaller scale to that provided at Langdale.

22. Expressing relation (generally or vaguely): In respect of, concerning, about, of, as to (see as *adv.* 33). Now only in special collocations.

In ***to name*** (obs.), ***to trade***, etc. (*Sc.* and *north. dial.*), now expressed by 'by'.

a **1300** *Cursor M.* 19806 Cornelius to nam he hight. **1450** *Rolls of Parlt.* V. 179/1 Reporte her advise what shuld be doon to the Articles comprised in the said Bille. **1481** Caxton *Reynard* xxxix. (Arb.) 105 He was lyghter to fote than he. **1513** Douglas *Æneis* i. v. 69 The ȝong child, quhilk now Ascanius hecht, And to suirname clepit Iulus. **1590** Shaks. *Mids. N.* iii. ii. 62 What's this to my Lysander? **1593** —— *Rich. II*, i. i. 110 What sayest thou to this? **1656** Burton *Diary* (1828) I. 136 There was one Mr. Thorne.. examined to the seal of the statute, whether the seal wanted not all the wax. **1693** J. Edwards *Author. O. & N. Test.* 308 Being conscious to my own inabilities. *a* **1716** Blackall *Wks.* (1723) I. 312 In speaking to the first of these Heads. **1724** Ramsay *Clout the Caldron* i, I am a tinkler to my trade. **1884** W. C. Smith *Kildrostan* 72 What will Doris say to it? **1892** *Guardian* 6 Jan. 8/3 Asking questions intended to show the untrustworthy character of a witness, or, as it is technically called, 'cross-examining to credit'.

23. Expressing relative position: esp. in *Geom.* In some instances allied to senses 5, 16.

1570- [see perpendicular A. 2]. **1600** Hakluyt *Voy.* III. 56 Parallel to the equinoctiall. **1660** Barrow *Euclid* iii. Prop. xvi. Coroll., A right line drawn from the extremity of the diameter of a circle, and at right angles, is a tangent to the said circle. **1796** [see asymptote]. **1813** Bakewell *Introd. Geol.* (1815) 58 Inclined to the horizon. **1848** J. H. Newman *Loss & Gain* 147 Unable to see how they lie to each other. **1887** *Encycl. Brit.* XXII. 718/1 Turned round so as to place the micrometer tangentially to the circle. **1892** [see right angle b].

VII. Expressing relations in which the sense of direction tends to blend with that of the dative.

24. After words denoting application, attention, or the like, indicating the object of this. Also (*arch.* or *rhet.*) with ellipsis of *go*, *betake oneself*, etc. (in imperative, or after an auxiliary).

a **1225** *Leg. Kath.* 115 Hire feder hefde iset hire earliche to lare. *c* **1290**- [see listen *v.* 2 b]. **1426** Lydg. *De Guil. Pilgr.* 10104 How that an Ampte, a best smal..To nouht elles doth entende, But on thys hylle vp tascende. *c* **1485** *Digby Myst.* iii. 758, I synful creature, to grace I woll a-plye. *a* **1553** Udall *Royster D.* iv. viii, Too it againe, my knightesses! **1616** *Marlowe's Faust.* vi, Let's to it presently. **1653** Walton *Angler* ii. 47 I'll to my own Art. **1710** Palmer *Proverbs* 254 To it they went with great fury. **1719** De Foe *Crusoe* (1840) I. xvii. 294 We fell to digging. **1843** *Blackw. Mag.* LIV. 219 Come, lads, all hands to work!

25. Expressing impact (cf. 1, 5 a) or attack: At, against, upon.

a **1225** *Ancr. R.* 62 Vre vo..scheot..mo cwarreaus to one ancre þen to seouene & seouenti lefdies iðe worlde. **1375** Barbour *Bruce* x. 312 [He] set a sege to the castele. *c* **1420** *Avow. Arth.* xxiv, Take thi schild and thi spere, And ride to him a course on werre. **1569** *St. Papers Eliz., Foreign* XI. 151 He had forces sufficient to make head to his enemies. **1641** Brome *Jov. Crew* iv. i, Heark! they knock to the Dresser. **1749** Fielding *Tom Jones* xviii. xii, Western.. with his hunting voice and phrase, cried out, 'To her, boy, to her, go to her'. **1832** Sir J. Campbell *Mem.* II. ii. 46, I presented it [the gun] to him without any other idea but that of intimidation. **1882** G. Macdonald *Weighed & Wanting* III. xviii. 256 His father's unmerciful use of the whip to him. **1888**, **1889** [see take *v.* 24 b].

b. After words denoting opposition or hostility: Against; towards (*obs.* or *arch.*). †In quot. 1670 *simply*: Against, so as to prevent (*obs.*).

Cf. *to one's face, teeth*, etc., in 5 b.

13.. *E.E. Allit. P.* B. 1230 Hade þe fader..neuer trepast to him in teche of mysseleue. **1388** Wyclif *Ps.* l. 6 [li. 4], I haue synned to thee aloone. *Ibid.* lxxxiv. 6 Whether thou schalt be wrooth to vs withouten ende? **1526** Tindale *Col.* iii. 13 If eny man have a quarrel to a nother. **1613** Shaks. *Hen. VIII*, i. i. 43 To the disposing of it nought rebell'd. **1670** Walton *Life Herbert* Pref., To embalm and preserve his sacred body to putrefaction. **1741** Middleton *Cicero* (1742) I. iv. 264 Clodius had an old grudge to the King, for refusing to ransom him. **1901** G. Douglas *Ho. w. Green Shutters* 261 He had a triple wrath to his son.

26. Indicating the object of speech, address, or the like; sometimes more vaguely: Before, in the presence (sight, hearing) of.

c **893** K. Ælfred *Oros.* vi. xxxiv. §2 He cwæð to ðæm folce. *c* **1000** Ælfric *Gen.* vi. 13 God cwæð þa to Noe. **1154** *O.E. Chron.* an. 1135 Durste nan man sei to him naht bute god. *c* **1230**- [see answer *v.* 12 b]. *a* **1300** *Cursor M.* 25312 If þou prais [= prayest] to godd þat he..þi sinnes forgiue to þe. *c* **1386** Chaucer *Sqr.'s T.* 208 Another rowned to his felawe lowe. **1609** Bible (Douay) *1 Kings* xviii. 6 The wemen came forth..singing and dancing to Saul the King. *a* **1625** Fletcher *Hum. Lieut.* i. i, Did you not mark a woman, my son rose to? **1711** Addison *Spect.* No. 60 ¶2 An Hymn in Hexameters to the Virgin Mary. **1820** Shelley *Skylark* i Hail to thee, blithe Spirit!

b. In honour of; for the worship of (as ***to build a temple*** or ***altar to***); in salutation of and expression of good wishes for (as ***to drink to***: see also 12 a, and drink *v.* 13 b).

1382 Wyclif *Acts* xix. 24 Sum man..makinge siluerene housis to Dian. **1388** —— *Acts* xvii. 23, Y..foond an auter, in which was writun, To the vnknowun God. **1530**- [see drink *v.* 13 b]. **1592**- [see here *adv.* 2 b]. **1611** Shaks. *Wint. T.* iv. iv. 62 Her face o' fire With labour, and the thing she tooke to quench it She would to each one sip. **1616** B. Jonson *Forest*, *To Celia* i Drink to me, only with thine eyes. **1712** Steele *Spect.* No. 462 ¶4 With continual toasting Healths to the Royal Family. **1838** Thirlwall *Greece* II. xvi. 353 They erected an altar to the father of the gods.

27. Expressing response or the like (of a voluntary agent); e.g. reply (*to* a statement, question, etc.), obedience or disobedience (*to* a command, etc.).

1297- [see assent *v.* 1, 4]. **1382**, *c* **1400**- [see answer *v.* 12 l, d]. *c* **1420** *Chron. Vilod.* 1123 Wylde bestes & folys of flyȝt To here clepynge wolde come. **1582** Allen *Martyrd. Campion* (1908) 68 A proclamation was red..and at the end thereof was said, God save the Queene. To which he said, Amen. **1641** R. Carpenter *Experience* i. ch. xvii. 116 When the silly Shepheard commeth to his call. **1754** Richardson *Grandison* V. xliv. 283, I will write to your letter. *a* **1766** Mrs. F. Sheridan *Sidney Bidulph* V. 115 Disobedience to his orders. **1897** *Badminton Mag.* Apr. 451 The next step is to take the pups out..and make them drop to hand.

b. Expressing reaction or responsive action (of an involuntary or inanimate agent); the object of *to* denoting the agent causing this.

1682 Otway *Venice Preserved* ii. i, My heart beats to this Man as if it knew him. **1768** Beattie *Minstr.* i. iii, His harp ..Which to the whistling wind responsive rung. **1805** Scott *Last Minstr.* ii. x, Full many a scutcheon and banner ..Shook to the cold night-wind. **1815** —— *Guy M.* iii, Little waves..sparkling to the moonbeams. **1850** Tennyson *In Mem.* Concl. 64 The dead leaf trembles to the bells.

28. Expressing exposure (of a thing *to* some physical agent).

1460-70 *Bk. Quintessence* 9 Sette it to the strong sunne in somer tyme. *c* **1500** *Melusine* xxx. 226 Mounted vpon a grete hors, his banere to the wynd. **1526** Tindale *Acts* xxvii. 40 They..hoysed vppe the mayne sayle to the wynde. **1852** Tennyson *Ode Dk. Wellington* 39 That tower of strength Which stood four-square to all the winds that blew.

VIII. Supplying the place of the dative in various other languages and in the earlier stages of English itself.

29. Introducing the recipient of anything given, or the person or thing upon whom or which an event acts or operates.

In OE. as in Latin, etc., expressed by the simple dative or indirect object; after *give*, *befall*, and various other verbs, *to* is still often omitted.

[*c* **893** K. Ælfred *Oros.* i. i. §13 Ohthere sæde his hlaforde, Ælfrede cyninge, þæt [etc.]. *Ibid.* iv. vi. §15 He him ȝeswor on his goda noman þæt [etc.]. *Ibid.* iv. x. §6 He hit het ðæm folce dælan. *c* **897** —— *Gregory's Past. C.* xlviii. 368 Godes æ, þe us forbiet deoflum to offrianne. *a* **900** *Ags. Ps.* (Th.) xxi[i]. 23 [25] Ic ȝylde min ȝehat Drihtne.]

1297 R. Glouc. (Rolls) 8183 Tancred & biaumond,..god herte hom nome to. *c* **1385** Chaucer *L.G.W.* 533 Mars ȝaf to hire corone red parde. **1477-9** *Rec. St. Mary at Hill* 89 Paid to the Skauagers..viijd. *a* **1533** Ld. Berners *Huon* cxlix. 568 All..were ioyful of that aduenture that was fallen to the emperoure. **1566** Painter *Pal. Pleas.* II. 336 Great dishonour would redound to us. **1667** Milton *P.L.* xii. 138 By promise he receaves Gift to his Progenie of all that Land. **1711** Addison *Spect.* No. 123 ¶4 Having a Son born to him. **1770** Goldsm. *Des. Vill.* 51 Ill fares the land, to hastening ills a prey, Where wealth accumulates, and men decay. **1850** R. G. Cumming *Hunter's Life S. Afr.* (1902) 47/1, I fired two shots at them..during the night, but none fell to my shots. **1887** A. Birrell *Obiter Dicta* Ser. ii. 156 He lost his heart to Peg Woffington.

b. Used esp. after *be*, *become*, *seem*, *appear*, *mean*, to indicate the recipient of an impression, the holder of a view or opinion; ***to be*** (something) ***to***, to be (something) in the eyes, view, apprehension, or opinion of; also, to be of importance or concern to: ***what is that to you?*** What does that matter to you? How does that concern you? What have you to do with that?

1362 Langl. *P. Pl.* A. Prol. 32 As hit semeþ to vre siht. **1565** T. Stapleton tr. *Staphylus' Apol.* 148 To these men Luther is a papist, and Caluin is the right..prophet. **1590-1908** [see seem *v.* 7]. **1798** Wordsw. *Peter Bell* i. xii, A primrose by a river's brim A yellow primrose was to him, And it was nothing more. **1850** J. H. Newman *Diffic. Anglic.* i. ii. (1891) I. 46 Faith has one meaning to a Catholic, another to a Protestant. **1856** Whyte Melville *Kate Cov.* xi, Scarcely big enough for a hunter to my fancy. **1862** [see appear *v.* 2]. *Mod.* To me it is simply absurd.

[*c* **950** *Lindisf. Gosp.* John xxi. 22 Huæd is ðe bi ðy? *vel* huæt is ðec ðæs? *Vulg.* Quid ad te?] *c* **1000** *Ags. Gosp.* ibid., Hwæt to þe? **1382** Wyclif ibid., What to thee? sue thou me. **1526** Tindale ibid., What is that to the? folowe thou me. **1526** —— *Matt.* xxvii. 4 What is that to vs? se thou to that. **1611** Bible *Lam.* i. 12 Is it nothing to you, all ye that passe by? **1674** Grew *Anat. Trunks* ii. ii. §3 What the Mouth is, to an Animal; that the Root is to a Plant. **1843** *Fraser's Mag.* XXVIII. 328 What's that to you? *Mod.* It means a great deal to him.

30. Indicating the person or thing for whose benefit, use, disposal, or the like, anything is done or exists: For; for the use or benefit of; for (some one) to deal with or dispose of (esp. after *leave* vb.); at the disposal of. ***to oneself*** (as pred.), to or at one's own disposal, free from the approaches or action of others.

1297 R. Glouc. (Rolls) 7136 Vpe holi relikes harald suor to willam bastard Treuliche to wite engelond to him. *c* **1330** R. Brunne *Chron. Wace* (Rolls) 1033 To mangeneles he dide make stones. **1382** WYCLIF *Rom.* xiv. 6-8 He that etith, etith to the Lord... No man of vs lyueth to hym silf, and no man deieth to him silf. Sothli where we lyuen, we lyuen to the Lord; where we deien, we deien to the Lord. *c* **1400** *Laud Troy Bk.* 17214 The Gregais wol not hir bodi grauen, But let hit ligge to roke & rauen. *c* **1425** tr. *Arderne's Treat. Fistula* 100 It availeþ to al woundez for to hold þam opne. **1474** *Acc. Ld. High Treas. Scot.* I. 70 Gevin to Johne of Murray.. to pay for clathis coft to Rannald gunnare. **1502** *Ibid.* II. 346 For ane gus to the Kingis halkis. **1586** MARLOWE *1st Pt. Tamburl.* II. v, I'll first assay To get the Persian kingdom to myself. **1611** BIBLE *Lev.* xxiii. 22 Neither shalt thou gather any gleaning of thy haruest: thou shalt leaue them vnto the poore, and to the stranger. **1653** WALTON *Angler* viii. 169 That hope and patience which I wish to all Fishers. **1695** DRYDEN *Parallel Poetry & Paint.* Ess. (ed. Ker) II. 153 The rest is left to the imagination. **1700** MARWOOD *Diary* in *Cath. Rec. Soc. Publ.* VII. 77 At 8 in the morn we took a Wagon to Our selves to Dunkerque. **1709-10** STEELE *Tatler* No. 118 ¶10 Your petitioner.. worked to the Exchange, and to several Aldermens wives. **1801** *Farmer's Mag.* Jan. 109 Topped and tailed [turnips].. which I hope to preserve as food to my ewes at lambing time. **1822** W. IRVING in *Life & Lett.* (1864) II. 84 In the country, where I can be more to myself. **1895** FROUDE *Erasmus* xv. 320 Religious houses were dissolved, their property seized to the State. *Mod.* We had the railway-carriage all to ourselves.

b. Indicating the person or thing towards which an action, feeling, etc., is directed; esp. as the object of conduct, behaviour, or demeanour.

to you, an elliptical phrase of courtesy or deference, = 'my service to you' or the like (quot. 1855).

c **970-***c* **1060** *Wifmannes Beweddung* c. 7 in Liebermann *Gesetze* 442 Ðæt hire man nan woh to ne do. *c* **1000** ÆLFRIC *Hom.* I. 240 Se is hyra and na hyrde, seðe.. næfð inweardlice lufe to Godes sceapum. *c* **1175** *Lamb. Hom.* 31 Nat ic hwer heo beoð þeo men þe ic þene herm to dude. **1297** R. GLOUC. (Rolls) 5824 To þe godnesse of þe holymon þe deuel adde enuye. *c* **1430** *How Gd. Wijf tau3te hir Dou3tir* 163 in *Babees Bk.* 44 To do to þem as þou woldist be doon to. **1712** STEELE *Spect.* No. 286 ¶1 That natural Horror we have to Evil. *a* **1758** DYER *Down Among the Dead Men* iii, Bacchus is a friend to Love. **1855** DICKENS *Holly-Tree* ii, 'I should wish you to find from themselves whether your opinion is correct'. 'Sir, to you', says Cobbs, 'that shall be done directly'.

31. Used in the syntactical construction of many intransitive verbs. (See also preceding senses, and the verbs themselves.)

1583 BABINGTON *Commandm.* viii. (1637) 73 Modesty in this hungry creature must yeeld to necessity. **1697** DRYDEN *Virg. Georg.* III. 817 'Tis in vain.. [to] trust to Physick. **1769** GOLDSM. *Hist. Rome* (1786) II. 61 That homage to which they had aspired. **1834** WORDSW. *Yarrow Revisited* viii, While they minister to thee. **1843** *Fraser's Mag.* XXVIII. 654, I have already alluded to the fact. **1875** POSTE *Gaius* I. Comm. (ed. 2) 87 The issue of a Denizen cannot inherit to him.

b. After *testify*, *witness*, *attest*, *swear*, *subscribe*, *confess*, *speak*, etc.: In support of; in assertion or acknowledgement of.

For *assent to* see 27; cf. also 21.

1630 PRYNNE *Anti-Armin.* 75 Conclusions which euery man must subscribe too. **1710** ADDISON *Tatler* No. 259 ¶6 The Prisoner brought several Persons of good Credit to witness to her Reputation. **1737** WHISTON *Josephus, Antiq.* IX. xiv. §2 Menander attests to it. **1771-** [see CONFESS *v.* 6]. **1776** *Trial of Nundocomar* 79/1 That is a fact to which I can speak. **1776** *Trial J. Fowke* c. 28/2, I took his affidavit to the truth of the contents of the Letters. **1802** MAR. EDGEWORTH *Moral T.* (1816) I. xix. 157 He would swear to the person from whom he received the note. **1884** *Manch. Exam.* 7 July 4/6 The hon. gentlemen spoke to a resolution congratulating the Government on the passing of the Franchise Bill.

c. In obsolete, archaic, or dialectal use: chiefly representing an OE. dative or French const. with *à*; now omitted, the verb being treated as *trans.*

a **1325-***c* **1450** [see PLEASE *v.* 1, 3 a]. *c* **1380** WYCLIF *Sel. Wks.* III. 362 Who shulde.. mor obe[i]she to þe pope þan to Crist? **1382** —— *Dan.* iii. 57 (Benedicite) Blesse 3e, alle the werkis of the Lord, to the Lord. *c* **1449** PECOCK *Repr.* I. xvi. 90 Serue to God. *Ibid.* II. xv. 234 Bileue thou to me. **1692** R. L'ESTRANGE *Josephus, Wars Jews* II. xxvi. (1733) 654 They should renounce to all manner of unlawful Violences. **1800** A. SWANSTON *Serm. & Lect.* (1803) II. 318 Titus and.. Timotheus also were present and assisting to the apostle. **1874** SWINBURNE *Bothwell* v. iv, If I did ill to seek to that strong hand.

32. In the syntactical const. of many transitive verbs, introducing the indirect or dative object. (See also preceding senses, and the verbs themselves.)

a **1300** [see sense 26]. *c* **1385** CHAUCER *L.G.W.* 2128 (*Ariadne*) Now be we duchessis.. And sekerede to the regalys of Athenys. *c* **1450** *Cov. Myst.* xiv. (1841) 141 To God in this case my cawse I have betaught. **1581** in Allen *Martyrd. Campion* (1908) 15 Her Maiestie will preferre him to great livings. **1666** PEPYS *Diary* 4 June, We fought them and put them to the run. **1779** *Mirror* No. 21 ¶1 This day's paper I devote to Correspondents. **1849** MACAULAY *Hist. Eng.* vi. II. 142 To admit Roman Catholics to municipal advantages.

b. In obsolete, archaic, or dialectal use; now replaced by other prepositions, or by different constructions. See under the vbs.

c **1500** *Melusine* vi. 32 Many.. shall axe to you tydynges of the Erle. **1534** CROMWELL in Merriman *Life & Lett.* I. 387 To answer unto suche thinges as then shalbe leyed and obiected to you. **1537** *Bury Wills* 130, I put them to the dysposycion of myne executo^rs. **1558** in Strype *Ann. Ref.* (1709) I. App. iv. 5 Not to pardon, till they.. put themselves wholly to her highness's mercy. **1660** F. BROOKE tr. *Le Blanc's Trav.* 37 We now had associated ourselves to a jolly company of Merchants. **1709** STRYPE *Ann. Ref.* I. xl. 410 The French hostages were put to liberty at Windsor. **1780** *Mirror* No. 87 ¶3 To masses and crucifixes, and images, were substituted a precise severity of manner, and long sermons, and a certain mode of sanctifying the Sabbath. **1794** G. ADAMS *Nat. & Exp. Philos.* I. xi. 465 If an alkali be substituted to the turnsole. **1823** F. COOPER *Pioneers* xii, His mild features were confronted to the fierce.. looks of the chief.

33. Expressing the relation of an adj. (or derived adv. or sb.) to a sb. denoting a person or thing to which its application is directed or limited.

In the construction of such adjs. as *accessible, adverse, agreeable, beneficial, common, complaisant, constant, difficult, due, easy, equal, essential, faithful, false, familiar, favourable, friendly, good, grateful, hostile, hurtful, impossible, incredible, injurious, kind, liable, manifest, natural, near, necessary, obedient, possible, proper, requisite, salutary, similar, subject, suitable, true, useful, visible, welcome*, etc., q.v., with their opposites; also, in a special sense, *alive, dead, deaf, blind, insensible*; also many adj. phrases, as *with child, in calf, of use, of value* (see the sbs.).

[In OE. mostly expressed by the dative: e.g. *c* **888** K. ÆLFRED *Boeth.* xiv. §3 þam neatum is ʒecynde. *c* **893** —— *Oros.* I. i. §3 þa sindon neh þæm garsecge. *Ibid.* I. vii. §1 Hy.. him ʒehyrsume wæron. *c* **897** —— *Gregory's Past. C.* xxxvi. 260 Hwa sceal.. Gode unðoncfull beon?]

c **888** K. ÆLFRED *Boeth.* xxiv. §2 Forðæm hit bið ofdælre ðærto. *c* **890** tr. *Bæda's Hist.* IV. xxv. [xxiv.] (1890) 348 Hwæþer heo ealle smolt mod &.. bliðe to him hæfdon. **971** *Blickl. Hom.* 103 Hi wæron to deaþe ʒearwe. *c* **1000** ÆLFRIC *Hom.* II. 60 þa wæs Abraham.. ʒearo to Godes hæse. **1303-** [see COMMON *a.* 3]. **1382-** [see NECESSARY *a.*] **1393-** [see DUE *a.* 5 a, 9]. **1393** LANGL. *P. Pl.* C. xx. 226 Beoþ nat vnkynde.. to 3oure emcristene. **1398** TREVISA *Barth. De P.R.* XII. xxviii. (Bodl. MS.), Hire crye is loþe and odios to oþer byrdes. *c* **1450-** [see OPEN *a.* 15]. **1451** CAPGRAVE *Life St. Gilbert* 112 He.. was in gret opinion both to þe Pope & þe court. **1576-** [see FAMILIAR *a.* 6]. **1593-** [see LIABLE 3 a]. **1601** SHAKS. *Jul. C.* II. i. 289 As deere to me, as are the ruddy droppes That visit my sad heart. **1607** [see DEAF *a.* 2]. **1610** SHAKS. *Temp.* I. ii. 303 Inuisible To euery eye-ball else. **1612-** [see ESSENTIAL *a.* 4]. **1632** MASSINGER *City Madam* v. iii, You are constant to your purposes. **1667** MILTON *P.L.* XI. 864 Grateful to Heav'n. **1711** [see COLD *a.* 7]. **1726** [see DEAD *a.* 3]. **1727** *Hartlepool Par. Reg.*, Mary Farding.. murdered by William Stephenson.. to whom she was pregnant. **1759** [see BLIND *a.* 2 b]. **1777** [W. MARSHALL] *Minutes Agric.* 14 Apr., This.. is new to me. **1824** SCOTT *St. Ronan's* viii, Induced to form conclusions not very favourable to his character. **1835** J. DUNCAN *Beetles* 151 Pervious to air and moisture. **1843** *Fraser's Mag.* XXVIII. 279 True to nature. **1881** BESANT & RICE *Chapl. of Fleet* II. xii, You are welcome to all my cast-off lovers. **1886** *Manch. Exam.* 3 Nov. 3/1 Comte.. lays himself specially open to attack. **1887** A. BIRRELL *Obiter Dicta* Ser. II. 80 He was always alive to the value of his wares. **1897** F. HALL in *Nation* (N.Y.) LXIV. 163/2 What is permissible to a critic is not impermissible to a counter-critic. **1905** *Oswestry & Border Cos. Advert.* 1 June (Advt.), The Cows and Heifers.. in-calf to a grand Pedigree Shorthorn Bull.

b. After pa. pples. of verbs of perception (now only with *known, unknown*; nearly = by). (Cf. *familiar to, visible to*, etc.) In OE. with dative.

[*c* **893** K. ÆLFRED *Oros.* I. i. §27 Hit is feawum mannum cuð.] *a* **1225** *Ancr. R.* 204 Heo beoð.. to monie al to kuðe. **13..** *Cursor M.* 10621 (Cott.) þaa þat þis maiden was to cuth. *c* **1380** WYCLIF *Sel. Wks.* III. 432 It is hyd to us whyche of hem ben seynts. *c* **1450** LOVE *Bonavent. Mirr.* lxi. (Gibbs MS.) lf. 115 þai weren no3t seen to hyre. **1539** BIBLE (Great) *1 Sam.* vi. 3 It shalbe knowen to you, why hys hand departeth not from you. **1548** UDALL, etc. *Erasm. Par. John* 47 God was seene and heard to Moses. **1598** SHAKS. *Merry W.* II. ii. 188 A man long knowne to me. **1770** GOLDSM. *Des. Vill.* 149 His house was known to all the vagrant train. **1855** MACAULAY *Hist. Eng.* xii. III. 157 They acted under no authority known to the law.

34. *Book-keeping.* Placed before debit entries, and followed by particulars of the goods or services for which money has been paid, or by the name of the account containing the corresponding credit entry. Cf. BY *prep.* 37.

1772 in *Country Life* (1973) 7 June (Suppl.) 104 To mending a Waiter & Candlestick & a Sauceboat 5s. **1803** G. COLMAN *John Bull* III i. 31 These charges are brought in like a bill!—To attending your ladyship at such a time—to dancing down twenty couple at another. **1876** *Encycl. Brit.* IV. 46 To J. Bevan and Co., for Bales, *ex* 'Mary Jane' £2349 0s. *od.* **1901** *Jrnl. R. Microsc. Soc.* 109 The Treasurer's Account for 1900... To Balance from 1899.. £195 11s. 3*d.* **1968** G. M. WHITEHEAD *Book-Keeping made Simple* v. 79 Whenever a debit entry is made on an account we begin with the word 'To' and follow with the name of the account where the other half of the double entry is to be found. **1978** J. KELLOCK *Elements of Accounting* i. 11 In many accounting text books the words 'To' and 'By' are used to preface debit and credit entries respectively in the ledger... These prefixes are now being discontinued in modern accounting systems.

35. Preceding the names of a person or group of persons who use a specified name or expression: in the language or usage of.

1922 P. S. O'HEGARTY *Terence MacSwiney* ii. 3 Terence James MacSwiney on the baptismal register, but Terry always to his friends and to Cork generally, was born in Cork City on March 28th, 1879. **1941** *Poor Souls' Friend* June 111 Her father, Edmund William Roe (Ted to his friends) was a man of character and great individuality. **1956** J. BRODRICK *St Ignatius Loyola* i. 12 In the Basque countries (to the Basques Euskalerria). **1970** *Outlook* Mar. 34 Owen Glyn Dwr—Glendower to the Anglo-Saxon—was the Welsh prince who made most of the mischief. **1977** *Transatlantic Rev.* LX. 118 Lindy (Miss Hoffmann to the kids) had to glide it back down to them.

B. to before an infinitive (or gerund: see 22).

History:—Beside the simple infinitive, or verbal substantive in *-an* (ME. *-en*, *-e*), OE., like the other WGer. languages, had a *dative* form of the same or a closely-related sb., which in OE. ended in *-anne*, *-enne*, in ME. reduced successively to *-ene*, *-en*, *-e*, and was thus at length levelled with the simple infinitive, and with it reduced to the uninflected verb-stem. This dative form was always preceded or 'governed' by the preposition *tó* 'to'. By many German writers it is called the 'gerund', after the Latin verbal sb. in *-ndum*. In mod.Eng. the functions of the Latin gerund are more properly discharged by the vbl. sb. in *-ing*, and it is therefore more convenient to speak of the OE. form in *-anne* as the 'dative infinitive' or 'infinitive with *to*'. Originally, *to* before the dative infinitive had the same meaning and use as before ordinary substantives, i.e. it expressed motion, direction, inclination, purpose, etc., toward the act or condition expressed by the infinitive; as in 'he came *to help* (i.e. to the help of) his friends', 'he went *to stay* there', 'he prepared *to depart* (i.e. for departure)', 'it tends *to melt*', 'he proceeded *to speak*', 'looking *to receive* something'. But in process of time this obvious sense of the prep. became weakened and generalized, so that *tó* became at last the ordinary link expressing any prepositional relation in which an infinitive stands to a preceding verb, adjective, or substantive. Sometimes the relation was so vague as scarcely to differ from that between a transitive verb and its object. This was esp. so when the vb. was construed both transitively and intransitively. There were several verbs in OE. in this position, such as *onginnan* to begin, *ondrǽdan* to dread, *bebéodan* to bid, order, *bewerian* to forbid, prevent, *ʒelíefan* to believe, *þencean* to think, etc.; these are found construed either with the simple (accusative) infinitive, or with *tó* and the dative infinitive. There was also a special idiomatic use (sense 13 a) of the infinitive with *tó* as an indirect nominative, where logically the simple infinitive might be expected. From these beginnings, the use of the infinitive with *to* in place of the simple infinitive, helped by the phonetic decay and loss of the inflexions and the need of some mark to distinguish the infinitive from other parts of the verb and from the cognate sb., increased rapidly during the late OE. and early ME. period, with the result that in mod.Eng. the infinitive with *to* is the ordinary form, the simple infinitive surviving only in particular connexions, where it is very intimately connected with the preceding verb (see below). To a certain extent, therefore, i.e. when the infinitive is the subject or direct object, *to* has lost all its meaning, and become a mere 'sign' or prefix of the infinitive. But after an intrans. vb., or the passive voice, *to* is still the preposition. In appearance, there is no difference between the infinitive in 'he proceeds *to speak*' and 'he chooses *to speak*'; but in the latter *to speak* is the equivalent of *speaking* or *speech*, and in the former of *to speaking* or *to speech*. In form, *to speak*, is the descendant of OE. *tó specanne*; in sense, it is partly the representative of this and largely of OE. *specan*.

(The simple infinitive, without *to*, remains: 1. after the auxiliaries of tense, mood, periphrasis, *shall, will*; *may, can*; *do*; and the quasi-auxiliaries, *must*, (and sometimes) *need, dare*: 2. after some vbs. of causing, etc.; *make, bid, let, have*, in sense 15 a; 3. after some vbs. of perception, *see, hear, feel*, and some tenses of *know, observe, notice, perceive*, etc., in sense 15 b; 4. after *had liefer, rather, better, sooner, as lief, as soon, as good, as well*, etc.: see HAVE *v.* 22, RATHER *adv.* 9 d, and the other words.)

The infinitive with *to* may be dependent on an adj., a sb., or a vb., or it may stand independently. To an adj. it stands in adverbial relation: *ready to fight* = ready for fighting; to a sb. it stands in adjectival or sometimes adverbial relation: *a day to remember* = a memorable day; to a vb. it may stand in an adverbial or substantival relation: *to proceed to work* = to proceed to working; *to like to work* = to like working.

I. With infinitive in adverbial relation.

* *Indicating purpose or intention.*

1. a. Dependent on a vb., *to* with inf. = *in order to*; equivalent to *that* or *in order that* with subjunctive, or to *for* or *for the purpose of* with gerund.

For *in order to, on purpose to*, see ORDER *sb.* 28 b (*b*), PURPOSE *sb.* 11 b.

The implied subject of the inf. may be either a subject or an object in the principal clause.

(*a*) Dependent on a verb of motion.

c **890** tr. *Bæda's Hist.* II. i. (1890) 96 Moniʒe cwomon to bicgenne þa ðing. *a* **900** *Ags. Ps.* (Th.) xxvi. 4 [xxvii. 3] þeah hi arisan onʒean me to feohtanne. *c* **950** *Lindisf. Gosp.* Mark iv. 3 Eode ðe sawende.. to sawenne. **971** *Blickl. Hom.* 165 To hwon eodan ʒe to westenne.. witʒan to secenne. **1205** LAY. 5238 Heo wolden fære to Rome to wreken o þon folke. **1297** R. GLOUC. (Rolls) 3523 þat he to him wende To helpe him in suche nede. **1388** WYCLIF *Matt.* iv. 1 Thanne Jhesus was led of a spirit in to desert, to be temptid of the feend. *Ibid.* xi. 8 Or what thing wenten 3e out to see [1382 for to seen]? **1577** B. GOOGE *Heresbach's Husb.* I. (1586) 3, I get me into my Closet to serue God. **1592** [see 10]. **1770** GOLDSM. *Des. Vill.* 180 Fools, who came to scoff, remained to pray. **1890** *Chamb. Jrnl.* 28 June 408/1 We made sail to return to Perim. *Mod.* She ran to meet her father.

(*b*) Dependent on other verbs.

Beowulf (Z.) 2562 Ða wæs hring-boȝan heorte ȝefysed sæcce to seceanne. *c* **890** tr. *Bæda's Hist.* IV. xiv. [xi.] (1890) 296 Ða ȝearwodon heo his lichoman to byrȝenne. *a* **901** *Laws of Ælfred* c. 62 §27 ȝif fyr sie ontended ryht to bærnenne. *c* **950** *Lindisf. Gosp.* Matt. ii. 13 Herodes sæcas ðone cnæht to fordoanne. *c* **1375** *Sc. Leg. Saints* xxxvi. (*Baptista*) 842 þan þe basare hewit on hicht His hand, to strik, gif he mycht. *c* **1425** WYNTOUN *Cron.* I. ix. 533 As men may be a roundall se, Merkit to be delt in thre. **1445** in *Anglia* XXVIII. 269 Bothe pore and riche labouryd righte sore, encrese to gete. *a* **1548** HALL *Chron., Hen. VI* 146 b, To have a Rowland to resist an Oliver. **1627** MILTON *Vac. Exerc.* 24 Thoughts that..loudly knock to have their passage out. **1724** DE FOE *Mem. Cavalier* (1840) 70, I gave a soldier five dollars to carry them news. **1787** COWPER *Stanzas Yearly Bill Mort.* 14 Like crowded forest trees we stand, And some are mark'd to fall. **1859** RUSKIN *Two Paths* iv. §110 As our bodies, to be in health, must be generally exercised, so our minds, to be in health, must be generally cultivated.

b. Dependent on an adj.; indicating the purpose or function to which the adj. refers.

c **890** tr. *Bæda's Hist.* II. i. (1890) 98 þæt he selfa ȝeara wære..þæt weorc to fremmenne. *a* **900** *Ags. Ps.* (Th.) xiii. 6 Heora fet beoð swiðe hraðe blod to ȝeotanne. *c* **1400** tr. *Secreta Secret., Gov. Lordsh.* v. 51 God..make cleer ȝoure vnderstondynge to persayue þe sacrament of þis science. **1578** LYTE *Dodoens* III. lxviii. 410 The lye..is very good to washe the scurffe of the head. *Mod.* Are they quite good to eat?

c. Dependent on a sb.; the inf. expressing the use or function of that which is denoted by the sb.

The advb. use may be explained as qualifying the adj. 'intended, adapted' before *to*.

c **890** tr. *Bæda's Hist.* III. xix. [xxvii.] (1890) 242 Bec on to leornienne [hi] ȝefon. *c* **893** K. ÆLFRED *Oros.* III. xi. §3 þonne seo leo bringð his hungreȝum hwelpum hwæt to etanne. **13..** *Minor Poems fr. Vernon MS.* xxiii. 771 To syke men made is he Medicyn, hem to mende. **1445** in *Anglia* XXVIII. 277 A plastir to cure þe wounde of Rome. **1526** TINDALE *Luke* ii. 32 A light to lighten the gentyls. **1609** BIBLE (Douay) *Numb.* iv. 16 The oyle to dresse the lampes. **1716** in J. O. Payne *Eng. Cath. Nonjurors of 1715* 348 One ciborium of silver, to preserve the consecrated Host. *a* **1845** HOOD *Lay of Labourer* i, A hook to reap, or a scythe to mow.

(*b*) After *time, room*, and words of similar meaning: equivalent to *for* with gerund (cf. a), or = at or in which (one) can or should..(cf. 11 b, c).

13.. *Cursor M.* 11814 (Cott.) Nu neghes tim to tak his lai. *c* **1385** CHAUCER *L.G.W.* 2000 (*Ariadne*) Rowm..To welde an axe. **1412–20** LYDG. *Chron. Troy* II. 658 To rekne hem alle I haue as now no tyme. **1597** J. PAYNE *Royal Exch.* 5 Now ys the tyme..to help one another. **1635** QUARLES *Embl.* I. vii. 3 Is this a time to pay thine idle vowes At Morpheus Shrine? **1858** MILL *Liberty* iv. (1873) 57 [There was] no time to warn him of his danger. **1887** 'L. CARROLL' *Game of Logic* iv. 96 The time to learn is when you're young.

2. In absolute or independent construction, usually introductory or parenthetic.

to be SURE, *to* WIT: see these words.

c **1305** *St. Kenelm* 266 in *E.E.P.* (1862) 54, & to telle hit wiþoute rym þuse wordes riȝt hit were. *c* **1386** CHAUCER *Knt's T.* 1037 And schortly to concluden, swich a place Was noon in erthe. *c* **1450** *Cov. Myst.* xiii. (1841) 129 Than ferther to oure matere to procede, Mary with Elizabeth abod. **1600** SHAKS. *A.Y.L.* I. i. 8 He keepes me rustically at home, or (to speak more properly) staies me heere at home vnkept. **1667** MILTON *P.L.* II. 922 Nor was his eare less peal'd With noises loud and ruinous (to compare Great things with small) then when Bellona storms [etc.]. **1711** ADDISON *Spect.* No 26 ¶6 But to return to our Subject. **1858** MILL *Liberty* iv. (1873) 53 The pleasure, not to say the useful recreation, of many, is worth the labour of a few. **1888** BRYCE *Amer. Commw.* III. VI. xcix. 387 All their ins and outs (to use an American phrase).

** *Indicating objectivity.*

3. Dependent on various verbs, chiefly transitive, passive, or reflexive, with weakened sense of purpose: indicating an action, etc. to which that of the principal verb is in some way directed. (See also the verbs themselves; and in particular, for specific uses, BE *v.* 16, HAVE *v.* B. 7 c, NEED *v.*[2] 8, OUGHT *v.* B. 5. Cf. also 14 below.)

The subject of the principal clause is also the implicit subject of the infinitive: so also in other senses below, except where the contrary is stated.

c **897** K. ÆLFRED *Gregory's Past. C.* xli. 302 Weorðen ȝeniedde hiera unðeawas to herianne & to weorðianne. *Ibid.* lvi. 433 Ða ðe ær ðenceað to syngianne. *a* **900** —— *Soliloquy* (1902) 46 Æall þæt þu wilnast to habbenne. *c* **1000** ÆLFRIC *Gen.* xi. 6 Hiȝ begunnon þis to wircanne. *Ibid.* xxvii. 41 Esau ..þohte to ofsleanne Iacob. *a* **1175** *Cott. Hom.* 227 Hi.. begunnon þa to worcen. *c* **1205** LAY. 18738-9 þu..þrattest hine to slænne, And his cun to fordonne. *Ibid.* 24722 þa..þe king gon to spekene. *c* **1290** *St. Gregory* 50 in *S. Eng. Leg.* I. 357 þou þencst..with þi conseil al rome to bi-traiȝe. *c* **1386** CHAUCER *Prol.* 12 Thanne longen folk to goon on pilgrimages. *c* **1400** *Destr. Troy* 312 The Emperour Alexaunder Aunterid to come. **1525** LD. BERNERS *Froiss.* II. xxi. 45 They determyned to crowne to their kyng this mayster Denyse. **1694** S. MEADE in *Jrnl. Friends' Hist. Soc.* (1912) IX. 182 Her Husband thinks to come downe tomorrow. **1746** P. FRANCIS tr. *Horace, Art Poet.* 36, I strive to be concise.

b. In obsolete, archaic, or dialectal uses; now replaced by various prepositions with the gerund, or by other constructions. (See the vbs.)

1525 LD. BERNERS *Froiss.* II. 627 Every man fell to make his prayers to God. **1533** CROMWELL in Merriman *Life & Lett.* (1902) I. 360, I shall aduyse yow to stay to doo [= refrain from doing] any thing. **1698** FRYER *Acc. E. India & P.* 58 Unless they would..content themselves to winter at the Mauritius. **1749** LAVINGTON *Enthus. Meth. & Papists* II. (1754) 34 Her Spouse insisting to play another Game. **1871** G. MEREDITH *H. Richmond* III. 109 Abstaining to write to her. **1885** J. HAWTHORNE *Love or Name* 111 We don't aim to establish a monopoly.

4. Dependent on various adjs. (and pples., and adjectival or predicative phrases): usually indicating the application of the adj., etc. For *going to*, used as future participle, see GO *v.* 47 b. (See also senses 1 b, 7–9, and the adjs. themselves.)

c **975** *Rushw. Gosp.* Matt. iii. 11 Æfter me cymeð se is me strængra þæt ic næm wyrþe scoas to beranne. *a* **1225** *Juliana* 5 (Bodl. MS.) þes ȝunge mon..wes iwunet ofte to cumen wið him. **1297** R. GLOUC. (Rolls) 1431 Gwider..is truage athuld sone Of rome þat is eldore were iwoned to done. **1340** HAMPOLE *Pr. Consc.* 8559 Certayne To have endelos ioy. *c* **1435** *Torr. Portugal* 1680 He is worthy to haue renown. **1513** DOUGLAS *Æneis* VI. xv. 3 The peple..Bene..moir sle To forge and carve lyflyk staturis of bras. **1651** W. DURHAM *Maran-atha* (1652) 4 Every man that is able to discipline souldiers. **1770** GOLDSM. *Des. Vill.* 161 Careless their merits or their faults to scan. **1832** TENNYSON *Love thou thy Land* 31 Not swift nor slow to change, but firm. **1838** THIRLWALL *Greece* V. xlii. 229 She was at liberty to enforce her claims. *Mod.* I am ready to go.

b. With inf. passive: altered from the active (see 9). *arch.*

c **1460** FORTESCUE *Abs. & Lim. Mon.* xi. (1885) 136 This was not possible to haue ben done. *c* **1483** *Vulg. Terent.* 02 b, Whatt is best to be doon now? **1693** EVELYN *De la Quint. Compl. Gard.* I. 5 The fittest to be chosen. **1779** *Mirror* No. 21 ¶3 Incidents still more frequent, and less easy to be foreseen. **1870** BURTON *Hist. Scot.* V. lxii. 382 She was hard to be entreated.

5. Dependent on various abstract sbs. (e.g. nouns of action from the vbs. in 3, or of quality from the adjs. in 4): usually indicating object or application, as in 3 and 4; also (after such words as *favour, honour, pleasure*) indicating an action which is the substance or form of that which is denoted by the sb., i.e. in which it consists: often replaceable by *of* with gerund.

For 'what has he to do, to..' (= 'what business has he to..') and the like, see DO *v.* 33 c.

c **888** K. ÆLFRED *Boeth.* xxxviii. §4 Ðæt hi..habbað leafe yfel to donne. **971** *Blickl. Hom.* 63 Us is mycel þearf to witenne þæt [etc.]. *c* **1000** *Ags. Gosp.* Mark ii. 10 þæt mannes sunu hæfð anweald..synna to forgyfanne. *c* **1200** *Trin. Coll. Hom.* 15 þat he geue us mihte and strengðe to forletene þesternesse, and to folȝie brictnesse. *c* **1300** *Harrow. Hell* 179 ȝef us leve,..To faren of this lothe wyke. **13..** *Minor Poems fr. Vernon MS.* l. 593 Haue non hope to liuen longe. **1470–85** MALORY *Arthur* xx. vii. 809 Ye haue no cause to loue sir Launcelot. **1525** BP. SAMPSON in Ellis *Orig. Lett.* Ser. III. I. 356 Means might be fownde to change hym. **1582** ALLEN *Martyrd. Campion* (1908) 113 This resolutnes of minde, and willingnes to die. **1665** BOYLE *Occas. Refl.* Introd. Pref. (1848) 13, I..took Pleasure to imagine two or three of my Friends to be present with me. **1737** SWIFT *Proposal for giving Badges*, etc. Wks. 1751 IX. 301, I had the Honour to be a Member of it. **1842** R. I. WILBERFORCE *Rutilius & Lucius* 249 As though in act to spring. **1859** GEO. ELIOT *A. Bede* xvi, Conscious of increased disinclination to tell his story.

*** *Indicating appointment or destination.*

6. Indicating destiny, or (expected or actual) event or outcome. Dependent on vb., adj., or sb.

See also COME *v.* 24 b, GET *v.* 32, LEAVE *v.*[1] 5 b, LIVE *v.*[1] 9.

a **1380** *St. Augustin* 108 in Horstm. *Altengl. Leg.* (1878) 63/2 þei [the Manichees] forsok þat alle men Schulde rise in flesch, to lyue aȝen. **1445** in *Anglia* XXVIII. 269 No theef iss suffrid to lyen in weyes there felawes him lyke to make. **1638** G. SANDYS *Paraphr. Job* xxvii. 34 Borne to begge their bread. **1725** *Bradley's Fam. Dict.* s.v. *July*, Plant out Colliflowers, to blow in September. **1750** GRAY *Elegy* xiv, Full many a flower is born to blush unseen. **1781** COWPER *Charity* 74 We come with joy from our eternal rest, To see the oppressor in his turn oppressed. **1808** BYRON *When we two parted* 4 When we two parted..To sever for years.

**** *Indicating result or consequence.*

7. Expressing result or consequence (potential or actual); esp. after *so* or *such* (now always with *as* before *to* = *that* with finite vb.: see AS *adv.* B. 20), or *enough*, For inf. after *than*, see THAN 1 c.

With *enough, too* (see b), the subj. of the principal clause may be either the implied subj. or obj. of the inf., or obj. of a following prep. (cf. constructions in sense 11), or the subj. of the inf. may be a sb. or pron. preceded by *for*, or may be unexpressed.

1303 R. BRUNNE *Handl. Synne* 5158 Ne be nat proude.. Yn þyn herte to make a rous. *c* **1386** CHAUCER *Can. Yeom. Prol. & T.* 308, I haue yow toold ynowe To reyse a feend. **1577** FULKE *Answ. True Christian* 95 Be not so impudent, to charge vs with these crimes aboue the Papistes. **1611** BIBLE *Gen.* iii. 22 The man is become as one of us, to know good & euill. **1742** FIELDING *Jos. Andrews* IV. iii, The Laws..are not so vulgar, to permit a mean Fellow to contend with one of your Ladyship's Fortune. **1865** RUSKIN *Sesame* i. §15 He has only to speak a sentence..to be known for an illiterate person. **1877** SPURGEON *Serm.* XXIII. 537 A man who has light enough to know he is wrong but not grace enough to forsake the evil. **1884** *Manch. Exam.* 14 May 5/1 The Government have..done much to excite against them the fiercest antipathies of the Opposition.

b. After *too*, with negative implication (*too..to* .. = *so..as not to*, or *so..that..not..*). See also TOO *sb.* 2 b.

Here *for* with the gerund may often be substituted.

a **1300** *A Sarmun* xxxv. in *E.E.P.* (1862) 5 Hit is to late whan þou ert þare To crie ihsu þin ore. ? *a* **1400** *Morte Arth.* 4031 We are..to fewe to feghte with them all. *c* **1538** R. COWLEY in Ellis *Orig. Lett.* Ser. II. II. 98 Too lamentable to expres. **1560** DAUS. tr. *Sleidane's Comm.* 113 b, It is nowe to late to examyne the licence. **1655** *Nicholas Papers* (Camden) II. 266 Cromwell hath too good a nose as to hunt vpon a false sent. **1665** [see TOO *sb.* 2 b]. **1712** BUDGELL *Spect.* No. 401 ¶4 My Answer would be too long to trouble you with. **1833** TENNYSON *Lady Clara Vere de Vere* ii, Too proud to care from whence I came. *Mod.* This tea is too hot to drink. The weight is too heavy for you to lift.

***** *Indicating occasion or condition.*

8. Indicating occasion (passing into ground, reason, or cause): equivalent to *at, in, on, for, of, by*, etc. with gerund, or *because* with finite vb.

? *a* **1366** CHAUCER *Rom. Rose* 122 Wonder glad I was to see That lusty place. **1380** *Lay Folks Catech.* 220 (MS. L.) And so myȝt pardoun be gotun to sey [= by saying] yche day a lady sawter. **1508** *Colyn Blowbol's Test.* 22 in Hazl. *E.P.P.* I. 93 An hors wold wepe to se the sorow he maide. **1535** COVERDALE *Ps.* xlvii[i]. 5 They marveled to se soch thinges. **1596** SHAKS. *1 Hen. IV*, II. iv. 343, I blush to heare his monstrous deuices. **1596** —— *Tam. Shr.* III. ii. 27 Goe girle, I cannot blame thee now to weepe. **1766** GOLDSM. *Vic. W.* iii, I could not but smile to hear her talk in this lofty strain. **1833** TENNYSON *Lady Clara Vere de Vere* ii, I know you proud to bear your name. **1843** MACAULAY *Lays, Horatius* xlix, All Etruria's noblest Felt their hearts sink to see On the earth the bloody corpses, In the path the dauntless Three.

9. With inf. after an adj. or (predicate) sb., in passive sense (equivalent to the L. supine in *-u*), the main sb. of the principal clause being the implied object of the inf., or of a preposition following (or in ME. preceding).

c **888** K. ÆLFRED *Boeth.* xxxiv. §11 Hi bioð swiðe eðe to tedælenne. *c* **950** *Lindisf. Gosp.* Mark ii. 9 Hwæt is eaður to coeðanne..? *c* **1200** *Trin Coll. Hom.* 31 Gode tiðinge and murie to heren. **13..** *K. Alis.* 6312 Heo buth the lothlokest men on to seon. **1340** HAMPOLE *Pr. Consc.* 705 A flour, þat es fayre to se. *c* **1400** MAUNDEV. (1839) xxvii. 274 Wylde men that ben hidouse to loken on. *c* **1435** *Torr. Portugal* 617 Gret Ruthe yt wase to se. **1535** COVERDALE *Gen.* xii. 11 Thou art a fayre woman to loke vpon. **1617** MORYSON *Itin.* II. 101 Ere it be good to eat. **1736** THOMSON *Liberty* v. 456 Oh! shame to think! **1805** SCOTT *Last Minstr.* I. i, Deadly to hear, and deadly to tell. **1899** W. T. GREENE *Cage-Birds* 71 Macaws.. very gorgeous creatures to look at.

10. With inf. expressing a fact or supposition which forms the ground of the statement in the principal clause, or is considered in connexion with it; equivalent to *in* with gerund, or *that, in that, considering that* (or sometimes *if*) with finite vb.

13.. *Seuyn Sag.* (W.) 2544 Sire, thou art wel nice, To leue [= believe] so mochel thin emperice. *c* **1489** CAXTON *Sonnes of Aymon* xxii. 481 He dothe wronge to leve me here. **1592** SHAKS. *Rom. & Jul.* IV. i. 23 *Par.* Come you to make confession to this Father? *Iul.* To answere that, I should confesse to you. **1610** —— *Temp.* III. i. 37, I haue broke your hest to say so. **1706** ADDISON *Rosamund* I. iii, Thou art a rustic to call me so. **1846** W. E. FORSTER in Reid *Life* (1888) I. vi. 186 What a strange little mortal he is, to be ruler of a mighty nation. **1884** R. W. CHURCH *Bacon* iii. 59 He was no mere idealist or recluse to under-value..the real grandeur of the world. **1887** 'L. CARROLL' *Game of Logic* i. §1. 15 You will do well to work out a lot more for yourself.

†**b.** With inf. equivalent to a conditional clause with indefinite subject (= *if one were to..*). *Obs.*

c **1386** CHAUCER *Miller's T.* 66 In al this world to seken vp and doun There nas no man so wys. *c* **1400** MAUNDEV. (1839) ix. 81 Fro that hospitall, to go toward the Est, is a full fayr chirche. **1591** SHAKS. *1 Hen. VI*, IV. vii 89 To keepe them here, They would but stinke, and putrifie the ayre. **1611** BEAUM. & FL. *Philaster* III. i, Bulls and Rams will fight, To keep their Females standing in their sight.

II. With infinitive in adjectival relation.

11. With inf. in adjectival relation to a sb.; either as predicate after the vb. *to be* (see BE 16, 17), or immediately qualifying the sb.

a. Expressing intention or appointment (cf. 1, 6), and hence simply futurity (thus equivalent to a future participle). (*a*) with inf. act.: *is to..* = intends or is intended to.., is going to.., will...

c **1000**- [see COME *v.* 33]. **1297** R. GLOUC. (Rolls) 287 Man þou art iwis To winne ȝut a kinedom. *c* **1420** *Sir Amadas* (Weber) 569 Yffe thou be a mon to wedde a wyfe, Y voche hyr save..On the. *c* **1460** *Oseney Reg.* 101 Thoo þat be present and to be. **1590** SHAKS. *Mids. N.* IV. ii. 29, I am to discourse wonders... I will tell you euery thing as it fell out. **1596** —— *Merch. V.* I. i. 5 Whereof it is borne, I am to learne. **1667** MILTON *P.L.* XII. 113 A Nation from one faithful man to spring. **1693** SOUTH *Serm.* II. 113 He who is to pray..has more to consider of, than..his Heart can hold. **1779** *Mirror* No. 23 ¶3 He was not suffered to play with his equals, because he was to be the king of all sports. **1864** BROWNING *Rabbi Ben Ezra* i, The best is yet to be.

(*b*) with inf. pass. (equivalent to Lat. gerundive): *to be done* = intended to be done, about to be done.

c **1450** *Cov. Myst.* x. (1841) 96 Here is to be maryde a mayde ȝynge. **1585** in *Cath. Rec. Soc. Publ.* V. 108 Articles to be ministred to Tho. Rowe. **1609** HOLLAND *Amm. Marcell.* XXVI. i, Having a presage..of the businesse to bee performed. **1719** DE FOE *Crusoe* (1840) II. xii. 245 The happy minute of our being to be seized by the Dutch.. ships. **1843** *Fraser's Mag.* XXVIII. 655 Leopold was to be appointed Viceroy.

(*c*) with inf. act., the sb. being the implicit object of the inf.; thus equivalent to the passive in (*b*).

As predicate, *obs.* in literary Eng. exc. in certain connexions, as *a house to let* (LET *v.*[1] 8); when following a sb., the sb. is usu. governed by *have* (see HAVE *v.* B. 7). *to let*, used *absol.* as *sb.*, is freq. applied *attrib.* to a board, sign, etc., indicating that premises are offered for rent.

c **1200** ORMIN Ded. 8 Witt hafenn takenn ba An reȝhellboc te follȝhenn. **14..** in *Rel. Ant.* I. 62 This poure man had suyn to selle. **1487–8** *Rec. St. Mary at Hill* 134 For a hoke to sett on his dorr. **1595** SHAKS. *John* I. i. 259 Were I to get againe,.. I would not wish a better father. **1771** SMOLLETT *Humph. Cl.* 26 Oct., He has a son to educate. **1797** CANNING *Knife-Grinder* ii, Knives and Scissars to grind O! **1852** M. ARNOLD *Empedocles* I. ii. 334 The mass.. Of volumes yet to read, Of secrets to explore. **1886** F. H. BURNETT *Little Lord Fauntleroy* xi. 174 He stopped opposite the empty house.. staring at the 'To Let', and smoking his pipe. **1894** A. MORRISON *Martin Hewitt, Investigator* ii. 80 The three shops.. appeared not yet to have been occupied. A dusty 'To Let' bill hung in each window. **1903** A. BENNETT *Truth about an Author* xv. 206 A To-let notice flourished suddenly in my front-garden. *a* **1912** *Mod. Notice.* This house to let or for sale. *a* **1912** *Mod.* I have much to tell. **1936** A. CHRISTIE *ABC Murders* vi. 46 A 'To Let' sign appeared in the windows. **1938** G. GREENE *Brighton Rock* III. iii. 122 A vista of To Let boards. **1976** J. BINGHAM *God's Defector* v. 54 One day they have hope, a basement, a letter-head, and the next their place is occupied by a 'To let' sign.

(*d*) with inf. followed (in ME. sometimes preceded) by a preposition, the sb. being the implicit obj. of the prep.

c **897** K. ÆLFRED *Gregory's Past. C.* xvii. 126 ȝif ðær ðonne sie ȝierd mid to ðreaȝeanne, sie ðær eac stæf mid to wreðianne. *c* **1200** *Trin. Coll. Hom.* 89 He..bed hem bringen a wig one te riden. **1408–17** in *Rec. St. Mary at Hill* Introd. 96 Item, .j. short fourme with a tapete and Quysshynes to knele at. **1577** B. GOOGE *Heresbach's Husb.* I. (1586) 13 These great roomes.. be Barnes to laye Corne in. **1611** COTGR. s.v. *Rosette*, Red Inke to rule bookes with. **1707** MORTIMER *Husb.* (1721) II. 366 A Dry Season.. is best to sow Barley and White Oats in.

b. Expressing duty, obligation, or necessity. (*a*) with inf. act.: ***is to..*** = is bound to, has to.., must.., ought to...

c **1450** HOLLAND *Howlat* 216 The Ravyne.. Was dene rurale to reid. *a* **1529** SKELTON *Phyllyp Sparow* 401 Robyn red breste He shall be the preest The requiem masse to syng. **1591** SHAKS. *Two Gent.* II. iii. 37 Thy Master is ship'd, and thou art to post after with oares. **1598** —— *Merry W.* IV. ii. 128 You are not to goe loose any longer, you must be pinnion'd. **1768** GOLDSM. *Good-n. Man* iii, I'm yet to thank you for choosing my little library. **1885** *Manch. Exam.* 13 July 5/2 The Southerners, with only one wicket to fall, were 259 runs to the bad. **1887** 'L. CARROLL' *Game of Logic* i. §1. 9 What, then, are you to do?

(*b*) with inf. pass. (= L. gerundive): ***is to be..*** = is proper to be, ought to be.., should be.., need be...

The inf. pass. is also occasionally used as adj. preceding the sb.; now with hyphens, as ***to-be-dreaded*** = dreadful.

1382 WYCLIF *John* xxi. 25, I deme neither the world him silf to mowe take tho bookis, that ben to be writun. *c* **1410** LOVE *Bonavent. Mirr.* (1908) 49 That is.. most profitable, and rather to be chosen. **1560–78** *Bk. Discipl. Ch. Scot.* (1621) 61 Unprofitable questions are to be avoided. **1611** BEAUM. & FL. *Knt. Burn. Pest.* v. iii, There's no more to be said. **1774** BURKE *Amer. Tax.* 32 If, Sir, the conduct of ministry.. had arisen from timidity.., it would have been greatly to be condemned. **1858** MILL *Liberty* v. (1873) 60 The taxation.. of stimulants.. is not only admissible, but to be approved of.

1548 UDALL, etc. *Erasm. Par. Matt.* 28* That same moste fortunate and moste to be desyred kyngdome. **1606** SHAKS. *Tr. & Cr.* I. iii. 157 Such to be pittied, and ore-rested seeming He acts thy Greatnesse in. **1779** *Sylph* II. 50 This shall be the last letter that treats on this to-be-forbidden theme. **1871** NAPHEYS *Prev. & Cure Dis.* III. vi. 835 The to-be-dreaded legacies of smallpox.

(*c*) with inf. act., of which the sb. is the implicit obj., as in 11 a (*c*).

As predicate, *obs.* exc. in ***to blame*** (BLAME *v.* 6); otherwise usu. with *have* before the sb., as in a (*c*); also with ellipsis of sb. in ***have to do*** (see DO *v.* 33 c, d).

971 *Blickl. Hom.* 63 Nis þæt no be eallum demum ȝelice to secȝȝenne. *c* **1122** *O.E. Chron.* an. 1083, þa munecas.. nyston hwet heom to donne wære. *Ibid.* an. 1086, Betwyx oðrum þingum nis na to forgytane þæt gode frið. *a* **1225** *Ancr. R.* 52 [Heo] wot betere þen ich wot, hwat heo haueð to donne. **1297** R. GLOUC. (Rolls) 3271 Hii slowe þere a þousend & mo.., & þat was to rywe sore. *Ibid.* 3318 Wat were to done. *c* **1380** WYCLIF *Sel. Wks.* I. 196 Confessioun of cowardise is to drede of men. **1390** GOWER *Conf.* I. 8 The hevene wot what is to done. *c* **1400** *Laud Troy Bk.* 6821 Ector bretheren weren mechel to prayse. **1503** HAWES *Examp. Virt.* vii. 104 A man without wytte is to dyspyse. **1634** W. TIRWHYT tr. *Balzac's Lett.* (vol. I.) 294 Having a thousand old debates to reconcile, and as many new ones to prevent. **1794** MRS. RADCLIFFE *Myst. Udolpho* l, They had no time to lose. **1870** ROGERS *Hist. Gleanings* Ser. II. 214 Everybody.. thought Horne to blame. **1888** W. S. GILBERT *Yeomen of Guard* I. 12, I have a song to sing, O! *Mod.* You are much to blame.

(*d*) with inf. and prep., as in 11 a (*d*).

1611 BIBLE *Luke* xii. 50, I haue a baptisme to be baptized with. **1779** *Mirror* No. 48 ¶10 The painter has yet more [difficulties] to struggle with. **1859** GEO. ELIOT *A. Bede* xvi, It was not.. a thing to make a fuss about. **1888** RIDER HAGGARD *Mr. Meeson's Will* xvii, Ladies need never wear anything to speak of in the evening.

c. Expressing possibility or potential action. (*a*) with inf. act.: that can or may...

a **1310** in Wright *Lyric P.* (Percy Soc.) 34 Heo hath a mury mouth to mele [= speak]. *c* **1380** WYCLIF *Wks.* (1880) 288 Men stable in bileue ben a þick walle to turnen aȝen þis þondir. *c* **1400** MAUNDEV. (1839) v. 45 In that contree [Egypt] ben the gode astronomyeres; for thei fynde there no cloudes to letten hem. **1526** TINDALE *Matt.* xi. 15 He that hath eares to heare, let him here. *a* **1533** LD. BERNERS *Huon* cxi. 385 There was no man to saye hym naye. **1625** BACON *Ess., Auger* (Arb.) 566 They haue so many Things to trouble them. **1782** COWPER *Alex. Selkirk* 2 My right there is none to dispute. **1799** WORDSW. *She dwelt among the untrodden ways* i, A maid whom there were none to praise And very few to love. **1890** 'L. FALCONER' *Mlle. Ixe* vi, There is no one to see us.

(*b*) with inf. pass.: = that can or may be..; often equivalent to an adj. in *-ble*, as *to be heard* = audible.

1533 ELYOT *Cast. Helthe* (1541) 24 The inner part therof is not to be eaten. **1590** SPENSER *F.Q.* II. vii. 30 In all that rowme was nothing to be seene But huge great yron chests. **1611** SHAKS. *Cymb.* III. i. 68 Looke For fury, not to be resisted. **1631** WEEVER *Anc. Fun. Mon.* 222 This inscription .. now hardly to be read. **1818** J. FLINT *Lett. Amer.* iv. 46 Not a sound was to be heard.

(*c*) with inf. act., of which the sb. is the implicit obj., as in 11 a (*c*): = that (one) can or may..; often nearly equivalent to *for* with gerund, as in 1 a.

Rarely in predicate (quots. 1297, *a* 1849 [2]). With *drink*, *eat*, sometimes as apparent obj. of the vb., with ellipsis of *something* or *anything* (*arch.*).

c **950** *Lindisf. Gosp.* Mark x. 40 Sitta.. to swiðra minra.. ne is min to sellanne. *c* **1000** ÆLFRIC *Gen.* xxviii. 20 Gif Drihten.. sylþ me hlaf to etenne and reaf to weriȝenne. *c* **1205** LAY. 13578 Nefden we noht to drinken. *Ibid.* 13583 Ʒe sculleð habben to drinken. **1297** R. GLOUC. (Rolls) 2747 He esste at is clerkes were it to leue [= to be believed, credible] were. *c* **1400** MAUNDEV. (1839) v. 47 There is no watre to drynke, but ȝif it come be condyt from Nyle. **1582** N. T. (Rhem.) *John* iv. 7 Giue me to drinke [so **1611**: *earlier vv.* Geue me drynke]. **1610** SHAKS. *Temp.* III. ii. 102 Without them [his books] Hee.. hath not One Spirit to command. **1736** *Gentl. Mag.* VI. 744/2 A taking pattern! to propose To our slim race of modern beaus. **1815** W. H. IRELAND *Scribbleomania* 190 The great Grecian youth, Who whimper'd for more worlds to conquer. *a* **1849** BEDDOES *Dream-Pedlary*, If there were dreams to sell. *Ibid.*, Were dreams to have at will. **1858** SEARS *Athan.* III. x. 332 Heathen nations.. who have had no truth given them to reject. **1897** KIPLING *5 Nations, Our Lady of Snows*, The gates are mine to open, As the gates are mine to close.

(*d*) with inf. and prep., as in 11 a (*d*).

c **1410** LOVE *Bonavent. Mirr.* (1908) 49 A pore wommanes sone, that skarsly hadde clothes to wrappe hym inne. **1423** JAS. I *Kingis Quair* clxxiv, Nor sekernes, my spirit with to glad. **1593** NASHE *Christ's T.* (1613) 54 Nere had you such a subiect to roialize your Muses with. **1593** SHAKS. *3 Hen. VI*, II. i. 68 Sweet Duke of Yorke, our Prop to leane vpon. **1784** BURNS *Ep. to J. Rankine* iv, Tak that, ye lea'e them naething To ken them by.

d. Expressing quality or character: = such as to.., fit to, such as would... (With various constructions as in a, b, c, but not used predicatively.)

14.. *Pol. Rel. & L. Poems* 217, I have herde of an erbe to lyss that peyne. **1610** SHAKS. *Temp.* II. i. 313 'Twas a din to fright a Monsters eare. **1735–6** THOMSON *Liberty* IV. 496 A sight to gladden Heav'n! **1824** SCOTT *Redgauntlet* ch. xix, Father Crackenthorp was not a man to be brow-beaten. **1833** T. HOOK *Parson's Dau.* I. ii, Is she a person to like? **1859** GEO. ELIOT *A. Bede* xxxii, She was not the woman to misbehave towards her betters.

12. With inf. equivalent to a relative clause with indicative; chiefly after *first*, *last*, or the like (in this case = *in* with gerund): as *the first to come* = 'the first in coming', 'the first who comes *or* came'.

1535 COVERDALE *2 Sam.* xix. 11 Why wyl ye be the last to fetch the kynge agayne vnto his house? **1591** SHAKS. *Two Gent.* II. i. 42 Not an eye that sees you, but is a Physician to comment on your Malady. **1667** MILTON *P.L.* x. 109 He came, and with him Eve, more loth, though first To offend. **1766** GOLDSM. *Vicar W.* viii, I have an interest in being first to deliver this message. **1821** F. COOPER *Spy* iii, Harper was the last to appear. **1835** LYTTON *Rienzi* I. v, Mine shall be the first voice to swell the battle-cry of freedom. **1855** KINGSLEY *Westw. Ho.* xxv, Why.. was I.. among the foremost to urge upon my general the murder of the Inca?

III. With infinitive in substantival relation.

Equivalent to a noun or gerund: *to* being ultimately reduced to a mere 'sign' of the infinitive without any meaning of its own.

13. a. with inf. as subject, or as object with complement, introduced by *it* or an impersonal verb; in quot. *c* 1205[1] without *it*.

Here the inf. app. originally depended on the adj. or sb. in the *it* clause (as in sense 9), or on the impersonal vb., and was therefore put in the form with *to*. Thus *hwilum ða leohtan scylda bioð beteran to forlætenne*, 'sometimes the slight sins are better to let alone' (K. Ælf. *Pa. C.* 457) might also be expressed *hwilum hit is betre ða leohtan scylda to forlætenne* (cf. *hit is god godne to herianne*, quot. *c* 890) 'sometimes it is better to let alone the slight sins'; and this easily passed into the later 'to let alone the slight sins is sometimes better', where the inf. clause becomes the subject as in b.

c **888** K. ÆLFRED *Boeth.* xvii, Nan þara þinga wyrcan þe him beboden is to wyrcenne. *Ibid.* xxxviii. §5 Þæt men sie alefed yfel to donne. *c* **890** tr. *Bæda's Hist.* Pref. (1890) 2 Forþon hit is god godne to herianne & yfelne to leanne. *a* **1175** *Cott. Hom.* 217 Hit is wel swete of him to specene. *c* **1200–** [see BEHOVE *v.* 4 a]. *c* **1205** LAY. 1848 Þa heo best wende to fleonne. *Ibid.* 31107 Hit is on mine rede To don þat þu bede. *a* **1230** [see BECOME *v.* 8 b]. **13..** *K. Alis.* 7346 (Laud MS.) Good it were to ben kniȝth. **1390** GOWER *Conf.* III. 341 Hem nedeth noght a Riff to slake. *c* **1430–** [see GRIEVE *v.* 5 b]. *a* **1440** *Sir Degrev.* 1498 Hyt was a mervelous thing To se the rydalus hyng. **1602** SHAKS. *Ham.* III. ii. 110 It was a bruite part of him, to kill so Capital a Calfe there. **1667** MILTON *P.L.* IV. 427 God hath pronounc't it death to taste that Tree. **1850** TENNYSON *In Mem.* xxvii. 15 'Tis better to have loved and lost Than never to have loved at all. **1880** SHORTHOUSE *J. Inglesant* xx, Many who will have it in their power to be of great use to you.

b. with inf. as direct subject or predicate, or in apposition with a sb. or pron., or after *than*: often replaceable by the gerund or vbl. sb. in *-ing*.

1303 R. BRUNNE *Handl. Synne* 6044 Ful wykkede ys þat coueytyse Wyþ oþer mennes gode falsly to ryse. **1388** WYCLIF *1 Sam.* xv. 22 To herkene Goddis word is more than to offre the ynnere fatnesse of rammes. **14..** *Chaucer's Pars. T.* ¶670 (Selden & Lansd. MSS.) Auarice is to with-holde & kepe suche thinges as thow hast withouten rightful nede. *c* **1450** tr. *De Imitatione* II. viii. 48 To be wiþoute ihesu is a greuous helle, and to be wiþ ihesu is a swete paradise. **1539** BIBLE (Great) *1 Sam.* xv. 22 Behold, to obeye [**1388** WYCLIF, **1535** COVERD. obedience], is better then sacrifice, & to herken, is better then ye fatt of rammes. **1557** NORTH *Gueuara's Diall Pr.* 126 A woman in nothing sheweth her sageness more then to dissemble with a foolish husband. **1601** SHAKS. *All's Well* I. i. 148 To speake on the part of virginitie, is to accuse your Mothers. **1667** MILTON *P.L.* I. 157 To be weak is miserable Doing or Suffering. **1709** POPE *Ess. Crit.* 525 To err is human, to forgive, divine. **1781** COWPER *Conversation* 8 Talking is not always to converse. **1865** E. BURRITT *Walk Land's End* 208 The Established Church could not do a better thing.. than to peopleise these magnificent edifices. **1878** ABNEY *Photogr.* (1881) 160 The result is to render such organic matter insoluble.

14. with inf. as direct object of a transitive verb. (See also GIVE *v.* 29 c.)

OE. normally had the simple inf., like mod.German: *Beowulf* 356 Þa andsware.. ðe me se goda agifan þenceð. [Cf. *c* **890** tr. *Bæda's Hist.* IV. xxiii. [xxii.] (1890) 330 Moniȝe men þa ðe þas þing ȝehyrdon secgan.]. *c* **893** K. ÆLFRED *Oros.* (Contents) I. ii, Her Ninus ongon monna ærest ricsian. *Ibid.* I. xii. §4 For ðon þe he him cweman þohte. *a* **900** —— *Solil.* (1902) 13 Ic wilneȝe cuman to þe. *a* **900** *Laws of Ælfred* c. 66 §7 And he bebead þone hlaford lufian swa hine selfne. *a* **900** *Ags. Ps.* (Th.) iii. 4 Þa ongan ic slapan. *c* **1000** *Ags. Gosp.* Luke i. 1 Maneȝa þohton þara þinga race ȝeendebyrdan. [*a* **1132** *O.E. Chron.* an. 1127, Þa muneces herdon ða horn blawen.]

Many of the vbs. which in OE. took the simple inf. could also be followed by *to* with the dative infinitive. But the auxiliary vbs. (see *History* above) have always been followed by the simple inf.; e.g. *Hwæt can ic sprecan?* What can I speak? *We maȝon ȝehyran*, We may hear.

c **888** K. ÆLFRED *Boeth.* xxxvi. §8 Swa hwa swa wilnað good to donne, he wilnað good to habbanne. *c* **897** —— *Gregory's Past. C.* lviii. 441 Đonne hi leorniað.. ða soðan god to secanne. *a* **900** —— *Solil.* (1902) 59 Ic wundriȝe hwi ðu swa swiðe ȝeorne.. þæt to witanne. *c* **1000** *Ags. Gosp.* Matt. i. 20 Nelle þu ondrædan Marian.. to onfonne [*Rushw.* onfoiæ]. *Ibid.* ii. 22 He ondred þyder to faranne [*Lind.* ðider fara *vel* to færenne]. **11..** *O.E. Chron.* MS. F. (12th c.) an. 40, Matheus on Iudea agan his godspell to writen. [Cf. anno 47, Marcus se godspellere in Egipta aginþ writan þæt godspell.] *c* **1200** ORMIN 11805 He forrsoc to don þe laþe gastess wille. *c* **1205** LAY. 4569 He þohte to habben [*c* **1275** he þohte habbe] Delgan to quene of Denemarke. **1377** LANGL. *P. Pl.* B. x. 90 Suche lessounes lordes shulde louie to here. *c* **1386** CHAUCER *Knt.'s T.* 1919 What asketh men to haue? *c* **1400** MAUNDEV. Prol. 2 He ches.. there to suffre his passioun. **1579** SPENSER *Sheph. Cal.* Feb. 186 Nought aske I, but onely to hold my right. **1601** B. JONSON *Poetaster* III. i. Wks. (Rtldg.) 114/2, I love not to be idle. **1611** BIBLE *Exod.* ii. 15 He sought to slay Moses. **1645** FULLER *Gd. Th. in Bad T.* xxii. (1841) 17 Give me to guard myself. **1727** DE FOE *Syst. Magic* I. iii. (1840) 74 If he would still refuse to grant their demands. **1754** A. MURPHY *Gray's-Inn Jrnl.* No. 83, I fancied to myself, to see my amiable Countrywomen [etc.]. **1812** CRABBE *Tales* xi. 314 He fear'd to die, yet felt ashamed to live. **1837** DICKENS *Pickw.* xxxii, Please, Mister Sawyer, Missis Raddle wants to speak to you. **1849** MACAULAY *Hist. Eng.* I. i. 62 The queen took upon herself to grant patents of monopoly. **1858** CARLYLE *Fredk. Gt.* II. v. (1872) I. 75 A talent.. for fighting.. and.. a talent for avoiding to fight.

b. rarely as object of another preposition, instead of the vbl. sb. or gerund. (Prob. imitating French use.)

For inf. with *about to*, *for to*, see ABOUT A. 10–12, FOR *prep.* 11.

1485 CAXTON *Paris & V.* (1868) 32 Vyenne salewed parys wythoute to make [Fr. *sans faire*] ony semblaunte of loue. **1591** SPENSER *Ruines of Time* 429 For not to have been dipt in Lethe lake, Could save the sonne of Thetis from to die. **1611** A. STAFFORD *Niobe* 76 The same difference.. that is betwixt to sin and not to sinne. **1868** TENNYSON *Wages* 5 Give her the glory of going on, and still to be. **1879** MALLOCK *Life Worth Liv.* 17 Not to affirm is a very different thing from to deny.

IV. With infinitive equivalent to a finite verb or clause.

15. With inf. as complement to a sb. or pron., forming a compound object or sb. phrase, corresponding to the 'accusative and infinitive' construction in Latin and Greek.

(But certain vbs. in a. and b. are followed (at least in the active voice) by the simple inf. without *to*: e.g. 'they made him come', 'I felt something move'. See *History* above.)

a. after verbs of commanding, teaching, desiring, causing, allowing, or the like; equivalent to a *that*-clause with the sb. or pron. governing a vb. in the subjunctive. Also after the passive of such verbs, the sb. or pron. then becoming the subject.

(Also in early OE. often with simple inf.: e.g. *c* **893** K. ÆLFRED *Oros.* IV. x. §11 Þa het he ænne mon stiȝan on þone mæst, & locian.)

c **888** K. ÆLFRED *Boeth.* Prayer (1899) 149 Tæc me þinne willan to wyrcenne. *c* **890** tr. *Bæda's Hist.* v. xx. [xxii.] (1890) 472 Đara þinga ðe he oðre lærde to donne. *c* **1000** *Ags. Gosp.* Matt. viii. 21 Alyfe me ærest to faranne & bebyriȝean [L. *permitte me primum ire et sepelire*] minne fæder. *c* **1200** ORMIN 10361 Acc wel itt maȝȝ hemm bringgenn onn To rihhtenn þeȝȝre dede. c1200- [see MAKE v.[1] 53b]. c1330 *Amis & Amil.* 1577 He was y-hote to go. c1400 MAUNDEV. (1839) iv. 25, I do þe to wytene, þat it is made be enchauntement. 1523 LD. BERNERS *Froiss.* I. cxxxiii. 161 The kyng..suffred them to passe through his host. 1611 CORYAT *Crudities* 268 Shee will..cause thy throate to be cut. 1704 SWIFT *T. Tub* ix. 170, I desire the Reader to attend. 1865 RUSKIN *Sesame* ii. §94, I know you would like that to be true. 1902 GAIRDNER *Hist. Eng. Ch. 16th C.* viii. (1903) 143 She was compelled to act as lady's-maid to her new-born half-sister.

b. after verbs of saying, thinking, knowing, perceiving, or the like; equivalent to a *that*-clause with vb. in the indicative. Also after the passive of such verbs, and after intr. verbs of like meaning, as *seem*, *happen*, etc.

(Also in early OE. with simple inf.: e.g. c890 tr. *Bæda's Hist.* v. ix. (1890) 408 Ðara cynna moniȝ he wiste in Germanie wesan.)

a1300- [see SEEM v. 4]. 13..- [see HAPPEN v. 3]. a1400- [see CHANCE v. 1c]. 1432-50 tr. *Higden* (Rolls) I. 167 Wyse men denye Eneas to have seen Cathago. a1450 *Cov. Myst.* xxxii. (1841) 324 We merveylyth..That ȝe wryte hym to be kyng of Jewys. 1566 PAINTER *Pal. Pleas.* I. 154 When hee sawe him to weepe. 1632 MILTON *Penseroso* 137 Where the rude Ax..Was never heard the Nymphs to daunt. 1726 SWIFT *Gulliver* IV. iii, The Houyhnhnms..could hardly believe me to be a right Yahoo. 1805 SCOTT *Last Minstr.* VI. xxiii, O'er Roslin..A wondrous blaze was seen to gleam. 1891 T. HARDY *Tess* xxxiv, Unlocking the case, they found it to contain a necklace. 1912 H. L. CANNON in *Eng. Hist. Rev.* Oct. 665 The English appear to have used all the methods [etc.].

†**c.** in other constructions, equivalent to a *that*-clause as subject, in apposition, or after a prep. or *than* (cf. THAT *conj.* 1, 1b, 1c). *Obs.* (now sometimes replaced by the const. with *for*: see d).

c1175 *Lamb. Hom.* 117 Þere bið uuel to wunienne eni wise men. 1382 WYCLIF *Matt.* xxiv. 6 It bihoueth thes thingis to be don. c1386 CHAUCER *Prol.* 502 If gold ruste, what shal Iren doo. For if a preest be foul,..No wonder is, a lewed man to ruste. c1460 *Towneley Myst.* xviii. 31 A madyn to bere a chyld,..that were ferly. 1470-85 MALORY *Arthur* I. xvi. 60 It is better that we slee a coward than thorow a coward alle we to be slayne. 1474 *Coventry Leet Bk.* 389 Vppon the peyn, who doth to þe contrarie to lose..vjs. viijd. 1535 COVERDALE *Ps.* cxxxii[i.] 1 Beholde, how good & ioyfull a thinge it is, brethren to dwell together in vnite. 1590 SHAKS. *Com. Err.* I. i. 33 A heauier taske could not haue beene impos'd, Than I to speake my griefes vnspeakeable. 1647 in Picton *L'pool Munic. Rec.* (1883) I. 143 Because of the rumour of sicknes to be begune in Warrington. 1678 CUDWORTH *Intell. Syst.* I. iv. §34. 534 *Qua pateat Mundum Divino Numine verti*..Whereby it may appear the World to be Governed by a Divine Mind.

d. preceded by *for* (with various constructions and shades of meaning): see FOR *prep.* 18.

16. With inf. after a dependent interrogative or relative; equivalent to a clause with *may*, *should*, etc. (Sometimes with ellipsis of *whether* before *or* in an alternative dependent question.)

a1300- [see HOW *adv.* 9]. c1386 CHAUCER *Man of Law's T.* 558 She hath no wight to whom to make hir mone. c1400 *R. Gloucester's Chron.* (Rolls) 9237 (MS. B.) Hii nuste wat to do. c1460 *Towneley Myst.* xxiii. 259 Godys son..Hase not where apon his hede to rest. 1470-85 MALORY *Arthur* XIII. xix. 639 He..wyst not what to do. 1564 STAPLETON tr. *Staphylus' Apol.* Pref. 3 Looking of him to be directed where, howe, and when to strike. 1602 SHAKS. *Ham.* III. i. 56 To be, or not to be, that is the Question. 1732 POPE *Ess. Man* II. 7 In doubt to act, or rest. 1896 A. AUSTIN *Eng. Darling* I. i, To know the worst Is the one way whereby to better it.

b. In absolute or independent construction after an interrogative, forming an elliptical question.

This may be explained as an ellipsis of the principal clause (sense 16), or of 'is one', 'am I', etc. before the inf. (sense 11b or c).

1713 ADDISON *Cato* III. vii, But how to gain admission? for Access Is giv'n to none but Juba, and her Brothers. 1821 SHELLEY *Hellas* 659 Whither to fly? 1835 J. H. NEWMAN *Lett.* (1891) II. 87 But..how to hinder vexatious prosecutions? 1841 *Ibid.* 347 Talk carries off a good deal of irritation; but how to make talk innocent? 1875 MORRIS *Æneid* XII. 489 Ah, what to do?

17. In absolute or independent construction, with subject expressed (in nom.) or omitted: in exclamations expressing astonishment, indignation, sorrow, or (after *O* or other interj.) longing.

a1450 *Cov. Myst.* viii. 77, I to bere a childe that xal bere alle mannys blyss,.. ho mythe have joys more? 1460 CAPGRAVE *Chron.* (Rolls) 141 Seynt Thomas hast thou killid; and now to forsake the proteccion of alle Cristen men! 1588 SHAKS. *L.L.L.* III. i. 202 And I to sigh for her, to watch for her, To pray for her, go to! 1596 —— *Merch. V.* III. i. 37 My owne flesh and blood to rebell. 1664 PEPYS *Diary* 27 Mar., But, Lord! to see how the trained bands are raised upon this. 1742 YOUNG *Nt. Th.* III. 93 O to forget her! 1832 R. H. FROUDE *Rem.* (1838) I. 257 Only to think that my stars should let me off so easily! 1842 TENNYSON *Locksley Hall* 175, I, to herd with narrow foreheads..! 1845 BROWNING *Home Thoughts*, Oh, to be in England! 1871 R. ELLIS *Catullus* lxv. 9 Ah! no more to address thee, or hear thy kindly replying, Brother!..Ne'er to behold thee again!

†**18.** With inf. immediately following the subject, in vivid narrative, equivalent to a past tense indic.; almost always with *go* and vbs. of like meaning.

? With ellipsis of *gan* (see GIN v.[1] 1), *took*, or the like; but cf. the 'historic infinitive' in Latin.

c1205 LAY. 21655 Ah Arður com sone mid selere strengðe, And Scottes to fleonne feor of þan ærde. a1300 *E.E. Psalter* ii. 2 Ogaine þair laverd þai come on ane, And ogaine his criste to gane. 1375 BARBOUR *Bruce* VIII. 351 He turnit his bridill, and to ga. c1385 CHAUCER *L.G.W.* 653 (*Cleopatra*) Antonye..put hym to the flyght And al his folk to go that best go myght. 1387 TREVISA *Higden* (Rolls) III. 161 Tarquinius..come uppon hire while sche slepte..and to lye by hire maugre hir teeþ. 1566 GASCOIGNE *Supposes* Wks. (1587) 34, I to fuge and away hither as fast as I could. 1668 PEPYS *Diary* 18 Sept., I..away home,..and there to read again and sup with Gibson.

V. Peculiar constructions.

†**19.** *To* was formerly often used with the second of two infinitives when the first was without it, esp. after an auxiliary, with words intervening between the infinitives. (See also note s.v. THAN *conj.* 1.)

c1205 LAY. 1220 Swa he gon slomnen & þer æfter to slepen. c1440 *Ipomydon* 1246 Bettyr is on huntynge goone, ..Than thus lyghtly to lese a stede. c1486 *Rec. St. Mary at Hill* 16 Euery persone..shall haue one of thise smale candelles brennyng in their handes & so to go on procession. a1533 LD. BERNERS *Gold. Bk. M. Aurel.* (1546) I iij, A good prince that wil..governe wel, and not to be a tyraunt. 1598 SHAKS. *Merry W.* IV. iv. 57 Then let them all encircle him about, And Fairy-like to pinch the vncleane Knight. 1611-1803 [see THAN *conj.* 1γ, δ].

20. Occasionally an adverb or advb. phr. (formerly sometimes an object or predicate) is inserted between *to* and the infinitive, forming the construction now usually (but loosely) called 'split infinitive'. (See Onions *Adv. Eng. Syntax* §177.)

13.. *Cursor M.* 8318 (Cott. & Fairf.) To temple make he sal be best. *Ibid.* 12965 (ibid.) He sal þe send Angels for to þe defend. c1400 tr. *Secreta Secret, Gov. Lordsh.* 66 To enserche sciences, and to perfitly knowe alle manere of Naturels þinges. 1606 G. W[OODCOCKE] *Hist. Ivstine* IV. 23 To quite rid himselfe out of thraldome. 1650 R. GENTILIS *Considerations* 137 Anniball was advised..to not go to Rome. 1779-81 JOHNSON *L.P., Milton* Wks. II. 100 Milton was too busy to much miss his wife. 1805 EMILY CLARK *Banks of Douro* III. 114 This answer seemed to seriously offend him. 1839 *Times* 15 Jan., This jack-in-office had taken upon himself..to more than insinuate [etc.]. 1893 J. A. HODGES *Elem. Photogr.* (1907) 114 The only way to successfully overcome it.

21. Used absolutely at the end of a clause, with ellipsis of the infinitive, which is to be supplied from the preceding clause. *rare* before 19th c.; now a frequent colloquialism.

13.. *Minor Poems fr. Vernon MS.* xxxiii. 74 Þe soules of synners,..Þer to take and resseyue so As þei on eorþe deserueden to. 1448 J. SHILLINGFORD *Lett.* (Camden) 114 He woll amende hit as sone as God well yeve hym grace and tyme to. c1450 *St. Cuthbert* (Surtees) 3330 Sayntes biddings forto do, Þof all' þare seme na resoun to. 1621 LADY M. WROTH *Urania* 7 She..obserued him, as well as she could bring her spirit to consent to. 1719 DE FOE *Crusoe* (1840) I. iii. 33 Going no oftener into the shore than we were obliged to for fresh water. 1828 R. H. FROUDE *Rem.* (1838) I. 229, I feel quite differently from what I ever used to. 1883 HOWELLS *Register* i, I kept on,..I had to. a1909 F. M. CRAWFORD *Uncanny Tales* (1911) 173, I wanted to turn round and look. It was an effort not to.

†**22.** Instead of the dative infinitive, the gerund in *-ing* was sometimes used after *to*: prob. originating in a phonetic confusion of *-en* and *-in(g)*, but later perh. with the notion of a future action (cf. 11a); as *to coming* = 'to come', or 'coming': see also COME v. 33β (after c). *Obs.*

1382 WYCLIF *Num.* xxxii. 7 Thei doren not passe into the place that the Lord is to ȝyuynge to hem. —— *Acts* xxii. 29 Thei that weren to turmentinge him. 1382-1490 [see COME v. 33β]. 1387 TREVISA *Higden* (Rolls) I. 73 Hit is not to trowynge. *Ibid.* 103 Damascus is to menynge 'schedynge blood'. *Ibid.* 153 They..taught hem to schetynge. 1393 LANGL. *P. Pl.* C. XVIII. 313 Iuwes..hopen þat he be to comynge þat shal hem releue. a1450 *Knt. de la Tour* xxxiv. (1868) 48 That is to menying that ye shulde loue and doute youre husbonde. 1471 FORTESCUE *Wks.* (1869) 530 Both titles, that is to saynge his auncient title,..and this new title.

†**C.** to *conj.* *Obs.*

1. To the time that; till, until.

a1300 *E.E. Psalter* xvii. 38, I sal filghe mi faas,..And noght ogain torne to þai wane swa. 13.. *K. Alis.* 5902 (Bodl. MS.) Þe kyng þere soiourned to he was hoole. c1400 MAUNDEV. (Roxb.) xx. 89 Þase..þai fede to þai be fatte. c1575 *Durham Depos.* (Surtees) 275 Umphray culd gett no reste of the said Thomas to he had cast hym doon on his bedd.

b. followed by *that*: cf. THAT *conj.* 7.

c1460 *Towneley Myst.* xx. 332 We shall hy vs before, To that we com to that cyte. 1509 *Sel. Cases Star Chamb.* (Selden) II. 7 [They] vsed..to haue commens..in the same vj closes to now of late that..thei be interupt. 1626 J. HAIG *Let.* 10 Nov., in J. Russell *Haigs* vii. (1881) 178 And to that I be into fashion, I am ashamed to presume.

2. During the time that; while; = TILL *conj.* 2. (Also with *that*.) *rare*.

1357 *Lay Folk's Catech.* 345 (MS. T.) For to lyve samen Withouten ony lousyng to thair life lastes. c1375 *Sc. Leg. Saints* i. (*Petrus*) 304 Mony..He helyt, to þat he was þare.

D. to (tuː) *adv.*

†**1.** Expressing motion resulting in arrival (cf. A. 1): To a place, etc. implied or indicated by the context. *Obs.* (Often the separable particle of a compound vb.)

c1000 ÆLFRIC *Hom.* II. 182 Gang to and arær hine. c1175 *Lamb. Hom.* 87 Þa on þere ilke nihte iwende godes engel to, and acwalde on elche huse [etc.]. 13.. *Cursor M.* 5530 (Cott. & Fairf.) Þis godds folk bar to þe clay. a1400-50 *Alexander* 1389 Þare presis to with paues peple withouten.

2. Expressing direction (cf. A. 2): Towards a thing or person implied; after *end*, *head*, etc., forming advb. phrases (cf. ON *adv.* 7b).

1889 *Amer. Nat.* Jan. 19 Three young owls with their feathers turned wrong end to. 1900 *Everybody's Mag.* III. 533 The Monitor came head-to when the cable brought her up.

b. In conjunction with other advbs. of direction: In one direction (as contrasted with the opposite one). Now only in TO AND FRO; see also 7, 9.

1375 BARBOUR *Bruce* x. 604 Him followit thai, With mekill payne, quhill to, quhill fra. c1421 HOCCLEVE *Complaint* 30 The grefe abowte my harte..bolned evar to and to so sore. 1560 ROLLAND *Crt. Venus* I. 356 Scho alteris ay to euerie kinde and stait: Quhylis to, quhylis fra. 1606 SHAKS. *Ant. & Cl.* I. iv. 46 This common bodie, Like to a Vagabond Flagge vpon the Streame, Goes too, and backe.

†**3.** Up to a time indicated by the context; till then: in phr. ***not be long to***. (Cf. A. 6.) *Obs.*

1468 J. PASTON in *P. Lett.* II. 318 When I come home, whyche, I tryst to God, shal not be long to. 1471 *Ibid.* III. 6 It shall not be longe to or then my wronges..shall be redressyd. 1538 HEN. VIII *Let. to Anne Boleyn* in *Select. fr. Harl. Misc.* (1793) 145 Till you repaire hydder, I keep something in store, trusting it shall not be long to.

4. Expressing contact (cf. A. 5): So as to come close against something; *esp.* with vbs. forming phrases denoting shutting or closing: see the vbs. Now *arch.* and *colloq.*

c1200 *Trin. Coll. Hom.* 181 Hie tuneð to hire fif gaten. a1225 *Ancr. R.* 96 Schutteð al þet þurl to. c1386 CHAUCER *Miller's T.* 554 Tehee quod she, and clapte the wyndow to. 1534 TINDALE *Luke* xiii. 25 When the good man of the housse..hath shett to the dore. a1619 FLETCHER *Mad Lover* III. ii, Put to the doors. 1620 J. DYKE in Spurgeon *Treas. Dav.* Ps. lxi. 2 This tower and rock were too high..and therefore he sets to the scaling ladder. 1855 MRS. GATTY *Parab. fr. Nat.* Ser. I. (1869) 61 The banging of the door, blown to by a current of wind. 1898 G. B. SHAW *Plays* II. *Arms & Man* 6 She goes out..and pulls the outside shutters to.

5. Expressing attachment, application, or addition (cf. A. 15, 16): after various verbs, as *put*, *set*, etc. (q.v.); also predicatively, *spec.* of a horse: = harnessed to a vehicle. Now *dial.* or *colloq.*

c1425 tr. *Arderne's Treat. Fistula* 84, I putte to regeneratyuez of flesch. c1450 *Oseney Reg.* 96 To this present writyng my seele I haue i-put to. 1530 PALSGR. Introd. 38 Lyke as we out of our adjectyves forme our adverbes..by adding to of ly. 1534 TINDALE *John* iii. 33 He that hath receaved hys testimonye hath set to his seale that God is true. 1596 SHAKS. *1 Hen. IV*, v. i. 133 Can Honour set too a legge? 1768 *Woman of Honor* I. 68 The horses are to. 1889 HISSEY *Tour in Phaeton* 97 We ordered the horses to, and resumed our pleasant pilgrimage.

b. In the senses 'in addition, besides, also', and 'in excess', now written as a distinct word, Too, q.v.

6. Expressing attention or application (cf. A. 24): after vbs., as *fall*, *go*, *set* (see the vbs.). In quot. 1606 *absol.* (with ellipsis of vb. in imperative).

c1200 ORMIN 6134 Forr þe birrþ don þin hellpe to Aȝȝ affterr þine fere. c1425- [see *set to*, SET v.[1] 152f]. 1606 SHAKS. *Tr. & Cr.* II. i. 119 To Achilles, to Aiax, to. 1610 —— *Temp.* III. iii. 49, I will stand to, and feede. *Ibid.* 52 Stand too, and doe as we. 1844 DISRAELI *Coningsby* VIII. i, It's difficult to turn to with a new thing.

†**7.** Expressing assent or adhesion (cf. A. 31b): In assent to or favour of something implied (opp. to *fra*, FRO *adv.*). Cf. 9b, TO AND FRO A. 3.

c1450 HOLLAND *Howlat* 270 Sum said to and sum fra, Sum nay and sum ȝa.

8. Used idiomatically with many verbs, as *bring*, *come*, *go*, *lay*, *lie*, etc.: see the verbs.

9. to and again.

a. To a place and back again; alternately in opposite directions; backwards and forwards: = TO AND FRO A. 1. *Obs.* exc. *dial.*

1627 CAPT. SMITH *Seaman's Gram.* ii. 6 A ship..hath sailed to and againe ouer the maine Ocean. 1628 DIGBY *Voy. Medit.* (Camden) 86 The wind shifted too and againe very vncertainely. 1628-1719 [see AGAIN A. 1c]. 1719 DE FOE *Crusoe* (1858) 240 Amazed when he saw me work the boat to-and-again in the sea by the rudder. 1760-72 H. BBOOKE *Fool of Qual.* (1809) II. 126 Walking..to and again. 1828 *Craven Gloss.*, *To and again*, backwards and forwards. 1888 ELWORTHY *W. Somerset Word-bk.* 763.

fig. 1736 NEAL *Hist. Purit.* III. 240 Such as had shifted their religion to and again.

†**b.** For and against a question: = TO AND FRO A. 3. *Obs.*

1656 *Burton's Diary* (1828) I. 3 All parties have been heard, too and again, in this last case. 1666 J. LIVINGSTONE in *Sel. Biog.* (1845) I. 181 Much debate too and again had been used.

†**c.** Again and again, repeatedly. *Obs.*

1659 *Burton's Diary* (1828) IV. 379 Your Committee too and again offered it as an expedient. 1666 PEPYS *Diary* 13 Aug., Sent him to and again to get me 1000*l*.

‖**to** (to), *sb.* Now *rare*. Pl. to. [Jap.] A Japanese unit of capacity equal to ten *sho*, equivalent to approximately 3·97 gallons (18·0 litres) or 0·496 bushel.

1871 A. B. MITFORD *Tales of Old Japan* II. 2 Each of these bags holds four tô (a tô is rather less than half an imperial bushel). 1884 *Murray's Handbk. Japan* (ed. 2) 18, 10 *shō* = 1 *to*. 1901 F. BRINKLEY *Japan* II. iii. 118 At the close of the sixteenth century,..the measure of capacity was exactly fixed, and its volume was called *tō*; ten *tō* (i.e. a sheaf of grain) being called a *koku*. **1956** R. J. SMITH in Cornell & Smith *Two Japanese Villages* 90 The most expensive *hōji*.. costs a minimum of 4,000 *yen* (one *koku* of rice). The least expensive costs 1,000 *yen* (1 *tō* of rice). **1959** R. K. BEARDSLEY et al. *Village Japan* 488/2 *Tō*, measure of volume; about 4 gallons.

to, obs. spelling of TOO *adv.*, TWO.

to-, *prefix*[1], the prep. and adv. TO used in combination with verbs, sbs., adjs., and advbs. in the sense of motion, direction, or addition to, or as the mark of the infinitive: see in their alphabetical places, TO-COME, TO-DO, TO-DRAUGHT, TO-GAINST, TOGETHER, TO-MIDST, TO-WHEN, TO-WHILE, etc. Also the following obs. verbs:

to-cast, to add, make addition: = L. *adicere*; **to-hang**, to append; **to-hear**, to hearken to, listen to; **to-knit**, to knit to, bind up: = L. *alligāre*; **to-lay**, to put forward, allege; **to-neighe**, to approach: = L. *accēdĕre*; **to-put**, to put to, add, affix: = L. *appōnĕre*; **to-set**, to set to, affix; **to-stand**, to stand to, post oneself, assist: = L. *astāre*, *assistĕre*; **to-step**, to step to, advance: = L. *aggredī*; **to-stick**, to stick to, adhere: = L. *adhærēre*; **to-tach**, to fasten to, attach; **to-yield**, to yield to, cede, give up.

a **1340** HAMPOLE *Psalter* cxiii. 23 Lord *tokast [L. *adiciat*] on ȝou, on ȝou & on ȝoure sunnys... Oure lord eke ȝoure noumbire. **1464** in *Acc. Fam. Innes* (1864) 78 To thir my present lettres I haf *to hungyn my sele. **1536** *Reg. Mag. Sig. Scot.* 343 *note*, I have subscrivit thir presentis with my hand, and has to hungin my proper sele of armes. *a* **1225** *Ancr. R.* 84 þet ȝe þe bet icnowen ham..*to-her hore molden. *a* **1300** *E.E. Psalter* cxlvi. 3 þat heles forbroken ofe hert for wa, And *toknittes [*alligat*] þar sorwes swa. *c* **1450** *Pol. Poems* (Rolls) II. 240 Auctoryteys for hem they *toleye. **1382** WYCLIF *Judith* xiv. 14 He wente *to-neȝhende to the curtin [*Vulg.* Accessit proximans ad cortinam]. **1420** in Pinkerton *Hist. Scot.* (1797) I. 455 The sealls of the for-said ..to thir indentures interchangablie are *toput. **1445** in *Charters rel. Glasgow* (1906) II. 440, I have procurit..the secrete sele of the burgh of Lithqw to be toput. *a* **1340** HAMPOLE *Psalter* lxxxviii. 22 þe sun of wickednes sall not *toset [*apponet*] him to noy. *c* **1375** *Cursor M.* 3498 (Fairf.) þer-to was he maste *to-sette. **1455** in *Charters, &c. Edinb.* (1871) 81 To the parte of this endentur remanand with the said toune the said Sir James sele is to sett. *a* **1340** HAMPOLE *Psalter* ii. 2 Tostode [L. *astiterunt*] þe kynges of erth. *c* **1205** LAY. 17406 þa cnihtes *to-stepen [*c* 1275 to-stapte] Mid muchelere strengðe. **1596** DALRYMPLE tr. *Leslie's Hist. Scot.* VI. (S.T.S.) I. 340 The capsell sa fast *tostack..that the force of man culde neuir sindir thame. **13..** *Gaw. & Gr. Knt.* 579 Queme quyssewes [cuisses]..with þwonges *to-tached. *c* **1350** *Will. Palerne* 3924 He a-liȝt, & wiȝtli to william his wepun vp *to-ȝelde.

to-, *prefix*[2]. *Obs.* exc. in rare *arch.* or *dial.* use. [OE. *to-*, ME. *to-* (*te-*) = OFris. *ti-*, *te-* (*to-*), OS. *ti-* (*te-*), OHG. *zi-*, *za-*, *ze-* and *zir-*, *zar-* (MHG. *ze-*, *zer-*, *zir-*, Ger. *zer-*):—WGer. **ti-*:—OTeut. **tiz-* = L. *dis-*, a particle expressing separation, 'asunder, apart, in pieces'.

The WGer. *ti-* (= L. *dis-*) in prehistoric times ran together in form with *ti* the unstressed prepositional form of *tó* (see TO *prep.*), with which it had no etymological connexion (being indeed almost opposite in sense); and when the latter was levelled in vowel with its stressed adverbial form *tó*, *ti-* (= *dis-*) also followed it, and appears constantly in OE. as *to-*. In most grammars and dictionaries this is written *tó-*, like the stressed form of TO *adv.* and *prep.* But as it was the *unstressed* form with which the prefix was formally confounded, and as it was itself always stressless (being sometimes written *te* as in OS. and OFris.), it seems more in accordance with the facts to spell it in OE. *to-* with short *o*, which is therefore done here.

In OE., about 125 compound verbs in *to-* are recorded; many of these did not survive in ME., where however so many new compounds appear (some formed even on vbs. from French) that their number in Early ME. was not less than in OE. In the 15th c. they rapidly disappeared and only a few are found after 1500. Many of the verbs which took the prefix *to-* had themselves the sense of separation or division; such were *break*, *burst*, *deal*, *melt*, *scatter*, *strew*, *tear*, etc.; in these *to-* added little but force to the notion: cf. *burst*, *burst asunder*, *tear*, *tear asunder*, etc. This led to the prefixing of *to-* to verbs which had no sense of partition, merely as a strengthening or emphasizing particle, as in *darken*, *to-darken*, *swink*, *to-swink*, etc. From an early time *to-* verbs were often strengthened by the qualifying adv. *all* (ALL C) in sense 'wholly, completely, altogether'; in later times this became universal. Consequently, the prefix began to be viewed as *all-to-* or *allto-*; and (verbal prefixes being very commonly written separate from the vb.) *all to* or *all-to* began to be treated as itself an adverb with the sense 'altogether, completely': see ALL C. 14, 15. Thus in the Bible of 1611, Judges ix. 53 'and all to brake his scull' was etymologically and historically *all to-brake*, i.e. 'all to-pieces-broke', but may have been understood as *all-to brake*, i.e. 'altogether' or 'completely broke'; Fairfax in 1674 by *all-to-be-deckt* can only have meant *all-to bedeckt*, 'completely bedecked'.]

1. With separative force: Asunder, apart, to or in pieces; also, away, about, abroad, here and there. Combined with verbs and derived adjs. and sbs. The more important of these appear in their places as main words: the following are obsolete words of single or rare occurrence. (All vbs. *trans.* unless otherwise stated.

† **to-bray** *v.*, to bray or beat to atoms; † **to-bust** *v.* [BUST *v.*[1]], to beat or thrash to pieces; † **to-crack** *v.*, to crack to pieces, shatter; † **to-dight** *v.*, to put apart, separate; hence † **to-dighting** *vbl. sb.*; † **to-flap** *v.*, to knock to pieces; † **to-gnide** *v.* [GNIDE *v.*], to crush to fragments; † **to-hale** *v.*, to haul or drag asunder; to pull about; to distend; † **to-heave** *v.*, to 'lift up' (one's eyes), to open; † **to-hene** *v.* [HENE *v.*], to mutilate by stoning; † **to-hurt** *v.*, to dash or knock asunder; † **to-leave** *v.*, to relinquish, to abandon; † **to-lithe** *v.* [LITHE *v.*[2]], to dismember; † **to-liver** *v.*, = DELIVER *v.*; † **to-melt** *v. intr.*, to melt away, dissolve; † **to-part** *v. intr.*, = DEPART *v.*; † **to-set** *v.*, to distribute, divide, arrange; † **to-shider** *v.*, [cf. SHIDE *sb.*] *intr.*, to break in pieces, to be shivered; † **to-shred** *v.*, to cut to shreds; † **to-skair** *v.* [SKAIR *v.*[2]], to scatter, disperse; † **to-skill** *v.*, to divide, distinguish; † **to-slent** *v.*[1] [SLENT *v.*[1]] *intr.*, to slip away; † **to-slent** *v.*[2] [SLENT *v.*[3]] *intr.*, split, burst; † **to-slive** *v.* [SLIVE *v.*[1]], to cleave; † **to-sned** *v.* [SNED *v.*], to cut to pieces; † **to-sparple** *v.*, to scatter abroad; = DISPARPLE; † **to-swinge** *v.*, to disperse by beating; to beat to pieces; † **to-thrust** *v.*, to thrust apart, to push open; **to-torve** *v.*, to hurl about; to dash to pieces; † **to-tose** *v.* [TOZE], to tear to pieces; † **to-twin** *v.*, to separate, divide; † **to-waver** *v. intr.*, to waver uncertainly; to wander; † **to-wawe** *v.*, [OE. *waȝian*] *intr.*, to move about; † **to-wowe** *v.* [OE. *wāwan*], to scatter by blowing; † **to-writhe** *v.*, (*a*) *trans.* to twist or wrench apart; (*b*) *intr.*, to twist or writhe about; † **to-wry** *v.*, to turn, twist about.

1382 WYCLIF *2 Chron.* xxxiv. 7 The mawmete wodus and grauen thingus he hadde *to-brayȝide in to gobetis. *a* **1250** *Owl & Night.* 1610 (Cott.) An euer euch man is wið me wroð ..An me *tobusteþ & tobeteþ. **13..** *Sir Beues* 4313 + 180 (MS. E.) þere men myȝte seen schafftys schake And mennys crownys al *tocrake. *c* **1450** LOVELICH *Grail* xiv. 196 Helmes and hawberkis to-kraked he then. **1340** *Ayenb.* 72 þanne þridde dyeaþ þet is þe *todiȝtinge of þe zaule and of þe bodie. **1382** WYCLIF *2 Sam.* xxii. 43 As cleye of streetis I sal breek hem, and *to-flappe [*confringam*]. *a* **1300** *E.E. Psalter* ci. 11 [cii. 10] For vp-heueand *to-gnodded þou me [*v.r.* for þou to-gnod me vpheuand: *Vulg.* elisisti; WYCLIF hurtledest me (down)]. **1387** TREVISA *Higden* (Rolls) V. 327 So was he al day to drawe and *to haled, i-scorned, and i-buffetted [*tractus et illusus colaphizatur*]. **1398** —— *Barth. De P.R.* XIX. liv. (Bodl. MS.), Raw hony not wele clarified.. streccheþ and to haleþ the bodie. *c* **1200** *Trin. Coll. Hom.* 201 Man þe nappeð [h]wile *to-heueð his eȝen, and þenne seð. *a* **1250** *Owl & Night.* 1119 Stones hi doþ in heore slytte [= pocket] & þe totorueþ & *toheneþ. *a* **1225** *Ancr. R.* 426 Sum nouhtunge hwar þuruh heo *to-hurteð [*v.r.* to hurren] eiðer urommard oðer. **1432-50** tr. *Higden* (Rolls) V. 69 The cardinalles supposede that he hade..to-lefte his benefice for the luffe of theyme. *c* **1000** ÆLFRIC *Hom.* II. 272 þa *toliðode se engel þæt cild on ðam disce. *c* **1205** LAY. 4216 Stater heo nom & al hene to-liðeden [*c* 1275 to-limekede]. *Ibid.* 25929 Nu hafeð be..Mine leomen al to-leðed [*c* 1275 a-liþede]. **13..** *Metr. Treat. on Dreams* in *Rel. Ant.* I. 266 Of sunne ant peril *to-lyvred he byth. *c* **1425** *Seven Sag.* (P.) 1976 Ham to-lywryd a man anon, And thider fast thay gone gone. *a* **1240** *Wohunge* in *Lambeth Hom.* 269 Hwat herte is swa hard þat ne mei *to-melte i þe munegunge of þe? *c* **1374** CHAUCER *Troylus* III. 249 (298) His olde wo..Gan tho for Ioye wasten and to-melte. *c* **1275** *Passion our Lord* 702 in *O.E. Misc.* 57 Hwanne hi schullen *to-party vt of lyue þisse. **1387** TREVISA *Higden* (Rolls) V. 265 Forto know rediliche þe meres and þe merkes of þe contrayes where þese men were *to set, loke in the firste book. *Ibid.* VII. 307 Eveniche celle is departed in foure, and to sette wiþ ynne for þe oratorie, þe dortour, þe fraytour, and þe werkhous. *c* **1450** *Guy Warw.* (C.) 1468 Faste þey smote þen togedur That þer sperys can *toschyder. *c* **1386** CHAUCER *Knt.'s T.* 1751 The helmes they tohewen and *toshrede. *c* **1200** ORMIN 1498 Till rihhte læfe turrnesst þatt flocc þatt was *toskeȝȝredd ær. *Ibid.* 9462 þatt Judisskenn follc þa shollde beon toskeȝȝredd..Forr heore depe sinne. *Ibid.* 18652 Illc an had iss oþerr fra *Toskiledd & todæledd. **14..** *Sir Beues* 2539 (MS. M.) Ascopard.. Smot Beues a strok gret, That his own fote *toslynt And he fel wiþ is owene dentte. *c* **1380** *Sir Ferumb.* 4940 þe ymage of Mahoun..Wiþ þe axe smot he oppon þe molde, þat al þat heued *to-slente [*pr.* to-flente]. *c* **1050** *Gloss.* in Wr.-Wülcker 406/29 *Findit*, *toslaf, tocleaf. *c* **1314** *Reinbrun* cv. in *Guy Warw.* (E.E.T.S.) 666 Helm and scheld,..þai gonne hem al to-schliue. *c* **1205** LAY. 4015 þe uniselie moder mid sexe hine *to-snæde. *Ibid.* 16148 Hengest..hafde..mid sæxen to-snædðe snelle þe þeines. **1387** TREVISA *Higden* (Rolls) V. 287 Hengistus..brouȝte to gydres his knyȝtes and men of arms þat were *to sparpled and to schad [L. *dispersis*]. *c* **1205** LAY. 1533 þer wes moni steap mon Mid stele *to-sw[u]ngen. *c* **1175** *Lamb. Hom.* 131 He *to-þruste þa stelene gate..of helle. *c* **1000** *Ags. Gosp.* Matt. xiv. 24 Witodlice wæs ꝥ scyp of þam yþum *totorfod, for-þam þe hyt wæs strang wind. *c* **1175** *Lamb. Hom.* 9 Ac me þe sculde nimen and al to-teon mid horse oðer þe al to-toruion mid stane. *a* **1250** [see *tohene*]. *a* **1250** *Owl & Night.* 70 þe sulue mose.. wolde þe *totose. *c* **1200** ORMIN 19060, & tiss lif unnderr Crisstenndom *Totwinneþþ & toshædeþþ All Cristess follc fra defless follc. *a* **1225** *Ancr. R.* 254 Euerichon to dealed [*Corpus* to twuned] from oðer. **1375** BARBOUR *Bruce* VII. 302 For thai trow we so scalit ar, And fled *to-vauerand her and thar. *c* **1350** *Will. Palerne* 19 þe child..spakly speke it couþe tho & spedeliche *to-wawe. **13..** in *Anglia* III. 279/89 þe wind hem wolde *towowen. *c* **1000** ÆLFRIC *Gram.* xxvi. (Z.) 155 *Torqueo*, ic wriðe,..*distorqueo*, ic *towriðe. *c* **1320** *Sir Tristr.* 3179 So wo was ysoude,..þat alle sche wald to wriþe. ? *a* **1400** *Morte Arth.* 3920 He al to-wrythes for woo. **1423** JAS. I *Kingis Q.* clxiv, So tolter quhilum did sche [Fortune] It *to-wrye.

2. Used as a mere intensive: Completely, entirely, soundly, greatly, severely, etc.

(A few of these show traces of the separative sense.)

All vbs. *trans.*, unless otherwise stated.

† **to-bent** *pa. pple.*, quite bent, bent low; † **to-bite** *v.*, to bite severely; † **to-blast** *v.*, to blast utterly; † **to-brain** *v.*, to brain completely; † **to-clout** *v.*, to cover with clouts; † **to-darken** *v.*, to darken greatly (rendering L. *contenebrare*); † **to-deraign** (**-dreyn**) *v.* [DERAIGN *v.*[1]], to maintain, vindicate (a cause, etc.) entirely; † **to-drunk** *pa. pple.*, thoroughly inebriated; † **to-dun** *v.* [DUN *v.*[2]], to strike with resounding blows; † **to-establish** *v.*, to establish perfectly or entirely; † **to-harrow** (**-harwe**) *v.*, to harrow completely; † **to-minish** *v.*, to make small, break up (rendering L. *comminuere*); † **to-pierce** (**-perse**) *v.*, to pierce entirely; † **to-punish** *v.*, to punish soundly; † **to-push** *v.*, to push about, to hustle; † **to-ray** *v.* [RAY *v.*[2] 5], to besmear; † **to-rot** *v. intr.*, to rot utterly (rendering L. *computrescere*); † **to-schrape** *v.* [SHRAPE], to scrape entirely; † **to-shell** *v.*, to peel entirely, to make bare of skin; † **to-smite** *v.*, to smite violently (in quot. *absol.*); † **to-spill** *v.*, to confound, ruin utterly; † **to-spreng** *v.*, to besprinkle completely; † **to-stick** *v.*, to prick all over; † **to-sting** *v.*, to sting severely; † **to-stink** *v. intr.*, to stink greatly; † **to-stir** *v.*, to move violently; † **to-stony** *v.*, to astound; † **to-swelt** *v. intr.*, to perish, die; † **to-swink** *v. intr.*, to toil hard; † **to-tar** *v.* (**-ter(re)** [TAR, TARRE *v.*[2]], to provoke greatly; † **to-teen** *v.* [TEEN *v.*[1]], to injure or annoy greatly: see quot. s.v. *to-tray*; † **to-threat** *v.*, to threaten violently; † **to-tray** *v.*, to torment exceedingly; † **to-trouble** *v.*, to trouble greatly, to afflict severly; † **to-turn** *v.*, to overthrow, upset, subvert; † **to-walt** *v. intr.*, to overflow; † **to-waste** *v.*, to waste greatly.

c **1401** LYDG. *Flour of Curtesye* 260 Over this, myn hertes lust *to-bente. **1375** *Creation* 640 in Horstm. *Altengl. Leg.* (1878) 132 An addre..al *to-bot Seth in þe face. **1382** WYCLIF *Job* Prol. 2 The boc shortid, and to-torn and to-bite. **1303** R. BRUNNE *Handl. Synne* 8866 þe syȝte of here myn herte *to-blaste. *c* **1330** —— *Chron. Wace* (Rolls) 9293 þe sight of hure hym al to-blast. *c* **1489** CAXTON *Blanchardyn* xliii. 164 He..*to brayned ther many one. *c* **1430** *Pilgr. Lyf Manhode* III. xxii. (1869) 148 That is thilke that hath thus to ragged me and *to clowted me as thou seest. **1382** WYCLIF *Lam.* v. 17 Therfore dreri mad is oure herte, therfore *to-dercned ben oure eȝen. *c* **1320** *Cast. Love* 974 For I chulle an ende ouercome þ[t] fiht, And *to-dreynen al þi riht. **1382** WYCLIF *Jer.* xlvi. 10 Deuouren shal the swerd,..and be *to-drunke with the blod of hem. *c* **1240** *Wohunge* in *Cott. Hom.* 281 Siðen ȝette buffetet and *to dunet i þe heaued wið þe red ȝerde. *a* **1562** CAVENDISH *Poems*, etc. (1825) II. 158 Your pryncely powers and hault dygnyties Assured me with suche perfection, *To-establyshed me in the hyest degrees. **1393** LANGL. *P. Pl.* C. XXII. 268 (MS. T.) Al þis hus oxen ereden thei *to harwen [*v.r.* to-harewide] after. **1382** WYCLIF *Isa.* xxviii. 28 Bred forsothe shal be *to-mynusht [1388 maad lesse]. *c* **1470** HENRY *Wallace* IV. 662 The trensand blaid *to persyt euirydeill Throu plaitt and stuff. *a* **1400-50** *Alexander* 4330 *To-ponyscht be-fore Fynd we na faute in na freke þat vs emange duellis. **13..** *Lament. St. Bernard* 198 in *Minor Poems Vernon MS.* 306 þe Iewes of harm hedde non ende, Mi sone to-beten and *to-pust. **1560** WHITEHORNE *Ord. Souldiours* (1588) 46 b, Putting Toe.. peeses of linnen cloth all *to-rayed therewith. **1382** WYCLIF *Jer.* xlvi. 15 Why *to-rotide [*v.r.* to-stank] thi stronge? *a* **1225** *Leg. Kath.* 1185 He..schrenchte þen alde deouel, & *teschrapet his heaued. **1377** LANGL. *P. Pl.* B. XVII. 191 Ac þough my thombe & my fyngres bothe were *to-shullen. **14..** *Beryn* 1456 Yeur wyff woll sikirliche..hir tuskis sharpe whet, And *to smyte with hir tunge. *a* **1300** *E.E. Psalter* xliii. 9 [xliv. 7] þou *tospilte vs hatand. **1382** WYCLIF *Jer.* vi. 26 Be thou gird with an heire, and *to-sprengd with asken. *c* **1315** SHOREHAM ii. 75 Hy *to-stek hys swete hefed Wyþ one þornene coroune. ? *a* **1300** *XI Pains Hell* 177 in *O.E. Misc.* 152 Olde men..neddren..Heom heo *to-styngeþ vychon. **1382** *To-stank [see *to-rot*]. **1382** WYCLIF *Isa.* xxiv. 20 With to-stering shal be *to-stired the erthe. **1375** BARBOUR *Bruce* XVIII. 547 His frendis..He couth ressawe,.. And his fais stoutly *to-stonay. ? *a* **1400** *Morte Arth.* 1436 Alle to-stonayede with þe strokes of þa steryne knyghtez. *c* **1205** LAY. 26810 Halmes to-hælden Hæhȝe men *to-swelten. *c* **1386** CHAUCER *Pard. T.* 191 In Erthe, in Eir, in Water man *to swynke. **1382** WYCLIF *2 Macc.* xii. 14 These that weren with ynne,..diden slow-licher, *to terynge [**1388** to-terrynge] Judas with cursyngis. **1377** *Pol. Poems* (Rolls) I. 218 The Frensche men..with heore scornes us *to-threte. *a* **1250** *Prov. Ælfred* 303 in *O.E. Misc.* 120 Ac heo hine schal steorne *To-trayen and to-teone. **1382** WYCLIF *Ecclus.* xxxv. 22 The strengeste shal not han in hem pacience, that he *to-truble the rigge of hem. —— *Isa.* xxviii. 17 The hail shal *to-turne vpsodoun the hope of lesyng. *c* **1470** *Golagros*

& *Gaw.* 704 All to-turnit thair entyre, traistly and tewch. **13..** *E.E. Allit. P.* B. 428 *To-walten alle þyse welle-hedez & þe water flowed. **1382** Wyclif *Jer.* xiv. 15 In swerd and hunger shul be *to-wastid tho profetus.

3. Hence **all to-, all to, all-to, † alto,** employed in middle and early modern Eng. as an intensive to any verb: see all C. 14, 15.

‖**toa**[1] ('təʊə). Also tooa. [Native name in many Polynesian langs.] A species of *Casuarina* (*C. equisetifolia*) found in the South Sea Islands.

Its wood, known from its colour and hardness as South Sea Ironwood, is traditionally used by the native islanders for their clubs.

1792 W. Bligh *Voy. South Sea* xii. 148 A wooden spear.. pointed with the toa wood. *Ibid.* xvi. 213 The soil is little other than sand, yet it produced small toa-trees. **1817** Mariner *Acc. Tonga Isl.* I. viii. 244 The whistling of the wind among the branches of the lofty *toa.* *Ibid.* 245 Restrictions respecting cutting down the Toa tree. **1823** Byron *Island* II. i, We will sit in twilight's face, and see The sweet moon glancing through the tooa tree.

‖**toa**[2] ('tɔːa). *N.Z.* [Maori.] A brave warrior.

1860 A. S. Atkinson *Jrnl.* 25 Dec. in *Richmond-Atkinson Papers* (1960) I. 671 A remark of Manuka's was rather good—Maori chiefs (leaders) were toas & went out at the head of their men, Pakeha chiefs stayed in Town & ate biscuit. **1881** C. W. Hursthouse *Let.* 12 June in *Ibid.* (1960) II. 486 Tuninia was a celebrated toa, and knew it. **1901** A. H. Grace in D. M. Davin *N.Z. Short Stories* (1953) 19 You can imagine what joy it is to become the wife of such a brave *toa.* **1949** P. H. Buck *Coming of Maori* (1950) III. i. 338 Those who had distinguished themselves in battle were termed *toa* and were usually of the *rangatira* class, for ruling chiefs had to lead in war as well as in peace.

toad (təʊd), *sb.* Forms: α. 1 **tádiȝe, tádie.** β. 1–5 **tadde,** (*pl.* 1 **-an,** 2–4 **en,** 3–7 **-es**). γ. ? 3, 4–6 *north.* **tade,** 5– *Sc.* **taid,** 9 *north. dial.* **teäde, tead, ted, tyed.** δ. 4–7 **tode,** 5–6 **toode,** 6 **tood,** 6–7 **toade,** 7– **toad.** [OE. *tádiȝe,* of unknown origin and unusual form, has no cognates in the other langs. (Da. and Norw. *tudse* are not connected.) The relation of *tadde* to *tádiȝe, tádie* is not clear: Björkman thinks it a hypocoristic form with shortened vowel and doubled cons.; it survived in s.w. ME. *tadde*; cf. also *tadpole* (see 7b), *tadpole.* The northern *tade, taid, teäde, ted* and midl. *tôde, tood, toad,* with long vowel and single cons., prob. represented *tádiȝe, tádie,* with its unusual ending reduced to *-e.*]

1. a. A tailless amphibian of the genus *Bufo*; primarily the common European species *Bufo vulgaris*; thence extended to many foreign species of the genus or of the family *Bufonidæ.* ***running toad,*** the natterjack.

α. *c* **1000** Ælfric *Voc.* in Wr.-Wülcker 122/11 *Buffo,* tadiȝe. *a* **1100** *Voc.* ibid. 321/23 *Rubeta,* tadie.

β. **11..** *Voc.* in Wr.-Wülcker 544/7 *(Ru)beta,* tadde. *c* **1175** *Lamb. Hom.* 51 Þer wunieð in-ne.. Blake tadden. *Ibid.* 53 Ah liggeð þer uppon, alse þe tadde deð in þere eorðe. *a* **1225** *Ancr. R.* 214 Schal ine helle iwurðen to him tadden & neddren. **1387** Trevisa *Higden* (Rolls) VIII. 18 A womman þat hadde a fende wiþ inne her.. caste up tweȝ blake taddes. **1398** —— *Barth. De P.R.* xvi. lxxi. (Tollen MS.), This stone is take oute of a tadde heed.

γ. *a* **1300** *Cursor M.* 23227 Fell dragons and tades [*v.r.* tadis] bath. *a* **1340** Hampole *Psalter* xc. 13 Þe snake werpis and þe tade nuryssis þe eg, and þarof is broght forth þe basilyske. *c* **1440** *York Myst.* xi. 271 For tadys and frosshis we may not flitte. *c* **1440** *Alphabet of Tales* 240 He drew oute a grete whik tade. *c* **1480** Henryson *Test. Cres.* 578 Heir I beteiche my Corps and Carioun With Wormis and with Taidis to be rent. **1508** Kennedie *Flyting w. Dunbar* 287 Tigris, serpentis, and taidis will remane In Dumbar wallis. **1725** Ramsay *Gentle Sheph.* II. ii, Mixt wi' the venom of black taids and snakes. **1818** Scott *Br. Lamm.* xxxv, A taid may sit on her coffin the day. **1823** Galt *Entail* II. xxix. 277 Ye would as soon think of likening a yird tead to a patrick. **1863** Robson *Bards Tyne* 353 Now, Geordy, my lad, sit as mute as a tyed.

δ. **12..** *St. Patrick's Purg.* 274 in Horstm. *Alteng. Leg.* (1875) 188 Eddren furi vpen hem sete, and toden grete al so. *c* **1325** *Song Mercy* 56 in *E.E.P.* (1862) 120 Þou seȝe me a monge todes blake Ful longe in harde prisoun lyng. **1370–80** *XI Pains of Hell* 60 in *O.E. Misc.* 224 As Fissches þei were in þat flod þo, Todus, Neddres, Snakes mony mo. **1422** tr. *Secreta Secret., Priv. Priv.* 152 Thay hym yaue pryuely a lytill toode in a drynke. **1530** Palsgr. 281/2 Tode, *crapault.* **1567** Maplet *Gr. Forest* 16 Nesorpora is a stone of Pontus ..found in a Todes heade. **1568** Grafton *Chron.* II. 116 Findyng there a most venemous toade. **1600** Shaks. *A.Y.L.* II. i. 13 Sweet are the vses of aduersitie, Which like the toad, ougly and venemous, Weares yet a precious Iewell in his head. **1667** Milton *P.L.* IV. 800 Him there they found Squat like a Toad, close at the eare of Eve. **1763** Churchill *Proph. Famine* Poems I. 112 Marking her noisome road With poison's trail, here crawled the bloated Toad. **1849** T. Bell *Brit. Reptiles* (ed. 2) 115 Few animals have ever suffered more undeserved persecution as the victims of an absurd and ignorant prejudice than the toad. *Ibid.* 126 Natter-jack Toad. **1895** Running Toad [see running *ppl. a.* 7c]. **1909** *Blackw. Mag.* Apr. 503/2 She was already on friendly terms with my mice and my toads and my snake.

b. As a type of anything hateful or loathsome.

a **1548** Hall *Chron., Edw. IV* 231 To whom the Frenche nacion was more odious then a tode. **1586** Day *Eng. Secretary* II. (1625) 125 It behoueth also that..he doe incline to good..that he abhorre flatterie as a Toad. **1606** Shaks. *Tr. & Cr.* II. iii. 170, I do hate a proud man, as I hate the ingendring of Toades. **1645** Milton *Colast.* Wks. 1851 IV. 360 To hate one another like a toad or poison.

c. In various figurative and proverbial uses. ***to eat (any one's) toads,*** to be a mean dependant, to toady (see toad-eater). ***toad under a harrow,*** a simile for a person under constant persecution or oppression.

1649 Bp. Reynolds *Serm. Hosea* i. 46 [As] impossible..as for a Toad to spit Cordials. **1788** Ld. Bulkeley in Dk. Buckhm. *Crt. & Cabinets Geo. III* (1853) I. 364 There is no man who eats Pitt's toads with such zeal, attention, and appetite. **1815** *Hist. J. Decastro,* etc. I. 252 [We] were e'en forced to eat our toads and be silent. **1855** Thackeray *Newcomes* liii, Don't they follow him to college: and eat his toads through life? **1802–12** Bentham *Rat. of Evidence* (1827) I. 385 *note,* Kept like toads under a harrow. **1825** Brockett *N.C. Words, Toad-under-a-Harrow,* the comparative situation of a poor fellow, whose wife, not satisfied with the mere hen-pecking of her helpmate, takes care that all the world shall witness the indignities she puts upon him. **1903** *Daily Chron.* 16 May 3/4 The 'toad-under-the-harrow' existence of a plain, middle-aged, but cultivated and fine-natured spinster, whose whole life was subordinated to an invalid and rather malignant old mother.

2. †Used erroneously for the frog (*obs.*); applied to other allied animals, as ***Surinam toad*** = pipa; ***horned toad:*** see horned 2b; ***midwife, obstetrical toad,*** the nurse-frog: see obstetrical.

a **1300** *E.E. Psalter* lxxvii. 50 [lxxviii. 45] And sent in am hundeflegh, and it ete þa; Tade [L. *ranam*], and it for-spilt þam swa. **1602** Marston *Antonio's Rev.* III. iii, Now croakes the toad. **1757–1894** [see pipa]. **1812–29, 1817** Surinam toad [see toadlet, toadling]. **1815** Kirby & Sp. *Entomol.* (1843) I. 305 Like the young of the Surinam Toad (*Rana pipa*) they attach themselves in clusters upon her back, belly, head, and even legs. **1901** P. Fountain *Deserts N. Amer.* viii. 158 The 'Californian toad' which is really a species of lizard.

3. a. Applied opprobriously to human beings and animals.

a **1568** *Bannatyne Poems* (Hunter. Cl.) 396/36 Ane fowle taid cairle. **1594** Shaks. *Rich. III,* IV. iv. 81 To helpe me curse That bottel'd Spider, that foule bunch-back'd Toad. **1605** *1st Pt. Ieronimo* II. v, *Ier.* Is not this a monstrous courtier? *Hor.* He is the court tode, father. **1634** Sir T. Herbert *Trav.* 159 All true Persians thinke of them as enemies to Mahomet..and that all their Disciples were Toades, the of-scum of the earth & vile Apostates. **1744** in Ozel *Brantome's Span. Rhodomontades* (ed. 2) Advert., A cursed Toad of a Horse..not only threw me but rolled over me. **1771** Foote *Maid of B.* III. Wks. 1799 II. 232 What a miserable poor toad is a husband, whose misfortunes not even death can relieve! **1853** R. Carmichael in *Whistlebinkie* Ser. III. 47 Sic a pridefu' taid Our Tibbie's grown. **1894** Astley *50 Years Life* II. 87 The silly toad had carelessly forgotten to pull the stirrup-irons up.

b. Applied to children. Cf. tad 2.

1836 T. C. Haliburton *Clockmaker* 1st Ser. xxvii. 178 Two little orphan children, the prettiest little toads I ever beheld. **1897** *Private Life of Queen* xi. 93 Jonathan Mace.. had been a day labourer at Frogmore... He always spoke of the Queen's spirited sons as 'rare young toads'. **1954** M. Sharp *Gipsy in Parlour* IV. xxiv. 234 Why shouldn't 'ee wed the poor toad? **1958** 'Miss Read' *Storm in Village* iii. 38 If our Billy has the nightmares, I shan't wonder! Poor little toad, and him so high strung! **1981** V. Canning *Boy on Platform One* vii. 108 I'll show you. Never seen a salmon! You poor little toad.

4. = toady *sb.* 2.

1831 [see toad *v.*]. **1834** Beckford *Italy,* etc. II. 159 Mrs. Guildermeester.. we found in a vast but dingy saloon, her toads squatting around her. *Ibid.,* Donna Genuefa, the toad-passive in waiting..Miss Coster, the toad-active,.. makes tea with decorum. **1959** I. & P. Opie *Lore & Lang. Schoolch.* x. 191 One who makes up to a teacher is recognized as being in a slightly different category from an outright sneak, although almost as nauseous. The usual epithets are 'toad' or 'toady', 'worms', 'crawler', or, in Camberwell, 'grease boy' or 'grease rat'.

†5. *Alchemy.* = bufo. *Obs.*

1471 Ripley *Comp. Alch.* I. xx. in Ashm. *Theat. Chem. Brit.* (1652) 134 Our Tode of the Erth whych etyth hys fyll. **1610** B. Jonson *Alch.* II. iii, Your toade, your crow, your dragon, and your panthar.

6. a. *Cookery.* ***toad in the (†a) hole:*** meat, now usu. sausages, baked in batter.

1787 Grose *Prov. Gloss., Pudding-Pye-Doll,* the dish called toad-in-a-hole, meat boiled in a crust. *Norf.* **1797** Mme. D'Arblay *Lett.* Dec., Mrs. Siddons and Sadler's Wells..seems..as illfitted as the dish they call a toad in a hole,..putting a noble sirloin of beef into a poor paltry batter-pudding. **1836** A. Fonblanque *Eng. under Seven Admin.* (1837) III. 314 'Toad-in-a-hole', a piece of meat baked in a pudding, with a pool of gravy round it. **1883** F. B. Harrison *Little Pretty* iv, I give you hashes, and toad-in-the-hole, and curry, and use up all the odds and ends. **1927** [see schooner *sb.*[1] 1b]. **1934** *Cassell's Mod. Practical Cookery* 145/1 Put in the sausages. Season the batter,..and pour it over them. Put the toad-in-the-hole into a good, moderately hot oven. **1934** T. S. Eliot *Rock* i. 40 Restaurants where you can get..sausage and mashed or toad-in-the-'ole for twopence. **1943** L. Chatterton *Mod. Cookery* 167/1 Toad in the hole without eggs... Milk,.. flour,..bicarbonate of soda,..vinegar,..salt,..sausages,.. dripping... Small sausages are best..., or..steak cut in two-inch pieces may be used. **1959** B. Nilson *Penguin Cookery Bk.* 330 Toad-in-the-hole is made like Yorkshire pudding, but 1lb. skinned sausages is heated in the fat for 5 minutes before adding the batter. **1971** *Guardian* 18 June 11/6 Although 'toad-in-the-hole' is an unprepossessing name it must be one of the few dishes which sounds even worse in French. I am sure no one would eat 'Le crapaud au trou'.

b. ***toad in the hole:*** a name applied to various games, esp. a form of hide-and-seek and a game in which lead discs are thrown at holes in a wooden structure.

1930 J. Dos Passos *42nd Parallel* 381 They got tired playing toad in the hole in the deep weeds. **1969** I. & P. Opie *Children's Games* iv. 154 When played after dark, as is not unusual, it [*sc.* Hide-and-Seek] may have a special name, such as..'Toad in the Hole' (Forfar). **1969** E. H. Pinto *Treen* 229 Toad-in-the-hole..probably originated in England in Tudor times. Since then, it has been played in many parts of the world, including Argentina, where it is known as *Sapo.* **1970** *Daily Tel.* 18 Mar. 15/6 Mr. P. N. Barnard's letter..about the 'charity game' known as toad in the hole..has provided me with a translation into English of this very old game which used to be played a great deal in France, where it is known as *tonneau.* **1975** *Country Life* 11 Dec. 1677/4, I am..looking for examples of the following regional inn sports:..twister (Suffolk), and toad in the hole (Sussex)... Every one of the games I have mentioned is actually played in English pubs today.

7. *attrib.* and *Comb.:* attributive, as ***toad-hole, -poison, -pond, -spawn, -venom;*** objective, similative, etc., as ***toad-bellied, -blind, -green, -housing, -legged, -shaped, -spotted, -swollen*** adjs., ***toad-like*** adj. and adv., ***toadwise*** adv.

1633 Ford *'Tis Pity* IV. iii, You *toad-bellied bitch! **1922** Joyce *Ulysses* 465 Beside him stands Father Coffey, chaplain, toadbellied, wrynecked. **1850** Kelly tr. *Cambrensis Eversus* II. 217 Giraldus, who was *toad blind (*talpâ cæcior*) to everything creditable to the Irish. **1890** *Daily News* 27 Sept. 2/1 A *toad-green cloth redingote. **1825** J. Neal *Bro. Jonathan* I. 108 Never seed a wood-chuck in a *toad-hole I guess? **1598** E. Gilpin *Skial.* (1878) 41 How *toad-housing sculs, and old swart bones, Are grac'd with painted toombs, and plated stones. **1843** *Jrnl. R. Agric. Soc.* IV. I. 190 The fact of wheat being broken down near the root, or '*toade-legged'. *a* **1586** Sidney *Arcadia* (1622) 126 A *tode-like retiredness, and closenesse of minde. **1812** *Religionism* 43 Then lay thy awkward, toad-like twists aside. **1839** Bailey *Festus* xxxiv. (1852) 550 My purpose..hath grown in me and lived on, Toad-like within a rock—vital where all Beside was death. **1869** *Zoologist* Sept. 1832 The ignorant of all ages have believed in the existence of this *toad-poison, the men of science have almost universally treated its existence as a fable. **1851** Borrow *Lavengro* iv. (1911) 30 The sludge in the *toad-pond. **1854** Badham *Halieut.* 507 These last acquired such celebrity in the knowledge of wheedling, as to be called parasite, or *toad-spawn. **1605** Shaks. *Lear* v. iii. 138 A most *Toad-spotted Traitor. **1915** W. Owen *Let.* Apr. (1967) 331 It's Measles!. .. Bloody eyes—toad-spotted, raw-meat-coloured skin. **1603** H. Crosse *Vertues Commw.* (1878) 82 So *toade-swolne with pride and ambition, that he is ready to burst in sunder. **1852** *Zoologist* X. 3658 The active principle of *toad-venom is alkaline in its character. **1867** Lanier *Strange Jokes* 17 Give lair and rest To him who *toadwise sits and croaks.

b. Special comb.: **toad-back** *a.*, of a stair-rail, etc., having a section of three-lobed shape held to resemble the back of a toad; **toad-bit,** a disease of cattle: see quot.; **toad-bug,** any species of the American genus *Galgulus* of small predaceous Hemiptera; **toad-cheese** (also **toad's cheese, † taddechese**), a poisonous fungus; **toad-flower,** an African plant, *Stapelia bufonia*; **toad-frog,** (*a*) a book-name for the genus *Pelobates* of tailless amphibians: see quot.; (*b*) *U.S. dial.* = sense 1a; **toad-grass** = *toad-rush*; **toad-head,** the American golden plover (*local U.S.*); **toad-lily,** (*a*) *Fritillaria pyrenaica*; (*b*) the American white water-lily (*local U.S.*); (*c*) the Japanese *Tricyrtis hirta*; **toad-lizard,** (*a*) the horned toad (*Cent. Dict.* 1891); (*b*) the labyrinthodon; **toad-marl,** a dark-coloured variety of marl; **toad-orchis,** a tropical West African orchid, *Megaclinium Bufo,* having purple-spotted flowers; **toad-pipe** († **tadpipe**), any one of various species of *Equisetum*; † **toad-pool,** a mass of corrupt poisonous matter; **toad-rock** = toadstone[2]; **toad-rush,** *Juncus bufonius*; † **toad's bread,** a fungus; **toad's cap,** a toadstool; **toad's eye,** a precious stone; ? = crapaud 2; **toad's eye tin,** a variety of cassiterite; † **toad's-guts,** a term of abuse; † **toad's hat,** a toadstool; † **toadskin** *N. Amer. slang.* (*obs.*), (*a*) a five-cent stamp; (*b*) a banknote; **toad's meat,** *dial.*, toadstools; **toad's mouth,** the snapdragon, *Antirrhinum majus*; **toad-snatcher,** the reed-bunting; **toad-spit, -spittle** = cuckoo-spit[2] 1; **toad-stabber** *slang* (chiefly *U.S.*), a large pocket-knife or jack-knife; **toad-sticker** *U.S. slang,* a large knife; formerly also, a sword; **toad-strangler** *U.S. dial.*, a heavy downpour of rain. See also toad-eater, etc.

1825 Brockett *N.C. Words,* **Toad-bit,* a disease among cattle..imputed to the poison of toads. **1902** L. O. Howard *Insect Book* 281 The *Toad Bugs..[These] odd and ugly little insects..have been appropriately termed the 'toad-shaped bugs'. The short, broad body,..the projecting eyes, ..the dull mottled colors, are toad-like. **14..** *Voc.* in Wr.-Wülcker 585/21 *Fungea..i. boletus*..a *taddechese. *Ibid.* 618/4 *Tubera,* taddechese. **1703** J. Whiting in C. Marshal *Sion's Trav.* (1704) b viij b, Several of which persecuting Justices soon after dyed with Eating of Tadcheese (alias Mushrooms). **1853** J. Lousley *Let.* 9 Jan. in *N. & Q.* (1962) Mar. 84/1 Toads cheeses are the poisenous Fungusses which grow in our hedgerows and woods. **1882** *Science Gossip* 165/1 'Toad's cheeses', rank fungi. **1884** Miller *Plant-n.* 137/2 African *Toad-flower. **1861** *Harper's Mag.* Aug. 421/1 Every body is a pitching into this matter like *toad-frogs into a willow swamp. **1896** Lydekker *New Nat. Hist.* V. 283 The fifth family..comprises eight genera, which may be collectively termed toad-frogs, since they come neither under the designation of toads or frogs. **1913** H. Kephart *Our Southern Highlanders* xiii. 295 In the Smokies a toad is called a frog or a toad-frog. **1964** J. H. Clarke *Harlem* 276 She just stood..swellin' up like a big toad frog. **1981** *Amer. Speech* LVI. 45 Toad-frog is

Southern and Midland. **1640** PARKINSON *Theat. Bot.* 1190 The Flemmings generally call [it] Padde grasse, that is, *Tode grasse. **1884** MILLER *Plant-n.* 137/2 *Toad-lily, *Fritillaria nigra.* Japanese Toad-lily, *Tricyrtis hirta.* **1899** *Edin. Rev.* Apr. 317 The Labyrinthodon, or monster *toad-lizard. **1764** *Museum Rust.* II. cx. 377 Called *toad marle, from its resemblance in colour to that animal. **1578** LYTE *Dodoens* I. lxviii. 101 The small [horsetail] is called..in English smal Shauegrasse, and of some *Tadpipes. **1607** CHAPMAN *Bussy d'Ambois* III. ii. 452 Thy gall Turns all thy blood to poison, which is cause Of that *toad-pool that.. makes thee..rot as thou livest. **1776** WITHERING *Brit. Plants* (1796) II. 348 [Juncus] bufonius..*Toad Rush. Wet Gravelly or sandy meadows and pastures. **1861** MISS PRATT *Flower. Pl.* V. 297 Toad Rush..sometimes called Toad-grass. **1624** T. SCOTT *Lawfulnesse Netherl. Warre* 17 Therefore Philip gaue him *fungos*, or *Toads-bread to eate. *a* **1825** FORBY *Voc. E. Anglia*, **Toad's-cap*, a fungus. **1747** DINGLEY in *Phil. Trans.* XLIV. 505 The *Toad's-Eye, black. **1850** ANSTED *Elem. Geol., Min.*, etc. §490 Toad's eye tin is the same variety [as wood tin] on a small scale. **1874** J. H. COLLINS *Metal Mining* 13 [In] Cornwall..valuable lumps of 'wood-tin' and 'toad's-eye' tin have been built into hedges. **1634** S. R. *Noble Soldier* IV. ii. in Bullen *O.P.* (1882) I. 317 *Toads-guts,..doe you heare, Monsire? *c* **1440** *Promp. Parv.* 495/2 *Todyshatte (or muscheron),..*tuber.* **1867** F.-H. LUDLOW *Little Brother* 251 'Why, ma, don't you know what a *toadskin is?' said Billy, drawing a dingy five-cent stamp from his pocket. 'Here's one... And don't I wish I had lots of 'em!' **1912** J. SANDILANDS *Western Canad. Dict. & Phrase-Bk.*, *Toadskin*, a dollar bill. Originally, in the States, a toadskin meant a five-cent stamp, and of a mean, grasping person it was said 'His purse is made of toad's skin.' **1926** Toadskin [see IRON-MAN I c]. **1886** P. S. ROBINSON *Valley Teet. Trees* 134 The rustic calls [toadstools] '*toad's meat'. **1839** PHILLIPS in *Sat. Mag.* 18 May 190/1 It has.. received various names, as Dog's Mouth,..*Toad's Mouth, and Snap-Dragon. **1848** *Zoologist* VI. 2290 The black-headed bunting..a '*toad-snatcher'. **1885** SWAINSON *Provinc. Names Birds* 72 Reed Bunting..Toad snatcher. **1751** WARBURTON *Pope's Wks.* IV. 24 *note*, Those frothy excretions, called by the people *Toad spits, seen in summer-time hanging upon plants. **1658** J. ROWLAND *Moufet's Theat. Ins.* 909 [Nature] hath infected the Sage with *Toad-spittle. **1885** G. SWEETMAN *Gloss. Wincanton*, **Toad-stabber*,..a bad knife. **1915** S. LEWIS *Trail of Hawk* x. 102 Carl..pried open a class-room window with his large jack-knife..known as a 'toad-stabber'. **1938** W. SMITTER *F.O.B. Detroit* 48 'There you are,' said Russ, snapping the blade open. 'A regular toad-stabber of a thing.' **1858** *Calif. Spirit of Times* 7 Aug. 1/8 The Judge put his *toad sticker atween his teeth, tuk a pistol in won hand, and a slung shot in the other, an sez thru his nose, 'cum on'. **1944** J. S. PENNELL *Hist. Rome Hanks* 293, I must have picked up this old toadsticker. **1938** M. K. RAWLINGS *Yearling* xix. 228 Hit's a *toad-strangler of a rain. **1980** *Knoxvill* (Tennessee) *News-Sentinel* 6 Apr. C4/5 'We say toad-strangler for a hard rain around here,' Farley said.

toad (təʊd), *v.* [f. prec., after *toad-eat*, etc.] *trans.* To act as a toady to; to toady. Also *intr.*

1802 G. COLMAN *Poor Gent.* II. ii, How these tabbies love to be toaded! **1826** F. REYNOLDS *Life & T.* II. 303 *note*, He could scarcely ever get anybody but dull toading tuft-hunters to remain there above four days. **1831** LADY GRANVILLE *Lett.* 21 Feb., All her toads toad on because they see that I toad her too. **1849** W. IRVING *Goldsmith* xxxix. 335 Boswell's inveterate disposition to *toad*, was a sore cause of mortification to his father.

toad, var. TODE *sb.*[1] *Obs.*, Dutch fishing-boat.

toad-eat ('təʊd,iːt), *v. rare.* [Back-formation from TOAD-EATER.] *trans.* To flatter, fawn upon (a person); to toady. Also *intr.* So **'toad-,eating** *vbl. sb.* and *ppl. a.*

1766 LADY S. LENNOX in *Life & Lett.* (1901) I. 199, I have got Charles into such order, that..he toad eats me beyond all conception. **1767** LADY S. BUNBURY in Jesse *Selwyn & Contemp.* (1843) II. 175, I toad-eat a little cur that is here, only because his name is Raton. **1791** EARL MORNINGTON in *14th Rep. Hist. MSS. Comm.* App. v. 7 Some verses which I took down..as being the excess of toad-eating. **1799** —— in Stanhope *Pitt* III. 191 The delight of being toad-eated by all India from Cabul to Assam. **1831** JEKYLL *Corr.* (1894) 273 Puffing himself in newspapers, and toad-eating Princes and Ministers. **1836–7** DICKENS *Sk. Boz, Horatio Sparkins*, 'Decidedly', said the toad-eating Flamwell. **1880** MISS BRADDON *Just as I am* xlv, A real sister has no motive for such toad-eating.

toad-eater ('təʊd,iːtə(r)).

1. One who eats toads; *orig.* the attendant of a charlatan, employed to eat or pretend to eat toads (held to be poisonous) to enable his master to exhibit his skill in expelling poison.

1629 J. ROUS *Diary* 45, I inquired of him if William Utting the toade-eater..did not once keepe at Laxfield; he tould me yes, and said he had seene him eate a toade, nay two. *a* **1704** T. BROWN *Sat. on Quack* Wks. 1730 I. 64 Be the most scorn'd Jack-pudding in the pack, And turn toad-eater to some foreign Quack. **1761** LADY S. LENNOX in *Life & Lett.* (1901) I. 53 Beckford, toad eater to the mountebank, as he has been not unaptly call'd.

2. *fig.* A fawning flatterer, parasite, sycophant; = TOADY *sb.* 2.

1742 H. WALPOLE *Let.* 7 July, Lord Edgcumbe's [place].. is destined to Harry Vane, Pulteney's toad-eater. **1807–8** W. IRVING *Salmag.* (1824) 177 Encouraged by the shouts and acclamations of..toad-eaters. **1859** GREEN *Oxf. Stud.* ii. §1 (O.H.S.) 33 Shabbily-genteel toadeaters, ready at his call. **1876** GEO. ELIOT *Dan. Der.* III. xxv, The toad-eater the least liable to nausea, must be expected to have his susceptibilities.

b. A humble friend or dependant; *spec.* a female companion or attendant. *contemptuous.* Now *rare.*

1744 FIELDING *David Simple* II. vii. I. 212 David begged an Explanation of what she meant by a Toad-Eater... Cynthia replied,..It is a Metaphor taken from a Mountebank's Boy's eating Toads, in order to show his Master's Skill in expelling Poison. It is built on a Supposition..that People who are..in a State of Dependance, are forced to do the most nauseous things that can be thought on, to please and humour their Patrons. **1746** H. WALPOLE *Let. to Mann* 21 Aug., I am retired hither like an old summer dowager; only that I have no toad-eater to take the air with me. **1750** COVENTRY *Pompey Lit.* I. v. (1785) 16/2 Such female companions, or more properly toad-eaters. **1808** ELEANOR SLEATH *Bristol Heiress* I. 139 Her.. Ladyship's confidential woman, or rather *toad-eater*, which is..the most fashionable phrase of the two. **1853** DE QUINCEY *Autobiog. Sk.* Wks. I. 351.

toader ('təʊdə(r)). *rare.* [f. TOAD *v.* + -ER[1].] A sycophant, parasite; = TOADY *sb.* 2.

1842 R. OASTLER *Fleet Papers* II. 415 The only remedy for any man not a toader, who may fall into difficulties.

'toadery. [f. TOAD *sb.* + -ERY.] A place where toads are kept or abound.

1763 ELIZ. CARTER in Pennington *Memoirs* (1808) I. 335 The dykes..with a perpendicular descent on each side to the toaderies and frogeries below. **1854** *Tait's Mag.* XXI. 695 He had what he called a Froggery and Toadery at the bottom of his orchard.

'toadess. *nonce-wd.* A female toad.

1871 SMILES *Charac.* iii. (1876) 80 The toad's highest idea of beauty is his toadess.

toad-fish ('təʊdfɪʃ). A name applied, from their appearance, to several distinct fishes; *esp.*

a. A swell-fish, or puffer, spec. *Tetrodon turgidus*, the common puffer of the Atlantic coast of the United States; also, a fish belonging to any of numerous other species of the family Tetraodontidæ, many of which are poisonous. **b.** The sea-devil, fishing-frog, angler, or wide-gab, *Lophius piscatorius.* **c.** ***American toad-fish***, the oyster-fish (*Sapo* of the Portuguese), *Batrachus tau*, of the Atlantic coast of U.S.A. **d.** ***Brazilian toad-fish***, *Chilomycterus geometricus.* **e.** ***poisonous toad-fish***, *Thalassophryne*, also species of *Tetrodon.* **f.** The mouse-fish, *Antennarius histrio*, or other species of *Antennarius.*

1612 CAPT. SMITH *Map Virginia* 15 The Todefish which will swell till it be like to brust, when it commeth into the aire. *a* **1642** SIR W. MONSON *Naval Tracts* VI. (1704) 534/1 There are many venomous Fishes upon that Coast [Brazil], as namely the Toad-fish, of a small bigness. **1668** CHARLETON *Onomast.* 130 *Rana piscatrix*..the Monk, Toad, Nass, or Devil-Fish, or Fishing-Frog. **1704** PETIVER *Gazophyl.* II. xx, *Piscis Brasilianus cornutus.* The American Toad-Fish. *Ibid.*, The Brasil Toad-Fish..found on the shores of Brasil, and several other Coasts of the West-Indies. **1736** *Gentl. Mag.* VI. 618/1 At Powderham, Devonshire, a Toad-Fish was thrown ashore; it is 4 Foot long, has a Head like a Toad,..and the Mouth opens 12 Inches wide. **1816** TUCKEY *Narr. Exped. R. Zaire* ii. (1818) 61 The only fish taken since we have been in muddy ground were two toad fish (*Diodon*) and several eels. **1845** GOSSE *Ocean* vii. (1849) 342 The Toad-fishes, or Anglers (*Antennarius*), whose pectoral and ventral fins have much of the form and also the functions of the feet of a quadruped. **1860** RICHARDSON in *Jrnl. Linn. Soc.* (1861) V. 213 The Toad-fish of the Cape is a *Diodon.* **1860** JAMESON *ibid.*, A poisonous fish, known at the Cape by the name of the Toad- or Bladder-fish. **1871** G. BENNETT in *N.S.W. Med. Gaz.* I. 176 (*title*) On the 'toad fish'..of New South Wales. **1923** *Med. Jrnl. Austral.* 1 Dec. 572/1 The toad fish belongs to the genus Tetraodon of which a number of species are known to be poisonous. **1974** [see TOADO].

toad-flax ('təʊdflæks). [f. TOAD *sb.* + FLAX, from the flax-like appearance of the foliage.] A popular name of the European plant *Linaria vulgaris*; hence extended as a generic name to other species of *Linaria*, as Ivy-leaved Toad-flax, *L. Cymbalaria*, Purple T., *L. purpurea.* ***bastard toad-flax***, a name for *Thesium linophyllum*, and the American genus *Comandra.*

1578 LYTE *Dodoens* I. liv. 79 Stanworte, wilde flaxe, or Tode flax, hath small, slender, blackish stalkes. **1630** DRAYTON *Muses' Elysium* iii. Wks. (1748) 448/1 By toad-flax which your nose may taste, If you have a mind to cast. **1776** LEE *Bot.* 353/1 Toad Flax, *Antirrhinum.* **1866** *Treas. Bot.*, Toadflax. Bastard, *Thesium linophyllum*; also an American name for *Comandra.* **1868** J. T. BURGESS *Eng. Wild Flowers* 211 The 'butter-and-eggs' of the country folk—the Yellow Toadflax. **1879** GEO. ELIOT *Theo. Such* ii. 50 A crumbling bit of wall where the delicate ivy-leaved toad-flax hangs its light branches. **1893** COUCH *Delect. Duchy* 21 A round stone wall, over which the toad-flax spread in a tangle.

'toadish, *a. rare.* [f. TOAD *sb.* + -ISH[1].] Of the nature of a toad; like a toad; †venomous.

1611 A. STAFFORD *Niobe* II. 76 Your toadish tongue would neuer haue sought to haue enuenom'd Vertue. **1665** SIR T. HERBERT *Trav.* (1677) 384 A speckl'd toadish or poyson fish as the Seamen from experience named it. **1822** BEDDOES *Bride's Trag.* II. iv, Something hath called me thrice, With a low muttering voice of toadish hisses.

toadless ('təʊdlɪs), *a.* [f. TOAD *sb.* + -LESS.] Devoid of toads.

1911 *Chambers's Jrnl.* July 435/2 When the garden was dug..it was toadless. **1922** M. TEMPLE *Shallowdale* iii. 39 No dog can be thoroughly happy in a toadless garden.

'toadlet. [f. TOAD *sb.* + -LET.] = next.

1817 COLERIDGE *Satyrane's Lett.* ii. in *Biog. Lit.*, etc. (1882) 252 Pretty little additionals sprouting out from it like young toadlets on the back of a Surinam toad. **1834** —— *Table-t.* 14 June, So many toadlets, one after another detaching themselves from their parent brute.

toadling ('təʊdlɪŋ). [f. as prec. + -LING[1].] A young or little toad.

c **1440** *Promp. Parv.* 495/1 Todelynge, *bufonulus.* **1779** JOHNSON in Mme. D'Arblay *Diary* Feb., I always knew you for a toadling. **1812–29** COLERIDGE in *Lit. Rem.* (1838) III. 121 A Surinam toad with a swarm of toadlings sprouting out of its back and sides. **1883** *Longm. Mag.* Oct. 643 A young toadling once hibernated within the empty rose of a large watering-pot.

toado ('təʊdəʊ). *Austral.* [f. TOAD(-FISH + -O[2].] A poisonous puffer-fish of the family Tetraodontidæ.

1943 G. P. WHITLEY in *Bull. Council Sci. & Industrial Res.* (Australia) CLIX. 8 Australia alone has more than 30 different species of Toadoes. **1953** *Copeia* I. 32/2 The terms 'tetrodon', fugu, globefish, toad-fish, toado, and puffer poisoning are synonymous. **1965** *Courier-Mail* (Brisbane) 11 Sept. 2/1 Few fish in the sea..pack such deadly poison as the Toadoes. **1974** J. M. THOMSON *Fish of Ocean & Shore* xv. 162 The common toadfish or toado..has a splotchy brown or green coat. *Ibid.*, The silver-cheeked toadfish or giant toado..attains a metre in length.

toad-pole, -poll, obs. forms of TADPOLE.

'toadship. *nonce-wd.* The personality of a toad.

1775 J. BERRIDGE *Wks.* (1864) 387 To hear one toad compliment another, and speak very handsome things of his toadship. **1885** C. F. HOLDER *Marvels Anim. Life* 89 Several lessons of this kind evidently made his toadship put on his thinking cap.

toadstone[1] ('təʊdstəʊn). [f. TOAD *sb.* + STONE.] A name (rendering Gr. and L. *batrachītēs*, or med.L. *bufonītēs*, *crapodinus*, F. *crapaudine* (13th c.): cf. Ger. *krötenstein*), formerly applied to various stones or stone-like objects, likened to a toad in colour or shape, or supposed to be produced by a toad; often credited with alexipharmic or therapeutic virtues, and worn as jewels or amulets, or set in rings. These, though of various origin, were all considered to be forms or species of the same 'stone', the most valued kind of which was fabled to be found in the head of the toad, a belief to which many allusions occur in literature: cf, TOAD *sb.* 1 δ, quot. 1600.

1558 *Gifts to Q. Eliz.* in Nichols *Progr.* II. 539 A iewell containing a Crapon or Toade stone set in golde. **1605** B. JONSON *Volpone* II. v, His saffron iewell, with the toade-stone in 't. **1645** EVELYN *Diary* 6 May, A ring..which seemed set with a dull, darke stone, a little swelling out, like what we call (tho' untruly) a toadstone. **1668** WILKINS *Real Char.* 63 As for that..styled a Toadstone; this is properly a tooth of the Fish called *Lupus marinus*, as hath been made evident to the Royal Society by..Dr. Merit. **1677** PLOT *Oxfordsh.* 128 By my Bufonites or Toad-stone, I intend not that shining polish'd stone,..but a certain reddish liver-colour'd real stone. **1679** *Lond. Gaz.* No. 1435/4 One gold Ring with a large counterfeited Toad stone. **1696** *Phil. Trans.* XIX. 199 These convex osseous Tubercules..are of the same kind with our English *Bufonites* or Toadstones. **1704** *Collect. Voy.* (Churchill) III. 658/1 The Toad-stone is found in the Head of a certain kind of Toads. **1776** PENNANT *Brit. Zool.* III. 15 It was distinguished by the name of the Reptile, and called the Toad-Stone, Bufonites, Crapaudine, Krottenstein; but all its fancied powers vanished on the discovery of its being nothing but the fossil tooth of the sea-wolf. **1812** SCOTT *Let. to Joanna Baillie* 4 Apr. in *Lockhart*, A toadstone—a celebrated amulet... It was sovereign for protecting new-born children and their mothers from the power of the fairies, and has been repeatedly borrowed from my mother, on account of this virtue. **1870** *Murray's Handbk. E. Counties* 291 At the feet [of an image of the Virgin] was a toadstone, indicating her victory over all evil and uncleanness.

attrib. **1855** tr. *Labarte's Arts Mid. Ages* xxvi, Toad-stone ring. **1877** W. JONES *Finger-ring* 156 A toadstone ring (the fossil palatal tooth of a species of Ray) was supposed to protect new-born children and their mothers from the power of the fairies.

toadstone[2] ('təʊdstəʊn). *local.* [Of uncertain origin; thought by some to be so named from the resemblance of its amygdaloidal spots to those on a toad's skin; by others to be a corruption of a Ger. *todtes gestein* 'dead rock', reduced perh. to **todt-stein.* But there appears to be no evidence of this, other than the fact that some Derbyshire mining terms appear to be of German origin.] A name given by the Derbyshire lead-miners to an igneous rock, occurring as irregular sheets of contemporaneous lava, interstratified with, or in connexion with the metalliferous mountain limestone.

1784 DARWIN in *Phil. Trans.* LXXV. 5 The vast beds of toad-stone or lava in many parts of this country. **1796** KIRWAN *Elem. Min.* (ed. 2) I. 229 *Toadstone* is of a dark brownish grey colour, abounding with cavities filled with crystallized spar. **1823** G. CHALMERS *Caledonia* III. II. iii. 52 The rock is covered occasionally by toadstone, called in that country coppercraig. **1859** Page *Handbk. Geol. Terms* 355 Some of these toadstone beds are compact and basaltic, others are earthy, vesicular, and amygdaloidal. **1888** *Derbysh. Archæol. Soc. Jrnl.* X. 2 The white patches of calcite give to a freshly fractured surface of the rock a peculiar appearance,.. considered so like the marks on the body of a toad that the rock is known as Toadstone.

toadstool ('təʊdstuːl), *sb.* Forms: see TOAD and STOOL. [f. TOAD *sb.* + STOOL, a fanciful name; cf. Sc. *paddo' stool*.]

A fungus having a round disk-like top and a slender stalk, a mushroom.

α. **1398** Trevisa *Barth. De P.R.* XVI. xxxi. (Tollem. MS.), It setteþ drye tadstoles a fyre. **1483** *Cath. Angl.* 377/1 A Tade stole, *boletus, fungus.* **1578** Lyte *Dodoens* 261 Them that are sicke with eating of venimous Tadstooles or Mousheroms. **1594** T. B. *La Primaud, Fr. Acad.* II. 97 Soft & like to the substance of a tad-stoole. **1601** Bp. W. Barlow *Serm. Paules Crosse* 50 Like the growth of a Tadstoole..a night's conceit, but vanished in the morning.

β. **1495** *Trevisa's Barth. De P.R.* XVII. cxxiv. (W. de W.), Yf perys ben sodde wyth tode stoles they take awaye fro them all greyf and malyce. **1519** Horman *Vulg.* 101 b, Todestolys, that be gethered from the tree be good to eate. **1530** Palsgr. 281/2 Tode stole, *eschampignon.* **1562** Turner *Herbal* II. Pref., Dark doctores..which soddenly lyke todestolles stert vp Phisiciones. *Ibid.* 29 b, A todstole..in a birche or a walnut tre, where of som make tunder. **1567** Maplet *Gr. Forest* 52 The Mushrom or Toadstoole..hath two sundrie kinds,..for the one may be eaten: the other is not to be eaten. **1579** Spenser *Sheph. Cal.* Dec. 69 The grieslie Todestoole growne there mought I se And loathed Paddocks lording on the same. **1601** Holland *Pliny* (1634) II. 133 The nearer that a Mushrome or Toadstoole commeth to the color of a fig hanging vpon the tree, the lesse presumption there is that it is venomous. **1707** Hearne *Collect.* 29 Nov. (O.H.S.) II. 76 The Dorians..us'd to write upon Toad-stools. **1872** Black *Adv. Phaeton* xxii, Moist odour of toadstools and fern. **1904** G. K. Chesterton *Browning* vi. 145 We are akin not only to the stars and flowers, but to the toadstools and the monstrous tropical birds.

b. Popularly restricted to poisonous or inedible fungi, as distinct from edible 'mushrooms'.

1607 Topsell *Four-f. Beasts* (1658) 204 The rennet is also commendable against Hemlock or Toad-stool. **1805** *Med. Jrnl.* XIV. 573 Toad stools and other species of the fungus kind are frequently eaten for mushrooms. **1859** *All Year Round* No. 19. 437 The delicious mushroom, the poisonous toad-stool.

c. *fig.* (in reference to its rapid growth and short duration: cf *mushroom*).

1823 in Cobbett *Rur. Rides* (1885) I. 286 This little toad-stool is a thing created entirely by the gamble: and the means have, hitherto, come out of the wages of labour. **1901** *Daily News* 2 Mar. 3/4 Some of the houses that were too solidly built to burn were blown up. Away off on a flank you would see a huge toadstool of dust, rocks, and rafters rise solemnly into the air and then subside in a heap of débris.

d. *attrib.* and *Comb.*, as ***toadstool-eater, -eating, -growth***; ***toadstool-like*** adj.

1886 P. S. Robinson *Valley Teet. Trees* 137 Some of these penny-reading toadstool-eaters would even turn a toad off its stool to eat its seat. **1887** W. D. Hay *Elem. Text-Bk. Brit. Fungi* Pref. 6 So far as 'toadstool eating' goes, I believe I have a right to speak with authority, since my own gastronomic experiments have been many, frequent, and varied. **1892** *Antidote* 20 Sept. 303 Wretched sects of toadstool growth, which spring up, fester and die out around us. **1903** *Westm. Gaz.* 30 Jan. 2/1 A writing-table (in the North Room) with numerous toadstool-like projections.. whose ugliness and inconvenience are only too obvious.

'toadstool, *v. rare.* [f. the sb.] *intr.* To grow up like a toadstool; to expand or increase rapidly and objectionably. Cf. MUSHROOM *v.* 4.

1939 R. Campbell *Flowering Rifle* I. 14 As limply fungoid in the idle rich As when it grimly toadstools from a ditch. **1971** M. McCarthy *Birds of America* 60 New little houses had toadstooled; they passed a trailer camp.

'toadstooled, *a. rare.* [f. as prec. + -ED[2].] Overgrown with toadstools.

1910 Kipling *Rewards & Fairies* 282 They hit an old toadstooled stump.

toady ('təʊdɪ), *sb.* Also 7 tody, 9 toadey. [f. TOAD *sb.*, with dim. or familiar suffix -Y, as in *slavey*, etc.; in sense 2 perh. sb. use of TOADY *a.*]

†**1.** A little or young toad. *Obs.*

c **1690** *Satire* in Kirkton *Hist. Ch. Scotl.* VI. (1817) 199 *note*, Beastly bodies, senseless nodies, venemous todies.

2. A servile parasite; a sycophant, an interested flatterer; also, a humble dependant; = TOADEATER 2, 2 b.

1826 Disraeli *Viv. Grey* II. xv, You know what a Toadey is? That agreeable animal which you meet every day in civilised society. **1834** Lytton *Pompeii* I. Notes 172 The umbra or shadow—who accompanied any invited guest—and who was..usually a poor relative, or a humble friend—in modern cant 'a toady'. **1848** Thackeray *Van. Fair* xi, When I come into the country..I leave my toady, Miss Briggs, at home. My brothers are my toadies here. **1883** W. J. Stillman in *Cent. Mag.* Oct. 827/1 A toady to the superior and a bully to the inferior grades.

toady ('təʊdɪ), *a. rare.* [f. TOAD *sb.* + -Y.]

1. Resembling a toad; toad-like, repulsive.

1628 Feltham *Resolves* II. [I.] xii. 30 Vice is of such a toady complexion, that shee cannot chuse but teach the soule to hate. **1719** Gordon *Cordial Low Spirits* I. 159 Gaffer Pitchfork is murder'd too, with thick same toady Clap of Thunder.

2. Infested with toads.

1882 Edna Lyall *Donovan* xxiv, The very froggiest and toadiest path in the garden. **1901** Meredith *Reading of Life* 76 A toady cave beside an ague fen.

toady ('təʊdɪ), *v.* [f. TOADY *sb.*]

1. *trans.* To play the toady to; to flatter, or attend to with servility from interested motives.

1827 Lady Granville *Lett.* (1894) I. 406 If her friends would..leave off toadying her. **1857** Hughes *Tom Brown* I. ii, Lots of us of all sorts toady you enough certainly. **1878** J. C. Collins *Tourneur's Plays* I. Introd. 28 That they might, in thus toadying the memory of a dead son, toady the patronage of a living parricide.

2. *intr.* To play the servile dependant; to pay deference from interested motives. Const. *to.*

1861 Hughes *Tom Brown at Oxf.* vii, Let them toady and cringe to their precious idols. **1873** M. Collins *Miranda* III. 8 She..toadied to her superiors when she really came face to face with them. **1881** C. E. Turner in *Macm. Mag.* Aug. 309/2 We never..toadied for a good place at Moscow, or sneaked into a ministry at Petersburg. **1906** *Times* 29 Aug. 4/2 He was toadying round Williamson like a lackey out of work.

Hence **'toadying** *vbl. sb.* and *ppl. a.*

1863 W. Phillips *Speeches* vi. 135 The toadying servility of the land. **1866** *Cornh. Mag.* Aug. 239 Needy toadying courtiers come to batten on the fatter south. **1897** H. Black *Friendship* iv. 82 They encouraged toadying.

toadyish ('təʊdɪɪʃ), *a.* [f. TOADY *sb.* + -ISH[1].] Characteristic of or resembling a toady; meanly servile.

1909 in Webster. **1955** M. Cooper in H. Van Thal *Fanfare for E. Newman* 50 A particularly toadyish begging letter. **1977** B. Pym *Quartet in Autumn* vi. 57 Only Marya, toadyish with her murmurs of 'such delicious coffee', accepted the offer.

toadyism ('təʊdɪɪz(ə)m). [f. TOADY *sb.* + -ISM.] The action or behaviour of a parasite or sycophant; mean and interested servility.

1840 Marryat *Olla Podr.* (Rtldg.) 303 A person of her consequence could never exist without..toadyism. **1857** Hughes *Tom Brown* I. viii, By dint of his command of money,..and his adroit toadyism, he managed to make himself..rather popular. **1898** Bealby & Hearn *Sven Hedin's Through Asia* I. 247 He would lash..everything that savoured of toadyism and servility.

'toadyship. *rare.* [f. as prec. + -SHIP.] The action or practice of a toady.

1839 *Times* 9 Sept., Their vanity flattered by the toadyship of some 1500 ignoramuses.

toagh, obs. f. TOW *sb.*

toa grass, var. of TWA(A-GRAS(S.

to-airn: see TEW-IRON.

toakin, obs. f. TOKEN.

toal, toale, toall, obs. ff. TOLL.

toal-pin, obs. f. THOLE-PIN.

toam, dial. var. TAUM.

to and fro, *phr.* (*adv., prep., sb., adj., vb.*) [TO *adv.* and *prep.*, FRO *adv.* and *prep.*]

A. *adv.* **1. a.** Successively to and from some place, etc.; hence more vaguely: In opposite or different directions alternately; with alternating movement; from side to side; backwards and forwards; hither and thither; up and down.

1340 Hampole *Pr. Consc.* 471 For a best when it es born, may ga Als tite aftir, and ryn to and fra. *c* **1412** Hoccleve *De Reg. Princ.* 543 Men passen by hym to and fro. *c* **1450** Lovelich *Grail* xlv. 464 Thus the schippe In the se gan to go On day & Oþer, bothe two & Fro as the wynd it Gan to blowe. **1560** Bible (Genev.) *Job* i. 7 The Lord said vnto Satan, Whence commest thou? And Satan answered.., From compassing the earth to and fro. **1660** F. Brooke tr. *Le Blanc's Trav.* 31 Having travelled to and fro, through very many towns and countries of Persia. **1798** Coleridge *Anc. Mar.* VII. xii, His eyes went to and fro. **1807** Crabbe *Parish Reg.* III. 617 Idle children, wandering to and fro. **1833** Ht. Martineau *Berkeley the Banker* I. vii, The messenger, who went to and fro between D—— and Haleham bank. **1855** Stanley *Mem. Canterb.* ii. (1857) 44 The pendulum which has been..swung to and fro, is at last about to settle.

b. after a verbal or other sb. denoting or implying movement. (Cf. D.)

c **1400** *Rom. Rose* 4134 With many a turnyng to and froo. **1582** N. Lichefield tr. *Castanheda's Conq. E. Ind.* xlvi. 102 They spent three daies with messages to and fro. **1688** S. Penton *Guard. Instr.* 59 Letters to and fro are some kind of Guard upon a Youth. **1840** Macaulay *Ess., Ranke* (1851) II. 131 A history of movement to and fro. **1888** Burgon *Lives 12 Gd. Men.* II. xi. 312 His rides to and fro.

†**2.** In places lying in opposite or different directions; here and there. *Obs.*

c **1440** *York Myst.* xx. 255 We haue þe sought both to & froo. **1513** Douglas *Æneis* VII. ix. 96 Bayth to and fro our all the cuntre syne Wemen and moderis..Thair ȝing childryng fast to thair breistis did braice. **1617** Moryson *Itin.* II. 272 The Northerne Borders, where his Lordship (with his retinue) lay to and fro. **1670–1** Narborough *Jrnl.* in *Acc. Sev. Late Voy.* I. (1711) 119 Many Whales spouting to and fro in these Bays. **1697** Dampier *Voy.* I. xv. 425 Many shoals scattered to and fro among them.

†**3.** *fig.* To or on opposite sides alternately (esp. in discussion or the like); for and against a question; pro and con. *Obs.*

[*c* **1374** Chaucer *Troylus* v. 1313 Troilus..rolleth in his herte to and fro How he may best discryven hir his wo.] **1568** Grafton *Chron.* II. 71 In multipliyng of wordes to and fro. **1583** Stubbes *Anat. Abus.* II. (1882) 110, I haue heard great disputation and reasoning pro and contra, to and fro. **1610** Holland *Camden's Brit.* (1637) 803 The victory waved alternately too and fro three or foure times. **1649** Milton *Eikon.* 239 Thus shall they be too and fro, doubtfull and ambiguous in all thir doings. **1690** W. Walker *Idiomat. Anglo-Lat.* 30 When there had been some little Arguing to and fro.

†**4.** So (in *lit.* and *fig.* senses, as above) **to or fro, to nor (ne) fro.** In quot. 1555[2], ***neither to nor fro*** = 'neither here nor there', indifferent, immaterial. *Obs.*

13.. *Cursor M.* 16762 + 123 (Cott.) His sely lyms miȝt he not rest. To put hom to ne fro. **13..** *E.E. Allit. P.* A. 347 When þou no fyrre may, to ne fro, þou most abyde þat he schal deme. *c* **1530** H. Rhodes *Bk. Nurture* 329 Cast not thyne eyes to ne yet fro. **1555** Philpot in Foxe *A. & M.* (1583) 1814/2 You stande dalying..and will neither answere to nor fro. **1555** Latimer *Let. to Morice* ibid. 1741/2 As it is called a fire, so it is called a Worme;..but that is neither to nor fro. **1579** Fulke *Heskins' Parl.* 297 Oecumenius saith little to the purpose, too or fro. **1652** Ashmole *Theat. Chem. Brit.* 204 Till thou hearest no manner of noyse rumbling to nor fro.

B. *prep.* To and from (a place); alternately to and from each of (two places): the latter now commonly expressed by *between* (BETWEEN *prep.* 9). Now *rare.*

1574 *Calr. Laing Charters* (1899) 225 Ane gait to cum and gang to and fra the same. **1598** Hakluyt *Voy.* I. 109 Messengers going and comming to and fro the Court of Baatu. **1860** Reade *8th Commandm.* 123 Counsel, who were continually flashing to and fro London and Croydon. **1885** Jefferies *Open Air* (1890) 126 The stream of lawyers.. rushing to and fro the Temple and the New Law Courts.

C. *sb.* (now with hyphens; but pl. *tos and fros*).

1. Alternating or reciprocating movement; the action of walking or passing to and fro.

1847 Tennyson *Princ.* II. 282 She, Like some wild creature newly-caged, commenced A to-and-fro. **1855** Browning *Lovers' Quarrel* xi, How was earth to know, 'Neath the mute hand's to-and-fro? **1906** *Westm. Gaz.* 14 Sept. 2/3 Watching the to-and-fro of a shuttle.

2. *fig.* Alternation generally; vacillation; †discussion for and against a question (*obs.*).

1553 Bale *Vocacyon* 40 In whose returne there was muche to and fro. For some wolde nedes to London..[and some] into Flaunders. *c* **1627** R. Cary *Mem.* (1905) 96 Many tos and fros there were before it was concluded. **1641** Earl Monm. tr. *Biondi's Civil Warres* II. 90 The incommodities and difficulties.., after many too's and fro's, caused a second peace. **1888** Gladstone in *19th Cent.* July 3 From the great national to-and-fro of the sixteenth century.

D. *adj.* (Usu. with hyphens). Executed, as movement, in opposite directions alternately; alternating, reciprocating; characterized by, or characterizing, such movement; passing to and fro.

1749 J. Cleland *Mem. Woman of Pleasure* I. 212 The sweet urgency of this to-and-fro friction. **1839** De la Beche *Rep. Geol. Cornw.*, etc. xv. 580 This to-and-fro motion. **1856** Dobell *Lyrics in War Time, Even. Dream*, The to and fro storm of the never done hurrahing. **1878** Huxley *Physiogr.* 146 The regular to-and-fro motion of the water in its estuary. **1898** *Allbutt's Syst. Med.* V. 755 As a rule pericardial friction-sound has a double, or to-and-fro rhythm.

E. as *vb. phr.* (only in pres. pple. and vbl. sb. ***toing and froing***, rarely ***to-and-froing***). **a.** *intr.* To pass to and fro, to go hither and thither.

1847 Le Fanu *T. O'Brien* 108 The clatter and bustle, the ..toing and froing of the soldiery. **1872** —— *In a Glass Darkly* I. 272 There were clerks to-ing and fro-ing. **1888** Morris *King's Lesson* (1890) 137 Unto him the King gave the job of toing and froing up and down the hill with the biggest dung-basket. **1904** *Westm. Gaz.* 28 Nov. 2/2 Why all this secrecy about these to-ings and fro-ings?

b. *trans.* To lead to and fro. *rare*[−1].

1852 R. S. Surtees *Sponge's Sp. Tour* xxxii, A cockaded servant was 'to and froing' a couple of hunters—a brown and a chestnut.

Toarcian (təʊ'ɑːsɪən), *a.* (*sb.*) *Geol.* [ad. F. *Toarcien*, f. L. *Toarcium*, F. *Thouars*, in western France.] Applied to a series of strata corresponding in position to the Upper Lias of England, which are extensively developed in Central and Southern France.

[**1859** Page *Handbk. Geol. Terms* 49 Upper Lias, Toarcien of d'Orbigny.] **1885** Geikie *Geol.* 802 In Normandy, the Toarcian stage is only about 20 feet thick. **1912** *Return Brit. Museum* 172 Crinoids from the Oxfordian of Var..from the Toarcian of the Balearic Islands. *Ibid.* 182 Seven Crinoid stem-fragments from the Toarcian rocks of Cabrera, Balearic Is.

toase, toaser, obs. ff. TOZE, TOZER.

toast (təʊst), *sb.*[1] Forms: see TOAST *v.*[1] [f. TOAST *v.*[1] Cf. OF. *tostée* (13th c.) toast = Sp. *tostada* (:—pop.L. **tostāta*).]

1. a. (With *a* and *pl.*) A slice or piece of bread browned at the fire: often put in wine, water, or other beverage. Now *rare* or *Obs.* except in India.

c **1430** *Two Cookery-bks.* (E.E.T.S.) 12 *Oyle Soppys*.. caste þer-to Safroune, powder Pepyr, Sugre, and Salt, an serue forth alle hote as tostes. *c* **1450** *Cov. Myst.* xix. (1841) 183 Ther is no lord lyke on lyve to me wurthe a toost. **1541** R. Copland *Guydon's Quest. Chirurg.* N j, Gyue hym a toste with wyne. **1573** L. Lloyd *Marrow of Hist.* (1653) 94 Alphonsus..took a toast out of his cup, and cast it to the dog. **1598** Shaks. *Merry W.* III. v. 3 Go, fetch me a quart of Sacke, put a tost in 't. **1617** Moryson *Itin.* III. 53 All within the sound of Bow Bell, are in reproch called Cocknies, and eaters of buttered tostes. *c* **1645** Howell *Lett.* (1688) IV. 489 This Drink..must be attended with a brown Tost. **1709** Steele *Tatler* No. 24 ¶8 A Toast in a cold Morning, heightened by Nutmeg, and sweetn'd with Sugar, has for many Ages been given to our Rural Dispensers of Justice, before they enter'd upon Causes. **1735** *Dict. Polygraph.* s.v. *China*, A very dry toast. **1769** Mrs. Raffald *Eng. Housekpr.* (1778) 291 Amulet... You may serve them up hot on buttered toasts. **1838** Dickens *Let.* 1 Feb. (1965) I. 366 We have had for breakfast, toasts, cakes, a yorkshire pie [etc.]. **1978** *Vishveshvaranand Indological Jrnl.* XVI. 218 He had stopped taking cereals after the age of sixty but after 85 he had to re-start on medical advice taking two toasts or some cornflakes.

b. As the type of what is hot or dry, ***as warm*** (*hot*, etc.) ***as toast***.

[*c* **1430**: see above.] **1546** J. Heywood *Prov.* (1867) 44 Loue had apeered in him to hir alway Hotte as a toste. **1694** Motteux *Rabelais* v. *Pantagr. Prognost.* x, Keep your selves as hot as Toasts, d'ye hear? **1842** J. Wilson *Chr. North* I. 83 The small brown Moorland bird, as dry as a toast. **1855** A. S. Stephens *Old Homestead* i. 16 Every thing nice and warm as toast. **1883** Stevenson *Silverado Sq.* 21 It keeps this end of the valley as warm as a toast.

2. a. As a substance (without *a* or *pl.*): Bread so browned by fire, electric heat, etc. (The ordinary current use.) ***French toast***: see French *a.* 3.

1730 Swift *Panegyrickon Dean* Wks. 1755 IV. I. 144 Sweeten your tea, and watch your toast. **1786** Mackenzie *Lounger* No. 89 ¶10 Putting him in mind where the toast stood. **1806** *Med. Jrnl.* XV. 454 The diet..consisted of tea and toast. **1807–26** S. Cooper *First Lines Surg.* (ed. 5) 15 The patient..confining himself to vegetable diet, gruels, slops, tea, acidulated drinks, dry toast, &c. **1886** Ruskin *Præterita* I. iii. 84 Quarrelling with her which should have the brownest bits of toast.

b. Coupled with the liquid in which the toast is immersed, as ***ale and toast, toast and ale, toast and water***; whence ***toast-and-watered*** adj., confined to a diet of toast and water.

[**1586** Day *Eng. Secretary* II. (1625) 47 How I drunk vp my grandams ale and toste.] **1719** D'Urfey *Pills* (1872) II. 324 Many a Night o'er Toast and Ale. **1778** Mme. D'Arblay *Diary* (1842) I. 97 Our biscuits and toast-and-water, which make the Streatham supper. **1800** *Med. Jrnl.* IV. 313, I then directed her to live on toast and water exclusively. **1810** Byron *Let. to Hodgson* 3 Oct., What can a helpless, feverish, toast-and-watered..wretch do? **1888** Mrs. H. Ward *R. Elsmere* xliv, Lunch was on the table—the familiar commons, the familiar toast-and-water.

c. ***on toast***, served up on a slice of toast. Also *fig.* ***had on toast*** (*slang*), done, swindled; ***to have*** (one) ***on toast*** (*colloq.*), to have (a person) at one's mercy or 'where one wants him'; to subject to anxiety; also with other verbs.

1842 Barham *Ingol. Leg.* Ser. II. *St. Medard*, Delicate Woodcocks served up upon toast. **1886** *St. James's Gaz.* 6 Nov. (Farmer), The High Court..took judicial cognizance of a quaint and pleasing modern phrase..'to be had on toast'. **1889** D. C. Murray *Danger. Catspaw* 273 We've got him now on toast. **1895** J. G. Millais *Breath fr. Veldt* (1899) 259 Thinking he had fairly got us on toast, he meant to blackmail us pretty freely. **1896** B. L. Farjeon *Betrayal of John Fordham* III. 288 'It's my night,' I sed. 'Didn't I tell yer? I've got 'im on toast.' **1916** E. F. Benson *David Blaize* xiv. 285 To think that half an hour ago that little squirt thought he had us on toast. **1929** D. H. Lawrence *Pansies* 127 But Tolstoi was a traitor To the Russia that needed him most... He shifted his job on to the peasants And landed them all on toast. **1942** 'R. Crompton' *William Carries On* v. 119 Well, let's have 'em on toast for a bit wonderin' what's happened to him. **1964** J. Creasey *Guilt of Innocence* xvii. 151, I think the time has come to tell the Press we want to interview him... That will get 'em both on toast. **1981** 'J. Ashford' *Loss of Culion* xix. 151 'You've been positively identified by Mr Barnard.'.. 'Then he's having you on toast.' 'He has no reason for lying.'

†**3.** *fig.* (usually *old toast*). One who drinks to excess, a soaker, a boon companion; a brisk old fellow fond of his glass. *slang. Obs.*

1668 R. L'Estrange *Vis. Quev.* 306 How often must I be put to the Blush too, when every Old Toast shall be calling me Old Acquaintance. *c* **1670** Cotton *Voy. Irel.* III. 128 There comes in my Host, A Catholick, good, and a rare drunken Tost. *a* **1688** Villiers (Dk. Buckhm.) *Confer.* (1775) 184. **1694** Motteux *Rabelais* v. xviii, Most of 'em of good Families; among the rest Harry Cottiral, an old Tost. *a* **1700** B. E. *Dict. Cant. Crew, Old-Toast*, a brisk old Fellow. **1709** *Rambling Fuddle-Cups* 14 Bring my Father a Quart; I'll be hang'd if 'twill do the old Toast any hurt.

4. *attrib.* and *Comb.*, as ***toast-burner, -crumb, -fork***; **toast-colour**, a light brown; so ***toast-coloured*** adj.; †**toast-iron**, a toasting-iron; **toast Melba**: see Melba; **toast-stand**, a stand for toast, etc. by the fire: see cat *sb.*[1] 9, quot 1806; **toast-water**, water in which toasted bread has been steeped, used as a drink for invalids, etc. Also toast-rack.

1483 *Cath. Angl.* 390/2 A Toste yren (*A.* Tostyrne), *assatorium.* **1801** Nemnich *Waaren-Lexicon* 687/1 Toast forks, *Röstgabeln, Tohstgabeln.* **1872** G. M. Hopkins *Let.* 22 Mar. (1956) 55 If you say the Mahâbhârata is your toast-crumb ordinary breakfast book I am jaundiced all marigold under the eyes. **1895** *Q. Rev.* Oct. 283 Cobbed by his fagmaster as an incorrigible toast-burner. **1898** *Daily News* 5 May 2/2 A toast-coloured straw toque trimmed with pink ribbon and roses. **1900** *Ibid.* 20 Jan. 6/5 Toast colour is again included among the fashionable tints. **1905** *Daily Chron.* 18 Dec. 4/6 Why should not toast-water become the temperance beverage for [drinking the health of the King]?

toast, *sb.*[2] [A figurative application of toast *sb.*[1], the name of a lady being supposed to flavour a bumper like a spiced toast in the drink.

See the *Tatler*, No. 24, of 2 June, and No. 31, of 18 June, 1709, in both of which *toast* is explained as a new name, upon the origin of which 'the Learned differ very much'. No. 24 says that 'many of the Wits of the last Age will assert' that the term originated in an incident alleged to have occurred at Bath in the reign of Charles II, 1660–1684. No. 31 is silent as to the incident, and gives the account cited below.]

1. A lady who is named as the person to whom a company is requested to drink; often one who is the reigning belle of the season. Now only *Hist.*

1700 Congreve *Way World* III. x, More censorious than a decayed Beauty, or a discarded Toast. **1705** Cibber *Careless Husb.* v. 63 Ay, Madam,..'t has been your Life's whole Pride of late to be the Common Toast of every Publick Table. **1709** Steele *Tatler* No. 24 ¶9 This Whim gave Foundation to the present Honour..done to the Lady we mention in our Liquors, who has ever since been called a *Toast. Ibid.* No. 31 ¶8 Then, said he, Why do you call live People Toasts? I answered, That was a new Name found out by the Wits to make a Lady have the same Effect as Burridge in the Glass when a Man is drinking. *Ibid.* No. 71 ¶8 A Beauty, whose Health is drank from Heddington to Hinksey,..has no more the Title of Lady, but reigns an undisputed Toast. **1711** Swift *Lett.* (1767) III. 185 Lord Rochester, and his fine daughter, lady Jane, just growing a top toast. **1713** Steele *Guard.* No. 85 ¶7 Was that the silly thing so much talked of? How did she ever grow into a toast? **1766** [C. Anstey] *Bath Guide* xi 34 'Tis she that has long been the Toast of the Town. **1779** Mme. D'Arblay *Diary* Oct., The present beauty,..a Mrs. Musters,..the reigning toast of the season. **1822** W. Irving *Braceb. Hall* iv. 35 She will often speak of the toasts of those days as if still reigning. **1888** Burgon *12 Gd. Men* II. 346 He..described how very lovely she was..when she was a toast at Northampton.

2. Any person, male or female, whose health is proposed and drunk to; also any event, institution, or sentiment, in memory or in honour of which a company is requested to drink; also, the call or act of proposing such a health.

1746 Fielding *True Patriot* No. 13 A toast, which you know is another word for drinking the health of one's friend ..or some person of public eminence. **1780** Cowper *Mod. Patriot* 10 When lawless mobs insult the Court, That man shall be my toast, If breaking windows be the sport, Who bravely breaks the most. **1831** Sir. J. Sinclair *Corr.* II. 84 (Tour in 1775) He then gave as a toast, 'Success to Scotland, and its worthy inhabitants'. The sentiment was drank with much enthusiasm. *a* **1860** T. Keightley cited in Worcester, When the toast went out of use, the sentiment took its place, and this I can remember myself. At length *toast* came to signify any person or thing that was to be commemorated: as 'The King', 'The Land we live in', etc. **1866** Geo. Eliot *F. Holt* ii, You'll rally round the throne —and the King, God bless him, and the usual toasts. **1884** *Marshall's Tennis Cuts* 229 Wine (..for doing honour to the toasts), cigars, etc. amounted to another 14*s.*

3. *attrib.* and *Comb.*, as ***toast-drinking, -list, -man***; **toast-master**, one who at a public dinner or the like is appointed to propose or announce the toasts; **toast-master('s) glass**, a drinking-glass having a thick bowl on a tall stem and thus giving the impression of having greater capacity than it really has; **toast-mistress**, a female toast-master.

1908 *Westm. Gaz.* 12 Aug. 8/1 The members..were pledged to abstain from toast-drinking. **1882** Ld. Dalhousie in *Daily News* 5 Jan. 2/3 Those gentlemen whose names are down on the toast-list to respond for the House of Commons. **1814** *Sporting Mag.* XLIV. 45 Oft amid the merry tattle, The toastman's empty cup would rattle. **1749** Fielding *Tom Jones* VII. xii, The lieutenant, who was the toast-master, was not contented with Sophia only. He said he must have her sirname. **1768** Goldsm. *Good-n. Man* III, No man was fitter to be a toast-master to a club. **1818** Scott *Let. to Ld. Montagu* 12 Nov. in *Lockhart*, I was at the cattle-show on the 6th, and executed the delegated task of toast-master. **1916** J. H. Yoxall *Collecting Old Glass* ix. 63 (*heading*) Toastmaster glasses. **1919** M. Percival *Glass Collector* 162 Toast-masters' [*sic*] glasses are found in many varieties. **1969** *Canad. Antiques Collector* Oct. 25/1 The tiny, clear toastmaster glass was usually solid except for a narrow v-shaped depression at the top capable of holding a bare half-ounce of liquor. **1921** *Daily Colonist* (Victoria, B.C.) 7 Apr. 7/5 The toast mistress, Mrs. Sutton, referred in very complimentary terms to the naval lads and their splendid services during the war. **1979** *Arizona Daily Star* 5 Aug. J 6/1 She..has been picked as 'Toastmistress of the Year'.

toast (təʊst), *sb.*[3] Chiefly *U.S.* (and *W. Indies*). [Perh. f. toast *sb.*[2]] **1.** A type of long narrative poem recited extempore by American and Caribbean Blacks.

1962 R. D. Abrahams in A. Dundes *Mother Wit* (1973) 300/1 Many of them [*sc.* insults] take the form of rhymes or puns, signaling the beginning of the bloom of verbal dexterity which comes to fruition later in the long narrative poem called the 'toast'. **1972** T. Kochman *Rappin' & Stylin' Out* 261 The best talkers from this group often become the successful streetcorner, barber shop, and pool hall storytellers who deliver the long, rhymed, witty narrative stories called 'toasts'. **1978** *Maledicta* II. 290 An extraordinary collection of black American folk poetry (*toasts*) collected by the author from lower-class black males (inmates of county jails, streetcorner gangs).

2. In reggae, a performance by a disc-jockey who speaks or shouts while playing a record.

1980 N. Kimberley in J. Collis *Rock Primer* 249 The wedding of John Holt's sentimental singing and Roy's effervescent toast..show [*sic*] us the new musical idiom in full flower. **1983** *Listener* 19 May 22/3 Loud and bass-heavy 'dub' music with a patois talkover 'toast' booms into the bus.

toast (təʊst), *v.*[1] Forms: 5–7 tost, 5–6 toste, tooste, (6 *Sc.* toyst), 6– toast. [ad. OF. *toster* (12th c. in Godef.) to roast or grill:—pop.L. **tostāre*, f. *tost-*, supine stem of L. *torrēre* to parch; cf. Sp., Pg. *tostar*, It. *tostare.*]

1. a. *trans.* To burn as the sun does, to parch; to heat thoroughly. *Obs.* exc. as *transf.* from 2.

1398 Trevisa *Barth. De P.R.* xv. lii. (Bodl. MS), Ethiopia ..þe sonne is nyȝe and rosteþ and tosteþ ham. **1582** N. Lichefield tr. *Castanheda's Conq. E. Ind.* I. ii. 6 b, They haue for armes or weapons certaine staues of an Oke tree bathed or toasted with fire. **1626** Bacon *Sylva* §665 The Earth whereof the grass is soon parched with the Sun and toasted. **1657** R. Ligon *Barbadoes* (1673) 106 Some flowers must be warmed, some toasted, and some almost scalded. **1860–1** Flo. Nightingale *Nursing* 56 A careful woman will air her whole bedding, at least once a week,..by hanging it out in fine weather in the sun and air, or by toasting it before a hot fire.

b. *fig.* To redden (by drinking).

1701 Cibber *Love makes Man* v. iii, Now, Charles, we'll e'en toast our Noses over a chirping Bottle.

c. *intr.* for *refl.* To warm oneself thoroughly.

1614 W. Browne *Sheph. Pipe* i. B iij b, I will sing what I did leere..Of a skilfull aged Sire, As we tosted by the fire. **1861** Holland *Less. Life* i. 10 Toasting in the sunlight is conducive rather to reverie than thought.

2. a. To brown (bread, cheese, etc.) by exposure to the heat of a fire, etc.

c **1420** *Liber Cocorum* (1862) 14 Loke thou tost fyne w[h]ete brede. *c* **1440** *Promp. Parv.* 497/2 Tooste brede, or oþer lyke, *torreo.* **1483** Caxton *G. de la Tour* cxxi. (1906) 170 Men must..toste and Rost them before the fyre. **1562** Turner *Herbal* II. 106 If it [Psillium] be perched or tosted at the fyre. **1582** Stanyhurst *Æneis* I. (Arb.) 23 Theyre corne in quernstoans thye doe grind and toste yt on embers. **1617** Moryson *Itin.* III. 130 Toasting of cheese in Wales and seething of Rice in Turkey will enable a man freely to professe the Art of Cookery. **1672** Grew *Anat. Plants, Idea Philos. Hist.* §42 The Root of Horse-Radish, toasted, tasteth like a Turnep. **1796** Mrs. Glasse *Cookery* xiv. 230 Toast a slice of bread brown on both sides. **1808** *Med. Jrnl.* XIX. 74 The seeds are by some people toasted, so as to be used in the manner of coffee. **1849** Dickens *Dav. Copp.* xxiv, I'll toast you some bacon in a bachelor's Dutch-oven.

b. *transf.* To warm (one's feet or toes) at a fire.

1860 Emerson *Cond. Life, Culture* Wks. (Bohn) II. 373 People..who toast their feet on the register. **1869** Lowell *Under the Willows, Prelude* i, My Elmwood chimneys seem crooning to me..As I sit in my arm-chair, and toast my toes. **1894** Crockett *Raiders* 240, I toasted my feet at the fire, setting them on the hot hearthstone to dry.

c. *intr.* for *pass.* To undergo toasting; to be toasted.

1845–51 [implied in toaster[1] 2 b]. *Mod.* This cheese toasts well.

†**3.** To destroy or disintegrate with fire. *Obs.*

1577 tr. *Bullinger's Decades* (1592) 174 Nabuchodonosor whose purpose was to toast with fire and vtterly destroy the martyrs of God. **1578** Lyte *Dodoens* II. xcvi. 279 The onely fume or smoake of Nigella tosted or burnt, driueth away Serpents.

Hence '**toasted** *ppl. a.*; '**toasting** *vbl. sb.*, also in comb., as ***toasting-jack, -pan***; **toasting-fork**, a fork used for toasting bread, etc.; *fig.* a rapier or sword; **toasting-iron** (*arch.*) = prec.

1584 B. R. tr. *Herodotus* II. 116 For their lyuery fiue pound of *tosted bread, two pounde of Beefe, and a gallon of wyne. **1614** Raleigh *Hist. World* I. (1634) 178 To draw out a Mouse with a piece of tosted Cheese. **1842** Loudon *Suburban Hort.* 606 Crumbs of toasted bread. **1541–2** *Acc. Ld. High Treas. Scot.* VIII. 51 For..ane kais to ane *toysting pan, and for ane kais to four ladillis. **1595** Shaks. *John* IV. iii. 99 Put vp thy sword betime; Or Ile so maule you, and your tosting-Iron. **1807** Southey *Lett. from Eng.* I. xvii. 185 Pocket-toasting-forks have been invented, as if it were possible to want a toasting-fork in the pocket. **1836** Gen. P. Thompson *Exerc.* (1842) IV. 164 An order ensued, that.. the Sir Charles Grandisons of the day should leave their toasting-irons in another room. **1838** Dickens *O. Twist* xiii, The Dodger snatched up the toasting fork, and made a pass at the merry old gentleman's waistcoat. **1861** Hughes *Tom Brown at Oxf.* xli, If I had given him time to get at his other pistol, or his toasting fork, it was all up. **1873** Holland *A. Bonnic.* viii, The girl with the toasting-jack dropped her implement to answer the unwelcome summons.

toast, *v.*[2] Also 7 tost. [f. toast *sb.*[2]]

1. *intr.* To name a person to whose health or in whose honour, or a thing or sentiment to the success of which or in honour of which, the company is requested to drink; to propose or drink a toast. Const. *to.*

a **1700** B. E. *Dict. Cant. Crew, Tost*, to name or begin a new Health. Who Tosts now? Who Christens the Health? **1701** F. Manning *Poems* 73 When ere I Toast..I'll begin No Giant's Health. **1709** Prior *Hans Carvel* 111 The Colonel toasted to the best. **1756** Toldervy *Hist. 2 Orphans* IV. 207 The sage of the cottage..toasted to the prosperity of his liberal benefactors!

2. *trans.* To name when a toast is drunk; to drink in honour of (a person or thing).

1700 Congreve *Way World* IV. v, *Mirabell.* That on no Account you encroach upon the Mens prerogative, and presume to drink Healths, or toast Fellows. *Millamant*... I toast Fellows! odious Men! **1703** Rowe *Fair Penit.* Epil., Ev'ry marry'd Man shall toast his Wife. **1712** Steele *Spect.* No. 462 ¶4 With continual toasting Healths to the Royal Family. **1775** Sheridan *Duenna* I. i, I love dearly to toast her. **1828** Macaulay *Ess., Hallam* (1851) I. 53 The cause for which Hampden bled on the field and Sidney on the scaffold is..toasted by many an honest radical. **1836** *Random Recoll. Ho. Lords* ix. 192 Times without number did he toast 'The Liberty of the Press'. **1852** THACKERAY *Esmond* I. x, They.. toasted past and present heroes and beauties in flagons of college ale.

Hence **'toasting** *vbl. sb.* and *ppl. a.*; **toasting glass**, a glass used for drinking toasts, formerly inscribed with the name of a belle or with verses in her honour.

1703 GARTH (*title*) Verses written for the Toasting-Glasses of the Kit-Cat-Club. *Ibid.* 28 When Jove to Ida did the gods invite, And in immortal toasting pass'd the night. **1821-30** LD. COCKBURN *Mem.* i. (1874) 34 In that toasting and loyal age, the King was never forgotten. **1855** MACAULAY *Hist. Eng.* xx. IV. 455 A few well turned lines inscribed on a set of toasting glasses. **1885** *Manch. Exam.* 14 May 5/1 The institution of dinners with elaborate toasting.

toast (təʊst), *v.*³ [See TOAST *sb.*³] *trans.* and *intr.* In reggae, to accompany (music) by speaking or shouting. Freq. **'toasting** *vbl. sb.*³

1976 *New Musical Express* 17 Apr. 17/5 Another bass riff that cracks foundations, knocks down walls, and brushes aside nine stone weaklings, but this and all the dubwise trickery in Trenchtown can't hide the absolute ordinariness of Woosh's toasting. **1980** N. KIMBERLEY in J. Collis *Rock Primer* 249 Much of the strength of 'Your Ace From Space', 'Version Galore', etc, lies in the original rhythm which Roy toasts. **1980** *Times* 19 May 9/4 A group of young London blacks whose lives centre on their reggae music—the technology of sound systems, the virtuoso techniques of improvisational 'toasting'.

'toastable, *a. rare.* [f. TOAST *v.*¹ + -ABLE.] Capable of being toasted.

1570 LEVINS *Manip.* 3/1 Tostable, *tostilis.*

toastee (təʊ'sti:). [f. TOAST *v.*² + -EE.] One who is toasted, or whose health is being drunk.

1840 *New Monthly Mag.* LVIII. 530 He had been eating the toastee's mutton throughout the whole oration. **1852** R. S. SURTEES *Sponge's Sp. Tour* xliv, The various intonations that mark the feelings of the speaker towards the toastee.

toaster¹ ('təʊstə(r)). [f. TOAST *v.*¹ + -ER¹.]

1. One who toasts anything by the fire.

1582 STANYHURST *Conceits* in *Æneis*, etc. (Arb.) 137 Chymneys fyrye be scorching Of Cyclopan tosters. **1861** J. PYCROFT *Agony Point* (1862) 233 Dear Willie should be made a fag..a toaster of muffins, with no time to eat his own.

2. a. A toasting-fork. Humorously, a rapier or similar weapon. Cf. *cheese-toaster*: CHEESE *sb.*¹ 7. **b.** A kind of cheese, bread, or the like, that toasts (well or otherwise, as expressed).

1695 in *Verney Mem.* (1907) II. 475 A Silver Toster to toast bread on. **1751** SMOLLETT *Per. Pic.* xxiv, His assailant ..desired he would lay aside his toaster [i.e. rapier] and take a bout with him at equal arms. **1838** MAGINN in *Fraser's Mag.* XVII. 8 Sliced into steaks,..Pierced on the toaster's point. **1845** *Jrnl. R. Agric. Soc.* VI. I. 107, I have tasted some of these cheeses, and find them..fair toasters. **1851** MAYHEW *Lond. Labour* I. II. 9/2 'Here's toasters!' bellows one with a Yarmouth bloater stuck on a toasting-fork.

3. An electric appliance for toasting bread; = *electric toaster* s.v. ELECTRIC *a.* 2 b. See also *pop-up toaster* s.v. POP-UP *a.* b.

1913 *Maclean's Mag.* Feb. 163/1 Electric cooking appliances—the shining nickel-plated or aluminum utensils, including coffee percolators, toasters, chafing dishes, each with its long connecting cord and plug for attachment to the electric light socket. **1948** *Clarke County Democrat* (Grove Hill, Alabama) 2 Dec. 4/4 Frigidaire Ranges, Water Heaters, Sunbeam Mixmasters, Toasters..are here. **1962** A. LURIE *Love & Friendship* x. 187 He has to have it quiet so he can fix our toaster for us. **1975** C. FREMLIN *Long Shadow* xi. 82 The second lot of crumpets were out of the toaster.

4. Special Comb.: **toaster-oven**, a small oven suitable for toasting, broiling, and baking.

1961 *Better Homes & Gardens* Sept. 74/2 Toasters come in family-fitting styles... New dual purpose styles: a toaster-oven and a toaster-broiler. **1976** *Woman's Day* (U.S.) Nov. 124 The island's taller side..houses a microwave oven, toaster-oven and..a waffle grill. **1980** *Redbook* Oct. 54/1 In the kitchen, use a small toaster-oven whenever possible rather than the main oven, particularly if the latter is electric.

'toaster². [f. TOAST *v.*² + -ER¹.] One who proposes or joins in a toast; in quot. 1896, = *toast-master* (see TOAST *sb.*² 3).

a **1704** T. BROWN *Amusem. Ser. & Com.* iv. Wks. 1709 III. I. 42 That Toaster there, is it Possible he can give a Judgment of the Beauties of a Play, while he is wholly taken up in Surveying those of the Ladies? **1720** *Humourist* 182 Chief Toaster at a Drinking-Match. **1896** E. P. POWELL in *Chicago Advance* 5 Nov. 614, I would arrange that..the sophomores occupy the special place of entertainers and toasters.

toaster³ ('təʊstə(r)). [f. TOAST *v.*³ + -ER¹.] In reggae, one who accompanies music by speaking or shouting.

1976 in Cassidy & Le Page *Dict. Jamaican Eng.* (1980) 507/2 The toaster has the microphone; he introduces the performers, comments, beats time and talks with the music —keeps things lively. **1977** *Melody Maker* 5 Feb. 16/2 New albums by two of Jamaica's most popular toasters. **1980** *Guardian* 6 Nov. 9/1 Blue..is a garage mechanic by day and a 'toaster' for a reggae group by night.

'toast-rack. [f. TOAST *sb.*¹ + RACK *sb.*² 4.] A contrivance for holding dry toast, keeping each piece on edge and separate. Also *transf.*, a vehicle, esp. a tram, having full-width seats and (usu.) open sides; also *attrib.*

1801 NEMNICH *Waaren-Lexicon* 687/1 Toast rack or waggon, *ein Tohstgestell.* **1807** *Specif. of Roberts' Patent* No. 3083 So constructing a toast rack or tray that it may be extended or contracted at pleasure. **1861** N. A. WOODS *Pr. of Wales in Canada* 104 The chief..wore something like a beadwork toastrack on his head. **1905** *Westm. Gaz.* 30 May 4/2 A vehicle of the 'toast-rack' type familiar on the Continent, consisting simply of a platform with seats going transversely. **1941** BAKER *Dict. Austral. Slang* 77 *Toastrack*, one of the old-style footboard trams still used in Sydney. **1957** *Railway Mag.* June 427/2 There are now 24 bogie motor cars and 25 bogie trailers. Toastrack and saloon types exist in both categories; the former, as befits a holiday line, are in the majority. **1966** P. MATHERS *Trap* 190 A tram now, it would be a toast-rack with ten or so compartments with the only physical intercommunication along the outside footboards, and the concertina doors. **1970** *Railway Mag.* Oct. 587/2 Only horse traction was used, and there were two four-wheel cars, a closed one for winter service, and an open 'toast-rack', used in the summer. **1976** *Country Life* 22 Jan. 191/4 Single-deck 'toast-rack' trams, so named because they closely resembled that table implement on wheels.

† **'toastree.** *Obs. rare.* [First element obscure; second element TREE.] A name used by Markham and Surflet for the main swingletree of a plough, to the end of which are attached the two smaller swingletrees or whipple-trees, to which the two horses or oxen are harnessed.

In the *Eng. Husbandman* Markham appears to use the term as equivalent to swingletree, calling the main swingle-tree 'the first' or 'hindmost toastree'.

1613 MARKHAM *Eng. Husbandman* I. I. v. C iv b, Presenteth the plough-cleuisse, which being ioyned to the plough-beame, extendeth, with a chaine, vnto the first Toastree... The hind-most Toastree..is, a broad piece of Ash-woode..which..hath the Swingletrees fastned vnto it ..Because this Toastree is such a notable Implement both in Plough, Cart, or Waine,..I think it not amisse to shew you the figure thereof. **1616** SURFL. & MARKH. *Country Farme* v. vi. 533 When they draw two and two together.. then there is needfull the plow, cleuise, and teame, the toastree, the swingle-trees, the treates, the harnesse, the collars [etc.].

toasty ('təʊstɪ), *a.* [f. TOAST *sb.*¹ + -Y.] Like toast, esp. in having a slightly burnt flavour. Now usu. *spec.*, warm and comfortable. Hence **'toastiness**, 'toasty' quality (of tea).

1890 BARRÈRE & LELAND *Dict. Slang* II. 357/1 *Toasty* (studios) is said of a picture painted in very warm tints. French painters call this *rôti.* **1892** WALSH *Tea* (Philad.) 100 The infusion is also darker in draw, but very 'toasty', that is 'burnt' in flavor, owing to too high firing. *Ibid.* 72 The finer grades [of Pakeong] yield a rich ripe flavor..but lacking in that 'toastiness' for which the former [kinds of tea] are so much admired. **1961** WEBSTER, *Toasty*, pleasantly or comfortably warmed. **1970** *New Yorker* 19 Sept. 14/1 (Advt.), A smart, double-breasted coat... In soft wool melton with..a toasty wool interlining for cold weather. **1977** *Time* 14 Feb. 32/2 His toasty (75°) office on Kutuzovsky Prospekt. **1978** *Nieman-Marcus Xmas Bk.* 80/2 Natural shearling ear muffs keep ears truly toasty in the bitterest weather.

toating, var. TOTING *Obs.*, prominent.

toatoa ('təʊə,təʊə). *N.Z.* [a. Maori.] = *celery pine* s.v. CELERY 2.

1831 G. BENNETT in *London Med. Gaz.* 12 Nov. 184/1 Toatoa, of the natives of New Zealand, is an unpublished species of Phyllocladus. **1845** E. J. WAKEFIELD *Adv. N.Z.* II. 120 The *toa toa*..is much prized by the natives for walking-sticks. **1910** L. COCKAYNE *N.Z. Plants* iii. 46 Confined to the north are..the toatoa (*Phyllocladus glaucus*) and some other trees. **1966** *Encycl. N.Z.* I. 730/1 In the same forests are rimu, tanekaha..and, in places, toatoa.

tob, variant of TOBE, Arab garment.

tobaccæan, -chian, etc.: see under TOBACCO.

tobacco (tə'bækəʊ, təʊ-). Forms: α. 6-8 **tabaco, tabacco,** (6-7 **tabacca**), 7 **tabaccho.** β. 6-7 **tobaccho,** 6-8 **tobaco, tobacca,** (6 **tobacko, tobackco,** 7 **tobako, tobaccha, tobbacco, towbaco, tobaccow,** 8 *erron.* **tobago**), 6- **tobacco.** γ. 7 **tabac, toback,** 7-9 **tobac.** [Altered from Sp. *tabaco*, according to Oviedo, the name in the Carib of Haiti of the **Y**-shaped tube or pipe through which the Indians inhaled the smoke; but according to Las Casas, 1552, applied to a roll of dried leaves which was kindled at the end and used by the Indians like a rude cigar. Even before Oviedo's date the name had been taken by the Spaniards as that of the herb or its leaf, in which sense it passed from Sp. into the other European langs.: Pg. *tabaco*, It. †*tabaco* (1578), *tabacco* (Florio, 1598), F. *tabac*, whence Du., Ger., Boh. *tabak*, Du. (17th c.) *taback*; Pol. *tabaka*, Russ. *tabak*ᵘ. The original forms *tabaco*, *tabacco*, were retained in Eng. to the 18th c., but gradually driven out by *tobacco*. Da. and Sw., and many Ger. dialects, have also *tobak*, Ger. 18th c. *toback*.

1535 OVIEDO *Hystoria de las Indias* (1851) I. 131 A aquel tal instrumento con que toman el humo, o a las cañuelas que es dicho, llaman los Indios Tabaco: e no a la yerva o sueño que les toma (como pensavan algunos).—IV. 96 En lengua desta isla de Haiti o Española se dice tabaco.

But Dr. A. Ernst of Caracas, in *Amer. Anthropologist* 1889, p. 133, criticizes Oviedo's account, citing from the Guarani Vocabolario of Almeida Nogueira (Rio Janeiro, 1879) *taboca* as the extant Guarani name for such a tube as that described by Oviedo, and used for inhaling through the nostrils not smoke but stimulating powders. He gives some reasons for holding that a Guarani tribe using this may have occupied the northern extremity of Haiti; and suggests that Oviedo, writing 43 years after the event, may have confused the use of this instrument with that of the tubular roll of leaves mentioned by Las Casas as *tabacos*.

The island of *Tobago*, after which the herb has been said by some to be named, according to '*Tobago, a Geogr. Description*' etc. (*c* 1750) p. 74, received the name from its resemblance in shape to the Indian pipe; but other accounts have been given: see quot. 1577 in sense 2.]

1. a. The leaves of the tobacco-plant (see 2) dried and variously prepared, forming a narcotic and sedative substance widely used for smoking, also for chewing, or in the form of SNUFF, and to a slight extent in medicine.

1588 HARRISON *Chronol.* in *England* (1877) I. App. i. p. lv, In these daies [1573] the taking-in of the smoke of the Indian herbe called Tabaco, by an instrument formed like a litle ladell, wherby it passeth from the mouth into the hed & stomach, is gretlie taken-vp & vsed in England. **1589** HAKLUYT *Voy.* 541 *margin*, Tabacco, & the great vertue thereof. **1597** *1st Pt. Return fr. Parnass.* I. i. 397 What, oulde pipe of Tobacco! why, what's to paye? **1598** B. JONSON *Ev. Man in Hum.* I. iv, He dos take this same filthy roguish tabacco, the finest, and cleanliest! *Ibid.* [see DRINK *v.*¹ 5]. **1600** SIR R. CECIL in *Calr. Carew MSS.* III. 485, I haue sent you tobacco, as good as I could procure any. **1601** *Ibid.* IV. 14 Tabacca. **1601** ? MARSTON *Pasquil & Kath.* I. 276 Ha, ha! Her loue is..just like a whiffe of Tabacco, no sooner in at the mouth, but out at the nose. **1608** A. WILLET *Hexapla in Exod.* 442 Taking with them strong beere..tobaccha. **1612** DEKKER *If it be not good* Wks. 1873 III. 293, I thinke the Diuell is sucking Tabaccho, heeres such a Mist. **1616** SYLVESTER (*title*) Tobacco battered; and the Pipes shattered (About their Eares that idlely Idolize so base and barbarous a Weed). **1622** R. HAWKINS *Voy. S. Sea* xvii. 39 With drinking of Tobacco it is said, that the Roebucke was burned in the range of Dartmouth. **1643** BAKER *Chron., Eliz.* 65 Drake brings home with him Ralph Lane, who was the first that brought Tobacco into England. *a* **1668** LASSELS *Voy. Italy* I. (1670) 235 A little Town, famous for perfumed Tobacco in Powder. **1686** *Rec. Co. Merch. Alnwick* in Gross *Gild Merch.* (1890) I. 131 Not to sell any grosser goods.. towbaco or pipes. **1689** W. BULLOCK in *11th Rep. Hist. MSS. Comm.* App. VII. 109, 2 rowles of chawing tobbacco. **1705** BEVERLEY *Virginia* I. iv. (1722) 56 The Duty of two Shillings per Hogshead on all Tobacco's. **1726** MRS. DELANY in *Life & Corr.* (1861) I. 120, I am sure tobacca is there in its full force. **1777** *Account of Island of Tobago* 8 *note*, Columbus gave this island the appellation of Tobago, or Tabago, from a whimsical notion that its form resembled that of a tubical instrument, so called by the Aborigines, with which they inhaled the fumes of tobacco—the Indian name of which plant was kohiba. **1823** BYRON *Island* II. xix, Sublime Tobacco! which from east to west Cheers the tar's labour or the Turkman's rest. **1847** DISRAELI *Tancred* III. ii, The choice tobaccoes of Syria. **1875** H. C. WOOD *Therap.* (1879) 364 Tobacco..has almost passed out of sight as a therapeutic agent.

b. A fashion shade; cf. TABAC *a.* Cf. sense 3 c below.

1923 *Daily Mail* 10 Jan. 1 Becoming Hat in good quality Petersham Ribbon... Colours: Grey, Cherry, Nigger, Tobacco, Peacock. *Ibid.* 5 June 6 In Pale and Mid Fawn,.. Sky, Tobacco, Lemon. **1954** [see ALIZARIN]. **1972** *Country Life* 7 Dec. (Suppl.) 24/2 Haroun Keshan [rug] with rich tobacco field. **1980** G. M. FRASER *Mr American* I. iii. 41 Socks, in the fashionable shades of tobacco, Leander, Wedgwood and crushed strawberry.

2. a. The plant whose leaves are so used: Any one of various species of *Nicotiana* (N.O. *Solanaceæ*), esp. *N. Tabacum*, a native of tropical America, or *N. rustica* (*green* or *wild tobacco*), now widely cultivated.

1577 FRAMPTON tr. *Monardes' Joyfull Newes* II. (*title*) The Seconde Part,..where is treated of the Tabaco, and of the Sassafras [*orig.* Seqvnda Parte... Do se trata del Tabaco, y dela Sassafras]. *Ibid.* 34 This hearbe which commonly is called Tabaco, is an Hearbe of muche antiquitie, and knowen amongest the Indians... The proper name of it amongest the Indians is *Piecielt*, for the name of Tabaco is geuen to it of our Spaniardes, by reason of an Ilande that is named Tabaco. **1588** HARRIOT in Hakluyt *Voy.* (1600) III. 271 There is an herbe [in Virginia] which is..called by the inhabitants Vppowoc: in the West Indies it hath diuers names... The Spanyards..call it Tabacco. **1590** SPENSER *F.Q.* III. v. 32 There, whether yt diuine Tobacco were, Or Panachæa, or Polygony, She fownd. *c* **1595** CAPT. WYATT *R. Dudley's Voy. W. Ind.* (Hakl. Soc.) 48 The high land of Paria, one of the fruitfullest places in the worlde for excellent good tobacco. **1660** *Act 12 Chas. II.* c. 34 §4 The planting of Tobacco in any Phisike Garden. **1767** J. ABERCROMBIE *Ev. Man his own Gard.* (1803) 172 Tender kinds of annual flowers such as..French and African marigolds, chrysanthemum, broad-leaved tobacco [etc.]. **1853** ROYLE *Mat. Med.* (ed. 2) 579 Tobacco..is now extensively cultivated in most parts of the world.

b. With defining words, applied to plants of other genera, as **Congo tobacco** (*Cannabis sativa*), found wild in the Congo (called by the natives *deiamba*), the narcotic flowers of which are used for smoking; **English tobacco**, †henbane, *dial.* colts-foot (also real tobacco grown in England); **Indian tobacco**, (*a*) *Lobelia inflata* of N. America, used medicinally, and having properties similar to those of tobacco; (*b*) Indian hemp, *Cannabis indica* (see HEMP); **mountain tobacco**, *Arnica montana* (see ARNICA); **riverside tobacco**, *Pluchea odorata*

(N.O. *Compositæ*) of the West Indies; **wild tobacco** = *Indian tobacco* (*a*), (*Cent. Dict.*); see also TOBACCO-PLANT.

1597 GERARDE *Herbal* II. lxii. 284 Of yellow Henbane or English Tabaco. **1653** *Sev. Proc. Parlt.* 9–16 Aug. No. 4. 48 (Stanf.) Reports..touching the Planting of English Tobacco in the County of Gloucester. **1678** *Anc. Trades Decayed* 15 (Stanf.) He hath laid the like Impost on our English Tobaccho too. **1846** [see MOUNTAIN 9 d]. **1851** [see INDIAN A. 4 b]. **1851** R. O. CLARKE in *Hooker's Kew Jrnl.* III. 9 (*title*) Short notice of the African Plant Diamba, commonly called Congo Tobacco. **1866** *Treas. Bot.* 1154 Tobacco, Indian, *Lobelia inflata*; also *Cannabis indica*... —, Riverside, *Pluchea odorata*.

3. *attrib.* and *Comb.* **a.** simple attrib., as ***tobacco-ash***, ***bag***, ***barn***, ***-breath***, ***-cask***, ***field***, ***-fume***, ***-garden***, ***-jar***, ***-juice***, ***-merchant***, ***-monger***, ***-powder***, ***-reek*** (Sc.), ***-smoke***, ***-stalk***, ***tin***, ***-whiff***; in *Path.* = caused by immoderate use of tobacco, as ***tobacco amaurosis***, ***angina***, ***disease***, ***vertigo*** (see also *tobacco heart* in d). **b.** objective and obj. gen., as ***tobacco-abusing***, ***-chewing***, †***-fuming***, ***-growing***, ***-smoking***, ***-taking*** sbs. and adjs.; ***tobacco-chewer***, ***-drier***, ***-planter***, ***-seller***, ***-smoker***, ***-taker***, ***-trader***, ***-whiffer***. **c.** similative, instrumental, etc., as ***tobacco-breathed*** (-brεθt), ***-coloured*** adj. ***-stained***, ***-stinking*** adjs.; ***tobacco-like*** adj. and adv. ***tobacco-brown*** sb. and adj. (cf. sense 1 b above); **d.** Special Combs.: †**tobacco bait**, ? a regaling with tobacco, a 'smoke' (cf. BAIT *sb.* 4); **tobacco baron** [BARON 2 b, c], (*a*) *colloq.*, a powerful tobacco merchant or manufacturer; (*b*) *slang*, a prisoner who dominates his companions because he is able to sell tobacco to them (cf. quot. 1950 s.v. BARON 2 c); **tobacco beetle**, a small beetle, *Lasioderma serricorne*, of the family *Ptinidæ*, which infests stores of tobacco and other pungent substances (*Cent. Dict.* 1891); †**tobacco clay** = *tobacco-pipe clay*, pipe-clay; **tobacco-cutter**, (*a*) a person employed in cutting tobacco; (*b*) a machine or knife for this purpose; †**tobacco-docks**, humorous name for a substitute for tobacco made of dock-leaves; **tobacco dove**, a small light brown ground-dove, *Columbina passerina*, native to central America; †**tobacco-fellow**, a companion in tobacco-smoking, a fellow-smoker; **tobacco fly**, a hawk moth of the genus *Protoparce*, either *P. quinquemaculata* or *P. sexta*, the larva of which feeds on tobacco leaves; **tobacco-grater**, a machine for grinding tobacco for smoking; **tobacco heart**, *Path.*, a heart functionally disordered by excessive use of tobacco, characterized by a rapid and irregular pulse; **tobacco house**, † (*a*) a public resort where tobacco was sold and smoked; (*b*) a building in which tobacco is stored; **tobacco housing** (see quot. 1965); **tobacco-knife**, 'a knife for cutting plug-tobacco into pieces convenient for the pocket' (Knight *Dict. Mech.*); **tobacco-leaf**, (*a*) a leaf of the tobacco plant; (*b*) used *attrib.* to designate eighteenth-century Chinese porcelain decorated with a floral pattern including tobacco-leaves; **tobacco-liquor** = *tobacco-water*; **tobacco lord** (now *Sc. Hist.*), a wealthy tobacco merchant of Glasgow; **tobacco-man**, a man who sells tobacco, a tobacconist (now *rare* or *Obs.*); **tobacco mosaic virus**, the virus that causes mosaic disease in tobacco and similar effects in other plants, much used as an experimental subject; **tobacco paper**, (*a*) paper in which tobacco is wrapped, or in which it is rolled for cigarettes; (*b*) paper impregnated with tobacco, used for fumigating; **tobacco-pouch**, a pouch for carrying tobacco for smoking or chewing; **tobacco press**, an apparatus for pressing tobacco into packages, or into a compact shape (Knight *Dict. Mech.*); **Tobacco Road**, the title of a novel (1932) and play by Erskine Caldwell, used allusively with reference to conditions of extreme poverty, esp. in rural districts of the Southern U.S.; **tobacco roll**, a roll of tobacco (see ROLL *sb.*[1] 6 c); **tobacco-roller**, a person employed in making up tobacco in rolls; †**to'bacco-room**, a room for smoking tobacco, a smoking-room; **tobacco-root**, a name for the root of the N. American plant *Lewisia rediviva*, used as food by the Indians; also = VALERIAN 1; **tobacco-shop**, a shop in which tobacco is sold; formerly a public resort for smoking; **tobacco-stick**, 'one of a series of sticks on which tobacco-leaves are hung to dry in curing-houses' (*Cent. Dict.*); **tobacco-stopper**, a contrivance for pressing down the tobacco in the bowl of a pipe while smoking; **tobacco streak**, a streak disease of tobacco (STREAK *sb.*[1] 7); **tobacco-stripper**, a person employed in stripping or tearing off the midribs of the leaves of tobacco; **tobacco tongs**, a light pair of tongs formerly used by smokers to pick up tobacco or a live coal for igniting it; **tobacco-twister**, a person employed in making twist tobacco (see TWIST *sb.*); **tobacco-water**, an infusion of tobacco in boiling water, used in veterinary medicine, and for sprinkling on plants to rid them of noxious insects; **tobacco-wheel**, a machine for making twist tobacco (see quot.); **tobacco worm**, the larva of the tobacco fly. See also TOBACCO-BOX, etc.

1643 [ANGIER] *Lanc. Vall. Achor* 20 Our..*Tobacco-abusing Commanders and Souldiers. **1879** HARLAN *Eyesight* v. 60 *Tobacco amaurosis is a form of partial paralysis of the optic nerve met with in excessive smokers. **1899** *Allbutt's Syst. Med.* VI. 29 *Tobacco angina is more prevalent amongst men. **1857** HUGHES *Tom Brown* II. ix, Soiled with the marks of toddy-glasses and *tobacco-ashes. **1643** R. WILLIAMS *Key into Lang. of America* vi. 44 Generally all the men throughout the countrey have a *Tobacco-bag, with a pipe in it, hanging at their back. **1864** K. CUMMING *Jrnl. Hospital Life* (1866) 120/2, I hinted to some of the ladies about having tobacco bags made. **1961** L. VAN DER POST *Heart of Hunter* vii. 115 He poured the capsules into an empty canvas tobacco bag. **1618** S. WARD *Jethro's Justice* (1627) 18 [They] cannot endure to hold out a forenoon or afternoone sitting without a *Tobacco bayte, or a game at Bowles. **1877** G. W. BAGBY *Old Virginia Gentleman* (1910) 3 Where is your plank to come from, and your logs for new cabins and *tobacco barns? **1971** *Country Life* 22 July 214/2 (*caption*) The tobacco barns are a characteristic feature of the landscape. **1961** *Spectator* 7 July 5/1 The brewers and the '*tobacco barons', who had recently raised their prices. **1964** *Daily Tel.* 15 Jan. 15/1 Powers to limit the activities of prison 'tobacco barons' are provided in modernised prison and Borstal rules. **1896**, **1959** *Tobacco beetle [see *cigarette beetle* s.v. CIGARETTE 2]. **1609** DEKKER *Gull's Horn-bk.* ii. 11 That thicke *tobacco-breath which the rheumaticke night throwes abroad. **1638** DRUMM. OF HAWTH. in *Bk. Scot. Pasquils* (1868) 69 Thesse *tobacco-breathed deuyns. **1908** *Sears, Roebuck Catal.* 437/1 We can furnish plain brocaded velour in solid color of myrtle green, deep red or *tobacco brown. **1940** R. CHANDLER *Farewell, my Lovely* xiii. 99 She was wearing a tobacco-brown suit. **1977** Tobacco-brown [see SMOKING *vbl. sb.* 2 c]. *a* **1832** F. TROLLOPE *Notebk.* in *Dom. Manners Amer.* (1949) 421 Doom to worse than death the spitter and *tobacco chewer. *Ibid.*, Whether a *tobacco-chewing age preceded that of Anacreon, my books do not say. **1878** H. B. BAKER *Our Old Actors* II. 95 Not the transpontine trouser-hitching, tobacco-chewing monster. **1675** EVELYN *Terra* (1729) 7 Vessels made of *Tobacco-Clay. **1972** D. BLOODWORTH *Any Number can Play* xiii. 113 A *tobacco-coloured dress of coarse linen. **1670** *Lond. Gaz.* No. 529/4 A *Tobacco-cutter, lately dwelling in Fryingpan Alley in Petticoat-lane without Bishopsgate-street. **1877** KNIGHT *Dict. Mech.*, *Tobacco-cutter.* 1. A machine for shaving tobacco-leaves into shreds for chewing or smoking. .. 2. A knife for cutting plug-tobacco into smaller pieces. **1899** *Allbutt's Syst. Med.* VI. 845 [We] are most familiar with *tobacco disease among seafaring men. **1599** H. BUTTES *Dyets drie Dinner* Ep. Ded. Aa j b, The Yorkers they will bee content with bald *Tabacodocks. [Cf. **1599** CHAPMAN *Humor. Day's Mirth* E j b, *Ber*... Haue you a pipe of good Tabacco?.. *Boy.* Theres none in the house sir. *Ve.* Drie a docke leafe.] **1891** *Cent. Dict.*, *Tobacco dove. **1954** SMILEY & WHITE *Hurricane Road* xi. 97 Blackbirds, tobacco doves, and a roseate tern fluttered about in bewilderment. **1662** R. MATHEW *Unl. Alch.* §101. 170 Have ready a *Tobacco-drier, & put upon it a spungy thin brown paper. **1616** SYLVESTER *Tobacco Battered* 148 These beastly, base *Tobacco-Fellowes. **1852** J. B. JONES *Adventures Col. Vanderbomb* 46 They rode by a large *tobacco field. **1981** B. HEALEY *Week of Scorpion* vi. 112 They turned aside along a quieter lane between tobacco fields. [**1688** *Phil. Trans. R. Soc.* XVII. 947 There be various Accidents and Distempers, whereunto Tobacco is liable, as the Worm, the Flie,..and the like.] **1807** JANSON *Stranger in Amer.* 339 The devastation produced by the *tobacco-fly which is of the beetle species, black and large enough to be seen committing its depredations. **1904** E. GLASGOW *Deliverance* 126 It was..mid-August—the time of the harvest moon and the dreaded tobacco fly. **1962** METCALF & FLINT *Destructive & Useful Insects* (ed. 4) xiii. 594 The parent 'tobacco flies', or hawk moths,..lay the eggs of the hornworm. **1609** DEKKER *Gull's Horn-bk.* vi. 28 Libertie to be there in his *Tobacco-Fumes. **1634** WITHER *Emblemes* 5 In sleeping drinking and *tobacco-fuming. *a* **1877** KNIGHT *Dict. Mech.* III. 2583/1 **Tobacco-grater*, a machine for grinding tobacco into small pieces suitable for smoking in pipes. **1824** *Deb. Congress U.S.* 13 Apr. (1856) 2324 The effect of this measure on the cotton, rice, and *tobacco-growing States will be pernicious in the extreme. **1884** H. M. JONES *Hints Health Senses* 144 A functionally affected heart,..resulting from Tobacco, and known as the '*Tobacco Heart'. **1611** RICH *Honest. Age* (Percy Soc.) 42 For *Tobacco houses and Brothell houses, (I thanke God for it) I doe not vse to frequent them. **1676** T. GLOVER in *Phil. Trans.* XI. 635 The greatest part..had their Tobacco-houses blown down and their Tobacco spoiled. **1960** *Encounter* Feb. 31/1 Those [G.I.s] who live in the semi-luxury of on-base '*tobacco' housing. **1965** *New Society* 22 Apr. 5/3 'Tobacco housing' constructed with sterling funds from sales of American tobacco in England. **1775** J. LOVELL *Let.* 26 June in *Essex Inst. Hist. Coll.* (1875) XIII. 186, 1 *Tobacco Jar; 1 Large Lead.ⁿ d.° **1857** T. B. GUNN *N.Y. Boarding-Houses* 26 Hair-brush and tobacco-jar jumbled among your shirt-collars. **1967** M. KENYON *Whole Hog* xxv. 252 A tobacco jar bounced..to the floor, where it exploded into fragments. **1833** MARRYAT *P. Simple* xiv, There were spitting-pans placed..that they might not dirty the planks with the *tobacco-juice. **1598** MARSTON *Sco. Villanie* (1599) 166 That neuer turn'd but browne *Tobacco leaues. **1705** tr. *Bosman's Guinea* xvi. 307 The Tobacco-Leaf here grows on a Plant about two Foot high. **1969** *Times* 25 Feb. 12/5 A magnificent tobacco leaf dinner service of 96 pieces. **1976** *Times* 27 July 14/5 A famille rose tobacco leaf part service, painted with a lady punting a lotus leaf of flowers. **1599** H. BUTTES *Dyets drie Dinner* P iv, Whose stomach..Sucks vp *Tobacco like the vpmost ayr. **1864** [see *tobacco-root*]. **1844** STEPHENS *Bk. Farm* III 875 A solution of corrosive sublimate, or a strong decoction of *tobacco-liquor. **1832** J. CLELAND *Enumeration Inhabitants of Glasgow* 258 When any of the most respectable master tradesmen of the city had occasion to speak to a *tobacco lord, he required to walk on the other side of the street till he was fortunate enough to meet his eye. **1975** T. M. DEVINE (*title*) The tobacco lords. **1618** N. FIELD *Amends for Ladies* III. i. in Hazl. *Dodsley* XI. 127 Her fortune, o' my conscience, would be To marry some *tobacco-man. *a* **1680** BUTLER *Rem.* (1759) II. 122 There was a Tobacco-Man, that wrapped Spanish Tobacco in a Paper of Verses. **1599** NASHE *Lenten Stuffe* Ep. Ded., By that time his *Tobacco merchant is made euen with. **1618** J. ROLFE in Capt. Smith *Virginia* IV. 126 There are so many sofisticating *Tobaco-mungers in England. **1914** *Bull U.S. Dept. Agric.* No. 40. 15, 15 healthy tobacco plants..were innoculated with *tobacco mosaic virus. **1947** *Ann. Rev. Microbiol.* I. 87 Ordinary tobacco mosaic virus consists of submicroscopic, rod-shaped particles..composed chiefly of nucleoprotein and possessing a high degree of resistance to heat, desiccation and deleterious chemicals. **1970** PASSMORE & ROBSON *Compan. Med. Stud.* II. xviii. 93/2 Plant viruses, such as tobacco mosaic virus (TMV), are more easily studied than animal viruses. **1877** KNIGHT *Dict. Mech.*, **Tobacco-paper.* **1882** *Garden* 21 Jan. 49/1 Fumigate with Tobacco paper on a calm day. **1775** *Amer. Husbandry* I. 66 Those who have dealings with London..are the *tobacco and rice planters. **1838** *Southern Lit. Messenger* IV. 197 A fine old specimen of the real Virginia tobacco planter, a half domesticated son of France. **1687** A. LOVELL tr. *Thevenot's Trav.* I. 30 They carry two Hankerchiefs at their girdle,.. their *Tobacco-pouch hangs also at it. **1818** SCOTT *Hrt. Midl.* xlv, He knocked the ashes out of his pipe,..returned the tobacco-pouch or spleuchan to its owner. **1672** *Phil. Trans.* VII. 5021 Washing the Sore..and strewing *Tobacco-powder thereon. **1815** SCOTT *Guy M.* xi. Is not the *tobacco-reek disagreeable to your honour? **1937** *Harper's Mag.* Nov. 566/1 Nobody in his senses wants slums, *Tobacco Roads, and undernourished, ragged schoolchildren in a land of potential economic plenty. **1961** Tobacco Road [see OVER-EXPLOIT *v.*]. **1679** M. RUSDEN *Further Discov. Bees* 108 Much like to a *Tobacco-roll standing upright. **1856** OLMSTED *Slave States* 361 All quiet housekeepers were kept in a state of excited alarm during the seasons when the *tobacco-rollers were in town. **1656** in *Westm. Gaz.* 17 Oct. (1902) 2/3 Uppon my returne into the Howse..I mett Major-General Desborough in the *tobacco roome. **1845** J. C. FRÉMONT *Rep. Exploring Exped.* 135, I ate here, for the first time, the *kooyah*, or *tobacco root, (*valeriana edulis*). **1864** *Chamb. Encycl.* VI. 109/2 *Lewisia.. rediviva*... Its roots are gathered in great quantities by the Indians... It is called Tobacco Root because, when cooked, it has a tobacco-like smell. **1919** E. L. STURTEVANT *Notes Edible Plants* 589 Tobacco Root. Valerian. Ohio to Wisconsin and westward. *c* **1645** in *Archæologia* LII. 137 Seriaunt Maior William Underwood a *Tobacco seller in Bucklersbury. **1605** CHAPMAN *All Fooles* I. i, Th'art known in Ordinaries, and *Tabacco-shops. **1974** J. AIKEN *Midnight is Place* v. 145, I have sold some [cigar] ends..to a man in a tobacco-shop. **1597–8** BP. HALL *Sat.* IV. iv. 41 Quaffs a whole tunnel of *tobacco smoke. **1848** tr. *Hoffmeister's Trav. Ceylon*, etc. iv. 174 Like our *tobacco-smokers lounging on their sofas. **1897** *Westm. Gaz.* 12 May 2/1 He would look at their *tobacco-stained tongues. **1704** LUTTRELL *Brief Rel.* (1857) V. 435 The officers of the customes burnt publickly in this citty 12 load of *tobacco stalks lately seized. **1616** SYLVESTER *Tobacco Battered* 763 Awefull Justice will..at one blow cut-off this Over-Drinking, And ever Dropsie, of *Tobacco-stinking. **1664** BUTLER *Hud.* II. III. 454 By his proper Figure, that's like *Tobacco-stopper. *a* **1701** CIBBER *Love makes Man* I. i, As inseparable Companions, as a Beau and a Snuff Box, or a Curate and a Tobacco-stopper. **1840** DICKENS *Barn. Rudge* lxxviii, He used the little finger..as a tobacco-stopper. **1936** *Tobacco streak [see STREAK *sb.*[1] 7]. **1968** *Times* 3 Oct. 13/5 Tobacco streak virus, so called because of the symptoms it produces in tobacco plants, infects a wide variety of plants, including French beans, peas and clover. **1725** *Lond. Gaz.* No. 6380/7 Elizabeth Sims,..*Tobacco stripper. **1599** NASHE *Lenten Stuffe* Wks. (Grosart) V. 240 Hee will needes be a man of warre, or a *Tobacco taker. **1666** W. BOGHURST *Loimographia* (1894) 55 *Tobacco-taking, Diemerbrook greatly commends; but how many thousand Tobacco-takers think you, dyed this year? **1930** J. S. HUXLEY *Bird-Watching & Bird Behaviour* v. Plate VII, A Black-headed gull contentedly brooding a *tobacco-tin which has been substituted for its eggs. **1975** M. BRADBURY *History Man* ix. 153 Ashtrays have been stolen, and replaced by..tobacco tins. **1669** BOYLE *Contn. New Exp.* I. xl. (1682) 139 We fastened a small pair of *Tobacco-Tongs to the inside of the Receivers Brass Cover. **1840** *Picayune* (New Orleans) 13 Sept. 3/1 The same Mac..[is] well known to the Western country *Tobacco Traders. **1808** *Cobbett's Weekly Pol. Reg.* XIII. 134 Thread-spinners and *tobacco-twisters. **1899** *Allbutt's Syst. Med.* VIII. 152 *Tobacco vertigo and the other nervous consequences of the weed. **1808** *Nicholson's Jrnl.* XIX. 298 (*heading*) On the Use of *Tobacco Water, in preserving Fruit Crops, by destroying Insects. **1851** *Birmingham & Midl. Gard. Mag.* Dec. 236 Mix up flour of sulphur,..and tobacco-water,..and dress the trees with the mixture. **1877** KNIGHT *Dict. Mech.*, **Tobacco-wheel*, a machine by which leaves of tobacco are twisted into a cord. **1611** [TARLTON] *Jests* (1628) C iij b, *Tobacco whiffes made them leaue him to pay all. *c* **1614** FLETCHER, etc. *Wit at Sev. Weap.* IV. i, Great *tobacco-whiffers. [**1688** Tobacco worm: see *tobacco fly* above.] **1737** J. BRICKELL *Nat. Hist. N. Carolina* 168 The *Tobacco-worm..has two sharp horns on its Head. **1773** *Hist. Brit. Dom. in N. Amer.* XI. iii. 190 The tobacco-worm is a caterpillar of the size and figure of a silk-worm. **1872** *Rep. Vermont Board Agric.* I. 319 The large night-flying moths..produce the large larvæ, as the potato-worm and the tobacco-worm. **1962** METCALF & FLINT *Destructive & Useful Insects* (ed. 4) xiii. 594 The best known of tobacco insects..are the large green tobacco worms with white bars on the sides and a slender horn at the end of the body.

Hence (chiefly *humorous nonce-wds.*) †**to'bacchian** (ta'backian, toba'ccæan), *a.* addicted to tobacco; *sb.* a person addicted to tobacco; †to'baccical (tabackicall), to'baccoic (-əʊɪk) *adjs.*, pertaining to, addicted to, or caused by tobacco; **to'baccoed** (-əʊd), **to'baccofied** *adjs.*, characterized by the use of tobacco; **to'baccoite** (-əʊaɪt), an advocate of tobacco; **to'baccoless** *a.*, without tobacco, not supplied with tobacco; **to'baccophil(e** [-PHIL], a lover of tobacco; **to'baccose** (-bacch-) *a.*, addicted to, or characterized by addiction to, tobacco; **to'baccoy** (-əʊɪ) *a.*, impregnated with or smelling of tobacco-smoke.

1597 GERARDE *Herbal* II. lxiii. §2. 286 It is not so thought nor receiued of our *Tabackians. **1615** SIR. E. HOBY *Curry-Combe* i. 25 Whom he describeth to be one of the Knights fellow tobaccæan Wrighters. **1637** VENNER *Tobacco* in *Via Recta* 359 Such..are no base Tobacchians: for this manner of taking the fume, they suppose to be generous. **1604** *Will W. Woodhall*, Perceiving his *tabackicall humor. **1893** *Granta* 2 Dec. 113 Luxurious and *tobaccoed ease. **1846** THACKERAY *Cornhill to Cairo* xv, A dreamy, hazy, lazy, *tobaccofied life. **1878** *Cope's Tobacco Plant* Jan. 130/1 Three hundred years..have failed to develop any distinct *Tobaccoic disease. **1898** *Daily News* 9 Sept. 5/1 Eventually the *tobaccoites completely routed their opponents. **1840** R. G. LATHAM *Norway* I. 189 It is better to be without a whip than *tobaccoless. **1889** *Sat. Rev.* 4 May 528/1 Left tobaccoless after dinner! **1882** M. HOWIE in *Knowledge* I. 343 The smaller appetite of the inveterate *tobaccophile. **1845** FORD *Handbk. Spain* I. II. 194/2 Many *tobacchose epicures who smoke their regular dozen. *Ibid.* II. 731 Tobaccose. **1840** J. T. HEWLETT *P. Priggins* xx, Taken..out of the *tobaccoy atmosphere into the open air.

to'bacco-box.

1. A box for holding tobacco, *esp.* a small flat box to be carried in the pocket.

1599 B. JONSON *Cynthia's Rev.* I. i, Pray Iove the perfum'd courtiers keep their casting-bottles..from you, or our more ordinary gallants their tobacco-boxes. **1654** GAYTON *Pleas. Notes* III. v. 100 A Tobacco box with a Burning Glasse. **1859** FAIRHOLT *Tobacco* 229 The old brass tobacco-box was generally oblong, and contained all the smoker required... There is a horn tobacco-box preserved in London.

2. Local name for two N. American fishes, from their flattened shape: (*a*) a species of skate or ray, *Raia erinacea*; (*b*) the common sunfish, *Lepomis gibbosus*, or other species of *Lepomis* (*Cent. Dict.*).

1877 C. HALLOCK *Sportsman's Gazetteer* I. 379 Black Perch, sometimes called 'tobacco-box'; found in ponds. **1903** *Outing* Apr. 134/1 He is content to lure to the surface ..the 'sunny', 'tobacco box', or 'pumpkin seed'. **1913** A. DOUGLAS *Fast Nine* 150 The commonest and smallest skate of the Eastern coast of the United States is the 'Tobacco Box'.

tobaccoed, -ic, -ite, etc.: see after TOBACCO.

tobacco'nalian, *sb.* and *a.* [f. TOBACCO, app. after *bacchanalian*.] **A.** *sb.* A person addicted to tobacco-smoking. **B.** *adj.* Relating to tobacco-smoking.

1835 J. H. INGRAHAM *South-West by Yankee* I. viii. 89 Every other gentleman we met was enveloped in a cloud, not of bacchanalian, but tobacconalian incense. **1855** THACKERAY *Newcomes* xxxv, We get very good cigars..for us cheap tobacconalians. **1889** *Sat. Rev.* 23 Nov. 573/2 A cake of golden-leaf..and other tobacconalian fantasies.

†to'bacconer. *Obs.* [f. as TOBACCON-IST + -ER[1].] = TOBACCONIST (senses 1 and 2). So **toba'cconian** *a.*, of or pertaining to tobacco; **†to'bacconing,** *vbl. sb.* tobacco-smoking; *pres. pple.* smoking tobacco.

1616 SYLVESTER *Tobacco Battered* 643 For Dumpier none then the *Tobacconer. **1701** *Reg. St. Andrew's, Canterb.*, Charles Jecks Tobackoner of Wapping. **1835** *Fraser's Mag.* XI. 39 The rattling of the diligence,..and..the *tobacconian flavour within. **1616** SYLVESTER *Tobacco Battered* 204 It shall suffice to say, *Tobacconing is but a smoakie play. **1647** BP. HALL *Hard Measure* Rem. Wks. (1660) 64 The Cathedrall..filled with Muskatiers,.. drinking and tobacconing as freely as if it had turn'd Alehouse.

tobacconist (tə'bækənɪst). Also 6 tabbacconist, 7 tabaccanist, -onist, tobackonist, -baconist, -bacchonist, -bacconiste. [f. TOBACCO + -IST, with inserted *-n-*, perh. suggested by such words as *Platonist*, with etymological *n*.]

†**1.** A person addicted to the use of tobacco; *esp.* a habitual tobacco-smoker. *Obs.*

1599 B. JONSON *Ev. Man out of Hum.* III. i, It pleases the world (as I am her excellent Tabacconist) to giue me the style of Signior Whiffe. **1615** H. CROOKE *Body of Man* 587 We see that cunning Tobacconistes..can driue the smoake out of their mouthes thorough their eare. **1686** PLOT *Staffordsh.* 302 Who though a great Tobacconist, never spits in the smoking of ten pipes together. *a* **1700** B. E. *Dict. Cant. Crew, Smoker*, a Tobacconist. **1757** MRS. GRIFFITH *Lett. Henry & Frances* (1767) II. 280 As phlegmatic as a Dutch tobacconist.

2. A seller of or dealer in tobacco; also, a manufacturer of tobacco.

1657 W. RAND tr. *Gassendi's Life Peiresc* VI. 195 That [the books] might..escape the danger of the Tobacconist and Grocer. **1700** T. BROWN *Amusem. Ser. & Com.* viii. 112 In the Tobacconist's Shops Men were sneezing and spawling. **1840** DICKENS *Old C. Shop* vii, Mr. Richard Swiveller's apartments were..over a tobacconist's shop.

Hence **tobacco'nistical** *a.*, belonging to or characteristic of a tobacconist. Also **to'bacconize** *v.*, (*a*) *intr.* to smoke tobacco; (*b*) *trans.* to impregnate with tobacco-smoke.

1839 *New Monthly Mag.* LVII. 118 Submitting this *tobacconistical list to the snuff-taking public. **1876** BLACKMORE *Cripps* III. xiii. 204 In picturesque attitudes of *tobacconizing. **1884** *American* VIII. 73 The necessity of enduring a tobacconized atmosphere.

tobaccophil, -e: see after TOBACCO.

to'bacco-pipe.

1. A pipe for smoking tobacco, made of clay, wood, or other material, of various shapes and sizes, consisting of a bowl in which the tobacco is placed and ignited, with a slender tube through which the smoke of it is drawn into the mouth by suction. ***King's (Queen's) tobacco-pipe***: see PIPE *sb.*[1] 10c.

1596 NASHE *Saffron Walden* Wks. (Grosart) III. 199 The pummell of a scotch saddle, or pan of a Tobacco pipe. **1597–8** BP. HALL *Sat.* v. ii, Nor half that smoke..Which one tobacco-pipe drives thro' his nose. **1632** LITHGOW *Trav.* v. 205 The Turkish Tobacco pipes are more than a yard long. **1861** WRIGHT *Ess. Archæol.* I. ii. 27 Tobacco pipes have been found..in very singular approximations with objects of remote antiquity.

2. *U.S.* Local name for a parasitic plant, also called *Indian pipe*: see INDIAN A. 4b.

1845 S. JUDD *Margaret* I. xvi, She found..the curious mushroom-like tobacco-pipe.

3. *attrib.* and *Comb.*, as ***tobacco-pipe bowl, maker***; **tobacco-pipe clay** = PIPE-CLAY; **tobacco-pipe fish** = PIPE-FISH.

1620–1 *Canterb. Marr. Licences* (MS.), John Lyne of Canterbury, tobacco-pipe-maker. **1667** *Lond. Gaz.* No. 156/4 One [vessel]..laden with Tobacco-pipe Clay, and Fullers-Earth. *a* **1672** WILLUGHBY *Ichthyogr.* (1686) Tab. 6 *Petinbuaba* Bras.: Tobacco pipe Fish. **1804** TINGRY *Paint. & Varnish. Guide* 280 A white earthy matter, commonly known under the name of tobacco-pipe clay. **1876** GOODE *Fishes Bermudas* 17 Petimbuabo Brazil (The Tobaccopipe-Fish) is *Fistularia tabaccaria*.

to'bacco-plant. The plant which yields tobacco; = TOBACCO 2.

1761 J. HILL (*title*) Cautions against the immoderate use of Snuff. Founded on the known qualities of the Tobacco Plant. **1796** STEDMAN *Surinam* II. xxv. 224 The tobacco plant grows here with large downy leaves, full of fibres. **1879** *Cassell's Techn. Educ.* VIII. 65/1 The tobacco plant is an annual, growing six feet high.

b. A general name for species of *Nicotiana.*

1884 MILLER *Plant-n.* 137 Tobacco-plant. The genus *Nicotiana*... Latakia, Syrian, or Wild T., *Nicotiana rustica*. .. Persian or Shiraz T., *N. persica*... Tuberose-flowered T., *N. affinis*... Virginian T., *N. Tabacum*.

c. Also applied to other plants.

1884 MILLER *Plant-n.* 137 English Tobacco-plant, an old name for *Hyoscyamus*... Indian T., *Lobelia inflata*... Mountain T., *Arnica montana*.

tobaccose, -coy: see after TOBACCO.

Tobagonian (təbeɪ'gəʊnɪən), *sb.* and *a.* [f. *Tobago* (see below and etym. of TOBACCO) + *-n-* + -IAN.] **A.** *sb.* A native or inhabitant of Tobago, an island in the West Indies, part of the nation of Trinidad and Tobago. **B.** *adj.* Of or pertaining to Tobago.

1955 *Caribbean Q.* IV. II. 158 The Tobagonian says *is go ah goin'* (it's go I'm going). **1957** C. MACINNES *City of Spades* II. xiii. 189 Word will reach the ear of this Tobagonian owner and I lose my good job. **1962** *Times* 31 Aug. (Trinidad Suppl.) p. iv/5 There are more Tobagonians living in Trinidad than in Tobago. **1972** [see *ring-play* s.v. RING *sb.*[1] 19a]. **1974** *Trinidad Guardian* (Port-of-Spain) 16 Oct. 24/9 Trinidadians and Tobagonians have an outstanding record in bodybuilding.

‖**tobe** (təʊb). Also tob, tope. [a. Arab. *thaub* (locally pronounced toːb, soːb) a garment.] A length of cotton cloth (see quot. 1889), worn as an outer garment by natives of Northern and Central Africa, and in some parts used as currency.

1835 *Court Mag.* VI. 34/1 His coat of divers colours, his decorated tobe, the panther skin he bestrode, his uplifted arm and threatening spear were seen throughout the field. **1843** MCWILLIAM *Med. Hist. Niger Exped.* 87 The articles exposed for sale were bags of salt.., tobes of various colours, country cloths [etc.]. **1858** SIMMONDS *Dict. Trade, Tob*, a piece of Dammour cotton cloth, sufficient to make a shirt, which passes as a currency money in Nubia. **1867** BAKER *Nile Tribut.* xiii. 333 The old Abou Do being resolved upon work, had divested himself of his tope or toga before starting. **1872** W. H. D. ADAMS *Land of Nile* IV. i. 278 They [Nubians] have no currency of their own; glass beads, coral, cotton, tobs or shirts, and samoor or cloth, they receive as money. **1889** *Edin. Rev.* Oct. 391 It consists, for men and women alike, of a 'tobe', or straight piece of cotton cloth,.. two breadths wide, and some twelve feet long, draped.. about the body, and fastened on the left shoulder.

to-be (tə'biː). [inf. of BE *v.* as *sb.* and *a.*; cf. BE *v.* B. 24.]

A. as *sb.* That which is to be; the future. Cf. *to-come*, s.v. COME *v.* 33c.

1819 BYRON *Venice* ii, The everlasting *to be* which *hath been*. **1838** LYTTON *Alice* VI. ii, The *To Be* is as the shadow of a far land in a mighty and perturbed sea. **1847** TENNYSON *Princess* VII. 273 These twain..Sit side by side,.. Dispensing harvest, sowing the To-be. **1900** MARIE CORELLI *Master-Christian* xvi, I work and write for the To-Be, not the Has-Been.

B. as *adj. phrase* (often following the *sb.*). That is yet to be or to come; future. Esp. following sbs. of kinship, as ***grandfather-, wife-to-be***; see also *mother-to-be* s.v. MOTHER *sb.*[1] 17a.

c **1600** SHAKS. *Sonn.* lxxxi, Toungues to be, your beeing shall rehearse. *a* **1804** NELSON in Nicolas *Disp.* II. 457 Marry..speedily, or the to be Mrs. Berry will have very little of your company. **1860** MRS. EDKINS *Chinese Scenes* (1863) 102 The four to-be priests I knew before. **1930** A. BENNETT *Imperial Palace* lxix. 581 The excited grandfather-to-be. **1969** L. HELLMAN *Unfinished Woman* xii. 174 The so-called good life for us is the to-be-good life for them. **1973** H. NIELSEN *Severed Key* iii. 33 My wife-to-be is going to be fabulously successful.

†to-'bear, *v. Obs.* [OE. *toberan*, f. TO-[2] + *beran*, BEAR *v.*[1]] *trans.* To carry in different directions; to carry off, take away; also *fig.* to separate (persons) in feeling, etc.; to part, sunder, set at variance. Also *refl.*

971 *Blickl. Hom.* 95 Þeah þe hie ær eorþe bewrigen hæfde, ..oþþe wildeor abiton, oþþe fuᵹlas tobæron. *c* **1000** ÆLFRIC *Hom.* I. 386 He is me ᵹecoren fætels, þæt he tobere minne naman ðeodum. *c* **1250** *Gen. & Ex.* 2146 Ðo was vnder him ðanne putifar, And his wif ðat hem so to-bar. *c* **1320** *Cast. Love* 522 Þe kynges sone al þis con heren, Hou his sustren hem to-beeren.

†to-'beat, *v. Obs.* [OE. *tobéatan*, f. TO-[2] + *béatan*, BEAT *v.*[1] So MHG. *ze-, zerbôzen*.] *trans.* To beat to pieces, to destroy by beating (OE.); to beat severely, belabour, thrash. Often emphasized by *all* (ALL C. 14). Also *absol.* or *intr.*

c **893** K. ÆLFRED *Oros.* IV. xiii. §3, & Scipia het ealle þa burᵹ toweorþan, & ælcne hiewestan tobeatan. *a* **1122** *O.E. Chron.* an. 1009 (Laud MS.) Þa com him swilc wind onᵹean ..and þa scipo ða ealle to beot. *a* **1250** *Owl & Night.* 1610 An euer euch man..me mid stone and lugge þreteþ, An me to-busteþ and to-beteþ. **1390** GOWER *Conf.* I. 283 Mi wofull harte is so tobete. *a* **1425** *Cursor M.* 1846 (Trin.) Þe wawes to bote bifore & bihynde. **1494** FABYAN *Chron.* v. cxxii. 99 He was all to betyn and arrayed in moost vyle maner.

†to-'bell, *v. Obs.* Also 4 te-belle. [f. TO-[2] + BELL *v.*[1]] *intr.* To swell exceedingly; also *fig.* to be puffed up with pride or swollen with anger. Chiefly in *pa. pple.* **to-bollen.**

c **1200** ORMIN 8080, & all himm wærenn fet & þeos To bollenn & to blawenn. *a* **1225** *Ancr. R.* 282 Heorte to-bollen & to-swollen, & ihouen on heih ase hul. **13..** *Sir Beues* (A.) 2832 His flesch gan ranclen & tebelle. **1377** LANGL. *P. Pl.* B. v. 84 His body was to-bolle [*v.rr.* to-bollen, to-bolne] for wratthe þat he bote his lippes.

tober ('təʊbə(r)). *Showmen's slang.* Also tobur. [a. Shelta; see TOBY *sb.*[2]] The site occupied by a circus, fair, or market.

1890 BARRÈRE & LELAND *Dict. Slang* II. 357/2 *Tobur, toba* (showmen, &c.), the ground or field at fairs, hired to put the waggons on for show or circuses, or other *al fresco* entertainments, which does not amount to much, so that a man or manager is considered very hard up if he has not enough to pay the *tobur*. Gypsy *tober*, the road, hence ground. **1933** E. SEAGO *Circus Company* vi. 85 How can I walk about the tober without me trousers, I'd be askin' ye? **1939** J. B. PRIESTLEY *Let the People Sing* x. 256 'It's not a bad tober—but what's 'is bunce?'.. 'It's all fair-ground slang... Micky..said this wasn't a bad market here, but what had Knocker made?' **1957** *Times Lit. Suppl.* 6 Dec. 742/1 She lived with it [*sc.* a circus] for some time as a privileged outsider, parking her caravan on the tober, as the site is called. **1968** [see JOINT *sb.* 14b].

tobermorite (təʊbə'mɔəraɪt). *Min.* [f. *Tobermory*, name of a village on the Isle of Mull, Scotland + -ITE[1].] A hydrated, basic calcium silicate occuring as masses of pale pinkish white translucent orthorhombic crystals.

1880 M. F. HEDDLE in *Mineral. Mag.* IV. 119 Tobermorite. This is a zeolite which I first found filling small druses in the cliffs of the shore immediately to the north of the pier of Tobermory in the Island of Mull. **1962** *Engineering* 3 Aug. 137 All tobermorites, natural or synthetic, are layer crystals having some similarity to vermiculite. **1978** *Mineral. Mag.* XLII. 229/1 Tobermorite minerals vary in some properties, most notably in whether loss of molecular water is accompanied by unidimensional lattice shrinkage... Tobermorites that show this lattice shrinkage have come to be called 'normal' and ones that do not, 'anomalous'.

Tobias night (təʊ'baɪəs naɪt). [tr. G. *Tobiasnacht*, which alludes to Tobit viii. 1–3.] (See quots.) Cf. *Toby-night* s.v. TOBY *sb.*[1] 6.

1960 C. WINICK *Dict. Anthropol.* 539/1 *Tobias nights*, in the Catholic church, postponing the consummation of a marriage for several nights. **1975** *Amer. Speech 1973* XLVIII. 73 One need not go all the way back to Semitic antiquity..nor to the derivative nineteenth-century Swiss and German custom of the 'Tobiasnächte', the 'Tobias nights', in which the next of kin slept between the newlyweds for the first three nights of marriage to protect them at a time when their resistance to evil would be at its lowest ebb.

Tobin bronze. An alloy invented by John A. Tobin of U.S. navy, composed mainly of copper, zinc, tin, with some iron, and lead; one kind is called *delta-metal* (see DELTA 4).

Used for articles of domestic use, parts of machines, parts of ships exposed to the constant action of salt water, etc.

[**1882** (Dec. 14) J. A. TOBIN *U.S. Patent Specif.* No. 309011 The essential elements of my alloy are copper, zinc, and tin.] **1891** *Jrnl. Franklin Inst.* CXXXII. 55 The

Ansonia Brass and Copper Company..are..the sole manufacturers of Tobin bronze. **1893** *Outing* (U.S.) XXII. 147/1 The fin [centre-board of a sailing boat] is of Tobin bronze, one-quarter inch thick, six feet long on upper edge. **1899** *Westm. Gaz.* 12 June 7/2 The quality of the skin material..has been the subject of much thought and experiment, resulting in the use of Tobin bronze, as contrasted with manganese bronze in *Defender* [a racing yacht].

† **to'bine.** *Obs.* [app. an altered form of TABINE, = Du. *tabijn*, ad. It. *tabino* (Florio), by-form of *tabi* (see TABBY), whence also Ger. *tabin*, of which *tobin* is cited by Heyse *Fremdwörterbuch* as an upper German variant.] = TABINE.

1755 *The Card* II. xi. 59 With superior lustre shine in simple lutestring or tobine. **1799** G. SMITH *Laboratory* II. 45 There are likewise lutestring tobines, which commonly are striped with flowers in the warp, and sometimes between the tobine stripes, with brocaded sprigs. **1858** SIMMONDS *Dict. Trade*, *Tobine*, a stout twilled silk.

Tobin's tube. Also **Tobin tube**. A device for admitting fresh air into a room in an upward direction, invented by Martin Tobin of Leeds.

[**1873** M. TOBIN *Patent Specif.* No. 1081 In some cases.. I pass a tube..into the apartment, and form or turn the mouth or inlet, so as to give the air..an upward or fountain-like direction.] **1884** BILLINGS *Ventilation*, etc. 102 Another form of inlet consists in what are often spoken of as Tobin's Tubes.

† **to-'blow**, *v. Obs.* Forms: see BLOW *v.*^{1} [OE. *tobláwan*, f. TO-^{2} + *bláwan*, BLOW *v.*^{1} So OHG. *zaplâen*, MHG. *ze-*, *zerblæjen*.] *trans.* **a.** To distend with wind, inflate, puff up; also *fig.* to puff up with an emotion. **b.** To blow in different directions, scatter by blowing, blow away.

c **1000** ÆLFRIC *Saints' Lives* vii. 139 On ðam [hell fire] ȝe beoþ toblawene. *c* **1000** *Sax. Leechd.* III. 58 ȝif he bið to-blawen se innoð. *c* **1200** [see TO-BELL]. **13..** *Sir Beues* (A.) 2696 For þe venim is on me þrowe, Her I legge al to-blowe. *Ibid.* 6872 Þat he no were anon y-slawe, For-brent, and þat dust to-blowe. *c* **1425** *Seven Sag.* (P.) 1523 Hys body was al to-blaw.

toboggan (tə'bɒgən), *sb.* Also **tabagane, ta-, tobognay, tarbog(g)in, treboggin, tobogin, -en, toboggen, tobaugan, tobogan, tabougin, tabogan.** [Adaptation of a Canadian Indian name of a sleigh or sledge; given in French spelling *tabaganne* by Le Clercq *Nouvelle Relation de la Gaspesie*, 1691, p. 70 (J. Platt in *N. & Q.* 9th Ser. XII. 467). The nearest Indian forms cited are Micmac (Lower Canada, New Brunsw., Nova Scotia) *tobâkun* (to'baːkən) (Rand *Micmac Dict.* 1888), and Abnaki (Quebec and Maine) *udãbãgan* (Trumbull). Other allied Algonquian langs. have, Montaignais *utapan*, Cree *otâbânâsk* (Lacombe), Odjibwa *odaban-ak*: cf. PUNG *sb.*^{2}]

1. Originally, a light sledge consisting of a thin strip of wood turned up in front, used by the Canadian Indians for transport over snow; now, a similar vehicle, sometimes with low runners, used in the sport of coasting (esp. down prepared slopes of snow or ice).

1829 G. HEAD *Forest Scenes N. Amer.* 64 After leaving Fredericton there was no town nor village at which the required articles could be procured: namely, a couple of tobogins, a tobogin bag, a canteen..two pairs of snow shoes. **1846** G. WARBURTON *Hochelaga* I. 122 One of the great amusements..is, to climb up to the top of this cone, and slide down again on a tarboggin. **1850** S. D. HUYGHUE in *Bentley's Misc.* XXVII. 152 Snow-shoes, mocassins, and tobaugans, for the use of the men. **1861** J. LEECH *Pict. Life & Char.* 78 (Punch Office publ.) Militaire recalls his Canadian experiences, builds a treboggin. **1863** H. Y. HIND *Labrador* I. 280 The tabognay is a little sledge upon which people in winter amuse themselves in descending hills covered with snow. **1865** P. B. ST. JOHN *Snow Ship* xv. 106 These tarbogins, or tabougins, as they are indifferently called, are small sleighs drawn by hand over the snow. **1874** SYMMONDS *Sk. Italy & Greece* (1898) I. i. 26 The little hand-sledge..which the English have christened by the Canadian term 'toboggan'. **1880** *Daily Tel.* 18 Feb., The 'toboggin' is a wooden car..which is curled up at the lower extremity, or prow, so as to constitute a seat holding a couple of sitters. **1885** *New Bk. Sports* 239 The steersman..gives the tobogan a start, and away they go down the hill. **1891** *Month* LXXIII. 24 Travelling with dogs and toboggans during winter.

2. a. [f. next.] The practice or sport of tobogganing.

1879 *Birmingham Weekly Post* 8 Feb. 1/4 We have heard of a new sport called toboggen, brought from Canada and adopted here when the ground is hilly enough by country house parties. **1896** R. S. S. BADEN-POWELL *Matabele Campaign* i, Madeira... Scramble up on horses to the convent, up the long, steep, cobbled roads, and the grand toboggan down again in sliding cars.

b. *U.S. slang.* A rapid decline, a progression towards disaster. Usu. in phr. ***on the toboggan.***

1910 E. A. WALCOTT *Open Door* xii. 153 Do you remember the time I got Conny Mulnix off, when the police had him on the toboggan for the Kinsley affair? **1947** *Christian Cent.* 20 Aug. 999/1 The United States is sliding down the toboggan with 75 per cent of the south a negroid population. **1950** J. DEMPSEY *Championship Fighting* 197 A veteran of thirty or thirty-one who is on the 'toboggan'. **1978** J. A. MICHENER *Chesapeake* 853 My daughter Clara's a little younger than you. For three years she's been on one hell of a toboggan.

3. *U.S.* A long woollen cap. Cf. *toboggan-cap*.

1929 *Amer. Speech* V. 152 *Toboggan*, a woolen cap. 'Take off your toboggan.' **1948** *Pacific Spectator* Winter 83 He had on faded overalls with new blue patches on the knees, and a sweater under the overalls, and a knitted blue toboggan on his head, against the cold. **1975** *Raleigh* (N. Carolina) *News & Observer* 6 Jan. 24/4 He [*sc.* a burglar] was wearing a red toboggan and tight pants, police said.

4. *attrib.* and *Comb.*, as ***toboggan-bag***, ***-cap***, ***-race***, ***-sleigh***, etc.; **toboggan-slide**, a steep incline for tobogganing, also called **toboggan-chute**, **-run**, or **-shoot**; also applied to an inclined series of rollers down which toboggans run.

1829 G. HEAD *Forest Scenes N. Amer.* 64 The tobogin bag [for luggage] when full is..laced tightly on the machine by means of a cord. **1881** *Standard* 22 Jan. 5/1 The Canadian ..considers the snowy season the period of enjoyment. It is the sleigh-driving, the 'coasting', and the 'taboggan season'. **1884** *Brandon* (Manitoba) *Blade* 21 Feb. 9/2 The several Toboggan Slides were illuminated every evening. **1887** O. W. HOLMES *100 Days in Europe* 150 Like what..would be a pretty steep toboggan slide. **1890** *Silverton* (Colorado) *Miner* 1 Mar. 3/2 During the storm, the big tree on Anvil, which was generally known as the starting point for snow shoers and the toboggan club, was blown down. **1902** *Sears, Roebuck Catal.* 1159/3 Toboggan Caps or Toques. **1902** A. C. LAUT *Story of Trapper* xiv. 196 Wrapping her husband in robes on the long toboggan sleigh, the squaw placed her younger child beside him and with the other began tramping through the forest drawing the sleigh behind. **1903** *Daily Chron.* 4 Feb. 6/1 He gets ready for the toboggan club's train, which leaves Davos for the village of Wolfgang every morning. **1904** *Times* 25 Aug. 7/5 The Royal party returned at noon in toboggan basket sleighs. **1907** C. HILL-TOUT *Brit. N. Amer.*, *Far West* v. 93 A toboggan-shaped basket with an opening near its curved end. **1913** W. P. EATON *Barn Doors & Byways* 223 One road runs along the ridge, the other plunges over it and crosses the intervale like the smooth, straight drop of a great toboggan chute. **1928** *Chicago Tribune* 11 June 10/5 Women and children in winter wore toboggan caps which wrapped two or three times around the neck and hung about a yard down the back. **1936** J. H. STREET *Look Away!* xiii. 91 Tiller wore a faded green coat, woolen stockings, and a toboggan cap. **1964** *Globe & Mail* (Toronto) 15 Dec. 32/3 Winter fun-seekers will take to ..two new toboggan chutes.

to'boggan, *v.* [f. prec. sb.] *intr.* To ride on a toboggan or sleigh; *esp.* to 'coast' or slide down a snowy (or other) slope on a toboggan. Hence **to'bogganing** *vbl. sb.*

1846 E. WARBURTON *Hochelaga* I. v. 68 They tarbogginned, slid, and trudged about merrily in the deep dry snow. **1849** J. E. ALEXANDER *L'Acadie* I. 186 An amusement of which Canadian boys, and sometimes ladies too, are passionately fond..is called 'toboggoning'. **1856** MISS BIRD *Englishwom. in Amer.* 264 With balls, and moose-hunting, and sleigh-driving, and 'tarboggining'. **1863** H. Y. HIND *Labrador* I. xvii. 280, I didn't want to break the canoe, so I sat down and slid as if I was tabognaying. **1874** SYMONDS *Sk. Italy & Greece* (1898) I. i. 27 On a run selected for convenience..tobogganing is a very Bohemian amusement. **1887** MARCHIONESS DUFFERIN *Viceregal Life India* 15 Sept., The children got three tin baths..and began to toboggan down the grassy slopes in them.

tobogganer (tə'bɒgənə(r)). [f. prec. + -ER^{1}.] One who toboggans.

1878 *Canad. Gentleman's Jrnl.* 8 Mar. 1/5 In fact, there has been so little snow this winter that the tobogganers have not had a good time. **1884** J. A. SYMONDS in *Pall Mall G.* 22 Feb. 1/2 The tobogginner sits rather to the back of his sledge; and when he is once in motion has only to steer. **1907** *Times* 19 Feb. 5/5 Expert tobogganers approach the junction at a speed of nearly 40 miles an hour.

So (in same sense) **tobogga'neer**, **to'bog-ganist**.

1880 *Daily Tel.* 18 Feb., Upon the toboggin..a cushion is placed, upon which the tobogginist either lies flat upon his stomach, or assumes a sitting posture, with stiffened knee-joints, the feet being firmly pressed against the roll of the curved prow. **1887** *Cornh. Mag.* Mar. 273 The costume of the tobogganeer differs in no respect from that of the snowshoer. **1910** *Times* 28 Jan. 10/5 All three tobogganists were hurled violently into the road.

to-bollen, to-bone: see TO-BELL, TO-BUNE.

to-bote, pa. t. of TO-BEAT.

† **to-'braid**, *v. Obs.* [OE. *tobreȝdan*, f. TO-^{2} + *breȝdan*, BRAID *v.*^{1}] *trans.* To wrench apart, pull to pieces, rend; also, to tear or snatch away.

c **893** K. ÆLFRED *Oros.* IV. ii, Þrie wulfas..brohton anes deades monnes lichoman binnan þa burȝ, & hiene þær siþþan styccemælum tobrudon. *c* **975** *Rushw. Gosp.* Matt. xii. 29 Þonne [he] hus his to-breȝdeþ. *a* **1250** *Owl & Night.* 1008 Suych wolues hit hadde tobroude [*v.r.* tobrode]. **1382** WYCLIF *Mark* ix. 25 He criynge, and moche to-breidynge him, wente out fro him. *c* **1400** *St. Alexius* 396 (Laud MS.) She..of hire bedd þe cloþes doun cast And siþen hem al to breyde.

Tobralco (təʊ'brælkəʊ). [f. the name of *To*otal *Br*oadhurst *L*ee *Co*mpany, Limited, the manufacturers.] The proprietary name of a type of cotton fabric.

1910 *Westm. Gaz.* 25 Jan. 9/3 (Advt.), 'Tobralco', a new material, made in White, Ecru, and Black. **1917** *Trade Marks Jrnl.* 26 Sept. 942 *Tobralco*... Textile fabrics (not included in other Classes) made from substances covered by Class 50, but not including Incandescent Gas Mantles and not including any goods of a like kind... Tootal Broadhurst Lee Company, Limited, 56, Oxford Street, Manchester, manufacturers and merchants. **1932** D. C. MINTER *Modern Needlecraft* 250 *Kimono Pinafore*... Gingham, zephyr, tobralco. **1961** D. STUART *Driven* xx. 200 The agent was a middle-aged man, sharp and alert, clean-shaven, in gaberdines and Tobralco shirt.

tobramycin (tɒbrə'maɪsɪn). *Pharm.* [f. *to-* (of unkn. origin) + L. *tene)brā(rius* belonging to darkness (see def.), f. *tenebræ* darkness: see -MYCIN.] An antibiotic related to streptomycin that is produced by the fungus *Streptomyces tenebrarius* and is active mainly against Gram-negative bacteria, being used esp. to treat *Pseudomonas* infections.

1971 *Appl. Microbiol.* XXII. 1147/2 Factor 6 of the nebramycin complex was originally given the generic name of ebbramycin in 1970. Subsequently, its official generic designation was changed to tobramycin. **1977** *Lancet* 19 Mar. 655/2 She had a *Pseudomonas æruginosa* skin infection which responded rapidly to tobramycin and carbenicillin. **1980** [see TICARCILLIN].

to-bread ('tubrɛd). *Sc.* [f. TO-^{1} + BREAD.] Additional bread; = IN-BREAD *sb.* Also *fig.*

1854 *N. & Q.* 1st Ser. X. 531/2 The Scotch baxter..may at times..give a farthing biscuit—as what is called 'too (or additional) bread'—on the purchase of a shilling's worth. **1868** SALMON *Gowodean* III. vii. 104 You were yoursel' the 'to-bread' to the gift.

† **to-'break**, *v. Obs.* Forms: see BREAK *v.* [OE. *tobrecan*, f. TO-^{2} + *brecan* to BREAK. So OHG. *zaprehhan*, *zibrechan*, Ger. *zerbrechen*.]

1. *trans.* To break to pieces; to shatter, rupture; to break down, destroy, demolish; cf. senses of BREAK *v.*

c **888** K. ÆLFRED *Boeth.* xxxv. §4 Woldon þa [the giants] tobrecan þone heofon under him. *c* **1000** ÆLFRIC *Hom.* I. 180 Tobrec ðinne hlaf. *c* **1000** *Sax. Leechd.* II. 22 ȝenim, wiþ tobrocenum heafde, betonican. **1056–66** *Inscr. Kirkdale Ch., Yorks.*, Hit wes al tobrocan & tofalan. *c* **1175** *Lamb. Hom.* 131 He to-þruste þa stelene gate, & to brec þa irene barren of helle. *c* **1275** *Passion our Lord* 490 in *O.E. Misc.* 51 We biddeþ þat heore þyes beon to-broken a to. **1387** TREVISA *Higden* (Rolls) VII. 257 His hors nekke was to brooke. *c* **1440** *Gesta Rom.* lxxxviii. 410 (Add. MS.) Here is my sone ..with his hede all to-broke. **1535** COVERDALE *Prov.* vi. 15 Sodenly shal he be all tobroken, and not be healed. **1611** BIBLE *Judg.* ix. 53 A..woman cast a piece of a milstone.. and all to brake his scull. **1623** LISLE *Ælfric on O. & N. Test.* Pref. 18 An old Colosse, All soiled, all to broke. *a* **1688** BUNYAN *Acceptable Sacr.* Wks. (ed. Offor) I. 698 This was it, that all to-brake his heart.

b. To rend, to tear (clothes or the like).

c **1200** *Trin. Coll. Hom.* 163 Þe chirche cloðes ben to-brokene and ealde. *c* **1275** *Passion our Lord* 315 in *O.E. Misc.* 46 Kayphas his weden he to-brek. **1382** WYCLIF *Matt.* vii. 6 Lest houndis turned to gidre al to-breke ȝou.

c. To break (a commandment, promise, etc.).

a **1067** *Charter of Eadweard* in Kemble *Cod. Dipl.* IV. 213 Ne ðat any man ðas mundbirdnesse tobreke. *a* **1175** *Cott. Hom.* 221 Gif þu þis litle bebod to-brecst. **1297** R. GLOUC. (Rolls) 9287 Asayli þen false king..þat þe grete oþ þat he suor so villiche [h]aþ to broke. **13..** *Guy Warw.* (A.) 572 Þine hest ichaue to-broke. **1393** LANGL. *P. Pl.* C. I. 69 Asoilie hem alle..of vowes to-broke.

2. *intr.* To break into pieces; to burst asunder; to be ruptured, shattered, or fractured.

c **1205** LAY. 1467 His hæfd-bon to-brec. *a* **1225** *Ancr. R.* 164 Vor gles ne to-brekeð nout bute sum þinc hit arine. *c* **1386** CHAUCER *Can. Yeom. Prol. & T.* 354 Ofte it happeth so The pot tobreketh, and farwel al is go. **14..** *Sir Beues* (M.) 1613 Me thinkyth, my hert wyll tobreke. *c* **1470** HENRY *Wallace* IV. 452 Wallace straik ane, with his gud sper of steill, ..the shafft to brak ilk deyll. **1510–20** *Wedn. Faste* (W. de W.) xxv, He tumbled ouer a clyffe, his body all to brake.

3. *intr.* To break away from restraint. *rare*$^{-1}$.

c **1475** *Partenay* 5731 But non retourned, ne myght thens to-breke.

† **to-'brede**, *v. Obs.* [OE. *tobrǽdan*, f. TO-^{2} + *brǽdan*, BREDE *v.*^{2} So OHG., MHG. *zebreiten*, Ger. *zer-*.] **a.** *trans.* To spread abroad, extend, make broad. **b.** *intr.* To spread, extend itself; to be diffused.

c **888** K. ÆLFRED *Boeth.* vii. §2 ȝif þu þines scipes seȝl onȝean þone wind tobrædest. *c* **1000** *Ags. Gosp.* Matt. xxiii. 5 Hiȝ to-brædaþ hyra heals-bec. *a* **1023** WULFSTAN *Hom.* x. (Napier) 68 Of ðyson eahta deofles cræftan ealle unþeawas up aspringað and syððan tobrædað ealles to wide. *a* **1300** *E.E. Psalter* iv. 2 Ife þat drouyng in I ware, Þou tobreddest to me þare.

† **to-'brenn**, *v. Obs.* Forms: see BURN *v.*^{1} [ME., f. TO-^{2} + *brennen*, *beornen* to BURN. So late MHG. *zerbrinnen* intr.] **a.** *trans.* To burn up; to consume or destroy by burning. **b.** *intr.* To burn, to be 'burning hot': = BURN *v.*^{1} 3.

a **1300** *E.E. Psalter* ii. 13 When in schorte his wreth tobrent has he; þat in him traisted alle seli be. **13..** *Cursor M.* 22921 (Fairf.) If his bodi ware alle tobrint. **1382** WYCLIF *Ps.* xlv. 10 Armys and sheeldis he shal to-brenne with fyr. —— *Jer.* xi. 16 To-brend ben alle his busshy places. *c* **1440** *Pallad. on Husb.* IV. 21 Ffor [= against] sonne and wynde hem make a tegument, Lest thai in this be shake, in that tobrent. *a* **1500** *Flower & Leaf* 358 The sonne so fervently Wex hoot, that..the ladies eek to-brent, That they [etc.].

† **to-'britten**, *v. Obs.* [ME. *tobritne-n*, f. TO-^{2} + *britnen*:—OE. *brytnian*, BRITTEN *v.*] *trans.* To cut in pieces.

c **1200** ORMIN 9468 Forrþi wass þeȝȝre kinedom Todæledd & tobrittnedd. *c* **1440** *Partonope* 596 Hys swerde..oute draweth he And alle to bryttenyth this wylde best.

a **1400–50** *Alexander* 3905 Oure kniȝtis.. Alto-bretind þaim on bent & broȝt þaim on fliȝt.

to-broken: see TO-BREAK.

† **to-'bruise**, *v.* *Obs.* Forms: see BRUISE *v.* [OE. *to-brýsan*, f. TO-[2] + *brýsan* to BRUISE.] *trans.* To crush to pieces, to smash; to bruise severely.

c **1000** *Ags. Gosp.* Matt. xxi. 44 Seþe fylþ uppan þysne stan he byð tobrysed [*c* **1160** to-brised]; & he to-brysð þone ðe he onuppan fylð. *c* **1200** ORMIN 12032 He munnde þær Tobrisenn all himm sellfenn. **1297** R. GLOUC. (Rolls) 6059 Hii.. henede him wiþ stones.. & tobrusede is smale bones. **1382** WYCLIF *Ecclus.* xxviii. 21 The wounde.. of a tunge shal to-broosen boenes. *a* **1400–50** *Alexander* 1274 All bebled & to-brissid [*Dubl.* to-brysed]. *c* **1450** *Merlin* x. 157 He.. hym threwe to the erthe so rudely, that he hym all to brosed. **1516** *Life St. Birgette* in *Myrr. our Ladye* p. lviii, There theyr Shyppe was all to Broysyd. **1609** HOLLAND *Amm. Marcell.* XXXI. x. 418 All to brused and broken.

† **to-'bryt, -'brit**, *v.* *Obs. rare.* [OE. *to-brýtan*, f. TO-[2] + *brýtan* to break: cf. BRIT *v.*] *trans.* To break in pieces.

c **1000** ÆLFRIC *Hom.* I. 568 Forðan ðe hi næron godas, ac .. treowene and stænene, and he hi forði tobrytte. *c* **1205** LAY. 1602 Corineus heom to-brutte [*c* **1275** to-brut] ban & heora ribbes.

† **to-'bune**, *v.* *Obs. rare.* Also 4 to-bone. [ME., f. TO-[2] + **bun-en* (perh. related to ME. *bunsen* BOUNCE *v.*).] *trans.* To beat severely, thrash, thump; to pelt.

a **1250** *Owl & Night.* 1166 (Cott. MS.) Heruore hit is þat me þe shuneþ An þe totoruep & tobuneþ Mid staue & stoone & turf & clute. *c* **1315** SHOREHAM ii. 85 For so to-bete and so to-boned, Hyȝt was wel reweleche and drery.

† **to-'burst**, *v.* *Obs.* exc. *dial.* Forms: see BURST *v.* [OE. *toberstan*, f. TO-[2] + *berstan* to BURST. So OS. *te-brestan*, OHG. *zibrestan*, MHG. *ze-, zerbresten*, Ger. *zerbersten*.]

1. *intr.* To burst asunder, to be shattered.

c **893** K. ÆLFRED *Oros.* v. x. §1 Sco eorþe tobærst. *c* **1000** ÆLFRIC *Hom.* I. 86 He eal innan samod forswæled wæs, and toborsten. *c* **1200** ORMIN 16147 Himm þinkeþþ þatt hiss herrte shall Tobressten. *c* **1205** LAY. 1921 Al þe feond to-barst. *a* **1225** *Ancr. R.* 214 Te ueond lauhweð þet he to-bersteð. *c* **1375** *Sc. Leg. Saints* xli. (*Agnes*) 60 His hart þane cane to-brist for bale. **14..** *Pol. Rel. & L. Poems* (1866) 246 Al to-broste synwe & veyne. **1513** DOUGLAS *Æneis* x. vi. 37 To bristis scho, and rivis all in sondyr. **1535** COVERDALE *2 Chron.* xxv. 12 They all to barst in sunder. **1881** MISS JACKSON *Shropsh. Word-bk.* s.v., If it freezes we sha'n 'ave it to-bost like the tother.

2. *trans.* To cause to burst asunder, to break or dash to pieces, to shatter.

c **1000** ÆLFRIC *Hom.* II. 258 þæs temples wah-ryft eac wearð toborsten. *c* **1205** LAY. 27520 þer iwurðen to-bursten eorles swiðe balden. *c* **1275** *Ibid.* 5926 Hii to-borste þe lokes. *a* **1300** *Cursor M.* 6615 (Cott.) þis golden calf he did to brest to pudre [*Tr.* to peces]. *c* **1374** CHAUCER *Troylus* IV. 1518 (1546) Attropos my thred of lif to-breste, If I be fals! **1470–85** MALORY *Arthur* VIII. xxx. 318 They.. alle to braste their speres. *c* **1530** REDFORD *Mor. Play Wit & Sc.* (Shaks. Soc.) 71 The fall wherof downe in the rest My joyntes and sinewes all to-brast!

toby ('təʊbɪ), *sb.*[1] [The familiar form of the Christian name Tobias, employed in various unconnected senses. (But some of the senses here grouped may have a different origin.)]

1. The posteriors, the buttocks: esp. in phrase *to tickle one's toby*. *slang.*

1681 [see TICKLE *v.* 6 b]. **1842** BARHAM *Ingol. Leg.* Ser. II. *Sir Rupert, Lay Naiads*, Throw us out John Doe and Richard Roe, And sweetly we'll tickle their tobies.

2. (With capital T.) A jug or mug (formerly common) in the form of a stout old man wearing a long and full-skirted coat and a three-cornered hat (18th c. costume). Also called ***Toby Fill-pot***, ***Toss-pot***. Also *attrib.* as ***Toby (Fill-pot) jug***.

1840 DICKENS *Barn. Rudge* iv, 'Put Toby this way, my dear'. This Toby was the brown jug of which previous mention has been made. *Ibid.* lxxx, When he had dined, comforted himself with a pipe, an extra Toby, a nap. **1852** SEWELL *Exper. Life* xix. (1858) 131 The great earthenware cup, the figure of a stout little man, which usually went by the name of Toby. **1857** HUGHES *Tom Brown* I. i, Pouring out his old ale from a Toby Philpot jug. **1901** *Pall Mall G.* 31 Aug. 3 (Cass. Supp.) The brown Toby jug was filled for him. **1908** *Daily Chron.* 3 Nov. 5/6 The Tobies are relics of the old coaching days.

3. The name of the trained dog introduced (in the first half of the 19th c.) into the Punch and Judy show, which wears a frill round its neck: hence ***Toby collar***, ***frill***, a turn-down pleated or goffered collar worn by women and children.

1840 DICKENS *Old C. Shop* xviii, Producing a little terrier .. 'He was once a Toby of yours, wasn't he?' **1882** [see FRILL *sb.*[1] 1]. **1885** *Pall Mall G.* 30 Apr. 6/1 A trailing dress with the Toby frill so favoured by these.. reformers. **1909** *19th Century* Mar. 446 A young gentleman in so-called skeleton trousers and a Toby frill. **1909** *Daily Chron.* 30 Aug. 7/5 A turn-down Toby collar of frilled lawn.

4. In full *toby tub*. A colour-printing machine for textiles.

1842 *London Jrnl. Arts & Sci.* XIX. 35 The printing [of the fabric] is to be done in an ordinary machine or press, the colours being furnished from what is called the 'toby tub'. **1876** *Encycl. Brit.* IV. 684/2 By means of a modern invention several colours may be applied at once on the cloth by means of one block. The machine used for this purpose, which is called a 'toby', consists of [etc.]. **1881** *Instructions to Census Clerks* (1885) 43 Toby and Rainbow Tub Maker.

5. An inferior kind of cigar. *U.S. slang.*

1894 T. B. SEARIGHT *Old Pike* 144 They [*sc.* cheap cigars] became very popular with the drivers, and were at first called Conestoga cigars; since, by usage, corrupted into 'stogies' and 'tobies'. **1896** *Columbus* (Ohio) *Dispatch* 18 July 15/3 A large supply of.. tobies. **1903** *Westm. Gaz.* 23 May 10/1 The railway ticket office clerk twists and swigs at a 'toby' as he asks you 'Where for, sir?'

6. ***Toby-night*** = TOBIAS NIGHT.

1910 T. M. PARROTT *Chapman's Plays & Poems* I. 699 The custom.. is the well-known 'Toby-night', or 'nights', ordained as a rule of the Church by the Council at Carthage, A.D. 398. The rule was authorized by the example of Tobith (Toby), who spent the first three nights of his marriage in prayer.

7. *Austral. slang.* A stick of ochre used for marking sheep which have not been shorn to the owner's satisfaction.

1912 in Stewart & Keesing *Old Bush Songs* (1957) 273 I've been shearing on the Goulburn side and down at Douglas Park, Where every day 'twas 'Wool away!' and toby did his work. **1964** H. P. TRITTON *Time means Tucker* 41 Raddle was a stick of blue or yellow ochre, also called 'Toby'. **1965** J. S. GUNN *Terminol. Shearing Indust.* II. 11 The raddle stick was also called 'Toby', and its improper use was one of the main reasons for the formation of the first Shearers' Union.

8. (With capital initial.) The name of a stock character of American comedy (see quot. 1961), used *attrib.*, esp. in ***Toby show***.

1946 *Theatre Arts* Nov. 652/1 Young actors who have played juveniles or ingenues with a Toby show seldom succumb to first-night nerves in later years. **1961** BOWMAN & BALL *Theatre Language* 393 *Toby*,.. a comic character type, a boisterous, blundering yokel as the protagonist. Hence *Toby play* (or *show*), a repertory favorite. **1964** *Tennessee Folklore Soc. Bull.* June 49 Bisbee's Comedians.. is one of the two surviving Toby Shows left in the entire country. **1967** *Oxf. Compan. Theatre* (ed. 3) 949/1 Most travelling dramatic tent-shows, playing one-week stands in rural communities, feature a Toby-comedian. *Ibid.*, Frederick R. Wilson, member of a touring tent-show company known as Horace Murphy's Comedians, was the first of a long line of actors to specialize in Toby roles. *Ibid.*, Toby-comedy includes generous use of the typical 'ad-lib'. **1978** *Chicago* June 56/2 We thought this [*sc.* donkey baseball] had gone the way of the Toby shows.

9. *Angling.* (With capital initial.) A type of lure used in spinning.

1969 V. CANNING *Queen's Pawn* i. 2 The river would be high... No use for a fly. He wanted.. a few small Tobies for spinning. *Ibid.* 3 He bought some.. four-gram golden Tobies, and the rod. **1973** A. ROSS *Dunfermline Affair* 139 Bayne's biggest lure—a six-inch metal Toby with a big triple hook.

toby ('təʊbɪ), *sb.*[2] *Thieves' slang.* [app. altered (? through *toba*', *toba*) from *tobar*, the word for 'road' in Shelta, the cant or secret language of the Irish tinkers: see Note below.] ***the toby***: the highway as the resort of robbers; 'the road'; also *transf.* highway robbery (called also ***the toby concern***, ***toby lay***); hence ***to ply*** or ***ride the toby***, to practise highway robbery; ***the high*** (or ***main***) ***toby***, highway robbery by a mounted thief; also, the highway itself; ***the low toby***, robbery by footpads.

1807 *Sessions' Papers* Feb. 133/1 He.. asked me if I had any objection of being in a good thing... I asked him when and.. he replied it was *low* toby, meaning a fotpad [*sic*] robbery. **1811** *Lex. Balatr.*, *Toby Lay*, the highway. **1812** J. H. VAUX *Flash Dict.* s.v., The toby applies exclusively to robbing on horseback; the practice of footpad robbery being properly called the *spice*, though it is common to distinguish the former by the title of *high-toby*, and the latter of *low-toby*. **1824** SCOTT *St. Ronan's* xxxi, Armed, as if he meant to bing folks on the low toby. **1830** LYTTON *Paul Clifford* I. iv. 76, I heered as ow Long Ned started for Hampshire this werry morning on a toby consarn! **1904** *Athenæum* 4 May 648/1 Travellers.. looked askance at its long, empty reaches, haunted maybe by gentlemen of the high toby. [**1890** J. SAMPSON in *Jrnl. Gypsy Lore Soc.* II. 217 *Tober* or *Toby*. This old word has found acceptance in every branch of cant. .. *Toba*, ground, is given as strolling-players' cant in the 'Sporting Chronicle'. Borrow in his 'Lavo-Lil' calls Tobbar 'a Rapparee word'.]

Hence **toby** *v.*, *trans.* to rob on the highway; **'tobyman**, a highwayman.

So *toby-gill*, *high toby gloak*, *high toby spice* (also *high spice toby*): see quots.

1811 *Lexicon Balatronicum* s.v. *galloper*, The toby gill clapped his bleeders to his galloper. *Ibid.* s.v. *Toby*, *High toby man*, a highway-man. *Low toby man*, a footpad. *c* **1812** in Byron *Juan* XI. xix. *note*, On the high toby-spice flash the muzzle, In spite of each gallows old scout. **1812** J. H. VAUX *Flash Dict.* s.v., To *toby* a man, is to rob him on the highway, a person convicted of this offence, is said to be *done* for a toby. *Ibid.*, *Toby-gill* or *Toby-man*, properly signifies a highwayman. *Ibid.*, *High-toby-gloak*, a highwayman. **1834** H. AINSWORTH *Rookwood* III. v, Jack Hall, a celebrated toby-man. **1876** HINDLEY *Adv. Cheap Jack* 4 Halting.. during the heat on the 'high spice toby', as we used to call the main road. **1881** *Daily News* 22 Dec. 1/3 When the footpad and 'high-tobymen' of ancient turnpike roads are replaced by male and female brigands armed with pistol and chloroform. **1902** *Illustr. Lond. News* 20 Dec. 951/3, I am a-looking anxiously for a tobyman that has wickedly robbed a lady.

[*Note.* For Shelta see J. Sampson in *Jrnl. Gypsy Lore Soc.* 1890, II. 217, also Kuno Meyer, *ibid.* 257. The latter holds Shelta or 'Sheldhru' to be 'a deliberate and systematic modification' of Irish Gaelic, of considerable antiquity, the words being altered by reversal, metathesis, substitution and addition of letters or elements. Hence *tobar* has been viewed as formed by metathesis from Irish *bothar* 'road'; though, if so, it must either have been formed from the *written* word, or be very ancient, since medial *th* has long been mute.]

toc (tɒk). Also **tock**. Used for *t* in telecommunication codes and in the oral transliteration of coded messages. Cf. TOC EMMA, Toc H.

1898 [see ACK]. **1913** [see PIP *sb.*[4]]. **1944** K. DOUGLAS *Alamein to Zem Zem* (1946) xvii. 100 This means they are hopelessly broken down and want the technical adjutant, known officially over the wireless as 'Tock Ack', to arrange their recovery.

toc, obs. f. *took*, pa. t. of TAKE *v.*

† **to-'carve, to-kerve**, *v.* *Obs.* [OE. *toceorfan* (ME. *tokerve*), f. TO-[2] + *ceorfan* to CARVE.] *trans.* To cut to pieces, cut up; to cut off.

c **950** *Lindisf. Gosp.* Mark xiv. 47 Sum monn.. ofsloȝ esne hehsacerdas & tocearf [*Ags. Gosp.* of acearf] him ða earelippríca. *c* **1000** ÆLFRIC *Minster Hom.* in *Leg. Rood* (1871) 105 (Cott. MS.) þeah þe se beam beo to-coruen. **13** .. *Guy Warw.* (A.) 3612 þer nas no man þat þer neye come, þat he ne was to corwen anon. **13..** *E.E. Allit. P.* B. 1700, & cowþe vche kyndam to-kerue & keuer. *c* **1500** *Lancelot* 868 His suerd atwo the helmys al to-kerwith.

‖ **toccata** (tok'kata; anglicized tɒ'kɑːtə). *Music.* [It. *toccata*, '*toccáta d'vn musico*, a preludium that cunning musitions vse to play as it were voluntary before any set lesson' (Florio 1611); lit. 'a touching', f. *toccare* to touch.] A composition for a keyboard instrument, intended to exhibit the touch and technique of the performer, and having the air of an improvisation; in later times loosely applied.

1724 *Short Explic. For. Wds. in Mus. Bks.*, *Toccata*, or *Toccato*, is of much the same Signification as the Word *Ricercata*. **1753** CHAMBERS *Cycl. Supp.* s.v., But what distinguishes the *Toccata* from other kinds of symphonies, is, first, its being usually played on instruments that have keys, as organs, spinnets, &c. Secondly, that it is commonly composed to exercise both hands. **1855** BROWNING *A Toccata of Galuppi's* 18 While you sat and played Toccatas, stately at the clavichord. **1875** STAINER & BARRETT *Dict. Mus. Terms* (1898), *Toccata*, (1) a prelude or overture... (2) Compositions written as exercises. (3) A fantasia. (4) A suite.

fig. **1903** *Trawl* May 22 A sigh of wind; and through the cool air sprang Toccatas of sharp patterings.

toccatina (tɒkə'tiːnə, ‖tokka'tina). *Mus.* [a. It., dim. of TOCCATA.] A short toccata. Also **toccatella** (-'tɛlə).

1740 J. GRASSINEAU *Mus. Dict.* 284 Toccatina, a small research when we have not time to perform it in all its parts. **1889** GROVE *Dict. Mus.* IV. 130/1 Dupont has published a little pf. piece entitled Toccatella. *Ibid.*, The same composer [*sc.* Rheinberger] has used the diminutive term Toccatina for one of a set of short pieces. **1938** *Oxf. Compan. Mus.* 937/1 Widor in his seventh Organ Symphony has a toccatina —a sort of *Perpetuum Mobile*.

toc emma (tɒk 'ɛmə). *Mil. slang.* Also **tock** (and **toch**) **emma** and with capital initials. [Representing T.M. (see T 6); see TOC, EMMA.] A trench mortar. Also *transf.*

1916 *B.E.F. Times* 1 Dec. f. 3/1 Completely oblivious of the dangers I encountered from our own artillery and Tock Emmas! **1918** J. H. DOUGLAS *Captured* ii. 25 He turned out to be Bombardier 'Chuck' Gibson who was with the sixty-pound 'Tock Emma' (Trench Mortar) Battery located on our frontage. **1928** R. C. SHERRIFF *Journey's End* (1929) II. ii. 57 Can't have men out there while the toch-emmas are blowing holes in the Boche wire. **1931** [see EMMA].

Toc H (tɒk eɪtʃ). [Representing T.H., initials of Talbot House (see sense 1 below), which was so called in memory of Gilbert W. L. Talbot (d. 1915); see TOC.] **1.** Colloq. abbrev. of the name of *Talbot House*, a rest-house and club for soldiers opened at Poperinghe, 15 Dec. 1915.

1918 in P. B. Clayton *Tales Talbot House* (1919) 138 Owing to the inconsiderate retirement of our old neighbours, the Boche, Toc. H. is in a pretty fix. **1925** FRASER & GIBBONS *Soldier & Sailor Words* 286 Poperinghe .. was visited by thousands of officers and men, for practically every one of whom 'Toc H', with its unique atmosphere and surroundings, proved alike a club and a home from home.

2. An association, orig. of ex-servicemen, founded by the Rev. P. T. B. Clayton after the war of 1914–18 to embody Christian fellowship and service.

1920 *Christmas Spirit 'Toc. H.' Ann.* 77 (*heading*) Toc. H. *Late* Talbot House. *Ibid.*, To open the club houses, Toc. H. asks for sympathy and help in many practical forms... H.R.H. The Prince of Wales has consented to open the H.Q. Club in London in 1921. **1930** *Toc H Jrnl.* Jan. 3 Toc H will indeed begin.. to be.. a power making for righteousness. **1954** P. TOYNBEE *Friends Apart* i. 17, I intended to work in a Toc H settlement. **1981** J. BRABAZON *Dorothy L. Sayers* xix. 241 An Anglican priest, chaplain to the Toc H hostel where I was staying.

3. ***Toc H lamp***: an oil lamp, an emblem of Toc H, used *iron.* as a type of dimness.

1977 *New Statesman* 9 Sept. 341/1 'He is as dim as a Toc H Lamp'.. is not yet rare as a phrase though members of the Toc H organisation may well be thin on the ground. **1977** J. PORTER *Who the Heck is Sylvia?* v. 46 Sometimes you can be dimmer than a Toc H lamp.

Tocharian (tə'kɛərɪən, -ɑːrɪən), *a.* and *sb.* Also **Tokharian**. [ad. F. *tocharien* (or next), f. Gr. *Τοχάροι* (Strabo) a Central Asiatic people formerly thought to speak Tocharian; see -IAN.]
A. *adj.* Of, pertaining to, or designating an extinct Indo-European language spoken in the latter half of the first millennium A.D., of which remains have been discovered in Chinese Turkestan. **B.** *sb.* This language; also, a member of the people or peoples speaking the language.
Two dialects of Tocharian are recognized: an eastern, *Tocharian A* (= TURFANIAN), and a western, *Tocharian B* (= KUCHAEAN, KUCHEAN).
1927 PEAKE & FLEURE *Peasants & Potters* 134 The Tocharian language of parts of Turkestan. **1934** A. TOYNBEE *Study of Hist.* I. I. iii. 113 One isolated language in the far north-east (the now extinct 'Tokharian', which has become known to Western scholars through the discovery.. of documents in this language.) **1950** *Trans. Philol. Soc. 1949* 9 The system of *r*-endings found in the verbal paradigms of various I[ndo-] E[uropean] languages..is clearly attested in Hittite, Indo-Iranian, Tocharian, Phrygian and Armenian, Italic, Celtic. **1960** PARTRIDGE *Charm of Words* 170 The *-k-* variation attested by Lett *aka*, a water-spring, and Hittite *eku-*, to drink, and dubiously Tokharian *yoko*, (a) thirst, should perhaps be aligned with certain OE and ON *-g-* words. **1966** G. S. LANE in Birnbaum & Puhvel *Anc. Indo-European Dial.* 218 If we could ever find out what non-Indo-European influence brought about the distinction in gender in A, we might know considerably more about the wanderings and contacts of the 'Tocharians'. **1975** *Language* LI. 141 Tocharian *-tsi*..is regularly added to a verbal stem, the present stem in East Tocharian and the subjunctive stem in West Tocharian. **1977** *Word 1972* XXVIII. 1 We have on one side Latin and Keltic, on the other Indo-Aryan, Iranian..and Tocharian.

Tocharish (tə'kɑːrɪʃ, -ɛərɪʃ). Also **Tokharish**. [ad. G. *tocharisch*; see TOCHARIAN *a.* and *sb.*, -ISH[1].] The Tocharian language.
1910 *Encycl. Brit.* II. 712/2 Up to 1909 only a preliminary account had been given of Tocharish, a hitherto unknown Indo-European language. **1926** J. R. R. TOLKIEN in *Year's Work in Eng. Stud. 1924* 27 The traditional Indo-European philology has suffered shocks in recent years, shocks from Tokharish and Hittite that begin at last to be felt even by the inexpert. **1939** [see KUCHAEAN, KUCHEAN]. **1956** J. WHATMOUGH *Language* ix. 179 Irish and Welsh have a middle or passive voice in *-r*, analogies to which are known in Hittite, Phrygian, Tocharish, Latin, [etc.].

toche, rare obs. form of TOUCH *sb.* and *v.*

tocher ('toxər), *sb.* *Sc.* and *north. dial.* Forms: 5–6 toquhir, -yr, 6 toquher, -eir, touchquhare, touchar, -er, towcher, (towher), tochar, 6–7 tochir, 7 tochare, tougher, 7–9 *dial.* towgher (9 togher), 6– tocher. [a. Irish and OGael. *tochar* (mod.Gael. *tochradh*) assigned portion, dowry, in OIr. assignment, f. *tochuirim* I put to, I assign, f. *cuirim* I put.] The marriage portion which a wife brings to her husband; dowry, *dot*.
1496 *Acc. Ld. High Treas. Scot.* I. 307 Giffen to Robert Lile, in his toquhyr of the Mertymes terme bipast jc markis. **1536** BELLENDEN *Cron. Scot.* (1821) II. 194 And [Rolland] in the name of Touchquhare, sall have all thay landis. **1546** *Reg. Privy Council Scot.* I. 43 The said Lord Governour sall gif in tocher with his said dochter to the said Eirle and his airis the soume of twa thousand, thre hundreith, and threttie thre pundis vi s viii d. **1568** *Durham Depos.* (Surtees) 86 The parties went..to hir frends, to demand towher. **1569** *Wills & Inv. N.C.* (Surtees) II. 314 *note*, He shall haue 100l..as towcher and mariadge money, whiche I gaue him with my dowghter Anne. *c* **1614** SIR W. MURE *Dido & Æneas* II. 192 Now Dido may be tyed to Trojane mate, And thow receave, in tougher, Carthage great. **1674** RAY *N.C. Words* 50 A *Towgher*, a Dower or Dowry. *Dial. Cumb.* **1692** *Sc. Presbyter. Eloquence* (1738) 149 Ye ken well enough..that Lads do not marry Lasses now, except they have a Tocher. **1796** BURNS *Hey for a Lass* i, Then hey, for a lass wi' a tocher; the nice yellow guineas for me. **1894** CROCKETT *Raiders* 22 He married a lass from the hills who brought him no tocher, but..a strong dower of sense and good health.
b. *attrib.* and *Comb.*, as *tocher-fee*, *-gear*; **tocher-band**, a marriage settlement; **tocher-good**, property given as tocher or dower.
1792 BURNS *Gallant Weaver* iii, My daddie sign'd my *tocher-band, To gie the lad that has the land. **17..** in Kinloch *Anc. Sc. Ballads* (1827) 85 'A clerk! a clerk!' the king cried, 'To sign her *tocher-fee'. **18..** *Cath. Jaffery* iv. in Child *Ballads* VII. (1890) 225/1 For *tocher-gear he did not stand. **1538** *Aberdeen Regr.* (1844) I. 158 To pay me the soume of thretty poundis..and that in *tochir gud for the mareage. **1609** SKENE *Reg. Maj.* I. 25 The mariage being dissolved, the tocher-gude returnes and perteins to the wyfe. **1822** SCOTT *Pirate* v, Though I fall heir to her tocher-good, I am sorry for it.

tocher ('toxər), *v.* *Sc.* and *n. dial.* [f. prec.] *trans.* To furnish with a tocher; to dower.
a **1578** LINDESAY (Pitscottie) *Chron. Scot.* (S.T.S.) I. 125 He..tocharit hir with the Lordschipe of Ballvenie. **1781** BURNS *Tarbolton Lasses* ii, Well he can spare't, Braid Money to tocher them a', man. **1829** HOGG *Sheph. Cal.* I. x. 304 It wad tocher a' our bonny lasses. **1878** *Cumberld. Gloss.* s.v. *Tokker, Togher*, 'He tokker't his dowter wi' twenty pund'.
Hence **tochered** ('toxəd) *ppl. a.* (qualified by adverbs, as *well-tochered*).
1728 RAMSAY *Give me a Lass with a Lump of Land* iii, Well tocher'd lasses or joynter'd widows. **1816** SCOTT *Antiq.* xii, Ye are a bonny young leddy, and a gude ane, and maybe a weel-tochered ane. **1881** *Blackw. Mag.* Apr. 524 The fairly tochered spinster.

'tocherless, *a.* *Sc.* [See -LESS.] Having no tocher or portion, portionless.
1790 SHIRREFS *Poems* 76 Wha bids the maist, is sure to win the prize, While she that's tocherless, neglected dies. **1820** SCOTT *Monast.* iv, I wasna sae tocherless but what I had a bit land at my breast-lace.

†**to-'chew**, *v.* *Obs.* [OE. *tocéowan*, f. TO-[2] + *céowan* to CHEW. So MHG. *zerkiuwen*.] *trans.* To chew to pieces; to tear with the teeth.
c **1000** ÆLFRIC *Hom.* II. 270 þæt husel is..betwux toðum tocowen. *a* **1225** *Ancr. R.* 202 þes laste bore hweolp..to-cheoweð & to-uret Godes milde milce. *a* **1240** *Sawles Warde* in *Cott. Hom.* 251 Oðer hwile [devils] torendeð ham & to cheoweð ham euch greot.

tochilinite (tə'tʃɪlɪnaɪt). *Min.* [ad. Russ. *tochilinít* (N. I. Organova et al. 1971, in *Zap. Vsesoyuznogo Min. Obshch.* C. 477), f. the name of M. S. *Tochilin* (1910–55), Russian geologist: see -ITE[1].] A mineral that is a complex of iron sulphide and magnesium and iron hydroxides, found as bronze-black grains and fibrous aggregates.
1973 *Mineral. Abstr.* XXIV. 186/2 A new mineral tochilinite..occurs in two habit modifications. **1976** *Papers Geol. Survey Canada* No. 76-1B. 66/1 Tochilinite is associated with clear and white calcites, some of which are coarse euhedral crystals.

†**to-chine**, *v.* *Obs.* [OE. *tocínan*, f. TO-[2] + *cínan*, CHINE *v.*[1]] *intr.* To split asunder or open; to be burst or cloven.
c **725** *Corpus Gloss.* (O.E.T.) 653 *Dehiscat*, tocinit. *c* **1000** *Sax. Leechd.* III. 18 ȝif hit ne tocine, tosleah hwon. *c* **1175** *Lamb. Hom.* 141 þe stan to-chan. *c* **1200** *Trin. Coll. Hom.* 199 þe nedre..drinkeð þat hie to-chineð. *a* **1250** *Owl & Night.* 1565 Wel neh min heorte wule to chine. *c* **1380** *Sir Ferumb.* 3001 þe schild to-chon.

tochus ('təʊxəs, 'tɒxəs). *slang* (chiefly *Jewish* and *N. Amer.*). Also **tochas** (-ess, etc.), **tuchus** ('tʊxəs), -as; *Anglicized* **tokus** ('təʊkəs), **tocus**, etc. [ad. Yiddish *tokhes*, ad. Heb. *taḥaṯ* beneath.] The backside, buttocks; the anus.
1914 *Dialect Notes* IV. 114 *Tookis, n.*, the anus:—said to be of Jewish origin. Also *tukis*. **1930** M. GOLD *Jews without Money* 250 I'll spit in his face..and tell him to kiss my *tochess* for his rent. **1934** J. T. FARRELL *Young Manhood of Studs Lonigan* i. 11 He was hurtled forwards by three swift kicks in the tocus. **1938** J. CURTIS *They drive by Night* xxiv. 269, I could do three months on me tochas. **1951** B. SCHULBERG *Disenchanted* xvii. 308, I don't go for all these fancy conferences and I don't kiss anybody's tochis. **1952** W. R. BURNETT *Vanity Row* v. 43, I was..getting my tokus pinched all over the place. **1963** 'R. L. PIKE' *Mute Witness* (1965) iv. 59 They call this stuff Sun-Bay Tinge... I'd call it Tuchus Pink myself. **1973** *Kingston* (Ontario) *Whig-Standard* 22 Dec. 7/3 Now get your tokus off my beat. You want to get killed go over on the next beat. **1975** R. H. RIMMER *Premar Experiments* (1976) i. 99 Your tuchas is smiling sideways at me.

tock (tɒk), *v.* [Echoic; cf. TICK-TOCK.] *intr.* To make a sound similar to TICK *sb.*[3] 2, but slightly lower and therefore more resonant. Esp. of a clock, and in phr. *to tick and tock*.
1913 J. MASEFIELD *Daffodil Fields* 72 A stately time-piece ticked and tocked. **1917** S. GRAHAM *Priest of Ideal* xxxi. 306 The comfortable grandfather clock ticked and tocked temperamentally. **1961** H. R. F. KEATING *Rush on Ultimate* iv. 69 There were tears in her eyes as Sebastian's second ball tocked against the peg. **1967** T. KENEALLY *Bring Larks & Heroes* iv. 24 Their ears, drenched by the south wind, tocked like clocks, thumped like sails. **1970** W. BROWN in Ramchand & Gray *West Indian Poetry* (1972) 14 The clock tocked and the stable dried.

tock, obs. f. TOQUE; obs. pa. t. of TAKE *v.*

tockay, var. TOKAY.

tocken, -in, obs. Sc. ff. TOKEN.

tocksaine, obs. f. TOCSIN.

†**to-'clatter**, *v.* *Obs.* [ME. *toclater*, f. TO-[2] + CLATTER *v.*] *trans.* To knock to pieces with a noise; to shatter.
c **1350** *Will. Palerne* 2858 þe komli kerneles were to clatered wiþ engines. *c* **1380** *Sir Ferumb.* 897 Ys scheld.. Sone þay had hit al to-clatrid; þe peeces leye on þe grounde. *c* **1440** *Partonope* 1078 Alle to clateryd and broken. *a* **1450** *Tourn. Tottenham* 160 in Hazl. *E.P.P.* III. 89 Ther were scheldis al to claterde, Bolles and disshis al to baterde.

†**to-cleave**, *v.* *Obs.* Forms: see CLEAVE *v.*[1] [OE. *tocléofan*, f. TO-[2] + *cléofan*, CLEAVE *v.*[1] So OS. *teklioban*, OHG. *zi-*, *zeklioban*.]
1. *trans.* To cleave asunder; to split open; to divide or separate into two parts.
c **888** K. ÆLFRED *Boeth.* xxxiv. § 11 ȝif þu þonne ænne stan toclifst, ne wyrð he næfre ȝegadrod swa he ær wæs. *c* **1000** ÆLFRIC *Saints' Lives* xxv. 55 þa nytenu sind clæne þe to-cleofað heora clawa. *c* **1200** ORMIN 14798 Drihhtin þær toclæf þe sæ. *a* **1375** *Joseph Arim.* 516 þer weoren..harde scheldes to-clouen. **1377** LANGL. *P. Pl.* B. XII. 141 For þe heihe holigoste heuene shal to-cleue.
2. *intr.* To split or fall asunder.
c **1205** LAY. 1920 Corineus..hine fusde mid mæine..þat his ban to-cluuen. **1377** LANGL. *P. Pl.* B. XVIII. 246 (MS. B.) The erthe..Quaked..and al to-clief þe roche. **1390** GOWER *Conf.* III. 296 The Schip toclef upon a roche. *c* **1430** *Hymns Virg.* 41 His herte to-cloue, and he for-bleed. **1571** GOLDING *Calvin on Ps.* xlvi. 3 The mountaines to clive from their rotes.

‖**toco**[1] ('təʊkə). *Ornith.* [Native name in Guyana; also in F. *le toco* (Buffon *Ois.* VII. 185).] The typical species of TOUCAN, *Rhamphastos toco*, a native of Guyana.
1781 LATHAM *Synopsis* I. 325 The Toco. The length of this bird is nine or ten inches from the head to the end of the tail... Inhabits Cayenne. *Ibid.* 323 Genus VI. *Toucan.* No. 1. The Toco. **1902** P. FOUNTAIN *Gt. Mts. & Forests S. Amer.* vi. 159 The native name of these birds is *toco*.

toco[2] ('təʊkəʊ). *slang.* Also **toko**. [ad. Hindi *ṭhōko*, imp. of *ṭhoknā* beat, thrash.]
Chastisement, corporal punishment. Also *fig.* and in phr. *to get toco for yam*.
1823 'J. BEE' *Slang* s.v., Yams are food for negroes in the West-Indies,..and if, instead of receiving his proper ration of these, Blackee gets a whip (*toco*) about his back, why 'he has caught *toco*' instead of yam. **1848** J. R. PLANCHÉ *Theseus & Ariadne* (1859) I. ii. 14 Toco from my father I instead of yam shall get. **1857** HUGHES *Tom Brown* I. v, The School leaders come up furious and administer toco to the wretched fags nearest at hand. **1885** W. S. GILBERT *Mikado* i. 16 To embrace you thus, *con fuoco*, Would distinctly be no gioco, And for yam I should get toco. **1903** J. COLEMAN *C. Reade* II. ii. (1904) 274 They both caught 'Toko' when they went back. **1910** KIPLING *Let.* in Ld. Birkenhead *R. Kipling* (1978) xvi. 252 The Teuton..prepares to give us toko when he feels good and ready. **1921** [see BOLSHY, BOLSHIE]. **1941** J. CARY *Herself Surprised* lviii. 143 You'd better tell people how I took your trousers down last time and gave you toko.

toco- (tɒkəʊ), combining form of Gr. *τόκο-ς* offspring, used as a verbal element in some terms (chiefly biological and obstetrical); as **,tocodyna'mometer**, an instrument for measuring uterine contractions during parturition (Webster, 1911); **tocoge'netic** *a.*: see quot.; **tocogony** (-'ɒgənɪ), propagation by parents as distinct from spontaneous generation; **toco'logical** *a.*, of or pertaining to tocology; **to'cologist**, one versed in tocology; an obstetrician; **to'cology**, the science of parturition, or of midwifery; obstetrics; **toco'mania**, puerperal mania (*Cent. Dict. Supp.*, 1909).
1903 L. F. WARD *Pure Sociol.* II. v. 96 The genetic succession of cosmic products..is not only genetic but *toco-genetic. The higher terms are generated by the lower through creative synthesis, and are thus affiliated upon them. **1876** E. R. LANKESTER *Haeckel's Hist. Creat.* I. 183 At present we must occupy ourselves with Propagation, or *Tocogony. **1902** *Amer. Anthropologist* Oct.–Dec. 739 This element in the story is not without its *tocological significance. *Ibid.*, This feature in the tale must be suggestive to the *tocologist. **1828** M. RYAN in *Lancet* 28 June 400/1 From much consideration on these deficiencies, I would propose the following nomenclature... *Τόκολογια*, *Tocology, on parturition. **1890** BILLINGS *Nat. Med. Dict.*, Tocology,..Tokology. **1895** ALICE B. STOCKHAM (*title*) Tokology: A Book for Every Woman.

†**'tocome**, *sb.* *Obs.* [OE. *tócyme*, f. TO *adv.* + COME *sb.*[1], rendering L. *adventus*: cf. OHG. *zôquimi*, *zôquemi*, 'conventus'.]
1. Arrival, advent, coming.
c **897** K. ÆLFRED *Gregory's Past. C.* xxxii. 212 For ðæm tocyme Dryhtnes Hælendan Cristes. **971** *Blickl. Hom.* 35 Foran to þon tocyme þæs eȝeslican domes dæȝes. *c* **1000** ÆLFRIC *Hom.* I. 404 Storc and swalewe heoldon ðone timan heora to-cymes. *a* **1175** *Cott. Hom.* 227 Christes to-cyme to þis life. *c* **1175** *Lamb. Hom.* 93 þurh þes halie gastes to-cume. *Ibid.* 153 For to bodien his tokume. *c* **1325** *Metr. Hom.* 8 Cristes to com mad endinge Of al our soru. *c* **1330** R. BRUNNE *Chron. Wace* (Rolls) 5576 (Petyt MS.) Mirth þei mad at þer tocome. *a* **1340** HAMPOLE *Psalter* cxxiv. 4 He prayes þat he wate is to cum. **1513** DOUGLAS *Æneis* XI. xii. 22 The contyr of first tocome..Full ardent wolx.
2. Means of access. *Sc. rare.*
1513 DOUGLAS *Æneis* IX. ii. 59 Gyf ony entre or tocom espy He myght, fortill assaill the cite by.

†**'to-come**, *v.* *Obs.* [f. TO *prep.* or *adv.* + COME *v.* Cf. OHG. *zuoqueman*, Ger. *zukommen*.]
1. *intr.* To happen, befall; cf. COME *v.* 9.
c **1200** *Vices & Virtues* 63 Alle unȝelimpes ðe him for his sennes to-cumeð. **1297** R. GLOUC. (Rolls) 7566 As is wille to com, þe eldore soster of þe tuo, in spoushod he nom. *c* **1300** *Beket* 1088 For him was to cominge sorwe ynouȝ.
2. *intr.* To approach, arrive, come *to*.
1393 LANGL. *P. Pl.* C. XXII. 343 These to-comen to conscience. **1455** *Charter in Liber Eccl. de Scon* 185 To all þaim to quhais knawlagis þir present lettres sal to-cum.
b. *trans.* To come to.
1596 DALRYMPLE tr. *Leslie's Hist. Scot.* IV. (S.T.S.) I. 206 He..wastes, burnes, and slayes al that he tocumis.
Hence †**'to-coming** *vbl. sb.*, coming, advent.
a **1300** *Cursor M.* 13676 Mi to-cumming In erth es jugement to bring. **1513** DOUGLAS *Æneis* X. viii. 44 On siclyke wys was Turnus tocummyng. *a* **1578** LINDESAY (Pitscottie) *Chron. Scot.* (S.T.S.) I. 75 [They] maid sa great slaughter at the first tocoming.
to come, to-come, *inf.* used as *sb.* That which is to come, the future: see COME *v.* 33 c.
So †**to-coming** *a.*, future: see COME *v.* 33 c β; also as *sb.* the future.
1556 *Aurelio & Isab.* (1608) Pj, Therefore, for the toe-comminge I shall have boldnesse to liffe joyfulley.

tocopherol (tə'kɒfərɒl). *Biochem.* [f. TOCO- + Gr. *φέρ-ειν* to bear + -OL.] Vitamin E: any or all of a group of closely related fat-soluble compounds that occur esp. in plant oils and are anti-oxidants essential in the diets of many animals and probably of man.

1936 H. M. EVANS in *Jrnl. Biol. Chem.* CXIII. 321 For this alcohol we propose the name 'α-tocopherol'. **1956** *Nature* 14 Jan. 86/2 (*heading*), η-Tocopherol (7-methyltocol): a new tocopherol in rice. **1968** PASSMORE & ROBSON *Compan. Med. Stud.* I. x. 9/1 Vitamin E is a mixture of tocopherols, which are yellow oily liquids remarkably stable to heat. **1972** *Daily Colonist* (Victoria, B.C.) 13 Feb. 27/4 Glib armchair vitamin experts discuss tocopherol, the chemical name of Vitamin E, as easily as they talked of ascorbic acid and riboflavin two years ago. **1979** *Nature* 19 Apr. 737/2 Vitamin E (α-tocopherol) and vitamin C (ascorbic acid) react rapidly with organic free radicals, and it is widely accepted that the antioxidant properties of these compounds are responsible in part for their biological activity.

tocornalite (tɒ'kɔːnəlaɪt). *Min.* [f. personal name Tocornal (see quot. 1896) + -ITE¹.] An iodide of silver and mercury occurring in pale-yellow granular masses, in Chile.

1880 DANA *Min.* App. 11, *Tocornalite*.. Amorphous, structure granular. Color a pale-yellow, by the action of the air it grows darker... Soft, easily reduced to a powder... From the mines of Chañarcillo, Chili. **1896** CHESTER *Dict. Names Min.*, *Tocornalite*,.. in honor of A. Tocornal.

tocque, obs. form of TOQUE.

†**to-crush**, *v. Obs.* [ME. f. TO-² + CRUSH *v.*] **a.** *trans.* To crush to pieces. **b.** *intr.* To be crushed, to break to pieces under pressure.

c **1300** *Havelok* 1992 Was non þat hauede þe hern-panne So hard, þat he ne dede alto-cruhsse, And alto-shiuere, and alto-frusshe. *c* **1380** *Sir Ferumb.* 5153 þe walles to-breke, & al to-crusschede. **1542** UDALL *Erasm. Apoph.* 111 b, I will at one stroke all to crushe thy hedde to powther.

tocsin ('tɒksɪn). Forms: 6 **tocksaine**, 7 **tocquesain, toxin**, 8 **toczin**, 8– **tocsin**. [a. F. *tocsin*, in OF. *toquassen* (1372 in Godef. *Compl.*), *toquesin*, *-sain*, *-saint* (16th c.), etc.; ad. Prov. *tocasenh*, f. *toca-r* (F. *touche-r*) to TOUCH, strike + *senh* 'signe, marque, appel de la cloche, cloche':—L. *signum* sign, in later Latin also a bell; 'campana, nola, Italis *Segno*' (Du Cange).]

1. A signal, esp. an alarm-signal, sounded by ringing a bell or bells: used orig. and esp. in reference to France.

1586 FULKE *Answ. to P. Frarine* 52 The priests then went vp into the steeple, and rang the bells backward, which they call Tocksaine, whereupon the people of the suburbs flocked togither. **1603** DEKKER *Wonderfull Yeare* Wks. (Grosart) I. 110 The Allarum is strucke vp, the Toxin ringes out for life. **1670** COTTON *Espernon* I. II. 89 At the same time that the Assault began, the Tocquesain rung throughout all the Churches in the City. **1795** HEL. M. WILLIAMS *Lett. France* II. 13 The signal for ringing that fatal tocsin, which was the knell of liberty. **1837** CARLYLE *Fr. Rev.* I. v. v, The tocsin.. is pealing madly from all steeples. **1861** STANLEY *East. Ch.* xii. (1869) 409 They rang a tocsin with the great bell of the ancient Novgorod.

b. *fig.*

1794 J. STEWART (*title*) The Tocsin of Britannia. **1802** —— (*title*) The Tocsin of Social Life. **1803** FESSENDEN *Terrible Tractoration* IV. ii, Sound Discord's jarring tocsin louder. **1832** A. CLARKE in *Life* xv. (1840) 572 He thought the seizure in my foot would turn to an attack of gout. This was a tocsin to me. **1877** MRS. OLIPHANT *Makers Flor.* Introd. 12 The tocsins of immemorial strife were sounding all about.

2. *transf.* A bell used to sound an alarm.

1842 LONGF. *Belfry of Bruges* xvii, The wild alarum sounded from the tocsin's throat. **1868** MILMAN *St. Paul's* iii. 63 The great bell of St. Paul's was the tocsin which summoned the citizens to arms. **1890** LECKY *Eng. in 18th C.* VIII. xxix. 60 Tocsins or alarm bells were set up in various parts of the town.

3. *attrib.*, as ***tocsin bell, note, sound***.

1822 BYRON *Juan* VI. lxxxiv, When all around rang like a tocsin bell. **1878** H. PHILLIPS tr. *Poems fr. Spanish & Germ.* 19 An Baeza's tocsin note Bellows forth from brazen throat. **1900** UPWARD *Eben. Lobb* 178 What meaning has the tocsin sound of liberty for ears like yours?

tocusso (təʊ'kʊsəʊ). Also **tocussa**. [a. Amharic.] A name used in Ethiopia for finger millet, *Eleusine coracana*, the ear of which is composed of several spikes resembling the fingers of a hand.

1790 J. BRUCE *Trav. Source of Nile* V. 79 In place of Teff .. there grows a black grain called Tocusso. **1866** LINDLEY & MOORE *Treas. Bot.* II. 1154/2 Tocusso. An Abyssinian corn-plant or millet. **1875** *Encycl. Brit.* I. 63/1 The low grounds produce also a kind of corn known as *tocussa*, of which a black bread is made.

†**to-'cut**, *v. Obs.* Forms: see CUT *v.* [f. TO-² + CUT *v.*] *trans.* To cut to pieces, to hew asunder; to cut greatly.

1382 WYCLIF *1 Chron.* xx. 3 Thei weren al to-kut and to-brosed alle. **1482** CAXTON *Trevisa's Higden* III. xxxiv. 161 Lete slee somme of the oxen,.. and to kytte [TREVISA kutte] reynes of the skynnes to teye with other oxen. *c* **1489** —— *Blanchardyn* xxxviii. 141 The Cassydonyens.. were slayne and all to-cutte and clouen. **1578** LYTE *Dodoens* II. xcvi. 277 His leaues be ashe colour, and all to cut. **1609** HOLLAND *Amm. Marcell.* xxv. iii. 264 Out went our light armed companies,.. and all to cut and hacked them.

tod (tɒd), *sb.*¹ *Sc.* and *north. dial.* Also 5 **tode**, 6 **todd(e**, **toad**, 7 **todd**. [A northern word of unknown origin; 'app. not from Norse' (Biörkman).

The suggestion that this word may be identical or connected with TOD *sb.*², and have reference to the bushy or tufted tail of the fox, is at variance with chronology and local distribution. TOD *sb.*² is essentially southern, while *tod* = fox is exclusively Scotch and Northumbrian, and was in use 400 years before *tod* = ivy-bush appears.]

1. A fox. Now only *dial.*

c **1170** REGINALD DUNELM. *Libellus* (Surtees) xv. 25 Pro caseo quem furto sustulit Tod agnomen accepit. *Ibid.* 28 Nam anglicæ linguæ.. tota illius familia stirpis, Tod, quod vulpeculam sonat, cognominantur eloquio. **1508** KENNEDIE *Flyting w. Dunbar* 288 Todis, wolffis and beistis wyle. **1535** LYNDESAY *Satyre* 3574 Birdis hes thair nestis and todis hes their den. **1536** BELLENDEN *Cron. Scot.* (1821) I. p. xli, Toddis will eat na flesche that gustis of thair awin kind. **1588** KING tr. *Canisius' Catech.* 113 Eschewed as theewes, murtherars, tods, dogs, and wolues. **1637** B. JONSON *Sad Sheph.* I. iv, Or strew Tods haires, or with their tailes doe sweepe The dewy grasse, to d' off the simpler sheep. **1721** RAMSAY *Richy & Sandy* 49 Had the tod Worry'd my lambs. **1825** SCOTT *Betrothed* Introd., I have a grew-bitch at hame will worry the best tod in Pomoragrains. **1871** E. PEACOCK *Ralf Skirl.* II. 150 I'll trap every tod that comes our way, and all t'other farmers.. 'll do th' same.

b. in proverbial and allusive expressions; cf. FOX *sb.* 1 b, c. (See also 2.)

c **1560** A. SCOTT *Poems* (E.E.T.S.) xxv. 29 Be scho wylie as ane tod, Quhen scho winkis I sall nod. **1583** J. MELVILL *Diary* (1842) 137 Bischope Adamsone keipit his castle, lyk a tod in his holl, seik of a disease of grait fetiditie. **1706** *Let. fr. Country Farmer* 2 (Jam.) This will be very odd, for.. Scotsmen to play their own Country sic a Tod's turn. **1820** SCOTT *Monast.* iv, Fear ye naething frae Christie; tods keep their ain holes clean.

2. *fig.* A person likened to a fox; a crafty person.

tod's birds, tod's bairns, an evil brood, children or persons of a bad stock.

1500–20 DUNBAR *Poems* xiii. 37 Sum in ane lamb skin is ane tod. **1581** J. HAMILTON in *Cath. Tractates* (S.T.S.) 74 The vnthankfull dealing of sik vylie [= wily] toddis. **1589** R. BRUCE *Serm.*, *2 Tim. ii. 22* (1591) Y viij, [The affections] wald ever be handled as Tods birds; for they ar aye the war of ouer great libertie. **1639** BAILLIE *Lett.* (1841) I. 196 To hold the islanders and these tod's-birds of Lochaber in some awe. **1721** KELLY *Scot. Prov.* 329 The Tod's Bairns are ill to tame. **1789** BURNS *Kirk's Alarm* viii, Daddy Auld, Daddy Auld, there's a tod in the fauld, A tod meikle waur than the Clerk. **1886** STEVENSON *Kidnapped* vi, Take care of the old tod; he means mischief.

b. *transf.* In the game of ***tod and lambs*** (in draughts), the piece representing the fox.

1812 W. TENNANT *Anster F.* II. lxx, Some force, t' inclose the Tod, the wooden Lamb on; Some shake the pelting dice upon the broad backgammon.

†**3.** *ellipt.* Fox-skin. *Obs.*

[**14..** tr. *Assisa David Reg. Scott.* in *Acts. Parl. Scot.* I. 667 Of a tymmyr of skynnis of toddis [*12th c. orig.* De tymbria wlpium].] **1503** *Kalender Sheph.* H v b, Gownys.. furryt wyth toddys for yt ys the most heyt furryng that they may wse. **1506** *Acc. Ld. High Treas. Scot.* III. 249 Item, for bordouring of it [goun to the King] with toddis,.. xxiijs. **1564** *Reg. Privy Council Scot.* I. 308 Ane gown, lynit with toddis of blak, begareit with velvot.

4. *attrib.* and *Comb.*, as ***tod-hunt***, ***-hunter***, †***-pult*** (***-powt***) (sense uncertain), ***-skin***; **tod-hole**, a fox's hole or den; *fig.* a secret hiding-place; **tod-lowrie** (also *Laurie Tod*), a familiar name for the fox; cf. *reynard*; †**tod-stripe**, a strip of woodland in which foxes have their holes; **tod-tails** (also **tods'-tails**), name for the club-moss, *Lycopodium clavatum*; **tod-tike** (**-tyke**), **-touzing**, **-track**: see quot. 1824.

c **1170** *Newminster Cartul.* (Surtees) 62 Usque ad *Todholes. **1844** W. CROSS *Disruption* vi, We maun.. try to find some tod-hole whaur the Doctor can ne'er get his clauts owre me. **1904** A. THOMSON *Remin.* II. v. 154 To go and have a *tod hunt in the Highlands. **1882** *Standard* 10 Feb. 5/3 The '*Tod-hunter', who last century was kept in the Western Isles for the purpose of exterminating the foxes. **1822** GALT *Sir. A. Wylie* II. xv. 144 His *tod-like inclination to other folks' cocks and hens. *c* **1470** HENRYSON *Mor. Fab.* v. (*Parl. Beasts*) xxii, The *tod lowrie luik not to the lam. **1725** RAMSAY *Gentle Sheph.* IV. i, As fast as flaes skip to the tate o woo Whilk slee tod-lowrie hauds without his mow. **1511** *Acc. Ld. High Treas. Scot.* IV. 198 Item, to Lance Ferry for ane lyning of *tod pultis to the samyn gowne.. xviij *li.* **1522** *Ibid.* V. 194 Item, for ane lynying of tod powtis to the Kingis nichtgoun.. viij *l.* v *s.* **1424** *Sc. Acts Jas. I* (1814) II. 6/1 Of ilke x of otter skynnis and *tode skynnis, vj d. *c* **1440** *Regr. Aberdon.* (Maitl. Cl.) I. 250 Robert Innes .. takis.. part fra þe *tode stripe to Edinglasse. **1820** *Blackw. Mag.* June 278/1 That singular and beautiful creeping ornament of the moorlands, called by the peasantry *tod tails. **1824** MACTAGGART *Gallovid. Encycl.*, **Tod-tykes*, dogs half foxes, half common dogs... **Tod-tracks*, the traces of the fox's feet in snow... **Tod-touzing*, the Scottish method of hunting the fox, by shooting, bustling, guarding, halloaing, &c.

tod (tɒd), *sb.*² [Known in sense 1 from 15th c.; app. the same word as mod.EFris. (= LG. dial.) *todde* 'bundle, pack, small load (of hay, straw, turf, etc.)': see Doornkaat-Koolman; also in dial. (Groningen, Guelderland, Overyssel) *tod* load. With this cf. Sw. dial. *todd* 'a conglomerated mass, esp. of wool' (Biörkman). Answering in form also (though not very satisfactory in sense) is MHG., Ger. *zotte* 'tuft of hair, matted or shaggy hair', also 'rag', mod.Du. *tod*, *todde* 'rag'. (The ON. *toddi* does not mean 'tod of wool' as erroneously stated in Vigf., but only 'bit, piece'.

An original sense of 'conglomerated mass', passing on the one hand into 'load', and on the other into 'bushy mass, bush', would perhaps suit the various senses. Sense 1 may have come to England in connexion with the wool trade with the continent; sense 2, on the other hand, which is a century later, seems to approach the sense 'tuft' or 'tufted mass'.]

I. 1. A weight used in the wool trade, usually 28 pounds or 2 stone, but varying locally.

1425 in Kennett *Par. Antiq.* (1818) II. 250 De xxiii todde lanæ puræ.. per le todde ix sol. vi den. **1467** in *Eng. Gilds* (1870) 384 Custom for euery todd j d. **1542** RECORDE *Gr. Artes* (1575) 203 In woolle, 28 pounde is not called a quarterne, but a Todde. **1696** *Phil. Trans.* XIX. 343 Three or four Fleeces usually making a Tod of Twenty eight Pound. **1776** ADAM SMITH *W.N.* I. xi. (1869) I. 242 One-and-twenty shillings the tod may be reckoned a good price for very good English wool. **1833** *Wauldy Farm Rep.* 115 in *Libr. Usef. Knowl.*, *Husb.* III, The agreement is made by the tod, which the dealers have contrived to enlarge to 28½ lbs. **1888** *Daily News* 23 July 2/7 The finest growths of home-grown produce.. changing hands at from 23s to 25s per tod.

b. A load, either generally, or of a definite weight.

1530 PALSGR. 281/2 Tode of chese. **1621** FLETCHER *Pilgrim* III. iv, A hundred crowns for a good Tod of Hay. **17..** *Songs Costume* (Percy Soc.) 248 There's the ladies of fashion you see.. With a great tod of wool on each hip. *a* **1722** LISLE *Husb.* (1757) 311 [They] allow three tod and an half of hay to the wintering of one sheep. **1863** W. BARNES *Poems* 3rd Coll. 73 Zoo all the lot o' stuff a-tied Upon the plow, a tidy tod. **1887** ROGERS *Agric. & Prices* V. 302 Prices of hay and straw... The cwt. and its subdivision, the tod, are the commonest of these exceptional measures. **1889** *Devon farmer* (E.D.D. s.v. *Tad*), I've a-got a middlin' tad [load of hay] here, sure 'nough.

fig. **1648** HERRICK *Hesper.*, *Conjuration to Electra*, By those soft tods of wooll [clouds] With which the aire is full.

II. 2. A bushy mass (esp. of ivy; more fully IVY-TOD, q.v.).

1553 BECON *Reliques of Rome* (1563) 53 b, Our recluses haue grates of yron in their spelunckes and dennes, out of the which they looke, as owles out of an yuye todde. **1592** WARNER *Alb. Eng.* VII. xxxvii. (1612) 183 Your Ladiship, Dame Owle, Did call me to your Todd. *a* **1619** FLETCHER *Bonduca* I. i, Men of Britain Like boading Owls, creep into tods of Ivie. **1626** BACON *Sylva* §588 Some [trees] are more in the forme of a Pyramis, and come almost to todd; As the Peare-Tree. **1709** *Brit. Apollo* II. No. 73. 3/1 What Tod of Ivy hath so long conceal'd Thy Corps? **1908** *Outlook* 4 Jan. 4/2 Ivy tods were covered with pollen in Christmas week and the smaller gorse is flowering freely.

III. 3. *attrib.* or *Comb.* †**tod-wool**, clean wool made up into tods.

1636 *Minute Bk. Exeter City Chamber* 5 Apr. (MS.), The weighing and sale of all toddwooll, rudge-washt wooll, and fleecewooll, and unwashed wooll.

tod, *sb.*³ *U.S. colloq.* Short for TODDY.

1862 T. WINTHROP *C. Dreeme* xiv, Selleridge's was full of fire-company boys, taking their tods after a run. **1903** J. LUMSDEN *Toorlo*, etc. 250, I spared nowther grub nor tod.

tod (tɒd), *sb.*⁴ *slang.* [Short for *Tod* Sloan (occas. used in full), name of a U.S. jockey (1874–1933), used as rhyming slang for 'own' in the phr. *on one's own*.] ***on one's tod***: alone, on one's own. Cf. PAT MALONE.

1934 P. ALLINGHAM *Cheapjack* vi. 56 'Are you on your tod?' I gathered that she was asking me if I was on my own. **1956** L. GODFREY in *Pick of Today's Short Stories* 91, I was in a small ward, and one evening some clot turned on the bloomin' wireless, and then went out, leaving me on my tod. **1959** J. WAIN *Travelling Woman* 7 Frequent visits to town on your Tod Sloan—no need to account for your doings. Leave her to keep the home fires burning. **1966** T. E. B. CLARKE *Wide Open Door* xi. 156 I'm on me Tod 'cept for the baby. **1972** J. BROWN *Chancer* v. 64 That left Sonny and me on our tod in the public. **1981** 'G. GAUNT' *Incomer* xiii. 71 Maybe they don't want your company... Never seen you on your tod before.

tod (tɒd), *v. dial.* ? *Obs.* [f. TOD *sb.*²] *intr.* Of (so many) sheep or fleeces: To produce a tod of wool; ***to tod threes*** (etc.), to produce a tod from every three (etc.) sheep; hence, To obtain a tod of wool from a specified number of sheep. In quot. *a* 1797 *trans.* (? erron.) to yield (so much wool).

1611 SHAKS. *Wint. T.* IV. iii. 34 Let me see, euery eleuen [*pr.* Leauen-] weather toddes, euery tod yeeldes pound and odde shilling: fifteene hundred shorne, what comes the wooll too? *a* **1797** R. FARMER *Note* (L.), Dealers in wool say, twenty sheep ought to tod fifty pounds of wool. **1799** A. YOUNG *Agric. Lincoln.* 311 Then sheap 'll tod threes; that is, the fleeces of three of them will weigh a tod... Of what was called Lincoln sheep, he todded all threes. *Ibid.* 327 His flock tods on an average half threes, half fours.

Toda ('təʊdə), *sb.* and *a.* **A.** *sb.* **a.** (A member of) a people of southern India. **b.** The language of this people, a Dravidian language closely related to Tamil. **B.** *adj.* Of or pertaining to this people.

1864 F. METZ *Tribes inhabiting Neilgherry Hills* 19 The Todas justify their belief in intermediate spiritual agencies by a reference to analogy. *Ibid.* 20 Great sanctity attaches to the person of the Pa'laul in the eyes of his Toda brethren. **1873** W. E. MARSHALL *Travels amongst Todas* xxiv. 208 Everything with the Toda is taken *au sérieux*. **1900** *Knowledge* 1 Mar. 67/1 On the clearances amid the dense and luxuriant primeval forest, or on the open grass-lands of the hill-tops, dwell a number of interesting aboriginal wild tribes, among whom the Todas and the Kotas are perhaps those whose names are the least unfamiliar to European ears. **1921** *Blackw. Mag.* July 28/1 The Toda puzzles and interests the Occidental because the Toda's origin is undiscoverable. **1938** [see MOIETY 4]. **1939** L. H. GRAY *Foundations of Language* 386 [Dravidian] falls into four great divisions, the first of which is *Tamil-Kurukh*, comprising Tamil..; Malayāḷam..; Ṭulu..; Koḍagu..; Kanarese, including Toda, Kōta, and Baḍaga..; and Kurukh. **1955** T. BURROW *Sanskrit Language* viii. 376 Besides the major languages there are numerous minor non-literary Dravidian languages spoken in various parts of India, namely: (i) Southern: Tulu, Coorg, Toda, Kota. **1976** *Language* LII. 259 This latest monograph..is most easily understood when studied in conjunction with his massive earlier tome on Toda songs. **1980** H. TREVELYAN *Public & Private* 7 The bee-hive huts of the Todas, the earliest known inhabitants of the [Nilgiri] hills who still lived there.

† **to-ˈdash**, *v. Obs.* [ME. *todaschen*, f. TO-² + *daschen* to DASH.] *trans.* To dash to pieces, to shatter by a violent blow or blows.

c **1205** LAY. 1469 His blod & his brain ba weoren to-dascte. **1297** R. GLOUC. (Rolls) 1186, & to dasste & drainte vourti ssipes þere. **13..** *Sir Beues* (A.) 3563 Wiþ his hint fot he him smot And to-daschte al is brain. *c* **1450** *Merlin* xv. 246 Theire sheildes were hewen and to daissht. **1582** BENTLEY *Mon. Matrones* i. 1 Thy right hand, O Lord, hath all to dashed the enimie.

b. *intr.* To split or burst asunder.

c **1305** *Judas Iscariot* 84 in *E.E.P.* (1862) 109 So þat he smot him wiþ a ston:..þat al þe sculle to-daschte, þe brayn ful out þerate.

today (təˈdeɪ), *adv.*, *sb.* and *a.* Forms: see DAY. Also as two words and with hyphen. [OE. *tó dæȝ*, TO *prep.* A. 7 + DAY. Cf. the parallel *tonight*, *tomorrow*, and dial. *to-year*; also Ger. *heut zu Tage*, *heutzutage*.]

A. *adv.* **1. a.** On this very day.

Freq. in phr. ***here today and gone tomorrow***: see HERE *adv.* 1 e.

In Scotland and Border counties of England expressed by *the day*: see THE *dem. adj.* B. 1 c, DAY *sb.* 13 b(*b*).

c **897** K. ÆLFRED *Gregory's Past. C.* lviii. 441 Ic hæbbe ðe nu todæȝ ȝesetne ofer rice & ofer ðioda. *c* **1000** ÆLFRIC *Hom.* II. 14 Þu eart min sunu, nu to-dæȝ ic ȝestrynde þe. *c* **1120** *O.E. Chron.* an. 656 (Laud MS.) Ic Wulfere gife to dæi Sce Petre [etc.]. *c* **1175** *Lamb. Hom.* 3 Hit is an heste dei to dei. *c* **1200** *Trin. Coll. Hom.* 27 Gif us to dai ure daihwamliche bred. *c* **1205** LAY. 5442 To daie a seouen nihte. **1382** WYCLIF *Luke* xiii. 32 Loo! I caste out fendis..to day and to morwe. **1483** *Cath. Angl.* 389/2 To day threday (*A.* Today thrydday), *nudius tercius*. **1535** COVERDALE *Josh.* xxii. 18 That he maye be wroth to daye or tomorrow. **1535** —— *Ps.* xciv. [xcv.] 7 To daye yf ye wil heare his voyce [etc.]. **1598** B. JONSON *Ev. Man in Hum.* IV. viii, And bade mee weare this cursed sute too day. **1680** OTWAY *Orphan* I. i, To day they chas'd the Boar. **1797** GODWIN *Enquirer* II. v. 225 He will plead for the plaintiff today. **1819** KEATS *Isabella* xxix, To-day thou wilt not see him, nor to-morrow. *Mod.* I have met them twice to-day.

b. *to-day..to-morrow* (†*to-morn*) = on one day..on the next day.

13.. *Cursor M.* 26769 (Cott.) þat ar to dai, to moru ar gan. **13..** *Minor Poems fr. Vernon MS:* 727/56 Here to-day, a-wey to-morn. **1510–20** *Compl. too late maryed* (1862) 7 To daye I had peas, rest, and unyte, To morowe I had plete and processe dyvers. **1567** *Gude & Godlie Ball.* (S.T.S.) 30 To day ane man, is fresche and fair, To morne he lyis seik and sair. **1710** PALMER *Proverbs* 273 A wise man will save himself to day for to morrow. **1738** GRAY *Propertius* II. 65 To-day the Lover walks, to-morrow is no more.

2. *transf.* At the present time, in the present age; in these times; nowadays.

a **1300** *Cursor M.* 2123 (Cott.) þe thrid part..hatt quar mast to day Regns o þe cristen lay. **1699** GARTH *Dispens.* IV. 47 Five Guinneas make a Criminal to Day. **1874** MORLEY *Compromise* i. (1886) 8 What great political cause..is England befriending to-day?

B. *sb.*

1. This day; also, any day considered as present.

1535 COVERDALE *Exod.* xvi. 25 To daye is yᵉ Sabbath of the Lorde. **1742** YOUNG *Nt. Th.* II. 316 Today is yesterday returned. **1802** MAR. EDGEWORTH *Moral T.* (1816) I. iv. 20 Here, for to day!..but, to morrow, it goes away for ever. **1846** LONGF. *Builders* iii, Our to-days and yesterdays Are the blocks with which we build. **1885** *Manch. Exam.* 22 Sept. 5/6 To-day has been beautifully fine throughout.

2. *transf.* This present time or age.

1848 THACKERAY *Van. Fair* xxx, From the story of Troy down to to-day, poetry has always chosen a soldier for a hero. **1889** *Tablet* 14 Dec. 947 The educated Scotchman of to-day. **1900** *Westm. Gaz.* 27 Sept. 10/1 A..tribute to the English girl of to-day. **1910** *Nation* 28 May 307/2 The fad of today is the orthodoxy of tomorrow.

C. *adj. colloq.* Modern, characteristic of or suitable for the present day.

1969 *Harper's Mag.* Oct. 65/2 I'm a today writer. **1976** A. CROSS *Question of Max* III. xiii. 154 It's old-fashioned and sentimental and altogether not 'today' to talk of restitution. **1980** J. WAINWRIGHT *Eye of Beholder* 24 The today song-smiths..wrote boy-girl-and-bed words.

Hence **to-ˈdayish** *a.*, of or pertaining to the present time; characteristically modern.

1864 J. D. CAMPBELL in *Glasgow Herald* 9 Nov., 'Old Boy', as a form of familiar address,..to-dayish as it may sound,..is at least a century old. **1885** BARING-GOULD *Court Royal* xviii, The new plate looks to-dayish; there is not the character about it that our ancestral store possesses.

todboat, -bote, var. *tode-boat*: see TODE *sb.*¹

Todd-AO (tɒd eɪ əʊ). *Cinemat.* [f. the name of Mike *Todd* (1907–58), U.S. stage and film producer, + the initials of *A*merican *O*ptical Co.] The proprietary name (in the U.S.) of a cinematic process producing a wide-screen image. Freq. *attrib.*

1955 *Times* 6 Aug. 3/5 The Todd-AO process uses 70mm. film instead of the standard 35mm. It has six sound tracks running at 30 frames a second as against the usual 24. The image is projected on to a huge curved screen presenting a picture about 25 ft. high and 65 ft. wide. **1955** *Official Gaz.* (U.S. Patent Office) 29 Nov. TM 239/2 *Todd-AO*. For motion picture equipment. Use since August 1953 on motion picture camera equipment... The Todd-AO Corporation, New York. **1958** *New Statesman* 26 Apr. 530/3 There can be no question about it; Todd-AO wipes the floor with Cinerama. **1958** *Observer* 27 Apr. 15/6 The Todd-AO screen is a huge, incurved affair, rather like the other side of a monstrous broken cup. **1976** *Oxf. Compan. Film* 692/2 His [*sc.* Todd's] main contribution to films..was his promotion of a new 70mm wide screen process, called Todd-AO, in the mid-fifties.

todder (ˈtɒdə(r)). *Obs.* exc. *dial.* Also **tother**. [Origin obscure.] Spawn of a frog or toad; slimy gelatinous matter.

1604 DRAYTON *Moyses* II. 116 The soile..Lies now a ley-stall as a common ditch, Where in their Todder loathly Paddocks breed. **1881** *Leicester. Gloss.*, *Tother*,..var. pron. of 'todder', slime; spawn.

todder, variant of TOTTER: cf. DODDER *v.* 3.

1871 *Daily News* 11 Sept., Enter..next a toddering old man—the feeble father.

toddle (ˈtɒd(ə)l), *sb.* [f. TODDLE *v.*]

1. An act or the action of toddling, as of a child or infirm person; *transf.* a leisurely walk, a stroll.

1825 C. M. WESTMACOTT *Eng. Spy* I. 32 After a toddle [*mispr.* toodle] of 3 miles. **1837–48** B. D. WALSH *Aristoph.*, *Knights* I. iii, Now falling and now on the toddle. **1871** BLACKMORE *Maid of Sker* v, The little thing..set off in the bravest toddle for the very bow of the boat. **1891** SARAH J. DUNCAN *Soc. Departure* 123 Her toddle was worth many strides of the female suffragist.

2. (Also **toddles.**) A toddling child.

1825 JAMIESON, *Toddle*, a designation given to a child, or to a neat person of a small size. *Angus.* **1828** *Craven Gloss.* *Toddles*, an endearing appellation of a child when just beginning to walk. **1854** THACKERAY *Wolves & Lamb* I, I have two girls—Amelia, quite a little toddles [etc.]. **1882** *Society* 18 Nov. 23/1 A..little pelisse..for a toddle of two-and-a-half.

Hence **ˈtoddlekins, ˈtoddleskin** = sense 2.

1852 C. J. MATHEWS (*title*) Little Toddlekins. **1879** SALA *Paris herself again* (1880) I. xvii. 287 There were many little manikins and toddlekins. **1890** *Century Mag.* Aug. 511/2 To return perhaps with a toddleskin or two born at sea. **1904** *Daily Record & Mail* 1 Jan. 4 The plump and laughing little toddlekins who can be seen in every home suburban street.

toddle (ˈtɒd(ə)l), *v.* Forms: 6–9 **todle**, (9 **taddle**), 8– **toddle**. [Originally *todle*, Scotch and northern Eng.; origin obscure. Not orig. connected with *tottle*; synonymous with DODDLE. (It is doubtful whether sense 1 belongs here.)]

†**1.** *intr.* To play or toy *with*. *Obs. rare*⁻¹.

1500–20 DUNBAR *Poems* xxxii. 11 He..todlit with hir lyk ane quhelp.

2. *intr.* To walk or run with short unsteady steps, as a child just beginning to walk, an aged or invalid person; also said of a similar walk or run of any animal.

c **1600** *Burel's Pilgr.* in Watson *Coll. Sc. Poems* (1709) II. 22 [The mole] Quhiles dodling, and todling, Vpon fowr prettie feit. **17..** *Allison Gross* x. in Child *Ballads* (1884) II. 315/1 She's turnd me into an ugly worm, And gard me toddle about the tree. **1783** JOHNSON 29 May in *Boswell*, I should like to come and have a cottage in your park, toddle about, live mostly on milk, and be taken care of by Mrs. Boswell. **1785** BURNS *Halloween* v, The vera wee things, todlin, rin Wi' stocks out owre their shouther. **1804** CHARLOTTE SMITH *Conversations*, etc. I. 23 It would be curious..if I was to be tied to my mother's apron string, and taddle about so. **1840** THACKERAY *Catherine* vii, When his strength enabled him to toddle abroad. **1859** HOLLAND *Gold F.* xxiii, The first little lambs of the season toddle by the side of their dams. **1879** H. GEORGE *Progr. & Pov.* IX. iv. (1881) 412 The child just beginning to toddle or to talk will make new efforts.

b. Hence, To walk or move with short easy steps; to go leisurely, to saunter, stroll; by playful or familiar meiosis, simply = walk, go.

1724 RAMSAY *Tea-t. Misc.* (1733) II. 167 Could na my love come todlen hame. **1803** R. ANDERSON *Cumberld. Ball.* 59 Now, wi' twee groats and tuppence, I'll e'en toddle heame. **1812** J. H. VAUX *Flash Dict.* s.v., Come, let us toddle, is a familiar phrase, signifying, let us be going. **1825** BROCKETT *N.C. Words*, *Todle* or *Toddle*, to walk, to saunter about. **1848** THACKERAY *Bk. Snobs* xlviii, We toddled into the Park for an hour. **1882** G. J. ROMANES *Anim. Intell.* xii. 359 It [the hare or rabbit] merely toddles along with the weasel toddling behind, until tamely allowing itself to be overtaken.

c. *fig.* Said of the hurried flow of a shallow stream (compared to the running of a child).

a **1774** FERGUSSON *Elegy Death Scots Music* x, Cou'd..todling burns that smoothly play O'er gowden bed, Compare wi' Birks of Indermay? **1838** J. STRUTHERS *Poet. Tales* 78 (E.D.D.) Owre hagg or hill, Whar Irvine todlin rins alang, A wee bit rill.

d. *trans.* To cause to toddle. *rare.*

1791 MME. D'ARBLAY *Diary* 4 June, Catching me fast by the arm..she safely toddled me back.

¶**3.** *intr.* To bubble gently in boiling. *Sc.* (Improperly for *tottle*.)

1797 A. DOUGLAS *N. Yr.'s Wish* Poems (1806) 67 A junt o' beef, baith fat and fresh, Aft in your pat be todlin!

Hence **ˈtoddling** *vbl. sb.* and *ppl. a.*

a **1774** [see 2 c]. **1861** *Star & Dial* 4 Nov., The poor little child, the toddling innocent. **1905** SIR F. TREVES *Other Side of Lantern* II. ix. (1906) 83 A toddling princess who was the joy of her father's life. *Mod.* Tired of toddling.

toddler (ˈtɒdlə(r)). [f. TODDLE *v.* + -ER¹.] One who toddles; *esp.* a toddling child.

1793 URE *Hist. Rutherglen* i. 95 She who sits next the fire, towards the east, is called the Todler. **1812** J. H. VAUX *Flash Dict.*, *Toddler*, an infirm elderly person or a child not yet perfect in walking. **1821** *Sporting Mag.* IX. 51 The road..exhibited a variety of toddlers eager to arrive at the destined spot. **1876** BESANT & RICE *Gold. Butterfly* III. 197 Little Phillis—a wee toddler of six or seven.

ˈtoddlerhood. [f. TODDLER + -HOOD.] The condition of being a toddler.

1966 'L. LANE' *ABZ of Scouse* Foreword, In his very toddlerhood his mother *lerned* him. **1967** *Punch* 15 Mar. 377/2 A normal childhood needs a good decade to run its full noisy course from toddlerhood to puberty. **1976** *Word 1971* XXVII. 37 The physical transition from infancy to early toddlerhood is marked by a qualitative transition in the nature of mother-child communication.

toddy (ˈtɒdɪ), *sb.* Forms: α. 7 **tarrie, tary**, 7–8 **terry**, 9 **taree, tarea**; β. 7 **tadie, -ee, taddy**; γ. 7 **toddey, toddie**, 7– **toddy**. [ad. Hind. *tāṛī* (with cerebral *r*, approaching English *d*), f. Hind. *tāṛ* palm-tree:—Skr. *tâla* palmyra.]

1. The sap obtained from the incised spathes of various species of palm, esp. *Caryota urens*, the wild date, the coco-nut, and the palmyra, used as a beverage in tropical countries; also, the intoxicating liquor produced by its fermentation.

α. **1609–10** W. FINCH in Purchas *Pilgrims* (1625) I. 436 A goodly Countrey..abounding with wild Date Trees..whence they draw a liquor called Tarrie or Sure. **1662** J. DAVIES tr. *Mandelslo's Trav.* 23 In this Village we found some Terry. **1687** A. LOVELL tr. *Thevenot's Trav.* III. I. vi. 16 They make a strong water also of tary which they distil. **1850** *Directions Rev. Off. N.W. Prov.* 225 The Taree or juice of the Palm Tree is liable to duty, in its fermented or unfermented state.

β. **1611** N. DOUNTON in Purchas *Pilgrims* (1625) I. III. xii. §4. 298 Palmita wine, which they call Taddy. **1615** in *Calr. Col. Pap., E. Ind.* (1862) 386 A wine called Tadie, distilled from the Palmetto trees. **1626** PURCHAS *Pilgrimage* v. (ed. 4) 539 Goodly Villages full of trees, yeelding Taddy. **1678** PHILLIPS (ed. 4), *Taddy*, a sort of pleasant juice issuing out of a spungy Tree.

γ. **1620** in Foster *Eng. Factories India* (1906) 185 Excessive drincking of toddy. **1622** *Ibid.* (1908) II. 144 All stragglinge libertyes and discontented toddey pott companyons. **1634** SIR T. HERBERT *Trav.* 6 [At Sierra Leone] they were often presented with Flowres, Fruits, Toddy, and like things. **1655** E. TERRY *Voy. E. Indies* 97 A very pleasant and clear liquor, called Toddie. **1732** PIKE in *Phil. Trans.* XXXVII. 235 Instead of Toddy, which is a Sort of Palm-Wine, the Liquor from the Birch-Tree comes near to it. **1770** COOK *Voy. round World* III. xi. (1773) 689 A kind of wine, called toddy, is procured from this tree [fan-palm], by cutting the buds which are to produce flowers, soon after their appearance, and tying under them small baskets, made of the leaves, which are so close as to hold liquids without leaking. **1885** G. S. FORBES *Wild Life in Canara* 253 The Khonds drink a great deal of 'toddy', drawn from the sago palm.

2. a. A beverage composed of whisky or other spirituous liquor with hot water and sugar.

Often distinguished by prefixing the name of the chief ingredient, as *brandy-*, *gin-*, *rum-*, *whisky-toddy*.

1786 BURNS *Holy Fair* xx, The lads an' lasses, blythely bent, To mind baith saul an' body, Sit round the table, weel content, An' steer about the toddy. [Brit. Mus. MS. copy of 1785 in Burns's own handwriting has lines 2 and 4 'Their lowan thirst an drowth tae quench',..'And steer about the punch'.] **1788** GROSE *Dict. Vulg. T.* (ed. 2), *Toddy*, originally the juice of the cocoa tree, and afterwards rum, water, sugar, and nutmeg. **1798** *Root's Amer. Law Rep.* I. 80 For giving her a dose in some toddy, to intoxicate and inflame her passions. **1808** *Sporting Mag.* XXXII. 215 Punch is certainly wholesomer than..toddy, which is grog with the addition of sugar. **1809** A. WILSON *Poems & Lit. Prose* (1876) I. 158 A tumbler of toddy is usually the morning's beverage of the inhabitants [Paisley]. **1818** TODD *J.'s Dict.*, *Toddy*..3. In low language, a kind of punch, or mixture of spirits and water. **1820** Rum-toddy [see RUM *sb.*¹ 3]. **1859** MRS. CARLYLE *Lett.* III. 7 A stiff tumbler of brandy toddy. **1861** HUGHES *Tom Brown at Oxf.* vi, They took to more toddy and singing Scotch songs. **1896** *Allbutt's Syst. Med.* I. 402 A few spoonfuls of hot brandy or whisky toddy.

b. With *a* and *pl.* A glass of this beverage.

1863 S. L. J. *Life in South fr. Commencement of War* I. xv. 299 Your parents do not encourage toddies. **1894** *Blackw. Mag.* July 75, I drank more than one toddy.

3. *attrib.* and *Comb.* **a.** From sense 1, *toddy-fruit*, *-shop*, *-wine*; **toddy-bird**, any of various E. Indian birds, as *Ploceus baya*, which feed on the sap of palms; see also *toddy-shrike*; **toddy-cat** = *palm-cat* a. (PALM *sb.*¹); **toddy-cuttter**, see quot.; **toddy-drawer** = *toddy-man*; † **toddy-fly**, see quot. *c* 1711; **toddy-maker** = *toddy-man*; **toddy-man**, a man engaged in the collection or preparation of toddy from palms; **toddy-palm**, any palm that yields toddy; spec. *Caryota urens*, and the wild date-tree of India, *Phœnix sylvestris*; also applied to the coco-nut tree and palmyra; **toddy-shrike**, the palmyra swallow (*Artamus fuscus*); **toddy-tapper** = *toddy-man*; **toddy-tapping**, the collection of toddy from palms; **toddy-tree**, a tree that yields toddy; = *toddy-palm*.

1698 FRYER *Acc. E. India & P.* 76 *margin*, The Ingenuity of the *Toddy Bird. **1864–5** WOOD *Homes without H.* xiii. (1868) 249 This is the nest of the Baya Sparrow, sometimes called the Toddy Bird. **1867** JERDON *Mammals India* 127 It [Tree-cat] is very abundant in the Carnatic and Malabar coast, where it is popularly called the *Toddy-cat, in consequence of its fondness for the juice of the palm. **1839** T. BEALE *Sperm Whale* 339 Persons.. called by the English sailors '*toddy-cutters', are employed.. for obtaining the juice of the cocoa nut tree. *Ibid.* 340 The 'Toddy-cutter'.. cuts off the end of the fructifying bud... He then places under the wounded part a long empty bamboo. **1839** URE *Dict. Arts* 1257 When the flowering branch is half shot, the *toddy-drawers bind the stock round with a young coco-nut leaf. **1681** GREW *Musæum* I. vii. §2. 162 The *Toddy-Fly.. hath but two Horns. *c* **1711** PETIVER *Gazophyl.* VII. 70 The Toddy Fly,.. 30 or 40 of them together, sawing thro' the Bark by the Help of their Snout-horn, will make themselves drunk with the Liquor that flows down. **1902** *Blackw. Mag.* May 606/2 An over-ripe *toddy-fruit fell off from a tall palm. **1821** J. LEYDEN tr. *Malay Annals* 151 There was a *toddy-maker, who went to amuse himself on the sea. **1866** *Treas. Bot.* 157/2 As soon as a spike makes its appearance.. a *toddyman.. securely binds it with thongs so that it cannot expand. **1900** *Daily News* 9 Mar. 6/2 A talking of the breezes in the tops of the *toddy palms. **1842** W. T. HUMPHREY *Let. to Presbyters in Madras* 10 With as little ceremony as if walking into a *toddy shop. **1937** *Discovery* May 143/2 It [*sc.* coconut shell] is an indispensable part of the *toddy-tapper's outfit, for it is in a coconut shell that he carries his cinnamon leaf paste and his lime for the pûrpose of stimulating the reluctant flowers to give up their sweet nectar. **1971** *National Geographic* Mar. 355/2 Ko Than Shwe, like many men around Pagan, is a toddy tapper. **1946** *Nature* 5 Oct. 493/2 *Toddy-tapping is a popular occupation as it only occupies a small portion of the day. **1958** *Contributions to Indian Sociology* II. 54 Toddy-tapping and the taking of animal life are associated with low status. **1632** R. CARTWRIGHT in *St. Papers Col., E. Ind.* 291 Order 2 pago[das] worth of *toddy trees. **1638** SIR T. HERBERT *Trav.* 29 The Toddy Tree is not unlike the Date or Palmeto. **1816** 'QUIZ' *Grand Master* II. 44 *note*, Toddy tree, the Indian name for the cocoa-nut tree. **1672** W. HUGHES *Amer. Physit.* 59 It is called by some the Mamin-Tree, or the Mamee-Tree; by others of the Planters Toddie-Tree: and the liquor or Wine that runneth out is called *Toddie-Wine, or Mamee-Wine. **1971** *National Geographic* Mar. 358/1 Juice collected at 8 a.m. ferments to toddy wine by 5 that evening.

b. From sense 2, ***toddy-drinker***, ***-drinking***, ***-glass***, ***-jug***, ***-maker***, ***-sap***, ***-stirrer***; **toddy-kettle**, see quot.; **toddy-ladle**, (*a*) see quot.; (*b*) a name for the American aloe (*Cent. Dict.*); **toddy-lifter**, a device used in the manner of a pipette to transfer hot toddy from a bowl to a glass; **toddy-stick**, a spatula, usually of glass or metal, for stirring toddy.

1882 MISS BRADDON *Mt. Royal* vii, In the North he may become a confirmed *toddy-drinker. **1838** *Chambers's Jrnl.* 3 Mar. 48/1 The universal practice of *toddy-drinking among the middle classes in the country towns. **1857** HUGHES *Tom Brown* II. ix, Soiled with the marks of *toddy-glasses and tobacco-ashes. **1865** ALEX. SMITH *Summer in Skye* I. 110 The *toddy-jugs were drained. **1858** SIMMONDS *Dict. Trade*, **Toddy-kettle*, a small hot-water kettle used in Scotland for making toddy. *Ibid.*, **Toddy-ladle*, a small deep spoon or ladle, used in Scotland for conveying whisky-toddy from a rummer or punch-bowl to a wine-glass. **1923** *Classical Q.* July–Oct. 173 The '*Toddy-lifter', known in Scotch and Irish households during the eighteenth and early nineteenth centuries, a bulbous glass cylinder, is exactly the instrument [*sc.* the clepsydra] described here. **1954** E. M. ELVILLE *Paperweights* x. 107 A toddy-lifter was something like a miniature decanter in shape, with a body large enough to hold a glassful of liquid. **1970** G. SAVAGE *Dict. Antiques* 430/1 The toddy-lifter was dipped into the bowl and allowed to fill through the hole in the bottom. The thumb was then placed over the upper orifice, air-pressure keeping the contents from flowing out. **1812** W. TENNANT *Anster F.* II. lxix. 50 By the social fires Sit many, cuddling round their *toddy-sap. **1840** *Picayune* (New Orleans) 4 Oct. 2/5 A '*toddy stick' is as spirit-stirring an article as any poet can boast. **1845** S. JUDD *Margaret* I. vi, A small counter covered with tumblers and toddy-sticks.

Hence **'toddy** *v.*, *trans.* to intoxicate with toddy; **'toddyize** *v.*, *trans.* to cause to drink toddy.

1836 T. HOOK *G. Gurney* (1850) III. iii. 362, I submitted myself to be toddyised according to his will and pleasure. *a* **1849** POE *W. E. Channing* Wks. 1864 III. 239 Better things than getting toddied are to be expected of Socrates.

†**tode**, *sb.*[1] *Obs.* Also 7 toad, (tod). [Origin obscure: no similar term is known in Dutch; but cf. Groningsche dialect *todden* to drag, tug, tow, *todde*, *tod*, as much as one can carry, burden, load (Molema); also Guelderland and Overyssel dial. (Gallée) *todden* to drag.] More fully **tode-boat**: A small Dutch fishing-vessel.

c **1600** J. KEYMER *Dutch Fishing* (1664) 2 The Hollanders have above 4100 fishing Ships and Vessels, whereof 100 Doggerbotes, 700 Pinks and Wellbotes, 700 Strandbotes, 400 Evers, and 400 Galliotts, Drivers and Todbotes, and 1200 Busses. **1614** T. GENTLEMAN *Eng. Way to Wealth* 14 Vessels of diuers fashions.. go.. onely for Herrings.., Sword-pinks, Flat-bottomes, Holland-toads, Crab-skuits, and Yeuers. **1616** CAPT. SMITH *Descr. New Eng.* 12 The poore Hollanders.. hauing 2 or 3000 Busses, Flat bottomes, Sword pinks, Todes, and such like. **1620** —— *New Eng. Trials* Wks. (Arb.) 239, 3600 [vessels] are fishermen, whereof 100 are Dogers.. 700 frand botes, 400 Enaces, 400 Galbotes, Britters and Todebotes, with 1300 Busses.

tode (təʊd), *sb.*[2] *U.S.* [Origin obscure; but cf. LG. *todden* to drag, in prec.] A rude sledge used in hauling logs, consisting of a tree-fork with a cross-piece on which the balk rests. Hence **tode** *v. trans.* and *intr.* to haul (logs) with a tode.

1895 in *Funk's Standard Dict.* **1911** in WEBSTER.

tode, obs. form of TOAD.

‖**Todea** ('təʊdiːə). *Bot.* [Named in honour of H. J. Tode, German botanist, 1733–97.] A small genus of ferns of the Southern hemisphere, related to *Osmunda*, often cultivated in greenhouses, and known as *crape-ferns*.

1882 *Garden* 25 Feb. 135/3 Todeas are often spoilt through being syringed overhead. **1892** *19th Cent.* Sept. 407 A carpet of maidenhair, umbrella, and brilliant todea ferns.

†**to-'deal**, *v. Obs.* [OE. *todǽlan*, f. TO-[2] + *dǽlan* to DEAL; = OS. *te-dêlian*, OHG. *zi-*, *zateiljan*, Ger. *zerteilen*.]

1. *trans.* To divide (into parts); to distribute, deal out; also, to separate, sever.

c **888** K. ÆLFRED *Boeth.* xxxiii. §4 þone anne noman þu todældest on feower ȝesceafta. *c* **893** —— *Oros.* I. i. §1 Ure ieldran ealne þisne ymbhwyrft þises middanȝeardes.. on þreo todældon. *c* **1000** ÆLFRIC *Hom.* II. 194 Astrece ðine hand ofer ða sæ, and todæl hi. **1154** *O.E. Chron.* an. 1137, Ac he to-deld it & scatered sotlice. *c* **1200** ORMIN 9468 Forrþi wass þeȝȝre kinedom Todæledd & tobrittnedd.. O fowwre feorþenn daless. *c* **1205** LAY. 2994 Ich wille mi dirhliche lod a þroe al to-dalen [*c* **1275** a þreo al to-deale]. *a* **1225** *Ancr. R.* Pref. 23 This an Boc is todealet in eahte lesse Boke. **1340** *Ayenb.* 164 þe filozofes.. to-delden þise uirtues ine zix deles. **1387** TREVISA *Higden* (Rolls) I. 185 þe hil mons Olympus.. to delep tweie londes.

2. *intr.* To divide, separate, part.

a **900** *O.E. Chron.* an. 885, Her to dælde se fore-sprecena here on tu, oþer dæl east, oþer dæl to Hrofes ceastre. *a* **1023** WULFSTAN *Hom.* xxx. (Napier) 149 Swa todæleð se lichoma and seo sawul. *c* **1175** *Lamb. Hom.* 131 Swa sone swa heore saulen and heore licoma to-delden heo ferden to helle. *c* **1205** LAY. 30833 Sone heo gunen to-delen. *c* **1275** *Passion our Lord* 480 in *O.E. Misc.* 50 þat huding-cloþ to-delde in þe temple a to.

3. *trans.* To decide (a contest). *rare.*

c **1205** LAY. 9519 He scal.. mit fehten hit to-dælen [*c* **1275** to-deale]. *Ibid.* 22799 We þis comp scullen to-delen wið þas uncuðe kempen.

toder, dial. variant of TOTHER.

†**'todly**, *a. Obs. rare*⁻¹. [f. TOD *sb.*[1] + -LY[1].] Foxy, crafty.

1571 *Satir. Poems Reform.* xxix. 33 The Ministre, far todlyar, his hure in houshold chereis.

to do, to-do, *sb.*: see DO *v.* 33.

†**to-'do**, *v. Obs.* [OE. *to-dón*, f. TO-[2] + *dón* to DO, to put. Cf. MHG. *zertuon*.] *trans.* **a.** To put asunder, divide, separate. **b.** To undo, open.

a **839** *Penit. Laws Ecgbert* II. c. 11 ȝif hwylc wif tweȝen ȝebroðru nimð hire to ȝemæccan, oþerne æfter oþrum, to-do man hiȝ. *a* **900** *Ags. Ps.* (Th.) xxi. 11 Hi todydon heora muð onȝean me. *a* **1000** *Ags. Hexameron St. Basil* iv. (1849) 8 Ðæt wæter and seo eorðe wæron ȝemengede oð ðone ðriddan dæȝ; ða todyde hi God. *c* **1205** LAY. 2945 Ic wlle mine riche to-don.. & twemen mine bearnen. *Ibid.* 6507 And þat deor to-dede [*c* 1275 vndude] his chæfles.. And for-bat hine amidden a twa.

todorokite (tɒ'dɒrəkaɪt). *Min.* [f. the name of the *Todoroki* mine, Hokkaidô, Japan + -ITE[1].] A hydrated oxide of manganese, calcium, and other elements occurring as soft black aggregates of minute, probably monoclinic laths having a metallic lustre; also, any of a group of minerals structurally related to this.

1934 T. YOSHIMURA in *Jrnl. Faculty Sci. Hokkaidô Univ.* Ser. IV. II. 297 The new mineral belonged to the purest species of crystalline manganomelane. As such a mineral had not yet been reported, this mineral was named 'todorokite' after the name of the mine where it had been first noticed. **1981** *Science* 29 May 1024/1 Todorokites are calcium-bearing manganese oxides found in terrestrial manganese ore deposits, in weathering products of manganese-bearing rocks, and in some manganese nodules.

todpole, obs. form of TADPOLE.

†**to-draught**. *Obs. rare.* [ME., f. TO-[1] + *draȝt*, DRAUGHT *sb.*] **a.** A following, train, retinue. **b.** A place that people draw to; a resort.

a **1300** *Cursor M.* 5961 þan sent godd þam on a flei,.. On pharaon and his to draght. *Ibid.* 14745 (Cott.) Mi hus.. yee mak it, witvten leue, A to-draght o reuer and thefe.

†**to-draw**, *v. Obs.* Forms: see DRAW *v.* [Early ME. *to-drawen*, f. TO-[2] + DRAW *v.*; = OHG. *zi-tragan*, MHG. *zertragen*.]

1. *trans.* To pull apart, draw or drag asunder; to tear to pieces; to destroy by tearing apart.

c **1205** LAY. 2603 Heo.. his leomen to-drowen & his hors al swa. *a* **1225** *Ancr. R.* 122 Ne to drauhð me þe eorðe? *c* **1250** *Gen. & Ex.* 191 Leunes and beres him wile to-draȝen. *a* **1300** *K. Horn* 181 His sloȝen and todroȝe Cristenemen inoȝe. **13..** *K. Alis.* 4613 (Bodl. MS.) Lete non houndes me to-drawe. *c* **1350** *Will. Palerne* 2086 He schal be honged heie & wiþ horse to-drawe. *c* **1425** *Seven Sag.* (P.) 877 How the naddir was y-slawe, That the grewhond hadde to-drawe.

b. *fig.*

c **1175** *Lamb. Hom.* 53 Heo.. heom to-twiccheð and to-draȝeð mid ufele weordes. **1297** R. GLOUC. (Rolls) 8729 þo men miȝte.. lybbe in Ioye & in riȝte, þat er were al to drawe. **1340** *Ayenb.* 57 þise ten boȝes.. ydelnesse, yelpinge, blondinge, todraȝinge, lyesynges, vorzueriinges, stryfinge, grochinge, wyþstondinge, blasfemye.

2. In various other senses of DRAW *v.* (*lit.* and *fig.*); to draw or drag away, about, or out.

a **1240** *Ureisun* in *Cott. Hom.* 199 Nis hit ðe no wurðscipe þet þe deouel me to-drawe. **13..** *Cursor M.* 28289 (Cott.) þe gode vous.. Broken ic haue or lang to-draun. *a* **1400–50** *Alexander* 5364 þis baratour.. Fand caratros & candoile at knyfes to-drawen. **1446** LYDG. *Two Nightingale Poems* i. 256 On euery syde to-togged and to-drawe.

†**to-drese**, *v. Obs.* Pa. pple. to-drore(n. [OE. *to-dréosan*, f. TO-[2] + *dréosan*, DRESE *v.*, to fall.] *intr.* To fall apart; to decay, fade.

a **900** *O.E. Martyrol.* 21 Dec. 222 þæt goldȝe-weorc todreas, swa swa hwæs ȝemylt æt fyre. *c* **1250** *Death* 62 in *O.E. Misc.* 173 (Jesus MS.) Er þe saule and þet body a two beon to-drefed [*v.r.* to-drehen]. *c* **1275** LAY. 9245 Portcastre.. mid hire bitere reses al he gan to-drese. ? *a* **1300** *XI Pains Hell* 182 in *O.E. Misc.* 152 Sum beoþ fur-brend & summe ifrore & alle þe bones beoþ to-drore.

†**to-dreve**, *v. Obs.* [OE. *todrǽfan*, f. TO-[2] + *drǽfan*, DREVE *v.*[2], to drive, impel.]

1. *trans.* To drive asunder or apart; to disperse, separate, scatter.

a **900** tr. *Bæda's Hist.* III. xviii. [xiv.] (1898) 227 (MS. O.) Hiora heriȝes þær wæs micel ofslaȝen.. & eal todræfed. *c* **1000** *Ags. Gosp.* Matt. xxvi. 31 þurh þæs hyrdes sleȝe byð seo heord to-dræfed. *c* **1175** *Lamb. Hom.* 155 He to-drefeð þe þonk þet erre weren to-gedere. *a* **1225** *Ancr. R.* 298 Schrift schent þene deouel.. & to-dreaueð his ferde. **13..** *Guy Warw.* (A.) 1483 On þe erþe liþ þi scheld to-dreued, Nouȝt o pece is wiþ oþer bileued. *c* **1400** *St. Alexius* (Laud 622) 326 And he fer from his frendes to dreued.

2. *intr.* To disperse, go or fly asunder.

c **1175** *Lamb. Hom.* 93 þi bileafden heo heore timbrunge and to dreofden ȝeond al middeleard. *c* **1400** R. *Gloucester's Chron.* (Rolls) App. XX. 121 (MS. *a*) His ost to drefde sone her & þer. *c* **1400** *Rowland & O.* 573 þat bothe þaire bodies wexen bare, þaire armours all to-dreues.

†**to-drive**, *v. Obs.* [OE. *todrífan*, f. TO-[2] + *drífan* to DRIVE; = OHG. *zi-*, *ze-trîban*, MHG. *ze-*, *zer-trîben*.]

1. *trans.* To drive asunder, disperse, rout, scatter; to drive away, dispel; to dissolve.

Beowulf 545 þa wit ætsomne on sæ wæron fif nihta fyrst oþ þæt unc flod to-draf. *c* **950** *Lindisf. Gosp.* John x. 12 Ðe ulf nimeð &.. todrifeð ða scip. *c* **1200** ORMIN 16397 Forr þatt hiss stren all shollde ben Todrifenn & toskeȝȝredd. **1297** R. GLOUC. (Rolls) 4722 At bedeford come þe saxons & smite an bataÿle & to driue [*v.rr.* to droue, to drofe] þe brutons. *c* **1330** R. BRUNNE *Chron.* (1810) 16 þe kyng was narow holden, his folk alle to dryuen. **1393** LANGL. *P. Pl.* C. XXIII. 174 Lechecraft lette sholde elde And to-dryue away deþ with drogges.

b. To dash or break in pieces. *rare*⁻¹.

c **1320** *Cast. Love* (Halliw.) 862 That ther shuld come a woman blyve That shuld all his hed to-dryve.

c. *intr.* To strike violently; to let drive. *rare*⁻¹.

c **1205** LAY. 8152 Euelin wes swiðe wrað & mid þan stæue to-draf And smat Herigal a þon ribben.

2. *intr.* To fly in pieces; to be splintered or shattered; to burst.

c **1205** LAY. 2895 þe king feol on þene rof þat he al to-draf. **13..** *S. Eng. Leg.* (MS. Bodl. 779) in Herrig's *Archiv.* LXXXII. 410/96 Witþ þat ilke word.. þe god of bras al to-drof so hit were of clay. *c* **1430** *Hymns Virg.* 122 Alle the worlle schalle to-dryve; Wo be þey þatt ben on lyve! *c* **1460** *Launfal* 482 Than myghte me se.. Speres to-breste and to-dryve.

tody ('təʊdɪ). *Ornith.* [ad. F. *todier* (1764 in Littré), ad. L. *todus*, name of some small bird, adopted by Linnæus as generic name.] Any member or species of the genus *Todus* or family *Todidæ* of small insectivorous birds, resembling and allied to the kingfisher; of which four species are found in the Greater Antilles.

1773 PENNANT *Genera Birds* 17 Tody, bill thin, depressed, broad... Inhabits the hot parts of America... The name first given it by Dr. Brown, I suppose, from Todi, small birds. **1834** tr. *Cuvier's Anim. Kingd.* I. 292. **1847** GOSSE *Birds Jamaica* 74, I have never seen the Tody eating vegetable food. **1879** E. P. WRIGHT *Anim. Life* 276 The Little Todies.. are only found in a few of the West Indian Islands.

toe (təʊ), *sb.* Forms: α. 1 tá, *pl.* tán; *sing.* 4–5 ta, taa; *Sc.* 6 ta, 9 tae, teae, *north. dial.* teea; *pl.* 3 tan, (4 taan); 4 tas, 4–5 taas, 5 taasse; *Sc.* 6 tais, taiss, tayis, tees, 6– taes, (9 *dial.* teaes, teaase). β. *sing.* 3–5 tô, 4–6 too, 5– toe; *pl.* 3–5 ton, 4–5 tone, toon, 5 toone; 4 tôs, 5 tose, tois, toose, 5–6 toos, 5– toes. [OE. *tá* (contr. f. **táhe*, in OMerc. *táhæ*), pl. *tán*, ME. *tô*, pl. *tôn*, *tôs* = OLG. **têha*, MLG. *tê*, MDu., mod.Flem. *tee*, OHG. *zêha* wk. fem. (MHG. *zêhe*, Ger. *zehe*, *zeh*), ON. *tá*, pl. *tǽr* (Da., Norw. *taa*, Sw. *tå*):—OTeut. **taih(w)ôn*.

Beside the above forms OFris. had *táne*, mod.WFris. *tean* (dial. *tane*, *teine*), NFris. *tuan*, EFris. *tône* (*tôn*), also MLG. *tene*, MDu., MFl. *teen*, mod.LG. and Du. *tên*, *teen*, also mod.Du. *toon* from Fris.; the origin of the final *-ne*, *-n* is uncertain: it may be from the pl. On the pre-Germanic relations, see Kluge, Franck, Dornkaat-Koolman, Falk & Torp. The OE. pl. in *-n* survived in s.w. till the 14th c.]

1. a. Each of the five digits of the human foot. ***big*** or ***great toe*** (†***mickle toe***), the thick inner toe; ***little toe***, the short outer toe. (See also d.)

α. *c* **725** *Corpus Gloss.* (O.E.T.) 141 *Allox*, tahae. *a* **901** K. ÆLFRED *Laws* c. 64 ȝif sio micle ta bið ofaslegen, ȝeselle him xx scill. to bote.. æfterre ta.. midleste ta.. feorþe ta.. sio lytle ta.. v scill. *c* **1000** ÆLFRIC *Voc.* in Wr.-Wülcker 161/8 *Allox*, micele tan. *a* **1225** *Juliana* 59 As þat istelede irn strac hire in.. from þe top to þe tan. *a* **1300** *Cursor M.* 12967 Witvten hurt o fote or ta. **1340** HAMPOLE *Pr. Consc.* 683 þe tas and þe fyngers alle. *Ibid.* 1910 In ilka taa and fynger of hand. *c* **1400** MAUNDEV. (Roxb.) xxii. 100 þai hafe on ayther fote viii. taasse. *c* **1440** Thomble ta [see THUMBLE-TOE]. **1500–20** DUNBAR *Poems* lx. 54 With his wawill feitt, and virrok taiss. **1513** DOUGLAS *Æneis* v. vi. 66 His tais [*v.r.* tayis] choppand on his heill. **1583** *Leg. Bp. St. And.* 300 Palme croces, and knottis of strease, The parings of a preistis auld te[a]es. **1816** SCOTT *Antiq.* xxv, Tak care o' your taes wi' that stane.

β. *c* **1290** *S. Eng. Leg.* I. 268/253 Heo orn and ne watte neuere a to. *c* **1315** SHOREHAM iii. 133 Ten fyngres and ten þine tone. **1340–70** *Alisaunder* 194 þe fairest feete.. With ton tidily wrought. *c* **1400** *St. Alexius* (Laud 463) 317 þe teres fellen to his tone. *c* **1400** *Lanfranc's Cirurg.* 177 þe bonys of þe toos. *Ibid.*, þe grete too.. haþ...ij. boones. *a* **1425** *Cursor M.* 6703 (Trin.) Foot for foot, to for to [*Gött.* ta for ta]. *c* **1440** *York Myst.* xxii. 108 þat þou schall on no stones descende to hurte þi tose. *c* **1450** *Cov. Myst.* xiv. (1841) 139 This olde shrewe may not wele gon,.. Lyfte up thi feet, sett forthe thi ton. **1526** *Pilgr. Perf.* (W. de W. 1531) 44 Euery hand and fote hath his fyngers & toos particularly distinct. **1591** NASHE *Pref. Sidney's Astr. & Stella*, 'Tis as good to goe in cut-fingerd Pumps as corke shooes, if one wore Cornish diamonds on his toes. **1632** MILTON *L'Allegro* 34 Com, and trip it as ye go On the light fantastick toe. **1741** MONRO *Anat.* (ed. 3) 301 The Flexors of the great Toe. **1878** GAMGEE tr. *Hermann's Hum. Physiol.* (ed. 2) 314 The toes.. are of use in maintaining the balance, particularly in walking.

†**b.** ***to stand upon one's toes***, i.e. on tiptoe.

a **1300** *Cursor M.* 24446 (Cott.) Apon mi tas of[t] sith i stod. *a* **1550** *Ane littill Interlud* 45 in *Dunbar's Poems* (S.T.S.) 315 He wald vpoun his tais vp stand, And tak the starnis doun with his hand. *c* **1572** GASCOIGNE *Fruites Warre* clxvi, Thus met we talkt, and stoode vpon our toes, With great demaundes whome little might content.

†**c.** Put for the foot as a whole, or the point of the foot. *Obs.*

c **1290** *Beket* 1444 in *S. Eng. Leg.* I. 147 A-non to is þies þe schuyrte tilde, þe brech riȝt to is to. *a* **1300** *Cursor M.* 5932 Man moght noght þeron sett his ta.

d. *fig.*

1607 SHAKS. *Cor.* I. i. 159 What do you thinke? You, the great Toe of this Assembly? **1649** DANIEL *Trinarch.*, *Rich. II* ciii, Soe was it here; these Petty toes of State, Who would haue Trod a Galliard of Designe.. Fell in a ligge. **1650** FULLER *Pisgah* I. iv. §9 Mustard, the little Toe of trees.

e. *Austral.* and *N.Z. slang.* Speed, energy.

1963 *Truth* (Wellington) 8 Oct., Happy Song has a fair share of toe in spite of her nine years and she was flying in fifth place after losing ground at the start. **1969** *Sun* (Melbourne) 12 July 58/1 The North half-forward line.. has a ton of toe and could give Richmond's novice half-back line a torrid afternoon.

2. a. Each of the digits of the foot of a beast or bird.

c **1386** CHAUCER *Nun's Pr. T.* 42 A Cok heet Chauntecleer.. Lyk Asure were hise legges and his toon. *Ibid.* 511 This Chauntecleer stode hye vp on his toos. *c* **1400** MAUNDEV. (1839) xxvii. 274 Psitakes.. þat speken.. and han v. toos vpon a fote. **1596** DALRYMPLE tr. *Leslie's Hist. Scot.* (S.T.S.) I. 63 As esie as to ken the lione be his taes. **1668** WILKINS *Real Char.* 161 That which hath two toes behind in each foot, with prominencies upon the head like ears,.. Chamelion. **1713** DERHAM *Phys.-Theol.* VII. i. (1727) 339 *note*, Two of the Toes are somewhat joined, that they [wading birds] may not easily sink in walking upon boggy Places. **1774** GOLDSM. *Nat. Hist.* (1776) IV. 262 The feet [of the elephant].. are divided into five toes, which are covered beneath the skin, and none of which appear to the eye. **1841–71** T. R. JONES *Anim. Kingd.* (ed. 4) 810 The Rhinoceros has only three toes to each foot. **1860** *All Year Round* No. 37. 247 Geckoes.. by help of padded toes can run up walls like a fly. **1894** *Nature's Meth. in Evol. Life* ii. 21 The Eocene antecessor of the horse possessed.. four separate toes, which subsequently became reduced to three, and at the beginning of the Quaternary Age the horse of the present day appeared with a single toe or hoof.

b. The front part of the hoof (or shoe) of a horse.

1566 BLUNDEVIL *Horsemanship* IV. cix. (1580) 50b, If a Horse.. halt.. in the heele, as by ouer reach, or otherwise, then he will tread most on the toe. **1831** [YOUATT] *Horse* 181 Cutting down.. at the union between the crust and the sole at the very toe. *Ibid.* 316 For work a little hard, the shoe shall still be light, with a bit of steel welded into the toe.

c. The ultimate joints of the tarsus of insects.

1826 KIRBY & SP. *Entomol.* III. 386 *Digitus* (the Toe),.. includes the *Allux* and *Ungula*.

3. *transf.* The part of a shoe or stocking which covers the toes; the hood or cap for the toe sometimes attached to a stirrup; a toe-piece.

1600 ROWLANDS *Lett. Humours Blood* vii. 13 From dish-crown'd Hat, vnto th' Shooes square toe. **1722** *Lond. Gaz.* No. 6119/4 Narrow square Toe Shoes with high Tops. **1828** SCOTT *F.M. Perth* xi, Place thy foot on the toe of my boot. **1842** J. AITON *Domest. Econ.* (1857) 262 A stirrup for the misses, with toes to be taken off or on as the boy or girl mounts. **1886** C. DICK *The Model*, etc. 95 Skirts, short and sweet, that deftly swing Round pointed heels and patent toes.

4. A part resembling a toe or the toes, in shape or position; (usually) the lower extremity or projection of anything; a point, tip; often identical with *foot* (FOOT *sb.* IV). (Cf. HEEL *sb.*[1] 5–7.)

a. Generally.

c **1440** *Pallad. on Husb.* XI. 49 Of vynes yonge The rootis.. kitte hem not to nygh, lest they abounde Three toon for oon, or feester into a wounde. ? *a* **1643** SANDYS tr. *Seneca's Œdipus*, About the mast the youthfull Ivy twines, The lofty toe imbrac'd with clustred vines. **1725** *Bradley's Fam. Dict.* s.v. *Saddle*, If.. the Toes of the Fore-bow be too narrow and streight. **1866** DARWIN in *Intell. Observ.* No. 56. 85 The toe of the labellum. **1869** SIR E. J. REED *Shipbuild.* iv. 71 The aftermost rivets were driven through the thin part of the toe, and knocked down in a countersink as usual. **1904** MAUD S. RAWSON *Apprentice* 140 The old man.. began to chip at the toes of the monster oak.

b. The lower extremity of a spindle or screw, as in a press; the projection on a lock-bolt or the like, against which the key or a cam presses.

1677 MOXON *Mech. Exerc.* ii. 27 The Toe or Nab of the Bolt, which rises.. above the straight on the Top of the Bolt. **1683** *Ibid.*, *Printing* x. ¶ 12 The very bottom of the Spindle.. is called the Toe, it is.. of an hemispherical form. **1833** J. HOLLAND *Manuf. Metal* II. 216 By the operation of the handle, the toe is made to act upon the inside bolt, and thus force down the piston. **1839** *Civil Eng. & Arch. Jrnl.* II. 242/1 The toe of the screw works in the fixed cross piece. **1877** KNIGHT *Dict. Mech.*, *Toe*, 1. a. The lower end of a vertical shaft, as a mill-spindle, which rests in a step, or ink. b. An arm on the valve-lifting rod of a steam-engine. A cam or lifter strikes the toe and operates the valve; such toes are known respectively as steam-toes and exhaust-toes.

c. A projection for the base of a wall; the foot or base of a cliff or embankment.

1838 *Civil Eng. & Arch. Jrnl.* I. 98/2 The mode pursued in blasting down high cliffs, by boring at the toe of the rock. **1839** *Ibid.* II. 433 Sheet piling at the toe of the wing walls. **1895** *Law Times Rep.* LXXIII. 156/2 Two vessels.. drifted.. on to the toe of a breakwater. **1901** *Daily News* 5 Jan. 6/5 A second chalk wall was built to form a watertight toe for the new bank.

d. The lower extremity of a gun-stock, rafter, organ-pipe, etc.

c **1860** H. STUART *Seaman's Catech.* 11 On the stock [of the rifle] is a toe. **1892** GREENER *Breech-Loader* 94 It is too straight or has too much toe upon the stock.

e. The thin end of a hammer-head, the peen; the tip of the 'head' of a golf or hockey club.

1873 E. SPON *Workshop Receipts* Ser. I. 412/1 Take an ordinary hammer,.. place the toe upon a piece of veneer previously glued on the under side. **1909** *Westm. Gaz.* 8 Feb. 12/4 The question of whether the toe of the club should point downwards at the top of the swing or somewhat skywards.

f. In full ***the toe of Italy***. The south-western extremity of that country. Cf. HEEL *sb.*[1] 6.

1894 A. J. EVANS in Freeman *Sicily* IV. 234 The coinage of Syracuse had now become the only coinage for the whole of Greek Sicily, and even for the toe of Italy. **1941** C. MILBURN *Diary* 15 Feb. (1979) 83 We have dropped parachutists.. on Italy's toe.. near Brindisi. **1974** *Times* 7 Jan. 3 The boy had been kept in various hideouts in the southwestern 'toe' of Italy. **1979** R. PERRY *Bishop's Pawn* iv. 68 The advancing Allied armies.. forced themselves northwards from the toe of Italy.

g. A flattish portion at the foot of an otherwise steep curve.

1940 *Wall's Dict. Photogr.* (ed. 15) 573 The method of speed-measurement used must.. depend on the position, not of the extreme under-exposed 'toe' of the curve, but of its straight-line portion. **1948** *Rep. Progress Physics* XI. 284 A pronounced toe can be obtained on a density-development-time curve by adding bromide ions to a hydroquinone developer. **1982** *Sci. Amer.* Apr. 41/2 The design of tension-leg platforms, like the design of guyed towers, is still at the toe of the learning curve and will undoubtedly go through several generations of improvement.

h. *Hort.* A section of a fleshy root.

1952 A. G. L. HELLYER *Sanders' Encycl. Gardening* (ed. 22) 169 Dracaena... Propagation: by cuttings or 'toes' of fleshy roots in sandy peat in spring. **1976** *Billings* (Montana) *Gaz.* 27 June 4-G/6 Rhizomes branching from the old toe will bear flowers next year. **1984** *Gardening from 'Which'?* (Consumers' Assoc.) Mar. 64/1 Remove the offsets.. known as yucca toes... Remove the 'toes' if new plants are needed.

5. Phrases (chiefly *colloq.* and *slang*).

†**a.** ***on old toes***, in old age. *Obs.*

a **1400** *Pistill of Susan* 305 þou dotest nou on þin olde tos [*v.r.* toes] in þe dismale. *c* **1460** *Towneley Myst.* xxx. 592 He that to that gam gose, Now namely on old tose.

b. ***the toe's length***, a very short distance.

1824 SCOTT *Redgauntlet* Let. x, No to be fit to walk your tae's-length.

c. ***toe and heel***, (*a*) a style of dancing in which the toe and heel tap rhythmically on the ground; also *attrib.*; (*b*) in walking: see quot. 1865; also *attrib.* Cf. *heel and toe* (HEEL *sb.*[1] 14).

1840 HOOD *Kilmansegg*, *Marriage* xxiv, The gaping people.. turn'd to gaze at the toe-and-heel Of the Golden Boys beginning a reel. **1842** J. WILSON *Ess.*, *Gymnastics* (1856) 103 A first rate walker,.. toe and heel—six miles an hour. **1865** *Routledge's Ev. Boy's Ann.* 434 When the heel of one foot is on the ground, the toe of the other must be upon it. This is called toe-and-heel walking. **1869** *Punch* 10 July 4/2 Hungarians.. dancing a toe-and-heel step to polka time.

d. ***from the crown to the toes, from head to (the) toe(s***, from head to foot, all over; ***from top to toe***: see TOP *sb.*

1297 R. GLOUC. (Rolls) 11177 þo stode hii I-armed fram heued to þe ton. *c* **1430** *Syr Gener.* (Roxb.) 3405 Fro the crovn to the toon Blak as cole thei were echoon. *c* **1489** CAXTON *Sonnes of Aymon* x. 274 All armed from hede to too.

†**e.** ***to claw one's toes***, to gratify or indulge oneself. *Obs.*

c **1460** *Towneley Myst.* xiii. 414 Dos noght but lakys and clowse hir toose.

†**f.** ***to cool one's toes***, to be kept waiting; cf. *to cool* (COOL *v.* 5) or ***kick one's heels*** (HEEL *sb.*[1] 18). *Obs.*

1665 BRATHWAIT *Comment Two Tales* 28 Cooling his Toes at the Blacksmith's door.

†**g.** ***to have*** or ***hold by the toe***, to have a secure hold of. *Obs.*

a **1548** HALL *Chron.*, *Hen. VIII* 186 The Bishop thinkyng that he had God by the too, when in deede he had.. the Deuell by the fiste. **1623** BP. HALL *Serm.* v. 139 While they think they have God by the finger, they hold a devil by the toe.

h. ***to kiss the pope's toe***, to kiss the golden cross of the sandal on the pope's right foot, as a mark of respect; formerly the customary salutation of those (excepting sovereigns) to whom audience was granted.

1768 EARL CARLISLE in Jesse *Selwyn & Contemp.* (1843) II. 296, I kissed the Pope's toe yesterday morning. **1782** PRIESTLEY *Corrupt Chr.* II. x. 253 All other persons.. must kiss the pope's toe.

i. ***to step*** or ***tread on the toes of***; also *fig.* to give offence to, to vex.

c **1394** *P. Pl. Crede* 649 For stappyng on a too of a styncande frere. **1866** TROLLOPE *Belton Est.* (ed. 3) I. iii. 71 'But you mustn't offend my father.'.. 'I won't tread on his toes.' **1868** BROWNING *Ring & Bk.* III. 1032 He could not turn about Nor take a step i' the case and fail to tread On someone's toe. **1879** GEO. ELIOT *Theo. Such* (1880) 119 A man who uses his balmorals to tread on your toes with much frequency.

j. ***to turn one's toes up***, to die; hence ***toes up***, lying dead.

1851 MAYHEW *Lond. Labour* II. 95/2, I thought I'd be by this time toes up in Stepney churchyard. **1857** LD. DUFFERIN *Lett. High Lat.* xiii. (ed. 3) 393 Ah, my Lord!—the poor thing!—toes up at last! **1860** READE *Cloister & Hearth* xxiv, 'Several arbalestriers turned their toes up, and I among them'. 'Killed..? come now!'

†**k.** ***to turn*** (a person) ***on the toe***, ? to turn off the ladder in hanging. *Obs.*

1594 NASHE *Unfort. Trav.* Wks. (Grosart) V. 36 He for his trecherie was turnd on the toe.

l. ***on one's toes***: alert, eager.

1921 J. DOS PASSOS *Three Soldiers* II. i. 56 If he just watched out and kept on his toes, he'd be sure to get it. **1958** B. NICHOLS *Sweet & Twenties* 94 You have to be on your toes to make the right sort of riposte on such an occasion. **1972** P. MARKS *Collector's Choice* ii. 123 Anavi was convinced that he had the right to delude even the most experienced connoisseurs; he was doing them a service because it kept them on their toes.

m. ***toe-to-toe***: (carried on) in close combat, at close quarters; also, neck and neck. Cf. *foot to foot* s.v. FOOT *sb.* 26 b.

1942 BERREY & VAN DEN BARK *Amer. Thes. Slang.* §701/14 *Toe-to-toe*, evenly matched. **1950** J. DEMPSEY *Championship Fighting* 199 Has each enough confidence in his own punching ability.. to engage the other in toe-to-toe exchanges? **1952** *Newsweek* 23 June 21/1 In the toe-to-toe fight for the Republican Presidential nomination, last week's round went to Sen. Robert A. Taft of Ohio. **1958** *Oxf. Mag.* 15 May 429/2 The sense of toe-to-toe negotiation with financial giants. **1971** *Flying* Apr. 42/1 My wife and I landed.. to top up the tanks and have a toe-to-toe talk with the weather guys. **1977** *Sounds* 9 July 23/3, I love real eccentric people, getting toe to toe with them.

n. ***to have it on one's toes***: to run away. *slang.*

1958 F. NORMAN *Bang to Rights* 53 They hold us responsable for anyone haveing it on their toes [*sic*]. **1976** 'P. B. YUILL' *Hazell & Menacing Jester* vi. 67, I had it across the road on my toes.

o. ***toes over*** (*Surfing*) (see quots.).

1962 T. MASTERS *Surfing made Easy* 65 Toes over, walking to the very front of the board during a ride on a steep hollow wave. **1965** J. POLLARD *Surfrider* ii. 19 Walking the board when you don't wish to put all your toes over you can still put a few over the edge—do a 'toes over'.

p. ***a toe in the door***: a position from which progress can be made.

1977 *Times* 7 Oct. 17/2 Gail Sheehy stopped her sample at 50... She says she now has a toe in the door of the 50's and 60's. **1978** *Dumfries Courier* 20 Oct. 6/5 He was only using the application for boating as a 'toe in the door' to sell something else. **1979** D. SANDERS *Queen sends for Mrs Chadwick* 11 He'd be thirty-five at the next election. Just the right age to get a toe in the door.

q. ***to dig in one's toes***: see DIG *v.* 11 c.

6. *attrib.* and *Comb.*, as ***toe-action***, ***-bone***, ***-calk***, ***-dresser***, ***-end***, ***-joint***, ***-turn***; ***toe-kissing***, ***-scraping***, ***-stretching***, ***-treading*** (*lit.* and *fig.*), sbs. and adjs.; ***toe-like*** adj.; **toe-ball**, the thickened fleshy pad under the toe; with quot. 1826 cf. sense 2 c; **toe-board**, a board for the feet to rest upon; also, a board marking the limit of the thrower's run in putting the weight and similar feats; **toe-boot**, a boot (BOOT *sb.*[3] 5) to protect the hind feet of a trotting horse from injury by the fore feet; **toe brake** *Aeronaut.*, in an aircraft, a brake that is operated with the foot; so **toe braking** *vbl. sb.*; **toe-cap**, a cap of leather covering the toe of a boot or shoe; hence **toe-capped** *a.*, furnished with a toe-cap; **toe-clip**, (*a*) an attachment to the pedal of a bicycle in which the toe of the shoe is placed to prevent the foot slipping; (*b*) a tip turned up at the toe of a horse-shoe, to keep the shoe in position (= CLIP *sb.*[1] 2); **toe-cover** *slang*, an inexpensive and useless present; **toe-crack** (*Farriery*), a sand-crack in the front of the hoof; **toe-dancer**, see quot.; **toe-dancing**, dancing on points; **toe-drop** (*Path.*), see quot. 1899; **toe-end** *v. trans.*, to kick with the point of one's foot; † **toe-gleek**, some variety of gleek; **toe-hardy**, a half-round hardy or cold-chisel; **toe-hold**: (*a*) in *Wrestling*, a hold in which the toe is seized and the leg forced backwards; (*b*) a place of support for the toe (of a boot) in climbing; hence *fig.*, a position of little significance or influence, esp. one seen as providing a base from which they may be increased; **toe-hole** *rare*, a place of support for the toe (of a boot) in climbing; **toe-jam** *slang*, dirt which accumulates between the toes; **toe jump** *Skating*, a jump initiated with the help of the toe of the non-skating foot; **toe-link**, a bottom end link; **toe loop**, (*a*) *Skating*, a loop jump that is also a toe jump (see quot. 1979); more fully *toe loop jump*; (*b*) a loop on a sandal through which a toe is placed; **toe-movement**, see quot., and cf. *toe-drop* and *toe-scraping*; **toe-nail** *sb.*, (*a*) the nail of a toe; also *fig.*; (*b*) an iron nail employed for the toe in shoeing; **toe-nail** *v.*, to fasten with toed nails: see TOED 2; **toe-narrow** *a.* (*Farriery*), having the fore feet too close when standing; **toe-piece**, a toe-cap; a toe-plate; in armour, the toe of a solleret; also, the lengthened tip of this; see also quot. 1879; **toe-plate**, (*a*) an iron plate under the toe of a boot or shoe; (*b*) a metal plate worn as a remedy for hammer-toe; **toe-puff**, a stiffener for the toe of the upper of a shoe; **toe rake** *Skating*, a set of teeth at the front of the blade of a skate; **toe-ring**, a ring worn on the toe; a stout ferrule on the end of a cant-hook (*U.S.*); **toe-rubber** *N. Amer.*, a rubber overshoe that covers only the front part of a shoe; **toe-scute** = *toe-plate* (*a*); † **toe-shell**, a species of cirriped, *Pollicipes mitella*; **toe shoe** *N. Amer. Ballet*, a shoe with a reinforced toe, worn for toe-dancing; a point shoe; **toe-spin** *Skating*, a spin performed on the toe; **toe-step** (*Mech.*), the socket in which the end of a spindle works; = FOOTSTEP 5 d; **toe-strap**, (*a*) a strap or thong which secures the toe of a sandal, skate, or the like; (*b*) a strap on a bicycle pedal to keep the foot from slipping off it; (*c*) a band fixed to a boat and serving to hold the foot of someone leaning out; **toe-string** = *toe-strap* (*a*); **toe-tapping** *vbl. sb.*, the tapping of feet in time to music; (in quot. 1929, a derogatory term for 'dancing'); *ppl. a.*, that makes one want to tap one's feet; **toe-thong sandal** = *thong sandal* s.v. THONG *sb.* 2; **toe-tights**, tights in which the toes are separated like glove-fingers; **toe-tip**, the extremity of a toe; cf. TIPTOE; also = *toe-plate* (*a*); **toe-tuft**, a tuft of hair covering the toe in some dogs; **toe-walking** *a.*, that walks on the toes, digitigrade; **toe wall** a low wall built at the foot of an embankment to help keep the earth in place; **toe-weight**, a small knob of metal attached to the hoof or shoe of a horse to modify the gait in trotting; **toe-wide** *a.* (*Farriery*), having the fore feet too far apart in standing; **toe-writer**, one who writes with his toes; in quot. *allusively*.

1826 KIRBY & SP. *Entomol.* III. xxxiii. 386 Allux (the *Toe-ball). The last joint but one of the Tarsus, when remarkable, as in Rhyncophorous beetles. **1856** AIRD *Poet. Wks.* 15 The big Toeball just resting on the stirrup. **1892** *Harper's Mag.* Jan. 271/1 The..bag..to put under his feet on the *toe-board. **1907** *Westm. Gaz.* 21 Jan. 2/1 Here had trudged the bloody pirate..about to step the dance of death without a toe-board under the gallows-tree up harbour. **1898** *Guide Mammalia* 11 The tarsus, or ankle-bones, corresponding to the carpus, and the metatarsals and *toe-bones to the metacarpals and finger-bones. **1898** *Daily News* 11 Nov. 5/1 An ill-formed boot with a foot inside, the toe bones all squeezed out of their natural shape. **1901** *Munsey's Mag.* XXV. 736/1 The hind feet were protected with the *toe boots, while the action of the front feet was stimulated by the weight of the quarter boots, made of soft sheepskin or leather. **1944** *Jrnl. R. Aeronaut. Soc.* XLVIII. 297 The *toe brakes are awkward to operate, and heavy pressure is needed on them to get the desired braking effect. **1976** B. LECOMBER *Dead Weight* ii. 32, I stood on the toe-brakes and opened the throttle. **1977** *R.A.F. Yearbk.* 29 Direction is maintained or altered by holding the rudder central and applying differential *toe-braking as required. **1877** KNIGHT *Dict. Mech.*, **Toe-calk*, a prong or barb on the toe of a horse's shoe, to prevent slipping on ice or frozen ground. **1797** WOLCOTT (P. Pindar) *Out at Last* Wks. 1812 III. 494 Come hobbling forth without one blush of shame With heel-taps, *toe-caps, soles for worn-out fame. **1907** *Daily News* 4 June 6 Shoes much the worse for wear, often broken across the toecaps. **1861** J. BROWN *Horæ Subs.* (1863) 378 His heavy shoes,..heel-capt and *toe-capt. **1895** *Army & Navy Co-op. Soc. Price List* 1379/2 The Courier *Toe Clips... For Rat Trap Pedals (adjustable), price 2/0. **1908** *Daily Chron.* 6 June 8/3 The N.C.U...leaves it permissible—not compulsory—for riders to use toe-clips, blocks on the shoes, or slots in the soles, or any other device for assisting to keep the feet in position. **1948** B. MACDONALD *Plague & I* xvi. 193 *Toecover is a family name for a useless gift. A crocheted napkin ring is a toecover. **1983** *Listener* 3 Feb. 21/2 Gifts are given, not only the completely useless trivia or 'toe-covers' which litter the surgery, but more substantial gifts, such as briefcases. **1903** *U.S. Dept. Agric., Rep. Dis. Horse* 405 The *toe-crack..extending from the coronary band to the sole. **1911** WEBSTER, *Sand-crack*, a fissure or lesion in the horn of the hoof wall, often causing lameness. When in the front wall it is known as toe crack. **1898** *Pall Mall Mag.* Nov. 419 Mrs. Draper was a *toe-dancer..a young lady..flitting hither and thither on the very tips of her tiny feet. **1924** SHARP & OPPÉ *Dance* 47 *Toe-dancing is perhaps the most extreme instance of the virtuosity achieved by the ballet-dancers of the last century. **1976** F. MUIR *Frank Muir Bk.* 42 About 1820 the ballerina Taglioni popularized toe-dancing, which called for special built-up shoes. **1725** *Lond. Gaz.* No. 6399/3 James Stubs,..*Toe-Dresser. **1899** *Syd. Soc. Lex.*, **Toe-drop*, inability to lift the toes, or the anterior part of the foot, due to a local paralysis, usually from peripheral neuritis. **1968** B. HINES *Kestrel for Knave* 98 He pivoted on his left foot and *toe-ended a lump of coke back across the asphalt. **1976** *Sunday Mail* (Glasgow) 21 Nov., Jonquin took a free-kick and the inside-right toe-ended the ball into the net. **1689** SHADWELL *Bury F.* III. i, Women, go pack into the drawing room and play at *Toe-gleek. **1911** WEBSTER, *Toe-hardy. **1880** 'MARK TWAIN' *Tramp Abroad* xxxiv. 379 One man's *toe-hold broke and he fell! **1918** *Observer* 10 Nov. 8/6 The enemy retains a toehold in the Rimeuse Valley. **1945** MENCKEN *Amer. Lang.* Suppl. I. 324 So many novelties swarm in... A large number come and go without the lexicographers so much as hearing of them... At least four-fifths of those which get any sort of toe-hold in the language originate in the United States. **1963** M. I. FINLEY *Ancient Greeks* ii. 12 Small groups of men began to migrate eastward across the Aegean to find toeholds on the Asia Minor coast. **1965** *Listener* 10 June 869/3 By Carletti's time Europe..retained only a toe-hold on the China trade. **1980** 'M. FONTEYN' *Magic of Dance* 155 A model rock about twelve inches high was dragged onto the stage by the corps de ballet. It had a special toehold into which I had to place my foot and balance for a moment on pointe. **1876** H. MELVILLE *Clarel* I. II. xix. 224 A ladder of steep stone With *toe-holes cut. **1934** R. CAMPBELL *Broken Record* 165 The stale smell of the *toe-jam of the shuffling pedestrian Charlot. **1973** *Black World* June 21 If you miss nose Picking time Then you collect Three and one half milograms Of toejam And give it to barbara's cat. **1897** MARY KINGSLEY *W. Africa* 606 He.. pointed to his distorted *toe-joints, and informed me that once he always wore boots. **1938** M. Y. VINSON *Primer Figure Skating* ix. 150 Another nice *toe jump is the 'ballet hop'. **1975** *Oxf. Compan. Sports & Games* 523/1 The split jump, a toe jump in which the skater takes off from a back inside edge, assisted by the toe-point of the free foot, half-turning in mid-air [etc.]. **1896** *Daily News* 9 Mar. 6/4 As I had said A—I was going to say B, too—and made up my mind to the *toe kissing. **1849** D. J. BROWNE *Amer. Poultry Yd.* (1855) 30 Their legs are..armed with one or more *toe-like claws. *c* **1850** *Rudim. Navig.* (Weale) 105 They are secured to the ship's side by a bolt through the *toe-link, called the *chain-bolt*. **1867** SMYTH *Sailor's Word-bk.*, *Chain-bolt*, a large bolt to secure the chains of the dead-eyes through the toe-link. **1964** J. NOEL *Figure Skating for Beginners* ix. 92 The *toe loop and double toe loop jumps are the ordinary loop and double loop jumps with the addition of toe-strikes. **1973** K. MARKANDAYA *Nowhere Man* iii. 18 Sandals on her smooth-skinned feet, with thongs and a toe-loop. **1976** *Times* 19 Jan. 9/6 Miss de Leeuw fell on her triple jump, a toe loop. **1979** M. HELLER *Illustr. Encycl. Ice Skating* 209 The toe loop is the simplest skating jump from the backward outside edge with the assistance of the free toe, a 360° turn to backward inside edge of the same foot. **1899** *Allbutt's Syst. Med.* VIII. 103 In some cases [of functional paralysis]..the *toe-movement does not occur. **1841** *Knickerbocker* XVII. 407 All the young ladies were on the very *toe-nail of curiosity. **1856** KANE *Arct. Expl.* I. 132 Bonsall was minus a big toe nail and plus a scar upon the nose. **1908** *Animal Managem.* (War Office) 238 The smith begins with the toenails first. *a* **1912** *Mod.* A chiropodist, attending to a defective toe-nail. **1900** *Yearbk. U.S. Dept. Agric.* 443 The braces are *toe-nailed in place to prevent the possibility of their becoming loosened and dropping down. **1903** *U.S. Dept. Agric., Rep. Dis. Horse* 560 The regular position, the base-wide or toe-wide position, or the base-narrow or *toe-narrow position. **1879** *Cassell's Techn. Educ.* IV. 131/1 The *toe-piece or extreme end of the body and boot [of a coach]. **1894** *Daily News* 4 May 6/4 A very enormous boot would be required to receive the *toe-plate, as well as the foot. **1898** *Ibid.* 19 Aug. 4/5 The camp.. contains everything needful down to the toeplates for the soldiers' boots. **1929** *Footwear Organiser* July 81/2 (Advt.), For unvarying high quality and thoroughly reliable service use Walker prepared *toe-puffs. **1958** *Observer* 21 Sept. 10/5 The modern toe-puff makes feeling the position of the toes impossible. **1963** T. D. RICHARDSON *Your Bk. of Skating* iii. 20 The strike must be from the edge of the blade —*and not from the point or* **toe* rakes of the skate. **1973** *Times* 3 Mar. 18/1 Towards the end of the programme..Miss Buck tripped over the toe rake of her skate. **1980** *Radio Times* 16 Feb. 33 The front of the blade has teeth (the toe-rake) to assist with spins, pivots and jumps. **1896** 'MARK TWAIN' *Diary* 30 Jan. in *Following Equator* (1897) xliv. 403 All the females among them [*sc.* Hindoos]..bejeweled with cheap and showy nose-rings, *toe-rings, leglets, and armlets. **1905** C. DAVENPORT *Jewellery* v. 87 Toe-rings were common in India, but, like all native customs of this sort, their use is practically dying out. **1948** *Sun* (Baltimore) 16 Jan. 7 (Advt.), Handy, dual-purpose umbrella that protects you top to toe! Its smart plastic handle holds a pair of excellent quality *toe-rubbers that fit any size foot. **1975** *Toronto Star* 25 Oct. H7/1 Who wouldn't develop a sense of humor in a country where some men have to wear toe rubbers half the year. **1899** *Allbutt's Syst. Med.* VII. 150 Instead of the *toe-scraping of ordinary spastic disease, the whole foot is shoved forwards in walking. **1899** QUILLER COUCH *Ship of Stars* v, A glint of daylight on the *toe-scutes of two dangling boots. **1753** CHAMBERS *Cycl. Supp.*, *Pollicipes*, the *toe-shell... They are multivalve flat shells, of a triangular figure, each being composed of several laminæ, which end in a sharp point. **1949** CHUJOY & MANCHESTER *Dance Encycl.* 480/2 *Toe-shoes are usually, but not always, made of silk and the toe of the shoe is re-enforced with a box made of several layers of strong glue between layers of material. **1979** T. GIFFORD *Hollywood Gothic* (1980) vi. 71, I played so much tennis that my sneakers actually got bloody, like toe shoes—like ballet. **1921** B. MEYER *Skating with Bror Meyer* 117 All the *toe-spins are beautiful if well executed. **1928** [see COUNTER *sb.*[4] 6]. **1960** M. V. OWEN *Fun Figure Skating* vii. 130 Back toe spins (with the free leg closing in in front) and back sit spins should be learned by all those expecting to go on to advanced free skating. **1888** *Lockwoods Dict. Mech. Engin. Terms* 147 *Foot step*, or *Footstep Bearing*, a bearing closed at its bottom end, to sustain the end thrust of a vertical shaft or spindle. It is, therefore, a bearing socket, called also a step, and *toe step. **1884** *Queen* 29 Nov. (Advt.), Superior polished wood skates with broad *toe-straps. **1910** *Cycling* 26 Jan. 66/1 The first time I ever essayed to climb Westerham I had no toe-straps, and I failed. **1911** *Blackw. Mag.* Dec. 780/1 The toe-strap of one of his rope-sandals broke. **1948** I. PROCTOR *Racing Dinghy Handling* vi. 56 At least one foot should be tucked under the canvas toe strap. **1966** [see CROSS-BAR *sb.* 1 a]. **1968** *Daily Tel.* 29 Jan. 7/8 Dean hit the buoy, and Hinton fell in when his toestrap broke. **1981** B. WEBB tr. *Schult's Sailing Dict.* 257/2 A crew can only sit out effectively if the boat has toe-straps or some other device to enable weight to be placed well outboard. **1862** *Catal. Internat. Exhib.* II. XXVII. 56 His new instep- and *toe-stretching boot tree. **1882** FLOYER *Unexpl. Baluchistan* 72 They all wore huge knitted list stockings, with a division for the *toe-string of the suāss, or grass sandals. **1929** 'SEAMARK' *Down River* iii. 46 You didn't think *I* wanted to come *toe-tapping in a shanty like this, did you? **1935** *Motion Picture* Nov. 4 (Advt.), Roaring comedy, warm romance, sensational song hits, toe-tapping dances. **1966** C. KEIL in T. Kochman *Rappin' & Stylin' Out* (1972) 87 The jazz audience now remains immobile save for some head-bobbing, toe-tapping, and finger-popping. **1975** *Broadcast* 3 Nov. 14/1 A charming presentation of..music in a toe-tapping reminiscent mood. **1966** M. LAURENCE *Jest of God* viii. 130 Her feet..slap with the rubbery sound of her royal-blue *toe-thong sandals. **1839** *Civil Eng. & Arch. Jrnl.* II. 318/2 Machinery for manufacturing shoe-heels, and *toe-tips. **1892** SYMONDS *Life Michel Angelo* (1899) I. iv. 168 His whole frame laboured to the toe-tips. **1842** *P. Parley's Ann.* III. 264 The elbowing, the *toe-treading. **1910** *Daily News* 4 Apr. 12 The practice of gibbeting one's enemies in fiction is not a form of toe-treading that one ought to encourage. *a* **1858** in Youatt *Dog* (N.Y.) iii. 138 The ball pads being well protected by the spaniel *toe-tufts. **1598** MARSTON *Sco. Villanie* III. xi. (1599) 225 He dreames of *toe-turnes: each gallant he doth meete He fronts him with a trauerse in the streete. **1894** *Pop. Sci. Monthly* June 284 All the other cats in the world excepting Australia are digitigrade (*toe-walking). **1934** WEBSTER, *Toe wall. **1947** *Sun* (Baltimore) 5 May 16/6 Concrete toe walls have been installed on both sides of the river. **1975** WINTERKORN & FANG *Foundation Engin. Handbk.* xi. 398/2 In England wide dry-stone toe walls have been used successfully to stabilize cuts in over-consolidated clay. **1901** *Scribner's Mag.* Apr. 422/1 A trotting dandy who sported ankle-boots and *toe-weights, pulled up before him. **1903** *Toe-wide [see *toe-narrow*]. **1845** J. KITTO in Eadie *Life* ix. (1861) 307 The danger of being mixed up with the *toe-writers and learned pigs of literature.

toe (təʊ), *v.* [f. prec. sb.]

1. *trans.* To furnish with a toe or toes; to make or put a new toe on (a stocking, etc.): cf. HEEL *v.*[1] 2; also with *off*, to complete (a sock, etc.) by knitting the toe and then casting off. Also *fig.*

1607–8 T. COCKS *Diary* 1 Feb. (1901) 26 Paide for heelinge & toynge a payer of iersy stockings vj d. **1660** HOWELL *Parly of Beasts* 39 They all bowed their snaky heads down to their very feet, which were toed with Scorpions. **1856** M. J. HOLMES *Homestead* 126 She..was toeing off the stocking only that morning commenced. **1870** G. M. HOPKINS *Jrnls. & Papers* (1959) 196 The next morning a heavy fall of snow. It tufted and toed the firs and yews.

2. To touch or reach with the toes; chiefly in *to toe a* or *the line, mark, scratch, crack, trig* (TRIG *sb.*[2]), to stand with the tips of one's toes exactly touching a line; to stand in a row; hence *fig.* to present oneself in readiness for a race, contest, or undertaking; also, to conform, esp. to the defined standard or platform of a party.

1813 'H. BULL-US' *Diverting Hist. John Bull & Bro. Jonathan* (ed. 2) xii. 62 He began to think it was high time to toe the mark. **1817** *Deb. Congress U.S.* 30 Jan. (1854) 792 The necessity appeared..of toeing the trig, and standing there at all hazards. **1826** W. N. GLASCOCK *Naval Sketch-Bk.* (ed. 2) I. 271 The brigades of seamen embodied to act with our troops in America, as well as in the north coast of Spain, contrived to '*ship a bagnet*' on a pinch, and to '*toe*' (for that was the phrase) 'a tolerable line'. **1833** MARRYAT *P. Simple* ix, He desired us to 'toe a line', which means to stand in a row. **1840** R. H. DANA *Bef. Mast* xxvii, The chief mate ..marked a line on the deck, brought the two boys up to it, making them 'toe the mark'. **1853** 'C. BEDE' *Verdant Green* II. iv, Toeing the scratch for business. **1862** MACLAREN *Milit. Syst. Gymnastic Exerc.* 37 There should be..a permanent mark to 'toe' at starting. **1895** *Westm. Gaz.* 15 Jan. 8/1 The phrase 'toeing the line' is very much in favour with some Liberals. **1905** *Eng. Dial. Dict.* VI. 235/2 The player may 'toe the trig', but may not overstep it. **1910** *Daily News* 30 Mar. 7 To-day they had decided to toe the line with the progressive workers of the country.

3. a. To kick with the toe. **b.** *Golf.* To strike (a ball) with the tip of the club: cf. HEEL *v.*[1] 5 c.

1865 NIXON *P. Perfume* 58 Tom toed them out. **1893** LANG in *Longm. Mag.* Apr. 651 They might toe or heel the ball.

4. *intr.* To move the toe, to tap rhythmically with the toe in dancing; *to toe and heel* (*it*), to dance.

1828 *Examiner* 630/1 A Sailor toe-and-heels it, and lock-steps and straddles. **1859** DICKENS *Haunted House* VIII. 48 There ensued such toe-and-heeling, and buckle-covering, and double-shuffling. **1882** *Punch* 27 Dec. 302/2 Fiddler, tune up merrily! Toe and heel it happily.

5. *trans. Carpentry.* To secure or join together by nails driven obliquely: see TOED *ppl. a.* 2.

6. orig. *U.S.* **a.** *intr.* To turn the toes *in* or *out.* Also *fig.*

1877 BARTLETT *Dict. Amer.* (ed. 4) 710 *To toe in*, to turn in the toes. **1894** *Vermont Agric. Rep.* XIV. 120 Avoid a horse which toes in or toes out. **1945** B. MACDONALD *Egg & I* (1946) i. 16 She toed out and had trouble with her arches. **1950** J. DEMPSEY *Championship Fighting* 70 If you toe-in slightly with the left foot, you'll get greater freedom in the whirl.

b. Of a pair of wheels: to have a slight forward convergence (***to toe in***) or divergence (***to toe out***). Also *trans.* (causatively).

1926 J. A. MOYER *Gasoline Automobiles* (ed. 2) i. 25 To facilitate steering, the front wheels of the conventional rear-wheel drive 'toe in' about $\frac{1}{4}$ to $\frac{3}{8}$ inch. **1929** NEWTON & STEEDS *Motor Vehicle* xxvii. 324 The alignment of the wheels should be checked occasionally since if the wheels should get to 'toe-out' the wear on the tyres will be excessive. **1939** *Automobile Engineer* XXIX. 40/1 In addition to a camber change, the wheel is 'toed-in' as it rises or falls in relation to the car. **1962** *Which? Car Suppl.* Oct. 139/1 Front wheel alignment [was] toeing out $\frac{1}{8}$ in. instead of toeing in $\frac{1}{8}$ in. **1976** CROUSE & ANGLIN *Pocket Automotive Dict.* 101 On a turn, the inner wheel turns, or toes out, more.

Hence **'toeing** *vbl. sb.*

1871 G. MEREDITH *H. Richmond* III. 188 Your French phrases and toeings! **1876** A. D. WHITNEY *Sights & Insights* I. 21 It is the 'toeing off' that is the satisfaction, after all, even whilst you knit the stocking. **1891** S. M. WELCH *Home Hist.* 116 That peculiar turn of the foot called 'toeing in' which in the white girl would be called 'pigeon toed'. **1904** M. E. WALLER *Wood-Carver of 'Lympus* 36 Ther ain't nothin' more ter learn but 'toein' off'. **1928** *Bureau of Standards Jrnl. Res.* (U.S.) I. 24 The common practice of cambering and toeing in of the front wheels of an automobile doubtless influences the tread wear. **1962** R. H. SMYTHE *Anat. Dog Breeding* 77 Such a dog might show no sign of toeing-in. **1970** K. BALL *Fiat 600, 600D Autobook* vii. 78/1 The final torque loading of the short arm mounting pin nut is determined after the toeing-in procedure.

toed (təʊd), *ppl. a.* [f. TOE *sb.* and *v.* + -ED.]

1. Having a toe or toes; mainly in compounds in which the first element specifies the number or kind of toes, as ***three-toed, black-toed.*** Of a stocking, Having separate divisions for the toes; of a clog, or the like, Having a (leather) toe-piece.

1611 COTGR., *Guillemot*, a certain three-towed fowle. **1757** JEFFERYS *Collect. Dresses* I. 29 The Slipper resembles a toed Clog. **1772–84** COOK *Voy.* (1790) I. 17 On the 25th this gentleman shot a black-toed gull. **1774** *Trinket* 37 In her little black bonnet, India handkerchief, and toed clogs. **1880** HAUGHTON *Phys. Geog.* vi. 281 They..possessed five-toed fore and hind feet. **1895** *Outing* (U.S.) XXVII. 200/1 That old man, upon his old-fashioned, curly-toed skates. **1910** *Daily Chron.* 15 Mar. 7/4 The stockings were toe-ed.

2. *Carpentry.* Secured or joined by nails driven obliquely; also of a nail, driven obliquely.

1877 KNIGHT *Dict. Mech.*, *Toed* (Carpentry), a brace, strut, or stay is said to be toed when it is secured by nails driven in obliquely and attaching it to the beam [etc.].

toeding, var. TOERING.

toe-in ('təʊɪn). [f. vbl. phr. *to toe in*: see TOE *v.* 6 b.] The inclination of a pair of wheels so that they are closer together in front than behind.

1929 NEWTON & STEEDS *Motor Vehicle* xxvii. 324 The distances between the marks at the front and at the rear should then be measured and the amount of toe-in determined. **1979** *Arizona Daily Star* 5 Aug. c 9/2 (Advt.), We'll set caster, camber and toe-in to manufacturer's original specifications.

toek, obs. f. *took*, pa. t. of TAKE *v.*

to-eke, to-eken: see TEKE, TEKEN.

toeless ('təʊlɪs), *a.* [-LESS.] Having no toes, esp. of footwear.

1891 BULLOCH in *Boston Mission Herald* May 208 His own feet are toeless. **1895** *Chamb. Jrnl.* XII. 628/1 Pity! pity! they cried, as they showed their fingerless hands, and toeless feet or stumps of feet. **1942** D. POWELL *Time to be Born* viii. 187 Her feet in toeless, heelless sandals. **1952** C. W. CUNNINGTON *Eng. Women's Clothing* vii. 248 (*caption*) Toeless sandal with low square heel.

‖**toenadering** ('tunadərɪŋ). *S. Afr.* [Du., f. *toe* TO *prep., conj., adv.* + *nadering* approach (f. *na* NEAR *adv.*[2]).] Rapprochement, esp. between political parties or factions.

1920 S. BLACK *Dorp* 187 All Oakley saw in any toenadering (coming together) of the bickering factions, was a trick to deprive King George and his heirs of their legitimate ownership of the country. **1947** *Forum* (Johannesburg) 3 May 3/2 The whole question of toenadering with the English-speaking section has..been.. an apple of discord in Nationalist-Afrikaner Party circles. **1957** *Cape Times* 18 June 8/7 He must draw a large Nationalist vote if he is to win those English-speaking people who want White *toenadering.* **1971** *Financial Mail* (Johannesburg) 26 Feb. 669/1 Michael Botha..revealed to shareholders..details of a deal with the Afrikaanse Pers... It certainly is a fairly ingenious bit of *toenadering.* **1973** *Star* (Johannesburg) 16 June 13, I have a feeling there is a good deal of public support for 'toenadering', particularly on the part of the unthinking and the wishful thinkers.

toe-out ('təʊaʊt). [f. vbl. phr. *to toe out*: see TOE *v.* 6 b.] The inclination of a pair of wheels so that they are closer together behind than in front.

1930 *Flight* 25 Apr. 460 Toe in or toe out of wheels should be carefully avoided. **1970** K. BALL *Fiat 600, 600D Autobook* ix. 112/2 With toe-in or toe-out correctly set, securely tighten the track rod clamps.

Toepler, var. TÖPLER.

toer, obs. variant of TOWER.

'toe-rag. [f. TOE *sb.* + RAG *sb.*[1]] **1.** A rag wrapped round the foot and worn inside a shoe, in place of a sock.

1864 J. F. MORTLOCK *Experiences of Convict* II. ix. 80 Stockings being unknown, some luxurious men wrapped round their feet a piece of old shirting, called, in language more expressive than elegant, a 'toe-rag'. **1932** F. JENNINGS *Tramping with Tramps* vi. 98 Socks are very seldom worn. Instead you get a winding of cotton rag round the ball and toes of the foot as a safeguard against blisters. Toe-rags, the tramp calls them. **1933** 'G. ORWELL' *Down & Out in Paris & London* xxvii. 197 Less than half the tramps actually bathed.., but they all washed their faces and feet, and the horrid greasy little clouts known as toe-rags which they bind round their toes.

2. A tramp or vagrant; a despicable or worthless person. Also *attrib.*

1875 T. FROST *Circus Life & Circus Celebrities* xvi. 278 *Toe rags* is another expression of contempt..used..chiefly by the lower grades of circus men, and the acrobats who stroll about the country, performing at fairs. **1903** 'T. COLLINS' *Such is Life* (1937) v. 229 'Come over to the wagon, and have a drink of tea,' says I. 'No, no,' says he, 'none of your toe-rag business.' **1912** D. H. LAWRENCE *Let.* (1962) I. 154 Remember, whatever toe-rag I may be personally, I am the person she livanted with. So you be careful. **1960** H. PINTER *Caretaker* I. 9 All them toe-rags, mate, got the manners of pigs. **1971** 'H. CALVIN' *Poison Chasers* xii. 168 Move, ya useless big toerag! **1978** M. KENYON *Deep Pocket* xiii. 165 Could she have loved this toe-rag sheikh out of the desert? **1980** J. WAINWRIGHT *Tainted Man* 171 The Law doesn't differentiate between you and the most miserable towrag [*sic*] on the face of the earth.

Hence **toe-ragger** *Austral. slang* = sense 2 above.

1896 *Truth* (Sydney) 12 Jan. (Morris), The bushie's favourite term of opprobrium 'a toe-ragger' is also probably from the Maori. Amongst whom the nastiest term of contempt was that of *tau rika rika*, or slave. **1919** V. MARSHALL *World of Living Dead* (1969) 82 Over the way a 'trial' man had tossed a 'chew' to a 'toeragger'. **1953** E. PARTRIDGE in I. Bevan *Sunburnt Country* 217 Some of the gold-diggers were tramps,..and several terms connected with them are worth recording—..*toe-ragger*, a dead-beat wanderer. **1966** G. W. TURNER *Eng. Lang. Austral. & N.Z.* vii. 144 The battler seems to have been the poorest itinerant. The toeragger was not much wealthier than the battler.

‖**toering** ('tu:rɪŋ). *S. Afr.* Also **toeding, toudang, tudong.** [Afrikaans, ad. Malay *tudong* (now *tudung*) cover, lid, sun-hat.] A wide-brimmed conical hat of straw, formerly worn by Cape Malays.

1855 J. S. MAYSON *Malays of Capetown* 10 The coloured cap, the *tudong* or hat, and the sandals of wood, formerly formed a part of the national dress; but being adopted by Mahometan converts of every class, are now regarded as badges of a common faith. **1909** *Cape* 25 June 9 There was ..the 'toeding' (sometimes spelt 'toering'), a conical, wide-brimmed hat of plaited straw. **1913** D. FAIRBRIDGE *That which hath Been* 52 The *toudang* of the old Malay coachmen is still to be seen at the Cape, but it is fast disappearing. **1944** I. D. DU PLESSIS *Cape Malays* iii. 48 The *toering* is still worn by Malay coachmen when driving the wedding group. **1965** A. GORDON-BROWN *C. W. Smith, Artist at Cape of Good Hope* iv. 18 Very small figures appear in some of the drawings... They are usually Malays in which the 'toering', or conical straw hat worn by the men, is prominent.

toe-toe, var. TOI-TOI.

toey ('təʊɪ), *a. slang* (chiefly *Austral.*). [f. TOE *sb.* + -Y[1].] Restive, anxious, touchy.

1930 *Bulletin* (Sydney) 8 Oct. 35/2 Wise Force [*sc.* a horse] was 'toey' before the race, and behaved in alarming fashion on his way to and at the post. **1961** *Coast to Coast 1959–60* 47 And the other umpire a bit toey out there at square leg. **1968** K. WEATHERLY *Roo Shooter* 91 He knew that the roos were toey, and, as they were drinking on the opposite side, they would be gone as soon as he moved a muscle. **1969** C. DRUMMOND *Odds on Death* viii. 175 The horse seemed to him a bit on the toey side. He looked down to see if saliva was dripping. **1974** *Sydney Morning Herald* 1 Jan. 2 He's that toey he's got us all nervous, too. **1981** *National Times* (Austral.) 25–31 Jan. 24/3 Dallas Jongs..had a hotel bouncer friend who could get as toey as a Roman sandal.

to-fall ('tu:fɔ:l), *sb.* Also 5 taw-, 5–6 tu-, 6 tuf-, (tul-), toy-, 7–9 too-, 9 two-, tee-, -fa, -fal, -falle. [f. TO *prep.* + FALL *v.* or *sb.* In sense 2 = MHG. *zuoval*, Ger. *zufall*, Du. *toeval*, LG. *tofal.*]

1. A supplementary building with its roof sloping up to and leaning on the wall of a main building; a lean-to; a penthouse; a shed. *Sc.* and *north. dial.*

c **1425** WYNTOUN *Cron.* IX. v. 568 Þe north ile and þe quere, Þe tofallis ii. war mad but were. **1435** *Nottingham Rec.* II. 359 A tawfall' yat standes on ye comon ground. *c* **1440** *Alphabet of Tales* 254 Þe kyngis nowte-hard..tuke provand..to his catell, & had it home vnto his tofall at he dwelte in. *Ibid.* 393 The erle..ffled with his wife in-to a wudd, and þer he hid hym in a tufall. *c* **1450** *St. Cuthbert* (Surtees) 7651 Þai made þaim tofalles To duell in vndir þe walles. **1512** *Nottingham Rec.* III. 402 The tofalle that ye chyldern lerne inne. **1518** *Burgh Rec. Edinb.* (1869) I. 178 Na tulfais be biggitt to the said wallis. **1523** in *Visit. Southwell* (Camden) 121 My tuffall of paysen the which standeth over myn oxen. **1642–3** in J. Watson *Jedburgh Abbey* (1894) 86 That ane roofe to-fa-wayis may theik vnder the eising of the body of the kirk. *a* **1670** SPALDING *Troub. Chas. I* (1851) II. 154 He tirrit the too-fallis of the haill office houssis..and careit rooff and sklait away. **1825** BROCKETT *N.C. Words, Toofall, Twofall,* or *Teefall*,..often pronounced *Touffa.* **1844** STEPHENS *Bk. Farm* II. 12 Piling them against a high wall, and thatching them like a to-fall. **1887** D. H. FLEMING *Tourist's Hand-bk. St. Andrews* 31 The slight raggle..marks the height of some to-fall.

b. *fig.* (*a*) A dependant. (*b*) A shelter.

1822 AINSLIE *Land of Burns* 209 He was a sort o' toofa' upon their kindness. **1871** WADDELL *Ps.* xviii. 2 The Lord my rock, my hainin-towir, an' my to-fa'.

†**2.** That which befalls or falls to any one; a chance, accident, casualty: cf. FALL *v.* 46. *Obs.*

1562 TURNER *Baths* 17 These that are rytche..may haue other remedies inough agaynst the forenamed tofalles. **1572** J. JONES *Bathes of Bath* III. 22 Accident is that, which the Greekes call *Symptoma*, and wee properly in English, to fall and with fall.

3. The act of falling to; ***to-fall of the day*** or ***night***, the close of day or beginning of night. *Sc.*

1749 COLLINS *Ode Superstit. Highl.* 123 For him in vain at to-fall of the day, His babes shall linger. *a* **1754** W. HAMILTON *Braes of Yarrow* xx, But ere the toofall of the night He lay a corps on the Braes of Yarrow. **1831** J. WILSON *Unimore* x. 165 Who only waits the to-fall of the night To wake the jocund sound of dance and song.

†**to-'fall**, *v. Obs.* [OE. *tofeallan*, f. TO-[2] + *feallan* to FALL; = OS. *te-fallan*, OHG. *zi-, zar-fallan.*] *intr.* To fall asunder or to pieces; to fall down, collapse; also, to fall to decay.

c **893** K. ÆLFRED *Oros.* VI. ii. §2 Þa hie æt hiora theatrum wæron.., þa hit eall tofeoll, & heora ofsloȝ xx M. **1056–66** *Inscr. Kirkdale Ch. Yorks.*, Hit wes æl tobrocan & tofalan. *c* **1205** LAY. 18867 Scullen stan walles Biuoren him to-fallen. *a* **1300** *Signa ante Judicium* 139 in *E.E.P.* (1862) 11 As heuen and erþe sold to-fal. *c* **1380** *Sir Ferumb.* 5011 Þe walle þat was so broken & to-falle. **1398** TREVISA *Barth. De P.R.* XVI. lxxiv. (Bodl. MS.), ȝif it [a stone] is not fattye it wolle alle to fall bi maistrye of druynes.

†**to-'fare**, *v. Obs.* [OE. *tofaran*, f. TO-[2] + *faran* to go, FARE; = OS. *to-faran*, OHG. *zi-, ze-, za-faran.*] *intr.* To go asunder, disperse.

a **900** *Cædmon's Gen.* 1691 Toforan þa on feower weȝas. *c* **1000** *Sax. Leechd.* I. 122 Drincan on win eal, þ attor tofærð. **14..** in *Anglia* III. 546/146 The folk..Shall tofare on every clyve.

†**to-'fere**, *v. Obs.* [OE. *toféran*, f. TO-[2] + *féran*, FERE *v.*[1]] *intr.* = prec.

c **1000** ÆLFRIC *Hom.* I. 22 Hi ða ȝeswicon þære ȝetimbrunge, and toferdon ȝeond ealne middanȝeard. *c* **1175** *Lamb. Hom.* 93 Ða apostoli siððan er þon þet heo to-ferden isetten iacob..on cristes setl [*MS.* selt].

tofet, variant of TOVET, measure of two pecks.

toff (tɒf), *sb. slang.* Also *rarely* **toft.** [Perh. a vulgar perversion of TUFT, as formerly applied to a nobleman or gentleman-commoner at Oxford.] **a.** An appellation, orig. given by the lower classes, to a person who is stylishly dressed or who has a smart appearance; a swell; hence, one of the well-to-do, a 'nob'.

1851 MAYHEW *Lond. Labour* I. 217/2. *Ibid.* (1864) II. 562/1 If it's a lady and gentleman, then we cries, 'A toff and a doll!' **1865** *Slang Dict.*, *Toft*, a showy individual, a swell. **1883** *Fortn. Rev.* Dec. 852 The poets who are here are tremendous proud toffs. **1900** UPWARD *Eben. Lobb* 130 Nonsense, man,..why, in these days a jockey is no end of a toff. **1901** *Essex Weekly News* 29 Mar. 2/1 She..declared that tramps were treated like toffs at Stanway Workhouse.

b. Sometimes applied in compliment to a person who behaves 'handsomely'; a 'brick'.

1898 *Brit. Weekly* 27 Jan. 306/2 A Paisley bailie let off a man easier than the culprit expected, and was addressed, 'Thank you, sir, you're an old toff'. This was meant for a compliment. **1906** *Daily Chron.* 25 May 4/7 One of the witnesses..spoke of a generous employer as 'a regular toff'. 'Toff' is perhaps the highest compliment, or the bitterest sneer, according to the tone, that a man who does not make any pretence to magnificence can aim at a man who does.

Hence **'toffish, 'toffy** *adjs.*, like or characteristic of a 'toff', stylish; also **'toffishness**, behaviour characteristic of a 'toff'.

1873 J. GREENWOOD *In Strange Company* 43 Thick slices, bear in mind: anything under an inch thick would be regarded with contempt by the bony young barrow-man, and perhaps with an uncomfortable suspicion that you have designs to inveigle him into the detestable ways of gentility. He calls it 'toffishness'. *Ibid.*, To affect thin bread and butter is undoubtedly 'toffish'. *c* **1876** J. ALBERY *Dramatic Wks.* (1939) II. 105 But only because his toffishness wexes me. **1898** *Westm. Gaz.* 13 Jan. 4/2 He wore a 'toffish' side pocket jacket, which fitted him like a glove. **1901** J. K. JEROME *Obs. Henry* 31 Toffy enough she looked in her diamonds and furs.

toff (tɒf), *v. slang.* [f. TOFF *sb.*] *trans.* and *refl.* To dress *up* like a 'toff'.

1914 D. H. LAWRENCE *Widowing of Mrs. Holroyd* I. i. 5 He'd got a game on somewhere—toffed himself up to the nines, and skedaddled off as brisk as a turkey-cock. **1928** *East End Star* Dec. 2/2 Notice the perfect stillness when the 'lovely lidy all toffed up' sings. **1932** L. GOLDING *Magnolia Street* II. ii. 298 The fellows come in [to a hair-dressing saloon] when they're on leave. They want to get toffed up for their girls.

toffee ('tɒfɪ), *sb.* and *a.* Also **toffy**. [Of uncertain origin: app. orig. dialectal, and sometimes spelt *tuffy*, *toughy*, as if named from its toughness; but the earlier form is the northern TAFFY, q.v.]

A. *sb.* **1. a.** A sweet-meat made from sugar or treacle, butter, and sometimes a little flour, boiled together; often mixed with bruised nuts, as ***almond*** or ***walnut toffee***.

a **1825** FORBY *Voc. E. Anglia, Toughy*, a coarse sweetmeat, composed of brown sugar and treacle; named from its toughness, though perhaps it should be spelled *tuffy*, and considered as another form of taffy, described in Wilbraham's *Cheshire Dialect* [1817] as compounded of the same ingredients. **1825** MRS. CAMERON *Seeds Greediness* in *Houlston Tracts* I. No. 22. 2 Some shining sticky stuff, which in some countries children call tuffy. **1828** *Craven Gloss.* s.v., 'To join for toffy', to club for making toffy, a custom still very frequent amongst young persons. **1862** DICKENS *Lett.* 28 Jan., I am going to bring the boys some toffee. **1877** BLACK *Green Past.* ii, Is it sixpence you want to buy toffy with?

b. *attrib.* and *Comb.*

1857 HUGHES *Tom Brown* I. iii, It being only a step to the toffy shop. **1896** *Westm. Gaz.* 30 May 2/1 The effect..that a toffee drop has on a churchwarden when he finds it in the bag.

c. A small, shaped piece of toffee, usu. sold wrapped.

1938 G. GREENE *Brighton Rock* I. iii. 52 'Have a toffee.' 'It's bad for the figure.' **1984** W. GARNER *Rats' Alley* x. 195 He..bought..a box of her favourite toffees from the shop next door.

2. Phr. ***not to be able*** (to do a thing) ***for toffee***: to be incompetent at it. *colloq.*

1914 *Illustr. London News* 12 Sept. 380/1 Their opponents cannot 'shoot for nuts' (or 'for toffee', as one Tommy more expressly put it). **1932** D. L. SAYERS *Have his Carcase* xii. 145 The Morgan wouldn't start, not for toffee. **1951** M. KENNEDY *Lucy Carmichael* II. 76 Those dreary girls you get in every Drama School who can't act for toffee. **1977** C. MCCULLOUGH *Thorn Birds* xiii. 325 You can't kiss for toffee. You open your mouth too wide.

3. Nonsense, rubbish.

a **1930** D. H. LAWRENCE *Phoenix* (1936) 588 The eternal flame of the high ideal is all my-eye. It's all toffee, my dear sirs. **1957** P. WILDEBLOOD *Main Chance* 220 Working-class to the backbone, just like us... And if he's been filling you up with a lot of toffee to the contrary, more fool you. **1970** M. TRIPP *Man without Friends* vii. 77 'It was all a lot of toffee,' I said, 'as Hardacre very well knows.'

4. A medium shade of brown. Cf. sense B below.

1960 *Woman's Own* 19 Mar. 42/2 In stone, toffee, scarlet, green. **1976** *Honolulu Star-Bull.* 21 Dec. A-12 (Advt.), In toffee, green or blue... Jacket with stitched back-belt.

5. ***toffee-coloured***, ***-like*** adjs.; **toffee apple**, (*a*) an apple coated with toffee and mounted on a stick; (*b*) *slang*, a bomb of similar shape that is fired from a trench mortar; **toffee-brown** = sense 4 above; **toffee hammer**, a miniature hammer such as may be used to break pieces of toffee; **toffee-nose** *slang*, a snob or supercilious person; also *attrib.*; **toffee-nosed** *a. slang*, snobbish, supercilious; **toffee paper**, a small piece of paper in which a toffee is wrapped.

1917 *B.E.F. Times* 25 Dec. f. 3/2 The planting of Toffee-apples on the border of your neighbour's allotment will seriously interfere with the ripening of his gooseberries. **1930** BROPHY & PARTRIDGE *Songs & Slang 1914–18* 171 Toffee Apples.—Trench mortar bombs, so called from the haft, like the skewer in a toffee-apple. **1937** 'R. CROMPTON' *William—the Showman* vi. 127 A little girl was leaning against the wall, eating a toffee-apple on a stick. **1957** *Times* 5 Sept. 11/4 We must kill the idea that Weymouth is just a candy-floss, toffee-apple resort. **1975** P. FUSSELL *Gt. War & Mod. Memory* (1977) ix. 313 Everything from shovels,..and rolls of barbed wire, to..the perverse toffee-apple. **1976** *Milton Keynes Express* 16 July 8/2 Toffee apples and ice-cream, sweets and raffles, pony rides and competitions—these were all part of the scene. **1961** M. KELLY *Spoilt Kill* I. 30 Creased forehead, receding toffee-brown hair. **1978** R. RENDELL *Sleeping Life* xvi. 129 Malina..wore jeans, of toffee-brown silk. **1948** M. ALLINGHAM *More Work for Undertaker* xiii. 167 The clear toffee-coloured pavements. **1979** D. MACKENZIE *Raven settles Score* 5 His long toffee-coloured hair. **1958** B. BEHAN *Borstal Boy* III. 230, I sometimes saw a fellow wearing overalls and walking round ..carrying brushes and paint and sometimes glazing tools; hacking knife, glazing knife, toffee hammer,..and rule. **1978** D. BLOODWORTH *Crosstalk* vii. 54 Toby jugs and toffee hammers. **1919** Toffee-like [see RAFT *v.*[1] 5]. **1944** K. DOUGLAS *Alamein to Zem Zem* (1946) 78 A tin of treacle, which had been well heated, contained a delicious black toffee-like substance. **1943** HUNT & PRINGLE *Service Slang* 67 *Toffee-nose*, another of the expressions chiefly heard amongst the W.A.A.F. This refers to a snob or someone who considers herself 'superior'. It is very apt since it implies that the nose is kept high to prevent it coming into contact with the mouth. **1958** *Woman* 12 Apr. 69/4 People thought I was a bit of a toffee-nose for the first few months because I didn't speak to them. **1962** *John o' London's* 29 Nov. 506/3 Christian was a gentleman, hence Mr. Brando's toffee-nose accent. **1974** Toffee-nose [see *Jew boy* s.v. JEW *sb.* 3 a]. **1925** FRASER & GIBBONS *Soldier & Sailor Words* 287 *Toffee-nosed*, stuck up. **1928** T. E. LAWRENCE *Let.* 20 Jan. (1938) 568 A premature 'life' will do more to disgust the select and superior people (the R.A.F. call them the 'toffee-nosed') than anything. **1960** K. AMIS *Take a Girl like You* iv. 60 She did not want any more chat, but could not think how to say so without running the risk of sounding both stagey and toffee-nosed. **1978** *Radio Times* 28 Jan.–3 Feb. 17/2 Let Elkan Allan and the rest of the toffee-nosed critics sneer; I shall be watching *Big Jim McLain* this Sunday and so, I am sure, will a lot of other people. **1958** G. BELLAIRS *Corpse at Carnival* i. 9 A little Manx cat..chasing a piece of toffee-paper. **1983** R. SUTCLIFF *Blue Remembered Hills* xii. 91 They ..flipped screwed-up toffee papers onto the heads of the orchestra.

B. *adj.* Toffee-coloured; medium brown. Cf. sense A. 4 above.

1962 J. D. MACDONALD *Key to Suite* (1968) vii. 116 A very pretty slender girl with toffee hair and dark-blue eyes. **1971** *Homes & Gardens* Aug. 57/1 The dining chairs are covered in a toffee and black houndstooth check. **1975** G. HOWELL *In Vogue* 259/2 (*caption*) A toffee and gold mesh sweater.

† **to-fleet**, *v. Obs.* [OE. *tofléotan*, f. TO-[2] + *fléotan*, FLEET *v.*[1]; = OHG. *zifliozan* 'defluere', to melt, MHG. *zervliezen*.] *intr.* To float away; to be carried away by or as by water.

a **1122** *O.E. Chron.* an. 1097, þa brycȝe þe forneah eall to flotan wæs. *a* **1225** *Ancr. R.* 72 Forstoppeð ouwer þouhtes ..þ heo climben & hien touward heouene, & nout..to uleoten ȝeond te world. *Ibid.* 74–6 Vor mid te fleotinde word, to fleoteð þe heorte.

† **'to-flight.** *Obs. rare.* [f. TO-[1] + FLIGHT *sb.*[2]: so OHG., MHG. *zuofluht*, Ger. *zuflucht*, Du. *toevlucht* refuge, shelter, resource.] A shelter, refuge.

a **1300** *E.E. Psalter* xvii[i]. 1 [2] Laverd mi festnes ai in nede, And mi to-flight [*v.r.* tofliht] þat es swa, And mi leser oute of wa.

† **to-fly**, *v. Obs.* Forms: see FLY *v.*[1] [OE. *tofléoȝan*, f. TO-[2] + *fléoȝan* FLY *v.*[1]; = OHG. *zefliogan*, MHG. *zevliegen*.] *intr.* To fly in different directions, to be dispersed in flight; also, to fly to pieces, be shattered.

c **1000** *Sax. Leechd.* I. 188 Sona hyt toflyð [*v.r.* flihð]. *Ibid.* III. 34 Woden..sloh ða þa næddran þæt heo on viiii to-fleah. *c* **1205** LAY. 28668 þa cnihtes alle..þa weoren wide to-floȝen. **13..** *Cast. Love* (Halliw.) 1559 The stones woll breke and all to-flyn. **1387** TREVISA *Higden* (Rolls) VII. 35 þe giestes and þe bemes of þe soler al to fligh, and þe soler fil doun.

† **to'fore**, *prep.*, *adv.*, and *conj. Obs.* Forms: α. 1–2 **tóforan**, (1 **-on**), 2–3 **toforen**, 3–5 **to foren**, 4–6 **toforn(e**, 4–7 **to forn(e**. β. 3 **to vore**, 3–4 **tovore**, 3–6 **to for**, (3 **te for**), 3–7 **to fore**, 4–6 **tofor**, 4–7 **tofore**, (5 **toffore**), 6 *Sc.* **to-foir**. γ. *Sc.* 5 **to forowe**, **toforowe**, 6 **to forrow**. [OE. *tóforan*, f. TO *prep.* + *foran* adv., deriv. of OTeut. **fora* fore, for: see BEFORE, also AFORE, ATFORE, HERETOFORE. Cognate with OFris. *tô-fora*, OS. *te foran*, MHG. *zevor*, *zuovor*, *-vorn*, Ger. *zuvor*.]

A. *prep.*

1. Of motion: To before, to the front of; of position: In front of; = BEFORE B. 2.

a **900** tr. *Bæda's Hist.* III. xii. [xiv.] (1890) 196 Se cyning.. stop ofostlice toforan [ðam] biscope, & feoll to his fotum. *c* **1000** *Ags. Gosp.* Luke x. 8 Etað þæt eow toforan aset ys. *c* **1275** LAY. 31548 þo stot him vp Penda: To-vore þan heȝe kinge. *c* **1300** *Beket* 2001 That bred..that tofore him lay. *a* **1325** *Prose Psalter* liii. [liv.] 3 [Thei] ne sett nouȝt God to-forn her syȝt. *c* **1489** CAXTON *Sonnes of Aymon* xiv. 346 He cast hym deed to fore his fete. *a* **1547** SURREY *Æneid* IV. 264 Tofore thaltars, in presence of the Gods.

b. Into or in the presence of; in the sight or cognizance of; = BEFORE B. 3.

c **1000** *Ags. Gosp.* Matt. xxv. 32 Ealle þeoda beoþ toforan hym ȝegaderude. **10..** *Leg. Rood* (1871) 11/4 þæt hio rædlice coman toforan þare mære cwenan þa hio beforan hire stodan. *c* **1070** *O.E. Chron.* an. 1070 (Parker MS.), Se arcebiscop..þæt ylce ȝefæstnode toforan þam papan Alexandre. *c* **1205** LAY. 14071 þan kinge he eode to-foren. **1340** *Ayenb* 218 þe ilke comþ to-uore god mid ydele honden. **1387** TREVISA *Higden* (Rolls) V. 347 He knowleched his trespas openliche tofore þe bisshop and al þe peple. **1493** *Festivall* (W. de W. 1515) 14 b, Anone tofore them he made a blynde man to se. **1600** FAIRFAX *Tasso* I. xxxv, All tofore their chieftaine mustred beene.

c. ***tofore God***: in the sight of God; at the tribunal of God; hence as an asseveration (also ***God tofore***), by God: cf. BEFORE B. 3 b, 4, 5.

c **1374** CHAUCER *Troylus* III. 800 (849) So shal I do to morw I-wis..And god to-forn. **1377** LANGL. *P. Pl.* B. v. 457 And made avowe to-fore god for his foule sleuthe. *a* **1450** MYRC *Par. Pr.* 213 That ys feyre to-fore god. *a* **1500** *Chaucer's Dreme* 1281 Madame..god tofore, ye shul be there.

2. Of position in motion: In advance of, ahead of: = BEFORE B. 1. (In quot. 1297 with a pursuer as object; cf. BEFORE B. 1 c.)

c **1000** *Ags. Gosp.* Luke i. 17 He gæð toforan him on gaste and Elias mihte. *c* **1250** *Old Kentish Serm.* in *O.E. Misc.* 26 Swo kam si sterre þet yede to-for hem in-to ierusalem. **1297** R. GLOUC. (Rolls) 2202 Ȝe ne conne bote fle Ase ssep to vore wolues. *a* **1450** *Knt. de la Tour* (1906) 63, .ij. yonge women ..wolde haue hasted hem tofore her felawes. **1600** FAIRFAX *Tasso* I. xxxvii, Their wonted ensigne, they tofore them bring.

3. Of time: Previously to, earlier than; = BEFORE B. 7–9.

a **1000** in Cockayne *Narrat.* (1861) 16 Hit wæs to foran dæȝes. *c* **1025** *O.E. Chron.* an. 1013, On þam ilcan ȝeare to foran þam monðe Augustus. *c* **1275** *Woman of Samaria* 5 in *O.E. Misc.* 84 A lutel te-for þe tyme. **1387** TREVISA *Higden* (Rolls) I. 165 Carthago was i-buld þre score ȝere and twelue to fore þe citee of Rome. **1440** in *Wars Eng. in France* (1864) II. 455 Not longe tyme tofore his deth. **1577–87** HOLINSHED *Scott. Chron.* (1805) II. 198 Rather..than we did tofore his fathers invasion.

4. Of rank, order, or preference: In precedence of or preference to; beyond, more than; rather than; = BEFORE B. 10, 11.

c **888** K. ÆLFRED *Boeth.* Prayer (at end), þæt ic mæȝe þe inweardlice lufian toforon eallum þingum. *c* **1000** ÆLFRIC *Deut.* vii. 14 Ðe beoþ ȝebletsod toforan eallum oþrum mannum. *c* **1000** —— *Hom.* I. 208 Assa is stunt nyten..and toforan oðrum nytenum unȝesceadwis. *c* **1175** *Lamb. Hom.* 117 He is on heuene on his kine setle to-foran oðer mennen. *a* **1272** *A Luue Ron* 155 in *O.E. Misc.* 98 Nys non betere vnder heouene grunde. He is to-fore alle oþre i-coren. *a* **1325** *Prose Psalter* xliv. [xlv.] 3 Fair artou..in fourme to-fore mennes sones. **14..** *Chaucer's Pars. T.* ¶677 (Harl. MS.) Thus is he an auerous man þat loueth his tresor toforn god.

b. Of serial order: Before, preceding.

1387 TREVISA *Higden* (Rolls) III. 61 þe peple putte hir owne names to fore þe names of hir felawes.

5. Besides, over and above. *rare.* (Cf. B. 5.)

c **1000** ÆLFRIC *Hom.* II. 584 Salomon eac forȝeaf þære cwene swa hwæs swa heo ȝyrnde æt him, toforan ðære cynelican lace ðe he hire ȝeaf.

B. *adv.* (not in OE.).

1. Of time: Previously, beforehand, earlier; heretofore, in the past; = BEFORE A. 5.

c **1175** *Lamb. Hom.* 121 Al swa þet writ seide bi him muchel to-foran. **1258** *Proclam. Hen. III*, þurȝ þe besiȝte of þan to foren iseide redesmen. **1340** *Ayenb.* 7 He deþ aye þe heste of god to uore yzed. *c* **1350** *Will. Palerne* 142 Ac his witt welt he after, as wel as to fore. *c* **1400** *Lanfranc's Cirurg.* 110 þat I have told to forn. **1423** JAS. I *Kingis Q.* ii, New partit out of slepe a lyte tofore. *Ibid.* xxiii, The way we tuke, the tyme I tald to-forowe [*rimes* morowe, borowe]. *a* **1425** *Cursor M.* 3010 (Trin.) Ysaac hir son..þat was longe bihet to forn [*earlier MSS.* biforn, be-forne]. **1481** CAXTON *Reynard* xxxiv. (Arb.) 100, I am more hongry now than I was to fore. **1546** *Supplic. of Poore Commons* (E.E.T.S.) 61 Not many yeres tofore. **1649** G. DANIEL *Trinarch., Hen. V* c, Mortimer, Earle of March, in the right Line Discendent, and to fore declared Heire.

2. Of position: In front; = BEFORE A. 2.

13.. *Guy Warw.* (A.) 1871 Sadok toforn haþ him smete Of his scheld a quarter wiþ gret hete. *c* **1400** *Lanfranc's Cirurg.* 105 þe senewis tofore ben drawe togidere. **14..** *Beryn* 155 It is a spere, yf thowe canst se, with a prik tofore.

3. Of motion: In advance, ahead; = BEFORE A. 1.

c **1330** *Arth. & Merl.* 1365 Now wendeþ to forn, on of ȝou, & tel anon þe king. **1426** LYDG. *De Guil. Pilgr.* 24570 Send hem toforne, on thy massage. **1470–85** MALORY *Arthur* II. ix. 85, xx of hem rode to fore to warne the lady. **1513** DOUGLAS *Æneis* I. Prol. 419 Saying he followit Virgillis lantern to forne, Quhen Eneas to Dido was forsworne.

4. Of rank: In precedence; cf. BEFORE A. 4.

c **1440** *Gesta Rom.* xci. 416 (Add. MS.) þe proude man wil all wey be sette aboue and be-fore oþer, he wil all way be putte tofore in Euery place. **1481** CAXTON *Godeffroy* cxci. 280 Without doubte the spyrituel thynges be more digne and worthy than the temporall. Therfore..the moost hye thynges ought to goo to fore.

5. Beforehand; in hand for the future; left over. Cf. mod.Sc. *to the fore*.

1597 *Trials for Witchcraft* in *Spalding Misc.* (1841) I. 95 Hir and hir guidman..suld newir haue frie geir tofoir.

C. *conj.* Of time: = BEFORE C. 1. **a.** with *that*: cf. BEFORE C. 1 a.

a **1325** *Prose Psalter* lxxxix. [xc.] 2 To-fore þat þe mounteins were made. **1388** WYCLIF *Matt.* x. 23 To fore that mannus sone come. **1484** CAXTON *Curial* 12 Tofore that thou hast ony offyces.

b. *simply*: cf. BEFORE C. 1 b.

1464 *Rolls of Parlt.* V. 563/2 Tofore it passe out of any of the seid Townes. **1477** SIR J. PASTON in *P. Lett.* III. 187 Iff I had hadde it toffore he wente. **1560** DAUS tr. *Sleidane's Comm.* 9 So cannot he condemne him for an Heretike tofore he be detected of errour.

c. ***tofore or*** (= ere): cf. BEFORE C. 1 c.

c **1440** LYDG. *Hors, Shepe & G.* 5 (Lamb. MS.) On shreffe thursday toforne or he was dede! **1474** CAXTON *Chesse* III. i, Tofore or Adam synned. **1485** —— *Paris & V.* (1868) 30 Alwaye tofore or he wente to hys bedde.

D. *Comb.*: **toforegoing** *a.*, foregoing, preceding, antecedent; **toforehand** *adv.*, beforehand, previously; **toforesaid** *a.*, previously mentioned, aforesaid; **toforetime** *adv.*, previously, aforetime.

1387–8 T. USK *Test. Love* III. iii. (Skeat) l. 180 That oon is *toforgoing necessite, whiche maketh thing to be. *Ibid.* viii. 30 Onely through grace tofornegooyng. **1387** TREVISA *Higden* (Rolls) III. 147 I-wrete of hym an hondred ȝere and twenty ȝere *to forehonde. *Ibid.* VI. 175 Seint Aldelyn was to forehonde abbot of Malteby, þat is Malmesbury. **1387–8** T. USK *Test. Love* I. vi. (Skeat) l. 154 Of errours coming herafter, men may lightly to forne hande puruaye remedye. *c* **1430** *Syr Gener.* (Roxb.) 3681 As ye haue herd tofore hond. **1258** *To foren iseide [see B. 1]. **1387–8** T. USK *Test. Love* III. iv. (Skeat) l. 261 If thou have knowing of these to-forn-said thinges. **1444** *Rolls of Parlt.* V. 121/2 Founden by an enquerre bi the Baillifs toforeseid. *c* **1400** *Three Kings Cologne* 82 (Cambr. MS.) þe sterre þat *tofore-tyme ȝede a-fore hem. *c* **1477** CAXTON *Jason* 46 Him semed that he hadde seen them tofore tyme.

Tofranil ('tɒfrənɪl). *Pharm.* [Of unknown origin.] A proprietary name for the drug imipramine.

1958 *Trade Marks Jrnl.* 4 June 564/2 *Tofranil*... Pharmaceutical preparations for human and veterinary use. .. J. R. Geigy..Basle, Switzerland. **1958** *Official Gaz.* (U.S. Patent Office) 16 Sept. TM 91/2 Geigy Chemical Corporation, Ardsley, N.Y... *Tofranil* for antidepressants. **1963**, **1965** [see IMIPRAMINE]. **1979** *Daily Tel.* 27 Nov. 12/7 Prescriptions for the brand leaders Tofranil and Tryptizol accounted for an estimated £5 million.

†to-fret, *v. Obs.* [ME. *tofreten*, f. TO-[2] + *freten* FRET *v.*[1]; cf. Ger. *zerfressen*.] *trans.* To gnaw, devour, consume.

a **1225** *Ancr. R.* 202 þes laste bore hweolp..to-cheoweð & to-uret Godes milde milce. *c* **1412** HOCCLEVE *De Reg. Princ.* 3226 Thy disese is lesse, Ffalle in þe daunger of lambes humblesse, Than he [who is] with cruel wolues al to-frete. *a* **1529** SKELTON *Garl. Laurel* 1450 This delycate dasy.. With frowarde frostis, alas, was all to-fret.

to-fro ('tuːˈfrəʊ), *a.*, *adv.*, and *sb. poet.* [f. TO AND FRO *phr.*] **A.** *adj.* = TO AND FRO *adj. phr.*

1879 G. M. HOPKINS *Poems* (1967) 81 To-fro tender trambeams truckle at the eye. **1936** R. CAMPBELL *Mithraic Emblems* 83 How shrill the long hosannahs of despair With which those to-fro scolopendras bear, Statesmen to conferences, troops to war. **1952** C. DAY LEWIS tr. *Virgil's Aeneid* XI. 253 It was like the to-fro rhythm of the sea, when a wave runs forward..then rapidly draws away. **1983** T. HUGHES in *Listener* 13 Jan. 21/1 The silent to-fro hurrying of nurses, The bowed stillness of surgeons.

B. *adv.* = TO AND FRO *adv. phr.* I. *rare.*

1920 BLUNDEN *Waggoner* 44 A sharp snatch, swirling to-fro of the line.

C. *sb.* = TO AND FRO *sb. phr.* I. *rare.*

1937 C. DAY LEWIS *Starting Point* 200 The rhythmic tap and to-fro of the white ball. **1960** —— *Buried Day* viii. 157 Almost from the start I seem to have been aware of a fidgetiness, and a constant to-fro made up of many individual, desultory movements.

†to-frush, *v. Obs.* [ME. *to-frusche(n*, f. TO-[2] + *frusch(e* FRUSH *v.* (from French).] *trans.* To smash or break to pieces; also, to drive violently *into* something as with a blow or blows.

c **1300** *Havelok* 1993 Was non..þat he ne dede alto-cruhsse, And alto-shiuere, and alto-frusshe. *a* **1330** *Syr Degarre* 381 Ac he..with his bat leid up an, And al to frusst him ech a bon. **1375** BARBOUR *Bruce* VIII. 303 Speris þat to-fruschyt war. *c* **1400** tr. *Secreta Secret., Gov. Lordsh.* 106 Here y dwelle all to-ffrushyd, & y haue gret myster of pytee. **1513** DOUGLAS *Æneis* II. viii. [vii.] 40 Hewit, hackit, smate doun, and all to fruschit. **1532** MORE *Confut. Tindale* Wks. 717/2 Christ shall come down..and all to frush & to breke those earthlye wretched heretikes like a sort of earthen pottes. **1586** WARNER *Alb. Eng.* II. xii. (1589) 51 Who, lying all to frusshed thus, the sonne of Ioue did bring His cruell Iades.

toft[1] (tɒft). Also 5–7 tofte, (7 tuft), 8–9 *Sc. dial.* **taft.** [Late OE. *toft*, a. ON. *topt*, *tupt*, later *toft*, *tuft* (Norw. *toft*, *tuft*, *tyft* 'ground attached to a house' (Aasen), early and dial. Swed. *toft*, Da. *toft*, *tofte*), existing beside and commonly identified with ON. *tomt*, OSwed. *tompt* (Vigfusson), Norw. *tomt* (Aasen), Swed. *tomt*, Da. *tomt* 'toft'; both forms:—OTeut. **tumft-*, **tumf(e)t-*, with which cf. Gr. *δά-πεδον*:—**dm-pedo-m*, a level surface, lit. 'a site for building'.]

1. Originally, a homestead, the site of a house and its out-buildings; a house site. Often in the expression ***toft and croft***, denoting the whole holding, consisting of the homestead and attached piece of arable land.

1001 in Kemble *Cod. Dipl.* III. 317 Healf þæt land æt Suðham, innur and uttur, on tofte and on crofte. *a* **1100** in *Sax. Leechd.* III. 286 An ic agnian wille to agenre ahte ðæt ðæt ic hæbbe, & næfre ðæt yntan, ne plot ne ploh, ne turf ne toft, ne furh ne fotmæl, ne land ne læse, ne fersc ne mersc, ne ruh ne rum. **12..** (orig. *a* **1000**) *Charter of Siflæd* in Birch *Cart. Sax.* III. 217 And ic [an] mine landsethlen here toftes to owen aihte and alle mine men fre. **1290** *Rolls of Parlt.* I. 62/1 Johanna..petit dotem..de VIII to Toftis et VIII to Bavatis terre. **1348** *Ibid.* II. 205/1 Un toft & cink acres de terre. **14..** *Customs of Malton* in *Surtees Misc.* (1888) 63 For every tofte þ[t] is nott beldydd j d. **1473** *Rental Bk. Cupar-Angus* (1879) I. 165 Ilke man sal kepe his pairt of his malyn and his toft that his nichtbur be nocht injuryt. **1592** WEST *Symbol.* II. *Fines* §55 A Toft is the place wherein a mesuage hath stand. **1607** NORDEN *Surv. Dial.* v. 207, I haue.. obserued..that many croftes, toftes, pightes, pingles, and other small quillits of land, about farme houses, and Tenements, are suffred to lie together idle. **1683** *Lond. Gaz.* No. 1800/4 A Tuft of Ground..by Thames-Street, will be disposed of by Lease for 61 years, by the Committee for Letting the City Lands. **1760** LD. MANSFIELD in *Burrow's Rep.* (1766) II. 1064 The Owner of a House may, if he pleases, pull it quite down, and convert it into a Toft. **1790** A. WILSON *To Eben. Picken* Poet. Wks. (1846) 107 And scores o' times, in kintra tafts, They've gart the fouk maist rive their chafts. **1809** BAWDWEN *Domesday Bk.* 614 But the riding say that he has only 9½ acres and one toft, the soke of which belongs to the King's Manor of Gayton. **1818** HALLAM *Mid. Ages* ix. I. (1819) III. 366 A house with its stables and farm-buildings, surrounded by a hedge or inclosure, was called a court, or..a curtilage; the toft or homestead of a more genuine English dialect. **1870** LADY VERNEY *Lettice Lisle* xiii. 146, I might ha' been a comfortable man by this; and now I'm like to have neither toft nor croft. **1955** *Times* 19 Aug. 8/5 Even a layman, with guidance, can recognize the signs pointing to medieval occupation: the hollow said to be the main street; the adjoining humps of the house enclosures, each with its 'toft' (garden) and croft, or small holding. **1965** AUDEN *About House* (1966) 17 A toft-and-croft Where I needn't, ever, be at home *to* Those I am not at home *with*.

2. Apparently including the croft, or applied to a field or piece of land larger than the site of a house.

c **1440** *Promp. Parv.* 459/1 Toft, *campus*. *c* **1450** *Godstow Reg.* 315, iij. mesis liyng to-gedir..with the toftis liyng therto..; also with two toftis I-closed in, of the which one strecchith hit-self in lengthe of the gardeyn of the seid Symond, and another in lengthe of the gardeyn of the said abbesse and Couent, in þe forsaid towne of karsynton. **1549** *Reg. Mag. Sig. Scot.* 82/2 Terras de Drumfyne nuncupatas the Toftis of Drumfyne. **1598** KITCHIN *Courts Leet* (1675) 151 One Tenement with a Toft adjoining. **1831** LANDOR *Fra Rupert* II. i, Though the parks and groves and tofts around, ..Open would be to her.

3. An eminence, knoll, or hillock in a flat region; esp. one suitable for the site of a house or tower. Cf. quot. 1863. Now *local.*

1362 LANGL. *P. Pl.* A. Prol. 14, I sauh a Tour on A Toft triȝely I-maket; A Deop Dale bi-neoþe. **1387** TREVISA *Higden* (Rolls) VII. 359 In þe myddel of þat playn was a litel toft as it were an hille [*colliculus turgescebat*]. **1558** PHAER *Æneid* VII. U iv, They, from their Fescen hilles, and from Faliscus equall toftes. **1863** BARING-GOULD *Iceland* xxii. 368 A farm named Tratharholt, crowning a toft which rises out of green meads and almost impossible swamps. **1887** FENN *Dick o' Fens* (1888) 23 Right up on a high toft with the river on one side and the fens for miles on the other.

†4. 'A small grove of trees' (E.D.D.). *dial.* (or ? error in Kersey's Phillips.) *Obs.*

1706 PHILLIPS (ed. Kersey), *Toft*..also a Grove of Trees. **1726** *Dict. Rust.* (ed. 3), *Toft*, a Grove of trees.

5. *attrib.* and *Comb.*, as ***toft field***, ***toftstead***; **toftman**, the owner or occupier of a toft.

1763 *Museum Rust.* I. 35 The soil of your upper *toft field. **1826** SCOTT *Jrnl.* 16 Mar., I shall have on the toft field a gallant show of extensive woodland. **12..** *Prior. Lewens.* 18 (Cowell's Interpr. 1684) *Toftmanni similiter operabantur. **1706** PHILLIPS (ed. Kersey), *Toft-man*, the Owner of a Toft. **1524** *Test. Ebor.* (Surtees) V. 180 An other *toftstede which I/haue in Lownd. **1773** *Burstwick Inclos. Act* 6 Gardens, orchards, toftsteads, crofts. **1839** STONEHOUSE *Axholme* 35 To the owners of ancient messuages, cottages, tofts, and toftsteads.

Toft[2] (tɒft). The surname of a Staffordshire family used *attrib.* to designate (a style of) lead-glazed slipware made there in the late-seventeenth cent., some of the best examples of which bear the name of Thomas Toft (d. 1689) or another Toft, usu. regarded as the maker of the piece.

1878 L. JEWITT *Ceramic Art of Gt. Brit.* I. iv. 103 Another Toft dish..bears a female figure..and the name Ralphoft, or Ralph Toft, the h and t being apparently conjoined. **1900** F. LITCHFIELD *Pottery & Porcelain* ii. 26 Those buff-coloured dishes which we now recognise as 'Toft ware'. **1957** MANKOWITZ & HAGGAR *Conc. Encycl. Eng. Pottery & Porcelain* 222/2 The name [of Ralph Toft] occurs on many typical large Toft-style dishes. **1961** L. G. G. RAMSEY *Connoisseur New Guide Antique Eng. Pottery* 20 Signed Toft pieces are known dated 1671 and 1674. **1975** *Country Life* 26 June (Suppl.) 56/1 Christie's... Fine English Porcelain and Pottery... Toft dated slipware bragget-pot.

toft, variant of *tought*, obs. form of TAUT *a.*

tofu ('təʊfuː). [a. Jap. *tōfu*, ad. Chinese *dòufu*, f. *dòu* beans + *fǔ* rotten.] A curd made in Japan and China from mashed soya beans; bean curd.

1880 *Trans. Asiatic Soc. Japan* VIII. 399 *Tôfu* is made by pounding the soy beans after soaking in water. **1905** *Bull. U.S. Dept. Agric.* CLIX. 46 The larger part of the leguminous food in the Japanese diet consists of the preparations of soy beans, such as miso, shoyu and tofu. **1934** BLUNDEN *Mind's Eye* 109 Two hawks have raided the *tofu*. **1936** K. TEZUKA *Jap. Food* 28 Tōfu (bean-curd) is made by soaking soy beans in water, mashing them, straining the mass through cloth and solidifying with the addition of magnesium chloride. **1979** *Sunset* Apr. 214/2 Arrange all tofu strips in the casserole and cover with ⅓ of the cheese. **1981** *Guardian* 14 Aug. 7/1 In the United States,.. tofu has become an 'in' food.

tofus, variant of TOPHUS.

tog (tɒg), *sb.*[1] *slang* or *colloq.* Usually *pl.* **togs.** [app. a shortening of TOGEMAN(S, TOGMAN, used in Vagabonds' Cant as early as the 16th c. Its currency in the 19th c. was no doubt aided by its obvious connexion with TOGA; cf. TOGE.]

1. *Cant* and *slang.* A coat; any outer garment; see also quot. 1809.

1708 *Memoirs Right Villanous John Hall* (ed. 4) 10/2 *Togge*, a Coat. **1718** C. HITCHING *Regulator* 20 The names of the flash words now in vogue among thieves... Togge, *alias* Coat. **1755** J. POTTS *Jrnl.* in R. Price *Howling Arctic* (1970) i. 16 Having no beaver coats in the factory to make their togs, mittens nor caps. **1798** TUFT *Gloss. Thieves' Jargon* (Cent. D.), *Long tog*, a coat. **1809** G. ANDREWES *Dict. Slang & Cant*, *Tatty togg*, a gaming cloth. **1812** J. H. VAUX *Flash Dict.*, *Tog*, a coat. **1821** *Sporting Mag.* IX. 27 Curtis, in a new white upper tog. **1911** *19th Cent.* Sept. 548 A tog and kicks is synonymous with a coat and breeches.

2. *pl.* **a.** Clothes. *slang* and *humorously colloq.*

1779 J. WEDGWOOD *Let.* 9 May (1965) 233 He determined to strip off his waistcoat, and put on the togs at once. *a* **1790** H. T. POTTER *New Dict. Cant & Flash* (1795) 59 *Toges* or *toggs*, cloaths for both sexes. **1809** G. ANDREWES *Dict. Slang & Cant*, *Toggs*, clothes. **1812** J. H. VAUX *Flash Dict.*, *Togs* or *Toggery*, wearing apparel in general. **1838** DICKENS *O. Twist* xvi, 'Look at his togs, Fagin!' said Charley... 'Look at his togs!—Super-fine cloth, and the heavy swell cut!'

b. Variously qualified: often humorous or depreciative; ***long togs*** (*Naut.*), landsmen's clothes.

1830 MARRYAT *King's Own* x, I retained a suit of 'long togs', as we call them. **1840** [see LONG *a.*[1] 18]. **1850** SMEDLEY *F. Fairlegh* iv. 34, I should have thought he had seen the sporting togs. **1860** *All Year Round* No. 66. 380 Three or four days..employed by us in providing sea-going togs, and other requirements. **1867** SMYTH *Sailor's Word-bk.* s.v., Sunday togs.

c. *Austral.* and *N.Z. colloq.* A swimming costume.

1930 V. PALMER *Passage* I. x. 83 'You nip in and get my togs.'.. He was much more at ease in his bathing-trunks than in his..suit and slippery shoes. **1935** J. GUTHRIE *Little Country* xiii. 216 We..tore down to a quiet beach, stripped off our clothes, and plunged in... We didn't bother about togs. **1944** G. TEXIDOR in D. M. Davin *N.Z. Short Stories* (1953) 313 Mum came over and said..they could put on their togs. But they mustn't stay in for long, it was getting chilly. **1959** M. SHADBOLT *New Zealanders* 96 'I forgot my togs. I left them at the other place.' 'Never mind, you can swim in your shorts, can't you?' **1971** *N.Z. Listener* 15 Feb. 14/5 'I haven't got a costume.'..'Go back and get your togs.'

3. A unit of thermal resistance used to express the insulating properties of clothes and quilts (see quots. 1945, 1978); so ***tog rating***, ***value***. [Modelled on the earlier U.S. term *clo*.]

1945 PEIRCE & REES in *Shirley Inst. Mem.* XIX. 343 So that practical clothing may be described conveniently by a range of small integers, the unit of thermal resistance, to be called the 'tog', is the resistance that will maintain a temperature difference of 0·1°C. with a flux of 1 watt per square metre, or in more practical terms, 10°C. with a flux of 1 watt per square decimetre. This is the resistance of a light summer suit, and 10 togs represents about the thickest clothing..practicable to wear. **1975** *Daily Tel.* 9 Dec. 13/4 White goose down: 10·5 togs (which means that it is extra-warm and light)... Terylene P.3: 8·5 to 9 togs (normal warmth). The heaviest quilt, I am told, gives the same tog warmth as five blankets at less than half the weight. **1977** *Observer* (Colour Suppl.) 25 Sept. 60/1 (Advt.), Genuine continental quilt luxury at bargain prices: Tog rating (warmth factor) 9·5+. **1978** *Textiles* VII. II. 50/2 The tog value of a textile is equal to ten times the temperature difference between its two faces when the flow of heat is equal to one watt per square metre. One tog is the thermal resistance of a fabric for a conventional man's suiting or of a blanket of medium quality.

4. *Comb.*, as ***tog-maker***.

1901 *Daily Tel.* 16 Apr. 5/2 Describing himself as a 'tog-maker', with no fixed abode.

tog (tɒg), *sb.*[2] *dial.* Local variant of TEG, perh. influenced by *hog*.

1851 *Jrnl. R. Agric. Soc.* XII. II. 333 A lamb eight or nine months old, and until his first shearing, is called a 'heder' or 'sheder', 'hog', 'hogget', or 'lamb-hog'. In other counties a 'teg', 'tog', 'gimmer', and 'dinmont', &c.

tog (tɒg), *v.* [Occurs first and chiefly as *togged* (tɒgd), prob. orig. from TOG *sb.*[1]: cf. *booted*, *hatted*, etc.] **a.** *trans.* To clothe, to dress. Const. *out*, *up*.

1793 *European Mag.* XXIII. 466 An old fine lady..Tog'd out in each extravagance of fashion. **1811** *Lex. Balatr.* s.v. *Togs*, The swell is rum-togged, the gentleman is handsomely dressed. **1812** J. H. VAUX *Flash Dict.* s.v., To *tog* is to dress or put on clothes; to *tog* a person, is also to supply them with apparel. **1824** SCOTT *St. Ronan's* iv, He was tog'd gnostically enough. **1862** *All Year Round* 13 Sept. 12/1 He was togged out in first-rate style. **1894** HENTY *Dorothy's Double* I. 202 You had better tog yourself up a bit. **1904** J. A. RIIS *Roosevelt* xiv. 344 Mrs. Cleveland when he was Governor, togged out his staff in the most gorgeous clothes.

b. *intr.* for *refl.* Also ***to tog it***.

1812 [see above]. **1844** ALB. SMITH *Adv. Mr. Ledbury* xvi, My pardner's going to tog it. **1869** J. GREENWOOD *Curses London* (Farmer), She's a dress-woman..they tog out that they may show off at their best, and make the most of their faces. **1903** 'MARJORIBANKS' *Fluff-Hunters* 132 It was a new experience—'togging up to meet a prospective landlady!

‖**toga** ('təʊgə). [L. *toga* = cloak or mantle, f. ablaut-stem of *teg-ĕre* to cover.]

Rom. Antiq. The outer garment of a Roman citizen in time of peace.

It consisted of a single piece of stuff of irregular form, long, broad, and flowing, without sleeves or armholes, and covered the whole body with the exception of the right arm. ***toga prætexta***, a toga with a broad purple border worn by children, magistrates, persons engaged in sacred rites, and later by emperors. ***toga virilis***, the toga of manhood, assumed by boys at puberty; hence in *fig.* context.

1600 HOLLAND *Livy* XXII. lvii. 467 All the younger sort above 17 yeares old, yea and some also under that age, that yet were in their *Pretexta*, and were not come to *Toga virilis*. **1638** JUNIUS *Paint. Ancients* 152 The gowne deserved by them,..that had overcome their enemies, was called Toga palmata. **1690** LOCKE *Hum. Und.* III. xi. §25 *Toga*, *Tunica*, *Pallium*, are Words easily translated by *Gown*, *Coat*, and *Cloak*; but we have thereby no more true Ideas of the fashion of those Habits..than we have of the Faces of the Taylors who made them. **1838–42** ARNOLD *Hist. Rome* II. xxxvii. 478 The white *toga* wrapped round the body like a plaid with its broad scarlet border. **1855** THACKERAY *Newcomes* xvii, During this period Mr. Clive assumed the *toga virilis*. **1867** BAKER *Nile Tribut.* iii. (1872) 46 There is a uniformity of dress throughout all the Nubian tribes of Arabs, the simple *toga* of the Romans.

b. *transf.* and *fig.* A robe of office; a professional gown, a cloak, a 'mantle'; a dress coat.

1738 *Gentl. Mag.* VIII. 435/2 There were found a Chalice, two Crucifixes, a Toga or Pall, with several Mass-Books Latin and English, and other Popish Relicks. **1828** [C. SWAN] tr. *Manzoni's Betrothed Lovers* I. vii. 200 Another ancestor, the dread of litigants; seated on a high stool of red velvet, and wrapped in an ample black *toga*—totally black, but for a white collar with two broad facings and lining of sable. **1855** J. STRANG *Glasgow & Clubs* (1856) 207 Lord Braxfield wore the scarlet toga of the Justiciary Court. **1867** J. MACFARLANE *Mem. T. Archer* v. 128 Can they be expected to don the togas of the geologist, the geographer, the chemist, the linguist, the political economist?

c. *Comb.*: **toga-folded** *a.*, folded like a toga; **toga-like** *a.*, resembling a toga; **toga-wise** *adv.*, in the manner of a toga.

1887 RIDER HAGGARD *Allan Quaterm.* xii. 132 The toga-like garment of brown cloth. **1902** *Westm. Gaz.* 5 Aug. 3/1, I saw my friend the artillery officer, wrapped in his long, pale blue cloak, one fold thrown over his left shoulder toga-wise. **1911** *Blackw. Mag.* Nov. 680/2 The Kapkoto were noticeable with their toga-folded blankets.

togaed (ˈtəʊgəd), *a.* Also toga'd. [-ED².] Clad in a toga; wearing the toga; togated.

1860 HAWTHORNE *Marb. Faun* xli, The togaed [i.e. Roman] nation. **1897** *Archæologia* Ser. II. V. 310 Fullers, a class in great request among a togaed people.

†**to-gains, -gainst, -yenst,** *prep.* (*conj.*) *Obs.* Forms: α. 1 **toȝæȝnes (-ȝeæȝnes, -ȝeeȝnes), 1-2 toȝeanes, -ȝenes, to ȝeȝnes, 2-4 toȝeines, 3 toȝenes, -ȝenys, toȝanes, (to janes, teȝenes), 3-4 to ȝeȝnes, to-ȝeynes, 4 to yans, to ayens, to ayans.** β. 5 **to ȝenst, -e.** γ. 1 **toȝeæȝn, 3 toȝæn, to ȝein, 3-5 to ȝen.** [OE. *tóȝæȝnes, tóȝéanes,* etc., formed, with advb. genitive *-es,* on the simpler **tóȝæȝn, tóȝeæȝn,* from TO *prep.* + *ȝæȝn*:—**gagn-, gegn-* 'against', the second element also of AGAIN, AGAINST. In this word, the simpler *tóȝeæȝn* was nearly superseded by the form in *-es,* and was rare both in OE. and ME.: see the γ-forms above. In the 15th c., *to-ȝenes* began to be strengthened by adding *-t,* as in *agains-t, amids-t, amongs-t* (app. after superlatives); if the word had survived into mod.Eng., its form would have been *to-yenst* or *to-yainst*; being entirely southern, it never had hard *g,* as in *again, against.*]

1. Towards with hostile intent; in opposition or hostility to, contrary to; = AGAINST A. 11, 12.

Beowulf 666 Hæfde kyning wuldor grendle to-ȝeanes.. sele-weard aseted. *a* **1000** *Ags. Ps.* (Spelm.) xl. 8 To-ȝeanes me runedon ealle fynd mine. *c* **1005** *O.E. Chron.* an. 1001 (Parker MS.), Him þær toȝeanes com Palliȝ. *c* **1200** *Trin. Coll. Hom.* 55 Flesliche lustes and fule sinnes flited eure toȝanes þe wreche saule. *c* **1205** LAY. 4536 Scip ærne to-ȝen [*c* **1275** to-ȝein] scip. *Ibid.* 9792 þer ute wes heom to-ȝæn þe kæisere Uaspasien. *a* **1225** *St. Marher.* 15 Ah þeo þ stalewurðe beoð ant starke to ȝein me. *c* **1275** *Passion* 83 in *O.E. Misc.* 39 If he ouht prechede to-ȝeȝnes þere lawe. *c* **1300** *Vox & Wolf* 95 in Hazl. *E.P.P.* I. 61 Hit wes to-ȝeines his wille. **1340** *Ayenb.* 6 Yef he zuereþ uals be his wytinde, he him uorzuereþ and deþ to ayans þise heste. *a* **1440** *R. Gloucester's Chron.* (Rolls) App. G. 197 þou to ȝenst kunde .. Bringest me in sorewe. *Ibid.* App. EE. 20 Charlemaines spere þat to ȝenste þe saracins he was ywoned to bere.

b. In defence or protection from; = AGAINST A. 13.

a **1225** *Ancr. R.* 66 God is þ ȝe asken red, & salue þ he teche ou to ȝeines fondunges. *a* **1300** *K. Horn* 56 þe king hadde al to fewe Toȝenes so vele schrewe. *c* **1380** *Sir Ferumb.* 172 He þat scholde me socoury to ȝen myn enymys. *a* **1440** *R. Gloucester's Chron.* (Rolls) App. XX. 380 þe castel of ȝipeswich.. þat huwe bigod hadde iholde to ȝen his kinedom.

2. Towards, forward to, so as to meet; = AGAINST A. 5.

c **950** *Lindisf. Gosp.* Mark xiv. 13 And toȝeæȝn iornað iuh monn. —— Matt. xxvii. 32 ȝemoeton monno cyriniscne cymmende toȝeeȝnas him [*L.* venientem obuiam sibi]. *c* **1000** ÆLFRIC *Hom.* I. 136 Se ealda man Symeon eode toȝeanes þam cilde. *a* **1200** *Moral Ode* 347 þos goð un-ieþe to-ȝeanes þe cliue aȝean þe heȝe hulle. *c* **1205** LAY. 3626 Aganippus.. Ferde him to-ȝenes.

3. Of time: Towards, at the approach of; towards the coming, arrival, or convenience of (a person); = AGAINST A. 18, 19.

971 *Blickl. Hom.* 53 þonne biþ hit eft him toȝeanes ȝehealden. *c* **1122** *O.E. Chron.* an. 1095 (Laud MS.), Toȝeanes Eastron com ðæs Papan sande. *c* **1200** *Trin. Coll. Hom.* 177 To-ȝenes sumere þis woreld floweð.. to-ȝanes wintre heo hebbeð. *c* **1250** *O. Kentish Serm.* in *O.E. Misc.* 26 To-janes þo sun risindde. *Ibid.* 34 To-ȝenes þan euen.

b. as *conj.* = AGAINST B.

a **1440** *R. Gloucester's Chron.* (Rolls) App. XX. 376 God him greiþede pes to ȝenst he bere croune.

4. Towards; with respect to; in regard to; = AGAINST A. 3.

c **1175** *Lamb. Hom.* 145 þos word he seide et sumtime toȝeines þet he walde þis lif forleten. *c* **1200** *Trin. Coll. Hom.* 9 Ure lif we ledeð richtliche toȝenes ure louerd ihesu crist. *Ibid.*, Teȝenes ure emcristene we sulle laden ure lif edmodeliche.

5. Opposite, facing; = AGAINST A. 1. *rare.*

c **1450** *Two Cookery-bks.* 112 Bray hit wel in a morter, & drie hit toȝenst ye sonne.

†**to-ˈgang,** *v. Obs.* [OE. *togangan,* f. TO-² + *gangan,* GANG *v.*¹ So OS. *ti-, te-gangan,* OHG. *za-, zi-gangan.*] *intr.* To go away, pass away.

a **900** tr. *Bæda's Hist.* IV. xxx. [xxix.] (1890) 372 Forðon ðe æfter þon ðe wit nu betwih unc nu togangne beoð. *c* **1000** *Riddles* xxiv. 10 (Gr.) Ne togongeð þas gumena hwylcum ænigum eaðe, þat ic þær ymb sprice. **1596** DALRYMPLE tr. *Leslie's Hist. Scot.* x. (S.T.S.) II. 286 Our folk, about the sone togangeng,.. met with thame at the fute of ane hill castne betueine.

togate (ˈtəʊgeɪt), *a.* [ad. L. *togāt-us,* f. TOGA: see -ATE².] = TOGAED; in quots., belonging to ancient Rome.

1851 BADHAM *Halieut.* (1854) 2 The existence of togate and eucnemic proficients in the art of angling is competently attested. **1853** WHEWELL *Grotius* II. 13 The Togate Provinces (*Provinciæ Togatæ*) [of the Roman Empire].

togated (ˈtəʊgeɪtɪd), *a.* [f. as prec. + -ED.]

1. Clad in a toga; wearing the toga; hence, associated with the idea of peace, peaceful.

1634 M. SANDYS *Prudence* x. 138 Now, I suppose, my Striplings are formally clad, and togated, newly arrived at the Vniversitie. **1651** HOWELL *Venice* 186* But touching maritime affaires,.. these grave men shake off their togated Habitts, and receave Martiall employment. **1695** KENNETT *Par. Antiq.* ix. 686 As he was a valiant Warrier, so was he a togated Senator. **1856** SMYTH *Rom. Fam. Coins* 193 A togated figure stands towards the left on rough ground.

2. Of words: Latinized; stately, majestic.

1868 LOWELL *Shaks. Once More* Wks. 1890 III. 13 What homebred English could ape the high Roman fashion of such togated words as 'The multitudinous sea incarnadine?'

togavirus (ˈtəʊgəvaɪərəs). *Med.* [f. L. *toga* TOGA + VIRUS.] Any of a group of RNA animal viruses with enveloped icosahedral capsids, many of which are arthropod-borne and including the viruses of rubella, yellow fever, dengue, and several forms of encephalitis.

1970 C. H. ANDREWES et al. in *Virology* XL. 1070/1 Togavirus (from the Latin toga = a cloak) is the name now proposed to cover what is likely to prove the great majority of arboviruses having taxonomic characters like those of the A and B groups. **1974** *Nature* 27 Sept. 343/1 We have examined only one virus outside the picornavirus family, the togavirus, Semliki Forest virus. **1980** R. W. SCHLESINGER *Togaviruses* i. 10 The rubiviruses, pestiviruses and other 'non-arbo' togaviruses are also of enormous medical or veterinary importance.

†**toge.** *Obs.* [a. F. *toge* (older *togue*), ad. L. *toga.*] A Roman toga; hence, a cloak or loose coat.

? *a* **1400** *Morte Arth.* 3189 In toges of tarsse fulle richelye attyryde. *Ibid.* 178 Alle with taghte mene and towne in toges [*MS.* togers] fulle ryche, Of saunke realle in suyte, sexty at ones. **1607** SHAKS. *Cor.* II. iii. 122 Why in this woolvish toge [Steevens' conj. for *tongue* of Fol. 1, *gown* of others] should I stand here To beg of Hob & Dick? *a* **1693** *Urquhart's Rabelais* III. vii. 65 Made after the manner of a *Toge,* which was the ancient fashion of the Romans in time of peace. *a* **1700** B. E. *Dict. Cant. Crew, Toge,* a Coat.

†ˈ**toged,** *a. Obs.* or *arch.* [f. prec. + -ED².] Clad in a toga, togated: hence, robed.

1604 SHAKS. *Oth.* I. i. 25 (Qo. 1) Unless the bookish theoric Wherein the toged [*folios* tongued] consuls can propose As masterly as he. **1862** KNIGHT *Pop. Hist. Eng.* VIII. xx. 365 To walk in toged state to church [as members of municipal corporations *a* 1836].

†ˈ**togeman(s, ˈtogman.** *Vagabonds' Cant. Obs. rare.* [app. f. F. *toge* or L. *toga* TOGA + the cant suffix *-man(s,* as in *crackmans* hedge, *darkmans* night, *lightmans* day, etc.] A cloak or loose coat.

1567 HARMAN *Caveat* (1869) 77 For want of their Casters and Togemans. *Ibid.* 82 A caster, a cloke.. a togeman, a cote. *Ibid.* 85, I towre the strummel trine vpon thy nabchet and Togman, I see the strawe hang vpon thy cap and coate. *a* **1700** B. E. *Dict. Cant. Crew, Togemans,* a Gown or Cloak. *Ibid.* s.v. *Nim,* Nim a togeman, to steal a cloak. **1785** GROSE *Dict. Vulg. T., Togmans,* a cloak.

together (təˈgɛðə(r)), *adv.* (*prep., sb.,* and *a.*) Forms (in most cases either as one word or two, or in mod. edd. of OE. and ME. with hyphen): α. 1 **togædere (to gædere, to-gædere), togadore, 3-4 togadere, togare, (3 to gaddre, to gaderen, 4 to gadir); 7 togather.** β. 2-5 **togedere,** 3 (*Orm.*) **togeddre, 4 to gedder,** *Sc.* **to geidir, 4-5 togeder, togedre, 4-6 togedir, 5 togedur, togedyr, to gedire, (to geyder, to gheder); 4-5 to gethir, 6 togeather, 7 togeither, 5- together.** γ. 3-5 **togider** (6 *Sc.*), **togydere, (3 to giddre, 4 to gidir), 4-5 togidere, togidre, 4-6 togyder, togiddir, (5 -yr), 4, 5-7** *Sc.* **togidder, 5 to gidur, to gydre, togyddyr, 6 togydur, to gydder** (*Sc.* **-ir**), **toguyder; 4 togiþer, 6 togyther, toguyther,** *Sc.* **togithir,** 6 (9 *dial.*) **togither;** *Sc.* 6 **þe gidder, 8-9 thegither.** [OE. *tógædere, tógadore,* f. TO *prep.* + *gædre* adv.:—**gaduri,* orig. locative or instr. of **gador, -ur,* OE. *geador* 'together', whence also *gaderian,* later *gæderian* to GATHER, q.v. So OFris. *togadera, -ere,* MDu. *te gader(e,* Du. *tegader* 'together', MLG. *gader,* MG. *gater* 'together', f. same root as OE. *gæd* companionship, fellowship, union, *ȝegada* companion, associate, Du. *gade,* MDu. *ghegade* companion, comrade, consort, mate. OE. had, beside *tógædre,* of motion or direction, a parallel compound *ætgædere,* of position. The derivatives of *gad-* appear only in the Saxon-Frisian or LG. group of WGer., OHG. substituting *zi-samane,* Ger. *zusammen*: see SAMEN; and cf. GATHER, GOOD. ME. had forms in *-gader* and *-geder,* which in North. ME. and Sc. became *-gidir.* In the 14th c. the *d* or *dd* began to change to (ð) written *th*: cf. GATHER, FATHER.]

A. *adv.* **1. a.** Into one gathering, company, mass, or body.

707 *Charter of Ine of Wessex* in Birch *Cart. Sax.* I. 149 Andlang Icenan þer Cendefer and Icene cumað to gædere; andlang Cendefer þer hit ær upeode. *c* **1000** *Ags. Gosp.* Matt. xv. 10 And he þa ðam meneȝum to-gædere ȝeclypedum þus cwæð. *c* **1200** ORMIN 1485, & gaddresst swa þe clene corn All fra þe chaff to geddre. *a* **1300** *Cursor M.* 2515 (Cott.) He did togeder samen his men. *c* **1386** CHAUCER *Prol.* 824 Vp roos oure hoost.. And gadrede vs togidre alle in a flok. **1482** *Monk of Evesham* (Arb.) 22 Than all the brethirne came to gedyr in to the chaptur hows. *a* **1547** SURREY *Æneid* II. (1557) D iij, A rout exiled, a wreched multitude, From eche where flockke together. **1552-3** *Inv. Ch. Goods, Staffs.* in *Ann. Lichfield* IV. 6 On other grett bell.. to call the parishonars to geather. **1611** BIBLE *1 Cor.* xiv. 23 If therefore the whole Church be come together into one place. **1766** GOLDSM. *Vic. W.* iii, My next care was to get together the wrecks of my fortune. **1818** SCOTT *Rob Roy* xxxii, Laying a' this thegither.

b. Of two persons or things: Into companionship, union, proximity, contact, or collision.

a **900** *Andreas* 1437 Heofon & eorðe hreosaþ togadore. **1154** *O.E. Chron.* an. 1135, & hi to gædere comen & wurðe sæhte. **1297** R. GLOUC. (Rolls) 8996 Hii were to gadere icome þis bataile to do. *c* **1380** WYCLIF *Sel. Wks.* III. 442 God and iche membre of his Chirche bene weddid togedre. *c* **1400** *Lanfranc's Cirurg.* 142 Brynge þe parties togidere of þe wounde & sowe hem. **1549** *Compl. Scot.* vi. 66 The rammis raschit there heydis to gyddir. **1600** HOLLAND *Livy* VI. xii. 224 When you see the battailes buckle together pell mell, and come to handstrokes. **1610** SHAKS. *Temp.* I. ii. 461 Ile manacle thy necke and feete together. **1703** MOXON *Mech. Exerc.* 194 To contain.. both the Cheeks when they are shut together. *a* **1704** [see ADD *v.* 4]. **1850** *Tait's Mag.* XVII. 498/1 Our last extract tells how Dr. Chalmers and Edward Irving came together. **1894** H. DRUMMOND *Ascent of Man* 251 Two flints struck together yielded fire.

2. a. In one assembly, company, or body; in one place. (Not in OE., which used *æt-gædere.*)

c **1220** *Bestiary* 369 in *O.E. Misc.* 12 Ðis wune he hauen hem bi-twen, Ðoȝ he an hundred to giddre ben. *c* **1250** *Gen. & Ex.* 1897 So riche were growen hise sunen, Ðat he ne miȝte to gider wunen. **1382** WYCLIF *John* xxi. 2 Ther weren to gidere Symount Petre, and Thomas, that is seid Didymus, and Nathanael [etc.]. *c* **1400** MAUNDEV. (1839) xxiii. 247 Here wyfes ne dwelle not to gydere, but euery of hem be hire self. **1526** *Pilgr. Perf.* (W. de W. 1531) 1 All christians gooth this pilgrymage all togyder in one company. **1607-12** BACON *Ess., Counsel* (Arb.) 324 If they take the opinions of theire Councell, both seperately, and togither. **1749** FIELDING *Tom Jones* XVIII. v, Shall we take a hackney coach, and all of us together pay a visit to your friend? **1826** J. WILSON *Noct. Ambr.* Wks. 1855 I. 244 We'll a' get fou thegither.

b. Of two persons or things: In each other's company; in union or contact.

c **1315** SHOREHAM I. 1912-8 þe sibbe mowe to gadere nauȝt þe foerþe grees wyþ-inne.. And ȝef oþer þe fifte of-takeþ, To-gare moȝe hy dwelle. **1393** LANGL. *P. Pl.* C. XVIII. 22 Loue and leel by-leuye heeld lyf and soule to-gedere. *a* **1425** *Cursor M.* 10571 (Laud) Sone after to-gethir [*Cott.* samen] they lay. **1483** *Rolls of Parlt.* VI. 241/1 The said King Edward,.. and the seid Elizabeth, lived together sinfully.. in adultery. **1596** SPENSER *F.Q.* VI. ii. 16 He and I together roade Upon our way. *c* **1645** HOWELL *Lett.* (1650) II. 113 You and I have eaten a great deal of salt together. **1726** in W. Wing *Ann. Steeple Aston* (1875) 54 Two lands lye together at Drywell. **1848** THACKERAY *Van. Fair* xxix, She gave George the queerest, knowingest look, when they were together.

c. In ideal combination; considered collectively; added or summed up. (Cf. PUT *v.* 54 e.)

1796 MACNEILL *Will & Jean* III. i, What this warld is a' thegither, If bereft o' honest fame! **1849** MACAULAY *Hist. Eng.* v. I. 645 Jeffreys boasted that he had hanged more traitors than all his predecessors together since the Conquest.

d. *pred.* †(*a*) In agreement, consonant (*obs.*); (*b*) Courting, or mutually engaged, as lovers.

1502 *Ord. Crysten Men* (W. de W. 1506) I. ii. 11 It behoueth that the wordes & the doynge.. be holly in ony wyse togyder. **1749** FIELDING *Tom Jones* VI. ii, She.. knew better than anybody who and who were together.

e. Used expletively in addressing a number of persons. *dial.* (*E. Anglia*).

a **1825** FORBY *Voc. E. Anglia, Together,*.. used in familiarly addressing a number of persons collectively. Ex. 'Well, together, how are ye all?' **1859** *N. & Q.* 1st Ser. II. 217/2 Where are you going together? (meaning several persons). What are you doing together? **1866** J. G. NALL *Gt. Yarmouth & Lowestoft* 517 It has been wittily observed, that .. 'together' is [the] plural [of 'bor'] [a single person, male or female, being addressed as *bor* or '*bo*', two or more persons as 'together'].

f. Colloq. phr. (*all*) *girls together*: see GIRL *sb.* 2 f.

3. In reference to a single thing. **a.** With union or combination of parts or elements; into or in a condition of unity; so as to form a connected whole.

***to pull, shake oneself together*:** see the verbs.

a **1300** *Cursor M.* 550 (Cott.) Of þir things.. was adam cors to gedir graid. *Ibid.* 582 Now haf i sceud yow til hider, How tua thinges halds man to gider. **1521** FISHER *Serm. agst. Luther* Wks. (1876) 324 Euery vertue that is gadred togyder is more stronger. **1562** TURNER *Herbal* II. 2 As runnynge or chese-lope maketh mylke runne together into cruddes. **1581** LAMBARDE *Eiren.* II. ii. (1588) 109 It standeth not well togither, that he should become bound to the Prince in x or xx pounds. **1652** NEEDHAM tr. *Selden's Mare Cl.* 161 The matter hang's well together, if wee say [etc.]. **1832** *Examiner* 562/1 While society holds together, while life and property are.. secure.

b. After such verbs as *fold, roll,* etc.: Of different parts (sides, ends, etc.): Into or in contact or junction, so as to form a compact body.

1480 [see FOLD *v.*¹ 1]. **1526** [see ROLL *v.*² 8]. **1578** LYTE *Dodoens* IV. vi. 552 His leaues be.. crompled, and drawen togither or curled. **1637** RUTHERFORD *Lett.* I. cxli. (1664) 279

Ye..shall one day see God take the heavens in his hands and fold them together like an old holly garment.

4. At the same time, at once, simultaneously. (Usually connoting 'in combination or association'.)

c **1200** *Vices & Virt.* 35 Đe hali apostel namneð ðese þrie haliȝe mihtes to gedere. *c* **1375** *Sc. Leg. Saints* ii. (*Paulus*) 806 þat he [Nero] mycht stand his towr in, And se all to-geidir byrne. **1508** FISHER *Penit. Ps.* xxxii. Wks. (1876) 33, I shall knowlege togyder all my synnes. **1610** HEALEY *Vives' Comm. St. Aug. Citie of God* XI. ix. 416 Basil and Dionysius, and almost all the Latines..hold that God made althings together. **1662** STILLINGFL. *Orig. Sacr.* III. iii. §4 We cannot believe that and the Scriptures to be true together. **1746** FRANCIS tr. *Horace, Epist.* II. ii. 270 If Death..must mow Down Great and Small together at a Blow. **1849** MACAULAY *Hist. Eng.* iv. I. 469 James found that the two things which he most desired could not be possessed together.

5. Without intermission, continuously, consecutively, uninterruptedly, 'running', 'on end'. (In reference to time, less commonly to space.)

c **1290** *S. Eng. Leg.* I. 280/73 In þe Cite of tolouse ten ȝer to gadere he was. **1450–1530** *Myrr. our Ladye* 29 Where the soulle was..sore tormented longe tyme togidre. **1580** E. CAMPION in Allen *Martyrd.* (1908) 21 Tarying for wind four daies together. **1615** W. LAWSON *Country Housew. Gard.* (1626) 8 Trees cannot beare fruit plentifully two yeeres together. **1630** *R. Johnson's Kingd. & Commw.* 44 That wall of China,..was continued and fortified for six hundred miles together. **1698** FRYER *Acc. E. India & P.* 124 Forests ..on Fire two or three Miles together. **1840** GRESLEY *Siege Lichf.* 242 He..never slept twice together in the same apartment. **1856** F. E. PAGET *Owlet Owlst.* 148 Her back aches..if she sits up for long together.

6. In concert or co-operation; with unity of action; unitedly; conjointly.

a **1300** *Cursor M.* 17351 (Cott.) Eftir þair sabat þai badd togedir, þat [etc.]. *c* **1330** R. BRUNNE *Chron.* (1810) 7 þe Scottes & þe Peihtes togider gan þei cheue, To waste alle Northumberland. **1474** CAXTON *Chesse* II. i, Birdes of whom the male and female haue to gyder the charge in kepynge and norisshinge of their yonge fowlis. **1538** STARKEY *England* I. i. 9 Conspyryng togydur in al vertue and honesty. **1807** WORDSW. *Alice Fell* viii, Together we released the Cloak. **1891** *Law Times Rep.* LXIII. 776/1 The contract and the label together constituted a written warranty within the meaning of the..section.

7. a. In the way of, into, or in mutual action (friendly or hostile); with or against each other; mutually, reciprocally.

†In quot. 1523 in reference to distance: = of each other.

c **1350** *Will. Palerne* 1011 þan eiþer hent oþer hastely in armes, & wiþ kene kosses kuþþed hem to gidere. **1377** LANGL. *P. Pl.* B. Prol. 46 Pilgrymes and palmers pliȝted hem togidere. *a* **1400** HYLTON *Scala Perf.* (W. de W. 1494) I. li, This is my biddynge that ye loue you togyder as I loued you. *c* **1400** *Laud Troy Bk.* 9244 With swerdes gode..Fauȝt thei to-gedur. **1477** EARL RIVERS (Caxton) *Dictes* 68 Why it is that tresour and Science may not accorde to gider. **1523** LD. BERNERS *Froiss.* I. xl. 55 They were within two leages toguyther. **1561** T. HOBY tr. *Castiglione's Courtyer* II. (1577) L vj b, Which..(as you knowe) are enimies togyther. **1686** tr. *Chardin's Coronat. Solyman* 107 He resolv'd to set the King's two Chief Eunuchs..together by the ears. **1766** GOLDSM. *Vic. W.* x, I could perceive..my wife and daughters in close conference together. **1855** LYNCH *Rivulet* XCVI. i, Yet sometimes, and in the sunniest weather, My work and I have fallen out together.

†**b.** After a trans. verb: = each other. *Obs.*

c **1330** R. BRUNNE *Chron. Wace* (Rolls) 4863 [Men] þat syþen han loued to gedre wel. **1483** *Vulgaria abs Terentio* 7 b, Scolers shulde loue to gyder lyke as thei were bredyr. **1525** LD. BERNERS *Froiss.* II. cxxviii. [cxxiv.] 364 When they mete, and haue nat sene toguyder longe before. *a* **1548** HALL *Chron., Hen. VIII* 200 After this day, the kyng and she neuer saw together.

†**c.** *well* or *ill together*: agreeing well or ill; friendly or unfriendly. *Obs.*

1741 CHESTERF. *Lett.* 30 May, I believe we are yet well enough together for you to be glad to hear of my safe arrival. **1765** *Ibid.*, Probably that is the Cause of their being so ill together. **1766** *Ibid.* 11 July, From the interview at Torgaw, ..they will be either a great deal better or worse together.

d. After *multiply*: By or into one another. Cf. *add together* (1 b).

1709, 1885 [see MULTIPLY *v.* 5 b]. **1894** *Act 57 & 58 Vict.* c. 60 Sch. 2 (3) The contents of the shaft trunk shall be ascertained by multiplying together the mean length, breadth, and depth of the trunk, and dividing the product by 100.

e. After *belong*: To one another; hence, to one or the same whole, company, or set. Cf. *to hang together* in 3.

1897 A. LANG *Bk. Dreams & Ghosts* i. 20 The two fragments, which you have published separately..belong together. **1908** *Expositor* Apr. 335 The whole is too closely connected and must, therefore, belong together.

8. together with (in various senses): Along with; in combination with, in addition to, or with the addition of; in company or co-operation with; at the same time as, simultaneously with.

1478 *Exch. Rolls Scotl.* VIII. 603 *note*, For his servandis mete, togiddir with his horse luveraye. **1596** DALRYMPLE tr. *Leslie's Hist. Scot.* (S.T.S.) I. 49 With a schip read, or hartsum hauining place, togithir with grene Cnowis upon the seysyde. **1608** TOPSELL *Serpents* (1658) 655 The labouring, that is the male Wasps, together with Autumn, make an end of their days. **1641** J. JACKSON *True Evang. T.* II. 120 Simon..entred Persia, together with Thaddeus. **1664** SOUTH *Serm.* (1697) II. ii. 69 He..never weighs the Sin, but together with it He weighs the force of the Inducement. **1686** tr. *Chardin's Trav. Persia* 21 The Gains and Advantages of a Constantinopolitan Embassie, together with the Splendor and Authority that belongs to it. **1858** *Penny Cycl.* XI. 41/1 The former principality of Haliczia or Galiczia, which, together with a considerable portion of Red Russia, once formed part of Hungary.

†**9.** Together with this; in addition, besides, at the same time, moreover. *Obs. rare.*

a **1648** LD. HERBERT *Hen. VIII* (1683) 147 This New invention of printing..as it had brought in and restored Books and Learning, so together it hath been the Occasion of those Sects and Schisms, which daily appeared in the World. *Ibid.* 236 The King understanding this, and together finding that their Numbers and Power did daily increase, advis'd to raise Forces.

†**10.** In nonce-combinations (chiefly with a vbl. sb. or agent-n.), after L. *con-* or *co-*: as ***together-binding, -healing, -speaking*** (= colloquy, conversation), ***-words*** (= context), ***-worker*** (= co-worker, collaborator). *Obs.*

1382–8 WYCLIF *Gospels* (K.O. I. 141), The *togidere bindingus. **1597** A. M. tr. *Guillemeau's Fr. Chirurg.* 45 b/2 The combinatione or *together healinge is hindered. *c* **1425** *St. Mary of Oignies* II. iv. in *Anglia* VIII. 163/12 Yuel *togedir-spekynges harmeþ good maners. *Ibid.* viii. 173/22 Homely and often togedir-spekynge of seyntes. *c* **1449** PECOCK *Repr.* III. ii. (Rolls) 283 The ful hool riȝt is expressid in these *to gidere wordis 'Ȝeue to the dekenis citees forto dwelle in hem'. **1581** J. BELL *Haddon's Answ. Osor.* 151 That the Apostles were *together workers with God: yet that those same together workemen should be hyred to worke in this Vyneard.

†**B.** *prep.* Along with, in addition to, with the addition of, with. *Obs. rare.*

1556 *Aurelio & Isab.* (1608) E iv, Withe suttell communications unto their maedens, to gether a thousande written thinges that you fynde. **1583** STOCKER *Civ. Warres Lowe C.* IV. 44 The Lordes Liutenauntes..together all Magistrates and Chief Officers..shall be bounde to promise to obserue..this vnion. **1657** R. LIGON *Barbadoes* 25 You shall finde..the worth and value of it, together the whole processe of the great work of Sugar-making.

C. as *sb.* Condition of being together, union; togetherness. *nonce-use.*

1880 G. MEREDITH *Tragic Com.* (1881) 271 In their secrecy: in the close and boundless together of clasped hands.

D. *adj.* **a.** Fashionable, up-to-date; hence used as a general term of commendation. *slang.*

1968 *Daily Mirror* 27 Aug. 7/5 No finer honour can be bestowed on a man down the King's Road than to be called a together cat. **1970** E. BULLINS *Theme is Blackness* (1973) 176 Honey, with the right clothes and a together front I'd be a knockout. **1971** *Jamaican Weekly Gleaner* 3 Nov. 5/1, I read in the Miami Herald that conditions in the women's jails [are] not so together.

b. Composed, self-assured; free of emotional difficulties or inhibitions. *colloq.*

1969 FABIAN & BYRNE *Groupie* ii. 19, I reckoned it was no good putting on a together image if you were all screwed up inside. **1971** *New Yorker* 18 Dec. 31 A young lady of twenty-two who's been through what Twiggy has been through has got to be a very together person to survive. **1974** A. LURIE *War between Tates* (1977) iii. 67, I forgot you, and me, and where I was—I felt very calm, very together. **1977** *O.D.* No. 3. 13/3 All free festivals dream of a together stage manager —try your best to get one, as on the day it's all up to him. **1978** I. M. GASKIN *Spiritual Midwifery* (rev. ed.) I. 41, I knew William was together enough to be there through the whole birthing and I was really excited that he was going to get to see such a heavy thing as a birth. **1979** *Amat. Photographer* 10 Jan. 67 (*caption*) Biddy and Eve—a very together cabaret act. **1983** *Times* 25 Mar. 13/3 An amateur flute player, well groomed and articulate, she looks a very together young woman.

Hence **to'getherhood** (*nonce-wd.*) = TOGETHERNESS; † **to'getherward, -wards** *adv.*, towards each other, together.

1896 MARY C. CLARKE *Long Life* 194 The most exquisite precision of tune, the most perfect *togetherhood in beginning and ending phrases. *c* **1205** LAY. 9869 *To-gædereward heo uusden alswa heo wolden fehten. **1530** PALSGR. Introd. 17 They bryng theyr chawes togetherwardes agayne. *a* **1553** UDALL *Royster D.* IV. ii. (Arb.) 60 Now I shrew their best Christmasse chekes both together-ward. *c* **1630** SANDERSON *Serm.* (1681) II. 253 We shall not now stand so much upon any nice distinguishing of the terms, but take them together-ward.

to'getherness. [f. TOGETHER *adv.* + -NESS.]

a. The state or condition of being together or being united; union, association.

1656 [? J. SERGEANT] tr. *T. White's Peripat. Inst.* 302 This togetherness must not be referr'd to the time but to the way of knowledge. **1892** *Monist* II. 218 Even if the link is a feeling it cannot be less than a feeling of the togetherness of two other feelings. **1909** R. BARCLAY *Rosary* xv. 156 Having been apart for a little while seemed to make this curious feeling of 'togetherness' deeper and sweeter than ever. **1912** [see COMPRESENCE]. **1920** A. S. PRINGLE-PATTISON *Idea of God* 354 Our primitive and basal experience of time is thus characterized by a togetherness of parts or elements. **1953** E. L. MASCALL *Corpus Christi* iii. 57 Assuming that the corporateness of the liturgy is produced by a merely geographical togetherness of the worshippers. **1966** J. PORTER *Sour Cream* ix. 123 'I thought I'd take Katia out somewhere.' 'How about making up a foursome?' This blasted Russian passion for togetherness! **1971** *Sci. Amer.* May 105/3 Bullheads often form a dense community, composed of hundreds of individuals, that is based not on a hierarchy or a collection of territories but on close togetherness, with the members swimming freely and peacefully throughout the pond.

b. The fact of getting on well together or being well suited to one another; a sense of belonging together, fellowship.

1930 D. H. LAWRENCE *A Propos of Lady Chatterley's Lover* 58 Class-hate and class-consciousness are only a sign that the old togetherness, the old blood-warmth has collapsed. **1930** *Times Lit. Suppl.* 13 Nov. 925/3 Characters ..must also be real in relation to each other... The personages of Tourneur have this togetherness. **1941** AUDEN *New Year Let.* 34 O cruel intellect that chills His natural warmth until it kills The roots of all togetherness! **1952** C. BARDSLEY *Bishop's Move* vi. 74, I wish I saw more of this 'togetherness' in church congregations. **1963** *Economist* 9 Mar. 876/2 The new togetherness [in the Ministry of Defence] is unlikely to mean that..controversies..will disappear. **1972** M. WILLIAMS *Inside Number 10* xiv. 352 So there we had social class divisions within the organization itself, so one can imagine how much 'togetherness' that encouraged. **1981** G. CLARE *Last Waltz in Vienna* II. 126 What mattered to me was the ideal of scouting, one for all and all for one, the togetherness in a good and just cause.

†**to'gethers**, *adv. Obs.* Forms (in many cases either as one word or two, or with hyphen: cf. TOGETHER): α. 3–4 **togaderes**, 5 **to gadders**; 6 **togathers**. β. 2–5 **togederes**, 4–6 **togeders**, 5 **togederis (-ys)**, to **gedrys**, **togedres**, 6 **togedirs**; 5–6 **togethers**, 6 **togetheres**, **togethirs**. γ. 4–5 **togidres**, **-eres**, **-ers**, (4 **-irs**, **-iris**, **togyderes**), 5 to **guyders**, **togyders**, 5–6 to **gidders**, 6 to **gydders**, **togydres**; 5–6 **togithers**, 6 **-gythers**. [f. TOGETHER *adv.* with *-s* of advb. genitive: cf. *besides*, *betimes*, *eftsoons*, *towards*, etc.] = TOGETHER (in its various senses).

c **1175** *Lamb. Hom.* 139 Sunne dei blisseð to gederes houeneware and horðeware. *c* **1275** LAY. 1834 Hii drowen alle to gaderes. *c* **1300** *Cursor M.* 21749 (Edin.) þu do togidiris ten and tua. **1362** LANGL. *P. Pl.* A. Prol. 46 Pilgrimes and Palmers Plihten hem to-gederes For to seche seint Ieme. **1387** TREVISA *Higden* (Rolls) I. 177 þe clergie and the chiualrie hilde so to giders. *c* **1430** *Two Cookery-bks.* 45 Stere it wel in þe panne tyl it come to-gederys wel. **1440** in *Wars Eng. in France* (1864) II. 590 Whiche of his saide retinue he shalle holde togithers. *c* **1450** *Brut* 427 There they foughten to-gederis. **1491** *Act 7 Hen. VII*, c. 22 To take to your remembraunce the wordes we spake to guyders in Seynt Petir Church. **1537** CROMWELL in Merriman *Life & Lett.* (1902) II. 87 Loyaltie and treason dwell seldome togethers. **1538** in *Lett. Suppress. Monast.* (Camden) 250 Everich of us severally and also alle togethers. *a* **1540** BARNES *Wks.* (1573) 224/1 So tooke they their counsell togithers. **1581** MARBECK *Bk. of Notes* 900 How releasement and payment cannot stand togethers. **1591** SYLVESTER *Du Bartas* I. ii. 330 All the Links of th' holy Chain, which tethers The many members of the World togethers. **1594** T. BEDINGFIELD tr. *Machiavelli's Florentine Hist.* (1595) 192 Being togithers..they alwaies talked thereof.

togge, obs. f. TUG.

toggel, obs. var. TOGGLE.

Toggenburg ('tɒgənbɜːg). Also Toggenburgh. The name of a valley in the canton of St. Gall, N.E. Switzerland, used *attrib.* and *absol.* to designate a hornless light brown goat belonging to a breed first developed in the region.

1886 H. S. H. PEGLER *Bk. Goat* (ed. 3) iii. 27 The Toggenburgh goat is generally hornless, and of a rather unusual colour, being a pale drab. **1891** *Goat-Keeper* Sept. 7/2 Champion Zampa, Swiss Toggenburg Goat, 5 years old, short-haired, hornless. **1921** *Blackw. Mag.* June 764/2 The white Nanny and her kid are Alpino goats, and the brown lot are Toggenburgs. **1937** E. B. WHITE *Let.* 9 Sept. (1976) 162 He lives there, with a wife, three children, and a Toggenburg goat. **1979** B. MALAMUD *Dubin's Lives* ix. 356 One of the Toggenburgs was killed in the goat pasture by a dog.

'Togger. *slang.* [Oxford undergraduates' perversion of TORPID: see -ER[6].] A boat rowing in the Oxford college races called 'Torpids'; in *pl.* the Torpids.

1891 P. S. ALLEN *Let.* Oct. (1939) 10, I hope to combine reading and rowing, for both I hugely desire to get into the Eight next summer and also they are rather hard up for men for the Togger. **1897** *Westm. Gaz.* 18 Aug. 2/1 He once rowed in his second Togger. **1903** *Oxford Mag.* 11 Feb. 213/1 Brasenose. The River.—Good luck to both Toggers.

toggery ('tɒgərɪ). *slang* or *colloq.* [f. TOG *sb.*[1] + -ERY: cf. *drapery*, *foolery*.]

1. Garments; clothes collectively.

1812 COL. HAWKER *Diary* (1893) I. 44 In spite of all coats, 'toggerys and upper benjamins'. *a* **1845** BARHAM *Ingol. Leg.* Ser. III. *Blasphemer's Warn.*, Had a gay cavalier Thought fit to appear In any such 'toggery'. **1894** FENN *Real Gold* 47 That's as much toggery as I can get in the..portmanter.

b. *esp.* Professional or official dress.

long toggery = long togs: see TOG *sb.*[1] 2 b.

1826 *Sporting Mag.* XVII. 378 These, with the squire's pad-groom (all in the same toggery). **1827** *Blackw. Mag.* XXII. 603 [He] is seen hebdomadally in the pulpit, adorned in clerical toggery. **1837** MARRYAT *Perc. Keene* xx, Cross had dressed himself in long toggery as a captain of a merchant vessel. **1861** *Court Life at Naples* I. 224 Officers in full toggery with clanging swords.

2. The trappings of a horse; harness.

1877 C. D. WARNER *Levant* vi. 128 The horse I rode on was not an animal to take advantage of the weakness of his toggery. **1890** 'R. BOLDREWOOD' *Col. Reformer* (1891) 104, I never thought of wanting the regular colts' toggery.

toggle ('tɒg(ə)l), *sb.* Also 8–9 toggel. [Said to be orig. in nautical use; of obscure etymology, but app. closely related to TUGGLE *v.*, to catch, hold fast, entangle, and to TAGLE *v.*, TAIGLE *v.*, and their nasalized form TANGLE. The use of a toggle was originally to catch or hold fast a rope or chain and prevent its slipping.]

1. *Naut.* A short pin passed through a loop or the eye of a rope, or a link of a chain, or through a bolt, to keep it in place, or for the attachment of another line.

1769–76 FALCONER *Dict. Marine, Toggel, cabillot*, a small wooden pin, about five or six inches in length, and usually tapering from the middle towards the extremities. It is used to fix transversely in the lower part of a tackle, in which it serves as an hook whereby to attach the tackle to a strop, slings, or any body whereon the effort of the tackle is to be employed. There are also toggels of another kind, employed to fasten the top-gallant sheets to the spar, which is knotted round the cap at the top-mast-head. **1775** ASH, **1828** WEBSTER, Toggel. **1829** MARRYAT *F. Mildmay* viii, The yard-ropes were fixed to the halter by a toggle in the running noose of the latter. **1854** HOOKER *Himal. Jrnls.* I. ix. 218 Tethered by halters and toggles to a long rope. **1898** F. T. BULLEN *Cruise Cachalot* vi, The strap of the second cutting tackle was inserted and secured by passing a huge toggle of oak through its eye.

fig. phr. **1835–40** HALIBURTON *Clockm.* (1862) 348 There's an eend to that; you've put a toggle into that chain.

2. *transf.* **a.** A cross-piece attached to the end of a line or chain (e.g. a watch-chain), or fixed in a belt or strap for attaching a weapon, etc. by a loop or ring; also, a cross-piece put through a loop to effect compression by twisting. Now freq. a short rod attached to one side of a garment to fasten it by being passed through a loop attached to the other side.

1873 E. SPON *Workshop Receipts* Ser. I. 310/2 This straightens the toggles, and causes a sharp impression of the stamp upon the leather. **1875** BEDFORD *Sailor's Pocket Bk.* x. (ed. 2) 380 A strop round the nose, hove short with a short stick or toggle, will rapidly tame an unmanageable horse. **1880** CLARK RUSSELL *Sailor's Sweetheart* viii, Around his waist was a broad leather belt with toggles for the reception of a knife or a pistol. **1887** *Q. Rev.* Jan. 97 The exquisite workmanship of the toggles and sword guards. **1903** W. F. PETRIE *Abydos* II. ii. 26/2, 141–3 appear to be toggles for fastening dress through a loop, like the frogs on a modern military cloak. **1905** MISS A. S. GRIFFITH tr. *Capart's Prim. Art Egypt* Index, Studs or toggles for cloaks, pp. 57, 59. **1916** *Chambers's Jrnl.* Sept. 617/1 He undid the toggles of his thick lammy coat. **1968** [see *duffle coat* s.v. DUFFEL, DUFFLE 3]. **1982** B. ALDISS *Helliconia Spring* ix. 231 She was buttoning up her tunic, looking down at the toggles.

b. A device for fixing an anchor: see quot.

1831 J. HOLLAND *Manuf. Metal* I. vi. 100 In 1821, R. F. Hawkins, a Kentish mariner, obtained a patent for an anchor, the arm and flukes of which turned round in eyeholes at the termination of the shank, until they formed therewith an angle of about sixty degrees, in which position they were detained by a thick piece of iron, called by the inventor a 'toggle'. When this anchor is let go, one of the ends of the toggle comes in contact with the ground, and puts both flukes in a position to enter; and when the strain comes on the cable, the other end of the toggle..sets the anchor in its holding position, not with one fluke only, as in the common anchor, but with both.

c. A movable pivoted cross-piece serving as a barb in a harpoon.

1881 *Sydney Morn. Herald* 24 Oct., The harpoon was a patent one, with a toggle, and opens when there is any strain on the line.

d. *Mech.* A toggle-joint.

1908 *Installation News* II. 22/2 This is done by connecting a bell and dry cell between the screw D and the toggle of the switch, so that when the piston rises and makes contact with the toggle the bell rings before sufficient pressure is exerted to throw off the switch.

e. *dial.* Each of the two short handles or 'nibs' of a scythe.

1885 *Reports Provinc.* (E.D.D.), I can't mow the lawn, sir, till I've got a new snead and toggles to my scythe.

f. A kind of wall fastener for use on open-backed plasterboarding, etc., having a part that springs open or turns through 90 degrees after it is inserted, so as to prevent withdrawal and aid gripping.

1934 in WEBSTER. **1964** *Practical Householder* Dec. 1369/1, I had an occasion to use Rawlplug ⅛ in. and $\frac{3}{16}$ in. gravity toggles... If you decide to remove the toggle at a later date, when the burr on the screw comes up against the swivel nut, the whole device will turn. **1977** *Reader's Digest Bk. Do-It-Yourself Skills & Techniques* v. 154 Gravity toggles have a swivel toggle that drops vertically when pushed through a hole bored in the wall... Spring toggles have two spring-loaded gripping arms which expand after the toggle is pushed through a hole.

g. *Electronics.* = LATCH *sb.*¹ 3 b. Also *toggle circuit.*

1953 *Proc. IRE* XLI. 1429/1 The toggles or other storage elements hold the accumulated count. **1955** *Sci. Amer.* June 93/2 In the logical circuits of a modern computer the memory units commonly consist of pairs of vacuum tubes connected in a circuit which is called a 'toggle' because of its analogy with a toggle switch. **1962** [see BISTABLE *a.*]. **1971** J. H. SMITH *Digital Logic* iv. 54 The latch or toggle circuit is used to hold signals fed momentarily into a system.

h. *Computers.* A key or command that is always operated the same way but has the opposite effect on successive occasions.

1982 *Personal Computer World* Dec. 138/1, I find that the 'Install' program is unable to make the best of configuring for my printer as Wordstar expects toggles where the Epson has separate control codes for turning on and off certain modes.

3. *attrib.* and *Comb.*, as ***toggle action, fastening, line, -noose, pattern***; ***toggle-like*** adj.; also **toggle-bolt,** (*a*) a bolt having a hole through the head to receive a toggle; (*b*) = sense 2 f; **toggle-chain,** a short chain fastened to a timber sledge, having a *toggle-hook* at the end by which the effective length of the binding chain is regulated; **toggle circuit**: see sense 2 g; **toggle-harpoon,** a harpoon with a pivoted toggle instead of barbs; **toggle-hole,** a hole made, as in blubber, for inserting a toggle (*Cent. Dict.*); **toggle-hook,** a long-shanked hook used on a *toggle-chain* (*Cent. Dict. Supp.*); **toggle-iron** = *toggle-harpoon*; **toggle-joint,** a joint consisting of two pieces hinged endwise, operated by applying pressure at the elbow; **toggle-lanyard**: see quot.; **toggle-pin** = sense 1; **toggle-press,** a press operated by means of one or more toggle-joints; **toggle switch,** an electric switch operated by means of a projecting lever that is moved with a snap action, usu. up and down.

1893 *Jrnl. R. Agric. Soc.* Dec. 716 The drawing together of the nave flanges..produces a *toggle action of the spokes. **1794** *Rigging & Seamanship* I. 152 **Toggle-bolt.* **c 1850** *Rudim. Navig.* (Weale) 99 The Toggle-Bolt has a flat head and a mortise through it, that receives a toggle or pin. **1934** WEBSTER, *Toggle bolt*, a bolt having a nut with pivoted flanged wings that close against a spring when passed through a constricted passage and open after emerging. **1968** *Trade Marks Jrnl.* 8 May 736/2 *Rawlplug*... Bolt anchoring devices, expansion bolts; toggle bolts, wall plugs and sockets. **1976** *Country Life* 29 Apr. 1143/1 Suit with *toggle fastenings. **1976** *Woman's Weekly* 6 Nov. 49/2 Plus a zingy crochet jacket in bold bright stripes with toggle fastenings. **1888** GOODE *Amer. Fishes* 249 What is known to whalers as a *toggle-harpoon is a modification of the lily-iron. **1884** KNIGHT *Dict. Mech., Suppl.*, *Toggle iron. **1888** *Encycl. Brit.* XXIV. 526/2 The hand harpoon is a light and efficient weapon..introduced by the Americans, to whom it is known as a 'toggle-iron'. **1847** WEBSTER, **Toggle-joint*, an elbow or knee-joint. **1869** *Routledge's Ev. Boy's Ann.* 412 The cranked knee or toggle joint. **1879** *Cassell's Techn. Educ.* IV. 12/2 A box of wooden soldiers, with a slightly jointed framework on which they can be stuck,..which elongates and contracts..is simply a combination of toggle-joints. **1874** SCAMMON *Marine Mammals* App. 312 It [the toggle] has a hole near one end, through which a rope is attached, which is termed the *toggle-lanyard. This lanyard is used in handling or confining the toggle. **1904** *Brit. & Col. Printer* 10 Mar. 14/2 Links pivoted to the lever are slotted to engage pins carried by the extension of the hand lever, which thus exerts a *toggle-like action on the lever. **1880** *Harper's Mag.* LX. 851 The engines, by means of the *toggle line, steadily haul the seine to the shore. **1883** *Century Mag.* Sept. 675/2 Attaching a *toggle noose where the trace joins the harness. **1885** C. G. W. LOCK *Workshop Receipts* Ser. IV. 210/1 The press employed may be either of the 'hydraulic' or of the '*toggle' pattern. **1877** KNIGHT *Dict. Mech.*, **Toggle-press*, one in which the platen is moved by the flexion or extension of two bars which unite to form a knee-joint. **1938** *Rev. Sci. Instruments* IX. 86/1 A *toggle switch allows application of the input pulses either..to the scaling circuit or to a thyratron pulse sharpener. **1962** *Times* 8 May 16/5 A steering column lever would be handier than the headlight toggle switch. **1976** *Gramophone* Apr. 1687/3 Neat toggle switches are provided for loudness, tape monitor, low and high filters and tone cancel.

toggle ('tɒg(ə)l), *v.*¹ [f. prec. sb.]

1. *trans.* To secure or make fast by means of a toggle or toggles. Also *fig.*

1836 *Knickerbocker* VIII. 207 What,..has the devil toggled you at last, Jacky? **1853** KANE *Grinnell Exp.* xi. (1856) 83 Each man..has a canvas strap..fastened to the tow-line; or, nautically,..toggled to the warp. **1899** W. CHURCHILL *R. Carvel* xiii, I..beheld him..toggle it [a flag] to the ensign halyard. **1899** *Outing* (U.S.) XXX. 229/1 In the *Mab* and other canoes employing this device, the stick is toggled at one end to the rudder yoke, and at the other to the collar of the deck tiller.

2. To furnish with a toggle or toggles.

1875 BEDFORD *Sailor's Pocket Bk.* vi. (ed. 2) 216 Toggle the bight with a stretcher. **1905** *Sat. Rev.* 14 Oct. 499/1 A Union Jack made of bunting..roped and toggled.

† **'toggle,** *v.*² *Obs. rare*⁻¹. [freq. of *tog*, TUG *v.*: see -LE 3.] *intr.* To tug, tussle.

a 1225 *Ancr. R.* 424 Heo ne schulen cussen nenne mon,.. ne toggen [*v.r.* toggle] mid him, ne pleien.

† **toggy, tuggy.** [? Connected with TOG *sb.*¹ or L. *toga* TOGA.] A kind of overcoat for the arctic regions.

1742 J. L. in *Naval Chron.* XII. 118 Our clothing is a beaver or skin tuggy, above our other clothes. **1768** WALES in *Phil. Trans.* LX. 122 We who stayed at the factory began to put on our winter rigging; the principal part of which was our toggy, made of beaver skins.

togh, toghe, obs. ff. TOUGH *a.*, TOW, TUG.

to-ȝe(i)n, to-ȝe(i)nes: see TO-GAINS.

togidashi (tɒgɪ'dæʃɪ). Also togi-dashi. [a. Jap., f. *togu* to whet, grind + *dasu* to produce, let appear.] A kind of Japanese lacquering in which several coats of lacquer, applied over gold or silver designs, are rubbed and ground down to let the underlying picture appear as if floating below the lacquer surface.

1881 *Trans. Asiatic Soc. Japan* IX. 26 For making *Togi-dashi*, gold dust of a slightly coarser quality is used than for ordinary *Hira-makiye.* **1911** *Encycl. Brit.* XV. 189/1 The togi-dashi design, when finely executed, seems to hang suspended in the velvety lacquer. **1911** [see NASHIJI]. **1972** *Times* 15 June 21/3 A two-case togidashi inro by Moei at £1,000.

togider, togither, etc., obs. ff. TOGETHER.

'togless, *a.* [f. TOG *sb.*¹ + -LESS.] Without togs or clothes; naked; also, without proper dress.

1857 E. M. WHITTY *Friends in Bohemia* II. 52 Till you are run down roofless and togless.

† **to-'glide,** *v. Obs.* [OE. *toglīdan*, f. TO-² + *glīdan* to GLIDE; = MHG. *zeglîten.*] *intr.* To glide or slip away or off; to pass away.

Beowulf 2486 Guð-helm toglad, gomela scylfing hreas blac. **a 1000** *Boeth. Metr.* vii. 34 Grundweal ȝearone; se toglidan ne þearf. **a 1046** *O.E. Chron.* an. 979 (MS. C.), Blodiȝ wolcen..wæs swyðost on middeniht oþywed..þonne hit dagian wolde þonne to glad hit. **a 1272** *Luue Ron* 43 in *O.E. Misc.* 94 Al so hwenne hit schal to-glide Hit is fals.

† **to-'gnaw,** *v. Obs.* Pa. t. **-gnew.** Pa. pple. **-gnowe(n).** [ME., f. TO-² + *gnawen, gnaȝen* to GNAW; = MHG., Ger. *zernagen.*] *trans.* To gnaw to pieces; to gnaw away.

13.. *K. Alis.* 4629 No let none houndes me to-gnawe [*Bodl. MS.* todrawe]. *Ibid.* 6119 And they al day..heore flesch to-gnowe. **c 1305** *St. Kath.* 248 in *E.E.P.* (1862) 96 Hi nome kene hokes of ire and hire flesche to-gnowe. **1340** HAMPOLE *Pr. Consc.* 863 Wormes þan sal it al to-gnaw. **14..** *Sir Beues* (M.) 2174 Into the caue cam lyons two,..anone they hym slewe And hym and his hors al to-gnewe.

† **to-'go,** *v. Obs.* [OE. *to-gán*, f. TO-² + *gán* to GO; = OHG. *za-, zigân*, MHG. *ze-, zergân*, Ger. *zergehen*, MLG. *togân.*] *intr.* To go in different directions, go asunder; to be divided, part, separate; to pass away, disappear.

c 1000 *Leg. Rood* 103 þa toeodon ða stanas, & ȝeopenode ðæt ȝet. **c 1000** ÆLFRIC *Hom.* II. 194 Seo sæ toeode on twa. **c 1175** *Lamb. Hom.* 141 þe see toeode and þet iraelisce folc wende ouer. **c 1275** LAY. 23980 Arthur..smot Frolle vppe þan helm þat he atwo toȝeode. **c 1315** SHOREHAM i. 790 Ȝet þaȝ þe fourme of brede togo, þat body bylefþ ȝet þanne. **13..** *Sir Beues* (A.) 1896 þow schelt nouȝt, whan we tegoþ, Lauȝande me wende fram. **1560** ROLLAND *Crt. Venus* IV. 704 My riding geir is all to gane and spent.

Togolese (təʊgəʊ'li:z), *a.* and *sb.* [f. *Togo* (see below) + -ESE, after F. *togolais.*] **A.** *adj.* Of or pertaining to the state of Togo (formerly Togoland) in W. Africa. **B.** *sb.* The people of Togo.

1957 *Keesing's Contemp. Archives* 27 Apr.–4 May 15511/1 Continued Togolese representation in the French National Assembly. **1962** A. LEJEUNE *Duel in Shadows* II. x. 142 The Togolese..are not too fond of Dr. Nkrumah. **1972** *Times* 9 Oct. (Nigeria Suppl.) p. ii/2 General Gowon visited Lome for the twelfth anniversary of Togolese independence. **1983** *Times* 25 Jan. 6/1 Thousands of Togolese and Beninese have already left Lagos.

† **to-grade,** *v. Obs. rare.* [f. TO-² + GRADE *v.*¹] *trans.* To degrade, put or bring down.

a 1440 *Sir Degrev.* 104 He hade a grete spyt of the knyght ..And thoght howe he best myght That dowghty to grade [*MS.* grode; *rimes* brade (*MS.* brode), hade, made].

† **to-grind,** *v. Obs.* [Late ME., f. TO-² + GRIND *v.*] *trans.* To grind to dust.

1393 LANGL. *P. Pl.* C. XII. 62 Good men for oure gultes he [God] al to-grynt to deþe. **c 1440** *Pallad. on Husb.* I. 1135 Eek oister shellis drie and al togrounde.

† **'to-grow,** *v. Obs. rare.* [f. TO-¹ + GROW *v.*] *intr.* To grow to or towards (something).

1422 tr. *Secreta Secret., Priv. Priv.* 230 Tho that haue a longe heede, and the eeris to-growynge to the forhede negh to the noose.

Hence † **to-'growing,** (*a*) *vbl. sb.*, a growth, an excrescence; (*b*) *ppl. a.*, growing on, attached.

[But in these the prefix is perh. TO-².]

1562 TURNER *Herbal* II. 31 The iuice..healeth outwaxynges or to growinges in the fleshe. *Ibid.* 70 b, Ornithogalum is a tendre stalk..with ij. or thre togrowyng branches in ye top.

togt (tɔxt). *S. Afr.* [a. Afrikaans, a. Du. *tocht* expedition, journey.] † **1.** A trading expedition or venture. *Obs.*

[**1816** C. I. LATROBE *Jrnl.* 6 May (1818) 265 The master.. was about to set off..on a trip..to dispose of it [*sc.* arrack] in barter... They call this, going *op de tocht.*] **1860** *Queenstown Free Press* 8 Feb., Horses have been discovered amongst those of 'smouses' who were returning..after a somewhat successful *togt.* **1862** LADY DUFF-GORDON *Lett.* (1921) 105 He has made a fortune by 'going on *Togt*'.

2. Casual labour, hired for a specific job.

1901 A. R. R. TURNBULL *Tales from Natal* 120 The black devils..so often put us about by deserting—without even the possibility of our being able to obtain togt even. **1948** *Rep. Native Laws Comm. 1946–8* (Dept. Native Affairs, S. Afr.) 37/1 Migrant labour tends to be casual and to produce less and earn less than stable labour. The supply of such labour is often badly adjusted to the demand... In Durban it is..a characteristic of so-called togt or daily labour.

3. *attrib.* and *Comb.*, as ***togt labour, labourer, work***; **togt boy,** a casual labourer; **togt-ganger** [ad. Afrikaans *togganger* (also used)], a travelling trader; **togt licence,** a licence authorizing the holder to undertake casual labour.

1898 *Port Elizabeth Tel.* (Weekly ed.) 2 Sept., A Chinaman refused to supply a small quantity of bread and sugar to a togt boy on Saturday. **1972** J. McCLURE *Caterpillar Cop* ix. 139 He had slunk up to the door..and informed the maid he was a *togt* boy. She..said there were no odd jobs going. **1879** *Cape Monthly Mag.* Feb. 88 For a long time he used to accompany the togtgangers (hawkers or traders). **1896** R. WALLACE *Farming Industr. Cape Colony* 91 The plant [*sc.* prickly pear] was first spread in the Colony by transport riders or 'togt-gangers'. **1957** L. G. GREEN *Beyond City Lights* 31 In slack times the clever speculators known as *toggangers* would drive out of Paarl with cavalcades of carts and wagons. **1951** *Cape Argus* 5 Jan. 5/7 Durban harbour had been crippled by a shortage of rail trucks and togt (casual) labour. *Ibid.*, A compound capable of housing up to 1,000 togt labourers should be set aside for this purpose. **1960** J. L. L. SISSON *S. Afr. Judicial Dict.* 121 Casual Labourer, in terms of Native Pass Laws, is synonymous with the term togt labourer. **1948** O. WALKER *Kaffirs are Lively* 172 A Native is required to carry on his person.. one or more of the following documents... 7. A receipt for *togt* (casual labour) licence. **1968** K. L. MCMAGH *Dinner of Herbs* xiv. 101 Is there work, togt work nearby?

togue[1] (təʊg). *rare.* [ad. L. *toga* gown, or a. OF. *togue* (14th c. in Godef. *Compl.*).] = TOGA 2.

1862 THOREAU *Yankee in Canada* iv. (1866) 70 He was lucky to have brought his togue, or frock coat with him.

togue[2] (təʊg). [Adaptation of Indian name in Maine and New Brunswick.] The great lake trout (*Salvelinus namaycush*) of North America; also called *lunge* or *longe* (LUNGE *sb.*[3]) and *namaycush.*

1877 HALLOCK *Sportsm. Gaz.* 304 The togue or gray trout of Maine and New Brunswick. **1884** L. L. HUBBARD *Woods & Lakes of Maine* 204 Lakers or togue, the largest of their lake fish. **1888** GOODE *Amer. Fishes* 466 The Togue or Lunge.. is held in much higher favor by the angler.

tog(u)yder, -ther, obs. ff. TOGETHER.

†**to-hack,** *v. Obs.* [OE. *tohaccian*, f. TO-[2] + *haccian* HACK *v.*[1]; = MHG., Ger. *zerhacken.*] *trans.* To hack to pieces.

c **1000** *Leg. Veronica* 166 in Grein *Angelsächs. Prosa* (1889) III. 186 Sume hiȝ wæron on feower dælas tohaccede. **1387** TREVISA *Higden* (Rolls) V. 281 He.. was alto hakked [L. *dilaniatus*] of Valentinianus his servauntes. *c* **1425** *Eng. Conq. Irel.* 82, & anoon-ryght the yonge man was al to-hakked to-for hym. **1597** *2nd Pt. Gd. Hus-wives Jewell* E vij, Take.. a knuckle of yong Veale.. and all to hack it.

toheroa (ˌtəʊəˈrəʊə). Also 9 tairoa. [a. Maori.] A large edible bivalve mollusc, *Amphidesma ventricosum*, native to New Zealand.

1873 J. E. TINNE *Wonderland of Antipodes* 66 She sent us a present of a basket of tairoas, a large white shell-fish from the coast, which is considered a delicacy... When roasted, or, better still, made into soup, they are not unlike the clams of New England. **1908** A. HAMILTON *Fishing & Sea-Foods Anc. Maori* 13 An enterprising firm in Auckland has recently started a factory for canning toheroa. **1934** *Bulletin* (Sydney) 18 Apr. 20/4 It is only quite recently that toheroa soup has had any standing in culinary circles. **1967** K. GILES *Death & Mr. Prettyman* i. 37 The number one has special black caviar, but the two has smoked Spanish swordfish and New Zealand toheroa patties. **1976** *Daily Colonist* (Victoria, B.C.) 1 Oct. 25/5 The toheroa has a distinctive flavor.

†**to-hew,** *v. Obs.* [OE. *to-héawan*, f. TO-[2] + *héawan* to HEW; = MHG. *zerhouwen*, Ger. *zerhauen.*] *trans.* To hew to pieces.

c **1000** ÆLFRIC *Saints' Lives* ii. 360 þæt basilla sceolde ȝebuȝan.. Oþþe hi man to-heowe mid heardum swurde on twa. *c* **1010** *O.E. Chron.* an. 1004 (Laud MS.), þa seonde he þ man sceolde þa scipu to heawan. *c* **1205** LAY. 178 þar Turnus feol Mid mechen to-heawen. **13..** *Sir Beues* (A.) 4407 þar hii were.. al to-hewe flesch & bon. *c* **1386** CHAUCER *Knt.'s T.* 1751 The helmes they tohewen and toshrede. **1494** FABYAN *Chron.* vi. clxxxviii. 191 The sayd felon.. at length was all to hewen and dyed forthwith.

†**to-hield,** *v. Obs.* [OE. *tóhieldan, f. TO-[1] + *hieldan*, HIELD *v.* Cf. OE. *tóheald* adj. inclined.] **a.** *trans.* To cause to incline, lean, bend, or fall over; to push or pull down. **b.** *intr.* To incline, heel over, bow down, fall, give way. **c.** *intr.* To bend one's course *to*, turn *to*, to approach.

c **1205** LAY. 1135 Ane burh swiðe stronge To-hælde [*c* 1275 to-haled] weoren þe walles. *Ibid.* 7522 þat þe helm to-hælde [*c* 1275 þat hit in wende]. *Ibid.* 14744 Bruttes heom æfter.. & heom to-heolden In æchere hælue. *Ibid.* 26809 þer me iseon mihte sorȝen inoȝe: sceldes scenen, scalkes fallen, halmes to-hælden.

to-ho (təʊˈhəʊ), *int. Sport.* A call to a pointer or setter to stop.

1825 *Sporting Mag.* XV. 348 It was no uncommon thing for him to call out 'To-ho', and sometimes, with increased emphasis, 'To-ho you devil', in his sleep. **1855** 'STONEHENGE' *Brit. Sports* (ed. 4) 32 The breaker should walk up to [the dog] quietly, crying 'Toho! toho! toho!' **1884** SPEEDY *Sport* 52 Hold up your hand and cry 'Toho'.

†ˈ**to-hope.** *Obs.* [OE. *tóhopa*, f. TO-[1] + *hopa* HOPE.] Hope, expectation.

c **888** K. ÆLFRED *Boeth.* x. §1 Seo godcunde lufu & se tohopa. *a* **900** *Ags. Ps.* (Th.) xxxix. 4 Eadiȝ byð se wer, þe his to-hopa byð to swylcum Drihtne. *c* **1175** *Lamb. Hom.* 155 Nimeð gode ileue to burne, to hope to helme. *a* **1240** *Ureisun* in *Cott. Hom.* 191 Mi lif and mi tohope.

tohoro, var. TAHARAH.

‖**tohu-bohu** (ˈtoːhuːˈboːhuː). Forms: 7 tohu and bohu, tohu-vavohu, -vabohu, 8–9 tohubohu. [a. Heb. *thōhū wa-bhōhū* 'emptiness and desolation', in Gen. i. 2, rendered in Bible of 1611 'without form and void'. So F. *thohu et bohu* (Rabelais 1548), *tohu-bohu* (Voltaire 1776).] That which is empty and formless; chaos; utter confusion.

[**1613** PURCHAS *Pilgrimage* (1614) 219 That Prophecie.. that the world should be two thousand yeares *Tohu* emptie and without Law.] **1619** —— *Microcosm.* xxviii. 275 It is.. not any figure, but a *Chaos*, a *Tohu and Bohu*, a meere confusion. **1643** TRAPP *Comm., Gen.* i. 24–5 (1867) I. 8/2 Man's heart is a mere emptiness, a very *Tohu vabohu.* **1645** A. HENDERSON *Serm. bef. Ho. Lords* in *Life* (1846) 105 That such a Tohu vavohu can be the face of the Kingdom of Christ. **1692** RAY *Disc.* I. ii. (1693) 5 The Earth.. which was made *tohu vabohu*, without form and void. **1875** GLADSTONE *Glean.* (1879) VI. 180 Yet a judge may.. be required to dive, at a moment's notice, into the tohu-bohu of inquiries, which have never yet emerged from the stage of chaos. **1883** BROWNING *Jochanan Hakkadosh* 721 How from this tohu-bohu—hopes which dive, And fears which soar. **1894** L. S. HOUGHTON tr. *Sabatier's St. Francis* iii. 36 That tohu-bohu of mystery and folly.

‖**tohunga** (ˈtɔhʊŋə, ˈtəʊhʊŋə). [Maori *tóhunga*, lit. one skilled in signs and marks, f. *tohu* sign, omen.

Cognate with Samoan *tufunga* tattooer, carpenter; in Tongan, artificer, skilled workman; in Horne Is. *tufuga* master workman, architect, etc.]

A Maori priest; a native doctor.

1831 G. BENNETT in *London Med. Gaz.* 12 Nov. 182/1 This species of Asplenium is a sacred plant among the New Zealanders..; it is used by the Tohunga, or Priest, when praying over a sick person. **1843** E. DIEFFENBACH *Trav. N.Z.* II. I. iv. 60 If a chief or his wife falls sick, the most influential tohunga.. attends. **1872** A. DOMETT *Ranolf* v. x, But he whose grief was most sincere.. Was Kangapo the Tóhunga—a Priest And fell Magician famous far and near. **1893** *Westm. Gaz.* 13 Feb. 10/1 His secret longings and natural tendencies are towards the tohungas, the only visible monuments of his old priestly *régime.* **1904** *Daily Chron.* 23 July 4/6 The methods of the 'tohungas', or Maori native doctors of New Zealand, are remarkable. **1928** [see ATUA]. **1938** R. D. FINLAYSON *Brown Man's Burden* 42 She was a witch all right—like her father the tohunga. **1943** [see RANGATIRA]. **1955** W. J. PHILLIPPS *Maori Carving Illustrated* 4 Some [carvings] were carried out under the instruction of the old tohunga. **1976–7** *Art N.Z.* Dec./Jan. 34/1 The art of kite making and flying played an important role in the lifestyles of the ancient Maoris. Their manufacture was a sacred and time-consuming affair, for, according to tradition, only a tohunga (priest) of some standing in the tribe could prepare them.

‖**toi** (ˈtɔi) [Maori.] Var. form of TI, q.v.

1861 BOWEN *Poems* 57 High o'er them all the toi waved, To grace that savage ground. **1909** *Auckland Weekly News* 29 May 17/4 A few other species are found, such as.. Toi (Cordyline indivisa)..; but these are few and scattered.

toich (tɔɪx). *Geogr.* [a. Dinka.] In Southern Sudan, a stretch of flat land near a river that is subject to annual flooding.

1948 J. D. TOTHILL *Agric. in Sudan* vii. 136 The 'toich' lands.. are primarily used as grazing lands. *Ibid.* 954 Toiches are a feature of Equatoria Province. **1955** P. A. BUXTON *Nat. Hist. Tsetse Flies* ix. 271 The same sharp edge may generally be observed in the southern Anglo-Egyptian Sudan, at the boundary of the 'toich' or grassy flood-plain on cotton soil, with deciduous woodland on ironstone. **1974** *Nature* 10 May 121/2 The site may have been subject to the type of annual flooding and partial drying which now occurs in 'toich' soils which adjoin rivers or 'khors' in the permanent swamps of the Sudd region in the southern Sudan.

Toidey (ˈtɔɪdɪ). Also toid(e)y. The proprietary name (in the U.S.) for a toilet-training apparatus that can be clipped or strapped on to an ordinary lavatory seat. Also *attrib.*

1924 *Official Gaz.* (U.S. Patent Office) 9 Dec. 300/2 Little Toidey... Water-Closet Seats for Infants, Attachable to Ordinary Water-Closet Seats. **1956** *Ibid.* 6 Mar. 42/2 Toidey. The Toidey Company, Gertrude A. Muller. **1963** M. MCCARTHY *Group* xiv. 323 She had set him on the new toidey-seat strapped to the regular toilet. *Ibid.*, She tried leaving him on the toidey. **1981** D. UHNAK *False Witness* xxiv. 164 It is the current day-by-day life we have to deal with, not mama and the toidy potty and papa and the primal scene.

toil (tɔɪl), *sb.*[1] Forms: 4–7 toyle, toile, (7 toiel), 7–8 toyl, 6– toil; see also the Sc. form TUILYIE. [a. AF. *toil, toyl* dispute, contention, forensic strife = OF. *tooil toeil, toel, touil, tueil* bloody mêlée, trouble, confusion, etc. (12th c. in Godef.), f. *tooillier*, etc.: see TOIL *v.*[1]]

1. †Verbal contention, dispute, controversy, argument (*obs.*); also, battle, strife, mêlée, turmoil (*arch.* or merged in 2).

(Quot. *a* 1450 may possibly belong to TOIL *sb.*[2] 3, but its date is in favour of this sense.)

[**1292** BRITTON I. xxvii. §6 Si soit le toyl entre eux et le viscounte. *Ibid.* II. xi. §21. *c* **1325** *Gloss. W. de Bibbesw.* in Wright *Voc.* 147 Entre pledoures sourd le toyl [*gloss* strif].] **13..** *K. Alis.* 2212 (Bodl. MS.) Gret & dedly was þe prees, Among þe toyle Hardapilon On of Alisaunders fon Seiȝ theoloman Alisaunders stiwarde Bryngen darryes folk dounwarde. ? *a* **1400** *Morte Arth.* 1802 The bolde.. Tittez tirauntez doune, and temez theire sadilles, And turnez owte of þe toile, whene hym tyme thynkkez. *c* **1400** *Destr. Troy* 6958 Toax þat tyme þurght the toile rode:.. And myche wo with his weppon wroght at þe tyme. [*c* **1425**–: see TUILYIE.] *a* **1450** *Bone Flor.* 1938 He was so tuggelde in a toyle. **1715** POPE *Iliad* I. 351 With these of old to toils of battle bred, In early youth my hardy days I led. **1746** FRANCIS tr. *Horace, Epist.* II. ii. 141 Like Gladiators, who with bloodless Toils Prolong the Combat, and engage with Foils. **1825** LONGF. *Burial of Minnisink* v, The weapons, made For the hard toils of war.

fig. **1642** ROGERS *Naaman* 136 Hence it is, that selfe hath so continuall a toile to hold correspondence with grace.

2. With *a* and *pl.* A struggle, a 'fight' (with difficulties); hence, a spell of severe bodily or mental labour; a laborious task or operation.

1576 GASCOIGNE *Steele Gl.* (Arb.) 74 Since al their toyles, and all their broken sleeps Shal scant suffize, to hold it stil vpright. **1589** PUTTENHAM *Eng. Poesie* III. xix. (Arb.) 215 To till it is a toyle. **1603** BRETON *Dial. Pithe & Pleas.* (Grosart) 7/1, I doo not loue so to make a toyle of a pleasure. **1735** SOMERVILLE *Chase* IV. 241 The Hunter-Horse, Once kind Associate of his sylvan Toils. **1832** HT. MARTINEAU *Life in Wilds* ix. 115 The toils of the day were done. **1855** KINGSLEY *Heroes* II. iv. (1868) 127 Many a toil must we bear ere we find it, and bring it home to Greece.

3. a. Without *a* or *pl.* Severe labour; hard and continuous work or exertion which taxes the bodily or mental powers.

1594 W. HAR[BERT] *Epicedium* 1 You that to shew your wits, have taken toyle. **1697** DRYDEN *Virg. Georg.* I. 24 Thou Founder of the Plough and Ploughman's Toyl. **1750** GRAY *Elegy* 29 Let not Ambition mock their useful toil. **1774** GOLDSM. *Nat. Hist.* (1776) VIII. 81 The toil of man is irksome to him, and he earns his subsistance with pain. **1860** TYNDALL *Glac.* I. xvii. 215 On the steeper slopes especially the toil was great. **1884** A. M. FAIRBAIRN in *Congregationalist* Apr. 276 You are many of you accustomed to toil manual; I a man accustomed to toil mental.

b. *transf.* The result of toil; that which is produced or accomplished by toil.

1713 ADDISON *Cato* IV. iv. 103 How is the toil of fate, the work of ages, The Roman Empire fallen!

4. *attrib.* and *Comb.*, as ***toil-assuaging, -beaten, -bent, -bowed, -hardened, -oppressed, -stained, -stricken, -won*** adjs.; **toil-drop**, a drop of sweat caused by toil. See also TOIL-WORN.

1726 POPE *Odyss.* xx. 452 This poor, tim'rous, toil-detesting drone. **1730–46** THOMSON *Autumn* 1223 The toil-strung youth, By the quick sense of musick taught alone. **1748** —— *Cast. Indol.* II. xxiii, The best and sweetest far, are toil-created gains. **1760** FAWKES tr. *Sappho, Epigr.* i. 2 The toil-experienc'd Fisher, Pelagon. **1781** COWPER *Conversat.* 732 The scenes of toil-renewing light. **1786** BURNS *Lament* viii, My toil-beat nerves, and tear-worn eye. **1791** COWPER *Odyss.* VII. 410 Ulysses toil-inured his words Exulting heard. **1805** SCOTT *Last Minstr.* II. xxviii, Till the toil-drops fell from his brows, like rain. **1839** CARLYLE *Chartism* x. 176 The toilwon conquest of his own brothers. **1847** MARY HOWITT *Ballads*, etc. 316 Toil-stricken, though so young. **1890** KIPLING *Poems 1886–1929* (1929) III. 289 They strove to stand to attention, to straighten the toil-bowed back. **1907** G. PARKER *Weavers* ix, The slave and the toil-ridden fellah.

toil (tɔɪl), *sb.*[2] Forms: 6 toyll(e, (tull, tole), 6–7 toyle, 6–8 toyl, toile, 6– toil. [a. OF. *teile, toile* (11th c. in Godef. *Compl.*), mod.F. *toile* cloth, web, etc.:—L. *tēla* web; F. pl. *toiles* 'large pieces of cloth bordered with thick ropes, stretched round an enclosure, for the purpose of capturing wild beasts; also, large nets stretched to take stags and other deer' (Littré).]

1. A net or nets set so as to enclose a space into which the quarry is driven, or within which the game is known to be. In later use usually *pl.*

sing. *a* **1529** SKELTON *How the douty Dk. of Albany* 269 About hym a parke Of a madde warke, Men call it a toyle. **1530** PALSGR. 281/2 Toyll for a prince to hunt with, *toille.* **1577–87** HOLINSHED *Chron.* III. 1120/2 A generall hunting with a toile raised of foure or fiue miles in length, so that manie a deere that day was brought to the quarrie. *a* **1667** COWLEY *Agric.* Wks. 1710 II. 722 He drives into a Toil the foaming Boar. **1827** D. JOHNSON *Ind. Field Sports* 18 The sudden jerk occasioned by an animal rushing at speed against the toil.

pl. **1530** PALSGR. 711/2, I sette, as a hunter setteth his hayes, or his toylles, or any other thinges to take wylde beestes with. **1554** in Kempe *Losely MSS.* (1836) 97 Yt hathe pleased the Quenes mat[ie].. to take yo[r] Accompt for the Revelles, Tentes, and Toyles. **1611** COTGR., *Toiles*, toyles; or a Hay to inclose, or intangle, wild beasts in. **1707** *Lond. Gaz.* No. 4358/3 The Toiles are already set round a large Lake. **1726** ARBUTHNOT *It cannot rain but it pours* Swift's Wks. 1755 III. I. 132 The wonderful Wild Man that was nursed in the woods of Germany by a wild beast, hunted and taken in toyls. **1852** MISS YONGE *Cameos* I. xxv. 200 His men-at-arms may come and catch me like a fox in the toils.

†**2.** A trap or snare for wild beasts. *Obs. rare.*

1607 TOPSELL *Four-f. Beasts* (1658) 574 The manner of taking of Wolfs.. an Iron toil which they still fasten in the earth with Iron pins. *a* **1629** HINDE *J. Bruen* x. (1641) 34 It is lawfull.. to set Toyles for Foxes. **1727** GAY *Fables* I. xxi. 21 Again he sets the poison'd toils.

3. *fig.* or in fig. context (*sing.* and *pl.*).

sing. *a* **1548** HALL *Chron., Rich. III* 56 Let vs not feare to enter in to the toyle where we may suerly sley hym. **1606** SHAKS. *Ant. & Cl.* v. ii. 351 As she would catch another Anthony In her strong toyle of Grace. **1671** MILTON *P.R.* II. 453 Extol not Riches then, the toyl of Fools. **1718** ROWE tr. *Lucan* I. 168 Who hope to share the spoil, And hold the World within on common toil. **1774** GOLDSM. *Nat. Hist.* (1776) VIII. 258 The spider's.. next care is to seize and secure whatever insect happens to be caught in the toil.

pl. *c* **1586** C'TESS PEMBROKE *Ps.* CXLII. i, Lord, thou.. knowest each path where stick the toyls of danger. **1648** HERRICK *Hesper., Disswasions fr. Idlenesse*, Armes and hands.. Are but toiles or manicles. *a* **1704** T. BROWN *On Beauties* Wks. 1730 I. 42 Each fair enchanter sets Toyles for my heart. **1738** WESLEY *Ps.* LVII. iii, While in the Toils of Hell I lie. **1810** SCOTT *Lady of L.* II. xxviii, Themselves in bloody toils were snared. **1897** B. STOKER *Dracula* iv. 41, I am surely in the toils... In the present state of things it would be madness to quarrel openly with the Count whilst I am so absolutely in his power. **1931** V. SACKVILLE-WEST *All Passion Spent* I. 69 Their mother quietly disentangling herself from their toils. **1958** E. BIRNEY *Turvey* v. 46 Soldiers in the toils of civilian law for thefts, burglaries, assaults, rapes and the odd murder. **1973** J. G. FARRELL *Siege of Krishnapur* vi. 91 How hopelessly Prejudice, on the point of throwing a net over Truth, had become enmeshed in its own toils.

4. *attrib.* and *Comb.*, as † **toil-house**, a building in which toils and other hunting equipments were housed; so † **toil-yard**.

1558 in Feuillerat *Revels Q. Eliz.* (1908) 48 One greate house called the Toyle house..with a Toyle yerde.

toil (tɔɪl), *v.*[1] Forms: 4-7 **toyle**, 5-7 **toile**, 7 **toyl** (toiel), 7- **toil**. See also TOLY *v.* and Sc. TUILYIE *v.* [a. AF. *toiler* to strive, dispute, wrangle = OF. *toeillier*, *tooillier*, *toillier*, *touellier*, mod.F. *touillier* (12th c. in Godef.), 'salir, souillier', to soil, stir up, agitate, in mod.F. dial. to mix, stir up; 'filthily to mix or mingle,..shuffle together, to intangle, trouble, or pester by scuruie medling; also, to bedurt, begrime, besmeare, etc.' (Cotgr. 1611); according to Hatz.-Darm.:—L. *tudiculāre* to stir, stir about, f. *tudicula* a machine for bruising olives. The development of sense was app. 'to stir up, make a stir or agitation, struggle, wrangle'.]

I. † **1.** *intr.* To contend in a lawsuit or an argument; to dispute, argue; also, to contend in battle; to fight, struggle. *Obs.*

[**1292** BRITTON v. x. §11 En ceo cas quant plusours heirs toillent entour heritage [etc.].] *c* **1330** [see TOILING *vbl. sb.*]. [*c* **1350** *Nominale Gall.-Angl.* (E.E.T.S.), *Homme plede et toile pur glebe*, M. motith and striuyth for rit of kyrke.] *c* **1380** *Anticrist* in Todd *Three Treat. Wyclif* (1851) 150 Crist wiþhelde no men of lawe ne pleders at þe barr for robes & fees..to toyle for worldly cause. *c* **1400** *Laud Troy Bk.* 6957 When Paris hadde with him thus toyled, Off his Armes he him dispoyled. *c* **1400** *Destr. Troy* 10160 The Troiens wiþ tene toiled full hard, Wiþ a Rumour full roide & a roght hate.

† **2.** *trans.* To pull, drag, tug about. *Obs.*

c **1325** *Body & Soul* 383 in *Map's Poems* (Camden) 344 Hit was in a deolful pleyt, Reuthliche i-toyled to and fro. *c* **1394** [see TOILING *vbl. sb.*]. *a* **1400** *Leg. Rood* (1871) 143 Þe dispitous Iewes nolde not spare Til trie fruit weore tore and toyled. *c* **1440** *Alphabet of Tales* 54 As Saynt Anton lay in a den in wildernes, a grete multitude of fendis come vnto hym and rafe hym, & toylid hym.

II. 3. *intr.* To struggle for some object or for a living; to engage in severe and continuous labour or exertion; to labour arduously. Often in the collocation ***toil and moil***: see MOIL *v.* 3.

c **1394** *P. Pl. Crede* 742 Y miȝt tymen þo troiflardes to toilen wiþ þe erþe, Tylyen & trewliche lyven. *c* **1400** *Langland's P. Pl.* A. XI. 183 (MS. T.) And alle kyne crafty men..toille for here foode. **1530** PALSGR. 758/2, I toyle, I stryve to gette my lyvyng, *je me estriue*... I toyle, I laboure, *je me trauaille*. **1548** FORREST *Pleas. Poesye* 57 The Pooreman to toyle for twoe pense the Daye. **1580**, etc. [see MOIL *v.* 3]. **1611** BIBLE *Luke* v. 5 Wee haue toyled all the night. *Ibid.* xii. 27 They toile not; they spinne not. **1654** GATAKER *Disc. Apol.* 17 For worldlie wealth, men can toil and moil all the week long. **1729** LAW *Serious C.* iv. (1732) 53 If he labours and toils, not to serve any reasonable ends of life. **1833** HT. MARTINEAU *Manch. Strike* ix. 101 Thirteen thousand workpeople—who toil for twopence halfpenny a day. **1909** R. NICOLL in *Mem. H. Bonar* 103 He toiled on till he was past eighty.

b. *fig.* To struggle mentally.

1788 V. KNOX *Winter Even.* I. ii. 22 Language toils in vain for expressions. **1831** SCOTT *Ct. Robt.* xxxi, Anna Comnena deeply toiled in spirit for the discovery of some means by which she might assert her sullied dignity.

c. *intr.* With adverbial extension: To move or advance toilsomely or with struggling and labour.

1781 COWPER *Truth* 457 The Soul reposing on assured relief..Forgets her labour as she toils along. **1836** W. IRVING *Astoria* I. 296 Trusting to his overtaking the barges as they toiled up against the stream. **1855** MACAULAY *Hist. Eng.* xii. III. 163 The road was deep in mire...the women and children weeping, famished, and toiling through the mud up to their knees. *Mod.* Toiling up the steep.

4. *trans.* To bring into some condition or position, or to procure, by toil; ***toil out***, to accomplish or effect by toil. Also with cognate obj. *rare.*

1667 MILTON *P.L.* x. 475, I Toild out my uncouth passage. **1796** COLERIDGE *Introd. to Sonn.* Poems 1877 I. 131 When, at last, the thing is toiled and hammered into fit shape. **1817** —— *Biog. Lit.* ix. I. 148 In Schelling..I first found a genial coincidence with much that I had toiled out for myself. **1823** PRAED *Troubadour* I. 487 'Toil yet another toil', quoth he.

5. To subject to toil, cause to work hard; to weary, tire, fatigue, esp. with work. ***toil out***, to tire out or exhaust with toil. *arch.* and *dial.*

1549 COVERDALE, etc. *Erasm. Par. Jas.* 36 You are vexed in your mynde, and..toyled with sondrye tumultes of cares. **1596** DANETT tr. *Comines* (1614) 328 The poore man that trauelleth and toileth his body to get foode. **1607** MARKHAM *Caval.* IV. (1617) 16 The very toyling him vpon the deep lands, will bring him to a weaknesse in his limbs. **1610** HOLLAND *Camden's Brit.* 55 The army was toiled out with cruell tempests. **1760** DODD *Hymn to Gd. Nat.* Poems (1767) 6 Steeds much toil'd, ill fed. **1825** SCOTT *Talism.* xvi, Physicians had to toil their wits to invent names for imaginary maladies. **1837** CARLYLE *Fr. Rev.* I. VII. ix, A man so tossed and toiled for twenty-four hours and more.

† **b.** *refl.* *Obs.*

1587 GOLDING *De Mornay* xi. (1592) 160 [For] the diuine Prouidence..to toyle it selfe in the cark and care of so many particular things. **1596** DANETT tr. *Comines* (1614) 220 What needed he thus to haue toiled himselfe? *a* **1677** HALE *Prim. Orig. Man.* IV. vi. 343 Let Men toyl themselves till their Brains be fired,..they will toyl in vain.

† **6.** *trans.* To labour upon; to work at; *esp.* to till (the earth, ground, or soil).

1552 HULOET, Toyle or labour the earth, *solicito*. **1614** W. B. *Philosopher's Banquet* (ed. 2) A ij, Like Alchemists toyling the Stone. **1616** SURFL. & MARKH. *Country Farme* 151 The Mules..are vsed to toile the earth.

III. † **7.** *trans. Cookery.* To stir, mix by stirring. *Obs.*

c **1430** *Two Cookery-bks.* 24 Toyle hem with Flowre, an frye hem. *Ibid.* 54 Toyle yt with þin hond al þes togederys. *c* **1550** LACY *Wyl Bucke's Test.* (Halliw.) 59 Sete him [the chine] on the fire, and toyle him with a pot staffe tyl he sethe for quailing and then he shal be browne of his owne kinde.

toil (tɔɪl), *v.*[2] [f. TOIL *sb.*[2]] *trans.* To trap or enclose in a toil; to drive (game) into a toil; also *fig.* to entrap, entangle; *dial.* to set (a trap); cf. TILL *v.*[1] 7.

1592 WARNER *Alb. Eng.* VIII. xli. (1612) 199 And hath he toyled vp his game? **1621** ELSING *Debates Ho. Lords* (Camden) App. 139 Seeing these poore men toyled in this maze of affliccions. **1887** T. HARDY *Woodlanders* xlvii, He laid the trap,..set it, or to use the local and better word 'toiled' it.

Hence **toiled** *ppl. a.*, netted, trapped, snared.

1852 JERDAN *Autobiog.* II. 16 The toiled bird had been liberated from its cage. **1854** S. DOBELL *Balder* xxiii. 85 Lying close like a toiled bird that with wide eyes Is mute and strange. *Ibid.* xxxvii. 186 Bind him down With the strong bonds of love..Naked and toiled.

toilanette: see TOILINET.

‖ **toile**[1] (twal). In 6 also toyl(e, Also 8 toille. [F. *toile* linen cloth, canvas:—L. *tēla* web.]

1. † **a.** Cloth; in quot. 1575, cloth or canvas used for painting on. *Obs. rare.*

1561 *Reg. Privy Council Scot.* I. 172 To persew for ane schip and toylis, quhilk is callit lynnyng clayth in oure language. **1575** LANEHAM *Let.* 51 By toile and pensill so lyuely exprest.

b. A painting on canvas.

1919 R. FRY *Let.* 6 Oct. (1972) II. 458 Her old studio.. was stacked with her husband's immense *toiles* of Majorca. **1949** N. MITFORD *Love in Cold Climate* II. v. 237 The dozens of *toiles* by him..are worthy of the Douanier himself.

2. A dress material: see quots. Also with Fr. defining addition; esp. ***toile de Jouy***, a fabric for upholstery or drapery with a characteristic floral, figure, or landscape design, usu. in one colour on a light background, orig. made at Jouy-en-Josas near Paris.

1794 A. YOUNG *Trav. France* (ed. 2) I. xix. 552 The linens ..are *toille de menage*; that exported to Spain is..called *toille de leon*. **1858** SIMMONDS *Dict. Trade*, *Toile* (French), linen cloth. **1873** *Young Englishwoman* Oct. 506/1 Paletot of grey-coloured toile de laine. **1899** *Westm. Gaz.* 22 June 3/2 A simple pretty afternoon gown of blue toile, that mixture of silk and linen. **1923** *Weekly Dispatch* 11 Feb. 14, 5,000 Yards of Toile de Chine. Made of finest Spun Silk. **1934** E. WAUGH *Handful of Dust* i. 16 She hasn't paid for the toile-de-jouy chaircovers we made her last April. **1958** I. MURDOCH *Bell* ix. 135 She saw the flat in Knightsbridge.. glowing with stripy wallpaper and *toile de Jouy*. **1983** *Harrods Mag.* Spring & Summer 143 'Toile de Jouy', a French pastoral scene in Deep Pink on Plain Pink.

3. A pattern for a garment made up in muslin, cotton, or the like, for fitting or for use in making copies.

1959 *Guardian* 18 Nov. 6/4 An excellent little collection of models made from toiles bought in Paris. **1982** *Times* 29 June 13/4, I spent seven months of a two-year couture course *just* making toiles for skirts.

‖ **toilé**[2] (twale). [Fr. *toilé*, f. *toile* TOILE[1].] In lace-making, an area with a closely-worked inwrought pattern.

1865 F. B. PALLISER *Hist. Lace* iii. 27 The flower or ornament..is called 'toilé', from the flat, close texture resembling linen, and also from its being often made of that material, or of muslin. **1902** [see BINCHE]. **1953** M. POWYS *Lace & Lace-Making* v. 41 The linen part or Toilé should show the effect of the raised work.

toile, obs. f. TUILLE, piece of body armour.

toile, obs. f. TOIL; obs. Sc. form of TOOL.

toiled (tɔɪld), *ppl. a.*[1] [f. TOIL *v.*[1] + -ED[1].]

1. Exhausted with toil; worn-out, weary. *arch.* and *dial.*

1592 WYRLEY *Armorie, Capitall de Buz* 144 His toyled mates do tend But how from death they may themselues defend. **1614** W. B. *Philosopher's Banquet* (ed. 2) A iij, Tedious howres and toyled braines. **1622** DRAYTON *Poly-olb.* xxv. 203 When the toyld Cater home them to the Kitchen brings, The Cooke doth cast them out, as most vnsauory things. **1791** COWPER *Iliad* II. 466 Ev'ry buckler's thong Shall sweat on the toil'd bosom.

Comb. **1895** J. L. MAXWELL *W. B. Thomson* iv. 41 A pale, toiled-looking young mother.

† **2.** Of plants or soil: Subjected to or improved by cultivation, tilled, cultivated. *Obs.*

1578 LYTE *Dodoens* III. lix. 399 There be two sortes of Hoppes, the manured or toyled Hop, and the wilde hedge Hoppe. **1601** HOLLAND *Pliny* (1634) II. 278 Cala..loueth to grow in toiled and ploughed grounds. **1616** SURFL. & MARKH. *Country Farme* 181 Sowne in a well toyled ground.

toiled, *ppl. a.*[2]: see TOIL *v.*[2]

toilenet, -ette: see TOILINET.

toiler ('tɔɪlə(r)). [f. TOIL *v.*[1] + -ER[1].] One who toils, a hard worker.

1549 COVERDALE, etc. *Erasm. Par. Peter* i. 2 Goodes (in getting and heaping together wherof the toylers of the world thinke themselfes fortunate). **1580** HOLLYBAND *Treas. Fr. Tong*, *Tracasseur*, a busie body, a toyler to little purpose. **1858** MISS MULOCK *Th. ab. Wom.* 86 'In all labour there is profit'—ay, and honour too, if the toilers could but recognise it. **1909** *Chr. Express* 1 Mar. 41/2 Any toiler in the field of sociology—black or white.

toilet ('tɔɪlɪt), *sb.* Forms: 6 *Sc.* **tulat, tolat**, 7-8 **toylet**, 8 **toylett**, 7-9 **toilette** (now usu. twɑːˈlɛt), (8 **toillette**), 7- **toilet**; also 7 **twil(l)et**, (7-9 **twilight**). (Cf. *twily* in *Eng. Dial. Dict.*, var. *toily*.) [a. F. *toilette* (twalɛt), dim. of *toile* cloth: see TOIL *sb.*[2] Cf. TILLET[1].

Most, if not all, of the English senses are to be found in Fr. (see Littré), esp. in 17th cent. use.]

† **1. a.** A piece of stuff used as a wrapper for clothes. *Obs.*

Also, in dictionaries, from Cotgrave, a night-dress bag; app. an error and never in Eng. use.

1540 in Pitcairn *Crim. Trials* (1830) I. 302 For pointis to þe Cote and brekis, and ane Tulat to þe Cote..iijs. **1541** *Ibid.* 318 For ix elnis blak freis, to lyne þe Cote... Item, for pointis and ane tolat to turs it to Sanct Johnestoune. **1611** COTGR., *Toilette*, a Toylet; the stuffe which Drapers lap about their clothes; also, a bag to put night-clothes, and buckeram, or other stuffe to wrap any other clothes, in.

[**1656** BLOUNT *Glossogr.*, *Toylet* (Fr. *toylette*), a bag or cloth to put night clothes in. **1858** SIMMONDS *Dict. Trade*, *Toilet*, a bag or case for night-clothes.]

† **b.** A towel or cloth thrown over the shoulders during hair-dressing; also, a shawl. *Obs. rare.*

1684 J. PHILLIPS in tr. *Plutarch's Morals* (1874) IV. 238 Pleasant..was the answer of Archelaus to the barber, who, after he had cast the linen toilet about his shoulders, put this question to him, How shall I trim your majesty? In silence, quoth the king. **1687** A. LOVELL tr. *Thevenot's Trav.* III. 37 When they go abroad, they wear a Chal which is a kind of toilet of very fine Wool made at Cachmir.

2. A cloth cover for a dressing-table (formerly often of rich material and workmanship); now usually called a *toilet-cover*.

1682 *Lond. Gaz.* No. 1739/4 A gold-coloured Tabby Twilet and Pincushion with Silver Lace. **1683** *Ibid.* No. 1811/4 Stolen the 20th Instant, a Toilet of blew Velvet, with a Gold and Silver Fringe. **1696** PHILLIPS (ed. 5), *Toilet*, a kind of Table-cloth, or Carpet of Silk, Sattins, Velvet or Tissue, spread upon a Table in a Bed-chamber. **1703** *Countrey Farmer's Catech.* (N. s.v. *Knit-knot*), Not to spend their time in knit-knots, patch-work, fine twilights. **1767** MRS. DELANY *Life & Corr.* Ser. II. (1862) I. 104 Your fancy about taking a gimp round the flowers on the toilet would be pretty, but too much work. **1858** SIMMONDS *Dict. Trade*, *Toilet*,..a cotton cover for a dressing-table.

3. *collective.* The articles required or used in dressing; the furniture of the toilet-table; toilet-service; also, †a case containing these (*obs.*).

1662 EVELYN *Diary* 9 June, The greate looking-glasse and toilet of beaten and massive gold was given by the Queene Mother. **1718** LADY M. W. MONTAGU *Let. to C'tess of Mar* 10 Mar., In her bedchamber, her toilet was displayed consisting of two looking-glasses [etc.]. **1727-41** CHAMBERS *Cycl.*, *Toilet*,..the dressing-box, wherein are kept the paints, pomatums, essences, patches, &c.; the pin-cushion, powder-box, brushes, &c. are esteemed parts of the equipage of a lady's toilet. **1815** *Chron.* in *Ann. Reg.* 53/2 A superb toilet of plate. *Ibid.* 55/1 His toilet is of silver. **1853** KANE *Grinnell Exp.* iii. (1856) 26 To one long string was fastened..my entire toilet, a tooth-brush, a comb, and a hair-brush.

4. The table on which these articles are placed; a toilet-table.

c **1695** PRIOR *Ode*, '*The merchant*', etc. 6 My darling lyre, Upon Euphelia's toilet lay. **1709** —— *Hans Carvel* 60 An untouch'd Bible grac'd her toilet: No fear that thumb of hers should spoil it. **1789** GIBBON *Autobiog.* (1854) 100 My book was on every table, and almost on every toilette. **1803** MARY CHARLTON *Wife & Mistress* I. 118, I have made up a twilight in her room, and put my white taffety pin-cushion upon it. **1818** SCOTT *Br. Lamm.* xxvi, On the toilette beside, stood an old-fashioned mirror, in a fillagree frame. **1838** W. WALLACE *Mackintosh's Hist. Eng.* VIII. v. 188 The letter of the princess Anne, said to have been left by her on her toilet, was not delivered.

5. a. The action or process of dressing, or, more recently, of washing and grooming.

Transf. from the table (sense 4) to the process there performed, app. through the phr. 'at her toilet'.

1681 tr. *Combes' Versailles*, etc. (1684) 32 She was given to understand, being at her Toilette, of the death of her Husband. **1712-14** POPE *Rape Lock* III. 24 The long labours of the Toilet cease. **1713** SWIFT *Cadenus & Vanessa* 50 Ev'ry trifle that employs The out or inside of their heads Between their toylets and their beds. **1777** MME. D'ARBLAY *Early Diary* (1889) II. 194 We were down before Mrs. Wall, whose toilette is an affair of moment. **1811** B. WYNNE *Diary* 18 Sept. in *Wynne Diaries* (1940) III. x. 340 We began our toilette which refreshed us much after the fatigue of having sat up the whole night. **1822** W. IRVING *Braceb. Hall* (1849) 51 She actually spent an hour longer at her toilette, and made her appearance with her hair uncommonly frizzed and powdered. **1826** in *Sheridaniana* 309 One morning, when finishing his toilet. **1858** LYTTON *What will he do* II. iv, Lionel's toilet was soon hurried over. **1890** G. GISSING *Emancipated* I. I. iii. 83 But when at length he appeared at the dinner-table, once more fresh from his toilet, then did a gleam of animation transform his countenance. **1939** T. S. ELIOT *Old Possum's Bk. Pract. Cats* 20 They make their toilette and take their repose.

b. The reception of visitors by a lady during the concluding stages of her toilet: very fashionable in the 18th c. Now *Hist.* (Cf. *toilet-call* in 9.)

1703 STEELE *Tend. Husb.* I. i, You shall introduce him to Mrs. Clerimont's Toilet. **1765** CHESTERF. *Let. to A. C. Stanhope* 21 Mar., I carried him a little time ago to a lady's toilette, who was delighted with him. **1786** MME. D'ARBLAY *Diary* 19 Aug., I am forced to deny all admission to my toilette, as it has never taken place without making me too late.

6. Manner or style of dressing; dress, costume, 'get-up'; also, a dress or costume, a gown.

1752 A. HERVEY *Let.* 27 Nov. in *11th Rep. Hist. MSS. Comm.* App. IV. 380 in *Parl. Papers 1887* (C. 5060-111) XLVII. 309 'Tis so long (tell Lady Caroline) since I have seen so spruce a Toylet as hers. **1821** SCOTT *Kenilw.* iii, His toilette had apparently cost him some labour, for his clothes ..were of the newest fashion, and put on with great attention. **1821** *Sporting Mag.* IX. 32 The lady was beautiful, her *tourneure* distinguished, her toilette elegant. **1849** THACKERAY *Pendennis* xxiv, Madame noted every article of toilette which the ladies wore. **1867** LATHAM *Black & White* 128 We observed some show of evening toilet. **1883** *Truth* 31 May 745/2 Lady Dudley's black toilette was much admired. **1889** GUNTER *That Frenchman* x, This toilet is a mass of fleecy muslin.

7. A dressing-room; in *U.S. esp.* a dressing-room furnished with bathing facilities. Hence, a bath-room, a lavatory; (contextually), a lavatory bowl or pedestal; a room or cubicle containing a lavatory.

1819 BYRON *Juan* I. cliii, There is the closet, there the toilet. **1858** SIMMONDS *Dict. Trade, Toilette* (French), a dressing-table; an ante-room for dressing. **1895** in *Funk's Stand. Dict.* **1909** in *Cent. Dict. Supp.* **1917** C. R. WADHAMS *Simple Directions for Chambermaid* 50 The toilet should be kept absolutely clean. Hot water with washing soda or cleanser is often needed to clean it thoroughly, using the chamber-cloth or toilet brush for that purpose. **1930** F. J. EBLE tr. *Grisar's Martin Luther* v. 108 In the second story of this tower there was a so-called hypocaust, i.e., a furnace-room, and beneath it the toilet (*cloaca*) of the monks. **1955** A. HUXLEY *Genius & Goddess* 109 She..poured the perfume into the toilet and pulled the plug. **1957** J. BRAINE *Room at Top* xxiv. 196 You could watch me on the toilet. **1959** S. GIBBONS *Pink Front Door* xviii. 222 Such a *gentleman*.. always pretended not to see you if he met you coming out of the toilet. **1968** B. HINES *Kestrel for Knave* 193 He struck a match. A moment while it flared, then two urinals, a toilet in a doorless cubicle, and the sink without a tap. **1979** L. & J. BROWN *Our Miracle called Louise* i. 16 A harsh voice beat against the door of a toilet at the home. I had bolted myself inside.

8. *transf.* from 5. **a.** *Surgery.* The cleansing of a part after an operation. **b.** The cleaning up of a street, a ship, etc. **c.** Preparation for execution (in Fr. form *toilette*: see Littré s.v. *Toilette* 10 a).

a. 1879 *Brit. Med. Jrnl.* 24 May 790 Spencer Wells, by his careful toilette of the peritoneum. **1890** BILLINGS *Nat. Med. Dict.*, *Toilet of the peritoneum*, cleansing the abdominal cavity after abdominal section.

b. 1901 *Daily Tel.* 9 Mar. 9/6 The toilet of London—to use the picturesque phrase of an authority consulted yesterday—cannot be satisfactory unless the streets are flushed with water every night. **1907** C. URBAN *Cinematograph* 21 The performance of the toilet of an ocean greyhound.

c. 1885 DU CANE *Punishm. & Prev. Crime* ii. 23 The hangman was not allowed to enter the gaol even to receive his wage, but was paid over the gates, the 'toilette' or pinioning being performed by the 'yeomen of the halter'. **1903** LD. R. GOWER *Rec. & Remin.* 281 The ghastly ceremony of his toilette [for the guillotine], as they call the pinioning and cutting off the hair at the back of his head.

9. *attrib.* and *Comb.* **a.** Of or pertaining to the toilet (mainly sense 7): as *toilet article, bucket, -call* (see 5 b), *-can, -chamber, jug, kit, -pail, -quilt, -service, -set, -soap, -stand, -tidy, ware,* etc.; *toilet block, bowl, lid, seat, stall, tank.*

1848 THACKERAY *Van. Fair* vii, [She] examined the dreary pictures and toilette appointments. **1868** *Mich. Agric. Rep.* VII. 351 Perfumery toilet articles. **1981** 'J. ROSS' *Dark Blue & Dangerous* iv. 23 He checked the essentially male shaver and toilet articles. **1976** *Star* (Sheffield) 26 Nov. 26/5 A two-classroom mobile unit and toilet block. **1947** E. HODGINS *Mr. Blandings builds his Dream House* II. xii. 164 One bathroom seemed all but finished... A toilet bowl was in place. **1983** *Out of Town* Dec. 16/3 We could at least instal the odd alligator in the toilet-bowl. **1957** H. ROOSENBURG *Walls came tumbling Down* 11 A guard would..open one cell, and allow two prisoners to come out, one with the toilet bucket, the other with the water jug. **1827** CARLYLE *Germ. Rom.* I. 26 Toilette calls were not in fashion. **1858** SIMMONDS *Dict. Trade, Toilet-can*, a tin can for water for a dressing-room... **1853** JAMES *Agnes Sorel* (1860) I. 87 When they had entered his toilet-chamber, the Duke cast himself into a chair. **1873** J. H. EWING *Flat Iron for Farthing* iv. 37, I fancied that I heard the familiar sound of Rubens lapping water from the toilette jug in my room at home. **1913** C. MACKENZIE *Sinister Street* I. II. iv. 198 After trying to soak a shadowy tomcat down below with water from the toilet-jug Michael and Alan would undress. **1922** S. LEWIS *Babbitt* xiii. 163 The leather seat piled with dingy toilet-kits, and the air nauseating with the smell of soap and toothpaste. **1982** D. BAGLEY *Windfall* xxii. 221 Stafford took his toilet kit and went into the bathroom. **1848** THACKERAY *Van. Fair* xxxi, He would make a present of the silver essence-bottles and toilet knicknacks to a young lady. **1971** J. D. MACDONALD *Seven* (1974) vi. 143 Turned toilet lid down. Sat on it. **1721** CIBBER *Refusal* II. i, Vanity is the only fruit of toilette lucubrations. **1909** ELIZ. BANKS *Myst. Frances Farrington* xiv. 162 Toilet odds and ends, such as hair-pins, safety-pins,..thread and needles. **1858** SIMMONDS *Dict. Trade, Toilet-pail*, a tin pail for holding slops in a bedroom. **1858** SIMMONDS *Dict. Trade, Toilet-quilt*, a bed-cover or cover for the dressing-table. **1941** N. LAST *Diary* 4 Aug. in *Nella Last's War* (1983) 165, I remember washing the floor and toilet seat. **1982** J. AIKEN *Whisper in Night* 114 A small round lavatory, with a mahogany Victorian toilet seat. **1855** GEO. ELIOT in *Fraser's Mag.* June 706/1 A decanter and a sugar-basin or pie-dish, are an ample toilette service for them. **1858** SIMMONDS *Dict. Trade, Toilet-set, Toilet-service*, earthenware and glass utensils for a dressing-room. **1890** O. WILDE *Picture of Dorian Gray* (1891) viii. 138 A chased silver Louis-Quinze toilet-set. **1977** G. MARTON *Alarum* 6 The *New Yorkers* on top of Claire's toilet set. **1839** URE *Dict. Arts* 1147 Ordinary soft toilet soap... The fat generally preferred is good hog's lard. **1978** R. LUDLUM *Holcroft Covenant* xxiii. 265 If they let the weapon through, he was to reassemble it immediately, in the toilet stall of a men's room. **1766** *Gentl. Mag.* Dec. 558/1 A beautiful alabaster..intended for..her toilet-stand. **1974** R. B. PARKER *Godwulf Manuscript* xvi. 126 There was nothing in the toilet tank. **1912** Toilet-tidy [used s.v. TIDY *sb.* c]. **1921** D. H. LAWRENCE *Let.* 10 Nov. (1962) 674, I haven't heard from him, so I can't send him..a set of toilet-tidies until I do. **1928** A. M. DAVIES *Bk. with Seven Seals* xvii. 380 Mary Anne was not inspired with any admiration for the antimacassars and toilet-tidies that she made. **1864** *Hist. North-Western Soldiers' Fair* (Chicago) 168, 1 set fancy toilet ware. **1977** *Western Morning News* 30 Aug. 2/3 Woolland, Son & Manico have received instructions from private vendors to sell by auction..toilet ware.

b. Special Comb.: **toilet-basket**, a wicker dressing-case; **toilet box**, a box containing toilet articles; **toilet brush**, (*a*) a brush used in washing and grooming; (*b*) a lavatory brush; †**toilet-cap**, a cap formerly worn by men of fashion while dressing; **toilet-case**, a dressing-case; **toilet-cloth**, a cloth for the toilet-table; **toilet club** (see quot. 1966); **toilet-cover**, *toilet-cloth*; **toilet-cup**, a cup, vase, or the like used as a receptacle for small articles of the toilet; **toilet-glass**, a looking-glass for dressing, a toilet-table mirror; **toilet humour** = *lavatory humour* s.v. LAVATORY *sb.* 8; **toilet paper**, soft paper prepared: †(*a*) for shaving, hair-curling, etc.; (*b*) for use in lavatories; also *attrib.*; **toilet powder**, a form of dusting powder employed in the toilet, talcum powder; **toilet roll**, a roll of toilet paper (*b*); also *attrib.*; **toilet-room**, a dressing-room; in *U.S. spec.* a lavatory or bath-room (*Funk's Stand. Dict.* 1895); **toilet-sponge**, a sponge of fine texture for washing; **toilet-table**, a dressing-table furnished with the utensils and materials of the toilet; **toilet tent**, a tent serving as a lavatory; **toilet tissue**, tissue for use as toilet paper (*b*); **toilet-training** *vbl. sb.*, the training of a child to adopt acceptable habits of urination and defecation; hence **toilet-train** *v. trans.*, **toilet-trained** *ppl. a.*; **toilet-vase**: see *toilet-cup*; **toilet-vinegar**, aromatic vinegar used as an emollient; **toilet-water**, perfumed liquid for the toilet.

1908 *Westm. Gaz.* 23 Jan. 4/2 The new automobile *toilet basket is just the thing to carry when touring... It contains ..everything necessary for the toilet. **1774** J. WEDGWOOD *Let.* 2 Mar. (1965) 158 We shall send you some *Toilet boxes. **1869** LADY C. SCHREIBER *Jrnl.* (1950) I. 10 A fan-shaped toilet box made of Chelsea china. **1936** *Burlington Mag.* July 26/1 The tall rectangular toilet-box bears the old standard hall-marks of 1723–24. **1897** *Sears, Roebuck Catal.* 33/2 Rubber *Toilet Brush. For the nails and hands. **1917** Toilet brush [see sense 7 above]. **1976** *Sunday Mail* (Glasgow) 26 Dec. 5/7 We went into a bar and found a toilet brush in the gents which still had a price label on it. **1660** PEPYS *Diary* 3 Sept., To get [my Lord]..a *toilet cap, and comb case of silk, to make use of in Holland. ?**1879** S. F. P. *Stepping Westward* 8 My *toilet case for my brush and comb. **1889** H. F. WOOD *Englishman of Rue Cain* xi, One of our governesses had a toilette-case sent her as a present. **1884** W. S. GILBERT *Princess Ida* ii. 69 He grew moustachios, and he took his tub, And he paid a gui-nea to a *toi-let club—And he paid a gui-nea to a toi-let club. **1966** J. S. COX *Illustr. Dict. Hairdressing & Wigmaking* 150/2 *Toilet club*, a barber's shop which, in the 19th cent., offered reduced charges to clients who paid a regular quarterly or yearly subscription. **1838** C. GILMAN *Recoll. Southern Matron* xxix. 207 The bride's chamber..neatly set off with white curtains and *toilet cover. **1858** SIMMONDS *Dict. Trade, Toilet-cover.* **1904** E. NESBIT *Phœnix & Carpet* xii. 226 He's pulled the toilet-cover off the dressing-table with all the brushes and pots and things. **1818** M. EDGEWORTH *Let.* 29 Oct. (1971) 132 Long rolling *toilette glass and every piece of furniture belonging to better times. **1848** THACKERAY *Van. Fair* lviii, The dreary little toilet-glass on the dressing-table. **1956** AUDEN & KALLMAN *Magic Flute* (1957) 60 Indulged in *toilet-humour with his cousin. **1884** *Stationers' & Booksellers' Jrnl.* 31 Mar. 3/1 An attractively put-up packet of *toilet paper. **1907** *Yesterday's Shopping* (1969) 340/1 Automatic toilet paper rack... Only one sheet of paper can be drawn at a time. **1956** [see *lavatory paper* s.v. LAVATORY *sb.* 8]. **1976** M. H. KINGSTON *Woman Warrior* (1977) 181 Her sister went into one of the stalls and got handfuls of toilet paper and wiped her off. **1840** *Picayune* (New Orleans) 28 July 4/1 [Merchandise includes].. perfumed *toilet and pearl powders. **1898** W. J. LOCKE *Idols* viii. 107 A delicate odour of toilette-washes and powder hung on the warmth of the room. **1934** A. P. HERBERT *Holy Deadlock* 172 Mr. Rigby..propped the door open with a *toilet roll. **1961** *Guardian* 20 Jan. 2/7, 17 toilet roll holders ..have been broken or stolen. **1982** *Times* 1 June 18/6 There would seem to be very little difference between one soft toilet roll and another. **1794** MAR. J. HOLROYD in *Girlhood of M. J. H.* (1896) 289 We have put a *Toilette Table and a neat Pembroke Table..in your own Room. **1902** *Daily Chron.* 20 June 10/4 Visitors to London..see her now at her toilet table. **1969** *Guardian* 2 Sept. 6/7 A crushed marquee, two burnt-out *toilet tents, and a partly demolished fence. **1968** N. GIOVANNI in W. King *Black Short Story Anthol.* (1972) 30 We'd get slightly used *toilet tissue with an article on it or brown paper bags with short sayings or just a note to say they dig us. **1982** *Verbatim* Summer 5/1 Take lavatory paper, or, in the genteel euphemism of Adspeak, toilet tissue. **1951** *Med. Jrnl. Austral.* XXXVIII. II. 111/2 Of our 73 children, 43 were *toilet trained with impatience. **1961** *Guardian* 8 May 6/1 When a baby shows signs of being 'toilet trained' a mother can look forward to the end of nappy washing. **1980** A. CORNELISEN *Flight from Torregreca* x. 202 The long process of toilet training her children. **1940** *Time* 15 Apr. 48/1 *Toilet Training. **1955** B. SPOCK *Baby & Child Care* 177 Sometimes parents make a great fuss about toilet training. **1964** M. ARGYLE *Psychol. & Social Probl.* i. 19 An example of a Freudian hypothesis which has been definitely refuted is the hypothesis that early or traumatic toilet training should lead to an anal personality. **1973** E.-J. BAHR *Nice Neighbourhood* ii. 19, I hope Women's Lib never gets to hear about it, but..it was like fun to sit and talk about toilet training. **1874** BIRCH *1st & 2nd Egypt. Rooms Brit. Mus.* 32 The present *toilet-vase is a remarkably fine example of this kind of ware [glazed steatite]. **1867** LADY HERBERT *Cradle L.* viii. 218 Even scented soap and *toilette vinegar were ransacked from his stores. **1855** DICKENS *Dorrit* II. xiv, A bottle of sweet *toilette water.

Hence **toi'letic** *a. nonce-wd.*, of or pertaining to the toilet.

1879 BAKER *Cyprus* 13 He..plunged into..their numerous small packages, rumpling clean linen, and producing a toilettic chaos.

toilet ('tɔɪlɪt), *v.* [f. prec. sb.] **a.** *intr.* To perform one's toilet, to wash and attire oneself. **b.** *trans.* To furnish with a toilet; to dress, attire.

1840 HALIBURTON *Letter Bag* i. 7 Rose and toileted, went on deck. **1850** 'PETER CROOK' *War of Hats* 52 A Guy Fawkes figure toiletted and chaired. **1893** LELAND *Mem.* II. 177 As soon as I had toiletted and gone below.

c. To assist or supervise in using a toilet (sense 7); *refl.* to use a toilet unaided.

1954 F. G. BLAKE *Child, his Parents & Nurse* v. 150 Some children stay awake after they have been toileted. **1973** *Lancet* 9 June 1301/1 The same type of elderly patient..may be..wheeled to the toilet in sanitary chairs, or toileted on these within the ward. **1976** *Listener* 19 Feb. 206/1 He is 100 per cent physically and mentally handicapped... He cannot walk, talk, feed or toilet himself.

Hence **'toileted** *ppl. a.*, dressed, costumed, garbed (chiefly as second element); **'toileting** *vbl. sb.*

1864 'P. PATERSON' *Glimpses of Real Life* xxx. 289 There is a gay cavalcade of exquisitely-'toileted' ladies. **1875** BRET HARTE *John Oakhurst* Wks. 1880 III. 120 And then the long hotel piazza came in view, efflorescent with the full-toileted fair. **1882** ANNIE EDWARDES *Ballroom Repentance* I. 3 There wasn't a well toiletted woman there. **1954** F. G. BLAKE *Child, his Parents & Nurse* v. 157 Until the child has thoroughly mastered his impulses to soil and has incorporated his mother's standards into his conscience, successful achievement in toileting is dependent upon his reward (mother's pride and acceptance). **1977** *Lancet* 17 Dec. 1294/2 She was found to be depressed, occasionally aggressive, and totally dependent on others in all self-care activities, including feeding, toileting, and grooming.

'toiletry. [f. TOILET *sb.* + -RY.] **a.** Performance of the toilet (sense 5 a). *nonce-use.*

1832 J. P. KENNEDY *Swallow B.* iv, Sundry evidences..of what—to coin a word,—I might call a scrupulous toiletry.

b. The apparatus of the toilet. *nonce-use.*

1892 *Edin. Rev.* Apr. 433 The claim to have dug up Priam's treasure and Helen's toiletry.

c. A preparation for use in washing or grooming. Chiefly in *pl.*

1927 *Glasgow Herald* 5 May 8 One really up-to-date shop coins a new and compact name for these indispensable odds and ends and calls them 'toiletteries'. **1927** *Hollis St. Theatre Programme* (U.S.) 19 Sept. (Advt.), Her keen individuality finds in the inimitable Djer-Kiss *odeur* a refreshing complement; she fastidiously insists upon it in *all* her toiletries! **1957** *Observer* 10 Nov. 11/2 'Men's toiletries' are now accepted here as they have been in America for years past. **1981** M. KENYON *Zigzag* iv. 23 The hold-all..held clothing and toiletries.

toilful ('tɔɪlfʊl), *a.* [f. TOIL *sb.*[1]] Full of toil.

1. Of an agent or his actions: Characterized by toiling; labouring; hard-working.

1596 SPENSER *Hymn Heavenly Love* 227 Betweene the toylefull Oxe and humble Asse. *a* **1789** MICKLE *Liberty* xvii, The fruitful lawns confess his toilful care. **1832** W. IRVING *Alhambra* I. 70 We behold the patient train of the toilful muleteer, slowly moving along the skirts of the mountain. **1839–40** —— *Wolfert's R., Mountjoy* (1855) 33 The wild-flowers were no longer..the resorts of the toilful bee. **1887** BLACKIE in *Blackw. Mag.* Oct. 536 The toilful monks of Croyland Clave the clod.

2. Of an action, condition, etc.: = TOILSOME I.

1614 SYLVESTER *Bethulia's Rescue* IV. 432 Hee..that..In Toil-full Fears will his own death procure. **1621** T. WILLIAMSON tr. *Goulart's Wise Vieillard* 105 Long trauell, tyrings, and toylefull labours. **1847** W. IRVING in *Life* IV. 11 This has been a toilful year to me. **1859** FARRAR *J. Home* 96 Climbing with toilful progress some steep and rocky hill.

Hence **'toilfully** *adv.*, in a toilful manner.

1832 tr. *Tour Germ. Prince* II. vii. 124 A white footpath winded along toilfully through the brown heather. **1860** FARRAR *Orig. Lang.* i. 3 We toilfully examine the unburied monuments of extinct nations. **1882** E. ARNOLD *Pearls of Faith* (1883) 144 There through toilfully, with steps of pain Went an old Jew.

'toilinet, -ette, toile'nette. Also 8 -enet, 9 -anette. [Origin unascertained: perh. a fancy trade-name; app. f. F. *toile* linen, cloth, the rest of the word being modelled on *satinet, -ette, sarsenet, -ette*, or the like (in which the *n* belongs to the root).] A kind of fine woollen cloth: used in the first half of the 19th c. for waistcoats of grooms, huntsmen, etc.; for later application see quot. 1858². Also *attrib.*

1799 *Hull Advertiser* 12 Jan. 2/2 Waistcoat of kerseymere or toilenet. **1801** NEMNICH *Waaren Lexicon* II. 687 *Toilinet*, ein feines Westenzeug von Wolle, das in Yorkshire verfertigt wird; *Striped*, gestreift; *Checked*, gewürfelt. Es ist dem Swansdown ähnlich. **1810** in *Spirit Pub. Jrnls.* XIV. 47 With the broad-cloth, toilinets, waistcoat and breeches-stuff. **1840** CHALMERS *Chr. & Civic Econ.* xxii, The making of shawls and the making of toilinette waistcoats. **1858** R. S. SURTEES *Ask Mamma* lxviii, His vest [was] a canary-coloured striped toilanette, with a slightly turned-down collar. **1858** SIMMONDS *Dict. Trade*, *Toilinet*, a kind of German quilting; silk and cotton warp with woollen weft.

toiling (ˈtɔɪlɪŋ), *sb.* ? *Obs. rare.* [f. TOIL *sb.*² + -ING¹; cf. NETTING *sb.*²] (See quot.)

1805 R. W. DICKSON *Pract. Agric.* II. 675 A sort of net-work, formed of small cord, called toiling.

ˈtoiling, *vbl. sb.* [f. TOIL *v.*¹ + -ING¹.] The action of TOIL *v.*¹ in various senses; struggling; tugging; labouring, working hard.

c **1330** *Arth. & Merl.* (Kölbing) 6083 Ac on hors in þis toiling Was brouȝt Sornigrex þe king. *c* **1394** *P. Pl. Crede* 753 His syre a soutere y-suled in grees, His teeþ wiþ toylinge of leþer tetered as a sawe. **1549** COVERDALE, etc. *Erasm. Par. Phil.* i. 3 b, To be losed frome the troublous toylynges of thys lyfe. **1587** HARRISON *England* I. iv. in Holinshed I. 7/2 When their toiling and drudgerie could not please them. **1644** MILTON *Areop.* (Arb.) 63 He..resolvs to give over toyling. **1831** CARLYLE *Sart. Res.* II. v, The Day of Man's Existence..with all its sick toilings. **1895** *Athenæum* 9 Mar. 307/3 The traveller..must make up his mind to..slow toiling along miserable..roads.

ˈtoiling, *ppl. a.* [f. TOIL *v.*¹ + -ING².] That toils, in various senses of the verb; struggling; labouring, laborious, hard-working.

1552 HULOET, Toylyng, *tuditans.* *c* **1592** MARLOWE *Massacre Paris* III. ii, Sorrow seize upon my toiling soul! **1642** FULLER *Holy & Prof. St.* IV. xix. 338 He..avoids a toyling and laborious industry. **1703** ROWE *Ulyss.* II. i, The Labours of the toiling Hind. **1844** LONGF. *Sea-weed* i, Landward in his wrath he [storm-wind] scourges The toiling surges. **1890** 'R. BOLDREWOOD' *Col. Reformer* (1891) 108 A toiling owner of a small station.

Hence **ˈtoilingly** *adv.*, in a toiling manner.

1812 W. TENNANT *Anster F.* III. vi, Toilingly each bitter beadle swung..his greasy rope. **1828** *Blackw. Mag.* XXIV. 351 Toilingly he raises his body.

toille, obs. Sc. form of TOLL *sb.*¹

toilless (ˈtɔɪllɪs), *a.* [f. TOIL *sb.*¹ + -LESS.] Without toil; apart or free from toil. †**a.** Entailing no toil. *Obs.* **b.** That is or acts without labour or exertion.

1606 SYLVESTER *Du Bartas* II. iv. *Magnif.* 664 There all grows toylless. **1839** BAILEY *Festus* xix. (1848) 207 Earth's luxurious toilless tribes. **1894** *Scott. Leader* 4 Jan. 3 And soar o'er life, and toilless comprehend Of flowers and all things dumb the silent speed.

Hence **ˈtoillessness,** freedom from toil.

1881 J. M. BROWN *Student Life* 4 They keep as a stimulus to toil the prospect of future toillessness.

† **toilous,** *a. Obs. rare.* Also 5 -ose. [f. TOIL *sb.*¹ + -OUS.] **a.** Contentious, disputatious, wrangling. **b.** Full of toil; toilsome.

c **1430** *A.B.C. of Aristotle* in *Babees Bk.* (1868) 12, T to toilose, ne to talewijs, for temperaunce is beest. *c* **1520** *Treat. Galaunt* (W. de W.) 17 As tyrauntes and traytours, toyllous in moote. **1530** PALSGR. 327/2 Toylouse, full of toyle and labour.

toilsome (ˈtɔɪlsəm), *a.* [f. TOIL *sb.*¹ + -SOME.] **1.** Of actions, conditions, etc.: Characterized by or involving toil; laborious, tiring.

1581 J. BELL *Haddon's Answ. Osor.* 23 b, O my ouer tedious and toylesome lucke, that hoped to dispute with a learned and discrete Diuine,..: but now finde all contrary. **1590** SPENSER *F.Q.* I. iv. 3 For she is wearie of the toilsom way. **1667** MILTON *P.L.* XI. 179 What can be toilsom in these pleasant Walkes? **1707** *Curios. in Husb. & Gard.* 111 The making of Cyder being Toilsom and expensive. **1855** MACAULAY *Hist. Eng.* xiii. III. 358 The ascent had been long and toilsome.

b. Of concrete things: Entailing toil.

1609 W. M. *Man in Moone* (Percy Soc.) 44 The toylsomest burden that combreth a man. **1791** COWPER *Odyss.* x. 94 Our force Exhausting ceaseless at the toilsome oar.

2. Of an agent: = TOILFUL I.

1655 H. VAUGHAN *Silex Scint.* II. *Quickness* v, Thou art a toylsom Mole. *a* **1841** SHEPARD in *Ess. Chr. Ministry* 66/2 Fervent, heroic, toilsome men. **1845** LONGF. *Rain in Summer* vii, In the furrowed land The toilsome and patient oxen stand.

†**3.** Caused by toil. *Obs. rare.*

1590 SPENSER *F.Q.* II. v. 30 Toylsom sweat. *Ibid.* xii. 29 Ne ever sought to bayt His tyred armes for toylesome wearinesse.

Hence **ˈtoilsomely** *adv.*, in a toilsome manner, laboriously; **ˈtoilsomeness,** laboriousness.

1614 BP. HALL *Contempl.*, *O.T.* VIII. v, Their life must be *toilesomely spent in hewing of wood, and drawing of water for all Israel. **1816** SCOTT *Bl. Dwarf* iv, Slowly and toilsomely labouring to pile the large stones one upon another. **1871** MACMILLAN *True Vine* ii. (1872) 61 Earning toilsomely his daily bread. **1586** STANYHURST *Ded. to Sir H. Sidney* in Holinshed (1808) VI. 274 The *toilsomnesse of the paine I refer to my priuat knowledge. **1630** *R. Johnson's Kingd. & Commw.* 89 A Peasant, disparaged in his drudgery and servile toilsomenesse. **1889** *Spectator* 30 Nov., All dwelt on the painful toilsomeness of manual work, and not one on the satisfaction it produces.

toil-worn (ˈtɔɪlwɔːn), *a.* [f. TOIL *sb.*¹ + WORN.] Worn by toil; showing marks of toil.

1751 MASON *Elfrida* Poems (1774) 122 Mean and pilgrim weeds, All like an ancient, toil-worn traveller. **1804** GRAHAME *Sabbath* 24 The toil-worn horse, set free. **1843** BETHUNE *Sc. Fireside Stor.* 124 The toil-worn countenance, and the anxious eye. **1898** J. ARCH *Story of Life* viii. 183 The farmers looked care-worn and toil-worn.

ˈto-inˌfinitive. [f. TO *prep.* + INFINITIVE *sb.*] The infinitive form of the verb immediately preceded by *to*.

1946 O. JESPERSEN *Mod. Eng. Gram.* V. 154 There is no reason to have a separate name for the to-infinitive. **1964** C. BARBER *Linguistic Change in Present-Day Eng.* vi. 135 Another auxiliary which is becoming extremely important is *be going* followed by a *to*-infinitive.

tois, obs. f. *toes*, pl. of TOE.

toise (tɔɪz), *sb.* In 6 toyse. [a. F. *toise*:—OF. *teise* = It. *tesa*:—Late L. *tēsa*, *tensa* (sc. *brachia*) 'the outstretched arms', taken as a fem. sing.: see also the ME. TEISE, TAISE.] A French lineal measure of 6 French feet, roughly equal to 1·949 metres, or 6⅜ English feet. Chiefly in military use. ***square toise***, a measure = about 4½ square yards.

1598 DALLINGTON *Meth. Trav.* B iv b, This great City..is within ten Toyses as large as Paris. **1644** EVELYN *Diary* 7 Mar., The Greate Garden, 180 toises long and 154 wide. **1759** tr. *Duhamel's Husb.* II. xi. (1762) 150, 1344 square toises of 36 feet. **1823** BYRON *Juan* VIII. vii, The column order'd on the assault scarce pass'd Beyond the Russian batteries a few toises [*rime* noises]. **1904** QUILLER-COUCH *Fort Amity* xiii, It was quadrilateral with a frontage of fifty toises.

Hence **toise** *v. rare* [ad. Fr. *toiser*] *trans.*, to measure with the eye, to eye from head to foot.

1889 STEVENSON *Master of B.* iv, At the same time he had a better look at me, toised me a second time sharply, and then smiled. *a* **1894** —— *St. Ives* xix, I am acquainted also with the properties of a pair of pistols, said I, toising him.

‖**toisech** (ˈtoʃəx). *Sc. Hist.* [Gaelic *tòisech* lord, chief; = Welsh *tywysog* 'dux, princeps': cf. *tòisich* to begin, *tùs*, *toiseach* beginning, front, and TAOISEACH.] A personage or officer of the third rank (in order *king*, *mormaer*, *tòisech*) in ancient Celtic Scotland, corresponding generally to the later chief of a clan.

1836 SKENE *Highlanders Scot.* (1902) I. vii. 114 There can be little doubt that the Gaelic title of Toisich was peculiar to the oldest cadet. **1885** *Edin. Rev.* Apr. 309 The Celtic 'Toisechs' took their corresponding place as Chiefs of Clans. **1900** WATT *Aberdeen & Banff* ii. 49 A few appear to have been descendants of the old toisechs.

‖**toison d'or** (twazɔ̃ dɔr). Also 7 toyson d'ore. [F., = fleece of gold; *toison*:—L. *tonsiōn-em* shearing (i.e. of a sheep), *or*:—L. *aurum* gold.]

a. The Golden Fleece: see GOLDEN *a.* 1; also *fig.* **b.** *Her.* The figure of this, giving name to an order of knighthood (see FLEECE *sb.* 1 c), and afterwards borne by certain families.

1623 LISLE *Ælfric on O. & N. Test.* Ded. xxii, Yea Weathers furr'd with her own Toyson d'Ore. **1704** J. HARRIS *Lex. Techn.* I, *Toison d'Or* (French), the Term in Heraldry for a golden Fleece, which is sometimes born in a Coat of Arms. **1854** THACKERAY *Newcomes* xxviii, She had done everything for Jason; she had got him the *toison d'or* from the Queen Mother.

toist (tɔɪst). Also **toyst**. App. a dial. form of TEISTIE: see quot. 1893 s.v.

a **1688** WALLACE *Descr. Orkney* (1693) 16 There are like-wise many Toists and Lyres, both Sea Fowls, very fat and delicious to eat. **1744** PRESTON in *Phil. Trans.* XLIII. 61 There are many Sorts of Wilk-fowl;..Solan Goose,..Whaps, Toists,..Plovers, Scarfs, &c.

‖**toi-toi** (ˈtɔɪtɔɪ, ˈtɒetɒe). Also toe-toe, tohi, toi. [Maori.] The native name for various tall reed-like grasses of the genus *Arundo*, esp. *A. conspicua*, natives of New Zealand.

1843 in A. Domett *Collect. Ord.* (1850) (Morris), Every building constructed wholly or in part of raupo, nikau, toi-toi, wiwi kakaho, straw or thatch of any description. **1867** LADY BARKER *Station Life N. Zealand* xv. (1870) 110 Thatching it with Tohi, or swamp-grass. **1892** *19th Cent.* Sept. 409 The Toe-toe, which closely resembles pampas grass. **1907** 'K. MANSFIELD' *Jrnl.* Nov.–Dec. (1954) 23 A clump of *toi-toi* waving in the wind, and looking for all the world like a family of little girls drying their hair. **1957** J. FRAME *Owls do Cry* 13 The place was like a shell with gold tickle of toi-toi around its edges. **1981** M. GEE *Meg* xxi. 244 Hedges of toi-toi and fields of fat spring grass.

tok, obs. pa. t. of TAKE *v.*

tokamak (ˈtəʊkəmæk). *Physics.* [a. Russ. *tokamák*, f. *toroidálnaya kámera s magnítnym pólem*, toroidal chamber with magnetic field.] One kind of toroidal apparatus for producing controlled fusion reactions in a hot plasma, distinguished by the fact that the controlling magnetic field is the sum of a toroidal field due to external windings and a poloidal field due to an induced longitudinal current in the plasma.

1969 *Nature* 1 Nov. 488/1 Measurements have been made of the electron temperature and density of the plasma in the toroidal discharge apparatus Tokamak T3..at the Kurchatov Institute. **1972** *Sci. Amer.* July 73/3 The first large Tokamak machine put into operation in the U.S. resulted from a conversion of the Model *C* stellarator in the Princeton University Plasma Physics Laboratory. **1980** *Ann. Rep. 1979/80* (U.K. Atomic Energy Authority) 31/1 In tokamaks, plasma is heated and confined by an electric current induced by transformer action, while a strong external field stabilizes the plasma. **1981** [see STELLARATOR]. **1984** *N.Y. Times Bk. Rev.* 1 Apr. 23/2 In the race to achieve commercial success, Princeton's tokamak (the original Russian acronym for a toroidal magnetic chamber) is pitted against..laser technology.

tokan, obs. form of TOUCAN.

Tokarev (ˈtɔːkəjɛf). The name of the Russian designer of firearms F. V. *Tokarev* (1871–1968), used *attrib.* and *absol.* to designate any of a range of automatic and semi-automatic firearms designed or developed by him.

1953 W. G. B. ALLEN *Pistols, Rifles & Machine Guns* iii. 33 Hotchkiss machine guns and the Russian Tokarev rifles provide examples of the cupped piston. *Ibid.* xi. 138 Modern manufacturing techniques permit the weight to be no greater than that of an orthodox rifle; the Russian Tokarev weighs 8¾ pounds. **1956** 'E. MCBAIN' *Cop Hater* (1958) xiv. 123, I keep a few guns... There's a Luger, and a Mauser, and I even got a Tokarev. **1981** S. DUNMORE *Ace* II. i. 150 The Russian was dead..a Tokarev pistol in his right hand.

Tokay¹ (təʊˈkeɪ). Also 8 tockay. [Name of a town in Upper Hungary.] **a.** (Also ***Tokay wine.***) A rich sweet wine of an aromatic flavour, made near Tokay in Hungary; hence applied to a Californian wine made in imitation of this, and similarly to an Australian vine, grape, and white wine. Also, in Alsace (more fully ***Tokay d'Alsace***) the Pinot Gris vine, grape, or white wine made from this.

1710 SWIFT *Jrnl. to Stella* vi, I dined at Stratford's in the City and had Burgundy and Tokay. **1714** MANDEVILLE *Fab. Bees* (1725) I. 260 When he has had a large Company, and thought it Extravagant to treat with Tockay. **1773** DOUGLASS in *Phil. Trans.* LXIII. 295 There are four sorts of wine made from the same grapes, which they distinguish at Tokay by the name of Essence, Auspruch, Masslasch, and the common wine. —— 296 The Auspruch is the wine commonly exported, and what is known in foreign countries under the name of Tokay. **1857** MILLER *Elem. Chem.* (1862) III. 160 Sherry yields from 1 to 5 per cent., port from 3 to 7 per cent., and Tokay as much as 17 per cent. of sugar. **1959** W. JAMES *Word-bk. Wine* 190 The tokay of Alsace bears no resemblance to the Hungarian wine; light and fruity, with sometimes a pink tinge, it is made from the pinot gris,.. Australia, too, has a vine called the tokay, which yields a good sweet white dessert wine. **1967** A. LICHINE *Encycl. Wines & Spirits* 67/2 Wines from the Pinot Gris (which, in this region, has for centuries been called the Tokay d'Alsace) and Gewürztraminer varieties. *Ibid.* 107/1 The versatility of Australian soil has been amply demonstrated.. by its ability to produce..from Tokay either a dry white or a luscious dessert wine. **1976** [see PINOT]. **1983** *Wine Soc. 1982/1983* (Ann. Rep., Internat. Exhib. Co-operative Wine Soc.) 21 These '82s..are good by any standard, the Gewürztraminer and Tokay particularly so.

b. ***Tokay grape,*** the variety of grape from which Tokay wine is made.

1896 *Godey's Mag.* Feb. 222/2 The luscious Tokay grapes, the golden oranges, and purple plums may be placed in separate dishes.

‖**tokay**² (ˈtəʊkeɪ). Also tokee, tockay, tookai. [a. Malay *tōkē*, also written *tōkeq*, *tĕkeq*, with final *q* often silent: see GECKO.]

A species of Gecko, or lizard of the family *Geckonidæ*, app. *G. verticillatus*, of Burma, Thailand, and the Malay region.

1753 CHAMBERS *Cycl. Supp.*, *Tockay*,..the name of a species of Indian lizard distinguished from the other kinds, by being spotted all over. **1774** GOLDSM. *Nat. Hist.* VII. 149 Directly descending from the crocodile, we find the Cordyle, the Tockay and the Tejuguacu, all growing less in order, as I have named them. **1899** *Proc. Zool. Soc.* 16 May 631 The Great House-Lizard or Tokay is recorded from Penang, Singapore, and the Malay Peninsula... In Siam, however, it is one of the commonest animals.

toke (təʊk), *sb.*¹ *slang.* [Origin uncertain.] (A piece of) bread; also *fig.* (see quot. 1967).

1843 DICKENS *Let.* 7 June (1974) III. 503 Now, we don't want none of your sarse—and if you bung any of them tokes of yours in this direction, you'll find your shuttlecock sent back as heavy as it came. **1874** M. CLARKE *His Natural Life* I. vii. 53 Sarah was standing on the poop throwing bits o' toke to the gulls... She..throwed crumbs and such like up in the air over the side. **1905** [see GROUND *ppl. a.* 1 a]. **1963** M. KENDON *Ladies College, Goudhurst* 8 Dripping..spread on 'tokes', was eaten for eleven o'clock lunch by schoolgirls for well nigh forty years. **1967** K. GILES *Death in Diamonds* v. 90 'If you fall foul of Tiny Holdsworth he gives you toke.' .. 'In the local dialect..toke used to be poor quality bread, hence toke and water equals punishment.'

toke (təʊk), *sb.*² *U.S. slang.* [Origin uncertain: cf. TOKE *v.*] An inhalation of smoke from a cigarette or pipe containing marijuana or other narcotic substance.

1968 *Harper's Mag.* Mar. 48 If he still took a toke of marijuana from time to time..still! Mailer was not in approval of any drug. **1973** R. L. Simon *Big Fix* xii. 87, I packed my pipe with..hashish... I took a good heavy toke and held it in as long as I could. **1976** *New Yorker* 17 May 34/3 The host shall light up and take the first toke. He will then offer the joint to the first woman on his left. **1980** *London Mag.* Aug.-Sept. 106/1 He takes huge tokes from a home-made hookah.

toke (təʊk), *sb.*³ *N. Amer. slang.* [Origin uncertain: perh. an abbrev. of TOKEN *sb.*] A gratuity or tip.

1971 *Daily Colonist* (Victoria, B.C.) 22 June 18/4 The prime advantage [of being a waitress] is instant money—tips or 'tokes' as they are known in the profession. **1981** *Miami Herald* 26 Mar. 30A/2 They have just gone in and hassled people on tips and tokes.

toke (təʊk), *v. U.S. slang.* [Origin uncertain: cf. TOKE *sb.*²] *intr.* and *trans.* To smoke (a marijuana cigarette). Also *const.* ***up***. Hence **'toker**.

1952 *Amer. Speech* XXVII. 30 *Toke v.*, to smoke a cigarette; to take a puff of a cigarette. **1973** *Newsweek* 1 Jan. 4 Bill Buckley says he went 'outside the 3-mile limit—I'm a law-and-order advocate, you know'—to toke up, but neglects to mention where he got the stuff. **1975** *High Times* Dec. 6/2 Thousands of tokers. *Ibid.* 13/2 This hash oil joint is one of the most satisfying ways of toking oil. **1979** N. Mailer *Executioner's Song* (1980) I. xxi. 339 He had been over at a friend of his selling drugs, a little crystal, some speed, toked a couple, got blasted.

toke, obs. pa. t. of TAKE *v.*; see TOQUE, TUCK.

token ('təʊkən), *sb.* Forms: α. 1–3 **tác(e)n**, 2 **takan**, 2–3 **takenn** (*Orm.*), 3–7 **taken**, 4 **takein**, 4–6 **takin, -yn**, 6 **taikin**, 8 **-en**, 7 **tackyn**. β. 2–4 **tocne**, 3 **tocken**, 3–5 **tokne**, 4 **-ene, -in, -un**, 5 **toocun, tookne, tokyng**, 5–6 **-yn, tooken**, (6 **tukne**), 7 **toakin**, 4– **token**. [OE. *tácen, tácn*; = OFris. *têken, têkn, teiken* (WFris. *teiken*, †*teeckne*), OS. *têcan* (MLG., MDu., LG. *têken*, Du. *teeken*), OHG. *zeihhan* (MHG., Ger. *zeichen*), ON. *teikn* (*tákn* from OE.), Sw. *tecken*, Da., Norw. *tegn*, all neuter:—OTeut. **taik-no*ᵐ (in Goth. *taikns* fem.:—**taiknis*), cognate with **taik-jan*, OE. *tǽcean* to show, TEACH.]

1. a. Something that serves to indicate a fact, event, object, feeling, etc.; a sign, a symbol. ***in token of***, as a sign, symbol, or evidence of.

c **890** tr. *Bæda's Hist.* I. viii. (1890) 42, & heora stowe bræddon & weorðodon, swa swa siȝefæst tacon. *c* **897** K. Ælfred *Gregory's Past. C.* xxviii. 196 To tacne ðæt he his ȝeweald ahte. *c* **1200** *Vices & Virt.* 135 Nis þat non god tocne of ripe manne. *a* **1300** *Cursor M.* 16574 Þe rode þai scop þan as þai wald, Als we þe taken se. *c* **1315** Shoreham vi. 15 In tokne þat pays scholde be By-tuexte god and manne. **1483** Caxton *G. de la Tour* lviii. E vij, [The queen] shewed hym many signes and tokenes of loue. *a* **1533** Ld. Berners *Huon* lxxxiv. 266 Charlemayne..kyssyd Huon in token of peace. **1585** T. Washington tr. *Nicholay's Voy.* III. xiii. 95 Bearing..a satchell ful of haye in token of their bondage and seruice. **1686** in *Verney Mem.* (1907) II. 409 Friendly cautions are Tokens of Love. **1778** Miss Burney *Evelina* (1784) II. i. 5 He gave him..a cordial slap on the back, and some other equally gentle tokens of satisfaction. **1833** Ht. Martineau *Briery Creek* iii, The hollow tree, from which the mists had drawn off, leaving a diamond token on every leaf.

†**b.** A sign of the zodiac. *Obs. rare.*

c **1000** *Sax. Leechd.* I. 164 Sy þæt ðonne þære sunnan ryne beo on þam tacne þe man uirgo nemneð. *c* **1050** *Byrhtferth's Handboc* in *Anglia* (1885) VIII. 303 Seo sunne wunað on þam twelf tacnum. **1535** Coverdale *2 Kings* xxiii. 5 Them that brent incense..to the Sonne, and the Mone, and the twelue tokens, and to all yᵉ hoost of heauen.

†**c.** An ensign, a standard. (Only OE.)

a **1000** *Gloss. Prudentius* 45 Eal werod ȝehwyrfedum tacnum [*versis signis*]..foron. *a* **1000** *Ags. Ps.* (Spelm.) lxxiii. 6 [lxxiv. 4] Hi asetton tacna heora tacna.

†**d.** The sign of an inn, etc. *Obs. rare*⁻⁰.

c **1440** *Promp. Parv.* 495/2 Tokne, or sygne of ane in, *idem quod* seny, *supra* (*P.* signe of an ostry).

e. *Coal-mining* (*S. Wales*). A thin seam of coal indicating the vicinity of a thicker bed.

1883 in Gresley *Gloss. Coal-mining.*

f. *Semiotics*, etc. A particular and individual sign, as opposed to the type of which it is an instance. Cf. TYPE *sb.*¹ 8 e.

1908 C. S. Peirce in *Coll. Papers* (1958) VIII. 240, I devoted much study to my ten trichotomies of signs... I..called..an Actisign a Token, a Famisign a Type. **1955** N. Chomsky *Logical Struct. Linguistic Theory* (microfilm, Mass. Inst. Technol.) i. 31 The assumption..that it is possible to assign a meaning to each utterance token to be compared with other meanings. **1971** J. B. Carroll et al. *Word Freq. Bk.* p. xix, A *type* is a particular word, counted just once, regardless of how many times it occurs; a *token* is any of the individual occurrences of the type. **1979** *Computers & Humanities* X. 135/1 Without further intervention concordances remain concordances of word tokens and not of headwords.

2. a. A sign or mark indicating some quality, or distinguishing one object from others; a characteristic mark.

c **1000** Ælfric *Gen.* iv. 15 God him sealde tacn, þæt nan þæra..hine ne ofsloȝe. *a* **1300** *Cursor M.* 6124 Bot in þat huse noght he yode þar he fand taken wit þe blode. **1398** Trevisa *Barth. De P.R.* vi. v. (Bodl. MS.), Whanne childrenne voice chaungeþ it is a tokene of Puberte. *c* **1400** Maundev. (1839) xxiii. 247 Þat beren the tokne vpon hire hedes of a mannes foot. **1456** Sir G. Haye *Law Arms* (S.T.S.) 281 A maister armoureur..in his werkis had a takyn that his werkis war knawin by. **1557** North *Gueuara's Diall Pr.* 95 The tokens of a valyant and renowmed captaine are, his woundes and hurtes. **1577** B. Googe *Heresbach's Husb.* III. (1586) 115 b, Virgill..doth..describe the tokens of a good Horse. **1814** Scott *Ld. of Isles* vi. xiv, The tokens on his helmet tell The Bruce, my Liege: I know him well. **1822** Lamb *Elia* Ser. I. *Chimney-Sweepers*, One unfortunate wight..by tokens was discovered to be no chimney-sweeper.

b. A spot on the body indicating disease, esp. the plague. Now *rare* or *Obs.*

1634 T. Johnson *Parey's Chirurg.* xxii. xiii. (1678) 500 [In Plague] spots (vulgarly called Tokens) appear over all the body. **1666** J. H. *Treat. Gt. Antidote* 5 The Tokens are, I am confident, Marks sent from God, and it is as impossible to cure any that have them, as to contradict the Divine Decree. **1722** De Foe *Plague* (1756) 225 Those Spots they call'd the Tokens were really gangreen Spots, or mortified Flesh in small Knobs as broad as a little silver Peny, and hard as a piece of Callus or Horn. **1896** *Allbutt's Syst. Med.* I. 932 In the seventeenth century they [purpuric patches] were known as the 'Tokens'. *Ibid.* 934 Petechial eruptions or 'tokens'.

3. a. Something serving as proof of a fact or statement; an evidence.

Beowulf (Z.) 1655 Beowulf maþelode..hwæt we þe þas sælac..brohton tires to tacne. *c* **1000** *Ags. Gosp.* John vi. 30 Hwæt dest þu to tacne þæt we ȝeseon & ȝelyfon? *c* **1200** *Vices & Virt.* 31 And wel ilieue be are tacne ðe he hafð iȝiuen me. *c* **1250** *Gen. & Ex.* 2860 Moyses tolde hem ðat bliðe bode, And let hem sen tockenes fro gode. *c* **1425** tr. *Arderne's Treat. Fistula* 28 Þis schal be to þe þe tokne of perfite curyng when þou seez þe linne cloutez..to be drye. **1517** in *Acts Parlt. Scotl.* (1875) XII. 38/1 And in takin of this oure consent and oblissing hereintill We..have [affi]xt to thir presentis oure Selis. *a* **1533** Ld. Berners *Huon* lxxxi. 246 He shal shew tokens that my sayenge is trewe. **1692** Washington tr. *Milton's Def. Pop.* iii. M.'s Wks. 1851 VII. 73 Money bears the Prince's Image, not as a token of its being his, but of its being good Metal. **1715** De Foe *Fam. Instruct.* I. i. (1841) I. 6 A token of his being, and of his being God. **1769** Cook *Voy. round World* I. viii. (1773) 79 These ..were brought as tokens of peace and amity. **1843** Mill *Logic* I. iii. §7 By what token could it manifest its presence?

†**b.** Something remaining as evidence of what formerly existed; a vestige, trace, 'sign'. *Obs.*

1555 Eden *Decades* To Rdr. (Arb.) 49 There remayneth at this daye no token of the laborious Tabernacle whiche Moises buylded. **1610** Holland *Camden's Brit.* (1637) 518 Yet wee with all our seeking could see no tokens of any such Wall. *Ibid.* 547 There be many tokens remaining of old antiquity.

†**4.** In biblical use, An act serving to demonstrate divine power or authority; = SIGN *sb.* 10. *Obs.* or *arch.*

c **897** K. Ælfred *Gregory's Past. C.* lviii. 443 Ðone Nazareniscan Hælend ðæt wæs afandon wer..on mæȝenum & tacnum. *c* **1000** *Ags. Gosp.* John x. 41 Witodlice ne worhte iohannes nan tacn [*c* **1160** *Hatton G.* takan]. *c* **1175** *Lamb. Hom.* 91 Þa warhte god feole tacne on þan folke þurh þere apostlan hondan. *c* **1200** Ormin 14068 Þiss takenn wrohhte Jesu Crist. **1382** Wyclif *Acts* ii. 22 Jhesu of Nazareth, a man prouyd of God in ȝou by vertues [*gloss* or myraclis], and wondris, and tokenes. **1535** Coverdale *Josh.* xxiv. 17 The Lorde oure God..did soch greate tokens [1611 signs] before oure eyes. **1611** Bible *Ps.* cxxxv. 9 Who sent tokens [1885 (R.V.) signs] and woonders into the midst of thee, O Egypt. *Ibid.* lxv. 8 They also that dwell in the vttermost parts are afraid at thy tokens [so **1885** (R.V.)].

5. A sign or presage of something to come; an omen, portent, prodigy. *Obs.* (exc. as included in 1).

971 *Blickl. Hom.* 117 Ealle þa tacno & þa forebeacno þa þe her ure Drihten ær toweard sæȝde. *c* **1175** *Lamb. Hom.* 91 Ic sende min tacna ȝeond þa eorðe. **1297** R. Glouc. (Rolls) 5927 Þis was as a tokne þat to comene was. **1340** Hampole *Pr. Consc.* 4733 Þe grete day of dome, Agayn whilk alle þir takens sal come. *c* **1400** Maundev. (Roxb.) vii. 27 If it brynne, it es a gude taken. *c* **1440** *Promp. Parv.* 495/2 Tokne, of a thynge to cumme or cummynge, *pronosticum.* **1594** Shaks. *Rich. III*, v. iii. 21 The weary Sunne..by the bright Tract of his fiery Carre, Giues token of a goodly day to morrow. *a* **1628** Sir J. Beaumont *Bosworth F.* 73 Some mark his Words, as Tokens fram'd t'express The sharp Conclusion of a sad Success. **1791** Cowper *Iliad* iv. 455 By unpropitious tokens interfered.

6. A signal given; a sign to attract attention or give notice. Now *rare* or *Obs.*

a **1000** *Prose Life Guthlac* xi. (Goodwin) 54 Comon þær þry men to þære hyðe, and þær tacn sloȝon. *c* **1440** *Promp. Parv.* 495/2 Tokne, wythe eye or wythe the hand, *nutus.* *c* **1450** *Merlin* xviii. 292 Thei sowned theire hornes and tymbres and trumpes, and that was token that thei wolde haue socoure. **1560** Daus tr. *Sleidane's Comm.* 452 As a token or watche worde, they cried that the Frenchemen were vp in harnesse. **1577–87** Holinshed *Chron.* I. 33/2 He gaue the token to fight vnto his souldiers. **1726** Swift *Gulliver* I. i, I gave tokens to let them know, that they might do with me what they pleased. **1833** Ht. Martineau *Fr. Wines & Pol.* iii. 43 Charles lifted his finger in token of silence.

7. a. A sign arranged or given to indicate a person; a word or material object employed to authenticate a person, message, or communication; a mark giving security to those who possess it; a password.

1377 Langl. *P. Pl.* B. xvi. 147 And [Judas] tolde hem a tokne how to knowe with ihesus. *c* **1440** *Gesta Rom.* xxiii. 80 (Harl. MS.), & told to hir all the prive tokyns þat were ysaid bytwene hem two. **1561** in *Exch. Rolls Scotl.* XIX. 460 Delyverit to Peter Cokburne, quha come with ane takin fra George Symson, the saidis George lettres. **1716** Hearne *Collect.* (O.H.S.) V. 189 Admitting no one..but one or two, to whom I had given tokens that I might know when they were at the Door. **1827** Roberts *Voy. Centr. Amer.* 270 It is customary for the King to give any person..travelling specially 'on King's business' a token [by which he may be known]. **1840** Dickens *Barn. Rudge* lxxi, You bring..some note or token from my uncle.

b. *Railways.* (See quot. 1936.)

1936 *Gloss. Terms Railway Signalling* (*B.S.I.*) 51 *Token*, the authority which must be carried by trainmen to permit a train to travel over a prescribed section of a single line. **1968** O. S. Nock *Railway Enthusiast's Encycl.* 273 The tokens are engraved with the stations at each end of the sections to which they apply. **1971** D. J. Smith *Discovering Railwayana* iv. 20 Tokens for single-line working were frequently fitted with a looped end and attached to a vertical post near a junction with the main line.

†**8. a.** A badge worn to indicate service or party.

1472 *Coventry Leet Bk.* 374 Noo Reteindres, lyuerees, signes ne tokenys of clothing, nor othir wyse be taken, had nor vsed. **1516** *Sel. Cas. Star Chamb.* (Selden) II. 115 Sworne..that he shall not be receyued ne were any lyuerey or token of or with any lord Gentilman or..other personne foreyn. **15..** *Battle of Balrinnes* in Maidment *Sc. Ball.* (1868) I. 253 He that thought not for to blyne His mistres' tockin taks; They kist it first, and set it syne Upone their helms and jackes.

†**b.** *pl.* Armorial bearings, heraldic arms. *Obs.*

1562 Leigh *Armorie* 28 b, In the first inuention of them, they were not called Armes, but Tokens.

9. Something given as an expression of affection, or to be kept as a memorial; a keepsake or present given especially at parting.

c **1385** Chaucer *L.G.W.* 1273 (*Dido*) Send hir letres tokens broches and rynges. **1463** *Bury Wills* (Camden) 36 For a tookne to remembre hire husbond. **1606** Shaks. *Tr. & Cr.* I. ii. 306 A token from Troylus. **1722** Ramsay *Three Bonnets* III. 62 Accept o' this love-taiken. **1848** Dickens *Dombey* v, I must present your friend with some little token.

10. a. Something given as the symbol and evidence of a right or privilege, upon the presentation of which the right or privilege may be exercised.

1538 Elyot, *Tessera*,..a token [*ed.* 1548 of leade, leather or other thyng] gyuen to people to receyue corne of the kinges almes. **1548** *Ibid.*, *Tesseræ nummariæ*, tokens geuen to men to receiue a summe of money by. **1552** Huloet, Token geuen vnto people in fayres and markets when they bye cattell..*tessera, tesserula.*

b. *spec.* A stamped piece of lead or other metal given (originally after confession) as a voucher of fitness to be admitted to the communion: in recent times used in Scotland in connexion with the Presbyterian Communion service, but now generally represented by a 'communion card'.

1534 in Kitts *Churchw. Acc. St. Martin in the Fields* 37 Item Receued and gathred for howssellyng tokons in the Churche xiijˢ vijᵈ. **1583** *Churchw. Acc. St. James' in Bristol past & pres.* (1881) II. 37 Paid for tokens to deliver to the howselynge people at Easter, vid. **1608** (Feb. 24) *Churchw. Acc. St. Martin in the Fields* 585 It is ordered That every Communicant, for the generall Communions at Easter, shall the day before Their Receiving, Repaire to the Minister, or Curate, and then and their pay his duties and take a token, and Restore his Token, at his Comming the next day to the Communion. **1611** Cotgr., *Marreau*, the token of lead, etc., giuen for a remembrance, in Churches, to such as meane to receiue the Communion. **1626** in Swayne *Sarum Churchw. Acc.* (1896) 184 The Clarke shall deliver out a token for euerye persone that will receyve [the Sacrament]. **1645** *Dalgety Sess. Rec.* in W. Rose *Past. Wk. in Covt. Times* vi. (1877) 135 All that wants tokens were forbidden to approoch the table. **1791** Boswell *Johnson* 27 Aug. an. 1773, Her husband was in the church distributing tokens. **1888** Barrie *Auld Licht Idylls* iii, Without a token, which was a metal lozenge, no one could take the sacrament. **1896** 'Ian Maclaren' *Kate Carnegie, A Moderate*, The women had their tokens wrapt in snowy handkerchiefs. *Ibid.*, Domsie went down one side and Drumsheugh the other, collecting the tokens, whose clink, clink in the silver dish was the only sound.

11. a. A stamped piece of metal, often having the general appearance of a coin, issued as a medium of exchange by a private person or company, who engage to take it back at its nominal value, giving goods or legal currency for it.

From the reign of Queen Elizabeth to 1813, issued by tradesmen, large employers of labour, etc., to remedy the scarcity of small coin, and sometimes in connexion with the truck-shop system. ***bank-tokens***, silver tokens for 5*s.*, 3*s.*, 1*s.* 6*d.*, were issued by the Bank of England in 1811: see quots. 1812, 1832.

1598–1604 Tauerne token [see TAVERN *sb.* 4]. **1614** B. Jonson *Barth. Fair* III. iv, Buy a tokens worth of great pinnes. **1638** Sir R. Cotton *Abstr. Rec. Tower* 25 Retailers of victuals and small wares..using their owne tokens; in and about London there are above three thousand that one with another cast yearely five pound a peice of leaden tokens. **1757** Jos. Harris *Coins* 65 To supply the want of very small silver coins, a kind of Tokens or substitutes have been instituted all made of copper. **1812** *Chron.* in *Ann. Reg.* 150/1 The Silver Tokens issued by the Bank of England.. Silver Tokens of 3*s.* each... The weight of the 1*s.* 6*d.* token is 4 dwts. 17½ grains. **1832** Babbage *Econ. Manuf.* xiv. (ed. 3) 131 Silver tokens for various sums were issued by the Bank of England.

b. A voucher exchangeable for goods or services; ***book token***: see BOOK *sb.* 19; ***gift-token***: see GIFT *sb.* 9 b; ***record token***: see RECORD *sb.* 14. Also, a small disc or other piece representing or resembling a coin, esp. one used to operate a machine or in exchange for goods or services. Freq. with defining word.

1908 R. Brooke *Let.* Mar. (1968) 123 Dear Mother, I am so sorry about the Boots token. I quite failed to realize..that it was wanted at once. **1934** Webster, *Token*,..the metal fare or ticket issued by a transportation company. **1942**

BERREY & VAN DEN BARK *Amer. Thes. Slang* §560/4 Scrip; tokens; coupons; etc. **1954** *Daily Progress* (Charlottesville, Va.) 26 July 16/2 If the Department of Urbiculture will hand out free bus tokens, I'm not too much against the ideas. **1961** WEBSTER, *Token*,..a game counter. **1965** AYLLON & AZRIN in *Jrnl. Exper. Anal. Behav.* VIII. 358/2 Special metal tokens were used as conditioned reinforcers. **1966** G. W. TURNER *Eng. Lang. Austral. & N.Z.* viii. 174 The *milk tokens*..are put out for milk last thing at night. **1968** *Listener* 29 Aug. 266/3 The patients are paid with tokens resembling money for acting normally, and..behaving inappropriately or psychotically results in a loss of tokens. **1973** *People's Jrnl.* (Inverness) 4 Aug. 16/4 A little boy who joined in the scramble collected, in addition to money, nine milk tokens, at that time each valid for 'a pinta'. **1976** *Southern Even. Echo* (Southampton) 18 Nov. 18/5 Those who come to watch the show and contribute nothing (or only fruit machine tokens!) if the show is to be held again. **1977** *Washington Post* 16 June DC3 The subway will no longer accept the 10-cent student bus tokens. **1978** *Times Lit. Suppl.* 1 Dec. 1400/3 Boards range in style from Cruikshank's 'Comic Game of the Great Exhibition of 1851' to the Mondrian simplicity of 'Quartette' and counters or tokens are provided. **1980** J. BARNES *Metroland* II. iv. 113 Orange ten-shilling notes at Christmas and Boots tokens. **1980** *Washington Post Mag.* 29 June 20 The valet reminds you to present your parking token to your waiter 15 minutes before you plan to leave so that your car will be waiting. **1981** M. GEE *Dying, in Other Words* 111 The milkman, who was dishonest, and sometimes stole Clothilde's token, leaving no milk. **1982** *Christian Sci. Monitor* 15 Nov. 1 A collector of transportation tokens. **1983** *N.Y. Times* 9 Oct. I. 1/1 The price of bus and subway tokens..must be increased.

12. *Printing.* A measure or quantity of presswork; a certain number of sheets of paper (usually 250 pulls on a hand-press) passed through the press.

token-sheet, the last sheet of each token, turned down to facilitate counting the whole number.

1683 MOXON *Mech. Exerc., Printing* xxv. ¶5 A Token.. for Half a Press, viz. a Single Press-man, is generally but five Quires..: But if it be for a Whole Press, it contains Ten Quires. *Ibid.* xxiv. ¶9 Having Wet his first Token, he doubles down a..corner of the upper Sheet of it..: This Sheet is called the Token-Sheet, as being a mark..to know how many Tokens of that Heap is Wrought-off. **1867** BRANDE & COX *Dict. Sc.*, etc., *Token*, in Printing [is] ten quires eighteen sheets of perfect paper, or 258 sheets. It is reckoned an hour's work for a hand press, of ordinary work. **1886** *Encycl. Brit.* XXIII. 707/1 It has been mentioned that 250 sheets or a *token* per hour, printed on one side only, represent the work of two men at the hand-press. **1896** T. L. DE VINNE *Moxon's Mech. Exerc., Printing* 427 It required much activity to pull a token in one hour... The full ream printed on both sides is rated as four tokens.

13. In the Isle of Man: A legal summons: see quotations.

1724 BP. WILSON in Keble *Life* xix. (1863) 638 If he owns it he is to have seven days' imprisonment and three penances in Church. If not he is to have a token to clear himself. **1726–31** WALDRON *Descr. Isle of Man* (1865) 40 When a person has a mind to commence a suit against his neighbour for debt, he has no more to do than to take out a token, which is a piece of slate marked with the governour's name on it; and it is the same thing with an arrest in England.

14. *Weaving.* (See quot.)

1878 BARLOW *Weaving* xv. 177 Several small bobbins with a little of the various colours of the weft that may be used, that is, when several kinds are employed. They are called tokens, and are raised by the Jacquard hooks attached, so as to remind the weaver which shuttle to use.

15. *Phrases* (in which the sense of *token* becomes vague). **a.** ***by the same token*** or (somewhat *arch.*) ***by this*** (or ***that***) ***token***: (*a*) on the same ground; for the same reason; in the same way; (*b*) (= F. *à telles enseignes que*), 'the proof of this being that'; introducing a corroborating circumstance, often weakened down to a mere associated fact that helps the memory or is recalled to mind by the main fact (now *arch.* or *dial.*).

Sense (a) represents the predominant modern use (and app. that current in the 15th c.). Sense (b) occurs from 1600.

1463 *Paston Lett.* II. 134 And to this [course] Maister Markham prayed you to agre by the same token ye mevyd hym to sette an ende be twyx you and my masters your brethern. **1463** *Will of Sir H. Stafford* in *Somerset Med. Wills* (1901) 200 When ye come to him by the same token that I said to thabbat, Sir, I have a goode quarrell, the which is the cause of my journey, by that token he will deliver the said writinges unto you. **1491** *Act 7 Hen. VII*, c. 22 Preamble, Ye may speke with him by the same token that he and y commyned toguyder of matiers touching your maisters sonne. **1606** SHAKS. *Tr. and Cr.* I. ii. 307 *Pand.* I, a token from Troylus. *Cres.* By the same token, you are a Bawd. **1607** R. C[AREW] tr. *Estienne's World of Wonders* I. xxxviii. 305 At Aix in Germany, they were accustomed to shew his breeches, together with the virgin Maries smocke, by the same token that [*orig.* à telles enseignes que] the smocke was big enough for a giant. **1659–60** PEPYS *Diary* 28 Feb., Up in the morning and had some red herrings to our breakfast, while my boot-heel was a-mending, by the same token the boy left the hole as big as it was before. **1662** *Ibid.* 13 Apr., I went to the Temple Church, and there heard another [sermon]: by the same tokens, a boy, being asleep, fell down a high seat to the ground. **1722** DE FOE *Plague* (1756) 280 Others caused large Fires to be made..; by the same Token, that two or three were pleased to set their Houses on Fire, and so effectually sweetened them by burning them down to the Ground. **1857** DICKENS in *Househ. Words* XVII. 46 Max..was a staunch Roman Catholic. (By this token: Many an argument have I had with him on religion). **1875** 'MARK TWAIN' in *Atlantic Monthly* Aug. 193/2 By the same token any person can see that seven hundred and forty-two years from now the Lower Mississippi will be only a mile and three quarters long. **1907** PHYLLIS DARE *School to Stage* vii. 126 To receive letters from people whom they do not know, and are, by the same token, never likely to know. **1945** B. MACDONALD *Egg & I* (1946) I. i. 11 If you marry a doctor, don't whine because he doesn't keep the hours of a shoe clerk, and by the same token if you marry a shoe clerk, don't complain because he doesn't make as much money as a doctor. **1970** 'D. HALLIDAY' *Dolly & Cookie Bird* v. 66 I've dined out on a few stories about her. But not ones that matter. By the same token, she could have made quite a good thing about telling how she saw you ..that night. **1978** *Jrnl. R. Soc. Arts* CXXVI. 701/1 By the same token, among the most interesting and valuable sections of this book are those which deal with technique.

b. ***more by token***: still more, the more so. *dial.*

1816 SCOTT *Antiq.* xl, Ane suldna speak ill o' the dead—mair by token, o' ane's cummer and neighbour. **1850** HAWTHORNE *Scarlet L.* xxi, Our only danger will be from drug or pill; more by token, as there is a lot of apothecary's stuff aboard. **1861** GEO. ELIOT *Silas M.* i, All this Jem swore he had seen, more by token that it was the very day he had been mole-catching on Squire Cass's land.

16. a. *attrib.* and *Comb.*: †**token-bell**, ? a signal- or alarm-bell; **token booth** *U.S.*, a booth from which tokens are sold, esp. those for obtaining tickets for a subway; **token coin**, **coinage**, **currency**: see TOKEN-MONEY c; **token economy**, in the treatment of behavioural disorders, the principle or practice of rewarding desirable behaviour with tokens which can be exchanged for goods or privileges and punishing undesirable behaviour by withholding or forfeiting such tokens; † **token-girdle**, ? a girdle mounted with amulets; **token pledge** = sense 7; **token-proprium**: see TOKEN-MONEY b; **token-reflexive** *a.* (*Logic*), denoting words the referent or temporal or spatial orientation of which is contextually determined, e.g. 'I', 'now', 'here', 'today'; also as *sb.*; **token-ring**, a ring worn in token of an engagement or pledge; **token-sheet** *Printing* (see 12); † **token-teller**, an indicator; **token value**: see TOKEN-MONEY c; † **tokenworth**, the worth of a token (sense 11), the very least amount.

1486 in J. R. Boyle *Hedon* (1875) App. 130 Soluti pro undecim les *tokyngbelles hoc anno, iij.s. xj. d. **1970** *New Yorker* 31 Oct. 123/1 Their reptile-papered basement..is a bit bigger than a *token booth. **1897** *Daily News* 30 Nov. 4/6 The shilling..is declared to be..the twentieth part of a pound. No evil results follow from this fiction, because the shilling is a *token coin and because silver is not a legal tender, except for a comparatively trivial amount. **1881** H. H. GIBBS *Double Stand.* 73 It would be necessary to re-coin all our silver *token-coinage. **1883** *Times* 14 July 5 Silver ..[is] in this country in the nature of a token coinage. **1893** *Daily News* 27 June 2/3 If so, the silver rupee will become '*token' currency. **1968** AYLLON & AZRIN *Token Economy* ii. 16 We first conceived of the *token economy and its use as a motivational system for therapy during the early part of 1961. **1981** W. REICH in Bloch & Chodoff *Psychiatr. Ethics* iv. 59 The development of aversive techniques of control, 'token economies' and other forms of behaviour modification. **1477** *Croscombe Churchw. Acc.* (Som. Rec. Soc.) 5 Sylver ryng gylt and a *token gyrdel of sylver. **1896** A. AUSTIN *Eng. Darling* I. iii, Only a *token pledge to make me free Of Alfred's camp at Athelney. **1716** M. DAVIES *Athen. Brit.* III. 78 The Traders were not oblig'd to take one anothers Penny-coyns or such like *Token-Propriums. **1947** H. REICHENBACH *Elem. Symbolic Logic* vii. 284 Words which refer to the corresponding token used in an individual act of speech, or writing..may therefore be called **token-reflexive* words. **1949** *Mind* LVIII. 356 Personal pronouns are to be distinguished from personal proper names such as 'Jones', or 'Fleur',.. by their different use, the former 'token reflexive', the latter 'proper name'. **1962** W. & M. KNEALE *Devel. Logic* ii. 53 A sentence containing a token-reflexive taken out of context expresses no proposition at all. **1968** A. J. AYER *Origins of Pragmatism* 156 With the exception of quantifiers and relative pronouns,.. designations are token-reflexive. That is to say, their use is determined by the context. **1840** MRS. NORTON *Dream*, etc. 296 By the true *token-ring upon thy hand. **1877** W. JONES *Finger-ring* 350 A pledge or token ring of remarkable interest. **1574** NEWTON *Health Mag.* 29 For smellinge is the discouerer and *token teller of tast. **1898** *Daily News* 30 Mar. 5/1 The closing of the Mints to the free coinage of silver, with the view of giving an artificial *token value to the coinage, was adopted. **1614** B. JONSON *Barth. Fair* I. ii, Why? he makes no loue to her, do's he? *Lit.* Not a *tokenworth that euer I saw.

b. passing into *adj.* Serving as a token; pro forma; (purely) symbolic; constituting a gesture (only); minimal, nominal, perfunctory; cf. STATUTORY *a.* 3 b; **token estimate**, a provisional statement of a sum of money, placed before Parliament to allow discussion to proceed; **token payment**, (*a*) the payment of a small proportion of a sum due, as an indication that the debt has not been repudiated; (*b*) a nominal payment; **token stoppage**, **strike**, a brief strike to demonstrate strength of feeling only; **token vote**, a vote of money on the basis of a token estimate.

1915 *Political Q.* May 147 For form's sake 'token' estimates were presented, on the basis of £1,000 for each vote and £100 for each appropriation in aid. **1923** *Times* 27 Feb. 18/3 On the Supplementary Vote of £10 for Diplomatic and Consular Services..the anticipated savings under various subheads were rather larger than £155,198, and would..be sufficient to cover the whole amount now asked for; but inasmuch as all but one of the subheads referred to new services, it had been thought right that a token vote of £10 should be put down in order to provide the opportunity for discussing these new services. **1933** *Sun* (Baltimore) 15 June 1/7 The British Government.. tendered a partial or 'token' payment of $10,000,000 to the United States 'as an acknowledgment of the (war) debts pending a final settlement'. **1937** *Ibid.* 19 Oct. 6/1 British and French authorities have expressed belief that there are at least 100,000 Italians serving under Generalissimo Francisco Franco and have urged a 'token' withdrawal on that basis as a guarantee of good faith. **1941** *Ibid.* 28 June 6/3 Less than a week after launching its aggression, Berlin has requested other European states to dispatch 'token forces' to the battlefield. *Ibid.* 29 Aug. 12/3 They [sc. the Persians] have insured themselves against this..by making a token resistance and yielding to demonstrated superior force. **1947** *Daily Mail* 22 May 1 Civil Servants in some sections are considering 'token' strikes if their wages claims continue to drag on without result. **1954** *Times* 20 Jan. 6/7 Twenty-six workers employed by a Manchester contractor have been dismissed for participating in Monday's token stoppage. **1958** *Listener* 12 June 978/1 Some London railway workers vote in favour of an unofficial 'token' strike in support of busmen. **1960** *Time* 12 Dec. 56 The schools took in token Negroes. **1962** *N.Y. Times Mag.* 5 Aug. 11 The current notion that token integration will satisfy his people, says Dr. King, is an illusion. **1968** C. BROOKE-ROSE *Between* 7 More often the bathroom..has a token window on the hotel corridor or no window at all, merely a ventilation shaft. **1970** J. G. FARRELL *Troubles* I. 10 For some reason—the poor quality of the soil or the proximity of the sea—vegetation has only made a token attempt to possess them. **1971** H. MACMILLAN *Riding Storm* xiv. 442, I..only agreed to a very small, almost a token, delivery of arms to Tunisia. **1972** D. E. WESTLAKE *Bank Shot* ix. 64 He and his wife Linda were the token whites at this dinner party..the three other couples all being black. **1974** *Times* 21 May 7/8 No tightly run business will have 'token' women on the board. Each director must be able to offer some exceptional contribution. **1976** *New Society* 7 Oct. 28/3 The resistance is little more than token. **1979** J. COOPER *Class* iv. 82 'We've even got two Punk Rockers' (rather like token blacks).

token ('təʊkən), *v.* Forms: *α.* 1 **tácnian**, 2 **tacnien**, 2–3 **tacnen** (*Orm.* **-enn**), 3 **taknen**, 4 **-nyn**, **takenen**, 4–6 **takin**, **-yn**. *β.* 3 **toknien**, **-ny**, **tocknen**, 3–4 **tokenen**, 3–5 **toknen**, (5 **tooken**), 3– **token**. [OE. *tácnian* (also *ȝe-*) = MLG. *têkenen*, OHG. *zeihhanôn* (Ger. *zeichnen*):—OTeut. **taiknôjan*, f. **taiknoᵐ*, TOKEN *sb.*]

1. *trans.* To be a token or sign of; to signify, represent, denote, mean, betoken.

*c***888** ÆLFRED *Boeth.* xxxix. §13 þon tacnað [se steorra] æfen. **971** *Blickl. Hom.* 19 Smeaȝean we nu..hwæt þæt tacnode. [*c***1175** *Lamb. Hom.* 7 Nu we wulleð seggen mare wet þis godspel itacnet.] *c***1205** LAY. 32115 To wulche þinge hit iteon wolde þat him wes itacned þere [*i.e.* in the dream]. *Ibid.* 32131 Al swa godd him hafde itakned to don. *c***1350** *Will. Palerne* 2957 What þat it tokeneþ telle wol ich sone. *c***1425** *Craft of Nombrynge* (E.E.T.S.) 5 A cifre tokens noȝt. *c***1425** tr. *Arderne's Treat. Fistula* 14 Suche pronosticacions sheweþ and tokneþ to þe pacient þat þe leche is experte in þe knowyng of þe fistule. **1535** STEWART *Cron. Scot.* (Rolls) II. 424 Quhat this takynnit I will nocht tell ȝow heir. **1889** C. C. R. *Up for the Season*, etc. 16 On fair leaves and ladies as yet there no shade is To token their coming decay.

2. To be a type, emblem, or symbol of; to typify, symbolize.

971 *Blickl. Hom.* 35 Þa Easterlican daȝas tacniaþ þa ecean eadiȝnesse. *c***1000** ÆLFRIC *Hom.* II. 280 Wæter ȝetacnað.. mennisc inȝehyd. *c***1220** *Bestiary* 763 in *O.E. Misc.* 24 Crist is tokned ðurȝ ðis der. *a***1300** *Cursor M.* 6341 (Cott.) Þis wandes takens persons thre. *Ibid.* 18644 He [Christ] es takend to leon. **1426** LYDG. *De Guil. Pilgr.* 809 And by thys dowe wych thow dost se,..I am tookenyd. **1552** GRINDAL *Fruitful Dial.* in Foxe *A. & M.* (1570) 1558/2 The token of the body of Christ is [not] the thing tokened; wherfore they are not one. **1863** KINGLAKE *Crimea* II. xiii. 195 The principle of the 'moveable column' would be well enough tokened by that simple skinful of water.

†**3.** To mark with a sign or significant mark.

*c***1300** *Cursor M.* 21713 (Edin.) Þe signe of taue in alde laiis Bitaknis cros nu in ure daiis. The men that tarwiþ takind ware Oft it helpid fra misfare. *c***1375** *Sc. Leg. Saints* xli. (*Agnes*) 30 With þe fare blud of his passione [He] taknys þar chekis vpe & done. **1483** CAXTON *Gold. Leg.* 431 b/1 He was marked or tokened on the lyppes of hym with an hote and brennyng yron. **1513** DOUGLAS *Æneis* XI. viii. 23 Quhen thou takynnit hes sa worthely With syng tropheall the feyldis.

†**4.** *intr.* To make a sign or signs. *Obs. rare.*

1535 COVERDALE *Prov.* vi. 12 He wyncketh with his eyes, he toketh with his fete, he poynteth with his fyngers.

5. *trans.* To betroth, promise in marriage. *dial.*

1880 in *W. Cornwall Gloss.* **1910** E. PHILLPOTTS *Thief of Virtue* I. ii. 10 'How can she throw over the man afore they'm tokened?'.. 'If they are tokened, does it follow they've let all the world know it?'

†**6.** ***token up***, to put up in writing, write out. *Obs. rare.*

1535 COVERDALE *Dan.* v. 23 Therfore is the palme off this honde sent hither..to token vp this wrytinge. —— *Ecclus.* l. 27, I Iesus the sonne of Sirac..haue tokened vp these informacions and documentes of wyszdome and vnderstandinge in this boke.

Hence **'tokened**, **'tokening** *ppl. adjs.*

1606 SHAKS. *Ant. & Cl.* III. x. 9 *Eno.* How appeares the Fight? *Scar.* On our side, like the Token'd Pestilence, Where death is sure. **1820** CLARE *Rural Life* (ed. 3) 109 We'll mix our wishes in a tokening tear.

† **tokener** ('təʊkənə(r)). *Obs.* Also 6 *Sc.* **takinar**, **taknair**. [f. prec. + -ER[1].]

1. One who or that which portends or prognosticates; a portent.

1513 DOUGLAS *Æneis* I. v. 114 The dreidful portis sal be schet,..Of Janus temple, the taknair of battail. *Ibid.* vii. 46 Thai, delvand, fand the takinar of Cartage, Ane mekle hors heid that was, I wene.

2. One who signs or marks.
1648 HEXHAM II, *Een Teeckenaer*, a Marker, a Noter, a Signer, or a Tokener.

tokening ('təʊkənɪŋ), *vbl. sb.* Now *rare.* [OE. *tácnung* (*ȝe-*), f. *tácn-ian*, TOKEN *v.* + -ING[1]: cf. OHG. *zeihnunga*, MHG. *zeichenunge*, Ger. *zeichnung*, Du. *teekening*, etc.]
1. The action of the verb TOKEN; representation, signification, meaning, symbolization, betokening, presaging, etc.: see the verb.
c **888** K. ÆLFRED *Boeth.* vii. §2 To hwæm cumað hi þon elles butan to tacnunge sorȝes &..sares? [*c* **1175** *Lamb. Hom.* 99 Þe helende ableu his gast on his apostlas for ðere itacnunge þet heo and alle cristen men scullan lufian heore nehstan.] *c* **1200** *Trin. Coll. Hom.* 91 Chirche haueð þe tocninge of bethfage. *a* **1300** *Cursor M.* 6337 Sum-kin takening suld þar be Loken in þir wandes thre. *c* **1410** *Sir Cleges* 217, I am aferd yt ys tokynnyng Of more harme that ys comynge. **1496** *Dives & Paup.* (W. de W.) I. xv. 48/1 Encensynge done..byfore the ymages in dyuerse sygnyfycacyons or tokenynges.
†**b.** *in tokening*, in token, as a token or evidence (*of*). *Obs.*
c **890** tr. *Bæda's Hist.* II. vi. (1890) 114 Þa he me in tacnunge his lufan bebead. **1297** R. GLOUC. *Chron.* (Rolls) 1165 Ibured it was uorþ wiþ him as in tokninge Of is prowesse. **1456** SIR G. HAYE *Law Arms* (S.T.S.) 39 A branch of ane olyve tree in takenyng of pes. ? *a* **1500** *Chester Pl.* xi. 147 A signe I offer..in tockeninge shee has lived oo in full devocion.
2. A token, emblem, sign, mark; a portent; a signal; †a zodiacal sign (*obs.*).
c **888** K. ÆLFRED *Boeth.* viii. §1 Hwæt syndon ða woruldsælða oðres buton deaðes tacnung? *a* **1300** *Cursor M.* 11252 Þar es þe king ouer al kinges Born to night wit þir takeninges. *c* **1320** *Sir Tristr.* 506 Hunters, whare be ȝe? Þe tokening schuld ȝe blowe. *c* **1400** tr. *Secreta Secret., Gov. Lordsh.* 73 Whenne þe sonne entrys yn to þe firste tokenynge of þe crabbe. *a* **1450** *Tourn. Tottenham* 85 A broche on hur brest..With the holy-rode tokenyng, was wrotyn for the nonys. **1553** *Douglas's Æneis* III. vi. 67, I sall the schaw taikynins [*ed. Small* takins] therof full mete. **1710** *Dict. Feudal Law* 151 *Taiknings*, are Signals given to forwarn people of the approach of the Enemy. **1867** MORRIS *Jason* III. 46 Bid him hearken, by this tokening, That I, who send thee to him, am the same.

tokenism ('təʊkənɪz(ə)m). orig. *U.S.* [f. TOKEN *sb.* 16b + -ISM.] The practice or policy of making merely a token effort or granting only minimal concessions, esp. to minority or suppressed groups.
1962 *N.Y. Times Mag.* 5 Aug. 11 (*heading*) The case against tokenism. **1963** *Times* 28 May 10/1 Tactics such as 'tokenism', which have been adopted in some southern states seeking to delay the process of desegregation without opposing the original court order. **1972** [see JOUAL]. **1976** R. BAXANDALL in Mitchell & Oakley *Rights & Wrongs of Women* viii. 265 Women are not encouraged to become leaders in unions. Tokenism is a standard practice. **1980** *Jewish Chron.* 12 Sept. 27/3 Philip Rosenthal..waffled on about 'tokenism' in his factory, where two workers sit on the board, as if real democracy had been achieved.
Hence **toke'nistic** *a.*, of the nature of tokenism.
1976 in *6,000 Words.* **1977** M. EDELMAN *Political Lang.* vii. 125 Disorder..invites a response that is only tokenistic or symbolic when the protest is narrow in scope and expressed through conventional tactics. **1983** *Daily Tel.* 14 Sept. 32/5 That was just a tokenistic load of knackers about gay rights.

'tokenless, *a.* [-LESS.] Without a token.
a **1763** BYROM *On Church Communion* III. ii, Heartless, and tokenless if it remain, It ought to pass, in Strictness, for profane. **1969** *Railway Mag.* Feb. 88 (*caption*) Introduction of tokenless-block working over this route will make these [*sc.* tablet-catchers], and associated lineside equipment, redundant.

'token-,money.
a. *Eccl.* The payment made or contribution given (by way of Easter Offering) by persons on receiving their token that they were duly prepared to make their Easter communion.
(See TOKEN 10b, quot. 1608, and *Churchw. Acc. St. Martin in the Fields* 37 *note*.)
1546 *Churchw. Acc. St. Martin in the Fields* 101 In primis Receued and gatherd of the Paryshyons ffor the pascall and tokyn money at Easter in the Church xlis. vjd. **1564** *Ibid.* 216 It'm Receyued the ix[th] of Aprile 1564 for the halfe of the token monneye at Easter xxvj[s] viij[d]. **1572** *Ludlow Churchw. Acc.* (Camden) 153 Imprimis receaved of the parishenars for the token money at Easter..xlij s. **1573** *Ibid.* 156 Receavede at Easter of token money..xlv s. x d. **1611** *Churchw. Acc. St. Margaret's Westm.* (Nichols 1797) 29 Received for the token-money for the whole year, ended the 11th day of May, 1611 £6. 5.
b. Private tokens (TOKEN *sb.* 11) issued by a trader or company to serve as a fractional currency and temporary medium of exchange between trader and customer; so *token-proprium* (TOKEN *sb.* 16).
1890 *Pall Mall G.* 9 Jan. 3/3 He has also grocery and provision stores all along the line, and pays all his employés in token-money which he mints himself—probably the most gigantic truck system which ever existed. **1900** M. PHILLIPS (*title*) The Token-Money of the Bank of England, 1797 to 1816.
c. State coinage of money not having the intrinsic value for which it is current, but bearing a fixed value relative to gold coin, for which it is exchangeable.
1889 *Spectator* 9 Nov. 641/2 They [gold and silver] perform different functions, and it is this fact which enables a State to use one of them as token-money, the demand for it practically neither rising nor falling according to its price, nor according to the activity of trade. **1892** *Pall Mall G.* 22 Dec. 2/3 The remedy lies not in increased use of token money, but in providing in gold-using countries a second currency for silver.

†**'toker.** *Obs.* A large variety of garden bean.
1786 J. ABERCROMBIE *Gard. Assist.* Feb. 32 *Beans.*—Plant ..a full crop of long-pods, Windsors, tokers, Sandwich, or other broad kinds, in rows a yard distance. **1802** *Eng. Encycl.* IV. 473/1 The Toker is the largest garden-bean, and somewhat of an oval shape.

toker, tokke, obs. ff. TUCKER, fuller, TUCK *v.*

to-kerve: see TO-CARVE.

‖**toki** ('tɔki). *N.Z.* [Maori.] A Maori war adze or axe, usu. of stone. Freq. with defining addition.
1860 A. S. ATKINSON *Let.* 9 Apr. in *Richmond-Atkinson Papers* (1960) I. 559 It was perfectly innocuous, I believe, in the ordinary way of guns and was probably intended not to hit us but to frighten us into a fit state for nobbling with the toki. **1905** W. B. *Where White Man Treads* 93 The Maori was..provided with no more efficient tool..than the 'toki panehe' (stone axe). **1949** P. BUCK *Coming of Maori* II. vi. 188 The ceremonial adze termed *toki pou tangata* was formed of a nephrite adze lashed to a carved haft.

toko, var. TOCO[2].

toko-: see TOCO-.

‖**tokoloshe** (,tɔkɔ'lɔʃɪ). *S. Afr.* Also **thikoloshe, tikolosh(e), tokolosh,** etc. [Sotho *thokolosi*, *t(h)ikoloshi*, Xhosa *uThikoloshe*, Zulu *utokoloshe.*] In African folklore, a mischievous and lascivious hairy dwarf.
1833 S. KAY *Trav. in Caffraria* xiii. 339 *Tikaloshi* also is much more frequently and familiarly talked about than amongst the more southern tribes. **1894** E. GLANVILLE *Fair Colonist* 82 Tikoloshe is supposed to be an evil spirit which takes the shape of a small man. **1911** *Daily Dispatch* (E. London, S. Afr.) 24 Nov. 7 One might be dragged into the watery den of the *tikolosh.* **1927** W. PLOMER *Notes for Poems* 30 The water spirits laughed at her, my friends the tokoloshes. **1949** *Handbk. Race Relations in S. Afr.* 561 The most widely believed in amongst many Nguni tribes is *thikoloshe.* **1959** L. G. GREEN *These Wonders to Behold* 22 Witchcraft has never lost its grip on the African native. Wherever you go, from Algiers to Cape Town..you will find black millions who are still ruled by the fear of djinns and demons,..ngogwe and tokoloshe. **1972** *Country Life* 10 Feb. 348/2, I was looking at a modern bronze..of a Tokoloshe, a Bantu evil spirit. **1974** *Stand. Encycl. S. Afr.* X. 504/2 The tikolosh (or tokolosh) is believed to be a dwarfish being, pitch-black, with a hairy body and baboon-like face..half-human and half-animal, having only one buttock, while the male has an enormous sexual organ.

‖**tokonoma** (,təʊkə'nəʊmə). Also 8–9 toko, tokko. [Jap.] In a Japanese house, a recess or alcove, usu. a few inches above floor-level, in which pictures, ornaments, etc., are displayed. Also *attrib.*
1727 J. G. SCHEUCHZER tr. *Kæmpfer's Hist. Japan* II. iv. 421 In the solid wall of the room there is allways a *Tokko*.. or a sort of a cupboard, raised about a foot..above the floor, and very near two feet deep. **1822** F. SHOBERL tr. *Titsingh's Illustrations of Japan* II. 202 Two cakes..which are placed as an ornament within the *toko.* **1871** A. B. MITFORD *Tales of Old Japan* II. 127 The *tokonoma*—that portion of the Japanese room which is raised a few inches above the rest of the floor, and which is regarded as the place of honour. **1929** *Periodical* Feb. 25 The whole set [of the *O.E.D.*] of mine is now sitting stately on the 'tokonoma' of my study in my residence by the side of a Japanese 'Oxford Dictionary'. **1957** C. BROOKE-ROSE *Languages of Love* 45 The recess on the left of the chimney-breast, which Georgina had turned into a *tokonoma.* **1980** J. MELVILLE *Chrysanthemum Chain* 14 In the *tokonoma* alcove a modest flower arrangement stood in a simple bowl.

Tok Pisin (tɒk 'pɪzɪn). Also **talk Pidgin.** [Pidgin, = talk pidgin.] A Melanesian pidgin English spoken in Papua New Guinea.
1943 R. A. HALL *Melanesian Pidgin Phrase-Bk. & Vocab.* 52 *Pidgin*,..talk Pidgin. **1976** *Language* LII. 631 We first began working on the problem of relativization in New Guinea Tok Pisin (Melanesian Pidgin English, Neo-Melanesian) in 1972. **1982** *Trans. Philol. Soc.* 103 Unfortunately, data about the use of Tok Pisin by the indigenous population is very scarce.

tol, obs. form of TOLL, TOOL.

‖**tola**[1] ('təʊlə). *East Ind.* Also 7 tolla; anglicized tole, toll; 9 tolah. [Hindī *tola*:—Skr. *tu'lā* balance, scale, weight, f. *tul-* to weigh.] An East Indian weight, chiefly used for gold or silver, varying at different times and places; (from 1833) in British dominions fixed at 180 grains (the weight of the rupee). Also, a coin of this weight.
1614 PURCHAS *Pilgrimage* V. xvii. (ed. 2) 544 Euery Tole is a Rupia of siluer, and tenne of those Toles is the value of one of golde. **1618** in Foster *Eng. Factories Ind.* (1906) 47, 52½ tole make a seere of 30 pices. **1683** W. HEDGES *Diary* (Hakl. Soc.) I. 83 They..tooke from them 4 or 5 tolas upon a Seer, over weight, on all their Silk brought into y[e] Ware-house. **1687** A. LOVELL tr. *Thevenot's Trav.* III. 18 All Gold and Silver is weighed by the Tole. **1800** *Misc. Tr.* in *Asiat. Ann. Reg.* 45/1 Each of these persons shall pay a fixed revenue of a tola of gold to the Rajah. **1803** GREVILLE in *Phil. Trans.* XCIII. 203 *note*, A tolah is about 180 grains, Troy weight. **1895** *19th Cent.* Aug. 255, I placed a piece of gold, weighing a tola, on his lap.

tola[2] ('təʊlə). [a. *ntola*, name used in Zaïre.] = AGBA.
1897 M. KINGSLEY *Trav. W. Afr.* iii. 58 The Bubi... His idea of decoration goes in the direction of a plaster of 'tola' pomatum over his body. **1959** *Archit. Rev.* CXXVI. 313 The table top and chair seats are covered with black imitation leather; the chair backs are of tola. **1962** *House & Garden* Jan. 45/2 (*caption*) 3-drawer desk in tola wood.

tolat, obs. Sc. form of TOILET.

tolazamide (tə'leɪzəmaɪd). *Pharm.* [f. *tol(uene* s.v. TOLU- + AZ(O- + AMIDE.] A hypoglycæmic sulphonylurea drug given orally in the treatment of diabetes; 1-perhydroazepin-1-yl-3-*p*-tolylsulphonylurea, $C_{14}H_{21}N_3O_3S$.
1963 *Canad. Med. Assoc. Jrnl.* LXXXIX. 669/1 Tolazamide is a new sulfonylurea compound which has hypoglycemic properties said to be six to eight times as potent as tolbutamide. **1974** M. C. GERALD *Pharmacology* xxv. 441 Several oral hypoglycemic sulfonylurea agents are currently used in the United States, including..tolazamide.

tolazoline (tə'leɪzəli:n). *Pharm.* [f. TOL(YL + *imid)azoline*, f. IMIDAZOL(E + -INE[5].] An adrenergic blocking agent and vasodilator, used esp. in the treatment of spasm of the peripheral arteries; 2-benzyl-2-imidazoline, $C_{10}H_{12}N_2$.
1952 *Martindale's Extra Pharmacopœia* (ed. 23) I. 605 Tolazoline hydrochloride is a sympatholytic and adrenolytic compound which also exerts a vasodilator effect. **1959** S. DUKE-ELDER *Parsons' Dis. Eye* (ed. 13) 582/1 (*heading*) Tolazoline ('Priscol') injection. **1972** [see PHENTOLAMINE].

tolbooth, var. TOLL-BOOTH.

†**'tolbot.** *dial. Obs.* **a.** Local name of some measure of capacity: according to some, a bushel. **b.** The tub or cask for the reception of meal taken in multure. [Cf. TOLL *sb.*[1] 2 a (*b*), and *boat* (*dial.*), a tub for meal or meat, a meal-boat (*Eng. Dial. Dict.*).]
1536 *MS. Acc. St. John's Hosp., Canterb.*, Payd for a tolbot off otemell vij d. **1589** R. HARVEY *Pl. Perc.* 3 Make meale of it, and take large tole to the enriching of the Tolbot.

tolbutamide (tɒl'bju:təmaɪd). *Pharm.* [f. *tol(uene* s.v. TOLU- + BUT(YL + AMIDE.] A hypoglycæmic sulphonylurea drug given orally in the treatment of diabetes; 1-butyl-3-tosylurea, $C_{12}H_{18}N_2O_3S$.
1956 *Metabolism* V. 801 (*heading*) Hypoglycemic actions of tolbutamide and carbutamide. **1974** M. C. GERALD *Pharmacol.* xxv. 436 Tolbutamide (Orinase) and related sulfonylurea compounds used for the oral treatment of diabetes act by enhancing the release of insulin from the pancreas.

told (təʊld), *ppl. a. rare.* [pa. pple. of TELL *v.*] Related, narrated, recounted; counted, reckoned; †esteemed: see the verb. Chiefly in Comb., as ***oft-told*** (OFT A. c), ***twice-told***, etc. †***by told tales***, as is said, as they say (cf. *by all accounts*).
c **1310** in Bödddeker *Altengl. Dicht.* 292 Ȝef þou art riche & wel ytold, Ne be þou noht þarefore to bold. *a* **1425** *Cursor M.* 18713 (Trin.) Alle þat wolde leue [= believe] þat tolde And bapteme receyue wolde. **1546** J. HEYWOOD *Prov.* (1867) 22 All is not golde that glisters by tolde tales. **1882** W. B. WEEDEN *Soc. Law Labor* 94 Capital is told wealth.
b. ***told out***, counted out; hence, played out, spun out, exhausted (*colloq.*).
1861 WHYTE MELVILLE *Mrkt. Harb.* xi. (1862) 89 He could not disguise from himself that the roan was about 'told out'.

tol-de-rol, tol de rol (tɒl dɪ rɒl). Also in extended form tol de rol lol. A combination of syllables used as the refrain of a song, and hence as an exclamation of jollity, or the like. Also as *sb.* and *attrib.*
1765 H. TIMBERLAKE *Mem.* 56 Just like the tolderols [*sic*] of many old English songs. **1782** MRS. H. COWLEY *Bold Stroke for Husb.* IV. ii, Tol-de-rol! Ah, that won't do—that won't do! You can't hide it. **1797** F. REYNOLDS *The Will* V. ii, What, Mandeville! Howard! all together! all reconciled! —Tol de rol lol! **1798** WOLCOTT (P. Pindar) *Tales of Hoy* Wks. 1816 IV. 18 Let us have something in the tol-de-roll-loll-way—funny. **1815** W. H. IRELAND *Scribbleomania* 40 Some scribes who write fast, and are flippant at rhymes, Think Genius is center'd in tol-de-rol chimes. **1861** DUTTON COOK *P. Foster's D.* i, The policeman sings a sort of a 'tol de rol'. **1889** *Grove's Dict. Mus.* IV. 805 *Ture-lure*.., or *Toure-loure*, a very ancient lyrical burden or refrain.. still survives in English popular music in the forms 'tooral-looral-looral', and 'tol-de-rol'.

‖**toldo** ('toldo). Also 9 tolda. [Sp. *toldo* awning, canopy, penthouse: cf. F. *taudis* a shelter, a hut, OF. *tauder* to shelter; see Körting 9422, 9519.]
a. A canopy. **b.** A tent, hut, or simple dwelling of the native Indians of South America.
a. 1760–72 tr. *Juan & Ulloa's Voy.* (ed. 3) I. 159 To avoid the tortures of the Moscitos..all persons..have *toldos* or canopies over their beds. **1852** TH. ROSS *Humboldt's Trav.*

II. xx. 286 We could not make use of mosquito-curtains (toldos) while on the Orinoco.

b. **1845** DARWIN *Voy. Nat.* iv. (1873) 65 The Cacique Lucanee constantly have their Toldos on the outskirts of the town. *Note.* The hovels of the Indians are thus called. **1864** *Reader* 9 Apr. 463/1 These *toldas* (or dwelling-places) are constructed only with branches of sticks, joined overhead at a height of about five feet from the ground. **1910** *Blackw. Mag.* June 850/1 An old revolver may find its way into their guanaco-skin toldos.

† **tole**, *sb.*[1] *Obs. rare.* [OE. *tál* (str. fem.), a by-form of *tǽl*: see TELE *sb.*[1]] Evil-speaking, calumny; blasphemy; reproach, blame.

c **1000** *Ags. Gosp.* Luke iii. 14 Ne tale ne doð. *c* **1000** ÆLFRIC *Hom.* I. 498 Ælc synn and tal bið forgifen. *a* **1023** WULFSTAN *Hom.* lvii. (1883) 299 þæt man god to tale habbe. *c* **1315** SHOREHAM i. 975 þer-fore ȝe mote þolyen hyt [pain] Wyþ-oute alle manere tole [*rime* hole = whole].

tole (təʊl), *sb.*[2] Also ‖tôle. [a. F. *tôle* sheet-iron, f. dial. *taule* table, f. L. *tabula* a flat board.]

a. Tin-plated sheet-iron which is first varnished and then ornamented by decorative painting. Also in phr. *tôle peinte*, painted sheet-iron.

1946 *National Button Bull.* (U.S.) Oct. 290 Let's consider these buttons of japanned or lacquered metals. First we have those of Tôle, which are really of tin... Tôle is composed of thinly rolled sheets of iron, tinned. **1958** *Times* 29 Nov. 8/6 A Regency library table decorated in *tôle peinte* ..made £540. **1973** *Canadian Antiques Collector* Jan.–Feb. 28/2 The French-Canadian workers in 'tole' or sheet iron.

b. *attrib.* and *Comb.*

1948 E. O. CHRISTENSEN *Popular Art in U.S.* 19 *Toleware Coffee-pot*... Though called Pennsylvania Dutch, it was of English production... The term 'japanned' tin-ware, or toleware, is applied to..household utensils..made of sheet iron, covered with a coating of tin. **1960** *Washington Post* 12 Mar. A-6 (Advt.), All metal tole lamps with brass accents. **1973** *New Yorker* 3 Feb. 40/3 Toleware—exquisite hand-painted tinware produced in the nineteenth century in Pennsylvania, New York State, Ohio, and New England. **1975** *Country Life* 11 Dec. (Suppl.) 22/1 Pair of Austrian tôle peinte figures of red Indians..sold at Christie's..for £4,200. **1976** *National Observer* (U.S.) 17 Jan. 10/2 The city's community-education system offers hundreds of classes that vary from appliance repair to tole painting.

tole (təʊl), repr. a U.S. dial. and Black English pronunc. of *told* pa. t. and pa. pple.

1797 J. BARTON *Let.* in *Amer. Speech* 1969 (1973) XLIV. 304 If I had a tole any such a story. *a* **1911** D. G. PHILLIPS *Susan Lenox* (1917) I. ix. 152 So you ain't tole her? Well, Keziah, I've been and gone and got married. **1935** Z. N. HURSTON *Mules & Men* (1970) I. i. 26 John tole him, 'Massa, he had two great big eyes lak balls of fire.' **1955** F. O'CONNOR *Wise Blood* iv. 72, I done tole you them tires won't bust. **1979** 'E. MCBAIN' *Calypso* ix. 122 She tole me what she'd been doin.

tole, obs. f. or var. of TOLA[1], TOLL (esp. *v.*[1]), TOOL.

Toledan (tɒˈleɪdən, tɒˈliːdən), *a.* and *sb.* [f. *Toledo* (see TOLEDO) + -AN.] **A.** *adj.* Of or pertaining to Toledo. Cf. TOLETAN *a.* **B.** *sb.* A native or inhabitant of Toledo.

1846 R. FORD *Gatherings from Spain* iii. 28 The Toledan chroniclers derive the name from Tagus, fifth king of Iberia. *Ibid.* 29 The performance has been contemplated by many *foreigners*, the Toledans looking lazily on. **1914** J. MASEFIELD *Philip the King* 47 Till their Toledan armour was burnt black. **1965** C. D. EBY *Siege of Alcazar* (1966) viii. 156 Once and for all the Toledan nightmare must be ended.

Toledo (təʊˈliːdəʊ). [Name of a city (toˈleðo) in Spain, long famous for its manufacture of finely tempered sword-blades.] Short for *Toledo blade* or *sword*: A sword or sword-blade made at Toledo, or of the kind made there.

1598 B. JONSON *Ev. Man in Hum.* II. ii, *Step.* How will you sell this rapier, friend? *Brai*... ''Tis a most pure Toledo. *c* **1626** *Dick of Devon* III. i. in Bullen *O. Pl.* II. 46 A hundred of the best Toledoes. **1645** MILTON *Colast.* Wks. 1851 IV. 357 What doe these keen Doctors heer but cut him over the sinews with their Toledo's? **1713** ADDISON *Ct. Tariff* ¶ 22 A long Toledo sticking out by his side. **1826** SCOTT *Woodst.* ii, Reach me my Toledo.

tolenar, variant of TOLNER *Obs.*

tolene (təʊˈliːn). *Chem.* [f. TOL(U + -ENE.] The oily constituent of tolu-balsam, $C_{10}H_{16}$.

1868 WATTS *Dict. Chem.* V. 851 Tolene is a colourless very mobile liquid, having a pungent odour... When exposed to the air, it quickly takes up oxygen, and becomes resinised.

toler, variant of TOLLER[2] 2.

toleraˈbility. *rare.* [f. TOLERABLE *a.*: see -ITY.] The quality or state of being tolerable; tolerableness.

1640 FULLER *Joseph's Coat* ix. (1867) 192 Let them labour also to ingratiate every pastor, who hath tolerability of desert, with his own congregation. **1655** —— *Ch. Hist.* IX. i. §35 Alas; tolerability was eminency in that age. **1810** W. TAYLOR in Robberds *Mem.* II. 294, I might fit up the lives of the German poets,..and so mend each into tolerability.

tolerable (ˈtɒlərəb(ə)l), *a.* (*adv.*) Also 5–7 toller-. [a. F. *tolérable* (14th c. in Godef. *Compl.*), ad. L. *tolerābilis* that may be borne, that can bear or endure, f. *tolerāre* to bear, endure: see -ABLE.]

1. a. Capable of being borne or endured; supportable (physically or mentally); bearable, endurable.

1422 tr. *Secreta Secret.*, *Priv. Priv.* 132 Suche a kynge is tollerabill, as many men thynkyn, for the more myschefe to Enchu. **1515** BARCLAY *Egloges* iii. (1570) B vj b/2 It were thing tollerable To becke and to bowe to persons honorable. **1582** N. T. (Rhem.) *Matt.* x. 15 It shall be more tolerable for the land of the Sodomites and Gomorrheans in the day of iudgement, then for that city. **1604** E. GRIMSTONE *Hist. Siege Ostend* 157 Nakednesse, by reason of the..colde..is not very tollerable. **1653** BAXTER *Worc. Petit. Def.* 39, I abhor as much as most do..not bearing with each other in tolerable differences. *a* **1704** T. BROWN *Two Oxf. Scholars* Wks. 1730 I. 9 He did not know how to maintain himself and his Family in any tolerable sort. **1834** SOUTHEY *Doctor* lxx. (1862) 149/2 The temperature of a glass-house is not only tolerable but agreeable to those who have their fiery occupation there. **1909** *Westm. Gaz.* 27 Aug. 2/2 Ideas..of making the motor less anti-social and more tolerable by the general public.

b. Of drugs: That may be endured, or of which the action may be resisted, by the human system: cf. TOLERANCE *sb.* 1 b, TOLERANT *a.* c.

2. Such as to be tolerated, allowed, or countenanced; sufferable, allowable. Now *rare.*

1531 ELYOT *Gov.* II. ii, That langage that in the chambre is tollerable, in place of iugement or great assembly is nothing commendable. **1597–1602** *W. Riding Sessions Rolls* (Yorks. Rec. Ser.) 27 Misdemeanours not tollerable by the lawes of the Realme. **1598** MANWOOD *Lawes Forest* xii. §4 (1615) 91 When there is no mast in the woods, then hogges nor swine are not tollerable there. **1619** T. CAMPION *Art of Descant* (1674) 41 If the Bass be sharp in F fa ut, it is not tolerable to rise from a sixth to an eight. **1625** BACON *Ess.*, *Revenge* (Arb.) 502 The most Tolerable Sort of Reuenge is for those wrongs which there is no Law to remedy. **1690** LOCKE *Govt.* II. xiii. §151 Where..the Executive is vested in a single Person,..that single Person in a very tolerable Sense may also be called Supream.

†**3.** *actively.* Capable of bearing or enduring; tolerant. Const. *of.* *Obs. rare.*

1555 EDEN *Decades* 99 The owlde souldiours..were.. exceadynge tollerable of labour, heate, hunger, and watchynge.

4. Moderate in degree, quality, or character; of middling quality, mediocre, passable; now *esp.* moderately good, fairly good or agreeable, not bad.

1548 UDALL, etc. *Erasm. Par. Matt.* v. 38 To the intent ye shoulde be of the meane and tollerable sorte. **1597** HOOKER *Eccl. Pol.* v. lxxxi. §5 Wee are to descend to a lower step, receiving knowledge in that degree, which is but tolerable. **1658** EVELYN *Diary* 9 June, The new front towards yᵉ gardens is tollerable, were it not drown'd by a too massie and clomsie pair of stayres of stone. **1693** DRYDEN *Disc. Orig. & Progr. Satire* Ess. (Ker) II. 110 We have yet no English *prosodia*, not so much as a tolerable dictionary, or a grammar. **1706** PHILLIPS (ed. Kersey), *Tolerable*,..also indifferent, passable. **1790** *Cook's Voy.* V. 1729 Some of it, which had adhered in lumps, was of a tolerable [*ed.* 1784 II. 235 sufficient] whiteness. **1833** L. RITCHIE *Wand. by Loire* 53 The staircase is all that now exists even in tolerable preservation. **1835** SIR J. ROSS *Narr. 2nd Voy.* xl. 538 Found a tolerable road. **1866** MRS. GASKELL *Wives & Dau.* xv, He had eaten a very tolerable lunch. **1868** M. PATTISON *Academ. Org.* v. 209 Leisure and tolerable freedom from the anxieties of straitened means.

5. As *adv.* **a.** = TOLERABLY 2. As *adv.*

(After 1750 chiefly in inferior writers and *dial.*)

1673 *Remarques Humours Town* 40 If you can but discourse tollerable of good Wine. **1711** STEELE *Spect.* No. 114 ¶ 1, I observed a Person of a tolerable good Aspect. **1796** MRS. E. PARSONS *Myst. Warning* III. 142 They halted at a tolerable large hamlet. **1823** F. COOPER *Pioneers* xxxviii, They..emerged at once into a tolerable clear atmosphere. **1884** 'MARK TWAIN' *Huck. Finn* i. 3 Her sister, Miss Watson, a tolerable slim old maid, with goggles on.

b. *pred.* In fair health; moderately or passably well: = TOLERABLY 2 b. *colloq.*

1812 J. CONSTABLE *Let.* 16 Feb. (1962) I. 77 Your Father looks well & is very tolerable as to his cough & breathing. **1847** C. BRONTE *J. Eyre* xxvi, We're tolerable, sir, I thank you.

ˈtolerableness. [f. prec. + -NESS.] The quality or fact of being tolerable.

1. Allowableness: cf. prec. 2.

1612 J. MASON *Anat. Sorc.* 69 Not so much to confirme the lawfulnesse..as to induce or insinuate a tolerablenesse in regard of the necessity..thereof. **1644** J. GOODWIN *Innoc. Triumph.* (1645) 33 Questioning the Orthodoxisme, yea, the tolerablenesse of the..Doctrine.

2. Capability of being borne or endured; bearableness, endurableness: cf. prec. 1.

a **1678** WOODHEAD *Holy Living* (1688) 39 Practising..the inconveniences and sufferings of poverty, to try by the tolerableness of these the unnecessariness of wealth.

ˈtolerablish, *a. rare.* [f. as prec. + -ISH[1].] Somewhat tolerable, pretty fair, just passable.

1798 [Given as a 'Hampshirism' in a letter from J. Jefferson to J. Boucher 23 Feb. (MS.)]. **1899** *Pall Mall Mag.* Jan. 80, I vow the music sounds tolerablish.

tolerably (ˈtɒlərəblɪ), *adv.* [f. TOLERABLE *a.* + -LY[2].] In a tolerable manner or way.

1. In a way that may be borne, endured, or permitted; bearably, supportably; allowably, permissibly.

1580 HOLLYBAND *Treas. Fr. Tong*, *Passablement*, tollerably, that may be borne withall. **1586** W. WEBBE *Eng. Poetrie* (Arb.) 65 What wordes may tollerably be placed in Ryme, and what not. **1597** HOOKER *Eccl. Pol.* v. lviii. §4 It may be tollerably giuen without them rather then any man without it should.. depart this life. **1643** MILTON *Divorce* II. viii. Wks. 1851 IV. 81 He might dismisse her whom he could not tolerably and so not conscionably retain.

2. In a moderate or passable degree; passably, moderately, fairly, pretty well.

1485 CAXTON *Paris & V.* Prol. (1868) 12 The matter is reasonable and tolerably credible. **1602** MARSTON *Ant. & Mel.* Induct., Ha! ha! ha! tolerably good; good faith, sweet wag. **1695** WOODWARD *Nat. Hist. Earth* III. i. (1723) 148 Bodyes that are still tolerably firm. **1712** ADDISON *Spect.* No. 275 ¶ 10 [He] had acquitted himself tolerably at a Ball or an Assembly. **1799** HT. LEE *Canterb. T.*, *Frenchm. T.* (ed. 2) I. 198 She had made rapid strides too in her education; she wrote tolerably. **1815** J. SMITH *Panorama Sc. & Art* II. 708 It will be easy to form a tolerably correct idea of the perspective appearance of any object. **1843** RUSKIN *Mod. Paint.* (1848) I. II. I. vii. §18. 93 He painted everything tolerably, and nothing excellently. **1894** LD. WATSON in *Law Times Rep.* LXXI. 103/1 Two things appear to their Lordships to be tolerably certain.

b. *pred.* Moderately well in health; pretty well. *colloq.* and *dial.*

1778 in *Mme. D'Arblay's Early Diary* (1889) II. 241 He is tolerably to-day.

tolerance (ˈtɒlərəns), *sb.* Also 5–6 toll-. [a. F. *tolérance* (14th c. in Hatz.-Darm.), ad. rare L. *tolerantia*, f. *tolerāre* to TOLERATE: see -ANCE. But from 16th c. prob. directly referred to the L.]

†**1. a.** The action or practice of enduring or sustaining pain or hardship; the power or capacity of enduring; endurance. *Obs.*

1412–20 LYDG. *Chron. Troy* II. 7014 Riȝt so convenient Is to þe wyse..with suffraunce, In al his port to haue tolleraunce. **1603** HOLLAND *Plutarch's Mor.* 230 Sage counsell and wisdome..in dangers and travels, we tearme tolerance, patience and fortitude. *a* **1626** BACON *Apophthegm.* 138 in *Resuscitatio* (1661) 311 Diogenes, one terrible frosty Morning, came into the Market-place; And stood Naked shaking to shew his Tolerance. **1650–3** tr. *Hales' Dissert. de Pace* in *Phenix* (1708) II. 366 [They] have omitted nothing to the most certain Hope of Salvation, and to all the toil of a pious Life, and to the tolerance of Christ's Cross. **1814** W. TAYLOR in *Monthly Mag.* XXXVII. 527 We do not ascribe superior tolerance to the protestant dissenters for enduring more patiently their privations.

b. *Phys.* The power, constitutional or acquired, of enduring large doses of active drugs, or of resisting the action of poison, etc.; hence diminution in the response to a drug after continued use. Also const. *to.* Cf. TOLERANT *a.* c, TOLERATE *v.* 1 b, TOLERATION 1 b.

1875 H. C. WOOD *Therap.* (1879) 153 By the aid of opiates and careful dilution a species of tolerance was often obtained for these heroic doses. **1876** BARTHOLOW *Mat. Med.* (1879) 236 When emetic doses even are continued in some subjects, this effect finally ceases, and the drug is borne without producing any gastric symptoms. To this state has been applied the term *tolerance.* **1890** BILLINGS *Nat. Med. Dict.*, *Tolerance*, power of endurance whereby a dangerous drug can be safely taken in excessive doses. **1951** A. GROLLMAN *Pharmacol. & Therapeutics* xviii. 362 A certain degree of tolerance to the nitrites is gained by man from their repeated administration. Especially is this true as regards the headache which they often produce. **1974** M. C. GERALD *Pharmacol.* iii. 62 For the heroin addict, tolerance represents a very real problem, for he is obliged to take larger and larger doses to get the same psychological response. **1982** *Sci. Amer.* Mar. 112/3 The body may accumulate the drug or develop a tolerance to it.

c. *Forestry.* The capacity of a tree to endure shade. More widely in *Biol.*, the ability of any organism to withstand some particular environmental condition. Const. *to.* Cf. TOLERANT *a.* d. orig. *U.S.*

1898 PINCHOT *Adirondack Spruce* 6 A provisional scale of tolerance is as follows, beginning with the species which demand most light: Tamarack, Poplar, Bird Cherry, White and Black Ash [etc.]. *Ibid.* 23 All species..are not equal in their tolerance of shade, their resistance to storm and disease [etc.]. *Ibid.* 30 Black Cherry stands about midway in the scale of tolerance among the trees in the Park. **1932** FULLER & CONARD tr. *Braun-Blanquet's Plant Sociol.* vi. 169 The higher plants have a more or less wide pH tolerance. **1939** *Ecology* XX. 71 (*heading*) A study of the tolerance of trees to breakage by ice accumulation. **1953** E. P. ODUM *Fund. Ecol.* iii. 29 Trees give way to grassland as the amount of available water drops below the limits of tolerance for forests. **1960** N. POLUNIN *Introd. Plant Geogr.* xiv. 428 The arborescent species..fall into groups having a particular height-limit and degree of tolerance to shading. **1961** *Biol. Abstr.* XXXVI. 6632/1 Restraint may affect altitude tolerance in the rat by hastening the body temperature fall. **1979** *Environmental Biol. Fishes* IV. 253/1 Cox..found differences in thermal tolerance of large and small 26°C acclimated bluegill sunfish warmed at 0·1 and 1·0° C min⁻¹.

d. *Biol.* The ability of an organism to survive or to flourish despite infection with a parasite or an otherwise pathogenic organism.

1904 *Q. Rev.* July 137 It is probable that the sleeping-sickness parasite flourished innocently in a state of adjustment due to tolerance on the part of the aboriginal men and animals of West Africa. **1951** R. H. PAINTER *Insect Resistance in Plant Crops* ii. 59 Corn strains that are tolerant to chinch bug infestation under the moisture conditions of Illinois may not show as much tolerance under drier conditions in Kansas. **1976** GIBBS & HARRISON *Plant Virology* xv. 226/1 The use of tomato plants containing a single gene for tolerance to TMV resulted in the selection and rapid spread of virus strains virulent for the plants.

e. *Immunol.* The ability to accept without an immunological reaction an antigen that normally produces one.

1951 *Heredity* V. 396 It may seem surprising that the interchange of red cell precursors should confer tolerance upon homografts of, effectively, skin epithelium. **1968** PASSMORE & ROBSON *Compan. Med. Stud.* I. xxvii. 21/2 Experimentally tolerance can be induced by exposure to antigens either in utero or..in the neonatal period. **1979** *Nature* 15 Mar. 257/2 It is pertinent to ask whether the induction and maintenance of specific immunological unresponsiveness (tolerance) to foreign antigens is also under genetic control.

†**2.** The action of allowing; licence, permission granted by an authority. *Obs.*

1539 *Act 31 Hen. VIII*, c. 13 §19 Without any other licence, dispensacion or tollerance of the kinges highnesse. **1567** *Reg. Privy Council Scot.* I. 571 Na persoun sould intromet thairwith..without his rycht licence and tollerance had thairto. **1580–81** *Ibid.* 357 Be the Kingis Majesties permissioun and tollerance.

3. The action or practice of tolerating; toleration; the disposition to be patient with or indulgent to the opinions or practices of others; freedom from bigotry or undue severity in judging the conduct of others; forbearance; catholicity of spirit.

1765 LOWTH *Let. to Warburton* 13 It admits..of no tolerance, no intercommunity of various sentiments, not the least difference of opinion. **1809–10** COLERIDGE *Friend* (1865) 56 The only true spirit of tolerance consists in our conscientious toleration of each other's intolerance. **1841** MYERS *Cath. Th.* III. §5. 15 It may not accord with the undisciplined instincts of some to associate the tolerance of Imperfection in connection with the instrumentality of Perfection. **1868** HELPS *Realmah* vi. (1876) 89 Tolerance, or to use a more Christian word, charity. **1902** C. LENNOX *J. Chalmers* xiv. (1905) 70/1 With the same large tolerance he satisfied the curiosity of the astonished black.

4. Technical uses. **a.** *Coining.* The small margin within which coins, when minted, are allowed to deviate from the standard fineness and weight: also called *allowance.* (Cf. TOLERATION 5, REMEDY *sb.* 4.)

1868 *Rep. Royal Commission on Internat. Coinage* 95 As to the minimum of remedy or tolerance to be allowed on coining, it will be observed that there is a near agreement among the Mints of different countries on this head. *Ibid.* App. xi. 228 Gold coins... The margin allowed for error in coining, known as the remedy or tolerance, is calculated upon the pound troy of coin, and amounts to 15 grains for the fineness, plus or minus, or $\frac{1}{16}$ of a carat, and 12 grains for the weight.

b. In *Mech.*, an allowable amount of variation in the dimensions of a machine or part. More widely, the allowable amount of variation in any specified quantity.

1909 *Cent. Dict. Supp.* s.v., A tolerance of ·00025 [= $\frac{1}{4000}$] of an inch is allowed above or below the exact dimension in fine machine parts. **1916** *Yorkshire Post* 28 Mar. 8/1 Permissible margins of error in workmanship are known as tolerances. **1937** *Times* 13 Apr. (Suppl.) p. xii/4 Visitors may see..how the metal cools and can be withdrawn a minute or two later, finally to be machined to within a tolerance of 0·001 in. on the inside and 0·0005 in. on the outside. **1957** R. W. G. HUNT *Reproduction of Colour* xii. 174 With this system, discrepancies..will result only in errors in chrominance and not in errors of luminance. The tolerances thus become slightly larger. **1965** *Economist* 28 Aug. 812/2 The Ministry will be able to tighten up on tolerances in the road building specifications which it is now rewriting. **1973** A. PARRISH *Mech. Engineer's Ref. Bk.* III. 17 A geometrical tolerance is applied to a feature when there is a requirement to control its variation of form or position. **1975** D. G. FINK *Electronics Engineers' Handbk.* I. 48 Stations must operate on an assigned carrier frequency..which must be maintained within specified limits of frequency tolerances.

5. *attrib.* and *Comb.*: **tolerance dose** *Med.*, a dose, esp. of radiation, believed to be received or taken without harm; **tolerance level**, the level that can be tolerated or is acceptable; *spec.* in *Med.* = *tolerance dose* above; **tolerance limit**, a limit laid down for the permitted variation of a parameter of a product.

1925 *Amer. Jrnl. Röntgenol.* XIII. 66/2 We will have then to decide upon a tolerance dose which can be considered harmless for the operator within a certain assumed period of time. **1958** W. D. CLAUS *Radiation Biol. & Med.* xvi. 390 The concept of 'tolerance dose' has changed somewhat to the thought that there is no such thing as a literally harmless dose of radiation. **1972** H. C. RAE *Shooting Gallery* III. 202 You know what controlled tolerance doses [of drugs] are?.. I had it under control. **1947** *Radiology* XLIX. 364/2 What are the first changes produced by exposures just above the tolerance level? **1964** F. G. W. & M. G. JONES *Pests of Field Crops* xvi. 361 The U.S.A. and Canada have laws determining the tolerance levels for those pesticides that leave residues on or in the crops. **1977** *New Yorker* 19 Sept. 82/2 It's very important to gauge your audience's tolerance level—decide what it's receptive to, what it can take. **1931** W. A. SHEWHART *Econ. Control of Quality of Manufactured Product* xvii. 249 The tolerance range for a given quality X is defined as the range between the maximum and minimum tolerance limits specified for this quality. **1963** BEGEMAN & AMSTEAD *Manuf. Processes* (ed. 5) xv. 356 The tolerance limits for a part are placed outside of the control limits.

tolerance ('tɒlərəns), *v. Engin.* [f. the sb.] *trans.* To specify a tolerance for (a machine part, etc.). So **'toleranced** *ppl. a.*, **'tolerancing** *vbl. sb.*

1950 W. STANIAR *Plant Engin. Handbk.* ii. 45 *(caption)* Quality-control chart—correct tolerancing of operations. **1953** F. ZOZZORA *Engin. Drawing* viii. 126/2 As a general rule, nonmating members are toleranced bilaterally, while mating surfaces are toleranced unilaterally. **1959** *B.S.I. News* Aug. 13 British proposals on dimensioning and tolerancing of tapers were generally approved. **1971** J. H. SMITH *Digital Logic* ii. 19 The designs are well toleranced and the reader will find that almost any small-signal transistor will function quite satisfactorily. **1973** A. PARRISH *Mech. Engineer's Ref. Bk.* III. 18 The concept of geometrical tolerancing is complex. *Ibid.* 19 The feature toleranced is indicated by a leader line.

tolerancy ('tɒlərənsɪ). *rare.* [ad. rare L. *tolerāntia*: see TOLERANCE *sb.* and -ANCY.] The quality or habit of being tolerant: cf. prec. 3.

a **1556** UDALL *Let.* in *Royster D.* (Shaks. Soc.) Introd., By their excedyng gret tolerancie brought them to goodnes. **1825** COLERIDGE *Aids Refl.* xxvi. (1848) I. 77, I shall believe our present religious tolerancy to proceed from the abundance of our charity and good sense.

tolerant ('tɒlərənt), *a.* (*sb.*) [a. F. *tolérant* (16th c. in Hatz.-Darm.), pr. pple. of *tolérer* to TOLERATE, ad. L. *tolerānt-em*, pr. pple. of *tolerāre.*] **A.** *adj.* **a.** Disposed or inclined to tolerate or bear with something; practising or favouring toleration.

1784 JOS. WHITE *Bampton Lect.* iii. 145 His [Gibbon's] eagerness to throw a veil over the deformities of the Heathen theology, to decorate with all the splendor of panegyric the tolerant spirit of its votaries. **1792** BURKE *Let. to Sir H. Langrishe* Wks. VI. 318 A tolerant government ought not to be too scrupulous in its investigations. **1796** MORSE *Amer. Geog.* I. 429 The religion of this Commonwealth [Massachusetts] is established..on a most liberal and tolerant plan. All persons, of whatever religious profession or sentiments, may worship God agreeably to the dictates of their own consciences, unmolested. **1838** LYTTON *Alice* I. xi, His own early errors made him tolerant to the faults of others. **1841** MACAULAY in *Four C. Eng. Lett.* (1880) 537 You were less tolerant than myself of little mannerisms. **1875** MANNING *Mission H. Ghost* ix. 237 Though we are to be tolerant towards the persons of heretics, we are intolerant of the heresies themselves.

b. *transf.* Of a thing: Capable of bearing or sustaining. Const. *of.*

1864 J. H. NEWMAN *Apol.* ii. 169 How far the Articles were tolerant of a Catholic, or even of a Roman interpretation.

c. *Phys.* Able to endure the action of a drug, an irritant, etc., without being affected; capable of resisting. Const. *of.* Cf. TOLERANCE *sb.* 1 b.

1879 *St. George's Hosp. Rep.* IX. 748 Chrysophanic acid having at first given rise to irritation, I diluted it... The skin in two or three weeks became tolerant of it. **1881** *Encycl. Brit.* XIII. 210/2 The amount [of ipecacuanha] required to produce its effect varies considerably, children as a rule being more tolerant than adults. **1899** *Syd. Soc. Lex.*, *Tolerant*, withstanding the use of a drug without injury.

d. *Forestry.* Capable of enduring shade. More widely in *Biol.*, capable of withstanding any particular environmental condition. Cf. TOLERANCE *sb.* 1 c. orig. *U.S.*

1898 PINCHOT *Adirondack Spruce* 5 A selection forest is usually composed of species tolerant of shade. *Ibid.* 6 Spruce, Hemlock, Balsam, the Maples [etc.] are tolerant. **1929** WEAVER & CLEMENTS *Plant Ecol.* xiii. 321 Tolerant species..retain their branches. **1943** D. V. BAXTER *Path. Forest Practice* viii. 478 Certain woody species tolerant of wet soil. **1979** *Austral. Jrnl. Bot.* XXVII. 531 *Coleochloa setifera* is a desiccation-tolerant sedge which becomes yellow during drying. **1980** SPURR & BARNES *Forest Ecol.* (ed. 3) xiv. 380 A forest tree that can survive and prosper under a forest canopy is said to be tolerant.

e. *Biol.* Of an organism: exhibiting tolerance (sense 1 d) to infection.

1904 E. R. LANKESTER in *Q. Rev.* July 128 A more precise nomenclature would describe the attacked organism..as 'tolerant', for it tolerates the presence and multiplication of the parasite without suffering by it. **1951** [see TOLERANCE *sb.* 1 d]. **1976** GIBBS & HARRISON *Plant Virology* xv. 225/2 In the western U.S.A., where beet curly top virus is widespread, the sugar-beet industry has been saved by introducing tolerant cultivars.

f. *Immunol.* Exhibiting immunological tolerance (sense 1 e). Const. *of, to.*

1951 *Heredity* V. 396 Not all dizygotic twins are completely tolerant to grafts of each other's skin. **1969** R. S. WEISER et al. *Fund. Immunol.* xviii. 227 The F_1 hybrid is an example of an allogeneic recipient which for genetic reasons is immunologically tolerant of parental grafts.

B. *sb.* (subst. use of the adj.: so in Fr.) One who tolerates opinions or practices different from his own; one free from bigotry; a tolerationist.

1780 J. BROWN *Lett. on Toleration* i. (1803) 35, I dare defy all the Tolerants on earth, to point out one thing.. competent to masters and parents [etc.]. **1872** MORLEY *Voltaire* iii. 144 Henry the Fourth was a hero with Voltaire, for no better reason than that he was the first great tolerant, the earliest historic indifferent.

†**tolerantial** (tɒlə'rænʃəl), *a. Obs. rare.* [f. L. *tolerāntia* TOLERANCE *sb.* + -AL[1].] Belonging or pertaining to tolerance.

1681 *Religio Clerici* 121 Till we have tried our Strength and Patience to the quick in sharp Exercises of Vertue's other branch, the Tolerantial part.

†**'tolerantism.** *Obs. rare.* [f. TOLERANT + -ISM.] The principles of a tolerant (see TOLERANT B).

1824 *Hist. Europe* in *Ann. Reg.* 196/1 This sect..professes tolerantism (for thus they call it), or indifference.

'tolerantly, *adv.* [f. as prec. + -LY[2].] In a tolerant manner; with tolerance; forbearingly.

1822 BYRON *Vis. Judg.* Pref., I have..treated them more tolerantly. **1883–4** J. G. BUTLER *Bible Work* II. 42 It is wise and right to deal tolerantly with errorists in sentiment.

†**'tolerat**, *ppl. a. Obs.* [ad. L. *tolerāt-us*, pa. pple. of *tolerāre* to TOLERATE.] Tolerated: in quot. as *pa. pple.*

1711 *Countryman's Let. to Curat* 24 He [Bacon] advised that Non-conformity should not meerly be conniv'd at, but even Tolerat by a Law.

tolerate ('tɒləreɪt), *v.* Also 6–8 toll-. [f. F. *tolérer* (15th c. in Godef. *Compl.*), ad. L. *tolerāre* to bear, endure: see -ATE[3].]

†**1.** *trans.* To endure, sustain (pain or hardship).

1531 ELYOT *Gov.* III. xiv, To tollerate those thinges whiche do seme bytter or greuous (wherof there be many in the lyfe of man). *a* **1548** HALL *Chron.*, *Rich. III* 37 The great dolour and sorowe that you haue suffred and tollerated by the cruel murther of your innocente children. **1599** A. M. tr. *Gabelhouer's Bk. Physicke* 39/1 Applye that same as warme as he may or can tollerate it on and rownde about his heade. **1616** BULLOKAR *Eng. Expos.*, *Tolerate*, to indure or suffer.

b. *Phys.* To endure with impunity or comparative impunity the action of (a poison or strong drug). Cf. TOLERANCE *sb.* 1 b, TOLERANT *a.* c.

1895 in *Funk's Standard Dict.* **1899** *Allbutt's Syst. Med.* VIII. 932 [Oil of santal wood has] the advantage of being usually well tolerated in reasonable doses by the stomach. **1911** WEBSTER, *Tolerate*, to endure or resist, esp. without injurious effect, the action of, as a poison.

c. *Forestry.* Cf. TOLERANCE *sb.* 1 c, TOLERANT *a.* d.

1898 PINCHOT *Adirondack Spruce* 20 This ability to tolerate heavy shade is common to large numbers of forest trees, among which both the Beech and the Hard Maple excel the Spruce in this regard.

2. To allow to exist or to be done or practised without authoritative interference or molestation; also *gen.* to allow, permit.

1533 MORE *Debell. Salem* Wks. 981/2 He can..be none other rekened but a plaine heretike.., whome to tolerate so long doth sometyme lyttle good. **1586** FERNE *Blaz. Gentrie* 149 This King ordained, that no person..within his dominions, should..tollerate the bearing of these signes vpon armes to any man. **1631** GOUGE *God's Arrows* I. §4. 7 Marke how farre such sinnes are winked at, or tolerated by Magistrates and Ministers. **1647** JER. TAYLOR *Lib. Proph.* xvi. 214 The question whether the Prince may tollerate divers perswasions, is no more than whether he may lawfully persecute any man for not being of his opinion. **1651** BAXTER *Inf. Bapt.* 143 A few of them are in some places tolerated, as Jews and Hereticks are. **1722** WOLLASTON *Relig. Nat.* ix. 217 If the expression may be tolerated. **1856** FROUDE *Hist. Eng.* I. ii. 142 England..was in no humour to tolerate treason. **1884** H. N. OXENHAM *Short Stud.* 142 To tolerate a religion does not mean to treat it as true,..but simply as having a fair claim to exist and enjoy civil rights.

†**b.** To allow, permit, suffer *to do* something.

c **1585** R. BROWNE *Answ. Cartwright* 15 Hee alloweth or tollerateth those officers..to haue the power and authoritie. **1635** QUARLES *Embl.* III. iii. (1718) 137 True Lord; yet tolerate a hungry Whelp To lick their crums. **1660** R. COKE *Power & Subj.* 143 Berta the wife of Ethelbert..was tolerated to observe the rites of Christian religion. **1709** *Lond. Gaz.* No. 4525/3 The Groom-Porter doth hereby declare, that he neither Licenses or Tolerates any Person to Game, or keep Gaming-Houses. **1817** JAS. MILL *Brit. India* I. II. ii. 111 The highest of the other classes are barely tolerated to read the will of God.

3. To bear without repugnance; to allow intellectually, or in taste, sentiment, or principle; to put up with.

1646 SIR T. BROWNE *Pseud. Ep.* v. xix. 262 We shall tolerate flying Horses, black Swans, Hydrae's, Centaur's, Harpies, and Satyres. **1822** WORDSW. *Sonn.*, *Old Abbeys*, By discipline of Time made wise, We learn to tolerate the infirmities And faults of others. **1841** BREWSTER *Mart. Sc.* i. (1856) 8 Nor could the Aristotelians tolerate the rebukes of their young instructor. **1875** H. C. WOOD *Therap.* (1879) 412 Children almost always learn to tolerate the taste of the oil. **1910** *Daily News* 9 Apr. 6 He cannot tolerate Buddhism. I use the word 'tolerate', of course, in an intellectual, not a political, sense.

†**4.** To relax. *Obs. rare*$^{-1}$.

1579–80 NORTH *Plutarch* (1656) 45 (*Lycurgus* xxii) In their time of Warre, they did tolerate [F. *ils relaschoyent*] their young men a little of their hard and old accustomed life, and suffered them to trim their haires.

Hence **'tolerated** *ppl. a.*, **'tolerating** *vbl. sb.* and *ppl. a.*; whence **'tole,ratingly** *adv.*

1644 MILTON *Judgm. Bucer* xxiv. Wks. 1738 I. 283 For whatsoever is contrary to these, I shall not persuade the least tolerating therof. **1692** PRIDEAUX *Direct. Ch.-wardens* (ed. 4) 109 Not Members of some of the said tolerated Assemblies. **1700** in *Westm. Gaz.* 9 Aug. (1907) 2/3 Notice is given, That the Tollerated Boats bear a Red Flagg in the Stern of each of them. **1711** SHAFTESB. *Charac.* (1733) I. 29 How barbarous..are we tolerating Englishmen. **1724** A. SHIELDS *J. Renwick* (1827) 146 All this never moved the tolerated Ministers. **1848** R. I. WILBERFORCE *Doctr. Incarnation* xi. (1852) 290 Its permission is the main point expressed in the tolerating edict issued by Galerius. **1893** *Pall Mall Mag.* II. 209 She spoke of his views toleratingly. **1902** C. LENNOX *J. Chalmers* v. (1895) 26/1 Tolerated wickedness inevitably cramps the religious consciousness.

toleration (tɒlə'reɪʃən). Also 6–8 toll-. [a. F. *tolération* (15th c. in Godef.), ad. rare L. *tolerātiōn-em*, f. *tolerāre* to TOLERATE.]

1. †**a.** The action of sustaining or enduring; endurance (of evil, suffering, etc.). *Obs.*

1531 ELYOT *Gov.* III. xxi, There is also moderation in toleration of fortune of euerye sorte, whiche of Tulli is called equabilite. **1616** BULLOKAR *Eng. Expos.*, *Toleration*, an induring; a sufferance. **1623** COCKERAM III, *Mutius Sceuola*, saued his life by the patient tolleration of the burning of his hand.

b. *Phys.* = TOLERANCE *sb.* 1 b. *rare.*

1877 CARNOCHAN *Operat. Surgery* 328 Military surgery supplies many illustrations of toleration of shock and mildness of collapse after severe injuries to the medullary substance of the hemispheres. **1882** A. WILSON *Facts & Fictions Zool.* 10 Suppose that the toleration of the toad's system to starvation and to a limited supply of air is taken into account. **1905** *Allbutt's Syst. Med.* I. 287 *Toleration.* When, on taking a drug continuously, the first effects decrease until they are no longer noticed, toleration is said to be established.

2. †**a.** The action of allowing; permission granted by authority, licence. *Obs.*

1517–18 *Rec. St. Mary at Hill* 296 Paid..for goyng to ffulham to my lorde of london..to haue tolleracion of Nasynges chauntry. **1565** JEWEL *Def. Apol.* VI. xxiii. (1579) 735 The yeerely perquisites that yᵉ Pope made of his Elections, Preuentions, Dispensations,..Tolerations. **1571–2** *Reg. Privy Council Scot.* II. 122 Na licencis or tolleratiounis grantit of befoir to have any strenth. **1612** BEAUM. & FL. *Cupid's Rev.* I. i, Would I had giv'n 100*l.* for a tolleration, That I might but use my conscience in mine Own house. **1660** R. COKE *Power & Subj.* 209 If any person or persons..should procure and obtain at the Court of Rome, or elswhere, any Licence or Licences, Union, Toleration, or Dispensation to receive or take any more Benefices with cure, then was limited by the said Act. **1727** A. HAMILTON *New Acc. E. Ind.* II. l. 224 Ordered the Hapoa or Custom-master to..take the Emperors customary Dues, and give me a free Toleration to Trade.

b. Locally in U.S. applied to a licence to gather oysters or keep oyster-beds.

1796 *Rec. Smithtown, N.Y.* (1898) 129 Any person not an inhabitant..taking Soft shelled clams within the limits of said Town shall pay six pence for every bushel as toleration for taking the same. **1881** E. INGERSOLL *Oyster-Industry* III. 249 Toleration.—License to gather oysters or operate beds. .. The money paid is called a Toleration fee. **1891** *Cent. Dict.* s.v., The fee is a toleration fee.

3. The action or practice of tolerating or allowing what is not actually approved; forbearance, sufferance.

1582 N. T. (Rhem.) *Rom.* iii. 26 The remission of former sinnes in the toleration [WYCLIF in the sustentacioun *or* bering vp, 1611 through the forbearance] of God. **1588** HUNSDON in *Border Papers* (1894) I. 367 His tolloracion of the mase in sondrie places of Scotland. *a* **1610** HEALEY *Epictetus' Man.* (1636) 84 Every thing may bee apprehended two waies, eyther with toleration, or with impatience. **1755** YOUNG *Centaur* v. Wks. 1757 IV. 220 Faults which are the natural growth of these distinct periods of life, may meet with some toleration. **1768** STERNE *Sent. Journ.* (1778) I. 201 (*The Rose*) Mutual toleration..taught us mutual love. **1890** *Hardwicke's Science-Gossip* XXVI. 186/1, I think, also, that a wise toleration might be extended to hawks and owls. **1907** *Verney Mem.* I. 571 A large hopefulness and toleration born of his wide acquaintance with human nature.

4. *spec.* **a.** Allowance (with or without limitations), by the ruling power, of the exercise of religion otherwise than in the form officially established or recognized.

1609 (*title*) An Humble Supplication for Toleration and Libertie..by some of the deprived Ministers and People. **1643** *Declar. Com., Reb. Irel.* 3 To bring in a more publique Tolleration of the Popish Religion. **1672** EVELYN *Diary* 12 Mar., To this succeeded the King's declaration for an universal toleration. **1689** POPPLE tr. *Locke's 1st Let. Toleration* ¶ 1 Since you are pleased to inquire what are my Thoughts about the mutual Toleration of Christians in their different Professions of Religion, I must needs answer you freely, That I esteem that Toleration to be the chief Characteristical Mark of the True Church. **1691** BURNET *Orig. Mem.* an. 1689, I. (1902) 317 At the same time that the toleration was proposed to both houses. **1780** BURKE *Corr.* (1844) II. 369, I have been a steady friend, since I came to the use of reason, to the cause of religious toleration. **1849** MACAULAY *Hist. Eng.* vi. II. 9 Locke..contended that the church which taught men not to keep faith with heretics had no claim to toleration.

b. *Act of Toleration*, *Toleration Act*, an act or statute granting such toleration; so *Bill of Toleration*, *Toleration Bill*; esp. in *Eng. Hist.* Act 1 Will. & Mary (1689) cap. 18, by which freedom of religious worship was granted, on certain prescribed conditions, to Dissenting Protestants.

1692 *Ho. Lords MSS.* (Hist. MSS. Comm.) 1 Feb., Moved that the Quakers shall not have the benefit of this Act before they take the Declaration in the Act of Toleration. **1714** BARRINGTON *Let. fr. Lay-man* Title-p., A Postscript, shewing How far the Bill to prevent the Growth of Schism is Inconsistent with the Act of Toleration. *a* **1715** BURNET *Own Time* an. 1689 (1823) IV. 16 The bill of toleration passed easily. It excused dissenters from all penalties,..for going to their separate meetings. **1769** BLACKSTONE *Comm.* IV. iv. 53 The statute 1 W. & M. st. 2. c. 18, commonly called the toleration act. **1799** DRYSDALE (*title*) Popery Dissected; or, a Speech against the Popish Toleration Bill. **1827** JOS. IVIMEY *Pilgr. 19th C.* iv. 139 'Hand me', said the judge, 'the new Toleration Act' [app. 52 Geo. III, c. 155]. **1855** MACAULAY *Hist. Eng.* xi. III. 81 The Toleration Bill passed both Houses with little debate. *Ibid.* 86 The sound principle..is, that mere theological error ought not to be punished by the civil magistrate. This principle the Toleration Act not only does not recognise, but positively disclaims. **1878** GARDINER in *Encycl. Brit.* VIII. 352/1 The Toleration Act..guaranteed the right of separate assemblies for worship outside the pale of the Church. **1910** A. MENZIES in *Encycl. Brit.* XXIV. 463/1 The Act of Toleration [Scotland] of 1712 allowed Episcopalian dissenters to use the English liturgy.

5. *Coining.* = TOLERANCE *sb.* 4 a.

1887 *Encycl. Brit.* XXII. 71/1 In Great Britain all silver coins are made of 'standard silver', the fineness of which by legal definition is 925. The toleration is 4 units of pure silver in 1000 of alloy. In Germany and in the United States all silver coins, in France and Austria the major silver coins, are of the fineness 900, with a toleration of three units.

tole'rationism. [f. prec. + -ISM.] Toleration of religious differences as a principle or system.

1898 *Cath. News* 24 Dec. 12/6 This was sometimes called ..Tolerationism—But they would understand it better as Free Trade [in religion].

tole'rationist. [f. as prec. + -IST.] One who advocates or supports toleration.

1830 W. TAYLOR *Hist. Surv. Germ. Poetry* I. 472 There lies The prating tolerationist unmask'd. **1899** S. R. GARDINER *Cromwell* 98 A fanatic might have objected that it was unfitting a tolerationist to support the most intolerant clergy in Protestant Europe.

†**'toleratist.** *Obs. rare.* [f. TOLERATE *v.* + -IST.] = TOLERATIONIST.

1716 M. DAVIES *Athen. Brit.* II. 335 Amongst our Nationalists and Toleratists, High and Low, or those that are indulg'd and others that are conniv'd at.

'tolerative, *a. rare.* [f. as prec. + -IVE.] Tending to toleration; permissive.

1891 E. L. WAKEMAN in *Columbus* (Ohio) *Dispatch* 29 Oct., It may be said that the English folk..universally make mental defense of the Halloween time and spirit,..while its recognition by the English is complete, its observance is tolerative rather than active.

tolerator ('tɒləreɪtə(r)). [f. as prec. + -OR.] One who tolerates.

1706 A. SHIELDS *Inquiry Ch. Commun.* (1747) 29 By that bargain and confederacy with the tolerator. **1791–1823** DISRAELI *Curios. Lit.*, *Toleration*, To this moment it is far from being clear, either to the tolerators, or the tolerated. **1826** SIR T. F. BUXTON in *Mem.* (1872) 90 If not a lover of the vices of the world, at least a tolerator of its vanities. **1884** *Macm. Mag.* Nov. 22/2 The moderate Conservatives or tolerators of progress.

†**tole'ratorist.** *Obs. rare.* [irreg. f. as prec. + -IST.] = TOLERATIONIST.

1654 E. JOHNSON *Wond.-wrkg. Provid.* 231 There is no room in his [Christ's] Army for toleratorists. **1845** T. W. COIT *Puritanism* 452.

toleress: see TOLLER *sb.*[4]

†**'tolerism.** *Obs. rare*$^{-1}$. [irreg. f. L. *toler-āre* to TOLERATE + -ISM.] = TOLERATIONISM.

1851 BORROW *Lavengro* iii, Thou wouldst be sadly out of place in these days of..universal tolerism. [**1851** *Fraser's Mag.* XLIII. 283 How can this master of words [Borrow] justify such a barbarous bit of patchwork as 'tolerism'?]

tolerize ('tɒləraɪz), *v. Immunol.* [f. TOLER(ANT *a.* (*sb.*) + -IZE.] *trans.* To render immunologically tolerant. So **'tolerizing** *ppl. a.*; also **toleri'zation,** the action of tolerizing.

1967 *Immunology* XIII. 156 Immunocompetent cells might not have been exposed to the tolerizing antigen. **1973** *Nature* 16 Mar. 161/3 Free IgT complexes are present and these effectively tolerize B cells. **1974** I. M. ROITT *Essent. Immunol.* (ed. 2) viii. 202 It may be that the tolerance-inducing regimen does truly tolerize T cells..but not all B-cells. **1978** *Jrnl. R. Soc. Med.* LXXI. 161/1 The interaction of bacteria with the adjuvant and tolerizing agents in plaque may induce immune responses which could enhance or inhibit the development of caries. **1979** *Nature* 15 Mar. 258/2 One day after tolerisation the recipient mice plus appropriate controls were sensitised by two paintings with DNFB.

tolerogen ('tɒlərədʒən). *Immunol.* [f. TOLER(ANCE + -O + -GEN.] A substance inducing immunological tolerance.

1967 *Immunochemistry* IV. 180 The multi-chain polymer was a very efficient tolerogen. **1980** *Nature* 28 Aug. 837/2 Both generations, neither of which had been intentionally exposed to the tolerogen, showed a wide range of response, from normal down to undetectable.

Hence **tolero'genic** *a.*, **ˌtoleroge'nicity.**

1967 *Immunochemistry* IV. 180 The protein carrier is not necessary to endow a molecule with tolerogenic capacity. **1970** *Nature* 11 July 176/1 There is much evidence for a reciprocal relationship between immunogenicity and tolerogenicity. **1979** *Jrnl. Immunol.* CXXII. 1886/2 Polyethylene glycol has been shown to serve as an effective tolerogenic carrier.

Toletan ('tɒlɪtən), *a.* Also 4–5 **tolletane, tollitane.** [ad. L. *Tolētān-us*, f. *Tolētum* Toledo.] Pertaining to Toledo; in ***Toletan tables***, 'the astronomical tables composed by order of Alphonso X, king of Castile (1252–82), from their being adapted to the city of Toledo' (Tyrwhitt in note to the passage in Chaucer); also called ALPHONSINE *tables.*

c **1386** CHAUCER *Frankl. T.* 545 Hise tables tolletanes [*Harl.* tollitanes] forth he brought Ful wel corrected. **1894** SKEAT *Chaucer's Wks.* V. 394 (*Notes Cant. T.*) The longitude of a planet at a given date is the 'root'; and its longitude..twenty-three years later can be obtained from the Toletan tables by adding (1) its change of longitude in twenty years,..and (2) its further change in three years.

tolfrædic (təʊl'friːdɪk), *a.* [f. Icel. *tólf-rǽðr* adj. only in comb. *tolfrætt hundrað*, a hundred of twelve tens (f. *tólf* twelve + *rǽða* (:—*rœ́ða*) to speak) + -IC.] Duodecimal: applied to the ancient Scandinavian system of reckoning, in which twelve tens were counted as a hundred (cf. HUNDRED 3).

[Cf. **1703** HICKES *Thesaurus* I. III. 43.] **1813** ELLIS *Brand's Pop. Antiq.* II. 325 The Doctor observes that this Tolfrædic mode of computation by the greater decads, or tens which contain twelve units, is still retained amongst us in reckoning certain things by the number twelve. **1905** *Daily Chron.* 16 June 4/6 The tolfraedic ten meant twelve, the tolfraedic hundred meant a hundred and twenty, and so on.

tolibant, tolipane, -pant, obs. ff. TURBAN.

tolidine ('tɒlɪdiːn). *Chem.* [f. TOL(YL + BENZ)IDINE.] A benzidine derivative, $(NH_2(CH_3)C_6H_3-)_2$, which is the parent compound of a group of azo dyes and is used (in the *ortho* form) as a reagent in chemical analysis.

1879 *Jrnl. Chem. Soc.* XXXVI. 235 (*heading*) The three isomeric tolidines (diamido-ditolyls). **1935** *Discovery* July 208/1 A minute sample of the bath water is taken and 'doped' by the mixture of few drops of 'O.T.' (Ortho-Tolidine), a chemical which turns chlorinated water yellow. **1964** *Kirk-Othmer Encycl. Chem. Technol.* (ed. 2) III. 414 *o*-Tolidine is used to a rather large extent in qualitative and quantitative analysis. It is employed for the detection..of such substances as chlorine..gold..and tungsten. *Ibid.* 415 Azo dyes prepared from *m*-tolidine..have little affinity for cotton, but are interesting dyes for wool.

†**toliduse,** illiterate spelling of TAILLE-DOUCE.

1715 *Grizel Baillie's Acc.* (MS.), For two pictures of King George in Toliduse 5/-.

†**to-'lie,** *v. Obs.* [OE. *tolicgan*, f. TO-[2] + *licgan*, LIE *v.*[1]] *intr.* To lie or extend in different directions.

c **893** K. ÆLFRED *Oros.* I. i. §9 þonne..west irnende heo toliþ on twa ymb an igland þe mon hæt Meroen. **938** in Birch *Cart. Sax.* II. 431 þær ða wegas to licgað. *c* **1320** *Cast. Love* 1000 þeose ne mowen Jhc̄ suwen wiþ, For heore dede al to-lyth.

†**to-'lim,** *v. Obs.* In 3–4 **to-lime(n.** [ME. f. TO-[2] + *lim* limb: cf. OE. *tolipian*, f. TO-[2] + *lip* limb. See also LIMB *v.* in same sense.] *trans.* To tear limb from limb, to dismember.

a **1225** *Ancr. R.* 84 Auh [he] lihted upon cwike fleschs, tetereð & tomlimeð hit. *a* **1225** *Juliana* 79 (Bodl. MS.) Wilde deor..to limeden eauer euch lið from þe lire. **13..** *Guy Warw.* 636 In his court he schal deme þe, & al to-lime.

Hence (*dim.*) †**to-'limeken** *v.*, to dismember.

c **1275** LAY. 4227 Stater hii nome And al hine to-limekede Leme fram oþer.

tolite ('tɒlaɪt). Also Tolite. [f. TOL(U- + -ITE[1].] Trinitrotoluene used as an explosive.

1909 O. GUTTMANN *Manuf. Explosives* i. 14 Trinitrotoluene has been introduced into the French Service under the name of Tolite. **1924** *Chem. Abstr.* XVIII. 2604 During the war..use was made of a cold, dil. soln. of Na_2SO_3 for the purification of crude trinitrotoluene (tolite) to produce TNT. **1953** J. Y. COUSTEAU *Silent World* 39 With one-pound tablets of German tolite explosive the effect was different. **1968** *New Scientist* 7 Nov. 304/3 Molène favours the use of classic explosives such as TNT, Tolite, Melinite or Trinitrophenylamine.

tolk, variant of TULK *Obs.*, man.

‖**tolkach** ('tolkatʃ). Pl. **tolkachi.** [Russ., f. *tolkat'* to push or jostle.] In the U.S.S.R., a person who negotiates difficulties or arranges things, a 'fixer'.

1955 H. HODGKINSON *Doubletalk* 129 *Tolkach* (from *tolkat*, to push or jostle), a 'fixer'; the man who knows a man; the man who can get it for you wholesale; who has *blat.* **1957** J. S. BERLINER *Factory & Manager in U.S.S.R.* xii. 215 The key figure in financing all these operations of the tolkachi is the accountant. **1963** *Economist* 29 June 1390/2 Plant directors..buy..supplies illegally from each other, through *tolkachi* or spivs. **1977** *Western Political Q.* XXX. 217 The premier practitioner of *blat* is the *tolkach.* He is the plant's representative who travels the country searching for needed supplies or unsnarling bureaucratic bottlenecks.

Tolkienian (tɒl'kiːnɪən), *a.* Also **Tolkinian** (tɒl'kɪnɪən). [f. the name *Tolkien* (see below) + -IAN.] Of or pertaining to the philologist and author of fantasy literature John Ronald Reuel Tolkien (1892–1973) or his writings.

1954 C. S. LEWIS in *Time & Tide* 14 Aug. 1083/1 In the Tolkinian world you can hardly put your foot down.. without stirring the dust of history. **1975** C. N. MANLOVE *Mod. Fantasy* v. 160 Escape merges into another Tolkinian criterion of the higher fairy-tale—Consolation. **1979** J. C. NITZSCHE *Tolkien's Art* 4 A pattern emerges upon an examination of the titles of other Tolkienian works. **1980** *Times Lit. Suppl.* 7 Nov. 1258/3 If nursery puddings, Tolkienian fantasy and public school cuddles are anything to do with politics at all, they are slightly more identifiable with the Right.

So **ˌTolkie'nesque** *a.* [-ESQUE], characteristic of or resembling Tolkien or his writings.

1970 *Nature* 18 July 215/2 Earlier this month it was announced that Loch Morar, too, would be screened for a monster, already christened with suitably Tolkienesque undertones, as Morag. **1977** *Sounds* 9 July 28/3 Tyrannosaurus Rex, a duo small in sound but big in Tolkienesque fantastical imagery.

toll (təʊl), *sb.*[1] Also 2-7 tol, 5-7 tolle, tole, (5-6 towl(e, 6 toule, towlle, *Sc.* toille, 7 toal(l, toale; 4 tholle, 5-6 tholl, 5 (7 *Sc.*) thoill, 6-7 thole); the *th*-forms chiefly in Latin context. [OE. *toll* = OFris., OS. *tol* (MLG., LG., MDu., Du. *tol*), OHG., MHG. *zol* (Ger. *zoll*); ON. *tollr* (Sw. *tull*, Da. *told*), all masc., which with their by-forms, OE. *toln*, OFris. *tol(e)ne*, OS. *tolna*, all fem. (see TOLNE), are generally referred to late pop. L. *tolōneum* (recorded in 3-4th c.) for L. *telōnium*, a. Gr. τελώνιον place of custom, toll-house, f. τελώνης farmer or collector of taxes, τέλος toll, tax, duty.

The form-history is in some points obscure, and some etymologists have sought to derive *toll* from an OTeut. **tulno-*, pa. pple. of **tal-*, root of TELL *v.* and of TALE. The derivation from Latin is supported by French, in which *teloneum*, becoming by metathesis **toneleum*, has given mod.F. *tonlieu*, Prov. *tolieu* 'toll'.]

1. a. Orig., a general term for: (*a*) a definite payment exacted by a king, ruler, or lord, or by the state or the local authority, by virtue of sovereignty or lordship, or in return for protection; more especially, (*b*) for permission to pass somewhere, do some act, or perform some function; or (*c*) as a share of the money passing, or profit accruing, in a transaction; a tax, tribute, impost, custom, duty.

In (*a*) *obs.* exc. *Hist.*; in (*b*) retained in special senses (see 2); in (*c*) still in vague or rhetorical use: see quots. 1832-1909.

c **1000** *Ags. Gosp.* Matt. xvii. 25 Hwæt þincð þe symon, æt hwam nymað cyningas gafol oððe toll? **1050-1100** in Earle *Land Charters* 273 Æilsiȝ bohte anne wifmann.. & hire sunu ..mid healfe punde..& sealde Æilsiȝ portȝereua[n] et Maccosse hundredes mann iiii. penȝas to tolle. *a* **1100** *Aldhelm Glosses* I. 1455 in Napier *O.E. Glosses* 39 *Fiscale tributum*, cynelic toll. *a* **1100** *O.E. Chron.* an. 1086 (Laud MS.), Hy arerdon unrihte tollas, and maniȝe oðre unrihte hi dydan. *c* **1100** in Earle *Land Ch.* 262 Her-kyð on þissere boc þ Leowine..&..his wif ȝebohton Ælfilde..to feower & sixtuȝe peneȝon, & Ælfric Hals nam þ toll..for þæs kynges hand. *a* **1300** *Cursor M.* 28438 (Cott.) Toll and tak, and rent o syse, Wit-halden i haue wit couettise. **13..** *K. Alis.* 1760 (Bodl. MS.) þat ich shal of olde & ȝonge Of þis midlerde tol afonge. *c* **1375** *Sc. Leg. Saints* x. (*Mathou*) 549 þis mathow ..wes tollar, and toll tuke. **1393** LANGL. *P. Pl.* C. I. 98 Boxes ..I-bounden with yre, To vnder-take þe tol [*v.rr.* tolle, tool] of vntrewe sacrifice. *c* **1400** MAUNDEV. (1839) xiii. 149 The tolle & the custom of his [Emperor of Persia's] marchantes is with outen estymacyoun to ben nombred. *c* **1440** *Promp. Parv.* 495/2 Tol, or custome, *guidagia*, ..*petagium, toloneum.* **1483** *Cath. Angl.* 389/2 A Tolle,..*talliagium.* **1485** *Rolls of Parlt.* VI. 345/2 The Graunte of the Tolle of oure Towne of Knyghton. **1535** COVERDALE *Ezra* iv. 13 Then shal not they geue tribute, toll, and yearly custome. **1570** LEVINS *Manip.* 218/17 Toule, *census.* **1577** tr. *Bullinger's Decades* (1592) 276 These Publicanes were such as liued vppon the publique toll and customes which they had farmed at the Romanes hands. **1642** FULLER *Holy & Prof. St.* v. xix. 438 Hereby the same commodity must pay a new tole at every passage into a new trade. **1832** TENNYSON *Œnone* 114 'Honour', she said, 'and homage, tax and toll, From many an inland town and haven large'. **1849** MACAULAY *Hist. Eng.* ix. II. 445 All fines, all forfeitures went to Sunderland. On every grant toll was paid to him. **1895** POLLOCK & MAITLAND *Hist. Eng. Law* I. 648 A large part of the borough's revenue was derived from tolls, if we use that term in its largest sense to include 'passage, pontage, lastage, stallage, bothage, ewage, tronage, scavage' and the like. **1909** *Daily News* 14 Sept. 4/2 Sir William Harcourt wished to establish the rule that property should pay toll once every generation, and he succeeded in establishing it.

†**b.** The taking of toll or tribute; the office of a tax-collector. *Obs.*

c **1000** ÆLFRIC *Hom.* II. 288 Oðer [is] þæt man ðurh toll feoh ȝegadriȝe. *Ibid.* 468 Matheus aras þærrihte fram his tolle, and filiȝde ðam Hælende. *Ibid.*, He hine ȝeseah sittan æt tolle.

c. In the obsolete law phrase ***sac and sóc, toll and team***, etc. (see SAC, TEAM *sb.* 8 b, c): The right to 'toll' included (among others) in the grant of a manor by the crown; see quot. 1895.

1017-1118 [see TEAM *sb.* 8 b]. **1130-35** *Laws Edw. Conf.* c. 22 §2 Tol, quod nos vocamus theloneum, scilicet libertatem emendi et vendendi in terra sua. *c* **1250** *Expos. Vocab.* in *Placita de Quo Warranto* 511 *Tol*..pro voluntate sua tallagium de villanis suis. *a* **1400** *Reg. Maj.* I. c. 2 in *Acts Parl. Scot.* (1844) I. 598/1 Qui habent et tenent terras suas cum soko et sako, furca et fossa, toll et them, et infangandthefe. **1456** [see TEAM *sb.* 8 d]. **1597** SKENE *De Verb. Sign.* s.v., He quha is infeft with Toll, is custome free, and payis na custome. **1607** COWELL *Interpr.*, *Toll*, alias *Tholl*..hath in our common lawe two significations: First it is vsed for a libertie to buy and sell within the precincts of a maner... Bracton..interpreteth [it] to be a libertie as well to take as to be free from Tolle. **1818** HALLAM *Mid. Ages* viii. I. II. 156 A charter of Edred grants to the monastery of Croyland soc, sac, toll, team and infangthef. **1871** [see TEAM *sb.* 8 b]. **1895** POLLOCK & MAITLAND *Hist. Eng. Law* I. 566 *Toll* is sometimes the right to take toll, sometimes the right to be free of toll; but often it is merely the right to tallage one's villeins.

2. *spec. uses.* **a.** A charge made for some service rendered: †(*a*) for passage in a ship, fare. *Obs.*

c **1000** ÆLFRIC *Saints' Lives* xxx. 168 þa..þæs scypes hlaford..ȝyrnde þæs scyp-tolles, ac ða hi nan þincg næfdon to syllanne, þa ȝyrnde he þæs wifes for þam tolle.

(*b*) A proportion of the grain or flour taken by the miller in payment for grinding. ? *Obs.* or *dial.*

c **1386** [implied in TOLL *v.*[3] 1]. *c* **1440** *Promp. Parv.* 496/1 Tol, of myllarys, *multa.* **1523** FITZHERB. *Husb.* §146 Mete it to the myll & fro the myll, & se y[t] thou haue thy measure agayne besyde the toll. **1589** [see TOLBOT]. **1638** PENKETHMAN *Artach.* G iv, If the Baker buy corne unground by the Quarter..he hath 68 l. Troy to the bushell, and is to pay the Millers tolle. **1888** ELWORTHY *W. Somerset Word-bk.*, *Toll*,..the quantity of meal kept by the miller for grinding another's corn.

†**b.** Rent paid for a house, mill, etc. *Obs.*

c **1000** ÆLFRIC *Saints' Lives* xix. 253 Hit ne ȝedafnað þæt man do godes hus anre mylne ȝ elic for lyðrum tolle.

c. A charge for the privilege of bringing goods for sale to a market or fair, or of setting up a stall.

c **1205** LAY. 13316 Her beoð chæpmen icumen of oðere londen..Heo habbeoð ibroht to me tol for heore æhte. *c* **1460** *Oseney Regr.* 10 Be quyte in all mercates of tol i-axid of thynges i-bowghte or solde. **1500** *Reg. Privy Seal Scotl.* I. 68/1 That the said erle..have tholl and uther small custumez of the fairis. **1567** *Expos. Termes of Law* (1579) 178 b/2 *Tolle* or *Tolne*, is most properlye a payment vsed in Cities, townes, markets & faires for goods and cattel brought thither to bee bought & solde. **1587** *Shuttleworths' Acc.* (Chetham Soc.) 41 Foure oxen in Prestone xj[li] xv[s] iiij[d]; towlle for the said besste, viij[d]. **1818** CRUISE *Digest* (ed. 2) III. 273 Toll is not of right incident to a fair or market, and can only be claimed by special grant from the Crown, or by prescription; and if the toll be unreasonable, the grant will be void. **1863** FAWCETT *Pol. Econ.* II. vii. (1876) 614 A market toll is paid for the accommodation which a market provides.

d. A charge for the right of passage along a road (at a turnpike or toll-gate: now abolished in Great Britain), along a river or channel, over a bridge or ferry; formerly also, through the gate or door of a building.

1477-8 *Acc. Exch. K.R.* Bundle 496 No. 17 (P.R.O.) Omnes summas monete..vel Toles pro dictis edificacionibus..solutas pro cariagio petrarum maeremii.. per terram vel per aquam. **1498** *Coventry Leet Bk.* 592 Howe the Citezenis of Couentre were trobled be there merchandisez in Bristoll, Gloucestre, & Worcestre & compelled to pay tholl & oþer customez contrarie to their liberteez. **1505** *Reg. Mag. Sig. Scot.* 603 Exceptis theoloneo finis pontis, viz. le tholl de le Brig-and de Are. *a* **1548** HALL *Chron.*, *Hen. VIII* 203 b, In this yere was an olde Tolle demaunded in Flaunders of Englysh men, called the Tolle of the Hounde, which is a Ryuer and a passage. The Tolle is .xii. pence of a Fardell. **1604** DRAYTON *Owle* 386 At his entrance he must pay them Tole. **1617** MORYSON *Itin.* I. 56 Here those which carried any merchandise paid tole. **1634** *Althorp MS.* in Simpkinson *Washingtons* (1860) App. p. xiv, For toale at Thrapston bridge 00 00 02. **1663** *Act 15 Chas. II*, c. 1 §5 Summes of money in the name of Toll or Custome, to be paid for all such Horses, Carts, Coaches, Waggons, Droves, and Gangs of Cattell, as..shall passe, bee ledd, or droven, in or through the said waye. **1838** *Murray's Hand-bk. N. Germ.* 254/1 A toll is here paid by all vessels navigating the Rhine, to the Duke of Nassau, the only chieftain remaining on the river who still exercises this feudal privilege. **1840** HOWITT *Visits Remark. Places* Ser. I. 234 The tolls at the doors of St. Paul's and the Tower have been relaxed. **1845** M[c]CULLOCH *Taxation* Introd. (1852) 33 The statute..imposed tolls, or duties collected at toll gates (called turnpikes), on all travellers along the great north road. **1883** 'OUIDA' *Wanda* I. 61 With a right to take toll on the ferry.

e. A charge for the right of landing or shipping goods at a port; formerly also, a customs duty. *Obs.* exc. *Hist.*

1680 MORDEN *Geog. Rect.*, *Germ.* (1685) 132 The place where Ships pay Tole. **1884** S. DOWELL *Taxes in Eng.* I. IV. v. 83 Of wine, a toll in the strictest sense of the term was taken by the king's officer from every ship having in cargo ten casks or more, on the arrival of the ship at a port in England.., unless the toll formed the subject of a composition in the way of a money payment.

f. A charge made for transport of goods, esp. by railway or canal. (Arising out of d.)

1889 *Standard* 21 Mar., Railway projectors were empowered to charge 'tolls', not exceeding a specified sum, for the use of their roads. Out of these 'tolls' rates were, in a manner, evolved, covering every service.

g. with defining words: **through toll** (also ***toll through, thorough***), **toll traverse**, **turn toll** (also ***toll turn***): see quots.

1567 *Expos. Termes of Law* (1579) 179/1 *Through tolle*, is where a Towne prescribes to haue tol for euery beast that goeth through their Towne. *Ibid.*, *Tolle trauers*, that is where one claimeth to haue a halfepeny, or such like toll of euery beast that is driuen ouer his ground. *Ibid.*, *Turne tolle* ..is where toll is paied for beasts that are dryuen to bee solde, although that they bee not solde. **1636** PRYNNE *Rem. agst. Shipmoney* 8 This Tax..layes a farre greater charge on the Subject then any new office, Murage, Toll-travers, or thorough-toll. **1670** BLOUNT *Law Dict.* s.v., *Toll-through*.. *Toll-travers*..; and *Toll-turn*, which is Toll paid at the return of Beasts from Fair or Market, though they were not sold. **1827** MACKENZIE *Hist. Newcastle* II. 649 The claim of toll thorough..is made by the corporation upon all goods.. of non-freemen, brought into or carried out of the town. **1911** G. R. HILL in Halsbury *Laws Eng.* XVI. 62 A toll-thorough is independent of any ownership of the soil by the original grantee, the consideration necessary to support it being usually the liability to repair the particular highway or bridge. *Ibid.*, A toll-traverse is a toll taken in respect of the original ownership of the land crossed by the public.

h. A charge for a telephone call. Usu. *attrib.* (see also *toll call*, sense 3 below, TOLL-FREE *a.*). *N. Amer.*

1886 *Jrnl. Soc. Telegr. Engineers* XV. 275 Another term also very largely used in America is 'toll line working'; i.e., communication between town and town..which is paid for by tolls per message, and not by annual subscription such as usually occurs in local exchanges. **1912** THIESS & JOY *Toll Telephone Pract.* i. 3 In Bell practice the terms 'suburban' and 'toll' are often used synonymously, but suburban business is always short haul..while toll business may be long haul but not exceeding 100 miles. The term 'long distance' in Bell practice implies any haul exceeding 100 miles and in many cases the toll and the long distance business are handled at different switchboards... The terms 'toll' and 'long distance' do not have this distinction in independent practice and are commonly synonymous. *Ibid.* iv. 43 When a toll subscriber desires to call central, he will operate his generator. *Ibid.* 44 If the jack of the subscriber wanted terminates in the toll position.., the toll operator will simply insert her calling plug and ring. **1921** *Telegraph & Telephone Jrnl.* VII. 180/2 It was eventually decided to remove all the short trunk lines (i.e. up to 25 miles in length) from the Trunk Exchange and to connect them to one or more Toll Exchanges. **1926** *Daily Colonist* (Victoria, B.C.) 11 July 16/1 The British Columbia Telephone Co...built the first toll line to Nanaimo. **1933** K. B. MILLER *Telephone Theory & Pract.* III. xi. 466 Telephone traffic between subscribers whose lines are connected to different local exchanges is ordinarily called 'toll traffic'... Toll traffic is generally classified as 'short haul' or 'suburban' for distances up to the neighborhood of about 50 miles, and 'long haul' or 'long distance' for connections between more widely separated points. **1970** N. ARMSTRONG et al. *First on Moon* xiv. 363, I had a telephone call yesterday. The toll wasn't..as great as the one I made to you fellows..on the moon. **1978** *Sci. Amer.* June 90/2 It may also provide paths between trunks, but this task is usually performed by special exchanges called toll exchanges.

i. *fig.* (Cf. *tribute*, similarly used.) Freq. in phr. ***to take its toll*** (esp. of death, loss, or injury).

c **1375** *Sc. Leg. Saints* xlii. (*Agatha*) 256 þane bad he.. brynnand cole Straw in þe floure..& nakyt þare-one hire rol, Til scho of ded had quyt þe tol.

1870 J. C. DUVAL *Adv. Big-Foot Wallace* p. xv, Wallace joined Colonel Hays's regiment..and was with it at the storming of Monterey, where he says he took 'full toll' out of the Mexicans for killing his brother and cousin..in 1836. *a* **1882** ROSSETTI *Ho. Life, Introd. Sonn.*, [Whether] In Charm's palm it pay the toll to Death. **1909** *Blackw. Mag.* July 19/2 Nott's gallant division..paid its toll of killed and wounded. **1927** W. E. COLLINSON *Contemp. Eng.* 34 The 'toll of the road' (often used by the Daily Mail in 1925-6) has been so heavy that some of the local authorities have adopted the expedient of the white line. **1929** *Daily Express* 7 Nov. 2/3 Miners' members were artists in presenting the toll of the mines in its most impressive form. **1959** *Listener* 6 Aug. 222/1 A thoroughly well-intentioned programme aimed at reducing the toll on the roads. **1962** E. ROOSEVELT *Autobiogr.* II. xv. 123 The war had taken from France a heavy toll of her young men from 1914 to 1918. **1972** N. FREELING *Long Silence* II. 189 In fact it had been very hardbought, some of the winnings, taking fearful tolls of nerve, straining every atom of him. **1974** F. FORSYTH *Dogs of War* xiv. 264 He felt tired and flat; the strain of the past thirty days was taking its toll. **1974** C. RYAN *Bridge too Far* III. ii. 147 Forty-five patients were dead (the toll would increase to over eighty), and countless more were wounded. **1981** *Times* 9 June 6/3 The death toll in the train disaster.. could be more than 1,000. **1982** S. BRETT *Murder Unprompted* xii. 113 The obscurity of the play, and the.. lack of star names—all the elements which pessimists had predicted would work against the show—were now beginning to take their toll.

3. *attrib.* and *Comb.*: **toll-bar** [BAR *sb.*[1]], a barrier (usually a gate) across a road or bridge, where toll is taken; in Scotland formerly often applied to the toll-collector's house; †**toll-bell**, a bell rung at the close of the collection of toll at a market; **toll-bridge**, a bridge at which toll is charged for passage; **toll call**: orig., † a telephone call which was not a local call and for which an individual charge was therefore made; in later (not British) use, a long-distance call, or a call between different telephone areas; **toll-clerk**, a clerk who keeps a record of tolls collected, e.g. at a market; **toll-collector**, (*a*) a person who collects toll, esp. the tolls at a turnpike, a market, etc.; (*b*) a device for indicating the number of persons passing a turnstile or gate and paying toll; (*c*) a device in the feeder of a mill for separating the toll of grain; **toll-corn**, corn retained by a miller as toll; †**toll-cote**, a toll-collector's cottage or shed; †**toll-customer** [CUSTOMER *sb.* 2], a toll- or tax-gatherer; **toll-farmer**, one who farms the tolls at a certain place; = FARMER[2] 1; †**toll-fat**, ? a vessel for toll-corn (in quot. 1222 a measure of capacity); **toll-gate**, a gate across a road at which toll was payable, a turnpike-gate; †**toll-hall**, ? = TOLL-BOOTH 2, guildhall, town hall; †**toll-hoop** [HOOP *sb.*[1] 5] = TOLL-DISH; **toll-keeper**, the keeper of a toll-gate or toll-house; **toll-lodge** = TOLL-HOUSE 2; †**toll-master**, the master of a toll-office; †**toll mere** [MERE *sb.*[2]], the boundary within which a local toll is payable; **toll-office**, an office where toll is taken; **toll penny**, a penny paid or charged as toll; †**toll-pin**, (?) a cylindrical stick used as a strake for the toll-dish; **toll plaza** *U.S.*, a row of toll booths on a toll road; †**toll-reeve**, an officer to whom tolls were payable; **toll-road**, a road maintained by tolls, a turnpike road (now chiefly *U.S.*); **toll-room**, a room or apartment where tolls are collected, as at a turnpike; †**toll-shop** = TOLL-HOUSE 2; †**toll-stock** (**tolstok**), ? = *toll-pin*; **toll**

television, TV = *pay television*, *-TV* s.v. PAY- 4; **tollway** *U.S.*, a highway for the use of which a charge is made; **toll-table**, a table of the toll-dues at a turnpike; **toll-taker**, one who takes tolls; a toll-collector, toll-gatherer; so **toll-taking** *sb.* and *a.* See also TOLL-BOOK, -BOOTH, -DISH, etc.

1813 *Examiner* 19 Apr. 243/1 The only light..was that shed by the *toll-bar lamp. **1825** JAMIESON, *Toll-bar*, a turnpike. [*Toll-bar* in *Calr. Inq. P.M.* V. 389, in a docmt. of 1315 is a misreading.] **1858** SURTEES *Ask Mamma* lxxvii, [He] trotted across the bridge,..and was speedily brought up at a toll-bar on the far side. **1736** DRAKE *Eboracum* I. vi. 219 No corn to be carried out of this market till the toll be gathered, and that the *toll-bell be rung. **1790** LUCKOMBE *Eng. Gaz.* III, *Sheperton*.. has a *toll-bridge over the Thames to Walton. **1912** THIESS & JOY *Toll Telephone Pract.* i. 3 Common usage among telephone men has led to the general classification of telephone service under four headings, as follows: local, suburban, toll and long distance. .. Any telephone call which is not local bears a special or toll charge and broadly may be termed a *toll call; hence it seems proper to use the term 'toll' to embrace all service of this class, whether it be suburban, toll, or long distance in the narrow sense. **1928** E. WALLACE *Again Three Just Men* x. 223 The telephone-bell rang. The voice of the porter informed him that a toll call had come through. **1965** S. T. OLLIVIER *Petticoat Farm* vi. 88 This ring was a toll call and would be costing a fortune. **1977** D. ANTHONY *Stud Game* vii. 45 Grant must have called the Bishop girl from here. She lives in Santa Monica, which makes it a toll call. **1878** BRAITHWAITE *Life & Lett. W. Pennefather* xi. 245 A young man who had been long employed as *toll-clerk. **1887** *Pall Mall G.* 25 Jan. 6/2 The toll clerk of Billingsgate Market. **1822** *Act 3 Geo. IV*, c. 126 §22 If the Owner or Driver of any Waggon..shall resist any Gate Keeper or *Toll Collector, in weighing the same,..[he] shall forfeit and pay..Five Pounds. **1877** KNIGHT *Dict. Mech.*, *Toll-collector*. 1. A counter at a turnstile or gate to indicate the number of persons passing. 2. A device attached to the feed of a grain-mill to subtract the toll. **1903** H. B. SWETE in *Expositor* Aug. 196 The rich and well-hated chief of the Jericho toll-collectors. **12..** *Reading Cartul.* (Harl. MS. 1708, lf. 107), Ego Willelmus babbe dedi..abbati et conuentui de Radinges vnam dimidiam summan bladi, scilicet de *tolcorn de molendino de Homstalle. **1701** *Cowell's Interpr.*, *Tolcorn*, Corn taken for Toll at grinding in a Mill. *c* **1460** *Play Sacram.* 540 Inquyre to þe *Tolkote, for ther ys hys loggyng. *a* **1681** WHARTON *Fasts & Fest.* Wks. (1683) 28 Saint Matthew, who being..a Publican or *Toll-customer by Profession, became a Disciple, an Apostle, an Evangelist, and Martyr. **1553** GRIMALDE *Cicero's Offices* I. (1558) 66 The gayne of *tolfarmers and misers. **1820** W. TOOKE tr. *Lucian* I. 469 Murderers, adulterers, toll-farmers,..and others of the same pack. [**1222** in J. Thorpe *Registrum Roffense* (1769) 369, xvj *tolfata faciunt unum quarterium salis.] **1547** in J. H. Glover *Kingsthorpiana* (1883) 93 That all thos persones that have quernes shall suffer noe body to grynde theirat above a Tolfatt, upon payn for every Tolfatt more then their owne..iii*d*. **1773** *Gentl. Mag.* XLIII. 441/1 They..shall pass upon any turnpike road, through any *toll-gate or bar, for half-toll. **1774** JOHNSON *Journ. West. Isl.* Wks. 1787 X. 17 It affords a southern stranger a new kind of pleasure to travel so commodiously without the interruption of toll-gates. **1884** PAE *Eustace* 95 The toll-gate was closed, but he vaulted over it. **1395** in *Cart. Abb. Whitby* (Surtees) II. 555 De *tolale de Hakeness v *s.* **1416-17** *Durham Acc. Rolls* 285, viij s. x d. de profect. curiæ et tolhale villæ de Hett. **1577-87** HOLINSHED *Chron.* II. 23/1 Skinners rew reaching from the pillorie to the tolehall, or to the high crosse. *c* **1270** *Customs Gt. Farringdon* (MS. Barlow 49, lf. 22 b), De consuetudine mercati..pro carectata salis dabitur vnus discus salis, qui continere debet unum *tolhop, uel vnus denarius. **1701** *Cowell's Interpr.*, *Tol-hop*, a Toll-dish, or small Measure by which they take Toll for Corn sold in an overt Market. **1822** *Act 3 Geo. IV*, c. 126 §22 *margin*, *Toll keepers permitting Waggons, &c. of greater Weight than allowed, to pass without Toll. Penalty 5 l. **1840** DICKENS *Barn. Rudge* iii, He..had cried a lusty 'good-night', to the toll-keeper. **1858** CARLYLE *Fredk. Gt.* III. i. (1872) I. 139 [They] continued their feuds, *toll-levyings, plunderings, and other contumacies. **1818-19** LEIGH *New Pict. Lond.* 313 The four *toll-lodges are neat doric structures. *a* **1649** DRUMM. OF HAWTH. *Hist. Jas. IV*, Wks. (1711) 70 These projectors and new *toll-masters, the king giving way to enrich his exchequer, awakened them [old laws]. **1500** *Nottingham Rec.* III. 450 Every shipp sayling with merchandise within the *toll meres. **1841** PUSEY tr. *Aquinas' Comm. Matt.* I. 94 He found a man sitting at the *toll-office. **1520** in W. H. Turner *Select. Rec. Oxford* (1880) 24 No person shall pay toll for his Catell..but only a *toll peny..if any catell be sold. **1623** FLETCHER & ROWLEY *Maid in Mill* III. i, The Miller has a stout heart Tough as his *toal-pin. **1948** *Sun* (Baltimore) 20 Nov. 14/2 All tolls for travel across the Chesapeake Bay Bridge will be paid at booths on the 1,000-foot *toll plaza on the Western Shore approach to the bridge. **1983** *N.Y. Times* 16 July 26/6 Connecticut state police have been stopping northbound trucks at the Greenwich toll plaza on the Connecticut Turnpike. **1433** *Rolls of Parlt.* IV. 477/2 *Tollèreves, to resceyve the Toll and..Custumes. **1444** *Ibid.* V. 124/1 Tolreves to resceyve and gedre the tolle, and such custumes as longeth to hem to take at the Yates of the seid Toun. **1825** JAMIESON, **Toll-road*, a turnpike road. **1883** STEVENSON *Silverado Sq.* 70 A dry water-course entered the Toll Road. **1749** in Feret *Fulham* (1900) I. 63 Paid for Whitewashing the offices and *Toll Room 5*s.* **1789** BRAND *Hist. Newcastle* I. 53 No houses, except *toll shops, were to be erected on the new bridge. **1316-17** *Chester Plea Roll* 9 & 10 Edw. II. m. 35 None partis cuiusdam proficui prouenientis del *Tolstok. **1806** *Chron.* in *Ann. Reg.* 405/1 The *toll-table, against the turn-pike house, at Whalley, in Yorkshire. **1555** *Act 2 & 3 Phil. & Mary*, c. 7 §4 The open Place appointed for the *Toll-Taker. **1647** TRAPP *Comm. Luke* iii. 12 These [publicans] were toll-takers, custom-gatherers for the Romans. **1882** MOZLEY *Remin.* I. iv. 30 A quaint little church..adjoining the toll-taker's shed. **1611** COTGR., *Peagerie*, *Toll-taking. **1956** *Britannica Bk. of Year* 492/2 *Pay T.V.*, **Toll T.V.*,..these phrases having been coined in America during a discussion of the possibilities of providing additional television programmes to viewers willing to pay for them on a subscription basis. **1960** *News Chron.* 13 Oct. 14/2 The pioneer Toll-TV service working in a suburb of Toronto. **1960** *Spectator* 30 Dec. 1039 The principle of toll television is that the viewer should pay only for films..he wants to see. **1955** *Britannica Bk. of Year* 490/1 Modern automobile transport continued to produce new words. Among these were **Tollway*, a modern version of the old toll road. **1958** *Times* 22 Nov. 7/6 To the other points of the compass the expressways—and even newer, faster, tollways—throw out rippling tentacles. **1969** 'E. LATHEN' *When in Greece* vi. 61 The new tollway along the coast..was..the only high speed road in Greece. **1982** S. PARETSKY *Indemnity Only* xvi. 214, I headed back to the tollway and Chicago.

toll (təʊl), *sb.*^{2} Also 7 **tole, towle.** [f. TOLL *v.*^{2}] The act of tolling a bell, or the sound made by a bell when tolled; (with *pl.*) a single stroke made in tolling or ringing a bell, or the sound made by such stroke.

1452 *Cal. Anc. Rec. Dublin* (1889) 276 The comone bell shuld toll iii. tollis iiii. tymes to warne the comones to harr semble. **1653** H. COGAN tr. *Pinto's Trav.* lxi. (1663) 250 At the sound of a bell which gave three toles, the Bonzes prostrated themselves all with their faces to the ground. **1775** S. J. PRATT *Liberal Opin.* civ. (1783) III. 253 The sermon-bell was upon the toll when I had not so much as penned a slip of paper. **1822** SCOTT *Nigel* iv, I should lose my good name for ever within the toll of Paul's were I to grant quittance. **1871** ROSSETTI *John of Tours* v, As it neared the midnight toll, John of Tours gave up his soul. **1875** *Encycl. Brit.* III. 537/2 At the news of Nelson's triumph and death at Trafalgar, the bells of Chester rang a merry peal alternated with one deep toll.

b. A sound resembling the tolling of a bell, as the note of the S. American bell-bird or campanero.

1825 WATERTON *Wand. S. Amer.* II. 118 No sound or song from any of the winged inhabitants of the forest..cause such astonishment, as the toll of the Campanero... You hear his toll, and then a pause for a minute, then another toll, and then a pause again, and then a toll, and again a pause.

†**toll**, *sb.*^{3} *Falconry. Obs.* [app. f. TOLL *v.*^{1} to lure.] ? A lure. (Cf. quot. 1653 in TOLL *v.*^{1} 1.)

1486 *Bk. St. Albans, Hawking* d j, An hawke flieth to the vew, to the Beke, or to the Toll. *Ibid.* d j b, A Goshawke or a tercell that shall flee to the vew, to the toll or to the beke.

toll, *sb.*^{4} Now *dial.* (Kent. to Hampsh.) Also 7 **tolle**, 9 **tole.** [Origin not ascertained.] A clump of trees.

1644 G. PLATTES in *Hartlib's Legacy* (1655) 245 Feeding of Cattel in racks under a tolle of trees. **1892** A. J. BUTLER tr. *Marbot's Mem.* I. ii. 13 My father stopped his carriage by the famous toll [*orig.* devant l'arbre remarquable] under which the Constable Montmorency was made prisoner by the troops of Louis XIII.

toll, tole (təʊl), *v.*^{1} Now *dial.* and *U.S.* Forms: 3-7 **tolle**, (4 **tulle**), 4-6 **tol**, (6 **toull**, 6-7 **toule, towle**, 7 **toul, toal**), 5-7, 9 **toll, tole.** [ME. *tollen*, *tullen*, implying OE. **tollian*, **tullian*:—**toll-*, *tullôjan*; from same root *tull-* as TILL *v.*^{3}:—OE. (*for*)*tyllan*:—**tulljan*.

Ulterior history and phonology obscure. Relation to stem *till-*, in OFris. *tilla*, MLG., MFlem., LG., Du., WFris. *tillen*, 'to raise, lift up, take up', is phonetically difficult.]

1. *trans.* To attract, entice, allure, decoy; †to incite, instigate (*obs.*).

In literary use in England down to 1690; in 18-19th c. in midl. and south. dialects (see *E.D.D.*), and U.S. literary use.

c **1220** *Bestiary* 545 in *O.E. Misc.* 17 Ðis deuel..Tolleð men to him wið his onde. *a* **1250** *Owl & Night.* 1627 An swa mai mon tolli him to Lutle briddes & iuo. *c* **1386** CHAUCER *Reeve's T.* 214 And we wil payen trewely atte fulle With empty hand men may none haukes tulle [*Camb. MS.* folle.. tolle]: Loo heere our siluer redy for to spende. *c* **1440** *Promp. Parv.* 496/1 Tollyn, or mevyn, or steryn to doon..a dede, *incito, provoco, excito.* **1548** UDALL, etc. *Erasm. Par. Mark* iv. 33 Which allure and tolle men vnto them. **1570** T. WILSON *Demosth.* Ded. 4 If by this meanes I could towle out some other to do this perfitely. **1593** *Tell-Troth's N.Y. Gift* (1876) 18 To tole in customers. **1594** CAREW *Tasso* (1881) 117 She..with sweet sighes them on doth toule. **1601** HOLLAND *Pliny* (1634) I. 261 She..by little and little tilleth and tolleth them so neere, that she can easily sease vpon them. **1611** COTGR., *Emmiellé*..inticed, inueagled, allured, tolled, or drawne on by sweet meanes. **1653** MILTON *Hirelings* (1659) 132 By that lure or loubel [he] may be toald from parish to parish all the town over. **1692** LOCKE *Educ.* §115 Whatever you observe him to be more frighted at..be sure to tole him on to by..Degrees. **1801** JEFFERSON *Writ.* (1830) III. 467 To toll us back to the times when we burnt witches. **1828** *Craven Gloss.*, *Toll-on*, to entice, to draw on by degrees. **1879** J. D. LONG *Æneid* I. 785 Now Dido, she Of Tyre, is toling him with tender words. **1879** T. HARDY *Wessex Tales* (1889) 248 'Tis all done to tole us the wrong way. **1885** HOWELLS *Silas Lapham* (1891) I. 271 I'm not going to have 'em say we..tolled him on.

2. *spec. U.S.* To lure or decoy (wild animals) for the purpose of capture; *esp.* (*a*) to decoy (ducks) by means of a dog trained for the purpose (see TOLLER^2 2); (*b*) to attract (fish) by means of bait thrown into the water (see TOLL-BAIT, also TOLLING *vbl. sb.*^{1} b, quot. 18..). Also *absol.* or *intr.*

1858 LEWIS in Youatt *Dog* iii. 90 In this simple branch of education, within the comprehension of any dog, consists the almost incredible art of toling the canvass-back. **1885** C. F. HOLDER *Marvels Anim. Life* 131, I..procured a large rabbit and placed it some way up from the pond, to toll her [a snake] away from the water. **1885** *Blackw. Mag.* July 108/1 Captain Kennedy's Indian attendant had toled: but neither stag paid any attention. **1901** *Ibid.* Nov. 691/2 He [a fox] is 'tolled'..by a noise made like two fighting crows.

b. *intr.* for *pass.* To admit of tolling.

1858 LEWIS in Youatt *Dog* iii. 90 The canvass-back toles better than any other duck. **1874** J. W. LONG *Amer. Wild-fowl* xxv. 251 The black-heads tole the most readily.

3. *trans.* To pull, drag, draw (physically). ? *Obs.*

a **1400-50** *Alexander* 3640 Þan preses in þe Persyns & of þe proud Medis..agayn all þe yndis, Tolls of þe tirantis.., Seȝes doun on aithire side a sowme out of nounbre. *c* **1440** *York Myst.* xlvi. 58 As a traytour atteynted þei toled hym and tugged hym [Jesus]. **1542** *Lam. & Piteous Treat.* in *Harl. Misc.* (Malh.) I. 243 Thynkynge that..he woulde with strength of men, tolle forth his shippes..into the depth of the see. **1654** GAYTON *Pleas. Notes* I. vi. 20 Mr. Nicholas ..toles downe the books with as little remorse, as a Carman does billets.

†**b.** *toll out*: (?) To stretch out to (a stated length) by being pulled. *Obs. rare*$^{-1}$.

1377 LANGL. *P. Pl.* B. v. 214 And put hem in a presse and pyn[n]ed hem þerinne, Tyl ten ȝerdes or twelue hadde tolled out threttene.

c. *intr.* for *pass.* To pull (itself), move, drift.

18.. SCOTT in Goode *Amer. Fishes* (1888) 89 The boat toles round from the tide toward the feeding-ground.

toll (təʊl), *v.*^{2} Also 6 **tolle**, 6-7 **towle, toul(e**, 6-7 (9 *dial.*) **towl**, 7 **toull**, 7-8 **tole.** [Found in this sense in 15th c.: nothing similar outside Eng. Prob. orig. a particular use of TOLL *v.*^{1} sense 3, 'to pull'; the sense having passed from 'pull the bell-rope', to 'pull the bell', and so to 'make the bell sound by pulling the rope'. The variant forms are exactly the same as in TOLL *v.*^{1}; but no distinct evidence of the transfer of sense from 'pull' to 'ring' appears in the quots., although these are compatible with it.]

1. *trans.* To cause (a great bell) to sound by pulling the rope, esp. in order to give an alarm or signal; to ring (a great bell). *arch.* or *rhet.*

(Since *to toll* is said of the bell itself (sense 3) in 1452, the transitive sense must have been in use before that date.)

1494 FABYAN *Chron.* (1811) 352 Sir Hughe le Spenser came..& desyred assystence of the fore named constables, the which commaunded the said belle to be tolled. **1568** GRAFTON *Chron.* II. 284 Syr John went into the market place, and there tolled the common Bell, and then incontinent men and women assembled. **1573** G. HARVEY *Letter-bk.* (Camden) 48 He accusid me of..præsumption for that I tooke uppon me to bid the butler toul the bel. **1684** *Foxe's A. & M.* III. 920/1 Let the Bell of the Church of S. German be touled. **1703** *Lond. Gaz.* No. 3749/4 The Bells were tolled at Caneto, and the Allarm was given on all sides by firing of Guns. **1849** JAMES *Woodman* viii, You run to the porter and tell him to toll the great bell with all his might. *a* **1873** DEUTSCH *Rem.* (1874) 255 The bells were tolled in an irregular and funereal fashion.

†**b.** *absol.* or *intr.* To ring. *Obs.*

1513 BRADSHAW *St. Werburge* II. 1592 The same glad tidyng shewed an honest woman Tollyng at the churche-dore the sayd day and hour.

2. *spec.* To cause (a large or deep-toned bell) to give forth a sound repeated at regular intervals by pulling the rope so that the bell swings through a short arc (in contrast to *ringing* it in full swing), or by striking it with a hammer or the like, or pulling the clapper; esp. for summoning a congregation to church, and **b.** (now) on the occasion of a death (the passing-bell) or funeral. Also *absol.* or *intr.*

1552 *Bk. Com. Prayer* Pref., The Curate..shall tolle a bell therto [i.e. to Morning and Evening Prayer] a conuenyente tyme before he begyn, that such as be desposed maye come ..to praye wyth hym. **1600** *Weakest goeth to Wall* G iij, Heere take the key and toll to Euening prayer. *a* **1604** HANMER *Chron. Irel.* (1633) 103 [They] wayted for divine service, they rung the Bell, they tould, they waited long. **1617** MINSHEU *Ductor*, *To toll* a Bell, which is to make him strike onely of one side. *c* **1618** MORYSON *Itin.* IV. v. i. (1903) 480 Some one [bell] (as that of Lincolne Minster) requiring the helpe of many men to toule it, and some dossen or twenty men to ringe it out. **1844** MRS. BROWNING *Rhyme Duchess May*, Toll slowly. **1868** DENISON *Clocks, Watches, & Bells* (ed. 5) 364 A large bell may be tolled easily by one man, if it is properly hung... I should hang a very large bell for tolling only, on wedge shaped gudgeons, so as to move with very little friction, and put a stop to prevent it from being pulled too far.

b. **1526**, *c* **1600** [see PASSING-BELL]. **1635** CRANLEY *Amanda* 88 My tongue doth faile, goe toule the passing bell. **1782** COWPER *Loss of Royal George* i, Toll for the brave! The brave that are no more! **1790** —— *Mother's Picture* 28, I heard the bell toll'd on thy burial day, I saw the hearse, that bore thee slow away. **1832** TENNYSON *Death Old Year* 3 Toll ye the church-bell sad and slow..For the old year lies a-dying. **1901** H. E. BULWER *Gloss. Techn. Terms Ch. Bells* 37 *Tolling*, causing a bell—generally the 'Tenor', or one of the heavier bells—to sound a number of times in slow succession, sometimes with marked intervals between every two or three 'blows', to announce a death or funeral. **1905** *Harmsworth Encycl.* 660/1 The passing bell was tolled when any one was passing out of life. This custom still survives in many parts of Britain, but the bell is now tolled after the death.

3. Said of a bell (also of the ringer): To sound (esp. a knell, etc.) by ringing as in sense 2; also of a clock, to strike (the hour) in a deep tone with slow measured strokes. Cf. KNOLL *v.*

1452 *Cal. Anc. Rec. Dublin* (1889) 276 The comone bell shuld toll iii. tollis iiii. tymes. **1651** T. BARKER *Art of Angling* (1653) 1 This man may come home..and cause the clerk to tole his knell. **1682** DRYDEN *Dk. Guise* IV. ii, Some crowd the

Spires, but most the hallow'd Bells, And softly Toll for Souls departing Knells, Each Chime thou hear'st, a future death foretells. **1750** GRAY *Elegy* 1 The Curfew tolls the knell of parting day. **1771** BEATTIE *Minstrel* I. xxxix, Slow tolls the village-clock the drowsy hour. **1805** SCOTT *Last Minstr.* VI. xxxi, And bells toll'd out their mighty peal, For the departed spirit's weal. **1818** —— *Br. Lamm.* xxii[i], She died just as the clock in the distant village tolled one. **1861** DUTTON COOK *P. Foster's D.* i, The clock of St. Paul's Covent Garden has just tolled out the hour of two.

4. *intr.* Of a bell: To give forth sounds of this character by being tolled; also quasi-*impers.* (quot. *c* 1729). Also said of a clock striking the hour on a deep-toned bell; in quot. 1826 of the hour.

1551 HOOPER *Injunctions* xxiii. Wks. (Parker Soc.) II. 137 In case..any of their friends will demand to have the bell toll whiles the sick is in extremes. **1592** KYD *Sp. Trag.* III. xii, The Windes blowing, the Belles towling, the Owle shriking,..and the Clocke striking twelue. **1599** SHAKS. *Hen. V*, IV. Prol. 15 The Countrey Cocks doe crow, the Clocks doe towle. **1653** H. COGAN tr. *Pinto's Trav.* lxi. 257 Then the same bell having tolled three times more, the two Priests descended. **1678** BUNYAN *Pilgr.* I. 189 If I heard the Bell Toull for some that were dead. *c* **1729** in *Cath. Rec. Soc. Publ.* VIII. 88 After compline the same day it toled to Chapter. **1745** R. LEVESON GOWER in Jesse *Selwyn & Contemp.* (1843) I. 76 The bells toll for prayers. **1816** J. WILSON *City of Plague* II. ii. 289 By day and night the death-bell tolls, And says, 'Prepare to die'. **1826** SCOTT *Woodst.* xxxiii, Midnight at length tolled. **1858** HAWTHORNE *Fr. & It. Note-bks.* I. 231 The great bell of St. Peter's tolled with a deep boom.

b. *intr. transf.* and *fig.* To make a sound like the tolling of a bell; to give forth a deep-toned or monotonously repeated note; *spec.* (*Sc.*) said of bees before swarming (see TOLLING *vbl. sb.*^{2} b).

1747 [see TOLLING *vbl. sb.*^{2} b]. **1839** BAILEY *Festus* xviii. (1852) 265 A thought comes tolling o'er the darkened soul Which we dare hardly guest. *a* **1849** J. C. MANGAN *Poems* (1859) 122 Sullen tolls the far-off river's flow. **1857** BORROW *Romany Rye* ix. (1858) I. 110 Oh, that's the cuckoo tolling. **1912** M. HEWLETT in *Eng. Rev.* Apr. 5 Then in clear sky the thunder tolled Sudden.

5. *trans.* To announce (a death, etc.) by tolling; to toll for (a dying or dead person).

1597 SHAKS. *2 Hen. IV*, I. i. 103 (Qo.) His tongue Sounds euer after as a sullen bell, Remembred tolling [*Folios* knolling] a departing friend. **1602** MARSTON *Ant. & Mel.* IV. Wks. 1856 I. 48 Groning like a bell, That towles departing soules. **1850** TENNYSON *In Mem.* lvii. 10 One set slow bell will seem to toll The passing of the sweetest soul That ever look'd with human eyes. **1858** O. W. HOLMES *Aut. Breakf.-t.* xii. (1883) 248 My room-mate thought..it was the bell tolling deaths, and people's ages, as they do in the country.

6. To summon or dismiss by tolling. Const. *in*, *out*, etc.

1611 SPEED *Hist. Gt. Brit.* IX. xxii. §21 To ring the Masse into England, and to towle Cardinall Poole from Rome. **1683** DRYDEN *Vind. Dk. Guise* 17 For Conscience or Heavens fear, religious Rules Are all State-bells to toll in pious Fools. **1697** —— *Virg. Georg.* IV. 277 When hollow Murmurs of their Ev'ning Bells, Dismiss the sleepy Swains, and toll 'em to their Cells. **1819** KEATS *Ode Nightingale* viii, Forlorn! the very word is like a bell To toll me back from thee to my sole self. **1841** THACKERAY *Gt. H. Diamond* iv, As she spoke, the bells were just tolling the people out of church.

b. *absol.* or *intr.* **toll in**: to summon a congregation to church by tolling (said of a person, or of the bell); *esp.* in reference to the change from ordinary ringing or chiming a few minutes before the commencement of worship.

1710 J. B. *Let. to Sacheverell* 13 The Bells were Tolling in. **1712** STEELE *Spect.* No. 372 ¶1, I was tolling in to Prayers at Eleven in the Morning. **1860** WARTER *Sea-board* II. 455, I had no time to lose, as the bell was tolling in.

toll (təʊl), *v.*^{3} Now *rare.* [f. TOLL *sb.*^{1}]

1. *intr.* To take or collect toll; to exact or levy toll.

a **1350** [see TOLLING *vbl. sb.*^{3}]. *c* **1386** CHAUCER *Prol.* 562 Wel koude he stelen corn, and tollen thries And yet he hadde a thombe of gold pardee. *c* **1440** *Promp. Parv.* 496/1 Tollyn, or make tolle.., *multo.* **1530** PALSGR. 759/1, I tolle, I take the tolle, as a baylyfe dothe in a fayre or market... I tolle, as a myller doth, *je prens le tollyu.* **1576** GASCOIGNE *Steele Gl.* (Arb.) 79 When millers toll not with a golden thumbe. **1595** SHAKS. *John* III. i. 154 No Italian priest Shall tythe or toll in our dominions. *a* **1658** CLEVELAND *Sing-Song* xxx, He toll'd for the rest of the Grist. **1886** [see TOLLING *vbl. sb.*^{3}].

2. a. *trans.* To take toll of (something); to exact a part of by way of toll.

1399 LANGL. *Rich. Redeles* III. 81 And tymed no twynte, but tolled her cornes, And gaderid þe grotus with gyle, as I trowe. **1546** [see TOLLING *vbl. sb.*^{3}]. **1591** *Troub. Raigne K. John* (1611) 62 Till I had tithde and tolde their holy hoords. **1686** W. HEDGES *Diary* (Hakl. Soc.) I. 230 Here we were mett by ye Customer of Diarbekeer, who tolled our loads, and tooke ye custom & dutys of all the 3 places. **1794** M. WOLLSTONECRAFT *Hist. View Fr. Rev.* I. 76 The poor husbandman,..afterwards forced to carry the scanty crop to be tolled at the mill of monseigneur. **1894** *Westm. Gaz.* 26 May 5/2 The company-promoting system, whereby the City sharper tolls the savings of the credulous investor.

b. To charge (a person, etc.) with a toll, impose a toll upon, exact a toll from.

1583 MELBANCKE *Philotimus* Dd ij b, Aegeon..doeth scoure the Seas, and toules the trafficke of trading merchauntes. **1592** tr. *Junius on Rev.* xiii. 1 What time the Empire of Rome..was mightily tolled, hauing euer and an one new heads. **1897** *Daily News* 2 Nov. 6/3 You have only to cross the bridge and you are sure to be tolled. **1912** M. HEWLETT in *Eng. Rev.* Apr. 10 All [must] be tolled By Charon in his dark-prowed boat.

c. To take or gather (something) as toll.

1597 SHAKS. *2 Hen. IV*, IV. v. 75 (Qo.) Like the bee toling from euery flower [*Folios* culling from euery flower] The vertuous Sweetes. **1820** W. IRVING *Sketch Bk.* I. 189 Writers, like bees, toll their sweets in the wide world.

d. To charge a toll for the use of (a bridge, crossing, etc.). Chiefly as *ppl. a.*

1978 *Financial Times* 24 Oct. 11/3 The tolled Humber bridge. **1978** in H. Wilson *Final Term* (1979) 247 Concessions to 'Orange Badge' holders at most tolled crossings.

†**3. a.** *intr.* To pay toll; *to toll for* (*spec.*), to enter (a horse, etc.) for sale in the toll-book of a market.

1393 LANGL. *P. Pl.* C. XIV. 51 For þe lawe askeþ Marchauns for here merchaundise in meny place to tollen. **1530** PALSGR. 759/1, I tolle..as they that come to the myll, *je paye le tollyu.* You shal tolle, or you go, or I wyll tolle for you. **1537** BOORDE *Let.* in *Introd. Knowl.* (1870) Fore-words 62 They þat bowght þem dyd neuer toll for them. **1596** BACON *Use Com. Law* (1636) 63 If hee bee a horse hee must bee ridden two houres in the market or faire, between ten and five a clock, and tolled for in the toll-book. **1601** SHAKS. *All's Well* v. iii. 149, I will buy me a sonne in Law in a faire, and toule for this. Ile none of him. **1664** BUTLER *Hud.* II. i. 698 Where, when, by whom, and what y'were sold for, And in the open Market toll'd for?

b. *trans.* (in same sense).

1697 *Lond. Gaz.* No. 3310/4 The Person who exposed him to Sale being required to Toll him withdrew himself, by which it was conjectured he was stole.

toll (təʊl), *v.*^{4} *Law.* [a. AF. *toller, toler, touller*, ad. L. *toll-ĕre* to take away.] *trans.* To take away, bar, defeat, annul. ***to toll an entry***, to take away the right of, or bar entry.

[**1292** BRITTON I. vi. §2 Ensint qe peyne ne lour toulle nule resoun. *Ibid.* xxvi. §1 Cum il avera tolet ai pieyntif. Et si.. ele avera tolu a homme ses membres.] **1467–8** *Rolls of Parlt.* V. 631/1 That the esson and..other delay of eny persone.. by this acte be not prejudiced nor tolled in any wise. **1495** *Act 11 Hen. VII*, c. 63 §4 Wherof their entres..shall be tolled and taken away by the Course of the Lawe. **1544** tr. *Littleton's Tenures* (1574) 86 b, Suche discent shall not tol the entre of the childe, but he may enter vpon the issue that is in by discent. **1642** J. M[ARSH] *Argt. conc. Militia* 18 The King may dissolve a Parliament and so totally toll their power. **1726** AYLIFFE *Parergon* 74 It..tolls the Presumption in Favour of a Sentence. **1818** HALLAM *Mid. Ages* (1878) III. 166 *note*, In what case this right of entry was taken away, or *tolled*, as it was expressed, by the death or alienation of the disseisor.

tollable ('təʊləb(ə)l), *a. rare.* [f. TOLL *v.*^{3} + -ABLE.] Subject to toll; on which toll is payable.

1611 COTGR., *Peageau*, tollable; of toll. *Chemin peageau*, wherein toll may be taken. **1912** *Daily News* 12 July 3 To take proceedings against the Clayton-square flower-girls for selling tollable articles.

tollage ('təʊlɪdʒ). Also 6 **-adge, toullage.** [? f. TOLL *v.*^{3} + -AGE; confounded with TALLAGE *sb.*^{1}]

1. = TOLL *sb.*^{1}; exaction or payment of toll.

1494 FABYAN *Chron.* VII. (1516) 27 b/2 That y^e Cytezyns shulde enioye the lybertyes of y^e Fayre euer after without paying of any Tollage [*some MSS.* tallage] or Tolle. **1579** in Willis & Clark *Cambridge* (1886) I. 312 The tolladge at bottle bridge off the cartes y^t shall carrye the sayd slate. **1591** *Rutland MSS.* (1905) IV. 398 Paid for swarfage and toullage, ij s. **1612** DRAYTON *Poly-olb.* xiii. 270 By Leofrick her Lord..The people from her Marts by tollage who expelld. *a* **1835** *Certificate of Freedom of City of Norwich* (MS.), Know ye, That..the Bearer hereof..is Free, and ought so to be from all kind of Tollage, Pontage, Passage, Murage [etc.] and from all other Customs in all the Sea-Ports throughout England. **1888** *Pall Mall G.* 24 Sept. 5/2 Carrying all at the stereotyped figure of 2*s.* 6*d.* per ton..the River Weaver Trustees charging another 1*s.* per ton tollage.

†**2.** = TALLAGE *sb.*^{1} *Obs.*

1551 (ed. Berthelet) *Act 23 Hen. VIII*, 1531–2, c. 10 §6 Taxes and Tollages [*Record ed.* Tallages] hereafter to be assessed and leuyed. **1583** STOCKER *Civ. Warres Lowe C.* I. 17 We..will faithfully paye all taxes, tollages, customes, impostes, subsidies, tenthes. **1610** HOLLAND *Camden's Brit.* I. 39 The revenewes comming by tollage and pondage and such like imposts. **1634** *Malory's Arthur* I. lxxxix. 155 They ..put this land to great extortions and tollages [1470–85 (v. ii. 161) extorcions & taylles].

†**to'llation.** *Obs. rare*$^{-1}$. [irreg. f. L. *tollĕre* to lift + -ATION.] The action of lifting.

1688 R. HOLME *Armoury* II. 387/1 An Ellevation, or Tollation, is the lifting up of a thing, which shews it to be light or heavy.

'toll-bait. *U.S.* [f. TOLL *v.*^{1} 2 + BAIT *sb.*] Chopped bait thrown into the water to 'toll' or attract fish; throw-bait.

1870 *Amer. Naturalist* IV. 516 The 'tole-bait' consists chiefly of Menhaden (*Alausa menhaden*) ground very fine. **1887** *Fisheries of U.S.* Sect. v. II. 594 In the old style of mackerel fishing,..clams were chopped up (often with a mixture of menhaden) and sprinkled overboard as 'toll-bait' to attract the mackerel to the surface.

†**'toll-book.** *Obs.* [TOLL *sb.*^{1}] A book containing a register of beasts or goods to be sold at a market or fair, and the tolls payable for them; ***in the toll-book***, in the market, for sale (in quot. 1607 *fig.*); also, a tax-collector's register or assessment-book. Also in Comb. ***toll-book keeper.***

1596 BACON *Use Com. Law* (1636) 63 [see TOLL *v.*^{3} 3]. *Ibid.*, And the seller must bring one to avouch his sale, knowne to the toll-book-keeper. **1607** TOURNEUR *Rev. Trag.* II. ii, Some that were Maides..are now perhaps i'th Toale-book. **1655** FULLER *Ch. Hist.* IV. iii. §36 Nor is it probable he was a Mendicant, who was rated in the Publicans Tole-Book, and paid Tribute unto Cæsar. **1679** *Lond. Gaz.* No. 1446/4 Whoever gives notice of the said Horse to John Warren aforesaid, or to John Davenport, Keeper of the Toll-Book in West Smithfield, shall have 20s. Reward.

toll-booth, tolbooth ('təʊlbuːð, -buːθ, 'tɒlbuːθ), *sb.* Chiefly *Sc.*, exc. (more recently) in sense 1. Forms: 4 **tolboþe**, 4–6 **tolbothe, tolbuth**, 5 **tolboythe, tolle buthe, tolbuthe, (towboth, -buthe)**, 5–7 **tolbuith**, 6 **tolboth, -boith, -buyth, tollboothe, -bouthe, (towbuyth**, 7 **toole-, towle-, tolebooth)**, 6– (*arch.* or *Sc.*) **tolbooth**, 7– **tollbooth, toll-booth.** [f. TOLL *sb.*^{1} + BOOTH, *lit.* the booth, stall, or shed of the tax-collector. Cf. Ger. *zollbude*, Da. *toldbod*, custom-house.]

1. A booth, stall, or office at which tolls, duties, or customs are collected; a custom-house. *spec.* a booth at which the toll for the right of passage across a bridge, along a road, etc., is collected.

[**1314–15** *Rolls of Parlt.* I. 331/1 Mandetur..Ballivis de Tolbotha de Lenne.] **13..** *Propr. Sanct.* (Vernon MS.) in Herrig's *Archiv* LXXXI. 309/4 Matheu cald was his name, In a Tol-boþe sat þe same. *c* **1375** *Sc. Leg. Saints* x. (*Mathou*) 8 Quhare in þe tolbuth set lewy. **1381** *Rolls of Parlt.* III. 108/1 Alerent jeske a Tolbothe du dite ville [Canterbury]. **1382** WYCLIF *Matt.* ix. 9 He seiȝ a man sittynge in a tolbothe, Matheu by name. *c* **1475** *Pict. Voc.* in Wr.-Wülcker 804/8 *Hoc toloneum*, a tolbothe. **1483** *Cath. Angl.* 390/1 A Tolle buthe. **1577–87** HOLINSHED *Chron.* III. 1186/1 The tolboth in the market of Durham all of stone. **1587** *Lanc. Wills* (Chetham Soc.) III. 116 Excepte onelie of the tollboothe the toll and stallages of Manchester. **1633** BP. HALL *Hard Texts, N.T.* 14 Sitting in the Tole-booth of the Publicans to gather up the rents. **1756** NUGENT *Gr. Tour, Germ.* II. 133 There is here a great toll-booth, or custom-house, where toll is paid for..black cattle that pass from Jutland into Germany. **1973** *Times* 8 May (Hong Kong Suppl.) p. iii/9 Fourteen toll booths can be seen from the control room. **1978** D. DEVINE *Sunk without Trace* xxvi. 243 The car halted at the toll. He jumped out..to question the man in the toll-booth.

2. A town hall or guildhall.

Often (esp. in Scotland) comprehending senses 1 and 3.

1440 *Sc. Acts Jas. II* (1814) II. 32/2 The Consale Generale haldyn at Strivilyn in the tolbuthe of that ilk. **1467** *Dunfermline Regr.* (Bann. Cl.) 358 þis inquisicion made at Berwik vpoun twede in þe tolbuth of þe samyn. **1593** *Reg. Mag. Sig. Scot.* 817/2 Ad edificandum pretorium, carcerem domumque ponderum et telonium (lie tolbuith, prissoun, weyhous and customehous)..ad publicos usus dicti burgi. **1596** DALRYMPLE tr. *Leslie's Hist. Scot.* x. (S.T.S.) II. 400 Publiklie be heraldis..scho [the Queen] commandis, that Johne Knox, Wilok, Douglas, and Paul Meffen, compeiring in the Tolbuith of Striuiling in Judgment to mak ansuer. **1665** J. BUCK in Peacock *Stat. Cambridge* (1841) App. B. 54 Upon Michaelmass day the Vice Chancellor with some of the Heads and Doctors..goe to the Toll Booth in their Scarlet Gowns, there to give the Maior his oath. **1820** LINGARD *Hist. Eng.* IV. ii. 74 Margaret..offered to conduct her son (he was only in his twelfth year) to the tolbooth of Edinburgh, and to announce by proclamation that he had assumed the government. **1828** *Craven Gloss., Toll-booth...* In this district it signifies a Town Hall, where the Court Baron is held, and the rents and amercements due to the Lord are paid. **1900** J. KIRKWOOD *United Presbyterians Ayr.* iii. 29 They had to perform the ceremony in the Tolbooth of Irvine.

3. A town prison, a gaol.

(Formerly usually consisting of cells under the town hall.)

c **1470** HENRY *Wallace* VII. 202 A bauk was knyt all full of rapys keyne; Sic a towboth sen syn was neuir seyne. *c* **1520** NISBET *N.T. in Scots, Acts* xxiii. 35 He comandit him to be kepit in the tolbuth of Herode. **1535** CROMWELL in Merriman *Life & Lett.* (1902) I. 432 The said universitie [Cambridge] hath hertefor had..the use of the kings prisoune there called the Tolbothe. **1581** N. BURNE *Disput.* in *Cath. Tractates* (S.T.S.) 109 Being impresoned first in the Castel of Sanctandrois, and nixt in the tolbuith of Edinburgh. **1655** FULLER *Hist. Camb.* vii. §25 The Maior refused to give them the keys of the Toll-booth, or Town-prison. **1661** BLOUNT *Glossogr.* (ed. 2), *Tolbuyth*, the name of the chief Prison at Edenburgh. **1738** (*title*) Captain Porteous's Ghost, giving an Account how he was dragged from the Tolbooth of Edinburgh, by the outrageous mob, and hung by the neck like a Dog. **1752** J. LOUTHIAN *Form of Process* (ed. 2) 67, I being incarcerate within the said Tolbooth, by Warrant of the Lord Justice-Clerk, for the Crime of Murder alledged committed by me. **1818** SCOTT *Hrt. Midl.* Note C, Since the year 1640..the Tolbooth was occupied as a prison only. **1855** [BURN] *Autobiog. Beggar Boy* (1859) 6, I am not without some pleasing reminiscences of the *gude toun* of Hawick, having been boarded and lodged in the tolbooth there for the space of seven days.

4. *attrib.*

1611 *Acc. Bk. W. Wray* in *Antiquary* XXXII. 214 The crosse of stone standing in the toolebooth garth. *c* **1737** in Scott *Hrt. Midl.* Note D, One Stoddart,..was charged of haveing boasted publickly, in a smith's shop at Leith, that he had assisted in breaking open the Tolbooth door. **1818** *Ibid.* iii[i], 'I would claw down the tolbooth door wi' my nails,' said Miss Grizel, 'but I wad be at him [Porteous]'. **1847** MRS. S. MENTEATH *Lays Kirk & Covt.* 65 A gleam is waking —more faintly now—Her Tolbooth prison-hold.

Hence †**'tolbooth** *v.* (*obs. nonce-wd.*), to imprison in a toll-booth.

a **1635** CORBETT *Poems* (1648) 35 (*Jas. I's Visit to Cambridge*) And well bestow'd he thought his hen, That they might Tolebooth Oxford men.

tollcester, erron. form of TOLSESTER *Obs.*

ˈ**toll-dish.** [TOLL *sb.*¹ 2 a (*b*).] A dish or bowl of stated dimensions for measuring the toll of grain at a mill; a multure-dish.

a **1550** *Mery Jest of Mylner of Abyngton* 50 in Hazl. *E.P.P.* III. 102 The mylner was so trewe and fele, Of each mannes corne wolde he steale More than his toledish by a deale. *c* **1585** *Faire Em* I. 168 You are too fyne to be a Millers daughter: For if you should but stoope to take vp the tole dish You will haue the crampe in your finger At least ten weekes after. **1623** FLETCHER & ROWLEY *Maid in Mill* III. ii, A Lord, a Miller? Take your toal-dish with ye. **1726** AYLIFFE *Parergon* 505 Corn Mills pay Tithes in Kind as Mills, which is the tenth Toll-dish. **1778** *Eng. Gazetteer* (ed. 2) s.v. *Farnham*, The toll-dish here was once reckoned worth 200 l. a year. **1820** SCOTT *Ivanhoe* xi, The thieves.. crying to their comrade, 'Miller! beware thy toll-dish'.

tolled, pa. t. of TOLL *v.*; also obs. f. TOLD.

tollenar, -er: see TOLNER *Obs.*

Tollens (ˈtɒlənz). *Chem.* [The name of B. C. G. *Tollens* (1841–1918), German chemist.] ***Tollens'(s) reagent***: a solution of ammoniacal silver nitrate and sodium hydroxide, used as a test for aldehydes with which it reacts to give a silver precipitate; so *Tollens' test* (described by Tollens in *Ber. d. deut. Chem. Ges.* (1882) XV. 1828).

1904 S. P. MULLIKEN *Method for Identification Pure Organic Compounds* I. 22 (*heading*) Compounds reducing silver from Tollen's [*sic*] reagent. **1946** F. SCHNEIDER *Qualitative Organic Microanalysis* vii. 198 A blank experiment should be run with the Tollens' reagent and the original substance. **1964** N. G. CLARK *Mod. Organic Chem.* x. 187 Tollens's reagent..gives a precipitate of silver, often in the form of a silver mirror. **1981** WINGROVE & CARET *Organic Chem.* xxi. 867 A simple chemical test to distinguish between aldehydes and ketones is based on aldehydes being readily oxidized to carboxylic acids whereas ketones are not. Tollens' test..is used most frequently.

tollent (ˈtɒlənt), *a. Logic. rare.* [ad. L. *tollent-em*, pres. pple. of *tollĕre* to lift, take away.] That 'takes away' or negatives: opp. to PONENT 3.

1770 tr. *C. F. von Wolff's Logic* 87 The Tollent mode. **1837-8** SIR W. HAMILTON *Logic* xviii. (1866) I. 344 A Tollent or Destructive syllogism. [See DESTRUCTIVE A. d.]

toller¹ (ˈtəʊlə(r)). Also 4 -ere, 4–5 -are, 4–6 -ar, 6 towler. [OE. *tollere*, f. TOLL *sb.*¹ + -ER¹.]

1. One who takes toll, a toll-collector (now *rare*); †a tax-gatherer, 'publican' (*obs.*).; ***toller of the sack***, a miller.

c **1000** ÆLFRIC *Hom.* I. 510 Hu ðæs caseres tolleras axodon Petrus. *Ibid.* II. 468 God..hine awende of tollere to apostole. *c* **1050** *Supp. Ælfric's Voc.* in Wr.-Wülcker 171/29 *Telonearius*, tolnere *vel* tollere. **13..** *Cursor M.* 25804 (Cott.) Matheu was first toller And siþen cristes gospeller. *c* **1375** *Sc. Leg. Saints* x. (*Mathou*) 9 In þe tolbuth set lewy, þat as a tollare þare wes sate. **1377** LANGL. *P. Pl.* B. Prol. 220 Taillours and tynkeres & tolleres in marketes. **1474** CAXTON *Chesse* III. iv. (1883) 108 The customers, tollers, and resseyuours of rentes & of money. *c* **1510** BARCLAY *Mirr. Gd. Manners* (1570) G iv, No towler, catchpoll nor customer No broker nor botcher, no somner nor sergeaunt. *c* **1550** CHEKE *Matt.* ix. 10 Mani tollers and sinners sat doun also with Jesus and with his discipils. **1591** GREENE *Conny-Catch.* II. Wks. (Grosart) X. 79 The Priggar when he hath stollen a horse..bringeth to the touler..two honest men, eyther apparelled like citizens, or plain country yeomen, and they ..offer to depose, that they know the horse to be his. **1724** A. SHIELDS *J. Renwick* (1827) 148 One of the Tollers or Waiters discovered the House. **1831** *Lincoln Herald* 6 May, Surely a tailor or shoemaker is as good as a printer's devil or a toller of the sack.

2. An apparatus for separating the toll of grain: = *toll-collector* (*c*) (TOLL *sb.*¹ 3).

1884 KNIGHT *Dict. Mech.* Supp., *Toller.* (Grist Mill.) The Tom Thumb toller is an automatic divider of the toll from the grist.

toller², **toler** (ˈtəʊlə(r)). Also 5 tollare. [f. TOLL, TOLE *v.*¹ + -ER¹.]

† **1.** One who 'tolls', entices, or instigates. *Obs.*

c **1440** *Promp. Parv.* 496/1 Tollare or styrare to do goode or badde, *excitator, instigator.*

2. A decoy; *spec.* a dog of a small breed used in decoying ducks: see TOLL *v.*¹ 2. Also *attrib. U.S.*

1831 I. T. SHARPLESS in *Cabinet of Nat. Hist.* I. 43/2 Most persons on these waters, have a race of small, white or liver coloured dogs, which are familiarly called the *toler* breed. **1874** J. W. LONG *Amer. Wild-fowl* iii. 72 For deep-water ducks, three or four decoys as tolers may be set out to leeward.

toller³ (ˈtəʊlə(r)). [f. TOLL *v.*² + -ER¹.] One who tolls a bell.

1562 J. HEYWOOD *Prov. & Epigr.* (1867) 118 The milner tolth corne, the sexton tolth the bell, In whiche tollyng, tollers thriue not a lyke well.

† **toller**⁴. *Law. Obs.* [Agent-n. f. TOLL *v.*⁴] One who tolls or bars the entry of another. Hence **tol-, tolleress**, a female toller.

1313-4 *Eyre of Kent* (Selden) II. 5 Ele entra com nostre toleresse. **1912** *transl.* She entered but as our toleress. *Note. A toleress is one who tolls the entry.*

toller-: see TOLER-.

ˈ**tollery.** *nonce-wd.* [f. TOLL *sb.*¹ or TOLLER¹ + -ERY.] A place at which tolls are collected.

1858 CARLYLE *Fredk. Gt.* II. v. (1872) I. 69 Zollern is equivalent to *Tollery* or Place of Tolls.

tolletane, obs. form of TOLETAN.

tolley (ˈtɒlɪ). [Var. of *taw-alley* (Eng. Dial. Dict. s.v. TAW *sb.*¹): see ALLY, ALLEY, ALAY *sb.*²] = TAW *sb.*² a.

1970 *Times* 18 Feb. 2 Playing marbles requires a player to bend double to flick the tolley. **1972** *Daily Tel.* (Colour Suppl.) 14 Jan. 25/1 You flick the tolley with your thumb.

toll-free, *a.* [TOLL *sb.*¹ + FREE *a.*] Free from toll; exempt from payment of toll. (Usually in predicative or adverbial construction.)

1052-67 *Charter of Eadweard* in Kemble *Cod. Dipl.* IV. 209 Tolfreo ofer ealle Engleland, wiðinne burhe and wiðutan. **1277** *Brit. Mus. Add. Charter* 51563 [Pannage and other rights are granted] cum hopirfre et tolfre in omnibus molendinis meis. **1494** FABYAN *Chron.* VII. 327 That yᵉ cytezens of London shulde passe toll fre thorough all Englande. **1523** FITZHERB. *Surv.* 10 Some men to be tole free, and some to be hopper fre. **1610** HOLLAND *Camden's Brit.* (1637) 493 He obtained that it might bee every where Toll-free. **1829** SCOTT *Anne of G.* x, Such wares will not pass toll-free where Archibald of Hagenbach hath authority.

b. Esp. (*N. Amer.*) of telephone calls, lines, etc.

1970 *Globe & Mail* (Toronto) 26 Sept. 31/1 (Advt), For reservations, call toll-free 368-7474. **1971** *Sci. Amer.* Oct. 7/2 (Advt.), When you buy a '72, you get the name and toll-free number of a person in Detroit. **1976** *National Observer* (U.S.) 13 Mar. 3/6 (Advt.), Write or call now. Our toll-free lines are open 24 hours daily, 7 days a week. **1979** *Arizona Daily Star* 5 Aug. (Advt. Section) 4/3 Make a toll-free call to Bill Jackson. **1984** *Gainesville* (Florida) *Sun* 28 Mar. 2A/3, I have called the same toll-free number I ordered from several times but these people will not return my call.

ˈ**toll-ˌgatherer.** Now *rare.* [f. TOLL *sb.*¹ + GATHERER.] One who collects tolls or dues; a tax-gatherer: = PUBLICAN *sb.*¹ 1.

1382 WYCLIF *Matt.* Prol., Fro the office of a tol gaderer he was clepid to God. **1474** CAXTON *Chesse* III. vii. (1883) 138 Kepars of townes customers and tolle gaderers. **1555** *Act 2 & 3 Phil. & Mary*, c. 7 §2 Every Toll-gatherer..shall..take their due and lawful Tolls. *a* **1610** HEALEY *Theophrastus* (1636) 25 Fit to keep an Alehouse or an Inne: to be a Pandar or a Tole-gatherer. **1766** BLACKSTONE *Comm.* II. xxx. 451 The horse shall be brought by both the vendor and vendee to the tollgatherer or bookkeeper of such fair or market. **1820** W. TOOKE tr. *Lucian* I. 365 The toll-gatherer Æacus would take it very ill.

So ˈ**toll-ˌgathering**, collection of tolls or dues.

1577 tr. *Bullinger's Decades* (1592) 277 Hee bad not these Publicanes to leaue off their toll-gathering, but willed them to bee content with their appointed duty.

ˈ**toll-house.** [f. TOLL *sb.*¹ + HOUSE: cf. OHG. *zolhûs*, Ger. *zollhaus*.] A house or building at which tolls or dues are collected.

1. = TOLL-BOOTH 1 (*obs.*) or 2 (now *local*).

c **1440** *Promp. Parv.* 496/1 Tolhowse, *teloneum.* **1506** GUYLFORDE *Pilgr.* (Camden) 49 Our Sauyor..sawe the publycan named Leui,..syttynge at the tolhous. **1530** PALSGR. 281/2 Tolle house, *mayson de decrepte.* **1889** *N. & Q.* 7th Ser. VIII. 213/1 The 'tolhouse' or 'tolbooth' (as our town halls were called in the Middle Ages). In this place [Great Yarmouth] the name of 'tolhouse' is still retained.

2. A house by a toll-gate or toll-bridge, occupied by the toll-taker; †a railway booking-office (*obs.*).

1763 *Chron.* in *Ann. Reg.* 91/1 Richard Watson, tollman of Marybone turnpike, was..murdered in his toll-house. **1841** *Civil Eng. & Arch. Jrnl.* IV. 322/2 The whole rise of the railway from its toll-house in Plymouth to the Prince-town terminus..is 1350 feet. **1906** T. SINTON *Poetry of Badenoch* 163 Her charms were proclaimed everywhere from the toll house to Castle Gordon.

3. *attrib.* and *Comb.*: **Toll House cookie** (also **toll-house cookie**) *U.S.*, the proprietary name of a kind of a biscuit containing chocolate chips.

1940 *Official Gaz.* (U.S. Patent Office) 18 June 591/2 *Toll House*.. For Cookies. Claims use since Apr. 10, 1940. **1962** *Trade Marks Jrnl.* 14 Feb. 179/1 *Toll House.* All goods included in Class 30. **1973** *Publishers Weekly* 22 Jan. 71/2 Henry begins suffering from dark spots that pop out all over his body; he soon looks like a toll-house cookie. **1978** R. NIXON *Memoirs* 316 After our meeting we had a delicious lunch of steak and fresh corn on the cob, followed by Lady Bird's homemade toll-house cookies.

tolliban, obs. form of TURBAN.

tolling, toling (ˈtəʊlɪŋ), *vbl. sb.*¹ Now *dial.* and *U.S.* [f. TOLL *v.*¹ + -ING¹.] **a.** The action of enticing, allurement; †incitement, instigation (*obs.*).

a **1225** *Ancr. R.* 116 þis is wowunge efter Godes grome, & tollunge of his vuel. *c* **1330** *Arth. & Merl.* (Kölbing) 5304 Bot Wawain, þat bi him cam, & he him of his tolling nam. *c* **1440** *Promp. Parv.* 496/1 Tollynge, styrynge, or mevynge to good or badde, *instigacio, excitacio.* **1496** *Dives & Paup.* I. x. 41/2 Suche richesses of clothynge of the ymages is but a tollynge of more offrynge.

b. *spec.* The luring or decoying of wild animals, as ducks or fish (see TOLL *v.*¹ 2); also *attrib. U.S.*

1838 J. J. AUDUBON *Ornith. Biogr.* IV. 6 The usual mode of taking these birds has been..by *toling*, as it is strangely termed, an operation by which the ducks are sometimes induced to approach within a few feet of the shore. **1858** LEWIS in Youatt *Dog* iii. 90 The toling season continues about three weeks from the first appearance of the ducks. **18..** ATWOOD in Goode *Amer. Fishes* (1888) 180 The present mode of catching mackerel by drifting and tolling with bait did not come into general use until 1812. **1879** *Dogs Gt. Brit. & Amer.* 271 The system pursued on the Chesapeake Bay and the North Carolina Sounds, and known as 'toling', is the most successful... A small dog..is trained to run up and down on the shore in the sight of the ducks. **1901** *Blackw. Mag.* Nov. 692/2 The judicious 'hough', 'hough' or tolling-call of the hunter.

ˈ**tolling,** *vbl. sb.*² [f. TOLL *v.*² + -ING¹.] The action of TOLL *v.*²; the sounding of a large bell by slow regularly repeated strokes; esp. that of the passing-bell.

1494 FABYAN *Chron.* VII. 352 [In 1264] by tollyng of the great belle of Paules, all the cytie shuld be redy shortly in harneys, to gyue attendaunce. **1526** [see PASSING-BELL]. **1599** MASSINGER, etc. *Old Law* III. i, I am afraid the tolling of the bell will wake her again. **1628** WITHER *Brit. Rememb.* IV. 69 My Fancy tuned so the Bell, As if her Towlings did the story tell Of my mortality. **1711** STEELE *Spect.* No. 14 ¶5, I..have not missed tolling in to Prayers six times in all those Years. **1874** SIR E. BECKETT *Denison's Clocks, Watches, & Bells* (ed. 6) 359 The great superiority of tone of bells ringing in full swing over tolling, and even of tolling over striking by a clock hammer, has been often noticed.

b. *transf.* A sound resembling this; *spec.* (*Sc.*) a special humming sound made by the queen bee before swarming (see quots. 1747, 1830).

1747 MAXWELL *Pract. Bee-Master* §147. 46 This Sound, commonly called Towling, proceeds, I suppose, from the young King, giving Signal to his Company to make ready for a March. **1830** *Edin. Encycl.* s.v. *Bee* II. 414/1 Most observers..affirm, that in the evening before swarming an uncommon humming or buzzing is heard in the hive, and a distinct sound from the queen, called tolling or calling. **1869** SIR V. BROOKE in *Life* (1894) 162 Nearer and nearer came the tolling of the grand old hound.

c. *attrib.* as **tolling-lever**, a lever attached to a bell or to the clapper by means of which the bell is tolled: see quot.

1874 SIR E. BECKETT *Denison's Clocks, Watches, & Bells* (ed. 6) 357-8 Tolling-levers... The great Worcester bell is hung on wedge-shaped gudgeons.., to enable it to be tolled, almost without friction, by a long lever; for the tower would not bear it in full swing... But..it answers equally well to toll it by a short lever..projecting from the top of the clapper, and pulled by a slight rope.

ˈ**tolling,** *vbl. sb.*³ Now *rare.* [f. TOLL *v.*³ + -ING¹.] The action of TOLL *v.*³; the taking or levying of toll; also payment to hop-pickers at so many bushels a shilling. Also *attrib.*

a **1350** *St. Matthew* 416 in Horstm. *Altengl. Leg.* (1881) 136 Saint Mathew..A toller was..With tolling mikell gude he gat. *c* **1440** *Promp. Parv.* 496/1 Tollynge, of myllarys, *multura.* **1509** BARCLAY *Shyp of Folys* (1874) I. 64 Brybours and Baylyes that lyue upon towlynge. **1546** in W. H. Turner *Select. Rec. Oxford* (1880) 179 The untrewe and excessyve tollinge of certayne quarters of wheate meale. **1562** PILKINGTON *Expos. Abdyas* 129 As though he were set to gather up Christs tolling money. **1886** J. CRAIG *Tollman's Lament* in R. Ford *Harp Perthshire* (1893) 346 Whan first my tollin' days began. **1888** *Pall Mall G.* 5 Oct. 5/1 If hops are pretty good, however, and the 'tolling' not too low—say, six bushels a shilling—an average hopper can live like a lord. *Ibid.* 5/2 When the hops are large and plentiful the farmer may commence his 'tolling' at twelve a shilling.

ˈ**tolling, toling,** *ppl. a.*¹ Now *dial.* and *U.S.* [f. TOLL *v.*¹ + -ING².] That 'tolls'; enticing, alluring; *spec.* used as a decoy (see TOLL *v.*¹ 2).

a **1225** *Ancr. R.* 50 Vor nabbe ȝe nout þene nome..of totinde ancres, ne of tollinde lokunges. **1642** MILTON *Apol. Smect.* Wks. 1851 III. 258 His own title; hung out like a toling signe-post to call passengers. **1868** R. B. ROOSEVELT *Florida & Game Water Birds* 336 Red is selected by the Southerners for their tolling dogs, but this is with the purpose of making them attractive.

ˈ**tolling,** *ppl. a.*² [f. TOLL *v.*² + -ING².] That tolls, as a bell.

1728 POPE *Dunc.* II. 228 With horns and trumpets now to madness swell, Now sink in sorrows with a tolling bell.

ˈ**tolling,** *ppl. a.*³ Now *rare.* [f. TOLL *v.*³ + -ING².] Taking toll; tax-gathering.

1641 J. JACKSON *True Evang. T.* II. 110 A greedy Wolfe, a tolling Publicane.

tollman (ˈtəʊlmən). Pl. **-men.** [f. TOLL *sb.*¹] A man who collects tolls; the keeper of a toll-gate.

1743 in Feret *Fulham* (1900) I. 63 It was agreed to take on Mr. Haines (tollman) again. **1763** [see TOLL-HOUSE 2]. **1782** COWPER *Gilpin* 243 The toll-men thinking as before That Gilpin rode a race. **1816** SCOTT *Tales my Landlord* Introd., The tollman at the well-frequented turnpike on the Wellbrae-head. **1886** W. J. TUCKER *E. Europe* 98 'You must pay toll', said the toll-man, stepping forward.

tol-lol (ˌtɒlˈlɒl), *a. slang.* Also **toll-loll.** [f. the first syllable of TOLERABLE, with riming extension.] Tolerable, pretty good, pretty well, passable, 'middling'.

1797 MRS. A. M. BENNETT *Beggar Girl* (1813) V. 137 Our lady did nothing..but stare at you all supper time; and he says you looked very toll-loll. **1809** *Sporting Mag.* XXXIII. 278 Lounged to the theatre..Kemble toll-loll. **1835** MARRYAT *Olla Podr.* iii, 'And how does..Maria find herself?'.. At last there was a reply. 'Oh! *tol, lol!*'

Hence **tol-ˈlol-ish** *a.*

1840 H. COCKTON *Valentine Vox* xxvii. 210 'And the ladies, how are they?' 'Why, they're only tollolish. You know what women are.' **1866** *Routledge's Every Boy's Ann.* 296 Two friends, who seemed rather tol-lol-ish. **1911** COUCH *True Tilda* ix, How do my bantlings find themselves this morning? Tol-lollish I trust.

tollon, var. TOYON.

tollsel: see TOLSEL.

tollutate, tollutation: see TOLUTATION.

tolly ('tɒlɪ). *School slang.* Now *arch.* or *Hist.* [app. f. TALLOW *sb.*] A (tallow) candle.

1890 BARRÈRE & LELAND *Dict. Slang.* II. 360/2 *Tolly* (public schools), a candle. **1905** *Daily News* 2 Aug. 4 Who does not recognise a living experience in Hugh working after prohibited hours for a scholarship, caught by the master and 'jawed for having a tolly alight'. **1924** E. MARSH tr. *La Fontaine's Fables* 77 The luckless tolly..Ended as a pool of grease.

Also as *v. intr.* (*Harrow*), to work by candle-light after the lights have been extinguished; to 'burn the midnight oil'; usu. with *up*.

1890 BARRÈRE & LELAND *Dict. Slang.* II. 360/2 *Tolly up, to* (Harrow School), to keep a candle alight after the gas has been turned off. **1894** WILKINS & VIVIAN *Green Bay Tree* I. 73 The process known as 'tollying up', or working by candle-light after the legal hours.

Tolman ('tɒlmən). Also **Tallman**. The surname *Tolman* used *ellipt.*, *attrib.*, or in the possessive in **Tolman('s) sweet(ing)**, to designate a yellow-skinned apple belonging to a variety originally developed in Rhode Island; also, the variety itself, or the tree bearing this fruit.

1822 J. THACHER *Amer. Orchardist* 139 Tolman sweeting ..is held in much estimation for family use during the autumn. **1838** *Genesee Farmer* 17 Mar. 81/1 Winter Fruit.. Tallman Sweeting. **1845** A. J. DOWNING *Fruits & Fruit Trees Amer.* viii. 137 The Tolman's Sweeting..is one of the most popular orchard sorts. **1867** J. A. WARDER *Amer. Pomology—Apples* 557 Tallman's Sweet..has traveled from Rhode Island wherever her hardy sons have gone westward. **1875** J. BURROUGHS *Winter Sunshine* 155 Now you have got a Tolman sweet. **1878** [see MCINTOSH]. **1893** A. M. DIAZ *William Henry Lett.* 7 He..set out Baldwins and Tallmans and Porters. **1909** S. B. GREEN *Pop. Fruit Growing* ix. 169 Some varieties..are adapted to a wide range as..Tolman Sweet. **1928** W. H. CHANDLER *N. Amer. Orchards* iv. 105 Tolman, the leading sweet apple to reach the market,..but few trees now being planted. **1949** *Boston Globe* 14 Aug. (Fiction Mag.) 11/4 We could look squarely at the tolman sweet standing all alone with the moonlight making its blossoms burn like candles. **1970** [see RUSSET *a.* 1 b].

†'**tolmen**. *Obs.* [Given by Borlase, 1754, as a common name in Cornwall, and explained by him as 'hole of stone', f. *tol* hole + *mên* stone; but app. the same word as Breton *taol men* or *tôl mên* 'table-stone', adopted by French archæologists (from the mutated *an dôl mên*) as DOLMEN, q.v.

Borlase app. interpreted the first element as Cornish *toll, toul, tewl*, = Welsh *twll*, 'hole', and was thus misled as to the meaning. (The three examples mentioned by him are app. all natural formations.) Some later writers have identified the second element as Eng. *man*, and made it sing. *tolman*, pl. *tolmen*. The word is now disused.]

See quots., and cf. DOLMEN, CROMLECH.

1754 BORLASE *Observ. Antiq. Cornw.* III. iii. 166 There is another kind of Stone-deity, which has never been taken notice of by any Author that I have heard of. It's common name in Cornwall and Scilly, is Tolmên; that is, the Hole of Stone. It consists of a large Orbicular Stone, supported by two Stones, betwixt which, there is a passage. *Ibid.* 167 The two Tolmêns at Scilly are Monuments..of the same kind with this. *Ibid.*, These Tolmens rest on supporters, and do not touch the Earth... Underneath these vast stones, there is a hole, or passage, between the Rocks. [*Note.* From this Hole they have the Name of Tolmen.] **1827** G. HIGGINS *Celtic Druids* Pref. 45 In Westphalia and East Friesland are some very curious examples of Tolmen. **1845** KNIGHT *Old Eng.* I. i. 18/2 Such are the remains which have been called Tolmen; a Tolman being explained to be an immense mass of rock placed aloft on two subjacent rocks which admit of a free passage between them.

†'**tol-me-'neer**. *Obs.* Also (? erron.) **tolmeiner, tol(l)meyner**. [app. = *toll* (= draw or attract) *me near*: see TOLL *v.*[1], and cf. COLMENIER.] A name for the Sweet William.

1578 LYTE *Dodoens* II. viii. 157 The floures grow at the toppe of the stalkes, many clustering togither after the manner of Tol-me-neers, or sweete Williams. *Ibid.* xiii. 334 They..are taken for Sweete Williams or Tolmeyners. **1597** GERARDE *Herbal* II. clxxiv. §4. 480 [The great Sweete William and the narrow leafed Sweete William are called] sweete Williams, Tolmeiners, and London Tuftes. **1629** PARKINSON *Paradisus* 320 *Armerius*, or *Armeria*... In some places they call the broader leafed kindes that are not spotted, Tolmeiners, and London tufts; but the speckled kinde is termed by our English Gentlewomen, for the most part, London pride.

tolmond, -mont(h, -mount, obs. forms of TWELVEMONTH.

†**tolne**. *Obs.* [OE. *toln* = OFris. *tolne, tolene*, OS. *tolna*, f. late L. *tolōneum*: whence also AF. *tolun(e.*] Tax, custom, duty; = TOLL *sb.*[1]

1023 in Thorpe *Charters* (1865) 318 Heore is þæt scip.. and se tolne of ealle scipen [L. *eorum est navicula..et theloneum omnium navium*]. **1038** *Ibid.* 339 Se þridda pænig of þære tolne on Sandwic. [**1292** BRITTON I. xvi. §5 De ceo [il] paya tolun as baillifs. *Ibid.* xxii. §13 Totes torcenouses prises..de travers ou de tolune.] *c* **1447–8** *Shillingford Lett.* (Camden) 93 All maner tolne of all maner marchaundyse. **1473** *Rolls of Parlt.* VI. 73/2 The Issues, Fermes, Tolnes, Revenuez, Amerciamentes and other Profittes.

†**tolner**. *Obs.* Forms: 1 tolnere, 5 tolenar, 5–6 tollenar, 6 tollener, tolner, 7 toulner. [OE. *tolner* = OFris., MLG. *tolner*, MDu. *tolnâre*, Du. *tollenaar*, OHG. *zol(l)anâri, zolneri*, MHG. *zolner*, Ger. *zöllner*:—late L. *tolōneāri-us*, for L. *telōniārius*, f. *telōnium* custom-house: see TOLL *sb.*[1]] A toll-taker, tax-gatherer, publican; = TOLLER[1] 1.

c **1050** *Suppl. Ælfric's Voc.* in Wr.-Wülcker 171/29 *Telonearius*, tolnere, *uel* tollere. **1481** CAXTON *Chesse* Contents, Receyuers of custum and tollenars [*ed.* 1474 toller]. **1483** —— *Gold. Leg.* 125/1 Why wepest yᵘ tolenar? **1546** *St. Papers Hen. VIII*, XI. 199 Somme of the tolleners war comme, and somme war not. **1563–87** FOXE *A. & M.* (1596) 295/2 The pope of them maketh his tolners and bankers to get in his monie. *a* **1603** T. CARTWRIGHT *Confut. Rhem. N.T.* 89 The Toulner..asking tribute house by house.

toloache (tɒl'wætʃɪ). Also **toloachi**. [a. Mexican Sp. *toloache*, a. Nahuatl *toloatzin*, f. *toloa* to bow the head + *tzin* reverential.] A preparation of a plant of the genus *Datura* used as an intoxicating and hallucinogenic drug.

1894 [see MARIJUANA, MARIHUANA 1 a]. **1948** A. L. KROEBER *Anthropol.* (rev. ed.) xiv. 567 Southern and south-central California: Initiation of youths with *toloache* or jimson-weed drug (*Datura* species). The narcosis is accompanied by visions, which were considered sacred. **1964** I. FLEMING *You only live Twice* vii. 93 Addiction to toloachi, a drink made from *D. tatula*, causes chronic imbecility.

†**toloney**. *Obs.* Also *Sc.* 6 **tholoney**, 7 **tholnie**. [ad. late and med.L. *t(h)olonēum* toll, for L. *telōnium*, a. Gr. τελώνιον toll, tax: see TOLL *sb.*[1] (In med.L. also *tholneum*, Du Cange, whence F. *tonlieu.*)] = TOLL *sb.*[1]

1517 in *Reg. Mag. Sig. Scot.* 1542. 644/2 We..grantis to him and his airis,..that thai..bruke ilk yeir..within the.. Toun of Clakmannane, commoun fairis in the feist of Sanct Bartilmo..with all tholoneis. **1563–87** FOXE *A. & M.* (1596) 297/2 Great taxes and tolonies and tenths were required of his subiects. **1633** *Sc. Acts Chas. I* (1870) V. 97/2 With all ..multurs frie ports or harberies customes tholnies and vthers.

†'**to-look**. *Sc.* Also **to-luyke, -luik**. [f. TO-[1] + LOOK *sb.*] A looking to, a prospect.

a **1572** KNOX *Hist. Ref.* III. Wks. 1848 II. 174 Thocht scho, the to-luyke of Ingland sall allure mony wowaris to me. *a* **1598** ROLLOCK *Serm.* Wks. 1849 I. 306 It is the to-luik to hevin that makis the saull of Paull to rejoyce. **1678** J. BROWN *Life of Faith* I. i. (1824) 14 The sure expectation and to-look for the better and more enduring substantial thing above.

To'losa-wood. [f. *Tolosa*, name of a place near Hobart.] A name in Tasmania of the wood of *Pittosporum bicolor*, also called *cheese-wood* in Victoria, and in both countries *white-wood*.

1866 *Treas. Bot.*, Tolosa-wood, *Pittosporum bicolor*. **1884** MILLER *Plant-n.*, *Pittosporum bicolor*, Cheese-wood or White-wood of Victoria, Tolosa-wood, White-wood of Tasmania.

†**to-louk, to-luke**, *v. Obs.* [OE. *tolúcan*, f. TO-[2] + *lúcan*, LOUK *v.*[2] to pull.] *trans.* To pull or tear to pieces; to pull apart, wrench asunder.

c **890** tr. *Bæda's Hist.* v. vi. (1890) 402 Forðon mine innoðas..fylle tolocene wæran. *c* **1205** LAY. 2602 Heo..to-luken þene king & his leomen to-drowen. *a* **1225** *Juliana* 12 (Roy. MS.) Ichulle leoten deor to teoren ant to luken þe.

†**tolowr**. *Obs. rare.* (Suggested to be the TILLER of a cross-bow.)

? *a* **1400** *Morte Arth.* 3619 Tolowris tentyly takelle they ryghttene, Brasene hedys fulle brode buskede one flones.

‖'**tolpatch**. Also **tolpatz**. [Ger. *tolpatsch*, earlier *tolpatz*: according to Kluyver (Beitr. XXX. 211), Magyar *talpas* foot-soldier, f. *talp* sole of the foot.] A foot-soldier. Hence '**tolpatchery** (*nonce-wd.*) infantry.

1705 *Lond. Gaz.* No. 4151/1 The Hungarian Horse were routed, and their Tolpatzes or Foot escaped. **1864** CARLYLE *Fredk. Gt.* XV. ii. IV. 21 Tolpatches, Pandours, Warasdins. *Ibid.* v. 65 The matter..not one of Tolpatchery alone.

tolpyn, obs. form of THOLE-PIN.

tolsel ('təʊlsəl), **tolzey** ('təʊlzɪ). *local.* Forms: α. 4 tol(l)seld, 5 tollsell, (6 tollsill, towllsill, 7 toll(e)shell, towlsell, towsell, towelshill, towellshell, 7–8 tholsel(l), (7 tolser, towlsher); β. 5- tolsey, 8- tolzey. [ME. *tolseld, tollsell*, f. OE. TOLL *sb.*[1] + OE. *seld* seat, or *sæl, sęle* hall: cf. OE. *tollsetl* 'tolbooth, custom-house'.]

The ancient name in some English and Irish towns for the guildhall, tolbooth, or borough court-house; also for the local court of justice (more fully *tolsel* or *tolzey court*) there held.

The original form, long retained in Ireland, has been reduced in some English towns to *tolsey* ('tɒlsɪ) (sometimes only the traditional name of the building), or *tolzey*, as in the existing *Tolzey Court* of Bristol: see quots. 1883–4, 1906.

α. [**1344** in *Litt. Red Bk. Bristol* (1900) I. 41 Constabularii, ballivi et alii ministri tenentes placita in Tols[eto].] **1373** *Charter Edw. III*, 8 Aug. (Seyer *Charters Bristol*, 1812, 50), Placita, quæ in curia nostra in dicta villa Bristoll' vocata Tollseld coram senescallo et aliis ministris nostris..teneri consuevere. **1486** *Galway Arch.* in *10th Rep. Hist. MSS. Comm.* App. v. 385 His matter or suite be pledid and tried in the Tollsell or Courte-housse befor the Mayor. **1584** *Ibid.* 435 To appeare in the Towllsill or court howse. **1621** *Ibid.* 469 The Towsell or Courthowse of Galwey. **1632** *Ibid.* 480 The Mayor..and Comonaltie of Galwey..assembled in their Towelshill. **1680** *Ibid.* 505 The concerne of the Corporation formerly acted by Tholsell was vested in the Council by charter. **1701** *Ibid.* 515 Nor doe they enjoy any houses..except the Tholsell and gaole thereunder. **1701** *Lond. Gaz.* No. 3721/3 *Dublin*... The Lord Mayor, with the Aldermen,..and Commons of the City, assembled at the Tholsell at Four a Clock. **1769** WESLEY *Jrnl.* 15 June, I.. preached in the Tholsel [Kilkenny].

β. **1479** in *Eng. Gilds* 421 The Maire and the Shiref of Bristowe..to assemble with all the hole counseill, at the Tolsey. **1656** BLOUNT *Glossogr.*, *Tolsey* or Toldsey is a place in the City of Bristow, answerable to the old Exchange in London, where the Merchants meet. **1697** *Lond. Gaz.* No. 3336/3 *Hereford, October* 26... Being returned to the Tolsey, the Mayor gave the Gentry an Entertainment. **1701** *Ibid.* No. 3709/4 The Fair will be kept [at Westbury]..on the first Friday in Lent, as formerly; and a Tolsey duly kept. **1706** *Ibid.* No. 4289/3 The Tolzey or Benefit of the Fair of Wellow aforesaid. **1883** *Wharton's Law Lex.*, *Tolsey*,..a local tribunal, usually spelt 'Tolzey', for small civil causes held at the Guildhall, Bristol. **1884** *Arrowsmith's Dict. Bristol* 278/1 In this Court of the Tolzey all actions of debt, assumpsit, covenant, trespass, trover, and other civil actions arising within the City [of Bristol] could be prosecuted by action, or by foreign attachment... The trial of the Court is by Jury. **1898** J. A. GIBBS *Cotswold Village* 190 The ancient building in the centre of the town [Burford] is called the 'Tolsey'. **1906** *Daily Chron.* 22 Aug. 4/6 Some quaint local courts which have survived innumerable Judicature Acts, such as the Tolzey Court of Bristol and the Court of Passage at Liverpool: courts which for expedition can put all others to the blush.

†**tol'sester**. *Obs.* Also **toll-**. [f. TOLL *sb.*[1] + SESTER.] A toll or duty of a sester of ale (SESTER 2) formerly payable in some manors to the lord of the manor for liberty to brew and sell ale.

1232 *Charter Roll* 16 Hen. III, m. 2 (P.R.O.) De singulis bracinis cerusie venalis vnum sexterium ceruisie quod dici consueuit Tolsester. **1499** *Rot. Plac.* in *Itin. apud Cestriam* 14 H. 7 (Blount 1670), Per Tolsester clamat esse quietum de reddendo unum Sextarium Cervisiæ quod continet xvi Lagenas. *c* **1640** J. SMYTH *Lives Berkeleys* (1883) I. 341 In the 13ᵗʰ of Edward the third, 284. tollcesters, which I call brewings. **1679** BLOUNT *Anc. Tenures* 153 If any Alewife brewed Ale to sell, she was bound to satisfy the Lord for Tolsester. **1701** *Cowell's Interpr.*, *Tolcestrum, Tolsaster*. **1706** PHILLIPS, Tolsaster or Tolsester.

Tolstoyan ('tɒlstɔɪən), *a.* and *sb.* Also **Tolstoian**. [f. proper name *Tolstoy* + -AN.]

A. *adj.* Of or pertaining to Count Leo N. Tolstoy, a famous Russian writer and social reformer (1828–1910). **B.** *sb.* A follower of Tolstoy or his teachings. So '**Tolstoyism**, the opinions or teachings of Tolstoy; '**Tolstoyist** = *Tolstoyan* b.

1894 *Westm. Gaz.* 12 Nov. 5/3 An article by a Russian correspondent on the harrying of Tolstoyists by the police in the Southern and Central provinces... the banishment of a certain Prince Khilkov..a rich landowner who had given up his estates to the poor in his neighbourhood, and was actively engaged in propagating the peculiar tenets known as Tolstoyism. **1898** *Daily News* 6 Oct. 5/4 Anything more distant from the Quaker, or Stundist, or Tolstoian view of military things..it would be difficult to imagine. **1900** *Westm. Gaz.* 22 Mar. 2/2 We are not converted to any Tolstoyan gospel by this book. **1901** *Daily Chron.* 30 May 3/1 Already the Tolstoyans are becoming a sect. **1905** *Contemp. Rev.* May 685 The Tolstoyan gospel of Christian morality apart from faith in the Supernatural.

tolt (təʊlt), *sb. Old Law.* [a. AF. *tolte, toulte* = med.L. *tolta*, f. L. *tollĕre* 'to take up, raise, lift', with the form of a sb. from pa. pple.] A writ by which a cause was removed from a court-baron to the county court.

[**1294** *Placita coram rege*, Easter 22 *Edw. I*, 18 *d*, Dicit quod..Alicia numquam toltam predicti placiti per probacionem..ei optulit tanquam vicecomiti. **1337** *Year-bks. 11–12 Edw. III* (Rolls) 307 Le vicomte manda qil navoit pas fait la toulte.] **1607** COWELL *Interpr.*, *Tolt* (*tolta*) is a writ whereby a cause depending in a court Baron, is remoued into the county court. **1647** N. BACON *Disc. Govt. Eng.* I. xlviii. (1739) 83 This Suit was originally begun and had its final determination in the County-Court, and not brought by a Tolt out of the Hundred-Court. **1768** BLACKSTONE *Comm.* III. iv. 34 The proceedings on a writ of right may be removed into the county court by a precept from the sheriff called a *tolt*, '*quia tollit atque eximit causam e curia baronum*.' **1876** DIGBY *Real Prop.* ii. §2. 73 *note.* **1912** *Eyre of Kent* (Selden) II. 87 The plea [1313–4] was removed by a tolt into the County Court.

Hence **tolt** *v.* (*nonce-wd.*), *trans.* to raise, lift up.

1896 *Calendar Inner Temple* I. Introd. 35 These [i.e. the clerks commoners], after certain probation, could be called or 'tolted' to the Masters' Commons table.

Toltec ('tɒltɛk), *sb.* and *a.* Also 8 **Tolteca**, 9 **Tolteck, Tultec**. [ad. Sp. *tolteca*, ad. Nahuatl *toltecatl*, pl. *tolteca*.] **A.** *sb.* (A member of) a Nahuatl people who dominated the valley of Mexico *c* 900–1150 A.D., before the arrival of the Aztecs. **B.** *adj.* Of or pertaining to this people.

1787, etc. [see OLMEC 1]. **1814** [see AZTEC *sb.* and *a.*]. **1843** W. H. PRESCOTT *Conquest of Mexico* I. I. i. 12 The Toltecs were well instructed in agriculture. **1875** *Encycl. Brit.* I. 696/1 The Toltec and Aztec races. **1939** G. Greene *Lawless Roads* iii. 104 Quetzalcoatl..was the white Toltec god of culture. **1955** *Sci. Amer.* May 82 To be a Toltec in Mexico was to be an exponent of civilization. **1977** *Time* 21 Feb. 19/1 He wrote his mystical novelette about the god Quetzalcoatl, who figures so largely in the Toltec legends of the Mexican people. **1979** P. Theroux *Old Patagonian Express* iii. 52 Towards Tula, a treeless desert..rose into peaks like pyramids. This was the capital of the Toltecs.

Hence '**Toltecan** *sb.* and *a.*

1839 *Penny Cycl.* XV. 165/1 The older..monuments of Mexico are..the productions..of the Toltecans. *Ibid.* 165/2 The extraordinary vastness of..these..Toltecan constructions.

tolter ('toltər), *a.* (*adv.*) *Sc.* and *dial.* Also 6 **towter**, 9 **toolter**. [Late ME.; goes with next; exact relation obscure.] Moving unsteadily; unsteady, unstable, tottering; insecure, precarious; in quot. 1430–40, giddy. Also as *adv.* unsteadily.

1423 Jas. I *Kingis Q.* ix, Sothe It is, that, on hir tolter quhele, Euery wight cleuerith In his stage. *Ibid.* clxiv, So tolter quhilum did sche it to-wrye. **1430–40** Lydg. *Bochas* iv. xxiii. (MS. Bodl. 263) 252/1 Tascende the mounteyn, feeble wer ther chynes Ther hedis toltir, & ther brayn gan faille. *c* **1470** Henryson *Orpheus & Eur.* 283 Before his [Tantalus'] face ane apill hang also, Fast at his mouth, apon a tolter threid. **1560** Rolland *Seven Sages* 29 That we may all prouyde Sum help, that may put by this towter tide. **1880** Dennison in *Orcadian Sketch-Bk.* 119 His bowie legs ..Wur trumblan' like twa toolter stoops.

'**tolter**, *v. dial.* [Early mod.Eng.: app. the same as MDu., Du. *touteren* to waver, totter, swing, *touter* a swing, representing an earlier OLG. or OS. **taltrōn* (cf. *oud:—ald*), which exists in a dial. Du. *talteren* (Franck), = OE. *tealtrian* to totter, stagger, be unsteady.] *intr.* To move unsteadily; to flounder; to turn or toss about; to hobble; to jolt along. Hence '**toltering** *ppl. a.*

1529 More *Suppl. Soulys* 43 You walter peraduenture and tolter in syknes fro syde to syde. **1533** —— *Answ. Poysoned Bk.* Wks. 1039/2 There lyeth he still tumblyng and toltryng in myre. **1821** Clare *Vill. Minstr.* II. 76 From..dusty lane, Where home the cart-horse tolters with the swain.

tolu (təʊ'l(j)uː, 'təʊl(j)uː). [From *Tolu* (to'lu) (now *Santiago de Tolu*) in the Republic of Colombia, whence obtained.] In **tolu balsam, balsam of Tolu**: A balsam obtained by incision from the bark of the **tolu-tree**, *Myrospermum* (*Myroxylon*) *toluiferum*, a leguminous tree of tropical S. America; used in medicine and perfumery.

1671 Salmon *Syn. Med.* iii. xxiii. 444 Balsam of Tolu.. hath the same virtue with the former. **1789** W. Buchan *Dom. Med.* App. (1790) 697 Tincture of the Balsam of Tolu. **1855** Bailey *Spir. Leg.* in *Mystic*, etc. (ed. 2) 81 Not less renowned Than lote, nepenthes, moly, or tolu. **1858** Hogg *Veg. Kingd.* 282 Balsam of Tolu is a stimulating tonic, with a peculiar tendency to the pulmonary organs. **1871** Garrod *Mat. Med.* (ed. 3) 210–11 *Balsamum Tolutanum.* Tolu Balsam..or Balsam of Tolu Tree. **1912** J. Terry & Sons *Let.*, We can trace their manufacture as Tolu Lozenges for about 100 years.

tolu-, the prec. word as a formative element in chemical terms (first in Ger. *toluin*, Berzelius 1842, whence in Eng. *toluol* 1845, *toluene* 1871). '**toluate**, a salt of toluic acid, as *toluate of calcium*, $C_{16}H_{14}Ca''O_4$. **toluene** ('tɒl(j)uːiːn, 'təʊl-) [so named because obtained by Deville 1841, by the dry distillation of tolu balsam], C_7H_8 = benzylic hydride, $C_7H_7.H$, a colourless very mobile strongly refracting liquid, with a smell like benzene and a burning taste; discovered by Pelletier and Walter, 1837; the source of many compounds and substitution products, into the names of which it enters, e.g. ***chlorotoluene***, ***methyltoluene***, ***toluene-sulphuric***, etc.; hence **tolu'enic** *a.*, as ***toluenic sulphydrate***. **toluic** ('tɒl(j)uːɪk, 'təʊl-) *a.* [tolu(ene + -ic], in ***toluic*** or ***toluylic acid***, $C_8H_8O_2$, an aromatic acid, homologous with benzoic acid, prepared from toluene, cymene, or xylene; so ***toluic aldehyde***, C_8H_7OH, ***toluic chloride***, C_8H_7OCl, ***toluic ether***, etc. '**toluides**, compounds homologous with the anilides, derived from toluidine salts by abstraction of water, e.g. ***aceto-toluide***. '**toluol**, earlier name of *toluene*. **tolu'oxyl**, C_8H_7O, the radical of toluic acid and its derivatives. **toluquinone** [quinone], the aromatic compound $CH_3C_6H_3O_2$; also, any of the derivatives of this compound. **to'luric** *a.* [uric], in ***toluric acid***, $C_{10}H_{11}NO_3$, also called ***toluglycic acid***, homologous with hippuric acid, produced in the passage of toluic acid through the animal body; its salts are **to'lurates**. **toluyl** ('tɒl(j)uːɪl, 'təʊl-) [-yl], the radical, C_8H_9; hence **tolu'ylic** *a.*, of or belonging to toluyl, as ***toluylic alcohol***, C_8H_9OH, etc.

1860 Kopp in *Phil. Trans.* CL. 262 *Toluate of Ethyl.. $C_{20}H_{12}O_4$. **1868** Watts *Dict. Chem.* V. 862 A mixture of toluate and formate of calcium yields by distillation toluic aldehyde, C_8H_8O. **1871** *Jrnl. Chem. Soc.* XXIV. 680 On the determination of the chemical position in some *Toluene derivatives. **1887** *Standard* 16 Sept. 3/3 The toluene was the root substance from which..saccharine was prepared. **1894** *Daily News* 26 Jan. 5/4 One ton of good cannel coal, when distilled in gas retorts, leaves twelve gallons of coal-tar, from which are produced a pound of benzine, a pound of toluene, a pound and a-half of phenol, six pounds of naphthalene, a small quantity of xylene, and half-a-pound of anthracene for dyeing purposes. **1857** Miller *Elem. Chem.* III. 430 In the benzoic series the existence of three homologous terms,.. the benzoic, the *toluic, and the cuminic series. *Ibid.* 475 But the acid.., the *toluic* (or toluylic), is known. **1873** Watts *Fownes' Chem.* (ed. 11) 816 Toluic Acid is derived from dimethyl-benzene. **1880** *Nature* XXI. 218/2 A toluic alcohol. **1845–8** Noad in *Mem. & Proc. Chem. Soc.* III. 422 Proposed the more appropriate name of *toluol. **1857** Miller *Elem. Chem.* III. 479 When balsam of tolu is distilled, it yields benzoic ether and a hydrocarbon..termed toluole. **1863** Tyndall *Heat* i. 20 Let us compare in this respect toluol and water. **1866** Roscoe *Elem. Chem.* 335 A series of bodies, isomeric with these toluol compounds, exists. **1891** *Anthony's Photogr. Bull.* IV. 415 Formula for the production of toluol matt varnish. [**1870** *Jrnl. Chem. Soc.* XXXIII. 135 (*caption*) Trichlorotoluquinone.] **1874** *Index Jrnl. Chem. Soc. 1848–72* 254/1 *Toluquinones. **1975** *Nature* 20 Nov. 194/1 The chemicals present in the glandular secretions of insects are often exceedingly diverse. .. They comprise..a great number of phenolic substances and quinones (such as phenol..and toluquinone). **1868** Watts *Dict. Chem.* V. 869 *Toluric acid crystallises from boiling water in colourless laminæ; from alcohol in trimetric prisms. *Ibid.*, *Toluyl. C_8H_9. The radicle of toluylic alcohol and its allied compounds; isomeric with xylyl. **1873** Ralfe *Phys. Chem.* Introd. 19 Benzene C_6H_6 and Toluene C_7H_8 are the most important members of this series... From them are derived the important monad radicals phenyl C_6H_5 and toluyl C_7H_7. **1896** *Allbutt's Syst. Med.* I. 196 The action on the blood of certain poisons, such as arseniuretted hydrogen and toluyl-endiamine. **1862** Miller *Elem. Chem.* (ed. 2) III. 462 *Toluylia is a fusible crystalline solid, which boils at 388°. **1857** *Toluylic [see *toluic*].

†**to-'lug**, *v. Obs.* Also 4–5 **to-logg**. [f. to-[2] + lug *v.*] *trans.* To lug or pull about.

1362 Langl. *P. Pl.* A. ii. 192 Liȝtliche Lyȝere leop a-wey þenne, Lurkede [*v.r.* lurkynge] þorw lones, to-logged [*v.r.* to-luggid, B. ii. 216 to-lugged] of Monye.

to'luidine. *Chem.* Also toluidene, -in. [f. tolu- + -idine.]

a. A crystalline base, $C_7H_7(NH_2)$, produced by the action of sulphuric acid on nitrotoluene, solidifying in snow-white crystals, which gradually turn brown on contact with the air: the source of numerous compounds, e.g. ***ˌazoto'luidine***, ***ˌphenylto'luidine***, etc. Also called *aˌmido'toluene*, and formerly *toluylia*.

1850 Daubeny *Atom. The.* viii. (ed. 2) 243 Methylaniline being identical with toluidine, an alkali obtained from the balsam of Tolu. **1857** Miller *Elem. Chem.* III. 467 Benzo-hydrochloric ether when heated in a sealed tube with ammonia furnishes the volatile base toluidine. **1866** Roscoe *Elem. Chem.* 348 A basic substance..analogous to aniline, and called amido-toluol, or Toluidine.

b. **toluidine blue**, a thiazine dye, $C_{15}H_{16}ClN_3S$, now used chiefly as a biological stain.

1898 *Philadelphia Med. Jrnl.* II. 343 Toluidin-blue is a member of the aniline group closely related chemically to methylene-blue. **1908** Toluidene blue [see metachromatically *adv.*]. **1947** *Ann. Rev. Microbiol.* I. 346 Both methylene blue..and toluidin blue..have shown therapeutic activity in experimental rickettsial infections in animals. **1981** J. A. Kiernan *Histol. & Histochem. Methods* xviii. 258/1 The procedure..for demonstrating metachromasia with toluidine blue gives excellent results when used as a Nissl stain.

†**To'lutan**, *a. Obs. rare.* [ad. mod.L. *Tolūtān-us* of Tolu.] Of Tolu, as ***Tolutan balsam***.

1681 tr. *Willis' Rem. Med. Wks.* Vocab., *Tolutan balsom*.. brought from the Indies.

†**tolu'tation**. *Obs. rare.* Also toll-. [f. stem of L. *tolūtim* adv. 'at a trot' + -ation; cf. *tolutārius* adj. trotting.] *prop.* Trotting; but used by Sir T. Browne, Butler, and others, for 'ambling'; in later use only as a humorous pedantry. So †**to'lutate** (**toll-**) *v.* (*humorous*), *intr.* to trot (or amble); †**tolu'tiloquence** (*rare*[−0]) [L. *tolūtiloquentia*], talking 'at a trot', voluble speech.

1646 Sir T. Browne *Pseud. Ep.* iv. vi. 193 Whether they move *per latera*, that is, two legs of one side together, which is Tollutation or ambling; or *per diametrum*,..which is Succussation or trotting. **1656** Blount *Glossogr.*, *Tolutation* .., an ambling pace, a going easie... *Tolutiloquence*.., a smooth or nimble kinde of speaking. **1663** Butler *Hud.* i. ii. 47 They rode, but Authors having not Determined whether Pace or Trot (That is to say, whether Tollutation, As they do term 't, or Succussation) We leave it, and go on. **1755** Johnson, *Tolutation*, the act of pacing or ambling. **1796** R. L. Edgeworth in *Life* (1821) II. 153 You compose in your chaise, and I on horseback, which..is the reason why your lines roll so smoothly, and mine partake so much of Tolutation. **1803** Fessenden *Terrible Tractoration* 39 We'll jog along in plain narration; And tollutate o'er turnpike path.

tolvet(t, variant of tovet, two-peck measure.

†**toly**, *v. Obs.* [Obs. by-form of toil *v.*[1] Cf. the similar 'oly or oyl', 'bolyyn or boylyn', 'spoylyn or spolyon', 'spoylyng or spolyynge'; also *assolye* = assoil, and the Sc. form *tulȝie*, tuilyie.] = toil *v.*[1] 1, to dispute, argue, *esp.* to contend or plead in a lawsuit.

c **1440** *Promp. Parv.* 345/1 Mootyn, or tolyon (*P.* motyn, or pletyn), *discepto, placito.* Motynge, or tolyynge, or pleytynge, *disceptacio. Ibid.* 496/1 Tolyon, or motyn.

toly, variant of tuly *a. Obs.*

tolyl ('təʊlɪl). *Chem.* [f. tolu + -yl.] A hypothetical monatomic radical, C_7H_7, isomeric with cresyl, called also benzyl, which may be supposed to exist in benzylic alcohol, toluene, and other compounds. Entering into the names of many compounds and substitution products, e.g. ***tolyl-*** (or ***benzyl-***)***acetamide***, ***tolyl-carbamide***, ***tolyl-sulphurous***, ***tolylene***, C_7H_6 = benzylene, ***tolylene-diamine***, etc. Hence **to'lylic** *a.*

1868 Watts *Dict. Chem.* V. 870 The name *benzyl* is the most convenient for it, as tolyl is too much like toluyl. *Ibid.*, Tolylic or benzylic bromide.

tolypeutine (tɒlɪ'pjuːtaɪn), *a.* and *sb. Zool.* [f. mod.L. *Tolypeutes* + -ine[1].] **a.** *adj.* Belonging to the genus *Tolypeutes* of armadillos. **b.** *sb.* An armadillo of this genus.

1885 *Stand. Nat. Hist.* (1888) V. 50 The Apars, or Tolypeutines, exhibit the extreme of modification in the family.

tolypyrin (tɒlɪ'paɪərɪn). *Pharm.* [f. tolyl, after *antipyrin*.] The compound $C_{12}H_{14}N_2O$ (*tolyl-dimethyl-pyr-azol-on*), the homologue of antipyrin.

1893 *Brit. Med. Jrnl.* 25 Mar. 47/3 In acute rheumatism tolypyrin produced a similar effect to that observed after antipyrin. *Ibid.*, Tolypyrin is excreted in the urine.

tolzey: see the historical form tolsel.

Tom (tɒm), *sb.*[1] Forms: 4–6 **tomme**, (5 **thomme**, 6 **thom**), 6– **Tom**; also, in general uses, with lower-case initial.

1. A familiar shortening of the Christian name *Thomas*; often a generic name for any male representative of the common people; esp. in ***Tom and Tib*** (cf. *Jack and Jill*); ***Tom, Dick, and*** (or *or*) ***Harry***, any men taken at random from the common run; ***Blind Tom***, blind-man's-buff.

1377- [see 7 c]. **1588** Shaks. *L.L.L.* v. ii. 924 Dicke the Shepheard blowes his naile; And Tom beares Logges into the hall. **1596** —— *1 Hen. IV*, ii. iv. 9, I am sworn brother to a leash of Drawers, and can call them by their names, as Tom, Dicke, and Francis. **1606** *Choice, Chance*, etc. (1881) 72 When Tom and Tib, were in their true delight, And he lou'd her, and she held him full deere. **1734** *Vocal Miscellany* (ed. 2) I. 332 Farewell, Tom, Dick, and Harry, Farewell, Moll, Nell, and Sue. **1749** Fielding (*title*) Tom Jones. **1762** J. Otis *Vindication House Representatives Massachusetts-Bay* 21 That I should die very soon after my head should be cut off..whether chopped off to gratify a tyrant by the christian name of Tom, Dick or Harry is evident. **1790** Dibdin *Song, Poor Tom* i, Here, a sheer hulk, lies poor Tom Bowling. **1815** *Farmer's Almanack* (Boston, Mass.) in Kittredge *Old Farmer* (1904) 88 So he hired Tom, Dick and Harry, and at it they all went. **1818** in *J. Adams' Wks.* (1856) X. 351 Tom, Dick, and Harry were not to censure them and their Council. **1857** Hughes (*title*) Tom Brown's School-days. **1864** Trollope *Can you forgive Her?* I. xxxii. 254 Didn't he want to squander every shilling of the property,..property which I could give to Tom, Dick, or Harry tomorrow, if I liked? **1865** Alex. Smith *Summer in Skye* I. 46 Thereafter Tom, Jack and Harry; for every cab, carriage and omnibus..is now allowed to fall in. **1891** Tom, Dick, and Harry [see Dick *sb.*[1] 1]. **1906** I. Zangwill *Let.* 29 Oct. in K. Gregory *First Cuckoo* (1978) 64 And have these wise and witty ladies less right than Tom, Dick or 'Arry to a direct influence on the government of their country? **1909** Healey *Sp. in Ho. of Comm.* 3 Sept., He never could understand this system of playing Blind Tom with the House of Commons—especially in a taxing statute. **1974** *New Statesman* 22 Nov. 740/3 There is no legislation for giving them a licence, so that any Tom, Dick or Harry can work as a guide and give..wrong information.

†**b.** = *Tom o' Bedlam*: see 7 c. *Obs.*

1561 Awdelay *Frat. Vacab.* 3 An Abraham man is he that ..fayneth hym selfe mad..and nameth himselfe poore Tom. **1605** Shaks. *Lear* iii. iv. 51 Who giues any thing to poore Tom? *Ibid.* 59 Blisse thy fiue Wits, Toms a cold.., Do poore Tom some charitie, whom the foule Fiend vexes. **1682–3** Dixon *Canidia* i. ii, We treat mad-Bedlams, Toms, and Besses, With ceremonies and caresses.

c. A clown; cf. tom-fool b.

1820 *Sporting Mag.* VI. 284 Two or three of the company called toms or clowns.

d. A girl or woman. *Austral. slang.*

[**1882** *Sydney Slang Dict.* 8 *Tom-tart*, Sydney, phrase for a girl or sweetheart.] **1906** E. Dyson *Fact'ry 'Ands* i. 8, I may be wrong in thinkin' your tom was tryin' t' mash ther man shootin' off ther camera. **1951** D. Stivens *Jimmy Brockett* 102 'You did, darling,' one of the little social toms said. She was a nuggety little sheila.

e. A prostitute. *slang.*

[**1914** Jackson & Hellyer *Vocab. Criminal Slang* 84 *Tommy*... A prostitute.] **1941** V. Davis *Phenomena in Crime* xix. 255 *Tom*, old prostitute. **1955** M. Hastings *Cork & Serpent* i. 12 I'll bet she's holding out on us. We know these toms, sir. **1957** H. Williamson *Golden Virgin* ix. 134 'Is Lily a tom?'.. 'Not within the meaning of the act. She works in Nett's Laundry, on the lower side of Randiswell Bridge. Of course, I don't say she doesn't have a bit of fun at times, but that's her business.' **1977** *Time Out* 17–23 June 18/1 What doesn't appear in the film but is very revealing about police mentality, is the filing room on prostitutes (or Toms as they are called).

f. Short for UNCLE TOM: a Black regarded, esp. by other Blacks, as behaving in a servile, ingratiating, or complaisant manner towards white people. *slang.*

1959 *Esquire* Nov. 122/1 *Tom*.., a Negro who does not try to maintain his complete dignity before whites. **1968** N. GIOVANNI in W. King *Black Short Story Anthol.* (1972) 26 Toms, I told him, only have power if we let them have power. I mean, if a tom says get off the streets and you get off the streets, then that's your fault, not his. **1973** R. LUDLUM *Matlock Paper* ii. 14 The African studies may be in trouble. That 'Tom' I recruited from Howard turned out to be..a little to the right of Louis XIV. **1975** *Publishers Weekly* 3 Feb. 72/1 By installing 'American Nigger Toms' as the Third World élite, the U.S. has controlled the angry hunger of the poor populace.

†2. The knave of trumps in the game of gleek.

1655, *a* **1659** [see TIB *sb.* 2]. **1680** COTTON *Compl. Gamester* vi. 65 The Ace [of trumps] is called Tib, the Knave Tom.

3. As the name of some exceptionally large bells, esp. in ***Great, Mighty Tom, Tom of Lincoln, Tom of Christ Church, of Oxford, Tom of Exeter***, etc.

1630 WHITE in Rimbault *Rounds, Catches*, etc. 30 (Farmer) Great Tom is cast; And Christ Church bells ring ..And Tom is last. **1635** R. JOHNSON *Tom a Lincolne* ii. (1682) B iij, He sent..a thousand pounds..to be bestowed upon a great Bell to be rung at his Funeral, which Bell he caused to be called Tom a Lincoln, after his own Name. **1682** H. ALDRICH *Upon Christ Church Bells Oxf.*, The Devil a man Will leave his can, Till he hears the mighty Tom. **1685** WOOD *Life* 7 July (O.H.S.) III. 151 And another [bonfire] in Ch. Ch. great quadrangle, at which time Great Tom rang out. **1705** HICKERINGILL *Priest-cr.* I. (1721) 63 Whose Tongue was as clamorous and loud almost as Tom a Lincoln. **1787** [see TINKLER 2]. **1839** *Penny Cycl.* XIV. 8/2 The old bell, called the Tom of Lincoln..being exceeded only by 'Mighty Tom' of Oxford..and 'Great Tom' of Exeter. **1886** RUSKIN *Præterita* I. xi. 369, I..amused myself till Tom rang in.

4. a. (Usually ***Long Tom***.) A long trough formerly used in gold-washing: see quot. 1859. Sometimes applied to the rocker or 'cradle'.

1855 [see LONG TOM 2]. **1859** CORNWALLIS *Panorama New World* I. 135 The Long Tom..consists of a trough ten or twelve feet in length, by sixteen inches in width, and tilted so that water may flow rapidly down it. **1874** RAYMOND *Statist. Mines & Mining* 20 Inefficient implements have been largely superseded..by the long-tom and the sluice. **1890** 'R. BOLDREWOOD' *Miner's Right* xiv, We drove and raised our wash-dirt.., and afterwards separated it..by the old-fashioned expedient of a 'tom'. **1891** E. ROPER *By Track & Trail* xxii. 326 They have to use quicksilver in their Long Toms and cradles to save it [gold].

b. ***Long Tom***: a long gun; *esp.* a naval gun mounted amidships, as distinct from the shorter guns of the broadside: see LONG TOM 1.

1867- [see LONG TOM 1]. **1888** CHURCHWARD *Blackbirding* 44 The ship was armed with four carronades on each side, and a 'long Tom' trained fore and aft, in the bows.

5. ***Old Tom***: a name for gin. *slang.*

1823 'JON BEE' *Slang Dict.* 130 *Old Tom*, he is of the feminine gender in most other nations than this: 'tis a cask or barrel, containing strong gin, and thence by a natural transition..the liquor itself. **1832** EGAN *Bk. Sports* 268 Tis the 'liquor of life', with 'spirits' to boot—'Old Tom', is better than gold. **1836-** [see OLD E. 4].

6. The male of various beasts and birds; perh. first for a male cat: see TOM CAT *sb.*; cf. also 8 a.

1791 HUDDESFORD *Salmag.* (1793) 141 Cats..Of titles obsolete, or yet in use, Tom, Tybert, Roger, Rutterkin, or Puss. **1826-8** [see TABBY *sb.* 2 b]. **1884** *Bazaar, Exch. & Mart* 17 Dec. 2205/2 Hamburghs... Redcaps, four hens and tom, prize strain, handsome birds. **1893** G. D. LESLIE *Lett. to Marco* xxxii. 214 The tom [swan] is very gallant in defence of his mate. **1898** *Blackw. Mag.* Nov. 663/2 He be a tom. I've heard him crow. **1905** *Daily News* 24 Jan. 8/1 Tiger, their cat (a beautifully marked tabby tom, aged five).

7. Combinations and phrases. **a.** *attrib.* and *Comb.*: **tom-pin**, a very large pin (Halliwell 1847–78); **tom-plough** (*local, E. Anglia*), a double breasted plough; also called *tommy* and **tom-tommy**; **† tom-rig** [RIG *sb.*[4]], a strumpet; a romping girl, a tomboy; **tom-toe**, the great toe; **Tom tower**, a tower in which a great bell hangs; *spec.* at Oxford, the western tower of Christ Church; **tom-trot (trot, tom-trod)**, home-made toffee stretched or drawn out as it cools (Halliwell).

1849 RAYNBIRD *Agric. Suff.* 301 The *tom or *tommy* plough is a plough with a double breast for ridging, or for clearing out furrows. **1668** SHADWELL *Sullen Lovers* Pref. a ij b, An impudent ill bred *tomrig for a Mistress. **1728** DENNIS *On Pope's Rape of Lock* 16 The author represents Belinda a fine, modest, well-bred lady: and yet in the very next canto she appears an arrant ramp and tomrigg. **1823** E. MOOR *Suffolk Words*, *Tom toe, the great toe of either foot. **1857** in DUNGLISON *Med. Lex.* **1853** 'C. BEDE' *Verdant Green* I. iii, As he looks across Christ Church Meadows and rolls past the *Tom Tower. **1844** DISRAELI *Coningsby* I. ix, I want toffy; I have been eating *Tom Trot all day. **1866** [CHARL. M. TUCKER] *Parlt. in Play-room* x. 93 A plateful of brown, tempting tom-trot, otherwise known by the title of toffy.

b. As the first element in a personal name applied allusively, as **Tom Astoner (Estenor)**, **Tom Brown**, (see quots.); **Tom Collins** orig. *U.S.*, a cocktail made of gin, lime or lemon juice, sugar, and soda water (cf. sense 5 and COLLINS[2]); **Tom Dingle** (see quot.); **Tom Farthing**, a fool, simpleton; **Tom Pepper** (*Naut.*), a liar; **Tom Tailor**, the tailor generically; **Tom Tiler, Tyler**, any ordinary man; also, a henpecked husband; **Tom Towly**, a simpleton; **Tom Tram**, a buffoon, jester; **Tom Walker** *U.S. dial.*, the Devil; also ***the Devil and Tom Walker***.

1706 E. WARD *Wooden World Diss.* (1708) 80 It's barbarous..to have the Bread thus pick'd from our Mouths by little *Tom Estenors. **1867** SMYTH *Sailor's Word-bk.*, *Tom Astoners*, dashing fellows; from astound or 'astony', to terrify. **1812** J. H. VAUX *Flash Dict.*, **Tom Brown*, twelve in hand, in crib. **1888** H. JOHNSON *New Improved Bartenders Man.* (rev. ed.) 227 *Tom Collins. **1906** L. MUCKENSTURM *Louis' Mixed Drinks* 99 (*heading*) Tom Collins. **1959** 'M. AINSWORTH' *Murder is Catching* xvi. 178 She made us both long cool Tom Collinses, the tumblers frosted with ice-chips. **1979** S. RIFKIN *McQuaid in August* (1980) ii. 7 The bartender would make me a tall tom collins without any cherry. **1711** *Brit. Apollo* III. No. 144. 3/1 Never yet Woman..had..such a poor wretched *Tom Dingle. **1689** SHADWELL *Bury F.* Prol. 21 For writing..silly Grub-street Songs worse than *Tom Farthing. **1867** SMYTH *Sailor's Word-bk.*, **Tom Pepper*, a term for a liar. **1820** SCOTT *Monast.* xxv, 'We rend our hearts, and not our garments'... 'The better..for yourselves, and the worse for Tom Tailor', said the baron. **1582** STANYHURST *Epitaphs* in *Æneis*, etc. (Arb.) 154 An Epitaph..such as oure vnlearned Rythmours ..make vpon thee death of euery *Tom Tyler. **1598** (*title*) Tom Tylere and his Wyfe. *a* **1625** FLETCHER *Woman's Prize* II. vi, She shall, Tom Tilers. **1582** STANYHURST *Æneis* Ded. (Arb.) 9 What *Tom Towly is so simple, that wyl not attempt, too bee a rithmoure? **1689** PRIOR *Ep. to F. Shephard* 172 All your wits, that fleer and sham, Down from don Quixote to *Tom Tram. *c* **1700** (*title*) The Mad Pranks of Tom Tram. **1739** 'R. BULL' tr. *Dedekindus' Grobianus* 39 To a Book..in Dutch, entituled, the Life of Uyle-Spegel, or Owl-glass; a Hero of equal Rank with Tom Tram in English. **1833** S. SMITH *Life & Writings J. Downing* 139 They always would have their way in spite of every body and *Tom Walker besides. **1914** *Dial. Notes* IV. 71 He wukked like the Devil an' Tom Walker. **1949** 'T. NELSON' *Backwoods Teacher* xiii. 136, I don't know nary charm, but they's an' old sayin' that some folks says but all it is is, 'Ol' Tom Walker [the devil] under yore hat, God the Father, God the Son, an' God the Holy Ghost.' **1958** *Virginia Q. Rev.* Spring 261 He whispered: 'Old Tom Walker under your hat. Father, son and holy ghost,' the way blue-eyed Dulcie would have done.

c. Followed by another word denoting or alluding to something (esp. the action or character) distinguishing the person to whom it is applied, forming a *quasi*-proper name or nickname, as in various phrases with specific sense: as ***Tom All-thumbs, Tom-ass, Tom (-a-)doodle, Tom Piper, Tom Tapster, Tom Tawny-coat, Tom Tell-troth (-truth), Tom Trifler, Tom True-tongue, Tom Truth, Tom Two-tongued***; **Tom-a-Stiles**: see quot. 1785, and cf. JOHN-A-STILES; **Tom Bray's bilk**, at Cribbage: see quot.; **Tom-come-tickle-me**, an old card-game; **Tom Cony (Conney)**, a simpleton, ninny; **Tom Cox's traverse** (*Naut.*): see quot. 1867; **Tom Double**, a shuffler, an equivocator; **Tom Drum**: see DRUM *sb.*[1] 3 b; **Tom Long**, one who takes a long time in coming, or in finishing his tale; **Tom of all trades**, a Jack of all trades; **Tom o' Bedlam**, a madman, a deranged person discharged from Bedlam (see BEDLAM 5) and licensed to beg; **Tom Pat** (*slang*), a parson, a hedge-priest (cf. PATRICO); also, a shoe; **Tom Poker, † Tom Po**, a nursery bugbear, a bogy; **Tom Pudding** *slang*, one of the box-like iron boats that are connected together and towed by a tug to carry coal on canals (see also sense 8 b); **Tom tumbler**, name for an imp or devil. See also TOM AND JERRY, TOM-FOOL, TOM-NODDY, TOM THUMB, TOM TIDDLER'S GROUND.

1598 I. M. *Health Gent. Profession Servingmen* B iij, The Clowne, the Slouen, and *Tom althummes. **1611** J. FIELD *Panegyr. Verses* in Coryat *Crudities*, *Tom-Asse may passe, but, for all his long eares, No such rich jewels as our Tom he weares. **1772** G. A. STEVENS *Songs Comic & Satyr.* 246 From John o' Nokes to *Tom o' Stiles, What is it all but Fooling? **1785** GROSE *Dict. Vulg. T.* s.v. *Nokes*, John-a-Nokes and Tom-a-Stiles.., fictitious names commonly used in law proceedings. **1812** J. H. VAUX *Flash Dict.*, **Tom Bray's Bilk*, laying out ace and deuce at cribbage. **1819–20** W. IRVING *Sketch-Bk., Litt. Brit.* (1865) 310 We played at All-Fours, Pope-Joan, *Tom-come-tickle-me, and other choice old games. *a* **1700** B. E. *Dict. Cant. Crew*, **Tom Conney*, a very silly fellow. **1840** R. H. DANA *Bef. Mast* xii, Every man who has been three months at sea knows how to 'work *Tom Cox's traverse'—'three turns round the long-boat, and a pull at the scuttled-butt'. This morning everything went in his way. **1867** SMYTH *Sailor's Word-bk.*, *Tom Cox's traverse*, up one hatchway and down another: others say 'three turns round the long boat, and a pull at the scuttle'. It means the work of an artful dodger, all jaw, and no good in him. **1708** E. WARD *Terræ-Fil.* v. 10 That one *Tom-doodle of a Son, who..if he happens to be Decoy'd ..to fling away Two Pence in Strong Drink, he Talks of nothing but his Mother. **1710** —— *Brit. Hud.* 31 Whether on him who'd..labour'd like a Tom-a-doodle, To place the Rump above the Noddle. **1705** *Charac. of Sneaker* 4 He's for a single Ministry, that he may play the *Tom Double under it. **1707** *Reflex. upon Ridicule* II. 145 Tom-doubles are to be avoided as Enemies that would betray you. **1577, 1603** *Tom Drum's entertainment [see DRUM *sb.*[1] 3 b]. **1609** C. BUTLER *Fem. Mon.* iv. (1623) I ij, They gently giue them Tom Drum's entertainment. **1631** W. FOSTER *Hoplochrisma-Spongus* 43 Surely this is *Tom Long the carrier, who will never doe his errand. **1785** GROSE *Dict. Vulg. T.*, *Tom Long*, a tiresome story teller; it is coming by Tom Long, the carrier, said of any thing that has been long expected. **1631** T. POWELL (*title*) *Tom of All Trades. *Ibid.* Ep. Ded. 13 Our Tom of all Trades hereupon Askt what was his condition. **1605** SHAKS. *Lear* I. ii. 148 *Tom o' Bedlam. **1671** GLANVILL *Disc. M. Stubbe* 28 [I] am afraid that some will think, that I am not well in my Wits, because I seriously answer such a Tom of Bedlam. *a* **1691** AUBREY *Nat. Hist. Wilts.* II. iv. (1847) 93 Till the breaking out of the civill warres, Tom ô Bedlam's did travell about the countrey. They had been poore distracted men that had been putt into Bedlam, where recovering to some sobernesse they were licentiated to goe a begging. **1880** SHORTHOUSE *J. Inglesant* (1881) I. 72 Wandering beggars and halfwitted people called 'Tom o' Bedlams' who were a recognised order of mendicants. *c* **1700** *Street Robberies Consider'd*, *Tom Pat, a parson. **1579** SPENSER *Sheph. Cal.* Oct. 78 *Tom Piper makes vs better melodie. **1616** W. BROWNE *Brit. Past.* II. ii. 32 So haue I seene Tom Piper stand vpon our village greene. **1744** GREY *Hudibras* II. 207 *note*, You are afraid that you shall meet *Tom Po. *a* **1825** FORBY *Voc. E. Anglia*, *Tom Poker*,..the great bugbear and terror of naughty children, who inhabits dark closets [etc.]. **1902** *Longm. Mag.* Nov. 41, I tells him them days o' Tom-pokers be gone. **1906** *Westm. Gaz.* ?8 Mar. 8/2 Trains of iron compartment boats, known locally as '*Tom Puddings', are towed all the way to Goole. **1949** *Archit. Rev.* CVI. 8/3 On the Aire and Calder, compartment boats, or Tom Puddings, are used. These are oblong iron boxes towed in trains up to 32 in number by steam tugs. **1970** *New Society* 19 Nov. 898/2 If you haven't seen a chain of tom puddings then you've missed one of the sights of England. **1592** GREENE *Upst. Courtier* Wks. (Grosart) XI. 275 Last to you *Tom tapster, that tap your smale cannes of beere to the poore, and yet fil them half ful of froth. *c* **1600** DAY *Begg. Bednall Gr.* I. iii, I think not but thou and this *Tom Tawny coat here gulls me. **1600** J. LANE *Tom Tel-Troth* 713 But sooth to say, *Tom-teltroth will not lie, We heere haue blaz'd Englands iniquitie. **1622** (*title*) Tom Tell Troath, or a Free Discourse touching the Manners of the Tyme. **1847–78** HALLIWELL, *Tom-tell-trouth*, a true guesser. **1377** LANGL. *P. Pl.* B. iv. 17 And also *tomme trewe-tonge-telle-me-no-tales. **1581** J. BELL *Haddon's Answ. Osor.* 68 b, They will all condemne you for *tomme trifler. **1542** UDALL *Erasm. Apoph.* II. 179 b, For his malaparte toungne called at home..Parrhesiastes, (as ye woulde saye in englyshe), *Thom trouthe, or plain Sarisbuirie. **1550** LATIMER *Serm. at Stamford* I. 94 Maister we know that thou art Tomme truth, and thou tellest the very truth, and sparest no man. **1580** G. HARVEY *Let. to Spenser* iv. Wks. (Grosart) I. 83 Tell me, in Tom Trothes earnest, what [he] sayth. **1393** LANGL. *P. Pl.* C. XXIII. 162 *note*, Here syre was a sysour þat neuere swor treuthe, Or *tomme [*v.r.* thomme] two-tounged ateynt at eche enqueste.

8. a. In names of animals, denoting the male; see also TOM CAT.

1762 T. BRYDGES *Homer Travest.* (1772) 192 And, like Tom puss, o'er pantiles dance. **1859** BARTLETT *Dict. Amer.* (ed. 2), *Tom-Dog*, male dogs, as well as cats, take the prefix 'tom', in some parts of the West. **1871** MRS. STOWE *Oldtown Stories* 92, I never heard that a tom-turkey would set on eggs. **1875** *Sussex Gloss.*, *Tom*, any cock bird, as a tom-turkey or a tom-parrot. **1890** *Glouc. Gloss.*, *Tom*, used to denote the male of birds, as 'tom-bird', 'tom-chicken', 'tom-pheasant'. **1893** G. D. LESLIE *Lett. to Marco* xxxii. 214 The tom-swan..landed on a likely spot. **1905** *Daily Chron.* 31 Oct. 4/7 In his part [Hampshire] people spoke of tom-rats, tom-rabbits, tom-mice, tom-hedgehogs [etc.].

b. In familiar or local names of species: **Tom-hoop** [cf. HOOP *sb.*[3] 2], **Tom-noup** [cf. NOPE *sb.*[1]] *dial.*, the great tit (*Parus major*); **Tom-pot, Tompot**, name in Cornwall for the gattorugine, a species of blenny; in Devonshire, for the guinea-fowl, from its cry; in Devon and Somerset, a well-known kind of red-cheeked apple (also called **tomput**); **Tom-pudding**, the little grebe; **Tom-tailor**, the crane-fly; in East Anglia, the stormy petrel; **Tom Titmouse**, = TOMTIT. See also TOM-COD.

1847–78 HALLIWELL, **Tom-Noup*, the titmouse. *Salop.* **1837** J. F. PALMER *Gloss. Dialog. in Devon Dial.* (E.D.D.), *Tom-put. **1863** COUCH *Brit. Fishes* II. 219 Gattorugine.. is known to fishermen of the west of England by the homely appellation of Tompot. **1891** *Hartland* (Devon) *Gloss.*, *Tom pot*, a name sometimes given to the guinea-fowl on account of its peculiar cry. **1904** *Longm. Mag.* Apr. 489 Cheeks as rosy as a 'tomput' apple. **1848** *Zoologist* VI. 2290 The little grebe or 'dipper' or 'dobber' or '*Tom pudding'. **1853** HICKIE tr. *Aristoph.* (1887) I. 37 A Bœotian might stick it in a *tom-tailor. **1856** P. THOMPSON *Hist. Boston* List Provinc., *Tom-tailor*, the Daddy-long-legs. **1885** SWAINSON *Provinc. Names Birds* 212 They [Stormy Petrels] are called Tom tailors by the Lowestoft and Yarmouth fishermen. **1576** GASCOIGNE *Philomene* 26 Sometimes I wepe To see *Tom Tyttimouse, so much set by. *c* **1776** *Roxb. Ball.* (1889) VI. 308 Says Tom Tit-Mouse then, 'There be some men That will change nine times a day'.

Hence **'tomling**, a small or young tom cat; **'tomship** (*humorous*), the personality of a 'Tom'.

1821 SOUTHEY *Let. to C. Bedford* 3 Apr., Moved by compassion (his [a cat's] colour and his tomship also being taken into consideration), I consented to give him an asylum. **1821** *Ibid.* 29 Apr., We are promised to succeed him a black Tomling.

tom (tɒm), *sb.*[2] Colloq. abbrev. of TOMATO.

1920 *Chambers's Jrnl.* 15 May 384/1 The acreage of 'outside toms' is increasing annually. **1935** [see CUE *sb.* 4]. **1976** *Coventry Evening Tel.* 27 Oct. 9/3 (*heading*) Summer of the giant toms.

tom (tɒm), *sb.*[3] Slang abbrev. of TOMFOOLERY (sense 2, = jewellery).

1955 P. WILDEBLOOD *Against the Law* 119 Two grand's worth of tom. **1970** G. F. NEWMAN *Sir, You Bastard* ii. 68 What d'you do with the tom and money you had out of

Manor Gardens this afternoon? **1980** *Times* 23 Feb. 3/3 One of thieves.. told police: 'When we found the tom (Cockney slang: tomfoolery jewellery) in the car we were amazed.'

tom (tɒm), *sb.*[4] Slang abbrev. of TOM-TOM *sb.* 1 d.

1970 J. WAINWRIGHT *Freeze thy Blood* 11 Fatso grinned and notched the buckle of a tom case. **1975** J. PIDGEON *Flame* v. 65 Around the drum kit he arranged four mikes, one for the bass drum, one for the floor tom, one for the snare, and one overhead.

tom (tɒm), *v.* [f. TOM *sb.*[1]] **1.** *trans.* To address familiarly as 'Tom'. *nonce-use.*

1900 S. J. WEYMAN *Sophia* xxiv, 'You may Tom me, you don't alter it', he answered.

2. *intr.* [f. TOM *sb.*[1] 1 f.] To behave in an ingratiating and servile way to someone of another (esp. white) race. Also *to tom it (up)*. *U.S. slang.*

1963 L. BENNETT in W. King *Black Short Story Anthol.* (1972) 161 They say you are going to chicken out, Papa... They're betting you'll 'Tom'. **1972** M. J. BOSSE *Incident at Naha* ii. 94 Virgil just smiled, Tomming it up. **1976** *Public Opinion Q.* XXXIX. 527 The respondent 'accommodates', or to use the colloquial term, 'toms', in order to get through the racial interaction with minimal tension.

3. *intr.* To practise prostitution, to behave promiscuously; also, to have sexual intercourse in such a context. Also *to tom (it) around*. *slang.*

1964 Z. PROGL *Woman of Underworld* iii. 35 They were perfectly willing to go 'tomming' on the streets to earn a few quid, but I never could. **1968** 'J. Ross' *Diminished by Death* i. 14 She's just tomming around. **1973** J. ROSSITER *Manipulators* ix. 102 This woman... Is she tomming it around with the local villains? **1981** A. SEWART *Close your Eyes & Sleep* xviii. 181 What was she doing? Tomming, to put it bluntly. She was having it off with a bloke.

Hence **'tomming** *vbl. sb.*

1968 J. LOCK *Lady Policeman* ii. 12 A prostitute was a 'tom'..and to practise prostitution was 'tomming'. **1973** *Black World* May 44 Afrikan People all over the world Conscious, unconscious, struggling, sleeping, Resisting, tomming, killing the enemy. **1981** 'J. Ross' *Dark Blue & Dangerous* ix. 55 His own tomming around had given him a charitable view of casual sex.

tom, var. TAUM; obs. form of TOOM *sb.*[1]

tomahawk ('tɒməhɔːk), *sb.* Also 7 **tamahauk(e, -hawk, tomahauke,** 8 **tommahauk, (tomahaw, tomhog),** 8–9 **tomohawk,** (9 **tommyhawk).** [a. Renâpe (N. Amer. Indian of Virginia) *tämähāk* (given by Capt. J. Smith as *tomahack*), apocopated form of *tämähākan*, 'what is used for cutting, cutting utensil', from *tämähāken* 'he uses for cutting', from *tämäham* 'he cuts' (W. R. Gerard in *American Anthropologist* X. 1908, p. 277). Cognate with Pamptico (Carolinian) *tommahick*, and with the full forms, Mohegan *tummahegan*, Delaware *tamoihecan*, Abenaki *tamahigan*, Micmac *tŭmeegŭn* (ta'migan), Passamaqoddy *tumhigen*.]

1. a. The axe of the North American Indians, used as a weapon of war and the chase, and also as a tool and agricultural implement; in English use the word is usually applied to it as the war-axe.

It consists of a wooden shaft about 2½ feet long, with a head originally formed of a long hard stone sharpened at one end, or of a piece of copper, or of the horn of a deer, but after the advent of white traders usually of iron (*trade tomahawk*). Sometimes the shaft was hollow, and a bowl was fashioned at the back of the head (*pipe-tomahawk*).

[**1612** CAPT. SMITH *Map Virginia* (Arb.) 44 *Tomahacks.* Axes. *Tockahacks.* Pickaxes.] **1634** W. WOOD *New Eng. Prosp.* II. i. 58 [They] beate them downe with their right hand Tamahaukes, and left hand Iavelins. [**1701** C. WOLLEY *Jrnl. New York* (1860) 36 They dig their ground with a Flint, called in their Language tom-a-hea-kan.] **1705** BEVERLEY *Virginia* I. iii. (1722) 39 Knocking the English unawares on the Head, some with their Hatchets, which they call *Tommahauks*, others with the Hows and Axes of the English themselves. **1715** *Phil. Trans.* XXIX. 308 Targets, Tomahaws, poisoned Daggers. **1716** B. CHURCH *Hist. Philip's War* (1865) I. 82 A great surly look'd fellow took up his Tomhog, or wooden Cutlash, to kill Mr. Church, but some others prevented him. **1756** WASHINGTON *Lett.* Writ. 1889 I. 393 The wampum and tomahawks I have purchased. **1780** EDMONDSON *Heraldry* II. Gloss., *Tomahawk*, an Indian war-ax. **1809** A. HENRY *Trav.* 41 They walked in single file, each with his tomahawk in one hand, and scalping-knife in the other. **1851** MAYNE REID *Scalp Hunt.* xxvii, They [Indians] break the shanks [of buffalo] with their tomahawks. **1865** LUBBOCK *Preh. Times* iv. (1869) 91 The North American stone axe or tomahawk served not merely as an implement, but also as a weapon.

b. erron. applied to a war-club or knobkerry.

1674 JOSSELYN *Voy. New Eng.* 147 Their other weapons are Tamahawks which are staves two foot and a half long with a knob at the end as round as a bowl. *a* **1817** T. DWIGHT *Trav. New Eng.*, etc. (1821) I. 118 Another of their principal weapons was the well known Tomahawk, or war-club... Since the arrival of the English, they have used fire-arms. To these they add a long knife: and a small battle-axe, to which they have transferred the name of Tomahawk.

c. *transf.* Applied to similar weapons used in primitive societies elsewhere; also *Naut.* a pole-axe used by sailors; in Australia, the usual word for *hatchet*.

1670 NARBOROUGH *Jrnl.* in *Acc. Sev. Late Voy.* I. (1694) 23 An Indian Club..called by the Caribbe-Indians at Surinam a Tomahauke. **1681** GREW *Musæum* IV. ii. 367 A Tamahauke, or Brazilian Fighting-Club. **1802** J. JONES in *Naval Chron.* VII. 348, I saw him chop at him with a.. tomahawk. **1833** MARRYAT *P. Simple* xxxv, In a moment, pikes, tomahawks, cutlasses, and pistols were seized,..and our men poured into the eighty-gun ship, and in two minutes the decks were cleared, and all the Dons pitched below. **1866** LIVINGSTONE *Last Jrnls.* (1873) I. i. 20 For they are accustomed to clearing spaces for gardens,..using tomahawks well adapted for the work. **1875** BEDFORD *Sailor's Pocket Bk.* vi. (ed. 2) 229 A couple of tomahawks will be found useful. **1880** FISON & HOWITT *Kamilaroi* 206 The [Australian] aborigines have obtained iron tomahawks. **1898** MORRIS *Austral Eng.* s.v., In Australia the word *hatchet* has practically disappeared, and the word *Tomahawk* to describe it is in every-day use. It is also applied to the stone hatchet of the Aboriginals.

d. Applied locally to various kinds of rural tools and agricultural implements: see quots.

c **1825** J. CLARE in M. Grainger *Nat. Hist. Prose Writings J. Clare* (1982) 88 The hookd bill usd by hedgers & calld by them a tomahawk. **1830** *Q. Jrnl. Agric.* III. 653 Mortises made by a centre-bit leave an intermediate piece between the apertures. This is taken out by the tomahawk, a tool made for the purpose. One end is a sharp stout pointed knife, which cuts each side of the middle piece left in the mortise, and the other end hooks out the piece not dislodged by the knife. **1881** MISS JACKSON *Shropsh. Word-bk.*, *Tummy-awk*, a dung-fork, carried at the back of the cart, and used to scrape out the manure, on the land, as it is required. **1893** *Wiltshire Gloss.*, *Tommy-hawk*, a potato hacker.

e. *fig.* As the imaginary instrument of a savage attack or vindictive onslaught.

1805 SURR *Winter in Lond.* (1806) II. 195 His meek nature ..would..sink beneath the tomahawk of such a barbarian as the writer of the article in question. **1836** H. ROGERS *J. Howe* vii. (1863) 183 Such a temper is rare at any period; but in that age of fierce and savage controversy, of the tomahawk and scalping-knife, it was indeed a phenomenon. **1897** *Daily News* 30 Sept. 8/2 He flourished the rhetorical tomahawk over 'those false teachers who say that the articles of Christian faith are illusions'.

2. Phrases. ***to blow tomahawks***, of the wind, to blow with cutting violence. ***to bury*** or ***lay aside the tomahawk***: to lay down one's arms, to cease from hostilities. ***to dig up, raise,*** or ***take up the tomahawk***: to take up arms in warfare, to commence hostilities. Cf. HATCHET *sb.* 2.

1705 R. BEVERLEY *Hist. Virginia* III. 27 They use..very ceremonious ways in concluding of Peace..such as burying a tomahawk. **1775** ADAIR *Amer. Ind.* 239, I persuaded the Choktah to take up the bloody tomohawk against those perfidious French. **1775** in *Virginia Hist. Coll.* (1887) VI. 80, I..resolve never to bury the Tomahawk untill liberty shall be fixed on an immovable basis thro' the whole Continent. **1806** PIKE *Sources Mississ.* (1810) 86 Grateful that the two nations had laid aside the tomahawk at my request. **1812** BRACKENRIDGE *Views Louisiana* (1814) 123 They may come here in peace, or for the purpose of trade, but it will be far hence that they will dare to raise the tomahawk. **1848** BARTLETT *Dict. Amer.* s.v., It was and is the custom of the Indians to go through the ceremony of burying the tomahawk, when they made peace; when they went to war, they dug it up again. Hence the phrases 'to bury the tomahawk', and 'to dig up the tomahawk',.. sometimes used by political speakers and writers. **1903** LD. R. GOWER *Rec. & Remin.* 297 The weather is boisterous; it blows tomahawks and tornadoes.

3. *attrib.* and *Comb.*, as ***tomahawk-blow, -critic, -dance, -pipe*** (quot. 1860), ***tongue***; **tomahawk improvement**, an 'improvement' of a slight character, made to secure a right of pre-emption (Thornton); so **tomahawk settler**.

1873 R. BROWN *Races Man.* I. 235 Until the *tomahawk-blow puts an end to him. **1886** J. PAYN *Heir of Ages* xxxviii, He was not..a *tomahawk critic; he thought less of being smart himself..than of doing justice to a book. **1856** EMERSON *Eng. Traits, Ability* Wks. (Bohn) II. 39 They have no Indian taste for a *tomahawk-dance. **1842** L. MUNSELL in *M. Cutler's Life*, etc. (1888) I. 133 They were determined to hold the lands by what is called '*tomahawk improvements'. **1860** DOMENECH *Deserts N. Amer.* II. 272 The Comanches, in Texas,..have *tomahawk-pipes (small hatchets, the head of which is made hollow like the bowl of a pipe, and the handle perforated in its whole length to serve for a tube). **1907** *Q. Rev.* July 161 A recipe for *tomahawk punch. **1788** M. CUTLER in *Life*, etc. (1888) I. 425 Stopped and breakfasted at a little clump of houses on the Indian side. They were *tomahawk settlers. **1849** C. BRONTË *Shirley* x, Of whose observant faculties and *tomahawk tongue Caroline stood in awe.

Hence **'tomahawked** *a.*, provided or armed with a tomahawk.

1895 K. GRAHAME *Golden Age* (1904) 3 A prairie studded with herds of buffalo, which it was our delight, moccasined and tomahawked, to ride down.

tomahawk ('tɒməhɔːk), *v.* [f. prec. sb.]

1. *trans.* To strike, cut, or kill with a tomahawk.

1755 *Gentl. Mag.* XXV. 579/2 Mac Swine was ordered by the Indian to make a fire, and upon his not doing it so readily or so nimbly as was expected, he was threatened to be tomohawk'd. **1769** *Middlesex Jrnl.* 14–16 Sept. 1/4 By six Indians, the man and woman were tomahawked and scalped. **1791** J. LONG *Voy. Ind. Interpr.* 96 The instant the animal drops they tomahawk it. **1829** SOUTHEY *O. Newman* IV. 45 Stragglers tomahawk'd And scalp'd, or dragg'd away that they may die By piecemeal murder. **1889** H. H. ROMILLY *Verandah in N. Guinea* 74 They..were treacherously tomahawked.

b. *fig.* To attack savagely or mercilessly in speech or (more usually) in writing; to 'cut up' or demolish in a review or criticism.

1815 'AGRESTIS' *Feudal Hall* xlv, [She] tomahawks me with sharp words. **1820** *Blackw. Mag.* VII. 388 He afterwards goes out of his way to tomahawk Dryden, for an allusion to Abraham in a dedication. **1895** *Daily News* 19 June 6/2 Her second daughter, Lady Charlotte,..wrote the book which Thackeray tomahawked.

2. To cut (a sheep) in shearing it. *Australia.*

1859 H. KINGSLEY *G. Hamlyn* xx, Shearers were very scarce, and the poor sheep got fearfully 'tomahawked' by the new hands. **1872** EDEN *My Wife & I in Queensland* iv. 96 Some men never get the better of this habit, but 'tomahawk' as badly after years of practice as when they first began. **1896** PATERSON *Man fr. Snowy River* 162 The novice who..had tommyhawked half a score.

Hence **'tomahawking** *vbl. sb.* and *ppl. a.*; also **'tomahawker**, one who tomahawks (*lit.* and *fig.*).

1819 *Metropolis* III. 69 The tomahawkers of the Edinburgh Review. **1833** *Boston*, etc. *Herald* 9 Apr. 2/1 We have not a tomahawking article in the whole number. **1839–40** W. IRVING *Wolfert's R.* i. (1855) 2 They recreated themselves occasionally with a little tomahawking and scalping. **1862** *Times* 8 Apr. 11/4 A large body of scalping and tomahawking Indians. **1886** *Pall Mall G.* 2 Oct. 6/1 My father,..noticing that the sheep were particularly badly shorn, remarked to the manager that 'it was mere tomahawking'. **1886** *Manch. Exam.* 3 Nov. 3/1 A return to a style of literary tomahawking which we had hoped was for ever extinct. **1897** *Athenæum* 20 Mar. 372 Lest he should find himself tomahawked instead of being the tomahawker.

tomal, variant form of TAMAL.

‖**tomalley** (tɒ'mælɪ, tɔː'mælɪ). Also **tomally, taumally, tomalline.** [According to J. Davies, 1666, a Carib word (see quot.); in F. *taumalin*, (Littré).] The fat or 'liver' of the North American lobster, which becomes green when cooked, and is then known as ***tomalley sauce***.

1666 J. DAVIES *Hist. Caribby Islands* II. xvi. 300 They call the inner part of the Crab *Taumaly*. *Ibid.*, *Carrib. Vocab.* Zz iv/1 Sauce, Taomali, or Taumali. **1864** WEBSTER, *Tomalley*, the liver of the lobster, which becomes green when boiled; called also *tom-alline*. **1882** OGILVIE, Tom-alley, Tomalline. **1950** R. MOORE *Candlemas Bay* 289 The lobsters boiled to a fine, even red. Grampie ate five. Then he wiped the tomalley off his jacknife. **1981** *Times* 13 June 12/7 The [lobster's] red coral and the creamy green liver, known as tomalley, are delicious.

¶ *erron.* A Spanish-American dish made of crushed Indian corn, etc.; properly TAMAL.

1860 BARTLETT *Dict. Amer.*, *Tamal*, or *Tamauli*, a peculiar Spanish-American dish made up of a paste of crushed or ground maize, sometimes with minced meat added, when it is wrapped in the husks of maize and baked on the coals. *c* **1900** C. W. GREENE *Let. to Editor*, When I was a youngster in Massachusetts, we called the gelatinous part of a baked maize pudding, the *tom-alley*. It somewhat resembles in appearance the *tom-alley* of the lobster; but in meaning it comes very near the Mexican, Cuban, and Southern U.S. use of *tamauli* or *tamalli* as the name of a kind of maize pudding.

‖**toman**[1] (taʊ'mɑːn, 'tʊmən, 'tʌmən). Forms: 7– **toman**; also 6 **tumen, thuman,** 7 **tomana, thoman, thoma(u)nd, tomin, tumain, tummon,** 7–9 **tomaun.** [a. Pers. *tūmān*, *tumān*, *tuman*, according to Devic, a Yuzbeg Tartar word (whence its unsettled form), lit. 'ten thousand'.]

1. Formerly among the Mongols, Tartars, etc., and thence in Persia and Turkey: The sum of ten thousand; also, a military division consisting of 10,000 men. Now *rare*.

1599 HAKLUYT *Voy.* II. I. 61 The lord of the same citie hath in yeerely reuenues for salt onely, fiftie Thuman of Balis, and one balis is worth a floren and a halfe of our coyne: insomuch that one Thuman of balis amounteth vnto the value of fifteene thousand florens. **1788** GIBBON *Decl. & F.* lxv. VI. 333 The fruitful territory of Cash, of which his fathers were the hereditary chiefs, as well as of a toman of ten thousand horse. **1877** J. M. PORTEOUS *Turkey* 54 Numbering in Turkish custom was by tomans, ten thousands or myriads.

2. A Persian gold coin issued until 1927, nominally worth 10 silver krans or 10,000 dinars; formerly a money of account, which was constantly depreciated in value from £3 13*s.* (or more) *c* 1600: its value *c* 1912 stood at 7*s.* 1*d.*: see quots.

1566 A. EDWARDS in Hakluyt *Voy.* (1589) 378, I haue receiued 6. tumens in readie money: 200. shaughes is a tumen, reckoning euery shaugh for 6. pence Russe. **1613** SHERLEY *Trav. Persia* 72 Marganobeague..brought mee.. a thousand Tomanas, which is sixteene thousand Duckets of our Money. **1623** *St. Papers, Col.* 212 Sold the Primrose for 400 tomans, every toman 3*l.* 6*s.* 4*d.* **1629** in Foster *Eng. Factories India* (1909) III. 354 Other men pay tre keale or quart uppon every tummon. **1662** J. DAVIES tr. *Olearius' Voy. Ambass.* 300 When they [the Persians] are to name great Sums, they accompt by Tumains. **1686** W. HEDGES *Diary* (Hakl. Soc.) I. 215 They were robbed of all their money, to the sum of 4 Tomauns. **1698** FRYER *Acc. E. India & P.* 222 He pays the King yearly Twenty two thousand Thomands, every Thomand making Three pound and a Noble in our Accompt. **1753** HANWAY *Trav.* (1762) I. v. lxiv. 292 The toman, bistie, and denaer are imaginary... A toman is 10 hazardenaers..Value in denaers, 10000. Weight in muscals, 50. **1811** PINKERTON *Mod. Geog.*, *Persia* ii. (ed. 3) 459 The whole revenue was by some estimated at 700,000 tomans, or about thirty-two millions of French livres. **1815** ELPHINSTONE *Acc. Caubul* (1842) II. 269 The sum to be paid for a substitute..generally is from five to seven tomauns (from 10*l.* to 14*l.*). **1845** BROWNING *Flight Duchess* xiv, The band-roll strung with tomans Which proves the veil a Persian woman's. **1858** SIMMONDS *Dict. Trade*, *Toman*, a conventional money of Persia of a very variable character..; it may be valued at about 12*s.* 6*d.* **1882** FLOYER *Unexpl. Baluchistan* 505 Ali Abker engages to hire a saddle horse and three mules to Mr. Floyer.. for fifteen days, for the sum of eight tomans (£3 16s.),.. at the rate of two tomans each.

‖**toman**[2] ('tomən). (*erron.* tomhan.) [Gaelic *toman* hillock, dim. of *tom* hill.] A hillock; a mound of earth. Often applied to mounds representing ancient glacial moraines, found in the heads of valleys in the Highlands.

1811 MRS. GRANT *Superstit. Highl. Scot.* I. vii. 282 The children's nursery tales are full of wonders performed by the secret dwellers of these *tomhans*, or fairy hillocks. **1830** J. WILSON *Noct. Ambr.* Nov., Wks. 1856 III. 86 The Queen of the Fairies among the tomans of her ancient woods. **1854** H. MILLER *Sch. & Schm.* v. (1858) 99 The western slopes of the valley are mottled by grassy tomhans—the moraines of some ancient glacier. **1876** D. GORRIE *Summ. & Wint. in Orkneys* iii. 121 Those huge boulders and gravel-knolls or tomans continued a mystery till the glacial theory.

Tom and Jerry. Names of the two chief characters in Egan's *Life in London*, 1821, and its continuation, 1828; whence in various allusive and attributive uses, esp. as name of a compound alcoholic drink, a kind of highly-spiced punch (U.S.); and *attrib.* in ***Tom and Jerry shop*** (Engl.), a low beer-house. Hence **Tom-and-Jerry** *v.*, *intr.* to drink and indulge in riotous behaviour, like young bloods of the Regency period; **Tom-and-Jerryism**, drunken roistering, window-breaking, and the like.

The title of Egan's original work (1821) is 'Life in London, or Days and Nights of Jerry Hawthorne and his elegant friend Corinthian Tom'; that of the continuation of 1828 is 'Finish to the Adventures of Tom, Jerry, and Logic', whence app. the order of the names in *Tom and Jerry*.

(*Tom and Jerry shop* was app. an expansion of the earlier *Jerry-shop* 'a low beer-house' (in *Preston Temperance Advocate* Mar. 1834, 18/2), which had no original connexion with Tom and Jerry.)

1828 *Lights & Shades* I. 124 No drinking and raking. No Tom-and-Jerrying in those days. **1829** W. IRVING in *Life & Lett.* (1864) II. 387 We are too apt to take our ideas of English life from such vulgar sources as Tom and Jerry, and we appear to be Tom and Jerrying it to perfection in New York. **1852** MUNDY *Our Antipodes* (1857) 207 As the glazier prays for hail-storms, civic riots, and the revival of 'Tom-and-Jerryism, for his own private ends! **1862** JERRY THOMAS *How to mix Drinks* (N.Y.) 69 [Recipe]. *Ibid.*, To deal out Tom and Jerry to Customers. *Ibid.*, Adepts at the bar in serving Tom and Jerry [etc.]. **1865** *Slang Dict.*, *Tom and Jerry* [ed. **1873** adds *shop*], a low drinking shop. **1880** *Barman's Man.* 47 [Recipe for Tom and Jerry]. **1884** S. DOWELL *Taxation* II. 277 Free trade in beer in over 31,000 'Tom and Jerry' shops, as the new beer-houses and shops were termed. **1894** *Northumbld. Gloss.*, *Tom-and-Jerry*, a catcall. **1899** MORROW *Bohem. Paris* 305 Sipping Manhattan cocktails with a cherry-brandy-and-soda, Tom-and-Jerry, and the rest. **1903** FARMER & HENLEY *Slang Dict.*, *Tom-and-Jerry days*, the period of the Regency (1810–20); also, 'when George IV was king'.

tomasha, -shaw, -sia, var. ff. TAMASHA.

tomatin ('tɒmətɪn). *Biochem.* Also -ine. [f. TOMAT(O + IN[1].] A steroidal alkaloid present as a glycoside in the stems and leaves of the tomato plant and some other members of the family Solanaceæ.

The distinction made in quot. 1948 was not generally adopted.

1946 [see LYCOPERSICIN b]. **1948** *Arch. Biochem.* XVI. 399 The crystalline compound has very low antibacterial activity.. and is designated tomatine to distinguish it from the crude or partially purified tomatin. **1959** H. MARTIN *Sci. Princ. Crop Protection* (ed. 4) ii. 19 Although tomatine effectively inhibits the growth of *F[usarium] lycopersici* in pure culture.., no direct evidence has been obtained that it is responsible for wilt resistance. **1973** L. P. MILLER *Phytochemistry* I. vi. 160 Lycobiose (4-*O*-β-D-glucopyranosyl-D-galactose) and the trisaccharide lycotriose were obtained from the tetrasaccharide tomatin in tomato leaf. **1980** *Phytochemistry* XIX. 1322/1 Tomatin in neutral or alkaline pH is highly membranolytic.. and forms a complex with cholesterol.

tomato (tə'mɑːtəʊ, təʊ-, U.S. -'meɪtəʊ). Forms: α. 7–9 **tomate**; β. 8– **tomato**; γ. 8–9 **tomata**; δ. 8 **tomatum**, 9 **-us**. *Pl.* 8 **tomatos**, 8– **tomatoes**. [In 17th c. *tomate*, a. F. *tomate* (2 syll.) fem., or Sp. and Pg. *tomate* (3 syll.) masc., ad. Mex. *tomatl*. *Tomato* is an English alteration, app. assumed to be Spanish, or perh. after *potato*; *tomata* a later change, app. assuming a Sp. **tomata* like *patata*; *tomatum*, *-us* are erroneous latinizations.

1572 GUILLANDINUS *De Papyro* 90 Americanorum tumatle. *Ibid.* 91 Tumatle.. recentiores fere pomum aureum, et pomum amoris nuncupant.]

1. a. The glossy fleshy fruit of a solanaceous plant (*Solanum Lycopersicum* or *Lycopersicum esculentum*), a native of tropical America, now cultivated as a garden vegetable in temperate as well as tropical lands. It varies when ripe from red to yellow in colour, and greatly in size and shape, the common form being irregularly spheroidal, while two smaller forms, considered by some as species, are named from their shape, *L. cerasiforme*, the cherry tomato, and *L. pyriforme*, the pear-shaped tomato. Formerly called *love-apple*, from supposed aphrodisiac qualities. Also the plant, an annual with a weak trailing or climbing stem, irregularly pinnate leaves, and yellow flowers resembling those of the potato.

α. **1604** E. G[RIMSTONE] *D'Acosta's Hist. Indies* VII. ix. 519 There was also Indian pepper, beetes, Tomates, which is a great sappy and savourie graine. **1775** R. TWISS *Trav. Portugal & Spain* 256 Its district produces.. radishes, endive, cucumbers and tomates. **1796** STEDMAN *Surinam* II. xxv. 224, I found plenty of tomaté, which being produced in many British gardens, I will not attempt to describe. **1846** SOYER *Cookery* 10 Preserved tomates.

β. **1753** CHAMBERS *Cycl. Suppl.*, *Tomato*, the Portuguese [*error*] name for the fruit of the lycopersicon or love-apple; a fruit.. eaten either stewed or raw by the Spaniards and Italians and by the Jew families in England. **1777** G. FORSTER *Voy. round World* II. 588 The *Solanum Lycopersicon*, the fruit of which they call tomatos. **1846** LINDLEY *Veg. Kingd.* 621 Tomatoes.. are a common ingredient in sauces. **1856** EMERSON *Eng. Traits, Voy. Eng.*, I find the sea-life an acquired taste, like that for tomatoes and olives.

γ. **1759** MILLER *Gard. Dict.*, *Lycopersicon*... Apple-bearing Nightshade, with a soft, round, striated Fruit, commonly called Tomatas [*error*] by the Spaniards. **1806** [see 3]. **1839** *Mag. Dom. Econ.* IV. 127 Directions for the various preparations of the Tomata. **1887** J. ASHBY STERRY *Lazy Minstrel* (1892) 107 The ruddy ripe tomata, In china bowl of ice.

δ. **1796** C. MARSHALL *Garden.* xvi. (1813) 276 *Tomatum*, or love apples, we have red, white and yellow fruited. **1822** *Lancaster* (Pa.) *Jrnl.* 6 Sept. (Thornton), The pies made of the Tomatus are excellent.

b. = *tomato-red*, sense 3.

1920 *Queen* 22 May (front cover), Colours:.. Apricot, Ivory, Mastic, Tomato, Suede, and Saxe. **1923** *Daily Mail* 29 Jan. 1 (Advt.), Striped suitings... On grounds of mole, grey, fawn, black and tomato. **1977** M. KENYON *Rapist* v. 56 Her rosy cheeks turned tomato with indignation. **1978** P. MCCUTCHAN *Blackmail North* viii. 93 She got into the tomato Mini and drove away.

c. An attractive girl. *slang* (orig. *U.S.*).

1929 D. RUNYON in *Hearst's Internat.* Nov. 74/1 Different guys have different names for dolls, such as broads,.. and tomatoes, which I claim are not respectful. **1962** J. HELLER *Catch-22* xvi. 153, I can rush back to that night club before Aarfy leaves with that wonderful tomato he's got without giving me a chance to ask about an aunt or friend she must have who's just like her. **1977** H. FAST *Immigrants* v. 303 This tomato is twenty-three years old and she's a virgin.

2. a. With qualifying words, applied to varieties of this fruit or plant, as ***cherry-***, ***currant-tomato***, or to other species resembling it, as ***cannibal's tomato***, ***strawberry-*** or ***husk-tomato***: see quots.

1867 BRANDE & COX *Dict. Sc.*, etc. III. 806/1 The *Solanum anthropophagorum*, which the Feejeans eat at their feasts of human flesh, is hence called the Cannibal's Tomato. **1884** MILLER *Plant-n.*, Cherry Tomato-plant, *Solanum Lycopersicum* var. *cerasiforme*. *Ibid.*, *Physalis Alkekengi*,.. Bladder Herb, Red Nightshade, Red Winter-cherry, Straw-berry-Tomato. *P. pubescens*, Barbadoes Cape-Goose-berry, Straw-berry Tomato. **1887** *Nicholson's Dict. Gard.* IV. 53/1 *Cherry and Red Currant Tomatoes*, these are chiefly grown for ornament, as their fruits are borne in great profusion in bunches or clusters. They represent, in general appearance, the Cherry and Red Currant, after which they are popularly called.

b. tree tomato, the shrub *Cyphomandra betacea*, N.O. *Solanaceæ*, a native of Colombia and Peru, now naturalized in many tropical and subtropical countries; also its fruit.

1880–81 MORRIS *Ann. Rep. Public Gardens Jamaica* 35 Tree Tomato. **1884** *Gard. Chron.* XXI. 510 Tree Tomato. This is the popular name of a fruit naturalized in Jamaica... It answers in every respect the purposes for which the ordinary Tomato is esteemed. **1887** *Standard* 16 Sept. 5/2 Here.. is the tree tomato,.. the Tomato de Paz, or the 'vegetable mercury'. **1944** *Living off Land* ii. 40 Tree-tomatoes will be found as garden-escapees. **1959** *N.Z. Listener* 8 May 22/3 Tree Tomato Sauce. Eight pounds tree tomatoes, 2 large onions, [etc.]. **1966** G. W. TURNER *Eng. Lang. Austral. & N.Z.* viii. 172 Tree tomato and Chinese gooseberry seem to be commoner in New Zealand than in other English-speaking countries. **1976** K. THACKERAY *Crownbird* v. 91 A separate table bore.. tree tomatoes, portions of yellow jackfruit and chilled mountain paw-paw.

3. *attrib.* and *Comb.*, as ***tomato-blight***, ***-can***, ***chutney***, ***-grafting***, ***-growing***, ***-ketchup***, ***-leaf***, ***-plant***, ***purée***, ***-rot***, ***salad***, ***sandwich***, ***-sauce***, ***-scab***, ***-seed***, ***soup***, ***-top***; ***tomato-coloured***, ***-red*** adjs; **tomato-gall**: see quot. 1891[2]; **tomato hawk-moth** or **sphinx**, an American sphingid moth, *Protoparce celeus*; **tomato hornworm** = *tomato worm*; **tomato juice**, the juice from tomatoes; also, a drink of this; **tomato paste**, thick, concentrated tomato purée; **tomato pinworm**, the larva of a small moth, *Keiferia lycopersicella*, which bores holes in the buds or fruit of the tomato plant; **tomato vine** *U.S.*, a tomato plant; **tomato-worm**, the caterpillar of this, which feeds on tomato leaves.

1868 'O. C. KERR' *Smoked Glass* xviii. 216 What mean these letters which I find imprinted upon.. the tomato can? **1914** *Sat. Even. Post* 4 Apr. 11/1 A gay-cat.. will turn against a friend when that friend is down to tomato cans. **1855** E. ACTON *Mod. Cookery* (rev. ed.) xxxii. 609 Tomata and other chatnies. **1963** A. L. SIMON *Guide Good Food & Wines* 133/1 (*heading*) Green tomato chutney. **1869** L. M. ALCOTT *Little Women* II. iii. 31 Brown rain, and purple clouds, with a tomato-coloured splash in the middle. **1891** MISS DOWIE *Girl in Karp.* 68 Her two tomato-coloured aprons. **1904** E. NESBIT *Phœnix & Carpet* xi. 206 Tomato-coloured Liberty silk. **1887** *Nicholson's Dict. Gard.* IV. 51/2 It is only in warm situations.. that the Tomato crop can be depended upon in the open air. **1887** *Ibid.* 52/1 Tomato culture. **1891** *Cent. Dict.*, *Tomato-gall*, a gall made upon the twigs of the grape-vine in the United States by the gall-midge *Lasioptera vitis*: so called on account of its resemblance to the fruit of the tomato. **1897** *Westm. Gaz.* 16 Dec. 12/2 To graft the tomato on the potato stalk... So far from taking from the strength of the tubers, the tomato-grafting, he thinks, improves them. He never grew such fine potatoes as with tomato-tops, nor such fine tomatoes as with potato roots. **1928** METCALF & FLINT *Destructive & Useful Insects* xvi. 488 The southern or tomato hornworm ranges from the northern states southward far into South America. **1972** SWAN & PAPP *Common Insects N. Amer.* xix. 263 Tomato hornworm... sometimes called the five-spotted hawk moth. **1935** M. MORPHY *Recipes of All Nations* 595 Tomato juice cocktail. **1936** 'R. WEST' *Thinking Reed* ii. 56 She ordered some tomato juice, for she would never again need a cocktail. **1981** P. VAN GREENAWAY *'Cassandra' Bell* iv. 47, I ordered another tomato juice to calm his nerves. **1845** E. ACTON *Mod. Cookery* v. 136 Tomato catsup. **1896** *Daily News* 25 Nov. 3/5 An alleged libel on the plaintiffs in their trade as sellers of tomato ketchup. *Mod. Breakfast Menu Card*, Tomato Omelettes. *c* **1938** *Fortnum & Mason Price List* 59/1 Tomato Paste. **1979** *Guardian* 25 Aug. 10/4 Pepsi's had been selling cola in Budapest.. but all the company had been able to get out of the country was tomato paste. **1931** *Monthly Bull. Calif. Dept. Agric.* XX. 458 (*heading*) Damage to tomatoes in Southern California by the tomato pin worm. **1972** SWAN & PAPP *Common Insects N. Amer.* xix. 323 The closely related Tomato Pinworm.. bores pinholes in the developing buds, green and ripening fruits of tomatoes. **1887** *Nicholson's Dict. Gard.* IV. 52/2 Tomato-plants are seldom very seriously injured by insects. **1877** E. S. DALLAS *Kettner's Bk. of Table* 122 Add to the sauce a tablespoonful of tomato purée. **1977** B. PYM *Quartet in Autumn* vii. 64 Tomato purée, stuffed vine leaves.. and tapioca pudding. **1892** *Daily News* 3 Sept. 2/1 Another tea jacket is in tomato red velvet. **1877** E. S. DALLAS *Kettner's Bk. of Table* 460 For the tomato salad a dash of mustard is not a bad addition. **1980** I. MURDOCH *Nuns & Soldiers* 176 Supper consisted of onion soup, black sausage with tomato salad, and a local cheese with herbs. **1911** W. J. LOCKE *Glory of Clementina Wing* ii. 17 Tomato sandwiches and plum-cake set out for a visitor's tea. **1978** F. OLBRICH *Desouza pays Price* xxv. 161 Delicate tomato sandwiches and fragrant Darjeeling tea. **1806** A. HUNTER *Culina* (ed. 3) 233 The only difference between this and the genuine tomata sauce, is the substituting the pulp of apple for the pulp of tomata. **1846** SOYER *Cookery* 9 Four tablespoonfuls of tomate sauce. **1897** *Allbutt's Syst. Med.* III. 885 Readily mistaken for tomato-seeds. **1846** *Jewish Manual, or Pract. Information Jewish & Mod. Cookery* v. 97 Dry tomato soup. **1974** 'E. LATHEN' *Sweet & Low* xvi. 154 The problem we have with tomato soup in my cannery. **1897** Tomato top [see *tomato-grafting* above]. **1876** 'MARK TWAIN' *Adventures Tom Sawyer* i. 18 [She] looked out among the tomato vines and jimpson weeds that constituted the garden. **1981** G. V. HIGGINS *Rat on Fire* xii. 92 You.. tromp all over the old people's tomato vines.

Hence **to'matoey** *a.*, having the taste or flavour of tomatoes.

1972 *Homes & Gardens* Aug. 101 (Advt.), The result is a tomato juice that's thicker, smoother and more tomatoey than any you've ever tasted. **1982** D. WILTSE *Wedding Guest* xv. 205 The shared appreciation of the wine, the spicy sausage, the tomatoey beans.

tomaun, variant of TOMAN[1].

†**tom-axe.** *Obs. rare.* [A mixture of TOMAHAWK and AXE.] = TOMAHAWK.

1759 JOHNSON *Idler* No. 40 ¶7 With his face and body painted, with his scalping-knife, tom-ax, and all other implements of war.

tomb (tuːm), *sb.* Forms: α. 3–6 **toumbe, tumbe**, 4–5 **toumb**, 4–6 **tumb**, 4–7 **tombe**, 5 **towmbe**, 6–7 **toombe**, 4– **tomb**. β. 4–5 **towme**, 4–6 **tome**, 5–6 **toume**, 6 *Sc.* **toim**, 6–7 **toome**. [Early ME. *toumbe*, *tumbe*, a. AF. *tumbe*, OF. *tombe* (12th c. in Godef.) = Sp., Pg. *tumba*, It. *tomba*:—late L. *tumba* (Prudentius), ad. Gr. τύμβος sepulchral mound.

The final *b* began to be mute in Eng. (cf. *lamb*, *dumb*) early in 14th c., but the spelling *tomb*, which never exactly represented the spoken word, has survived, and from the 17th c. been the accepted form.]

1. a. A place of burial; an excavation in earth or rock for the reception of a dead body, a grave. Also, a chamber or vault formed wholly or partly in the earth, and, in early times, a tumulus or mound raised over the body.

(In quot. 1275, perhaps a coffin or sarcophagus.)

c **1275** LAY. 6080 Hii makede one tumbe [*c* 1205 tunne] of golde and of gimmes. þane kinge hii dude þar ine.. and leide hine mid honure heȝe in þan toure. *c* **1290** *Beket* 2341 in *S. Eng. Leg.* I. 173 Riȝt so he wende to þe stude þere seint thomas lai At is toumbe he feol a-doun a-kneo wepinde wel sore. *a* **1300** *Cursor M.* 17798 (Cott.) Yee sal find þair tumbs [*Gött.* tumbes] tome [= toom]. *c* **1400** *Destr. Troy* 12113 þis burd was broght to þe bare toumb. **1474** CAXTON *Chesse* 93 Thenne they took the body out of the tombe. **1513** DOUGLAS *Æneis* v. vii. 16 At the tumbe [L. *tumulum*].. Quhair beryit was Hector of maist renoun. **1642** FULLER *Holy & Prof. St.* III. xiv. 187 Tombes are the clothes of the dead. **1756–7** tr. *Keysler's Trav.* (1760) II. 232 The church-yard is so full of tombs. **1838** THIRLWALL *Greece* II. xvi. 389 A tomb.. which was generally believed to contain his bones.

b. *transf.* Anything that is or may become the last resting-place of a corpse.

1812 J. WILSON *Isle of Palms* I. 646 The sails now serve them for a shroud, And the sea-cave is their tomb.

c. *fig.*

1816 SHELLEY *Sunset* 42 The tomb of thy dead self. **1818** —— *The Past* 9 Memories that make the heart a tomb. **1907** *Nation* (N.Y.) 12 Sept. 222/2 The office of mayor has been the tomb of many political ambitions.

2. A monument erected to enclose or cover the body and preserve the memory of the dead; a sepulchral structure raised above the earth. Hence sometimes a cenotaph. Also formerly, a tombstone erected over a grave.

c **1290** *S. Eng. Leg.* I. 102/33 þoruȝ touchingue of seinte Agace toumbe þouȝ schalt beo hol a-non. **1297** R. GLOUC. (Rolls) 2617 He bad þat.. me is bodi nome & burede it.. In an tumbe suiþe hey, þat hii miȝte hit ver yse. *Ibid.* 4594 At glastinbury.. at uore þe heye weued,.. As is bones liggeþ, is toumbe wel vair is. *c* **1330** R. BRUNNE *Chron. Wace* (Rolls) 7791 Byrieþ me þere.. & doþ make a toumbe þat longe may last. **1470–85** MALORY *Arthur* II. xi. 88 Kyng Arthur lete make the tombe of kynge Lot passyng rychely. **1545** *Test. Ebor.* (Surtees) VI. 234 Fortie poundes.. to make a tombe over my grave. **1613** PURCHAS *Pilgrimage* (1614) 304 The common sort haue their Tombes of marble engrauen with letters. **1657** in Swayne *Sarum Churchw. Acc.* (1896) 234 To make a Toombe ouer his wiues Graue. *a* **1717** PARNELL *Night Piece on Death* 39 The Marble Tombs that rise on high, Whose Dead in vaulted Arches lye. **1820** W. IRVING *Sketch Bk., Westm. Abbey*, I paused to contemplate a tomb on which lay the effigy of a knight in complete armour.

3. Regarded as the final resting-place of every one; hence sometimes used for the state of death.

1559 *Mirr. Mag., Hen. VI* vi, Would god the rufull toumbe had been my royall trone. **1690** LOCKE *Hum. Und.* II. x. §5 Our Minds represent to us those Tombs, to which we are approaching. **1769** GRAY *Install. Ode* 50 Charity, that glows beyond the tomb. **1777** J. RYLAND in Palmer *Bk. Praise* (1862) 226 He that formed me in the womb, He shall guide me to the tomb. **1822** BYRON *Heav. & Earth* I. iii, Than to behold the universal tomb.

4. *R.C. Ch.* Designating a cavity in an altar, where relics are deposited; an altar-cavity.

1886 *Encycl. Brit.* XX. 357/2 Every altar used for the celebration of mass must, according to Roman Catholic rule, contain some authorized relics. These are inserted into a cavity prepared for their reception, called 'the tomb', by the bishop of the diocese, and sealed up with the episcopal seal.

5. *The Tombs*: New York City prison. *U.S. slang.*

1840 *Daily Picayune* (New Orleans) 27 Aug. 2/3 Poor Chapman.. is in the 'Tombs', charged with false swearing at an election. **1842** DICKENS *Amer. Notes* I. vi. 199 What is this dismal-fronted pile of bastard Egyptian?.. A famous prison, called the Tombs. **1935** A. G. MACDONELL *Visit to Amer.* iii. 53 A criminal had been brought from the Tombs ..to be examined in the 'Line-Up'. **1981** M. C. SMITH *Gorky Park* III. iii. 330 It's the Tombs... Night Court's open now.

6. *attrib.* and *Comb.* **a.** attrib., as ***tomb-board, -burglar, -burglary, -cave, -chamber, -chapel, chest, -dweller, figure, figurine, furniture, -house, monument, -painting, -palace, -relief, -slab, -temple***, etc. **b.** objective, as ***tomb-breaker, -haunter, -maker, -robber***. **c.** instrumental, etc., as ***tomb-paved, -strewn***; ***tomb-black, -like*** adjs. See also TOMB-BAT, -STONE.

1590 SPENSER *F.Q.* II. viii. 16 To decke his herce, and trap his *tomb-blacke steed. **1594** ? GREENE *Selimus* Wks. (Grosart) XIV. 269 When thus they see me with religious pompe, To celebrate his tomb-blacke mortuarie. **1785** T. CUMBER *Diary* in *Home Counties Mag.* (1902) IV. 226 The following inscription on a *tomb board. **1631** WEEVER *Anc. Fun. Mon.* 51 These *Tombe-breakers, these graue-diggers. **1654** WHITLOCK *Zootomia* 408 *Tomb-Burglary in this kind, being so uncouth a Case, as Law never made Provision against it. **1891** G. F. X. GRIFFITH tr. *Fouard's Christ* I. 310 *note*, Numerous *tomb-caves are still to be seen hollowed out of the mountain-side. **1906** PETRIE *Relig. Anc. Egypt* iii. 12 In Upper Egypt at present a hole is left at the top of the *tomb chamber; and I have seen a woman remove the covering of the hole, and talk down to her deceased husband. **1908** *Blackw. Mag.* July 59 Solid *tomb-chapels had to be constructed in honour of the more important dead. **1955** M. D. ANDERSON *Imagery Brit. Churches* II. ii. 44 The late medieval *tomb chests often have small figures arranged in niches all round them. **1925** B. RACKHAM in R. Fry et al. *Chinese Art* 13 In his wonderful *tomb figures.. we come to the very border-line of sculpture. **1970** Tomb figure [see HANIWA]. **1933** *Burlington Mag.* Nov. 233/2 There are several *tomb figurines which show vivacity and able characterization. **1976** 'M. DELVING' *China Expert* v. 56 Tashjian.. had.. unloaded an extremely dubious Han tomb figurine on an unsuspecting German dealer. **1908** *Chambers's Jrnl.* July 527/2 We were in the midst of such a medley of *tomb-furniture. **1977** *Times* 23 Apr. 13/3 The increasing vogue for tomb 'furniture' among the lower echelons of T'ang society. **1939** W. B. YEATS *Last Poems* 20 What great *tomb-haunter sweeps the distant sky. **1975** G. EWART *Be My Guest!* I. 15 But stay! who is this totally melodramatic opium-smoking tomb-haunter? **1762–71** H. WALPOLE *Vertue's Anecd. Paint.* (1786) I. 176 Leland says that.. Henry VII. pulled it down, and erected the present *tomb-house in it's place. **1963** E. M. JOPE in Foster & Alcock *Culture & Environment* xiii. 338 It is an area where hog-backed tomb-houses are to be found. **1845** HIRST *Com. Mammoth*, etc. 18 No murmur broke The silence of that *tomb-like spot. **1906** DK. ARGYLL *Autobiog.* I. ix. 203 The lower church is essentially tomblike. **1580** in *Archæol. Jrnl.* (1851) VIII. 185 Richard Roiley.. *Tumbe maker. **1619** *Rutland MSS.* (1905) IV. 517 Paid to Nycholas Johnson, tombmaker, for the finishing of the monument for the late Earle Roger of Rutland, 100 li. **1948** D. DIRINGER *Alphabet* II. iv. 261 *Tomb-monuments in various countries. **1887** MAHAFFY & GILMAN *Alexander's Empire* xxix. (1890) 271 Objects represented in the *tomb-paintings with their names written over them. **1901** *Edin. Rev.* Jan. 33 The *tomb-palaces of long-dead kings. **1804** J. GRAHAME *Sabbath* (1805) 14 Slowly the throng moves o'er the *tomb-paved ground. **1906** *Macm. Mag.* Oct. 896 Such an almost pathetic beauty is the dominant note of the later *tomb-reliefs of Athenian sculpture. **1853** HICKIE tr. *Aristoph.* (1872) II. 592 He would thus be a *tomb-robber. **1908** *Athenæum* 21 Mar. 360/3 A tomb-robber could.. remove the jewellery and other valuable objects buried with the corpse. **1889** HISSEY *Tour in Phaeton* 329 Ancient and curious *tomb-slabs. **1906** *Daily Chron.* 20 July 5/5 In a quiet *tomb-strewn graveyard among the winding lanes of Welwyn. **1904** H. SPENCER *Autobiog.* II. XII. lvii. 335 The thing which impressed me was the *tomb-temple in which we picnic'd.

tomb (tuːm), *v.* Now *rare.* Forms: see the sb. [f. TOMB *sb.*: cf. It. *tombare* to entomb.]

1. *trans.* To deposit (a body) in the tomb; to lay in the grave, bury, inter, entomb.

c **1330** R. BRUNNE *Chron.* (1810) 48 He lies a Glastenbire toumbed, as I wene. **14..** *Sir Beues* (M.) 4321 He towmbed ham to geder in ffere, Kyng and quene as they were. **1475** *Bk. Noblesse* (Roxb.) 45 And there made his faire ende at Rone, where he liethe tombid. **1591** GREENE *Maidens Dreame* Wks. (Grosart) XIV. 316 Let that [body] be earthed and tombed in gorgeous wise. *c* **1611** CHAPMAN *Iliad* XXIII. 305 Imagine them some monument, of one long since tomb'd there. **1759** W. MASON *Caractacus* Poems (1773) 256 Ye can tomb me in this sacred place. **1899** J. LUMSDEN *Poems* 16 In the Atlantic's bed Tombed ten leagues deep.

b. in *fig.* senses of 'bury'.

1611 HEYWOOD *Gold. Age* I. i. Wks. 1874 III. 13 I'le toombe th' usurper in his Infant bloud. **1613** MARSTON *Insat. Countess* I. i, [I'll bury thee] In the Swans downe, and tombe thee in mine armes. **1813** SCOTT *Rokeby* II. xviii, There dig and tomb your precious heap, And bid the dead your treasure keep.

2. To enclose or contain as a tomb; to serve as a tomb for. Hence **'tombing** *ppl. a.*

a **1586** SIDNEY *Arcadia* III. Wks. 1724 II. 512 The Stone that tombs the Two. **1865** TENNYSON *On a Mourner* vi, And when no mortal motion jars The blackness round the tombing sod,.. Comes Faith from tract no feet have trod.

tombac ('tɒmbæk). Forms: 7 **tombaga, tambaycke, tumbeck, 8 tombago, tambaqua, tumbanck, tambac,** 9 **tombec, tombak,** 8– **tombac.** [The current form is a. F. *tombac* (1700 in Hatz.-Darm.) = It. *tombacco*, Pg. *tambaca*, Sp. *tumbaga*, a. Malay *tambâga* copper.]

a. An alloy, of East Indian origin, of copper and zinc, in various proportions, containing from 82 to 99 per cent. of copper. Used in the east for gongs or bells; in Europe, under various names, as Prince's metal, Mannheim gold, etc., as a material for cheap jewellery.

red tombac, that containing above 92 per cent. of copper. ***yellow tombac***, that containing 82 to 90 per cent. ***white tombac***, an alloy of copper and arsenic.

1602 LANCASTER *Voy. India* in Purchas *Pilgrims* (1625) I. III. iii. §3. 153 All the dishes.. were, either of pure Gold, or of another Mettall.. called Tambaycke, which groweth of Gold and Brasse together. **1602–5** SCOTT *Disc. Java* ibid. iv. §5. 180 Their drummes are huge pannes made of a metall called Tombaga. **1727–41** CHAMBERS *Cycl.*, *Tambac*, or *Tambaqua*, a mixture of gold and copper which the people of Siam hold more beautiful.. than gold itself. **1760–72** tr. *Juan & Ulloa's Voy.* (ed. 3) I. 121 Round their arms, they [women of Panama] wear bracelets of gold and tombac. *Ibid.* II. 60 Jewels set in gold, or for singularity sake, in tombago. **1815** J. SMITH *Panorama Sc. & Art* I. 43 Tombac has still more copper, and is of a deeper red than pinchbeck. *Ibid.* II. 399 Copper combines with five-sixths of arsenic, forming a white, hard, and brittle alloy;.. it is called white tombac, and is much used in the manufacture of buttons. **1825** J. NICHOLSON *Operat. Mechanic* 710 Tombac. 16 lb. of copper, 1 lb. of tin, and 1 lb. of zinc. Red Tombac. 5½ lb. of copper, and ½ lb. of zinc... White Tombac. Copper and Arsenic. **1853** URE *Dict. Arts* I. 243 Tombak, or Red Brass, in the cast state, is an alloy of copper and zinc, containing not more than 20 per cent. of the latter constituent. **1864–72** WATTS *Dict. Chem.* II. 47 The most ductile of all the alloys of copper and zinc are those which contain 84·5 per cent. of copper to 15·5 of zinc (tombac), and 71·5 copper to 28·5 zinc (brass)... Karsten.

(*b*) In *Archæol.* usu. **tumbaga, -bago.**

1931 E. NORDENSKIÖLD *Compar. Ethnogr. Stud.* IX. 104 The awl.. has been analyzed by Dr. K. G. Almström, and found to contain 33% Au, 12% Ag and 55% Cu. This is the composition generally known in archaeological literature as tumbaga. **1936** *Nature* 4 Jan. 29/1 In Antioquia, in Colombia,.. objects are found made particularly of the gold alloy.. which is known as 'tumbago'. **1974** S. E. MORISON *European Discovery of America*: *Southern Voy.* vii. 152 As ornaments they [*sc.* Venezuelan Indians] displayed great polished disks made of an alloy of copper and gold that they called *guanin*, and which modern archaeologists have named *tumbaga*.

†**b.** A musical instrument made of this. *rare.*

1662 J. DAVIES tr. *Mandelslo's Trav.* I. (1669) 30 A Tumbeck, or Timbrel, a Haw-boy, and several Tabours.

c. *attrib.*, as **tombac-brown** adj.

1796 KIRWAN *Elem. Min.* (ed. 2) I. 30 (Colours) Tombac brown—metallic yellowish brown. **1811** PINKERTON *Petralogy* I. 194 Granite, with tombac brown mica.

tombal ('tuːmbəl, 'tɒmbəl), *a. rare.* [f. TOMB *sb.* + -AL[1].] Of or pertaining to a tomb.

1900 *Daily News* 3 Aug. 5/1 A beautiful tombal monument, shut in, according to French fashion, by an iron grille.

‖**tombarolo** (tomba'rolo). Pl. tombaroli. [It.] A grave-robber.

1973 *New Yorker* 7 Apr. 98/2 A skilled *tombarolo* knows the surface indications of a tomb and pilfers the treasure inside after using an ingenious probing device known as an *asta* ('lance') or *chiave* ('key'). **1975** *Listener* 11 Dec. 793/2 The ware.. had been illegally excavated from an Etruscan tomb.. by a gang of grave robbers, the notorious *tombaroli*.

†**tombazite** ('tɒmbəzaɪt). *Min. Obs.* [Named in Ger. *tombazit* by Breithaupt 1838, in allusion to its tombac colour.] An obsolete synonym of GERSDORFFITE, a sulph-arsenide of nickel.

1850 ANSTED *Elem. Geol., Min.*, etc. §468 Nickel green, Tombazite, Arsenate of nickel, with 36 per cent. of the oxide.

'tomb-bat. A name for bats of the genus *Taphozous*, family *Emballonuridæ*, which frequent tombs as their dwelling-places.

1883–96 *List Anim. Zool. Soc.* (ed. 9) 105 *Taphozous nudiventris.* Naked-bellied Tomb-Bat. Hab. Africa.

tombe, obs. f. TOOM *a.* empty, TOME, TOMBO.

tomberel, -ell, obs. forms of TUMBREL.

tombestere, early form of TUMBESTER.

tombic ('tuːmbɪk, 'tɒmbɪk), *a.* [f. TOMB *sb.* + -IC.] Of, pertaining to, or connected with tombs, sepulchral: esp. in reference to the view that the Great Pyramid was a tomb.

1874 PIAZZI SMYTH *Inherit. in Gt. Pyramid* (new ed.) vi. 96 Different from either the treasure-theory of the East, or sepulchral, i.e. tombic, theory of Western minds. *Ibid.* 92 The Tombic Theory. **1883** R. A. PROCTOR *Gt. Pyramid* iii. 172 There are the strongest possible objections against the credibility of the merely tombic theory (to use a word coined, I imagine, by Professor Piazzi Smyth, and more convenient perhaps than defensible).

tomble, -ed, -er, obs. forms of TUMBLE, etc.

tombless ('tuːmlɪs), *a.* [f. TOMB *sb.* + -LESS.] Having no tomb or sepulchral monument, destitute of a grave; unburied. Also *fig.*

1594 BARNFIELD *Affect. Sheph.* II. xxxvi, Fame is toombles, Vertue liues for aye. **1599** SHAKS. *Hen. V*, I. ii. 229 Or lay these bones in an vnworthy Vrne, Tomblesse, with no remembrance ouer them. *a* **1814** *Orpheus* III. i. in *New Brit. Theatre* III. 298 Shades of the tombless dead! **1823** PRAED *Australasia* 231 The bleak desert, or the tombless sea. *a* **1849** J. C. MANGAN *Poems* (1859) 373 And scorn shall point at our tombless graves. **1855** O. W. HOLMES *Poems* 188 Shroudless and tombless they sank to their rest.

tomblet ('tuːmlɪt). *rare.* [f. as prec. + -LET.] A small tomb or burial-mound.

1855 BAILEY *Spir. Leg.* in *Mystic*, etc. 128 Earth heaves with tomblets, as the sea with waves.

‖**tombo** ('tɒmbəʊ). Also 8 in F. form **tombe.** [Native name.] General African W. Coast name of the fruit of the wine palm, *Raphia vinifera*; also, a native palm wine obtained from it.

1704 *Barbot's Guinea* in *Churchill's Voy.* V. 144 The fruit produced by the tombe tree, from which they also draw the wine called bourdon or tombe. **1819** REES *Cycl.* s.v. *Ivory*, A species of fruit growing on a sort of palmtree, which the natives call tombo or bourbon. **1908** *Daily Chron.* 7 Dec. 4/4 Considerable evidence.. adduced to show that intoxication is more frequent from drinking tombo and other native brews than from drinking imported spirit.

tombola (tɒm'bəʊlə, 'tɒmbələ). [a. F. *tombola* (1878 in *Dict. Acad.*), or It. *tombola*, f. *tombolare* to turn a somersault, fall upside down, tumble.] A kind of lottery resembling lotto.

1880 'OUIDA' *Moths* xv, You have a tombola for a famine, you have a dramatic performance for a flood, you have a concert for a fire. **1883** *Daily News* 19 July 5/7 There were various other Chinese articles for sale, and a tombola with all prizes and no blanks. **1883** *World* No. 471. 13 One of the features of the Savage Club, which is not advertised, on account of the Lottery Act, is a tombola. **1907** *Daily Chron.* 7 June 7/3 The law has now stepped in, and forbidden the tombola, on the ground that it would be a contravention of the Gaming Act. The tombola was arranged on the novel principle of no blanks, and a prize for every ticket-holder.

tombolo ('tɒmbələʊ). *Physical Geogr.* [a. It. *tombolo* sand dune, tombolo.] A bar joining an island to the mainland.

1899 F. P. GULLIVER in *Proc. Amer. Acad. Arts & Sci.* XXXIV. 189 Upon the coast of Italy where island-tying.. is beautifully shown, such a bar is called a tombolo. For convenience in distinguishing island-tying bars from those of other kinds, the writer proposes to call every bar of this kind a tombolo, giving an English plural tombolos. **1937** *Geogr. Jrnl.* XC. 190 The writer goes on to discuss bars, spits, and tombolos along the more sheltered shores of the Firth of Clyde. **1960** B. W. SPARKS *Geomorphol.* viii. 201 In the British Isles a fine example of a tombolo is provided by Chesil Beach, an eighteen-mile-long ridge connecting the Isle of Portland to the mainland. **1977** A. HALLAM *Planet Earth* 94/3 In high-latitude, previously glaciated areas, tombolos are often formed of shingle, the commonest beach material in such regions.

tomboy ('tɒmbɔɪ). [f. TOM *sb.*[1] + BOY *sb.*]

†**1.** A rude, boisterous, or forward boy. *Obs.* (Generally so taken in quot. *a* 1553; certainly so in 1599.)

a **1553** UDALL *Royster D.* II. iv. (Arb.) 37 Is all your delite and ioy In whiskyng and ramping abroade like a Tom boy? **1599** MASSINGER, etc. *Old Law* III. ii, Must young court tits [= young gentlemen courtiers] Play tomboys' tricks with her, and he live?

†**2.** A bold or immodest woman. *Obs.*

1579 TOMSON *Calvin's Serm. Tim.* 203/2 Sainte Paule meaneth that women must not be impudent, they must not be tomboyes, to be shorte, they must not be vnchast. **1611** SHAKS. *Cymb.* I. vi. 122 To be partner'd With Tomboyes hyr'd with that self exhibition Which your owne Coffers yeeld. **1619** FLETCHER, etc. *Knt. Malta* II. i, Ye Filly, Ye Tit, ye Tomboy! *a* **1700** B. E. *Dict. Cant. Crew*, *Tom-boy*, a Ramp, or Tomrig.

3. A girl who behaves like a spirited or boisterous boy; a wild romping girl; a hoyden.

1592 LYLY *Midas* I. ii, If thou shouldest rigge vp and downe in our iackets, thou wouldst be thought a very tomboy. **1622** T. STOUGHTON *Chr. Sacrif.* xii. 169 Of such short-haired Gentlewomen I find not one example either in Scripture or elsewhere. And what shall I say of such poled rigs, ramps and Tomboyes? **1656** BLOUNT *Glossogr.*, *Tom-boy*, a girle or wench that leaps up and down like a boy. **1730–6** BAILEY (folio), *Tom-boy*, a ramping, frolicsome, rude girl. **1802** in *Spirit Pub. Jrnls.* VI. 72 The violent exercise of the skipping-rope, which is..only fit for some Miss Tomboy. **1830** MISS MITFORD *Village* Ser. IV. Introd. Let. 7 He had no taste for giantesses, and a particular aversion for hoydens and tomboys and women who trespassed against the delicacy of their sex. **1888** MRS. H. WARD *R. Elsmere* x, As a rough tomboy of fourteen, she had shown Catherine.. a good many uncouth signs of affection.

4. *attrib.*

1657 HOWELL *Londinop.* 398 Stool-ball, though that stradling kind of Tomboy sport be not so handsome for Mayds. **1675** HAN. WOOLLEY *Gentlewom. Comp.* 52 To laugh, or express any Tom-boy trick is as bad or worse. **1874** MRS. H. WOOD *Mast. Greylands* iv, He saw a great deal to find fault with in her rude, tomboy ways. **1882** *Atlantic Monthly* LI. 87 Having..practiced them in a mere romping, 'tom-boy' spirit when she was a young girl.

Hence **tomboy'ade** *nonce-wd.*, an escapade in the manner of a tomboy; **tom'boyful** *a.*, **'tom,boyish** *a.*, like or having the character of a tomboy; hence **'tom,boyishness**; **'tomboyism**.

1886 *Blackw. Mag.* Apr. 516 Reminiscences of scrambles and *tomboyades when they were girls together. **1887** J. ASHBY STERRY *Lazy Minstrel* (1892) 82 Careless and joyful. .. Pet in short petticoats—Truly *tomboyful! **1862** MISS YONGE *C'tess Kate* iv, A child..certainly *tom-boyish except for a certain timidity. **1887** 'EDNA LYALL' *Knt.-Errant* (1889) 227 A rather tomboyish young person of fourteen. **1883** L. WINGFIELD *A. Rowe* III. vii. 130 Under the roughness and *tomboyishness was a heart of real gold. **1876** MISS YONGE *Womankind* ii, What I mean by '*tomboyism' is a wholesome delight in rushing about at full speed, playing at active games, climbing trees, rowing boats, making dirt-pies, and the like.

tombrell, -il, obs. forms of TUMBREL.

tombstone, tomb-stone ('tu:mstəʊn).

1. a. A horizontal stone covering a grave; in early use, the cover of a stone coffin, or the stone coffin itself.

1565 STAPLETON tr. *Bede's Hist. Ch. Eng.* 125 The very same tombestone was found to be of a fyt length for the quantitie of the bodie. **1672** WILKINS *Nat. Relig.* 28 Suppose he should dig up a large stone of the shape of an ancient tomb-stone. **1696** PHILLIPS (ed. 5), *Tomb-stone*, a Stone that is laid over a Grave, with an Inscription upon it. **1715–20** POPE *Iliad* XVII. 492 Still as a tombstone, never to be mov'd, On some good man or woman unreprov'd, Lays its eternal weight. **1840** DICKENS *Barn. Rudge* i, Sitting down to take his dinner on cold tombstones. **1898** *Saga-Bk. of Viking Cl.* Jan. 34 Two hog-back or coped tomb-stones, supposed to be one thousand years old.

b. A stone or monument of any kind placed over the grave of a deceased person to preserve his memory; a gravestone; including a headstone (or the like of wood). (Early quots. may be in sense 1.)

1711 ADDISON *Spect.* No. 26 ¶5 When I meet with the Grief of Parents upon a Tomb-stone, my Heart melts with Compassion. **1712** STEELE *ibid.* No. 518 ¶3 There is not a Gentleman in England better read in Tomb-stones than my self, my Studies having laid very much in Church-yards. **1793** SMEATON *Edystone L.* §98 A well shaped Tomb-stone of Granite. **1820** W. IRVING *Sketch Bk.* I. 84 (*Rip Van Winkle*) There was a wooden tombstone in the church yard that used to tell all about him. **1843** BETHUNE *Sc. Fire-side Stor.* 160 That species of erect tombstone which some one has..designated as spectral. **1870** F. R. WILSON *Ch. Lindisf.* 35 The churchyard is crowded with tombstones.

c. *fig.*

c **1611** CHAPMAN *Iliad* III. 60 For which thou well deserv'st A coat of tombstone not of steel in which thou serv'st. **1658** (*title*) Mistris Shawes Tomb-stone,..Beeing a Narrative of Remarkable Passages in the Holy Life and Happy Death of Mrs. Dorothy Shaw, of Brampton. **1755** SMOLLETT *Quix.* II. IV. x. (1803) IV. 212, 'I swear to that condition', answered Don Quixote: 'and, for the greater security, will put a tomb-stone over whatever you shall communicate'. **1819** J. MONTGOMERY *Greenland* v. 186 One frozen plain, The mighty tombstone of the buried main. **1902** *Daily Chron.* 24 May 3/1 It puts tombstones to the reputations of many good officers, and buries the blunders of others under cairns of apologetic explanations.

2. *slang.* **a.** A pawn-ticket. **b.** See quot. 1903.

1883 J. GREENWOOD *Odd People in Odd Pl.* 168 The..bag in which the 'tombstones' or pawn-tickets were deposited. *c* **1889** *Sporting Times* (Farmer), The collection for master amounted to $4\frac{1}{2}d.$, and a tombstone for ninepence on a brown Melton overcoat. **1903** FARMER & HENLEY *Slang Dict.*, *Tombstone*, a projecting tooth, a snaggle-tooth.

3. *Comm.* An advertisement displaying the names of the underwriters or firms associated with a new issue or the like. Also ***tombstone ad(vertisement.***

1968 *Times* 27 Feb. 22/3 'Tombstones'..are getting bigger. I am referring, of course, to the new issue advertisements. **1972** *Times* 24 Oct. 2 The Times is now able to offer financial advertisers an exclusive service for the placing of Tombstone advertising (public announcements and notices of redemption) in Europe. **1977** *National Times* (Austral.) 17 Jan. 40/2 The advertising of trusts is limited to 'tombstone' advertising. **1981** *U.S. Banker* Dec. 56/1 The old tombstone ad, promoting a service and basing the appeal largely on price,..is long gone, according to advertising men. **1983** *Marketing* 24 Mar. 39/1 Financial advertising columnage, i.e. tomb-stones, company meetings, prospectuses, takeovers, etc.

4. *attrib.* and *Comb.*

1751 B. LYNDE *Diary* 16 Oct. (1880) 176 Yesterday Cox and Stacy ½ day abo. Tombstone monument. *a* **1845** HOOD *Valentine* ii, Just stopped before The tomb-stone steps that lead us to death's door. **1905** *Daily Chron.* 24 Apr. 4/5 An elderly man was sitting dejectedly on the tombstone-shaded bench.

tom cat, tom-cat ('tɒm'kæt), *sb.* [See TOM *sb.*[1] 6.

In 1760 was published an anonymous work 'The Life and Adventures of a Cat', which became very popular. The hero, a male or 'ram' cat, bore the name of Tom, and is commonly mentioned as 'Tom the Cat', as 'Tybert the Catte' is in Caxton's Reynard the Fox. Thus Tom became a favourite allusive name for a male cat (see quot. 1791 s.v. TOM *sb.*[1] 6); and people said 'this cat is a Tom' or a 'Tom cat'.]

A male cat.

[**1760** *Life & Adv. of a Cat* 11 Chap. iv. Tom the Cat is born of poor but honest parents. *Ibid.* 31 The single adventures of Tom the Cat only.] **1809** MALKIN *Gil Blas* II. vii. ¶27 The devil fetch that tom cat! **1825** *Univ. Songster* (*title*) The Tortoiseshell Tom-cat. **1838** DICKENS *Nich. Nick.* xii, It's enough to make a Tom cat talk French grammar. **1881** J. HAWTHORNE *Fort. Fool* I. xxvii, A cur.. unexpectedly confronted by a large tomcat.

'tom-cat, tomcat, *v. U.S. slang.* [f. the sb.] *intr.* To pursue women promiscuously for sexual gratification. Freq. const. *around*. Hence **'tomcatting** *vbl. sb.*

1927 *Dial. Notes* V. 478 *Tom catting*, v., to seek illicit sexual adventure. 'Jeff he's out a-tomcattin' roun' some 'ers.' **1932** W. FAULKNER *Light in August* xii. 259 So this is where you tomcat to every night. **1939** J. STEINBECK *Grapes of Wrath* xvi. 239, I was goin' out an' dance, an' I was gonna go tom-cattin'. **1953** W. P. MCGIVERN *Big Heat* ii. 23 A guy tom-catting around while his wife's away. **1962** H. GREEN *Time to pass Over* iii. 42 Don't drink, don't chew, don't tomcat with the women so far as I know. **1975** *New Review* May 20/1 'He had a very strong tendency to be doing a lot of tomcatting.'..Would go out looking for women. **1980** G. THOMPSON *Murder Mystery* (1981) xxii. 172 A man who's been tom-catting around with three women all day long.

tom-cod ('tɒm'kɒd). Name for several small fishes. In U.S.: **a.** The frost-fish (FROST *sb.* 7 c); also, loosely, one of various small fishes confused with this. **b.** In California, the Jack-fish (*Sebastodes paucispinis*), a rock-fish. **c.** = KING-FISH d. In Great Britain: **d.** A young codfish.

1795 J. SULLIVAN *Hist. Maine* 21 The people have tom cod, or what they call frost fish, smelts, and also alewives in great plenty. **1838** HALIBURTON *Clockm.* Ser. II. v. 65 [They] used to..catch herrin' and tom cods, and such sort o' fish. **1854** LOWELL *Leaves fr. Jrnl.* Wks. 1890 I. 108 An old fisherman, browner than a tomcod. **1883** *Fisheries Exhib. Catal.* (ed. 4) 174 Tom Cods, the young of Cod Fish. **1888** GOODE *Amer. Fishes* 123 The King-Fish,..also known..as the 'Tom-cod' on the coast of Connecticut.

tome (təʊm). (Also 7 **tombe.**) [app. a. F. *tome* (16th c. in Godef. *Compl.*), ad. L. *tomus*, a. Gr. τόμος volume, section of a book, f. ablaut series τεμ-, τομ-, τμ-, to cut.]

†**1.** Each of the separate volumes which compose a literary work or book; rarely, one of the largest parts or sections of a single volume. *Obs.*

1519 HORMAN *Vulg.* 84 A *tome* proprely is but a peace vnperfecte of a boke, neuer the lesse, it is taken for a great quantyte of a whole warke. **1548** UDALL (*title*) The first tome of the Paraphrase of Erasmus vpon the newe Testamente. **1549** *Ibid.*, The second tome or volume of the Paraphrase of Erasmus vpon the newe testament. **1563** *Homilies* (title-p.) The seconde Tome of Homelyes, of such matters as were promysed and Intituled in the former part of Homelyes. **1600** J. PORY tr. *Leo's Africa* II. 53 The said volume is diuided into three tomes. **1659** BAXTER *Key Cath.* xxv. 151 A large volume containing six Tomes. **1672** J. FRASER *Polichron.* (S.H.S.) 503, I read over to him my own Triennial Travells abroad, in 3 tombes. **1731** *Hist. Litteraria* II. 493 To the IVth Tome will be prefixed a Collection of..Pieces, relating to the Life and Writings of the Author.

2. A book, a volume; now usually suggesting a large, heavy, old-fashioned book.

1573 (*title*) The whole workes of..Tyndall..Frith, and.. Barnes..collected and compiled in one Tome together. **1621** BURTON *Anat. Mel.* I. ii. IV. vii. (1651) 167 To what end are such great Tomes? **1730** SHENSTONE *Ode to Health* 30 Adieu, Ye midnight lamps! ye curious tomes! **1789** J. WHITE *Earl Strongbow* I. 159 Father Hugh..prayed my acceptance of a little tome, covered with fine vellum. **1849** MISS MULOCK *Ogilvies* iv, Ponderous tomes, in century-old bindings,—dusty piles of newspapers. **1890** HALL CAINE *Bondman* II. ix, 'Bring me the Statute Book', and the great tome was brought.

3. *fig.*

1622 DONNE *Serm.*, *Job xxxvi. 25* (1649) II. xxxi. 273 Who knowes..how many volumes of Spheares involve one another, how many tomes of Gods Creatures there are? **1654** FULLER *Two Serm.* 54 Seventhly, the Booke of men's Afflictions. Some account this onely a distinct Tome, or Volume, of the former Booke [Book of Men's Actions]. **1867** BAILEY *Univ. Hymn* 9 He through your space-spread tome ..His starry rede To man predictive speaks.

4. A papal letter or epistle. *Hist.*

[ad. L. *tomus*, a. Gr. τόμος, applied esp. to synodical and pontifical letters or epistles: see Du Cange.]

1788 GIBBON *Decl. & F.* xlvii. (1836) 827 The tome of Leo was subscribed by the Oriental bishops. **1867** MANNING *Petri Privilegium* (1871) 73 The Council of Chalcedon was directed by S. Leo to condemn Eutyches, whom he had already condemned. The Fathers of the Council would define nothing until they had heard the Tome, or dogmatic letter of the Pontiff.

Hence (*nonce-words*) **'tomecide** ('təʊmɪ-) [-CIDE 1], a destroyer of books; **'tomeful** ('təʊmfʊl), as much as fills a tome; **'tomelet**, a small volume.

1849 CURZON *Visits Monast.* 382, I ought, perhaps, to have slain the *tomecide. **1859** SALA *Tw. round Clock* (1861) 141 How many *tomesful [*error for* tomefuls] of gossiping scandal will be talked! **1846** WORCESTER cites *Q. Rev.* for *Tomelet. **1884** *Irish Monthly* Jan. 52 This dainty tomelet.

tome, obs. f. TAUM, TOOM.

-tome (təʊm), terminal element: (*a*) f. Gr. -τόμον, neut. of -τόμος that cuts (see -TOMY), used in names of instruments for cutting, esp. ones used in surgical operations denoted by the corresponding word in *-tomy*, as in *cystotome* s.v. CYSTO-, HYSTEROTOME, MICROTOME; (*b*) f. Gr. τομή a cutting, used in words denoting a distinct section or segment of a body or part, as in MYOTOME 1, *gonotome* s.v. GONO-.

to-melt: see TO-[2] 1.

tomentigerous, etc.: see under TOMENTUM.

tomentose (təʊ'mɛntəʊs), *a.* [ad. mod.L. *tōmentōs-us*, It. *tomentoso*, f. L. *tōment-um* stuffing for cushions + -OSE.]

1. *Bot.* Closely covered with down or short hairs; pubescent, downy. Also as second element, in ***albo-tomentose***, covered with white down, ***farinose-tomentose***, covered with mealy down, etc.

1698 FRYER *Acc. E. India & P.* 40 (*Plate*) Nutts..whose tomentose husk taken off, leaves the Areca nut. **1699** SLOANE in *Phil. Trans.* XXI. 116 Pappous and tomentose Seeds of *Hieracium, Lisymachia*. **1785** MARTYN *Rousseau's Bot.* xxix. (1794) 455 The surface..tomentose or nappy underneath. **1872** OLIVER *Elem. Bot.* App. 307 Stem.. glabrous or sparsely tomentose. **1887** W. PHILLIPS *Brit. Discomycetes* 61 *Peziza grandis*..externally olivaceous-umber, with a lacunose albo-tomentose base. *Ibid.* 269 Externally farinose-tomentose, pale red or dilute-cinnamon.

2. *Entom.* and *Anat.* Flocculent, flossy, woolly.

1826 KIRBY & SP. *Entomol.* IV. xlvi. 276 *Tomentose*... Covered with short interwoven inconspicuous hairs. **1852** DANA *Crust.* I. 240 The pubescence or tomentose covering is exceedingly short. **1859** *Todd's Cycl. Anat.* V. 636/1 A tomentose or..villous condition of the surface. **1872** PEASLEE *Ovar. Tumors* 35 If the latter be purulent, it becomes fungous, tomentose, reddish.

to'mentous, *a.* [ad. mod.L. *tōmentōs-us* or F. *tomenteux*: see -OUS.] = TOMENTOSE.

1806 GALPINE *Brit. Bot.* §285 Leaves cordate, doubly-serrated, tomentous beneath. **1822** J. PARKINSON *Outl. Oryctol.* 40 Soft, tomentous, very jagged and porous. **1900** B. D. JACKSON *Gloss. Bot. Terms.*

‖**tomentum** (təʊ'mɛntəm). [L.: see above.]

1. *Bot.* The soft down or pubescence growing on the stems, leaves, or seeds of certain plants.

1699 SLOANE in *Phil. Trans.* XXI. 115 Having very soft hairs, down, or tomentum, much longer in proportion to the Seed, then any tomentum I know. **1793** G. WHITE *Selborne* (1853) 375 (*Observ. Wild Bee*) A sort of wild bee frequenting the garden-campion for the sake of its *tomentum*. **1866** *Treas. Bot.* s.v. *Centaurea*, Leaves clothed on both surfaces with a white silky tomentum.

2. *Anat.* A downy covering or investment; *spec.* the flocculent inner surface of the pia mater, consisting of numerous minute vessels entering the brain and spinal cord (in full ***tomentum cerebri***).

1811 in HOOPER *Med. Dict.* **1841** RAMSBOTHAM *Obstetr. Med.* (1855) 62 The ovum..is completely surrounded by a thick tomentum of minute filamentous, mossy villi.

Hence **tomen'tigerous, tomen'titious, to'mentulose** *adjs.*: see quots.

1860 MAYNE *Expos. Lex.*, *Tomentiger*.., *Entom.*, having the body hairy or downy: *tomentigerous. **1656** BLOUNT *Glossogr.*, **Tomentitious* (*tomentitius*), made of flocks or wool. **1895** *Funk's Stand. Dict.*, *Tomentulose. **1900** B. D. JACKSON *Gloss. Bot. Terms* 272 *Tomentulose*, slightly tomentose.

tomerel, obs. form of TUMBREL.

'tom-'fool, *sb.* [f. TOM *sb.*[1] + FOOL *sb.*[1]]

†**a.** As quasi-proper name, *Tom Fool*: a man mentally deficient; a half-witted person. *Obs.*

1356–7 *Durham Acc. Rolls* (Surtees) 719 Pro funeracione Thome Fole [from 1337 frequently mentioned as 'Thomas fatuus']. **1565** CALFHILL *Answ. Treat. Crosse* 103 b, I might byd them tell them, as Tom foole did his geese. **1611** J. FIELD *Panegyr. Verses* in Coryat *Crudities*, Tom-Foole may goe to schoole, but nere be taught. ? **1640** *New Serm. of newest fashion* (1877) 32 A foole reall..such ffooles wee commonlie expresse by the names of Tom ffoole, Dick ffoole, and Jack ffoole. **1865** *Cornh. Mag.* Oct. 391 Now though he didn't know Hannah, Hannah knew him. 'More folks know Tom Fool, than Tom Fool knows', asking Mr. Preston's pardon.

b. One who enacts the part of a fool in the drama, etc.; a buffoon; *spec.* a buffoon who accompanies morris-dancers; also, a butt, laughing-stock.

1650 H. MORE *Observ.* in *Enthus. Tri.*, etc. (1656) 91 Come out Tom-Fool from behinde the hangings,..and put off your vizard, and be apert and intelligible. **1677** W. HUGHES *Man of Sin* II. ix. 139 But poor Thomas is made a Tom-fool of; for they make a bridge of his Nose, for ought I find, and leave him nothing. **1796** MRS. M. ROBINSON *Angelina* II. 131 'So then I am to be the only properly drest person at the wedding?' In short, the Tom fool of the company', said he. **1846** THACKERAY *Snob Papers* Wks. 1886 XXIV. 319 A theatre manager..walking backwards in a Tom-Fool's coat. **1894** *S.E. Worc. Gloss.* s.v. *Morris-dance*, In the neighbourhood of Pershore the morris-dancers go out for about ten days at Christmas-tide, accompanied by their musician and a 'tom-fool'.

c. A foolish or stupid person; one who behaves foolishly. (More emphatic than *fool*.)

1721 AMHERST *Terræ Fil.* No. 44. (1754) 233 From this tom-fool proceed we to the second, entitled Joseph. **1835** MARRYAT *Pacha* x, I came with the rest of the tom-fools. **1860** MAYHEW *Upp. Rhine* iv. §1. 173 A titled tom-fool, that some crowned head has been pleased to nickname noble. **1881** BESANT & RICE *Chapl. of Fleet* I. 78 If they were not clergymen, I should say they were all tom-fools.

d. *attrib.* (in senses b and c).

1762 STERNE *Tr. Shandy* V. xxx. 107 'Twas a Tom-fool-battle. **1819** SCOTT *Fam. Let.* 25 Nov., I had some regret in putting him into that Tom Fool dress, which is so unlike that of a British soldier. **1879** SALA *Paris herself again* (1880) I. x. 151 You may..wear whatever tomfool costume you like to assume. **1903** *Sat. Rev.* 7 Feb. 172/2 The absolute tom-fool nonsense in which Fielding could indulge.

Hence **'tom-fool** *v., intr.* to play the fool; whence **'tom-'fooling** *vbl. sb.*

1825 T. HOOK *Sayings* Ser. II. *Man of Many Fr.* I. 181 She began lecturing and tom-fooling with as great a quack as herself. **1836** —— *G. Gurney* i, All the lovers and their ladies were to be flirting and tom-fooling about in the costume of the then present day. **1881** *Daily Tel.* 27 Dec., In this scene there is very good tomfooling on the part of King Hoity-Toity..and the Nigger Chamberlain.

tom'foolery. [f. prec. after FOOLERY.] **1. a.** The action or behaviour of a tom-fool; foolish or absurd action; silly trifling.

1812 H. & J. SMITH *Rej. Addr., Punch's Apotheosis*, Round let us bound, for this is Punch's holyday; Glory to Tomfoolery, huzza! huzza! **1899** A. DOBSON *Paladin of Philanth.* iii. 65 That solemn tomfoolery, the Stratford Jubilee of 1769.

b. With *a* and *pl.* An instance of this; an action, practice, or thing of a foolish or absurd kind.

1840 T. A. TROLLOPE *Summ. in Brittany* I. 58 One of those solemn tom-fooleries which so much delighted the middle ages. **1862** MISS YONGE *C'tess Kate* xii, Come, don't make a tomfoolery of it. **1885** HUXLEY in L. Huxley *Life* (1900) II. vi. 91 How grown men can lend themselves to such elaborate tomfooleries.

2. *Rhyming slang.* Jewellery. Cf. TOM *sb.*[3]

1931 C. RIMINGTON *Bon Voyage Bk.* xv. 88 *Tomfoolery*, jewelry. **1943** M. HARRISON *Reported Safe Arrival* 52, I wouldn' be surprised if you both done a stretch fer knockin' orf some ole bloke's tom-foolery. **1975** *Sunday Times* 30 Mar. 49/2 He will have contacts in 'tomfoolery', or jewellery outlets.

So **'tom-'foolish** *a.*, of, pertaining to, or of the nature of a tom-fool; hence **'tom-'foolishness.**

1799 SOUTHEY *Nondescripts* viii, A man he is by nature merry, Somewhat Tom-foolish, and comical, very. **1889** J. K. JEROME *Three Men in Boat* v, Of all the irritating silly tomfoolishness by which we are plagued, this 'weather-forecast' fraud is about the most aggravating.

tomhog, obs. form of TOMAHAWK.

'tomial, *a. Ornith.* [f. TOMI-UM + -AL[1].] Of or pertaining to the tomia or to a tomium.

1872 COUES *N. Amer. Birds* 30 'Commissural edge' of either mandible (equivalent to 'tomial edge'). **1895** *Proc. Zool. Soc.* 7 May 369 The lamella of bone between each nostril and the tomial margin is relatively wider.

‖**tomice** ('tɒmɪsiː, -kiː). *rare.* [f. Gr. type *τομική (sc. τέχνη), f. τομικός that cuts.] The art of carving.

1662 EVELYN *Chalcogr.* (1769) 16 As to working in wood or ivory, *tomice.* **1710** in J. HARRIS *Lex. Techn.* II.

†**to-'mid,** *prep. Obs.* [ME. *to myd*, f. TO *prep.* + MID.] In or into the midst of, amid.

c **1420** *Liber Cocorum* (1862) 19 Be sleȝe and powre in water þenne To myd þo pot, as I the kenne.

†**to-mids,** *adv.* and *prep. Obs.* [OE. *tó-middes*, ME. *to-medis*, f. TO *prep.* + *middes*: see MIDS.]

A. *adv.* In or into the midst.

Beowulf 3141 [Hie] Aleȝdon ða to middes mærne þeoden. *c* **1000** *Sax. Leechd.* III. 56 Sete on feower healfe þæs ceapes, and an to middes. *a* **1400** *Sir Perc.* 1202 He roghte wele the lesse Awther of lyfe or of dede, To-medis that he were in a stede, Thar he myghte riste hym in thede A stownde in sekirnes!

B. *prep.* In or into the midst of. (Only OE.)

c **1000** *Ags. Gosp.* John i. 26 Tomiddes eow stod þe ȝe ne cunnon. *c* **1000** ÆLFRIC *Saints' Lives* xxiii. 609 Hine þanon ealle atuȝan tomiddes þære cypinge.

‖**tomin** (to'min). Also 6 -yne, 7 -ine. [Sp.] A Spanish measure of weight for silver, equivalent to 9.26 grains; also, **b.** in Spain and Spanish America, the name of various small silver coins.

'In Bolivia, a coin equal to one-fifth of the Bolivian dollar, i.e. about eightpence; in Paraguay, a coin worth 2 reales or nearly fivepence' (*Cent. Dict., Supp.*).

[**1599** MINSHEU *Span. Dict.*, *Tomin*, a kinde of weight weighing the quantity of a Reall in Spaine, neere sixpence English.] **1600** HAKLUYT *Voy.* III. 454 Fiue Tomynes, that is, fiue Royals of plate, which is iust two shillings and sixe pence. **1604** E. G[RIMSTONE] tr. *D'Acosta's Hist. Indies* IV. xxii. 272 In Potozi it is readily worth foure peeces, and five Tomines.

†**c.** As the name of a weight used by jewellers.

1658 PHILLIPS, *Tomin*, a certain weight among Jewellers, weighing about three Carrats. **1717** *Blount's Law Dict.*, *Tomin*, a Weight so called amongst Goldsmiths and Jewellers, and is twelve Grains.

tominorie: see TOM-NODDY I.

tomiparous (təʊ'mɪpərəs), *a. Biol. rare.* [f. mod.L. *tomipar-us* (f. Gr. τομή cutting, section + L. *-par-us* producing) + -OUS.] Multiplying (as a cell or organism) by division; fissiparous.

1860 MAYNE *Expos. Lex.*, *Tomiparus*.., applied by Bory to plants and animals which are multiplied by cuttings or division, i.e. by separation of parts: tomiparous. **1887** W. PHILLIPS *Brit. Discomycetes* 272 The external papillæ are formed by the ends of short, hair-like, tomiparous cells, which are remarkable from their habit of breaking off at the joints under slight pressure.

Tomistic, variant of THOMISTIC.

‖**tomium** ('təʊmɪəm). *Ornith.* Pl. tomia (-ɪə). [mod.L., f. Gr. τομ-ός cutting, sharp + L. *-ium* (cf. Gr. τόμιον a sacrifice cut up, also τομεῖον incision).] Each of the cutting edges of a bird's bill.

1834 R. MUDIE *Brit. Birds* (1841) I. 349 They..do not peck..or grind hard substances between the oblique *tomia.* **1874** COUES *Birds N.W.* 622 Bill greenish-yellow, chrome along the tomia. **1890** —— *Field & Gen. Ornithol.* II. 152 The mandibular *tomium.*

tomjohn, corruption of TONJON.

Tom Jones. The name of the hero of Fielding's novel *History of Tom Jones* (1749), used *attrib.* to designate dress and hair styles represented in the film version of 1963 and considered suggestive of eighteenth-century styles.

1964 *Glamour* May 186 Wonderful way to wear hair that's fit and silky: Brush it back from the brow, catch it at the nape, tie in a Tom Jones queue. **1967** *Observer* 14 May 28/6 A chiffon scarf in a Tom Jones bow. **1971** *Jamaican Weekly Gleaner* 10 Nov. 15/2 Looking..beautiful in belted tan tailored pants with chocolate Tom Jones blouse.

tomkin, -king, obs. variants of TAMPION, plug.

tomling, a young tom cat: see under TOM *sb.*[1]

tommahauk, obs. form of TOMAHAWK.

‖**tomme** (tɒm). Also (erron.) tome. [Fr.] The name given to a variety of cheeses made in Savoy, a region of S.E. France.

1946 A. L. SIMON *Conc. Encycl. Gastron.* IX. 24/2 [One of] the best known *Tommes* of Savoy [is]..*Tomme au Fenouil.* **1958** *Catal. County Stores, Taunton* June 9 Cheese. .. Tome de Savoie—each 7/6. **1966** P. V. PRICE *France* II. 310 There are several *tommes* in the region and this is the most famous. **1972** *Sat Rev.* (U.S.) 24 June 77/3 In Savoy I sampled..*reblochon*..and the famous *tomme aux raisins*, a blander cheese coated on the outside with dried grape pips.

tommelaitje, var. TAMELETJIE.

Tommy[1] ('tɒmɪ). In senses 2–5 usu. **tommy.** [dim. or pet form of TOM *sb.*[1]: cf. *baby, dolly, Bobby, Teddy*, etc.]

1. a. Familiar form of *Thomas.*

b. A simpleton; also, short for *tommy-noddy* (= TOM-NODDY I). *dial.*

1829 BOWLES *Days Departed* 44 The tandem-driving Tommy of a town. **1833** P. J. SELBY *Illustr. Brit. Ornithol.* II. 439 Puffin..Tommy-nodie, Tommey. **1847–78** HALLIWELL, *Tommy*..a simple fellow. **1899** *Leeds Mercury*, *Suppl.* 6 May (E.D.D.), He's as big a Tommy as iver I knew.

c. Short for *Tommy Atkins*: see 7.

1884 KIPLING in L. L. Cornell *Kipling in India* (1966) iii. 83 (*title*) The story of Tommy. **1893** —— *Many Invent.* 28, I was..with sixty Tommies—private soldiers, that is. **1898** *Westm. Gaz.* 26 Jan. 7/1 An occasional detachment of Tommies with the attendant coolies and sweepers. **1901** *Daily Graphic* 23 Feb. 7/4 A vigorous protest is being made on behalf of the dignity of the British line against the use of the too familiar sobriquet 'Tommy'. **1907** *Blackw. Mag.* Nov. 651/2 A group of Tommies in uniform.

2. a. A soldiers' name for the brown bread formerly supplied as rations (also ***brown tommy***); with *a* and *pl.*, a loaf of bread (*dial.*); among workmen, Food, provisions generally, *esp.* those carried with them to work each day. ***soft tommy, white tommy***: see quot. 1796. See also TAMMIE.

App. personified as *Tommy Brown*, altered to *brown Tommy* and *tommy.* Similarly a hunk of grey bread distributed at Minto House, as part of a Hogmanay gift to the village children, used to be called *Tam Gray.*

1783 [see quot. 1830]. **1796** GROSE *Dict. Vulg. T.* s.v., Soft Tommy, or white Tommy; bread is so called by sailors, to distinguish it from biscuit. **1803** in *Spirit Pub. Jrnls.* VII. 352 A high sea,..without a bit of soft Tommy to put into your lantern jaws. **1811** *Lex. Balatr.* s.v., Brown Tommy; ammunition bread for soldiers; or brown bread given to convicts at the hulks. **1825** BROCKETT *N.C. Words*, *Tommy*, a little loaf. 'A soldier's tommy'. **1830** in W. Cobbett *Rur. Rides* (1885) II. 353 When I was a recruit at Chatham barracks, in the year 1783, we had brown bread served out to us twice in the week. And, for what reason God knows, we used to call it *tommy*... Any one that could get white bread called it 'bread', but the brown stuff..was called 'tommy'. **1846** *Camp & Barrack-Room* ii. 16 After I had breakfasted upon tommy and insipid coffee. **1865** *Slang Dict.*, *Tommy*, bread,—generally a penny roll. Sometimes applied by workmen to the supply of food which they carry ..as their daily allowance. **1911** H. F. RUTTER *Let. to Editor*, Used in provincial dialects and invariably by English navvies as a synonym for food. 'I was that bad I couldn't eat my tommy'. 'Go into the stable and give that old horse his tommy'.

b. Goods; *esp.* provisions supplied to workmen under the truck system; also, short for *tommy-shop*, and for the truck system.

1830 [implied in *tommy-shop, system* in 6]. **1845** DISRAELI *Sybil* III. i, Diggs' tommy is only open once a-week. *Ibid.* III. iii, What are you doing here, little dear?; very young to fetch tommy. **1856** *Househ. Words* 21 June 545/1 The navvy knows that he is a helpless being if he cannot get his tommy; and this word..signifies beef, bacon, cheese, coffee, bread, butter, and tobacco. **1860** *Slang Dict.*, *Tommy*, a truck, barter, the exchange of labour for goods, not money.

3. As the name of something small of its kind. **a.** See quot. *a* 1825. **b.** = *tommy bar*, sense 6 below.

a **1825** FORBY *Voc. E. Anglia*, *Tommy*, a small spade to excavate the narrow bottoms of under-drains [**1895** *Gloss. E. Anglia* adds 'Also a small wrench used by engineers']. **1843** J. J. GREER *Brit. Patent 9811* (1856) 2 My invention.. consists..first, in working a double screw..from a central axis into two separate boxes or cases, either by a lever commonly called a tommy, or by a spanner. **1844** *Civil Eng. & Arch. Jrnl.* VII. 35/1 On giving motion to the screw, which is effected by means of a tommy, or spanner. **1881** HASLUCK *Lathe Work* 179 Hooked tommys are employed to actuate all those capstan headed screws and nuts which from insufficiency in the depth of the holes do not afford a hold for the ordinary straight forward tommy.

c. The smallest of the gazelles, Thomson's gazelle, of East Africa. [Here orig. from *Thomson.*]

1906 *Westm. Gaz.* 2 June 2/2 It is a pretty sight to see a herd of the graceful little Thomson's gazelle (locally called Tommies) mingling with a flock of sheep and goats. **1912** *Comtemp. Rev., Lit. Suppl.* Jan. 137 Mr. Barnes came across the gigantic eland..Grant's gazelle, Tommy, oryx [etc.].

4. A gold-washing trough; = TOM *sb.*[1] 4 a.

1892 *Pall Mall G.* 10 Aug. 2/1 At the end of the tiny creek, where a 'tommy' was..set in motion to wash the alluvial soil and extract the tiny glittering particles of gold.

5. (Usually **soft tommy.**) Pewter solder (PEWTER 6) used by jewellers.

1877 G. E. GEE *Practical Gold-worker* 137 'Soft solder'.. commonly called in the jewellery trade 'soft tommy'. **1912** *Let. from Jeweller to Editor*, Tommy or soft tommy means the ordinary lead or pewter solder that is in common use for repairing Britannia metal or lead articles.

6. *attrib.* and *Comb.*; chiefly in senses 2, 2 b, as ***tommy-box, -master, system***; **tommy-bag**, a bag in which a workman or school-boy carries his day's food; **tommy bar** *Mech.*, a short bar that can be inserted into a hole in a box-spanner or screw to assist in turning it; **tommy-book**, an account book of goods supplied on the truck system; **tommy-cod** = TOM-COD a; **Tommy('s) cooker** *Mil. slang*, a small portable spirit stove; also, a piece of rolled-up canvas soaked in grease used in place of this; **tommy-day**, a day on which a *tommy-shop* is open; **Tommy Dod(d**, the 'odd man' in odd-man-out (ODD D. 2); **tommy-hole**, one of two or more holes in a nut, into which steel pins can be inserted to turn it; **tommy-long-legs**, the daddy-long-legs; **tommy-noddy, -norie** = TOM-NODDY; **tommy-plough** = *tom-plough* (TOM *sb.*[1] 7 a); **tommy-'rot**, nonsense, bosh, twaddle; hence **tommy'rotic** *a.* [after *erotic*], nonsensical; **'tommy-shop**, a store (esp. one run by the employer) at which vouchers given to employees instead of money wages may be exchanged for goods; a truck-shop; also *attrib.*; **Tommy talker** *colloq.* = KAZOO; **Tommy-touchwood**, the game of 'touch wood'.

1873 *Slang Dict.* s.v. *Tommy*, *Tommy-Bag is the term for the bag or handkerchief in which the [workman's tommy or] 'daily bread' is carried. **1983** P. NASH *Coup de Grass* ii. 23 He was wearing overalls and carrying a canvas tommy-bag. **1920** WEBSTER, *Tommy bar. **1930** *Engineering* 25 Apr. 538/1 The cylinder is removed bodily from its supporting bracket, by unscrewing a hinged fixing pillar by means of a tommy bar. **1953** E. HYAMS *Vineyards in England* 226 Pass a tommy-bar through the hole at the top of the screw and spin the screw to bring the piston down on to the grapes. **1973** D. LEES *Rape of Quiet Town* vii. 121 He fixed each jack separately..then gave the tommy bars a few..twists until they were tight. **1845** DISRAELI *Sybil* III. i, You know as how Juggins applied for his balance after his *tommy-book was paid up. **1906** *Westm. Gaz.* 2 July 5/2 The rescuers ultimately found the two men alive in the old workings... Without food, their '*tommy' boxes having been washed away by the flood, they subsisted on a few candles. **1879** J. BURROUGHS *Locusts & W. Honey, Halcyon* (1884) 310 From Rivière du Loup, where we passed the night and ate our first '*Tommy-cods'. **1917** W. OWEN *Let.* 4 Feb. (1963) 430 We had 5 *Tommy's cookers between the Platoon, but they did not suffice to melt the ice in the water-cans. **1919** *N.Y. Times* 23 Feb. IV. 12/2 When 4 o'clock came around every manjack of us would take out his Tommy-cooker and begin making his tea. **1948** A. BARON *From City, from Plough* xviii.

165 On the little tommy-cookers that they sheltered between their feet they brewed .. tea in their mess-tins. **1845** DISRAELI *Sybil* III. iii, It's grand *tommy-day you know. **1870** A. STEINMETZ *Gaming-Table* II. 221 Not long ago a returned tradesman .. allowed himself to be induced to play at *Tommy Dodd with two low sharpers. **1873** *Slang Dict.*, *Tommy-Dodd*, in tossing when the odd man either wins or loses, as per agreement. **1884** *Punch* 16 Feb. 73/2 A gambling game known as 'Tommy Dod' is extensively practised. **1897** PEMBERTON *Compl. Cyclist* 125 The head nut, which could be made with a milled edge, and with *tommy holes to start it if stuck beyond finger power. **1863** ATKINSON *Stanton Grange* (1864) 84 Large flies, may-flies, *tommy-longlegs, and grasshoppers. **1860** *Slang Dict.*, **Tommy-master*, one who pays his workmen in goods, or gives them tickets upon tradesmen, with whom he shares the profit. **1849** W. & H. RAYNBIRD *Agric. Suffolk* 301 The *tom* or **tommy* plough is a plough with a double breast for ridging, or for clearing out furrows. **1884** MOORE *Mummer's Wife* (1887) 25 Bill .. said it was all '*Tommy rot'. **1899** MARY KINGSLEY *W. African Stud.* ii. 41 My fellow new-comers .. thought nothing of calling some of our instructor's best information 'Tommy Rot'! **1895** *Chicago Advance* 4 July 4/1 A whole school of what has been humorously called erotic and *tommyrotic realists .. asserting that progress in art requires the elimination of moral ideas. **1830** in W. Cobbett *Rur. Rides* (1885) II. 354 A *tommy shop: a .. place containing every commodity that the workman can want, liquor and house-room excepted. **1833** WADE *Hist. Mid. & Working Classes* (1835) 113 An effort was made by 1 & 2 Wm. IV. c. 37 to put an end to what are termed tommy shops, and the practice so general .. of paying wages in goods, in lieu of coin and banknotes. **1845** DISRAELI *Sybil* III. i. *note*, The Butty generally keeps a Tommy or Truck shop, and pays the wages of his labourers in goods. **1882** *Standard* 26 Dec. 2/3 The 'foggers', or 'Tommy shop' men, live lives of contentment, .. at the expense of the poor nail-workers. **1830** in W. Cobbett *Rur. Rides* (1885) II. 352 In the iron country .. the truck or *tommy system generally prevails. **1938** *Tommy Talker [see KAZOO]. **1976** S. BARSTOW *Right True End* I. iii. 38 Learn the piano... Well, the french horn, clarinet, fiddle, trombone; mouth-organ, jew's harp, tommy-talker. **1876** MISS BRADDON *J. Haggard's Dau.* ix, The children playing *Tommy Touchwood under the chestnuts.

7. Tommy Atkins. Familiar form of *Thomas Atkins*, as a name for the typical private soldier in the British army: for origin, see THOMAS 3; hence *transf.* a private in any army; also, one of the rank and file in any organization.

1883 SALA in *Illustr. Lond. News* 7 July 3/3 Private Tommy Atkins, returning from Indian service. **1887** *St. Andrews Citizen* (Dixon), In the privacy of his house Tommy Atkins may .. hold his baby in his arms. **1892** KIPLING *Barrack-r. Ballads*, *Tommy*, God bless you, Tommy Atkins, We're all the world to you. **1893** F. ADAMS *New Egypt* 101 The Egyptian Tommy Atkins inspires one rapidly with feelings of sheer affection. **1898** E. J. HARDY in *United Service Mag.* Mar. 646 Some years ago, Lord Wolseley .. said, 'I won't call him Tommy Atkins myself, for I think it is a piece of impertinence to call the private soldier Tommy Atkins'. *Ibid.* 649 From talks with these men, I have learned to know and respect Tommy Atkins.

Hence **'tommy** *v.*, *trans.* to subject to the tommy system; to enforce the truck system on; **'tommyhood**, the condition or state of a Tommy.

1845 DISRAELI *Sybil* III. i, The fact is we are tommied to death. **1857** J. MILLER *Alcohol* (1858) 66 *note*, The razor is kept from Tommy in his Tommyhood.

'tommy[2]. *Austral.* and *N.Z. colloq.* [Shortened f. TOMAHAWK *sb.*] A hatchet. Also **tommy-axe**.

1873 M. A. BARKER *Station Amusements N.Z.* ix. 148, I had to get the tommy (*anglicé*—tomahawk) and *chop* his boots off. **1898** MORRIS *Austral Eng.* 474/2 *Tommy-axe*, a popular corruption of the word *Tomahawk*. **1939** X. HERBERT *Capricornia* xxii. 328 Cutting a strip of bark from the tree with the tommy-axe.

'tommy-gun. *colloq.* (orig. *U.S.*). Also Tommy- and as two words. [f. TOMMY[1], repr. the name of J. T. *Thompson*: see THOMPSON.] A Thompson or other sub-machine-gun.

1929 *Sat. Even. Post* 13 Apr. 54/3 There are three types of machine gun used—Tommy guns, Browny guns and Louie guns. **1934** E. HEMINGWAY in *Cosmopolitan* Apr. 23/2 The nigger shot him in the belly with the Tommy gun. **1941** *Times* 21 Nov. 3/4 Twelve of the enemy were killed with bayonets and tommy-guns. **1955** M. BANKS *Commando Climber* iii. 40 He survived the war by a combination of good fortune and adroitness with a tommy-gun. **1973** D. LEES *Rape of Quiet Town* vii. 111 A wild assortment of weapons, including a couple of tommy guns and a cavalry sabre.

Hence as *v. trans.*; also **'tommy-gunner**.

1942 *Times* 3 Oct. 4/1 A party of our tommy-gunners penetrated enemy barbed wire entanglements. *Ibid.* 24 Nov. 4/1 When one Soviet tank was engaged in pursuing the retreating Germans its crew leapt out and tommy-gunned them. **1973** A. MANN *Tiara* iii. 22 Thirty years ago he was the best tommy-gunner in the Appennines. **1978** T. GIFFORD *Glendower Legacy* (1979) 144 Maybe they're waiting for me to leave so they can come in and tommy-gun you.

Tom-noddy ('tɒm'nɒdɪ). Also tom-noddy. [f. TOM *sb.*[1] + NODDY *sb.*[1]]

1. A local name of the Puffin (*Fratercula arctica*). Also ***Tommy Noddy***, ***Tom*** or ***Tommy norie***, and ***Tammie-norie***: see TAMMIE 2.

1702 Tominories [see TAMMIE 2]. **1771** PENNANT *Tour Scotl. in 1769* 36 Puffins, called here Tom Noddies. **1793** *Statist. Acc. Scot.* V. 189 Tomnorries, lyres, calloos. **1805** BARRY *Orkney* III. i. 305 The Puffin .. or tommy noddie of this place, is seen very often. **1822** HIBBERT *Descr. Shetl. Isl.* iii. 401 Numberless flocks of birds, such as gulls and scarfs; and along with these, .. the Tomnorry. **1885** SWAINSON *Provinc. Names Birds* 219 Puffin .. Tom noddy, or Tommie norie (Farn Islands; Scotland).

2. A foolish or stupid person; = NODDY *sb.*[1] 1.

1828 *Craven Gloss.*, *Tom-noddy*, .. a tom-fool. **1833** T. HOOK *Parson's Dau.* II. xiv, Why, what a tom-noddy you have made yourself! .. that is, if you care for the Parson's Daughter. **1863** COWDEN CLARKE *Shaks. Char.* vi. 144 Our brother John does at times contrive to make a prodigious Tom-noddy of himself.

tomo ('təʊməʊ). *N.Z.* [a. Maori.] A depression or hole in limestone terrain.

1952 *Arena* (N.Z.) XXXI. 3 See him drag a gully full of tomos and patches of scrub. **1961** R. PARK *Hole in Hill* (1962) x. 76, I fell down a big hole... Not just a hole, but a *tomo*, a limestone shaft. **1975** *N.Z. Jrnl. Agric.* Sept. 24/2 It may be located in a tomo or natural depression down the back, or in a corner, of a paddock.

tomography (tə'mɒgrəfɪ). *Med.* [f. Gr. τόμος slice, section + -GRAPHY.] Radiography in which an image of a predetermined plane in the body or other object is obtained by rotating the detector and the source of radiation in such a way that points outside the plane give a blurred image. Also in extended use, any analogous technique using other forms of radiation.

1935 *Brit. Jrnl. Radiol.* VIII. 750 The most significant field of application for the method of reproducing body layers (tomography) will, in practice, be lung diagnosis. **1949** *Ibid.* XXII. 627/1 Today, sectional röntgenography, commonly called tomography has indeed, in many places, found recognition as a method of radiological diagnosis. **1968** *Brit. Med. Bull.* XXIV. 242/1 With the advent of transverse tomography, it is now possible to get much more accurate estimations of the various volumes and areas of tissues of differing density, in any cross-section of the body. **1977** 'E. TREVOR' *Theta Syndrome* iii. 40 The axial tomography revealed bilateral subdural hematomas. **1982** *New Scientist* 21 Jan. 155/1 Paul Carson and others .. have been comparing the new-developed technique of ultrasonic computed tomography (UCT) with pulse echo imaging. **1983** *Ibid.* 17 Mar. 725/3 Tree physiology and dendrochronology are just two of the possible applications for portable computer tomography. **1984** *McGraw-Hill Yearbk. Sci. & Technol. 1985* 335/1 Positron emission tomography (PET scan) now allows scientists to measure noninvasively the functional activity of the living human brain.

So **'tomogram**, an X-ray picture taken by tomography; **'tomograph**, (*a*) a tomogram; (*b*) an apparatus for carrying out tomography; **tomo'graphic** *a.*, **tomo'graphically** *adv.*

1935 *Brit. Jrnl. Radiol.* VIII. 736 The new tomographic method is also based upon the principle of the method already mentioned. *Ibid.* 750 Three tomographs are generally sufficient for lung diagnosis. *Ibid.*, A new device, the tomograph, is described, which permits the radiography of body layers of any size and variable thickness. **1936** *Lancet* 25 July 185/2 For all practical purposes three tomograms are ample for accurate diagnosis. **1949** *Radiography* XV. 242/1 (*caption*) Aneurysm demonstrated by lesion of dorsal vertebræ tomographically. **1950** *Times* 22 Nov. 6/6 The infection was discovered, thanks to the use of a tomograph, a new X-ray apparatus, apparently during Sir Stafford Cripps's last stay at Zurich. **1955** D. B. FRY in B. I. Evans *Stud. in Communication* 156 The internal action of the larynx was for a long time inaccessible to X-ray photography but the development of the tomogram technique has enabled Ardram and Kemp to obtain remarkable pictures of the larynx in action. **1968** Tomographic [see LAMINAGRAPHIC *a.*]. **1975** *Radio Times* 1–7 Nov. 7/1 The EMI ('Emmy')-scanner is a machine for taking axial X-ray tomograms. **1975** *Sci. Amer.* Oct. 56/3 In most tomographic instruments the X-ray source moves in one direction and the photographic film simultaneously moves in the opposite direction. The patient lies in between. **1976** *Physics Bull.* Oct. 436/3 X-ray tomography has become a popular method of medical imaging over the past few years... A M Cormack and A M Koehler have come up with an alternative idea for improving the density resolution of tomographs. **1982** *Times* 26 July 2/3 Using the tomograms, the interior of the helmet has now been excavated.

to-morn (tə'mɔːn), *adv.* and *sb.* Now *dial.* or *arch.* Forms: α. 1 **to morȝ(en)ne**, 1–2 **to morȝen** (**to morhȝen**), 3 **to morȝen**, 3–4 **to morwen**, 4 **to morewen**, 5 **to morowen**, **to moroun**. β. 4–5 **tomorne**, 4–6 **to morne**, 4– **to-morn**; 6, 9 **tomorn**, 9 *dial.* **to moorn**. γ. 1 **to merne**, **to męrȝen**, 2 **to marȝan**, 3 **to marȝen**, **marhen**, **mærȝen**, **marwen**, **marewene**. [f. TO *prep.* 7 + OE. *morȝenne*, dative of *morȝen*, *męrȝen*, MORN, which see for ulterior etymology. The syncopated *to morn* appears first in northern dial., and is still the vernacular form in a great part of northern England. (In Sc. *the morn*: see MORN 3 d.)

Beside *tó morȝ(en)ne*, OE. had also *on morȝne* (*Beow.* 2484), *on morne* (*Bæda's Hist.* II. vi) in the sense 'on the morrow'.]

A. *adv.* = TOMORROW *adv.* 1. *Obs.* in literary Eng. *c* 1500. Revived as poetical archaism *c* 1850.

α. *c* **897** K. ÆLFRED *Gregory's Past. C.* xliv. 324 Ga, & cum to morȝen [*Hatton MS.* to morȝenne]. *c* **1000** To-morhȝen [see quot. *c* 950 in γ]. *c* **1050** *Byrhtferth's Handboc* in *Anglia* VIII. 323 We nyton hwæðer we moton to morȝen. *a* **1225** *Ancr. R.* 278 He to dai, ich to morwen. *c* **1330** R. BRUNNE *Chron. Wace* (Rolls) 9081 To morewen schul þey boþe be schent. **13..** in *Pol. Rel. & L. Poems* (1866) 222 To morwen y mai beon wiþoute. **1413** *Pilgr. Sowle* (Caxton) IV. xxxviii. (1859) 63 Abydeth for to morowen.

β. *a* **1300** *Cursor M.* 11248 (Cott.) Yee ga to morn wen it es dai To bethleem. **1375** BARBOUR *Bruce* I. 124 Alss weill to-morn as ȝhisterday. *c* **1420** *Anturs of Arth.* 437 Yet þou shalt be mached by mydday to morne. *c* **1475** *Rauf Coilȝear* 85 To-morne, on the morning, quhen thow sall on leip. **1483** CAXTON *Gold. Leg.* 58 b/1 To morn ye shal see ye glorye of our lord. *a* **1547** SURREY *Æneid* IV. 150 To morne as soon as Titan shall ascend. **1855** ROBINSON *Whitby Gloss.* s.v., 'I'll see thee to moorn'. **1856** DOBELL *Lyrics in War Time*, *Tommy's Dead*, Stop the mill to-morn, boys. **1870** MORRIS *Earthly Par.* II. III. 125 Bide thou with us to-morn.

γ. *c* **950** *Lindisf. Gosp.* Luke xiii. 32 Hælo ic ðerh-doe .. todæȝ & tomerne [*c* **1000** *Ags. Gosp.* to-morhȝen; *c* **1160** *Hatton* to-morȝen]. *c* **1000** ÆLFRIC *Gram.* xxxviii. (Z.) 224 *Cras*, to merȝen. *c* **1175** *Lamb. Hom.* 21 To marȝan hit [bote] him is awane. *c* **1205** LAY. 16066 Heo cumeð to-mærȝen. *Ibid.* 23661 þat scal beon tomarȝen. *a* **1225** *Leg. Kath.* 645 Sete, Iesu, swucche sahen i mi muð to marhen.

b. In antithesis to *to-day*: see TODAY 1 b.

c. Followed by ***day***, ***eve*** (*obs.*), by ***morn***, ***morning***, ***night*** (*dial.*). Cf. Sc. *the morn's mornin'*, *the morn's nicht*.

c **1205** LAY. 17732 Ær to marwen eue. *a* **1300** *Cursor M.* 15343 (Cott.) To-morn dai sal i be dempt On rode tre to hang. **1801** ANDERSON *Cumberld. Ball.* 18 To mworn-o'mworn, i' this seame pleace, We'll hae the stwory out. **1855** ROBINSON *Whitby Gloss.*, *To Moorn't moorn*, or *To Moorn't moorning*, to-morrow morning. *Ibid.*, *To Moorn't neight*, to-morrow night.

B. *sb.* = TOMORROW *sb.* 1.

Truly substantival uses are late, but they were led up to by uses of the adv. in which it might be taken as sb., e.g. when preceded by *till*, *from*; cf. *till then*, *from now*.

c **1205** LAY. 26393 Nu to-morȝen is þe dæi. **13..** *Cursor M.* 3758 (Fairf.) In þe deu and gresse of thorne Sal be þi blessinge fra to-morne. **1375** BARBOUR *Bruce* I. 621 Tharwith awysit be, Till to morn, that ȝe be set. *c* **1420** *Avow. Arth.* viii, I may haue my leuynge Her tille to-morne atte day. *c* **1440** *York Myst.* xxxvi. 276 To-morne is our dere sabott daye. *c* **1450** *St. Cuthbert* (Surtees) 2873 To morne haly sonday is. **1870** MORRIS *Earthly Par.* II. III. 161 Eager, bright-eyed, and careless of tomorn.

tomorrer (tə'mɒrə(r)), *adv.* Also **to-morrer**. Repr. a dial. and slang pronunc. of TOMORROW *adv.*

1901 M. FRANKLIN *My Brilliant Career* iii. 16 Only I promised to stick to the missus a while, I'd scoot tomorrer. **1921** H. WILLIAMSON *Beautiful Yrs.* 81 Go when you like, miboy. Only I shall be a-mowing to-morrer. **1959** [see SICKIE 1]. **1970** T. HUGHES *Crow* 63 O do not chop his winkle off His Mammy cried with horrer Think of the joy will come of it Tomorrer and tomorrer.

tomorrow (tə'mɒrəʊ), *adv.* and *sb.* Forms: α. 3 **to moruwe**, 3–5 **to morewe**, 3–6 **to morowe**, **to morwe**, 4 **to morȝe**. β. 4 **to moru**, 5 **to morw**, **to morow**, 5–6 **to morrowe**, 6 **tomorow**, 6–8 **to morrow**, 6– **tomorrow**, **to-morrow**. Regularly written as two words till 1500 and usually so till *c* 1750. [ME. from *to morȝen*, *to morwen* (see TO-MORN), with dropping of final *-n*, and later of *-e*, as in inflexions of nouns and vbs., etc. When the final *e* was lost, *w* was vocalized to *-ow*, as in *arrow*, *borrow*, *sorrow*. Cf. MORROW.]

A. *adv.* **1. a.** For or on the day after today; for or on the morrow.

c **1275** *Passion our Lord* 140 in *O.E. Misc.* 41 Er hit beo day to morewe al oþer hit schal go. *c* **1290** *S. Eng. Leg.* I. 393/29 þus time to-moruwe cum aȝein. **1297** R. GLOUC. (Rolls) 2838 Hii walleþ tomorwe ariue at te hauene of toteneys. *c* **1320** *Sir Tristr.* 2089 To morwe y schal hir se. *c* **1380** *Sir Ferumb.* 3513 To-morȝe on þe spryng of þe day .. to þe pauyllouns take þe way. **1382** WYCLIF *Ecclus.* xx. 16 To day leeneth a man, and to moru [**1388** to morewe] he asketh it bi ple. *c* **1386** CHAUCER *Knt.'s T.* 1544 Thanne helpe me lord tomorwe in my bataille. **1426** AUDELAY *Poems* 25 To-morw or hit be day. **1484** CAXTON *Fables of Æsop* V. viii, To morowe on the mornyng .. sende me a dyssh ful of mylk. **1568** GRAFTON *Chron.* II. 368 Euery day in the weeke it was sayde, he departeth to morwe. *a* **1628** PRESTON *New Covt.* (1634) 435 This doing of it now, and now, and to morrow, and to morrow, these little distances deceive us, and delude us. **1709** PRIOR *Song 'If wine & music have the power'*, But She to Morrow will return. **1897** *Outing* (U.S.) XXIX. 383/2 'Sometime; not to-day; to-morrow'. This is the stereotyped answer which a Turk has always at his tongue's end.

b. in antithesis to *to-day*: see TODAY A. 1 b.

c. *fig.* In the (near) future.

1871, etc. [see *jam tomorrow* s.v. JAM *sb.*[2] b]. **1957** *Listener* 15 Aug. 223/1 An accelerated movement towards independence: Ghana yesterday; Nigeria, French West Africa, the Cameroons, tomorrow.

†**2.** On the morrow after the day mentioned. *Sc. Obs.*

a **1699** KIRKTON *Hist. Ch. Scot.* (1817) 126 After he hade drunk liberally in the Advocate's house that same day, went to bed in health, but was taken up stark dead to-morrow morning. **1717** WODROW *Let. to J. Hart* 8 Oct., A committee for peace was proposed to-morrow, who heard the ministers and Mr. Anderson upon the heads of complaint.

B. *sb.* **1.** The day after this day; the next succeeding day; the morrow. **a.** after *till*, *unto*, *from*, where it may be adv. **b.** clearly sb.

a. *c* **1386** CHAUCER *Melib.* ¶829 The goodnesse þat thou mayst do this day, do it, .. ne delaye it nat til to morwe. **1485** CAXTON *Chas. Gt.* II. II. xi. 121 It is better to abyde tyl to morowe. **1526** *Pilgr. Perf.* (W. de W. 1531) 98 b, Knowest thou whether he shall liue vnto to morowe.

b. **1535** COVERDALE *Prov.* xxvii. 1 Make not thy boost of tomorow. **1600** FAIRFAX *Tasso* VI. v, To morrowes sun shall spread his timely raies. *a* **1667** COWLEY *Ess. in Verse & Prose*, *Danger Procrastination*, Our Yesterdays To morrow now is gone. **1711** ADDISON *Spect.* No. 163 ¶11 A .. Story .. which I shall relate at length in my To-morrow's Paper. **1758** FRANKLIN *Prel. Addr. Pennsylv. Alm.*, One to-day is worth two to-morrows. **1832** TENNYSON *May Queen* i, To-morrow 'ill be the happiest time of all the glad New-year. **1838** LONGF. *Psalm Life* iii, To act, that each to-morrow Find us farther than to-day.

2. *fig.* The (near) future. Freq. in the possessive.

1943 J. B. PRIESTLEY *Daylight on Saturday* ii. 5 He belonged to tomorrow's new ruling class. **1959** *Brno Studies in English* I. 73 Progressive poets preferred to look forward into distant future and dreamed..of a better to-morrow. **1979** *Guardian* 30 Oct. 32/8 The Prime Minister..told the Wales TUC that British industry was not going to get tomorrow's jobs 'unless we move into tomorrow's world'.

3. *attrib.* with times of the day: ***tomorrow morning, forenoon, afternoon, evening, night, dinner-time***; also †***tomorrow day***. The combination is used both as *sb.* and as *adv.*

c **1275** LAY. 17732 Are to morewe heue. **1382** WYCLIF *Acts* xxiii. 20 That to morwe day thou bringe forth Poul into the counceil. **1470–85** MALORY *Arthur* I. xxiii. 70 He commaunded that..his best hors and armour..be withoute the cyte or to morowe daye. **1539** BIBLE (Great) *Matt.* vi. 34 Care not then for the morow, for to morowe day shall care for it selfe. **1588** SHAKS. *L.L.L.* III. i. 161, I wil come to your worship to morrow morning. **1596** —— *1 Hen. IV*, II. iv. 564, I will by to morrow Dinner time, Send him to answere thee. **1681** OTWAY *Soldier's Fort.* III. i, He shall be Crows-meats by to-morrow Night. **1782** MISS BURNEY *Cecilia* VIII. iii, To-morrow morning I shall but call to see how she is. *Mod.* Can you spend to-morrow evening with us?

4. Phrase. ***tomorrow come never***, a day that will never arrive; 'when two Sundays meet together'; 'on the Greek Kalends'.

1725 BAILEY *Erasm. Colloq.* (1878) I. 70 He shall have it in a very little Time... When? To morrow come never? [orig. *ad Calendas Græcas*]. **1770** COLMAN *Man & Wife* III. 46 *Marc.* Very soon, my dear! to-day, or to-morrow, perhaps. *Sally.* To-morrow come never, I believe. **1825** BROCKETT *N.C. Gloss.* s.v. *Nivver*, To-morrow come nivver—when two Sundays meet together.

5. ***as if there were no tomorrow*** and varr., recklessly, with no regard for the future.

1862 WHYTE-MELVILLE *Queen's Maries* II. xxii. 10 Why should you thus risk your life as if there was no to-morrow? **1980** *Guardian Weekly* 3 Feb. 1/3 Oil supplies that Americans at home continue to consume as though there were no tomorrow.

6. Proverb. ***tomorrow is another*** (or †***a new***) ***day***.

c **1527** J. RASTELL *Calisto & Melebea* sig. C1ᵛ, Well mother to morrow is a new day. **1603** FLORIO tr. *Montaigne's Ess.* II. iv. 57 A letter..beeing delivered him..at supper, he deferred the opening of it, pronouncing this by-word, *To morrow is a new day.* **1824** SCOTT *St. Ronan's* III. vii. 192 We will say no more of it at present... To-morrow is a new day. **1927** P. GREEN *Field God* I. 148 Go to it, you Mag and Lonie! To-morrow's another day, and you'll need all you can hold. **1956** M. DICKENS *Angel in Corner* vi. 90 'You can run along now... Those few letters will keep until the morning.'.. 'But there will be a whole heap of new ones by the morning.' .. 'I know, dear... If the letters didn't come, that would be the time to start worrying. But tomorrow is another day.' **1980** B. PYM *Few Green Leaves* xiii. 107 He would probably have said nothing and so missed his opportunity. Still, tomorrow was another day.

Hence (*nonce-wds.*) **to'morrower**, one who puts off till tomorrow; a procrastinator; **to'morrowing** *a.*, that procrastinates; **to'morrowness**, the distinctive quality of being tomorrow.

1810 COLERIDGE *Lett., to Wife* (1895) 563 He is as great a to-morrower to the full as your poor husband. **1880** G. MEREDITH *Tragic Com.* xiv, The postponer, the deferrer, or, as we might say, the to-morrower. **1824** J. MCCULLOCH *Scotl.* IV. 300 The *Cras hoc fiet* of this tomorrowing country. **1897** *Bookman* Nov. 235 If to-morrow..in its essential to-morrowness, has no objective existence.

tomp, obs. form of TUMP.

tompeon, -ping, -pion, tompkin: see TAMPION.

Tompion ('tɒmpɪən). ? *Obs.* [From the name of Thomas Tompion, a noted watchmaker in the reign of Queen Anne.] A watch made by Tompion or of the same type. Also *attrib.*, as ***Tompion clock, watch.***

1727 POPE, etc. *Art of Sinking* x. 94 Lac'd in her Cosins new appear'd the bride, A Bubble-bow and Tompion at her side. **1727** SWIFT *Circumcision E. Curll* Wks. 1755 III. I. 164 A Tompion's gold watch (which was given her by Mark Anthony). **1729** *Art of Politicks* 10 Think we that modern words eternal are? Toupet, and Tompion, Cosins, and Colmar Hereafter will be called by some plain man A Wig, a Watch, a Pair of Stays, a Fan. **1837** DICKENS *Pickw.* xxxvi, A spacious saloon ornamented with..a music gallery and a Tompion clock. **1871** MISS BRADDON *R. Ainsleigh* xii, I looked at my watch, a bulky Tompion with a clumsy outer case of leather.

Tom Piper, Tom Poker: see TOM *sb.*[1] 7 c.

tompon, variant of TAMPON.

Tom-pudding, tom-rig: see TOM *sb.*[1] 7 a, c, 8 b.

†**tom-pung**, original form of PUNG *sb.*[2], q.v.

Tom Thumb. [In reference to diminutive stature: cf. THUMB *sb.* 3.]

1. A dwarf or pigmy of popular tradition or fable, whose history was common as a chap-book; hence a name for a dwarf or diminutive male person; also contemptuously, a petty or insignificant person, a pigmy holder of a high position. Also *attrib.*

1579 FULKE *Heskins' Parl.* 235 They feigned him to be a little child like Tom Thumb. **1621** R. JOHNSON (*title*) The History of Tom Thumbe. **1630** (*title*) Tom Thumbe, his Life and Death. **1661** NEEDHAM *Hist. Eng. Reb.* 74 Princes are brav'd by Jack and Jill, Wat Tilers and Tom Thums. **1665** *Surv. Aff. Netherl.* 93, Jan. 20. 1651. they Voted our Tom Thombs a free State forsooth, and Commonwealth. *a* **1700** B. E. *Dict. Cant. Crew, Tom-thumb*, a Dwarf. **1806** *Naval Chron.* XV. 159 The Tom Thumb egotism..of the Corsican Usurper. **1889** *N.W. Linc. Gloss., Tom Thumb*, a small and insignificant person. **1907** *Daily Chron.* 6 Feb. 5/5 'Tom Thumb' is a name generally given by showmen to liliputians. The first holder of this 'title' was Charles Stratton, who was brought to London by Barnum.

2. *attrib.* Applied to dwarf varieties or specimens of animals or plants; also, *ellipt.* or *absol.* as *sb.* **a.** A kind of dwarf oyster. **b.** A dwarf variety of cabbage, lettuce, or other vegetable, of antirrhinum, nasturtium, or other flower.

1876 *Rep. Sel. Committee Oyster Fisheries* 49/2 Those oysters which you call buttons, I believe, or which some people call Tom Thumbs. *Ibid.* 77/2 A sort of dwarf oyster, or Tom Thumb oyster, would pass through the two-inch ring. **1898** *Westm. Gaz.* 29 Oct. 1/3 He had gone on sowing radishes and broccoli—making odd signs with pieces of stick and coloured paper to mark 'tom-thumb' or 'giant', 'early' or 'late' [varieties]. *Mod.* The Tom Thumb nasturtiums are preferable to the long straggling forms. Are the antirrhinums Tom Thumbs?

3. A popular name of some British wild flowers.

1886 BRITTEN & HOLLAND *Eng. Plant-n.*, Tom Thumb, *Lathyrus pratensis*. Berks... Suss. *Ibid.*, Appendix, Tom Thumb,..*Lotus corniculatus*. Oxf.

Tom Tiddler's ground. Also *dial.* **Tom Tickler's, Tittler's, Tinker's ground.** Name of a children's game.

One of the players is Tom Tiddler, his territory being marked by a line drawn on the ground; over this the other players run, crying 'We're on Tom Tiddler's ground, picking up gold and silver'. They are chased by Tom Tiddler, the first, or sometimes the last, caught taking his place.

1823 E. MOOR *Suffolk Wds. & Phr.* 437 *Tom Tickler's ground*, a juvenile sport. **1861** MISS YONGE *Stokesley Secret* ii. 34 She heard the joyous cry behind her—'I'm on Tommy Tittler's ground, Picking up gold and silver'. **1880** MRS. LYNN LINTON *Rebel of Family* II. xvi, Squalid children played about the door and made their Tom Tiddler's ground of the steps and street.

b. *transf.* Any place where money or other consideration is 'picked up' or acquired readily; also, a disputed or 'debatable territory, a no man's land between two states' (*Slang Dict.*).

1848 DICKENS *Dombey* xxxvi, Now, the spacious dining-room with the company seated round the glittering table,.. might have been taken for a grown-up exposition of Tom Tiddler's ground, where children pick up gold and silver. **1861** —— *Tom Tiddler's Ground* i, 'And why Tom Tiddler's ground?' said the Traveller. 'Because he scatters halfpence to Tramps and such-like', returned the Landlord, 'and of course they pick 'em up'. **1890** 'R. BOLDREWOOD' *Col. Reformer* (1891) 290 He..had come on to..Tom Tidler's ground,..gold..was sticking out of the soil everywhere. **1910** W. SICHEL *Glenbervie Jrnls.* i. 6 Ireland was then the Tom Tiddler's ground of parliamentary fortune hunters.

tom-tit, tomtit ('tɒm'tɪt). Also 8 **Tom teet.** [See TIT *sb.*[3] 3.] **1. a.** A common name of the Blue Titmouse (*Parus cæruleus*); also *locally*, of the Coal Titmouse (*P. ater*), the Great Tit, (*P. major*), and the American *P. atricapillus*; incorrectly of other small birds, as the Wren, and the Tree-creeper.

1709 STEELE *Tatler* No. 112 ¶2 To spare the Life of a Tom-Tit. **1711** ADDISON *Spect.* No. 5 ¶7 The Singing Birds will be Personated by Tom-tits. **1796** MORSE *Amer. Geog.* I. 211 Tom Teet, *Parus atricapillus*. **1812** COMBE *Picturesque* XXII, I must breathe my dogs a-bit, And try my gun at some tom-tit. *a* **1825** FORBY *Voc. E. Anglia, Tom-tit*,..by us it is applied to the wren.., *tom-tit* seems to belong indiscriminately to both sexes. **1909** *Athenæum* 20 Mar. 347/1 Magee characterized somebody's religion as insufficient for a tomtit. **1965** *Jrnl. Lancs. Dial. Soc.* Jan. 19 Great Tit... Tom Tit. Accrington. **1972** *Guardian* 23 Feb. 12/2 An octogenarian farm worker..pointed out that, just as one's largest toe is the 'tom toe', so it followed naturally that the largest tit was the tom-tit.

b. *transf.* applied to a little man or boy.

1741 RICHARDSON *Pamela* (ed. 2) I. Introd., I have told you the History of this Tom-tit of a Prater. **1909** *Daily News* 19 July 11 A veritable little tomtit of a man in his jerky little ways and lively good humour.

2. A small sailing boat.

1857 A. W. HABERSHAM *My Last Cruise* xvii. 333 Some of us also took the tomtit, (a boat smaller even than the dingy). **1925** A. B. ARMITAGE *Cadet to Commodore* xx. 278 Out with the 'Tom-tits' in the harbour on a breezy Saturday afternoon was another delightful sport.

3. Rhyming slang for 'shit'. Freq. with *the* in *fig.* use: 'the willies'; also, nonsense.

1943 'R. LLEWELLYN' *None but Lonely Heart* xx. 116 'You're always doing it, you shower of tom tit, you.' **1944** L. GLASSOP *We were Rats* 67 'Break it down,' said the corporal. 'You'll give these blokes the tomtits before they get their first lot of C.B.' **1967** J. GARDNER *Madrigal* I. iii. 54 You can cut the Tom Tit, sergeant. **1970** C. WOOD '*Terrible Hard,' says Alice* vii. 91 Perhaps 'e stopped for a tomtit. **1973** P. A. SMITH *Barcoo Salute* 14 What's the matter, got the tom tits? **1982** L. CODY *Bad Company* xii. 80, I was just sitting there, trousers round me ankles... If I hadn't been doing it already, he'd 've given me the tom-tits.

tom-tom ('tɒm,tɒm), *sb.* Also 8–9 **tam-tam**, 9 **tum-tum, tong-tong.** [a. Hindūstānī or other E. Indian vernacular *tam-tam*: cf. Sinhalese *tamaṭṭama*, Malay *tong-tong*; all imitations of the sound of the instrument.]

1. a. A native East Indian drum; extended also to the hand-beaten drums of Asia and Africa generally.

1693 in Wheeler *Madras* (1861) I. 268 That to-morrow morning the Choultry Justices do cause the Tom Tom to be beat through all the streets of the Black Town. **1764** in J. Long *Select. Rec. Govt.* (*Fort William*) (1869) 391 (Y.) You will give strict orders to Zemindars to furnish Oil and Musshauls, and Tom Toms and Pikemen, &c., according to custom. **1782** W. F. MARTYN *Geog. Mag.* I. 249 The music is composed of small drums called tamtams. **1804** WELLINGTON in Gurw. *Desp.* (1837) IV. 186 Let the cause of their punishment be published in the Bazaar by beat of tom tom. *c* **1813** MRS. SHERWOOD *Stories Ch. Catech.* iv. 20 They were almost deafened by the sound of their tum-tums and trumpets. *Ibid.* (*Explan. Ind. words*), *Tum-tums*, small drums. **1860** TRISTRAM *Gt. Sahara* xi. 184 The chief characteristic of the affair was the noise of drums and tomtoms. **1864** ENGEL *Mus. Anc. Nat.* 63 The other class of Oriental small drums consists of those which are of a barrel-form, covered at each end with skin, carried obliquely, and beaten with one hand at each end. Such drums are best known by the name tom-tom.

b. *transf.* Anything beaten like a drum so as to make a loud noise. Chiefly *fig.*

1885 *Pall Mall G.* 7 Apr. 1/1 Those preparations about which the journalistic tom-tom is being beaten so vigorously. **1891** *Scott. Leader* 2 July 5 Mr. Parnell was greeted with such a vigorous beating of tom-toms that he gave up the attempt to speak.

c. A low-toned drum (without snares), used in Western music.

1934 E. LITTLE *Mod. Rhythmic Drumming* (rev. ed.) 26 No outfit is complete without at least one tomtom. **1977** *Rolling Stone* 30 June 97/2 Ringo slams away on his tom-toms.

2. The beating of a drum; an imitation of the sound of this.

1898 ALDERSON *Mounted Infantry Mashonaland* v. 90 Then 'Tom-tom, tom-tom, tom, tom-a-tom, tom', go the war drums; out go the fires. **1912** *Eng. Rev.* Mar. 615 The tom-tom of the watchman could be heard.

3. *attrib.* and *Comb.*

1857 WILKINSON *Egypt Time of Pharaohs* 28 The trumpet was chiefly confined to the military band; to which also belonged, though not exclusively, the tomtom drum, the clappers, and a few others. **1884** J. COLBORNE *Hicks Pasha* 59 The band consisted of three fiddlers and a tam-tam beater. **1908** SIR H. JOHNSTON *Grenfell & Congo* II. xxv. 719 A drum of the tom-tom form is used.

'tom-tom, *v.* [Partly f. prec. sb., partly directly echoic.] **a.** *intr.* To beat a tom-tom or drum; to drum. **b.** *trans.* To give notice of or call attention to by beating a tom-tom. **c.** To perform on a tom-tom or drum; *transf.* to play in a monotonous way, to 'drum', 'strum'. Hence **'tom-tomming** *vbl. sb.*, **'tom-tommer.**

1857 S. HISLOP in G. Smith *Life* v. (1888) 166 It had been tom-tomed in the city that all who are too poor to lay in a supply of provisions should leave. **1859** R. F. BURTON in *Jrnl. Geog. Soc.* XXIX. 414 A man tom-toming lustily upon a kettle-drum shaped like an European hourglass. **1860** TRISTRAM *Gt. Sahara* ix. 146 While preparing for the night we heard a loud tomtomming without. **1872** 'ALIPH CHEEM' *Lays of Ind* (1876) 6 The dancer..Keeping time to the piper's and tom-tommer's strains. **1884** J. COLBORNE *Hicks Pasha* 118 My friends..trumpet, bugle, and 'tam-tam' all day long. **1898** BARKER *Comic Side School Life* 29 Able to tom-tom easy accompaniments on the piano.

tom-trot, tom-turkey: see TOM *sb.*[1]

-tomy, a. Gr. -τομία, often through mod.L. *-tomia*, used to form abstract sbs. from adjs. in -τομος cutting; f. verbal ablaut-series τεμ-, τομ-, τμ-, in τέμ-ν-ειν to cut, τομή, τμῆσις cutting: entering into numerous technical terms, as *anatomy*, lit. 'cutting up', *cystotomy*, *dichotomy*, *lithotomy*, *phlebotomy*, *thymotomy*, *tracheotomy*, *zootomy*, etc.

tomyll, obs. form of TUMBLE.

ton[1] (tʌn). Forms: 4–6 **tonne**, 5 **toun**, 6 **toonne**, (**tune**), *Sc.* **twn**, 6–7 **tunne**, 6–8 **tun**, 7 **tunn**, 5– **ton**. See also TUN *sb.* [In origin the same word as TUN (OE. *tunne*, OF. *tonne*) a cask. In ME. this was commonly spelt, as in French, *tonne*; in 16–17th c., more often *tun*; from *c* 1688 the two spellings have been differentiated, *tun* being appropriated to the sense 'cask' and the liquid measure, and *ton* to the senses here treated, which, it will be seen, are partly measures, and partly weights.]

†**1.** A large wine-vessel, a cask; hence, a measure of capacity used for wine: now spelt TUN, q.v.

2. A unit used in measuring the carrying capacity or burden of a ship, the amount of cargo, freight, etc. Originally, the space occupied by a tun cask of wine (see explanatory quot. 1894 on *ton tight* s.v. TIGHT *a.* 14, and quot. 1539 here). Now, for the purposes of registered tonnage, the space of 100 cubic feet. For purposes of freight, usually the space of 40 cubic feet, unless that bulk would weigh more than 20 cwt., in which case freight is charged by weight. But the expression 'ton of cargo' is also used with regard to special packages which are conventionally assumed as going so many packages to the ton. Cf. also TONNAGE.

1379–1603 Tonne tight, etc. [see TIGHT *a.* 14]. **1509** HAWES *Past. Pleas.* XIX. xxii. (Percy) 92 The shyp was great, fyve c. tonne to charge. **1530** PALSGR. 460/1 A shyppe of a hundred tonne. [**1539** in R. G. Marsden *Sel. Pl. Crt. Adm.* (Selden) I. 89 Unam naviculam vocatam a shippes boat oneris trium doliorum.] **1544** *Ibid.* 126 Ladyn . . 35 butts wynes wich goith for fyeftey tons ladinge. **1555** EDEN *Dec. New World* 349 (*Second Voyage to Guinea*) (Arb.) 379 A shyppe of the burden of seuen score toonne. **1582** N. LICHEFIELD tr. *Castanheda's Conq. E. Ind.* I. ii. 4 b, The King then bought . . a Caruell of fiftie tunne. **1587** HARRISON *England* II. xvii. (1877) I. 285 A ship of ours of six hundred tun. **1657** R. LIGON *Barbadoes* (1673) 2 We . . had with us a small ship of about 180 tunns, called the *Nonesuch*. *a* **1687** PETTY *Pol. Arith.* iii. (1690) 54 The King of Englands Navy consists of about seventy thousand Tuns of Shipping. *Ibid.* 56 In France . . there are not above one hundred and fifty thousand Tun of Trading Vessels, and consequently not above fifteen thousand Seamen, reckoning a Man to every ten Tun. **1769** FALCONER *Dict. Marine* (1789) Zj, A ton in measure is generally estimated at 2000 lb. in weight. **1821** J. Q. ADAMS in C. Davies *Metr. Syst.* (1871) III. 98 The casks of Bordeaux wine were then [1423] and still are made for stowage in such manner that four hogsheads occupy one ton of shipping. The ton was of thirty-two cubic feet by measure, and of 2,016 English pounds, of fifteen ounces to the pound, in weight; equal to 2,560 of the easterling tower pound. **1858** SIMMONDS *Dict. Trade* s.v., The ton of freight or merchandise varies with the article and the locality from whence shipped. **1867** SMYTH *Sailor's Word-bk.*, *Ton*, or *Tun*. . . In the cubical contents of a ship it is the weight of water equal to 2000 lbs., by the general standard for liquids. *Ibid.*, 42 cubic feet of articles equal one ton in shipment.

3. A measure of capacity: **a.** for timber; usually equivalent to 40 cubic feet (or for hewn timber, 50).

1521 *MS. Acc. St. John's Hosp., Canterb.*, For hewyng of a tune and xvj fote of tymber. **1707** MORTIMER *Husb.* (1721) II. 88 To sell your Timber . . by the Ton, Load or Foot, forty Foot being reckoned a Ton, and fifty a Load, and in some places just the contrary. **1774** PENNANT *Tour Scotl. in 1769* (ed. 3) 107 The tenant is obliged to work 150 tuns of timber annually, paying eighteen shillings and six-pence per tun. **1813** T. DAVIS *Agric. Wilts.* Gloss., *Ton* of Rough Timber, 40 feet, the load 50 feet, is only used when timber is hewn for the navy.

b. for various solid commodities, as stone, gravel, lime, plaster, wheat, cheese, etc.

1428–9 *Rec. St. Mary at Hill* 70 A tonne tyght of northerin ston. *a* **1500** *How Plowman lerned Pater-Noster* 110 in Hazl. *E.P.P.* I. 213 Of whete amonge them they gate an hole tunne. **1504** *Acc. Ld. High Treas. Scot.* II. 277 For xx twn of plaistir brocht hame be Dorange, Franchman. **1538** in R. G. Marsden *Sel. Pl. Crt. Adm.* (Selden) I. 82 For the freight of every ton tight of the saide wheate, accompting fyve quarters to every ton. **1667** PRIMATT *City & C. Build.* 68 Half a Tun of Plaister of Paris will lay fifteen yards of Lath-work. *a* **1674** CLARENDON *Hist. Reb.* VII. §335 Threescore and fifteen Barrels of Butter, and fourteen Tun of Cheese. **1821** J. Q. ADAMS in C. Davies *Metr. Syst.* (1871) III. 127 Before the statute of 1496, the London quarter of a ton was the one measure, to which the bushel for corn, the gallon, deduced by measure, for ale, and the gallon, deduced by weight, for wine, were all referred. **1858** SIMMONDS *Dict. Trade* s.v., A ton of flour, in commerce, is 8 sacks or 10 barrels; a ton of potatoes, 10 bushels.

4. a. A measure of weight, now generally 20 cwt.; in Great Britain legally 2240 lbs.; in the United States and elsewhere, for most purposes 2000 lbs. 'Tons' of different amounts were formerly in use and are still so locally for some commodities. (Where two weights are so known and used, the heavier is distinguished as the ***long*** or ***gross ton*** and the lighter as the ***short ton***.) ***metric ton*** (Fr. *tonne*) = 1000 kilogrammes (2204·6 lbs. avoirdupois).

1485 *Cely Papers* (Camden) 183 Item the sam day payd for vj toun of balast, ij s. **1539** in R. G. Marsden *Sel. Pl. Crt. Adm.* (Selden) I. 89, lxxj kintalls of yron in ends 44 . . . And it goes for iij tone and xj kintalls. **1545** *Rates of Custome-ho.* b v, Iron called Lukes Iron the tonne conteynynge .xx. C. pounde iii. li. vi.s. viii.d. **1588** GREENE *Pandosto* (1607) 6 A pound of goold is worth a tunne of leade. **1670** EACHARD *Cont. Clergy* 115 Unless we had some vent for our learned ones beyond the sea, and could transport so many tunn of divines yearly, as we do other commodities, with which the nation is over-stocked. **1725** *Bradley's Fam. Dict.* II, *Tun*, a Measure in Averdupois, consisting of twenty hundred Weight, each Hundred being a Hundred and twelve Pounds. **1793** SMEATON *Edystone L.* §154 Every thing stood fast with eight ton weight upon the tackle-blocks. **1829** *Glover's Hist. Derby* I. 100 It [pure white gypsum] sells at 10s. per long ton. (*Note.*—120 lb. to the Cwt.) *Ibid.* 265 It was agreed that weighing-houses should be erected upon the several canals, and that the ton should be fixed at 2,400 lbs. **1858** SIMMONDS *Dict. Trade* s.v., In Great Britain, the legal ton by weight is usually 20 cwt., or 2240 lbs., but in long weight it is 2400 lbs. . . In Cornwall, the miner's ton is 21 cwt., or 2352 lbs. **1881** RAYMOND *Mining Gloss.* s.v., For many things, such as coal and iron, the ton in use [in U.S.] is the long ton of 20 hundred-weight at 112 pounds avoirdupois. . . In gold and silver mining, and throughout the Western States, the ton is the short ton of 2000 pounds. **1894** *Times* 10 Sept. 6/1 The total quantity which exploded was about 3,700 lb., or not far short of two tons, 2,000 lb. being reckoned as a ton in measuring explosives.

b. (*colloq.*) A very large amount: cf. LOAD *sb.* 6. Mostly in *pl.*

1770 P. FRENEAU in Brackenridge & Freneau *Father Bombo* (1975) I. iii. 13 My head stuck a considerable time in a ton of mud. **1895** *Daily News* 25 Apr. 6/3 'Is there any culture at Chicago?' asked a young lady of Boston of a damsel of the former city. 'You bet your sweet life! . . Tons of it', was the reply. **1899** H. SWEET *Pract. Study Languages* x. 115, I am told that the great English lexicographers of the present day look down with contempt on anything less than a ton of such materials. **1911** BARRIE *Peter & Wendy* iv, 'I say! Do you kill many [pirates]?' 'Tons'. **1971** *Scope* (S. Afr.) 19 Mar. 38/1 Fine, thanks a ton, Len. I won't be a sec. **1977** *Belfast Tel.* 28 Feb. 20/8 This has brought the lass on a ton.

c. *pl.* As *adv.* qualifying comparative or (*U.S.*) positive adjs.: much; very. *colloq.*

1908 S. WILSON *Let.* 17 Aug. in R. S. Churchill *Winston S. Churchill* (1969) II. Compan. II. 804. I feel tons better for being in the wonderful air. **1970** 'D. HALLIDAY' *Dolly & Cookie Bird* viii. 127 He was looking tons better, with his ribs done up in crèpe. **1977** *Amer. Speech 1975* L. 68 *Tons adv*, very, extremely. 'Her outfit is tons neat.'

d. Phr. ***to come down*** (***on*** or ***upon***) (a person) ***like a ton of bricks***: see COME *v.* 60 g.

5. *trans.* **a.** *colloq.* A score of one hundred in a game, *spec.* in *Cricket* (= CENTURY 3 b) and *Darts*.

1936 R. CROFT-COOKE *Darts* vi. 42 *Ton*, the word means simply 100. While in more gentlemanly games they speak of Centuries, in Darts we curtly say 'One Ton'. **1946** J. MOORE *Brensham Village* III. 95 Darts has its own esoteric terminology. . . A hundred is a 'ton', of course, all over England. **1958** *Punch* 9 July 40/2, I owe everything to Cambridge. I got a ton in the Freshman's Match of 1941. **1973** *Atlantic Monthly* Aug. 73 Now he's averaging 60 or more, frequently throws a 'ton'—a round of 100 or more points—and can put a dart into a fifty-cent piece area every time. **1978** *Lancashire Life* Apr. 41/3 Scoring a century didn't mean a hoot to me then. . . Now, as an experienced pro, I know I must make a 'ton' and then keep going to get another.

b. *slang.* A hundred pounds.

1946 *People* 7 Apr. 2/6 A red-faced punter . . whose conversational powers were limited to . . jargon, which translated fivers as 'flims' . . ; £100 as a 'ton' [etc.]. **1960** 'A. BURGESS' *Doctor is Sick* 164 'And what's the first prize?' asked Edwin. 'A ton,' screamed Harry Stone. ''Undred nicker an' a film test.' **1981** P. TURNBULL *Deep & Crisp & Even* vii. 131 The old man would charge three ton for this but me and the boys will do it for half-price.

c. *colloq.* A speed of one hundred miles per hour (esp. with reference to motor cycles). Freq. in phr. ***to do the*** (or ***a***) ***ton***. Cf. TON-UP *sb.* and *a.*

1954 G. SMITH *Flaw in Crystal* iv. 36 At eighty I felt a wild sense of elation. . . I watched to see if Several would triumphantly lead Teddy onwards at a majestic full ton. **1959** *News Chron.* 17 Dec. 3/1 The dangerous noddles who boast about doing the ton on the public roads. **1964** *New Statesman* 21 Feb. 288/3 We do the ton sometimes, but not where any one's goin' to get 'urt. **1973** *Hansard Lords* 5 Dec. 684 In that case, you must have been doing a 'ton', if very few cars passed you.

d. In other miscellaneous colloq. uses to denote one hundred.

1962 *Electronics Weekly* 21 Nov. 3/1 Elliott reach a ton. The 100th National Elliott 803 computer has been installed. **1970** *Sunday Tel.* 22 Mar. 13/3 Blissful summer breezes . . ease the discomfort of temperatures which occasionally threaten to make the ton. **1980** *Financial Rev.* (Sydney) 29 Aug. 29/1 Australians staying at the best capital city hotels . . will have reached 'the ton' in their room rates—accommodation will be costing $100 a night.

†**6. ton mascull** (**tonne maskyll**), app. a tun cask of 252 gallons: = TUN *sb.* 2. *Obs.*

[*Mascull* may represent a Latin or Romanic *masc(u)la* = It. *maschia* 'male, large, big, huge', as a description of the largest *tunna* or *tonna*.]

1432 *Rolls of Parlt.* IV. 405/2 Wynes . . not havyng of lyes overe iiij or v ynches in a tonne maskyll. **1531** in R. G. Marsden *Sel. Pl. Crt. Adm.* (Selden) I. 36 Lade the sayd shypp with wynes to the fful number of lvij tonnes . . accounttyng always a ton mascull for a ton, ij pipes for a ton, iiij hoggesheдds for a ton, and vj tercys for a ton, and twenty hundred Englyshe weyght for a ton. **1541** *Ibid.* 113 So many thowsand orenges as makyth by account and custom of Galizia, all with the forsaid xlvj hogsheds whales grece and oyle, xlvj ton mascull.

7. a. *attrib.* and *Comb.*, as ***ton-burden***, ***-load***; esp. with measures of distance, forming units measuring the work done in the conveyance of heavy bodies, esp. in reference to its cost; as **ton-fathom**, the equivalent of the work done in raising a ton through the depth of a fathom, as in the shaft of a mine; **ton-force** (pl. *tons-force*), a unit of force equal to the weight of a mass of one ton, esp. under standard gravity; **ton-mile**, the same in carrying a ton the distance of a mile, as by a railway-train or motor-car; so **ton-mileage**, amount of or reckoning in ton-miles, or charge per ton-mile; **ton weight**, the weight of one ton; usu. *fig.*

1805 *Act 45 Geo. III*, c. 10 §3 For every *ton burthen of every such ship or vessel, which shall have so arrived without a clean bill of health, fifteen shillings. **1874** J. H. COLLINS *Metal Mining* (1875) 77 About 1-50th of a penny per *ton-fathom or less. **1961** *B.S.I. News* Oct. 26/2 A similar distinction is made between . . ton (no abbreviation) and *ton-force (tonf). **1972** *Physics Bull.* May 285/1 The 50 tonf dead-weight standard was originally designed to give forces only in units of tons-force. *a* **1400** *MS. Cott. Vesp. B. xxii.* lf. 97 in *Blk. Bk. Adm.* (Rolls) I. 400 Accustumez de doner pur chascun *tonnelode, que le vesseau purra porter . . douze deniers. **1894** *Outing* (U.S.) 393/1 Were the *ton mileage of each contrasted, the waterways would make much the greater showing. **1900** *Engineering Mag.* XIX. 734 Two horses harnessed to one waggon may achieve 35 nett *ton miles daily in regular work. **1902** *Monthly Rev.* Aug. 35 Obtaining the average per ton-mile from other canals. **1906** *Westm. Gaz.* 28 Aug. 4/2 The 10-h.p. [motor car] . . ran . . at the rate of 41.7 ton miles per gallon. *a* **1855** C. BRONTË *Professor* (1857) I. vi. 87 This liability is a *ton weight at least. **1893** H. FREDERIC *Return of O'Mahony* I. x. 83 Then would come . . the fierce buffeting of ton-weight blows as the boat staggered blindly at the bottom of the abyss. **1936** *Discovery* Feb. 37/2 The power developed per ton-weight of the engine. **1960** H. PINTER *Caretaker* I. 18 I'll give you a hand. (*They lift it.*) It's a ton weight, en't? **1981** J. WAINWRIGHT *All on Summer's Day* 198 She'd been like a ton weight across his shoulders. Her and her infernal daughters.

b. ton tight: see TIGHT *a.* 14.

†**ton**[2]. *Obs.* [a. F. *taon* (pronounced tã, earlier tɔ̃) gad-fly (12th c. in Littré), later also applied in the environs of Paris to the larva of the cockchafer (Littré):—pop.L. **tabōnem*, for L. *tabānum* (*-us*) gad-fly, whence Prov. *tavan*, Sp. *tábano*, Pg. *tavão*, It. *ta'fano*, *tabano*, †*tavano*, gad-fly.] The larva of the cockchafer, which lives underground and feeds on the roots of plants.

1693 EVELYN *De la Quint. Compl. Gard.* II. 100 Kitchen-Plants, especially Lettuce, and Succory, &c. constantly have some of those Tons, or other little reddish Worms which gnaw them about the neck, and kill them [*margin* Those usually called by the Name of Cock-Chafers]. *Ibid.* 202 The great Enemies of Straw-berry Plantations are the Ton's which are great White Worms, that in the Months of May and June, gnaw the necks of their Roots. **1712** J. JAMES tr. *Le Blond's Gardening* 173 The great Enemies to Trees, are . . Snails, Tons, Turks, and abundance of Worms.

‖**ton**[3] (tɔ̃, †tɒn). [Fr. *ton* manner in general:—L. *ton-us*, TONE in colouring, etc.]

a. The fashion, the vogue, the mode; fashionable air or style.

See also *bon-ton* s.v. BON.

1769 *Lloyd's Evening Post* 18–20 Dec. 589 The present fashionable *Ton* (a word used at present to express every thing that's fashionable) is a set of French puppets. **1775** SHERIDAN *Rivals* I. i, None of the London whips of any degree of ton wear wigs now. **1778** MISS BURNEY *Evelina* (1791) II. xxxvii. 244 Don't we all know that you lead the *ton* in the *beau monde*? **1812** H. & J. SMITH *Rej. Addr.*, *Beautiful Incend.* ix, And if she were here all alone, Our house might nocturnally boast A bumper of fashion and ton. **1812** COMBE *Picturesque* XI, A mantle, too, is all the ton, And therefore I have order'd one. **1881** BESANT & RICE *Chapl. of Fleet* II. i, In everything . . make my niece an accomplished woman, a woman of ton. **1939** D. CECIL *Young Melbourne* viii. 220 Some humble country acquaintances and a few persons of ton. **1978** J. KRANTZ *Scruples* ii. 39 And these Bostonians . . did own a gratifying number of mills and plants and banks and brokerage firms. Also they had *ton*.

b. *transf.* People of fashion; fashionable society; the fashionable world.

c **1770** in de Vries & Fryer *Venus Unmasked* (1967) 33 Miss P. . . D. . . will only . . take engagements from billiard table gentlemen, gentlemen of the ton, and young shop-men. **1815** *Sporting Mag.* XLVI. 93 All the 'Ton's' a stage, And Fashion's motley votaries are but play'rs. **1854** J. S. C. ABBOTT *Napoleon* (1885) I. xiv. 255 The princess, the nobles, and all the *ton* had disappeared. **1969** H. ELSNA *Abbot's House* 99 A waste, when all the *ton* will flock here for this event. *Ibid.* 103 The *ton* are here in force.

†**ton**[4]. *Obs.* [a. OF. *ton* (14–16th c.), F. *thon*:—L. *thunn-us*, TUNNY.] A sea-fish, a tunny.

1624 MIDDLETON *Game at Chess* v. iii, You may eat kid, cabrito, calf, and tons. **1624** [T. SCOTT] *Vox Populi* II. 22 A peece of leane Kid, or Cabrito, a Tripe, Tone's or such like. **1672** JOSSELYN *New Eng. Rarities* 31. **1768** BOSWELL *Corsica* i. (ed. 2) 37 There is the greatest variety of all the best kinds, and in particular a sort of ton or sturgeon.

ton, obs. ME. pl. of TOE; var. TONE *pron.*; obs. f. TOWN, TUN; dial. var. of *tan*, obs. pa. pple. of TAKE (see TAKE *v.* 5 γ, TO *v. Obs.*).

tonacle, -culle, tonage, obs. ff. TUNICLE, TONNAGE.

‖**tonadilla** (tɒnaˈdiːjə). [Sp., dim. of *tonada* tune, song.] A light operatic interlude of the mid-eighteenth to early-nineteenth cent., orig. forming an intermezzo between the acts of a serious play or opera, but later performed independently.

1830 W. C. STAFFORD *Hist. Music* xviii. 263 The Tonadilla, originally a simple and popular song, sung in the *Zarguela* and *Saynette*, now frequently represents an entire action, consisting of a whole scene, or even of an act. **1876** STAINER & BARRETT *Dict. Mus. Terms* 435/2 *Tonadilla* (*Sp.*), a short tune, an interlude, ritornello, symphony to a song. **1920** C. VAN VECHTEN *Mus. Spain* v. 82 The *tonadilla* . . accompanied by a guitar or violin and interspersed with dances, was very popular for a number of years. **1947** A. EINSTEIN *Mus. Romantic Era* xvii. 329 The works decisive in bringing out this national style were . . *zarzuelas* in the realistic manner of the *tonadilla*. **1973** *Oxford Times* 30 Mar. 14/4 The scenic tonadilla in the 18th century can be described as miniature comic opera.

tonal (ˈtəʊnəl), *a.* and *sb.* [ad. med.L. *tonāl-is* (St. Bernard of Cluny), f. *ton-us* TONE: see -AL[1]; cf. mod.F. *tonal* (Littré).]

A. *adj*., Of or pertaining to tone or tones.

1. *Mus*. †a. Pertaining to the ecclesiastical modes.

1776 HAWKINS *Hist. Mus.* III. ix. I. 354 The first [discourse]..is on..Guidonian music.., the one [part] treating of Manual, i.e. elementary music..and the other of Tonal music, containing the doctrine of the ecclesiastical tones.

b. Applied to a fugue, or a sequence, in which the repetitions of the subject in different positions are all in the same key, and therefore vary in their intervals: opp. to REAL *a.* 3 c.

1869 OUSELEY *Counterp. Canon & Fugue* xix. 160 *note*, In the early days of counterpoint a tonal fugue was one in which the relations of the subject and answer were governed by the old Church modes. **1879** —— in Grove *Dict. Mus.* I. 567 In most cases the answer [to the subject of a fugue] has to be modified according to certain rules to avoid modulating out of the key... An answer so treated is called a 'tonal answer', and the fugue is called a 'Tonal fugue'. **1889** PROUT *Harmony* v. §138 The intervals..differ in quality according to their position in the scale... Such a sequence is termed a *tonal* sequence.

c. Of tonality; pertaining to music written in keys. Opp. ATONAL *a.*

1884 G. OAKEY *Text Bk. Harmony* viii. 51 A sequence.. in which the intervals belong to one scale, is termed..a Tonal Sequence. **1922** [see ATONAL *a.*] **1957** *Encycl. Brit.* XI. 205/1 With the development of polyphony, tonality becomes as important as the concord-discord system itself; and, indeed, that system could not have existed without tonal guidance at every point. **1978** P. GRIFFITHS *Conc. Hist. Mod. Music* ii. 23 Sibelius's long silence..may suggest the difficulty of maintaining tonal composition in the twentieth century.

2. Of, pertaining, or relating to the tone or tones. Of speech or a language: expressing difference of meaning by variation of tone.

1866 *Athenæum* 24 Mar. 404/1 The multiplicity of tonal divagations. **1867** MACFARREN *Harmony* i. 11 Ambrose.. called the modes he adopted according to their tonal ascent, 1st, 2nd, 3rd, 4th. **1886** C. TROTTER in *Encycl. Brit.* XXI. 774/1 But [Shan] is a tonal language, and the vowel sounds are few, so that some have two or three values assigned them. **1896** F. NIECKS *Paper bef. Congr. Incorp. Soc. Mus.*, The Association of Tonal and Verbal Speech.

3. Pertaining to or characterized by shades of colour or effects of light and shade. Cf. TONE *sb.* 10 a, b.

1910 S. J. SOLOMON *Practice of Oil Painting* vi. 62 The same method is applicable in arriving at a similar decision with regard to the relation of shadows, all intervening tones, and the general tonal aspect of the whole figure. **1931** J. H. BROWN *Water-Colour Guidance* x. 192 Present-day colour work..has tended to divert the colourist's attention from the *tonal* aspect of painting. **1967** E. SHORT *Embroidery & Fabric Collage* i. 4 (*caption*) As one fabric is used throughout, there are no contrasts of colour or texture, and the design relies for interest on the tonal pattern made by the shadows. **1980** *Economist* 20 Aug. 62/1 Plain and tonal designs— mingled colours, but no pattern—are the fashion. *Ibid.* 62/2 Tonal carpets are what the customer wants.

†**B.** *sb.* (med.L. *tonāle*). A book containing a summary of the rules governing ecclesiastical music, with examples. Cf. the *tonārius* 'liber de tonis seu cantu' (Du Cange). *Obs. rare*$^{-0}$.

c **1475** *Pict. Voc.* in Wr.-Wülcker 755/20 (Nomina ecclesie necessaria) *Hoc tonale*, a tonal.

Hence **'tonally** *adv.*, in respect of tone.

1883 GURNEY *Tertium Quid* (1887) II. 22 Bits that are rhythmically and tonally coherent.

tonalite ('tɒnəlaɪt). *Min.* [ad. G. *tonalit* (G. vom Rath 1864, in *Zeitschr. der deutsch. geol. Ges.* XVI. 249).] Orig., a particular variety of quartz-diorite; later used for any quartz-diorite. Now *spec.* a rock in which quartz represents 20–60 per cent of quartz plus feldspars (a higher proportion than in quartz-diorite) and alkali feldspar is less than 10 per cent of total feldspars.

1879 RUTLEY *Stud. Rocks* xii. 244 The rock termed tonalite by Vom Rath, which occurs in the Tonale Pass in the Tyrol,..formerly regarded as a variety of granite, is a micaceous quartz-diorite. **1885** LYELL *Elem. Geol.* (ed. 4) 571 *Tonalite*..consists of quartz, oligoclase, and hornblende. **1913** *Jrnl. Geol.* XXI. 213 Lindgren has defined tonalite (or quartz diorite), as containing less than 8 per cent of alkali feldspar, granodiorite as containing 8–20 per cent of alkali feldspar. **1932** A. JOHANNSEN *Descr. Petrogr. Igneous Rocks* II. 379 Diorites with less than 5 per cent of quartz may be called quartz-bearing-diorites. With more than 5 per cent, they become quartz-diorites (tonalites). **1962** W. T. HUANG *Petrology* iv. 91 From granite, granodiorite, tonalite to diorite, the proportional amounts of quartz and alkalic feldspar decrease, while that of sodic plagioclase increases. **1976** *Earth-Sci. Rev.* XII. 14 For field 5 the term *tonalite* is recommended, whether hornblende is present or not, in agreement with Johannsen ..; whereas quartz diorite, frequently used for this field, is restricted to field 10*. *Ibid.* 27, 20–60% of light-colored minerals... Plag 90–100% of total feldspar: (5) tonalite. **1977** *Sci. Amer.* Mar. 94/1 The average chemical composition [of gneisses] resembles that of the common igneous rocks diorite and tonalite.

Hence **tona'litic** *a.*

1963 *Revista de la Asociación Geológica Argentina* XVIII. 97 In the Pampean Ranges, tungsten ore deposits are related to tonalitic-granitic intrusives of the pre-Cambrian tectomagmatic cycle. **1978** *Nature* 16 Mar. 241/1 Although the gneiss belts show great structural complexity.. granodioritic and tonalitic compositions greatly predominate.

tonalitive (təʊ'nælɪtɪv), *a. Mus. Obs.* or *rare.* [f. TONALIT(Y + -IVE.] Of or pertaining to tonality.

1907 M. H. GLYN *Rhythmic Conception of Music* iii. 64 Nothing would seem more natural than that tonality should suggest 'tonalitive', but the word has not hitherto appeared. **1918** *Mus. Assoc. Proc. 1917–18* 162, I should expect the new tonalitive schemes of such composers as Debussy and Ravel to bring about great changes in composition. **1924** T. H. Y. TROTTER *Music & Mind* 237 The old major and minor tonalitive schemes are giving way.

tonality (təʊ'nælɪtɪ). [f. TONAL *a.* + -ITY: so mod.F. *tonalité* (1866 in Littré).] Tonal quality.

1. *Mus.* **a.** The relation, or sum of relations, between the tones or notes of a scale or musical system; *spec.* in modern music, = KEY *sb.* 7 c; hence *transf.* a particular scale or system of tones; in modern music = KEY *sb.* 7 b.

1838 G. F. GRAHAM *Mus. Comp.* App. 68 The peculiar tonalities of many old national airs. **1855** *Fraser's Mag.* LI. 568 Grafting..more elegant melodic forms, improved rhythm, and the modern 'tonality' on the sustained grandeur of the old masters. **1867** BRANDE & COX *Dict. Sc.*, etc., *Tonality*..is used generally to denote that peculiarity which modern music possesses, in consequence of its being written in definite keys, thereby conforming to certain defined arrangements of tones and semitones in the diatonic scale. **1875** OUSELEY *Mus. Form* ii. 5 A Melody, if it is to produce a pleasing effect..must be written in some definite tonality.

b. The principle or practice of organizing musical composition around a key note or tonic.

1932 J. YASSER *Theory Evolving Tonality* 375 *Tonality*, a principle which organically and tonocentrically unites the function of a certain number of systematically arranged sounds..in their melodic and harmonic aspects. **1957** *Encycl. Brit.* XI. 205/2 Palestrina's tonality is one of the most mature and subtle things in music. **1978** P. GRIFFITHS *Conc. Hist. Mod. Music* iii. 39 Berg's opera differs from Schoenberg's monodrama in its direct references back to tonality.

2. *Painting.* The quality of a painting in respect of tone; the general tone or colour-scheme of a picture: see quots.

1866 *Sat. Rev.* 27 Jan. 117/1 Much of the value of a painting depends on the completeness of its tonality... The *tonalité* of a picture is the proportionate arrangement, and especially the accurate subdivision of tones, both with regard to colour and to relative lightness and darkness. **1884** *Athenæum* 24 May 668 The tonality of the picture is very good, although the illumination is in a low key. **1890** TALBOT ARCHER in *Anthony's Photogr. Bull.* III. 218 By 'tone' or 'tonality' is here meant the correct rendering, in black and white, of any natural object—as a landscape, a portrait, etc.

3. *Linguistics.* The differentiation of words, phrases, or syllables by a change in the pitch of the voice.

1948 R. A. D. FORREST *Chinese Lang.* i. 26 All the languages which we group under the term Sinitic have..a tendency to develop significant tonality. **1956** JAKOBSON & HALLE *Fundamentals of Lang.* iii. 29 All the inherent features are divided into two classes that might be termed sonority features and tonality features,..the latter [akin] to the prosodic pitch features. **1973** *Archivum Linguisticum* IV. 23 The 'paratonality system' determines the relationship between sentences and paratone groups in the same way as the tonality system relates clauses and tone-groups.

to-name ('tu:neɪm), *sb.* Now *dial.* Also 3–4 tuo-, tou-, 4 tow-, 4, 7 too-, 9 *Sc. dial.* tee-name. [OE. *tó-nama*, f. TO-[1] + NAME *sb.* So MLG. *toname*, Du. *toenaam*, MHG. *zuoname*, G. *zuname*.] A name or epithet added to an original name; a cognomen, surname, nickname; now in *Sc.* a name added to distinguish one individual from another or others having the same Christian name and surname, a 'by-name'.

c **950** *Lindisf. Gosp.* Mark v. 9 [Hælend] ȝefreȝn hine huætd ðe tonoma is? & cuæð to him here tonoma me is, forðon moniȝ we sindon. *c* **1200** *Trin. Coll. Hom.* 143 Ðes wimman hadde ec on toname magdalene..Nu ȝie habbeð iherd þes wimmanes name & ec hire toname. **1303** R. BRUNNE *Handl. Synne* 4741 Þe bysshope Seynt Roberd; Hys toname ys 'Grostest Of Lynkolne'. **1382** WYCLIF *Ecclus.* xlvii. 19 The name of the Lord, to whom is the toname [1388 surname] God of Irael. **1567** SIR R. MAITLAND *Complaynt* vii, Thay theifis that steillis and tursis hame, Ilk ane o' them has ane to-name; Will of the Lawis, Hab of the Schawis. **1636** in Ld. A. Campbell *Rec. Argyll* (1885) 5 Archibald, Earl of Argyle, his too name was Gillispick Dow. **1823** SCOTT *Quentin D.* iii. **1870** F. BUCKLAND in Bompas *Life* xi. 243 There were no less than seven men every one of whom was a 'David Main', hence the necessity of Tee names, to distinguish one person from the other.

Hence **'to-name** *v. trans.*, to give a to-name to.

1775 BUCHANAN *Inquiry Anc. Scott. Surnames* 49 Brian Kennedy, to-named Boraimh, or Taxer.

†**tonance** ('təʊnəns). *Obs. rare*$^{-1}$. [f. as next: see -ANCE.] A loud or echoing sound.

1778 H. BROOKE *Antony & Cl.* III. iii, The emperor's trumpet—I do know it, By the pride of its tonance.

tonant ('təʊnənt), *a.* [ad. L. *tonānt-em*, pr. pple. of *tonāre* to thunder, make a loud noise.] Thundering, loud-sounding.

1891 G. MEREDITH *Reading of Life* (1901) 122 Nay, nor so tonant thunders the stress of the gale in the oak-trees. **1898** —— *Napoleon* xiii, The penetrant, the tonant, tower of towers, Striking from black disaster starry showers.

‖**tonari gumi** (to'nari 'gumi). Also tonari-gumi, tonarigumi. [Jap.] A neighbourhood association in Japan, formed of groups of families who assume responsibility for their own community affairs.

1947 R. BENEDICT *Chrysanthemum & Sword* iv. 82 Japan had, like China, tiny units of five to ten families, called in recent times the *tonari gumi*, which were the smallest responsible units of the population. **1958** W. J. H. SPROTT *Human Groups* 93 In Japanese cities they have associations called *tonari-gumi*, made up of from ten to twenty households. **1980** J. MELVILLE *Chrysanthemum Chain* 119 People who lived nearby..members of Murrow's *tonari-gumi* or neighbourhood association.

†**to'nation.** *Obs. rare*$^{-1}$. [f. TONE *sb.* or *v.* + -ATION.] The action of toning or producing musical tones; the tones or notes so produced.

1728 R. NORTH *Mem. Music* (1846) 13 To observe the various tonations, and reduce them to a certain order, or scale.

tonca bean: see TONKA.

‖**tondino** (ton'dino). [It. *tondino*, dim. f. *tondo* round: see next. In Fr. *tondin*.]

1. *Arch.* (See quot. 1823.)

1704 J. HARRIS *Lex. Techn.* I, *Tondino*, a Term in Architecture. See *Astragal*. **1823** P. NICHOLSON *Pract. Build.* 595 *Tondino*, a round moulding resembling a ring.

2. *Ceramics.* Pl. **tondini.** A plate with a wide flat rim and deep centre made of majolica.

1885 [see FAENZA]. **1900** F. LITCHFIELD *Pott. & Porc.* ii. 16 A set of round plates or *tondini*. **1958** M. WYKES-JOYCE *7000 Years Pottery* vi. 76 What we may term useless wares, a particular kind of *piatto con fondo*, the *tondino*, which would be sent by a gallant to his current inamorata, filled with candied flower petals... A flirtatious signorina would have some dozen or score of the *tondini* on display. **1971** *Times* 30 Nov. 24/3 (Advt.), A Faenza tondino by the 'Green Man'.

‖**tondo** ('tondo). Pl. **tondi** ('tondi). [It. *tondo* 'a round, circle, compass; also a round trencher, plate, or little dish' (Florio); in mod.It. a studio term used in relation to paintings, Della Robbia ware, and other fine art work; shortened from *rotondo* round.] An easel painting of circular form; also a carving in relief within a circular space.

1877 GEO. ELIOT *Let.* 29 Mar. (1956) VI. 359 The little *tondi* on the covers of the 3/6 edition are charming. **1890** *Blackw. Mag.* Jan. 140 A medal representing the great tondo of Botticelli. **1892** SYMONDS *Michel Angelo* (1899) I. III. v. 111 Michel Angelo found time to carve the two tondi, Madonnas in relief enclosed in circular spaces which we still possess. **1901** *Athenæum* 9 Nov. 635 A catalogue..of the Della Robbia monuments and..tabernacles, tondos, reliefs, medallions, and the like. **1909** *Times, Lit. Suppl.* 7 Oct. 361/2 One of the most beautiful of Michelangelo's works, the tondo in the Bargello.

tone (təʊn), *sb.* Forms: 4 ton, 4– tone; (5 toun, toyn, 5–6 toyne; 6 toone). [Partly a. OF. *ton* (of voice, 13th c. in Littré) = Prov. *ton*, Cat. *to*, Sp. *ton, tono*, Pg. *tom, tono*, It. *tuono*:—L. *ton-um*, acc. of *ton-us*; and partly directly f. L. *tonus* 'stretching, quality of sound, tone, accent, tone in painting', in med.L. esp. as a term of music, a. Gr. *τόνος* 'stretching, tension, raising of voice, pitch of voice, accent, musical mode or key, exertion of physical or mental energy'; f. strong grade of vbl. ablaut series *τεν-, τον-, τα-*, in *τείν-ειν* to stretch. In musical senses, much influenced by med.L. uses of *tonus*, and in more recent uses, largely influenced by Greek.

The early phonology is far from clear, the obscurity being increased by the changing values of the spellings *o, oo, ou, oy*, and their ambiguity at certain periods. The normal course of Fr. *-on* was to become *-oun* (= -u:n) in ME., and diphthongal *-oun, -own* (as in *soun(d, noun, renown, bounty*) in mod.Eng. An example of this appears *c* 1407 in sense 1, where Lydgate rimes *toun, sown*. But earlier than this we find *tōn, tone* (perh. a more learned or technical formation) direct from L. *tonus*, so well known in mediæval music, which became the prevalent form, and appears *c* 1325 in sense 2 b, riming with *nōn* 'noon'. The normal fate of this was to become in 15–16th c. *toon* (= tu:n); cf. 1570 in sense 1, where Levins rimes *toone* with *boone, moone, noone, soone*, etc. But here again the influence of L. *tonus* appears to have prevailed, so as to make *tone* (to:n) the finally accepted form. The sound of *toyn, toyne*, in *c* 1460, 1521, is doubtful: *-oy, -oi* in Sc. and north. dial. generally meant long *ō*. The Sc. examples of *tone* in sense 2 c are also doubtful; they may be precursors of mod.Sc. (tøn, tʏn), and more properly belong to TUNE, a divergent form of *tone* which has finally been differentiated as a distinct word, q.v. *Tone, toon*, and *toun*, might thus be viewed as separate words; but as the two latter are obs., and all the forms go back directly or indirectly to L. *tonus*, they are here treated as one, under the current spelling, but with the quotations separated.]

I. 1. a. A musical or vocal sound considered with reference to its quality, as acute or grave, sweet or harsh, loud or soft, clear or dull.

1340 HAMPOLE *Pr. Consc.* 9296 Ilkan þat sal won þar, Sal syng with angels,..In swilk tones þat sal be swete to here. **1667** MILTON *P.L.* v. 626 Harmonie Divine So smooths her charming tones, that Gods own ear Listens delighted. **1797** MRS. RADCLIFFE *Italian* xvii, The deep tone of a bell, rolling on the silence of the night. **1855** BAIN *Senses & Int.* II. ii. §5 (1864) 213 Instruments and voices are distinguished by the sweetness of their individual tones.

β. *c* **1407** LYDG. *Reson & Sens.* 5211 The wherbles, nor the vnkouth touns, Nor the ravysshinge sowns, Nor the sugryd melodye Of ther soot[e] armonye.

γ. **1521** J. T. in Bradshaw *St. Werburge* Prol. 1 Honour, ioye, and glorie, the toynes organicall.
δ. **1570** LEVINS *Manip.* 168/37 A Toone, *tonus* [*rimes* boone, moone, noone, soone, etc.].

b. (Without *a* or *pl.*) Quality of sound.

1663 BUTLER *Hud.* I. I. 459 Though Writers, for more lofty Tone Do call him Ralpho, 'tis all one. **1732** LEDIARD *Sethos* II. VIII. 219 The tone of your voice has become more masculine. **1908** [MISS E. FOWLER] *Betw. Trent & Ancholme* 82 You may get much variation of tone, by change of speed [with a THUNDERER].

γ. *c* **1460** *Towneley Myst.* xv. 13 A! myghtfull god, what euer this ment, so swete of toyn?

2. a. *Mus.* and *Acoustics.* A sound of definite pitch and character produced by regular vibration of a sounding body; a musical note.

difference-tone (or ***differential tone***), ***summation-tone*** (or ***summational tone***), the secondary or resultant tones produced when two notes of different pitch are sounded together with sufficient force, having rates of vibration equal respectively to the difference and the sum of those of the primary tones. ***combinational, fundamental, partial, resultant*** (etc.) ***tone***: see the adjs.

c **1400** tr. *Secreta Secret., Gov. Lordsh.* 98 Fyue tones er of Musyke. **1579** E. K. *Gloss. Spenser's Sheph. Cal.* Oct. 27 The Arcadian Melodie.. being altogither on the fyft and vij tone, it is of great force to molifie and quench the kindly courage. *a* **1650** CRASHAW *Music's Duel* 23 She Carves out her dainty voice.. Into a thousand sweet distinguish'd tones. **1666** PEPYS *Diary* 8 Aug., Mr. Hooke.. having come to a certain number of vibrations proper to make any tone, he is able to tell how many strokes a fly makes with her wings .. by the note that it answers to in musique. **1867** TYNDALL *Sound* vii. 282 Helmholtz inferred.. that there are also resultant tones formed by the sum of the primaries, as well as by their difference. He thus discovered his summation tones before he had heard them. **1875** *Encycl. Brit.* I. 118/2 These resultant tones.. are termed *difference-tones.* **1876** BERNSTEIN *Five Senses* 280 Besides the difference tone, Helmholtz has pointed out a much weaker summational tone. **1881** BROADHOUSE *Mus. Acoustics* 130 By a simple tone is meant a musical sound in which no upper partials are present... By a compound tone is meant a tone where not only the fundamental note is present, but where upper partials are found in addition.

(*b*) Also, such a sound produced electrically; cf. *pure tone* s.v. PURE *a.* 1 e. In *Teleph.*, a pure tone or a more complex sound generated automatically to convey to a calling subscriber information about the line or the number required (see *busy, dial, dialling, engaged,* etc., *tone* under the first elements).

1878 G. B. PRESCOTT *Sp. Telephone* (1879) 6 A series of vibrations, a definite number of which are produced in a given time, and of which we thus become cognizant, is called a tone. **1919** J. POOLE *Pract. Telephone Handbk.* (ed. 6) xxi. 364 The tones and interruptions required are as follows:—(1) A 'tone' of 24 interruptions per revolution of the armature or 400 interruptions per second, [etc.]. **1958** G. HIGGS in E. Molloy *High Fidelity Sound Reproduction* i. 10 The specification of a definite acoustical or electrical level necessarily involves reference to a steady-value test-tone of the stipulated frequency. **1962** A. NISBETT *Technique Sound Studio* v. 103 To calibrate for this, the most accurate method is to replay a reference tone (or some other steady sound). **1973** T. J. GLATTKE in F. D. Minifie et al. *Normal Aspects of Speech* viii. 329 A series of three tones at 800 Hz.. followed by a series at 800, 1,000, and 800 Hz.. was differentiated by cats following cortical ablation. **1976** T. H. FLOWERS *Introd. Exchange Syst.* iii. 67 Each tone is generated by a tone generator common to the whole exchange.

†**b.** (Without *a* or *pl.*) Pitch of a musical note; correct pitch, 'tune'. *Obs.*

c **1325** *Song* in *Rel. Ant.* I. 292 Thu holdest nowt a note by God in riht ton [*rime* non, 'noon']. *c* **1440** *Alphabet of Tales* 88 A prowde yong monke began at sett it vp abown þaim iij notis;.. yit som þat was on his syde fell in tone vnto hym and helpyd hym. **1704** J. HARRIS *Lex. Techn.* I, *Tone,* a Term in Musick, signifying a certain Degree of elevation, or depression of the Voice, or some other Sound.

†**c.** *fig.* in phr. ***in tone***, 'in tune', in harmony or accordance; also, in good condition (quot. 1500-20); ***out of tone***, out of order, in a state of disarrangement. *Obs.* [perh. belongs to TUNE.]

a **1400-50** *Alexander* 1343 So ware þai troubild out of tone quen þai þaire tild miste. **1500-20** DUNBAR *Poems* xxix. 16 Quhen men that hes purssis in tone, Passes to drynk or to disione. **1513** DOUGLAS *Æneis* Prol. 159 For Caxtoun puttis in his buik out of tone The storme furth sent be Eolus and Neptone. **1571** *Satir. Poems Reform.* xxix. 15 All is owtte of tone. **1647** WARD *Simp. Cobler* (1843) 84 When things and words in tune and tone doe meet.

γ. *c* **1460** *Towneley Myst.* xiii. 477 Hard I neuer none crak so clere out of toyne.

3. *Mus.* **a.** In plainsong, any of the nine psalm-tunes (including the ***peregrine tone***), each of which has a particular 'intonation' and 'mediation' and a number of different 'endings'; commonly called ***Gregorian tones***: see GREGORIAN A. 1.

1776 HAWKINS *Hist. Mus.* I. 358 The essential parts of each of the tones, that is to say, the beginning, the mediation, and the close. **1850** HELMORE *Psalter Noted* Pref., The intonation (beginning), mediation (middle), and cadence (ending) of the Tones. **1872** [see GREGORIAN A. 1]. **1893** *Blackw. Mag.* Aug. 253 The plainsong to which Psalms were sung was the 2nd Tone.

†**b.** Applied to the ecclesiastical modes (in which the Gregorian tones were composed). *Obs.*

1776 HAWKINS *Hist. Mus.* I. 347 The tones, as they stood adjusted by Saint Ambrose, were only four. *Ibid.*, The ecclesiastical tones.. answer exactly to the several keys, as they are called by modern musicians. **1782, 1839** [see MODE *sb.* 1 a (*b*)].

4. a. *Mus.* One of the larger intervals between successive notes of the diatonic scale; a major second; sometimes called ***whole tone***, as opposed to *semitone*.

1609 DOULAND *Ornith. Microl.* 18 A Tone.. is the distance of one Voyce from another by a perfect second,.. a Tone is made betwixt all Voyces excepting *mi* and *fa*. **1651** J. F[REAKE] *Agrippa's Occ. Philos.* 191 There are six Tones of all harmony, viz. 5 Tones, and 2 half Tones which make one Tone, which is the sixt. **1752** tr. *Rameau's Treat. Musick* 89 The Sixth may be taken upon the Second of two Notes that ascend a whole Tone, or a Semitone. **1881** MACFARREN *Counterp.* ii. 3 A Tone is the interval of a major semitone and a minor semitone, either of which may be above or below the other.

†**b.** *transf.* Applied to the space between planets: see quots. *Obs.*

1601 HOLLAND *Pliny* (1634) I. 14 Pythagoras otherwhiles vsing the termes of Musicke, calleth the space betweene the earth and the Moone *Tonus,* saying that from her to Mercurie is halfe a tone and from him to Venus in manner the same space. **1660** STANLEY *Hist. Philos.* IX. (1701) 386/2 Pythagoras by Musical proportion calleth that a Tone, by how much the Moon is distant from the Earth.

5. a. A particular quality, pitch, modulation, or inflexion of the voice expressing or indicating affirmation, interrogation, hesitation, decision, or some feeling or emotion; vocal expression.

a **1610** HEALEY *Theophrastus* (1636) 25 To whom they speak in a great broken Tone, rayling on them. *a* **1654** SELDEN *Table-T., Preaching* (Arb.) 92 The tone in Preaching does much in working upon the Peoples Affections. **1697** DRYDEN *Virg. Past.* IX. 6 The grim Captain in a surly Tone Cries out, pack up ye Rascals, and be gone. *a* **1739** JARVIS *Quix.* I. I. iv. (1742) 13 He raised his voice and with an arrogant tone cried out. **1796** MME. D'ARBLAY *Camilla* II. 355 She asked in a tone of displeasure, who was there? **1817** JAS. MILL *Brit. India* II. v. iv. 456 He tried the tone of humility; he tried that of audacity. **1824** L. MURRAY *Eng. Gram.* (ed. 5) I. 368 There is not.. an emotion of the heart, which has not its peculiar tone, or note of the voice, by which it is to be expressed. **1834** MACAULAY *Ess., Pitt* (1887) 311 Every tone, from the impassioned cry to the thrilling aside was perfectly at his [Pitt's] command.

b. The distinctive quality of voice in the pronunciation of words, peculiar to an individual, locality, or nation; an 'accent'.

a **1680** BUTLER *Rem.* (1759) I. 204 Strangers never leave the Tones, They have been us'd as Children to pronounce. **1683** WOOD *Life* 19 May (O.H.S.) III. 50 Dr. Robert Morison.. hath no command of the English [tongue], as being much spoyled by his Scottish tone. **1711** ADDISON *Spect.* No. 29 ¶4 The Tone, or (as the French call it) the Accent of every Nation in their ordinary Speech is altogether different from that of every other People. **1837** LOCKHART *Scott* I. ii. 88 The tone and accent remained broadly Scotch.

c. Intonation; *esp.* a special, affected, or artificial intonation in speaking.

1687 A. LOVELL tr. *Thevenot's Trav.* I. 36 The greatest part of their Poems and songs are in the Persian Tongue, which they sing, not musically as we do, but with a certain tone, which though at first.. not pleasing, yet by custom becomes agreeable enough to the ear. **1720** WATTS *Art of Reading* xiv, Let the Tone and Sound of your Voice in reading be the same as it is in speaking. **1748** J. MASON *Elocut.* 16 There are some Kinds of Tone, which, tho' unnatural, yet, as managed by the Speakers, are not very disagreeable. **1795** MASON *Ch. Mus.* (L.) You hear nobody converse in a tone, unless they have the brogue of some other country, or have got into a habit of altering the natural key of their voice when they are talking of some serious subject in religion. **1891** *19th Cent.* Nov. 828 The 'tones' are a short sermon.. in which the principal tones taken by a preacher are given one after another.

d. *transf.* A particular style in discourse or writing, which expresses the person's sentiment or reveals his character; *spec.* in literary criticism, an author's attitude to his subject matter or audience; the distinctive mood created by this. (Cf. 9.)

1765 T. HUTCHINSON *Hist. Mass.* I. 138 At first, the Naragansets gave kind words to the messengers.. but they soon changed their tone. **1844** H. WILSON *Brit. India* II. 108 He determined,.. to adopt a tone of conciliation. **1866** J. MARTINEAU *Ess.* I. 147 His book.. is bright and joyous in tone. **1929** I. A. RICHARDS *Pract. Crit.* III. i. 183 A man writing a scientific treatise, for example, will put the *Sense* of what he has to say first... His *Tone* will be settled for him by academic convention. **1950** F. B. MILLETT *Reading Fiction* 11 This tone, the general feeling which suffuses and surrounds the work, arises ultimately out of the writer's attitude toward his subject. **1959** H. GARDNER *Business of Crit.* 40 The tone of the close of the play. **1973** G. W. TURNER *Stylistics* vi. 186, I shall use.. *tone* for the range of variation reflecting adjustments to an audience. **1977** *N.Y. Rev. Bks.* 15 Sept. 40/2 His practical criticism is not much concerned with the structure of an individual poem except as an embodiment of crisis; it has little to say of diction, the metres, rhythm, syntax, or tone.

6. *Phonetics.* **a.** A word-accent; a rising, falling, or compound inflexion, by which words otherwise of the same sound are distinguished, as in ancient Greek, modern Chinese, and other languages.

1679 R. HOOKE *Diary* 14 May (1935) 412 At Garways, Chinese Language Tones. **1763** FOSTER *Accent & Quantity* Introd. 20 In Dionysius.. accounts of high and low tones.. assigned to certain syllables. **1791-1823** DISRAELI *Cur. Lit., Chinese Lang.,* [The Chinese] can so diversify their monosyllabic words by the different tones which they give them, that the same character differently accented signifies sometimes ten or more different things. **1906** PINCHES *Relig. Babyl. & Assyria* i. 2 [They] ask themselves whether the people who spoke it were able to understand each other without recourse to devices such as the 'tones' to which the Chinese resort. **1909** JESPERSEN *Progress Lang.* 86 In the Danish dialect spoken in Sundeved.. two.. tones are distinguished, one high and the other low... These tones often serve to keep words.. apart that would be perfect homonyms but for the accent.

b. The stress accent (Fr. *accent tonique*) on a syllable of a word; the stressed or accented syllable.

1874 DAVIDSON *Hebr. Gram.* (1892) 46 *A* in the pretone, or *a* in the tone, or *a* in both places. **1891** *Cent. Dict., Tone.* In *Gram.* A stress of voice on one of the syllables of a word.

II. 7. *Physiol.* The degree of firmness or tension proper to the organs or tissues of the body in a strong and healthy condition. Also in reference to a plant (quot. 1671).

This seems to be in part a distinct derivative from Gr. τόνος, with reference to the tension of the muscles or nerves. Cf. the Physiol. use of TONICAL 1 (1586) and TONIC A. 1 (1649). (Matth. Sylvaticus, *a* 1480, has 'tonus, id est vigor'.)

1669 W. SIMPSON *Hydrol. Chym.* 139 This astringeth and keepeth up the right tone of the membranous parts. **1671** GREW *Anat. Plants* I. ii. §23 With which Sap, the Cortical Body being dilated as far as its Tone.. will bear. **1704** F. FULLER *Med. Gymn.* (1711) 27 Exercise.. affects the Solids [by] restoring the true Tone of the Parts. **1780** *Mirror* No. 86 ¶2 Of sovereign efficacy in restoring debilitated stomachs to their proper tone. **1802** MAR. EDGEWORTH *Moral T.* (1826) I. Pref. 8 Thus, by alternate exercise and indulgence, their limbs acquire the firmest tone of health and vigour. **1888** J. PAYN *Myst. Mirbridge* (ed. Tauchn.) II. x. 104 The douche.. would restore her tone.

fig. **1835** I. TAYLOR *Spir. Despot.* ix. 374 There is little tone in our church and chapel ethics. **1860** MAURY *Phys. Geog. Sea* (Low) xi. §517 How, by this operation, tone is given to the atmospherical circulation of the world.

8. A state or temper of mind; mood, disposition.

a **1744** BOLINGBROKE *Let. to Pope* Wks. 1754 III. 316 The strange situation I am in, and the melancholy state of public affairs,.. drag the mind down by perpetual interruptions, from a philosophical tone, or temper. **1779** *Mirror* No. 60 ¶3 Acquiring.. a tone of mind which will render him incapable of going through the common duties of life. **1820** W. IRVING *Sketch Bk.* I. 127 These hardy exercises produce also a healthful tone of mind and spirits.

9. A special or characteristic style or tendency of thought, feeling, behaviour, etc.; spirit, character, tenor; *esp.* the general or prevailing state of morals or manners in a society or community.

Partly from 7; but influenced also by 5.

a **1635** NAUNTON *Fragm. Reg.* (Arb.) 57 As the tone of his house, and the ebbe of his fortune then stood. **1747** CHESTERF. *Lett.* 16 Oct., Take the tone of the company that you are in, and do not pretend to give it. **1754** RICHARDSON *Grandison* III. xii. 188, I complained to one, and to another; but all were in a [= one] tone: And so I thought I would be contented. **1850** TENNYSON *In Mem.* lx. 1 A soul of nobler tone. **1884** *Times* 5 Feb. 11/6 The tone of the market is.. dull. **1908** *Westm. Gaz.* 26 Sept. 2/1 In our elementary schools.. the inculcation of a good moral tone is of the greatest importance.

III. 10. a. The prevailing effect of the combination of light and shade, and of the general scheme of colouring, in a painting, building, etc.

c **1816** FUSELI in *Lect. Paint.* viii. (1848) 512 The tone, that comprehensive union of tint and hue spread over the whole. **1843** RUSKIN *Mod. Paint.* I. II. II. i. §2, I understand two things by the word *Tone*: first, the exact relief and relation of objects against and to each other in substance and darkness, as they are nearer or more distant, and the perfect relation of the shades of all of them to the chief light of the picture..: secondly, the exact relation of the colours of the shadows to the colours of the lights, so that they may be at once felt to be merely different degrees of the same light [etc.]. **1844** DISRAELI *Coningsby* III. iv, The tone of rich and solemn light that pervaded all.

b. A quality of colour; a tint; *spec.* the degree of luminosity of a colour; shade.

1821 CRAIG *Lect. Drawing* iii. 143 Tone, then, is the degree of dark that any object has compared with white, independently of its kind of colour. **1870** F. R. WILSON *Ch. Lindisf.* 69 The tone of the interior is a tender silvery grey. **1874** SYMONDS *Sk. Italy & Greece* 212 (*Athens*) The tones of the marble of Pentelicus have daily grown more golden. **1879** *Cassell's Techn. Educ.* IV. 212 Tones, often called shades, signify colours mixed with varying proportions of white or black. **1893** J. A. HODGES *Elem. Photogr.* (1907) 91 A tone a little darker than the desired colour.

11. *attrib.* and *Comb.*, as (sense 2) ***tone-quality***; (sense 6) ***tone-curve, -group, -mark, -pattern, -sequence, -unit; tone-bearing*** adj.; (sense 9) ***tone-setter; tone-setting*** adj.; (sense 10) ***tone-production, -quality, -reinforcer, relation, -relationship, scheme, study, value, -work; tone-producing*** adj.; **tone-arm**, †(*a*) the tubular arm connecting the sound-box of a gramophone to the horn (*obs.*); (*b*) = *pick-up arm* s.v. PICK-UP *a.* a; **tone burst**, an audio signal used in testing the transient response of audio components; **tone cluster** *Mus.*, a group of adjacent notes on a piano played simultaneously by placing the forearm or flat of the hand on the keys; cf. *note-cluster* s.v. NOTE *sb.*[2] 21; **tone-colour** (after Ger. *tonfarbe*), timbre; hence ***tone-coloured*** adj., ***-colouring***; **tone control**, the adjustment of the proportion of high and low frequencies in reproduced sound; a device or manual control for achieving this; **tone-deaf** *a.*, deaf to the tones of music; also *transf.* and *fig.*, insensitive, lacking in perception; hence **tone-deafness**; **toneful**, **tone-full** *a.*, full of musical or vocal sound; cf. TUNEFUL *a.*; **tone generator**, an apparatus for electronically producing tones of a desired frequency; **tone language** *Linguistics*, a language which uses variations in pitch, in addition to different consonants and vowels, to distinguish words, e.g. Chinese; **tone-long** *a.*, in *Hebrew Grammar*: see quot.; **tone-master**, a master or expert in the use of tones, an experienced musical composer; **tone-measurer**, = MONOCHORD 1; **tone-on-tone** *a.*, applied to designs, textiles, etc., composed of toning rather than contrasting shades of colour; **tone-painting**, the art of composing descriptive music; hence **tone-painter**; **tone-picture**, a descriptive piece of music; **tone poem** *Mus.* = *symphonic poem* s.v. SYMPHONIC *a.* (*sb.*) 3; **tone poet**, (*a*) [Ger. *tondichter*] a musical composer; (*b*) *spec.* one who composes tone poems; hence **tone poetry**; **tone-row** *Mus.*, the twelve notes of the chromatic scale arranged in a fixed order to form the basis of a composition; **tone sandhi** *Linguistics* [SANDHI], in tone languages: the differences between the tones of words through the influence of contiguous tonal patterns; **tone separation** *Photogr.* = POSTERIZATION; **tone-syllable**, the stressed syllable; **tone-tester**, an instrument for determining the differential sensibility for (musical) tones.

1907 *T. Eaton & Co. Catal.* Spring & Summer 249/1 Columbia Graphophone..patent aluminium *tone-arm. **1923** *Gramophone* Apr. p. vii/2 (Advt.), 18 models of Tonearms with and without Goosenecks. **1946** [see *record groove* s.v. RECORD *sb.* 13 b]. **1981** *Popular Hi-Fi* Mar. 85/3 This is a direct drive, quartz locked, fully automatic turntable with integrated tonearm. **1971** B. Mafeni in J. Spencer *Eng. Lang. W. Afr.* 107 There is a syllabic nasal /*N*/ [in Nigerian Pidgin] which is *tone-bearing and is always homorganic with the succeeding consonant. **1981** *Word 1980* XXXI. 186 Other syllables..may be higher, lower, or on the same level relative to the onset of the tone-bearing syllable. **1967** *Electronics* 6 Mar. 82/1 (Advt.), See the little boxes. See what they can do... *Tone burst..trigger.. sweep. **1978** *Gramophone* Jan. 1336/1 The toneburst oscillogram..shows that the output across an 8-ohm dummy load is virtually identical with the input signal. **1921** *Freeman* 13 Apr. 112/2 The significance of the *tone cluster, like that of the single tone, is to be found in its possibility of combinations with other tone clusters. **1937** N. Slonimsky *Music since 1900* 122 [12 March 1912] At the San Francisco Music Club Henry Cowell performs for the first time in public, on the day after his fifteenth birthday, piano tone-clusters on white or black keys, struck with the forearm. **1973** *Daily Tel.* 24 Nov. 11/2 He watched the Sinfonietta's resident pianist..elbowing his way through the tone clusters of an early Roberto Gerhard. **1983** *Listener* 28 July 30/3 The music abounds in such special effects as tone-clusters like smudged chords, microtones, fragmentation of the text, whistling, whispers, shouts. **1881** A. J. Hipkins in Grove *Dict. Mus.* III. 193 The tone of the Ruckers clavecins has never been surpassed for purity and beauty of *tone-colour (timbre). **1895–6** *Cal. Univ. Nebraska* 216 No other instruments require so much patient and unremitting toil in their mastery as [the violin, viola, violoncello]; and none are so well adapted for the expression of all shades of musical feeling or so nearly resemble the human voice with all its possibilities of *tone-coloring. **1930** *Electronics* July 195/1 *Tone control was the most evident technical idea at the Trade Show of the Radio Manufacturers Association in June. **1934** *Discovery* Nov. 324/2 The models..have effective tone and volume controls fitted. **1974** *Harrods Christmas Catal.* 70/3 Electric Guitar..with volume and tone controls. **1922** H. E. Palmer *Eng. Intonation* i. 3 That part which is concerned chiefly with the *tone-curves irrespective of their meanings has been called *Tonetics*. **1953** C. E. Bazell *Linguistic Form* 99 'Questioning intonation' (a special tone-curve) in English. **1894** Du Maurier *Trilby* I. 169 She was quite *tone-deaf, and didn't know it. **1932** R. Knox *Broadcast Minds* iv. 85 When we ask him precisely what it is which 'religion' can give us that is inaccessible to a nature..tone-deaf to religion, he has nothing to point to except those moments themselves. **1972** F. Warner *Lying Figures* III. 35 We are spiritually tone-deaf. Mum's the word! **1884** T. Barr *Man. Dis. Ear* IV. ii. 459 If this partial *tone-deafness is not connected with disease of the conducting apparatus, the anomaly is probably due to cochlear disturbance. **1941** F. Matthiessen *Amer. Renaissance* I. iv. 34 The honesty of Whittier's effort was somewhat vitiated by the tone-deafness that robbed his verse of any full variety of cadences. **1973** *Listener* 14 June 786/3 Mr Nixon..has persistently shown..a disturbing tone-deafness to the legal restraints which..are built into the American system. **1977** *Proc. R. Soc. Med.* LXX. 134/1 Tone deafness is a defect of pitch discrimination in which the relationship of one musical tone to others cannot be accurately assessed or imitated. **1838** Keightley *Grk. Mythol.* 338 (Odyssey XIX. 518) She..poureth forth her voice *Tone-full, lamenting her son Itylos. **1925** T. Dreiser *Amer. Trag.* I. I. xi. 77 The none too toneful piano. **1927** *Observer* 10 Apr. 24 The short, quick flutter of the wing and the most toneful croak of satisfaction. **1942** *Brit. Jrnl. Psychol.* XXXII. 292 We now have in the laboratory a *tone generator capable of sounding tones of any desired harmonic structure. **1980** *Sci. Amer.* Oct. 74/1 Each phoneme is generated by a particular setting of various tone generators, noise generators and acoustic filters. **1922** H. E. Palmer *Eng. Intonation* i. 6 The more serious difficulty is the teaching of the semantic values of the *tone-groups. **1977** *Bull. School Oriental & African Stud.* XL. 654/2 The structure of the basic intonational unit, the *tone-group*, consists of an obligatory *tonic*, i.e. the syllable where the pitch movement identifying the *tonic type* begins, and an optional *pretonic* element. **1930** R. Paget *Human Speech* 188 In the *Tone-languages, the melody of phonation is tied to the articulation. **1971** G. Ansre in J. Spencer *Eng. Lang. W. Afr.* 157 Most of the languages of the region [*sc.* West Africa] use pitch in their phonological patterning in a way which has earned them the term 'tone languages'. **1978** *Sci. Amer.* Nov. 96/1 Many African and Asian languages are tone languages. **1874** Davidson *Hebr. Gram.* (1892) 14 [Vowels] called **Tone-long, ā, ē, ō*, that is vowels not long by nature but from occupying a certain position in relation to the place of tone, and therefore changeable, when their relation to the tone alters. *Ibid.* 15 The final accented short syllable and the pretonic open have tone-long vowels. **1924** H. E. Palmer *Gram. Spoken Eng.* 6 When *tone-marks are provided, the use of the sign ['] may therefore be entirely dispensed with. **1964** M. Schubiger in D. Abercrombie et al. *Daniel Jones* 265 The tone-marks are mine. **1939** *Country Life* 11 Feb. p. xxxviii/2 This Matita two-piece redingote and dress is in a *tone-on-tone effect in light and dark grey. **1965** 'L. Egan' *Detective's Due* i. 10 Beige tone-on-tone carpet. **1979** *Arizona Daily Star* 5 Aug. A-12/3 (Advt.), From the tip of its tone-on-tone toe to its sleek, stacked heel, it's everything you'd expect from Evan Picone. **1903** A. W. Patterson *Schumann* 49 How first the pianoforte, next the orchestra, and lastly the string quartet suggested sound pictures to the *tone-painter. **1897** *Daily Tel.* 31 Mar. 10/4 Even great musicians do not appear at their best in *tone-painting. **1905** *Q. Rev.* July 103 Tone-painting, he [Wagner] admits, may be used in jest. **1931** T. H. Pear *Voice & Personality* 74 The *tone-pattern of the Welsh sentence. **1961** *Amer. Speech* XXXVI. 221 Tone patterns illustrated by Kingdon's tonetic stress marks. **1901** *Pall Mall G.* 3 May (Cass. Supp.), What may be called the ground-work of his *tone-picture. **1889** G. B. Shaw *London Music 1888–89* (1937) 68 A long, scrappy movement which is neither bravura nor *tone poem. **1942** E. Paul *Narrow St.* xviii. 142 Jacques Benoit-Mechin, who wrote tone poems about South America. **1977** *Gramophone* Apr. 1561/3 Nor does the performance..really project the work as the blazing tone poem that it self-evidently is. **1983** *Listener* 3 Nov. 36/4 At seven and a half minutes it is perhaps a little short-winded for a full-blown tone poem. **1874** F. J. Crowest (*title*) The great *Tone-poets. **1892** *Review of Reviews* Sept. 289/1 A most original tone-poet. **1901** *Pall Mall G.* 1 Apr. 5 The great English word-poet and the great German tone-poet seemed to meet together on that imminent verge. **1903** A. W. Patterson *Schumann* p. viii, The writer..has endeavoured..to let the great tone poet speak to the readers through his own thoughts. **1890** *Tone poetry [see *absolute music* s.v. ABSOLUTE *a.* 16]. **1899** *Allbutt's Syst. Med.* VI. 528 A continuous, though variable, stream of *tone-producing energy. **1889** Brinsmead *Hist. Pianoforte* 172 The *tone-pulsator, patented 1878,..connects the ring-bridge with the continuous rim. **1934** Webster, *Tone quality. **1936** *Discovery* July 224/1 The tone-quality [can] be very considerably altered. **1961** *Times* 10 Mar. 22/2 No conductor in my experience has shaped a melody with more tenderness and lustre of tone-quality. **1884** A. J. Hipkins in Grove *Dict. Mus.* IV. 143/1 These bars..promote the elasticity of this most important *tone reinforcer. **1903** R. Fry *Let.* 6 Mar. (1972) I. 204 The *tone relations are nearer to Moretto's in breadth. **1955** *Times* 9 May 3/5 He was before everything a colourist, and all the machinery of his art —composition, drawing, tone relation, and touch— was organised in the interests of his ruling passion. **1936** *Musical Q.* XXII. 14 (*title*) Schoenberg's *tone-rows and the tonal system of the future. **1958** *Times* 6 June 4/3 Composition in tone-rows of 12 notes. **1967** A. L. Lloyd *Folk Song in England* i. 38 The scale of a folk tune is the series of notes used, the tone-row and no more. **1925** E. Sapir in *Language* I. 45 In Sarcee, an Athabaskan language..there is a true middle tone and a pseudo-middle tone which results from the lowering of a high tone to the middle position because of certain mechanical rules of *tone sandhi. **1968** P. Kratochvíl *Chinese Lang. Today* ii. 38 One of the factors which cause modifications of these general tendencies of tones in continuous speech is the influence of the tone environment of the given syllable. This is what is known as tone sandhi. **1943** *Tone separation [see POSTERIZE *v.*]. **1977** Tone separation [see POSTERIZATION]. **1924** H. E. Palmer *Gram. Spoken Eng.* 21 Any pair or more of tone-groups in one sentence constitutes a *tone-sequence. **1973** *Archivum Linguisticum* IV. 17 Halliday..though he describes certain tone sequences..implies that these are no more than chance associations of tones. **1973** *Publishers Weekly* 9 July 44/2 A *tone-setter on the field, he contributed to five Packer championships and two Super Bowl wins. **1979** C. E. Schorske *Fin-de-Siècle Vienna* p. xxiii, The intellectual tone-setters among college students. **1962** Y. Malkiel in Householder & Saporta *Probl. Lexicogr.* 11 Many *tone-setting Academy dictionaries. **1978** *Language* LIV. 430 Condillac and other tone-setting figures were concerned solely with generalities. **1893** Sir G. Reid in *Westm. Gaz.* 4 Feb. 2/1 My own way of working is to make a *tone study with the utmost rapidity, to seize the impression of the moment, if possible, and then, for the knowledge of form and detail to make a careful and accurate drawing. **1847** Webster (citing Stuart), *Tone-syllable. **1905** *Athenæum* 29 July 140/3 One of its main characteristics is that the nature of the metre is determined by the tone-syllable alone. **1893** *Yale Psychol. Studies* 81 The instrument used in making the experiments was composed of an adjustable pitchpipe with an index-arm moving over a large scale. The instrument..may for brevity be called the *tone-tester. **1964** Crystal & Quirk *Prosodic & Paralinguistic Features in Eng.* iv. 50 We come now to the system which has the *tone-unit..as its actual matrix. **1981** *Word 1980* XXXI. 154 The vertical bar marks the 'onset' of the tone unit. **1927** R. H. Wilenski *Mod. Movement in Art* 35 Taught successfully to draw 'by the shadows' and paint 'by the *tone values'. **1967** E. Short *Embroidery & Fabric Collage* i. 9 It is easy to assess the relative tone values of strong contrasts, such as black and white. **1894** Creighton & Titchener *Wundt's Hum. & Anim. Psychol.* v. 76 *note*, The vibration-rate of these new *tone-waves is the sum of the vibration-rates of the original tones. **1894** Herkomer in *Daily News* 28 Apr. 6/7 To use process work for the reproduction of line alone, leaving *tone-work to express the more complete work of the artist, which must be rendered again by an artist-engraver.

tone, *pron.* and *a.* Now only *dial.* Forms: α. (*north. dial.* and *Sc.*) (3 **þat an**), 4 **þe tan**, 4–5 **þe tane**, 4–6 **the tayne**, 6 **the taine**, 4–9 **the tane**, (9 **the taen**). β. 3–5 **þe ton**, (4 **þe tonn**), 4–5 **þe toon**, **þe tone**, 4–6 **the ton**, 4–7 **the tone**, 5 **the toon**, (6 **the tonn**, 7 **the t'one**). γ. (without *the*) 6–7 **ton**, 6–8 **tone**, 8 **t'on**, 9 **t'one**, (**t'an**). [Early ME. *þe tān*, *þe tôn*, for earlier *þet* or *þat ān*, 'the one' (see THAT *dem. adj.* 5); the *t* of *þet* being attached to *ān*, *ôn*, when *þe* became the general form of the definite article. Normally used in antithesis to *þe toþer*, *the tother*, which had a similar origin: see TOTHER. This usage cannot have arisen until the OE. antithesis of *óðer...óðer*, as in L. *alter ...alter*, gave place to *án...oðer*, as in Fr. *l'un ...l'autre*; nor until *þæt* (*þet*, *þat*) was usable for masc. and fem. as well as neuter, i.e. between 1200 and 1250: see ONE *numeral* 18, OTHER *a.* B. 1, 2. Used absolutely or pronominally, *the tone* is found in literature down to *c* 1600, and in many dialects to the present day; in Sc. *the tane* is in ordinary use. But as an adj., preceding a sb., esp. before a consonant, it was reduced at an early date to *þe tā*, *þe tô*, still in Sc. *the tae* (see TO *a.*); although the full *the tone...the tother* was also frequent, until gradually superseded in literary Eng. by *the one...the other*, dialectally and colloquially also *tone...tother*, later sometimes written *t'one...t'other*. This, in the northern Eng. dialects in which the definite article regularly appears as *tĕ*, *tă*, *t'*, may really stand for *t'one*, *t'other*; but elsewhere, where the article is not *te*, *t'*, it is perhaps rather *'t one... 't other*, due to the dropping of *the* from *the tone ...the tother*. In both *the tone* and *the tother*, *the* is omitted after a possessive pronoun or case, as *dial. his tone* or *to hand*, Sc. *his tae hand* = 'one of his hands'. For full illustration of existing dialect use, see *Eng. Dial. Dict.* s.v. *Tone*.]

The one (of two): often opposed to *tother*.

1. as *pron.*

α. [*a* **1225** *Leg. Kath.* 1373 (MS. C) þa ȝeide þus ꝥ an, & elnede þe oðre.] **13..** *Cursor M.* 1533 (Cott.) Tua pilers þai mad, o tile þe tan, þe toþer it was o merbul stan [*Gött.* and *Fairf.* þat an, þe toþer; *Trin.* þat oon, þat oþer]. *c* **1440** *Alphabet of Tales* 167 Me thoght att ij angels led þe tane of you vnto hevyn & þe toder vnto hell. **1513** Douglas *Æneis* v. vi. 25 The tane born of Epiria, And the todir was of Archadia. *a* **1774** Fergusson *Drink Ecl.* Poems (1845) 49 Brandy the tane, the tither whiskey. **1816** Scott *Old Mort.* xxxviii, They will neither want the tane nor the tother while Lord Evandale lives.

β. **1303** R. Brunne *Handl. Synne* 4005þe toon men calle Eutycyus, þe touþer hyght Florentyus. *c* **1380** Wyclif *Wks.* (1880) 190 Neiþer þe ton ne þe toiþer. [*c* **1386** Chaucer *Pard. T.* 479 That oon spak thus vn to that oother Thou knowest wel thou art my sworn brother.] *a* **1425** *Cursor M.* 13966 (Trin.) His sistres two, þe toon was martha to seyn And þat oþere Maudeleyn. **1426** *Rolls of Parlt.* V. 409/1 My said ii Lordes or the toon of hem. **1522** More *De quat. Noviss.* Wks. 79/2 Within a litle while die the tone may, the tother muste. **1591** Harington *Orl. Fur.* Pref. ¶vj, The tone begins, *Arma virumque cano*. The tother [begins] [etc.]. **1891** Miss Jackson *Shropsh. Word-bk.* 448 Both the tone an' the tother on 'em.

γ. **1573** Tusser *Husb.* (1878) 123 Vse ton for thy spinning, leaue Mihel the tother. *c* **1590** Marlowe *Faust.* ix. 19 Well, tone of you hath this goblet about you. **1632** Brome *Court Beggar* III. i. Wks. 1873 I. 230 I'le jowle your heads together, and so beat ton with tother. *a* **1800** Pegge *Suppl. Grose*, *T'on T'other*, one another. Derb. **1825** Brockett *N.C. Words* s.v. *Tane*, Gi me t'an or tother. **1900** [see *Eng. Dial. Dict.* s.v. TONE].

2. as *adj.* preceding a sb.

α, β. *c* **1250** *Gen. & Ex.* 2196 Al but ðe ton broðer symeon. **13..** *Cursor M.* 7074 (Gött.) Bot as þe tonn half a-gayn þat oþer. *c* **1380** Wyclif *Serm.* Sel. Wks. II. 284 Men speken now of Crist bi þe toon kynde and now by þe toþer. *c* **1400** *Destr. Troy* 13206 The ton Egh in the toile lost tynt he belyue. **1529** More *Dyaloge* III. i. Wks. 206 The hole church had neuer taken all the tone sorte and reiected all the tother. **1535** Stewart *Cron. Scot.* (Rolls) I. 254 At the tonn end set Cesar in his trune, And at the tother stude king Caratac. **1552** *Lyndesay's Poems* To Rdrs. (E.E.T.S. p. 318), The quhilkis ar verray fals, And wantis the tane half. **1584** Cogan *Haven Health* ccxli. (1636) 274 That wee lie on the tone side. **1622** Mabbe tr. *Aleman's Guzman d'Alf.* II. I. v. 48 The t'one halfe of an old broken great Pitcher.

γ. *a* **1765** *K. Estmere* xxvii. in Child *Ballads* III. (1885) 53/1 Tone day to marrye Kyng Adlands daughter, Tother daye to carrye her home. *a* **1800** Pegge *Suppl. Grose* s.v. *T'on-End*, It must be set a t'on end.

tone (təʊn), *v.* [f. TONE *sb.*]

I. 1. *trans. Mus.* †**a.** To sound with the proper tone or musical quality; to intone. *Obs.*

c **1325** in *Rel. Ant.* I. 292 Thu tones nowt the note ilke be his name, Thu bitist a-sonder bequarre, for bemol I the blame. **1570** Levins *Manip.* 168/38 To Toone, *modulari*.

b. To give a good or proper tone to.

1891 *Advt.*, Pianos toned and repaired.

2. *intr.* To issue forth in musical tones. *rare.*

1447 Bokenham *Seyntys* (Roxb.) 74 Wyth ympnys and psalmys wel tonyng Thousandis of aungells aftyr hym dyd goon. **1850** L. Hunt *Autobiog.* ix. 160 The sounding words came toning out of his dignified utterance like 'sonorous metal'.

3. *trans.* To utter with a musical sound, or in a special or affected tone; to intone.

1660 SOUTH *Serm., Matt. xiii. 52* (1727) IV. i. 52 Those strange new Postures used by some in the Delivery of the Word. Such as shutting the Eyes,..speaking through the Nose, which I think cannot so properly be called Preaching, as Toning of a Sermon. **1704** SWIFT *Mech. Operat. Spirit* §2 Misc. (1711) 295 Tuning and toning each Word, and Syllable, and Letter to their due Cadence. **1719** D'URFEY *Pills* (1872) III. 334 With pleasing Twang he tones his Prose,..And draws John Calvin through the Nose. **1796** SOUTHEY *Lett. fr. Spain* (1799) 399 He sung or toned his verses. **1852** MRS. STOWE *Uncle Tom's C.* i, The boy.. commenced toning a psalm-tune through his nose with imperturbable gravity. **1883** W. C. SMITH *N. Country Folk* 185 The Common prayer Was sweetly toned to the fishers there.

†**4.** To lay the accent or stress upon, to accent (a word or syllable). *Obs.*

1683 MOXON *Mech. Exerc., Printing* xxii. ¶5 If it be Set thus, that that That that that Man would have stand at the beginning of the Line should stand at the end; it will, by toning and laying Emphasis on the middlemost That become good Sense.

II. 5. To alter or modify the tone or general colouring of; to give the desired tone to (also const. *down*: cf sense 6 b); *spec.* (*a*) To cover (a painting) with oil or varnish so as to soften the colouring; (*b*) To alter the tone or tint of (a photograph) in the process of finishing it. Also *absol.*

1831 J. CONSTABLE *Let.* 13 Oct. (1966) IV. 357, I think the *large sail*..much too light. I shall like it toned down very considerably. **1859** GULLICK & TIMBS *Paint.* 215 It was not unfrequent for the possessors of old pictures to have them toned, as it was called. **1868** M. C. LEA *Man. Photogr.* xiii. 219 This bath tones much like the preceding; gives brown, purple-black, or black tones, and by overtoning, blue. *Ibid.* 220 Landscapes should be toned only with the acetate or benzoate bath. **1893** J. A. HODGES *Elem. Photogr.* (1907) 49 A gold bath will only tone when in a neutral or slightly alkaline condition. **1902** *Westm. Gaz.* 13 Mar. 2/2 One can always send the lace..and get it toned exactly.

b. *intr.* To receive or assume a tone, tint, or shade of colour; *esp.* in *Photogr.*

1868 M. C. LEA *Man. Photogr.* xiii. 218 If a washed print be simply thrown into a dilute solution of chloride of gold, it will tone. **1873** E. SPON *Workshop Receipts* Ser. I. 257/2 If delayed many hours the prints will not tone readily.

c. To harmonize *with* in colouring. Also with *in* and without const.

18.. *St. Louis Spectator* (U.S.) XI. 327 (Cent.) Beaded passementerie, which tones in with the delicate shades of blue, and pink chiffon, and dark velvet. **1904** *Westm. Gaz.* 20 Jan. 3/2 In each case her hat tones with the dress. **1907** *Ibid.* 25 Sept. 2/1 The red- or brown-tiled wooden chalets at once tone in with Nature. **1976** W. J. BURLEY *Wycliffe & Schoolgirls* i. 31 The colour scheme was old gold from the carpet to the wallpaper, cushions and curtains. Everything was 'to tone' as Mrs Clarke would..have said.

III. 6. *trans.* To impart a tone to (in various senses of the sb.); to modify, regulate, or adjust the tone or quality of; to give physical or mental tone to, to brace.

1811 SHELLEY *St. Irvyne* viii, A degree of solemnity, mixed with concealed fierceness, toned his voice as he spoke. **1859** J. CUMMING *Ruth* ii. 18 The husband tones into a loftier pitch the spiritual and moral character of the wife. **1871** L. STEPHEN *Playgr. Eur.* xiii. (1894) 334 Your mind is properly toned by these influences. **1884** W. C. SMITH *Kildrostan* I. ii. 11 Nor many years had toned his heedlessness.

b. ***tone down***, to lower the tone, quality, or character of; to soften, make less emphatic. ***tone up***, to raise or improve the tone of, to give a higher or stronger tone to.

1847 DICKENS *Dombey* (1848) xx. 197 The Native.. handed him..his hat; which..the Mayor wore with a rakish air on one side of his head, by way of toning down his remarkable visage. **1860** TYNDALL *Glac.* II. xxvi. 371 These [ice-ridges]..become more and more toned down by the action of sun and air. **1864** *Reader* No. 98. 603/1 By toning up public sentiment. **1884** *Times* (weekly ed.) 29 Aug. 14/1 These rosy impressions were decidedly toned down on closer inspection. **1896** *Chatauqua Mag.* Dec. Advt., Some remedy that will tone-up the nervous system. **1906** F. L. DODD *Municip. Milk* 9 A custom has grown up called 'toning down the milk', which consists in the addition of skimmed milk to such an extent as just to reduce the percentage of fat to the legal minimum.

c. *intr.* for *pass.* ***tone down***, to become lowered, weakened, or softened in tone; ***tone up***, to rise or improve in tone.

1850 KINGSLEY *Alt. Locke* xiii, The ivory and vermilion of the complexion had toned down together into still richer hues. **1865** DICKENS *Mut. Fr.* I. ix, Gradually toning down to a motherly strain. **1881** *Chicago Times* 14 May, Trade toned up considerably under the influence of warm weather. **1885** *L'pool Daily Post* 11 Apr. 5/2 Public excitement with respect to Russia has considerably toned down.

d. The vb.-stem in Comb. **'tone-up**, an act or means of raising to a higher tone; a strengthening or improvement.

1943 W. S. CHURCHILL *Second World War* (1951) IV. 852 It is time to have another tone-up of security arrangements. **1950** *Times* 2 Feb. 2/7 He was a man of 37, and if I had known he was going on this course I should have advised a period of drill training as a tone-up.

tone, Sc. var. of TUNE; obs. f. DHONEY, TEEN *sb.*[1], TOWN, TUN; obs. pa. pple. of TAKE *v.* (see TO *v.* *Obs.*); obs. pl. of TOE.

tonecle, obs. f. TUNICLE.

toned (təʊnd), *ppl. a.* and *adj.*

I. *ppl. a.* [f. TONE *v.* + -ED[1].]

1. a. Sounded with the proper, or a specified, tone.

c **1460** *Towneley Myst.* xii. 419 Thay [notes] were gentyll and small, And well tonyd with all. **1533** BELLENDEN *Livy* v. xviii. (S.T.S.) II. 208 The cryis & evill tonyt sangis of þe gaulis.

b. Of body or mind: Brought into tone (TONE *sb.* 7); braced, strung. Chiefly with adv., as ***well-toned, toned-up***.

1742 YOUNG *Nt. Th.* VIII. 1285 Juices, thro' the well-ton'd Tubes, well-strain'd. **1855** MACAULAY *Hist. Eng.* xiv. III. 432 A human being whose mind was quite as firmly toned at eighty as at forty. **1879** H. SPENCER *Data of Ethics* vi. §36. 90 Showing by toned-up face and vivacious manner..greater energy.

2. a. Slightly or finely coloured or shaded; tinted. ***toned paper***, paper which is not quite white, but cream-coloured or slightly buff.

1864 *N. & Q.* 3rd Ser. VI. 454/1 That yellowish-coloured, or what is now called toned paper, is..more beautiful and pleasant to the eyes than the glaring white paper of modern times. **1869** *Advt.* in *A. Stafford's Fem. Glory*, Toned paper, limp cloth, red edges. **1877** MRS. OLIPHANT *Makers Flor.* iv. 117 Soft shades of those toned marbles which fit so tenderly into each other.

b. *Photogr.* Treated with chemicals so as to acquire the desired tone or shade of colour.

1861 *Photogr. News Alm.* in *Circ. Sc.* (*c* 1865) I. 155/1 Imperfectly-toned patches will be the result. **1892** *Photogr. Ann.* II. 97 The toned and fixed prints are immersed in a strong solution of common salt.

3. ***toned-down***, modified, reduced in intensity.

1974 *Listener* 24 Jan. 122/2 The dances are in effect toned-down Bartok. **1981** V. GLENDINNING *Edith Sitwell* v. 83 Edith published two very similar accounts of Wyndham Lewis..both toned-down versions of a provocative essay she wrote.

II. *adj.* [f. TONE *sb.* + -ED[2].] In combination: Having a tone (in various senses) of a specified kind or quality; e.g. ***deep-, fine-, high-, low-toned***. See also the adjs.

1790 GOUV. MORRIS in Sparks *Life & Writ.* (1832) I. 350 A higher toned Government than that of England. **1812** W. TENNANT *Anster F.* III. xli, The brass-ton'd clarion gave the air a thump. **1870** ROCK *Text. Fabr.* vi. (1876) 54 A fine toned yellow as a ground. **1896** *Idler* Mar. 291/2 The deep-toned, old-fashioned furniture of the housekeeper's room.

tonee, var. DHONEY, E. Indian sailing vessel.

†**tonekin.** *Obs. rare.* [? dim. of *ton* or *tun*; ? a. Flem. *tonneken*.] ? A small cask or barrel.

1546 O. JOHNSON in Ellis *Orig. Lett.* Ser. II. II. 174, ij small tonekins of capers q[t] 4½ lb. cost 4[s] 6[d].

tonel, -ell, obs. forms of TONNEL, TUNNEL.

toneless ('təʊnlɪs), *a.* [f. TONE *sb.* + -LESS.] Destitute of tone.

1. Soundless, mute; of a body: without resonance.

1773 KENRICK *Rhet. Gram.* ii. §3 in *Dict.* 35 This sound.. in oratorial and poetical stile..is contracted and rendered almost toneless in speech. **1899** *Allbutt's Syst. Med.* VI. 129 The side of the chest is completely dull and toneless.

2. Having no distinctive quality; (*a*) of sound: without modulation or expression; (*b*) of colour: dull.

(*a*) **1833** *Philol. Museum* II. 386 The Old English..the Middle English, and the New, inflect all these verbs in a plain and toneless -ed. **1847** *Fraser's Mag.* XXXVI. 105 The harsh roar of his toneless, irritating voice. **1861** S. BROOKS *Silver Cord* viii, 'Mrs. Empson is my aunt..', said Mrs. Berry, in a toneless voice.

(*b*) **1843** RUSKIN *Mod. Paint.* I. II. III. i. §19 In paintings, they [the skies] are commonly toneless, crude, and wanting in depth and transparency. **1856** *Ibid.* III. IV. xv. §6 The Apennine limestone is so grey and toneless. **1883** GRANT WHITE *W. Adams* 80 Her hair, a toneless brown.

3. Lacking tone in body or mind; void of energy; listless, dull.

1854 F. L. MACKENZIE in Miles *Mem.* (1856) 263 Must I ..withered, toneless..Trudge on through life. **1899** *Allbutt's Syst. Med.* VI. 39 The fibres of the heart are not primarily diseased, but are merely more or less toneless and atrophied.

Hence **'tonelessly** *adv.*; **'tonelessness.**

1873 EARLE *Philol. Eng. Tongue* (ed. 2) §438 When this adverbial *-ly* was superadded to the adjectival the latter shrank into tonelessness. **1888** tr. *Ibsen's Ghosts* (Camelot Classics) 198 Oswald (tonelessly as before) The Sun. **1891** G. MEREDITH *One of our Conq.* II. v. 105 Her present tonelessness of blood and being. **1895** ZANGWILL *Master* III. vii, 'I see he calls you Eleanor', he observed tonelessly.

toneme ('təʊniːm). *Linguistics.* [f. TONE *sb.* + -EME.] A tone or set of tones functioning as a distinctive unit in a tone language (cf. PHONEME 1 b). Hence **to'nemic** *a.*; **to'nemically** *adv.*

1923 D. M. BEACH *Phonetics of Pekingese* (London Univ. thesis) ii. 9 Corresponding to the phoneme is the *toneme*, which is a group of tones no one of which may be used in the same position as any other. **1924** —— in *Bantu Stud.* Dec. 90 The key to all tonetic transcription is the principle of the *toneme*,..a group of tones within a given language. **1926** C. M. DOKE in *Ibid.* July 218 Words tonemically different and differing in meaning may under certain morphological circumstances become tonemically alike. **1930** J. R. FIRTH *Speech* iii. 27 A proper understanding and use of the tonemes of these languages would appear to be a *sine qua non.* **1944** *Internat. Jrnl. Amer. Linguistics* X. 123/2 The tonemic changes are by no means always substitution of a high for a mid toneme. **1957** D. JONES *Hist. & Meaning of Term 'Phoneme'* 12 One day—..about February 1921—he [*sc.* D. M. Beach] gave a lecture in the Department of Phonetics at University College, London,..in the course of which he demonstrated that each of the four so-called 'tones' of that language [*sc.* Pekingese] had 'variants' conditioned by the tones of syllables adjoining them in connected speech, and sometimes by other factors. The word 'toneme' was coined at my suggestion: it was readily accepted by Beach and the..staff of the Department. **1965** [see INTONEME]. **1976** *Word 1971* XXVII. 379 The toneme distinction in Swedish (accent 1 and accent 2), differentiating words like *stegen* [steːgen] with accent 1 'the ladder' and *stegen* [*steːgen] with accent 2 'the steps', however, is not mastered at an early stage. **1978** *Language* LIV. 245/2 R. W. Wilkinson..argues that mid tone is tonemic.

toner ('təʊnə(r)). [f. TONE *v.* + -ER[1].] **I. 1.** One who or that which tones: see the verb.

1888 *Medical News* LIII. 499 Sulphuric and nitric acids have..some claim to be regarded as toners of the vasomotor nerves. **1904** *Daily Chron.* 25 Mar. 10/7 Pianos.—Experienced tuner and toner wanted in factory.

II. In specific uses. **2.** *Photogr.* A chemical bath used to change the tone or colour of a (black-and-white) photographic print.

1920 E. J. WALL *Dict. Photogr.* (ed. 10) 661 There are many alternative toners for different colours which may be used alone or in combination on the same print. **1950** O. R. CROY *Compl. Art Printing & Enlarging* IV. 201 Immerse the print in the toner until the desired tone is reached. **1977** J. HEDGECOE *Photographer's Handbk.* 275 (*caption*) The already stark appearance of the print..was further accentuated by processing in a blue toner.

3. Particles of pigment used in xerographic processes to render an electrostatic image visible.

1954 *RCA Rev.* XV. 471 Developing consists in bringing fine positively charged particles of developer powder, or toner, close to the surface, so that they will be attracted to those areas which are still charged. **1977** *Sci. Amer.* Nov. 69/1 (Advt.), Develop in a second or two by a dip through any of at least three makes of commercial electrographic liquid developers that carry positive-charging toner particles.

4. *Hairdressing.* (See quot. 1966.)

1966 J. S. COX *Illustr. Dict. Hairdressing* 151/1 *Toner*, a substance which when applied to the hair effects a change of tone or an accentuation of an existing tone. **1969** E. TASHO *Hair Styling for Women* x. 182 Temporary rinses can be used as toners on bleached hair. **1976** *Wymondham & Attleborough Express* 10 Dec. 6/3 Brassiness in blondes can be cured by an application of one of the latest ash blonde toners—or by a visit to your hairdresser.

5. = ***toning lotion*** s.v. TONING *vbl. sb.* and *ppl. a.*

1970 *Vogue* Jan. 5/2 (Advt.), Toners that polish, purify, pep up circulation. **1983** *Harrods Mag.* Spring–Summer 74 Skin care products..Refresher Toner..£15·75.

tonetic (təʊ'nɛtɪk), *a.* *Linguistics.* [f. TONE *sb.*, after *phonetic.*] Of or pertaining to the use of tones in languages. So **to'netics**, the study of tones; **to'netically** *adv.*

1921 in *Trans. Philol. Soc. 1921–4* (1928) 11 A paper on Tonetics by Mr. D. H. [*sic*] Beach. **1921** H. E. PALMER *Princ Lang.-Study* i. 37 Learned specialist in 'tonetics' (or whatever the science of tones will come to be called). **1922** —— *Eng. Intonation* i. 6 The teacher articulates one or more syllables and calls upon the students to write down in tonetic symbols what they think they have heard. **1924** [see TONEME.] **1926** *Bantu Stud.* July 198 Phonetics treats of phones, phone-groups, and phonemes: tonetics treats of tones, tone-groups, and tonemes. **1934** WEBSTER Tonetically. **1938** D. M. BEACH *Phonetics Hottentot Lang.* ix. 125 In Hottentot, as in Chinese, two roots which are identical *phonetically* may differ *tonetically* when pronounced in isolation. **1958** R. KINGDON *Groundwork Eng. Intonation* p. xxix, The tonetic stress-mark system used in this book was developed..in an endeavour to find the most practical system of marking intonation. **1964** M. SCHUBIGER in D. Abercrombie et al. *Daniel Jones* 256 Even without extra tonetic prominence, it [*sc.* the self-pronoun] increases the weight of the head. **1975** *Language* LI. 561 A considerable residue of cases still remains which must be analysed in terms of underlying homonyms yielding tonetically distinct forms in many environments. **1981** *Word 1980* XXXI. 151 (*heading*) Intonation: tonetic stress marks *versus* levels *versus* configurations.

tonette (təʊ'nɛt). [f. TONE *sb.* + -ETTE.] A simple end-blown wind-instrument resembling a small flute.

1958 E. BIRNEY *Turvey* i. 10 'Plays tonette.' Some kind of a whistle, wasn't it? **1963** *Guardian* 29 Oct. 7/1 [He] is able to produce notes from a small flute, called a Tonette, by sticking the mouthpiece in his nostrils. **1979** *Arizona Daily Star* 1 Apr. K10/1 Tonettes, recorders, triangles and tambourines are the types of instruments needed.

tone-up, *sb.*: see TONE *v.* 6 d.

toney, variant of TONY; obs. f. DHONEY.

1622 in Foster *Eng. Factories Ind.* (1908) II. 154 One of their toneyes.

toney, var. TONY *a.*

tong (tɒŋ), *sb.*[1] [Echoic: cf. *ting, tang, dong*, etc.] A deep ringing sound produced by a stroke on a large bell, deeper than that denoted by TANG *sb.*^{2}, but sharper than that denoted by *dong*; the stroke producing this.

1881 MISS JACKSON *Shropsh. Word-bk.*, *Tong*, the sound produced by a slow single stroke on a church-bell; the stroke itself... 'The bell gies a tong or two w'en they comen out o' Church'. **1883** C. S. BURNE *Folk-Lore* xxxvii. 604 Giving a few tongs on the bell.

tong (tɒŋ), *sb.*^{2} Also **Tong**. [ad. Cantonese *tohng* hall, meeting place.] **a.** An association or secret society of Chinese in the U.S., orig. formed as a benevolent or protective society but freq. associated with underworld criminal activity.

1883 *Harper's Mag.* May 831/1 This burial-place..is parcelled off by white fences into enclosures for a large number of separate burial guilds, or *tongs*, as the Fook Yam Tong [etc.]. **1913** [see HATCHET-MAN 2]. **1924** *Glasgow Herald* 29 Oct. 8 Rival Tongs, whose principal object seems to be mutual extermination. **1948** P. JOHNSTON *Lost & Living Cities of California Gold Rush* 15/2 Chinese who were members of two tongs, the Sam-yap and the Yan-wo, were working side by side at Two-mile Bar, on the Stanislaus River. **1968** *New York City* (Michelin Tire Corp.) 83 Chinatown was then an area rife with debauchery and vice, the scene of 'tong wars' fought by rival 'tongs' to win control over opium dens, gambling haunts and houses of ill fame. **1972** K. BONFIGLIOLI *Don't point that Thing at Me* xv. 128 The Chinese Tongs used to favour a six-inch nail, the Japanese use a sharpened umbrella-rib. **1977** *Time* 12 Dec. 28/2 The famous Tongs were something else, more mysterious—secret societies similar to Mafia families. They ran gambling, prostitution, drugs, and offered merchants 'protection'.

b. *attrib.*, esp. in ***tong war***.

1927 *Daily Express* 25 Mar. 2/1 Chinese Tong (secret society) warfare broke out at midnight throughout the United States. **1928** H. ASBURY *Gangs of N.Y.* 301 The tong wars appeared to have begun about 1899, and..were all caused by conflicting gambling interests. **1950** *Los Angeles Times Home Mag.* 26 Mar. 5/2 The servants of 70 years ago were mostly Chinese whose favorite outdoor sports were tong wars. **1962** 'K. ORVIS' *Damned & Destroyed* ii. 20, I was called in by a tong leader. **1966** 'G. BLACK' *You want to die, Johnny?* iii. 51 The police are not neutrals in the little wars. Our interests are not entirely focussed on Tong feuds. **1972** J. BALL *Five Pieces of Jade* xvi. 220 He had the idea that he could get rid of the two Chinese by..making it look like a ritual killing or a tong murder. **1976** J. O'CONNOR *Eleventh Commandment* viii. 101 The screws weren't standing for Tong warfare. **1980** G. V. HIGGINS *Kennedy for Defence* xvii. 149 We are liable to have a nice little tong war on our hands.

tong (tɒŋ), *v.*^{1} [Goes with TONG *sb.*^{1}] **a.** *intr.* To emit a deep ringing sound, as a bell when struck. Also with cognate object. Cf. TANG *v.*^{2} 1, 3. **b.** *trans.* To cause (a bell, or other resonant body) to emit such a sound. ***tong out***, to sound forth by tonging. Hence '**tonging** *vbl. sb.*

1584 R. SCOT *Discov. Witchcr.* XII. xviii. (1886) 218 Trusting rather to the tonging of their belles, than to their own crie unto God. **1881** MISS JACKSON *Shropsh. Word-bk.*, *Tong v.a.* and *v.n.*, to cause to sound,—to sound in one tone, as of a church-bell. **1883** *Hampshire Gloss.* s.v., The bells be tonged', i.e. are being tolled. **1907** *Scribner's Mag.* Feb. 151 The great bell of the cathedral tonged out the vespers.

tong (tɒŋ), *v.*^{2} *U.S.* [f. TONGS.] **a.** *trans.* To grasp, gather, or handle with tongs; *spec.* to gather (clams or oysters) with oyster-tongs. **b.** *intr.* To use or work with tongs.

1868, etc. [implied in TONGING *vbl. sb.*]. **1887** [implied in TONGER].

c. *trans.* To lift or move (a log) with skidding tongs.

d. To style (hair, etc.) with curling tongs.

1932 'E. M. DELAFIELD' *Thank Heaven Fasting* I. ii. 35 Monica's hair had been tonged into waves. **1953** P. L. FERMOR *Violins of Saint-Jacques* 48 His moustache was crisply tonged. **1976** 'D. HALLIDAY' *Dolly & Nanny Bird* iii. 37 She had her hair waved to her ears, and then tonged out sideways.

Hence **tonger** ('tɒŋə(r)), one who gathers oysters with oyster-tongs; '**tonging** ('tɒŋɪŋ) *vbl. sb.*, the use of tongs; *spec.* the taking of oysters with tongs.

1868 *Rep. U.S. Commissioner Agric.* (1869) 342 Eleven million bushels [of oysters] taken in the legitimate way of dredging and tonging. **1887** *Fisheries of U.S.* Sect. v. II. 552 As soon as a tonger has caught as many as his small boat will carry he sells out to the runner and returns to work. *Ibid.*, The size of the tonging-canoe ranges from 15 or 16 feet to 30 feet or more. **1891** W. K. BROOKS *Oyster* 2 There were 1000 boats engaged in dredging and 1500 canoes engaged in tonging. **1901** *Munsey's Mag.* XXV. 386/1 Before it reaches the mill..a saw log is moved four times in four different ways. First, it has to be 'tonged' a distance of anywhere from ten to a hundred feet.

tong, var. TANG *sb.*^{1}; obs. f. TONGUE; see also TONGS.

‖**tonga** ('tɒŋgə), *sb.*^{1} *E. Indies.* Also **tanga**. [a. Hindī *tāngā*.] **a.** A light and small two-wheeled carriage or cart used in India.

1874 *Settlement Rep. Nasik* (Yule), Driving light tongas drawn by ponies or oxen. **1882** F. M. CRAWFORD *Mr. Isaacs* ix, The Himalayan *tonga* is a thing of delight. **1894** IRENE PETRIE in *Life* vii. (1900) 136 A tonga resembles a squat dog-cart with a hood. **1904** *Times* 6 Jan. 5/2 The Indian tongas used in South Africa were very suitable over even ground.

b. *attrib.* and *Comb.* as ***tonga cart***, ***-driver***, ***-horn***, ***road***; **tonga wallah**, the driver of a tonga.

1881 *Let. fr. Bombay Govt. to Govt. of India* 17 June (Yule), Gallantly defending the mail tonga cart. **1882** F. M. CRAWFORD *Mr. Isaacs* ix, Every tonga-driver is provided with a post horn. **1886** KIPLING *Departm. Ditties*, etc. (1899) 86 So long as 'neath the Kalka hills The tonga-horn shall ring. **1894** IRENE PETRIE in *Life* vii. (1900) 141 The tonga road was demolished by recent snows. **1942** M. R. ANAND *Sword & Sickle* i. 27 A tonga wallah called rudely. **1955** R. P. JHABVALA *To whom she Will* xiv. 98 The tonga-walla in his stained turban cursed and muttered and whipped his horse. **1978** 'M. M. KAYE' *Far Pavilions* II. x. 155 Tell the tonga-wallah to wait.

‖**tonga** ('tɒŋgə), *sb.*^{2} [An arbitrary name, said in *Pharm. Jrnl.* to have been invented by Mr. Ryder, who first sent specimens to Europe.] A drug extracted from the root of the Fijian plant *Epipremnum pinnatum*, Engler, used by the natives of Fiji as a remedy for neuralgia; also known in England and America. Also *attrib.*

(For its introduction into England, see *The Lancet* for March, 1880, 360, 361, also 445, and the *Pharmaceutical Journal* for April, 1880. A full history in *Gardeners' Chron.* 1882, XVII. 180, and *Journal of Bot.* 1882, 332.)

1880 S. RINGER in *Lancet* 6 Mar. 360/2 (*heading*) On Tonga: a remedy for neuralgia, used by the natives of the Fiji Islands. **1880** *Kew Report* 55. **1882** N. E. BROWN in *Gard. Chron.* XVII. 180/2 The Tonga plant is an ornamental climber of rapid growth, with bold dark green pinnatisect leaves. **1883** *Science* I. 80/2 The drug tonga is shown..to be the product mainly of a climbing aroid (*Epiprem*[*n*]*um mirabile*).

Hence **tongine** ('tɒŋgaɪn), *Chem.*: see quot.

1890 BILLINGS *Nat. Med. Dict.*, *Tongine*, a volatile alkaloid found by Gerrard in tonga.

‖**tonga** ('tɒŋgə), *sb.*^{3} [Native name in Peru.] A beverage inducing stupefaction and delirium, prepared from the seeds of *Datura sanguinea* by the Indians of Peru. Also in *comb.*

1852 KINGSTON *Manco* iii. (1853) 36 Our brother has but drunk the tonga; his spirit has departed for a season. *Ibid.* 37 The group of Indians..collected round the tonga-drinker. **1857** DUNGLISON *Med. Lex.* s.v. *Datura*, A narcotic drink called *Tonga*.

Tonga ('tɒŋə), *sb.*^{4} and *a.* [Native name: cf. Zulu *i*(*li*) *Thonga* member of the Tonga people, perh. f. *-thonga* member of a subject race.] **A.** *sb.* The name of several African peoples living chiefly in southern Mozambique, Malawi, and Zambia; a member of these peoples. Also, the Bantu language spoken by them. Cf. TSONGA. **B.** *adj.* Of, pertaining to, or designating these peoples or their language.

1866 in A. Mackenzie *Memorials Henrietta Robertson* 247 He might make beginnings both in the Amaswazi and Amatonga countries. **1872** *Cape Monthly Mag.* Feb. 117 The Tonga does not own a single head of cattle. **1875** *Jrnl. R. Geogr. Soc.* XLV. 53 The Portuguese..must have found conquest south of the Zambesi an easy matter when the country was entirely peopled by these industrious natives, called generally by the Zulus by the contemptuous title of Tongas. *Ibid.* 93 We found..the poor Tonga Chief at his wit's end. **1910** *Jrnl. Afr. Soc.* IX. 305 The Tonga of the Zambezi is..a different language from the one just mentioned [*sc.* Thonga], and also distinct from the Tonga of Lake Nyasa. **1910** *Encycl. Brit.* III. 360/1 The *Ronga* (*Tonga*) languages of Portuguese South-East Africa..are almost equally related to the *Nyanja* group..and to *Zulu*. **1929** [see NGUNI *sb.* and *a.*]. **1951** COLSON & GLUCKMAN *Seven Tribes Brit. Central Africa* II. i. 94 The Plateau Tonga, a matrilineal people, occupy a large portion of the Southern Province of Northern Rhodesia. *Ibid.* 95 Within the Tonga group itself slight changes accumulate. **1968** C. BURKE *Elephant across Border* iii. 79 Roger broke the silence, translating his discussion in Tonga dialect to Gomez. **1968** *Guardian* 15 Apr. 9/4 In Zambia..there are four strong tribal vernaculars—Bemba, Tonga, Lozi and Nyanja. **1970** [see ILA *sb.* and *a.*]. **1977** *Times Lit. Suppl.* 30 Sept. 1109/3, I am a chi-Tonga speaker from the lakeside Tonga of Malawi, and I should say that the so-called Tongas of Zambia, Mozambique, Malawi, etc., are one people.

tonga bean: see TONKA.

Tongan ('tɒŋən), *a.* and *sb.* [f. *Tonga* (see def.) + -AN.] **A.** *adj.* Of or pertaining to the island kingdom of Tonga in the south-west Pacific Ocean. **B.** *sb.* A native of Tonga. Also, the Polynesian language spoken in Tonga.

[**1818** J. MARTIN in Mariner & Martin *Acct. Natives Tonga Islands* p. iii, Having written down sundry examples in English,..I gave them to Mr. Mariner to translate into Tonga.] **1853** J. E. ERSKINE *Jrnl. Cruise Western Pacific* iv. 119 The group has from time immemorial formed part of the Tongan dominions. *Ibid.* iv. 157 In imitation of the Feejeeans, the Tongans have occasionally practised cannibalism. **1897** S. W. BAKER *Eng. & Tongan Vocab.* II. iii. 35 The present tense in the Tongan language..for which we have two forms in English... In Tongan..there is but one form. **1901**, etc. [see NIUEAN *sb.* and *a.*]. **1927** J. S. HUXLEY *Relig. without Revelation* vi. 183 The Tongans became..the most virulent Sabbatarians. **1939** G. BLAMIRES *Little Island Kingdom of South* 13 We had at least five anthems that evening, some of Tongan composition, others European, in the latter case the words being translated into Tongan. **1951** R. FIRTH *Elem. Social Organization* iii. 105 Every male Tongan is entitled by law when he becomes a taxpayer to receive a residential plot of land in a village or town. **1966** *Listener* 13 Jan. 62/1, I wrote it out in Tongan. **1972** *Vogue* June (Special no.) 135/1 Rate of exchange: 2·14 Tongan dollars to £1. **1976** S. R. ANDERSON in *Symposium on Subject & Topic* 3 A language in which ergativity is indicated by case marking alone is Tongan. **1978** *Times* 17 Jan. 17/4 Captain Cook..noted that Tongans boxed in much the same way as the English.

tonger, tonging: see under TONG *v.*^{2}

tongkang (tɒŋ'kæŋ). Also **tongkan, tonkang**. [a. Malay.] A sea-going barge used as a cargo boat in the Malay archipelago.

1834 *Singapore Chron.* 2 Jan. 3/2 The fourth [race] was a sailing match, between several tonkangs or cargo-boats. **1858** P. L. SIMMONDS *Dict. Trade Products* 383/2 *Tongkang*, a kind of boat or junk used in the seas of the Eastern archipelago. **1892** *Nautical Mag.* Dec. 1155 *Hydra*, s.s. and a tongkang, in collision in Singapore Harbour. **1922** *Chambers's Jrnl.* 8 July 503/1 A string of big, heavy *tongkangs*, towed by a puffing launch. **1950** *People* (Austral.) 11 Oct. 16/2 It was a hazardous adventure but they brought it off in spectacular fashion, first by sampan and then by tongkan. **1972** *Straits Times* (Malaysian ed.) 25 Nov. 87/2 Liew Kim..later became a trishaw puller and a tongkang builder.

Tongkinese, var. TONKINESE *sb.* and *a.*

tongman: see TONGS 4.

Tongrian ('tɒŋgrɪən), *a. Geol.* [f. *Tongres*, in Belgium, where developed + -IAN.] Name for marine strata of the Lower Oligocene of Belgium.

1883 [see RUPELIAN]. **1885** GEIKIE *Text-bk. Geol.* (ed. 2) 864 The Tongrian deposits contain an abundant marine fauna = the Egeln beds of Germany. **1885** LYELL *Elem. Geol.* xv. 202 The lower division [of the Oligocene], or Tongrian, includes the sands in the neighbourhood of Tongres, and..corresponds with the upper part of the Gypseous series of Montmartre, and with the Headon series of England.

tongs (tɒŋz), *sb. pl.* Forms: α. *sing.* 1 **tang**, 1–5 **tange**; *pl.* 1 **tangan**, 2–4 **tangen**; 4 **tangs**, (5 **tangys**, **-is**, **tang(g)es**, 6 *Sc.* **tang(g)is**, **taingis**, **tayngis**), 6– *Sc.* **tangs**, **tayngs**; 6 *Sc.* double pl. **tangisis**. β. *sing.* 1 **tǫng**, 3–5 **tonge**, (4 **toenge**, 5 **tongge**), (9 **tong**); *pl.* 3 **tongen**; 4 **tunges**, 4–5 **tongys**, 5 **toonges**, **tongges**, 5–7 **tonges**, (6 **tonkes**, **thounges**, 7 **tungs**), 7–8 **tongues**, 5– **tongs**. [OE. *tang* (str. f.), *tange* (wk. f.) = OLG. *tanga* (MDu. *tanghe*, Du. *tang*), OFris. *tange*, OHG. *zanga* str. fem. (MHG., Ger. *zange*), ON. *tǫng* str. f.,:—**tangu* (Norw. *tong*, Swed. *tång*, Da. *tang*):—OTeut. **tangṓ-* (also, with weak inflexion, *tangṓn-*):—Indo-Eur. **dankā́-*, referred to the root **dak-*, *dank-* to bite (Skr. *damç*, *daç*, Gr. δάκνειν); cf. OHG. *zangar*, MLG., LG. *tanger*, MDu. *tangher* sharp, biting.]

1. An implement consisting of two limbs or 'legs' connected by a hinge, pivot, or spring, by means of which their lower ends are brought together so as to grasp and take up objects which it is impossible or inconvenient to lift with the hand. Examples of different forms are seen in a smith's tongs, domestic fire-tongs, and sugar-tongs.

A particular use or shape is often indicated by a prefixed word, as ***blacksmith's t.***, ***curling-t.***, ***gas-fitter's t.***, ***pipe t.***, ***sugar-t.*** When not otherwise particularized usually applied to ***fire-tongs***. In early quots. often not distinguishable in sense from *pincers* or *forceps*.

†**a.** in sing. form **tong**. *Obs.*

c **725** *Corpus Gloss.* (O.E.T.) 905 *Forceps*, tong. *a* **1000** *Ags. Gloss.* in Wr.-Wülcker 218/37 *Delebra*, tang. *Ibid.* 272/34 *Forceps*, tang. *c* **1050** *Byrhtferth's Handboc* in *Anglia* (1885) VIII. 325 Mid his gyldenan tange. *a* **1250** *Owl & Night.* 156 Þu twengest þar mid so doþ a tonge. *c* **1305** *St. Dunstan* 77 in *E.E.P.* (1862) 36 He droȝ forþ his tonge And leide in þe hote fur. *c* **1380** *Sir Ferumb.* 1308, & het to brynge wiþ him anon anuylt, tange, & slegge. **1382** WYCLIF *Isa.* vi. 6 A cole, that with the toenge [**1388** a tonge] he toc fro the auter. *c* **1440** *Promp. Parv.* 496/2 Tongge, fyyr instrument. *c* **1483** CAXTON *Dialogues* 8/9 *Ung estenelle, ung greyl*, a tonge, a gredyron.

b. in pl. form with plural construction: the usual current use. ***pair of tongs*** is used when qualification by a numeral or an indefinite article is wanted.

α. *c* **890** tr. *Bæda's Hist.* v. xiii. [xii.] (1890) 428 Hæfdon heo fyrene eaȝan..ond fyrene tangan him on handa hæfdon. *c* **1000** ÆLFRIC *Hom.* II. 352 Woldon me ȝelæccan mid heora byrnendum tangum. *c* **1300** Tangen [see quot. *c* 1290 in β]. **1384–5** *Durham Acc. Rolls* (Surtees) 265, j par de Tangs. **1412–13** *Ibid.* 610, j pare belowys et tangys empt. *c* **1425** *Voc.* in Wr.-Wülcker 657/11 *Hec forceps*, tangges. **1483** *Cath. Angl.* 378/1 A paire of Tanges, *jn plurali numero*, *tenalia*. **1500–20** DUNBAR *Poems* lii. 14 The wyff..That with the taingis wald brack his schinnis. **1547** *Reg. Mag. Sig. Scot.* 20 *note*, Tua pair of tayngis. **1595** DUNCAN *App. Etym.* (E.D.S.), *Forceps*, tayngs. **1718** RAMSAY *Christ's Kirk Gr.* III. iv, Her aunt a pair of tangs fush in. **1816** J. BOSWELL, etc. *Justiciary Opera* 5 To seize on anither man's geer (As the tangs ance a Highlandman fand). **1825** JAMIESON s.v. *Tangs*, 'You fand that whar the Highlandman fand the tangs' S. Prov. [Cf. quot. 1721 in β.]

β. *c* **1290** *St. Brendan* 480 in *S. Eng. Leg.* I. 233 With tongen [*Harl. MS.* 2277 (*c* 1300) tangen] and with hameres brenninde mani on. **1352–3** *Ely Sacr. Rolls* (1907) II. 155 In j pari de Tongys pro plumbario. **1392–3** *Earl Derby's Exp.* (Camden) 158 Pro tunges et aliis necessariis. **1426** LYDG. *De Guil. Pilgr.* 16144 And with thy Toonges pynche hem so. **1483** *Act 1 Rich. III*, c. 12 §2 Andyrons, Cobbardes, Tongges, Fireforkes. **1495** *Naval Acc. Hen. VII* (1896) 205 Tongges of yron..j payre. **1530** PALSGR. 251/1 Payre of tonges, *tenailles*. *Ibid.*, Payre of smythes tonges, *gresses*.

1531 *Rec. St. Mary at Hill* 37 A payre of andi[r]onis and a payre of tonkes with a fyer Raike. **1586** *Rates of Custome* E viij b, Tongs for fire the dosen vj. s. **1599** *Acc. Bk. W. Wray* in *Antiquary* XXXII. 243 One pair of thounges. **1605** ROWLANDS *Hell's Broke Loose* 47 Their flesh torne from the bones with fiery tongs. **1614** *Liber Depos. Archidiaconat. Colcestr.* lf. 71 (MS.) To saye he would laye her on the pate with the tungs. **1663** PEPYS *Diary* 7 Sept., Dogs, tongues, and shovells, for my wife's closett. **1697** DRYDEN *Virg. Georg.* IV. 255 With Tongs they turn the Steel. **1721** KELLY *Scot. Prov.* 383 You found it where the Highland Man found the Tongs. **1815** J. SMITH *Panorama Sc. & Art* II. 171 Grasping the tongs with the right hand a little below the middle. **1845** JAMES *Arrah Neil* ii, He was as thin and spare, too, as a pair of tongs.

c. In pl. form *tongs* const. as sing.; with rare pl. *tongisis*, *tongses*, pairs of tongs. Chiefly *Sc.*

1489 *Act. Dom. Conc.* (1839) 132/1 Twa axis, a wowmill.. a tangis, price xl d. **1542** *Rec. Elgin* (N. Spald. Cl. 1903) I. 71 The masterfull streking of Ellene Murray with ane tanggis. **1576** *Reg. Mag. Sig. Scot.* 691 *note*, 2 pair of tangisis, 3s. apiece. **1596** DALRYMPLE tr. *Leslie's Hist. Scot.* VII. (S.T.S.) II. 46 The rest of his body.. the pynouris raue with an yrne tangs. **1708** *Caldwell Papers* (Maitl. Cl.) I. 216, I must also have a tongs and shovel. **1796** BURNS *On Life* vii, Like a sheep-head on a tangs. **1849** W. IRVING *Crayon Misc.* 254 A relic.. which, if I recollect right, he pronounced to have been a tongs.

d. in sing. form *tong*: One leg of a pair of tongs. *humorous nonce-use*.

1862 THACKERAY *Philip* xxxii, He keeps a tong to the present day, and speaks very satirically regarding that relic. **1864** *Daily Tel.* 26 Aug., With the half of a pair of tongs, or perhaps I should say with a tong, in his tiny fist. **1897** in *Westm. Gaz.* 7 Dec. 4/1 The beetle trotted down the kitchen tong.

2. a. *fig.* and in *phrases*: e.g. ***not to touch with a pair of tongs***, expressing repugnance to have anything to do with.

c **1386** CHAUCER *Pars. T.* ¶481 Thanne stant Enuye and holdeth the hoote Iren vpon the herte of man with a peire of longe toonges of long rancour. **1579** FULKE *Refut. Rastel* 714 [It] maketh M. Rastel.. to gnaw the tonges for anger. **1643** J. CARYL *Expos. Job* ii. 8 A man would scarce touch such an one with a pair of Tongs. *a* **1688** BUNYAN *Jerus. Sinner Saved* (1886) 112 We are scarce for touching of the poor ones .., no not with a pair of tongs. **1828** *Craven Gloss.* s.v. *Tangs*, 'He brades of a pair o' tangs', this is applied to a person with long limbs. **1882** MISS BRADDON *Mt. Royal* III. vii. 136, I wouldn't touch it with a pair of tongs.

b. As used in burlesque music.

1590 SHAKS. *Mids. N.* IV. i. 32 *Clowne.* I haue a reasonable good eare in musicke. Let us haue the tongs and the bones. **1678** RYMER *Trag. Last Age* 139 The tintamar and twang of the Tongs and Jewstrumps. **1885** DOBSON *Sign of Lyre* 123 Well, our immortal Shakespear owns The Oaf preferred the 'Tongs and Bones'!

c. ***snapping tongs***, a game: see quot.

1844 BARNES *Poems Rural Life* Gloss., *Snappen tongs*, a game of forfeits.. [played] in a room in which are seats for all but one,.. when the tongs are snapped all run to sit down, and the one that fails to get a seat pays a forfeit. **1847** in HALLIWELL.

d. Short for *sugar-tongs*, *curling-tongs*, *oyster-tongs*: see these words; also LAZY-TONGS.

1713 *Lond. Gaz.* No. 5086/3, 6 gilded Tea Spoons with Forks and Tongs. **1837** THACKERAY *Ravenswing* i, He was twiddling the [curling-] tongs with which he had just operated on Walker. **1870** *Standard* 19 Oct., A party of Maryland oystermen were caught sinking their tongs into the Virginia beds.

3. In various transferred and technical applications. †**a.** Name for an ancient surgical forceps: see quot. *Obs.* †**b.** A weeding-tool: see quot. *Obs.* **c.** The pincer-like organs of a scorpion. **d.** In a pile-engine, the forceps which grips the staple in the head of the ram. **e.** In diamond-cutting, a stand having at its upper end a vice-like device for holding the dop in which the diamond is imbedded for cutting. **f.** *Railway*. A pincer-like device for grasping the rail on which a vehicle is standing, thus holding it still (Forney *Car-builder's Dict.* 1884). **g.** 'A name for pantaloons and roundabouts [short jackets] formerly in use in New England' (Bartlett *Dict. Amer.* 1848); a skeleton suit. **h.** *Oil Industry*. A large pipe wrench used for making up or breaking out lengths of pipe or casing.

a. *c* **1425** tr. *Arderne's Treat. Fistula* 35 Whiche y-do, be þe lure y-opned wiþ tonges so y-shape þat when þe vtward endes bene streyned togidre þe inner endes be opned & agaynward.

b. 1523 FITZHERB. *Husb.* §21 The chyefe instrument to wede with, is a pairc of tonges made of wode, and in the farther ende it is nycked, to holde the wed faster.

c. 1608 TOPSELL *Serpents* 223 The sixt is like a Crabbe, and this is called by Elianus a flamant Scorpion, it is of a great body, and hath tonges and takers very solide and strong, like the Gramuell or Creuish.

d. 1776 G. SEMPLE *Building in Water* 36 The Tongs are opened by the two inclined Planes. *Ibid.* 37 The Ram.. with the Staple, that the Tongs take hold of. **1825** J. NICHOLSON *Operat. Mechanic* 310 Forceps or tongs are lowered down speedily, and instantly of themselves again lay hold of the ram and lift it up.

g. 1845 S. JUDD *Margaret* I. vi, The boys dressed in 'tongs', a name for pantaloons or overalls, that had come into use.

h. 1922 F. M. TOWL in D. T. Day *Handbk. Petroleum Industry* I. 411 When the friction becomes so great that this method cannot be used, the tongs are placed on the line. **1972** L. M. HARRIS *Introd. Deepwater Floating Drilling Operations* v. 46 The normal rig-floor tools, such as, tongs, slips, and small hand tools.

4. *Comb.*: **tongs-carriage**, a carriage which supports the tongs used in glass-making, foundry-work, and the like; **'tongsman**, (*a*) = *tongman*; (*b*) *Oil Industry*, one who handles the large pipe wrench used for making up or breaking out lengths of pipe; **'tongman**, one who uses the tongs in oyster-fishing (*U.S.*).

1839 URE *Dict. Arts* 590 Glass-making... Two powerful branches of iron united by a bolt, like two scissar blades,.. form the tongs-carriage, which is mounted upon two wheels like a truck. **1887** *Fisheries of U.S.* Sect. v. II. 525 In midwinter, when the heavy planters are busy marketing their crops, the tongmen are idle, or are attending to their own little cove-beds. **1891** W. K. BROOKS *Oyster* 140 They are exposed to the depredations of both tongmen and dredgers. **1891** *Cent. Dict.* (citing DAVIDSON), Tongsman. **1974** *China Reconstructs* July 47/1 Before long he became a skilled tongsman.

tong-tong, variant of TOM-TOM.

tongue (tʌŋ), *sb.* Forms: 1–6 tunge, (3 tunke, tonke), 3–6, 7 *Sc.* tonge, (4 tungge, tongge), 3–8 tounge, 4 *Sc.* towng, -e, 4–6 tung (also 8 *Sc.*), *Sc.* twng, 4–7 toung, tong, (5 tounghe), 5–7 toong, (6 toongue, 6–7 toungue), 5– tongue. [OE. and ME. *tunge* wk. f. = OFris. *tunge*, OS. *tunga* (MLG., LG. *tunge*, MDu. *tonghe*, Du. *tong*), OHG. *zunga*, *zunka* (MHG., Ger. *zunge*), ON. *tunga* (Da., Norw. *tunge*, Sw. *tunga*), Goth. *tuggô*:—OTeut. **tungôn-*, held to be cogn. with L. *lingua* tongue, for older **dingua* (as *lacrima*:—*dacrima*: see TEAR *sb.*[1]).

The natural mod.Eng. repr. of OE. *tunge* would be *tung*, as in *lung*, *rung*, *sung* (and as the word is actually pronounced); but the ME. device of writing *on* for *un* brought in the alternative *tonge* with variants *tounge*, *townge*; app. the effort to show that the pronunciation was not (tundʒ(ə) led to the later *tounghe*, *toungue*, *tongue*, although it is true that these hardly appeared before final *e* was becoming mute, so that its simple omission would have been equally effective. The spelling *tongue* is thus neither etymological nor phonetic, and is only in a very small degree historical.]

I. The bodily member.

1. a. An organ, possessed by man and by most vertebrates, occupying the floor of the mouth, and attached at its base to the hyoid bone; often protrusible and freely movable. In its development in man and the higher mammals, it is tapering, blunt-tipped, muscular, soft and fleshy, important in taking in and swallowing food, also as the principal organ of taste, and in man of articulate speech.

In some mammals, as the ant-eaters, it is attenuated, long, and worm-like; in most birds it is pointed, hard, and horny; in fishes, hard and immovable; in snakes and many lizards, cylindrical, slender, and forked, and an important tactile organ; in some amphibia, it is fixed at the front and free at the hinder end, and (as also in chameleons) used in licking up their prey.

c **897** K. ÆLFRED *Gregory's Past. C.* xliii. 309 Ðætte he ʒewæte his ytemestan finger on wættre, & mid ðæm ʒecele mine tungan. *c* **1000** *Sax. Leechd.* II. 272 Do hwon on þine tungan. *c* **1200** *Trin. Coll. Hom.* 181 Teð hine grindeð, tunge hine swoleȝeð. *c* **1250** *Gen. & Ex.* 372 And atter on is tunge cliuen. *c* **1290** *S. Eng. Leg.* I. 206/206 For Anguische þe eorþe heo freten, and hore tongene gnowen al-so. **13..** *Cursor M.* 16767 + 15 (Cott.) He tast it with tonge Bot þer-of toke he noght. *c* **1380** WYCLIF *Serm.* Sel. Wks. I. 29 Crist touchide his tonge.. and þe bonde of his tonge was opened for to speke. *c* **1380** —— *Wks.* (1880) 110 He schal make his tounge cleue faste to þe roof of his mouþ. **1398** TREVISA *Barth. De P.R.* v. xxiii. (Bodl. MS.), Soune.. is yschape with þe wraaste of þe tunge and þanne wise men clepeþ it a voice. **1530** PALSGR. 284/1 Tunge to speke with, *langue*. **1604** SHAKS. *Oth.* II. iii. 221, I had rather haue this tongue cut from my mouth. **1697** DRYDEN *Virg. Georg.* III. 666 A Snake.. Erect, and brandishing his forky Tongue. **1828** STARK *Elem. Nat. Hist.* I. 29 The tongue in the Mammalia is always fleshy, and attached to the hyoid bone, which bone is suspended by ligaments to the cranium. **1831** R. KNOX *Cloquet's Anat.* 586 The Tongue, a symmetrical organ,.. situated in the interior of the mouth, extending from the hyoid bone and epiglottis to behind the incisive teeth.

b. In reference to invertebrate animals, applied to various organs or parts of the mouth having some of the functions of the tongue of vertebrates, or some analogy to it.

1753 CHAMBERS *Cycl. Supp.*, *Tongue of a Mussel*,.. an organ by means of which it spins a sort of threads.. to fix itself to the rocks by. **1826** KIRBY & SP. *Entomol.* III. 358 *Lingua* (the Tongue). The organ situated within the *Labium* or emerging from it, by which insects in many cases collect their food and pass it down to the *Pharynx*. **1870** ROLLESTON *Anim. Life* Introd. 87 'Odontophorous' Mollusca.. possessing the peculiar dentigerous rasping organ known as the tongue.

c. Erroneously regarded as the 'stinging organ'.

1581 J. HAMILTON in *Cath. Tractates* (S.T.S.) 78/30 Venemous serpentis to stang thame with the fyrie edge of thair tungis. **1595** SHAKS. *John* III. i. 258. **1599** —— *Much Ado* v. i. 90 Villaines, That dare as well answer a man indeede, As I dare take a serpent by the tongue.

2. A figure or representation of this organ. **a.** A symbolic figure or appearance as of a tongue, as those that appeared on the day of Pentecost.

[*c* **1000** ÆLFRIC *Hom.* I. 314 And wæs æteowed bufon heora ælcum swylce fyrene tungan.] *c* **1175** *Lamb. Hom.* 89 Biforan heore elche swilc hit were furene tungen. **1382** WYCLIF *Acts* ii. 3 And tungis dyuersely partid as fyer apperiden to hem. **1526** TINDALE *Acts* ii. 3 And there apered vnto them cloven tonges, as they had bene fyre..: and they ..began to speake with other tonges. *a* **1740** WATTS *Remnants of Time* xi[i], On that day when the tongues of fire sat on his twelve apostles. **1792** HAWEIS *Hymn*, *'Enthroned on high'* ii, Though on our heads no tongues of fire Their wondrous powers impart.

b. A delineated or artificial figure of a tongue.

1488–92 *Acc. Ld. High Treas. Scot.* I. 81 A grete serpent toung set with gold, perle and precious stanes. **1536** *Register of Riches* in *Antiq. Sarisb.* (1771) 199 Having.. two white Leopards and two dragons facing them as going to engage, their tounges are done in curiousest wyse. **1577–87** HOLINSHED *Chron.* III. 849/1 Then entered a person called Report, apparelled in crimsin sattin full of toongs, sitting on a flieng horsse.. called Pegasus. **1886** *Edin. Rev.* July 151 The classical 'egg and tongue' and 'tongue and dart' patterns are branches from the same stem.

3. The tongue of an animal as an article of food; *esp.* an OX-TONGUE or NEAT'S TONGUE.

c **1420** *Liber Cocorum* (1862) 26 Take tho ox tonge and schalle hit wele. **1598** *Epulario* C iv, To seeth Tongues. **1653** WALTON *Angler* viii. 165 The tongues of Carps are noted to be choice and costly meat. **1740** SOMERVILLE *Hobbinol* III. Poems (1749) 158 Black Hams, and Tongues that speechless can persuade To ply the brisk Carouse. **1869** 'L. CARROLL' *Phantasm.* 112 Dispense the tongue and chicken.

II. In reference to speech.

4. a. Considered as the principal organ of speech; hence, the faculty of speech; the power of articulation or vocal expression or description; voice, speech; words, language. Also *fig.*

In many contexts it is impossible to separate the sense of the organ from that of its work or use.

c **890** tr. *Bæda's Hist.* IV. xxv. [xxiv.] (1890) 348 Seo tunge, þe swa moniȝ halwende word in þæs scyppendes lof ȝesette. *c* **1000** ÆLFRIC *Exod.* IV. 10 þa cwæþ Moises.. ic hæfde þe lætran tungan. *c* **1200** ORMIN 4879 þuss spacc þe Laferrd Jesu Crist þurrh his prophetess tunge. *a* **1250** *Prov. Ælfred* 282 in *O.E. Misc.* 118 Wymmon is word-woþ & haueþ tunge [*v.r.* tunke] to swift. *c* **1290** *Beket* 645 in *S. Eng. Leg.* I. 125 No tounge telle ne may. **13..** *Cursor M.* 8404 (Gött.) þou salamon mi sone be ȝong, He es wijs and of redi toung. **1414** *26 Pol. Poems* xiii. 100 He wolde trouþes tonge were tyȝed. **1573** G. HARVEY *Letter-bk.* (Camden) 6 A hie point for them to beat there heds and whet there tungs about. **1587** *Mirr. Mag.*, *Brennus* xxxiv, What tong can tell thy mothers griefe. **1600** SHAKS. *A.Y.L.* II. i. 16 This our life.. Findes tongues in trees, bookes in the running brookes. **1888** F. HUME *Mme. Midas* I. Prol., As you have not even a tongue to contradict.

b. In many colloquial and proverbial expressions of obvious meaning.

c **1375** *Sc. Leg. Saints* l. (*Katerine*) 257 Na man of ws had tuth na towng To conclud hir, þocht scho be ȝounge. *c* **1425** *Eng. Conq. Irel.* 46 Tong breketh bon, thegh hym-self ne hawe none. **1484** CAXTON *Fables of Auian* xxii, The felauship of the man whiche hath two tongues is nought. **1546** J. HEYWOOD *Prov.* (1867) 64 Her tong ronth on patens. **1562** —— *Prov. & Epigr.* 163 Thy tounge runth before thy wit. **1607** T. WALKINGTON *Opt. Glass* i. (1664) 2 Pythagoras ..had this golden Poesie ever on his tongues end. **1677** W. HUGHES *Man of Sin* III. iii. 77 For a Tongue to pierce an Inch-Board, commend me to Tursellinus. **1820** SCOTT *Abbot* iv, I would.. give him a lick with the rough side of my tongue. **1859** READE *Love me Little* x, Wasn't your tongue a little too long for your teeth just now? **1870** DICKENS *E. Drood* ii, Have you lost your tongue, Jack? **1890** MAJOR-GEN. A. F. BOND in Rogerson *Hist. Rec. 53rd* (*Shropshire*) *Regt.* 206 Having.. given them a taste of his rough tongue. **1895** *E. Anglia Gloss.* s.v. *Length*, *To give one the length of your tongue*, to slang. **1899** RAYMOND *Two Men o' Mendip* xv. 248 Vather'll.. call ee everything he can lay his tongue to. **1911** H. H. HARPER *Bob Hardwick* 88, I was so angry at her that I.. made no answer... Presently she said, 'Has the cat got your tongue?' **1940** 'J. FALSTAFF' *Jacoby's Corners* vi. 69 The cat has got his tongue. **1981** I. ST. JAMES *Balfour Conspiracy* vi. 229 Shaughnessy shook his head. 'Cat got your tongue?'

c. ***to hold one's tongue***, to refrain from speech, keep silence, say nothing. † ***to keep one's tongue***, (*a*) to keep one's word; (*b*) to hold one's tongue.

c **897** K. ÆLFRED *Gregory's Past. C.* xxxviii. 276 Se mon se ðe ne mæȝ his tungan ȝehealdan sie ȝelicost openre byriȝ. **1377** LANGL. *P. Pl.* B. XVIII. 146 Hold þi tonge, mercy! It is but a trufle þat þow tellest. **1390** GOWER *Conf.* III. 143 Ther schal a worthi king beginne To kepe his tunge and to be trewe. *c* **1440** *Alphabet of Tales* 83 þe toder.. flate with hym agayn & bad hym hold his tong. **1535** COVERDALE *Matt.* xxvi. 63 Iesus helde his tonge. **1596** SHAKS. *Tam. Shr.* I. i. 214, I will charme him first to keepe his tongue. **1605** —— *Macb.* II. iii. 125 Why doe we hold our tongues? **1672** *Mede's Wks.* p. xvii, It was a frequent Proverbial speech of our Author's, He that cannot hold his tongue can hold nothing; and he practis'd accordingly. **1749** LADY LUXBOROUGH *Let. to Shenstone* 28 Nov., Shocked to hear in rough English Hold your tongue. **1833** HT. MARTINEAU *Loom & Lugger* I. vii, Hold your impertinent tongue, Sir. **1884** GEORGIANA M. CRAIK *G. Helstone* 26 Here is your father who knows it is, though he thinks it best to hold his tongue.

d. Phr. ***to put***, or ***speak with***, ***one's tongue in one's cheek***, to speak insincerely. Also in phr. ***to stick*** (or ***thrust***) ***one's tongue in one's cheek***, as a gesture of sly or †contemptuous humour; hence ***with*** (one's) ***tongue in*** (one's) ***cheek***, with sly irony or humorous insincerity. Cf. TONGUE-IN-CHEEK *a.* and *adv.*

1748 [see CHEEK *sb.* 2]. **1828** SCOTT *Fair Maid of Perth* in *Chron. Canongate* 2nd Ser. I. viii. 153 The fellow who gave this all-hail thrust his tongue in his cheek to some scapegraces like himself. **1842** BARHAM *Ingol. Leg.* Ser. II. *Black Mousquetaire* II. xv, He.. Cried *'Superbe!—Magnifique!'* (With his tongue in his cheek). **1849** *Blackw. Edin. Mag.* Oct. 450/2 Hows'ever, I just sticks my tongue in my cheek,..watches my chance, an' off by a track-boat..to New Orleans. **1869** M. ARNOLD *Cult. & An.* Pref. 56 If statesmen, either with their tongue in their cheek or through a generous impulsiveness, tell them [etc.]. *Ibid.* 123 He unquestionably..knows that he is talking clap-trap, and, so to say, puts his tongue in his cheek. **1887** R. H. ROBERTS *In Shires* i. 10 [He] sticks his tongue in his cheek, and whispers to his neighbour. **1898** SIR E. W. HAMILTON *Gladstone* 10 There was no speaking 'with his tongue in the cheek'. He spoke straight from the heart. **1928** *Observer* 19 Feb. 5/1, I must confess my utter inability to grasp what Mr. B. Nicholson is after, though I am loath to believe that he painted his apparently flippant still life arrangements with his tongue in his cheek. **1951** *Sport* 30 Mar.–5 Apr. 9/3 Walsall fans will tell you, with tongue in cheek, that the Fellows Park club is always on the alert where transfer of players is concerned.

e. ***with*** **(one's)** ***tongue hanging out*** and varr., with great thirst or (*fig.*) eager expectation. *colloq.*

1897 KIPLING *Day's Work* (1898) 102 They've been waiting for this youth with their tongues hanging out. **1928** WODEHOUSE *Money for Nothing* x. 222, I should hurry. His tongue was hanging out when I left him. **1967** E. LEMARCHAND *Death of Old Girl* xii. 141 My tongue was hanging out, so I thought I'd..see if there was any sherry going. **1974** L. LAMB *Man in Mist* ii. 16, I don't have to run round to them with my tongue hanging out the moment I am promised something.

5. a. The action of speaking; speech, talking, utterance, voice; also, what is spoken or uttered; words, talk, discourse.

c **897** K. ÆLFRED *Gregory's Past. C.* i. 27 Ac sio tunge bið ȝescended on ðæm lareowdome ðonne hio oðer lærð, oðer hio ȝeleornode. *c* **1020** *Rule St. Benet* (Logeman) 4 Se ðe na deþ facn on his tungan. *a* **1225** *Ancr. R.* 78 Wite ich wel mine tunge, ich mei wel holden þene wei toward heouene. **1362** LANGL. *P. Pl.* A. I. 86 Hose is trewe of his tonge..is a-counted to þe gospel. *c* **1470** HENRY *Wallace* I. 294 He was wondyr fayr, Nocht large of tong. **1520** WHITINTON *Vulg.* (1527) 3 b, He is full of tonge [*linguax*]. **1604** S. HARRISON *Archs of Triumph* B j, Their lastingnes should liue but in the tongues and memories of men. **1667** DRYDEN *Sir Martin Mar-All* III. iii, Sometimes you have tongue enough; what, are you silent? **1835** MONTGOMERY *Hymn, 'For ever with the Lord'*, The choral harmonies of Heaven Earth's Babel tongues o'erpower.

b. Speech as distinguished from or contrasted with thought, action, or fact; mere words.

1382 WYCLIF *1 John* iii. 18 Loue we not in word, nether in tunge, but in werk and treuthe. *c* **1400** *Apol. Loll.* 54 Þe tung a lone is not to be axid, but the lif. *c* **1560** A. SCOTT *Poems* (S.T.S.) iii. 23 Bot offir thame ȝour daly observance Be tung, thoᵗ naþir hairt nor mynd consentis. **1853** LYNCH *Self-Improv.* iv. 102 If religion begins with your tongue, it is very likely only to end there; but if religion is in your heart, it must needs come to your tongue sometimes. **1866** CARLYLE in *Morn. Star* 4 Apr. 5/4 It seems to me the finest nations of the world—the English and the American—are going all away into wind and tongue.

†**c.** Spoken as distinct from written or other communication; ***by tongue***, by word of mouth. *Obs.*

1549 *Compl. Scot.* xi. 94 The messengeir gat nay ansuer be tong fra ald tarquine. **1553** JANET BETHUNE in *Maitl. Cl. Misc.* (1840) I. 41 *note*, I haif committit sum part of my mynd be toung to my broder.

†**d.** A 'voice', vote, suffrage. *Obs. rare.*

1607 SHAKS. *Cor.* II. iii. 216 Have you, ere now, deny'd the asker: And now againe, [? on] him that did not aske,.. Bestow your su'd-for Tongues?

†**e.** Eulogy, fame. *Obs. rare.*

c **1616** FLETCHER *Thierry & Theod.* v. (last sp.), And because She was born Noble, let that Title find her A private grave, but neither tongue nor honor.

6. Manner of speaking or talking, with regard to the sense or import of what is said, the mode of expression or form of words used, or the sound of the voice.

c **1460** *How Gd. Wif thaught hir Doughter* 19 in Hazl. *E.P.P.* I. 181 Be of a good berynge and of a good tonge. **1595** *Enq. Tripe-wife* (1881) 147 Keepe a good tung in your head, least it hurt your teeth. **1596** SHAKS. *Tam. Shr.* Induct. i. 114 With soft lowe tongue, and lowly curtesie. **1596** —— *Merch. V.* II. vi. 27 Who are you? tell me for more certainty, Albeit Ile sweare that I do know your tongue. **1664** in *Verney Mem.* (1907) II. 204 She gros very malisas in hur toung to us all. **1724** RAMSAY *Tea-t. Misc.* (1733) I. 86 Ye.. ha' na learn'd the beggars tongue. **1828** *Trial of W. Dyon at York Assizes* 10, I knew him by his tongue.

7. Of a dog. **a.** In phrases: ***to move (its) tongue***, to bark (*arch.*); ***to give tongue, to throw (its) tongue***, properly of a hound: to give forth its voice when on the scent or in sight of the quarry. Also *transf.* of persons.

1535 COVERDALE *Josh.* x. 21 No man durst moue his tunge agaynst the children of Israel. **1539** BIBLE (Great) *Exod.* xi. 7 But amonge all the children of Isrl' shal not a dogg moue his tonge, nor yet man or beast. **1737** HERVEY *Mem.* II. 374 To speak in the sportsman's style, he has not given tongue often. **1742** FIELDING *Jos. Andrews* III. vi, Ringwood..never threw his tongue but where the scent was undoubtedly true. **1843** R. PALMER in *Mem.* (1896) I. xxiv. 353, I nearly picked a quarrel with a Repealer, who opened tongue to the people in the market place of Larne. **1857** GEO. ELIOT *Scenes Clerical Life, Amos Barton* ii, When Papa opened the door Chubby was giving tongue energetically. **1859** *Art of Taming Horses* xii. 203 When a hound throws his tongue he is said to speak. **1871** FREEMAN *Norm. Conq.* IV. xx. 518 He was for a moment undisputed lord, without a dog moving his tongue against him, from the Orkneys to the Angevin march. **1893** *Black & White* 15 July 81/1 He has a tendency to throw his tongue too freely, to speak without fair warrant.

b. Hence, the hunting-cry or 'music' of a hound in pursuit of game.

1787 HUNTER in *Phil. Trans.* LXXVII. 266 Others, as the Hound, have a peculiar howl, which, by huntsmen, is called the tongue. **1879** *Dogs Gt. Brit. & Amer.* 56 (Cent.) The tongue [of the bloodhound should be] loud, long, deep, and melodious. **1890** *The Tongue of the Hound* in *Sat. Rev.* 1 Feb. 134/2 It is odd that the English hound, alone of hounds, should have this melodious tongue. *Ibid.* 135/1 How the squires of bygone times valued the tongues of their hounds.

8. a. The speech or language of a people or race; also, that of a particular class or locality, a dialect.

c **1000** *Ags. Gosp.* Mark xvi. 17 Hi sprecaþ niwum tungum. *a* **1300** *Cursor M.* 233 Þis ilke boke is translate In to Inglis tong to rede. **1423** JAS. I *Kingis Q.* vii, Editing In his faire latyne tong. **1485** *Rolls of Parlt.* VI. 375/1 Maister Stephen Fryon', our Secretary in Frensh tonge. *a* **1560** ROLLAND *Seven Sages* (1837) A ij, In vulgar toung he bure the bell that day To mak meter. **1570–6** LAMBARDE *Peramb. Kent* (1826) 233 Erasmus compareth the English toong to a Dog's barking that soundeth nothing els but Baw waw waw in Monosillable. **1667** MILTON *P.L.* XII. 501 To speak all Tongues, and do all Miracles. **1689–90** TEMPLE *Ess. Learning* Wks. 1731 I. 165 The three modern Tongues much esteemed, are Italian, Spanish and French. **1711** ADDISON *Spect.* No. 1 ¶3 Celebrated Books, either in the learned or the modern Tongues. **1868** GLADSTONE *Juv. Mundi* iii. (1869) 89 There were many races in Crete, and there was a mixture of tongue. **1908** [MISS E. FOWLER] *Betw. Trent & Ancholme* 307 Now the local tongue is becoming too 'correct' to be characteristic and picturesque.

b. ***the tongues***, foreign languages; often *spec.* the classical or learned languages; † ***the three tongues***, Hebrew, Greek, and Latin.

[*c* **1450** CAPGRAVE *Life St. Aug.* 4 The Barbar tonge is euery tonge in þe world whech is fer fro þe iij principall tongis, Hebrew, Grek, & Latyn.] **1535** JOYE *Apol. Tindale* (Arb.) 11 A man of grete lerning..both in the scriptures and the tongues. **1560** DAUS tr. *Sleidane's Comm.* 37 Excellencie in the knowledge of all three tonges. **1577** HARRISON *England* II. iii. (1877) I. 71 In..Cambridge & Oxford..the vse of the toongs..are dailie taught and had. **1591** SHAKS. *Two Gent.* IV. i. 33 Haue you the Tongues?..My youthfull trauaile, therein made me happy. **1617** MINSHEU *Ductor* Title-p., The Guide into the tongues. With their agreement and consent one with another..in these eleuen Languages, viz. [etc.]. **1691** RAY *Creation* I. (1692) 162 We content ourselves with the knowledge of the Tongues. **1907** A. LANG in *Blackw. Mag.* July 17 He was well-educated, familiar with 'the tongues'. **1912** *Bodleian Library, Man. for Readers* 4/1 The rooms once used for the teaching of..the two Tongues (Greek and Hebrew).

c. The knowledge or use of a language. Esp. in phrases ***gift of tongues, to speak with a tongue (tongues)***, in reference to the Pentecostal miracle and the miraculous gift in the early Church; also simply ***tongues*** (*pl.* in *collect.* sense).

1526 TINDALE [see 2 a]. —— *1 Cor.* xii. 30 Do all speake with tonges? *Ibid.* xiii. 8 Though that prophesyinge fayle, other tonges shall cease, or knowledge vanysshe awaye. **1533** GAU *Richt Vay* 48 The halie spreit..gaif to thayme ye gift to speik with al twngis. **1538** CROMWELL in Merriman *Life & Lett.* (1902) II. 144 Ioynyng wyth you Maister Mason.. to declare your purpose for that having the tongue he may doo..it more fully thenne you could percace easly vtter the same. **1593** R. HARVEY *Philad.* 3 Neither can you proue that hee had not wealth enough to serue his vses, or tongue enough in euery place of his trauell. *a* **1637** B. JONSON *Underwoods, Execration upon Vulcan* 75 Their..bright stone that brings Invisibility, and strength, and tongues. **1879** FARRAR *St. Paul* I. 96 The glossolalia or 'speaking with a tongue', is connected with 'prophesying', that is, exalted preaching. **1965** *Sunday Mail* (Brisbane) 5 Dec. 31/5 Some parishioners have complained to the Diocesan authorities.. about Mr. Schofield's interest in speaking with tongues. **1972** S. TUGWELL *Did you receive Spirit?* v. 40 Some manifestation, usually tongues, is generally expected; indeed, strict Pentecostals demand it. **1976** *Church Times* 5 Mar. 14/2 Tongues is a personal and devotional gift as opposed to the others, which are intended to help people.

9. *transf.* in biblical use: A people or nation having a language of their own. Usually in plural: ***all tongues***, people of every tongue.

1382 WYCLIF *Rev.* v. 9 In thi blood, of al lynage, and tunge, and puple, and nacioun. **1526** TINDALE *ibid.*, Thou.. haste redemed vs by thy bloud, out of all kynreddes, and tonges, and people, and nacions. **1535** COVERDALE *Isa.* lxvi. 18, I wil come to gather all people and tonges. **1587** GOLDING *De Mornay* xxvii. (1592) 433 All People, Nations, and Toungs shal serue that Kingdome. **1745** *Scot. Paraphr.* XVIII. ii, To this the joyful nations round, all tribes and tongues shall flow. **1875** MANNING *Mission H. Ghost* ix. 234 Throughout all lands, and people, and tongues.

III. Anything that resembles or suggests the human or animal tongue by its shape, position, function, or use; a tapering, projecting, or elongated object or part, esp. when mobile, or attached at one end or side.

10. Any tongue-like part or organ of the human or animal body. † ***tongue of the throat***, the uvula.

1398 TREVISA *Barth. De P.R.* v. xxiv. (Bodl. MS. lf. 13 b/1), [Þis] þe phisicians clepiþ þe tunge of þe throte and Cataracta also. **1483** *Cath. Angl.* 396/2 A Tunge in the throte, *vua*; or ye palase of ye mowthe. **1831** R. KNOX *Cloquet's Anat.* 253 The *Trachelo-Mastoideus* (*Complexus Minor*),..arises from the last four transverse processes of the neck, and three or four of the back, by tendinous and fleshy tongues. **1897** *Allbutt's Syst. Med.* IV. 527 A projecting tongue [of splenic tissue] becoming pedunculated.

†**11.** A wedge, an ingot of gold or silver. *Obs.*

(In quot. a lit. rendering of Heb. *l'shōn zahab.*)

1535 COVERDALE *Josh.* vii. 21 And two hundreth Sycles of syluer and a tunge of golde, worth fiftye Sycles in weight.

12. (= *tongue-fish.*) A young or small-sized sole.

[So, in same sense, early mod.Du. *tonghe* (Kilian), Ger. *zunge*, Da. *tunge*, Sw. *tungfisk*.]

a **1825** FORBY *Voc. E. Anglia, Tongue*, a small sole, from its shape. **1881** *Daily News* 4 Mar. 4/6 Large soles are put at the top and bottom of the box, and the 'tongues' stowed cleverly in the middle, so that the sole buyer..has but scant opportunity of fairly judging its contents. **1881** *Daily Tel.* 11 Mar., The fishermen know the ground on which little else than tongues can be caught, and they should be prevented fishing over that ground. **1884** F. DAY *Fishes Gt. Brit.* II. 40 Sole..slips, or tongues, the market terms for the young.

13. A tongue-like projecting piece of anything. **a.** A narrow strip of land, running into the sea, or between two branches of a river, or two other lands; also a projecting horizontal point or spit of ice in the sea, a narrow inlet of water running into the land, etc. **b.** A narrow and deep part of the current of a river, running smoothly and rapidly between rocks. **c.** A tapering jet of flame. **d.** *Geol.* A part of a formation that projects laterally into the material of an adjacent formation, becoming thinner in the direction of its length. **e.** *gen.*

a. 1566 in *Reg. Mag. Sig. Scot.* 1577. 735/1 Duas acras vocatas *the kirk-dur-keyis* (..descendendo cum uno *lie tung* inter terras de Erlishall). **1615** G. SANDYS *Trav.* 231 There is a double haven devided by a tongue of rocke. **1682** WHELER *Journ. Greece* I. 27 You see the Sea on both sides of this long Tongue of Land. **1693** LUTTRELL *Brief Rel.* (1857) III. 89 The Windsor Castle run on the tongue of the Goodwin sands. **1766** J. BARTRAM *Jrnl.* 12 Jan. 33 A long tongue of marsh comes from the N.E. end. **1771** *Chron.* in *Ann. Reg.* 73/1 Whitehaven..the tide..overflowed the quays and tongues, and ran..into the market-place. **1775** ROMANS *Florida* App. 48 To the westward of Stirrup's Key is a tongue of ocean water shooting into the bank. **1820** SCORESBY *Acc. Arctic Reg.* I. 228 A tongue is a point of ice projecting nearly horizontally from a part that is under water. Ships have sometimes run aground upon tongues of ice. **1832** *Act 2 & 3 Will. IV*, c. 64 Sched. O, 16 The tongue of land in the river just above Kingsbury fish-pond. **1839** MURCHISON *Silur. Syst.* I. x. 134 A..smaller tongue of the coal measures passes from the Forest of Wyre to the left bank of the Severn. **1857** LIVINGSTONE *Trav.* xx. 404 A tongue of rather high land, formed by the left bank of the Lucalla, and right bank of the Coanza. **1895** MARY KINGSLEY *W. Africa* 573 Tongues of forest go up the mountain in some places a hundred yards or more above the true line of the belt.

b. 1891 *Cent. Dict.* s.v., A tongue is well-known to anglers as a favorite resting-place of salmon in their laborious ascent of rapid streams.

c. 1797 COLERIDGE *Christabel* I. 159 A tongue of light, a fit of flame. **1849** MRS. SOMERVILLE *Connex. Phys. Sc.* xxxiii. (ed. 8) 370 The flame of a taper..is immediately divided into two tongues by the electric current. **1872** HANNA *Resurrection* ix. 178 That broad strong tongue of flame.

d. 1917 L. W. STEPHENSON in *Jrnl. Washington Acad. Sci.* VII. 245 It is..proposed that such features as *x* and *y* in figure 1 be designated 'tongues'... A tongue is not a member nor a lentil, either one of which differs lithologically from the typical material composing the formation of which it forms part. **1953, 1970** [see LENTIL 5].

e. 1881 E. A. FREEMAN *Sk. Subject & Neighbour Lands Venice* 207 Columns with richly carved capitals, and..with tongues of foliage at their bases. **1954** F. T. PRINCE *Soldiers Bathing* 7 Letting the sea-waves coil Their frothy tongues about his feet. **1965** E. L. MYLES *Emperor of Peace River* II. iv. 226 The frantic bawling of a calf in the edge of a tongue of brush near the river's bank. **1966** D. BAGLEY *Wyatt's Hurricane* v. 129 They emerged on to an open place, an incursive tongue of the countryside licking into the suburbs.

14. In many technical applications.

a. The pin of a buckle or brooch. **b.** The pointer of a balance; also of a dial. **c.** A thin elastic vibratory strip of metal, covering the aperture of a reed in an organ-pipe: = REED 8 c; hence *transf.* an analogous device in a seed-sowing machine (*obs.*); also, a reed in the oboe or bassoon: = REED 8 a; the vibrating fork in the Jew's harp or 'trump'; hence *fig.* the essential or principal person in a company or the like; also, a plectrum or jack in the harpsichord (= JACK *sb.*[1] 14). **d.** The clapper of a bell; hence, the pistil or a stamen of a bell-flower. **e.** The pole of a wagon or other vehicle; †the head of a plough (*obs.*). **f.** A projecting piece of leather or the like forming a tab or flap, or means of fastening; the strip of thin leather or kid closing the opening in a boot which is laced or buttoned; hence, any similar appendage. †**g.** In *Fortification*, a pointed horn-work; see quot. *Obs.* **h.** The movable tapered piece of rail in a railway switch. **i.** The wedge-shaped or tapered end of a scion in grafting. **j.** A projecting tenon along the edge of a board, to be inserted into a groove or mortise in the edge of another board; also, a connecting slip, often of iron or steel, which joins two grooved boards; in *Mech.* a projecting flange, rib, or strip for any purpose (*Cassell's Encycl. Dict.* 1888). **k.** The tapered end of a pole, etc. by which it is fixed in a socket; also, the upper main-piece of a made mast. **l.** A short piece of rope spliced into the upper part of the standing backstays, etc. **m.** Of a sword or knife: see quots. **n.** Of a bevel: see quot. **o.** *Mus.* = PLAQUE 1 d.

a. *c* **1325** *Gloss. W. de Bibbesw.* in Wright *Voc.* 150 Einsy doyt le hardiloun [*gloss*, the tungge]. Passer par tru de subiloun [*gloss*, a bore of an alsene] [nalkin]. *c* **1440** *Promp. Parv.* 506/1 Tunge of a bocle, *lingula.* **1483** *Cath. Angl.* 396/2 A Tunge of ye belte, *lingula.* **1524** in G. Oliver *Hist. Coll.* (1841) App. 15 A silver bokyll without a tong. **1530** PALSGR. 281/2 Tong of a buckell, *hardillon.* **1608** in *Archæologia* XI. 93 Sixteen gold buckles with pendants and toungs. **1802** *Trans. Soc. Arts* XX. 334 A buckle, with its double tongue received in a groove. **1851** D. WILSON *Preh. Ann.* (1863) II. 258 The acus or tongue is wanting.

b. 1429 *Rolls of Parlt.* IV. 349/1 So yat ye tunge of ye balance encline not to on party. **1530** PALSGR. 281/2 Tong of a balaunce, *languette.* **1626** MASSINGER *Roman Actor* v. ii, As I can move this dial's tongue to six. *a* **1691** BOYLE *Hist. Air* (1692) 91 The scales being gently stirred, the tongue would play altogether on that side, at which the bubble was hung. **1896** M. Rutherford *Cath. Furze* vi, It was just a tremble of the tongue of the balance.

c. **1551** Turner *Herbal* I. E ij, Ther are dyuerse kyndes of reedes, some are thicke redes; wherof arrowes are made, .. some serue for to make tonges for pypes. **1727–41** Chambers *Cycl.* s.v. *Organ*, The degree of acuteness and gravity in the sound of a reed pipe, depends on the length of the tongue. **1733** Tull *Horse-Hoeing Husb.* xxii. 319 The Tongue of the Seed-Box .. differs from that in the Sound-Board of an Organ .. in Shape. **1786** Jefferson *Writ.* (1859) I. 503 The last invented tongue for the harpsichord. **1795** Burns *Election* ii, An' there will be black-lippit Johnnie, The tongue o' the trump to them a'. **1854** Bushnan in *Orr's Circ. Sc.* I. *Org. Nat.* 127 The air throws the tongue .. into a state of vibration. **1879** Stainer *Music of Bible* 78 The real difference between an oboe and a clarinet is, that the former has a double tongue which vibrates, the latter a single tongue. **1898** Stainer & Barrett *Dict. Mus. Terms* s.v. *Organ Construction* 345 The *reed* is a brass tube .. having a narrow orifice over which lies the *tongue*, a thin elastic piece of brass large enough to cover the orifice and its edges... The lower end of the tongue is .. perfectly free.

d. **1577** B. Googe *Heresbach's Husb.* II. (1586) 65 By plucking out the little yellowe toongs from the bell. **1578** *Burgh Rec. Glasgow* (Maitl. Club) 104 For ane tong to Sanct Mungowes bell 2/. **1590** Shaks. *Mids. N.* v. i. 370 The iron tongue of midnight hath told twelue. **1595** —— *John* III. iii. 38. **1690** *Vestry Bks.* (Surtees) 258 For leather to the bell tongues, 2s. 8d. **1721** Wodrow *Sufferings Ch. Scot.* (1838) I. I. iv. §i. 333/1 The bell's tongue in some places was stolen away, that the parishioners might have an excuse for not coming to church. **1842** *Belfast & Environs* 71 This fine bell, which—except that the tongue is wanting—is in as fine preservation as at the moment it was originally cast.

e. **1591** Percivall *Sp. Dict.*, *Pertiga de carreta*, the toong of a plowe, (L.) *temo*. **1792** Belknap *Hist. New Hampsh.* III. 106 The oxen which are nearest to the tongue are sometimes suspended. **1827** F. Cooper *Prairie* I. ii. 27 The men .. applied their strength to the wagon, pulling it by its projecting tongue. **1858** Lewis in Youatt *Dog* (N.Y.) ii. 54 Constantly by the side or at the heels of the horses, or under the tongue of the vehicle.

f. **1597** A. M. tr. *Guillemeau's Fr. Chirurg.* 32 b/1 The hornes hauinge internally a little leatherne tunge which stoppeth the hoales. **1643** Sir T. Hope *Diary* 25 June (1843) 191 Quhil I wes pulling on my left buit both the tungis of it brak. **1830** Marryat *King's Own* x, He passed the leathern tongue of the [pocket-] book through the strap. **1840** J. Devlin *Shoemaker* 65 A further closing .. beginning at the turn of the .. counter, and going right round, along the range, and up the tongue. **1912** W. H. Stevenson in *Eng. Hist. Rev.* Jan. 7 The writs of Edward the Confessor have pendent seals affixed to a tongue of the parchment.

g. **1688** R. Holme *Armoury* III. xvi. (Roxb.) 99/1 Tongues .. are outworks that differ from Horn-works only in this, that in two halfe Bulworks they haue only an acute angle: and this sort is called the Single Tongue: it is called a double Tongue work, when it hath two outward angles with one inward.

h. **1841** *Penny Cycl.* XIX. 257/1 Switches are moveable rails placed at the point where two tracks fall into one, .. to guide vehicles from the single track into either of the two... In the old railways this was effected by short tongues of iron, moved by hand. **1877** Knight *Dict. Mech.*, *Tongue* .. the short movable rail of a switch, by which the wheels are directed to one or the other lines of rail.

i. **1832** *Planting* 30 in *Libr. Usef. Knowl., Husb.* III, The upper division of the scion made by the slit, termed the tongue or wedge, is then inserted into the cleft of the stock. **1887** *Nicholson's Dict. Gard.* s.v. *Tongue-grafting*, A small, thin tongue is cut in an upward direction in the scion, and also a notch the opposite way in the stock.

j. **1842** Francis *Dict. Arts*, etc., *Tongue*, a projecting part at the edge of a board, to be inserted into a groove ploughed in the edge of another. **1902** *How to Make Things* 57/1 Then add the other boards, fitting the tongue of one into the groove of the other.

k. **1815** Burney *Falconer's Dict. Marine* 568/1 *Tongue*, in mast-making, the taper part of the lower end of a spindle, or of a scarph.

l. **1815** Burney *Falconer's Dict. Marine*, *Tongue*, a short piece of rope spliced into the upper part of standing backstays, &c. to the size of the topmast-head.

m. **1853** Stocqueler *Milit. Encycl.*, *Tongue of a Sword*, that part of the blade on which the gripe, shell, and pummel, are fixed. **1869** Boutell *Arms & Arm.* ix. (1874) 170 The tongue .. is the spike .. which is fixed into the hilt in order to join the hilt and the blade together.

n. **1867** Smyth *Sailor's Word-bk.*, *Tongue of a bevel*, .. by which the angles or bevellings are taken. **1877** Knight *Dict. Mech.*, *Tongue*, .. the movable arm of a bevel, the principal member being the stock, which forms the case when the instrument is closed.

o. **1953**, **1957** [see plaque 1 d]. **1977** Goossens & Roxburgh *Oboe* iii. 34 The scraping tongue (or plaque). A flat oval plate of steel... Some players prefer a narrower plate to prevent the knife from coming into contact at the edges.

IV. *attrib.* and *Comb.* (very numerous: the following are examples).

15. a. Simple attrib., as ***tongue-battery***, ***-battle***, ***-bolt***, ***-bully***, ***-combat***, ***-compliment***, ***-craft***, ***-debate***, ***-drill***, ***-fire***, ***-government***, ***-grace***, ***-itch***, ***-metal***, ***-part*** (of a top-boot), ***-plague***, ***-play***, ***-position***, ***-powder***, ***-prayer***, ***-root***, ***-saw***, ***-sin***, ***-skirmish***, ***-squib***, ***-structure***, ***-tangle***, ***-tattle***, ***-tip***, ***-toil***, ***-valour***, ***-vice***, ***-war***, ***-warrior***, ***-weapon***. **b.** objective and obj. genitive, as ***tongue-biting***, ***-cutting***, ***-lolling***, ***-paralysing***, ***-scraper***, ***-taming***, ***-wagger***, ***-wagging*** (so ***tongue-wag*** vb. intr.), sbs. and adjs. **c.** instrumental, as ***tongue-bang***, ***-hammer***, ***-kill***, ***-lash***, ***-taw*** vbs., ***tongue-baited***, ***-bitten***, ***-rent*** adjs., ***tongue-lashing***, ***-murdering***, ***-scourging***, ***-smiting***, ***-travailing*** sbs. and adjs., ***tongue-banger***, ***-smiter*** sbs. **d.** locative, similative, etc., as ***tongue-bound***, ***-doughty***, ***-dumb***, ***-flowered***, ***-free***, ***-gilt***, ***-haltered***, ***-leaved***, ***-like***, ***-proof***, ***-puissant***, ***-valiant***, ***-wanton*** adjs.

1750 *Student* I. 304 Socrates was too much *tongue-baited. **1880** Tennyson *North. Cobbler* iv, Sally she turn'd a *tongue-banger, an' räated me. **1824** Miss Mitford *Village* Ser. I. (1863) 97 The feminine accomplishment of scolding, (*tongue-banging, it is called in our parts, a compound word which deserves to be Greek). **1881** *Good Wds.* 842/2, I heerd her tonguebanging o' ye as I cum past the house. **1671** Milton *Samson* 404 Mustring all her wiles, With blandisht parlies, feminine assaults, *Tongue-batteries. *a* **1743** Ozell tr. *Brantome's Span. Rhodomontades* (1744) 84 He did by no means like Handy-blows, but only your *Tongue-Battles. **1898** J. Hutchinson in *Arch. Surg.* IX. No. 34. 126 It [an epileptic fit] came without warning, and was attended by *tongue-biting. **1615** Day *Festivals* xii. 335 Now for us .. who are thus *Tongue-bitten and Reviled in such sort. **1611** Beaum. & Fl. *Philaster* II. ii, Look well about you and you may find a *tongue-bolt. **1856** R. A. Vaughan *Mystics* (1860) II. VIII. iv. 52 The .. doctors of Lyons hurled back his tongue-bolts with the dreaded cry of heresy. **1906** E. A. Abbott *Silanus* xxix, I stood silent, .. as it were *tongue-bound. *a* **1834** Coleridge *Notes & Lect.* (1849) I. 283 Such a mouthing Tamburlane, and bombastic *tongue-bully as this Cethegus of his! **1897** *Allbutt's Syst. Med.* III. 354 The most important factors in the *tongue-coating of fever. **1623** Hexham (*title*) A *tongve-combat, lately happening be-tweene two English Souldiers in the Tilt-boat of Grauesend. **1660** Fuller *Mixt Contempl.* (1841) 198 The rent-completing of the one, and the *tongue-compliments of the other. **1837** C. Lofft *Self-formation* I. 220 Despatch .. is a surpassing quality in *tonguecraft. **1697** Dryden *Æneid* XI. 588 Ever foremost in a *tongue-debate. **1671** Milton *Samson* 1181 *Tongue-doubtie Giant, how dost thou prove me these? **1886** Tupper *My Life as Author* 73 That was the sort of *tongue-drill and nerve-quieting recommended and enforced. **1556** *Aurelio & Isab.* (1608) H ij, You thoughte .. to rendre me *tonge domme. **1876** Swinburne *Erechtheus* 642 *Tongue-fighters, tough of talk and sinewy speech. **1690** C. Nesse *O. & N. Test.* I. 19 This raging *tongue-fire causeth great confusion. **1890** *Cent. Dict.* s.v. *Serapias*, *S. Lingua* is known as the *tongue-flowered .. orchis. **1617** Bp. Hall *Quo Vadis* xxi, Others more capricious, some more *tongue-free; few euer better. **1907** 'J. Halsham' *Lonewood Corner* 116 John Board .. to the last degree tongue-free. **1608** Machin & Markham *Dumb Knight* III. i. F j b, Thus are the pauement stones before the doores Of these great *tongue guilt Orators, worne smoth With clients. **1656** E. Reyner *Rules Govt. Tongue* 97 *Tongue-government is needfull to prevent Miseries from our selves. **1637** Rutherford *Lett.* clxxxi. (1881) 314 O that He would give me more than .. *tongue-grace. **1847** *Fr. Oxford to Rome* (ed. 2) 105 The din of word-battles and *tongue-hammers. **1836–48** B. D. Walsh *Aristoph., Knights* II. iii, Handed it o'er To us to be *tongue-hammered loudly. **1540** Cranmer *Pref. to Bible*, Wherof commeth all this *tongue itche, that we haue so moch delight to talke & clatter. **1676** Dryden *Aureng-zebe* II. i, My Ears still ring with Noise, I'm vex'd to Death: *Tongue-kill'd. **1887** Baring-Gould *Red Spider* ii, Let yourself be led and *tongue-lashed by your housekeeper. **1881** 'Mark Twain' *Prince & Pauper* xix. 222 She promptly brought the King out of his dreams with a brisk and cordial *tongue-lashing. **1885** H. C. McCook *Tenants Old Farm* 74 You .. deserve a little tongue-lashing. **1822** *Hortus Angl.* II. 374 *C. Myconis*. *Tongue-leaved Chrysanthemum. Leaves tongue-shaped, obtuse, serrate. **1832** *Planting* 31 in *Libr. Usef. Knowl., Husb.* III, The scion [should be] split .. so as to form the two divisions into *tongue-like processes. **1826** J. Wilson *Noct. Ambr.* Wks. 1855 I. 256 Smoking, and leering, with *tongue-lolling cheek. **1847** L. Hunt *Men, Women, & B.* I. iii. 44 The yelps and tongue-lollings of the dog. **1611** *Coryat's Crudities, Char. Authour*, He is alwaies *Tongue-major of the company. **1608** *Pennyless Parl.* in *Harl. Misc.* III. 79 A quart or two of fine Trinidado shall arm us against the gun-shot of *tongue-metal. **1599** *Broughton's Let.* v. 18 Such a *tongue-murthering Cain .. cannot withhold. **1841** *Penny Cycl.* XXI. 410/2 It .. goes twice through the hands of the workman; the first time to do what is called the *tongue part, the closing of the vamp and counter to the leg. **1617** Lane *Cont. Sqr.'s T.* IV. 159 What faleshode (which this witch termes veritie)! what *tonge-plages (cowardlie scurrilitie)! **1872** Swinburne *Ess. & Stud.* (1875) 52 The pur-blind .. policy of sword-play and *tongue-play. **1918** D. Jones *Outl. Eng. Phonetics* vi. 16 We examine the *tongue positions of these five classes [of vowels]. **1977** *Word 1972* XXVIII. 321 The most important feature for the correct perception of this phoneme from the viewpoint of the listener is high tongue position. **1589** R. Harvey *Pl. Perc.* (1590) 7 He that hath most *toong powder hopes to driue the other out of the field first. **1604** Hieron *Wks.* I. 491 Blind deuotions and *tong-prayers, which the hart doth not conceiue. **1652** Bp. Hall *Invisible World* III. v, Another while he bids him be *tongue-proof. **1566** Drant *Horace, Sat.* vii. D vij, Two *tongue puisante knyghts. **1607** Hieron *Defence* I. 3 b, Miserably slandered & *tongue-rente. *a* **1300** *Cursor M.* 1375 Bot þou sal tak þis pepins thre .. And do þam vnder his *tong rote. **1825** Jamieson s.v., *It was juist at my tongue-roots*, .. intimating either that a person was just about to catch a term that had caused some degree of hesitation, or that he was on the point of uttering an idea in which he has been anticipated by another. *a* **1711** Ken *Edmund* v. 82 Thus Dipsychus when he most Kindness feigns, With his *Tongue-Saw licks Mortals to their Banes. **1599** A. M. tr. *Gabelhouer's Bk. Physicke* 88/1 Then scrape your tunge with a wooden *tungescraper. **1710** Steele *Tatler* No. 245 ⁋2 [She] carried off .. a Silver Tongue-Scraper. **1897** *Star* 20 Apr. 4/7 A curious instrument possessed by everyone in China above the extremely poor is the tongue-scraper. **1713** M. Henry *Check to Ungoverned Tongue* Wks. 1853 I. 149 Peter resolved against a *tongue-sin in his own strength. **1822** T. Mitchell *Aristoph.* II. 214 What, my friends, if we quit This *tongue-skirmish of wit? **1647** Trapp *Comm. Matt.* v. 11 There are *tongue-smiters, as well as hand-smiters. **1690** C. Nesse *O. & N. Test.* I. 18 *Tongue-smiting is as smart as any hand-smiting. **1628** Feltham *Resolves* II. [I.] ii. 6 As for the crackers of the braine, and *tongue-squibs, they will dye alone, if I shall not reuiue them. **1861** *Proc. Amer. Phil. Soc.* VIII. 281 The *tongue-structure of folded anticlinals. **1901** *Westm. Gaz.* 29 Nov. 2/3 He generally got into a *tongue-tangle over the word. **1592** Lyly *Midas* v. ii, I feare nothing so much as to be *tongue tawde. **1896** A. Morrison *Child of the Jago* 299 His *tongue-tip passed quickly over them. **1900** H. Sutcliffe *Shameless Wayne* ix, Martha had a keen answer on her tongue-tip. **1609** Boys *Expos. Script. Eng. Liturg.* Wks. (1629) 29 He praiseth God but little, who makes it a *tongue-toile and a lip labour only. **1603** Dekker *Wonderfull Yeare* B iv, *Tongue-trauelling Lawyers faint at such a day. **1556** J. Heywood *Spider & F.* lx. Dd j, For the feare, that his *tongtromp (to you did sowne:) By thus manie flies: to thus few spiders seene. *a* **1700** Dryden *Iliad* I. 336 *Tongue-valiant hero, vaunter of thy might, In threats the foremost, but the lag in fight! **1838–42** Arnold *Hist. Rome* II. xxx. 186 The Greeks being a tongue-valiant people returned an insulting refusal. **1629** Maxwell tr. *Herodian* (1635) 383 You wel know what weather-cocks the Roman people are: and how great their *tongue-valour is. **1628** Feltham *Resolves* II. [I.] xxx. 96 For the *tongue-vice, talkatiuenesse, I see not, but .. Men may very well vie words with them [women]. **1913** D. H. Lawrence *Sons & Lovers* i. 16 He was blab-mouthed, a *tongue-wagger. **1885** B. Harte *Maruja* vi, No .. *tongue-wagging gossip. **1887** *Pall Mall G.* 27 Jan. 1/1 It is not necessary that he should say anything wise or true or new. All that he needs do is to keep on tongue-wagging. **1820** T. Roscoe *Gonzalo* III. i, Being *tongue-wanton of his noble friend, And crying up his many excellences. **1730** B. Martyn *Timoleon* IV. iii, I hate This Female *Tongue-War, and will end it thus. **1820** T. Mitchell *Aristoph.* I. 190 A man in tongue-war His superior by far. **1742** R. Blair *Grave* 297 The *tongue-warrior .. cannot tell his ails. **1681** Colvil *Whigs Supplic.* (1751) 131, I .. have both will and wit to reckon, And beat thee at thy own *tongue weapon. **1849** Miss Mulock *Ogilvies* xviii, The sharpest tongue-weapons that sarcasm ever forged. **1575** R. B. *Appius & Virg.* B j b, Content, for I shall repent it, for this my *tonge wralling.

16. Special combs.: **tongue aloe**, *Aloe linguæformis*; **tongue-and-groove**, applied (chiefly *attrib.*) to boards in which a tongue along one edge fits into a groove along the edge of its neighbour, and to joints, etc., so made; also *fig.*; **tongue-bar**, each of the processes separating the gill-slits in *Balanoglossus* and *Amphioxus*, suggesting the tongue of a jews' harp (*Cent. Dict.*, *Suppl.* 1909); **tongue-bird**, local name of the wryneck, from its long retractile tongue (Swainson *Provinc. Names Birds* 1885); **tongue-bit**, a bridle bit having a plate attached so as to prevent the horse from putting his tongue over the mouthpiece (Knight *Dict. Mech.* 1877); †**tongue-blade**, the shrub *Ruscus Hypoglossum*; = double-tongue 2; **tongue-bleed**, **-bleeder**, the Goose-grass or Cleavers (*Galium Aparine*); **tongue-bone**, the hyoid bone; †**tongue-butt** [butt *sb.*[6]], a butt or odd corner of land at the end or side of a field; **tongue-case** (*Entom.*), the part of a pupa-case enclosing the 'tongue'; **tongue-chain**, the pole-chain of a vehicle: = team *sb.*[1]; **tongue-cheek** (*Entom.*), a side-piece of a moth's mouth; **tongue-compressor**, a clamp for retaining the tongue during dental operations; **tongue-curve**, a figure showing position and movement of the tongue in speech, etc.; **tongue-depressor**, a surgical instrument for depressing the tongue during operations on the mouth or throat; †**tongue-evil** [evil *sb.* 7], a disease of the tongue; in quot. *fig.*; **tongue-fence**, argument, debate; **tongue-fencer**, a debater, skilful disputant; **tongue-fish**, the sole: cf. 12; in southern U.S., *Aphoristia* (*Symphurus*) *plagiusa*, a small sole-like fish; **tongue-flower**: see quot.; **tongue-grafting**, whip or splice grafting, in which a thin wedge-shaped tongue of the scion is fitted into a cleft in the stock; **tongue-grass**, name for garden cress (*Lepidium sativum*); **tongue-hero** (*nonce-wd.*), a braggart (transl. G. *wortheld*); **tongue-holder**, an instrument for holding the tongue during dental operations; **tongue-hound** [hound *sb.*[2] 2], one of the 'hounds' by which the tongue of a vehicle is braced (*Cassell's Encycl. Dict.* s.v. *tongue-support*); **tongue-joint**, a joint formed in metal by welding a tongue in one piece into a recess in the other; **tongue-key**, in *Exper. Psychol.*, a reaction-key which is opened or closed by movement of the tongue; **tongue-membrane** = *tongue-ribbon*; **tongue-mole** (*Her.*): see quot., and cf. hurt *sb.*[2]; **tongue-oxen** *sb. pl.*, the pair of oxen harnessed to the tongue of a plough, etc.; **tongue-pipe**, a reed-pipe in an organ or similar instrument; **tongue-ribbon**, the odontophore of a mollusc; †**tongue-ripe** *a.*, garrulous, loquacious, voluble, glib (of a person or his utterance); **tongue-scapular**, a scapular on which tongues of red cloth were fastened, worn by the Cistercians as a punishment for evil-speaking (*Funk's Stand. Dict.* 1895); **tongue-sewer**, one who stitches the tongues into boots; **tongue-shell**, a brachiopod of the family *Lingulidæ*; **tongue-shot**, speaking or talking distance, voice-range; **tongue-slip**, a slip of the tongue; †**tongue-sore**, *fig.* evil-speaking; cf.

tongue-evil; **tongue-spatula** = *tongue-depressor* (Knight); **tongue-speaker**, one who speaks with tongues (see sense 8 c); **tongue-speaking**, (*a*) oral as distinct from written communication; (*b*) speaking with tongues (see sense 8 c); **tongue-tacked, -it** *a. Sc.* = TONGUE-TIED (*lit.* and *fig.*); so **tongue-tack** *v. trans.*, to put to silence; **tongue-test**, a test of the existence or strength of an electric current by applying the tongue to a break in the circuit; **tongue-tooth**, one of the teeth of the odontophore of a mollusc; **tongue-tree**, the pole of a wagon; **tongue-triangle**: see quot.; **tongue-twist** *sb.*, a mispronunciation, a provincialism; **tongue-twist** *v. intr.*, to twist the tongue; in quot. to prevaricate; **tongue-twister**, one or that which is said to twist the tongue; *spec.* a sequence of words, often alliterative, difficult to articulate quickly; **tongue-twisting** *a.*, difficult to articulate; **tongue-violet**, name for *Schweiggeria parviflora* (N.O. *Violaceæ*), an erect Brazilian shrub bearing white stalked violet-shaped flowers in the axils; **tongue-walk** *v. trans.*, to scold, abuse; hence **tongue-walking** *vbl. sb.*; **tongue-work**, (*a*) work in 'the tongues', philological labour; (*b*) debate, discussion, dispute; (*c*) chatter, gossip, babble; **tongue-worm**, †(*a*) disease of the tongue (*fig.*); cf. *tongue-evil*; (*b*) a tongue-shaped parasite which becomes adult in the nasal fossæ and frontal sinuses of the dog or wolf; a pentastom; (*c*) the 'worm' of the tongue in dogs; = LYTTA. See also TONGUEMAN, -PAD, -TIE, etc.

1731 MILLER *Gard. Dict.*, *Aloe, Africana flore rubro,*.. The *Tongue Aloe. **1882** W. J. CHRISTY *Practical Treat. Joints* III. 52 Joggle Joint.—This term is applied to a square, semi-circular,..or otherwise shaped *tongue and groove joint generally of equal depth the full way through. **1929** W. FAULKNER *Sound & Fury* 353 He emerged carrying a sawn section of tongue-and-groove planking. **1939** —— *Wild Palms* 19 The flimsy walls (they were not even tongue-and-groove..but were of ship-lap). **1976** *Southern Even. Echo* (Southampton) 11 Nov. (Advt. Suppl.) 4/2 End terr. house, built 1972,..d. glazing, tongue and groove floors, etc. **1977** *Time* 3 Oct. 53/1 Despite its style and tongue-and-groove plotting, *The Honourable Schoolboy* sometimes displays a Balzacian tendency to turn urges into passions. **1902** *Encycl. Brit.* XXVI. 85/1 The *tongue-bar is the essential organ of the gill-slit in Balano-glossus. **1578** LYTE *Dodoens* VI. xiv. 676 *Tongueblade or double tongue, his nature is to asswage payne. **1611** COTGR. s.v. *Langue*, Tong-blade, Double-tongue, Horse-tongue. *c* **1450** *Alphita* (Anecd. Oxon.) 157 *Rubea minor*, cliure [= cleavers] uel *tongebledes. **1853** G. JOHNSTON *Bot. E. Bord.* 100 *G. aparine*... Children, with the leaves, practise phlebotomy upon the tongue..hence they call the plant Bluid-tongue or *Tongue-bluiders. **1841** *Penny Cycl.* XX. 456/1 The body of the *tongue-bone is most frequently of a rhomboidal form. **1906** *Westm. Gaz.* 17 Apr. 10/2 These sounds are produced in a bony cavity formed by an enlargement of the hyoid, or tongue-bone. **1220–51** *Cockersand Chartul.* (Chetham Soc.) II. I. 450 Et insuper super Waldemurfeld, duas *Tunge-buttes quæ jacent ex utraque parte terræ. **1826** KIRBY & SP. *Entomol.* III. xxxi. 250 Before from the middle [proceeds] the *tongue-case (*Glosso-theca*) [of pupæ]. **1885** H. C. MCCOOK *Tenants Old Farm* 73 The long, slender object which you mistook for the cord by which a cocoon hangs is a tongue-case. **1890** JUL. P. BALLARD *Among Moths & Butterfl.* 108 The deep, rich, velvety side-pieces, or *tongue-cheeks. **1902** E. W. SCRIPTURE *Exper. Phonetics* 469 Phonograms, palatograms, breath records, *tongue curves, etc. **1872** COHEN *Dis. Throat* 6 A *tongue-depressor, with a handle which is out of the line of vision, is the proper instrument. **1662** T. I. (*title*) A Cure for the *Tongue-Evill. Or, A Receipt against Vain Oaths. **1644** MILTON *Divorce* II. xxi, To have her unpleasingness..bandied up and down and aggravated in open Court by those hir'd masters of *Tongue-fence. **1850** BLACKIE *Æschylus* I. Pref. 18 Euripides, the great master of tongue-fence. **1675** CROWNE *Country Wit* II, The most admirable *tongue-fencer I have heard! **1655** MOUFET & BENNET *Health's Impr.* (1746) 260 Soles or *Tongue-fishes are counted the Partridges of the Sea. **1672** JOSSELYN *New-Eng. Rarities* 30 Soles, or Tonguefish, or Sea Capon, or Sea Partridge. **1884** MILLER *Plant-n.*, *Tongue-flower, *Glossula tentacula*; Australian [Tongue-flower], the genus *Glossodia*. **1710** J. HARRIS *Lex. Techn.* II, **Tongue Grafting*, is a way of Grafting in Roots. **1719** LONDON & WISE *Compl. Gard.* 183 Tongue or Whip Grafting, is proper for small Stocks, of an Inch, half an Inch, or less Diameter. **1844** N. PATERSON *Manse Gard.* 118 This is supposed to resemble a tongue, and hence this mode of operation is called tongue grafting. **1726** THRELKELD *Synopsis Stirp. Hibern.* G viij, *Nasturtium Hortense*, the Garden Cresses, is..sold by the silly Name of **Tongue-grass*, and used as a Sallet. **1887** *Nicholson's Dict. Gard.*, *Tongue Grass*, a common name for *Lepidium sativum*. **1800** COLERIDGE *Piccolom.* IV. vii, I Am no *tongue-hero, no fine virtue-prattler. **1902** *Baldwin's Dict. Philos. & Psychol.* II. 419/2 The most common form of motor response is the act of pressing a telegrapher's key with the finger or hand. Other forms are with the lip key, *tongue key, and mouth or voice key. **1562** LEIGH *Armorie* (1597) 87 b, These appeare light blewe, and come by some violent strok on men, they are called hurtes, but on women they are commonly called *Tongue-molles. **1851** *Harper's Mag.* III. 518 It would be impossible for the *tongue-oxen to resist the pressure of the load. **1874** WOOD *Nat. Hist.* 638 Feeding..on little bivalves, which they can assault with their short but strongly armed *tongue-ribbon. **1610** HEALEY *St. Aug. Citie of God* V. xxvii. 234 Their *tongue-ripe Satyrisme may more easily disturbe the truth of this world. **1627** [R. BERNARD] *Guide agst. Witches* II. ii. 93 They [women] are more tongue-ripe, and lesse able to hide what they know from others. **1891** *Cent. Dict.*, *Tongue-shell. **1895** *Edin. Rev.* Oct. 355 Tongue-shells and helmet-shells and lamp-shells. **1905** W. J. SOLLAS *Age Earth* i. 26 The little tongue-shell, *Lingula*, has endured ..from the Cambrian down to the present day. **1656** S. HOLLAND *Zara* (1719) 82 Who was no sooner within *Tongue-shot of him, but alighting..she made most humble and lowly obeysance. **1860** READE *Cloister & H.* lii, She would stand timidly aloof out of tongue-shot. **1913** *Tongue-slip [listed in *N.E.D.* at sense 15 a]. **1948** *Sunday Pictorial* 18 July 5/2 Freud took up this pioneer work and showed how the half-forgotten world of dreams and tongue-slips could be explored. **1978** *Canadian Jrnl. Linguistics 1977* XXII. 179 The penultimate chapter of AM whips through pauses, tongue slips, and other topics in the science of word-botching. **1542** UDALL *Erasm. Apoph.* I. 22 b, Imputyng his *toungsore, not vnto maliciousnesse: but vnto the defaulte of right knowelage. **1910** *Encycl. Relig. & Ethics* III. 370/2 The '*tongue-speaker' needed as his complement the 'interpreter'. **1978** *Amer. Speech* LIII. 59 They.. associate these utterances with the inspiration of the Holy Spirit, although tongue-speakers differ in their beliefs about the significance of the gift of tongues. *c* **1545** LD. MORLEY *Hyst. Masscutio* 12 b, Neyther with pen wrytyng nor with *tunge spekynge. **1902** SELWYN in *Expositor* Nov. 391 They continue tongue-speaking, which is such a marked feature of the Holy Apostolic Church. **1685** R. HAMILTON in A. Shields *Faithf. Contendings* (1780) 218 It..hath *tongue-tacked many a valiant hero for Christ in our day. **1727** P. WALKER *Remark. Passages* (1827) 211 That sharp Challenge, which would strike our Mean-spirited Tongue-tacked Ministers dumb. *Ibid.* 228 If ever he saw such an Occasion, he should not be tongue-tacked. **1814** W. NICHOLSON *Peacock* IV. 44 Till fairly tongue-tack'd wi' a pension. *a* **1877** P. P. CARPENTER cited in *Cent. Dict.* for *Tongue-tooth. **1829** T. MOORE *Hist. Devon* I. IV. i 510 **Tongtree*, the pole of an ox-cart. **1899** *Syd. Soc. Lex.*, **Tongue-triangle*, the triangular or wedge-shaped red arch at the tip of a coated tongue seen in typhoid. **1898** *Tit-Bits* 21 May 150/2 These little *tongue-twists..are of such small import. **1836–48** B. D. WALSH *Aristoph.*, *Clouds* II. i, I shall be lost, unless I learn to *tongue-twist. **1898** *Echo* 1 July 1/5 *Tongue-twisters had..composed a sketch called 'The Race'. **1904** *Speaker* 4 June 229/1 The famous tongue-twister, Miss Smith's fish-sauce shop. **1949** KOESTLER *Insight & Outlook* vii. 109 Its name, too, is funny—foreign and *tongue-twisting. **1961** E. S. TURNER *Phoney War* viii. 109 Each new campaign brought them a crop of tongue-twisting place names. **1884** MILLER *Plant-n.*, *Schweiggeria*, *tongue-violet. **1841** HARTSHORNE *Salopia Antiqua* Gloss., **Tongue Walk v.* to abuse or scold. Ex. 'Pretty well tongue-walked him'. **1888** *Illustr. Lond. News* Christmas No. 3/2 Give him a *tongue-walking. I would. **1598** FLORIO *Dict.* To Rdr. 12 His labours ..which..he may as iustly stand vpon in this *toong-work, as in Latin Sir Thomas Eliot, Bishop Cooper, and after them Thomas Thomas, and Iohn Rider. *a* **1661** HOLYDAY *Juvenal* (1673) 137 Seek then some other Law-courts..: tongue-work there may fill thy purse. **1866** GEO. ELIOT *F. Holt* xx, If a man takes to tongue-work it's all over with him. *a* **1899** R. WALLACE *Life & Last Leaves* (1903) 6, I have done a considerable amount of penwork and tongue-work. **1645** USSHER *Body Div.* (1647) 359 Those *tongue-wormes of swearing, blasphemy, and unreverent speaking of God. **1896** *Yearbk. U.S. Dept. Agric.* 161 The Tongue worm is found encysted in the viscera of cattle, sheep, and other animals. It is about a quarter of an inch long, and when eaten by dogs grows to be 2 to 5 inches long.

tongue (tʌŋ), *v.* [f. TONGUE *sb.*]

1. *trans.* To assail with words; to reproach, scold; to discuss or talk about injuriously. In quot. 1388, to drive *out* by talking against.

1388 in *Wyclif's Sel. Wks.* III. 493 If ony of þese curatus were trewe aungelis of God,..þai myȝtten sone be tongide out of court. **1603** SHAKS. *Measure for M.* IV. iv. 28 But that her tender shame Will not proclaime against her maiden losse, How might she tongue me? **1702** C. MATHER *Magn. Chr.* II. App. (1852) 224 Sir William was very hardly handled (or tongued, at least), in the liberty which people took to make most..injurious reflections upon his conduct. **1872** H. COWLES in Spurgeon *Treas. Dav.* (1877) IV. 413 He that tongueth his neighbour secretly. **1901** *Dundee Advert.* 14 Feb. 2 She met him in Small's Wynd, and 'tongued' him.

2. a. *intr.* To use the tongue, talk, speak; *esp.* to talk volubly, to prate. (Chiefly *tongue it.*)

1624 *Gd. News fr. N. Eng.* in *Story Pilgr. Fathers* (Arb.) 571 Shewing how base and womanlike he was, in tonguing it, as he did. **1679** DRYDEN *Troil. & Cress.* Pref., He shall tongue it as impetuously, and as loudly as the errantest hero in the play. **1885** FORFAR *Cornish Poems* 19 The more they parley voo'd, the more Our maidens tongue'd away. **1898** *Tit-Bits* 21 May 150/2 [When] they tumble across a person who 'tongues' it different to them, they grimly smile.

b. Of a hound: To give tongue.

1832 [see TONGUING *vbl. sb.*]. **1885** *Househ. Words* 20 June 142/2 'What's thee tonguing like that for, Dick?'..'What's amiss?' **1888** ELWORTHY *W. Somerset Word-bk.* s.v. *Tongy*, I yeard the hounds tongy, and tho I zeed the fox gwain on under the hedge.

c. *Mus.* To move the tongue when playing a woodwind instrument so as to interrupt the air flow briefly. Also *trans.*, to produce (a note) repeatedly interrupted in this way. Cf. TONGUING *vbl. sb.* a.

1936 F. B. CHAPMAN *Flute Technique* iv. 18 The student must..ultimately aim at producing notes by multiple tonguing..: he should..be able to tongue them continuously and quite clearly at the rate of nine or ten to the second. **1953** E. ROTHWELL *Oboe Technique* iii. 30 To 'tongue' a note pronounce the consonant 'T' with your tongue on the reed. **1977** *Early Music* July 343/1 Do not tongue too much or you may dislodge the reed from its staple.

3. *trans.* To utter or turn *over* with the tongue; to say; also, to pronounce, articulate (*dial.*).

1611 SHAKS. *Cymb.* V. iv. 148 'Tis still a Dreame; or else such stuffe as Madmen tongue, and braine not. **1841** GEN. P. THOMPSON *Exerc.* (1842) VI. 12 He took up the phrase, and tongued it over in his damning way. **1860** O. W. HOLMES *Elsie V.* vii, The Colonel raged..and tongued a few anathemas inside of his shut teeth. **1876** *Whitby Gloss.* s.v., 'I can't tongue 't', cannot say the word.

4. a. To touch with the tongue; also, to lick *up*.

1687 WOOD *Life* (O.H.S.) III. 247. *a* **1700** B. E. *Dict. Cant. Crew* s.v. *Velvet*. **1837** S. B. HARPER in *Fraser's Mag.* XVI. 191 An icy shudder shook me through—it stuck there, As you'd tongued iron on a December morn. **1888** H. S. MERRIMAN *Young Mistley* II. vi. 76 Fairy [a horse]..gently tongued the bit. **1894** BARING-GOULD *Kitty Alone* II. 149 The fire..was tonguing up the heap, sending the tips of its flames tastingly towards him.

b. To push *out* or distend with the tongue. *rare.*

1768 *Woman of Honor* I. 160 Exposing him..by winking with one eye, and tonguing out his cheek.

5. *intr.* To project as a protruding tongue; to throw out tongues (of flame).

a **1814** [see *tonguing* ppl. a. below]. **1856** KANE *Arct. Expl.* I. xxiii. 282 Old ices bulge and tongue out below. **1859** MASSON *Brit. Novelists* iv. 303 Scattered through all, is the fiercer element of Fire, here tonguing over the earth wherever it may be kindled, there flashing through the ether. **1871** G. MEREDITH *H. Richmond* xi, It really did look as if they [the firemen] were engaged in slaying an enormous dragon, that hissed and tongued at them. **1942** *Bull. U.S. Geol. Survey* No. 936. 374 In places a thick shale lens lies within, or tongues into, an ore-bearing sandstone lens. **1973** *Nature* 2 Mar. 41/2 The patch reef, 13 m long and over 2 m high, tongues out to the west. **1980** D. CREED *Scarab* III. xix. 183 A low spit of land tongued out into the shallow water.

6. *trans.* To furnish with a tongue (*lit.* or *fig.*).

[In this sense perh. a back-formation from TONGUED *a.*].

a. To give a speaking tongue or utterance to.

1602 DEKKER *Satirom.* K ij, Yes, yes, true chastity is tongu'd so weake, 'Tis overcome, ere it know how to speake. **1807** J. BARLOW *Columb.* VIII. 323 What avails..To tongue mute misery, and re-rack the soul With crimes oft copied from that bloody scroll? **1838** S. BELLAMY *Betrayal* III. 102 This Nazarene..hath tongued With a strange speech this talking world of ours.

b. (*a*) To cut a tongue on (a plank, etc.). (*b*) To slit or shape a tongue in (a plant-stem or shoot) for grafting or layering.

1733 W. ELLIS *Chiltern & Vale Farm.* 101 Make a Groove in each Plank, and put in a Slip of Wood, like a Lath, which the Carpenters call Tongueing it. **1766** *Compl. Farmer* s.v. *Layer*, Cut a slit upwards at a joint, as is practised in laying of carnations, which, by gardeners, is called tonguing the layers. **1825** *Greenhouse Comp.* I. 229 Let neither stock nor scion be tongued, but apply the scion to the stock..so that their barks on both edges and below may join. **1908** *Daily Chron.* 13 Nov. 6/5 Each length of maple..is tongued and grooved both at the side and ends.

c. To join or fit together by means of a tongue and groove or tongue and socket.

1823 P. NICHOLSON *Pract. Build.* 163 The sections of two pieces of stuff, grooved and tongued together. **1835** SIR J. ROSS *Narr. 2nd Voy.* iv. 55 Some convenient anchorage.. where we could fish or tongue the foremast. **1862** *Illustr. Catal. Exhib.* I. 26 The gallery floor..was closely boarded and tongued, to prevent the passage of dust.

d. To furnish with a tongue-like projection.

1900 *Westm. Gaz.* 6 July 5/2 Great curling clouds of black smoke, tongued with red and yellow where the light from the fire struck it.

Hence **ˈtonguing** *ppl. a.* (in quot., throwing out tongues).

a **1814** *Apostate* IV. iv. in *New Brit. Theatre* III. 336 The sense of guilt, With keener agony than tonguing flames Lick to the bone.

tongued (tʌŋd), *a.* (*ppl. a.*) [f. TONGUE *sb.* or *v.* + -ED.] Having or furnished with a tongue or tongues (in various senses); ***tongued and grooved***, furnished with a tongue and groove joint (see TONGUE *sb.* 16). Also *fig.*

Also in numerous parasynthetic combs., as ***double-tongued***, ***true-tongued***, etc., for which see the first element.

c **1369** CHAUCER *Blaunche* 927 Ne trewer tonged, ne scorned lasse. **1390** GOWER *Conf.* I. 218 This false tunged Perseus. **1413** *Pilgr. Sowle* (Caxton 1483) III. iii. 51 Somme were by the eyen hanged with hookes, and som by the tonges, whiche as me semyd were tonged double. **1611** L. BARRY *Ram Alley* IV. i. G ij, Nosd like a Goose, and toungd like a woman. **1635** A. STAFFORD *Fem. Glory* (1860) 185 Were all..the Starres of Heaven tongued, they could not all expresse thee so well, as a silent Extasie. **1666** J. DAVIES *Hist. Caribby Isles* 55 Two kinds of Tobacco Plants, commonly call'd..Green-Tobacco and Tongu'd Tobacco, from the figure of its leaf. **1773** *Bristol* (Va.) *Vestry Bk.* (1898) 238 A Dwelling House [shall] be built..[with] Good flouring Plank, well Tong'd & Groved. **1839** URE *Dict. Arts* 966 The boring tools are..16. The tongued chisel. *a* **1847** ELIZA COOK *Silence* 108 The soul..Shall keep an eloquence all, all her own, And mock the tongued interpreter. **1854** BUSHNAN in *Circ. Sc.* (*c* 1865) I. 284/1 Reeded and tongued instruments. **1884** *Northern Echo* 11 Aug. 2/5, 24,000 Feet of Grooved and Tongued Flooring Boards. **1886** *Archæol. Cantiana* XVI. p. xlv, The tongued or leaf-like ornament, so common in the period of Transition between pure Norman and pure Early English. **1897** F. C. MOORE *How to build Home* 15 The sheathing should be tongued and grooved and planed on one side. **1955** J. S. CHAPPELL *Woodworking* x. 136 A..stronger form of tongued and grooved joint is made by ploughing a groove in both edges to be joined.

tongueful (ˈtʌŋfʊl). [See -FUL 2.] As much as the tongue will hold or carry.

1892 M. DODS *Israel's Iron Age* 43 A dog..snatching mouthfuls or tonguefuls of water.

tongue-in-cheek, *a.* and *adv.* [See TONGUE *sb.* 4 d.] **A.** *adj.* Ironic, slyly humorous; not meant to be taken seriously. Also **tongue-in-the-cheek**.

1933 *Times Lit. Suppl.* 30 Mar. 223/4 *Shooting the Bull*.. is a tongue-in-the-cheek march through newspaperdom. **1937** M. COVARRUBIAS *Island of Bali* xi. 375 A typical tongue-in-cheek Balinese answer to dodge a complicated explanation for outsiders. **1953** *Spectator* 13 Mar. 320/2 This.. novel.. seems too facile, too tongue-in-cheek. **1959** *Times* 4 Sept. 5/1 Though the piece was energetic and often exuberant it was certainly not tongue-in-the-cheek or humorous in style. **1976** *National Observer* (U.S.) 27 Mar. 10/1, I enjoyed Wesley Pruden's tongue-in-cheek suggestion.. that every man, woman, and child in the United States be given a college degree so they 'become equal'. **1982** *Listener* 16 Dec. 28/1 Angela Carter translated Perrault's fairy tales.. with absolute fidelity to the understatement, the tongue-in-cheek charm of the originals.

B. *adv.* = *with tongue in cheek* s.v. TONGUE *sb.* 4 d.

1934 in WEBSTER. **1976** *Listener* 18 Mar. 334/3 Someone told Muhammad Ali, tongue-in-cheek, that his book made him come over as a 'deep thinker'. **1979** H. MCLEAVE *Borderline Case* xi. 113 'You mean you're a spy.' 'Only for those people who have something sinister to hide,' he said, tongue-in-cheek.

tongueless ('tʌŋlɪs), *a.* [See -LESS.]

1. *lit.* Having no tongue, without a tongue.

1398 TREVISA *Barth. De P.R.* XVIII. xxxii. (Bodl. MS.), Amonge beestes of þe londe he [the crocodile] is tungles. **1570** LEVINS *Manip.* 91/16 Tonguelesse, *elinguis, e.* **1611** COTGR., *Gouttreuse*, a certain white, long-beaked, and tonglesse bird [a pelican]. **1738** *Gentl. Mag.* VIII. 524/1, I doubt very much, whether a Tongueless Person, or one that is without a Roof to the Mouth, can Taste. **1876** L. STEPHEN *Eng. Th. in 18th C.* I. IV. vi. 267 The miracle of the tongueless confessor is mentioned by Gibbon as resting on remarkably good evidence. **1879** BODDAM-WHETHAM *Roraima & Brit. Guiana* 171 *note*, Herodotus, too, who was a keen observer of the crocodile, repeats the idea that it is tongueless. **1907** *Q. Rev.* July 201 The most revered objects in the *ti* are the bells, usually tongueless.

2. Without the faculty of voice or speech, dumb, mute; also, without speaking, speechless, silent.

1447 BOKENHAM *Seyntys* (Roxb.) 196 Why stonde ye thus stylle, be ye tunglees? **1542** UDALL *Erasm. Apoph.* 287 b, That persone, by whose benefite thou art made of a tounglesse bodye, eloquente. **1630** J. TAYLOR (Water P.) *Anagrams & Sonn.* Wks. II. 256/2 Now chirping birds are all turn'd tounglesse mutes. **1630** LENNARD tr. *Charron's Wisd.* I. xxxi. (1670) 90 We go with our heads hanging,.. our mouths tongueless. **1824** J. SYMMONS tr. *Æschylus' Agam.* 73 The mighty judges heard the tongueless plea.

b. Said of things.

1593 SHAKS. *Rich. II*, I. i. 105 Euen from the toonglesse cauernes of the earth. **1624** F. WHITE *Repl. Fisher* 92 The consent of the Church alone.. ought to be of greater esteeme .. than all mute and tonguelesse Bookes. *a* **1822** SHELLEY *Ess. & Lett.* (1852) I. 138 There is eloquence in the tongueless wind. **1868** J. H. NEWMAN *Verses Var. Occas.* 9, I cannot bear those sullen walls, Those eyeless towers, those tongueless halls.

†**3.** Not spoken of; unmentioned. *Obs. rare.*

1611 SHAKS. *Wint. T.* I. i. 92 One good deed, dying tonguelesse, Slaughters a thousand, wayting vpon that.

tonguelet ('tʌŋlɪt). [f. TONGUE *sb.* + -LET.] A little tongue or tongue-like object; *spec.* **a.** in *Entom.* = LIGULA 1 b; **b.** = *tongue-worm* (*b*): see TONGUE *sb.* 16 (*Cent. Dict.* 1891).

1840 E. WILSON *Anat. Vade M.* (1842) 384 The Linguetta laminosa is a thin tonguelet of grey substance, marked by transverse furrows, which extend forwards.. from the grey substance of the cerebellum. **1840** tr. *Cuvier's Anim. Kingd.* 529 The tonguelet consists of two small hairy setæ, extending beyond the large horny mentum. **1866** J. K. LORD in *Intell. Observ.* No. 48. 431 In this tube is the tonguelet [of a Cicada]. **1878** BROWNING *Poets Croisic* v, I shall not sulk If yonder greenish tonguelet [of flame] licked from brass Its life.

tongueman, tongue-man ('tʌŋmən). ? *Obs.* [f. TONGUE *sb.* + MAN *sb.*[1]] A speaker, an orator.

1594 NASHE *Unfort. Trav.* Wks. (Grosart) V. 69 Our present incorporation.. by me the tongue-man of their thankfulnes.. bid you welcome. **1611** SPEED *Hist. Gr. Brit.* IX. xxiv. (1623) 1175 Poysonous tonguemen and libellous Pen-men. **1627** E. F. *Hist. Edw. II* (1680) 55, I am no tongue-man, nor can move with language; but if we come to act, I'll not be idle.

tongue-pad ('tʌŋpæd), *sb. slang* or *dial.* [f. TONGUE *sb.* + PAD *sb.*[2] 3, 4.] A talkative person.

a **1700** B. E. *Dict. Cant. Crew, Tongue-pad*, a smooth, Glib-tongued, insinuating Fellow. **1709** O. DYKES *Eng. Prov. & Refl.* (ed. 2) 230 'Twas pleasant enough to hear two Tongue-Pads a-scolding, and giving one another the Lie. **1821** *Joseph the Book-Man* 70 Determin'd every ear t'engage Thus spoke the tonguepad of a sage. **1882** JAGO *Cornw. Gloss., Tongue-pad*,.. a chatterer, a very talkative person.

Hence '**tongue-pad** *v.*, *trans.* to assail with words; to scold; also *intr.* (with *it*) to tattle, chatter; whence '**tongue-padder** = ? *tongue-pad* (see quot.); '**tongue-padding** *vbl. sb.*, scolding.

1707 J. STEVENS tr. *Quevedo's Com. Wks.* (1709) 422 They would all *Tongue-pad him at once. **1825** SCOTT *Betrothed* xxx, My wife Gillian, who will tongue-pad it with any shrew in Christendom. **1676** *Warning for Housekprs.* Title-p., Budg and Snudg, File-lifter, *Tongue-padder, The private Theif. **1876** *Whitby Gloss., Tongue-whaling*, or **Tongue-padding*, a scolding lecture.

'**tonguer.** [f. TONGUE *v.* + -ER[1].] **1.** An utterer, a speaker.

1822 *New Monthly Mag.* IV. 297 Ceaseless tonguers of 'words of no tone', they lisp.

†**2.** *N.Z.* (See quots.) *Obs.* exc. *Hist.*

1836 in R. McNab *Old Whaling Days* (1913) 436 Some mention of what are called tonguers... When the whale is cut in they are entitled to the carcass and the tongue. **1843** [see CUTTER *sb.*[1] 1 b]. **1845** E. J. WAKEFIELD *Adventure N.Z.* I. xi. 323 The proper officers have been selected—such as cooper, carpenter, cooks, painter, and 'tonguer'.. [who] takes his name from having an exclusive right to the oil obtained from the tongue.. in payment of his duty of 'cutting-in', or dissecting, the whale. **1941** BAKER *N.Z. Slang* ii. 13 A tonguer was a native or white living in New Zealand who assisted a whaling crew to cut up whales... These men earned their name.. from the fact that they were given the whale's carcass and tongue to dispose of as they wished.

tongue-shaped ('tʌŋʃeɪpt), *a.* Shaped like a tongue; linguiform.

1776 J. LEE *Introd. Bot.* Explan. Terms 386 *Lingulatum*, Tongue-shaped, linear, fleshy. **1776** WITHERING *Brit. Pl.* (1796) II. 55 A small tongue-shaped glandular substance. **1837** KEITH *Bot. Lex.* 286 The [Mistletoe] leaves are.. tongue-shaped, entire, smooth. **1898** *Allbutt's Syst. Med.* V. 464 At each systole of the ventricles the tongue-shaped valve-flaps pendent.. are moved together towards those orifices.

'**tonguesman.** *rare.* [Cf. *swordsman, townsman*, etc.] = TONGUEMAN.

1596 FITZ-GEFFRAY *Sir F. Drake* (1881) 5 So he, and I his tongues-man, doe require Thy Sanctuarie. **1610** *Chester's Tri., Sp. Fame* 22 (Chetham Soc.), [To Mercury] Descend then Tongue's man of the universe. **1837** C. LOFFT *Self-formation* I. 252 Certain rough and ready tonguesmen.. spoke, if not absolutely well, yet forwardly and fluently.

tonguester ('tʌŋstə(r)). [f. TONGUE *sb.* + -STER.] A talkative person; a great talker; a gossip.

1871 TENNYSON *Last Tourn.* 392 The tonguesters of the court she had not heard. **1877** —— *Harold* v. i. 47 The simple, silent, selfless man Is worth a world of tonguesters. **1899** *Q. Rev.* Apr. 478 Two such formidable tonguesters as George Borrow and Thomas Carlyle!

attrib. **1885** *Punch* 11 Apr. 169/1 Thee, Great heart, whose silent grandeur seems to shame Our tonguester time. **1889** TENNYSON *To Mary Boyle* ix, Lowly minds were madden'd to the height By tonguester tricks.

tongue-tie ('tʌŋtaɪ), *sb.* [f. TONGUE *sb.* + TIE *sb.*] That which ties the tongue, or restrains speech; also, the condition of being tongue-tied (*lit.* and *fig.*); *spec.* (*Path.*): see quot. 1890.

1641 BROME *Jovial Crew* II. Wks. 1873 III. 374 And asks a stronger tongue-tie then tearing of Books. **1849–52** *Todd's Cycl. Anat.* IV. 1162/1 Tongue-tie.. is a congenital malformation. **1890** BILLINGS *Nat. Med. Dict., Tongue-tie*, abnormal shortness of the frænum linguæ, or adhesion of the tongue to the floor of the mouth.

tongue-tie ('tʌŋtaɪ), *v.* [f. TONGUE *sb.* + TIE *v.*, or more prob. a back-formation from next.] *trans.* To tie or confine the tongue of; to restrain or debar from speaking; to render speechless.

1555 J. ROGERS in Foxe *A. & M.* (1563) 1032/2 Your wycked lawes can not so tongue tye vs, but we will speake the truth. **1611** HEYWOOD *Gold. Age* I. i. Wks. 1874 III. 14 Let euerlasting silence Tong-tye the world. **1833** LAMB *Elia* Ser. II. Pref., The ligaments, which tongue-tied him, were loosened. **1851** D. JERROLD *St. Giles* xxxii. 335 Her face was livid with agony, that seemed to tongue-tie her.

Hence '**tongue-ˌtier**, that which ties the tongue: see quots.; '**tongue-ˌtying** *vbl. sb.* (*lit.* and *fig.*).

1754–64 SMELLIE *Midwif.* I. 428 Tongue-tying is easily remedied by introducing the forefinger into the child's mouth, raising up the tongue, and snipping the bridle with a pair of Scissars. **1869** *Routledge's Ev. Boy's Ann.* 469 This tongue-tying was the severest part of our watch. **1883** *Athenæum* 24 Nov. 675/3 [It] shows a woman wearing a branks, or tongue-tier. **1905** *Daily Chron.* 29 Aug. 4/6 There are names.. that demand shortening, tongue-tiers such as Giggleswick, which almost necessarily dwindles into Gilzick.

tongue-tied ('tʌŋtaɪd), *ppl. a.* [Locative comb. f. TONGUE *sb.* + TIED *ppl. a.*; becoming at length pa. pple. of TONGUE-TIE *v.*] Tied as to or in the tongue.

1. Having the frænum of the tongue too short, so that its movement is impeded or confined; incapable of distinct utterance from this cause; also, unable to speak, dumb (*poet.*).

1530 PALSGR. 282/1 Tongetyed, *qui a le filet.* **16..** SWINBURNE *Spousals* (1686) 19 Until that time they are as it were Tongue-tied, being unable to speak. **1707** J. STEVENS tr. *Quevedo's Com. Wks.* (1709) 389 If she were deaf, and Tongue-ty'd. **1849–52** *Todd's Cycl. Anat.* IV. 1153/2 The tongue may be unnaturally fixed.. the individual thus circumstanced being *tongue-tied*.

2. *fig.* Restrained or debarred from speaking or free expression from any cause; speechless, mute, dumb, silent; also reticent, reserved.

1529 MORE *Dyaloge* I. Wks. 107/2 He is of nature nothing tonge tayed. **1571** GOLDING *Calvin on Ps.* iii. 5 He himselfe was not tungtyde, but rather lifted up his voyce. **1576** GASCOIGNE *Steele Gl.* (Arb.) 57 Nor none serue God, but only tongtide men. **1600** HOLLAND *Livy* X. xix. 364 A dumbe and tongue-tide [*elinguis*] Consull. **1640** YORKE *Union Hon.*, *Commend. Verses*, Criticks be tongue-ti'd, stand, admire. **1734** tr. *Rollin's Anc. Hist.* XVIII. i. (1827) VII. 357 Fear kept them all tongue-tied and dumb. **1886** STEVENSON *Kidnapped* xxvi, I was.. sitting tongue-tied between shame and merriment.

Hence '**tongue-tiedness.**

1597 A. M. tr. *Guillemeau's Fr. Chirurg.* 24/2 When as we would cut the tunge-tyednes in yonge children nuely borne. **1661** LOVELL *Hist. Anim. & Min.* 348 The ancylosis, or tongue-tiednesse, caused, by the vinculum; it's cured, by cutting the same with a pair of cisers or sharp knife. **1894** MRS. H. WARD *Marcella* I. 59.

tonguey ('tʌŋɪ), *a.* Also 4–5 tungy, 7–9 tonguy. [f. TONGUE *sb.* + -Y.]

1. Full of 'tongue' or talk; talkative, loquacious (now *U.S.* and *dial.*); of hounds, 'giving tongue'.

1382 WYCLIF *Ecclus.* viii. 4 Striue thou not with a tungy man. *a* **1774** R. FERGUSSON *Sandie & Willie* 55 A tonguey woman's noisy plea. **1836** *Life on the Lakes* I. 54 (Thornton) We had on board a very tonguey Yankee lawyer. **1855** EGERTON-WARBURTON *Hunting Songs* (1877) 102 Your babblers draft, as we our tonguey hounds. **1896** HOWELLS *Impressions & Exp.* 39 There were some men.. tongueyer than the rest.

2. That is so 'in tongue' or 'in word', not 'in deed' (cf. 1 John iii. 18). *nonce-use.*

1612 W. SCLATER *Chr. Strength* 10 Alas! how many bare, tonguy Christians! Linguists only, in religion.

3. Of the nature of the tongue; produced or modified by the tongue; lingual.

1859 F. FRANCIS *Newton Dogvane* (1888) 25 He set that tonguey pendulum of his going. **1885** H. C. DEACON in Grove *Dict. Mus.* IV. 321/1 The quality of the voice.. will be tonguey, throaty, palatal, or veiled, according to the part thus unnecessarily brought into play.

Hence '**tonguiness.**

1607 COLLINS *Serm.* (1608) 77 Some mens silence profits the Church of Christ more than all their tonguinesse can doe it hurt. **1910** *Boston* (Mass.) *Transcript* 16 July 2/3 The natural gift of what the old Yankee horse traders would have called tonguiness.

tonguing ('tʌŋɪŋ), *vbl. sb.* [f. TONGUE *v.* + -ING[1].] The action of the verb TONGUE in various senses (see the verb); *spec.* in playing the flute and other wind instruments: see quot. 1880.

1682 D'URFEY *Injured Princess* II. iv, Tonguing, fingering and fighting, don't please her, The Devil's in her. **1687** WOOD *Life* (O.H.S.) III. 247. **1763** MILLS *Pract. Husb.* IV. 217 The third method [of whip-grafting], which is an improvement of the last, is properly named *tipping* or *tonguing*. **1832** J. P. KENNEDY *Swallow B.* xli, The tonguing of this dog was followed by the quick yelping of four or five others. **1862** *Times* 7 Mar., The tonguing and grooving by which the Warrior's plates are dovetailed together. **1880** W. H. STONE in Grove *Dict. Mus.* I. 459/2 s.v. *Double tongueing*, Single tongueing,.. signifies the starting of the reed-vibrations by a sharp touch from the tip of the tongue... Single tongueing is phonetically represented by a succession of the lingual letter T, as in the word 'rat-tat-tat'. Double tongueing aims at alternating the linguo-dental explosive T with another explosive consonant produced differently, such as the linguo-palatals D or K, thus relieving the muscles by alternate instead of repeated action. **1895** H. CALLAN *Fr. Clyde to Jordan* 136 You must give them a right good 'tonguing'.

b. The furnishing of boards with tongues (TONGUE *sb.* 14 j); *concr.* the tongues of boards collectively.

1841 *Civil Eng. & Arch. Jrnl.* IV. 22/2 Although the deal tongueing has been destroyed by the worms, the green-heart planking remains untouched and perfectly sound.

toni ('təʊnɪ). *India.* Also **tonee, tony.** [a. Tamil: see DHONEY, DONEY.] †**a.** A small South Indian sailing vessel. **b.** A dug-out boat. **c.** A ferry boat.

1582 N. LICHEFIELD tr. *Castanheda's Conq. E. Ind.* I. xxiv. 60 There came towarde him to yͤ number of lx. Tonys full of Souldiers. **1704** *Collect. Voy.* (Churchill) III. 734/2 Four Fishermen were coming to us in a *Tony* or Fisher-boat. **1881** *Naval Encycl.* 811/2 *Tonee*, a canoe formerly used on the coast of Malabar. **1914** *Yachting Monthly* June 83/2 Inshore the flood tide had already turned the tony and bunder boats, the former a canoe-like craft hollowed straight out from the tree. **1917** *Ibid.* Sept. 268/2 The large Tonis are between 25 and 30 feet long. **1946** *Mariner's Mirror* XXXII. 209 The ordinary Malabar dug-out, called *toni* in Bombay. **1978** *Times of India* 15 Jan. 3/5 Contraband radios and cassettes .. were seized from a toni, Laxmi, on Thursday at the Ferry Wharf.

-tonia ('təʊnɪə), also anglicized as **-tony**, terminal element [f. Gr. τόν-ος TONE *sb.* + -IA[1]] with the sense 'tone, condition' in terms in *Med.*, as HYPOTONIA, SYMPATHICOTONIA.

tonic ('tɒnɪk), *a.* and *sb.* [ad. Gr. τονικ-ός of or for stretching, f. τόν-ος: see TONE *sb.* Cf. mod.L. *tonicus*, F. *tonique* (16th c. in Godef. *Compl.*).]

A. *adj.*

1. *Phys.* and *Path.* **a.** Pertaining to, consisting in, or producing tension: *esp.* in relation to the muscles.

tonic contraction, continuous muscular contraction without relaxation. ***tonic convulsion*** or ***spasm***, one characterized by such contraction (opp. to CLONIC). † ***tonic motion***, a former term for a state of continuous tension in the muscles such as that which keeps the body erect (cf. quot. 1646 s.v. TONICAL 1).

1649 BULWER *Pathomyot.* II. i. 83 Action without motion of the Muscle, is called a Tonique motion. **1666** J. SMITH *Old Age* (1676) 62 They [muscles] can perform adduction, abduction; flexion, extension; pronation, supination, the Tonick motion, circumgiration. **1756** P. BROWNE *Jamaica* 381 Of worms or insects that have no solid props within themselves, but perform all their weakly motions by a mere tonic or muscular power. **1799** *Med. Jrnl.* II. 340 The increased tonic motion of the vessels which the Stahlians.. considered as the efficient cause of inflammation. **1830** R. KNOX *Béclard's Anat.* 135 Motions of tonic contraction, augmented in many places by the action of the elastic tissue.

1834 J. Forbes *Laennec's Dis. Chest* (ed. 4) 375 We cannot regard the tonic spasm of the bronchi, or even perhaps of the air-cells, as impossible; since every muscle is susceptible of spasm. **1899** *Allbutt's Syst. Med.* VII. 351 Tonic or clonic convulsions sometimes occur [in positive hæmorrhage].

b. Pertaining to, or maintaining, the tone or normal healthy condition of the tissues or organs (cf. tone *sb.* 7). See also 2.

1684 T. Burnet *Th. Earth* I. 207 The tone or tonick disposition of the organs whereby they perform their several functions. **1813** J. Thomson *Lect. Inflam.* 65 Stahl's ideas respecting the tonic or vital action of the capillary vessels. **1855** H. Spencer *Princ. Psychol.* (1873) I. I. v. 93 This pervading activity of the muscles is called their tonic state.

2. *Med.*, etc. Having the property of increasing or restoring the tone or healthy condition and activity of the system or organs; strengthening, invigorating, bracing. (Of remedies or remedial treatment, and hence of air, climate, etc.) Also ***tonic water***, a non-alcoholic carbonated drink containing quinine or another bitter as a stimulant of appetite and digestion; a drink or glass of this; ***tonic wine***, weak, flavoured wine sold as a medicinal tonic.

1756 C. Lucas *Ess. Waters* III. 205 Their vapor..is found to be more tonic. **1800** *Med. Jrnl.* IV. 160 A long course of steel, in conjunction with tonic bitters. **1867** Aug. J. E. Wilson *Vashti* xxiv, Be sure she takes that tonic mixture three times a day. **1885** G. Meredith *Diana* v, She spoke of the weather—frosty, but tonic. **1899** *Graphic* 11 Mar. 320/1 (Advt.), His Holiness the Pope writes that he has fully appreciated the beneficent effects of this Tonic Wine. **1926** *Daily Colonist* (Victoria, B.C.) 6 July 9/6 (Advt.), Schweppes famous British table waters. Soda water,.. ginger beer, tonic water. **1958** S. Hyland *Who goes Hang?* xi. 53 'What will there be to drift?' asked Mrs. Kimmis.. over the top of a tonic water. **1970** G. Greer *Female Eunuch* 276 Perhaps she can try a glass or two of tonic wine? More likely her G.P. will..prescribe a happiness pill. **1982** G. F. Newman *Men with Guns* x. 74 He drank gin swamped with Indian tonic water.

fig. **1848** Kingsley *Saint's Trag.* II. ix, God brings thee The tonic cup I feared to mix. **1867** H. Latham *Black & White* p. viii, One great benefit to be derived from a visit to America is its tonic effect upon the mind.

3. *Mus.* **a.** Formerly applied to the key-note of a composition (*tonic note*), now called simply *tonic* (see B. 2); now (*attrib.* use of B. 2), Pertaining to or founded upon the tonic or key-note: as ***tonic chord***, a chord having the tonic for its root; ***tonic pedal***, the key-note sustained as a pedal (*sb.* 4).

1760 Stiles in *Phil. Trans.* LI. 773 Two modes with the same tonic note, the one neither acuter nor graver than the other, make no part of the old system of modes. **1867** Macfarren *Harmony* (1892) 56 A tonic pedal..has the effect of confirming the conclusion indicated by a perfect cadence. **1880** Stainer *Composition* §14 The third degree of the scale can form a portion of a tonic chord, or chord of the relative minor.

b. *Tonic Sol-fa*: name of a system of teaching music, esp. vocal music, introduced by the Rev. John Curwen about 1850, in which the seven notes of the ordinary major scale in any key are sung to syllables written *doh, ray, me, fah, soh, lah, te* (modifications of the older *do, re, mi, fa, sol, la, si*: see these words and gamut), and indicated in the notation by the initials d, r, m, etc.; *doh* always denoting the tonic or key-note, and the remaining syllables indicating the relation to it of the other notes of the scale. Chiefly *attrib.* Hence **Tonic Sol-faist** (-fɑːist), one who advocates or uses the Tonic Sol-fa system.

1852 J. Curwen (*title*) Pupils' Manual of the Tonic Sol-Fa Method of teaching to sing; and the Tonic Sol-Fa School Music. **1883** *American* VI. 174 At the annual meeting in London..of the Tonic Sol-Fa College.

1881 Broadhouse *Mus. Acoustics* 372 We agree most cordially with our friends the tonic sol-faists. **1895** *Daily News* 30 Dec. 5/2 So many of the Welsh are Tonic Solfaists.

4. a. Pertaining to musical tone or quality.

1795 Mason *Ch. Mus.* i. 42 This solemn instrument [the organ]... In point of tonic power, I presume, it will be allowed preferable to all others.

b. Pertaining or relating to tone or accent in speech; indicating the tone or accent of spoken words or syllables; characterized by distinctions of tone or accent. ***tonic accent*** (= F. *accent tonique*), the stress-accent of a word.

1849 *Jrnl. Indian Archipelago* III. 668 The influence of this habit of the tonic languages is still largely impressed on their Malay-Polynesian and Turonian descendants and congeners. **1859** S. W. Williams (*title*) A Tonic Dictionary of the Chinese language in the Canton dialect. **1867** Howells *Ital. Journ.* 72 In their divine language, and with that ineffable tonic accent which no foreigner perfectly acquires. **1868** Max Müller *Stratif. Lang.* 42 The Thibetan is..tonic and monosyllabic. **1894** A. H. Keane in *Church Mission. Intell.* Oct. 723 Thus the monosyllable *pa* will be toned in six or more different ways to represent so many original dissyllables, *pada, pake, pana, pasa, pata*.. and some of the Chinese and Shan dialects have..as many as ten or twelve such tones... Hence these languages are now called isolating and tonic rather than isolating and monosyllabic. **1896** —— *Ethnol.* xii. 324 A far more important feature than the length of the words is their tonic utterance.

B. *sb.*

1. a. *Med.* A tonic medicine, application, or agent.

[**1693** tr. *Blancard's Phys. Dict.* (ed. 2), *Tonica*, those things which being externally applied to, and rubb'd into the Limbs, strengthen the Nerves and Tendons.] **1799** *Med. Jrnl.* II. 116 When..the hectic symptoms were subdued, and only weakness remained, tonics completed the cure. **1875** H. C. Wood *Therap.* (1879) 54 Substances..which, when taken internally, act upon the nutrition of the various tissues so as to restore lost tone... Such substances are known as tonics. **1897** *Badminton Mag.* IV. 380 My hair tonic costs eight-and-sixpence a bottle.

b. *fig.* An invigorating or bracing influence.

1840 Clough *Early Poems* i. 8 The tonic of a wholesome pride. **1868** Farrar *Silence & V.* viii. (1875) 136 It is the strongest of moral tonics.

c. Tonic water.

1935, 1949 [see *gin and tonic* s.v. gin *sb.*[2] 2 a]. **1972** M. J. Bosse *Incident at Naha* ii. 108 We all had vodka and tonics.

2. *Mus.* **a.** = key-note *sb.* 1.

tonic major or *minor*: that key (major or minor) which has the same key-note as a given key (minor or major).

1806 Callcott *Mus. Gram.* II. iv. 131 The Tonic Minor must have in its Signature another flat. **1889** E. Prout *Harmony* i. §12 The first note of the scale is called the Tonic, or Key-note. This is the note which gives its name to the scale and key.

b. The principal key of a musical composition or passage; the home key.

1896 G. Grove *Beethoven & his Nine Symphonies* 8 The *Coda* which closes the first movement, after repeating in the tonic the phrase already quoted as No. 5, combines the wind instrument passage with the first subject. **1923** E. Evans *Beethoven's Nine Symphonies* I. 177 At the third portion we have a new treatment of the first part of the same subject.. leading to a triumphant cadence in C as tonic. **1961** A. Hopkins *Talking about Symphonies* i. 20 The key you start in is called the 'Tonic'. **1979** D. R. Hofstadter *Gödel, Escher, Bach* v. 130 With the inversion of the theme for our melody, we begin in D as if that had always been the tonic—but we modulate back to G after all, which means that we pop back into the tonic, and the *B*-section ends properly.

Hence **'tonic** *v.*, *trans.* to act as a tonic upon, to invigorate, 'brace up'; to administer a tonic to; whence **'tonicking** *vbl. sb.*

1825 *New Monthly Mag.* XV. 199/1 It tonicked the sedentary stomach into unwonted vigour. **1889** Mrs. C. Praed *Romance Station* 126 She needed..tonicking;..her blood didn't nourish her brain properly.

Tonica, var. Tunica[2].

† **'tonical**, *a.* *Obs.* [f. tonic *a.*: see -ical.]

1. = tonic A. 1.

1586 Bright *Melanch.* xxvi. 149 The spirits..are the authors by tonicall motion of erection [of muscles]. **1646** Sir T. Browne *Pseud. Ep.* III. i. 105 One kinde of motion, relating unto that which Physitians (from Galen) doe name extensive or tonicall. **1693** J. Beaumont *On Burnet's Th. Earth* II. 88 The Tone or tonical Disposition of the Organs, whereby they perform their several Functions. **1733** Cheyne *Eng. Malady* II. xii. §2 (1734) 240 A Defect in their [Muscles] innate Power of Contraction and Tonical Nature.

2. = tonic A. 4.

1656 Blount *Glossogr.*, *Tonical*, pertaining to tone, note, tune, or accent. **1677** Plot *Oxfordsh.* 7 Tonical [Echoes], such as return the voice but once, nor that neither, except adorned with some peculiar Musical note. **1737** *Gentl. Mag.* VII. 9/1 Whatever Musical or Tonical Notes were expressed in the Accents of the Text.

tonically ('tɒnɪkəlɪ), *adv.* [f. tonic *a.* or tonical: see -ically.] In a tonic manner.

1. By or in relation to tension; in the way of tonic contraction (see tonic A. 1).

1885 Romanes *Jelly-Fish* viii. 209 In..Sarsia the irritability of the tonically contracting manubrium is higher than that of the rhythmically contracting bell. **1904** *Brit. Med. Jrnl.* 17 Dec. 1627 The muscles on the right side are somewhat more tonically contracted than those on the left.

2. As a tonic (see tonic B. 1 a, b); so as to invigorate or 'brace up'.

1873 Curwen *Hist. Booksellers* 304 The difficulty..might act tonically. **1889** Crouter in *Amer. Ann. Deaf* July 182 The agreeable labor of planting and harvest, which tonically would be of service to them.

tonicity (təʊ'nɪsɪtɪ). [f. tonic + -ity. So mod.F. *tonicité* (Roquefort, 1829).] **1.** *Phys.* and *Path.* **a.** Tonic quality or condition; the property of possessing tone (see tone *sb.* 7); the normal state of elastic tension of living muscles, arteries, etc., by which the tone of the organs is maintained.

1824 Bostock *Elem. Syst. Physiol.* I. iii. 176 Besides contractility,.. the muscular fibre has been supposed to possess another specific..quality, which has been called tone or tonicity. **1834** *Good's Study Med.* (ed. 4) I. 242 Even the tonicity of the skin seems to be quite destroyed. **1851** Carpenter *Man. Phys.* (ed. 2) 212 These same muscles exhibit a tendency to a moderate and permanent contraction, which is not shown by them when they are dead ..; this endowment..is called Tonicity. **1899** *Allbutt's Syst. Med.* VIII. 75 An apparently increased tonicity of the muscles.

b. Of spasm: see tonic *a.* 1.

1897 *Allbutt's Syst. Med.* II. 695 Tetanus..may be distinguished by the shorter incubation period, the tonicity of the spasms [etc.].

2. *Linguistics.* The fact or property of having a phonetic emphasis at a certain place in an intonation pattern.

1963 M. A. K. Halliday in *Archivum Linguisticum* XV. 13 Second [is]..the placing of the tonic syllable..—the location, in each tone group, of the pretonic and tonic sections... I propose to call these three systems 'tonality', 'tonicity' and 'tone'. **1966** G. N. Leech *Eng. in Advertising* ix. 88 Devices of graphic emphasis such as underlining and italics can be used to represent special tonicity in speech. **1973** [see nucleus *sb.* 12 a].

tonicize ('tɒnɪsaɪz), *v.* [f. as prec. + -ize.] *trans.* **a.** To render tonic, give tone to. **b.** To invigorate as with a tonic. Hence **'tonicizing** *ppl. a.*

1884 *Brachet's Aix-les-Bains* I. 96 Thus more effectually tonicizing the cutaneous covering. **1890** *N. & Q.* 7th Ser. IX. 141/2 This would spread a tonicizing analeptic influence throughout our English world of readers.

tonico-, combining form from Gr. τονικός tonic, used to form compounds in sense 'combining a tonic and (some other) quality': see quot.

1840 Pereira *Mat. Med.* II. 1189 In its remote effects myrrh partakes of both the tonic and stimulant characters, and hence some have denominated it a *tonico-stimulant*; and as its stimulant powers are analogous to those of the balsams, it has also been called a *tonico-balsamic*.

'tonify, *v.* [app. f. F. *ton* (ton[3]) or Eng. tone + -i)fy: in mod.F. *tonifier*.]

† **1.** ('tɒnɪfaɪ.) *trans.* To impart a good 'ton' to; to make fashionable or stylish. *Obs.*

1786 Mrs. Grant *Lett. fr. Mountains* (1807) II. xxiii. 118 You can imagine no set of people more polished, powdered, tonified and englified, than they are.

2. ('təʊnɪfaɪ.) = tonicize a.

1858 J. H. Bennet *Nutrition* vi. 185 The cutaneous circulation is tonified and vitalized. **1892** *Star* 29 Aug. 4/1 Tepid water..tonifies the skin and prevents wrinkles.

tonight (tə'naɪt, tʊ-), *adv.* and *sb.* Forms: see night. Also as two words and with hyphen. [OE. *tó niht*, to *prep.* A. 7 + night. Cf. today.]

A. *adv.*

1. On this very night (i.e. the night now present).

a **1300** *Cursor M.* 11246 (Cott.), I bring yow word wit ioi and blis, Born to night your sauueour es! **1670** Narborough *Jrnl.* in *Acc. Sev. Late Voy.* I. (1711) 83 Much Wind to Night at Northwest. **1797** Nelson in Nicolas *Disp.* (1846) VII. p. cxlv, Half past 3 A.M. I was merely a spectator to-night. **1832** Tennyson *May Queen* II. ii, To-night I saw the sun set. **1842** —— *Audley Court* 69, I go to-night: I come to-morrow morn.

b. On any night (as contrasted with the next day). Cf. today A. 1 b.

1500–20 Dunbar *Poems* xxiii. 5 And with thy nychtbouris glaidly len and borrow His chance to nycht it may be thyne tomorrow. **1557** North *Gueuara's Diall Pr.* I. xxviii. (1568) 41 For many are layde to nighte into their graue, which the next day following [are] thought to be aliue.

2. On the night following this day.

c **1000** Ælfric *Numb.* xxii. 19 Ac beoþ her toniht, and abidaþ andsware. *c* **1000** —— *Hom.* II. 104 Ðu stunta, nu toniht [Luke xii. 20 on þisse nihte] ðu scealt ðin lif alætan. *c* **1205** Lay. 709 Anacletus leofe freond to-niht þu scalt faren. *c* **1275** *Passion of Our Lord* 104 in *O.E. Misc.* 40 He me schal bitraye to nyht er he slepe. *c* **1470** Henry *Wallace* XI. 495, I sall cum out..to morn, Or ellys to nycht. **1539** Bible (Great) *Ruth* iii. 2 Beholde, he wenoweth barleye to nyght in the thresshyng floure. **1596** Shaks. *Tam. Shr.* IV. i. 201 Last night she slept not, nor to night she shall not. **1605** —— *Macb.* I. v. 59 Duncan comes here to Night. **1876** Morris *Sigurd* (1877) 237 Tonight shall be the weaving, and tomorn the web shall ye win.

† **3.** On the night just past; last night. (Perhaps only said in the morning.) *Obs.* exc. *dial.*

c **1205** Lay. 28011 Þa axede hine an uæir cniht, Lauerd hu hauest þu iuaren to-niht? *c* **1290** *Beket* 1542 in *S. Eng. Leg.* I. 150 To-niȝt ase ich was a-slepe a wonder metinge me com. **1390** Gower *Conf.* I. 73 No mannes myht Mai do that he hath do to nyht. **1592** Shaks. *Rom. & Jul.* I. iv. 50. I dreampt a dreame to night. **1610** B. Jonson *Alch.* I. ii, *Sub.* .. The Queene of Faerie do's not rise, Till it be noone. *Fac.* Not, if she daunc'd to night. **1641** Brome *Jovial Crew* III. Wks. 1873 III. 393 Ease call'st thou it? Didst thou sleep to night? **1798** J. Jefferson *Let. to J. Boucher* 23 Feb. (MS.), [Hampshire expressions] *To-night* for *last night*, or *yesternight*.

B. *sb.* This night, or the night after this day.

a **1300** *Cursor M.* 3543 (Cott.) Þou sal neuer forth fra to night In þi forbirth do claim na right. **1601** Shaks. *Twel. N.* II. iii. 142 Sweet Sir Toby be patient for to night. **1709** Prior *Thief & Cordelier* ix, He that's hang'd before noon, ought to think of to-night. **1799** Wordsw. *Lucy Gray* iv, To-night will be a stormy night—You to the town must go. **1908** [Miss E. Fowler] *Betw. Trent & Ancholme* 212 To-night is cloudy and dull.

Tonikan, var. Tunica(n.

'toning, *vbl. sb.* and *ppl. a.* [f. tone *v.* + -ing.]

a. In various senses: see the vb.

1660 [see tone *v.* 3]. **1708** Ozell tr. *Boileau's Lutrin* IV. (1730) 192 The Toning of the Tenebrae. **1796** Southey *Lett. fr. Spain* (1799) 399 The defects of metre are disguised by toning. **1843** Ruskin *Mod. Paint.* I. II. II. ii. §15 This toning down and connection of the colours actually used. **1861** *Photogr. News Alm.* in *Circ. Sc.* (*c* 1865) I. 155/1 Sufficient water tends..to secure regular toning. *Ibid.*, Several different forms of the alkaline gold toning bath have been proposed. **1878** Abney *Photogr.* (1881) 140 A trace of hypochlorous acid was found in the toning solution. **1891** Meredith *One of our Conq.* xxxv, She struck a toneing warmth through his intelligence.

b. *spec.* Having or being a colour that tones in (with something previously mentioned). ***toning lotion***, a lotion, usu. slightly astringent, used for cosmetic purposes to refine the texture of the skin.

1960 *Harper's Bazaar* (U.K. ed.) Aug. 22/2 An easy seven-eighths suit, that wraps around a simple toning dress. **1965** *Ibid.* (U.K. ed.) June 40 A toning lotion beneath base provides a protective film beneath make-up. **1970** *Cabinet Maker & Retail Furnisher* 30 Oct. 204/1 It is available in toning shades of browns, blues, reds and greens. **1977** *Sunday Times* 6 June 43/1 The attack on the Cooper pores was maintained with Fresh Toning Lotion. **1982** BARR & YORK *Official Sloane Ranger Handbk.* 31/1 She has, naturally, a kilt, which she wears with toning tights.

tonish, tonnish (ˈtɒnɪʃ), *a.* Now *rare.* Also 8 ton-ish. [f. TON³ + -ISH¹.] Having 'ton'; fashionable, modish, stylish. Hence **ˈtonishly** *adv.*, **ˈtonishness**.

1778 *Crt. of Adultery* 6 The finer features of a Ton-ish face. **1779** MME. D'ARBLAY *Diary* 26 May, Lord Mordaunt, ..a pretty, languid, tonnish young man. **1780** *Ibid.* Apr., The young lady..half tonish, and half hoydenish. *Ibid.* May, Mrs. North, who is so famed for tonishness, exhibited herself in a more perfect undress than I ever before saw any lady..appear in. **1802** COLERIDGE *Lett.* I. 368, I should be a thing in vogue,—the very tonish poet. **1804** EUGENIA DE ACTON *Tale without Title* III. 14 Our elevated, spirited, and tonnish readers. **1825–9** MRS. SHERWOOD *Lady of Manor* I. vi. 242 The Dashwood family..spending their money in the most lavish and tonish style. **1872** C. D. WARNER *Saunterings* (1873) 11 A footman..wore the same colors; and the whole establishment was exceedingly tonnish. **1895** *Funk's Stand. Dict.*, Tonishly.

tonist (ˈtəʊnɪst). [f. TONE *sb.* + -IST.] An artist skilled in giving the proper tone to pictures.

1883 *Academy* 17 Mar. 193/1 Wilson was a wonderful tonist, a subtle colourist, a painter of *chiaroscuro*, a master of artificial and elegant composition. **1883** *St. James' Gaz.* 11 Apr., His powers as a draughtsman, modeller and tonist.

tonit, obs. Sc. form of TONED.

tonite (ˈtəʊnaɪt), *sb.* [f. L. *ton-āre* to thunder + -ITE¹.] A high explosive composed of pulverized gun-cotton impregnated with barium nitrate; cotton powder. Also *attrib.*

1881 RAYMOND *Mining Gloss.*, *Tonite*, a nitrated gun-cotton, used in blasting. **1883** V. D. MAJENDIE in *Standard* 19 Apr. 5/6 Explosives (such as dynamite, blasting gelatine, ..tonite, potentite). **1893** *Star* 28 Aug. 2/4 A tonite cartridge with a lighted fuse was thrown into the garden of a farmhouse at Euxton... An explosion occurred which almost wrecked the front of the house.

tonite (təˈnaɪt), *adv.* Simplified spelling of TONIGHT *adv.*, after NITE *sb.*², used chiefly in advertisements.

1968 R. CLAPPERTON *No News on Monday* iv. 35 Another placard announced..'Tonite, for one nite only, the fabulous Lisa Mundt.' **1971** *Black World* Mar. 55/1 They wud be up all nite tonite if they didn't wake up soon. **1976** *Leicester Mercury* 16 July (Advt.), Riverside disco. Tonite. All welcome.

tonitrual (təʊˈnɪtruːəl), *a. rare*⁻¹. [ad. rare late L. *tonitruāl-is* (L. Appuleius), f. *tonitru-s* thunder.] Pertaining to, or loaded with, thunder. So **toˈnitruant** *a.*, less regularly **tonitrant** (ˈtɒnɪtrənt) [ad. late L. *tonitruānt-em*, pres. pple. of *tonitruāre* to thunder (*Vulg.* Ps. lxxvi.)], thundering (*fig.*); **toˈnitruate** *v.* (less regularly **ˈtonitrate**) [late L. *tonitruāre*: see -ATE³], to thunder (*intr.* and *trans.*); **tonitruˈation**, thundering (in quot. 1689, ? explosion, or ? = FULMINATION 3); **ˈtonitruˌone**, a device for imitating thunder (see quot.); **toˈnitruous** *a.* (less regularly **ˈtonitrous**), full of or characterized by thunder, loud noise, or violent utterance; thundery; thundering.

a **1693** *Urquhart's Rabelais* III. li, They may..charging those *Tonitrual Guns afresh, turn the whole force of that Artillery against ourselves. **1861** M. COLLINS in *Temple Bar Mag.* I. 576 *Tonitrant writer in leading journal. **1907** *Times* 5 Sept. 8/1 Mr. Asche's robust personality and tonitruant style. **1623** COCKERAM, **Tonitrate*, to thunder. **1630** RANDOLPH *Shirley's Gratef. Servant* Pref. Verses, I cannot fulminate nor tonitruate words To puzzle intellects. **1656** S. HOLLAND *Zara* (1719) 60 This potent..Incantation ..was no sooner utter'd by the Inchantress, but it tonitruated horribly. **1666** G. HARVEY *Morb. Angl.* iv. 42 Winds and rumblings..whose tonitruating noise might have been heard at a great distance. **1658** PHILLIPS, **Tonitruation* (Lat.), a thundring. **1689** G. HARVEY *Curing Dis. by Expect.* xvii. 132 Minerals are to be disrobed of their Venom..by Tonitruation, Sublimation [etc.]. **1909** *Times* 13 Feb. 8/1 The '*tonitruone',..a piece of iron fastened to a wooden frame and shaken by hand, produces a strange thunderous sound—and is of M. Paderewski's own invention. **1606** DRUMM. OF HAWTH. *Answ. to Challenge* Wks. (1711) 233 Most *tonitruous, astonishing chevaliers, re-know ye, that we..do allow you this for answer. **1646** SIR T. BROWNE *Pseud. Ep.* II. v. 88 This tonnitruous and fulminating report of gunnes. *a* **1704** T. BROWN *Walk round Lond.*, *Thames* Wks. 1709 III. III. 64 By whom Billingsgate was much outdone in..tonitrous Verbosity, and malicious Scurrility. **1882** J. NICHOL *Amer. Lit.* ii. 51 Increase [Mather] had a tonitruous cogency in his perorations.

‖**tonjon** (ˈtɒndʒɒn). *E. Indies.* Also **tomjohn.** [Origin uncertain.] A kind of sedan chair slung on a pole and carried by four bearers.

c **1804** MRS. SHERWOOD *Autobiog.* xvi. (1854) 300, I had a tonjon, or open palanquin, in which I rode. **1838** *Lett. fr. Madras* (1843) 132 After dinner he took us out to see the town: we in our palanquins, and he in his tonjon. [*Note.* A kind of open sedan-chair.] **1885** G. S. FORBES *Wild Life in Canara* 132 It was not practicable to take a horse,..and I began the journey in a tonjon.

tonk (tɒŋk), *sb.*¹ *slang* (chiefly *Austral.*). [Etym. unknown.] **a.** A term of abuse: a fool, an idiot.

1941 BAKER *Dict. Austral. Slang* 77 *Tonk*, a simpleton or fool. (2) A dude or fop. (3) A general term of contempt. **1963** *New Society* 22 Aug. 5/1 'Bleg', 'thick boot', 'tonk', and 'greb' are all of uncertain origin, but probably have euphemistic backgrounds. **1965** [see NANA²].

b. A homosexual man.

1943 *Penguin New Writing* XVII. 83 The cook got my goat when he started trying to do the same thing. He was a tonk all right, just a real old auntie. **1965** H. PORTER *Stars Austral. Stage & Screen* 280 During the last ten years or more, there have been imported a coterie of *untalented* English homosexuals, English tonks unheard of outside their home country. **1970** *TV Times* (Austral.) 15 July 41/3 There was also a homosexual (who was referred to as a 'tonk' —thereby dating Mr Porter rather badly).

tonk (tɒŋk), *sb.*² Colloq. abbrev. of HONKY-TONK.

1937 [see *smoke-shop* s.v. SMOKE *sb.* 11]. **1948** *Common Ground* VIII. 38 The man who owned the little country Tonk was named Hamp... It was a one-room shanty store that doubled as a country bar room at night. **1960** C. HAMBLETT in J. Pudney *Pick of Today's Short Stories* XI. 138 None of the other rundown bars and tonks had anyone remotely like Lia.

tonk (tɒŋk), *v. colloq.* (chiefly *Sport*). [Echoic.] *trans.* **a.** To strike. **b.** To beat or defeat. Freq. *pass.*

1910 A. A. MILNE *Day's Play* 114 Wanting four to win, I fairly tried to tonk the leather. **1926** GALSWORTHY *Silver Spoon* III. i. 224 'He seems to enjoy the prospect of getting tonked,' murmured Michael. **1945** BAKER *Austral. Lang.* 207 Here are a few general expressions concerned with school life:..*to get tonked*, to receive corporal punishment. **1963** A. ROSS *Australia 63* ii. 55 Our spinners have been tonked about yet again by uncouth country batsmen.

‖**tonka** (ˈtɒŋkə). Also 8–9 **tonquin,** (9 **tonkin**), 9 **tonca, tonqua, tonga,** (**tonkay, tongo**). [*Tonka*, according to Focke, *Neger-Engelsch Woordenboek* 1855, the Negro name in Guyana of the bean (the Arawak Indian name being *cumaru*). So Fr. *tonka* or *tonca*, also *tongo* (Littré). Ulterior origin unknown. From the 18th century erroneously referred to *Tonquin* in Further India, and called *Tonquin bean*, in Du. 1770 *tonquin-boontje* (Hartsinck I. 82).]

1. tonka bean (Pg. *fava de tonca*, F. *fève tonka*, Du. *tonka-boon*): the black, fragrant, almond-shaped seed of a large leguminous tree, *Dipterix odorata* (also, according to Taubert in Engler & Prantl, 1894, of *D. oppositifolia*), of Brazil, Guyana, and adjacent regions, used for scenting snuff, and as an ingredient in perfumes. Also the tree itself.

1796 STEDMAN *Surinam* (1813) II. xxix. 388 The tonquin beans are said to grow in a thick pulp, something like a walnut, and on a large tree. **1830** LINDLEY *Nat. Syst. Bot.* 92 The volatile oil of the Coumarcouma odorata, or Tonka Bean, has been ascertained to be a peculiar principle called Coumarin. **1832** MACGILLIVRAY tr. *Humboldt's Trav.* xvii. (1836) 284 The fruit is known in Europe by the name of tonkay or tongo bean. **1833** *Penny Cycl.* I. 446/2 The fragrant tonga bean, which is..employed for perfuming snuff. **1852** TH. ROSS *Humboldt's Trav.* II. xix. 224 This fruit,..under the name of tonca, or Tonquin bean, is regarded as poisonous. **1862** *Contrib. fr. Br. Guiana to London Exhib.*, Cuamara or Tonka..yields the Tonquin bean. **1888** *Encycl. Brit.* XXIII. 443/2 Tonqua beans are used principally for scenting snuff. **1902** *Westm. Gaz.* 29 Oct. 4/2 When first engaged as pilot, Gatiño was gathering tonga beans in the forest.

2. tonka-bean (or *tonga-bean*) **wood**, the wood of *Alyxia buxifolia*, a Tasmanian evergreen shrub, also called *tonquin bean-tree*; scentwood.

1862 W. ARCHER *Products Tasmania* 41 Tonga Bean Wood (*Alyxia buxifolia*, Br.). The odor is similar to that of the Tonga Bean. A straggling sea-side shrub, three to five inches in diameter. **1866** *Treas. Bot.*, Tonga-bean wood, *Alyxia buxifolia*.

Tonkawa (ˈtɒŋkəwə), *sb.* (*a.*) [ad. Sp. *tancagueis, tancahues*, etc., prob. ad. Wichita (Waco dial.) *tonkawéya*, said to mean 'they all stay together'.] **a.** (A member of) an Indian people of Texas. **b.** The language of this people. Also *attrib.* or as *adj.*

1806 J. SIBLEY in *Message from President of U.S., communicating Discoveries made in exploring the Missouri by Captains Lewis & Clark* 74 Tankaways..have no land,.. but are always moving. **1870** J. C. DUVAL *Adventures Big-Foot Wallace* xxv. 148, I got it from 'Puppy's Foot', the Tonkawa chief. *Ibid.* xl. 245 My old friend 'Bah-pish-na-ba-hoo-tee' (which means 'Little blue whistling thunder' in the Tonkawa language). **1933** H. HOIJER *Tonkawa* (thesis, Columbia Univ.) p. ix, The Tonkawa appear to have been an important and warlike tribe living in central Texas during most of the 18th and 19th centuries. *Ibid.* p. x, Tonkawa is now spoken by only six persons—all of them past middle age. **1974** *Encycl. Brit. Micropædia* X. 43/3 By the 1970s the Tonkawa reservation in Oklahoma was reported to have a total population of about 60.

Tonkinese (tɒŋkɪˈniːz), *sb.* and *a.* Also 7–9 **Tonquinese,** 9 **Tong-, Tungkin(g)ese.** [f. *Ton-kin* (*Tongking*) + -ESE.] **A.** *sb.* **a.** The people of Tongking, a region of northern Vietnam on the border with China; also, a member of this people. **b.** The language of the Tonkinese. **B.** *adj.* Of or pertaining to the Tonkinese.

1697 [see BALACHONG]. **1726** SWIFT *Gulliver* II. III. i. 4 Several sorts of Goods, wherewith the Tonquinese usually trade to the Neighbouring Islands. **1806** J. BARROW *Voy. Cochinchina* ix. 251 The *Tung-quinese*, being in fact of the same character and disposition as the Chinese, were little able to cope with the hardy and disciplined troops. **1845** *Encycl. Metrop.* XXV. 673/1 In self-sufficiency and jealousy of strangers, the Tonkinese do not yield to their neighbours in China. **1884** W. MESNY *Tungking* xviii. 115 The protracted struggle that has been going on for long months is quite as much due to the action of China as to the Tungkingese themselves. **1885** J. G. SCOTT *France & Tongking* i. 11 Garnier and his lieutenants..enrolled many thousand Tongkinese auxiliaries. **1890** J. FRAZER *Golden Bough* I. i. 36 Many other peoples (Tonquinese, Hindoos, Chuwash, etc.) have adopted the same test of a suitable victim. **1926** H. A. FRANCK *East of Siam* xii. 220 In the mess that followed the Manchu conquest of China, a Tonkinese fisherman founded a new dynasty. **1934** WEBSTER, *Tonkinese*, the Annamese dialect of Tonkin. **1951** M. B. EMENEAU *Stud. Vietnamese (Annamese) Gram.* p. v, Tonkinese and Chochin Chinese are slightly differentiated from one another by differences of pronunciation and of vocabulary. **1983** C. MCCARRY *Last Supper* 172 Christopher met a fellow poet, a Tonkinese who had studied at the Sorbonne... The Tonkinese poet was a female.

tonlet (ˈtʌnlɪt). [ad. MF. *tonnel(l)et* short, full skirt, (also) *tonlet*, dim of *tonneau* cask (see TONNEL, -ELL).] A short skirt of armour; also, each of the overlapping horizontal bands of which this was sometimes made.

[*a* **1480** *Traictié de la Forme et Devis d'ung Tournoy* in *Œuvres Complètes du Roi René* (1844) II. 11 Le harnoys de corps est come une cuirasse ou comme ung harnoys à pié qu'on appelle tonnellet.] *a* **1486** in *Archaeologia* LVII (2nd Ser. VII. 1900) 43 *To arme a man...* Firste ye muste sette on Sabatones..& þe the breche of mayle And thē tonletis And thē brest And þē vambras [etc.]. **1894** *Antiquary* Jan. 26/2 Another suit, or rather part of one, of Henry VIII...is that which has been called the tonlet, or, as in the Tower inventories it is written, the trundlet suit. **1910** *Encycl. Brit.* II. 587/2 The surcoat being gone we see him armed in breast and back plate, his loins covered by a skirt of 'tonlets', as the defence of overlapping horizontal bands comes to be named. **1934** G. C. STONE *Gloss. Construction, Decoration & Use of Arms & Armor* 622/2 The tonlet suit was used mainly for fighting on foot, but was sometimes used in place of other leg armor when jousting at the barrier. It had wide, bell-shaped skirts of plate which were often solid and elaborately fluted with deep vertical folds... Sometimes it was made of horizontal plates. **1975** *Country Life* 3 July 45/3 The superb 'tonlet' or skirted armour made for King Henry VIII for foot combat in about 1512. **1983** *Daily Tel.* 18 Oct. 10 (*caption*) Henry VIII's tonlet armour ready to go on view at the Burlington House Fair.

tonnage (ˈtʌnɪdʒ), *sb.* Also 5–6 **tonage,** (6 **to(u)ndage, t(o)unage**), 7– **tunnage,** (8 **tunnige**). [In sense 1, a. OF. *tonnage* (1300 in Du Cange), *tonaige* (1374 in Godef.), *tonage* (1477 ibid.), f. *tonne* TUN: see -AGE, also med. (Anglo-)L. *tonnāgium* (Du Cange); in senses 2–7, f. TON *sb.*¹ + -AGE.]

I. Charge, duty, or payment of so much per tun or ton.

1. *English Hist.* A tax or duty formerly levied upon wine imported in tuns or casks, at the rate of so much for every tun. Commonly in association with *poundage*: see POUNDAGE *sb.*¹ 1.

By some historical writers and in some dictionaries written *tunnage* for distinction's sake, and to emphasize the connexion with TUN *sb.*; but *tonnage* is the more usual form.

Tonnage and poundage were first levied in the 14th c., and were granted for life to several sovereigns, beginning with Edward IV. They were abolished by 27 Geo. III c. 13, in 1787.

1422 *Rolls of Parlt.* IV. 173/2 A subsidie of Tonage and Poundage.., that is to sey of every Tunne iii s; and xii d of every Pounde. *c* **1460** FORTESCUE *Abs. & Lim. Mon.* vi. (1885) 123 Pondage and tonnage mey not be rekenned as parcell off the revenues wich the kynge hath ffor the mayntenance off his estate, bi cause it aught to be applied only to þe kepynge off the see. **1568** GRAFTON *Chron.* II. 509 *margin*, This is the custome whiche we nowe paye, called Tonnage and poundage. **1640** PYM in Rushw. *Hist. Coll.* III. (1692) I. 22 There is First Tunnage and Poundage, and the late new Book of Rates taken by Prerogative, without Grant of Parliament. **1647** CLARENDON *Hist. Reb.* III. §215 Great Complaint had been made, 'that Tonnage and Poundage' (which is the duty and subsidy paid by the Merchant upon Trade) 'had been taken by the King without consent of Parliament'. **1765** BLACKSTONE *Comm.* I. viii. 304 Tonnage was a duty upon all wines imported, over and above the prisage and butlerage aforesaid. **1845** MᶜCULLOCH *Taxation* II. v. (1852) 235 The duties of tonnage and poundage, of which mention is so frequently made in English history, were customs duties. **1875** STUBBS *Const. Hist.* II. xvi. 424 The custom of tunnage and poundage, two shillings on the tun of wine and sixpence on the pound [i.e. pound's worth] of merchandise which had been granted the year before [1371] for the protection of the merchant navy.

†**2.** A charge for the hire of a ship of so much a ton (of her burden) per week or month. *Obs.*

1512 *French Wars of 1512–13* (Navy Rec. Soc. 1897) 5 (*Charge of the Marie Roose*)..Also for toundage, after 3d. a ton a weke, 500 tons: nihil, quia navis regis. *Ibid.* 7 Also for toundage of 400 tons: 60*l.* *Ibid.* 12 Somme total of the charges of the 22 shippes afore said, as in vitayle, wages, deddeshares and toundage for the first 3 mounthes: 5608*l.* 2*s.* *Ibid.* 34 Toundage after 12d a ton a mounth, for 9 shippes tyght 1790 tons, amountyng for 3 mounthes to 268*l.*

10s. *c* **1525** in *Archæologia* (1883) XLVII. 335 To David Miller apon the wages and vitailles and tondage of the *Vyncent*, of Eryth, xxxvij. li. ix. s. iij. d... To Christofer Coo apon wages and vitailles and tonage of diverse shippes, dclxxix. li. vj. s. viij. d. **1587** *Spanish War* (Navy Rec. Soc.) 237 For tonnage of the 6 ships for 3 months 141 0 0.

3. A charge or payment per ton on cargo or freight; e.g. that payable at any port or wharf, or on a canal; also, sometimes, that received or earned by a railway (quot. 1838).

1617 MINSHEU *Ductor, Tonnage*.. I haue heard it also a Dutie due to the Mariners for vnloading their shippe arriued in any Hauen, after the rate of euerie Tonne. **1649** G. DANIEL *Trinarch., Hen. IV*, cccxiv, The French.. surprised as they stood In harbour, by some English Lords, make out The Tunnage lost, & forfeit stock to boot. **1708** J. C. *Compl. Collier* (1845) 53 What other Additions and Allowances of Tunnige for other Wares and Merchandize as are paid at the Ports aforesaid. **1789** *Constitution U.S.* I. §10 No state shall, without the consent of the Congress, lay any duty of tonnage. **1806** *Gazetteer Scotl.* 409 [Paisley] to defray the expence by a tonnage of 8d per ton upon all vessels navigating the Cart, except those loaded with coal. **1828** WEBSTER, *Tonnage*.. a duty, toll or rate payable on goods per tun, transported on canals. **1838** *Civil Eng. & Arch. Jrnl.* I. 322/2 It was admitted.. that the amount of tonnage received by the Railway Company.. was 1,236*l.* 0*s.* 6*d.* per mile. *Ibid.*, They would allow.. 30*l.* 18*s.* per mile, or 2¼ per cent. for the collection of the tonnage.

II. Carrying capacity, weight, etc., in tons.

4. The carrying capacity of a ship expressed in tons of 100 cubic feet (see TON[1] 2).

Originally the number of tun casks of wine which a merchant ship could carry. Afterwards estimated by measurements and calculations which gave rough approximations to the actual cubic content (*Old Measurement*). Later arrived at by measurements of breadth and depth at determinate distances, from which by a mathematical calculation (see Merchant Shipping Acts from 1854 onward, and subsequently Merchant Shipping (Tonnage) Regulations) the cubic content of the space under the tonnage-deck (***under-deck tonnage***) is obtained. To this is added the volume of certain specified enclosed spaces above this deck, the result being the ***gross (register) tonnage***. A deduction is made from the latter for those parts of the ship which are deemed to be non-earning, to give the ***net (register) tonnage*** or ***register tonnage***, for which vessels are registered, and on which the assessment of dues and charges on shipping is based. Systems of measurement vary from country to country, but there have been moves towards international standardization. The ***Suez Canal tonnage*** makes a smaller deduction for engine-space, etc., and approximates more closely to the gross tonnage. ***dead-weight tonnage*** represents the ship's carrying capacity, expressed in tonnes. ***displacement tonnage***, the weight of water in tonnes displaced by a fully-laden ship, formerly used to express the tonnage of warships; superseded by *standard displacement*.

1718 STEELE *Acc. Fishpool* 170 There is a great difference between a shipwright's and merchant's way of calculating the tonnage of a ship. *Ibid.*, The shipwright's way is to multiply the length of the keel by the middle-breadth, and that product by half the breadth and then they divide the last product by 94, and the quotient is the tunnage. **1748** *Anson's Voy.* III. vii. 354 The duty.. paid by all ships.. according to their tunnage. **1751** LABELYE *Westm. Br.* 86 Of more Tonnage or Capacity than a Man of War of 40 Guns. **1836** W. IRVING *Astoria* III. 133 Coasting vessels.. of small tonnage and draft of water, fitted for coasting service. **1838** *Civil Eng. & Arch. Jrnl.* I. 384/2 She is 271 tons old measurement,.. and has 99 ft. 9 in. [length] for tonnage. **1858** E. B. TINLING in *Merc. Marine Mag.* V. 306 She had a registered American tonnage of 1035, corresponding with 997 British. **1888** *Encycl. Brit.* XXIII. 442/2 There are three terms used in respect of the tonnage of ships,—namely, tonnage under decks, gross tonnage, and register tonnage... In obtaining the tonnage under tonnage deck, ships are divided in respect of their length into five classes. *Ibid.* 443 This formula is also applicable for finding displacement tonnage of ships, that is, the external displacement measured by taking transverse areas to the height of the load water-line to find the cubic content, which divided by 35 gives the displacement in tons weight. **1894** *Pall Mall Mag.* Nov. 388 Gross tonnage means a vessel's actual burthen;.. registered tonnage is her burthen when the capacity of all the space in which cargo is not carried has been deducted.

b. *fig.* (Used of mental capacity or bodily size.)

1806–7 J. BERESFORD *Miseries Hum. Life* (1826) I. Introd., To settle the comparative tonnage of their minds. **1869** 'MARK TWAIN' *Innoc. Abr.* ii, A dignitary of that tonnage. **1897** FLANDRAU *Harvard Episodes* 323 A person, female, aged—say forty-five; of abundant tonnage and affable manners.

5. *transf.* Ships collectively, shipping (in relation to their carrying capacity, or together with the merchandise carried by them).

1633 T. STAFFORD *Pac. Hib.* II. xxiv. (1821) 443 Victuals, and tonnage for the victualling and transporting of three thousand and two hundred men. **1748** in Hanway *Trav.* (1762) I. v. lxxvi. 348 He should not otherwise be able to give us any tonnage. **1808** WELLINGTON in Gurw. *Desp.* (1837) IV. 24 If the additional Tonnage does not arrive tomorrow, I shall settle to leave behind the veteran battalion or the 36th. **1809** *Ibid.* V. 212 To send to Lisbon that part of the coppered tonnage of the country which can be spared from service elsewhere. **1833** HT. MARTINEAU *Vanderput & S.* i. 16 The tonnage of this country is more than half that of all Europe. **1844** H. H. WILSON *Brit. India* I. I. viii. 515 The amount of tonnage then provided for the private trade had never been fully occupied. **1849** MACAULAY *Hist. Eng.* ix. II. 484 The tonnage [of Brixham] exceeds many times the tonnage of the port of Liverpool under the kings of the House of Stuart. **1858** CARLYLE *Fredk. Gt.* III. xviii. (1872) I. 250 The Friedrich-Wilhelm's Canal.. still carries tonnage from the Oder to the Spree. **1898** *Daily News* 14 Feb. 9/5 An inadequate supply of tonnage has prevented the shipments coastwise being carried on on the large scale which the demand would undoubtedly warrant. **1909** *Daily Chron.* 22 Jan. 1/3 The tonnage built in German yards amounted to only 201,000, against 311,000 in 1907 and 338,000 in 1906.

6. a. Weight in tons. *rare.*

1793 SMEATON *Edystone L.* Contents 7 Tonnage of the Stone. *Ibid.* 8 The Moorstone considered as ballast. Its tonnage.

b. Weight of (iron or other heavy merchandise) in the market.

1898 *Daily News* 14 Feb. 9/5 Production has.. been curtailed with a view to raising prices, but no impression is made upon the tonnage on offer, the Lancashire and Welsh makers being serious rivals.

7. Mode of reckoning the ton of cargo for freightage.

1913 *Handbk. Conference of W.I. Atlantic S.S. Comps., Genl. Regulations*, All goods to be freighted at actual measurement, or at actual gross weight, which ever tonnage be the greater.. the measurement to be taken at 40 cubic feet to the ton, and the weight at 2240 pounds or 1000 kilos to the ton.

8. *attrib.* and *Comb.*, as ***tonnage bounty***, ***capacity***, ***due***, ***duty***, ***length***, ***money***, ***tax***; **tonnage annuity**, a government annuity payable out of the proceeds of tonnage duties: see *Act 5 & 6 Will. & Mary*, 1694, c. 20 §§16–18; **tonnage-cheater**, term applied to a vessel built so as to cheat the rules for tonnage measurement, esp. a yacht with a 'dog's-leg' stern-post, by which its length was diminished; **tonnage-deck**, in a ship, the second deck from below in all vessels of two or more decks; the only deck in a vessel of one deck; **tonnage-displacement** = *displacement tonnage*, in 4.

1698 *Lond. Gaz.* No. 3374/4 The Purchasers may satisfie the Purchase-Money by Arrears, incurred.. on the *Tunnage-Annuities or by Lottery-Tickets, which became due within the same Time on the Salt Act. **1846** M^cCULLOCH *Acc. Brit. Empire* (1854) I. 631 A high *tonnage bounty was granted upon every buss fitted out for the deep-sea fishery. **1901** *Munsey's Mag.* XXIV. 463/2 Commercial competition demanded that *tonnage capacity should be secondary to speed. **1912** DU BOULAY *Compl. Yachtsman* 474 Many yachtsmen attributed her [a yacht's] success to her evading the rule of length-measurement, and she was [1874] commonly known as a '*tonnage-cheater'. **1888** *Encycl. Brit.* XXIII. 442/2 In obtaining the gross measurement the space under the *tonnage deck is first measured; then the space or spaces, if any, between the tonnage deck and the upper deck. **1888** *Daily News* 8 Sept. 2/1 The smaller of the two ironclads will be named the Texas... Her *tonnage displacement is 6,300, and she will steam about 17 knots. **1834** *Tait's Mag.* I. 71/2 At present the orders in Council fix 2s. for the *tonnage dues [in China], and 7s. per cent. on the export and import cargo. **1846** M^cCULLOCH *Acc. Brit. Empire* (1854) II. 65 The tonnage dues and other revenues being generally insufficient to defray the ordinary expenditure. **1697–8** *Act 9 Will. III*, c. 37 (*title*) Annuities.. payable out of *Tunnage Duties. **1801** A. HAMILTON *Wks.* (1886) VII. 217 Rather let the tonnage duty on American vessels be abolished. **1705** SIR C. WREN *Let.* in *N. & Q.* 3rd Ser. IV. 103/2, I am sorry M[r]. Wood has p[d] you the *Tunnage-money, but.. I shal endeavor that you be made to refund it. **1882** D. A. WELLS *Our Merchant Marine* vii. 179 *Tonnage-taxes on shipping are not levied by Great Britain, nor, it is believed, by any other of the maritime states of Europe, except Spain. Prior to the war, also, there were no tonnage-taxes in the United States. **1899** *Daily News* 19 Aug. 6/6 The challenging yacht is subject to tonnage tax, and must enter and clear at the Custom House like a regular merchant vessel.

'tonnage, *v.* [f. prec. sb.]

1. *trans.* To impose tonnage upon (see prec. 1); hence **'tonnaging** *vbl. sb.*: in quot. *fig.*

1644 MILTON *Areop.* (Arb.) 64 Nothing.. but what passes through the custom-house of certain Publicans that have the tunaging and the poundaging of all free spok'n truth.

2. To have a tonnage of (so much): see prec. 4.

1850 SCORESBY *Cheever's Whalem. Adv.* i. (1858) 8 Six hundred and fifty ships, barks, brigs, and schooners, tonnaging two hundred thousand tons. **1874** SCAMMON *Marine Mammals* 241 Sixteen vessels, which tonnaged in the aggregate 1,871 tons.

tonne (tʌn, 'tʌnɪ). [a. Fr.: = TON[1].] The French word for ton, adopted in English use to denote a metric ton of 1000 kilogrammes (TON[1] 4).

1877 *Rep. Brit. Assoc. Adv. Sci. 1876* II. 32 The Tonne is the mass or quantity of matter contained in a cubic metre of water, and is very nearly the same as the British Ton. **1930** *Engineering* 25 July 119/3 Each of the two high-pressure turbines takes some 224 tonnes of steam per hour. **1953** *Economist* 28 Mar. 902/1 The country's refining capacity, in terms of crude oil throughput, was about 23 million tonnes a year. **1972** *Which?* May 130/3 The British Steel Corporation, going metric but realising the possible confusion between a ton and a tonne (1,000 kilograms) has directed its staff to pronounce 'tonne' 'tunnie'. **1975** *B.S.I. News* Apr. 5/1 Our units committee has been asked to advise how, in speech, confusion between 'tonne' and 'ton' can best be avoided. Their advice is simply this: when saying the word 'tonne' never say it alone; always say 'metric tonne'. **1977** A. HALLAM *Planet Earth* 24/2 Meteorites vary in weight from a few tens of grammes to several tonnes. **1981** *Southern Horticulture* (N.Z.) Spring 3 It should be possible to achieve yields of 5 tonne/ha or more from mature roots.

tonne, obs. form of TON, TUN.

‖**tonneau** ('tɒnəʊ). [F. *tonneau*, specific application of *tonneau* cask, tun: see TONNEL.]

1. The rounded rear body of a motor-car (orig. with the door at the back); the rear part of a car with front and rear compartments or of an open car. Also, a car having a tonneau. Hence **tonneau cover**, a removable, flexible cover for protecting the rear or passenger seats in an open car when they are not in use; also *transf.*

1901 *Daily Record & Mail* 26 Dec. 7 The tonneau, which is of the roomiest and most comfortable description, is designed to hold six passengers. **1904** KIPLING *Traffics & Discov.* 322 She knelt at the bottom of the tonneau telling her beads without pause. **1905** A. M. BINSTEAD *Mop Fair* 118 With the entrancing little green *tonneau* which a railway rustic delivered.. next morning, it was entirely different. So winsome was the diminutive car [etc.]. **1907** *Westm. Gaz.* 19 Mar. 4/2 A good tonneau seat is as comfortable as anyone could wish. **1931** GARRARD & GEDDES *Practical Motoring* 643/1 *Tonneau.* The rear part of an open four or five seater motor car body was at one time commonly referred to as the tonneau but this term is now rarely used by itself. When the front seats only are used, a special cover known as the tonneau cover is sometimes stretched across the whole of the rear part. **1976** *Glasgow Herald* 26 Nov. 21/6 (Advt.), 16ft cabin cruiser... Complete with tonneau cover and canopy, £3000. **1978** *Sat. Rev.* (U.S.) 1 Apr. 45 That leaves London [taxis]. Ah, how civilized... There is room in the tonneau for five, with two on jump seats. **1979** J. LEASOR *Love & Land Beyond* vi. 88 Victoria brought the plane down... Love helped her batten down tonneau covers over the two cockpits. **1980** *Times* 1 Nov. 14/3 (*caption*) During the 1975 run, an 1898 Daimler wagonette.. overtakes a 1903 de Dietrich tonneau. **1981** *West Lancs. Evening Gaz.* 25 Feb. 15 (Advt.), Sports boat.., complete with trailer, tonneau cover, etc.

2. (A gallicism.) A barrel or cask; a measure of capacity for wine, equal to one tun (198 gallons).

1794 A. YOUNG *Trav. France* (ed. 2) I. xviii. 535 Wine has increased in its export to England..; before the treaty it was 8000 tonneaux a year. **1851** [see QUEUE *sb.* 6]. **1978** S. SHELDON *Bloodline* iv. 69 We should get three hundred thousand francs a *tonneau* for the first pressings.

Hence **'tonneaued** *a.*: of a motor-car, having a tonneau.

1904 KIPLING *Traffics & Discov.* 200 It was a big, black, black-dashed, tonneaued twenty-four horse Octopod [motor-car].

† **'tonnel, -ell.** *Obs.* Also 4 tonele, 4–7 tonel, 5 tonell. [Earlier form of TUNNEL, a. OF. *tonel*, *tonnel*, mod.F. *tonneau*, deriv. of *tonne* cask, med.L. *tonna*, *tunna*. The corresponding med.L. form was *tonnellus* masc., but the more usual and normal form was *tonnella* fem., dim. of *tonna*, *tunna*. See further under TUNNEL.]

1. A cask or barrel for wine or other commodities.

[*c* **991–***c* **1002** *Laws Æthelred* IV. ii. §10 Duos caballinos tonellos aceto plenos. **1341–2** *Ely Sacr. Rolls* (1907) II. 117 In xij hopes pro tonelis... In iij staues pro uno tonele. **1390–1** *Earl Derby's Exp.* (Camden) 24 Johanni Clerk pro ij tonnellis, pris de tonnello iijs... Willelmo Franch pro j tonella j pipa de Rynen vjs.] **1483** *Act 1 Rich. III*, c. 13. §1 Every Tonell to hold xij[xx] xij galons. **1483** CAXTON *Gold. Leg.* 111 b/1 A good woman whyche had but a lytyl wyn in her tonnel or vessel. **1582** N. LICHEFIELD tr. *Castanheda's Conq. E. Ind.* I. xxix. 72 A fish which y[e] sea did cast a land. y[t] was greater then any Tonel. **1601** TATE *Househ. Ord. Edw. II* (1876) 61 If any tonel be found to be corrupt.. let the botome of the tonel be knocked out, and the wine spilt. **1880** O. CRAWFURD *Portugal Old & New* 256 [The wine] is drawn into tonels [= Pg. *toneles*], huge casks often with a capacity of over thirty pipes. **1884** DOWELL *Hist. Taxation* I. II. ii. 28 The Bishop of Winchester owes a tonell of good wine for not reminding the king (John) about a girdle for the countess of Albemarle.

b. *Comb.* **tonnel-hoop**, a hoop of a cask.

1341–2 *Ely Sacr. Rolls* (1907) II. 117 In iiij staues pro uno tonele et iij tonelhopes. Item pro j tonelhope et ij paylhopes.

†**2.** Early spelling, in various senses, of TUNNEL.

‖**tonnelle** (tɔnɛl). [Fr., = TUNNEL *sb.*] An arbour. Also *fig.*

1861 THACKERAY *Roundabout Papers* (1863) 219 Those who sit down under my *tonnelle*, and have a half-hour's drink and gossip. *a* **1922** H. JONES *Old Memories* (1923) 160, I can even yet see him sitting peaceably, sheltering from the heat in our vine *tonnelle*. **1947** *Horizon* Feb. 106 The Queen is looking back along the flowery *tonnelle* of her day.

tonner ('tʌnə(r)). [f. TON[1] + -ER[1]: cf. POUNDER *sb.*[4]] In comb. with prefixed numeral: a vessel of (so many) tons burden; e.g. ***forty-tonner***, a vessel of forty tons burden: see TON[1] 2. Also, a lorry of (so many) tons weight.

1851 A. O. HALL *Manhattaner in New Orleans* 177 A seven hundred tonner,.. full of Dutch emigrants. **1883** *Harper's Mag.* Aug. 443/1 The forty-tonners.. carried off most of the prizes. **1891** E. KINGLAKE *Australian at H.* 78 There is generally a race of some description, either for forty tonners, ten tonners, half-deckers, or the plain open sailing boat. **1891** *Lit. World* 20 Nov. 419/2 The Vancouver, one of the splendid 5,000 tonners of the White Star Line. **1959** I. JEFFERIES *Thirteen Days* iv. 43 The Arab six-tonner driver. **1978** R. MARK *Office of Constable* iii. 38 Came the great day when the survivors were packed with their kit into a three-tonner en route for Sandhurst.

tonnie, tonny, obs. ff. TUNNY.

tonnish: see TONISH, TUNNISH.

tono-, repr. Gr. τονο-, combining form of τόνος stretching, tension, TONE, combining element in many technical words. **tono'fibril** *Histology* [ad. G. *tonofibrille* (M. Heidenhain 1899, in *Arch. f. mikrosk. Anat.* LIV. 212)], a bundle of tonofilaments; **tonofi'brilla,** (*a*) *Histology* = prec.; (*b*) *Ent.*, a non-contractile fibril in an insect that passes from a myofibril through the epidermis into the cuticle; **'tonofilament** *Histology*, one of the minute supportive or non-contractile filaments that occur aggregated into networks in the cytoplasm of many epithelial cells, esp. in the epidermis; **tonogram** ('tɒnəgræm) [-GRAM], the record of a tonograph; **'tonograph** [-GRAPH], a recording tonometer; see also quot. 1890; so **tono'graphic** *a.*, **to'nography**; **to'nology**, the study of tones or of intonation in speech; hence **tono'logical** *a.*; **tono'mitter** [L. *mittĕre* to send]: see quot.; **'tonophant** [Gr. -φάντης one who shows], a device whereby acoustic vibrations are rendered visible; **'tonoplast**, *Bot.* [-PLAST]: see quots.; **tono'tactic** *a.*, of or pertaining to tonotaxis; **tono'taxis** [TAXIS]: see quot.: also called *osmotaxis*; **tono'topic, -topical** *adjs. Anat.* [Gr. τόπος place], exhibiting a spatial correspondence with the frequency of heard sound; hence **tono'topically** *adv.*

1901 *Jrnl. R. Microsc. Soc.* 512 (*table*) *Tonofibrils or resistance fibrils, e.g. in intestinal epithelial cells, epidermis cells. **1964** G. H. HAGGIS et al. *Introd. Molecular Biol.* v. 120 In the stratified squamous epithelium of the skin, tonofibrils arch through all the cells like scaffolding and they are attached to numerous desmosomes over the entire surface of the cells. **1976** *Path. Ann.* XI. 220 At a fine structural level, the cells of thymoma contain tonofibrils and complex desmosomes, but no neurosecretory granules. **1925** E. B. WILSON *Cell* (ed. 3) i. 41 The greater number of writers have ..accepted the conclusion..that they are of the nature of supporting or skeletal structures, hence the term *tonofibrillæ (Heidenhain). **1935** R. E. SNODGRASS *Princ. Insect Morphol.* iii. 63 It frequently appears not only that the tonofibrillae traverse the epidermal layer, but that they penetrate a varying distance into the cuticula. **1969** R. F. CHAPMAN *Insects* xii. 211 In *Musca* each myofibril is attached to the cuticle by about twelve tonofibrillae. **1964** *Jrnl. Investigative Dermatol.* XLIII. 278/1 In pemphigus vulgaris, a severe necrotizing injury of unknown etiology leads to complete destruction of the *tonofilaments with ensuing loss of desmosomes. **1978** *Sci. Amer.* May 145/1 The tonofilaments are not contractile but seem to form a tensile, structural framework for the cell cytoplasm. **1980** *Nature* 17 Jan. 249/1 Electron microscopy shows that bundles of keratin tonofilaments often terminate in membrane-bound desmosomes. **1899** *Syd. Soc. Lex.*, *Tonogram. **1911** WEBSTER, *Tonogram*, a curve showing graphically a muscle's isometric contraction. **1890** *Pall Mall G.* 21 Mar. 5/2 Some specimens of a new photographic process, called '*Tonographs', were exhibited by Messrs. Mayall. **1899** *Syd. Soc. Lex.*, *Tonograph*, a machine for recording the tension of the arterial blood-current. **1867** MACFARREN *Harmony* i. 31 The vibrations of the air inducing musical sounds, by a process which might be called *tonography, imprint their [etc.]. **1934** WEBSTER, *Tonological. **1975** *Language* LI. 565 The nouns in the two classes with L final vowels show tonological behavior parallel to that of the nouns in the two classes with Ø final vowels. **1983** *Word 1982* XXXIII. 230 With regard to other tonological features in the area, one can mention a number of languages with four-tone systems. **1874** H. SWEET in *Trans. Philol. Soc. 1873–4* 98 What is wanted, then, is a comparative '*tonology' of the Danish dialects. **1924** D. M. BEACH in *Bantu Studies* Dec. 77 An entirely new field..is lying open before us—the comparative and historical study of tones. This study..will be called tonology. **1970** *Stud. Afr. Linguistics* I. 100 (*heading*) Nupe tonology. **1978** *Language* LIV. 245/2 There are ten papers on phonology, seven of which deal specifically with tonology. **1899** *Syd. Soc. Lex.*, **Tonomitter*, an instrument to improve the hearing near the opening of the Eustachian tube. **1895** *Funk's Standard Dict.*, **Tonophant*, a device in which two thin pieces of steel welded together are used to exhibit acoustic vibrations to the eye. **1895** *Ibid.*, *Tonoplast. **1903** PORTER tr. *Strasburger's Text-bk.* 57 Since the vacuole wall regulates the pressure exerted by the cell sap contained in the vacuole, Hugo de Vries has applied the name Tonoplast to this layer. **1909** *Cent. Dict. Supp.*, *Tonotactic. **1900** B. D. JACKSON *Gloss. Bot. Terms*, **Tonotaxis*,..sensitiveness to osmotic variation. **1942** *Anat. Rec.* LXXXII. 430 In the monkey and chimpanzee.. surface positive potentials evoked by various pitches indicate *tonotopic localization within the primary auditory cortex. **1983** *Nature* 10 Feb. 463/1 This 'tonotopic' organization is preserved in all levels of the central auditory pathway. **1948** A. BRODAL *Neurol. Anat.* ix. 314 Pfeifer (1936)..was led to conclude that if there exists any *tonotopical localization in the primary acoustic cortex, tones of the highest pitch must be represented medially, those of lowest pitch laterally. **1963** *Jrnl. Neurophysiol.* XXVI. 294 (*heading*) Tonotopical organization, relation of spike counts to tone intensity, and firing patterns of single elements. **1971** *Brain Res.* XXVI. 402 There is good evidence that cells in the cochlear nucleus, superior olivary nuclei, nuclei of the lateral lemniscus, and inferior colliculus are organized according to their best frequencies, or *tonotopically. **1978** *Nature* 9 Mar. 139/2 Spatial analyses of the evoked potentials indicate that the auditory centre in the midbrain is organised tonotopically.

tonometer (təʊ'nɒmɪtə(r)). [f. TONO- + -METER.]

1. *Music.* An instrument for determining the pitch of tones; *spec.* a tuning-fork, or a graduated set of tuning-forks, as that made by Scheibler about 1833, for determining the exact number of vibrations per second which produce a given tone.

1725 A. WARREN (*title*) The Tonometer, explaining and demonstrating.. all the 32 distinct and different Notes, adjuncts or Supplements contained in each of four Octaves inclusive, of the Gamut. **1840** WHEWELL *Philos. Induct. Sc.* I. I. IV. iv. 312 The monochord is a complete and perfect tonometer. **1876** A. J. ELLIS in *Athenæum* 2 Dec. 731/1 Tonometry was first placed on a scientific basis in a.. pamphlet..published at Essen, 1834, and entitled 'The Physical and Musical Tonometer' (*Tonmesser*), which proves by the pendulum, visibly to the eye, the absolute vibrations of tones,..invented and executed by Heinrich Scheibler. **1881** BROADHOUSE *Mus. Acoustics* 104 Appunn's reed tonometer is a mode of measuring the pitch by means of harmonium reeds. **1885** *Athenæum* 18 Apr. 513/3 A class is devoted to..tuning-forks, pitch-pipes, sirens, tonometers, and other appliances for the determination of pitch.

2. An instrument for measuring (*a*) tension of the eyeball in glaucoma, (*b*) intravascular blood-pressure, (*c*) strains within a liquid.

(*a*) **1876** *Catal. Sci. App. S. Kens.* §3674 Tonometer, for Measuring the Hardness and Convexity of the Eye. **1879** P. SMITH *Glaucoma* 14 A distinct indication of a different tension was given by the tonometer.
(*b*) **1898** *Allbutt's Syst. Med.* V. 924 If the ventricle of a frog beat in a tonometer under a supply of blood from a pressure bottle, at varying heights, curves may be taken to measure the volume of the ventricle.
(*c*) **1909** in *Cent. Dict. Suppl.*

Hence **tonometric** (tɒnəʊ'mɛtrɪk) *a.*, of or pertaining to tonometry; **to'nometry**, the using of a tonometer; measurement of vibrations of sound or of tension.

1901 *Nature* 24 Oct. 630/2 He also presents a *tonometric apparatus, consisting of about 670 diapasons or tuning forks. **1902** *Encycl. Brit.* XXX. 61/1 At the Philadelphia Exposition of 1876 great admiration was expressed for a tonometric apparatus of his [König's] manufacture. **1876** *Tonometry [see TONOMETER 1]. **1899** *Syd. Soc. Lex.*, *Tonometry*, measurement of tension, as of the eyeball.

tonour, variant of TUNNER *Obs.*

tonous ('təʊnəs), *a. rare.* [f. L. *tonus* TONE + -OUS.] Having a full tone or sound; sonorous.

1773 KENRICK *Rhet. Gram.* in *Dict.* 39 The last is much clearer and tonous in English than in French. **1846** in WORCESTER, and in later Dicts.

tonquin bean: see TONKA.

Tonquinese, obs. var. TONKINESE *sb.* and *a.*

tonse, *v. Obs.* or *dial.* [f. L. *tons-*, ppl. stem of *tondēre* to shear, clip.]

†**1.** *trans.* To cut the hair of. *Obs.*

1555 W. WATREMAN *Fardle Facions* App. 333 Before that she (being tonsed, and hauing taken on her mourning wiede) haue bemoned her kinsfolke. **1676** in *Vicary's Anat.* (1888) App. xv. 282 If any Brother of the said Company shall.. tonse, barbe, or trim any person on the Lord's day.

2. To trim; to dress up. *dial.*

1828 *Craven Gloss.*, *Tonse*, to dress, to deck, to trim. *Tonsed*, dressed up. 'Thou's finely tonsed this morning.

tonsil ('tɒnsɪl). Usually in pl. **tonsils** ('tɒnsɪlz). Also 7 **-ell.** [ad. L. *tonsillæ* (pl.); cf. F. *tonsilles* (Paré, 16th c., *les tonsilles ou amygdales*).]

1. Each of two oval lymphoid glands situated one on each side of the fauces between the anterior and posterior arches.

1601 HOLLAND *Pliny* XXIII. Proem 146 Ulcers that happen in moist parts, and namely those of the mouth, Tonsils or Almond-kernels on either side of the throat. **1603** —— *Plutarch's Mor.* 1022 The glandulous parts or kernelles called tonsells. **1776** CRUIKSHANK in *Phil. Trans.* LXXXV. 183 The tonsils were considerably inflamed. **1840** G. V. ELLIS *Anat.* 238 The tonsil is a collection of mucous follicles, situated between the pillars of the soft palate, above the side of the tongue, and below the velum.

2. Each of the two lobes of the cerebellum; also called *amygdala*.

1891 in *Cent. Dict.* **1899** in *Syd. Soc. Lex.*

3. ***abdominal tonsil***: a name sometimes applied to the lymphatic tissue of the appendix vermiformis.

4. *attrib.* and *Comb.*

1767 GOOCH *Treat. Wounds* I. 425 The operation [was] easily performed, with an instrument a little more curved than a tonsil-needle, having an eye towards the point. **1898** J. HUTCHINSON in *Arch. Surg.* IX. No. 36. 349 There may also..be a difference in proneness to tonsil affections in different races.

†**tonsile** ('tɒnsɪl, -aɪl), *a. Obs.* Also 8 **tonsil.** [ad. L. *tonsil-is*, f. *tons-*, ppl. stem of *tondēre* to shear: see -IL, -ILE.] That may be clipped or shorn.

1664 EVELYN *Sylva* (1776) 321 The Shrub [Juniper] is tonsile and may be shorn into any form. **1707** MORTIMER *Husb.* (1721) II. 366 In mild Weather, clip Phillyrea and other tonsil Shrubs. **1791** GILPIN *Forest Scenery* I. 93 The yew is of all other trees the most tonsile. **1847–78** HALLIWELL, *Tonsile-hedge*, a hedge cut neat and smooth. *North.*

tonsillar ('tɒnsɪlə(r)), *a.* [ad. med. or mod.L. *tonsillār-is*, f. *tonsillæ*: see TONSIL and -AR.] Of or pertaining to the tonsils; affected by the tonsils, as, a ***tonsillar voice.***

1831 R. KNOX *Cloquet's Anat.* 589 The arteries of the tongue are furnished by the lingual branches of the external carotid arteries, and by the palatine and tonsillar twigs of the labial. **1899** *Allbutt's Syst. Med.* VIII. 467 Tonsillar, pharyngeal, or bronchial congestion.

tonsillary ('tɒnsɪlərɪ), *a.* [f. as prec. + -ARY[2]. Cf. F. *tonsillaire* (Roquefort 1829).] = prec.

1842 F. H. RAMADGE *Curability Consumption* (1850) 9 Preternatural tonsillary development. **1860** MAYNE *Expos. Lex.*, *Tonsillaris*, of or belonging to the tonsil: tonsillary.

tonsillectomy (tɒnsɪ'lɛktəmɪ). *Surg.* Also **tonsilectomy.** [f. TONSIL + -ECTOMY.] Removal of the tonsils.

1899 *Jrnl. Amer. Med. Assoc.* 23 Sept. 768/2 What then are the general results of tonsillectomy, as compared with those obtained by the usual operation of tonsillotomy? **1932** *Oxford Times* 23 Sept. 22/7 It would be a mistake to suppose that tonsilectomy..is indicated only where there is throat trouble. **1961** J. HELLER *Catch-22* (1962) xvii. 164 He could come through other people's tonsilectomies without suffering any postoperative distress. **1977** *Rolling Stone* 16 June 43/2 They told him he was going to the circus but instead took him for a tonsillectomy.

tonsillitic (tɒnsɪ'lɪtɪk), *a.* [f. next + -IC.]

a. (Irregularly used.) Of or pertaining to the tonsils; = TONSILLAR. ? *Obs.* **b.** Affected with tonsillitis.

1839–47 *Todd's Cycl. Anat.* III. 953/1 The tonsillitic branches of the glosso-pharyngeal. **1856** TODD & BOWMAN *Phys. Anat.* II. 116 Tonsillitic branches are numerous. **1879** *St. George's Hosp. Rep.* IX. 162 There was but one tonsillitic patient who possessed a healthy constitution.

‖**tonsillitis** (tɒnsɪ'laɪtɪs). *Path.* [f. L. *tonsill-a* TONSIL + -ITIS.] Inflammation of the tonsils; when suppuration takes place, called *quinsy*.

1801 E. DARWIN *Zoon.* III. 361 By tonsillitis, the inflammation of the tonsils is principally to be understood. **1878** T. BRYANT *Pract. Surg.* I. 534 Tonsillitis as an acute affection is known as quinsy, and is characterized by the rapid swelling of the part, acute pain, foul tongue, and fever.

ton'sillolith. *Path.* [-LITH.] A concretion in the substance of the tonsil.

1903 *Buck's Handbk. Med. Sc.* VI. 599 The same fungi have been found in fœtid bronchitis, tracheal ozæna, pulmonary gangrene, rhinoliths, tonsilloliths, vesical calculi.

ton'sillotome. [irreg. f. L. *tonsilla* TONSIL + -TOME; cf. F. *tonsillitome* (Littré).] A surgical instrument for excising the tonsil.

1857 in DUNGLISON *Med. Lex.* **1872** COHEN *Dis. Throat* 128 When the organ is not very large, it may be excised by the tonsillotome. **1897** *Allbutt's Syst. Med.* IV. 744 The hypertrophy should be reduced..by the lingual tonsillotome.

So **tonsi'llotomy** (now *rare*), excision of the tonsils; usu. applied to partial removal of the tonsils, in contrast to TONSILLECTOMY.

1876 *Louisville Med. News* I. 280 (*heading*) Dangerous hemorrhage after tonsillotomy. **1897** *Allbutt's Syst. Med.* IV. 778 No belief is too foolish and groundless to be advanced against tonsillotomy. **1901** *Lancet* 27 Apr. 1211/1 Six minor operations (opening of abscesses and two double tonsillotomies). **1899** [see TONSILLECTOMY]. **1902** C. JOYES (*title*) Tonsillotomy or tonsillectomy, which? **1924** W. D. HARMER in H. W. Carson *Mod. Operative Surg.* II. 272 The question whether it is better to cut away part of the tonsils (tonsillotomy) or to remove them entirely with their capsules (tonsillectomy) has been hotly discussed.

tonsilly ('tɒnsɪlɪ), *a. rare.* [f. TONSIL + -Y.] Affected by the tonsils. (Cf. *throaty*.)

1894 *Westm. Gaz.* 31 Aug. 7/2 His voice..is..weak and tonsilly to the ear.

tonsion, variant of TUNSION, beating.

tonsor ('tɒnsə(r)). [a. L. *tonsor* barber, agent-n. f. *tondēre* to shear, clip.]

1. A barber.

1656 [see TONSORIOUS]. **1721** BAILEY, *Tonsor*, a Barber. **1749** FIELDING *Tom Jones* VIII. vi, 'So, tonsor', says Jones, 'I find you have more trades than one'. **1866** R. CHAMBERS *Ess.* Ser. II. 16 When we sit under the tonsor..we fall into chat.

†**2.** A clipper of coin. *Obs.*

1697 EVELYN *Numism.* vii. 225 Not our Tonsors only, Clippers and False Moneyers.

tonsorial (tɒn'sɔərɪəl), *a.* [f. L. *tonsōri-us* pertaining to a barber + -AL[1].] Of or pertaining to a barber or his work; often used humorously, as 'a tonsorial artist'.

1813 MOORE *Post-bag* ii. 22 During that awful hour or two Of grave tonsorial preparation. **1851** THACKERAY *Contrib. to Punch* Nov., Wks. 1894 XIII. 575 Under the roof of a tonsorial practitioner in the Waterloo Road. **1910** *Daily News* 15 Dec. 6 American 'tonsorial artists' are furious at the popularity of the safety razor.

Hence **ton'sorialist** *humorous*, a 'tonsorial artist', a barber; also †**ton'sorian,** †**ton'sorious** *adjs.*, tonsorial.

1656 BLOUNT *Glossogr.*, *Tonsorious*.., of or belonging to a barber or tonsor. **1658** in PHILLIPS. **1705** ELSTOB in Hearne *Collect.* 30 Nov. (O.H.S.) I. 107 Worthy a Prince of the Tonsorian Race, The best that er'e with steel mow'd human face. **1869** *New North West* (Deer Lodge, Montana) 6 Aug. 3/1 Mr. Plummer, the colored tonsorialist..has the misfortune to be a 'bloody Hinglishman'. **1898** A. M. BINSTEAD *Pink 'Un & Pelican* xi. 253 One of them [*sc.* constables]..gazed..at the abstracted sign of the tonsorialist.

tonstein ('tɒnstaɪn). *Geol.* [a. Ger., lit. 'clay stone'.] A rock composed mainly of kaolinite which is commonly found in association with certain coal seams, or a thin band of such a rock (see quots.).

1961 I. A. WILLIAMSON in *Mining Mag.* CIV. 9 Tonsteins are essentially argillaceous rocks containing kaolinite in a variety of forms together with occasional detrital and carbonaceous material. **1971** *Nature* 6 Aug. 371/2 The thin, curious, kaolinitic bands called tonsteins discovered more recently in the coalfields of Western Europe have provided welcome additional markers for coalfield correlation.

'tonsurate. [ad. med.L. *tonsūrāt-us*, f. L. *tonsūra* TONSURE: see -ATE¹.] The state or quality of being tonsured, esp. in preparation for orders, or while only in the lowest order of Reader.

1897 *Tablet* 8 May 725 Cranmer and his associates abolished the Tonsurate and all the minor orders.

tonsure ('tɒnsjʊə(r)), *sb.* Also 5 tonsur, -our. [a. F. *tonsure* (14th c. in Godef.), or ad. L. *tonsūra* a shearing or clipping, f. *tondēre*, *tons-um*: see TONSE.]

1. *gen.* The action or process of clipping the hair or shaving the head; the state of being shorn.

1390 GOWER *Conf.* III. 291 For unlust of that aventure Ther was noman which tok tonsure. **1616** BULLOKAR *Eng. Expos.*, *Tonsure*, a clipping or cutting of the haire. **1650** BULWER *Anthropomet.* ii. 56 We..reduce our Tonsure to a just moderation and decency. **1770** LANGHORNE *Plutarch* (1851) I. 3/1 This kind of tonsure, on his account was called Theseis. **1876** C. M. DAVIES *Unorth. Lond.* 183 The 'county crop'—that species of tonsure which all had undergone.

2. *spec.* The shaving of the head or part of it as a religious practice or rite, esp. as a preparation to entering the priesthood or a monastic order.

In the Eastern Ch. the whole head is shaven (*tonsure of St. Paul*); in the Roman Ch. either a circular patch on the crown, as in secular priests, or the whole upper part of the head so as to leave only a fringe or circle of hair, as in some monastic orders and friars (*t. of St. Peter*); in the ancient Celtic Ch. the tonsure 'consisted in shaving the head in front of a line drawn from ear to ear' (*t. of St. John*). A form of tonsure was also practised by the priests of Isis.

1387 TREVISA *Higden* (Rolls) VI. 167 He took tonsure and habit of clerk, þe ȝere of his age foure and twenty. *c* **1450** *St. Cuthbert* (Surtees) 1366 And ȝaf him tonsour and habite. **1530** PALSGR. 183 *Les ordres*..benet the first tonsure. **1655** FULLER *Ch. Hist.* II. ii. §96 No mention herein of settling the Tonsure of Priests..according to the Roman Rite. **1753** CHALLONER *Cath. Chr. Instr.* 153 The Clerical Tonsure..is not properly an Order, but only a Preparation for Orders. The Bishop cuts off the Extremities of their Hair, to signify their renouncing the World and its Vanities; and he invests them with a Surplice, and so receives them into the Clergy. **1829** J. DONOVAN tr. *Catech. Counc. Trent* II. vii. §14 In tonsure the hair of the head is cut in form of a crown, and should always be worn in that form, enlarging the crown as one advances in orders. **1842** HOOK *Ch. Dict.* 558 A clerical tonsure was made necessary about the 5th or 6th century. **1846** SHARPE *Hist. Egypt* xiv. 431 In Rome he was very partial to the Egyptian superstitions, and he had adopted the tonsure, and had his head shaven like a priest of Isis. **1849** ROCK *Ch. of Fathers* I. I. ii. 186 Of the ecclesiastical tonsure ..the Roman form was perfectly round; the Irish was made by cutting away the hair from the upper part of the forehead in the figure of a half-moon, with the convex side before.

b. The part of a priest's or monk's head left bare by shaving the hair.

[**1351-2** *Rolls of Parlt.* II. 244/2 Gentz de Religion portantz tonsure.] **1430-40** LYDG. *Bochas* IX. xiv. (MS. Bodl. 263) lf. 418/2 As a prest she [Joan] had a brod tonsure. *a* **1625** SIR H. FINCH *Law* (1636) 65 But if he shew cause which our law alloweth not (as because hee hath not his tonsure, or *ornamentum Clericale*, &c.) he shall pay a fine, and yet be driuen to take the felon. **1768** STERNE *Sent. Journ.*, *Monk, Calais* i, The monk, as I judged from the break in his tonsure,..might be about seventy. **1849** JAMES *Woodman* xiii, You must cover the tonsure with this peasant's bonnet.

†**3.** The clipping (*a*) of coin; (*b*) of shrubs or hedges. *Obs. rare.*

1621 BOLTON *Stat. Irel.* 12 (Act 25 Hen. VI) Ireland is greatly impoverished..by the..carriage..into England of the silver plate, broken silver Bullion and wedges of silver made of the great Tonsure of the money. **1691** in *Archæologia* (1796) XII. 185 His yew hedges with trees of the same..kept in pretty shapes with tonsure. *Ibid.* 186 A fair gravel walk betwixt two yew hedges with rounds and spires of the same, all under smooth tonsure.

4. *attrib.* and *Comb.*, as ***tonsure-cap***, ***tonsure-plate*** (see quot.).

1889 *Pall Mall G.* 23 July 2/1 His rank..distinguished by the scarlet sash which he wears..and by his tonsure-cap, which is of the same colour. **1891** *Cent. Dict.*, *Tonsure-plate*, a round thin plate slightly convex so as to fit the top of the head, used to mark the line of the tonsure according to the Roman rite.

'tonsure, *v.* [f. prec. sb. or ad. F. *tonsurer* (14-15th c. in Hatz.-Darm.) or med.L. *tonsūrāre* (845 in Du Cange).] *trans.* To clip or shave the hair of; to confer the ecclesiastical tonsure upon.

1793 *Minstrel* I. 90, I must tonsure those fine tresses to the due form. **1843** CARLYLE *Past & Pr.* II. xiv, Now tonsured into a mournful penitent Monk. **1872** O. SHIPLEY *Gloss. Eccl. Terms* 459 The Greeks tonsured their whole heads, like St. James and the other Apostles. **1878** MACLEAR *Celts* viii. (1879) 123 They..were tonsured from ear to ear,—that is, the fore part of the head was made bare, and the hair was allowed to grow only on the back part of the head.

b. *fig.* To make bald-headed.

1876 W. B. SCOTT *Sonn.* 9 And now that age hath shriven and tonsured me.

Hence **'tonsuring** *vbl. sb.* and *ppl. a.*

1811 *Henry & Isabella* I. 3 He manifested a sufficient genius at the tonsuring business. **1906** *Reader* 24 Nov. 123/2 He..gladly followed her advice to remedy with a curled scalp the 'tonsuring action of middle age'.

'tonsured, *ppl. a.* [f. prec. + -ED¹.]

1. That has received tonsure; hence, in orders.

1706 tr. *Dupin's Eccl. Hist. 16th C.* II. III. xxii. 395 By which, Tonsured Clerks..are exempt from Lay-Jurisdiction. **1827** HALLAM *Const. Hist.* (1876) I. ii. 58 The immunity of all tonsured persons from civil punishment for crimes. **1873** M. ARNOLD *Lit. & Dogma* (1876) 370 The cowled and tonsured Middle Age.

b. *fig.* Bald or partially bald.

1855 TENNYSON *Brook* 110 Bowing o'er the brook A tonsured head in middle age forlorn.

2. Clipped, as a yew or box. *rare.*

1837 HOWITT *Rur. Life* I. vii. (1862) 70 Walpole overturned this ancient fondness for pleached walks and tonsured trees.

†**tonsword.** *Obs. rare.* (?)

1575 LANEHAM *Let.* (1871) 29 Captin Cox.., very cunning in fens, and hardy az Gawin; for hiz tonsword hangs at his tablz eend. [See Editor's Note.] *Ibid.* 31 Captain Cox cam marching on valiantly before..floorishing with hiz ton-swoord, and another fensmaster with him.

tontine (tɒn'tiːn), *sb.* (*a.*) [a. F. *tontine*, from name of Lorenzo Tonti, a Neapolitan banker, who initiated the scheme in France *c* 1653.]

A. *sb.* **1.** A financial scheme by which the subscribers to a loan or common fund receive each an annuity during his life, which increases as their number is diminished by death, till the last survivor enjoys the whole income; also applied to the share or right of each subscriber.

Introduced first in France as a method of raising government loans. Afterwards tontines were formed for building houses, hotels, baths, etc.

1765 *Chron.* in *Ann. Reg.* 71/2 The house of Commons came to a resolution of raising £300,000..by way of tontine, or annuities upon lives, at 3 per cent. with benefit of survivorship. **1777** SHERIDAN *Sch. Scand.* I. i, I hear he pays as many annuities as the Irish tontine. **1791** *Gentl. Mag.* Jan. 27/2 This gentlewoman had ventured 300 livres in each Tontine; and in the last year of her life she had for her annuity..about 3600*l.* a year. **1827** HONE *Every-day Bk.* II. 1533 During a scarcity of money which prevailed in 1644, Lawrence Tonti came from Naples to Paris, and proposed that kind of life-rents, or annuities, which are named after him *Tontines*: though they were used in Italy long before his time. **1871** *Daily News* 4 Jan., It is proposed to organize a tontine, to purchase the Alexandra Palace, with the park of about 100 acres, and utilise them for public recreation. The sum required is 650,000*l.*, which it is intended to raise in shares of 20s. each.

fig. **1796** BURKE *Regic. Peace* iv. Wks. IX. 67 The murderers of Robespierre, besides what they are entitled to by being engaged in the same tontine of Infamy,..have inherited all his murderous qualities.

2. A game of cards played on the tontine principle: see quots.

1798 *Sporting Mag.* XI. 24 Tontine may be played by twelve or fifteen persons; but the more the merrier. *Ibid.*, Tontine..is played with an entire pack of fifty-two cards.. every one is to take a stake. *Ibid.* 25/1 He who outlives all the rest, by having counters left, when theirs are gone, wins the party, and enjoys what the others have deposited.

¶**3.** Applied to a friendly society which shares out its unexpended funds at the end of the year. (*Erroneous use.*)

1871 *2nd Rep. Comm. Friendly Soc.* II. (1872) 38/1 It is curious..that they [these sharing out clubs] call themselves tontines; I do not know why; of course it is a wrong name. **1898** BRABROOK *Provid. Societies* 69 The Dividing Societies ..exist in great numbers, under a variety of names, as Slate Clubs, Tontines, Birmingham Benefit Societies, &c.

B. *adj.* (or *attrib.* use of the sb.). Of, pertaining to, or of the nature of a tontine.

1790 J. WOODFORDE *Diary* 3 Sept. (1927) III. 211 Mr. Custance brought some Papers for me to sign respecting all his Children being put into the new Tontine Annuities. **1824** SCOTT *St. Ronan's* i, At length a tontine subscription was obtained to erect an inn. **1834** HT. MARTINEAU *Farrers* i, Some of the lot of lives with which her father and she were joined in a tontine annuity had failed. **1863** KIRK *Chas. Bold* II. IV. ii. 222 The destined survivor of a tontine partnership. **1876** *Haydn's Dict. Dates* (ed. 15) 719 A Mr. Jennings was an original subscriber for a 100*l.* share in a tontine company; and being the last survivor.., his share produced him 3000*l.* per annum. He died aged 103 years, 19 June, 1798, worth 2,115,244*l.* **1891** *Cent. Dict.*, *Tontine policy*, a policy of insurance, in which the holders agree to receive no dividend for a term of years called the *tontine period*. The money is allowed to accumulate till the end of the period, when it is divided among those who have maintained their insurance in force.

Hence **tontiner** (tɒn'tiːnə(r)), a shareholder in a tontine.

1881 *Times* 1 June 6/2 [Two survivors] claimed the whole fund, in their respective classes, as against the representatives of the deceased tontiners in the same class.

Tonton Macoute (tɔ̃tɔ̃ mæ'kuːt). Also Ton Ton Macoute and with small initials. [a. Haitian French, of uncertain origin.] **a.** A militia which was formed by President Duvalier in Haiti and became notorious for its brutal and arbitrary behaviour; also, a member of this. Also *ellipt.* as **Tonton.**

1962 S. E. FINER *Man on Horseback* ix. 133 Duvalier took office in October 1957... Instead of relying upon the *Garde Nationale*, he has built himself up a 5,000 strong counterforce of palace guards, civilian militia, and civilian hoodlums called '*tonton macoute*'. **1965** J. E. FAGG *Cuba, Haiti & Dominican Republic* 136 A gang of ruffians known as *Tonton Macoute* murdered or beat citizens who complained. **1966** G. GREENE *Comedians* I. i. 16 The Tontons Macoute. .. The President's bogey men. They wear dark glasses and they call on their victims after dark. *Ibid.* ii. 47 He was believed by some to have connections with the Tontons. *Ibid.*, He exchanged some words with a Tonton Macoute at the door. **1972** *Times* 23 Nov. 10/8 Mr Luckner Cambronne, former Haitian Minister of Defence and of the Interior, who organized the dreaded Ton Ton Macoutes, has sought asylum in the Colombian Embassy in Port-au-Prince. **1976** *Globe & Mail* (Toronto) 5 Nov. 7/2 Rather than fire his father's tontons, (and risk sending a bunch of disgruntled triggermen underground) the young President found them jobs in public institutions such as hospitals. **1981** PLATE & DARVI *Secret Police* ii. 47 There is no agreement among scholars of Haiti about what 'Tonton Macoutes' means. Some claim the name refers to a primitive bad figure in Haitian voodoo culture who takes you away when you misbehave.

b. *fig.*

1970 'D. CRAIG' *Young Men may Die* xi. 83 Our two people..have on Tonton Macoute sunglasses. **1973** *Publishers' Weekly* 8 Jan. 34/1 'Veronica Ganz', the one-girl *ton ton macoute*.

'ton-up, *sb.* and *a. slang.* [f. TON¹ + UP *adv.*² 12 c.] **A.** *sb.* A speed of 100 m.p.h.; a motor-cyclist who achieves this. Also in the sense of TON¹ 5 a and *fig.*

1961 *Daily Tel.* 11 Feb. 1/2 The term 'Ton Up' is used by young motor-cyclists to indicate doing 100 m.p.h. **1964** *New Statesman* 21 Feb. 288/3 Many made a point of..assuring me that the ton-ups weren't as black as they thought I'd painted them. **1964** in Hamblett & Deverson *Generation X* 146 Of course, there were the Tonups (now Rockers) who mustn't be forgotten, but then they have always been an untouchable group on their own, kinkily keen on their bikes. **1972** J. BLACKBURN *For Fear of Little Men* xiv. 147 Eighty miles an hour, ninety, a ton-up—as the motorcycle maniacs call a hundred. **1976** J. SNOW *Cricket Rebel* 44 My return read nought for 117. I got a ton-up in my next Test at Headingley as well. **1978** *Gramophone* Aug. 329/3 The sleeve photograph shows Perényi in action, head, hands and cello blurred as if moving at too great a rate for even the fastest stop on the camera. There is indeed an element of the 'ton-up' about his performance.

B. *attrib.* **1. a.** Applied to young motor-cyclists who enjoy travelling at high speed.

1961 *Harper's Bazaar* May 104/2 Gangs, rebels without a cause and ton-up kids. **1961** *Times* 1 Sept. 11/1 A reasoned defence, of the 'throttle-potties' or 'ton up boys' was submitted to the psychology section. **1965** G. MCINNES *Road to Gundagai* xiii. 225 Dad wore leather hip boots and jacket, goggles and a cap with its peak at the rear... The Ton-Up kids on the M1 had nothing on him. **1982** 'C. AIRD' *Last Respects* iii. 31 I'm not stupid enough to want that boy Crosby behind the wheel of one of Traffic Division's vehicles... He'd be after a ton-up kid.

b. *fig.* Applied to a person who incongruously imitates the dress or behaviour of such people.

1964 *Economist* 13 June 1246/2 The ton-up type of vicar who is trying to be 'with it'.

2. Achieving a speed or score of 100 in other contexts.

1967 *Daily Tel.* 17 Feb. 1/4 Plans are being made to cut BEA's Manchester-to-London air service..as a result of big passenger losses to British Railways 'ton-up' trains. **1976** *Southern Even. Echo* (Southampton) 6 Nov. 13/4 After his two records for the number of winners trained in a season on the flat, it is the North Country that has the ton-up trainers of the jumping game. **1977** *News of World* 17 Apr. 19/1 'Ton-up' Taylor—he landed 100 winners last season for the first time.

‖**tonus** ('təʊnəs). *Physiol.* and *Path.* [L. *tonus*, a. Gr. *τόνος* TONE.]

1. The condition or state of muscular tone; the proper elasticity of the organs; tonicity.

1876 tr. *Wagner's Gen. Pathol.* (ed. 6) 162 In a reflex manner the arterial tonus is reduced or increased. **1882** BURDON SANDERSON in *Lancet* 29 Apr. 678 The paralysed artery recovers, and sometimes over-recovers its normal state of contraction, or, as we call it, its *tonus*. Tonus..is one of the independent endowments of arteries. **1899** *Allbutt's Syst. Med.* VII. 109 Whence comes this loss of tonus?

2. A tonic spasm.

1891 in *Cent. Dict.* **1899** *Allbutt's Syst. Med.* VII. 890 The clonic spasm may..pass into slight tonus of very short duration. **1899** *Syd. Soc. Lex.*, *Tonus*, tonic spasm.

3. (See quot.)

1902 *Encycl. Brit.* XXXI. 740/1 A continuous lesser 'change' or stream of changes sets through the neuron, and is distributed by it to other neurons in the same direction and by the same synapses as are its nerve impulses. This gentle continuous activity of the neuron is called its *tonus*.

4. *Comb.*, as ***tonus-producing*** adj.

1897 *Allbutt's Syst. Med.* III. 317 Any failure of the circulation dependent upon the absence from the blood-stream of this tonus-producing substance.

Tony ('təʊnɪ), *sb.*¹ Also 8 toney. [In sense 1, a particular application of *Tony*, used as short for *Antony*. In sense 2, the nickname of Antoinette Perry (1888–1946), U.S. actress, manager, and producer, arbitrarily used.] †**1.** A foolish person; a simpleton. *Obs. slang.*

For possible origin, cf. MIDDLETON *Changeling* (1623) I. ii.

1654 GAYTON *Pleas. Notes* III. x. 141 Their Friends and Wives have took them for Tonies or Mad-men. **1699** R. L'ESTRANGE *Erasm. Colloq.* (1711) 148, I saw once an errant Tony, with a Gown to his Heels. *a* **1700** B. E. *Dict. Cant. Crew*, *Tony*, a silly Fellow, or Ninny. *a* **1784** JOHNSON in Piozzi *Anecd.* (1786) 195 Teaching such tonies is like setting a lady's diamonds in lead.

2. One of the medallions that have been awarded annually since 1947 by the American Theatre Wing (New York) for excellence in some aspect of the theatre. Freq. in ***Tony award***.

1947 *N. Y. Times* 7 Apr. 40/1 The award already has been dubbed a 'Tony', as her associates called Miss Perry. **1948** *Ibid.* 29 Mar. 23/6 John Garfield represented the Experimental Theatre in accepting a 'Tony' for 'experiment in theatre'. **1975** *Times* 10 May 9/3 The Tonys have been awarded, and the 1974/75 New York theatre season is over. **1976** *Time* 27 Dec. 5/3 He later starred in several musicals, including his 1963 Tony Award-winning performance in *She Loves Me*.

tony ('təʊnɪ), *a.* (and *sb.*[2]) *colloq.* (orig. *U.S.*). Also toney. [f. TONE *sb.* + -Y.] **1.** Having a high or fashionable tone; high-toned, stylish; 'swell'.

1877 R. J. BURDETTE *Rise & Fall of Mustache* 177 He's a toney old cyclopedia on the patter. **1880** *Harper's Mag.* Jan. 209/2 He just put on heaps of style..you know—regular tony. **1886** *Pall Mall G.* 24 Sept. 5/1 Nevern-square, with its comfortable and, as the Americans have it, 'tony' residences. **1895** S. R. HOLE *Tour Amer.* 270 Well you see, it is so toney. **1901** H. LAWSON in *Blackw. Mag.* Apr. 478/1 The furniture looked as if it had belonged to a tony homestead at one time. **1920** D. H. LAWRENCE *Lost Girl* xii. 299 The really toney women of the place came to take tea. **1922** JOYCE *Ulysses* 158 Theodore's cousin in Dublin Castle. One tony relative in every family. **1959** D. BARTON *Loving Cup* I. iii. 60 Have you got your dinner-jacket with you, old man?.. I'm afraid we're very toney these days. We seem to get tonier. **1966** 'J. HACKSTON' *Father clears Out* 84 Father, dignified and collected,..entered the calm, cool tony atmosphere of the Commercial Hotel. **1982** A. H. GARNET *Maze* (1983) iii. 14 He was charming..what Cyrus's mother used to call a 'toney fella'.

2. A fashion colour between red and brown; also as *sb. temporary*.

1921 *Punch* 4 May 357/1 Ladies' artificial silk stockings. In black, white, nigger, grey and toney. **1927** W. E. COLLINSON *Contemp. Eng.* 61 Brogues..sometimes of ox-blood or tony red colour. **1965** *Guardian* 31 Mar. 15/1 Toney was a colour of the twenties which died with the twenties.

† **'tony**, *v. Obs. rare.* [f. TONY *sb.*[1]] *trans.* To make a fool of; to fool, cheat, swindle.

a **1652** BROME *Damoiselle* I. ii. Wks. 1873 I. 391 You, that had all these once,..To be wrought on, and tonyed out of all.

tony, obs. form of TUNNY, a fish.

tony: see TONI.

-tony [-Y[3]], anglicized f. -TONIA.

tonycle, tonyd, obs. ff. TUNICLE, TONED.

Tony Curtis ('təʊnɪ 'kɜːtɪs). The film-name of Bernard Schwarz (b. 1925), U.S. actor, used *attrib.* and *absol.* to designate a style of haircut in which the hair at the sides of the head is combed back and that on the forehead is combed forward.

1956 *People* 13 May 10/2 The blokes with crew cuts or Tony Curtises. **1961** J. I. M. STEWART *Man who won Pools* iv. 48 His girl had..made him quit that Duck's Behind for a straight sleeking back with oil. George Pratley had his Tony Curtis still. **1969** *It* 13–28 June, She had seen him.. with a well slicked back Tony Curtis style complete with DA at the back.

too (tuː), *adv.* Forms: 1 tó, 2–7 to, (3 tu, 6 toe), 6– too. [Stressed form of TO *prep.*, which in the 16th c. began to be spelt *too*.]

I. 1. a. In addition (cf. TO *adv.* 5); furthermore, moreover, besides, also.

The use of *too* in this sense at the beginning of a clause, formerly common, was rare or obsolete by the nineteenth cent. It was revived in the twentieth cent., at first in the U.S.

c **888** K. ÆLFRED *Boeth.* xli. §5 Þa styriendan netenu.. habbað eall þæt ða unstyriendan habbað, and eac mare to. *a* **1240** *Ureisun* in *Cott. Hom.* 183 Tu art se softe and se swote ȝette to swa leoflic. *c* **1330** R. BRUNNE *Chron.* (1810) 229 Þe envenomed knyfe [he] out braid, & gaf Edward a wounde. To, I wene, he lauht. ? **1400** *Arthur* 532 Seyþ a Pater noster more to. **1533** MORE *Debell. Salem* Wks. 997/1 Wold not the iudges..geue them yᵉ hearing; yes yes I dout not, and the iury to. **1590** SHAKS. *Com. Err.* III. i. 110 Prettie and wittie; wilde, and yet too gentle. **1627** HAKEWILL *Apol.* (1630) 296 Not the bodie only but the minde to..is sickish & indispos'd. **1641** J. SHUTE *Sarah & Hagar* (1649) 156 Too, we professe our selves the Redeemed of the Lord. **1766** GOLDSM. *Vic. W.* iii, Take..this book too. **1821** SCOTT *Kenilw.* xx, I too have sometimes that dark melancholy. **1891** *Law Times* XC. 315/1 If you sell the mansion-house in which the heirlooms are to be kept, you must sell the heirlooms too. **1930** *Publishers' Weekly* 17 May 2514/2 Too, chain store merchandising tactics are the result..of the keenest..retailing brains in this country. **1956** GARDNER & SMITH *Geneal. Res. Eng. & Wales* I. iv. 46 Many births and deaths were not recorded in the parish registers of England and Wales. Too, some of the other denominations kept poor records. **1969** *Daily Tel.* (Colour Suppl.) 17 Oct. 59/1 And, too, is there any future for the Dunebuggy in Britain? **1976** *National Observer* (U.S.) 7 Mar. 13/2 Too, supermarket officials note, the projected 10 to 20 per cent saving..covers only part of the..bill. **1978** R. LUDLUM *Holcroft Covenant* vii. 89 Too, the windows were not that close to one another.

b. Used after a vb. to emphasize a reassertion of a denied statement. orig. and chiefly *U.S.*

1914 B. TARKINGTON *Penrod* xiv. 122 'No, I didn't.'.. 'He did, too! Didn't he, Sam?' **1936** M. MITCHELL *Gone with Wind* xlvii. 843 'Surely you can't be thinking of marrying a man who wasn't in the army..?' 'He was, too, in the army.' **1937** WODEHOUSE *Summer Moonshine* (1938) v. 59 'Do you know the Princess?' 'My stepmother.' 'She isn't!' 'She is, too. I have documents to prove it.' **1939** *Reader's Digest* Dec. 25 'She hasn't got appendicitis.' The husband became even wilder, insisting that she did too have appendicitis. **1963** L. DEIGHTON *Horse under Water* xxi. 92 'How do you think she guessed?' 'No idea,' I said. 'You have too. Please tell me,' said Jean. **1969** tr. *Godard's Masculine Feminine* 60 *Madeleine*: You don't care, but for me my first record is very important. *Paul*: I do too care. **1978** A. MALING *Lucky Devil* xxxiii. 181 'Well, you can't really believe in both,' she said. 'You can too!' Frances said hotly.

II. 2. In excess; more than enough; overmuch, superfluously, superabundantly. (Preceding and qualifying an adj. or adv.) **a.** *gen.* In excess of what ought to be; more than is right or fitting.

a **900** CYNEWULF *Crist* 1567 Ac hy to sið doð gæstum helpe. **971** *Blickl. Hom.* 41 ȝe eow ondrædaþ þæt ȝe onfon to lytlum leanum. *a* **1200** *Moral Ode* 28 in *Lamb. Hom.* 161 Al to muchel ich habbe ispent, to litel ihud in horde. **13..** *E.E. Allit. P.* B. 182 For mon-sworne, & men-sclaȝt, & to much drynk. **1535** COVERDALE *Num.* xvi. 3 Ye make to moch a doo. **1604** SHAKS. *Oth.* v. ii. 345 One that lou'd not wisely, but too well. **1605** —— *Lear* I. iv. 279 Woe, that too late repents. **1766** GOLDSM. *Vic. W.* vi, I delivered this observation with too much acrimony. **1852** MRS. STOWE *Uncle Tom's C.* xvi, A fellow's taking a glass too much, and sitting a little too late over his cards.

b. More than enough for the particular case in question; in excess of what is consistent with or required by something expressed by the context.

Usually const. *for* with sb. (cf. FOR *prep.* 13 b); *to* with inf. (cf. TO *prep.* B. 7 b); or *for* with sb. + *to* with inf. (cf. FOR *prep.* 18).

a **1300**– [see TO B. 7 b]. *c* **1350** *Will. Palerne* 5024 Of here a-tir for to telle to badde is my witte. *c* **1489** CAXTON *Blanchardyn* xlvi. 177 Blanchardyn shal neuer come ayen at thys syde; kyng alymodes is to myghty a lorde in his lande. *c* **1518** SKELTON *Magnyf.* 1892 All worldly Welth for hym to lytell was. **1599** SHAKS. *Much Ado* v. ii. 72 Thou and I are too wise to wooe peaceablie. **1653** WALTON *Compl. Angler* vii. 160 This dish of meat is too good for any but Anglers. **1665** MANLEY *Grotius' Low C. Warres* 791 The Castle..was too mean a prize for so great an Army to look after. **1710** STEELE *Tatler* No. 200 ¶2 Men of Letters know too much to make good Husbands. **1804** WORDSW. *She was a phantom of delight* ii, A Creature not too bright or good For human nature's daily food. **1908** R. BAGOT *A. Cuthbert* xix, Too large an apartment for two people not to feel somewhat lost in it.

c. Expressing, sorrowfully or indignantly, regret or disapproval: To a lamentable, reprehensible, painful, or intolerable extent; regrettably, painfully, esp. as ***too true***, ***just too bad***: see JUST *adv.* 6 c. Cf. 5 c.

c **1205** LAY. 5268 To late heom þuȝte are heo þer to comen. **1297** R. GLOUC. (Rolls) 4618 Ac to prout he was & to fals, þat ssende þis lond alas. *c* **1380** WYCLIF *Wks.* (1880) 454, & þus ech siche were herde of ech, but þis abusioun were to straunge. **1447** *Rolls of Parlt.* V. 137/1 It apperith to openly in som persones. **1568** GRAFTON *Chron.* II. 501 The old prouerbes be to true. **1592** CHETTLE *Kinde-harts Dr.* (1841) 24 Either witles, which is too bad, or wilfull, which is worse. **1648** *Petit. Eastern Assoc.* 15 Which is too well pleasing to the adverse partee. **1721** WODROW *Suffer. Ch. Scot.* (1838) I. I. iv. §1. 333/2 Some of them, alas too many, were heard swearing very rudely. **1839** THACKERAY *Fatal Boots* Aug., This was too cool. **1849** MACAULAY *Hist. Eng.* v. I. 663 It is indeed but too true that the taste for blood is a taste which ..men..may..speedily acquire. **1855** MACAULAY *Hist. Eng.* xvii. IV. 87 At best a blunderer, and too probably a traitor. **1900** C. M. YONGE *Modern Broods* I. 5 'I am considered quite passée——' 'My dear! With your art, and music, and all!' 'Too true!' **1930** 'E. QUEEN' *French Powder Mystery* xxxi. 261 'The presumption is that he slept home all night and therefore couldn't have committed the crime. Yet physically it was possible.'.. 'Too true, too true,' murmured Ellery. **1976** N. FREELING *Lake Isle* x. 67 'Rare, that sort of saint.' 'Too true.'

d. Rarely used to qualify a verb: Too much, to excess. (See also 4 b.)

1509 BARCLAY *Shyp Folys* 59 Whyle one is ladyd to the others backe is bare. **1833** BROWNING *Pauline* 937–8, I have too trusted my own lawless wants, Too trusted my vain self. **1873** —— *Red Cott. Nt.-cap* III. 790 The causes,..Would too distract, too desperately foil Enquirer.

3. As a mere intensive: Excessively, extremely, exceedingly, very.

('Now chiefly an emotional feminine colloquialism'—N.E.D.; but see also 5 c and d.)

1340 *Ayenb.* 95 The wel greate loue and to moche charite of god þe uader. **1697** tr. *C'tess D'Aunoy's Trav.* (1706) 79 He..had not lost nothing of whatever made me heretofore fancy him too Lovely. **1825** T. HOOK *Sayings* Ser. II. *Man of Many Fr.* I. 273 'We shall see you at dinner, perhaps', said the Colonel... 'I shall be too happy', replied Noel. **1868** PR. ALICE *Mem.* 4 Sept. (1884) 203 How too delightful your expeditions must have been.

4. Reduplicated for emphasis: *too too* (formerly occas. written as one word, *toto*, *totoo*, *tootoo*).

a. Qualifying an adj. or adv.; chiefly in sense 2 c. (Very common *c* 1540–1660.)

c **1489** CAXTON *Blanchardyn* liv. 213 Ah ! to to well I suspected..that my captiuitie would bring her callamity. **1542** UDALL *Erasm. Apoph.* 271 It was toto ferre oddes yᵗ a Syrian born should in Roome ouer come a Romain. **1582** in Hakluyt *Voy.* (1904) V. 233 Threed..some tootoo hard spun, some tootoo soft spun. **1586** DAY *Eng. Secretary* I. (1625) 5 Vsed *bona fide*, it was too too bad. **1602** SHAKS. *Ham.* I. ii. 129 Oh that this too too solid Flesh would melt. **1654–66** EARL ORRERY *Parthen.* (1676) 547 Her fears were but too-too well grounded. **1745** *Gentl. Mag.* Oct. 550/1 Not apt to toy, and yet not too too nice. **1821** SCOTT *Kenilw.* xxxvi, It is too, too apparent. **1885** LELAND *Brand-new Ballads* (ed. 2) 109 Perishing to find Something which was not too-too-utter-ish To serve for dinner. **1887** *N. & Q.* 7th Ser. III. 109/2 The too-too painfully ceremonious manners ..of the French.

† **b.** Qualifying a verb, as in 2 d; also *absol.*

c **1518** SKELTON *Magnyf.* 872 He doth abuse Hym self to to. **1533** J. HEYWOOD *Merry Play* (1903) 183 By my soule I love thee too too. **1534** MORE *Comf. agst. Trib.* III. Wks. 1247/2, I cannot then see, that the feare..shold any thing sticke with vs, & make vs toto shrinke. *c* **1537** *Thersites* (1820) 66 It is to to, mother, the pastyme and good chere That we shall see and haue.

c. As *adj.* in predicative or attributive use: Excessive, extreme; extremely good, highly exquisite.

An affectation, connected with the 'æsthetic' craze of *c* 1880–90. In quot. 1891 = characterized by the use of 'too too'.

1881 *Punch* 26 Mar. 138 (*caption*) 'Have you seen the Old Masters at Burlington House?'.. 'Are they not really quite *too* TOO!!' **1891** *N. & Q.* 7th Ser. XI. 30/2 Let the exclusive too-too æsthetes tolerate the remark that music and painting do not exist for them. **1893** MRS. A. KENNARD *Diogenes' Sandals* i. 12 The piece is nowhere; but my frocks are too too!

5. In special collocations. † **a.** ***too much*** (besides its ordinary use) was formerly sometimes used instead of the simple *too* to qualify an adj. or adv. *Obs.*

c **1449** PECOCK *Repr.* I. xi. 53 To miche homeli dele with him. **1530** RASTELL *Bk. Purgat.* III. i, When the bodye is to mych hote or to mych colde, or to mych drye or to mych moyste. **1593** SHAKS. *Rich. II*, II. ii. 1 Your Maiesty is too much sad. **1638** JUNIUS *Paint. Ancients* 230 His minde is kept too much busie.

b. ***too much*** (as predicate): (*a*) more than can be endured, intolerable: also ***too much of a good thing***; (*b*) orig. *U.S.*, excellent, first-rate; ***too much for***: more than a match for; such as to overcome or subdue: so ***too many for*** (see MANY A. 5 f), ***too hard for***, etc. Chiefly *colloq.*

1533 J. HEYWOOD *Merry Play* (1830) 30 Shall we alway syt here styll, we two? That were to mych. **1692–1872** [see MANY A. 5 f]. **1777** SHERIDAN *Trip to Scarb.* v. ii, Don't be frightened, we shall be too hard for the rogue. **1794** A. RADCLIFFE *Myst. Udolpho* I. ix. 251 The sight of this poor old woman would have been too much for Emily. **1796** MME. D'ARBLAY *Camilla* I. 233 O too much! too much! there's no standing it! **1809** SYD. SMITH *Wks.* (1867) I. 175 This (to use a very colloquial phrase) is surely too much of a good thing. **1832** HT. MARTINEAU *Life in Wilds* v, The light had been too much for him. **1861** DICKENS *Gt. Expect.* xlviii, Mr. Jaggers was altogether too many for the Jury, and they gave in. **1937** *Metronome* Mar. 55/1 Man, if you didn't you really missed something. That man's too much! What great bass drum work he shows. **1958** G. LEA *Somewhere there's Music* xviii. 155, I want to make it to the City... Man, like the City is too much—and that's where I want to be. **1966** *Melody Maker* 15 Oct. 19, I just can't wait for his Spring return with Earl Hines, Budd Johnson and the rest. This could be too much. **1967** [see LEAN *v.*[1] 6 d]. **1968** *Scottish Daily Mail* 3 Jan. 6 They got 'Absolutely divine'; we get 'Too much'... One day 'Too much' will sound as old fashioned as 'ripping'.

c. ***but too..***, ***only too***: Here *too* is app. = 'more than is desirable' (cf. 2 c), or 'more than is or might be expected', while *but* (BUT C. 6) or *only* (ONLY A. 1) = 'nothing but', 'nothing else than', app. emphasizes the exclusion of any different quality or state of things such as might be desired or expected.

1639 MASSINGER *Unnat. Combat* II. i, I have Discourse and reason, and but too well know I can nor live, nor end a wretched life. **1654–66** [see 4]. **1817** CASS. AUSTEN in *Jane Austen's Lett.* (1884) II. 334, I loved her only too well. **1818** SCOTT *Rob Roy* viii, Stay, then, rash, obstinate girl..you know but too well to whom you trust.

d. ***only too*** in recent use, is often a mere intensive, = 'extremely'. (Cf. 3.)

1889 'J. S. WINTER' *Mrs. Bob* (1891) 245 Mrs. Trafford will only be too glad to come and pay you a visit. *Mod.* I shall be only too pleased.

e. ***none too..*** is used by meiosis for 'not quite.. enough', 'somewhat insufficiently'; also rather less than; only moderately; not very.: see also NONE C. 3. Also in other negative contexts, esp. ***not too***— (cf. NOT *adv.* 15 d).

1842 E. A. POE in *Graham's Mag.* Feb. 126/2 The mind of the not-too-acute reader. **1866** GEO. ELIOT *Felix Holt* I. iii. 86 They were not too hopeful about Protestants who adhered to a bloated and worldly Prelacy. **1866**, etc. [see NOT *adv.* C. 2 d]. **1885** *Manch. Exam.* 21 May 5/3 The vast territories of the Dominion have hitherto been none too coherent. **1892** E. G. WHITE *Steps to Christ* (1908) 108 We do not pray any too much, but we are too sparing of giving thanks. **1909** GALSWORTHY *Fraternity* xxxvii. 313 There were not too many people in London who..would have behaved with such seemliness—not too many so civilised as they! **1912** J. SANDILANDS *Western Canad. Dict. & Phrase-Bk.*, *Not too bad*, a characteristic Canadian reply to an inquiry regarding one's health or circumstances. *a* **1913** *Mod.* Money is none too plentiful with us. **1947** *Sun* (Baltimore) 5 Nov. 2/7 There is little incentive for him to do more than seek a mere existence for himself and family, without too keen a regard for the plight of others. **1956** *English* Summer 45 The English Association..having survived half a century and two world wars..has not done too badly. **1967** L. DEIGHTON *Expensive Place to Die* 19 'Can I have a shower?' she asked. 'The water's not too warm I'm afraid,' said Byrd. **1984** A. BROOKNER *Hotel du Lac* i. 10 My intervention did not seem to be too welcome.

f. ***quite too..***: see QUITE 4 c.

g. *too right*: expressing emphatic agreement or assertion. orig. *Austral.*

1926 'J. DOONE' *Timely Tips to New Australians*, Too right!—A slang term expressing agreement or corroboration. **1934** T. WOOD *Cobbers* v. 76 What I says is, give 'em an axe and send 'em into the bush. Then they'd work, or starve. Too right they would. **1951** J. FLEMING *Man who looked Back* xi. 145 'We should have thought of that before we started out.' 'Too right,' Joe agreed. **1961** *Lancet* 5 Aug. 311/2 The chairman agreed it was thumbs down for Dr. Y., too right it was. **1978** P. McCUTCHAN *Blackmail North* viii. 95 'He'll see you now sir.' 'Too right he will.'

6. In combination. **a.** With an adj. or adv., forming a (nonce) sb. phr., as ***a too-late***, ***a too-little***, ***a too-much***.

1602 SHAKS. *Ham.* IV. vii. 119 Goodness, growing to a plurisy, Dies in his own too much. **1637** C. DOW *Answ. to H. Burton* 158 There may be a too-much even in the best things. **1784** R. BAGE *Barham Downs* I. 346 [One] who complains of the Too-much of things he does not value, and of the Too-little of things he does. **1860** PUSEY *Min. Proph.* 542 There will be a 'too late'; not a final 'too late',.. but.. a 'too late' to avert that particular judgment. **1905** *Daily Chron.* 14 Apr. 5/4 We have suffered greatly in our national life from the domination of the 'too-lates'; political procrastination is the thief of opportunity.

b. With an adj. or adv., forming an adj. phr. preceding and qualifying a sb., or an adv. phr. qualifying an adj., as ***too-anxious***, ***-celebrated***, ***-familiar***, ***-fervent***, ***-near***, ***-piercing***, ***-trusting***, ***-willing***, ***-wise*** adjs.; ***too-early***, ***-late***, ***-long***, ***-much*** (in quot. 1620 = too great *obs.*; see also 5 a) adjs. and advs. Hence derivatives (*nonce-wds.*), as ***too-bigness***, ***-lateness***, ***-muchness***, ***-soonness***.

1612 *Two Noble K.* II. ii. 32 Like a too-timely Spring. **1620** VENNER *Via Recta* vi. 100 It.. represseth the too-much tenuity.. of the bloud. **1624** DONNE *Devot.* 221 Those sentences, from which a too-late Repenter will sucke desperation. **1793** HOLCROFT *Lavater's Physiog.* xxvi. 127 The gentleness of his voice [will] temper thy too-piercing tones. **1838** LYTTON *Alice* II. ii, The good man was quite shocked at the too-familiar manner in which Mrs. Merton spoke. **1842** TENNYSON *Day-dream* Prol. 18 Turn your face, Nor look with that too-earnest eye. **1849** MISS OTTÉ tr. *Humboldt's Cosmos* II. II. v. 596 My lamented and too-early deceased friend. **1855** KINGSLEY *Heroes* II. I. (1868) 82 Only one walked apart.. Asclepius, the too-wise child. **1887** *Spectator* 16 Apr. 532/1 A too-fervent patriotism.

1858 DE QUINCEY in 'H. A. Page' *Life* (1877) II. xviii. 142 In midst of too-soonness he shall suffer the killing anxieties of too-lateness. **1875** BLACKIE *Let.* in *Biog.* (1895) II. xviii. 122 An everlasting too-muchness. **1904** S. E. WHITE *Forest* iii. 30 Everything was wrinkled in the folds of too-bigness.

too, variant of TEW *v.*, to bustle round (*U.S.*).

1866 LOWELL *Biglow Papers* Introd., Poems 1890 II. 199 'Ther's sech a thing ez bein' *tu*'.. hence the phrase *tooin' round*, meaning a supererogatory activity like that of flies.

too, obs. f. TOE, TWO; var. of TO *v.*, to take.

tooa: see TOA[1].

‖**tooart** ('tuːət). Also **tewart**, **tuart**. [Native name in Australia.] A West Australian tree, *Eucalyptus gomphocephala*, which furnishes a very hard heavy durable timber used in ship-building.

1870 BRAIM *New Homes* iv. 181 Another valuable tree is the tooart, a kind of white gum. **1875** LASLETT *Timber & Timber Trees* xxvi. 187 The Tewart Tree (*Eucalyptus*). A variety of the White Gum... The wood is.. hard, heavy, tough, strong, and rigid... It is used in ship-building for.. keelsons,.. and for other works below the line of flotation.

tooche, obs. form of TOUGH.

toocke, **toocun**, obs. ff. TOQUE, TOKEN.

toocker, variant of TUCKER *Obs.*, a fuller.

tood(e, obs. forms of TOAD.

toodle ('tuːd(ə)l), *v.* ? *dial.* [In sense 1 echoic (cf. TEEDLE, TOOTLE).]

1. *intr.* To hum or sing in a low tone (as to a baby).

1865 W. G. WILLS *D. Chantrey* xxxii. III. 140 She shall have the toodling and the cooing and a sequestered spot, and be spared these foolish accessions of nerves.

2. See quot 1904. [perh. a different word.]

1890 A. LANG *Sir S. Northcote* I. i. 11 In winter [at Eton] they 'toodled'. **1904** J. A. THOMSON *Eighty Years' Reminiscences* I. i. 19 [At Eton in 1832] One of our great amusements in winter was toodling—hunting birds in the hedges and chasing them till they were blown, when we captured them.

So **'toodle-'loodle**; † **toodle-toodle** [cf. Ger. *dudeldudel*], an imitation of the sound of a pipe or flute; **toodle-pipe**, a pipe making such a sound.

1542 UDALL *Erasm. Apoph.* 223 b, His instrumente wheron to plaie toodle loodle bagpipe. *a* **1553** —— *Royster D.* II. i. (Arb.) 32 Then to our recorder with toodleloodle poope As the howlet out of an yuie bushe should hoope. *a* **1566** R. EDWARDS *Damon & Pithias* (1571) F iv b, Wyll singes, Too nidden, and toodle toodle doo nidden. *Ibid.* G j, Todle todle. **1890** DOYLE *White Company* xviii, A Scotch army, where every man fills himself with girdle-cakes, and sits up all night to blow upon the toodle-pipe.

toodle-oo (tuːd(ə)l'uː), *int. colloq.* [Origin unknown; perh. f. TOOT *sb.*[2]] Goodbye. Cf. PIP-PIP.

1907 *Punch* 26 June 465 'Toodle-oo, old sport.' Mr. Punch turned round at the amazing words and gazed at his companion. **1908** T. E. LAWRENCE *Let.* 16 Aug. (1938) 62 Tootle 'oo. E.L. **1931** D. L. SAYERS *Five Red Herrings* vi. 64 Well, toodle-oo! **1960** [see BLOT *sb.*[1] 1 c]. **1981** R. BARNARD *Sheer Torture* xi. 121 I'll be downstairs. Toodle-oo.

Also **toodle-**, **tootle-pip**.

1977 A. C. H. SMITH *Jericho Gun* v. 67 Well, tootle-pip for now. **1983** *Standard* 26 Oct. 23 (*heading*) Toodlepip to the poor British Exec.

toofan, variant of TYPHOON.

toofer, var. TWOFER.

toogh, obs. f. TOUGH.

too-hoo, var. of TOO-WHOO, owl's cry.

took, pa. t. of TAKE *v.*; obs. form of TUCK.

tooken, obs. f. TOKEN; obs. pa. pple. of TAKE *v.*

tool (tuːl), *sb.* Forms: 1 tól, 2–4 tol, 4–7 tole, toole, (5 tule, toyel, 5–6 toile, 5–7 toyle, 6 toyll, towle, 7 tooell), 4– tool. [OE. *tól* neut., = ON. *tól* n. pl. (cf. Norw. *tøler*):—OTeut. **tôwlo*[m], *tôlo*[m], f. **tôw-* to prepare, make (cogn. with Goth. *taujan*: see TAW *v.*[1]) + agent-suffix *-lo*[m], -EL[1].]

1. a. 'Any instrument of manual operation' (J.); a mechanical implement for working upon something, as by cutting, striking, rubbing, or other process, in any manual art or industry; usually, one held in and operated directly by the hand (or fixed in position, as in a lathe), but also including certain simple machines, as the lathe; sometimes extended to simple instruments of other kinds, as in quot. 1893. See also EDGE-TOOL.

c **888** K. ÆLFRED *Boeth.* xiv. §1 þæt mete and drync & claðas, & tol to swelcum cræfte. *c* **1000** ÆLFRIC *Exod.* xx. 25 Gif þu þin tol ahefst ofer hyt, hit biþ besmiten. *a* **1100** *Gerefa* in *Anglia* (1886) IX. 262 He sceal fela tola to tune tilian. *c* **1205** LAY. 29253 Nettes.. and þa tolen þer to. **13..** *E.E. Allit. P.* B. 1342 Formed with handes Wyth tool out of harde tre, & telded on lofte. *a* **1400–50** *Alexander* 4708 A pelare of marble Quare-on a tulke wiþ a toile þis titill vp he wrate. *c* **1440** *York Myst.* xxxiv. 298, I warand all redy Oure tooles bothe lesse and more. **1497** *Naval Acc. Hen. VII* (1896) 89 Carpenters toles.. j chest. **1501** *Bury Wills* (Camd.) 84 To .. Margarett my wyff all my stuff of houshold.. excepte my werkyng toole, weche I wyll that John my sone haue. **1570** LEVINS *Manip.* 214/45 A Toyle, *instrumentum.* **1573** TUSSER *Husb.* (1878) 31 Few lends (but fooles) their working tooles. **1597** *Knaresborough Wills* (Surtees) I. 207 One lowme with the towles yr unto belonginge. *a* **1660** *Contemp. Hist. Irel.* (Ir. Archæol. Soc.) II. 172 All theire bagage, tooells, and instruments. **1667** MILTON *P.L.* XI. 572 Moulds.. from which he formd First his own Tooles. **1706** E. WARD *Wooden World Diss.* (1708) 62 His [the Surgeon's] Tools are of various Sorts and Sizes. **1818** BYRON *Juan* I. cci, Good workmen never quarrel with their tools. **1877** KNIGHT *Dict. Mech.* s.v., Of late it has become usual to embrace in the general term *machine tools*, such machines as the lathe, planer, slotting-machine, and others employed in the manufacture of machinery. **1893** HODGES *Elem. Photogr.* (1907) 22 The anastigmat [lens] will.. prove the more useful tool.

b. A weapon of war, *esp.* a sword. *arch.*

[*c* **1000** *Ags. Gloss.* in *Haupt's Zeitschrift* IX. 424 *Instrumenta bellica*, wiȝlice tol.] *c* **1386** CHAUCER *Nun's Pr. T.* 96 We alle desiren.. no fool Ne hym þat is agast of euery tool. ? *a* **1400** *Morte Arth.* 3617 The toppe-castelles he stuffede with toyelys, as hyme lykyde. *c* **1400** *Destr. Troy* 938 Iason.. gryppet a grym toole, gyrd of his hede. **1592** SHAKS. *Rom. & Jul.* I. i. 37 Draw thy toole, here comes of the house of Mountagues. **1671** H. FOULIS *Hist. Rom. Treasons* (1681) 228 Pope John xxii.. pulls out his tools against Lewes. **1706** E. WARD *Wooden World Diss.* (1708) 63 He's somewhat prouder of that long Tool of his, that hangs without board. **1821** SCOTT *Kenilw.* iv, Draw thy tool, man, and after him.

(*b*) Hence in *Criminals' slang*, any weapon.

1938 F. D. SHARPE *Sharpe of Flying Squad* xix. 209 'Here they are, boys; get your tools ready.'.. As they ran they pulled weapons from under their coats, hatchets, knuckle-dusters, hammers, and bars of iron. **1971** J. MANDELKAU *Buttons* i. 28 We grabbed our tools and by then the Mods were at the bottom of the street.

† **c.** The cutting part of a knife, the blade. *Obs.*

1653 URQUHART *Rabelais* I. xxvii. 129 Little hulchback't demi-knives, the iron toole whereof is two inches long, and the wooden handle one inch thick.

d. *spec.* in technical use: (*a*) *Bookbinding.* A small stamp or roller used for impressing an ornamental design upon leather book-covers: cf. TOOLING 2 b. (*b*) A large kind of chisel. (*c*) A generic name for any kind of paint-brush used by house-painters or decorators; also, a large brush used by picture-painters. (*d*) An abbreviated form of *grafting-tool*, etc.

(*a*) **1727–41** CHAMBERS *Cycl.* s.v. *Book-binding*, These ornaments are made with each its several gilding-tool, engraven in relievo. *Ibid.*, To apply the gold, they glaze those parts of the leather, whereon the tools are to be applied, lightly over [etc.]. **1837** WHITTOCK, etc. *Bk. Trades* (1842) 37 (Bookbinder) The tools that produce the figures or letters are applied hot. **1895** ZAEHNSDORF *Short Hist. Bookbinding* 13 He cut most of these tools himself,.. because he could not find a tool cutter of sufficient skill.

(*b*) **1815** [see TOOLING 2]. **1823** P. NICHOLSON *Pract. Build.* 341 Of the two kinds of chisels.. the tool is the largest. **1842–76** GWILT *Encycl. Arch.* §1910 The tools used to work the face of a stone are, successively, the point, the inch tool, the boaster.. and the broad tool. *Ibid.*, The broad tool 3½ inches at the cutting edge.

(*c*) **1859** GULLICK & TIMBS *Paint.* 198 The larger brushes .. made of hog-hair.. are called 'tools'. **1860** PIESSE *Lab. Chem. Wonders* 153 A painter calls a paint-brush 'a tool'.

2. *fig.* **a.** Anything used in the manner of a tool; a thing (concrete or abstract) with which some operation is performed; a means of effecting something; an instrument.

c **1000** *Eccles. Inst.* c. 21 þis synt þa lara and þa tol gastlices cræftes. **1555** PHAER *Æneid* II. E j b, At last Those toles for shift at death extreme, to fend them selfs they cast. **1611** SIR W. MURE *Misc. Poems* ii. 46 He [Cupid].. left behind his tort'ring toyle [*rime* spoyle; *cf.* l. 40 Ye bow, ye schafts, ye quaver and ye brace]. **1651** HOBBES *Leviath.* II. xxv. 132 They.. make use of Similitudes.. and other tooles of Oratory. **1674** GREW *Disc. Mixture* ii. § 5 As the World, taken together, is Natures Shop; so the Principles of Things are her Tools, and her Materials. **1749** SMOLLETT *Gil Bl.* VIII. ix. III. 161 You have (to use the expression of our tennis-court) the universal tool: that is to say, you are qualified for every thing. **1847** L. HUNT *Men, Women, & B.* I. i. 7 Mechanical knowledge is a great and a glorious tool in the hands of man. **1884** B. PRICE in *Contemp. Rev.* Mar. 381 Money.. is a pure tool—nothing more.

b. A bodily organ; *spec.* the male generative organ (or *pl.* organs). Now *slang.* [So ON. *tól*.]

1553 BECON *Reliques of Rome* (1563) 18 All his toles that appertayne vnto the court of Venus. **1613** SHAKS. *Hen. VIII*, v. iv. 35 Or haue wee some strange Indian with the great Toole, come to Court? **1687** SHADWELL *Juvenal* 307 What pleasure can the weak Old Doting Fool, Expect from that infirm and Aged Tool? **1885** R. F. BURTON *Arab. Nts.* III. 7, I was become even as a woman, without manly tool like other men. **1922** JOYCE *Ulysses* 299 The poor bugger's tool that's being hanged. **1966** L. COHEN *Beautiful Losers* (1970) I. 114 You uncovered his nakedness!—You peeked at his tool! **1971** J. STEWART tr. *Simenon's Rich Man* iii. 64 A little slut of a girl.. who had not protested when he had put his tool in her hand.

3. *fig.* **a.** A person used by another for his own ends; one who is, or allows himself to be, made a mere instrument for some purpose; a cat's-paw.

1663 BUTLER *Hud.* I. i. 35 Which made some take him for a tool, That knaves do work with, call'd a fool. **1688** BP. PARKER in *Magd. Coll.* (O.H.S.) 240 To set me here to make me his tool and his prop! **1711** HEARNE *Collect.* (O.H.S.) III. 133 Charlett and his Tools have got Rogers advanc'd. **1769** *Junius Lett.* xxiv. (1770) 153 If there be any tool of administration daring enough to deny these facts. **1849** MACAULAY *Hist. Eng.* iv. I. 494 The sheriffs were the tools of the government. **1874** GREEN *Short Hist.* vii. §4. 379 Mary had used Darnley as a tool to effect the ruin of his confederates.

b. (esp. qualified by *poor* or the like.) An unskilful workman; a shiftless person. *slang* or *dial.*

a **1700** B. E. *Dict. Cant. Crew*, *Slug*, a drone, or dull Tool. **1722** G. VERTUE *Diary* in *N. & Q.* (1861) 2nd Ser. XII. 81/1 The organists are poor tools and very deficient. **1863** MRS. TOOGOOD *Yorks. Dial.* (MS.), You are a poor tool, your work is not done as it ought to be.

c. A pickpocket; the member of a pair or team of pickpockets who actually picks pockets; = WIRE *sb.* 13.

1865 *Leaves from Diary Celebr. Burglar* xviii. 62/1 They were getting uneasy about the absence of their 'tool'. **1886** A. PINKERTON *Thirty Yrs. a Detective* 38 The man who is to do the actual stealing is called the 'tool' or 'hook' and the others are known as 'stalls'. **1936** *Evening News* 9 Dec. 8/5 Modern pickpockets are either 'tools' or 'stalls.'.. Really clever tools work alone, disdaining the assistance of a stall. **1955** *Publ. Amer. Dial. Soc.* XXIV. 60 The tool selects the mark to be robbed, and actually takes the score.

4. *Bookbinding.* (*transf.* from 1 d (*a*).) A tooled design on a book-cover.

1881 CUNDALL *Bookbindings* 76 He began with a small number of dotted tools, foliage, and the so-called seventeenth-century tools. **1885** C. G. W. LOCK *Workshop Receipts* Ser. IV. 252/1 A book on Natural History should have a bird, insect, shell or other tool indicative of the contents.

5. *attrib.* and *Comb.*, as **tool bag** (also *fig.*), ***-basket***, ***-box***, † ***-budget*** (BUDGET *sb.* 2 b), ***-chest***, ***-cutter***, ***-dressing***, ***-extractor***, ***-gauge***, ***-handle***, ***-kit***, ***-maker***, ***-making*** sb. and adj., ***-pouch***, ***-rack***, ***-roll***, ***-room***, ***-seller***, ***-shed***, ***-shop***, ***-tray***, ***-user***, ***-using*** sb. and adj.; **tool-bar**, a frame fitted to a tractor on which interchangeable implements may be mounted; **tool-box**, *spec.* the steel box (BOX *sb.*[2] 15) in which the cutting tool of a planing or other machine is clamped; **tool-car** (*U.S.*), a car used on a railway equipped with tools and appliances for clearing the line after an accident; a breakdown car; **tool-coupling**, a screw coupling by which the operating part of a tool is fastened to the handle (Knight); **tool-crib**, a place from which tools or other stores are issued to workmen; **tool-dresser** *Oil Industry* = ROUSTABOUT 3; **tool head**, a part of a machine that carries the tool or tool-holder and can be moved to bring the tool to bear on the work; **tool-holder**, (*a*) a handle by which a tool is held in the hand, esp. a detachable handle for various tools; (*b*) a tray with a rack for holding a set of tools; (*c*) a device for holding a tool firmly in place, as in a lathe, or when being ground upon a grindstone; **tool-house**, a building in which tools are kept, a tool-shed; **tool-man**, (*a*) a worker with tools; a toolroom worker; (*b*) *Criminals' slang*, a lock-picker or (*U.S.*) safe-breaker; **tool-mark**, the mark of a tool upon any object that has been shaped or worked by it; **tool-marking**, the etching of a mark or lettering upon a steel tool; **tool-post**, an upright piece in the tool-rest of a lathe, with a slot and a screw for holding the cutting-tool; **tool-pusher** *Oil Industry*, someone in charge of a drilling rig; **tool-rest**, a part of a lathe serving to support a hand-tool, or to hold a mechanical tool in place (in the latter case often having various adjustments for different positions of the tool); **tool slide**, a sliding machine part which carries a tool; **toolsmith**, a man who makes steel tools; **tool-stack** = *tool-post*, *tool-holder* (*c*); **tool-stay**, a tool-holder in a lathe-rest, with a slot for a drill or other tool (Knight); **tool steel**, steel of the quality used for tools; **tool-stock** = *tool-post*; **tool-stone**, name for a palæolithic implement consisting of a natural stone very slightly adapted to be held in the hand, or used as a rude tool; **tool subject** *Educ.*, a subject taught or studied as a help to a main subject.

1892–3 *T. Eaton & Co. Catal.* Fall & Winter 95/1 Bicycle Accessories... *Tool Bags—Flat pouch with fastener. **1970** *New York* 16 Nov. 42/2 Talk is the most unreliable and over-reacted-to weapon in the black revolutionary toolbag. **1960** *Farmer & Stockbreeder* 8 Mar. 74/3 In a great many cases they are designed as units to be carried on an ordinary *toolbar. **1858** Simmonds *Dict. Trade*, *Tool-basket*, a carpenter's or other workman's basket, for holding tools. **1832** *Chambers's Edin. Jrnl.* I. 236/2 Lifting his *tool-box, and going through all the operations of horse-shoeing. **1841–4** Emerson *Ess.*, *Prudence*, [He] builds a work-bench, or gets his tool-box set in the corner of the barn-chamber. **1904** *Lineham's Text-bk. Mech. Eng.* 171 The tool box is fixed to a ram, the sliding of which in saddle gives the cut. **1794** W. Felton *Carriages* (1801) I. 223 *Tool budget is a small convenience made to hang by straps under the hind part of a carriage. **1778** Cook *Voy. Pacific* iv. v. (1784) II. 373 As well and ingeniously made, as if they were furnished with the most complete *tool-chest. **1936** J. Dos Passos *Big Money* 19 In six years he rose from machinist's helper to keeper of *toolcribs. **1973** T. Pynchon *Gravity's Rainbow* i. 160 It must have been the wind that was carrying him down a dirt road.. among the shacks and tool cribs to a wire fence with a gate. **1896** B. Redwood *Petroleum* I. v. 258 The drilling 'crew' consists of two drillers and two *tool-dressers. **1976** M. Machlin *Pipeline* iv. 53 His Daddy started him as a tool dresser—same way I started. **1882** *Rep. to Ho. Repr. Prec. Met. U.S.* 594 It includes tools, *tool-dressing and grinding. **1877** Knight *Dict. Mech.*, *Tool-extractor*, an implement for recovering from drilled holes broken tools or portions of rods. *Ibid.* 2594/1 Nasmyth's *tool-gage, for testing the angularity of the cutting-face of iron-turning tools. **1887** Moloney *Forestry W. Afr.* 207 Red wood used for *tool-handles and mallets. **1950** W. Cooper in A. W. Judge *Centre, Capstan & Automatic Lathes* I. iv. 212 Independent feed for the *tool heads is provided at each [work] station. **1977** *Sci. Amer.* Sept. 188/1 The appropriate toolhead was selected automatically by a punched-paper-tape program that was read by an electronic computer-controller. **1877** Knight *Dict. Mech.* 2594/1 A *tool-holder for dentists. **1887** D. A. Low *Machine Draw.* (1892) 110 Tool-holders must be drawn in their proper positions in the ram, and not separate as in the diagram. **1905** *Athenæum* 14 Oct. 510/1 The needles used were European, fitted into watchmaker's tool-holders. **1818** Scott *Rob Roy* xiv, Before he trundled them off to the *tool-house. **1908** *Betw. Trent & Ancholme* 10 A lattice-gate, into the tool-house. **1963** A. Lubbock *Austral. Roundabout* 108, I took.. a *tool-kit, a box of spare parts, two spare wheels, [etc.]. **1977** C. McFadden *Serial* (1978) iv. 14/2 Did she have enough cash in her Swedish carpenter's tool kit? **1844** Mill *Ess. Pol. Econ.* iv. 98 The producer.. must set aside a portion of the produce to replace not only the wages paid both by himself and by the tool-maker, but also the profits of the *tool-maker. **1858** Simmonds *Dict. Trade*, Tool-maker. **1888** E. Clodd *Story Creation* xi. 217 If he is not the only tool-user, he is the only tool-maker among the Primates. **1785** Boswell *Jrnl. Tour Heb.* 25 *n.*, Dr. Franklin said, Man was 'a *tool-making animal', which is very well; for, no animal but man makes a thing, by means of which he can make another thing. **1893** Eliza R. Sunderland in Barrows *Parl. Relig.* I. 630 Religion is an attribute of humanity, as reason and language and tool-making are. **1909** Webster, *Toolman, one who works with or makes tools. **1949** W. R. Burnett *Asphalt Jungle* vii. 47 We need an expert toolman. **1970** R. Busby *Frighteners* xvi. 157 The toolman.. got his nickname and reputation by proving there wasn't a lock made that he couldn't tickle. **1977** *Whitaker's Almanack 1978* 577 British Leyland was given 28 days to get the striking toolmen back to work. **1979** K. Bonfiglioli *After you with Pistol* xxiv. 149 Every sound, professional team of thieves has.. a 'toolman' who knows how to neutralize burglar-alarm systems and to open locks. **1865** J. F. Campbell *Frost & Fire* I. x. 94 Before a craftsman can recognise a *tool-mark, he must be familiar with the tool. **1864** Webster, *Tool-post, the part of a tool-rest that holds a stationary cutting-tool;—called also tool-stock. **1932** *Amer. Speech* VII. 271 *Tool pusher, a foreman in charge of drilling operations—distinct from driller. **1976** M. Machlin *Pipeline* xlii. 460 Around daylight a tool-pusher comes out and he tells us we better shut down our rig and put out the fire because the crew on the next well's going to change their control head. **1864** Webster, *Tool-rest (*Machine-tools*), the part that supports a tool-post or a tool. **1917** *Harrods Gen. Catal.* 1059/4 Motor car *tool roll.. containing 19 best quality tools. **1979** W. H. Canaway *Solid Gold Buddha* xxii. 146 Pete spread a toolroll on the spillway. **1878** Aylward *Transvaal* ii. (1881) 18 Everywhere one may observe that older houses are being used as waggon shelters, coach-houses, *tool-rooms. **1937** *Times* 13 Apr. p. xv/2 This checking is the function of the tool room staff in which are to be found the finest craftsmen in the factory. **1963** *Times* 28 May 5/2 More than 1,400 toolroom workers in 10 Birmingham factories of the Joseph Lucas group took part in a 24-hour token strike today. **1976** *Milton Keynes Express* 16 July 13/4 (Advt.), Toolmaker and toolroom miller required. **1875** Sir T. Seaton *Fret-Cutting* 71 The *tool-seller has to pay the workman for dressing the wood. **1840** Dickens *Barn. Rudge* lv, To break open a *tool-shed in the garden. **1875** Sir T. Seaton *Fret-Cutting* 71 Unprepared wood bought at the *tool-shop. **1919** G. W. Burley *Lathes* vii. 108 In some special forms of vertical turning and boring mills the *tool-slide is of the non-swivelling variety,.. and only vertical and horizontal movements are possible. **1936** Colvin & Stanley *Turning & Boring Practice* vii. 101 When the cut is completed the spindle stops, the flow of coolant is shut off, and the tool slides return.. to the starting point. **1963** Tool slide [see semi-automatic *sb.* 1]. **1884** C. G. W. Lock *Workshop Receipts* Ser. iii. 269/2 A *toolsmith usually heats cast steel to what he terms a cherry-red. **1868** Joynson *Metals* 90 For *tool-steel, from 1·5 to 1·7 per cent [of charcoal being required]. **1894** Bowker in *Harper's Mag.* Jan. 419 Too costly.. to be in demand except for tool steel. **1864** *Tool-stock [see *tool-post*]. **1865** Lubbock *Preh. Times* iv. 76 The oval *tool-stones.. are oval or egg-shaped stones, more or less indented on one or both surfaces... Some antiquaries suppose that they were held between the fingers and thumb, and used as hammers or chippers. **1934** Webster, *Tool subject. **1966** *Rep. Comm. Inquiry Univ. Oxf.* II. 456 Teaching in any 'ancillary' or 'tool' subject (e.g. languages for historians or mathematics for economists). **1888** *Tool-user [see *tool-maker*]. **1831** Carlyle *Sart. Res.* i. v, This Definition of the *Tool-using Animal appears to us, of all that Animal-sort, considerably the precisest and best. **1862** D. Wilson *Preh. Man* vi. (1865) 96 Man was created with a tool-using instinct.

tool, *v.* [f. prec. sb.]

1. a. *trans.* To work or shape with a tool; *spec.* to smooth the surface of a building stone with the chisels called 'tools': cf. quot. 1842 in tool *sb.* 1 d (*b*).

1815 [see tooling 2]. **1828** *Craven Gloss.*, *Tool*, to make a level surface on a stone. **1842** *Civil Eng. & Arch. Jrnl.* V. 211/1 The whole exterior.. will be faced with stone from the Summit delphs, which is to be neatly hammer-dressed, except the ashlar dressings, which are to be neatly tooled. **1873** Sir T. Seaton *Fret-Cutting* (1875) 56 The stems and branches look very well when simply rounded and tooled with the V-tool, or tooling-gouge, which is the smallest sized round gouge. **1876** Preece & Sivewright *Telegraphy* 238 Chatterton's compound should be warmed, and a small quantity put on the copper and joint, and properly tooled over, so as to cover the joint equally. Before applying the tooling-iron it should be well wiped. **1895** *Daily Chron.* 15 Jan. 6/7 Aluminium.. is ductile, but difficult to tool.

b. *Bookbinding.* To impress an ornamental design upon the binding of (a book) with a special tool (see prec. 1 d (*a*)). Most usually in pa. pple.; see also tooled.

1836 *J. R. Smith's Catal. Bks.* Feb. 14/1 A remarkable fine copy, russia extra, tooled on sides, gilt. **1881** A. Lang *Library* 65 Leather tooled with geometrical patterns. **1885** C. G. W. Lock *Workshop Receipts* Ser. iv. 246/1 Another method is to tool the edge before burnishing.

c. *intr.* To work with a tool or tools; *spec.* in *Bookbinding*: see prec. sense and tooling 2 b.

1890 *Daily News* 2 July 5/1 'The Tasmanians'.. the very last people who 'tooled' with rudely chipped flints. **1892** *Sat. Rev.* 16 Jan. 64/2 They are a ferocious people.. and 'tool' with spears almost as broad in the head as shovels.

d. *trans.* To equip (a factory) with the machine tools needed for a particular product; to provide the tools needed for (a new product); also *intr.* Usu. with *up*. Also *fig.*

1927 *Observer* 25 Sept. 4 The work of tooling up the Manchester and Cork factories may result in production within the next two months. **1933** *Flight* 27 Apr. 392 It is standard practice to 'tool up' for a certain type as soon as the size of the order warrants the expenditure on jigs and dies. **1939** *Times* 4 Nov. 6/3 The United States National Defence Council is taking steps to see that American plants shall not be tooled to fit European needs at the expense.. of the United States' own later military needs. **1940** E. J. H. Jones *Production Engin.* i. 6 The expression to 'tool up' a component means to design and supply all jigs, fixtures, cutting tools, and gauges required for the manufacture and inspection of the piece. **1957** *Observer* 3 Nov. 11/4 Makers must be given a chance to sell models already tooled-up. **1959** *Times Rev. Industry* Apr. 57/3 Much expenditure had to be faced for tooling new models. **1962** *Listener* 13 Sept. 375/1 The automobile factories have tooled up for their new models. **1972** M. Kaye *Lively Game* v. 23, I saw all of the specs.. and I helped to tool it up.

e. *intr.* *to tool up* (*fig.*): to arm oneself. *slang.*

1959 *Times* 7 Apr. 6/3 There seemed a general agreement that the fashion of carrying dangerous weapons was more widespread to-day than formerly. One read all too often about groups of young men 'tooling up' before setting off for a showdown with a rival gang. **1971** J. Mandelkau *Buttons* xiii. 142 We tooled up with pieces of wood and iron bars and hiked over towards their main camp. **1978** H. Wouk *War & Remembrance* xxi. 213 We might have closed the Mediterranean and forced England to her knees even while.. we tooled up for our summer Caucasus thrust.

2. *slang.* **a.** *trans.* To drive (a team of horses, a vehicle, or a person in a vehicle); of a horse, to draw (a person) in a vehicle.

1812 *Sporting Mag.* Oct. 10/2 She intends to tool the Liverpool expedition to-morrow night. **1840** J. T. Hewlett *P. Priggins* xv, He would only drive to Benson, and 'tool' the down mail back again. **1849** Lytton *Caxtons* xiii. iv, He could tool a coach. **1865** Dickens *Mut. Fr.* i. xi, She was on most days solemnly tooled through the park.. in a great tall custard-coloured phaeton. **1881** Jessopp *Arcady* (1887) i. 13 The high-stepping mare that tools him along through the village street. **1882** H. C. Merivale *Faucit of B.* II. ii. ii. 158, I tooled the little mare over from Luscombe Abbey—the six miles in the half-hour.

b. *intr.* Orig., to drive, to travel in a horse-drawn vehicle; also said of the vehicle, or team. Subsequently, by extension, to travel in any kind of vehicle, and (of the vehicle) to travel, go *along*.

1835 Dickens *Let.* 11 Jan. (1965) I. 53, I wish.. you could have seen me tooling in and out of the banners, drums,.. and go-carts. **1839** J. Frazer in *Haileybury Observer* I. 53 The road was so good.. as to enable us to 'tool along' in a well-hung britschka, at the rate of ten miles an hour. **1849** Thackeray *Pendennis* iii, I thought I'd just tool over, and go to the play. **1877** Mar. M. Grant *Sun-Maid* xi, The Marquis's frisky chestnuts are tooling rapidly through the town. **1893** W. A. Shee *My Contemp.* iii. 77 Went to Ascot.. and we 'tooled' down in very good style. **1923** Wodehouse *Inimitable Jeeves* xiii. 155, I borrowed a bicycle from one of the grooms and tooled off. **1964** *Manhunt* May 134/1, I was tooling home from the Mexican border in a light blue convertible. **1977** D. Anthony *Skid Game* xix. 114, I tooled down the Coast Highway to Sunset.

c. Of a person: to go (or come) in an easy manner; to go *off* quickly.

1862 A. J. Munby *Diary* 23 Feb. (1972) 116 Near S. Martin's Lane, I met W. M. Thackeray; 'tooling' along quietly, alone, with hands in pockets. **1881** *Punch* 17 Dec. 285/2 Now we'll just tool off to some quiet sort of a place where we can divide this 'ere shining swag without fireworks. **1936** Wodehouse *Laughing Gas* xxviii. 293 Well, I know when I'm licked. I tooled straight round to the Temple of the New Dawn and asked for an entrance form. **1937** D. L. Sayers *Busman's Honeymoon* 25 The Dowager saw them and was quite nice to them, so they tooled off, fairly happy. **1940** Wodehouse *Eggs, Beans & Crumpets* 58 Bingo was tooling along the road with the Peke in his arms. **1945** 'A. Gilbert' *Don't open Door!* xix. 176 Citizens come tooling up to the Police Station.. to give information. **1955** E. Waugh *Officers & Gentlemen* 8 Tool off to Headquarters and get the gen about tonight's do. **1977** 'E. Crispin' *Glimpses of Moon* vi. 90 Then along comes the boy-friend.. and tools off without the least idea that anything's seriously wrong.

d. To play *around*; to behave in an aimless or irresponsible manner.

1932 F. Iles *Before the Fact* i. v. 77 'Well, anyhow, what are you doing with yourself.'.. 'Oh, tooling around, you know. Nothing much.' **1957** *New Yorker* 21 Sept. 37/3 Let him stay parched or get a head cold tooling around in ferryboats. **1973** 'A. Hall' *Tango Briefing* ii. 22 We were tooling around in Malta on a friendly visit. **1981** J. Wainwright *All on Summer's Day* 8 Tool around long enough with the paper work and.. half the night has slipped by.

toold, obs. f. *told*, pa. pple. of tell *v.*

tooled, *a.* [f. tool *sb.* + -ed².] In parasynthetic comb.: Having or furnished with a tool.

1577 Grange *Golden Aphrod.* M ij, Priapus the great tooled god. **1935** [see *middle leg* s.v. middle *a.* 6].

tooled (tu:ld), *ppl. a.* [f. tool *v.* + -ed¹.]

1. Worked or shaped with a tool; *spec.* in *Bookbinding*: see tool *v.* 1 b.

1815 [see tooling 2]. **1837** *Civil Eng. & Arch. Jrnl.* I. 72/1 Tooling is also practised upon wall stones, when they cost as much as common hewing or tooled work. **1856** Mrs. Browning *Aur. Leigh* viii. 895 A copy bound in scarlet silk, Tooled edges, blazoned with the arms of Leigh. **1893** *Q. Rev.* July 200 Specimens of their handiwork in tooled morocco.

2. *tooled up*: equipped with an offensive weapon. *slang.*

1959 *Observer* 1 Mar. 10/1 They sit in all-night cafés, 'tooled up' sometimes with knives and 'choppers' and crank handles. **1973** *Time Out* 2–8 Mar. 13/2 They had knives, chains, house-bricks, iron bars, and everything. We weren't tooled up, because we were coming out of school, and so couldn't get ready properly. **1982** J. Barnett *Marked for Destruction* v. 58 Smith brandished the shotgun.. to let the minder know he was tooled up.

tooler ('tu:lə(r)). [f. as prec. + -er¹.]

1. A broad chisel used by stone-masons for random tooling; a drove.

1828 *Craven Gloss.*, *Tooler*, a broad chissel.

2. *Bookbinding.* A workman who tools the covers of books: see tool *v.* 1 b.

1834 De Quincey in *Tait's Mag.* I. 28/2 The King.. coming into the binding-room and minutely inspecting the progress of the binder and his allies—the gilders, toolers, &c. **1865** *Englishm. Mag.* Sept. 220 The most finished specimens of the tooler's art in these days.

toolie ('tu:lɪ). *Oil Industry. slang.* [f. tool *sb.* + -ie.] = *tool-dresser* s.v. tool *sb.* 5.

1932 *Amer. Speech* VII. 271 *Toolie*.., a tool-dresser—i.e., the assistant of a cable-tool driller, who dresses bits, fires the boilers, and maintains the rig in order. **1976** L. St. Clair *Fortune in Death* i. 13 He wouldn't be the first wildcatter to end up a toolie, a roustabout.

toolies ('tu:lɪz), *sb. pl. Canad.* [Respelling of *tules*, pl. of tule.] Backwoods; remote or thinly populated regions.

1961 R. P. Hobson *Rancher takes Wife* i. 22 We're plenty far back in the toolies at Batnuni. **1976** M. Machlin *Pipeline* xii. 141 This here's a program they got for people out in the toolies.

tooling ('tu:lɪŋ), *vbl. sb.* [f. tool *sb.* and *v.* + -ing¹.]

†**1.** Provision of tools; tools collectively. *Obs.*

1673 KIRKMAN *Unlucky Citizen* 210 By such time as he and his are fitted with Clothing, Teething and Tooling, his money is gone.

2. The action of the verb TOOL; workmanship performed with some special tool; *spec.* **a.** The dressing of stone with a broad chisel; also, elaborate ornamental carving in stone or wood.

1815 J. SMITH *Panorama Sc. & Art* I. 218 The larger sizes of chisels obtain the name of tools, the act of using them is called tooling, and the stone to which they have been applied is said to be tooled. **1840–1** DE QUINCEY *Style & Rhet.* Wks. 1858 XI. 31 The fine tooling, and delicate tracery of the cabinet artist. **1891** *Edin. Rev.* July 110 The tooling of the Haram stones is peculiar, and is the same found on the later Carthaginian monuments.

b. *Bookbinding.* The impressing of ornamental designs upon the covers of books by means of heated tools or stamps; also applied to the designs so formed: either with gilding (*gold-* or *gilt-tooling*) or without it (*blind-tooling*: BLIND *a.* 16).

1821 G. ORMEROD *Let. to J. G. Nichols* May (in *Pearson's Catal.* (1886) No. 60), I would not have any lettering or tooling on the back. **1847** L. HUNT *Men, Women, & B.* II. vi. 78 The charms of vellums, tall copies, and blind tooling. **1875** KNIGHT *Dict. Mech.*, *Gold-tooling*, ornaments impressed by the hot-tool upon gold-leaf laid on book-covers. **1893** *Q. Rev.* July 187 The tooling in gold introduced at this time..came originally from the East.

c. The process of designing and supplying the machine tools needed for a product or model; also *concr.*, these tools collectively.

1939 *Daily Tel.* 18 Dec. 12/3 (Advt.), Experience should include the setting up and tooling of automatic and turret lathes. **1940** *Sun* (Baltimore) 9 Dec. 14/8 War plants emerge from the 'tooling up' phase into production. **1958** *Times Rev. Industry* June 57/2 A minimum of three-year development time is necessary..through all stages of design, prototypes, testing and tooling. **1963** *Wall St. Jrnl.* 1 Oct., Dayton Reliable Tool & Manufacturing Co... has switched 90% of its manufacturing to making tooling for turning out pull-open devices. **1967** L. B. ARCHER in Wills & Yearsley *Handbk. Management Technol.* 125 Should we begin to sell at a high price to recover our tooling costs quickly? **1977** G. V. HIGGINS *Dreamland* xii. 150, I had earned commissions in hand, from cleaning out Vulcan's obsolete tooling.

3. *Comb.*, as ***tooling-gouge***, ***-iron***.

1873 Tooling-gouge, **1876** Tooling-iron [see TOOL *v.* 1].

toolless ('tu:llɪs), *a.* [f. TOOL *sb.* + -LESS.] Having no tools; destitute of tools.

1831 *Fraser's Mag.* III. 13 Art thou lonely, idle, friendless, toolless? **1889** H. O. PENTECOST in *20th Cent.* (N.Y.) 30 Mar., So low has the landless and toolless man fallen that work seems to him now the greatest boon in life.

toolsee, -si, -sy, variant forms of TULSI.

toolsman ('tu:lzmən). *rare*$^{-1}$. A man who uses tools, a craftsman.

1821 T. G. WAINWRIGHT *Ess. & Cr.* (1880) 193 *note*, That mannered petty toolsman, Raffaëlle Morghen—the admiration of fallen, immaculate Italy.

toolter: see TOLTER *a.*

tooly, obs. f. TEWLY *a.*, sickly.

tooly, -lye, var. TUILYIE.

†**toom,** *sb.*^{1} *Obs.* (in later use only *Sc.*) Forms: 3–6 tome, 4 tom, (toume, towme, toym), 5 toom, 6 tume. [a. ON. *tóm* sb. neut. emptiness, vacuity, leisure, OSw. *tōm* leisure, occasion, ODa. *tōm* time, occasion; f. *tómr* adj. empty: see TOOM *a.*] Vacant or unoccupied time; time free or sufficient for doing something, leisure; a space or interval of time, a while.

1297 R. GLOUC. (Rolls) 11656 In hor bed hii founde hom in toune þo hii come.. Vor to wel cloþi hom hii ne ȝeue hom no tome. *a* **1300** *Cursor M.* 14595 Haf i na tome at ga þar-to. *c* **1315** SHOREHAM I. 2119 Þaȝ he by hyre ne ligge nouȝt, Oþer halt hys ine hys house, In tome. **13..** *E.E. Allit. P.* A. 134 More.. Þen I cowþe telle þaȝ I tom hade. **1375** BARBOUR *Bruce* v. 642 Or þe topir had toym to tak His suerde, þe king sic swak him gaiff. *c* **1430** *Syr Gener.* (Roxb.) 3126 Of Generides dome To speke had thei nomore tome. **1535** STEWART *Cron. Scot.* (Rolls) II. 18 3it will I tell, for I haif space & tume, How efterwart he set ane seig to Rome.

b. Time convenient or proper for doing something; opportunity, occasion.

13.. *E.E. Allit.* P. B. 1153 3if 3e wolde tith [*MS.* ty3t] me a tom telle hit I wolde. **1390** GOWER *Conf.* I. 249 His Bacheler, which hadde tome, Whan that his lord be nihte slepte, This Ring,.. Out of his Pours awey he dede. *c* **1440** *York Myst.* xl. 18 Atte townes for to tarie take we no tent, But take vs tome at þis tyme to talke of sume tales. *c* **1450** *Bk. Curtasye* 10 in *Babees Bk.* 299 Ther-to the nedys to take the tome.

toom, *sb.*^{2} *Sc.* [f. TOOM *v.*] A place where rubbish is or may be emptied out; a 'coup'.

1882 JAMIESON, *Toom*, a place into which rubbish is emptied. **1884** *Blackw. Mag.* June 817/1 The piled-up rubbish of millions of years which has been cast out here as into one vast 'toom'. **1894** CROCKETT *Raiders* 226 Great tails [of stones] that spread down the mountain steep, like rubble from a quarry toom.

toom (tu:m; in mod.Sc. tøm, tʏm), *a.* Now only *Sc.* and *north. dial.* Forms: α. 1 tóm, 3–6 tōme, (5 tombe, toyme, 6 towme), 5–7 toome, 5– toom. β. 4 tum, 4–7 tume, 6 twme, (?) twyme, 9 *Sc.* tume, tuim. γ. 8–9 teem, 9 *dial.* teeam. [OE. *tóm* = ON. *tómr* (Norw., Da., Sw. *tom*); also OS. *tômi, tômig*, OHG. *zuomîg*:—OTeut. **tôm-o*^{z} or **tôm-u*^{z} (OS. *tômia-*); ulterior origin unknown. Hence TEEM *v.*^{2}]

1. Empty, vacant, containing nothing, void of contents; destitute (*of* something).

a **900** CYNEWULF *Christ* 1211 þæt hy mostun man-weorca tome lifȝan. *a* **1300** *Cursor M.* 17798 And yee sal find þair tumbs tome [*Gött.* tume]. *Ibid.* 17815 Þai sagh þaa tumbs, tum war þai. *a* **1340** HAMPOLE *Psalter* cxliii. 16 Ful of riches and tome of goednes. *c* **1400** MAUNDEV. (Roxb.) xxxiii. 149 When þai see þe toome vessellez, þai ga and fillez þam with gold. **1435** MISYN *Fire of Love* II. iv. 76 Certan of godis lufe þat ar toyme. *c* **1440** *Promp. Parv.* 496/2 Toom, or voyde, *vacuus.* *c* **1470** HENRYSON *Mor. Fab.* I. (*Cock & Jasp*) iv, As draf, or corne, to fill my tume Intraill. **1508** KENNEDIE *Flyting w. Dunbar* 365 Thow has a tome purs. **1560** ROLLAND *Seven Sages* (1837) 1 Of all vertew that Ceitie was maid tome. **1727** P. WALKER *R. Cameron* in *Biog. Presbyt.* (1827) I. 241 There were many toom pulpits in Scotland. **1786** BURNS *Earnest Cry & Prayer* vii, Her mutchkin stoup as toom's a whissle. **1831** CARLYLE *Sart. Res.* III. vi, The man John Baliol being quite gone, and only the 'Toom Tabard' (Empty Gown) remaining. **1855** ROBINSON *Whitby Gloss.* s.v., As toom as an egg-shell.

γ. *a* **1774** FERGUSSON *Hallowfair* Poems (1845) 14 Here, tak a rug, and show your pose Forseeth, my ain's but teem And light the day. **1861** E. WAUGH *Lake Country* 180 He was as helpless as a teeam seck.

2. *fig.* Empty, insubstantial, vain, void, futile.

a **1250** *Owl & Night.* 1672 Me þuncþ þu ledest ferde tome. **1513** DOUGLAS *Æneis* VI. iv. 120 The tume schaddowis smytyn to haue slane. **1568** *Satir. Poems Ref.* xlvi. 27 Till deif 3ow wt tome clatter. **1721** RAMSAY *Prospect of Plenty* 46 O'er lang, with empty brag, we have been vain Of toom dominion on the plenteous main. **1786** G. FRAZER *Fall of Man* 157 Blown up with the toom wind of a flattering empty sound.

†**b.** Idle, unoccupied. *Obs.*

a **1340** HAMPOLE *Psalter* xlix. 21 Sitand tome [*MS.S.* ydel], for it likes þe to speke ill. *c* **1460** *Towneley Myst.* xxx. 125 To stand thus tome thou gars me grete.

3. *Comb.*, as ***toom-handed***, ***-headed***, ***-skinned*** adjs.

c **1400** MAUNDEV. (Roxb.) xxv. 120 Na man comme in my sight tome hand. **1629** Z. BOYD *Balme of Gilead* 21 (Jam.) A man as we say that hath not harnes, or brain, a toome headed man. **1768** ROSS *Helenore* Introd. 4 Ye're nae toom handed gin your heart be free. **1824** MACTAGGART *Gallovid. Encycl.*, *Toom-skin'd*, hungry.

toom, *v. Sc.* and *north. dial.* Forms: see prec. [f. TOOM *a.*, taking the place of the earlier TEEM *v.*^{2}]

1. *trans.* To empty (a vessel, receptacle, etc.); *esp.* to empty by drinking, to drink off the contents of.

1500–20 DUNBAR *Poems* xxvi. 64 Ay as thay tomit thame of schot, Ffeyndis fild thame new vp to the thrott With gold of allkin prent. **1580** *Burgh Rec. Edinb.* (1882) IV. 187 The inhabiteris.. maist filthely castes furth and tomes thair closettis and pottis on the hie gaitt. **1583** *Leg. Bp. St. Androis* Pref. 136 Concluding this, we toome a tass of wyne. **1721** RAMSAY *Prospect of Plenty* 106 They'll toom their banks before you reap their crap. **1896** 'IAN MACLAREN' *Kate Carnegie* 71 Toom.. yir mooth this meenut and say the twenty-third Psalm to the minister.

2. To empty out, discharge, pour out (water, the contents of a vessel, etc.).

1535 STEWART *Cron. Scot.* (Rolls) II. 630 This ilk Banquho, the quhilk the aill gart brew,.. Amang the aill gart tume thame in the fat. **1816** SCOTT *Antiq.* xxxvi, She.. was like to hae toomed it a' out into the slap-basin. **1818** —— *Hrt. Midl.* xxviii, Our gawsie Scots pint.. toomed doun the creature's throat wi' ane whorn.

toomatoogooroo, variant of TUMATA-KURU.

toomble, obs. form of TUMBLE.

†'**toomhead.** *Obs. rare.* In 3 tomehed(e. [f. TOOM *a.* + -HEAD.] Emptiness, vanity. ***over tomehed***, uselessly, to no purpose.

a **1300** *E.E. Psalter* xxiv. 4 Schente be alle are quede doand Ouer tomehed in ani land. *Ibid.* xxxiv. 7 Ouer tomehede vpbraided þai.

'**toomly,** *adv. Sc.* and *north. dial.* [f. TOOM *sb.*^{1} and *a.* + -LY^2.]

1. In a leisurely way; somewhat slowly; without haste.

c **1400** *Destr. Troy* 2447 When he told hade his tale tomly to the ende. *Ibid.* 11488 Antenor his tale tombly began.

2. †**a.** Idly, without occupation. *Obs.* **b.** Emptily, vainly, to no purpose.

c **1400** *Destr. Troy* 4580 Ye haue tarit ouer tyme tomly at home. **1606** BIRNIE *Kirk-Buriall* (1833) 5 Rather to teach what the kirk should doe nor toomely to talke what hes beene done.

3. With empty saddle.

17.. '*Willie's drowned in Gamery*' xi. in Child *Eng. & Sc. Ball.* VII. (1890) 181/2 And every one on high horse sat, But Willie's horse rade toomly.

toompe, obs. form of TUMP.

†'**toomsome,** *a. Obs. rare*$^{-1}$. [f. TOOM *sb.*^{1} + -SOME.] Leisurely, free from haste.

13.. *Cursor M.* 26350 (Fairf.) Shrift.. þer ar xv pointis to shaw.. Clene & reuful.. wreiande, tomsome [*Cott.* (*erron.*) turnsum] propre, stedefast [etc.].

‖**toon**^{1}, **tun** (tu:n). *E. Ind.* [a. Hindī *tun, tūn*, Skr. *tunna.*] An East Indian tree, *Cedrela Toona*, which yields a timber resembling mahogany but softer and lighter, used for furniture and cabinet-work: the wood of this tree, also called *Indian mahogany*. Also *attrib.*, as ***toon-tree***, ***-wood***.

1810 MARIA GRAHAM *Jrnl. Resid. India* (1812) 101 The toon, or country mahogany, which comes from Bengal. **1843** HOLTZAPFFEL *Turning* I. 108 Toon-wood has already been mentioned under the head of Cedar. **1879** MRS. A. E. JAMES *Ind. Househ. Managem.* 28 The wood they use mostly in the Punjaub is toon... It is valuable from its durability, and is reddish in colour.

toon^2 (tu:n), repr. a dial. pronunc. of TUNE *sb.*

1901 M. FRANKLIN *My Brilliant Career* iii. 16 Some of us wuz always good for a toon on the concertina. **1977** *New Musical Express* 12 Feb. 17/1 How the mighty are fallen. Shel Talony.. is reduced to dealing with a non-voice churning out four mock country toons for a 99p line.

toon, obs. pl. of TOE; obs. f. TONE, TUN; north. dial. f. TOWN.

toondra, var. TUNDRA.

toonie ('tu:nɪ). [f. *toon*, repr. Sc. pronunc. of TOWN *sb.* (in Shetland, *spec.* = the arable land on a croft) + -IE.] In full ***toonie dog***: = *Shetland sheepdog* s.v. SHETLAND 1 d.

1910 J. A. LOGGIE in J. S. Turner *Kennel Encycl.* III. 1249 The 'Shetland Sheep-dog'.. was originally known as the 'Shetland Collie' or 'Toonie Dog'.. from the fact of its being used to drive the sheep off the township, croft, or what is known in Shetland as the 'Toon'. **1958** O. GWYNNE-JONES *Shetland Sheepdog Handbk.* i. 4 The 'Toonie' dogs ('Toonies' or Shetland Sheepdogs) are of great service to the farmer. **1971** [see PEERIE *sb.*].

toopick, obs. f. TOPIC.

toor, toore, var. TOR *a.*, *Obs.*, difficult.

tooraloo (tu:rəˈlu:), *int. colloq.* [Var. TOODLE-OO *int.*] 'Goodbye.'

c **1921** D. H. LAWRENCE *Phoenix II* (1968) 121 So long! See you soon! Too-ra-loo! **1922** JOYCE *Ulysses* 229 Tooraloo, Lenehan said, see you later. **1974** J. JOHNSTON *How Many Miles to Babylon?* 22 I'll have to be off... Tooraloo.

toord, obs. f. TURD.

toorkes, obs. f. TURQUOISE.

toos(e, obs. f. *toes*, pl. of TOE.

toose, obs. f. TOZE.

toosie, toosy, var. TOSY, TOUSY.

toost, obs. pa. pple. of TOSS *v.*

toot, tote (tu:t), *sb.*^{1} *local.* Also 5–9 tout. [f. TOOT *v.*^{1}]

I. 1. An isolated conspicuous hill suitable as a place of observation; a look-out hill; perh. short for TOOT-HILL, q.v. Chiefly *south-western*.

1387 TREVISA *Higden* (Rolls) III. 85 Temples þat were on groues vppon hiȝe totes [CAXTON or hilles], to worschippe mawmetes inne. *Ibid.* V. 163þe eorþe aroos in þe manere of a tote [so *MSS.* α, β, γ, and CAXTON; *Camb. MS.* tufte]. **1884** D. CLAYFIELD IRELAND *Let.*, In the west of England I think 'fairy toot' is a tolerably common topographical expression. And there is a curious jagged and pointed hill a few miles from Bristol known as Cleeve toot. **1904** *Daily News* 15 June 5 In the West of England.. 'toot' signifies hill. **1905** *Eng. Dial. Dict.*, *Toot*,.. a hilly promontory, on which there is a coast-guard watch-station and flag. *Mod.* (South Dorset) There's one of the preventive-men on the tout.

†**2.** An elevated structure, or part of one, used as a look-out. *Obs.*

1770 GRAY *Jrnl. in Lakes* 12 Oct., I went up a winding stone staircase.., and at the angle is a single hexagon watch-tower rising some feet higher, fitted up in the taste of a modern Toot, with sash-windows in gilt frames, and a stucco cupola. **1785** GROSE *Dict. Vulg. Tongue*, *Tout*, a look out house, or eminence.

II. 3. A peep or glance. *dial.*

1865 E. WAUGH *Lanc. Songs* (1871) 56 Th' cat pricks up her ears at th' sneck, Wi' mony a leetsome toot.

4. *Comb.*: †***tote-hole***, a hole for spying: cf. *tooting-hole* (TOOTING *vbl. sb.*^{1} b).

1561–6 *Child-Marriages* 113 Lokid in at a tote hole.

toot (tu:t), *sb.*^{2} Also *Sc.* **tout** (tu:t). [f. TOOT *v.*^{2}] An act of tooting; a note or short blast of a horn, trumpet, or other wind instrument. Also *fig.*

1641 *D. Ferguson's Scot. Prov.* (1785) 7 A new tout in an old horn. **1714** RAMSAY *Elegy on J. Cowper* vi, Fame, Wi' tout of trumpet, Shall tell. **1721** KELLY *Scot. Prov.* 28 An old Tout in a new Horn. Spoken when we hear (perhaps in other words) what we have heard before. **1765** BOSWELL in Ramsay *Scot. & Scotsm.* (1888) I. ii. 172 James has taken a tout on a new horn. **1787** BURNS *Tam Samson's Elegy* 59 Now he proclaims, wi' tout o' trumpet, 'Tam Samson's dead!' **1822** SCOTT *Nigel* xxvii, It is just a new tout on an auld horn. **1874** D. MACRAE *Amer. at Home* xlii. 327 She gave two 'toots' with her steam-pipe.

b. Reduplicated ***toot-toot***; so ***toot-tootling***.

1883 S. C. HALL *Retrospect* I. 7 How pleasant.. the jovial toot-toot of the guard's horn. **1904** MARIE CORELLI *God's Good Man* xx, With a weird toot-tootling of his horn he guided the car at quite a respectable ambling-donkey pace. **1905** *Daily Chron.* 19 May 4/7 Of all the noises of London the 'toot-toot' of the motor-car is the most hideous.

toot, tout (tu:t), *sb.*[3] *Sc.* and *U.S.* [f. TOOT, TOUT *v.*[3] *Tout* is Sc. spelling of (tu:t).]

1. An act or fit of tooting; a copious draught.

1787 SHIRREFS *Jamie & Bess* I. ii, Were he ay [sober], he then wad ay be kind, But then, anither tout may change his mind. **1816** G. MUIR *Clydesdale Minstr.* 56 (E.D.D.) To your health I'll drink a tout Frae out the whisky gill. **1902** OGILVIE *J. Ogilvie* 96 (ibid.) Sit doon an' tak a hearty tout.

2. A drinking match; a drunken fit, a spree (*U.S. slang*); esp. in the phrase ***on the toot***; hence, a tea-party.

1790 SHIRREFS *Poems* Gloss., *Tout*, a drinking-bout, a drinking match. **1891** *Century Mag.* Nov. 54 Grubbsy's went off on a toot, and they've got nobody to ride. **1897** HOWELLS *Landl. Lion's Head* 228 To-day I found him at Mrs. Bevidge's altruistic toot. **1900** LYNCH *High Stakes* xxxii. (Farmer *Slang*), I'd never 'a' carried 'em..if I 'adn't been on a regular toot for the last week.

3. Cocaine; a 'snort' of cocaine. *U.S. slang.*

1977 *Maclean's Mag.* 2 May 24 They slink into some of the finer furnished bathrooms of the city for a quick toot. **1978** *Detroit Free Press* 16 Apr. (Parade Suppl.) 21/1 Cocaine—also called 'coke', 'C', 'snow' and 'toot'. **1979** *Daily News* (N.Y.) 23 Sept. 5 Each man dipped a spoon into the white powder and got his toot. **1981** W. SAFIRE in *N.Y. Times Mag.* 15 Mar. 1981 The familiar 'to go on a toot', or to drink heavily and thereby lose a weekend, has been replaced by 'to blow a toot', or to inhale a 'line' of cocaine.

toot (tu:t), *sb.*[4] *dial.* and *U.S.* [Origin obscure.]

1. An idle or worthless person; a simpleton, fool.

1888 *Harper's Mag.* Oct. 801/1 Marsh Yates, the 'shif'less toot', and his beautiful, energetic wife. **1889** T. E. BROWN *Manx Witch*, etc. 118 Be off, you brute!..you donkey! you thundh'rin toot! **1894** HALL CAINE *Manxman* 157 Success to the fine girl,..lucky they kept her from the poor toot.

2. *dial.* 'The devil, *Linc.*' (Halliw.).

toot (tu:t), *sb.*[5] [Anglicized form of the Maori name *tutu*.] **a.** A shrub or small tree, *Coriaria arborea*, of New Zealand. It bears shining pulpy black berries containing poisonous seeds, with an action similar to that of strychnine. See also TUTU[1].

1851 E. WARD *Jrnl.* 18 Feb. (1951) 131 Found poor Novice had taken the 'toot' and had been very ill. **1857** R. WILKIN in C. Hursthouse *N. Zealand* xiii. 372 The plant called 'tutu' or 'toot'..appears to be universal over New Zealand. **1872** *Routledge's Ev. Boy's Ann.* 40/2 Toot is a poisonous shrub of which cattle are very fond. **1949** F. SARGESON *I saw in my Dream* 126 There wasn't even any fern, only a few pieces of the tutu which everybody called toot.

b. *to eat* (one's) *toot*: see TUTU[1] b. *N.Z. slang* (now *Obs.* exc. *Hist.*).

Hence **'tooted** (*ppl.*) *a.* = TUTUED *a.*; also as *pa. pple.*

1879 in H. Guthrie-Smith *Tutira* (1921) xvi. 123 Two bullocks dead at Troutbeck's. One 'tuted', the other bogged. **1930** L. G. D. ACLAND *Early Canterbury Runs* 1st Ser. vii. 169 A travelling showman had the bad luck to get his elephant tooted near the Waitaki.

‖**toot**, *sb.*[6] [Hindī *tut*.] The White Mulberry of India (*Morus alba*).

1879 MRS. A. E. JAMES *Ind. Househ. Managem.* 59 Nectarines, plums, tamarinds, toots, bairs, are all more or less grown. **1898** *Globe* 15 Jan. 1/4 The 'toot' is a ridiculous-looking Indian fruit, which some hold to be an excellent corrective of overnight intoxication.

toot (tu:t), *v.*[1] Now *dial.* Forms: 1 **tótian**, 3–4 **tōten**, 4–7 **tote, toote**, 5– **toot**. [OE. *tótian*, a word of single occurrence (see quot. *c* 897), of which ME. *tōte, toote*, and mod. *toot* are the regular representatives. OE. had also *týtan* (:—*tūtjan*) to peep out, become visible, as a star; and ME. had *tūten*, mod. TOUT *v.*[1] These indicate two synonymous OE. and OTeut. stems, *tôt*, and *tût-*, the relation between which is obscure. See Note below.]

1. *intr.* To protrude, stick *out*, 'peep *out*', so as to be seen; in *mod. dial.*, of a plant, to begin to appear above ground.

*c***897** K. ÆLFRED *Gregory's Past C.* xvi. 104 Se ceac.. oferhelede ða oxan ealle, butan þa heafdu totodun ut. *c***1394** *P. Pl. Crede* 425 Wiþ his knopped schon clouted full þykke His ton toteden out as he þe londe treddede. *c***1400** *Destr. Troy* 9540 He was brochit þurgh the body with a big speire, þat a trunchyn of þe tre tut out behynd. **1519** *Four Elements* (1905) 38 Now rise up, Master Huddypeke, Your tail toteth out behind. **1593** [see *tooting* below]. *c***1645** [see TOTING *ppl. a.*]. **1777** *Antiq.* in *Ann. Reg.* 149/2 When pease in Derbyshire first appear they are said to toot. **1808–18** JAMIESON, *Tute*, to jut out, to project. [North of Sc.] *c***1880** *Northampt. Dial.*, I can just see the taters tooting out of the ground.

2. *intr.* To peep, peer, look out; to gaze; = TOUT *v.*[1] 1.

*a***1225** *Ancr. R.* 52 Is hit nu so ouer vuel uor to toten [*MS. T.* lokin] utward? Auh toten vt wiðuten vuel ne mei nouðer of ou. *c***1300** HAVELOK 2106 He stod, and totede in at a bord. **1377** LANGL. *P. Pl.* B. XVI. 22 Pieres þe plowman..bad me toten on þe tree. *c***1400** *Destr. Troy* 862 Sho went vp..To the toppe of a toure, & tot ouer the water For to loke on hir luffe. **1529** MORE *Dyaloge* III. Wks. 225/1 Into the one [wallet]..he putteth other folkes faultes, and therein he toteth and poreth often. **1553** BRADFORD *Serm. Repent.* (1574) D ij b, Get thee Gods law as a glas to toote in. **1603** SIR C. HEYDON *Jud. Astrol.* iv. 140 While the Astrologer tooteth vpward, and examineth in what signe is the Moone. **1884** DOHERTY *N. Barlow* iv. 27 Let cheeky folk as come wi' stools to toot Sit theer an' stare.

b. To look inquisitively; to pry.

1390 GOWER *Conf.* III. 29 Riht so doth he, whan that he pireth And toteth on hire wommanhiede. **1546** J. HEYWOOD *Prov.* (1867) 57 On my maydes he is euer tootyng. **1550** LATIMER *Serm. Stamford* I. B ij b, Those obseruauntes were spyinge, totynge, and lookynge, watchynge and catchinge what they myghte heare or se against the sea of Rome. **1579** SPENSER *Sheph. Cal.* Mar. 66 With bowe and bolts..For birds in bushes tooting. **1593** B. RICH *Greenes Newes* E iij b, One..who was walking by himselfe, prying and tooting in every corner. **1597–8** BP. HALL *Sat.* IV. ii. 45 Nor toot in Cheapside baskets earne and late To set the first tooth in some nouell-cate. **1829** in HUNTER *Hallamshire Gloss.* **1888** *Sheffield Gloss.*, *Toot*, to pry into anything.

†**c.** *trans.* To peep or look at; to behold, view.

*c***1200** *Trin. Coll. Hom.* 211 Ech man þe þerto cumeð pleie to toten, oðer to listen, oðer to bihelden. *c***1394** *P. Pl. Crede* 142 Whow myȝt-tou in thine broþer eiȝe a bare mote loken, And in þyn owen eiȝe nouȝt a bem toten. *Ibid.* 219 þanne turned y aȝen, whan y hade all y-toted.

Hence **tooting** *ppl. a.*[1], in 3 **totinde**, looking out, peeping, prying, spying; protruding, sprouting.

*a***1225** *Ancr. R.* 50 Vor nabbe ȝe nout þene nome..of totinde ancres. **1593** *Tell-troth's N. Y. Gift* (1876) 33 If there be any that hath a tooting head [of 'horns'], and would not haue it sene, let him keepe it secretely to himselfe. *c***1645–1676** [see TOTING *ppl. a.*].

[*Note.* Words app. connected with OE. *tótian, týtan*, ME. *tōte, tūte*, mod. *toot, tout*, are Du. *tuit* spout, snout, MDu. *tûte* nipple, pap, early mod.Du. (Kilian) *tote, tuyte* horn, apex, cone, also *tote* nipple, teat, LG. *tote*, point, teat; also MLG. *tûte* horn, funnel, LG. *tûte, tût* spout, EFris. *tûte* pipe, spout, snout. Cf. also ON. *túta* 'teat-like prominence' (Vigf.), *tota* teat, toe of a shoe, Norw. dial. *tota* something projecting, as a spout; Da. *tud* spout of a cask, Sw. *tut*, mod.Norw. *tût* also snout, horn; with many other derivatives all pointing to an original sense of something projecting or sticking out. Except Norw. *tyte*, 'to trickle or ooze out', the verbs appear only in Eng., where also the special sense of 'look or peep out' has been developed.]

toot (tu:t), *v.*[2] Also 6 tute, 6–7 tote, toote; 6 towt, 6, 7–9 *Sc.* tout. [Known only from *c* 1510. Cf. MLG., LG. *tûten*, also Ger. *tuten*, Du. *tuyten, toeten* to blow a horn; perh. originally echoic, imitating the sound of a horn, etc. Not related to ON. *þjóta* to blow a horn, whistle (see THEOTEN, in Ormin *þûtenn*, to howl); the Norw. *tûta*, Sw. *tūta*, Da. *tūde*, in same sense, are perh. influenced by LG., whence also the Eng. may have been taken.]

I. *intr.* **1.** Of a person: To sound or blow a horn or similar wind instrument. Also with extensions, ***to toot it, to toot on, along, one's way***, etc.

1549 CHALONER tr. *Erasmus' Moriæ Enc.* H j b, That foule musike, whiche a horne maketh, being touted in. **1570** LEVINS *Manip.* 196/4 To Tute in a horne, *cornucinère.* **1693** J. H. tr. *Juvenal's Sat.* x. 4 See here a Troop of Horn-pipes toot along. **1698** FRYER *Acc. E. India & P.* 108 Tooting with their Trumpets, and beating with their Drums. **1707** E. WARD *Hud. Rediv.* II. VI. vi. 7 These led the Van, each crown'd with Feather Tooting harmoniously together. **1709** MRS. MANLEY *Secret Mem.* I. 149 A great many of 'em..can toot, toot, toot, it upon a Pipe. **1880** SPURGEON *J. Ploughm. Pict.* 29 We can all toot a little on our own trumpet. **1903** *Daily Chron.* 11 Nov. 4/5 The motor-car..tooting its way through London.

2. Of a wind-instrument: To give forth its characteristic sound; to sound.

*c***1510** *Kalender of Sheph.* li. M vij b, Take hede of my horne, totynge al alowde. **1595** MORLEY *1st Bk. Ballets* xi. C iij b, While as the Bagpipe tooted it. *a***1800** *Lord Barnaby* xiii. in Child *Ballads* II. 250/2 O lady, I heard a wee horn toot, And it blew wonder clear. **1894** *Daily News* 12 Mar. 2/1 The guard's long tapering horn never toots more merrily.

3. Of an animal: To make a sound likened to that of a horn, etc.; to trumpet as an elephant, bray as an ass; *spec.* of grouse, to 'call'.

1817 COBBETT *Wks.* XXXII. 10 The trick answered very well 'till the Ass began to bray, or toot. *a***1835** HOGG *Ringan & May* 39 The storm-cock touts on his towering pine. **1877** HALLOCK *Sportsman's Gazetteer* 119 The 'tooting' is the call of the male bird. *Ibid.* 124 The (pinnated) Grouse in the spring commences about April to 'toot', and can be heard nearly a mile. **1890** *Century Mag.* Feb. 613/1 The elephants ..raised their trunks, and tooted as no locomotive could toot.

b. Said of a person, esp. a child: see quots.

1808–18 JAMIESON, *Toot*, to make a plaintive noise, as when a child cries loud or mournfully. **1847–78** HALLIWELL *Toot*, to whine or cry.

II. *trans.* **4.** To cause (a horn, etc.) to sound by blowing it. Also *transf.* of an animal.

1682 FOUNTAINHALL *Decis.* (1759) I. 182 Suffering Brown then preaching and praying, to be affronted by boys, who touted horns. **1841** FARADAY in B. Jones *Life* (1870) II. 131 At the call of the goat-herd, who tooted a cow's horn. **1890** *Century Mag.* Feb. 613/2 The elephant..tooting his trumpet as though in great fright. **1899** *Daily Graphic* 19 Aug. 7 The Monmouth's whistle was tooted vigorously, and the passengers crowded her rail.

5. To sound (notes, a tune, etc.) on a horn, pipe, or the like.

1614 W. BROWNE *Sheph. Pipe* II. C vij b, He..That sits on yonder hill, And tooteth out his notes of glee. *c***1662** F. SEMPILL *On Birth Princess Mary*, But let those brosie pack tout on..They'll tout anuther tune I true. **1842** BARHAM *Ingol. Leg.* Ser. II. *St. Aloys*, With eight Trumpeters tooting the Dead March in Saul.

6. To call out aloud, to shout (something).

1582 STANYHURST *Æneis* IV. (Arb.) 107, In this eare hee towted thee speeche. **1653** URQUHART *Rabelais* II. xx. 143 They to toote, Draw, give (page) some wine here reach hither. **1756** MRS. CALDERWOOD in *Coltness Collect.* (Maitl. Club) 249 You will see them [beggars] standing at a door, and touting a Pater noster through the key-hole.

b. To proclaim loudly; to trumpet abroad. *Sc.*

*a***1810** TANNAHILL *Poems* (1846) 57 Ilk rising generation toots his fame, And hun'er years to come, 'twill be the same. **1887** SERVICE *Dr. Duguid* III. iv. 258 There were plenty to carry the news... It was tootit owre a' the kintra-side.

toot, tout (tu:t), *v.*[3] *Sc.* and *U.S.* [In Sc. *tout* (tu:t), in Anglicized spelling *toot*. Of obscure origin, perh. orig. thieves' cant. Cf. Sw. (vulgar or familiar) *tūta* to drink grog; but this is perh. from Eng.]

1. *intr.* 'To drink copiously; to take a large draught' (Jam.).

1676, *a***1700** [see *tooting* below]. *a***1774** R. FERGUSSON *Drink Ecl.* 64 At thee they toot, an' never spear my price. **1813** A. CUNNINGHAM *Songs* 7 She sat singing..And touting at the rosie wine.

2. *trans.* 'To empty the vessel from which one drinks, to drink its whole contents' (Jam.). Const. *off, out, up.*

*a***1774** R. FERGUSSON *Leith Races* xiii, They'll ban fu' sair the time That e'er they toutit aff the horn. **1788** G. TURNBULL *Poet. Ess.* 199 He leugh and toutit up the liquor Out ilka drap. **1811** C. GRAY in Whitelaw *Bk. Scot. Song* 260 'Tis sweet to tout the glasses out.

3. *intr.* To go on a spree; to make a night of it. *U.S.*

1890 GUNTER *Miss Nobody* xvii, Spreeing, gaming, and tooting all night.

4. *trans.* To inhale (cocaine). *U.S. slang.*

1975 *High Times* Dec. 110/2 Counterculture advocates of cocaine sniffing now have public confirmation of what they've known for a long time: the chief drawbacks to tooting coke are high costs and the law. **1979** *Ibid.* Jan. 52 You'll feel better knowing that what you toot is cut with the original Italian Mannite Conoscenti.

Hence **'tooting, 'touting** *vbl. sb.*[3], drinking, toping; in † ***touting-ken*** (*obs. slang*), a drinking-house.

1676 COLES *Dict.*, *Touting-ken*, tavern-bar. *a***1700** B. E. *Dict. Cant. Crew*, *Touting-ken*, a Tavern or Ale-house Bar.

toot, too't, to't, coalesced form of *to it.*

1596 SHAKS. *Tam. Shr.* I. ii. 195 Too't a Gods name. **1605** CHAPMAN *All Fooles* Plays 1873 I. 170, I will not set my hand toot. **1607** SHAKS. *Timon* III. vi. 37 We shall too't presently. **1828** in *Craven Gloss.*

toot, toots, Sc. forms of TUT, *tuts* interj.

tootanag, obs. form of TUTENAG.

†**'tooter**[1]. *Obs.* [f. TOOT *v.*[1] + -ER[1].]

1. One who gazes; a watchman; a prier or peeper.

1382 WYCLIF *Isa.* xxi. 6 Go, and put a tootere [1388 lokere]; and what euere thing he shal see, telle he. *Ibid.* lii. 8 The vois of thi tooteres. **1550** LATIMER *Serm. at Stamford* I. B ij b, Obseruantes, y[t] is watchers, toters, spies. **1583** STUBBES *Anat. Abus.* II. (1882) 57 As these foolish starre tooters promised. **1598** FLORIO, *Bugigattolo*, a sneaker, a pryer into corners, a tooter.

2. Something that projects; in quot., a prominent nose.

1638 SHIRLEY *Duke's Mistr.* IV. i, *Val.* Examine but this nose. *Scol.* I have a toter. *Val.* Which placed with symmetry is like a fountain I' the middle of her face.

tooter[2] ('tu:tə(r)). Also 7 to(a)ter. [f. TOOT *v.*[2]]

1. One who toots, or plays on a wind-instrument; a trumpeter or piper.

1620 THOMAS *Lat. Dict.*, *Vocalis*..a tooter, a piper. **1623** FLETCHER & ROWLEY *Maid in Mill* III. i, Hark hark! these Toaters tell us the King's coming. **1633** B. JONSON *Tale Tub* V. v, Come, Father Rosin, with your fiddle now, As two tall toters; flourish to the masque. **1907** *Daily Chron.* 29 Jan. 4/7 A tutor who tootled a flute Tried to teach two young tooters to toot.

2. A horn or other wind-instrument.

1860 O. W. HOLMES *Prof. Breakf.-t.* viii, A boy..loves to ..blow squash 'tooters'. **1896** D. S. MELDRUM *Grey Mantle* 108 The guard's blowing it about like a blast on his tooter. **1897** KIPLING *Captains Courageous* 169 'Gimme the tooter.' Dan took the tin dinner-horn, but paused before he blew.

3. One who proclaims loudly; *spec.* = TOUTER 1. *U.S.*

1863 *Rio Abajo Weekly Press* (Albuquerque, New Mexico) 19 May 2 The nameless party's tooter speaks confidently of the success of its nominee. **1886** *Harper's Mag.* Aug. 417/2 The wharf..was alive with vehicles and tooters for the hotels. **1897** R. E. ROBINSON *Uncle Lisha's Outing* 297 Noisiest of all were the tooters, vociferously proclaiming the wonders of the side shows.

tooth (tu:θ), *sb.* Pl. **teeth** (ti:θ). Forms: see below, sense 1. [OE. *tóþ, tóð* (:—**tanþ*), Com. Teut. and Com. Indo-Eur.; OFris. *tôth, tond*, (NFris. *tôth*, EFris. *tond*); OS. *tand* (MLG. *tand, tan*, LG. *tan*; MDu. *tant* (*d*), Du. *tand*; OHG. *zana, zan* (MHG. *zant, zan*, Ger. *zahn*); ON. *tǫnn* (:—*tanþuz*; Sw., Da. *tand*, NNorw. *tonn*); beside Gothic *tunþus*;:—OTeut. **tanþ-* and **tunþ-*:—Indo-Eur. *dent, dont, dnt*, whence Skr. *dan, danta*, Gr. *ὀ-δούς* (*ὀ-δόντ-ς*), L. *dens* (*dent-s*), OIr. *dét* (**dent*), W. *dant*, Lith. *dantìs.* The termination agrees with that of pr. pples., whence Pott conjectured an original **ed-ont-*, pr. pple. of *ed-* to eat; i.e. 'an eater'. OE. *tóþ* was originally a masculine consonantal stem, with dative sing. *téþ* (:—*tóþi*), pl. nom. *téþ* (:—**tóþiz*), gen. *tóþa*, dat. *tóþum* (in early ME. *toþen*). A rare pl. *tóþas* after masc. -*o*^{2} stems also occurs. An umlaut pl. is seen also in OFris. *têth*, MLG. *tene*, LG. *täne*, OHG. *zeni*, MHG. *zene*, Ger. *zähne*. In use the plural is much more frequent than the singular, and in some dialects the latter is sometimes assimilated to it as 'a teeth'.

A double plural *teeths* was formerly (and is still *dial.*) used in speaking of a number of persons; e.g. *in spite of their teeths*, pl. of *in spite of his teeth*: see senses 4 d, 5.]

I. 1. a. In plural, the hard processes within the mouth, attached (usually in sockets) in a row to each jaw in most vertebrates except birds (but also in some extinct birds), having points, edges, or grinding surfaces, and serving primarily for biting, tearing, or trituration of solid food, and secondarily as weapons of attack or defence, and for other purposes; in singular, each of these individually.

In mammals usually consisting of dentine coated with cement around the root and with enamel in the exposed part; but in some cases horny, chitinous, or osseous. In some animals, also occurring on other parts, as the tongue or pharynx. Also, applied to similar or analogous structures occurring in the mouth or alimentary canal in some invertebrates.

Sing. 1 **tóð** (*dat.* **téð**), 1–4 **tóþ** (3 **toþþ** *Orm.*), 4–5 **toþe**, 4–6 **toth, tothe, tuth**; 5 **tooþ** (**thothe, toyth, toeth, tuthe**), 5–6 **toothe**; 5– **tooth.** (Also 6 **touthe**, *Sc.* **twth, twith, twithe**, 6–7 **touth**, 6– *Sc.* **tuith.** The shortened vowel in Ormin's *toþþ* is anomalous: see TOTH.)

a **900** K. ÆLFRED *Laws* c. 19 Selle his aȝen fore, toð fore teð. *c* **975** *Rushw. Gosp.* Matt. v. 38 Eȝe for eȝe toð for toþ. *c* **1250** *Gen. & Ex.* 4148 Ðoȝ him lestede hise siȝte briȝt, And euerilc toð bi tale riȝt. *a* **1300** *Cursor M.* 23798 To tell þe soth, Bath me wantes tung and toth [*v.r.* toþe, toþ]. **1382** WYCLIF *Matt.* v. 38 It is said Eiȝe for eiȝe, toth for toth. *a* **1425** *Cursor M.* 6040 (Trin.) A litil beest Of tooþ is not vnfoulest. **1481** CAXTON *Reynard* viii. (Arb.) 15 Olde wymen that..had not one toeth in her heed. **1483** *Cath. Angl.* 398/1 A Tuthe, *dens.* **1530** PALSGR. 282/1 Tothe, *dent.* **1562** TURNER *Herbal* II. 107 b, Pylletoris is good for the tuth ach if the tuth be wasshed with vinegre. **1620** SHELTON *Quix.* (1746) IV. ii. 11 Meddle not with a hollow Tooth. **1709–10** STEELE *Tatler* No. 127 ¶ 11 She has not a Tooth in her Head. **1852** THACKERAY *Esmond* I. ii, She was lean, and yellow, and long in the tooth.

Pl. 1 **tóeþ**, 1–4 **téþ, téð**, (*dat.* 1 **tóþum, -an**, 2–3 **-en**), (3 **tieth**), 4 **teþe** (**teþþe**, *Sc.* **tetht**), 4–5 **teeþ**, 4–6 **teth, tethe**, 5–6 **teethe, teithe**, 6 **teath**, (**tithe**), 5– **teeth** (*Sc.* 6– **teith**); also 1 **tóþas**, 6 **tothes.**

c **725** *Corpus Gloss.* (O.E.T.) 1967 *Suaeder*, butan toðum. *c* **825** *Vesp. Psalter* iii. 8 Toeð synfulra ðu forðræstes. *c* **1000** *Life Guthlac* v. (1848) 34 Heora toþas wæron ȝelice horses twuxan. *c* **1000** *Sax. Leechd.* III. 104 Oft man smeaþ hwæþer teþ bænene beon. *c* **1200** *Vices & Virt.* 19 Ðar is chiueringe of toðen. *a* **1225** *Ancr. R.* 288 His teð beoð attrie, ase of ane wode dogge. *c* **1290** *S. Eng. Leg.* I. 206/228 With kene tieth al fuyrie. *a* **1300** *Cursor M.* 19354 For tene þair tethe [*v.rr.* teþþe, teþ, teth, teeþ] to gnast. *c* **1375** *Sc. Leg. Saints* i. 25 Vith his tetht he wald haf refyn sone. **1390** GOWER *Conf.* II. 245 A furgh of lond, in which a-rowe The teth of thaddre he moste sowe. **1483** *Cath. Angl.* 380/2 To drawe oute Tethe, *edentare.* **1486** *Bk. St. Albans* f vij, A Rage of the teethe. **1552** HULOET s.v., *Dentosus*, full of teath, or hauyng many teath. **1577** tr. *Bullinger's Decades* (1592) 54 [They] whet their teeth for anger. **1597** A. M. tr. *Guillemeau's Fr. Chirurg.* b iij b/2 These artificialle teethe are sometimes made of Ivorye. **1598** Q. ELIZ. *Plutarch* xv. 3 When the think ther handz to slow the ad to ther tithe. **1653** WALTON *Compl. Angler* viii. 166 The Carp is..amongst those..fish which..have their teeth in their throat. **1705** VANBRUGH *Confed.* I. iii, There's the woman..that sells paint and patches, iron-bodice, false teeth, and all sorts of things, to the ladies. **1812** *Examiner* 23 Nov. 752/2 Mrs. G. Gatehouse, in the 101st year of her age;..cut her teeth about two years since. **1872** MIVART *Elem. Anat.* vii. (1873) 238 Our teeth are dermal structures..developed from the deeper layer or enderon. **1888** ROLLESTON & JACKSON *Anim. Life* 115 A..lingual membrane bearing transverse rows of teeth [in the snail]. *Ibid.* 217 The three muscular jaws..bear at their edges in the medicinal Leech about 80–90 fine chitinoid teeth. *Ibid.* 348 New teeth in succession to old teeth are either formed without limit of numbers, as in most *Pisces, Amphibia, Reptilia*, or are restricted to a second set in some *Mammalia.*

b. *spec.* An elephant's tusk (projecting upper incisor tooth), as a source of ivory.

c **1050** *Gloss.* in Wr.-Wülcker 397/27 *Eburneus dens*, elpend toþ. **1483** CAXTON *Gold. Leg.* 73/3 The nauye.. brouht..teeth of Olyphauntes. **1533** ELYOT *Cast. Helthe* (1539) 70 The olyphantes tothe. **1681** R. KNOX *Hist. Ceylon* 21 But few [elephants] have Teeth, and they males onely. **1720** DE FOE *Capt. Singleton* vi, The ground was scattered with elephants' teeth. **1897** MARY KINGSLEY *W. Africa* 325 Ivory is everywhere an evil thing... A very common way of collecting a tooth is to kill the person who owns one.

c. In expressions referring to speech (now esp. biting or angry speech).

a **1300** *Cursor M.* 13941 Sal yee na leis here o mi toth. **13..** *Guy Warw.* (A.) 4385 Þou lexst amidward þi teþ, & þer-fore haue þou maugreþ. **1864** TENNYSON *Aylmer's Field* 328 So stammering 'scoundrel' out of teeth that ground As in a dreadful dream. *Mod.* Hissing 'Traitor!' through his clenched teeth.

2. *fig.* or in figurative expressions: **a.** referring to eating, esp. to the sense of taste; hence often = taste, liking (cf. *palate*). See also various phrases in 8.

c **1386** CHAUCER *Wife's Prol.* 449, I wol kepe it for youre owene tooth. **1435** MISYN *Fire of Love* 36 My toyth continuly to myrth of songe was chaungyd. **1555** LATIMER in Strype *Eccl. Mem.* (1721) III. App. xxxvi. 103 For all theis things make you the meter for Gods tothe. **1579** LODGE *Def. Poetry* (Hunter. Cl.) 8 Will you haue all for yon owne tothe? **1598** LODGE & GREENE *Looking Glasse* G iij, The Smith and the diuel hath a drie tooth in his head. **1615** BP. HALL *Contempl., Old Test.* XI. vii, A wanton tooth is the harbinger to luxurious wantonnesse. **1634** *Ibid., N.T.* IV. iv, Well did Herodias know, how to fit the tooth of her paramour. **1675** COTTON *Scoffer Scoft* 6 And keep the best o' th' meat (forsooth) For your own Worships dainty tooth! **1704** J. PITTS *Acc. Mohammetans* ix. (1738) 210 He had a great Tooth for the Dey-ship. **1851** *Beck's Florist* Sept. 213 What a tooth for fruit has a monkey!

b. referring to biting or gnawing; hence denoting a hurtful, hostile, destructive, or devouring agency or quality. See also various phrases in III.

1546 PHAER *Bk. Childr.* (1553) A ij, It is impossible to auoide the teethe of malicious enuy. **1603** SHAKS. *Meas. for M.* V. i. 12 It deserues..A forted residence 'gainst the tooth of time. *a* **1659** OSBORN *Ess.* ii. Wks. (1673) 560 Out of fear of the Iron-teeth of the Law. **1742** GRAY *Eton* 66 Jealousy with rankling tooth. *a* **1765** YOUNG *Statesman's Creed*, Records that defy the tooth of time. **1816** BYRON *Prisoner of Chillon* ii, That iron is a cankering thing, For in these limbs its teeth remain, With marks that will not wear away. **1874** D. GRAY *Poet. Wks.* 89 'Tis April, yet the wind retains its tooth.

(*b*) *pl.* denoting the ability to compel or enforce, esp. by the exaction of penalties, etc.

1925 *Country Gentleman* 25 July 15/1 How many teeth can you put in a grower's contract of membership with a cooperative marketing association? **1931** *Week-End Rev.* 14 Mar. 380/1 It is even more urgent to take steps which will lead to the success of the Disarmament Conference next February than to 'give teeth' to the Paris Peace Pact. **1935** *Evening Sun* (Baltimore) 27 May 13/3 (*heading*) Coal control bill with teeth studied. **1949** *Economist* 16 Apr. 694/2 It is well that President Truman should have made quite clear, not only that the Atlantic Pact is meant to have teeth in it, but also what sort of teeth. **1963** *Listener* 7 Mar. 432/3 It needed guts to fight a battle against an Establishment with teeth. **1964** *Daily Tel.* 20 Mar. 24 (*heading*) 'Teeth' put in scheme for fair coal sales. **1976** *Howard Jrnl.* XV. I. 29 The Magistrates' Association..asked for an order stronger than a care order to show that 'in the last resort the law has teeth'.

(*c*) *spec.*, denoting the combatant personnel of an armed service or military unit. Cf. TAIL *sb.*^{1} 4 c.

1946, 1961 [see TAIL *sb.*^{1} 4 c]. **1962** *Daily Tel.* 26 Sept. 12/2 There is, indeed, room for a 'teeth' role for certain units [of the Territorial Army]. **1967** M. AYUB KHAN *Friends, not Masters* iv. 45 These changes gave the infantry more teeth and less tail. **1968** *Listener* 25 July 99/3 As for recruiting, the 'teeth arms' of the three Services are likely to go on attracting young men of high quality. **1977** J. HAINES *Politics of Power* ii. 24 He knew..that the Labour Government's great 'defence review' had left a vast area of spending—administrative 'tail' as opposed to front-line 'teeth'—almost untouched and unharmed.

II. 3. *transf.* A projecting part or point resembling an animal's tooth; esp. one of a row or series of such. **a.** As an artificial structure, in an implement, machine, etc.; e.g. one of the pointed projections of a comb, saw, file, rake, harrow, fork, etc.; a prong, tine; one of the series of projections on the edge of a wheel, pinion, etc., which engage with corresponding ones on another; a cog.

1523 FITZHERB. *Husb.* §24 If the rake be made of grene woode,..the tethe wyll fall out, whan he hath mooste nede to them. **1577** B. GOOGE *Heresbach's Husb.* II. (1586) 106 b, [These] doe more fill the teeth of the Sawe. **1591** PERCIVALL *Sp. Dict., Pua*,..the tooth of a combe. **1611** COTGR. s.v. *Allochons*, The teeth, or toothing, of a wheele, in a clocke, &c. **1639** T. BRUGIS tr. *Camus' Mor. Relat.* 169 But iron is never..brighter than when it hath been under the sharp teeth of the file. **1680** MOXON *Mech. Exerc.* x. 189 A great Iron Wheel, having Teeth on its edge. **1793** *Statist. Acc. Scotl.* VIII. 48 The teeth, or wooden pins [of a harrow] must be made long. **1807** ROBINSON *Archæol. Græca* IV. xv. 412 Anchors were made of iron, and furnished with teeth,.. fastening to the bottom of the sea. **1829** *Nat. Philos.* I. *Mechanics* II. vii. 27 (Usef. Knowl. Soc.) The cogs on the surface of the wheel are generally called teeth, and those on the surface of the axle are called leaves. **1966** B. MALAMUD *Fixer* VII. iii. 239 He combed his hair and beard until the teeth of the comb fell out.

b. As a natural structure, in animals, plants, etc.; e.g. the odontoid process of the axis vertebra; a projecting point in the upper mandible of the bill in certain birds (cf. DENTIROSTER); each of a row of small projections on the edge of one valve of the shell in some bivalve molluscs; each of the pointed processes on the margin of leaves or other parts in many plants (cf. DENTATE), or of those forming the peristome of the capsule in mosses; also, generally, a projecting point of rock, etc.

1694–1815 [see AXIS^1 2]. *c* **1711** PETIVER *Gazophyl.* vii. 63 A small rugged Shell... Its Navel small with a Tooth or Knag in the Mouth. **1796** WITHERING *Brit. Plants* I. 253 Cal[yx]. Cup 1 leaf, concave, but expanding, with 5 teeth, permanent. **1847** CARPENTER *Zool.* iv. §361 Its [the upper mandible of a bird of prey] edge is notched, so as to form a kind of projecting tooth on either side. *Ibid.* xviii. §932 This hinge [in the shell of a bivalve mollusc] is sometimes formed ..by a number of little projections or teeth, which fit into corresponding hollows in the opposite valve. **1861** MISS PRATT *Flower. Plants* IV. 88 (Toad-flax)..capsule swollen, ..opening by valves or teeth. **1871** L. STEPHEN *Playgr. Eur.* v. (1894) 125 Great rocky teeth, striking up through their icy covering, like the edge of a saw. **1887** J. BALL *Nat. in S. Amer.* 210 The long stiff leaves, edged with sharp teeth.

c. An accidental jag or uneven projection at the edge of something.

1612 BRINSLEY *Lud. Lit.* 29 You may make your pen of the best of the quil, & where you see the cleft to be the cleanest, & without teeth.

d. A rough surface on paper, canvas, etc., such as to enable pencil-marks, colours, etc. to adhere; a roughness made by a toothing-plane on surfaces to be glued together, to promote adhesion of the glue. (Only in *sing.*)

1811 *Self Instructor* 525 The tooth or grain of the paper catching the crayons in dots. **1884** *Century Mag.* XXIX. 205/2 The substance worked upon being commonly rough paper, to the 'tooth' or burr of which the color partially adheres. **1894** MASKELYNE *Sharps & Flats* 232 [It] is roughened by rubbing it with coarse glass paper. This gives it a kind of 'tooth'. **1906** R. C. BAYLEY *Compl. Photogr.* 382 A polished sheet of copper..has its surface treated in some way to give it a very fine grain or tooth... Fine bitumen dust is generally employed.

e. *pl.* The lower zone of facets in a rose-diamond.

1877 in KNIGHT *Dict. Mech.*

f. *pl. fig.* A ship's guns. *Naut. slang.*

1806 J. DAVIS *Post-Captain* iv. 19 'She looks, sir, like a whacking frigate.' 'Can you see her teeth?' 'Yes, sir; she has a very heavy tire of teeth.' **1810** B. SILLIMAN *Jrnl. Trav.* (1820) III. 291 The ship had no teeth, as the sailors say, when they mean great guns. **1833** MARRYAT *P. Simple* xlvi, They were..large schooners,..showing a very good set of teeth. **1849** W. S. MAYO *Kaloolah* ii, There's at least three rows of teeth beneath that mass of spars.

III. Phrases.

4. in the teeth, in (one's) **teeth. a.** In direct (local) opposition or attack; ***in the teeth of***, in direct opposition to, so as to face or confront, straight against.

1297 R. GLOUC. (Rolls.) 8404 Our lord..þe smoke þat hii made..Riȝt in hor owe teþ bigan hom euene sende. **1581** A. HALL *Iliad* VIII. 138 A Hector, who no lesse desires to meete them in the teeth. **1669** STURMY *Mariner's Mag.* I. ii. 18 The Wind is right in our teeth. **1737** WHISTON *Josephus, Wars* III. x. § 5 Others..met the enemy in the teeth. **1833** L. RITCHIE *Wand. by Loire* 160 They..had run into the teeth of a heavy barge full of armed men. **1892** EMILY LAWLESS *Grania* II. 7 He..had run across in the teeth of the rising gale.

b. ***in the teeth of***, in direct and manifest opposition to, in defiance of, in spite of.

1792 GOUV. MORRIS in Sparks *Life & Writ.* (1832) II. 160 State necessity will be urged in the teeth of policy, humanity, and justice. **1818** SCOTT *Hrt. Midl.* xxii[i], In no civil case would a counsel have been permitted to plead his client's case in the teeth of the law. **1847** L. HUNT *Jar Honey* x. (1848) 128 Why do you continue to live here, in the teeth of these repeated warnings? **1885** *Law Times* 13 June 113/1 A judge has no right to enter judgment in the teeth of the finding of a jury.

c. ***in the teeth of***, in the presence of, in the face of; usually implying hostility or danger; threateningly confronted by.

1825 LAMB *Elia* Ser. II. *Barbara S.*, They were in fact in the very teeth of starvation. **1867** PARKMAN *Jesuits N. Amer.* xxvii. (1875) 381 His post was in the teeth of danger. **1876** BLACKMORE *Cripps* i, The Carrier scarcely knew what to do in the teeth of so urgent a message.

d. *to cast* (one) ***in the teeth with*** (something), later *to cast* (a thing) ***in one's teeth*** (see CAST *v.* 65), †*to hit* (one) ***in the teeth with*** (*obs.*), *to throw in* (one's) *teeth*: to reproach, upbraid, or censure with; to bring up in reproach against. (In quot. 1596 *to throw in* (one's) *teeth* = to send or direct defiantly against: cf. 4 b, 6 b.) Also in similar phrases expressing reproachful or defiant utterance.

1535 COVERDALE *Matt.* xxvii. 44 The murtherers also that were crucified with him, cast the same in his tethe. **1548** PATTEN *Exped. Scotl.* Pref. b iv b, Take it not that I hit you here in the teeths with oure good turnes. **1581** PETTIE tr. *Guazzo's Civ. Conv.* III. (1586) 147 Some..will not sticke to hit him in the teeth, that he was the sonne of [etc.]. **1596** SHAKS. *1 Hen. IV*, V. ii. 42 To Armes, for I haue thrown A braue defiance in King Henries teeth. **1614** DAY *Dyall* Ep. Ded., Caius of Cambridge did twit us in the teeth with some of our Founders here in Oxford that had been them-selves Cambridge Men. **1619** W. WHATELEY *God's Husb.* ii. (1622) 53 He giueth to all liberally, and hitteth no man in the teeth. **1640** SIR W. BOSWELL in *Abp. Ussher's Lett.* (1686) App. 27 The main things that they hit in our teeth are, our Bishops to be called Lords. **1694** F. BRAGGE *Disc. Parables* xiii. 441 This neglect of family-devotions is often thrown in our teeth. **1819** KEATS *Otho* IV. ii. 105 In thy teeth I give thee back the lie! **1850** *Tait's Mag.* XVII. 441/2 Perpetually throwing in the teeth of the second wife the unrivalled virtues..of the first.

5. in spite of (despite, maugre, etc.) **one's teeth**: notwithstanding one's opposition or resistance; in spite of one, in defiance of one. Now *rare* exc. *dial.*

c **1230** *Hali Meid.* 47 He ȝarkeð þe unþonc hise teð þe blisse & te crune of cristes icorene. **13..** *K. Alis.* 5840 (Bodl. MS.) He..maugre þe teeþ of hem alle Sette his rigge to þe walle. *c* **1489** CAXTON *Sonnes of Aymon* iii. 86 He putte theym to flight, magre their teeth. **1549** LATIMER *2nd Serm. bef. Edw. VI* (Arb.) 73 A greate man keepeth certaine landes..and wilbe hyr tenaunte in the spite of hyr tethe. **1551** ROBINSON tr. *More's Utop.* II. viii. (1895) 260 Spyte of there tethes wrestynge owt of theire handes the sure and vndowbted victory. **1586** J. Hooker *Hist. Irel.* in *Holinshed* II. 115/1 Which perforce and maugre of his teeth compelled him to retire with shame. **1586** T. B. *La Primaud. Fr. Acad.* I. (1594) 414 Compelling him..to be liberall in despite of his teeth. **1596** Danett tr. *Comines* v. xv. (1614) 169 Constrained them spite of their teeths to depart the towne. **1598** Greneway *Tacitus' Ann.* iv. ix. (1622) 103 Noble men which maugre thy teeth mount to authority. **1689** Hickeringill *Ceremony-Monger* iii. Wks. 1716 II. 482 Let the People go whistle, they are their Feeders and Pastors in Spight of their Teeths. **1712** Arbuthnot *John Bull* iv. vii, [We] will go on with the Lawsuit in spite of John Bull's teeth. **1835** *Court Mag.* VI. 74/2 Pleasing herself before his very eyes, in spite of his teeth.

6. to the teeth. a. So as to be completely equipped; very fully or completely: in ***armed to the teeth***; so ***entrenched up to their teeth***.

c **1380** *Sir Ferumb.* 2707 þey wern y-armed in-to þe teþ & araid wel for þe fiȝt. **14..** *Lybeaus Disc.* 460 All yarmed to the teth. **1708** Luttrell *Brief Rel.* (1857) VI. 328 The French..are intrench't up to their teeth. **1845** Ford *Handbk. Spain* I. xi. 43 Everybody in Spain travels armed to the teeth.

b. *to* (one's) ***teeth, to the teeth of***: intensive of 'to one's face'; directly and openly; defiantly; also, so as directly to face, confront, or oppose.

1542 Udall *Erasm. Apoph.* 319 Cicero mocked hir to the harde teeth with sembleyng that he graunted hir saiyng [etc.]. **1583** Melbancke *Philotimus* L iv b, Though I praise you to your teeth. **1602** Shaks. *Ham.* iv. vii. 57 That I shall liue and tell him to his teeth; Thus diddest thou. **1677** W. Hughes *Man of Sin* III. iii. 79 Which..plainly gives them the lye unto their Teeths. **1680** Otway *Caius Marius* I. i, Now Romes last Stake of Liberty is set, And must be push'd for to the Teeth of Fortune. **1724** De Foe *Mem. Cavalier* II. 189 The Foot.., coming close up to the Teeth of one another.., fought with great Resolution.

c. So as to be utterly committed; ***up to the teeth***: heavily involved or absorbed.

1934 T. E. Lawrence *Let.* 8 June (1938) 805 At the moment we are all up to the teeth in 5 more target boats. **1974** *Spartanburg* (S. Carolina) *Herald* 25 Apr. A11/6 A young farmer who is starting out and he's mortgaged to the teeth at the bank would not look at it the same way.

d. ***fed*** (***up***) ***to the*** (***back***) ***teeth***: see fed *pa. pple.*

7. a. tooth and nail (orig. ***with tooth and nail***), advb. phr.: *lit.* with the use of one's teeth and nails as weapons; by biting and scratching: almost always *fig.*, in the way of vigorous attack, defence, or action generally; vigorously, fiercely, with one's utmost efforts, with all one's might.

1534 More *Comf. agst. Trib.* III. xxii. (1573) 193 They would faine kepe them as long as euer they might, euen with tooth and naile. **1562** Winȝet *Cert. Tract.* Wks. (S.T.S.) I. 16 Contending with tuith and naill (as in the prouerb). **1568** V. Skinner tr. *Montanus' Inquisition* 46 b, To perswade them tooth and naile, not to cleaue vnto that doctrine. **1579** W. Wilkinson *Confut. Familye of Love* 51 M. Harding fighteth for it tooth and nail. **1651** Culpepper *Astrol. Judgem. Dis.* (1658) 118 He will helpe it forward with tooth and naile. **1692** L'Estrange *Josephus, Antiq.* xv. xi. (1733) 413 Salome and her Faction were Tooth and Nail for dispatching her out of Hand. **1719** D'Urfey *Pills* IV. 156 She flew in her Face Tooth and Nail. **1827** Scott *Jrnl.* 26 July, To-morrow I resume the Chronicles, tooth and nail. **1892** Huxley in *Life* (1900) II. xviii. 312, I am ready to oppose any such project tooth and nail.

attrib. **1872** B. Jerrold *London* xiv. 116 Honourable instinct making a tooth-and-nail fight against adverse circumstances. **1900** *Century Mag.* Feb. 509/1 The tooth-and-nail fight to which they and their children were condemned.

†**b.** So ***with teeth and all***. *Obs.*

a **1600** Hooker *Eccl. Pol.* viii. vi. §2 Even with teeth and all they that favour the papal throne must hold the contrary.

8. Various phrases.

†**a. to have the teeth cold, to have cold at the teeth,** to suffer hunger, go hungry (*obs.*). **b. from the teeth forward(s** or **outward(s** (also *simply* **from one's teeth,** and *ellipt.* **teeth outward(s)**, formally or feignedly, in profession but not in reality (opp. to *from the heart*). †**c. to hide one's teeth,** *fig.* to conceal malice or hostile intention under a show of friendliness (opp. to *to show one's teeth*) (*obs.*). †**d. to love the tooth,** to be fond of eating, to be an epicure (*obs.*). **e. to set one's teeth,** to press or clench one's teeth firmly together from indignation, or fixed resolution as in facing danger, opposition, or difficulty; hence *fig.* or *allusively*; see also set *v.*[1] 95. **f. to show one's teeth,** *lit.* to uncover the teeth by withdrawing the lips from them, esp. as a beast in readiness for biting or attack; usu. *fig.* to show hostility or malice, to behave in a threatening way. **g. the teeth water,** a variant of *the mouth waters*: see mouth *sb.* 2 c (? *obs.*). **h. to get one's teeth into,** to become engrossed in; to come to grips with, to begin serious work on.

a. **1484** Caxton *Fables of Æsop* II. xv, Suche weren fayre gownes and fayr gyrdels of gold that haue theyr teeth cold at home. *Ibid.* IV. xvii, He that werketh not..shal haue ofte at his teeth grete cold.

b. **1570–6** Lambarde *Peramb. Kent* (1826) 420 They met ..and from the teeth forwarde departed good friends againe. **1588** J. Udall *Diotrephes* (Arb.) 27 Manye of them like vs but from the teeth outwarde. **1647** Lilly *Chr. Astrol.* lxxxviii. 459 They love not [one another], or but teeth outward. **1815** J. Hogg *Let.* 28 Feb., in Lockhart *Scott* xxxvi, To be friends from the teeth forwards is common enough.

c. **1714** T. Ellwood in *Life* 230 The Goaler..hid his Teeth,..putting on a shew of Kindness.

d. **1610** Holland *Camden's Brit.* (1637) 543 Meates.. greatly sought for by these that love the tooth so well.

e. **1599** Shaks. *Hen. V*, III. i. 15 Now set the Teeth, and stretch the Nosthrill wide. **1672** Dryden *Marriage-à-la-Mode* Epil. 28 You..set your teeth when each design fell short. **1823** Scott *Quentin D.* xxxii, 'If this should prove truth', said the Duke, setting his teeth, and pressing his heel against the ground. **1859** Geo. Eliot *A. Bede* xxxvii, She set her teeth when she thought of Arthur: she cursed him. **1870** Morris *Earthly Par.* II. III. 350 Her teeth were set hard, and her brow was knit.

f. **1615** J. Chamberlain in *Crt. & Times Jas. I* (1848) I. 361 It were to no purpose to show our teeth unless we could bite. **1710** O. Sansom *Acc. Life* 330 He somewhat appeared at the Sessions at Wantage; shewing his Teeth in what he could; and thereby discovering what lodged in his Heart against us. **1742** Young *Love Fame* I. 17 When the law shews her teeth, but dares not bite. **1837** Carlyle *Fr. Rev.* II. I. i, Such Patriotism as snarls dangerously and shows teeth.

g. **1600** Holland *Livy* VII. xxx. 269 At it their teeth water, that most goodly and beautifull cittie will they either destroy, or be LL. thereof themselves. **1698** Farquhar *Love & Bottle* V. i, Oh, my little green gooseberry, my teeth waters at ye! **1724** Littleton *Lat. Dict.* (ed. 5) s.v., It makes my teeth water. *Salivam mihi movet.* [**1879**: see *teeth-watering* in 9 b.]

h. **1935** D. L. Sayers *Gaudy Night* i. 23 If one could work here steadily..getting one's teeth into something dull and durable. **1961** B. Fergusson *Watery Maze* vi. 140 American eagerness to get their teeth into the enemy. **1983** G. Mitchell *Cold, Lone, & Still* x. 111 He's not the man to let go while he's got his teeth into a suspect.

i. For other phrases see the words involved, as *to take the bit in one's teeth* (bit *sb.*[1] 8 d), *to carry a bone in the teeth* (bone *sb.* 14 b), *colt's tooth* (colt *sb.* 8), *to cut one's teeth* (cut *v.* 39), *to set the teeth on edge* (edge *sb.* 4), *to grind one's teeth* (grind *v.*[1] 10), *to have the run of one's teeth* (run *sb.* 32 b), *long in the tooth* (long *a.*[1] 1 c), *by* or *with the skin of one's teeth* (skin *sb.* 6 g), *a sweet tooth* (sweet *a.*). For *to lie in one's teeth*, see 1 c.

9. a. *attrib.* and *Comb.*, as ***tooth-dint, -dye, -extraction, -point, -stainer, -stump; tooth-bred, -chattering, -extracting, -like, -setting, -shaped, -tempting*** adjs.; with many others of obvious meaning. Special combs.: **tooth-axe**, 'a stone-cutters' axe the edges of which are divided into blunt teeth' (*Cent. Dict. Suppl.*); **tooth-back**, a moth of the family *Notodontidæ*, or its larva, which has a tooth-like prominence on the back; so **tooth-backed** *a.*; **tooth-bearer** = odontophore; †**tooth-blanch**, a substance for whitening the teeth, a dentifrice; **tooth-block**, a block forming part of a machine for moulding in sand the iron teeth of a gear-wheel; **tooth-bone**, (*a*) = dentine; (*b*) the bony substance or 'cement' of the teeth; **tooth-chisel**, a chisel with a toothed or serrated cutting edge, used by stone-masons; **tooth-cleaner**, a machine for dressing and finishing the teeth of cog-wheels (Knight *Dict. Mech.* Suppl. 1884); **tooth-comb**, (*a*) a small-tooth comb; usu. in *fig.* use; also *attrib.* and as *v. trans.*, to investigate minutely; cf. fine-tooth *a.*; (*b*) *Zool.*, a group of procumbent lower front teeth found in tree shrews and lemurs; **tooth-coralline** = sertularia; **tooth-cress** = toothwort 3; **tooth-doctor**, a dentist; **tooth-edge**, the sensation of having the teeth 'set on edge' (see edge *sb.* 4); **tooth fairy**, a fairy believed by children to take away milk teeth and leave a small sum of money; also *transf.*; **tooth-fern**, a rendering of *Odontopteris*, a genus of fossil ferns; **tooth-fever**, fever accompanying teething; **tooth-flower**, a name for *Dentella repens*, a small creeping herb found in Australia, Polynesia, etc., having a tooth-like process on each petal of the flower; **tooth-forceps**, a forceps used by a dentist for extracting teeth; **tooth-germ**, the 'germ' or growth of tissue from which a tooth is developed; **tooth-glass**, (*a*) (see quot. 1858); (*b*) a glass used to hold false teeth; †**tooth-iron**, ? an instrument for extracting teeth; **tooth-ivory** = dentine; †**tooth-key**, a dentist's instrument, turned like a key, formerly used for extracting teeth; **tooth-mark**, a mark made by a tooth in biting, or *transf.* by an edged tool; so **tooth-marked** *a.*; **tooth-mill**, a dentist's drill-stock or drilling-machine; **tooth-mug** = *tooth-glass* (*b*); **tooth ornament** *Arch.*, a kind of ornament or moulding suggesting a tooth or teeth: = dog-tooth 3; †**tooth-pain** = toothache; **tooth-paste**, a paste used for cleaning the teeth; freq. *attrib.* in ***tooth-paste tube***; also in fig. phr. ***to put the toothpaste back in the tube***, illustrating the futility of trying to restore a stable state of affairs in the light of subsequent events; **tooth-plane** = toothing-*plane*; **tooth-plate** (*Dentistry*) = plate *sb.* 4 f; **tooth-plugger**, an instrument for filling or stopping decayed teeth (Knight 1884); tooth-powder, a powder used for cleaning the teeth, a dentifrice; also *attrib.*, as ***tooth-powder box***; †**tooth-proof** *a.*, having teeth of tried strength or efficiency (cf. proof *a.* 1); **tooth-puller**, one who extracts teeth; **tooth-pulling**, extraction of a tooth or teeth; **tooth-pulp**, the soft cellular tissue around which the hard parts of a tooth are developed, and which fills the cavity of the fully formed tooth; **tooth-rail**, a tramway rail having teeth or cogs; **tooth-rake**, †(*a*) a toothpick (*obs.*); (*b*) a rake with teeth; **tooth-rash**, an eruptive disease incident to infants when teething; **tooth-ribbon**, the lingual ribbon or odontophore of certain molluscs; **tooth-root** = toothwort 3; **tooth-sac**, a sac or hollow structure of connective tissue, within which a tooth is developed; **tooth-saw** (*Dentistry*), a fine frame-saw for sawing off portions of the teeth (Knight 1877); †**tooth-scrape** (*obs.*), **tooth-scraper**, an instrument for scraping the teeth, as a toothpick, or a dentist's instrument; **tooth-set** *a.*, set with teeth, having tooth-like projections; †**tooth-shaken** *a.*, having the teeth loosened, as by age; **tooth-soap**, a preparation for cleaning the teeth; **tooth-stick**, †(*a*) a dentifrice in shape of a stick; (*b*) a stick used for cleaning the teeth; **tooth(ed)-violet** = toothwort 1; **tooth-wark** (now *dial.*) [cf. head-wark], toothache (cf. *teeth-work* in 9 b); **tooth wash**, a liquid dentifrice; **tooth-wheel**, a wheel with teeth, a toothed wheel, cog-wheel; **tooth-winged** *a.*, having the wings toothed or notched on the outer margin, as certain butterflies; **tooth-work**, (*a*) ornamental work resembling teeth; (*b*) work done with the teeth, i.e. eating (*nonce-use*); **tooth-wound**, a wound inflicted by the tooth of an animal (cf. *teeth-wound* in 9 b); †**tooth-wrest**: see quot. See also tooth-brush, -pick, -shell, etc.

1872 Wood *Insects at Home* 470 A family of Moths called Notodontidæ, or *Tooth-backs. **1585** Higins *Junius' Nomenclator* 260/2 *Dentifricium*,..tooth powder: tooth sope, or *tooth blanch. **1857** Dunglison *Med. Lex.* s.v. *Tooth*, The ivory of the tooth or Dentine,..proper tooth substance, bone of the tooth, osseous substance of tooth, *tooth bone. **1878** T. Bryant *Pract. Surg.* I. 557 The portion of the case that forms the root or roots is covered by 'crusta petrosa' or tooth-bone. **1642** A. Ross *Mel Heliconium* (1643) 68 And then the Dragon, he did wound And all his *toothbread sonnes confound. **1887** Rider Haggard *Allan Quaterm.* 73 A *tooth-chattering cook. **1889** Stevenson *Master of B.* 80 Alone..in this tooth-chattering desert. **1893** *Westm. Gaz.* 24 Apr. 4/3 The force was a mere *toothcomb in the face of the rioters. **1902** *Sat. Rev.* 1 Nov. 556/1 The rake with which Mr. Nield gathers together his authors is a very tooth-comb. **1918** *Daily Chron.* 25 Jan. 3/7 The Army behind the front is being tooth-combed of all men fit for the fighting line. **1924** *Glasgow Herald* 28 Aug. 4/2 She was a strong woman, well accustomed to 'toothcomb' her husband's MS. **1931** *Times Lit. Suppl.* 1 Oct. 749/3 Whatever the 'tooth-combs' of Dr. Hotson's fellow-scholars may leave of it, he must be congratulated on his discovery. **1958** *N.Y. Times Mag.* 6 Apr. 68/4 The three officers start their own toothcomb check of their huge ship. **1962** *Amer. Jrnl. Physical Anthropol.* XX. 128/1 The closely spaced incisors [of lemurs] seem to scrape the fur rather than comb it. The use of the term 'tooth comb' may be, therefore, objectionable. **1972** *Times Lit. Suppl.* 11 Aug. 946/1 A novel which has been picked over with toothcombs, in search of clues to 'The Mystery'. **1977** *Listener* 7 Apr. 442/1 Decides whether the bid is contentious enough to be toothcombed by the mergers panel. **1980** J. Gardner *Garden of Weapons* I. xi. 110 The four men and one woman trained after a toothcomb selection. **1981** *Times* 16 Feb. 14/4 Tooth combs are found today in tree shrews..as well as in the lemurs and lorises. **1873** Dawson *Earth & Man* iv. 73 The Sertulariæ or *tooth-corallines. **1863–79** Prior *Brit. Pl.*, *Tooth-cress, or Tooth-Violet,..*Dentaria bulbifera.* **1767** S. Paterson *Another Trav.* I. 300 'Tis the celebrated *tooth-doctor—he takes out your old teeth without any pain. **1884** C. G. W. Lock *Workshop Receipts* Ser. III. 312/1 Adding to crude or branch lacquer, about 5 per cent. of the *tooth dye (haguro) used by women. **1794** E. Darwin *Zoon.* I. iii. 22 The disagreeable sensation called the *tooth-edge. **1898** P. Manson *Trop. Diseases* iv. 89 In such patients..*tooth extraction..may prove a dangerous matter. **1977** *Age* (Melbourne) 18 Jan. 15/5 Who do you suppose pays for the $50 billion difference? The *tooth fairy? Hardly. You do. **1977** *Rolling Stone* 7 Apr. 45/4 Anyone who thinks they acted alone must also believe in Santa Claus, the Easter Bunny and the Tooth Fairy. **1978** J. Hyams *Pool* xi. 163 Alan had ceased to believe in miracles at about the same age he stopped believing in the Tooth Fairy. **1867** W. W. Smyth *Coal & Coal-mining* 37 The Odontopteris, or *tooth-fern. **1788** Charlotte Smith *Emmeline* (1816) IV. 179 The child was very ill once with a *tooth-fever. **1884** Miller *Plant-n.*, *Tooth-flower, Australian, *Dentella repens.* **1844** Dufton *Deafness* 91 A pair of *tooth-forceps was..employed. **1841** *Penny Cycl.* XX. 460/2 The number of successive *tooth-germs..behind the..functional teeth. **1858** P. L. Simmonds *Dict. Trade Products* 384/2 **Tooth-glass*, a toilet water-glass for washing the mouth. **1915** Kipling *Diversity of Creatures* (1917) 411 That plate of the four lower ones in the blue tooth-glass. **1978** G. Greene *Human Factor* v. iii. 286 The toothglasses were swathed in plastic. **1483** *Cath. Angl.* 398/1 A *Tuthe yren, *dentaria.* **1851** Mantell *Petrifact.* III. §5. 255 The central body of dentine or *tooth-ivory. **1827** N. Arnott *Physics* I. 247 The *tooth-key is an instrument found in many hands. **1835–6** *Todd's Cycl. Anat.* I. 312/1 A *tooth-like process on either side [of the bill]. **1839** Bailey *Festus* ix. (1852) 99 The toothlike aching ruin of the body. **1889** C. C. R. *Up for the Season*, etc. 53 A *tooth-mark left me by her black-and-tan. **1831** Trelawny *Adv. Younger Son* I. 52 Buttered toast, half eaten, and *tooth-marked. **1879** Thomson & Tait *Nat. Phil.* I. I. §109 The dentist's *tooth-mill is an..illustration of the elastic universal flexure joint. **1891** *Outing* (U.S.) Dec. 244/2 Some drank their champagne out of *tooth mugs. **1935** *Discovery* Apr. 114/1 To this communal tooth-mug débris and food particles get transferred. **1979** A. Morice *Murder in Outline* ix. 77 Why not repair to..our room, where tooth mugs abound, and push the boat out? **1840** *Civil Eng. & Arch. Jrnl.* III. 2/1 A narrow lancet opening, having the *tooth ornament in the hollow surrounding the same. **1592** Chettle *Kinde-harts Dr.* (1841) 30 The only remedy for the *tooth paine, either to haue patience, or to pull them out. **1832** *Amer. Railroad Jrnl.* I. 607/3 (Advt.), Seidlitz powders, chloride of soda, chlorine *tooth paste. **1857** Dunglison *Med. Lex.*, *T[ooth] Paste*, Dentifricium. **1966** A. Sachs *Jail Diary* vi. 62, I get up off the floor, fetch my toothpaste-tube. **1975** *Listener* 9 Jan. 44/3 Haldeman says to him: 'John, you ought to think about that, because once the toothpaste is out of the tube, it is awfully hard to put it back again.' **1978** F. King *Action* xxxi. 105 Pinching at an exhausted toothpaste tube. **1823** P. Nicholson *Pract. Build.* 246 The *Tooth-plane is fitted with a blade or iron, on the steel side of it covered with rakes or small grooves. **1880** M. Mackenzie *Dis. Throat & Nose* I. 411 Teeth, real or artificial, or *toothplates, become loosened during sleep. **1542** *Acc. Ld. High Treas. Scot.* VIII. 89 Ane stoppell to keip the kingis grace *twithe pulder. **1823** J. Badcock *Dom. Amusem.* 25 As a tooth-powder, nothing can exceed the virtues of charcoal. **1654** Gayton *Pleas. Notes* iii. v. 101 The..more crusty meats fell to Sancho's share, who was *tooth-proofe. **1839** J. Brown *Lett.* (1907) 46 A good *tooth-puller can pull with any key or claw. **1850** Thackeray *Pendennis* lxi, No more than *tooth-pulling, or any other pang, eternal. **1854** R. Owen *Skel. & Teeth* in *Orr's Circ. Sc.* I. *Org. Nat.* 265 The primary basis of the tooth, called '*tooth-pulp'. **1862** Smiles *Engineers* III. 85 Mr. Blenkinsop of Leeds, in 1811, took out a patent for a racked or *tooth-rail. **1585** Higins *Junius' Nomenclator* 260/2 *Dentiscalpium*... Curedent. A tooth scraper, or *tooth-rake. *c* **1830** *Pract. Treat. Roads* 17 in *Libr. Usef. Knowl., Husb.* III, Scratching it [the surface], with a tooth-rake regularly all over, as occasion requires. **1818–20** E. Thompson *Cullen's Nosol. Method.* (ed. 3) 321 *Strophulus confertus*, sometimes called the rank red gum and the *tooth rash. **1883** J. G. Wood in *Gd. Words* Sept. 603/2 The still more curious '*tooth-ribbon' set with its hundreds of hooked toothlets. **1818** *Tooth-root [see dentaria]. **1890** Billings *Nat. Med. Dict.*, **Tooth-sac*, connective-tissue structure enclosing the dentine germ and enamel-organ in the fœtal development of the teeth. **1552** Huloet, *Tothscrape instrument, *dentiscalpium*. **1585** *Tooth-scraper [see *tooth-rake*]. **1860** Mayne *Expos. Lex.*, Tooth-scraper. **1860** *Artist & Craftsman* 125 The *toothset edge of those eternal hills. **1650** Bulwer *Anthropomet.* 140 Tooth-drawers and *Tooth-setting Chyrurgions. **1549** Chaloner *Erasm. on Folly* F ij, Wrincled, *totheshaken..so desyrous yet of life. **1674** Josselyn *Voy. New Eng.* 185 The Women are pittifully Tooth-shaken. **1837** P. Keith *Bot. Lex.* 292 Peristomium..consists of a circular and double row of fine and *tooth-shaped substances. **1607** Topsell *Four-f. Beasts* (1658) 401 That excellent powder, for the scowring and clensing of the teeth called *Tooth-soap. **1762** Goldsm. *Cit. W.* iii, Your nose-borers, feet-swathers, *tooth-stainers, eye-brow-pluckers. **1729** *MS. Accounts* in *N. & Q.* 7th Ser. VII. 30/1 Disbursed at London..a silver *tooth-stick, 8*d.* **1859** R. F. Burton *Centr. Afr.* in *Jrnl. Geog. Soc.* XXIX. 323 Some of the more civilized have learned..to use a toothstick. **1862** *Catal. Internat. Exhib., Brit.* ii. No. 3533, Improved *tooth-stump instrument. **1634** Fowldes *Homer's Batt. Frogs & Mice* B v, No *tooth-tempting fare. **1863–79** *Tooth-Violet [see *tooth-cress*]. *c* **1375** *Sc. Leg. Saints* xxii. (*Laurentius*) 567 A man sa disesyt..Of *tuth-wark. **1871** 'Mark Twain' in *Galaxy* Aug. 284/2 He tendered me a *tooth-wash atrocity of his own invention. **1895** *Army & Navy Co-op. Soc. Price List* 716/2 Tooth-wash. **1949** E. Pound *Pisan Cantos* lxxx. 104 Pepitone was wasting toothwash. **1862** *Catal. Internat. Exhib.* II. xii. 2 A series of shaftings and *tooth-wheels. **1891** *Cent. Dict.*, *Tooth-winged. **1681** Grew *Musæum* i. vi. i. 133 The ridges also of the rounds are wrought with *Tooth-Work. **1899** *Syd. Soc. Lex.*, **T[ooth] wounds*, wounds inflicted by the teeth of animals which do not owe their gravity to poison, but to the laceration of the tissues. **1706** Phillips (ed. Kersey), **Tooth-wrest*, an Instrument to draw, or pull out Teeth.

b. Combs. with the pl. *teeth* (most of which have corresponding forms in *tooth-*: see above), as ***teeth-ache*** (= toothache), ***-brush*** (= toothbrush), ***-chatter***, ***-chattering*** sb. and adj., ***-dints*** (double pl. of *tooth-dint*), ***-edging*** adj. (setting the teeth on edge), ***-filing***, ***-gnashing*** sb. and adj., ***-grinding*** adj., ***-like*** adj., ***-mark***, ***-plate***, ***-pulps*** (double pl. of *tooth-pulp*), ***-ridge***, ***-watering*** (cf. phr. *the teeth water* in 8 g), †***-wind*** (? a wind meeting one in the teeth), †***-work*** (= *tooth-wark*), ***-wound***.

1890 P. H. Emerson *Wild Life* xxii. 96 For *teeth-ache we rub the inside wi' rum. **1651** *Verney Mem.* (1894) III. 39 A gift of the new Paris luxury—'the *Teeth Brushes and boxes'. **1751** Smollett *Per. Pic.* (1779) III. lxxx. 63 Waiting-women..who clean your teeth-brushes. **1834** *Tait's Mag.* I. 43/2 He has managed to get up a masterly *teeth-chatter. **1796** Coleridge *Blossom 1st Feb.* 3 This dark..*teeth-chattering month. **1887** Rider Haggard *Allan Quaterm.* 91 He nearly aroused the Masai camp with teeth-chattering. **1839** Bailey *Festus* xviii. (1852) 241 The foul fiend's *teeth-dints may be seen. **1603** Florio *Montaigne* ii. xii. (1632) 336 That sharp, harsh, and *teethedging noise that Smiths make in filing of brasse. **1897** Mary Kingsley *W. Africa* 477 The *teeth-filing I think undoubtedly does arise from this. *a* **1711** Ken *Hymnotheo* Poet. Wks. 1721 III. 90 *Teeth-gnashing Envy at the Saints above. **1642** A. Ross *Mel Heliconium* (1643) 175 *Teeth-grinding anger, with fierce-glowing eyes. **1969** Fabian & Byrne *Groupie* (1970) xxvi. 173 Teeth-grinding teenagers from Muswell Hill picking you up in Cortinas. **1884** W. S. B. McLaren *Spinning* (ed. 2) 6 Seeing the *teeth-like edges which thus catch the fingers. **1898** R. Blakeborough *Wit*, etc. *N. Riding Yorks.* 202 *Teeth-marks were found on..part of their body. **1900** *Edin. Rev.* Apr. 362 Their works bear the teethmark of their own age. **1897** *Allbutt's Syst. Med.* III. 346 A badly fitting artificial *teeth-plate. **1859** J. Tomes *Dental Surg.* (1873) 4 The depth of these bony cells is only sufficient to contain the developing teeth and *teeth-pulps. **1928** I. C. Ward *Phonetics of Eng.* xiii. 117 *T* and *d* before *r* are articulated on the teeth, not on the *teeth-ridge. **1966** J. Derrick *Teaching Eng. to Immigrants* iii. 127 The tip or blade (i.e. the very front part) of the tongue is just behind the upper gums ('the teeth ridge'), i.e. towards the front of the mouth. **1879** Calderwood *Mind & Br.* 273 That result known as '*teeth-watering', which may be described as a reminiscence of taste. *a* **1732** T. Boston *Crook in Lot* (1863) 45 What a sad thing must it then be to lose this *teeth-wind for Immanuel's land! *c* **1440** *Thornton MS.* lf. 176 (E.E.T.S.) A charme for þe *tethe worke. **1856** Kane *Arct. Expl.* II. xv. 164 Five were scarred by direct *teeth-wounds of bears.

tooth (tuːθ), *v.* Forms: see prec. [f. prec.]

1. *intr.* To develop, grow, or 'cut' teeth; to teethe. ? *Obs.*

c **1410** *Master of Game* vii. (1904) 32/1 þei tothen [*pr.* tochen; *MS. Digby 182* teth] ii tymes in þe yere whan þei be whelpes. *c* **1440–1796** [see toothing 1].

2. *trans.* To furnish or supply with teeth; to fit or fix teeth into; to cut teeth in or upon, to indent.

1483 *Cath. Angl.* 398/1 To Tuthe, *dentare.* **1523** Fitzherb. *Husb.* §24 Than maye he..tothe the rakes with drye wethy wode. **1611** *Shuttleworths' Acc.* (Chetham Soc.) 196 Making thre huckes and toothing nyne sicles, xv^{d}. **1745** Arderon in *Phil. Trans.* XLIV. 170, I toothed two Pieces of Brass..to fit each other. **1833, 1884** [see toothing 3]. See also toothed.

3. To exercise the teeth upon; to bite, gnaw. Also *absol.*

1579 Gosson *Sch. Abuse* (Arb.) 19 The Syracusans vsed such varietie of dishes..they were many times in doubt, which they shoulde touth first, or taste last. **1858** H. W. Beecher *Life Th.* (1859) 32 The pragmatic prophecy-monger and the swinish utilitarian have toothed its fruits and craunched its blossoms. **1871** R. Ellis *Catullus* xxiii. 4 Each for penury fit to tooth a flint-stone.

4. To fit or fix into something by projections like teeth, or in the manner of teeth. **a.** *trans.*

[**1672**: cf. toothing 2 b.] **1703** T. N. *City & C. Purchaser* 51 'Tis common to Tooth in the stretching Course 2 Inches with the Stretcher only. **1793** W. H. Marshall *W. England* (1796) II. 341 By toothing the one into the other..the whole settles..into one corporate mass. **1888** *Law Rep., Weekly Notes* 77/1 The defendant..might use it..by putting a lean-to against it, or by toothing a door support into it.

b. *intr.* for *pass.* To interlock.

1703 Moxon *Mech. Exerc.* 260 Whereas if the Header of one side of the Wall, toothed as much as the Stretcher on the other side, it would be a stronger Toothing. **1865** Masson *Rec. Brit. Philos.* 321 The one [mind] might have a conviction that it toothed at some points into the independent constitution of the other [matter].

toothache (ˈtuːθeɪk). Forms: see tooth *sb.* and ache *sb.*; also 4–7 **-ake**, 6 *Sc.* **-aike**, **-ȝaik**, 7–9 **-ach**. An ache or continuous pain in a tooth or the teeth. (As a malady, commonly ***the tooth ache*** down to 19th. c. See the 8.)

1377 Langl. *P. Pl.* B. xx. 81 Coughes, and cardiacles, crampes, and tothaches. *c* **1489** Caxton *Sonnes of Aymon* ix. 215 The Kyng..sayd he had the tooth ache. *a* **1585** Montgomerie *Flyting* 321 The phtiseik, þe twithȝaik [*v.r.* toothaike], þe tittis, and þe tirrillis. **1599** Shaks. *Much Ado* iii. ii. 21, I haue the tooth-ach. *Ibid.* v. i. 36 There was neuer yet Philosopher, That could endure the tooth-ake patiently. **1649** Jer. Taylor *Gt. Exemp.* iii. Disc. xvi. 56 Some persons used certain verses of the psalter as an antidote against tooth-ach. **1711** Addison *Spect.* No. 7 ¶4 She lay ill of the Tooth-ach. *a* **1774** Tucker *Lt. Nat.* (1834) II. 581 Engaged at home by a violent toothache. **1791** Burke *App. Whigs* Wks. VI. 221 A charm for the tooth-ach. **1887** *Times* 26 Aug. 7/4 All that is the matter with him is a fit of toothache.

b. *attrib.*, usually denoting something used as a remedy for toothache, as ***toothache spell***, ***tincture***; **toothache-grass**, a N. American grass (*Ctenium americanum*) having a very pungent taste; **toothache-tree**, (*a*) name for several N. American species of the genus *Xanthoxylon*, having pungent aromatic fruit, esp. *X. fraxineum*, also called *prickly ash*; (*b*) the similar N. American *Aralia spinosa*, also called *angelica-tree*.

1616 Sylvester *Tobacco Battered* 655 It is but like some of our Tooth-ake Spells, Which for the present seem to ease the Pain. **1730** Mortimer in *Phil. Trans.* XXXVI. 428 *Zanthoxylum spinosum*,..the Pellitory or Tooth-ach Tree. **1860** Mayne *Expos. Lex.*, *Tooth-ache Tree*, a common name for the tree *Aralia spinosa*. **1860** Worcester, *Toothache-grass*.

Hence **ˈtoothˌachy** *a.* (*colloq.*), affected with toothache. So **ˈtooth-ˌaching**, aching of the teeth, toothache.

1709 *Brit. Apollo* II. No. 7. 3/2, I was taken With a vi'lent Tooth-aching. **1838** Lady Granville *Lett.* (1894) II. 269 Toothachy and tired, I have been writing this letter. **1900** El. Glyn *Visits Elizabeth* (1906) 72 That is how she got the toothachy look.

tooth and egg, obs. corr. of tutenag, zinc.

toothbill (ˈtuːθbɪl). The tooth-billed pigeon.
1862 [see next].

tooth-billed (ˈtuːθbɪld), *a.* *Ornith.* [See billed.] Having one or more tooth-like projections on the edge of the bill; dentirostral or serratirostral.

tooth-billed bower-bird, a rare Australian bower-bird, *Scenopœus dentirostris*. *tooth-billed pigeon*, *Didunculus strigirostris*, of the Samoan Islands.

1862 Wood *Illustr. Nat. Hist.* II. 593 Tooth-billed Pigeon... The whole contour of the Tooth-bill is remarkable. **1872** Coues *N. Amer. Birds* 223 Didunculidæ consists of the only less singular tooth-billed pigeon, *Didunculus strigirostris*. **1905** *Westm. Gaz.* 18 Nov. 7/2 The didunculus, or tooth-billed pigeon,..if native accounts are to be believed,..has only saved itself from extinction by changing its habits in one of the islands.

ˈtooth-brush. **a.** A small brush with a long handle, used for cleansing the teeth.

[**1651**, **1751**: see *teeth-brush*, tooth *sb.* 9 b.] **1690** Wood *Life* (O.H.S.) III. 319 [Bought] toothbrush [of] J. Barret. **1807** J. Beresford *Miseries Hum. Life* 236 While you are waiting..for a fresh supply of tooth-brushes. **1844** W. H. Maxwell *Sports & Adv. Scotl.* ii. (1855) 35 My chattels are safe,..even to a tooth-brush.

b. *attrib.*, as ***tooth-brush glass***, ***handle***, ***holder***, ***rack***. **tooth-brush moustache** (*humorous*), a bristly moustache; **tooth-brush tree**, a name for *Salvadora persica*, from the use of its twigs for cleaning the teeth.

1931 H. E. L. Mellersh *Salt of Earth* vii. 159 Put them [*sc.* flowers] in the toothbrush glass or something till May can see to them. **1979** R. Jaffe *Class Reunion* (1980) i. 30 Go get your toothbrush glasses and we'll lock the door. **1886** Fenn *Master Cerem.* i, That peg was an old tooth-brush handle. **1911** *T. Eaton & Co. Catal.* Spring & Summer 199/2 Combination tumbler and tooth brush holder, nickel-plated. **1979** M. Millar *Murder of Miranda* ii. 85 The chrome toothbrush holder was empty. **1904** *Daily Chron.* 31 Aug. 4/4 Clothes of outlandish cut, toothbrush moustache. **1926–7** *Army & Navy Stores Catal.* 121/2 Bath bracket outfit consisting of..tumbler ring, tooth brush rack. **1969** Hurd & Osmond *Smile on Face of Tiger* v. 184 [He] stood leaning against the toothbrush rack, cup in hand. **1891** *Cent. Dict.* s.v. *Salvadora, S. Persica*..in India furnishes *kikuel-oil*, and from the use of its twigs is sometimes called *toothbrush-tree*.

Hence **ˈtoothbrushing** *vbl. sb.*; **ˈtoothbrushy** *a.* *nonce-wd.*, resembling a tooth-brush; bristly.

1904 'A. Hope' *Double Harness* xiii, His toothbrushy hair had..more than usual of its suggestion of comical distress. **1920** A. Huxley *Limbo* 168 A foam of tooth-brushing. **1976** J. Philips *Backlash* (1977) ii. ii. 93 Go into the bathrooms. .. Time for tooth brushing.

ˈtooth-ˌdrawer.

1. One who 'draws' or extracts teeth; a dentist. Now *contemptuous*.

1393 Langl. *P. Pl.* C. vii. 370 Of portours and of pyke-porses and pylede toþ-drawers. *c* **1440** *Promp. Parv.* 498/1 Toothe drawere, *edentator.* **1529** More *Dyaloge* ii. Wks. 194/2 Sainct Apoline we make a toth drawer. **1601** Sir W. Cornwallis *Ess.* ii. xliii. (1631) 199 To heare Tooth-drawers or Rat-catchers sweare themselves the best in the world. **1654** Whitlock *Zootomia* 291 Enough to make a Tooth-drawer, or Corn-cutter passe for a generall Physitian. **1833** L. Ritchie *Wand. by Loire* 40 The only rumbustious individual in the whole crowd was an itinerant tooth-drawer.

2. A dentist's instrument for extracting teeth.

1597 A. M. tr. *Guillemeau's Fr. Chirurg.* 27/2 We must gently and easyly crushe the tooth-drawer together. **1694** *Acc. Sev. Late Voy.* ii. (1711) 123 He hath two Claws before, ..somewhat like the Phangs of a Tooth-drawer.

So **ˈtooth-ˌdrawing**, *sb.* extraction of a tooth or teeth; *adj.* that extracts teeth.

1610 Healey *St. Aug. Citie of God* 120 The third, sonne to Arsippus,..first inventor of..tooth-drawing. **1764** Foote *Mayor of G.* i, You blood-letting, tooth-drawing,.. glistering ——. **1779** Warner in Jesse *Selwyn & Contemp.* (1844) IV. 260 The tooth-drawing must have been a curious scene. **1860** Thackeray *Lovel* vi, My bleeding, bolusing, tooth-drawing rival.

toothed (tuːθt, *poet.* ˈtuːθɪd), *a.* [f. tooth *sb.* or *v.* + -ed.] Furnished with teeth (or a tooth).

1. *lit.* of an animal: Having teeth; with defining words, Having teeth of a specified kind.

13.. *K. Alis.* 5392 (Bodl. MS.) Hij weren toþed als a man. **1413** *Pilgr. Sowle* (Caxton) ii. xlv. (1859) 51 Somme of them were tothyd as boores. **1592** Shaks. *Ven. & Ad.* 1117 Had I been tooth'd like him, I must confesse, With kissing him I should haue kild him first. **1661** Lovell *Hist. Anim. & Min.* Introd., The teeth are wanting in some, others are toothed. **1860** Wraxall *Life in Sea* i. 3 The Cetacea are subdivided into the 'toothless' and the 'toothed'.

b. *fig.* cf. tooth *sb.* 2. *rare.*

1584 B. R. tr. *Herodotus* i. 63 The basest sorte of yonkers that were not so deyntely toothed.

c. *fig.* 'Biting', pungent, corrosive. ? *Obs.*

1628 Feltham *Resolves* ii. [i.] lxi. 175 Dab it with aqua fortis, toothed waters, and corroding Minerals. **1675** V. Alsop *Anti-sozzo* ii. 65 Those Severe and Toothed Satyrs wherewith he has Torn and Lasht poor Honest Men.

2. Having natural projections or processes like teeth; dentate; indented; jagged: *esp.* of leaves or other parts of plants; also of the bill of birds, the margin of shells, etc.

toothed vertebra, a name for the axis vertebra, from its tooth or odontoid process (*Syd. Soc. Lex.* s.v. *Vertebra*).

1387 Trevisa *Higden* (Rolls) II. 383 Perdix..took a plate of iren..and made it i-toþed as a rugge boon of a fische. **1610** Shaks. *Temp.* iv. i. 180 Through Tooth'd briars, sharpe firzes, pricking gosse, & thorns. **1796** Withering *Brit. Plants* (ed. 3) III. 679 Leaves smooth, notched and acutely toothed. **1802** Paley *Nat. Theol.* xiii. §3 (1819) 221 The middle claw of the heron and cormorant is toothed and notched like a saw. **1859** W. S. Coleman *Woodlands* (1866) 27 The leaves..doubly toothed at the edges. **1895** *Oracle Encycl.* I. 594/2 The wing-margin is denticulated or irregularly toothed.

3. Made or fitted artificially with teeth or tooth-like projections: *spec.* of a wheel, cogged.

toothed ornament (*Arch.*) = tooth-ornament: tooth *sb.* 9.

1387 [see 2]. **1573** Tusser *Husb.* (1878) 37 A barlie rake toothed. **1577** Googe *Heresbach's Husb.* 42 They holde their leaft hande full of Corne, and..with toothed Syckles they cut it. **1641** MILTON *Animadv.* i. Wks. 1851 III. 191 A toothlesse Satyr is as improper as a toothed sleekstone, and as bullish. **1797** *Encycl. Brit.* (ed. 3) I. 92/2 The toothed wheel D, fixed on the axis EF. **1815** J. SMITH *Panorama Sc. & Art* I. 163 The ribs were often enriched by the toothed ornament. **1834–6** BARLOW in *Encycl. Metrop.* (1845) VIII. 101/2 A toothed wheel is generally understood to be one in which the teeth are cast or cut on the wheel itself, forming one whole. **1862** RICKMAN *Goth. Archit.* 294 An ornament almost as peculiar to the Decorated style as the toothed ornament [is] to the Early English. **1905** *Westm. Gaz.* 20 June 4/2 The protest..against the use of the spring toothed-trap.

4. *Comb.*, as ***toothed-billed*** (= TOOTH-BILLED); also freq. as the second element in parasynthetic combinations, as ***buck-toothed***, ***sweet-toothed***.

1523 FITZHERB. *Husb.* §136 A graffynge sawe..very thyn and thycke tothed. **1670** NARBOROUGH *Jrnl.* in *Acc. Sev. Late Voy.* I. (1694) 64 They are smooth and even toothed. **1706** S. SEWALL *Diary* 25 Dec., I bought me a great Tooth'd Comb at Dwight's. **1841** *Penny Cycl.* XXI. 416/2 The..tribe of *Dentirostres*, or toothed-billed birds.

toothenague, -aque, obs. ff. TUTENAG, zinc.

'toother. [f. TOOTH *v.* + -ER[1].] One who makes the teeth of saws; a machine for doing this.

1881 *Instr. Census Clerks* (1885) 45 Saw Making: Parer. Toother. Backer.

'tooth-fee. [Literal rendering of ON. *tann-fé*, f. *tọnn*, *tann-* tooth + *fé* money.] A gift to an infant on cutting its first tooth, a custom mentioned in Old Norse, and still observed in Iceland (Vigfusson). Also **'tooth-gift, -money, -piece.**

1851 THORPE *North. Mythol.* I. 25 Alfheim was given to him [Frey] by the gods as tooth-money. **1868** G. STEPHENS *Runic Mon.* II. 538 This fine Gold-bracteate..was probably a Tooth-fee or Birthday gift. *Ibid.* 529 It would seem to have been struck as a Birth-day- or Tooth-piece for some highborn child. **1875** R. B. ANDERSON *Norse Mythol.* 445 Alfheim was given him as a tooth-gift. **1884** YORK POWELL in *Academy* 23 Feb. 128/2 What Sigmund gave his son was a sword, *imon-lauk*, a very fitting tooth-fee, or name-gift, to one who was to live and die in arms.

toothful ('tu:θfʊl), *sb.* [f. TOOTH *sb.* + -FUL 2.] *lit.* As much as would fill a tooth; a small mouthful, esp. of liquor.

a **1774** FERGUSSON *Drink Ecl.* 69 Tho' lairds tak toothfu's o' my warming sap. **1821** *Joseph the Bk.-Man* 132 When Joseph landed, A potent toothful he commanded. **1839** *Fraser's Mag.* XIX. 474 Wiping each platter, so as not to leave One toothful of the garlic sauce behind. **1882** MRS. RIDDELL *Pr. Wales' Garden-P.* 115 If he would be persuaded to take a toothful of brandy before beginning the evening's duties.

toothful ('tu:θfʊl), *a.* [f. TOOTH *sb.* + -FUL 1.]

1. Full of teeth; having many teeth. *rare.*

1591 SYLVESTER *Du Bartas* I. iii. 834 Our mealy grain..being covered by the tooth-full Harrow.

†2. Pleasant to the taste: = TOOTHSOME. *Obs.*

1622 MASSINGER & DEKKER *Virg.-Mart.* v. i, What dainty relish on my tongue This fruit hath left! Some angel hath me fed: If so toothfull, I will be banqueted.

tooth-gift: see TOOTH-FEE.

toot-hill ('tu:thɪl). Also 4 **tote-**, 4–5 **tute-**, 6–8 **tout-hill.** Preserved in many forms *toot-*, *tote-*, *tot-*, *tut-* in place-names. [ME. *tōte-hill*, f. TOOT *v.*[1] (or *sb.*[1]) + HILL.] A natural or artificial hill or mound used for a look-out place; a prominent hill; = TOOT *sb.*[1] 1. (In quot. 1250 a place-name.)

[**1250** *Pat. Roll 34 Hen. III*, m. 1 Concessimus..quod illa feria que consuevit esse in eorum cimeterio apud Westmonasterium..fit singulis annis apud Tothull'.]

1382 WYCLIF *2 Sam.* v. 7 Forsothe Dauid took the tote [*v.rr.* toot, tute] hil [1388 tour of] Syon; that is the citee of Dauid. —— *Isa.* xxi. 8 Vpon the toothil of the Lord I am stondende. *c* **1440** *Promp. Parv.* 498/1 Tote hylle, or hey place of lokynge, *conspicillum*. **1483** *Cath. Angl.* 398/1 A Tute hylle, *aruisium montarium*. **1532–3** *Durham Househ. Bk.* (Surtees) 181 Pro factura unius muri circa le toythyll 5s. 10d. **1535** *Goodly Prymer* (1834) 163 Sion by interpretation signifieth a tout-hill, or a place where a man may see far about him. **1609** HOLLAND *Amm. Marcell.* XVIII. viii. 118 A certaine high Barbican or Toot-hill [*specula*]. **1827** HODGSON *Northumbld.* II. I. 286 *note*, In a field, a little to the north-east of Hartington, there is a small conical hill, apparently natural, but artificially terraced, which is called the Tote-hill. **1886** *Chester Gloss.*, *Toot Hill*, prop. name, a steep hill near Alvanley. **1894** O. HESLOP *Northumbld. Gloss.*, *Tuthill, Tote-hill*, an eminence. Of frequent occurrence in place-names. The Tuthill-stairs in Newcastle ascend the eminence (called Tout-hill in Bourne's map, 1736) from The Close to Clavering Place... In old formal gardens a tout-hill was an artificial mound formed for the purpose of commanding a prospect.

toothily ('tu:θɪlɪ), *adv.* [f. TOOTHY *a.* + -LY[2].] In a toothy manner; so as to display the teeth.

1930 R. MACAULAY *Staying with Relations* xiii. 193 She stared at her master tied up in his chair,..and sunnily and toothily grinned. **1939** A. HUXLEY *After Many a Summer* i. 4 The chauffeur.., slightly over-acting the part of an old-world negro retainer, bowed, smiled toothily. **1977** P. D. JAMES *Death of Expert Witness* IV. 190 A studio photograph of Miss Willard herself, young, toothily coy.

toothing ('tu:θɪŋ), *vbl. sb.* [f. TOOTH *sb.* or *v.* + -ING[1].]

1. Development or 'cutting' of the teeth, dentition: = TEETHING *vbl. sb.* 1. *Obs.* or *rare.*

c **1440** *Pallad. on Husb.* I. 665 As seek ar they [peacocks] as children in tothynge. **1656** RIDGLEY *Pract. Physick* 323 Toothing of Children is about the seventh Moneth. **1796** E. DARWIN *Zoon.* II. 51 The pain of toothing often begins much earlier than is suspected.

2. A structure or formation (natural or artificial) consisting of teeth or tooth-like projections; such teeth collectively; dentation, serration.

1611 COTGR., *Allochons d'un rouët*, the teeth, or toothing, of a wheele, in a clocke. **1753** BAKER in *Phil. Trans.* XLVIII. 122 The toothing in the middle thereof almost proves that part to have been the palate of some animal. **1845** LINDLEY *Sch. Bot.* i. (1858) 9 If the toothings are..like those of a saw, the leaves are serrate. **1872** COUES *N. Amer. Birds* 236 A toothing of the under mandible.

b. *spec.* in *Building.* Bricks or stones left projecting from a wall to form a bond for additional work to be built on; the bond or attachment thus formed; the construction of this. Also *fig.*

1672 *Phil. Trans.* VII. 4081 In the first Wall there are Stones in toothings, from the top to the bottom. **1674** BLOUNT *Glossogr.*, *Toothing*, the working in of Bricks in a party-wall. **1769** H. MALDEN in Willis & Clark *Cambridge* (1886) I. 490 On the outer wall, may be perceived Toothings, where the Building was formerly joined. **1841** *Civil Eng. & Arch. Jrnl.* IV. 395/1 Regular half brick toothings were inserted, at intervals of 2 feet 3 inches apart.

3. The process of forming teeth or serrations; the furnishing (of a saw, etc.) with teeth.

1833 J. HOLLAND *Manuf. Metal* II. 56 The toothing [of a sickle] is effected by a small well tempered chisel and a hammer. **1884** C. G. W. LOCK *Workshop Receipts* Ser. III. 287/1 After toothing comes hardening [of saws].

4. *attrib.* and *Comb.*, as ***toothing-course***, ***-stone*** (see 2b); **toothing-plane**, a plane having the iron almost upright, with a serrated edge, used to score and roughen a surface; see TOOTH *sb.* 3d.

1703 T. N. *City & C. Purchaser* 51 Lay it on the last Toothing Course to bear it. **1847** SMEATON *Builder's Man.* 95 Made somewhat rough with either a rasp or toothing-plane. **1875** BRASH *Eccl. Archit. Irel.* 18 The chancel has disappeared; toothing-stones..show it to have been 12 ft. wide.

toothless ('tu:θlɪs), *a.* Forms: see TOOTH *sb.* [See -LESS.] Having no teeth; destitute of teeth.

1. *lit.* a. That is naturally without teeth; not developing teeth. b. Having the teeth still undeveloped; that has not yet cut its teeth. c. Having lost the teeth, as from age.

1398 TREVISA *Barth. De P.R.* VI. ix. (Bodl. MS.), þe norise ..chewith mete in hire owne mowþe and makeþ it redie to þe toþeles child. *Ibid.* XVIII. xviii. (ibid.), Bestes þat beþ toþeles in þe ouer iowe. *c* **1440** *Promp. Parv.* 498/1 Tootheles, for age, *edentatus*. *Ibid.*, Tootheles, for ȝungthe. **1581** DERRICKE *Image of Irel.* (1883) 19 Let the toothlesse crabbed queane boyle in her owne despight. **1673** HICKERINGILL *Greg. F. Greyb.* 185 A toothless dog bites not much more than a dead dog. **1784** COWPER *Task* IV. 81 Teeth for the toothless, ringlets for the bald. **1810** SOUTHEY *Kehama* XIII. xii, The Tygress leaves her toothless cubs. **1880** GÜNTHER *Fishes* 170 The toothless buccal cavity is surrounded by a semi-circular upper lip.

2. *transf.* Destitute of tooth-like formations or projections; not jagged or serrated.

1812 *New Bot. Gard.* I. 8 Follicles oblong, acuminate, toothless. **1822** J. PARKINSON *Outl. Oryctol.* 153 The aperture [of the shell] long, narrow, toothless. **1883** *Gd. Words* Aug. 505/2 There are grooves of the portcullis still, but it is toothless now.

3. *fig.* a. Destitute of keenness or 'edge'; not biting or corrosive; also *fig.*

1592 NASHE *Four Lett. Confut.* Wks. (Grosart) II. 203 Poore secular Satirist..that with the toothlesse gums of his Poetry so betuggeth a dead man. **1597** BP. HALL (*title*) Virgidemiarum, Sixe Bookes. First three Bookes, Of Toothlesse Satyrs. **1650** BAXTER *Saints' R.* III. ii. §14. 295 If a drunken..Preacher did..read the Common Prayer, or some toothless Homily, instead of a searching..Sermon. *a* **1764** LLOYD *Epist. to C. Churchill* Poet. Wks. 1774 I. 86 No toothless spleen, no venom'd critic's aim. **1882** MRS. OLIPHANT *Lit. Hist. Eng.* I. 312 The 'Lyrical ballads', at which every toothless critic sneered.

†b. *loosely.* Tasteless; not toothsome. *Obs.*

1679 JANE *Serm. at St. Margarets* 11 Apr. 17 This.. renders all his most exquisite pleasures toothless and insipid.

c. Lacking the means of compulsion or enforcement; ineffectual. Cf. TOOTH *sb.* 2b(*b*).

1961 in WEBSTER. **1966** *Federal Suppl.* (U.S.) CCXLIV. 823/2 Congress might as well have legalized the closed shop as have enacted such a cynical and toothless provision. **1971** *Nature* 23 Apr. 486/1 Reasons for the failure include unenforceable and toothless laws,..foot dragging by local and state authorities, [etc.]. **1973** *Guardian* 16 Feb. 13 The EEC's social and economic committee..is a toothless organisation... Its views are not seriously taken into account. **1984** *N.Y. Times Mag.* 22 Jan. 46/4 If we do not do what we propose to do, we shall be reviled as toothless and irrelevant.

Hence **'toothlessly** *adv.*; **'toothlessness.**

1631 *Celestina* IV. 49 That toothlessnesse of the gummes. **1855** H. SPENCER *Princ. Psychol.* (1872) II. VI. vi. 62 In the infant, toothlessness coexists with the power of developing thirty-two teeth at maturity. **1891** *Harper's Mag.* Sept. 537/1 Toothlessly smiling.

toothlet ('tu:θlɪt). [f. TOOTH *sb.* + -LET.] A small tooth or tooth-like projection; a denticle.

1800 *Misc. Tr.* in *Asiat. Ann. Reg.* 264/2 Calyx very small, tubular, five toothed; toothlets short. **1884** W. K. PARKER *Mammal. Descent* vii. 177 Notched..into eight or nine toothlets like a comb.

Hence **'toothleted** *a.*, denticulate.

1812 *New Bot. Gard.* I. 47 The other [stems] having the bases of the petioles toothleted. **1845** LINDLEY *Sch. Bot.* vi. (1858) 74 Leaves heart-shaped, with 5 angles, toothletted.

tooth-money: see TOOTH-FEE.

toothpick ('tu:θpɪk). Forms: see TOOTH *sb.*; also 5–6 **-pike**, 6 **-picke**. [See PICK *sb.*[1] 5.]

1. An instrument for picking the teeth: usually a pointed quill or small piece of wood; sometimes of gold, silver, or other material.

1488 *Acc. Ld. High Treas. Scot.* I. 81 Twa tuthpikis of gold with a chenȝe. **1538** ELYOT, *Nitella*, a toothe pike [1545 tothe pykar]. Sometyme it signifyeth elegancy in speche. **1562** TURNER *Herbal* II. 34 b, Stickes and strawes and other tooth pickes. **1579** *N.C. Wills* (Surtees) II. 93 To Mr Roberte Toutte a tothe pyke of silver. **1635** SWAN *Spec. M.* ix. §1 (1643) 450 Of these [porcupine] quills men make wholesome tooth-picks. **1775** BLACK in *Phil. Trans.* LXV. 125 Stirring it gently with a quill tooth-pick. **1873** DORAN *Lady of last Cent.* xi. 298 A welcome which extended..from the manufacturer of toothpicks to the writer of an epic poem.

2. A name for the umbelliferous plant *Ammi Visnaga*, the hardened rays of the umbel of which are used as toothpicks: also called ***Spanish toothpick***, ***toothpick bishop-weed*** (see 6b).

1598 FLORIO, *Bisacuto*, the hearbe toothpick, or cheruill. **1760** J. LEE *Introd. Bot.* App. 330 Tooth-pick, *Daucus*. **1884** MILLER *Plant-n.*, *Ammi Visnaga*, Spanish Tooth-pick, Tooth-pick Bishop's-weed.

3. *pl.* Splinters, small elongated fragments, 'matchwood': in hyperbolic phr. ***smashed*** (etc.) ***into toothpicks***.

1839 MARRYAT *Phant. Ship* ix, The..ship will be beaten into toothpicks. **1899** *Daily News* 9 Mar. 5/3 The Pavonia tried to lower a boat, but it was smashed into toothpicks on the ship's side.

4. A bowie-knife: also ***Arkansas toothpick***. *U.S. slang.*

1867 LOWELL *Biglow P.* Ser. II. i. 151, I didn't call but jest on one, an' he drawed toothpick on me, An' reckoned he warn't goin' to stan' no sech doggauned econ'my. **1881** A. B. GREENLEAF *Ten Y. in Texas* 27 With..an Arkansas 'toothpick' suspended to a raw-hide belt buckled around their waists.

5. A very narrow pointed boat. *slang.*

1897 KIPLING *Captains Courageous* iv. 104 'You should see one o' them toothpicks histin' up her anchor on her spike outer fifteen-fathom water'. 'What's a toothpick, Dan?' 'Them new haddockers an' herrin' boats'. **1909** J. DALZIEL *High Life in East* 201 The Magistrate got smartly into his 'toothpick', the attendant boat-boys..gave him carefully the necessary offing, he swung forward on his sculls.

6. *attrib.* and *Comb.* a. *attrib.* or as *adj.* †(*a*) in reference to the use of the toothpick as an idle occupation; (*b*) denoting objects of narrow and pointed shape.

1761 CHURCHILL *Night* 109 Or if in tittle-tattle, tooth-pick way, Our rambling thoughts with easy freedom stray. **1767** S. PATERSON *Another Trav.* II. 168 To enjoy uninterrupted, listless, toothpick ease. **1880** 'MARK TWAIN' *Tramp Abroad* I. 235 A heaped-up confusion of red roofs, quaint gables,.. toothpick steeples. **1895** S. B. KENNEDY in *Outing* (U.S.) XXVII. 6/1 [She] gave me the go-by for a patent medicine drummer with tooth-pick shoes.

b. *Comb.*, as ***toothpick-box***, ***-case***; ***toothpick-shaped*** adj.; **toothpick bishop-weed** (see 2); †**toothpick chervil** = prec., or allied species.

1866 *Treas. Bot.* 51 *Tooth-pick Bishop-weed, *A*[*mmi*] *Visnaga*, is so called on account of the use made in Spain of the rays or stalks of the main umbel. These, after flowering, shrink, and become so hard that they form convenient tooth-picks. **1669** R. MONTAGU in *Buccleuch MSS.* (Hist. MSS. Comm.) I. 448, 2 knives, a *toothpick-box, and a tiremoelle. **1684** *Lond. Gaz.* No. 1972/4 A *tooth pick Case of Black wood, tipt on both ends, and at the opening with Silver. **1578** LYTE *Dodoens* V. i. 615 This herbe is called..in Spayne, Visnaga:..it may be called *Toothpick Cheruill. **1905** W. E. GEIL *Yankee in Pigmy Land* v. 64 We tramped past many trees armed with long, white *toothpick-shaped thorns.

'tooth-,picker. †1. = prec. 1. *Obs.*

1545 *Rates Custome House* b j b, Ere pikers or tothe pikers of bone the groce xii d. **1591** FLORIO *2nd Fruites* 61, I praie thee giue me a little stick, or a tooth picker. **1655** CULPEPPER *Riverius* VI. ii. 134 To preserve the Teeth, first clense them with a Tooth-picker of Mastich Wood. **1707** MORTIMER *Husb.* (1721) II. 185 Lentisc is a beautiful evergreen..; it makes the best Tooth-pickers in the World.

2. One who picks the teeth; in first quot. used of a bird which was fabled to pick the teeth of the crocodile; in second quot. with allusion to this.

1612 WEBSTER *White Devil* IV. iii, Away flies the pretty tooth-picker from her cruell patient. *a* **1653** G. DANIEL *Idyll.* iii. 37 The Civetts of an Officer, Whose Tooth-picker, like ye Officious Bird Betrayes him Sleeping.

'tooth-,picking, *a.* Picking the teeth; *fig.* careless, *nonchalant*: cf. TOOTHPICK 6a(*a*).

1814 L. HUNT *Feast of Poets*, etc. (1815) 63 Here we have the plainest, tooth-picking acknowledgements, that Charles was a pensioner of France.

tooth-piece: see TOOTH-FEE.

ˈtooth-shell. The long tubular shell, in shape like a tooth or tusk, of any gastropod mollusc of *Dentalium* or other allied genus; also the mollusc itself. **b.** *false tooth-shell*, the similar shell (or animal) of the molluscous genus *Cæca*, or the family *Cæcidæ*. **c.** 'In Australia, the shell of *Marinula pellucida*, a small marine mollusc used for necklaces' (Morris *Austral Eng.*).

*c*1711 PETIVER *Gazophyl.* vii. 65 Small English Tooth-shell... It's smooth, white, and somewhat crooked with purplish Tips. **1777** PENNANT *Zool.* IV. 127 *Dentalium*, tooth-shell. **1850** MISS PRATT *Comm. Things Sea-side* v. 314 The old shell of the mollusk, commonly called Tooth-shell (*Dentalium entalis*),.. so common on our coasts, shaped like a small horn. **1879** E. P. WRIGHT *Anim. Life* 548 The Tooth-shells are animal feeders, devouring foraminifera and minute bivalves.

toothsome (ˈtuːθsəm), *a.* [See -SOME[1].]

1. Pleasant to the taste, savoury, palatable: cf. TOOTH *sb.* 2 a.

*c*1565 SPARKE *Sir J. Hawkins' 2nd Voy.* (Hakl. Soc.) 46 We..found water, which although it were neither so toothsome as running water..yet did we not refuse it. **1584** COGAN *Haven Health* cc. (1636) 189 Vineger, that is not onely toothsome, but wholesome also. **1604** E. G[RIMSTONE] *D'Acosta's Hist. Indies* IV. xviii. 260 The Patattoes, which they eate as a delicate and toothsome meate. **1733** CHEYNE *Eng. Malady* III. iv. (1734) 340, I began to find a Craving.. for more solid and Toothsome Food. **1899** E. CALLOW *Old Lond. Tav.* II. 286 Hard to please if they cannot select something toothsome from the menu.

b. *fig.* or in *fig.* context: Pleasant, 'palatable'.

1551 T. WILSON *Logike* (1580) 83 Speaking thinges nothing tothsome. *a*1568 COVERDALE *Carrying Christ's Cross* iv. 59 Seeing our phisician..(Iesus Chryst I meane) telleth vs that it is veri wholsome, how so euer it be toothsome. **1648** in Rushw. *Hist. Coll.* IV. (1701) II. 1047 Your only News is not very Toothsom but it may prove wholesom. **1805** J. RAMSAY *Scot. & Scotsm. in 18th C.* (1888) I. 287 Elegant and toothsome sermons were most in request.

2. Having a 'dainty tooth'; fond of savoury food.

1837 R. NICOLL *Poems* (1842) 95 She kent na, douse woman! how toothsome was he. **1848** LYTTON *Harold* VII. i, The Earl is a toothsome man.

†**3.** Resembling a tooth; 'biting', sharp. *Obs.*

1601 T. MORLEY *Madrigales*, etc. Ded., Whose malice (being as toothsome as the Adders sting).

Hence **ˈtoothsomely** *adv.*; **ˈtoothsomeness**.

1612 T. TAYLOR *Comm. Titus* ii. I. (1619) 336 Others stand so much vpon toothsomnes of their meate. **1871** 'MARK TWAIN' *Let.* 25 Dec. in C. Clemens *My Father Mark Twain* (1931) 53 Gossip of any kind, and about anybody is one of the most toothsomely Christian dishes I know of. **1880** MRS. ROLLINS *New Eng. Bygones* 12 Here..apples mellowed toothsomely under the matted grass. **1887** BESANT *The World went* xxxvii, I live sufficiently, and..with toothsomeness.

toothwort (ˈtuːθwɜːt). [f. TOOTH *sb.* + WORT.] Name given to several different plants.

1. *Lathræa squamaria* (N.O. *Orobanchaceæ*), a leafless fleshy herb, parasitic on the roots of hazel and other trees, bearing a double row of flesh-coloured drooping flowers, and having tooth-like scales upon the root-stock.

1597 GERARDE *Herbal* III. clxiii. 1386 Great Toothwoorth, or Clownes Lungwoort..in forme like vnto Orobanche, or the Broome Rape,..hauing a tender, thicke, tuberous..bodie, consisting as it were of scales like teeth (whereof it tooke his name). **1778** G. WHITE *Selborne* 3 July, *Lathræa squammaria*, tooth-wort. **1905** E. STEP *Wild Flowers* I. 23 John Ray died exactly two hundred years ago, but the Toothwort still flourishes in Westhumble Lane [Mickleham].

†**2.** A name for Shepherd's purse, *Capsella Bursapastoris. Obs. rare.*

1597 in GERARDE *Herbal* App.

3. A plant of the genus *Dentaria* (N.O. *Cruciferæ*), characterized by tooth-like projections upon the creeping root-stock; *esp.* the British species *D. bulbifera*, occurring locally in woods; also called *coralwort*.

1668 WILKINS *Real Char.* II. iv. §5. 100 Dames Violet, Double Rocket Toothwort. **1678** PHILLIPS (ed. 4), *Toothwort*, a sort of Herb, called in Latin, *Dentaria*. **1786** ABERCROMBIE *Arr.* in *Gard. Assist.* 73 *Dentaria*, toothwort. **1866** *Treas. Bot.* 393/2 Closely allied to Cardamine, from which it differs in having broad seed-stalks, and in its creeping roots being singularly toothed; hence the systematic name [*Dentaria*], and the English one of Toothwort.

4. A name for *Plumbago europæa* and the Central American and West Indian *P. scandens*, whose pungent leaves and roots are used as a remedy for toothache.

1760 J. LEE *Introd. Bot.* App. 330 Tooth-wort, *Plumbago*. **1884** MILLER *Plant-n.*, *Plumbago scandens*, Devil's-herb, or Tooth-wort, of the W. Indies.

toothy (ˈtuːθɪ), *a.* [f. TOOTH *sb.* + -Y.]

1. Having numerous, large, or prominent teeth (in quot. 1881 connoting 'devouring, ravenous').

1530 PALSGR. 327/2 Toothye as one that hath great tethe or plenty of tethe, *denteux*. **1799** CORSE in *Phil. Trans.* LXXXIX. 208 *note*, *Dauntelah* signifies toothy; having large or fine teeth. **1881** F. G. LEE *Reg. Baront.* II. iv, Toothy wolves in lambswool.

2. Furnished with or full of teeth or tooth-like projections; toothed.

1611 COTGR., *Dentelé*,..toothed, toothie; full of iags resembling little teeth. **1705** J. PETIVER in *Phil. Trans.* XXV. 1960 Its [a shell's] Toothy part is finely variegated with red and black. *a*1770 SMART *Hop-Gard.* II. Poems (1810) 41/1 Next expand The smoothest surface with the toothy rake.

3. *fig.* 'Biting', ill-natured, peevish. (Cf. TEETHY *a.*[1]) *north. dial.* and *Sc.*

1691 RAY *N.C. Words, Toothy*, peevish, crabbed. **1787** BURNS *Willie's Awa* vi, Toothy critics by the score, In bloody raw! **1824** MISS FERRIER *Inher.* xxiv. 'I suspect that's your case..', retorted Miss P., in a very toothy manner.

4. Toothsome, palatable. *rare.*

1864 *Athenæum* 8 Oct. 456/2 A most toothy meal I had of it! **1889** *Alien. & Neurol.* July 459 Meat or game, which is at first tough, becomes more tender and toothy.

ˈtoothy-peg. Also toospeg. [f. **toothy*, dim. of TOOTH *sb.* + PEG *sb.*[1]] Nursery word for 'tooth'. Also used *joc.* in other contexts.

1828 HOOD *Kilmansegg, Childh.* iv, Cutting her first little toothy-peg. **1921** 'K. MANSFIELD' *Let.* 3 Feb. (1928) II. 91 When the time comes just put your toospeg brush, pyjamas and a collar..into a handkerchief. **1931** A. CHRISTIE *Sittaford Mystery* xxi. 171 [He] took his elephant's trotters and his hippopotamus's toothy pegs and all the sporting rifles and what nots. **1977** J. WILSON *Making Hate* vi. 71 It's those toothypegs, isn't it, my lovey, those naughty old toothypegs.

tooting (ˈtuːtɪŋ), *vbl. sb.*[1] Now *dial.* In 4-6 totyng; 6 towting. [f. TOOT *v.*[1] + -ING[1].] The action of TOOT *v.*[1]; spying, peeping, looking.

1553 *Respublica* I. iii. 5 Theare was suche tooting, suche looking and suche priinge. **1598** FLORIO, *Osolamento*, a spying, a peeping, a tooting.

b. *attrib.* as **tooting-glass**, looking-glass; **tooting-hill** = TOOT-HILL; so ***tooting-hole***, peep-hole; ***tooting-place, -tower***, etc.

1382 WYCLIF *Jer.* xxxi. 21 Ordeyne to thee a toting place. **1388** —— *Isa.* xxi. 8 Y stonde contynueli bi dai on the totyng place of the Lord. *c*1460 *Med. Gramm., Speculare*, a totynge hylle and a bekyne. *a*1548 HALL *Chron., Hen. VI* 105 Thei with in the citee [Orleans] perceiued well this totyng hole, and laied a pece of ordynaunce directly against the wyndowe. **1552** HULOET, Towtynge hoole to loke out at in a wall or wyndowe. **1556** PHAER *Æneid* IV. L ij, As dawning waxed white from tooting towres on hie. *c*1560 GEST *Serm.* in Dugdale *Life* (1840) 182 Senec..wryteth that tootyng glasses be founde to know our selfes and to rule our lyfes by. .. O that we Christen men and women thus used our tootinge glasses. **1894** O. HESLOP *Northumbld. Gloss.*, *Tooting-hole*, a spyhole or loophole.

ˈtooting, *vbl. sb.*[2] Also 7-9 *Sc.* touting. [f. TOOT *v.*[2] + -ING[1].] The action of TOOT *v.*[2]; the sound made by blowing a horn or other wind-instrument.

1568 *Hist. Jacob & Esau* I. ii. A iij b, Then maketh he with his Horne such tootyng and blowing. **1603** HOLLAND *Plutarch's Mor.* 665 Another mercenary minstrell..kept a foolish and ridiculous tooting. **1630** J. LEVETT *Order. Bees* (1634) 30 You shall heare a touting in manner like the sounding of a Bewgle horne amongst the Bees. **1712** NEVILL in *Phil. Trans.* XXVIII. 270 Will not admit of any sound by Blast as a Horn doth, but by the articulate Voice of tooting it will. **1880** W. NEWTON *Serm. for Boys & Girls* (1881) 410 Tootings innumerable from the steam whistle.

b. *attrib.* and *Comb.*, as ***tooting-horn, -trumpet***.

1737 RAMSAY *Scots Prov.* xx. 75 It is ill making a silk purse of a sow's lug, or a touting-horn of a tod's tail. **1805** J. NICOL *Poems* I. 2 *note* (Jam.), A touting horn (the horn of an ox perforated at the small end) by blowing on which they made a loud..sound. **1889** W. G. DICKSON *Glean. fr. Japan* xiii. 251 The boy behind is provided with a small tooting-trumpet to warn other travellers on the road.

tooting, touting, *vbl. sb.*[3]: see TOOT, TOUT *v.*[3]

tooting *ppl. a.*[1]: see TOOT *v.*[1]

tooting (tuːtɪŋ), *ppl. a.*[2] [f. TOOT *v.*[2] + -ING[2].]

1. That toots, as a horn, siren, etc. See also *rootin' tootin'* s.v. ROOTING *ppl. a.*[2] 2.

1652 BENLOWES *Theoph.* XI. xxx, Still to have toting Waits unseal thine eyes. **1668** SHADWELL *Sullen Lovers* I. i, Those rogues that..upon their toting instruments make a more hellish noise than they do at a play-house. **1909** *Daily Chron.* 16 Sept. 1/1 No tooting whistles signalled our departure.

2. *U.S. slang.* Used, usu. with preceding adv. or adj. (as *damn* or var.), as a strong affirmative or intensive.

1932 *Amer. Speech* VII. 338 You're damn tootin', emphatic affirmative. **1933** E. CALDWELL *God's Little Acre* i. 12 'After the albino, Pa?' Buck asked. 'You're durn tooting, son,' he said. **1952** B. MALAMUD *Natural* 36 You're plumb tootin' crazy. **1970** E. BERCKMAN *She asked for It* xi. 134 You're goddam' tootin' I'm on that again. Y'say I've been prying, you admit there's something to pry into. **1981** G. MCDONALD *Fletch & Widow Bradley* xviii. 72, I got pregnant, when you said I wouldn't... You tol' me a tootin' lie.

tooting, var. TOUTING *vbl. sb.*[1]

tootle (ˈtuːt(ə)l), *sb.* [f. TOOTLE *v.*]

1. An act or the action of tootling or sounding a horn or similar wind-instrument.

1852 R. S. SURTEES *Sponge's Sp. Tour* xli, Bragg's queer tootle of his horn..now sounded at the low end of the cover. **1889** *Scott. Leader* 6 Dec. 5 The sudden and shrill tootle of a trumpet. **1894** *Daily News* 12 Mar. 2/1 The guard's inspiriting tootle wakes the echoes.

2. Speech or writing of more sound than sense; verbiage, twaddle.

1883 *Cornh. Mag.* May 542 Sometimes..the tootle becomes a middle in a weekly paper, sometimes it assumes the guise of an amusing review. **1888** *Scott. Leader* 8 Mar. 7 The good old order of English prose which used to be called at the English Universities 'tootle', and for which there are other names, older and more recent, but hardly any more expressive.

So **tootle-te-ˈtootle, tootle-tootle**, a piece of continuous tootling.

1855 BROWNING *Up at a Villa* ix, *Bang, whang, whang* goes the drum, *tootle-te-tootle* the fife. **1884** *Pall Mall G.* 24 July 4/2 The musical powers of most of the bands, whom no amount of entreaty could divert even for a moment from their prearranged and wholly meaningless tootle-ti-tootle. **1910** *Sat. Rev.* 10 Sept. 322/1 Footle-footle-footle goes the clarinet with a fragment of a theme; tootle-tootle-tootle echoes the flute.

tootle (ˈtuːt(ə)l), *v.* [freq. f. TOOT *v.*[2] + -LE 4.]

1. *intr.* **a.** To toot continuously; to produce a succession of modulated notes on a wind-instrument.

1842 S. LOVER *Handy Andy* xviii, The fifer..tootled with some difficulty. **1878** STEVENSON *Inland Voy.* 4 Tootling on the sentimental flute. **1879** SALA *Paris herself again* II. iv. 53 The sable minstrel..begins to tootle most sweetly.

b. Of birds: To make a similar noise.

1820 CLARE *Rural Life* (ed. 3) 207 When tootling robins carol-welcomes sing. **1827** —— *Sheph. Cal.* 25 To hear the robin's note once more, Who tootles while he pecks his meal. **1899** O. SEAMAN *In Cap & Bells* (1900) 21 The lark is tootling in the sky.

c. *fig.* To write twaddle or mere verbiage.

1883 [see *tootling* below]. **1894** *Daily News* 28 Feb. 5/1 Mr. Skeat's 'Life of Chaucer' is entirely businesslike. He does not 'tootle' over what Chaucer may have done, and seen, and said.

2. *trans.* To play music on (a wind instrument). Also *transf.* and with music as direct obj. *colloq.*

1890 J. SERVICE *Thir Notandums* xiv. 99 Heralds clad in green tootled glorious musick frae their siller horns. **1895** G. MORTIMER *Like Stars that Fall* iii. 28 'There's no need for the cornet in this piece,' said Jenny. 'No, only Abrahams is so fond of tootling his bloomin' instrument,' said Larpenti. **1939** [see SMOKER 4 b]. **1978** J. GALWAY *Autobiogr.* xiv. 164, I had tootled my flute to some purpose with Herbert von Karajan.

3. *intr.* To walk, to wander casually or aimlessly; usu. const. *along, around*, etc. Also *transf.* with reference to motor transport; ***to tootle off***, to go, to depart. *colloq.*

1902 *Cornh. Mag.* July 102, I tootled down to Cooney's a half-hour before time. **1914** M. & J. FINDLATER *Crossriggs* xx. 149 Take that beast and stop all his work, feed him fat and let him sleep on the rug and tootle around the garden. **1918** *Punch* 3 Apr. 222 Well, I must tootle off now. **1951** J. B. PRIESTLEY *Festival at Farbridge* II. ii. 272 You're going to be tootling round to a lot of big houses. **1956** N. COWARD *South Sea Bubble* II. i. 52 It's getting late... It is time for me to tootle off home. *a*1974 R. CROSSMAN *Diaries* (1975) I. 532 We had a real honeymoon holiday..tootling round in a Volkswagen which Helga Greene's villainous friend Johnnie in Heraklion had rented to us. **1978** E. O'BRIEN *Mrs. Reinhardt* 55 He would work for an hour or so and then tootle off. **1983** *Listener* 20 Oct. 31/3 Veteran cars tootle down country lanes.

Hence **ˈtootling** *vbl. sb.* and *ppl. a.*; also **ˈtootler**, a writer of 'tootle', verbiage, or twaddle; **tootle-too** *v.*, **tootle-tootle** *v.* = TOOTLE *v.* 1.

1821 CLARE *Vill. Minstr.* I. 30 He heard the tootling robin sound her knell. *Ibid.* 36 The tuteling fife, and hoarse rap-tapping drum. **1857** HUGHES *Tom Brown* I. v, Here's Rugby, ..said the old guard, pulling his horn out of its case, and tootle-tooing away. **1879** JEFFERIES *Wild Life in S.C.* 105 The tootling of pan-pipes in front of the shows. **1883** *Cornh. Mag.* May 542 The sort of scribblers..whom I am wont to call in my own private dialect the tootlers, that is to say the good folk who write a tootle about nothing in particular. *Ibid.* 543 The consumer who takes a delight in the perusal of tootling. **1892** *Pall Mall G.* 16 Dec. 3/1 The drumming and the tootle-tooting, even the skirling of the Hallelujah maidens.

tootman: see under TOOT-NET.

tootnague: see TUTENAG.

toot-net (ˈtuːtnɛt). *Sc. local.* [f. TOOT *v.*[1] + NET.] 'A large fishing net anchored' (Jam.), which is watched in order to be drawn in when the fish enter it. More fully ***toot and haul net***.

1805 *Case Ho. Lords, Gray of Carse* (Jam.), The fishing-tackle..sometimes consisted of a common moveable net or siene; sometimes of a toot-net, much larger and stronger than the former, extending to an indefinite length from the beach into the water, and secured at its extremity by an anchor. **1840** LEIGHTON *Hist. Fife* II. 82 The mode of fishing is now confined..to what is called the toot-net. **1898** *Glasgow Herald* 19 May 4 To fish in..the river and estuary of the Tay for salmon kind with toot and haul nets. **1900** *Law Rep., App. Cas.* 410 The First Division..declared fishing with the nets of the description of toot and haul..an illegal method.

So **ˈtootman, ˈtootsman**, one who watches a toot-net.

1805 *Case Ho. Lords, Gray of Carse* (E.D.D.), A man stands in a coble, or small fishing-boat; and when he sees the fish enter the net, calls the fishers to haul it. He is designed the Tootsman. **1840** LEIGHTON *Hist. Fife* II. 82 The tootman is seated to watch the net.

too-too (tuːˈtuː), *v.* [Echoic: usually depreciatory.] *intr.* To make an instrumental or vocal sound resembling these syllables. Hence **too-ˈtooing** *vbl. sb.*; so also **too-too** *adv.* and *sb.*, **too-ˈtooer**.

1812 H. & J. SMITH *Rej. Addr., The Theatre* 25 Tang goes the harpsichord, too-too the flute. **1828** MOIR *Mansie Wauch* xi. (1849) 74 The old flute was for Benjie, poor thing, too-tooing on. **1836–9** DICKENS *Sk. Boz, Public Dinners*, The singers..begin too-tooing most dismally. **1840** THACKERAY *Pict. Rhapsody* Concl., Wks. 1900 XIII. 345 Punchman is tootooing on the pipes, and banging away on the drum. **1843** —— *Irish Sk. Bk.* xxviii, An unequal and disagreeable tootooing on a horn. **1862** MISS YONGE *C'tess Kate* ix, Kate..came up too-tooing through her hand with all her might. *a* **1884** CALVERLEY *Verses & Transl., To Mrs. Goodchild* x, Checked by that absurd Too-too [of a person practising on a horn].

too-too: see TOO *adv.* 4.

toots (tʊtz). *slang* (orig. and chiefly *U.S.*). Also **Toots**. [Prob. abbrev. of TOOTSY 2.] A woman, a girl; freq. used as a familiar form of address, esp. to a female.

1936 *Amer. Speech* XI. 375/2 *Toots* used to be used in families here and there as a nickname, or a term of endearment, the vowel sounded as in 'boots'... Is this term the ancestor of the present mode of address in 'O.K., toots!', 'Hello, toots!' etc., the vowel shortened into that of 'full'? **1936** *Mademoiselle* Jan. 63 Out here everyone who isn't 'Toots' or 'Cookie' is 'Darling'. **1941** H. A. SMITH *Low Man* iii. 30, I..raised my hand in a clumsy wave and cried out: 'Hiya, toots!'... I had called J. P. Morgan 'toots' to his face. **1946** E. LINKLATER *Private Angelo* xii. 143 'Hiya, toots,' repeated the Count. 'I like that. It is the felicitous expression of a young people who are making their own language.' **1951** J. B. PRIESTLEY *Festival at Farbridge* III. 565 'Wasting it on you, Toots,' said Smith reproachfully. **1975** *New Yorker* 29 Dec. 33/2 'Hi, toots,' Ducky said in Donald's voice a few minutes later to a tiny girl. **1981** G. HAMMOND *Revenge Game* xv. 161 Maybe it's in his mind to come back for you and dig a quiet grave... How does that grab you, Toots?

tootsicum, a whimsical expansion of TOOTSY.

1860 LEECH *Pict. Life & Char.* Ser. III. 18 The brutality of connecting..such words [as 'Beetle-crusher'] with the feminine Tootsicums. **1877** BESANT & RICE *With Harp & Crown* xxxiv, Beer is the real magnet for the male feet. Champagne..draws the feminine tootsicums.

Tootsie Roll (ˈtʊtsɪ rəʊl). *U.S.* A proprietary name for a type of sweet or candy bar.

1925 *Official Gaz.* (U.S. Patent Office) 7 Apr. 19/1 The Sweets Company of America, Incorporated, New York, N.Y. Filed Oct. 24, 1924. Tootsie Rolls... Claims use since September, 1908. **1955** W. GADDIS *Recognitions* I. v. 177 And so brown. Like a tootsie roll. **1969** L. HELLMAN *Unfinished Woman* ii. 22, I bought a few Tootsie Rolls and a half loaf of bread. **1980** J. KRANTZ *Princess Daisy* xxiv. 421 Her Tootsie Roll brown eyes sparkling.

tootsman: see under TOOT-NET.

toot sweet (tuːt swiːt), *adv.* Also **toot and sweat, toots sweet**; *compar.* **the tooter the sweeter.** [Repr. colloq. anglicization of F. *tout de suite*.] Straightaway; promptly, quickly; freq. used as *imp.*

1917 A. G. EMPEY *Over Top* 311 '*Toots Sweet.*' Tommy's French for 'hurry up', 'look smart'. **1917** *Punch* 5 Dec. 389 (*caption*) Tommy (to inquisitive French children): 'Nah, then, alley toot sweet, an' the tooter the sweeter.' **1929** [see FUCK *v.* 3]. **1942** 'N. SHUTE' *Pied Piper* v. 109 Get them kids dressed toot and sweet—I ain't going to wait all night. **1959** R. POSTGATE *Every Man is God* xxiii. 216 'The tooter the sweeter' was an adjuration to do something, usually bringing a drink, more *tout de suite*, more promptly. **1967** *Guardian* 16 May 2/8 Your two brace of crocodiles[' eggs] have arrived—Yes. I'll get 'em incubated toot sweet. **1978** D. WILLIAMS *Treasure up in Smoke* xiii. 118 The Governor wanted him toot sweet this morning but he hasn't shown up.

tootsy, tootsy-wootsy. **1.** A playful or endearing name for a child's or a woman's small foot. Cf. FOOTSY. *colloq.*

1854 THACKERAY *Rose & Ring* xi, As for the shoe, what was she to do with one poor little tootsey sandal? **1865** E. C. CLAYTON *Cruel Fortune* III. 90 His poor little tootsies peeping out from the tips of his boots. **1897** GUNTER *Susan Turnbull* v, Yer [a young lady of 19]..little tootsy-wootsies will be as safe as if they were tucked in yer little cot bed upstairs. **1906** CHARLOTTE MANSFIELD *Girl & Gods* xii, But if you are walking along a muddy road with old shoes on, all the idealistic thought in the world won't keep the damp away from your poor tootsies.

2. Also **tootsie, tootsey-wootsey, tootsie-wootsie**, etc. A woman, a girl; a sweetheart; occas. applied to a male lover. Freq. as a familiar form of address. *slang* (chiefly *U.S.*).

1895 W. STEVENS *Let.* 23 July (1967) 6, I can be your own dearest tootsey wootsey. **1901** 'H. MCHUGH' *John Henry* 88 One of the kind that's anxious to lead you away from your own tootsie-wootsie, in the hope that you may have a spare bunch of sweet talk you can hand her on the quiet. **1905** E. M. FORSTER *Purple Envelope* in *Life to Come* (1972) 48 'Well, she's not my idea of a tootsy!' said Howard, and clenched his criticism by a coarse and vapid jest. **1920** D. H. LAWRENCE *Lost Girl* vi. 114 Underneath the oak-tree nice and shady Calling me your tootsey-wootsey lady? **1930** *Sat. Even. Post* 5 Apr. 72/4 'Hello, tootsie,' Rusty Charley says. **1938** 'E. QUEEN' *Four of Hearts* ii. 23 The future Mrs. Butcher wouldn't throw her tootsie, would she? **1952** B. WOLFE *Limbo* xvi. 239 'What's the matter, tootsie?' she whispered. **1952** *Sat. Even. Post* 1 Mar. 21/2 What about one of those tootsy-wootsies? **1968** G. DE FRAGA *Murder at Cookout* xv. 71 Don't bother to kiss me. Save that for the little tootsies who think you're as marvellous as you do yourself. **1979** 'P. O'CONNOR' *Into Strong City* xx. 74 Two chicks. One for me. .. One of the hot-time tootsies.

tooward, tooze, obs. ff. TOWARD, TOZE.

too-whit, too-whoo, cry of the owl: see TU-.

toozle, toozy, dial. ff. TOUSLE, TOUSY.

top (tɒp), *sb.*[1] Forms: 1 top, 3–6, (?) 7 toppe, *pl.* **toppes**, 4–6 **tope**, 4–7 **topp**, 6– *Sc.* and *north.* **tap**, 3– **top**. [OE. *top* (*topp-*), Com. WGer. and Norse; = OFris. *topp* (WFris. *top*, NFris. *top*, *tup*), OLG. **topp* (MDu., Du. *top(p)*, MLG., LG. *top*), OHG. (MHG., Ger.) *zopf* top, summit, a crest or tuft of hair; ON. *toppr* top, tuft, Sw. *topp* top, pinnacle, Da. *top* top, point, MDa. also tuft of feathers, plume, mod.Norw. also *tupp*:—OTeut. **tuppoᶻ*; not known in Gothic. Outside Teutonic known only in Romanic derivatives: cf. TOUPET.]

I. A tuft, crest, or bush of hair, etc.

1. a. The hair on the summit or crown of the head; the hair of the head. *Obs.* exc. *Sc.*

foreward top = FORETOP. ***to take*** (†***hent***, †***nim***) ***by the top***, to seize by the hair, lay hold violently (also *fig.*).

c **1205** LAY. 684 Bi þone toppe [*c* 1275 bi þe coppe] he hine nome Al swa he hine walde of-slean. **1297** R. GLOUC. (Rolls) 5619 He..hente þis lof bi þe top, & fram þe bord him drou. *c* **1386** CHAUCER *Prol.* 590 His tope [*v.rr.* top, toppe] was doked lyk a preest biforn. *c* **1386** —— *Reeve's Prol.* 15 This white tope writeth myne olde yeris. *c* **1440** *Promp. Parv.* 496/2 Top, or fortop (*K.*, *P.* top of the hed), *aqualium*. **1535** COVERDALE *Bel. & Dr.* 36 Then the angel..toke him by the toppe, and bare him by the hayre of the heade. **1601** SHAKS. *All's Well* v. iii. 39 Let's take the instant by the forward top: For we are old. *a* **1643** CARTWRIGHT *Ordinary* II. ii. **1884** D. GRANT *Lays & Leg.* 21 Eppie got him by the tap..Quo' Davit then,..'Lat go my puckle hair'.

b. The crest or 'topping' of a bird; the forelock of a horse, etc. Now *Sc.* and *north. dial.*

a **1225** *St. Marher.* 12 And toc him [the dragon] bi þe ateliche top. **13..** *K. Alis.* 5186 (Bodl. MS.) Ypotame a wonder beest..; Toppe, & rugge, & croupe, & cors, Is semblablel to an hors. *c* **1450** HOLLAND *Howlat* 837 The Golk ..Tit the Tuchet be the tope, ourtirvit his hed. **1578** in Feuillerat *Revels Q. Eliz.* (1908) 296, viᵈ for iii hearons toppes which were burnte with Torches. **1585** JAS. I *Ess. Poesie* (Arb.) 43 Euen so, had Nature,..Giuen her [the phœnix] ane tap, for to augment her grace. **1650** EARL MONM. tr. *Senault's Man bec. Guilty* 353 We deck ourselves with birds feathers, the tops of herons. **1756** MRS. CALDERWOOD *Jrnl.* iii. (1884) 66 The horses have..a large top betwixt their ears. **1808–25** JAMIESON, *Tap*..3. The tuft on the head of some fowls. Hence the phrase, *tappit hen*.

2. a. A tuft or handful of hair, wool, fibre, etc.; *esp.* the portion of flax or tow put on the distaff (in full, *top of flax*, *lint* (†*line*), *tow*). Also *fig.* Now only *Sc.* and *north. dial.* [Cf. med.L. *toppus lini* (top of flax).]

to tak one's tap in one's lap: see quot. 1825.

[But some refer this sense to TOP *sb.*[2], as having reference to the shape; cf. quot. 1891 in 36.]

a **1250** *Owl & Night.* 428 Ne rouhte þe þeyh flockes were Imeynd bi toppes & bi here. *c* **1325** *Gloss. W. de Bibbesw.* in Wright *Voc.* 144 E serencez du lyn le toup [*gloss*] hekele, a top of flax. **14..** *Nom.* in Wr.-Wülcker 696/3 *Hoc lapsum*, a top of lin. **1558** in Feuillerat *Revels Q. Eliz.* (1908) 25 Into vi nighte cappes & toppes of turkes heddes peces. **1681** COLVIL *Whigs Supplic.* 258 A Top of Lint for his Panash. **1794** BURNS *Weary Pund o' Tow* iv, Gae spin your tap o' tow! **1818** SCOTT *Hrt. Midl.* xxxvii[i], 'And does your honour think', said Jeanie, 'that will do as weel as if I were to take my tap in my lap, and slip my ways hame again?' **1825** JAMIESON s.v. *Tap, To tak one's tap in one's lap, and set aff*, to turse up one's baggage, and be gone..from the practice of women accustomed to spin from a rock, who often carried their work with them to the house of some neighbour. **1894** *Northumbld. Gloss.*, *Top*, in spinning, the quantity of flax put on the 'rock' at a time.

b. *spec.* A bundle of combed wool prepared for spinning. Chiefly *pl.* (also *collect. sing.*).

1637 *Bury Wills* (Camden) 169, I owe John Brightall for combeing of ten skore poundes and ten of tops. **1759** *Overseers' Acc., Holy Cross, Canterb.*, To 1 Top of wool for worsted deliver'd to Mrs. Hawley..0. 2. 0. **1844** G. DODD *Textile Manuf.* iv. 129 The wool generally comes to the factories in narrow bundles or 'tops', about eighteen inches long, and weighing about a pound and a half or two pounds each. **1882** *Worc. Exhib. Catal.* III. 31 Combing process, separating long wool from short, the long wool being then called combed tops. **1888** ELWORTHY *W. Somerset Word-bk.*, *Top*, a bundle of combed wool as made up by the comber for spinning, usually weighing about 28lbs... At present the word is applied to the bundles of combed wool from the machine—hand combing having been quite superseded.

II. The highest or uppermost part.

3. a. The highest point or part of anything; perh. originally a pointed or peaked summit, an apex or peak; but now applied to the uppermost part, whatever its nature or shape; the highest place or limit *of* something. Also *pl.*, mountain tops, high moorland, etc.

to swim at the top (fig.), to maintain a high social position.

c **1000** *Ælfric's Voc.* in Wr.-Wülcker 143/26 *Apex, summitas galeæ*, helmes top. *c* **1205** LAY. 1339 He hihte hondlien kablen Teon seiles to toppa [*c* **1275** toppe]. *a* **1250** *Owl & Night.* 1422 Vp to þe toppe from þe more. *c* **1275** LAY. 7781 In þan grunde of þe tur mihte sitte Sixti hundred cnihtes And þe toppe [*c* **1205** þa turres cop] mihte wreie On cniht mid his cope. **13..** *K. Alis.* 1417 (Bodl. MS.) Hii drawen sayl to top of mast. *a* **1400–50** *Alexander* 2110 þan vp he clame to a cliffe..þare fand he tildid on þe top & tild vp a cite. **1459** *Paston Lett.* I. 488 Pottis of sylver,.. enamelyd on the toppys withe hys armys. **1560** DAUS tr. *Sleidane's Comm.* 54 b, Reaching from Thuringe..vnto the toppe of the Alpes. *c* **1630** RISDON *Surv. Devon* §215 (1810) 223 Trees..no taller than a man may touch to top with his hand. **1686** tr. *Chardin's Trav. Persia* 74 The Door is made ..with an opening at the Top. **1691** HARTCLIFFE *Virtues* 229 This Sentence should be writ on our Houses Tops. **1781** COWPER *Truth* 549 From Sinai's top Jehovah gave the law. **1825** SCOTT *Talism.* i, The flat top of his cumbrous cylindrical helmet was unadorned with any crest. **1873** J. RICHARDS *Wood-working Factories* 116 Everything about the top of a bench must be strong and simple. **1930** L. G. D. ACLAND *Early Canterbury Runs* 1st Ser. viii. 190 A wedge-shaped block of ninety thousand acres of high tops, mostly bush-bound. **1948** A. PATON *Cry, Beloved Country* I. x. 65 He would tell him of..the mist that shrouded the tops above Ndotsheni. **1951** E. COXHEAD *One Green Bottle* ii. 45 Cathy saw the great Welsh tops at last..four great blue mountains grouped at its farther end. **1976** *Lancs. Evening Post* 7 Dec. 8/3 There's no collective name for these tops but I've always known them as the Troutbeck Fells. **1980** J. WAINWRIGHT *Kill of Small Consequence* xiv. 109 Up on The Tops the first snows of winter had already etched the dry-stone walls.

b. That part of anything portable which, when it is in use, occupies the highest place; e.g. the top of a page, map, etc.

1593 SHAKS. *2 Hen. VI*, IV. ii. 107 They vse to writ it on the top of Letters. **1681** S. FELL in *Jrnl. Friends' Hist. Soc.* July (1912) 136 You may see at the Topp of every leafe, which Meetings testimonies followes. **1817** *Parl. Deb.* 430 Lord Cochrane..knew persons in office had frequently procured signatures to petitions without a top. **1859** LANG *Wand. India* 388 'Order a fresh bottle of our wine for him, Blade', said the Colonel, 'and let him taste the top of it'.

c. The higher end of anything on a slope; †the head or source of a river (*obs.*), the head of a lake (*arch.*), of a street, etc.; also that end of anything which is conventionally considered the higher, as of a room or dining-table; the end of a billiard-table opposite the baulk.

1624 CAPT. SMITH *Virginia* II. 23 The third navigable river is called Toppahanock... At the top of it inhabit the people called Mannahoacks amongst the mountaines. **1782** MRS. COWLEY *Which is the Man* v. ii, Coming down from the Top [of the room], addressing the Company. **1811** T. WILSON *Country Dancing* (ed. 2) 129 The top of the Dance or Set..is known thus:—the Ladies will always have the top of the Set on their right hands, and the Gentlemen on their left. **1849** MRS. CARLYLE *Lett.* (1883) II. 41 In the omnibus to the top of Sloane Street. **1896** W. BROADFOOT *Billiards* i. 51 McNeil..certainly played the 'top of the table' game better than any of his contemporaries. **1906** ALICE WERNER *Natives Brit. Cent. Africa* xii. 282 They..went on to the north, and round the top of the lake. **1927** *Observer* 20 Mar. 29 Prior..is essentially an all-round player with a tendency to make the top of the table game his chief scoring medium.

d. In the war of 1914–18, with reference to the parapet of a trench; esp. in phr. ***(to go) over the top*** (at the start of an attack). Also *fig.*

1916 *War Illustr.* 9 Sept. 80/1 Some fellows asked our captain when we were going over the top. **1917** 'CONTACT' *Airman's Outings* 184 When, at a scheduled time, the infantry emerge over the top behind a curtain of shells, the contact patrol buses follow their doings. **1923** *Publishers' Circular* 24 Nov. 703/2 If Canada, metaphorically speaking, 'goes over the top', it will be against the wishes of the rest of the Empire and against the wishes of her own authors and publishers. **1933** J. BUCHAN *Prince of Captivity* II. i. 154 Life's a perpetual affair of going over the top. **1962** [see AUNTIE, AUNTY b]. **1971** S. HILL *Strange Meeting* 120 Armstrong went over the top with the first wave and was hit almost at once. **1978** T. WILLIS *Buckingham Palace Connection* ix. 179 'This is it, then.' 'Yep... Over the top and the best of luck.'

4. a. The uppermost division of the body; the head; *esp.* the crown of the head. Chiefly, now only, in alliterative expressions: see 25, 26, and in slang phrases, as ***to blow one's top***: see BLOW *v.*[1] 24 i; ***to be off one's top*** (chiefly *Austral.*) = *to be off one's nut* s.v. NUT *sb.*[1] 7 b; ***to do one's top*** = *to do one's nut* s.v. NUT *sb.*[1] 7 d. Also ***up top***, with reference to brains, intelligence.

a **1225** *Juliana* 59 Ouer al & from þe top to þe tan. **1303**, *c* **1330** [see 25, 25 d]. **13..** *E.E. Allit. P.* C. 229 Tyd by top & bi to, þay token hym synne. *a* **1400–50** *Alexander* 752* And toton owt of hys top als tyndis of hornes. ? *a* **1500** *Chester Pl.* (Shaks. Soc.) II. 176 Thou take hym by þe toppe and I by þe tayle. ? *a* **1500** *Debate Carpenters Tools* 188 in Hazl. *E.P.P.* I. 86 Methinke gode ale is in ȝour tope. **1611** SHAKS. *Cymb.* IV. ii. 354 Soft hoa, what truncke is heere? Without his top? **1821** SCOTT *Kenilw.* ix, The pains I have bestowed on the top and bottom of..Dickie, whom I have painfully made to travel through the accidence.

1916 C. J. DENNIS *Songs Sentimental Bloke* vi. 48 'E's fair orf 'is top wiv love. **1945** BAKER *Austral. Lang.* vi. 130 The state of being stupid is described variously as being *off one's ..tile, top* or *saucer*. **1961** *She* Oct. 28/3 Peg, you've got enough up top for both of us. **1972** F. WARNER *Lying Figures* III. 32 Mousey little creature, bless her, not much up top if y'know what I mean. **1977** *Shoot* 18 June 22 (*caption*) Always does his top when he scores, you know.

b. The uppermost branch of a deer's horn: esp. in phr. ***on*** (***upon***) ***top***.

1486 *Bk. St. Albans* e j b, When he hath Awntelere with owt any lett Ryall and Surriall also there Isett, And that in the toppe so. **1801** in C. P. Collyns *Notes Chase Wild Red Deer* (1862) App. 211 The remaining horn had three on top with all his rights. **1886** *Wellington* (Som.) *Weekly News* 19 Aug., A large, heavy deer, with two upon top on each side.

5. Usually *pl.* The part of a plant growing above ground as distinct from the root; esp. of a vegetable grown for the 'root', as ***turnip-tops***. Also the tender tips of branches or shoots.

[1377 LANGL. *P. Pl.* B. XVI. 22 Pieres..bad me toten on þe tree on toppe and on rote.] **1523** FITZHERB. *Husb.* §28 Thanne he taketh the barley or otes by the toppes. **1552** HULOET, Toppe of an herbe, *capillamentum*. **1639** O. WOOD *Alph. Bk. Secrets* 10 Then take the young tops of Rosemary, Marigolds [etc.]. **1725** WATTS *Logic* I. vi. §3 If the buds are made our food, they are called heads, or tops. **1766** *Complete Farmer* s.v. *Radish* 6 I 1/1 They will run up in tops, and not increase in their roots. **1844** H. STEPHENS *Bk. Farm* II. 5 Tops of turnips make good feeding at the beginning of the season. **18..** *U.S. Dispensatory* (ed. 14) 827 (Cent. Dict.) The fruits and tops of juniper are the only officinal parts.

6. *pl.* (also *collect. sing.*). The smaller branches and twigs of trees as distinct from the timber.

Often with *lop*, as ***top(s and lop(s, lop(s and top(s, lop(s, top(s, and bark*** (or ***crop(s***).

1485–6 *Durham Acc. Rolls* (Surtees) 98 Rec. xvjs. pro corticibus et Toppys in silva de Rylley. **1523** FITZHERB. *Husb.* §154 If thou haue any woode to selle..sell the toppes as they lye. **1669**, etc. [see LOP *sb.*[2] 1]. **1858** SIMMONDS *Dict. Trade* s.v. *Lop*, In a sale of standing timber trees they are advertised with their 'lop, top, and bark'.

7. The extremity of a growing part (which is often the highest and usually the most slender point); hence the narrower end (of anything tapering), the point, tip. ***top and butt*** (*Shipbuilding*), a method of working long tapering planks together in pairs with the top of one to the butt of another, so as to maintain a constant width.

1538 ELYOT, *Sagitta*, an arow, also the top of a twygge or rodde. **1573–80** BARET *Alv.* T 290 The sharpnesse of the top, or tippe of the nose... The tops, or tips of the fingers. **1754** SHEBBEARE *Matrimony* (1766) I. 76 My Lord stept off lightly, on the Tops of his Toes. **1815** BURNEY *Falconer's Dict. Marine*, *Top and Butt*, in ship-building, a general method of working the English plank (except in the topside) to make good work and conversion, which is done by disposing of the top-end of every plank, within six feet of the butt-end of the plank above or below it. **1866** *Chambers' Encycl.* VIII. 684/2 Top-and-butt.

8. In various applications. **a.** In *Gem-cutting*: see quot. **b.** The inside of a roof; a ceiling; *spec.* the roof of a coal-mine or tunnel. **c.** ***tops and bottoms***: the flattish halves of small rolls sliced lengthways, and browned in the oven; rusks. **d.** See quot. 1905, and cf. BOTTOM *sb.* 8 a. **e.** *Mining*. See quot. **f.** orig. *U.S.* A circus tent. Cf. *big top* s.v. BIG *a.* B. 2.

a. 1877 KNIGHT *Dict. Mech.*, *Top*, that portion of a cut gem which is between the girdle, or extreme margin, and the table or flat face.

b. 1706 SWIFT *Baucis & Philemon* 58 The kettle to the top was hoist, And there stood fasten'd to a joist. **1830** T. WILSON *Pitman's Pay* (1843) 13 For if maw 'top' comes badly down. **1844** F. W. SIMMS *Pract. Tunnelling* ix. 83 This stage of progress, which is technically called 'getting in the top' [of a tunnel]. **1889** *N.W. Linc. Gloss.*, *Top*, the ceiling, as 'th' room top', 'th' kitchen top'. **1894** *Northumbld. Gloss.*, *Top*, in mining, the portion of coal that has been kirved and nicked, and is ready to be blasted or wedged down.

c. 1765 *Univ. Mag.* XXXVII. 371/2 The biskets called tops and bottoms, or rusks. **1866** *Routledge's Ev. Boy's Ann.* 55 Some nice tops-and-bottoms for its supper.

d. 1905 *Daily Chron.* 17 July 4/7 The labourers who board the steamers inquire anxiously for 'tops and bottoms'—that is, everything that has been left undrunk in the passengers glasses.

e. 1894 *Northumbld. Gloss.*, *Top*, the blue flame above a candle or lamp.., whose appearance indicates the presence of fire-damp in the mine.

f. 1931 *Amer. Mercury* Nov. 354/2 *Top*, a tent. **1942** D. POWELL *Time to be Born* xii. 291 A perpetual rain cloud spread like a circus top. **1959** *Manch. Guardian* 16 July 5/1 He supervises the erection of the 'top'.

III. A piece or part placed upon or fitted to anything, and forming its upper part or covering.

9. a. A platform near the head of each of the lower masts of a ship. In early fighting ships, a platform at the head of the mast, fenced with a rail (cf. *top-armour*, 35), stored with missiles and occupied by archers, etc., called more fully TOP-CASTLE; later, a similar platform on which musketeers or riflemen were stationed (cf. TOPMAN[1] 3); in a modern warship, an armoured platform on a short mast, for machine-guns, signalling, etc.; more fully ***fighting-top***, ***military top***. In a sailing ship, a framework and platform serving to extend the rigging of the topmast, and for convenience in making sail.

c **1420** ? LYDG. *Assembly of Gods* 342 A shyp with a toppe & seyle was hys crest. *a* **1533** LD. BERNERS *Huon* cvii. 360 He caused one of the maryners to mounte vp into the toppe to se yf he myght se any lond. **1561** EDEN *Arte Navig.* I. vii. 9 If you stande in the toppe of the shyppe. **1697** DAMPIER *Voy. round World* (1699) 208 We saw the light in the Admirals top, which continued about half an hour. **1764** VEITCH in *Phil. Trans.* LIV. 291 The top, or round scaffolding on the mast..in this ship it was 18 feet broad. **1859** *All Year Round* No. 17. 399 We literally raced for the lubber's hole, through which we crept, and then stood in the top to survey the scene. **1867** SMYTH *Sailor's Word-bk.*, *Half-top*, the mode of making ships' tops in two pieces, which are afterwards secured as a whole by what are termed sleepers.

b. *Naut.* Short for *topsail*: see quots.

† ***to pull*** or ***take down, bow,*** or ***vail one's top***, to lower one's topsail in token of submission or respect; said of a ship, hence *fig.* of a person. *Obs.*

1513–42 *Hist. Sir W. Wallace* x. (1881) 54 All the shipis.. pulling down ther topis, did obeysance vnto the read Lyon. *a* **1600** HOOKER *Serm. Justif.* §28 Let the Pope take downe his top and captiuate no more mens soules. **1694** MOTTEUX *Rabelais* IV. lxiv. (1737) 264 A fresh gale..began to fill the.. Tops, and Top-gallants.

c. ***top and topgallant***, short for *topsail and topgallant sail*; hence *fig.* (also *attrib.*); as *advb.* with all sail set, in full array or career.

1593 NASHE *Christ's T.* 71 b, Theyr heads, with theyr top and top gallant Lawne-baby caps. **1594** PEELE *Battle of Alcazar* III. iii, He cometh hitherward amain, Top and top-gallant, all in brave array. **1607** *Merry Devil Edmonton* I. i. 34 Heele be here top and top-gallant presently. **1626** BACON *Sylva* §646, I have seen..one Rose grow out of another, like Honey-suckle, that they call Top and Top-Gallants. **1662** OWEN *Animadv. Fiat Lux* xiii. Wks. (ed. Gould) XIV. 111 They carry their top and top-gallant so high that they will go to heaven without Christ. **1812** SCOTT *Rokeby* II. xi, Top and top-gallant hoisted high,..The Dæmon-frigate braves the gale. **1819** —— *Let.* in *Lockhart* (1837) IV. viii. 239, I did not lose my senses,..but I thought once or twice they would have gone over-board, top and top gallant.

10. a. The uppermost part of the leg of a high boot or riding-boot, *spec.* when widened out or turned over (as in 17th c.); now, on hunting-boots and the like, a broad band of material (simulating the turned-over part), white, light-coloured, or brown. Also *pl.* short for TOP-BOOTS.

1629 *Disc. Leather* 13 The manner of cutting Bootes out with huge, slouenly, vnmannerly, and immoderate tops. **1683** *Lond. Gaz.* No. 1869/4 A pair of Boots without Tops. **1835** SIR G. STEPHEN *Adv. Search Horse* xv. 193 Boots, that once had tops, approach within six inches of the knee. **1836–9** DICKENS *Sk. Boz, First of May*, Knee-cords and tops superseded nankeen drawers and rosetted shoes. **1837** —— *Pickw.* x, Mr. Samuel Weller happened to be..engaged in burnishing a pair of painted tops. **1846–79** EGERTON WARBURTON *Hunting Songs* lix. (1883) 162 Above the boots' jet polish Was a top of tender stain, Nor brown nor white, but a mixture light, Of rose-leaves and champagne. **1904** *Blackw. Mag.* Nov. 675/2 They had red waistcoats, white breeches, white tops, black velvet caps and white gloves.

b. The gauntlet part of a glove; the turned-down top part of men's hose.

1819 SCOTT *Leg. Montrose* ii, A pair of gauntlets,..the tops of which reached up to his elbow. **1906** in *Daily Chron.* 20 Aug. 3/3 The Highland regiments introduced complications with five different tartans, and three different patterns of hose-tops.

11. In various technical applications: †**a.** A piece (perh. a socket) fitted to the upper end of a torch-staff. *Obs.* **b.** The terminal joint of a fishing-rod. **c.** A jewel worn in the lobe of the ear, often with a 'drop' or pendant; usually in ***tops and drops***. †**d.** A lady's high 'head': see HEAD *sb.* 5. *Obs.* **e.** *pl.* A framing which increases the capacity of a cart; shelvings, cart-ladders, load-trees. **f.** *Spinning*. The top-cards in a carding-engine. **g.** The glass or metal stopper of a scent-bottle or the like; also, an inverted tumbler used as a cap to cover a decanter; also, the lid of other kinds of container, esp. the metal-foil cover of a milk bottle, the colour of which may indicate the kind or quality of the milk, as ***gold top***, ***silver top***, etc. **h.** The hood or cover of a carriage. Subsequently also of a motor-car (chiefly *U.S.*): see *hard top* s.v. HARD *a.* 23 a, *soft top* s.v. SOFT *a.* 29. **i.** *Typog.* See quot. **j.** Orig., a piece of female dress covering the neck and shoulders, worn with a certain kind of gown made without this part. Now usu. a blouse or similar upper garment for wearing with a skirt, trousers, etc.; cf. *sun-top* s.v. SUN *sb.* 11 d, *tank-top* s.v. TANK *sb.*[1] 5, etc.

a. 1453 *Mem. Ripon* (Surtees) III. 162 Pro faccione ij torchearum novarum et pro ij toppes magn. torch.

b. 1676 WALTON & COTTON *Angler* II. xii. 101 Though I have taken with the Angle..some thousands of Trouts..my top never snapt, though my Line still continued fast. **1706** R. H[OWLETT] *Angler's Sure Guide* 79 The Stock [of the Rod] bored no wider than to carry a Ground-top therein, or a Flie-top.

c. 1703 *Lond. Gaz.* No. 3942/4 Stolen.., a pair of Diamond Ear-Rings, with 4 large Faucet Diamonds (Tops and Drops). **1761** COLMAN *Genius* No. 3 in *Prose on Sev. Occas.* (1787) I. 34 To humour my wife, little Tubal was ordered to furnish her with a pair of diamond tops. **1825** T. HOOK *Sayings* Ser. II. *Sutherl.* I. 79 In her ears hung pendant diamonds, top and drop.

d. 1780 MRS. DELANY in *Life & Corr.* Ser. II. (1862) II. 524 Rows upon rows of fine ladies with towering tops.

e. 1844 STEPHENS *Bk. Farm* III. 1087 The common cart.. mounted with a framing called tops, is used in some parts of the country.

f. 1845 *Statist. Acc. Scot.* VI. 147 In 1815 Mr. Smith constructed a carding-engine, having the flats or tops moveable on hinges. **1851** L. D. B. GORDON *Art Jrnl. Illustr. Catal.* p. iv**/2 The large card-drum is generally surmounted by urchin or squirrel cards instead of tops.

g. 1862 MISS BRADDON *Lady Audley* xvi, Do you suppose that because people don't wear vinegar tops, or part their hair on the wrong side..by way of proving the vehemence of their passion? **1889** *Anthony's Photogr. Bull.* II. 361 This stopper is of tin, has a top screw with two holes. Whenever this top is a little unscrewed the liquid can come out of the bottle by drops. **1893** *N. & Q.* 8th Ser. III. 233/2 A carafe and 'top' is the shop-name for such a vessel [*i.e.* tumbler] and the bottle ministrant. **1958** A. SILLITOE *Saturday Night & Sunday Morning* ii. 35 Screwing the top back on the flask. **1959**, **1972** [see *milk bottle* s.v. MILK *sb.* 9 a]. **1979** *Daily Mirror* Nov. 8/3 (*caption*) Lisa Faulkner..displays the 10,000th Gold Top Milk Gymnastics Award Scheme double gold certificate. **1980** *Ibid.* Feb. 1/1 The retail price of a pint of ordinary silver top milk goes up from 15p to 16½p. **1981** J. BARNETT *Firing Squad* v. 48 What do you think this is, laddie? The top off a Fry's cocoa-tin?

h. 1617 MORYSON *Itin.* III. 54 The top of the Coaches is made with round hoopes. **1884–1898** [implied in *top-buggy*, *-phaeton*, *-wagon*: see 27]. **1910** *Sears, Roebuck Catal.* 1143/2 Three-bow skeleton automobile top of heavy moroccoline. **1942** D. POWELL *Time to be Born* ii. 51 Ted would never put the top down when he drove. **1977** H. FAST *Immigrants* III. 199 They argued about putting up the top.

i. 1888 JACOBI *Printer's Vocab.* 142 *Tops*. In stacking work as printed off, the warehouseman places a few sheets of each signature on the top, so that they may be at hand if a set of advanced sheets are asked for, thereby obviating the lifting of a quantity of work.

j. 1902 *Westm. Gaz.* 14 Aug. 3/2 The main thing is to have several well-fitting slips and a selection of tops... I saw a very pretty creamy chiffon top the other day. **1922** JOYCE *Ulysses* 341 His little man-o'-war top and unmentionables were full of sand. **1949** N. MITFORD *Love in Cold Climate* II. i. 186 A jersey top, however Parisian, was obviously unacceptable for evening wear in high Oxford society. **1968** *Daily Mirror* 20 Aug. 9/2 And I got a couple of bright flowery roll-neck tops..and some super things for the beach, stretch bikini bottoms and loose towelling tops in hectic colours.

12. Short for *top-button*: see 34.

1852 W. HUTTON in *Househ. Words* V. 108/1 The long coats of our grandfathers, covered with half a gross of high-tops. **1860** TOMLINSON *Arts & Manuf.* Ser. II. *Buttons* 38 The buttons [are] stirred about in the solution for all-overs; or brushed on the face for tops. **1874** KNIGHT *Dict. Mech.* 416/1 When the face only is gilt, the buttons are technically known as tops.

IV. *fig.* and *transf.* The part of anything which has the first place in time, order, or precedence.

13. Of time: The earliest part of a period; the beginning.

For *the top of the morning*, as a greeting, see 17.

c **1440** *Pallad. on Husb.* III. 1000 In thende of Octob'r, or in the toppe [*orig.* inicio] Of Novemb'r. **1669** WORLIDGE *Syst. Agric.* (1681) 98 A mellifluous Army of Bees, from the top of the morning, till the cool and dark evening. **1825** HONE *Every-day Bk.* I. 403/1 The dawn is awakened by a cry in the streets of 'Hot-cross-buns; one-a-penny buns..!' This proceeds from some little 'peep-o'-day boy', willing to take the 'top of the morning' before the rest of his compeers.

14. a. The highest, chief, or leading position, place, or rank; the head, forefront; now freq. in ***the top of the tree*** (*fig.*). Also in Journalism, Broadcasting, etc., the leading position in a news bulletin, or the top of a column in a newspaper.

1627 HAKEWILL *Apol.* Pref. 5 By vertue..being come to the top, they lost it againe by vice. *a* **1677** BARROW *Serm.* Wks. 1716 II. 143 We who are placed in the top of nature. **1699** LOCKE *Educ.* (ed. 4) §70. 104 Take a Boy from the top of a Grammar-School. **1782** MISS BURNEY *Cecilia* IV. x, I thought to have seen him at the top of the tree, as one may say! **1879** B. TAYLOR *Stud. Germ. Lit.* 136 The medieval passion for song began at the top and worked downwards. **1885** W. S. GILBERT *Mikado* I, I'm right at the top of the school. **1908** *Times* 3 Aug. 11/6 Brilliancy and determination..brought them to the top of the tree. **1973** L. HEREN *Growing up Poor in London* vi. 163 The first flashes were coming through on the attempt to get an abandoned ship in tow somewhere in the Atlantic... The story rated a top. **1979** 'A. HAILEY' *Overload* I. iv. 23 On the radio,..a news bulletin. The item Nim had been waiting for was at the top.

b. One who or that which occupies the highest or chief position; the head (of a clan, family, etc.); also *spec.* in Journalism: cf. sense 14 a.

1612 DAY *Festivals* ii. (1615) 27 Adam the Top of our Kin. **1646** J. GREGORY *Notes & Obs.* (1650) 30 Muazzus the Toppe of the Fatimæan family, caused the City of Gran Cairo to be set up. **1695** J. EDWARDS *Perfect. Script.* 332 Lastly man, the top and glory of the creatures. **1741** BETTERTON *Eng. Stage* vi. 116 He looks upon himself as the Top of his Family. **1856** LEVER *Martins of Cro' M.* xxxviii, They barred out the master to make 'the head usher' top of the school. **1960** R. ST. JOHN *Foreign Correspondent* x. 195, I..dictated a new 'top' for Sunday papers.

c. *ellipt.* for *top sergeant*, sense 34 below. *U.S. Mil. slang.*

1898 E. H. BLATCHFORD *Let.* 30 July (1920) 53 The 'top' said he wanted us to sign the pay-roll and be back at ten to-night. **1930** T. FREDENBURGH *Soldiers March!* ii. 12 The Top says he'll pass the word along. **1970** W. JUST *Military Men* iii. 95 Don't worry, Top.

15. a. The highest pitch or degree; the height, summit, zenith, pinnacle; now esp. in ***the top of one's bent*** (see BENT *sb.*[2] 9), ***the top of one's voice***, and ***at the top of one's form*** (FORM *sb.* 16 a).

1552 in *Vicary's Anat.* (1888) App. xvi. 294 What thyng at the first can atteyne to the toppe of perfectnesse. **1602** SHAKS. *Ham.* III. ii. 383 From my lowest Note, to the top of my Compasse. **1602–1875** [see BENT *sb.*[2] 9]. **1671** MILTON *Samson* 167 By how much from the top of wondrous glory, ..To lowest pitch of abject fortune thou art fall'n. **1711** STEELE *Spect.* No. 32 ⁋2 High Shoulders, as well as high Noses, were the Top of the Fashion. **1737** BRACKEN *Farriery Impr.* (1757) II. 195 Let him be kept to the Top of his Speed. **1881** BESANT & RICE *Chapl. of Fleet* I. iv, All the drivers were swearing at each other at the top of their voices. **1933** A. POWELL *From View to Death* iii. 89 It had come at a time when he was not feeling at the top of his form. **1947** L. P. HARTLEY *Eustace & Hilda* vii. 138, I can't pretend that she was at the top of her form.

b. One who or that which is or represents the highest pitch or degree; the most perfect example or type of something. (The constr. in quot. 1682 is *obs.* and *rare.*)

1593 Q. ELIZ. *Boeth.* 80 All such referd to greatest good, as to the top of Natures best. **1594** T. B. *La Primaud. Fr. Acad.* II. 570 His goodnesse, bountie, grace, and fauour towardes vs, which is the toppe of happinesse. **1603** SHAKS. *Meas. for M.* II. ii. 76 If he, which is the top of Iudgement, should But iudge you, as you are. **1682** DRYDEN *Mac Fl.* 167 But write thy best and top; and in each line Sir Formal's oratory will be thine. **1711** HICKES *Two Treat. Chr. Priesth.* (1847) II. 297 The episcopate is the top of all the honours among men. **1885–6** SPURGEON *Treas. Dav.* Ps. cxxx. 8 Redemption is the top of covenant blessings.

c. (absol. use of *top* as adj.: see 28–31). *Motoring slang.* The top or highest gear; esp. ***in(to) top*** (formerly also ***on (the) top***).

1906 *Westm. Gaz.* 21 Aug. 4/2 It was only found necessary twice during the journey to change to the second speed, most of the run being done on the 'top'. **1909** *Ibid.* 30 Nov. 5/2 In this machine the driving is..always done on top. **1925** *Morris Owner's Man.* 10 When changing gear up from first to second, or second to top, the clutch pedal should be pressed down. **1932** S. GIBBONS *Cold Comfort Farm* xvi. 217 They heard him change into top. **1953** [see CHANGE *v.* 6 d]. **1958** [see GEAR *sb.* 7 b]. **1970** N. FLEMING *Czech Point* (1971) viii. 107 Melanie rammed the car into top and kept up the acceleration.

d. *Bridge.* (*a*) Either of the two highest cards of a suit; (*b*) the best score made in the play of a particular hand.

1929 M. C. WORK *Compl. Contract Bridge* Gloss. 246 *Tops*, Aces and Kings. **1945** 'S. J. SIMON' *Why you lose at Bridge* ix. 103 As the Clubs didn't break, and he took the Heart finesse to try and save something from the wreck, he went six down. A cold top for us. **1958** *Listener* 23 Oct. 669/2 To ask whether, at match points, East-West should try for Seven Hearts is like asking whether a golfer should play for a birdie or a bogey: it all depends on the state of the game. If they need a 'top' they take the chance. **1977** *Hongkong Standard* 12 Apr. 10/3 Romik was able to claim all 13 tricks for an outright 'top' on the hand.

16. The highest point reached in a progression or series; the culminating point; esp. in ***the top of high water, of the tide***; ***top of the market***, the moment at which prices are highest.

a **1670** SPALDING *Troub. Chas. I* (1850) I. 341 Grevous to the people, now in top of harvest. **1719** DE FOE *Crusoe* I. 299 It was just at the Top of High-Water when these People came on Shore. **1759** DILWORTH *Pope* 131 The hackney scribblers seizing the top of the market, had quite run down the subject. **1801** *Naval Chron.* VI. 76 At the top of the tide she turned off the stocks. **1899** MACMANUS *Chimney Corners* 168 They'll insure me the top of the market.

(*b*) In fig. phr. ***on top of the world***, at the peak of well-being, prosperity, or elation; hence ***top of the world*** attrib. phr. (also with hyphens).

c **1920** D. HAMMETT in W. F. Nolan *Dashiell Hammett* (1969) ii. 19 A Samuels diamond puts you on top of the world! **1930** WODEHOUSE *Very Good, Jeeves!* ix. 226 If ever a bird was sitting on top of the world, that bird was Bingo. **1946** E. S. GARDNER *Case of Borrowed Brunette* xi. 132 This time Gulling, with this new evidence making him feel he's sitting on top of the world, slapped my proposition right back in my face. **1962** D. FRANCIS *Dead Cert* vii. 79 His eyes were alight with that fantastic, top-of-the-world elation. **1978** D. DEVINE *Sunk without Trace* v. 51 Last time I spoke to Liz she was on top of the world. **1979** *Guardian* 12 Jan. 9/8 As Colt's say in their publicity handout: 'This top of the world feeling can now be reproduced in a factory, office or shop.'

17. a. The best or choicest part; the cream, flower, pick. Now esp. in ***the top of the morning***, as an Irish morning greeting (cf. 13).

1663 BP. PATRICK *Parab. Pilgr.* xiv. (1687) 96 A conjunction of the very top and flower of the mind with the beginning and original of all good. **1668** BP. HOPKINS *Serm., Vanity* (1685) 99 The soul, next to angels, is the very top and cream of the whole creation. **1757** W. THOMPSON *R.N. Advoc.* 44 Which their..Friends, the top of the Physical Faculty can verify. **1815** SCOTT *Guy M.* iv, The top of the morning to you, sir. **1843** LEVER *J. Hinton* lviii, Captain, my darling, the top of the morning to you! **1894** *Westm. Gaz.* 10 Apr. 2/3 A 'top of the basket' young lady, like Lady Anne, would have been married long before the curtain rises.

b. *spec. pl.* (*a*) The best sheep or lambs in a flock.

1831 *Sutherland Farm Rep.* 80 in *Libr. Usef. Knowl. Husb.* III, The tops (the most choice and best breed) possess the outskirts of the ewe herding. **1886** C. SCOTT *Sheep-Farming* 19 When a lot of sheep are drafted, they are assorted. The best lot are called 'tops'.

(*b*) Members of the highest social class.

1887 *Pall Mall G.* 24 Aug. 11/1 Here..were given the dances when a party of London 'Tops' were invited to spend the Christmas holidays or to enjoy a week's shooting.

(*c*) The better quality of grain, separated from the *tails* (TAIL *sb.*[1] 7 b, q.v.).

1906 J. PATTERSON *Wamphray* vii. 193 It threshes, separates 'tops from tails', bags each separately, and bundles the straw.

(*d*) In gen. colloq. use (predicatively): the best. Freq. with *the*. orig. *U.S.*

1935 *Motion Picture* Nov. 41/1 *Top Hat* is tops—it has everything! **1937** R. STOUT *Red Box* xv. 249 Your conversation is an intellectual and esthetic delight. It's the tops. **1942** N. STREATFEILD *I ordered Table for Six* 243 He didn't go near your mother until he was the tops, so to speak. **1948** C. DAY LEWIS *Otterbury Incident* 94 Toppy is tops at spur-of-the-moment tactics. **1958** *Punch* 9 July 44/3 Cooney's Cassocks stand the test, Choosy Churchmen say they're best. Sure-fire sermons, never flops; Cooney's Cassocks are the tops. **1976** 'W. TREVOR' *Children of Dynmouth* i. 36 'You're easily tops, lad,' Hughie Green was enthusing, putting an arm round his shoulder. **1979** L. MEYNELL *Hooky & Villainous Chauffeur* i. 14, I always looked up to him... I just thought he was the tops.

18. *Particle Physics.* [An arbitrary choice of name.] The name of (a quark carrying) a possible sixth flavour, with a charge of $+\frac{2}{3}$. Freq. *attrib.*

1977 *Sci. Amer.* Oct. 74/2 The new quarks will apparently be called 'top' and 'bottom', the names being meant to suggest properties surpassing those of the up and down quarks found in ordinary matter. **1978** *Nature* 2 Feb. 407/2 Similarly if top quarks exist then 'naked top'—or 'topless' states will eventually be found. The prudish may care to note that t and b are said to stand for truth and beauty, rather than top and bottom, by some physicists. It is predicted that..top decays to bottom. **1980** J. S. TREFIL *From Atoms to Quarks* xii. 184 As I write (spring 1979), there is no evidence to indicate that particles made from a top quark have been seen. **1982** *Sci. Amer.* Mar. 64/2 The member of the top family that should be easiest to identify would be made up of a top quark bound to a top antiquark. **1984** *Nature* 12 July 97/1 Last week, the 80-strong collaboration..announced the discovery of the missing sixth quark, called *top*. *Ibid.* 97/3 The discovery of the *top* quark. *Ibid.*, The discovery of *top*.

V. Applied to actions.

19. The action of TOP *v.*[1]; the putting of a top on something; ***top-up***, a finish or conclusion. *rare.*

1883 *Three in Norway* 146 He thought this a grand top-up for a successful day.

20. Forward spin imparted to a ball by the mode of its impulsion or delivery (in billiards, by striking it above the centre; hence in cricket and tennis). Cf. TOPSIDE d, and *top-twist* in 34.

1901 *Westm. Gaz.* 13 Aug. 2/3 A vertical twist given by friction against the ground analogous with 'top' on a billiard ball. **1903** H. G. HUTCHINSON *Cricket* iv. 88 A ball..which ..is simply propelled with a large quantity of 'top on'. **1907** C. B. FRY in *Daily Chron.* 18 July 7/2 Schwarz's off-break, being produced by a perversion of leg-break action, contains an inordinate amount of 'top'.

†**21.** *Dice-play.* A cheating trick in which one of the dice was retained at the top of the box.

1709 *Tatler* No. 68 ¶ 5 There is lately broke loose from the London Pack, a very tall dangerous Biter... His Manner of Biting is new, and called the Top. **1711** PUCKLE *Club* 22 *note*, Supposing both box and dice fair, gamesters have the top, the peep, eclipse, thumbing.

VI. Phrases.

22. a. at, on top: see prec. senses and quots.; *fig.* supreme; dominant; **on (the) top of**, (*a*) above, upon, close upon, following upon; in addition to; (*b*) too close to; esp. ***on top of one another***, in crowded conditions; (*c*) burdensome to, too much for; ***to get on top of***: to overwhelm, harass, depress; (*d*) in control of. Also (**† in**), **upon (the) top of** = *on (the) top of* (*a*).

1602 SHAKS. *Ham.* II. ii. 355 Little Yases, that crye out on the top of question. *Ibid.* 459 Others, whose judgement in such matters, cried in the top of mine. **1603** KNOLLES *Hist. Turks* (1621) 394 Hee was vpon the top of his marriage. **1756** C. LUCAS *Ess. Waters* II. 125 With this inscription, at top. **1796** MME. D'ARBLAY *Camilla* II. 62 One thing heaped o'top of t'other. **1824** M. WILMOT *Let.* 5 Feb. (1935) 207, I came home hungry, took some hot tea on the top of a cold ice which I got there, got an indigestion. **1886** *St. Stephen's Rev.* 13 Mar. 11/2 Two heavy falls in a week, and a bad cold on the top of them. **1898** N. GOULD *Landed at Last* iv, This year I fancy I shall be on top with my pair of brothers. **1903** FARMER & HENLEY *Slang* s.v., *To come out on top*, to be successful. **1911** MARETT *Anthropol.* ii. 43 On top of the Wealden dome. **1947** A. L. ROWSE *Tudor Cornwall* xvi. 434 There was little privacy, for they lived on top of one another. **1952** *Chambers's Jrnl.* May 267/1 Our work consisted, mainly, in safeguarding road convoys from attack by hostile tribesmen. By no stretch of the imagination could it have been termed exhausting, but it was always on top of you. **1952** M. ALLINGHAM *Tiger in Smoke* x. 167 This time there was..no faltering. He was on top of himself and them. **1955** —— *Beckoning Lady* iv. 55 None of us saw her until she was right on top of us. **1962** B. COBB *Murder: Men Only* ix. 109 Oh, Kitty, it's Thursday and I know we agreed, but how? With everything on top of me. **1965** *New Society* 11 Nov. 7/1 People..do not necessarily want to live 'on top of each other'. **1968** *Listener* 4 July 5/1 On top of all this there are the continuing constitutional negotiations. **1974** A. MORICE *Killing with Kindness* ii. 21, I didn't mean to be rude. It's all got so much on top of me that I don't know what I'm saying half the time. **1977** M. ALLEN *Spence in Petal Park* xxxiii. 158 He still lives in Downsea. Near enough for me to babysit but not so close that we're on top of him. **1977** 'A. YORK' *Tallant for Trouble* vi. 87 He really felt he was getting on top of the situation. **1981** *Sunday Express Mag.* 2 Aug./33 Lord Mackan has had a busy programme of special ceremonial events on top of his normal Household chores.

b. at the top: in a position of power or authority. Cf. sense 14 and *room at the top* s.v. ROOM *sb.*[1] 2 a.

1936 G. B. SHAW *Millionairess* I. 145 That's what keeps him at the top in the city. **1962** J. BRAINE (*title*) Life at the top. **1979** A. FOX *Threat Warning Red* iii. 41 The machines ..hadn't made life easier at the top.

c. over the top, beyond reasonable limits, too far, into exaggeration.

1968 C. WATSON *Charity ends at Home* x. 129 For instance, you said at our first interview that your wife got so worked up about some things that she was in danger of going 'over the top', as you put it. **1974** *Times* 6 Mar. 2/8 We agreed to give every possible support to the Labour Government, including not going over the top with wage claims. **1981** 'D. JORDAN' *Double Red* i. 11, I could summon less and less response to Magnus's more rhetorical flights: so here we are, going over the top again, I was thinking.

23. a. (**† in**), **on, upon one's top**, attacking or assailing one, esp. from a superior position; 'coming down upon one', 'about one's ears'. So ***never off one's top***. **† in tops with**, in or into conflict or antagonism with. Now chiefly *Sc.*

1494 FABYAN *Chron.* VII. ccxxiii. 249 He..suffered for a season, leste he hadde brought all in his toppe atones. **1519** HORMAN *Vulg.* 137 Euery man is in my toppe [*omnibus sum infestus*]. **1560** DAUS tr. *Sleidane's Comm.* 125 b, To styre vp cruell warres, and set one in an others toppe. **1570** G. HARVEY *Letter-bk.* (Camden) 8 Strait wais M. Nevil was on mi top. *a* **1658** J. DURHAM *Expos. Rev.* xi. 2 (1680) 416 Fear to come in tops with this Word; it is a sword with two edges. **1680** ARCHD. ALESON in *Cloud of Witnesses* (1810) 46 Ye have Kirk and State upon your top. **1710** J. WILSON in Calderwood *Dying Test.* (1806) 155 Who would have thought that those builders..would have so soon flown upon one anothers tops? **1825** JAMIESON s.v. *Tap*, *To be on one's tap*, to assault, literally; especially by flying at one's head, or attempting to get hold of the hair. **1888** in *Scott. Leader* 3 May 5/1 It's a most singular thing that Bailie Lawson is always on my top about paltry things of that sort.

b. off the top of one's head and varr., impromptu, without consideration, superficially; hence ***top-of-the-head*** attrib. phr.

1939 H. L. ICKES *Secret Diary* (1954) II. 718 He was impetuous and inclined to think off the top of his head at times. **1959** 'E. MCBAIN' *'Til Death* xiii. 169 The jokes.. took on an ad lib quality, each prankster..coming up with top-of-the-head advice on the proper hotel-room behaviour. **1967** *Listener* 20 Apr. 518/2 His [*sc.* Bertrand Russell's] political activities..are not something that is coming out of the top of his head, they are coming from his nature. **1972** J. RIPLEY *My Word you should have seen Us* 159 You're talking out of the top of your head, mac. **1977** W. J. BATE *Samuel Johnson* (1978) xi. 173 *London*..seems breezy, as if written off the top of the head..; it lacks the sublime moral elevation of the *Vanity*. **1981** C. DEXTER *Dead of Jericho* xxviii. 160 A bit of bread-and-butter investigation was worth a good deal more than some of that top-of-the-head stuff.

24. top..bottom. a. ***top to bottom*** (also ***bottom to top***), so that the highest part becomes the lowest; with complete inversion. **b.** ***from top to bottom*** = *from top to toe* (26). **c.** ***top or bottom*** = *top or tail* (25 b). **d.** ***top and bottom***, (*a*) = *top and tail*, 25 a (*a*); (*b*) short for *at top and bottom* (of table).

[*a* **1250** *Owl & Night.* 1328 Of clerkes lore top ne more [= root]. *Ibid.* 1422 [see 3].] **1621** BURTON *Anat. Mel.* II. ii. III. (1651) 245 Turned.. top to bottom, or bottom to top. **1666** PEPYS *Diary* 10 June, The management..was bad from top to bottom. **1887** *S. Cheshire Gloss.* s.v., 'That's the top an' the bottom on it' corresponds to 'that is the long and the short of it'.

25. top..tail. a. ***top and tail*** (also † ***tail and top***). (*a*) The whole, everything without exception, every part. (*b*) The long and short of it, the substance, upshot (also ***the top, tail, and mane***). (*c*) *advb.* From head to foot, from beginning to end; all over. (*d*) Bottom upwards, topsy-turvy (now *dial.*). **b.** ***top or tail***, also ***top, tail, or mane*** (***root***), (in negative statements), any part; anything definite or intelligible; head or tail. **c.** ***from top to tail*** = *top and tail* (*c*); also *fig.* wholly, absolutely.

1303 R. BRUNNE *Handl. Synne* 5416 þarfor shul þey..Go to helle, both top and tayle. *c* **1384** CHAUCER *H. Fame* II. 371 (Fairf. MS.) Toppe and tayle and euery del..euery word that spoken ys. *c* **1440** *York Myst.* xxxi. 193 Tell hyme fro toppe vnto tayle. **1550** BALE *Apol.* 106 b, It is in the whole, toppe and tayle, length and bredth, begynnynge and endynge. **1558** PHAER *Æneid* v. Nj b, Headlong down in dust he ouerturnyd tayle and topp. **1727** P. WALKER *Remark. Passages* (1827) 212 His Sermon had neither Top, Tail, nor Mane. **1822** CARLYLE *Early Lett.* (1886) II. 32 They will..make neither 'top, tail, nor root out of it'. **1874** T. HARDY *Far fr. Madding Crowd* lvi, The top and tail o't is this. **1888** ELWORTHY *W. Somerset Word-bk.* s.v., The pony put his foot in a rabbit's hole and proper turned top-on-tail.

d. ***top over tail***, app. an inversion of *tail over top* (which also occurs: cf. *head over heels*, HEAD *sb.*[1] 46): upside down, topsy-turvy. Also *attrib.* Chiefly *north. dial.*

c **1330** R. BRUNNE *Chron.* (1810) 70 Into þe waise þam fro he tombled top ouer taile. *c* **1400** *Laud Troy Bk.* 16727 He bar him tayl ouer top, That he lay ther as a sop. **1535** LYNDESAY *Satyre* 3744 Bot this fals world is turnit top ouir taill. **1786** *Pogonologia* 6 The *Culbute* (the flying-top-over-tail hoop). **1819** W. TENNANT *Papistry Storm'd* 200 Cam tumblin' tap-owr-tail. **1881** MISS JACKSON *Shropsh. Word-bk.*, *Top o'er tail*, head over heels—completely over.

26. top..toe. a. ***from top to*** (***†into, †unto***) ***toe***, from head to foot, in every part; also *fig.* from beginning to end, throughout, entirely.

[*a* **1225** *Juliana* 59 Ouer al & from þe top to þe tan.] *c* **1375** *Sc. Leg. Saints* xxiii. (*Sleperis*) 121 Malchus..tald þame fra tope to ta Quhow decius þame socht to sla. *c* **1425** *Cast. Persev.* 615 in *Macr. Plays* 95, I holde þee trewe ffro top to þe too. **1526** *Pilgr. Perf.* (W. de W. 1531) 241 b, Thou art made abhominable from the toppe of [? to] the too. **1545** RAYNOLD *Byrth Mankynde* Prol. Bij, I..reuisying from top to too the sayde booke. **1613** PURCHAS *Pilgrimage* (1614) 267 After this follow fifteene other most faire Camels,..couered from top to toe with Silke. **1718** MRS. DELANY in *Life & Corr.* (1861) I. 45 Top-a-Toe, my dear Niece, Your most affectionate, Faithful, humble servant, Lansdowne. **1887** LOWELL *Democr.* 87 English from top to toe.

†**b.** ***neither top nor toe***, no part or vestige; = *top nor tail* (see 25 b). *Obs. rare*$^{-1}$.

1610 HOLLAND *Camden's Brit.* (1637) 269 there stood in old time a citie, but now neither top nor toe, as they say, remaineth of it.

VII. Combinations and collocations.

* *attrib. uses, passing into adjective* in 28–31.

27. Having a top, fitted with a top, as ***top-buggy***, ***-phaeton***, ***-stocking***, ***-wagon***; ***top-ship*** (see 35).

1849 *Knickerbocker* XXXIV. 266 An ordinary '*top-buggy' wagon. **1866** 'MARK TWAIN' *Lett. from Hawaii* (1967) 45 His 'turnout', as he calls a top buggy that Captain Cook brought here in 1778. **1894** HOWELLS in *Harper's Mag.* Feb. 381 Grocers don't drive round in top-buggies. **1898** —— *Open-eyed Conspir.* 52 Buoyant *top-phaetons and surreys, with their light-limbed horses. **1686** *Lond. Gaz.* No. 2126/4 Light-coloured *Top-Stockings striped with black. **1852** C. A. BRISTED *Upper Ten Thousand* 208, I have a *top-wagon. **1880** W. WHITMAN *Daybks. & Notebks.* (1978) III. 639 Many queer old one-horse top-wagons. **1884** ROE *Nat. Ser. Story* x, He hastened to harness Thunder to his light top-wagon. (See also TOP-BOOT.)

28. Of or pertaining to the top, belonging to the top; situated, placed, or growing at or on the top of something; topmost, upper, uppermost. Now usually written separate as *adj.*

1593 SHAKS. *3 Hen. VI*, v. ii. 14 Whose top-branch ouerpeer'd Ioues spreading Tree. **1610** HEALEY *St. Aug. Citie of God* 225 Nero..got first of all to the top-turret of all this enormity. *c* **1611** CHAPMAN *Iliad* xx. 211 These twice-six colts had pace so swift, they ran Upon the top-ayles of corn-ears, nor bent them any whit. **1656** EARL MONM. tr. *Boccalini's Advts. fr. Parnass.* I. lxxvii. (1674) 99 If they fall to cut down the top-boughs. **1676** MOXON *Print. Lett.* 6 The Top-line is the line that bounds the top of the Ascending Letters. **1707** MORTIMER *Husb.* (1721) II. 139 An Herb whose top Leaves are a Sallet of themselves. **1769** MRS. RAFFALD *Eng. Housekpr.* (1778) 91 It is proper for a top dish at night, or a side dish for dinner. **1805** R. W. DICKSON *Pract. Agric.* I. 34 Advantages in carrying top-loads. **1827** STEUART *Planter's G.* (1828) 328 The topshoots of the former year will inevitably be cut down. **1833** T. HOOK *Parson's Dau.* I. vii, A five pound fish..had snapped off the top-joint of his four guinea rod. **1851** MRS. BROWNING *Casa Guidi Wind.* I. 700 How..we may..as we reach Our own grapes, bend the top vines to supply The children's uses. **1865** *Sat. Rev.* 21 Jan. 80/2 the want of protection of the top-shifts against fire. **1875** KNIGHT *Dict. Mech.* 1465/2 A crowning molding is a top member. **1888** H. MORTEN *Sk. Hosp. Life* 46 There were two doors on the top landing. **1904** J. SWEENEY *At Scotl. Yard* v. 110 The carriages..passed..along the top side, passing out at the left hand top corner. **1906** *Athenæum* 15 Dec. 777/3 A top stop was equivalent to a stop..in the upper focal plane of the objective. *Mod.* The top end of the tube is sealed.

29. Forming or constituting the top, or the exterior surface, or layer; upper, outer.

Now usually separate, as in prec. sense.

1603 FLORIO *Montaigne* II. xii. (1632) 275 A light stroke that dooth scarce the top-skin wound. **1634–5** BRERETON *Trav.* (Chetham) 96 They cutt and flea top-turves with linge upon them. **1707** MORTIMER *Husb.* (1721) II. 384 Take away some of the Top exhausted Earth. **1838** *Civil Eng. & Arch. Jrnl.* I. 97/2 Walls of rubble,..which support a top covering of flat stones. **1874** CROOKES *Dyeing & Calico-Print* 526 Putting a top bloom on blacks. **1879** B. TAYLOR *Stud. Germ. Lit.* 38 Hollow spaces cut in the top-slab of his tombstone. **1883** R. HALDANE *Workshop Receipts* Ser. II. 236/2 Aniline colours..are now usefully employed as top colours..brushed in very dilute solution over vegetable colours. **1891** *Daily News* 11 July 5/4 Top milk and bottom milk have been proved to be practically the same. **1912** *Nation* 10 Feb. 779/2 Good farming increases the humus or productive 'top spit' of the land.

30. First in rank, order, or quality; principal, chief, most eminent, best; of high standing. See also TOP PEOPLE *sb. pl.*

1647 N. BACON *Disc. Govt. Eng.* I. vi. 22 Bishops, who are now..the very top-flowers of wisdom and learning. **1649** ROBERTS *Clavis Bibl.* 292 The flourishing or Top-glory of Israels Kingdome under K. Solomon. **1657** AUSTEN *Fruit Trees* II. 45 This is the top priviledg of beleivers. **1697** COLLIER *Immor. Stage* iv. (1698) 242 These Sparks generally marry the Top-ladies. **1712** E. COOKE *Voy. S. Sea* 73 The Top Nation of all that Part of the World for Bravery. **1713** STEELE *Englishman* No. 40. 261 When they grow up, Dancing is the top Accomplishment. **1727–41** CHAMBERS *Cycl.* s.v. *Physiognomy*, The top modern authors on physiognomy. **1733** SWIFT *Let. to Pope* 2 Apr., They are certainly the top wits of the Court. **1750** R. POCOCKE *Trav.* (Camden) I. 50 One of their top merchants. **1774** J. HAWLEY in *J. Adams' Wks.* IX. 345 Our top Tories here give out..that he will certainly be taken up before the Congress. **1794** GODWIN *Cal. Williams* 291 Regarded as the top gentry of the place. **1819** KEATS *Let.* (in *Daily Chron.* 26 Mar. (1904) 9/2) Fine writing is, next to fine doings, the top thing in the world. *c* **1926** [see RUNNING *vbl. sb.* 2 e (*b*)]. **1936** *Publishers' Weekly* 21 Nov. 1965/2 Publishers involved in recent top-seller crises. **1938** E. AMBLER *Cause for Alarm* xiii. 213 The prisons would be overflowing..and most of the top men would be with them. **1939** *Supervision* Feb. 1/1 The whole related circle which reaches from top management down to the worker. **1945** *Richmond* (Va.) *Times-Dispatch* 25 Oct. 12/1 The A-bomb has aroused so much interest a complex technical tome on that subject is now a top-seller. **1958** *Observer* 3 Aug. 5/1 Grouse-shooting, it must be conceded, is the top sport. **1965** *Mod. Law Rev.* XXVIII. v. 587 Corporations, seemingly, will be liable for the acts and omissions of 'top management'. **1972** L. DEIGHTON *Close-Up* viii. 166 They are going to spend a hundred thousand dollars just on this one story. They'll get a top outside photographer to do it. **1981** R. SAMUEL *East End Underworld* xi. 133 Cockney Cohen was the favourite; he was regarded as the top man of the two [boxers]. **1982** *Lakeland Echo* 18 Mar. 6/7 Peter Frankl was going to play there..on May 1, and other top performers were lined up for the future.

31. Highest (in degree), greatest (in amount); very high, very great; also in weakened sense, first-rate, tip-top, excellent.

1714 G. LOCKHART *Mem. Scot.* 229 Obliged to go off at a top Gallop. **1736** DUCHESS PORTLAND in *Mrs. Delany's Life & Corr.* (1861) I. 563 The Speaker was in top good humour. **1769** LADY M. COKE *Jrnl.* 6 Aug., The Duchess..said she was in a top sweat. *a* **1774** FERGUSSON *Caller Oysters* xi, The fisher-wives will get top livin. **1806–7** J. BERESFORD *Miseries Hum. Life* XVIII. xii, His common trot is just a match for your top speed. **1872** MICHIE *Deeside Tales* v. 49 He reached the house 'in a top sweat'. **1894** *Lit. World* 13 Apr. 341/2 One [who] commands 'top prices' for serial rights. **1902** *Daily Chron.* 20 Dec. 7/5 Half a dozen hounds went at top pace towards Tugby.

** *Locative, etc., combinations.*

32. In sense 'at or to the top', as ***top-draining***, ***lacing***, ***-pruning***; ***top-dry***, ***-feeding***, ***-filled***, ***-ironed***, ***-laden***, ***-loose***, ***-opening***, ***-shackled***, ***-tempestuous***, ***-turned*** adjs. See also TOP-DRESS, TOP-FULL, TOP-HAMPER, TOP-HEAVY, TOPKNOT, etc.

1860 WORCESTER, **Top-draining*, the act or the practice of draining the surface of land. **1933** *Sun* (Baltimore) 20 Apr. 5/6 Some 200,000 of the American *top-feeding minnow species Gambusia were dumped into some of the ponds. *c* **1611** CHAPMAN *Iliad* XVI. 219 From a coffer..*top-fild with vests; warme robes to checke cold wind. **1691** tr. *Emilianne's Observ. Journ. Naples* 104 The Treasuries of their Churches are top fill'd with these kind of precious Relicks. **1910** *Daily Chron.* 12 Jan. 5/7 One with perfect nailing, beautifully executed, *top-ironed, and with exquisitely finished edging. **1925** F. SCOTT FITZGERALD *Great Gatsby* i. 8 He seemed to fill those glistening boots until he strained the *top lacing. **1831** CARLYLE *Sart. Res.* I. iii, There, *topladen,..rolls in the country Baron and his household. **1887** *Pall Mall G.* 28 June 6/1 On each side of the hall are aisles, *top-lighted. **1905** *Daily Chron.* 17 May 8/5 Private offices are arranged along the back and top-lighted. **1747** HOOSON *Miner's Dict.* U ij b, This being *Toploose, gives more Liberty for the cutting thereof than the taking of a whole Roof. **1926–7** *Army & Navy Stores Catal.* 409/2 *Top-opening handbag. **1963** *Which?* 6 Feb. 36/1 The chest top-opening freezer. **1842** LOUDON *Suburban Hort.* 343 Ringing..may often serve as a substitute both for root pruning and *top pruning. **1612** N. FIELD *Woman a Weathercock* III. ii. E iv, Oh good old woman, she is *topshackeld. **1632** LITHGOW *Trav.* (1906) 346 Like to a halfe ballast ship tottering on *top-tempestuous waves. **1902** *Westm. Gaz.* 5 July 2/3 Black crowns Of wind-worn pines..*top-turned by gales that weighed Them eastward.

33. In sense 'highest or first'. **a.** With nouns forming attrib. phr., as ***top class***, ***quality***, ***rank***, etc. See also *top drawer*, *flight*, sense 34 below.

1948 J. TOWSTER *Political Power in U.S.S.R.* III. xiii. 318 'Stakhanovites', that is, top-efficiency workers. **1950** *N.Y. Times* 20 Apr. 1/3 Virtually every top bracket job..could be filled from the proposed register. **1950** *Times* 23 May 5/6 Time and again one reads..of top grade British films which will never be shown here at all. **1953** *Newsweek* 30 Mar. 81/2 Higgins-built mine sweepers..became the top-priority ships on the Navy's program. **1959** *Times* 29 Oct. 2/2 Position calls for top-calibre executive with experience of marketing. **1960** *Farmer & Stockbreeder* 9 Feb. 74/3 These ..would only be interested in top-quality products tailor-made to suit their demand. **1960** *Times* 12 July 13/4 It isn't only the field events that are a poor show at top-class athletics meetings. **1961** *Lancet* 9 Sept. 598/1 We have very few top-rate managers. **1962** L. DEIGHTON *Ipcress File* i. 15 It makes eight top rank Disappearances in..six and a half weeks. **1972** J. AIKEN *Butterfly Picnic* x. 190 [He] is doing forty years in a top-security prison for handing over state secrets. **1973** *Country Life* 29 Nov. 1773/1 No champagne is made exclusively from top-price grapes. **1975** G. ST. GEORGE *Proteus Pact* i. 36 An urgent matter, a top-priority project. **1977** *National Observer* (U.S.) 8 Jan. 7/1 They conclude that there are no significant differences in intellectual and social development between young children reared at home and those placed in a top-quality day-care center. **1978** K. HUDSON *Jargon of Professions* v. 122 X is a top-class product manager because his father and mother were top-class product managers. **1979** *Jrnl. R. Soc. Arts* July 504/2 Something should be done to encourage a really efficient and top-grade display of arts and crafts. **1982** *Lakeland Echo* 18 Mar. 6/4 Special attention has been paid to acoustics and lighting so that really top-rank artistes can be persuaded to play there.

b. Adverbially with adjs. or ppl. adjs., as ***top-ranking***, ***-rated***, ***-secret***, etc.

1936 *Time* 19 Oct. 67/1 Adapting a story which is to be played by four top-ranking film personalities. **1944** *Top secret* [see CLASSIFIED *ppl. a.* c]. **1946** KOESTLER *Thieves in Night* 194 Turning to the urgent blue and so to the top-urgent red tray. **1958** *People* 4 May 19/7 Top-rated American Davey Moore said yes. **1960** *Farmer & Stockbreeder* 22 Mar. 83/3 Top-priced bull at Hereford last week was Haven Possible. **1962** *Guardian* 13 July 8/1 Drambuie..ranks with Benedictine and Cointreau among the world's five top-selling digestifs. **1975** *Listener* 17 July 69/1 Top-paid people should agree to limit their incomes. **1976** *Billings* (Montana) *Gaz.* 16 June 3-c/2 The victory by the third-rated Hurons left top-rated Arizona State one defeat from elimination. **1976** *Scotsman* 25 Nov. 14/5 A commercial paper nowadays would have to be less 'Left-of-centre'..to be read by the top-earning businessmen and stockbrokers who justify expensive advertising. **1976** H. WILSON *Governance of Britain* iv. 92 The Churchill and Macmillan appointees inevitably had the same access to secret and top-secret documents as any civil service appointee. **1978** *N.Y. Times* 30 Mar. D22/1 In a postponed first-round match, top seeded Vitas Gerulaitis..defeated Ray Moore. **1978** *Observer* (Colour Suppl.) 9 Apr. 30 These two were 'top rankin'' gunmen in the ghetto for Jamaica's two main political parties. **1980** *Washington Star* 17 Dec. E2/6 Mississippi State jumped into national prominence with its big win over top-ranked Alabama.

*** *Special combinations and collocations.*

34. In general senses of *top*.

(When *top* is adjectival properly without hyphen.)

top banana *Theatr. slang* (chiefly *U.S.*), the leading comic in a burlesque entertainment; also *fig.*; **top-beam** = COLLAR-BEAM 1; **top-binder**, ?a branch serving to bind the upper part of a hedge; **top-block**: see quot. (see also 35 b); **top board** *Chess*, the principal player of a team in a tournament; **top box**, on a motor-cycle, a carrier box for baggage, etc., placed on top of the cycle behind the saddle (as opp. to panniers at the sides); **top brass**: see BRASS *sb.* 2 e; **top breadth**, the breadth of the ship at the level of the top-timbers; **top-breadth line**, a line in a plan showing the longitudinal curve of the ship's side at the level of the top-timbers; **top-button**, † (*a*) a metal button of which the top or face is gilt or silvered; (*b*) an ornamental knob on the top of a mast; **top-card** *Spinning*, a flat strip of wood covered with hooked teeth set over the drum of a carding-engine; **top-cast** [CAST *sb.* 18] = *top-swarm*; **top coal**, an important seam, which in the southern part of the Shropshire coalfield is the topmost; **top-coat**, (*a*) overcoat, great-coat, outer coat; (*b*) any of the finishing layers of paint applied after undercoat; hence **top-coated** *a.*; **top-contact**, contact at the top or upper surface; **top copy**, the original typescript of a document, of which the under-sheets are carbon copies; also *ellipt.*; **top-crop**, (*a*) see *top-fruit*; (*b*) *Mining*, an outcrop; **top-cross** *Horse-breeding*, a cross in which one parent is of pure or superior blood (*U.S.*); **top-cut**, reduction of the strength of the higher-frequency components of a signal; **top cutter** *U.S. Mil. slang* = *top sergeant* below; **top cymbal** *Mus.* = *ride cymbal* s.v. RIDE *sb.*[1] 7; **top dead centre** (see quot. 1978); **top deck**: see DECK *sb.*[1] 3 d; **top dog**, *lit.* the dog uppermost or 'on top' in a fight; *fig.* the victorious or dominant party; **top dollar** *N. Amer. colloq.*, a high price; **top-down** *a.*, (*a*) *Computers*, working from the top or root of a tree towards the branches (with or without backtracking); (*b*) that proceeds from the top downwards; authoritarian, hierarchical; occas. as *adv.*; (*c*) (of planning or design) starting with the overall structure and going on to successively more detailed parts of it; **top drawer**, the upper-most drawer in a cabinet or the like; also *fig.*, freq. with reference to social standing; also *attrib.* or as *adj.*, first-class, of the highest level; **top-drive** *Mech.* = *top-gear* (*b*); **Top End** *Austral. colloq.*, the Northern Territory of Australia; hence **Top-Ender**; **top fermentation** *Brewing*, a process in which the yeast rises to the surface during fermentation; **top flask** *Founding*, the upper part of a moulder's flask when made in two parts; the 'cope' when a 'drag' is used (*Cent. Dict. Suppl.* 1909); **top-flat** *Spinning* = *top-card*, FLAT C. 8 d (Knight *Dict. Mech.* 1877); **top flight**, the highest rank or peak of excellence; also *attrib.* or as *adj.*; hence **top-flighter**; **top-fruit**, fruit growing on trees, as distinct from bush-fruit and ground-fruit (strawberries, etc.); **top-fuller**, a *top-tool* having a narrow rounded edge (Knight 1877); **top-gear**, (*a*) the rigging, sails, and spars of a ship; (*b*) (without hyphen) in power transmission, the alternative gearing which produces the highest speed in proportion to that of the motor; also *fig.*, a fast pace, full speed; **top-graft** *v. trans.* (*Horticulture*) = *top-work* vb. below; hence **top-grafting** *vbl. sb.*; **top hand** *N. Amer. colloq.*, a cowboy who is an experienced or first-rate ranch-worker; also *fig.*; **top-hard (coal)**: see quot. 1834–5, and cf. *top coal*; **top-head** *Mining*: see quot.; **top-heat** *Horticulture*, heat generated in a frame or greenhouse; cf. *bottom heat* s.v. BOTTOM *sb.* 20; **top-hole**, (*a*) *Mining*, = *top-head*; (*b*) = *top-notch*; *attrib.* first-rate, 'tip-top' (*slang*); †**top-honours** *nonce-use*, the topsails of a ship, in reference to the custom of lowering them in token of respect; **top-house** *Naut.*, a deck-house; **top iron**, the upper iron in a carpenter's plane, adjusted so as to stiffen the cutter and turn up the shavings; the break-iron; **top kick** *U.S. Mil. slang* = *top sergeant* below; also **top kicker**; **top-land**, high or elevated land, highland; **top-latch** *dial.*, the strap or thong used to fasten the hames together at the top; **top lift**, (*a*) [LIFT *sb.*[2] 5], the uppermost working in a cutting, etc.; (*b*) the external layer of a boot or shoe heel; see also 35 a; **top light**, a pane of glass affording illumination from overhead; a skylight; hence **top-lighted**, **top-lit** *adjs.*; **top-loader**, (*a*) *Lumbering*, one who works at the top of a load of logs (*N. Amer.*); (*b*) a machine or device designed to be loaded from the top; opp. *front-loader* s.v. FRONT *sb.* (and *a.*) 14; hence **top-loading** *vbl. sb.*; **top minnow**, a small, often brightly coloured, fish belonging to the family

Cyprinodontidæ or Poeciliidæ; **top notch**, the highest notch; *fig.* the highest point attainable; also *attrib.* first-rate, 'tip-top'; hence **'top-'notcher**, a first-rate person or thing, a 'tip-topper'; **top note**, the highest note in a singer's compass; also *fig.*; **top of the bill** *Theatr.*, the chief place on a bill of entertainment; also (with hyphens) *attrib.* and *fig.* (cf. *to top the bill* s.v. TOP *v.*[1] 16 a); **top-of-the-line** *a.* (chiefly *U.S.*), designating a commercially produced commodity that is the best, most expensive or luxurious, etc., of its kind; **top of the milk**, the cream that rises to the top of milk when left undisturbed; **top of the pops**: see POP *a.* (*sb.*[8]) 1 b; **top-onion**, the Canada or tree onion (*Allium Cepa proliferum*), bearing a cluster of small green bulbs at the top of the stem, instead of flowers and seed; **top plate**, the back plate of a watch-movement; **top-proud** *a.*, proud to the highest degree; **top-rail** *Carpentry*: see quot. 1823 (also 35 b); **top-rider** *Shipbuilding*: see quot.; † **top-right** *a. nonce-wd.*, upright, erect; **top rock** *Coal-mining*, the uppermost stratum of (hard) rock; **top-roll**, some part of a bridle-bit; **top saw**, the upper of a pair of circular saws, cutting down to meet the kerf of the lower; **top-score** *v. intr.* (*Cricket*), to make the greatest number of runs of an innings; hence **top scorer**; **topscript** [*nonce-wd.* after *postscript*], something written at the top of a letter; **top sergeant** *U.S. Mil. slang*, first sergeant; **top-set** *sb.*, the top section of a vein of ore, which has sections of different width at different depths; **top-set** *a.*, set or deposited at the top, or above something else; in *Mining* and *Geol.*, *spec.* of a bed, layer, or stratum; **top-sew** *v.*, *trans.* to hem by oversewing; **top shelf**, the uppermost and least accessible shelf; also *attrib.* in *fig.* expressions: (*a*) as in *top-shelf book*, a book seldom used, or that is to be kept out of the way; (*b*) first-rate; cf. *top-notch*; hence **'top-'shelfer**, a person or thing of the highest class; **top-slicing** *vbl. sb.*, (*a*) *Mining*, a method of working in which successive slices up to 12 feet thick are mined from the top of an ore body, working downwards, the material overlying each slice being made to cave after its completion; so **top-slice** *v. trans.*, to work in this way; (*b*) a method of assessing income- or surtax chargeable on a lump sum by averaging it out over the years for which it has accrued and charging tax accordingly; **top-soil** *sb.*, the (cultivatable) surface layer of the soil, as distinct from the subsoil; in *Archæol.*, the soil covering a site being investigated; **top-soil** *v.*, to pare off the top soil; **top soldier** *U.S. Mil. slang* = *top sergeant* above; **top-spin** = OVERSPIN *sb.*; see also sense 20; also *fig.*; **top-spinner** = *overspinner* s.v. OVERSPIN *sb.*; also **top-spun** *a.*; **top-stitch** *v. trans.*, to make a row of stitches on (the right side of a garment or other piece of sewn work), usu. as a form of decoration; so **top-stitched** *ppl. a.*; **top-stitching** *vbl. sb.*; **top storey**, the uppermost storey of a house; *fig.* the head as the seat of intellect; also *attrib.*; **top-string** *dial.* = *top-latch*; **top-swarm** *Sc.* and *north. dial.*, the first swarm of the season thrown off by a hive of bees; also *fig.*; hence **top-swarmer**; **top table**, at a formal dinner, the table at which the chief guests are placed; also *fig.*, esp. in *Pol.*; **top-tail** *v.*, *intr.* to turn the tail up and head down, as a whale in diving (*Cent. Dict.*); **top ten** *Popular Music*, the first ten tunes or gramophone records in the popularity charts (CHART *sb.* 3 c) at a particular time; also *transf.*; similarly **top twenty**, etc.; **top-, tap-thrawn** *a.*, *Sc.*, perverse, obstinate, wrong-headed; **top-tool**, any smith's tool which is held upon the work while being struck, as distinct from a *bottom-tool*, which is socketed in the anvil; **top-turnip**, the turnip-cabbage, KOHLRABI (*Cent. Dict. Suppl.*); **top-twist** = sense 20; **top view** = *plan view* s.v. PLAN *sb.* 6; **top wall** (*Mining*): see quot.; **top-water**, (*a*) *Mining*: see quot. 1894; (*b*) as *adj.* (of a lure) that floats on top of the water; **top-weight**, the heaviest weight carried by a horse in a race; also *transf.* a horse carrying this weight; **top-work** *v. trans.*, *Horticulture*, to replace part or all of the top of (a fruit tree) by grafts of another variety; so **top-worked** *ppl. a.*, **-working** *vbl. sb.*; **top-yeast**, the yeast which forms on the top of fermenting liquor (*Cent. Dict. Suppl.*). See also TOP-BOOT, etc.

1953 BERREY & VAN DEN BARK *Amer. Thes. Slang* (1954) §583/12 **Top banana*, the burlesque comedian who gets top billing. **1956** *Picturegoer* 21 July 29/3 'Top banana' is the comic-in-chief of a burlesque show. **1974** *Time* 21 Jan. 53/3 Dentsu Advertising Ltd.. has become the new top banana of world-wide advertising. **1978** *N.Y. Times* 29 Mar. C27/1 Miss Burnett is a.. very, very funny woman. She is a superb top banana. **1679** MOXON *Mech. Exerc.* viii. 147 *Top-beam. **1823** P. NICHOLSON *Pract. Build.* Gloss., *Top-beams*, the collar-beam of a truss;.. formerly called *wind-beam* or *strut-beam*, and now *collar-beam*. **1883** PENNELL-ELMHIRST *Cream of Leicestersh.* 402 A horse.. will make short work of an ordinary *topbinder when once the sap of the thorn has gone to the roots. **1877** KNIGHT *Dict. Mech.*, **Top-block*,.. a projecting piece on which the bows of a carriage rest when down. **1910** *British Chess Mag.* XXX. 463 A *top-board winning seven times successively might find himself temporarily or unjustly displaced in the ninth match. **1976** *Milton Keynes Express* 28 May 55/7 The competition was won.. by county top board Norman Stephenson. **1976** *Eastern Daily Press* (Norwich) 19 Nov. 5/6 (Advt.), 1975 Yamaha FS1E, excellent condition, low mileage, winkers, *topbox. **1846** A. YOUNG *Naut. Dict.* 278 the Top-timber Line, or *top-breadth Line, a curve describing the height of the top-timbers, which gives the sheer of the vessel. **1574** in Feuillerat *Revels Q. Eliz.* (1908) 243 *Topp Buttons and frenge Lace. **1856** EMERSON *Eng. Traits* ii. 34 The mainmast, from the deck to the top-button, measured 115 feet. **1874** KNIGHT *Dict. Mech.* 470/1 These slats are called card-tops, *top-cards, or top-flats. **1827** G. HIGGINS *Celtic Druids* ii. §37. 78 It seems reasonable to expect that from these great *top casts, smaller ones should be found branching off to different countries. **1803** PLYMLEY *Agric. Shropsh.* 56 *Top-coal. **1841** HARTSHORNE *Salop. Antiq.* Gloss. **1879** MISS JACKSON *Shropsh. Word-bk.* 90. **1804** F. ASBURY *Jrnl.* 18 Apr. (1821) III. 136, I had heedlessly thrown off my *top-coat for a few hours, and caught cold. **1821** *Blackw. Mag.* Jan. 406/2 He had twa tap-coats and a plaid on. **1858** RAMSAY *Remin.* vi. (1870) 235 [He] offered the beggar an old top-coat. **1959** *Sears, Roebuck Catal.* Spring & Summer 1182/3 House paint undercoat... Insures longer wear.. and a smoother appearance of top coat. **1977** *Custom Car* Nov. 26/3 After three undercoats and four topcoats of Dulux Golden Yellow Coach Paint,.. Chris describes the finish as 'not bad'. **1819** R. ANDERSON *Cumberld. Ball.* 63 *Top-cwoatet squire. **1849** D. J. BROWNE *Amer. Poultry Yd.* (1855) 114 Artificial heat most ingeniously applied by '*top contact'. *Ibid.*, The difference ..between top-contact heat and that received from radiation as applied to hatching. **1919** H. ETHERIDGE *Dict. Typewriting* 68 If an error is made whilst taking carbon copies, it is a lengthy process to make the correction, as, in erasing the original or *top copy, the pressure of the eraser will make a bad smudge on the copies. **1967** L. MEYNELL *Mauve Front Door* vii. 89 If you could possibly do a top and two carbons of these notes. **1979** G. MITCHELL *Mudflats of Dead* II. xvi. 162 The bill is for typing a top copy and two carbons of a book. **1889** *Daily News* 29 June 6/3 He foresees a corresponding depression in what he calls 'the *top crops'. **1895** G. HUNTINGTON in *Chicago Advance* 19 Dec. 910/3 And it ain't top-crop rock, anyhow. **1890** *Breeder's Gaz.* (Chicago) 28 Mar. (Cent.), A filly with three *top crosses or a horse with four top crosses can be registered [in the stud-book]. **1957** *Practical Wireless* XXXIII. 706/1 Simple switched bass-boost and *top-cut compensation is provided by S1 and S2 respectively. **1962** A. NISBETT *Technique Sound Studio* ii. 35 There is no worse microphone defect.. for emphasizing any slight sibilance which may be present (and you cannot get rid of it by top cut if the emphasis lies in upper middle peaks). **1917** *Editor* 13 Jan. 33 **Top cutter*, first sergeant. **1930** T. FREDENBURGH *Soldiers March!* 279 It's a damn good book. Lots of swell dope for Top Cutters in it. **1948** *Record Changer* July 12/1 The *top cymbal has become the main tool of the bebop drummer. **1956** M. STEARNS *Story of Jazz* (1957) xviii. 234 Clarke made the single right-hand 'ride' or 'top' or 'front' cymbal the rhythmic center... The top cymbal was the only regular and continuous sound made by the drummer. **1924** E. C. M. SHEPHERD *Motor Car* ii. 23 When a piston is at the top of its stroke.. on the point of changing from an upward motion to a downward motion, it is said to have reached *top dead centre. **1978** *Vocab. Reciprocating Int. Combust. Engines* (*B.S.I.*) (1979) 7 *Top dead centre*, dead centre when the piston is farthest from the crankshaft. **1900** *Speaker* 28 Apr. 97/1 The most popular argument in favour of the war is that it will make the individual Briton *top dog in South Africa. **1906** P. WHITE *Eight Guests* (Tauchn.) I. 66 Marcus had never had a tussle yet without coming out 'top dog!' **1906** *Daily Chron.* 26 Mar. 6/4, I recall.. many in which I started as under-dog and came out top-dog. **1970** *Toronto Daily Star* 24 Sept. 15/9 He said Sault residents 'are paying *top dollar for a second-rate flight'. **1978** M. PUZO *Fools Die* xvi. 170 A lot of those guys.. had paid him top dollar to buy their enlistment in the six months' program. **1964** *Communications Assoc. Computing Machinery* VII. 80 [What are your general views regarding the merits of doing the syntax analysis from the 'top down' as against the 'bottom up'?] *Ibid.*, My analyzer is bottom-up and Warshall's is *top-down. **1969** R. BLACKBURN in Cockburn & Blackburn *Student Power* 178 Its officials are robbed of all real initiative by the requirements of rule obedience, top-down control and hierarchy. **1972** O. J. DAHL et al. *Structured Programming* p. v, Structured programming principles can be equally applied in 'bottom-up' as in 'top-down' program design. **1975** *Nature* 16 Oct. 548/1 Many somewhat different algorithms are properly classified as top-down parsing algorithms. **1976** *Eastern Daily Press* (Norwich) 16 Dec. 8/6 You take the familiar top-down view, pointing out the various problems which always beset constitutional changes. **1977** *N.Y. Rev. Bks.* 13 Oct. 28/1 The students were intent on showing that.. 'every decision was made top-down by the power structure'. **1979** *Personal Computer World* Nov. 74/2 The approach we shall take in programming this problem is known as 'Top-Down Design'. **1980** *Times* 9 Feb. 17/2 The emphasis in the latest public spending round has shifted from 'bottom up' planning, where spending totals are built up from the individual elements in the programmes, to 'top down' planning. **1905** H. A. VACHELL *The Hill* i, Such boys as a rule don't come out of the *top drawer. **1920** R. MACAULAY *Potterism* I. i. 10 The Potter family, however respectable now, wasn't really 'top-drawer'. **1946** *Sun* (Baltimore) 10 Oct. 12/2 The National Bureau of Economic Research, a top-drawer group of research economists. **1958** 'A. BRIDGE' *Portuguese Escape* iii. 42 The composed decision that somehow had so much distinction. 'She *is* out of the top drawer, isn't she?' **1959** *Vogue* Dec. 61 Vedonis also make ladies' underwear, sweaters, nightwear and bed jackets. They're top-drawer because everything about Vedonis is so good. **1960** *Guardian* 25 June 4/4 The word 'Hampstead' with all its associations of top-drawer socialism. **1976** *Time* 20 Dec. 10/3 Tanaka and four other Diet members linked to Lockheed's scheme to buy top-drawer influence and stimulate sales with more than $2 million in bribes were re-elected by loyal rural constituencies. **1977** C. MCCULLOUGH *Thorn Birds* vii. 149 Quite respectable, socially admissible, but not top drawer. Never top drawer. **1909** *Westm. Gaz.* 16 Nov. 5/2 The gear ratios are given as: 1st, 15 to 1; 2nd, 8.4 to 1; and on the *top-drive 4.7. **1933** F. E. BAUME *Tragedy Track* 93 She.. left again for the more human.. regions of the *Top End, where at least one could drink fresh water occasionally. **1969** *Northern Territory News* (Darwin) *Focus '69* 81/1 Beef roads.. will criss-cross the Top End with 665 miles of good bitumen. **1941** C. BARRETT *Coast of Adventure* 14 The old *Top-ender drank beer, which, to the men up there, is more desirable than iced nectar is to gods. **1961** T. RONAN *Only a Short Walk* 52 Any 'Top-Ender' who wanted ..a tip for the races.. went to Billy. **1902** *Encycl. Brit.* XXVI. 367/1 The system is called **top-fermentation*, because the type of yeast employed develops on the surface of the liquid, forming the 'head'. **1905** [see *bottom fermentation* s.v. BOTTOM *sb.* 20]. **1974** *Encycl. Brit. Macropædia* III. 161/2 Top fermentations are usually carried out using selected strains of *Saccharomyces cerevisiae*, botanically identical with bakers' yeast. **1874** *Top-flats [see *top-card*]. **1939** R. CHANDLER *Big Sleep* xx. 150 *Top-flight racketeers have business brains. **1958** *Times* 19 July 3/4 Lifting himself into the top flight of English batsmen. **1959** J. THURBER *Years with Ross* viii. 138 Reporters.. joined the staff, all of them top flight. **1967** *Punch* 20 Dec. 951/3 Good though it is, it isn't top-flight. **1979** E. NEWMAN *Sunday Punch* xv. 123 Every successful fighter when he reaches a point just below the top flight. **1981** *Beautiful Brit. Columbia* Fall 37 The University of Victoria, with its new, acoustically exuberant auditorium, is the scene now for many top-flight performances. **1950** 'M. INNES' *Hare sitting Up* II. ii. 52 He lives on his nerves, as so many *top-flighters do. **1959** J. DEMPSEY *Championship Fighting* v. 21 If you boast only nine professional fights, there's little danger of your being tossed in with a top-flighter or a champion. **1884** *Pall Mall G.* 15 Aug. 2/1, (1) *Top fruit, such as apples, pears, plums, cherries, medlars, and quinces; (2) bush fruit..; (3) ground fruit. **1903** *Q. Rev.* Oct. 390 A plantation of top and bottom fruit. **1884** PAE *Eustace* 100 He's a trim craft as I would not like to damage in the *top-gear. **1909** *Westm. Gaz.* 28 Jan. 4/1 Handcross and Reigate, both of which the Napier can stealthily scale on top-gear and think nothing of it. **1910** *Ibid.* 21 Apr. 5/2 The extraordinary top-gear hill-climbing powers of the Ford. **1932** E. BOWEN *To North* xxii. 235, I can't live at top gear. **1973** *Nature* 13 Apr. 440/1 The coal industry must now put its research and development programmes into top gear. **1897** BAILEY *Princ. Fruit-growing* 342 It will probably pay to *top-graft them. **1912** F. A. WAUGH *Beginners' Guide Fruit Growing* i. 13 Trees for *top-grafting may be of almost any age. **1975** W. E. SHEWELL-COOPER *Compost Fruit Grower* viii. 118 Many of the trees consist of quite unsuitable varieties... It is, therefore, worth realising that top-grafting methods may be adopted which will convert one variety into another. **1912** 'B. M. BOWER' *Flying U Ranch* 201 We can both safely consider ourselves *top-hands when it comes to lying. **1955** R. P. HOBSON *Nothing too Good for Cowboy* i. 12 It will be impossible to line up enough top hands to carry on. **1972** T. A. BULMAN *Kamloops Cattlemen* iii. 19 They were all top hands with either saddle or work horses. **1834–5** J. PHILLIPS *Man. Geol.* (1855) 190 The thickest coal in the district, called the '*top hard', is the same bed as that called the thick or ten-foot coal in Yorkshire. **1867** W. W. SMYTH *Coal & Coal-mining* 56 Cutting the top-hard coal at 510 yards deep. **1883** GRESLEY *Gloss. Coal Mining*, **Top Heads* (S.S.), passages driven in the upper part of the Thick coal for draining off the gas. **1842** LOUDON *Suburban Hort.* 501 That lively heat within the frame, which is usually called *top-heat. **1905** *Dundee Advert.* 23 Jan. 5 The victims.. at the time of the explosion were engaged widening the '*tophole' between No. 6 and No. 7 levels. **1899** DOYLE *Duet* vi. 74 We certainly did ourselves up to the top hole last night. **1908** E. V. LUCAS *Over Bemertons* ii, 'A top-hole idea', he called it. **1909** *Blackw. Mag.* Sept. 409/1 A piece like the Merry Widow.. would be top-hole. **1700** PRIOR *Carmen Seculare* 478 Let all the naval world due homage pay; With hasty reverence their *top-honours lower. **1803** T. NETHERTON in *Naval Chron.* XV. 220 Shipwrights employed in the capstern and *top house. **1815** J. SMITH *Panorama Sc. & Art* I. 108 It is always necessary to make the *top-iron fit the blade so correctly that no shaving can get between them. **1918** J. E. RENDINELL *Diary* 28 Mar. in *One Man's War* (1928) viii. 63 The old *top-kick would make a running dive for the dugout. **1976** L. DEIGHTON *Twinkle, twinkle, Little Spy* vii. 70, I was a gunner, nineteen —youngest top-kick in the group. **1979** *Arizona Daily Star* 22 July A8/1 The president's appointment of Hamilton Jordan as the White House topkick. **1919** L. L. LINCOLN *Company C, Eleventh Engineers* 8 Veeder was our first *top-kicker. **1877** KINGLAKE *Crimea* VI. vi. 71 The high ..*topland or spine of Mount Inkerman. *Ibid.* 446 The Inkerman toplands. **1842** *Civil Eng. & Arch. Jrnl.* V. 60/1 The '*top lift' was deposited in spoil bank. **1901** *Daily Record & Mail* 28 Nov. 2 A new machine.. will do heel-shaving, rough scouring, fine scouring, heel-edge blacking, top-lift blacking, heel-burnishing, top-lift burnishing, and breasting. **1843** J. BALLANTINE *Gaberlunzie's Wallet* ix. 199 The speck of sky overhead looked not larger than a common *top-light or cupola. **1873** *Young Englishwoman* July 342/2 The top-lights were.. removed.. and whitewashing and painting were done. **1924** GALSWORTHY *White Monkey* II. ii. 131 A high room with rafters and a top light, and lots of pictures. **1972** P. DIAMAND in D. Sutton *Lett. R. Fry* I. 60 On the top floor was Roger's studio... It had a top light. **1911** W. J. LOCKE *Glory of Clementina Wing* xxiv. 374 The room, spacious and *top-lighted, was converted into a studio. **1932** F. L. WRIGHT *Autobiogr.* II. 152 The top-lighted interior created the effect of a great official family at work in day-lit, clean airy quarters. **1962** *Times* 16 May 5/5 The great, *top-lit room of the Whitechapel Gallery. **1979** *Jrnl. R. Soc. Arts* CXXVII. 655/1 The new galleries should be on the same level as the old and top-lit by natural light. **1904** *Amer. Inventor* 15 Apr. 184 The *toploader is the man who runs the greatest risks. **1968** *Which?* May 149/1 This machine is a top loader, but has a horizontal stainless steel drum—you have to lift the top lid before being able to open the doors of the wash drum. **1976** *Gramophone* Dec. 1084/3 Included in the 1977 Tandy catalogue..are..two new stereo cassette decks with Dolby—a front-loader..and a top-loader. **1978** *Nature* 18 May p. xviii/3 The Sartorius 3802MP electronic balance is a toploader of large capacity and high readability. **1976** *CB Mag.* June 59/1 (Advt.), And *top loading eliminates vehicle body obstructions, a common problem for base loaded antennas. **1884** *Bull. U.S. Nat. Museum* No. 27. 471 *Gambusia patruelis*..*Top Minnow..Southern United States, from Virginia to Texas. **1962** K. F. Lagler et al. *Ichthyology* vi. 180 The mouths are superior in most of the topminnows. **1848** *N. York Com. Adv.* 16 Oct. (Bartlett), To-day the editor of the *Union* is cheered to the very *top notch of joyous exultation..; to-morrow he is horrified. **1888** *N. York Herald* (Dixon), The effect of their [locusts'] blighting touch has not yet reached the top notch. **1900** *Billboard* 29 Dec. 8/1 The last is a top-notch figure, and it is reached no oftener than can be helped. **1910** I. K. Bangs *Pursuit of House-boat* iii. 51 My seamanship, which was top-notch for my day. **1928** *Amer. Speech* IV. 244 Some successful criminals escape getting a monicker, for they, especially top-notch con men and syndicate members, think it adds 'class' to be without one. **1902** *13th Rep. Kansas State Bd. Agric.* 64 There are not a sufficient number of '*top-notchers' to go around, the result being..the use of many inferior specimens. **1896** *Daily News* 28 Dec. 3/2 Another even more popular ballad (or whatever he calls it), known as 'Mary Jane's *Top-note'. **1908** A. Noyes *W. Morris* 54 Never once do we feel that he is exerting himself, or on his top-note. **1912** *Music Hall & Theatre Rev.* 7 Mar. 157/1 The divided '*top' of the bill happens with these two artistes. **1933** P. Godfrey *Back-Stage* xviii. 222 The London theatre queues provide a great variety of performances. At the top of the bill are a few well-organized teams of strolling players. **1965** *Times Lit. Suppl.* 25 Nov. 1047/4 The..top-of-the-bill entertainer. **1963** *Economist* 19 Oct. 301/1 The *top-of-the-line sporty version [of a car]. **1981** *Sci. Amer.* Feb. 4/1 (Advt.), The new, top-of-the-line HP 3000 Series 44 computer has up to double the throughput power and memory size of its predecessor. **1942** C. Spry *Come into Garden, Cook* v. 51 Make a mixture of tomato sauce..and a little '*top of the milk' cream. **1958** *Listener* 21 Aug. 287/2 Serve hot or cold, with cream or top of the milk. **1979** A. Parker *Country Recipe Notebk.* viii. 103 The milk..pasteurized..has no 'top of the milk'. **1884** Britten *Watch & Clockm.* 47 The full cap to full plate watches covers the *top plate. **1885** C. G. W. Lock *Workshop Receipts* Ser. iv. 327/1 Push out the pillar pins, and remove the top plate. **1613** Shaks. *Hen. VIII*, i. i. 151 This *top-proud fellow..I doe know To be corrupt and treasonous. **1679** Moxon *Mech. Exerc.* viii. 147 *Top-rail of the Balcony. **1823** P. Nicholson *Pract. Build.* Gloss., *Top-rail*, the upper rail of a piece of framing or wainscotting. **1867** Smyth *Sailor's Word-bk.*, *Upper* or **top-rider futtocks*, these timbers stand nearly the same as breadth-riders, and very much strengthen the topside. **1562** Phaer *Æneid* ix. Ddj, His *topright crest from crown downe battred falles. **1803** Plymley *Agric. Shropsh.* 56 *Top-rock 7 yds. 0 ft. 0 in. *a* **1879** in Miss Jackson *Shropsh. Word-bk.* 89 Soil,..Clay, ..Loose Rock,..Coal,..Blue Clod,..Red Clunch,..Top Rock,..White Clod,..Brown Clunch. **1728** Chambers *Cycl.* s.v. *Bit*, The several parts of a snaffle or curb bit are.. Trench, *Top-roll, Flap, and Jeive. **1877** Knight *Dict. Mech.* 2597/2 The *top-saw is a little in advance or rear of the under one, to make the kerf complete without collision of the teeth of the respective saws. **1960** J. Fingleton *Four Chukkas to Australia* 29 Huntington.. *top-scored with 73. **1977** *World of Cricket Monthly* June 26/3 Mohsin Khan batted well to top-score with 55. **1860** *Baily's Mag.* Aug. 367 The *top scorer for the Midland was Mr. J. H. Marshall. **1976** *Milton Keynes Express* 30 July 41/1 Arnold Mann was top scorer with a patient knock of 24. **1731** Lady B. Germain *Let. to Swift* 4 Nov., So much for your *topscript, not postscript;..I heartily thank you for remembering me so often. **1898** J. Bowe *Diary* 2 June in *With 13th Minnesota in Philippines* (1905) 12 The *top sergeant went around with a lantern. **1969** I. Kemp *Brit. G.I. in Vietnam* vii. 150 My immediate superior was First (or Top) Sergeant Rutledge, a dour and somewhat autocratic professional soldier in his early forties. **1747** Hooson *Miner's Dict.* Sij, There are some Veins when once discover'd, carry Ore of a whole Stool-end, twenty or thirty Yards in Depth..; then the Ore cuts off on the Sole, and the Vein becomes hard and streat, ..and endures so many Yards in Sinking, and then at last breaks over again, and the Ore proves to be as good and stronge as..before; these Levells are called Sets, as the first is the *Top-Set, the second which is found out by Sinking through the Deadness, is called the Under-Set. **1905** Chamberlin & Salisbury *Geol.* I. iii. 191 Deposition is also taking place on the top of the delta. These top-set beds are laid down in a nearly horizontal position. **1876** Miss Braddon *J. Haggard's Dau.* x, The sheets and table-cloths we *top-sewed when we were children. **1808** G. Ellis *Let.* in Lockhart *Scott* (1837) II. iv. 145, I should have ranked it ..on the very *top shelf of English poetry. **1882** Top-shelf [implied in *top-shelfer*]. **1891–2** *Lupton Bros. Catal.* Dec. and Jan., Gentlemen requiring scarce and top-shelf books. **1905** Hornung *Thief in Nt.* (Tauchn.) 12 'Nice house?' said Raffles... 'Top shelf,' said I. **1882** *N. York Tribune* 12 July, The rich tourist, or as the frontiersman calls him, 'the *top-shelfer', who goes about with guides and a luxurious outfit. **1905** Ihlseng & Wilson *Man. Mining* (ed. 4) i. iii. 79 (*heading*) *Top-slicing and caving. *Ibid.* (*caption*) A system of top-slicing the ore. **1963** *Economist* 23 Mar. 1141/2 Other taxpayers..deserve some form of relief by 'top-slicing'. **1973** L. J. Thomas *Introd. Mining* vi. 209 Top slicing is more suitable for large horizontal deposits. *Ibid.*, Small pillars that could be top sliced are more likely to be recovered by cut and fill methods or to be abandoned. **1983** *Sunday Tel.* 5 June 28/7 If the recipient pays tax above the basic, 'top slicing' relief is provided to mitigate the effect of taxing the whole gain in one year. **1836, 1850** *Top-soil [see encallow *sb.*]. **1868** *Rep. U.S. Commissioner Agric.* (1869) 169 Mild loamy top soil, with a subsoil more tough. **1904** *Archæol. Æliana* XXV. ii. 253 A foot-and-a-half of blackish top-soil. **1967** *Antiquaries Jrnl.* XLVII. 188 In 1965 the stripping of the turf and topsoil from the rampart defences ..exposed the top of the wall and an internal tower. **1975** J. G. Evans *Environment Early Man Brit. Isles* vi. 128 Chalk waste bringing about the burial of topsoil and the destruction of what may have been valuable pasture or arable land. **1860** Worcester, **Top-soiling*, the act of taking off the top-soil. **1926** Anderson & Stallings *What Price Glory?* in *Three Amer. Plays* i. 10 I'm the new *top soldier here. **1935** *Our Army* Nov. 39 Top Soldier Rawhide was sitting in the NCO club. **1913** *Daily Mail* 7 July 9/2 A good straight ball, with *top spin, that comes off the ground very quickly. **1934** *Punch* 7 Feb. 141/1 She has thrown her husband out of the house sixty-one times, but he always returned. It looks as if she put too much top-spin on him. **1977** *Time* 4 July 10/3 Guillermo Vilas,..winner of the French Open last month, never could get his big topspin game going on grass. **1980** *Times Lit. Suppl.* 12 Sept. 983/5 Such existentialist propositions..sound pedestrian when summarized. The kind of intellectual top-spin required to give them philosophic solemnity is supplied. **1921** P. F. Warner *My Cricketing Life* x. 194 A. R. Littlejohn.. bowled an occasional *top spinner which came very quickly off the ground. **1975** *Times* 13 Aug. 6/8 Intikhab..beat him with a top-spinner and hit his middle stump. **1969** *New Yorker* 14 June 44/3 He just can't hit a heavily *top-spun backhand. **1977** *Sunday Times* (Perth, Austral.) 16 Jan. 11/4 The large crowd..reserved their warmest applause for some Wilkinson top-spun forehand lobs. **1960** *Lebende Sprachen* V. 35/3 **Top stitch*, Steppstich, steppen. **1964** *McCall's Sewing* vii. 100/2 Faced edges should be top-stitched to keep them flat. **1976** N. C. Anders *Appliqué Old & New* v. 104 Bind edge of each potholder with double fold bias tape. Cut two 2½″ strips for loops. Topstitch edges. Attach to potholder. **1934** A. L. Hird *Needlework & Dressmaking* v. 100 List of seams..plain lapped = *top stitched. **1975** *New Yorker* 17 Nov. 138/2 Bottega Veneta has some splendid wrist-length styles..in topstitched pigskin. **1947** C. Talbot *Compl. Bk. Sewing* xxi. 145/1 *Top-stitching is the frank use of stitching on the outside of a dress, suit or coat to emphasize lines that are important in the design. **1979** *Tucson* (Arizona) *Citizen* 20 Sept. 2b/1 Remove any top-stitching to 4 inches above the 'new' hemline. **1855** Macaulay *Hist. Eng.* xiii. III. 347 From a window in the *top story of one of the loftiest of those gigantic houses. **1903** [Ld. W. Neville] *Penal Servitude* 150 [Prisoners] who are more or less touched in the top story. **1904** *Daily Chron.* 9 May 8/4 In every top-storey window the machinery can be seen working. **1690** J. Wodrow in *Life* (1828) 112 These may be named the *Tap-swarm. *a* **1905** *Eng. Dial. Dict.* s.v. *Top*, Twea topswarms 'll mak' a strang hive. **1856** Aird *Poet. Wks.* 404 The unfinished skep For June *top-swarmers. **1964** *Guardian* 7 Oct. 10/1 (*heading*) At the *top table in Washington. *a* **1974** R. Crossman *Diaries* (1976) II. 125 We found ourselves at the top table. I was sitting opposite the Bishop of London and next to the wife of a City alderman. **1977** 'J. le Carré' *Hon. Schoolboy* i. viii. 191, I have a standing instruction..to repair our American liaison. .. 'To get us back at the top table.' **1983** *Daily Tel.* 1 Mar. 16/4 A late guest [at the St. David's Day banquet] will be Simon Hughes, Liberal victor of Bermondsey—too late to get a place on the top table. **1839** *Knickerbocker* XIII. 385 'There she *top-tails! there she blows!' added he,..after taking a long look at the sporting shoal. **1958** J. Asman in P. Gammond *Decca Bk. Jazz* xiv. 174 Traditional jazz records vie with the accepted 'pop' *Top Ten in selling power. **1960** *News Chron.* 7 May 3/5 Buxton will have to change..to make the tourist top ten. **1979** E. H. Gombrich *Ideas & Idols* 157 It [*sc.* a Beethoven Quartet] will never belong to the top ten. But it does belong to the canon. **1981** R. D. Edwards *Corridors of Death* v. 22 One of the country's top ten management whizz-kids. **1808–18** Jamieson, **Tapthrawn*, adj.,..having the..top or head distorted; or in allusion to the hair of the head lying in an awkward and unnatural manner. **1819** W. Tennant *Papistry Storm'd* (1827) 194 A tap-thrawn monk wi' roundit cap. **1877** Knight *Dict. Mech.*, **Top-tool*, a blacksmith's tool..used above the work, being struck by a hammer. **1959** 'F. Newton' *Jazz Scene* (1960) xiii. 236 Jazz has until recently simply not been big business in Britain, in the terms in which those who prepare records for the 'hit parade' of the 'top ten' or '*top twenty' think of it. **1962** *Listener* 20 Sept. 451/3 TAM puts the repeats of *Steptoe and Son* in the top twenty week after week. **1982** *Daily Tel.* 15 Apr. 16/6 All we need now is a royal baby named George.., and the name may be back in the top 20 once more! **1895** T. S. Lawley *Lessons in Woodwork Drawing* 10 The *top view of a penny ..placed on a table will be a circle. **1912** V. C. Getty *How to Read a Drawing* i. 8 As we were..looking at the top of the object, this view would be known as the top view, or plan view. **1953** A. C. Parkinson *Pictorial Drawing for Engineers* vi. 44/1 We commence by drawing a true-shape top view or plan view of the object. **1881** Raymond *Mining Gloss.*, **Top-wall*. See *Hanging-wall*. *Ibid.*, *Hanging-side* or *Hanging-wall*, or *Hanger* (Cornw.), the wall or side over the vein. **1778** W. Pryce *Min. Cornub.* 21 A very large proportion of our Mine Water is temporary; and..is denominated *Top Water. **1894** *Northumbld. Gloss.*, *Top-watter*, water percolating through the roof of a coal mine. **1945** *Richmond* (Va.) *Times-Dispatch* 21 Sept. 18/2 It is well to try your top-water lures first, and if they fail, then try the under-water varieties. **1980** *Hunting Ann. 1981* 36/2 Rather than look for a long stick or get clothing and boots wet and muddy, the hunter can use a multihooked topwater lure and cast for his bird. **1892** *Daily News* 28 Mar. 3/5 It looks as if the *top-weights are in the Grand National precluded from winning... It is time the top-weights had a chance in this event. **1896** *Ibid.* 19 Feb. 2/6 Another top-weight got home safely in the February Hurdle Handicap, Doge, about whom as little as 3 to 1 was taken. **1883** *Maine Agric. Rep.* XXVI. 342 The Bourassa..does well *top-worked on a strong stock, and then produces bountifully of apples. **1910** Paddock & Whipple *Fruit-Growing in Arid Regions* ix. 150 It seldom pays to top-work any crab. **1968** *Punch* 27 Mar. 466/2 Though apples can be 'top worked' by grafting another kind on the sawn off branch ends, no peach will stand this treatment. **1934** Webster, *Top-worked. **1974** *Country Life* 28 Nov. 1660/1 Topworked trees, that is those which are grafted at the top of a standard stem and trunk. **1897** L. H. Bailey *Princ. Fruit-Growing* v. 235 Some persons have proposed to sow seeds in the very spot where the trees are to stand, and thereby to raise stocks for *top-working without transplanting them. **1946** *Nature* 28 Dec. 941/2 There is a particularly good chapter on top-working and frame-working, but that on pruning might have been improved.

35. From senses 9 and 9 b; (*top* being also short for *topsail* or *topmast*), as: **a.** ***top-bowline***, ***-lift*** (lift *sb.*[2] 7; see also 34), ***-sheet***, ***-shroud***, ***-stay***, ***-yard***. **b.** †**top-arming**, **top-armour**, †**top-arms** (*pl.*): see quots. *a* 1625, 1867; **top-block**, a large block suspended below the cap of the lower mast, used in hoisting or lowering topmasts (see also 34); **top-brim**: see quot. 1794, and cf. *top-rim*; **top-burton**: see quot. 1867 and burton[1]; also *attrib.*; **top-chain**, a chain used to sling the yards in action, in case the ropes by which they are hung should be shot away; **top-cloth**: see quot. and cf. *top-armour*; **top-lantern**, **top-light**: see quot. 1867; **top-lining**, topsail-lining: see quots.; also 'a platform of thin board nailed upon the upper part of the cross-trees on a vessel's top' (Smyth); **top-maul**: see quot. 1867; †**top-nail**, ? = fid *sb.*[2]; **top-nettings** *sb. pl.*: see *top-armour* (quot. 1867); **top-pendant**, a pendant used in hoisting and lowering topmasts (*Cent. Dict.* 1891); **top-rail**: see quot. (also 34); **top-rim** = *top-brim*; **top-rope**: see quot. *a* 1625; ***to sway*** (erron. ***swing***) (***away***) ***on all top-ropes***, to go to great lengths; so ***to be on*** (***the***) ***top-ropes***; †**top-royal**, short for *top-gallant royal*: see topgallant; †**top-ship**, a ship having tops; = topman[1] 1; **top-tackle**, a tackle used in raising or lowering topmasts. See also top-castle, topgallant, topman[1], topmast, topsail.

1486 *Naval Acc. Hen. VII* (1896) 14 A *Top Armyng of say. **1867** Smyth *Sailor's Word-bk.*, *Top-armings*, hammocks stowed inside the rigging for the protection of riflemen. **1485** *Cely Papers* (Camden) 184 Item ij ȝerdes di rede..for the *topearmer... Item an ȝerde of wyght for the same. **1514** *Inv. Henri Grace de Dieu* in Oppenheim *Admin. Roy. Navy* (1896) I. 377 Top Armours..vii. *a* **1625** *Nomenclator Navalis* (Harl. MS. 2301), *Topparmors* are the clothes which are tied aboute the Tops of the mastes for shewe and also for to hide menn in the Fight which lie there to fling fire-potts [etc.]. **1823** Crabb *Technol. Dict.* s.v. *Top*. **1867** Smyth *Sailor's Word-bk.* s.v. *Top*, This top was formerly fenced on the afterside by a rail about three feet high, between the stanchions of which a netting was usually constructed, and stowed in action with hammocks. This was covered with red baize, or canvas painted red, and called the top-armour. *c* **1599** *MS. Otho E. ix.* in Bree *Cursory Sk. Nav., Mil. & Civ. Estab.* (1791) I. 217 For waste cloaths and *top-arms. **1769** Falconer *Marine Dict.* (1776) s.v. *Block*, The *top-block is used to hoist up or lower down the top-masts, and is for the purpose hooked in an eye-bolt driven into the cap. **1762** —— *Shipwr.* ii. 149 The halyards and *top-bow-lines soon are gone. **1730** Capt. W. Wriglesworth *MS. Log-bk. of the 'Lyell'* 30 Nov., Arm'd the fore Shrouds, Matted the *Top-brims. **1794** *Rigging & Seamanship* I. 90 *Top-brim*, a space in the middle of the foot of a topsail, containing one-fifth of the number of its cloths, ..so called from..being near the fore part of the top,.. when the sail is extended. **1797** *Encycl. Brit.* (ed. 3) XVII. 433/2 The holes for marling the clues of sails and the top-brims of topsails have grommets of log-line. *c* **1860** H. Stuart *Seaman's Catech.* 46 The topmen will hand out the *top burtons. **1867** Smyth *Sailor's Word-bk.*, *Burton*, a small tackle..generally used to set up or tighten the shrouds, whence it is frequently termed a top-burton tackle. **1698** in *MSS. Ho. Lords* N.S. (1905) III. 344 Asked if the *top-chains, davits and fishes were made use of to make a boom. **1772–84** Cook *Voy.* (1790) VI. 1989 The boats were moored with top-chains. **1815** Burney *Falconer's Dict. Marine*, **Top-Cloth*, a large piece of canvas, used to cover the hammocks which are lashed in the top when prepared for action. **1748** *Anson's Voy.* i. x. 98 the main top-sail shook so strongly in the wind, that it carried away the *top lanthorn. **1867** Smyth *Sailor's Word-bk.*, *Top-lantern*, or *Top-light*, a large signal lantern placed in the after-part of a top. **1485** *Naval Acc. Hen. VII* (1896) 48 Toppe yerdes..j, *Toppe lyftes..ij. **1809** J. Thicknesse in *Naval Chron.* XXII. 57, I carried a *top-light. **1794** *Rigging & Seamanship* I. 93 The *toplining of topsails is of canvas, No. 6 or 7. **1882** Nares *Seamanship* (ed. 6) 11 *Top lining.*—Double part on the after side of a topsail, to take the chafe of the top, etc. **1726** Shelvocke *Voy. round World* 214 The *top mall, which being made fast to the head of the main-mast, was wash'd ashore. **1867** Smyth *Sailor's Word-bk.*, *Top-maul*, a large hammer used to start the topmast fid, and to beat down the top, when setting up topmast-rigging. **1352** *Acc. Excheq. Q.R.* Bundle 20 No. 27 (P.R.O.) Pro quadam clav[o] ferri vocato **toppenaill*' pro eodem mast. **1769** Falconer *Dict. Marine* (1789), *Cercles de hune*, the *top rails, which formerly surrounded the tops, when circular. *Ibid.* (1780) s.v. *Out-rigger*, It is then thrust out to it's usual distance beyond the *top-rim, where it is securely fastened. *a* **1625** *Nomenclator Navalis* (Harl. MS. 2301), **Top-Roapes* are those Roapes wherewith wee sett or strike the Top-mastes. **1762** Falconer *Shipwr.* ii. 259 At each mast-head the top-ropes others bend. **1864** Burton *Scot Abr.* I. iii. 119 Apt to attempt feats..in nautical phrase, 'to swing on all top-ropes'. **1867** Smyth *Sailor's Word-bk.* s.v., 'Swaying on all the top-ropes', figuratively, 'going the whole hog' in joviality or any trickery. **1868** W. Pengelly in H. Pengelly *Life* xii. (1897) 188 The veteran..was on the top ropes about the meeting. **1500–20** Dunbar *Poems* lxxxviii. 30 Thy Ryuer..Where many a ship doth rest with *toppe-royall. **1485** *Naval Acc. Hen. VII* (1896) 48 Toppe lyftes.. ij, *Toppe shetes..ij. **1562** Phaer *Æneid* viii. Ziv, His crowne couragious shines with garland wun from *topshipsnout. **1631** Weever *Anc. Fun. Mon.* 718 Two and fifty religious structures, as many wind-mils, and as many toppe Ships in Dunwich. **1485** *Naval Acc. Hen. VII* (1896) 48 Toppe mastes..j, *Toppe shrowdes..vj. **1751** Smollett *Per. Pic.* (1779) IV. xcviii. 275 'Split my *topstay-sail', said he. **1769** Falconer *Dict. Marine* (1789) Bbiij, To the lower end of the top-rope is fixed the *top-tackle. **1485** *Naval Acc. Hen. VII* (1896) 48 Toppe mastes ..j, Toppe shrowdes..vj, *Toppe yerdes..j.

36. In sense 2 b, as ***top-dyeing***, ***-maker***, ***-making***, ***-master***, (***tops-***)***mill***; †**topwork**, wool-combing.

1888 *Daily News* 16 Apr. 2/7 Merino tops are firm in price, ..though *top makers are said to have little margin for profit. **1891** *Labour Commission* Gloss. s.v., Some woolstaplers are also 'top-makers', i.e., woolcombers. In woolcombing the long smooth fibres are combed out into 'tops', so called from the form in which the 'ribbon' of wool is coiled upon its spindle being like a spinning top. **1896** *Balme & Co. Wool Brokers Circular* 15 May, Long-stapled parcels which..were largely purchased by the Bradford Topmakers. **1884** W. S. B. McLaren *Spinning* (ed. 2) 116 Balling or *Top-Making.—One other process follows combing..namely, balling, or making into 'tops'. **1902** *Times* 6 Nov. 10/5 *Top-masters report a fair trade during the week at satisfactory prices. **1909** *Edin. Rev.* Oct. 284 He was building the largest *tops mill in the United States. **1637** *Bury Wills* (Camden) 169 A great deale of *topworke abroad at spynners.

top (tɒp), *sb.*[2] Also 4–6 toppe, 4 topp (toop); (7– *Sc.* tap). [A word of difficult history, found (app.) in late OE. (*c* 1060) as *top*, also *c* 1325 in Walter de Bibbesworth (AFr. and Eng.), and common from late 14th c. onward. There are words coinciding in sense, and app. related in form, both in German and French, but their phonological relations are not normal: see Note below.]

1. a. A toy of various shapes (cylindrical, obconic, etc.), but always of circular section, with a point on which it is made to spin, usually by the sudden pulling of a string wound round it; the common ***whip-*** or ***whipping-top*** is kept spinning by lashing it with a whip.

Other tops, as the peg-top, are spun in the same way, but not whipped; some are spun by the action of a spring. ***humming-top***, a hollow top, usually of metal, with perforations, which makes a humming noise in spinning. ***parish top***, ***town top***, a large top kept for public use, which two players or parties whipped in opposite directions. See also quot. 1911.

[*c* **1060** *Apollonius of Tyre* (Thorpe) 13 Mid ʒelæredre handa he swang þone top mid swa micelre swiftnesse, þæt þam cynge wæs ʒeþuht swilce he of ylde to iuʒuðe ʒewænd wære.] *c* **1325** *Gloss. W. de Bibbesw.* I. 39 (Camb. MS.) En la rue iuez au toup [*All Souls MS.* a toop]; *Gloss. All Souls* [In the] strete plaies þe toop, *Camb. MS.* atte toppe, *B.M. Arundel* a top of tre. **13..** *K. Alis.* 1727 (Bodl. MS.) þere fore, ich habbe þee ysent, A top and scourge to present. *Ibid.* 1756 þe Top þat is rounde aboute, Signefieþ also saunz doute, þat þe werlde þat þe rounde is, Shal be myne also I wys. **1398** Trevisa *Barth. De P.R.* iii. xvii. (1495) d iiij b/1 All þe lynes pt ben drawe fro all pe partyes of þe thynge pt is seen, make aperaunce, shapen as a toppe, and the poynt therof is in pe black of the eye, and the brode ende in þe thynge pt is seen, as in this fygure & shappe. *c* **1400** *Destr. Troy* 1624 Soche soteltie þai soght to solas hom with; The tables, the top, tregetre also. *c* **1425** *St. Christina* xxiv. in *Anglia* VIII. 128/36 Whirlynge about as a scoprelle or a toppe þat childer pleye with. *c* **1440** *Promp. Parv.* 496/2 Top, of chylderys pley, *trochus.* **1567** Drant *Horace, Art Poet.* B iv, The stoole ball, top, or camping ball if suche one should assaye. **1581** Mulcaster *Positions* ix. (1887) 54 Fensing, and scourging the Top. **1601** [see parish *sb.* 7]. **1616–61** Holyday *Persius* iii. (1673) 311 For the scourgstick I did strive, That none his top with greater art might drive. **1623** [see town 10]. **1628** Wither *Brit. Rememb.* Pref. 209 Are no more worthy of my serious hopes, Then Ratles, Pot-guns, or the Schoole-boyes Tops. **1697** R. Peirce *Bath Mem.* i. x. 235 To play at Trap, and Top and Scourge, with the Boys. **1838–43** C. Knight *Pict. Shaks., Twel. N.* i. iii. *note*, The *town-top* and the *parish-top* were one and the same. The custom..existed in the time of Elizabeth, and probably long before, of a large top being provided for the amusement of the peasants in frosty weather. **1851** [see humming *ppl. a.* 1 c]. **1868** Lockyer *Guillemin's Heavens* (ed. 3) 457 The motion of our globe has often been compared..to that of a top. **1911** *Encycl. Brit.* XXVII. 47/2 Other kinds of tops are made as supports for coloured disks which on revolving show a kaleidoscopic variation of patterns. The top is also used in certain games of chance, when it is generally known as a 'teetotum'.

b. As the type of a sound sleeper, in reference to the apparent stillness of a spinning top when its axis of rotation is vertical: cf. sleep *v.* B. 3 c; esp. in ***to sleep like*** (***as sound*** or ***as fast as***) ***a top***: cf. sleep *v.* B. 1 e. †Rarely *fig.* = sound sleeper.

c **1616** Fletcher & Massinger *Thierry & Theod.* v. ii, I will assure you, he can sleep no more Than a hooded Hawk; a centinel to him, Or one of the City Constables are tops. **1693** Congreve *Old Bach.* i. 8 'Tis but well lashing him, and he will sleep like a Top. **1711** Ramsay *On Maggy Johnstoun* x, I took a nap..As sound's a tap. **1763** Mrs. F. Sheridan *Discov.* i. ii, In two minutes I was as fast as a top. **1909** G. Tyrell in *Q. Rev.* July 106 Its [a perfect life's] quiet is that of a sleeping top,—the ease of intense well-balanced activity.

2. A marine gastropod having a short conical shell; any species of the genus *Trochus* or family *Trochidæ*; a top-shell. In earliest use, ***sea top***.

a **1682** Sir T. Browne *Norf. Fishes* Wks. 1835 IV. 332 Also *trochi, trochili*, or sea tops, finely variegated and pearly. **1856** Gosse *Mar. Zool.* ii. 118 *Trochus* (Linn.), Top. Shell pyramidal, nearly flat at the base. **1857** Wood *Com. Objects Sea Shore* 25 Little shells, called Tops from their form... One of the most beautiful of these shells, the Livid Top (*Trochus ziziphinus*).

3. *Rope-making.* (Also ***laying-top***.) See quots.

1794 *Rigging & Seamanship* I. 58 *Tops*, to lay ropes,..are conical pieces of wood, with three or four grooves..from the butt to the end, for the strands to lie in, and form a triangle. **1797** *Encycl. Brit.* (ed. 3) XVI. 485/1 The top comes away from the swivel..and the line begins to lay. **1841** *Penny Cycl.* XX. 154/2 A piece of wood called a *top*, in the form of a truncated cone, being placed between the strands, and kept during the operation gently forced into the angle formed by the strands, where they are united by the closing or twisting of the rope. **1877** Knight *Dict. Mech.* s.v., The top is forced as far as possible toward the sledge-hook, so as to allow the twist to commence at that end, the top giving way as the twist crowds it forward to the head end of the yarns.

[Some would refer to this word 'top of flax or wool': see top *sb.*[1] 2.]

4. *attrib.* and *Comb.*, as ***top-fashion***, ***-shape***, ***-spinner***, ***-spinning*** (sb. and adj.), ***-string***; ***top-giddy***, ***-like***, ***-shaped*** adjs.; **top minor** (*Ropemaking*): see quot. 1835–6; **top-shell** = sense 2; **top-wise** *adv.*, like a top, in the manner of a top. See also topman[2].

1824 J. Symmons tr. *Æschylus' Agam.* 60 They vanish'd in deep night, *Top-giddy, whirl'd about, or scatter'd wide. *c* **1711** Petiver *Gazophyl.* vii. 65 A small Pyramidal or *Toplike Shell. **1895** I. B. Richman *Appenzell* xi. 195 To execute..a series of top-like revolutions about the room. **1793** J. D. Belfour *Specif. Patent* No. 1939. 10 To prevent the strand from being twisted too quick, I have introduced an instrument which I call the *top minor. **1835–6** *Encycl. Metrop.* (1845) VIII. 754/2 The yarns were all united.. round the notches of an implement which he [J. D. Belfour] called a *top minor*. **1776** J. Lee *Introd. Bot.* Explan. Terms 394 *Turbinatum*, *top-shaped, like an obverse cone. *c* **1711** Petiver *Gazophyl.* Dec. vii. Tab. 70 The large Barbadoes Magpye *Top-shell. **1885** C. F. Holder *Marvels Animal Life* 83 Usually a Top-shell (*Trochus*). *a* **1913** *Top-spinning [listed in *N.E.D.*]. **1964** *Catal. National Mus. Kuala Lumpur* 3/1 Dioramas present aspects of Malay dances, Kelantan top spinning, [etc.]. **1979** *Arizona Daily Star* 5 Aug. b 5/3 For relaxation, the brothers have taken up juggling, motocross bike-riding and top-spinning. **1855** Mrs. Gaskell *Lizzie Leigh & Other Tales* 247 He had been the..Robin Good-fellow of the neighbourhood..whose *top-strings were always hanging in nooses to catch the unwary. **1398** Trevisa *Barth. De P.R.* iii. xvii. (Tollem. MS.), þe syȝte is nouȝt mad but by a piramys schape a *top wise [orig. *per piramidem*; **1535** shapen top wise] pt comeþ to þe ye. *Ibid.* x. v, In the moost ouermest poynt of his shappe that is a topwyse the flamme is moost hote. **1900** F. T. Bullen *Idylls of Sea* v. 27 The angry currents..whirling us topwise in defiance of wind and helm.

[*Note.* The meaning of *top* in the OE. quot. is only inferential, as the OE. *Apollonius* here diverges from the Latin original, which contains no such terms as *turbo*, *trochus* or other word meaning 'top'; but it is difficult to see what else the OE. word could mean. In *c* 1325 the sense is clear. On the continent, the name of the toy in Holland generally is now *tol*; but *top* is used in East and West Flanders, Antwerp, and parts of Brabant; also in Friesland, Groningen, and Drente, in the North Netherlands; but this has not been found earlier than 1500. In Brussels, Mechlin, South Brabant generally, and Limburg, the form used is *dop*. *Dop*, *doppe*, was also the MDu. form, occurring from 13th c., and was the normal LG. equivalent of OHG. *topfo*, *topf*, MHG. *topfe*, *topf*, Ger. dial. *topf* (= Ger. *kreisel*) in this sense. Of this comparatively late substitution of *top* for *dop* in Flemish, etc., no explanation appears, and it does not help to account for the use of *top* in English in 1060 or even in 1325. The most that could be suggested would be that the word meaning *turbo* or *trochus* has in both cases run together in form with that meaning *apex* (top *sb.*[1]). On the other hand, the use in 1325 of an Anglo-French *toup* (*toop*) in this sense seems to form a link with F. *toupie* (also †*topie*) and its kindred words, OF. *topet*, or *toupet*[2], *obs. F. toupin*, and the derivative vbs. OF. *topier* or *toupier*, *topiner* or *toupiner*, and *toupiller*. But the etymology of *toupie* and its family is beset by as many difficulties as that of *top*; it does not answer in form to either OHG. *topfo* or MLG. *doppe*.]

†**top**, *sb.*[3] *Obs.* Also 5 toppe. [a. MLG., MFl. *toppe*, *top* (14–15th c.) basket (as a measure of raisins, figs, etc.): cf. MLG. *top* basket, as a measure of grapes (Walther-Lubben), MDu. *topkine* (*c* 1334), *toppen* (1486), *top van vijghen* basket of figs (Kilian); OF. (Picard) *toppe* (cf. *trois toppes ou vaisseaulx*). See also toppet[2] and cf. tap *sb.*[3], *topnet*, tapnet.] A basket, as a measure of grapes or figs.

1440–1 *Durham Acc. Rolls* (Surtees) 78 It. in ij sorttes ficuum et racemorum magnorum cum viij toppes racemorum magnorum. **1530–1** *Durham Househ. Bk.* (Surtees) 44, 7 fraylls ficuum et 1 tope racemorum magnorum.

top (tɒp), *v.*[1] Also (5 toppyn), 6–7 toppe, (7 tope). [f. top *sb.*[1], in various senses.]

I. †**1.** *intr.* To fight, struggle, strive. *Obs.*

[For the original sense of this and its connexion with that of the sb., cf. obs. Du. '*toppen*, *tobben* crines pugnando invadere, crinibus apprehendere' (Kilian); Ger. *zupfen*, formerly *zopfen* to pull by the hair, pull, pluck.]

c **1305** *Pilate* 15 in *E.E.P.* (1862) 111 þat child..and pilatus also..to-gadere were ido As hi wexe hi toppede ofte, þer nas bituene hem no loue Ac þat child riȝt biȝute euer was aboue. *c* **1315** Shoreham vii. 577 Ac þo hy hedde ine heuene y-topped Wy nedde hy be ine helle y-stopped For evere mo. *c* **1440** *Promp. Parv.* 496/2 Toppyn, or fechte be the nekke (..*P.* feightyn by the nek).

II. To deprive of the top.

†**2.** *trans.* To cut *off* (the hair of the head), poll (the head), crop (a person). *Obs.*

c **1330** *Arth. and Merl.* (Kölbing) 7715 For diol he topped of his hare And him self tobete and tare. **14..** *Beryn* 2917 Getith a peir sisours, sherith my berd..And aftirward lete top my hede. **1632** *Star Chamb. Cases* (Camden) 112 Lord Privy Seale..found great fault with his long ruffian-like haire, and would have topped him if the vote of the Court had been for it.

3. a. To cut off the top of (a growing tree, a plant, or the like); to poll or pollard (a tree); to lop, prune, or shorten back (branches or shoots); to cut or break off the head, flower, or ear of (a plant), the withered calyx from (a gooseberry or other fruit); often in phr. ***to top and lop***, ***top and tail***.

1509 *Brasenose Coll. Doc.* C[2] 40 He shall toppe ne byhede Elme Asshe ne Oke. **1616** *MS. Acc. St. John's Hosp., Canterb.*, Payd for toping of treses. **1637** Earl Monm. tr. *Malvezzi's Romulus & Tarq.* 225 Hee tops off the heads of the highest flowers. **1649** Lovelace *Grass-hopper* iv, Sharpe frosty fingers all your Flow'rs have topt. **1688** J. Clayton in *Phil. Trans.* XVII. 982 They top their Tobacco, that is, take away the little top-bud. **1794** *Rigging & Seamanship* I. 58 *Topping and Tailing* is the clearing both ends of the hemp with the hatchell. **1824** L. M. Hawkins *Mem.*, etc. II. 52 A gentleman..was topping and tailing gooseberries for wine. **1894** R. H. Elliot *Gold, Sport*, etc. *in Mysore* 387 Some planters top [the coffee trees] at from three to three and a half feet.

b. *transf.* and *fig.*, or in *fig.* context.

1605 *1st Pt. Ieronimo* iii. ii, Ile top thy head for that ambitious word. **1633** P. Fletcher *Purple Isl.* x. xxii, Topping rank desires which vain exceed. **1690** Locke *Govt.* i. vi. (Rtldg.) 60 Just as Procrustes did with his guests, top or stretch them. **1840** Dickens *Barn. Rudge* vii, Those prejudices of society which lop and top from poor handmaidens all such genteel excrescences.

(*b*) ***to top and tail*** *colloq.*, to wash the face and bottom of (a baby or small child); also *absol.*; hence ***top-and-tail*** *attrib. phr.*, ***top-and-tailing*** *vbl. sb.* Cf. topping *vbl. sb.*[1] 1 h.

1924 H. de Sélincourt *Cricket Match* ii. 22 She topped and tailed each small boy with the same rubber sponge. **1931** P. W. Yeomans *Happy Motherhood* vii. 61, 5.50 to 6.20 p.m. —Top-and-tail wash, and feed baby. **1960** C. Day Lewis *Buried Day* ii. 31 We did not go in for a desperate amount of washing—top-and-tailing twice a day, and a hip-bath once a week. **1964** *Guardian* 24 June 6/2 Freda showed me how to top and tail (which is done on the lap because these babies do not get enough cuddling). **1983** *Woman's Weekly* 8 Jan. 53/3 There is no need to bath your new baby more than twice a week, 'topping and tailing' on the other days.

†**4.** To snuff (a candle). *Obs.*

1594 Plat *Jewell-ho.* iii. 50 The candle..after it is newly topped. **1607** Middleton *Your Five Gallants* i. i, Top the candle, sirrah. **1785** Grose *Dict. Vulg. T.*, *Top*, the signal among taylors for snuffing the candles. **1840** Marryat *Poor Jack* xxii, Let us top this glim a bit.

5. To pare off the surface soil of (land).

1638 A. Cant *Serm.* in Kerr *Covenants & Cov.* (1895) 120 The mountain must not be pared or topped.

6. Orig., to put to death by hanging; perh. originally to behead; cf. topsman. Now usu. simply, to kill (someone); chiefly *refl.*, to commit suicide. *slang.*

1718 C. Hitchin *Regulator* in F. J. Lyons *Jonathan Wild* (1936) 238 He, being known to be an old practitioner, will certainly be *cast* and *top'd*, *alias* hang'd for the same. **1811** *Lexicon Balatr.* s.v., The cove was topped for smashing queer screens. **1851** Mayhew *Lond. Labour* (1861) III. 387/1 Thirty-six were cast for death, and only one was 'topped'. **1904** A. Griffiths *50 Y. Public Service* xxii. 337 [One] hoped the day would be fine when he was to be topped. **1958** F. Norman *Bang to Rights* 30 He also took my tie and belt so that I could not top myself. **1961** [see slag *sb.*[1] 5 (*b*)]. **1983** *Listener* 3 Feb. 18/3, I have to try and get a key to it all, otherwise I'll just top myself. **1984** M. Litchfield *See how they Run* xvii. 157 That shooter..wasn't used to top Frost.

7. To shorten the teeth of (a toothed or cogwheel, etc.); cf. topper *sb.*[1] 1.

1874 [implied in topper *sb.*[1] 1]. **1884** F. J. Britten *Watch & Clockm.* 74 Very slightly top the wheel by holding a piece of Arkansas stone against the teeth. *Ibid.* 152 If the lockings are too deep..the wheel is too large and should be topped.

III. To put a top on or form a top to.

8. To furnish with a top; to put a top on; to cover or surmount, crown, cap (*with*). Also *fig.* Cf. sense 16, with which this sometimes blends.

1581 A. Hall *Iliad* vii. 133 When as their towres they topt aloft, and rampires great did raise. **1583** Melbancke *Philotimus* U iij b, I suppose that..Nanes and Dwarfes muste needes be topped with such heades. **1679** O. Heywood *Diaries*, etc. (1881) II. 188 To Roger Stocks, topping orchard wal. **1705** Addison *Italy, Tirol* 527 The little *Notredame*..topp'd with a Cupola. **1864** Burton *Scot Abr.* I. v. 294 The practice..of topping the flanking round towers with conical roofs.

9. a. To complete by putting the top on, or forming the top of (a stack, etc.): often *to top up*; hence (*colloq.*) to put the finishing touch to (a process); to finish *off*, round *off*, crown.

1504 [see topping *vbl. sb.*[1] 1 a].

1641 Best *Farm. Bks.* (Surtees) 35 The other comming behinde with a rake, to correckt, toppe up, and finish the cocke [of hay]. **1787** M. Cutler in *Life*, etc. (1888) I. 231 Her hair in front is craped at least a foot high,..and topped off with a wire skeleton in the same form covered with black gauze. **1837** W. Irving *Capt. Bonneville* I. 162 The chiefs leading the van, the braves following in a long line, painted and decorated, and topped off with fluttering plumes. **1872** O. W. Holmes *Poet Breakf.-t.* ii, He has topped off his home training with a..foreign finish. **1892** *Cornh. Mag.* Oct. 363 One [governess] grounded and another topped. **1903** Morley *Gladstone* III. viii. xii. 217 The sea voyage that was to 'top up' the rest and the treatment.

b. *absol.* or *intr.* To finish *up* or *off*, wind *up*, conclude (*with* something). *colloq.*

1836 J. H. Newman *Lett.* 15 Apr. (1891) II. 189 Before they would venture to top up with such a..startling enunciation. **1840** R. H. Dana *Bef. Mast* xxv, We had the usual southeaster..and finally topped off with a drenching rain of three or four hours. **1848** THACKERAY *Bk. Snobs* xxxix, They absorb pale-ale.., and top-up with glasses of strong waters. **1870** *Daily News* 6 Oct., Then you..find the inmates of another room topping off with chocolate or coffee. **1885** RIDER HAGGARD *K. Solomon's Mines* i, Everything went wrong that trip, and to top up with I got the fever badly.

c. *to top* (*up*) *one's fruit*, *punnet*, etc., to put the best fruit on the top of the basket, punnet, etc. *Market slang.*

1888 [see TOPPING *vbl. sb.*^{1} 1 a]. **1891** *Brit. Workman* Aug., I mean..that you're a topper... You've been topping your punnets. **1896** *Jrnl. R. Hortic. Soc.* Nov. 209 A grower who does not top up his fruit deserves to be canonised.

10. *trans.* **a.** *Dyeing.* To give a final bath of colour to; to finish *off* (a dyeing process) with a certain dye. **b.** To top-dress land. **c.** To stain the tips of the hair of (fur).

1856 *Jrnl. R. Agric. Soc.* XVII. I. 188 A friend of mine always tops from $1\frac{1}{2}$ to 2 cwt. [of salt] per acre before ploughing the clover leys. **1874** CROOKES *Dyeing & Calico-Print.* 526 Such increase of oxalic acid is not recommended for topping blacks. **1875** F. J. BIRD *Dyer's Handbk.* 35 Top-off with serge blue to shade. **1882** CROOKES *Dyeing & Tissue-Print.* 118 Lift, and top in a fresh water with magenta and a little alum. **1910** W. PARKER in *Encycl. Brit.* XI. 352/2 The paler skins from all districts in Siberia are now cleverly coloured or 'topped', that is, just the tips of the hair are stained dark.

11. To 'cover', copulate with. Cf. TUP *v.* Now only *U.S.*

1604 SHAKS. *Oth.* III. iii. 396. *Ibid.* V. ii. 136. **1633** FORD *Love's Sacr.* III. i, Oh, for three Barbary stone-horses to top three Flanders mares! **1959** W. FAULKNER *Mansion* i. 14 My young bull topped her last week.

IV. To exceed or come up to in height.

12. a. *trans.* To exceed in height; to overtop; also to exceed in weight, amount, number, etc.

1582 STANYHURST *Æneis* II. (Arb.) 50 Two serpents.. charg Laocoon..His neck eke chayning with tayls, hym in quantitye topping. **1686** PLOT *Staffordsh.* 380 When they come to top them, [they] will quickly shade, and so kill them. **1747** *Gentl. Mag.* Dec. 589/1 The sea ran so high at Rotterdam, as to top two stories of many houses. **1760** R. BROWN *Compl. Farmer* II. 82 White oats..come up sooner, and top the weeds better than black. **1867** F. FRANCIS *Angling* iii. (1880) 57 Many of them topped two pounds. **1887** BESANT *The World went* ix, She was so tall that she topped her father..by a head. **1901** *Daily Express* 21 Mar. 5/4 Thames..topped the Trinity high water mark by $3\frac{1}{2}$ feet.

b. To surpass, excel, outdo; to cap.

1586 MARLOWE *1st Pt. Tamburl.* II. iii, But, when you see his actions top his speech Your speech will stay. **1607** SHAKS. *Cor.* II. i. 23 Topping all others in boasting. **1787** BURKE *Corr.* (1844) III. 55 A measure, if possible, to top the former. **1852** THACKERAY *Esmond* III. v, [One] who for fun and humour seemed to top them all.

13. a. To rise above; to mount beyond the level of.

1773 *Poetry* in *Ann. Reg.* 233 Another bird, just flushing at the sound, Scarce tops the fence, then tumbles to the ground. **1869** BLACKMORE *Lorna D.* xviii, My head topped the platform of rock. **1870** MORRIS *Earthly Par.* III. IV. 159 At last the low sun topped the garden-wall. **1883** *Century Mag.* XXVI. 376 The sun was just topping the maples when [etc.].

b. To get or leap over the top of, to surmount.

1735 SOMERVILLE *Chase* II. 164 With Emulation fir'd They..top the barr'd Gate, O'er the deep Ditch exulting bound. **1826** *Sporting Mag.* XVII. 242 Topping a high paling, he makes play over the country. **1835** SIR G. STEPHEN *Adv. Search Horse* xvi. 241 Many a little horse will top a fence that he cannot put his nose over.

14. To reach the top of, ascend to the top of.

1600 W. WATSON *Decacordon* (1602) 75 Their harts were inflamed with flashes of conspiracies, how to top the highest place. *a* **1668** DENHAM *Of Prudence* Poems 157 Wind about, till thou have topp'd the Hill. **1775** BURKE *Sp. Conc. Amer.* Wks. III. 63 Already they have topped the Apalachian mountains. **1807** J. BARLOW *Columb.* I. 204 The sun's blue ray Topt unknown cliffs and call'd them up to day. **1865** KINGSLEY *Herew.* vi, A pale yellow line, seen only as they topped a wave. **1886** CORBETT *Fall of Asgard* I. 61 As they topped the crags that overhung the tarn.

15. *Theatr. to top one's part*, to play one's part to its utmost possibilities or to perfection; also, to transcend the character assigned to one; *transf.* to sustain (a character) with success. *to top the officer* (*Naut.*): see quot. 1867.

1672 VILLIERS (Dk. Buckhm.) *Rehearsal* III. i. (Arb.) 71 He does not hit me in't: he does not top his part. **1697** DENNIS *Plot & no Plot* A iij, But are you sure, Daughter, that you can act a fit of the Mother well?.. Ay, and top my part too, Mother. **1761** CHURCHILL *Rosciad* 46 Palmer! Oh! Palmer tops the janty part. **1786** EARL MALMESBURY *Diaries & Corr.* II. 219 Warm as I am in wishing to see her [England] once more topping her part on the Continent. **1797** MRS. A. M. BENNETT *Beggar Girl* (1813) IV. 212 Delighted to be queen of the company where she might top the great personage. **1827** HARE *Guesses* Ser. II. (1848) 72 By diligently performing the part assigned to him, by topping it, as the phrase is. **1831** *Examiner* 177/1 The Opposition.. are acting up to their character—nay, topping their parts. **1833** MARRYAT *P. Simple* lii, I've been hail-fellow well met with the ship's company so long, that I can't top the officer over them. **1867** SMYTH *Sailor's Word-bk.*, *Top the officer, to*, to arrogate superiority.

16. a. To be at the top of, constitute the top of. (In literal sense often running together with 8.) Also *fig.* to be the first, chief, or best of, to be at the head of, to take the lead in. Freq. in phr. *to top the bill*: to be at the top of a bill of entertainment (BILL *sb.*^{3} 8 c); to be the star of a show; also *fig.* and with the entertainment as object.

1615 G. SANDYS *Trav.* 42 Rhodope still topt with snow. **1629** WADSWORTH *Pilgr.* iii. 14 A Dormitory, which containes three long Galleries topping the house. **1707** *Reflex. upon Ridicule* 21 They kindle against such as will be Topping and Monopolizing the Conversation. *a* **1734** NORTH *Lives* (1826) I. 46 His youthful habits were never gay, or topping the mode. **1770** GOLDSM. *Des. Vill.* 12 The decent church that topt the neighbouring hill. **1802** MRS. J. WEST *Infidel Father* xvii. II. 208 It came in two winters ago for very high ladies to stand godmothers to the natural children of all their relations. Lady Random topped the fashion. **1850** BLACKIE *Æschylus* II. 160 Mount the battlements: Top every tower; crown every parapet. **1861** DIXON *Pers. Hist. Ld. Bacon* xii. §7 In character as in intellect Bacon tops the list. **1910** WODEHOUSE *Psmith in City* 3 He is a man of hobbies... When I left the house this morning he was all for cricket... Cricket seems still to be topping the bill. **1933** P. GODFREY *Back-Stage* xiv. 179 The old favourites, when they still topped the bill, had to revise the material they had formerly worked. **1959** [see BILL *sb.*^{3} 8 c]. **1977** *Sounds* 9 July 4/4 Led Zeppelin remain favourites to top a one-day festival at Wrotham Park.

b. To have the supremacy over; to get the better of. Now freq. in *U.S. Sport.*

1633 SHIRLEY *Gamester* III. ii, I'll..send my nephew; he shall top and top him, And scourge him like a top too. **1681** HICKERINGILL *Black Non-Conf.* ii. Wks. 1716 II. 18 Legions of Lordly Priests and Cardinals that topt the whole world. **1832** AUSTIN *Jurispr.* (1879) I. xxii. 462 Our aversion from the sanction tops the conflicting wish. **1951** *Amer. Speech* XXVI. 230/2 Dartmouth tops Harvard. **1974** *State* (Columbia, S. Carolina) 27 Feb. 3-B/1 The Panthers demolished both, topping Duquesne, 82–65, and trouncing Davidson in Charlotte, 90–63. **1979** *Tucson* (Arizona) *Citizen* 20 Sept. 8D/3 Boston topped Toronto, 8–0.

†**c.** *intr.* To have the supremacy. *Obs. rare*$^{-1}$.

1718 W. WRIGHT in *Wodrow's Corr.* (1843) II. 353 But.. the magistrates..were in as great danger as ever, for now the Cocceians begin to top.

V. Idiomatic uses, and phrases. (Chiefly *slang.*)

†**17. a.** *Dice-play. trans.* and *intr.* To retain one of the dice at the top of the box by unfair manipulation, to palm the die: cf. TOP *sb.*^{1} 21; hence, to cheat, trick (a person). *Obs.*

1663 [see TOPPING *vbl. sb.*^{1} 1 c]. **1671** [implied in TOPPER *sb.*^{1} 1 b]. **1678** DRYDEN *Limberham* IV. i, I think in my Conscience he's Palming and Topping..before he comes into the World. *a* **1700** B. E. *Dict. Cant. Crew*, *Top*, to Cheat, or Trick any one; also to Insult. *What do you Top upon me?* do you stick a little Wax to the Dice to keep them together, to get the Chance? *He thought to have Topt upon me*, he design'd to have..Sharpt me,..or Affronted me. **1726** [see TOPPING *vbl. sb.*^{1} 1 c].

†**b.** *intr.* To practise cheating or trickery; to impose *upon*; in quots. 1697, 1709, with mixture of sense 'to encroach or obtrude upon'. *Obs.*

1664 ETHEREDGE *Com. Revenge* II. iii, How neatly I could tope upon him! **1676** SHADWELL *Virtuoso* I. i, A Rascal.. that would Slur and top upon our Understandings. **1697** COLLIER *Ess. Mor. Subj.* I. (1709) 49 When a Man finds his Hopes disappointed, himself unsupported, and topp'd upon by Persons of meaner Pretences and Employments. *a* **1700** B. E. *Dict. Cant. Crew*, *To Passe upon one*, to top upon him, or impose upon him. *Ibid.* [see a above]. **1709** J. JOHNSON *Clergym. Vade M.* II. p. lxxxvii, Patriarchs..did, in the latter end of the 4th, and in the 5th century top upon the Metropolitans, and reduced many great Provinces with their Bishops under the direction of one. *Ibid.* 118 They were still growing and topping upon their neighbours.

†**c.** *trans.* To impose (a thing) *upon* a person; to foist, fob *off*, palm *off upon*. *Obs.*

1672–5 COMBER *Comp. Temple* (1702) 558 It is no less than Blasphemy to Top a device of Men upon the People whom they were to lead into all Truth. **1682** T. FLATMAN *Heraclitus Ridens* No. 73 (1713) II. 199 'Tis but topping upon 'em a Sermon now and then about Mortification. **1712** in Somers *Tracts* (1815) XIII. 211 As to the topping a king upon the throne of Spain, so by the same reason the king of France by his power may top the Pretender on England. **1733** *Revolution Politicks* II. 63 The Pope and his Jesuits.. were going to top Popery and Slavery upon us in good earnest.

†**d.** To insult. *Obs. slang.*

a **1700** [see a above]. **1785** GROSE *Dict. Vulg. T.*, *Top*,.. to insult.

†**e.** *trans.* To oppose. Cf. *in tops with* (TOP *sb.*^{1} 23). *Obs. rare*$^{-1}$.

1641 R. BAILLIE *Lett.* (1841) I. 390 Whill Argyle topes this nomination, as of a man unmeet, because of irresponsableness to the law for his debts.

18. a. *to top a ball* (*Golf*), to hit the ball above its centre; so *to top one's drive*, *to top*. **b.** *to top a clout* (*Thieves' slang*): see quot. **c.** *to top the deck* (*Card-sharping*): to cause a particular card to fall on the top of the pack. **d.** *to top a saw* (*U.S.*): to fix a stiffening piece or a gauge for limiting the depth of the cut (*Cent. Dict.*).

a. 1881 FORGAN *Golfer's Handbk.* 24 For ball I when struck will be 'topped' with the result of lacerating the turf. **1889** *Scott. Leader* 20 Apr. 6 He who never, or hardly ever, 'tops' a ball does not undergo the temptations to cast all his clubs into the whins. **1893** A. LANG in *Longm. Mag.* Apr. 652 My cleek seems merely made to top. **1894** *Times* 28 Apr. 13/3 Playing to the first hole Mr. L—— topped his drive, and Mr. B—— won the hole in 4 to 5.

b. 1812 J. H. VAUX *Flash Dict.*, *Top*, to top a clout or other article (among pickpockets) is to draw the corner or end of it to the top of a person's pocket, in readiness for..taking out, when a favourable moment occurs.

c. 1894 MASKELYNE *Sharps & Flats* v. 83 [The cuff holdout] is a neat invention to top the deck. *Ibid.* 86 The cards are simply slipped between the jaws, where they are held until required. The hands being crossed..the lever is pressed and the cards fall upon the top of the pack... This operation is termed technically 'topping the deck'.

VI. Idiomatically combined with adverbs. (See also sense 9.)

19. top off. a. *intr.* Of a ship, aircraft, etc.: to fill up or complete a cargo. Cf. sense 20 b below. *colloq.* (chiefly *U.S.*).

1937 G. S. DOORLY *In Wake* 22 A tramp steamer..called in to the Gulf to top-off with sugar. **1950** *Sun* (Baltimore) 3 July 14/2 Ships go to other ports to 'top off'. **1961** *Aeroplane* C. 761/2 Since the passenger carriers..'top-off' with cargo, it..seems fair and reasonable to permit the all-cargo carriers to carry cargo and to 'top-off' with passengers. **1978** H. WOUK *War & Remembrance* v. 46 We top off, take on provisions and torpedoes, and go.

b. *trans.* To fill up to the top (a tank already partly full) with fuel. *U.S. colloq.*

1943 F. J. BELL *Condition Red* 16 There'll be a fuel barge alongside some time tonight to top us off. **1953** C. A. LINDBERGH *Spirit of St. Louis* II. vi. 182 The fuel tanks would need topping off again. **1970** N. ARMSTRONG et al. *First on Moon* iii. 65 White streaks of vapor were emitted by the fuel tanks—which were constantly being 'topped off'. **1979** *Farmington* (New Mexico) *Daily Times* 27 May 3C/6 If everyone in New Mexico topped off their tank, that would use about 10 million gallons of gasoline.

c. *intr.* = *top out*, sense 20 c below.

1970 *Toronto Daily Star* 24 Sept. 4/2 If wage rates show signs of topping off, the Cabinet can face Parliament. **1976** *Survey* Spring 60 The progressive character of the scale tops off at 3 per cent of earnings for any income over 300 R/mo.

20. top out. a. *trans.* To put the finishing touch to (the roof of a building, etc.), freq. (in modern times) accompanied by some form of ceremony. *colloq.*

1834 W. SEWALL *Diary* 22 Dec. (1930) 160 Topped out house chimney, and went to saw mill. **1962** *Engineering* 16 Nov. 640 The dome was 'topped out' on 2 November. **1969** *Daily Tel.* 18 Apr. 27 (*caption*) Ald. Walter C. Dennis, Mayor of Lambeth, toasting the workmen..when the G.L.C.'s..Lambeth Walk development was 'topped out' yesterday. **1979** *Guardian* 25 July 3/2 Britain's most expensive new homes in Knightsbridge, London, were 'topped out' at a champagne reception yesterday.

b. Of a ship: to fill up or complete (its cargo). Also *absol.* Cf. sense 19 a above. *U.S. colloq.*

1940 *Sun* (Baltimore) 16 Apr. 24/6 Preparations were being made to tow her into the stream to 'top out' a 12,500-ton cargo. **1941** *Ibid.* 24 June 22/4 Every ship ..'topped out' with scrap, if there was any room left.

c. *intr.* To reach a peak, to cease rising. Cf. sense 19 c above and BOTTOM *v.* 4 c.

1972 *Sunday Tel.* 26 Mar. 30/4 Gilts now look as though they have topped out, and this is another sign that we are in the late stages of this bull market. **1972** *Guardian* 24 June 10/6 World population, he says, will probably top out at 10,000 millions sometime in the twenty-first century. **1979** *Sci. Amer.* Feb. 28/1 From the 10th century to the Mongol Wars, numbers rose, topping out in A.D. 1200.

21. top up. *trans.* **a.** To bring (something) up to its full capacity; to fill to the top (a partly full container, *spec.* (the cells of) a motor vehicle's battery). Used esp. with reference to a drinker's glass, freq. with the person as object. Occas. *absol.* and *transf.*

1937 *Times* 13 Apr. p. xxii/2 In order to help the owner-driver to look after his battery, a combined acid-level indicator, vent plug and filler cup has been introduced, thus enabling the cells to be 'topped up' accurately and visibly, without removing the vent plugs. **1946** *Happy Landings* July 12/1 Failure to..top-up brake pressure..and to check the voltage readings of batteries, are common examples. **1958** *Times* 1 Mar. 6/3 Liquid oxygen..to top up its [*sc.* a missile's] fuel tanks. **1960** 'N. SHUTE' *Trustee from Toolroom* ix. 237 We'll need water, and top up with diesel fuel. **1965** *Listener* 18 Nov. 800/3 Tea is expensive..so you economize by topping up your mug with hot water. **1969** 'R. PETRIE' in *E. Queen's Mystery Mag.* Mar. 33/1 Jim Morris tiptoed over to the sideboard for the bottle of brandy... Top him up, he told himself. **1971** 'E. FERRARS' *Stranger & Afraid* iii. 40 She..picked up the glass of sherry that she had started earlier. He said at once, 'Shall I top that up?' and..filled the glass to the brim. **1976** J. I. M. STEWART *Memorial Service* i. 14, I tried to teach him how to translate Tacitus, but had more success in topping him up with madeira. **1981** G. BOYCOTT *In Fast Lane* xi. 79 There was at least three feet of water in the main channel, constantly topped up by torrential showers.

b. *fig.*

1968 *Listener* 27 June 835/3 They..topped up the Welfare State with plenty of money for its more exquisite and bizarre excrescences. **1973** *Times* 20 Oct. 20/3 (*heading*) Topping up a mortgage with a loan from a life office. **1976** *Scotsman* 27 Dec. 1/2 It proposes a Scottish Assembly of 100 members... An Assembly member elected for each of the 71 parliamentary constituencies, 'topped up' by 29 additional members.

top (tɒp), *v.*^{2} Forms: 5–6 **toppe**, 6– **top**; see also TOPE *v.*^{1} [Of uncertain origin: appears doubtfully in 1497, certainly in 1549; in regular nautical use in 1627 and onward. So mod.Du. and Ger. *toppen*. Possibly a special application of TOP *v.*^{1}, or an independent deriv. of TOP *sb.*^{1}; but the difficulty is increased by the synonymous TOPE *v.*^{1} It is also possible that branch II is a distinct word; but TOPE *v.*^{1} also has both senses.]

I. *Naut.* **1.** *trans.* To tip *up* or slant (a yard), by tilting up one arm and depressing the other; sometimes = PEAK *v.*^{3}, to tilt up vertically or nearly so; but sometimes more loosely, to alter the position of (a yard), whether by raising, depressing, or levelling it.

The exact meaning in quot. 1497 is not clear; ? to shore the ship up.

[**1497** *Naval Acc. Hen. VII* (1896) 249 To Retourne the seid mastes to Portesmouth where they served to toppe the Regent in the dokke at euery tyde bothe ebbe & flowde.] **1549** *Compl. Scot.* vi. 41 Than the master cryit, top ȝour topinellis. **1627** CAPT. SMITH *Seaman's Gram.* v. 24 The Lifts are two ropes which belong to all yards armes, to top the yards; that is, to make them hang higher or lower at your pleasure. **1688** R. HOLME *Armoury* III. xv. (Roxb.) 51/1 Top the yards, that is make them hang euen. **1762–9** FALCONER *Shipwr.* II. 261 Topp'd and unrigg'd, they [top-gallant yards] down the backstays run. **1769** —— *Dict. Marine* (1789), *Apiquer une vergue*, to top a sail-yard, or peek it up. **1802** *Eng. Encycl.* VIII. 431/1 'Top the yard to port!' the order to make the larboard extremity of a yard higher than the other. **1816** TUCKEY *Narr. Exped. R. Zaire* ii. (1818) 39 The Portuguese vesels putting themselves in mourning by topping their yards up and down. **1844** *Hull Dock Act* 91 No vessel shall enter..except the same have her yards topped up. **1867** SMYTH *Sailor's Word-bk.* s.v. *Boom, To top one's boom*, to start off.

2. *intr.* To assume a slanting position, tip *up*, tilt *up*; = TIP *v.*[2] 9.

c **1860** H. STUART *Seaman's Catech.* 57 A martingale is sometimes used to prevent the davit from topping up.

II. 3. *intr.* To fall over, or to one side, by overbalancing; to tumble head foremost; = TOPPLE *v.* 1, TIP *v.*[2] 8. ***to top over tail*** (cf. *to towp tail over end*, dial), to turn head over heels; cf. *topple up tail* (TOPPLE *v.* 3 b).

1545 ASCHAM *Toxoph.* I. (Arb.) 47 To tumble ouer and ouer, to toppe ouer tayle..may be also holesome for the body. **1620** SHELTON *Quix.* II. xxix. 194 Don Quixote and Sancho topted [*ed.* 1746 top'd; (? error for *topled* = *toppled*)] into the Riuer.

4. *trans.* To tip or throw over, overturn, upset; = TOPPLE *v.* 3, TIP *v.*[2] 1. *Obs.* exc. *dial.*

1662 HIBBERT *Body Div.* I. 135 A little ship without ballast ..is soon either dasht against the rocks, or topped over. *c* **1890** W. S. PASMORE *Song of Press Gang* 5 They took'd me up both neck and heels, And topped me into the zay.

† **top**, *v.*[3] *Obs.* [Origin obscure: known 1598. Perhaps identical with prec. vb., with the primary sense 'to tip up into the mouth', whence 'to drink in large draughts': cf. *tip, tip off*, TIP *v.*[2] 5. See also TOPE *v.*[2], which is identical in sense, though, as in prec., the phonetic relation is difficult.]

1. *trans.* = TOPE *v.*[2] 1; ***to top off***, to drink off, quaff; cf. *tip off* (TIP *v.*[2] 5).

1598 R. BERNARD tr. *Terence's Adelphi* I. i, It's no heinous offence for a young man to hunt harlots, to toppe of a canne roundly. **1690** D'URFEY *Collin's Walk thro. London* i. 41 This said, they top'd off t'other quart.

2. Only in pa. pple. (**topt**): Made tipsy, intoxicated, drunk. Cf. TIP *v.*[2] 4.

a **1632** T. TAYLOR *God's Judgem.* vi. II. (1642) 82 When she with her son were together topt with wine. **1637** HEYWOOD *Dial., Vulcan & Jupiter* Wks. 1874 VI. 220 She leaps and capers, topt with rage divine.

top, *v.*[4] *rare.* [f. TOP *sb.*[2] 3.] *trans.* To lay (a rope) with a top: see TOP *sb.*[2] 3.

1825 [see TOPPING *vbl. sb.*[3]].

† **top**, *prep. Obs. rare.* In 4 **toppe**. [From TOP *sb.*[1]: app. either aphetic for ATOP B., or elliptical for *top of*.] Above, beyond, more than.

1340 *Ayenb.* 6 Hi ssolden him..toppe all þinges louie. *Ibid.* 248 þise uirtue me ssel loky toppe alle þinges.

top, obs. Sc. form of TAP *v.*[1]

‖ **topalgia** (təʊ'pældʒɪə). *Path.* [mod.L., f. Gr. τόπ-ος place + -αλγία, f. ἄλγ-ος pain: cf. *neuralgia*.]

1896 *Allbutt's Syst. Med.* I. 829 Local pain, allied to local neurasthenia (topalgia of Berequi) is occasionally noticed. **1899** *Syd. Soc. Lex., Topalgia*, pain in a circumscribed area, not referable to the distribution of any particular nerve.

† **'top-'annual.** *Sc. Law. Obs.* [f. TOP *sb.*[1] + ANNUAL.] An annual sum payable out of the rent of a building or buildings as distinct from the land: cf. GROUND-ANNUAL. So † **top-'annualler**.

(The distinction appears to have disappeared soon after the date of the Act cited; and after 1693 there was no legal way of making such a distinction.)

1555 *Sc. Acts Mary* (1814) II. 490/2 [Mentions] few annuellaris [and] tope annuellaris. **1597** SKENE *De Verb. Sign.* s.v. *Annuel*, Top-annuel, is ane certaine duty, given and disponed furth of ony bigged tenement or land, of the quhilk tenement the propertie remainis with the disponer, and he is onely oblished to pay the said annuel. **1681** STAIR *Instit.* xv. §7. 320 The case being there of Tenements within Burgh, the *Feu Annual* is [etc.]; *Ground-annuals* is a distinct several annualrent, Constitute upon the Ground, before the House was built; and the *Top*-annualrent is out of the House.

toparch ('tɒpɑːk). [ad. Gr. τοπάρχης ruler of a small district, f. τόπ-ος place + -αρχης ruler. Cf. mod.F. *toparque*.] The ruler or prince of a small district, city, or petty state; a petty 'king'.

1640 FULLER *Joseph's Coat* 11 By those many Kings mentioned in the old Testament, thirty and one in the little land of Canaan,..is meant onely Toparchs, not great Kings, but Lords of a little Dition, and Dominion. **1646** SIR T. BROWNE *Pseud. Ep.* VII. viii. 353 Toparks, Kings of Cities or narrow territories, such as were the Kings of Sodome and Gomorrah, the Kings of Jericho and Ai. **1737** WHISTON *Josephus, Antiq.* XI. iii. §2 The toparchs of India and Ethiopia. **1852** MISS YONGE *Cameos* (1877) I. xxii. 162 The top-arch, Turlogh O'Connor, was the friend of O'Rourke.

So **to'parchical** *a.* [-ICAL], of, pertaining to, or of the nature of a toparch or toparchy.

1650 FULLER *Pisgah* II. xiv. 302 Communicating it to the Sons and Nephews of Toparchicall Princes.

toparchy ('tɒpəkɪ). Also in L. form **toparchia**. [ad. L. *toparchia*, a. Gr. τοπαρχία, f. τοπάρχης TOPARCH. So mod.F. *toparchie*.] The small district or territory under the rule of a toparch.

1601 HOLLAND *Pliny* (1634) I. 100 It is diuided into ten gouernments or territories, called Toparchies..: to wit, that of Hiericho..: Emmaus,..Lydda, Ioppica, Accrabatena, Gophnitica, Thamnitica, Betholene, Tephena, and Orine, wherein stood Jerusalem. **1737** WHISTON *Josephus, Hist.* I. i. §5 Judas..fled to the toparchy of Gophna. **1848** A. HERBERT in Todd *Irish Nennius* Notes p. lxiii, When the general name is improperly added to *ri* [king], instead of the name of the toparchy. **1883** EDERSHEIM *Life Jesus* I. 87 Judæa proper, to which Galilee, Samaria, and Peræa were joined as Toparchies. These Toparchies consisted of a group of townships under a Metropolis.

† **to-'part**, *v. Obs.* [ME., f. TO-[2] + PART *v.*]

1. *trans.* To dispart, separate, divide, distribute.

c **1325** *Poem Times Edw. II* 202 in *Pol. Songs* 332 And he shal ben to-parted..From his wif. **1340** *Ayenb.* 170 Saynt Ion..topartep zeue ouercomeinges and zeue corounes. **1387** *E.E. Wills* (1882) 1 Or my godes be to-partyd.

2. *intr.* To depart: see TO-[2] 1.

topass ('təʊpəs). *E. Indies.* Also 7–8 **topaz**. [a. Pg. *topaz* (to'pas), Lucena, 1600; said in *Madras Manual of Administration*, 1893, to be ad. *tōpāshé*, Malayālam form of Hindī *dōbāshī*, man of two languages, interpreter (in which capacity these men of mixed descent were employed): see DUBASH. (A fancied derivation from Hindī *tōpī* hat, making the term = *tōpī-wālā* 'hat-man', European (see TOPI) has been current since the middle of the 18th c.)] A person of mixed Black and Portuguese descent; often applied to a soldier, or a ship's scavenger or bath-attendant, who is of this class.

[**1648** *Van Spielbergen's Voy.* (Dutch) 34 (transl. in Yule) We saw to seaward another Champaigne (Sampan) wherein were 20 men, Mestiços and Toupas.] **1680** in J. T. Wheeler *Madras* (1861) I. 121 It is resolved and ordered to entertain about 100 Topasses or Black Portuguese into pay. **1727** A. HAMILTON *New Acc. E. Ind.* II. xlviii. 199 There are about two hundred Topasses, or Indian Portugueze settled and married in Cambodia. **1758** *Ann. Reg.* 283/2 A Topaz. [*Note*] A black Christian soldier; usually termed subjects of Portugal. **1766** J. H. GROSE *Voy. E. Ind.* (ed. 2) I. xiv. Gloss., *Topasses*, a tawny race of foot-soldiers, descended from Portuguese marrying natives, and called Topasses, because they wear hats. **1865** *Daily Tel.* 24 Oct. 5/1 Thirty 'topasses' on board the deserted ship launched a boat and got to Port Canning as soon as the steamer.

topaz ('təʊpæz). Forms: 3 **tupace**, 3–7 **topace**, 4–6 **topias**, 5 **thopas, topeus, tapace, (topyes)**, 5–7 **topas, topaze, topase**, 6– **topaz**. β. 4 **topasie; (topazius)**, 7 **topasius**. [ME. a. OF. *topaze, topace, -ase* (Roland, 11th c.), mod.F. *topaze* = Prov. *topazi*, Sp. *topacio*, Pg. *topazio*, It. *topazio*, ad. L. *topazus* (also later *topazius, -ion*), a. Gr. τόπαζος, -ιον, a foreign word; according to Pliny named from an island in the Red or Arabian Sea, where it abounded; but thought by some to be connected with Skr. *tapas* heat, fire.]

1. The name given (with or without distinguishing adjunct) to several highly valued precious stones. **a.** According to King, *Antique Gems* 26, given by the Greeks and Romans to the ***yellow*** or ***oriental topaz***, a yellow sapphire or corundum; by Pliny, also to the modern chrysolite. **b.** In modern use (***true*** or ***occidental topaz***), a fluo-silicate of aluminium, usually in prismatic crystals, transparent and lustrous, yellow, white, pale blue, or pale green, found in Brazil, Mexico, Saxony, Scotland, the Ural Mountains, etc.

Also with distinctive adjuncts: **false topaz**, a transparent pale yellow variety of quartz; **pink t.**, pink or rose-coloured topaz, artificially produced from the yellow Brazilian stone by exposure to strong heat; **Scottish** or **smoky t.**, the smoky variety found in Scotland; **Siberian t.**, a bluish white variety; **Spanish t.**, a golden brown variety of smoky quartz; **star-topaz**, a yellow asteriated sapphire.

a **1272** *Luue Ron* 172 in *O.E. Misc.* 98 Hwat spekstu of eny stone..Of Amatiste, of calcydone, Of lectorie, and tupace? *a* **1300** *Floriz & Bl.* 287 And suþþe riche cassidoines And Jacinctes and topaces. *c* **1375** *Sc. Leg. Saints* vi. (*Thomas*) 279 With brycht & schenand preciuse stanys, As sardiane, topias fyne, Iaspis. **1382** WYCLIF *Job* xxviii. 19 Topasie of Ethiope. *c* **1400** *Emaré* 91 Of topaze and rubyes, And oþur stones of myche prys. *c* **1407** LYDG. *Reson & Sens.* 6719 Hyr Rokys..Wer makyd of a ryche stoon, Of a Thopas. *c* **1420** *Anturs of Arth.* xxviii, The tassellus were of topeus, that was ther-to tiȝte. *a* **1440** *Sir Degrev.* 635 With topyes and trechoure Overtrasyd that tyde. **1481** CAXTON *Myrr.* II. vii. 79 A stone called Topace whiche is of colour lyke vnto fyn golde. **1567** MAPLET *Gr. Forest* 22 The Topaze..Plinie sayth, is a Gem of grassie colour: although that in Germanie it is found like to Golde. **1584** R. SCOT *Discov. Witchcr.* XIII. vi. (1886) 239 A topase healeth the lunaticke person of his passion of lunacie. **1645** EVELYN *Diary* 21 May, Many pearls, diamonds, amethysts, topazes. **1738** GLOVER *Leonidas* IV. 266 The flaming topaz with its golden beam. **1888** *Encycl. Brit.* XXIII. 446 The topaz of modern mineralogists was unknown to the ancients.

c. The dark yellow colour of topaz.

1908 *Sears, Roebuck Catal.* 360/2 These colors are.. sapphire blue, emerald green, topaz, etc. **1942** W. FAULKNER *Go down, Moses* 237 A horse stands, blinking his sleepy topaz eyes at nothing. **1974** *Times* 2 Dec. (Wines & Spirits Suppl.) p. iii/5 Pale topaz with a gentle grapey aroma ..it [*sc.* a wine] costs less than £12 a dozen.

2. *Her.* In blazoning by precious stones, the designation of the tincture Or.

1562 LEIGH *Armorie* 4 b, That precious stone, which y[e] Herhaughts do vse in blason, for, and in y[e] name of this metall [or] and Planett [the sun] that is called a Topace. **1572** BOSSEWELL *Armorie* II. 56 The field is parted per fesse embattyled, Topaze and Emeraude, two Lyciskes passant conterchanged of the fielde. **1766–87** PORNY *Heraldry* Gloss., *Topaz*, the name of a precious Stone used instead of Or, in blazoning the Arms of the English Nobility only.

3. *attrib.* and *Comb.*, as ***topaz-colour, -fire, -gleam, -seal, -stone; topaz-coloured, -tailed, -throated, -tinted*** adjs.; also **topaz humming-bird**, two S. American species of humming-bird of brilliant colours, *Topaza pella* and *T. pyra*; **topaz-pycnite** *Min.*, a variety of topaz, occurring in columnar aggregations; **topaz-rock**: see quot. 1796.

1902 *Westm. Gaz.* 2 Aug. 2/1 The yellow cat lay motionless and supine, its *topaz-coloured eyes rolling from one to the other. **1816** J. SCOTT *Vis. Paris* App. (ed. 5) 321 An infinity of glass lamps..sparkling with green, crimson, and *topaz fires. **1782** LATHAM *Synopsis Birds* I. II. 746 *Topaz Humming-Bird. This bird is not much inferior to a Wren in size. **1839** URE *Dict. Arts* 1243 The rare mineral called *topaz pycnite is found in this mine. **1796** KIRWAN *Elem. Min.* (ed. 2) I. 368 **Topaz rock*..presents a compound of topaz, quartz, shorl, and lithomarga, confusedly compacted together. **1812** SCOTT *Let. to J. B. S. Morritt* 10 Dec. in *Lockhart*, A pretty *topaz seal, with a talisman which secures this letter. *c* **1470** HENRY *Wallace* VII. 77 Off *topastone him thocht the plumat was. **1595** *Locrine* II. i. 24 Enthronized in seates of Topace stones. **1811** SHAW *Gen. Zool.* VIII. 335 *Topaz-tailed Humming-bird. .. Length four inches: Native of Paraguay. *Ibid.* 274 *Topaz-throated Humming-bird... The throat..is of the most splendid *topaz yellow. **1867** AUG. J. E. WILSON *Vashti* xiv, The glassy stretch of *topaz-tinted sea. **1845** LINDLEY *Veg. Kingd.* (1846) 114 Barley-straw melts into a glass of a topaz yellow colour.

Hence **'topazy** *a.* (*nonce-wd.*) [see -Y], like topaz.

1892 STEVENSON *Vailima Lett.* xxii. (1895) 224 The colour ..is a topazy yellow.

topazine ('təʊpəzɪn, -aɪn), *a.* [f. TOPAZ + -INE[2], after *amethystine, crystalline*, etc.] That resembles topaz; topaz-coloured.

1826 KIRBY & SP. *Entomol.* IV. xlvi. 283 Topazine... The yellow splendour of the topaz. **1829** *Glover's Hist. Derby* I. 94 Amethystine and topazine fluors. **1888** *Harper's Mag.* Aug. 338 How the emerald and the topazine eyes glow!

† **to'pazion.** *Obs.* Also 4 **topasiune**, 4–5 **-ion**, 5 **topazyon**, 6 **topatioun, -ason**. [a. late L. *topazion*, a. Gr. τοπάζιον, dim of τόπαζος TOPAZ.] An early name for a topaz.

c **1305** *Land Cokayne* 92 þer is saphir and uniune..Beril, onix, topasiune. *c* **1430** LYDG. *Min. Poems* (Percy Soc.) 188 Lyke topasion of colours sonnyssh bright. *c* **1460** *Play Sacram.* 168, I haue..topazyons smaragdis of grete degre. **1560** ROLLAND *Crt. Venus* I. 109 With Iacinth fine, and Topazion sa fair. **1622** PEACHAM *Compl. Gent.* (1661) 169 The first colour is *Or, i.e.* Yellow, and signifieth in Plannets the Sun, in Pretious Stones, Topazion and Chrysolith.

topazolite (təʊ'pæzəʊlaɪt). *Min.* [f. Gr. τόπαζο-ς topaz + λίθος stone: see -LITE.] A variety of garnet resembling topaz in colour.

1819 W. PHILLIPS *Introd. Min.* (1823) 31 Topazolite... This variety of the garnet has been discovered within the last few years. It occurs in remarkably well-defined dodecahedral crystals, of a topaz yellow colour. **1823** URE *Dict. Chem.* (ed. 2) 1 *Topazolite*, a variety of precious garnet, found at Mussa in Piedmont.

top-boot ('tɒpbuːt). [f. TOP *sb.*[1] 10 + BOOT *sb.*[3] 1.] **1.** *properly.* A high boot, having a top of white, light-coloured, or brown leather or the like (TOP *sb.*[1] 10), formerly habitually worn by gentlemen, yeomen, and farmers, in riding or country dress; now by hunting men, jockeys, grooms, and coachmen. Usually in *pl.*

1768 J. R. PEYTON *Let.* 10 Apr. in J. L. Peyton *Adventures of my Grandfather* (1867) ii. 17, I found my heavy top-boots of immense service. **1813** J. F. REES *Art & Myst. Cordwainer* 103 How to take the measure..for a jockey or top boot. **1821** *King in Ireland* in *New Monthly Mag.* II. 407 [The priest] in his black satin breeches and bright top-boots. **1836** E. HOWARD *R. Reefer* ii, He has purchased a pair of *top* boots, a swell *top* coat, and..thinks himself..a topping gentleman. *c* **1868** G. PRYME *Autobiog. Recoll.* xiv. (1870) 220 [In 1782] the County Members went up to the Throne —according to their privilege—in leather breeches and top-boots, instead of Court-dress. **1875** W. S. HAYWARD *Love agst. World* 73 In hunting-dress, buckskin, top-boots and scarlet coat. **1893** VIZETELLY *Glances Back* I. iii. 81 Burdett, in his customary buckskins and top boots. **1910** O. BARRON in *Encycl. Brit.* VII. 243/2 Men of fashion [in late 18th c.] walked the streets in short top-boots of soft black leather.

1911 *Ibid.* XXIV. 993/1 Such forms as jack-boots, top-boots, Hessian boots and Wellington boots. **1912–13** *Civil Serv. Co-op. Soc. Price List* 916 Coachman's Top Boots. Any Colour Top.

2. Improperly applied to any long or high boots which partly cover the leg.

1891 *Cent. Dict., Top-boot*, a boot having a high top; spec. [as in sense 1]. **1906** G. W. CHRYSTAL tr. *Mem. Pr. Chlodwig of Hohenlohe-Schillingsfuerste* II. 260 She appeared in pink stockings, black top-boots. **1906** *Athenæum* 19 May 606/3 The new heresy which, to the horror of makers and wearers of 'top-boots', gives to the military boot of Eastern Europe that time-honoured name. **1907** *Ibid.* 13 Apr. 440/1 We.. dislike the practice of writers on Russia of using for the boot of Eastern Europe the classical term 'top-boot', which has in our literature a special meaning. For the British hunting boot there is no other term.

3. *attrib.* and *Comb.*

1854 KNIGHT *Once upon a Time* xxxvii. (1859) 497 The top-boot wearers.

Hence **'top-'booted** *a.*, wearing top-boots.

1829 G. GRIFFIN *Collegians* I. viii. 169 A stout top-booted elderly gentleman. **1831** CARLYLE *Sart. Res.* II. ii, Topbooted Graziers from the North; Swiss Brokers, Italian Drovers, also topbooted, from the South.

†**top-castle.** *Obs.* [Cf. TOP *sb.*[1] 9 and CASTLE *sb.* 7.] An embattled platform at the head of a ship's masts, from which missiles were discharged: later called also *top* (TOP *sb.*[1] 9).

1335 *Exch. Acc., K.R.* 19/14 m. 6 (P.R.O.) In paracione de guerra et arraiamenta cuiusdam magni Navis vocat' la Trinite, vt in Ofcastel, Topcastel et Forcastel... In cordis emptis pro petris tractandis apud Topcastel. xviij d. Rendered, in Nicolas *Hist. Royal Navy* (1847) II. 170 The 'Trinity', of two hundred tons, was prepared for war with an 'ofcastle, topcastle, and forecastle'; the 'ofcastle' being the aftcastle, and the 'topcastle' the 'top' or stage at the top of the mast; and ropes were bought for pulling stones up to the topcastle.] **13..** *Coer de L.* 2539 Sterne strokes with harde stones Out off the top-castel on hygh. *a* **1400** *Siege of Troy* 695 in *Archiv neu. Spr.* LXXII. 27 Vche maste hade top castel And asayliþ þe cite harde and wel. **1411** *Exch. Acc., K.R.* 44/17 La barge appelle la Marie de la Toure..ove lapparail..une mast, un trief ove iiij. bonetz, un topchastiell, un seilyerde. *c* **1450** *Chron. London* (Kingsford 1905) 145 Beryng the standard of Seynt Jorge in the topcastell lyke Englissh schippes. **1555** EDEN *Decades* 27 The foreshyppe and the sterne, the toppe castel, the maste [etc.].

b. *transf.* and *fig.*

1548 UDALL *Erasm. Par. Luke* xi. 110 To sytte euen in the high topcastell of true seruyng of God. **1556** *Chron. Gr. Friars* (Camden) 84 There was a man made too tope-castelles above the crosse of the stepulle, and there stode with a flagge in hys honde and viij flagges hangynge besyde. **1688** R. HOLME *Armoury* III. xxi. (Roxb.) 252/1 He beareth Vert, the top castle of a Loome, with its pullaces, issueing out of base, Or.

‖**topchee** ('təʊptʃiː). Also 7 topagee, toptchi, 9 topechee, topdji, topgi; topgey. [Hind. *topcī*, Pers. *topchī*, Turk. *topçu* artilleryman, f. Pers., Turk. *top* gun, cannon.] A term used in the former Ottoman Empire for a gunner or artilleryman.

1623 in W. Foster *Eng. Factories India* (1908) 234 They delivered mee..into the hands of the Topagee. **1668** P. RYCAUT *Present State Ottoman Empire* III. x. 200 The Toptchi. These are Gunners, called so from the word *Tope*, which in Turkish signifies a Cannon. **1828** J. B. FRASER *Kuzzilbash* I. 337 The men..bore down like lightning on the topechees. **1854** R. CURZON *Armenia* 73 He brought four guns with him, and a number of topgis, or gunners, to work these instruments of destruction. **1892** P. L. SIMMONDS *Dict. Trade Products* (new ed.) Suppl. 502/1 *Topdjis*, militia artillerymen in Turkey. **1918** E. S. FARROW *Dict. Mil. Terms* 620 *Topgeys*, the term for Turkish artillerymen or gunners. Also written *topgis*.

'top-ˌdress, *v.* [f. TOP *sb.*[1] + DRESS *v.* 13 c.] *trans.* To manure on the surface, as land, grass, or any crop. Also *absol.*

1733 W. ELLIS *Chiltern & Vale Farm.* 15 Much better than top-dressing the Grain after it is in the Ground. **1764** *Museum Rust.* III. xii. 47 The advantages of top-dressing wheat in the spring with soot, or other light manure. **1852** *Beck's Florist* June 117 To enable us to 'top-dress', as it is termed; *i.e.* to clean the surface, and cover it with a mixture of half-rotten manure and loam.

b. *transf.* and *fig.*

1834 *Tait's Mag.* I. 381/2 Before I was sixteen, [I] grinded, and partly top-dressed the Autobiography and Opinions of Men and Things, at home and abroad, of Stephen Fox, Esq. **1849** F. B. HEAD *Stokers & Pokers* i. (1851) 13 The wealth..almost without metaphor top-dressed the greater portion of the old as well as of the new world. **1862** WHYTE MELVILLE *Ins. Bar* 342 Plumtree was a mere boy,..actually shaving for whiskers, top-dressing with balm of Columbia, and raising an abundant crop of pimples as the result.

'top-ˌdressing, *vbl. sb.* [f. as prec. + DRESSING *vbl. sb.* 4 c.] **a.** The application of manure to the surface of the soil; *concr.* the manure or fertilizer so applied.

1744 W. ELLIS *Mod. Husbandman* Mar. i. 7 The Top-dressing of a powdered Manure is far more preferable on this Account to the Top-dressing of Dung. **1764** *Museum Rust.* III. ii. 5, I bestow on it a top-dressing of wood ashes, soot,..or coal ashes. **1770–4** A. HUNTER *Georg. Ess.* (1803) I. 324 Pigeon dung, and rape-dust are considered as top-dressings. **1799** J. ROBERTSON *Agric. Perth* 311 When this powerful top-dressing..with sheep dung and urine has been completed. **1892** *Garden* 27 Aug. 195/2 The top-dressing was put on early in spring before the plants began to grow.

b. *transf.* and *fig.*

1846 MRS. CARLYLE *Let. to Carlyle* 7 Sept., Helen has been most diligent in my absence, and left nothing for me to do but a little 'top-dressing'. **1884** J. PAYN *Lit. Recoll.* 35 Culture is more common, but very little comes of such 'top dressing'. **1906** *Edin. Rev.* Jan. 196 Stimulated..by this top-dressing of the northern energy.

†**tope,** *sb.*[1] *Obs.* [Origin obscure.] A measure (of hay, corn, etc.).

1530–1 *Durham Househ. Bk.* (Surtees) 263 [In threshing and winnowing account] Item 4 topez of pyese. **1618** *Inv. F. Banks* in W. F. Irvine *Hist. Rivington, Lanc.* 65 Item, a tope of haye. **1676** *Will of Jas. Kenyon of Middleton, Lanc.* (Prob. Reg. Chester), In the Barne. A tope of Wheate 10s. od. 2 topes of Barley 14s. od. A tope of Oates 3l. 6s. 8d.

tope (təʊp), *sb.*[2] [Etymology not ascertained. ? Cornish name.] A small species of shark, *Galeus galeorhinus* or *G. canis*, native to British seas, especially off the coast of Cornwall. Called also *dog-fish, penny-dog, miller's-dog*.

1686 RAY *Willughby's Hist. Pisc.* I. xii. 22 Canis galeus Rondeletii & aliorum. Cornubiensibus, ni fallor, *A Tope* dicitur. **1774** GOLDSM. *Nat. Hist.* (1862) II. II. i. 269 The Dog Fish, the Zygæna, the Tope, the Cat Fish. **1846** OWEN *Compar. Anat. Vertebr.* iii. 56 In the Tope..may be seen the highest stage of vertebral ossification in the Chondropterygian Fishes. **1909** *Daily Chron.* 9 Oct. 7/3 Another kind of shark..is the tope, an ugly and rapacious brute, attaining an average length of about six feet.

b. The Australasian species, *Galeus australis*.

1898 MORRIS *Austral English*, *Tope*, an Australasian Shark, *Galeus australis*, Macl... Called also School-Shark.

tope (təʊp), *sb.*[3] A local name for the Wren.

1813 G. MONTAGU *Suppl. Ornith. Dict.*, *Tope*. Vide *Wren, common*. **1831** *Ibid.*, *Tope*, a name for the Wren. **1885** SWAINSON *Provinc. Names Birds* 35 Tope (Norfolk, Cornwall).

‖**tope** (təʊp), *sb.*[4] *East Indies.* [ad. Tamil *tōppu*, Telugu *tōpu*.] A clump, grove, or plantation of trees; in Upper India, chiefly of fruit-trees; *esp.* a mango grove or orchard.

1698 FRYER *Acc. E. India & P.* 41 The Country is.. plentiful in Provisions; in all Places Topes of Trees. **1792** Q. CRAUFORD *Sk. Hindoos* (ed. 2) II. 104 *note*, Topes are very frequent, and some..containing perhaps 100 acres of land. **1826** *Soldier's Album* 82 The word 'tope' means clump... We encamped nightly in the topes of Mangoe trees. **1834** *Penny Cycl.* II. 233/1 The 'toddy topes', or coco-nut tree orchards, are very extensive in Ceylon.

‖**tope** (təʊp), *sb.*[5] *East Indies.* [a. Hind. (Panjābī) *tōp*, held to be:—Prākrit or Pālī *thūpo*:—Skr. *stūpa*.] An ancient structure, in the form of a dome or tumulus of masonry, for the preservation of relics or in commemoration of some fact; numerous specimens, usually of Buddhist or Jain origin, exist in India and south-eastern Asia.

A tope containing relics is specially called a DAGOBA.

1815 ELPHINSTONE *Caubul* I. 80 *note*, Tope is an expression used for a mound or burrow as far west as Peshawer. **1853** —— in *Calcutta Rev.* July–Dec. 266 The famous Tope at Manikhyla. **1882** *Edin. Rev.* Oct. 360 A tope may be described as a domed structure, not unlike the dome of St. Paul's if it were lifted from the cathedral and placed on the ground. **1886** *Guide Galleries Brit. Mus.* 202 A Tope is a shrine peculiar to the Buddhist religion... In the centre is a solid dome-shaped structure, termed a *dagoba*, enclosing one or more small chests, with relics of Buddha or of his principal followers. This is generally surrounded by an elaborately carved rail. **1903** *Athenæum* 26 Sept. 405/2 A notable feature of these towns, the dagabas, or topes, are not themselves especially Buddhist monuments.

tope (təʊp), *v.*[1] Also *dial.* towp, toup; cf. TOP *v.*[2] [Known from 1669; of obscure origin. Synonymous with TOP *v.*[2], which occurs much earlier; but the long *o* is difficult to account for.]

†**1.** *Naut. trans.* To tilt, tip (a yard): = TOP *v.*[2] 1.

1669 STURMY *Mariners Mag.* I. ii. 17 Tope your Sprit-sail Yard.

2. To tilt over, cause to slope or lean to one side; to overturn, turn upside down; = TOP *v.*[2] 4. *Obs.* exc. *dial.*

1684 *She-Wedding* ¶6 in *Harl. Misc.* (1810) VI. 404 When the good wives are together, toping their noses over the brandy-bottle. **1701** FARQUHAR *Sir H. Wildair* IV. i, Here, boy.—No Nants left.—(Topes the Glass.) **1901** F. E. TAYLOR *Folk-sp. S. Lancs.* (E.D.D.), Hoo [= she] tope't her yed o' one soide.

b. *intr.* To incline, nod, or fall to one side; to topple or fall over; to fall asleep; to die. *dial.*

1796 W. MARSHALL *Rur. Econ. Yorks.* (ed. 2) Gloss., To *Towp*, to heel; to towp-over; to topple. **1800** *Spec Yorks. Dial.* 24 (E.D.D.) T'ows [the ox] towpt ower hedge intil a lang dyke. **1863** BRIERLEY *Waverlow* 168 If her father would 'just tope o'er' [doze off, fall asleep]..she could steal out. **1876** *Whitby Gloss.*, *Towp*, *Towple*, or *Towple down*, to fall over. *c* **1900** in *Eng. Dial. Dict.* (E. Yorks.), Old you [ewe] 'z boon te toup ower.

tope, *v.*[2] Now only *literary* or *arch.* [Known 1654; origin obscure. Synonymous with the earlier TOP *v.*[3], but, as in prec., the substitution of long *o* offers difficulties. See Note below, and that to TOPE *int.*]

1. *trans.* To drink, *esp.* to drink copiously and habitually.

1654 GAYTON *Pleas. Notes* IV. ix. 230 Tope it about mine Host; the wine bags now Had been as good, as milke of the red Cow. *c* **1679** *Roxb. Ball.* (1890) VII. 13 They tope the brandy, beer, and ale. **1719** D'URFEY *Pills* (1872) I. 41 And could we tope an ocean His due we hardly give. **1772** MRS. DELANY in *Life & Corr.* Ser. II. (1862) I. 410 Fat John will no more..snore by the great kitchen fire or tope Staffordshire ale! **1876** T. S. EGAN tr. *Heine's Atta Troll*, etc. 250 Our Rhine-wine constantly toping.

2. *intr.* To drink largely or in large draughts.

1667 DRYDEN *Maiden Queen* V. i, I'll Tope with you, I'll Sing with you, I'll Dance with you. **1671** CROWNE *Juliana* I, I can go into the Cardinal's cellar and tie my nose to one barrel, and my horse to another, and tope who shall tope most for a wager. *a* **1701** SEDLEY *Toper* Wks. (1766) 27 Let's tope and be merry, Be jolly and cheery. **1754** *Connoisseur* No. 9 ¶4 On Sundays, while the husbands are toping at the alehouse,..their wives..go to church. **1827** HOOD *Don't you Smell Fire* 7 Now where can the turn-cock be drinking?.. But he still may tope on, for I'm thinking That the plugs are as dry as himself.

Hence **'toping** *vbl. sb.* (also *attrib.*) and *ppl. a.*

(The word in first quot. may be for TOPPING.)

1667 DRYDEN & DK. NEWCASTLE *Sir Martin Mar-all* V. iii. (1668) 68 A rare toping health this. *a* **1680** BUTLER *Epigr. on Club of Sots*, The jolly Members of a toping Club. **1690** DRYDEN *Don Sebast.* I. i, This Mufty..is some English Renegade, he talks so savourly of toping. *a* **1701** SEDLEY *To Phillis* Wks. (1766) 20 A club of witty, toping boys. **1709** O. DYKES *Eng. Prov. & Refl.* (ed. 2) 298 Tipling, and Toping, and Bouzing above measure is as bad as Bouncing in our Liquor. **1753** *Scots Mag.* Oct. 491/2, I had..got by heart several toping..songs. **1855** KINGSLEY *Westw. Ho!* ii, To amuse themselves in something more intellectual than mere toping in pot-houses. **1884** *Edin. Rev.* Oct. 314 The country squires who sang Durfey's songs at their 'toping-tables'.

[*Note.* One theory would identify this with TOP *v.*[2], TOPE *v.*[1], with the primary sense 'to tilt a bottle or vessel in drinking', hence 'to drink with great draughts, or copiously'; another would connect this vb. with TOPE *int.*, for which there is someting to be said; only that TOP *v.*[3] occurs a good deal earlier.]

†**tope,** *int.* *Obs.* [See Note below.] An exclamation used in drinking; app. = I pledge you.

1651 STANLEY *Excit. Anacreon* Poems 94 By thy tall Majestic Flaggons; By Mas, Tope, and thy Flap-dragons.. To thy frolick Order call us, Knights of the deep Bowle install us. **1659** SHIRLEY *Hon. & Mammon* V. i, *2nd Sol.* To my Colonel, honest Squanderbag. (*Drinks.*) *1st Sol.* Who wants my colonel? *2nd Sol.* I want it, tope: give me 't. **1663** COWLEY *Cutter of Coleman St.* II. viii, Fill us t'other Quart, That we may drink the Colonel's Health... Why dost thou frown, thou arrant Clown? Hey Boys—Tope. **1664** ETHEREDGE *Love in Tub* II. iii, Lend me your hand, Sir..; here's a good health To all that are so: Tope..here pledg me.

[*Note.* Generally held to be a. F. *top, tope, tôpe*, according to Littré ellipt. for *je tope*, from *toper, tôper, tauper*, 'to accept a stake or wager', orig. a word of dice-play (cf. Littré s.v. L'un des joueurs ayant dit: mâsse dix pistoles, l'autre a dit, tôpe); hence, to accept an offer or proposal; = It. *toppa* 'done!', a word said to signify acceptance of a bet, *toppare* 'to say " done" when another offers to lay a wager'; orig. to strike against, 'give a counter-shock' (Florio), Sp. *topar* to meet, to run or strike against. Its use in drinking is cited in It. 1659 (see quot. below), and in F. in 1671 (see Littré). The Fr. *tope* has passed into Du. *top*, Ger. *topp*, Sw. *topp*, in sense 'done!', 'agreed', and for the acceptance of a pledge in drinking. Hence some would derive TOPE *v.*[2] to drink deeply.

1659 TORRIANO *Ital. Dict.*, *Topa*, a word among Dicers, as much to say, 'I hold it, done, throw', or 'I see the By'; also by good fellows, when they are drinking: 'I'll pledge you'.]

tope, obs. Sc. f. TAP *v.*[1]; var. TOBE.

topectomy (tə'pɛktəmɪ). *Surg.* [f. TOP(O- + -ECTOMY.] An operation in which specific areas are removed from the frontal lobe of the cerebral cortex as a treatment for mental illness.

1948 *Newsweek* 29 Mar. 47/3 In the new operation, called a topectomy, the brain fibers are not cut. **1967** [see GYRECTOMY].

topee, var. TOPI.

topen, var. TO-UP *Obs.*, above.

to-pens, obs. f. TWOPENCE.

toper ('təʊpə(r)). Now chiefly *literary*. [f. TOPE *v.*[2] + -ER[1].] One who topes or drinks a great deal; a hard drinker; a drunkard.

1673 *S' too him Bayes* 56 Your right topers now, when a friend begins to flag..use to rouse him up again. **1675** COTTON *Scoffer Scofft* 60 A sturdy piece of flesh, and proper, A merry Grig, and a true Toper. **1768** TUCKER *Lt. Nat.* (1834) I. 41 The cobbler..sits among his fellow topers at the two-penny club. **1816** J. WILSON *City of Plague* I. iv. 153 Bacchanalian song By toper chaunted o'er the flowing bowl. **1844** DICKENS *Mart. Chuz.* xxxvi. **1898** *Allbutt's Syst. Med.* V. 162 Topers are prone to tuberculous affections.

Hence **'toperdom, 'toperism** (*nonce-wds.*).

1891 *Scott. Leader* 30 Dec. 4 Much rejoicing has..been caused in London toperdom by the issue by certain enterprising publicans of 'free insurances'. **1896** *Speaker* 6 June 618 The besotted toperism of so many of his companions.

topet, topeus, obs. ff. TOPPET, TOPAZ.

†**'topful,** *a.* *Obs. rare.* [f. TOP *sb.*[1] + -FUL.] High, lofty, towering.

c **1611** CHAPMAN *Iliad* V. 761 Soone they wonne The top of all the topfull heauens. *Ibid.* VIII. 4 In top of all the topfull heights, that crowne th' Olympian hill.

top-full ('tɒp'fʊl), *a.* Now *rare.* Also *erron.* topful. [f. TOP *sb.*[1] + FULL *a.*]

Full to the top; brim-full.

1553 BALE *Gardiner's De vera Obed.* G vj b, As it were a vessell being toppe full of water. **1617** MORYSON *Itin.* III. 49 A huge great purse top full of gold. **1762** STERNE *Tr. Shandy* V. xxxviii, My father drew in his lungs topfull of air. **1827** G. DARLEY in *Q. Rev.* July (1902) 186 Both go tottering, tattling home Topful of wine as well as glee.

†**b.** *transf.* Said of that which fills (to the top): brimming. *Obs. rare.*

1602 DOLMAN *La Primaud. Fr. Acad.* (1618) III. 769 If one cast into the same so toppefull water, some heauy thing, the water..will swell onely. **1608** SYLVESTER *Du Bartas* II. iv. IV. *Decay* 52 Achab's House, whose cursed wickednesse Was now top-full.

c. *fig.*

1579 TOMSON *Calvin's Serm. Tim.* 944/1 We shall haue the measure of our perfection and of all good workes toppefull. **1648** DARNELL in *I. Basire's Corr.* (1831) 74 Topfull of busines as I am. **1751** R. PALTOCK *P. Wilkins* xiv. (1883) 46/1 Top-full of these thoughts, I re-entered my grotto. **1881** FAIRBAIRN *Stud. Life Christ* v. 86 She, unsexed, filled from crown to toe, topfull of direst cruelty.

topgallant (tɒp'gælənt, tə'gælənt), *sb.* and *a.* Also 6 **-galand.** [f. TOP *sb.*[1] 9 + GALLANT *a.*, as making a brave or gallant show in comparison with the lower tops. The guess that the name was orig. *top-garland* (from GARLAND *sb.* 8) is disproved by the early evidence, and does not suit the sense.]

A. *sb.*

†**1.** *Naut.* A top (TOP *sb.*[1] 9) at the head of the topmast, and thus in a loftier position than the original top-castle or top. *Obs.*

The thing was in use before the name: see quot. 1497, where it is described without a name. The name was prob. *obs.* by 1600, when sense 2 came in.

[**1497** *Naval Accts. Henry VII* 278 *The Regent*, Also a Toppe maste aboue the mayne Toppe maste, Rotteyn perused & consumyd to noght. A sayle to the same.. Also viij Shrowdes belongyng to the same.] **1514** *Inv. Henri Grace de Dieu* in Oppenheim *Admin. Roy. Navy* I. 374 Toppe Galant apon the foretopmast..j. *Ibid.* 375 The top Galant apon the mayne topmast..j. **1514** *Inv.* in *United Serv. Mag.* (1910) Mar. 581 The top galant. The mast to the same .j. The sayle yerd. **1569** SPARKE *Sir J. Hawkins' 2nd Voy.* (Hakl. Soc.) 50 The *Jesus* also bare a light in her toppegallant. **1590** SPENSER *Vis. World's Van.* ix, A goodly ship with banners bravely dight, And flag in her top-gallant, I espide.

2. *pl.* Short for *topgallant sails* (see B. 1 a below), the sails above the topsail and topgallant.

This use appears to have come in as sense 1 became obs.

1599 DALLAM in *Early Voy. Levant* (Hakl. Soc.) 9 They.. made away with all the sayle they had, drablings and topgalands, but..we came nearer and nearer unto them. **1647** WARD *Simp. Cobler* (1843) 49 When Kings are hailing up their top-gallants, Subjects lay hold on their slablines. **1694** MOTTEUX *Rabelais* IV. lxiv, A fresh gale..began to fill the..Top-gallants. **1833** MARRYAT *P. Simple* xlix, She had ..got up..jury-masts, with topgallants for topsails.

3. a. *transf.* (from 1 and 2) The most elevated (*lit.* or *fig.*) part or member *of* anything; see quots., and also *top and topgallant* (TOP *sb.*[1] 9 c).

1581 J. BELL *Haddon's Answ. Osor.* 388 If these two gallaunt Gyaunts apply no stronger pillers..to vphold the Majesticall State of theyr toppegallaunt of Rome. **1618** G. STRODE *Anat. Mortalitie* 83 The Peacocke..when he..seeth his black feete,.. vaileth his top-gallant, and seemeth to sorrow. **1656** I. BOURNE *Def. Script.* 15 A faith in Christ.. was the top gallant of a Christian. **1878** STEVENSON *Edinburgh* (1889) 29 A few spires, the stone top-gallants of the city.

b. *fig.* The highest point or pitch; summit.

1592 SHAKS. *Rom. & Jul.* II. iv. 202 Which to the high top gallant of my ioy, Must be my conuoy in the secret night. **1666** SANCROFT *Lex Ignea* 17 The very Top-gallant of all our Glory. **1679** C. NESSE *Antichrist* 149 From..the top-gallant of his Luciferian pride. **1862** CARLYLE *Fredk. Gt.* XIII. ix. (1872) V. 92 He seems to himself a man at the topgallant of his wishes.

†**c.** Used for the nonce as an intensive of *gallant.*

1701 FARQUHAR *Sir H. Wildair* IV. ii, And such as he are all those topgallants that daily haunt my house, ruin your honour, and disturb my quiet.

B. *attrib.* or *adj.*

1. a. Of, pertaining to, or having the position of top-gallant: ***topgallant mast, sail, yard,*** the mast, sail, or yard above the topmast and topsail; the third mast, sail, or yard above the deck; †**topgallant royals,** early name for *royals* (ROYAL B. 5).

Often forming with the sb. an attrib. phrase, as ***topgallant-mast head, topgallant-sail yard, topgallant-yard man.***

1514 *Inv. Henri Grace de Dieu* in Oppenheim *Admin. Roy. Navy* I. 374 Bowlynes to the topgalant yerd... Lyftes to the foretopgalant yerd with iiij single polies. *Ibid.* 377 Topgalant Sayle. **1514** *Inv. Kateryn Forteleza* in *United Serv. Mag.* Mar. (1910) 581 Top galant, top galant mast, shrowdes to the same .vj. **1588** *State Papers Dom. Eliz.* CCXX. lf. 54 (P.R.O.), The Revendge..A mayne topgallant saile made of an olde myzon. *Ibid.* lf. 71 The Dreadnoughte..one mayne topgallant saile, servic[eable]. **1626** CAPT. SMITH *Accid. Yng. Seamen* 12 The top gallant mast, the marine top gallant sayle yeard, the trucke or flagge staffe. **1627** —— *Seaman's Gram.* vii. 31 There is also your maine top-saile, and fore top-saile, with their top-gallant sailes. **1634** SIR T. HERBERT *Trav.* 7 Sometimes the surges or sea-flashes doe rebound top-gallant height. **1671** *Lond. Gaz.* No. 544/3 He caused his Top-gallant Masts and Yards to be taken down, and his Galleries and Quarter Decks to be covered with Canvas made for the purpose, to the end they might take him for a Merchant man. **1692** in *Capt. Smith's Seaman's Gram.* I. xiv. 64, 7 Main Topsail Lifts, 8 Topgallant Lifts. **1704** J. HARRIS *Lex. Techn.* I, *Top-Gallant-Masts* of a Ship, are two, viz. *Maintop-gallant-Mast*, and *Foretop-gallant-Mast*; And these two are small round Pices of Timber, set on to their respective Top-Masts; on the Top of which Masts are set the Flagg-staffs. **1756** *Gentl. Mag.* XXVI. 506/1 Making all the sail they possibly could set to get from us, with top gallant ryalls, lower top-mast, and top-gallant steering sails, keeping a good full. **1835** SIR J. ROSS *Narr. 2nd Voy.* iii. 32 There were two seamen on the topgallant yard. **1840** R. H. DANA *Bef. Mast* iv, We sprang aloft immediately, and furled the royals and topgallant-sails. *c* **1860** H. STUART *Seaman's Catech.* 45 The topgallant yard men..will go aloft. **1891** *Times* 21 Oct. 7/4 The *Hoffnung*,..having..foretopmast and topgallant, with yards and sails attached, carried away; also main topgallant mast with yards.

b. See quotations.

1839 MARRYAT *Phant. Ship* viii, On her forecastle another small deck ran from the knight-heads, which was called the top-gallant forecastle. **1869** SIR E. J. REED *Shipbuild.* xii. 238 It is customary to complete the topsides above this gunwale by, what is termed, a top-gallant bulwark formed of wooden berthing and stanchions.

2. Allowing topgallant sails to be used, as ***topgallant gale, breeze, weather.***

1697 DAMPIER *Voy. round World* (1699) 79 We had it [wind] at E.S.E. where it stood a considerable time and blew a fresh Top-gallant gale. **1769** FALCONER *Dict. Marine* (1789), *Tems à perroquet*, a top-gallant gale; top-gallant weather. **1798** *Authentic Narrative Battle of Nile* 21 The wind was at this time N.N.W. and blew what Seamen call a Top-gallant breeze. **1806** A. DUNCAN *Nelson* 68 The wind.. blew what seamen call a top-gallant breeze. It was necessary to take in the royals when the squadron hauled upon a wind. **1873** *Routledge's Yng. Gent. Mag.* July 494/1 A good 'topgallant breeze' sprung up.

3. *fig.* Lofty, grand, fine, topping: cf. A. 3.

1613 SYLVESTER *Lachr. Lachr.* B iv, Stript..Of guiddie-Gaudes, Top-gallant Tires and Towers. **1650** FULLER *Pisgah* IV. vi. 108 Sure I am, the Babylonians were more top-gallant then the Jews, and quite put them down with bravery. **1735** POPE *Donne's Sat.* IV. 230 Top-gallant he, and she in all her trim. **1849** CUPPLES *Green Hand* ix, Here he [the sailor] came out with a regular string of top-gallant oaths.

toph[1], **tophe** (təʊf). Now *rare.* [ad. L. *tōph-us*, more correctly *tōf-us*: see TOPHUS.]

1. Usually ***toph stone***: Travertin, or other soft stone: = TOPHUS 1.

a **1552** LELAND *Itin.* VI. 72 A Quarre of Tophe Stone by Driselege, wherof much of the Castelle was buildid. **1577** HARRISON *England* III. xv. (1878) II. 61 For Tophe stone, not a few allow of the quarrie that is at Drisley, diuerse mislike not of the veine of hard stone that is at Oxford, and Burford. **1811** J. MILNER *Eccles. Archit. Eng. Mid. Ages* 95 Arched with hard stone for the ribs and light toph stone for the interstices.

2. *Path.* A calcareous deposit or calculus formed within the human or animal body: = TOPHUS 2.

1584 T. BASTARD *Chrestoleros* (1880) 10 Phisition Mirus talkes of saliuation, Of Tophes and Pustules, and Febrication. **1651** BIGGS *New Disp.* § 141 A neutrall nature of a tophe, between a Cartilage and a Stone. **1694** SALMON *Bate's Dispens.* (1713) 64/2 It softens, dissipates, yea, and dissolves the chalky Concretions..pocky Nodes, Tophs, Gums, and Swellings. *Ibid.* 682/1 It cleanses the Skin,.. takes away Gouty Tophs, cures the Leprosie. **1706** PHILLIPS (ed. Kersey), *Toph*, a word us'd by some Chirurgical Writers for a kind of Swelling in the Bones. **1822–7** GOOD *Study Med.* (1829) IV. 532 Some structural irritation within the cavity of the skull, such as a node or toph. **1843** R. J. GRAVES *Syst. Clin. Med.* xxviii. 355 Exanthemata..nodes, tophes, syphilitic gout and rheumatism.

‖**toph**[2] (to:f). [Heb. *tōph*, f. *tāphaph* to sound or beat the timbrel; app. echoic.] A Hebrew instrument of music, of the nature of a timbrel or tabret.

[**1749** Thoph: see TOPHET 1.] **1864** ENGEL *Mus. Anc. Nat.* 222 This deff may have been the *toph* of the Hebrews, as well as the square tambourine of the ancient Egyptians. **1879** STAINER *Music of Bible* 155 Among the instruments which the company of prophets bare..was a toph.

tophaceous (təʊ'feɪʃəs), *a.* [ad. L. *tōf-, tōphāce-us*, f. TOPHUS: see -ACEOUS.]

1. Of the nature of tophus or toph; sandy, gritty; rough, stony.

1672 *Phil. Trans.* VII. 4064 It is scabrous or rough, sand-like, although the substance is Tophaceous. **1692** RAY *Disc.* II. iv. (1732) 128 The Tophaceous Hills and Cliffs about Andria in Apulia. **1749** *Phil. Trans.* XLVI. 221 The Waters of these hot Springs..are so replete with tophaceous Matter, that where ever they run, Masses of Tophus are formed. **1777** LIGHTFOOT *Flora Scot.* II. 535 *Chara.* Incrusted with a kind of tophaceous coat, which is like sand between the teeth. **1819** H. BUSK *Vestriad* IV. 698 Sapphire brooks on beds tophaceous play.

2. *Path.* Gritty or calcareous, as the matter deposited in gout.

1687 *Phil. Trans.* XVI. 553 The Generation of the Tophaceous Matter in the nodose Gout. **1728** *Ibid.* XXXV. 493 That tophaceous gouty Substance commonly found about the Joints. **1879** *St. George's Hosp. Rep.* IX. 643 Gouty, or so-called tophaceous, deposits.

‖**tophaike** (təʊ'feɪk). [ad. vulgar Turkish *tüfek* (literary *tufeng*) musket: cf. Pers. *tufak* blow-pipe.] A (Turkish) musket.

1813 BYRON *Giaour* viii, Though too remote for sound to wake In echoes of the far tophaike (*note* 'Tophaike', musquet). **1816** *Sporting Mag.* XLVII. 285 Their coming was announced by the firing of their tophaikes. **1882** ARMSTRONG *Garl. Greece, Last Sortie* 268 At my new-found foe I sprung, And clutched with both my hands the raised tophaike.

'top-'hamper. [f. TOP *sb.*[1] + HAMPER *sb.*[2] 2.] *Naut.* Weight or encumbrance aloft: orig. said of the upper masts, sails, and rigging of a ship; later, also, weight or encumbrance on the deck, as in a steamer, ironclad, etc.

1791 *Jrnl. Barth. James* (Navy Rec. Soc.) 207 The ship being very uneasy from the loss of so much top hamper. **1800** *Naval Chron.* IV. 52 The objects of this invention are: ..The great reduction in top-hamper, height, and size of masts. **1829** MARRYAT *F. Mildmay* xiv, To disengage this enormous top hamper, was to us an object more to be desired than expected. **1840** R. H. DANA *Bef. Mast* xxxi. 114 To see our noble ship dismantled of all her top-hamper of long tapering masts and yards. **1857** MAURY in Corbin *Life* (1888) 135 She was a side-wheel steamer, with not a little top hamper, and therefore an ugly thing to manage in such a situation. **1870** *Daily News* 16 Sept., One cannot but suspect that the enormous top hamper, consisting of 4 25-ton guns with her immense turrets, had something to do with her heeling over.

b. *transf.* and *fig.* An encumbrance on the top or upper part of anything; something that makes it 'top-heavy'; the 'head-piece'.

1861 SMILES *Engineers* II. 269 Though the top-hamper of houses had long been removed, and the piers patched and strengthened at various times, the [London] bridge was becoming every year less and less adapted for accommodating the increasing traffic to and from the City. **1881** G. W. CABLE *Mme. Delphine* viii, The returned rover was a trifle snarled in his top-hamper. **1894** SALA *Things I have seen* I. iv. 147 The luggage..was piled..on the roof of the machine; and the whole tophamper was covered with a thick tarpaulin. **1905** W. P. KER *Ess. Mediæval Lit.* i. 11 Many of Hakluyt's men..carry more rhetorical top-hamper than Ohthere.

top hat. Also top-hat. **1. a.** A man's silk or beaver hat with high cylindrical crown; a tall or high hat.

1881 MISS BRADDON *Asph.* xvi, She liked to have her son well-dressed and in a top-hat. **1883** E. F. KNIGHT *Cruise of Falcon* (1887) 222 Black men in coats and top-hats. **1886** J. K. JEROME *Idle Thoughts* xiii, How I do hate a top hat! **1905** A. R. WALLACE *My Life* I. 17 He always wore a top-hat—a beaver hat as it was then called, before silk hats were invented.

b. *transf.* A person of the kind or class that wears a top hat; an important or senior person (see also quot. 1938).

1936 *Amer. Speech* XI. 221 The ermines and top-hats, the carriage trade of the early part of the century. **1938** F. D. SHARPE *Sharpe of Flying Squad* xix. 209 It's no good here, boys, there are too many top-hats (detectives). **1974** *Globe & Mail* (Toronto) 4 Oct. 7/1 Mr. White brought Mr. Benoit along to the Albany Club, and the Tory party tophats liked what they saw.

2. *attrib.* **a.** With reference to the wearing of top hats. **b.** Shaped like a top hat.

1902 R. HICHENS *Londoners* 159 Another top-hat Ascot! I wish the Prince would set the fashion of billycocks. **1958** *Engineering* 14 Mar. 344/2 Shallow 'top-hat' sections are used for the horizontal rails. **1966** MRS. L. B. JOHNSON *White House Diary* 13 Dec. (1970) 461 Lyndon made a splendid toast. He said he wanted American art to be enjoyed at the grass-roots level, just as it is by the top-hat crowd. **1967** M. CHANDLER *Ceramics in Mod. World* ii. 83 (*caption*) A 'top-hat' kiln loaded for firing.

3. Passing into *adj.* Designating insurance or pension schemes devised as a means of deferred payment for senior executives.

1952 *Economist* 8 Nov. 417/1 'Top-hat' contracts for higher executives. **1964** *Daily Tel.* 16 Apr. 23/1 The annual check on senior executives under the 'top-hat scheme', because of the neurosis it created, was a pernicious plan. **1979** *Guardian* 18 June 10/4 It would be good to know that the company car, the top hat pension,..will not survive the axe next spring.

Hence **'top-'hatted** *a.*, wearing a top-hat; **'top-'hatter**, one who wears a top-hat.

1892 *Spectator* 27 Feb. 305/1 To wonder at pig-tailed China and top-hatted Japan. **1892** R. BUCHANAN in *Pall Mall G.* 19 July 3/2 Far from the realms of hansoms and top-hatters all. **1900** *Westm. Gaz.* 21 Aug. 8/1 Of every social standing, from the top-hatted City man to the picturesque newspaper urchin.

tophe, variant of TOPH[1].

top-heavy (ˌtɒp'hɛvɪ), *a.* **a.** Disproportionately heavy at the top; having the upper part so heavy as to overbalance the lower; hence, unstable and inclined to topple. Also *transf.* and *fig.*

a **1533** FRITH *Answ. More* (1829) 184 They have made it so top-heavy, that it is surely like to have a fall. **1641** BEST *Farm. Bks.* (Surtees) 36 That they make theire loades broade, and large, but not over high and toppe-heavy, for feare of throwinge over..the waine. **1647** H. MORE *Song Soul* I. II. lxxvii, Top heavy was his head with earthly policy. **1707** MORTIMER *Husb.* (1721) II. 81 If your Trees grow too top heavy, you must abate the Head to lighten them. **1862** T. A. TROLLOPE *Lenten Journ.* xvi. 259 We were top-heavy with eight or nine great sacks of letters on the roof [of the vehicle]. **1889** *Anthony's Photogr. Bull.* II. 118 Do not make your picture topheavy with clouds. **1895** K. GRAHAME *Gold.*

Age (1904) 20 Harold,..top-heavy with eagerness of possession, had fallen into the pond.

b. Said of an intoxicated person: tipsy.

1687 in *Dk. Buckhm.'s Wks.* (1705) II. 120 Jack was too top-heavy to escape undiscovered. *a* **1700** B. E. *Dict. Cant. Crew, Top-heavy*, Drunk. **1823** T. W. L. in Hone *Everyday Bk.* (1827) II. 859 Being top-heavy with liquor, he..lost his balance.

c. *fig.* Of a business, organization, etc.: (*a*) overcapitalized; (*b*) having a disproportionately large number of people in senior administrative positions.

1934 in WEBSTER. **1945** A. HUXLEY *Let.* 8 Aug. (1969) 531 A country with a decentralized..economy could not compete as a military power with countries having a top-heavy capital goods industry. **1962** *Rep. Comm. Broadcasting 1960* in *Parl. Papers 1961–2* (Cmnd. 1753) IX. 259 Some witnesses alleged..that the BBC was 'top-heavy': that is, it spent too much on administration at the expense of programme production. **1963** *Listener* 7 Mar. 417/1 Petty officials multiplied till the administration became top-heavy. **1976** M. MACHLIN *Pipeline* vi. 71 Even now his firm was top-heavy on distribution and transportation.

Hence **'top-'heavily** *adv.*; **'top-'heaviness**; **'top-'heavyish** *a.*

1843 H. JAMES *Let.* 11 May in R. B. Perry *Tht. & Char. W. James* (1935) I. 46 Thought heaped up to top-heaviness and inevitable lopsidedness. **1853** G. J. CAYLEY *Las Alforjas* II. 204 A noble top-heavyish Gothic tower. **1869** SIR E. J. REED *Iron-Clad Ships* vii. 137 To the unprofessional eye there does appear to be a 'top-heaviness' in armoured ships. **1889** WELCH *Text Bk. Naval Archit.* iii. 63 The mistaken view..that 'top-heaviness' was the cause of the excessive rolling. **1926** FOWLER *Mod. Eng. Usage* 504/2 What reads well & what reads..jerkily, lopsidedly, topheavily, or otherwise badly. **1947** *Penguin New Writing* XXXI. 172 In the cottage gardens the crumpled, bunchy flowers of double daffodils waved top-heavily in the wind.

Tophet ('təʊfɪt). Also 4 tofeth, 4–9 topheth. [a. Heb. *topheth* pr. name, of uncertain etymol.

For conjectures, see references in *Oxford Heb. & Eng. Lex.* s.v., One of the most ancient sought to connect it with TOPH², or its vb.: see quots. 1388, 1749, 1865.]

1. *orig.* Proper name of a place near Gehenna or the Valley of the Son or Children of Hinnom, south of Jerusalem, where, according to Jer. xix. 4, etc., the Jews made human sacrifices to strange gods. Later it was used as a place for the deposit of refuse, and became symbolic of the torments of hell.

1382 WYCLIF *2 Kings* xxiii. 10 Forsothe he defoulide Topheth, that is in the valeye of the sone of Ennon, that no man schuld sacryn his sone or his douȝtre thorȝ fyr to Moloch [**1388** has *marg. note*..Tophet signefieth tympan.. for the prestis of this idol, maden noyse with timpans, lest fadres and modris schulden here the cry of her sones, diynge bi fier in the hondis of the idol]. **1535** COVERDALE *ibid.*, He suspended Tophet also in the valley of the children of Ennon [etc.]. **1611** BIBLE *ibid.*, He defiled Topheth. **1667** MILTON *P.L.* I. 404 [Moloch] made his Grove The pleasant valley of Hinnom, Tophet thence And black Gehenna call'd, the Type of Hell. **1749** STACKHOUSE *Hist. Bible* VI. iv. II. 911 *note*, It is the general Opinion of the Jews, that the Word *Tophet* comes from *Thoph*, which, in their Language, signifies a Drum. **1865** GROSART *Lambs all Safe* 117 (tr. Pintus 1582) That the parents of the child might not hear its wailing, the priests beat drums, from which cause the place was called Tophet, or a drum.

2. The place of punishment for the wicked after death; the place of eternal fire; hell, Gehenna.

1388 WYCLIF *Isa.* xxx. 33 For whi Tophet [**1382** Tofeth], *that is, helle*, deep and alargid, is maad redi of the kyng fro ȝistirdai. **1611** BIBLE *ibid.*, For Tophet [**1885** *R.V.* a Topheth] is ordained of olde..the breath of the Lord, like a streame of brimstone doeth kindle it. **1678** BUNYAN *Pilgr.* I. 2, I fear that this burden..will sinck me lower then the Grave; and I shall fall into Tophet. *a* **1708** BEVERIDGE *Priv. Th.* I. (1816) 95, I never did see..the flaming tophet that is below. **1825** SCOTT *Talism.* xviii, Whose ashes, when this earthly fuel is burnt out, must yet be flung into Tophet.

3. *fig.* A place, state, condition, or company likened to hell. **a.** A 'hell upon earth'.

1618 J. TAYLOR (Water P.) *Pennyles Pilgr.* E ij b, Yet all I saw was pleasure mixt with profit, which prou'd it to be no tormenting Tophet. **1849** MACAULAY *Hist. Eng.* iv. I. 498 The chief of this Tophet [Claverhouse], a soldier of distinguished courage and professional skill, but rapacious and profane. **1883** MISS BRADDON *Gold. Calf* xxv, If she could..lead her husband's footsteps out of this Tophet into which he had sunk himself.

b. A place or state of wild chaos and warring elements; a roaring furnace; a raging whirlpool, a maelstrom.

1837 HAWTHORNE *Twice-told T.* (1851) I. x. 172 Converted quite to steam, in the miniature tophet, which you mistake for a stomach. **1856** MRS. BROWNING *Aur. Leigh* I. 418 Shuffling off The hearer's soul through hurricanes of notes To a noisy Tophet. **1912** *Daily News* 4 July 1 The officer barked out the short order, 'Load twelve-inch gun'... Instantly tophet was let loose in the turret.

4. *Comb.*, as ***Tophet-black, -red*** adjs.

1837 CARLYLE *Fr. Rev.* III. v. iv, Simultaneously with this Tophet-black aspect, there unfolds itself another aspect, which one may call a Tophet-red aspect, the Destruction of the Catholic Religion; and indeed, for the time being, of Religion itself.

Hence (*nonce-wds.*) **To'phetic, -ical** *adjs.*, of, pertaining to, or of the nature of Tophet; **'Tophetize** *v.*, *trans.* to make a Tophet or hell of; **'Tophetism**, hellishness.

1684 N. S. tr. *Crit. Enq. Edit. Bible* xxv. 226 All the stratagems of Popery, all the tophitical Tyranny of the School-men. **1698** C. MATHER *Magn. Chr.* VII. (1702) 105 A Room Tophetized with Smoke, and Rhume, and Spittle, and Malice, and Lies. **1859** M. NAPIER *Mem. Visct. Dundee* I. 20 It is brutality rendered dangerous and Tophetical by excessive bumptuousness. [Cf. quot. 1849 in 3 a.] *Ibid.* 38 The idealized Tophetism of a trooper's 'damning'.

tophic ('təʊfɪk), *a.* [f. TOPH-US + -IC.] Of the nature of toph or tophus; tophaceous.

1789 J. WILLIAMS *Min. Kingd.* II. 383 There are great quantities of the concreted substance called *tufa* in many parts of Scotland... The process of nature, in the formation of this tophic substance, is to be explained upon the same principles as the stallactites.

†**to'phose**, *a.* [f. as next: see -OSE.] = next.

1752 J. HILL *Hist. Anim.* 581 The Capra, with a tophose bunch on the head.

†**'tophous**, *a. Obs.* [ad. rare L. *tōph-*, *tōfōsus*, f. TOPHUS, *tōfus*: see -OUS.] Of the nature of a stony or calcareous concretion: **a.** in the body, **b.** in deposits from springs, etc. (cf. next).

1634 T. JOHNSON *Parey's Chirurg.* XIX. iii. (1678) 432 You shall find them [pustules] stuffed with a certain plaister-like and tophous matter. **1692** RAY *Disc.* 110 Now these Teeth being burnt, pass presently into a Coal, but the tophous substance adhering to them, doth not so. **1699** MISAURUS *Hon. Gout* (1720) 8 And threw off the tophous Injury. **1754–64** SMELLIE *Midwif.* II. 79 Bones..perfectly sound with a few spots of tophous concretions on them. **1756** C. LUCAS *Ess. Waters* II. 141 A..petrifying incrusting or tophous water, which rises in several large springs.

tophus ('təʊfəs). Also 6–7 tofus, 7 tophis, -as. *Pl.* ‖tophi; also 7 tophy, tophoes, tophuses, tofusses. [a. L. *tōphus*, better *tōfus*, a general name for loose porous stones of various kinds, whence It. *tufo* (also *tofo* in Florio, 'a kind of soft, crumbling, or mouldring stone, to build withall'), Fr. *tuf* (16th c. in Hatz.-Darm.), 'generic name of porous stones, produced in the form of sediment or incrustation, as calcareous, siliceous, volcanic *tuf*' (Littré): see also TUFF, TUFA.]

1. A soft porous stone, arenaceous, calcareous, or volcanic; *esp.* a stony substance deposited by calcareous springs.

1555 EDEN *Decades* 19 The stone cauled *Tofus* whiche is soone resolued into sande. **1615** G. SANDYS *Trav.* 161 (tr. Juvenal) How much more venerable had it beene, If grasse had cloth'd the circling banks in greene, Nor marble had the natiue tophis marr'd. *Ibid.* 272 The artificiall rocks, shells, mosse and tophas, seeme euen to excell that which they imitate. **1621** —— *Ovid's Met.* III. (1632) 84 A natiue Arch she drew, With Pumice and light Tofusses, that grew [III. 160 nam pumice vivo, Et levibus tophis nativum duxerat arcem]. **1692** RAY *Disc.* 111 Among Tophi and Stones in those dry places. **1696** *Phil. Trans.* XIX. 194 He produces one Echinus, bruised in the Tophus in which it lay. **1789** PILKINGTON *View Derby.* I. vii. 316, I have seen a stag's head ..which was found in the tophus at Alport. **1842** BRANDE *Dict. Sc.*, etc., *Tophus*, the term has been applied to porous deposits of calcareous matter from water.

2. *Path.* A concretion which forms on the surface of the joints, the teeth, the pinna of the ear, etc. in gout; a gouty deposit; also gravel, or a stone or calculus, formed within the body.

1607 TOPSELL *Four-f. Beasts* (1658) 65 In the second venter of a cow there is a round black tophus found, being of no weight. **1612** WOODALL *Surg. Mate* Wks. (1653) 71 *Amoniacum*..dissolveth Tophoes or hard stones grown in the flesh. **1663** BOYLE *Usef. Exp. Nat. Philos.* II. iii. 77 With a very few Doses..the Merchant was quickly free'd, not onely from his Pains, but from his Gouty Tophy. **1698** TYSON in *Phil. Trans.* XX. 132 These Hairy Tophi are frequently to be met with in the Stomachs of Bruits. **1860** MAYNE *Expos. Lex.*, *Tophus*... *Med.* A name for the matter concreted in the joints of the gouty; also the calculous matter concreted in the kidneys and urinary bladder; also the tartar on the teeth. *Surg.* Term for a swelling particularly affecting a bone, or the periosteum: a toph. **1866** A. FLINT *Princ. Med.* (1880) 1103 These gouty concretions are called tophi or chalk-stones.

3. *Comb.* **tophus-stone** = TRAVERTIN.

1830 LYELL *Princ. Geol.* I. 211 Pallas..enumerates a great many hot springs, which have deposited monticules of travertin precisely analogous in composition and structure to those of the baths of San Filippo, and other localities in Italy... Speaking of the tophus-stone, as he terms these limestones, he often observes that it is snow-white.

‖**topī**[1], **topee** ('təʊpɪ, older təʊ'piː). *East Ind.* [a. Hindī *ṭopī* hat; prob. the word mentioned in the Vocab. of *Linguagem de Calicut* in the *Roteiro de Vasco da Gama* 1497, 'barrete: *tupy*', related to Hindī '*top* helmet or hat' (Yule). (But some think the latter is an adaptation of Pg. *topo* top.)] Originally applied by Indian natives to the European hat; now specialized in Anglo-Indian, as a name for the *sola topī*, sola hat or helmet: see SOLA *sb.*

1835 *Court Mag.* VI. 207/2 The white *sombrero* solah topee, was supplanted by a raking cocked hat. **1845–** Sola topi [see SOLA *sb.* (*b*)]. **1849** E. B. EASTWICK *Dry Leaves* 2 And there is need of many a fold of twisted muslin round the white topi to keep off his [the sun's] importunacy. **1872** 'ALIPH CHEEM' *Lays of Ind* (1876) 41 The boat came back in a little space, With Grant and the topee blue. **1889** *Blackw. Mag.* Aug. 245 You wear a pith topee. **1904** *Daily Record & Mail* 1 Jan. 4 The white topee, green-lined, is a favourite hat.

Comb. **1880** A. M. RUTHQUIST in *Life* xi. (1893) 201 A rather lengthy lesson in topee-making was given.

Hence ‖**topī-**, **topee-wallah** (ˌtəʊpɪ'wɒlə, təʊpiː'wɑːlɑː), also **-wala** [a. Hindī *ṭopīwālā*, one who wears a hat, f. *topī* + WALLAH fellow], the Indian name for a European, because he wears a hat.

The term is used 'by the natives with a shade of disparagement', while 'all persons claiming European blood' take pride 'in wearing a hat' (Yule s.v. *topaz*). R. Drummond says that in his time (before 1808), *Topeewala* and *Puggrywala* were used in Guzerat and the Mahratta country for 'European' and 'Native'. So 'the author of the Persian *Life of Hydur Naik* calls Europeans *Kalāh-posh* hat-wearers' (*Ibid.* s.v.).

1826 HOCKLEY *Pandurang Hari* vi. I. 88 It was now evident we should have to encounter the *Topee Wallas*. **1834** A. PRINSEP *Baboo* I. viii. 126 The Topee-walas are within matchlock shot of this grove! **1864** TREVELYAN *Compet. Wallah* (1866) 44 The idea got about that they were to be forcibly turned into topee-wallahs, hat-fellows, a synonym for the hated name of Frank or Christian.

topi[2] ('təʊpɪ). [a. Mende.] A glossy dark brown antelope belonging to a race of the korrigum, *Damaliscus lunatus*, found in the coastal region of East Africa.

1894 SCLATER & THOMAS *Bk. Antelopes* I. 68 The 'Topi', as we propose to designate another local representative of the Korrigum, from the name given to it by the Swahili, has been known for some years. **1910** R. E. DRAKE-BROCKMAN *Mammals Somaliland* 59 The Topi Hartebeest..is purplish brown. *Ibid.*, The Topi I have never seen in large herds. **1959** A. MOOREHEAD *No Room in Ark* iv. 91 The topi is a fairly mad animal.., a large brown gleaming antelope with gun-metal blazes on its legs and an air of continual stage-fright. **1976** K. THACKERAY *Crownbird* i. 9 They were now doing fifty..and overhauling the topi fast.

‖**topia** ('təʊpɪə). *Rom. Antiq.* [L. *topia*, a. Gr. τόπια, pl. of τόπιον, diminutive of τόπος a place.

But others (e.g. Casaubon) suppose it to be the pl. of τοπεῖον, a 'rope' or 'cord' (used of the cordage of a ship).]

Interior wall-decorations in the style of those found at Pompeii, consisting usually of landscapes or figures of trees and bowers; fanciful mural fresco.

1891 in *Cent. Dict.*; and in other mod. Dicts.

‖**topiaria** (təʊpɪ'ɛərɪə). [L. *topiāria*, fem. sing. (sc. *ars*) of TOPIARIUS.] The art of cutting trees and shrubs into quaint devices.

1599 R. LINCHE *Fount. Anc. Fict.* K iv, This Statue was.. supported by foure Images of Victoria, hewen out..with inimitable skill of the art Topiaria. **1706** PHILLIPS (ed. Kersey), *Topiaria*, the Art of making Arbours with Trees or Twigs cut and plaited. **1900** B. D. JACKSON *Gloss. Bot. Terms* 272/1 *Topiaria*,..ornamental gardening.

topiarian (təʊpɪ'ɛərɪən), *a.* [f. L. *topiāri-us*: see below and -AN.] = TOPIARY.

1694 MOTTEUX *Rabelais* IV. i. 3 A small Vine of large Indian Pearl, of Topiarian work. **1816** SCOTT *Antiq.* iii, Tall clipped hedges of yew and holly, some of which still exhibited the skill of the topiarian artist, and presented curious arm-chairs, towers, and the figures of St. George and the dragon. **1880** *Q. Rev.* Apr. 334 The most famous specimen of Topiarian work in England is probably that at Levens Hall in Westmoreland.

So **'topiarist** = next.

1910 *Athenæum* 15 Jan. 65/3 To the ordinary tourist, however, the place is noteworthy for the art of the topiarist.

‖**topiarius** (təʊpɪ'ɛərɪəs). [L. adj. 'of or belonging to ornamental gardening'; sb. 'an ornamental gardener': see TOPIA and -ARY[1].] One skilled in fanciful landscape-gardening.

1706 PHILLIPS (ed. Kersey), *Topiarius*, a Gardener that orders Arbours or Bowers; or that makes divers Kinds of Knots and Devices in Plants, as they grow. **1896** *Edin. Rev.* July 162 The zeal of the *topiarius*..tortured the bushes into extravagant forms. **1907** *Ibid.* Jan. 150 The shrubs clipped and pruned by the 'topiarius'.

topiary ('təʊpɪərɪ), *a.* (*sb.*) *Gardening.* Also 6–7 -arie. [ad. rare L. *topiāri-us*: see prec. Cf. F. *topiaire* adj. and sb. (Rabelais, 1548).] Consisting in clipping and trimming shrubs, etc. into ornamental or fantastic shapes.

1592 R. D. *Hypnerotomachia* 51 By a turnyng downe the transomes, did joyne decently one with the other with a Topiarie woorke. [Cf. F. *ouvrage topiaire.*] **1644** EVELYN *Diary* 22 Oct., There was much topiary worke, and columns in architecture about the hedges. *a* **1680** BUTLER *Rem.* (1759) I. 184 No topiary Hedge of Quickset Was e're so neatly cut. **1838–9** HALLAM *Hist. Lit.* IV. IV. v. §52 Rapin was a great admirer of box and all topiary works, or trees cut into artificial forms. **1902** *Lond. Mag.* June 474 A topiary garden is by no means an inexpensive hobby to indulge in.

b. *sb.* The topiary art; the training and clipping of trees into artificial shapes.

1908 *Sphere* 10 Oct. 30/1 Topiary is essentially the art of a leisurely age, for it takes a long time to develop a tree into the acquired shape.

topias, obs. variant of TOPAZ.

topic ('tɒpɪk), *a.* and *sb.* Also 6 topicke, (toopick), 7 topike, -ique, -yc, 7–8 -ick. [As adj., ad. Gr. τοπικ-ός of or pertaining to τόπ-ος a place (see -IC); local, or concerning τόποι commonplaces. As sb., ad. L. *topica*, a. Gr. τοπικά adj. neuter pl., in τὰ τοπικά, title of a work of Aristotle, lit. matters concerning τόποι commonplaces.

The use of τόπος 'place' for a class of considerations which would serve as a 'place' in which a rhetorician might look for suggestions in treating his theme, goes back to Isocrates. By Aristotle τόπος was especially appropriated to classes of considerations of a general character, *common* to many kinds of subjects, the use of which was open to any one dealing with his subject as a rhetorician or dialectician, not with special knowledge, with a view to scientific demonstration. Such were more fully described as κοινοὶ τόποι, *loci communes*, COMMONPLACES. Aristotle's treatise on *probable* (as distinguished from *demonstrative*) reasoning, which started from such general considerations and dispensed with special knowledge, was referred to as τὰ τοπικά; and such general considerations and arguments based thereon as were treated of in that work were called *topic axioms, rules*, or *maxims, topic arguments*, or simply *topics*; sometimes with less, sometimes with more emphasis on the general character of such arguments. (C. C. J. Webb.)]

A. *adj.*

I. †1. a. Pertaining to or of the nature of a 'commonplace' (COMMONPLACE A. 1) or general maxim. ***rule topic***, a general rule, which may fail to apply in a particular case, so that its application is only probable and not certain: see above. *Obs.*

1581 J. BELL *Haddon's Answ. Osor.* 117 b, You fayle in the rule Topicke: whereby we are taught to apply true proper Causes, to true effectes. And therefore your consequent is faultie. **1589** *Marprel. Epit.* (1843) 18, I marveile upon what topike place this reason is grounded. **1627** WREN *Serm. bef. King* 17 Feb. 26 That's the first, and it is a Topick rule that; particularly applied by him upon this ground, because of the generall Image of God, which is upon a mans brother. **1645** HOWELL *Twelve Treat.* (1661) 360 The Topique Axiome tells us, that *Dolus versatur in universalibus*, there is double dealing in universals. **1645** RUTHERFORD *Tryal & Tri. Faith* xxi. 231 Uncertain and topick arguments to conclude a God-head and a golden heaven in the creature. **1650** *Vind. Dr. Hammond's Addr.* §58. 23 Would it not be a strange reply, to say, That this consequence depended on the Authority of a Topick Maxime? The word (Topicke) I suppose to be here prefixt by him upon a designe of diminution, as Topicall is equivalent with probable, and oppos'd to demonstrative. **1653** R. BAILLIE *Dissuas. Vind.* (1655) 3 Such aerious and Topick arguments can give no strength to a cause.

†b. Containing 'commonplaces'; ***topic folio***, a commonplace-book. *Obs.*

1644 MILTON *Areop.* (Arb.) 64 To finish his circuit in an English concordance and a topic folio, the gatherings and savings of a sober graduatship, a Harmony and a Catena.

II. †2. a. Of or pertaining to a particular place or locality; local. *Obs.*

1610 HOLLAND *Camden's Brit.* I. 691 These Locall or Topick Gods doe never passe unto other Countries. **1683** E. HOOKER *Pref. Pordage's Mystic Div.* 79 That Topic Proverb among the Spaniards, There are two Magicians in Segura, the one Experience, the other Wisdom. **1793** HELY tr. *O'Flaherty's Ogygia* II. 195 Solemn conventions..to appease the topic deities.

†b. *Med.* Of or pertaining to a particular part of the body; designed for external local application.

1601 HOLLAND *Pliny* XXIX. vi. II. 364 The places ought before the application of those topicke medicines, to be well prepared with the razour. **1671** SALMON *Syn. Med.* III. xxvii. 474 *Linimentum* is a fat topick Medicine.

B. *sb.*

I. Representing Gr. τοπικά. (See note in etymol.)

1. *pl.* As title of the treatise of Aristotle, or as name for a work of the same nature, or for a set of general rules or maxims.

a **1568** ASCHAM *Scholem.* II. (Arb.) 131 Aristotle..when he had written that goodlie booke of the Topickes, did gather out of stories and Orators, so many examples as filled xv. bookes, onelie to expresse the rules of his Topickes. **1599** NASHE *Lenten Stuffe* D iv, Had I my topickes by me in stead of my learned counsell to assist me, I might haps marshall my termes in better aray. **1603** HOLLAND *Plutarch* Explan. Words, *Topicks*, That part of logicke which treateth of the invention of arguments, which are called *Topi*, as if they were places, out of which a man might redily have sufficient reasons to argue and dispute with *Pro & contra*. **1783** BLAIR *Lect.* xxxii. II. 180 These Topics or Loci, were no other than general ideas applicable to a great many different subjects, which the Orator was directed to consult, in order to find out materials for his Speech.

fig. **1644** BULWER *Chiron.* 9 For the Hands are those common places and Topiques of nature.

†2. a. A kind or class of considerations suitable to the purpose of a rhetorician or disputant: passing into the sense 'consideration', 'argument'. *Obs.*

1634 JACKSON *Creed* XI. xxvii. §4 A new topic or frame of arguments which they draw from this. **1652** HEYLIN *Cosmogr.* II. 137 Acts of Violence and Force..justified onely by the false Topick of success. **1662** BOYLE *Seraph. Love* (ed. 4) *Refl. on Let.* 170 When we have employed the loftiest hyperboles, and exhausted all the celebrating Topicks and Figures of Rhetorick. **1669–96** AUBREY *Brief Lives* (1898) I. 170 Judge Richardson harangued against him long, and like an orator, had topiques from the Druides, etc. **1692** BENTLEY *Boyle Lect.* vi. 179 This first Topic was very fitly made use of by our Apostle. **1719** W. WOOD *Surv. Trade* 96 The most general Topick made use of by the Advocates for it, was, That by prohibiting the French Trade, we only hurt our selves. **1756** HUME *Hist. Eng.* II. xxi. 29 These strong topics, in favour of the house of Lancaster, were opposed by arguments no less convincing on the side of the house of York. **1825** SCOTT *Betrothed* xxviii, Interrupting those tears to suggest topics of hope and comfort, which carried no consolation to her own bosom. **1840** J. H. NEWMAN *Par. Serm.* (1842) V. xxiii. 351 How cold and dreary do all such topics prove, when a man comes into trouble?

†b. A head under which arguments or subjects may be arranged. (This passes imperceptibly into 3.) *Obs.*

a **1661** FULLER *Worthies, Linc.* (1662) II. 150 What remaineth concerning Mastiffes is referred to the same Topick in Somerset-shire. *a* **1677** HALE *Prim. Orig. Man.* II. i. 131 These are the Heads of those Evidences of Fact which I shall use in this Argument.., whereunto possibly other occasional Topicks of the like nature may be added. **1705** ADDISON *Italy* Pref., There are still several of these Topicks that are far from being exhausted. *a* **1806** HORSLEY *Serm.* (1811) 375 It is a new kind of argument against the truth of a proposition..that it hath been asserted and maintained by wise and good and learned men... This is a new way of managing the topic of authorities.

3. a. The subject of a discourse, argument, or literary composition; a matter treated in speech or writing; a theme; also, a subject of admiration, animadversion, satire, mockery, or other treatment.

1720 SWIFT *Intelligencer* No. 3 Wks. 1761 III. 363 It is allowed that Corruptions in religion, politics, and law, may be proper topics for this kind of satire. *a* **1768** SECKER *Serm.* (1771) VII. xvi. 364 We are much to blame, that we banish religious Topics from our Discourse. **1770** *Junius Lett.* xxxvi. (1820) 172 The sovereign should..not..make them a topic of jest and mockery. **1797** MRS. RADCLIFFE *Italian* i, He had exhausted every topic of conversation. **1874** GREEN *Short Hist.* vi. §4. 308 The New Testament of Erasmus became the topic of the day.

b. *Gram.* The part of a sentence which is marked as that on which the rest of the sentence makes a statement (comment), asks a question, etc.

Topic sometimes corresponds to *subject*, but the *topic/comment* contrast is not necessarily the same as that of *subject/predicate*.

1958 C. F. HOCKETT *Course in Mod. Linguistics* xxiii. 201 In English and the familiar languages of Europe, topics are usually also subjects, and comments are predicates. **1972** HARTMANN & STORK *Dict. Lang. & Linguistics* 239/1 Some languages, e.g. Japanese, have special particles to mark the topic of the sentence, and for such languages the topic/comment is a more satisfactory analysis than the subject/predicate division. **1976** *Archivum Linguisticum* VII. 123 'Topicalization'..will here be used to denote a process of both foregrounding of information..and selection of the 'topic' of information, that is a process which singles out certain elements in a sentence and makes them the 'topic' on which some 'comment' is made. **1979** *Canad. Jrnl. Linguistics* XXIV. I. 42 Topics are created by a rule of Topic Formation, and preposed by a rule of Topic Preposing.

II. †4. *Med.* An external remedy locally applied, as a plaster or blister. *Obs.*

1587 *Burgh Rec. Edin.* 12 Apr. (1882) IV. 489 Ane vlcer.. applying thairto toopickis and vtheris emplasteres. **1621** BURTON *Anat. Mel.* II. v. III. i, Amongst topics or outward medicines none are more precious than baths. **1668** CULPEPPER & COLE *Barthol. Anat.* man. III. i. 323 To which part of the Back-bone Topicks are to be applied. **1758** J. S. *Le Dran's Observ. Surg.* (1771) 241 Phlebotomy, and emollient Topicks, are our principal Resources.

†5. App. used as = Gr. τόπος 'place'. *Obs.*

1650 FULLER *Pisgah* IV. iii. 60 Their Cities being one of David's Topicks or place where he haunted.

III. *Comb.*, as (sense 3 b) ***topic-neutral*** adj.; **topic-(and-)comment**, (based on) the dichotomy in grammar of topic and comment.

1964 E. A. NIDA *Toward Sci. Transl.* iv. 66 It has been found that all languages seem to have something equivalent to subject-predicate constructions. These may in some instances be more aptly termed *topic-comment, but essentially they are very similar from one language to another. **1978** *Language* LIV. 231 He [*sc.* R. Scollon] then suggests that topic-comment structures themselves may arise from discourse. **1979** *Amer. Speech 1978* LIII. 279, I think the basic type of openness in human language behavior is that of the topic-and-comment pattern. **1951** *Mind* LX. 541 There are..some forms of inference which can occur only in a restricted field of discourse... There are others, depending on the meaning of what Professor Ryle has called '*topic-neutral words', which can occur in the handling of any kind of subject matter. **1961** D. S. SHWAYDER *Modes of Referring* iii. 81 A distinguishing use may be more or less topic-neutral.

topical ('tɒpɪkəl), *a.* (*sb.*) [f. as TOPIC + -AL[1].]

A. *adj.* 1. a. Of or pertaining to a place or locality; local.

1588 J. HARVEY *Disc. Probl.* 121 Is it..to be supposed, that the Verticall, Perpendicular, or Topicall stars haue now conspired together to desolate, or oppresse the seuerall regions which they aspect? **1610** HEALEY *St. Aug. City of God, Vives' Comm.* II. xxiii. (1620) 89 The Topicall gods, that is, the locall gods of such and such places. **1624** BP. MOUNTAGU *Gagg* 44 Particular and topical churches have erred. **1664** H. MORE *Myst. Iniq.* 473 Rites or Opinions that are but Temporary or Topical. **1722** WOLLASTON *Relig. Nat.* v. 92 If [the flood] was only topical, affecting some one tract of the globe. **1870** LOWELL *Among my Bks.* Ser. I. (1873) 177 Their truth is not topical and transitory, but of universal acceptation.

b. *Med.* That belongs or is applied to a particular part of the body.

1608 TOPSELL *Serpents* (1658) 621 First I will speak of such means as are topical, or such as are outwardly applyed. *c* **1645** HOWELL *Lett.* (1688) IV. 503 This..Powder heals at a distance without topical Applications to the place affected. **1733** G. CHEYNE *Eng. Malady* I. vii. §4. 65 Small and Topical Disorders of the Nervous Kind. **1800** *Med. Jrnl.* IV. 173 The symptoms..may be divided into topical and general. **1871** GARROD *Mat. Med.* (ed. 3) 157 It [creasote] is ..used as a topical styptic in hæmorrhages.

fig. **1673** O. WALKER *Educ.* (1677) 98 In Religion lies the universal and never failing remedy of all the evils of the Soul. But many times particular and topical ones are also to be applied.

c. ***topical colour, colouring***: see quot. 1877.

1839 URE *Dict. Arts* 234 After printing-on the topical colour, the goods must be dried at a gentle heat. **1877** KNIGHT *Dict. Mech., Topical coloring*, a term used in calico-printing to indicate that the color or mordant is applied to specific portions of the cloth forming the pattern.

†2. Pertaining to a topic or general maxim; hence, not demonstrative but merely probable.

1594 CAREW *Huarte's Exam. Wits* iii. 24 Aristotle..with a purpose of crossing Plato..turned to reuiue the former opinion, and with topical places to make it probable. **1624** BEDELL *Lett.* v. 86 This Argument is..but Topicall and probable. *a* **1677** HALE *Prim. Orig. Man.* II. i. 132 It cannot be expected in an Argument of this nature,..that Evidences of Fact can be no more than topical and probable. **1697** tr. *Burgersdicius his Logic* II. xv. 65 A Syllogism Dialectical is also..called Topical,..because its Propositions tho' true, are yet Contingent. **1710** NORRIS *Chr. Prud.* viii. 385, I am now upon the larger and more topical part of my Subject.

3. a. Of or pertaining to a general heading, a topic or subject of discourse, composition, etc.

1856 MASSON *Ess., Milton's Youth* 40 He passes, by a very slight topical connexion, into an account of himself, his education, his designs, and his relations to the matter in question. **1879** MORLEY *Burke* vi. 122 Conversation..was ..ever taking new turns, branching into topical surprises. **1890** *Nature* 2 Jan. 196/2 The writer expects that the topical skeleton furnished by him will be clothed upon by the lessons of the intelligent teacher.

b. Of or pertaining to the topics of the day; containing local or temporary allusions.

1873 *Punch* 15 Mar. 111/1 The popular 'topical' song which delights music-hall politicians. **1881** *Daily News* 8 Nov. 5/2 A great many 'topical' allusions to events of the hour, and rough political hits. **1899** *Month* Apr. 410 A review accustomed to bestow articles on topical subjects as they came up. **1905** *Westm. Gaz.* 18 Jan. 12/1 M. Combes, whose resignation makes him topical, is a man with few recreations.

B. as *sb.* 1. = TOPIC B. 4. *Obs. rare*$^{-1}$.

1656 RIDGLEY *Pract. Physick* 98 Apply purgative Topicals.

2. A film dealing with topical events. (Now *disused.*)

1912 F. A. TALBOT *Moving Pictures* 123 This point of view is responsible for the apathetic American attitude toward the 'topical', as it is called in Great Britain. **1915** B. E. JONES *Cinematograph Bk.* 33 Something may here be said about topicals or 'newsy' films. **1917** C. N. BENNETT *Guide to Kinematogr.* 123 Fourpence or fivepence a foot will be the most a country showman will pay for a local topical. **1976** *Oxf. Compan. Film* 500/2 The early 'topicals' were very short, often less than a minute long, each dealing with a single event. The regular issue of newsreels in the conventional sense—several short items grouped under no general heading other than topicality—was begun by Pathé in 1908.

Hence **topi'cality**, the quality of being topical (see 3 b); an instance of this, a topical allusion.

1904 *Longm. Mag.* Nov. 93 The Beck case gives the subject a curious topicality. **1905** *Westm. Gaz.* 10 June 2/2 Fair actresses recite, and Pantomimes Rattle with Fiscal topicalities.

'topicalize, *v.* [f. TOPICAL *a.* + -IZE.] *trans.* To make into a grammatical topic. Usu. *pass.*

1970 *Language* XLVI. 375 In 47, *le tama* is topicalized out of the objective case. **1976** *Archivum Linguisticum* VII. 132 It must be some other quality inherent in *pay*, the 'abstract predication'.., or more precisely, the act, action, or activity, which is topicalized and appears on the surface as *-ment.* **1977** *Amer. Speech 1975* L. 71 One important aspect of this argument is that those proposing it..question the underlying verbal status of *have* and regard it instead as a surface form that serves to topicalize the possessor, which in other languages would be a locative or dative.

Hence **topicali'zation**; **'topicalized** *ppl. a.*

1967 *Foundations of Lang.* III. 47 Topicalization..means that some major constituent of a sentence, such as a noun phrase, which is identical with (or has the same referent as) a constituent in the given sentence, may be generated before or after this sentence. **1970** *Language* XLVI. 375 Reversing the order of the two topicalized noun phrases is not possible; the sentence cannot be interpreted 'the girl loves the boy'. **1978** [see *preposing* vbl. sb. s.v. PREPOSE *v.* 2 a]. **1980** *English World-Wide* I. 249 In the structure, only the plural marker, the locative copula, and the topicalized predicator were found to be of African origin. **1983** *Studies in Eng. Lit.: Eng. Number* (Tokyo) 158 Topicalization is a stylistic rule.

topically ('tɒpɪkəlɪ), *adv.* [f. TOPICAL *a.* (*sb.*) + -LY[2].] In a topical manner.

1. a. In respect to place; locally. *rare.* b. *Med.* In respect to some particular part of the body.

1646 SIR T. BROWNE *Pseud. Ep.* III. iii. 109 Their dung and intestinall excretions..Topically applyed become a.. Rubifying medecine. **1648** EVELYN *Let. to Sir R. Browne* 15 June, And now for the news. The scene is Essex, more topically Colchester. **1741** *Compl. Fam.-Piece* I. i. 73 An excellent Medicine to be used topically in Gleetings. **1803** *Med. Jrnl.* IX. 100 Bleeding, either generally or topically, I never had recourse to. **1845** GARROD *Mat. Med.* (1855) 23 It acts topically on the mucous membrane of the respiratory passages.

2. In reference to topics.

1881 *Gentl. Mag.* Feb. 252 These letters are arranged topically not chronologically. **1896** W. D. MACKENZIE in *Chicago Advance* 26 Mar. 445/1 A man who has only preached topically for five years.

‖**topinambou** (tɒpɪ'næmbuː). Also 9 -bour, -bar. [a. F. *topinambou* (16th c.), now *topinambour*, from the name of a people of

Brazil.] A name for the Jerusalem Artichoke, *Helianthus tuberosus*, a native of tropical America.

1666 J. DAVIES *Hist. Caribby Isles* 56 Topinambous or artichokes which are now not only very common in most parts but cheap. **1698** OSBORNE tr. *Froger's Voy. Straits Magellan* 60 The potato and ighname are roots very like the toupinanbous. **1858** SIMMONDS *Dict. Trade, Topinambar*, a name for the Jerusalem artichoke. **1866** *Treas. Bot.*, Topinambour, (Fr.) *Helianthus tuberosus.*

[**topinch**, a spurious word, founded on an erroneous emendation of *to pinch*, in Shaks. *Merry W.* IV. iv. 57. See TO *prep.* B. 19, quot. 1598.]

†**topinel.** *Obs. rare*$^{-1}$. app. = *topping-lift*: see TOPPING *vbl. sb.*^{2}

1549 *Compl. Scot.* vi. 41 Than the master cryit, top ȝour topinellis, hail on ȝour top sail scheitis.

toping, *vbl. sb.* and *ppl. a.*: see TOPE *v.*^{2}

topit ('tɒpɪt). [app. f. phrase *top it* (TOP *v.*^{1}).] An attachment at the top of a boring rod by means of which it is withdrawn.

1839 URE *Dict. Arts* 966 The boring tools .. 13. The topit, or top-piece. *Ibid.*, The runner, for taking hold of the topit. **1883** GRESLEY *Gloss. Coal Mining, Topit*, a kind of bracehead, but much smaller, which is screwed on to the top of boring rods when withdrawing them from the hole. It is attached to a rope worked from a jack-roll.

Topkhana ('təʊp,kɑːnə). Also 7 **Tophana**, 8 **Tope Khonnah**; 9 **Tope Khâna**; **top-khana**. [a. Pers. and Hind., ad. Turk. *tophane* (also used), f. *top* (see TOPCHEE) + Pers. *khāna* house.]

a. In Turkey, a gun-factory or arsenal, *spec.* the gun-factories in Galata, Constantinople (Istanbul), during the Ottoman Empire; hence (the current sense) the district of Istanbul adjoining them. **b.** In India, artillery; ordnance department.

1656 W. JESSON *Let.* 4 Dec. in W. Foster *Eng. Factories in India 1618–69* (1921) X. 73 The King, being resolved to renue the warr against Candahor, dispeeded Cossom Ckawn .. with the tobeconah [*tōp-khāna*, artillery] for Lahore. **1668** P. RYCAUT *Pres. State Ottoman Empire* 200 Their quarters are at Tophana, or the place of Guns in the Suburbs of Constantinople. **1765** J. Z. HOLWELL *Hist. Events* (1766) I. 96 By the treachery of the *Tope Khonnah Droger*, the cannon were loaded with powder only. **1842** C. MASSON *Baluchistan, Afghanistan & Panjab* II. 256 From the court of the Dafta Khâna the Tope Khâna, or artillery ground, is entered. **1901** KIPLING *Kim* iii. 67, I have known Him since he was a lieutenant in the *top-khana* (the Artillery). **1969** D. WALDER *Chanak Affair* xix. 350 An enormous Turkish flag floated over the Tophana naval depot. **1972** D. K. PALIT *Hist. Regiment of Artillery* i. 8 Although Shivaji had a regular department of *Topkhana* .. he never had a foundry of his own. He managed to obtain some guns from the foundries at Surat .. but by and large his *Topkhana* was described as a collection of 'old and defective' guns. **1974** J. F. GUILMARTIN *Gunpowder & Galleys* i. 44 The cannon foundries of the *Tophane* were directly dependent upon English tin which they could get only through Genoese entrepreneurs.

topknot ('tɒpnɒt). [f. TOP *sb.*^{1} + KNOT *sb.*^{1}]

1. a. A knot or bow of ribbon worn on the top of the head by ladies towards the end of the 17th and in the 18th century; later, a bow of ribbon worn in a lace cap; ? also of flowers, feathers, etc.

c **1686–8** *Roxb. Ball.* (1890) VII. 21 The lofty Top-knots on her crown, .. Makes me with care, alas! look down. **1688** R. HOLME *Armoury* III. xiv. (Roxb.) 12/1 Glasses .. used by Lady's .. to see how to dress their heads, and set their top knotts on their fore heads vpright. **1716–20** *Lett. fr. Mist's Jrnl.* (1722) I. 51 Let me beg thee .. to insert a polite History of Hoop-Petticoats, Top-Knots, .. and all that. **1831** SCOTT *Nigel* Introd., Obliged to compel .. a fellow-knight or squire to restore the top-knot of ribbon which he had stolen from a fair damsel. **1910** O. BARRON in *Encycl. Brit.* VII. 242/2 A cap [late 17th c.] whose top-knot or commode stood up stiff and fan-shaped.

b. A tuft of hair on the top or crown of the head of a person or animal; a knob of hair worn on the crown of the head in some styles of hair-dressing; also, a plume or crest of feathers or filaments on the head of a bird; *Austral.* and *N.Z.*, wool shorn from the top of the head of a sheep.

1700 T. BROWN *Amusem. Ser. & Com.* 22 A .. Trumpeter calling in the Rabble to see a Calf with Six Legs and a Top-knot. **1849** D. J. BROWNE *Amer. Poultry Yd.* (1855) 12 Unacquainted with fowls with topknots. **1867** BAKER *Nile Trib.* iii. (1872) 41 A Bishareen Arab wears his hair in hundreds of minute plaits .. surmounted by a circular bushy topknot upon the crown. **1894** GLADSTONE *Odes of Horace* II. xi. 24 Her hair be dressed like Spartan maid, With comely top-knot upwards tied. **1902** O. WISTER *Virginian* i, Have you ever seen a cockatoo—the white kind with the top-knot —enraged by insult? **1950** *N.Z. Jrnl. Agric.* Oct. 313 (*caption*) Pick over lambs' wool. Pick out stained wool, face pieces, leggings, and top-knots. **1972** J. S. GUNN in G. W. Turner *Good Austral. Eng.* iii. 61 One thing I did notice about shearing was that two terms for the one idea sometimes shared popularity, for example *rouseabout/shedhand*, .. *topknot/wig*, [etc.].

c. The head. *slang.*

1869 E. WAUGH *Hermit Cobbler* iii, I doubt it's unsattle't his top-knot a bit. **1889** 'J. S. WINTER' *Mrs. Bob* (1891) 63 The little tip-tilted nose and curly top-knot.

2. *transf.* **a.** One who wears a topknot.

1697 ISOBEL WRIGHT in *Collect. Dying Test* (1806) 42 Like gowkhorns, topeknots and I know not what to call them. **1909** *Bible in World* Feb. 60/1 Dirty children, and everywhere dreamy 'Top-knots', as the Korean men are called because they wear their hair in a top-knot.

b. One of several species of small European flat-fish, with a tapering filament on the head.

1832 JOHNSTON in *Proc. Berw. Nat. Club* I. No. i. 7 The most remarkable [fishes] .. were .. the top-knot, the toothed gilt-head. **1843** *Zoologist* I. 106 Description of Muller's Top-knot .. taken from a fresh specimen. **1880** GÜNTHER *Stud. Fishes* 555 'Bloch's Top-knot', *Rh*[*ombus*] *punctatus. Ibid.*, The 'Top-knot' (*Ph*[*rynorhombus*] *unimaculatus*) occurs occasionally on the south coast of England.

3. *attrib.*, as **topknot duck**: see quot.; **topknot pigeon**, an Australian crested fruit-pigeon, *Lopholaimus antarcticus*.

1849 D. J. BROWNE *Amer. Poultry Yd.* (1855) 197 Also the 'crested', or 'topknot duck', a beautiful ornamental tame variety. **1891** F. ADAMS *J. Webb's End* I. ii. 33 Flying for a moment by a lovely, melodious top-knot pigeon.

Hence '**topknotted** *a.*, having a topknot.

1859 GEO. ELIOT *A. Bede* vi, The old top-knotted hens, scratching with their chicks among the straw. **1868** DARWIN *Anim. & Pl.* I. viii. 295 There are topknotted canaries, and it is a singular fact, that, if two topknotted birds are matched, the young, instead of having very fine topknots, are generally bald, or even have a wound on their heads.

Töpler (tɜːplə(r)). *Physics.* Also **Toepler**. [The name of A. J. I. *Töpler* (1836–1912), German physicist, who invented the pump in 1862.] ***Töpler*** (or †***Töpler's***) ***pump***: a pump in which the reservoir to be evacuated is connected by a glass tube containing a valve to a second reservoir, which in turn is connected by a flexible U-tube to a reservoir of mercury, so that lowering the last draws gas out of the first reservoir into the second and raising it expels gas from the second reservoir into the atmosphere. Also *absol.*

1883 *Encycl. Brit.* XVI. 31/1 In Töpler's pump this is attained by using .. for the inlet and the outlet vertical capillary glass tubes. **1922** GLAZEBROOK *Dict. Appl. Physics* I. 8/1 The working of a Töpler by hand is extremely tedious, for several hours may be required to reach the limit of pressure. **1932** [see SPRENGEL]. **1976** A. ROTH *Vacuum Technol.* v. 201 With the Toepler pump, pressures down to 10^{-5} Torr can be obtained, except the mercury vapour pressure which is about 10^{-3} Torr.

topless ('tɒplɪs), *a.* [f. TOP *sb.*^{1} + -LESS.]

1. Having no top; without a top or summit.

1596 *Edw. III*, IV. v. 114 There is a loftie hill, Whose top seems toplesse. **1614** C. BROOKE *Trag. Rich. III*, ii, Thou toplesse builder of great Babel's Spyre, (Damnéd Ambition!). **1859** G. MEREDITH *R. Feverel* xliii, Gray topless ruins. **1910** *Daily Chron.* 14 Jan. 6/7 Statues to well-known Parsees wearing their topless hats.

2. a. *fig.* Seeming to have no top or summit; immensely or immeasurably high; unbounded.

1589 GREENE *Menaphon* (Arb.) 39 The glister of the Sunne vpon the toplesse Promontorie of Sicilia. **1602** MARSTON *Antonio's Rev.* I. i, And even adore my toplesse villany. *a* **1656** BP. HALL in Spurgeon *Treas. Dav.* Ps. lxviii. 19 Oh the boundless, topless, bottomless, load of divine benefits. **1707** WATTS *Hymn, 'Lord, we are blind'* ii, Where neither wings nor souls can fly, Nor angels climb the topless throne. **1863** *Pilgr. Prairies* II. 134 Where topless cliffs frown down on the intruder, forbidding further passage.

†**b.** Than which there is nothing higher; having no superior; supreme, paramount. *Obs. rare*$^{-1}$.

1606 SHAKS. *Tr. & Cr.* I. iii. 152 Sometime great Agamemnon, Thy toplesse deputation he puts on.

3. a. Designating or pertaining to a garment, esp. a (woman's) bathing-suit or dress, having little or no material above the waist; that does not cover the breasts and upper body.

1937 *Time* 21 June 53/1 With another bathing-suit season at hand, local lawmakers are aiming their ordinances at males on the score of topless suits rather than at underclad females. **1964** *San Francisco Chron.* 16 June 4/1 Saigis introduced San Francisco's first topless bathing suit for women. **1964** *Punch* 1 July 20/2 The topless look. **1964** *New Statesman* 24 July 116/1 A girl who wears a topless dress in the streets of Coventry or Nottingham could be doing as much for her sex as any Mrs Pankhurst. **1966** C. MACKENZIE *Paper Lives* xii. 166 And those topless dresses they're going in for now aren't nearly as topless as those dresses they were wearing about 1500 B.C. **1971** S. JEPSON *Let. to Dead Girl* xvii. 195 Her jeans were covered with dirt, and her shirt torn into topless decolleté. **1978** P. GLYNN *In Fashion* iv. 97 Rudi Gernreich's topless bathing suit had appeared in 1964.

b. Of a person (esp. a woman): naked or almost naked above the waist; bare-breasted.

1966 *Observer* 13 Nov. 2/8 The appearance of topless waitresses. **1968** 'R. RAINE' *Night of Hawk* xxvi. 125 Various acts, the main one being African girl dancers who perform topless. **1969** *Observer* 7 Dec. 25/3 Topless boys with shoulder-length hair pause as they cycle past you: 'Wanna buy some acid?' **1970** *Daily Progress* (Charlottesville, Va.) 29 May 19/5 (*heading*) Topless girl is acquitted. **1981** *Birds* Summer 55/2 New reserve records included nude female bathers on Loch Garten, a 'topless' woman picking blackberries, [etc.].

c. Applied to a place or area in which women are permitted to appear naked above the waist; esp. of bars, etc., employing bare-breasted waitresses or dancers, and of beaches at which women sunbathe topless. Hence also of entertainments, sunbathing, etc., so conducted.

1967 F. WARNER *Madrigals* 30 Draining down screwdrivers in topless Broadway. **1970** G. R. TAYLOR *Doomsday Bk.* x. 246 Fairbanks has become a boom-town with topless entertainment in the bars and saloons. **1972** G. BAXT *Burning Sappho* ii. 41 For Chrissakes not one of them topless joints. Who wants flabby tits hanging over my shrimp cocktail. **1976** P. CAVE *High Flying Birds* iii. 36 This section of the beach was strictly topless. **1978** *N.Y. Times* 30 Mar. B2/4 He has campaigned against marijuana decriminalization, 'topless' bars, [etc.]. **1979** *Globe & Mail* (Toronto) 26 Jan. 5 Toronto City Council probably will move on Feb. 5 to restrict new bars offering topless or nude entertainment. **1983** *Times* 6 July 32/1 Topless sunbathing is a well-established practice on a great many British beaches.

Hence '**toplessness**, the condition of being topless (sense 3).

1964 *Punch* 22 July 117/3 His pronouncement on toplessness. **1982** C. CASTLE *Folies Bergère* iii. 127 Today, the question of toplessness .. evokes little excitement in an age of naked beaches.

top level. orig. *U.S.* [f. TOP *sb.*^{1} + LEVEL *sb.*] The highest degree of importance, prestige, or ability; usu. (with hyphen) *attrib.*, designating that which belongs to or takes place at such a level.

1951 *Sci. Amer.* Sept. 43/2 The story is even less favorable when we examine what proportion of able people obtain the Ph.D. degree—today a requirement for many of our top-level intellectual occupations. **1952** *Times* 29 Jan. 3/2 It is estimated by the assistant director of public relations at American University that 'there must be more than 150 ghost writers at the top level in Washington alone'. **1955** *Times* 16 May 4/1 No one can say for certain that the results of a top-level meeting will fulfil our hopes. **1956** WALLIS & BLAIR *Thunder Above* (1959) xii. 116 They'll probably engage you .. as a top-level consultant. **1957** *Ann. Reg. 1956* 23 It was announced that a meeting 'at top level' between union officials and the management of Standard Motors had been arranged for 13 May. **1967** C. BERNERS-LEE in Wills & Yearsley *Handbk. Management Technol.* 15 In due course [a really good technical salesman] will find himself inundated with as much top-level work as he can cope with. **1969** *Daily Tel.* 17 Dec. 2/6 Top-level talks to discuss the threatened unofficial strike at 63 power stations .. are being held .. between employers and unions. *a* **1974** R. CROSSMAN *Diaries* (1976) II. 125 This Lord Mayor's dinner was the first top-level invitation which Anne and I have accepted since I was a Minister. **1979** *Yale Alumni Mag.* Apr. 8/2 The desire to watch top-level squash competition has also increased.

†**topliffe.** *Obs. rare*$^{-1}$. (See quot.)

1602 CAREW *Cornwall* I. 13 b, They measure their black Tynne, by the Gill, the Topliffe, the Dish, .. which containeth a pint, a pottell, a gallon.

top line. [f. TOP *sb.*^{1} + LINE *sb.*^{2}]

1. (In cattle), the profile line of the back from the centre of the shoulders to the end of the hip-bones.

2. The head item on a bill of entertainment; the headline of a newspaper; freq. (with hyphen) *attrib.*; also *fig.*

1906 *N.Y. Times* 6 May IV. 2/1 The rumor of a new $30,000,000 vaudeville act—a regular 'top-line' combination—has been giving Broadway a good deal to talk about. **1922** A. HADDON *Green Room Gossip* vi. 138 His .. duets with Miss Muriel George have reached a top-line position on the halls. **1928** *Boston Even. Transcript* 30 Mar. 15/6 This big 'top line' caught my eye: 'The Pocasset filicide.' **1928** *Daily Express* 31 July 13/7 The top-line contest on Saturday next is that between Jack Stanley of Deptford and Gipsey Daniels. **1947** [see CARE *v.* 4 a]. **1958** *New Statesman* 23 Aug. 211/3 The *Daily Mail* has recently been the most persistent in putting news first in its public appeal and in tying its 'top line' features much more closely to it than most. **1981** B. HEALEY *Last Ferry from Lido* i. 17 A real, top-line Venetian socialite.

3. ***on the top line***: in the highest state of perfection, readiness, etc. *slang* (orig. Naval). Phr. ***to sweat on the top line***: see SWEAT *v.* 9 c.

1916 'TAFFRAIL' *Pincher Martin* ix. 155 I've 'eard tell, too, that that there Kayser bloke o' theirs 'as gingered 'em up somethin' crool, an' a navy wot's been gingered up must be on th' top line same as us, mustn't it? **1942** *Tee Emm* (Air Ministry) II. 81 There are a lot of ways of navigating these days; you ought to be on the top line in them all. **1958** *Punch* 9 July 57/3 The famous scene in which he has to serve both his masters with dinner at the same moment becomes a juggling turn on the top line. **1972** *Times* 30 Nov. 17/4 It cannot be but harmful to the patient to be attended by a doctor who through sheer exhaustion is not on the top line.

4. *Mus.* In music divided into four parts for singing, the highest (usu. soprano) line.

1965 *Listener* 1 July 33/3 The top line could be sung by sopranos and altos in unison, while the baritones .. could dodge from the bass line to the tenor line. **1968** E. R. BUCKLER *Ox Bells & Fireflies* iv. 73 We sang—with the teacher always taking what was known as 'top line'.

Hence **top-'liner**, one who or that which appears in the top line, or in the first or principal place.

1901 *Munsey's Mag.* Nov. 247/1 Grand opera in this and other countries sadly needs a new bright particular star, a 'top liner', as they say in the music halls. **1901** *Daily Colonist* (Victoria, B.C.) 1 Nov. 3/1 One of the four schooners which returned to port yesterday morning was the top-liner of the fleet, the Otto. **1928** *Daily Express* 19 June 16/1 Every Ascot race is a top-liner. **1950** *Sport* 7–11 Apr. 9/1 For months past people have been trying to grab tickets for this match, which is always a top-liner. **1970** *Daily Tel.* 29 Apr. 13/1 On the club circuit there are top-liners .. making up to £400 a week. **1982** R. HILL *Who guards a Prince* IV. vi. 227 A journalist .. a top-liner as well as an old friend.

toploftical (ˌtɒp'lɒftɪkəl, -ɔː-), *a. humorous colloq.* [app. f. *top loft*, topmost gallery or story + -ICAL, after words like *magnifical*, *tyrannical*, etc.] High-flown, 'high and mighty', 'highfalutin', 'stuck-up'; also *lit.* lofty, elevated.

1823 *Blackw. Mag.* XIV. 104 Very toploftical to be sure. *c* **1824** MRS. CARLYLE *Early Lett.* (1889) 84 At the first she was quite intolerable with her fine-lady airs, and toploftical notions. **1884** J. BURROUGHS *Birds & Poets* 74 Our toploftical brilliancy and cleverness. **1892** *Century Mag.* Apr. 837/2 Whose turban handkerchief towered in a toploftical structure. **1894** *Harper's Mag.* May 940/2 A few days of toploftical strutting around town. **1898** *Speaker* 22 Jan. 100/2 Eaten up by pride and a toploftical sense of independence.

toplofty (ˌtɒp'lɒftɪ, -ɔː-), *a. humorous colloq.* [app. f. TOP *sb.*[1] + LOFTY *a.*, or f. *top loft*: see prec.; said in Farmer *Slang* to be of American origin.] Lofty in manner or character; elevated; haughty, 'high and mighty'. Hence **top'loftiness**.

1859 F. FRANCIS *Newton Dogvane* (1888) 218 Everything was very toplofty in the landlord and waiters' parts. **1889** *Pall Mall G.* 13 July 6/1 Lord F—— is dignity itself... There is a 'toploftiness' about him which is meant to be very impressive. **1896** *Chicago Advance* 25 June 941/2 The council sermon... A little top-lofty perhaps for children. **1898** *Contemp. Rev.* Jan. 17 They were snubbed with rather toplofty denials.

top-maker, -making: see TOP *sb.*[1] 36.

topman[1] ('tɒpmən). [f. TOP *sb.*[1] + MAN *sb.*[1]]

†**1.** A ship (MAN *sb.*[1] 14) with a top on its mast; = *top-ship* (TOP *sb.*[1] 35). *Obs.*

1513 N. WEST in Ellis *Orig. Lett.* Ser. I. I. 67, I found none but ix. or x. small topmen,..and other small balyngiers and crayers,..one little topman of the burdon of threescore tonne. **1577** HARRISON *England* II. xvii. (1877) I. 290 There are 135 ships that exceed 500 tun; topmen vnder 100, and aboue fortie, 656.

†**2.** A hangman: = TOPSMAN 2. *slang. Obs.*

1607 W. N. *Barley-Breake* D iv b, A nimble Ape his topman strait will be And hangs vp Streton.

3. *Naut.* A seaman stationed in one of the tops, to attend to the upper sails, or in a fighting ship as a marksman.

1748 *Anson's Voy.* III. viii. 379 Her topmen..made prodigious havock with their small arms, killing or wounding every officer..on the quarter-deck. **1825** H. B. GASCOIGNE *Nav. Fame* 74 The Topmen now the Backstays well attend, To lesser duties all attention lend. **1830** MARRYAT *King's Own* xvi, Topmen, aloft! loose top-gallant sails. **1898** NEWBOLT *Isl. Race* 8 One morning the topmen reported below The old Agamemnon escaped from the foe.

4. a. The upper man in a saw-pit: = TOP-SAWYER a; cf. PITMAN 3.

1678 MOXON *Mech. Exerc.* v. 98 With the Pit-Saw they enter the one end of the Stuff, the Top-man at the Top, and the Pit-man under him. *Ibid.* vi. 113 Of the two Sawyers, the uppermost is called the Top-man. **1881** *Lumber World* Mar., The frame or sash saw is operated in the same manner by a top-man and a pit-man.

b. A miner or pitman working at the top of the shaft.

1890 'R. BOLDREWOOD' *Miner's Right* iii, The bucket appeared slightly above the brace at the shaft, and was taken by the topman. **1912** *Scotsman* 5 Apr. 5/2 There was..no settlement of the banksmen's or topmen's question.

c. (See quot. 1964.)

1961 *Evening Standard* 3 Aug. 21/4 (Advt.), Topmen reqd. for demolition trade. **1962** PARKER & ALLERTON *Courage of his Convictions* i. 22 He's a top man, and don't you forget it... When derelict buildings were being knocked down he was one of those on the roof. **1964** J. S. SCOTT *Dict. Building* 94 *Demolisher* or *mattock man* or *topman* or *housebreaker*, a skilled man who pulls down a wall by standing on top of it and breaking pieces off below him, or by pulling a loose wall with a winch and rope, or by means of a concrete breaker. **1973** *Daily Tel.* 7 Mar. 13/2 Pulling down the YMCA dome, 120ft. or about 15 storeys high, had to begin with a topman..picking away with mattock.

'topman[2]. *rare.* [f. TOP *sb.*[2] 3 + MAN *sb.*[1]] A man who is engaged in laying rope.

1851-4 TOMLINSON *Cycl. Arts* (1866) II. 465/2 The motion of the top requires to be regulated so as to ensure equal hardness in the rope: the topman, therefore, before putting in the top, makes a mark across the strands of every beam: if, when the top reaches a beam the mark be above the bearer, the topman knows that the turning at the foretop has been too fast.

topmast ('tɒpmɑːst, -mæst, -məst). A smaller mast fixed on the top of a lower mast; *spec.* the second section of a mast above the deck, which was formerly the uppermost mast, but is now surmounted by the topgallant mast.

1485 *Naval Acc. Hen. VII* (1896) 48 Toppe mastes..j, Toppe shrowdes..vj. **1497** *Ibid.* [see TOPGALLANT A. 1]. **1556** W. TOWRSON in Hakluyt *Voy.* (1599) II. II. 43 Perceiuing the Admirall to be farre a sterne of his company, because his maine top-mast was spent. **1610** SHAKS. *Temp.* I. i. 37 Downe with the top-Mast: yare, lower, lower, bring her to Try with Maine-course. *a* **1625** *Nomenclator Navalis* (Harl. MS. 2301) s.v., The Top-mastes are ouer halfe soe long as the Mastes vnto which theie belong. **1764** VEITCH in *Phil. Trans.* LIV. 287 In great ships the masts are composed of three parts,..the lowermost part is called by its proper name, the middlemost part is called the top-mast, and the uppermost part the top-gallant-mast. **1795** NELSON in Nicolas *Disp.* (1845) II. 21 The Ça Ira lost her topmasts, which enabled the Agamemnon and Inconstant to close in with her. **1873** C. ROBINSON *N.S. Wales* 98 Every ship in port, from whatever clime, is decorated with flags of all colours, from stem to stern, from top-mast to hull.

b. *attrib.*, as *topmast-block*, *-head*, etc.

1672 *Lond. Gaz.* No. 690/1 Who carried the Union Flags on their Topmast-head, and each a White Flag in their Poupe. **1709** DAMPIER *Voy.* III. II. 37 This Island..may be seen from a Ship's Topmast-head about ten Leagues. **1840** R. H. DANA *Bef. Mast* xi, The topmast-studding-sail boom ..broke off at the boom-iron. **1897** *Daily News* 7 June 2/3 Through the thinner veil overhead..the gilded topmast-blocks could be seen gleaming in sunshine.

topmost ('tɒpməʊst, -məst), *a.* [f. TOP *sb.*[1] + -MOST.] Uppermost, highest. Also *absol.*, highest part.

1697 DRYDEN *Æneid* VII. 99 A swarm of bees..Upon the topmost branch in clouds alight. **1768** TUCKER *Lt. Nat.* (1834) I. 668 An ambition of..gaining the topmost summit of it. **1807** CRABBE *Par. Reg.* I. 442 Susan..had some pride Among our topmost people to preside. **1827-35** WILLIS *Scholar of Thebet Ben Khorat* 228 Wisdom sits alone, Topmost in heaven. **1875** MORRIS *Æn.* XII. 493 The eager-driven spear Smote on his helm, and shore away the topmost of his crest. **1899** E. J. CHAPMAN *Drama of Two Lives* 17 The topmost peaks were still aflame With the red sunset's dying glow.

topnet, obs. form of TAPNET.

topo, U.S. colloq. abbrev. of TOPOGRAPHIC *a.* Also *ellipt.* for 'topographic map'.

1970 N. ARMSTRONG et al. *First on Moon* xi. 256 The best we can do on topo features is to advise you to look to the west of the irregularly shaped crater. **1977** *Chicago Tribune* 2 Oct. III. 10/3 'Topos' show land contours, elevations, marshes, lakes, streams. **1979** *Amer. Alpine Jrnl.* XXII. I. 35 Japan's foremost mountain magazine..contains..valuable maps, diagrams and topos with English captions. **1981** *Northeast Woods & Waters* Jan. 16/2 You can buy topos most anywhere in Maine, but they are dated and won't show all the logging roads built in the past 25 years.

topo-, before a vowel **top-**, a. Gr. τοπο-, combining form of τόπος place, as in τοπο-γράφος topographer; a formative element in various words.

topo'centric *Astronautics*, (of a parameter of a spacecraft or an orbit) measured relative to a point on the earth's surface (rather than its centre); **'topocline** [CLINE *sb.*], a cline associated with variations in the locality of the species concerned; **to'pogenous** *a.*, formed as the result of a combination of geographical features; **ˌtopoinhi'bition** *Biol.*, the inhibition of cell multiplication by contact with other cells; **topoi'somerase** *Biochem.*, any enzyme that alters the supercoiled form of a DNA molecule; **to'polatry** [-LATRY], excessive reverence for a place; **'topomorph** [Gr. μορφή form]: see quot.; **toponar'cosis**, local narcosis; **topo'neural** *a.*, having separate marginal sense-organs; as in the *Toponeura*, a proposed division of *Hydrozoa*; **topo'phobia**, a morbid dread of certain places; **topo'politan** *a.* [Gr. πολίτ-ης citizen: cf. *cosmopolitan*], that inhabits a definite or restricted locality; **'topotype**, a specimen from the locality where the original type-specimen was obtained; hence **topo'typic, -ical** *adjs.*, of or pertaining to a topotype.

1965 P. R. ESCOBAL *Methods Orbit Determination* vii. 241 The *topocentric right ascension-declination of the unknown orbit at the three times..can be obtained as follows. **1976** *Sci. Amer.* June 70/2 Since the tracking stations are on the earth's surface, the direct measurements they provide of the spacecraft's radial parameters (range, velocity and acceleration) are topocentric rather than geocentric. **1939** J. W. GREGOR in *New Phytologist* XXXVIII. 317 Prefixes can be used to denote clines of different types, for example *topocline. **1953** J. HESLOP-HARRISON *New Concepts Flowering-Plant Taxon.* v. 68 Independent topoclines exist for different morphological features. **1970** *Watsonia* VIII. 140 The two subspecies may be regarded as the relatively extreme end-points of a topocline. **1939** A. G. TANSLEY *Brit. Islands & their Vegetation* xxxv. 719 Valley bog-*topogenous, formed in valleys and depressions where water..stagnates, and bog plants establish themselves. **1975** J. G. EVANS *Environment Early Man Brit. Isles* iv. 76 Essentially there are two types of peat, topogenous and ombrogenous. Topogenous peat forms in places of impeded drainage. **1970** *Nature* 22 Aug. 806/1 *Topoinhibition is probably an important mechanism regulating cell multiplication in organisms in normal conditions. **1975** *Ibid.* 29 May 371/3 The loss of topoinhibition at wound edges in culture is apparently not due to loss of junctional communication. **1978** *Devel. Biol.* LXIV. 273/2 The enzyme has been referred to as ω-protein .., swivelase.., untwisting enzyme.., relaxing activity.., relaxing protein.., nicking-closing activity.., and DNA *topoisomerase. **1979** WANG & LIU in J. H. Taylor *Molecular Genetics* III. ii. 66 We propose that they be called DNA topoisomerases. **1980** *Sci. Amer.* July 109/2 These nicking-closing enzymes, which are also called topoisomerases, generally require no energy source to function. **18..** *Macm. Mag.* (Ogilvie), This little land [Palestine] became the object of a special adoration, a kind of *topolatry, when the Church mounted with Constantine the throne of the Cæsars. **1897** SCLATER in *Geog. Jrnl.* June 673 Various areas [of the earth] are characterized by the presence of certain forms of animal life which do not occur elsewhere. These forms it is proposed to call '**Topomorphs*'. Thus the giraffe is a 'Topomorph' of the Æthiopian region. **1860** MAYNE *Expos. Lex.*, **Toponarcosis*. **1890** BILLINGS *Med. Dict.*, *Toponarcosis*, local anæsthesia. **1899** *Syd. Soc. Lex.*, **Topophobia*. **1897** SCLATER in *Geog. Jrnl.* June 673 The sloths and anteaters are confined to tropical America, and the polar bear to the North Polar lands. Such animals may be called '**topo-politan*'..in contradistinction to those that are universally distributed, or '*cosmo-politan*'. **1893** O. THOMAS in *Proc. Zool. Soc.* 14 Mar. 242 The word *topo-type (or place-type)..should..be restricted to specimens collected within, say, a few miles of the original typical locality. **1900** *Ibid.* 3 Apr. 405 The Mice of Hilleröd, in Zealand (an almost *topotypical locality for the former name), belong to the latter form.

topochemical (tɒpəʊ'kɛmɪkəl), *a.* [f. TOPO- + CHEMICAL *a.*] **1.** *Ent.* Of, pertaining to, or denoting an insect's capacity to perceive spatial relationships through the sense of smell (see quots.).

1908 M. YEARSLEY tr. *A. Forel's Senses of Insects* x. 237 It is..a question of a chemical sense which gives the exact relations between the different parts of space... The faculty of smell-by-contact could be called chemaphesthesia and relational smell topochemical sense. **1967** J. H. SUDD *Introd. Behaviour Ants* ii. 17 Because the antennae are moveable and have sense organs all over the surface it has been suggested that ants can perceive spatial arrangements of chemical stimuli, rather as we can perceive patterns of colour or texture. This is the so-called topochemical sense.

2. *Chem.* [ad. G. *topochemisch* (Kohlschütter & Tüscher 1920, in *Zeitschr. f. anorg. u. allgemeine Chem.* CXI. 193).] Of or pertaining to topochemistry.

1920 *Chem. Abstr.* XIV. 3202 The term topochemical is proposed as a designation of 'locally confined' reactions. **1945** *Electronic Engin.* XVII. 425 Not only pressure and quality of the gas play an important part in vacuum measurement but also its quantity... It may be altered by 'topophysical' or 'topochemical' effects. **1948** *Research* I. 262/2 The topochemical significance is that corrosion is almost always an electrochemical process, in which the anodic localities of corrosion are small surface elements. **1967** [see BIOGENESIS 3].

Hence **topo'chemically** *adv.*

1962 *Jrnl. Physical Chem.* LXVI. 2442/1 Photochromy in this series is a topochemically determined phenomenon, *i.e.*, ..the packing arrangement in the crystal is of importance. **1967** *Science* 26 May 1123/2 When the construction [of the termites] reaches a certain critical density it attracts other termites topochemically.

topochemistry (tɒpəʊ'kɛmɪstrɪ). [f. TOPO- + CHEMISTRY.] The chemistry of reactions as affected by local variations in the structure of the medium on or in which they occur.

1948 *Research* I. 260/2 Topochemistry, derived from the Greek τόπος meaning 'location',..and topochemical processes are localized reactions in every sense. **1971** *Nature* 16 July 194/1 We have demonstrated a new method for the study of the topochemistry of membrane surfaces. **1975** *Ibid.* 31 Jan. 310/3 Topochemistry is concerned with the nature and kinetics of chemical reactions, including polymerisation reactions, between adjacent molecules in crystals.

'top-off, *sb. Austral. slang.* [Of obscure origin: cf. TOP *v.*[1] 6 and TIP *v.*[5] 2.] An informer. Also ***top-off merchant*** (MERCHANT *sb.* 3).

1941 BAKER *Dict. Austral. Slang* 77 *Top-off*, a police informer. **1944** L. GLASSOP *We were Rats* 133 He pooled me with the Q.M. Just a top-off merchant, that's all he is. **1966** B. COLLINS *Copper Crucible* 14 About four o'clock in the morning some top-off rings the cops. **1973** *Sunday Mail* (Brisbane) 4 Mar. 4/2 He believed him to be a prison 'top-off'.

'top-off, *a.* [f. the vbl. phr. *to top off*: see TOP *v.*[1] 19 a.] Of a passenger: carried in a freight aircraft that would not otherwise be full.

1961 *Flight* CXXX. 864/2 Seaboard World Airlines is continuing to press hard its proposal to carry 'top-off' passengers on its..cargo flights across the Atlantic. *Ibid.*, 'Top-off' passengers would..afford the necessary extra revenues without interfering with the basic objective of profitable transatlantic freight services. **1962** *Aeroplane* CIII. 5/3 Application to carry 'top-off' passengers on scheduled cargo flights to be rejected.

topograph ('tɒpəgrɑːf, -græf). [f. Gr. τόπ-ος place + -(ό)γραφος and -γράφος: see -GRAPH I.]

1. *rare.* **a.** A representation or description of localities. **b.** Name given to a surveying instrument. **c.** (See quot. 1911.)

1833 CARRINGTON (*title*) The Topograph, or the bye-ways within 9 miles of Devonport and Plymouth. **1865** *Athenæum* 7 Oct. 472/2 On the Topograph, a New Surveying Instrument, by Capt. Lendy. **1865** *Reader* 7 Oct. 409/2 A useful little instrument, called by the inventor a 'Topograph'..combines a plane table, prismatic compass, level, and clinometer. **1911** WEBSTER, *Topograph*, a model or draft of a place.

2. *Cryst.* A photograph taken in such a way, usu. with X-rays, as to exhibit the variation over the surface of a crystal of some physical or structural characteristic.

1944 G. N. RAMACHANDRAN in *Proc. Indian Acad. Sci.* A. XIX. 292 Eighteen such 'topographs' of cleavage plates of diamond..are reproduced. **1963** G. L. CLARK *Encycl. X-Rays & Gamma Rays* 1053/2 Topographs may be taken that show, for example, the distribution of optical absorption or optical fluorescence in a specimen. **1971** *Physics Bull.* Sept. 553/2 X ray topographs..were used by many authors to assess accurately the quality of their crystals.

topographer (tə'pɒgrəfə(r)). [f. Gr. τοπογράφ-ος topographer + -ER[1]. Cf. F. *topographe* (16th c. in Godef. *Compl.*).] One who is skilled in topography; one who describes or delineates a particular locality.

1603 FLORIO *Montaigne* I. xxx. (1632) 101 We had need of Topographers to make us particular narrations of the places they have beene in. **1625** N. CARPENTER *Geog. Del.* II. i. (1635) 2 Topographers, who spend their stocke in the description of some particular place or Region. **1774** WARTON *Hist. Eng. Poetry* Diss. ii. (1840) I. p. cxxiv, Giraldus Cambrensis.. was an historian, an antiquarian, a topographer,.. and a poet. **1884** *Manch. Exam.* 18 July 4/6 The Russian topographers are.. correcting the existing maps.

topographic (tɒpəʊˈgræfɪk), *a.* (*sb.*) [ad. Gr. τοπογραφικ-ός studious of topography, f. stem of τοπογραφ-ία TOPOGRAPHY: see -IC. Cf. F. *topographique* (16th c. in Godef. *Compl.*).] Of or pertaining to topography; = TOPOGRAPHICAL I.

1632 E. ROBERTSON in Lithgow *Trav.* B iv, Townes Topographick view, and Riuers courses. **1638** SIR T. HERBERT *Trav.* (ed. 2) 1 If I have made no Topographic mistakes. **1730–6** BAILEY (folio), *Topographic, topographick*, pertaining to the art of topography. **1803** W. TAYLOR in *Ann. Rev.* I. 437 Some displays of topographic knowledge. **1883** *Daily News* 1 Sept. 5/3 A lieutenant employed in the topographic service.. perished by the eruption of the 27th inst. **1898** *Jrnl. Sch. Geog.* (U.S.) Oct. 289 The lines followed by pioneer settlement.. are greatly influenced by topographic configuration.

b. = TOPOGRAPHICAL 2.

1899 *Syd. Soc. Lex., Topographic anatomy*, descriptive anatomy; or, used in the restricted sense, surface anatomy.

B. *sb. pl.* **topoˈgraphics**, the science of topography. *rare.*

1831 CARLYLE *Sart. Res.* II. viii, Statistics, Geographics, Topographics came.. almost of their own accord.

topographical (tɒpəʊˈgræfɪkəl), *a.* [f. as prec. + -AL[1]: see -ICAL.]

1. Of, pertaining to, or dealing with topography.

1570–6 LAMBARDE *Peramb. Kent* Introd. (1826) 6 Which collection (bicause it was digested into Titles by order of Alphabet, and concerned the description of places) I called a Topographicall Dictionarie. *a* **1586** SIDNEY *Lett.* Misc. Wks. (1829) 280 The topographical description of each country. *a* **1646** J. GREGORY *Maps & Charts* Posth. (1650) 323 A particular Description and Topographical Table of Middlesex. **1710** *Stillingfleet's Wks., Life* 56 An unusual variety of.. topographical observations. **1803** WELLINGTON in Gurw. *Desp.* (1837) II. 104, I am also desirous of having .. any general topographical account of the country. **1860** MAURY *Phys. Geog. Sea* (Low) xxi. §871 The topographical features and the climates of the antarctic regions.

†**b.** *topographical instrument*, the name given by Digges to a combined surveying instrument, such as is now called a THEODOLITE. *Obs.*

1571 DIGGES *Pantom.* I. xxxiv. K iij b, Set vp your Instrument Topographicall on his staffe. **1611** A. HOPTON *Topogr. Glass* vi. 27 To work as the Theodelitus, and Topographicall Instrument... If you make this instrument like to that which Maister Digges called the Topographical Instrument, then is there a Boxe and a Needle.. in the center of the Planisphere, over which there doth stand a perpendicular, whereon is placed a Semicircle.. to move about with the Alhidada.

2. Pertaining to the description of the parts or regions of the body: cf. TOPOGRAPHY 3.

1857 DUNGLISON *Med. Lex.* s.v. *Anatomy*, Topographical anatomy. **1890** BILLINGS *Med. Dict.* s.v. *Anatomy*, Topographical anatomy, describing them [the organs] by regions.

topoˈgraphically, *adv.* [f. prec. + -LY[2].] In a topographical way; in relation to topography.

1625 N. CARPENTER *Geog. Del.* II. i. (1635) 3 To the constitution of a place (as it is here Topographically taken). **1797** DALLAWAY *Constantinople* xxi. 341 That it is topographically [exact], an examination of the present face of the country will amply prove. **1893** W. CHOATE in *Home Mission.* (N.Y.) Sept. 264 Topographically, it [New Mexico] is composed of lofty plateaus, crossed by mountain ranges. **1899** *Allbutt's Syst. Med.* VII. 414 No actual proof .. that the centre for writing-movements is topographically distinct.

topoˈgraphico-, combining form of TOPOGRAPHIC, as in ***topoˈgraphico-ˈmythical***, of or pertaining to a topographical or local myth.

1892 A. NUTT in *Folk Lore* III. 41 The 'Dindseuchas', a topographico-mythical poem of the 10th.. century.

toˈpographist. *rare.* [f. as TOPOGRAPH-ER + -IST.] One versed in topography; a professional topographer.

1776 DA COSTA *Conchol.* II. 46 This author is a topographist, or describer of a particular country, *viz.* Senegal. **1870** *Daily News* 18 Oct., The most accurate and rapid military topographist I have ever known.

toˈpographize, *v.* [f. as prec. + -IZE.] **a.** *trans.* To describe or treat topographically. **b.** *intr.* To make topographical researches.

1792 W. B. STEVENS *Jrnl.* 30 May (1965) 25 Shaw was topographising around Shenstone Church. **1810** BYRON *Let. to H. Drury* 3 May, We had topographised Attica. **1837** SOUTHEY *Doctor* Interch. xiv. IV. 44 Leaving.. Sir William Gell to genealogise, if he pleases, as elaborately as he has topographized,.. I proceed with my promised explanation. **1876** (*title*) Cuninghame, Topographized by Timothy Pont, A.M., 1604–1608.

to͵pographoˈmetric, *a.* [f. as TOPOGRAPH + METRIC.] Of or pertaining to topographical measuring or surveying.

1911 WEBSTER, *Topographometric*, connected with, or devised for, the measurement of heights, angles, and distances, as for topographical maps.

topography (təʊˈpɒgrəfɪ). [ad. late L. *topographia* (in Servius and Jerome), ad. Gr. τοπογραφία, f. τοπογράφ-ος (see TOPOGRAPHER) + -ία, -Y. Cf. F. *topographie* (16th c.).]

1. The science or practice of describing a particular place, city, town, manor, parish, or tract of land; the accurate and detailed delineation and description of any locality.

1549 *Compl. Scot.* vi. 46 Al them that hes studeit in cosmographie, geographie, and in topographie. **1570–6** LAMBARDE *Peramb. Kent* (1826) 474 We might at the last by the union of many partes and papers compact one whole and perfect bodie and booke of our English Topographie. **1621** HEYLIN *Microcosmus* Introd. 10 Topographie which is the description of a particular place, be it Towne, Citie or Village. **1642** FULLER *Holy & Prof. St.* II. vii. 75 Acquainted with Cosmography, treating of the world in whole joynts; with Chorography, shredding it into countries; and with Topography, mincing it into particular places. *a* **1646** J. GREGORY *Maps & Charts* Posth. (1650) 323 The late Geographers.. call these Kind of Descriptions (of small Parcels of the Earth..) *Topographie.* **1864** BURTON *Scot Abr.* I. iv. 164 *note*, He.. explains how lifeless all history is without topography.

b. A detailed description or delineation of the features of a locality.

1432–50 tr. *Higden* (Rolls) I. 329 Irlonde.. whom Giraldus describenge in his Topographye, extollethe hit with mony laudes. **1586** J. HOOKER *Hist. Irel.* Pref. A iv b, in *Holinshed*, In our Topographie we haue at large set foorth and described the site of the land of Ireland. **1659** R. KILBURNE (*title*) A Topographie, or Survey of the County of Kent. **1665–6** *Phil. Trans.* I. 121 A Map of the Moon.. with a Topography as it were.. of all the considerable places therein.

c. Localization, local distribution; the study of this.

1658 SIR T. BROWNE *Hydriot.* ii. (1736) 31 If according to Learned Conjecture, the Bodies of Men shall rise where their greatest Relics remaine, many are not like to err in the Topography of their Resurrection. **1658** —— *Gard. Cyrus* i, Of deeper doubt is its Topography, and locall designation. **1835** URE *Phil. Manuf.* iii. 67 The topography of the textile manufactures is a most interesting subject of philosophical research. It investigates the causes why one district is occupied chiefly with cotton fabrics, a second with flax, a third with wool, and a fourth with silk.

2. The features of a region or locality collectively.

1847 LYTTON *Lucretia* II. xxvi, Towards that [staircase] used by the servants, and which his researches into the topography of the mansion had.. made known to him. **1858** GLADSTONE *Homer* III. 519 [Virgil] is not less neglectful of the actual topography; for he implies that Ilium is among the hills. **1873** G. C. DAVIES *Mount. & Mere* xxv. 224 The water is often very clear, and the frost has cut the weeds down so that one learns the topography of the river bed and the exact locale of the 'homes' of the fish.

fig. **1642** MILTON *Apol. Smect.* Wks. 1851 III. 262 Having rambl'd over the huge topography of his own vain thoughts. **1764** REID *Inquiry* vi. §11. 155, I confess I am not so well acquainted with the topography of the mind.

3. *transf.* **a.** *Anat.* The determination of the position of the various parts and organs of the body; regional anatomy. **b.** *Zool.* The determination and naming of the different regions or parts of the surface of an animal.

1847 LEWES *Hist. Philos.* (1867) II. vi. 408 The organs are definitely indicated both as to position and size, by the topography of the skull. **1891** *Cent. Dict.* s.v., The topography of a bird, a crab, an insect.

topoi: see TOPOS.

topoˈlogical, *a.* [f. TOPOLOG(Y + -ICAL.] **1.** Of or pertaining to topology (esp. in sense 2).

1715 M. DAVIES *Athen. Brit.* I. 183 Another noted Historian.. publish'd two *Topological Pamphlets, containing the Description of Britanny and Ireland. **1716** *Ibid.* III. *Diss. Physick* 37 Ancient Chiron.. the most direct Predecessor, at least in the topological Line, of the Great Hippocrates. **1836** *For. Q. Rev.* XVII. 286 Except the following somewhat ingenious topological (not phrenological) explanation of Richter's genius. **1903** *Times* 4 Apr. 7/2 The Azores.. have a topological importance.

2. *Math.* Of or pertaining to topology; such as is dealt with by topology (sense 3); ***topological invariant***, something invariant under a topological mapping; ***topological mapping*** or ***transformation*** = HOMŒOMORPHISM 2; ***topological space*** [tr. G. *topologisch raum* (F. Hausdorff *Grundzüge der Mengenlehre* (1914) vii. 213); the sense is due to M. Fréchet (*Compt. Rend.* (1925) CLXXX. 421)], an abstract space together with a topology (sense 3 c) on it.

1913 *Amer. Jrnl. Math.* XXXV. 189 (*heading*) On some topological properties of plane curves and a theorem of Möbius. **1926** *Proc. Sect. Sci. K. Akad. van Wetenschappen te Amsterdam* XXIX. 462 Any normal, not absolutely closed topological space $\mathscr{R}$ can be extended to a normal topological space $R = \mathscr{R} + \xi$ by adjunction of a non isolated point ξ. **1939** M. H. A. NEWMAN *Elem. Topol. Plane Sets of Points* iii. 51 The correlation is called a homoeomorphism between the spaces, or a topological mapping of the one space on the other. **1946** E. LEHMER tr. *Pontryagin's Topological Groups* iii. 53 For any two elements p and q of the group G there exists a topological transformation $f(x)$ of the space G into itself which transforms p into q. **1956** [see HOMŒOMORPHISM 2]. **1961** A. E. FARLEY tr. *Alexandroff's Elem. Concepts Topology* 16 A simple closed curve (i.e., the topological image of a circle). **1968** E. T. COPSON *Metric Spaces* vii. 92 Properties of a metric space which depend only on its open sets.. are called topological properties. **1975** I. STEWART *Concepts Mod. Math.* x. 144 Straightness is not a topological property.

Also **topoˈlogic** *a.*; **topologically** *adv.*

1716 M. DAVIES *Athen. Brit.* III. *Diss. Physick* 12 They were distinguish'd topologically or Geographically. **1872** M. COLLINS in *Lett. & Friendships* I. 113, I might go on with topologic lore, Until you voted me an awful bore. **1903** *Cornh. Mag.* Feb. 259 The topologic compass keeps his prow true. **1915** *Trans. Amer. Math. Soc.* XVI. 153 A manifold.. topologically equivalent to the boundary of an n-dimensional complex. **1938** *Mind* XLVII. 126 Tests are gauged 'topologically' by the extent to which they succeed in grouping together men who are also grouped together in respect of their performances in life. **1969** R. B. FULLER *Operating Man. Spaceship Earth* v. 67 All the system's paths must be topologically and circularly interrelated. **1975** I. STEWART *Concepts Mod. Math.* x. 156 Now topologically a dog is a sphere (assuming it keeps its mouth shut and neglecting internal organs) because all we have to do is shrink its legs and fatten it up a bit.

topologize (təˈpɒlədʒaɪz), *v.* *Math.* [f. TOPOLOG(ICAL *a.* + -IZE.] *trans.* To make into a topological space. So **toˈpologized** *ppl. a.*; **to͵pologiˈzation**, the process of topologizing.

1946 E. LEHMER tr. *Pontryagin's Topological Groups* iii. 56 The abstract group G admits one and only one topologization under which the system Σ^* is a complete system of neighborhoods of the identity. *Ibid.*, If the group G can be topologized in such a way that [etc.]. **1963** D. BUSHAW *Elem. Gen. Topol.* ii. 29 It is no great step to convert each of these methods of topologization into an alternative definition of the concept of a topological space. **1964** A. P. & W. ROBERTSON *Topological Vector Spaces* i. 8 The real numbers and the complex numbers can both be topologised by taking $d(x, y) = |x - y|$. **1979** *Proc. London Math. Soc.* XXXVIII. 231 For any closed subspace S of ER^n; we topologize the space of continuous maps of S into ER^n with the compact open topology.

topology (təʊˈpɒlədʒɪ). [f. TOPO- + -LOGY. Cf. F. *topologique* adj., Littré, related to sense 1 b.] A term meaning 'science of place', which has been tentatively proposed or used in various senses.

1. †**a.** The department of botany which treats of the localities where plants are found. *Obs.*

1659 LOVELL *Compl. Herball* Pref., The Topologie or place of gathering them. Thus, Herbes, are to be gathered in mountaines, hills and plain places.

†**b.** The art of assisting the memory by associating the thing to be remembered with some place or building, the parts of which are well known. *Obs.*

1860 WORCESTER cites FLEMING. Hence in later Dicts.

c. *Anat.*: see quot.

1899 *Syd. Soc. Lex., Topology*, topographic anatomy. The relation of the presenting part of fœtus to the pelvic canal.

2. The scientific study of a particular locality: see quot. 1905[1].

1850 S. TYMMS *Bury Wills* (Camden) Introd. 12 The selection of wills.. has been made more with a view to illustrate the peculiar customs and language of the period than the topology or genealogy of the district. **1902** *Cassell's Encycl. Dict. Suppl., Topology*, the study of the places or localities in a given district. **1903** *Cornh. Mag.* Feb. 251 The fact that topology is not synonymous with topography, but bears the same relation to topography as geology does to geography. **1905** *Q. Rev.* Apr. 346 The comparatively new study of topology, the science by which, from the consideration of geographical facts about a locality, one can draw deductions as to its history. **1905** *Spectator* 10 June 856/1 We need a knowledge not only of topography, but.. of that.. sister science which has been christened 'topology'.

3. a. The branch of mathematics concerned with those properties of figures and surfaces which are independent of size and shape and are unchanged by any deformation that is continuous, neither creating new points nor fusing existing ones; hence, with those of abstract spaces that are invariant under homœomorphic transformations. [ad. G. *topologie* (J. B. Listing 1847, in *Göttinger Studien* I. 814).]

1883 *Nature* 1 Feb. 316/2 The term Topology was introduced by Listing to distinguish what may be called qualitative geometry from the ordinary geometry in which quantitative relations chiefly are treated. **1895** *Funk's Standard Dict., Topology*.. 2. *Geom.* The geometrical theory of situation without respect to size or shape, including the theory of knots in a closed curve and the relations of the bounding parts of a solid. **1929** *Trans. Amer. Math. Soc.* XXXI. 290 Analysis situs or topology is primarily concerned with invariants under homeomorphic transformations of a space into itself. **1952** F. BAGEMIHL et al. tr. *Pontryagin's Found. Combinatorial Topol.* i. 1 Combinatorial topology studies geometric forms by decomposing them into the simplest geometric figures, simplexes, which adjoin one another in a regular fashion. **1959** E. M. PATTERSON *Topology* i. 1 Nowadays mathematicians are in fairly general agreement that topology is a study of continuity. **1970** *Observer* (Colour Suppl.) 15 Feb. 19/2 Topology is one of the most recent and rapidly advancing branches of mathematics, and is a kind of universal geometry of surfaces. **1972** M. KLINE *Math. Thought* l. 1158 Topology, as it is understood in this century, breaks down into two somewhat separate divisions: point set topology, which is concerned with geometrical figures regarded as collections of points..; and combinatorial or algebraic topology, which treats geometrical figures as aggregates of smaller building blocks. **1975** I. STEWART *Concepts Mod. Math.* x. 146 The basic objects studied in topology are called topological spaces.

b. (The study of) the topological properties *of* something. Also *transf.*

1913 *Amer. Jrnl. Math.* XXXV. 189 An application..of the transformation by inversion to the topology of plane curves. **1930** *Proc. Nat. Acad. Sci.* XVI. 240 (*heading*) Combinatory topology of convex regions. **1959** *Ibid.* XLV. 1607 (*heading*) On the topology of the genetic fine structure. **1972** *Sci. Amer.* Jan. 65/1 With careful dissection techniques one can expose deep-lying sections of bulk specimens so that their topology can be studied by scanning electron microscopy. **1980** D. L. COHN *Measure Theory* p. vii, Chapters 1 through 5..presuppose only the familiarity with the topology of Euclidean spaces that a student should acquire in an advanced calculus course.

c. A family of open subsets of an abstract space such that the union of any of the subsets and the intersection of any two of them are members of the family, together with the space itself and the null set.

1946 E. LEHMER tr. *Pontryagin's Topological Groups* iii. 55 A topology can be introduced into any abstract group *G* whatsoever in such a way that *G* becomes a discrete group. **1963** M. J. MANSFIELD *Introd. Topol.* ii. 21 The topologies $\mathscr{S}$ and $\mathscr{U}$ for *R*..were defined, in effect by specifying neighborhoods for each point and then declaring a set to be a member of the topology if and only if the set contains a neighborhood of each of its points. **1976** *Physics Bull.* Sept. 388/2 A useful way to think of a topology for a space is as a specification of which functions on it are to be continuous.

d. *gen.* The way in which constituent parts are interrelated or arranged.

1967 *Electronics* 6 Mar. 149/1 If consideration is restricted to bipolar gate topologies..there are just three basic forms of IC logic schemes. **1970** *Nature* 7 Nov. 553/1 These data have been used to construct a topology based on the minimal mutation distance method... This topology places castor.. closest to sesame.., then mung bean.., then sunflower. **1971** *Physics Bull.* Dec. 717/3 Having an axisymmetric topology permits an easier study [of tokamaks] than, say, stellarators. **1972** *Computer Jrnl.* XV. 204/1 The resulting list structure has the same topology as the old, so that re-entrancy and sharing of common substructure are preserved.

Hence **to'pologist**, one versed in topology.

1903 *Cornh. Mag.* Feb. 258 The French topologist has shown that the Odyssey is subsequent to a vanished Phœnician sea power. **1905** *Spectator* 10 June 856/1 To the topographist..the site..is a mystery; to the topologist..it is full of meaning. **1954** *Sci. News* XXXIII. 56 If you cross the curve..you must go from one part to another—you cannot stay inside or stay outside. I think that anyone who is not a topologist will accept this as a self-evident fact. **1967** G. STEINER *Lang. & Silence* 33, I have watched topologists, knowing no syllable of each other's language, working effectively together at a blackboard. **1971** I. G. GASS et al. *Understanding Earth* iv. 77/1 It is not what the topologists call a simply connected body; it is like a Henry Moore statue: it has a hole in it. **1975** I. STEWART *Concepts Mod. Math.* x. 146 The oft-quoted assertion that to a topologist a doughnut is the same as a coffee-cup provides an example.

toponium (tɒ'pəʊnɪəm). *Particle Physics.* [f. TOP *sb.*[1] + -ONIUM, after POSITRONIUM.] A bound state of a top quark and a top anti-quark.

1978 *Nature* 28 Sept. 268/2 This gives the prospect of detailed investigation of quark dynamics by studying transitions among these levels of 'toponium' analogous to transitions among levels of positronium and hydrogen in atomic physics. **1984** *New Scientist* 17 May 15/1 Theory suggests that if there is an electrically neutral Higgs boson whose mass is less than that of toponium, then we should be able to observe toponium decaying into a photon and a Higgs.

toponomastic (tɒpɒnəʊ'mæstɪk), *sb.* and *a.* [f. TOPO- + ONOMASTIC *a.* and *sb.*] **A.** *sb.* (also *pl.*) = TOPONYMY. **B.** *adj.* Of or pertaining to place-names.

1916 T. TAYLOR *Celtic Christianity of Cornwall* iv. 54 Professor Loth, as the result of a careful study of Breton toponomastic, has arrived at the conclusion that the Armorican parishes were placed as early as the sixth and seventh century under the invocation of the saints..whose names they still bear. **1922** JOYCE *Ulysses* 673 Their.. toponomastic, historical and religious literatures. **1971** W. F. H. NICOLAISEN in A. J. Aitken et al. *Edin. Stud. Eng. & Scots* 211 There is no basic difference in the proper handling of the Scottish toponomastic material in this respect. **1977** *Maledicta* I. 41 (*heading*) Macedonian toponomastics.

'toponym. [f. as TOPONYMY.]

1. (See quot.)

1891 *Cent. Dict.*, *Toponym*,..the technical designation of any region of an animal, as distinguished from any organ.

2. a. A place-name; a name given to a person or thing marking its place of origin. **b.** = TOPONYMIC *sb.* 2.

1939 *Antiquity* Sept. 311 Important also are certain long lists of personal names followed by those of the cities from which these persons came... The toponyms include Byblus (*G-b-'l*, the *Gebal* of the Old Testament). **1958** [see ANTHROPONYMY]. **1973** *Times Lit. Suppl.* 5 Jan. 3/3 *The Manchester Guardian* (before it dropped the toponym). **1978** *Regional Lang. Stud.—Newfoundland* VIII. 3 The surname of the original author of this list, Jeddore, occurs as a toponym in Nova Scotia, and..Jeddore's Harbour is about 40 miles east of Halifax. **1980** *Sci. Amer.* Feb. 48/1 The Zapotec people also used toponyms, glyphic 'place signs' for important places or landmarks, mountains in particular.

topo'nymic, *a.* and *sb.* [f. TOPONYM(Y + -IC.] **A.** *adj.* Of or pertaining to toponymy.

1891 in *Cent. Dict.* **1896** *Nat. Geog. Mag.* (U.S.) VII. 222 We miss in the works of a government board of names all evidence of acquaintance with toponymic literature.

B. *sb.* **1.** See quot. 1906: cf. *patronymic.*

1906 *Cornish N. & Q.* 142 Toponymics, i.e. personal names derived from the place where a particular ancestor lived.

2. A descriptive place-name, usu. derived from some topographical feature of the place.

1933 *Times Lit. Suppl.* 20 Apr. 280/2 With a few.. exceptions..all Sussex place-names..ought to be explained as toponymics, i.e., as containing descriptive words. **1956** A. H. SMITH *Eng. Place-Name Elements* I. 6 Village names which were originally toponymics. **1957** H. H. JENKINS *Diction of 'Yank'* (Univ. Florida thesis) v. 45 Some of the GI's toponymics are banal and unimaginative; others are witty and colorful. **1977** *Word 1972* XXVIII. 117 (*heading*) Celtic toponymics in Scotland.

toponymy (təʊ'pɒnɪmɪ). Also *erron.* **toponomy.** [f. TOPO- + Gr. -ωνυμία, f. ὄνομα name: cf. *homonymy, synonymy.*]

1. The place-names of a country or district as a subject of study.

1876 W. K. SULLIVAN in *Encycl. Brit.* V. 306/2 The substitution of vague descriptions of dress and arms, and a vague toponomy, for the full and definite descriptions and precise toponomy of the primitive poems. **1887** *Athenæum* 20 Aug. 240/3 This book..does not deal at all with topography in the proper sense, but merely (if the word may be tolerated as English) with 'toponymy'. **1893** *Academy* 22 July 72/3 These papers are of interest for Basque toponymy and language. **1900** DENNIKER *Races of Man* xiii. 557 The pre-Columbian aborigines of Porto Rico, Haiti, Jamaica, and Cuba were Arawaks, to judge from the toponymy of these islands.

2. *Anat.* (See quot.)

1882 WILDER & GAGE *Anat. Techn.* 20 Terms of Position and Direction—Toponymy. *Ibid.* 23 The Intrinsic Toponymy... We..shall designate the aspects and regions of the body by terms derived from names which have been applied to the parts themselves. **1899** in *Syd. Soc. Lex.*

So **to'ponymal** *a.*, of or pertaining to toponymy; **topo'nymical** *a.* = prec. adj.; **to'ponymist**, one who deals with place-names.

1891 *Cent. Dict.*, **Toponymal.* **1882** WILDER & GAGE *Anat. Techn.* 20 Such terms constitute a *Toponymical Vocabulary which is based upon intrinsic instead of purely extrinsic and accidental relations. *a* **1852** MACGILLIVRAY *Nat. Hist. Dee Side* (1855) 235 Appropriately named by the Celts—who were famous *toponymists,..*Na claisean*—The Furrows.

topophone ('tɒpəfəʊn). [f. TOPO- + Gr. -φωνος sounding, φωνή voice, sound.] (See quots.)

1880 *Patent Specif.* No. 495, A topophone, or instrument for locating sounds, applicable more especially to the navigation of a vessel in a fog. **1881** *Standard* 1 Jan., The topophone of Professor Mayer..is intended to determine the direction and approximately the distance of a fog-horn. **1902** *Harper's Mag.* Feb. 498 Another wireless telephone for maritime use is known as the topophone. *Ibid.* 499 By the use of the topophone,..sounds can be heard which are inaudible to the unassisted ear.

topos ('tɒpɒs). Pl. topoi. [a. Gr. τόπος place: cf. etym. note s.v. TOPIC *a.* and *sb.*] A traditional motif or theme (in a literary composition); a rhetorical commonplace, a literary convention or formula.

1948 L. SPITZER *Linguistics & Lit. Hist.* v. 201 In a proem there is generally present a second topos. **1957** N. FRYE *Anatomy of Criticism* 103 The *topoi* or rhetorical commonplaces..are so dull when stated as propositions, and so rich and variegated when they are used as structural principles in literature. **1957** *Medium Ævum* XXVI. 148 We have identified the *topos* of the sixth age of the world (and its approaching end) in our two OE poems. **1962** D. A. PEARSALL *Floure & Leafe* 68 The submission formula is a *topos* of classical rhetoric. **1966** *Eng. Stud.* XLVII. 150 There must be few literary historians who have traced with such thoroughness the development of a single *topos* through two centuries. **1976** *Classical Q.* XXVI. 246 Kinds of anecdotes which Herodotus loved to include: raiding parties, espionage.., tales of bravery and cowardice, and other such *topoi.* **1981** *Times Lit. Suppl.* 16 Jan. 60/4 It is a common *topos* to remark that thanks are due to the editor or author for raising weighty questions.

toposcope ('tɒpəʊskəʊp). [f. TOPO- + -SCOPE.] **1.** A device (as a horizontal circular dial) showing the direction of designated features of the landscape and usu. erected on a hilltop.

1907 [see INDICATOR 1 a]. **1968** V. WAITE *Malvern Country* vi. 77 The direction indicator—or toposcope, to give it the technical name—was set up on the Beacon summit to commemorate the reign of Queen Victoria. **1974** *Victorian* (Victoria, B.C.) 22 Mar. 45/3 Nearby is a panoramic viewing area with a toposcope, giving details of all the islands dotted around in the sparkling blue China Sea 1,800 feet below.

2. *Med.* An instrument used for toposcopy.

1951 WALTER & SHIPTON in *Electroencephalogr. & Clin. Neurophysiol.* III. 282/2 Because it provided a visual display of topographic detail this device was called a Toposcope. **1965** *Math. in Biol. & Med.* (Med. Res. Council) IV. 159 The 'toposcope'..depicts each EEG electrode as a spot on a cathode ray tube. **1977** *Lancet* 21 May 1114/1 He devised the first on-line frequency analyser, which with subsequent modifications led to the 'toposcope'.

toposcopy (tə'pɒskəpɪ). *Med.* [f. as prec. + -Y[3].] Examination of the electrical activity at different points in the brain simultaneously by means of a number of electrodes each connected to a separate oscilloscope or the like. Hence **topo'scopic** *a.*

1950 *Electroencephalogr. & Clin. Neurophysiol.* II. 97/2 The split disc neon lamp method of toposcopy is particularly attractive. **1951** *Ibid.* III. 283/1 The mark I Toposcope was too limited in its resolution, but the results obtained with it were sufficiently encouraging to warrant the initiation of a development programme with the aim of investigating the general problem of toposcopic display. **1974** *Ibid.* XXXVI. 566/2 (*heading*) Current thoughts on toposcopy. *Ibid.*, Many of the toposcopic display devices used in EEG are products of the age of analog computers and devices.

topotaxy ('tɒpəʊtæksɪ). *Cryst.* [f. TOPO- + *-taxy*, after EPITAXY.] (See quot. 1959[3].) So **topo'tactic, -ical** *adjs.*; **topo'tactically** *adv.*

1959 F. K. LOTGERING in *Jrnl. Inorganic & Nucl. Chem.* IX. 115 For these reactions the name 'topotactical reactions' ..is proposed. *Ibid.* Plate facing p. 120 Photo-micrographs of topotactically oriented $Co_{0.5}Zn_{0.1}Z$. *Ibid.* 123 We propose the term 'topotaxy' for all chemical solid state reactions that lead to a material with crystal orientations which are correlated with crystal orientations in the initial product [*read* substance]. **1969** *Nature* 9 Aug. 609/1 Studies of the topotaxy of solid state precipitation from spinel crystalline solutions. **1976** *Ibid.* 19 Aug. 721/1 Dislocations in molecular crystals..have been studied on the microscale chiefly with a view to establishing their role in..topotactic transformations. **1982** *Ibid.* 22 Apr. 730/1 (*caption*) Electron micrograph of a fault-free β-phase grain, topotactically replacing faulted ring-woodite.

† **to-'poune,** *v. Obs.* Also 4 to-powne, (pone, -poyne). [f. TO-[2] + -ME. *pounen*, POUND *v.*[1]] *trans.* To pound to pieces.

c **1290** *S. Eng. Leg.* I. 39/181 þis desciples forthe wende And to-pouneden it [the dragon] al to deþe. **1382** WYCLIF *Ps.* civ. [cv.] 16 Alle fastnesse of bred he to-ponede [1388 wastide; Vulg. *contrivit*]. **1382** —— *Matt.* xxi. 44 Vpon whom it shal falle, it shal togidre poune [*v.r.* al to-powne] hym.

† **top over terve,** *vb. phr.* [Cf. TOPSY-TURVY.] *intr.* To topple over, fall topsy-turvy.

a **1450** *Brut* ccxliv. 378 Our stakez made hem top ouyr terve, eche on oþer, þat þay lay on hepis.

topped (tɒpt), *ppl. a.*[1] Also 5-6 *Sc.* toppit, 7-9 topt. [f. TOP *sb.*[1] and *v.*[1] + -ED.]

1. Having or furnished with a top or tops (see the senses of TOP *sb.*[1]). Also in parasynthetic comb., as ***large-topped, sharp-topped***, etc.

c **1450** HOLLAND *Howlat* 186 Heronnis contemplatif.. With toppit hudis on hed. **1513** DOUGLAS *Æneis* IV. x. 86 The seis large, All wmbeset with toppit schip and barge. **1567** MAPLET *Gr. Forest* 35 The other is rather Spearelike and sharpe topped. **1632** LITHGOW *Trav.* II. 44 Taking their directions from the topped hills of the maine continent. **1675** HAN. WOOLLEY *Gentlew. Comp.* 58 The large-topt stockings with supporters to bear them up. **1681** W. ROBERTSON *Phraseol. Gen.* (1693) 1240 To make topped, or sharp at the top. **1826** HOGG *C. Dinmont* in *Lit. Souvenir* 257 He had huge topped boots, all of one colour. **1852** R. S. SURTEES *Sponge's Sp. Tour* ix. 38 A pair of..brown topped boots.

2. Having the top removed; of a tree: polled, pollarded; of hemp: see TOP *v.*[1] 3, quot. 1794.

1712 J. JAMES tr. *Le Blond's Gardening* 169 Some topped Elms..in five or six Years time have form'd a handsome.. Head. **1794** *Rigging & Seamanship* I. 62 Ropes made from topt hemp will not stretch so much. **1844** STEPHENS *Bk. Farm* II. 8 The topped and tailed turnips. **1890** W. A. WALLACE *Only a Sister* 322 Under that topped willow.

topped (tɒpt), *ppl. a.*[2] *Golf.* [pa. pple. of TOP *v.*[1] 18 a.] Struck, as a ball, in the upper half; in which the ball is so struck.

1901 *Westm. Gaz.* 16 Aug. 2/2 If you put forward that plea for the foundered drive, the topped approach, or the putt that 'gangs agee', your partner must accept it. **1902** *Ibid.* 17 Oct. 4/2 The topped stroke with an iron, that sent the ball no great distance when gutta-percha was employed, answers nearly as well as a perfectly aimed shot when the 'Haskell' or 'Kempshall' is in use. **1907** *Ibid.* 13 Sept. 3/1 The natural penalty of an errant shot or a topped shot.

top people, *sb. pl.* Also with capital initials. [TOP *sb.*[1] 30.] The aristocracy; leaders and people of rank and influence in the arts, politics, the professions, etc. Occas. *sing.* as ***top person.***

The expression gained wide currency from the advertising slogan used by *The Times* in 1957.

1752 in M. M. Verney *Verney Lett.* (1930) II. xxxiv. 250 When they get in liquor they are very troublesome and noisy. They kept it up all night, several of the top people. **1957** *Economist* 21 Sept. 929/3 Like the *Times*, it [sc. *Punch*] has been read by top people for a long time. **1959** C. MACINNES *Absolute Beginners* 103 He had a very sharp top-person suit on. **1960** *Sunday Times* 21 Feb. 9/5 (Advt.), The man who gets on is he who makes himself bigger than his job... Top People take *The Times.* **1963** *Punch* 4 Sept. 356/2 Southerners, satiated with Top People prissiness. **1977** *News of World* 17 Apr. 2/3 The top people's directory, Who's Who. **1981** R. D. EDWARDS *Corridors of Death* vi. 29 The need for tact and sensitivity in handling the Top People involved.

topper ('tɒpə(r)), *sb.*[1] [f. TOP *v.*[1] + -ER[1].]

1. a. A person or thing that tops; one who cuts off the top of a tree; an instrument for topping (TOP *v.*[1] 4, 7); a candle-snuffer; a comb-maker's equilateral single-cut file or float.

1688 R. HOLME *Armoury* III. 381/2 A pair of Snuffers, or a pair of Toppers. **1874** KNIGHT *Dict. Mech.* s.v. *Float*, A single-cut file, or one in which the teeth are parallel and unbroken by a second row of crossing teeth... The floats of comb-makers and ivory-carvers..are known by specific names, as graille, found, carlet, topper. **1883** H. WALKER in *Leisure Hour* 505/1 Beeches unscathed by topper and lopper. **1895** *Oracle Encycl.* II. 125/1 Finished off with wedge-shaped files, called the graille, carlet, topper, &c.

†**b.** One who 'tops' (TOP *v.*[1] 17 a) at dice; a cheating gamester. *Obs. rare.*

1671 SHADWELL *Humourist* III. Wks. 1720 I. 174 Nor is it five months, since I saw you..by help of a dozen men, chastise one poor Topper or Palmer.

c. A horse or rider that tops a fence.

1854 WARTER *Last of Old Squires* xii. 133 A fence that would have baulked a Leicestershire topper.

2. One who makes or adds the top to something; one who works at the upper part of a garment.

1884 E. SIMCOX in *19th Cent.* June 1041 A shirtmaker proper, otherwise called a 'topper'. **1905** *Daily Chron.* 23 June 8/7 Shirt Hands.—Wanted a few good button-holers and toppers.

3. An action, remark, etc., that puts a finishing touch to what has gone before, *esp.* an outrageous one or one that cannot be capped. Cf. TOP *v.*[1] 12 b.

1939 J. O'HARA *Pal Joey* (1940) 98 It was a famous historical topper when Josephine was informed that the poor people did not have any bread and she said 'Why don't they eat some cake'. **1973** *Black Panther* 6 Oct. 6/3 The topper is that Foster completes this vicious cycle with a cold beg..to get his money under the..Law Enforcement Assistance Act. **1977** *Amer. Film* July-Aug. 18/1 The shot was part of a gag..a 'topper' that Keaton used to finish off a duel between two Civil War locomotives. **1977** *New Yorker* 12 Sept. 92/3 'Will you do me a favor and take me over to the Carnegie Deli..?' The driver said sure, swung off his bus route, and deposited Henny at the door. Henny's topper? He got off the bus and said, 'Pick me up in twenty minutes.'

topper ('tɒpə(r)), *sb.*[2] Chiefly *slang* or *low colloq.* [f. TOP *sb.*[1] + -ER[1]; in some uses perh. f. senses of TOP *v.*[1]]

1. a. A 'top' thing or person; a person or thing surpassingly or exceptionally good or excellent; the best or one of the best of the kind. *colloq.*

1709 *Brit. Apollo* II. No. 2. 3/2 A Bowl that is full of Punch, of all these is the Topper. **1802** R. ANDERSON *Bards of Tyne* 22 The king's meade a bit of a speech, And gentle-fwok say it's a topper. **1825** BROCKETT *N.C. Words, Topper*, any thing superior—a clever, or extraordinary person. **1828** *Craven Gloss.* s.v., This coat's a topper for turning rain. **1891** A. LANG *Angling Sk.* 115 He gets flurried with a big fish... And this one is a topper. **1894** ASTLEY *50 Years Life* I. 59 He was a real good fellow then, and..he is a topper now.

b. *U.S. Mil. slang.* A first sergeant. Cf. *top sergeant* s.v. TOP *sb.*[1] 34.

1918 *Radiator* 22 Aug. 2 Sergeant Hulbert, the 'topper' of 95. **1937** *Our Army* (U.S.) Jan. 19 'I'm sure there's no Lieutenant McGonigle here,' replies the Topper.

2. a. A top-hat, a tall hat. *slang* and *colloq.*

1820 *Sporting Mag.* VI. 269 The wind blew his white topper out of the ring. **1885** JESSOPP in *19th Cent.* July 48 We all wear black coats and dark trousers and 'toppers', at least in London. **1905** H. A. VACHELL *The Hill* v, The 'topper' you wear on Sunday.

b. A kind of loose-fitting jacket or short coat worn by women or children. orig. and chiefly *U.S.*

1937 *Los Angeles Times* 2 Sept. 5/1 (Advt.), Soft, fluffy casual toppers tailored in the best British way. **1938** *Sears, Roebuck Catal.* Spring/Summer 20/2 The absolutely perfect topper coat. **1948** *N.Y. Times Mag.* 8 Feb. 38 (Advt.), A boxy topper with cardigan neckline. **1960** *News Chron.* 22 July 6/4 Attractive little top jackets ('toppers'). **1972** *Country Life* 30 Nov. 1533 Printed dress..worn with a topper jacket in orange wool. **1978** *Detroit Free Press* 4 Mar. D 10/4 (Advt.), There are girls' topper sets and perky dresses.

3. A blow on the 'top' or head. *slang.*

1785 *Sessions Papers* 6 Apr. 571/2 One of them said, damn his eyes, *give him a topper at once.* **1803** in *Occasional Papers Univ. Sydney Austral. Lang. Res. Centre* (1980) No. 18. 44 He..had 'knocked him down and given him a topper for luck!' **1834** H. AINSWORTH *Rookwood* IV. ii, Vile Jem.. Straight threatened Tommy with a topper. **1887** FENN *Dick o' Fens* xvi, How I should have liked to give him a topper with the pole.

4. *pl.* The largest and finest fruit (esp. strawberries) displayed at the top of a punnet or package; cf. *to top one's fruit* (TOP *v.*[1] 9 c). *slang.*

1839 MOGRIDGE *Old Humphrey's Observ.* 252 There are toppers in dress,..and toppers in religion, as well as toppers in strawberries. **1891** *Brit. Workman* Aug., The punnet was a very bad case of what is generally bad enough at the best —of 'toppers'. The few good berries at the top were the only good ones. **1898** *Daily Tel.* 2 Mar. 5/4 Has a keen eye for 'toppers'..the attractive oranges which are displayed in the first row in order to entice buyers.

5. A large wave with curling or breaking summit.

1863 N. MACLEOD *Remin. Highl. Parish* iii, Quick as lightning the little craft, having again gathered way,..is spinning over the third topper, not a drop of water having come over the lee gunwale.

6. A cigar-stump or cigarette-end; also, the remains of tobacco in a pipe-bowl. *slang.*

1874 HOTTEN *Slang Dict.* 327 *Topper*, the tobacco which is left in the bottom of a pipe-bowl..; or the stump of a smoked cigar. **1888** in *Cassell's Encycl. Dict.* **1902** *Westm. Gaz.* 13 Nov. 5/1 It was his custom to rise before daybreak every morning and search the streets of the West End,.. picking up the ends of cigarettes and cigars commonly known as 'toppers'.

Hence '**topper** *v.*, *trans.* to knock on the head; to kill by a 'topper' or blow on the head. '**toppering** *vbl. sb. slang.*

1829 P. EGAN *Boxiana* 2nd Ser. II. 671 The *topper*-ing system was in full practice, till *poor* Cock Robin went down quite exhausted! **1869** E. FARMER *Scrap Bk.* (ed. 6) 128 Full ninety [rats] had died, Without counting seven they'd topper'd outside.

topper, obs. dial. form of TAPPER[1].

†**toppet**[1]. *Obs.* [ME. *topet*, app. a. OF. *topet*, *toupet* (12–13th c.) tuft, dim. of *top*, *toup* top, crest: in Eng. perh. eventually taken as dim. of TOP *sb.*[1]] Top, summit, tip.

1439 in *Archæologia* XXI. 37, ij Salers of Gold, whereof yt oon ys a man..garnysshed wt vij rubees and vij troches, every troche of iij perles, and upon ye topet is a saphur. **1561** HOLLYBUSH *Hom. Apoth.* 8 Take..the parynge of the toppet of hertes horne. *Ibid.* 23 Lyke vertue..hath Fenell, Penyreal, the floures of Hoppes. Branck vrsyne the toppets of the floure. *Ibid.* 38 Take the toppet of an onyon.

†**toppet**[2]. *Obs.* Also 5 **topet**, 6 **tappet**. [Late ME., dim. of *toppe*, TOP *sb.*[3] basket (of fruit); analogous to MFl. *topkin* ('viij topkine rosinen' 1334), OF. (Picard) *toppequin* (15th c. in Godef.). Cf. also TAP *sb.*[3], TAPNET.] = TOP *sb.*[3], TAPNET.

1481–90 *Howard Househ. Bks.* (Roxb.) 22 There cam from London x. lb. coton & a toppet figges. *Ibid.* 351 A topet of fygge dodes [see FIG-DOTE]. **1510–11** *Durham Acc. Rolls* (Surtees) 290 Et in quinque lez toppettis Racemorum parvorum ad ij s. viij d. **1511–12** *Ibid.* 291 In 4or le tapettes racemorum magnorum ad 2 s. 8 d., 10 s. 8 d. **1516** in Rogers *Agric. & Prices* III. 535/1 [Figs] Toppet.

toppie ('tɒpɪ). [perh. f. TOPKNOT.] A small brown bulbul of the genus *Pycnonotus*, found in southern Africa, either the Cape bulbul, *P. capensis*, or the red-eyed bulbul, *P. nigricans.*

1899 G. RUSSELL *Hist. Old Durban* viii. 176 Doves cooed and 'Toppies' answered each other obtrusively. **1940** A. ROBERTS *Birds S. Afr.* 225 Cape Bulbul, or Toppie..is not such a common bird as the Layard's Bulbul found further east. **1951** R. CAMPBELL *Light on Dark Horse* x. 142 The commonest bird in Africa, the Toppie as we call him.., is a great character. **1964** D. VARADAY *Gara-Yaka* xv. 126 His best friends became the Toppies, the conical-helmeted small dark birds that disclose the presence of snakes. **1971** J. DRUMMOND *Farewell Party* vi. 35 There were birds.. finches and toppies and a collared sunbird.

top-piece, *sb.* The piece that forms or is at the top of anything; *spec.* †**a.** The best or finest piece; the *chef-d'œuvre*, masterpiece. *Obs. rare.* **b.** The head. *colloq.* **c.** = TOPIT. **d.** *Shoe-making*: see quots.

a. 1682 BUNYAN *Greatness of Soul* Wks. (ed. Offor) I. 122 The soul is the..top-piece that He hath made in all the visible world. **1682** —— *Holy War* i. 3 The Top-piece beyond any thing else that he did in that country.

b. 1838 in *Eng. Dial. Dict.* **1864** LOWELL *Fireside Trav.* 180 The Acephali, with whom Herodotus..wound up his climax of men with abnormal top-pieces.

c. 1839 URE *Dict. Arts* 966 The topit, or top-piece.

d. 1911 *Encycl. Brit.* XXIV. 993/1 Lifts and top-pieces for the heels. *Ibid.* 993/2 The top-pieces, similar to the outsoles, are put on and nailed down to the lifts.

top-piece, *v. trans.* To put a top-piece on.

1830 GALT *Lawrie T.* IV. iv, In less time than Dick the Cobbler takes to top-piece an old shoe.

'**topping**, *vbl. sb.*[1] [f. TOP *v.*[1] + -ING[1]. In some concrete senses associated with TOP *sb.*[1]]

1. The action of TOP *v.*[1] in various senses.

a. The making, formation, putting on, or adding of a top or tops (see TOP *v.*[1] III).

1504 *Acc. Ld. High Treas. Scot.* II. 279 His task of the ending and topping of the chimnais of Halyrudhous. **1883** R. HALDANE *Workshop Receipts* Ser. II. 228/1 This colour may be modified by topping with small quantities of magenta, &c. **1888** *Times* 8 Sept. 9/2 The practice of what is known..as topping, that is of putting good fruit at the top, and of filling the rest of the hamper with rubbish. **1896** *Jrnl. R. Horticult. Soc.* Nov. 209, I believe the old system of ..'topping-up' is not quite as prevalent as it was some years ago. **1908** *Toilers of Deep* Sept. 185/2 The herrings have also shrunk and settled down—'pined', as it is called—and several more layers have now to be added in order to fill the barrel again. This is called 'topping'. **1909** *Daily Chron.* 18 Jan. 9/5 Trousers.—A smart girl wanted for topping and seams.

b. The cutting off of the top (of a tree or plant).

1513 *MS. Acc. St. John's Hosp., Canterb.*, For toppyng of xij treys & broshyng. **1550** CRANMER *Def. Sacrament* Pref. *iij b, The cuttyng away wherof is but like toppyng and loppyng of a tree. **1657** W. MORICE *Coena quasi Κοινὴ* ii. 37 Those that could not be satisfied with the topping, but wished the cutting down of the..Tree. **1797** A. YOUNG *Agric. Suffolk* 109 Take up [carrots] at 14d. to 16d. a load, topping included. **1807** J. HALL *Trav. Scot.* II. 445 Hedges frequently require topping.

†**c.** A method of cheating at dice (TOP *v.*[1] 17 a).

1663 *Proposal to use no Conscience* 3 Holding one or two Dice at the top of a Dice-Box, which we Gamesters call Topping. **1680** KIRKMAN *Eng. Rogue* IV. xvi. 226 You must sometimes use Topping; that is, by pretending to put both Dice into the Box, whereas you have dropt but one, holding the other between your fore-fingers. **1680** COTTON *Compl. Gamester* (ed. 2) II. [Fully described.] **1726** *Art & Myst. Mod. Gaming* (title-p.), Working with a grate Box, Eclipsing, Sighting, Waxing, and Topping.

d. Levelling the teeth of a wheel or a saw.

1884 BRITTEN *Watch & Clockm.* 152 The wheel is so fragile that care is required in topping.

e. *topping up*, completing, bringing to perfection; also, filling up or bringing to capacity. Cf. TOP *v.* 21.

1890 'R. BOLDREWOOD' *Col. Reformer* (1891) 403 It was not thought advisable to wait longer for the ultimate 'topping up' of the beeves. They were good enough. **1919** *Gloss. Aeronaut. Terms* (R. Aeronaut. Soc.) 54 *Topping up*, the operation of replenishing the balloon with fresh gas. **1935** *Motor Commerce* Jan. 8 (Advt.), Acid-level indicator.. shows when the maximum level is reached on 'topping-up', and so safeguards against over-filling. **1941** *Illustr. London News* CXCIX. 308 (*caption*) Interior contents of the rubber dinghy: bailer, 'topping-up' pump, chocolate, paddles, stoppers or plugs, and sea-drogue. **1959** *Engineering* 6 Feb. 192/3 An infra-red heater provides a focal point for 'topping-up' if required. **1963** *Motor* 17 July 3/1 The automatic gearbox of my 3.4 Jaguar was in need of topping up. **1972** HILLIER & PITTUCK *Fund. Motor Vehicle Technol.* 534 A further check is the need for topping up.

f. *topping of the land*, the sighting of the land from a ship's top; the limit or distance at which this is possible.

1666 *Lond. Gaz.* No. 77/1 Whitby, August 3. Several of our Fisherboats inform us that the Dutch Busses, and Doggers are fishing, a little off the Topping of the Land.

g. *slang.* Execution by hanging.

1699 B. E. *New Dict. Canting Crew, Topping cheat*, the gallows. *Topping cove*, the hangman. **1846** *Swell's Night Guide* 134/2 *Topping*, hanging. **1968** *Daily Tel.* 15 Nov. 24/7, I wish they still had topping..because if I get bird.. for this I will get 30 years and I will top myself anyway. **1971** *Times* 6 Oct. 3/8, I deserve topping for shooting a copper.

h. *topping and tailing*, the action or practice of washing a baby's face and bottom; a sketchy wash. Also *top-and-tailing*: see TOP *v.*[1] 3 b.

1931 P. W. YEOMANS *Happy Motherhood* vii. 69 A.. recommendation of the evening tub comes when the baby crawls and gets really grubby. Topping-and-tailing is not then sufficient. **1941** U. ORANGE *Tom Tiddler's Ground* xi. 205 The next hour was a busy one, what with Norman's 'topping and tailing', Norman's bottle and Marguerite's bath. **1972** *Times* 9 Aug. 7/7 Washing and changing a baby ..can be a problem... Topping and tailing is all that is required.

i. *topping out* (*ceremony*), (the ceremony accompanying) the finishing of the roof of a building. Cf. TOP *v.*[1] 20 a.

1961 *Times* 9 Sept. 16/5 Mr. H. R. Lake, New Zealand Minister of Finance,..performed the topping-out ceremony. **1962** *Guardian* 3 Nov. 6/6 The mystical ceremony of 'topping out' was performed this morning on the domed roof of the new Smithfield Market. A green bough was nailed to the roof..as a means..of warding off evil spirits and protecting the future inhabitants. **1973** *Times* 19 Mar. 11/4 A topping-out ceremony of a new shopping centre being built for Ravenstone Securities.. took place in Glasgow. **1977** P. VAN GREENAWAY *Destiny Man* i. 9 For any building, there must be some sort of topping out. **1984** *Daily Tel.* 26 Jan. 6/4 Some concrete words of advice from Mr Gow..as he performed the 'topping-out' ceremony for the International Conference Centre in Westminster yesterday.

2. a. A distinct part or appendage which forms a top to anything, a crest; the top-lock or forelock of the hair of the head; the forelock of a horse or other beast; the crest of a bird. Also the erect tassel of a Scotch cap, and *humorously* the head (*dial.* usually *toppin*).

13.. *Gaw. & Gr. Knt.* 191 þe tayl & his [a horse's] toppyng twynnen of a sute, & bounden boþe wyth a bande of a bryȝt grene. *c* **1400** *Rule St. Benet* 146 þen sal þe prelete with a payr of schers be-gyn forto kut hir hair befor at þe toppyng. **1483** *Cath. Angl.* 390/1 A Toppynge, *cirrus, cirritus, crista, coma.* **1593** *Bacchus' Bountie* in *Harl. Misc.* (1809) II. 268 Shee..tooke him roundly by the topping. **1688** J. CLAYTON in *Phil. Trans.* XVII. 997 [In Virginia] The Tewits are smaller than the English, and have no long Toppins. *a* **1720** SHEFFIELD (Dk. Buckhm.) *Wks.* (1753) II. 140 A little Indian Bird is call'd a Pope, only because there grows a high Topping upon his head. **1751** MRS. DELANY in *Life & Corr.* (1861) III. 39 A black cock and hen with white toppings. **1814** W. NICHOLSON *Peacock* II. Poet. Wks. 91 Wi' frills an' feathers on his tappin'. **1817** *Lintoun Green* II. xvi. Notes 154 His bonnet..Has tappin [1685 button] either nane. **1828** *Craven Gloss., Topping*, a crest, a plume or tuft of feathers on the head of birds; also, the hair on a person's forehead. **1872** J. HARTLEY *Yorks. Ditties* Ser. II. 66 Thi toppin's grown whiter nor once.

†**b.** *Typog.* The fine line or serif at the top of a letter. *Obs.*

1676 MOXON *Print Lett.* 7 The Topping is the small Arch above the Letter, as the Arches in the Tops of the Letter V are the Toppings of that Letter. **1683** —— *Mech. Exerc., Printing* xiv. ¶2 The Topping, is the straight fine Stroak or Stroaks that lie in the Top-Line of Ascending Letters.

c. Local term in Yorkshire for a hill.

1876 *Whitby Gloss., Topping*, a high hill. 'Roseberry topping'. 'Blakey topping'. *a* **1904** *Summer Holidays in N.E. Eng.* p. xi, Hills and mountains..are anything and everything, from hopes, laws, fells and nabs, to howes..and toppings.

3. †**a.** Arming for the tips of bows and arrows. *Obs. rare.* †**b.** A high head-dress or coiffure; cf. TOP *sb.*[1] 11 d. *Obs.* **c.** That which is put on the top of anything to complete it; a top layer; cf. TOP *v.*[1] 9. **d.** *Angling*: see quots. 1856, 1877.

1495 *Trevisa's Barth. De P.R.* XVIII. xiii. (W. de W.) 773 Of oxe hornes ben made tappynge [*Bodl. MS.* tippinges] and nockes to boowes..and arowes to shete ayenst enmyes. *c* **1690** *Roxb. Ball.* (1891) VII. 481, I wear my Topping, Lace, and Fan, and am on daintys feeding. **1700** T. BROWN

Amusem. Ser. & Com. 57 They..touch the Clouds with their proud Toppings. *a* **1704** —— *Walk round Lond., Quaker's Meet.* (1709) 23 High Topping and Lace in a Woman, they abominate, as Ensigns of Vanity. **1839** URE *Dict. Arts* 580 The pot is now ready for receiving the topping of cullet, which is broken pieces of window glass. *a* **1856** 'STONEHENGE' *Brit. Sports* I. v. ii. §4. 247/1 Tail of two slips of brown mallard's feather, with a thin topping of golden-pheasant's crest. **1877** HALLOCK *Sportsman's Gaz.* 599 The tail [of a salmon fly] is what is usually called a 'topping', *i.e.* feather from the crest of the golden pheasant. **1895** *Westm. Gaz.* 23 Nov. 7/2 From five to twelve score of whiting, with a topping of codling, form average baskets.

4. *pl.* **a.** Cuttings from the tops of trees: cf. TOP *sb.*¹ 6; also, the tops of hemp removed in hatchelling. **b.** The second skimmings of milk. *dial.* **c.** The best bran. *dial.*

1668 ROLLE *Abridgm., Tit. Action sur Case* (N.) pl. 22. 108 Les toppings del arbers cresent sur son Copihold. **1774** FOOTE *Cozeners* I, You are to have all the loppings and toppings. **1794** *Rigging & Seamanship* I. 62 The toppings of all hemp..is made into spun-yarn. **1801** *Farmer's Mag.* Apr. 231 Many individuals have used heath and toppings of whins for their cattle. *a* **1825** FORBY *Voc. E. Anglia*, *Toppings*, the second skimming of milk; the first being properly called cream. **1880** JEFFERIES *Hodge & M.* I. vi. 122 Old Hodson..would not even fatten a pig, because it cost a trifle of ready money for 'toppings', or meal.

5. A top layer or garnish put on food, esp. dessert (see also quots. 1926, 1927). Chiefly *U.S.*

1926 *Amer. Speech* I. 653/2 *Toppings*, pastry or cakes. **1927** *Ibid.* II. 389/2 *Toppings* refers to pastry, because it is used to top off a meal. **1950** *Manch. Guardian Weekly* 31 Aug. 5 Sundae 'toppings'. **1978** *Chicago* June 248/2 Toppings—including sausage, pepperoni, green peppers, anchovies, and fresh mushrooms are generously applied [to pizzas]. **1981** *Living Trends* (U.S.) Summer 6 Ice cream plus one or two toppings, such as crushed peanuts, toasted coconut, maple syrup, cherries.

'topping, *vbl. sb.*² [f. TOP *v.*² + -ING¹.] The action of TOP *v.*² ***topping-lift*** (*Naut.*), each of a pair of lifts (LIFT *sb.*² 7) by which a yard may be topped; in quot. 1841 *transf.*

1743 BULKELEY & CUMMINS *Voy. S. Seas* 117 We made the Signal for her, by hoisting an Ensign at the Topping-Lift. **1769** FALCONER *Shipwr.* II. 261 *note*, To raise one yard-arm higher than the other..is..called *topping.* **1841** *Civil Eng. & Arch. Jrnl.* IV. 56/2 The shaft rotates in a bearing, and can be raised or lowered by means of a topping lift. **1882** NARES *Seamanship* (ed. 6) 51 The sprit-sail-gaff topping lift [is] fitted with an eye splice.

'topping, *vbl. sb.*³ [f. TOP *v.*⁴ + -ING¹.] The twisting of the strands over a top (TOP *sb.*² 3) in laying a rope. ***topping sledge***, the loaded sledge or carriage to which one end of the strands is attached in laying, which advances as they are shortened by twisting.

1825 J. NICHOLSON *Operat. Mechanic* 438 The forward movement of the stranding, topping, and dragging sledges, is that slow progressive movement necessarily required..by the shortening or shrinking up of the strands in twisting,..and of the strands and cordage, either common or patent, whilst hardening and topping.

'topping, *ppl. a.* [f. TOP *v.*¹ + -ING².] That tops, in various senses of TOP *v.*¹

1. *lit.* That exceeds in height; very high. *Obs.*

1681 HICKERINGILL *Vind. Naked Truth* II. 4, I never heard of a King shut out even from the Topping-Pulpit, if he had a mind to climb so high. **1691** RAY *Creation* I. (1692) 205 Chains of lofty and topping Mountains. **1705** HICKERINGILL *Priest-cr.* II. v. 48 Every little Domine (when mounted over our heads in the topping Pulpit) is as positive..and pragmatical, as any Woman.

2. a. *fig.* Very high or superior in position, rank, degree, amount, or estimation; chief, principal; pre-eminent, distinguished; over-hanging; 'towering'.

c **1685** DK. BUCKHM. *Conference* Wks. 1705 II. 51 She was able to buy out her Lease, and is now the Topping Dame of the Parish. **1690** LOCKE *Hum. Und.* II. xxi. §38 All the thoughts of the mind..are uninterruptedly employed that way,..influenced by that topping uneasiness. **1698** J. CRULL *Muscovy* 306 The topping Saint of all Muscovy for Miracles, is one Sergius. **1703** E. WARD *Lond. Spy* v. (1706) 119 More Money..than the Topping'st Taylor in Town ever got by a Young Heir. *a* **1716** SOUTH *Serm.* (1720) II. iv. 48 Some of the topping Sinners of the World. *Ibid.* xxii. 319 Wheresoever in any topping degree it finds them. **1722** WOLLASTON *Relig. Nat.* iii. 46 Just as men learn rules in arithmetic..and grow very ready and topping in the use of them. **1840** MRS. F. TROLLOPE *Widow Married* v, Taking her to court, and to a few other topping places. **1893** *Daily News* 6 June 7/3 Some prime animals which took the topping rates of the day's trade. **1893** KATE D. WIGGIN *Cathedral Courtship* 3 Fondness for the very toppingest High Church ritual.

b. Ironically used; cf. 'fine', 'pretty'.

1693 SIR T. P. BLOUNT *Nat. Hist.* Pref. 5 Let these high-flown Topping Sparks, swell and strut as much as they please. **1706** E. WARD *Wooden World Diss.* (1708) A vj, Some ..topping Dawber of Sign-Posts. **1847** ALB. SMITH *Chr. Tadpole* xix, One of those topping gents you see in the slips of the play-houses at half price.

3. Of high quality; very fine, excellent; tip-top, first-rate. *colloq.* and *slang.*

1822 GALT *Provost* xlvi, Instead of being drowned..in debt, it might have been in the most topping way. **1841** LEVER *C. O'Malley* lxix, We came on at a topping pace. **1861** HUGHES *Tom Brown at Oxf.* xxiii, He may have made topping averages in first-rate matches of cricket.

4. Domineering; confident, boastful. *U.S.*

1815 D. HUMPHREYS *Yankey in Eng.* 30 She's lofty—topping—has her highs—sometimes. **1852** MRS. STOWE *Uncle Tom's Cabin* II. xxix. 147 She'd..have me know..that I wasn't going to be so topping as I had been. **1885** M. E. WILKINS in *Harper's Mag.* Mar. 595/1 He was awful toppin' at first. **1890** *Harper's Mag.* Apr. 769/1, 'I never saw such nerve. It was superb.' 'Perhaps a little topping', I suggested. 'Yes, perhaps a little topping... But still, it was a toppingness that could have consisted only with the most perfect conscience.'

5. Swelling into crested billows; crested.

1857 W. COOK in *Merc. Marine Mag.* (1858) V. 42 The sea ..changed to a kind of boil, or topping sea, as if surged up from beneath.

6. quasi-*adv.* = next.

1683 *Lond. Gaz.* No. 1860/8 [He] rides very topping, and hath all his paces. **1694** *Ibid.* No. 2959/4 A Bay Nag,.. carries his head very topping. **1706** *Ibid.* No. 4209/4 A very dark bay Gelding.., lean, but rides bold and topping.

'toppingly, *adv.* [f. prec. + -LY².] In a topping manner; gallantly, splendidly; in excellent condition or health. ? *Obs.* or *dial.*

a **1739** JARVIS *Quix.* II. III. xviii, I mean to marry her toppingly when she least thinks of it. **1828** *Craven Gloss.*, *Toppingly*, excellently. **1829** BROCKETT *N.C. Words*, *Toppenly*, in good health. 'He's toppenly to day'.

So **'toppingness.**

1890 [see TOPPING *ppl. a.* 4].

†**'toppingly,** *a. Obs. rare*⁻¹. [app. f. TOPPING *vbl. sb.*¹ 4 b + -LY¹.] ? Pertaining to 'toppings', skimmings of milk; hence, pertaining to cheese-making or cheese.

1573 TUSSER *Husb.* (1878) 107 A lesson for dairie maid Cisley, of ten toppings gests... These toppingly gests be in number but ten, As welcome in dairie as Beares among men.

†**'topple,** *sb.*¹ *Obs.* In 5 **topylle.** [f. TOP *sb.*¹ + -LE I.] ? A crest, tuft: cf. TOPPING *vbl. sb.*¹ 2.

14.. *Nom.* in Wr.-Wülcker 675/29 *Hic cirrus*, a topylle.

topple ('tɒp(ə)l), *sb.*² *rare.* [f. next.] An act of toppling or overbalancing and falling.

1907 *Blackw. Mag.* Aug. 272/2 This ain't the topple over of the Coll building yet.

topple ('tɒp(ə)l), *v.* [f. TOP *v.*¹ + -LE 3.]

1. a. *intr.* To fall top foremost, or as if top-heavy; to fall headlong, tumble or pitch over. Also *fig.*

1590 SHAKS. *Mids. N.* II. i. 53 The wisest Aunt.. Sometime for three-foot stoole, mistaketh me, Then slip I from her bum, downe topples she. **1605** —— *Macb.* IV. i. 56 Though castles topple on their Warders heads. **1621** T. WILLIAMSON tr. *Goulart's Wise Vieillard* 200 Although you bee ready to topple into your grave, and haue not much longer to liue. **1786** tr. *Beckford's Vathek* (1868) 108 The watch-towers were ready to topple headlong upon them. **1853** KANE *Grinnell Exp.* xxvi. (1856) 211 When these [bergs] attain their utmost height, still pressed on by others, they topple over. **1884** *Pall Mall G.* 16 Feb. 5/2 Water stocks toppled all round yesterday.

†**b.** ? To roll or tumble about; in quot. 1568, ? to wrestle, to 'try a fall' *with*. *Obs.*

1542 UDALL *Erasm. Apoph.* I. 146 b, When ye must lye toppleyng in the dust. **1568** *Jacob & Esau* II. ii. C j b, *Esau.* .. I will not eate thee Ragau... *Ragau.* No... Being in your best lust I woulde topple with ye, And plucke a good crowe, ere ye brake your fast with me.

c. To turn somersaults. *dial.*

1801 BLOOMFIELD *Rural T., Rich. & Kate* xxx, The Children toppled on the green. **1802** W. TAYLOR in Robberds *Mem.* I. 411 A boy about eleven..was toppling beside the Diligence in hope of halfpence. *a* **1825** FORBY *Voc. E. Anglia*, *Topple*, to tumble; to bring the head to the ground and throw the heels over.

2. *intr.* To lean over unsteadily, as if on the point of falling; to overhang threateningly.

1827 POLLOK *Course T.* v. 585 Toppling upon the perilous edge of Hell. **1850** TENNYSON *In Mem.* xv. 19 Yonder cloud That..topples round the dreary west, A looming bastion fringed with fire. **1860** TYNDALL *Glac.* I. vii. 47 Masses of granite..toppling above the terminal face of the glacier.

3. a. *trans.* To cause to tumble over or fall headlong; to thrust over, overturn, throw down. Also *fig.*

to topple up one's heels, to die: see HEEL *sb.*¹ 24.

1596 SHAKS. *1 Hen. IV*, III. i. 32 (Qos.) Vnruly wind.. which..Shakes the old Beldame earth, and topples [*Fol.* tumbles] down Steeples and mossegrown towers. **1599** NASHE *Lenten Stuffe* 13 In one year, seauen thousand and fifty people toppled vp their heeles there. **1809** W. IRVING *Knickerb.* VII. xi. 434 At the moment when the victorious legions of Titus had toppled down their bulwarks. **1856** MISS MULOCK *J. Halifax* ix, Don't..topple us at once down the slope. **1907** C. HILL-TOUT *Brit. N. Amer., Far West* vii. 136 They topple over the biggest trees in this way. **1951** *Amer. Speech* XXVI. 230/2 California topples Washington. **1970** A. TOFFLER *Future Shock* (1971) viii. 177 Research topples older conceptions of man and nature. **1976** *Evening Post* (Nottingham) 15 Dec. 23 They beat Scotland 6-3 (one drawn) in the semi-finals and went on to topple England 'A' 6-1 (three drawn) in the final. **1979** *Daily Tel.* 26 May 14/4 A painting by Burne-Jones..made £48,000, toppling the artist's previous best price of £33,000. **1983** *Times* 15 Feb. 7/1 The revolution that toppled the regime of Emperor Haile Selassie eight years ago.

b. ***topple*** (***tapple***) ***up tail, topple tail***: in phr. † ***to play tapple up tail***, ? to die (cf. *topple up one's heels* in 3); ***to turn topple-tail***, to turn a somersault (cf. 1 c).

1573 TUSSER *Husb.* (1878) 57 Take heede..To thresher for hurting of cow with his flaile, Or making thy hen to plaie tapple vp taile. **1828** *Craven Gloss.*, *Topple*, 'to turn topple tail ower', to turn topsy turvy. **1884** *Pall Mall G.* 6 Mar. 11/2 How many..have you..who can turn topple-tail accurately?

4. To cause to tip or tilt so as to be in danger of being upset. *rare.*

a **1656** BP. HALL *Breathings Devout Soul* (1851) 187 Like some little cock-boat in a rough sea, which every billow topples up and down, and threats to sink.

Hence **'toppled** *ppl. a.*, overturned, thrown down; **'toppler**, one who topples; *dial.* a tumbler, acrobat.

1871 J. MILLER *Songs Italy* (1878) 23 *Toppled old columns that tumble across. **1897** *Daily News* 30 Sept. 5/4 Toppled cartloads of..bricks. *a* **1825** FORBY *Voc. E. Anglia*, **Toppler*, a tumbler, who, among various antic postures, throws his heels over his head.

'toppling, *ppl. a.* [f. TOPPLE *v.* + -ING².] That topples.

1. Overhanging or leaning as if about to fall.

1804 J. GRAHAME *Sabbath* 259 Back from the toppling edge his fancy shrinks. **1817** BYRON *Manfred* I. ii. 74 Ye toppling crags of ice! Ye avalanches, whom a breath draws down. **1883** SYMONDS *Ital. Byways* v. 83 The storm-clouds ..climbing the heavens with toppling castle towers.

2. Falling headlong (*lit.* and *fig.*).

1812 H. & J. SMITH *Rej. Addr., Archit. Atoms* xvi, Jill.. Head over heels begins his toppling track. **1884** BROWNING *Ferishtah, Pillar at Sebzevar* 14 Gain, to-day, Was toppling loss to-morrow.

topply ('tɒplı), *a.* [f. TOPPLE *v.* + -Y¹.] Liable to topple over.

1913 J. VAIZEY *College Girl* xvii. 236 The screen's..a topply one. **1950** G. GREENE *Third Man* ix. 67 The inadequate too-fancy topply table.

toppy ('tɒpı), *a.* *colloq.* [f. TOP *sb.*¹ + -Y.]

†**a.** Having or characterized by a top or tops; peaked. *Obs.*

c **1557** ABP. PARKER *Ps.* lxviii. 185 Why leape ye so: to spyte thys mounte, ye toppy hillockes gay?

b. Top-heavy, inclined to tip over; in quot., tipsy.

1885 *Times* 6 Aug. 3 The lady gave her some whisky..and it made her 'toppy'.

c. Showy, stylish.

a **1905** H. S. H. in *Eng. Dial. Dict.* s.v., She looks toppier to-day.

d. *U.S.* Of animals: of superior quality.

1893 *Columbus* (Ohio) *Dispatch* 8 Apr., On military or civic parades the horse has been conspicuous for several years for its toppy appearance. **1927** J. LOMAX *Cowboy Songs* 303 I've cut your toppy mounts, boys. **1938** *Sun* (Baltimore) 24 Oct. 13/1 Firm rates were paid for vealers..and indications at times suggested that more of the 'toppy' offerings would have met with good reception. **1960** A. WEST *Trend is Up* (1961) v. 145 He turned to his favorite page in the book which showed a nice toppy lot of young lambs.

e. *Mus.* Containing too much treble.

1956 B. EDWARDS in S. Traill *Play that Music* vi. 63, I should want from a side-drum plenty of response and life —without being too 'toppy' so that the drum has a certain amount of 'guts' when it comes to playing in large places. **1969** W. RUTHERFORD *Gallows Set* vi. 85 'What the hell's "toppy sound"?' 'Sound with too much treble in it. It's caused by the camera running slow when the film was taken so when its projected the sound is speeded up.' **1976** *Gramophone* Aug. 360/2 It could be argued that some modern discs are too toppy.

f. *Stock Exchange.* Of a market currency, etc.: high and unstable.

1961 *Spectator* 26 May 774 When markets became 'toppy' he should be busy switching from vulnerable to stronger positions. **1968** *Economist* 5 Oct. 81/2 What could be developing in London is a 'toppy' situation for a few months as the market consolidates the laurels it has earned. **1979** *Daily Tel.* 2 Aug. 17 Sterling suddenly looked toppy. **1983** *Times* 28 Apr. 16/2 If, however, the market looks 'toppy', it is the highest-rated sectors which are likely to suffer most.

†**top-root,** obs. var. of TAP-ROOT; hence †**top-rooted** *a.*, = *tap-rooted.*

1651 N. BACON *Disc. Govt. Eng.* II. xxxvii. 283 Edward the sixth came in like a storm that tore up Episcopacy by the Roots, yet a Top-Root remained intire with the stock. **1669** WORLIDGE *Syst. Agric.* vi. §9 (1681) 105 Leave as much of the Root on as you can, abating only the top-Root, or downright Roots. **1765** A. DICKSON *Treat. Agric.* (ed. 2) 278 The top-rooted plants, that is, such as push one principal root perpendicularly downwards.

TOPS (tɒps). [Acronym f. the initial letters of *T*raining *Op*portunities *S*cheme.] A system of vocational training programmes established in 1972, and organized by the Training Services Agency within the Manpower Services Commission. Also *attrib.*

1975 *Ann. Rep. Manpower Services Comm. 1974–75* 8/3 The government's vocational training programmes, which were to be developed into the Training Opportunities Scheme (TOPS) to meet the needs of individuals. *Ibid.*, The initial target for the TOPS scheme was to increase the number of people trained each year. **1979** *Jrnl. R. Soc. Arts* Dec. 10/1 The Board arranged for TOPS candidates to be provided with special examinations in a limited range of subjects.

topsail ('tɒpseıl, 'tɒps(ə)l). *Naut.* [f. TOP *sb.*¹ 9 + SAIL *sb.* So LG. *toppsegel.*] A sail set above the lower course, orig. the uppermost sail (cf. TOPGALLANT A. 1). In a square-rigged vessel, orig. a single square sail set next above the lower sail or yard; now, in larger ships, divided for convenience in handling into an ***upper*** and a ***lower topsail*** (***double topsails***). In a fore-and-aft rig, a square or triangular sail set above the gaff.

1390 [see d]. [**1399** LANGL. *Rich. Redeles* IV. 72 They bente on a bonet, and bare a topte saile Affor þe wynde ffresshely to make a good ffare.] *c* **1420** ? LYDG. *Assembly of Gods* 129 [Eolus] With hys boystous blast,..other whyle he brak top seyle and mast. **15..** *Sir A. Barton* in *Surtees Misc.* (1888) 67 Full soone he let his toppe-saill fall. **1622** R. HAWKINS *Voy. S. Sea* (1847) 126 Bearing up before the winde wee put out our topsayles and spritsayles. **1674** *Lond. Gaz.* No. 891/4 He met..with part of the Dutch Fleet,..having with them a Vice-Admiral, who upon sight of the Fregat lowred his Flag and Topsails, and saluted. **1762** FALCONER *Shipwr.* I. 361 The topsails low'r and form a single reef. **1820** SCORESBY *Acc. Arctic Reg.* I. 402 The ship could only bear close-reefed topsails and courses. **1860** MAURY *Phys. Geog. Sea* (Low) xix. §807 At 8 P.M. took in fore and mizen top-sails.

b. *fig.* esp. in ***to hoist, lower, strike the topsail.***

a **1629** HINDE *J. Bruen* xli. (1641) 128 For the practice and power of Religion, the very Topsaile of all England. **1745** J. MASON *Self Knowl.* I. vii. (1853) 53 The Sin, to which not our Vertues only, but Vices too, lower their Topsail, and submit. **1805** SOUTHEY *Madoc in W.* xv. 114 You may tell Your Pope, that..I shall not strike a topsail for the breath Of all his maledictions!

†**c.** Phrases, etc. (*a*) ***topsails over*** (also simply ***topsail***), head over heels, topsy-turvy. ***topsail walten***, upside down. (*b*) ***with topsail***, with topsails set; under all sail, in full career. *Obs.*

Those in (*a*) may have some bearing upon TOPSY-TURVY.

(*a*) *c* **1400** *Destr. Troy* 1219 Mony turnyt with tene top-sayles ouer, þat hurlet to þe hard vrthe, & þere horse leuyt. *c* **1400** *Sege Jerus.* 706 þe lered men of þe lawe a litel bynyþe Weren tourmented on a tre, topsail walten. *c* **1430** *Chev. Assigne* 320 And eyther of hem so smerlye smote other,.. And eyther of hem topseyle tumbledde to yᵉ erthe.

(*b*) *c* **1400** *Sc. Trojan War* II. 1963 Tharfor with topsall all & sum Vpon þe craggis suld cum.

d. *attrib.* and *Comb.*, of or pertaining to the topsail, as ***topsail halyard, sheet, truss, yard***; carrying a topsail or topsails, as ***topsail barge, schooner, vessel***; allowing a vessel to carry topsails, as ***topsail breeze***, †***cole, gale***.

(With *topsail cole* cf. quots. under COOL *sb.*[1] 2.)

1390 GOWER *Conf.* II. 231 The wynd stod thanne noght amis Bot evene topseilcole it blew. *Ibid.* III. 338 Thei hadden wynd at wille tho, With topseilcole and forth they go. **1549** *Compl. Scot.* vi. 41 Hail on ȝour top sail scheitis, vir ..ȝour top sail trossis,..hail out the top sail boulene. **1673** *Lond. Gaz.* No. 807/4 The Wind has been all this day between the South and the South-West, a fine Topsail Gale. **1711** W. SUTHERLAND *Shipbuild. Assist.* 109 Top-sail Yards [are] ⅞ of the Main-yards.., the Top-gallant Yards ½ the Top-sail Yards. **1796** MORSE *Amer. Geog.* I. 766 The number of top-sail vessels..is about 150. **1840** R. H. DANA *Bef. Mast* ii, The topsail halyards had been let go. **1867** SMYTH *Sailor's Word-bk.*, *Topsail-schooner*, is full schooner-rigged, but carries a square-topsail on the foremast.

'top-'sawyer. **a.** The sawyer who works the upper handle of a pit-saw; cf. TOPMAN[1] 4 a, ***pit-sawyer*** (PIT *sb.*[1] 15), and SAW-PIT. Hence, **b.** *fig.* One who holds a superior position; the best man. **c.** *loosely.* A first-rate hand at something; a distinguished person.

a. **1823** *Grose's Dict. Vulgar T.*, *Top-sawyer*, signifies a man that is a master genius in any profession. It is a piece of Norfolk slang and took its rise from Norfolk being a great timber country, where the top sawyers get double the wages of those beneath them. **1836** E. HOWARD *R. Reefer* ii, The top-sawyer had been..pleased to toss his arms up and down over the pit.

b. **1826** *Sporting Mag.* XVIII. 215 To ascertain which of two competitors is top-sawyer. **1869** BLACKMORE *Lorna D.* xxxvi, 'See-saw is the fashion of England always, and the Whigs will soon be the top-sawyers'. 'But', said I,..'the King is the top-sawyer, according to our proverb; how then can the Whigs be?'

c. **1823** [see a]. **1829** *Sporting Mag.* XXIII. 412 Many a top-sawyer will speedily give me 'the go by'. **1854** THACKERAY *Newcomes* xv, How he had paid the post-boys, and travelled with a servant like a top-sawyer. **1880** DISRAELI *Endym.* xxxiii, There are some top-sawyers here to-day, Ferrars!

So **'top-'sawing** *vbl. sb.*, top-sawyer's work.

1894 *Times* 11 Sept. 16/7 A decayed wheelwright who had done top-sawing in his young days.

†**topset downe**, *adv. Obs.* = *topside down* (TOPSIDE e); upside down.

1569 J. SANFORD tr. *Agrippa's Van. Artes* xlvii. 62 A certaine Greekishe Cabala, turninge topset downe all the misteries of the Christian faith.

topset turvie, etc., obs. var. TOPSY-TURVY.

topsey, *adv.*: see TOPSY-TURN, quot. 1664.

topside ('tɒpsaɪd), *sb.* (*adv.*) [f. TOP *sb.*[1] + SIDE *sb.*[1]] **A.** *sb.* **a.** *gen.* The upper side of anything.

1677 MOXON *Mech. Exerc.* i. 27 This Bolt must be wrought straight on all its sides, except the Topside. **1980** *Family Handyman* Sept. 85/1 Did you just smear caulk over the topside crack and hope for the best?

b. *Shipbuilding.* The upper part of a ship's side: cf. TOP-TIMBER. Also *attrib.*

1815 [see TOP *sb.*[1] 7]. **1836** MARRYAT *Pirate* iv, She is.. taking it in at the topsides. **1874** THEARLE *Naval Archit.* 49 At the present day we hear only of topside planking, wales, bottom plank, and garboards. **1877** KNIGHT *Dict. Mech.*, *Topside-line*,..a sheer line drawn above the top timber at the upper side of the gunwale. **1889** WELCH *Text Bk. Naval Archit.* vi. 96 The transverse frames..are continuous from topside to topside across the keel. **1903** *Daily Chron.* 21 Feb. 9/4 With nickel-steel top-sides and a bronze under-body, the boat will be the first composition yacht since the Defender.

c. *Butchering.* The outer side of a round of beef, cut from the haunch between the 'leg' and the 'aitch-bone'; the bottom of this is the 'silver-side'.

1896 *Girl's Own Paper* 8 Feb. 295/1 Braised beef.—A piece of 'top-side' is best for the purpose. **1898** *Westm. Gaz.* 25 Feb. 5/2 In schools, where topsides and legs of mutton are the chief supply, the price would be proportionately less.

d. *Billiards.* = TOP *sb.*[1] 20.

1904 MANNOCK *Billiards Expounded* I. 163 'Top side' is, as its title would suggest, gained by hitting the cue-ball as high up as possible.

e. Phr. ***topside down, topsides under***, upside down. *rare.*

1725 *Bradley's Fam. Dict.* s.v. *Miroton*, Let it be well clear'd from the Fat, and laid Topside-down in the Dish. **1872** W. MORRIS in Mackail *Life* (1899) I. 288 Unless the world turns topsides under, some day.

f. *Oil Industry.* (See quot. 1948.) Now usu. with reference to the equipment and installations above water in offshore drilling. Freq. *attrib.*

1948 *Dialect Notes* IX. 60 *Top side*, any place above ground or ground level... Borrowed from nautical usage. **1975** *Offshore* Aug. 136/3 The system consists of a neutrally buoyant helmet mounted camera assembly and topside controls. **1977** *Offshore Engineer* Aug. 38/2 The manufacture of topside equipment. **1981** *Daily Tel.* 2 June 2/7 He [*sc.* a diver] complained of 'poor topside management'. **1982** *Sci. Amer.* Apr. 35/1 In designing platforms for North American conditions one can assume extended periods of calm for fastening the platform to the sea floor and erecting the topsides.

g. (With capital initial.) The upper or ruling classes, the Establishment. Freq. *attrib.* passing into *adj.*

1958 J. B. PRIESTLEY *Topside* 5 Topside people. *Ibid.* 8 Topside..takes and uses power, controls all patronage, imposes whatever pattern it prefers on the life of the nation. **1959** *New Statesman* 10 Jan. 47/2, I make this criticism as one who, in general, agrees with Priestley. What he calls Topside, what others call the Establishment, and what others, including myself, still call the capitalist ruling-class, does indeed..behave very much as Jordan asserts. **1962** *Guardian* 6 Oct. 5/2 J. B. Priestley, quite an attraction even in Topside Cheltenham. **1973** *Listener* 7 June 742/3 Jazz in the thirties in Topside circles was synonymous with vulgarity.

h. *Meteorol.* The part of the ionosphere above the height at which the concentration of free electrons is greatest, viz. about 300 km. Freq. *attrib.*

1962 *Canad. Jrnl. Physics* XL. 1692 The sounder is part of the 'Alouette' satellite.., which was launched at 0605 GMT on September 29, 1962... Several unfamiliar phenomena appear on the top-side ionograms... The top-side sounder project is an international one. **1965** HEIKKILA & AXFORD in C. O. Hines et al. *Physics of Earth's Upper Atmosphere* v. 114 Most recently, the technique of 'topside sounding' from a satellite has been accomplished. *Ibid.*, Better geographical coverage can be obtained now for the topside than for the bottom. **1976** *Nature* 19 Aug. 675/1 It may be possible to consider this process as a means of modifying the topside ionosphere by using a high power, low frequency transmitter at high latitudes. **1979** J. K. HARGREAVES *Upper Atmosphere* iii. 39 To study the 'topside', an ionosonde may be carried on a satellite.

B. *adv.* On the top. Also *fig.* Freq. with reference to the upper deck of a ship. Also, to the top, and in form ***topsides***. *colloq.*

1873 LELAND *Egypt. Sketch Bk.* 89 Will the big nigger sit ..top-side of the carriage, or on the locomotive? **1898** *Westm. Gaz.* 29 Sept. 2/3 Straining every nerve to keep 'top-side' in China. **1899** F. T. BULLEN *Way Navy* 85 All the privileges attaching to those who work 'topside' in a ship of war. **1946** P. CARTER in Aldiss & Harrison *Decade 40s* (1975) 115 Chief [Navigator] Schmidt..relayed data topside. **1971** H. T. WALDEN *Anchorage Northeast* i. 27 While the ferry awaited its capacity load of eight vehicles a band topsides serenaded the passengers with martial airs. **1976** L. SANDERS *Hamlet Warning* (1977) II. xix. 164 On the third level below the main deck, they met four men..fleeing topside in panic. **1977** *New Yorker* 15 Aug. 54/3, I bring two of the sandwiches topside. **1978** *Guardian Weekly* 2 Apr. 24/5 A carrion crow..who, though damaged, can get top-sides of the noisy pack of winds who winter near here.

'Top-sider. Also topsider. [f. TOPSIDE *sb.* + -ER[2].] A kind of casual shoe, freq. of canvas with a rubber sole.

A proprietary term in the U.S.

1937 *Official Gaz.* (U.S. Patent Office) 13 Apr. 261/1 Top-sider. For boots and shoes made of a combination of rubber or rubber substitute in combination with either fabric or leather or both. **1958** S. A. GRAU *Hard Blue Sky* (1959) 17 He waited perched on the railing picking the shells from the soles of his topsiders. **1968** [see SPANDY *a.*]. **1977** *New Yorker* 10 Oct. 121/1 Standing in Topsiders and white ducks.

topside-turn: see TOPSY-TURN.

topside turvy, etc.: see TOPSY-TURVY *adv.* ¶γ, δ.

'topsman. *dial.* and *slang.* Also *Sc.* taps-. [f. *top's*, genitive of TOP *sb.*[1] + MAN *sb.*[1]]

1. *Sc.* and *north. dial.* A head man, bailiff, principal servant; *esp.* the chief drover in charge of a herd of cattle on the road.

1825 BROCKETT *N.C. Words*, *Topsman*, the head man or manager, the chief hind or bailiff. **1827** SCOTT *Two Drovers* i, Many large droves were about to set off for England, under the protection of their owners, or of the topsmen whom they employed. **1844** STEPHENS *Bk. Farm* II. 92 Some dealers' top's-men, that is, the men who take charge of their master's lots after delivery.

2. *slang.* A hangman. Cf. TOP *v.*[1] 6, HEADSMAN.

1825 *Celebrated Trials* IV. 171 R. Turpin..after speaking half an hour to the topsman, threw himself off the ladder, and expired in about five minutes. **1836** MILNER *Turpin's Ride to York* I. iii. (1885) 5/2, I shall never come to the scragging-post, unless you turn topsman. **1883** A. DOBSON *Old World Idylls* 29 Waved to the crowd with his gold-laced hat; Talked to the Chaplain after that; Turned to the Topsman undismayed.

topsoltiria, tops o're tiria: see TOPSY-TURVY A. ¶ι.

topstar, -er, obs. ff. TAPSTER.

'top-stone. A stone which is placed upon or forms the top of something; a cap-stone: chiefly *fig.* Also, the upper end-stone or jewel in a chronometer.

1658–9 in *Burton's Diary* (1828) III. 222 Our kings: those that know history, know they were kings before the Parliament declared them so, their top-stone. **1662** JER. TAYLOR *Serm. to Univ. Dublin* 51 Humane learning is an excellent Foundation; but the top-stone is laid by Love and Conformity to the will of God. **1707** MORTIMER *Husb.* (1721) I. 3 Where are abundance of flat Stones, they make Fences of them by laying of them one upon another like a Wall, and only lay the Top-stones in Clay to keep them together, the weight of which secures the under ones. **1871** *Routledge's Ev. Boy's Ann.* Sept. 513 Religion, that indispensable top-stone of every social edifice. **1901** *N. Amer. Rev.* Feb. 292 The strict observance of the rules of Caste, with the Brâhman as the top-stone of the social pyramid, was everything.

Topsy ('tɒpsɪ). The name of a character in Mrs. H. B. Stowe's novel *Uncle Tom's Cabin*; used allusively as the type of something that seems to have grown of itself without anyone's intention or direction (see quot. 1851).

[**1851** MRS. STOWE *Uncle Tom's Cabin* in *Nat. Era* 6 Nov. 1/5 Have you ever heard anything about God, Topsy?.. Do you know who made you?' 'Nobody, as I knows on,' said the child... 'I spect I grow'd. Don't think nobody never made me.'] **1885** KIPLING *Let.* in Ld. Birkenhead *Rudyard Kipling* (1978) vi. 81, I have really embarked..on my novel *Mother Maturin*—Like Topsy 'it growed' while I wrote. **1936** C. ROUSE *Old Towns* i. 17 The planning of towns in medieval England can be said to have followed no given rule —they were like Topsy who 'just growed'. **1955** *Times* 30 Aug. 9/7 It may be that political parties must emulate Topsy and just grow. **1967** *Boston Sunday Herald* 9 Apr. 27/4 This practice [*sc.* bugging] has grown like Topsy. **1973** 'J. RYDER' *Trevayne* (1974) xxv. 201 Are you implying that it [*sc.* a business] just grew—a Topsy? **1982** *Oxford Times* 30 Apr. 31/1 The garden, like Topsy, 'just growed'.

'topsy-'turn, *v.* Now *rare.* Also 7 topside-turn. [f. *topsy* as in TOPSY-TURVY + TURN *v.*: cf. the form *topsiturnie* s.v. TOPSY-TURVY *adv.* ¶θ. Sometimes hyphened; also used analytically, *to turn topsy.*] *trans.* To turn topsy-turvy, turn upside down; *fig.* to throw into confusion. Hence **'topsy-'turning** *vbl. sb.*

1573 TWYNE *Æneid* x. Dd iv b, Than graue Auletes went, and with his hundred beating ores, He topsy turnes vp streames [L. *centenaque arbore fluctus Verberat assurgens*]. **1605** SYLVESTER *Du Bartas* II. iii. I. *Vocation* 744 He..by his travell topsi-turneth then The live and dead, and half-dead horse and men. **1608** *Ibid.* II. iv. III. *Schisme* 919 Now the furious waues All topsie-turned by th' Æolian slaues Do mount & roule. **1632** HEYWOOD *Iron Age* v. i. Wks. 1874 III. 341 This obiect..Which topsiturnes my braine. **1637** —— *Dialogues* IX. ibid. VI. 214 All things are topside-turn'd. **1664** COTTON *Scarron.* 108 Then turning't [a mug] Topsey on her Thumb Says look, here's *Supernaculum*. **1870** S. BOWLES in Merriam *Life* xxxviii. (1885) II. 159 In the presence of such wickedness, of such suffering, of such topsy-turning of right and wrong.

†**topsy-turve**, *v. Obs. rare*$^{-1}$. In 7 topsie-. [Back-formation from next: cf. TIRVE *v.*[2]] = prec.

1603 FLORIO *Montaigne* II. xii. 337 Confounding and topsie-turving the visage of all things.

topsy-turvy (ˌtɒpsɪ'tɜːvɪ), *adv.* (*a.*, *sb.*, and *v.*) Forms: α. 6 topsy tervy, tyrvy, turuie, turvy; 6– topsy-turvy, (8–9 -turvey). Also 6 topsituruie, -turuy, 7 -turvy, -turvie, topsi-turvi, top-si-turvy; 6 topsie turuie, -vie, -vey, 6–7 -turuy, 7 -turvie, -turvy; 7 topse-turvie. See also the inverted TURVY-TOPSY. (Now almost always hyphened; in early use more usually two words; sometimes (in every century) as one word.) β–ι: see below. [A kind of alliterative or assonant combination, known in print from 1528, but prob. in popular use from an earlier period. The early spelling was *topsy-tervy* or *-tirvy*, from *c* 1540 written *-turvy*, *-turvie*. (Cf. the pronunciation of *nerve*, *curve*.) As to the actual components no external evidence has been found, and numerous conjectures and suggestions (many of them absurd and impossible) have been offered. Some of the more plausible of these, taking *topsy* as representing *top-set* or *top-side*, have been introduced (by those who favoured them) into the spelling; but amid all these aberrations, the typical form, with mere spelling variants, as *topsy*, *topsie*, *topsi-*, and *tervy*, *tirvy*, *turvy*, *turvie*, has remained practically constant. It seems certain that the first element contains *top* (or *tops*) and probable that the second is related to *terve* or TIRVE *v.* to turn, turn over, overturn; but the *-sy* of the first and *-y* of the second still want explanation: the former is viewed by some as representing an earlier *so*, as in *up-so-down*, now *upside-down*, *so* becoming *sy* under the influence of *turvy*, the *y* of which is apparently as in *hitty-missy*, *hurly-burly*, *arsy-versy*. A suggestion that *turvy* was connected with *turf* or *turve*, and referred to the laying of cut turfs or turves face downward, to keep them fresh, is now discarded, as is the earlier notion that *turvy* might have been altered from *t'other way*.

(There is a certain parallelism between the series *up-so-down*, later *upset-down*, *upside-down*, and **top-so-tervy*, *topsy-tervy*, *topset-tervy*, *topside-tervy*; but the former has not become *upsy-down*, nor has any trace of **top-so-tervy* been yet found, so that the analogy is incomplete.)]

A. *adv.* **a.** With the top where the bottom should be; in or into an inverted position; upside down, bottom upwards; also less definitely, In or into the position of being toppled over, overturned, overthrown, or upset; right over. (Most commonly qualifying the vb. *turn*, or used predicatively after *be*, *lie*, etc.)

1530 PALSGR. 843/1 Topsy tyrvy, *ceu dessus dessoubz*. **1555** EDEN *Decades* 46 They say that.. they see the houses turne topsy turuye, and men to walke with theyr heeles vpwarde. **1615** G. SANDYS *Trav.* III. 205 The huge wals and arches turned topsie turuey, and lying like rockes vpon the foundation. **1747** MRS. DELANY in *Life & Corr.* (1861) II. 450 As soon as I got into my chair, the chairmen fairly overturned it:.. Lord Westmoreland.. found me topsy turvy. **1847** ALB. SMITH *Chr. Tadpole* ix, Wondering how the flies could walk topsy-turvy on the ceiling. **1848** DICKENS *Dombey* vi, A chaos of carts, overthrown and jumbled together, lay topsy-turvy at the bottom of a.. hill. **1871** R. ELLIS *Catullus* xvii. 9 Catullus adjures thee Headlong into the mire below topsy-turvy to drown him. **1907** *Verney Mem.* I. 297 He writes topsy-turvy in sympathetic ink, between the lines of a letter ostensibly full of public news.

b. *fig.* With the higher where the lower should be; in or into a reversed condition; with inversion of the natural or proper order; less definitely, With things all in wrong places or positions; in or into utter confusion, dislocation, or disorder.

1528 ROY *Rede me* (Arb.) 51 He tourneth all thynge topsy tervy. *c* **1540** tr. *Pol. Verg. Eng. Hist.* (Camden) I. 283 The deathe of Canutus didd noe lesse turne all thinges topsieturvie in Denmarcke. **1579** FULKE *Heskins' Parl.* 215 This comparison is topsituruie. *a* **1623** FLETCHER *Love's Cure* II. ii, Custom hath turn'd Nature topsy-turvy in you. **1670** G. H. *Hist. Cardinals* II. I. 128 Turning all Europe as it were top-si-turvy. **1713** ADDISON *Guard.* No. 154 ¶2, I found nature turned topsy-turvey, women changed into men, and men into women. **1833** HT. MARTINEAU *Fr. Wines & Pol.* viii. 125 How strangely the values of things are turned topsy-turvy! **1866** R. M. BALLANTYNE *Shift. Winds* xxvii, A world of inconsistencies, where things are all topsy-turvy, so to speak.

¶ Also in various altered or corrupt forms, mostly indicating popular or conjectural etymologies: see above.

β. 6 **topset tourvie, toruie, turvie, -tirvi.**

1549 CHALONER *Erasm. on Folly* A iij, Bothe holy and vnholy thyngs be tourned topset touruie. **1553** GRIMALDE *Cicero's Offices* I. (1558) 12 Who tourned topset toruie all the lawes of God. **1573** G. HARVEY *Letter-bk.* (Camden) 53 Thus within a few years al shuld be turnid topset tirvi.

γ. 6 **top syd turuye, (topside turfway),** 6–8 **topside turvy,** 6–9 **-vey.**

1582 STANYHURST *Æneis* II. (Arb.) 59 Top syd turuye be turned Al thee Princelye thrasholds. *c* **1586** C'TESS PEMBROKE *Ps.* LVIII. vii, With whirlwinds topside turfway blown. **1596** SPENSER *F.Q.* V. viii. 42 At last they have all overthrowne to ground Quite topside turvey. **1686** GOAD *Celest. Bodies* III. iv. 499 Dreadful Tempest, turned several Villages.. Topside-turvy. **1761** STERNE *Tr. Shandy* IV. xix, How was my system turned topside turvy! **1815** MRS. PILKINGTON *Celebrity* III. i. 25 The world must be turned topside-turvey.

δ. 6 **topside thother-way,** 7 **topside t'other way,** 8 **topside the other way.**

1577 HOLINSHED *Chron.* I. *Descr. Irel.* 14 b/1 The estate of that flourishing towne was tourned arsye versye, topside thother-way. **1654** H. L'ESTRANGE *Chas. I* (1655) 75 Thus were all things strangely turned in a trice topside t'other way. **1768** TUCKER *Lt. Nat.* (1834) I. 456 His [Socrates'] words are to be turned topside the other way to understand them.

ε. 6 **typsiturvy, typsy tyrvye,** 8 **tipsy-turvy.**

1581 J. BELL *Haddon's Answ. Osor.* 324 b, The generall fraylty of nature will violently carry you away typsiturvy. *Ibid.* 569 Typsy tyrvye. **1766** [C. ANSTEY] *Bath Guide* ii. 35 Their Systems.. all turn'd tipsy-turvy [*later edd.* topsy-].

ζ. 7 **tupsiturvie.**

1640 HOWELL *Dodona's Gr.* 50 They would have turned up tupsiturvie the very kingdome of Satan.

η. 6 **top turuye.**

1582 STANYHURST *Æneis* (Arb.) 33 His launce staffe thee dust top turuye doth harrow.

θ. 7 **topsiturnie, topsie turnie.**

1617 MINSHEU *Duct. Ling.*, *Topsiturnie*, the topside turned.. Arsiuersie. **1655** in *Clarendon Papers* No. 1753, [They] would assuredly turne all that hath been ajusted topsie turnie.

ι. *Sc.* (? associated with *topsail*: see TOPSAIL c.) 7 **topsoltiria, tops o're tiria,** 8–9 **tapsalteerie,** 9 **tapsal-, tapsil-, tapsul-teerie, -teery, tapseeteerie, topsieteerie.**

1623 LITHGOW *Trav.* 202 Let all the misticall drifts and ambiguous designes.. turne topsoltiria, or upside downe, I care not. **1684** in Maidment *Bk. Scott. Pasquils* (1868) 326 There was a duke so full of pryde There durst no man come neeria Till cam a monkey out of Fife And dang him tops o're tiria. **1784** BURNS '*Green grow the Rashes*' iv, An' warly cares, an' warly men, May a' gae tapsalteerie, O! **1801** MACNEILL *Poet. Wks.* (1844) 90 And dealing round strong punch and joke, Good-humoured mad, near twa o'clock, Turns a' things tapsilteery! **1805** A. SCOTT *Poems* (1808) 100 For tapsee-teerie lie the sheaves. **1827** J. WILSON *Noct. Ambr.* July, Wks. 1855 II. 10 Wi' ae desperate wallop we baith gaed tapsalteerie.

B. *adj.* Turned upside down; inverted, reversed; *fig.* utterly confused or disorderly.

1618 BP. W. BARLOW *Breife Disc.* 8 With those topsituruy motions. **1710** SWIFT *On a Broomstick* ¶ 2 Wks. 1755 II. I. 181 What is man, but a topsy-turvey creature.. his head where his heels should be? **1748** RICHARDSON *Clarissa* (1811) II. xxxiv. 248 Dear! what a topsy-turvy house is this! **1856** F. E. PAGET *Owlet Owlst.* 1 This queer topsy-turvy world. **1873** MISS BRADDON *L. Davoren* I. i, It was the topsy-turviest kind of thing I ever heard in my life. **1887** *Spectator* 6 Aug. 1050/2 A very topsy-turvy way of reasoning. **1904** *Westm. Gaz.* 3 June 8/1 Inventor and engineer of the topsy-turvy railway.

C. *sb.* The act of turning or fact of being turned upside down; inversion of the proper order; state of utter confusion or disorder.

1655 tr. *De Parc's Francion* IV. 10 They played topsy turvy excellently well, for there was not a book in all the Study which.. they had not thrown on the ground. **1683** E. HOOKER *Pref. Pordage's Mystic Div.* 24 The whol frame of the world seemeth to me.. to circumgyrate, to wheel, whirl, and turn round about in a Topsi-Turvi. **1692** tr. *Sallust* 3 Nor should we see such Topsy-Turvies in the World. **1823** MOORE *Fables, Holy Alliance* iv. 2 Of all that, to the sage's survey, This world presents of topsy-turvey. **1879** GEO. ELIOT *Theo. Such* x. 181 Finds matter for screaming laughter in mere topsy-turvy.

D. as *vb. trans.* To turn topsy-turvy or upside down; to invert; *fig.* to reverse; to throw into utter confusion, upset or disorder greatly. Hence ˌ**topsy-'turvied** *ppl. a.*, ˌ**topsy-'turvying** *vbl. sb.* and *ppl. a.*

1626 T. H[AWKINS] *Caussin's Holy Crt.* 163 They had.. one sole action in this life, which is to topsy-turuy all things, and to do nothing. **1741** RICHARDSON *Pamela* (1824) I. 119 My poor mind is all topsy-turvied. **1807** SOUTHEY *Let. to J. May* 30 Mar., In this topsey-turveying of ministers. **1834** —— *Doctor* xxxix. II. 59 In the topsy-turveying course of time. **1863** SALA *Capt. Dangerous* II. iv. 148 He.. Topsy-turvies his goblet. **1967** [see SKOOB].

Hence (chiefly *nonce-wds.*) **topsy-'turvical** *a.*, of a topsy-turvy character; **topsy-turvifi'cation**, a making or turning topsy-turvy, reversal of the natural order; **topsy-'turvify** *v.*, *trans.* to make or turn topsy-turvy; **topsy-'turvily** *adv.*, in a topsy-turvy manner; **topsy-'turviment**, act of turning or condition of being turned topsy-turvy; **topsy-'turviness**, topsy-turvy quality or condition; † **topsy-'turvyan**, an inhabitant of an imaginary 'Topsy-turvy Island'; **topsy-'turvydom**, the realm of topsy-turvy, inversion, or confusion; also, topsy-turvy condition or state; **topsy-'turvyhood** = *topsy-turviness*; **topsy-'turvyism**, topsy-turvy system or method; **topsy-'turvyist**, an advocate of something (considered to be) topsy-turvy; **topsy-'turvyize** *v.*, *trans.* to turn topsy-turvy, throw into confusion, upset.

1882 *Pall Mall G.* 10 Oct. 6 Its *topsy-turvical fun is characteristic of the author. **1840** THACKERAY *Paris Sk.-Bk.* xvii. Wks. 1900 V. 191 A regular *topsyturvyfication of morality. **1879** G. SAINTSBURY in *Fortn. Rev.* No. 151. 55 One of the oddest topsyturvifications of a noble sentiment to be anywhere found. **1886** *Sat. Rev.* 27 Feb. 286/1 We have *topsyturvified the whole theory of politics. **1887** SAINTSBURY *Hist. Elizab. Lit.* iv. (1894) 146 The topsy-turvified conceits which came to a climax in Crashaw. **1886** *Daily Tel.* 5 Feb. (Cassell), [He] might well be employed for Faust viewed *topsyturvily. **1908** *Athenæum* 29 Aug. 233/1 All the MSS. topsy-turvily give μὲ... γὲ σοῦ, with the exception of one, which has σὲ... γὲ σοῦ, whence Brunck restored σὲ... γέ μου. **1884** *Daily News* 28 Mar. 5 The *topsy-turvyment of the house. **1842** *Fraser's Mag.* XXVI. 544 Full of sport and fun, frolic and '*topsy-turvyness'. **1892** *Times* 22 Dec. 9/3 They lost all perception of the topsy-turvyness of the situation. **1745** ELIZA HEYWOOD *Female Spect.* No. 19 (1755) IV. 11 The present race of the *Topsy-Turvyans are.. too indolent to reflect on their misfortunes. **1870** W. S. GILBERT in *Fun* 19 Mar. 15/1, I dreamt that somehow I had come To dwell in *Topsy-Turveydom! **1878** L. WINGFIELD *Lady Grizel* III. v. 107 A faint hope that topsy-turvydom might bring with it the glorious bygone days. **1904** *Edin. Rev.* Apr. 469 The most absurd instance of Japanese topseyturveydom. **1791** H. WALPOLE *Let. to Miss M. Berry* 19 May, That *topsy-turvy-hood which characterizes the present age. **1855** DICKENS *Lett.* (1880) I. 408 In that state of topsy-turvyhood. **1880** F. G. LEE *Church under Q. Eliz.* I. p. xv, Disorder and *topsy-turvyism must certainly have risen to a perfect climax. **1890** *Illustr. Lond. News* 9 Aug. 166/2 The new school of *topsy-turvyists. **1893** *Daily News* 24 July 6/2 Something like an unusual *topsy-turvyising of this great throughfare might be looked for.

'topsy 'versy, colloq. alteration of TOPSY-TURVY *adv.*, after ARSY-VERSY.

1767 D. GARRICK *Peep behind Curtain* (1772) 9 Damn all these new vagaries, that put us all upon our heads topsy versy. **1911** J. MASEFIELD *Everlasting Mercy* 46 Joe, and Si, and Nick, and Percy I rolled together topsy versy.

topt, var. TOPPED; obs. var. TAP *v.*[1]

†topteler. *Obs. rare*$^{-1}$. (Derivation and meaning uncertain.)

a **1440** *Sir Degrev.* 1182 Greyþ myn hors on hore gere, And lok þat þei be gay; þat þey be trapped a get In topteler and in mauntolet.

'top-ˌtimber. *Shipbuilding.* One of the uppermost timbers in the side of a ship: see quot. *c* 1850. Also *attrib.*

1626 CAPT. SMITH *Accid. Yng. Seamen* 8 Then plancke your out-side and inside vp, with your Top timbers. **1664** E. BUSHNELL *Compl. Shipwright* 20 Marke it on the foot of the Toptimber Mould. **1769** FALCONER *Dict. Marine* (1789) C iv b, The top-timbers, which are.. united to the floor-timbers. **1797** *Encycl. Brit.* (ed. 3) XVII. 378/1 The top-timber line, is a curve [drawn along the top of the ribs] limiting the height of the ship at each timber. *c* **1850** *Rudim. Navig.* (Weale) 156 *Top-timbers*, the timbers which form the topside: those which reach the tops are called the long top-timbers, and those below.. the short top-timbers.

†top'tyre. *Obs. rare*$^{-1}$. (Derivation and meaning uncertain.)

c **1400** *Laud Troy Bk.* 5740 Thei sclow ther many a gret sire, When thei were comen In that toptyre.

†to-'pull, *v.* *Obs.* [f. TO-[2] + ME. *pullen*, PULL *v.*] *trans.* To pull to pieces. Also *fig.*

c **1330** R. BRUNNE *Chron. Wace* (Rolls) 10210 [The eagles] feighte to-gydere.. & al to-pulle þe feþeres, & ryue. **1382** WYCLIF *Isa.* xviii. 7 Fro the puple to-pullid and to-torn, fro the ferful puple. **1390** GOWER *Conf.* I. 61, I am to-pulled in my thoght, So that of reson leveth noght. *c* **1430** *Pilgr. Lyf Manhode* III. xvi. (1869) 143 When the poore ben skorched thus and topulled. **1565** CALFHILL *Answ. Treat. Crosse* 37 Silvester.. was killed, all to pulled, of the promoter of his, the Diuel.

to-punish, to-put: see TO- *pref.*[1], [2] 2.

†top-'up, *adv.* *Obs. rare.* [f. TOP *sb.*[1] + UP *adv.*] Up to the top, to the brim.

1581 A. HALL *Iliad* III. 52 With good wine.. of Goate a ful great hide They fild top vp.

'top-up, *sb.* [f. the vbl. phr. *to top up* s.v. TOP *v.*[1] 21.] An addition; that which serves to complete an amount or a number; a filling up to the top of something already partly full (esp. a glass of alcoholic drink). Freq. *attrib.*

1967 N. FREELING *Strike Out* 55 Fifty children that already had their top-up shots [against polio] in February. **1968** J. LOCK *Lady Policeman* xvi. 138 Cypriots.. predominated, then a fair sprinkling of Italians, with a top-up of every nationality under the sun. **1971** A. MORICE *Death of Gay Dog* vii. 85 'Time for a top-up.' 'No more, thank you.' **1977** *Proc. R. Soc. Med.* LXX. 160/2 Post-operative analgesia occurs for a few hours after short operations, but is otherwise much as after other methods, unless 'top-up' doses are given through a catheter. **1978** A. BAINES in J. M. Thomson *Future of Early Music in Britain* 23 The next stage should be.. to.. get the Associated Board to accept this instrument—but excluding the crumhorns etc. save perhaps as optional top-ups. **1983** *Truckin' Life* Aug. 66/1 We.. were looking for some improvement in consumption at the top-up point, the Ampol station. **1984** *Times* 13 July 2/5 Moneylenders.. offer 'top-up' loans.. before the original debt has been settled.

topwork: see TOP *sb.*[1] 36.

topyc, topylle, obs. forms of TOPIC, TOPPLE.

†topynett, obs. variant of *topnet*, TAPNET.

1530–1 *Durham Househ. Bk.* (Surtees) 44, 1 topynett ficuum. **1532–3** *Ibid.* 227, 2 topynetts feggs 5s.

†to-'quake, *v.* *Obs.* [f. TO-[2] + ME. *cwacien*, OE. *cwacian*, to QUAKE.] *intr.* To quake violently.

c **1275** LAY. 15946 þe eorþe gan to-cwakie. *c* **1400** *Rom. Rose* 2527 And eke thy blode shal al to-quake. *c* **1410** *Sir Cleges* 353 Ar wyth a staffe I schall the wake, That thy rebys schall all to-quake.

†to-'quash, *v.* *Obs.* Also 4 to-quassen. [f. TO-[2] + ME. *quaschen*, QUASH *v.*] *trans.* To crush or squash to pieces.

c **1375** *Sc. Leg. Saints* xlviii. (*Juliana*) 160, & syne hir banys sa to-quassyt, þat þe self merch out passyt. **1494** FABYAN *Chron.* VII. 598 A gunne was leuellyd out of the cytie.. whiche brake yᵉ tymber or stone of the wyndowe with suche vyolence, that the pecys therof all to quasshed yᵉ face of the noble erle. **1583** STUBBES *Anat. Abus.* (ed. 2) 126 Some had their braines dasht out, some their heades all to quasht.

toque (tɔʊk, ‖tɔk). Forms: 6 toocke, tock, *Sc.* towk, 7, 9 tocque, 9 toque, (toke). [a. F. *toque* (15th c. in Godef.), app. the same word as It. *tocca* cap, 'tinzell cloath of Gold or siluer' (Florio), Sp. *toca* a female head-dress, '*toca* or *tocado*, a womans kerchiefe or coife' (Minsheu),

Pg. *touca* a woman's coif. Ulterior origin uncertain.]

1. a. A kind of small cap or bonnet worn by men and women in various countries. (In quot. 1505, a large tippet.)

1505 *Acc. Ld. High Treas. Scot.* III. 42 Item, for vij quartaris taffetj to be ane gret tepat to the King, callit ane towk. **1582** N. LICHEFIELD tr. *Castanheda's Conq. E. Ind.* I. ii. 29 The hayre of their heades is long lyke vnto womens, and pleited vnder theyr toockes, which they weare on theyr heades. **1599** HAKLUYT *Voy.* II. I. 244 On their heads they weare a small tock of three braces, made in guize of a myter, and some goe without tocks, and cary (as it were) a hiue on their heades. **1644** EVELYN *Diary* 23 Nov., The Knight Gonfalonier and Prior of the R.R. in velvet tocques. **1823** SCOTT *Quentin D.* vii, To confound our Scottish bonnets with these pilfering vagabonds' *tocques* and *turbands*, as they call them. **1864** BABBAGE *Passages Life Philos.* 366 A kind of head-dress called a toke.

b. †A cushion or pad worn by women to raise up the hair (*obs.*, quot. 1817); also, a kind of headdress (quot. 1835); after *c* 1880, a kind of bonnet, cap, or small hat without a projecting brim, or with a very small or closely turned-up brim.

1817 MAR. EDGEWORTH *Harrington* xiii, A sort of triangular cushion, or edifice of horse hair.. called I believe a *toque* or a *system*, was fastened on the female head.., and upon and over this system the hair was erected, and crisped, and frizzed [etc.]. **1835** *Ladies' Cabinet* Jan. 68 Ball Dress. .. Head-dress a white satin toque, profusely trimmed with white ostrich feathers. *Ibid.* Mar. 202 The head-dress is a *toque* of pink terry velvet,.. the brim very deep. **1837** THACKERAY *Ravenswing* iv, Her hats, toques,.. marabouts, and other fallals. **1881** MISS BRADDON *Asph.* xxvii, Her neat travelling-gown of darkest olive cashmere, and coquettish little olive-green toque. **1903** *N. & Q.* 9th Ser. XI. 366/1 The term 'bonnet', as applied to the costume of ladies, may be taken to mean either bonnets or tocques, but not hats.

attrib. **1844** *West. Daily Press* 29 May 3/7 The toque hat is too comfortable, too convenient, and too becoming to be lightly laid aside.

c. *Canad.* = TUQUE.

1890 S. M. ST. MAUR *Impressions Tenderfoot* 265 [He] was .. made picturesque by a red cap 'toque', sash and red duffel overall stockings. **1906** G. LAWRENCE *Let.* 20 Jan. in R. E. Watters *Brit. Columbia* (1958) 7 With his toque pulled down .. he looked for all the world like one of the small gnomes we children used to see pictures of. **1945** K. M. HAIG *Brave Harvest* 170 They were matched by toques and mittens, and tied in with gay voyageur sashes streaming like banners against the snow. **1972** *Daily Tel.* (Colour Suppl.) 8 Dec. 10/4 He wore a woollen ski toque on his head. **1977** *Westworld* (Vancouver, B.C.) Jan.—Feb. 44/2 A few other clothing essentials to remember are an extra pair of wool socks, some wool mitts, with a waterproof outer mitt, and a woolen toque.

d. A kind of tall white hat worn by chefs. In full ***toque blanche***. orig. *U.S.*

[**1965** C. KLEIN *Professional Cook* ii. 28 The origin of the high white hat (*la toque blanche*) that has been the cook's trademark for centuries is in the monastery.] **1966** *McCall's* June 168/4 The symposium ended with a discussion about the shape of the chef's hat, the *toque blanche*. **1975** *N.Y. Times* 1 Nov. 18/1 The wearer of the toque blanche.. is among a handful of women now presiding over restaurant kitchens here. **1977** *Guardian Weekly* 9 Oct. 19/1 France's two super-gourmets.. found only 21 restaurants worth a chef's toque, their mark of at least qualified approval. **1978** R. CONDON *Bandicoot* i. 2 His cook.. was a man of great height, made taller still by the two-foot-high, fluted *toque blanche* he wore to ventilate his head. **1981** *Listener* 17 & 24 Dec. 772/1 When the celebrated Swiss *chef de cuisine*.. retired.. he handed his toque to another Swiss.

2. ***toque monkey***, also simply *toque*: the bonnet-monkey or bonnet-macaque, *Macacus pileatus*, a native of Ceylon (see BONNET *sb.* 10).

1840 *Curvier's Anim. Kingd.* 59 The Bonneted Macaque (*Macacus sinicus*) and the Toque (*M. radiatus*) have the hairs on the top of the head disposed as radii. **1882** OGILVIE (Annandale), *Toque*.. 2. A name given to the bonnet-macaque. **1883** *List Anim. Zool. Soc.* 16 *Macacus pileatus* (Shaw), Toque Monkey. **1892** *Pall Mall G.* 28 Sept. 3/1 The Guinea baboons and the toque monkeys.

to-queme, toquher: see QUEME *sb.*, TOCHER.

toquilla (to'kiʎa). [a. Amer. Sp.] = JIPIJAPA a.

1877 *Encycl. Brit.* VII. 647/2 The leaves of the toquilla.. furnish material for the well-known hats. **1924** *Countries of World* III. 1713/1 The toquilla palm yields the leaf-fibre for the famous 'Panama' hats of Ecuador.

tor (tɔː(r)), *sb.* Forms: 1, 6- torr, 4-7 **torre**, 4- tor. [Occurs as an element in topographical names in early West Saxon charters; also, as a local term for a topographical feature from OE. onward. Generally held to be Celtic; but, though frequent in place-names in Cornwall, Devon, etc., not recorded as a 'common noun' in Cornish or Breton. In Welsh the nearest word is app. *tŵr* (= tur), OW. *twrr* 'heap, pile' (rare in place-names, but cf. *Mynydd Twrr*, old name of Holyhead Mountain, Rhŷs). Prob. cognate with Gaelic *tòrr* 'hill of an abrupt or conical form, lofty hill, eminence, mound, grave, heap of ruins' (Macleod and Dewar), primarily 'heap, pile', cf. *tòrr* vb. 'to heap up, pile up, bury', Ir. *torraim* 'I heap up', and the deriv. Gael. *torran* 'little hill, knoll, hillock', Ir. *torrán* 'heap, pile, hillock'. Cf. also quot. 1905.]

1. a. A high rock; a pile of rocks, *gen.* on the top of a hill; a rocky peak; a hill. In proper names of eminences or rocks in Cornwall, Devon, Peak of Derbyshire; also sporadically in some other counties, e.g. *Glastonbury Tor*, in Somerset.

847 *Grant by K. Æthelwulf* in Birch *Cart. Sax.* II. 34 Ærest on merce cumb [in Dorset], ðonne on grenan pytt, ðonne on ðone torr æt merce cumbes æwielme. *a* **1000** *Boeth. Metr.* v. 17 Oð him [a brook] oninnan felð muntes mæȝenstan.. atrendlod of ðæm torre [in *Prose* vi, Micel stan wealwiende of þam heohan munte]. *a* **1400-50** *Alexander* 4863 So hedous & so hoge hillis þam beforn, Cloȝes at was cloude he [cloud-high] clynterand torres, Rochis & rogh stanes, rokkis vnfaire. **1539** POLLARD in *Lett. Suppress. Monast.* (Camden) 261 The late abbott of Glastonberye.. was drawyn thorowe the towne apon a hurdyll to the hyll callyd the Torre, wheare he was putto execucion. *a* **1552** LELAND *Itin.* (1711) II. 38 Camallate, sumtyme a famose Toun or Castelle, apon a very Torre or Hille, wunderfully enstrengthenid of nature. **1610** NORDEN *Spec. Brit., Cornw.* (1728) 38 Mount St. Michaells, a steepe and most craggie torr. *c* **1630** RISDON *Surv. Devon* (1810) 6 A chain of hills.. whose tops and torrs are in the winter often covered with a white cap. **1681** COTTON *Wond. Peake* (1702) 42 Tor in that Country-Jargons uncouth sense, Expressing any Craggy Eminence. **1806** GOUGH *Camden's Brit.* II. 423/2 Matlock great Torr is 140 yards perpendicular. **1894** BARING-GOULD *Kitty Alone* II. 160 Tors rise to the height of from twelve to fifteen hundred feet. **1905** *Eng. Dial. Dict.* s.v. *Torr*, In E. Cornw. 'Tor' means a pile of rocks, and is never used for a hill, or the top of a hill, unless the hill or top is so very rocky that the whole may be considered one pile of rocks. **1913** *Let. to Editor*, A high hill in Haslingden, Lancashire, is simply called 'The Tor'.

b. Locally in Scotland, applied to an artificial mound; a burial mound.

1794 BUCHANAN *Def. Scott. Highl.* 142 What are the Torrs .. but burrying hills? **1845** *Statist. Acc. Scot.* VI. 887 Its name [Torrance] was taken from an artificial mound of earth, still known by the name of the Tor, which is situated a quarter of a mile from the present house of Torrance.

†**2.** ? A heavy mass of cloud. *Obs.*

(But the sense 'rock mass' seems also possible.)

13.. *E.E. Allit. P.* A. 874 A hue fro heuen I herde þoo, Lyk flodez fele laden, runnen on resse, & as þunder þrowez in torrez blo. *Ibid.* B. 951 Torres, þat þe þik þunder þrast þirled hem ofte.

3. *attrib.* **tor grass**, a perennial grass, *Brachypodium pinnatum*; cf. TORE *sb.*[3]; **tor ouzel**, local name of a bird, the ring ouzel, *Turdus torquatus*.

1770 G. WHITE *Selborne* xxxi. (1789) 84 [The ring ousels] breed in great abundance all over the Peak of Derby, and are called there *Tor-ousels*. **1885** SWAINSON *Provinc. Names Birds* 8 Ring Ouzel (*Turdus torquatus*).. Tor ouzel (Devon). Rock, or crag ouzel (Craven). **1954** C. E. HUBBARD *Grasses* 71 Tor grass.. A worthless grass of neglected open grassland on chalk and limestone. **1976** *Times* 28 June 14/8 Coarse Tor and Erect Brome grasses have supplanted the grazed pastures.

†**tor**, *a. Obs.* Forms: 3-5 **tor**, 4 **toor**, 4-5 **toore**, 5 **tore**, **toure**. See also TERE *a.* [The Old Norse and OE. adverbial particle *tor-* 'hardly, with difficulty, ill-', used esp. with verbal adjs. as in ON. *tor-fengr* hard to get, *tor-næmr* hard to learn, *tor-sýnn* hard to see, *tor-talinn* pple., counted with difficulty, *tor-tryggr* hard of belief; also OE. *tor-cyrre* hard to turn or convert, *tor-beȝéte* hard to get. In ME., esp. in those parts in which the Norse influence was strong, this particle was treated as a separate word, in the sense 'hard, difficult, ill', and was used esp. with the infinitive, as *tor (for) to tell*, *tor for to ken*; the former of these was a favourite phrase of the alliterative poets. In some instances, as already in Ormin, *tor* alone was used attributively. ON. and OE. *tor-* were cognate with OHG. *zur-*, Gothic *tuz-*, Gr. δυς-, Skr. *dus-*, hard, evil, ill-: with the ON. and OE. words cf. Gr. δυσαής ill-blowing, δύσβρωτος hard to eat, δυσμαθής difficult to learn. Senses 2 and 3 appear to be the same word, but the change of sense is remarkable.]

1. Difficult, hard, toilsome; irksome, tedious; = TERE *a.*

c **1200** ORMIN 6350 Harrd & strang & tor & hefiȝ lif to ledenn. *a* **1225** *Ancr. R.* 108 (MS. T.) Ho is grucchere, & ful itohen: dangeruse & tor for to paien. *Ibid.* 254 An honful ȝerden arn tor to breken [*v.r.* boeð erueð forte breken]. **13..** *Cursor M.* 14085 (Cott.) O þair gladnes war tor to tell. *c* **1350** *Will. Palerne* 5066 It were toor forto telle treuli al þe soþe. *c* **1400** *Destr. Troy* 644 But this tyme is so tore & we no tome haue.

2. Strong, sturdy. (? Hard to conquer.)

a **1400-50** *Alexander* 5500 Ser Tarbyn, a tulke with many toore thousandis. *c* **1400** *Destr. Troy* 320 Grete toures full toure all þe toune vmbe. *Ibid.* 1035 Of the tidiest of Tessaile, tore men of strenght. *Ibid.* 1131 Telamon, þat is a tore kyng. *Ibid.* 6156 Dissyrus.. Of all the Troiens to tell torest in armys.

3. In vague or loose uses: **a.** Full, replete; **b.** Great, violent, excessive.

c **1400** *Destr. Troy* 3348 Trowe ye not Troy is tore of all godis, As plaintiouse in yche place as þe prouynse of Achaia? *Ibid.* 13723 þis proud in hir yre.. Bad hym turne vnto tessail in a tore hast.

tor, erron. spelling of TAW *sb.*[2], a marble; obs. pa. t. of TEAR *v.*[1]

tora ('tɔərə). [a. Amharic.] In full, ***tora hartebeest***. A light brown hartebeest, *Alcelaphus buselaphus tora*, found in parts of north-eastern Africa.

1873 J. E. GRAY in *Nature* 4 Sept. 364 The British Museum has just received a series of skins of a new Bubale from Abyssinia called Tora... I propose to call it *Alcephalus tora*. **1873** —— in *Ann. Mag. Nat. Hist.* XII. 341 The male of the Tora.. has a large, round, convex tuft.. of darker hair in front of each eye. **1894** [see TETEL]. **1912** J. STEVENSON-HAMILTON *Animal Life Afr.* vii. 102 The Tora Hartebeest.. is found in Abyssinia and the Blue Nile Valley. **1970** DORST & DANDELOT *Field Guide Large Mammals Afr.* 220 The Tora Hartebeest.. is pale tawny.

† **to-'race, to-'rance, to-'rase,** *v. Obs.* Forms: 3-4 **to-rauncen, -rancen, -rassen**; 3-5 **-racen, -rasen**. [ME. *to-racen*, etc., f. TO-[2] + RACE *v.*[3], RANCH *v.*[2], RASE *v.*[1]] *trans.* To hack, slash, cut, or tear to pieces.

1297 R. GLOUC. (Rolls) 524 He was al to ranced pecemele in a stounde, Ech lime fram oþer, among þe rockes, ar he com to gronde. *Ibid.* 4412 Hor king.. Wiþ woundes to Raunced so þat he moste nede deye. **13..** *Gaw. & Gr. Knt.* 1168 What wylde so at-waped wyȝes þat schotten Watz al to-raced & rent, at þe resayt. *c* **1386** CHAUCER *Clerk's T.* 516 Burieth this litel body in som place, That beestes ne no briddes it to-race. *a* **1400-50** *Alexander* 2088 þai haue hedid of oure hathils.. Bet doun oure bachelers, my banir to-rased. *c* **1450** *Mirour Saluacioun* 4370 With breres and with sharpe thornes thaire bodyes alto racyng.

Toradja (tɒ'rɑːdʒə). Also **Toraja**. [Native name.] **a.** An Austronesian people living in central Sulawesi (formerly Celebes); a member of this people. **b.** The language of the Toradja.

1911 J. FRAZER *Golden Bough*: *Magic Art* (ed. 3) I. iii. 109 The Toradjas of Central Celebes believe that things of the same sort attract each other by means of their indwelling spirits. **1937** M. COVARRUBIAS *Island of Bali* ii. 16 The ancient inhabitants of the Malay Archipelago were 'Indonesians', also called Malayo-Polynesians,.. and so forth. Of these, pure branches are to be found today in the Dyak of Borneo, the Batak of Sumatra, the Toradja of Celebes. **1957** *Encycl. Brit.* V. 89/2 The Toraja are a collection of tribes, living in central, southeast and east Celebes. **1964** E. A. NIDA *Toward Sci. Transl.* ix. 208 In east Toradja, spoken in Indonesia, 'they mentioned his-he-ness' is a way of rendering 'they spoke about him'. **1979** *Radio Times* 5-11 May 61/1 It's in the mountains of central Sulawesi that you find the land of the Torajas.

† **to-'rag,** *v. Obs.* [ME., f. TO-[2] + RAG *v.*[1]] *trans.* To tear the clothes of, to make very ragged.

c **1430** *Pilgr. Lyf Manhode* III. xxii. (1869) 148 That is thilke that hath thus to ragged me and to clowted me. *a* **1550** *Friar & Boy* 266 in Hazl. *E.P.P.* III. 72 All to ragged and to rente, And torne on euery syde.

‖**Torah** ('tɔəraː, 'təʊ-). Forms: 6, 9 **thora**, 7 **tora**, 7, 9 **thorah**, 9 **torah**. [Heb. *tōrāh* 'direction, instruction, doctrine, law', f. *yārāh* 'to throw', in Hiphil 'to show, direct, instruct'.] **a.** The teaching or instruction, and judicial decisions, given by the ancient Hebrew priests as a revelation of the divine will; the Mosaic or Jewish law; hence, a name for the five books of the law, the Pentateuch.

1577 tr. *Bullinger's Decades* I. (1592) 9 The lawe of Moses, which is in deede the lawe of God, and is most properly called Thora, as it were the guide and rule of faith. **1842** BONAR & M'CHEYNE *Narr. Mission to Jews* iv. (1843) 215 The [Samaritan] priest agreed to shew us the copy of the Torah, or five books of Moses.. so famed for its antiquity. **1875** M. ARNOLD *God & Bible* iv. 188 Thus the Pentateuch, or five books of Moses, stood alone as the 'Thora'. **1890** P. H. HUNTER *After the Exile* xiv. 273 The word Torah.. signifies doctrine, instruction. This wider sense is lost in the usual translation by νομος or law.

b. *attrib.* and *Comb.*, as ***Torah scroll***; esp. denoting ornaments or accoutrements of the parchment scrolls of the Torah, as ***Torah breastplate, crown, curtain, finial, mantle, pointer, wrapper***.

1901 *Ann. Rep. Board of Regents Smithsonian Inst. 1899* 545 *Torah scroll*, parchment scroll of the Pentateuch in Hebrew mounted on wooden rollers. **1941** F. LANDSBERGER in *Hebrew Union College Ann.* XVI. 374 The ritual implements used in the synagogues, above all the Torah crowns.. must have been made by Jews. *Ibid.* 398 The desire of German Jews for costly.. ceremonial objects was strong, and there were.. a few wealthy benefactors who could donate rich Torah curtains, Torah mantles, Torah finials, Torah breastplates, pointers.. and the like. **1950** S. S. KAYSER in *Ibid.* XXIII. II. vii. 498 The final benediction of the Brith Milah ceremony and therefore.. the text on Torah wrappers. **1968** *N.Y. City* (Michelin Tire Corp.) 112 Jewish Museum.. admirable examples of Torah Scrolls, the sacred texts of the Pentateuch... You can also admire.. Torah wrappers, in finely engraved silver, and Torah mantles with silk and gold embroidery,.. and Torah pointers, used by rabbis to follow the text. **1976** Y. L. BIALER *Jewish Life* 100 (*caption*) Torah crown, hammered, gilded silver with precious stones.. Poland, 18th century. *Ibid.* 120 (*caption*) Torah breastplate, pierced and engraved silver, Turkey, 19th century.

Toraja, var. TORADJA.

‖**toran** ('toːran). [Hindī *tōran*:—Skr. *toraṇa* arched portal.] A sacred Buddhist gateway, of wood or stone, consisting of a pair of uprights with one or more (often three) cross-pieces; sometimes elaborately carved.

1886 E. C. ROBINS *Temple of Solomon* (1887) 27 A design ..based on the Japanese and Indian *toran*, like those forming gateways to the Great Tope at Sanchi.

to-rance, to-rase, by-forms of TO-RACE *v.*

†**to-'rat**, *v. Obs. rare*$^{-1}$. [f. TO-[2] + RAT *v.*[3]] *trans.* To break up, scatter.

?*a.* **1400** *Morte Arth.* 2235 Thane þe Romayns..alle to-rattys oure mene with theire riste horsses.

‖**torba** ('tɔːbə). [ad. Arab. *turba* dust, earth, soil.] A primitive kind of cement made with broken pottery, traditionally used in Malta for the floors of buildings. Freq. *attrib.*

1910 *Ann. Rep. Valetta Mus. 1909–10* 4 The original 'torba' floor existed at a depth of about 15 cms. **1923** M. A. MURRAY *Excavations in Malta* I. v. 33 The beaten-earth floor, known as *torba*, is made as follows: the pots are broken ..or..pounded; [etc.]. **1953** *Proc. Prehistoric Soc.* XIX. 43 They were found only on the lowest torba floor at Santa Verna and Kordin III. **1968** J. D. EVANS in S. Rossiter *Malta* 13 Remains of huts..were found at Skorba... The floors were of beaten earth or *torba* (a plaster made of crushed limestone).

torbanite ('tɔːbənaɪt). *Min.* [f. *Torbane Hill* in Linlithgowshire, where found: see -ITE[1] 2 b.] A deep brown shale, allied to cannel coal; also called **Torbane Hill mineral** or *Boghead coal*; valuable for the production of petroleum and gas, and famous as the subject of a great lawsuit hinging upon the dispute whether or not it was legally 'coal'.

1858 GREG & LETTSOM *Man. Mineral.* 16 Torbanite... Boghead mineral. Boghead coal. *c* **1865** LETHEBY in *Circ. Sc.* I. 139/2 Mr. James Young..has..been engaged in producing an oil..from a shale known as the Torbanehill mineral. **1867** W. W. SMYTH *Coal & Coal-mining* 18 It is by no means easy..to draw a distinct line of demarcation between cannel and the black basses, bats, or crisp shales, which occur in the coal measures... And between all these and the torbanite, or 'Boghead mineral', there exists a relationship which makes the difference only one of degree.

torbant, obs. form of TURBAN.

torbel, torble, obs. ff. TROUBLE *sb.* and *v.*

torbernite ('tɔːbənaɪt). *Min.* Also **torberite**. [ad. Ger. *torbernit* (Werner 1792), orig. *torberit*, f. *Torbernus*, latinized form of the name of the chemist Torber Bergmann: see -ITE[1].] A native phosphate of uranium and copper, found in bright green tabular crystals; also called *copper-uranite*, and (erroneously) *chalcolite*.

1852 BROOKE & MILLER *Phillips Introd. Min.* 517 Torberite.—Uranite (in part)..is found in attached crystals, massive, and investing other minerals, in veins in slate and in granite. **1868** DANA *Min.* 585 Torbernite.

torbith, obs. form of TURBIT.

torc: see TORQUE *sb.*[1]

torcas, obs. f. TURQUOISE.

torcasse, var. TURKIS, -E *v. Obs.*, to distort, transform.

torce, variant of TORSE[1], *Her.*, wreath.

†'**torcenous**, *a. Obs. rare*$^{-1}$. *erron.* torcencious. [a. AF. *torcenous*, OF. *torçonos* (also *torçonereus*), f. *torçon*, *torcion* extortion, *torçoneor* extortioner.] Extortionate, exacting.

[**1292** BRITTON I. xxii. §13 Et ausi de totes torcenouses prises fetes par nos ministres. **1314–15** *Rolls of Parlt.* I. 292/2 Dont il prient qe tiel torcenouse demaunde soit oste.] **1387–8** T. USK *Test. Love* I. vi. (Skeat) l. 131 The gouernementes..of your citee, left in the handes of torcencious citezins, shal bring in pestilence and distrucion to you.

torch (tɔːtʃ), *sb.* Forms: 3–6 **torche**, (4 **torge**, **thorche**, 5 **tourche**, 6 **tortche**, **towrge**, *pl.* **torchesse**), 6– **torch**. [ME. a. OF. *torche* = Pr. *torcha*, according to Diez:—late pop. L. **torca*, from stem **tork-* of *torquēre* to twist; cf. also It. *torcia* (Veronese, and Venetian *torzo*), Sp. *antorcha*, earlier *entorcha*, Pg. *tocha* 'torch'. The primary sense is taken to have been 'a twist', 'something twisted', torches having been made of twisted tow dipped in pitch, or the like. Cf. also TORTIS.

(The derivation of the Eng. from F. *torche* is certain, but the etymology of the latter, and of the Romanic forms as a whole, is still in dispute: see Diez s.v. *Torciare*, Gröber *Archiv f. Lat. Lexicog.* VI. 128, Körting *Lat. Rom. Wbch.* 1901 s.v. *Tortica* 9616.)]

1. a. A light to be carried in the hand, consisting of a stick of resinous wood, or of twisted hemp or similar material soaked with tallow, resin, or other inflammable substance. Also applied to a lamp carried on a pole or similar appliance, and now also = *electric torch* (*b*) s.v. ELECTRIC *a.* 2 b.

c **1290** *S. Eng. Leg.* I. 467/187 With-oute liȝht of torche. *c* **1330** *Assump. Virg.* 598 (B.M. MS.) Loke þat ȝe haue candele Torches boþe faire & fele. **13..** *Sir Beues* (A.) 1659 þar inne he seȝ torges [*v.r.* torches] i-liȝt. **1377** LANGL. *P. Pl.* B. XVII. 203 To a torche or a tapre þe trinitee is lykned; As wex and a weke were twyned togideres, And þanne a fyre flaumende forth oute of bothe. **1483** *Cath. Angl.* 390/1 A Torche, *torticius*, *torchia*. **1546–7** in Swayne *Sarum Churchw. Acc.* (1896) 274, viij lb. of waxe to make twoo torches agaynst Alholoutyde. **1555** in *Shropsh. Par. Documents* (1903) 56 Peyde towrd byying of ii towrges. **1606** SHAKS. *Tr. & Cr.* v. i. 92 Follow his Torch, he goes to Chalcas Tent. **1721** BAILEY, A *Torch*..a Staff of Deal on which Wax-Candles are stuck, to be lighted on several Occasions. **1821** SCOTT *Kenilw.* xxx, Onward came the cavalcade, illuminated by two hundred thick waxen torches. **1901** E. W. HORNUNG *Black Mask* xii. 253, I saw Raffles on my right striking with his torch; a face flew out of the darkness to meet the thick glass bulb with the glowing wire enclosed. **1906** *Daily Chron.* 14 July 5 The ordinary tarred-rope torch. **1936** W. FAULKNER *Absalom, Absalom!* ix. 370 He..saw the light of the torch approaching along the upper hall. **1967** P. SHAFFER *Black Comedy* 48 The Colonel takes the torch from Harold and shines it pitilessly in Schuppanzigh's face.

b. *fig.* or *allusively.* Something figured as a source of illumination, enlightenment, or guidance, or of heat or 'conflagration'. Also in phrs.: ***to hand*** **(*pass*, etc.)** ***on the torch*** (and varr.), to pass on a tradition, etc., esp. one of enlightenment (after L. *lampada tradere*, Gr. *λαμπάδα παραδιδόναι*, a metaphor from the ancient Greek torch-race; cf. LAMP *sb.*[1] 1 c and see sense 3 below); ***to carry*** (etc.) ***a torch for*** (someone), to feel (esp. unrequited) love for, to feel lingering affection for.

1621 BURTON *Anat. Mel.* III. ii. VI. i. (1651) 545, I light my Candle from their Torches. **1664** JASZ-BERENYI (*title*) A new Torch to the Latine Tongue. **1775** SHERIDAN *Rivals* Epil., The torch of love. **1878** BOSW. SMITH *Carthage* 19 The torch of Greek learning and civilisation was to be extinguished. **1887** *Q. Rev.* Oct. 276 Her [*sc.* Italy's] work has been done among the nations, and in their turn France, England and Germany hand on the torch. **1912** E. GOSSE *Portr. & Sk.* p. viii, They were all..engaged in keeping bright, and in handing on unquenched, the torch of literary tradition. **1927** *Vanity Fair* (N.Y.) Nov. 132/3 When a fellow 'carries the torch' it doesn't imply that he is 'lit up' or drunk, but girl-less. His steady has quit him for another or he is lonesome for her. **1932** L. GOLDING *Magnolia Street* I. xi. 189 He had sometimes hoped that in Max a son was born to him who would take the torch from his dying hand and jump on to the platform he had vacated. **1953** L. Z. HOBSON *Celebrity* vi. 78 Jim's still carrying a torch for Roosevelt. **1959** *Manch. Guardian* 16 June 5/2 She was carrying a torch for someone. **1969** J. GROSS *Rise & Fall Man of Lett.* iv. 104 Dante was the poet of Catholicism, who handed over the torch to Shakespeare, the poet of Feudalism, who passed it on to Milton, the poet of Protestantism. **1977** H. FAST *Immigrants* v. 305 Maybe you got a torch for her, maybe not. But we both got her interest at heart.

c. = *blow-torch* s.v. BLOW-.

1909 WEBSTER, *Torch*, 3... Any of various devices for emitting a hot flame, as for vaporizing oil to start an oil engine, burning off old paint, melting solder, or the like. **1931** *Writer's Digest* Oct. 28 A keister torch is an acetylene torch which can be carried in a suitcase. **1961** *Sheet Metal Industries* XXXVIII. 613/1 The high rating of the water cooled models..is made possible by the design which permits the circulation of cooling water right to the tip of the torch. **1978** S. BRILL *Teamsters* vi. 225 Our theory is that the car was hidden there and then cut up with torches and carted out.

d. An arsonist. *U.S. slang.*

1938 *Reader's Digest* Mar. 71/1 The torch is now serving a 20-year sentence. **1977** *Time* 31 Oct. 28/3 Blazes are set by quasi-professional 'torches' hired by landlords, real estate brokers, store owners, or welfare tenants who want to be relocated.

2. *transf.* **a.** A spike composed of spikelets; also *fig.* said of a red or flame-coloured flower.

1578 LYTE *Dodoens* I. lxiii. 91 Of this kinde, there is founde an other, the Spikes, eares, or torches wherof, are very dubble,..in steede of the little knappes or heades, it bringeth forth a number of other smal torches, wherof eche one is lyke to the spike or torch of great Plantayne. **1862** B. TAYLOR *Poet's Jrnl.* II. *Lost May*, And burns in meadow-grass the phlox His torch of purple fire.

b. (Usually in *pl.* **torches.**) The Great Mullein, *Verbascum Thapsus* (or other species): from its tall spike of yellow flowers (or, according to some, from the use of its thick woolly leaves and stalks as material for torches).

1552 COOPER *Elyot's Dict.*, *Blattaria*, an herbe called Moleyne, or a kinde of Moleine called Torche. **1578** LYTE *Dodoens* I. lxxxi. 120 Mulleyn is called..in English also.. Hig[h]taper, Torches, and Longworte. [Cf. 118 The whole top with his pleasant yellow floures sheweth like to a waxe Candell or taper cunningly wrought.] **1657** W. COLES *Adam in Eden* cxii, Called of the Latines *Candela Regia* and *Candelaria*, because the elder age used the stalks dipped in Suet to burn... In English also some call it Torches. **1861** MISS PRATT *Flower. Pl.* IV. 135 Its tall tapering spike of light yellow flowers..suggested..the old names of High Taper.. and Torches.

†**c.** Applied to a species of cactus or cactaceous plant: prob. = TORCH-THISTLE. *Obs.*

1597 GERARDE *Herbal* 1015 The torch or thornie Euphorbium..called of the Indians *Vragua*..a torch, taper, or waxe candle, whereupon..in Latine of those that understoode the Indian toong, *Cereus*, or a torch. **1666** J. DAVIES *Hist. Caribby Isles* 62 The Plant..some of the European Inhabitants of these Islands call the Torch: it is a kind of great Thistle.

3. *attrib.* and *Comb.*, as ***torch battery***, ***-blaze***, ***-brand***, ***-carrier***, ***-flame***, ***-flare***, ***-glare***, ***-stick***, ***-waving***, ***-wick***; **torchlike** adj. and adv., ***torch-lighted*** ppl. adj., ***-lit*** adj.; also, **torch-blade**, the Great Mullein (= 2 b); **torch-carrying** *vbl. sb.* (*fig.*), the harbouring of (esp. unrequited) love (see sense 1 b above); **Torch Commando** *S. Afr.*, (see quots.); **torch-course** = *torch-race*; **torch-dance**, a dance in which some of the performers carry lighted torches; **torch-fish**, a deep-sea fish, *Linophryne lucifer*, having a luminous bulb upon the first dorsal spine, above the eye; **torch-fishing**, fishing by torch-light at night (also called *torching*: see TORCH *v.*[1] 3); **torch-flower**, any bright red or yellow flower resembling or suggesting a torch, e.g. the *torch-lily*; †**torch-herb**, the great mullein; **torch-holder**, one who or that which holds a torch; *spec.* a device for supporting a torch; also, a gas-bracket or the like imitating this; **torch igniter** (see quots.); **torch-lily**, the liliaceous genus *Tritoma*, having spikes of bright scarlet flowers; also called 'red-hot poker'; **torch-man**, a man who carries a torch, a torch-bearer; also *fig.*; **torch-pine**, *Pinus rigida* of N. America; = *pitch pine*; **torch-plant** = TORCH-THISTLE; **torch-race**, in *Gr. Antiq.*, a race held at certain festivals, in which the runners carried lighted torches, and (in some cases) passed them on to other runners posted at certain points: = LAMPADEDROMY; **torch singer** orig. *U.S.*, a singer of torch songs; **torch singing** *vbl. sb.* (orig. U.S.), the singing of torch songs; **torch song** orig. *U.S.*, a popular song on the subject of unrequited love; a sad sentimental or romantic song; **torch-staff** (*pl.* **-staves**), a staff upon which a torch is carried; †**torch-tree**, rendering L. *tæda*, a resinous species of pine, the wood of which was used for torches; also *Ixora parviflora*, an East Indian shrub with showy flowers. See also TORCH-BEARER, etc.

1926–7 *Army & Navy Stores Catal.* p. xxii/3 (Index), *Batteries, Torch. **1957** C. SMITH *Case of Torches* x. 128 Bring in the..report on the torch batteries. **1861** MRS. LANKESTER *Wild Flowers* 102 Great Mullein,..'*Torch-blade', or 'King's Taper'. **1818** MILMAN *Samor* 317 A *torchblaze, meet to search Earth's utmost. **1825** SCOTT *Talism.* iii, I am Theodorick of Engaddi—I am the *torch-brand of the desert—I am the flail of the infidels. **1864** TREVELYAN *Compet. Wallah* (1866) 220 The other half are.. listening to the disquisition of the *torch-carrier. **1970** E. R. JOHNSON *God Keepers* (1971) iii. 26 When does the *torch-carrying stop..and work itself into hate? **1951** *Sun* (Baltimore) 9 Nov. 13/1 South Africa's *Torch Commando, an organization of war veterans pledged to uphold the Dominion Constitution, is building up into a potent opposition to Prime Minister Daniel F. Malan's Nationalist Government. **1971** L. BLACKWELL *Blackwell Remembers* xviii. 158 The Torch Commando, a militant organization which strongly opposed the policy of the Nationalist Government relating to the coloured voters at the Cape. **1839** T. MITCHELL *Aristoph., Frogs* 124 *note*, From.. Pausanias we learn that three *torch-courses were held in the Ceramicus. **1907** *Discovery* Oct. 122 The *Torch-fish. .. On the upper jaw..there is a larger ovate bulb supported on a tentacle... It possesses powerful phosphorescent properties, the light being under the control of the fish. This is the 'torch'. **1840** BROWNING *Sordello* I. 80 Like a *torch-flame turned By the wind. **1910** W. DE LA MARE *Three Mulla-Mulgars* xv. 205 All the Men of the Mountains came out with their little ones in the starlight and *torch-flare to see them go. **1959** E. POUND *Thrones* cii. 82 Lit by the torch-flare. **1849** [W. M. CALL] *Reverberations* I. 59 The *Torch-flower burning by the river. **1905** in *Daily Chron.* 28 Dec. 3/2 It is now ablaze with the red torch flowers of an aloe. **1908** L. BINYON in *Academy* 14 Mar. 553/1 He stands on high in the *torch-glare. **1598** FLORIO, *Lunaria*, the herbe called *torch herbe or woollblade. **1874** tr. *Hugo's Ninety-Three* III. I. xix, They stuck an iron *torch-holder into the wall. **1948** *Jrnl. R. Aeronaut. Soc.* LII. 170/2 The simple expedient of fitting an igniter plug in the flame tube was not sufficient to cater for the more arduous duties of ignition, such as under flight conditions at over 20,000 feet. The *torch igniter was designed..to get over these problems. This unit was an ordinary igniter plug, with a subsidiary supply of fuel to it. The fuel was injected through a small hole on to the plug points. **1970** *Gloss. Aeronaut. & Astronaut. Terms* (*B.S.I.*) VIII. 17 *Torch igniter*, a combined igniter plug and fuel atomizer for initiating combustion when starting the turbine. **1881** 'MARK TWAIN' *Prince & Pauper* xxxii. 365 We find the *torch-lighted galleries already filling up with people. **1975** R. H. RIMMER *Premar Experiments* (1976) ii. 164 In every direction you looked, torchlighted faces were swaying to the music. **1579** J. JONES *Preserv. Bodie & Soule* I. xl. 87 [Comets] Swordlike, hornelike, *torchlike. **1897** *Daily News* 25 June 2/6 Meanwhile our [Jubilee] bonfires [on Skiddaw]..burned torch-like downwards with a grand head of flame. **1884** MILLER *Plant-n.*, *Torch-lily, the genus *Tritoma*. **1842** SIR A. DE VERE *Song Faith* 186 The *torch-lit gloom of Auchen's aisle. *a* **1618** SYLVESTER *Mayden's Blush* 364 The sacred *Torch-man (to that end imploy'd). **1856** J. M. KAYE *Sir J. Malcolm* I. vii. 162 The bearers or torchmen who ran by his side. *a* **1845** HOOD *Incendiary Song* xviii, Burn all *torch-parading elves! **1890** *Cent. Dict.* s.v. *Pine*, *Pitch-pine*, (*a*) in America, *Pinus rigida*... Also called **torch-pine*. **1696** *Phil. Trans.* XIX. 296 The Dildoe-tree is the same with the Cereus or *Torch-Plant. **1812** C. DUNSTER tr. *Aristoph., Frogs* I. ii. *note*, In [Ceramicus] was situated the academy, where the *torch-race was held. **1875** JOWETT *Plato* (ed. 2) III. 12 The promise of an equestrian torch-race in the evening. **1934** J. O'HARA *Appointment in Samarra* vii. 210 Taking that dame out, that *torch singer. **1973** *Times* 15

Dec. 10/1 She is sometimes a movie vamp, or a torch singer. **1947** E. JENKINS *Young Enthusiasts* 163 Jazz bands, *torch singing and swing. **1983** *Listener* 9 June 35/4 If this is 'torch' singing, then Julie London is not a flimsy key-ring flashlight. **1927** *Vanity Fair* (N.Y.) Nov. 132/3 'Sing a *torch song' is commonly used in Broadway late-places as a request for a ballad in commemoration of the lonesome state. Tommy Lyman is said to have created the slang and he announced one night: 'My famous torch song: "Come To Me, My Melancholy Baby".' **1939** G. GREENE *Lawless Roads* x. 256, I was grateful for the darkness and the torch songs. **1977** *Listener* 13 Oct. 481/2 The songs are pleasant parodies of Nashville, of torch songs and even of grand opera. **1599** SHAKS. *Hen. V*, IV. ii. 46 The Horsemen sit like fixed Candlesticks, With *Torch-staues in their hands. **1601** HOLLAND *Pliny* XVI. x. I. 462 A sixt sort.. of these trees.. is properly called Teda (i. the *Torch-tree): the same yeeldeth more plentie of moisture and liquor than the rest. **1862** BALFOUR *Timber Trees Asia* (ed. 2) 135 *Ixora parviflora*:.. Torch Tree.. A small tree.. more used for torches than for any other purpose, as it burns very readily and clearly. **1706** PHILLIPS (ed. Kersey), **Torch-weed*, a kind of Herb. **1444** *Compota Domest.* (Abbotsf. 1836) 18 In vij petris di... huiusmodi *torchweke emptis.

torch (tɔːtʃ), *v.*[1] [f. TORCH *sb.*]

1. a. *trans.* To furnish, or light, with a torch or torches.

(See TORCHED, and cf. TORCHER[1] 1.)

b. To set alight, to set fire to, *esp.* in order to claim insurance money. *slang* (orig. and chiefly *U.S.*).

1931 *Writer's Digest* Oct. 29, I had just lit a match to torch the squib when I heard steps behind me. **1971** *Wall St. Jrnl.* 16 Aug. 1/3 Two bombs were planted in a university dormitory, part of a Belfast soccer stadium was torched, and snipers attacked army patrols. **1977** *Time* 31 Oct. 34/1 Griffith relied on an arsonist turned informant.. who worked as a 'broker' for landlords eager to torch their property. **1979** *Arizona Daily Star* 22 July E4/4 BIA police suspected a night of violence.. when a group of people ran a car into Pike Creek... The car was then torched. **1983** *Granta* VII. 37 Halfway through the first pint of coffee, I torched a cigarette. Mmm, tasted good.

2. *intr.* To flare like a torch; to rise like smoke from a torch. *dial.*

1847–78 HALLIWELL s.v., Recently heard at Boyton, ..'Law! how them clouds torch up, we shall ha rain'.

3. To catch fish, etc., by torch-light. *U.S.*

1887 *Fisheries of U.S.* Sect. v. II. 502 Another method, known as 'torching',.. is practiced principally by negroes. Having provided themselves with torches they visit the sandy shores at night and catch the terrapins as they come upon the beach to spawn.

torch (tɔːtʃ), *v.*[2] [a. F. *torcher* to wipe, daub, rough-cast, build or plaster with clay mixed with chopped straw, etc., f. *torche* twisted straw, etc. (the same word originally as *torche* TORCH *sb.*).] *trans.* In *plastering*, To point the inside joints of slating laid on lath with lime hair mortar.

a **1850** [Remembered in use by workmen in Oxford]. **1851** [implied in TORCHER[2]]. **1882** in OGILVIE (Annandale). **1895** *Jrnl. R. Inst. Brit. Archit.* 14 Mar. 351 The roof should be torched—not bedded.

Hence **'torching** *vbl. sb.*, pointing or daubing of this kind: see also TORCHER[2].

torch, var. of TROCH, -E, tine of stag's horn.

torch-bearer ('tɔːtʃ,bɛərə(r)). One who carries a torch. Also *fig.*

1538 ELYOT, *Facularii*, torche bearers. **1596** SHAKS. *Merch. V.* II. vi. 40 Descend, for you must be my torch-bearer. **1624** BEDELL *Lett.* xi. 140 As if all that are made Priests among you were Psalmists, Sextons, Readers, Exorcists, Torch-bearers, Subdeacons, and Deacons before. **1814** SCOTT *Ld. of Isles* II. xxii, Twelve sandall'd monks, who reliques bore, With many a torch-bearer before. **1847** GROTE *Greece* II. xxxii. IV. 272 The enterprising mariners who inhabited it had been the torch-bearers of Grecian geographical discovery in the west. **1853** DALE tr. *Baldeschi's Ceremonial* 189 The Torch-bearers having genuflected, consign their torches to the first they meet in choir.

So **'torch-,bearing** *sb.* and *a.*

1721 STRYPE *Eccl. Mem.* III. xxi. 175 There he saw torch-bearing in day-light, at mass. **1881** RUSKIN *Bible of Amiens* ii. 88 No torch-bearing maid of battle, like Clotilde.

torched (tɔːtʃt, *poet.* 'tɔːtʃɪd), *a.* [f. TORCH *sb.* or *v.*[1] + -ED.] Furnished with a torch or torches; lighted with torches.

1819 KEATS *Isabella* xiv, In torched mines and noisy factories. **1901** *Harper's Mag.* CII. 774/1 Whirling six-foot sticks, torched at each end, in circles of fire.

torcher[1] ('tɔːtʃə(r)). [f. TORCH *v.*[1] + -ER[1].]

†**1.** One who gives light, as by carrying a torch. *Obs. rare*$^{-1}$.

1601 SHAKS. *All's Well* II. i. 165 Ere twice the horses of the sunne shall bring Their fiery torcher his diurnall ring.

2. One who fishes by torch-light: see TORCH *v.*[1] 3. *U.S.*

1891 in *Cent. Dict.*

'torcher[2]. [f. TORCH *v.*[2] + -ER[1].] A workman employed in torching.

1851 TURNER *Dom. Archit.* I. 25 The wages of workmen .., as.. mud-plasterers, torchers, excavators, and barrow-men.

'torcher[3]. *U.S. slang.* [f. TORCH *sb.* + -ER[1].] = *torch singer* s.v. TORCH *sb.* 3.

1940 R. CHANDLER *Farewell, my Lovely* xli. 317 A handsome.. torcher who could sing as if she meant it. **1975** J. GORES *Hammett* xxii. 147 A colored band.. was backing a torcher.

‖**torchère** (tɔrʃɛr). [Fr., f. *torche* TORCH.] A tall ornamental candlestick or lamp-stand.

1910 *Sale Catal.*, Boudoir and Bed-room Furniture, Louis XVI. carved console table,.. pair Adam torchères.

†**'torchet.** *Obs.* Also 5–6 -ett(e. [= OF. *torchete*, dim. of *torche*: in med.L. *torchetta* (1420 in Du Cange).] A small torch; also *fig.*

1470–1 *Mem. Ripon* (Surtees) III. 214 Nec r. de aliquo proficuo proveniente de torcheis sive torchettis consimili modo oblatis ad corpora mortuorum. **1497** in W. M. Williams *Ann. Founders' Co.* (1867) 48 Paid to the Wax-chandler for ij torchets weynt iij quarters, vj d. **1535** in *Rep. Hist. MSS. Comm.*, *Var. Coll.* IV. 218 That then the said torches and torchettes to be in a redynes, light with convenyent berers. **1604** in *Househ. Ord.* (1790) 305 Mortores, Torchetts, Torches, Quarrioures, Waxelights, Sizes, and Pricketts. **1614** GORGES *Lucan* VI. 429 Where Leos sparkling torchets are In enterchange with Cancers starre.

torchless ('tɔːtʃlɪs), *a.* [f. TORCH *sb.* + -LESS.] Without a torch; not lighted by a torch.

1814 BYRON *Lara* II. xii, Consenting Night Guides with her star their dim and torchless flight. **1901** tr. *Hugo's Notre-Dame* (ed. Nelson) 388 Showing the interior of the Church ..torchless and voiceless.

'torch-,light. **a.** The light of a torch; illumination by a torch or torches.

c **1425** *Brut* ccxliii. 367 He was brouȝt to London on an hors beere, with myche torche lyghte. **1470–85** MALORY *Arthur* XVII. ii. 691 The mayde.. armed hym by torche lyght. **1555** *Coventry Leet Bk.* 813 Euery of them to haue a man weytinge vppon hym with torche-light. **1619** MIDDLETON *Love & Antiq.* Wks. (Bullen) VII. 329 His lordship returns by torchlight to his own house. **1726** POPE *Odyss.* XVIII. 401 The shining baldness of his head survey, It aids our torch-light. **1855** MACAULAY *Hist. Eng.* xvi. III. 629 He made a final inspection of his forces by torchlight.

fig. **1847** WHITTIER *Lost Statesman* 25 Yet firmer hands shall Freedom's torchlights trim.

b. The time when torches are lighted; dusk.

a **1656** BP. HALL *Hard Meas.* Rem. Wks. (1660) 47 It now grew to be Torch-light. **1798** SOPH. LEE *Canterb. T.*, *Yng. Lady's T.* II. 323, I faintly recollect, that it was torch-light.

c. *attrib.* Performed or carried on by torch-light.

1837 *New Yorker* 30 Sept. 441/3 A Loco-Foco 'Torch-Light Meeting', auxiliary to the larger concern in Tammany, was held in the Park on Thursday Evening. **1876** BANCROFT *Hist. U.S.* III. xix. 521 In the evening, a torch-light procession. **1884** *West. Morn. News* 15 Sept. 5/4 Lord Fife gave a torchlight ball at Mar Lodge.

‖**torchon** (tɔrʃɔ̃). [F., f. *torcher* to wipe.] The French word for a duster or dish-cloth: used *attrib.* in **torchon board**, a board covered with *torchon paper*, used in water-colour drawing; **torchon lace** (also abbreviated ***torchon***, pl. **-ons**), a coarse bobbin lace, of loose texture; **torchon mat**, a picture-frame mat (MAT *sb.*[2] 3) made of torchon paper; **torchon paper**, a kind of paper with a rough surface, used for water-colour drawing and for picture-frame mats.

1865 F. B. PALLISER *Hist. Lace* iv. 53 But Venice point is now no more. The sole relic of this far-famed trade is the coarse torchon lace of the old lozenge pattern offered by the peasant women of Palestrina. **1879** MRS. A. E. JAMES *Ind. Househ. Managem.* 10 But laces certainly would not, not even the 'Torchon' now so much in vogue: the very first wash they are torn, look ragged and unsightly. **1891** *Times* 1 Oct. 9/3 Operations in torchon and cheap Maltese laces are still on a small scale. **1908** *Athenæum* 16 Feb. 198/3 From Russian lace to torchon is not a wide step, but the latter is superior, shading off.. into Maltese.

torch-thistle ('tɔːtʃ,θɪs(ə)l). A name for a columnar cactus of the genus *Cereus*.

1731–3 MILLER *Gard. Dict.* s.v. *Cereus*, The Torch-Thistle. Call'd Cereus, because it is, as it were, a kind of taper or torch.. because when these plants have been cut down and dry'd upon the ground, they dip them into oil, and burn them as torches. *Ibid.* s.v. *Greenhouse*, Euphorbiums, Torch-Thistles, and other tender succulent Plants. **1753** HOGARTH *Anal. Beauty* viii. 44 The indian-fig or torch-thistle,.. as well as all that tribe of uncouth shaped exotics. **1884** MILLER *Plant-n.* 177 *Cereus*, Torch-thistle.

torchwood, torch-wood ('tɔːtʃwʊd).

1. (*torch-wood*) Resinous wood of which torches are made.

1601 HOLLAND *Pliny* XXIV. vii. II. 184 As for Tæda or Torch-wood, if it be sodden in vinegre, it maketh a singular collution for to wash the teeth withall when they ake. **1603** —— *Plutarch's Mor.* 685 Trees that yeeld torch-wood and pitch, as pines, cone trees, and such like. **1842** BONAR & M'CHEYNE *Narr. Miss. to Jews* vi. (1843) 343 The Jews [there] are much employed in gathering and selling torch-wood.

2. (*torchwood*) Name for several plants. **a.** A tree of the genus *Amyris*, N.O. *Rutaceæ*, having resinous wood, as *A. sylvatica* and *A. balsamifera*, of West Indies and Florida. **b.** A West Indian shrub, *Casearia* (*Thiodia*) *serrata*, N.O. *Samydaceæ*. **c.** A species of cactus, *Cereus heptagonus*.

1866 *Treas. Bot.*, Torchwood, *Cereus heptagonus*: also *Thiodia serrata*. Torchwood, Mountain, *Amyris balsamifera*. **1880** *Libr. Univ. Knowl.* (N.Y.) VI. 65 There are [in Florida] splendid flowering magnolias,.. palmette, mangrove, torchwood.

torchwort ('tɔːtʃwɜːt). [f. TORCH *sb.* + WORT.] The Mullein: = TORCH *sb.* 2 b, *torch-herb*.

1642 H. MORE *Song of Soul* I. II. lix, At either end of this well raised sod A stately stalk shot up of Torchwort high.

torchy ('tɔːtʃɪ), *a.* [f. TORCH *sb.* + -Y.] **1.** Full of torches; in which torches are used. *rare.*

1629 F. LENTON *Gallant's Whirligigg* 16 All his spangled rare perfum'd attires, Which once so glistred in the Torchy Fryers, Must to the Broakers to compound his debt.

2. Of, pertaining to, or characteristic of a torch song or torch singer. *colloq.* (orig. and chiefly *U.S.*).

1941 W. C. HANDY *Father of Blues* xxi. 285 The torchiest of all torch songs, *Melancholy Baby*. **1962** [see SLINKY *a.*]. **1977** *Time* 25 July 60/2 He is married to Actress Diahnne Abbott, whose torchy rendition of *Honeysuckle Rose* in *New York, New York* upstages Liza Minnelli's belting.

torcion, torcious: see TORSION, TORTIOUS.

‖**torcular** ('tɔːkjuːlə(r)), *sb.* [L., a press for wine or oil; also an oil-cellar.]

1. *Anat.* (in full *torcular Herophili*) = *press of Herophilus*: see PRESS *sb.*[1] 12 b.

1657 *Physical Dict.*, *Torcular*, a press. **1693** tr. *Blancard's Phys. Dict.* (ed. 2), *Torcular Herophili*, that place where the four Cavities of the thick Skin of the Brain [*Dura Mater*] are joyned. **1840** G. V. ELLIS *Anat.* 56 Its opening into the torcular Herophili is sometimes double. **1879** *St. George's Hosp. Rep.* IX. 152 A pus-laden clot extending to the neighbourhood of the torcular.

2. *Surg.* A TOURNIQUET.

1727–41 CHAMBERS *Cycl.*, *Torcular*, among chirurgions, a contrivance for stopping bleedings in amputations. **1860** MAYNE *Expos. Lex.*, *Torcular*.. applied to the tourniquet.

'torcular, *a.* [ad. L. *torculārius*, f. *torcular*: see prec. (In 2 arbitrary f. *torques*: see TORQUE *sb.*[1])]

1. *Anat.* Pertaining to or connected with the *torcular Herophili*: see prec. 1.

1656 BLOUNT *Glossogr.* s.v. *Vein*, *Torcular vein* (*vena torcularia*), the second branch of the outward throat vein. **1899** *Allbutt's Syst. Med.* VII. 602 Never plug the torcular end of the sinus if it can possibly be helped.

†**2.** Twisted, spiral, torqued. *Obs. rare*$^{-1}$.

1661 LOVELL *Hist. Anim. & Min.* Introd., The Turbinate have a torcular shell, out of the middest whereof commeth the head with two hornes.

So †**torcu'larious,** *a. Obs. rare*$^{-0}$. (See quots.)

1656 BLOUNT *Glossogr.*, *Torcularious*.., of, or belonging to a Presse that squieseth grapes. **1658** PHILLIPS, *Torcularious*, belonging to a Vine presse.

tord, torde, obs. ff. TOWARD, TURD.

tordion ('tɔːdɪən). Now *hist.* Forms: 6 **turdion**, **turgion**, 9- **tourdion**, 20- **tordion**. [a. F. *tordion*, OF. *tourdion*, *-eon*, deriv. of *tord-re* to twist.] A lively dance, said to be of the nature of a galliard; 'a round' (Cotgrave).

1531 ELYOT *Gov.* I. xx, We haue nowe base daunsis, bargenettes, pauions, turgions, and roundes. **1549** *Compl. Scot.* vi. 66 Base dansis, pauuans, galȝardis, turdions, braulis and branglis, buffons, vitht mony vthir lycht dancis. **1895** L. GROVE *Dancing* viii. 244 The 'Danse basse' was very grave. .. It was performed to the accompaniment of psalms. It consisted of three parts—(1) the *Danse basse* proper, (2) the *Retour*, (3) the *Tourdion*. **1914** T. & M. W. KINNEY *Dance* iii. 54 The *Tordion* is another dance of lively origin. Sometimes it was made a vehicle for the grotesque. **1924** SHARP & OPPÉ *Dance* 15 The Tordion was danced with the same steps as the Galliard but more quietly, without spring. **1957** G. B. L. WILSON *Penguin Dict. Ballet* 267 *Tordion*, third section of the Basse Danse. **1974** *Early Music* July 164/2 The tordion, a restrained form of galliard.

tore (tor), *sb.*[1] *Sc.* Also 6, 9 tor, 7 torre, 8 torr. [Origin uncertain: Welsh *torr* belly, bulge, boss, knob, has been compared.]

†**1.** An ornamental knob upon a piece of furniture, as a chair or a cradle. *Obs.*

1560 ROLLAND *Seven Sages* 55 Betuix thame twa, the Creddill ouir thay cast, With boddum vp, and on the Toris it stude.. That the four Toris sauit the Childis face. *a* **1572** KNOX *Hist. Ref.* IV. Wks. 1848 II. 404 The Quene.. wes placeit in the chyre, haifing twa faithfull supportis, the Maister of Maxwell upoun the ane tor, and Secretour Lethingtoun on the uther tor of the chyre. *a* **1825** *Balankin* xi. in Child *Ballads* IV. (1886) 323/2 Till all the tores of the cradle wi the red blood down ran.

2. The pommel of a saddle. *rare* or *Obs.*

a **1671** SIR A. BALFOUR *Lett.* ii. (1700) 33 To Carry one.. in a Carpet Bag.. tyed to the Tore of my Saddle. **1751** in Burton *Crim. Trials Scot.* (1852) I. 62 Placing her body across the horse upon the torr or forepart of the saddle. **1828** *Thomas o' Yonderdale* in Whitelaw *Scot. Ball.* (1874) 147/1 On the tor o' her saddle A courtly bird did sweetly sing.

tore (tɔə(r)), *sb.*[2] [a. F. *tore*, ad. L. *torus*.]

1. *Arch.* See quot. 1704; = TORUS 1.

1664 EVELYN tr. *Freart's Archit.*, etc. I. vii. 24 He thinks fit to deck the Tore's with I know not what delicate foliages. **1704** J. HARRIS *Lex. Techn.* I, *Tore*, and *Torus*.. is that round Ring which encompasses in the Column, between the Plinth, and the List. This is the third Member of the Base of a Column. **1723** CHAMBERS tr. *Le Clerc's Treat. Archit.* I. 66 The preceding Orders.. have two Tores. **1850** INKERSLEY *Roman. & Pointed Archit. in France* 182 A central tore flanked by a smaller parallel one.

2. *Geom.* = TORUS 4.
1867 TAIT *Quaternions* ix. §322 An immediate proof of the very singular property of the ring (or tore) discovered by Villarceau. 1890 EAGLES *Descript. Geom.* 248 This surface is known as a tore or anchor ring.

tore (tɔə(r)), *sb.*^{3} *local.* Also toar (*Eng. Dial. Dict.*). [Origin unascertained.] Long coarse grass remaining in the field in winter or spring. Also *attrib.*
1707 MORTIMER *Husb.* (1721) I. 234 Which you must proportion according to the quantity of Rowen or Tore that you have upon the Ground; The more Tore you have, the less quantity of Hay will do. *Ibid.*, When your Tore is quite eaten up, which it will commonly be about February, you must house your Milch-Cows, that you give Hay to in your Cow-house all Night. 1766 *Compl. Farmer*, *Tore*, rowen, or winter-grass. 1836 SIR G. HEAD *Home Tour* 253, I found fields over-run with coarse tore grass, in many parts blotchy and covered with thistles. 1904 in *Eng. Dial. Dict.* from Kent, Sussex, Surrey, Hampshire.

tore, pa. t. and obs. and dial. pa. pple. of TEAR *v.*^{1}

tore, *a.* *Obs.*: see TOR *a.*

toreador (tɒriːəˈdɔə(r), ˈtɒrɪədɔə(r)). Also 8 tauridore, tawridore, 8–9 torreadore, 9 torreador, tauridor, (tauréador). [Sp. *toreador* 'a bull-baiter' (Minsheu), mod.Sp. 'a bull-fighter on horseback'; so in Fr. The forms in *taur-* agree with earlier Fr. *tauréador* and with L. *taurus.*]
a. One who engages in a (Spanish) bull-fight, esp. on horse-back; a bull-fighter.
1618 T. LORKIN in *Crt. & Times Jas. I* (1848) II. 82 The Conde de Cantilliana, that excellent Toreador, hath stolen away the wife of a Procurador de Corte. 1797 *Encycl. Brit.* (ed. 3) III. 771/1 When the price of the horses and bulls, and the wages of the Torreadores, have been paid. 1823 BYRON *Age of Bronze* vii, Up! up again! undaunted Tauridor! 1825 T. HOOK *Sayings* Ser. II. *Passion & Princ.* xii. III. 263 As the Matador puts the finishing stroke to the..victim of the lighter efforts of the Picadores and Torreadores who have preceded him. 1884 *Pall Mall G.* 3 June 3/2 The entertainment commenced with a flourish of trumpets as the tauréadors, five in number, marched in, bowed to the public, and ranged themselves.
¶**b.** Erroneously used for 'bull-fight'. *Obs.*
1728 ? DE FOE *Capt. Carleton's Mem.* 304 A Diversion less to be complained of than their Tauridores; because attended with less Cruelty to the Beast, as well as Danger to the Spectator.
c. *attrib.*: esp. in fancy names of styles of women's hats or dresses. **toreador pants** chiefly *U.S.*, women's tight-fitting trousers, tapering to mid-calf.
1892 *Daily News* 14 Nov. 6/3 The Zouave is as great a favourite as it has been for some seasons, and though it varies in form—being sometimes a bolero, sometimes a toreador, and sometimes a cross between an Eton jacket and a Zouave. 1899 *Westm. Gaz.* 5 Oct. 3/2 The toreador toque is another very popular species just now—a toque, or really a hat, of rounded crown and rounded brim that is always much tilted to one side by a broad bandeau. 1956 E. BAIN *Mugger* x. 83 She wore a white blouse, and black toreador pants, which tapered down to her naked ankles and feet. 1960 'A. BURGESS' *Right to Answer* ii. 22 Veronica..went off, slim as a blade in toreador pants. 1974 R. B. PARKER *God save Child* vi. 48 She was dressed for a bull fight. Tight gold toreador pants... A ruffled red shirt,..a bronze wide-brimmed vaquero hat.

†**to-ˈreave**, *v.*^{1} *Obs.* [f. TO-^{2} + ME. *reve*, REAVE *v.*^{1}] **a.** *intr.* To commit robbery or plunder. **b.** *trans.* To rob, plunder, deprive by violence *of.*
13.. *Minor Poems fr. Vernon MS.* xxxvii. 515 Wel wynnen he may, But Robbe ne to-reue Nouþer niht ne day. 1393 LANGL. *P. Pl.* C. IV. 203 Religion hue [Law] al to-reueþ. 1563 *Mirr. Mag.* II. Induct. Rjb, We sawe..pale death..to reve her of her breath.

†**to-reave**, *v.*^{2} *Obs. rare.* Also 5 torafe. [f. TO-^{2} + REAVE *v.*^{2}] *trans.* To break, shiver, or tear in pieces.
a1400 *Sir Beues* (E.) 2753 + 87 Hys helme, was al toreuyd, To gedere he ffastnyd on hys heuyd. c1400 *Destr. Troy* 7629 þe grym windes..al to rafet & rent all the riche clothes.

torel, -elle, obs. forms of TOURELLE.

†**ˈtorely**, *adv.* *Obs.* [f. *tore*, TOR *a.* + -LY^{2}.] Stoutly, sturdily.
c1400 *Destr. Troy* 8015 The Troiens, on the tothir syde torely withstode.

toren, obs. f. *torn*, pa. pple. of TEAR *v.*^{1}

†**to-ˈrend**, *v.* *Obs.* [OE. *torendan*, f. TO-^{2} + *rendan* to REND. So OFris. *to-*, *te-renda.*] *trans.* To rend in pieces.
c950 *Lindisf. Gosp.* Mark xiv. 63 Se heh ðonne sacerd torende woedo his. a1000 *Ags. Ps.* (Th.) cxxiii[i]. 7 Grin bið on sadan grame torænded. a1225 *Ancr. R.* 362 He..þet to-tereð his olde kurtel, & to-rendeð þe olde pilche of his deadliche uelle. c1330 R. BRUNNE *Chron. Wace* (Rolls) 2145 Lym fro lym hym al to-rent. 1388 WYCLIF *Matt.* xxvii. 51 The veil of the temple was to-rent in twey parties. —— *Acts* xiv. 13 Whanne the apostlis..herden this, thei to-renten her cootis. 1430–40 LYDG. *Bochas* VIII. xiii, Hir clothes to rent, bedewed with weepyng. 1596 DANETT tr. *Comines* (1614) 266 Their nauie all to rent and torne. 1631 WEEVER *Anc. Fun. Mon.* 306 He..plucked the other out of his place, and all to rent his casule, Chimer, and Rochet.
Hence †**to-ˈrent** *ppl. a.*, †**to-ˈrending** *vbl. sb.*
1388 WYCLIF *Isa.* xxxvi. 22 Eliachym..and Sobna.. entriden with to-rent clothis to Ezechie. —— *Nahum* iii. 1 Wo to the citee of bloodis, al of leesyng, ful of to-reendyng [*dilaceratione*].

torenia (tɒˈriːnɪə). [mod.L. (Linnæus *Nova Plantarum Genera* (1751) 45), f. the name of the Rev. Olof *Torén* (1718–53), chaplain to the Swedish East India Company + -IA^{1}.] An annual herb of the genus of this name, belonging to the family Scrophulariaceæ, native to sub-tropical or tropical Africa and Asia, and bearing racemes of yellow, blue, or purple flowers.
1840 *Curtis's Bot. Mag.* LXVI. 3715 (*heading*) Heart-leaved Torenia. 1902 L. H. BAILEY *Cycl. Amer. Hort.* IV. 1822/1 Torenias are of easy cultivation. 1978 *Detroit Free Press* 16 Apr. (Gardening Guide) 12/1 Torenia or wishbone flower and browallia perform well in considerable shade.

†**to-rent**, *v.* *Obs.* [f. TO-^{2} + RENT *v.*^{2}] = TO-REND.
c1410 *Master of Game* (MS. Digby 182) x, She altorenteth hem with hyr tethe. 1526 TINDALE *Matt.* vii. 6 Lest..the other tourne agayne and all to rent you. 1608 DOD & CLEAVER *Expos. Prov.* ix–x. 21 Christ saith, that hogs will all to rent them that so offer to feede them.

†**to-ˈreose**, *v.* *Obs.* [OE. *to-hréosan*, f. TO-^{2} + *hrēosan*, REOSE (where see Forms).] *intr.* To fall to pieces, fall into ruins; to decay.
a900 tr. *Bæda's Hist.* I. xi. [xiii.] (1890) 48 Moniȝe oðre ceastre tohrorene wæron. a1023 WULFSTAN *Hom.* xlix. (Napier) 263 þonne bið..þa lichaman tohrorene and to duste ȝewordene. c1205 LAY. 9245 Al heo gunnen to-reosen. *Ibid.* 9426 þus Port-chæstre to-ræs [*c* 1275 to-reos].

tore-out (ˈtɔəraʊt). [f. *tore*, dial. pa. pple. of TEAR *v.*^{1} + OUT *adv.*] A small inferior type of sailing-boat.
1923 *Yachting Monthly* Jan. 145/1 Wave was of the genus usually referred to by East Coast watermen as 'little old toreouts', being, in fact, a small converted ship's boat. 1956 A. DAVISON *My Ship is so Small* ii. 19 Most of the boats in the yard were old tore-outs like the one I lived in. 1979 *Yachts & Yachting* 9 Nov. 1443/3 Let it be hastily explained that the Sirens in the title of this book are all boats: old toreouts, yachts and ultimately a 117ft ex-trading schooner.

‖**torero** (toˈrero; anglicized ˈtɒrɛərəʊ). Also 8 tauriro. [Sp.] A (Spanish) bull-fighter (on foot). Cf. TOREADOR.
1728 ? DE FOE *Capt. Carleton's Mem.* 264 So that the poor Creature may be said to fight, not only with the Tauriro (or Bull-hunter..) but with the whole Multitude in the lower Class at least. *Ibid.* 267 The Tauriroes are very well paid. 1832 MACGILLIVRAY tr. *Humboldt's Trav.* xix. 287 They observe the manners of the crocodile as the torero studies those of the bull.

†**to-ˈrese**, *v.*^{1} *Obs.* [ME. *to-ræsen*, *-reasen*, *-resen*, f. TO-^{2} + *ræsen*, OE. *rǽsan* to rush, RESE *v.*^{1}] *intr.* To make a violent assault or attack.
c1205 LAY. 18682 Ofte heo to-ræsden [*c* 1275 hii to-resde]. *Ibid.* 26813 Bruttes heom to-ræsden. *Ibid.* 26964 Romleoden ræsden to [*c* 1275 to-reasde].

†**to-ˈrese**, *v.*^{2} *Obs.* [ME. *to-rusien*, *to-rese*, f. TO-^{2} + RESE *v.*^{2}] *intr.* To shake, to quake; to be shaken to pieces.
c1205 LAY. 15946 þe eorðe gon to rusien & þi wal to-reosen. c1275 *Ibid.*, þe eorþe gan to-cwakie and þin wal to-rese. a1225 *Juliana* 58 Swa þat hit al to resde [*v.r.* to reasde].

†**toret**, ? *pa. pple.* *Obs.* Of doubtful meaning.
13.. *Gaw. & Gr. Knt.* 960 Hir frount folden in sylk.. Toret & treieted with tryflez aboute.

toret, -ett(e, obs. forms of TORRET, TURRET.

toreumatography (tɒruːməˈtɒgrəfɪ). *rare*$^{-0}$. [ad. med.L. *toreumatographia*, f. Gr. τόρευμα(τ-, embossed work, etc. (f. τορεύειν: see TOREUTIC) + -GRAPHY.] Description of the toreutic art, or of works done in it: see TOREUTIC. So **toreuma-ˈtology**, *rare*, the science or study of toreutics.
1727–41 CHAMBERS *Cycl.*, *Toreumatography*, a Greek term, signifying the knowledge, or rather description, of ancient sculptures, and basso-relievo's... The invention of *toreumatographia* is owing to Phidias, and its perfection to Polycletes. 1842 BRANDE *Dict. Sc.* etc., *Toreumatology*.. signifies either the science or art of sculpture, or a description of ancient and modern sculpture and bas-relief. 1846 WORCESTER, *Toreumatography*, *Toreumatology* [cites *Brande*].

‖**toreutes** (tɒˈruːtiːz). [a. Gr. τορευτής, f. τορεύειν: see next.] A worker in toreutics; an artist in metal or ivory.
1840 tr. *C. O. Müller's Hist. Lit. Greece* xiii. §15 *note*, Anacreon's advice to the toreutes, who is to make him a cup. 1847 LEITCH tr. *C. O. Müller's Anc. Art* §85 *note*, The designation of toreutes hovers between caelator or enchaser and artist in gold and ivory. *Ibid.* §173 The work of the toreutes..was especially prized in Etruria.

toreutic (tɒˈruːtɪk), *a.* and *sb.* [ad. Gr. τορευτικός, f. τορεύειν to work in relief, etc.]
A. *adj.* Of or pertaining to toreutics (see B.); chiefly in phr. *toreutic art* = toreutics; also, of figures, etc., executed according to the toreutic art; of an artist, working in toreutics.
1837 *Antiq. Athens* 38 The Minerva of the Parthenon, also by Phidias, wrought in ivory and gold, the noblest example of the *toreutic* art. 1854 GANTILLON tr. *Propertius*, *Elegies* 87 *note*, *Mys.*—A toreutic artist who lived B.C. 444. 1874 *Edin. Rev.* July 187 The best toreutic representations of children are those of the Flemish artist du Quesnoy. 1910 D. G. HOGARTH in *Encycl. Brit.* I. 248/2 The..free sculpture and toreutic handiwork of Crete.
B. *sb.* [rendering Gr. τορευτική (sc. τέχνη) toreutic art: the Romanized form *toreuticē* occurs in 17th c. Eng. use]. Chiefly in pl. **toreutics**: The art, esp. the ancient art, of working in metal or ivory, including embossing, work in relief, chasing, etc.
[1662 EVELYN *Chalcogr.* (1769) 16 Then the *toreutice*..for I can only name them briefly.] 1847 LEITCH tr. *C. O. Müller's Anc. Art* §85 This species of work..is reckoned as a branch of toreutics, by which is meant sculpture in metals ..and also this combination of metal with other materials. 1900 *Year's Work Class. Stud.* 45 Pernice continues his notes on toreutic.

torey (ˈtɔərɪ), *a.* *nonce-wd.* [for *tory*, f. TORE *sb.*^{3} + -Y.] Of the nature of or consisting of 'tore' or coarse grass.
1893 *Blackw. Mag.* Mar. 392 The bleached torey grass of a sheltered hillside suits him.

torf, obs. form of TURF.

torfaceous (tɔːˈfeɪʃəs), *a.* *Bot. rare.* [f. assumed mod.L. *torfa* TURF + -ACEOUS.] 'Growing in bogs or mosses' (*Treas. Bot.* 1866).

†**torfer.** *Obs.* Forms: 4 torfere, (-phere), -fir, 4–5 -fer, -fare, 5 torfor, tourfer, torfoyr, *Sc.* torfeir. [Northern ME., a. ON. *tor-fœra* fem., or *torfœri* neut. (mod.Norw. *torføre*), a difficult or dangerous passage, f. *torfœrr* adj. hard or difficult to pass, f. *tor-* TOR *a.* + *fōr*, pret. stem of *fara* to go.] Hardship, trouble, distress; harm, mischief, injury.
13.. *Cursor M.* 6498 (Cott.) þat he sal hald vs hale and fere, And warn vs fra ilkin tor-fere [*Fairf.* alkin torfere]. *Ibid.* 20002 Ful mani torfer [*Trin.* mony turment] sufferd þai. c1325 *Metr. Hom.* (1862) 158 For than pin we our bodye, With torfir and with martyrye. ? a1400 *Morte Arth.* 1956 That schalle turne the to tene and torfere for ever. a1400–50 *Alexander* 3729 Quat tene & torfare may tide & tent to þine ende. c1440 *York Myst.* xl. 174 Suche torfoyr and torment of-telle herde I neuere. c1470 *Golagros & Gaw.* 876 Ye sall nane torfeir betyde, I tak vpone hand.

torfle (ˈtɔːf(ə)l), *v.* *dial.* Also 7–9 -fell, 9 -fil. [Origin unascertained. Cf. TORPLE.] *intr.* To founder, go lame (? *obs.*); to decline in health, pine away, languish; *fig.* to lose interest in or draw back from an undertaking.
(Hogg's use of the word is vague.)
1575–6 *Durham Depos.* (Surtees) 285 This deponent..had an ox that torfled. 1818 HOGG *Brownie of B.*, etc. II. 149 It was reportit, that there was to be seen every morning at two a clock, a naked woman torfelling on the Alemoor loch, wi' her hands tied behind her back, and a heavy stane at her neck. 1820 —— *Bridal of Polmood* viii, I..fleechyt Eleesabett noore to let us torfell in the waretyme of owir raik [in the springtime of our life's journey]. 1825 —— *Q. Hynde* I. 439 She saw him swathed in bloody red, And torfell'd on the monster's head. 1876 [see TORPLE 2].

ˈtorgant, *a.* *Her.* Also **targant**. [app. an erroneous form of *torquent*, L. *torquent-em*, or for TORQUED.] = TORQUED 2.
c1828 BERRY *Encycl. Her.* I. Gloss., *Targant, Torgant*, or *Torqued*, bending and rebending, like the letter S. 1890 ELVIN *Dict. Her.*, *Targant*, see Torqued.

‖**torgoch** (ˈtɔrgɔx). Also 7 torcoch; (*erron.*) 7 torcoth, 8 torgotch. [Welsh *torgoch*, f. *tor* belly + *coch* red.] The red-bellied char, a variety of the common char, found in the Welsh lakes.
1611 SPEED *Theat. Gt. Brit.* (1614) 123/2 In the poole Lin-Peris, there is a kinde of fish called there Torcoch, having a red belly, no where else seene. 1756 in *Gentl. Mag.* XXVI. 616/2 Torgotch, or Red-belly, which distinguishes the female. 1787 BEST *Angling* (ed. 2) 4 The English fishes that we have in our ponds, rivers, &c. are as follow: Umbla minor, Gesn. The Red Charr, or Welch Torgoch. 1924 *Glasgow Herald* 8 Feb. 8 Among the fish got in the Clyde at that time (about 1840) was the..torgoch or char. 1936 J. T. JENKINS *Fishes Brit. Isles* (ed. 2) 237 The Torgoch..inhabits two lakes near Llanberis.

torgsin (ˈtɔːgsɪn). Also Torgsin. [a. Russ., contraction of *vsesoyuznoe ob''edinenie po torgovle s inostrantsami*, the All-Union Association for Trade with Foreigners.] A Soviet trading organization in the 1920s and 1930s which sold goods only in return for foreign currency. Used *attrib.*
1933 *Sun* (Baltimore) 24 Nov. 18/5 Sale of 200,000 pounds of bacon to the 'torgsin' stores, which cater only to foreigners in Soviet Russia, has been announced by Polish exporters. 1934 H. G. WELLS *Exper. Autobiogr.* II. ix. 819 All over Moscow and Leningrad you can bribe with foreign currency because of the absurd *Torgsin* system. 1968 *Listener* 3 Oct. 434/2 It was fairly easy for us because of those Torgsin shops where you could really get everything.

Torgut (ˈtɔːgʊt). Now *Hist.* Also Torgod, Torgot, Torgud. [Native name.] A migratory Mongol people now absorbed into China; a member of this people. Also *attrib.*
1883 *Encycl. Brit.* XVI. 745/1 It was with no great difficulty..that his brother Ki Wang detached the greater

part of the Kerait tribes from his banner, and founded the Torgod chieftainship. *Ibid.*, The position of the Torgod at this time..was rapidly becoming unbearable. **1947** AUDEN *Age of Anxiety* (1948) v. 103 The Timurids and Torguts. **1957** *Encycl. Brit.* VIII. 351/1 Some of them [*sc.* the western Mongols], notably the Torgots (Torgud) migrated as far west as the Volga, whence they returned, and their descendants are settled in the Ili district. **1962** E. SNOW *Other Side of River* (1963) xix. 142 In the past three centuries there had been no similar armed migration of a nation in Asia, with the exception of the amazing Flight of the Torgut from the Caucasus to Mongolia.

†**torht**, *a.* *Obs.* [OE. *torht* bright, splendid, illustrious.] Bright, clear.

a **1000** *Phœnix* 96 Æþelast tungla... Torht tacen godes. **12..** *Prayer to our Lady 20 OE. Misc.* 193 Mi brune her is hwit bicume..& mi to[r]hte rude iturnd al in-to oðre dehe.

tori, pl. of TORUS.

toric (ˈtɔərɪk, ˈtɒrɪk), *a.* (*sb.*) [f. TOR-US + -IC.] Of or pertaining to a torus (see TORUS 4); having the form of a torus or a portion of one; *spec.* in *Ophthalm.*, applied to a lens with one surface curved like part of a torus, the radius of curvature having a minimum value in one direction and a maximum value in the direction at right angles to it; also as *sb.*, such a lens.

1890 *Trans. Amer. Ophthalm. Soc.* V. 708 Such toric surfaces are concave, and, when sunk in a plate of glass, afford typical examples of concavo-plane toric lenses. **1900** *Buch's Handbk. Med. Sc.* I. 595 A concave spherical combined with a convex toric surface. **1954** S. DUKE-ELDER *Parsons' Dis. Eye* (ed. 12) iv. 41 A regularly astigmatic surface is said to have a toric curvature. **1962** L. S. SASIENI *Princ. & Pract. Optical Dispensing* x. 264 'Commercial' torics of minus powers are usually transposed to the form which provides a plus cylinder. **1973** *Nature* 21/28 Dec. 479/2 A toric segment of bore diameter *d*, generator circle diameter *D* and length *s* measured along the central axis. **1978** J. PARR *Introd. Ophthalmol.* ii. 44/1 A cylindrical curvature can be combined with a spherical curvature in a lens which is then called a toric surfaced lens. In astigmatism the surface of the cornea is toric instead of spherical.

torify: see TORYFY.

‖**torii** (ˈtorii). Also tori, torij. [Jap., f. *tori* bird, fowl + *i* to sit, perch.] A ceremonial gateway in front of a Japanese Shintō shrine, consisting of two uprights and two crosspieces of which the lower is straight and the upper usu. curved and projecting. Also *attrib.*

Occas. erron. interpreted as *pl.*

1727 J. SCHEUCHZER tr. *Kæmpfer's Hist. Japan* III. ii. 208 At the entry of the walk, which leads to the temple, stands ..a particular fashioned gate, called *Torij*, and built either of stone or wood. **1874** C. HOEY tr. *Humbert's Japan & Japanese* I. ii. 14 A long avenue of fir-trees, headed by a sacred gate called a Tori. **1874** *Trans. Asiatic Soc. Japan* II. 116 The *torii* gradually assumed the character of a general symbol of *Shintô*. **1904** D. SLADEN *Playing the Game* II. v. 231 Tall torii, those mystic arches of Japan. **1911** *Encycl. Brit.* XV. 182 Originally designed as a perch for fowls which sang to the deities at daybreak, this torii subsequently came to be erroneously regarded as a gateway characteristic of the Shintō shrine. **1960** B. LEACH *Potter in Japan* ii. 55 Torii gateway leading to cryptomeria-shaded steps climbing to little empty Shinto Shrines. **1977** *Amer. Speech 1975* L. 69 Mills..must be almost as exotic to most younger Americans as torii or dagobas.

‖**toril** (toˈril). Pl. toriles. [Sp.] One (*spec.* the last) of a series of pens in which a bull at a bullfight is confined before being released into the ring. Also *attrib.*

1893 CHAPMAN & BUCK *Wild Spain* v. 65 The noble bulls will be lured in their company away from their native plains, ..to the entrance of the fatal *toril*. **1932** E. HEMINGWAY *Death in Afternoon* vi. 61 The alguacils ride up to under the president's box to ask for the key to the red door of the toril where the bull is waiting. **1961** *Times* 8 July 10/6 The *toril* gates open and out bounds the animal. **1974** *Encycl. Brit. Macropædia* III. 477/1 The *presidente municipal*..throws down to one of the *alguaciles* the key to the *toriles* or bull pens.

Torinese (tɒrɪˈniːz), *a.* and *sb.* Also Turinese. [a. It. *Torinese*, f. *Torino* Turin: see -ESE.]

A. *adj.* Of, pertaining to, or characteristic of the city of Turin in Piedmont, north-west Italy, its natives and inhabitants, or their dialect. **B.** *sb.* **a.** A native or inhabitant of Turin. **b.** The dialect of Italian spoken in Turin.

1883 H. JAMES *Little Tour in France* (1885) xix. 132 The shops are probably better than the Turinese, but the people are not so good. **1886** WEBSTER, Torinese *a.* and *sb.* **1960** A. COLQUHOUN tr. *di Lampedusa's Leopard* i. 19 The Piedmontese... Wouldn't things be just the same? Just Torinese instead of Neapolitan dialect; that's all. **1975** R. COBB *Paris & its Provinces* 2 The famous café..that unkind Torinese have sometimes called *il caffè della mennapausa*. *Ibid.* 3 Two louts engage the auburn beauty in the coarsest Torinese. **1977** *Times* 26 Mar. 10/1 Turinese cooking. **1980** *Times* 16 Oct. 7/2 As the five acts of the *opera* drifted their way onwards the Torinese decided they had had enough.

Toriness, Toryness (ˈtɔərɪnɪs). *nonce-wd.* [f. TORY *a.* + -NESS.] Tory quality or condition.

1890 *Sat. Rev.* 12 Apr. 425/1 Mr. Gladstone deplored the Toriness of Hertfordshire.

Torism, obs. form of TORYISM.

‖**torista** (toˈrista). [Sp.] An enthusiast for bullfighting who is chiefly interested in the performance of the bull.

1957 A. MACNAB *Bulls of Iberia* p. xii, The more solid Spanish *aficionados*, especially those known as *toristas* because their primary interest is in the Bull rather than the Bullfighter. **1967** MCCORMICK & MASCAREÑAS *Compl. Aficionado* ii. 31 The torista exalts the toro over the torero to the point where he will ignore and despise the man's best achievements.

†**to-ˈrit**, *v.* *Obs.* [ME., f. TO-² + *ritten*, RIT *v.*¹] *trans.* To cut or tear asunder.

13.. *Orfeo* (Auchinleck MS.) 43 Hir riche robe hye al to rett [*Ashm. MS.* to-rytte] And was reneyd out of hir witt.

†**to-ˈrive**, *v.* *Obs.* [ME., f. TO-² + RIVE *v.*¹]

1. *trans.* To rive or tear asunder; to split open, cleave. Also *fig.*

c **1300** *Havelok* 1953 Hwo haues the thus ille maked, Thus to-riuen, and al mad naked? **13..** *K. Alis.* 6216 (Bodl. MS.) Schippes..Ful ycharged of her clay, þat men clepeþ Butumay, þat water non ne may to Ryue Ne irne ne steel ne metal to dryue. **13..** *E.E. Allit. P.* A. 1196 þer-for my ioye watz sone to-riuen. *Ibid.* C. 379 His ryche robe he to rof of his rigge naked. **13..** *Sir Beues* (A.) 2159 þat hors..His rakenteis he al te-rof. *c* **1400** *Destr. Troy* 1234 The king..the rod all-to roofe right to his honde. **1470–85** MALORY *Arthur* I. xxviii. 75 The shyp..was al to ryuen.

2. *intr.* To burst asunder; to split, cleave, splinter, shiver.

c **1275** LAY. 7844 Mani sip al to-rof. *c* **1330** R. BRUNNE *Chron.* (1810) 170 þat schip salle alle toryue. **1390** GOWER *Conf.* III. 296 The mast tobrak, the Seil torof. *c* **1440** *York Myst.* xiii. 153 Was neuer wight sa wa, for ruthe I all to ryff. *c* **1470** HENRY *Wallace* II. 52 The tre to raiff & fruschit euiredeille. **1470–85** MALORY *Arthur* VIII. xxxviii. 330 A wynde drofe hem..vpon this yle of seruage..and there the Barget all to rofe.

tork, variant of TORQUE *sb.*¹

torkes, var. TURKIS *v.* *Obs.*, to distort, alter.

torma (ˈtɔːmə). Pl. **torma, tormas.** [a. Tibetan.] A sacrificial offering burned in a Tibetan Buddhist ceremony.

1895 L. A. WADDELL *Buddhism of Tibet* xii. 297 Another food-offering is a high conical cake of dough, butter and sugar, variously coloured, named *tormā*.., that is, holy food. It is placed on a metal tray supported by a tripod. **1929** D. MACDONALD *Land of Lama* xvii. 205 Everyone makes offerings in the temples, while the monks of the monastery prepare *torma*, symbolic emblems made of butter, on thin wooden or leather backing, often eight or ten feet high. **1958** *Illustr. London News* 13 Dec. 1041/1 A set of such figures, known as *torma* and representing divine personages, spirits and demons, as well as offerings of various forms, are required for every rite conducted by lamas. **1970** R. D. TARING *Daughter of Tibet* x. 135 On a certain day they burnt *tormas* (cone-shaped religious sweets). **1979** J. NORBU *Horseman in Snow* 46 The grass..yields a red dye that is used to colour sacrificial offerings called tormas.

tormaline, tormarith, obs. ff. TOURMALINE, TURMERIC.

torment (ˈtɔːmɛnt), *sb.* Forms: 3–6 **turment**, (4 **-te**), **tourment**, (5–6 **-te**), 3– **torment**, (*pl.* 3–4 **-menz, -mens**). (Also *β.* 5 **torna-, tourne-, turna-, turnement**, 6 **tornement.**) [ME. a. OF. *tor-, tourment*, ONF. *turment* (11th c.) = It., Sp., Pg. *tormento*:—L. *torment-um* (:—**torqu(e)mentum* something operated by twisting, f. *torquēre* to twist). In sense 5, a. F. *tourmente* fem. from L. *tormenta* neut. pl., which became fem. sing. in Romanic, sometimes with final *-e* in ME. The *β*-forms show confusion with TOURNAMENT.]

†**1.** An engine of war worked by torsion, for hurling stones, darts, or other missiles. *Obs.*

1382 WYCLIF *1 Macc.* vi. 51 And ordeynede there balistis, and engynes, and dartis, or castyngis, of fyr, and tourmentis for to cast stoons and dartis. **1398** TREVISA *Barth. De P.R.* XVIII. ix. (Bodl. MS.), Regulus þe Emperoure slowe an addre..þat was xx. fote longe wiþ alblastes and tormentes. **1531** ELYOT *Gov.* I. viii, All turmentes of warre, whiche we cal ordinance. [**1866** J. B. ROSE tr. *Ovid's Met.* 229 Like the bolt from the tormentum cast, Smiting the wall.]

2. An instrument of torture, as the rack, wheel, or strappado (*rare* or *doubtful*); hence, the infliction of torture by such an instrument as a form of punishment, a means of extracting information, etc.; torture inflicted or suffered.

c **1290** *S. Eng. Leg.* I. 84/33 Heo bad ore louerd..þat he ire ȝeue þere Studefaste bi-leue..And in hire tormenz treowe heorte. *c* **1300** *Seyn Julian* 49 þe more turment þat hi hire dude þe bet hi hire paide. **1340** *Ayenb.* 166 We redeþ of zaynte Agase, þet mid greate blisse hi yede to torment alsuo ase hi yede to feste. *c* **1384** CHAUCER *H. Fame* I. 445 And euery turment eke in helle Saugh he. **1413** *Sat. agst. Lollards* 113 in *Pol. Poems* (Rolls) II. 246 And namly James among hem alle, For he twyes had turnement. **1483** CAXTON *Gold. Leg.* 289/2 He dyde doo strayne and payne them in the torment of Eculee. **1494** FABYAN *Chron.* IV. lxviii. 46 [Mexencius] pursued ye Christen with all kynde of turment. **1550–1** *Acts Privy Counc.* (1891) III. 230 Order shalbe given that he may be sent up hither to be put to tornement. **1610** SHAKS. *Temp.* I. ii. 289 It was a torment To lay upon the damn'd. **1668** CULPEPPER & COLE *Barthol. Anat.* IV. ii. 161 That torment which the Italians call *Tratta de corda*, the Strappado. **1709** J. JOHNSON *Clergym. Vade M.* II. 169 Those who had done sacrifice thro' the violence of torment in time of persecution. **1725** POPE *Odyss.* IX. 454 They swift let fall The pointed torment on his visual ball.

b. *spec.* The punishment of hell.

1852 MRS. STOWE *Uncle Tom's C.* xviii, 'I knows I'm gwine to torment', said the woman, sullenly.

3. A state of great suffering, bodily or mental; agony; severe pain felt or endured.

c **1290** *Beket* 434 in *S. Eng. Leg.* I. 119 So þat þe preost was i-brouȝt In tormenz bi þe meste. **13..** *Guy Warw.* (A.) 325 Thus he lay in grete turment, Til þat þe fest was al to-went. *c* **1386** CHAUCER *Knt.'s T.* 440 That doubleth al my torment [*v.r.* turment] and my wo. *c* **1489** CAXTON *Sonnes of Aymon* I. 34 Ye haue broughte me in grete sorowe and tournement irrecouerable. **1500–20** DUNBAR *Poems* lxxvi. 6 A schoirt torment for infineit glaidnes. **1590** SPENSER *F.Q.* I. x. 28 In which his torment often was so great, That like a Lyon he would cry and rore. **1732** POPE *Let. to Swift* 5 Dec., In acute torment by the inflammation in his bowels and breast. **1861** KINGSLEY *Lett.* (1878) II. 134 The feeling of being always behind-hand..is second only in torment to that of debt.

†**b.** *spec.* A griping or wringing pain in the bowels: = TORMINA. *Obs.*

1578 LYTE *Dodoens* II. xcii. 273 The seede of Ameos is very good against the griping payne and torment of the belly. *c* **1610** *Women Saints* 112 She..endured moste sharpe payne and torment of stomacke. **1688** R. HOLME *Armoury* II. 172/1 Swelling and Torment in the Belly [of Cows]..if not speedily helped, is Death to the Beast.

4. An action, circumstance, or condition which causes extreme pain or suffering of body or mind; a source of pain, trouble, or anguish, or in weakened sense, of worry or annoyance.

1599 SHAKS. *Much Ado* II. iii. 130 No, and sweares she neuer will, that's her torment. **1611** B. JONSON *Catiline* v. vi, Why, death's the end of evils, and a rest Rather than torment. **1789** MRS. PIOZZI *Journ. France* II. 364 Want of language, our still recurring torment. **1825** T. HOOK *Sayings* Ser. II. *Passion & Princ.* vii. III. 102 The conviction that he had made himself absurd..was his torment. **1841** HELPS *Ess., Aids Contentm.* (1842) 13 A habit of mistrust is the torment of some people.

b. Applied to a person who causes trouble. Cf. PLAGUE *sb.* 2 c.

1784 COWPER *Task* IV. 632 That instant he [a recruit] becomes the serjeant's care, His pupil, and his torment, and his jest. **1873** 'OUIDA' *Pascarèl* I. 32 They were the pride and torment of Mariuccia's life. **1881** 'RITA' *Lady Coquette* i, Will you be quiet, you torment.

c. In jocular use: An instrument of irritation or annoyance: = TORMENTOR 3 f. (In quot. *attrib.*)

1882 *Daily News* 30 May 2/1 The Vale of Health was..the most frequented spot of all,..the 'torment' and squirt fun rather too buoyant.

5. A violent storm; a tempest, tornado. *Obs.* (exc. in Fr. form: see TOURMENTE).

a **1300** *Fragm. Pop. Sc.* (Wright) 184 For þeras the weder is, þer is turment strong Of wynd, of water, and of fur. *c* **1330** R. BRUNNE *Chron.* (1810) 148 In to þe se of Spayn wer dryuen in a torment. **1471** CAXTON *Recuyell* (Sommer) 540 Ther roose so a grete torment in the see [*orig.* si grant tormente leva de vent]. **1530** PALSGR. 282/1 Torment a storme on the see, *tourmente, tempeste*. **1604** E. G[RIMSTONE] *D'Acosta's Hist. Indies* III. xxvi. 199 Vpon the coast of Peru, there be no torments from heauen, as thunder and lightning.

6. *attrib.* and *Comb.*, as ***torment-house, robe.***

1649 J. E[LLISTON] tr. *Behmen's Epist.* v. 62 Being in the torment-house of the stars. **1846** T. AIRD *Poet. Wks.* (1856) 240 With torment-pointed threatenings. **1890** E. HATCH *Fields of Light* 55 Saints who were wafted to the skies In the torment robe of flame.

torment (tɔːˈmɛnt), *v.* Forms: see prec. sb.; also 5 *pa. pple.* (*contr.*) **tor-, turment.** [a. OF. *tor-, turmenter* (12th c.), *tourmenter*, f. *tor-, turment* sb.: cf. med.L. *tormentāre*, f. *tormentum*, Pr. *turmentar*, Sp. *tormentar*, It. *tormentare*.]

1. *trans.* To put to torment or torture; to inflict torture upon.

c **1290** *St. Edmund* 181 in *S. Eng. Leg.* I. 436 Fiet and hondene þat neren nouȝt i-tormentede with þat here Necke and face and al is heued. *c* **1300** *St. Brandan* 595 Oure maister ous hath i-turmented so grisliche allonge niȝt. **1382** WYCLIF *Rev.* xiv. 10 This..shal be tourmentid [**1388** turmentid] with fijr and brunston. *c* **1440** *Alphabet of Tales* 177 When a devull had turment horrebly a man þat he was in. **1475** *Bk. Noblesse* (Roxb.) 66 They turmentid hym in prison in the most cruelle wise to dethe. **1560** DAUS tr. *Sleidane's Comm.* 168 To moue the Frenche kynge, that innocente persones be not tormented, for Religion. **1651** HOBBES *Leviath.* III. xxxviii. 238 For what offences..men are to be Eternally tormented.

2. To afflict or vex with great suffering or misery, physical or mental; to pain, distress, plague.

1297 R. GLOUC. (Rolls) 4920 + 36 Seynt Petur to hym come, as þe slep hym toke, & tormented hym sore ynou. **1382** WYCLIF *Acts* v. 33 Whanne thei herden thes thingis, thei weren turmentid, and thouȝten for to sle hem. *c* **1420** *Chron. Vilod.* 2902 þo whyche was wᵗ sekenesse so tourmentyd. *a* **1450** *Knt. de la Tour* (1906) 41 The pepille that were..oute of her mynde and turmented. **1514** BARCLAY *Cyt. & Uplondyshm.* (Percy Soc.) 6 Whan the northe wynde..Hath brought cold wynter pore wretches to turment. *a* **1548** HALL *Chron., Rich. III* 28 b, What ys he.. that wil not..be moued & tormented with pitie and mercie? **1713** STEELE *Englishm.* No. 48. 308 Great Evils..torment the Life of Man. **1804** *Med. Jrnl.* XII. 143 A disease which had tormented me for sixteen years. **1856** [see TORMENTING *ppl. a.*].

b. In lighter sense: To tease or worry excessively; to trouble, 'plague'.

1718 LADY M. W. MONTAGU *Let. to Abbé Conti* 19 May, We are tormenting our brains with some scheme of politics. **1862** MAURICE *Mor. & Met. Philos.* IV. vii. §44. 373 He tormented the Rabbins with questions.

†**3.** To throw into agitation; to toss, disturb, shake up, or stir physically. *Obs.* (exc. as a Gallicism).

1491 CAXTON *Vitas Patr.* (W. de W. 1495) II. 246 Lyke.. raymentes when the foller fulleth them & tourmenteth them often vnder his fete. *a* **1533** LD. BERNERS *Huon* xlvi. 156 The shyppe was so sore tormentyd, that the shyppe brast all to peces. **1667** MILTON *P.L.* VI. 243 That warr..then soaring on main wing Tormented all the Air; all Air seemed then Conflicting Fire. **1784** COWPER *Task* II. 101 The fixed and rooted earth, Tormented into billows, heaves and swells. **1822** [see TORMENTED *ppl. a.*]. **1908** *Academy* 27 June 927/2 After madame had 'tormented' the ingredients—the salad was a dish from fairyland.

b. *fig.* To twist, distort (sense, style, etc.).

1647 HAMMOND *Power of Keys* iii. 26 Sure this is to peruert and torment the sense. *a* **1680** BUTLER *Rem.* (1759) I. 230 And pay 'em for tormenting Texts. **1895** *Daily News* 18 Oct. 4/7 In Mr. Pater we had a writer of singular natural gifts, who..ended by embroiling and tormenting his style.

Hence **tor'mentable** *a.*, capable of being tormented, susceptible of torment; †**tormen'tation** *Obs.*, tormenting, torment; †**tor'mentative**, †**tor'mentive** *adjs. Obs.*, that torments, tormenting.

1876 EMERSON *Ess.*, *Circles* Wks. (Bohn) II. 263 The great man is not convulsible or *tormentable. **1789** A. C. BOWER *Diaries & Corr.* (1903) 53, I shall have no more *Tormentations. **1654** GAYTON *Pleas. Notes* III. viii. 124 From Furies, and things worse *tormentative. **1653** F. G. tr. *Scudery's Artamenes* VIII. I. (1655) IV. 3 His presence is so *tormentive unto me.

tor'mented, *ppl. a.* [f. TORMENT *v.* + -ED[1].]

1. In senses of the vb.

1552 HULOET, Tourmented, *cruciatus, excruciatus.* **1686** HORNECK *Crucif. Jesus* v. 72 A fiery serpent..a symbol of God's presence and power to heal the tormented Israelites. **1808** G. EDWARDS *Pract. Plan* iii. 16 Evils, which our tormented imaginations apprehend. **1822** SCOTT *Pirate* vii, More than once, large fragments..gave way before him, and thundered down into the tormented ocean.

2. *U.S. slang.* Used adjectivally and adverbially as a mild equivalent of DAMNED *ppl. a.* 4.

1825 J. NEAL *Brother Jonathan* I. 138 They hadn't come such a tormented long piece. **1867** J. R. LOWELL *Biglow Papers* 2nd Ser. p. lix, *Tormented*, euphemism for damned, as, 'not a tormented cent'. **1903** G. S. WASSON *Cap'n Simeon's Store* 86 It don't look right for nobody..to take and hang on to them tormented ole witch-bridles so-fashion! **1938** M. K. RAWLINGS *Yearling* xi. 119 'Look at him,' she said. 'Tormented Yankee. His feet drag like a 'gator's tail.'

Hence **tor'mentedly** *adv.*

1891 *Longm. Mag.* Mar. 531 She was going to break out tormentedly, pleadingly: 'For God's sake tell me!'

†**'tormentful**, *a. Obs.* [f. TORMENT *sb.* + -FUL.] Full of, or fraught with torment.

1596 R. L[INCHE] *Diella* (1877) 30 My most tormentfull case. **1647** TRAPP *Comm. Matt.* vi. 31 Carefulness is a tormentful plodding upon businesses. *a* **1694** TILLOTSON *Wks.* (1717) II. 199 In what Nature soever they [malice, envy, revenge] are, they are as vexatious and tormentful to it self, as they are troublesome and mischievous to others.

tormentil ('tɔːməntɪl). Forms: 5 **tormentille**, **-ylle**, 6 **-yll**, 6–8 **-ill**, **-ile**, (8 **tormentle**), 6– **tormentil**; 5 **turmentylle**, 5–6 **-ill**, 6 **-yll**. [= F. *tormentille* (1314 in Hatz.-Darm.), ad. med.L. *tormentilla*, in form dim. of *tormentum*: see TORMENT *sb.* Reason of name obscure: cf. quot. 1616; according to others from its being used to relieve the gripes, L. *tormina*.] A low-growing herb, *Potentilla Tormentilla* (*Tormentilla repens*), N.O. *Rosaceæ*, of trailing habit, common on heaths and dry pastures, bearing small four-petalled yellow flowers, and having strongly astringent roots; in use from early times in medicine, and in tanning. Also called *septfoil*.

[*a* **1387** *Sinon. Barthol.* (Anecd. Oxon.) 42/1 Tormentilla pilos, pentafilon non habet ullos.] *a* **1400–50** *Stockh. Med. MS.* 6 Water of turmentill. **1530** PALSGR. 284/1 Turmentyll an herbe, *tourmentine.* **1578** LYTE *Dodoens* I. lvii. 83 Tormentill is much like vnto Sinckefoyle. **1610** FLETCHER *Faithf. Sheph.* II. i, This Tormentil, whose vertue is to part All deadly killing poyson from the heart. **1616** SURFL. & MARKH. *Country Farme* 204 Called Tormentill, because the powder or decoction of the root doth appease the rage and torment of the teeth. **1698** M. MARTIN *Voy. St. Kilda* (1749) 56 Their Leather is tanned with the roots of Tormentil. **1906** *Daily Chron.* 4 May 6/7 Tormentil and potentil, names fulfilled of pleasure, Set the world in tune again with the May Day measure.

b. *attrib.*, as *tormentil-root.*

1712 tr. *Pomet's Hist. Drugs* I. 43 The best Tormentil Roots come from grassy, wet Places about the Alps and Pyrenees. **1811** A. T. THOMSON *Lond. Disp.* (1818) 400 Tormentil root is a powerful astringent.

So †**'tormentine** [from F.] in same sense.

14.. *Nom.* in Wr.-Wülcker 713/6 *Hec tormentilla*, tormentyne [cf. 1530 PALSGR. above].

tor'menting, *vbl. sb.* [f. TORMENT *v.* + -ING[1].] The action of the verb TORMENT; torturing, vexing; an instance of this.

c **1290** *S. Eng. Leg.* I. 12/389 His soule wende to þe Joye of heouene After is tormentingue. **1382** WYCLIF *Isa.* xiii. 8 Tormentingus and sorewes thei shul holde. **1535** COVERDALE *Wisd.* ii. 19 Let vs examen him with despitefull rebuke and tormentinge, that we maye knowe his dignite & proue his pacience. **1633** P. FLETCHER *Elisa* II. iv, So sat she, as when speechlesse griefs tormenting Locks up the heart. **1884** *Athenæum* 6 Dec. 732/2 [They] suffer from no fancied ills and self-conscious tormentings.

tor'menting, *ppl. a.* [f. as prec. + -ING[2].] That torments, in various senses of the verb.

1575 [implied in TORMENTINGLY]. **1594** SHAKS. *Rich. III*, I. iii. 226 While some tormenting Dreame Affrights thee. **1637** PRYNNE *Passages Star Chamb.* in *Harl. Misc.* (1809) IV. 234 Let me be put to the tormentingest death they can devise. **1667** MILTON *P.L.* IV. 505 Sight hateful, sight tormenting! **1780** *Mirror* No. 74 ¶9 Haunted with the most tormenting thoughts. **1856** KANE *Arct. Expl.* II. viii. 87 The eruption, a tormenting and anomalous symptom.

Hence **tor'mentingly** *adv.*; **tor'mentingness**.

1575 GASCOIGNE *Dan Barthol. of Bathe* Wks. 1907 I. 105 He bounst and bet his head tormentingly. **1727** BAILEY vol. II, *Tormentingness*, tormenting Quality or Faculty. **1857** *Chamb. Jrnl.* VII. 397 Visits were tormentingly delayed.

†**tormen'tise.** *Obs.* Torment, torture.

c **1386** CHAUCER *Monk's T.* 527 But nathelees this Seneca the wise Chees in a Bath to dye in this manere Rather than han any oother tormentise.

tormentor (tɔːˈmɛntə(r)). Also 5–9 **-er**. [ME. and AF. *tormentour* = OF. *tor-*, *tourmenteur*, earlier *-teour*, *-teor* (*c* 1150 in Godef.):—L. type **tormentātōr-em*, agent-n. from *tormentāre* to TORMENT.] One who or that which torments.

1. An officer who inflicts torture or cruelty; an official torturer; an executioner. Also *transf.*

c **1290** *St. Edmund* 43 in *S. Eng. Leg.* I. 298 His luþere tormentores þat beoten him so sore. *a* **1350** *St. Andrew* 171 in Horstm. *Altengl. Leg.* (1881) 6 þe turmentours..Toke his bodi with bitter brayde, Vnto þe cros þai gun it bend. **1382** WYCLIF *Matt.* xviii. 34 His lord wroth, tok hym to tourmenturs [**1388** turmentouris; **1582** (Rhem.) tormenters; **1611** tormentors], til that he paiede al the dette. **1483** CAXTON *Gold. Leg.* 185b/2 The tormentour as he had smyten of his heed both his eyen sterte out of his heed. **1513** MORE *Rich. III* (1883) 79 He that playeth the sowdayne is percase a sowter. Yet if one should..calle him by his owne name.., one of his tormentors might hap to breake his [= one's] head. **1581** PETTIE *Guazzo's Civ. Conv.* I. (1586) 25 Such, who..are holden for infamous, as Sergeants, Hangmen, Tormentours. **1895** RIDER HAGGARD *Hrt. of World* xxv, That your souls be handed over to the tormentors of the under-world.

2. One who or that which persistently inflicts intense pain, suffering, vexation, or annoyance.

In quot. 1642 *humorously*: = TEASER[1] 2.

1553 BECON *Reliques of Rome* (1563) 199 They dissent both in the tormentours and in the tormentes of the soules. **1593** SHAKS. *Rich. II*, II. i. 136 These words heereafter, thy tormentors bee. **1642** MILTON *Apol. Smect.* Pref., Wks. 1851 III. 274 Certainly this tormentor of Semicolons is as good at dismembring and slitting sentences. **1712** ADDISON *Spect.* No. 447 ¶10 They will naturally become their own Tormentors. **1751** *Affecting Narr. of Wager* 84 The Prospect of that horridest Tormenter, Famine, [was] continually before our Eyes. **1846** J. BAXTER *Libr. Pract. Agric.* (ed. 4) I. 419 A host of tormentors, in the shape of flies,..persecuting the poor animal. **1897** 'OUIDA' *Massarenes* viii, The person whose instructress and tormentor she was.

3. An instrument that torments in some way. †**a.** Some device for catching fleas. *Obs.* **b.** *pl.* A long-handled fork used for taking the meat from the coppers on board ship; also, *Sc.* 'an implement on which to toast bannocks, etc.' (*E.D.D.*); in quot. 1866 (*sing.*), a piercing implement carried by excise officers. **c.** A wheel-harrow of which each tine is a small share or hoe, for breaking up stiff soil. **d.** *pl.* A slang name for riding-spurs. **e.** *Theatre.* (See quots.) **f.** A device used to annoy at pleasure-fairs (freq. a device for squirting liquid): cf. TICKLER 2b, SCRATCH-BACK 2. *colloq.*

a. **1609** HEYWOOD *Rape of Lucrece*, *Cries of Rome* Wks. 1874 V. 254 Buy a very fine Mouse-trap, or a tormentor for your Fleaes. **1614** B. JONSON *Barth. Fair* II. iv. *a* **1619** FLETCHER *Bonduca* II. iii, *Daughter.* Are they not our Tormentors? *Car.* Tormentors? flea-traps! **1622** J. TAYLOR (Water P.) *Trav. Twelve-pence* (1635) Bvij b, Of Mowse Traps, and tormentors to kill Fleas.

b. **1706** E. WARD *Wooden World Diss.* (1708) 84 He [a sea-cook] is never without a Pair of Tormentors in his Hand. **1823** GALT *Gilhaize* I. ii. 22 Toasting an oaten bannock on a pair of tormentors. **1866** FITZPATRICK *Sham Sqr.* 18 Sham made a violent pass at Peck with his tormentor. **1898** F. T. BULLEN *Cruise Cachalot* 186 The cook uncovered his coppers, plunged his tormentors therein, and produced such a succession of ugly corpses of fowls as I had never seen before.

c. **1807** VANCOUVER *Agric. Devon* (1813) 121 Scarifiers, scufflers, shims, and broad-shares of various constructions, ..called under the general name of tormentors. **1882** JAGO *Cornw. Gloss.*, *Tormentor*, an agricultural implement for breaking up the clods of a ploughed field.

d. **1875** WHYTE MELVILLE *Riding Recoll.* iv. (1879) 59 Fordham..wholly repudiates 'the tormentors', arguing that they only make a horse shorten his stride, and 'shut up'.

e. **1886** *Stage Gossip* 70 The 'tormentor' is the name for a door, placed in the R.I.E. and L.I.E., and which prevents anybody from obtaining a view of the performance from either of the entrances named, and also prevents the actor being seen by the 'house'—these doors are annoying at times. **1893** *N. York Herald* 25 Dec. 26/2 (Funk) The first wing has been known to the stage as 'tormentor' wing from time whereof memory of man runneth not to the contrary. **1898** *Westm. Gaz.* 12 Jan. 9/3 A strip of white bunting is waved by a master of the ceremonies from a wooden hutch in the 'tormentor' wing.

f. **1891** in *Cent. Dict.* **1903** FARMER & HENLEY *Slang Dict.*, *Tormentor*..3 (common), a back-scratcher. **1894** A. MORRISON *Tales of Mean Streets* 34 The ladies' tormentors are larger, and their contents smell worse than at any other fair. *Ibid.* 36 Billy bought a ladies' tormentor and began to squirt it at Lizerunt. **1912** J. MASEFIELD *Widow in Bye St.* 19 One's so safe with such a son to con her Through all the noises and through all the press, Boys daredn't squirt tormenters on her dress.

†**tor'mentous**, *a. Obs. rare.* [f. L. *torment-um* TORMENT + -OUS: cf. OF. *tormentos.*] Of tormenting nature; torturing. Hence †**tor'mentously** *adv.*

1583 STOCKER *Civ. Warres Lowe C.* II. 47 His body being trysed vp into the ayre with a tormentous [*printed* tormentrous] Engine, they bynd to his feete instruments of Yron. **1657** THORNLEY tr. *Longus' Daphnis & Chloe* 195 Astylus was not to learn that Love was a tormentous fire. **1669** *Address Hopeful Yng. Gentry Eng.* 87 Why so tormentously [do they] rend their weary throats?

So †**tor'mentuous** *a.* [ad. late L. *tormentuōsus.*]

1597 J. PAYNE *Royal Exch.* 44 So ys yt a moste bitter and tormentuouse estate to such as love not to gethers. **1860** MAYNE *Expos. Lex.*, *Tormentuosus*, having or full of racking pains: tormentuous.

tormentress (tɔːˈmɛntrɪs). [a. AF. *tormenteresse*, fem. of *tormentour* TORMENTOR.] A female tormentor.

1426 LYDG. *De Guil. Pilgr.* 11691 A gret turmenteresse Wych doth to ffolk fful gret dystresse. **1601** HOLLAND *Pliny* XXVIII. iv. II. 301 Fortune..ordinarily commeth after..as the scourge and tormentresse of glorie and honour. **1895** R. Y. TYRRELL *Latin Poetry* 103 He [Catullus]..breaks down in a wild burst of rage against his tormentress.

'tormentry. [a. OF. *tourmenterie* (1427 in Godef.), office of a tormentor or executioner, f. *tormenteur* TORMENTOR: see -RY.]

†**1.** A company or body of tormentors or executioners. *Obs.* [Cf. *Jewry*, *yeomanry*.]

a **1350** *St. Andrew* 108 in Horstm. *Altengl. Leg.* (1881) 5 Egeas þan..Sent efter al his turmentry, And bad þam.. ordan a cros. *Ibid.* 208 Both he and al his turmentri.

†**2.** The infliction or suffering of torture or torment, as by executioners or fiends. *Obs.*

1375 *XI Pains of Hell* 159 in *O.E. Misc.* 215 A sorouful syȝt, a hore hold mon, Be-twene iiij fyndis in turmentre. *c* **1412** HOCCLEVE *De Reg. Princ.* 2825 He snybbed is, and put to tormentrie. **1534** MORE *Comf. agst. Trib.* III. xvii. (1847) 253 All the tormentry that the devil..could devise.

3. Tormenting feeling; severe suffering, pain, or vexation. Now *rare.*

c **1386** CHAUCER *Wife's Prol.* 251 Thanne seistow it is a tormentrie To soffren hire pride and hire malencolie. **1434** MISYN *Mending of Life* i. 106 Ioy or turmentry we sal resayfe. **1509** FISHER *Serm. Funeral Hen. VII*, Wks. (1876) 279, I founde in them all but vanyte & turmentry of soule. **1885** R. F. BURTON *Arab. Nts.* III. 19 O joy of Hell and Heaven! whose tormentry enquickens frame and soul.

tormeryke, tormican, obs. ff. TURMERIC, PTARMIGAN.

‖**tormina** ('tɔːmɪnə), *sb. pl. Path.* [L. *tormina* gripes, griping of the bowels, pl. of **tormen*, for **torqmen*, f. *torquēre* to twist.] Acute griping or wringing pains in the bowels; gripes. Also *fig.*

1656 R. ROBINSON *Christ All* 106 They have not those tormina and gripings in their consciences which other Sinners have. **1658** PHILLIPS, *Torminous*, troubled with Tormina, i. gripings of the Belly. **1843** R. J. GRAVES *Syst. Clin. Med.* vi. 75 They have costive or irregular bowels, diarrhœa, tormina. **1866** A. FLINT *Princ. Med.* (1880) 413 Griping or colic pains which are called *tormina.*

Hence **'torminal**, †**'torminous** *adjs.*, of the nature of or characterized by tormina; †affected with tormina.

1656 BLOUNT *Glossogr.*, *Torminous*,..that frets the guts, or that hath torments and frettings in the guts. **1666** G. HARVEY *Morb. Angl.* x. 85 A torminous diarrhé. **1822–34** *Good's Study Med.* I. 198 A few slight torminal pains.

tormit, dial. form of TURNIP.

tormodont ('tɔːmədɒnt), *a. Ornith.* [f. Gr. τόρμο-ς hole, socket + ὀδούς, ὀδοντ- tooth.] Of a tooth or teeth: Set each in a separate socket or alveolus, as in certain fossil birds; of a bird: having socketed teeth.

1888 GADOW in *Nature* 20 Dec. 178/2 Ichthyornis and Apatornis..differ from recent Carinate birds in degree only, viz. by their tormodont teeth and amphicœlous vertebræ.

tormoyl, -e, obs. forms of TURMOIL.

torn (tɔːn), *ppl. a.* [pa. pple. of TEAR *v.*[1], q.v. for Forms.] **a.** Rent or riven by being pulled violently asunder; wearing torn garments.

1362 LANGL. *P. Pl.* A. v. 111 In A toren Tabart of twelue Wynter Age. *c* **1425** *Cast. Persev.* 109 in *Macro Plays* 80 þer schal com a lythyr ladde with a torne hod. **1552** HULOET, Torne garmentes, *lacides.* *a* **1631** DONNE *Hymn to Christ* I In what torne shipp soever I embark. **1693** DRYDEN *Juvenal*

I. 159 Tho born a Slave, tho my torn Ears are bor'd. ?*a* **1750** *Nursery Rime, 'House that Jack Built'* viii, This is the man all tattered and torn, That kissed the maiden all forlorn. **1818** SCOTT *Rob Roy* xxxiii, A rent and torn ravine resembling a deserted watercourse. **1839** DARWIN *Voy. Nat.* x. (1873) 210 Masses of rock and torn-up trees. **1860** READE *Cloister & H.* lxxi, The poor torn, worn creature wept. **1861** J. BARR *Poems* 119 (E.D.D.) Like some torn-doun play actor, That had sung for his bread thro' a fair.

b. *spec. Bot.*: see quots.; also in comb.

[**1760** J. LEE *Introd. Bot.* (1776) 384 *Lacerum*, lacerate, where the Margin is variously divided, as if torn.] **1888** *Cassell's Encycl. Dict.*, *Torn*,.. *Bot.*, irregularly divided by deep incisions. **1895** *Funk's Standard Dict.*, *Torn-crenate*, *Bot.*, crenate by a torn margin.

c. In combination with adverbs, as ***torn-off***, ***-out***, ***-up***; also **torn-down**: (*a*) that has been rent or pulled down; (*b*) *fig.* rough, riotous, boisterous, disorderly (*dial.* and *U.S.*); reduced in circumstances (*Sc.* and *dial.*); also *sb.*, a rough riotous person.

1870 W. M. BAKER *New Timothy* xxxii. (U.S.). **1877–88** in *N.W. Linc. Gloss.* **1886** in *S.W. Linc. Gloss.* **1933** S. SPENDER *Poems* 40 Through torn-down portions of old fabric. **1953** K. REISZ *Technique Film Editing* i. 35 Other fragments of the torn-down statue of the Czar reassembling.

torn, obs. f. TOURN (sheriff's court), TURN.

‖**tornada** (tor'nada). [Prov., from pa. pple. of *tornar* to turn.] An envoy of three lines, in which the verse-endings of all the preceding stanzas recur.

[Cf. Littré, *Tornade*, se dit, dans les chansons provençales, de la ritournelle.]

1823 ROSCOE *Sismondi's Lit. Eur.* (1846) I. vi. 173 The songs are usually in seven stanzas, followed by an envoy, which he calls a tornada. **1874** BREYMANN in *Ess. Owens Coll. Manch.* xi. 384 The Troubadours borrowed from the Saracens several of their poetical forms as, for instance, the Tornada. **1880** [see ENVOY *sb.*[1] 1].

†**tor'nade.** *Obs. rare.* Also 7 **tornathe.** Anglicized form of TORNADO.

1638 Tornathe [see TORNADO 1]. **1727** BAILEY vol. II, *Tornade*, a sudden and violent Gust of Wind or Storm. **1813** SCOTT *Rokeby* I. viii, Inured to danger's direst form, Tornade and earthquake, flood and storm.

tornadic (tɔː'nædɪk), *a.* [f. next + -IC.] Of, pertaining to, or of the nature of a tornado.

1884 *Amer. Meteorol. Jrnl.* I. 7 Four series of storms of tornadic character have passed over the states east of the Mississippi River since the beginning of the year. **1890** *Columbus* (Ohio) *Dispatch* 13 June, These are tornadic conditions. **1898** H. W. LUCY in *Daily News* 18 Feb. 2/2 Mr. Orchardson's portrait..presenting the ex-Speaker in one of his not unfamiliar tornadic moods.

tornado (tɔː'neɪdəʊ). Forms: (6–7 **ternado**), 7– **tornado**; also 7–8 **turnado**, (7 **tornatho**, **tornada**, 8 **tournado**). See also TORNADE. [In Hakluyt and his contemporaries, *ternado*; from Purchas 1625 onward, *turnado*, *tournado*, *tornado*. In none of these forms does the word exist in Spanish or Portuguese. But the early sense makes it probable that *ternado* was a bad adaptation (perh. orig. a blundered spelling) of Sp. *tronada* 'thunderstorm' (f. *tronar* to thunder), and that *tornado* was an attempt to improve it by treating it as a derivative of Sp. *tornar* to turn, return; cf. *tornado* pple., returned. It is notable that this spelling is identified with explanations in which, not the thunder, but the turning, shifting, or whirling winds are the main feature. This is emphasized in the variants *turnado*, *tournado*. Mod.F. *tornado* is from Eng. (not Portuguese, as in Littré).]

1. A term applied by 16th c. navigators to violent thunderstorms of the tropical Atlantic, with torrential rain, and often with sudden and violent gusts of wind. Now *rare* or passing into 2.

1556 W. TOWERSON in Hakluyt *Voy.* (1589) 100 The 4.day we had terrible thunder and lightning, with exceeding great gusts of raine, called Ternados. **1599** HAKLUYT *Voy.* II. II. 103 We had nothing but Ternados, with such thunder, lightning, and raine, that we could not keep our men drie. **1600** *Ibid.* III. 719 The ternados, that is thundrings and lightnings. **1634** SIR T. HERBERT *Trav.* 216 We crost the Æquator, where we had too many Tornathoes [*ed.* **1638**, 355 wee were pesterd with continuall Tornathes; a variable weather compos'd of lowd blasts, stinking showers, and terrible thunders; *ed.* **1677**, 393 Tornado's]. **1697** DAMPIER *Voy. round World* (1699) 31 We had fine weather while we lay here [an. 1681], only some Tornadoes or Thunder-showers. **1727** A. HAMILTON *New Acc. E. Ind.* II. xliv. 140 The Coast is subject to frequent Tornadoes, or Squalls of Wind and Rain, introduced with much Thunder and Lightning. **1788** J. MATTHEWS *Voy.* iii. (1791) 30 Had at least one tornado every twenty-four hours, which are always attended with violent gusts of wind, thunder, lightning, and excessive rain; but which greatly purify the air. **1832** G. DOWNES *Lett. Cont. Countries* I. 71 The return of the storm, swooping down in its various elements of thunder, lightning, and rain, with all the fierce grandeur of an Alpine tornado.

†**b.** *transf.* Chiefly in *pl.* The season at which such storms are prevalent. *Obs. rare.*

In quot. 1657 perh. associated with the 'turning' of the sun at the tropic.

1634 SIR T. HERBERT *Trav.* 5 Nor is this weather rare about the Æquinoctiall; by Mariners termed the Tornadoes: and tis so vncertaine, that now you shall haue a quiet breath and gale, and suddenly an vnexpected violent gust. **1657** R. LIGON *Barbadoes* (1673) 9 The time of our stay there, being the Turnado, when the Sun..became Zenith to the Inhabitants. **1698** FRYER *Acc. E. India & P.* 10 These Seasons the Seamen term the *Tornados.*

2. A very violent storm (now without implication of thunder), affecting a limited area, in which the wind is constantly changing its direction or rotating; a whirling wind, whirlwind; loosely, any very violent storm of wind, a hurricane. *spec.* **a.** On the west coast of Africa, a rotatory storm in which the wind revolves violently under a moving arch of clouds; **b.** In the Mississippi region of U.S., a destructive rotatory storm under a funnel-shaped cloud like a water-spout, which advances in a narrow path over the land for many miles.

(Quot. 1625 shows the transition from 1 to 2.)

[**1625** PURCHAS *Pilgrims* II. IX. vi. §1. 1463 We met with winds which the Mariners call The Turnadoes, so variable and vncertaine, that sometime within the space of one houre, all the two and thirtie seuerall winds will blow. These winds were accompanied with much thunder and lightning, and with extreme rayne.] **1626** CAPT. SMITH *Accid. Yng. Seamen* 17 A gust, a storme, a spoute, a loume gaile, an eddy wind, a flake of wind, a Turnado. **1656** BLOUNT *Glossogr.*, *Tornado*, (from the Span. *Tornada, i.* a returne, or turning about) is a sudden, violent and forcible storme of raine and ill weather at sea, so termed by the Mariners; and does most usually happen about the Æquator. **1688** R. HOLME *Armoury* II. 23/1 A Turnado [is] a fierce Wind. **1693** SIR T. P. BLOUNT *Nat. Hist.* 434 The Tornados are variable Winds, call'd in the Portugal Language Travados. **1710** J. HARRIS *Lex. Techn.* II, *Tornado*, is the Name given by the Seamen for a violent Storm of Wind, and sometimes followed by Rain; it usually swifts or turns about to almost all Points of the Compass, whence I suppose its name. **1719** DE FOE *Crusoe* I. 47 When a violent Tournado or Hurricane took us quite out of our Knowledge. **1727** [DORRINGTON] *Philip Quarll* 51 Several Storms and Turnadoes. **1755** JOHNSON, *Tornado*, a hurricane, a whirlwind. **1760–72** tr. *Juan & Ulloa's Voy.* (ed. 3) I. 13 From what quarter these tornadoes or squalls proceed, I cannot positively affirm. **1770** GOLDSM. *Des. Vill.* 357 While oft in whirls the mad tornado flies. **1788** COWPER *Negro's Compl.* 33 Hark! He answers—Wild tornadoes..Wasting towns, plantations, meadows. **1815** J. SMITH *Panorama Sc. & Art* II. 45 This tract is subject to frequent calms, and to sudden gusts of winds called tornadoes which blow from all points of the horizon. **1849** COL. HAWKER *Diary* (1893) II. 296 The gale increased to an absolute tornado.

b. 1849 LYELL *2nd Visit U.S.* (1850) II. 199 This tornado checked the progress of Natchez, as did the removal of the seat of Legislature to Jackson. **1883** *Encycl. Brit.* XVI. 130/1 The region of most frequent occurrence of tornadoes is the region where a large number of the cyclones of the United States appear to originate. *Ibid.* 130/2 The wind of the tornado reaches a velocity probably never equalled in cyclones.

c. *fig.*; cf. *tempest*, *storm*, *whirlwind*.

1818 LADY MORGAN *Autobiog.* (1859) 28 We live in a sort of tornado between business and pleasure, and my head literally turns round. **1840** THACKERAY *Pict. Rhapsody* Wks. 1900 XIII. 334 Beneath one of Turner's magnificent tornadoes of colour. **1849** CLOUGH *Bothie* I. 156 On this passage followed a great tornado of cheering. **1863** COWDEN CLARKE *Shaks. Char.* xvii. 416 The tornado of the north—Harry Percy, most commonly surnamed 'Hotspur'.

3. *attrib.* and *Comb.*, as ***tornado cloud***, ***mood***, ***night***, ***oath***, ***pitch***, ***rain***, ***spirit***, ***wind***; ***tornado-breeding***, ***-haunted*** adjs.; **tornado-cellar**, **-pit**, an underground place of refuge from tornadoes (in sense 2b); a cyclone-pit; **tornado-funnel**: see 2b; **tornado-lamp**, **tornado-lantern**, a hurricane-lamp, storm-lantern.

1861 H. ANGUS *Serm.* 150 The death-distilling, *tornado-breeding atmospheric stagnation of the tropics. **1899** MARY KINGSLEY *W. Afr. Stud.* ii. 48 If..you see that well-known *tornado-cloud arch coming..the sooner you get her [the ship] ready to run, the better. **1896** *Westm. Gaz.* 28 Dec. 7/1 Her ascent..to the bleak summit of a *tornado-haunted volcano. **1897** *Dublin Rev.* Oct. 299 Saner counsels prevailed over Gordon's *tornado mood. **1897** MARY KINGSLEY *W. Africa* 312 Particularly vigilant has he got to be on *tornado nights. *Ibid.* 396 When the wet season's *tornado rain comes down on it. **1863** COWDEN CLARKE *Shaks. Char.* xiii. 330 His *tornado spirit hurries him at once into a quarrel with the Duke of Austria. **1669** *Phil. Trans.* IV. 1003 These North-East-Winds hold most commonly to 8 degrees North-Latitude, and then begin the *Tornado Winds. **1671** R. BOHUN *Wind* 236 So variable and unsteady are the Tornado-winds, so little obliged to any certain law.

Hence **tor'nadoish** *a.* [-ISH[1]]. (*nonce-wd.*)

1889 *Columbus* (Ohio) *Dispatch* 16 Jan., Its [a storm's] powerful warm, wet, tornadoish right, and cold, snowy, blizzardy left hand.

tornadoed (tɔː'neɪdəʊd), *ppl. a. nonce-wd.* [f. TORNADO + -ED[2].] Affected by tornadoes. (In quot. *fig.*)

1851 H. MELVILLE *Moby Dick* III. i. 19 Even so, amid the tornadoed Atlantic of my being, do I myself still for ever centrally disport in mute calm.

tornal: see TORNUS.

tornament, obs. f. TOURNAMENT, TORMENT.

‖**tornaria** (tɔː'nɛərɪə). *Zool.* [mod.L., f. Gr. τόρν-ος or L. *torn-us* a turner's wheel, in reference to the shape of the larva.] The larval form of species of the Sea-acorn, *Balanoglossus*. Hence **tor'narian** *a.*, of or pertaining to a tornaria.

1888 ROLLESTON & JACKSON *Anim. Life* 592 Tornaria requires a fresh examination... Balfour regarded Tornaria as intermediate in structure between the Echinoderm larva and the Trochosphere. **1891** *Cent. Dict.*, Tornarian. **1892** THOMSON *Outl. Zool.* xvi. 355 The Tornaria becomes pelagic, acquires a proboscis, loses its special bands of cilia, and becomes diffusely ciliated, but has not yet a mouth or anus.

†**'tornatil**, *a. Obs. rare*$^{-0}$. [ad. L. *tornātil-is* turned in a lathe.] (See quot.)

1661 BLOUNT *Glossogr.* (ed. 2), *Tornatil* (*tornatilis*), that is turned, or made with a wheel.

tornay, obs. form of TOURNEY.

‖**torne** (tɔːn). *Obs.* [MLG., LG. *torn* = MDu., Du. *tōren*, MHG. *turn*, Ger. *turm.*] A tower.

1637 R. MONRO *Exped.* II. 80 Their Leaders..pursued the enemy so hard, till they had beaten them out of a *Torne*, they had fled unto. [**1871** WADDELL *Isa.* xxix. 4 (*pseudoarch.*) Tornes I sal bigg fornenst yo.]

torne, obs. f. TORN, TOURN, TURN.

torneament, **tornebroche**, obs. ff. TOURNAMENT, TURNBROACH.

tornel, **-elle**, var. TOURNELLE *Obs.*

tornement(e, obs. ff. TOURNAMENT, TORMENT.

tornepyke, **torner**, obs. ff. TURNPIKE, TURNER.

‖**tornese** (tor'neze). Pl. **tornesi** (-'ezi). [It., = F. *tournois*, L. *turonens-is*, lit. (money) of Tours. Cf. TOURNOIS.] An obsolete subsidiary coin of the Two Sicilies, $\frac{1}{300}$ of a ducat.

torne-seke, **tornesol(e**, **-solt**, obs. forms of TURN-SICK, TURNSOLE.

†**torney.** *Obs.* exc. *dial.* Aphetic f. ATTORNEY.

1490 *Acc. St. Dunstan's, Canterb.* (1885) 13 Payde for one torneys labor ij s... the recorde of the torney ij d.

torney, obs. form of TOURNEY.

tornhexactine (tɔːnhɛk'sæktaɪn, -ɪn). *Zool.* [f. Gr. τόρν-ος turner's wheel + HEXACTINE.] A six-rayed sponge-spicule in which the rays are abruptly pointed.

1909 in *Cent. Dict. Suppl.*

tornil, obs. form of TURNEL.

‖**tor'nillo**, **tor'nilla.** *U.S.* [Sp. *tornillo* screw, dim. of *torno* turn.] A tree, the screw-pod mesquite (*Prosopis pubescens*) of Texas, New Mexico, and California.

1866 *Treas. Bot.* 930 The Tornillo of the Sonora Mexicans. **1891** in *Cent. Dict.*

tornit, obs. Sc. f. *turned*, pa. pple. of TURN *v.*

tornly ('tɔːnlɪ), *adv. rare*$^{-0}$. [f. TORN *ppl. a.* + -LY[2].] In a torn condition, raggedly, in pieces.

1548–67 THOMAS *Ital. Dict.*, *Squarsiatamente*, toarnely, or peacemeale.

'tornote, *sb.* (*a.*) *Zool.* [ad. Gr. τορνωτ-ός adj. rounded with the τόρνος (see TORNUS).] A form of sponge-spicule: see quot.

1888 SOLLAS in *Challenger Rep.* XXV. p. lv, When the rhabdas is very abruptly pointed at each end a *rhabdus amphitornota* results, which we shall call a 'tornote'.

tornour, **tornoye**, obs. ff. TURNER, TOURNEY.

tornsell, **-sole**, obs. forms of TURNSOLE.

‖**tornus** ('tɔːnəs). *Entom.* Pl. **-i** (-aɪ). [L. *tornus* turner's wheel or lathe, a. Gr. τόρνος a tool for rounding.] The inner or anal angle of the wing of an insect, esp. of the secondary wing of a tineid moth. Hence **'tornal** *a.*, of or pertaining to the tornus.

1897 LD. WALSINGHAM in *Proc. Zool. Soc.* 19 Jan. 76 A creamy-ochreous dorsal streak..runs from the base through the tornal cilia. *Ibid.* 96 The apical and tornal angles of the cell;..cilia with a slight ochreous tinge about the tornus. **1904** SIR G. F. HAMPSON in *Annals & Mag. Nat. Hist.* Sept. 176 Hind wing..a fiery red stigma on termen near tornus.

toro ('tɔːrəʊ, ‖'toro). [Sp.] A bull used in bullfighting. Also, a child's bullfighting game.

1660 in T. Mathews *Collection of Lett.* 172 But, in a word, me-thinks, that not onely in their sports of Cannas and Toros, but even in some more solemn and serious things than those, they are not free from having still somewhat of the Moor. **1846** R. FORD *Gatherings from Spain* xxi. 291 The young urchins in the streets play at '*toro*', as ours do at leap-frog. **1932** R. CAMPBELL *Taurine Provence* 66 Novillos (bulls that are full grown but lack the ultimate footsureness of the toros). **1958** L. VAN DER POST *Lost World Kalahari* i. 29 The rhinoceros, angry like a pricked toro with the rosette of blood that comes to it in adolescence vivid on the flank. **1967** MCCORMICK & MASCAREÑAS *Compl. Aficionado* i. 4 He might be compared to the actor but for the fact that he writes his own script, in collaboration with the *toro*.

toroid ('tɒrɔɪd). [f. TOR(US + -OID.] An object having the shape of a torus (sense 4); a toroidal object.

1886 G. S. CARR *Synopsis Elem. Results Pure & Applied Math.* I. II. 932/1 (Index), Toroid. **1903** *Astrophysical Jrnl.* XVIII. 339 Each reflecting surface.. would be part of a parabolic toroid. **1916** G. KAPP *Princ. Electr. Engin.* I. xi. 211 The term 'toroid' in this connection means a circular coil of *n* turns of wire wound so that the cross-section is a circle. **1954** *Electronic Engin.* XXVI. 196 Magnetic toroids could.. be used.. for random access information storage at the rate of one core per digit. **1973** *Nature* 15 June 386/2 This field is supplemented by an additional field produced by a coil wound on the toroid.

to'roidal, *a. Geom.* [f. L. TOR-US + -OIDAL.] Resembling or pertaining to a torus (TORUS 4). Also = TORIC *a.*

1881 *Phil. Trans. R. Soc.* CLXXII. 609 By 'toroidal functions' are understood functions which satisfy Laplace's equation and which are suitable for conditions given over the surface of tores. **1889** *Cent. Dict.* s.v. *Function, Toroidal function*, a function serving to express the potential of an anchor-ring. **1895** *Scotsman* 3 Dec. 4/6 Professor Tait made a communication on, 'The application of net-work to a surface, in particular to a toroidal surface'. **1946** [see POLOIDAL *a.*]. **1948** *Electronic Engin.* XX. 28 The problem.. was solved by using a very few turns of concentrically wound copper tape and achieving the necessary self-inductance by winding on a high permeability toroidal core. **1962** CORSON & LORRAIN *Introd. Electromagn. Fields* v. 200 (*caption*) Toroidal coil of square cross section carrying a current *I*. **1973** *Sci. Amer.* Aug. 111/1 Optical surfaces are far from spherical these days; even our spectacle lenses are toroidal. **1975** *New Yorker* 12 May 84/2 Wind instruments were bolted to a toroidal buoy.

Hence **to'roidally** *adv.*

1961 *Technology* Mar. 72/1 A variable-ratio toroidally-wound transformer. **1970** *Nature* 26 Sept. 1299/1 Toroidally contained fusion plasmas. **1978** *Gramophone* Aug. 396/3 To the right of the PCB is a massive, toroidally wound mains transformer.

Torontonian (tɒrɒn'təʊnɪən), *sb.* [f. *Toronto*, capital of the province of Ontario in Canada + *-n-* + -IAN.] A native or inhabitant of Toronto.

1875 *United Service Mag.* Dec. 500 'No great thing after all!' exclaimed a Quebecker or Torontonian. **1967** *Economist* 29 July 396/3 Torontonians are often suspected of believing that money decides everything. **1975** *Globe & Mail* (Toronto) 16 July 7/3 Many Torontonians are probably not aware of the Western Guard's propaganda.

torope: see TERRAPIN[1].

‖**Torosaurus** (tɒrəʊ'sɔːrəs). *Palæont.* [mod.L., f. stem of Gr. τορός adj. piercing, τόρος borer (f. τείρειν to pierce) + σαῦρος lizard.] A genus of horned dinosaurs, occurring in the Laramie formation in U.S.

1891 MARSH in *Amer. Jrnl. Sc.* XLII. 266. **1892** *Ibid.* XLIII. 82 The open perforations in the parietal which have suggested the name *Torosaurus*. **1908** *Daily Chron.* 20 Feb. 4/6 The largest skull of any known land animal,.. is the skull of a new horned dinosaur, the torosaurus, and is 8 ft. 6 in. long and 5 ft. 8 in. across.

torose (tɒ'rəʊs), *a. Nat. Hist.* [ad. L. *torōs-us*, f. *torus* bulge, brawn: see -OSE.] Bulging, swollen, protuberant: said of an approximately cylindrical body swollen here and there.

1760 J. LEE *Introd. Bot.* III. xxii. (1765) 229 The *Pericarpium* is.. torose. **1785** MARTYN *Rousseau's Bot.* xxiii. (1794) 322 Radish has a cylindric, jointed, torose or swelling silique. **1829** LOUDON *Encycl. Plants* (1836) 461 Caps[ules] subglobose torose hispid.

So †**to'rosity** *Obs. rare*[−0], torose condition.

1656 BLOUNT *Glossogr.*, *Torosity* (*torositas*), fleshiness, fatnesse, brawninesse. **1727** BAILEY vol. II, *Torosity*, Fatness, Grossness.

torous ('tɔərəs), *a.* [ad. L. *torōs-us* TOROSE, as if through a F. **toreux*: see -OUS.] = TOROSE.

1657 R. CARPENTER *Astrol.* 35 The solid and succous body of Divinity still grows more and more torous and quadrangular. **1684** tr. *Bonet's Merc. Compit.* v. 139 Whole torous Muscles, and long tendons. **1828** WEBSTER, *Torous*, in botany, protuberant; swelling in knobs, like the veins and muscles; as, a torous pericarp.

tor-ouzel: see TOR *sb.* 3.

torp (tɔːp), slang abbrev. of TORPEDO *sb.* 2 and *torpedo juice* s.v. TORPEDO *sb.* 6. Cf. TORPS.

1929 *Papers Mich. Acad. Sci., Arts & Lett.* X. 330 *Torp*, a torpedo. **1945** J. BRYAN *Diary* 23 Apr. in *Aircraft Carrier* (1954) 193 Someone brought a pint of torp. **1967** B. KNOX *Blacklight* ii. 42 If anyone does find a stray torp, then they'll make damn' sure it stays lost.

†**torpedinal** (tɔː'piːdɪnəl), *a. Obs. rare.* [f. L. *torpēdin-em*, TORPEDO + -AL[1].] Of or pertaining to the torpedo or electric ray.

1772 WALSH in *Phil. Trans.* LXIII. 465 The vigour of the fresh taken Torpedos at the Isle of Ré, was not able to force the torpedinal fluid across the minutest tract of air. *Ibid.*, Notwithstanding the weak spring of the torpedinal electricity, I was able.. to convey it through a circuit, formed from one surface of the animal to the other, by two long brass wires, and four persons. **1800** *Med. Jrnl.* IV. 118 He.. offers his own new and striking apparatus as more nearly resembling the torpedinal organ.

torpedineer (tɔːpiːdɪ'nɪə(r)). *rare.* [f. as prec. + -EER[1]: cf. *engineer.*] One who is engaged in the management of marine torpedoes.

1881 *Times* 18 Jan. 4/1 The young Prince of Naples, in the sailor's dress of his rank as corporal of Torpedineers.. was on the bridge.

torpedinoid (tɔː'piːdɪnɔɪd), *a. Zool.* [f. as prec. + -OID.] Of the form or kind of the torpedo or electric ray; belonging to the *Torpedinoidea* or *Torpedinidæ* considered as a group distinct from the true rays and the saw-fishes.

torpedinous (tɔː'piːdɪnəs), *a. rare.* ? *Obs.* [f. as prec. + -OUS.] Having the quality of a torpedo; benumbing, paralysing; also = TORPEDINAL.

1774 PRINGLE *Torpedo* 23 Nor in this circumstance only did the similitude between the electric and torpedinous fluids appear. **1845** DE QUINCEY *Coleridge & Opium-eat.* Wks. 1859 XII. 92 First came Dr. Andrew Bell.. Fishy were his eyes; torpedinous was his manner.

torpedism, -ist: see after TORPEDO *sb.*

torpedo (tɔː'piːdəʊ), *sb.* Also 6 -ido. Pl. -oes. [a. L. *torpēdo* stiffness, numbness, also the cramp-fish or electric ray, f. *torpēre* to be stiff or numb; = Sp., Pg. *torpedo*, It. *torpedine*. Cf. F. *torpille*, It. *torpiglia* from the same verb.]

1. a. A flat fish of the genus *Torpedo* or family *Torpedinidæ*, having an almost circular body with tapering tail, and characterized by the faculty of emitting electric discharges; the electric ray; also called *cramp-fish*, *cramp-ray*, *numb-fish*.

c **1520** L. ANDREWE *Noble Lyfe* xcii. in *Babees Bk.* (1868) 239 Torpido is a fisshe, but who-so handeleth hym shalbe lame & defe of lymmes that he shall fele no thyng. **1589** R. HARVEY *Pl. Perc.* (1860) 13 Like the fish Torpedo, which being towchd sends her venime alongst line and angle rod, till it cease on the finger, and so mar a fisher for euer. **1603** SIR C. HEYDON *Jud. Astrol.* xxiii. 547 Neither doth the Torpedo benumme other things, though it benummeth the fishers hand. **1646** SIR T. BROWNE *Pseud. Ep.* III. vii. 119 Torpedoes deliver their opium at a distance, and stupifie beyond themselves. **1772** *Chron.* in *Ann. Reg.* Nov. 136/1 Mr. Walsh touched the back of the torpedo; when all the five persons.. felt a shock at the same instant, which differed in nothing from the Leyden experiment. **1815** J. SMITH *Panorama Sc. & Art* II. 253 The torpedo is a flat fish, of the ray tribe, very seldom exceeding twenty inches in length, and twenty pounds in weight... It inhabits the Mediterranean and the North Seas. **1879** E. P. WRIGHT *Anim. Life* 465 The Torpedo (*T. vulgaris*), is found occasionally on the south coasts of England and Ireland.

b. *fig.* One who or that which has a benumbing influence.

1590 MARLOWE *Edw. II*, I. iv, Fair queen, forbear to angle for the fish.. I mean that vile torpedo, Gaveston. **1762** GOLDSM. *Nash* 34 He used to call a pen his torpedo whenever he grasped it, it numbed all his faculties. *c* **1855** B. S. HOLLIS *Hymn-bk. C'tess Huntingdon's Conn.* Pref., The torpedo of formality had benumbed the churches.

2. a. orig. A case charged with gunpowder designed to explode under water after a given interval so as to destroy any vessel in its immediate vicinity; later also, a self-propelled submarine missile, usually cigar-shaped, carrying an explosive which is fired by impact with its objective.

The original torpedo was a towed or drifting submarine mine, used to defend channels, harbours, and the like (*drifting* or *moored torpedo*); it was towed at an angle by means of a spar extending at right angles (*otter* or *towing torpedo*), or carried on a ram or projecting pole (*boom-*, *out-rigger-*, *spar-torpedo*).

1776 J. THACHER *Military Jrnl.* (1823) 75 Mr. Bushnell gave to his machine the name of American Turtle or Torpedo. **1807** (Aug. 14) W. IRVING *Salmag.* xiii. (1855) 135 A torpedo; by which the stoutest line-of-battle ship.. may be.. decomposed [i.e. blown up] in a twinkling. **1807** (Sept. 6) *Admiralty Secretary In-Lett.* No. 4353 (P.R.O.) A description of the machine invented by Mr. Robert Fulton for exploding under ships' bottoms and by him called the torpedo. **1810** FULTON *Torpedo War* (N.Y.) 4. **1868** *Daily News* 3 Nov., The particular kind of torpedo used on this occasion is an American invention, which was found very effective in the defence of the harbour of Charleston. **1877** KNIGHT *Dict. Mech.* s.v., The drifting torpedo.. is carried against the enemy's works or vessels by the current,.. the tide, or.. the wind... Anchored torpedoes are attached to mooring piles or anchors. **1880** *Standard* 29 Dec. 6/1 In 1777 a schooner was destroyed in the harbour of New London, Connecticut, by a drifting percussion torpedo.

b. See *aerial torpedo* s.v. AERIAL *a.* 5. Also without specifying adj.

1922 W. RALEIGH *War in Air* I. 467 The hope of using the torpedo, launched from the air, against ships which are sheltered and protected from naval attack, was never long absent from the minds of those who directed the activities of the Royal Naval Air Service. **1943** *Jane's Fighting Ships 1942* 5, 18 inch torpedoes are used by the torpedo bombers of the Fleet Air Arm.

3. a. *Milit.* A shell furnished with a percussion or friction device buried in the ground, which explodes when the ground is trodden upon; a petard. *U.S.* **b.** A toy consisting of fulminating powder and fine gravel wrapped in thin paper, which explodes when thrown on a hard surface. **c.** A cartridge exploded in an oil-well to cause a renewal or increase of the flow. *U.S.* (In use 1873: see *torpedoed* s.v. TORPEDO *v.*) **d.** A detonator placed on a railway line, as a fog-signal, etc. *U.S.*

1786 tr. *Beckford's Vathek* (1883) 127, I will spring mines of serpents and torpedos from beneath them, and we shall soon see the stand they will make against such an explosion. **1831** T. P. JONES *Convers. Chem.* xix. 197 Those dangerous playthings called torpedoes, which explode when thrown upon the floor, derive this property from some preparation of silver. **1877** KNIGHT *Dict. Mech.* s.v., Torpedoes for opening the fissures of oil-wells... 4. (*Railway.*) A cartridge placed on a rail to be exploded by a passing train. **1909** *Westm. Gaz.* 28 July 2/1 The use or abuse of Roman candles, paper-caps, display pieces, small crackers, or.. torpedoes.

4. *slang.* **a.** *U.S.* A professional gunman. **b.** A tablet or capsule of a narcotic drug.

1929 G. L. HOSTETTER *It's a Racket!* 241 *Torpedo*, a professional gunman or bomb tosser. **1940** R. CHANDLER *Farewell, my Lovely* xxxvi. 239 There's yellow cops and there's yellow torpedoes. **1971** *Go ask Alice* (1972) 28 He introduced me to torpedoes on Friday and Speed on Sunday. **1973** P. EVANS *Bodyguard Man* iii. 24 Ask Al Capone. Mention his torpedoes to most people and they conjure up mental sketches of middle-aged heavyweights. **1978** M. RUSSELL *Daylight Robbery* xv. 154 The phial.. contained more tablets... He tried to estimate how long.. it took a couple of the torpedoes to send him off.

5. = *torpedo-body*. Also, a car with such a body.

1909 *Daily Chron.* 13 Nov. 9/6 There is a general tendency.. to utilise the form of body known as the 'torpedo'. **1930** V. PALMER *Passage* III. i. 213 Another car coming! They.. watched with strained eyes as the dusty torpedo shot into view. **1968** *Compl. Encycl. Motorcars* 624 *Torpedo*,.. an open touring car with an unbroken line from bonnet to windscreen, and from windscreen right through to the back of the car, the seats being flush with the body sides. Bodies of this design began to appear in about 1910.

6. *attrib.* and *Comb.*; in sense 1, as ***torpedo-fish***, ***-ray***; esp. *fig.* in allusion to its benumbing power, as ***torpedo history***, ***narrative***, ***quality***, ***touch***; ***torpedo-like*** adv.; in sense 2, as ***torpedo armament***, ***bomber***, ***coxswain***, ***craft***, ***department***, ***flat*** (FLAT C. 10 b), *-fuse* (Knight *Dict. Mech.* 1877), ***gunner***, ***-instructor***, ***-launch***, ***plane***, ***room***, ***school***, ***ship***, ***-vessel***, ***-works***; ***torpedo-carrying***, ***-launching***, ***-proof***, ***-shaped*** adjs.; also **torpedo-anchor**, an anchor for mooring a stationary torpedo (Knight, 1877); **torpedo beard**, a pointed beard; **torpedo-body**, a motorcar body tapered at the ends; **torpedo-boom**, 'a spar bearing a torpedo on its upper end, the lower end swiveled and anchored to the bottom of the channel' (Knight, 1877); **torpedo-catcher**, (*a*) see quot. 1877; (*b*) a torpedo-boat catcher; **torpedo-cruiser**, a cruiser which serves also as a torpedo-boat; **torpedo destroyer**, a torpedo-boat destroyer (officially called simply 'a destroyer'); **torpedo director**, an instrument by which the direction for aiming a locomotive torpedo is determined; **torpedo-drag**, a cable with a grapple or drag for clearing a channel of torpedoes (Knight, 1877); **torpedo gun** = *torpedo-tube*; **torpedo juice** *slang*, intoxicating liquor extracted from torpedo fuel; any strong home-made alcoholic liquor; **torpedo-lieutenant**, a naval officer in charge of torpedoes; **torpedo man**, in the British navy, a man who has passed certain courses of training in torpedo-work, to whom a non-substantive rating is granted; (*U.S.*), one whose business is the clearing of oil-wells by means of torpedoes (see 3 c); **torpedo-net**, a steel-wire netting suspended round a ship on projecting booms as a protection against torpedoes; **torpedo-ram**, a ram (RAM *sb.*[1] 3 c) provided with torpedo-tubes; **torpedo-spar**, a spar rigged to a torpedo boat, to which a torpedo is attached; **torpedo-tube**, a kind of gun from which torpedoes are discharged by compressed air or gunpowder. See also TORPEDO BOAT.

1896 *Daily News* 4 Nov. 7/2 As to the *torpedo armament, it is instructive to quote Commander Bacon's words. **1899** SOMERVILLE & ROSS *Irish R.M.* 29 A saturnine young man with a black *torpedo beard. **1924** *Motor* 21 Oct. 630 (*caption*) A handsome *torpedo body, on a Voisin chassis, by H. J. Mulliner. **1930** *Flight* 16 May 535/2 The aircraft equipment consists of.. two flights of two-seater fleet *torpedo bombers. **1970** *Times* 24 Mar. 2/4 (*caption*) Using engine cylinders taken from an exhibit at the Imperial War Museum, the last air-worthy Swordfish torpedo bomber in the Royal Navy. **1922** W. RALEIGH *War in Air* I. 466 The *torpedo-carrying aeroplane or seaplane would outrival the submarine as a weapon of offence against enemy shipping. **1877** KNIGHT *Dict. Mech.*, **Torpedo-catcher*, a forked spar or boom extending under water, ahead of a vessel, to displace or explode torpedoes. **1888** *Encycl. Brit.* XXIII. 451/2 Special vessels, called 'torpedo catchers', are being built by most nations. **1903** *Windsor Mag.* XIX. 6/2 Speakin' as a *torpedo-coxswain,.. I presume we fall in. **1918** KIPLING *Land & Sea Tales* (1923) 107 If his torpedo-coxswain had ever allowed anyone to look there. **1885** *Times* 30 Apr. 10/6 The four first-class *torpedo craft which have hoisted the white ensign are being fitted with Nordenfelt guns. **1901** *Daily Graphic* 12 July 6 The *torpedo-cruiser Kapitan Sacken. **1896** *World* 12 Feb. 29/1 It would not cost us much—not so much, in the long run, as a single *torpedo-destroyer. **1899** *Westm. Gaz.* 8 Mar. 9/2 The torpedo destroyer instructional flotilla. **1825** J. NEAL *Bro. Jonathan* I. 29 Lying in wait like a *torpedo-fish. **1885** *Times* 30 Apr. 10/6 Each boat will have five *torpedo guns or tubes. **1903** *Windsor Mag.* XIX. 9/2 What's a *torpedo-gunner more or less to a full lootenant? **1928** C. F. S. GAMBLE *Story N. Sea Air Station* xiv. 234 The crew consisted of the pilot, the observer, the torpedo-gunner, and a machine-gunner for the back seat. **1845** CARLYLE *Cromwell* (1871) I. 3 Dryasdust, who wishes merely to compile *torpedo Histories. **1946** *Seafarers' Log* 31 May 13/5, I have known many Navy men who were chronic drinkers at sea as well as ashore. Some have gone blind from drinking *torpedo juice. **1961** *Guardian* 26 Sept. 9/5 Torpedo juice is a combination of these [*sc.* bush beer and toddy] and acquires its name from its lethal effect. The original torpedo juice was the neat alcohol extracted from torpedoes during the war by American servicemen and sometimes mixed with local bush beers to soften the blow. **1878** *N. Amer. Rev.* CXXVII. 384 Dispatched their *torpedo-launches against their intended victim. **1895** *Daily News* 29 May 6/4 She still has..quick-firing guns, and two *torpedo-launching tubes. **1718** *Entertainer* No. 12. 74 'Tis the way to lay waste the Fences of Virtue,..and *Torpedo-like, petrify and benum us. **1839** BAILEY *Festus* xix. (1852) 307 As though to touch but on that topic had, Torpedo-like, numbed thought. **1883** *Century Mag.* July 330/2 The '*torpedo man'..travels about in a light vehicle with his tubes and his nitro-glycerine can. **1885** *Times* 30 Apr. 10/6 The Colossus is coaled and has been fitted with *torpedo nets. **1917** *Flying* 1 May 317/2 Admiral Fiske declared that *torpedo-planes in the battle of Jutland would have given a tremendous advantage to the side employing them. **1981** G. MACBETH *Kind of Treason* xi. 106 The *Prince of Wales* and the *Repulse* had been sunk by Japanese torpedo planes. **1914** H. H. ASQUITH *Let.* 27 Oct. in M. Gilbert *W. S. Churchill* (1972) III. Compan. I. 220 *Torpedo-proof harbours and refuges. **1828** CARLYLE *Misc.* (1857) I. 82 The old man has a *torpedo quality in him. **1877** KNIGHT *Dict. Mech.*, **Torpedo-ram.* **1900** *Daily News* 4 May 2/5 The Polyphemus, torpedo-ram, arrived at Sheerness yesterday from the Mediterranean. **1804** SHAW *Gen. Zool.* V. 297 *Torpedo Ray. **1822–34** *Good's Study Med.* (ed. 4) IV. 214 The torpedo-ray was well known by the Romans to possess this extraordinary power. **1889** WELCH *Text Bk. Naval Archit.* xii. 133 The air finally reaches the under-water *torpedo room. **1899** *Westm. Gaz.* 29 June 1/3 A telephone chamber communicating with the *torpedo-school ship and also with the target. **1903** *Ibid.* 2 July 7/3 The *torpedo-shaped blue Mors cars. **1873** *Illustr. London News* 29 Mar. 294/2 It is also proposed to build a small *torpedo-ship of 214 tons burden by way of trying experiments. **1911** *Q. Rev.* Oct. 476 This gradual merging of the essential features of the gun-ship and the torpedo-ship is now about to find expression in the submarine. **1792** S. ROGERS *Pleas. Mem.* I. 278 What tho' the fiend's *torpedo-touch arrest Each gentler, finer impulse of the breast. **1809–10** COLERIDGE *Friend* I. xvi. (1865) 220 Benumbed into selfishness by the torpedo touch of extreme want. **1893** *Souvenir World's Fair: Naval Exhibit*, The battery mounted comprises..two Gatling guns, and six *torpedo tubes or torpedo guns. **1898** KIPLING in *Morn. News* 10 Nov. 5/1 We are blessed with a pair of deck torpedo-tubes, which weigh about ten tons, and are the bane of our lives. **1877** *Illustr. London News* 16 June 556 Steel *Torpedo-vessel used by the Russians on the Danube. **1878** *N. Amer. Rev.* CXXVII. 230 The torpedo-vessel has been successfully developed.

Hence **tor'pedoic** *a.* (*nonce-wd.*), of a torpedo, like that of a torpedo; **tor'pedoism (tor'pedism)**, (*a*) action or quality like that of a torpedo or electric ray; (*b*) the use of the torpedo (sense 2) in warfare; **tor'pedoist (tor'pedist)**, one who is employed or skilled in, or advocates, the use of torpedoes; **tor'pedo-less** *a.*, having no torpedoes.

1893 H. W. LUCY in *Strand Mag.* Feb. 201 Mr. Gladstone leaped to his feet with *torpedoic action and energy. **1845** CARLYLE *Cromwell* (1871) I. 68 Dilettantisms, Dryasdust *Torpedoisms. **1880** *Athenæum* 21 Aug. 242/2 Readers must not expect to find..an elaborate treatise on torpedism, nor ..the so-called secret of the Whitehead torpedo. *Ibid.* 242/1 During..1877, the Russian *torpedists made a night attack upon the Ottoman squadron lying off Batoum. **1883** *19th Cent.* May 796 The naval officer should be a perfect navigator, a good artilleryman, torpedoist, and electrician, a steam engineer, &c. **1886** *Pall Mall G.* 29 Dec. 6/2 The command of a small *torpedo-less cruiser in the Indian Ocean.

tor'pedo, *v.* [f. prec. sb.]

†**1.** *trans.* To benumb, deaden; = TORPEFY. *Obs.*

1771–2 *Ess. fr. Batchelor* (1773) I. 269 The faculties of that consummate orator..may be torpedoed by that wicked weed, before he has half delivered the following abstract of his sentiments.

2. To destroy or damage by means of a torpedo; to attack with a torpedo.

1879 in WEBSTER *Suppl.* **1881** P. ROBINSON *Under the Punkah* 221 If..an ironclad were to be run down, accidentally torpedoed, or suffer from an explosion. **1898** *Westm. Gaz.* 1 Apr. 7/2 In action the battleship would have been torpedoed before she could have fired a gun.

b. *fig.* To paralyse, destroy: cf. *to explode.*

1895 SIR W. HARCOURT *Sp. Ho. Comm.* 18 Feb., The consummate speech..might be described as having torpedoed the amendment. **1899** *Folk-Lore* Mar. 105 It seems effectually to have torpedoed the enemies' arguments.

c. *intr.* To discharge torpedoes.

1896 *Westm. Gaz.* 15 Jan. 2/1 In four hours they'd be inside the Isle of Wight, torpedoing away right and left.

d. *trans.* To lay (a channel, etc.) with torpedoes or submarine mines; to defend with torpedoes.

1877 *Daily News* 16 Nov. 5/7 The Russians are supposed to have immediately torpedoed the river in his front and rear. **1890** *Sat. Rev.* 11 Jan. 29/1 The *canard* that German officers have been torpedoing the Tagus.

3. To explode a 'torpedo' at the bottom of (an oil-well) to increase the output by shattering the rock or clearing the passage. Also *intr. U.S.*

1873 [see *torpedoed* below]. **1883** *Century Mag.* July 330/1 When a well fails it is usually 'torpedoed' to start the flow afresh. A long tin tube containing six or eight quarts of nitro-glycerine, is lowered into the hole and exploded by dropping a weight upon it. *Ibid.* 330/2 Sometimes well-owners 'torpedo' their wells..by night to avoid paying the ..price charged by the company.

Hence **tor'pedoed** (-əʊd) *ppl. a.*, **tor'pedoing** *vbl. sb.*; **tor'pedoer** (-əʊə(r)), one who operates torpedoes.

1873 HOWELLS *Chance Acquaint.* vi, As if I were..an inflammable naiad from a torpedoed well. **1884** *Pall Mall G.* 1 Sept. 8/1 It may be said torpedoing is a game at which two can play. **1903** *Contemp. Rev.* Aug. 186 Captain Sigsbee, formerly commander of the torpedoed 'Maine'. **1905** *Edin. Rev.* Oct. 322 Our torpedoers, operating in the open sea, were at no small disadvantage.

tor'pedo boat. A vessel carrying one or more torpedoes; now a small, fast war-ship from which torpedoes are discharged. Hence **torpedo-boat** *v.* (*nonce-wd.*), *trans.* to furnish or arm with torpedo boats.

1810 FULTON *Torpedo War* (N.Y.) 44 It would be difficult for a Torpedo boat to depart from any port of America, and return without being detected. **1865** in *Morn. Star* 2 Feb., They took advantage of the storm and darkness to send down a fleet of eight vessels of war and three torpedo boats. **1880** *Standard* 29 Dec. 6/1 The first [torpedo boat] ever known being a very primitive model, invented by Captain David Bushnell, of the Engineer Corps, United States Army, and launched in New York harbour in 1776. **1898** *Harper's Mag.* XCVI. 830 She is building twelve new first-class torpedo-boats and four destroyers. **1884** *Pall Mall G.* 8 Dec. 5/2 To torpedo boat our coast on the German, Russian, or Austrian scale we should require not 100 torpedo boats, but 1,000.

b. *attrib.* and *Comb.*, as ***torpedo-boat engagement, workshop***; **torpedo-boat catcher, torpedo-boat destroyer**, two types of small, fast warships, originally designed to prevent torpedo boats from operating against a fleet.

(The *torpedo-catcher*, officially termed *torpedo-gunboat*, was superseded in 1893 by the *torpedo boat destroyer*, a larger, faster, and more powerful torpedo boat, designed for offensive purposes; the *torpedo boat* being appropriated to coast and harbour defence.)

1893 *Daily News* 14 Feb. 8/7 They are to be termed Torpedo-boat Destroyers, and in size will be between a torpedo catcher of the sharpshooter class and a first-class torpedo boat. **1899** F. T. BULLEN *Way Navy* 59 But torpedo-boat people are accustomed to put up with many things of which landsmen have little idea. **1901** F. T. JANE in *New Penny Mag.* 30 Nov. 205/1 We had..a number of torpedo-boat catchers, which..were unable to catch the craft they were intended to chase.

torpedoic, -ism, -ist: see after TORPEDO *sb.*

torpefy ('tɔːpɪfaɪ), *v.* (erron. **torpify**). [ad. L. *torpefacĕre*, f. *torpē-re* to be numb + *facĕre* to make.] *trans.* To render torpid, benumb, deaden, paralyse. Also *fig.* Hence **'torpefying** *ppl. a.*

1808 *Nat. Hist.* in *Ann. Reg.* 117/2 The common eel, when equally frozen and torpefied, is capable of being conveyed a thousand miles up the country. **1822–34** *Good's Study Med.* (ed. 4) III. 203 Sternutatories, which exhaust, weaken and torpefy the nerves of smell. *Ibid.* 432 Carbonic acid,.. chiefly found in the guise of a torpefying vapour, in close rooms where charcoal has been burnt. **1829** SOUTHEY *Sir T. More* II. 117 To stablish, and to quicken his belief, not to shake, or torpify it. **1875** JOWETT *Plato* (ed. 2) I. 280 Like the flat torpedo fish, who torpifies those who come near him with the touch.

†**'torpel.** *Obs. rare*⁻¹. [var. of TIRPEIL, *-pell.*] Turmoil, throng of battle, mêlée.

c **1400** *Laud Troy Bk.* 16736 Thei put hem certes In gret perel To saue her lord In that torpel. But al was not that thei coude do, For thei no-wyse myght come him to.

†**torpelness.** *Obs. rare*⁻¹. [app. f. prec. + -NESS.] ? State of turmoil.

a **1225** *Ancr. R.* 322 Ure Louerd sulf seid to his deciples ..'Go we eft..into Iudee'. Judee speleð schrift... Galilee speleð hweol, uorte to leren us þet we of þe worldes torpelnesse, & of sunne [= sin's] hweol, ofte gon to schrifte.

torpent ('tɔːpənt), *a.* and *sb. rare.* [ad. L. *torpēnt-em*, pr. pple. of *torpēre* to be torpid.]

a. *adj.* = TORPID *a.* **b.** *sb. Med.* See quots.

1647 H. MORE *Song of Soul* Notes 342 Let..anon an universall soul flow into this torpent masse. **1699** EVELYN *Acetaria* (1729) 126 Cresses..quicken the torpent Spirits, and purge the Brain. **1882** OGILVIE (Annandale), *Torpent, n.*, a medicine that diminishes the exertion of the irritative motions. **1899** *Syd. Soc. Lex.*, *Torpent*, incapable of the active performance of a function. A medicine or agent that reduces or subdues any irritative action.

†**tor'pescent**, *a. Obs. rare.* [ad. pr. pple. of L. *torpēscĕre* to become torpid.] That grows torpid; becoming numb. Hence †**tor'pescence** [see -ENCE], the process of becoming torpid.

c **1750** SHENSTONE *Economy* I. 139 Their torpescent soul Clenches their coin. **1784** JOHNSON in *W. Windham's Diary* (1866) 19 Torpescence, much of the faculties of man-kind lost in them.

torpex ('tɔːpɛks). [Blend of TORPEDO *sb.* + EXPLOSIVE *sb.*] An explosive consisting largely of T.N.T., cyclonite, and aluminium, used for depth charges.

1948 *Jane's Fighting Ships 1947–48* 6/1 These charges could be set to explode at any depth, the former [*sc.* hedgehog] employing torpex, and the latter minol. **1974** [see RDX].

torpid ('tɔːpɪd), *a.* (*sb.*) Also 7 **torpide.** [ad. L. *torpid-us* benumbed, f. *torpē-re* to be numb.]

1. Benumbed; deprived or devoid of the power of motion or feeling; in which activity, animation, or development is suspended; dormant.

1613 PURCHAS *Pilgrimage* I. v. 22 If he descend not lower, to become torpide and lifelesse. **1621** BURTON *Anat. Mel.* I. iii. III. i, Drinesse, which makes the nerues of the tongue torpid. **1784** COWPER *Task* III. 468 When..November dark Checks vegetation in the torpid plant Expos'd to his cold breath. **1860** EMERSON *Cond. Life, Fate* Wks. (Bohn) II. 323 Some animals became torpid in winter, others were torpid in summer.

b. *Path.* Sluggish in action or function.

1807 *Med. Jrnl.* XVII. 72 Complaints of phlegmatic and torpid constitutions. **1843** SIR C. SCUDAMORE *Med. Visit Gräfenberg* 41 Digestive functions torpid. **1899** *Allbutt's Syst. Med.* VIII. 477 Gout and tendency to torpid liver.

2. *fig.* Wanting in animation or vigour; inactive; slow, sluggish; dull; stupefied; apathetic.

1656 BLOUNT *Glossogr.*, *Torpid*, slow, dull, drowzy, astonied. *a* **1677** HALE *Prim. Orig. Man.* I. ii. 63 They [connatural principles] lye more torpid, and inactive, and inevident. **1703** T. N. *City & C. Purchaser* 92 The Workmen are taken to be torpid Operators. **1764** GOLDSM. *Trav.* 171 No vernal blooms their torpid rocks array. **1778** JOHNSON 9 Apr., in *Boswell*, It is a man's own fault..if his mind grows torpid in old age. **1834** MACAULAY *Ess., Pitt* (1865) I. 293/2 To a small, a torpid, and an unfriendly audience. **1885** DUNCKLEY in *Manch. Weekly Times* 7 Feb. 5/5 In the counties..the population is comparatively torpid and inert.

3. Causing torpidity; torporific. *rare.*

1830 WHITTIER *Frost Spirit* iv, The Frost Spirit comes! and the quiet lake shall feel The torpid touch of his glazing breath, and ring to the skater's heel.

B. *sb.* **1.** At Oxford: (*pl.*) The races rowed in Lent term in eight-oared clinker-built open boats: originally designating the boats; later also the crews.

'The "Torpid boats" were originally the second boats of a college, which until 1837 rowed with the "Eights". They are understood to have started *c* 1827, when Christ Church put a second boat on the river; but no record of the name has been found till 1838, when it was app. well established. In that year, the Torpids were made a class by themselves, and raced in the days between the Eight-oared Races (which were not then continuous). In 1852 they were moved to the Lent Term, and reorganized on their present basis.' (W. E. Sherwood.)

1838 *Trin. Coll. Boat Club Bk.*, It was determined at a meeting of Strokes that no Torpid should put on with the racing boats. **1839** *Oxford Herald* 31 May, A race between the Torpids, or second crews, took place on Thursday Evening. **1839** *O.U.B.C. President's Bk.*, [After the Chart of] The Eights [is one of] The Torpid Races. **1853** 'C. BEDE' *Verdant Green* II. vi, The little gentleman..did not join with the 'Torpids' (as the second boats of a college are called). **1861** HUGHES *Tom Brown at Oxf.* xxvii, The torpids being filled with the refuse of the rowing-men—generally awkward or very young oarsmen. **18..** *Inscr. on picture of Exeter White Boat in O.U.B.C. barge*, 'Presented..by the Honourable John Joclyn, late of Exeter College, and stroke oar of the Torpid in 1827'. **1866** *Oxf. Undergraduates' Jrnl.* 20 Brasenose went head in Torpids as well as Eights. **1869** BRADWOOD *O.V.H.* (1870) 4 He had..done two years hard duty in the college torpid. **1910** *Westm. Gaz.* 24 Feb. 4/1 Oxford 'Torpids'..were so named about 1827, when Christ Church staggered humanity by putting a second crew on the river.

2. At Harrow: see quots.

1903 FARMER & HENLEY *Slang Dict.*, *Torpid* (Harrow), a boy who has not been two years in the school. **1905** H. A. VACHELL *The Hill* ii. 39 Scaife expects us to be Torpids. [*Note*] Boys [at Harrow] who have not been more than two years in the school are eligible as 'torpids'; out of each house a Torpid football eleven is chosen.

C. *Comb.* **a.** of the adj., as ***torpid-minded***; **b.** of the sb., as ***Torpid eight, -race.***

1884 *Pall Mall G.* 19 Feb. (Farmer), Twenty-six *Torpid eights were out at Oxford in training for the races. **1909** *Nation* 18 Sept. 878/2 The average man..may be..less ignorant and *torpid-minded than in the older countries. **1858** 'M. SPLENE' *Almæ Matres* 49, I see myself now.. pulling for very life in the *torpid-race.

Hence **'torpidly** *adv.*, in a torpid manner; **'torpidness**, torpidity, torpor.

a **1677** HALE *Prim. Orig. Man.* I. i. 3 It keeps it from rust and torpidness. **1820** C. R. MATURIN *Melmoth* (1892) III. xxvii. 107 The aged father and mother, retreating torpidly to their seats. **1831** TRELAWNY *Adv. Younger Son* xii, A death-like torpidness came over me. **1845** DAY tr. *Simon's Anim. Chem.* I. 227 The torpidly circulating blood.

torpidity (tɔː'pɪdɪtɪ). [f. prec. + -ITY.] The condition or quality of being torpid; torpor, sluggishness, numbness.

1614 PURCHAS *Pilgrimage* VII. xi. (ed. 2) 710 You see one Retrograde..vnto a stonie torpiditie they obserued in the same plant. **1772** BARRINGTON in *Phil. Trans.* LXII. 298 As the swallows were found in the winter, they must have been in a state of torpidity. **1843** R. J. GRAVES *Syst. Clin. Med.* xxx. 388 A torpidity of the kidneys supervened. **1887** A. BIRRELL *C. Brontë* ix. 100 In a world of torpidities any rapid moving thing is hailed somewhat extravagantly.

‖**torpilleur** (tɔrpijœr). *Obs.* exc. *Hist.* [Fr., f. *torpille* torpedo.] A torpedo boat or destroyer in the French navy.

[**1894** W. Le Queux *Great War in England in 1897* xiv. 88 The reinforcements consisted of the French battleships.. together with nine cruisers, and thirty-eight *torpilleurs de haute mer*.] **1950** *Jane's Fighting Ships 1949–50* 181/2 (*caption*) 3 ex-German Type (Classed as *Torpilleurs*.)

torpitude (ˈtɔːpɪtjuːd). Now *rare*. [Irregularly for **torpetude*, f. L. *torpē-re* + -tude: the L. form, if existent, would be **torpetūdo*: cf. *consuētūdo, hebetūdo*. (Perh. by false analogy with *turpitude*, f. L. *turpi-s*.)] = torpidity.

1713 Derham *Phys.-Theol.* iv. vii. 158 In a Torpitude, or sort of Sleep, or middle state between Life and Death. **1788** Jefferson *Writ.* (1859) II. 396 The Russians seem not yet thawed from the winter's torpitude. **1817** J. Gilchrist *Intell. Patrimony* 24 His Elysian torpitude of many weeks duration. **1822–34** *Good's Study Med.* (ed. 4) IV. 105 In some cases there is great torpitude or sluggishness in the growth..of the ovaries.

torple, turple, *v. Obs.* exc. *dial.* [Early ME.: origin obscure. Cf. topple *v.* and torfle.]

†**1.** *intr.* To fall, tumble; = topple *v.* 1. *Obs.*

a **1225** *Ancr. R.* 266 Ant, ȝif a miracle nere..heo hefde iturpled [*v.r.* torplet] mid him, boðe hors & lode, adun into helle grunde. *Ibid.* 322 Mid al þet schendlac, þu schalt trussen & al torplen into helle. *Ibid.* 324.

2. Of an animal; To die; = torfle. *dial.*

1876 *Mid-Yorksh. Gloss.*, *Torple*,.. *Turple*,.. *Torfle*,..or *Turfle, v.n.*, to die. The term is only used in connection with animals.

torpor (ˈtɔːpə(r)). [a. L. *torpor, -ōrem*, f. *torpēre* to be numb.] Torpid condition or quality; torpidity. **a.** Absence or suspension of motive power, activity, or feeling; †inertia (*obs.*); suspended animation or development; in *Path.* morbid inertia or insensibility, stupor.

1626 Bacon *Sylva* §763 Motion doth discusse the Torpour of Solide Bodies Which..have in them a Natural Appetite, not to move at all. **1681** tr. *Willis' Rem. Med. Wks.* Vocab., *Torpor*, a numness, heaviness,..and unaptness for any motion. **1774** Goldsm. *Nat. Hist.* (1862) I. v. 443 Strictly speaking.., these animals cannot be said to sleep during the winter; it may be called rather a *torpor*, a stagnation of all the faculties. *a* **1854** H. Reed *Lect. Brit. Poets* ii. (1857) 63 Why does the earth break forth from its winter's torpor in all the luxuriance of Spring?

b. *transf.* Intellectual or spiritual lethargy; apathy, listlessness; dullness; indifference.

[*a* **1225** *Ancr. R.* 202 Þe Bore of heui Slouhðe haueð þeos hweolpes: Torpor is þe uorme þet is wlech heorte..þe oðer is Pusillinimitas.] **1607** *Schol. Disc. agst. Antichr.* i. i. 38 What meaneth our torpor? what our frozen coldnesse in zeal? **1789** Belsham *Ess.* I. xvii. 333 A universal torpor of the mental faculties must take place. **1878** Lecky *Eng. in 18th C.* I. i. 62 That intellectual torpor which we are accustomed to associate with ecclesiastical domination.

c. Comb., as *torpor-shedding* adj.

1806 J. Grahame *Birds Scot.*, etc. 140 Till noon-tide pour the torpor-shedding ray.

torporific (tɔːpəˈrɪfɪk), *a.* (*sb.*) [ad. L. type **torpōrific-us*, f. *torpōr-em* torpor + *-ficus* making: see -fic.] Causing torpor; producing numbness; paralysing; also *fig.* stupefying, deadening. †*torporific eel*, the gymnotus or electric eel (*obs.*).

1769 E. Bancroft *Guiana* 190 There is one of the Eel tribe,..which I shall beg leave to call the Torporific Eel. **1825** *New Monthly Mag.* XV. 77/2 The torporific sway of Austria. **1852** *Fraser's Mag.* XLV. 632 Galen..tells the Torpedo affects by a torporific action peculiar to itself.

b. *absol.* as *sb.* Something causing torpor.

1840 Manning *Let.* in Purcell *Life* (1895) I. ix. 169, I find the want of such opportunities of conversation a great torporific.

torporize (ˈtɔːpəraɪz), *v.* [f. torpor + -ize.] *intr.* To cause torpor. Hence ˈ**torporizing** *ppl. a.*

1822 *New Monthly Mag.* VI. 223/2 The..torporizing effects of the Lancastrian system of education.

torps (tɔːps), slang abbrev. of *torpedo-lieutenant* s.v. torpedo *sb.* 6. Cf. torp.

1914 'Bartimeus' *Naval Occasions* xxiv. 237 The Torpedo Lieutenant (hereinafter known as 'Torps') was awakened by the June sunlight. **1943** C. S. Forester *Ship* 20 Torps and Lightfoot, the Officers of the Watch.

†ˈ**torpulent,** *a. Obs. rare*$^{-1}$. [irreg. f. torpor, after *corpulent*, etc.: see -ulent.] Torpid. So †ˈ**torpulency** *Obs. rare*$^{-1}$, torpidity, torpor.

1657 Reeve *God's Plea* 350 Lay aside neglect, awake from torpulency. *Ibid.* 142 Our prayers do show, what an oscitant and torpulent people we are.

torquate (ˈtɔːkweɪt), *a. Zool.* [ad. L. *torquāt-us* adorned with or wearing a *torques*: see torques and -ate[2].] Having a ring-like marking, formed by hairs or feathers of special colour or texture, round the neck; collared.

1661 Lovell *Hist. Anim. & Min.* Introd., The pigeon, ring-dove,..wild, torquate, juglandine.

ˈ**torquated,** *a.* [f. as prec. + -ed[1].]

1. Wearing a torque: see torque *sb.*[1]

1623 Cockeram, *Torquated*, one wearing a chaine. **1656** Blount, *Torquated*.., that weares a collar or chain.

2. Formed as or like a torque; twisted from a narrow strip or band.

1851 D. Wilson *Preh. Ann.* (1863) I. 113 The parish of Shapinsay..in which was found a beautiful torquated ring. *Ibid.* ii. vi. 470 The discovery of..torquated neck and arm rings. *Ibid.* II. iv. iii. 258 The torquated hoop.

3. *Zool.* = torquate.

1891 in *Cent. Dict.*

torque, torc (tɔːk), *sb.*[1] Also **tork.** [ad. L. *torquēs, -is* (see torques); so mod.F. *torque*.] A collar, necklace, bracelet, or similar ornament consisting of a twisted narrow band or strip, usually of precious metal, worn especially by the ancient Gauls and Britons.

1834 Planché *Brit. Costume* 10 The Britons..who could not procure them of the precious metals wore torques of iron. **1851** D. Wilson *Preh. Ann.* (1863) II. iv. vi. 472 The torc may be regarded as the most characteristic relic of primitive Celtic and Teutonic art. **1877** Ll. Jewitt *Half-hrs. among Eng. Antiq.* 226 Having torn a torque of gold from the neck of a vanquished Gaul.

attrib. **1877** W. Jones *Finger-ring* 66 This might be denominated a torque ring.

torque, *sb.*[2] *Physics.* [f. L. *torquēre* to twist.] The twisting or rotary force in a piece of mechanism (as a measurable quantity); the moment of a system of forces producing rotation.

1884 (Apr.) Jas. Thomson in *Sci. Papers* (1912) p. civ. **1884** S. P. Thompson *Dynamo-electric Mach.* xvii. 308 The torque or turning-moment is, in a series dynamo, both when used as generator and when used as a motor, very nearly proportional to the current. **1906** *Daily Chron.* 21 Apr. 3/7 Torque is the amount of force in a rotary direction—the power of the twist. If you hold one end of a rod and I hold the other, and I twist it round in your hands, that is because I am giving it a torque greater than you can resist. **1907** *Installation News* Oct. 9/1 This small boss takes up the torque due to screwing up the tube.

b. A proposed unit of this: see quot.

1899 Jude *Physics, Exper. & Theor.* I. i. i. §46. 33 In the French system, the absolute unit of moment would be the moment of a force of one dyne, about a point at one centimetre perpendicular distance from its line of action; this unit we shall call one *torque*.

c. *attrib.* and *Comb.* **torque converter**, a device that varies or multiplies torque; **torque meter, torquemeter** = *torsionmeter* s.v. torsion 3; **torque motor** *Electr. Engin.*, an electric motor designed to exert a torque without continuous rotation; **torque wrench**, a device to set and adjust the tension of nuts and bolts.

1934 Webster, *Torque converter. **1944** *Machine Design* July 117 The Lysholm-Smith torque converter.. incorporates multiple-stage turbine blading. **1970** *Commercial Motor* 25 Sept. 65/3 Its 190 bhp is passed through a two-stage torque-convertor which in its hydraulic stage multiplies the engine torque by 4·7 and in its mechanical stage has a ratio of 1·046 to 1, a slight overdrive. **1909** *Westm. Gaz.* 30 Nov. 5/1 Intended as a *torque-increasing mechanism to propel motor-cars within reasonable limits without the intervention of change-speed gears. **1911** H. M. Hobart *Dict. Electr. Terms* II. 564/1 *Torque meter. **1955** *Electronic Engin.* XXVII. 430/1 Several types of torquemeter are known but..it has sometimes proved difficult to obtain reliable results in this particular application [*sc.* in aircraft]. **1926** *Gloss. Terms Electr. Engin.* (Brit. Engin. Stand. Assoc.) 54 *Torque motor. **1946** *Nature* 13 July 54/2 As a torque motor, the machine was required to operate on 333 c./s. and works continuously under standstill conditions, with a temperature rise at 20 volts/phase of about 30°C. **1979** *Engin. Materials & Design* Oct. 43/1 Torque motors are those which are designed to provide their maximum torque under the conditions of 'stall' or 'locked rotor'. **1907** *Westm. Gaz.* 9 Nov. 16/2 The propeller shaft casing..fitted with a massive hinged bracket to form its own *torque rod. **1948** A. W. Judge *Automobile Engine Overhaul* (ed. 3) x. 187 It is important to tighten each nut a little at a time... A *torque wrench is here an advantage. **1979** G. Hammond *Dead Game* v. 55 Janet was still working on the hydraulics of the tractor... She pulled gently on the torque-wrench.

torque, *v.* [f. torque *sb.*[2]] *trans.* To apply torque to. So ˈ**torquing** *vbl. sb.*

1954 *Fasteners* IX. v. 3 The subject of bolt torquing. **1960** D. A. Halperin *Building with Steel* xii. 163/2 He then checks the bolts to verify that they have been torqued to at least specified minimum tension. **1978** *Nature* 12 Oct. 517/1 Perhaps these radio galaxies are systems where a pre-existing central black hole is gradually being torqued into alignment with the angular momentum of newly supplied fuel that has reactivated the nucleus. **1981** *Ibid.* 24 Sept. 261/2 Drilling conditions were rugged... Cave-ins and torquing finally caused them to abandon the hole well above their oceanic crustal target.

torqued (tɔːkt), *a.* Also 6 torquet. [after obs. F. *torqué*, pa. pple. of *torquer*, ad. L. *torquēre* to twist: see -ed[1].]

1. Twisted, convoluted; formed like a torque.

1577 D. Settle *M. Frobisher's Voy.* ii. in Hakluyt *Voy.* (1589) 625 We found a dead fishe..which had in his nose a horne streight and torquet, of length two yardes lacking two ynches. **1857** *Archæologia* XXXVII. 102 A pair of ear-rings of base silver, the large torqued circles of which were closed by a sort of hook and eye.

2. *Her.* Twisted or bent into a double curve like the letter S: said of a serpent or dolphin used as a bearing. (In quot. 1572 app. Bent into a coiled form.)

1572 Bossewell *Armorie* ii. 63b, The fielde is of the Saphyre, a Serpente torqued, Topace. **1688** R. Holme *Armoury* iii. xvii. (Roxb.) 119/1 A Fasce, or fiue arrowes in fasce, with a serpent Torqued about the same. *c* **1828** [see torgant]. **1894** *Parker's Gloss. Her.*, *Torqued*, bowed-embowed, especially of a serpent's tail; also *wreathed*.

‖**torques** (ˈtɔːkwiːz), *sb.* and *a.* Also 6 torquess, 7, 9 torquis. [L. *torquēs, torquis* a twisted neck-chain or collar, f. *torquēre* to twist.]

A. *sb.* **1.** = torque *sb.*[1]

1693 Pepys in *Lett. Lit. Men* (Camden) 211 Your account of the *Torquis* spoken of in your..Letter. **1695** Gibson *Add. to Camden* 658 In..1692 an ancient golden Torques was dug up..near this castle of Harlech. **1778** *Eng. Gazetteer* (ed. 2) s.v. *Pattingham*, Where, in 1700, was found a large torques of fine gold, 2 feet long, 3 pounds 2 ounces weight... These torqueses were worn by the ancient Britons. **1865** *Pall Mall G.* 24 Oct. 5 There is no torques, no finger ring..nothing but 'the seal of Tirhaka, King of Æthiopians'.

2. *Zool.* A collar or ring-like marking round the neck of an animal, formed by hair, feathers, etc. of special colour or texture.

1891 in *Cent. Dict.*

†**B.** *adj.* Twisted, bent. *Obs. rare*$^{-1}$.

a **1568** Wedderburn in *Bannatyne Poems* 695/27 With ane bow torquess diuerss Greikis did scho kill.

torquey (ˈtɔːkɪ), *a.* [f. torque *sb.*[2] + -y[1].] Of the engine of a motor vehicle: producing plenty of torque; able to pull well.

1977 *What Car?* Apr. 59/1 Tractable, torquey engine. **1981** *Motor* 27 June 9/2 The torquey, sweet engine.

torr (tɔː(r)). *Physics.* Also Torr. [f. the name of *Torricelli* (see Torricellian *a.*).] A unit of pressure used chiefly in measuring partial vacuums (see quot. 1958); 133·32 newton/sq. metre.

1949 S. Dushman *Sci. Foundations Vacuum Technique* i. 4 In German literature, 1 Tor (or 1 Torr) is used to designate 1 mm Hg pressure. **1958** *Gloss. Terms Vacuum Technol.* (*B.S.I.*) 7 *Torr*, a unit of pressure defined by the relationship: 760 torr = 1 standard atmosphere (atm) = 1 013 250 dyn/cm² exactly. 1 torr is equal to the conventional barometric millimetre of mercury..within 1 part in 7 × 10⁶. *Ibid.* 20, 1 torr = 1·333 22 millibar (mb) approximately. **1981** J. B. Adams in J. H. Mulvey *Nature of Matter* vii. 151 It is necessary to achieve a very low pressure in the vacuum chamber; pressures of 10⁻¹¹ Torr are essential.

torr(e, obs. form of tor *sb.*

†**torreˈfacted,** *ppl. a. Obs. rare.* (*irreg.* torri-.) [f. L. *torrefact-us*, pa. pple. of *torrefacĕre* to torrefy + -ed[1].] Torrefied, roasted.

1601 Holland *Pliny* xxx. viii. II. 385 Sheepes tallow incorporat with salt torrifacted.

torrefaction (tɒrɪˈfækʃən). [n. of action f. L. *torrefacĕre* to torrefy: see -tion and cf. F. *torréfaction*.] The process of drying or roasting by fire; the state or condition of being roasted.

1612 Woodall *Surg. Mate* Wks. (1653) 274 Torrefaction like siccation, but more violent. **1648** Bp. Hall *Serm. at Higham* Rem. Wks. (1660) 196 Here was not a scorching and blistering but a vehement and full torrefaction. **1758** Reid tr. *Macquer's Chym.* I. 155 The term calcination is generally used to express this torrefaction of antimony. **1829** Togno & Durand *Man. Mat. Med.* 189 The torrefaction to which coffee is subjected..gives it a light brown colour. **1839** De Quincey *Casuistry Rom. Meals* Wks. 1859 III. 252 Ping.. now for the first time tasted it [pig] in a state of torrefaction.

torrefiˈcation (torri-), erron. form for prec.

1763 Horne in *Phil. Trans.* LIII. 53, I gave it a very powerful torrification (or roasting). **1853** Soyer *Pantroph.* 314 The Italians extract from cocoa more exalted qualities by torrefication.

torrefied (ˈtɒrɪfaɪd), *ppl. a.* [f. torrefy *v.* + -ed[1].] Roasted; dried or parched by the action of fire; scorched.

1612 Woodall *Surg. Mate* Wks. (1653) 21* Any torrified or dry powdred medicaments. **1670** Capt. J. Smith *Eng. Improv. Reviv'd* 290 Some torrefied Rhubarb. **1796** Kirwan *Elem. Min.* (ed. 2) II. 373 He also extracted Copper from the torrefied Ore. **1829** Togno & Durand *Man. Mat. Med.* 189 The stimulating influence of torrefied coffee. **1857** Miller *Elem. Chem.* (1862) III. 99 This soluble torrefied starch is known under the name of British gum.

torrefy (ˈtɒrɪfaɪ), *v.* Also *irreg.* torrify. [a. F. *torréfi-er* (1566 in Hatz.-Darm.), ad. L. *torrefacĕre* to dry by heat, f. *torrēre* to dry, parch, roast + *facĕre* to make: see -fy. (The spelling *torrify* follows *terrify, horrify*.)]

1. *trans.* To roast, scorch, or dry by fire.

1601 Holland *Pliny* xxiii. Proem II. 147 To bring it into ashes, it must be torrified in an oven. **1661** Lovell *Hist. Anim. & Min.* Introd., It's hardly concocted..and torrifieth the bloud. **1819** H. Busk *Banquet* i. 234 The housewives..on the embers torrify their cake. **1883** R. Haldane *Workshop Receipts* ii. 159/2 Taking care not to torrefy them too much.

b. To deprive of all moisture by heating, as a chemical or drug.

1601 Holland *Pliny* xxvii. iv. II. 272 It [Aloe] ought to be torrefied in an earthen vessell. *Ibid.* xxxi. x. 422 Torrifie nitre untill it begin to looke blacke. **1713** *Phil. Trans.* XXVIII. 230 They torrify a Spoonful of white Cummin-seed.

c. *Metallurgy.* To roast, as ores, in order to deprive of sulphur, arsenic, or other volatile substance.

1686 PLOT *Staffordsh.* 188 *Pyrites aureus* (which if torrefy'd..prove all Iron Ores). **1806** FORSYTH *Beauties Scotl.* III. 100 To prepare iron-stone for the furnace, it must be roasted, or torrified, to expell all volatile matters. **1840** *Civil Eng. & Arch. Jrnl.* III. 415/1 It contains carbonaceous matter enough to torrify the stone and make it fit for the furnace.

2. *intr.* To become reduced to a cinder or ash; to become calcined.

1615 CROOKE *Body of Man* 89 This Fat..is not melted by fire, but rather torrifieth.

† **torrelite** ('tɒrəlaɪt). *Min.* [Named after Dr. J. Torrey: see -LITE.] Obs. syn. of COLUMBITE.

1836 T. THOMSON in *R. D. & T. Thomson's Rec. Gen. Sc.* IV. 408 Torrelite. I give this name to the new species, which I have just received from New York, by the liberality and kindness of Dr. Torrey.

Torrens ('tɒrənz). The name of Sir Robert *Torrens* (1814–84), first Premier of South Australia, used *attrib.* in ***Torrens system***, a system of land title registration devised by him, and adopted in Australia and elsewhere outside the U.K.

1863 R. R. TORRENS (*title*) Transfer of land by 'registration of title', as now in operation in Australia under the 'Torrens system'. **1905** J. E. HOGG (*title*) The Australian Torrens system. *Ibid.* p. v, The system of land transfer and registration known as the Torrens system has now been in operation in Australasia more than forty-six years. **1976** S. R. SIMPSON *Land Law & Registration* v. 68 Outside Great Britain the system of registering title..is widely known as the 'Torrens system', for it was Sir Robert Torrens who in 1858 introduced registration of title into South Australia, the first jurisdiction (at least of jurisdictions using English land law) to establish such a system.

torrent ('tɒrənt), *sb.* (*a.*) [a. F. *torrent* (*a* 1200 in Godef. *Compl.*), ad. L. *torrĕnt-em* burning, boiling, rushing, impetuous, pr. pple. of *torrēre* to scorch, burn; also as sb. a torrent. Cf. the sense-transition of L. *æstus* fire, fierce heat, the surging or flowing of the sea, the tide.]

1. A stream of water flowing with great swiftness and impetuosity, whether from the steepness of its course, or from being temporarily flooded; more esp. applied (as in Fr.) to a mountain stream which at times is full of rushing water and at other times is more or less dry: cf. WINTER-BOURN.

[**1398** TREVISA *Barth. De P.R.* XIII. iii. (Bodl. MS.), Of ryuers beþ twei manere kindes..one is icleped a lyuynge ryuer; þat oþer manere ryuer hatte Torreens and is a water þat comeþ wiþ swifte rees and passeþ; and hatte torrens for it creseþ in grete rayne and fordruyeþ in druye wedeir. **1506** GUYLFORDE *Pilgr.* (Camden) 31 So firste we come to Torrens Cedron, which in somer tyme is drye. [Cf. Vulgate *John* xviii. 1, trans torrentem Cedron, in *Lindisf. gl.* þ uinterburna cedron.]] **1601** SHAKS. *Jul. C.* I. ii. 107 The Torrent roar'd, and we did buffet it With lusty Sinewes. **1609** BIBLE (Douay) *Gen.* xxvi. Comm., *Torrent*, the chanel where sometimes a vehement streame runneth, sometimes none at al. **1697** DRYDEN *Virg. Georg.* I. 160 The wary Ploughman, on the Mountain's Brow, Undams his watry Stores, huge Torrents flow. **1760** JOHNSON *Idler* No. 97 ¶5 He observed among the hills many hollows worn by torrents. **1835** THIRLWALL *Greece* I. i. 14 The *Ilissus*..is a mere brook, which is sometimes swollen into a torrent. **1856** STANLEY *Sinai & Pal.* vii. 299 This green thread is the course of the torrent now called Kelt, possibly the ancient Cherith. **1858** HAWTHORNE *Fr. & It. Note-Bks.* I. 247 We discerned the dry beds of mountain torrents, which had lived too fierce a life to let it be a long one.

2. a. *fig.* A violent or tumultuous flow, onrush, or 'stream', e.g. of words, feelings, opposition, etc.; a 'flood'.

1647 CLARENDON *Hist. Reb.* I. §1 Those, who out of Duty and Conscience have opposed..that Torrent which did overwhelm them. *Ibid.* §70 The torrent of his Impetuous Passions. **1784** MME. D'ARBLAY *Let.* 14 Nov., She poured forth again a torrent of abuse. **1826** MARGRAVINE OF ANSPACH *Mem.* I. viii. 304 He was forced to follow the torrent of his notes [in music]. **1845** S. AUSTIN *Ranke's Hist. Ref.* I. 249 The near approach of the resistless torrent of Turkish power.

b. *transf.* A forcible stream or rushing body (of various physical things, as lava, loose stones, wind, light); also, a violent downpour of rain.

1781 MORE in *Phil. Trans.* LXXII. 52 The force of those violent torrents of wind. **1806–7** J. BERESFORD *Miseries Hum. Life* (1826) II. xiv, A soaking torrent of rain. **1821** R. TURNER *Arts & Sc.* (ed. 18) 37 Torrents of smoke and of flames, rivers of melted metals. **1839** DE QUINCEY *Recoll. Lakes* Wks. 1862 II. 11 The moon arose, and shed a torrent of light upon the Langdale fells. **1840** R. H. DANA *Bef. Mast* x. 23 The rain coming down in torrents. **1858** LARDNER *Hand-bk. Nat. Phil.* 360 The torrents of liquid lava which flow from volcanos. **1860** TYNDALL *Glac.* I. viii. 58 A torrent of what appeared to me to be stones and mud.

c. A mass of hanging foliage, drapery, etc. resembling in appearance a descending stream.

1864 LOWELL *Fireside Trav.* 284 A cliff over which the ivy pours in torrents. **1880** 'OUIDA' *Moths* II. 271 A loose white gown that was all torrents and cascades of lace.

3. *attrib.* and *Comb.* **a.** Simple attrib., as ***torrent-action, -bed, -flood, -line, -scar, -sound, -stream, -voice, -water; torrent-wise*** adv.; **b.** objective, as ***torrent-braving*** adj.; **c.** instrumental, as ***torrent-bitten, -borne*** adjs.; **d.** similative, etc., as ***torrent-like, -mad*** adjs. **e.** Special combs.: **torrent-bow**, a rainbow formed in the spray of a torrent; **torrent-duck**, any species of duck of the South American genus *Merganetta*.

1856 KANE *Arct. Expl.* II. xiv. 150 The evidences of *torrent-action were unequivocal. **1867** LADY HERBERT *Cradle L.* vii. 203 We rode through this same *torrent-bed, at this time of the year, dry. **1863** ATKINSON *Stanton Grange* (1864) 258 The huge sweeping wave whirling the *torrent-borne sticks and boughs. **1832** TENNYSON *Pal. of Art* ix, In misty folds, that, floating as they fell, Lit up a *torrent-bow. **1777** WARTON *Odes* VIII. vi, The foam-beat pier, and *torrent-braving mound. **1899** *Camb. Nat. Hist.* IX. 116 This peculiar and tame *torrent-duck is rarely seen on the sea, though it can fly from one gorge to another. **1825** J. WILSON *Poems* II. 209 Each misty cataract, and *torrent-flood. **1769** PENNANT *Zool.* III. 241 Salmon..gain the sources of the Lapland rivers in spite of their *torrent-like currents. **1865** ALEX. SMITH *Summ. Skye* I. 287 They stand with all their scars and *torrent-lines bare to the blue heavens.. **1728** D. MALLET *Excurs.* Wks. 1759 I. 92 A hundred *torrent-streams, Each ploughing up its bed. **1898** *Westm. Gaz.* 1 Nov. 7/2 The feeding torrents might be diverted or blocked, and the Abyssinian *torrent-water might be so interfered with as largely to deprive the river of the fertilising matter which it carries in suspension. **1862** CARLYLE *Fredk. Gt.* XII. xii. III. 379 These..fly *torrent-wise along the winds.

B. *adj.* Rushing like a torrent.

1667 MILTON *P.L.* II. 581 Fierce Phlegeton, Whose waves of torrent fire inflame with rage. **1859** TENNYSON *Enid* 1020 As one That listens near a torrent mountain-brook.

Hence **'torrentful** *a.*, full of torrent or rush of words (whence **'torrentfulness**); **'torrentless** *a.*, void of torrents.

1873 SYMONDS *Grk. Poets* Ser. I. vi. 162 The *torrentfulness, the intoxicating charm of Pindar. **1911** B. W. BACON in *Expositor* Mar. 205 The rainless, *torrentless, alluvial valley of the Nile.

torrential (tɒ'rɛnʃəl), *a.* [f. L. *torrĕnt-em* TORRENT + -IAL: cf. *tangential*.]

1. Of, pertaining to, or of the nature of a torrent; produced by the action of a torrent.

torrential months, months characterized by torrents.

1861 J. H. BENNET *Winter Medit.* I. i. (1875) 11 A series of hills..rent by numerous ravines and torrential valleys. **1873** J. GEIKIE *Gt. Ice Age* xxvi. 362 The denuded and partially rearranged portions of old torrential gravel and sand. **1880** V. BALL *Jungle Life in India* ii. 57 These rivers are..fed by thousands of torrential streams which, when there is no rain, completely dry up. **1892** *Daily Graphic* 8 Jan. 7/3 The torrential months of January and February.

2. Like a torrent in rapidity or violence; torrent-like; rushing; falling in torrents, as rain.

1849 *Fraser's Mag.* XL. 605 No eddying groups; no torrential processions. **1863** TYNDALL *Heat* 388 The condensation of the vapour, and its torrential descent to the earth. **1865** *Morn. Star* 21 July, To the intense heat,..has succeeded torrential rain. **1894** *Scotsman* 27 Aug. 7 A rainstorm which the newfangled appellation 'torrential' only feebly describes.

b. *fig.* As copious or impetuous as a torrent.

1877 D. M. WALLACE *Russia* xxv. 396 The poetasters poured forth their feelings with torrential recklessness. **1879** G. MEREDITH *Egoist* III. xiv. 293 He could woo, he was a torrential wooer. **1897** in *Academy* 13 Mar. 308/2 A man of torrential eloquence. **1909** *Blackw. Mag.* Aug. 232/1 They broke and fled with the British in torrential pursuit.

Hence **torrentiality** (tɒ,rɛnʃɪ'ælɪtɪ), torrential character or condition; **to'rrentially** *adv.*, in a torrential way; in torrents, or like a torrent.

1882 PROCTOR in *Nat. Stud.* (N.Y.) 52 Since the woods were cleared the rain falls more torrentially than before. **1891** *Cent. Dict.*, Torrentiality. **1901** *Daily Chron.* 4 Nov. 5/7 To the stern, where sailors and marines rushed torrentially, called for 'three cheers, and one cheer more'.

† **torrentille.** *Obs. rare*⁻¹. App. var. of next.

c **1460** J. RUSSELL *Bk. Nurture* 548 ȝiff ye haue salt purpose, ȝele, torrentille, deynteithus fulle dere, Ye must do afture þe forme of frumenty, as y said while ere.

† **'torrentine**, *sb. Obs. rare*⁻¹. [In note to passage quoted, said to corresp. to an Ital. *torrentina*, a fish so called because it abounds in mountain streams.] A kind of fish; perh. trout.

c **1460** J. RUSSELL *Bk. Nurture* 835 in *Babees Bk.* (1868) 173 Vynegur is good to salt purpose & torrentyne, Salt sturgeon, salt swyrd-fysche savery & fyne.

† **'torrentine**, *a. Obs. rare.* [f. L. *torrĕnt-em* TORRENT + -INE[1].] (See quot.)

1656 BLOUNT *Glossogr.*, *Torrentine*, belonging to, or abiding in torrents, or swift and violent streames. **1864** in WEBSTER; and in later Dicts.

torrentuous (tɒ'rɛntjuːəs), *a.* [= mod.F. *torrentueux* (neologism in Littré), f. L. *torrĕnt-em* TORRENT: see -UOUS, and cf. *tempestuous*.] Torrent-like, impetuous.

1840 THACKERAY *Paris Sk.-bk.* vii. *Fr. Fash. Novels*, Wks. 1900 V. 84 My affairs whirl onwards together in such a torrentuous [orig. *torrentueux*] galopade. **1897** F. THOMPSON in *Academy* 6 Feb. 180/2 Womanly and unstayed of nature, torrentuous of golden talk.

torrepine: see TERRAPIN[1].

torret, turret. *Obs.* or *dial.* Forms: 4–5 toret, 5 torett, touret, 5–6 torrett, turet(t, turrett, 5–8 torret, 6 (9) turret. [ME. *toret, touret*, a. OF. *toret*, dim. of *tor* (12th c.), *tour* a round, circuit, circle, ring: see TOUR. From the 15th c. this word is also formed as *ter(r)et, tyret, tyrret*, which in senses b and d are the ordinary forms: see TERRET.] **a.** A swivel ring on a dog's collar by which a string can be attached.

c **1386** CHAUCER *Knt.'s T.* 1294 Aboute his Chaar ther wenten white Alauntz..with mosel faste ybounde Colored of gold, and tourettes [*v.rr.* turrettes, torettys, torettes, torrettes, turettes, torettz] fyled rounde. **1552** HULOET, Turret of a dogges collare, *vertibulum*.

b. Each of the two rings by which the leash is attached to the jesses of a hawk. See TERRET b.

[Cf. *c* **1247** *Emperor Fredk. II's 'De arte venandi cum avibus'* (1596) II. xl. (*heading*) De tornetto, qualiter factum sit, et ad quid sit utile.]

c. A ring or the like, often moving on a swivel, whereby an object can be attached to a chain.

c **1391** CHAUCER *Astrol.* I. §2 Thyn Astrelabie hath a ring to putten on the t[h]owmbe of thy ryht hand in takyng the heyhte of thynges... This ring rennyth in A Maner turet, fast to the Moder of thyn Astrelabie. **1463** *Bury Wills* (Camden) 16 My lityll bagge of blakke ledyr with a cheyne and toret of siluyr. **1554** in *Shropsh. Par. Doc.* (1903) 55 For three cheynes and two turettes for the sensor viii[d]. **1900** *N. & Q.* 9th Ser. VI. 235/2 Turettes, tirrets, tirets, or tyrritts, swivels (of metal), a term also used in heraldry. In the trickings of arms in many early heraldic MSS. these are represented as a ring at the end of a chain. **1910** *Let. to Editor*, The term 'turret' (pronounced 'torret') is still in use at Winterton, North Lincolnsh., though obsolescent, to indicate the bow and pendant of a watch case. The word is used principally by farm men. It is the local name for the swivel with which all plough traces are furnished to prevent them from becoming twisted.

d. In horse-harness, A ring on the harness of a horse through which a rein passes: see TERRET d.

1429–30 *Durham Acc. Rolls* (Surtees) 230 In iiij Renes, ij colers de coreo novis cum Turettes emptis. **1849** DE QUINCEY *Eng. Mail Coach* Wks. 1863 IV. 306 Inspecting professionally the buckles, the straps, and the silvery turrets of his harness. [*Note*] The little devices through which the reins are made to pass... This same word..I heard uniformly used by many scores of illustrious mail-coachmen.

torret, obs. form of TURRET.

torreyite ('tɒrɪaɪt). *Min.* [f. the name of John *Torrey* (1796–1873), U.S. scientist + -ITE[1].] A hydrated basic sulphate of magnesium, manganese, and zinc, $(Mg, Mn)_5Zn_2SO_4(OH)_{12}{\cdot}4H_2O$, found as massive aggregates of white to colourless monoclinic crystals.

1949 J. PREWITT-HOPKINS in *Amer. Mineralogist* XXXIV. 595 A new name, torreyite, is proposed to replace the name delta-mooreite. **1979** *Ibid.* LXIV. 952/2 Torreyite in fine-grained aggregates resembles hardened granular sugar.

Torricellian (tɒrɪ'tʃɛlɪən, tɒrɪ'sɛlɪən), *a.* [f. the name of *Torricelli*, an Italian physicist (1608–1647) + -AN.] Of or belonging to Torricelli.

Torricellian experiment, that by which, in 1643, Torricelli proved that the column of mercury in an inverted closed tube is supported by the pressure of the atmosphere on the mercury in the vessel, and that the height of the column corresponds exactly to the atmospheric pressure. ***Torricellian tube***, early name for the tube of the mercurial barometer. ***Torricellian vacuum***, the vacuum above the mercurial column in the barometer, produced by filling the tube with mercury and then inverting it in a cup of mercury.

1660 BOYLE *New Exp. Phys. Mech.* xvii. 123 We are unwilling to examine any further the Inferences wont to be made from the Torricellian Experiment. **1663** —— *Usef. Exp. Nat. Philos.* I. iv. 69 Nor did it appear that by repeated Suctions..it could at all be rais'd above the seven and twenty Digits at which it us'd to subsist in the Torrecellian Experiment *De Vacuo*. *a* **1680** BUTLER *Rem.* (1759) I. 162 Or measuring of Air upon Parnassus With Cylinders of Torricellian Glasses. **1682** H. MORE *Annot. Glanvill's Lux O.* 130 The Quicksilver in a Torricellian Tube will sink deeper in an higher or clearer Air. **1753** *Phil. Trans. R. Soc.* XLVII. 371 The Torricellian vacuum then occupied a space of about thirty inches. **1812** SIR H. DAVY *Chem. Philos.* 97 Even the best Torricellian vacuum must contain elastic matter. **1812–16** PLAYFAIR *Nat. Phil.* (1819) I. 243 The weight of air is known from the Torricellian experiment, or that of the barometer. **1835** *Penny Cycl.* III. 483/2 It is a Torricellian barometer.

torrid ('tɒrɪd), *a.* Also 7 *erron.* torred. [ad. L. *torrid-us*, f. *torrēre* to dry with heat: see -ID. Cf. F. *torride* (Rabelais 1546), Sp., Pg. *tórrido, -a*, It. *torrido, -a*.]

1. Scorched, burned, exposed to great heat; also, intensely hot, burning, scorching.

1611 COTGR., *Torride*, torride, scorched, burned, parched; also,..dried by the extremitie of heat. **1613** PURCHAS *Pilgrimage* VIII. i. 603 A torrid and scorched earth. **1658** J. ROBINSON *Endoxa* ix. 48 Exotick simples..corrupted by the long and torrid space of the Voyage. **1667** MILTON *P.L.* XII. 634 Fierce as a Comet; which with torrid heat..Began to parch that temperate Clime. **1798** CANNING in *Anti-Jacobin* No. 27. 146 All in the town of Tunis, In Africa the torrid. **1809** BYRON *Ch. Har.* I. xxviii. *note*, Such torrid weather. **1876** MERIVALE *Rom. Triumvirates* vii. (1877) 146 The march through this torrid and trackless region occupied seven days.

b. *esp.* in ***torrid zone***, the region of the earth between the tropics. (Orig. in L. form, *torrida zona* or *zona torrida*; cf. Virg. *Georg.* I. 234.)

[**1398** TREVISA *Barth. De P.R.* XI. iii. (Bodl. MS.), þe cercle þat hatte Torrida zona [L. orig. *a* 1350] vnder þe whiche þe sonne meueþ alwei. **1553** EDEN *Treat. Newe Ind.* (Arb.) 33 The burning lyne called *Zona Torrida*.] **1586** MARLOWE *1st Pt. Tamburl.* IV. iv, Thence by land unto the torrid zone. **1794** SULLIVAN *View Nat.* I. 156 Why, under the torrid zone, have the little islands a temperature always supportable..? **1834** MRS. SOMERVILLE *Connex. Phys. Sc.* xxvii. 272 In the valleys of the torrid zone, where the mean annual temperature is very high.

c. *transf.* Inhabiting the torrid zone.

1771 PENNANT *Syn. Quadr.* 297 Torrid jerboa.

†**d.** Of colour: Burned, blackened with burning.

1634 SIR T. HERBERT *Trav.* 24 Their colour is (answerable to the Zone they breathe in) blacke and Torrid. **1650** CHARLETON *Paradoxes* 18 It grows not black and torrid.. by the affriction of the Saphire.

2. *fig.* **a.** In reference to the 'heat' of persecution, or sometimes to the burning of heretics.

a **1635** CORBET *Poems* (1807) 48 Had shee bin then In Maryes torrid dayes engend'red, when Cruelty was witty. **1702** C. MATHER *Magn. Chr.* III. I. iii. (1852) 316 The countries which the bloody Popish inquisition has made a clime too torrid for a Protestant.

b. Hot in temper or passion; ardent, zealous, enthusiastic.

1646 CRASHAW *Steps to Temple* 84 Temper'd 'twixt cold despair and torrid joy. **1685** in Maidment *Bk. Scott. Pasquils* (1868) 287 But I was ne'er in love so torrid As to miscarry with my mate. **1909** *Nation* 16 Oct. 129/2 Mr. Finck is about as torrid a hot gospeller as one could meet with.

Hence ˌ**torridly** *adv.*; ˈ**torridness**.

1657 R. LIGON *Barbadoes* (1673) 9 Finding the Air so *torridly hot, I thought good to make tryal of the water. **1638** SIR T. HERBERT *Trav.* (ed. 2) 36 The [ayre] inflamed by the *torridnesse of the Zone. *a* **1656** USSHER *Ann.* vi. (1658) 271 Their horses being all spent.. with the length and torridnesse of the way.

torridity (tɒˈrɪdɪtɪ). [f. prec. + -ITY, corresp. to a L. type **torriditās*.] The state, condition, or quality of being torrid; intense heat.

1846 in WORCESTER. **1890** *Columbus* (Ohio) *Dispatch* 23 June *heading*, Torridity likely to continue for the coming 24 hours. **1901** *Wide World Mag.* VIII. 131/1 There is no relief by night from the torridity of the daylight hours.

Torridon (ˈtɒrɪdən). *Geol.* The name of Loch *Torridon* on the NW. coast of Scotland, used *attrib.* to designate Torridonian rocks (see next), which are well exposed there.

1873 *Q. Jrnl. Geol. Soc.* XXIX. 334 The lowest conglomerate bed of the Torridon sandstone is seen in fine section in a cliff north-west of Brochel castle. **1896** [see next]. **1930** PEACH & HORNE *Chapters Geol. Scotl.* iii. 83 The various groups of Torridon Sandstone are not equally developed along the belt from Cape Wrath to Skye. **1963** D. W. & E. E. HUMPHRIES tr. *Termier's Erosion & Sedimentation* i. 7 In this field the studies of British scientists ..extend over rocks of all ages back to the Torridon Sandstone (Precambrian).

Torridonian (tɒrɪˈdəʊnɪən), *a. Geol.* [f. prec. + -IAN.] Of, pertaining to, or designating the later of the two main series of Pre-Cambrian rocks in NW. Scotland, which occur in a narrow belt running from Cape Wrath to Skye and consist chiefly of sandstones, grits, and shales; also the time of their deposition. Also *absol.*, the Torridonian series.

1896 J. W. JUDD *Student's Lyell* xxviii. 435/1 The Torridon Sandstone or Torridonian. *Ibid.* 435/2 The Cambrian strata being found lying on every portion of the Torridonian series. **1934**, etc. [see MOINE]. **1938**, etc. [see MOINIAN *a.*]. **1952** *Geol. Mag.* LXXXIX. 70 The possibility of a Torridonian age for this very isolated outlier should not be excluded. **1969** BENNISON & WRIGHT *Geol. Hist. Brit. Isles* iii. 46 Resting with marked unconformity upon the Lewisian of the foreland is the Torridonian Series, an enormous thickness of dominantly arenaceous rocks. **1971** *Country Life* 18 Nov. 1349/3 The fertile oolite soil gives way to Torridonian sandstone just north of James Gillie's croft. **1976** T. R. OWEN *Geol. Evolution Brit. Isles* ii. 19 Radiometric datings (1000–800 m.y.) now confirm that the Torridonian and the Moine are the lateral equivalents of one another.

torrify, erron. form of TORREFY.

†ˈ**torrion.** *Obs.* [a. obs. F. *torrion*, ad. It. *torrione* 'any great towre, or strong keepe' (Florio), augm. of *torre* tower.] A large tower (in Italy).

1652 HOWELL *Giraffi's Rev. Naples* II. 144 Hereupon there went off from the Torrion of Carmine, twenty six shot of Ordinance. *Ibid.* 191 That the said Torrion or Bastion should be put into his hands.

torrit, obs. form of TOWERED *a.*

torrock, local form of TARROCK, a gull.

1752 J. HILL *Hist. Anim.* 449 The Larus, with a white head, with a spot of black on each side..; Our common people in Cornwall call it the Torrock.

‖**To'rrubia.** *Bot.* [mod.L., named after Joseph Torrubia (d. 1768).] A genus of ascomycetous fungi, parasitic on living insects: a synonym of *Cordyceps*, but frequent in Eng. use.

1883 R. TURNER in *Gd. Words* Nov. 731/2 The Red Torrubia, growing from the pupa of a moth.

torry (ˈtɒrɪ), *v.* [ad. Sp. *torear* to fight (a bull), to be a bullfighter.] *trans.* To provoke and fight (a bull).

1936 R. CAMPBELL *Mithraic Emblems* 52 The white Torero—him who took the toss Sky-high upon the black horns of the Cross, For torrying the hornèd prince of Death. **1957** A. MACNAB *Bulls of Iberia* viii. 81 To give passes to a bull is not the same as to 'torry' it (*torear*). *Torear* means to exercise control over the bull at all times, and to work on it as desired. *Ibid.* 263 *Torear*, to 'torry', neologism.. adopted from Roy Campbell.. who has used it in print for twenty years.

torsade (tɔːˈseɪd). [a. F. *torsade* a twisted fringe, f. L. stem *tors-* twisted: see TORSE[1] and -ADE.] A twisted fringe, cord, or ribbon, used as an adornment in head-dresses, curtains, etc.

1872 *Young Englishwoman* Nov. 593/1 The black velvet bonnet is trimmed with a torsade of violet faille ribbon. **1882** *Society* 14 Oct. 24/1 Another.. hat was composed of cream white felt,.. trimmed with.. torsades of cream velvet. **1889** *Harper's Mag.* Apr. 753/1 Little children,.. with their heads shaven, and on the crown a tuft of hair bound up and lengthened out with torsades of red wool. **1894** *Season* X. 35/2 A velvet and silk torsade.

torsal (ˈtɔːsəl), *a. Geom.* [f. TORSE[3] + -AL[1].] Of or pertaining to a torse: see quot.

1869 CAYLEY *Math. Papers* VI. 334 If there is at each point of the line one and the same tangent plane, then the section of the surface by the tangent plane contains the line at least twice; if it contain it twice only, the line is *torsal*; if three times the line is *oscular*, and the tangent plane containing the torsal or oscular line may in like manner be termed a torsal, or an oscular tangent plane.

‖**Torschlusspanik** (ˈtoːrʃlʊsˌpanɪk). [Ger., lit. 'shut door (or gate) panic'.] A sense of alarm or anxiety (said to be experienced particularly in middle age) caused by the suspicion that life's opportunities are passing (or have passed) one by; *spec.* that manifested in an ageing woman who longs to (re)discover the (sexual) excitement of youth, and who fears being left 'on the shelf'.

1963 P. BRACKEN *I Hate to Housekeep Bk.* ix. 92 The random housewife is often prone to Torschlusspanik, or fear of being locked in the park at night, after the gates are closed. **1977** *Time* 8 Aug. 21/3 She was haunted by *Torschluss-panik* (mid-life crisis). **1980** *Times Lit. Suppl.* 14 Mar. 287/2 She [*sc.* Mme de Staël] is perhaps history's most outstanding case of *Torschlusspanik*: the panic at the shutting of the door.

torse[1] (tɔːs). *Her.* Also 6–9 torce. [a. obs. F. *torse, torce*, fem. a wreath:—Romanic type **torsa*, f. stem *tors-* for L. *tort-* from *torquēre* to twist.] An occasional term for the twisted band or wreath by which the crest is joined to the helmet.

1572 BOSSEWELL *Armourie* II. 60 b, For the Creaste uppon the Helme an Hiricion passante, of the Diamonde, charged with Grapes propre, sett on a torce, Pearle and Emeraude. **1652** J. WRIGHT tr. *Camus' Nat. Paradox* x. 265 A Milk-white Plume shadowed the Torse of his glittering Helmet. *a* **1700** B. E. *Dict. Cant. Crew, Wreath*,.. a Torce between the Mantle and the Crest. **1892** E. CASTLE *Eng. Bk.-plates* 92 The crest is supported by a plain torce. **1910** E. R. SUFFLING *Eng. Ch. Brasses* 124 A torse, or wreath of two bands of coloured silk.

Hence **torsed** (tɔːst) *a.*, also **torced**, furnished with a torse.

1892 EGERTON CASTLE *Eng. Book-plates* 51 The crested, torced, and mantletted helm.

torse[2] (tɔːs). [a. F. *torse* masc. (16th c.), ad. It. *torso*.] = TORSO.

1622 PEACHAM *Compl. Gent.* xii. (1634) 110 To Painters for the picturing of some excellent arme, leg, torse or wreathing of the body, or any other rare posture. **1762** GOLDSM. *Cit. W.* xxxiv, The torse.. is at last discovered to be a Hercules spinning, and not a Cleopatra bathing. **1892** LD. LYTTON *King Poppy* v. 78 The necessary quantity of heads To suit the growing torse.

torse[3] (tɔːs). *Geom.* [f. med.L. *tors-us, -um*, for L. *tort-us* twisted.] A developable surface; a surface generated by a moving straight line which at every instant is turning, in some plane or other through it, about some point or other in its length.

1863 CAYLEY *Math. Papers* (1892) V. 182 By Torse (*m, n*) I denote the developable surface or 'Torse' generated by a line which meets each of the curves *m* and *n*. **1879** —— in *Encycl. Brit.* X. 417 If the system be such that a line does not intersect the consecutive line, then the surface is a skew surface, or scroll; but if it be such that each line intersects the consecutive line, then it is a developable, or torse.

torsel: see TASSEL *sb.*[2]

torsi'bility. [f. **torsible* (f. *tors-*, ppl. stem (see prec.) + -IBLE) + -ITY.] Capability of being twisted; esp. in reference to degree or amount.

1864 WEBSTER s.v., The torsibility of a rope. **1884** A. DANIELL *Princ. of Physics* x. 234 Torsibility of a body is measured in the simplest case—that of a rod or wire—in terms of the angle through which a unit of force, applied at the distance of one cm. from the axis.. can twist it.

torsile (ˈtɔːsɪl, -aɪl), *a.* [f. L. *tors-*, ppl. stem (see prec.) + -IL, -ILE.] Of the nature of torsion.

1882 *Athenæum* 25 Mar. 385/1 A process for increasing the resistance of iron to tensile, torsile, and transverse strains.

torsiograph (ˈtɔːʃɪəʊgrɑːf, -æ-). *Mech.* [f. late L. *torsiō* (see TORSION) + -GRAPH.] An instrument for measuring torsional oscillations of the crankshaft of an engine.

1930 *Engineering* 25 Apr. 551/3 The handiest instrument, and therefore the most widely used, is the torsiograph. **1950** *Ibid.* 1 Sept. 204/1 It was decided.. to carry out torsiograph tests on the engines under specially standardised conditions with specified instrumentation.

torsi'ometer. *Ophthalm.* [f. late L. *torsio* (see next) + -METER.] An instrument for investigation of the declination of the meridians of the eye.

1904 in *Dunglison's Med. Lex.* (ed. 23).

torsion (ˈtɔːʃən). Also 5 torcion, 6 -syon, 7 tortion. [a. F. *torsion* (1314 in Littré, in sense 2 below), ad. late L. *torsiōn-em* (Vulg.), by-form of *tortiōn-em*, n. of action from L. *torquēre, tort-um* to twist, wring. Cf. Pr. *torsio*, Sp. *torsion*, Pg. *torsão*; also It. *torzione*, ad. L. *tortiōnem*.]

1. a. The action of twisting, or turning a body spirally by the operation of contrary forces acting at right angles to its axis; also the twisted condition produced by this action; twist.

angle of torsion, (*a*) the angle through which one end of a rod or other body is twisted while the other end is held fast; (*b*) *Geom.* the infinitesimal angle between two consecutive osculating planes of a tortuous curve. ***balance of torsion*** = torsion-balance: see 3.

1543 TRAHERON *Vigo's Chirurg.* VI. i. 180 Yf the dislocation be lytle, so that the bone be not out all togyther, it is called dislocation not complete, and it is it which commonly is called torsion, or wresting. **1658** PHILLIPS, *Torsion*, a wresting, or wringing of any thing. **1807** T. YOUNG *Lect. Nat. Phil.* I. 140 Torsion, or twisting, consists in the lateral displacement, or detrusion, of the opposite parts of a solid, in opposite directions, the central particles only remaining in their natural state. *Ibid.* 141 The force of torsion, as it is determined by experiment, varies simply as the angle of torsion. **1814** R. BUCHANAN *Shafts Mills* 24 *note*, Journals, or journeys, are gudgeons subject to torsion. **1834** *Nat. Philos.* III. *Hist. Astron.* xxi. 105/2 (Usef. Knowl. Soc.) By means of a delicate instrument, called the balance of torsion, the attraction of a leaden sphere, eight inches in diameter, was made sensible. **1835** URE *Philos. Manuf.* 106 With very short filaments like those of wool, cotton, and cachemire, a thread of the greatest length may be formed by torsion. **1859** J. TOMES *Dental Surg.* 163 Torsion, or twisting of the central incisors upon their axis, is far from rare. **1867** THOMSON & TAIT *Nat. Phil.* I. I. §608 The fundamental principle that spiral springs act chiefly by torsion seems to have been first discovered by Binet in 1814.

b. A twisting of the body or a part of it; contortion, distortion. *rare.*

1660 F. BROOKE tr. *Le Blanc's Trav.* 89 They ejulate, weep, and lament with exotick gestures, and tortions. **1899** *Allbutt's Syst. Med.* VII. 242 During the flexions and torsions of the vertebral column.

c. *Surg.* The twisting of the cut end of an artery to stop hæmorrhage.

1835–6 *Todd's Cycl. Anat.* I. 224/2 The successful employment of torsion of the arteries as a means of suppressing hæmorrhage. **1878** T. BRYANT *Pract. Surg.* (1879) II. 5 Any bleeding taking place can usually be checked by cold styptics, or torsion.

d. *Bot.* The condition of being twisted spirally.

1875 BENNETT & DYER *Sach's Bot.* 772 A distinction must be drawn between two kinds of torsion; firstly, that of erect organs; and secondly, that of organs.. in a horizontal or oblique position. In the former case the torsion results from internal conditions of growth, and especially from the outer layers growing more rapidly than the inner ones.

e. *Math.* The degree to which a curve departs from being planar at any given point, measured by the rate of change of the angle of the osculating plane or the binormal with respect to distance along the curve; ***radius of torsion***, the reciprocal of this.

1862 G. SALMON *Treat. Analytic Geom. Three Dimensions* xi. 269 The angle made with each other by two consecutive osculating planes.. we shall call the angle of torsion, and denote by $d\eta$. *Ibid.* 270 Following the analogy of the radius of curvature which is $ds/d\theta$, the later French writers denote the quantity $ds/d\eta$ by the letter r, and call it the radius of torsion. **1939** BURINGTON & TORRANCE *Higher Math.* vi. 711 Torsion is agreed to be positive when the rotation (with s increasing) of the binormal increases in the same sense as that of a right-handed screw traveling in the direction of t. **1978** E. C. YOUNG *Vector & Tensor Analysis* ii. 106 The torsion of a plane curve is zero, just as the curvature of a straight line is zero.

f. *Zool.* The twisting of the visceral hump of gastropod molluscs through 180 degrees when the embryo reaches a certain stage of development.

1888 ROLLESTON & JACKSON *Forms Animal Life* (ed. 2) 475 In.. the *Streptoneura*, the posterior union of the visceral nerves.. is situated dorsally to the intestine, and the loop is therefore twisted with the torsion of the visceral dome. **1930** G. R. DE BEER *Embryol. & Evol.* vii. 53 The limpet develops into a more or less symmetrical Veliger larva which suddenly undergoes a twist through 180°, the process of torsion occupying two or three minutes. **1972** M. S. GARDINER *Biol. of Invertebrates* ii. 59/2 Torsion appears to be a reversible process, for in some genera the anus and the organs on either side of it lie posteriorly and the nerve commissures are untwisted.

g. *Chem.* Restricted rotation of an atom or group about a bond joining it to another atom.
1932 *Physical Rev.* XL. 445 (*heading*) The torsion oscillator-rotator in the quantum mechanics. **1978** *Nature* 14 Dec. 674/1 Although in some cases, rotation of a rigid molecular structure cannot lead to superposition, this may be possible as a result of torsion about certain bonds.

†**2.** *Path.* A wringing or griping of the bowels; tormina. *Obs.* (The earliest sense in Eng.)
c **1425** tr. *Arderne's Treat. Fistula* 78 It availeþ..to euery inflacion of þe wombe, and to ventositе of it, and torcions, i.[e.] gryndyng. **1543** TRAHERON *Vigo's Chirurg.* III. *Wounds* I. ii. 100 Knowen by the greate payne, and torsyon or grypynge of the bellie. **1626** BACON *Sylva* §39 All Purgers have in them a raw Spirit, or Winde; which is the principall Cause of Tortion in the Stomach, & Belly. **1689** MOYLE *Sea Chyrurg.* III. vii. 109 Sometimes there is..intolerable tortion of the Bowels.

3. *attrib.* and *Comb.*, as ***torsion arm, axis, circle, pendulum, screw, spring***; **torsion-balance**, an instrument for measuring minute horizontal forces, consisting of a wire or filament having a horizontal arm to the end of which the force is applied so as to make it revolve and twist the wire, etc., through an angle proportional to the twisting moment of the force; **torsion bar**, a bar that is subject to torque; *spec.* one in the suspension of some motor vehicles, fixed to the frame at one end and the wheel assembly at the other so that up-and-down motion of the latter tends to twist the bar and is thereby absorbed; **torsion-basin** *Geol.*, a basin formed by torsion of the earth's crust in any region; **torsion-curve**, a curve caused by torsion; **torsion electrometer**, an electrometer that measures by means of a torsion-balance; **torsionmeter**, **torsion meter**, an instrument which measures the torsion in a rotating shaft, thus providing information about the power output of the engine driving it; **torsion test** *Engin.*, a test in which a material is subjected to torsion (see quot. 1936).
1831 HOLLAND *Manuf. Metal* I. 199 It does not appear that these torsion nails have ever found much favour. **1837** BREWSTER *Magnet.* 15 The torsion balance, for measuring small forces. **1873** MAXWELL *Electr. & Magn.* §38 The torsion-balance was devised by Michell for the determination of the force of gravitation between small bodies, and was used by Cavendish for this purpose. *Ibid.* §215 The angle through which the electrical force twisted the torsion-arm. *Ibid.* §725 The torsion-screw, which turns the torsion-head round a vertical axis. **1884** F. J. BRITTEN *Watch & Clockm.* 265 Small clocks..are made with torsion pendulums. **1891** W. G. KIRCALDY *Strength & Properties of Materials* vii. 196 Some examples of Twisting, or torsion, tests have been given to show in a graphic way the behaviour of different metals. **1899** MAR. M. OGILVIE-GORDON in *Nature* 7 Sept. 445/1 Two great internal torsion-basins, within the Alpine systems of southern Europe, are the Hungarian and the west Mediterranean. **1901** —— *Ibid.* 24 Jan. 294/1, I wrote my paper on the 'Torsion-structure of the Dolomites' in 1898. *Ibid.* 295 The torsion-curves round the northern periphery of the Adriatic crust-basin. **1905** *Engineering* 7 Apr. 440 (*heading*) Denny and Johnson's torsion meter. **1936** P. F. FOSTER *Mech. Testing of Metals & Alloys* vii. 115 Torsion tests are carried out to determine the modulus of rigidity of a material..or to ascertain its ultimate torsional strength. **1937** *Daily Herald* 15 Jan. 16/6 The action of the torsion-bar controlled shock-absorbers preventing roll and pitch. **1969** DIVAKARAN & GARG *Strength of Materials* i. 27 In a torsion test on the same specimen the angle of twist was found to be 0.43°. **1978** L. PRYOR *Viper* viii. 150 He'd nodded and set to work ordering adjustments to the tires, wings and torsion bars. **1983** *Sci. Amer.* Jan. 120/2 The strength of the gravitational force is measured from the magnetic force that is required to prevent the rotation of a torsion bar when an additional mass is brought close to it. **1970** *Jrnl. Physics E* III. 105/1 The only practicable way to measure the power [of a ship's main engine] is by the use of a torsionmeter, ie an instrument that measures the twist put in the propeller shaft by the torque it transmits.

Hence **'torsionless** *a.*, not subject to torsion.
1858 HERSCHEL *Outl. Astron.* I. iv. (ed. 5) 160 A metallic arc..supported from its middle..by a torsionless suspension.

torsional ('tɔːʃənəl), *a.* [f. prec. + -AL[1].] Of, pertaining or relating to, or caused by or resulting from torsion.
1861 FAIRBAIRN *Iron* 195 Experiments..on the torsional strength of iron cast in various forms. **1873** MAXWELL *Electr. & Magn.* §215 The torsional elasticity of a glass fibre or metal wire. **1879** THOMSON & TAIT *Nat. Phil.* I. I. §435 The torsional rigidity of iron, copper, and brass wires is diminished about ½ per cent. with 10° elevation of temperature. **1882** *Rep. to Ho. Repr. Prec. Met. U.S.* 583 There is..considerable torsional strain upon the shaft, depending on its length. **1909** *Athenæum* 6 Mar. 292/1 Interesting experiments are described on the energy dissipated through torsional hysteresis.

Hence **'torsionally** *adv.*, in respect of torsion.
1890 *Nature* 2 Jan. 198 The internal friction of a torsionally oscillating iron wire.

torsive ('tɔːsɪv), *a. Bot.* [f. med.L. *tors-us* twisted + -IVE.] Twisted spirally; = CONTORTED 2: see quot.
1866 *Treas. Bot.*, *Torsive*, twisted spirally. The same as Contorted, except that there is no obliquity in the form or insertion of the pieces as in the petals of *Oxalis*.

torsk, var. TUSK *sb.*[3]

torso ('tɔːsəʊ). *Pl.* **torsos.** [a. It. *torso* stalk, stump (e.g. of a cabbage), core (of apple or pear), trunk of a statue:—L. *thyrsus* stalk, stem (of a plant), a. Gr. θύρσος the THYRSUS (q.v.) or Bacchic wand. The common Romanic form was **turso-*, whence also OF. *tors, tros, trous*, Pr. *tros*, Sp. *trozo* stem, stump.]

1. *Sculpture.* The trunk of a statue, without or considered independently of head and limbs; also, the trunk of the human body. Also *attrib.*
1797 HOLCROFT *Stolberg's Trav.* (ed. 2) II. xlvii. 144 The thigh, and *torso*, or body, from the neck to the hip, are inimitable. **1805** W. TAYLOR in *Monthly Mag.* XX. 43 An antique female statue, or rather the torso of a statue, had formerly stood in the library at Wolfenbüttel. **1833** ELLIS *Elgin Marbles* II. 29 The torso of Apteral Victory is 4 ft. 9 in. in height. **1860** HAWTHORNE *Marb. Faun* v, Headless and legless torsos. **1865** DICKENS *Mut. Fr.* I. ii, With..too much torso in his waistcoat. **1875** F. WEY *Rome* xxiii. 300 The Torso of the Belvedere, a colossal fragment of Herculean stature... Michelangelo studied it to such a degree that he was wont to call himself pupil of the Torso. **1899** F. T. BULLEN *Log Sea-waif* 296 Clad only in a waist-cloth, his torso was fully revealed.

2. *fig.* Something left mutilated or unfinished.
1825 T. MOORE *Life R. B. Sheridan* xvi. 534 And exhibit little more than the mere *Torso* of his eloquence. **1852** LONGFELLOW in *Life* (1891) II. 240 We have seen only the brief and mutilated torso of your speech. **1892** STEVENSON *Across the Plains* 132 Headless epics, glorious torsos of dramas. **1906** H. BLACK *Edin. Serm.* 56 Without Christ the Old Testament is only a torso.

3. *Comb.*: **torso-tosser** *slang*, a hootchy-kootchy dancer.
1927 *Vanity Fair* (N.Y.) XXIX. 134/2 A kootch or hootchie kootchie dancer is a 'torso tosser'. **1954** F. P. KEYES *Royal Box* 361 Barbara Villiers, a torso-tosser who got to be no less than the Duchess of Cleveland.

torsocclusion (tɔːsɒ'kluːʒən). *Surg.* [f. med.L. *tors-us* twisted + OCCLUSION.] Treatment by acupressure combined with torsion.
1899 *Syd. Soc. Lex.*, *Torsoclusion*, a form of acupressure in which the point of the pin is pushed through a portion of tissue parallel to the course of the vessel to be secured, then carried over its anterior surface, and..swept round until it is brought to a right angle to the course of the artery, when its point is thrust into the soft parts beyond.

tort (tɔːt), *sb.* Also 6–7 **torte.** [a. OF. *tort* (11th c. in Hatz.-Darm.) = Pr. *tort*, Sp. *tuerto*, It. *torto*, med.L. *tortum*, wrong, injustice (cf. *tortum facere*, 864, in *Capitul. Caroli II*), sbst. use of L. *tortus*, *-um* twisted, wrung, pa. pple. of *torquēre* to twist, wring.]

†**1.** Injury, wrong. *Obs.* [see TORTIOUS *a.* 1].
1387–8 T. USK *Test. Love* II. ii. (Skeat) l. 71 Than wer tort & forthe [? force] nought worthe an haw about. **1585** JAS. I *Ess. Poesie* (Arb.) 33 So Iob and Ieremie, preast with woes and wrongs, Did right descryue their ioyes, their woes and torts. **1590** SPENSER *F.Q.* II. v. 17 It was complained that thou hadst done great tort Unto an aged woman, poore and bare. **1591** —— *M. Hubberd* 1078 No wild beasts should do them any torte. **1632** LITHGOW *Trav.* x. 425 To show King Iames, my torments, pangs, and tort. **1748** MELMOTH *Fitzosb. Lett.* lxxii. (1749) II. 215 Deem not, ye plaintive crew, that suffer wrong, Ne thou, O man! who deal'st the tort, miswean The equal gods.

†**b.** Physical injury or pain; torment. **c.** A false or wrong statement. *Obs. rare.*
1632 LITHGOW *Trav.* v. 193 Good t'expell all sorts Of burning Feauers, in their violent torts. *Ibid.* x. 488 No Tort I introduct,..I Organize the Truth.

2. *Eng. Law.* The breach of a duty imposed by law, whereby some person acquires a right of action for damages.
1586 FERNE *Blaz. Gentrie* 214 Ministers of the Gospell, to whome the keyes of right do apperteine (for the others did by dissenin and tort, hold the possession of them). **1609** SKENE *Reg. Maj.*, *Stat. Robt. I*, 23 Saifeand the Law and consuetude of Burghis, quhilk is, to defend preciselie torte and non reason, that is wrang and vnlaw. **1622** CALLIS *Stat. Sewers* (1647) 184 If two be admitted to a Copyhold by Tort, or to an Office in a Court of Justice unlawfully. **1647** N. BACON *Disc. Govt. Eng.* I. lxvii. (1739) 162 In case it concerned only a Tort done to the party, he was amerced. **1714** SCROGGS *Courts-leet* (ed. 3) 59 This is a private Tort to the particular Inhabitants of this Vill. **1768** BLACKSTONE *Comm.* III. viii. 117 Personal actions are such whereby a man claims a debt, or personal duty, or damages in lieu thereof; and, likewise whereby a man claims a satisfaction in damages for some injury done to his person or property. The former are said to be founded on contracts, the latter upon *torts* or wrongs. **1887** SIR F. POLLOCK (*title*) The Law of Torts. **1895** POLLOCK & MAITLAND *Hist. Eng. Law* II. 510 *note*, *Tort* again is [in 13th c. A.-Fr.] a large, loose word. Britton, I. 77, heads a chapter on some of the smaller offences present in the eyres by the title *De plusours tortz*. **1909** SIR F. POLLOCK in *Encycl. Laws of Eng.* (ed. 2) XIV. 134 What we now understand by a tort is a breach of some duty between citizens, defined by the general law, which creates a civil cause of action. The duty must be founded in common right... It must be a duty assigned by law, not dependent on the will of the parties... There must be a private right of action.

†**tort**, *ppl. a. Obs.* [ad. L. *tort-us*, pa. pple. of *torquēre* to twist.] Twisted; in quot. 1513, ? tortured (const. as *pa. pple.*).
1513 DOUGLAS *Æneis* X. xi. 30 Now sall he perisch,..be Troianis tort and rent. **1568** GRAFTON *Chron.* II. 210 Henry Erle of Lancaster with yͤ wrie neck, called Tort coll. **1765** J. LEE *Introd. Bot.* I. xii. 28 *Tort*, twisted, as in *Nerium*.

tort, erroneous variant of TAUT *a.*

‖**torta** ('torta). *Mining.* [Sp. *torta*: see next.] One of the large flat circular heaps or 'cakes' of ore spread upon the floor or *patio* (PATIO 2) in the Mexican amalgamation process.
1839 URE *Dict. Arts* 1119 The *patio*, or amalgamation floor..is capable of containing 24 *tortas*, or flat circular collections of *lama*, of about 50 feet diameter, and 7 inches deep. **1881** RAYMOND *Mining Gloss.*, *Torta*, a flat heap of silver ore (slime or pulp) prepared for the patio process.

tortayes, tortays: see TORTIS.

torte (sense 2: 'tɔːtə). [In sense 1, ad. F. *tourte*, dial. *torte* = Sp. and It. *torta*:—late L. *tōrta* (Vulg. 1 Chron. xvi. 3 *tortam panis*, Wyclif 'a kake of brede'). A different word from L. *torta* twisted: see also TOURTE[1] and TART; in sense 2, a. G. *torte*, of same origin.] †**1.** A round cake (of bread). *Obs.*
1555 EDEN *Decades* 194 They drawe a mylke thereof [i.e. of the coco-nut]..The which the Christian men of those regions put in the tortes or cakes which they make of the grayne of *Maizium*..by reason of the sayde mylke of *Cocus*, the tortes are more excellent to be eaten withowt offence to the stomake.

2. Pl. **torten** or **tortes.** An elaborate sweet cake or tart.
1748 H. GLASSE *Art of Cookery* (ed. 3) viii. 142 To make a Tort. First make a fine Puff-paste. **1957** [see PASTRY 1 c]. **1967** V. NABOKOV *Speak, Memory* (rev. ed.) x. 205 Wedges of slightly salty mokka *torte* with whipped cream. **1972** F. B. MAYNARD *Raisins & Almonds* 20 Mama produced meringues..puff paste..tortes layered with nut creams and Turkish delight.

‖**torteau** (tɔrto). *Pl.* **torteaux** (tɔrtoz). Also *pl.* 5 **tortellis**, 6 **tourteaulx, torteaulxes**, 6–8 **torteauxes**, 7 **tortauxes**, 8 **torteaux's, tourteaux, tourteauxes.** [a. F. *tourteau* 'a large round cake or flat bannock of bread', a mass of oilcake, a wooden disk used as a crusher, and in heraldry as below; in OFr. *tortel* (12th c. in Hatz.-Darm.), in Guernsey *tourtel* (= Pr. *tortelh*, Cat. *tortell*), deriv. of *tourte* (TOURTE[1], TORTE).]

1. *Her.* A roundle gules; the specific name of a small red circular figure charged upon a shield, supposed to represent a cake of bread.
1486 *Bk. St. Albans, Her.* e vj, Ther be also tortellis yͭ be litill Cakys the wich be grettir then ballys & [= if] tharmys be truly made as here it is opyn... *Portat tres tortellas rubias in campo aureo*... He berith golde & iij. Cakys of gowles. **1530** in *Ancestor* XI. (1904) 180 A lymmers hede rased sable with a coller siluer full of tourteaulx. **1562** LEIGH *Armorie* 151 b, He beareth or, x torteauxes... These haue been called of olde blazoures, wastelles, and are cakes of breade. **1725** COATS *Dict. Her.*, *Tourteaux*, according to the French, and *Tourteauxes*, as we make the Plural Number in English, are small Rounds..in England,..they are always Red; but the French give the same Name to such as are of any other Colour, expressing the same... The *Tourteaux* in Latin are call'd *Tortellæ*. **1825** *Gentl. Mag.* XCV. I. 305/1 Sir Thomas Dacre..used these arms: Argent, a chevron Sable between three Torteaux, on each an escallop Argent. **1894** *Parker's Gloss. Her.*, *Torteau*..: the name now always applied to a *roundle gules*... The figure is said to have been intended to represent the sacred Host.

†**2.** A flat cake, a pancake. *Obs.*
(Cf. quot. 1562 in 1.)
1625 PURCHAS *Pilgrims* II. IX. xix. §3. 1652 Torteaux and Bignets, and many other sorts of food... They make pottage, and Torteaux and Galletus.

torteaux, torteise, tortesse, obs. ff. TORTOISE.

tortel, early f. TORTEAU; obs. f. TURTLE.

tortellini (tɔːtɪ'liːniː), *sb. pl.* Also *erron.* tortelloni. [a. It., pl. of *tortellino*, dim. of *tortello* cake, fritter, dim. of *torta*: see TORTE.] Small squares of pasta rolled round a filling and then formed into a ring shape.
1937 M. MORPHY *Good Food from Italy* 5 One of the characteristic features of Italian soups is their garnish..—*ravioli, tortellini, gnocchi* and plain dumplings or forcemeat dumplings. **1954** E. DAVID *Italian Food* 102 Although tortellini are always to be had in the restaurants of Bologna, in private houses they are still the great dish for Christmas Eve. **1975** J. CLEARY *Safe House* iv. 172 Charlie Lincoln ate the now-just-warm tortelloni he had bought. **1980** *Times* 18 Oct. 11/8 The Bolognese invented tagliatelle, tortellini and lasagne.

tortes: see TORTIS.

†**tortey.** *Obs.* Variant of TORTEAU 1.
1688 R. HOLME *Armoury* I. 103/3 Our old English terms were..Torteys for Torteauxes.

tortfeasor ('tɔːt,fiːzə(r)). *Law.* [a. OF. *tortfesor*, *tort-faiseur*, *torfesor*, f. *tort* wrong, evil + *-fesor*, *faiseur* doer. (In OF. *tortfesor*, *tort* is an adj.

qualifying *fesor*; hence pl. *torzfesors*.)] One who is guilty of a tort; a wrong-doer, trespasser.

1659 CROKE *Reports* II. (1669) 383 He is meerly a *Tortfeasor*, and that Trespass liable against him to recover damages. **1670** BLOUNT *Law Dict.*, *Tortfeasor*, a Doer of wrong, a Trespasser. Hence in later Law Dicts. **1883** *Law Times Rep.* XLIX. 11/2 Waiving the tort and bringing an action of *indebitatus assumpsit* for work and labour done against the tort feasor. **1886** *Times* 27 Jan. 4 The father and son were here being sued by the plaintiff as joint tortfeasors.

‖**torticollis** (tɔːtɪˈkɒlɪs). *Path.* [mod.L., f. L. *tort-us* crooked, twisted + *collum* neck. Cf. obs. F. *torticolis*.] A rheumatic or other affection of the muscles of the neck, in which it is so twisted as to keep the head turned to one side; wry-neck.

1811 HOOPER *Med. Dict.*, *Torticollis*, the wry neck. **1857** DUNGLISON *Med. Lex.*, *Torticollis*..*Stiffneck, Wryneck*.., a variety of rheumatism, seated in the muscles of the neck. **1859** SEMPLE *Diphtheria* 347 There was also painful torticollis. **1897** *Allbutt's Syst. Med.* III. 63 In cases of rheumatic torticollis there is conspicuous muscular spasm.

tortie (ˈtɔːtɪ). [dim. of TORTOISE-SHELL.] = *tortoise-shell cat* s.v. TORTOISE-SHELL 4b. Also *attrib.*

1948 P. M. SODERBERG *Cat Breeding* 312 The three colours required in the Tortie are black, red and cream. **1958** E. F. DAGLISH *Pet-Keeper's Man.* 1 Tortoise shell cats are almost invariably females... Anyone owning a male 'tortie' may pride himself on the possession of a feline rarity. **1960** *Times* 17 Mar. 1/4 (Advt.), Must find home for beautiful tortiecat. **1976** POND & SAYER *Cats* 25 Bi-Colours, bred from Tortie and White mothers,..could be produced.

tortile (ˈtɔːtɪl, -aɪl), *a. rare.* [ad. L. *tortilis*, f. *tort-*, ppl. stem of *torquēre* to twist: see -IL, -ILE.] Twisted, coiled; winding; capable of being twisted.

1658 SIR T. BROWNE *Gard. Cyrus* iii. 59 He..may observe it in the Tortile and tiring stroaks of Gnatworms. **1760** J. LEE *Introd. Bot.* III. xxii. (1765) 227 The Arista is tortile, twisted, when it has a twisted Joint in the Middle. **1819** H. BUSK *Vestriad* IV. 116 Each in her arms two fiery dragons holds, With slender limbs restrains the tortile folds. **1835** URE *Philos. Manuf.* 62 Tortile fabrics used for making webs of various kinds.

Hence **torˈtility**, the quality of being tortile.

1835 URE *Philos. Manuf.* 62 Under tortility must likewise be considered..fulling, felting, and the manufacture of hats. **1846** WORCESTER cites *Monthly Review*.

‖**tortilla** (torˈtiʎa). Also 9 tortillia. [Sp. dim. of *torta* cake: see TORTA.] In Mexico, A thin round cake made of maize-flour, baked on a flat plate of iron, earthenware, etc. and eaten hot.

1699 DAMPIER *Voy.* II. II. 43 Tartilloes are small Cakes made of the Flower of Indian Corn. **1828** LYON *Mexico* x. II. 142 Obliged to seek..for some woman, who will make a few tortillas or a dish of black beans. **1842** *New World* 11 June 373/3 Maiz..is chiefly used in the Tortillia cakes, of which we hear so much in Mexico..a tortillia is indispensable at least once a day for all classes. **1854** J. LL. STEPHENS *Centr. Amer.* 29 The people live exclusively upon tortillas, flat cakes made of crushed Indian Corn, and baked on a clay griddle. **1888** LEES & CLUTTERBUCK *Brit. Columbia 1887* xxii. (1892) 239 One of our favourite luxuries is the tortilla (pronounced torteea).

tortillon (tɔːˈtɪljɔ̃). [a. F. *tortillon*, f. *tortiller* to twist, twirl.] = STUMP *sb.*[2]

1885 F. FOWLER *Drawing in Charcoal and Crayon* ii. 12 The other form of paper stump, known as the tortillon, is made of strips of paper rolled to a point like spills. **1895** *Army & Navy Co-op Soc. Price List* 674/2 Stumps for chalk drawing... Tortillons, White. **1970** *Oxf. Compan. Art* 1111/2 *Stump*, also called *tortillon*. A short tapered stick usually of cork or tightly rolled leather or paper, used to soften the edges of a drawing or spread the chalk, crayon, or pencil in shading. It was used in 18th-c. France.

tortilly (tɔːˈtɪlɪ), *a. Her.* [ad. F. *tortillé* twisted, (in heraldry) wreathed, pa. pple. of *tortiller* to twist closely, f. *tort*, pa. pple. of *tordre* to twist.] (See quots.)

[*c* **1828** BERRY *Encycl. Her.* I. Gloss., *Tortillé*, a French term for nowed, twisted, or wreathed. **1889** ELVIN *Dict. Her.*, *Tortille*, nowed, twisted, or wreathed.] **1894** *Parker's Gloss. Her.*, *Tortilly*,..a term applied to Ordinaries which are wreathed,..the term *wreathy* is also found... Or, a lion rampant gules, a chief tortilly gules and vert..Macritchie.

†**torˈtiloquy.** *Obs. rare*[−0]. [ad. late or med.L. *tortiloquium* (Du Cange), f. *tortus* crooked + *loqui* to speak.] (See quot.)

1656 BLOUNT *Glossogr.*, *Tortiloquy*,..crooked talk.

tortion, obs. form of TORSION.

†**ˈtortionary**, *a. Obs. rare*[−1]. [ad. med.L. *tortiōnāri-us* unjust, injurious (1394 in Du Cange), F. *tortionnaire*, f. L. *tortiōn-em* 'torment, torture', in med.L. 'exercise of violence': see -ARY.] Wrongful, illegal.

1694 FALLE *Jersey* vii. 215 A Prize made by one Pointy,..was..pronounced Tortionary, and Illegal, and Pointy adjudged to make Restitution.

tortious (ˈtɔːʃəs), *a.* Also 4–6 torcious, 6 torteouse. [a. Anglo-Fr. *torcious* (14th c.), f. stem of *torcion*, *tortion*: see prec. and -IOUS. In use associated with TORT *sb.*, as if from *tort* + *-eous*: cf. *righteous*, *wrongous*, etc.]

†**1.** Wrongful, injurious, hurtful; illegal. *Obs.*

1387–8 T. USK *Test. Love* II. ii. (Skeat) l. 73 Than wer tort & forthe [? force] nought worthe an haw about, and pleasen no men, but thilke greuous and torcious been in might and in doinge. *a* **1548** HALL *Chron.*, *Edw. IV* 217b, A cruell man and a torcious vsurper. **1583** STUBBES *Anat. Abus.* I. (1879) 36 The deuil..inticed him (oh, torteouse serpent!) to eat of the forbidden fruite. **1590** SPENSER *F.Q.* II. ii. 18 Ne ought he car'd whom he endamaged By tortious wrong, or whom bereav'd of right. **1742** SHENSTONE *Schoolmistress* xv, When ..tortious death was true Devotion's meed.

2. *Law.* Pertaining to or of the nature of a tort. (Early quots. show the gradual development of sense.)

1544 tr. *Littleton's Tenures* 90 The more..that he came to the dede by a lawfull meane, than by a torcyous meane. **1619** DALTON *Country Just.* xciii. (1630) 237 Where the arrest is tortious,..there the killing of him that maketh such an unlawful arrest, is..manslaughter onely. **1671** F. PHILLIPS *Reg. Necess.* 259 The parties..endeavouring such breaches of Priviledge, should not take advantage *de son tort*, of their own wrongs or tortious doings. **1766** BLACKSTONE *Comm.* II. ix. 150 Unless the owner..will declare his continuance to be tortious, or, in common language, wrongful. **1863** H. COX *Instit.* II. viii. 500 To restrain threatened irremediable injuries to property by acts of a tortious kind. **1907** *Law Rep.* in *Cycl. Tour. Club Gaz.* June 220 The animal..would have done no harm but for the tortious act of a third person.

†**3.** Wrong, incorrect, improper. *Obs. rare.*

1644 [H. PARKER] *Jus Pop.* 66 A tortious, unnatural sense of the words. **1657** W. MORICE *Coena quasi Κοινὴ* I. ii. 106 It seemes a very Tortious and improper answer.

¶**4.** Misused for TORTUOUS.

1682 in R. Burthogge *Argt. Infants Bapt.* iv. (1684) 170 The most involved, tortious, intricate, that ever you heard of, except Origens Allegorical and Mystical Commentaries.

ˈtortiously, *adv.* [f. prec. + -LY[2]: cf. AF. *torciousement* (Godef.).] Wrongfully, illegally; by tort.

a **1812** LD. THURLOW in G. D. Collinson *Idiots & Lunaticks* (1812) I. 577 (Jod.) An application, where timber was cut by a stranger tortiously, to have the produce restored to the estate. **1818** CRUISE *Digest* (ed. 2) IV. 461 If a purchaser is tortiously evicted..he has his remedy at law. **1882** *Times* 22 Feb. 9/5 Not because the House had tortiously debarred Mr. Bradlaugh from taking his seat, but because Mr. Bradlaugh was disqualified by law from so doing.

†**ˈtortis.** *Obs.* Forms: 4 ? *pl.* tortyse, 4–5 *sing.* and *pl.* torteys, 5 *sing.* and *pl.* tortes, *sing.* tortays, *pl.* tortayes, torteies, 5–6 *sing.* and *pl.* tortys, 6 *pl.* tortaysez, 7 *sing.* and *pl.* tortis, *pl.* tortiz. [a. OF. *tortis*, *-iz* masc. (*a* 1200), also perh. *tortise*, *-isse* (*a* 1377), *-ice*, *-iche* fem., twisted thing, torch, in med.L. *tortīcius* (? 11th c. in Du Cange), *-īsius*, *-ītius* masc., also *tortīcia* fem. (*a* 1400) a torch, f. L. *tort-us* twisted, or med.L. *tortia* TORCH + *-īcius*, *-īcia*: see -ITIOUS. The forms in *-eys*, *-ays* are from OF. *torteis*, alteration of *tortis* after such words as *semeis*, for *semeis*:—**semināticius*.]

1. A kind of very large wax candle. (Usually distinguished from a *torch*: cf. quot. 1611.)

A note to Way's ed. of *Promp. Parv.* s.v. *Percher*, mentions *torticios*, 2 ells long and weighing 5 lb. each.

c **1375** *Sc. Leg. Saints* x. (*Mathou*) 250 Vith incense & lampis lycht And tortyse al brynnand brycht. **1404–5** *Abingdon Rolls* (Camden) 68 In j torteys empto xxij d. **1413** *Pilgr. Sowle* (Caxton) II. lx. (1859) 58 This wycked sauour, and smoke of the torteys when the fyre is oute. **1421–2** *Durham Acc. Rolls* (Surtees) 141 In candelis cerijs et albis.. cum ij torchis, ij tortys, iiij prikettys & factura eorundem. *c* **1450** *Bk. Curtasye* 492 in *Babees Bk.* 315 Fyrst to þe chaundeler he schalle go, To take a tortes lyȝt hym fro. *a* **1483** *Liber Niger* in *Househ. Ord.* (1790) 22 iii torches, one tortays, and iii prickettes. *Ibid.* 41 And he [a Grome of Chambyr] setteth nyghtly, after the seasons of the yere, torchys, tortays, candylles of wax, morters. **1506–7** *Burgh Rec. Edinb.* (1869) I. 111 That they have ilk ane ane new tortys reddy. **1533–4** *Durham Househ. Bk.* (Surtees) 249 Pro factura 4 le torchez et 4 tortaysez 16 d. **1601** F. TATE *Househ. Ord. Edw. II* (1876) 6 This stewarde..shall take everi night for his chamber, one sextier of wine, xij candels, two tortis, one tortis for wine, and one torche. [**1611** COTGR., *Tortis de cire*, a wreathed Linke or great candle of wax; most in vse about Candlemas.]

2. A twisted chain; a wreath. [mod.F. *tortis*.]

1688 R. HOLME *Armoury* IV. ix. (Roxb.) 390/2 A tortis or double chaine of gold.

tortive (ˈtɔːtɪv), *a. rare.* [ad. L. *tortīv-us*, f. *tort-*, ppl. stem of *torquēre* to twist: see -IVE.] Twisting, twisted, tortuous.

1606 SHAKS. *Tr. & Cr.* I. iii. 9 Tortiue and errant from his course of growth. **1656** BLOUNT *Glossogr.*, *Tortive* (*tortivus*), that is wrung or pressed out. *Br.* **1880** SWINBURNE *On Cliffs* 12 Between the tortive serpent-shapen roots.

So †**tortivous** *a. Obs.*, in same sense.

14.. LYDG. *Temple of Glas* (E.E.T.S.) p. 14 Ielusye, The vile serpent, the snake tortyvous.

tortle, obs. form of TURTLE.

†**ˈtortlet.** *Her. Obs.* [dim. of *tortel* TORTEAU.] A little cake of bread.

1486 *Bk. St. Albans, Her.* b iv b, Tortlettis be calde in armys wastell.

†**ˈtortness**, obs. f. TAUTNESS: cf. TAUT *a.* 2γ.

1727 BAILEY vol. II, *Tortness* (spoken of a Rope, etc.) Straightness, Tightness, by being hard pulled.

tortoise (ˈtɔːtəs, -tɪs). Forms: see below. [Found in 15th c. in forms *tortuca*, *tortuce*, *tortuge*, *tortu*, *tortuse*, *tortose*. *Tortūca* (*c* 1255 in Albertus Magnus *Animal.* 24 §126, 25 §59) was the late popular L. name (see below), which later regularly became, as still in Prov. and Sp., *tortuga*, and in F. *tortue*. (Diefenbach cites also med.L. *turtus*, *tortus*.) Of the Eng. forms, *tortuce* evidently represented the Latin, *tortue* and *tortu* the French, and the 16th c. *tortuga* the Sp. form. *Tortuse* was prob. a mere variant of *tortuce* (cf. *lettuce*, *letuse* below); *tortose* and the later forms in *-esse*, *-ise*, *-oise*, being further variants, partly at least due to shifting of stress and obscuration of the vowel. The forms in final *-s* may have arisen simply from dropping *-e* mute; but some of them may have come from taking the possessive *tortu's*, *tortou's*, in *tortou's skin*, *tortue's shell*, as the nominative. The form *tortoise* appears *c* 1569, preceded by *tortoyse*, 1552.

The late popular L. or Romanic *tortūca* is commonly held to be a derivative of L. *tortus* twisted, with the formative suffix seen in L. *carrūca*, *festūca*, *lactūca*, *verrūca*, and to refer to the crooked feet of the south European species (Diez). With L. *tortūca*, F. *tortue*, Eng. *tortuce*, *tortuse*, cf. L. *lactūca*, F. *laitue*, Eng. *lettuce*, *letuse*, and the variant forms of the last. The classical L. name was *testūdo*, from *testa* shell, whence It. *testudine*, *testuggine*.]

1. a. A four-footed reptile of the order *Chelonia*, in which the trunk is enclosed between a carapace and plastron, formed by the dorsal vertebræ, ribs, and sternum; the skin being covered with large horny plates, commonly called the shell.

The *Chelonia* are usually divided into Land-tortoises (*Testudinidæ*), Marsh-tortoises (*Emydæ*), River-tortoises (*Trionycidæ*), and Marine tortoises (*Chelonidæ*), in which the feet are compressed into flippers or paddles. The last are now commonly distinguished as *turtles*; but this name is sometimes extended to species of the *Emydæ* and *Trionycidæ*. By some zoologists the name 'tortoise' is confined to the terrestrial genus *Testudo* and its immediate congeners; see also TERRAPIN[1].

α. 5 tortuce, tortuge, (tortuca, 6 tortuga).

1398 TREVISA *Barth. De P.R.* XVIII. cviii. (Bodl. MS. *c* 1450) lf. 287b/1 The tortuge [*ed.* 1495 tortuse] is acounted amonge snailles for he is closed bitwene twey hard schellis.. and of tortuca is double kinde þat one woneþ in ryuers & þat oþer in londe. *c* **1440** *Promp. Parv.* 497/2 Tortuce, beest.., *tortuca*. **1577** FRAMPTON *Joyfull Newes* II. 73b, [Lagartos] take out their yonglynges, as the Tortugas of the sea doeth. **1596** RALEIGH *Discov. Guiana* 54 We found thousands of Tortugas egs, which are very wholesome meate. [**1832** MACGILLIVRAY tr. *Humboldt's Trav.* xvii. 223 The arraw or tortuga is a large fresh water tortoise.]

β. 5 tortu, turtu, tortou; 6–7 tortue.

c **1440** *Pallad. on Husb.* I. 874 The sedis in a tortous skyn [*testudinis coreo*] thou drie. *a* **1450** *Knt. de la Tour* (1906) 15 In sayeng youre praiers..be not like the crane or the tortu; ..thei are like the crane and the turtu that turnithe her hede and fases bacward, and lokithe ouer the shuldre. **1587** MASCALL *Govt. Cattle, Horses* (1627) 184 If Sinews or Nerues bee broken or bruised,..Yee shall lay thereon the flesh of a Tortue,..beaten with the powder of Mullenherbe.

γ. 5 tortose, 5–7 tortuse, 6 -tuous, -tueis, 7 -tuis, -tus.

1484 CAXTON *Fables of Auian* ii, The..fable..of the tortose and of the other byrdes. **1495** *Trevisa's Barth. De P.R.* XVIII. cviii. (W. de W.) gg iv b/1 The londe Tortuse [*Bodl. MS.* tortuge] dwellyth in houses and in wodes and is clene and good to etynge. **1565** COOPER *Thesaurus* s.v. *Tegimen*, The Tortuous, when she is shronke into hir shelle. **1590** TARLTON *News Purgat.* (1844) 76 She that..hath the tortueis under her feet, and gads not abroad. **1598** YONG *Diana* 49 Their shields..were broad shels of monstrous Tortuses. **1630** LENNARD tr. *Charron's Wisd.* (1658) 39 In the sense of Hearing, the Hart excelleth all others..; of Feeling the Tortuis. **1651** Tortus [see TORTOISE-SHELL 4].

δ. 6 torteyse, torteaux, 6–7 tortesse, -teise, 7 tortise, (-ties).

1545 ELYOT, *Chelys*, a torteyse. **1567** MAPLET *Gr. Forest* 106 The Tortesse is reckned one amongst the Snaile or Wormes. **1581** PETTIE *Guazzo's Civ. Conv.* I. (1586) 3, I goe to it as the Torteise to the inchantment. **1600** *E. de Jonghe's True Declar. Army by Sea* 22 There they saw verie great Torteauxes. *Ibid.*, The same day they took a Torteaux. **1615** G. SANDYS *Trav.* 205 The brooke it selfe abounding with Tortesses. **1661** LOVELL *Hist. Anim. & Min.* Introd., Having shells, as the Torteise. *Ibid.* 124 Tortise. In the deserts of Africa, Lybia, and Mauritania.

ε. 6–7 tortoyse, 6–8 -tois, (6 -toys, 7 -toisse, turtois), 6– tortoise.

1552 HULOET, Tortoyse fyshe, *chelys*. **1555** EDEN *Decades* 200 In..Cuba, are founde great Tortoyses (which are certeyne shell fysshes) of such byggenesse that tenne or fyfteene men are scarsely able to lyfte one of them owt of the water. **1569** Tortoises [see 2]. **1589** GREENE *Menaphon* (Arb.) 39 Venus standeth on the Tortoys, as shewing that Loue creepeth on by degrees. **1601** HOLLAND *Pliny* VI. xxii. I. 131 Tortoisses..so great..that one of their shels will serve to cover an house. **1611** BIBLE *Lev.* xi. 29 The Weasell, and the Mouse, and the Tortois, after his kinde. **1617** KEYMIS in *Raleigh's Apol.* 34, I have sent..one roule of Tobacco, one Tortoyse. **1648** Turtoises [see b]. **1666** J. DAVIES *Hist. Caribby Isles* 133 There are Land-Tortoises, Sea-Tortoises, and Fresh-water Tortoises, which are of different figures. **1699** GARTH *Dispens.* II. 19 And there, the Tortois hung her Coat o' Mail. **1719** DE FOE *Crusoe* I. 102 Going down to the Sea-side, I found a large Tortoise or Turtle. **1841–71** T. R. JONES *Anim. Kingd.* (ed. 4) 737 The perfect and typical Reptile, as the Lizard, the Tortoise, and the Serpent, breathes air, and air only.

b. A figure or image of a tortoise.

1648 J. RAYMOND *Il Merc. Italico* 42 Two Marble Pyramids that stand on brasse Turtoises. **1853** HUMPHREYS

Coin-Coll. Man. iii. (1876) 21 The coins of Ægina are easily recognized by the tortoise which is their invariable type. **1897** *Westm. Gaz.* 22 Apr. 3/3 Two metal tortoises—probably tobacco-jars?..were lying at hand on the table.

c. Taken as a type of slowness of motion; hence, applied to a very slow person or thing.

[**1670** G. H. *Hist. Cardinals* II. III. 198 He is slow in his Negotiations, advancing like a Tortoise.] **1825** SCOTT *Talism.* xxii, The speediest horse he had ever mounted was a tortoise in comparison to those of the Arabian sage. **1842** I. WILLIAMS *Baptistery* II. xvii. (1874) 6 One is travelling with a tortoise by his side, How slowly doth he wend.

2. a. A sort of penthouse, under which besiegers were protected as a tortoise by its shell; = TESTUDO 3.

1569 STOCKER tr. *Diod. Sic.* III. viii. 113/2 He had also many other Engines..and two great and puissaunt Tortoises to helpe them. **1610** W. FOLKINGHAM *Art of Survey* I. xiii. 45 Battering-Rams, Sowes, Horses, Tortuses. **1795** SOUTHEY *Joan of Arc* VIII. 159 Tortoises, beneath whose roofing safe, They, filling the deep moat, might for the towers Make fit foundation. **1856** GROTE *Greece* II. xcii. XII. 129 His soldiers, protected from missiles by moveable penthouses (called Tortoises).

b. = TESTUDO 3 b.

1697 DRYDEN *Æneid* II. 601 Their Targets in a Tortoise cast, the Foes Secure advancing, to the Turrets rose. **1734** tr. *Rollin's Anc. Hist.* XIX. iv. (1827) VIII. 139 They came forward in the form of the testudo, or tortoise. **1863** WHYTE MELVILLE *Gladiators* 408 He bade them form with their shields the figure that was called 'the Tortoise'.

3. Short for TORTOISE-SHELL. Usually *attrib.* or as *adj.*

1654 DOROTHY OSBORNE *Lett. to Sir W. Temple* (1888) 240 The ring..is very well, only a little of the biggest. Send me a tortoise one that is a little less. **1702** *Lond. Gaz.* No. 3833/4 A Gold Snuff-Box,..the bottom Tortoise. **1902** *Fur & Feather* 19 Sept. 232/2 The Young Brindle or Tortoise class [of Cavies].

4. a. *attrib.* (sometimes = adj.) and *Comb.*, as ***tortoise broth, -feeder, god, -heart, -myth, pond***; ***tortoise-headed, -shaped*** adjs., ***-like*** adj. and adv.; ***tortoise-fashion*** adv.; esp. with reference to the slow gait of the tortoise, as ***tortoise-hours, -pace, race***; ***tortoise-footed, -paced*** adjs.; also **tortoise-beetle**, a leaf-beetle of the family *Cassididæ*, from the resemblance of the wing-cases and prothorax to the carapace of a tortoise; **tortoise core** *Archæol.*, a core (CORE *sb.*[1] 5) resembling a tortoise in shape; †**tortoise encrinite**, a fossil crinoid of the genus *Marsupites*; **tortoise-flower**, a plant of the genus *Chelone*, from the resemblance of the corolla to the head of a tortoise (also called *turtle-head*); †**tortoise-iron**, ? a peg for tethering captured tortoises; **tortoise-lyre**, a lyre made of a tortoise-shell; **tortoise-plant**, a South African plant, *Testudinaria elephantipes*, allied to the yam, having a large fleshy root-stock growing above ground, the surface of which becomes deeply cracked so as to suggest the carapace of a tortoise; also called *elephant's foot* and *Hottentot's bread*; **tortoise race**, a race in which the last person home wins; **tortoise-roof** = sense 2; **tortoise-roofed** *a.*, having a roof resembling a tortoise-shell; **tortoise rotifer**, a rotifer or wheel-animalcule of the family *Brachionidæ*, having a broad shield-shaped body; **tortoise tent**, a kind of tent with a roof shaped like the shell of a tortoise; **tortoise-wood**: see quot.

c **1711** PETIVER *Gazophyl.* VI. lix, Brasil *Tortoise Beetle.. Its Legs and Body of a golden green, with Copper Edges, it creeps softly, and is slow to fly. **1826** KIRBY & SP. *Entomol.* III. xxix. 74 *Cassida viridis*, a tortoise beetle,..covers her group of eggs with a partially transparent membrane. **1861** HULME tr. *Moquin-Tandon* II. III. 178 *Tortoise broth is prepared from the flesh of the Testudo Græca... Some of the fresh-water tortoises may be substituted. **1919** R. A. SMITH in *Man* July 101 *Tortoise-cores have been found on the bank of the ancient river to the south-east. **1972** K. P. OAKLEY *Man the Tool-maker* 52 Viewed on its outer face an oval flake thus detached from a tortoise-core has the appearance of a flat, finely worked hand-axe. **1808** PARKINSON *Org. Rem. Former World* II. xxii. 225 The extraordinary fossil, which, from the disposition of the plates of which it is formed, may be termed the *Tortoise Encrinite. **1894** A. BEARDSLEY *Let.* Oct. (1971) 75 The Tannhaüser gets on *tortoise fashion but admirably for all that. **1921** W. DE LA MARE *Crossings* 71 Ann slowly thrusts her head out of the snow-house, tortoise-fashion. **1855** KINGSLEY *Heroes, Theseus* II. 213 Holla, thou *tortoise-feeder. **1818** MILMAN *Samor* 83 Thou *tortoise-footed sluggard! **1750** PARSONS in *Phil. Trans.* (1753) XLVII. 120 The *tortoise-headed seal. On the shores of many parts of Europe. **1865** J. H. INGRAHAM *Pillar of Fire* (1872) 223 A tortoise-headed god. **1873** E. BRENNAN *Witch of Nemi*, etc. 163 Fain would I beguile the *tortoise-hours. **1697** DAMPIER *Voy. round World* (1699) 37 The Moskito-men make their own striking Instruments as Harpoons, Fish-hooks, and *Tortoise-Iron or Pegs. *c* **1630** DRUMM. OF HAWTH. *Poems* Wks. (1711) 36 Stone-rolling Tay, Tine *tortoise-like that flows. **1645** BP. HALL *Remedy Discontents* 141 What is this, but Tortoise-like to be clogg'd with a weighty shel? **1804** [see TORTOISE-SHELL 4 b]. **1956** P. H. JOHNSON *Last Resort* xxiii. 143 His aged, stilted stride, his tortoise-like out-thrusting of the head. **1982** 'J. Ross' *Death's Head* iv. 22 The traffic once more moving, though at a tortoise-like crawl. **1820** SHELLEY *Hymn to Mercury* xxv, With his left hand about his knees—the right Held his belovèd *tortoise-lyre tight. **1865** TYLOR *Early Hist. Man.* xii. 334 The *Tortoise-myths of North America and India. **1690** DRYDEN *Don Sebast.* III. i, Thou mov'st a *tortoise-pace to my relief. *a* **1649** DRUMM. OF HAWTH. *Cypress Grove* Wks. (1711) 122 Swift and active pilgrims come to the end of it in the morning or at noon, which *tortoise-paced wretches..scarce..crawl unto at midnight. **1866** *Treas. Bot.*, *Tortoise-plant. **1913** *Tortoise race [listed in Dict]. **1914** ROWE & WEBB *Guide to Study of Eng.* iii. 126 This is a 'tortoise' race, the last man to receive the prize. **1855** SINGLETON *Virgil* I. 288 Leaguered by the *tortoise-roof. **1886** *Pall Mall G.* 12 Oct. 4/1 They [Mormons] convene within that hideously ugly, *tortoise-roofed building called the Tabernacle. **1826** KIRBY & SP. *Entomol.* III. xxix. 77 Those singular immovable *tortoise-shaped insects. **1911** *Archæologia* LXII. II. 523 Tortoise-shaped cores. This is perhaps the most striking group in the enormous series from Northfleet. **1890** *Daily News* 8 Apr. 3/2 The patients found every care bestowed upon them in the *tortoise tent. **1901** *Daily Chron.* 23 July 3/2 A good case made out for the 'tortoise' tent as used by the Portland Hospital. **1866** *Treas. Bot.*, **Tortoise-wood*, a variety of Zebra-wood.

b. (With capital initial.) A proprietary name for a type of solid-fuel-burning stove.

1884 *Trade Marks Jrnl.* 5 Nov. 1025 The Tortoise... Slow combustion stoves. Charles Portway & Son, 'Tortoise' Stove Works, and High Street, Halstead, Essex; Stove Manufacturers. **1895** *Army & Navy Co-op Soc. Price List* 336 (*heading*) 'Tortoise' heating stoves. **1948** J. BETJEMAN *Few Late Chrysanthemums* (1954) 10 The Tortoise stove is lit again. **1981** *Country Life* 12 Feb. 411/3 (Advt.), The old world appeal of the Tortoise Ornamental Stove... Accepts wood, coal or smokeless fuel.

tortoise-shell ('tɔːtəsˌʃɛl, *colloq.* 'tɔːtəʃɛl), *sb.* (*a.*)

1. The shell, esp. the upper shell or carapace, of a tortoise, consisting of horny scales covering the dermal skeleton. **a.** with *a* and *pl.*

1601 HOLLAND *Pliny* IX. x. I. 241 Among the Islands principally in the red sea, they use Tortoise shells..for boats and wherries. **1644** EVELYN *Diary* 21 Mar., Curiosities of ivory and tortoise-shells. *a* **1843** SOUTHEY *Common-pl. Bk.* Ser. II. (1849) 570 In Yucatan they made a musical instrument of the tortoise-shell, preserved whole. **1863** W. C. BALDWIN *Afr. Hunting* 388 A drink of muddy water..out of a dirty tortoise-shell.

b. As a material (without *a* or *pl.*): The shell of certain tortoises, esp. that of the hawk's-bill turtle, *Chelone imbricata*, which is semi-transparent, with a mottled or clouded coloration, and is extensively used in ornamental work, as inlaying, etc.

1632 EARL OF CORK *Diary* in *Lismore Papers* Ser. I. (1886) III. 132 A cabbonett of Torties shell. **1688** R. HOLME *Armoury* II. 206/1 The Turks have a kind of Tortois-shell.. of which they make hafts for Knives. **1703** DAMPIER *Voy.* III. I. 81 The Hawksbill-Turtle..of Brazil is most sought after..for its Shell, which..is the clearest and best-clouded Tortoise-shell in the World. **1756** MRS. CALDERWOOD in *Coltness Collect.* (Maitl. Club) 199 A bit of horn or tortyshell. **1768** HOLDSWORTH *On Virgil* 131 Some of the Romans were so extravagant as to cover their doors and door-cases with Indian tortoise-shell. **1779** FORREST *Voy. N. Guinea* 112 At Krudo, and the islands near it, may be got much tortoiseshell. **1838** DICKENS *Nich. Nick.* xv, The tortershell would have affected the brain. **1841** LANE *Arab. Nts.* I. 123 Made of wood,..inlaid with mother-of-pearl, tortoise-shell, etc.

†**2.** = TORTOISE 2 a and b. *Obs.*

a **1661** HOLYDAY *Juvenal* ii. (1673) 29/2 Like souldiers,.. when..they cast themselves..into the military figure of the testudo, or the torteise-shell. **1726** LEONI *Alberti's Archit.* I. 68 The ditch..will hinder the moveable Tortoise-shell.. from approaching the wall.

3. Short for (*a*) *tortoise-shell cat*, (*b*) *tortoise-shell butterfly*: see 4 b.

1840 *P. Parley's Ann.* 113 Oh, what a pretty little kitten! what a beautiful little dear tortoiseshell! **1884** *Pall Mall G.* 12 Aug. 3/2 A splendid specimen of the large tortoise-shell was fluttering about Westminster Bridge. **1903** *Westm. Gaz.* 11 Aug. 10/2 Of all flowers..that which the Red Admirals, Peacocks, and Tortoiseshells seem to like best is peppermint. **1903** F. SIMPSON *Bk. Cat* xvii. 208 Real tortoiseshells may be called tricolour cats, for they should bear three colours.., namely black, red, and yellow, in distinct patches or blotches.

4. *attrib.* or as *adj.* **a.** Made of tortoise-shell.

1651 in *Verney Mem.* (1904) I. 480 His toilet equipment includes..12 Tortus shell Agendas, 2 gold picktooths. **1652** in *10th Rep. Hist. MSS. Comm.* App. I. 38 Fyue torter shell spoones. **1683** *Lond. Gaz.* No. 1809/4 A great Tortoise-shell Comb, in a Case of the same. **1689** *Ibid.* No. 2416/4 A very large Tortoise-shell Tobacco Box. **1836–9** DICKENS *Sk. Boz, Doctors' Commons*, A very fat and red-faced gentleman, in tortoise-shell spectacles.

b. Having the colouring or appearance of tortoise-shell; mottled or variegated with black, red, and yellow, or similar colours; *spec.* **tortoise-shell butterfly**, one of several butterflies, esp. the European *Vanessa urticæ* and *V. polychlorus*, and the American *Aglais milberti*; **tortoise-shell cat**, a domestic cat of this colour; **tortoise-shell goose** (see quot. 1885); **tortoise-shell palm** (see quot. 1902); **tortoise-shell tiger** (see TIGER *sb.* 1 b); **tortoise-shell ware**, a fine kind of pottery coloured with oxide of copper and manganese.

1782 W. CURTIS *Brown-tail Moth* 6 The *Papilio Urticæ*, and *Iö*, small Tortoise-shell and Peacock Butterflies. **1791** HUDDESFORD *Salmag., Monody death Dick* 141 Cats..sable, sandy, grey, and tortoiseshell. **1803** SHAW *Gen. Zool.* IV. 471 Tortoise-shell Sparus..: colour brown, with a strong suffusion of pale yellow. **1804** *Ibid.* V. 444 Tortoise-shell Tetrodon... The Linnæan name [*Tetrodon testudineus*] of this fish is supposed to have been given from its tortoise-like beak, but perhaps, with more propriety, from its variegated skin. **1858** LYTTON *What will he do* I. xiv, They kept a tortoise-shell cat and a canary. **1879** [see *agate-ware* s.v. AGATE 6]. **1885** SWAINSON *Provinc. Names Birds* 148 White-fronted Goose (*Anser albifrons*)... Tortoise-shell goose (Ireland). From the mottled markings on the abdomen. **1902** P. FOUNTAIN *Mounts. & Forests S. Amer.* x. 270 The tortoise-shell palm..the leaves of which are so hard, and withal flexible, that combs, spoons, and ornamental articles are made of it. **1903** F. SIMPSON *Bk. Cat* xxv. 284 The tortoiseshell tom is a most rare and uncommon animal. **1975** *Country Life* 9 Oct. 898/2 (*caption*) 19th-century teapot similar to Whieldon's tortoiseshell ware.

c. Producing tortoise-shell: **tortoise-shell turtle**, the hawk's-bill turtle, or other species from which tortoise-shell is obtained.

1886 MIVART in *Encycl. Brit.* XX. 446/2 In the other Chelonians there are large epidermal shields, which may overlap, as in the Tortoise-shell Turtle (*C[helonia] imbricata*) and others.

5. *Comb.*, as ***tortoiseshell-producing*** adj., ***tortoise-shell worker***.

1883 W. S. KENT in A. J. Adderley *Fisheries Bahamas* 31 (Fish. Exhib. Publ.) The edible turtle (*Chelone midas*) and the tortoiseshell-producing variety (*Caretta imbricata*).. among the marine products of the Bahamas. **1903** [see CEMENTER]. **1931** P. A. S. PHILLIPS (*title*) John Obrisset Huguenot: carver, medallist, horn and tortoiseshell worker.

Tortolan (tɔː'təʊlən), *a.* and *sb.* [f. *Tortola* + -AN.] **A.** *adj.* Of or pertaining to Tortola, the largest of the British Virgin Islands. **B.** *sb.* A native or inhabitant of Tortola.

1923 C. F. JENKINS *Tortola* xi. 67 Captain Tittley, the commander of the Tortolan navy. **1953** *Caribbean Q.* III. II. 112 Most of Tortola's exports go to St. Thomas and most of her imports come from the island, and Tortolans go frequently by sloop or launch merely to do their marketing. *Ibid.* 113 In the Tortolan countryside..no one is seen at work between ten and four o'clock. **1980** *Washington Post* 20 July K6 Almost certainly, the government worker is a native St. Thomian, the taxi driver a Tortolan by birth.

Tortoni (tɔː'təʊnɪ). Also tortoni. The name of an Italian café-owner in Paris in the 18th cent., used *attrib.* and *absol.* to designate a kind of ice-cream.

1911 LEITER & VAN BERGH *Flower City Cook Bk.* xxiv. 128 *Tortoni pudding*, Scald 1 pint milk..; add 1 tablespoon of flour..; 1 egg and 1 cupful sugar... Add ½ pound chopped almonds, 7 macaroons..and a little vanilla. Cool. Add 1 pint whipped cream. Freeze. **1958** *Sunday Times* 27 Apr. 22/4 A raspberry Tortoni (raspberries plus cream, macaroons and a touch of kirsch). **1979** *Tucson Mag.* Sept. 61/2 Then try tortoni (made on the premises).

Tortonian (tɔː'təʊnɪən), *a.* *Geol.* [ad. G. *Tortonien* sb. (K. Mayer 1857, in *Verhandl. der allgemeinen schweiz. Ges. für die gesammten Naturwiss.* 171), f. *Tortona*, name of a town in N. Italy: see -IAN.] Of, pertaining to, or designating a stage of the upper (or middle) Miocene in Europe. Also *absol.*, the Tortonian age.

1885 A. GEIKIE *Text-bk. Geol.* (ed. 2) 873 Italy... The Tortonian stage (3) is made up [of] blue marls, reaching the great thickness of 3900 feet. **1931** GREGORY & BARRETT *Gen. Stratigr.* xii. 192 The volcanoes of the Rhine began in the Tortonian. **1974** *Nature* 22 Mar. 312/2 We suggest that the separation of Calabria from Sardinia took place in the middle Miocene, and that Tortonian deformation in Sicily indicates a collision that terminates this phase of separation.

†'**tortor**. *Obs.* Also 6–7 -our(e. [L., agent-n. from *torquēre*, *tort-um* to twist, torture.] A torturer, tormentor; an executioner.

1570 FOXE *A. & M.* (ed. 2) 125/2 The boucherlye tortoure pluckte the skynne from the crowne of hys head. **1606** tr. *Rollock's Lect. on 1 Thess.* 305 The conscience..as a tortor within thee to torment thee. **1610** HOLLAND *Camden's Brit.* I. 410 The Tortor proudly did the feat, but cleere he went not quit; That holy Martyr lost his head, this cruell wretch his sight. **1619** PURCHAS *Microcosmus* xlii. 401 Tortures and Tortours, Deuills and Deuillish Plagues.

tortor, tortou, obs. ff. TORTURE, TORTOISE.

tortour, var. TORTOR *Obs.*; obs. f. TORTURE.

tortricid ('tɔːtrɪsɪd), *a.* and *sb.* [f. mod.L. *Tor'tricidæ* pl., f. TORTRIX: see -ID[3].] **a.** *Entom. adj.* Belonging to the family *Tortricidæ* of *Lepidoptera*, comprising the leaf-roller moths, typified by the genus *Tortrix*; *sb.* a moth of this family. **b.** *Zool. adj.* Belonging to the family *Tortricidæ* of snakes, typified by the genus *Tortrix* or *Ilysia*; *sb.* a snake of this family. So '**tortricine** (-saɪn), *a.* and *sb.* = tortricid; '**tortricoid** (-kɔɪd) *a.*, belonging to the suborder *Tortricoidea* of *Ophidia*, including the family *Tortricidæ* (see b above).

1889 MARY E. BAMFORD *Up & Down Brooks* 113 The small tortricid moths that as caterpillars, curl the leaves of rose-bushes.

‖**Tortrix** ('tɔːtrɪks). Pl. tortrices (-'aɪsiːz). [mod.L. *tortrix*, *-īcem*, fem. of TORTOR, but taken in the literal sense 'twister', in reference to the leaf-rolling habits of the larvæ.]

1. *Entom.* A genus of moths, typical of the family *Tortricidæ* (see prec. a); a moth of this genus or family, a leaf-roller moth.

1797 *Encycl. Brit.* (ed. 3) XIV. 263/2 (Families of Moths) 5. The tortrices. The wings are exceeding obtuse, their exterior margin is curve, and declines towards the sides of the body. **1819** G. SAMOUELLE *Entomol. Compend.* 425 *Tortrix Avellana.* The hazel Tortrix. **1834** R. MUDIE *Brit. Birds* (1841) I. 347 The eggs and larvæ of the tortrices and other insects which they [tits] pick up. **1909** *Daily News* 31 Mar. 5 The rook..preys largely on the larvæ and pupæ of the oak tortrix, a most destructive insect.

2. *Zool.* A genus of snakes, also called *Ilysia*, including the coral-snake of Guyana, *T.* (*I.*) *scytale*.

1843 *Penny Cycl.* XXV. 79/2 *Tortrix.* Oppel's name for a genus of serpents. **1864** in WEBSTER.

tortu, tortuce, tortue, obs. ff. TORTOISE.

†**tortue,** *a. Obs. rare*$^{-1}$. [a. F. *tortu, -ue* (1314 in Hatz.-Darm.), f. L. *tortus*, F. *tort* twisted.] = TORTUOUS 1.

c **1450** *Merlin* xiv. 206 He bar [on a banner] a dragon..and the taile was a fadome and an half of lengthe tortue.

tortueis, tortuga, tortuis: see TORTOISE.

[**tortulous,** erron. form of TORULOUS.
1864 in WEBSTER.]

tortuose (ˈtɔːtjuːəʊs), *a. rare*$^{-1}$. [ad. L. *tortuōs-us*: see TORTUOUS.] = TORTUOUS 1.

1829 LOUDON *Encycl. Plants* (1836) 471 Stem tortuose.

tortuosity (tɔːtjuːˈɒsɪtɪ). [ad. L. *tortuōsitās*, from *tortuōs-us* TORTUOUS: see -ITY. Cf. F. *tortuosité*, Pr. *tortuositat*, It. *tortuosità*.] The quality or condition of being tortuous; twistedness, crookedness, sinuosity; an instance of this.

1. *lit.*: cf. next, 1.

1603 HOLLAND *Plutarch's Mor.* III. 686 The tortuositie of the bodie and branches. **1658** PHILLIPS, *Tortuosity*,..a winding, or crooking in and out. **1793** R. MYLNE *Rep. Thames* 40 The crookedness or tortuosity of its course. **1851** LANDOR *Popery* xiv. 42 A thread which has long been twisted carries with it when untwisted the tortuosity of its entanglement. **1887** *Proc. R. Geog. Soc.* Apr. 253 The extreme tortuosity of the river Yang-tsze.

b. *Geom.*: see quot. 1867, and cf. next, 1 c.

1867 THOMSON & TAIT *Nat. Phil.* I. I. §7 There are not two curvatures, but only a curvature..of which the plane is continuously changing... The course of such a curve is, in common language, well called 'tortuous'; and the measure of the corresponding property is conveniently called Tortuosity. **1898** A. N. WHITEHEAD *Univ. Algebra* I. 131 A curve locus of any order of tortuosity.

2. *fig.* Mental or moral crookedness: cf. next, 2.

1621 T. GRANGER *Comm. on Eccl.* ii. 14. 63 Hee discerneth the vprightnesse of godlinesse, and the tortuosity of wickednesse. **1767** A. CAMPBELL *Lexiph.* (1774) 62 To convict him of the tortuosity of his imaginary rectitude. **1818** BYRON *Juan* I. ccviii, Led by some tortuosity of mind. **1851** *Fraser's Mag.* XLIV. 336 The charge of deliberate tortuosity of action and double-dealing.

3. with *a* and *pl.* An instance of this, or something that exemplifies it; a twisted or crooked object, a twist, turn, winding. **a.** *lit.*: cf. 1.

1646 SIR T. BROWNE *Pseud. Ep.* v. v. 239 That tortuosity or complicated nodosity we usually call the Navell. **1853** KANE *Grinnell Exp.* xvii. (1856) 131 The linear distance, including tortuosities, is but three hundred miles.

b. *fig.*: cf. 2.

1677 GALE *Crt. Gentiles* II. IV. 109 Sin is said to be a Tortuositie or wresting of the Law. **1751** JOHNSON *Rambler* No. 122 ¶3 The tortuosities of imaginary rectitude. **1837** CARLYLE *Misc., Mirabeau* (1840) V. 139 The strangest of styles..distracted into tortuosities, dislocations. **1856** DORAN *Knts. & their Days* viii. 126 In tracing the tortuosities of this chivalric romance.

tortuous (ˈtɔːtjuːəs), *a.* [a. AF. *tortuous* (12–13th c. in Hatz.-Darm.) = 14th c. F. *tortueux*, ad. L. *tortuōs-us*, 'full of crooks or turns or twists', f. *tortu-s* a twisting, f. *tort-*, ppl. stem of *torquēre* to twist.]

1. Full of twists, turns, or bends; twisted, winding, crooked, sinuous.

1426 LYDG. *De Guil. Pilgr.* 18320 A camell..is so encomerous Off bak corvyd and tortuous. *c* **1450** *Merlin* xxii. 393 The dragon..be-tokened the kynge Arthur and his power;..and the taile that was so tortuouse be-tokened the grete treson of the peple. **1551** RECORDE *Pathw. Knowl.* I. Defin., Paralleles tortuouse, whiche bowe contrarie waies with their two endes. **1667** MILTON *P.L.* IX. 516 Hee..of his tortuous Traine Curld many a wanton wreath in sight of Eve. **1768** STERNE *Sent. Journ., Riddle Explained*, The most difficult and tortuous passages of the heart! **1811** A. T. THOMSON *Lond. Disp.* II. (1818) 317 The root is perennial, woody, and tortuous. **1839** DARWIN *Voy. Nat.* ix. (1879) 186 We found the river-course very tortuous.

†**b.** *Astron.* Applied to the six signs of the zodiac from Capricornus to Gemini, which (in northern latitudes) rise more obliquely than the other six. *Obs. rare*$^{-1}$.

c **1391** CHAUCER *Astrol.* ii. §28 Thise same signes, fro the heued of capricorne vnto the ende of geminis, ben cleped tortuos signes or kroked signes, for they arisen embelif on owre Orisonte.

c. *Geom.* Applied to a curve of which no two successive portions are in the same plane; also called a *non-plane curve, curve in space*, or *curve of double curvature* (see CURVATURE 1 b).

1867 [see TORTUOSITY 1 b].

2. *fig.* Not direct or straightforward; indirect, irregular, devious, circuitous, crooked: esp. in a moral sense. (In quot. 1801 app. Dealing in quaint 'turns' (of speech or expression).)

[**1682**: see TORTIOUS 4.] **1801** LD. CALTHORPE *Let.* in *Wilberforce's Priv. Papers* (1897) 104 Sir W. Scott..was very tortuous and amusing. **1823** SCOTT *Quentin D.* viii, The unscrupulous cunning with which he assisted in the execution of the schemes of his master's tortuous policy. **1858** SEARS *Athan.* III. vii. 319 A narrow and tortuous criticism. **1865** MILL *Exam. Hamilton* 415 The tortuous phraseology by which our author evades recognising the ideas of truth and falsity. **1911** *Times* 2 Nov. 3/4 A more tortuous way of trying to get possession of goods he had never heard of.

¶**3.** Malign (*obs.*); wrongful. (Misused for or confused with TORTIOUS.)

1594 GREENE & LODGE *Looking Glasse* (1598) E iv b, What tortuous planets..Hath made the concaue of the earth vnclose? **1839** *Times* 13 May, Keeping tortuous possession of premises after their several gentlemen had departed. **1839** *Morn. Herald* 3 June, The first action ever brought against a returning officer for the tortuous refusal of a vote for members of parliament.

Hence **ˈtortuously** *adv.*, in a tortuous manner (*lit.* and *fig.*; in quot. 1839 misused for TORTIOUSLY); **ˈtortuousness**, the quality or condition of being tortuous, tortuosity.

1824 *New Monthly Mag.* X. 175 Musty precedents..which an ingenious tortuousness may call in. **1839** *Morn. Herald* 3 June, Any person, whose vote has been..tortuously refused at an election. **1853** KANE *Grinnell Exp.* xlv. (1856) 413 We wound our way tortuously among them. **1862** H. SPENCER *First Princ.* II. ix. §80 (1875) 245 In proportion to the complexity of social forces is the tortuousness of social movements. **1884** *Pall Mall G.* 8 Aug. 5/1 Puget Sound..runs southward tortuously from Vancouver Island far into the rugged heart of the Washington territory.

torturable (ˈtɔːtjʊərəb(ə)l), *a. rare.* [f. TORTURE *v.* + -ABLE.] Capable of being tortured. Hence **ˈtorturableness** (*rare*).

1655–87 H. MORE *App. Antid.* v. §4. 193, I..assert that a torturable being is a Spirit incorporate. **1727** BAILEY vol. II, *Torturableness*, capableness of Torture. **1852** BURTON *Crim. Trials Scot.* I. 229 Long confinement having reduced the extent of his torturable strength.

torture (ˈtɔːtjʊə(r), -tʃə(r)), *sb.* Also 6–7 tortour, tortor. [a. F. *torture* (12th c. in Hatz.-Darm.), ad. L. *tortūra* twisting, wreathing; torment, torture; f. *torquēre, tort-* to twist, torment.]

1. The infliction of severe bodily pain, as punishment or a means of persuasion; spec. ***judicial torture***, inflicted by a judicial or quasi-judicial authority, for the purpose of forcing an accused or suspected person to confess, or an unwilling witness to give evidence or information; a form of this (often in *pl.*). ***to put to*** (***the***) ***torture***, to inflict torture upon, to torture.

1551 *Acts Privy Counc.* (1891) III. 407 Assisting to the sayd Commissioners for the putting the prisoners..to suche tortours as they shall think expedient. **1593** SHAKS. *2 Hen. VI*, III. i. 131 You did deuise Strange Tortures for Offendors. **1608** D. PRICE *Chr. Warre* 21 To punish the bad, and to prouide some sharpe and fearful tortors for them. **1653** H. COGAN tr. *Pinto's Trav.* iv. 10 We put the Captain and Pilot to torture, who instantly confessed. **1708** *Act 7 Anne* c. 21 §5 After [1 July 1709] no Person accused of any Capital Offence or other Crime in Scotland, shall suffer, or be subject or liable to any Torture. **1769** BLACKSTONE *Comm.* (1830) IV. xxv. 326 They erected a rack for torture. **1838** THIRLWALL *Greece* III. xxv. 393 Pisander moved that the persons..should be put to the torture, that all their accomplices might be known. **1849** MACAULAY *Hist. Eng.* i. (1871) I. 16 According to law, torture..could not..be inflicted on an English subject. **1882** GARDINER *Hist. Eng.* (1884) VI. lxv. 359 *note* 2 Torture had been allowed [in England] by custom as inflicted by the prerogative, but not by law... Torture was inflicted as late as 1640 by prerogative.

†**b.** *transf.* An instrument or means of torture.

1601 SHAKS. *All's Well* IV. iii. 135 He calles for the tortures, what will you say without em? **1621** G. SANDYS *Ovid's Met.* IX. (1626) 178 To teare the torture [*letiferam vestem*] off, he striues. **1721–2** R. WODROW *Suffer. Ch. Scot.* II. xiii. §5 (1837) II. 458/2 His leg being in the torture [i.e. the boot].

2. Severe or excruciating pain or suffering (of body or mind); anguish, agony, torment; the infliction of such.

c **1540** tr. *Pol. Verg. Eng. Hist.* (Camden) I. 269 Doe you preferre the horrible tortures of warre beefore tranquillitee? **1593** SHAKS. *Lucr.* 1287 And that deepe torture may be cal'd a Hell, When more is felt than one hath power to tell. **1612** WOODALL *Surg. Mate* Wks. (1653) 185 Pain and torture of the intestines. **1659** H. MORE *Immort. Soul* II. x. §6. 220 Who would bear the tortures of Fears and Jealousies, if he could avoid it? **1734** BP. PETRE *Let.* in E. H. Burton *Life Challoner* (1909) I. 93 He wasted away by degrees under the torture of the Strangury. **1744** M. BISHOP *Life & Adv.* 52 They were in such great Torture, wishing they had never come to Sea. **1797** MRS. RADCLIFFE *Italian* ii, He determined to relieve himself from the tortures of suspense. **1878** BROWNING *La Saisiaz* 353 As in one or other stage Of a torture writhe they.

b. *transf.* A cause of severe pain or anguish. (In quot. 1859 *humorous*.)

1612 BRINSLEY *Ludus Lit.* viii. (1627) 106 The labour of learning..Authours without booke..is one of the greatest tortures to the poore schollers. **1859** *Habits Gd. Society* xi. 300 Never was a more solemn torture created for mankind than these odious dinner-parties. **1873** HAMERTON *Intell. Life* II. i. (1875) 52 An ugly picture was torture to his cultivated eye. **1908** R. BAGOT *A. Cuthbert* xxvii, Do not make me put it into words, it is torture!

3. *transf.* and *fig.* with various allusions: Severe pressure; violent perversion or 'wresting'; violent action or operation; severe testing or examination.

1605 BACON *Adv. Learn.* II. xvii. §9 All the kernell [is] forced out and expulsed with the torture and presse of the Methode. *c* **1670** HOBBES *Dial. Com. Laws* (1681) 147 This Statute cannot by Sir Edw. Cokes Torture be made to say it. **1691** RAY *Creation* I. (1692) 87 All the Tortures of Vulcan or corrosive Waters. **1818** BYRON *Ch. Har.* IV. lxix, The hell of waters! where they howl and hiss, And boil in endless torture. **1855** BREWSTER *Newton* I. iv. 91 Experimental results, that may put his own views to the torture. **1887** *Spectator* No. 3067. 491/2 Much so-called wit of the present day is nothing more than the systematic torture of words.

4. *attrib.* and *Comb.*, as ***torture-chamber, -house, -monger, -rack, -room, -wheel; torture-scored*** adj.

1615 J. STEPHENS *Ess. & Char.* (1857) 133 An Impudent Censurer—Is the torture-monger of Wit, ready for execution before Judgement. **1829** SCOTT *Anne of G.* x, Building castles with dungeons and folter-kammers, or torture-chambers. **1837** CARLYLE *Fr. Rev.* I. I. ii, Torture-wheels and conical *oubliettes*. *a* **1847** ELIZA COOK *Silence* 2 Poverty has a sharp and goading power To wring the torture cry. **1898** S. COLERIDGE *Step by Step* 4 The guardian of the secret of the torture-house. **1899** *Westm. Gaz.* 9 Feb. 2/1 The torture-instinct (common alone to human and feline).

ˈtorture, *v.* Also 6 -or, 7 -er. [f. prec. sb.: cf. F. *torturer* (1480 in Hatz.-Darm.).]

1. *trans.* To inflict torture upon, subject to torture; *spec.* to subject to judicial torture; put to the torture. Also *absol.*

1593 SHAKS. *2 Hen. VI*, III. i. 376 Say he be taken, rackt, and tortured; I know, no paine they can inflict vpon him, Will make him say, I mou'd him to those Armes. **1594** *First Pt. Contention* (1843) 35 A murtherer or foule felonous theefe..I tortord above the rate of common law. **1611** BIBLE *Heb.* xi. 35 Others were tortured [*16th c. versions* racked], not accepting deliuerance. **1632** LITHGOW *Trav.* x. 480 Hee thought hee saw a man Torturing [*i.e.* being tortured]. **1651** HOBBES *Leviath.* I. xiv. 70 What is in that case confessed, tendeth to the ease of him that is Tortured. **1847** MRS. A. KERR tr. *Ranke's Hist. Servia* x. 203 Shall I live to see thee slowly tortured to death by the Turks? **1896** 'M. FIELD' *Attila* II. 48 You will not torture? *Placidia.* We use that to extort confession, not As punishment.

2. To inflict severe pain or suffering upon; to torment; to distress or afflict grievously; also, to exercise the mind severely, to puzzle or perplex greatly. Also *absol.* to cause extreme pain.

1588 SHAKS. *L.L.L.* v. ii. 60 That same Berowne Ile torture ere I goe. **1611** SPEED *Hist. Gt. Brit.* IX. xvi. (1623) 842 To consider how Writers torter us with the diuersities of reports. **1715–20** POPE *Iliad* XI. 985 The closing flesh..ceas'd to glow, The wound to torture, and the blood to flow. **1769** *Junius Lett.* xxix. (1797) I. 203 When the mind is tortured, it is not at the command of any outward power. It is the sense of guilt which constitutes the punishment, and creates that torture. **1849** MACAULAY *Hist. Eng.* vi. II. 67 Jeffreys was..tortured by a cruel internal malady. **1855** *Ibid.* xii. III. 167 It was rumoured..that he was tortured by painful emotions.

3. *fig.* **a.** To act upon violently in some way, so as to strain, twist, wrench, distort, pull or knock about, etc.

1626 BACON *Sylva* §137 The Bow tortureth the String continually, and thereby holdeth it in a Continuall Trepidation. **1743** DAVIDSON *Æneid* VII. 198 A top whirling under the twisted lash, which boys..exercise and torture in a large circuit. **1822** SHELLEY *To Jane—the Recollection*, Pines..Tortured by storms to shapes as rude As serpents interlaced. **186.** B. HARTE *My Other Self* in *Fiddletown*, etc. (1873) 120, I stood at the glass in the desperate attempt to torture my hair after the fashion of young Wobbles.

b. To 'twist' (language, etc.) from the proper or natural meaning or form; to distort, pervert. Also with *into*.

1648 JENKYN *Blind Guide* i. 8 To torture Scripture for the defending of his errors. **1682** DRYDEN *Mac Fl.* 208 There thou mayst..torture one poor word ten thousand ways. **1789** J. MOORE *Zeluco* I. ix. 80 What he said was excusable; to endeavour to torture it into mutiny would be absurd. **1803** VISCT. STRANGFORD *Camoens' Poems* Notes (1810) 127 It is surprising that this idea has not been more ramified and tortured by the English metaphysical poets of that school. **1840** POE *Tales of Mystery* (1905) 365 An unredeemed dreariness of thought which no goading of the imagination could torture into aught of the sublime. **1869** BALDW. BROWN *Chr. Policy Life* (1880) 281 There might be a sentence here and there which might be tortured to bear that meaning. **1956** E. H. HUTTEN *Lang. Mod. Physics* vi. 232 It is possible to torture almost any statement into the logical form of an implication.

4. To extract by torture; to extort. *rare.*

1687 tr. *Sallust's Wks.* (1692) 29 They..by all manner of extortions hale and torture money to themselves. **1818** KEATS *Endym.* III. 256 Like a wretch from whom the rack Tortures hot breath, and speech of agony.

tortured (ˈtɔːtjʊəd, -tʃəd), *ppl. a.* [f. prec. + -ED^{1}.] Subjected or put to torture (*lit.* and *fig.*); tormented; wrested, etc.: see the verb.

1603 DRAYTON *Bar. Wars* IV. xxxix, Eu'ry cadence as a torturde cry. **1687** DRYDEN *Hind & P.* II. 119 The tortur'd Text. **1743** FRANCIS tr. *Hor., Odes* II. xiii. 44 Charm'd by the melodious Strain The tortur'd Ghosts forget their Pain. **1814** SCOTT *Ld. of Isles* IV. xi, Scarba's isle, whose tortured shore Still rings to Corrievreken's roar. **1838** LYTTON *Leila*

I. vi, Thy father filled his treasuries from the gold of many a tortured Hebrew.

'torturer. Also 6–7 -or. [f. TORTURE *v.* + -ER[1].] One who or that which inflicts or causes torture; a tormentor; *spec.* one who executes judicial torture.

1593 SHAKS. *Rich. II*, III. ii. 198, I play the Torturer, by small and small To lengthen out the worst, that must be spoken. **1597** A. M. tr. *Guillemeau's Fr. Chirurg.* 52 b/2 Two torturors will deprive a man of life.. the torturer of greefe and sorrowe is the most cruellest. **1611** SHAKS. *Cymb.* v. v. 215 Thou King, send out For Torturors ingenious. **1780** BECKFORD *Italy* (1834) I. 69 That respectable corps, the torturers of butterflies. **1805** SOUTHEY *Madoc in Azt.* II. 114 Thou know'st how manfully These tribes.. in bonds Defy their torturers. **1830** SCOTT *Ayrshire Trag.* III. i, A torturer of phrases into sonnets.

'torturesome (-səm), *a. rare.* [f. TORTURE *sb.* + -SOME.] Characterized by, or causing torture; extremely painful or distressing.

1889 E. SALTUS *Tristrem Varick* 146 The enforced inactivity was torturesome as suspense. **1906** CHARL. MANSFIELD *Girl & Gods* viii, Your life in every way must be one of exquisite or torturesome emotion.

'torturing, *vbl. sb.* [f. TORTURE *v.* + -ING[1].] The action of the verb TORTURE; infliction of torture; tormenting; *fig.* wresting, perversion.

1633 P. FLETCHER *Purple Isl.* XII. lxv, He soon was led Unto a thousand thousand torturings. **1638** DRUMM. OF HAWTH. *Irene* Wks. (1711) 170 Ruines of noble houses,.. confiscation of estates, torturing of bodies. **1753** W. STEWART in *Scots Mag.* Mar. 135/2 What strange.. torturing of.. upright actions must there be, to make this criminal? **1765** BLACKSTONE *Comm.* (1830) I. i. 133 Prohibition not only of killing and maiming, but also of torturing (to which our laws are strangers). **1855** MAURICE *Patriarchs & Lawg.* xii. (1882) 223 These are not inferences drawn from the story by an unnatural torturing.

b. *attrib.* **'torturing-stock** (*nonce-wd.*), one upon whom torture is inflicted.

1622 BP. HALL *Serm. bef. Jas. I* 15 Sept., Wks. (1624) 493 Yet.. were these poor torturing-stocks higher.. than their persecutors.

'torturing, *ppl. a.* [f. as prec. + -ING[2].] That tortures; inflicting or causing torture; tormenting, excruciating.

1611 SIR W. MURE *Misc. Poems* ii. 46 He [Cupid].. fled away..; But, (woes me,) left behind his tort'ring toyle. **1669** A. THOROLD in *St. Papers, Dom.* 505 An eminent French Protestant.. put to a torturing death. **1794** MRS. RADCLIFFE *Myst. Udolpho* xxiii, This state of torturing suspense. **1817** SHELLEY *Rev. Islam* x. viii, [He] bade the torturing wheel Be brought. **1867** AUG. J. E. WILSON *Vashti* xvii, Her past.., of which the bare memory was so torturing.

Hence **'torturingly** *adv.*

a **1625** FLETCHER & MASSINGER *Laws of Candy* III. ii, An host of furies Could not have baited me more torturingly. **1882** T. HARDY *Two on a Tower* ix, He was there a torturingly long time.

torturous ('tɔːtjʊərəs), *a.* Also 5, 7 torterous. [a. AF. *torturous* = OF. *tortureus, -eux*, f. L. *tortūra* TORTURE: see -OUS.] Full of, involving, or causing torture; tormenting, excruciating; in first quot., given to inflicting torture.

c **1495** *Epitaffe*, etc. in *Skelton's Wks.* (1843) II. 392 O turmentoure, traytoure, torterous tyraunte. **1600** ABP. ABBOT *Exp. Jonah* 199 Dying he must live and living he must dy in a torturous execution. **1618** M. BARET *Horsemanship, Cures*, They follow the torterous inventions of hard snaffles. **1711** SHAFTESB. *Charac.* II. II. ii. (1737) II. 146 The assuaging of the most torturous Pain. **1871** R. ELLIS *Catullus* lxv. 1 Outworn with sorrow, with hours of torturous anguish.

b. *fig.* Involving perversion or violent dislocation (of words, etc.): cf. TORTURE *sb.* 3, *v.* 3 b.

1841 D'ISRAELI *Amen. Lit.* (1859) II. 27 Their torturous arrangement of words without rhythm or cadence. **1890** *Standard* 23 Aug. 3/2 Tortuous, as well as torturous, renderings of Psalms, Te Deums, Canticles, and responses.

Hence **'torturously** *adv.*, very painfully.

1857 W. ARNOT *Let.* in Mrs. A. Fleming *Life* vi. (1877) 320 They make the carriages torturously hard. *c* **1873** J. ADDIS *Eliz. Echoes* (1879) 77 A fate Through all thy Future torturously throbbing.

tortus, -use, obs. forms of TORTOISE.

tortys, tortyse: see TORTIS.

‖**torula** ('tɔːjuːlə, 'tɒruː-). *Biol.* Pl. -æ (-iː). [mod.L. dim. (with change of gender) of TORUS (sense 3): cf. F. *torule* masc.] *lit.* A small rounded swelling or bulge. **a.** Each of the minute rounded cells of various fungi or microbes, as the yeast-plant and certain endoparasitic organisms; also, a chain of such cells. **b.** (With capital initial.) A genus of fungi, chiefly fermentative. (Introd. by Persoon, 1796.)

1833 HOOKER *Brit. Flora* II. II. 359 (Genus) *Tórula*. Pers. *Sporidia* chained together into moniliform erect flocci. **1860** BERKELEY *Brit. Fungology* 326 Torula, P. Spores tomiparous, simple. **1861** H. MACMILLAN *Footn. Page of Nat.* 243 In all saccharine fluids undergoing the alcoholic and even the acetous fermentation these minute torulæ or yeast-cells make their appearance. **1875** HUXLEY & MARTIN *Elem. Biol.* i. 2 Each granule [of yeast] (which is termed a *Torula*) is.. a round, or oval, transparent body... The *Torulæ* are either single, or associated in heaps or strings. *Ibid.* iv. 26 *Bacteria*, like *Torulæ* and *Protococci*, are not killed by drying up, and from their excessive minuteness they must be carried about still more easily than *Torulæ* are.

Hence **torulaceous** (-'leɪʃəs) *a.*, consisting of torulæ; belonging to the order *Torulacei* of fungi; **'toruli,form** *a.* (erron. **torulaform**: see -FORM), having the form of a torula or chain of rounded cells, moniliform; **'toruloid** *a.*, resembling a torula; belonging or allied to the genus *Torula*; hence **toru'losis** *Path.* [-OSIS] = CRYPTOCOCCOSIS.

1876 tr. *Schützenberger's Ferment.* 205 The *torulaceous growth is developed with difficulty, and the transformation is very slow. **1876** tr. *Wagner's Gen. Pathol.* (ed. 6) 92 The filaments are not constricted at the joints, like the moniliform chains (*torulaform) of the globular bacteria. **1874** COOKE *Fungi* 120 Formation of networks of mycelium, or masses of *toruloid cells. **1929** *Jrnl. Amer. Med. Assoc.* 9 Feb. 438/1 Acute miliary *torulosis of the lungs follows a blood stream dissemination of the torula organisms from some chronic lesion. **1974** S. L. ROBBINS *Pathologic Basis of Dis.* xxxii. 1494/1 European blastomycosis is known more commonly as cryptococcosis or torulosis... It is caused by a blastomyces known as *Cryptococcus hominis* or *Torula histolytica*.

†**torulin.** *Biochem. Obs.* [f. TORUL(A + -IN[1].] = THIAMINE 3.

1912 E. S. EDIE et al. in *Biochem. Jrnl.* VI. 242 The substance isolated we propose to call Torulin. **1931** SHERMAN & SMITH *Vitamins* (ed. 2) ii. 81 The symptom of opisthotonus in pigeons appears to be due to excess of lactic acid in the brain and is cured most quickly by injecting concentrated preparations of torulin locally.

torulose ('tɔːjuːləʊs, 'tɒruː-), *a. Nat. Hist.* [f. TORULA + -OSE (after L. type **torulōsus*): cf. mod.F. *toruleux*.] Having at intervals small rounded swollen parts, as a stem, pod, tube, antenna.

1806 J. GALPINE *Brit. Bot.* §309 Arabis... Silique linear, torulose. **1826** KIRBY & SP. *Entomol.* IV. xlvi. 325 Torulose... When they [joints of the antennæ] are a little tumid. **1835** LINDLEY *Introd. Bot.* (1848) I. 154 Thickened slightly at the articulations (torulose). **1887** W. PHILLIPS *Brit. Discomycetes* 103 The paraphyses were septate, and nearly torulose at the upper part.

So **'torulous** *a.*, in same sense.

1752 J. HILL *Hist. Anim.* 11 The Brachionus, with a conic torulous body. **1860** MAYNE *Expos. Lex.*, *Torulosus*,.. swelled, or bulged out in a slight degree here and there, like knotted cord: torulous.

‖**torulus** ('tɔːjuːləs, 'tɒruː-). *Entom.* Pl. toruli (-aɪ). [mod.L. dim. of *torus* in sense 'couch, bed, seat'.] A cavity or orifice in the head of an insect, forming the socket of the antenna.

1826 KIRBY & SP. *Entomol.* III. xxxiv. 511 In considering the insertion of antennæ.. we must advert first to the orifice (*Torulus*) that receives them. This is a perforation of the crust of the head; commonly.. circular... In.. *Rhipicera*.. it is a long process..: in another Coleopterous genus, *Priocera*, it has somewhat of the shape of a trumpet. *Ibid.* 512 A membranous ligament is attached by which it is affixed to the torulus.

‖**torus** ('tɔərəs). Pl. tori ('tɔəraɪ). [L. *torus* a swelling, bulge, knot; muscle, brawn; bolster, cushion, couch, etc.: in *Arch.* a round moulding.]

1. *Arch.* A large convex moulding, of semicircular or similar section, used especially at the base of a column: resembling the astragal, but much larger.

1563 SHUTE *Archit.* 11 The Torus, beneth shalbe yᵉ forth part greater then the Torus aboue. **1768** SPENCE in Holdsworth *Remarks Virgil* 16 The plant which we see sometimes carved on the Torus of Pillars. **1854** H. MILLER *Sch. & Schm.* xiii. (1858) 271 Stairs of polished stone, ornamented in front and at the outer edge by the common fillet and torus. **1873** *Proc. Amer. Phil. Soc.* XIII. 210 The tori were rudely cross-barred.

2. *Bot.* The swollen summit of the flower-stalk, which supports the floral organs: = RECEPTACLE 3 b, THALAMUS 2 a.

1829 LOUDON *Encycl. Plants* (1836) 537 *Sisymbrium*. Silique roundish, sessile upon the torus. **1880** GRAY *Struct. Bot.* vi. §1. 167 The Torus or Receptacle of the flower, also named Thalamus, is the axis which bears all the other parts.

3. a. *Zool.* A protuberant part or organ, as the ventral parapodia in some annelids. ***torus angularis***, a single ossicle which articulates with a pair of interambulacral plates in some starfishes. **b.** *Anat.* 'A smooth rounded ridge or elongated protuberance, as of a muscle; *spec.* the *tuber cinereum* of the brain' (*Syd. Soc. Lex.*).

1877 HUXLEY *Anat. Inv. Anim.* ix. 564 The free surface of the torus angularis lies in the walls of a sort of vestibule in front of the mouth.

4. *Geom.* Orig., a surface or solid generated by the revolution of a circle or other conic about any axis; e.g. a solid ring of circular or elliptic section. In mod. use, a surface or solid conceived of as generated by the circular motion of a circle about an axis outside itself but lying in its plane; also, any body topologically equivalent to this, having one hole in it but not necessarily circular in form or cross-section.

1870 CAYLEY *Math. Papers* VII. 246 The 'Conic Torus', or surface generated by the rotation of a conic about a line whether not in or in the plane of the conic. **1871** *Ibid.* VIII. 25 The general Torus, or surface generated by the rotation of a conic about a fixed axis anywise situate. **1958** *Times* 25 Jan. 4/5 The Zeta apparatus is essentially a ring-shaped metal tube, or torus,.. containing deuterium gas at low pressure. **1966** E. H. SPANIER *Algebraic Topology* 148 The surface with one handle is topologically the torus. **1976** *Offshore Platforms & Pipelining* 49/1 The base structure consists of a torus through which the piles are placed. **1977** *Time* 6 June 54/3 Tokamaks are toruses, or doughnut-shaped chambers, surrounded by huge electromagnets.

5. *attrib.* and *Comb.* (chiefly in sense 1).

1697 EVELYN *Archit.* Misc. Writ. (1825) 378, I take a fillet to be more flat and torus-like. **1789** *Gentl. Mag.* Dec. 1101/2 The torus cap that bears the plinth of the balustrade. **1842** GWILT *Archit.* §2129 The distinction between torus mouldings and beads in joinery is, that the outer edge of the former always terminates with a fillet, whether the torus be single or double. **1877** KNIGHT *Dict. Mech.*, *Torus Bead-plane*, a certain form of plane for making the semicircular convex molding known as a torus.

†**to-'rush,** *v. Obs.* [ME. *to-ruschen*, f. TO-[2] + *ruschen*, RUSH *v.*[2]] *trans.* To dash in pieces; to disperse with force; to rout.

1387 TREVISA *Higden* (Rolls) IV. 399 Al þis was by Goddis ordinaunce so sodeynliche destroyed, so to russhed and to broke. ? *a* **1400** *Morte Arth.* 1428 The Romaynes.. arrayez þame better, And al to-ruscheez oure mene withe theire ryste horsez. **1470–85** MALORY *Arthur* v. x. 176 He.. al to russhed and brake the precious stones.

torve (tɔːv), *a. rare.* [ad. L. *torv-us* grim, frowning: cf. obs. F. *torve* (Cotgr.), Sp., Pg., It. *torvo*.] Stern in aspect; grim, fierce-looking.

1650 BULWER *Anthropomet.* 72 [They] become thereby dim-sighted, and of a torve or crooked aspect. *a* **1661** FULLER *Worthies, Linc.* (1662) II. 153 He [the devil] is supposed to have overlook'd this Church.. with a torve and tetrick countenance, as maligning mens costly devotion. **1862** J. BROWN *Horæ Subs.* Ser. IV. *Our Dogs* 144 Toby made straight at him with a roar too, and an eye more torve than Scrymgeour's. **1894** BLACKMORE *Perlycross* 405 A man,.. torve of aspect.

So **'torvid** (also 7 *erron.* **-ed**) [ad. late L. *torvidus*], **'torvous** *adjs.*, in same sense; **'torvity** [ad. L. *torvitās*], grimness, fierceness of aspect.

a **1639** WEBSTER *Appius & Virg.* v. iii, But yesterday his breath Aw'd Rome, and his least *torved frown was death. **1656** BLOUNT *Glossogr.*, *Torvid*, cruel and spightful in looks, stern, grim, sowre, unpleasant. **1706** E. WARD *Hud. Rediv.* I. XII. 19 Whose torvid Aspect made him show so Like some revengeful Furioso. **1866** J. B. ROSE tr. *Ovid's Met.* iv. 110 With torvid brow Saturnia gazed upon Ixion. **1620** FELTHAM *Resolves* lxxxix. 290 To shew us the inticing spots of this Panther, concealing the *torvitie of her countenance. **1787** *Minor* IV. i. 204 This.. increased my governor's natural torvity. **1825** W. TENNANT in Conolly *Mem.* iii. (1861) 75 Terrible John, with his countenance of Sabine torvity. **1694** R. BURTHOGGE *Reason & Nat. Spir.* 162 Some Ludicrous, some *Torvous. **1713** DERHAM *Phys.-Theol.* IV. xiv. 242 It is natural for many Quadrupeds, Birds and Serpents.. to put on a torvous angry Aspect, when in Danger. **1833** PALMERSTON *Let.* 7 May, in Bulwer *Life* II. x. 160 Sefton looks torvous when I meet him, that I have not appointed Molyneux.

†**torve,** *v. Obs.* [OE. *torfian* to throw, cast.] *trans.* To throw, cast.

c **1000** *Ags. Gosp.* Mark xii. 41 Ða sæt se hælend.. & ȝeseah hu þæt folc hyra feoh torfude on þone toll-sceamul, & maneȝa weliȝe torfudon fela. *c* **1122** *O.E. Chron.* an. 1083, þa Frencisce men bræcen þone chor & torfedon to wærd þam weofode þær ða munecas wæron. *c* **1175** To-toruion [see TO-[2] 1]. *c* **1205** LAY. 16703 Samuel þ sweord an-hof.. & al to-swadde þene king.. & þa stucchen tarueden [*c* **1275** toruede] Wide ȝeond þa straten. *a* **1250** *Owl & Night.* 1119 Stones hi doþ in heore slytte & þe to-toruep.

torves, obs. pl. of TURF.

torvid, torvity, torvous: see after TORVE *a.*

Tory ('tɔərɪ), *sb.* and *a.* [Anglicized spelling of Irish **tóraidhe, -aighe* (tɔːrije) 'pursuer', implied in the derivative *tóraigheachd, tóraidheachd* pursuit: cf. the syncopated Sc. Gaelic *tòrachd* pursuit, pursuing with hostile intent, f. Ir. *tóir* to pursue, *tóirighim* I pursue.

The OIr. agent-nouns in -(*a*)*id* and -(*a*)*ige* fall together in mod. Irish in -(*a*)*idhe* or -(*a*)*ighe*, whence the uncertainty of the spelling; the native form has not been found in writing, outside of dictionaries. In some Irish Dictionaries, the meaning is given as 'a pursued or persecuted person', hence an 'outlaw', which is not without historical suitability: but the best Irish etymologists agree that the form of the word is that of an agent-noun.

The following passage has what at first sight appears to be the same word, but the date makes this impossible. The writer is treating of the diversity of North American Indian languages, and *Torries* was possibly an Indian word:—

1634 W. WOOD *New Eng. Prosp.* II. xviii. 92 When any ships come neare the shore, they [Tarrenteens, Indians of Maine] demand whether they be King Charles his Torries, with such a rumbling sound [of *r*], as if one were beating an unbrac't Drumme.]

A. *sb.* **1. a.** In the 17th c., one of the dispossessed Irish, who became outlaws, subsisting by plundering and killing the English settlers and soldiers; a bog-trotter, a rapparee; later, often applied to any Irish Papist or Royalist in arms. *Obs.* exc. *Hist.*

1646 (Jan. 22) *Exam. P. Congan* in *Cal. Ormonde MSS.* N.S. (1902) I. 105 Some others of the Irish called Tories. **1646** (May 17) MAJ. W. CADOGAN in *Calr. Ormonde MSS.*

(1899) II. 39 Divers that had served under Finglas, Rowen and Welsh and such as had been Tories. **1647** *Proclamation* 2 Nov. (MS. Trinity Coll. Dublin, F. 3. 18. No. 22) Roberies..comitted by the Tories and Rebells upon the Protestants and others adhering to the Protestant partie. **1650** WHITELOCK *Mem.* 12 July (1732) 464/1 That eight Officers..riding upon the Highway [in Ireland], were murder'd by those bloody Highway Rogues called the Tories. **1652** (Dec. 18) in *Cal. St. Papers, Dom.* 41, I took the little island in Waterford river, and beat off Sturlock, the great Tory. **1656** BLOUNT *Glossogr., Banditi*,..in the north of England, Moss-Troopers; in Ireland Tories. **1657** BURTON *Diary* 10 June, *Major Morgan*... We have three beasts to destroy, that lay burdens upon us,—1st, is a public Tory, on whose head we lay 200*l.*, and 40*l.* upon a private Tory's... 2d. beast, is a priest, on whose head we lay 10*l.*, if he be eminent, more. 3d. beast, the wolf, on whom we lay 5*l.* a head if a dog; 10*l.* if a bitch. **1675** *Essex Papers* (Camden) I. 307 Wee, the undernamed parrish priests in the County of Kyery,..doe undertake and faithfully promise..That in our respective congregations wee shall publike and solemnly declare, and denounce, all toreys, murtherers, thieves & Robors. **1676** COLES *Dict., Tories*, Irish Out-laws. **1681** E. MURPHY *State Ireland* §1 Being a cruel Murderer, Rebel and Tory. **1693** G. STORY *Contn. Hist. Wars Irel.* 50 They [Rapparees] never can be reputed other than Tories, Robbers, Thieves, and Bogg-trotters. **1707** *Irish Act 6 Anne*, c. 11 An Act for the more effectual suppression of tories, robbers, and rapparees. **1769** *Dublin Merc.* 16–19 Sept. 3/2, 24 heifers..were..driven..into a bog by tories, robbers and rapparees out in arms. **1849** MACAULAY *Hist. Eng.* ii. I. 257 The bogs of Ireland..afforded a refuge to Popish outlaws, much resembling those who were afterwards known as Whiteboys. These men were then [*temp.* Chas. II] called Tories.

†**b.** Extended to (*a*) robbers or bandits of other races, as Border moss-troopers, Scottish Highlanders, (*b*) Rajput marauders or outlaws. Also (*c*) *fig. Obs.*

(*a*) [**1651** *Mercurius Scoticus* 28 Oct., The Highlanders under Marquesse Huntley and Lord Balcarras..are now betaking themselves to the High-wayes to play the Tories and Robbers.] **1653** COL. LILBURNE *Let. to Cromwell* 16 Oct. (Clarke MSS. LXXXVI. lf. 109b), Argyll tells mee hee cannott advise mee to advance further, though hee suffer never soe much by those Tories. **1654** R. BAILLIE *Lett. & Jrnls.* (1841) III. 255 The discussing of the Northern Tories would cost him bot a few weeks labour. *a***1661** FULLER *Worthies, Cumbld.* (1662) I. 216 The..Earl of Carlisle, who routed these English-Tories [*i.e.* moss-troopers] with his Regiment. **1680** KIRKTON *Hist. Ch. Scot.* ii. (1817) 67 Among the tories in the Highlands. **1690** *Ibid.* v. 158 Middleton had undertaken to command the tories on the hills in Cromwell's time.

(*b*) **1662** J. DAVIES tr. *Mandelslo's Trav.* I. 25 These Racboutes are a sort of High-way men or Tories. *Ibid.* 237 The distractions which then shook the State wherein there were eight Armies of Tories, or common Rogues.

(*c*) **1687** KIRBY & BISHOP *Marrow of Astrol.* I. 43 And now I must..drop down a little lower to the Sphere of Mars, who is termed a Tory amongst the Stars.

2. With capital T: A nickname given 1679–80 by the Exclusioners (q.v.) to those who opposed the exclusion of James, Duke of York (a Roman Catholic) from the succession to the Crown.

According to Roger North *Examen* (1740) II. v. ¶9 The Bill of Exclusion 'led to a common Use of slighting and opprobrious Words; such as *Yorkist*. That..did not scandalise or reflect enough. Then they came to *Tantivy*, which implied Riding Post to Rome... Then, observing that the Duke favoured Irish Men, all his Friends, or those accounted such by appearing against the Exclusion, were straight become *Irish*, and so *wild Irish*, thence *Bogtrotters*, and in the *Copia* of the factious Language, the Word *Tory* was entertained, which signified the most despicable Savages among the Wild Irish'. See also WHIG.

1681 [see TANTIVY B. 2]. **1681** O. HEYWOOD *Diaries*, etc. 24 Oct. (1881) II. 285 A new name lately come into fashion for Ranters calling themselves by the name of Torys... A gentleman..had a red Ribband in his hat,..he said it signifyed that he was a Tory, whats that sd. she? he ans. an Irish Rebel... I hear further since that..instead of Cavalier and Roundhead, now they are called Torys and Wiggs. **1681** DRYDEN *Abs. & Achit.* To Rdr., Wit and fool are consequents of Whig and Tory; and every man is a knave or an ass to the contrary side. *a***1685** EARL OF DORSET *Whigs & Tories* in *Coll. Poems* 15 The Fools might be *Whigs*, none but Knaves shou'd be *Toryes*. *a***1734** NORTH *Exam.* II. v. (1740) 321 Thus the Anti-exclusioners [*c* 1679] were stigmatised with Execration and Contempt, as a Parcel of damn'd *Tories*, for diverse Months together. *Ibid.* 324 The Faction..had found a sarcasmous Name to fling upon the Loyallists,..that of *Tory*, the same as savage Brute and Idiot.

3. a. Hence, from 1689, the name of one of the two great parliamentary and political parties in England, and (at length) in Great Britain.

The party sprang from the 17th century Royalists or Cavaliers, and its members at first were more or less identical with the Anti-Exclusionists or 'Tories' in sense 2. For some years after 1689 the Tories leant more or less decidedly towards the dethroned House of Stuart; but upon the accession of George III they, as a party, abandoned this attitude, retaining the principle of strenuously upholding the constituted authority and order in Church and State, and of opposing concessions in the direction of greater religious liberty. In opposition to the growing demands of Liberalism (see LIBERAL 5), a consistent antagonism to measures for widening the basis of parliamentary representation, or tending to impair the exclusive privileges of the Church as by law established, became their most marked characteristic; but this has in course of time undergone many modifications. As a formal name, 'Tory' was superseded *c* 1830 by CONSERVATIVE, merged after 1886 (when the Conservatives were joined by many who had previously belonged to the Liberal party, in opposing Home Rule for Ireland) in that of UNIONIST. But 'Tory' is still retained (1) colloquially; (2) as expressing attachment to a policy either more old-fashioned (cf. *old* or *high Tory* in b), or more positive and constructive than that of ordinary Conservatism (cf. *Tory democracy*, C. 3); (3) in hostile usage, identifying the party with the bigotry and opposition to reform and progress charged upon earlier Toryism. Opposed originally and during the 18th c. to WHIG; later to LIBERAL, and (still more) to RADICAL.

1705 G. LOCKHART *Let. to Dk. Athole* 15 Oct. in *12th Rep. Hist. MSS. Comm.* App. VIII. 62 Her Majesty having now, more than ever before, devoted herself and interest to the Whigs, the Torys have no hopes of being succesfull in allmost anything..during this parliament. **1710** SWIFT *Jrnl. to Stella* 7 Nov., The Queen passed by us with all Tories about her; not one Whig:..and I have seen her without one Tory. **1711** ADDISON *Spect.* No. 126 ¶8 The Knight is a much stronger Tory in the Country than in Town, which..is absolutely necessary for the keeping up his Interest. **1718** [see HIGH-FLYER 3]. **1735–8** BOLINGBROKE *Parties* viii. Wks. 1809 III. 132 The real essences of Whig and Tory were thus [in 1689] destroyed, but the nominal were preserved. **1741** HUME *Ess., Parties Gt. Brit.* (1758) 45 A Tory, therefore, since the revolution, may be defined in a few words, to be a lover of monarchy, tho' without abandoning liberty; and a partizan of the family of Stuart. **1755** JOHNSON, *Tory*. (A cant term, derived, I suppose, from an Irish word signifying a savage.) One who adheres to the ancient constitution of the state, and the apostolical hierarchy of the church of England: opposed to a whig. **1781** —— in *Boswell* (1906) II. 396 The prejudice of the Tory is for establishment; The prejudice of the Whig is for innovation. A Tory does not wish to give more real power to Government; but that Government should have more reverence. **1806** T. W. COKE *Let.* 23 Sept. in *Parr's Wks.* (1828) VII. 246 It was..a glorious victory of the Whigs over the Tories. **1827** HALLAM *Const. Hist.* III. xvi, To a tory the constitution, inasmuch as it was the constitution, was an ultimate point,..from which he thought it altogether impossible to swerve; whereas a whig deemed all forms of government subordinate to the public good. **1830** MACAULAY *Ess., Southey's Coll.* (1865) I. 115/2 A Tory of the Tories..won and wore that noblest wreath, 'Ob cives servatos'. **1831** ARNOLD Apr., in *Life & Corr.* (1845) I. vi. 303 The old state of things is gone past recall, and all the efforts of all the Tories cannot save it. *c***1832** BORROW in Knapp *Life* (1899) I. xiv. 144 As the question is, or will shortly be, Tory or Radical, we say Tory! and advise every honest man to say so too. **1833** GEN. P. THOMPSON *Exerc.* (1842) II. 329 The Tories in Great Britain are defunct;..they are all vaccinated into 'Conservatives'. **1839** Q. VICTORIA *Jrnl.* 9 May, I said..that I never talked politics with them [the Ladies], and that they were related, many of them, to Tories. **1843** *Penny Cycl.* XXV. 82/2 From the Revolution down to the present time the struggle between the two parties..has been a struggle by the Tories on behalf of the Church, to invest it with political power and privileges, and against the increase of the power of the people in the state, through the House of Commons. **1844** MACAULAY *Ess., Chatham* (1865) II. 361/2 If.. we look at the essential characteristics of the Whig and the Tory, we may consider each of them as the representative of a great principle... One is, in an especial manner, the guardian of liberty, and the other of order. One is the moving power, and the other the steadying power of the state. **1882** M. ARNOLD *Irish Ess.*, etc. 164 The Conservatives, or, as they are now beginning to be called again, the Tories. **1886** T. E. KEBBEL *Hist. Toryism* viii. 364 The Tories are for administrative reform: the Radicals for social revolution. **1892** SAINTSBURY *Earl of Derby* Pref. 5, I define a Tory as a person who would, at the respective times and in the respective circumstances, have opposed Catholic Emancipation, Reform, the Repeal of the Corn Laws, and the whole Irish Legislation of Mr. Gladstone. **1895** OMAN *Hist. Eng.* xxxix. 636 The generation of Tories who had grown up during the great French war, had forgotten the old liberal doctrines of their great leader Pitt. *Ibid.* xlii. 700 Down to 1865, the Liberals and the Conservatives alike retained in a great measure the characteristics of their forefathers the Whigs and Tories.

b. With various qualifications, as

high, high-flying T., a Tory of 'high' principles; in 17–18th c. a High-Church Tory, a 'Church and King' man: cf. HIGH-FLYER 3a; later, a thorough, old-fashioned, or reactionary Tory; *Jacobite T.*, a Tory of Jacobite principles, or tending to Jacobitism; *old T.*, a Tory of a non-modern type; in quot. 1827, a Jacobite Tory; *ultra T.*, a Tory of extreme principles or opinions.

1713 SWIFT *Jrnl. to Stella* 9 Apr., The Bishop of Chester, a *high Tory, was against the Court. **1827** SCOTT *Jrnl.* 3 Sept., The King..probably looks with no greater [favour] on the return of the High Tories. **1842** *Mem. M. T. Sadler* x. 335 One..whom it is customary..to hold up to popular abhorrence as a 'bigot', a 'borough-monger', and a 'high Tory'. **1863** G. PRYME *Autobiog. Recoll.* 12 Nov., I have been told by at least two high Tories that they could not discover by my lectures what political sentiments I held. **1738** BOLINGBROKE *Lett.* ii. *Patriot King* (1856) 165 What gives obstinacy without strength..to the *Jacobite-tories at this time? **1827** HALLAM *Const. Hist.* (1876) III. xv. 125 *note*, The thorough-paced royalists, or *old Tories [*c* 1690]. **1850** HT. MARTINEAU *Hist. Peace* I. III. xi. 555 We have, what the old Tories have not and cannot conceive of. **1886** T. E. KEBBEL *Hist. Toryism* viii. 366 The first Factory Bill..was introduced by the typical old Tory, Mr. Sadler. **1895** OMAN *Hist. Eng.* xxxix. 646 When O'Connell's agitation grew formidable, and the old Tories urged him to repress it by force, he [Wellington] refused. **1833** CROKER 25 Mar., in Kebbel *Hist. Toryism* v. (1886) 254 [Sir R. Peel] foresaw that Radicals and *ultra-Tories would unite against him. **1862** KNIGHT *Pop. Hist. Eng.* VIII. vi. 109 The measures..hardly came up to the expectation of the ultra-Tories of that day [1819].

4. a. *U.S. Hist.* A member of the British party during the Revolutionary period; a loyal colonist.

(These were orig. 'Tories' in the English political sense, who naturally continued loyal to the King.)

[**1774** J. ADAMS in *Fam. Lett.* (1876) 7 Dr. Gardiner, arrived..from Boston, brings news of a battle at the town meeting, between Whigs and Tories. **1774** —— *Wks.* (1854) IX. 336 The tories were never, since I was born, in such a state of humiliation as at this moment.] **1775** *Pennsylvania Even. Post* 1 July 278/1 The Whigs and Tories at Georgia are disputing with each other, and Governor Wright is much alarmed for his safety. *Ibid.* 18 July 309/2 The Tories in Georgia are now no more, the province is..about to choose Delegates to send to the Congress. **1776** M. CUTLER in *Life*, etc. (1888) I. 54 The ships lay down below the castle with the soldiers and tories and their families on board. **1776** *Ann. Reg.* 29 Many of the well-affected (or Tories, which was the appellation now given to them throughout America) thought it prudent..to seek the same asylum. **1777** [implied in *Toryess* below]. **1821** J. F. COOPER *Spy* xxix, Washington will not trust us with the keeping of a suspected Tory, if we let this rascal trifle in this manner with the corps.

b. During the American civil war, applied in the Confederate states to a Union sympathizer.

1862 *Southern Confederacy* (Atlanta, Georgia) 3 May 3/1 The other prisoners..are all sharp, intelligent-looking men—no hard looking cases like Yankee prisoners, and East Tennessee tories usually are. **1866** W. REID *After the War* 402 Ef you fetch any d—— tories heah, that went agin their State, and so kin take the oath,..'twill soon be too hot to hold 'em. **1953** T. C. BRYAN *Confederate Georgia* ix. 152 In the fall of 1864 bands of Tories were plundering northeast Georgia.

5. *transf.* Applied to any one in foreign countries or former ages holding views analogous to those of the English Tories; also, one who is by temperament or sentiment inclined to conservative principles.

1797 J. BOUCHER *View Amer. Rev.* Pref. 22 Every man capable of forming an opinion..is, in some degree, either a Whig or a Tory. Now the American revolution was clearly a struggle for pre-eminence between Whigs and Tories. **1827** HALLAM *Const. Hist.* (1876) III. xvi. 201 The names whig and tory are often well applied to individuals. **1836** ARNOLD *Let.* 28 Nov., in *Life & Corr.* (1845) II. 65 Men are all Tories by nature, when they are tolerably well off. **1841** *Ibid.* 26 June *ibid.* I. ix. 267 After all, those differences in men's minds which we express, when exemplified in English politics, by the terms Whig and Tory, are very deep and comprehensive,..they seem to be the great fundamental difference between thinking men. **1860** RUSSELL *Diary India* II. x. 191 Purrus Ram and Khoom Dass..fear greatly..that the Tories of Bussahir will triumph.

B. *adj.* **1. a.** That is a Tory; of, pertaining to, or characteristic of a Tory or Tories; consisting of or constituted by Tories; also, having the principles or aims of a Tory; supported or recognized by the Tory party; Conservative.

1682 DRYDEN *Loyal Brother* Epil. 3 He's neither yet a Whigg nor Tory-Boy. **1682** —— *Dk. Guise* Epil. 44 A kind of Bat..With Tory Wings, but Whiggish Teeth and Claws. **1689** EVELYN *Diary* 15 Jan., There was a Tory party (as then so call'd) who were for inviting his Majesty [Jas. II] againe upon conditions. **1693** ROKEBY *Diary* 15 Aug., It is a Tory complaint ag^t a Whigg. **1694** *Ibid.* 2 Apr., A Tory Bigot. **1710** SWIFT *Jrnl. to Stella* 5 Dec., [They] drank Mr. Harley's, Lord Rochester's, and other Tory healths. **1711** ADDISON *Spect.* No. 81 ¶2 [She] has most unfortunately a very beautiful Mole on the Tory Part of her Forehead. *a***1734** NORTH *Exam.* II. v. (1740) 322 He has split the former Church of England into two Churches, the Tory Church, and the Whig Church of England. **1735–8** BOLINGBROKE *On Parties* viii. Wks. 1809 III. 136 This inconsiderable faction could not be deemed the tory party, but received the name of jacobite with more propriety. **1738** —— *Lett.* ii. *Patriot King* (1750) 165 Men who had sense,..before that moment, thought of nothing, after it, but of setting up a tory King against a whig King. **1776** *Pennsylvania Even. Post* 18 July 356/1 Yesterday several Tory prisoners were sent to Halifax jail. **1791** BOSWELL *Johnson* 11 June an. 1784, We drank 'Church and King' after dinner, with true Tory cordiality. **1826** SCOTT *Jrnl.* 15 Dec., The Tory interest was weak among the old stagers, where I remember it so strong. **1830** GEN. P. THOMPSON *Exerc.* (1842) I. 306 The advice of the English High Church and Tory party has been taken; and the Bourbons are driven from France. **1886** T. E. KEBBEL *Hist. Toryism* viii. 398 The Tory revival was but the twin sister of the Anglican revival. *Ibid.* ix. 468 In its defence of the Monarchy, the Church, and the territorial Constitution of the country, the Tory party has never faltered.

b. With various qualifications: see A. 3b.

1791 BOSWELL *Johnson* 11 June an. 1784, A sermon (1772)..full of high Tory sentiments. **1827** SCOTT *Jrnl.* 11 Aug., A High Tory Administration would be a great evil at this time. **1850** HT. MARTINEAU *Hist. Peace* II. v. xvii. 445 It was cheering to see..high tory and deep radical chemists helping out one another's information about soils and manures. **1854** EARL ABERDEEN 6 Jan. in *Lett. Q. Victoria* (1908) III. xxiii. 2 The base and infamous attacks made upon the Prince..chiefly..in those papers which represent ultra-Tory or extreme Radical opinions. **1862** KNIGHT *Pop. Hist. Eng.* VIII. xviii. 320 The expectations of the ultra-Tory party that the Reform Bill [1832] would be repealed. **1895** OMAN *Hist. Eng.* xl. 667 Benjamin Disraeli,..who combined high Tory notions on Church and State with extreme Radical views on certain social questions. **1908** *Lett. Q. Victoria* I. i. 6 The ultra-Tory party, who had opposed to the last the Emancipation of the Catholics and the Reform Bill.

2. In extended or transferred senses: see A. 5.

1832 GEN. P. THOMPSON *Exerc.* (1842) II. 7 The Catilinarian conspiracy..was manifestly a plot in a green bag, and Cicero a Tory Secretary for the Home Department. **1837** *Ibid.* IV. 367 To pick holes in the history of the Greek republics, on the strength of the remains of the Tory poets of that time. **1899** R. H. CHARLES *Eschatology* v. 162 It [Ecclesiasticus] is uncompromisingly tory, and refuses to admit the possibility of the new views as to the future life. *Ibid.* vi. 204 The still orthodox and tory view found in the Old Testament.

C. Phrases and combinations.

1. Used advb. in phr. ***to talk, vote Tory***.

1827 SCOTT *Jrnl.* 21 July, Nobody talks Whig or Tory just now. **1913** *Ch. Q. Rev.* Jan. 452 He had the manhood to stand by his chapel and refuse to vote Tory.

2. *Comb.*, as ***Tory-Radical*** sb. and adj.; ***Tory-Irish, -leaning, -ridden, -voiced*** adjs.; ***Tory-***

Williamite, a Tory who supported or adhered to William III.

1696–7 ROKEBY *Diary* (Surtees) 51 Mr. Ratcliff, sheriff of Devonshire, is a Tory-Williamite. **1834** *Tait's Mag.* I. 387/2 The Governor, save on the question of slavery, the black niggers, and the Church, latterly became a sort of Tory-Radical. **1836** K. OF BELGIANS 18 Nov., in *Lett. Q. Victoria* (1908) I. v. 53 An infamous Radical or Tory-Radical paper, the *Constitutional*, which seems determined to run down the Coburg family. **1894** *Westm. Gaz.* 21 Sept. 2/3 Cases like mine, where in Tory-ridden villages the overseers resent both Liberal and women voters. **1898** *Ibid.* 24 Mar. 2/2 It must in the long run be a new Tory-Irish understanding. **1908** W. CHURCHILL in *Nation* 7 Mar. 812/2 The pressure of Tory-voiced discontent.

3. a. Tory democracy, combination of Toryism with democracy; democracy under Tory leadership; new or democratic Toryism; progressive Conservatism.

1867 LD. SALISBURY in *Q. Rev.* CXXIII. 539 It was not till the earlier struggles of the session were over..that the project of Tory democracy, which had been so long and so sedulously concealed, was at last given to the world. **1879** *Spectator* 21 June 776 Tory democracy—Jingoism is its proper name. **1884** *Pall Mall G.* 29 Nov. 3/2 We would venture to lay very long odds that Tory Democracy is much more likely to come in with a boom than to go out with a fiz. **1885** GLADSTONE *Let. to Ld. Acton* 11 Feb. in Morley *Life* (1903) III. VIII. x. 173 'Tory democracy'..is no more like the conservative party in which I was bred, than it is like liberalism. In fact less. It is demagogism, only a demagogism..living upon the fomentation of angry passions, and still in secret as obstinately attached as ever to the evil principle of class interests. **1910** S. J. LOW in *Encycl. Brit.* VI. 346/2 (Lord Randolph Churchill) By this time [1882] he had definitely formulated the policy of progressive Conservatism which was known as 'Tory democracy'. He declared that the Conservatives ought to adopt, rather than oppose, reforms of a popular character, and to challenge the claims of the Liberals to pose as the champions of the masses.

b. So **Tory democrat**, one who professes or supports Tory democracy. Also **Tory democratic** *a.*

1868 *Daily News* 2 Dec., Constitutionalist, tory, and tory democrat, are the names between which their choice wavers. **1885** E. W. HAMILTON *Diary* 15 June (1972) II. 885 It was R. Churchill's way of protesting publicly against a revival of the old Tory Cabinet..without any infusion of fresh (Tory-democratic) blood. **1902** *Daily Chron.* 29 Aug. 4/5 The policy of the advanced Tory Democratic section. **1903** *Westm. Gaz.* 14 Jan. 2/2 Recommended..to the electors..on the ground that he is a 'Tory Democrat', in which hybrid political creature it is roundly declared 'there is really more of true, old-fashioned Liberalism than in the Liberal Party to-day'. **1910** *Encycl. Brit.* VI. 976/2 Lord Randolph Churchill called himself a 'Tory democrat'.

Hence (chiefly *nonce-wds.*) † **'Torycal** *a.* [after *historical*] = *Tory* adj.; **'Torydom**, the realm or rule of Tories; **'Toryess**, a female Tory (in quot. in sense 4); **Tory'istic** *a.*, inclined to Toryism; **'Toryize** *v.*, *trans.* = TORYFY; **'Toryship** (*humorous*), the personality of a Tory.

1682 THORESBY *Diary* 14 July, Had some ineffectual discourses..with the *Torycal Papists. **1859** W. CHADWICK *Life De Foe* ii. 104 The bill passed; and, thanks to *Torydom, there it remains! **1908** M. BARING *Russian Ess.*, etc. Ded. 11 Here, they thought, was the voice of officialdom, Torydom, and hypocrisy speaking. **1777** FRANKLIN *Let.* Wks. 1889 VI. 67 You must know she is a *Toryess as well as you, and can as flippantly call *rebel*. **1899** HOWELLS in *Literature* 1 July 692 By a curious irony of fate he came to stand in later years for something *toryistic to men who were fighting other anti-slavery battles. **1887** *L'pool Mercury* 5 Jan., He was the first to show that London might be *Toryised. **1890** *Pall Mall G.* 22 Aug. 2/1 A narrow little clique—fossilized and Toryized to an almost incredible degree. **1793** PARR *Let. to Routh* 12 June, Wks. 1828 VII. 652 Farewell, and believe me..your *Toryship's friend and servant.

† **Tory**, *v. Obs.* [f. TORY *sb.*]

1. *intr.* To live as an Irish Tory or outlaw.

1651 G. RAWDON *Let.* 24 Dec. in *St. Pap., Irel.* CCLXXXII. 104 (P.R.O.) Sir Phill and Cormack Mulhallon Torye about Braintree woodes; soe that they cannot stirr out of Charlemount but with a considerable strengthe. **1655** [V. GOOKIN] *Gt. Case Transpl. Irel.* 21 Many Inhabitants, who are able to subsist on their Gardens in their present Habitations,..will rather choose the hazard of Torying, than the apparent danger of starving [in Connaught].

2. *trans.* To becall or nickname *Tory*.

1681 T. FLATMAN *Heraclitus Ridens* No. 34 (1713) I. 218 [They] shall pass for white Boys, and have never a word said to them for Torying, Tantivying and Masquerading his Majesty's most loyal and dutiful Subjects.

Toryfy, Torify ('tɔərɪfaɪ), *v. humorous.* [f. TORY + -FY.] *trans.* To make a Tory of, convert to Toryism (*generally dyslogistic*). Hence **'Toryfied**, **'Toryfying** *ppl. adjs.*; also **,Toryfi'cation**, conversion to Toryism.

1763 WILKES *N. Brit.* No. 37 (1766) 212 The strict harmony subsisting between the whiggified Tories, the torified Whigs, and the amphibious North Britons. **1834** LADY GRANVILLE *Lett.* (1894) II. 177 Neither of the Clanricardes seems pleased, or Tory-fied at the news. **1853** SIR G. C. LEWES *Lett.* 262 Most of his [Gladstone's] High church supporters stick to him, and..he is Liberalizing them, instead of their Torifying him. **1876** G. MEREDITH *Beauch. Career* xxviii, Mr. Tuckham was..prophesying the Torification of mankind. **1901** A. BIRRELL in *N. Amer. Rev.* Feb. 251 The Toryfication..of London and of so many of our great towns..is one of the most striking political facts of recent times. **1902** *Academy* 11 Jan. 667/1 Lowell was born and bred in a Toryfied old country seat at Elmwood, Cambridge, New England.

Toryish ('tɔərɪɪʃ), *a.* [f. TORY *sb.* or *a.* + -ISH[1].] Somewhat Tory; inclined to Toryism. So **'Toryishly** *adv.*

1681 T. FLATMAN *Heraclitus Ridens* No. 41 (1713) II. 17 The Mistress of the House being, it seems, Toryishly affected, would have two Pence the Dish for true Protestant Coffee. **1684** (Mar. 26) *Let. fr. Irel.* in T. Hutchinson *Hist. Mass.* (1764) I. ii. 343 *note*, I suspect you of the Massachusets, are more whiggish, and your neighbours more toryish, to express it in the language of late in use. **1794** PARR *Let. to Routh* 22 July, Wks. 1828 VII. 658 Manners which you would call Toryish, because they were at once correct, elegant, and dignified. **1826** *New Monthly Mag.* Jan. 20 He must not be too whiggish for his Tory customers, nor too toryish for his Whigs. **1876** G. MEREDITH *Beauch. Career* xiv, I fancy he is Toryish.

Toryism ('tɔərɪɪz(ə)m). Also 7–8 **Torism**. [f. as prec. + -ISM.] The principles, practices, and methods of Tories: *spec.* **a.** those of the British Tory party; Conservatism.

1682 in *Westm. Gaz.* 22 Jan. (1909) 2/3 [The *Loyal London Mercury* declared that it would not go with either] Whigism or Torism. **1711** *Medley* No. 24. 279 Put Torism instead of it, and it sits exactly in all its Parts. **1713** (*title*) Torism and Trade can never agree. **1735–8** BOLINGBROKE *On Parties* ii. Wks. 1809 III. 47 An inquiry into the rise and progress of our late parties; or a short history of toryism and whiggism from their cradle to their grave. **1786** MRS. PIOZZI *Anecd. Johnson* 40 Of Mr. Johnson's toryism the world has long been witness. **1791** BOSWELL *Johnson* 22 Mar. an. 1776, I felt all my Toryism glow in this old capital of Staffordshire. *Ibid.* 3 June an. 1784, Oxford, that magnificent and venerable seat of Learning, Orthodoxy, and Toryism. *c* **1832** BORROW in Knapp *Life*, etc. (1899) I. xiv. 144 The chief reason for Toryism, a reason sufficient by itself, is that within it are comprised love of country and pride of country. **1862** KNIGHT *Pop. Hist. Eng.* VIII. xxix. 528 The principle of ultra-Toryism. **1886** T. E. KEBBEL *Hist. Toryism* viii. 335 Lord Beaconsfield carried Toryism into the next stage. *Ibid.* 337 The Toryism of the future must be popular Toryism or nothing. **1895** OMAN *Hist. Eng.* xlii. 709 Disraeli, seated firmly in power, was able to display the characteristics of the 'New Toryism'. **1910** S. J. LOW in *Encycl. Brit.* VI. 346/2 He was actively spreading the gospel of democratic Toryism in a series of platform campaigns. *Ibid.*, In 1884 the struggle between stationary and progressive Toryism came to a head, and terminated in favour of the latter. **1913** F. E. SMITH in *Daily Express* 12 Feb. 2/4 Not the least potent method of preserving it [the State] is to link the conception of State Toryism with the practice of Social Reform.

b. of the American Tories or Loyalists at the War of Independence: see TORY *sb.* 4.

1777 J. ADAMS *Diary* 18 Sept., We are yet in Philadelphia, that mass of cowardice and Toryism. **1888** BRYCE *Amer. Commw.* III. ciii. 468 Because the Anglican Clergy were prone to Toryism (as attachment to the British connection was called).

c. Applied generally to principles analogous to those of English Toryism: cf. TORY *sb.* 5.

1832 GEN. P. THOMPSON *Exerc.* (1842) II. 7 Why will nobody re-write the Greek and Roman histories, and give us an insight into the Toryism of antiquity? **1837** *Ibid.* IV. 367 Toryism..is not a thing of modern date, but goes back to the earliest histories. **1837** ARNOLD *Let.* 3 Mar., in *Life & Corr.* (1845) II. 79 If I dared, I would put in a word for 'As in præsenti', perhaps even for 'Propria quæ maribus'. Is not this a laudable specimen of Toryism?

torymid ('tɒrɪmɪd), *a.* and *sb. Entom.* [f. mod.L. *Torymidæ* pl., f. *Torymus*, name of the typical genus: see -ID[3].] **a.** *adj.* Of or pertaining to the *Torymidæ*, a group of chalcididan parasitic hymenoptera. **b.** *sb.* An insect of this group.

1895 *Camb. Nat. Hist.* V. 547 Some of these Torymid fig-Insects have winged males, as is normal in the family.

toryn, obs. f. *torn*, pa. pple. of TEAR *v.*[1]

† **'tory-'rory**, *a.* (*adv.*) *Obs.* [Origin obscure: perhaps orig. a reduplication or riming expansion of *rory*, ROARY, f. ROAR *sb.* or *v.* The Eng. Dial. Dict. cites it from S. Lancash. as meaning 'a state of hurry or excitement'. After 1680 it was sometimes abusively associated with TORY *sb.*; but there can hardly have been any original connexion. Reference to the Irish *Tories* or outlaws and marauders is chronologically possible, but not evidenced.]

1. Roaring, uproarious, roistering, boisterous; in quots. 1694, 1716 with allusion to TORY A. 2, 3.

1678 DRYDEN *Limberham* I. i, And, before George, I grew tory rory, as they say. *Ibid.* IV. i, Sing like nightingales, you tory-rory jades. **1678** OTWAY *Friendship in F.* II. i, Methinks you look like two as roring, ranting tory rory Sparks as one would wish to meet withal. [**1681** O. HEYWOOD *Diaries*, etc. 24 Oct., Theres a book called the character of a Tory wherin it runs, A Tory, a Whory, a Roary, a Scory, a Sory.] **1694** MOTTEUX *Rabelais* v. *Pantagr. Progn.* v. 237 Swaggering Huffsnuffs,..Tory-rory Rakes and Tantivy-boys. **1716** M. DAVIES *Athen. Brit.* II. 337 From a Tory-Rory-Boy, he is become a cool-temper'd Wig.

2. Ruffianly (like the Irish Tories, or Judge Jeffreys).

1682 MRS. BEHN *City Heiress* 52 Some damn'd Tory-rory Rogues, to rob a man at his Prayers! **1822** PARR *Let. to Hill* 25 Jan., Wks. 1828 VII. 605 Servile and corrupt judges, prejudiced and perjured juries, merciless jailors and a tory-rory hangman.

B. *adv.* In a roaring or uproarious manner; boisterously, rantingly, roisteringly.

It may have been the name of a rowdy song or tune.

1664 COTTON *Scarron.* IV. (1715) 97 Roaring and drinking tory-rory. [**1667** DRYDEN & DAVENANT *Tempest* IV. iii, I found her an hour ago under an elder tree,..singing Tory Rory, and Rantum Scantum, with her own natural brother.] **1673** SHADWELL *Epsom Wells* II. i, We were at it Tory Rory, and Sung old Rose, the Song that you love so.

Hence † **'tory-'rory** *v. Obs.*, *intr.* to behave uproariously.

1685 CROWNE *Sir C. Nice* IV. 43 Well the house is our own, and the Night our own,..we'l Tory-rory, and 'tis—a fine Night, we'l Revel in the Garden.

Tosa ('təʊsə), *sb.*[1] The name of an aristocratic Japanese family of court painters used *attrib.* to designate (the products of) a school of painting characterized by the use of traditional themes and techniques, which flourished from the mid-fifteenth to the late-nineteenth century.

1879 *Trans. Asiatic Soc. Japan* VII. 355 The reputation of the Tosa school was maintained during the progress of the Kano riu. **1909** L. BINYON *Jap. Art* ii. 10 The typical Tosa picture was a long scroll (makimono) portraying scenes of battle, adventure, scenes of court life, or the lives of saints. **1952** L. WARNER *Enduring Art of Japan* vi. 64 It had been appropriate enough, for narrow Tosa scrolls..to use small patches of opaque colour set in cells of black ink. **1972** *Times* 18 May 21/5 An album of hand paintings of the Tosa school..dating from the turn of the seventeenth and eighteenth centuries.

Tosa ('təʊsə), *sb.*[2] [a. *Tosa*, the former name of a province on the island of Shikoku, Japan.] A black, tan, or brindle mastiff of the breed of this name, originally developed as a type of fighting dog in Japan. Also *attrib.*

1945 C. L. B. HUBBARD *Observer's Bk. Dogs* 191 The Tosa..has been known for at least six centuries. **1966** 'G. BLACK' *You want to die, Johnny?* ii. 39 Taro, my Japanese Tosa hound..is a big brindle fighting dog. **1971** DANGERFIELD & HOWELL *Internat. Encycl. Dogs* 309/2 Little effort has been made to keep the Tosa purebred until quite recently. *Ibid.*, The modern Tosa dogs are about 28 inches tall..and weigh well over 100 lb.

† **to-'same, to-'samen**, *adv. Obs.* Forms: 1 **tosǫmne, tosamne**, 2–3 **to somne**, (*Orm.*) **tosamenn**, 2–4 **to same**, 3 **to somnen**, 3–4 **to samen**, 4 **to samyn**. [OE. *tósamne*, *tósǫmne*, f. *tó*, TO *prep.* + SAMEN together. Cf. OFris. *to samene*, OS. *tô samane*, *te samne* (MDu. *te-zamen*, Du. *samen*), OHG. *saman*, *zi samane* (MHG. *zesamene*, Ger. *zusammen*); also ON. *til-samans*.

The element *samen* represents an orig. sb., of which *saman, samane, samans* were case-forms: cf. Skr. *samana* concourse, assembly, *samana* adv. together; also OIr. *samain* assembly, the Tara-festival.]

Together; into or in one body or company.

c **893** K. ÆLFRED *Oros.* IV. xi. §9 Raðe þæs þe hie tosomne comon. **971** *Blickl. Hom.* 191 þa coman þær tosamne unari-medlico menȝeo. *c* **1000** ÆLFRIC *Hom.* II. 100 Moyses fæste feowertiȝ daȝa and feowertiȝ nihta tosamne. *c* **1200** *Trin. Coll. Hom.* 23 Boðe to same þe sowle and þe lichame. *c* **1200** ORMIN 649 Forrþi shulenn alle þa..Tosamenn stanndenn att te dom. *c* **1205** LAY. 8597 To-somnen we scullen gliden. *c* **1315** SHOREHAM i. 116 Crist is mid ous to-same. **13..** *Cursor M.* 11461 (Cott.) And did he suith to samen call þe maisters of his kingrik all. *c* **1375** *Ibid.* 3073 (Fairf.) To-samyn dwelled þai þare.

‖ **tosaphoth** ('təʊsəfəʊθ). Also **tosafoth**. [Heb. *tōsāphōth*, pl. of *tōsāphāh* addition, f. *yāsaph* to add.] Critical and explanatory notes on the Talmud. Hence **'tosaphist (-fist)**, a writer of tosaphoth.

1887 H. ADLER in *Papers Anglo-Jewish Hist. Exhib.* 272 The marvellously exhaustive list of Tosafists (authors of comments on the Talmud) contained in Zunz's 'Zur Geschichte und Literatur'.

† **'tosard.** *Obs.* Some kind of fire-wood, or a form in which it was sold in 14th to 16th c.

1336 in Rogers *Agric. & Prices* (1866) II. 396 (Farley, Surrey) Tosards 1250 at 2/-. [*Ibid.* 393 *note*, Tosards..are sold by the hundred]. **1339** *Ibid.*, Tosards 50 at 2/-. **1341** *Ibid.*, Tosards 1000 at 2/-. **1429** *Ibid.* III. 257 (Charles & Rowhill) Tosards 15[c] at 2/-. **1550** in Strype *Stow's Surv.* (1755) II. v. xxii. 422/2 If any Freeman of this City use to resort into the Countries near to this City, and there to ingross and buy up much Billet, tall Wood, Faggot, Tosard, or other Fire-wood.

‖ **tosca** ('tɒskə). Also **tosco, toska**. [Sp. *tosca*, fem. of *tosco* coarse.] A soft dark-brown limestone occurring embedded and sometimes stratified in the surface formation of the Pampas.

Also applied to various lavas in southern Italy and Sicily; and in Colombia, S. America, to a surface rock of supposed volcanic origin (*Cent. Dict.*).

1818 *Amer. St. Papers, For. Relat.* (1834) IV. 277 This concretion, as it projects along the water's edge of the Rio de la Plata at the city of Buenos Ayres, is called *tosca*, or rough earth. **1846** DARWIN *Geol. Observ. S. Amer.* iv. 77 For convenience sake, I will call the marly rock by the name given to it by the inhabitants, namely, Tosca-rock. **1859** PAGE *Handbk. Geol. Terms*, *Tosca-Rock*, a name given by the inhabitants of Buenos-Ayres to a marly arenaceous rock found imbedded in layers and nodular masses among the argillaceous earth or mud of the Pampas.

Toscan, obs. or alien form of TUSCAN.

† **to-'scatter**, *v. Obs.* [ME. *to-scater-en*, f. TO-² + *scateren*, SCATTER *v.*] *trans.* To scatter abroad, disperse.

1382 WYCLIF *2 Chron.* xxxiv. 7 Whanne the auters he hadde to-scaterede..he is turnede aȝein in to Jerusalem. —— *Jer.* vi. 5 To-scatere wee ther houses. *c* **1386** CHAUCER *Sompn. T.* 261 Lo ech thyng that is oned in it selue Is moore strong than whan it is toscatered. **1494** FABYAN *Chron.* VI. ccxvii. 236 Lastely Harolde was wounded in the iye with an arowe..& was slayne, and his people to scatered.

b. *intr.* To part asunder, go to pieces. *rare.*

13.. *Cast. Love* (Halliw.) 1556 Castell, toure, boure ne halle, But thei shulle to-skatur and downfalle.

toschach, tosche: see TOSHACH, TUSH.

to-schrape, to-set: see TO- *pref.*¹, ².

tose, toser, etc.: see TOZE *v.*¹, TOZER.

tose, obs. f. *toes*, pl. of TOE.

tosh (tɒʃ), *sb.*¹ *School slang.* A bath; a footpan. Also *tosh-can*, *-pan*.

1881 LEATHES in Pascoe *Life Publ. Sch.* ii. 20 A 'tosh' pan ..is also provided. **1883** Tosh-can [see TOSH *v.*²]. **1905** H. A. VACHELL *The Hill* i, We call a tub a tosh. *Ibid.* iii, His feet were thrust into a 'tosh' filled with steaming water.

tosh (tɒʃ), *sb.*² *slang.* Bosh, trash; nonsense, rubbish, twaddle; in *Cricket*, see quot. 1898.

1892 *Oxf. Univ. Mag.* 26 Oct. 26/1 To think what I've gone through to hear that man! Frightful tosh it'll be, too. **1898** *Tit-Bits* 25 June 252/3 Among the recent neologisms of the cricket field is 'tosh', which means bowling of contemptible easiness. **1906** E. V. LUCAS *Listener's Lure* (1909) 36 This London business seems to me the most awful tosh.

Hence **toshy** ('tɒʃɪ) *a. slang*, trashy, rubbishy.

1902 BELLOC *Path to Rome* 163 The poor public..is driven back to toshy novels about problems, written by cooks.

tosh (tɒʃ), *sb.*³ *slang.* [Cf. TOSHER¹.] Items of value retrieved from drains and sewers.

a **1852** [see TOSHER¹]. **1974** J. AIKEN *Midnight is Place* v. 164, I am present engaged in fishing for tosh in the sewers of Blastburn.

tosh (tɒʃ), *sb.*⁴ *slang.* Also **tush**. Abbrev. of TOSHEROON. Also used *loosely* for two shillings, money.

1912 J. W. HORSLEY *I Remember* xii. 253 'Tush', for money, would be an abbreviation of 'tusheroon', which in old cant, and also in tinker dialect, signified a crown. **1937** *Night & Day* 22 July 14/3 A couple of grafters had the courage..to bat for a straight tush. **1961** J. MACLAREN-ROSS *Doomsday Bk.* I. v. 63 Here's a tosh to buy yourself some beer. **1964** A. PRIOR *Z Cars Again* ix. 74 'You can give me three blacks for a tush,' he said. 'Two blacks for a half a dollar,' was Mr. Thistlethwaite's reply.

tosh (tɒʃ), *sb.*⁵ *slang.* [Origin uncertain; perh. f. TOSH *a.* (*adv.*).] Used as a neutral or joc. form of address.

1954 E. HYAMS *Stories & Cream* 175 'Ere, tosh, you bin at Cha'ham? **1978** M. KENYON *Deep Pocket* vi. 75 'Sortin' you out for a start, tosh!' came a voice.

tosh, *a.* (*adv.*) *Sc.* [Origin not ascertained.]

1. Neat, clean, tidy, trim.

1776 D. HERD *Coll. Songs* Gloss., *Tosh*, tight, neat. **1794** RITSON *Scot. Songs* I. 99, I gang ay fou clean and fou tosh, As a' the neighbours can tell. **1823** J. WILSON *Trials Marg. Lyndsay* xxxiii. 271 The hedges will do—I clipped them wi' my ain hands..and, nae doubt, they make the avenue look a hantle tosher.

2. Agreeable, comfortable; friendly, intimate.

1821 *Blackw. Mag.* X. 4 We were a very tosh and agreeable company. **1887** *Suppl. to Jamieson*, s.v., 'They're unco tosh wi' ither'.

B. as *adv.* = *toshly* (see below).

1780 MAYNE *Siller Gun* I. xxiii, Shouther your arms; o! ha'd them tosh on, And not athraw! **1828** MOIR *Mansie Wauch* vi, Matters were..settled full tosh between us.

Hence **'toshly** *adv.*, neatly, tidily, trimly; snugly; **'toshy** *a.*, neat, tidy, pretty.

1788 PICKEN *Poems* 176 Row't toshly up, an' franket. **1827** J. WILSON *Noct. Ambr.* Wks. 1855 II. 21 Phrenologists.. hae nae slicht o' haun in curlin their hair toshly. **1856** J. BALLANTINE *Poems* 47 And see how it's keepit sae toshy and clean. **1881** JESSIE SIMPSON in *Mod. Sc. Poets* III. 263 Nae mair wee toshie feet to bath, nor gowden locks to kaim.

tosh (tɒʃ), *v.*¹ *Sc.* [f. TOSH *a.*] *trans.* To make 'tosh'; to tidy, trim.

1826 J. WILSON *Noct. Ambr.* Wks. 1855 I. 266 Hoo she wad try to tosh up..her breest. **1886** A. WARDROP *Mid Cauther Fair* 9 Let's tosh yer plaid a wee.

tosh, *v.*² *School slang.* [f. TOSH *sb.*¹] **a.** *trans.* To splash, souse. **b.** *intr.* To bath, 'tub'.

1883 J. P. GROVES *Fr. Cadet to Capt.* iii. 227 'Toshing' was the name given to a punishment inflicted by the cadets on any one of their number who made himself obnoxious. The victim, dressed in full uniform, was forced to run the gauntlet of his brother cadets, who, as he passed, emptied the contents of their 'tosh-cans' (small baths holding about three gallons of water) over the wretched lad's head. **1903** FARMER & HENLEY *Slang* s.v., He toshed his house beak by mistake, and got three hundred. **1905** H. A. VACHELL *The Hill* i, I believe he toshes now—once a month or so.

tosh, obs. and dial. form of TUSH, tusk.

toshach, -och, toschach, phonetized forms of TOISECH.

1836 W. F. SKENE *Highl. Scot.* (1902) II. vi. 289 Toshoch being unquestionably the title anciently applied to the oldest cadets of the different clans. **1861** C. INNES *Sk. Early Scot. Hist.* 396 The magistrate and head man of a little district known among his Celtic neighbours as the Toshach. **1872** —— *Lect. Scot. Legal Antiq.* iii. 97 Some of the inferior executors of the law had Celtic names long preserved as Maor and Toschach.

† **to-'shake**, *v. Obs.* Forms: see SHAKE *v.* [OE. *tosceacan*, f. TO-² + *sceacan*, SHAKE *v.*]

1. *trans.* To shake to pieces, shake asunder; to disperse or destroy by shaking.

a **1000** *Gloss.* in Wr.-Wülcker 214/34 *Concutit*, i. *turbat, terreat*, toscæcþ. *c* **1000** ÆLFRIC *Hom.* I. 570 He ðа tosceoc þone liȝ of ðam ofne. *a* **1250** *Owl & Night.* 1647 Þu seyst þat gromes þe ivoþ..& þe to twicceþ & to schakeþ. **13..** *Sir Beues* (A.) 742 Man and houndes, þat he tok Wiþ his toskes he al to-schok. **1382** WYCLIF *Isa.* xxiv. 20 With shaking shal be to-shaken the erthe. *c* **1440** *Pallad. on Husb.* II. 240 The plauntis bigge a depper delf desireth And larger space, as wynd may hem to shake. **1584** R. SCOT *Disc. Witchcr.* XII. xviii. (1886) 222 In the bloud of Adam death was taken, In the bloud of Christ it was all to shaken.

2. *intr.* To tremble, quiver, shiver violently.

a **1300** *Cursor M.* 22552 All þe erth it sal toscak. **1303** R. BRUNNE *Handl. Synne* 2528 He broghte on þat brynnyng croke, A brennyng soule þat al to-shoke. **14..** *Gosp. Nicodemus* 797 Þe erth trembled and al toschoke. **1508** DUNBAR *Gold. Targe* 231 With the blast the leuis all to-schuke.

† **to-'shatter**, *v. Obs.* [ME. f. TO-² + SHATTER *v.*] *trans.* To break into small pieces.

1494 FABYAN *Chron.* VI. clxiii. 156 Whan yᵉ shote was spent and the sperys to shateryd, than bothe hoostis ran to gyther with Rowlandys songe, so yᵗ in shorte whyle the grene feelde was dyed into a parfyte redde.

† **to-'shed**, *v. Obs.* Forms: see SHED *v.*¹ [OE. *tosceādan*, f. TO-² + *sceādan*, SHED *v.*¹: = OHG. *za-*, *zisceidan*.] *trans.* To separate, divide, diffuse, scatter, part; in OE. also, to discriminate, discern, distinguish.

c **888** K. ÆLFRED *Boeth.* xxxiv. §3 Ælc þing þe tosceaden bið from oðrum bið oðer, oþer þæt þing. *Ibid.* xl. §7 Se þe ȝesceadwisnisse hæfð, se mæȝ deman & tosceadan hwæs he wilniȝan sceal. *c* **1000** ÆLFRIC *Hom.* II. 106 He toscæt hi on twa, swa swa scephyrde toscæt scep fram gatum. *c* **1200** ORMIN 19862 Forr þatt he wollde hire & te king Todælenn & toshædenn. *c* **1205** LAY. 30262 He nom his lauerdes hefd ..& his lockes he to-scædde. **1387** TREVISA *Higden* (Rolls) III. 241 Leonida..fil vppon the oþer deel anyȝt..and to schad hem euerich oon from oþer. **1398** —— *Barth. De P.R.* XIX. xiv. (Bodl. MS.) lf. 295 b/2 Depe rede toschedeþ þe siȝt as liȝt doþe.

b. *intr.* To divide, separate, fall apart.

c **1330** R. BRUNNE *Chron. Wace* (Rolls) 6276 So þat þe Romayns route to-schadde, & dide hem to þe hauene fle. **1387** TREVISA *Higden* (Rolls) I. 133 Þe hepes of grauel to schedeþ and to falleþ.

† **to-'shend**, *v. Obs.* [f. TO-² + SHEND *v.*] *trans.* To ruin or destroy utterly.

1382 WYCLIF *Ps.* lvi. [lvii.] 1 In to the ende, ne destroȝe thou or shend [*v.r.* to-sheende] Dauid. *c* **1425** *Cast. Persev.* 794 in *Macro Plays* 101 Now schal careful Couetyse, Mankende trewly al to-schende. *c* **1500** *Lancelot* 1221 His face was al to-hurt and al to-schent.

† **to-'shene**, *v. Obs.* Forms: 1 to-scǽnan, 3 to-scænen, to-scenen, to-schenen. [OE. *to-scǽnan*, f. TO-² + *scǽnan* to break: see SHENE.] *trans.* To break or dash to pieces; also, to disperse, break up (an army).

c **950** *Lindisf. Gosp.* Mark v. 4 Ða fattro [he] forbræc *vel* tosceænde [*c* **975** *Rushw.* feoturo..toscænde]. —— John xix. 36 Ban ne to-scænas *vel* ni ȝebræcȝað ȝe from him. *c* **1000** ÆLFRIC *Saints' Lives* xxiii. 496 Ne furðon an næfde he mid oþrum, ac toscænede ofer eall laȝon. *a* **1250** *Owl & Night.* 1120 Stones hi doþ in heore slytte..& þine fule bon toscheneþ.

b. *intr.* To come or break in pieces.

c **1205** LAY. 2309 Al þu scalt to-scæne Mid scearpe mire eaxe. *Ibid.* 2315 þe stan al to-sceande. *c* **1275** *Ibid.* 4537 Sip orn to-ȝein sip þat hit al to-scende.

tosher¹ ('tɒʃə(r)). *Thieves' Cant.* **a.** A Thames thief who purloins copper sheathing from the bottoms of vessels in the river or from the docks.

1859 *Slang Dict.*, *Toshers*, men who steal copper from ships' bottoms in the Thames.

b. One who searches for valuable refuse in drains and sewers.

a **1852** H. MAYHEW *London Labour* (1861) II. 150/2 The sewer-hunters were formerly, and indeed are still, called by the name of 'Toshers', the articles which they pick up in the course of their wanderings along shore being known among themselves by the general term 'tosh', a word more particularly applied by them to anything made of copper. **1870** D. J. KIRWAN *Palace & Hovel* xxi. 331 These men.. search the sewers..for..whatever is of value... They are called 'Toshers' or 'Shore-men'. **1974** J. AIKEN *Midnight is Place* v. 154 Gudgeon's your mate, boy, he's my other tosher.

So **'toshing**, the practice of a 'tosher'.

1867 SMYTH *Sailor's Word-bk.*, *Toshing*, a cant word for stealing copper sheathing from vessels' bottoms, or from dock-yard stores. **1974** J. AIKEN *Midnight is Place* vi. 180 You tend to the toshing, let Mester Hobday tend to the dealing.

'tosher². [Origin uncertain; ? from TOSH *v.*²] A small fishing smack.

1885 *Daily Tel.* 26 Nov. (Farmer), A tosher is not a longshore driver, though both little vessels are employed in catching what they can close into the land. **1911** *Daily News* 10 Oct. 4 Time after time her stout-hearted skipper thrashed the smaller craft (she is but a 'tosher' of 23 tons, carrying only three hands), to windward.

tosher³ ('tɒʃə(r)). *Undergraduates' slang.* [A humorous deformation from *unattached*: cf. FOOTER *sb.*¹ 3 b, RUGGER², SOCKER, etc.] An 'unattached' or non-collegiate student at a university having residential colleges.

1889 *Durham Univ. Jrnl.* 9 Nov. 216 The 'toshers' as they are called in 'Varsity slang—the term is a corruption of the word 'unattached'—have been looked down upon in the past. **1891** DUNCAN *Amer. Girl in Lond.* 254 The man.. being an unattached student, a 'tosher'. **1897** *Blackw. Mag.* May 724 A third deemed that the millennium had arrived with the advent to Oxford of the humble 'tosher'.

tosheroon (tɒʃə'ruːn). *slang.* Also **tusheroon**. [Etym. unknown.] Half-a-crown; a coin of this value (in quot. 1859 erron. said to be a crown).

1859 HOTTEN *Dict. Slang* 112 *Tusheroon*, a crown piece, five shillings. **1933** 'G. ORWELL' *Down & Out in Paris & London* xxix. 214 A tosheroon (half a crown) for the coat, two 'ogs for the trousers. **1960** 'A. BURGESS' *Doctor is Sick* xvi. 125 'I haven't got three nicker,' said Edwin, 'nor one nicker, nor half a bar, nor a tosheroon, nor,' he added, 'a solitary single clod. I can't buy anything.' **1978** *Daily Mirror* 18 Feb. 19/1 All sorts of things, places and creatures we believed were everlasting have vanished, like trams, tosheroons and Constantinople.

† **to-'shift**, *v. Obs.* Forms: see SHIFT *v.* [OE. *tosciftan*, f. TO-² + *sciftan* to divide, SHIFT.] *trans.* To divide, separate, distribute.

c **1122** *O.E. Chron.* an. 1085, Ac se cyng let to scyfton þone here ȝeond eall þis land to his mannon. *Ibid.* an. 1095, He.. into Wealan ferde & his fyrde to scyfte. *c* **1315** SHOREHAM i. 721 For þer he hys, he hys al y-hol Ne mey me hym to-schifte. **1387** TREVISA *Higden* (Rollsl) I. 97 Noþer water noþer fire myȝte ham to schifte noþer to dele. *Ibid.* II. 251 Þere..þe longages and tonges of þe bulders were i-schad and to schift. *c* **1400** tr. *Higden* (Rolls) VII. 528 (MS. *β*) So thei beth departed and to schufte [*γ* scheft] atweyne.

† **to-'shiver**, *v. Obs.* Also **to-shever**. [f. TO-² + SHIVER *v.* So MHG. *ze-*, *zer-schiveren*.]

1. *trans.* To break into shivers, shatter, splinter.

c **1200** *Trin. Coll. Hom.* 113 Ure helende..alto shiurede þe ȝiaten and in wende. *c* **1300** [see TO-CRUSH]. *c* **1435** *Torr. Portugal* 1172 Hors and man down he bore, And alle to-sheverd his sheld. **1470–85** MALORY *Arthur* II. x. 87 They.. smoten to gyders and al to sheuered their speres.

2. *intr.* To fly to shivers, break into splinters.

13.. *K. Alis.* 2728 The scharpe spere gynneth al to-schivere. *c* **1381** CHAUCER *Parl. Foules* 493 The noyse of ffoules..So loude ronge..þat wele y went þe wode had Al to-sheuered [*v.r.* Alto-shyuered]. *c* **1430** *Syr Gener.* (Roxb.) 5156 His sheld to-sheuered euen in twoo. *c* **1530** LD. BERNERS *Arth. Lyt. Bryt.* (1814) 270 Bothe theyr speres all to sheuered to theyr fystes.

† **to-'shoot, to-'shete**, *v. Obs.* [OE. *to-scēotan*, f. TO-² + *scēotan*, SHOOT *v.* Cf. MHG. *zeschiezen*, Ger. *zerschiessen* to destroy by shooting.] *intr.* To spring apart; to burst asunder.

c **1000** ÆLFRIC *Hom.* II. 352 Þa toscuton ða deoflu sona þe me mid heora tangum ȝelæccan woldon. *c* **1122** *O.E. Chron.* an. 1083, Þa munecas..to scuton, sume urnon in to cyrcean. **1340–70** *Alisaunder* 1008 þe ai [= egg] fell on þe flore..And þe shell to-shett on þe schire grounde.

to-shred, to-skair, to-skill: see TO- *pref.*² I.

toshy, *a.*¹, ²: see under TOSH *sb.*², *a.*

tosie, tosily, tosiness: see TOSY.

Tosk (tɒsk), *sb.* and *a.* Also **Toshke**. [a. Alb. *Toskë*.] **A.** *sb.* (A member of) one of the major ethnic groups of Albania, living mainly in the south of the country. Also, the Albanian dialect spoken by this people. **B.** *adj.* Of or pertaining to the Tosks or their language. Cf. GHEG.

1835 [see GHEG]. **1900** 'ODYSSEUS' *Turkey in Europe* ix. 397 The Southern Albanians differ from the Northerners... Their generic name is Tosk. *Ibid.* 401 The whole of the Tosk country has been strongly influenced by Greece. **1908** T. G. TUCKER *Introd. Nat. Hist. Lang.* ix. 195 A number of dialects, usually grouped under the two heads *Ghegh* (to the north) and *Tosk* (to the south), spoken by the Albanians.. are admitted to belong to the Indo-European stock. **1939** L. H. GRAY *Foundations of Lang.* 331 The language [*sc.* Albanian] falls into two groups, each with a number of sub-dialects: *Geg* (with colonies in Dalmatia) to the north and *Tosk* (with colonies in Greece, Italy, and Sicily) to the south of the Shumbi River. **1958** [see GHEG]. **1966** E. P. HAMP in Birnbaum & Puhvel *Anc. Indo-Europ. Dial.* 98 Rosetti, however, mistakenly repeats the myth that some Tosk dialects show Geg characteristics. **1980** *Word* 1979 XXX. 27 Within Albania the proportion of northerners (Gegs) to southerners (Tosks) is almost equal. *Ibid.* 41 The imposition of Tosk upon a population that was not entirely Tosk-speaking. **1983** *Ibid.* XXXIV. 26 Arvanítika is the form of Tosk Albanian spoken in Greece; it is closely related to the southernmost variety of Albanian.

tosk, dial. var. TUSK *sb.*³

toske, obs. f. TUSK.

†**to-ˈslay**, *v. Obs.* Forms: see SLAY. [OE. *tosléan*, f. TO-² + *sléan* to strike, SLAY. So OS. *te-slahan*; OFris. *to-slâ*, OHG. *za-*, *zi-slahan*, MHG. *zerslahen*, *zerslân*, Ger. *zerschlagen*.]

trans. To strike or knock to pieces; to strike down violently; also, to kill outright.

a **700** *Epinal Gloss.* (O.E.T.) 195 *Concidit*, tisloȝ. *c* **725** *Corpus Gloss.* 516 Tosloȝ. *c* **893** K. ÆLFRED *Oros.* IV. ii. §1 þunor tosloȝ heora hiehstan godes hus Iofeses. *c* **1000** ÆLFRIC *Hom.* II. 450 Swiðlic wind..tosloh þæt hus. *c* **1430** *Syr Tryam.* 372 Why dyd he the to-slon? **14..** *Sir Beues* (C.) 2712 And had caste on hym venome, And the knyght all to-sloon.

†**to-ˈslift**, *v. Obs. rare*⁻¹. [ME. *toslyfte(n*, deriv. vb. f. OE. *to-slifan* to split, cleave, cut to pieces: cf. SLIVE *v.*¹] *trans.* To break to pieces.

c **1315** SHOREHAM i. 726 To-slyfte A myrour þou myȝt fol wel, Bote nauȝt þe ymage schifte.

†**to-ˈslit**, *v. Obs.* [ME. *to-slitte(n*, f. TO-² + *slitte(n*, SLIT *v.*] *trans.* To slit open, split.

a **1250** *Owl & Night.* 694 Ac ȝif þat he forlost his wit, þonne is his red purs al toslit. *c* **1300** *Seyn Julian* (Ashm.) 146 þe bones hi to slitte & þe marw out drowe. *c* **1400** *Laud Troy Bk.* 16808 Many a baly scho ther rittes And many a scheld sche al to-sclittes. **14..** *Sir Beues* (M.) 520 There was no sarzin, that hym hitte, But he is body all to-slitt.

to-slive, to-smite, to-sparple, etc.: see TO- *pref.*²

to-souse (*all to souse*): see ALL C. 15, and SOUSE *v.*¹

†**to-spread**, *v. Obs.* Forms: see SPREAD *v.* [OE. *tosprǽdan*, f. TO-² + *sprǽdan*, SPREAD *v.* So OHG. *za-*, *zi-*, *zarspreitan*, MHG. *ze-*, *zerspreiten*.] *trans.* To spread abroad, spread open; to expand, stretch out; also, to disperse, scatter.

a **1000** in *Techmer's Zeitschr.* II. 122 (B.-T.) Tosprǽd ðine fingras. *c* **1200** *Trin. Coll. Hom.* 21 His holie lichame was tospred on þe holie rode. *Ibid.* 205 Was to sprad. *a* **1225** *Ancr. R.* 402 To luuien þene king of blisse þet tospret so touward ou his ermes. **1297** R. GLOUC. (Rolls) 4317 þo þe romeyns..to spradde hom her & þer. **1390** GOWER *Conf.* II. 260 With..fot al bare, Hir her tosprad sche gan to fare.

†**to-ˈspring**, *v. Obs.* [OE. *tospringan*, f. TO-² + *springan*, SPRING *v.* So OHG. *zispringan*, MHG. *ze-*, *zerspringen*; Ger. *zerspringen*.] *intr.* To spring apart; to burst asunder.

c **1000** ÆLFRIC *Hom.* II. 156 Se niðfulla deofol..wearp ða ænne stan to ðære bellan, þæt heo eall tosprang. *Ibid.* 382 þæt [isene ȝeat] tosprang þærrihte him toȝeanes. **1303** R. BRUNNE *Handl. Synne* 10672 þe bondes to-braste, and alle to-sprunge. *c* **1320** *Cast. Love* 593 Er him ouȝte þe herte to springe þen he scholde him wraþþe for eny þinge. *c* **1400** *St. Alexius* 1020 Myne herte wil to-sprynge.

†**to-ˈsquat**, *v. Obs.* [ME. f. TO-² + SQUAT *v.*] *trans.* To flatten, crush, squash.

c **1325** *Poem Times Edw. II* (Percy) lxxii, Trechery is imeynteynd And trewth is al tosqwat. *a* **1380** *St. Ambrose* 544 in Horstm. *Altengl. Leg.* (1878) 16 Wiþ seknes he was al to squat. *c* **1380** WYCLIF *Wks.* (1880) 461 She shal al tosquatte þyn heed. **14..** *Sir Beues* (N.) 3563 Arondel.. Wiþ his hinder fot him smot þat he al tosquat is brain.

toss (tɒs, -ɔː-), *sb.*¹ [f. TOSS *v.*] An act of tossing.

1. A pitching up and down or to and fro.

1634 SIR T. HERBERT *Trav.* Ded., This poore Barque.. hath endurde many tosses at Sea, and is now tost on Land. **1801** SOUTHEY *Thalaba* XI. xl, The little boat rides rapidly, And pitches now with shorter toss Upon the narrower swell. *a* **1849** SIR R. WILSON in *Life* (1862) I. iii. 139 The continual toss almost made me mad. **1859** *Habits Gd. Soc.* ix. 286 The man who gives your hand one toss, as if he were ringing the dinner-bell.

†**2.** A state of agitation or commotion. *Obs.*

1666 PEPYS *Diary* 2 June, This put us at the Board into a tosse. **1667** *Ibid.* 10 Oct., Lord! what a tosse I was for some time in. *a* **1734** NORTH *Lives* (1826) II. 319 You can easily imagine what a toss I was in, to lie about a week aboard the ship for want of pratique. **1837** LONGF. in *Life* (1891) I. 278 The Little-Pedlington community of Boston is in a great toss,..first about the college, and then about Dr. Channing and the abolitionists.

3. a. An act of casting, pitching, throwing, or hurling; a throw, a pitch. ***full toss***, in *Cricket*, the delivery of a ball which does not touch the ground in its flight between the wickets.

1660 F. BROOKE tr. *Le Blanc's Trav.* 119 The Criminal.. expected death, a tosse or two at the least. **1833** NYREN *Yng. Cricketer's Tutor* 81 By one stroke from a toss that he hit behind him, we got ten runs. **1862** PYCROFT *Cricket Tutor* 52 Some balls of a loose sort—Volleys, Long-hops, and Tosses.

b. ***to take a toss***, to suffer a fall from a horse; also *fig.*

1917 [see HALF *sb.* 7 h]. **1926** GALSWORTHY *Silver Spoon* I. xiv. 101 The Government had 'taken their toss' over the Editor. **1949** M. STEEN *Twilight on Floods* IV. x. 699 By Jove, old boy, she's taken a toss for you! **1966** [see LEAGUE sb.¹ 1 e]. **1973** 'M. INNES' *Appleby's Answer* v. 47 The red-haired Lady Curricle, who had 'taken a toss', you will remember, over a hedge.

c. *U.S. slang.* A search (of a building or person) conducted by the police. Cf. TOSS *v.* 1 c.

1970 L. SANDERS *Anderson Tapes* xciv. 220 The author was allowed to attend as an observer but not active participant in the search. The toss of the above premises.. was..conducted with professional skill. **1972** J. MILLS *Report to Commissioner* 86 You wanta give her a toss, give her a toss, but let's not stand here all night.

4. a. A sudden jerk; *esp.* a quick upward or backward movement of the head.

1676 DRYDEN *Man of Mode* Epil. 22 His various modes from various fathers follow; One taught the toss, and one the new French wallow. **1718** *Free-thinker* No. 17 ¶8 She throws up her Head with a scornful Toss. **1836** J. GILBERT *Chr. Atonem.* viii. (1852) 242 The question is dismissed from the minds of some with an indignant toss. **1848** THACKERAY *Van. Fair* xlviii, She walked in..with a toss of the head which would have befitted an empress.

b. A spread or fall (of hair).

1946 D. C. PEATTIE *Road of Naturalist* i. 13 My wife lay hiding from the light in the toss of her hair. **1978** J. UPDIKE *Coup* (1979) vi. 233 Ezana looked at her and saw beyond the brassy toss of her hair.

†**5.** A bout, an encounter. *Sc. Obs.*

1730 T. BOSTON *Mem.* x. (1899) 316, I had a toss with Mr. Murray, he affirming and I denying that I had given them ground by word or deed. **1730** —— *View of this & other World* (1799) 399 You may get enough ado even to die through a vehement toss of sickness.

6. a. An act of tossing a coin: see TOSS *v.* 9, 15; a decision arrived at by this means: see *toss-up* in 10, and cf. PITCH AND TOSS.

1798 T. JEFFERSON *Writ.* IV. 227 The question of war and peace depends now on a toss of cross and pile. **1838** DE MORGAN *Probabilities* 75 Let us find the probability that, out of 200 tosses with a halfpenny, there shall be exactly 100 heads and 100 tails. **1859** *All Year Round* No. 13. 305 The town won the toss for innings. **1887** L. STEPHEN in *Dict. Nat. Biog.* XI. 467/2 They..decided by the toss of a halfpenny that Concanen should defend the ministry.

b. ***to argue the toss***, to dispute a decision or opinion.

1925 FRASER & GIBBONS *Soldier & Sailor Words* 288 *Toss, to argue the*, to dispute: wrangle: to have too much to say. **1945** *Penguin New Writing* XXIV. 84 Poetry was never much in my line, except Shelley, and Terry didn't think much of him, so..we argued the toss about it. **1958** *Economist* 11 Jan. 92/2 The Prime Minister's..venture.. cannot do more than clear the way... More is involved than just arguing the tosses of the moment. **1978** 'M. UNDERWOOD' *Crooked Wood* iv. 61 He was not in a strong position to argue the toss.

c. *fig.* In negative contexts: a jot, a whit, a very small amount. Usu. in phr. ***not to care*** (or ***give***) ***a toss***. *colloq.*

1876 GEO. ELIOT *Dan. Der.* xxviii, I don't care a toss where you are. **1925** P. GIBBS *Unchanging Quest* xviii. 132 She..didn't care a toss what people thought of her. **1973** *Time Out* 2–5 Mar. 13/1, I don't give a toss whether he's black, white or purple. **1979** *Bull. Yorks. Dial. Soc.* No. 26. 11 Ah deean't odd wi them as mooan As prices mak em cross. Then spend ther brass on eeaps o things Wat isn't woth a toss.

7. The throwing off of homing pigeons in a trial of their flight and homing powers.

1882 J. L. BURGESS *Homing Fancier's Ann.* 11 The intermediate tosses were Redhill, 184 miles from Brussels, and Worcester, 280 miles. **1897** *Westm. Gaz.* 1 June 9/2 As some of the 'tosses' numbered 6,000 birds at one time, the sight was a remarkable one. **1899** G. J. LARNER in *19th Cent.* XLV. 819 The first of these two experimental tosses took place on the 17th of December last year.

†**8.** (?) A payment. *Obs.*

1630 MASSINGER *Picture* II. ii, Yet, not to take From the magnificence of the King, I will Dispense his bounty too, but as a page To wait on mine: for other tosses, take A hundred-thousand crowns.

9. A measure for sprats: see quot.

1851 MAYHEW *Lond. Labour* I. 69/2 They [sprats] are sold at Billingsgate by the 'toss' or 'chuck', which is about half a bushel, and weighs from 40 lbs. to 50 lbs.

10. a. toss-up. The throwing up of a coin to arrive at a decision: see TOSS *v.* 15.

17.. *Laws of Cricket* in Grace *Cricket* (1891) 14 The party that wins the toss-up shall go in first at his option. **1802–12** BENTHAM *Ration. Judic. Evid.* (1827) V. 64 What charity-boy..was ever at a loss to know that the toss-up of a half-penny was worth a farthing. **1868** 'S. DARYL' *Quoits & Bowls* 48 A toss-up decides which party is to play first.

b. *fig.* A chance where the probability either way is equal; an even chance. *colloq.*

1809 MALKIN *Gil Blas* XI. vii. (Rtldg.) 407 It is a toss up who fails and who succeeds. **1844** DICKENS *Mart. Chuz.* xii, It was a toss-up with Tom Pinch whether he should laugh or cry. **1862** J. SKELTON *Nugæ Crit.* vi. 257 It is generally the merest 'toss-up' what verdict the..critic pronounces on any work. **1888** *Times* (weekly ed.) 14 Sept. 15/1 It was a toss up whether Lord Salisbury was going to offer them an Irish Government or a Coercion Act.

11. toss-off. An act of masturbation. Cf. TOSS *v.* 13 d. *coarse slang.*

1735 *Rake's Progress* III. 19 Or loudly sing some bawdy Song, Then drops into St. D—n's C—h, And take a *Toss-off* in the Porch.

12. *Comb.*: **toss pillow** *U.S.* = *scatter cushion* s.v. SCATTER *v.* 7 b.

1956 *Sears, Roebuck Catal.* Fall & Winter 897 (*heading*) Toss pillows .. new colors .. styles .. shapes. **1978** *Washington Post Mag.* 26 Mar. 20/2 (Advt.), Matching toss pillows $10 each.

toss, *sb.*² *dial.* [A variant of TASS¹.] A heap, stack; = TASS¹.

1695 KENNETT *Par. Antiq.* II. Gloss. s.v. *Thassare*, To lay up hay or corn into a tass, toss, stack or mow. *Ibid.*, A mow of corn in a barn is called in Kent the toss. **1847–78** HALLIWELL, *Toss*, the mow or bay of a barn into which the corn is put preparatory to its being threshed.

†**toss**, *sb.*³, var. of or misprint for TASS².

1698 FRYER *Acc. E. India & P.* 231 A Silver Toss, or Cup. *Ibid.* 399 Bowls of Wine,..most of Silver, some of Gold, which we call a *Toss*, and is made like a Wooden Dish.

toss (tɒs, -ɔː-), *v.* Pa. t. and pple. **tossed** (tɒst, -ɔː-), also 6– **tost**. [In use soon after 1500, and current in nearly all its senses by 1550. Origin uncertain: the only cognate word appears to be the Norw. and Sw. dialect *tossa* to spread, strew (Aasen); Welsh *tosio* is from Eng.]

I. *trans.* **1.** To throw, pitch, or fling about, here and there, or to and fro: expressing the action of wind or wave, or the light, careless, or disdainful action of a person, on something easily moved.

1506 GUYLFORDE *Pilgr.* (Camden) 73 Howbeit the wroughte sees tossyd and rolled vs ryght greuously. **1526** TINDALE *Matt.* xiv. 24 The shippe was in the myddes of the see, and was toost with waves. —— *Jas.* i. 6 Lyke the waves off the see, tost off the wynde. **1526** *Pilgr. Perf.* (W. de W. 1531) 301 Not restynge, they dyd cary the & tosse the from place to place. **1603** *Miracles Our Saviour* in Farr *S.P. Jas. I* (1848) 356 The Shaking ships amid the seas ytost. **1634** SIR T. HERBERT *Trav.* 19 The shippes are tossed they know not where. **1782** COWPER *Parrot* i, A native of the gorgeous east, By many a billow tost. **1852** THACKERAY *Esmond* II. vii, Mistress Beatrix,..tossing her rustling flowing draperies about her, and quitting the room, followed by her mother. **1887** BOWEN *Virg. Æneid* I. 524 We Troy's ill-starred sons, long tossed by the winds on the deep.

b. *fig.* or in fig. context.

1545 BRINKLOW *Compl.* 21 b, How men be tossed from one court to another. *Ibid.* 59 b, He that denyeth them but one grote.. how will thei tosse hym in the lawe. **1569** W. SAMUEL *vii Chapter of Job* ii, Both night and day they haue their toyl With work and dreames itost. **1592** G. HARVEY *Four Lett.* iii. Wks. (Grosart) I. 195 He tost his imagination a thousand waies. **1611** BIBLE *Eph.* iv. 14 That we..be no more children, tossed to and fro, and caried about with euery winde of doctrine. **1633** P. FLETCHER *Purple Isl.* XII. lii, Though I poore changeling rove, Tost up and down in waves of worldly floud. **1727** GAY *Fables* I. xvi. 17 Here, there, by various fortune tost. **1823** CHALMERS *Serm.* I. 245 This unhappy man thus tost and bewildered and thrown into a general unceasing Frenzy. **1862** MRS. H. WOOD *Mrs. Hallib. Troub.* I. i, I have been tossed about a good deal of late years.

c. *U.S. slang.* To search (a building or person) in the course of a police investigation. Cf. TOSS *sb.*¹ 3 c.

1939 *Fortune* July 102/2 [He] sent a couple of detectives across town to 'toss their flat' (i.e. search their apartment). **1969** 'P. KAVANAGH' *Such Men are Dangerous* vii. 82 They tossed the room while I had breakfast. **1972** B. GARFIELD *Line of Succession* III. 186 He had been tossed seven times.. but no drugs had been found on him. **1980** 'E. MCBAIN' *Ghosts* iii. 56 We ought to try for an order to toss his apartment.

†**2.** To turn over and over, to turn the leaves of (a book, etc.). *Obs.*

1555 W. WATREMAN *Fardle Facions* Ded. 2 The searche of wisedome and vertue, for whose sake either we tosse, or oughte to tosse so many papers and tongues. **1579** LYLY *Euphues* (Arb.) 99, I will to Athens, there to tosse my books. **1581** PETTIE *Guazzo's Civ. Conv.* III. (1586) 159 Whether in tossing ouer your bookes, you haue light vpon that place where Cicero giueth a nip to his daughter. **1597** MORLEY *Introd. Mus.* Pref., What labour it was to tomble, tosse, and search so manie bookes. **1730** T. BOSTON *Mem.* xi. (1899) 373 The huge toil in tossing lexicons and the Hebrew concordance.

3. To shake, shake up, stir up.

1557 N. T. (Genev.) *Matt.* xxiv. 29 The powers of heauen shall be tossed. **1610** HOLLAND *Camden's Brit.* (1637) 208 Thomas..was much tossed and shaken. **1811** *Ora & Juliet* I. 205 She tossed the cup after breakfast, and read the fortunes of the maid-servants. **1834** M. SCOTT *Cruise Midge* (1859) 391 A tall solitary palm shot up and tossed its wide spreading fan like leaves in the night wind.

†**b.** To fling (hay, wool, etc.) abroad, so as to loosen the mass. *Obs.* exc. as in 1.

1557 TUSSER *100 Points Husb.* xci, With tossing and raking, and setting on cox: The grasse that was grene, is now hay for an ox. **1573** —— *Husb.* (1878) 131 No turning of peason till carrege ye make,.. By turning and tossing they shed as they lie. **1581** A. HALL *Iliad* VI. 118 Of some Greeke thou shalt become the slaue Who to his country shal thee leade to tease and tosse his wul.

c. *Tin-refining.* (See quot.)

1884 C. G. W. LOCK *Workshop Receipts* Ser. III. 452/1 The refining [of tin] may be divided into two stages, liquation and tossing... The same effect is sometimes produced by 'tossing', or raising the metal in ladles, and pouring, from some height through the air, back again into the pan.

¶**d.** *Tin-mining.* Erron. used for TOZE *v.*², q.v.

e. In cookery, to stir or turn (food) over, esp. so as to coat it with butter, oil, etc.

1723 J. NOTT *Cook's & Confectioner's Dict.* No. 107A Artichokes with cream... Toss them up with butter. **1877** E. S. DALLAS *Kettner's Bk. of Table* 120 The fillets..are to be lightly tossed in butter, taking care not to colour them. **1913** C. M. PEARSE *Kitchen Garden & Cook* 197 Separate the endive into tufts. Toss these in the salad dressing. **1952** G. W. BRACE *Spire* (1953) viii. 69 The salad was tossed amid murmurs of pleasure. **1976** 'TREVANIAN' *Main* (1977) v. 109 You don't stir a salad. You toss it.

4. *fig.* To disturb or agitate socially or politically.

1552 ASCHAM *Germany* 36 Cæsar..also tossed the whole world with battle & slaughter, even almost from the sun setting unto the sun rising. **1618** BOLTON *Florus* (1636) 250 Hee tossed both Sea, and Land with mixture of his miseries. **1796** BURKE *Regic. Peace* ii. Wks. VIII. 256 The..

speculator Harrington, who has tossed about society into all forms.

b. To disquiet or agitate in mind; to set in commotion, as by shifting opinions, feelings, circumstances, or influences; to disturb, disorder.

1526 *Pilgr. Perf.* (W. de W. 1531) 172 b, To be exercised and tossed in dyuerse temptacyons. **1561** T. Norton *Calvin's Inst.* I. 53 Contrary motions do tosse and diuersly draw his soule. **1590** Spenser *F.Q.* I. i. 55 That troublous dreame gan freshly tosse his braine. **1632** Lithgow *Trav.* v. 199 Thus was I tost.. With strugling doubts. **1833** Ht. Martineau *Tale of Tyne* iv, The seamen were tossed in spirit through fear of the press gang. **1834** J. MacDonald in Tweedie *Life* iii. (1849) 238 My mind is tossed by various considerations.

II. *intr.* (Related to I.)

†**5.** To be in mental agitation or distraction; to be disquieted in mind or circumstances. *Obs.*

1509 Hawes *Past. Pleas.* ii. (Percy Soc.) 14 So forthe I went, tossynge on my brayne. **1513** More *Rich. III*, Wks. 35/1 Katheryne whiche longe tyme tossed in either fortune sometime in wealth, ofte in aduersitye. **1582** N. Lichefield tr. *Castanheda's Conq. E. Ind.* I. viii. 20 b, The Captaine generall and the other Captaines thus tossing vp and downe, to and fro, as well with their ships, as also in their mindes, determined to beare towards the Ilande of Mombassa.

6. a. for *refl.* To fling or jerk oneself about; to move about restlessly.

1560 Bible (Genev.) *Job* vii. 4, I am euen ful with tossing to and fro vnto the dawning of the day. **1575** *Gamm. Gurton* I. v. 11 See how Hodg lieth tomblynge and tossing amids the floure. **1638** Junius *Paint. Ancients* 151 Burning fevers shall leave you never a whit sooner,.. if you tosse in woven imagerie,.. than if you lie under.. ordinarie coverings. **1754** Gray *Pleasure* 45 Wretch, that long has tost On the thorny bed of Pain. **1886** *Tip Cat* xix, The child was tossing and turning and talking in her sleep.

b. for *pass.* To be flung or rocked about; to be kept in motion; to be agitated.

1582 [see 5]. **1596** Shaks. *Merch. V.* I. i. 8 Your minde is tossing on the Ocean. **1809** Jas. Moore *Camp. Spain* 2 The soldiers.. remained tossing on board the crowded transports. **1827** Pollok *Course T.* x. 471 The unfathomable lake, Tossing with tides of dark, tempestuous wrath. **1835** Macaulay *Hist. Eng.* xviii. IV. 131 A fleet of merchantmen tossing on the waves. **1884** W. C. Smith *Kildrostan* I. i. 20 Roots that cling as the branches toss.

III. *trans.* * To throw in a specified direction.

7. To throw, cast, pitch, fling, hurl (without any notion of agitation).

1570 Googe *Pop. Kingd.* IV. (1880) 47 b, The Dice are shakte and tost, and Cardes apace they teare. **1611** Bible *Isa.* xxii. 18 He will surely violently turne and tosse thee, like a ball into a large countrey. **1670** Cotton *Espernon* II. VI. 283 Had he known his temerity, he would have caus'd Marsillac to have been tost out of the Windows. **1700** S. L. tr. *Fryke's Voy. E. Ind.* 139 We lost one Man, who was Tossed off the Maintop Mast into the Sea. **1718** Lady M. W. Montagu *Let. to Abbé Conti* 31 July, The governor's daughter.. tossed a note to him over the wall. **1810** Scott *Lady of L.* III. xiv, The falc'ner tossed his hawk away. **1830** in Cobbett *Rur. Rides* (1885) II. 308 Two or three, or even one man, may, if not tossed out at once, disturb and interrupt every thing. **1853** Kingsley *Hypatia* xvi, He tossed his purse among the crowd. **1857** *G. Bird's Urin. Deposits* (ed. 5) 217 It seems now to run some risk of being tossed aside as a thing of no consequence.

b. *absol.* To fling oneself (like a body tossed).

1728 Young *Love Fame* v. 477 They throw their persons with a hoydon-air Across the room, and toss into the chair. **1852** Thackeray *Esmond* I. xiii, She tossed out of the room, being in one of her flighty humours then.

8. *esp.* Of two players: To throw, or impel by hitting (a ball, etc.) to and fro between them: cf. *to toss from pillar to post* (pillar *sb.* 11). Often *fig.* or in fig. context.

1514 Barclay *Cyt. & Uplondyshm.* (Percy) 67 From poste unto piller tossed shalt thou be. *a* **1533** Frith *Another Bk. agst. Rastell* Pref. A v, It is not Inoughe for a man playinge at tennes to tosse the ball agayn, but he must so tosse it that the tother take it not. **1550** Crowley *Last Trump.* 562 To play tenise, or tosse the ball. **1570–6** Lambarde *Peramb. Kent* (1826) 248 This Ball was busily tossed betweene the King and the Pope. **1879** Stainer *Music of Bible* 83 Shrill echoes ever and anon tossed from side to side.

b. *fig. spec.* To bandy (a subject or question) from one side to the other in debate; to discuss; to make the subject of talk.

c **1540** tr. *Pol. Verg. Eng. Hist.* (Camden) II. 8 The Frenche, somewhat appalled,.. tossed the matter amongst themselves what best were to do. **1637** Gillespie *Eng. Pop. Cerem.* III. viii. 177 When questions and controversies of Faith, are tossed in the Church. **1700** Blair in W. S. Perry *Hist. Coll. Amer. Col. Ch.* I. 68 There is nothing more usual among schollars.. than to toss an argument, and that sometimes to too great a height of heat and animosity. **1795** Burke *Corr.* (1844) IV. 325 If we were to toss the matter about.. for twenty days, we could only end as we began. **1859** Tennyson *Lanc. & El.* 233 Then she, who.. heard her name so tost about, Flush'd slightly at the slight disparagement.

** *spec.* To throw up.

9. To throw up, throw into the air; *esp.* to throw (a coin, etc.) up, to see how it falls; = *toss up*, 15 a.

to toss in a blanket, to throw (a person) upward repeatedly from a blanket held slackly at each corner: see blanket *sb.* 2. ***to toss a pancake***, to throw it up so that it falls back into the pan with the other side up.

1526 *Pilgr. Perf.* (1531) 166 As a ball, whiche yf it be tossed and cast vp streyght, it falleth down directly.. in the hande of hym that cast it vp. **1597**, **1682** [see blanket *sb.* 2]. **1598** Florio, *Zombata*, a tossing in a blanket. **1619** [see pancake 1]. **1687** A. Lovell tr. *Thevenot's Trav.* I. 45 He that has a minde to be tossed in the Air, sits down on a good seat of Wood, that is fastened to the end of the Ropes. **1688** in Ellis *Orig. Lett.* Ser. II. IV. 125 Capt. Ouseley is said to be come to town to give his reasons for tossing the Mayor of Scarborough in a blanket. *a* **1711** Ken *Blondina* Poet. Wks. 1721 IV. 526 A mad furious Bull.. Who gor'd and toss'd her to the Sky. **1713** Young *Last Day* I. 250 The foaming surges, tost on high. *a* **1756** Mrs. Haywood *New Present* (1771) 206 Turn it [a pancake] or, if you can, toss it, which is much better. **1841** Catlin *N. Amer. Ind.* I. iv. 25 Mons. Chardon 'tossed the feather' (a custom always observed to try the course of the wind). **1863** Kingsley *Water Bab.* i, He was tossing halfpennies with the other boys. **1900** G. C. Brodrick *Mem. & Impress.* 4 The newly-elected members were bound to undergo the ceremony of 'chairing', and were regularly 'tossed' at a particular spot.

fig. **1791** Boswell *Johnson* 8 May an. 1778, I don't care how often, or how high, he tosses me, when only friends are present. **1843** Lytton *Last Bar.* IV. ii, He thinks he tosseth all London on his own horns.

b. *absol.* = *toss up*, 15 b. (Cf. toss *sb.*[1] 9.)

1833 Nyren *Yng. Cricketer's Tutor* 20 The parties shall toss for the choice of innings. **1893** D. J. Rankin *Zambesi Basin* iv. 66 We tossed who should have first shot. My friend won.

c. To wager with (a person) on the toss of a coin. Usu. const. *for* (something).

1851 H. Mayhew *London Labour* I. 196/1 To 'toss the pieman' is a favourite pastime with costermongers' boys... If the pieman win the toss, he receives 1*d.* without giving a pie. **1858** G. H. Lewes *Sea-Side Stud.* IV. i. 271 We used to 'toss' the pieman for epicurean slices of pudding—a vulgar, but seductive form of juvenile gambling. **1942** Wodehouse *Money in Bank* (1946) xv. 128 He was in the frame of mind when he would have patted a small boy on the head and given him sixpence, though it is probable that a moment later he would have tossed him for it and won it back again. **1983** 'D. Shannon' *Exploit of Death* (1984) i. 18 'I'll toss you for the job.' Conway produced a quarter and flipped it.

d. To release (a homing pigeon) in a race or trial flight. Cf. toss *sb.*[1] 7.

1882 J. L. Burgess *Homing Fancier's Ann.* 10 Five hundred and eighty-nine birds were tossed at 4 a.m. **1911** *Encycl. Brit.* XXI. 596/2 Training.. consists in taking it [*sc.* the bird] out in a closed wicker basket and liberating or 'tossing' it at gradually increasing distances from its loft.

10. To throw or jerk up suddenly without letting go; †*spec.* to brandish (arms) (*obs.*). ***to toss oars***, 'to throw them up out of the rowlocks, and raise them perpendicularly an-end' (Adm. Smyth).

1590 Spenser *F.Q.* I. vii. 48 Sword,.. speare,.. Where haue yee left your lord, that could so well you tosse? **1598** Barret *Theor. Warres* III. i. 37 The good Picquier ought to learne to tosse his pike well. **1626** Gouge *Serm. Dignity Chivalry* §11 More fit.. to lift a pitchforke then to tosse a pike. **1697** Dryden *Alexander's Feast* vi, Behold how they toss their torches on high. **1718** Pope *Iliad* III. 323 Paris thy son, and Sparta's King advance, In measur'd lists to toss the weighty lance. **1830** Marryat *King's Own* xxx, The boats' crews tossed their oars while the cheers were given. **1894** C. N. Robinson *Brit. Fleet* 181 The junior salutes the senior, if the latter be royalty, or a flag-officer, by tossing oars.

†**b.** To drink out of (a cup, etc.), tilting it up; hence, to empty by drinking; = *toss off*, 13 a. *Obs.*

1568 Fulwel *Like will to Like* B iv, From morning til night I sit tossing the black bole. **1695** Congreve *Love for L.* III. xv, For my Part, I mean to toss a Can, and remember my Sweet-Heart, a-fore I turn in. **1708** Hudson in Hearne *Collect.* 3 Aug. (O.H.S.) II. 123 Who wth our merry Greek tosst a bottle.

11. To lift, jerk, or throw up (the head, etc.) with a sudden, impatient, or spirited movement.

1591 Sylvester *Ivry* 119 Some Savage Bull.. tosses his head on high. **1678** Dryden *All for Love* I. i, Sea-horses.. Toss'd up their heads, and dash'd the ooze about 'em. **1756** C. Smart tr. *Horace, Sat.* I. vi. (1826) II. 55 Do you.. toss up your nose at obscure people. **1822** Scott *Nigel* i, Tossing his head as one who valued not the raillery to which he had been exposed. **1849** Miss Mulock *Ogilvies* i, The first speaker tossed her head.

IV. With adverbs.

12. toss in. To finish, to give up. *N.Z. slang.*

1956 D. M. Davin *Sullen Bell* II. iv. 128 I'd toss it in for tonight, Miss Simm. It's an ugly night and you should get your train home. **1971** *N.Z. Listener* 19 Apr. 56/5 In the end they saw some hogsbacks up above the col so they tossed it in and glissaded down back to their bivvy.

13. toss off. a. To drink off with energetic action. **b.** To dispose of in an off-hand manner. **c.** To do or make easily, without effort. **d.** *trans.* and *intr.* To masturbate. *slang.*

c **1590** Greene *Fr. Bacon* i. 15 Tossing off ale and milk in country cans. **1816** T. L. Peacock *Headlong Hall* xi, Having ..insisted on every gentleman tossing off a half-pint bumper. **1840** Dickens *Old C. Shop* lxii, Drink that... Toss it off, don't leave any heel-tap. **1845** Judd *Margaret* II. i, Have you read Cynthia?.. It is a delightful thing to toss off a dull hour with. **1874** L. Troubridge *Life amongst Troubridges* (1966) 80 A new rage.. for painting the panels of the shutters of our bedrooms.. and they only take a jiffy to toss off. **1884** G. Allen *Philistia* II. 32 Herbert, having tossed off his coffee. **1879–80** *Pearl* (1970) 258, I don't like to see, though at me you might scoff, An old woman trying to toss herself off. **1915** L. Strachey *Let.* 12 Mar. in P. N. Furbank *E. M. Forster* (1979) II. i. 16 A propos of Maurice tossing himself off.. you say—'He knew what the price would be—a creeping apathy towards all things.' **1927** Joyce *Let.* 25 July (1966) III. 162 The verb 'to toss off' an expression for 'to masturbate'. **1937** M. Hillis *Orchids on your Budget* (1938) vi. 109 Any man worth anything could toss off a rarebit or an omelet. **1969** *Jeremy* I. III. 22/1 All they want to do is toss off in the cottage while they look at my prick. **1979** *Church Times* 17 Aug. 7/1 [These books] do not provide bibliographical support for the learned references tossed off in the articles. **1981** 'D. Kavanagh' *Fiddle City* iv. 82 Would you like me to toss you off?.. It's ten if you're worried about the price.

14. toss out. See prec. senses and out; in quot., to dress smartly, 'trick out'.

1759 Goldsm. *Bee* 13 Oct. (*On Dress*), A damsel, tossed out in all the gaiety of fifteen.

15. toss up. a. See also prec. senses and up.

1588 Deloney *Q. Eliz. at Tilbury* Poems (1912) 476 Tossing up her plume of feathers to them all as they did stand. **1602** Marston *Ant. & Mel.* III. Wks. 1856 I. 36 Rubbing my quiet bosome, tossing up A gratefull spirit to Omnipotence! **1719** De Foe *Crusoe* I. 59 The Boat.. lay as the Wind and the Sea had toss'd her up upon the Land. **1743** in Howell *St. Trials* (1813) XVII. 1179 One's hair is now tossed up in such a manner that its hard to distinguish between a person's own hair and a wig. **1840** Marryat *Poor Jack* vi, We tossed up our oars, and laid by. **1859** *Habits Gd. Society* vii. 249 The head should.. not [be] tossed up nor jerked on one side with that air of pertness.

b. *absol.* To toss a coin or some object in the air to wager on which side it will fall, or to determine a question by this: see head *sb.* 3 b.

1704 *Hymn Vict.* lviii, Victoria Tosses-up for Cross or Pile. **1762** Wilkes *Let. to Earl Temple* (1769) I. 31 They tossed up, and it fell to my adjutant to give the word. **1809** Malkin *Gil Blas* I. v. ¶9 Tossing up for heads or tails was not my ruling passion. **1861** Dickens *Gt. Expect.* xxxi, Some inclining to both opinions said 'toss up for it'.

†**c.** To cook or dress (food, a meal) hastily; to prepare, to serve up. Also *fig. Obs.*

c **1685** Villiers (Dk. Buckhm.) *Confer.* Wks. 1705 II. 54 Our ancient Matron had tossed up a nice Breakfast, out of the remainders of the Capons. **1710** *Tatler* No. 258 ¶1 To toss up the Fragments of a Feast into a Ragoust. **1737** Bracken *Farriery Impr.* (1757) II. 137 The Booksellers.. had a better Knack at tossing up a Title [for a book]. **1818** Scott *Rob Roy* viii, But you have not dined—we'll have something nice and ladylike, sweet and pretty like yourself, tossed up in a trice.

toss, tosser, etc., erron. ff. toze, tozer, etc.

toss-, the vb.-stem and sb. in Comb.: **toss-about** *a.*, that tosses about; **toss-ball**, a ball that is tossed; **toss-blade**, one who 'tosses' a blade or sword; **toss-cup**, one who tosses off drink; **toss-halfpenny, -penny**, the tossing of money in gambling, pitch and toss; **toss-loser**, the loser of a toss; so ***toss-winner***; **toss-pan**, a pan used for tossing in cooking. See also tosspot.

1844 J. T. Hewlett *Parsons & W.* lv, That dreamy, *toss-about sort of slumber. **1681** W. Robertson *Phraseol. Gen.* (1693) 1078 Fortunes *toss-ball. **1659** Torriano, *Accoltellatore*, a fighter, a *tosse-blade, a swash-buckler. **1883** G. H. Boughton in *Harper's Mag.* Apr. 684/2 The merry, liquid-eyed *toss-cup of Ostade. **1849** Thackeray *Pendennis* v, A little scamp of a choir-boy, who played *toss-halfpenny. **1906** *Daily Chron.* 8 Sept. 3/2 When that has been the case the writer cannot remember the *toss-losers failing to win the event. **1796** Mrs. Glasse *Cookery* v. 57 Put half a pint of gravy into a *toss-pan. **1874** Symonds *Sk. Italy & Gr.* (1898) I. v. 96 Men and boys play for the most part at bowls or *toss-penny.

†**'tossant,** *a. Obs. rare*[−1]. (*pseudo-arch.*) [irreg. f. toss *v.* + -ant[1] of F. pr. pple.] Tossing.

1616 Lane *Cont. Sqr.'s T.* xi. 267 His tossant plume, which sublimeth his head, All colors wore, save white, that mote bee read.

tossed (tɒst, -ɔː-), *ppl. a.* Also **tost.** [f. toss *v.* + -ed[1].] Thrown about, hurled this way and that; disordered; disturbed, troubled: see the vb.

1621 Bp. Hall *Heaven upon Earth* §4 The galled soule.. after many tossed and turned sides, complaines of remedilesse and vnabated torment. **1659** R. Cromwell in *Clarke Papers* (Camden) IV. 297 Oh,.. that poore tossed England might at laste finde a quiet harbour! **1780** A. Young *Tour Irel.* I. 265 Wild tossed-about ground. **1807** Crabbe *Village* I. 116 On the tost vessel bend their eager eye. **1825** Scott *Talism.* vi, His tossed couch and impatient gestures showed.. the energy and the reckless impatience of a disposition, whose natural sphere was [etc.]. **1844** H. G. Robinson *Odes of Horace* I. xxxii, His toss'd bark made fast to the watery shore.

b. Of a salad: stirred or turned, esp. so as to be coated with dressing (see toss *v.* 3e).

1947 M. Given *Mod. Encycl. Cooking* II. 1315 Whole meal tossed salad... Wash and clean all vegetables, chill thoroughly. **1962** H. Hood in R. Weaver *Canad. Short Stories* (1968) 2nd Ser. 207 It was a good hot-weather supper, tossed greens with the correct proportions of vinegar and oil. **1978** H. C. Rae *Sullivan* I. ii. 15 Artichokes, tossed green salad and cold lake trout.

tossel, -ell, obs. ff. tassel *sb.*[1], [2], tercel.

tosser ('tɒsə(r), -ɔː-). [f. toss *v.* + -er[1].]

1. a. One who or that which tosses. Also with *adv.*

1612 T. Taylor *Comm. Titus* ii. 12 (1619) 475 Scoffers of such as walke in these straite waies of God, tossers of reproaches against them. **1623** Fletcher & Rowley *Maid in Mill* II. ii, As satisfaction to the blustring god, To send his tossers forth. **1837** *New Monthly Mag.* LI. 195 Ticket-porters are.. such.. tossers-off of beer. **1846** Mrs. Gore *Eng. Char.* (1852) 109 The hapless tosser-up of omelets. **1896** A. Morrison *Child of the Jago* 130 The last of the tossers stuffed away his coppers. **1905** *Daily Chron.* 7 Sept. 4/4 As a caber tosser he has never been equalled.

b. [Prob. f. sense 13 d of the vb.] A term of contempt or abuse for a person; a 'jerk'. Cf. BUGGER *sb.* 2 b. *slang.*

1977 *Zigzag* Apr. 40/3 She came on in a big mac and flashed her legs like an old tosser before throwing it off. **1983** P. INCHBALD *Short Break in Venice* xviii. 172 It's a right pig's job.. Poor little tosser. As if he wasn't suffering enough already.

2. A cooking-vessel, a tossing-pan.

1884 *Hand & Heart* Oct. 123/2 Cut the other parts in small bits, put them in a small tosser with a grate of nutmeg, the least white pepper and salt,..simmer a few minutes before you fill.

3. A penny, a coin of small value. Cf. TOSS *v.* 9, TOSS *sb.*[1] 6 c.

1935 [see CARVE-UP]. **1964** J. AIKEN *Black Hearts in Battersea* (1965) vi. 70 Shall we play for money?.. I haven't a tosser to my kick. **1966** *New Statesman* 4 Nov. 662/1 There's no one mumming today whose opinion is worth a tosser on the cut of a dressing-gown. **1980** J. GERSON *Assassination Run* xi. 158 Your people don't give a tosser for me!

tossicate, variant of TOSTICATE.

tossily, *adv.*: see TOSSY *a.*

'tossing, *vbl. sb.* [-ING[1].] The action of TOSS *v.* in various senses. Also with *adv.*

1557 [see TOSS *v.* 3 b]. **1578** LYTE *Dodoens* 367 The other ..stirreth vp tossinges, wamlings, windinesse, and vomiting. *a* **1586** SIDNEY *Arcadia* II. (Sommer) 173 When Basilius after long tossing was gotten a sleepe. **1642** FULLER *Holy & Prof. St.* III. x. 174 Like the tossing of a pike, which is..to shew the strength and nimblenesse of the arm. **1711** ADDISON *Spect.* No. 63 ¶1 The Tossings and Fluctuations of the Sea. **1801** *Sporting Mag.* XIX. 115 No cards, dice, odd-horse or tossing-up to be permitted.

b. *attrib.*: †**tossing iron**, some cooking utensil; **tossing-pan**, a pan for tossing food in cooking.

a **1625** FLETCHER *Woman's Prize* II. v, They heave ye stool on stool, and fling main pot-lids Like massy rocks, dart ladles, tossing irons And tongs like thunder-bolts. **1769** MRS. RAFFALD *Eng. Housekpr.* (1778) 75 Put them all in your tossing-pan, and shake it over the fire till it boils, then put in your woodcock. **1796** MRS. GLASSE *Cookery* v. 47 Put it into a tossing-pan with a tea-spoonful of lemon-pickle.

'tossing, *ppl. a.* [f. TOSS *v.* + -ING[2].] That tosses: see the vb.

1575 *Gamm. Gurton* II. iv, My goodly tossing sporyars neele, chaue lost ich wot not where. **1742** YOUNG *Nt. Th.* I. 167 How I dreamt.. Of stable pleasures on the tossing wave! **1816** J. WILSON *City of Plague* II. iv. 106 Beside the couch of tossing agony. **1896** 'H. S. MERRIMAN' *Flotsam* iv, A fine boy with tossing fair curls.

Hence **'tossingly** *adv.*

1620 THOMAS *Lat. Dict.*, *Volutatim*..rollingly, tumblingly, tossingly.

†**'tossment.** *Obs.* [f. TOSS *v.* + -MENT.] The action of tossing or fact of being tossed.

1650 T. B. *Worcester's Apoph.* lix. 108 After so long a voyage as threescore and sixteen years tossement upon the waves of this troublesome world.

tosspot ('tɒspɒt, -ɔː-). [f. phr. *to toss a pot*, TOSS *v.* 10 b.] One accustomed to toss off his pot of drink; a heavy drinker; a toper, drunkard.

1568 FULWEL *Like Will to Like* D j b, I wil pledge Tom tospot, til I be as drunk as a mouse a. **1577** tr. *Bullinger's Decades* (1592) 153 Come not in companie of blasphemous tossepots. **1674** JOSSELYN *Voy. New Eng.* (1675) 76 The eggs of an owl put into the liquor that a tospot useth to be drunk with, will make him loathe drunkenness. **1809** W. IRVING *Knickerb.* VI. v. (1861) 204 They were sturdy toss-pots of yore. **1890** BESANT *Demoniac* iv, He is..a brother tosspot.

b. *Comb.*, as **'tosspotlike** adv.

1580 H. GIFFORD *Gilloflowers* (1875) 150 Doste thinke that such as tospotlike Set all at sixe and seuen, Are in a ready way to bring Their sinfull soules to heauen?

'tossy, *a. rare.* [f. TOSS *sb.*[1] or *v.* + -Y.] Contemptuous, pert. Hence **'tossily** *adv.*

1851 KINGSLEY *Yeast* vii, Argemone answered by some tossy commonplace. *Ibid.*, She answered tossily enough.

†**tost**, *v.* Corruption of TOSS *v.*

1606 tr. *Rollock's Comm. on 2 Thess.* 138 (Jam.) Thou shalt be beatten and tosted here and there. **1632** LITHGOW *Trav.* v. 215 The Whirlwind of Time, still so speedy posts, That like it selfe, all things therein, it tosts.

tost, var. TOSSED, pa. t. and pple. of TOSS *v.*, also *ppl. a.* Still frequent in poetry, and as second element in compounds, as *tempest-tost.*

tost, obs. form of TOAST.

tostada, tostado (tɒ'stɑːdə, -əʊ). [a. Sp., pa. pple. of *tostar* to toast.] A deep-fried cornmeal pancake topped with a seasoned mixture of beans, mincemeat, and vegetables.

1945 E. FERGUSSON *Mexican Cookbk.* (ed. 2) p. v, Mexican food has, even since the 'American Occupation', been a part of the Southwestern diet... In every Southwestern town *tostados* are served with cocktails. **1958** *McCall's Mag.* Aug. 9/2 The tortilla is the basis of many famous Mexican dishes: Enchiladas, Tacos, Tostadas. **1972** *Times* 6 May 12/7 Wait for the crunch of tostados—for the next culinary invasion.. will be Mexican. **1975** 'S. MARLOWE' *Cawthorn Journals* xxiv. 235 Maruja fed tostadas into the hot splattering oil.

to-stand, to-step: see TO- *pref.*[1]

tosticate ('tɒstɪkeɪt), *v.* Also 9 *dial.* tossicate. Usually in pa. pple. *tosticated*, app. originally a mispronunciation of *intoxicated* and so used, but later also associated with *tossed*, *tost*, and used as = tossed about, distracted, perplexed. So **tosti'cation.** Common dialectally; cited in E.D.D. for many counties from W. Yorksh. to Somerset.

1650 J. REYNOLDS *Flower of Fidelity* 3 His tosticated conceits fixt upon renowned travel. *Ibid.* 42 Being tosticated with the beauty. **1691** MRS. D'ANVERS *Academia* 8 Madam's most sadly tosticated, Knowing her Boy but empty-pated, Lest the soft Squire might starv'd be, When e're he's sent to th' 'Versity. **1712** SWIFT *Jrnl. to Stella* xlviii, I have been so tosticated about since my last. **1748** RICHARDSON *Clarissa* xvii. (1810) V. 181, I want these tostications (thou seest how women and women's words fill my mind) to be over. **1811** *Ora & Juliet* I. 32 Get thee to bed ..and sleep off that odious strong liquor that has tosticated thy senses. **1828** *Craven Gloss.*, *Tossicated*, tossed, perplexed. Also, drunk. **1881** MISS JACKSON *Shropsh. Word-bk.*, *Tossicated*, harassed; worried,—'upset', as by vexation or trouble.

to-stick, to-sting, to-stink, etc.: see TO- *pref.*[1], [2].

†**tostock(e, -stok(e**, shortening of TAVISTOCK, q.v. *Obs.*

1511-12 *Act 3 Hen. VIII*, c. 6 §3 Wollen Clothes called Tostokes made in the Countie of Devonshire. **1523** *Act 14 & 15 Hen. VIII*, c. 11 Any Clothes callyd Tostokkes.

‖**toston** (tos'ton). [(Amer.) Sp.: cf. TESTON, TESTOON.] A silver coin formerly in use in various Latin American countries; in Mexico, equivalent in value to half a peso.

1884 A. R. CONKLING *Appleton's Guide to Mexico* xv. 61 Mexico has followed the example of Spain in adopting the decimal system of coinage, of which the *real* is the basis. The current coins are as follows: *Silver.* One *peso*, or dollar, containing 8 *reales*, or 100 cents. Four *reales*, or one *toston*, 50 cents. **1932** H. CRANE *Let.* 22 Apr. (1965) 412 The telegraph office paid us off in six hundred and some odd 'Tostons' (about like getting it all in dimes) and neither the Ward Line office nor the official Banco de Mexico would accept them. **1947** M. LOWRY *Under Volcano* vii. 240 Laying a tostón on the counter. **1980** in S. Terkel *Amer. Dreams* 6 My father's father came from Mexico... He paid a *toston*, a half-dollar. That automatically made him a U.S. citizen.

tosudite ('təʊsjʊdaɪt). *Min.* [ad. Russ. *tosudít* (V. A. Frank-Kamenetsky et al. 1963, in *Zap. Vsesoyuz. Min. Obshch.* XCIII. 563): see quot. 1964 and -ITE[1].] A blue mixed-layer clay mineral (see quots.).

1964 *Mineral. Abstr.* XVI. 549/2 This newly characterized mixed-layer mineral consisting of unusual aluminian chlorite and montmorillonite is named tosudite, in honour of Toshio Sudo, who described the Japanese occurrences. **1976** *Clays & Clay Minerals* XXIV. 142/1 The name tosudite is usually used for a regularly interstratified mineral with dioctahedral or di-trioctahedral chlorite component.

†**to-'swell**, *v. Obs.* [OE. *toswellan*, f. TO-[2] + *swellan*, SWELL *v.* So OHG. *ziswellan*, MHG. *ze-*, *zerswellen.*] *intr.* To swell out; also *fig.* to be puffed up, as with an emotion. Chiefly in pa. pple. **to-swolle(n.**

c **1000** ÆLFRIC *Saints' Lives* iii. 481 He hæfde ænne lic-ðrowere.. Egeslice to-swollen. *c* **1205** LAY. 17815 Al ic æm to-swollen.. Nu nan ich wurðe dæd. *a* **1250** *Owl & Night.* 145 Þeos vle.. Sat toswolle & tobolewe So heo hedde one frogge iswolwe. *c* **1330** R. BRUNNE *Chron. Wace* (Rolls) 10876 Þem þoughte for wo þey al to-swal. **1382** WYCLIF *Jer.* v. 22 To-swelle shul his flodis. *c* **1400** *Lanfranc's Cirurg.* 311 Humouris fel so myche þerto þat his leggis & his hipis to-swollen al greet.

to-swelt, to-swinge, to-swink: see TO- *pref.*[2]

tosy, tosie ('tozɪ), *a. Sc.* Also tozie, -y. [Origin uncertain: it can hardly be the same as TOZY *a.*]

1. Warm; comforting or comfortable, snug, cosy.

Sometimes app. = 'fresh, refreshing'.

1720 RAMSAY *Patie & Rodger* I. i, How tosie is't tae snuff the cauller air. **1722** HAMILTON *Wallace* III. i. (1774) 58 He ..brought them wealth of meat and tosie drink. **1890** J. SERVICE *Notandums* x. 71 As tozie a howff as you would fin' in a' Glesco.

2. Slightly intoxicated; tipsy. Also *tosy-mosy.*

1727 P. WALKER *R. Cameron* in *Biogr. Presbyt.* (1827) I. 278 The Magistrates gave him Drink and kept him tozy. **1794** *Poems Eng., Sc., & Lat.* 95 (Jam.) What puir man, whan he's tozy, But spends as he ware bein and cozy? **1828** MOIR *Mansie Wauch* xvii. (1849) 111 We had another jug, after which we were both a wee tozy-mozy.

Hence **tosily, -lie**, *adv.*; **'tosiness.**

1825 in JAMIESON.

tosyl ('tɒsɪl). *Chem.* [a. G. *tosyl* (Hess & Pfleger 1933, in *Ann. d. Chemie* DVII. 48), f. *to*luol*sulfonyl*: see *toluol* (s.v. TOLU-), SULPHONYL.] The *para* isomer of the univalent radical toluenesulphonyl, $H_3C \cdot C_6H_4 \cdot SO_2$—.

1938 *Jrnl. Amer. Chem. Soc.* LX. 398/1 The unimolar tosylation of α- and β-methyl-*d*-glucosides in pyridine solution with tosyl chloride, followed by acetylation results in the formation of 6-tosyl-triacetyl-α-methyl-*d*-glucoside. **1975** *Nature* 30 Oct. 763/1 There is no evidence for a hydrophobic binding pocket or tosyl hole as seen in the α-chymotrypsin structure.

Hence **'tosylate** *sb.*, an ester of the tosyl group; *v. trans.*, to introduce a tosyl group into (a compound) or add one to (an atom); **'tosylated, 'tosylating** *ppl. adjs.*; **tosy'lation**, the process of tosylating.

1938 *Jrnl. Amer. Chem. Soc.* LX. 1203/2 The structure of this compound may be considered proved since it is identical with that obtained..upon tosylating 2,3,4,2',3'-pentaacetyl-β-methylcellobioside. **1938** [see TOSYL above]. **1963** I. L. FINAR *Org. Chem.* (ed. 4) I. xxv. 612 Tosylates are useful for preparing, *e.g.*, ethers. **1972** *Jrnl. Chem. Soc.: Chem. Communications* 1148/1 We have found that *N*-methyl-*N*-tosylpyrrolidinium perchlorate.. can be used as a selective tosylating reagent. *Ibid.* 1149/1 We assumed that only nitrogen would be tosylated if both amino- and hydroxy-groups were present in the substrate. **1974** *Jrnl. Org. Chem.* XXXIX. 635/2 A greater chemical shift difference was observed for the C-2 ring protons adjacent to the tosylated nitrogen. *Ibid.*, Tosylation was carried out with tosyl chloride in the usual basic media of pyridine or aqueous sodium bicarbonate. **1978** J. M. & D. J. CRAM *Essence Org. Chem.* vi. 150 The name *p*-toluenesulfonyl group (Ar—SO_2—) is shortened to the 'tosyl' group, and the ester is ethyl tosylate.

†**tot**, *sb.*[1] *Obs. rare.* In 5 totte, 7 toute. [Origin unascertained.] A person of disordered brain, a simpleton, a fool.

c **1425** *Cast. Persev.* 2880 in *Macro Plays* 162 Werldlys good þou hast for-gon, & with tottys þou schalt be torn. *c* **1440** *Promp. Parv.* 497/2 Totte, *supra in* folte. *Ibid.* (MS. Winch.), *Totte*, fowle, supra in ff. [*Ffolt* idem quod *folet*, *ffolette*, ffatuellus]. *a* **1660** *Contemp. Hist. Irel.* (Ir. Archæol. Soc.) I. 278 Whoe answeared like a toute, or a maddman, as he was, that he was for the Kinge.

†**tot** (tɒt), *sb.*[2] *Obs.* Also 6–7 tott(e. [f. TOT *v.*[1] (or its source).] The word *tot* or letter T written against an item in an account to indicate that the amount specified has been received; hence, an item in an account; also generally, a note, jotting, or comment written down.

1529 GARDINER *Let. to Wolsey* in *St. Papers Hen. VIII* I. 345 The copy.. I sende unto Your Grace,..adding in the margyne tottes, wherby Your Grace may perceyve omne consilium rei gestæ. *a* **1601** SIR T. FANSHAWE *Pract. Exch.* (1658) 71 After his said Secondary hath made up the Sheriffs second summ upon his *De debitis plurimum*, which be his Tots and upon his *De pluribus debitis* charge which be his greene wax, and his whole as before, or so many of them as he is charged with, hee causeth the Sheriffs forraigne accounts to be cast up. *Ibid.* 80 He maketh speciall *tot* against the same summe thus [etc.]. **1642** C. VERNON *Consid. Exch.* 32 The greatest part of the Sheriffes totts and summes of money by him taken in charge at his apposals, would be set off and discharged. **1798** T. FARRER in Manning *Exch. of Pleas.* (1819) II. App. 267 Such fines, recognizances and amerciaments, as each sheriff has received he answers by saying *Tot*, whereupon I [deputy clerk] mak that answer upon the roll of the estreat. When the sheriff receives part and not the whole, he answers Tot as to part, and Nil as to the rest.

tot (tɒt), *sb.*[3] *colloq.* [Short for *total* or L. *totum*: see also TOTE *sb.*[1]] The total of an addition, sometimes having *tot.* written against it; hence, an addition sum; also (*tot-up*) the action of TOT *v.*[2]: adding up, totalling. Also *gen.*, the total number or amount.

[**1690** PEPYS *Mem. Royal Navy* 36 Repaires, *l.* 132000, Sea-stores, *l.* 88000. Tot, 220,000.] **1755** C. CHARKE *Narr. Life Mrs. C. Charke* 260 The above-mentioned notable Gentleman, with his wife and a young Fellow, besides our two selves, made up the whole *Totte.* **1857** *Londonderry Standard* 26 Feb. 2/2 Forty monopolists whose numerical 'tot' is so oddly coincident with the history of Ali Baba. **1866** *Times* 28 Apr. 5/6 He added up the gross 'tots' of the several poll books himself. **1871** *Standard* 13 Feb., The task of going over the cards..and comparing the lists, and doing the general tot-up, is very arduous. **1879** C. MARVIN *Our Public Offices* 11, I fell upon the row of 'tots' with the same vigour. **1894** *Daily News* 14 July 5/1 He has seen children in Standards IV and V using their fingers freely during the examination, and even trying to do 'tots' by this cumbrous method.

tot, *sb.*[4] *colloq.* or *local.* [app. a recent word; recorded 1725. Origin uncertain. *Tottr* occurs in Icel. as the nickname of a dwarfish person, and *tommel-tot* as Danish for Tom Thumb; but no connexion has been traced.]

1. a. A very small or tiny child.

1725 RAMSAY *Gentle Sheph.* I. ii, Wow! Jenny, can there greater pleasure be Than see sic wee tots toolying at your knee? **1865** *Cornh. Mag.* Mar. 355 Her tiny trembling tot with yellow hair. **1896** 'IAN MACLAREN' *Kate Carnegie* 25 I've had it since I was a little tot and could remember anything.

b. *tot-o'er-seas*, a local name of the Goldcrest.

1885 SWAINSON *Provinc. Names Birds* 25 Goldcrest... From its tiny size. *Tot o'er seas.* **1895** NEWTON *Dict. Birds*, *Tot-o'er-seas*, a name by which *Regulus cristatus* is said to be known on some parts of the east coast.

2. A very small drinking-vessel; a child's mug. (See also quot. 1845.) Chiefly *dial.*

1828 *Craven Gloss.*, *Tot*, a cup or glass. **1845** SIR H. B. EDWARDES in *Mem.* (1886) I. 33 That half-mad camel, who is overladen with tents and tots. [*Note.* Tin pots, out of which the European soldiers drink.] **1872** *Daily News* 5 Sept., Dark figures [soldiers]..throw themselves down on the straw, and investigate into the contents of the mug or of the tot. **1890** 'R. BOLDREWOOD' *Miner's Right* xxvii, Give me that 'tot' that I see tied to your saddle. **1891** *Sale Catal. Glass Wks. Stourbridge*, Twenty-seven tots. Two flower bowls.

3. A minute quantity of anything, esp. of drink; a dram; also, anything very small.

1828 in *Craven Gloss.* **1847-78** HALLIWELL, *Tot*, anything very small. *East.* **1856** KANE *Arctic Explor.* II. vii. 78 We jabbed the stopper down the whiskey-tin and gave you a tot of it. **1878** F. S. WILLIAMS *Midl. Railw.* 527 The hole is charged with gunpowder,—about a pint—or two 'tots'.. being usually enough. **1908** *Times* 30 July 8/3 The issue of 'tots of rum' on cold nights was not only not desirable, but absolutely pernicious.

4. *Comb.*: **tot lot** *N. Amer.*, a playground for small children; **tot system** *S. Afr.*, a system of paying agricultural workers, esp. in vine-growing districts, part of their wages in 'tots' (usu. mugs) of wine.

1944 *Sun* (Baltimore) 15 July 13/3 (*heading*) Pall Mall *tot lot open daily except Saturday. **1968** *Daily Colonist* (Victoria, B.C.) 6 Dec. 41/4 Snow fails to stop Gold River children from enjoying recently completed tot-lot behind the community hall. **1977** *Ottawa Citizen* 19 May 2/2 The plan includes..a 'tot lot' for pre-schoolers. **1926** *Eastern Province Herald* (Port Elizabeth) 12 Feb. 7 (*heading*) Liquor bill under fire—evils of the *tot system. **1953** P. ABRAHAMS *Return to Goli* II. 77 The vicious 'tot'-system which obtains in the wine-growing Cape valley..is ruining the health..of a very large number of Coloureds. **1974** *Sunday Times* (Johannesburg) 24 Feb. 14 Asked whether he made use of the tot system, Mr. — said: [etc.].

tot, *sb.*^{5} *slang.* [Origin unascertained: cf. TAT *sb.*^{5}, *v.*^{3}] A dust-heap picker's name for a bone; whence by extension, anything worth picking from a refuse-heap or elsewhere. Hence **'totter**, a rag-and-bone collector; **'totting**, dust-heap picking.

1873 *Slang Dict.* s.v., 'Tot' is a bone, but chiffoniers and cinder-hunters generally are called *Tot-pickers* nowadays. *Totting* also has its votaries on the banks of the Thames, where all kinds of flotsam and jetsam, from coals to carrion, are known as *tots*. **1880** *Law Rep.*, 5 *Q.B.D.* 369 The contents of the dust-bins consisted chiefly of cinders and ashes and the sweepings of the houses, but they also contained a number of articles thrown into them as refuse by the occupiers of the houses, and known as 'tots'. **1891** *Daily News* 11 Mar. 3/3 Costermongers, wood-cutters, and 'totters', men who lounged about areas in the hope of getting old bottles and things from servants. **1910** *Lond. City Mission Mag.* May 85/2 The Totters. Up betimes, these queer people set out by the dozen, with sack or barrow, in quest of rags and bones, rubber, and bottles, scrap iron and cast-off clothing. *Ibid.*, When all else fails, and one can stoop so low, a day's totting is bound to yield the cost of a night's lodging.

†**tot**, *v.*^{1} *Obs.* [f. L. *tot* so much, so many; acc. to Blount, short for *tot pecuniæ Regi debentur* 'so many sums of money are due to the king'.]

1. *trans.* To mark (an item in the sheriff's list) with the word *tot* or the letter T, showing that the amount had been levied, and was to be accounted for, by him. Cf. NICHIL, O.NI. Also used in certain accounts between the Exchequer and other persons: see quot. 1785. Hence **totting** *vbl. sb.*

[**1368** *Act 42 Edw. III*, c. 9 Est ordene..qe homme veie les dites estretes enseallees, & qe ce qest paie soit tottee, et meismes les estretes mandez as Viscontes sur la receite. *transl.* a Man shall see the same Estreats sealed, and that the same which is paid, be totted, and the same Estreats sent to the Sheriffs upon the Receipt.] **1530–1** *Act 22 Hen. VIII*, c. 15 All other yssues and amercyamentes..whether they be totted or not totted, taken to the charge of the Shyryff or not taken to his charge. **1620** J. WILKINSON *Coroners & Sherifes* 75 An ignorant Undersherif may both undoe his high Sherife and himselfe, both in this world and in the world to come by totting and nichiling. *Ibid.*, If it bee totted, that is charged, though it can never be levied, it will now hardly be avoided, but it must be paid. *a* **1726** SIR G. GILBERT *Treat. Crt. Exchequer* vii. (1758) 115 If the Sheriff has levied any Part of these Debts he Totts it, and the Letter T is set upon such Sum. **1785** *MS. Dean's Bk. Canterb. Cathedr.* lf. 129 Agreed that the process called Totting, in the Exchequer, for a share of the Post Fines, attended with great expence, and little or no advantage, be in future discontinued. **1798** T. FARRER in Manning *Exch. of Pleas* (1819) II. App. 267 As to such sums as are totted by the sheriff.

2. *transf.* To note or distinguish (a name in a list) by some mark or a prick, e.g. to prick the sheriffs; also to make a note against a name in a list or a sum or item in an account; also, to write down by way of note, to jot down in writing.

1444 *Paston Lett.* I. 55 Sir, ther arn xv. jurores abowe to certifie ye, as many as ye will: but lete these men that be tottid be certified, for thei be the rewleris. **1522** WOLSEY *Let. to Hen. VIII* in *St. Papers* I. 115 The Judges procedyd to election of your Schreffes..for thys yere; whos namys be comprisid in a byll of parchement herin closid; desyring Your Grace to tot and marcke suche oon of thre namyd for every schire, as may stand with your gracious pleasure. **1524** *Ibid.* 150 The copy.., with my poore opinion upon the same, totted in the margyne. **1587** FLEMING *Contn. Holinshed* III. 1545/1 Such as were absent, had no allowance that daie: if they came late, their wages was totted at the expenditors good discretion. **1612** *Manch. Crt. Leet Rec.* (1885) II. 270 Those ffreeholders..whose names are not totted in the Courtbooke.

tot (tɒt), *v.*^{2} *colloq.* [f. TOT *sb.*^{3}] **a.** *trans.* To add *together* and bring out the total of; to sum *up*.

1760–72 H. BROOKE *Fool of Qual.* (1809) IV. 82 These, totted together, will make a pretty beginning of my little project. **1839** T. HOOK *Gurney Married* 403 Now, ma'am, if you will just tot up your account for schooling and that, I'll arrange the whole matter. **1876** FARJEON *Love's Vict.* xiv, When he totted up the figures, he was rather serious. **1895** STUART & PARK *Variety Stage* ii. 31 A waiter totting up the account as you passed through.

b. *intr. to tot up*: to amount, 'come' (*to*).

1882 BESANT *All Sorts* iv, I..wondered how much it would tot up to. Something, I thought, in four figures. **1892** *Idler* July 719 Three stalls a week tot up frightfully in a year.

Hence **'totting** *vbl. sb.*

1823 *Monthly Mag.* LV. 237 All the items were tenaciously preserved in the toting up. **1863** COWDEN CLARKE *Shaks. Char.* vi. 152 The very 'totting up' of his qualifications creates a 'real presence' of the man. **1865** *Standard* 31 July, The totting [of the votes] was not concluded by Mr. Dames until half-past two. **1963** *Guardian* 2 May 5/1 The 'totting up' procedure is a new principle, and Mr Marples explained that its sole purpose was to make anyone who had two endorsements in two years drive extra carefully. **1976** *Deeside Advertiser* 9 Dec. 24/1 Hamilton had been disqualified by Chester City Magistrates in October for six months under the totting up procedure because of previous endorsements of his licence. **1978** R. MARK *Office of Constable* xxii. 273 'Totting up'..is the arrangement under the 1972 Road Traffic Act authorizing the endorsement of a driving licence after conviction for any one of a number of offences. The endorsement lasts three years and two further endorsements during that period mean mandatory disqualification from driving for a minimum of six months.

tot (tɒt), *v.*^{3} *Sc.* [Not recorded before 19th c.; ?playful shortening of *totter* or *tottle*. Connexion with TOT *sb.*^{4} 1 'tiny child' uncertain.] *intr.* 'To move with short steps as a child does' (Jamieson 1825); to totter; to toddle; also playfully, to walk, go, move.

1824 W. JAMESON in *Mem. & Lett.* (1845) 46 My little Benoni is gathering strength and totting about. **1844** A. MCKAY in *Mod. Sc. Poets* II. 377 When ye were wee bairnies, tot, totting about. *c* **1850** *Whistle-binkie* (1890) II. *Songs Nursery* 81 Awa they tot wi' ane anither.

tot (tɒt), *v.*^{4} [Back-formation f. *totting* s.v. TOT *sb.*^{5}] *intr.* To pick anything saleable from a dustbin or tip; †to pick up bones.

1884 J. GREENWOOD *Little Ragamuffins* xiv. 121 'P'r'aps he's going a-tottin'' (picking up bones,) said Ripston. **1922** JOYCE *Ulysses* 422 On a step a gnome totting among a rubbishtip crouches to shoulder a sack of rags and bones. **1969** *Guardian* 6 Feb. 5 The right to tot or sell salvage is the cause of a 10-day-old strike of 267 dustmen. **1976** M. RUSSELL *Double Deal* iv. 32, I could earn as much, totting for the corporation.

tot, in phr. *tot and quot*: see TOT-QUOT.

†**to-tag.** *Obs.* In 3 to tagge, (to tage). [app. f. TO-^{1} + *tagge*, TAG *sb.* pendant or addition, or *v.* to append. But the simple sb. and vb. are not known bef. *c* 1400, and then not in abstract sense.

It is to be remembered however that *tag* was prob. a word not likely to occur in literature; and that there are other words in which the compound with *to-* is known much earlier than the simple word, e.g. *to-crush*, *to-touse*.]

Something 'tagged' or attached to a fact; a circumstance.

c **12..** *Ancr. R.* 316 (Corpus MS.) Six þinges O Latin circumstances: On Englisch to tagges mahe beon icleopede [*MS. Cott. Nero* On Englisch heo muwen beon ihoten to-tagges; persone, stude, time, manere, tale, cause]. *Ibid.* 346 þurh sum uuel to tagge þe lið þer biseden. *Ibid.*, Efter þe to tagges [*Nero* circumstances] þe beoð iwriten þruppe. [So in 8 instances in Corpus, in 2 of which Cott. Nero has *circumstances* without a gloss.]

total ('təʊtəl), *a.* and *sb.* [a. F. *total* (14th c. in Hatz.-Darm.) = Sp., Pg. *total*, It. *totale*, ad. Schol.L. *tōtāl-is* (in St. Bernard 1150), f. L. *tōt-us* entire: see -AL^1.]

A. *adj.* **1.** Of, pertaining, or relating to the whole of something. Now *rare*, exc. in

total eclipse, an eclipse of the sun or moon in which the whole of the disk is obscured. (Often taken as sense 3.)

c **1386** CHAUCER *Pars. T.* ¶218 His contricion..shal be vniuersal and total. **1594** BLUNDEVIL *Exerc.* II. (1636) 105 The total Sine, which is the whole Semidiameter, and greatest right Sine. **1627** W. SCLATER *Exp. 2 Thess.* (1629) 172 There are two kindes or degrees of it [faith]. 1. Totall respecting the whole word of God... 2. Partiall. *a* **1653** GOUGE *Comm. Heb.* ii. 9 (1655) 170 He was a totall Saviour. He saveth soul and body. **1671** MILTON *Samson* 81 Irrecoverably dark, total Eclipse Without all hope of day. **1683** *Phil. Trans., Abr.* II. 604 Total Eclipse of the Moon, Feb. 11–21, 1682, observed at Paris and Copenhagen. **1697** tr. *Burgersdicius his Logic* I. xv. 51 That Cause is total, which in its Species wholly causes the Whole Caused. **1715** HALLEY in *Phil. Trans.* XXIX. 245 Observations on the.. Total Eclipse of the Sun..22nd of April. **1857** WHEWELL *Hist. Induct. Sc.* (ed. 3) I. 362 The eclipse must have been one decidedly total.

2. a. Constituting or comprising a whole; whole, entire.

c **1400** *Plowm. T.* 418 Goodes frendship hem makes, They toteth on hir somme totall. **1474** *Acc. Ld. High Treas. Scot.* I. 72 Sum totale of bath thir sidis, lix li. xv d. *c* **1477** CAXTON *Jason* 7 b, The veray and sewre foundement vpon which my total espayr and hope resteth. *c* **1586** C'TESS PEMBROKE *Ps.* XCVIII. iii, Thou totall globe and all that thee enjoy. **1610** DONNE *Pseudo-martyr* 201 The whole totall body..of the points of their profession. **1709** LADY M. W. MONTAGU *Let. to Mrs. Hewet* 12 Nov., This is the sum total of all the news I know. **1807** J. BARLOW *Columb.* III. 174 The flaming deluge..Sweeps total nations from the staggering world. **1810** in Sir W. Napier *Penins. War* (1878) II. App. 418 Total number of bayonets..4924. **1833** HT. MARTINEAU *Cinnamon & P.* vi, Its total revenue does not pay its expenses. **1903** *Daily Chron.* 25 Mar. 8/7 The percentage of total rainfall which reaches the river is diminishing, as well as the total rainfall itself.

b. *total heat* (Physics): = ENTHALPY; *spec.* (see quot. 1853).

1851 *Phil. Mag.* II. 4 We often hear of the total heat of bodies, and of gases and vapours in particular, this term being meant to express the sum of the sensible and latent heat. **1853** *Trans. R. Soc. Edin.* XX. 172 If to the latent heat of evaporation at a given temperature, is added the quantity of heat necessary to raise unity of weight of the liquid from a certain fixed temperature (usually that of melting ice) to the temperature at which the evaporation takes place, the result is called the total heat of evaporation from the fixed temperature chosen. **1927**, **1962** [see ENTHALPY].

c. *total impulse* (Astronautics): (see quot. 1949).

1949 G. P. SUTTON *Rocket Propulsion Elements* i. 18 The impulse (often called total impulse) is the integral of the thrust over the firing duration. For a constant thrust it is the product of thrust and duration. **1979** J. W. CORNELISSE et al. *Rocket Propulsion & Space Flight Dynamics* vi. 115 The specific consumption is defined as the ratio of propellant weight consumed and the total impulse delivered.

3. a. Complete in extent or degree; absolute, utter. *total recall*: see RECALL *sb.*^{1} 2.

1647 CLARENDON *Hist. Reb.* I. §1 Nothing less..could have produced such a total and prodigious Alteration and Confusion over the whole kingdom. **1769** *Def. Locke's Opin. Pers. Identity* 31 After a total interruption of thought.. during sound sleep. **1770** *Aberdeen Burgh Rec.* in Bulloch *Pynours* (1887) 76 To put a total stop to the rolling of all sorts of Casks. **1816** COLERIDGE *Human Life* 1 If total gloom Swallow up life's brief flash for aye, we fare As summer-gusts, of sudden birth and doom. **1837** LOCKHART *Scott* I. iv. 127 Notwithstanding all that Scott says about the total failure of his attempts in the art of the pencil,..they proved very useful to him afterwards. **1838–9** FR. A. KEMBLE *Resid. in Georgia* (1863) 24 A total absence of self-respect.

b. *total abstinence*: *spec.* entire abstinence from the use of alcoholic drinks. So *total abstainer*; also (rare) *total abstinent*, *total abstention*.

1831 J. TUCKERMAN *Let. respecting a City Temperance Soc., Boston, Mass.* 5 A total abstinence from intoxicating stimulants, except for medicinal purposes. **1856** VAUGHAN *Mystics* (1860) II. 219 How much easier is total abstinence from scenes of amusement than temperance in money-getting. **1862** Total-abstainers [see ABSTAINER]. **1880** RICHARDSON in *Med. Temp. Jrnl.* 71 In their allegiance to 'total abstention'. **1882** (in a *Magazine*), Very few public men..care to order a bottle of wine at a public table. It is not because they are total abstinents.

c. Complete in nature; involving all resources; manifesting every characteristic or the whole nature of an activity, person, etc.; all-encompassing, all-inclusive; fully co-ordinated or integrated. *total diplomacy*, diplomacy conducted with the consent or participation of all citizens and institutions; *total institution* (see quot. 1962); *total theatre*, (*a*) a theatre designed for maximum involvement of performers and audience; dramaturgy which achieves this; (*b*) theatre involving a wide range of techniques and conventions; *total war*, a war to which all resources and the whole population are committed; loosely, a war conducted without any scruples or limitations; *total woman*, spec. a woman who conforms to the female 'ideal' or stereotype of complete self-abnegation and devotion to the interests of a man.

1935 W. GROPIUS in S. Giedion *W. Gropius* (1954) I. 61 The aim of this 'Total Theater' is to draw the spectator into the drama. All technical means have to be subordinated to this aim and must never become ends in themselves. **1937** W. L. SHIRER *Berlin Diary* (1941) 86 Total war means the complete and final disappearance of the vanquished from the stage of history! **1940** GRAVES & HODGE *Long Week-End* i. 13 The philosophy of 'total war', that a war can best be won by complete ruthlessness, was of German origin. **1942** Total war [see *people's war* s.v. PEOPLE *sb.* 9]. **1950** *World-Telegram-Sun* (N.Y.) 14 Mar. 12 He [*sc.* D. Acheson] defines 'total diplomacy' as the full use of Congress,.. government agencies, as well as business, labor and agriculture. **1951** E. A. WALSH (*title*) Total empire: the roots and progress of world communism. **1957** *Sat. Rev.* (U.S.) 26 Jan. 22/1 M. [Jean-Louis] Barrault..describes it as follows: '"Total Theatre" is simply the true and traditional theatre, the one which makes use of man "in his totality", his gestures, pantomime, dances, breath, cries, articulation, speech, poetry, and singing.' **1957** J. D. MACDONALD *Man of Affairs* iii. 43, I did not see how any platonic relationship between Mike and this total woman would be possible. **1957** E. GOFFMAN in *Symposium on Preventive & Soc. Psychiatry* 44 [These institutions'] encompassing or total character is symbolized by the barrier to social intercourse with the outside that is often built right into the physical plant: locked doors, high walls, barbed wire, cliffs and water, open terrain, and so forth. These I am calling total insititutions. **1962** —— *Asylums* p. xiii, A total institution may be defined as a place of residence and work where a large number of like-situated individuals, cut off from the wider society for an appreciable period of time, together lead an enclosed, formally administered round of life. **1963** I. FLETCHER in B. Sewell *Two Friends* 63 *Spiritual Poems* is a fine example of 'total art', its paper and typography reflecting the eclecticism and scholarly caprice of content. **1966** *Listener* 29 Dec. 959/2, I still think the best kind of Christmas show for children is pantomime. It is a form of total theatre—story, spectacle, ballet, song, revue sketch, comedians' jokes, audience-participation, even circus acts. **1966** SCHWARZ & HADIX *Strategic Terminology* 132 *War, total*, conflict in which the issue is a threat to survival and in which all weapons of the combatants are used. Many modern definitions of total war used the term for war involving nuclear weapons or the direct confrontation of the great powers on the assumption that it would be unlimited or become unlimited. **1967** *Boston Sunday Herald* 26 Mar. I. 34/2 Rather he is thought of as a human being who needs dentistry badly and one for whom total care is now available. **1969** *Times* 17 Oct. 17/4 Carlo Palazzi, who is a past-master of the total look.. had all his men wearing saffron coloured clothes which mixed and, of course, matched. **1972** A. BRYANT *Bless this House* iv. 44 Marabel Morgan.. talked about her course entitled 'The Total Woman'. **1973** M. MORGAN *Total Woman* (1975) iv. 60 A Total Woman caters to her man's special quirks, whether it be in salads, sex, or sports. **1973** *Times* 30 July 20/3 They became convinced that developers and local authorities ought to concern themselves with engineering a 'total' environment for a community, of which the buildings themselves are only a part. **1974** *Howard Jrnl.* XIV. 86 Most total institutions leave their mark on those who devote their lives to them—the colonel, the sea captain, the public school headmaster, the monk and the nun are popular cultural stereotypes. **1975** *Times Lit. Suppl.* 2 May 477/5 The approach throughout is scholarly and thorough, no one period receiving less attention than any other. As one might expect, Roman and medieval features are fully treated, but so too are post-medieval and recent... This is total archaeology at its best. **1977** *N.Y. Rev. Bks.* 27 Oct. 46/3 (Advt.), Professional man, 60, needs slender, total woman over 30 for September, 1978, fortnight Alaskan cruise. **1978** *New Yorker* 7 Aug. 45/1 In the past few years the Dutch have been the most thrilling [soccer] side to watch, playing a running game—'total football', it is called—with players interchanging positions and functions but always pressing forward on the attack. **1980** R. MOODY *Devil you Don't* iv. 45 In the fight against Hitler, we progressed to the concept of Total War, no quarter given, no humanity expected, victory at any price.

†**4.** Summary, concise, brief. *Obs. rare*⁻¹.

a **1586** SIDNEY *Astr. & Stella* xcii, Or do you meane my tender eares to spare, That to my questions you so totall are? When I demaund of Phœnix-Stellas state, You say, forsooth, you left her well of late: O God, thinke you that satisfies my care?

5. *total float* (see quot. 1967).

1964 K. G. LOCKYER *Introd. Critical Path Anal.* v. 49 *Total float*, the time by which an activity can expand. **1967** S. WOODGATE in Wills & Yearsley *Handbk. Management Technol.* 80 Total float is.. the maximum amount of spare time which can be made available to any activity.

B. *sb.* **a.** (the adj. used absolutely). The aggregate, the whole sum or amount; a whole.

1557 RECORDE *Whetst.* Cc ij b, The totalle will bee (as here in worke appeareth) 335,016. **1621** BP. MOUNTAGU *Diatribæ* 65 To cast vp these particulars into one totall. **1656** EARL MONM. tr. *Boccalini's Advts. fr. Parnass.* II. xi. 224 Here.. is a business in which consists the total of our safety. **1772** BURKE *Corr.* (1844) I. 380 But I must say with as great, as just suspicions of him and his, as with attachment to you, on the total. **1841** MARRYAT *Poacher* xxii, You can.. sum up totals. **1849** GROTE *Greece* II. xlii. V. 218 The grand total was not less than 110,000 men.

b. *in total*, all together, entirely.

1965 *Listener* 7 Jan. 3/1 Does the Government mean incomes in total cannot go up by more than production..? Or does it mean that all incomes should go up by the same percentage? **1969** R. BUCKMINSTER FULLER *Operating Man. Spaceship Earth* iv. 52 We have not been seeing our Spaceship Earth as an integrally-designed machine which to be persistently successful must be comprehended and serviced in total.

Hence **'totalness**, totality. *rare.*

1727 BAILEY vol. II, *Totalness*, the Wholeness, or whole Sum. Hence **1818** in TODD; and in later Dicts. *c* **1864** E. DICKINSON *Poems* (1955) II. 619 All I may, if small, Do it not display Larger for the Totalness—'Tis Economy To bestow a World And withold a Star.

total ('təʊtəl), *v.* [f. TOTAL *a.* and *sb.*]

1. a. *trans.* To reach the total of, amount to.

1859 *All Year Round* No. 13. 305 One of our adversaries scored 70 off his own bat: they totalled 138. **1884** *Pall Mall G.* 22 Aug. 2/2 The proofs actually issued in neither case totalled 1,000. **1901** *Cycl. Tour. Cl. Gaz.* Oct. 389 A list [of accidents].. totals no less than twenty.

b. *intr.* To amount *to*, mount *up to*.

1880 *Scotsman* 24 Jan., For the whole of 1879 they probably totalled up to between 16 and 17 millions. **1896** *Daily News* 23 Jan. 7/5 Even the 5s. or 10s. required as deposit on each ticket must total to a large amount.

2. *trans.* To bring to a total, add up, complete. Also (*U.S.*) with *out*.

1716 M. DAVIES *Athen. Brit.* III. 99 One, if not both of those Collectors dy'd.. before those Collections were total'd. **1863** P. BARRY *Dockyard Econ.* 23 The rating, valuing, totalling, and proving of workmanship notes in the Accountant's department. **1894** *Cath. News* 16 June 4/5 The heavy legal costs.. if totalled up, would strike our readers with surprise. **1966** *Word Study* Dec. 2/2 How long did I control on fly-by-wire?.. That is something we want to total out. **1977** *New Yorker* 13 June 30/1 We weren't going to wait until the Police Department could total out what it would cost them.

3. To damage beyond repair (esp. a motor vehicle, in an accident); to destroy, to demolish, to wreck; to kill or injure severely; also *fig.*, and with *out*. Freq. in *pass.* and as *pa. ppl.* Chiefly *N. Amer.*

1895 W. RYE *Vocab. E. Anglia* 232 Totald [sic], killed or injured. **1954** *Amer. Speech* XXIX. 103 Bob totaled his car last night. **1965** *Ibid.* XL. 159 Her son was hospitalized because of an automobile accident and.. his car was 'totalled'. **1966** *Newsweek* 13 June 48C/3 Amazingly, no drivers were 'totaled'. **1966** *Current Slang* (Univ. S. Dakota) Summer 4 *Totalled out*, intoxicated... Tom was *totalled out* by midnight. **1966** *Ibid.* Winter 8 *Totalled*, adj., mentally upset... After one semester, he was *totalled.* **1970** E. SEGAL *Love Story* iii. 24 Did you at least total the guy that hit you? **1971** *Wall St. Jrnl.* 17 Mar. 1/1 He has had 44 planes, three of which were 'totaled' in accidents. **1971** *New Yorker* 28 Aug. 81 Townshend did total his instrument during his last song. **1971** M. TAK *Truck Talk* 169 *Total it out*, to wreck a truck completely. **1972** C. WESTON *Poor, Poor Ophelia* x. 52 You think it's a fantasy my car's totaled? **1973** *New Yorker* 16 July 34/3 A streak of sudden tire skids,.. a totalled car at the bottom of a ravine. **1974** *Publishers Weekly* 1 Apr. 50/1 Water from fire engines and hydrants cascaded into the burning ruins. Eighteen businesses were totaled. **1974** J. GOLDMAN *Man from Greek & Roman* xxiii. 211 'Totalled out.'.. Big gash along the side, hood all barged up. **1975** *Times Lit. Suppl.* 12 Dec. 1486/5 'The Execution of Lady Jane Grey'... Lady Jane is about to be totalled by the axe. **1977** *Time* 10 Jan. 42/2 He can still total a liquor store in the course of rescuing hostages. **1979** *Yale Alumni Mag.* Apr. (Suppl.) cn10/3 Little Robert was totaled by a bus that ran a red light but escaped with fractures of collar bone and right hand. **1979** G. SWARTHOUT *Skeletons* 98 I'm too totalled to hate anyone... This has been the worst week of my life. **1981** J. D. MACDONALD *Free Fall in Crimson* xx. 230 'He's the one that beat the old man to death.'.. 'They *think* he totaled the movie lady.' **1982** *Guardian* 26 Oct. 8/7 Daddy's BMW which she can drive any time she wants as long as she doesn't total it.

'totalist, *sb.* (and *a.*) [f. TOTAL *a.* and *sb.* + -IST.] One who inclines to treat or regard things as a whole; one concerned with the whole social environment, esp. as a means of thought-control; one concerned with the whole person. Also *attrib.* or as *adj.*

1956 J. S. BRUNER et al. *Study of Thinking* v. 128 The totalists have wanted to stay as close as possible to the whole cortex as an explanation, and it is only with the greatest reluctance that they will subtract any of its attributes as irrelevant. **1961** R. J. LIFTON *Thought Reform* xxii. 420 Through this milieu control the totalist environment seeks to establish domain over not only the individual's communication with the outside.., but also.. over what we may speak of as his communication with himself. *Ibid.* 422 Ideological totalists do not pursue this approach *solely* for maintaining a sense of power over others. **1964** R. WILKINSON *Gentlemanly Power* xiii. 184 A 'totalist ideology'.. refers to any doctrine which attempts a complete, unified explanation of world and society. **1969** *Political Q.* XL. 472 Only that which is known by the 'whole being' is sound and healthy... The origins of this totalist view of knowledge.. are no doubt various.

So **tota'listic** *a.*

1932 H. H. PRICE *Perception* vi. 151 The perceptual act still has this totalistic character. **1942** *Mind* LI. 316 Some writers are frightened by the word *intuition*, and admittedly it has bad associations... Again, under, I believe, Croce's influence, it has come to mean the apprehension of a whole as a whole, a 'totalistic' apprehension. **1976** *Brit. Jrnl. Sociol.* XXVII. 88 A totalistic rejection of the contemporary order is not encountered. **1979** *Jrnl. R. Soc. Arts* Nov. 772/1 The idea of collage city was dualism itself, an incorporation of opposite qualities which Modern city planning in its utopian, or totalistic phase, had denied.

totalitarian (təʊtælɪ'tɛərɪən), *a.* and *sb.* [f. TOTALITY + -ARIAN, after It. *totalitario* complete, absolute; totalitarian.] **A.** *adj.* Of or pertaining to a system of government which tolerates only one political party, to which all other institutions are subordinated, and which usu. demands the complete subservience of the individual to the State. Also *transf.* Cf. TOTAL *a.* 3 c.

1926 B. B. CARTER tr. *Sturzo's Italy & Fascismo* ix. 220 Anti-Fascism.. has, however, a positive sense if it is taken to represent an element antagonistic to the 'totalitarian' and absolute position of Fascism. **1929** *Times* 2 Nov. 7/5 A reaction against parliamentarism.. in favour of a 'totalitarian' or unitary state, whether Fascist or Communist. **1936** E. UNDERHILL *Worship* xii. 251 This cultus is, in origin, an acknowledgement of the corporate and totalitarian character of the Christian response to God. **1937** E. POUND in *Germany & You* 25 Apr. 95 (*heading*) Totalitarian scholarship and the new paideuma. *Ibid.* 96/2 In 1937 we are concerned with the reintegration of the arts in totalitarian synthesis. **1940** *Hutchinson's Pictorial Hist. War* 2 Oct.–26 Nov. 183 We have all heard lately about total or totalitarian war. It has been defined as conflict between nations taking the place of armed forces. Every citizen is in a sense a combatant and also the object of attack. **1951** H. ARENDT *Burden of Our Time* III. x. 303 Totalitarian movements aim at and succeed in organizing masses—not classes. **1964** H. MARCUSE *One Dimensional Man* i. 3 'Totalitarian' is not only a terroristic political coordination of society, but also a non-terroristic economic-technical coordination which operates through the manipulation of needs by vested interests. **1977** M. WALKER *National Front* i. 15 The totalitarian society is a single-minded structure. It mobilizes all its resources under one authority to achieve one goal.

B. *sb.* A leader or member of a totalitarian party; an advocate or supporter of totalitarianism.

1938 *Times* 20 Oct. 15/3 The new methods of the totalitarians. **1944** A. HUXLEY *Let.* 10 Apr. (1969) 504 The Left-wing Intellectuals and the Labour Party are eager totalitarians. **1958** R. LIDDELL *Morea* II. vi. 149 Sparta has one of the finest romantic backgrounds in Greece; this is not surprising, for only romantics can successfully be totalitarians. **1978** L. DEIGHTON *SS-GB* xiv. 115 The totalitarians of right and left have constantly to describe the faith they have in common.

Hence **totali,tariani'zation**, the action or process of rendering totalitarian; the fact of becoming totalitarian.

1941 'G. ORWELL' in *Partisan Rev.* July–Aug. 321, I don't believe that the ordinary man cares a damn about the totalitarianisation of our economy. **1954** *Encounter* Dec. 32/2 Professor Hayek originated the phrase, 'the Road to Serfdom', to describe the progressive totalitarianisation of a whole *society* by a government that only wanted at first to control the *economy*, but finds more and more human obstacles to this aim. **1958** M. FAINSOD *Smolensk under Soviet Rule* xxiii. 446 The stately procession includes urbanization, industrialization, collectivization, secularization, bureaucratization and totalitarianization.

totali'tarianism. [f. prec. + -ISM.] Totalitarian theory and practice; the advocacy of totalitarian government. Also *loosely*, authoritarianism; *transf.* monolithic character.

1926 B. B. CARTER tr. *Sturzo's Italy & Fascismo* ix. 233 This would mark the end of Fascist 'totalitarianism' and the renewal of political dualism. **1937** *Times* 9 Nov. 12/6 Nothing could be worse than to introduce totalitarianism into literature and to try to breed in a single country races of men and women fundamentally incapable of understanding one another. **1944** J. S. HUXLEY *On Living in Revolution* iii. 31 It [*sc.* Japan] has transformed itself from tribal and feudal totalitarianism to a modern technological totalitarianism. **1952** J. L. TALMON *Origins of Totalitarian Democracy* 6 The starting-point of totalitarianism of the Left has been and ultimately still is man, his reason and salvation, that of the Right totalitarian schools has been the collective entity, the State. **1967** G. STEINER *Lang. & Silence* 408 Soviet totalitarianism is most extreme not in the claims it makes on the utopian future, but in the violence it would do to the past, to the vital integrity of human remembrance. **1974** *Guardian* 2 Dec. 14/1 Most Swedish companies must have at least two elected representatives of workers on their boards of directors... Yet there was general agreement that the work place is the last bastion of totalitarianism in an otherwise democratic society.

totality (təʊ'tælɪtɪ). [ad. Schol.L. *tōtālitās* (*a* 1141 in Hugo de S. Victor, also in Albertus Magnus, Aquinas, Duns Scotus), f. *tōtālis* TOTAL: cf. F. *totalité* (14th c. in Hatz.-Darm.).]

1. The quality of being total; entirety.

1627 DONNE *Serm.* xliv. (1640) 443 God the Father, God the Son, and God the Holy Ghost, whom this day we celebrate, in the Ingenuity, and in the Assiduity, and in the Totality, recommended in this text. **1684** BAXTER *Answ. Theol. Dial.* 4 We will not be cheated by it to believe that it causeth any more than Totality or Integrality. *c* **1819** COLERIDGE in *Rem.* (1836) II. 149 Instead of unity of action I should greatly prefer the more appropriate, though scholastic and uncouth, words homogeneity, proportionateness, and totality of interest. **1869** INGLEBY *Introd. Metaph.* II. ii. 171, I remark, *obiter*, that Totality is plurality in unity.

b. *Astron.* Total obscuration of the sun or moon in an eclipse; the moment of occurrence or time of duration of this.

1842 G. B. AIRY in *Mem. R. Astron. Soc.* (1846) XV. 12 About six minutes before the totality. *Ibid.* Plate ii. Fig. 1 Appearance of the sun a short time before totality. **1860** F. GALTON in *Vac. Tour.* 439 About twenty-five minutes before totality they gave place to our wishes. **1871** TYNDALL *Fragm. Sc.* (1879) I. vi. 208 The appearance of the corona and prominences at the moment of totality.

2. That which is total; a whole; the total number or amount, the aggregate.

1598 FLORIO, *Totalita*, a totalitie or whole sum. **1602** WARNER *Alb. Eng.* XIII. lxxix. (1612) 327 Whence, and to which Totalitie begins and ends alone. **1654** JER. TAYLOR *Real Pres.* xi. 224 There is a new heap of impossibilities, if we should reckon that which flowes from the multiplication of totalities. **1660** R. COKE *Justice Vind.* 35 The will of the major part cannot be the will of the totality, but plurality. **1789** GOUV. MORRIS in Sparks *Life & Writ.* (1832) I. 336 The totality of the public debt here is about 4,700,000,000 livres. **1864** BOWEN *Logic* iv. (1870) 76 'The universe'.. means only the totality of that class of objects which we are thinking of. **1884** H. SPENCER in *Contemp. Rev.* XLVI. 33 The totality of all powers and rights originally existed as an undivided whole in the sovereign people.

totali'zation. [f. TOTALIZE *v.*: see -ATION. Cf. F. *totalisation* (neologism in Littré).] The action or process of totalizing, or the condition of being totalized; calculation of the total.

1888 *Sci. Amer.* 29 Dec. 404/1 The totalization of the slight liftings due to the repetition of this maneuver on each of the cables finally effected a general lifting of four inches. *Mod.*, The totalization of the returns from different parts.

totalizator ('təʊtəlaɪzeɪtə(r)). [f. as if from a L. **totalizāre* to totalize: prob. ad. mod.F. *totalisateur* (1869 in Littré, in scientific use).]

1. A machine or apparatus for registering and showing the total of operations, measurements, etc.; *spec.* an apparatus for registering and indicating the number of tickets sold to betters on each horse in a race; also, on each greyhound, etc., in a race; also, a system of betting based on the totalizator.

1879 *S. Australian Independ. & Presbyt.* Nov., The passing through Parliament of the Totalizator Bill—a measure to legalise a certain form of betting. **1881** *Standard* 7 Sept. 5/2 'Paris mutuals'.. would perhaps be better understood by English people under their other appellation of 'totalisators', instruments much in vogue upon the race-courses of Australia. **1885** *Q. Rev.* Oct. 455 A board is exhibited, containing the names of the horses starting. A person who wishes to back a horse pays in a pound, or as many pounds as he likes, to the officer in charge of the totalisator. When the race is over, all the money staked is divided between the backers of the winning horse, less ten per cent, which is the profit of the management. **1890** *Times* 26 Feb. 5/3 The Lower House of the Reichsrath to-day adopted a resolution in favour of increasing the tax on the totalisator, or *pari-mutuel*, used on Austrian race-courses, from 3 to 5 per cent. **1910** *Encycl. Brit.* III. 827/1 On all French racecourses.., a system of betting known as the *Pari-Mutuel* or Totalizator, is carried on. **1935** *Encycl. Sports* 321/1 In 1931 and 1932 most of the licensed tracks in England were equipped with the most up-to-date all-electric totalisators; but in the February of 1933, following a High Court decision of December 17, 1932, that a totalisator on a greyhound track constituted a place within the meaning of the Act, these machines ceased to operate. **1975** *Oxf. Compan. Sports & Games* 445/2 Punters betting with a totalisator endeavour to select the dog or dogs they think will either win or obtain a place.

2. *Comb.*: **Totalizator Agency Board**, in Australia and New Zealand, an official organization, with local offices, for off-course betting on horses.

1950 *N.Z. Statutes 1949* 496 There shall be a board to be known as the Totalizator Agency Board. **1957** D. Glover *Since Then* 16 We are equals all in the sight of the Lord And the Totalizator Agency Board. **1957** *Weekly News* (Auckland, N.Z.) 6 Nov. 48/1 With the virtual extermination of the illegal bookmaker in the Dominion and the establishment of the Totalisator Agency Board as a firm medium for off-course bettors. **1983** *Austral. Encycl.* (ed. 4) X. 75 In Australia, the Totalizator Agency Boards are the government agencies which control legal off-course betting in the respective States and in the Australian Capital Territory.

totalize ('təʊtəlaɪz), *v.* [f. total *a.* + -ize: cf. F. *totaliser* (neologism in Littré).] *trans.* To make total; to combine into a total or aggregate. Hence **'totalized** *ppl. a.*; **'totalizing** *vbl. sb.* and *ppl. a.*; ***totalizing machine***, a totalizator.

1818 Coleridge in *Rem.* (1836) I. 223 To place these images totalized and fitted to the limits of the human mind so as to elicit from..the forms themselves the moral reflexions to which they approximate. **1855** Bain *Senses & Int.* iii. ii. §33 (1864) 525 This force, or impulse, of mind that resists the totalizing influence of a complex object, and isolates for study and comparison its individual effects. **1865** Grote *Treat. Mor. Ideas* iv. (1876) 43 A number of partial views which we cannot harmonize and totalize or bring into a whole. **1888** *Daily News* 27 Aug. 3/5 [At Baden] Betting is now strictly prohibited, except by the medium of the totalising machine, which is worked under State supervision. **1888** *Sci. Amer.* 29 Dec. 404/1 The cables.. constituted a totalizing apparatus that permitted of moving million-pound masses by means of..successive stresses never exceeding 15 tons.

'totalizer. [f. prec. + -er[1].] That which totalizes; in quot. = totalizator.

1887 *Daily News* 18 Apr. 3/6 The Jockey Club and the National Steeplechase Society have applied for permission to make use of the betting-machines known as 'totalisers', which are in use throughout the Continent.

totally ('təʊtəlɪ), *adv.* [f. total *a.* + -ly[2]: cf. Schol.L. *tōtāliter*, OF. *totalement* (Oresme, 14th c.).] In a total manner or degree; wholly, completely, entirely, altogether.

1509 Hawes *Past. Pleas.* xliv. (Percy Soc.) 216 Lyke as the worlde was distroyed totally By the virgins sone, so it semed well A virgins sone to redeme it pyteously. **1647** Clarendon *Hist. Reb.* i. §32 The Imprudence and Presumption..of carrying the Prince into Spain, was totally Forgotten. **1660** Blount *Boscobel* 23 Thus was the Royal Army totally subdued, thus dispersed. **1711** Addison *Spect.* No. 121 ¶6 Tho' the Mole be not totally blind (as it is commonly thought). **1815** W. H. Ireland *Scribbleomania* 30 *note*, He seems to be at present totally eclipsed by Walter Scott. **1882** Mrs. Pitman *Mission L. Greece & Pal.* 155 It is totally beyond human effort to control the memory.

†**b.** In a body, collectively, in one lot. *Obs. rare.*

1676 *Lond. Gaz.* No. 1073/4 Divers Watches and Pocket Clocks..are to be Sold, either totally or severally, at his late shop,..on the back-side of the Royal Exchange, London.

†**totangle.** *Obs. nonce-wd.* [f. L. *tōt-us* whole, entire + *angulus*, angle *sb.*[2]] A figure that is 'all angle': applied to a circle as the limit of regular polygonal figures when the number of angles is infinite.

1628 Jackson *Creed* vi. xxi. §3 The circle likewise is as truly ἰσόπλευρος and ἰσογώνιος, of equal sides and equal angles, as ὁλόπλευρος and ὁλογώνιος, a totangle or totilater.

totanine ('tɒtənaɪn), *a. Ornith.* [f. mod.L. *Totanīnæ* f. *Totan-us*, name of a genus of birds, including the redshanks: see -ine[1].] Of or pertaining to the *Totaninæ*, a subfamily of the *Scolopacidæ*; called by some the tattlers (tattler 3).

‖**totara** ('təʊtərə, təʊ'tɑːrə). Also *erron.* totarra. [Maori *to'tăra* (Morris).] A large New Zealand coniferous tree, *Podocarpus Totara*, producing light, durable, tough timber of a dark red colour, highly valued for building, piles, cabinet work, etc.

1832 G. Bennett in Lambert *Genus Pinus* II. 190 (Morris) This is an unpublished species of *Podocarpus*, called Totara by the natives. **1840** J. S. Polack *Mann. & Cust. N. Zealanders* I. xx. 227 The *totarra* or red-pine. **1860** Donaldson *Bush Lays* 38 A ponderous totara down on them doth bear. **1872** A. Domett *Ranolf* vi. i. 107 One lone totára-tree that grew Beneath the hill-side. **1892** E. Reeves *Homeward Bound* 73 Totara piles immersed in salt water for forty years have been taken up at Wellington sound as the day they were put down.

tote (təʊt), *sb.*[1] Now *dial.* Also *Sc.* tot (tɔːt, toːt). [Short for *total*: cf. tot *sb.*[3]]

1. The total amount, number, or sum. Mostly in pleonastic phrase ***the whole tote***.

1771–2 *Ess. fr. Batchelor* (1773) II. 40 That this was the whole tote of his case is notoriously known. **1774** Foote *Cozeners* iii. Wks. 1799 II. 180 My bill?..what is the tote? *a* **1801** R. Gall *Poems, Tint Quey* (1819) 37 Where the hale tot, for fear o' skaith, Were fley'd to speak aboon their breath. **1810** Bentham *Mem. & Corr.* Wks. 1843 X. 460 Let me have the whole tote. **1825** J. Neal *Bro. Jonathan* III. 384 Our gals—the whole tote of them. **1830** Galt *Lawrie T.* i. iv, Only myself of the whole tot was accustomed to the handling of iron. **1905** in *Eng. Dial. Dict.* (from Northumbld. to E. Anglia and Cornwall, with long *ō*).

2. Dial. and colloq. abbrev. of *total abstainer* (also *tot*). Also *colloq.* (orig. *Austral.*) of totalizator; *loosely*, a lottery; hence ***tote board, double, -man, -shop, ticket***.

c **1870** *Music Hall Song* (Farmer), By all of his mates called the Tote. **1887** Mather *Nor'ard of the Dogger* 239 The fishermen are all 'totes'. **1891** E. Kinglake *Australian at H.* 74 Altogether, bookmakers, 'tote' proprietors, sweep promotors, in spite of occasional fines of £50 and £100.. drive a roaring trade in Australia. **1901** *Westm. Gaz.* 8 Mar. 5/1 One of his audience called out: 'Are you a 'tot.'?' 'Yes', the Bishop replied. 'All right, go on, then; if you wasn't I wouldn't listen to you'. **1902** *Ibid.* 25 July 1/3 You..walk into the money order department and deposit the amount you would have invested on the Tote. **1906** *Daily Chron.* 3 Aug 4/7 Nearly 2,000..entering the gambling dens or 'tote-shops'. **1926** *Spectator* 9 Jan. 45/2 The 'tote' goes steadily on and the bookies do a roaring trade secretly. **1927** *Glasgow Herald* 30 Apr. 9 Information will be given on the legal and practical aspects of the 'tote'. **1930** *Cambridge Daily News* 25 Sept. 5/7 In the Tote Double on the 2.30..the winning dividend was £10 13s. 9d. **1933** *Sun* (Baltimore) 3 May 14/4 (*heading*) Ticket a second expected of electric 'tote' at racing meet. **1945** *Daily Herald* 31 Aug. 3/4 A fraud by which a considerable sum..was obtained with forged Tote tickets at Harringay Greyhound Stadium..is thought to have been carefully planned by a gang. **1950** *Amer. Speech* XXV. 304/2 A tote board is a board where odds, payoffs, time of race and numbers of winners are posted in electric lights. **1966** *Listener* 27 Oct. 605/1 Further along there was a board showing the latest stock prices on Wall Street:..Zurichers watch them in much the same spirit as race-goers watch the tote. **1974** *Times* 26 Nov. 16/4 Young women were selling tote tickets through the window. **1975** *Ox. Compan. Sports & Games* 495/2 The Tote also operates 'doubles', 'trebles', and 'jack-pot' prizes for correct forecasts. **1976** *Star* (Sheffield) 30 Nov., The money was raised through totes and the fund is being wound up with a final pay-out because income was not enough to keep it going. **1977** *N.Z. Herald* 5 Jan. 2-8/4 The tote at Ellerslie, in line with the general trend this year, was up 22 per cent.

tote (təʊt), *sb.*[2] Also 9 toat. [app. f. *tote*, obs. and dial. form of toot *v.*[1] to project, stick out. (R. Holme belonged to Cheshire, where the vb. is still *tote*.)] The handle of a carpenter's plane.

1678 Moxon *Mech. Exerc.* iv. 61 A Fore Plain. *a* The Tote. **1688** R. Holme *Armoury* iii. 352/2 All the difference is in the Tote or Handle, which every Workman maketh according to his own Fancy. **1823** P. Nicholson *Pract. Build.* 243. **1873** *Routledge's Yng. Gentl. Mag.* July 503/1 The handle [of a jack plane] is called a toat or horn. **1901** *J. Black's Illustr. Carp. & Build., Home Handicr.* 10 The jack plane is used by grasping the 'tote', or handle, firmly with the right hand, placing the left hand on the fore part of the plane [etc.].

†**tote,** *sb.*[3] *Obs. rare*[−1]. Of doubtful origin and meaning; recorded only in the passage quoted. Prob. = MDu. *tote*, pl. *toten*, 'the point or toe of a shoe'; from the same root as prec.

The suggestion has also been made that *totez* is a verb (viz. *tote*, toot *v.*[1]), and that *toez* or *totz* 'toes' has been omitted before it, the reading being *his toez totez oute* 'his toes peep out': cf. *his ton toteden oute* 'his toes peeped out' (*P. Pl. Crede* 425).

13.. *E.E. Allit. P.* B. 41 His tabarde to-torne and his totez oute.

tote, *sb.*[4] [f. tote *v.*] **a.** An act of carrying or transporting (Webster, 1911). **b.** *ellipt.* = *tote bag* below.

1959 *Sears, Roebuck Catal.* Spring-Summer 68 Cowhide Bag... 2 side zip pockets in this top-zipper tote. Rayon lined. **1967** *Observer* 24 Dec. 15/7 A Twiggy Fashion Tote, 'for shopping and surfing'. **1979** *Kingston* (Ontario) *Whig-Standard* 5 Apr. 24/6 Remember that an open bag, like a tote may make access to its contents easier for you, but it also means access is easier for a pickpocket.

c. tote bag, a large hand-bag or shoulder-bag; **tote box**, a portable box for small items.

1900 in *N. & Q.* (1904) 27 Aug. 162/1 The Watson *Tote Bag..best thing..for carrying coat, camera,..lunch, &c. **1969** *Daily Colonist* (Victoria, B.C.) 24 Sept. 2/6 Tote Bags —Great for knitting supplies, shopping. **1982** M. Millar *Mermaid* x. 108 A girl entered, carrying an oversized canvas tote bag with the name Gretchen printed on it. **1917** *Machinery* (N.Y.) July 957/1 The New Britain Machine Co. ..makes these *tote boxes of steel, and they are designed in such a way that they may be stacked up to economize in floor space. **1951** Urquhart & Boyle *Materials Handling Case Bk.* 7/1 If the parts are small and are handled in a tote box, then each operator must: 1. Position the totebox of pieces to be worked [etc.]. **1966** *Guardian* 18 Apr. 6/1 Tote boxes are also available with cushion tops and back cushions.

tote (təʊt), *v. colloq.* (orig. *U.S.*) Also toat. [In current use 1676–7; origin unascertained.

For an alleged Negro origin there is no foundation; the quot. 1676–7 from Virginia does not refer to Negroes; later the word is found well-established in the New England States; evidence for an Indian origin is also wanting.]

a. *trans.* To carry as a burden or load; to transport, esp. supplies to, or timber, etc. from, a logging-camp or the like. Also, to wear or carry regularly as part of one's equipment; to take (a person) with one; ***to tote fair***, to carry one's fair share; *fig.* to act or deal fairly or honestly.

For catena of quots. see Mr. A. Matthews in *N. and Q.* 10th Ser. II. 161, and Thornton *Amer. Gloss.* s.v.

1676–7 (Feb.) *Grievances of Glouc. Co.* (Va.), (Col. Office Rec., P.R.O. 5/1371, p. 326), They [Governor's out-guard] were by Beverly comanded to goe to work, fall trees and mawle and toat rails, which many..refusing to doe, he presently disarm'd them. **1769** *Boston Gaz.* 7 Aug. 3/2 The next Morning he was toated on board the Rippon, in a Canoe..or some other small boat. **1781** J. Witherspoon *Wks.* (1802) IV. 470 *Tot* is used for *carry*, in some of the southern states. **1803** J. Davis *Trav. U.S.* 389, I..cart all the wood, tote the wheat to the mill. *Note*, Tote is the American for to carry. **1807** W. Irving *Life & Lett.* (1864) I. 189 At Baltimore I made a stay of two days, during which I was toted about town. **1809** *Monthly Anthology* VII. 264 *Tote* is marked by Mr. Webster 'Virg.' But we believe it a native vulgarism of Massachusetts. **1812** J. J. Henry *Camp. agst. Quebec* 38 (Arnold's Exped. 1775) We slided glibly along, over passages where a few days previously, we had toted our canoes. **1823** J. A. Quitman in J. F. H. Claiborne *Life Quitman* (1860) I. 85 The belles..'tote' their fans with the air of Spanish señoritas. **1828** J. Hall in *Western Souvenir for 1829* 269 This is a poor shooting-iron..it might do for young men to 'tote' in a settlement, but it is of no use in the woods. **1852** Mrs. Stowe *Uncle Tom's C.* vii, Is that ar man going to tote them bar'ls over to-night? **1866** C. H. Smith *Bill Arp, so Called* 147, I don't think you tote fair. **1883** A. Forbes in *Contemp. Rev.* Oct. 605 His lordship and the lady had toted the trunk on to a cart. **1892** Kipling *Barrack-r. Ballads* 117 The Government Bullock Train toted its load. **1896** *Current Hist.* (Buffalo, N.Y.) VI. 865 The trust maintained a regular force of inspectors to keep all the members of the pool 'toting fair'. **1909** R. Parrish *My Lady of South* viii. 95 Thar warn't many Danielses left able ter tote a gun. **1909** H. G. Wells *Tono-Bungay* ii. iii. 194 The old merchant used to tote about commodities. **1952** C. Day Lewis tr. *Virgil's Aeneid* iv. 89 One who, men say, totes round his home-gods Everywhere. **1975** *Nation* 20 Dec. 659/1 Others wear official-looking uniforms and tote service revolvers. **1977** C. McCullough *Thorn Birds* vi. 110 He toted the infants with easy familiarity. **1979** *Chatelaine* (Canada) Jan. 24/3, I toted a canvas bag over one shoulder. **1983** E. Reveley *In Good Faith* iii. 59 They still tote the two original evangelists around with them but I think that's mostly so's they can keep getting money from the mother church.

b. The verb-stem in combination with a sb.; as ***tote-pole, -team, -wagon***; **tote-load** (see quot. 1859); **tote-road**, a rough temporary road for conveying goods to or from a settlement, camp, etc.

1857 Thoreau *Maine W.* (1894) 296–7 The Indian was greatly surprised that we should have taken what he called a 'tow' (i.e., tote or toting or supply) road, instead of a carry path. **1859** Bartlett *Dict. Americanisms*, *Tote-load*, as much as one can carry. *Southern.* **1887** M. Roberts *West. Avernus* 71 On this 'toat' or freight-road the wagons went east during one part of the day and west during the other. **1895** F. A. C. Emerson in *Century Mag.* July 478/2 One might visit every one of the hundreds of logging camps [in Maine]..and he would find each one furnished with its separate 'tote road', 'tote team' and 'toter'.

Hence **'toter**, one engaged in toting, a carrier, teamster, etc.; **'toting** *vbl. sb.*

1857 Toting [see b. above]. **1860** Olmsted *Journ. Back Country* i. 48 Each gang was attended by a 'water-toter'. **1895** Toter [see b. above]. **1911** *Blackw. Mag.* Sept. 362/2 So accustomed are some of them to this 'toting' of loads.

tote, var. toot *sb.*[1]; obs. or dial. f. toot *v.*[1]

†**to-'tear,** *v. Obs.* Forms: see tear *v.*[1] [OE. *to-teran*, f. to-[2] + *teran*, tear *v.*[1] So MHG. *zerzern*.] *trans.* To tear to pieces.

c **893** [see to-tee]. *a* **900** *Ags. Ps.* (Th.) xxix. 11 þu totære min hwite hrægl. *c* **1000** Ælfric *Hom.* II. 238 Ða næddran hi totæron. *c* **1205** Lay. 4994 Heo nom hire on anne curtel þe wes swiðe to-toren [*c* **1275** al to-tore]. *a* **1225** *Ancr. R.* 84 Ȝet wolde he teteren & pileken, mid his bile, roted stinkinde fleshs. **13..** *K. Alis.* 4658 Alisaundre his clothes to-tare. *c* **1380** Wyclif *Serm.* Sel. Wks. II. 204 þis spirit..al to-teerynge him, wente oute from him. *c* **1440** *Partonope* 4452 Why be your clothes thus to tore? *c* **1485** *Digby Myst.* (1882) iv. 305 The tormentours..With sharp scowrges te-terre his fleshe. **1520** *Treat. Galaunt* (W. de W.) xiv, In our wanton werynge of clothes to-torne. **1605** Sylvester *Du Bartas* ii. iii. 111. *Law* 784 Their shields, and staves, and chariots (all-to-tore).

†**to-'tee,** *v. Obs.* [OE. *to-téon*, f. to-[2] + *teon*, tee *v.*[1] to draw, pull. So OHG. *ziziohan*, MHG. *zerziehen*.] *trans.* To pull to pieces.

c **893** K. Ælfred *Oros.* iii. xi. §3, & his æfterfolȝeras feowertiene ȝear hit siþþan totuȝon & totæron. *a* **1000** *Ags. Ps.* (Th.) cxxiii. 5 þam þe us mid toðum toteon woldan. *c* **1175** *Lamb. Hom.* 9 Ac me þe sculde nimen and al to-teon mid horse. **13..** *Guy Warw.* (A.) 517 Al mine limes it wil to-te. **13..** in *Rowland & V.* (1836) p. xxiii, Ther men might reuthe y-sen, Mani baroun her here to ten.

totel, -er, var. tutel, -er *Obs.*, to whisper.

totem ('təʊtəm), *sb.* Also 8 totam, 9 otem. [From Odjibewa, or some kindred Algonkin dialect. Mentioned (apparently) in 1609 by Lescarbot as *aoutem* (in Acadia); by Long 1791 as *totam*, by Henry *a* 1776, Cooper 1826, Catlin 1841, as *totem*, by Rev. P. Jones (a native Odjibewa) 1861, as *toodaim*, by Francis Assikinak (an Ottawa Indian) as *Ododam*, while the Abbé Thavenel gives the simple form as *ote*, 'the possessive of which is *otem*'. The initial *t* is explained by some as the final letter of a prec. possessive pronoun. The meaning given by most of these is 'mark'; by the younger Henry 'tribe'; Thavenel gives 'mark' and 'family or tribe', app. meaning 'that which marks the family or tribe'. Lescarbot and Long explain it as applied to a familiar spirit.]

1. a. Among the American Indians: The hereditary mark, emblem, or badge of a tribe, clan, or group of Indians, consisting of a figure or representation of some animal, less commonly a plant or other natural object, after which the group is named; thus sometimes used to denote the tribe, clan, or division of a 'nation', having such a mark; also applied to the animal or natural object itself, sometimes considered to be ancestrally or fraternally related to the clan, being spoken of as a brother or sister, and treated as an object of friendly regard, or sometimes even as incarnating a guardian spirit who may be appealed to or worshipped.

[**1609** LESCARBOT *Hist. Nouvelle France* vi. 683 Son dæmon appellé Aoutem, lequel ceux de Canada nomment Cudonagni.] **1760–76** A. HENRY (the elder) *Travels* (1809) 305 To these are added his badge, called, in the Algonquin tongue, a totem, and which is in the nature of an armorial bearing. **1791** J. LONG *Voy. Indian Interpr.* 86 One part of the religious superstition of the Savages, consists in each of them having his *totam*, or favourite spirit, which he believes watches over him. This *totam* they conceive assumes the shape of some beast or other, and therefore they never kill, hunt, or eat the animal whose form they think this totam bears. *Ibid.*, One of them, whose totam was a bear. **1799–1808** A. HENRY (the younger) *Journals* (1897) I. 106 Should he not belong to the clan (totem). **1826** F. COOPER *Mohicans* (1829) II. x. 162 There was one chief of his party who carried the beaver as his peculiar symbol, or 'totem'. **1841** CATLIN *N. Amer. Ind.* II. liv. 168 Here are to be seen (and will continue to be seen for ages to come), the totems and arms of the different tribes, who have visited this place for ages past. *Ibid.* 170 We [a Mandan chief and his tribe] left our *totems* as marks on the rocks. We cut them deep in the stones, they are there now. **1851** SCHOOLCRAFT *Indian Tribes* 294 A single element in the system attracted early notice. I allude to the institution of the Totem, which has been well known among the Algonquin tribes from the settlement of Canada. **1855** LONGF. *Hiaw.*, *Picture Writing* 23 From what old, ancestral Totem, Be it Eagle, Bear, or Beaver, They descended, this we know not. **1865** J. G. HODGINS *Hist. Canada* 101 The *totem*, or outline of some animal, (from *do-daim*, a family mark,) was always the chief's signature to a treaty. **1861** P. JONES *Hist. Ojebways* 138 Each 'nation' is subdivided into a number of tribes or clans called 'toodaims', and each tribe is distinguished by certain animals or things, as for instance: the Ojebway nations have the following toodaims:—the Eagle, Reindeer, Otter, Bear, Buffalo, Beaver, Catfish, Pike, Birch-bark, White Oak Tree, Bear's liver, etc., etc. The Mohawk nation have only three divisions or tribes—the Turtle, the Bear, and the Wolf. **1865** TYLOR *Early Hist. Man.* x. 281 The Indian tribes are usually divided into clans, each distinguished by a *totem* (Algonquin *do-daim*, that is 'town-mark') which is commonly some animal, as a bear, wolf, deer, etc., and may be compared on the one hand to a crest, and on the other to a surname. **1885** CLODD *Myths & Dr.* I. vi. 106 The Dacotahs would neither kill nor eat their totems. **1887** L. OLIPHANT *Episodes* 72 Twelve of these placed their totems opposite my signature; each totem consisting of the rude representation of a bear, a deer, an otter, a rat, or some other wild animal. **1893** A. LANG *Custom & Myth* 105 Prof. Max Müller (Academy, Jan., 1884) says the word should be, not Totem, but Ote or Otem. Mr. Tylor's enquiries among the Red Men support this.

b. By anthropologists the name has been extended to refer to other peoples and tribes, which (though they may not use totem marks) are similarly divided into groups or clans named after animals, etc.; such animals, animal-names, or animal-named groups, being spoken or written of as their totems, and their organization, their complex system of mutual and marriage relations and religious usages, being styled TOTEMISM, q.v.

There are also said to be among certain races (as the Australian Aboriginals) *sex-totems*, peculiar to men or to women, and *personal totems*, pertaining to the individual and not hereditary.

[**1851–9** PRICHARD in *Man. Sci. Enq.* 263 The institution of the *Totem* as it was termed among the North American nations has its counterpart among the nations of Australia.] **1874** LUBBOCK in *Manch. Sci. Lect.* Ser. v. & VI. 248 In Australia we seem to find the Totem, or, as it is there called, the 'kobong', in the very process of deification. **1879** A. LANG in *Academy* 11 Jan. 24/3 A man or woman is born of such or such a totem, and choice has nothing whatever to do with the matter. **1883** —— in *Contemp. Rev.* Sept. 415 The totem was but a badge worn by all the persons who found themselves existing in close relations. **1887** J. G. FRAZER *Totemism* 52–3 Clearly these sex totems are not to be confounded with clan totems... The sex totem seems to be still more sacred than the clan totem; for men who do not object to other people killing their clan totem will fiercely defend their sex totem against any attempt of the opposite sex to injure it. **1888** —— in *Encycl. Brit.* XXIII. 467/1 A totem is a class of material objects which a savage regards with superstitious respect, believing that there exists between him and every member of the class an intimate and altogether special relation. **1905** *Athenæum* 21 Jan. 87/1 They have no special word answering to 'totem' for such animals. *Ibid.*, M. van Gennep.. uses 'totem' only in the sense of the hereditary name-giving animal or other object of the kin. **1909** tr. *Hopf's Hum. Species* 300 The necessity for setting up sub-totems first arose from the great extension of the totem in a single tribe, and it was convenient to take the sub-totem from the father who transferred his totem-name to his son.

c. *fig.*

1890 *Pall Mall G.* 30 June 7/2 The vulgar embroidered smoking-cap, which used to be the distinctive totem of the bazaar debauchee. **1893** *Times* 11 May 9/5 Mr. Bryce, whose totem is very different, threatened the Unionists that their vote against a bogus second chamber would be remembered against them.

d. *ellipt.* = *totem-pole* (*a*), esp. in fig. phr. ***low on the totem***. *colloq.*

1974 K. MILLETT *Flying* (1975) II. 167 Counting on faculty privilege. Almost too low on the totem even to deserve it. **1977** D. BAGLEY *Enemy* xviii. 148 'What's your status here?' 'Low man on the bloody totem... I have a line into the Embassy but that's for emergency use only.'

2. *attrib.* and *Comb.*, as ***totem ancestor***, ***animal***, ***clan***, ***figure***, ***god***, ***group***, ***kin***, ***name***, ***people***, ***plant***, ***soul***, ***stage***, ***system***, ***tree***, ***worship***, etc.: **totem exogamy**, the custom of marrying only one of a different totem or totem-clan; **totem-pole**, (*a*) a post carved and painted with totem figures, erected by the Indians of the north-west of North America in front of their houses; also *fig.*, esp. in colloq. phr. ***low on the totem pole***, of lowly status (see also sense 1 d); (*b*) *Electronics*, an arrangement of two output transistors or valves in which one takes the place of the load of the other, the output being taken from between the two; also **totem-post**; **totem-stone**, a stone with markings supposed to be prehistoric totemic figures.

1869 M'LENNAN in *Fortn. Rev.* Oct. 408 Men in, what we may call, the Totem stage of developement. **1870** *Ibid.* Feb. 213 The tribesmen.. esteem themselves as of the species of the Totem-god. **1871** TYLOR *Prim. Cult.* II. xv. 213 Some accounts describing the totem-animal as being actually regarded as the sacred object. *Ibid.* 214 Considering it [animal-worship] as inherited from an early totem-stage of society. *Ibid.* 215 The systematic division of a whole people into a number of totem-clans. **1872** MORLEY *Voltaire* v. 241 The needs and aspirations.. of the developed polytheist [would not be satisfied] by totem-worship. **1880** S. JACKSON *Alaska & Missions on North Pacific Coast* ix. 263 Daylight found us near Fort Tongas... From the water there seemed to be a whole forest of.. *totem* poles. **1882** *Athenæum* 22 Apr. 501/3 Even ethnologists.. will maintain that the totem-kin became the *gens*. **1888** J. G. FRAZER in *Encycl. Brit.* XXIII. 468/1 The Bechuanas in South Africa.. have a well-developed totem system. *Ibid.* 470/1 The fundamental rules of totem societies. *Ibid.* 470/2 The Australian ceremony at initiation of pretending to recall a dead man to life by the utterance of his totem name. **1889** W. ROBERTSON SMITH *Relig. Semites* viii. 276 Among totem peoples.. the sacred animal is forbidden food, it is akin to the men who acknowledge its sanctity. **1891** *Cent. Dict.* s.v., Totem Posts, Canadian Pacific Coast. **1896** F. B. JEVONS *Introd. Hist. Relig.* xx. 294 The sacramental eating first of totem-animals and then of totem-plants. **1897** B. W. JAMES *Alaska* 75 It has ever been an unanswerable question as to the origin of these totem poles. **1901** *Athenæum* 7 Dec. 779/1 Mr. N. W. Thomas exhibited a collection of 'totem-stones'. **1902** *Folk-Lore* Dec. 363 To savage reasoners, the totem-soul may perhaps seem to tenant each plant or animal of its species. **1907** C. HILL-TOUT *Brit. N. Amer., Far West* ix. 177 The family or kin totem-figures which are customarily carved on the beams or painted on the sides of their houses. **1910** SELIGMANN *Melanesians of Brit. N. Guinea* Introd. 10 Totem exogamy is still generally observed. **1910** A. F. CHAMBERLAIN in *Encycl. Brit.* XIV. 470/1 The wood art of the Indians of the North Pacific coast (masks, utensils, houses, totem-poles, furniture, &c.). **1937** *Jrnl. Anthrop. Inst.* XL. 413 It is thus clear that the gi is nothing other than the totem-ancestor. **1940** L. MACNEICE *Last Ditch* 18 And under the totem poles—the ancient terror—between the enormous fluted Ionic columns There seeps.. The guttural sorrow of the refugees. **1945** *Sun* (Baltimore) 3 Sept. 1/7 The lowest brass to sign the surrender documents was Colonel L. Moore Cosgrave... 'He's low man on the totem pole,' murmured an Australian correspondent. **1949** J. CAMPBELL *Hero with Thousand Faces* 390 An unconscious identification took place, and this was finally rendered conscious in the half human, half-animal, figures of the mythological totem-ancestors. **1967** *Electronics* 6 Mar. 155/2 High leakage of the multiple-emitter transistor may load a circuit excessively. To offset this.. the totem pole output stage is used. **1973** 'B. MATHER' *Snowline* iii. 36 Just how far up the Departmental totem pole was Hallaby? **1978** *Jrnl. R. Soc. Arts* CXXVI. 456/2 In looking at the heritage of ideas or values we are looking at the totem poles of the heritage, symbols that are of more importance to us for what they represent than for themselves. **1978** D. BAGLEY *Flyaway* xxxiii. 311 Kissack.. was pretty low on the totem pole—a hired hand. **1981** P. M. CHIRLIAN *Analysis & Design Integrated Electronic Circuits* v. 114 The load resistance of Fig. 5–10 has been replaced by an enhancement MOSFET. This 'load' is called an active load or active pull-up... The circuit is also called a totem pole because the elements are drawn one above the other in the schematic diagram.

Hence **ˈtotem** *v.*, *trans.* to draw, paint, or tattoo (a totem mark).

1894 S. JACKSON *Educ. in Alaska* in *Educ. Rep.* (U.S.) 1891–2, 890 Some [Tchuktchi men] have a small mark or figure totemed on their cheek.

totemic (təʊˈtɛmɪk), *a.* [f. prec. + -IC.] Of, pertaining to, or of the nature of a totem or totems; characterized by or having totems.

1846 H. R. SCHOOLCRAFT *Notes on Iroquois* 79 It will be necessary to go back, and examine.. the curious and intricate principles of the Totemic Bond. **1865** LUBBOCK *Preh. Times* xiv. (1878) 528 The totemic tie that binds relationships together. **1867** PARKMAN *Jesuits N. Amer.* Introd. (1875) 68 The names of the totemic clans, borrowed in nearly every case from animals. **1885** CLODD *Myths & Dr.* I. vi. 99 The belief of the Moquis of Arizona, that after death they live in the form of their totemic animal. **1905** *Athenæum* 21 Jan. 87/1 Mr. Haddon derives totemic names from such surnames as 'Eaters of Turtle'. **1906** *Ibid.* 17 Mar. 332 There are many tabous on food which are certainly not totemic in origin.

Hence **toˈtemically** *adv.*, in reference to totems or totemism; after the manner of a totem.

1902 *Folk-Lore* Dec. 373 Two cases in which Australian totem-groups averred that they were named totemically after a small species of opossum. **1910** *Athenæum* 11 June 707/3 We may regard Africa, totemically speaking, as an unexplored continent.

totemism (ˈtəʊtəmɪz(ə)m). [f. TOTEM + -ISM.] The use of totems, with the clan division, and the social, marriage, and religious customs connected with it.

1791 J. LONG *Voy. Indian Interpr.* 87 This idea of destiny, or, if I may be allowed the phrase, 'totamism',.. is not confined to the Savages. **1870** LUBBOCK *Orig. Civiliz.* v. (1875) 199 Nature-worship or Totemism, in which natural objects are worshipped. **1883** A. LANG in *Contemp. Rev.* Sept. 414 Totemism is the name for the custom by which a stock (scattered through many local tribes) claims descent from some plant, animal, or other natural object. *Ibid.*, Totemism.. is a widespread institution prevailing all over the north of the American continent. **1905** *Westm. Gaz.* 13 Dec. 3/1 Here is the beginning of totemism—'the bearing of the name of an object by a human group', as Mr. Howitt says. 'Naming' is the 'original germ', says Mr. Lang, 'of totemism'.

ˈtotemist. [f. TOTEM + -IST.]

1. One who belongs to a totem clan, or has a totem.

1881 *Cornh. Mag.* Sept. 332 Our Aryan ancestor in person was a most undoubted totemist. **1883** F. SEEBOHM *Eng. Vill. Community* 362 The hasty conclusion that the Saxons were 'totemists'. **1887** A. LANG *Myth, Ritual & Relig.* I. 73 Totemists.. spare the beasts that are their own.. kin. **1905** *Athenæum* 21 Jan. 87/1 If the people were once true totemists, the traces thereof are indistinct.

2. One who is versed in the history of totemism.

1897 *Edin. Rev.* July 239 Some of the highest authorities on the myths and customs of savage races are by no means on the side of the thoroughgoing totemist. **1902** *Folk-Lore* Dec. 361, I am not aware that any totemists do make this assertion.

So **toteˈmistic** *a.*, of, pertaining to, or characterized by totemism.

1873 *Fortn. Rev.* May 631 They have lost whatever meaning their totemistic forefathers may have had. **1881** *Sat. Rev.* 12 Feb. 216/2 Why were the 'primary divisions', as Mr. Fison says they were, totemistic? **1882** *Athenæum* 22 Apr. 502/1 While Huitzilopochtli had many features of the magician, he had also elemental and totemistic sides to his complex nature. **1884** *Pall Mall G.* 18 Oct. 5/1 Their society is Totemistic; that is to say, they are divided into stocks of kin (real or assumed), each designated by the name of its Totem plant, animal, or what not. **1905** C. SQUIRE *Mythol. Brit. Isl.* 20 An agricultural.. people, still in the Stone Age, dwelling in totemistic tribes on hills.

totemite (ˈtəʊtəmaɪt). [f. TOTEM + -ITE[1].] = TOTEMIST 1.

1904 HOWITT *Native Tribes S.E. Australia* iii. 145 To dream about his own totem means that some one has done something to it for the purpose of harming the sleeper or one of his totemites. **1911** MARETT *Anthropol.* vi. 167 Sometimes the totem is thought of as an ancestor, or as the common fund of life out of which the totemites are born and into which they go back when they die.

‖**Totenkopf** (ˈtotənkɔpf). [Ger., = 'death's head'.] Used *attrib.* and *absol.* to designate (a member of) one of the divisions of the SS in Nazi Germany, having a death's head as its badge; *spec.* in the war of 1939–45, designating a unit (*Verband*) of concentration-camp guards.

1943 W. NECKER *German Army of To-day* iv. 164 During the war some formations of the *Totenkopf-Verbände* or *Death's-head (Skull) Detachments* were incorporated into the *Waffen-SS*. Originally, these formations were guards at concentration camps. *Ibid.* 167 The *Totenkopf-Division*, or 'Death's Head' Division. **1953** G. REITLINGER *Final Solution* ii. 43 Later there developed a strong distinction between the *Totenkopfverbaende* and the SS *Totenkopf* Division, which.. became a field division like any other. **1975** tr. *Melchoir's Sleeper Agent* II. 81 You and me both know what those *Totenkopf* bastards are. Concentration camp guards, that's what! **1977** D. JAMES *Spy at Evening* vii. 45 Eicke was.. a *Waffen SS* divisional commander... He commanded The Death's Head, Totenkopf division. **1981** 'E. TREVOR' *Damocles Sword* xv. 149 The Totenkopf and the Gestapo keep extensive records.

‖**Totentanz** (ˈtotəntants). Also 8 Toden Tans; (*hist.*) Todtentanz. [Ger.] = *dance of death* s.v. DANCE *sb.* 6 c. Also *fig.*

1789 *Emblems of Mortality* p. xxiv, He [*sc.* Holbein] also engraved several things upon wood, among which are his *Scripture Cuts*, and *Dance of Death*, vulgarly called *Toden Tans*. **1937** *Jrnl. Archæol. Assoc.* I. 249 Switzerland, which was once rich in representations of the Dances of Death, has suffered grievous losses. All that remains are a few.. fragments in Museums. The earliest of these—the Klingental Totentanz at Basle—.. was destroyed.. about 1850. **1950** A. WILSON *Such Darling Dodos* 144 (*heading*) Totentanz. *Ibid.* 163 Your first big reception, duckie, shall be a Totentanz. **1964** W. G. RAFFÉ *Dict. Dance* 50/1 The popular play and mime dance of the *Todtentanz* was then [*sc.* in 1535] still extant in its ritual or miracle play form. **1966** J. FOWLES *Magus* xix. 113 Dupes of the reality of war, of the ultimate *Totentanz*. **1982** P. DICKINSON *Last House-Party* (1983) ii. 18 Time emerged.. no friendly old gaffer with a scythe, but close kin to the skeleton reaper of the *Totentanz*.

†**toth.** *Obs. rare.* [Only in Ormin, *toþþ*. Origin unknown: the short *o* makes connexion with OE. *tóþ*, TOOTH, highly improbable.] Exact meaning uncertain: the context implies some kind of wrong-doing.

c **1200** ORMIN 7186 Alle þa þatt lufenn toþþ & woh & unnsahhtnesse. *Ibid.* 9317 ȝiff þatt ȝe wel ȝuw lokenn Fra clake & sake, & fra þat toþþ þat follȝheþþ ȝifernesse.

tother (ˈtʌðə(r)), *pron.* and *a.* Now *dial.* Forms: α. (3 **þet oþer**), 3–5 **þe toþer**, 4–6 **the tothir, the toder,** etc. (see OTHER), 4–7, 9 **the tother,** 7–8 **the t'other,** 8–9 *Sc.* **the tither.** β. 4 **þat toþer, þat toiþer.** γ. (without *the*) 6 **tothir,** (*dial.* toore), 6–7, 9 **tother,** 7–9 **t'other.** [ME. *þe toþer*, for earlier *þet oþer*, *þat oþer* 'the other'; formed in the same way as *þe tone* from *þet* or *þat one*: see TONE *pron.* and *a.* *The tother* is still used in Sc. and in north. Eng. dialects, but in general Eng. is replaced by *the other*, and often in familiar use by the simple *tother*, also written *t'other*. Cf. the similar use of *tone*, *t'one*. When a possessive pronoun or case took the place of *the*, *tother* remained, e.g. *his tother hand*, in literary Eng. 'his other hand'.]

A. *pron.*, or *adj.* used absolutely.

1. The other (of two): often opposed to *tone* (see TONE *pron.*). Phr. ***to tell tother*** (or ***t'other***) ***from which*** (joc.), to tell one from the other or (loosely) another; to distinguish or tell apart.

α. [*a* **1225** *Leg. Kath.* 101 Ane dale ha etheold..& spende al þ oðer. **1340** *Ayenb.* 16 þet uerste heaued of þe beste of helle ys prede, þet oþer is enuie.] *c* **1250** *Gen. & Ex.* 2724 Ðis on wulde don ðe toðer wrong. *a* **1300** *Cursor M.* 11056 þe tan was leuedi maiden ying, þe toþer [*Gött.* toder] hir hand-womman kerling. *c* **1380** WYCLIF *Sel. Wks.* III. 248 þe toon pope fallip þe toþurs bullis. **1382** —— *Isa.* vi. 3 Thei crieden the tother to the tother. **1388** *Ibid.*, Thei crieden the toon to the tother. *c* **1440** *Anc. Cookery* in *Househ. Ord.* (1790) 435 Dresse up the tone with the tother. **1533** J. HEYWOOD *Play Wether* (1903) 1200 Nother wyll we do the tone nor the tother. **1613** FLETCHER, etc. *Captain* II. ii, *Fran.* What's the tother? *Clor.* What tother? *Fran.* He that lyes along there. **1715** M. DAVIES *Athen. Brit.* I. 7 Two small Dissertations, the one upon Noe's arrival..the t'other was about the Origin of the Druids. *a* **1774** FERGUSSON *Drink Ecl.* Poems (1845) 49 Brandy the tane, the tither whiskey. **1816** SCOTT *Antiq.* xxvii, My lord cares as little about the tane as the tother.

β. **13..** *Cursor M.* 84 (Cott.) And in þat toþer [*v.rr.* þe toþer, þat oþer] scho lastes ever. *Ibid.* 2032 'þi fader slepand', said þat toiþer [*other MSS.* þe toþer], 'Liggus here-oute'. *Ibid.* 3494 His moder him luued mare þan þat toþer [*other MSS.* þe toþer].

γ. **1587** FLEMING *Contn. Holinshed* III. 1339/1 Tone gone to God,..still reigning tother. **1632** BROME *North. Lasse* I. iv, Here's one, there's tother. **1688** PRIOR *On Exod. III* vi, He on t'other's Ruin rears his Throne. **1710** PALMER *Proverbs* 129 Securing the vogue on one side and t'other. **1800** MAR. EDGEWORTH *Lame Jervas* i, I saw the ghost..with the light in one hand, and a chain dragging after him in t'other. **1870** LOWELL *Study Wind.* 259 You cannot tell one from tother.

Phr. **1874** M. CLARKE *His Natural Life* (1975) III. xxii. 24 You're so much alike one can't tell t'other from which. **1904** KIPLING *Traffics & Discoveries* 258 We've mixed the whole show up..till you can't tell t'other from which. **1979** D. FRANCIS *Whip Hand* ii. 27 He calls them all Tommy, because he doesn't know tother from which.

†**2.** The second (of two or more): cf. OTHER B. 3. (Cf. Ger. *der andere.*) *Obs.*

a **1300** *Cursor M.* 1629 (Cott.) þe first was sem, cham was the toþeir [*other MSS.* þe toþer], And Iaphet hight þat yongest broþer. **1380** *Lay Folks Catech.* 332 (Lamb. MS.) þe fyrst ys syȝt of eye, þe toþer heryng of Ere. *c* **1450** *Merlin* ii. 24 Thre sones, the first hight Moyne, and the tother Pendragon, and the thirde Vter.

3. *pl.* (*the tother* obs., *tothers* rare): The others, the rest: cf. OTHER B. 4.

c **1330** R. BRUNNE *Chron. Wace* (Rolls) 45 þat were Maysters of alle þe toþire, Hengist he hight, & Hors his broþire. **13..** *Cursor M.* 4948 (Gött.) þan spac ruben þe eldest broder Stille menand til þe toder. **1494** FABYAN *Chron.* VII. 339, xviii. were conuycte and hangyd, & the tother remayned longe after in pryson. **1691** J. WILSON *Belphegor* v. iii, When t'others shall..break themselves, on what they fall.

B. as *adj.* preceding a sb.

1. a. The other (of two). In early use often opposed to TO, TONE *a.*: see these.

α. *a* **1300** *Cursor M.* 6305 (Cott.) In sirie apon þe toiþer side. *Ibid.* 16721 þe toþer [*Laud MS.* the todir] theif him gaf ansuer. **1303** R. BRUNNE *Handl. Synne* 3993 Yn þe toþer worlde þer þey shul be, þey are nat wurþy any ioye to se. *c* **1385** CHAUCER *L.G.W.* 325 (*Balade*) Or he haue herd the tothyr partye speke. **1419** *Munim. de Melros* (Bann. Cl.) 502 Betwix..Dauid abbot..and hys Conuent on þe ta part and Nychole of Wedale on þe toþer part. **1465** *Cal. Anc. Rec. Dublin* (1889) 320 The tothyr half to the cowrte. **1482** *Monk of Evesham* (Arb.) 71 He..brought certen worde to the todyr man that tolde me. **1522** MORE *De Quat. Noviss.* Wks. 75/1 On the tother syde wher as one doth such spiritual busines with a dulnes of spirite & werines. *a* **1578** LINDESAY (Pitscottie) *Chron. Scot.* (S.T.S.) I. 149 He dissaweit baith the tuddar twa. **1681** DRYDEN *Span. Friar* v. ii, No! the t'other old gentleman in black shall take me if I do. **1716** M. DAVIES *Athen. Brit.* II. 172 In requital to the t'other Prelate's Urias's Letter. **1816** SCOTT *Antiq.* xxxix, I heard Puggie Orrock, and the tother thief of a sheriff-officer..speaking about it.

γ. **1627** W. SCLATER *Exp. 2 Thess.* (1629) 299 Wee, Britans of t'other race. **1720** WHITE *Monit. Clergy Peterbo.* I. 27 This, that, and t'other invented Order of their Church. **1727** GAY *Begg. Op.* II. xiii, How happy could I be with either, Were t'other dear Charmer away!

†**b.** After a possessive: Other. *Obs.*

1482 *Cely Papers* (Camden) 108 Accordyng as hit specyfyeth in my toder letter. **1549** *Compl. Scot.* 6 The grit armye of enemeis valkand on ther tothir syde. **1613** HEYWOOD *Silver Age* II. i. Wks. 1874 III. 113 Vnlesse it were my tother selfe, I haue no hand in it. **1721** D'URFEY *Two Queens Brentford* v. i, Now you shall have my t'other Walk.

c. ***tother school, 'un*** (Public School slang), a preparatory school, a school one attended before one's public school.

1880 TROLLOPE *Dr. Wortle's School* (1881) I. ii. 34 The old prescribed form of education..must be followed,—a t'other school, namely, then Eton... Therefore Bowick was chosen as the t'other school. **1940** M. MARPLES *Public School Slang* 179 'Where's your t'other 'un?' a question generally addressed to new boys. **1958** *Sunday Times* 25 May 8/3 Mr. Kenward's totherun (if the reviewer may be permitted to adopt, for the moment, his own public-school terminology) is named Ripple.

†**2. a.** The second (of two or more): cf. OTHER A. 3. *Obs.*

a **1300** *Cursor M.* 1627 *heading* (Cott.) Her bigins at noe þe lede þe toþer werld right for to del. *c* **1400** MAUNDEV. (1839) xxi. 225 The first statute was, that [etc.]... The tother Statute was, that [etc.]. *a* **1400** *Relig. Pieces fr. Thornton MS.* (1867) 3 The toþer artecle es þat we sall trowe. **1456** SIR G. HAYE *Law Arms* (S.T.S.) 2 The ferde is of the first angel...The fyft is of the tothir angel.

b. The second, another, one more. *Obs.* exc. *Sc.*

1600 ROWLANDS *Lett. Humours Blood* xix. 25 He calleth: Boy, fill vs the tother quart. **1653** WALTON *Angler* xi. 218 Then each man drink the tother cup and to bed. **1733** RAMSAY *Tea-t. Misc.* (ed. 9) I. 9 The lover he ga'e her the tither kiss, Syne ran to her dady and tell'd him this. **1785** BURNS *Jolly Beggars* ii, And aye he gies the tozie drab The tither skelpin' kiss.

3. (***the***) ***tother*** (***day***, etc.). †**a.** The second; the following, the next (day, etc.): cf. OTHER A. 3 b (*a*). *Obs.* †**b.** The preceding (day, etc.): cf. OTHER A. 3 b (*b*). *Obs.* **c.** The other (day, night, etc.); a few (days, etc.) ago: cf. OTHER A. 3 b (*c*).

a. *a* **1300** *Cursor M.* 7619 (Cott.) þe toþer morn [*Gött.* day] her after-ward þe warlau trauail saul ful hard. *Ibid.* 13249 In aueril þe toþer dai. *c* **1330** R. BRUNNE *Chron.* (1810) 38 þe toþer ȝere next of his coronment. **13..** *Cursor M.* 5993 (Gött.) Moyses praid þe toder day, All þe flijs wair quit a-way. *c* **1430** *Syr Tryam.* 508 The tother day, on the same wyse, As the kynge fro the borde can ryse. *a* **1765** *K. Estmere* xxvii. in Child *Ballads* III. (1885) 53/1 Tone day to marrye Kyng Adlands daughter, Tother daye to carrye her home.

b. *c* **1470** HENRY *Wallace* v. 908 Schir Jhone the Grayme, ..To the Corhed come on the tothir nycht.

c. **1575** *Gamm. Gurton* III. iv, Did not Tom Tankard rake his Curtal toore day standing in the stable? **1680** SIR C. LYTTELTON in *Hatton Corr.* (Camden) 232 Tother day, in shifting of a cabinet. **1711** STEELE *Spect.* No. 153 ¶1 An old Gentleman t'other Day in Discourse with a Friend. **1779** *Mirror* No. 12 ¶8, I confess, I could not help being in a passion t'other day. **1863** *Tyneside Songs* 31 Tuther Seturday neet aw saw a grand foot race Alang at the Victoria grund.

C. *Comb.*: **tother-day** *a. nonce-wd.* (see B. 3 c), that happened or existed a few days ago, very recent; **'tother,sider**, one from the other side; *spec.* of Australia.

1662 OWEN *Animadv. Fiat Lux* Wks. 1851 XIV. 65 Do we talk of t'other-day things? **1896** H. LAWSON *Let.* 3 Sept. (1970) 62 W.A. is a fraud... The old Sand-gropers are the best to work for or having dealings with. The Tothersiders are cutting each other's throats. **1900** H. LAWSON *Over Sliprails* 72 We were all T'othersiders, and old mates, and we worked things together. It was in Westralia—the Land of T'othersiders. **1903** 'T. COLLINS' *Such is Life* (1944) 276 The ancient t'other-sider [*sc.* Vandemonian Jack] oscillated his frame-saw. **1929** J. RAESIDE *Golden Days* 224 The population of Hannans, although mostly composed of t'othersiders, included not a small sprinkling of West Australians. **1949** *Geographical Mag.* Feb. 373 *Tothersider*, a Western Australian. **1950** K. S. PRICHARD *Winged Seeds* 30 Unemployed from all over the country swarmin' here, t'other siders as well as W.A. blokes. **1963** X. HERBERT *Disturbing Element* 2 My parents..were what were called T'othersiders, meaning people who had come to West Australia from the other side of the continent.

toðing(e, obs. form of TITHING *sb.*

to-threat, to-thrust: see TO- *pref.*[2]

†**to-throw,** *v. Obs.* Forms: see THROW *v.*[1] [ME. f. TO-[2] + *thrawe(n, throwe(n*, OE. *þráwan*, to twist, THROW *v.*[1] Cf. MHG. *gedræjen, gedræn.*] *trans.* To wrench asunder; to separate, part.

c **1315** SHOREHAM I. 1740 þe tyme is, wane aþer can Oþer fleschlyche y-knowe; For wanne hy habbeþ þet y-do, Ne mowe hi be to-þrowe. **1340** *Ayenb.* 256 þe norþene wynd to-þrauþ þe raynes.

‖**totidem verbis** (ˈtɒtɪdɛm ˈvɜːbiːs), *adv. phr.* [L.] In so many words.

1659 N. HARDY *First Ep. John* VI. 101 We do not read (*totidem verbis*) in the Scripture that the Apostle Baptized Infants, yet it is very probable. **1704** SWIFT *Tale of Tub* 64 'Tis true, said he, there is nothing here in this Will, *totidem verbis*, making mention of Shoulder-knots. **1844** MILL *Ess. Pol. Econ.* ii. 47 This object, under the varying names of an extensive demand, a brisk circulation, a great expenditure of money, and sometimes *totidem verbis* a large consumption, was conceived to be the great condition of prosperity. **1902** L. A. BURD in *Cambr. Mod. Hist.* (1907) I. vi. 202 These [fundamental beliefs or hypotheses] are rarely stated *totidem verbis* in any passage, though implied in nearly all.

totient (ˈtəʊʃənt). *Math.* [irreg. f. L. *totiēs, totiens*, f. *tot* so many, after QUOTIENT.] The number of numbers (including unity) less than and prime to a given number. So **totitive** (ˈtɒtɪtɪv) [irreg. f. L. *tot* + *-itive* in such words as *primitive, unitive*], any one of such numbers in relation to the given number.

1879 SYLVESTER *Math. Papers* (1909) III. 337 Understanding by the 'totitives' of *k* the numbers less than *k* and prime to it, these totitives may be arranged in (among others) the natural groups hereunder written. **1883** *Ibid.* (1912) IV. 102 The sum of the totients of all the natural numbers up to *j* inclusive—a totient to *x* (which I denote by *τx*) meaning the number of numbers less than *x* and prime to it. **1891** *Athenæum* 21 Mar. 383/1 'Some Theorems concerning Groups of Totitives of *n*', by Prof. L. Tanner.

‖**toties quoties** (ˈtəʊʃiːz ˈkwəʊʃiːz), *adv.* Also **totiens quotiens** (ˈtəʊʃɪɛnz ˈkwəʊʃɪɛnz). Also 6 **tociens quociens, tossyens quossyens.** [L., 'so often as often'.] As often as something happens or occasion demands; repeatedly.

In quot. 1845 applied to a jubilee of the Latin Church, at which a general pardon was granted.

1525 *Order Com. Counc. Lond.* in *Vicary's Anat.* (1888) App. viii. 214 Commaundyd & compelled vppon the payne of imprisonament of xx days, tociens quociens, that they shall no more occupie phisike till they be examyned. **1555** MACHYN *Diary* (Camden) 94 He declaryd..clen remyssyon of all ther synes *tossyens quossyens* of all that ever they dyd. **1569** *Reg. Privy Council Scot.* I. 685 He sall na wyis..troubill Alexander Quhitlaw..under the pane of V^c li. toties quoties. **1698–9** *Act 11 Will. III*, c. 2 §141 And such Assignee may in like manner assigne again and soe toties quoties. *a* **1734** NORTH *Exam.* I. ii. §165 Grand Juries may enquire *toties quoties* of the same Offence. **1845** FORD *Handbk. Spain* II. 771/1 Hence the jubilee was called 'toties quoties', for it was an annual benefit.

†**to-'tight,** *v. Obs.* [ME. *to-tuhten*, f. TO-[2] + *tuhten*, OE. *tyhtan*, TIGHT *v.*[1] to draw.]

1. *trans.* To stretch or spread out; to extend.

c **1200** *Trin. Coll. Hom.* 205 His lichame beð to-spred and to-tiht on þe rode. *Ibid.*, þeh his lichame..ne beo to-spred ne to-tuht on lichamliche rode.

2. To pull or draw asunder.

13.. *Guy Warw.* (A.) 511 Mi sorwe is euer cominge,..al mi limes it hath to-tiȝt; Swiche liif y lede day & niȝt. *Ibid.* 3711 Her armes & legges he to-tiȝt, [*C.* to-twighte = twitched] & cleped hem wreches [*MS.* wroches] anon riȝt.

†**toti'later.** *Obs. nonce-wd.* [f. L. *tōt-us* whole, entire + *latus, later-* side: cf. QUADRILATER.] A figure that is 'all side', or consists of an infinite number of sides: applied to a circle as the limit of regular multilateral figures when the number of sides is infinite.

1628 [see TOTANGLE].

†**to-tilde,** ? *sb.* (? *a.*). *Obs.* [f. ME. *tot-en*, TOOT *v.*[1], to peep out, pry, + (perh.) *-ild*, fem. suffix, as in *beggild, begenild, cheapild, fostrild*, etc.] ? A peeping, peering, or prying woman.

a **1225** *Ancr. R.* 102 Hweðer eni totilde [so also *Corpus*] ancre uondede euer þis, þet bekeð [*C.* breakeð] euer utward ase untowe brid ine cage?

[But the attrib. or adj. use, and the final *-e*, suggest that *totilde* here is perh. a scribal error for *totinde*, pr. pple. of *toten*, TOOT *v.*[1]: cf *totinde ancres*, ibid. 50 and 100.]

†**'toting,** *ppl. a. Obs.* [pr. ppl. of *tote*, earlier form of TOOT *v.*[1]; see also *tooting* under the verb.] Protruding, projecting, sticking out.

c **1645** HOWELL *Lett.* (1650) I. III. xxxi. 91 Though perhaps he had never a shirt to his back, yet would he have a toting huge swelling ruff about his neck. *Ibid.* (1655) IV. vii. 19 A poor shallow-brain'd puppy, who..would have men to have a priviledg to change their Wives,..deserves of all other to wear a toting horn. **1648–60** HEXHAM, *Geneust*, Nosed, or he that hath a great Nose, or a toting Nose. **1650** HOWELL *Giraffi's Rev. Naples* I. 87 With a toting plume of feathers in his hat all white. **1676** WISEMAN *Chirurg. Treat.* I. xxvi. 141 Rendring the Visage fiery, and in progress of time make those toting Copper-noses, as we generally express them.

totipalmate (təʊtɪˈpælmeɪt), *a.* (*sb.*) *Ornith.* [f. L. *tōti-*, from *tōt-us* whole + PALMATE.] Wholly webbed; having all the toes connected by membrane which reaches to the extremities; steganopodous. **b.** *sb.* A totipalmate bird. Hence **,totipal'mation**, the condition of being totipalmate.

1872 COUES *N. Amer. Birds* 48 Goatsuckers, some Western swifts, loons, and all the totipalmate swimmers. *Ibid.* 296 Feet totipalmate, with three full webs; hind toe semi-lateral,..connected with the inner toe by a complete web reaching from tip to tip. **1884** *Ibid.* (ed. 2) Index, Totipalmation.

totipotent (təʊˈtɪpətənt), *a. Biol.* [f. L. *tōti-* (see prec.) + POTENT: cf. *omnipotent.*] Capable of developing into or generating a complete organism: said of a cell. Also, able to differentiate into any other related kind of cell. So **to'tipotence, toti'potency, ,totipotenti'ality,** the quality of being totipotent; **totipo'tential** *a.* = TOTIPOTENT *a.*

1901 T. H. MORGAN *Regeneration* xii. 243 If we substitute the term 'totipotence', meaning that any meridian of the egg had the possibility of becoming the median plane of the embryo. **1904** *Amer. Nat.* July–Aug. 504 While in this species also the material is totipotent, yet when the determining influence of polarity is removed the stronger tendency is to produce a tail. **1909** J. W. JENKINSON *Experim. Embryol.* 281 In very many, though not in all, instances the parts of the ovum—blastomeres or egg fragments—are totipotent... The totipotence is, however, sooner or later lost. *Ibid.* 76 From other sources also there is evidence of a progressive loss of totipotentiality of the parts. **1911** —— *Sea Urchin* 292. **1918** *Jrnl. Exper. Zool.* XXV. 500 Totipotency is restricted to those girdle-forming cells which become implanted along with the limb bud. **1934** *Discovery* Aug. 220/1 There must be some power which controls and regulates the powers of these turbulent totipotential cells and this is exactly what Driesch called the 'entelechy'. **1942** M. M. WINTROBE *Clin. Hematol.* i. 30 According to the monophyletic school.. the lymphocyte of lymphatic tissue is identical with the primitive blood cell and is thus totipotential, giving rise under proper stimulation to any other type of blood cell. **1959** W. ANDREW *Textbk. Compar. Histol.* xii. 458 These cells are 'totipotent' and, according to need, can give rise to any other type of cell in the body of the sponge. **1967** *Amer. Jrnl. Med.* XLII. 932/1 Yoffey and Courtice.. believe that a major function of the small lymphocyte is that of a circulating totipotential cell. **1979** *Sci. Amer.* Apr. 93/2 Totipotency equivalent to that of early embryonic cells was thereby established unequivocally for individual embryonal carcinoma cells.

† **toti'present**, *a. Obs. nonce-wd.* [f. as prec. + PRESENT: cf. *omnipresent.*] Present throughout the whole of a space. So † **toti'presence**, the fact of being totipresent.

1768 TUCKER *Lt. Nat.* (1834) I. 337 Our own manner of existence in a sphere or portion of space sufficient to receive the action of many corporeal particles, we may term a *totipresence* throughout the contents of that sphere... A totipresence throughout all immensity amounts to the same as omnipresence. *Ibid.* 409 There is a certain portion of space throughout which we are totipresent, because we can receive the action of many corporeal particles at once which cannot be brought into contact with a mathematical point.

totitive: see TOTIENT.

totive ('təʊtɪv), *a. nonce-wd.* [f. L. *tōt-us* whole + -IVE.] Denoting a whole: see quot.

1874 KEY *Language* xviii. 225 A leading use of the genitive is that called 'partitive', but might more fitly be called 'totive', for the genitive here denotes the whole whence a part is taken.

totle, Totnam: see TOTTLE *v.*[1], TOTTENHAM.

‖**toto** ('təʊtəʊ), *a.* Abl. sing. masc. and neut. of L. *tōtus* all, whole, entire: occurring in a few phrases in literary use, as **toto cælo** ('təʊtəʊ 'siːləʊ, 'kaɪləʊ), 'by the whole heaven', by as much as the distance between the poles, diametrically; in quot. 1844 *attrib.* entire, absolute; **toto genere** ('dʒenəriː), in the whole nature or character; **toto orbe** ('ɔːbiː), 'by the whole world'; = *toto cælo*.

1727 POPE *Art of Sinking* i. Wks. 1751 VI. 167 In their others [pieces] they differ'd **toto cælo* from us. **1844** W. G. WARD *Ideal Chr. Ch.* (ed. 2) 272 The toto-coelo difference in kind between [etc.]. *a* **1878** SIR G. G. SCOTT *Lect. Archit.* xvi. (1879) II. 234 The dome [of the Pantheon].. differs *toto cælo* from the normal mode of construction. **1672** BOYLE *Orig. & Virt. Gems* I. 49 Bodies, that differ **toto genere*, as Metals and Stones. *a* **1834** COLERIDGE in *Lit. Rem.* (1839) IV. 232 Here I differ **toto orbe* from Waterland.

toto ('təʊtəʊ), *sb.*[1] [ad. Swahili *mtoto* offspring, child.] In East Africa: a child; a baby; a young animal; a young servant.

1916 *Chambers's Jrnl.* Nov. 719/2 Poor little 'toto', bereft of his mother. **1927** *Ibid.* Nov. 762/1, I was a 'toto' then. How old I cannot say. In my tribe there is no record of birth or death. **1937** K. BLIXEN *Out of Africa* IV. 336, I was.. a long way in front of the waggons, with Farah, my dog Dusk and the Toto who looked after Dusk. **1964** C. WILLOCK *Enormous Zoo* v. 90 At first he ran out in front as is the custom with white rhino *totos*. **1979** *Observer* (Colour Suppl.) 9 Sept. 43/1 We hear goat-bells, and tiny herd-boys emerge cautiously from the bush. 'Give those *totos* a bowl of maize meal,' Thesiger orders.

toto ('təʊtəʊ), *sb.*[2] *Mil. slang* (of the 1914–18 war). [a. Fr. mil. argot.] A louse.

[**1917** G. CLOVER *Stop at Suzanne's* (1919) 223 They were all covered with lice—*les totos* they call them.] **1918** *Radiator* 30 May 1 Dr. Kent Hagler.. saw no evidence of flea or toto. *a* **1919** in E. C. Garrett *Trench Ballads* (1919) 78 Some people call 'em Totos—Some people call 'em lice. **1929** HALL & NILES *One Man's War* 46, I do not know who developed lice first, but I noticed them on that march. We called them 'totos'.

toto, totoo (16th c.), i.e. *too too*: see TOO.

toto-, used as combining form of L. *tōtus* whole, in certain cases, instead of the normal form *toti-* (see -O[1]), forming compound adjs., **a.** in sense 'entirely, wholly, utterly' (see -O[1] 1), as '**toto-con'genital, 'toto-'mute, 'toto-o'fficious**; **b.** in sense 'total and..' (see -O[1] 2), as '**toto-'partial** *Logic*, applied to a proposition in which one term is universal and the other particular; so '**toto-'total**, having both terms universal.

1890 *Q. Rev.* Jan. 68 The marriage of *toto-congenital deaf mutes. **1893** F. W. BOOTH *World's Congr. Instruct. Deaf* 59 The German semi-mute brought to a study of English has a decided advantage over his *toto-mute brother. **1586** in J. Morris *Troub. Cath. Forefathers* (1877) 69 Condemned as rude, troublesome, and *toto-officious. **1833** SIR W. HAMILTON *Discuss.* (1852) 162 *Toto-total—all is all... *Toto-partial—all is some.

to-tog, variant of TO-TUG *v. Obs.*

† **to-'toll**, *v. Obs.* [ME. f. TO-[2] + TOLL *v.*[1] to draw.] *trans.* To pull or drag hither and thither.

c **1325** *Poem times Edw. II* (Percy) lix, Hit schal be to-tolled, hit schal be totwyȝt [*v.r.* Hit shal be forpinched, totoilled & totwiht]. *Ibid.* lxi, Hit is so to-tolled, bothe heder & theder Hit is halfendel istole, ar hit be brout togeder. *c* **1330** *Arth. & Merl.* (Kölbing) 8531 Þe heþen me tok & totoiled, Tobeten, todrawe & defoiled.

Totonac (təʊtə'næk). Also † **Totonaca**. [ad. Sp. *Totonaca*, f. Nahuatl *Totonacatl*, pl. *Totonaca.*] An Indian people of east central Mexico; a member of this people. Also, their language. Also *attrib.*

1787 C. CULLEN tr. *Clavigero's Hist. Mexico* II. VIII. 18 Five men.. said in Mexican.. that they were of the nation of the Totonacas, and sent by the lord of Chempoalla. **1852** B. MAYER *Mexico* I. iii. 29 The Tlascalans were not so easily won as his allies, the Totonacs. **1900** *Proc. Davenport Acad. Sci.* VIII. 187 Some of the.. Totonac women in the Plaza.. are really gay with hair ribbons. **1908** F. STARR *In Indian Mexico* xx. 245 In Tlaxco, a small village in this *municipio*, four idioms are spoken—Aztec, Otomi, Totonac and Tepehua. **1940** F. JOHNSON in C. L. Hay et al. *Maya & their Neighbors* vi. 109 The area on the map in which Totonac was spoken remains practically identical with that originally drawn by Orozco y Berra. **1948** A. L. KROEBER *Anthropol.* (rev. ed.) xviii. 794 Along the Gulf Coast in Tabasco nd Vera Cruz, a series of peoples known as Olmec, Totonac, and Huastec, in order from south to north. **1977** T. A. SEBEOK *Native Lang. Americas* II. 153 The Totonac.. were the first to become allies of Cortez when he disembarked on the coast of Veracruz and set out to conquer Mexico. **1977** *Language* LIII. 262/2 The publication of these volumes.. makes Totonac an unusually well-documented language.

Hence **Toto'nacan** *a.*, of or pertaining to the family of languages that comprises Totonac and Tepehua.

1933 J. E. THOMPSON *Mexico before Cortez* viii. 259 The Tajin pyramid is in Totonacan linguistic territory. **1940** F. JOHNSON in *Maya & their Neighbors* vi. 109 (*heading*) Totonacan family [of languages]. **1977** T. A. SEBEOK *Native Lang. Americas* II. 153 There are.. well over 130,000 speakers of Totonacan dialects in Veracruz and Puebla.

totora (təʊ'tɔərə). [a. Quechua, Aymara.] A perennial bulrush, *Scirpus totora*, native to alpine lakes in Peru and Bolivia. Also *attrib.*

1936 *Discovery* Dec. 372/2 The 'totora'.. is still used by the Indians of Lake Titicaca to make nets and cordage. **1958** A. TOYNBEE *East to West* vi. 17 The cattle wade out, breast-deep, to crop the tender shoots of the totóra reed. **1971** P. CRAMPTON tr. *Heyerdahl's Ra Exped.* vi. 110, I knew that the *totora* reed in America was capable of long sea voyages. **1974** T. MORRISON *Land above Clouds* 142 For centuries, the Indians around Titicaca have used the Totora for making their reed boats.

to-torve, to-tose, to-tray, etc.: see TO-[2].

† **tot-quot**. *Obs.* [L. *tot quot* as much or as many as (there may be).]

1. *Eccl.* A dispensation or licence to hold as many ecclesiastical benefices as the holder pleases or can get; hence, the holding of such benefices, unlimited pluralism; *pl.* benefices so held.

1509 BARCLAY *Shyp Folys* (1570) 60 He hath hope To haue another benefyce of greater dignitie, And so maketh a false suggestion to the pope, For a tot quot or els a pluralitie. **1522** SKELTON *Why not to Court?* 125 We shall haue a tot quot From the Pope of Rome. *a* **1550** *Image Ipocr.* I. in *Skelton's Wks.* (1843) II. 420/2 Ye drawe and cast lottes, In hattes and in pottes, For tottes and for quottes. **1583** STUBBES *Anat. Abus.* II. (1882) 79 They purchase a dispensation, a licence,.. by vertue whereof they may hold totquots so manie, how manie soeuer. **1637** BASTWICK *Litany* II. 9 The Pope selleth nonresidences, pluralityes, trialityes, totquots, the Prelats doe the same.

b. *transf.* One who holds tot-quots; an unlimited pluralist.

1628 P. SMART *Serm. Durh. Cath.* 7 July 21 The same will be also a notorious Non-resident, a very Tot-quot. **1677** W. HUGHES *Man of Sin* II. iv. 82 S. Wereburga,.. being Governess of three Nunneries (being no more, she was no Tot-quot then).

2. An indefinite or infinite number; as many as you like.

1565 JEWEL *Repl. Harding* xiii. (1611) 360 He pleadeth his toties, quoties, and thereby would erect a whole totquot of Masses, sans number... By these words, M. Hardings Totquot is much abridged.

3. A rate or tax assessed in proportion to income.

1611 COTGR., *Quottité*, an euen assessement, a rate or totquot imposed; the laying on euerie one his share.

† **to-'tread**, *v. Obs.* [OE. *totredan*, f. TO-[2] + *tredan*, TREAD *v.* So OS. *te-tredan*, OHG. **zatretan*, MHG. *ze-, zertreten*, Ger. *zertreten.*] *trans.* To trample down, trample upon. Hence † **to-treading** *vbl. sb.*

[*c* **725** *Corpus Gloss.* (Hessels) D 77 *Desicit* [? *Deficit*], tetridit.] *c* **1175** *Lamb. Hom.* 133 Sum [feol] bi þe weie and werð to-tredan and fuȝeles hit freten. **13..** *K. Alis.* 3946 (Bodl. MS.) Horses totraden alle þe Boukes Of noble Barouns & of Dukes. **1382** WYCLIF *Prov.* xxvii. 7 The soule fulfild shal to-trede the hony comb. **1535** COVERDALE *Isa.* xxviii. 18 The greate destruction.. shal all to treade you.

totsane, tott(e, obs. ff. TUTSAN, TOT.

‖**tot siens** (tɔt sins). *S. Afr.* Also **totsiens**. [Afrikaans *tot (weer)siens* 'until we meet again', f. Du. *tot* until + *zien* to see.] A formula of farewell: au revoir, till I see you again.

1937 S. CLOETE *Turning Wheels* ix. 142 'Tot Siens. Tot siens,' they cried, their voices growing fainter. **1948** H. V. MORTON *In Search S. Afr.* ii. 52 We said good-bye, with a *tot siens* or two and one 's' long folks'. **1963** A. DELIUS *Day Natal took Off* 72 This is, then, not good-bye, only totsiens. **1974** *Argus* (Cape Town) 30 July 22/9 Tot siens! May you come back to Britain soon.

totsy ('tɒtsɪ). *slang.* [f. TOT *sb.*[4] + -SY.] = TOTTY *sb.* 2.

1938 G. GREENE *Brighton Rock* IV. i. 142 The atmosphere of innumerable roadhouses, of totsies gathered round swimming pools.

† '**totted**, *ppl. a. Obs. rare*[−1]. [? related to TOT *sb.*[1]] ? Muddle-headed; or = TOTTY *a.*[2]

c **1480** *Kyng & Hermyt* 348 in Hazl. *E.P.P.* I. 26 And you schall here a totted frere Say *Stryke pantnere*; And in yᵉ cope leve ryȝt nouȝt.

Tottenham ('tɒt(ə)nəm). In 6 **Totnam**. Name of a northern suburb of London.

† **a.** ***Tottenham is turned French***, a proverb used in reference to any unlikely or remarkable change. *Obs.*

1546 J. HEYWOOD *Prov.* (1867) 14 Their faces told toies, that Totnam was tournd frenche. **1581** A. HALL *Iliad* IV. 60 Do what thou canst, the time wil come that Totnam French shal turn; The Gods and I will so prouide. *a* **1661** FULLER *Worthies, Middlesex* (1662) II. 178.

b. ***Tottenham Pudding***, feed for pigs or poultry, consisting of sterilized kitchen waste.

1944 HALNAN & GARNER *Princ. & Pract. Feeding Farm Animals* (ed. 2) xvi. 329 In the process of cooking the waste.. sets to a firm.. 'pudding' which finds a ready market for feeding to pigs and poultry. Since this pudding was first produced in.. Tottenham.. such prepared food is known as 'Tottenham Pudding'. **1966** K. NICHOLSON *Hook, Line & Sinker* viii. 91 He's a Large White... In the winter, he has his quota of Tottenham Pudding—that's concentrated swill, sterilised by steam. **1980** *Good Housekeeping* Dec. 226/6 The days of muck and mystery, when poultry were fed on 'Tottenham Pudding'—kitchen waste from hotels and restaurants, boiled up and sterilised.

totter ('tɒtə(r)), *sb.*[1] Forms: 4–5 **totre**, 5 **totyr**, **totoure**, 6– **totter**. [f. TOTTER *v.* Cf. Flem., Du. (and WFris.) *touter* in sense 1.]

† **1.** A swing; a board suspended by two ropes, on which a person sits and is swung to and fro.

1387 TREVISA *Higden* (Rolls) II. 387 Whan men [fel] of þe totres and were i-herte sore, it was ordeyned among hem þat images i-liche to þe bodies schulde be sette in þe totros, and meue and totery in stede of hem þat were a-falle. Þat game is cleped ocillum in Latyn. *c* **1440** *Promp. Parv.* 498/1 Totyr, or myry totyr, chylderys game.., *oscillum*. **1468** *Medulla Gram.*, *Oscillum*, genus ludi, cum funis suspenditur a trabe in quo pueri et puelle sedentes impelluntur huc et illuc,—a totoure. *Petaurus*, quidam ludus, a totre. **1483** *Cath. Angl.* 390/2 A mery Totyr (*A.* A Totyr), *petaurus*, & *cetera*. **1552** HULOET, Totter playe, betwene two bell ropes to tottre to and fro, *petaurum*.

2. The action, or an act, of tottering; wavering, oscillation; an unsteady or shaky movement or gait as of one ready to fall.

1747 E. POSTON *Pratler* I. 1 My Mind is so on the Totter between For and Against. **1751** JOHNSON *Rambler* No. 109 ¶8, I.. had his bend in my shoulders, and his totter in my gait. **1830** *Chron.* in *Ann. Reg.* 35/2 He seemed all of a totter and tremble. **1898** WATTS-DUNTON *Aylwin* II. iv, Without raising an arm to balance her body, without a totter or a slip.

3. *attrib.* and *Comb.* (or from the verb-stem), as **totter-arse**, † (*a*) the game of see-saw; = TITTER-TOTTER 1; (*b*) one who totters (*dial.*); **totter-grass**, quaking-grass, *Briza media*, or sometimes another grass with slender stalk; '**totter-,headed** *a.*, light-headed, frivolous, changeful; **totter-kneed** *a.*, yielding, 'weak-kneed'.

1611 COTGR., *Baccoler*, to play at titter-totter, or at *totter-arse; to ride the wild Mare; as children who sitting vpon both ends of a long Pole, or Timber-log (supported only in the middle) lift one another vp and downe. **1888** ELWORTHY *W. Somerset Word-bk.* s.v., I ant a-zeed no such two double totterarse 'is longful time. **1821** CLARE *Vill. Minstr.* II. 198 And *totter-grass, in many a trembling knot. **1909** *Spectator* 10 July 48/2 The ox-eye daisies white among the totter-grass and sorrel. **1662** PETTY *Taxes* ii. §14 The things which cause animosities among the *totter-headed multitude. **1887** G. MEREDITH *Ballads & P.*, *Whimper of Sympathy*, The feelings of the *totterknee'd.

totter, *sb.*[2]: see TOT *sb.*[5]

† **totter**, *a. Obs. rare*[−1]. In 4 **totyre**. [If genuine, goes with TOTTER *v.* (but it may be a copyist's error for TOLTER).] Tottering, shaky, unstable, insecure.

c **1375** *Sc. Leg. Saints* xxviii. (*Margaret*) 42 Þe wikit warld scho ourcom als, Þat ay is totyre, fekil, & fals.

totter ('tɒtə(r)), *v.* Also 3–5 **toter**, 6 **tottre**. [Appears first *c* 1200; has the form of a frequentative from a stem *tot-*, expressing instability or unsteady movement. Perh. from Norse: cf. Norw. dial. *tutra*, *totra* to quiver, shake (Ross), Sw. dial *tuttra* (Rietz). The sense is found in Flem. & Du. *touteren* to swing, though it is difficult to connect this phonologically: cf. TOLTER *v.*]

†**1.** *intr.* To swing to and fro, esp. at the end of a rope; *fig.* to waver, vacillate. *Obs.*

c **1200** *Vices & Virtues* 135 Ne mid fote sitten toterinde. **1387** TREVISA *Higden* (Rolls) II. 387 Men of Athene heng vp ropes in þe ayer and men totrede þeron and meued hider and þider [*orig.* huc et illuc agitabantur]. *Ibid.* [see TOTTER *sb.*[1] 1]. *c* **1440** *Promp. Parv.* 498/1 Toteron, or waveron, *vacillo.* **1552** [see TOTTER *sb.*[1] 1]. **1594** PLAT *Jewell-ho.* III. 47 It should seem that before the breaking of the yolke, that the yolke did hang playing or tottering within the white. **1601** SHAKS. *All's Well* I. iii. 129 Manie likelihoods..which hung so tottring in the ballance.

†**b.** *spec.* To swing from the gallows, to be hanged. *Obs.*

c **1530** *Hickscorner* B ij b, That is a knauysshe sight to se them totter on a beme. **1542** UDALL *Erasm. Apoph.* 122 Diogenes..had a greate zele..to see theim euery one swyngyng & tottreyng in halters. **1556** J. HEYWOOD *Spider & F.* xv. 13 If they be had, they shall hang therupone, And yet if they totter twenty togyther, Still do theeues rob there. **1623–33** FLETCHER & SHIRLEY *Night-Walker* III. v, I would lose a limb, to see their rogueships totter.

†**c.** To play at see-saw. Cf. TITTER-TOTTER.

1530 PALSGR. 760/1, I totter to and fro, as chylder do whan they play.., *je ballance*... Totter nat to moche leste you fall.

†**2.** To move up and down or to and fro, as a ship on the waves; to toss, to pitch. *Obs.*

13.. *E.E. Allit. P.* C. 233 þenne þaȝ her takel were torne, þat totered on yþeȝ. *c* **1400** *Laud Troy Bk.* 4294 Other..In the water swam and flotered, And there schippis a-boute totered. **1596** *Edward III*, III. i. 170 Then might ye see the reeling vessels split, And tottering sink into the ruthlesse floud.

3. To rock or shake to and fro on its base, as if about to overbalance or collapse; †in quot. *c* 1400, to tremble.

c **1400** *Laud Troy Bk.* 9717 Thei sat toterynge as it were gece—What for the strokes & the hete. **1522** MORE *De Quat. Noviss.* Wks. 99 The hands trimbling..and the feete totteryng. **1576** PETTIE *Petite Pallace* 33 As a tree hewen downe with axes, redy to fal.., tottereth euery way, being vncertayne which way to fal. **1697** DRYDEN *Æneid* II. 384 Troy nods from high, and totters to her fall. **1775** SHERIDAN *St. Patr. Day* II. ii, I was..taken with a sudden giddiness, and Humphrey seeing me beginning to totter, ran to my assistance. **1836** MARRYAT *Midsh. Easy* xxx, Her main-mast was seen to totter, and then to fall over the side.

b. *fig.* or in fig. context.

1610 SHAKS. *Temp.* III. ii. 8 If th'other two be brain'd like vs, the State totters. **1641** MILTON *Ch. Govt.* I. Wks. 1851 III. 100 So long as the Church is mounted upon the Prelaticall Cart..it will but shake and totter. **1719** YOUNG *Revenge* IV. i, O forbear! You totter on the very brink of ruin. *a* **1774** TUCKER *Lt. Nat.* (1834) II. 173 Their faith..will be apt to shake and totter grievously in the storms of opposition. **1874** GREEN *Short Hist.* v. §1. 221 From the day of Cressy feudalism tottered slowly but surely to its grave.

†**c.** To oscillate, vibrate, rock (without any notion of falling). *Obs. rare.*

1668 CULPEPPER & COLE *Barthol. Anat.* I. xi. 27 The use of which bones, is to hinder that the valve do not easily totter. **1678** MOXON *Mech. Exerc.* iv. 64 Not letting the Plain totter to or from you-wards.

4. To walk or move with unsteady steps; to go shakily or feebly; to toddle; also, to walk with difficulty; to reel, stagger.

1602 MARSTON *Ant. & Mel.* I. Wks. 1856 I. 17 He totterd from the reeling decke. **1796** MORSE *Amer. Geog.* II. 489 Chinese women..may be said to totter rather than to walk. **1797** DOWNING *Disorders Horned Cattle*, etc. 106 When the staggers and convulsive symptoms arise, the horse..is feeble, reels and totters about as he moves. **1818** SCOTT *Br. Lamm.* xix, The old blind woman arose, assumed her staff, ..tottering to her hut. **1863** W. C. BALDWIN *Afr. Hunting* vii. 280 Three niggers staggering after us with as much as ever they could totter under.

b. *trans.* (*nonce-uses.*) (*a*) To make (one's way) totteringly. (*b*) To carry with tottering steps.

1846 MRS. GORE *Eng. Char.* (1852) 57 Poor Corney tottered his way from the miserable cellar of St. Giles's.. towards the fashionable quarter of the town. **1864** LOWELL *Fireside Trav.* 280 After our little bearers [mules] had tottered us up and down the dusky steeps.

†**5.** *trans.* To cause to shake to and fro, to rock; to render unstable. Also *fig. Obs.*

1615 T. ADAMS *White Devill* 45 There is some disobedient and fugitive Jonasses that thus totter our ship. *a* **1625** FLETCHER *Hum. Lieut.* I. i, Earthquakes To shake and totter my designs. *a* **1693** *Urquhart's Rabelais* III. Prol. 7 He.. totter'd it, lifted it,..transpos'd it, transplaced it.

totterdemal(l)ion, obs. f. TATTERDEMALION.

†**tottered** ('tɒtəd), *ppl. a. Obs.* [Orig. a variant of TATTERED, and used in that sense (cf. Norw. dial. *totra* rag); subsequently associated with TOTTER *v.*, and more or less assimilated in sense.]

1. = TATTERED 2, 3.

1570 FOXE *A. & M.* (ed. 2) 1357/1 He..was not so disguised in hys tottered attyre, but that hys countenaunce gaue signification [etc.]. **1596** SHAKS. *1 Hen. IV*, IV. ii. 37 A hundred and fiftie totter'd Prodigalls, lately come from Swine-keeping. **1657** S. PURCHAS *Pol. Flying-Ins.* 118 [They] have their wings tottered and torn. *a* **1693** *Urquhart's Rabelais* III. xvii, The ragged and tottred Equipage of her Person.

2. Of a building or a ship: Battered and shaken, rendered ruinous and liable to fall; in a tottering condition.

1615 G. SANDYS *Trav.* 178 A tottered Tower doth challenge regard for the waste receiued in that places protection. **1649–50** in Swayne *Sarum Churchw. Acc.* (1896) 221 Carpenter pulling down yᵉ tottered seiling over yᵉ East end of the Chancell. **1689** SHERLOCK *Disc. Death* (1715) 26 Merciless waves even overwhelm his tottered and decayed vessel. **1808** SCOTT *Marm.* IV. xi, Thy turrets rude, and tottered Keep, Have been the minstrel's loved resort.

3. Made to totter, shaken, reeling. *rare.*

1621 G. SANDYS *Ovid's Met.* xv. (1626) 317 The hot horses..O'r ragged rocks the totterd charriot driue: While I to curb their furie vainly striue.

totterer ('tɒtərə(r)). [f. TOTTER *v.* + -ER[1].] One who totters, or walks with tottering steps.

1711 SWIFT *Jrnl. to Stella* 21 Apr., I am much better than I was, though something of a totterer. **1827** *Blackw. Mag.* XXII. 702 He snatched the little totterers..up in his arms. **1890** [see next].

'**tottering**, *vbl. sb.* [f. TOTTER *v.* + -ING[1].] The action of the verb TOTTER; oscillation, wavering, shaking as if about to fall.

1387 TREVISA *Higden* (Rolls) II. 387 That game is cleped ocillum in Latyn,..of cilleo cilles þat is forto mene toterynge. *c* **1440** *Promp. Parv.* 498/1 Toterynge, or waverynge, *vacillacio.* **1577** B. GOOGE *Heresbach's Husb.* 40 The Wayne or Cart must be lyned with sheets, lest with iogging and tottring of the carryage, the seede fall thorowe. **1672** CLARENDON *Contempl. Ps.* Tracts (1727) 280 The prodigious tottering and instability of that [church] they are about to enter. **1890** J. H. STIRLING *Gifford Lect.* xii. 262 If you totter already, the tottering against you of ever so many totterers will only floor you.

'**tottering**, *ppl. a.* [f. TOTTER *v.* + -ING[2].] That totters, in various senses of the verb.

1534 MORE *Comf. agst. Trib.* IV. xxiv. (1847) 298 The three feet of this tottering stool. **1585** ABP. SANDYS *Serm.* xiv. 232 Our tottering boate is tossed in the stormie seas. **1610** HOLLAND *Camden's Brit.* (1637) 642 The tottering walles of Caer-philli Castle. **1700** T. BROWN *Amusem. Ser. & Com.* ii. 12 The tottering Earth made them Giddy and Stumble. **1801** SOUTHEY *Thalaba* IX. xvii, She leans on her staff With a tottering step. **1877** BLACK *Green Past.* xxxv, A tottering white-headed old man.

fig. **1554** LATIMER *Disput. Oxford* in Foxe *A. & M.* (1563) 980/1 That thys world hath bene, and yet is, a tottering world. **1649** MILTON *Eikon.* v. Wks. 1851 III. 375 A tottring and giddy Act rather then a settling. **1796** BURKE *Regic. Peace* i. Wks. VIII. 158 The tottering imbecility of a new government. **1870** H. SMART *'Race for Wife* iii, Tottering coronets must be propped by wealthy alliances.

Hence '**totteringly** *adv.*

1660 INGELO *Bentiv. & Ur.* I. (1682) 82 It seem'd to stand totteringly upon a pitiful foundation. **1891** L. KEITH *Lost Illusion* II. xii. 41 An old man totteringly and feebly cleaning a little vegetable-bed.

totterish ('tɒtərɪʃ), *a. rare.* [f. TOTTER *a.* or *v.* + -ISH[1].] Inclined to totter; somewhat tottery.

1817 SCOTT *Let. to Mrs. M. Clephane* 23 Mar., in *Lockhart*, I am still very totterish and very giddy. **1819** —— *Let. to Southey* 4 Apr. *ibid.*, My health is at present very totterish.

tottery ('tɒtərɪ), *a.* [f. TOTTER *v.* + -Y.] Given to tottering; shaky; unsteady.

1861 HUGHES *Tom Brown at Oxf.* vi, When I looked up and saw what a tottery performance it was, I concluded to give them a wide berth. **1880** MISS BRADDON *Just as I am* xviii, Frances felt very faint and tottery. **1907** *Speaker* 19 Jan. 484/2 Stocks have been distinctly 'tottery' this week.

Tottie ('tɒtɪ). Also Totty. Familiar diminutive of HOTTENTOT.

1849 E. E. NAPIER *Excurs. S. Africa* I. 55 To portray..the Hottentot of the time of Van Riebeck, and the 'Totty' of the present day. **1863** W. C. BALDWIN *Afr. Hunting* ix. 366, I have..five horses, six Kaffirs, and one Tottie, and have every comfort in my wagons. **1883** *Gd. News in Africa* viii. 110 The Hottentots are a miserable little race, sometimes called 'Totties' in contempt.

tottie, variant of TOTTY.

totting: see TOT *sb.*[5], *v.*[1] and [2].

tottle ('tɒt(ə)l), *a. dial.* [? f. *tot-* in TOTTER *v.* + -LE 1, as in *brittle.*] Weak-headed, silly, dazed.

1894 BARING-GOULD *Kitty Alone* II. 94 Wi' the death of her little maid, gone almost tottle (silly). **1897** —— *Furze-Bloom* (1899) 13, I reckon. Genefer, the old lady be gone quite tottle (dazed).

tottle ('tɒt(ə)l), *v.*[1] Chiefly *dial.* Also 8–9 totle. [In sense 1 app. onomatopœic, representing the motion and sound involved. In senses 2 and 3 perh. by-form of TODDLE or TOTTER, and TOPPLE.]

1. a. *intr.* To move and bubble, as a boiling liquid; also said of the vessel; and applied to the somewhat similar motion and sound of a rivulet over a stony bed. *Sc.* Hence '**tottling** *vbl. sb.*

1717 *Lament for Ld. Maxwell* in *Jacob. Songs & Ball.* (1887) 103 'Side the sang o' the birds, where some burn tottles owre. **1739** A. NICOL *Nat. without Art* 100 In Winter-time a Piece fat Beef to tottle. **1835** MONTEATH *Dunblane* (1887) 32 The woman..cast a longing eye at the kail-pot 'tottling on the fire'. **1864** A. LEIGHTON *Myst. Leg. Edinb.* (1886) 68 They heard the sound of..the sweltering and tottling of the pot.

b. *trans.* To cause to simmer or boil. *Sc.*

a **1774** FERGUSSON *To Principal, etc. St. Andrews* 40 Imprimis, then, a haggis fat, Weel tottl'd in a seything pat. **1776** HERD *Collect. Scot. Songs* II. 182 Ye's get a cock well totled i' the pat, An ye'll come hame, an ye'll come hame.

2. *intr.* To move unsteadily and with short tottering steps; to toddle.

1821 GALT *Sir A. Wylie* III. xxxiii. 287 Their bairns.. when they begin to tottle about the house. **1824** —— *Rothelan* VI. iii, The tidy grand-dame..is seen with a pitcher slowly tottling across the fields to the dairy. **1873** HALE *In His Name* i. 4 The twin babies who could hardly tottle along the road.

3. *intr.* = TOPPLE *v.* 1. *dial.*

1830 HOGG in *Blackw. Mag.* XXVIII. 895 Off flew the English warder's head, And tottled into Foxton burn. *a* **1905** in *Eng. Dial. Dict.* s.v., (N. Yorks.) T'oad fella nearly tottled of t' steul 'at he was set on wi' laughing.

Hence '**tottledom**, *nonce-wd.* (for *toddledom*), the sphere of toddlers or toddling; babyhood, infancy; **tottlish** ('tɒtlɪʃ), '**tottly** *adjs.*, unsteady, totterish.

1889 *Anthony's Photogr. Bull.* II. 354 There not being the least fear of its..ever exceeding the limits of cameraic *tottledom. **1835** *Knickerbocker* VI. 6 Had she not been obliged..to steady her *tottlish bark with the paddle which now loitered behind the stern. **1853** MRS. MOODIE *Life in Clearings* 16 This was the first time he had ever ventured upon the water in such a tottleish machine [as a birch-bark canoe]. **1889** C. F. WOOLSON *Jupiter Lights* xxviii, She'll soon fill it full of tottlish little tables and dimity. **1905** *Eng. Dial. Dict.* VI. 203/1 **Tottly*,..ready to fall, unstable. **1910** KIPLING *Rewards & Fairies* 155 My legs are pretty tottly, but I made shift to go on deck.

'**tottle**, *v.*[2], altered form of TOTAL *v.*, with shortened vowel. (Common *dialectally.*)

1891 GOSSE *Gossip in Library* xiii. 164 She did not tottle up her milk-scores on the bastard-title [of a book].

'**tottling**, *ppl. a.* [f. TOTTLE *v.*[1] + -ING[2].] That tottles; moving unsteadily; apt to tip or topple; shaky; crazy; also *fig.* feeble or shaky in intellect. Cf. TOTTY *a.*[2]

1746 *Exmoor Scolding* (E.D.S.) 53 A toteling, wambling, zlottering, zart-and-vair yheat-stool. **1849** DANA *Geol.* ii. (1850) 31 Safe navigation for the tottling canoe. **1873** E. H. CLARKE *Sex in Educ.* 35 The girl..will caress a doll, that her tottling brother looks coldly upon. **1880** MRS. PARR *Adam & Eve* xxxvi, Th' ole chap was gone reg'lar totlin' like, and can't tell thickee fra that.

totty ('tɒtɪ), *sb.* (*a.*[1]) Also tottie, totie.

1. Affectionate diminutive of TOT *sb.*[4]; a tiny tot or little child. Also as *adj.* Tiny, wee. Hence '**tottykins** = TODDLEKINS.

1821 GALT *Sir A. Wylie* III. xxxiii. 287, I would be blithe to see the wee totties spinning about the floor like peeries. **1849** J. MILNE *Let.* in Bonar *Life* ix. (1868) 129 There is not a day that I don't think of our poor little totty. *Ibid.* 128 Bonnie wee totikins, Bricht as a bee. **1906** A. MCCORMICK *Tinkler Gipsies Galloway* ii. 89 The fairies,—totie wee bodies a' cled in red.

2. *slang.* A girl or woman, *esp.* a 'good-time' girl.

1890 BARRÈRE & LELAND *Dict. Slang* II. 368/2 *Tottie*.., a girl, a fast girl. **1914** JOYCE *Dubliners* 29 He asked us which of us had the most sweethearts. Mahony mentioned lightly that he had three totties. **1957** J. BRAINE *Room at Top* xxviii. 230 She has a pal, some old tottie that lends her a flat. **1968** 'O. MILLS' *Sundry Fell Designs* viii. 86 All Dan's Manchester-type ladies were only totties. This marriage wasn't going to make any difference to them. **1977** C. WATSON *One Man's Meat* iv. 34 Showing off. Certainly, why not? There were a couple of totties just behind.

3. *Comb.*: **totty-pot** = POTTY *sb.* 1.

1966 'L. LANE' *ABZ of Scouse* II. 83 *Potty* or *totty-pot*, a child's chamber-pot. **1971** *Daily Tel.* (Colour Suppl.) 22 Oct. 17/2 Room in boot for pram, pushchair, totty-pots, picnic gear.

totty ('tɒtɪ), *a.*[2] Now *dial.* Forms: 4–6 toty, 6 tottye, -ie, 6– totty. [app. f. *tot-*, as in *totter* and *tottle* + -Y.] Unsteady, shaky, tottery (physically or mentally); dizzy, dazed; tipsy, fuddled.

c **1386** CHAUCER *Reeve's T.* 333 Myn heed is toty of my swynk to-nyght. **1412–20** LYDG. *Chron. Troy* II. 5752 Somme also so toty in her hede þat þei..haue no foot for to stonde vp-riȝt. **1522** MORE *De Quat. Noviss.* Wks. 97 What good can the great gluton do wᵗ..his noll toty with drinke? **1570** LEVINS *Manip.* 112/11 Totty, *vacillans, ebriolus, a.* **1594** O. B. *Quest. Profit. Concern.* 23 b, I thought his head was but tottie. **1652** *Season. Exp. Nether1.* 10 Who proving totty, They thought to ballast him. **1819** SCOTT *Ivanhoe* xxxiii, I was somewhat totty when I received the good knight's blow, or I had kept my ground. **1828** *Craven Gloss.*, *Totty*, half drunk, tipsy. **1890** DOYLE *White Company* xvii, Nay, nay, your head I can see is still totty.

b. *Comb.*: **totty-grass**, totter-grass, quaking-grass; **totty-head**, an imbecile; **totty-headed** *a.*, light-headed, silly, frivolous; dizzy, giddy.

1901 *Speaker* 20 Apr. 86/2 Who ever saw a child that did not love to gather primroses, horse daisies, or *totty-grass? **1680** *Honest Hodge & Ralph* 28 Not such *Totty-heads yet, as to be led by the Nose by him. *a* **1700** B. E. *Dict. Cant. Crew*, **Totty-headed*, Giddy-headed, Hare-brain'd. *a* **1825** FORBY *Voc. E. Anglia*, *Totty*, *totty-headed*, dizzy. Particularly from the effect of too much drink.

Totty, variant of TOTTIE.

†**to-'tug**, *v. Obs.* Also 3 te-, 5 to-togge. [ME. f. TO-[2] + *toggen, tugge*, TUG *v.*] *trans.* To pull to pieces.

c **1220** *Bestiary* 420 in *O.E. Misc.* 13 [He] tetoggeð and tetireð hem mid hire teð sarpe. *c* **1400** *Destr. Troy* 8042 All fadit that faire of hir fyn coloure,..All to tugget hir tresses of hir triet here. **1446** LYDG. *Two Nightingale Poems* i. 256 On euery syde to-togged and to-drawe.

totum[1] ('təʊtəm). Now *dial.* [a. L. *tōtum* all, the whole, the initial T of which was one of the four letters inscribed on the teetotum: cf. F. *toton*, in Cotgr. and *Dict. Acad.* 1694–1740 *totum*, pronounced (tətɔ̃).] = TEETOTUM, q.v.

[**1500–20** DUNBAR *Poems* xxii. 74 He playis with *totum* and I with *nichell*.] **1706** PHILLIPS (ed. Kersey), *Totum*, a Whirl-bone, a kind of Die that is turned about. **1734** CHESTERF. in *Lett. C'tess Suffolk* (1824) II. 116 A couple of totums set a spinning. **1825** JAMIESON, *Totum* sb. 1, the game of *Te-totum*. [See *Eng. Dial. Dict.*, TOTUM[2].]

'**totum**[2]. *Sc.* [perh. a humorous extension of TOT *sb.*[4]; but generally associated with prec.] A little child, a wee tot.

17.. *Cauld Kail in Aberdeen* in Aitken *Scott. Song* (1874) 146 Whene'er the totums cry for meat She curses aye his cogie. **1844** A. COCHRANE in Whitelaw *Bk. Scott. Song* (1875) 73/1 Our twa bits o' totums are toddlin their lane. **1898** *Westm. Gaz.* 6 Oct. 3/2 That the fact.. that had generated so critical an eyesight in this 'totum' of three.

‖'**totum**[3]. [L.: See TOTUM[1].] A whole.

1657 J. SMITH *Myst. Rhet.* A viij b, *Totum*, is whatsoever hath parts:..and so parts are such as make up the whole. *a* **1658** CLEVELAND *On little Gentleman* 22 How comes it that she thus converts So small a *Totum*, and great Parts? **1678** CUDWORTH *Intell. Syst.* I. i. §31 The *totum* or *compositum* of a man or animal may be said to be generated and corrupted, in regard of the union and disunion, conjunction and separation of those two parts, the soul and body.

†'**totuple**, *a.* *Obs.* [f. L. *tot* so many, after QUADRUPLE, etc.] So many-fold: = TANTUPLE.

1656 HOBBES *Six Less.* iii. Wks. 1845 VII. 240 The antecedents are of their consequents totuple or tantuple, that is, equimultiple. *a* **1696** SCARBURGH *Euclid* (1705) 201 Therefore..Totuple shall AB, CD together, be of E, F together.

to-turn, to-twin: see TO- *pref.*[2]

†**to-'tuse**, *v.* *Obs. rare*[−1]. [ME. f. TO-[2] + **túsen*, TOUSE *v.* (The later ME. form would have been *to-touse.*)] *trans.* To pull asunder; to dishevel.

c **1300** *Havelok* 1948 Al to-tused and al to-torn.

†**to-'tween**, *prep. Obs. rare.* [f. TO-[1] + *-tween* in BETWEEN.] Between.

c **1440** *Partonope* 4170 And cleuyd hys forhed to twene þe yen.

†**to-'tweme**, *v. Obs.* Forms: see TWEME. [OE. *totwǽman*, f. TO-[2] + *twǽman*, TWEME *v.* to separate, part.] **a.** *trans.* To separate, divide; also to distinguish, discriminate.

c **893** K. ÆLFRED *Oros.* III. vii. §6 Hie eft totwæmde wæron. *a* **1225** *Ancr. R.* 396 Auh ure Louerd willeliche totweamede [*v.r.* to-twinnede] his soule urom his bodie.

b. *intr.* To separate, part asunder.

c **1205** LAY. 26593 Ær heo to twemden [*pr.* to-tweinden] þe wurse wes Rom-leoden. *a* **1225** *St. Marher.* 17 Wið þe ilke þe eorðe to twemde ant bitunde him.

†**to-'twitch**, *v. Obs.* [ME. *to-twicchen*, f. TO-[2] + TWITCH *v.*] *trans.* To pull apart or away with a sudden jerk or twitch. Also *fig.*

c **1175** *Lamb. Hom.* 53 Swa sone se hi beoð iturned awey from heom, [hi] heom to-twiccheð & to-draȝeð mid ufele weordes. *a* **1250** *Owl & Night.* 1647 Gromes þe ivoþ..& þe to twiccheþ & to schakeþ. *c* **1350** *Will. Palerne* 2097 His berde & his briȝt fax for bale he to-twiȝt.

‖'**toty**. *Anglo-Ind.* [Tamil and Canarese *toṭi*.] A man of low caste employed as messenger and odd man of a South Indian village. Also **totyman**.

1800 in Gurw. *Wellington's Suppl. Desp.* (1858) I. 452 Washerman, barber, and totyman. **1886** YULE & BURNELL *Hobson-Jobson*, Toty.

toty, totyr, obs. ff. TOTTY *a.*[2], TOTTER.

‖**tou** (dou, tou). *Chinese Antiq.* [Chinese *dòu*.] A hemispherical pedestalled bowl with a lid of similar shape, used as a container for food.

1899 S. W. BUSHELL *Oriental Ceramic Art* xvii. 491 The twelve bowls (*pien*) on the right being made of closely woven slips of bamboo, lacquered yellow, the twelve (*tou*) on the left of carved wood, gilded. **1909** B. LAUFER *Chinese Pottery of Han Dynasty* iv. 122 The ears are not essential to the type of the *tou*, as there are also bronze *tou* which lack them. **1973** *Genius of China* 52/2 Red Pottery tazza *tou*, with undulating ornament painted in black.

tou, toual(l, obs. forms of TOUGH, TOWEL.

Touareg, var. TUAREG.

touart, toubbe, obs. forms of TOWARD, TUB.

toucan (tuːˈkɑːn, ˈtuːkən). Also 8 **tokan**, 9 **toukan**. [= F. *toucan*, Sp. *tucan*, Pg., It. *tucano*, a. Brazilian, Tupi *tucana*, Guarani *tucà*, *tucãn* (*a* nasal), the native name, prob. from its cry or call; but other suggestions have been offered.

The statement of Buffon that the name means 'feather' arose from his misunderstanding a statement of Léry *c* 1558: see J. Platt in *N. & Q.* 9th s. VII. 486–VIII. 250.]

1. A Neotropical bird of the genus *Rhamphastos*, or, in a wider use, of the family *Rhamphastidæ*, inhabiting the tropical parts of South America, a few species being also found in Central America and Mexico. They are noted for the enormous size of the beak and their striking colouring. The species originally so named was app. *R. toco*.

[**1558** THEVET *Sing. France Antarctique*, D'un oyseau qu'ils appellent en leur langue Toucan.] **1568** tr. *Thevet's New-found. World* 73 Of a birde named toucan. **1634** T. JOHNSON *Parey's Chirurg.* XXV. xxii. (1678) 621 He saw a Bird in America, which in that Countrey Speech is called Touca,..that the beak in length and thickness exceeds the bigness of the rest of the body. **1668** CHARLETON *Onomast.* 115 *Tucana*..Toucan. **1677** PLOT *Oxfordsh.* 178 In..1644 the *Pica Brasiliensis*, or Toucan, whose beak is near as big as its whole body, was found within two miles of Oxford. **1681** GREW *Musæum* I. IV. i. 59 The Head of the Toucan, so called by the Indians. **1796** STEDMAN *Surinam* I. vi. 117 The toucan is not larger than a tame pigeon, and yet its beak is no less than six inches in length. **1863** BATES *Nat. Amazon* xii. (1864) 404 Toucans... Two of them are often heard yelping alternately, and in different notes. These cries have a vague resemblance to the syllables Tocáno, Tocáno, and hence the Indian name of this genus of birds. **1875** WHITNEY *Life Lang.* vii. 120 The cuckoo and the peewee and the toucan were named from their notes.

b. Sometimes applied or misapplied to other birds with large or curious beaks; esp. in the East Indies to species of Hornbill (*Buceros*).

But the word in the latter case is said to be the Malay *tukang* 'workman' or 'artificer', and entirely distinct from the Brazilian: see Yule & Burnell *Hobson-Jobson*.

1816 TUCKEY *Narr. Exped. R. Zaire* iii. (1818) 82 Several varieties of the king fisher, a toukan, and many small birds. **1862** JERDON *Birds of India* I. 242 They [the hornbills] are, indeed, popularly called *Toucans* throughout India; and this appears to be their name in some of the Malayan isles; the word signifying 'worker', from the noise they make.

2. *Astron.* Name of a southern constellation.

1669 STURMY *Mariner's Mag.* VI. iii. 128 The Bird Toucan [*pr.* Taican], or Brasilian Pye, in which Constellation is 7 Stars. **1868** LOCKYER *Guillemin's Heavens* xii. (1872) 319 The splendid cluster in Toucan, quite visible to the naked eye.

3. *Comb.*, as ***toucan skin***, etc.; **toucan-beak**, the beak of the toucan, or the substance of this used as a decorative material.

1862 *List Contrib. fr. Brit. Guiana to Lond. Exhib.* in Veness *El Dorado* (1866) App. 145 Tassel of Toucan Skins, worn by the Accawai Indians..hanging down the back. **1886** *Art Jrnl., Exh. Suppl.* 26/2 Some clever and minute carvings in toucan-beak set with alternate links in gold.

Hence **toucanet** ('tuːkəˌnɛt), any of the smaller kinds of toucan, as those of the genera *Pteroglossus* and *Selenidera*; **toucanity** (tuːˈkænɪtɪ), *nonce-wd.*, the character of a toucan.

1825 WATERTON *Wand. S. Amer.* II. 118 There are three species of Toucans in Demerara, and three diminutives, which may be called Toucanets. **1892** *Cornh. Mag.* May 525 A large bill..a mark of perfect and advanced toucanity.

touch (tʌtʃ), *sb.* Forms: see TOUCH *v.* [Originally a. OF. *touche*, f. *toucher* to TOUCH: cf. Pr., It. *tocca* stroke, blow, touch; also Prov. *toc*, It. *tocco* knock, stroke; f. *toccare* to hit, strike. In some later uses, directly from TOUCH *v.*]

I. Literal and directly connected senses.

1. a. The action or an act of touching (with the hand, finger, or other part of the body); exercise of the faculty of feeling upon a material object. †In quot. 1340, ? a tactile organ (*obs.*). In quot. 1591, Hold, grasp, embrace (*nonce-use*).

1340 HAMPOLE *Pr. Consc.* 779 Fyngers and taes, fote and hande, Alle his touches [*MS. Lansd.* lymmes] er tremblande. **1390** GOWER *Conf.* II. 136 For he..preide, That wherupon his hond he leide, It scholde thurgh his touche anon Become gold. **1398** TREVISA *Barth. De P.R.* XVI. vii. (Bodl. MS.), Quyke siluer..semeþ ful colde in touche. **1513** DOUGLAS *Æneis* III. iv. 36 The Harpyes..with thair laithlie tuiche all thing file thai. **1591** SHAKS. *Two Gent.* V. iv. 60 Ruffian: let goe that rude vnciuill touch. **1614** PURCHAS *Pilgrimage* IX. vii. (ed.2) 864 He toucheth the face and breast with cold touches. **1681** H. MORE *Exp. Dan.* iv. Notes 120 He healed the Blind and the Lame with Spittle and touch. **1705** *Lond. Gaz.* No. 4126/3 They never had before received the Royal Touch. **1841–71** T. R. JONES *Anim. Kingd.* (ed. 4) 464 The antennæ..may be regarded as special instruments of touch. **1842** TENNYSON '*Break, break, break*' iii, But O for the touch of a vanish'd hand! **1898** G. B. SHAW *Widowers' Houses* I. 6 The porter..receives it with a submissive touch to his cap.

b. *euphem.* Sexual contact.

a **1300** *Cursor M.* 2985 (Cott.) Fra toche of hir i saued þe. **1412–20** LYDG. *Chron. Troy* I. 2860 Sche Ay kepte hir clene from touche of any man. **1603** SHAKS. *Meas. for M.* V. i. 141 Who is as free from touch or soyle with her As she from one vngot.

c. *Med.* Examination by feeling, esp. of a cavity of the body; palpation.

1805 *Med. Jrnl.* XIV. 245 Had we..trusted to the touch, it might have been said we were deceived. **1860** MAYNE *Expos. Lex.*, *Touch..Obstet.* Term for the examination of the womb, or mouth and neck of the womb.

d. *Milit.* Contact between the elbows of a rank of soldiers; see quots. and cf. TOUCH *v.* 2 g.

1877 *Man. Field Artillery Exerc.* 23 The right-hand or left-hand man being first placed, the remainder will fall in in line one after the other, closing lightly towards him, turning the elbow slightly outwards. Soldiers must be carefully instructed in the 'Touch', as, in this formation, it is the principal guide when marching. *Ibid.* 25 During the march ..the dressing is kept by the touch.

e. ***within*** or ***in touch***, near enough to touch or be touched; within reach (*of*); accessible; also *fig.*

1854 S. DOBELL *Balder* v. 29 Tottering..In touch of the inestimable prize. **1858** HAWTHORNE *Fr. & It. Note-Bks.* I. 119 The rough-hewn roof was within touch. **1896** *Times* 16 Dec. 5/3 [He] is not yet within touch of the telegraph.

†**f.** The act of touching at a port (TOUCH *v.* 11); a passing call during a voyage. *Obs. rare*[−1].

1603 KNOLLES *Hist. Turks* (1621) 1331 His first touch was upon the Island of Cerigo.

g. A boys' game in which one player touches another, who then chases and tries to catch him; in full ***touch-and-run***; also allusively (cf. TOUCH AND GO). Cf. TIG.

1815 LADY GRANVILLE *Lett.* (1894) I. 80 His favourite has hit the line between good-humoured frankness and vulgarity, just touch and run. **1912** *Daily News* 4 Nov. 2/2 The lad was playing 'touch-and-run' with a number of others.

2. a. The act, fact, or state of touching or being touched (of inanimate objects, or as an involuntary act: see TOUCH *v.* 3); contact.

13.. *E.E. Allit. P.* C. 252 With-outen towche of any tothe he tult in his þrote. *a* **1586** SIDNEY *Arcadia* II. (1590) 149 b, The touch of the cold water made a prettie kinde of shrugging come ouer her bodie. **1596** SHAKS. *Merch. V.* III. ii. 273 And not one vessell scape the dreadfull touch Of merchant-marring rocks? **1667** MILTON *P.L.* VI. 520 Part incentive reed Provide, pernicious with one touch to fire. **1784** COWPER *Task* II. 11 The flax That falls asunder at the touch of fire. **1874** O'SHAUGHNESSY *Music & Moonlight* 40 Her passing touch was death to all, Her passing look a blight.

†**b.** *Geom.* Contact; point of contact. *Obs.*

a **1400** in Halliwell *Rara Mathem.* (1841) 62 Counte þe poyntes fro þe begynnyng of þe side of þe vmbre to þe touche of þe perpendicle. **1551** RECORDE *Pathw. Knowl.* I. xxix, In the very poynte of the touche muste I make an angle. **1570** BILLINGSLEY *Euclid* III. def. iii, Such a touch of circles is euer in one poynt onely.

c. A small quantity of some substance brought into contact with a surface so as to leave its mark or effect; a dash, as of paint; a mark or stain so produced. See also 10.

In quot. 1581 with figurative allusion: cf. PITCH *sb.*[1] 4, and quot. 1382 s.v. TOUCH *v.* 1. So *a touch of the tar-brush*: see TAR-BRUSH b, quot. 1864.

1581 PETTIE *Guazzo's Civ. Conv.* I. (1586) 24 Of one selfe pitch, we all haue a touch. **1664** POWER *Exp. Philos.* I. 31, I ..glew'd them to the object-plate, as I do stronger Insects with a touch of Turpentine. **1818** SCOTT *Hrt. Midl.* xvii, Maybe a touch o' a blackit cork, or a slake o' paint.

d. A very close approach, a 'shave': cf. TOUCH *v.* 14, TOUCHER 4.

18.. DICKENS (Ogilvie), The hind coach passed my engine by a shave. It was the nearest touch I ever saw.

e. ***no touch to*** (*U.S. colloq.*): 'nowhere near', nothing approaching to.

1838 HALIBURTON *Clockm.* Ser. II. vi. (1862) 206 Our sea sarpant was no touch to it. **1840** —— *Letter Bag* ii. 18 You ab seen fourth July day,..well he [is] no touch to it.

3. a. That sense by which a material object is perceived by means of the contact with it of some part of the body; the most general of the bodily senses, diffused through all parts of the skin, but (in man) specially developed in the tips of the fingers and the lips.

c **1394** *P. Pl. Crede* 537 þanne haue y tynt all my tast, touche and assaie! **1599** DAVIES *Immort. Soul* ccxxii, By touch the first pure qualities we learn Which quicken all things, hot, cold, moist, and dry. *a* **1704** LOCKE *Elem. Nat. Philos.* xi. (1754) 50 The fifth and last of our senses is touch; a sense spread over the whole body, tho' it be most eminently placed in the ends of the fingers. **1764** REID *Inquiry* vi. §8. 213 That figure and that extension which are objects of touch have been tortured ten thousand ways for twenty centuries. **1851** CARPENTER *Man. Phys.* (ed. 2) 551 There is strong reason to regard the sense of Taste as only a refined kind of Touch, combined with the sense of Smell.

b. The sensation caused by touching something (considered as an attribute of the thing); tactile quality, feel.

1674 DRYDEN *Epil. opening of New House* 4 A Country Lip may have the Velvet touch. **1804** J. GRAHAME *Sabbath* (1805) 37 The smooth birch With rind of silken touch. **1839** URE *Dict. Arts* 1202 Most decide by 'the touch', that is, the feel and appearance of a drop of the syrup..drawn into a thread between the thumb and fore-finger. **1844** *Jrnl. R. Agric. Soc.* V. I. 259 The first token..for the purpose of ascertaining the feeding properties of an ox, is technically called the touch.

4. a. A hit, knock, stroke, blow; *esp.* a very slight blow or stroke.

[Quot. 1297 here appears to be the earliest example of the word in Eng., and perh. shows the original sense, as 'hit, stroke, blow'.]

In quot. *c* 1375, ? a slight wound or abrasion such as might be produced by a blow or scratch.

1297 R. GLOUC. (Rolls) 12020 So þat þe erl of wareine slou atte verste touche Biuore þe iustises atte bench sir alein de la souche. *c* **1375** *Cursor M.* 14012 (Fairf.) þer ho fande any touche of sare [*Cott.* ani breck or sare; *Trin.* chyn or soore] Wiþ hir þingus anoynt hit þare. *c* **1420** *Anturs of Arth.* 605 (Thornton MS.) Swylke a touche at þat tyme he taughte hym in tene. **1581** T. HOWELL *Deuises* (1879) 216 For some perchance will byde a toutch or two, And will not seeme to flye when you shall fall. **1879** F. W. ROBINSON *Coward Consc.* II. xvii, 'It requires the finest touch', said Mr. Slitherwick, shutting one eye to admire the position of the balls, 'one of your very best touches, Mr. Oliver'.

b. *fig.* A 'hit', stroke (of wit, satire, etc.); a 'knock'; a 'blow'.

1522 *World & Child* (1817) Cj, How sayeste thou now folye hast thou not a touche? **1667** MILTON *P.L.* IX. 1144 To whom soon mov'd with touch of blame thus Eve. *c* **1720** PRIOR *Paulo Purganti* 29 It yet may feel the nicer touch Of

Wycherley's or Congreve's wit. **1852** THACKERAY *Esmond* II. v, There was a hard touch for his Grace, .. in the concluding sentence of the Don.

II. Technical and allied senses.

* *Relating to the touchstone.*

5. a. The action or process of testing the quality of gold or silver by rubbing it upon a touchstone. [So OF. *touche*, It. *tocco*.]

1436 *Pol. Poems* (Rolls) II. 187 Whereof was fyned metalle gode and clene, At the touche, no bettere coude be sene. **1587** *Mirr. Mag., Runa* ii, Good metall bides the touch that trieth out the gold. **1686** W. DE BRITAINE *Hum. Prud.* xx. 94 He is like Gold, which hath too much Allay, that feareth the Touch. **1837** WHITTOCK, etc. *Bk. Trades* (1842) 279 This test, by the touch, is performed at the present day... Touch needles are small bars made of compound metals, the proportions whereof are accurately marked on each.

b. An official mark or stamp upon gold or silver indicating that it has been tested, and is of standard fineness; also, a die, punch, or stamp for impressing this. Also, an official mark stamped upon pewter.

1423 [see TOUCH *v.* 8 b]. **1443** *Test. Ebor.* (Surtees) II. 132 A quart pot of silver with the touche of Parys. **1522** *Will J. Surdevall* (Somerset Ho.), Which spones hath the toche of the Goldesmythes. **1526–7** in Welch *Hist. Pewterers' Co.* (1902) I. 118 A fyn for delieueryng vessell vn-markyt w^t his towch .. v s. [**1564–1750** *ibid. passim.*] *a* **1553** UDALL *Royster D.* II. ii. (Arb.) 34 If he haue not one Lumbardes touche, my lucke is bad. **1594** PLAT *Jewell-h.* III. 79 Plate as either carieth no touch, or so old a touch as the buier shall not bee acquainted withall. **1697** *View Penal Laws* 142 If the Keeper of the Touch mark such harness with the Leopards head. **1852** A. RYLAND *Assay of Gold & Silver* 38 The *Touch* is used in the old Statutes to denote in some places the Standard, in some the punch used in marking the wares, and in others the mark impressed upon the plate. **1860** J. SCARTH *12 Yrs. China* 116 Of the enormous amounts of gold .. the greater part is guaranteed by a certain touch.

c. The quality or fineness of gold or silver (or other metal) as tested with the touchstone and indicated by the official mark. [Cf. OF. *touche de Paris*, etc.]

a **1325** *MS. Rawl. B.* 520 lf. 53 b, þat is to witen golde of certein touche. *Ibid.*, Ant þat non ne wurche worse gold þan þe touche of paris. **1465** *Paston Lett.* I. 134, j. herneyse complete of the touche of Milleyn. **1601** HOLLAND *Pliny* XXXIII. ix. II. 479 An act .. for the proofe and allowance of silver deniers, what touch and what poise they should have. **1697** *Observ. on Money & Coin* 9 Gold shall be of the fineness of the Touch of Paris. **1766** T. BROOKS *Coins E. Indies* 6, 1 Madrass Rupee .. is Country Touch 9⅝. China Touch 98⅞. **1908** H. B. MORSE *Trade Chinese Emp.* 149 'Pure silver' of the Kuping tael touch is actually 987 fine when reduced to the Western standard of chemically pure silver.

d. *fig.* Quality, kind, sort, 'stamp'. In quot. 1878 *transf.* Quality or degree of purity (of opium).

1388 *Pol. Poems* (Rolls) I. 274 Fresch of the newe towch, *incedunt ridiculose*, Lityl or noght in her powch, *pascuntur deliciose*. **1579** J. STUBBES *Gaping Gulf* A vij, To be of one assaie or touche with the idolatrous and trayterous Israelits. **1607** SHAKS. *Cor.* IV. i. 49 Come my sweet wife, my deerest Mother, and My Friends of Noble touch. **1821** LAMB *Elia* Ser. I. *Imperfect Sympathies*, He never stoops to catch a glittering something .. before he quite knows whether it be true touch or not. **1878** BABER *Rep. Chinese Opium* (Parl. Paper Eng. C. 3378, 1882, 29) The advantage of 'touch', or percentage of extract, possessed by the Indian drug.

†**6.** Short for *touchstone* (see TOUCHSTONE 2); *esp.* applied to black marble or some similar black stone used in monumental work. *Obs.* [So OF. *touche* for *pierre de touche* (Godef.).]

a **1509** *Will. of Hen. VII* (Parker *Gloss. Archit.* 1845), In which place we wol, that .. be made a Towmbe of Stone called Touche, sufficient in largieur for us booth. *a* **1548** HALL *Chron., Hen. VIII* 96 b, Gates all like Masonrie, of White and Blacke, like Touche and White Merbell. **1577** STANYHURST *Descr. Irel.* in *Holinshed* (1808) VI. 41 Such notable quarries of greie marble and touch. *c* **1625** BACON *Will* Wks. 1874 XIX. 541 Also the armour, and also all tables of marble and towch. *a* **1661** FULLER *Worthies, York* (1662) II. 186 Vulgar eyes confound the inlayings made of black Marble .. with Touch, Geat, and Ebony. **1665** SIR T. HERBERT *Trav.* (1677) 143 Several parts of it were as bright and splendent as Touch or Steel-mirrour.

7. *fig.* (from 5). An act of, or thing that serves for, testing; a test, trial, proof; a criterion, 'touchstone'. Now chiefly in phr. *to put to the touch*.

1581 MULCASTER *Positions* iii. (1887) 12, I will binde vpon proofe, and let triall be the tuche. **1594** SHAKS. *Rich. III*, IV. ii. 8 Ah Buckingham, now doe I play the Touch, To trie if thou be currant Gold indeed. **1624** QUARLES *Job* VII. med. xiii, Affliction is the Touch, whereby we proove, Whether 't be Gold, or guilt. **1688** R. HOLME *Armoury* III. 206/1 Verity is not ashamed of the Light, nor afraid to come to the touch. **1706** KENNETT *Compl. Hist. Eng.* III. 561/1 That when it came to the Touch, they wou'd never bear the Brunt of a Battle. **1886** STEVENSON *Kidnapped* 10 Till I had put the matter to the touch of proof.

** *In instrumental music.*

8. *Mus.* The act or manner of touching or handling a musical instrument, so as to bring out its tones; now *esp.* the manner of striking or pressing the keys of a keyboard instrument so as to produce special varieties of tone or effect. Hence *transf.* (chiefly *poet.*) a single sound produced by touching an instrument; a note or brief strain of instrumental music.

13.. *Gaw. & Gr. Knt.* 120 Nwe nakryn noyse with þe noble pipes, Wylde werbles & wyȝt wakned lote, þat mony hert ful hiȝe hef at her towches. **1591** SHAKS. *Two Gent.* III. ii. 79 Orpheus Lute, .. Whose golden touch could soften steele and stones. **1596** —— *Merch. V.* V. i. 67 With sweetest tutches pearce your Mistresse eare, And draw her home with musicke. **1628** MILTON *Vac. Exerc.* 38 Listening to what unshorn Apollo sings To th' touch of golden wires. **1667** —— *P.L.* IV. 686 With Heav'nly touch of instrumental sounds. **1828** SCOTT *F.M. Perth* x, I hear no unpleasing touch of minstrelsy. **1879** A. J. HIPKINS in Grove *Dict. Mus.* I. 647 A sensitive instrument of touch, instead of one of mere percussion. **1884** F. TAYLOR *ibid.* IV. 152 Pianoforte music demands two distinct kinds of touch, the one adapted for .. brilliant passages, the other for sustained melodies.

b. As an attribute of the performer: Capacity, skill, or style of playing; now esp. on a keyboard instrument, in relation to the action of the fingers upon the keys (see above).

1601 ? MARSTON *Pasquil & Kath.* I. 15, I had the best stroke, the sweetest touch, but now .. I am falne from the Fiddle. **1613** FLETCHER, etc. *Captain* I. iii, You had a pleasant touch o' th' cittern once, If idleness have not bereft you of it. *a* **1913** *Mod.* He has a remarkably delicate touch, and excels in *pianissimo*.

c. As an attribute of a keyboard instrument, referring to the manner in which its keys and action respond to the touch of the player.

1816 JANE AUSTEN *Emma* II. viii. 147 Having so much to ask and to say as to tone, touch, and pedal. **1884** W. PARRATT in Grove *Dict. Mus.* IV. 153 It is rare to find any two [organ] manuals with a similar touch, and the amount of force required to press down the key varies within wide limits. Even on the same keyboard the touch is appreciably heavier in the bass. **1885** C. G. W. LOCK *Workshop Receipts* Ser. IV. 279/2 The next item, and one claiming serious attention, is the 'touch', for on this depends in a great measure the pleasure and comfort of the performer. **1906** *Edin. Rev.* Apr. 412 It has a flexibility, what musicians call a sense of touch. *a* **1913** *Mod.* This piano (or organ) has a very stiff (or, a very light) touch.

†**d.** app. = TOCCATA. *Obs.*

a **1623** in Grove *Dict. Mus.* IV. 154 (*title of MS. in Brit. Mus.*) A touche by Mr. Byrd. *a* **1782** *Ibid.* (*title of MS. in Lib. Roy. Coll. Music*), Mr. Kelway's touches.

9. *Bell-ringing.* Any series of changes less than a peal.

1872 ELLACOMBE *Ch. Bells Devon*, etc. ix. 471 A peal .. means the performance of the full number of changes which may be rung on a given number of bells; any less number of changes would be called 'a touch'. **1898** G. S. TYACK *Bk. about Bells* viii. 141 Five thousand changes .. is the smallest number to which the name of a peal is technically allowed, less than that number merely constitutes a 'touch'.

*** *In artistic work.*

10. a. An act of touching a surface with the proper tool in painting, drawing, writing, carving, etc.; a stroke or dash of a brush, pencil, pen, chisel, or the like; hence, a stroke or dash of colour in a picture, etc., or a detail of any artistic work, as in literary description; a slight act or effort added in doing or completing a piece of work of any kind.

1607 SHAKS. *Timon* I. i. 38 It [a picture] tutors Nature, Artificiall strife Liues in these toutches, liuelier then life. **1693** DRYDEN *Juvenal* Ded. (1697) 5 Some few Touches of your Lordship, some secret Graces which I have endeavour'd to express after your manner. **1712** ADDISON *Spect.* No. 357 ¶8 Milton never fails of .. bestowing the last finishing Touches to every Incident. **1768** W. GILPIN *Ess. Prints* 39 Unless the pencil add those high-blown touches, which mark the passion. **1847** L. HUNT *Men, Women, & B.* II. x. 212 She might be suspected of having given it some after touches. **1894** J. T. FOWLER *Adamnan* Introd. 74 Eddius's graphic touch about St. Wilfrid .. some life-like touches in Colgan's *Vita Secunda*.

b. Capacity of using the brush, pencil, pen, or other instrument; artistic skill or faculty; style or quality of artistic work; method of handling, execution. (Cf. 8 b, 18.)

1815 J. SMITH *Panorama Sc. & Art* II. 748 Painting in crayons .. may serve to teach him a masterly freedom of touch. **1880** WARREN *Book-plates* iv. 35 In Mountaine's early Chippendale style, and with that engraver's touch.

**** *In Magnetism.*

11. The action or process of magnetizing a steel bar or needle by contact with one or more magnets; different methods are known as *single, double*, and *separate touch*.

1705 DERHAM in *Phil. Trans.* XXV. 2143 This gave so vigorous a Touch, that I am almost of opinion, It is the best way of Touching. **1837** BREWSTER *Magnet.* 15 The science of magnetism is .. indebted to Mr. Michell for his invention of the method of double touch. **1849** NOAD *Electricity* 308 Mr. Michell states that two magnets will, by his process of double touch, communicate as strong a magnetic virtue to a steel bar, as a single magnet of five times the strength, when used in the process of single touch.

***** *In Amer. and Rugby Football.*

12. The act of touching the ground with the ball behind the goal, usually the opponents' goal (see TOUCH *v.* 30, also *touchback*, s.v. TOUCH- 2, TOUCHDOWN 1); *transf.* (esp. in phr. *in* or *into touch*), that part of the ground outside the bounding lines of the field of play (*touch-lines* and *goal-lines*); *touch-in-goal*, that part of this behind the goal-line.

1857 [see PLAY *sb.* 10 d]. **1864** *Field* 5 Nov. 331/1 The School .. managed to keep the ball close to their opponents' goal, till at length a long drop of Poole's took the ball into touch-in-goal. *Ibid.* 19 Nov. 354/2 [see TOUCH *v.* 2 f]. **1877** *Ibid.* 24 Feb. 220/2 Clifton scored a touch in goal. **1886** *Ibid.* 9 Oct. 535/2 An easy victory .. by eight goals, three tries, and six touches to one goal. **1889** H. VASSALL *Rugby Football* 18 Our full-back .. should always bear in mind that he must send it [the ball] into touch at all costs, as that means so much ground gained for his side for the next line out. **1895** *Outing* (U.S.) XXVII. 250/1 The ball is thrown out from touch by the side that carried it in, or by the opposite team to that which kicked it in.

III. Various figurative senses. (See also 1 e, 2 e, 4 b, 5 d, 7.)

13. *fig.* The act of touching or fact of being touched (in *fig.* senses of the vb.). **a.** A stroke, action, or influence (esp. slight, or momentary); a slight or instantaneous act producing some effect.

c **1586** C'TESS PEMBROKE *Ps.* XC. i, Free From all touch of age and yeare. **1602** MARSTON *Ant. & Mel.* III. Wks. 1856 I. 35, I will .. strike her thoughts with the pleasing touch of my voice. *c* **1742** GRAY *Ignorance* 21 With damp, cold touch forbid it [spark of wit] to aspire. **1780** BURKE *Sp. Econ. Reform* Wks. III. 261 That their ancient .. castles should moulder into decay, under the silent touches of time. **1799** *Monthly Rev.* XXX. 490 The Cartesian hypothesis melted away under the touch of geometry. **1819** SCOTT *Leg. Montrose* xvi, Curing me, in respect that I had got a touch of the wars in my retreat. **1878** BROWNING *La Saisiaz* 329 Death's kindly touch .. gave Soul and body both release. **1884** H. JAMES *Little Tour France* xxvii. 173 Vineyards red with the touch of October.

b. *spec.* An impression upon the mind or soul; a feeling, sense (*of* some emotion, etc.); †a feeling of interest or concern *in* something (cf. TOUCH *v.* 20, 21).

c **1586** C'TESS PEMBROKE *Ps.* CIII. viii, And looke how much The neerly touching touch The father feeles towards his sonne most deare. **1591** SHAKS. *Two Gent.* II. vii. 18 Didst thou but know the inly touch of Loue. **1690** C. NESSE *O. & N. Test.* I. 210 If the Holy Spirit doth not touch us with his divine touches, the unclean spirit will with his deadly touches. **1866** B. TAYLOR *Over Possession* Poems 270, I wait the touch of song. **1869** TOZER *Highl. Turkey* II. 232 One occurrence, or idea, or touch of feeling, is selected, and .. seldom treated at any great length. **1873** BLACK *Pr. Thule* xii, Some touch of compunction smote him.

c. The condition of being mentally 'touched' or affected (TOUCH *v.* 23 b); slight derangement. *rare*$^{-1}$.

1710 STEELE *Tatler* No. 178 ¶2 My Friend the Upholsterer, whose Crack towards Politicks I have heretofore mention'd. This Touch in the Brain of the British Subject is .. owing to the reading News-Papers.

d. A close relation of communication, agreement, sympathy, or interest; chiefly in phr. *in* or *out of touch with*, also *to keep* or *lose touch with* (rarely *of*). [Perh. orig. in literal use, in military drill; cf. 1 d.]

1884 CHURCH *Bacon* vi. 153 The Kingship of the Tudors .. always seeking .. to be in touch and sympathy with popular feeling. **1884** *Pall Mall G.* 25 Jan. 4/2 Sir Henry Parkes has always kept himself in touch with English public opinion. **1884** *Christian World* 15 May 369/2 He had never lost touch with his brethren. **1887** A. FLEMING in *Libr. Mag.* 29 Jan. 325 To bring religion into touch with conduct. **1891** G. MOORE *Impressions & Opinions* 88 He is out of touch with them; he cannot make them understand. **1901** EARL SPENCER in *Parl. Deb.* 5 July 948 But they are not in touch .. with all the best information which the Board of Admiralty have at their command. **1969** H. PERKIN *Key Profession* i. 4 By then Newman was out of touch with what universities were becoming. **1980** D. LODGE *How Far can you Go?* iv. 121 Most of them had been out of touch with him for many years, but he spoke to them as if it was only yesterday.

14. (*fig.* from 3.) A faculty or capacity of the mind analogous or likened to the sense of touch; mental or moral perception or feeling.

1656 STANLEY *Hist. Philos.* IV. (1701) 134/1 They held that .. those things only can be perceived which are felt by inward touch as grief and pleasure. **1872** LIDDON *Elem. Relig.* v. 179 An accuracy and delicacy of intellectual touch. **1904** H. BLACK *Pract. Self Cult.* vii. 168 You will develop tact, which is just the faculty of touch, fineness of sensation.

15. A stroke of action, an act; a brief turn or 'go' *at* some occupation; †in early use, a sly, mean, or deceitful act, a trick (*obs.*). Now *rare*.

1481 CAXTON *Reynard* xxv. (Arb.) 56 O what false touches can he, how can he stuffe the sleue wyth flockes. *a* **1521** J. HEYWOOD *Pard. & Friar* Plays (1905) 21 If thou play me such another touch I sh' knock thee on the costard. **1530** PALSGR. 640 It is no good felowes touche to stande mouching in a cornar. **1572** GASCOIGNE *Counc. to B. Withipoll* 7 Beleeue me now it is a friendly touch, To vse fewe words where friendship doth remaine. *a* **1591** H. SMITH *Wks.* (1867) II. 406 Mahomet .. went and first took part with the Romans, but afterwards served them a sly touch, and forsook them. **1598** T. BASTARD *Chrestoleros* (1880) 36 Some will giue sixe pence for a witty touch, And some to see an Ape will giue as much. **1681** T. FLATMAN *Heraclitus Ridens* No. 37 (1713) I. 246 We'll have a Touch with him for it one of these Days. **1791** O'KEEFFE *Wild Oats* II. ii, I'll take a touch at the London theatre. **1833** HT. MARTINEAU *Loom & Lug.* II. i, She might not only clean her husband's loom in peace but have a touch at the old man's.

16. a. An act of touching upon or mentioning something; a mention, reference, allusion, slight notice, hint; a brief statement or narration. Now *rare* or *Obs.*

13.. *Gaw. & Gr. Knt.* 1301 Bot he had craued a cosse, bi his courtaysye, Bi sum towch of summe tryfle, at sum talez ende. **1460** CAPGRAVE *Chron.* Ded. (Rolls) 1 Whanne I loke upon hem, and have a schort touch of the writing, I can sone dilate the circumstaunses. **1600** O. E. *Repl. Libel* I. vi. 169 He passeth this ouer without touch, and onely telleth vs [etc.]. **1628** COKE *On Litt.* (1629) 289 Two ancient Records .. whereof to my remembrance, I neuer read any touch in our Bookes. **1653** H. MORE *Antid. Ath.* II. ii. §7 (1712) 43 First I shall recurr and give a touch upon the nature of gravity. **1685** BAXTER *Paraphr. N.T.* Mark xvi. 14 Mark doth but give us a brief touch of some of Christ's appearances, and leaves much, recorded by others. **1706** J. LOGAN in *Pa. Hist. Soc. Mem.* X. 120, I cannot think it becomes me when I write about thy business to give it by hints and touches. **1855** W. ARNOT *Let.* in Mrs. A. Fleming *Life* vi. (1877) 295, I can on short warning give you a little touch, with a moral in it like the two papers I have sent you.

†**b.** The fact or quality of touching, affecting, concerning, or relating to something; relation, reference, concern. *Obs. rare.*

1612 BACON *Ess., Discourse* (Arb.) 21 Speech of touch toward others, should bee sparingly vsed; for discourse ought to bee as a field, without comming home to any man. **1625** *Ibid., Anger* 566 Opinion of the Touch of a Mans Reputation, doth multiply and sharpen Anger.

†**17.** The quality or fact of affecting injuriously; reproach, blemish, stain, taint. *Obs.*

1567 Q. ELIZ. *Let. to Throgmorton* in Robertson *Hist. Scot.* (1759) II. App. 47 We..cannot but think them to have therein gone so far beyond the duty of subjects, as must needs remain to their perpetual touche for ever. *c* **1580** WALSINGHAM in Digges *Compl. Ambass.* (1655) 366 They did not see how their Monsieurs honour..could be salved, without great touch to both. **1588** *Copy of Let.* in *Harl. Misc.* (Malh.) II. 71 Reported, to the dishonour of the Duke of Medina..and to a great touch to the commanders of the Spanish navy. **1616** SIR R. DUDLEY in *Fortescue Papers* (Camden) 16 That I have lived these nine yeares abroade, without all tutche of disloyalty.

18. a. A distinguishing quality, characteristic, trait. (Cf. 5 d; but app. partly *fig.* from 10.) In later use often passing into 'trace': see 19.

1539 TAVERNER *Erasm. Prov.* (1552) 38 It is theyr owne maners, theyr owne qualities, touches, condicions, & procedynges that shape them this fortune. **1603** B. JONSON *Sejanus* I. i, But he had other touches of late Romans, That more did speak him: Pompey's dignity, The innocence of Cato, Cæsar's spirit. **1606** SHAKS. *Tr. & Cr.* III. iii. 175 One touch of nature makes the whole world kin [= One natural trait proves the kinship of all mankind]: That all with one consent praise new borne gaudes. **1679** J. GOODMAN *Penit. Pard.* II. i. (1713) 144 As if men had forgone all touches of humanity and were become a kind of walking-ghosts. **1856** EMERSON *Eng. Traits, Ability* Wks. (Bohn) II. 35 You shall trace those Gothic touches at school, at country fairs, at the hustings, and in Parliament. **1897** H. NEWBOLT *Admirals All* 30 But cared greatly to serve God and the king, And keep the Nelson touch.

b. (*fig.* from senses 8 b, 10 b.) A person's characteristic skill or aptitude in any activity, *spec.* a sport; ***to lose one's touch, to be out of touch***, not to show one's customary skill; similarly ***to be in touch***.

1927 *Sat. Rev.* 9 July 60/1 But in the extended character-drawing of Ferdinand Banting and Tom Lord, who are not indigenous to the King's Cross scene, he seems to lose his touch. **1933** *Times* 18 Nov. 5/7 Success depended on being in touch for his drop shots, and yesterday his touch failed him. *Ibid.* 8 Dec. 6/2 He lost his touch and made but one more ace before the match was over. **1939** *Punch* 4 Oct. 378/1 That fatal hour when Hitler lost his touch. **1955** *Times* 13 July 8/5 It is one of the signs of greatness to be able to stay in for a long time without finding touch, and yet without looking exactly like getting out. **1959** *Times* 29 May 4/2 Nicholls, who has been out of touch, is a tall, stylish player. **1976** *Liverpool Echo* 6 Dec. 17/2 It was..stalemate until Ipswich found the touch which produced the winner 15 minutes from the end. **1977** *World of Cricket Monthly* June 28/3 The presence of Kallicharran in his best touch for the series..encouraged a little West Indian optimism entering the last day. **1979** A. MORICE *Murder in Outline* v. 44 She may not be in the pink of health, but she has not lost her touch.

19. A slight amount or trace *of* some quality, attribute, or ingredient; 'a small quantity intermingled' (J.); a trace, spice, smack.

1594 SHAKS. *Rich. III*, IV. iv. 157 Madam, I haue a touch of your condition, That cannot brooke the accent of reproofe. **1643** J. M. *Soveraigne Salve* 21 Hath not even the Lord Chancellour a little touch of such a power? **1707** NORRIS *Treat. Humility* vi. 282 The bashful and blushing speaker must have a touch of vanity in his constitution. **1821** SCOTT *Kenilw.* vii, She hath in her a touch of her father Henry. **1835** LINDLEY *Introd. Bot.* (1839) 477 Grey with a touch of red.

b. *spec.* A slight affection or attack *of* illness or disease; a twinge. (Cf. 4.) Also ***a touch of the sun***, a mild attack of sunstroke.

1662 J. DAVIES tr. *Olearius' Voy. Ambass.* 259 Monsieur Mandelslo was the onely person who had no touch of sicknesse all along our Travels. **1687** A. LOVELL tr. *Thevenot's Trav.* I. 260 Every one threatned me with that Distemper, and yet..I never had the least touch of it. **1791** 'G. GAMBADO' *Ann. Horsem.* viii. (1809) 102, I have a touch of the gout in my knees. **1890** BESANT *Demoniac* ii, He said he had had a touch of sore throat. **1890** KIPLING *Life's Handicap* (1891) 165, I judge no man this weather... He had a touch of the sun, I fancy. **1915** R. BROOKE *Let.* Apr. (1968) 680 When I had a touch of the sun, in Egypt. **1965** M. SPARK *Mandelbaum Gate* v. 118 'A touch of the sun,' Freddy said. Amnesia, was the doctor's conclusion... Nonsense, I'm suffering from sunstroke.

c. Without *of*: A very little, a slight amount; in advb. const. = slightly, somewhat, 'a little bit'.

1786 BURNS *Twa Dogs* 81 Ye maist wad think, a wee touch langer, An' they maun starve o' cauld and hunger. **1827** SCOTT *Surg. Dau.* vii, Still this story..seems a touch even beyond Tom Hillary. **1868** FREEMAN in Stephens *Life & Lett.* (1895) I. 405, I really think that the Great Unpaid are a touch more sensible.

20. a. *slang* or *colloq.* An article or 'affair' that will touch or move purchasers to the extent of a certain price.

1712 SWIFT *Pref. to Burnet's Hist. Ref.* Wks. 1738 VI. 53, I desire you to print in such a form, as in the Bookseller's phrase will make a Sixpenny touch. **1720** SIR E. PHILIPPS *Diary* 22 Sept., At night went to the Ball at the Angel. A guinea touch. **1815** SCOTT *Let. to J. B. S. Morritt* 2 Oct., in *Lockhart*, I think..the Poems of David [Hume] would make a decent twelve-shilling touch. **1865** *Slang Dict.*, *Touch*, a slang expression in common use in phrases which express the extent to which a person is interested or affected, as 'a fourpenny touch', i.e. costing that amount.

b. *slang.* An act of stealing or theft, esp. of pocket-picking; also, the act of getting money from a person, esp. by persuasion or glib talk; *transf.* a sum of money gained or got at once, esp. by theft; ***to make a touch***, to obtain money thus. (Cf. TOUCH *v.* 15, 16 b.)

1846 *Nat. Police Gaz.* (U.S.) 18 July 390/1 Ingenious Touch... Phillsburg..felt for his money, and..found in its place another pocket-book filled with newspaper instead of money. *Ibid.* 25 July 389/1 The Read Street Touch Case. Ann Henry, the keeper of a den of infamy and..one of her syrens, have been fully committed on the charge of robbing Townsend W. Hetherington. **1865** *Leaves from Diary of Celebrated Burglar & Pickpocket* xv. 48/2 The most splendid 'touch' of the campaign was already in our grasp! *Ibid.* xvii. 58/2 They took a furnished room in..Seven Dials, until a lucky 'touch' came off, when they took larger apartments. **1888** 'R. BOLDREWOOD' *Robbery under Arms* xliv, A thousand ounces of gold was no foolish touch. **1896** ADE *Artie* v. 43 Next day they had to make a hot touch for a short coin so as to get the price of a couple o' sinkers and a good old 'draw one'. **1900** *Westm. Gaz.* 13 Dec. 12/2 Returns of pocket-picking. He estimates twenty-five dollars a 'touch' as a fair record if there is much money in the crowd, and five or six touches a day as a good average. **1912** *Nation* 7 Dec. 428/2 No two thefts are ever absolutely alike, and no 'touch' of any merit is brought off but with study and preparation. **1914** *Automobile Topics* 4 July 638/3 His story of not being able to find employment..has enabled him to make many a successful 'touch'. **1939** R. CHANDLER *Big Sleep* xvi. 114, I figure it's a good time to..make a quick touch on the Sternwoods for travel money. **1953** *Essays in Crit.* III. 111 The poet might regard the patron as an intimate,..or simply as a public Maecenas, good for a 'touch' of three guineas a dedication. **1964** C. CHAPLIN *Autobiogr.* xvii. 299 It seemed obvious from the tone of the letter that it was all leading up to a 'touch'. So I thought I would take along $500.

c. ***soft*** or ***easy touch***: a person easily manipulated; *spec.* one easily induced to part with money; also, a task or opponent easily handled. *colloq.*

1940 J. O'HARA *Pal Joey* 44 You get the reputation of being a soft touch. **1945** *Sun* (Baltimore) 4 Oct. 1/1 Newhouser.., who figured to be the outstanding pitcher of the season, proved..to be the softest sort of a touch for Manager Charlie Grimm's National Leaguers. The second Cub to bat belted him cleanly. **1955** H. KURNITZ *Invasion of Privacy* (1956) xii. 80 Dorsey's appetite for easy money..was honed to a razor edge... He sensed a vast soft touch. **1959** H. P. TRITTON *Time means Tucker* vi. 45/1 He was an easy touch for any hard-luck story. **1972** *Police Rev.* 1 Dec. 1562/2, I would also warn any university student regarding the Police as a 'soft touch' for graduates. **1976** *Eastern Even. News* (Norwich) 29 Nov., Caravan dwellers are on the increase and they will keep on increasing while Norwich remains an easy touch; the complacency regarding this problem is alarming.

d. ***to cut up*** (***old***) ***touches***: see CUT *v.* 60 r.

IV. Concrete senses. (See also 2 c, 6, 10, 20.)

21. Short for TOUCH-POWDER, TOUCHWOOD, or the like. *Obs.* exc. *dial.*

1541–2 *Act 33 Hen. VIII*, c. 6 §1 Little handguns, ready furnished with..Gunpouder, fyer, & touche. **1619** H. HUTTON *Follies Anat.* (Percy Soc.) 18 Where's your tobacco box, your steele and touch? **1649** G. DANIEL *Trinarch., Hen. IV* cclviii, The fangle which Fires the drye touch of Constitution. **1887** *Suppl. to Jamieson, Touch, touche*, short for *touch-wood*, but applied to amadou and other materials used as tinder: 'as sharp as touch', as quick [to 'fire up'] as touch-wood, quick-tempered.

†**22.** = TOUCH-PIECE 2. *Obs.*

1659 LEAK *Waterwks.* 26 When the Barrel turns the pins Q and R, they may make the said conveiances open..according to..the disposition of the Pins and Touches Q and R.

23. *Shipbuilding.* In a plank tapering both ways, the projecting angle at the broadest part (near one end if worked top-and-butt, in the middle if worked anchor-stock fashion); also, each of the angles of the stern-timbers at the counters.

1711 W. SUTHERLAND *Shipbuild. Assist.* 25 Set off the exact Length forward and aftward from the Observation of the rising of the Keel, by Shipwrights called the Touch, or Place where the Keel's upper Part ends to be streight. **1797** *Encycl. Brit.* (ed. 3) XVII. 392/1 On the pencil line set off the distance the touch of the lower counter is abaft the aft side of the wing transom. *c* **1850** *Rudim. Navig.* (Weale) 128 This work is the best when the touch or knuckle is at the planksheer.

V. Phrases.

†**24.** ***to keep touch.*** **a.** To keep covenant, keep faith, keep one's promise, or engagement, act faithfully. Also ***to hold touch***. (? From the practice of striking hands, or of touching something sacred (cf. TOUCH *v.* 1, quot. 1491), in making a covenant.) So ***to break touch***. *Obs.*

13.. *Gaw. & Gr. Knt.* 1677, I schal..halde þe towchez. *a* **1529** SKELTON *Mann. World* 90 Amonge them that are riche, No frendshyp is to kepe tuche. **1540–1** ELYOT *Image Gov.* (1556) 159 By kepyng his promise and touche. *c* **1557** ABP. PARKER *Ps.* lxxviii. 219 They kept not true tutch wyth God hys pact they overyed. **1594** *Death of Usurie* 4 If a shop-keeper lend mony..to his neighbour.., if he breake touch the shop-keeper may lawfully take so much as he sustained losse. **1663** BUTLER *Hud.* I. I. 847 Quoth Hudibras, Thou offer'st much, But art not able to keep touch. **1706** *Reflex. upon Ridicule* 47 To promise every body and keep touch with no body. **1825** LAMB *Elia* Ser. II. *Superannuated Man*, When the week came round did the glittering phantom..keep touch with me?

b. To keep up communication, keep in touch *with*: so ***to lose touch***: see 13 d.

†**25.** ***to flee touch***, to make off, to escape; also = ***break touch*** (see 24 a). *Obs.*

c **1530** *Hickscorner* B j b, A strype he gaue me, I fledde my touche, And frome my gyrdle he plucked my pouche. *a* **1569** KINGESMYLL *Man's Est.* x. (1580) 56 He was fain to flee touche and avoide from Bethlehem into Egypt. **1583** GOLDING *Calvin on Deut.* xxvi. 153 They were vnconstant and fled touch anon after.

†**26.** ***true*** (***good, sure***) ***as touch***: perfectly or absolutely true, etc. (? from sense 5.) *Obs.*

1590 SPENSER *F.Q.* I. iii. 2 To thinke how she through guyleful handeling, Though true as touch,..Is from her knight divorced. **1620** SHELTON *Quix.* (1746) IV. x. 77 Of Sancho's Proceeding in his Government, with other Successes as good as Touch. *a* **1670** HACKET *Abp. Williams* I. (1692) 187 And that was sure as touch, because the House was to be past by Act of Parliament to the King's Majesty.

†**27.** ***rum touch***: an odd or queer fellow. *Obs. slang.*

1804 T. CREEVEY in *C. Papers*, etc. (1904) I. 22 To meet Brogden and Col. Porter, two cursed rum touches that he has persuaded to vote with him and to desert Fox. **1806** S. GRILDRIG *Miniature* (ed. 2) II. 9 The last whom I shall mention is an Odd Fellow, or according to the language of the day, 'a rum touch'. *Ibid.* 10 Whereas many young fellows..have..attempted to sustain the character of a Rum Touch, and have..failed most miserably, notice is hereby given [etc.].

28. ***in*** or ***out of touch***: see 13 d, 18 b. ***in*** or ***within touch***: see 1 e. ***to put to the touch***: see 7.

VI. Combinations: see TOUCH- in comb.

touch (tʌtʃ), *v.* Forms: *α.* 3–6 **touche**, 3–7 **towche**, (4 **tuoche**), 4–6 **toche**, **tuche**, (**tuouche**), 4–7 **tuch**, 5–7 **towch**, (6 **twoche**, 6–7 **toutch**, **tutch**(**e**, 7 **towtch**), 6– **touch**. *β.* (chiefly *Sc.*) 4–6 **twech**(**e**, 5–6 **twich**(**e**, **twych**, **tuiche**, **tuech**(**e**, 5–7 **tuich**, 6 **tweich**, **tueiche**, **tuitch**, 6–7 **twitch**; 7–9 *dial.* **titch**. [ME. a. OFr. *tochier*, *tuchier* (11th c. in *Chanson Roland*), mod.F. *toucher* 'to touch' = ONF. *toquer*, Pr. *toquar*, *tocar*, *tochar*, Sp. and Pg. *tocar*, It. *toccare* 'to strike, to smite, to hit, to touch' (Florio), Romanian *tocà* to knock.

The passage of the sense 'knock, strike' into that of 'touch' (in Fr., etc.), is like that of Eng. 'thrust, push' into 'put': a stroke at its lightest is a mere touch. The Romanic *toccare* has been held, after Diez, to be from an OLG. **tokkôn*, **tukken*, MLG. *tocken*, *tucken*, = OHG. *zocchôn*, *zucchen*, 'to draw or pull with force, pluck'; but a change of sense from 'pull' to 'knock' is inexplicable, and it is a more probable view that *toccare* was not from German, but an onomatopœic formation of the Romanic langs. from the syllable *toc* imitating a knock. *Tocken*, in its own sense 'draw', is still in use in LG. and in parts of Holland on the German frontier, but not in Dutch itself. But the South Netherlands (Flanders, Antwerp, etc.) use now, as in Kilian's time, a vb. *tokken* in the same sense as the *toquer*, *touker* of Old Northern French and its modern dialects, whence this has prob. been taken over. There is thus a gap in local continuity, as well as in sense, between the German and Romanic words. (Cf. Diez s.v. *Toccare*, Scheler s.v. *Toucher*, Körting 9802 *Tukkôn*; Gaston Paris in *Romania* XXVII. 626.)]

I. The simple verb.

* *Physical senses.*

1. a. *trans.* To put the hand or finger, or some other part of the body, upon, or into contact with (something) so as to feel it; 'to exercise the sense of feeling upon' (Phillips, 1696). Also with the hand, etc., as subject of the verb.

Usually denoting a momentary and slight act: cf. TOUCH *sb.*

c **1300** *Beket* 2229 And ho miȝte him enes tuochi, he was glad ynouȝ. **13..** *Cursor M.* 24498 (Cott.) Þat i moght toche him hand and fote. **1382** WYCLIF *Ecclus.* xiii. 1 Who shal touche pich, shal be defoulid of it. **1382** —— *Matt.* viii. 3 And Jhesus holdynge forthe the hond, touchide hym, sayinge, I wole, be thou maad clene. **1491** *Regr. Aberdon.* (Maitl. Cl.) I. 328 Þe parteis..ar oblist..be þe haly ewangell tuechet befor þir vytnes. **1526** TINDALE *John* xx. 17 Jesus sayde vnto her: touche me not. **1528** LYNDESAY *Dreme* 1088 All that he twychit, but delatioun, Turnit in gold. **1570** LEVINS *Manip.* 182/30 To Tutche, *tangere*. **1599** DAVIES *Immort. Soul* cxcvi, And in those fiue All things their Formes expresse, Which we can touch, tast, feele, or heare, or see. *a* **1657** SIR W. MURE *Misc. Poems* xi. 5 Hands, forbeare to tuich Oght 30ʳ tuiching can bewitch! **1764** REID *Inquiry* v. vi. 127 My two hands touch the extremities of a body. **1800** tr. *Lagrange's Chem.* I. 22 When I touch a warm body, the caloric passes from the body into my hand. **1847** KINGLAKE *Eothen* xvi, With tremulous boldness she touches—then grasps your hand.

Constructions. **b.** To touch (a thing) *with* the hand or other part, or *with* some instrument.

c **1375** *Cursor M.* 20759 (Fairf.) Ga to þa men..& touche ham he saide wiþ hit. **1598** SHAKS. *Merry W.* v. v. 88 With Triall-fire touch me his finger end. **1643**- [see TONGS 2 a]. **1667** MILTON *P.L.* IV. 811 Him thus intent Ithuriel with his Spear Touch'd lightly. **1704** POPE *Messiah* 6 O thou my voice inspire, Who touched Isaiah's hallow'd lips with fire. **1839** URE *Dict. Arts* 582 (Glass-making) The..workman..touching its tubular neck with an iron chisel dipped in cold water. **1847** KINGLAKE *Eothen* xviii, She has touched the poor Levantine with the hem of her sleeve.

c. To touch (the hand or other part, or something held) *to* (†*till*) something, = to bring it into contact with something; with *pl. obj.* to bring (two things) into mutual contact.

a **1300** *Cursor M.* 21549 (Cott.) Þe thred [third cross] þai toched til his hide, And up he ras wit-vten bide. *c* **1460** *Play Sacram.* 775 And towche thyn hand to thy saluacon. **1715** PRIOR *Down-Hall* 173 Now let us touch thumbs, and be friends ere we part. **1760–72** H. BROOKE *Fool of Qual.* (1809) IV. 141 He then touched his white wand to the neck of his steed. **1897** *Outing* (U.S.) XXX. 378/2 Touch a match to it, and you will presently have a fire.

d. *absol.* or *intr.* (in general sense).

1388 WYCLIF *Isa.* lix. 10 We as with outen iȝen touchiden. *a* **1648** DIGBY *Chym. Secr.* II. (1682) 232 Dip a Straw or Feather in it, and touch all round about the borders of the Sore with it. *a* **1897** G. MEREDITH *Marian* i, She can talk the talk of men, And touch with thrilling fingers.

2. Specific applications of sense 1.

a. To have sexual contact with. *trans.*, or (obs.) *intr.* with *to* (*till*).

13.. *Cursor M.* 10877 (Gött.) Þe womman þat neuer touchid man, How sal scho conceyue? tel me þan. *Ibid.* 11139 (Cott.) Als quen he fand wit barn his wijf, Þat he neuer had toched till. *c* **1375** *Ibid.* 2422 (Fairf.) Þat muȝt na mon of lecchery hir body touche wiþ velany. **1512** *Helyas* in Thoms *Prose Rom.* (1828) III. 40 Your noble person hath touched often times to hers after the constitucion of the sacrament of mariage. **1762** BRYDGES *Burlesque Homer* (1772) 361 May I for cats and dogs turn butcher, If ever yet she'd let me touch her.

(*b*) = *to touch up*, sense 34 c (*b*) below; *refl.*, to masturbate.

1903 FARMER & HENLEY *Slang* VII. 177/2 *Touch*... verb. .. (or *to touch up*), to grope a woman. **1927** F. HARRIS *My Life & Loves* (1934) IV. ix. 182 You want to know if I have touched myself. Sure, all girls have. **1973** *Family Circle* July 114/1 Little girls are told not to touch or play with themselves, and later their sexual parts are associated with urination and menstruation, which are considered 'dirty'.

b. To lay the hand upon (a diseased person) for the cure of the 'king's evil' or scrofula, as formerly practised by French and English sovereigns. Also *absol.*

1606 J. MELVILL *Diary* (Wodrow Soc.) 657 The Royall ceremonie of tuiching of some diseased childrein for hailling off sume of the escrolles. **1660** EVELYN *Diary* 6 July, His Majestie began first to touch for the evil, according to costome. **1705** *Lond. Gaz.* No. 4126/3 All Persons who shall ..apply to be Touched, shall bring a Certificate. **1716** HEARNE *Collect.* (O.H.S.) V. 359 He said the King touched many for yᵉ Evil..and that they recovered. **1791** BOSWELL *Johnson* (1906) I. 17 His mother..carried him to London, where he was actually touched by Queen Anne. **1880** DIXON *Windsor* IV. xxxi. 298 The King began to touch for scrofula.

c. *Sc. Hist.* referring to the touching of an Act of Parliament with the sceptre in token of the royal assent.

1694 FOUNTAINHALL in M. P. Brown *Suppl. Decis.* (1826) IV. 179 This act was not touched; and so the Lords thought they could not supply the royal assent, nor make it an act. **1855** MACAULAY *Hist. Eng.* xviii. IV. 186 He [William] had ..suffered the law which abolished patronage to be touched with his sceptre. **1907** A. LANG *Hist. Scot.* IV. i. 3 Of the Acts passed by the Estates at this time, hardly one was 'touched' with the sceptre by the Commissioner. *Ibid.* ii. 29 He was to 'touch' and pass the Acts of 1689 for restoring Presbyterian preachers.

d. *Med.* To examine by touch or feeling: see TOUCH *sb.* 1 c. Also *absol.*

1734 E. HODY *W. Giffard's Cases Midwif.* lxxxi. 192, I thought it proper to touch her. **1754–64** SMELLIE *Midwif.* III. 424 Upon touching I found the os uteri a little more dilated.

e. To bring by touching *into* some condition.

1813 MONTGOMERY *World bef. Flood* II. 207 Time had but touch'd her form to finer grace. **1892** TENNYSON *Making of Man* 4 Shall not æon after æon pass and touch him into shape?

f. *Rugby Football*: = Touch down: see 30.

1864 *Field* 19 Nov. 354/2 When the ball is touched inside goal-line, must it be touched down dead? that is, is it fair touch if the ball move or roll afterwards? **1877** *Ibid.* 24 Feb. 220/1 Hutchinson..safely touched the ball behind the home team's line.

g. *absol.* or *intr.* Of soldiers in the rank: To close up until the elbows are in contact.

1803 DICKINSON *Instr. Infantry* 79 The leading man of the Front Rank..marks Time, the Rest wheel up to him, dressing by the Left, and touching lightly to the Right. **1877** *Man. Field Artillery Exerc.* 26 During the wheel, each man must touch lightly..towards the pivot flank.

h. *intr.* for *pass.* (with descriptive extension): To 'feel' to the touch; to cause a specified sensation when touched.

1770–4 A. HUNTER *Georg. Ess.* (1803) IV. 575 We say this beast touches nicely upon its ribs. **1885** JEFFERIES *Open Air* (1890) 104 They touch rough—dusty rough, as books touch that have been lying unused.

3. a. *trans.* To come into, or be in, contact with. (Expressing an involuntary act or state of a person or part of the body, or of an inanimate thing.)

c **1330** R. BRUNNE *Chron.* (1810) 190 He smote him in þe helm, bakward he bare his stroupe. Þe body he did ouerwhelm, his hede touched þe croupe. **1382** WYCLIF *Numb.* xxxi. 19 Who sleeth a man, or a man sleyn touchith. **1398** TREVISA *Barth. De P.R.* XVI. vii. (Bodl. MS.), Quike siluer..cleueþ nouȝt to þinge þat it toucheþ. **1506** GUYLFORDE *Pilgr.* (Camden) 65 If the galye had ones towched the rok, we had ben all perysshed. **1653** H. COGAN tr. *Pinto's Trav.* iv. 10 The ends of their sailyards, whereof some were so long that they touched even the very water. **1771** LUCKOMBE *Hist. Print.* 385 Its touching the letters underneath may be prevented. **1860** TYNDALL *Glac.* II. viii. 263 Loose shingle..falls upon the ice where it touches the rocks.

b. *intr.* or *absol.*: usually of two things, in reciprocal sense.

1615 W. LAWSON *Country Housew. Gard.* (1626) 23 That no tree..drop vpon, or touch his fellowes... If they touch, the winde will cause a forcible rub. **1821** SHELLEY *Epipsych.* 578 Those spheres..Touch, mingle, are transfigured. **1832** TENNYSON *Dream Fair Wom.* 116 The bright death quiver'd at the victim's throat; Touch'd; and I knew no more. **1842** —— *Talking Oak* 131 So fleetly did she stir, The flower, she touch'd on, dipt and rose. *Mod.* Place them close together, but do not let them touch.

4. a. *trans.* To be in contact with, or immediately adjacent to; to adjoin, border on; to skirt.

c **1391** CHAUCER *Astrol.* II. §5 Waite wel wher as thin Almury toucheth the bordure, & set ther a prikke of ynke. **1630** *R. Johnson's Kingd. & Commw.* 361 This State, touching the Apenine mountaines on the South, and the Adriatike Sea upon the North. **1865** DICKENS *Mut. Fr.* III. viii, A part of the road where it touched the river. **1896** BADEN-POWELL *Matabele Campaign* x, The Transvaal border touches ours near Tuli.

b. *intr.* †To be contiguous *to* (obs.); *fig.* to have mutual contact; (with *upon*) to succeed continuously.

c **1400** MAUNDEV. (1839) vii. 80 The vale of Josaphathe, þat touchethe to the walles, as thoughe it were a large dyche. **1669** FLAVEL *Husb. Spir.* III. iii. (1674) 211 There are several particulars in which this..design..and the pains of Husbandmen..do meet and touch. **1794** PALEY *Evid.* I. ix. §4 (1817) 238 A series of writers touching upon one another.

c. *Geom.* (*trans.*) Of a line (straight or curved) or a surface: To meet (another line or surface) at a point so that when produced it does not (ordinarily) intersect or 'cut' it at that point; to be tangent to. Also *absol.* or *intr.* in reciprocal sense.

(A straight line may exceptionally both *touch* and *cut* a curve or curved surface at the same point, viz. at a point of inflexion, where the curvature changes from convex to concave or *vice versa*. In some cases also two surfaces (e.g. a cylinder and a plane, or two cylinders) may touch *along a line* instead of at a single point. See TANGENT A. 1, B. 1 b.)

1570 BILLINGSLEY *Euclid* III. def. ii. 81 A right line is sayd to touch a circle, which touching the circle and being produced cutteth it not. **1840** LARDNER *Geom.* 52 The straight line joining the centres of circles which touch externally, must pass through their point of contact. **1885** EAGLES *Constr. Geom. Plane Curves* 136 To describe an ellipse to touch five given lines. **1885** LEUDESDORF *Cremona's Proj. Geom.* 147 An infinite number of conics can be drawn to touch a given straight line at a given point, and to touch two other given straight lines.

5. To strike or hit lightly (esp. with the spur, or in *Fencing*); in quot. *c* 1550, to hit, beat. Also (*rare*) *fig.* in pa. pple., = TOUCHÉ b.

a **1330** *Otuel* 84 Wiþ þat word þe kinges a non Touchede here stedes & made hem gon. *c* **1550** R. WEVER *Lusty Juventus* D iij b, If thou tel not truth, I wil not be behind, To touch you as well agayne. **1596** DALRYMPLE tr. *Leslie's Hist. Scot.* IX. (S.T.S.) II. 181 As a noble horss tuechte with the spur is mair quik. **1809** ROLAND *Fencing* 124 At no time should you endeavour to touch your adversary while thrusting carte and tierce. **1831** SCOTT *Ct. Robt.* iii, Achilles ..touched the door with a rap, distinct at once and modest. **1853** E. SEWELL *Experience of Life* xviii. 183 'I dislike this kind of bantering very much, Horatia,' I said... Horatia laughed merrily. 'Touched, I declare!'

6. To affect physically in some way by contact.

a. To make an impression upon; to stain, scratch, abrade, corrode, decompose, etc.

touched with the tar-brush (fig.): see TAR-BRUSH b.

c **1440** *Gesta Rom.* xii. 40 (Harl. MS.) If ȝe hadde on your cloke, the reyne shulde not haue y-towchid your clothing. **1677** MOXON *Mech. Exerc.* i. 3 So hard that a File will not touch it (as Smiths say when a File will not cut or race it). **1725** *Bradley's Fam. Dict.* s.v. *Silver*, The Aqua Regalis, which dissolves Gold, will not touch Silver. **1881** YOUNG *Every Man his own Mechanic* §1438 No file or cutting tool will 'touch' it.

†**b.** *intr.* with *upon*, in same sense. *Obs.*

a **1626** BACON *Phys. Rem.* Wks. 1879 I. 245/1 For dissolution into liquor, we are to inquire..what will touch upon the one [metal] and not upon the other.

c. *trans.* To magnetize by contact or rubbing with a magnet. ? *Obs.* (Cf. TOUCH *sb.* 11.)

1627 CAPT. SMITH *Seaman's Gram.* ii. 12 The darke Compasse hath the points blacke and white, and the other onely touched for the true North and South. **1698** BALLARD in *Phil. Trans.* XX. 418, I took my Knife, which had been formerly toucht..and profering it to the Needle, it drew the North Pole. **1706** E. WARD *Wooden World Diss.* (1708) 13 The Loadstone,..tho' never so well touch'd, will often point from its true Pole. **1769** FALCONER *Dict. Marine* (1789), *Toucher un compas*, to touch the needle of a compass with a magnet. **1795** HUTTON *Math. Dict.* s.v. *Magnet*, This vertical way of touching a bar will not give it quite so much of the magnetic virtue.

d. To apply some substance lightly to (a part of the body, etc.) by contact, esp. for medicinal purposes (const. *with* the substance); *spec.* (*Med.*) ***to touch the gums***, to induce salivation, as by the use of mercury.

1602 SHAKS. *Ham.* IV. vii. 147 Ile touch my point, With this contagion, that if I gall him slightly, It may be death. **1843** R. J. GRAVES *Syst. Clin. Med.* xxvi. 332 The raw surface itself..touched with zinc ointment. **1893** W. R. GOWERS *Man. Dis. Nerv. Syst.* (ed. 2) II. 358 The patient should be brought slightly..under its [i.e. mercury's] influence, so as just 'to touch the gums' as the phrase is.

7. To affect injuriously in some physical way (e.g. by fire or frost), esp. in a slight degree; to communicate disease to by contagion, to infect, taint; also *spec.* in reference to a horse's 'wind' or breathing. (Usually in *pa. pple.*) Also (*colloq.*), *pass.*, to be slightly affected by drink.

1595 SHAKS. *John* V. vii. 2 It is too late, the life of all his blood Is touch'd corruptibly. **1601** W. LEIGH *Soules Solace* (1617) 7 When..he [Job] was toucht in his own person, so as his bone claue to his flesh. **1681** *Lond. Gaz.* No. 1584/4 Lost.., A bright Bay Gelding,.. all his Paces,..his Wind touch'd. **1772** R. GRAVES *Spir. Quix.* (1820) I. 82 A horse which was touched in the wind. **1794** MRS. RADCLIFFE *Myst. Udolpho* xxviii, An icy coldness touched her cheeks, and her fears for awhile overcame her judgment. **1834** C. BRONTË *My Angria & Angrians* in W. Gérin *C. Brontë* (1967) vi. 84 Two bottles of..ale, and a double quart of Porter..and I'm not a bit touched—only light and smart and active. **1884** ROE *Nat. Ser. Story* ii, The plants that were touched with frost. **1888** 'R. BOLDREWOOD' *Robbery under Arms* II. xi. 180, I wasn't no ways drunk; but I must have been touched more or less, because I felt myself to be so sober.

8. a. To test the fineness of (gold or silver) by rubbing it upon a touchstone (see TOUCHSTONE 1); †*fig.* to test, try, make trial or proof of (*obs.*).

a **1548** HALL *Chron., Hen. VIII* 193 There the crounes were wayed and touched. **1595** SHAKS. *John* III. i. 100 A counterfeit Resembling Maiesty, which being touch'd and tride, Proues valuelesse. **1607** —— *Timon* III. iii. 6 They haue all bin touch'd, and found Base-Mettle. **1745** P. THOMAS *Jrnl. Anson's Voy.* 136 They..then carry [the bars of Silver] to be touch'd and mark'd. **1908** H. B. MORSE *Trade Chinese Emp.* 160 It is then 'touched' and the difference..from a certain standard, as indicated by the colour on the touchstone, is written on the other side.

b. To mark (metal) as of standard purity, etc., with an official stamp, after it has been tested.

1423 *Rolls of Parlt.* IV. 257/1 That no..Man that werketh Selver Hernois, put noon therof to the sale..or [= ere] that it be touched wyth the touche of the Liberdisheed, that he that may resonabli bere the touche. **1697** *View Penal Laws* 142 None shall put to sale any Silver Harness in London before it is touched. **1746–7** in Welch *Hist. Pewterers' Co.* (1902) II. 193 That all..wares capable of a large Touch shall be touched with a large Touch. **1772–3** *Act 13 Geo. III*, c. 52 §6, I will touch no silver but what shall be of the goodness of and according to the standard of this kingdom. **1852** A. RYLAND *Assay Gold & S.* 72 The silver-smiths..were under great difficulties..for want of assayers in convenient places to assay and touch their plate.

c. *intr.* for *pass.* To appear or prove to be of standard fineness on testing; to undergo or stand the test. *lit.* and *fig.* ? *Obs.*

1618 FLETCHER *Loyal Subject* I. v, And now you are brought to th' test; touch right now, soldier, Now shew the manly pureness of thy mettle. **1701** COLLIER *M. Aurel.* 31 His honesty is right sterling, and touches as well as it looks. **1705** tr. *Bosman's Guinea* 81 These Lumps or Pieces are called Mountain-Gold; which being melted, touch better than Dust-Gold.

9. a. *trans.* To strike the strings, keys, etc. of (a musical instrument) so as to make it sound; to play on, esp. to play a few notes on; to sound (a horn, a bell). [Cf. Fr. *toucher la lyre*, Sp. *tocar la lira*.] †Also *intr.* with *on* (quot. *c* 1470).

c **1470** HENRYSON *Orpheus & Eurydice* 611 Than Orpheus our ressoun is full wo, And twichis on his harp. **1484** CAXTON *Fables of Æsop* VI. vii, A fyssher..somtyme touched his bagpype nyhe the Ryuer for to make the fysshe to daunce. **1580** LYLY *Euphues* (Arb.) 473 Instruments sound sweetest when they be touched softest. **1633** MASSINGER *Guardian* II. iv, I'll touch my horn (Severino blows his horn): they know my call. **1697** DRYDEN *Alex. Feast* 22 Timotheus..With flying fingers touched the lyre. **1779** *Mirror* No. 43 ¶6 The organ was touched with a hand less firm. **1818** PEACOCK *Melincourt* xxi, Touch the bell for the waiter. **1830** SIR J. BARRINGTON *Pers. Sk. own Times* (ed. 2) II. 164, I recollect Moore one night..touching the pianoforte in his own unique way. **1888** BURGON *Lives 12 Gd. Men* II. ix. 214 Having touched the piano, [he] was requested to sing.

b. *transf.* To produce (musical sounds) by 'touching' an instrument; to play (an air).

1823 SCOTT *Peveril* xxx, A person in the royal retinue touched a light and lively air on the flageolet. **1848** THACKERAY *Van. Fair* lix, Touching, to the best of her simple art, melancholy harmonies on the keys. **1848** DICKENS *Dombey* xviii, Her low voice in the twilight, slowly and stopping sometimes, touched the old air to which he had so often listened.

10. a. In drawing, painting, etc.: To mark, draw, delineate (a detail of the work) by touching the surface with the pencil, brush, etc.; also, to modify or alter by such touches. Hence *transf.* in literary composition. (See also *touch in*, 31, *touch up*, 34.)

1675 A. BROWNE *App. Art of Limning* 10 The next you touch the Tips of the Ears with the forementioned Temperature. **1709** POPE *Ess. Crit.* 22 The lines, tho' touch'd but faintly, are drawn right. **1780** COWPER *Let.* 2 July, To touch and retouch is..the secret of almost all good writing especially in verse. **1890** *N. & Q.* 7th Ser. X. 118/2 My impression [of the engraving] is unequal, being faint in some parts, very dark in others. If the plate was worn, it has been 'touched' afterwards.

†**b.** *intr.* with *upon*: To add touches to, modify by touching, touch up. *Obs.*

1675 BENTLEY in *Dryden's Mistaken Husb.* To Rdr., If a great Master have but touch'd upon an ordinary Piece, he makes it of Value. **1762–71** H. WALPOLE *Vertue's Anecd. Paint.* (1786) III. 219 A French painter who was suffered to alter and touch upon his pictures.

c. *fig.* (*trans.*) To mark slightly or superficially *with* some colour or aspect: chiefly in *pa. pple.* Also said of the colour, etc.

c1600 Shaks. *Sonn.* xvii, Such heauenly touches nere toucht earthly faces. **1829** Scott *Anne of G.* xiii, The dawn had scarce begun to touch the distant horizon. **1847** L. Hunt *Jar Honey* xii. (1848) 158 The rock on the woody promontory..is touched with rose-colour. **1883** F. M. Peard *Contrad.* xix, A faint smile touched her lips as she wondered.

11. a. *intr.* Of a ship, or those on board: To arrive and make a short stay in passing at a port or place on the way; to call in passing. Also *transf.* (of a traveller), and *fig.* Usually with *at.* Also in legal formula *to touch and stay.*

1517 Torkington *Pilgr.* (1884) 16 Many Shippys and galyes towche ther rather thanne at Parence. **1582** N. Lichefield tr. *Castanheda's Conq. E. Ind.* i. xlii. 96 That in his way he should touch at the Ilande of S. Blaze. **1697** Dryden *Æneid* vii. 29 Lest the Trojan's pious host Should bear, or touch upon th' inchanted coast. **1725** De Foe *Voy. round World* (1840) 58 Whenever any ship touched at that port. **1745** P. Thomas *Jrnl. Anson's Voy.* 59 For the Ships who frequently touch here. ?**1796** in *Eng. Reports* (1927) CLXX. 471 Liberty to sail to, touch and stay at any port or ports whatsoever on her passage out..without prejudice to the insurance. **1828** Duppa *Trav. Italy*, etc. 206 We touched at Panaria..on account of its warm baths of which there are numerous vestiges. **1870** Kingsley in *Gd. Words* 203/1 Our own mail steamers..could as easily touch at Terceira now, as they did a few years since. **1895** W. Gow *Marine Insurance* iii. 59 The liberty to touch and stay is limited by its close application to the main object of the voyage. **1969** E. R. H. Ivamy *Marine Insurance* xiii. 142 It was formerly held that 'liberty to touch and stay' did not permit of trading at the port of call.

b. *trans.* with the port or place as obj.: To land upon; to visit in passing; also *transf.* and *fig.*

1593 Shaks. *Rich. II*, ii. i. 288 All these..With eight tall ships..meane to touch our Northerne shore. **1632** J. Hayward tr. *Biondi's Eromena* 7 Supposing that they could not touch land in Sardegna. **1774** Johnson *Let. to Boswell* 26 Nov., Shall we touch the continent? **1850** Tennyson *In Mem.* xiv. 2 If one should bring me this report, That thou hadst touch'd the land to-day.

** *Physical, passing into non-physical.*

12. a. To handle or have to do with in any or the slightest degree; to meddle or interfere with however slightly; to 'lay a finger on'. (Usually with negative expressed or implied.)

1377 Langl. *P. Pl.* B. xviii. 192 Þat Adam & Eue..Shulde deye doune riȝte..If þat þei touched a tre, and þe fruite eten. c**1400** *Destr. Troy* 1337 All loste þe lyfe þat þe lede touchet. **1591** Spenser *M. Hubberd* 702 He so light was at legierdemaine, That what he toucht came not to light againe. **1655** Fuller *Ch. Hist.* i. ii. §1 Being conscientiously scrupulous, not to take or touch a thread which is none of our own. **1711** Hearne *Collect.* (O.H.S.) III. 103 Five hundred Pounds..wch he said he never did or would touch. **1886** Ruskin *Præterita* I. xi. 345, I had never touched a card.

b. *spec.* To lay hands on or meddle with so as to harm; to injure, hurt, in any or the least degree.

1297 R. Glouc. (Rolls) 10369 In þe popes half he sede, ich uorbede..þat no man ne touchi þulke clerc. c**1400** Maundev. (1839) ix. 76 The Soudan hath do make a wall aboute the sepulcre, þat noman may towche it. **1596** Shaks. *1 Hen. IV*, ii. iv. 300 The Lion will not touch the true Prince. **1716** Hearne *Collect.* V. 271 He stood [in the Pillory]..on Wednesday, and was not touch'd; but yesterday..he was pelted miserably. **1812** Ld. Wellington in *Examiner* 23 Nov. 742/2 No officer was touched. **1836** J. Gilbert *Chr. Atonem.* vii. (1852) 204 The hand of violence must not touch them. **1888** *Times* (weekly ed.) 21 Dec. 4/2 Enemy in full retreat... No English officers touched.

c. To take (food or drink); to 'taste': usually (with negative), not to take any at all. (Cf. L. *tangĕre* to touch, in this sense.)

c**1400** *Destr. Troy* 466 That euyn full was þat fre and no fode touchet. c**1450** *St. Cuthbert* (Surtees) 3346 Þe forsaide gose þai touched noȝt. **1600** Shaks. *A.Y.L.* ii. vii. 98 He dies that touches any of this fruite, Till I, and my affaires are answered. **1766** Goldsm. *Vic. W.* xxi, If a spoonful of liquor were to cure me of a fever, I never touch a drop. **1886** W. J. Tucker *E. Europe* 191, I could not touch another drop, unless more of the gentlemen join me.

†**d.** *intr.* with *with, at, on*: To meddle with, have to do with (slightly or at all); to deal with cursorily (quot. 1693); to come into contact with.

a**1656** Bp. Hall *Revelation Unrev.* viii, That they ever offered to touch with any either secular or sacred business, we never find. **1693** Locke *Educ.* §175 Studies which a Gentleman should not barely touch at, but constantly dwell upon. **1697** Collier *Ess. Mor. Subj.* ii. (1709) 29 He will never touch at a great Proposal; nor run any generous Hazards for his Friends or Country. **1701** *Col. Rec. Pennsylv.* II. 63 But they refused to touch with it unless it was intirely surrendered to ym [them]. **1746-7** Hervey *Medit.* (1818) 214 Our purity is of so delicate a complexion, that it scarce touches on the world without contracting a stain.

13. a. *trans.* To get or go as far as; to reach, attain (*lit.* and *fig.*).

c**1384** Chaucer *H. Fame* iii. 285 And with hir hed she touched hevene. **1613** Shaks. *Hen. VIII*, iii. ii. 223, I haue touch'd the highest point of all my Greatnesse. **1713** Steele *Guard.* No. 82 ¶1 Mr. William Peer [an actor] distinguished himself particularly in two characters, which no man ever could touch but himself. **1842** Tennyson *Vis. Sin* 23 The music touch'd the gates and died. **1864** —— *En. Ard.* 57 Ere he touch'd his one-and-twentieth May. **1883** *Manch. Exam.* 3 Dec. 4/1 The price, after touching 88, fell back on French sales to 86.

b. *fig.* To attain equality with, 'come up to', rival, compare with. *colloq.*

1838 Dickens *O. Twist* xliii, Is there one of you that could touch him or come near him on any scent? **1902** Violet Jacob *Sheep-Stealers* viii, I thought there was nothing that could touch that mare of mine.

†**c.** *intr.* with *to*, in same sense. *Obs.*

1450-1530 *Myrr. our Ladye* 198 Tyl there were rysen a starre..that myght with hys heate touche to the heate of the sonne.

14. a. *intr.* with *at, to, on, upon* (also *absol.*): To approach closely, draw very near; to verge upon; †in quot. 1615, to resemble closely (*obs.*).

1451 Capgrave *Life St. Gilbert* 75 Thus seknes growyng, and age of an hundred ȝere touching, he was in party compelled for to passe fro þis lif. **1615** Chapman *Odyss.* i. 326 Thy forehead and fair eyes at his form touch. **1791** Burke *App. Whigs* Wks. VI. 116 During the course of a political life just touching to its close. **1801** *Lusignan* IV. 224 Brother Ambrose touches at that dreadful hour, which delivers us to the sentence of an incorruptible judge! **1819** Lady Morgan *Autobiog.* (1859) 315 He sometimes touched on the very verge of meanness. **1832** Lytton *Eugene A.* iv. iii, At length the time touched upon dinner.

b. *Naut.* (*trans.*) To keep as close to (the wind) as the vessel will sail. Also *absol.*

1568 *Satir. Poems Reform.* xlvi. 54 Syne treveiss still, and lay abowt, And gar hir top twiche wind and waw. **1627** Capt. Smith *Seaman's Gram.* ix. 37 Touch the wind, and warre no more, is..to bid him at the Helme to keepe her so neere the wind as may be. **1692** *Ibid.* i. xvi. 76 In keeping the Ship near the Wind, these terms are used,..*Veer no more,..touch the Wind.* c**1860** H. Stuart *Seaman's Catech.* 85 Keep your eye on the weather leech of the sails, and just keep them touching.

15. *trans.* To take in the hand, take, receive, draw (money) [cf. F. *toucher de l'argent* (16th c. in Littré)]; sometimes, to get by underhand means; hence (*Thieves' cant*), to steal. Also *absol.* Now chiefly *slang* or *colloq.*

1654 in *Nicholas Papers* (Camden) II. 153 He will give you a good account of Mr. Lovell and that he hath touched..over £1000 sterling to his owne use. **1691** Wood *Ath. Oxon.* I. *Fasti* 859 Out of which, he had, I think, 1000l., which, with 200l. more, was all he touched in the said 19 years. **1720** Swift *Elegy on Demar* 27 He touch'd the pence when others touch'd the pot. **1758** Smollett *Hist. Eng.* III. ii. vii. 82 For secret service money during the last ten years the Earl of Orford had touched £1,453,400 of public money. **1833** Marryat *P. Simple* xxxii, I proved the [will]..at Doctors' Commons, and touched the whole of her money. **1855** Thackeray *Newcomes* xxxi, The..matrimonial arrangement is concluded (the agent touching his percentage). [**1898** Bodley *France* II. iii. v. 238 The average annual ministerial salaries touched by French legislators.]

16. a. To fee, 'tip', bribe, tamper with. ? *Obs.*

1752 Fielding *Amelia* xi. iv, He had heard that the great man must be touched; for he never did anything without touching. **1754** J. Shebbeare *Matrimony* (1766) I. 95 Mr. N——..having 'scaped the Servants..without touching one of them. **1770** Foote *Lame Lover* iii. Wks. 1799 II. 84 The court may proceed... But..I hope no gentleman has been touch'd on both sides.

b. To 'come down upon', 'get at', or 'tap' (a person) *for* money, to succeed in getting money from, to obtain a loan or gift of money from (*colloq.*); also, to rob (*thieves' cant*); in *Australian slang*, to swindle, cheat.

1760 C. Johnston *Chrysal* (1822) II. 43, I am quite broke up; his grace has touched me for five hundred. **1807** H. Tufts in E. Pearson *Autobiogr. of Criminal* (1930) ii. iv. 293 *Touching a cly*, robbing a pocket. **1809** E. S. Barrett *Setting Sun* III. 105 If you could get me a commission, I could touch Dad for a few hundreds. **1888** in Farmer & Henley *Slang* (1903) VII. 177/1 A dip [*sc.* pick-pocket] touched the Canadian sheriff for his watch and massive chain while he was reading the Riot Act. **1898** *Tit-Bits* 21 May 139/3 Well, old boy, I've just touched Reggy for another tenner. **1898** *Westm. Gaz.* 14 Nov. 8/1 L.'s going to touch the public to a pretty tune for this. **1928** [see knock *v.* 15 d]. **1950** *Austral. Police Jrnl.* Apr. 110 To touch a person is to steal from him, but to touch him for a loan is to ask him for one. **1951** G. Greene *End of Affair* v. iv. 197 'If you would lend me a pound.'..Had she 'touched' Henry once too often? **1963** T. Parker *Unknown Citizen* i. 32 He wants some money... Don't you send it to him, let him touch somebody else for a change.

c. To lay hold upon, to arrest.

1791 O'Keeffe *Wild Oats* ii. i, Knock [at his door], and when he comes out touch him.

*** *Non-physical senses.*

17. a. *trans.* To apprehend, succeed in getting at, 'hit', hit upon; to guess or state correctly. ? *Obs.*

c**1325** in *Rel. Ant.* I. 292 Thu tuchest nowt the notes [in singing], thu bites hem on sonder. **13..** *Cursor M.* 18940 (Cott.) Als gaf to þaim þe haligast Alkin wiit to tuche and tast. **1606** Shaks. *Tr. & Cr.* ii. ii. 194 There you toucht the life of our designe. **1715** De Foe *Fam. Instruct.* i. iii. (1841) I. 58 O you have touched it! there it lies. **1797** Ht. Lee *Canterb. T., Old Wom. T.* (1799) I. 380 He had at length, then, touched the point of truth.

†**b.** *intr.* with *at*: To succeed in hearing, to 'catch'. *Obs.*

c**1611** Chapman *Iliad* xix. 77 Hard it is, in such a great concourse (Though hearers' ears be ne'er so sharp) to touch at all things spoke.

18. a. *trans.* To speak or write of, treat of, mention, tell, relate; now always, to mention briefly, casually, or in passing; to refer to, allude to. Now *rare* or *arch.*

13.. *E.E. Allit. P.* B. 1437 Þenne towched to þe tresour [= treasurer] þis tale watz sone. **1380** *Lay Folks Catech.* (Lamb. MS.) 266 The secunde part of þis Crede..towchis xiiij artyculis. c**1440** *Gesta Rom.* i. 1 (Harl. MS.) And shortly for to touche þis mater; he tooke his leve. **1585** T. Washington tr. *Nicholay's Voy.* iii. xi. 91 b, I will not forgette to touch the manner of the apparrell. **1669** Sturmy *Mariner's Mag.* v. xii. 67, I shall come to touch how to make a good Shot. a**1704** T. Brown *Sat. agst. Wom.* 120 Nor shall I touch their secret murders. **1895** Gladstone *Psalter* 170 Subjects specially touched in particular passages of the Psalms. a**1903** 'H. S. Merriman' *Last Hope* v, She gave a curt laugh, as if he had touched a topic upon which they would disagree.

b. *intr.*, usually with †*of*, †*at* (obs.), *on, upon*, in same sense. Now the more usual construction.

c**1320** *Cast. Love* 1309 Sumwhat touchen Ichulle fonde Of þat Ich may vnderstonde. c**1400** Maundev. (1839) xxx. 303 The roundenesse of the erthe, of the whiche I haue towched to ȝou of before. **1549** [see 26]. **1573** L. Lloyd *Marrow of Hist.* (1653) 39 To omit..to touch any more of women. **1610** Healey *St. Aug. Citie of God* 139, I thought good to touch at this Asian luxurie. **1638** R. Baker tr. *Balzac's Lett.* (vol. II) 39 One cannot touch upon any point where he is not ready for you. **1665** J. Sergeant *Sure Footing* 85 We will briefly touch at some of the Advantages which those Assistances..give the Church. **1746** Wesley *Answ. Ch., Princ. Methodist* 8 To touch only on what seems of the most Importance. **1875** Jowett *Plato* (ed. 2) IV. 5 He touches on the same difficulties and he gives no answer to them. **1883** *Manch. Guard.* 22 Oct. 5/2 The matter was touched upon in a general way at the Leeds Conference.

†**19. a.** *trans.* (? *fig.* from 5.) To take to task, rebuke, reprove, censure; to charge, accuse. *Obs.*

1526 *Pilgr. Perf.* (W. de W. 1531) 142 Yf we be touched with a sharpe worde, we shal yelde a benigne & gentyll answere. **1570** *Darrell Papers* in H. Hall *Soc. Eliz. Age* (1886) App. 248 Sur Water Hungerfo, and his brother hathe touched me in iij thinges. **1596** Dalrymple tr. *Leslie's Hist. Scot.* x. (S.T.S.) II. 474 Gif tha tuouche ouer scharplie, tha be suspected of Jnuious persounis. **1643** *5 Years K. James I* in *Select. fr. Harl. Misc.* (1793) 306 He is stung with fear to be touched with Overbury's death. a**1677** Barrow *Serm.* (1687) I. xxii. 307 Our Saviour..touched Martha for being troubled about many things.

b. With mixture of senses: To say something apt or telling about, esp. in censure; to 'hit' by some apt or smart saying. Also *to touch to the quick* (cf. 25 b).

a**1529** Skelton *Agst. Scottes* 86 Thalia, my Muse, for you also call I, To touche them with tauntes of your armony. **1548** Udall *Erasm. Par. Luke* x. 92 b, The Pharisee beeyng somewhat touched with ye aunswer of our Lorde,..woulde not acknowelage his owne faulte. a**1566** R. Edwardes *Damon & Pithias* Prol., In commedies the greatest skill is this, rightly to touche All thinges to the quick. **1693** *Humours Town* A vj, If, therefore any find themselves touch'd, they ought to make a Right Use of it. **1733** Pope *Hor. Sat.* ii. i. 41 Ev'n those you touch not, hate you. **1831** Scott *Ct. Robt.* xxxiii, 'Marry, you touch me there', said the centurion.

20. a. *trans.* To pertain or relate to; to have bearing upon; to be the business of; to concern. *Obs.* or *arch.* (passing into next sense).

a**1325** *MS. Rawl. B. 520* lf. 52 b, That þer ne passe no writ..vnder þe kinges lutele seal þat tuchi þe commune lawe. c**1350** in *Eng. Gilds* (1870) 349 Þinges þat toucheþ the rewle of þe town. **1428** *Surtees Misc.* (1888) 7 Yis mater touched all ye gude men of ye consell. **1535** Coverdale *Eccl.* xii. 14 Feare God, and kepe his comaundementes, for that toucheth all men. **1697** Bentley *Phal.* (1699) 128 [These] Arguments touch only those particular Epistles. **1883** *Manch. Guard.* 22 Oct. 5/3 This..touches us not as Liberals or Conservatives, but as citizens.

†**b.** *intr.* with *to, unto, upon*, in same sense.

c**1325** *Poem times Edw. II* (Percy Soc.) xxxix, Ʒut ther is another craft That toucheth to clergy. **1390** Gower *Conf.* I. 225 That oght unto my ladi toucheth. **1456** Sir G. Haye *Law Arms* (S.T.S.) 220 The offence touchis to the realme, and to the citee anerly of thair propre burges. **1523** Ld. Berners *Froiss.* I. cccxcv. 682 [It was] the duke of Lancastre, to whome the matere moost touched. **1673** *Essex Papers* (Camden) 104 This may a little touch upon his Father in Law, my Lord Chancellr. **1816** Scott *Antiq.* xxxiv, Ne'er a man should steer a hair touching to Monkbarns while Steenie and I could wag a finger.

c. To have affinity with. †*intr.* with *at* (*obs.*), or *trans.* (*obs.* or *arch.* exc. as directly *fig.* from 3 or 4).

c**1611** Chapman *Iliad* xxi. 103 None now of all the brood of Troy..shall any breath enjoy.., specially that touch at Priam's race. **1774** Burke *Corr.* (1844) I. 505 To secure the attendance of those whom they touched the most nearly. **1888** Burgon *Lives 12 Gd. Men* II. v. 6 He never identified himself with any school of religious thought, though he touched them all.

21. *trans.* To be felt as the concern of or important to; to be a matter of moment to; to affect, make a difference to.

c**1470** *Golagros & Gaw.* 1177 It tuichis myne honour sa neir. **1491** *Act 7 Hen. VII*, c. 16 §8 That this Acte..in no wise extend to ne touche the warde ne mariage of Henry Erle of Essex. **1523** Ld. Berners *Froiss.* I. cxv. 136 A thynge..which herafter may sore touche the Countrey of Flaunders. **1613** Shaks. *Hen. VIII*, ii. ii. 54 His Curses and his blessings Touch me alike: th' are breath I not beleeue in. **1882** Pebody *Eng. Journalism* xxi. 156 Till the publication of penny newspapers a few years ago the position of the Provincial Press was hardly touched.

†**22.** To produce an impression on, strike, impress (the senses, or organs of sense). *Obs.*

c**1400** *Destr. Troy* 1668 Bright Aumbur, þat..smellis full swete, With taste for to touche the tabull aboute. **1596** Shaks. *Merch. V.* v. i. 76 If..any ayre of musicke touch their eares. **1607** —— *Cor.* ii. i. 61 If the drinke you giue me, touch my Palat aduersly, I make a crooked face at it. **1629** Milton *Morn. Christ's Nativity, Hymn* xiii, Ring out ye

Crystall sphears, Once bless our human ears, (If ye have power to touch our senses so). **1667** —— *P.L.* IX. 987.

23. a. To affect mentally or morally, to imbue *with* some quality; in bad sense, to infect, taint (cf. 7). Also predicated of the quality. Usually in *pa. pple.*

13.. *Cursor M.* 11328 (Cott.) þis symeon þat had his tast Toched o þe hali gast. **13..** *E.E. Allit. P.* A. 897 For neuer lesyng ne tale vntrwe Ne towched her tonge for no dysstresse. *a* **1568** *So Fremmit is my Fortoun* 14 in *Bannatyne Poems* (Hunter. Cl.) 717 Hairtles I am, for slewth twichis me so. **1600** SHAKS. *A.Y.L.* III. ii. 366, I thanke God, I am not a Woman to be touch'd with so many giddie offences as hee [my uncle] hath generally tax'd their whole sex withal. **1640–1** SIR B. RUDYARD *Sp.* in Rushw. *Hist. Coll.* (1721) IV. 167 The Scots being truly touched with Religion, according to their Profession. **1850** TENNYSON *In Mem.* cix. 10 High nature amorous of the good, But touch'd with no ascetic gloom. **1871** MORLEY *Crit. Misc.* Ser. I. *Byron* (1878) 211 Byron was touched by the same fire.

b. *pass.* To be deranged mentally in a slight degree; in *pa. pple.* slightly insane or crazy, 'cracked'. Also in phr. ***touched in the head*** or ***the upper story***.

[**1603** SHAKS. *Meas. for M.* v. i. 51 With that opinion That I am touch'd with madnesse.] **1704** STEELE *Lying Lover* v. iii, Pray mind him not, his Brain is touch'd. **1705** VANBRUGH *Confed.* v. ii, You see master's a little—touched, that's all. **1810** *Sporting Mag.* XXXV. 292 He thought he was a little touched, or insane. **1867** TROLLOPE *Last Chron. Barset* I. xx. 172 We tried to get him through as being a little touched in the upper story. **1873** MISS THACKERAY *Old Kensington* xxviii, What an extraordinary creature poor Sarah is! touched, certainly. **1902** E. NESBIT *Five Children & It* ii. 61 Touched in the head, eh?.. All the more shame to you boys dragging the poor afflicted child into your sinful burglaries.

24. a. To affect with some feeling or emotion; to move or stir the feelings of; to produce an emotion in; *spec.* to affect with tender feeling, as pity or gratitude. Const. *with.*

c **1340** HAMPOLE *Prose Tr.* 2 þe mynd towchede with þe souerayne swettnes. *c* **1500** *Three Kings Sons* 188 He thought it touchid hir hert somwhat. **1603** H. CROSSE *Vertues Commw.* (1878) 119 [He] heareth a buzzing sound in his eares, but is neuer truly toucht in his heart. **1631** GOUGE *God's Arrows* III. §50. 277 It is inhumanity not to be touched with others needs. **1711** STEELE *Spect.* No. 11 ¶7, I was so touch'd with this Story.. that I left the Room with Tears in my Eyes. **1833** TENNYSON *Poems* 133 That man, of all the men I ever knew, Most touched my fancy. **1860** THACKERAY *Round. Papers, Nil nisi bonum* 227, I can't say how much the thought of that fidelity has touched me.

b. With the feeling as subject; in *passive* const. *with* the feeling.

1560 DAUS tr. *Sleidane's Comm.* 371 They are neither touched with the gilt of conscience, nor haue given none any occasion of displeasure. **1663** BP. PATRICK *Parab. Pilgr.* xii. 70, I know this touches you with a strong inclination to it. **1718** POPE *Iliad* XXI. 105 If ever yet soft pity touch'd thy mind. **1810** SCOTT *Lady of L.* I. ix, Then, touched with pity and remorse, He sorrowed o'er the expiring horse.

c. To influence, move (in mind or will).

1570 T. WILSON *Demosth. Orat., Life* 127 As for corrupting him wyth giftes or rewardes, he is no more to be touched that way, than was Aristides. **1667** MILTON *P.L.* x. 45 No Decree of mine Concurring to necessitate his Fall, Or touch with lightest moment of impulse His free Will.

25. a. To grieve, vex; to injure, harm: esp. in a slight degree. ? *Obs.* (or merged in 23). Cf. 5.

1535 STEWART *Cron. Scot.* (Rolls) II. 262 As ressone wald, it tuechit him full soir. **1581** *Reg. Privy Council Scot.* III. 401 Be the violatioun and brek of the same his Hienes is sumquhat twitchit and offendit unto. **1608** *Yorks. Trag.* I. ii, Shall I stand idle And see my reputation touch'd to death?

b. To hurt or wound in mind or feelings, as if by touching a sore or tender part; to irritate, sting, nettle. Often in *fig.* phrases, as ***touch to the quick.*** (Cf. 5, 19 b.)

1589 *Love & Fort.* A ij b, He hath been lately rubde and toucht perhaps too neere. **1600** E. BLOUNT tr. *Conestaggio* 85 They touched the ministers of iustice to the quicke. **1711** ADDISON *Spect.* No. 99 ¶7 Telling a Man he lyes, is touching him in the most sensible Part of Honour. **1820** HOGG *Tales & Sk., Bridal of P.* II. 66 He feared it would be.. touching the king upon the sore heel. **1898** J. ARCH *Story of Life* xi. 257 It touched scores and scores of labourers on the raw.

II. Phrases.

26. a. Phrases with other verbs or sbs. **touch and go**: to touch for an instant and immediately go away or pass on; to deal with momentarily or slightly. (See also TOUCH AND GO *sb.* and *a.*)

1549 LATIMER *1st Serm. bef. Edw. VI* (Arb.) 26 As the text doeth ryse, I wyl touche and go a lyttle in euery place, vntyl I come vnto to much. **1600** ABP. ABBOT *Exp. Jonah* 446 Therefore it shall be enough for me, now to touch and go. *c* **1670** in *Roxb. Ball.* (1891) VII. 486 A Taylor in the Strand .. Most finely was Trappan'd, touch and go.

b. ***touch and run***: see TOUCH *sb.* 1 g.

27. touch and take: in various senses (see above and TAKE *v.*); in quot. 1793, to take fire at a touch.

1670 NARBOROUGH *Jrnl.* in *Acc. Sev. Late Voy.* I. (1694) 14 One blinded with a Cloth serv'd every Man as they were called to touch and take. **1793** *Regal Rambler* 40 Our hero laid in a large cargo of fresh fuel, ready to touch and take like phosphorus. **1805** NELSON *Let. to J. D. Thomson* 5 Sept., The Enemy have a shoal of frigates with their fleet and other Small Vessels, which will take their Crippled Ships in Tow. My Motto shall be Touch and Take.

28. In comb. with *sb. **to touch one's hat***: to raise the hand to the hat and touch it in token of salutation (an abbreviated form of the act of taking off or raising the hat). Const. *to* (the person saluted).

1782 MISS BURNEY *Cecilia* VII. ix, And, touching his hat, he was riding away. **1820** W. IRVING *Sketch Bk.* II. 149 Not a stage coach-man.. but touches his hat as he passes. **1840** HALIBURTON *Letter Bag* iv. 54 We bow and touch our hats with much formality. **1863** KINGSLEY *Water-Bab.* i, So Mr. Grimes touched his hat to him.

29. In ***to touch wood***. **a.** In a children's game: see quots. 1849, 1888. **b.** In folk-lore, or *quasi*-superstitious use: To touch wood as a charm to avert apprehended misfortune, esp. that apt to follow untimely boasting or self-gratulation: cf. L. *absit omen!* (OMEN *sb.*, quot. 1637).

1849 *Boy's Own Bk.* 37 This.. game [TOUCH *sb.* 1 g] is sometimes called 'Touch-iron' or 'Touch-wood'; in these cases the players are safe only while they touch iron or wood, as may be previously agreed. They are liable to be *touched* only when running from one piece of wood or iron to another. **1888** *Berksh. Gloss., Touch 'ood.* Boys have games called 'touch 'ood' and 'touch-iron', where anyone not touching either of the substances named is liable to be caught by the one standing out and has to stand out accordingly. **1908** *Westm. Gaz.* 30 Dec. 2/3 On the next occasion when we read of Christmas with spring weather or of the changing seasons we shall 'touch wood'.

III. In combination with adverbs.

30. touch down. a. *Rugby Football, Amer. Football*, etc. *trans.* To touch the ground with (the ball) behind the goal, usually that of the opposing side; also *absol.* See also TOUCHDOWN.

1864 *Field* 5 Nov. 331/1 The Old Rugbeians.. soon touched the ball down in the School goal. *Ibid.* 19 Nov. 354/2 [see TOUCH *v.* 2 f]. **1882** *Standard* 20 Nov. 2/8 The Military had.. to touch-down several times in self-defence. **1891** *Football: Rugby Union Laws* §19 A Maul in Goal is when the ball is held inside the goal line and one of the opposing sides endeavours to touch it down. **1897** *Sportsman* 16 Dec., [B.] took a shot at goal.. but the ball went wide and J. touched down.

b. *Aeronaut. intr.* To alight on the ground from the air; to land; also *transf.* Also (*rare*) *trans.*, to land (an aircraft).

1935 C. DAY LEWIS *Time to Dance* 41 M'Intosh touched her down. **1938** *Jrnl. R. Aeronaut. Soc.* XLII. 498 A successful flight down the beam.. gives the feeling that if the ceiling had been only 50 feet one could have held on.. longer before finally touching down. **1942** P. BRENNAN et al. *Spitfires over Malta* (1943) ii. 55, I touched down and swung my aircraft away from the pitted landing path, braking violently. **1955** *Times* 22 Aug. 5/4 The first aircraft to touch down brought an official party from Kallang. **1962** *Listener* 8 Feb. 260/2, I send this dove from the ark Where she must never touch down. **1970** N. ARMSTRONG et al. *First on Moon* xiv. 369 At 12.45 A.M. Houston time, Apollo 12's lunar module Intrepid touched down on the moon. **1979** *Arizona Daily Star* 1 Apr. E9/1 14 persons were injured when a tornado touched down near Glasgow, Ky.

31. touch in. *trans.* In drawing, painting, etc.: To insert (a detail) by touching with the pencil, brush, etc.

1871 *Routledge's Ev. Boy's Ann.* Oct. 615 The dry leaves in the hedges.. may be touched in with burnt sienna. **1892** *Photogr. Ann.* II. 262 Touching in as small a portion of top edge as possible.

32. touch off. *trans.* **a.** To represent exactly, to 'hit off' (cf. 17); also ***to touch it off***, to do exactly right, hit the mark exactly; in quot. 1766, to 'take the measure of' correctly, 'size up'; hence to be a match for (*obs.*).

1758–65 GOLDSM. *Ess.* i. ¶5, I was [told].. that I should now see something touched off to a nicety, for Mr. Spriggins was going to give us 'Mad Tom' in all its glory. **1766** GOLDSM. *Vic. W.* xii, I knew you would touch them off. **1821** GALT *Ayrshire Legatees* viii, He's such a funny man! and touches off the Londoners to the nines.

b. To fire off (a cannon, etc.), orig. by putting a match to the touch-hole. Hence *fig.*, to provoke (a reaction), to spark off.

1884 'MARK TWAIN' *Huck. Finn* xxviii. 282 It does seem most like setting down on a kag of powder and touching it off. **1907** *Daily Chron.* 6 Dec. 7/3 The only delay.. is due to a fear that a dispatch of the troops will touch off the magazine. *a* **1934** in WEBSTER s.v., These terms.. have become push buttons which touch off emotional reflexes. **1943** *Sun* (Baltimore) 12 Feb. 6/2 Senator Truman touched off the debate with a speech in which he assailed the supplanting of Lou Holland as chairman of the SWPC. **1950** *N.Y. Times* 20 Apr. 1/6 The surprise proposal.. touched off several outbursts of denunciation of the Soviet action. **1958** *Listener* 29 Nov. 813/1 The Bundestag declaration has touched off a chain-reaction of inquiry, proposal, examination, plan. **1966** *Ibid.* 10 Feb. 221/2 All these insights the piano touched off with its single hollow note struck over and over again. **1979** *Tucson* (Arizona) *Citizen* 20 Sept. 5C/1 A $1·8 million error may touch off a legal challenge.

33. touch out. *trans.* To clean out (corners) by touches or light strokes, as in wood-carving.

1879 *Cassell's Techn. Educ.* IV. 71/2 Tools.. for fancy work, and for touching out corners difficult of access.

34. touch up. a. *trans.* To improve, finish, or modify by adding touches or light strokes.

1715 ADDISON *Freeholder* No. 44 ¶3 What he saw was.. her natural Countenance, touched up with the usual Improvements of an aged Coquette. **1748** *Phil. Trans.* XLV. 173 All the illuminated Sets were.. touch'd up and finish'd by his own Hand. **1860** THACKERAY *Round. Papers, Screens*, Suppose the Editor.. never 'touched up' one single line of the contribution. **1863** BARING-GOULD *Iceland* 277 It is touched up, but it is for the most part quite trustworthy.

b. To stimulate by striking lightly or sharply, as with a whip; hence *fig.* to remind, 'to gently jog the memory' (Farmer *Slang*). Also, to exert influence upon; to rouse the emotions of.

1810 *Sporting Mag.* XXXV. 34 (*Single Stick*) Maslen set to with great confidence, sharply touching up the right arm of his antagonist. **1811** JANE AUSTEN *Sense & Sens.* III. iv. 88 We must touch up the Colonel to do something to the Parsonage. **1817** M. EDGEWORTH *Harrington* I. iii. 55 You will see.. how cleverly I will get myself out of the scrape with her. I know how to touch her up. **1838** DICKENS *Nich. Nick.* xxxii, He let out his whip-lash and touched up a little boy on the calves of his legs. **1846** —— *Let.* 28 Mar. (1977) IV. 528, I hope you mean to go to the General Theatrical Fund Dinner on Monday Week... Let me know, that I may touch up the Committee to place you near me. *c* **1863** T. TAYLOR in M. R. Booth *Engl. Plays of 19th Cent.* (1969) II. 140 The roughs adore music.. and as for sentiment and sensation, if you could hear Miss St. Evremond touch them up with the 'Maniac's Tear', the new sensation ballad [etc.]. **1884** E. W. HAMILTON *Diary* 10 Mar. (1972) II. 573 Slavery is a matter which specially touches up the British public. **1902** 'MRS. ALEXANDER' *Stronger than Love* viii, She touched up the ponies, and brought them over the bridge.. at a great pace.

c. † (*a*) (See quot. 1785.) *Obs.* (*b*) To finger or caress so as to excite sexually. *slang.*

1785 GROSE *Dict. Vulgar T., To touch up a woman*, to have carnal knowledge of her. **1903** [see sense 2 a above]. **1923** J. MANCHON *Le Slang* 318 *To touch up a woman*, caramboler une femme. **1961** H. S. TURNER *Something Extraordinary* vii. 135 She.. went in for a crass practice.. known as 'touching up'. It is.. a quick flick, in passing, from the crotch upwards... When a girl 'touches up' a boy it seems to be a very casual signal,.. nowhere near a definite proposition. **1966** P. WILLMOTT *Adolescent Boys E. London* iii. 49 They would often try to move on from kissing to sexual play: as they put it, they.. went up her skirt or 'touched her up'. **1973** C. EGLETON *Seven Days to Killing* iv. 48 Good-looking tart... I wouldn't have minded her touching me up.

touch- *sb.* or *vb.* in combination.

1. a. Simple attrib. combinations of the sb., as ***touch-feeling***, ***-knowledge***, ***-pleasure***, ***-sensation***, ***-stimulus***; ***touch-sensitive*** adj. **b.** Special combinations of the sb. (or in some cases directly from the vb.-stem): **touch-bodies, -corpuscles** *Anat.*, minute bodies of connective and nervous tissue occurring in the skin of the hands, feet, lips, and other parts, supposed to be connected with the sense of touch; also called *tactile corpuscles*; **touch-cell** *Anat.*, a nerve-cell at the end of a sensory nerve in a touch-corpuscle; **touch-dancing** orig. *U.S.*, dancing in which the partner is held close; hence (as a back-formation) **touch-dance** *v. intr.*; **touch-finder** *Rugby Football*, one who or a kick which succeeds in driving the ball into touch (TOUCH *sb.* 12); so **touch-finding** *vbl. sb.* and *ppl. a.*; **touch football** *U.S.*, a form of American football in which a player carrying the ball may be stopped simply by touching him, instead of tackling; **touch judge**, in *Rugby Football*, an umpire who marks when and where the ball goes 'into touch' (TOUCH *sb.* 12), corresponding to a *linesman* in the Association game; **touch-key**, name given to an instrument for scientific experiments on the sense of touch; **touch-kicking** *Rugby Football*, the action of kicking the ball into touch (TOUCH *sb.* 12); hence (as a back-formation) **touch-kick** *v. intr.*; so **touch-kick** *sb.*; **touch-mark**, an official stamp on pewterware, esp. one identifying the maker; cf. TOUCH *sb.* 5 b; **touch-needle**, a slender bar or rod of gold or silver, one of a set of different standards of fineness, used in conjunction with a touchstone for testing the fineness of gold or silver; **touch pad** *Computers*, a computer input device in the form of a small touch panel; **touch panel**, a panel containing different areas that need only to be touched to operate an electrical device; **touch-plate**, one of a set of plates bearing the 'touches' or official marks of the company of pewterers (TOUCH *sb.* 5 b); † **touch-point** *Geom.*, point of contact; **touch preparation** *Microscopy*, a preparation made by lightly touching cultured or freshly cut tissue with a slide so that a thin layer of cells adheres to it; **touch-proof**, in *Sugar Manuf.* a method of testing the degree of crystallization of the syrup by touching a drop of it, laid on the thumb, with the forefinger, and drawing it out to a thin thread; **touch rugby** or **rugger**, a version of rugby football in which touching takes the place of tackling; **touch screen** *Computers*, a VDU screen that is also an input device operated by touching it; **touch shot** *Lawn Tennis*, a shot without any force; **touch spot** *Physiol.*, one of the spots on the skin specially sensitive to touch or pressure; **Touch-Tone** *U.S.*, a proprietary name for telephone apparatus in which push-buttons take the place of a dial; **touch-typing,**

the art of typing without looking at the keys; hence (as a back-formation) **touch-type** *v. intr.*; so **touch-typist**; †**touch-warden**: see quot. 1676 (cf. TOUCH *sb.* 5, *v.* 8); also *fig.*; **touch watch**, a watch so contrived that the time by it can be ascertained by touch, e.g. in the dark; **touch-weight**, one of a set of weights used in experiments on the sense of touch; **touch-writer** = *touch-typist* above. **c.** Connected with the notion of ready ignition: see TOUCH-POWDER; **touch-pan**, the pan of an old-fashioned gun, into which the touch-powder was put; **touch-paper**, paper steeped in nitre so as to burn slowly on being touched by a spark, used for firing gunpowder, etc.; **touch-place**, the metal plate in which was the touch-hole of a culverin; **touch-string**, string steeped in nitre used as a fuse (cf. *touch-paper*). See also TOUCH-BOX, TOUCH-HOLE, TOUCHWOOD.

1889 *Cent. Dict.* s.v. *Corpuscle*, Tactile corpuscles.. Also called..touch-corpuscles, *touch-bodies, palpation-corpuscles. **1897** PARKER & HASWELL *Zool.* II. 100 Touch-corpuscles are formed of an ovoidal mass of connective tissue containing a ramified nerve, the terminal branches of which end in *touch-cells. **1876** DUHRING *Dis. Skin* 26 Tactile corpuscles are also called *touch corpuscles. **1899** *Allbutt's Syst. Med.* VI. 641 A trophic centre in a touch corpuscle. **1972** *Harper's Bazaar* Oct. 72/1 Dance experts agree that, as the East goes, so goes the nation, and what you've heard by now is true—'*touch', 'partner', 'ballroom' dancing is back. *Ibid.* 72/3 Freddie doesn't *touch dance at all. **1974** *Courier-Mail* (Brisbane) 23 Feb. 18/4 The latest craze among young people in the U.S. is 'touch dancing', which their mums and dads used to call 'dancing cheek-to-cheek'. **1884** tr. *Lotze's Metaph.* iv. 507 *heading*, How can *Touch-feelings form a series? **1939** *Daily Tel.* 18 Dec. 11/1 Jenkins..alternated long *touch-finders with sliced shots. *Ibid.*, Ellis was allowed a lot of latitude in..putting in *touch-finding kicks. **1960** *Times* 30 Nov. 3/6 The small, durable halves were dedicated touch-finders. **1976** *Leicester Mercury* 14 Oct. 46/1 It was a very solid display of good catching, good touch-finding and some probing entries into the line. **1933** *Jrnl. Health & Physical Educ.* Oct. 41/1 *Touch football is now a scientific and standardized game. **1951** J. STEINBECK *Burning Bright* i. 37, I was..just playing around with some of the fellows—touch football. **1977** *Transatlantic Rev.* LX. 119 You often see Winterville kids playing touch football along the parkway. **1893** *Daily News* 14 Dec. 2/6 Messrs. Temple Gordon and Percy Christopherson were *touch judges. **1894** *Westm. Gaz.* 11 Jan. 5/3 Altogether 14 players were injured, the touch-judge was threatened, and the referee reported that it had never been his lot to witness such a shameful exhibition. **1905** TITCHENER *Exper. Psychol.* II. I. 159 Fig. 60. Scripture's *touch key. **1954** J. B. G. THOMAS *On Tour* vi. 71 They.. saved and counter-rushed and *touch-kicked with unerring accuracy. **1960** *Times* 31 Oct. 4/4 Long *touch-kicks. **1978** *Morecambe Guardian* 14 Mar. 11/3 Glover took a while to find his usual accuracy with his touch kicks. **1936** *Times* 9 Jan. 4/3 Some excellent *touch-kicking by Morris forced the Navy back into their own '25'. **1884** *St. James' Gaz.* 13 June 4/2 The true dealer's *touch-knowledge of Oriental antiquities. **1904** H. J. L. J. MASSÉ *Pewter Plate* xiv. 190 The *touch-marks usually were the initials of the maker of the pewter, and various other devices such as the Company's quality mark. **1959** L. GROSS *Housewives' Guide to Antiques* viii. 103 Some, but not all, pewter will be found with a touch-mark. **1974** L. KOENIG *Little Girl* iii. 34 A pewter tankard..seemed to demand examination. She..turned it over to study the touchmark. **1763-6** W. LEWIS *Comm. Phil.-Techn.* 124 Accustoming himself to compare the colours of a good set of *Touch needles. **1884** F. J. BRITTEN *Watch & Clockm.* 266 Touch needles are small bars of gold, one each of all the different standards likely to be tested. **1980** *Displays* I. 206/1 These experimental studies, conducted during the development of the *Touch-pad, demonstrate the viabiity of an off-display touch input device. **1983** *Your Computer* Aug. 32/2 Once out of its package the Wizzard takes on the appearance of a quite simple, compact unit, complete with two joysticks, touch pads and firing buttons. **1591** SYLVESTER *Du Bartas* I. vii. 36 Down falls the Cock, up from the *Touch-pan flies A ruddy flash. **1974** *Physics Bull.* June 225/2 One of these is a *touch panel made of a glass plate on which capacitors are thinly etched in copper. A TV tube behind the panel 'names' the capacitors in an array of 4 × 4 and these 'buttons' can be 'pushed' by merely touching the panel. **1981** J. B. ADAMS in J. H. Mulvey *Nature of Matter* vii. 156 The operator..can send instructions to any component of the machine by means of a touch panel, which identifies the component, and one knob, which determines the required action. **1750** *Phil. Trans.* XLVI. 449 Neither these, nor those of Cheltenham, will deflagrate or flash in *Touch-Paper. **1832** MISS MITFORD *Village* Ser. v. 113 Why dost thou not fire?.. So please your worship, the wind hath extinguished the touch-paper. **1873** E. SPON *Workshop Receipts* Ser. I. 131/2 Touchpaper..placed..round the mouth of the firework, and twisted into a point. **1778** PRYCE *Min. Cornub.* 178 [The miners] have a *touch-pipe, that is, rest..half an hour to smoke a pipe. **1508** *Acc. Ld. High Treas. Scot.* IV. 122 For vernesing of ane lang culveryn and gilting of the end of it and the *twich plaith. **1902** WELCH *Hist. Pewterers' Co.* I. Introd. 1 The..inventories of the Company's goods show that touch-plates existed at an early date. *a* **1618** SYLVESTER *Spectacles* xii, How soon doe Odours from thy Nostrils fly! How short, *touch-Pleasures (tipt with pain and fear)! **1602** BLUNDEVIL *Theoriques Seuen Planets* 29 The *Touch-point, otherwise called the point of conjunction. *Ibid.* 73 The right line BHP sheweth the Touch-point. **1956** *Nature* 7 Jan. 47/1 *Touch-preparations of spleen and lung on slides were fixed in 95 per cent ethanol at 37°C. for 30 min. **1975** *Ibid.* 17 July 225/2 Spleens were sectioned sagittally and touch preparations were made and stained with the Wright-Giemsa stain or benzidine. **1977** *Arab Times* 14 Dec. 9/7 Both [games] entail constant running, both in defence and attack, especially *touch rugby. **1942** C. MILBURN *Diary* 16 Dec. (1979) 161 He talks of hockey, soccer and *touch-rugger, describing the latter game. **1974** *Management Informatics* III. 70/1 As a first step, a prototype *touch screen was designed and constructed in our Laboratory by Mr. Stephen Salter. **1983** *Austral. Personal Computer* Aug. 60/2 The touch-screen and light-pen both have the limitation that the user must first identify the location that has to be touched, and then a physical movement has to be made... Also, touch screens do get finger-marked. **1865** S. HODGSON *Time & Space* ii. 78 A combination of a whole series of *touch-sensation into a solid whole is apparently possible..in grasping a small object, where the fingers meet each other. **1899** *Allbutt's Syst. Med.* VII. 35 The transmission of ordinary touch sensations being unimpaired. **1969** *Bull. Radio & Electr. Engin. Div. Nat. Res. Council Canada* July–Sept. 15 (*heading*) An *X-Y* *touch sensitive position encoder for computer input. **1979** *Washington Post Mag.* 25 Mar. 5/3 The clavichord changed. Its keyboard widened... 'It got louder and more touch-sensitive,' says Tom. **1983** *Listener* 12 May 3/2 You controlled your route by pressing buttons on a touch-sensitive screen. **1959** *Touch shot [see [DINK *sb.*[2]]. **1969** *New Yorker* 14 June 56/2 A loose, liberal, infuriating touch shot. **1906** C. S. SHERRINGTON *Integrative Action of Nervous System* ix. 324 The retina is thus a group of glorified 'warm-spots,' and the cochlea a group of glorified '*touch-spots'. **1927** HALDANE & HUXLEY *Animal Biol.* v. 122 The fineness of discrimination for touch depends mainly on the closeness of touch-spots. **1968** D. F. HORROBIN *Med. Physiol. & Biochem.* xxv. 150/2 There are touch spots, cold spots and warm spots, each particularly sensitive to one modality. **1927** HALDANE & HUXLEY *Animal Biol.* xii. 268 Most..of the group possess nerves, and at least scattered sense-organs for perceiving *touch-stimuli. *a* **1860** ALB. SMITH *Lond. Med. Stud.* (1861) 61 Crackers..contrived to explode at any period..by attaching graduated pieces of *touch-string to them. **1962** *Official Gaz.* (U.S. Patent Office) 19 June TM 122 American Telegraph and Telephone Company, New York... **Touch-Tone*. For providing telephone communication service. **1970** O. DOPPING *Computers & Data Processing* xi. 163 If the telephone is of the touch-tone type, the same buttons that are used for dialling can be used also for putting questions, expressed in numerical form, to the computer. **1972** *Sci. Amer.* Sept. 112/3 The first telephone switching systems were actuated by human operators; today the job is done automatically by means of a dial or 'Touch-Tone' terminal on the user's telephone. **1976** *National Observer* (U.S.) 10 Apr. 9/4 Touch-tone converters. This device changes your dial telephone to a touch-tone telephone. **1962** *Punch* 8 Aug. 191/1 If you will learn to *touch-type, I will give you a new, feather-light portable. [**1897** in *Story of Typewriter* (1923) 113 Omaha has become the storm centre of the commotion over the touch method of typewriting.] **1947** K. JAEDIKER *Tall, Dark & Dead* viii. 117 All I know about *touch-typing is that there are home keys and if you don't put your fingers on them, you go haywire. **1976** 'J. FRASER' *Who steals my Name?* iv. 46 Many coppers had done touchtyping courses. **1929** *Telegr. & Telephone Jrnl.* XVI. 13/1 Attention was concentrated upon touch-typing with the object of turning out highly-skilled *touch-typists. **1972** 'J. & E. BONETT' *No Time to Kill* vii. 90 I'm not a touch typist. Very few writers are. **1644** BULWER *Chirol.* 172 The grape of the Index [finger]..is..chiefe *Touch-warden to the King of the five senses. **1676** B. W[ILLIS] *Man. Goldsm.* 30 The Wardens that are to make the Assays and mark the Silver, are now called the Touch-Wardens. **1862** *Catal. Internat. Exhib., Brit.* II. No. 3324 *Touch watches, regulators, and railway clocks. **1884** F. J. BRITTEN *Watch & Clockm.* 33 *Blind Man's Watch*... A watch in which the progress of the hands may be ascertained by touch... The objection to this form of touch watch is that if the pointer is pressed hard against the finger it is apt to advance the hands of the watch. **1905** TITCHENER *Exper. Psychol.* II. II. 46 The *Touch-Weights. Sets of these weights were made, a few years ago, by Willyoung. **1915** *Literary Digest* (N.Y.) 21 Aug. Advt. p. i, Great numbers were so-called *touch-writers—yet there has hardly been a single one who hasn't doubled or trebled his or her speed and accuracy.

2. Substantival phrases consisting **a.** of the vb. in combination with an advb.: **touch-back** (*Rugby Football*), the act of touching the ground with the ball on or behind the player's own goal-line after it has been driven there by the opposing side; also, a similar action in some other ball games; **touch-last**, a children's game, = TOUCH *sb.* 1 g; **touch-up**, an act of touching up (see TOUCH *v.* 34 a); a stroke added by way of improvement or finish; also a slight incitement or reminder; **b.** of the vb. with object; **touch-no-wall, -s**, *Real Tennis*: see quots.

a. 1891 W. CAMP *Amer. Football* 172 A *touch-back is made when a player touches the ball to the ground behind his own goal, the impetus which sent the ball across the line having been received from an opponent. **1941** *Daily Progress* (Charlottesville, Va.) 14 Jan. 11 This used to be an automatic touchback and the ball was placed in play on the 20-yard line. **1976** *Webster's Sports Dict.* 455/2 *Touchback.* Speedball. A situation in which the ball is driven over the end line by an offensive player without scoring. **1825** JAMIESON Suppl. II. 568/2 *Tig*, a game among children, in which one strikes another and runs off... This game in S[cotland] is the same with *Touchlast in E[ngland]. **1902** [see HE *pers. pron.* 6 b]. **1927** *Sunday Express* 17 July 8/2 The younger and sprightlier guests..played 'touch last' on the lawn. **1951** E. GRAHAM *My Window looks down East* iv. 29 He walks sideways away from her, like a child playing 'touch-last'. **1885** *Athenæum* 1 Aug. 144/3 Tom Moore did not..give the great novelist a retrospective *touch-up with his poetic pencil. **1907** *Times* 3 May 4/1, I ask your lordship to give a sort of a kind of 'touch-up' to these people.

b. 1777 [T. SWIFT] *Gamblers* I. 221 Now sounds the Grill; 'tis Setts, and Touch-no-wall, And Chaces echo thro' the lattic'd Hall. **18..** *Laws Tennis* §33 in J. Marshall *Ann. Tennis* (1878) 166 When the odds of touch-no-walls, or touch-no-side-walls, are given, a ball returned by the giver of the odds, which makes a nick, is counted for the striker. **1878** J. MARSHALL *Ann. Tennis* 160 Touch-no-walls, or All-the-walls: a point of cramped-odds, by which the giver of the odds loses a stroke whenever a ball, returned by him, touches a wall or a gallery-post, or enters an opening, before falling on the floor.

touchable ('tʌtʃəb(ə)l), *a.* [f. TOUCH *v.* + -ABLE.] Capable of being touched.

1. a. Affecting the sense of touch; tangible.

c **1400** *Wyclif's Bible* Heb. xii. 18 ȝe han not come to the tretable fyer, or able for to touche [*v.r.* or toucheable]. **1572** J. JONES *Bathes of Bath* II. 18 The truest touchestone, of all properties, trying both toucheable and tasteable qualities. **1656** W. D. tr. *Comenius' Gate Lat. Unl.* §469. 135 To the end that things touchable may in lying down gently affect us. **1829** JAS. MILL *Hum. Mind* (1869) I. 13 In that case, we should have no idea of objects as seeable, as hearable, as touchable, or tasteable.

b. Fit to be touched or tasted. *nonce-use.*

1751 SMOLLETT *Per. Pic.* lxxxvii. **1881** BLACK *Beautiful Wretch*, etc. III. 177 The butter was not touchable.

2. Capable of being affected in mind or feeling.

1822 *Examiner* 154/2 Every mind touchable by musical sounds. **1890** *Church Union* (N.Y.) May, Such of our readers as are touchable by the appeal of this writer.

Hence **toucha'bility**, suitability to be touched; **'touchableness.**

1620 T. GRANGER *Div. Logike* 66 Also visiblenesse, touchablenesse, which are inseparable both in state of mortalitie, and in the state of glory. **1674** BLOUNT *Glossogr.*, *Tangibility*, touchableness. **1937** L. MACNEICE in *Essays & Stud.* XXII. 157 Spender..believes in 'touchability'... It means..the belief that people in themselves are worth knowing and touching, just as for Auden facts are worth remembering. **1944** [see MARRIAGEABILITY].

'touch and 'go, *sb.* and *adj. phr.* (Also with hyphens.) [The vbl. phrase *touch and go* (TOUCH *v.* 26) used as sb. or adj.]

A. *sb.* **1.** The act of touching for an instant and quitting immediately; something done quickly or instantaneously.

1655 MOUFET & BENNET *Health's Impr.* (1746) 59 Howsoever we may taste of it to bring on Appetite, let it be but a touch and go.

2. Applied to a person of hasty temper or disposition. *nonce-use.*

1675 DUFFETT *Mock Temp.* III. i, Old touch and go, why so hasty?

3. A risky, precarious, delicate, or ticklish case or state of things (such that a mere touch may cause disaster); a narrow escape, 'near shave'.

1815 R. WARDLAW *Let.* in Alexander *Life* vi. (1856) 166 'Twas touch and go—but I got my seat. **1831** MISS FERRIER *Destiny* iv, So it was with Glenroy and his lady. It had been touch-and-go with them for many a day; and now..ended in a threatened separation. **1858** C. HUNT in *Merc. Marine Mag.* V. 84 Passing so close, that it is often a 'touch and go'. **1867** SMYTH *Sailor's Word-bk.*, *Touch-and-go*, said of anything within an ace of ruin; as in rounding a ship very narrowly to escape rocks, &c., or when, under sail, she rubs against the ground with her keel, without much diminution of her velocity. **1887** 'H. SMART' *Cleverly Won* iii, She caught [the horse]..by the mane, and though it was touch and go she managed to retain her seat.

B. *adj.* **1.** Involving or characterized by rapid, slight, or superficial execution; sketchy; casual, careless; instantaneous; expeditious.

1812 H. & J. SMITH *Rej. Addr.* Pref. 11 There is an art of writing for the Theatre, technically called *touch and go*,.. indispensable when we consider the small quantum of patience which..a London audience can be expected to afford. **1832** MOORE *Mem.* (1854) VI. 247 Free to introduce anecdotes, quotations, and all such touch-and-go things as the formality of an essay would not admit of. **1832** J. P. KENNEDY *Swallow B.* xii, It was a touch-and-go manner which spoke volumes. **1879** STEVENSON *Trav. Cevennes* (1886) 98 In the neighbourhood of women, it is but a touch-and-go association that can be formed amongst defenceless men. **1885** MISS BRADDON *Wyllard's Weird* iv, A murder of that kind must be touch and go—no sooner thought of than done. **1891** *Spectator* 14 Feb. 246/2 They are 'touch-and-go' sketches, and impressions such as a clever man may throw off at will.

2. Risky, of the nature of a narrow escape: cf. A. 3.

1856 ALEXANDER *R. Wardlaw* vi. 168 His getting off at all was generally a 'touch and go' matter. **1897** BLACKMORE in *Blackw. Mag.* Sept. 361 Some touch and go adventure he has been through.

†**'touchangle.** *Obs. rare.* ? = ANGLE-TWITCH, worm used as bait in angling.

1581 J. BELL *Haddon's Answ. Osor.* 291 With this touch-angle he may fishe a good while, and catch a foole at the last.

†**'touchant**, *prep. Obs. rare.* [a. F. *touchant* prep. use of pr. pple. of *toucher* to TOUCH.] = TOUCHING *prep.*

c **1375** *Cursor M.* 26439 (Fairf.) Touchant dedeli synne say we. **1425** *Paston Lett.* I. 21, I send yow..the copie of unfrendly lettre..sent to me late, touchant the same matier. ? **1430** *Ibid.* 30 My clerke, to wham I prey yow to gyve feith and credence touchant this matier. **1457** HARDING *Chron.* in *Eng. Hist. Rev.* Oct. (1912) 751 His greuance..touchant the Euydence of the souereynte of Scotlonde.

touchar, obs. form of TOCHER.

†**'touch-box.** *Obs.* exc. *Hist.* [for *touch-powder box*: see TOUCH-POWDER.] A box for 'touch-powder' or priming-powder, formerly forming part of a musketeer's equipment.

1549 *Acts Privy Council* (1890) II. 348 Flaskes, cviij; touche boxes, c. **1564** *Wills & Inv. N.C.* (Surtees) I. 226 One dagg wth flask and tutchbockes vs. **1590** SIR J. SMYTH *Disc. Weapons* 21 The touchpowder in the touch-boxes also. **1591** *Garrard's Art Warre* 3 Hys Flaske and Tutchboxe must keepe hys Pouder. **1598** BARRET *Theor. Warres* III. i. 34 To haue his touchboxe fastened by the string..and to prime his peece with touch-powder. **1627** CAPT. SMITH *Seaman's Gram.* xiv. 68 A Horne is his touch-box. **1660** *Act 12 Chas. II.* c. 4 Sched. s.v. *Boxes*, Touch-boxes of iron or other mettal, guilt, the dozen..j. l. **1902** FIRTH *Cromwell's Army* iv. 81 A fine powder for priming..in what was termed a touch-box or primer, and a coarser powder for loading..in his flask.

'touchdown. Also touch-down. [f. phr. *to touch down* (TOUCH *v.* 30.)]

1. *Rugby Football*, *Amer. Football*, etc. The act of touching the ground with the ball behind the goal-line, usually that of the opposing side, to score points; ***safety touchdown***, the same done behind the player's own goal-line after it has been driven there by his own side, in order to prevent the opposing side from making a touchdown.

1864 *Field* 29 Oct. 315/1 The School..obtaining two 'touches down', which Poole..was unable to turn into a goal. **1876** in P. H. Davis *Football, Amer. Intercollegiate Game* (1911) 462 A match shall be decided by a majority of touchdowns. **1895** *Outing* (U.S.) XXVII. 249/2 Canadian system of scoring... A 'touch-down' or 'try' consists of four points with the privilege of trying a kick at the goal, which, if successful, nets the team which scored two points more. **1949** *Desplaines Valley News* (Summit, Illinois) 28 Oct. 7/3 Harvard could not push across a touchdown in the first half. **1977** *New Yorker* 9 May 122/2 A figure holding hands overhead like a referee indicating a touchdown.

2. *Aeronaut.* The action of coming into contact with the ground during landing.

1935 P. W. F. MILLS *Elem. Pract. Flying* vii. 102 [The purpose] of causing the actual touchdown, when it takes place, to take place with the aeroplane in its natural position on the ground. **1948** *Sun* (Baltimore) 3 Nov. 11/3 You are 50 feet above glide path and one quarter of a mile from touchdown. **1961** H. H. KOLBE *Handbk. Astronaut. Engin.* XXVII. 7 The term *landing*, when used in a discussion of space flight, actually can be considered as four phases: i.e., the exit from orbit, the reentry, the letdown, and the touchdown. **1975** *Daily Tel.* 11 Aug. 11/4 One vehicle will make a soft touchdown on Mars while the large spacecraft which carried it on its journey will remain in orbit.

‖**touché** (tuʃe), *int.* Occas. *fem.* touchée. [Fr., pa. pple. of *toucher* to hit.] **a.** *Fencing.* An exclamation used to acknowledge a hit.

1904 *Red Book* Feb. 382/1 '*Touché!*' Jarsac growled sharply. **1958** A. WEST *Princ. & Persuasions* 202 These cosy thrusts will never slip between the ribs into the lungs; the weapons are not rapiers but buttoned foils that will bend double against a jacket and at most produce a murmur of '*Touché*'.

b. A pleasant admission of a valid point or justified accusation made by another person.

1907 *Everybody's Mag.* XVI. 221/1 They did not cry *touché*, but the House cheered to the echo. **1912** E. C. BENTLEY *Trent's Last Case* xv. 322 '*Touché*', Trent said, with a dry smile. **1928** *Sat. Rev.* 17 Nov. 649/1 Touché—I apologize to Messrs. Brown and Phillips for my lack of technical discernment. **1952** H. INNES *Campbell's Kingdom* I. iv. 81 'I'd my own reasons, the same as you have.' ..'Touchée,' she said softly. **1981** A. PRICE *Soldier no More* 50 '*Touché*...' he nodded, accepting the rebuke.

touched (tʌtʃt), *ppl. a.* Also 7-8 **toucht**. [f. TOUCH *v.* + -ED¹.] **a.** In various senses corresponding to those of TOUCH *v.*

In quot. *a* 1625, tried, proved (sense 8); in quot. 1667, magnetized (sense 6c); in quot. 1660 *absol.* from sense 2b.

touched gold, the touch-piece given by the sovereign when he touched for the 'king's evil', supposed to retain a healing virtue. **touched proof**, a 'proof' from an engraved or etched plate approaching completion, submitted to the artist of the picture copied, for his approval or criticism.

a **1400** HYLTON *Scala Perf.* (W. de W. 1494) II. ii, It was impossyble goddis sone to be borne of towchyd woman. *a* **1586** SIDNEY *Arcadia* (1622) 461 To repay the touched honour of her house. *a* **1625** FLETCHER *Women Pleased* II. i, Ye shall be sure I am a touch'd friend. **1660** EVELYN *Diary* 6 July, The other Chaplaine..., having Angel gold strung on white ribbon on his arme, delivers them one by one to his Majestie, who puts them about the necks of the touched as they passe. **1667** H. OLDENBURG in *Phil. Trans.* II. 423 Whether touched Needles move otherwise, when the Veins of Iron do not lie North and South. **1715** E. BETTS 1 Mar. in *The Betts of Wortham* xvi. (1912) 167 My mother lent Coz Mary Betts ye piece of toucht gold with ye Britaine and this motto [etc.]. **1831** J. CONSTABLE *Let.* 13 Apr. (1966) IV. 348, I send you the *twelve pounds*, and a touched proof of the Heath. **1861** THORNBURY *Turner* I. 408 Turner was always quarrelling with the engravers about his touched proofs. He wanted every proof on which he had written directions to be returned.

b. With adv., as ***touched-up***: see TOUCH *v.* 34.

1875 tr. *Vogel's Chem. Light* vi. 48 A single touched-up negative gave hundreds of unexceptionable impressions.

Hence **'touchedness** (in quot., state of being mentally 'touched', slight insanity).

1883 F. W. ROBINSON *Hands of Justice* II. v, Clambering out of the window in the middle of the night was a striking example of his 'touchedness'.

toucheous, var. TOUCHOUS *a.*

toucher ('tʌtʃə(r)). [f. TOUCH *v.* + -ER¹.] One who or that which touches, in senses of the verb.

1. *gen.* **a.** *lit.* or in physical sense.

1435 MISYN *Fire of Love* I. xxv. 54 Qwhils þe hart of þe toucher in dyuers desires is takyn. **1495** *Trevisa's Barth. De P.R.* VII. lxvi. (W. de W.) Siij, Yf he [torpedo] be touchyd with a spere, the towcher shall fele the vyolence of the venym. **1548** UDALL, etc. *Erasm. Par. Matt.* ix. 59 [Jesus] loked about hym as seking for the priuy toucher. **1680** C. NESSE *Church Hist.* 340 Touch a great man upon the sore.. he fumes and casts the toucher into prison. **1763** *Life Swift* in *Wks.* XI. 265 A thistle is the Scotish arms Which to the Toucher threatens harms. **1904** *Times, Lit. Suppl.* 1 Apr. 97/2 That high sort..means death to the profane toucher.

b. *fig.*

1601 DEACON & WALKER *Spirits & Divels* 121 This argument..is a toucher. **1709** MRS. MANLEY *Secret Mem.* (1720) III. 323 A Heart truly touch'd, values nothing in comparison with the Toucher. **1846** HAYDON in Gullick & Timbs *Paint.* (1859) 235 The touchers..are the great men who had discovered the optical principles of imitating nature to convey thought.

c. With adv., as ***toucher-up***.

1908 *Westm. Gaz.* 28 Jan. 4/1 Taken..advantage of by the wily dealer and his ally, the 'toucher-up'.

d. One who †robs or seeks to obtain gifts or loans of money for himself. *slang.*

1849 G. G. FOSTER *New York in Slices* 25 The other places in the cotillion are occupied by a notorious kracksman [*sic*] with his 'pal'—a celebrated 'toucher'. **1904** *Chicago Tribune* 30 Oct. (Worker's Mag.) 4/2 The salaried clerk who keeps his wife..at a fashionable hotel is, usually, a toucher of the kind that makes a good front. **1919** WODEHOUSE *My Man Jeeves* 91 Many's the time in London, I've hurried along Piccadilly and felt the hot breath of the toucher on the back of my neck. **1961** 'F. O'BRIEN' *Hard Life* xii. 101 The streets aren't crawling with touchers like Dublin.

2. *Bowls.* A bowl which touches the jack.

1600 NASHE *Summer's Last Will* 1178 Ho, wel shot, a tutcher, a tutcher! **1659** FULLER *App. Inj. Innoc.* (1840) 552, I expected when the Animadvertor had knocked away my bowl, he would have laid a toucher in the room thereof. **1868** 'S. DARYL' *Quoits & Bowls* 51 A bowl which touches the Jack at any time during its course..is called a 'toucher'.

3. An instrument for touching: see quot.

1885 C. G. W. LOCK *Workshop Receipts* Ser. IV. 327/2 By means of a little strip of brass—called a 'toucher'—the crossings are found [in examining a watch].

4. *colloq.* or *slang.* **a.** A case of close contact, an exact fit. **b.** A very near approach, a 'near go'; in phr. ***as near as a toucher***, very nearly, all but; ***within a toucher***, within an inch *of* doing something (only in Wodehouse).

1827 W. CLARKE *Every Night Bk.* 73 The cock which takes your fancy..is..to all appearance, right-thorough bred, or 'as near it as a toucher'. **1828** *Craven Gloss.* s.v., An exact fit. 'It hits to a toucher', i.e. so exactly that the joints touch each other. **1840** J. T. HEWLETT *P. Priggins* ix, 'So Dick and Tripes were nearly being rusticated this morning'... 'As near as a toucher'. **1860** SALA *Baddington Peerage* I. xvii. 298 It was a near toucher, though! **1894** ASTLEY 50 *Years Life* II. 199, I was as near as a toucher turning too short, through mistaking the post. **1932** WODEHOUSE *Doctor Sally* viii. 78, I came within a toucher of saying, 'pause before it is too late!' **1954** —— *Jeeves & Feudal Spirit* xviii. 173 The hand of doom within a toucher of descending.

toucher, obs. form of TOCHER.

'touch-hole. [f. TOUCH- in *touch-powder* + HOLE.] A small tubular hole in the breech of a fire-arm, through which the charge is ignited; the vent.

1501 *Acc. Ld. High Treas. Scot.* II. 25 Item, for casting of the erd fra Mons [Meg], and to turne hir and lay the twych hole vp,..iij s. ij d. **1560** WHITEHORNE *Ord. Souldiours* 33 Putting sum poulder in the touchehole and aboute the touchhole, the Gunne is then charged. **1618** in Foster *Eng. Factories Ind.* (1906) 31 The fire out of hir toutchole (as yt is most likely) tooke hold of the bandeleros. **1709** DAMPIER *Voy.* III. II. 81 Six bad Guns..whose Touch-holes..are so enlarg'd..that a great part of the strength of the Powder flies away there. **1837** W. IRVING *Capt. Bonneville* (1849) 193 Some of the more knowing..contrived to stop the touch-holes of the field-pieces with dirt.

b. *fig.* or *allusively*.

1602 MARSTON *Ant. & Mel.* II. Wks. 1856 I. 19 The match..will presently set fire to the touch-hole of intemperance. **1617** MIDDLETON & ROWLEY *Fair Quarrel* II. ii. *a* **1625** FLETCHER & MASS. *Cust. Country* III. iii. **1664** BUTLER *Hud.* II. II. 830 Like linstock, to the horse's touch-hole.

touchily ('tʌtʃɪlɪ), *adv.* [f. TOUCHY + -LY².] In a touchy manner; irritably, testily; †saucily.

1653 WATERHOUSE *Apol. Learn.* 251 The King answered only, Say what I can do acceptable to the Athenians; the Varlet Democrates replyed touchily, Nothing better then to hang thy selfe. **1844** WARDLAW *Prov.* II. xxxix. 47 The hasty spirit..startles touchily at every word. **1888** MRS. H. WARD *R. Elsmere* xlv, Rose..had grown so touchily sensitive.

touchiness ('tʌtʃɪnɪs). [f. as prec. + -NESS.] The quality of being touchy.

1. Sensitiveness of temper, irritability, testiness.

1653 GAUDEN *Hierasp.* To Rdr. 26 Nor is he ignorant of the touchinesse, and roughnesse..of many mens spirits in these times. **1660** HICKERINGILL *Jamaica* (1661) 96 Their discontents had heated them to so (tinder-like) a Touchinesse, that they were ready to take fire on all occasions. **1828** *Lights & Shades* II. 52 She is known only by her one absorbing quality of touchiness, and is dreaded and hated accordingly.

2. Ticklishness, precariousness.

1648 *Eikon Bas.* iii. 14 My friends resented it as a motion ..not guided with such discretion, as the touchinesse of those times required.

3. *Painting*, etc.: see TOUCHY 4.

1813 *Examiner* 8 Feb. 90/2 The heads and hands have.. a rich touchiness of pencil. *Ibid.* 1 Mar. 141/1 The trees.. have perhaps too minute a touchiness of foliage. **1821** *New Monthly Mag.* III. 391 It is too much limited to the outline of the body: it wants a good filling up, a breaking and touchiness in the intermediate spaces.

touching ('tʌtʃɪŋ), *vbl. sb.* [f. TOUCH *v.* + -ING¹.] The action of the verb TOUCH.

1. a. The action, or an act, of feeling something with the hand, etc.; the fact or state of being contiguous; touch, contact; a touch; *spec.* for the 'king's evil' (quot. 1704).

c **1290** *St. Lucy* 33 in *S. Eng. Leg.* I. 102 þoruȝ touchingue of seinte Agace toumbe þouȝ schalt beo hol a-non. *a* **1450** *Knt. de la Tour* (1906) 58 Leude touchinge and handelyng sterithe and chafithe the flesshe. **1561** T. NORTON *Calvin's Inst.* IV. xix. (1634) 723 Some he healed with touchings, other some with his word. *a* **1657** SIR W. MURE *Misc. Poems* xi. 6 Hands, forbeare to tuich Ought 30ʳ tuiching can bewitch! **1704** *Lond. Gaz.* No. 4020/4 Her Majesty thinking it necessary to discontinue Touching for this Season. **1842** TENNYSON *Locksley Hall* 38 Our spirits rush'd together at the touching of the lips.

†b. The sense of touch. *Obs.*

c **1460** *Wisdom* 1105 in *Macro Plays* 72 By towchynge, I felte peyne smerte. **1500–20** DUNBAR *Poems* ix. 12 My wittis fyve,—In hering, seing, gusting, twiching, and smelling. **1656** STANLEY *Hist. Philos.* v. (1701) 189/1 The sense of Touching. **1774** GOLDSM. *Nat. Hist.* (1776) II. 179 The closer senses, if I may so call them, such as smelling, tasting, and touching, are..as simple as they are limited.

c. In various *spec.* senses: see the verb; also with *up*: see TOUCH *v.* 34c.

1671 MILTON *P.R.* II. 370 No interdict Defends the touching of these viands pure. **1705** DERHAM in *Phil. Trans.* XXV. 2143 This way of Touching [with a magnet]. **1833** T. HOOK *Parson's Dau.* III. xii, The only difference between the passages is the frequency of touching in the one case. **1908** H. B. MORSE *Trade Chinese Emp.* 148 A lot of sixty [silver ingots] of which I saw the weighing and touching. **1973** C. MULLARD *Black Britain* vii. 87 Both employees had for some months been practising a mild form of homosexuality—'touching up'. **1980** J. SCOTT *Gospel Lamb* iii. 51 Touchings-up were frequent—the girls seemed as eager as the boys.

d. In reference to painting, or artistic or other work; also with *up*: see TOUCH *v.* 10, 34a.

1781 SIR J. REYNOLDS *Journ. Flanders*, etc. Wks. 1797 II. 87 [Tenier's] manner of touching, or what we call handling, has perhaps never been equalled. **1825** J. NICHOLSON *Operat. Mechanic* 465 The several touchings and retouchings requisite. **1902** *Athenæum* 26 Apr. 538/3 The touchings-up of the Gavotte were in the worst possible taste. **1936** *Burlington Mag.* May 208/1 The artist's later touching-up. **1957** *Practical Wireless* XXXIII. 558/1 'Look Back to Lyttleton' was a novel by Caryl Brahms, which had been laid aside for touching up and taken out as suitable material for a radio play.

e. *slang.* Getting hold of money, as by theft, or pocket-picking; also bribery (? *obs.*): see TOUCH *v.* 15, 16.

1726 C. D'ANVERS *Craftsman* No. 32 (ed. 3) 299 If once he gives himself up to touching..I give him over as incurable. **1896** A. MORRISON *Child of the Jago* 231 It would never do to go home without touching.

2. In various *fig.* senses: Mention, treatment or discussion; affecting or injuring; †charging, accusation, etc.

a **1400** HYLTON *Scala Perf.* (W. de W. 1494) I. ii, Made bi the presence and the touchyng of a good angell. **1410** in *Proc. Privy Council* (1834) I. 326 And yf by that mocioun and touchyngge the forseide Emonde may fele the forseide Duc be ther of righte desirous. **1590** SIR J. SMYTH *Disc. Weapons* Ded. 13 Is no other but a blaspheming and offending of God in the highest degree, a touching of the honour of the Princes. *a* **1625** SIR H. FINCH *Law* (1636) 185 The touching of him with some hainous crime. **1711** ADDISON *Spect.* No. 34 ¶6 To commend my Prudence in not touching upon the Army.

†3. *Building.* (*pl.*) Projections from the foundations of a building, from which those of the adjoining building are begun. *Obs.*

1663 GERBIER *Counsel* 50 To cause the foundation of the intended building to be generally laid, without leaving any touchings.

4. *attrib.*, as ***touching-distance***; ***touching-distant*** adj. (*poet.*); **touching-stuff**, in engraving, a composition of cork ashes, ivory-black, gall, and treacle, used for touching up the dark parts of a plate (*Cent. Dict.*).

1881 W. WHITMAN *Leaves of Grass* (new ed.) 352 Thy touching-distant beams. **1884** J. TAIT *Mind in Matter* (1892) 314 'Criticism' has never reached nearer than touching-distance to the extreme outworks of divine truth.

'touching, *ppl. a.* Forms: see TOUCH *v.* [f. as prec. + -ING².] That touches: in various senses of the verb.

1. *lit.*: chiefly of things: Coming into, or being in contact.

1674 N. FAIRFAX *Bulk & Selv.* 113 Because this touching draught is more broken in some, and more tight in others. **1875** KNIGHT *Dict. Mech.* s.v. *Riding-part*, The joint part of a scissors-blade which forms the touching portion back of the rivet.

2. *fig.* That touches the feelings or emotions; such as to excite tender feeling or sympathy; affecting, pathetic. (The usual sense.)

In quot. 1508, ? 'sharp', satirical or reproachful.

1508 DUNBAR *Tua Mariit Wemen* 303, I wald ryght tuichand in talk be. **1601** SHAKS. *Jul. C.* IV. iii. 151 O insupportable, and touching losse! **1742** YOUNG *Nt. Th.* III. 240 If not forgot my touching tale. **1823** SCOTT *Peveril* xiii, So touching, also, in her simplicity and purity of thought. **1870** HUXLEY *Lay Serm.* iii. (1874) 30 A touching faith in the efficacy of acts of parliament.

'touching, *prep.* Now somewhat *arch.* Forms: see TOUCH *v.*; also 4 -end(e, 4, 5 *Sc.* -and(e. [The pres. pple. of TOUCH *v.* used prepositionally; cf.

CONCERNING *prep.* Prob. after F. *touchant*, used in the same way: see also TOUCHANT.]

1. (*introd.*) Where *touching* is in concord with a prec. sb. or pron., and may be rendered 'that refers or relates to' (TOUCH *v.* 18, 20). In later use passing into 2. (Cf. CONCERNING *prep.* 1.)

c **1350** *Will. Palerne* 1383 For þe tyding þat þei told touchend hire fader. **1456** SIR G. HAYE *Law Arms* (S.T.S.) 10 The visioun touchand the first tyme of the sorouful persecucioun. **1542** HEN. VIII in *Buccleuch MSS.* (Hist. MSS. Comm.) I. 221 Certeine thinges..towching vs and..our Realme. **1621** ELSING *Debates Ho. Lords* (Camden) 129 There was debate touching Sir Gyles Mompesson. **1709–10** STEELE *Tatler* No. 145 ¶1 A late Request..touching the Care of a young Daughter. **1867** FREEMAN *Norm. Conq.* I. iv. 196 *note*, The dealings of the Assembly touching the abdication of Rolf.

2. Without concord, becoming entirely prepositional: In reference or relation to; as to, respecting, regarding; in the way of mentioning or treating of; concerning, about. (Cf. CONCERNING *prep.* 2.)

c **1375** *Cursor M.* 23011 (Fairf.) Saint austin sais touchand [*C., G.* enent, *T.* of] þat day Is nane can goddis consail say. *c* **1400** MAUNDEV. (Roxb.) xxiii. 107 Wonder sutell of witte towchand any thing þat þai will do. **1513** DOUGLAS *Æneis* XII. Prol. 271 Twichand the lattyr buke of Dan Virgill. **1594** T. B. *La Primaud. Fr. Acad.* II. 49 The composition of the head touching the bones thereof. **1611** BIBLE *Transl. Pref.* 5 This may suffice touching the Greeke translations of the old Testament. **1771** SMOLLETT *Humph. Cl.* 17 Apr., The master of the company being sent for, and examined touching the said Wilson. **1855** DICKENS *Dorrit* II. xxviii, Touching the bargain, your..mother was a little too calm.

3. Preceded by *as.* (Cf. CONCERNING *prep.* 3.)

c **1386** CHAUCER *Frankl. T.* 685 Mo than a thousand stories..Koude I now telle as touchynge this mateere. **1428** *Munim. de Melros* (Bann. Cl.) 521 As twichand þe plew of land in þe husbandry..þe assis saide it nedit na departisoun. *a* **1533** LD. BERNERS *Huon* lix. 203 What counsell wyl ye geue me as touchyng yᵉ admyrall? **1601** HOLLAND *Pliny* x. xxxii. I. 287 As touching the Guls or Sea-cobs, they build in rockes. **1780** M. MADAN *Thelyphthora* (1781) I. 105 The exceeding ignorance of mankind as touching the acts and dispensations of that infinitely wise Being. **1890** FREEMAN in W. R. W. Stephens *Life & Lett.* (1895) II. 420 Your facts are very valuable, specially as touching your own stay in Crete.

†**4.** Followed by *of* or *to* (and mostly preceded by *as* as in 3), forming a prepositional phr. *Obs.*

as touching for in *Paston Lett.* is app. a confusion between *as touching* and *as for.*

1390 GOWER *Conf.* I. 307 Now tell me forth if ther be more As touchende unto Wraththes lore. *Ibid.* III. 174 And as touchende of this bataille, Thou schalt noght of the sothe faile. **1417–19** *Paston Lett.* I. 10 As towchyng to the derth of vytayles withyn thys..Cytee. ?**1450** *Ibid.* 161 As towchyng for tydyngs, I can none. **1523** [COVERDALE] *Old God & New* (1534) P j, Speake as towchyng to yᵉ workes of theym selues.

touchingly (ˈtʌtʃɪŋlɪ), *adv.* [f. TOUCHING *ppl. a.* + -LY².] In a touching manner; so as to touch the feelings; affectingly, pathetically.

1717 GARTH *Ovid's Met.* Pref., This last fable shows how touchingly the poet argues in love affairs, as well as those of Medea and Scylla. **1824** *Examiner* 246/2 Sympathy..makes the scene tell more touchingly. **1884** Q. VICTORIA *More Leaves* 210 He prayed most touchingly for me.

So **ˈtouchingness**, touching or affecting quality, pathos.

a **1750** A. HILL *Wks.* (1753) II. 355 He..charm'd me infinitely..by a peculiar touchingness, in cadency of voice. **1823** *Examiner* 411/1 Her medium notes have a touchingness about them which is not common. **1841** *Fraser's Mag.* XXIII. 315 To..prove The simple touchingness of Morn. **1876** G. MEREDITH *Beauch. Career* II. v. 79 Beauchamp had the history..recounted to him, with a mixture of Gallic irony, innuendo, openness, touchingness, ridicule, and charity novel to his ears.

touchit, Sc. obs. var. TEWHIT, the lapwing.

touchless (ˈtʌtʃlɪs), *a.* [f. TOUCH *sb.* + -LESS.] **a.** Devoid of the sense of touch. **b.** Incapable of being touched, intangible: cf. *viewless.*

1813 T. BUSBY *Lucretius* I. III. 936 As the touchless space, they're free from blow. **1871** HUXLEY *Crit. & Addr.* xiii. (1873) 343 Of course our touchless man would be devoid of any notion of resistance. **1888** B. W. RICHARDSON *Son of Star* xii, Touchless with human hands, Sightless with human eyes.

ˈtouch-line. Also touchline, touch line. [f. TOUCH *sb.* or *v.* + LINE *sb.*²]

†**1.** *Geom.* A straight line that touches a curve; a tangent. *Obs.*

1551 RECORDE *Pathw. Knowl.* I. Defin., A touche lyne, is a line that runneth a long by the edge of a circle, onely touching it, but doth not crosse the circumference of it. **1593** FALE *Dialling* 7 Which shall be called the touch line or line of Contingence. **1675** COLLINS in Rigaud *Corr. Sci. Men* (1841) I. 217 If you conceive a chord line to join R, T, and a touch-line to be drawn at either of those.

2. A line in a diagram representing the touch of the counter of a ship: see TOUCH *sb.* 23.

1797 *Encycl. Brit.* (ed. 3) XVII. 392/1 Take the round up of the upper counter from the dimensions, and set it below the touch at the middle, and with a pencil draw a level line; take also the round aft, and set it forward from the touch on the touch line, and square it down to the pencil line.

3. *Football.* The boundary line on each side of the field of play, extending from goal-line to goal-line: cf. TOUCH *sb.* 12. Also in some other ball games, and *fig.*

1868 *Boy's Own Bk.* 132 [Diagram of football ground]. The goals at either end;..the goal lines;..touch, the touch lines. **1889** *Pauline* VIII. 38 The kick, which was very near the touch-line, was not successful. **1895** *Outing* (U.S.) XXVII. 247/2 The Canadian football field... Along the edges, from one end to another, run the 'touch lines', and when the ball goes over these it is not in play. **1932** AUDEN *Orators* II. 46 The two-faced, the obscure and amazed, the touch-line admirers. **1964** *Sunday Times* 25 Oct. 22/5 A charming touchline companion called the [hockey] match 'grotty'. **1973** PARK & FAHEY *Team Handball* 50 The Boundary-Lines on the long sides shall be termed the Touch-lines. **1973** *Nature* 9 Nov. 108/2 From the touchlines the editor does, however, bias the issue by setting H. G. Haas's article on 'Active Ion Transport' immediately before that on the sinoatrial node.

ˈtouch-me-ˌnot, *sb.* [phrase used as *sb.*]

1. Name for two different kinds of plants with seed-vessels which burst at a touch. †**a.** The Squirting Cucumber: see CUCUMBER 3. *Obs.*

1597 GERARDE *Herbal* II. cccxxvii. 766 *Cucumis asininus.* Wilde Cucumber... Called..wilde Cucumber..and Touch me not. **1611** in COTGR. s.v. *Coucombre.* **1760** J. LEE *Introd. Bot.* App. 330 Touch me not, *Momordica.*

b. The Yellow Balsam (*Impatiens Noli-tangere*), or other species of *Impatiens*, the ripe capsules of which split open with a jerk on being touched.

1659 GAUDEN *Tears Ch.* ***ij, Presbytery seeming like the plant called Touch me not, which flies in the face, and breaks in the fingers of those that presse it. **1760** J. LEE *Introd. Bot.* App. 330 Touch me not, *Impatiens.* **1885** HORNADAY *2 Yrs. in Jungle* xxv. 300 A bed of touch-me-nots took me back like a flash to the terrace flower-beds at college. **1888** *Harper's Mag.* Dec. 153/2 The 'touch-me-not' or 'snapweed' of the loitering school-boy, with its touchy, jumping pods, popping even at a hard look or breath.

2. A name for the disease Lupus.

1860 MAYNE *Expos. Lex.*, *Touch-me-not*, common name for the disease *Noli me tangere.*

3. a. *gen.* A person or thing that must not be touched; in quot., a forbidden topic.

1893 *Daily News* 8 May 5/5 Military matters..are a 'touch-me-not' here.

b. *attrib.* or as *adj.*

1817 M. EDGEWORTH *Harington* I. v. 112 Lady de Brantefield, the *touch-me-not* mistress of the mansion. **1852** THACKERAY *Esmond* III. iv, The saucy little beauty carried her head with a toss..and assumed a touch-me-not air, which all her friends very good-humouredly bowed to. **1880** 'OUIDA' *Moths* 43 Just the old-fashioned, prudish, open-air, touch-me-not Englishwoman.

Hence **ˌtouch-me-ˈnot-ish** *a.* [-ISH¹], having a 'touch-me-not' character; whence **ˌtouch-me-ˈnot-ishness** (*nonce-wd.*). Cf. *stand-off-ish.*

1837 DICKENS *Pickw.* viii, There was a dignity in the air, a touch-me-not-ishness in the walk, a majesty in the eye of the spinster aunt.

touch-no-wall, -s: see TOUCH- 2 b.

touchous (ˈtʌtʃəs), *a. dial.* Also **toucheous.** [f. TOUCH *sb.* or *v.* + -OUS.] Easily offended, sensitive, touchy.

1867 P. KENNEDY *Banks of Boro* xxv. 190 By the time I got home, however, I was very cross and *touchous.* **1933** C. MILLER *Lamb in his Bosom* iv. 28 The ill-temper worked in her body like a slow fever... Lonzo called her toucheous. **1960** H. LEE *To kill Mockingbird* viii. 72 He said Atticus was still touchous about us and the Radleys and it wouldn't do to push him any. **1973** *N.Y. Times* 3 June L-19/1 [In the Caribbean] an overly sensitive person is 'touchous', not touchy.

ˈtouch-piece. [f. TOUCH *v.* or *sb.* + PIECE *sb.*]

1. A coin or medal (originally a gold angel, in later times specially struck for the purpose in gold or silver) given by the sovereign to each person touched for the 'king's evil' (TOUCH *v.* 2 b).

1844 *Chron. Seasons* II. 26 Touch-pieces were a sort of coins, of which the king, when he touched a person in order to cure the evil, used to hang one round the neck of the patient. **1855** SMEDLEY, etc. *Occult Sc.* 341 The touch-pieces were generally preserved with great care, and worn as amulets. **1908** *Athenæum* 20 June 769/1 There are varieties of gold and silver touch-pieces of the time of James II.

2. A piece of mechanism operated by a touch.

1897 *Daily News* 7 June 6/4 The observer taps a little touch-piece by the side of the instrument, and this movement is conveyed by galvanic wire to the chronograph.

3. A piece of music designed to exhibit the touch of the performer, a toccata. (*nonce-use.*)

1900 *New Cent. Rev.* VII. 394 A Toccata (or touch-piece).

†**ˈtouch-powder.** *Obs.* [This appears to be the earliest of the series of compounds mentioned in TOUCH- 1 c, in which *touch-* signifies the ready kindling or setting fire to something; app. from OF. *tochier* (*le feu*), *touchier* to set fire. *Touch-powder* prob. represented an OF. **poudre-à-toucher* (*le feu*). Thence *touch-box, -hole, -pan*, etc., and the parallel *touch-wood*, etc.] A fine kind of gunpowder placed in the pan over the touch-hole in an old-fashioned fire-arm; priming-powder. Also *attrib.*

1497 *Naval Acc. Hen. VII* (1896) 88 Towchepoudre..j barell. **1508** *Acc. Ld. High Treas. Scot.* IV. 137 Item, for double gilting of the Kingis twich powdir horn, xxvj s. **1591** *Garrard's Art Warre* 6 Let him make hys Tutch Pouder. **1598** [see TOUCH-BOX].

touchquhare, obs. form of TOCHER.

touchstone (ˈtʌtʃstəʊn). Forms: see TOUCH *v.* [f. TOUCH- 1 + STONE: cf. OF. *touchepierre*, F. *pierre de touche*, Sp. *piedra de toque.*]

1. A very smooth, fine-grained, black or dark-coloured variety of quartz or jasper (also called BASANITE), used for testing the quality of gold and silver alloys by the colour of the streak produced by rubbing them upon it; a piece of such stone used for this purpose.

1530 PALSGR. 282/1 Touch stone to prove golde with. **1754** *Phil. Trans.* XLVIII. 664 The difference in colour of these compositions was much less conspicuous on the touchstone. **1812** J. SMYTH *Pract. of Customs* (1821) 262 Touchstone is the Basaltes, a heavy hard stone, of a very fine texture, of a deep glossy black, resembling that of polished steel. **1908** H. B. MORSE *Trade Chinese Emp.* 149 A silver commercially pure, as shown by the crude methods of the touchstone.

b. *fig.* That which serves to test or try the genuineness or value of anything; a test, criterion.

a **1533** FRITH *Another Bk. agst. Rastell* (1829) 216 Lay them to the touchstone, and try them with God's word. **1535** COVERDALE *Ecclus.* vi. 21 Vnto soch she is as it were a twichstone, & he casteth her from him in all the haist. **1677** *Govt. Venice* 106 Therefore it is that Venice is called the School and Touchstone of Embassadors. *a* **1720** SHEFFIELD (Dk. Buckhm.) *Wks.* (1753) II. 207 Time..in all matters of writing, is the only true touchstone of merit. **1822** HAZLITT *Table-t.* I. xi. 253 Well-digested schemes will stand the touchstone of experience. **1871** BLACKIE *Four Phases* i. 42 The touchstone..to distinguish the true man..from the false pretender.

2. Applied to other stones of similar texture and colour, as black marble or basalt. (Cf. TOUCH *sb.* 6.)

1481–3 *Acc. Exch. K.R.* Bd. 496. No. 26 (MS.), Ultra lv dolijs lapidum de Cane,..et xxxiij doliis de Touchestone. **1509** HAWES *Past. Pleas.* xxxv. (Percy Soc.) 184 Into the castell of olde foundacion, Walled about with the blacke touche stone. **1584** in Willis & Clark *Cambridge* (1886) I. 294 The pece of tutch stone wᶜʰ my Ladye Bacon hath gyven vnto this woorke. **1607** TOPSELL *Four-f. Beasts* (1658) 377 Upon the steps of the Capitol of Rome, there were two Lions of black Marble touch-stone. *a* **1647** HABINGTON *Surv. Worc.* in *Worcs. Hist. Soc. Proc.* I. 102 All..wrytten in Tuchstone with letters of goulde. **1670** PETTUS *Fodinæ Reg.* I If common Stones onely are found (as Marble, Touchstone, Freestone, etc.) we call them Quarries, and not Mines. **1845** PARKER *Gloss. Archit.*, *Touch-stone* [is] a name sometimes applied to compact dark-coloured stones, such as Purbeck and Petworth marble..frequently used for fine work in Gothic architecture.

touchwood (ˈtʌtʃwʊd). [f. TOUCH- 1 c + WOOD *sb.*] Wood or anything of woody nature, in such a state as to catch fire readily, and which can be used as tinder. **a.** The soft white substance into which wood is converted by the action of certain fungi, especially of *Polyporus squamosus*, and which has the property of burning for many hours when once ignited, and is occasionally self-luminous.

By confusion the name is sometimes applied to the powdery snuff-coloured mass into which wood is sometimes converted without the agency of fungi, by a process of slow chemical combustion (*eremacausis*), which is not distinguishable from the effects of dry rot, except by the absence of fungous spawn. (M. J. Berkeley in *Treas. Bot.* (1866).)

1579 LYLY *Euphues*, (Arb.) 62, I, but Euphues, hath she not hard also that the dry touchewoode is kindled with lyme ..that the fire quickly burneth the flaxe? **1621** BURTON *Anat. Mel.* III. ii. II. i. (1651) 450 As match or touchwood takes fire, so doth an idle person love. **1646** SIR T. BROWNE *Pseud. Ep.* II. v. 89 To make white powder... The best I know is by the powder of rotten willowes; spunck, or touchwood prepared, might perhaps make it russet. **1706** E. WARD *Wooden World Diss.* (1708) 14 He had rather see the whole Fleet parch'd up like Touchwood, for want of Water. **1799** *Med. Jrnl.* II. 298 Observations..on the luminous property of touchwood. **1809** MALKIN *Gil Blas* IV. vii. ¶13 Gonzales, dry as touchwood, with all its inflammability. **1887** T. HARDY *Woodlanders* III. ix. 183 The rain had imparted a phosphorescence to the pieces of touchwood. **1898** WATTS-DUNTON *Aylwin* XV. vi, A fallen willow tree, the inside of which was all touchwood.

b. A name given to various fungi, esp. two species of *Polyporus* (*P.* or *Fomes fomentarius* and *P.* or *F. igniarius*), also called ***touchwood boletus***, or to the tinder called 'amadou' made from them. Cf. TINDER.

The former of these is found on oak, beech, birch, lime, etc., the latter (which requires a process of preparation) on ash, poplar, willow, plane, fir, etc.

1598 FLORIO, *Pano*..touchwood, or a spungie swelling on trees like a mushrume. **1666** PEPYS *Diary* 12 Nov., His skeleton [is here seen], with the flesh on; but all tough and dry like a spongy dry leather, or touchwood all upon his bones. **1688** R. HOLME *Armoury* II. 85/2 Touchwood [is] a kind of hard, dry, spungy Mushroom. **1778** LIGHTFOOT *Flora Scot.* (1789) II. 1034 *Boletus igniarius.* Touchwood Boletus... An excellent touchwood is made from this Fungus by..pounding and boiling it up with saltpetre. **1845–50** MRS. LINCOLN *Lect. Bot.* 199 The genus Boletus contains the touchwood, or spunk, which is sometimes used as tinder.

c. *fig.* Said of a thing or person that easily 'takes fire', or which, like tinder, 'kindles' something else (quot. 1601); *esp.* an irascible or passionate person, one easily incensed. Now *rare*.

[**1601** DENT *Pathw. Heaven* 204 Sins of oppression..be the very fire-brands of Gods wrath, and as it were touch-wood, to kindle his anger.] **1617** MIDDLETON & ROWLEY *Fair Quarrel* II. i, The Colonel, soon enrag'd, as he's all touchwood. *c* **1620** FLETCHER & MASSINGER *Lit. French Lawyer* II. iii, Peace touchwood. **1761** G. COLMAN *Jealous Wife* I. i, She is all Impetuosity and Fire.—A very Magazine of Touchwood and Gunpowder. **1840** *Life of Origen* vii. 66 Wood, hay, stubble, and that which soonest burns of anything, the touchwood of denial.

d. *attrib.* and *Comb.*

1784 COWPER *Task* VI. 688 From his touchwood trunk the mulberry-tree Supplied such relics as devotion holds Still sacred. **1864** TENNYSON *Aylmer's F.* 514 There the manorial lord too curiously Raking in that millennial touchwood-dust Found for himself a bitter treasure-trove.

touchy ('tʌtʃɪ), *a.* Also 7 **tutchie**. [f. TOUCH *sb.* or *v.* + -Y; but in sense 1 perh. an alteration of TETCHY.]

1. Easily moved to anger; apt to take offence on slight cause; highly sensitive in temper or disposition; irascible, irritable, testy, tetchy.

1605 *King Leir & Daughters* D j, She breeds yong bones, And that is it makes her so tutchy sure. **1619** BEAUM. & FL. *Maid's Trag.* III. ii, Y'are touchie without all cause. *a* **1652** BROME *Queen* I. iv, Ther's the old tutchie testie Lord. **1656** H. JEANES *Fuln. Christ* 79 If earthly Potentates be so tender, and touchy in the point of their Embassadours honour and safety. **1702** C. MATHER *Magn. Chr.* I. ii. (1852) 50 Avoid all discoveries of a touchy humour. **1843** LE FEVRE *Life Trav. Phys.* I. I. viii. 170 She was most touchy upon the subject of age. **1903** G. H. BIRCH *Lond. on Thames* ii. 18 The citizens wanted no foreigners—they were always very touchy on that subject.

2. Sensitive to touch; physically irritable.

Quot. 1618 perh. belongs rather to 1.

1618 LATHAM *2nd Bk. Falconry* xiv. 57, I perceiued her to bee very tutchie and coy to bee handled. **1658** A. FOX *Würtz' Surg.* I. vi. 25 As often as a vein or sinew is toucht.. is a new pain caused; for they are very touchy and full of sense. **1710** T. FULLER *Pharm. Extemp.* 209 Those whose Guts being wove up of fine-spun Fibrillæ, are touchy and irritable. **1806–7** J. BERESFORD *Miseries Hum. Life* (1826) XI. xv, Jarring the touchy part of your elbow against the edge of the table. **1888** [see TOUCH-ME-NOT 1 b].

b. Taking fire when touched with a spark; easily ignited.

In quots. 1660 and 1766 combining this sense and 1.

1660 [implied in TOUCHINESS 1]. **1679** *Phil. Collect.* XII. 7 Our Colliers assure me that those touchy Works which are continually apt to take Fire, do it most..in the Winter. **1766** *Goody Two-Shoes* iv. (1882) 111 You are both as touchy as Tinder, and very often make your own House too hot to hold you.

3. Ticklish, risky, precarious; not to be touched without danger. (Cf. 2 b.)

1620 WOTTON in *Reliq.* (1672) 500 In such a touchy time as this, I had almost had my share. **1651** N. BACON *Disc. Govt. Eng.* II. vi. (1739) 36 It is a touchy thing to have to do with fire, lest it get too high. **1697** COLLIER *Ess. Mor. Subj.* I. (1709) 53 You are upon a touchy Point, and therefore I hope you will treat so nice a Subject..with proportionable Caution. **1884** *Graphic* 15 Nov. 518/2 These were, of course, very touchy subjects to ask of courtiers.

4. *Painting*, *Drawing*, etc. Characterized by or composed of distinct touches or light strokes.

1820 *Examiner* No. 651. 634/1 One of the prime beauties ..is its extensiveness of touchy marking, whereby in all the parts the eye is most satisfactorily entertained. **1826** *Ibid.* 342/1 Indifferent anatomical drawing and a want of touchy pencilling. **1839** CHATTO & JACKSON *Wood Engraving* viii. 649 The drawing, which originally may have been clear and touchy, loses its brightness, and becomes indistinct from its frequent contact with the soft pliable paper.

5. Involving a mere light touch. *nonce-use.*

1879 G. MACDONALD *Sir Gibbie* xiv, As if some gentle hand had..dipped them—just a tiny touchy dip, in a molten ruby.

†**6.** 'Touched' or slightly affected in the head; slightly crazed or crack-brained, 'cranky': in comb. *touchy-headed*.

1666 J. SMITH *Old Age* To Rdr. A iij b, The Author..is himself as willing, as any touchy-headed Decryers of Anatomy and Anatomists..that all the shame..should return upon his own pate. **1675** E. WILSON *Spadacrene Dunelmensis* Pref. 17 Those touchy headed Chymists, who pretend to Panacæa's, Universal Medicines, Secrets, and such like whimsical Remedies.

touck, -e, toucker, obs. ff. TUCK *sb.* and *v.*, TUCKER.

toudang, var. TOERING.

touel, touele, obs. ff. TOWEL, TEWEL.

touffan, -on, obs. forms of TYPHOON.

‖**toug** (tuːg). [a. F. *toug*, ad. Turk. *tūgh* tail of a horse.] The Turkish standard, consisting of a horse's tail fixed at the end of a short pike.

1687 A. LOVELL tr. *Thevenot's Trav.* I. 81 The *Toug* is a Horses Tail fastened to the head of a Pike: It is neuer put out but in extreme necessity, and then all the Militia must take the Field. **1902** R. W. CHAMBERS *Maids of Paradise* v, I could still hear..the tinkle of the silver chimes on their *toug*.

tough (tʌf), *a.* (*adv.*, *sb.*) Forms: *α.* 1 **tóh, tóch,** 3 **tou,** 3–5 **touȝ, toȝ,** 3–6 **tow,** 4 **touh, towh, towȝ, toȝe,** 4–5 **togh, towe,** 5 **touȝe, towȝe, toghe, towghe, toogh, touhe, (towhe),** 5–6 **towgh, toughe,** 4– **tough.** *β. Sc.* 5–9 **teuch, teugh,** (5–6 **tewch,** 6 **tuich, tewgh, teoch, twch, -e, twich**). *γ.* (with inorganic *-t*) 3 **toht,** 3–4 **toȝt,** 3–5 **touȝt,** *Sc.* 4 **tucht,** 5 **touȝte, tout;** 6 *Sc.* **tewcht.** *δ.* 4–5 **tuf,** 7 **tuffe,** 7–8 **tuff.** [OE. *tóh*:—**tǫnh*:—**tanh*, OTeut. **taŋχu-z*; NFris. *toch, tuch*. From an OTeut. stem **taŋχ-*, *taŋg-*, whence OE. *ȝe-tęnge*. Cf. (with ending of *-ja* decl.) OS. **tâhi* (MLG. *tâ*, *tei*, LG. *taa, tage, tau*, Du. *taai*); OHG. *zâhi* (MLG. *zâhe, zæhe, zæch*, Ger. *zähe, zäh*).]

A. *adj.* **1. a.** Of close tenacious substance or texture; strongly cohesive, so as to be pliable or ductile; not easily broken, divided, or disintegrated; not fragile, brittle, or tender; of food, difficult to masticate.

α. *a* **700** *Epinal Gloss.* (O.E.T.) 581 *Lenta, tarda vel* toch. *Ibid.* 614 *Lentum vimen*, toch ȝerd. *c* **725** *Corpus Gloss.* 1207 *Lentum vimen*, toh ȝerd. *c* **1275** LAY. 5865 Keruep ȝoure speres lang and makeþ heom toȝe an strang. **1340–70** *Alex. & Dind.* 691 Hue tilede in hur time on þe touh erþe, & whete soþliche sew. **13..** *E.E. Allit. P.* B. 630 [Abraham] a calf bryngez þat watz tender & not toȝe; bed..þat he hit seþe faste. **1387** TREVISA *Higden* (Rolls) IV. 317 Temperynge of glas to make þe glas tough i-now to bende. *c* **1400** *Laud Troy Bk.* 10877 The spere was tow & long. *c* **1400** *Destr. Troy* 7495 Telamon, the tore kyng, with a togh speire. *c* **1440** *Promp. Parv.* 498/1 Towhhe, not tendyr (*A.* tow, *P.* tough). **1552** HULOET, Towgh, *tenax*. **1612** *Two Noble K.* II. v. 2, I have not seene..a man of tougher synewes. **1697** DRYDEN *Virg. Georg.* II. 628 The tougher Yeugh Receives the bending Figure of a Bow. **1769** E. BANCROFT *Guiana* 209 Its body is tough and fibrous. **1827** FARADAY *Chem. Manip.* v. (1842) 151 A wrought-iron mortar..would be too tough.

β. *c* **1470** HENRY *Wallace* XI. 1061 With seuir cordys.. Bath scharp and tewch. **1513** DOUGLAS *Æneis* VII. xiii. 65 Knyt wyth a teuch string. *a* **1584** MONTGOMERIE *Cherrie & Slae* 328 The Cherries..grewe On trimbling twistis tewch. *a* **1758** RAMSAY *Address of Thanks* xii, That setting-dog his man, May..use a teugh St. Johnston ribbon.

γ. **1297** Touȝt [see 8]. *c* **1586** *Dunbar's Poems* xxxii. 24 Na ȝowis auld, twch [*Maitl. MS.* tewcht] and sklender.

δ. *a* **1400–50** *Alexander* 319 Tachid in his for-top—twa tufe hornes. *a* **1602** Tuffe [see sense 4]. **1653** WALTON *Angler* xii. 223 Gentles..is a good bait..being lively and tuffe. **1665** HOOKE *Microgr.* 51 The pure parts of metals are of themselves very flexible and tuff. *a* **1679** R. BOYLE *Guzman* II. Dram. Wks. 1739 II. 267 Let his Skin be tuff as Wall. **1683** PETTUS *Fleta Min.* I. (1686) 3 Silver which is tuff or hard. **1733** W. ELLIS *Chiltern & Vale Farm.* 8 Being tuffer, and more tenacious than any other.

b. Phr. ***tough as* (*old*) *boots*** or ***leather***. Freq. *fig.*, implying sense 4.

1843 MRS. CARLYLE *Lett.* (1883) I. 219 The 'cold fowl' was..as tough as leather. **1870** As tough as old boots [see BOOT *sb.*[3] 1 b]. **1946** J. B. PRIESTLEY *Bright Day* iv. 111 Joe Ackworth's more the type. He's as tough as old leather. **1967** *Listener* 7 Dec. 765/1 This is no sweet old dolly... She is tough as old boots, working for a living. **1981** M. HATFIELD *Spy Fever* I. iii. 31 Colonel Theakston was..as the saying goes, as tough as old boots.

2. Of viscous consistence or nature; sticky, adhesive, tenacious; glutinous.

c **1000** *Sax. Leechd.* III. 16 Gnid ða buteran on ðæm hwetstane mid copore þæt heo beo wel toh. **1382** WYCLIF *Gen.* xi. 3 Thei hadden..towȝ cley for syment. *c* **1440** *Pallad. on Husb.* I. 66 Tough to glue ayein though thowe it delve. **1460** CAPGRAVE *Chron.* (Rolls) 30 Tow erde, cleped bitumen. **1530** TINDALE *Answ. More* IV. xii. Wks. (1573) 338/1 A carte that is ouer laden..in a tough mire maketh them [the horses] stand still. **1658** A. FOX *Würtz' Surg.* III. iv. 228 Clear water, somewhat tuff and slimie. **1789** W. BUCHAN *Dom. Med.* (1790) 675 Tough viscid saliva. **1800** *Med. Jrnl.* III. 154 The first class possess tough, glutinous juices.

3. *fig.* Stiff; severe, violent; †(sometimes) grievous, painful; of a contest, etc.: stoutly maintained, strenuous, vigorous and stubborn.

α. *c* **1205** LAY. 9319, & Hamun him to strac Mid toȝen [*c* 1275 luþer] his mæine. **1297** R. GLOUC. (Rolls) 10605 Wan tueye stronge comeþ to gadere, it is somdel tou [*rime* slou]. ? *a* **1300** *Cursor M.* 24439 (Cott.), I sagh him dei, i sorud ai,..mi tening es sa togh. *c* **1430** *Hymns Virg.* 120 With wawys grete, & stormys towe. **1539** TAVERNER *Erasm. Prov.* (1552) 3 They wil giue much tougher and more ernest strokes. *a* **1661** FULLER *Worthies, Warwick* (1662) II. 122 There was a tough contest betwixt the South and Northern-men in that university. **1865** GOSSE *Land & Sea* (1874) 4 A tough breeze from the westward. **1891** C. ROBERTS *Adrift Amer.* 153 In spite of the tough racket I had had.

γ. **13..** *R. Gloucester's Chron.* (Rolls) 517 þe wrastlinge bitvene hom was somdel toȝt [*rime* ibroȝt]. **1400–40** *Ibid.* App. H. 41 þat bataile was wel towȝt [*rime* nouȝt]. *Ibid.* App. XX. 150 Sumdel þat was tout [*rime* nout].

4. Capable of great physical endurance; strongly resisting force, injury fatigue, etc.; not easily overcome, tired, or impaired; hardy, stout, sturdy.

c **1330** R. BRUNNE *Chron. Wace* (Rolls) 13038 Petron had go, hat Beofs be tow. **1393** LANGL. *P. Pl.* C. XIII. 187 Ac seedes þat been sowen and mowe suffre wyntres, Aren tydyour and tower to mannes by-hofthes. **1451** CAPGRAVE *Life St. Gilbert* 73 His witte as fresch,..his mynde as tow,.. as euyr þei were. **1571** *Satir. Poems Reform.* xxv. 100 They know I am ane tuilȝeour teoch. **1576** FLEMING *Panopl. Epist.* 258 A painefull and laborious fellowe, and such a one as is hard and toughe, and able to indure toile. *a* **1602** in Campion *Art Eng. Poesie* v. 18 All the glebe His tuffe hands manur'd. **1697** DRYDEN *Virg. Georg.* II. 322 A Glebe that asks Tough Teams of Oxen, and laborious Tasks. **1775** SHERIDAN *Rivals* I. i, There is an old tough aunt in the way. **1818** SCOTT *Br. Lamm.* xxi, That was what tough old Sir Evan Dhu used to say. **1856** EMERSON *Eng. Traits, Ability*, Even the..sots of England are of a tougher texture.

5. a. Having great intellectual or moral endurance; difficult to influence, affect, or impress; steadfast, firm, persistent; also, stubborn, obstinate, hardened.

c **1400** *26 Pol. Poems* xxv. 521 Yef myn hert be styf and towe, To thanke the in wele and woo. **1411** *Ibid.* x. 35 My loue to man it was so tow. **1519** HORMAN *Vulg.* 142 b, The stewarde of the house is harde and toughe. **1603** KNOLLES *Hist. Turks* (1621) 965 A man of ripe yeares, but yet fierce of courage, tough in opinion. **1780** COWPER *Table-Talk* 458 Obduracy takes place; callous and tough, The reprobated race grows judgment proof. **1848** DICKENS *Dombey* x, You'll find him tough, Ma'am. Tough, Sir, tough is Joseph. **1898** *Daily News* 25 Jan. 6/2 As a witness before Parliamentary Committees he was what is called 'a tough customer'.

b. Resolute in dealing with opposition; vigorously uncompromising; severe; esp. in phr. ***to get tough*** (cf. GET *v.* 81 d). *colloq.* (orig. *U.S.*).

1906 U. SINCLAIR *Jungle* i. 11 He affects a 'tough' aspect, wearing his hat on one side and keeping a cigarette in his mouth all the evening. **1930** E. H. LAVINE *Third Degree* ii. 17 A conscientious, or 'tough', [police] sergeant was assigned to a west-side precinct. **1935** WODEHOUSE *Blandings Castle* vi. 151 In all villages, of course, there must ..be an occasional tough egg. **1938** E. AMBLER *Cause for Alarm* vii. 116 Vagas got tough. They had a showdown. **1964** in Hamblett & Deverson *Generation X* 10 The funniest thing was seeing the cops getting tough. If they want a fight we'll give it to them. **1972** J. SYMONS *Bloody Murder* xii. 159 The behaviour of the private detective may be tough, but is based on ethical standards. **1978** J. IRVING *World according to Garp* i. 14 They initiated a get-tough policy with Jenny Fields. It was a staff decision—'for her own good', of course. **1984** *N.Y. Times* 12 Feb. (Late City Final) I. 1. 35/1 My policy is to be tough but fair with the gaming industry... Federal law-enforcement officials have greater access to data on Nevada.

c. Of laws or rules: strict, inflexible. Of an institution: marked by strict enforcement of discipline.

1961 in WEBSTER s.v., When the law gets too tough the courts don't convict. **1971** J. OSBORNE *West of Suez* I. 42 Father decided I needed 'toughening up' at a really tough school. **1977** *National Observer* (U.S.) 22 Jan. 1/1 Reformers want a tougher code of ethics for Presidential appointees. *Ibid.*, The environmentalists want a tougher line on automobiles that pollute.

6. a. Difficult to do, accomplish, perform, or deal with; hard, trying, laborious, troublesome.

1619 VISCT. DONCASTER *Let.* in *Eng. & Germ.* (Camden) 133 To perswade them to hearken to a treaty would prove a tough piece of worke. *c* **1645** HOWELL *Lett.* (1650) I. IV. xv. 117 [The town of Breda] hath yeelded.., after a tough siege of thirteen months. **1797** MRS. RADCLIFFE *Italian* xiii, They should find tough work of it. **1828** SCOTT *F.M. Perth* xv, 'It will be a tough job', growled the assassin. **1853** KINGSLEY *Hypatia* xxv, [He] comforted his troubled soul with a tough problem of astronomy.

b. Hard to believe or understand; taxing credulity or comprehension.

1820 W. IRVING in *Life & Lett.* (1864) I. xxvii. 459 When your boy grows large enough to understand tough stories. **1840** BARHAM *Ingol. Leg.* Ser. I. *Acc. New Play*, Tell us tough yarns, and then swear they are true. **1861** DU CHAILLU *Equat. Afr.* xii. 155 This seemed to them the toughest yarn of all.

c. Of circumstances, etc.: imposing hardship, distress, or injustice. *colloq.* (orig. and chiefly *U.S.*).

1890 *Stock Grower & Farmer* 8 Mar. 4/2 The recent blizzard..was pretty tough on range cattle. **1901** S. E. WHITE *Claim Jumpers* 256 I've been a little tough on you occasionally. **1929** WODEHOUSE *Mr. Mulliner Speaking* i. 34, 'I suppose it's because I'm rather an out-size and modelled on the lines of Cleopatra.' 'Tough!' 'You bet it's tough. A girl can't help her appearance.' **1933** P. GODFREY *Back-Stage* xvii. 216 The 'tough breaks' in their gipsy life soon weed out the weaklings. **1942** E. PAUL *Narrow St.* xxix. 265 You know you're likely to be bumped off?.. Things are tough down there, and they won't get any better. **1959** H. P. TRITTON *Time means Tucker* (1965) i. 11 Work was scarce and wages low, and conditions all round were tough. **1962** J. H. CUTLER *Honey Fitz* xx. 291 Joe [Kennedy] made his children stay on their toes... 'He would bear down on them and tell them, "When the going gets tough, the tough get going."' **1982** *Church Times* 30 Apr. 11/1 The life of a nun is extremely tough and involves a lot of physical hard work.

d. ***tough luck*** (*colloq.*, orig. *U.S.*), hard luck, misfortune; esp. as an expression of (sometimes ironic) commiseration; also (chiefly *U.S. slang*) ***tough shit***, ***stuff***, or ***tiddy*** (***titty***).

1912 Tough luck [see *old top* s.v. OLD *a.* 8 a]. **1932** *Kansas City* (Missouri) *Times* 14 Jan. 18 It may be Mr. Hoover's tough luck to be both renominated and re-elected. **1934** J. T. FARRELL *Calico Shoes* 143 You have to take your chances, and if you can't swim, you sink. It's just your tough tiddy. **1944** in A. M. Taylor *Lang. World War II* 198 Beachhead chaplains are carrying a special 'tough stuff' ticket these days which they issue to guys with complaints about which nothing can be done. **1946** *Amer. Speech* XXI. 249 [Army vocabulary.] *Tough shit*, something which is unfortunate, but about which nothing can be done. **1958** S. A. GRAU *Hard Blue Sky* ii. 89 'And the whole building near to going down with the next strong wind.' 'Tough titty, man.' **1971** 'A. BURGESS' *MF* ii. 32 [I got] robbed and rumpled.—Tough titty she said with little sympathy. **1974** *Black World* Jan. 10/2 Is Mr. Gayle exasperated by the fact that I do not give clear-cut answers to these questions? Tough luck: I do not have them. **1976** *New Yorker* 1 Mar. 74/2 I'm awfully sorry to hear about your tough luck. **1978** J. CARROLL *Mortal Friends* II. v. 200 Tough shit, Lady! Morning wears to evening and hearts break.

7. *U.S.* Of criminal or vicious proclivities. Cf. B.

1884 J. MILLER *Mem. & Rime* i. 9 And oh! but this is a tough town! **1894** STEAD *If Christ Came to Chicago* 35 An oasis of cleanliness and light in the midst of a district which was decidedly tough. *Ibid.* 36 One of the toughest of the toughs in the slums.

†**8.** Phrase. ***to make it tough.*** **a.** To make it difficult; to make difficulties about doing something; to show reluctance. *Obs.*

1297 R. Glouc. (Rolls) 10498 þe king glosede her & þer & made it somdel touȝt, Ac þo it com to þe strengþe he nolde it graunti nouȝt. *c* **1369** Chaucer *Dethe Blaunche* 531 Lo howe goodly spake this knyght.. And made it neyther tough ne queynt. *c* **1400** *Rowland & O.* 118 Þou may Iangill & make it toughe. *c* **1412** Hoccleve *De Reg. Princ.* 3516 'Iulius', quod he, 'make it noght so tow [*v.r.* tough]'. *c* **1470** *Golagros & Gaw.* 1069 It may nocht mend the ane myte to mak it so teugh. **1530** Palsgr. 624/2, I make it tough, I make it coye, as maydens do, or persons that be strange if they be asked a questyon... Mary, you make it toughe, *Marie, vous faitez le dangereux.*

†**b.** To be persistent or obstinate. *Obs.*

a **1549** in *Laneham's Let.* (1871) Pref. 151 Albeit ye mak it never sa tewch, To me your labour is in vane. *c* **1560** A. Scott *Poems* (S.T.S.) ii. 154 Quhen thai saw Sym sic curage ta, And Will mak it sa twche.

9. quasi-*adv.* †**a.** Vigorously, stoutly; persistently. *Obs.*

1398 Trevisa *Barth. De P.R.* xi. xviii. (Tollem. MS.), Yf it be touȝe [*ed.* 1535 strongly] blowe, and þanne broke. *c* **1470** *Golagros & Gaw.* 704 The wyis.. All to-turnit thair entyre, traistly and tewch. **1581** *Satir. Poems Reform.* xliv. 125 Quhen as he draue and Knox held steue the pleuch, And Methuen seu adulterie so teuch. **1805** A. Douglas *Poems* (1806) 12 At Luncarty they fought fu' teuch. **1827** W. Taylor *Poems* (ed. 2) 98 (E.D.D.) The carle he did play sae teugh.

b. In an uncompromising, aggressive, or unyielding manner.

1943 R. Chandler *Lady in Lake* iv. 25 You fellows [*sc.* cops] ever flash a buzzer—or is acting tough all the identification you need? **1968** *Globe & Mail* (Toronto) 3 Feb. 7/5 Saskatchewan's Premier Ross Thatcher, while he talks tough in private, is apparently willing to make at least a gesture.

10. As an epithet of commendation: very good, 'great'. *U.S. slang* (orig. *Blacks*').

1937 [see catch *v.* 35 b]. **1960** R. G. Reisner *Jazz Titans* 167 *Tough*, great. **1965** Mrs L. B. Johnson *White House Diary* 3 June (1970) 282 'Pat Nugent.. he's just tons, Mother—he's a tough guy!' ('Tough' means great, wonderful, nice, attractive, it seems.) **1972** J. Hudson in T. Kochman *Rappin' & Stylin' Out* 422 Now my singing ain't none too tough, but I can sell some dope.

11. a. In special collocations, as **tough baby, boy** *slang* (orig. *U.S.*), a person given to hard-headed, violent, or lawless behaviour; **tough-cake**: see quots. 1881, 1896; **tough guy** *colloq.* (orig. *U.S.*), a person not easily injured or thwarted; freq. *attrib.*; **tough-iron**: see quot. 1686; **tough movement** *Transformational Grammar*, a transformation applied to a sentence moving words of a certain class (of which *tough* is one), from one part of the sentence to another (e.g. *to convince John is hard*: *John is hard to convince*); **tough nut** *colloq.* (orig. *U.S.*), a person difficult or dangerous to deal with; **tough pitch**, commercially pure copper in which the amount of cuprous oxide was reduced by poling to the value at which it would produce minimum brittleness; usu. *attrib.* or as *adj.*; **tough-stone** = *puff-stone* (puff *sb.* 9 b).

1932 E. Wallace *When Gangs came to London* xxiii. 234, I've had real *tough babies on their knees to me in a police station, begging me to be put in a cell. **1946** Wodehouse *Joy in Morning* ii. 12 Scanning the roster of the females I've nearly got married to in my time, we find the names of some tough babies. **1958** F. Newton in P. Gammond *Decca Bk. Jazz* v. 68 It is no use being censorious about the atmosphere of..*tough boys and sleezy vaudevilles in which the great blues singers were nurtured. **1974** T. P. Whitney tr. *Solzhenitsyn's Gulag Archipelago* I. i. vii. 294 The interrogators and their tough-boy helpers dashed in from the interrogation prison. **1881** Raymond *Mining Gloss.*, **Tough-cake*, refined or commercial copper. **1896** *E. Durham Gloss.*, *Toughcake*, a water-cake, or white-cake, baked on the girdle. No currants used. **1932** *Tough guy [see clean *v.* 6 b]. **1938** L. MacNeice *Mod. Poetry* viii. 149 E. E. Cummings, the 'tough-guy' American poet. **1946** R. Chandler *Let.* 30 May (1981) 75 Bogart, of course, is.. much better than any other tough-guy actor... Ladd is..a small boy's idea of a tough guy. **1946** H. Croome *Faithless Mirror* vii. 75 Tough guys with a heart of gold. **1981** J. Dunning *Deadline* (1982) xix. 187 At the bottom of that tough-guy facade, you're just like all the rest... Scared to death. **1686** Plot *Staffordsh.* 161 The fourth and best sorts of Iron they call *tough-Iron of which they make all sorts of the best wares. **1971** P. M. Postal *Cross-Over Phenomena* iii. 27 There is a class of adjectives in English, *hard, tough, easy, difficult, impossible, simple*, which have played a prominent role in discussions of the need for a transformational grammar of English... The contrast between sentences like..*a* Throneberry is easy to please. *b* Throneberry is eager to please..is by now well known... There is a special rule defined for this class..which involves the movement of an NP out of the predicate of the complement sentence. Let us refer to this rule as *tough-movement. **1977** *Canad. Jrnl. Linguistics* 1976 XXI. 157 Consider (24), resulting from Passive, and (25), resulting from Tough-Movement, as answers to the question 'Why was John arrested?' (24) That he robbed a store was reported in the newspaper. (25) That he robbed a store is hard for us to believe. **1862** in E. W. Pearson *Lett. from Port Royal* (1906) 81 There are a great many men of twenty-five to forty, '*tough-nuts' many of them. **1892** 'Mark Twain' *Amer. Claim.* xxv. 263 His father was rather a tough nut. **1922** E. O'Neill *Hairy Ape* viii. 83 Say, yuh're some hard-lookin' guy, ain't yuh? I seen lots of tough nuts dat de gang called gorillas, but yuh're de foist real one I ever seen. **1950** *Times* 12 May 7/7 For the 'tough nut' the youth club as at present constituted offered no fold. **1977** C. McCullough *Thorn Birds* x. 236 Meggie was going to be a tough nut to crack and he couldn't afford to frighten or disgust her... He'd woo her the way she obviously wanted. **1881** Raymond *Mining Gloss.*, **Tough-pitch*, see *Tough-cake*. **1903** *Engineering* 4 Dec. 753/3 When the right amount of oxygen is present, the copper is said to be 'tough-pitch'. **1949** P. C. Carman *Chem. Constitution & Properties Engin. Materials* vii. 220 The product is a 'tough-pitch' copper of over 99·9% purity. **1964** H. Hodges *Artifacts* iv. 70 Correctly poled copper, tough pitch copper, still contains a little cuprous oxide. *c* **1640** J. Smyth *Hundred of Berkeley* (1885) 175 In this toune [Dursley] is a rocke of a strange stone called a Puffe stone or as some pronounce it a *tough stone.

b. In comb. (chiefly parasynthetic) with other adjs., as ***tough-backed, -hided*** (in quots. *fig.*), ***-looking, -metalled, -necked, -shelled, -skinned, -strung.***

a **1625** Fletcher & Massinger *Elder Brother* v. i, A true tough-metall'd blade. **1682** N. O. *Boileau's Lutrin* ii. 14 A tough-back't Knave. **1768** Tucker *Lt. Nat.* (1834) I. 644 Their solid bones, their tough-strung muscles, their strong-bounding blood. **1825** Coleridge *Lett., to J. Gillman* (1895) 743 Nature is..tough-lived as a turtle. **1826** Miss Mitford *Village* Ser. ii. 132 A tall, spare, tough-looking woman, with a long bony face. **1872** Browning *Fifine* xxxi, Unsensitive, tough-thonged In lieu of our fine nerve. **1925** D. H. Lawrence *St. Mawr* 158 She felt a peculiar tough-necked arrogance in him. **1930** R. Lehmann *Note in Music* vi. 249 It would take a good deal..to harm a tough-hided old hippopotamus like Uncle Tom. **1933** C. S. Lewis *Pilgrim's Regress* vii. v. 146, I always think it is possible for a place to be *too* bracing. They call it the land of the tough-minded—tough-skinned would be a better name. **1964** *Listener* 30 Apr. 731/3 A tough-hided, soft-centred, north-country, working-class dramatist.

B. *sb.* **1.** orig. *U.S.* A person given to rough or violent behaviour.

1866 Howells *Venet. Life* ii, The toughs of the distant alleys. **1884** J. Miller *Mem. & Rime* i. 9 Another 'tough'.. helped them hustle me in. **1897** *Outing* (U.S.) XXX. 429/1 It has spoiled our football, ruined our baseball, except for the 'tough'. **1903** C. Lumholtz *Unknown Mexico* I. 3 A raid on the camp by some toughs in the neighbourhood. **1929** 'G. Daviot' *Man in Queue* iii. 25 The missing man..was, in the opinion of the Durham inspector, a tough. **1946** R. Lehmann *Gipsy's Baby* 145 Can't think how your parents put up with it—all that gang of young toughs in and out all day. **1972** E. Grierson *Confessions of Country Magistrate* ix. 86 Certainly the treatment of the teenage tough..is a problem to which no one has ever hazarded an optimistic answer. **1982** I. Hamilton *Robert Lowell* (1983) ii. 16 He graduated to the status of school tough via a series of spectacular playground victories.

2. A person of uncompromising or aggressive views.

1928 C. Connolly *Let.* July in *Romantic Friendship* (1975) 321, I am becoming a tough, an anglophobe, and reverting to intolerance and intellectual pride. **1931** H. Nicolson *Diary* 21 Aug. (1966) 89 The latter asked whether Tom would join him and the Tory toughs in opposition. **1980** *Times* 23 June 31/1 The so-called 'toughs' who support Mrs Thatcher's policy—like Sir Keith Joseph..against the 'wets' led by Jim Prior.

tough (tʌf), *v. slang* (orig. and chiefly *U.S.*). [f. tough *a.*] **a.** intr. *to tough it* (*out*): to withstand (to the end) difficult conditions or adverse circumstances without flinching. Cf. *to rough* (*it*) *out* s.v. rough *v.*[1] 4 b.

1830 *Mass. Spy* 27 Jan. (Th.), Judy with whom he had toughed it three years. **1852** *Knickerbocker* XXXIX. 26 You don't need no medicine; you'll tough it out, I dare say. **1873** C. Thaxter *Isles of Shoals* 64 (Th.), Our brave little schooner 'toughed it out' on the distant ledge. **1939** L. M. Montgomery *Anne of Ingleside* xviii. 121 She darkly opined that it would be a miracle if he toughed it out till spring. **1956** T. Raddall *Wings of Night* (1957) xxxii. 241 She was a great ol' lady... Just kep' her chin up and..toughed it out to the end. **1982** H. Lieberman *Night Call* xvi. 94 We'll tough it out, but sacrifices will have to be made.

b. *trans.* With obj. in place of *it*: to withstand to the end.

1974 *Newsweek* 20 May 23/2 Everybody..was pressed into service denying that Mr. Nixon planned to quit; his daughter Julie vowed that he would tough out the impeachment process to its end in the Senate. **1979** *Courier-Mail* (Brisbane) 27 Sept. 1/6 Mr. Sinclair signalled he would try to tough out the crisis. **1981** *Observer* 26 Apr. 15/4 Fraser, it is assumed, will tough out this latest crisis.

tough, obs. variant of tow *v.*[1]

†**toughe, towghe.** *Irish Hist. Obs.* Also 6 toghe. [repr. Ir. *tuath* (*-th* = *-h*) territory, district.

Joyce *Irish Names of Places* ser. 2 (1875) 212, cites *Tuoghnafall* and *Tuogh of the Fall* from early 17th c. grants, as name of a district south of Belfast, now known as 'The Falls'; the orig. Irish being *Tuath-na-bhfál*, district of the *fáls*, i.e. hedges or enclosures.]

A territory or district in Ireland.

[.. Old Ir. doct., cited in G. Hill *Plantation in Ulster* (1877) 102 This is the number of Tuaths [districts] that are in Tirconnell.] **1584** *Calr. Carew MSS.* II. 391 The towghe of the two towghes, called the barony of Clonballykernan. **1586** *Ibid.* 428 The three toughes of Donseverige, Loghgill, and Toghe Ballamonyn. **1906** *Proc. R. Irish Acad.* XXVI. 58 Ancient Castles of Co. Limerick... These baronies were divided into Toghes, 'tuaths', or cantreds.

toughe, variant of tow *sb.*[3] *Obs.*

toughen (ˈtʌf(ə)n), *v.* [f. tough *a.* + -en[5].]

1. *trans.* To make tough.

1582 Stanyhurst *Æneis* iii. (Arb.) 76 O my son Æneas, with Troian destenye toughned. **1703** T. N. *City & C. Purchaser* 213 To toughen his Nails that were brittle. **1739** G. Smith *Laboratory* (1799) I. ii. 69 *heading*, Method of testing, refining, separating, allaying, and toughening [gold and silver]. **1901** F. W. Maitland *Rede Lect.* 27 Any scheme better suited to harden and toughen a traditional body of law. **1906** *Mem. Abp. Temple* I. 471 The experience of life had toughened the fibre of thought.

2. *intr.* To become tough.

1707 Mortimer *Husb.* (1721) I. 185 Lay them in some Room three or four Weeks or more, that they may cool, give and toughen. **1801** Southey *Thalaba* ix. xxx, Ere the green beauty of their brittle youth Grows brown, and toughens in the summer sun.

Hence **toughened** (ˈtʌf(ə)nd) *ppl. a.*, **toughening** (ˈtʌf(ə)nɪŋ) *vbl. sb.* and *ppl. a.*; **toughener** (ˈtʌf(ə)nə(r)), one who or that which toughens.

1876 *Encycl. Brit.* V. 754/2 *Toughened glass invented. **1894** *Chicago Advance* 25 Oct. 118/1 [They] went away.. with a toughened propensity to be bad. **1895** C. W. Lyman in *Voice* (N.Y.) 5 Dec. 7/2 Recommended as a *toughener of the constitution. **1868** Joynson *Metals* 45 The *toughening of cast-iron. **1869** Sir E. J. Reed *Shipbuild.* xxi. 317 The toughening effect produced on a mass of Steel when it is heated, and plunged into a bath of oil. **1881** Raymond *Mining Gloss.*, *Toughening*, refining, as of copper or gold.

tougher, obs. form of tocher.

toughie (ˈtʌfɪ), *sb.* (and *a.*) *colloq.* (orig. *U.S.*). Also **toughy**. [f. tough *a.* + -ie, -y[6].]

1. A tough person. **a.** = *tough guy* s.v. tough *a.* 10 a. **b.** A person of aggressive or uncompromising views.

1929 *Princeton Alumni Weekly* 24 May 981/2 The *toughie* is the man of the hour when the policeman's whistle blows. It is always nice to be close to him when the riot calls are turned in. **1938** *New Republic* 21 Sept. 188/1 Getting the toughies off the street. **1940** R. Chandler *Farewell, my Lovely* xxvii. 168 A toughie..came in and showed me a blackjack. **1959** *She* May 65/2 Luxury-lovers had better stick to planes or boats. A trip in the 'Bombay Bus' is definitely one for the toughies. **1960** *Sunday Express* 24 July 16/5 Mr. Butlin is a toughie too... A man who has learned to cater for the mood of the people and take full advantage of their longer purses... I think he will continue to prosper despite credit squeezes, Chancellors, the rain, and other vexations. **1971** J. Mandelkau *Buttons* x. 121 A group of bikers riding out for kicks every Friday and Saturday night, getting drunk and swinging back and forth over the white line behind the toughie they would call 'our leader'. **1980** I. Murdoch *Nuns & Soldiers* i. 84 Daisy had women friends ..'Women's Libbers', and left wing toughies. **1984** *Observer* 8 Apr. 12/4 Mondale may think that he makes a good political toughie.

2. A difficult problem, enterprise, or contest.

1945 *Good Housekeeping* June 230/2 How about the $80 question?..Think now. This is a toughie. **1947** *Sun* (Baltimore) 18 Jan. 1/7 West has another toughie for Congress... Would it be O.K. if the District used tax money to buy uniforms for the policemen's band? **1972** J. L. Dillard *Black English* vii. 281 Children who speak Standard English may react to words like *island*,..with 'That's a toughie!' **1972** D. Lees *Zodiac* 6 It sounded, as Harry put it, 'a doddle', but even if it had looked a toughy the Riviera would have sold it.

3. *attrib.* or as *adj.*

1962 *John o' London's* 9 Feb. 138/4 The nice, 'toughie' Irishman. **1974** *Times Lit. Suppl.* 14 June 644/3 Admirers of Stephen Becher's urbane *When the War is Over* will be surprised at the toughie metaphysics of the opening of his new novel. **1977** *Film & Television Technician* Jan. 9/3 Bob was one of those 'toughie' production managers, greatly concerned not only with the budget, but with the film and the people working on it.

toughish (ˈtʌfɪʃ), *a.* [f. tough *a.* + -ish[1].] Somewhat tough.

1776 Da Costa *Conchol.* v. 121 A kind of toughish coriaceous or leather-like substance. **1840** Darwin In *Life & Lett.* (1887) I. 271 A toughish argument. **1882** *Standard* 26 Sept. 2/1 The limpet is..a toughish comestible.

toughly (ˈtʌflɪ), *adv.* [f. tough *a.* + -ly[2].] In a tough manner (in various senses of tough); strenuously; persistently; stoutly; vigorously.

c **1400** *Apol. Loll.* 68 [Þei] þat he knawiþ to stond touȝly in þer synnis þat þei han don. *c* **1450** tr. *De Imitatione* iii. viii. 74 Not to cleue ouer touȝly to þis affeccion. **1589** Greene *Menaphon* (Arb.) 83 They fell toughly to blowes. **1635** Shirley *Coronat.* i, Cassander,.. oppos'd him toughly with his faction. **1728** Ramsay *Fables* xi. 32 He..laid till 't teughly tooth and nail. **1821** Joanna Baillie *Metr. Leg., Lady G. B.* liii, Strong and toughly nerved. **1883** Stevenson *Silverado Sq.* iii. (1886) 20 We struggled toughly upward.

tough-ˈminded, *a.* In the philosophy of William James: marked by a purely empirical, sceptical, non-metaphysical approach to questions; opp. tender-minded *a.* Hence more widely: free from excessive sensitivity, realistic, unsqueamish, etc. Also *absol.*

1907 W. James *Pragmatism* i. 12 You will..recognize the two types of mental make-up that I mean if I head the columns..*The Tender-Minded.* Rationalistic (going by 'principles'), Intellectualistic, Idealistic, Optimistic, Religious, Free-willist, Monistic, Dogmatical. *The Tough-Minded.* Empiricist (going by 'facts'), Sensationalistic, Materialistic, Pessimistic, Irreligious, Fatalistic, Pluralistic, Sceptical. **1927** J. S. Huxley *Relig. without Revelation* iv. 116 Youth wakes to the fact of social inequality, and, if not one of the tough-minded, to remorseful distress of its own privileged position. **1945** Auden *Coll. Poetry* 123 Tough-minded men get mushy in their sleep. **1952** C. P. Blacker *Eugenics* 240 The scientist, or at least the scientist's camp-followers, may become tough-minded and contemptuous: the word 'mysticism' expresses what they most passionately abjure. **1960** *Guardian* 17 Dec. 6/2 The tough-minded and unromantic pragmatism of the new President. **1974** *Sci. Amer.* Jan. 113/2 Tough-minded skeptics. **1980** F. K. PROCHASKA *Women & Philanthropy in Nineteenth Cent. Eng.* vi. 191 Reclaiming prostitutes was a daunting prospect for charitable women however tough-minded.

Hence **tough-'mindedness**.

1907 W. JAMES *Pragmatism* vii. 267 One misunderstanding of pragmatism is to identify it with positivistic tough-mindedness. **1936** *Mind* XLV. 218 The sort of tough-mindedness which, on principle, excludes ethical, aesthetic and religious considerations from metaphysical thinking, is wilfully blind. **1961** *Guardian* 3 Apr. 12/7 The first fruits of tough-mindedness [in U.S. policy in Laos] are..encouraging. **1975** *Nature* 10 Apr. 470/2 In addition to being careful in this way, we have also to be sensitive and observant, and not to react with a preconceived pattern of tough-mindedness.

toughness ('tʌfnɪs). Forms: see TOUGH *a.* [f. TOUGH *a.* + -NESS.] The state or quality of being tough, in various senses of the adjective.

c **1440** *Promp. Parv.* 498/2 Towghenesse (*K.*, *A.* townesse, *P.* toughnes), *tenacitas*. **1573–80** BARET *Alv.* T 307 *Lentor*, toughnesse: a clammie, or gluish humour. **1597** A. M. tr. *Guillemeau's Fr. Chirurg.* 48 b/2 The great toughenes of the ..Pituita. **1613** FLETCHER, etc. *Honest Man's Fort.* v. ii, Stock fish.., If it be well drest, for the tuffness sake. **1674** GREW *Veget. Trunks* vii. §12 Hence likewise we may understand the Cause of the Toughness of Flax. **1732** ARBUTHNOT *Aliments*, etc. (1736) 422 The Viscosity or Toughness of the Fluids. **1733** W. ELLIS *Chiltern & Vale Farm.* 9 Red Clays..stand in the front..for..Tuffness, Coldness, and Moistness. **1830** HERSCHEL *Stud. Nat. Phil.* III. i. (1851) 238 The toughness of a solid, or that quality by which it will endure heavy blows without breaking. **1845** J. COULTER *Adv. in Pacific* xi. 141 From its extreme toughness, we could not eat it. **1895** R. P. HERRICK in *Boston* (U.S.) *Pilgr. Missionary* June 11/1 You have gained a very good idea of the toughness of these mining towns.

‖**toughra** ('tugra). Also **toghra, tughra, tuğra**. [a. Turkish *tura*, *tuğra*.] An ornamental monogram incorporating the name and title of the Sultan.

1888 S. LANE-POOLE *Turkey* 36 [1365] It is said that Murād signed the treaty, for lack of a pen, with his open hand, over which he had smeared some ink, in the manner of Eastern seals. This veritable sign-manual is believed to be the origin of the *tughra* or Sultan's cipher, which has ever since appeared on the coinage and the official documents of the Turks. **1903** *Amer. Jrnl. Numismatics* Jan. 73 The principal device on the gold coins of the present Sultan..is the imperial *toghra*. **1954** *Stamp Lover* XLVI. 136/1 Turkey was introduced by an official document of 1840 bearing the manuscript Toughra or signature of the Sultan. **1962** R. A. G. CARSON *Coins* 488 The tughra, the monogram of the sultan's names and titles which is a feature of later Turkish coinage.., appeared for the first time under Suleyman I. **1974** *Encycl. Brit. Macropædia* III. 664/2 A distinctive *tuğra* was created for each sultan and affixed to imperial decrees by a skilled calligrapher.

tought. Now *dial.* Also 7 **towght**, 9 *dial.* **towt** (taʊt). [Origin obscure. It answers in form, but barely in sense, to OFris. *tocht*, EFris. *tocht*, *togt*, MDu. *tocht*, *togt*, Du. *togt*, draught, drawing.] A length or section of an angler's hair-line, a link, a trace; also a piece of spun yarn (*E.D.D.*).

1676 COTTON *Angler* II. v. 39 Take a strong small silk.. and then whip it twice or thrice about the bare hook..both to prevent slipping, and also that the shanck of the hook may not cut the hairs of your Towght. **1681** CHETHAM *Angler's Vade-m.* ii. §6 (1689) 10 When you make lines, especially 4 or 5 of the lowermost links, Gildards or toughts. **1905** *Eng. Dial. Dict.*, *Towt, tout, towght*, old rope, a piece of spun yarn, or a single strand of tarred rope used as a lashing.

tought, -e, obs. ff. TAUT, TOUGH.

toughy, dial. var. TOFFEE *sb.*, var. TOUGHIE.

touh, -e, obs. ff. TOUGH.

touit(t: see TOVET, two-peck measure.

‖**toujours** (tuʒur), *adv.* (and *sb.*) [Fr., = always.]

1. *toujours gai* (ge), 'always cheerful'; cheerful under all circumstances; also as *sb.*, an unfailingly cheerful disposition. Occas. partially anglicized as *toujours gay*.

1711 ADDISON in D. Piper *Eng. Face* (1957) vii. 163 A certain smirking Air..bestowed indifferently on every Age and Degree... The *Toujours Gai* appeared even in Judges, Bishops and Privy-Counsellors. **1899** KIPLING *From Sea to Sea* I. viii. 263 They [*sc.* prostitutes] spoke of themselves as 'gay'... A night's reflection has convinced me that there is no hell for these women in another world... It was my duty to watch through the night a patient—gay, *toujours* gay, remember—quivering on the verge of the 'jumps'. **1927** D. MARQUIS *archy & mehitabel* xiv. 56 Well archy the world is full of ups and downs but toujours gai is my motto. **1972** M. KENYON *Shooting of Dan McGrew* xxi. 174 He was 'toujours gai' (I wonder is he on drugs?).

2. *toujours perdrix* (perdri), lit. 'always partridge', an allusive phr. used to imply that one can have too much of a good thing. [For an explanation see A. M. Hyamson *Dict. Eng. Phrs.* (1922) 346/1.]

1818 *Blackw. Mag.* Feb. 569/2 A partridge is a good thing; and yet even '*Toujours Perdrix*' is not to be borne. **1877** L. W. M. LOCKHART *Mine is Thine* (1879) xvii. 163 He wanted a rest, a change from this *toujours perdrix* of ladies' society, polite small-talk, boredom. **1927** D. H. LAWRENCE *Let.* 12 Dec. (1962) II. 1026 I'm sick of Jesus... We might have somebody else born for a change. *Toujours perdrix!*

3. Used simply: always.

1902 G. MEREDITH *Let.* 19 Jan. (1970) III. 147 If it is *toujours* Goethe, that is because I share the *culte*.

touk(e, obs. form of TUCK (of drum).

toul, toule, toull, obs. forms of TOLL.

touladi, var. TULADI.

tould(e, obs. f. *told*, pa. t. and pple. of TELL *v.*

toulner, toulsell: see TOLNER, TOLSEL.

Toulousain (tuluzɛ̃), *sb.* and *a.* Fem. **-aine** (-ɛn). [Fr., f. *Toulouse* + *-ain* -AN.] **A.** *sb.* A native or inhabitant of Toulouse, in SW France. **B.** *adj.* Of, pertaining to, or characteristic of Toulouse.

1883 H. JAMES in *Atlantic Monthly* Oct. 461/1 A big, brown, expansive woman... This terrible Toulousaine of today. *Ibid.* 462/1 Saint-Sernin..dedicated to Saint Saturninus—the Toulousains have abbreviated—is, I think, alone worth the journey to Toulouse. **1970** *Sat. Rev.* (U.S.) 3 Oct. 45/1 A young Toulousaine from the local tourist office. **1972** R. COBB *Reactions to Fr. Revolution* iii. 119 To do the opposite to what the Bordelais did was an ancient rule of Toulousain conduct. **1980** 'M. HARRIS' *Treasure of Ste. Foy* v. 54 Serge Gaspar is a Toulousain, dark, with a Spanish look to him. *Ibid.* 55 She is the same Toulousain type as Gaspar, with dark hair..and a clear olive complexion.

†**toum**, obs. variant of TAUM, fishing-line, etc.

1670 *Bk. Barony of Urie* (1892) 90 Showe them wher they ar to cast in ther severall toumes.

†**toumbe**, *v.* *Obs. rare*⁻¹. [ad. F. *tomber* to fall. Cf. TUMB *v.*] *intr.* To fall.

1297 R. GLOUC. (Rolls) 10830 þe king..bigan nei vor pite isuowe vpriȝt toumbe.

toun(e, obs. f. TON[1], TONE, TOWN, TUN, TUNE.

tounder, -ire, obs. Sc. forms TINDER.

toundra, var. TUNDRA.

†**toung**, obs. f. TONGUE.

toungya, var. TAUNGYA.

†**toup, to-'up**, *prep.* *Obs. rare.* Also 4 **topen**. [f. TO-[1] + UP, *uppan*: cf. OE. *on-uppan*.] Above, beyond, in addition to.

c **1315** SHOREHAM v. 284 Ac toup alle oþren ys y-blessed, Soþe wyf and mayde. **13..** *Guy of Warw.* (A.) 2735, & topen al þis, ȝif Gij wer ded, We miȝten haue þe lesse dred.

toup (tu:p), *sb.* Slang abbrev. of TOUPEE.

1959 P. BULL *I know the Face* viii. 138 'Say, Padre, is that a toup?' he naïvely enquires. **1973** R. HAYES *Hungarian Game* xxxiv. 205 He picked a blond wig... He slipped the toup over his gray hair and adjusted it to cover the high forehead.

toup, toupe, obs. forms of TUP.

toupee (tu:'pi:, 'tu:peɪ, 'tu:pi:). Also 8 **toupé**, **tupee, toppee**, 9 **towpee**, 20 **toupée**. [app. ad. F. *toupet*: see next.] **a.** A curl or artificial lock of hair on the top of the head, esp. as a crowning feature of a periwig; a periwig in which the front hair was combed up, over a pad, into such a top-knot, worn by both sexes in the 18th c.; also the natural hair dressed in this mode; (now the usual sense) a patch of false hair or small wig to cover a bald place.

1731 FIELDING *Grubstreet Op.* III. xv, Love in his lac'd coat lies, And peeps from his toupee. **1742** POPE *Dunc.* IV. 88 Whate'er of dunce in College or in Town Sneers at another, in toupee or gown. **1753** in Fairholt *Costume in Eng.* (1885) I. 376 A tye-wig is banished for a pigeon-winged toupée. **1770** BARRETTI *Journ. fr. Lond. to Genoa* I. 137, I hate to see a little girl with a tupee. **1778** F. MARION in *Harper's Mag.* Sept. (1883) 546/1 The Lt. Col. recomends to every Soldier to have..the fore top short without toppee & short at the sides. **1843** MACAULAY *Ess.*, *Mme. D'Arblay* (1887) 740 He stalked about the small parlour, brushing the ceiling with his toupee. **1862** *Catal. Internat. Exhib.*, *Brit.* II. No. 4586 Fronts, partings, and toupées on the same novel principle. **1973** M. AMIS *Rachel Papers* 81 My hair hung on my head as if it were a cut-price toupée. **1980** V. S. PRITCHETT *Tale Bearers* 20 He is having his toupee fixed and his hair dyed.

attrib. **1817** COLERIDGE *Satyrane's Lett.* iii. 241 In the portrait of Lessing there was a toupee perriwig.

†**b.** One who wears a toupee; a person of fashion; a beau, a spark, a buck. *Obs.*

1727 POPE, etc. *Art of Sinking* x. 94 Then oh! she cries, what slaves I round me see? Here a bright Redcoat, there a smart Toupee. **1747** *Gentl. Mag.* Nov. 537/2 Here swiftly move toupee's, in spruce undress.

Hence **tou'peed** *a.*, wearing a toupee.

1847 R. CHAMBERS *Traditions of Edinburgh* 45 Their toupeed and deep-skirted beaux.

‖**toupet** (tupɛ, 'tu:peɪ, 'tu:pɪt). [a. F. *toupet* (tupɛ) tuft of hair, esp. over the forehead, deriv. (in form dim.) of OF. *toup*, *top*, *tup*, tuft of hair, foliage, etc.; ad. *LG. *topp-* = OHG. *zopf* top, tuft, summit; cf. OFris. *top* tuft, top, ONorse *toppr* top, tuft, lock of hair: see TOP *sb.*[1]]

1. = TOUPEE.

1729 *Art of Politicks* 10 Think we that modern words eternal are? Toupet, and Tompion, Cosins, and Colmar Hereafter will be called by some plain man A Wig, a Watch, a Pair of Stays, a Fan. **1818** SCOTT *Rob Roy* vi, These *fadeurs*, which every gentleman with a toupet thinks himself obliged to recite to an unfortunate girl. **1863** *Cornh. Mag.* VII. 395 Wigs are dangerous unless frankly avowed. A toupet may easily escape detection.

†**b.** *transf.* = TOUPEE b. *Obs.*

1728 FIELDING *Love in Sev. Masques* Epil., From you then —ye toupets—he hopes defence. **1748** RICHARDSON *Clarissa* Wks. 1883 VII. 495 A couple of brocaded or laced-waistcoated toupets..with sour screwed up half-cocked faces.

2. †The forelock of a horse or other animal (*obs.*); a thick head of hair (in quot., of a Negro).

1797 *Sporting Mag.* X. 295 The *Tuft* or *Toupet*, that part of the mane which lies between the two ears. **1834** SOUTHEY *Doctor* iii. (1862) 5 Some of the inhabitants of Congo make a secret fob in their woolly toupet.

3. *attrib.*, as **toupet-coxcomb, -man, -wig**; **toupet-titmouse**, the Crested Titmouse.

1731 FIELDING *Mod. Husb.* I. ix, I meet with nothing but a parcel of toupet coxcombs, who plaster up their brains upon their periwigs. **1748** RICHARDSON *Clarissa* (1811) VII. vi. 35 No mere toupet-man; but all manly. *a* **1784** PENNANT *Arct. Zool.* (1785) II. 423 Titmous. Toupet..feathers on the head long, which it erects occasionally into a pointed crest, like a toupet. **1884** E. YATES *Rec. & Exper.* II. 238 A carefully arranged toupet-wig.

Hence **toupeted** *nonce-wd.* ('tu:pɪtɪd, 'tu:peɪd) *a.*, wearing a toupet.

1903 *Smart Set* IX. 53/2 We go in to dinner with the toupeted colonels.

toupinambou, obs. form of TOPINAMBOU.

tour (tʊə(r)), *sb.* Also 7 **toure, tower**: see also sense 4. [ME. a. F. *tour*, in OF. and Prov. *tor*, back-formation from nom. *tors*:—L. *tornus*, a. Gr. τόρνος a tool for describing a circle, a turner's wheel, a circle. The orig. acc. form was *torn*, *tourn*:—L. *tornum*; cf. Prov., Cat. *torn*, Sp., Pg., It. *torno*. In some of the Fr. and English senses, perh. n. of action f. *tourner* to turn.]

I. 1. One's turn or order (to do something). Also, a spell of work or duty; a shift: see TURN *sb.*; freq. in *tour of duty*. Now mainly *Mil.* and (with pronunc. taʊə(r)) in *Oil Industry*. †*by tour*, *by tours*, by turns (*obs.*).

[**1292** BRITTON IV. ii, Si soen tourn soit a cele foiz de presenter ou noun.] *c* **1320** *Cast. Love* 1334 He was a-bated of his tour [Fr. *Il est de son torn abatuz*]. **1546** *Reg. Privy Council Scot.* I. 57 To cum and remane at the assege of the Castell.., ilk quarter in his tour. **1640** *Sc. Acts Chas. I* (1817) V. 311/1 If any of these whose tour fallis to be present shalbe absent. **1781** in Simes *Mil. Guide* (ed. 3) 9 That..each [may] march in their tour. **1800** WELLINGTON *Suppl. Desp.* (1858) I. 464 This tour of duty to commence at morning parade on halting days. **1868** *Regul. & Ord. Army* ¶837 When an Officer is in the performance of a duty, and his tour for another duty occurs, he is not to make good that other duty, but his tour is to pass him. **1887** *Harper's Mag.* June 129/2 The 'machine-tenders'..work in 'tours' or 'shifts' twelve hours each. **1903** *Dialect Notes* II. 345 The morning *tour* lasts from midnight until noon. **1939** D. HAGER *Fund. Petroleum Industry* ix. 212 These men work in shifts or 'tours' (pronounced *towers*) of 6 or 8 hrs. **1946** *R.A.F. Jrnl.* May 153 The existing Editor having performed his tour of duty and taken up other duties in the Service. **1975** L. CROOK *Oil Terms* 60 The Driller is responsible for his crew and the running of the rig during his eight or twelve hour 'tour'. **1981** 'J. ROSS' *Dark Blue & Dangerous* xxvii. 158 He's too soft, and..I don't know how he did the rest of his tour of duty without showing it on his face.

2. †**a.** A turning round, circular movement, revolution (in quot. 1688 *fig.*). *Obs. rare.*

1477 CAXTON *Jason* 95 b, They go to the masse..for to make their tours and signes thenne for ony deuocion. **1688** BURNET *Lett. conc. St. Italy* 175 After the many tours, that the matter made in the many Ballotings, it came to the fixing of the last three out of whom the Doge was to be chosen. **1712** BLACKMORE *Creation* II. 77 The Tours by Heav'nly Bodies made. **1719** DE FOE *Crusoe* xix. (1840) I. 349 He made so many Tours..and led us by such winding Ways.

b. *Dancing.* Also with pronunc. (‖tur). In a cotillion, a circular movement by the dancers. In *Ballet*, a turn by a solo dancer; *tour en l'air*, such a turn while leaping in the air.

1841 MRS. GASKELL *Lett.* (1966) 822 The cotillion was so pretty—such amusing & graceful *tours*. **1930** CRASKE & BEAUMONT *Theory & Pract. Allegro Class. Ballet* 94 (*heading*) Series of tours en dedans en diagonale. **1948** A. H. FRANKS *Approach to Ballet* iii. 45 Used sparingly, *tours* can become most effective highlights in a male solo. **1958** [see PLIÉ]. **1960** M. WOOD *Advanced Historical Dances* 93 The refrain had been replaced by a fixed series of movements called Tours, forming a framework into which the figures were fitted. The Tours in order of performance were these: (1) Grand Rond. All take hands in a ring and go round both ways. [Etc.] **1963** *Times* 29 May 13/4 Mr. Flindt..can produce effortless, waist-high *cabrioles*, yet is often constricted, even rough, in *tours*. **1977** *Times* 5 May 11/8 The skill with which she sustained the series of *tours en l'air* in her solo.

3. A going or travelling round from place to place, a round; an excursion or journey including the visiting of a number of places in a circuit or sequence; often qualified, as *cycling*,

walking, wedding tour; *esp.* a circuitous journey embracing the principal places of the country or region mentioned. Also, †an account of such a journey. ***on tour***, touring: see TOUR *v.* 2.

the (grand) tour, a journey through France, Germany, Switzerland, and Italy, formerly fashionable, esp. as a finishing course in the education of young men of rank: see GRAND TOUR.

1643 DENHAM *Cooper's H.* 183 Visits the World, and in his flying towers Brings home to us, and makes both Indies ours. **1652** EVELYN *St. France* Misc. Writ. (1805) 46 A traveller.. making the tour as they call it. **1688** BURNET *Lett. conc. St. Italy* 155 He made the Tower of Italy with him this year. **1697** DAMPIER *Voy. round World* (1699) 104 Having made a Tour, or Semi-circular March they return to the Sea again. **1748-1869** [see GRAND TOUR]. **1779** *Mirror* No. 57 ¶15 Manly and I.. had set out together to make the tour of Europe. **1812** COMBE (*title*) Dr. Syntax's Tour in Search of the Picturesque. *Ibid.* I, I'll make a tour—and then I'll write it. **1815** SCOTT *Guy M.* xiv, He.. resolved.. to make a short tour of a fortnight. **1817** JANE AUSTEN *Sanditon* (1925) viii. 110 He read all the Essays, Letters, Tours & Criticisms of the day. **1821** BYRON *Don Juan* v. lii. 161 Nature.. Resigns herself with exemplary patience To guide-books, rhymes, tours, sketches, illustrations. **1887** *Graphic* 15 Jan. 62/1 An actor.. 'on tour' in the *Vetah* company. **1888** *Spectator* 28 Apr. 561/1 President Carnot is on tour in the Gironde. *Mod.* We made the tour of the town and saw all the places of interest.

b. *transf.* and *fig.* A round.

1704 SWIFT *T. Tub* Pref., Thrice have I forced my imagination to make the tour of my invention. **1718** LADY M. W. MONTAGU *Lett.* (1887) I. 238 After having made their tour, the bride was again led.. round the rooms. **1746** COETLOGON (*title*) A Tour through the Animal World; or an historical and accurate Account of near 400 Animals, Birds, Fishes, Serpents, Insects, &c. **1857** JAS. HAMILTON *Less. Gt. Biogr.* (1859) 152 Making another tour of the company, each disciple filled his basket.

†**c.** A short outing taken for exercise, recreation, as a social function, or the like; also, the route taken on such occasions; in 17th c., in London, the drive round Hyde Park. *Obs.*

1656 DUCHESS OF NEWCASTLE *True Relation* in *Life* (1886) 309, I go sometimes abroad.. in my coach.. about some of the streets, which we call here a tour, where all the chief of the town go to see and to be seen. **1665** PEPYS *Diary* 19 Mar., Mr. Povy and I in his coach to Hyde Parke, being the first day of the tour there. **1667** DUCHESS OF NEWCASTLE *Life Dk. of N.* (1886) II. 99 Whereas at first there were no more but four coaches that went the Tour,.. all those that had sufficient means, and could go to the price, kept coaches, and went the Tour for their own pleasure. **1725** DE FOE *Voy. round World* (1840) 250 Now and then making a little tour about the fields, and towards the mountains. **1773** *Life N. Frowde* 46 Whilst the Ship staied at Cork we were perpetually diverted with Visits,.. Tours into the adjacent Country, and Entertainments at Home.

d. The circuit *of* an island, etc.; a round.

1719 DE FOE *Crusoe* (1840) I. x. 162 My next design was to make a tour round the island. **1748** *Anson's Voy.* III. v, He one day, attended by some of his officers, endeavoured to make the tour of the Island. **1756-7** tr. *Keysler's Trav.* (1760) II. 124 The tour is something above fifteen Italian, or three German miles.

†**4. a.** A crescent front of false hair (F. *tour de cheveux*). *Obs.* exc. *Hist.*

Cf. also TAURE. Also, in this sense, by confusion with TOWER *sb.*[1], spelt 7 **towr**, 7-8 **tower**.

1674 *Lond. Gaz.* No. 900/4 Lost.., a Red Russia leather Trunk about two foot long..; a very light curled Tower and Locks,.. with.. other wearing apparel in it for Women. **1676** ETHEREDGE *Man of Mode* II. i, Her Tour wou'd Keep in Curl no longer. *a* **1700** B. E. *Dict. Cant. Crew, Tower*, a Woman's false Hair on their Fore-heads. **1727-41** CHAMBERS *Cycl., Tour of hair*, a tress or border of hair, going round the head, which mingled dextrously with the natural hair, lengthens and thickens it. *a* **1732** GAY *Toilette* Poems 1737 II. 81 Ancient matrons with their frizled tow'rs. **1837** THACKERAY *Ravensw.* vii, People in tours and pig-tails.

b. See also TOWER *sb.*[1] 6 b.

II. Figurative uses (mostly from French).

†**5.** A course to turn to; a shift, device, expedient.

1555 PHAER *Æneid* II. D iij b, What shift? what tour is best we take? **1699** VANBRUGH *False Friend* III. iii, We are still in the dark. I have one tour yet. Impudence be my aid!

†**6.** A mode of phraseology; a 'turn' given to a phrase or sentence, etc. *Obs.*

1685 BOYLE *Enq. Notion Nat.* ii. 39 A dextrous Writer may oftentimes be able to give such a Form (or, as the Modern Frenchmen speak), such a Tour to his many-ways variable Expressions, as to avoid the necessity of making use of the Word Nature. **1751** J. BROWN *Shaftesb. Charac.* 32 With regard to the oratory of the bar,.. it is easy to observe, what a different tour the learned council takes, in addressing himself to the judge or jury.

†**7.** Manner of presenting or exhibiting anything; an aspect given to a matter. *Obs.*

1687 BURNET *Reply to Varillas* 28 Yet Mr. Varillas has a sublime tour in every thing, so that instead of setting before us the reasons which led him to depend upon such an Author,.. he gives one, which indeed no man beside himself would ever have thought on. *Ibid.* 119, I find I judged too well of his Invention, in ascribing to him those Romantick Tours that he gave matters. *a* **1734** NORTH *Exam.* III. vi. §22 (1740) 438 The next Tour of the Author.. is to demonstrate, that although there were very good Reasons for the King to indulge the Fanatics.., yet he did it for none of those, but for other Reasons that were abominably bad.

†**8.** The course or compass of anything; what it amounts to; range, scope. *Obs.*

1697 BENTLEY *Phal.* (1699) 81 The latter part of his Life was the whole Tour and Compass that the Sophist designed to write of. **1713** —— *Free-thinking* xviii. 36 The whole Tour of the Passage is this: A man given to Superstition can have no security, day or night, waking or sleeping. **1737** WATERLAND *Eucharist* vii. 232 Such is the Tour of the Argument, such the Chain of Ideas that forms it.

†**9.** Manner or mode of being. *Obs.*

1702 FARQUHAR *Inconstant* v. ii, Something I saw of a well-furnished, careless, agreeable tour about you. **1736** MRS. MANLEY *Secret Mem.* III. 204 The new-fashion Tour of Religion and Politicks.

†**10.** A round, a course (of engagements, etc.).

1711 STEELE *Spect.* No. 156 ¶4 Scarce one of all the Women who are in the Tour of Gallantries ever hear any thing of what is the common Sense of sober Minds.

11. One of the several trills, variations, or changes in the song of a trained canary.

1906 *Daily Chron.* 20 Oct. 6/7 There are.. in all, some twenty known trills or 'tours' in the song of a really accomplished roller canary.

III. 12. *attrib.* and *Comb.*, as ***tour-book, bus, director, guide, -making, operator, party, -writer, -writing***; **tour-money**, money paid for travelling fare and accommodation on a tour.

1767 BUSH *Hibernia Cur.* (1769) p. vi, Neglected by the.. tour-writers. **1793** W. ROBERTS *Looker-On* No. 74 (1794) III. 171 The rage for tour-writing, which prevails in the female world. **1824** MCCULLOCH *Highl.*, etc. *Scot.* I. 41, I shall be obliged to write a tour book myself. **1869** P. LANDRETH *Life & Min. A. Thomson* i. 1 This occasional tour-making did not break up the continuity of his energetic life. **1909** *Daily Chron.* 5 Aug. 4/4 A third member of the party took fright.. and requested the return of the tour-money. **1952** *Galaxy* June 56/2 I'm the tour director. Can I help you? **1965** J. A. MICHENER *Source* (1966) 22 That afternoon the first excursionists stopped at the tell, asking to see the Candlestick of Death, and the next morning a tour bus arrived. **1971** M. MCCARTHY *Birds of America* 107 Their tour director, who had met them at Le Havre. **1973** P. THEROUX *Saint Jack* xviii. 219 The tour-guide had started his spiel. **1976** J. SNOW *Cricket Rebel* 47, I could only wait anxiously for the announcement of the names of the tour party to visit the West Indies that winter of 1967-68. **1981** *Sunday Express Mag.* 11 Oct. 9/1 (Advt.), We've taken more British holiday-makers here than any other tour operator. **1981** M. KENYON *Zigzag* xi. 67 He was agonizingly shy... Guiding tour parties petrified him.

tour (tʊə(r)), *v.* [f. TOUR *sb.*]

†**1. a.** *intr.* To 'take a turn' in or about a place, esp. riding or driving. *Obs.*

1746 MRS. DELANY in *Life & Corr.* (1861) II. 443 The coach is ready for D. D. and me to tour in the park, and to see my lord's improvements. **1760** *Ibid.* III. 619 The Duchess has carried us to tour about the park and to see her hot-house.

b. To turn, direct one's steps. *dial.*

1768 ROSS *Helenore* I. 33 Aff I scours Blessing my lucky stars, an' hame I tours.

2. *intr.* To make a tour or circuitous journey, in which many places are visited, usually without retracing one's steps; to make a prolonged excursion for recreation or business; *spec.* of an actor, a theatrical company, or the like: to go 'on tour', to travel from town to town fulfilling engagements.

1789 A. C. BOWER *Diaries & Corr.* (1903) 97 We are all got thus far touring for Health. **1799** COLERIDGE *Lett., to T. Poole* (1895) 306 The man who toured with me in Wales and afterwards published his 'Tour'. **1858** CARLYLE *Fredk. Gt.* x. vii. (1872) III. 276 Algarotti.. has been touring about as a celebrity these four years past. **1886** *Cyclist's Tour. Club Gaz.* IV. 126 A word of advice to those about to tour at Easter. **1897** *Literature* 13 Nov. 123/2 [He] has made up his mind to take up once again lecturing work, and he will tour in several of the large American towns. **1907** H. WYNDHAM *Flare of Footlights* xii, Godfrey Deane has decided not to tour,.. so I shall ask Antony for the part.

3. a. *trans.* To make the tour or round of, to tour in (a country or district).

1885 J. COLEMAN in *Longm. Mag.* VII. 67 Barrett organised a company with which.. he toured the provinces. **1887** *Bicycling News* 8 Oct. 3/2 He landed at Melbourne, and toured the colonies with great success. **1898** *Westm. Gaz.* 25 Jan. 5/3 Mr. R. is this week touring his constituency. **1899** *Ibid.* 2 Feb. 9/1 To tour India.. with an English amateur cricket team.

b. To cover (a distance) in touring.

1891 in *Pall Mall Gaz.* 12 Feb. 1/2 One good performance on the path does more to arouse attention than 20,000 miles quietly toured.

4. *spec.* (*Theatr.*) To take (a play or entertainment) on tour; to tour with. Also with a performer as obj.

1897 *Westm. Gaz.* 22 May 8/1 'The County Fair', the American drama.. now being toured in the provinces by Mr. Neil Burgess's Company. **1904** *Ibid.* 12 Feb. 5/2 It is the intention of the lecturer to tour his illustrated entertainment in the provinces. **1910** *Stage Year Bk.* 52 This production [Peter Pan] was magnificently staged in Sydney, but the business was poor, and it was never toured. **1920** *Glasgow Herald* 10 June 7 Mr. Quinlan.. recently toured Madame Tetrazzini and Signor Caruso. **1922** JOYCE *Ulysses* 92 The idea is to tour the chief towns... Mary Anderson is up there now... Louis Werner is touring her.

¶ *Touring* in Capt. Smith *Virginia* (1624) VI. *New Eng.* 212 is an error for *turning* in the earlier *Descr. New Eng.* (1616) 17.

Hence **'touring** *ppl. a.*, that tours.

1832 F. TROLLOPE *Dom. Manners Amer.* II. xxxiii. 236 To this frail shelter.. nearly all the touring gentlemen.. find their way. **1867** *Harper's Mag.* Dec. 96/1 As railways have multiplied, the formation of what are called Touring-parties, for the purpose of giving concerts and operas in the provinces, has become the business of many. **1870** *Athenæum* 15 Oct. 506 A touring troupe of singers from this country. **1883** *Pall Mall Gaz.* 27 Oct. 4/1 Town-abiding and touring Americans. **1888** J. PENNELL *ibid.* 25 Oct. 5 From the standpoint of a touring cycler. **1895** ROBERTS & MORTON *Adventures Arthur Roberts* xiii. 159 Whether from preference or economy,.. this touring company generally slept at night on the beach. **1969** G. GREENE *Travels with my Aunt* I. xi. 105 The touring company.. came after my Paris days. It was in Paris that I was spotted by Mr Visconti... 'He was a great amateur of.. the stage.' **1983** *Times* 7 Sept. 3/4 Scunthorpe is a regular stop-off point for touring companies.

tour, obs. form of TOWER, TWIRE.

touraco, var. TURACO.

‖**Tourangeau** (turɑ̃ʒo), *sb.* and *a.* Pl. **-x.** [Fr.] (A native or inhabitant) of Touraine, a former province of France corresponding more or less to the modern department of Indre-et-Loire, or of Tours, its chief town.

1883 H. JAMES in *Atlantic Monthly* July 25/1 The real Tourangeau will not make an effort.. to go in search of a pleasure. **1969** B. ARTHAUD tr. *Martin-Demézil's Loire Valley* 9 The Tourangeaux gave it the wonderful name of '*le Jardin de France*'. **1973** *Listener* 22 Mar. 372/3 Motifs from this Tourangeau château or that, from Florentine palazzi or Classical temple architecture.

‖**Tourangeois** (turɑ̃ʒwa), *a.* and *sb.* [Fr.] = prec.

1857 C. KINGSLEY *Two Years Ago* III. vi. 155 Balzac's old Tourangeois judge. **1958** C. COCKBURN *Crossing the Line* ii. 37, I took a terrible chance by recommending to him—a Tourangeois—a certain Catalan wine I had discovered.

tourbe, var. TURB *Obs.*, a troop.

tourbillion (tʊə'bɪljən), ‖**tourbillon** (turbijɔ̃). Also 5 **turbilloun**, 8 **-billion**. [a. F. *tourbillon* whirlwind, in OF. *torbeillon* (12th c. in Hatz.-Darm.), *torbillon*, app., from the sense, an irregular derivative of L. *turbo, -inem* 'whirlwind'; though the form seems to connect it with vulgar L. *turbēla, turbella* 'bustle, stir', deriv. of *turba* crowd. See Hatz.-Darm., Littré, and Scheler.]

1. A whirlwind; a whirling storm. Also *fig. rare.* ? *Obs.*

c **1477** CAXTON *Jason* 57 A meruaillous turbilloun of winde roose in the see. **1585** T. WASHINGTON tr. *Nicholay's Voy.* I. xi. 13 A wind called.. vulgarly Tourbillon or whirlewinde. **1751** ELIZA HEYWOOD *Betsy Thoughtless* III. 138 With the more violence those tourbillions of the mind rage for a while, the sooner they subside. **1819** W. TENNANT *Papistry Storm'd* (1827) 57 A scharp-ee'd man, whase sicht was clear, Beneath the stowry tourbillon Micht see [etc.].

2. *transf.* A whirling mass or system; a vortex; a whirl; an eddy, a whirlpool. Also *fig.*

1712 STEELE *Spect.* No. 472 ¶4 Each of them [the fixed stars] is a Sun moving on its own Axis in the Centre of its own Vortex or Turbillion. **1753** CHESTERF. *Lett.* 26 Nov., I am very glad, that you are whirled in that *tourbillon* of pleasures. **1779** H. WALPOLE *Let. to C'tess Ossory* 27 Oct., The *tourbillon* of Ranelagh surrounds you. **1824** SCOTT *St. Ronan's* iii, All things were engaged in the *tourbillon*, of which she formed the pivot and centre. **1891** 'MARK TWAIN' *Lett.* (1917) II. xxxi. 557 We were allowed to go through the wrong arch, which brought us into a tourbillon below which tried to make this old scow stand on its head. **1931** R. GRAVES *To whom Else?* 19 Such portents are not to be wondered at Being tourbillions in Time made By the strong pulling of her bladed mind Through that ever-reluctant element. **1972** J. WAIN in Cox & Dyson *20th-Cent. Mind* I. xi. 374 In the history of any art there are unexpected eddies and tourbillions.

3. A kind of firework which spins as it rises, describing a spiral.

1749 *Descr. Machine for Fireworks* 15 Tourbillons.. 88. **1765** R. JONES *Fireworks* IV. 121 When you fire tourbillons, lay them on a smooth table, with their sticks downwards. **1842** G. FRANCIS *Dict. Arts*, etc., s.v., Fire will issue from four holes; that from the two lower holes will drive the tourbillion into the air, and that from the side holes will spin it round. **1873** E. SPON *Workshop Receipts* Ser. I. 135/1 The tourbillon is a species of firework very ingeniously contrived to represent a spiral column of fire.

4. (See quot.)

1884 F. J. BRITTEN *Watch & Clockm.* 266 *Tourbillon*.. a carriage in which the escapement of a watch is fitted so that it revolves round the fourth wheel. The idea of the tourbillon.. is to get rid of position errors.

tourbine, tourche, tourcheman, tourd(e: see TURBINE, TORCH, TRUCHMAN, TURD.

‖**tour de force** (turdəfɔrs). [F. *tour* turn, feat, *de* of, *force* force, strength.] A feat of strength, power, or skill.

1802 LD. ELGIN *Let.* 18 Feb. in *Paget Papers* (1896) II. 41 To exult over what is styled a *tour de force* of the British Influence here. **1802** M. BERRY *Jrnl.* 16 Mar. (1865) II. 137 Women now dance in the style of men, that is to say, with all the difficult steps and *tours de force* possible. **1805** G. ELLIS *Let.* in Lockhart *Scott* (1837) II. ii. 80 Leyden's breakfast was only a *tour de force* to astonish Ritson. **1818** LADY MORGAN *Fl. Macarthy* II. v. 234 Each should try a tour de force with the other. **1870** RUSKIN *Lect. Art* i. (1875) 15 The execution of the best Artists is always a splendid tour-de-force. **1895** SALMOND *Chr. Doctr. Immort.* VI. iii. 640 It is only by a tour de force that they can be driven that length.

‖**Tour de France** (tur də frɑ̃s). [Fr., lit. 'tour of France'.] The name of an annual cycling stage race on the public roads of France (with some crossing into adjoining countries), now typically over about 4,000 kilometres including mountainous terrain.

1922 *Times* 24 July 7/5 The 'Tour de France' cyclist competition.. ended to-day. **1926** E. HEMINGWAY *Sun also Rises* III. xix. 247 Bicycle road-racing was the only sport in the world, he said. Had I ever followed the Tour de France? **1967** *Guardian* 14 July 1/2 Tommy Simpson, the British cyclist, died early this evening after collapsing during a mountain stage of the Tour de France. **1978** *Listener* 6 July 15/1 These days find Paris in a sort of limbo... There is, it is true, the Tour de France to distract us in the weeks ahead.

‖**tour d'horizon** (tur dɔrizɔ̃). [Fr., lit. 'tour of the horizon'.] An extensive tour. Usu. *fig.*, a broad, general survey.

1952 *Ann. Reg. 1951* 181 General Eisenhower, returning from his European *tour d'horizon*, was able to give Congress ..a report. **1964** *Economist* 5 Sept. 929/1 A fascinating *tour d'horizon* of the main theories. **1979** T. SKYRME *Changing Image Magistracy* xii. 162 Lord Widgery, in the course of a *tour d'horizon* in 1973 said: [etc.]. **1984** *Oxf. Univ. Gaz.* 22 Mar. 584/1, I hope it is not invidious, in an avowedly personal *tour d'horizon*, to single out here the museums for mention.

tourdion: see TORDION.

toure, variant of TOR *a. Obs.*, difficult, tedious; obs. form of TOWER, TWIRE *v.* (to peep).

tourelle (‖turɛl, tʊ'rɛl). Also 4 **torel, -elle, tourel, towrelle, turel, -eile.** [a. F. *tourelle*, dim. of *tour* TOWER.] A turret.

13.. *Cursor M.* 10005 (Cott.) Þe four torels [*v.rr.* turret, trettis, turrettes] on hei er sett. *c* **1330** R. BRUNNE *Chron.* (1810) 178 A darte..com fro þat tureile, þat R[ichard] had doun smyten. **13..** *K. Alis.* 7173 (Bodl. MS.) He haþ taken myne castels, He haþ afelled myne Tourels [*v.r.* torellis]. **13..** *Coer de L.* 1841 A castel..With six stages ful of towrelles, Wel flourished with cornelles. **1840** LOUIS S. COSTELLO *Summer amongst Bocages* II. 218 Two beautiful and exquisitely carved tourelles. **1895** CROCKETT *Men of Moss-Hags* 391 In the little sunlit tourelle at Earlstoun.

tourer ('tʊərə(r)). [f. TOUR *v.* + -ER[1].]

1. a. A touring-car.

1927 *Sunday Pictorial* 28 Aug. 8/4 Two and five-seater tourers will be £495. **1948** G. H. JOHNSTON *Death takes Small Bites* v. 102 Through a great rent in the tourer's flapping hood she could see Cavendish hunched over the wheel. **1978** *Hot Car* June 91/3 The *Munster Koach*, a wild '27 Model T tourer with a gung-ho Cobra engine.

b. A kind of caravan for touring.

1970 *Guardian* 25 Apr. 15/3 There are three basic types of caravans... There are tourers tacked on to the back of family cars, [etc.].

2. One who tours or goes on tour.

1931 *Times Lit. Suppl.* 1 Oct. 746/3 Mürren..tends to breed racers, the other [*sc.* Malója] 'tourers'. **1981** *Beautiful British Columbia* Summer 5 The first thing that bicycle tourers learn about British Columbia is that it is all up and down.

touret, -ette, obs. forms of TORRET, TURRET.

tourette (tʊə'rɛt). [f. TOUR *sb.* + -ETTE.] A little or short tour; an excursion.

1881 HARE *Story of Life* (1900) V. xxii. 332, I made a tourette into Norfolk. **1906** BUMPUS *Cathedr. Eng. & Wales* II. 197 Charming tourettes may be made in one direction to Rushden..in another to Chelveston.

tourify ('tʊərɪfaɪ), *v. colloq.* [f. TOUR *sb.* + -(I)FY.] *intr.* To make a tour; to tour. Hence '**tourifying** *ppl. a.* So **tourifi'cation**, a touring.

1802 R. COUPER *(title)* The Tourifications of Malachi Meldrum, Esq. **1819** MISS MITFORD in L'Estrange *Life* (1870) II. iii. 71 Mr. Hofland is just now setting out on a tourification along the banks of the Seine. **1820** *Ibid.* 116 Dr. Nott..has been tourifying about Normandy. **1825** W. TAYLOR in *Monthly Rev.* CVI. 14 In this tourifying age.

'**touring,** *vbl. sb.* [f. TOUR *v.* + -ING[1].] The action of the verb TOUR.

1818 *Sporting Mag.* II. 225 Some persons call this touring. **1827** SOUTHEY *Lett.* (1856) IV. 76 It was in the summer season of touring and visiting. **1874** BLACKIE *Self-Cult.* 44 The modern habits of travelling and touring can be made to subserve the double end of health and culture.

b. *attrib.*, as ***touring bag, centre, club, ground***; **touring-car**, a motor car designed for touring purposes, with accommodation for passengers and luggage.

1858 CARLYLE *Fredk. Gt.* VII. iii. II. 181 Touring expeditions; which are now..done by steam, without even eye-sight, not to say intelligence. *c* **1878** *Prospectus*, The Bicycle Touring Club, founded at the North of England Meet held at Harrogate on the 5th August, 1878. **1885** *Manch. Exam.* 11 Nov. 3/2 Norway has become such a.. popular touring ground. **1903** *Encycl. Amer.* II. s.v. *Automobile*, Gasoline touring cars. **1908** *Westm. Gaz.* 23 July 4/1 The Grand Prix was in no sense a touring-car race. **1930** *Cycling* 4 July p. iii, Touring bag. **1978** *Exchange & Mart* (South ed.) 20 Apr. 133/3 (Advt.), Motor cycle tank touring bag. **1981** *Nordic Skiing* Jan. 4/2 A group of Appalachian Mountain Club members went for a hike on trails established by a touring center for cross country skiing.

tourism ('tʊərɪz(ə)m). Also ‖**tourisme** (turizm). [f. TOUR *sb.* + -ISM.] The theory and practice of touring; travelling for pleasure. (Orig. usually depreciatory.) Also, the business of attracting tourists and providing for their accommodation and entertainment; the business of operating tours.

1811 *Sporting Mag.* XXXVIII. 251 Sublime Cockey Tourism. **1843** THACKERAY *Irish Sk.-bk.* xvii, No doubt, ere long..the rush of London tourism will come this way [West of Ireland]. **1872** JERNINGHAM tr. *Hübner's Sixtus the Fifth* I. vi. I. 87 Tourism was born in the seventeenth century, and Englishmen were the first to practice it. **1903** C. WHIBLEY *Thackeray* iii. 44 The literature of 'tourism' is ever increasing. **1910** *Blackw. Mag.* Feb. 207/2 He thus inaugurated veritable aerial tourism. **1930** *Time & Tide* 2 May 555 The office of the commissioner of *tourisme* in France..was organized to clip as many petty annoyances as possible from the routine activities of visitors. **1954** H. F. M. PRESCOTT *Jerusalem Journey* v. 127 A mosque, to the Christian pilgrim, was forbidden ground, unless..he were ready to risk martyrdom in the cause of 'tourisme'. **1955** *Times* 24 May 9/3 In addition to the importance of the Kariba project for power and irrigation, emphasis is being laid on its potentialities with regard to fishing and tourism. **1976** J. ARCHER *Not a Penny More, Not a Penny Less* xii. 128 Tourism is the chief source of income for the Principality, and the Monégasques take the welfare of their visitors very seriously. **1981** I. MCEWAN *Comfort of Strangers* i. 12 They dutifully fulfilled the many tasks of tourism the ancient city imposed, visiting its major and minor churches, its museums and palaces, all treasure-packed.

tourist ('tʊərɪst). [f. TOUR *sb.* + -IST.]

1. One who makes a tour or tours; *esp.* one who does this for recreation; one who travels for pleasure or culture, visiting a number of places for their objects of interest, scenery, or the like; *spec.* a member of a touring sports team (usu. *pl.*).

1780 *Ode to Genius of Lakes in North of England* 3 (Advt.), He throws the piece only into the way of *actual tourists*. *c* **1800** PEGGE *Anecd. Eng. Lang.* (1814) 313 A Traveller is now-a-days called a Tour-*ist*. **1803** SYD. SMITH *Wks.* (1850) 34 An agricultural tourist will faithfully detail the average crop per acre. **1824** SCOTT *St. Ronan's* i, It provoked the pencil of every passing tourist. **1855** H. SPENCER *Princ. Psychol.* §66. 246 The Swiss tourist whose inquiries respecting distances are answered in '*stunden*', or hours. **1873** SMILES *Huguenots Fr.* III. i. (1881) 383 Dauphiny.. lying completely out of the track of ordinary tourists. **1975** *Cricketer* May 11/2 On the fourth day Julien joined the feast, hitting a scintillating 101 and helping the tourists to an 87-run first-innings lead.

b. *ellipt.* = *tourist class* (see sense c below).

1936 [see *cabin class* s.v. CABIN *sb.* 8]. **1939** T. S. ELIOT *Family Reunion* 42, I was down in the Tourist..and you could see the corner of the upper deck. **1939** G. GREENE *Lawless Roads* 297 A middle-aged American woman, who should have been travelling tourist. **1976** V. CANNING *Doomsday Carrier* vii. 117 A few men could fly tourist to any country and plague would fly in with them. **1981** J. RATHBONE *Base Case* i. 8 The service in tourist had been appalling.

2. *attrib.* and *Comb.*, as **a.** ***tourist agency, agent, attraction, board, bureau, bus, camp, circuit, country, hotel, industry, office, rendezvous, resort, route, season, shop, tax, ticket, trade, traffic, visa; tourist-crammed, -crowded, -haunted, -laden, -mobbed, -ridden, -trodden,*** adjs.; **tourist cabin,** *(a)* the tourist-class accommodation on a ship; *(b)* a cabin for tourists; **tourist-car**, a railway carriage with special accommodation for tourists; **tourist card**, an identity card substituting for a passport or visa for a short visit to certain countries; **tourist centre**, a place much frequented by tourists; **tourist class**, a low-charge class of passenger accommodation in a ship, aircraft, etc.; also *attrib.*; also adverbially, in the class of accommodation so designated; **tourist court** *U.S.*, a group of self-contained living units with service buildings, for tourists; **tourist flight**, a flight in the tourist class of a passenger aircraft, or in an aircraft which has only tourist-class seating; **tourist guide**, *(a)* = *tour guide* s.v. TOUR *sb.* 12; *(b)* a guide-book which introduces tourists to a region or locality; **tourist park** *U.S.*, a park or camp-site with facilities for overnight campers, etc.; **tourist track**, *(a)* a route from place to place frequented by tourists; *(b) N.Z.*, a track through the bush for walkers; **tourist trap**, *(a)* a type of object sold to tourists at an excessively high price; *(b)* a place where tourists are exploited; **Tourist Trophy**, the name of a trophy awarded to the winner of motor-cycle races held annually on the Isle of Man since 1907; freq. *attrib.*; also *ellipt.* one of these races; usu. abbrev. as *TT* (see T II. 6).

1895 P. HEMINGWAY *Out of Egypt* I. ii. 22 It was no good applying to the hotels or *tourist agencies. **1884** *Queen* 16 Feb. (Advt.), Mr H. Laurence..Oculist Optician... Testimonials from..Thomas Cook, Esq., the well-known *tourist agent, [etc.]. **1918** E. POUND *Pavannes & Divisions* 41, I knew a tourist agent, one whose art is To run such tours. **1867** J. G. FENNELL *(title)* The Rail and the Rod; or, *Tourist-Angler's Guide to Waters and Quarters around London. **1959** A. H. MCLINTOCK *Descr. Atlas N.Z.* p. xix, The..geysers and boiling pools have long been a *tourist attraction. **1978** *Times* 5 Aug. 5/6 Belsen had become almost a tourist attraction for visitors to Germany. [**1948** *Wales* (Tourist & Holidays Board Wales) 3 The Tourist and Holidays Board for Wales and Monmouthshire has pleasure in presenting its second Annual National Holiday Guide.] **1957** JACK & BLAIR *Chambers's Guide to Scotland* 13 An excellent publication (2s. 6d.) of the Scottish *Tourist Board. **1972** 'R. CRAWFORD' *Whip Hand* I. viii. 44 Ballycroom might be as pretty in summer as the Tourist Board said all Kerry was. **1935** G. GREENE *Basement Room* 108, I opened a *tourist bureau. Trips to the London underworld. Limehouse and all that. **1978** J. IRVING *World according to Garp* vi. 122 'I am from the Tourist Bureau,' Father announced. **1964** L. DEIGHTON *Funeral in Berlin* xvii. 105 In Horse Guards Avenue..*tourist buses were parked. **1928** H. CRANE *Let.* Dec. (1965) 332, I have been the only native American in the whole *tourist cabin. The rest being Britishers, Canadians, Australians, [etc.]. **1937** A. HUXLEY *Let.* 7 May (1969) 421 Are now at Del Rio, on the Mexican frontier, in a tourist cabin. **1943** J. S. HUXLEY *TVA* ix. 61 Cove Lake Inn, with its group of tourist cabins, ..has become..an important overnight stopping place for tourists. **1923** *Outlook* Aug. 591/3 The University of Iowa has published a bulletin on the *tourist camps of that State. **1968** C. BURKE *Elephant across Border* vi. 217 Tourist camps with hot and cold running. **1895** J. C. WAIT *Car-Builder's Dict.* 134 **Tourist car*, a car roughly built and furnished for the transportation of men alone, such as bodies of troops, parties of excursionists, emigrants, etc. **1908** *Westm. Gaz.* 9 May 3/1 His [ticket] had the tourist-car ticket appended as a portion of the fare. **1971** *Daily Nation* (Nairobi) 10 Apr. 5/3 Visitors now travelling to several Latin-American countries like Mexico require only a *Tourist Card, which is issued by an airline authorised by the respective government. **1922** W. J. LOCKE *Tale of Triona* xxvi. 292 The hiring garages, in anything like *tourist centres, found their resources strained. **1978** N. FREELING *Night Lords* xxvi. 123 The Loire country..a centre for tourism... Normandy.. another natural tourist centre. **1962** E. SNOW *Other Side of River* (1963) lxxv. 577 The city is after all on the main '*tourist circuit' — Peking-Shanghai-Hankow-Canton. **1936** *New Yorker* 22 Feb. 63/2 In *Tourist Class, too, you find typical American standards. **1939** F. SCOTT FITZGERALD *Let.* Aug. (1964) 107 Only the rich now can do the things you and I once did in Europe—it is a tourist-class world. **1951** *Word Study* Feb. 5/1 People sailed to Europe *cabin class* or *tourist class*. **1952** *Shell Aviation News* No. 164. 4/2 Tourist class fares are being introduced and are going to lead to a doubling of passenger air travel in two years. **1964** MRS. L. B. JOHNSON *White House Diary* 20 Jan. (1970) 55, I left early this morning..tourist class on a commercial airline for New York. **1978** J. A. MICHENER *Chesapeake* xii. 712 At the Sunday meal many of the first-class passengers came down to the tourist class..to urge that Paxmore conduct the services. **1892** *Pall Mall G.* 16 July 2/1 A *tourist country like Switzerland. **1937** *Amer. City* Oct. 115 *(heading)* House trailer and *tourist court regulations. **1979** R. THOMAS *Eighth Dwarf* iii. 27 A cluster of fishing shacks..and the odd tourist court. **1897** MRS. E. L. VOYNICH *Gadfly* ii, The glaring white streets and dusty, *tourist-crammed promenades. **1872** R. BROUGHTON in *Temple Bar* XXXVI. 340 The great glaring Schweizerhof, with its colonnaded, *tourist-crowded porch. **1881** I. E. B. COX *(title)* The Angler's Diary and *Tourist Fisherman's Gazetteer of the Rivers and Lakes of the World. **1959** A. HUXLEY *Let.* 9 Jan. (1969) 861 The *tourist flights are relatively cheap and I will treat you to the ticket. **1969** G. LYALL *Venus with Pistol* xxxii. 207 Maybe old Georgy-boy used to pop over to Germany on the cheap tourist flights. **1924** R. CUMMINS *Sky-High Corral* 15 You cut me down because you leased eighty acres of Hay Fork Meadow to that measly *tourist guide to fence for horse feed. **1925** W. DEEPING *Sorrell & Son* iii. 26 Medlum..kept the book-shop and sold..pretty-pretty art tourist guides. **1977** J. VAN DE WETERING *Japanese Corpse* (1978) xi. 109 He speaks English fairly well. He used to be a tourist guide. **1927** G. ADE et al. *Let.* 4 Mar. (1973) 118 We went to a most attractive *tourist hotel above the town [*sc.* Gibraltar]..surrounded by palms and tropical plants. **1980** R. CONNOLLY *Sunday Kind of Woman* xxix. 194 She was staying in an ordinary tourist hotel just off Gloucester Road. **1938** *United Empire* Sept. 398 With peace achieved, the Government is fostering the *tourist industry. **1977** *Times* 5 Apr. 16/6 The stately homes of England have been..making an important contribution to the tourist industry. **1898** *Edin. Rev.* Oct. 521 The beautiful but now.. hackneyed and *tourist-mobbed route to Chamonix. **1875** *Cooks Continental Timetable* (1973) Mar. p. iv/1 (Advt.), Cook's Waterloo Coach Tickets..may be obtained at any of their *tourist offices. **1977** *Times* 14 May 12/5 The tourist office put us in touch with the guest house association. **1927** F. F. VAN DE WATER *Family Flivvers to Frisco* iii. 52 There is money in well-run *tourist parks. **1977** *Chicago Tribune* 2 Oct. XII. 27/8 (Advt.), Facility has been updated with boat launch, tourist park and public beach nearby. **1887** RUSKIN *Præterita* II. 379 Ruin was inevitable in the valley after it became a *tourist rendezvous. **1906** 'MARK TWAIN' *Autobiogr.* (1924) II. 215 Mr. Richmond had become possessed of Tom Sawyer's cave in the hills three miles from town, and had made a *tourist-resort of it. **1959** A. H. MCLINTOCK *Descr. Atlas N.Z.* 74 New Zealand..has roads of high quality leading to the principal tourist resorts. **1905** E. CANDLER *Unveiling of Lhasa* xiii. 242 Just as one is dragged into a church in some *tourist-ridden land. **1874** *Cooks Continental Timetable* (1973) Mar. p. ii/2 (Advt.), List of the Principal Hotels on the *Tourist Routes in Europe. **1976** BOTHAM & DONNELLY *Valentino* xx. 147 He and Natacha followed the tourist routes to Windsor Castle, the Tower of London, Hampton Court, the theatre. **1884** MRS. F. F. MILLER *Harriet Martineau* viii. 135 Hunters of celebrities were wont, in the *tourist season,..to walk round her garden. **1980** I. MURDOCH *Nuns & Soldiers* ii. 139 Now the tourist season's starting it's better to have someone there, like a caretaker. **1969** 'E. LATHEN' *When in Greece* x. 112, I call Athens... I have business with the *tourist shops there. **1946** P. BOTTOME *Lifeline* vi. 61 It was two years since Mark had seen them, two years of grinding poverty under the [Nazi] *Tourist tax. **1963** *Times* 21 Jan. 5/4 The tourist tax proposal appears to have had its brief, controversial highland fling. **1977** *Times* 22 Aug. 13/2 Proponents of a tourist tax really mean for it to be imposed only on foreign tourists. **1887** M. CORELLI *Thelma* I. xiii. 288 She wad send a' her relations there wi' *tourist tickets, not available for the return journey. **1912** 'SAKI' *Chron. Clovis* 137 Continental travel..away from the great *tourist tracks, was a favoured hobby. **1959** M. SHADBOLT *New Zealanders* 110 Ted.. moved about the country from season to season..sheelite-mining in the Alps, cutting tourist tracks at Milford sound. **1969** *Guardian* 7 July 8/3 The Piazza Navona, right on the Roman tourist track. **1936** *Discovery* Sept. 264/1 That trade which cannot survive without peace—the *tourist trade. **1946** J. S. HUXLEY *Unesco* ii. 53 An unregulated tourist trade in 'curios'. **1979** V. S. NAIPAUL *Bend in River* xv. 254 London is destroying itself for its tourist trade. **1892** KIPLING & BALESTIER *Naulahka* xiii. 156 Some towns might think we had a little *tourist traffic now. **1979** *Tucson Mag.* June 54/1 Some extremists might seek out.. Hell on Earth. But, judging by the light tourist traffic into El Paso, these extremists are a small minority. **1939** G. GREENE *Lawless Roads* iv. 117 Different stations had their different *tourist traps—at Apizaco hideous hand-painted clubs..at Rinconada little grey stone mortars. **1942** E. PAUL *Narrow St.* xxvii. 241 The Oubliette Rouge was a small tourist-trap ..where..the drinks were watered to such an extent that temperance was automatically accomplished. **1967** O. WYND *Walk Softly, Men Praying* x. 157 The village..[was] now a tourist trap almost entirely given over to eating houses and souvenir shops. **1981** C. STORR *Vicky* xiv. 99 Vicky's eye was caught by something in one of the tourist-trap shop windows. **1907** *Motor Cycle* 1 May 358/1 Cash prizes will be awarded to the drivers of machines taking part in the International Auto Cycle *Tourist Trophy Race. **1913** [see *TT* s.v. T II. 6]. **1968** S. E. ELLACOTT *Everyday Things in England 1914–68* V. xii. 174 The Isle of Man..Tourist Trophy races..began in May 1907. **1973** S. JACKMAN *Guns covered with Flowers* iv. 40 The Immigration Officer... issued him with a *Tourist visa.

b. Of a foreign language: of that degree of proficiency required by a tourist or to communicate with a tourist.

1938 E. AMBLER *Cause for Alarm* ii. 30, I have seen six gentlemen before you. Three of them could speak tourist French and insisted that most Italians would understand it. **1953** S. BEDFORD *Sudden View* I. iii. 36, I had a small deposit of past tourist Spanish..equal to ordering the *comida corrida*, the table d'hôte luncheon. **1975** A. WORBOYS *Lion of Delos* ii. 23 Most of the [Greek] people you will come across talk Tourist English.

Hence (mostly *nonce-wds.*) **'tourist** *v. intr.*, to travel for pleasure, as a tourist; **'touristdom**, the realm or collective body of tourists; **'touristing**, the practice or habit of touring; **'touristry** = *touristdom* or *touristing*; **'touristship**, the quality or position of a tourist. Also **'touristy** *a.*, *colloq.*, characteristic of the tourist; also, designed for or likely to appeal to tourists, consisting of tourists, frequented by tourists; freq. with derog. connotation, superficial, trashy.

1953 E. M. FORSTER *Hill of Devi* 27, I continued my tour —I was *touristing—and I did not expect to see my delightful host again. **1971** K. WHEELER *Epitaph for Mr. Wynn* xxviii. 364 He wasn't just touristing around. **1888** *Pall Mall G.* 28 Aug. 13/2 Ere those Circe's sties, the Club-huts, harboured *touristdom in flocks. **1883** A. STEWART *Nether Lochaber* xxxviii. 233 Never before were all the conveniences for '*touristing' so perfect. **1878** STEVENSON *Inland Voy.* 32 All the ruck and rabble of British *touristry. **1883** —— *Silverado Sq.* 27 It was a pure little isle of touristry among these solitary hills. **1894** *Speaker* 7 Apr. 390/2 A Venice vulgarised by Cook's touristry. **1849** *Fraser's Mag.* XL. 375 He was rather a tourist than a traveller, and this *touristship was the worse for his scientific crotchets. **1906** *Athenæum* 8 Sept. 278/3 The letterpress..is..slight, sketchy, '*touristy', but genial. **1937** A. CHRISTIE *Death on Nile* vi. 86 This trip..feels somehow, so much less touristy —as though we were really going into the heart of Egypt. **1958** *Listener* 25 Sept. 454/1 Its rushing rivers leaping with salmon; its canyons; its glaciers;..steam from thermal springs..all these are perhaps the 'touristy' things. **1961** I. FLEMING *Thunderball* xii. 125 A tepid, touristy breakfast on his balcony. **1967** [see STRIP *sb.*[2] 1 h.] **1969** E. MCGIRR *Entry of Death* iii. 59 There's a little 'ostelry wot only the helite know of. None of yer touristy trash. **1973** *Daily Tel.* (Colour Suppl.) 16 Feb. 31/3 They've turned out so many phoney things—touristy things about the Civil War, say.

touristic (tʊə'rɪstɪk), *a.* [f. TOURIST + -IC.] Of or pertaining to tourists or touring.

1848 *Blackw. Mag.* LXIV. 373 The touristic hordes, who paddled up and down the well-known old banks. **1865** LD. STRANGFORD in *Lett. & Papers* (1878) 98 There is no such thing as a record of touristic journeying in Crete. **1894** *Athenæum* 26 May 672 It has importance from another than the touristic point of view.

So **tou'ristical** *a.*, in same sense. **tou'ristically** *adv.*, from the point of view of a tourist; as regards tourists or tourism.

1863 W. CORY *Lett. & Jrnls.* (1897) 98 A long quiet walk, only one touristical carriage all the way. **1893** *Sat. Rev.* 18 Feb. 189/3 His discursive record is chiefly 'touristical'. **1928** *Sunday Dispatch* 16 Dec. 4/2 Asked to show a young French boy of fifteen the 'sights' of London... But he had one ambition, touristically, and one only. **1959** *Encounter* May 30/2 The girls..go anywhere, do anything sexually or touristically interesting. County Dublin, Positano, Ibiza, Tangier. **1971** *Daily Tel.* 10 Sept. 14/4 Replicas of the castle could also be erected not only in London but at touristically under-privileged places like Leeds and Merthyr Tydfil. **1983** *Which?* Nov. 515/1 The qualities I look for in a country house hotel—a tranquil location in a touristically rewarding area, [etc.].

tourize ('tʊəraɪz), *v.* [f. TOUR *sb.* + -IZE.] *intr.* To make a tour, to go touring.

1837 SIR J. PAGET *Let.* 22 Mar., in *Mem.* v. 102, I think, if we are spared to tourize together, our first trip shall be to Fontainebleau. **1864** *Macm. Mag.* Apr. 521 Let him tourise out of the beaten track.

tourmaline ('tʊəməlɪn, -iːn). *Min.* Also **tour-, turmalin, -ine, (tormaline).** [= F. *tourmaline* (1771 in *Dict. Trev.*), Ger. *turmalin* (1707, Garmann), Du. *toermalijn* (1778), It., Sp. *turmalina*; all ultimately f. Sinhalese *tòramalli*, according to Clough 'a general name for the cornelian'. The origin of the European final *-n(e* is obscure: cf. *mandarin, talapoin*, etc. The better (18th c.) English spelling was *tour-, turmalin*; the spelling *-ine* is in imitation of French, in which the *e* merely supports the *n.*]

a. A brittle pyro-electric mineral, occurring in crystals, also massive, compact, and columnar, originally obtained from Ceylon (Sri Lanka); a complex silicoborate with a vitreous lustre, usually black or blackish and opaque (SCHORL), but also blue (INDICOLITE), red (RUBELLITE), green, or colourless, and in various rich transparent or semi-transparent shades, known as ***precious tourmaline***, and much used as a gem. Also formerly called, from its electrical properties, *ash-drawer*, Du. *aschentrecker*, Ger. *aschenzieher*, F. *tire-cendre*.

1759 B. WILSON in *Phil. Trans.* LI. I. 308, I have the pleasure to communicate to you some experiments made upon the Tourmalin, or Ashstone. **1794** SULLIVAN *View Nat.* I. 440 The tourmaline is a variety of the schoerl. **1798** EDGEWORTH *Pract. Educ.* (1811) II. 294 A small electrical stone called tourmalin. **1799** KIRWAN *Geol. Ess.* 121 All.. lose some part of their weight when exposed to a strong heat ..; turmaline loses 15 per cent. **1812** SIR H. DAVY *Chem. Philos.* 131 There is a stone..called tourmaline, which is sometimes crystallized as a nine-sided prism, terminated by a three-sided and a six-sided pyramid. **1825** HEBER *Jrnl.* xxvii. (ed. 2) 189 The topaz, ruby, tormaline, diamond, and various others. **1853** TH. ROSS *Humboldt's Trav.* III. xxxii. 382 The granite is traversed by..veins..abounding with rock-crystal, black tourmalin, and pyrites. **1866** RUSKIN *Eth. Dust* ix. 179 This black thing,..one of the prettiest of the very few pretty black things in the world, is called 'Tourmaline'. **1888** RUTLEY *Rock-Forming Min.* 38 A plate of tourmaline cut parallel to the principal axis.

b. With *a* and *pl.* A specimen or gem of this mineral; also a transparent plate of tourmaline cut parallel to the vertical crystal axis, used in polariscopes, etc.

1816 P. CLEAVELAND *Min.* 261 When a Tourmaline is viewed perpendicularly to the sides of the prism, it is more or less transparent, but, if observed in the direction of the axis, it is opaque. **1843–54** PEREIRA *Pol. Light* (ed. 2) 211 If the two tourmalines be crossed the rays are suppressed—if they coincide the rays are transmitted. **1890** *Academy* 12 Apr. 252/1 It [a bracelet] consists of a broad and heavy band of Californian gold, set with two large tourmalines.

c. (See quot. 1957.)

1957 J. H. F. STEVENSON *Mink in Britain* (ed. 2) 101 *Tourmaline*, EMBA [*sc.* Mutation Mink Breeders of America] brand name for high quality natural pale beige mutation mink skins. **1959** *Vogue* 1 Oct. 188/3 You'd see the all-important minks..from the very dark ranch mink through the lighter, lovely Emba mutations to the pales, which include a pearly blondness, 'Tourmaline'. **1959** *Official Gaz.* (U.S. Patent Office) 27 Oct. TM 127 Mutation Mink Breeders Association... Tourmaline. For Mink Fur Pelts. First use Dec. 11, 1956. **1965** P. O'DONNELL *Modesty Blaise* iii. 32 A Dior-designed mink coat in emba tourmaline.

d. *attrib.* and *Comb.*, as ***tourmaline crystal, granite, mink, pendant***; **tourmaline pincette, tongs**, a simple polariscope, consisting of tongs having a plate of tourmaline mounted in each grasping jaw; **tourmaline-rock, -schist**: see quots. 1882.

1843–54 PEREIRA *Pol. Light* (ed. 2) 213 The two sets of rays..successively pass through the tourmaline analyzing plate. **1879** RUTLEY *Stud. Rocks* x. 138 The terminations of tourmaline crystals are frequently composed of a great number of faces. **1882** GEIKIE *Text-bk. Geol.* (1885) 73 Tourmaline..with quartz forms tourmaline-rock. *Ibid.* 131 Tourmaline-schist.., a blackish, finely granular, quartzose rock with abundant granules and needles of black tourmaline. **1888** RUTLEY *Rock-Forming Min.* 59 The tourmaline pincette, or tongs. **1959** *Vogue* Dec. 25 (Advt.), Tourmaline mink coat. **1973** 'R. MACDONALD' *Sleeping Beauty* x. 51 Elizabeth Somerville came to the front door in a tourmaline mink which almost matched her blonde head.

Hence **tourma'linic** *a.*, pertaining to, of the nature of, or consisting of tourmaline; **'tourmaliˌnite** *Min.*, tourmaline.

1879 DANA *Man. Geol.* (ed. 3) 70 *Tourmalinic*, containing tourmaline. **1896** CHESTER *Dict. Names Min.*, *Tourmalinite*, variant of tourmaline.

'tourmaliˌnize, *v.* [f. TOURMALINE + -IZE.] *trans.* To impregnate or charge with tourmaline. Hence **'tourmalinized** *ppl. a.*, **'tourmalinizing** *vbl. sb.*; **ˌtourmalini'zation**, the process or state of being tourmalinized.

1899 *Bull. Geol. Soc. Amer.* X. 23 As the vein widens the tourmalinizing of the schist becomes less and less marked. *Ibid.*, Fragments of this tourmalinized schist are thickly strewn along both sides of the road. *Ibid.* 24 A more intense tourmalinization is to be noticed in the immediate vicinity of the veins. *Ibid.* 26 The hornfels..has been tourmalinized on both sides of the vein. **1908** *Amer. Jrnl. Sc.* Apr. 323 Along the margin..the granite is often strongly tourmalinized. **1946** *Geol. Survey Nigeria Bull.* No. 17. 56 The altered country-rock on the hanging-wall has been recrystallized and tourmalinized to form a rock composed of brown biotite ..and tourmaline. **1982** D. S. SUTHERLAND *Igneous Rocks of Brit. Isles* xxiii. 318/2 The second stage of tourmalinization followed the second stage of greisening, using the same channels. *Ibid.* 524/1 The tourmalinized varieties of the granitic rocks are of such striking appearance that they have given rise to several special names.

tourment, etc., obs. form of TORMENT, etc.

‖**tourmente** (turmɑ̃t). [Fr.: see TORMENT *sb.*] A whirling storm or eddy (of snow): cf. TORMENT *sb.* 5.

[**1843** J. D. FORBES *Trav. through Alps* 187 The strong west wind..raises the snow into fearful eddies, called *tourmentes* in the French.] **1847** G. B. CHEEVER *Wand. Pilgr.* xii. 90 The fury of these tourmentes is inconceivable. **1909** *Blackw. Mag.* Sept. 341/1, I reached it..in a more than usually objectionable tourmente of snow. **1924** J. BUCHAN *Three Hostages* xii. 177, I could see that it was blowing hard, for my glass showed me little *tourmentes* of snow. **1928** *Blackw. Mag.* May 601/1 Above the howl of the *tourmente* came the crash of falling rocks.

tourn (tʊən). *Eng. Hist.* Also 6–7 **tourne, turne,** 6–8 **torn,** 6–9 **turn,** 7–8 **torne.** [a. Anglo-Fr. *tourn*, TURN, n. of action f. *tourner* to turn, go round; in med.L. *turnus*. In the ordinary senses the sb. and vb. have become *turn*; but in this historical sense the Anglo-French spelling is usually retained, though Pollock and Maitland prefer to call it 'the sheriff's *turn*'.]

The tour, turn, or circuit formerly made by the sheriff of a county twice in the year, in which he presided at the hundred-court in each hundred of the county; the great court leet of the county, held by him on these occasions; it was a court of record.

[**1217** *Magna Carta, 2nd Reissue* c. 42 Nec aliquis vicecomes vel baillivus suus faciat turnum suum per hundretum nisi bis in anno,..semel post Pascha et iterum post festum Sancti Michaelis. **1292** BRITTON I. xix. §3 Sutes dues a noster Counté, et a nos hundrez, et a nos maners, et a tourns de noster viscounte. *Ibid.* xxx. §1 Les..pletz sount apelez tourns de viscounte; qi deus foiz par an les deit tener par mi chescun hundred de soen counté.] **1432** *Rolls of Parlt.* IV. 403/1 By cause the Decennare and Decennes.. comen noght hole and full unto the Sherrefes tourn. **1531** *Dial. on Laws Eng.* I. vii. 16 In euery shyre..there is a courte ..that is called the Shyryffes torne. **1542–6** in *14th Rep. Hist. MSS. Comm.* App. IX. 272 Bobbingworth Village come to the Turne aforesaid by iiii men, Tennants by coppie, and the Reeve of the village there. **1608** BACON *Office Constables* etc., *Sheriffs*, [The sheriff] hath authority to hold two several courts of distinct natures: the one called the tourne, because he keepeth his turn and circuit about the shire. **1765** BLACKSTONE *Comm.* I. 368 The sheriff's tourn, which is the court-leet of the county. **1875** STUBBS *Const. Hist.* II. xiv. 27 The 42nd article orders..the sheriff's tourn, which now first appears in the charters, [to be held] twice a year. **1895** POLLOCK & MAITLAND *Hist. Eng. Law* I. 515 Twice a year the sheriff makes a tour or turn (*turnus vicecomitis*) through all the hundreds of the country. He holds each of the hundred courts, and on these occasions many persons besides the ordinary suitors ought to be present.

tourn, tournado, obs. ff. TURN, TORNADO.

Tournai ('tʊəneɪ). Also **Tournay.** [F. *Tournai, Tournay* (Flem. *Doornik*), name of a town in Belgium. Cf. DORNICK[1].] **a.** See quot.

1858 SIMMONDS *Dict. Trade*, *Tournay*, a printed worsted material used for furniture. Hence in mod. Dicts.

b. Used *attrib.* and *absol.* to designate products of the town, *esp.* the porcelain manufactured there from 1751.

1873 C. SCHREIBER *Jrnl.* (1911) I. 207 He..prides himself upon his Tournai. **1874** *Ibid.* 292 One Tournai plate, gold marked. **1907** C. H. WYLDE *How to collect Continental China* 119 Birds..had always been a favourite subject as a *motif* of decoration on Tournay porcelain. **1959** *Listener* 22 Jan. 179/1 The more familiar tombstone of a bishop in Tournai 'marble'. **1980** *Times* 5 Feb. 16/5 A Tournai shaped oval dish of about 1765..made £11,000.

Tournaisian (tʊə'neɪzɪən), *a. Geol.* [ad. Fr. *tournaisien* of Tournai: see prec., -IAN.] Of, pertaining to, or designating the lower of the two divisions of the Lower Carboniferous (Dinantian) in Europe. Also *absol.*

1910 *Rep. Brit. Assoc. Adv. Sci. 1909* 187 A minute exposition of the coral sequence in the Tournaisian. *Ibid.*, The Tournaisian Beds of this fine coast section. **1923** L. D. STAMP *Introd. Stratigr.* ix. 129 The lower three zones constitute the Tournaisian or Lower Carboniferous Limestone, the upper zones the Visean or Upper Carboniferous Limestone. **1969** BENNISON & WRIGHT *Geol. Hist. Brit. Isles* ix. 187 The Tournaisian is..exposed in a continuous section in the gorge of the River Avon. *Ibid.* 205 The Upper Old Red Sandstone may be in part of Tournaisian age.

tournament ('tʊənəmənt), *sb.* Forms: α. 3 **tornei-,** 3–5 **torne-,** 4–7 **tornea-,** 5–7 **tornament.** β. 3–5 **turne-,** 4–8 **turna-,** 5–6 **turnei-, turney-,** 7 **turneament.** γ. (5 **tournoy-**), 5–7 **tourne-,** 7 **tournea-,** 6– **tournament.** (Also 4–6 **-mente,** *pl.* 3–5 **-mens.**) [a. OF. *torneiement* (*Enéas, c* 1150), *torney-, tornee-, torniement*; central and later OF. *tornoie-, tornoiment, tournoie-, tournoyement*; also *turnoie-, turneie-, turneement*, f. *tourneier, -oier*, etc., TOURNEY *v.*: see -MENT. Cf. Pr. *torneiament*, It. *tornia-*, †*torneamento*; the later Eng. spellings *tornea-, turna-* were app. due to the influence of med.L.

Cf. med.L. *torneamentum* (fr. Fr.), 1157 in Reims Synod, Canon iv, and 1179 in Lateran Council, Can. xx 'detestabiles illas nundinas vel ferias, quas vulgo torneamenta vocant'.]

1. a. Originally, A martial sport or exercise of the middle ages, in which a number of combatants, mounted and in armour, and divided into two parties, fought with blunted weapons and under certain restrictions, for the prize of valour; later, A meeting at an appointed time and place for knightly sports and exercises.

According to Roger of Hoveden III. 268, first introduced into England by Richard I.

α. **1297** R. GLOUC. (Rolls) 2896 In ioustes & in tornemens. *Ibid.* 11041 Sir edward..hauntede torneimens [*v.r.* (C.) turnemens] with wel noble route. **13..** *Sir Beues* (A.) 3766 þai ben come for a tornement þat is cride for a maide faire. *c* **1440** *Promp. Parv.* 497/1 Torneament, *torneamentum.* **1612** SELDEN *Illustr. Drayton's Poly-olb.* iv. 70 Torneaments and jousts were their exercises.

β. *a* **1225** *Ancr. R.* 390 He dude him ine turnement, & hefde uor his leofmonnes luue, his schelde ine uihte. **13..** *Guy Warw.* (A.) 821 He schal bring to þe turment [*v.r.* turnement] þat day (Wele is him þat it winne may) A gerfauk þat is milke white. *Ibid.* 829 Who so winneþ þe turnament al Bi aiþer half, þe priis have schal. *c* **1450** *Merlin* ix. 133 After they be-gonne a turnemente, and departed hem in two partyes. **1590** SPENSER *F.Q.* I. v. 1 That doughtie turnament. **1596** *Ibid.* IV. iv. 12 Against the Turneiment. *Ibid.* 13 Unto the place of Turneyment. *a* **1700** DRYDEN *Theodore & Hon.* 18 He..At tilts and turnaments obtained the prize, But found no favour in his lady's eyes.

γ. **1470–85** MALORY *Arthur* I. v. 41 Vpon newe yeersday the barons lete maake a Iustes and a tournement. *c* **1483** CAXTON *Dialogues* 25/1 For suche ladies Ben the tournemens. **1485** —— *Paris & V.* 11 Ioustes and tournoyment doon in his cyte of vyenne. **1552** HULOET, Tournamente or iuste. **1656** BLOUNT *Glossogr.* (1674), *Tournement*, or *Tourneament.* **1756–7** tr. *Keysler's Trav.* (1760) IV. 291 A cuirass used by the elector Augustus in tournaments. **1801** STRUTT *Sports & Past.* III. i. 103 Every kind of military combat made in conformity to certain rules ..was anciently called a tournament. **1818** HALLAM *Mid. Ages* ix. II. (1819) III. 502 Tournaments..may be considered to have arisen about the middle of the eleventh century; for..the name of tournaments, and the laws that regulated them, cannot be traced any higher. **1841** JAMES *Brigand* i, Henry the Second [of France]..closed his career in the last tournament [1559] which Europe was destined to witness. **1888** *Encycl. Brit.* XXIII. 489/1 Tournaments and jousts differed from one another principally in the circumstance that in the first several combatants on each side were engaged.., and in the second the contention was between two combatants only.

b. A modern imitation of the mediæval pastime.

1701 *Lond. Gaz.* No. 3734/2 The Imperial Court continues at the Palace at Favorita, where they were entertained yesterday with a Turnament. **1839** LD. COCKBURN *Jrnl.* (1874) I. 239 In August last the display called the *Tournament* took place at Eglinton Castle.

c. Applied to the Olympic and other ancient games or contests.

1387 TREVISA *Higden* (Rolls) I. 11 After þe strif, ioustes, and turnementis of Olympy. *Ibid.* II. 381 Theseus..slowȝ Minotaurus in þe tornemente [*in agone interemit*]. **1610** HOLLAND *Camden's Brit.* (1637) 703 Severus..His body was..committed to the flames, honoured with Justs and Turneaments of his souldiers and his owne sonnes. **1866** FELTON *Anc. & Mod. Gr.* II. v. 358 They..utterly disappeared from the face of Hellas, with their language, their manners, their jousts and tournaments.

2. *fig.* An encounter or trial of strength.

1638 BP. REYNOLDS *Peace Ch.* 31 Happy..the Church of God, when curious novelties, and as it were Tourneaments in sacred things are esteemed prophane. **1659** *Gentl. Calling* (1696) 118 They keep, as it were, solemn Justs and Turnaments of Debauchery. **1901** *Empire Rev.* I. 370 When this dogmatic tournament has spent its force. **1902** R. BAGOT *Donna Diana* xx, In the rose-gardens below, the nightingales were holding a tournament of song.

3. *transf.* A contest in any game of skill in which a number of competitors play a series of selective games, e.g. a *chess* or *lawn tennis tournament.*

military or ***naval tournament***, an athletic meeting at which there are a large proportion of contests especially adapted for soldiers or sailors.

1761 *Ann. Reg.* 152 A naval tournament, or race upon the waters, resembling those practised at Venice in the carnival season. **1852** H. STAUNTON (*title*) The Chess Tournament. A collection of the games played at this celebrated assemblage. **1869** in J. D. Heath *Croquet-Player* (1874) 95 N.C.C. Open tournament at Highgate (6 inch hoops). **1872** R. C. A. PRIOR *Croquet.* 55 The Gardener's Chronicle announced last year a 'Potato Tournament'. **1885** *Sat. Rev.* 24 Jan. 113 If..the old Counties Chess Association..holds its tournaments in the provinces. **1888** *Daily News* 15 Sept. 3/5 Lawn Tennis. The Essex Open Tournament was resumed yesterday at the Connaught Grounds.

4. *Math.* A set of points each of which is joined to every other point by a line having a direction. Also ***tournament graph.***

1959 F. HARARY in *Management Sci.* V. 398 Consider a tournament in which there are *n* players, every pair of players play each other once, and none of the games ends in a draw. For brevity let us call the resulting digraph *D* itself a tournament. **1972** R. J. WILSON *Introd. Graph Theory* vii. 108 Let *T* be a tournament on *n* + 1 vertices, and let *T'* be the tournament on *n* vertices obtained by removing from *T* a vertex *v* and every arc incident to *v*. **1980** *Sci. Amer.* Mar. 18/3 Tournament graphs provide a convenient means of modeling a person's pairwise preferences for any set of choices, such as brands of coffee or candidates in an election.

5. *attrib.*

1848 THACKERAY *Van. Fair* lii, It had been a Cistercian Convent in old days, when the Smithfield, which is contiguous to it, was a tournament ground. **1902** *Munsey's Mag.* XXVI. 476/2 When the skater has become proficient in all of them, he is ready to proceed to the simpler combinations of the tournament figures.

Hence **'tournament** *v.* (*nonce-wd.*), *intr.* to ride as in a tournament, to tilt; **tourna'mental** *a.*, of or pertaining to a tournament; † **ˌtournamen'teer**, *Obs. rare*, a combatant at tournaments.

1884 J. SHARMAN *Hist. Swearing* i. 10 They bestrode chairs and benches,..and *tournamented about the room. **1801** STRUTT *Sports & Past,* III. i. 127 When the grand *tournamental conflict was finished. **1896** *Daily News* 28 May 3/1 The rumour..that there was tournamental antagonism between the Navy and Army. **1737** OZELL *Rabelais* II. 221 Great Tilters and *Turnamenteers.

tournasin ('tʊənəsɪn). [a. F. *tournasin, tournassin* (Littré), f. *tournaser, -nasser* to turn (pottery) on the wheel, derivative of *tourner* to TURN.] A knife or spatula used to remove excess of slip from decorated pottery when partially dried.

1839 URE *Dict. Arts*, etc. 1017 The excess of the paste is removed by an instrument called a *tournasin*, till the ornamental figure produced by the stamp be laid bare. **1874** KNIGHT *Dict. Mech.* 308/1 Excess of slip is removed, after a certain amount of drying, by a spatula or knife, known as a *tournasin.*

tournay, obs. form of TOURNEY.

Tournay, var. TOURNAI.

tourne, obs. form of TOURN, TURN.

‖**tourné** ('tʊəneɪ), *a. Her.* [Fr., pa. pple. of *tourner* to turn.] = REGARDANT A. 2.

1725 COATS *Dict. Her.*, *Tourné* is used by French Heralds for what we call Regardant, that is, looking back, or behind. **1882** in OGILVIE; and in later Dicts.

‖**tournedos** (turnədo, 'tʊənədəʊ). *Gastronomy.* [Fr., f. *tourner* to turn + *dos* back: acc. to Littré and Robert, so called because the dish is traditionally not placed on the table, but is passed behind the backs of the guests (see quots. for this and another account).] A fillet steak of beef with a surrounding strip of fat; ***tournedos Rossini***, such a fillet served with a *croûton* and pâté, and a Madeira sauce.

1877 E. S. DALLAS *Kettner's Bk. of Table* 460 A tournedos is a thin collop, which..is done on one side before the cook has had time to turn round. **1937** G. FRANKAU *More of Us* v. 53 Italy! Twice ten thousand special pleaders Present your case—and tournedos Rossini, Whose rich appeal 'spite facial controlling Still sets these eyes in a fine frenzy rolling. **1958** *Times* 29 Nov. 7/6 Tucking into scampi and tournedos. **1966** P. V. PRICE *France: Food & Wine Guide* 124 About [1869]..the word tournedos came into use... Rossini was dining at the Café Anglais and..suggested an alternative method of cutting and preparing the steak... The horrified *maître d'hotel* announced that he could not..present a dish that was..unpresentable. 'Very well,' said Rossini, 'then don't let us see you do it—I'll turn my back' (*tourne le dos*). **1979** C. CURZON *Leaven of Malice* xi. 126 *Tournedos Rossini* with salad and a reasonable Valpolicella.

tournee ('tʊənɪ), ‖**tournée** (turne). [a. F. *tournée* round.] A round, circuit, tour.

1794 B. WYNNE *Diary* 8 Oct. (1952) xiii. 163 We did today what is called the *Tournee* and which is visits to all the ministers and *Grand* Families. **1834** W. F. TOLMIE *Jrnls.* (1963) 298 Made an unsuccessful tournee in the S. plain in quest of deer. **1961** *Times* 13 Oct. 10/5 When Louis Armstrong and Dave Brubeck come to Germany their tournées take them to sold-out concert halls.

tournell, var. TURNEL *Obs.*, ring, terret.

‖**tournelle** (turnɛl). *Obs.* Forms: 4, 6 tornel, 6 tornelle, 6–7 tournel, 7 tornil, tournell, 6–8 tournelle; also 5 turnelle. [a. OF. *tornele*, F. *tournelle*, according to Hatz.-Darm. deriv. of *tour* TOWER, influenced by *tourner* to turn.] A small tower; a turret. With capital T, name in the 16–18th c. of the building in Paris in which the criminal court sat; hence applied to this court, its prison, and other courts.

a **1400** *Siege of Troy* 1015 in *Archiv neu. Spr.* LXXII. 33 Vche tornel of þe toun þey gonne assaile. **1532** *Yatton Churchw. Acc.* (Som. Rec. Soc.) 147 Payd to R. Grenefelde for poyntyng a tornelle of yᵉ cherche ijˢ. viijᵈ. **1586** T. B. *La Primaud. Fr. Acad.* (1589) 646 There also is the Tournel, or place where criminall actions are judged, and the Treasure-Chamber for causes touching the Kings revenues. **1611** SPEED *Hist. Gt. Brit.* IX. xvi. §29 All runne to the Bastile. The Tournels are presently seized, and all approaches vnto the Bastile are soone wonne. **1689** tr. *Jurieu's Past. Lett.* ii. 43, I was carried to the Tournel, where they put the persons condemned to the Gallies. **1771** *Ann. Reg.* 102 Eleven members of the great council, who composed part of the great chamber and the Tournelle of the new parliament, have resigned their places.

tournement, tourner, -erie, tournesoll, -soule, tournsol, obs. ff. TOURNAMENT, TORMENT, TURNER, -ERY, TURNSOLE.

tournette (tʊə'nɛt). *Archæol.* [a. Fr., f. *tourner* to turn.] A rotating disc resembling a potter's wheel. Also *attrib.*

1927 PEAKE & FLEURE *Peasants & Potters* iv. 47 The pots were made on a tournette, a slow wheel turned by hand. **1952** V. G. CHILDE *New Light on Most Anc. East* xi. 235 Centrally perforated stone discs some 20 cm. in diameter have been called 'tournettes'. **1964** H. HODGES *Artifacts* i. 27 Ring or coil-built pots are generally flat-bottomed since they are frequently formed on a turn-table, or tournette. **1977** *Antiquaries Jrnl.* LVII. 317 The upper fills of such pits can often be seen as discarded rubbish relating to the use of clay: pot sherds,..loom-weight, and tournette fragments.

tourney ('tʊənɪ, 'tɜːnɪ), *sb.*[1] Forms: α. 4 **torneie, -aie,** 5 **-eye, -oye,** 5–6 **-ey, -oy,** 6 **-ay.** β. 4–7 **turnay,** 4–8 **-ey, -y,** 6 **-ei(e, -oye, -oi.** γ. 4 **tourneie,** 4–9 **-ay,** 5 **-eye, -oy,** 6 **-ai,** 6–7 **-oi,** 4– **tourney.** [ME. a. OF. *tornei* (*Enéas, c* 1150), *turnei, tornai, tournay*, F. *tournoi*, vbl. sb. f. *tornei-er*, TOURNEY *v.* So Prov. *tornei*, It., Sp., Pg. *torneo.*]

1. a. = TOURNAMENT 1.

α. *c* **1374** CHAUCER *Troylus* IV. 1641 (1669) In werre or torney [*v.r.* tournay] Marcial. *c* **1440** LOVELICH *Merlin* 9614 There departed the Torneye anon. *c* **1483** CAXTON *Dialogues* 45/27 Reyner the squyer Is atte Justes At the tornoye. *a* **1533** LD. BERNERS *Huon* xxi. 62, I..hauntyd the iustes & tornoys. *a* **1548** HALL *Chron., Edw. IV* 197b, These ij valeant persones coped together in the tornay. **1579** FENTON *Guicciard.* III. (1599) 107 The King..amused the time about iustes, torneys, and other pleasures of Court.

β. **13..** *K. Alis.* 141 Ladies loven solas, and play · Swaynes, justes; knyghtis, turnay [*Bodl. MS.* tournay]. **1516** *St. Bridget* in *Myrr. our Ladye* p. lv, In turneys and in vanytes of the worlde. **1550** J. COKE *Eng. & Fr. Heralds* §125 (1877) 95 Assaultes, turnois, scremuses and syeges. **1556** *Chron. Gr. Friars* 27 The kynge helde ryall justes, turnayes, & bankettes six dayes after. **1558** in Feuillerat *Revels Q. Eliz.* (1908) 70 The apparell & Trappers.. appointed..for his Justes & Turneis. **1585** T. WASHINGTON tr. *Nicholay's Voy.* IV. xxvii. 146 All sortes of turnoyes and cumbates. **1632** MILTON *Penseroso* 118 Great Bards..have sung, Of Turneys and of Trophies hung. **1742** COLLINS *Ode Poet. Char.* 7 The magic Girdle..At solemn Turney hung on high.

γ. **13..** *Seuyn Sag.* 719 In a mede was this tourney Of men that were of gret noblai. **1523** LD. BERNERS *Froiss.* I. xix. 27 There was also great iustes, tourneys, daunsyng, carolyng, and great feastis euery day. **1552** HULOET, Tournay, *vide in* turnay. **1556** *Aurelie & Isab.* (1608) E iv, She can not keape hir from the danses, jostes, tournois. **1569** STOCKER tr. *Diod. Sic.* III. xviii. 134 For the sportes, tournais, and diuerse other pastimes. **1625** BACON *Ess., Masques & Triumphs* (Arb.) 540 For Iusts, and Tourneys. **1820** W. IRVING *Sketch Bk.* I. 193 The suit of armour..embellished as if to figure in the tournay. **1868** FREEMAN *Norm. Conq.* (1877) II. viii. 265 Not justing with his lance as in a mimic tourney.

fig. **1878** E. JENKINS *Haverholme* 33 A few days' trial, a tournay of keen lawyers..and the poor man walked out of court beat.

†**b.** Applied to ancient games; = TOURNAMENT 1 c. *Obs.*

1485 CAXTON *Trevisa's Higden* II. xxxii. (1527) 87b, There the Iliens haue theyr tornamentes from iiij yere to iiij yere, so that iiij yere was bytwene the tornoyes. **1586** T. B. *La Primaud. Fr. Acad.* I. (1594) 103 Cæsar the first Romane emperor..not sparing any cost upon plaies, turneies, feastes, largesses, and other baits to curry favour. **1600** HOLLAND *Livy* XXIX. xxii. 726 The land souldiours, running and charging one another at turney. **1601** —— *Pliny* VIII. ii. I. 192 In the late solemnitie of tournois & sword-fight at the sharpe, which Germanicus Cæsar exhibited to gratifie the people.

c. = TOURNAMENT *sb.* 3.

1890 J. RAYNER *Chess Problems* 15 If..one should creep into a problem deemed by him..to be fit for a tourney, it will be useful..to know that the German school of problematists is less puritanical than the English. *Ibid.* 28 In solution and problem tourneys..it is necessary to throw aside all conventionalities. **1950** *Sun* (Baltimore) 20 June 21/6 It was really rather astonishing to watch this youth club his way through the tourney to a sturdy victory..in a 36-hole grind. **1951** *Sport* 30 Mar.–5 Apr. 10/2 J. Parsons..outscored Billy McHale, newly-crowned Northern Counties A.B.A. champion, in the miners' divisional tourney. **1971** *Rand Daily Mail* 4 Sept. 2/9 The Government's new sports policy ..has guaranteed a welcome for all teams for next year's Federation Cup tennis tourney. **1976** *Star* (Sheffield) 3 Dec. 28/8 Last week with the results boosted by the netball tourney..there were 140 results in the Hotline columns.

2. *attrib.* and *Comb.*, as ***tourney-day, -fall, -field, -fight, -prize***; †**tourney-head**, ? a blunt spearhead used in a tournament; **tourney-helm**, a helmet worn in tournaments, with light open bars across the face; distinguished from a *tilting-helm*; **tourney-queen**, the 'queen of beauty' at a tournament.

1813 SCOTT *Trierm.* III. xxxvii, Forgot was that fell *tourney-day. **1886** J. RICHMOND *Pref. Notice to Chatterton's Poet. Wks.* 25 The gay crowd of the *tourney-field. **1872** TENNYSON *Gareth & Lyn.* 88 In those brain-stunning shocks and *tourney-falls. **1814** SCOTT *Ld. of Isles* IV. xxv, Victor in Woodstock's *tourney-fight. **1506–7** *Acc. Ld. High Treas. Scot.* III. 364 Tua tournay suordis, four *tournay hedis to the tournay. **1872** TENNYSON *Last Tourn.* 32 Take thou the jewels of this dead innocence, And make them..a *tourney-prize. **1848** KINGSLEY *Saint's Trag.* IV. iii. 97 Now ruffling up like any *tourney queen.

†**tourney, -ay,** *sb.*[2] *Obs.* Also 5–6 turn-. [a. OF. *tornee* (13th c. in Hatz.-Darm.), F. *tournée*, It. *tornata*, ppl. sb. from *tourner, tornare* to TURN; lit. a turning, going round, circuit.]

†**1.** The sheriff's tourn: see TOURN. *Obs. rare.*

a **1500** in *Arnolde's Chron.* (1811) 181 All maner preuylegis frauncheses hundredis wapentakes leetis rapis vyew of frank-pledge sherefs turnays sherefgyldes amerciamentis.

†**2.** One's turn in order or rotation. *Obs. rare.*

1523 FITZHERB. *Surv.* 29b, Also what lordes or Gentylmen haue their tourneyse [**1539** turneys] with them in the same benifyce..who shall haue next.

tourney ('tʊənɪ, 'tɜːnɪ), *v.* Forms: see TOURNEY *sb.*[1] [ME. a. OF. *tornei-er, -ey-er, tornai-er, -ay-er* (later *tornoi-ier, -oy-er, tournoy-er*, etc. = Pr. *torneiar, -ejar, torniar*, Cat. *tornejar*, Sp., Pg. *tornear*, It. *torneggiare*:—Romanic type **tornizāre*, **tornidiāre*, f. *torno*, L. *torn-us* sb. or *torn-āre* vb.: see TURN *sb.* and *v. Tornizāre* was a secondary formation, with a specific sense, referring to wheeling or evolutions.] *intr.* To take part in a tourney; to contend or engage in a tournament.

α. **13..** *Sir Beues* (A.) 611 Mani a gentil kniȝt Torneande riȝt in þe feld. *Ibid.* 3774 Þanne seide Beues vnto Terry: 'Wile we tornaie for þat leuedy?' **1390** GOWER *Conf.* I. 126 On jousteth wel, on other bet, And otherwhile thei torneie. *c* **1440** LOVELICH *Merlin* 7177 Þere eche man torneyed with oþer. **1470–85** MALORY *Arthur* VII. xi. 228 His custome is.. to lye in this medowe to Iuste and torneye.

β. *c* **1435** *Torr. Portugal* 2591 They justyd and turneyd there. **1513** DOUGLAS *Æneis* V. x. 10 Bid hym bring hiddir his rowtis to turnay. **1567** DRANT *Horace, De Arte Poet.* B iv, He dare not turney, not yet tilte which neuer knew the play. **1600** HOLLAND *Livy* XXVI. li. 624 He conversed among the legions, and turnoied with them.

γ. **13..** *K. Alis.* 195 (Bodl. MS.) Þer was kniȝttes tourneying [*v.r.* turnyng]. **1470–85** MALORY *Arthur* I. v. 41 Alle knyȝtes that wold Iuste or tourneye. *a* **1533** LD. BERNERS *Gold. Bk. M. Aurel.* (1546) D iij, Yf he vse armes, all wil tourney. **1570** LEVINS *Manip.* 197/15 To Tournay, *hastis concurrere.* **1577–87** HOLINSHED *Chron.* III. 803/1 So presented themselues.. readie to tourneie. **1622** MABBE tr. *Aleman's Guzman d'Alf.* I. 86 Because he might not Tourney. **1715** tr. *Pancirollus' Rerum Mem.* I. IV. xviii. 227 There were.. tourneying together with coursing Chariots. **1855** SINGLETON *Virgil* I. 189 They tourney; in high heaven a din is raised.

b. *transf.*

a **1400–50** *Alexander* 5429 Ilka twelmonth a turne þai [snakes] turnay to-gedire.

'tourneyer. Also 4 tourn(e)our, 8 turnier. [ME. a. OF. *tornoieor, tournoieur, -ieur*, f. *torneier*: see prec.] One who engages in a tourney.

1303 R. BRUNNE *Handl. Synne* 4615 For wymmen sake knyghteys tournaments make.. loke now whedyr swyche tournours [*v.r.* tourneours] Mow be kalled turmentours? **1738** [G. SMITH] *Curious Relations* II. 358 Forty-eight Turniers, dress'd after the ancient German manner, in yellow Liveries, trim'd with black Velvet, and small Gold Lace. *Ibid.* 359 Twenty-eight Turniers on Horse-back, after the ancient Manner. **1846** H. W. TORRENS *Rem. Milit. Hist.* 191 Mere fantastic tourneyers breaking a lance for the bright eyes of their lady.

'tourneying, *vbl. sb.* [f. TOURNEY *v.* + -ING[1].] The action of the verb TOURNEY. Also *attrib.*

13.. *K. Alis.* 1045 (Bodl. MS.) Carolyng & turneieyng And wrestlyng & skirmyng. *c* **1386** CHAUCER *Knt.'s T.* 1699 No lenger shal the turneiynge [*v.rr.* torneyenge, turnyinge, tourneying] laste. **1483** CAXTON *G. de la Tour* g viij b, The Ioustynge and the tornoyeng was fayre to see. **1503** *Acc. Ld. High Treas. Scot.* II. 202 To the turnaying at Fasteringis evin. **1548** UDALL, etc. *Erasm. Par. Mark* Pref., To proue masteries with wagoners in the listes or turneiyng place called Circus. *a* **1631** DONNE *Paradoxes* (1652) 75 No way.. to win a Lady but by Tylting, Turnying, and riding in Forrests. **1657** C. BECK *Univ. Char.* L vij b, Tournaying or tilting. **1843** CARLYLE *Past & Pr.* II. xv, A liberty of tourneying.

tourniquet ('tʊənɪkɛt, -keɪ, ‖turnikɛ). Also 7 turneke, 8 turniket, tournequet. [a. F. *tourniquet*, dial. *torniquai*, deriv. of *tourn-er* to TURN.]

1. A surgical instrument, consisting essentially of a bandage, a pad, and a screw, for stopping or checking the flow of blood through an artery by compression; also, a bandage tightened by twisting a rigid bar put through it.

1695 W. W. *News Lt. Chirurg. put out* 53 His.. slacking the Turneke.. caused such an additional Expence of Blood. **1721** NAISH in *Phil. Trans.* XXXI. 227 Upon slackening the Turniket. **1756** *Gentl. Mag.* XXVI. 381 The offender is.. strangled by putting a cord twice round his neck, and twisting it tight with a piece of stick behind, like a tournequet. **1806** *Med. Jrnl.* XV. 149 Remarks.. on the screw tourniquet. **1869** *Latest News* 10 Oct. 7 He strangled himself in bed with a tourniquet made of a handkerchief and a piece of stick. **1877** ERICHSEN *Surg.* I. 34.

attrib. **1767** GOOCH *Treat. Wounds* I. 443 When such a wound happens in a limb, the leaving a tourniquet ligature loose about it,.. till the Surgeon can be called, is a precaution. **1820** *Sporting Mag.* VII. 108 The tourniquet [hand] shake is the next in importance.

2. a. A turnstile. *rare.* **b.** = BARKER'S MILL (Ogilvie, 1882).

1706 PHILLIPS (ed. Kersey), *Tourniquet*, a Turn-Still. **1768** STERNE *Sent. Journ.* (1775) I. 56 Seek some winding alley, with a *tourniquet* at the end of it, where chariot never rolled or flambeau shot its rays. **1876** RUSKIN *Fors Clav.* lxiv. VI. 113 We.. are to work outside, here, for your dinners, and hand them through the wall to you at a tourniquet.

tournit, -yt, obs. Sc. forms of TURNED.

‖**Tournois** (turnwa), *a.* (*sb.*) *Hist.* Forms: 4–5 Tourneys, 5 Turneis, 6 Tornois, 7 Tor-, Turnoys, 7– Tournois. [Fr. *Tournois* adj.:—L. *Turonēnsis*, of Tours, *Turonēs*, a city of France.] Of or pertaining to Tours: esp. said of the money coined at Tours, one-fifth less in value than that struck at Paris.

1475 *Bk. Noblesse* (Roxb.) 32 To the yerely valeu of .x.M[l]. marcs yerely, whiche was .lx.M[l].li. Turneis. **1523** LD. BERNERS *Froiss.* I. cliv. 184 The french kyng shall delyuer to the kyng of Nauer, xxxviii.M.li. tornois of lande. **1625** in Rushw. *Hist. Coll.* (1659) I. 331 The sum of Two hundred and thirteen thousand Livres Turnoys. **1769** *Chron.* in *Ann. Reg.* 85 The ship of war.. has on board.. about an hundred thousand crowns tournois in piastres. **1852** MISS YONGE *Cameos* (1877) III. iii. 27 Sufficient to pay nine thousand soldiers at the rate of ten livres tournois per month.

b. *sb.* Money or a coin of Tours: see quots.

13.. *Coer de L.* 2856 They myghte have none othir thyng For whyt tourneys, ne for sterlyng. **1426** LYDG. *De Guil. Pilgr.* 17664 To tourne, by hys sotylte, A Tourneys to A parysee. **1656** BLOUNT *Glossogr.*, *Tournois*.., a French penny, the tenth part of a penny sterling... In France they say so much money *Tournois*, as we say *sterling*. **1893** *Antiquary* Mar. 105 Coins found in St. Queran's Well, 1869. .. Double Tournois.

‖**tournure** (turnyr). [F. *tournure*, earlier *tournedre*:—late pop.L. *tornātūra*, f. *tornāre* to TURN; in Fr. (1) rounded form given to anything; (2) manner in which anything is fashoned.]

1. (Graceful) manner or bearing; cultivated address.

1748 CHESTERF. *Let.* 12 Oct., The easy manners and *tournure* of the world. **1816** *Sporting Mag.* XLVII 118 That ease and *tournure* so indispensable in the composition of a gentleman. **1832** MRS. F. TROLLOPE *Domest. Mann. Amer.* ii. (1839) 7 Her manner was easy and graceful, with a good deal of French *tournure*. **1878** *Cornh. Mag.* June 687 She had the tournure of a princess.

2. The turning of language or of a phrase; mode of expression. *rare.*

1816 J. SCOTT *Vis. Paris* (ed. 5) 194 The *tournure* of the phrase, when a woman is spoken to, cannot be mistaken.

3. Contour, outline, shape (of a limb, etc.).

1827 DISRAELI *Vivian Grey* III. v. xv. 299 Touched in with freedom—a grand *tournure*—great *goût* in the swell of the neck. **1841** LADY BLESSINGTON *Idler in France* I. xv. 354 There was the same classic *tournure* of heads and profiles. **1848** CLOUGH *Bothie* v. 112 The tournure of the elbow is shapely. **1864** *Daily Tel.* 5 Nov., You have.. the exquisite tournure of a figure, the subtle trick of a ridiculous expression.

4. A pad worn round the waist or hips to give shapeliness to a woman's figure; also = BUSTLE *sb.*[2] Also, a kind of corset.

1831 H. GRANVILLE *Let.* Jan. (1894) II. 75 Very fat, but squeezed into a *tournure*. **1872** *Young Englishwoman* Dec. 646/2 The tournure is high indeed behind... It has superseded the crinoline. **1874** *Echo* 30 Dec. (Stanf.), The tournure.. is still worn. **1882** *Daily News* 3 June 3/1 The tournure is a small horse-hair pad, worn under the dress at the waist. It throws out the skirt from the figure.

tourrette, obs. form of TURRET.

†**Tours** (turz). *Obs.* Also 6 Towres, 6–7 Towers. [Name of a city in France.] Used *attrib.* in names of things made at or associated with Tours; as ***Tours taffeta*** (also ***taffeta Tours***).

1558 in Feuillerat *Revels Q. Eliz.* (1908) 31 Taffita Towers white xix yardes. *Ibid.* 38 The gownes lyned with white towres taffita. **1572** *Ibid.* 187 Of Taffata crimsin thirtie two yardes, of Taffata Tawnie Towers thirtie and sixe yardes. **1586** *Rates of Custome* E vij b, Taffata, called Towers Taffata the yarde iii. s. iiij. d. **1640** in Entick *London* (1766) II. 169 Tabbies of silk, towers taffaty, the dozen yards, *2d.*

b. ***Tours sorrel,*** buckler-shaped or French sorrel, *Rumex scutata.*

1578 LYTE *Dodoens* v. ix. 558 *Oxalis Romana*, Tours Sorrel or Romayne Sorrel. [*Ibid.* 559 Romayne Sorrel.. in Frenche *Ozeille Romaine*, and *Ozeille de Tours.*] **1611** COTGR., *Ozeille Romaine*, Roman Sorrell,.. Tours Sorrell.

‖**tourte**[1] (turt). Also tourt. [mod.F. *tourte*, now, a piece of pastry containing meat, fish, etc., eaten hot, a pie; *dial.* bread in the form of a disk, a round flat cake, also in transferred senses; in dial. F. *torte*, Sp. and It. *torta*:—late L. *tōrta* a cake of bread, of uncertain origin. Cf. also TORTA.] (See quots.)

1706 PHILLIPS (ed Kersey), *Tourte*, (in *Cookery*) a kind of Pastry-work bak'd in a Pan; a Pie. **1725** *Bradley's Fam. Dict.*, *Tourte* or *Pan-pie*, in general a Pie bak'd in a Pan, of which there are several Sorts. *Ibid.*, To make a Tourte of Veal Sweet-Breads. **1762** *Char.* in *Ann. Reg.* II. 34 The pheasant tourt was a discovery he made in Spain. **1895** *Funk's Stand. Dict.*, Tourte.

Tourte[2] (tʊət, ‖turt). The name of the French violin-bow maker François *Tourte* (1747–1835), who perfected the modern bow, used *attrib.* and *absol.* to designate bows made according to his model.

1889 GROVE *Dict. Mus.* IV. 155 The Tourte bow greatly facilitated the new development of violin music. *Ibid.* 156 A very fine Tourte has been recently sold for £30. **1896** H. SAINT-GEORGE *Bow* vi. 51 What a marvellous thing a fine Tourte is! What a revelation the first time a player handles one! **1908** *Sears, Roebuck Catal.* 233/2 This [professional violin] outfit includes:.. One Tourte model bow, full German silver trimmings and best quality Brazil wood stick. **1950** *Musical Q.* Jan. 16 French and Italian bows shown in early 18-century sources seem lighter in construction than the Tourte bows. **1980** *Early Music* Apr. 200/1 Illus. 1c shows a genuine Tourte bow and 1d an English bow stamped FORSTER.. one of the types of so-called 'transitional' bows in vogue about 1775, some ten years before the invention of the Tourte.

tourteaux: see TORTEAU.

tourtière (tʊətɪ'ɛə(r), ‖turtjɛr). [a. Fr., lit. 'tart-tin', f. *tourte* TOURTE[1] tart.] **a.** *Fr. Canad.* A kind of meat pie traditionally eaten at Christmas. **b.** A tart-tin or round baking-sheet.

1953 WATTIE & DONALDSON *Nellie L. Pattinson's Canad. Cookbk.* (rev. ed.) xxv. 467 Tourtière (Pork Pies). These pies are traditional Christmas Eve fare. **1959** J. DONON *Classic French Cuisine* IX. 303 Pour into a well-buttered *tourtière*, or pie plate. **1960** E. DAVID *French Provincial Cooking* 69 *Tourtière*, a shallow tart tin... In former times a *tourtière* was a heavy iron or earthenware dish, much deeper than a tart tin, in which many things besides pastry could be cooked. **1975** *Globe & Mail* (Toronto) 3 Dec. s8/5 A meat pie of Christmas Eve fame in Quebec, the tourtiere is traditional fare at the reveillon after midnight mass. **1978** *N.Y. Times* 29 Mar. c8/6, I like to bake crust in flan rings set on round black baking sheets called tourtières.

touse (taʊz, taʊs), *sb. dial.* [f. TOUSE *v.*]

1. Rough pulling about, horse-play; a 'row', commotion, uproar; an outcry, a fuss.

1795 WOLCOTT (P. Pindar) *Lousiad* IV. 173 Let's have no more touse. **1802** —— *Middlesex Elect.* II. vi, Amongst the derty, lowzy crew, There's zich a touse and hallibulloo. **1835–40** HALIBURTON *Clockm.* (1862) 28 Marm Lecain makes such an eternal touss about her carpets. **1882** JAGO *Cornwall Gloss.*, *Touse*, fuss, row, uproar, hurry. 'Making such a touse'.

2. A tousled mass: in quot. of hair.

1894 CROCKETT *Lilac Sunbonnet* v. 43 With a touse of lint-white locks blowing out in the gusts.

touse (taʊz), *v.* Now *rare.* Forms: (3 to-tuse, 4–5 be-touse), 6–7 towse, 6–8 touze, towze, 6– touse, 8–9 *Sc.* and *north. dial.* toose (tuz). [The simple vb. is known only from *c* 1509; but the compounds with *be-* and *to-* are found in ME. from *c* 1300, pointing to an unrecorded OE. **túsian*, ME. *túsen, tousen*, cognate with OHG. *-zûsôn* in *zir-zûsôn* to pull to pieces, MHG. *er-zûsen, er-zousen*, Ger. *zausen*; also LG. (EFris.) *tûsen* to pull or shake about, tease, treat roughly, NFris. *tuuse* to pull by the hair:—OTeut. vb. stem **tŭs-*, closely allied in sense to **tais-*, whence TEASE and TOZE.]

1. *trans.* To pull roughly about; to drag or push about; to handle roughly; of a dog: to tear at, worry.

[*c* **1300** *Havelok* 1948 Bernard sone ageyn [him] nam Al to-tused and al to-torn. *c* **1400** *Laud Troy Bk.* 12944 Thei were alle thorow wet... Al be-rayned and be-toused.] **1509** HAWES *Conv. Swearers* xii, Beholde my body with blody proppes endewed.. Towsed and tugged with othes cruelly. **1567** MAPLET *Gr. Forest* 83 b, There was a Dog.. which at the first dash or onset.. daunted and toused the Lyon. **1590** SPENSER *F.Q.* II. xi. 33 As a Beare, whom angry curres have touzd. **1633** HEYWOOD *Eng. Trav.* II. Wks. 1874 IV. 26 The Cooke.. did so Towse them and Tosse them, so Plucke them and Pull them. **1736** MRS. DELANY in *Life & Corr.* (1861) I. 556 To Court, where we were touz'd and hunched about to make room for citizens in their fur gowns. **1869** PEACOCK *Lonsdale Gloss.*, *Touze*, to tug or pull about. **1898** T. HARDY *Wessex Poems* 66 When she used to sing and pirouette And touse the tambourine.

†**b.** To pull out of joint, to rack. *Obs. rare.*

1603 SHAKS. *Meas. for M.* v. i. 313 To th' racke with him: we'll towze you Ioynt by ioynt, but we will know his purpose.

†**c.** To pull (a woman) about rudely, indelicately, or in horse-play; to tousle. *Obs.*

1623 MASSINGER *Bondman* I. iii, They are rough, Boisterous, and saucy, and at the first sight Ruffle and touze us. **1638** FORD *Fancies* III. iii, He towzes the lady-sisters as a tumbling dog does young rabbits. **1675** HOBBES *Odyssey* XVI. 105 Maids tous'd ill-favouredly. **1719** D'URFEY *Pills* (1872) I. 93 And she.. Still gave him leave o towze her. **1751** ELIZA HEYWOOD *Betsy Thoughtless* I. 71 He.. began to kiss and touze me so, that.. I was frighted almost out of my wits.

2. To disorder, dishevel (the hair, dress, etc.); to tumble, rumple (bed-clothes, sheets, etc.).

1598 FLORIO, *Sparpagliare*, to desheuell, to vnkembe, to touze a womans haire. **1647** STAPYLTON *Juvenal* 215 Though her.. hair be tows'd, her face and eares do glow. **1682** D'URFEY *Butler's Ghost* 149 A Rampant shaver,.. with licentious hands does touze The Bridal Vesture of your Spouse. **1693** CONGREVE *Old Bach.* IV. viii, Oh the most inhumane barbarous Hackney-Coach! I am jolted to a Jelly! —Am I not horribly touzed? **1912** R. MACDONALD *First of Ebb* xi, Upon the lap of Clothilde.. lay the toused, sleeping poll of the little Antoinette.

3. *fig.* To abuse or maltreat in some way compared to the literal senses. Now *rare* or *Obs.*

1530 TINDALE *Answ. More* III. xiii. Wks. (1573) 311/1 There he biteth, sucketh, gnaweth, towseth, and mowseth Tyndall. **1593** DRAYTON *Eclogues* i. 59 Fortune, the World that towzes to and fro. **1609** BP. W. BARLOW *Answ. Nameless Cath.* 86 Hee hath rowsed her in her Death-bed; now hee runnes backe 70. yeeres, to towse her in her Cradle. *c* **1680** HICKERINGILL *Hist. Whiggism* I. Wks. 1716 I. 37 If they get a piece of a Text by the end.. they do so tear it, and towze it, and towzer it.. that they lose themselves. **1844** *Blackw. Mag.* LVI. 212 Invite especially those that have hitherto tightly toused, mocked, and scorned thee.

†**4.** To tease (wool); = TOZE *v.*[1] 1. *Obs.*

1599 T. M[OUFET] *Silkwormes* 4 Deuising beetles, hackels, wheeles, and frame, Wherwith to bruse, touse, spin, and weaue the same. **1601** HOLLAND *Pliny* IX. xxxviii. I. 259 They let the wooll lie to take the liquor..: then they have it forth, touse, and card it. **1706** PHILLIPS (ed. Kersey), To *Towz* or *Toze Wooll*, is to Card or dress it.

†**5.** *intr.* To touse each other, tussle; also *fig.*; in quot. 1607, to pull things about in disorder, rummage. *Obs.*

1542 UDALL *Erasm. Apoph.* 25 While she & I be touzyng & topplyng together. **1606** FORD *Hon. Tri.* (1843) 16, I touze to gaine me fame and reputation. **1607** DEKKER & WEBSTER *Northw. Hoe* III. Wks. 1873 III. 41 Sondry times shee.. opend her chests, touz'd among her linnen. **1681** OTWAY *Soldier's Fort.* I. i, To see a pretty Wench and a young Fellow touze and rouze and frouze and mouze.

Hence **toused** (taʊzd) *ppl. a.*, **'tousing** *vbl. sb.* and *ppl. a.*

a **1550** *Jack Juggler* (1873) 66, I haue forgotten with tousing by the here, What I deuised to say a lytle ere. **1582** STANYHURST *Æneis* I. (Arb.) 21 Hee noted Aeneas his touzdtost nauye to wander. **1682** MRS. BEHN *City Heiress* 21 Be sawcy, forward, bold, towzing, and lewd. **18..** MOORE *Moral Positions* iii, To guard the frail package from tousing and routing. **1912** Toused [see sense 2].

'tousle (see next), *sb.* Also † **touzle.** [f. next.]

1. A struggle, a tussle; a rough romping with a woman. *Sc.*

1788 R. GALLOWAY *Poems* 214 For tho' I be baith blyth and canty, I ne'er get a touzle at a'. **1814** J. BOSWELL *Justiciary Op.* (1816) 11 A chield had taen a glass, and had A towzle wi' a gauger. **1830** GALT *Lawrie T.* VII. vi, Ye're no' a pin the worse of all the bit touzle.

2. A tousled mass or mop (of hair).

1880 *Daily Tel.* 26 Nov., The eyes peeping out from under the overshadowing touzle, like young birds through a hedge. **1887** FLO. WARDEN *Scheherazade* ii, The thick tousle of hair ..was entirely innocent of curling tongs.

3. *attrib.* and *Comb.*, as ***tousle-haired, -headed*** adjs.; ***touslehead.***

1880 *Cornh. Mag.* Feb. 136 A couple of bare-armed touzle-headed viragoes. **1898** *Westm. Gaz.* 8 Dec. 2/1 Cattle of all kinds... Touzle-haired, tawny Highlanders with great sweeping horns, polled Galloways with coats like black astrachan. **1900** M. HEWLETT *Life & Death Richard Yea-and-Nay* II. xi. 364 The townsmen of Gratz, hoarse-voiced touzle-heads mostly, divined her to be an anchoress. **1981** *Sunday Express Mag.* 7 June 12/1 The breathlessness of a touslehead at a school concert.

tousle, touzle ('taʊz(ə)l, *Sc.* 'tuz(ə)l), *v.* Forms: 5, 8 tousel, (5 *Sc.* towsill, 7 -ell, 9 towsel), 6– tousle; 7– touzle, (8–9 towzle, 9 -zel, *Sc.* and *north.* toozle). [Iterative of TOUSE *v.*: see -LE 3. Cf. LG. *tûseln* (*Brem. Wbch.*); Oberd. *zusseln, züsseln* (Doornkaat-Koolman).]

1. *trans.* To pull about roughly; to handle (esp. a woman) rudely or indelicately; to disorder, dishevel (the hair, clothes, etc.); = TOUSE *v.* 1, 1 c, 2.

a **1440** *Sir Degrev.* 1492 Fayre schetus of sylk..Quyltus poyned of that ylk Touseled they ware. *c* **1475** *Rauf Coilȝear* 432 For to towsill me or tit me, thocht foull be my clais, Or I be dantit on sic wyse, my lyfe salbe lorne. *a* **1585** MONTGOMERIE *Flyting* 362 Tousled and tuggled with towne tykes. **1642** H. MORE *Song of Soul* II. I. xiv, His rugg'd flowing mane, Which the fierce winds do tosse and tousell sore. **1725** RAMSAY *Gentle Sheph.* IV. i, I have towzled his harigalds a wee! **1764** FOOTE *Mayor of G.* I. i, Come, Jane, give me my wig; you slut, how you have touzled the curls. **1839–40** W. IRVING *Wolfert's R.* xiii. (1855) 181 [He] kissed and tousled the young vrouws. **1884** *Harper's Mag.* Aug. 464/1 Romping with the dogs, tousling a big St. Bernard.

b. With *about, out, up.*

1816 SCOTT *Antiq.* ix, After they had touzled out mony a leather poke-full o' papers. **1822** W. IRVING *Braceb. Hall* xxxviii, Mrs. Hannah..being tossed and tousled about by the crowd. **1883** *Mem. S. Miller* Pref. 20 [She] requested us ..if she should be drowsy to be sure and 'touzle' her up.

c. *fig.* = TOUSE *v.* 3.

1826 J. WILSON *Noct. Ambr.* Wks. 1855 I. 260 Hoo your een sparkle as you touzle the clergy. **1900** HARE *Story my Life* VI. xxv. 188 Religion worried and touzled by a thousand million vagaries of personality.

2. *intr.* To toss oneself about; also, to rout, rummage (cf. TOUSE *v.* 5).

1852 MRS. STOWE *Uncle Tom's C.* xxxvii, Tom Loker we left groaning and touzling in a..clean Quaker bed. **1880** BARING-GOULD *Mehalah* xxiv, Do you think she is to come here toozling about among the wittles in her best gown?

Hence **'tousling, 'touzling** *vbl. sb.*

1749 FIELDING *Tom Jones* XVIII. xii, Damn me, if he shan't ha the tousling her. **1771** E. LONG *Trial Dog 'Porter'* in Hone *Every-day Bk.* (1827) II. 202 Tearings, woundings, pullings,..touzleings,..maliciously inflicted. **1865** E. BURRITT *Walk Land's End* 284 What tugging and touzling, and pinching and pulling at the tail he [a dog] will take.

tousled, touzled ('taʊ-, *Sc.* 'tuz(ə)ld), *ppl. a.* [f. TOUSLE *v.* + -ED[1].] Disarranged, dishevelled, tumbled; also shaggy, matted.

1848 DICKENS *Dombey* xxv, Rob the Grinder..stood then, panting at the captain, with a flushed and tousled air of bed about him. **1852** MRS. STOWE *Uncle Tom's C.* ix, A very heavy mat of sandy hair, in a decidedly tousled condition. **1861** *Crt. Life at Naples* II. 1 Prudent mammas carried off reluctant daughters, whose touzled dresses, disordered hair, and heavy eyelids bore witness..to the wisdom of the measure. **1890** W. BOOTH *Darkest Eng.* 104 A grimy footsore tramp..with filthy shirt and towselled hair.

b. *Comb.*, as ***tousled-headed, -looking*** adjs.

1860 DICKENS *Uncomm. Trav.* xiii, The touzled-headed man..hadn't got his coat on yet. **1883** CLELAND *Inchbracken* xiii. 105 A damp and tousselled-looking youth, who grasped his dripping 'Tam o' Shanter' tightly in his hands.

‖**tous-les-mois** (tulemwa). [F., = 'all the months, every month'; but probably a popular perversion of *toloman*, according to Duss and Jumelle the name in the French Antilles, prob. of native S. American origin.] The name in St. Kitts, etc., of species of *Canna*, esp. *C. edulis*, and of the starch obtained from its root-stocks, also called ***tous-les-mois starch.***

Canna coccinea was introduced into W. Indies from S. America in 1731; *C. edulis* from Peru in 1820 (A. W. Hill, Kew). Samples of the farina were sent to England from St. Kitts in 1835–6: see Ryan's *Med. & Surg. Jrnl.* Aug. 1836, and *Morning Chron.* 4 Aug. 1837.

1839 OLPHERS *Let.* cited in *Pharm. Jrnl.* VII. 56 (On the *Canna Achira* or Tous les Mois). **1858** HOGG *Veg. Kingd.* 787 The article known as *Tous-les-mois* is obtained from the root-stocks of some species of *Canna*... The substance is prepared in the island of St. Kitts. **1861** BENTLEY *Man. Bot.* 669 One or more species of this genus [*Canna*] yield 'Tous les mois', a very pure and useful starch, now largely consumed in this country and elsewhere. **1867** J. HOGG *Microsc.* I. ii. 153 The larger-grained starches form splendid objects; tous-les-mois being the largest may be taken as a type of all the others.

tously ('taʊzlɪ), *a.* Also formerly **touzly, touzley, towsly.** [f. TOUSLE *sb.* or *v.* + -Y.] Characterized by being tousled or dishevelled; having tousled hair or dress.

1832 *Chambers's Edin. Jrnl.* I. 193/2 Ye may be as touzly as ye like i' the outside o' your claes. **1891** *Pall Mall G.* 14 Feb. 6/2 Hither came the women, a blowsy, touzley crew, with mouth agape. **1905** *Daily News* 2 Aug. 6 One [humble-bee] with a tously yellow head and thorax and dark brown abdomen. **1911** *Ibid.* 7 Mar. 4 Why should a man send many men and teams of horses..to fetch towsly brown grass to clothe his town lawn?

‖**Toussaint** (tusɛ̃). [Fr., f. *tous*, pl. of *tout* all + *saint* saint.] The feast of All Saints (1 November).

1930 K. BOYLE *Plagued by Nightingale* (1931) xxv. 246 They would linger in the country..perhaps even until the *Toussaint.* **1955** *Caribbean Q.* IV. II. (*verso front cover*) In many West Indian Islands, especially but not exclusively those under Catholic influence, it is customary to keep the Festival of All Saints, or Toussaint. **1979** N. FREELING *Widow* xxxiv. 210 The flowers for mum's birthday or the Toussaint.

†**toust**, *sb. Sc. Old Law.* Also 6–7 **towst,** 6 **towist.** [a. AF. *toste, touste* (13–14th c. in Godef.), var. spelling of *tôte, toute, toulte, tolte,* 'enlèvement' = med.L. *tolta*, f. OF. *toldre*, L. *tollĕre* to lift, take away, raise: see TOLT.] An impost, rate levied, tax.

1574 *Reg. Privy Council Scot.* II. 408 Gif ony towst sould be takin of thair gudis. *Ibid.*, The said towist and impositioun. **1596** in *Munim. Burgh Irvine* (1890) I. 85 Grant to the provost, bailies, council and community of Irving..the toust, exactioun and impoist of all the following sorts of merchandise. **1598** in *Reg. Mag. Sig. Scot.* 1603. 513/1 Pro receptione cujusdam taxationis lie toust and taxatioun. **1620** *Ibid.* 777/2 Cum potestate..recipiendi parvas custumas..*lie towst* aliasque devorias nundinarum et portus.

Hence † **toust** *v.*, *Sc. Obs. rare*, *trans.* to tax; whence † **'tousting** *vbl. sb.*

1565 in Calderwood *Hist. Kirk* (1843) II. 574 The taxing and tousting of her Majestie's barons and other lieges, which are tousted for repairing of that which was so indiscreitlie of the patrimonie forsaid dilapidated.

tousy, towsy ('taʊzɪ, 'tuzɪ), *a.* Chiefly *Sc.* and *north. dial.* Also 8– **touzie,** 9– **touzy,** 9 **towzy, -sie, toosy.** [f. TOUSE *v.* + -Y.] **1.** Dishevelled, unkempt, tousled; shaggy, rough. Also in *Comb., transf.*, and *fig.*

[**1500–20** DUNBAR *Poems* xviii. 32 And be I ornat in my speiche, Than Towsy sayis, I am sa streiche.] **1786** BURNS *Twa Dogs* 33 His breast was white, his touzie back Weel clad wi' coat o' glossy black. **1820** *Blackw. Mag.* May 159/1 Like yere ain towsie hassock o' hair, that has nae been kamed since Kate Kimmer kamed it with the three-footed stool. **1826** J. WILSON *Noct. Ambr.* Wks. 1855 I. 180 What an outlandish, toosy-headed, wee sun-brunt deevil o' a lassie that. **1871** C. GIBBON *Lack of Gold* xiv, His hair was long and 'touzy'. **1873** A. G. MURDOCH *Lilts* 57 Tell him, when in the touzie key, A nicht wi' him I wadna gie. **1897** H. OCHILTREE *Out of Shroud* xxiv. 331, I was oot gey late ae nicht—a touzie nicht it was. **1925** G. B. CUMMING *A'anside Lilts* 71 The times then were touzie to live in. **1955** *Times* 9 May 6/3 A campaign that is already showing signs of developing into a tousy fight. **1972** *Listener* 27 July 104/3 (*heading*) Glory goals rock tousy Rangers.

2. Abundant, prolific; *esp.* in *Comb.*, **tousy tea,** a knife-and-fork tea, high tea.

1835 *Glasgow Jrnl.* 31 Oct. 44 Mrs Stewart had laid what she styled a 'touzie tea'. **1895** H. OCHILTREE *Redburn* ix. 90 It's no very great place for yits or barley, but a gye tousie place for gress. **1934** T. SMELLIE *Tea-Pairty* 12 Next to a touzie tea there's naething like maesic tae soothe a savage beast.

tout (taʊt), *sb.*[1] Also 8 **toute.** [f. TOUT *v.*[1]]

1. A thieves' scout or watchman. *slang.*

1718 C. HIGDEN *True Disc.* 13 (Farmer) He is a pushing toute, alias thieves' watchman, that lies scouting in and about the City to get and bring intelligence to the thieves.

2. One who solicits custom; = TOUTER 1.

1853 *Household Words* VII. 26/1 Touts and spungers to foreign hotels and on foreign visitors. **1879** SALA *Paris herself again* (1880) II. xi. 163 A regular house to house visitation was made..by touts or agents of the insurers. **1881** BESANT & RICE *Chapl. of Fleet* I. vi, Ludgate Hill, where the touts of the Fleet parsons ran up and down. **1881** HUGHES *Rugby, Tennessee* 34 The hotel touts rush on you.

3. (More fully ***racing tout.***) One who surreptitiously watches the trials of race-horses, so as to gain information for betting purposes: = TOUTER 2.

1865 *Slang Dict.*, Tout, in sporting phraseology..signifies an agent in the training districts, on the look-out for information as to the condition and capabilities of those horses entering for a coming race. **1887** BLACK *Sabina Zembra* I. vi. 80, I..don't object to seeing the touts coming about; it shows they think we have some horses worth watching.

4. The action of TOUT *v.*[1]; in phrase ***to keep (the) tout,*** to watch. *slang.*

1812 J. H. VAUX *Flash Dict.* s.v., *To keep tout*, is to look out or watch, while your pall is effecting any private purpose. *A strong tout*, is strict observation, or eye, upon any proceedings, or persons. **1834** H. AINSWORTH *Rookwood* IV. ii, [They] on each other kept the tout.

5. A spy; an informer. Cf. TOUT *v.*[1] 2. *N. Ireland* and *Sc.*

1959 I. & P. OPIE *Lore & Lang. Schoolch.* x. 189 The tell tale is..a tout, traitor, quisling, or widemouth. **1973** *Times* 6 June 1/5 The body of a young man..was found..shot through the head 800 yards from the southern Irish border. .. A label with the word 'Tout' written on it was attached to his neck. **1977** W. MCILVANNEY *Laidlaw* xl. 186 'What's his business?' 'Same as any tout's. Other people's.'

tout (taʊt), *sb.*[2] *Sc.* Also **towt.** [Origin obscure: cf. TOUT *v.*[2]]

1. A fit of ill humour; a transient displeasure; a pet.

1787 SHIRREFS *Jamie & Bess* I. ii, Were he ay sae, he then wad ay be kind, But then, anither tout may change his mind. **1818** SCOTT *Br. Lamm.* xi[i], He taks the tout at every bit lippening word. **1835** CARRICK *Laird of Logan* (1841) 76 Leezie was..discontented, and subject to bits o' touts now and then.

2. A fit or slight bout of illness.

1808–18 JAMIESON, *Tout, towt*, an ailment of a transient kind. **1823** GALT *Entail* II. ii. 12 It's neither the t'ane nor the t'ither, but just..a bit towt that's no worth the talking o'. **1831** MISS FERRIER *Destiny* lxxvi, The baby had a sad towt with its teeth. **1855** MUCKLEBACKIT *Rhymes* 219 (E.D.D.) She teuk the tout, near Galashiels,..She dee'd that vera nicht.

tout, *sb.*[3] [? Fr. *tout* all.] A term for a specially successful result in certain games: see quots. and cf. Littré s.v. *Tout* 47.

1678 DRYDEN *Limberham* IV. ii, Well, I have won the Party and Revenge however: A Minute longer, and I had won the Tout. **1687** SEDLEY *Bellamira* IV. i, I lost three sets at back-gammon, and a tout at trick-track, all ready money. **1891** *Cent. Dict., Tout*[1] 3. In the game of solo, a play when one person takes or proposes to take all the tricks.

‖**tout** (tu), *adv.*, *sb.*[4], and *a.* [Fr.] **A.** *adv.* Quite, entirely: ***tout au contraire*** (tut o kɔ̃trɛr), quite the contrary; ***tout court*** (tu kur), in short, in little, simply, without qualification or addition; ***tout de suite*** (tu də sɥit) [*de suite* in sequence], at once, immediately; cf. TOOT SWEET; ***tout seul*** (tu sœl), quite alone, on its (or his, etc.) own; ***tout simple, simplement*** (tu sɛ̃pl, sɛ̃pləmɑ̃) quite simply, just that.

1841 M. EDGEWORTH *Let.* 23 Mar. (1971) 590 Scandal but not by any means ill natured tout au contraire. **1982** E. DEWHURST *Whoever I Am* i. 18 'You find it obvious that I've been on the amateur stage?' '*Tout au contraire...* But I know.'

1747 H. WALPOLE *Let.* 26 June (1955) XIX. 420 My eagle is arrived—my eagle *tout court*, for I hear nothing of the pedestal. **1888** KIPLING *Wee Willie Winkie* 38 Judy was officially 'Miss Judy'; but Black Sheep was never anything but Black Sheep *tout court.* **1928** C. DAWSON *Age of Gods* xii. 262 There are grave objections to the identification *tout court* of the Nordic race with the Indo-European stock. **1958** *Oxf. Mag.* 15 May 435/1 Hove, instead of asking for Psychology *tout court*, has a course by a Harley Street psychiatrist. **1981** J. SUTHERLAND *Bestsellers* xxiv. 240 Len Deighton's..history *tout court* of the Second World War (*Bomber* and *Fighter*).

1895 E. DOWSON *Let. c* 13 Nov. (1967) 319 If you see Moore tell him that I am writing tout de suite. **1971** *Ink* 12 June 14/3 Some of the underwriters quietly told their clients to resell their shares *tout-de-suite.*

1926 H. CRANE *Let.* 19 Aug. (1965) 273, I have encountered him in the road, talking again tout seul and examining pebbles. **1954** *Essays in Criticism* IV. 272 The danger in self-exploration *tout seul* is that it can lead to loss of urgency.

1930 *Harvard Law Rev.* XLIII. 881 Strict or liberal construction or interpretation is therefore the ordinary process of interpretation, *tout simple.* **1977** *Times* 14 Apr. 14/6 The event was listed as a variety show, *tout simple.* **1939** *Burlington Mag.* Mar. 142/2 The most probable explanation..is, *tout simplement*, faulty recollection. **1973** E. BERCKMAN *Victorian Album* 114 There it was. There, *tout simplement*, as they say, was my murder.

B. *sb.*[4] and *a.* All: ***tout compris*** (tu kɔ̃pri), all included, inclusive; ***tout ensemble***: see ENSEMBLE *sb.* 1; ***tout le monde*** (tu lə mɔ̃d), all the world, everyone; (***le***) ***tout Paris*** (lə tu pari), all Paris, i.e. Parisian society; also *transf.*, of other cities, social circles, etc.

1901 LD. MILNER *Let.* in J. A. Smith *John Buchan* (1979) 34/2 You will have to pay your own way out—about £60 *tout compris.* **1960** *Harper's Bazaar* Aug. 63/1 A day in one of these hotels..can cost under 15 shillings, *tout compris.*

1825 H. WILSON *Memoirs* III. 110 Tout le monde seemed so very much to admire my person. **1944** AUDEN *Sea & Mirror* in *For Time Being* iii. 29 She invites..just *tout le monde* to drop in at any time.

1894 G. DU MAURIER *Trilby* III. VII. 15 'Tout Paris' passed them; but they were none the wiser, and agreed that the show was not a patch on that in Hyde Park during the London season. **1921** G. BELL *Let.* 5 May (1927) xx. 480 'Le tout' Bagdad was there—the Arab world. **1965** N. FREELING *Criminal Conversation* II. xix. 183, I married her..for the introduction she could give me into what I thought of as 'the club'. Le tout-Paris. **1975** P. Moyes *Black Widower* ii. 21 *Tout Washington* tends to arrive late at diplomatic cocktail parties. **1980** T. Morgan *Somerset Maugham* III. 221 He wanted a hostess, who knew the tout-Londres. **1982** *Times* 14 Jan. 15/3 It is the talk of le tout Paris in the French business world. Who will be getting the plum jobs?

tout, (taʊt), *v.*[1] Forms: 4–5 tute(n, 7– tout. [ME. *tūte-n*, pointing to an OE. **tútian*, synonymous with OE. *tótian*, TOOT *v.*[1], and OE. *týtan* :—**tûtjan*. (For etymological relations, and cognate words in the other Germanic langs., see under TOOT *v.*[1]) As used in ME., *tūte-n* was identical in sense with *tōten*, TOOT *v.*[1], sense 2; the two forms occur even as textual variants: see the first quotation in sense 1. The mod.Eng. form *tout* was in use before 1700 as a cant or slang word, whence the later sense-development, which has differentiated the word from TOOT.]

†**1.** *intr.* To peep, peer, look out; to gaze; = TOOT *v.*[1] 2. *Obs.*

a **1400–50** *Alexander* 694 (Ashmole) Anec[tanabus].. treyned doune fra þe toure to tute in þe sternes [*Dubl. MS.*, to tote on þe sternes]. *Ibid.* 4776 (Ashm.) Þe kyng in his caban with his kniȝtis he ligis, Tutand out of his tents. *a* **1603** T. Cartwright *Confut. Rhem. N.T.* (1618) 192 Dare you also affirme, that the soules in hell haue the same knowledge, by touting into the diuell? **1676** Coles *Dict.*, *Tout*, to look out or upon.

b. To keep a sharp look-out or watch; to take heed; to be on the look-out. *Thieves' cant.*

a **1700** B. E. *Dict. Cant. Crew*, *Tout*, to look out Sharp, to be upon one's Guard. **1728** [De Foe] *Street Robberies Consider'd*, *Tout*, take heed.

2. *trans.* To watch, spy on. *slang.*

a **1700** B. E. *Dict. Cant. Crew*, *Tout the Culls*, Eye those folks which way they take. **1812** J. H. Vaux *Flash Dict.*, *Tout*, to tout a person, is to watch his motions. **1832** *Examiner* 67/1 Two of them were sent forward.. in disguise, to tout (watch) the door of the house. **1870** *Sat. Rev.* 2 Apr. 445 But.. the Prince of Wales is touted, Mr. Gladstone is touted, their minutest actions are eagerly watched and regularly reported; why should not we be allowed to procure similar information about race-horses?

b. To watch furtively or spy upon (a race-horse or his trainer) with a view to using or disposing of the information for betting purposes.

1812 *Sporting Mag.* XXXIX. 283 He made it his business to be at the Wheat Sheaf public-house.. to tout Mr. Prince, who had the mare under his training. **1870** *Sat. Rev.* 2 Apr. 445 The touting of race-horses is practised, not to gratify curiosity, but as an aid to gambling. **1894** M. H. Hayes *Men & Horses* vi. (ed. 2) 94 With the fear of being touted ever on them, the Newmarket trainers are.. shy of strangers. **1895** *Westm. Gaz.* 2 Oct. 7/3 One of the most assiduously 'touted' animals at Newmarket during the last fortnight has been M. Aumont's Dormeuse.

3. a. *intr.* To look out busily for customers; to solicit custom, employment, etc. importunately; also, *U.S.*, *Austral.*, etc., to canvass for votes.

1731–54 [see TOUTING, TOUTER 1]. **1837** Dickens *Pickw.* x, Doctors' Commons... Two porters.. as touts for licences... Two coves in vhite aprons—touches their hats ven you walk in—'Licence, sir, licence?' **1847** Alb. Smith *Chr. Tadpole* xix, He used to go backwards and forwards.. to tout for customers. **1857** Kingsley *Two Y. Ago* x, I am to tout for introductions for you? **1869** Rogers *Hist. Gleanings* (1870) II. 200 Before Lord Hardwicke's Marriage Act, a particular class of clergymen, not.. in very good repute, touted for marriage-fees. **1881** *Nation* (N.Y.) XXXII. 397 It has never occurred to him that people would be shocked by seeing him 'tout' at Albany. **1891** *Melbourne Argus* 28 Sept., He should have gone round cap in hand and touted for votes. **1898** J. Hollingshead *Gaiety Chron.* ii. 119 The same way as postmen tout for Christmas boxes.

b. *trans.* (*a*) To importune (a person) in a touting manner; (*b*) to solicit custom for (a thing), to try to sell; also (*U.S.*) in extended sense, to recommend.

1920 S. Lewis *Main Street* xvi. 199 Why, you're always touting these Greek dancers. **1928** *Daily Tel.* 5 May 9/6 It strikes one as.. unfair for bankers to tout their clients for.. investment business. **1930** R. H. Mottram *Europa's Beast* vii. 164 He was involved in the ghastly job of touting motor cars. **1948** M. Laski *Tory Heaven* i. 14 Touting vacuum-cleaners at back doors. **1974** *Nature* 11 Jan. 81/1 Such deposits of geothermal energy have long been touted as potential sources of power. **1978** *Detroit Free Press* 2 Apr. 6E/1 Any team that touts Jerry Augustine as the ace of its staff is in serious trouble.

Hence **'touted** *ppl. a.* (*U.S.*), (usu. with qualifying advb.) vaunted, extolled; **'touting** *ppl. a.*

1812 *Sporting Mag.* XXXIX. 283 An object worthy the consideration of the touting firm. **1895** [see 2b]. **1953** *Manch. Guardian Weekly* 5 Feb. 3 The much touted Nationalist 'offensive' on the Chinese mainland. **1978** *Sci. Amer.* Aug. 32/2 The highly touted system of separating isotopes by laser excitation.

tout (taʊt, tut), *v.*[2] *Sc.* Also towt. [Origin of sense 1 obscure. Sense 2 evidently goes with TOUT *sb.*[2], and may be a different word from 1.]

1. *trans.* To toss or throw about in disorder. Also *fig.* to canvass, discuss.

a **1568** *Bannatyne Poems* (Hunter, Cl.) 408/18 To spill the bed it war a pane, Quoth he, the laird will nocht be fane, To fynd it towtit and ourtred. **1596–7** J. Melvil *Diary* (Wodrow Soc.) 410 We perceave the purpose is bot to canves and towt our maters heir a whyll, that thairefter men of lytle skill and les conscience may decern in to tham as they pleis. **1812** P. Forbes *Poems* 38 (E.D.D.) [He] lang an' sair the claise did tout, Dreaming o' an invasion An' fights yon night. **1899** J. Lumsden *Edin. Poems & Songs* 250 Their waters mountain high Uprear in never-ending wars And tout the ships an' flout the sky As if they'd quench the eternal stars.

2. To irritate, vex, tease. Cf. TOUT *sb.*[2]

1725 *Ramsay's Gentle Sheph.* 718 (E.D.D.) Losh preserve us, Bess! At thys tym; and swa towtit! **1832** Carrick in *Whistle-Binkie* Ser. II. (1853) 124 Weel, weel, Janet, dinna be sae toutit about it—I was awa' at a burial. **1887** P. M'Neill *Blawearie* 61 If Bob toutit you, very likely ye hae been toutin' him too.

b. *intr.* (See quot.)

1825 Jamieson, *Tout*, to be seized with a sudden fit of sickness [or] ill humour.

tout, obs. f. TAUT, TAUGHT; var. TOOT.

toutch, obs. form of TOUCH.

†**toute.** *Obs.* Also 5–6 towte. [Derivation obscure: ME. *toute* answers to an OE. **túte*, belonging to the root **tút-*, to stick out, project: see NOTE to TOOT *v.*[1]] The buttocks, fundament, posteriors, rump.

c **1305** *Land Cokayne* 136 He [the abbot] takeþ maidin of þe route And turniþ vp her white toute And betiþ þe taburs wiþ is hond To make is monkes liȝt to lond. *c* **1386** Chaucer *Miller's T.* 626 Of gooth the skyn an hande brede aboute, The hoote kultour brende so his toute. *c* **1450** *Cokwolds Daunce* 120 in Hazl. *E.P.P.* I. 43 To vse we[l]e the lechers craft, With rubyng of ther toute. *c* **1460** *Towneley Myst.* ii. 63 Com nar, & other drife or hald, and kys the dwillis toute.

toute, var. TOT *sb.*[1] *Obs.*, fool; obs. f. TOUT *sb.*[1]

touteaul, obs. erron. form of TORTEAU.

touter ('taʊtə(r)). [f. TOUT *v.*[1] + -ER[1].]

1. One who touts or canvasses for customers or clients; = TOUT *sb.*[1] 2.

a **1754** Richardson *Corr.* (1804) III. 316 Here [Tunbridge Wells] are a parcel of fellows, mean traders, whom they call touters, and their business touting.. riding out miles to meet coaches and company coming hither, to beg their custom while here. **1762** Derrick *Lett.* (1767) II. 49 The tradesmen of Tunbridge Wells, who use this silly practice [of waylaying visitors to solicit their custom] are called Tooters or Touters. **1844** Thackeray *Wand. Fat Contrib.* i, Touters were about seizing upon the passengers and recommending their hotels. **1881** *Nation* (N.Y.) XXXII. 397 His performances at Albany as a touter for votes.

2. A spy upon race-horses; = TOUT *sb.*[1] 3.

1812 *Sporting Mag.* XL. 200 A touter, that is, a person who hides up between the furzes on the heath to see the trials of horses.

3. A thief's scout; = TOUT *sb.*[1] 1.

1844 Dickens *Mart. Chuz.* xxxvii, Thimble-riggers, duffers, touters, or any of those.. sharpers,.. known to the Police.

†**4.** One who or that which watches: see quot. and cf. TOOTER[1] 1. *Obs.*

1867 Smyth *Sailor's Word-bk.*, *Tout*, an old term for looking out, or keeping a prying watch; whence the revenue cruisers and the customs officers were called touters.

touting ('taʊtɪŋ), *vbl. sb.*[1] [f. TOUT *v.*[1] + -ING[1].] The action of TOUT *v.*[1]

1731 *Gentl. Mag.* Sept. 399/1 Soon as they set Eyes on you, off flies the Hat, Does your Honour want this, does your Honour want that?.. Now this, please your Honour, is what we call *Tooting*, A Trick in your Custom to get the first footing. **1777** *Antiq.* in *Ann. Reg.* II. 149/2 Tooting at Tunbridge-wells means.. inviting and bringing guests to their master's house. **1820** W. C. Oulton *Pict. Margate* 47 This practice, called by the inhabitants touting, is exceedingly troublesome to strangers upon their first landing at Margate. **1883** *Manch. Exam.* 26 Nov. 5/1 If there was any touting for the Irish vote at York. **1894** M. H. Hayes *Men & Horses* vi. (ed. 2) 93 The disease of touting is endemic in Newmarket.

touting, *vbl. sb.*[2], in *touting-ken*: see TOOT, TOUT *v.*[3]

toutou ('tu:tu:). [Fr. nursery term.] A pet name for a dog, esp. a lap-dog. Cf. LOULOU.

1894, **1916** [see LOULOU].

‖**tou ts'ai** (tu tsaɪ). *Ceramics.* Also doucai. [Chinese (Wade-Giles), *duōcǎi* (Pinyin), lit. 'multi-coloured', f. *tou* many + *ts'ai* colours.] Used *attrib.* and *absol.* of a kind of enamel painting on Chinese porcelain, developed in the reign of Ch'êng Hua (1465–87), and of (pieces of) porcelain so decorated.

1953 S. Jenyns *Ming Pottery & Porcelain* vi. 90 Another problem piece is the famous Kitchener bowl... Brankston is uncomfortably non-committal. 'There are some points', he says, 'on which it differs from other known Ch'ê ng Hua *tou ts'ai* pieces.' **1960** H. Hayward *Antique Coll.* 285/1 *Tou ts'ai* ('*contrasting colour*') *enamels*, delicate, sparing designs on Chinese porcelain in under-glaze blue, set off by transparent enamel colours. **1972** *Trans. Oriental Ceramics Soc.* 109 A globular jar.. painted in *tou-ts'ai* style in underglaze blue. **1980** *Catal. Fine Chinese Ceramics* (Sotheby, Hong Kong) 104 A rare doucai (tou ts'ai) Vase, brightly enamelled with a formal pattern of lotus scrolls.

toutsayne, early form of TUTSAN.

touward, touzle: see TOWARD, TOUSLE.

tovarish, tovarich (tɒ'vɑːrɪʃ). Also tav-; -isch, -ishch, -istch, -itch. Pl. -i. [ad. Russ. *továrishch* comrade.] In the U.S.S.R., comrade (freq. as a form of address).

1918 C. E. Russell *Unchained Russia* ii. 95 After the Revolution everybody in Russia was 'tavarisch'. **1930** E. Pound *XXX Cantos* xxvii. 127 And these are the labours of tovarisch, That tovarisch lay in the earth, And rose, and wrecked the house of the tyrants. **1935** N. Mitchison *We have been Warned* III. 236 I'm rather looking forward myself to the first time someone calls me tovarish... It seems much more romantic in Russian. **1938** E. Hemingway *Fifth Column* III. ii. 86 Hurry up, Tovaritch, and tape good the mouths. **1968** L. Smith *Fear & Dead Man* x. 80 The Russian grinned slyly. 'Now you know I cannot tell you why I wanted you brought here, *tovarich*.' **1976** M. Barak *Secret List of Heinrich Roehm* xi. 120 The KGB Chairman shrugged. 'Very well... We shall take care of Tovarishch Joe Gonen.' **1977** *Time* 28 Feb. 12/3 To compensate for her lost lover, she found at least one more torrid *tovarish*.

tove (təʊv). A factitious word introduced by 'Lewis Carroll' (see quot. 1855[2]).

Quot. 1855[1] also occurs in the first verse of 'Jabberwocky' in *Through the Looking-Glass* (1871) i. 21.

1855 [see SLITHY *a.*]. **1855** 'L. Carroll' *Rectory Umbrella & Mischmasch* (1932) 142 Tove, a species of Badger. They had smooth white hair, long hind legs, and short horns like a stag: lived chiefly on cheese. **1928** [see SLITHY *a.*]. **1937** G. Frankau *More of Us* 2 While the free-versifier gyres and gimbles The slithy tove—with his own 'private symbols'.

†**tovet.** *Obs. local.* Forms: 6 tolvet, -vett, 7 talvett, tovit(t, 7–8 tof(f)et, 7–9 tovet; also 9 tavort, tobit, tofet, tofiet (*Eng. Dial. Dict.*). [A local word of Kent; evidently the same as *tollfat* (see TOLL *sb.*[1] 3).] A measure of two pecks or half a bushel.

[**1222** [see *tollfat* s.v. TOLL *sb.*[1] 3].] **1520** *MS. Acc. St. John's Hosp.*, *Canterb.*, Paied.. for a tolvet of malt in drynk vj d. **1527** *Ibid.*, For iij tolvettis of otemele xviij d. **1547** [see *tollfat*, as above]. **1618** *MS. Acc. St. John's Hosp.*, *Canterb.*, When he brought the iij tovitis of wheat, ij d. **1629** *Ibid.*, For a taluett of wheate ij s ij d. **1639** *Ibid.*, Payed for mendinge of a touitt ij d. **1674** Jeake *Arith.* (1696) 81, 1 Bushel 2 Tovits or Half Bushels, 1 Tovit 2 Pecks. **1674** Ray *S. & E.C. Words* 77 A *Tovet* or *Tofet*, half a bushel: Kent. **1695** *Birchington Par. Acc.* in *Archæol. Cant.* XII. 407 For three tovets of hair. **1777** *Ann. Reg.* II. 149 Tovet.. in Kent means two pecks.

tovore, variant of TOFORE *Obs.*, before.

tow (təʊ, *Sc.* tʌu, tou), *sb.*[1] Forms: 4–7 towe, (5 toow, 6 toa, 7–8 toe), 5–6 tawe, 5– tow. [Known only from last quarter of 14th c. Origin doubtful: perh. related to ON. *tó* n. uncleansed wool or flax, unworked fibre of thread; which is doubtfully connected with OE. **tow-* spinning, weaving, in *towcræft*, *towhús*, and *towlíc* fit for spinning, textile, and obs. MDu. *touwen* to knit, to weave (Kilian). The original sense may have been 'textile fibre' generally.

Kilian has '*Touw* Fris. Ang. j. *werck*, Stupa'; and '*Tauw* j. *touw*'; also, '*Werck*, Stupa, lini stupa, linum vile, lini purgamentum, lana crassior & recrementitia'; which evidently agrees with our word; but *touw* has not been found in Fris., and the value of Kilian's entry is uncertain.]

†**1.** *app.* The unworked stem or fibre of flax, before it is heckled. *Obs. rare*[−1].

c **1400** Maundev. (Roxb.) xi. 49 Raab.. þat ressayued þe messangers of Israel.. and seled [*pr.* feled] þam in hir hous amang towe of lyne [cf. *Vulgate* Josh. ii. 6 operuitque eos stipula lini; Wyclif, couerd hem with stuble of flaxe].

2. a. The fibre of flax, hemp, or jute prepared for spinning by some process of scutching.

1377 Langl. *P. Pl.* B. XVII. 245 Ac hew fyre at a flynte fowre hundreth wyntre But þow haue towe to take it with tondre or broches Al þi laboure is loste. *c* **1385** Chaucer *L.G.W.* 2004 (*Ariadne*) Ballis ek also Of wex & tow [*v.r.* towe].. To slake his hungir & encombre his teth. *c* **1440** *Promp. Parv.* 498/2 Toow, of a rok, or roket (.. K. towe of hempe, or flax, or othyr like), *pensum.* **1545** *Rates of Customs* c vij b, Towe fyne the C. pounde v.s. Towe the .c. pounde iij s. iiij.d. **1599** A. M. tr. *Gabelhouer's Bk. Physicke* 38/2 Madefye heerin hempen toa, and applye.. rownde about his heade. **1616** Surfl. & Markh. *Country Farme* 568 To the end that.. in beating it with beetles, heckling and spinning of it, such filth may not remaine among the tow. **1674** Grew *Anat. Trunks* II. vii. §13 The Qualities of the best Tow,.. are that the Staple be long, small, tough, and white. **1725** Ramsay *Gentle Sheph.* II. i, Gae break your wheel, and burn your tow, And set the meiklest peat-stack in a low. **178..** Burns (*title*) The weary pund o' tow. *Ibid.* i, I think my wife will end her life Before she spin her tow. **1825** Jamieson, *Tow*, hemp in a prepared state. **1839** *Cumbld. & Westmorld. Dial.* 13 Tae.. spin tow for bord claiths en sheets.

b. *fig.*; esp. in phrase ***to have tow on one's rock*** (***distaff***), to have business to attend to.

c **1386** Chaucer *Miller's T.* 588 This Absolon.. hadde moore tow [*v.r.* towe] on his distaf Than Gerueys knew. *c* **1460** *Towneley Myst.* xiii. 389, I haue tow on my rok more then euer I had. **1756** Mrs. Calderwood in *Coltness Collect.* (Maitl. Club) 155 'In good faith', says John, 'the Dutch has some other tow in their rock'. **1890** Doyle *White Company* v, They may find they have more tow on their distaff than they know how to spin.

3. More strictly, the shorter fibres of flax or hemp, which are separated by heckling from the fine and long-stapled, called *line*; = HARDS, *hurds.*

1530 Palsgr. 183 *Unes estovpes*, a locke of towe or hurdes. *Ibid.* 282/1 Towe, *estouppes.* **1552** Huloet, Tow, *stipa, æ, stupa, æ.* **1601** Holland *Pliny* XIX. i. II. 4 That part.. which is utmost and next to the pill or rind, is called Tow or Hurds, and it is..good for little or nothing but to make lampe-match or candle-wicke. **1844** G. Dodd *Textile Manuf.* v. 165 The flax ceases to be called by that name after it has passed through the heckling-machines; the good portion is then called '*line*', and the inferior '*tow*'. **1893** *Daily News* 14 July 3/7 Prices of lines and tows unchanged. **1896** *Ibid.* 12 Dec. 8/6 Flax, tow, and codilla quiet.

4. A bundle of untwisted natural or manmade fibres.

1950 B. E. Hartsuch *Introd. Textile Chem.* viii. 237 The filaments from several coagulating baths or cabinets (acetate) are combined to form a thick strand known as tow. **1969** [see prepreg *sb.* (*a*)]. **1971** *New Scientist* 8 July 68/2 The material [*sc.* carbon fibres] was in the form of 'tows'—14 inch long bundles containing 10 000 filaments each of 1½ denier. **1973** *Materials & Technol.* VI. iv. 302 In the case of viscose rayon the thick tows are sometimes supplied to mills which desire to do their own cutting into staple lengths.

5. *attrib.* and *Comb.* **a.** *attrib.* 'Of or for tow', as ***tow-beetle*** (beetle *sb.*¹), ***-card*** (card *sb.*¹ 2 a), ***-quality***, ***-waste***; 'consisting or made of tow', as ***tow cloth***, ***goods***, ***hards***, ***-linen***, ***rope***, ***-sack***, ***sheeting***, ***string***, ***thong***, ***weft***, ***yarn***. **b.** Comb., as ***tow-heckler***; ***tow-coloured***, ***-haired***, ***-like***, ***-made*** adjs. **c.** Special combs.: **tow-head**, a light-coloured head of hair; also an unkempt or tousled head; a person having such hair; *spec.* a local name in southern U.S. for *Mergus cucullatus*, the Hooded Merganser of North America, the male of which has a semicircular crest with a white patch; also (*U.S.*), a sand-bar or other obstruction causing ripples in a river or stream; hence **tow-headed** *a.*, having whitish or tousled hair; **tow-wheel**, a large spinning-wheel for making coarse tow yarn.

1601 Holland *Pliny* xix. i. II. 4 To be beaten and punned ..with an hurden mallet or *tow-beetle made for the purpose. **1655** *Essex County, Mass. Probate Rec.* (1916) I. 201 A pair of *tow cards, 1s. **1801** Jas. Thomson *Willy Weir's Legacy* xxv, A pair o' gude tow-cards. **1775** Cooke in Sparks *Corr. Amer. Rev.* (1853) I. 27 Such a demand for *tow-cloth for family use. **1822** J. Flint *Lett. Amer.* 232 A tent was dismantled of its tow cloth covering. **1887** J. Ashby-Sterry *Cucumber Chron.* 5 There are six *tow-haired children playing beneath a guide-post. **1617** J. Barbier *Jan. Ling.* 98 The remnants of *tow-hards..are turned into smoke, or burned in the chimney. **1829** S. Cummings *Western Pilot* 7 There are..a great number of *tow-heads and sand-bars. **1830** A. Royall *Southern Tour* I. 92 One insolent little tow-head. **1883** 'Mark Twain' *Life on Miss.* xxiii. 262 A large town which lay shut in behind a tow-head (*i.e.* new island). **1888** G. Trumbull *Names & Portraits of Birds* 75 The name Tow-Head..was heard in one of our Southern States. **1901** A. H. Rice *Mrs. Wiggs of Cabbage Patch* vii. 95 Little Europena, with baby wisdom, put her tow head under the cloth. **1960** *Guardian* 5 Nov. 1/6 The abominable tow-head from Massachusetts. **1977** *Verbatim* Dec. 6/2 Even the most casual student of American literature should have no trouble with..*tow-head* ('sand bar with cottonwoods'). **1850** S. Judd *R. Edney* xlix. 450 Bronze-faced and *tow-headed Wild Olive boys. **1884** G. H. Boughton in *Harper's Mag.* Sept. 530/2 The tow-headed children rolling about in the orchards. *a* **1800** Pegge *Suppl. Grose*, **Tow-Heckler*, a dresser of tow for spinning. North. **1907** *19th Cent.* Apr. 584 Her *tow-like hair was tied up with white tape. **1779** *New Jersey Archives* (1906) 2nd Ser. III. 154 [A] blue long elk saddle cloth lined with *tow linen. **1884** 'Mark Twain' *Huck. Finn* xx. 196 Some of the children didn't have on any clothes but just a tow-linen shirt. **1921** J. Buchan *Path of King* xiii. 259 He wore an old skin shirt and a pair of tow-linen pants. **1896** *Daily News* 12 Dec. 8/6 *Tow-made goods are selling freely in heavy makes for unions. **1336** *Acc. Exch., K.R.* 19/31 m. 4 (P.R.O.) In x. petris cordis de canabo..pro vno *towerope inde faciendo. **1902** Crockett *Dark o' Moon* xxxix, Saunders Lennox's tow rape will break mony a promise on Monday mornin' by nine o' Kirkcudbright clock. **1930** W. Faulkner *As I lay Dying* 48 The soaked *towsack tied about his shoulders. **1976** J. Lee *Ninth Man* 243 He anchored the tow-sack bundle on his left arm. **1806** *Balance* V. 5/3 Our worthy old friend..sometimes wears a *tow string round his hat. **1892** *Harper's Mag.* Mar. 649/2 What was known as the 'tow-string survey' offered him an excellent opportunity for the display of his peculiar talents. **1776** *Pennsylv. Even. Post* 25 May 264/2 A pair of *tow trowsers. **1837** *Civil Eng. & Arch. Jrnl.* I. 79/2 Bags filled with clay and *tow-waste. **1900** Mary E. Wilkins *Parson Lord* (ed. Tauchn.) 26 The great arc of an old *tow-wheel. **1780** A. Young *Tour Irel.* I. 262 The warp of *tow-yarn.

tow (təʊ, *Sc.* tʌu, tou), *sb.*² Also 5–7 towe. [Known in Sc. use *c* 1470: not in OE. (exc. perh. in '*tóh-line* remulcus', tow-line, in Wr.-Wülcker 182/32). Corresponds to OFris. *tow* (from 15th c.), WFris. *tou*, NFris. *tau*, *tāw*, mod.Du. *touw*, early mod.Du. *touwe* (Kilian), MLG. *touwe*, *touw*, LG. and EFris. *tau*, whence mod.Ger. *tau* (1663 in Kluge); generally identified (at least the monosyll. forms) with ON. *tog*, Norw. *tog*, Sw. *tåg*, Da. *toug*, *tov*, all meaning 'rope, cable, cord': akin also to ON. *taug* f., OE. *téag*, *téah* string, rope, tie *sb.* The fundamental meaning was app. 'means for drawing', f. ablaut stem *teuh-*, *tauh-*, *tuȝ-* (*tog-*) to draw: see tee *v.*¹] A rope. Chiefly *Sc.*

c **1470** Henryson *Mor. Fab.* v. (*Parl. Beasts*) xii, With towis proud ane palȝeoun can thay picht. **1513** Douglas *Æneis* v. xii. 163 Thair cabillis new, and thar heid towis reparis. **1534** *Acc. Ld. High Treas. Scot.* VI. 234 Cabillis and towis brocht hame to the Kingis schip. *a* **1578** Lindesay (Pitscottie) *Chron. Scot.* (S.T.S.) I. 175 His handis bund witht sic ane tow of hempt. **1646** *Alloa Kirk Session Rec.* in *North. N. & Q.* 18 For towes to the bell. *a* **1670** Spalding *Troub. Chas. I* (1829) 12 Upon Monday..at night, he came down over the castle wall, upon tows brought to him secretly by his wife, and clearly wan away. **1785** Burns *Holy Fair* xxvi, Now Clinkumbell, wi' rattlin tow [= bell-rope] Begins to jow and croon. **1888** J. M. E. Saxby *Lads of Lunda* 117 She was scudding out the Voe, Erik steering, Bill at the tows.

b. *spec.* A hangman's rope, a halter.

1596 Dalrymple tr. *Leslie's Hist. Scot.* viii. cii. (S.T.S.) II. 66 The tow, quhilke he maid to hang vtheris in, him selfe was first caught in. **1822** Scott *Pirate* xviii, It can end in naething but trees and tows [= gallows]. **1886** Stevenson *Kidnapped* 50 There's many would like to see him girning in a tow.

c. In various specific or contextual uses (*Sc.* or *Eng. dial.*): e.g.

The rope or chain by which the weights of a clock are suspended (*Sc.*); a line or rope for sea-fishing (*Orkney & Shetl.*); the winding-cable for raising and lowering the cage, etc. in a coal-pit (*Sc.* and *north. Eng.*); a rope or chain for hauling timber (*Eng. dial.*); a line attached to the horns of the leading oxen in a South African team (also *fore-tow*).

1834 A. Smart *Rhymes* 136 Just pou' the tow up when ye beddit. **1844** W. H. Maxwell *Sports & Adv. Scot.* xv. (1855) 136 They prepare to set their *tows*, or lines, provided with ling hooks... The whole of the *packies* a boat carries is a fleet of *tows*. **1850** R. G. Cumming *Hunter's Life S. Afr.* (1902) 8/1 The twelve oxen are soon all securely yoked in their proper places; the leader has made up his 'fore-tow', which is a long spare rheim attached round the horns of each of the fore or front oxen. **1863** W. C. Baldwin *Afr. Hunting* viii. 357 When the front oxen had reached the boys, I shouted, 'Let go the tow, and get out of the road'. **1883** Gresley *Gloss. Coal-mining*, *Tow*,..2. A winding rope of hemp. **1884** *W. Worc. Gloss.* (Upton-on-Severn), *Tow*, a chain for hauling timber. **1893** Heslop *Northumbld. Gloss.*, *Tow*, a small rope or painter. **1898** *Daily News* 25 Feb. 3/1 He went down with the first tow and found the fireman there.

†**tow**, *sb.*³ *Obs. local.* Forms: 5 toughe, 7 tawe, 8 tow. [Agrees in form and sense with Norw. *toge* (for *togje*), Aasen.] Orig. an iron chain, later, a large iron link, attached to the heel of the turn-wrest plough, and by which this is drawn. Also called **tow-chain**.

1407 in Kennett *Par. Ant.* (1818) II. 213 (Oxf. & Bucks.) Pro uno vomere et una cultura et dimid. Toughe cum uno Plowsho emptis, xxiii[d]. **1607** J. Carpenter *Plaine Mans Plough* 160 The Tawe, or that yron Rope which embracing the Beame, assureth it to the Tractory or Lambe. **1733** Tull *Horse-Hoeing Husb.* xxi. 301 The Tow-Chain which fastens the Plow-Tail to the Plow-Head. **1796** J. Boys *Agric. Kent* (1813) 52 The plough there being drawn by a long large iron link, called a tow, which comes from the axle of the carriage round the heel of the plough.

tow (təʊ), *sb.*⁴ Also 7 tawe. [f. tow *v.*¹]

1. A rope used for towing, a tow-line.

1600 Hakluyt *Voy.* III. 585 [The Phenix] kept her company vntil the next morning, then taking in a small cable from her for a towe: but by 9..she spent her maine mast and split her foreyard, breaking also her towe. **1625** J. Glanvill *Voy. Cadiz* 61 Wee could not thus have fastned a towe unto her. **1669** Sturmy *Mariner's Mag.* i. ii. 16 Those that be on Shore may have a Towe, and be blest with a Ruther; for we will stay for no man.

2. a. The action of towing or fact of being towed; chiefly in ***in tow***, in the condition of being towed (*of* or *by* the towing vessel); esp. ***to take in tow*** (said of a ship, etc.): to begin and continue to tow, to tow.

1622 R. Hawkins *Voy. S. Sea* (1847) 226 The *Daintie* sayled badly,..and with the advantage which all the South-sea shippes have of all those built in our North-sea, the admirall gave her a tawe. **1704** J. Harris *Lex. Techn.* I. s.v., Whatever is drawn after a Ship, or Boat with a Rope, &c. is said to be Towed after a Ship, or to be in her Tow. **1720** De Foe *Capt. Singleton* i. (1840) 4 As they were sailing away with our ship in tow as a prize. **1793** Smeaton *Edystone L.* §109 One of these blocks..is by a strong chain attached to the carriage,..which is then drawn forward with the block in tow. **1865** Livingstone *Zambesi* xvi. 324 We took the hippopotamus in tow. **1900** F. T. Bullen *With Christ at Sea* viii. 151 The long upward tow was nearly at an end. **1902** *Westm. Gaz.* 11 Apr. 5/2 The worst weather experienced during the tow was a fresh gale and lumpy sea.

b. *fig.*, esp. ***to take in tow***, to take under one's guidance or patronage; to take charge of; ***in tow*** (***with***) in extended sense: in company (with), accompanying, following.

1722 *New-England Courant* 17–24 Sept. 1/1 Their eager and amorous Emotions of the Body, occasion'd by taking their Mistresses *in Tow*, they call'd *wild Steerage*. **1789** Dibdin *Poor Jack* ii, Providence takes us in tow. **1790** Wolcott (P. Pindar) *Advice to Future Laureat* ii. xxiii, Too proud for bards to take in tow my name. **1804** Fessenden *Democr.* (1806) II. 30 Till he will condescend, I trow Our commonwealth to take in tow. **1883** Gilmour *Mongols* (1884) 226 A young lama..took me in tow, and conducted me to all the tents. **1896** Mrs. Caffyn *Quaker Grandmother* 28 She set off..to explore the world, with a one-eyed old aunt in tow, and a prize bull-dog. **1907** C. S. Ross *Early Otago* 169 He had got in tow with a young lady. **1937** C. Day Lewis *Starting Point* i. 14 Oh, he's got one of his Swedish blondes in tow. **1965** M. Shadbolt *Among Cinders* xiv. 117 I'm in tow with my parents. **1979** S. Brett *Comedian Dies* i. 18 'Come along, Paul.' And Walter Proud, with his writer in tow, hurried along to join them.

3. a. A vessel taken in tow; also, string of boats, barges, etc., being towed. Hence also, a string of barges that is pushed rather than pulled.

1805 in Nicolas *Disp. Nelson* (1846) VII. 189 *note*, Trinidada in tow. Employed knitting fore and mizen rigging, and securing the masts and tow. **1883** *Fisheries Exhib. Catal.* (ed. 4) 175 Methods of Crossing a Channel with Tows of Seals. **1883** *Law Times* 24 Nov. 62/1 The *R.R.*, by reason of the inefficiency of the *V.S.* to command the seven tows, stranded and became a total wreck. **1885** *Law Times Rep.* LIII. 53/2 The schooner..having come into collision with a tug and her tow. **1897** *Outing* (U.S.) XXX. 120/1 The tow consisted of thirty-four boats towing four abreast, a floating village with its houses and families and small children. **1906** *Roy. Comm. Canals, Min. Evid.* 59, I have seen a tow of as many as 23 boats in the Blisworth tunnel on the Grand Junction. **1976** *Sci. Amer.* July 124/3 The U.S. has a network of inland waterways that carries roughly a sixth of all the nation's freight in multiple-barge 'tows' that are usually pushed, rather than pulled, by powerful tugs. **1977** *Washington Post* 4 Sept. A12/1 They [*sc.* towboats] push the barges ahead of them. But the nest of barges that is pushed is called the 'tow'.

b. A vessel that tows; a tug.

1874 Bedford *Sailor's Pocket Bk.* vi. 172 The heaviest boats should be nearest the tow. Weighted boats tow best.

4. *attrib.* and *Comb.* (or perh. from tow *v.*¹), as ***tow-barge***, ***hook***, ***-horse***, ***-man***, ***-truck***, ***-vessel***; **tow-bar**, a bar used in towing; *spec.* the bar by means of which a trailer, caravan, etc., is attached to the vehicle that tows it; **tow-boat**, a boat used in towing; *spec.* a small vessel built for towing others, a tug; **tow-boating** *U.S.*, the piloting or operating of a tow-boat; **tow-car**, on street-railways in *U.S.*, a car which is towed by another, a trailer (*Funk's Stand. Dict.* 1895); **towfish**, a housing with measuring or detecting instruments in it or attached to it and designed to be towed underwater behind a ship; **tow-iron**, in *Whaling*, the toggle-iron or harpoon to which the tow-line is attached (*Cent. Dict.* 1891); **tow-plane**, an aircraft that tows gliders; **tow-post**, a towing-post; **tow-rail**: see quot.; **tow-start** *v. trans.*, to tow (a motor vehicle) in order to start the engine. See also tow-line, -net, -path, -rope.

1956 *Archit. Rev.* CXIX. 259 Small trucks are coupled to it by a quick-action *towbar. **1959** '*Motor*' *Manual* (ed. 36) xiii. 270 Don't be misled by the Unladen Weight which is stamped on the towbar. **1960** *Guardian* 19 Sept. 2/4 For sailing families, boat-cradle, mast support, and long tow-bar can be bought as extras. **1980** *West Lancs. Even. Gaz.* 5 June 16/4 (Advt.), Tow-bars supplied and fitted with electrics to suit every caravan and trailer requirement. **1681** W. Robertson *Phraseol. Gen.* (1693) 1085 A *tow-barge. **1815** *Massachusetts Statute* 7 Feb., His patent steam *tow-boats ..said patent bearing date the 2 day of April 1814. **1860** *Merc. Marine Mag.* VII. 99 Two powerful tow boats..are stationed at the bar. **1887** *Courier-Jrnl.* (Louisville, Kentucky) 7 Feb. 3/3 Theodore Brooks..will try his hand at *tow-boating this season. **1977** *Amer. N. & Q.* XV. 153/1 For more than 300 years its [*sc.* New London's] people were involved in just about every activity related to the sea including fisheries,..towboating, [etc.]. [**1973** *Jrnl. Marine Res.* XXXI. 73 An alternative solution..is the replacement of the weighted fish with a lighter tow body having a controllable fin.] **1975** *McGraw-Hill Yearbk. Sci. & Technol.* 292/1 The..*towfish..continuously monitors the depth of a preselected isotherm by towing at about 5 knots ..two depth-controlled instrument packages which bracket an isotherm. **1876** Knight *Amer. Mech. Dict.* 2604/2 *Tow-hook, an artillery-man's hook, used in unpacking ammunition-chests. **1971** M. Tak *Truck Talk* 170 *Tow hooks*, hooks, generally found on a tractor's bumper, by which it can be towed or pulled. **1978** J. McNeil *Consultant* xx. 180 He unclipped the tow hook from the back of the car. **1865** *Harper's Mag.* Apr. 571/1 It requires as much judgment to drive *tow-horses up the Alleghany as to pilot a steamboat down the Mississippi. **1864** Carlyle *Fredk. Gt.* xvii. vii. IV. 590 New boatmen, forty new *towmen. **1940** *Aeronautics* Nov. 42/1 If the glider is more heavily loaded than the *towplane, the latter will unstick first. **1973** 'A. Hall' *Tango Briefing* viii. 107 The change in the engine-note of the tow-plane. **1908** *Daily News* 29 July 4 He braced his back against the *tow-post as he flicked the cleanings overboard. **1894** *Pall Mall Mag.* Nov. 380 A stout arched timber, reaching from bulwark to bulwark [of a tug], termed a *tow-rail. **1976** A. Schroeder *Shaking it Rough* i. 4 We passed a trio of youths trying to *tow-start an old Chevrolet. **1957** *Tow-truck [see *shopping plaza* s.v. shopping *vbl. sb.* 2]. **1972** *Sat. Rev.* (U.S.) 17 June 6/2 A tow truck..came for the crippled car. **1698** T. Savery *Navig. Impr.* 10 The *Tow Vessel in [16]82 drew but four and a half Water the Outside.

b. With advbs.: **towaway** *U.S.*, the towing away of an illegally parked vehicle; freq. *attrib.* as ***towaway zone***, an area from which such vehicles may be towed away; **tow-out**, the action of towing a drilling platform out to an oil-field at sea.

1956 *Sun* (Baltimore) 31 Jan. 32/6 Such cars parked in the 'tow-a-way' zones would be hauled off to the police impounding lot. **1967** *N.Y. Times* 5 Mar. 75 Despite the published warnings about illegal parking—towaways averaged close to 200 cars daily during February. **1975** *Petroleum Rev.* XXIX. 303/1, 56 steel cylinders..provide buoyancy during tow-out. **1977** *Offshore Engineer* July 55/2 Initial plans were for flat tops to the storage tanks, but these were redesigned to increase the deck loading capacity, at tow-out, by 10,000t, to 24,000t.

†**tow**, *sb.*⁵ *Obs. rare. local.* Forms: 5 togh, 6 tow, towe, tawe. [Origin obscure: it cannot easily be connected with tye, *tie* in same sense.] A pillow-case; cf. tye *sb.*¹ 4.

a **1490** Botoner *Itin.* (Nasmith 1778) 268 Unam cimbam cum una togh de raycloth. **1535** in Weaver *Wells Wills* (1890) 95 A coffer, ij pelowtowes, a salte, a gyrdell. **1542–3** (Jan. 29) *Will J. Dowdynge, widow* (Wells Prob. Reg.), A syller, price of 7s; a pelow with a tawe. **1543** (Sept. 8) *Will R. Antell* (Ibid.), A pillow with the tow.

tow (təʊ), *v.*[1] Forms: 1 **toȝian**, 3 **toȝen**, 4 **towen**, 4–6 **tou(e**, 4–8 **towe**, (6 **toagh**, **toogh**, **tough**, 6–7 **togh**, **toe**; 6 **taw**, 6–7 **tawe**), 6– **tow**. [OE. *toȝian* to draw or pull by force, to drag, ME. *toȝen*, *towen* = OFris. *toga* to pull roughly, pull about, MLG. *togen* (early mod.Du. *togen* (Kilian)), OHG. *zogôn* to draw, tug, drag (MHG. *zogen*), ON. and Norw. *toga* to draw, pull:—OTeut. **togôjan*, deriv. vb. from *tog-*, weak grade of ablaut-series *teuh-*, *tauh-*, *tug-* (*tog-*) to draw: see TEE *v.*[1]]

†**1.** *trans.* To draw by force; to pull, drag.

c **1000** *Passio St. Margaret* in Assmann *Ags. Hom.* 178 And þa godes wiðerwinnan þa fæmnan ȝenamon, ut of þære byriȝ unȝerædelice hi toȝoden. *c* **1275** LAY. 7536 Julius þat sweord heold; and Nemnius þane sceald and longe þus i toȝede. ? *a* **1400** *Morte Arth.* 3655 The marynerse.. Towyne trvsselle one trete, trvssene vpe sailes. **1494** *Acc. Ld. High Treas. Scot.* I. 248 Item, for a rape.. quhilk was brokyne wyth towen of the tymmyr.. ij s. iiij d. **1581** STUDLEY *Agamemnon* III, They tough their oars and with their toyle they helpe the wynd and weather.

fig. **1583** STUBBES *Anat. Abus.* II. (1882) 50 What tricking & toying, and al to tawe out mony, you may be sure.

†**b.** To convey, carry. *Obs. rare.*

13.. *E.E. Allit. P.* C. 100 Jonas.. Maches hym with þe maryneres, makes her paye, For to towe hym in-to Tarce, as tyd as þay myȝt. *a* **1375** *Joseph Arim.* 374 þenne þei taken þis mon and towen him to þe temple.

c. To draw *up* or let *down* with a tow or rope. *Sc.*

In this sense perh. directly from TOW *sb.*[2]

1596 DALRYMPLE tr. *Leslie's Hist. Scot.* (S.T.S.) I. 27 With lang towis and Lathiris laitth doune thay ar towit vpe. **1755** *Edom o' Gordon* xxii. in *Percy Reliques* (1765) I. 104 O row me in a pair o' sheits, And tow me owre the wa.

2. *spec.* To draw or drag (a vessel, persons in a boat, etc.) on the water by a rope.

to tow (a boat) *under water*, to swamp by towing.

[**1290**: ? implied in TOWAGE 1.] **1391** *Earl Derby's Exp.* (Camden) 23 Pro touyng navem domini de la hauen apud Boston. *a* **1500** in *Arnolde's Chron.* (1811) 133 After tyme she was weyed and toued to the hauyn at Caleis. **1553** in Hakluyt *Voy.* (1904) V. 92 The boat (which we toed asterne from Jaffa). **1557** W. TOWRSON *ibid.* (1589) 117 Her rudder was broken, so that the *Hart* was glad to towe her. **1562** J. SHUTE tr. *Cambini's Turk. Wars* 34 b, They tawed the palandre after them. **1589** WARNER *Alb. Eng.* VI. xxix. (1612) 144, I will.. toogh the Pinnesse of my thoughts to kenning of your eyes. **1591** SYLVESTER *Du Bartas* I. i. 578 He that.. toghes against the tide His laden barge. **1597** J. KING *On Jonas* (1618) 56 They.. labored.. to toagh their ships to land. **1620** R. COCKS *Diary* (Hakl. Soc.) II. 113, I sent out 4 barkes to helpe to toe her. **1630** DRAYTON *Muses Elizium* II. 343 Swans vpon the Streame to tawe me, Stags vpon the Land to draw me. **1644** Z. BOYD *Gard. Zion* in *Zion's Flowers* (1855) App. 7/1 In thy great Barge me togh against the tide. **1743** BULKELEY & CUMMINS *Voy. S. Seas* 143 We took from the Indians a Canoe, made of the Bark of Trees, but soon towed her under Water. **1769** *De Foe's Tour Gt. Brit.* (ed. 7) I. 153 King's Ferry, where a long Cable of about 140 Fathom,.. fastened at each End across the Water, serves to get over the Boat by Hand... The Ferry-keeper.. is obliged to tow all Travellers over free. **1877** A. B. EDWARDS *Up Nile* vii. 174 Barges towed by government steam-tugs.

b. *intr.* To pull or tug as in trying to move.

1884 *Law Times* 10 May 26/2 A tug towed at her for an hour and a half before she was got off.

3. *trans.* To drag by or as by a line. (*humorous.*)

1663 BUTLER *Hud.* I. II. 1125 The Knight himself did after ride Leading Crowdero by his side, And tow'd him, if he lagg'd behind. **1767** LADY MARY COKE *Jrnl.* 29 July (1889) II. 68 Monsieur Wangenheim was towing up Lady Sarah, and complain'd it was hard work. **1803** SCOTT *Let. to Ellis* 14 Oct., in *Lockhart*, A rosy lass.. entered our cottage, towing in a monstrous sort of bulldog. **1883** W. H. BISHOP in *Harper's Mag.* Mar. 503/1 A mounted Mexican towing a bull. **1884** *Nonconf. & Indep.* 12 June 578/1 Mr. Cumberland, blindfolded, towed another dignified gentleman through the streets by a silken cord.

4. *intr.* or *absol.* To advance or proceed by towing or being towed.

1612 DRAYTON *Poly-olb.* ii. 451 When toghing vp that streame.. shee yet conceales her name. **1624** CAPT. SMITH *Virginia* III. vi. 61 He would.. cause.. divers of his Countrymen helpe vs towe against winde or tyde. **1667** *Lond. Gaz.* No. 186/4 One of them endeavoured to tow after him. **1695** BLACKMORE *Pr. Arth.* VI. 371 At last King Octa.. Commanding all to follow, tows away. **1720** DE FOE *Capt. Singleton* v. (1840) 90 We towed up as far as.. our boats would swim. **1813** SOUTHEY *Nelson* I. iii. 143 The French vessels were allowed to tow out of the port of Genoa. **1874** [see TOW *sb.*[4] 3 b].

Hence **towed** (təʊd), **towing** ('təʊɪŋ) *ppl. adjs.*

1898 *Daily News* 4 Aug. 5/3 The river journey in *towed barges from Shellal to Wady Halfa. **1901** *Westm. Gaz.* 8 July 9/3 One tug, and one towed raft, two self-propelled rafts. **1795** *Act 35 Geo. III*, c. 106 §23 For the making.. a Way or Road for the *Towing Horses. **1842** BRANDE *Dict. Sc.*, etc. s.v. *Tow*, As the vessel towed affects the motions of the other, much attention is required on her part to second the intentions of the towing vessel.

transf. **1909** *Westm. Gaz.* 2 Feb. 4/1 To couple up a towing machine to a fully equipped [motor-] car by means of a strap.

tow (təʊ), *int.* and *v.*[2] **a.** *int.* A word used in calling a hawk, and in urging on greyhounds. **b.** *vb. trans.* To urge (greyhounds) *on* with this call.

1575 TURBERV. *Falconrie* 182 Make them come from it to your fist.. with calling and chirping to them, saying: *Towe, Towe*, or *Stowe, Stowe*, as Falconers vse. **1793** F. GROSE *Olio* (1796) 178 Towing on two greyhounds, the constant attendants on his steps, pursued the game. *Note.* Tow, Tow, used in setting on greyhounds in Gloucestershire.

tow (təʊ), *v.*[3] [f. TOW *sb.*[1]] *trans.* To comb or card flax; also, to reduce to the state of tow or fibre. Hence '**towing** *vbl. sb.*[2], *spec.*: see quot. 1891; †**towing-mill**, a carding-machine: see quot. 1789.

1615 MARKHAM *Eng. Housew.* II. v. (1668) 134 That which comes from the flaxe being a little towed again in a pair of Wooll Cards, will make a course harding. **1789** *Trans. Soc. Arts* VII. 195 Mills.. in Yorkshire.. called Towing-Mills.. worked by men turning them backward and forward, till the wool is sufficiently opened for use. **1891** *Cent. Dict.*, *Towing*, in *curled-hair manuf.*, the operation of picking to pieces the ropes of hair after they have been steeped in water and then subjected to slow heat [to give a permanent curl to the hair].

tow, *v.*[4] *Pottery manuf.* [f. TOW *sb.*[1]] *trans.* To smooth the surface of (earthenware or china) when in the dry clay state before firing, by rubbing it with tow, sand-paper, or flannel. Hence '**tower**, '**towing** *vbl. sb.*[3]

1892 *Daily News* 23 July 5/4 Mr. Brewer, a factory inspector in the Derby district, calls attention to the probable extension of the method of putting a finer surface on earthenware, which is known as 'towing'. **1894** *Labour Commission Gloss.*, *Towers*,.. pottery workers, who, when plates that are still unfired are dried till nearly all the moisture is out of them, pass over the surface while they.. are rotating on a wheel a piece of 'tow', or sandpaper, to make them smooth.

tow, obs. form of TOUGH, TWO.

towable ('təʊəb(ə)l), *a.* [f. TOW *v.*[1] + -ABLE.] That may be towed.

1927 *Glasgow Herald* Jan. 7 The dock.. is towable to any part of Australia. **1967** [see DRACONE, DRACONE]. **1982** *Social Trends 1983* viii. 114/2 Towable caravans and house-boats.

towage ('təʊɪdʒ). [Used in 13th c. in med.L. form *towāgium*, in 13th or 14th c. in F. form *touage*, implying verbs med.L. *towāre*, F. *touer*. These verbs, however, have not yet been found at that date, and Hatz.-Darm. consider Fr. *touer* to be a deriv. of ON. *toga* to draw, pull; it might also be from MLG. *togen*: see TOW *v.*[1] The Eng. form *towage* appears in L. context *a* 1327. In mod. use it is felt as a direct derivative of TOW *v.*[1]]

1. The charge or payment for towing a vessel (in quot. 1670, for permission to tow along the bank). Also *attrib.*

[**1286** Towagium (Du Cange). **1290** *Rolls of Parlt.* I. 27/1 Cum Dominus Rex habeat & habere debeat Towagium navium & batellorum majorum & minorum in Aqua de Tyne, ascendendo versus Novum Castrum.] **1562** in R. G. Marsden *Sel. Pl. Crt. Adm.* (Selden) II. 64 Towage, sownage, and petye lodemanshippe with all other accustomed averages. **1670** BLOUNT *Law Dict.*, *Towage*.. is the towing or drawing a Ship... Also, that Money or other recompence, which is given by Bargemen to the owner of the Ground, next a River where they tow a Barge, or other Vessel. *a* **1688** DALLAS *Stiles* (1697) 414 Merchant of the said Towage, Rowage, Anchorage,.. and other dues. **1755** MAGENS *Insurances* I. 72 To the petty, or accustomary Average.. belong Lodemanage, Towage, and Pilotage.

2. The action or process of towing or being towed.

[**1297** *Boston Customs Acc. Customs, K.R.* Bd. 5 No. 5 *dorso* (P.R.O.), In frectagio pro .lij. saccis et .xx. petris lane ..et in touwagio dictarum lanarum et in loadesmanagio .lxxj.s... Item in primagio .ij.s.] *a* **1327** *Acc. Exch. K.R.* 17/34 m. 3 (P.R.O.) In towage eorundem [xl doleorum vini] per aquam.. de lostwithiel vsque Fawe ad nauem .xiij.s. .iiij.d. **1611** COTGR., *Toüaige*, Towage, the towing of a ship by boats, or at the sterne of another ship. *a* **1640** JACKSON *Creed* XI. xliv. §1 There is no possibility for two to go on breast, nor any room for steerage, but only towage. **1670** [see sense 1]. **1827** *Blackw. Mag.* XXI. 244 Under his towage we made way at a tolerably rapid rate. **1894** *Times* 12 Feb. 4/2 The Mosquito proceeded to tow the Cathay towards the Humber. The Cathay continued to labour heavily, and the towage required great care.

‖**towai** ('tɔːwai). Also **towhai**. [Native Maori name. (Not to be confused with TAWHAI.)] A large New Zealand timber tree, *Weinmannia racemosa*, N.O. *Saxifragaceæ*, also called by colonists *black birch*.

1845 WAKEFIELD *Adv. N. Zealand* II. 95 (Morris) Its banks.. are covered almost wholly with the towai. This tree has very small dark leaves. It is used for ship-building, and is called by Englishmen the 'black birch'. **1851** MRS. WILSON *N. Zealand* 43 The ake.. and towai (*Leiospermum racemosum*) are almost equal, in point of colour, to rosewood. **1883** J. HECTOR *Handbk. N. Zealand* 132 (Morris) Towhai, Kamahi. A large tree; trunk two to four feet in diameter, and fifty feet high.

towail(e, **-aille**, **-ale**, **-all**, obs. ff. TOWEL.

towan ('taʊən). *Cornw.* Also **towin**, **tewen**, **tuan**, **tûyn**. [Cornish *towan*, Welsh *tywyn* in same sense.] A coast sand-hill.

1803 POLWHELE *Hist. Cornw.* I. v. 161 The green hillocks or levels of our downs in the vicinity of the sea. We call them *towans*. **1859** M. WALCOTT *Guide Devon & Cornw.* 529 The neighbourhood of Hayle is remarkable for sands composed of shells, the towans. **1882** JAGO *Cornw. Gloss.*, *Towan, towin, tewen, tuan*, or *tûyn*.. are Celtic Cornish words for a dune or heap of sand. **1899** QUILLER COUCH *Ship of Stars* iv, He heard a horn blown somewhere high on the towans behind him.

†**towanite** ('taʊənaɪt). *Min.* [Named 1852, from Huel Towan in Cornwall: see -ITE[1].] An obsolete synonym for CHALCOPYRITE.

1852 BROOKE & MILLER *Phillips' Introd. Min.* 182 Bornite .. occurs in beds and veins in the older rocks with towanite [etc.]. **1878** GURNEY *Crystallogr.* 79 Towanite or Copper Pyrites is a double sulphide of copper and iron.

towar, obs. Sc. form of TOWER *sb.*[2], [3].

toward ('təʊ(w)əd, 'tɔːəd), *a.* and *adv.* Forms: see next. [OE. *tóweard* adj., f. *tó*, TO *prep.* + *-weard*, -WARD. So OS. *tôward*, *-werd*, OHG. *zuowart*, *-wert*, adjs. In OE., when used attributively, inflected like other adjs.; when in the predicate, uninflected exc. with pl. *-e*. The advb. use appears to arise out of the predicative use of the adj., or from the neuter adj.]

A. *adj.* †**1.** That is to come, coming, future. *Obs.*

c **888** K. ÆLFRED *Boeth.* xxxix. §11 Tacn þæs toweardan welan. **971** *Blickl. Hom.* 15 Be þisse ondweardan tide, ȝe eac be þære toweardan. *c* **1000** *Ags. Gosp.* Mark x. 30 On toweardre [*Hatt. G.* towearde] woruld ece lif. **11..** *12th Cent. Hom.* xiv. 136 Næfð he næfre þærof forȝyfenesse, ne on þisse weorlde, ne on þa towearden. **1590** SPENSER *F.Q.* II. iv. 22 He, either envying my toward good, Or of him selfe to treason ill disposd. **1613** CHAPMAN *Rev. Bussy D'Ambois* I. i, The toward victor of the whole low Countryes.

†**b.** *predicatively.* Coming or going (to be), about to be, future. *Obs.*

c **888** K. ÆLFRED *Boeth.* xi. §1 He nat hwæt him toweard bið, hwæðer þe god þe yfel. *c* **1000** ÆLFRIC *Gen.* xviii. 18 He ys toweard on micelre mægðe. *Ibid.* xlix. 1 Ic eow cyðe þa þing þe eow towearde synd. —— *Deut.* xxix. 15 Eallum mannum, þam þe nu sint and þam þe towearde sint. *c* **1530** LD. BERNERS *Arth. Lyt. Bryt.* (1814) 48 And she grew and amended dayly, so that she was towarde to be fayrest creature of ye worlde.

†**2.** Approaching, imminent, impending. *Obs.*

c **890** tr. *Bæda's Eccl. Hist.* IV. i. (1890) 256 Hy nedde se toweardα winter, þæt heo stille wunedon. **971** *Blickl. Hom.* 195 Forþon þe he ær nolde onȝytan þone towerdon deaþ. **1586** J. HOOKER *Hist. Irel.* in Holinshed II. 154/2 Dispatching also a messenger to hir maiestie of these toward broiles and rebellion.

b. *pred.* Now *rare* or *Obs.*

c **890** tr. *Bæda's Eccl. Hist.* IV. xiv. [xi.] (1890) 294 Mid þy he.. onȝet þæt him deaðes dæȝ toweard wæs. *a* **1000** *Læceboc* II. xlvi. in *Sax. Leechd.* II. 256 Tacn hu sio adl toweard sie. **1387** TREVISA *Higden* (Rolls) V. 101 Also for werre and batailles þat were toward [L. *propter imminentia bella*]. **1462** J. PASTON in *P. Lett.* II. 121 Mak as merry as ye can, for ther is no joperte toward not yet. **1494** FABYAN *Chron.* VII. 387 For so moche as wynter was towarde. **1582** N. T. (Rhem.) *Acts* xxvii. 20 No smal storme being toward [*imminente*] al hope was now taken away. **1600** SHAKS. *A.Y.L.* v. iv. 35 There is sure another flood toward, and these couples are comming to the Arke. **1795** *Montford Castle* II. 50 There was a trifling banquet toward, at which they would be glad of his company. **1877** MACQUOID *Doris Barugh* xviii. (E.D.D.), Ah knawed fower weeks sin' at ther war a wedding toward.

c. In progress, going on; being done.

1838 CAROLINE FOX *Old Friends* (1882) 229 Louis Buonaparte has reached France from London to see what is toward. **1892** A. MURDOCH *Yoshiwara Episode* 60 News of the encounter that was toward had spread.., and all the inmates.. had pushed into the ante-room where the contest was in progress. **1893** RIDER HAGGARD *Montezuma's Dau.* xxi, A fierce hope smote me.. when I saw what was toward.

d. 'Getting on', forward, advanced.

1893 *Cornh. Mag.* Nov. 522 Glidders's operations were well toward.

3. Of young persons: Promising, 'hopeful', forward; making good progress in learning or practice; disposed, apt, or willing to learn; docile. = TOWARDLY *a.* 2. *Obs.* or *arch.*

c **1290** *S. Eng. Let.* I. 42/278 Swuch a child touward as þou art i-loked. **1538** CROMWELL in Merriman *Life & Lett.* (1902) II. 163 On the behalfe of a ryght towarde yonge man, Edwarde Bashe, this Berer. **1598** B. JONSON *Ev. Man in Hum.* II. i, Where proving A toward Imp. **1600** HEYWOOD *1st Pt. Edw. IV*, Wks. 1874 I. 5 There was neuer mother had a towarder son. **1625** B. JONSON *Staple of N.* II. i, Vouchsafe my toward kinsman, gracious madam, The favour of your hand.

†**4.** Disposed to do what is asked or required; willing, compliant, obliging, docile. (The opposite of FROWARD *a.* 1.) *Obs.* or *arch.*

c **1440** *York Myst.* xxvi. 159 Goode sir, be toward þis tyme, And tarie noght my trace, For I haue tythandis to telle. **1472–3** *Rolls of Parlt.* VI. 6/1 Of their fre wille, toward, herty and lovyng dispositions. **1532** CROMWELL in Merriman *Life & Lett.* (1902) I. 350 What shalbe your towarde mynde herin I pray you to Aduertise me. **1592** SHAKS. *Ven. & Ad.* 1157 Peruerse it shall be, where it showes most toward, Put feare to valour, courage to the coward. **1713** STEELE *Guard.* No. 142 ¶3 Miss hath hitherto been very tractable and toward. **1738** tr. *Guazzo's Art Conversation* 233 A Child of a toward Disposition.

b. Of things: Favourable, propitious: the opposite of *untoward*. *rare.*

1850 GLADSTONE *Homer* II. 100 She can order out a rattling zephyr.. or simply a toward breeze. **1868** —— *Juv. Mundi* viii. (1870) 281 He too sends for the Greek ship a toward breeze. **1902** *Daily Chron.* 29 May 3/2 There are plenty of what we may call toward coincidences in Mr. Yoxall's book.

5. Left, as opposed to right. *dial.*

[From the fact that the left side of a horse, etc., is toward the person who mounts or leads it. Cf. NEAR *a.* 3.]

1866 BLACKMORE *Cradock Nowell* xxii, 'Mark, does Mr. Cradock Nowell generally shoot with cartridges?' 'He laiketh mostways to be with a curtreege in his toard barryel, sir'. 'Oh, keeps a cartridge in his left barrel, does he; and fires first the right, I suppose?' **1879** MISS JACKSON *Shropsh. Word-bk.* s.v. *Frommet*, A harvest-field term. *Toërt* is left hand... 'Theer, now yo'n chucked it down toërt way'.

†**6.** ? Forthcoming, ready at hand; in existence, 'going'. *Obs.* (Quotations obscure.)

c **1350** *Will. Palerne* 1101 Of proude princes sones, douȝti men toward, Fulle foure schore. *Ibid.* 1443 He has a sone dere, On þe triest man to-ward of alle douȝti dedes, þat any man vpon molde may of here. **1393** LANGL. *P. Pl.* C. I. 214 And ȝe, route of ratons of rest men a-wake, Ne were þe cat of þe court And ȝonge Kytones to-warde. *c* **1530** LD. BERNERS *Arth. Lyt. Bryt.* cxiv. (1814) 540 And this chyld was the most fair chyld toward of the world, and wel fourmed, byg and myghty. [*orig.* & si estoit l'enfant le plus beau qu'oncques fut veu grand & gros & bien forme.] **1559** AYLMER *Harborowe* 12, I shewed you the lyke towarde in a man of late.

B. *adv.* [Cf. MHG. *zuowart* adv.]

1. In a direction toward oneself, or toward something aimed at. *Obs.* or *arch.* †***toward and froward*** (dial. *fromward*), to and fro.

a **1300** *E.E. Psalter* cxviii[i]. 8 To-ward, fra-ward, forlete me noght. *a* **1400** in Halliwell *Rara Mathem.* (1841) 58 Come toward and go froward til þe perpendicle.. falle vpon þe mydel lyne of þe quadrant. *Ibid.* 66 Go toward and froward til þou se þe toppe of þat thing in þe mydel of þat myrure. **1470–85** MALORY *Arthur* XIII. xvi. 634 He rode many Iourneyes bothe toward and froward. **1858** BUSHNELL *Serm. New Life* xi. (1869) 148 The motion is outward and not toward, as we conceive it to be in happiness.

b. To the left or near side (of a horse, etc.). *dial.*

1711 *Lond. Gaz.* No. 4917/4 The forepart of his Mane longest, the one part being short, lies toward, the other fromward. [Gloucester, Hampsh., Wilts, in *Eng. Dial Dict.*]

2. Onward (in a course), forward (*lit.* and *fig.*).

1426 LYDG. *De Guil. Pilgr.* 12159 Al that thow wendyst ha be toward, Ys but a passage that goth bakward. **1509** HAWES *Past. Pleas.* xxx. (Percy Soc.) 148 The time renneth toward right fast. **1529** MORE *Dyaloge* Wks. 110/1 By that way, yᵉ faith went well toward, and one heritique so tourned did turne many other. **1888** *Berksh. Gloss.*, *Towart*, towards; forward. When a come a little tow-art I could zee as 'twas a pawle cat.

toward ('təʊəd, 'tɔːəd, tɔəd; tə'wɔːd), *prep.* Forms: 1–2 **toweard**, 2 **towaard**, 2–3 **touward**, 2–4 **to-ward**, 2, 4–6 *Sc.* **towart**, (4 **tawart**, 6 *Sc.* **touart**), 3 (*Orm.*) **towarrd**, (3–4 **to(-)war**), 4–5 **taward(e**, 4–6 **towarde**, 5 **tooward**, **to-warde**, **to ward**, **to warde**, (**towor**, 6 **towerde**, **towrd**, **tward**, **torde**), 3– **toward**, (8–9 **tow'rd**, 9 *dial.* **toard**). [OE. *tóweard*, f. *tó*, TO *prep.* + *-weard*, -WARD; orig. the uninflected form or singular neuter of TOWARD *a.* In OE., originally followed by a genitive; later by a dative like the simple *to*.

'The first pronunciation figured above is now chiefly northern and (app.) American; the fourth is not recognized in any modern dictionary, British or American, nor app. by any orthoepist; but it appears to be the prevailing one in London and the south of England.'—N.E.D.

See Walker on the word. It was app. referred to in 1749 by Chesterfield *Lett.* 27 Sept.: 'The vulgar man goes *to wards* and not *towards* such a place'. It may have arisen from the analytical form in *to us ward*, *to heaven ward*, in which *to* has its ordinary stressless pronunciation as a preposition; and, if so, may have existed locally or as an alternative form, esp. in verse, from the 16th c. So with TOWARDS.]

1. Of motion (or action figured as motion): In the direction of; so as to approach (but not necessarily reach: thus differing from TO *prep.* 1).

c **893** K. ÆLFRED *Oros.* I. i. §22 þonne ærnað hy ealle toweard þæm feo. *c* **897** —— *Gregory's Past. C.* ix. 59 Ða ðe gað on ryhtne weȝ toweard ðæs hefonrices. *c* **1175** *Lamb. Hom.* 3 þe helend nehlechede to-ward ierusalem þare burh. *c* **1290** *S. Eng. Leg.* I. 18/589 þo þe deuelene comen toward him, huy ne miȝten come him neiȝ. *c* **1375** *Cursor M.* 3356 (Fairf.) Quat mon ys he þat comande tawarde [*v.r.* tilward] vs I se. *c* **1375** *Sc. Leg. Saints* xxxiii. (*George*) 844 Dacyane .. Towart his palace went. *c* **1400** *Destr. Troy* 6112 þo ledys .. gon tooward þe grekis. *c* **1470** HENRY *Wallace* I. 98 Towart Dunbar without restyng thai raid. **1552** HULOET, Torde, *vide* in toward. **1611** BIBLE *Phil.* iii. 14, I presse toward the marke. **1715–20** POPE *Iliad* XI. 641 The steeds with sounding feet Shake the dry field, and thunder tow'rd the fleet. **1807** J. BARLOW *Columb.* I. 504 Tow'rd the Northern sky.. the Hero cast his eye. **1870** MORRIS *Earthly Par.* (1890) 233/2 The company of maidens drew Toward where they stood.

†**b.** *pred.* after *to be*: On the way to. *Obs.*

1297 R. GLOUC. (Rolls) 3569 þe king was toward scottlond. *c* **1425** *Seven Sag.* (P.) 660 Toward the deth as he was.. He mette with myster Baucillas.

†**c.** With implication of reaching; to. *Obs.*

c **1386** CHAUCER *Prol.* 27 Pilgrimes were they alle That toward Caunterbury wolden ryde. *c* **1425** *XI Pains of Hell* 238 in *O.E. Misc.* 218 Vp taward heuen þai con him bryng. **1440** *Paston Lett.* I. 40 This same weke shall he to ward Fraunce. *c* **1500** *Melusine* 102 They departed fro Lusynen and camme to Poytiers toward the Erle. **1596** SHAKS. *Merch. V.* IV. i. 403, I must away this night toward Padua. **1611** —— *Wint. T.* V. i. 232 Vpon which Errand I now goe toward him.

2. Of position: In the direction of; on the side next to; turned or directed to, facing.

13.. *Cursor M.* 2474 (Cott.) Abram chese him toward þe est. **1387** TREVISA *Higden* (Rolls) I. 235 Alway his face was toward þe sonne. *c* **1400** MAUNDEV. (Roxb.) xxxii. 147 þat tyme occupied Cristen men many cuntreez toward þase partiez. *c* **1482** J. KAY tr. *Caoursin's Siege of Rhodes* (1870) ¶10 Atte fote of a hylle toward the Weste. *a* **1548** HALL *Chron. Hen. V* 55 When he entred into the chambre the dukes backe was towarde him. **1610** HOLLAND *Camden's Brit.* (1637) 306 Under Suth-rey toward the South lieth.. Suth-sex. **1760–72** H. BROOKE *Fool of Qual.* (1809) I. 75 This needle.. [was] three-square toward the point. **1853** M. ARNOLD *Scholar Gypsy* xiii, Have I not passed thee on the wooden bridge.. Thy face toward Hinksey and its wintry ridge?

†**b.** Beside, near; about, in attendance upon; in the possession of; with. *Obs.*

c **1400** tr. *Secreta Secret., Gov. Lordsh.* 110 And þe gretteste with-holde toward þe. *c* **1400** *Brut* cxxxii. 136 Harolde.. wolde nouȝt departe with his peple of þing þat he hade gete, but helde it al toward [*v.r.* towards] him-self. **1433** *Rolls of Parlt.* IV. 423/1 Makyng þo þat beth toward hym to do the same. **1469** in *Archæologia* XV. 170 The oon key shall abyde toward the wardeyn, and the second toward the maister aboveseid. **1601** BP. ANDREWES *Serm., Matt. xxii. 21* (1631) II. 88 Herod and they that were toward him, being all that they were by Cæsar.

3. In the direction of (in *fig.* senses). **a.** *gen.*: esp. with words expressing tendency or aim, and followed by an abstract noun expressing state, condition, etc. (In quots. 13.. and 1553 'on the way to': cf. 1 b; in quot. 1600, 'to': cf. 1 c.)

[*a* **1225** *Ancr. R.* 120 Tu schalt demen þi suluen wod, þo þu þer touward þouhtest.] **13..** *Cursor M.* App. ii. 790 (B. M. Add. MS.) What þinges þat I say may To myn felawis.., That I was toward þi buriynge. **1426** LYDG. *De Guil. Pilgr.* 75 That folk may the Ryhte weye se Best assuryd to-warde ther passage. **1553** *Respublica* IV. iv. 1126 So ye though oppressed with longe aduersitee, Yet doubte not, are towarde wealth & prospiritee. **1600** SHAKS. *A.Y.L.* II. vii. 162 His bigge manly voice, Turning againe toward childish trebble, pipes And whistles in his sound. *a* **1677** BARROW *Serm. Eccl.* ix. 10 Wks. 1686 III. 224 Incessantly working toward the end for which it was designed. **1818** SOUTHEY *Ess.* (1832) II. 135 There is no danger of our tending toward the same extreme. **1875** WHITNEY *Life Lang.* ii. 18 Tracing the history of words toward their origin. **1891** MRS. MAUDE *Pyrography* i. 7 An immense advance has been made toward perfection.

b. With a noun or pronoun denoting the object of action or feeling: To; against.

c **1175** *Lamb. Hom.* 17 Gif we suneȝieð towaard him we sculen gan to bote. *c* **1200** ORMIN 2601 Forr ȝho wass.. milde & meoc & bliþe, ȝa towarrd Godd, ȝa towarrd mann. **1390** GOWER *Conf.* I. 122 Bot wolde god that grace sende, That toward me my lady wende, As I towardes hire wene. *c* **1400** *Laud Troy Bk.* 10049 He is wel wroth toward his wiff. *c* **1460** *Oseney Reg.* 123 The seruice.. that þe saide chanons schall aquite towarde the Chefe lordes. *c* **1500** *Melusine* xxxvii. 297 Now haue I betrayed you.. and haue forsworne my self toward you. **1601** SHAKS. *Twel. N.* III. ii. 13 This was a great argument of loue in her toward you. **1785** *Liberal Amer.* II. 226 To explain the real motives of his conduct toward me in America. **1813** SOUTHEY *Nelson* II. vi. 84 The policy which ought to be pursued toward the French in Egypt. **1867** R. COLLYER *Nat. & Life* xiii. 247 This is the way in which I act toward my own children.

†**c.** With regard to, in reference to, respecting, concerning, about. Also ***as toward*** (cf. *as to*). *Obs.*

a **1240** *Lofsong* in *Cott. Hom.* 211 Opene ham [my wits] heouenliche king touward heouenliche þinges. *c* **1300** *Becket* 765 If thu wolt owȝt toward me, thu wost wel y ne mai noȝt fiȝte. **1390** GOWER *Conf.* II. 34 Wel me qwemeth, That thou thiself hast thus aquit Toward this vice, in which no wit Abide mai. **1433** *Rolls of Parlt.* IV. 423/2 As toward his abode here.. he saide þat he knoweth [etc.]. *a* **1548** HALL *Chron., Hen. VI* 96 b, And as towarde the letter sent.. vnto my lorde of Bedford of the whiche the tenor is before rehersed. **1564** *Reg. Privy Council Scot.* I. 285 Swa that na complaint salbe.. maid to the Quenis Majestie towart the saidis contraversiis and debattis. **1670–1** MARVELL *Corr.* Wks. (Grosart) II. 360 On Monday next, when the House will probably proceed severely toward their penaltyes.

d. In comparison with: = TO 18. Now *dial.*

1527–8 in Strype *Eccl. Mem.* (1721) I. App. xvii. 38 Which bookes.. be not to be regarded toward the new printed Testament in Englishe. **1887** *S. Chesh. Gloss.*, *To'art as*, in comparison with.

4. Of time: So as to approach; at the approach of, nearly as late or as far on as, shortly before, near.

14.. *Torr. Portugal* (E.E.T.S.) Fragm. ii. 511 It drewe towarde the nyght. ? *a* **1500** *Wycket* (1828) p. ii, Towarde the laste dayes the kynge of the northe shall come. **1797** HOLCROFT tr. *Stolberg's Trav.* (ed. 2) III. lxxx. 240 Toward the conclusion of their independence. **1802** M. CUTLER in *Life*, etc. (1888) II. 89 Gentlemen most accustomed to speaking.. were principally to wait till toward the close of the debate. **1844** SOUTHEY *Life A. Bell* I. 54 Toward the close of October letters.. had reached him by way of Glasgow. **1876** STEDMAN *Victorian Poets* 103 At dates well toward the middle of this century.

5. †**a.** Of condition or quality: Verging upon, near; somewhat like, nearly, as if; ***toward blackness***, somewhat or nearly black. *Obs.*

1533 ELYOT *Cast. Helthe* (1541) N iij, Whan the bladder is towarde any syckenes. **1562** TURNER *Herbal* II. 153 The Thlaspi yᵗ cometh out of Cappadocia is toward blacknes, and the sede is not fully rounde. **1566** BLUNDEVIL *Horsemanship* IV. iv. (1580) 3 It is best knowne, whether a Horse be sicke or not, or toward sicknesse, by these signes.

b. Of quantity: Nearly as much as, nearly.

c **1449** PECOCK *Repr.* I. iv. (Rolls) 20 Welnyȝ or weel toward the al hool lawe with which Cristen men ben chargid. **1879** S. C. BARTLETT *Egypt to Pal.* xxi. 453 They rise.. toward a hundred feet above the plain.

6. In prospect of; in the imminence of; (as predicate) in preparation for. *Obs.* or *arch.*

1542 UDALL *Erasm. Apoph.* 327 b, When Crassus was towarde a iourney into Syria. **1576** GASCOIGNE *Steele Gl.* (Arb.) 79 Towarde shipwracke, many men can pray. **1865** SWINBURNE *Atalanta* 877, [I] stand, girt as they toward hunting.

†**b.** Coming upon, 'in store for'; usually of evil: ready to fall upon, threatening. *Obs.*

1375 BARBOUR *Bruce* I. 82 þai couth nocht persawe þe skaith þat towart þaim wes apperand. **1606** G. W[OODCOCKE] *Hist. Ivstine* XXVI. 94 By the inwardes of those beasts, perceiuing.. that there was toward them a great slaughter. **1609** HOLLAND *Amm. Marcell.* 399 All which.. plainely shewed, that this kind of death was toward him.

7. In the way of contribution to; as a help to; for the purpose of making up, promoting, assisting, or the like; for.

1468 in Blades *Caxton* (1882) 151 Hit is accorded that [they] shall haue in honde xl li sterling towarde thoire costs & charges. **1483** *Cely Papers* (Camden) 144 To pay thys hallff ȝerys wages.. here ys nothyng toward hytt. *c* **1530** H. RHODES *Bk. Nurture* 655 in *Babees Bk.* 100 Giue the pore of thy good; Part thou therof toward their want. **1662–3** MARVELL *Corr.* Wks. (Gros.) II. 83, I have writ this same.. to prepare our correspondence toward your service. **1710** SWIFT *Jrnl. to Stella* 5 Oct., Here is two and eight-pence halfpenny toward your loss. **1828** SOUTHEY *Ess.* (1832) II. 273 Raising a fund.. toward the expenses of removing paupers by emigration.

8. For *to ...-ward*, separated by the sb. or pron., as in *to us-ward*, *to God-ward*, see -WARD, and cf. TO *prep.* 2 e.

'towardliness (see next). Now *dial.* or *arch.* [f. TOWARDLY *a.* + -NESS.] The quality or character of being 'towardly'.

1. Good disposition towards something, willingness; *spec.* aptness to learn, docility, tractableness; forwardness in learning, 'promise'; ingenuity, proficiency: = TOWARDNESS 1, 2.

a **1569** KINGESMYLL *Confl. Satan* (1578) 25 Such as haue no towardlinesse nor framing of their hearts.. to do the will of God. **1603** KNOLLES *Hist. Turks* (1621) 360 [He] appointed eight hundred of the Christian children, in whom appeared most towardlinesse, to be brought up for Ianezaries. **1612** BRINSLEY *Lud. Lit.* p. xxv, All schollars of any towardlinesse and diligence may be made absolute Grammarians, and euery way fit for the Vniuersitie, by fifteen yeares of age. **1735–6** CARTE *Ormonde* I. Introd. 65 The loss of his only son, a noble young gentleman and of great towardliness. **1830** GODWIN *Cloudesley* III. i. 3, I had children that improved every day in towardliness and beauty.

2. Favourableness, friendliness, affability.

1566 Q. MARY *Let.* in *Sir J. Melvil's Mem.* (1735) 144 Touching our Towardliness to them of the Religion. **1603** KNOLLES *Hist. Turks* (1621) 573 The great towardlinesse and courteous nature of the Turkish emperour.

3. Furtherance, advancement, promotion.

1553 S. CABOT *Ordinances* in Hakluyt *Voy.* (1589) 262 In towardlinesse of beneficiall traffike. **1653** MANTON *Exp. James* iv. 16 Wks. 1871 IV. 394 If God suspend his concurrence, the creatures cannot act, at least not with any towardliness and success.

†**4.** Likelihood, likely condition or position, prospect; in such phrases as ***in great towardliness***, very likely. (Cf. TOWARDNESS 3.) *Obs.*

1579–80 NORTH *Plutarch* (1676) 297 Cato put out of the Senate also, one Manlius, who was in great towardliness to have been made Consull. **1655** OWEN *Vind. Evang.* Wks. 1853 XII. 192 The signs.. that he would be exalted to a Kingdom. He was by them in a good towardliness for it.

towardly ('təʊ(w)ədlɪ, 'tɔədlɪ), *a.* [f. TOWARD *a.* + -LY¹: cf. OE. *tóweardlic* that is to come, future (which did not survive into ME.).]

1. Likely to lead to a desired result; promising success, propitious; helpful, favourable, advantageous; seasonable, befitting. (Cf. TOWARD *a.* 4 b.)

1520 *St. Papers Hen. VIII*, II. 34 After ye shall have atteyned.. any towardly comfourte, this yere, to bring our rebellious subjecttes there to summe obedience. **1644** MILTON *Areop.* (Arb.) 69 What wants there to such a towardly and pregnant soile, but wise and faithfull labourers? **1704** SWIFT *T. Tub* Concl. ¶6, I have observed many a towardly word to be wholly neglected. **1825** MRS. CARLYLE in Froude *Life Carlyle* (1882) I. 322 Your circumstances.. may be in the process of time rendered more towardly. **1884** *Athenæum* 15 Mar. 340 He must choose a towardly hour.

2. Promising, 'hopeful', forward; apt to learn, docile: chiefly of young persons or their dispositions.

1528 J. LONDON *Let. to Bp. Lincoln* 25 Feb., in *Lett. & Papers Hen. VIII*, XLVII. 90 (P.R.O.) Neuer.. to calle hym nor any other cambridge manne vnto hys most towardely colledge [Christ Church, Oxford]. **1561** T. HOBY tr. *Castiglione's Courtyer* I. (1577) C ij b, One of the best fauoured, and towardlyest personages in the worlde, deformed and marred in his greene age. **1587** FLEMING *Contn. Holinshed* III. 959/1 They.. rode to Enfield to see the prince,.. greatlie reioising.. to behold so proper and towardlie an impe. **1627** ABP. ABBOT *Narr.* II. in Rushw. *Hist. Coll.* (1659) I. 451 He was my Pupil at Oxford, and a very towardly one. **1670** MILTON *Hist. Eng.* V. Wks. 1738 II. 90 Them also I wish.. mistaken, who write that Athelstan, jealous of his younger Brother Edwin's towardly Virtues,.. caus'd him to be drown'd in the Sea. **1712** STEELE *Spect.* No. 263 ¶1, I am the happy Father of a very towardly Son. **1863** *Sat. Rev.* 21 Mar. 368/2 He will be a towardly scholar under a willing teacher.

b. Of plants: Promising, forward. ? *Obs.*

1580 LYLY *Euphues* (Arb.) 451 Easterly windes blasteth towardly blossoms. **1664** EVELYN *Sylva* (1776) 303 Purge them of all superfluous shoots and cions, reserving only the most towardly for the future stem. **1676** HALE *Contempl.* II. 98 Towardly Plants, are by Death Transplanted into another Region, a Garden of Happiness and Comfort.

3. Well-disposed, dutiful, tractable.

1513 DOUGLAS *Æneis* III. viii. 70 Sen the sammyn four futtit beistis eik Bene oft vsit, full towartlie and meik, To draw the cart, and thoill bridill and renȝe. **1601** R. JOHNSON *Kingd. & Commw.* (1603) 234 [A slave's] faithfulnesse and towardly disposition. *a* **1629** HINDE *J. Bruen* xx. (1641) 64 If hee saw them any more towardly, in duties of Religion. **1672** EACHARD *Hobbs' State Nat.* (1705) 13 I'le promise you to be very towardly for the future.

b. Favourably disposed, friendly, affable. (Cf. TOWARD *a.* 4.)

15.. in Maton *W. Counties* (1797) I. 55 The ladi Elizabeth so towardli with the kinges honorable counselers. **1649** DAVENANT *Love & Hon.* III. iii, Good heart, it is As towardly an old thing! *a* **1674** CLARENDON *Hist. Reb.* XIV. §41 England proved not yet so towardly as he expected. **1893** *Nat. Observ.* 18 Feb. 340/2 The men.. were very courteous, and the women very towardly.

'towardly (see prec.), *adv.* Now *dial.* or *arch.* [f. TOWARD *a.* + -LY^{2}. Cf. OE. *tóweardlíce*, in time to come, in the future (which did not survive in ME.).] In a 'toward' or 'towardly' manner; with favourable disposition; willingly, compliantly, obligingly; docilely, tractably, submissively; with promise of good progress, promisingly: see the adj.

1481 *Coventry Leet Bk.* 484 Wherin ye shewed yewe ryght benyvolent and towardly disposed. **1523** HEN. VIII in Ellis *Orig. Lett.* Ser. I. I. 238 Thanks unto all the lords, capitains, and other whiche.. have right towardly, benivolently, and conformably served as under you in this Jorney. **1562** J. HEYWOOD *Prov. & Epigr.* (1867) 195 Wyll you reedes shrinke still to all windes towardly? **1597** MORLEY *Introd. Mus.* 55 To see my schollers go towardlie forward in their studies. **1704** PENN in *Pa. Hist. Soc. Mem.* IX. 342 If our friends will not behave towardly, I shall be constrained to break it. **1819** R. ANDERSON *Cumbld. Ball.* 43 How tow'rtly she com heame! **1874** *Daily News* 12 Aug., Postmaster-General Lord John Manners hands in the Twentieth Annual Report of his office as towardly as if he had done nothing but deliver letters all his life.

towardness ('təʊ(w)ədnɪs, 'tɔədnɪs). Now *Obs.* or *arch.* [f. as prec. + -NESS.] The quality or condition of being 'toward'.

†**1.** Disposition, inclination towards or to do something; readiness, willingness. *Obs.*

1461 *Coventry Leet Bk.* 316 Trustyng.. that ye in so doyng shall thynke your true hertis and towardnesse right welle be-sette. **1530** TINDALE *Answ. More* IV. xi. Wks. (1573) 337/2 What good towardnes can we haue vnto the will of God while we hate it and be ignoraunt therof? **1563** RANDOLPH in Robertson *Hist. Scot.* II. App. vii. (1759) 14 This queen being before advertized of his towardness, by many means, hath sought.. to know my lord of Murray's mind herein. **1610** E. SKORY *Extr. Hist. Hen. IV of France* 2 His qualitie drewe him into the knowledge of the world; where his royall towardnesse begot him estimation. **1692** BURNET *Past. Care* viii. 101 [This] may put some of them in a greater towardness to hear Reason.

2. *spec.* Willingness and aptness to learn; natural aptitude and good disposition; docility, tractableness; forwardness in learning or practice, 'promise', proficiency.

1509 FISHER *Funeral Serm. C'tess Richmond* Wks. 1876 I. 292 In her tendre aege she beynge endued with so grete towardnes of nature, & lyklyhode of enherytaunce. **1564** HAWARD *Eutropius* IX. 98 A yonge man of a wonderful towardnesse. **1601** FULBECKE *1st Pt. Parall.* 24 Knighthoode is bestowed in regard of precedent merite, or of some eminent prowesse and towardnesse. **1671** F. PHILLIPS *Reg. Necess.* 222 That none should be admitted into any place within his House.. but such as be of good towardness, likelihood, behaviour, demeanour and conversation.

†**3.** Condition or appearance of approaching in time, coming on or impending; imminence; likelihood, prospect. *Obs.*

1549 in Strype *Eccl. Mem.* (1721) II. 310 If there should be any towardness of a meeting.. likely to take any good effect, they would certify him of it. *a* **1586** SIDNEY *Arcadia* IV. (1598) 392 O Mopsa,.. here am I thine owne father Dametas, neuer in such a towardnesse of hanging, if thou canst not helpe mee. **1660** SHARROCK *Vegetables* 12 When the great frosts breake, at the first towardnesse to spring. **1721** STRYPE *Eccl. Mem.* II. 310 If there appeared any towardness of a good conclusion, he should be certified of it.

†**4.** State of advancement or forwardness; *in* (*a*) *good* (etc.) *towardness*, making good progress, getting on well. *Obs.*

1475 SIR J. PASTON in *P. Lett.* III. 122 All suche coumfforte as ye ffynde or heer off the towardnesse theroff. **1577** VAUTROUILLIER *Luther on Ep. Gal.* 107 All things were in a happie course and great towardnes with you. **1579–80** NORTH *Plutarch* (1676) 225 All his doings, which were now so far onwards in good towardness.

towards ('təʊədz, 'tɔːədz, tɔədz; tə'wɔːdz), *prep.* and *adv.* Forms: 1 toweardes, 1, 6 to wardes, 3–7 towardes, (5 -is, -ys, tawardes, 6 towerdys, *Sc.* towartis, 7 towardst), 5– towards, (7–8 tow'rds). [OE. *tóweardes*, f. *tóweard*, TOWARD *a.*, with *-es*, *-s* of adverbial genitive: see -WARDS.
(As to varieties of pronunciation see TOWARD *prep.*)]

A. *prep.*

1. Of motion, etc.: In the direction of, on the way to: = TOWARD *prep.* 1.

c **888** K. ÆLFRED *Boeth.* xxxix. §1 Hwy ne maȝon ȝe ȝebidan ȝecyndelices deaðes, nu he eow ælce dæȝ toweardes onet? *c* **1122** *O.E. Chron.* an. 1094, Se eorl innon Normandiȝ .. mid þam cynge of France.. ferdon to wardes Ou þær se cyng Willelm inne wæs. *c* **1205** LAY. 515 Brutus iherde seggen.. þat Pandrasus þe king him towardes com Mid muchelere ferde. **1442** T. BECKINGTON *Corr.* (Rolls) II. 190 Maister John de Batute departed hens on Saturday at noon towards his cuntrey. **1538** in R. G. Marsden *Sel. Pleas Crt. Admiralty* (1894) I. 73 They made saile towards their owne countrey. **1552** HULOET, Towardes and toward... Yet marke the maner of phrase as you dyd in amonge & amongest. **1766** GOLDSM. *Vic. W.* x, The procession marching slowly forward towards the church. **1816** J. WILSON *City of Plague* I. i, Every step I take Towards the city. **1860** TYNDALL *Glac.* I. viii. 59, I turned towards home.

†**b.** *pred.* after *to be*: On the way to: = TOWARD *prep.* 1 b. *Obs.*

1601 SHAKS. *All's Well* III. ii. 71 Towards Florence is he?

†**c.** To (with implication of reaching): = TOWARD *prep.* 1 c. *Obs.*

1467 *Coventry Leet Bk.* 335 Also þat [they] sufficiently amende þe fotewey towardes Crab-tre-feld. **1585** T. WASHINGTON tr. *Nicholay's Voy.* I. xxii. 29 Too dispatche and sende away the knight.. towardes the court, too aduertise the king. **1611** SHAKS. *Wint. T.* IV. iii. 121, I will .. pace softly towards my Kinsmans. **1613** T. MILLES tr. *Mexia's*, etc. *Treas. Anc. & Mod. T.* 698/1 Pope Innocent.. sent verie Learned and Religious men towards Baty.

2. Of position: In the direction of; on the side next to; directed to, facing: = TOWARD *prep.* 2.

1423 JAS. I *Kingis Q.* civ, Benignely sche turnyt has hir face Towardis me. **1503** in *Lett. Rich. III & Hen. VII* (Rolls) I. 202 The said bishop as he stode.. towardes the quere. **1555** BRADFORD in Strype *Eccl. Mem.* (1721) III. App. xlv. 129 To make all our Haven-Townes mor stronger towardes the Land, than they be towardes the Sea. **1611** BIBLE *Ps.* xxv. 15 Mine eyes are euer towards the Lord. **1662** J. DAVIES tr. *Olearius' Voy. Ambass.* 58 Canon, with the mouths towards that street. **1726** LEONI *Alberti's Archit.* I. 99/2 Hills towards the North.. encrease the heat. **1727** SWIFT *Let. Eng. Tongue* Wks. 1755 II. I. 186 The Northern parts lying towards the Euxine. **1851** HELPS *Comp. Solit.* vi. 85, I sat upon a garden seat in a sheltered nook towards the south.

†**b.** Beside, near; in attendance on, about; in the possession of; with: = TOWARD *prep.* 2 b. *Obs.*

? **1447** *Lett. Marg. Anjou & Bp. Beckington* (Camden) 94 We.. praye yow hertely, that.. ye wil have oure said secretary towards yow. **1459** *Rolls of Parlt.* V. 367 Persones of grete myght, havyng towardes theym of their lyverey.. such multitude of Robbers, Rioters, and myschevous persones. **1614–15** *Archdeaconry of Essex Minutes* lf. 103 b (MS.), The prince his landresse and a man towards the prince were by the harbenger placed to lodge in his house. **1664** MARVELL *Corr.* Wks. (Grosart) II. 166 Had chosen his Excellence the Earle of Carlisle.. for his Ambassador Extraordinary towards him.

3. In the direction of (*fig.*). **a.** *gen.* = TOWARD *prep.* 3 a.

1634 SIR T. HERBERT *Trav.* 49 Their beauties are.. such as preuaile in my iudgement, towards chastitie, more then Ouids Remedy of Loue. **1692** E. WALKER *Epictetus' Mor.* lxxi, He that labours on Towards Perfection. **1763** J. BROWN *Poetry & Mus.* xiv. 241 In all polished States, these Arts have a natural Tendency towards Corruption. **1849** MACAULAY *Hist. Eng.* ii. I. 231 The king was suspected by many of a leaning towards Rome. **1871** R. H. HUTTON *Ess.* v. (1888) 118 The absolute will towards right.

b. Introducing the object of action or feeling: = TOWARD *prep.* 3 b.

1390 GOWER *Conf.* II. 32, I mai wel.. Excuse me of necgligence Towardes love in alle wise. **1483** in *Lett. Rich. III & Hen. VII* (Rolls) I. 48 Good will towardes hir housband. *c* **1495** *Ibid.* II. 57 To ordre that matier towardis hym as he shalbe right well contented. **1536** *Cal. Anc. Rec. Dublin* (1889) I. 498 Thankes off hys grett goodnes towerdys me. **1536** in *Lett. Suppress. Monasteries* (Camden) 99 How I shal use me self towardes thaim. **1596** SPENSER *F.Q.* VI. ii. 11 To blame him for such cruelty Towards a Ladie. **1682** NORRIS *Hierocles* 32 Friendship ought to be exercised towards all, but especially toward good men. **1713** BERKELEY *Guard.* No. 3 ¶1 A sense of piety towards heaven. **1802–12** BENTHAM *Ration. Judic. Evid.* (1827) IV. 53 He has as good a pretence and (as towards the public) a justification, as heart can wish. **1885** *Manch. Exam.* 10 July 5/2 The sentiments of the Thibetans towards us.

†**c.** In favour of; favourable to: = FOR *prep.* 7. *Obs. rare.*

1472 *Paston Lett.* III. 52 To have thys Parlement as for one of the burgeys of the towne of Maldon, syche a man of worchep and of wytt as wer towardys my seyd Lady. **1477** *Ibid.* 171 And [= if] ye come and fynde the mater no more towards you then ye dyd afortyme.

d. Compared to, in comparison with: = TO *prep.* 18, TOWARD *prep.* 3 d. Now *dial.*

a **1568** COVERDALE *Bk. Death* xxv. (1579) 113 In comparison whereof.. myrthe and cheere vpon earth is scarce to be esteemed as castinge counters towardes the finest coynes of Golde. **1685** TRAVESTIN *Siege Newheusel* 27 They fought with such desperation and courage towards what they had done before. **1887** *S. Cheshire Gloss.*, To'arts *as*, in comparison with.

e. In expression of good wishes for (a person, or his health): = TO *prep.* 12 a, 26 b. *dial.*

1766 GOLDSM. *Vic. W.* xxi, Drinking towards my good health. **1855** THACKERAY *Newcomes* xi, Here's towards you, my buck.

4. Of time or succession: = TOWARD *prep.* 4.

1594 SHAKS. *Rich. III*, III. v. 101, I goe, and towards three or foure a Clocke Looke for the Newes. **1661** LOVELL *Hist. Anim. & Min.* Introd., Snailes, which some count most dainty sweet and nourishing meat, and are best towards winter. **1754** SHERLOCK *Disc.* (1759) I. ix. 251 These Words stand towards the Close of St. John's Gospel. **1836** *Backwoods of Canada* 208 The skins are very thick and glossy towards winter. **1886** C. E. PASCOE *Lond. of To-day* xxxi. (ed. 3) 282 In Whitehall Gardens.. Beaconsfield lived for a short time towards the latter part of his life.

5. 'Getting on for', verging upon, nearly as much as; tending to: = TOWARD *prep.* 5.

1570 FOXE *A. & M.* (ed. 2) 2276/2 Being iudged by the common people, more then an hundreth yeare of age, and by her own estimation well towardes a c. **1619** HALES *Gold. Rem.* II. (1673) 84 When Gomarus had spoken towards an hour and a half. **1626** BACON *Sylva* §77 Water, thicker, and more towards Ice, than Common Water. **1712** STEELE *Spect.* No. 437 ¶1 She was gay, airy, and a little towards Libertine in her Carriage. **1777** BURKE *Corr.* (1844) II. 195 Where there are towards six hundred persons. **1845** J. H. NEWMAN *Ess. Developm.* 41 When he is towards fifty, Mr. Wesley marries.

†**6.** In prospect of, approaching: = TOWARD *prep.* 6. *Obs.*

1523 LD. BERNERS *Froiss.* I. cccxxvii. 512 He was towardes a treaty for a maryage for him with the doughter of y^{e} kyng of Castell. **1541** *St. Papers Hen. VIII*, VIII. 599 As towching ony maryage that she was towardes, I harde of non. **1611** TOURNEUR *Ath. Trag.* II. v, What, is not thy mistresse towards a husband yet? *a* **1624** BP. M. SMITH *Serm.* (1632) 141, I did not know that thou hadst a cause towards hearing. **1661** in *Verney Mem.* (1907) II. 175, I here your son is towardes a good fortewen. **1688** SHADWELL *Sqr. Alsatia* v, Your brother has heard of this great match you are towards.

†**b.** Coming upon, in store for: = TOWARD *prep.* 6 b. *Obs.*

1560 DAUS tr. *Sleidane's Comm.* 14 b, There was muche trouble towardes him, what by the Turkes, and what by the Frenche men. **1633** BP. HALL *Hard Texts, N.T.* 123 Jesus.. well knew what evill was towards him. **1719** YOUNG *Busiris* v. i, I fear some ill is tow'rds me. **1749** FIELDING *Tom Jones* VIII. vi, I dreamed.. that I stumbled over a stool without hurting myself; which plainly showed me something good was towards me.

7. In contribution to; for making up, promoting, etc.: = TOWARD *prep.* 7.

1474 *Coventry Leet Bk.* 412 Such benivolence as his louyng subgettes there schall shewe vnto hym towardes his grete viage in-to ffraunce. **1521** in *Essex Rev.* XIII. 221 Item I bequeth to Bryghtlyngsey Church towards lengthing of our Lady Chapell.. iii. quarters of the ship called the Trinitie. **1639** S. DU VERGER tr. *Camus' Admir. Events* 77 Nothing could have prevailed towards the saving of his life. **1729** LAW *Serious C.* viii, She pays their rent, and gives them something yearly towards their clothing. **1806** *Act 46 Geo. III*, c. 132 (*title*) To advance a certain sum.. towards that purpose. **1908** *Month* Mar. 317 This is a contribution towards what is now denominated 'Methodology'.

8. For *to ..-wards*, separated by the sb. or pron., see -WARDS. Cf. TO *prep.* 2 e, TOWARD *prep.* 8.

B. *adv.* or predicative *adj.*

I. Predicative, or following a sb.: cf. predicative uses of TOWARD *a.*

†**1.** In preparation, at hand, coming on, imminent: cf. TOWARD *a.* 2 b. *Obs.*

1468 SIR J. PASTON in *P. Lett.* II. 328 If ye undrestond that any assawte schold be towardys. **1585** T. WASHINGTON tr. *Nicholay's Voy.* I. xxii. 28 There was no danger towards. **1592** SHAKS. *Rom. & Jul.* I. v. 124 We haue a trifling foolish Banquet towards. **1637** SUCKLING *Aglaura* II. i, If there be not some great storme towards, Ne'er trust me. **1652** DOROTHY OSBORNE *Lett.* (1888) 30 His marriage, which I hear is towards, with a daughter of [etc.]. **1697** VANBRUGH *Relapse* III. ii, Take heed my heart, for there are dangers towards.

†**2.** Favourable, compliant, forward, ready. *Obs.*

c **1525** ABP. WARHAM in Ellis *Orig. Lett.* Ser. III. I. 366 Seing men grudgeth to be towardes in graunting, it is to be feared they will make more murmur and busynes in the tyme of payment.

†**3.** At hand, ready, present: cf. TOWARD *a.* 6.

1548 UDALL, etc. *Erasm. Par. John* 71 b, Being redy and towardes at his call. **1564** HAWARD *Eutropius* VI. K vij b, Hys Sonne also, a valyaunte and worthye yonge man towardes.

II. 4. In the direction of some person or thing indicated by the context (cf. TOWARD *adv.* 1, *forwards*, *onwards*). *Obs.* or *arch.*

1590 SPENSER *F.Q.* I. ii. 15 The knight.., when him he spide,.. Gan fairely couch his speare, and towards ride. *Ibid.* II. iv. 37 A varlet ronning towards hastily. **1592** *Arden of Feversham* III. vi, At your dags discharge Make towards. **1818** KEATS *Endym.* III. 494 This fire, like the eye of gordian snake, Bewitched me towards; and I soon was near A sight too fearful for the feel of fear.

†**b.** ? Towards some end or purpose; (as a contribution) towards something. *Obs.*

1473 SIR J. PASTON in *P. Lett.* III. 104, I pray yow sende me worde.. iff I have Caster ageyn, whethyr she [my modre] wolle dwelle ther or nott, and I wyll fynde hyr a prest towardes at my charge.

†**5.** Onwards, on (in quot., of time): cf. TOWARD *adv.* 2. *Obs. rare*$^{-1}$.

1586 J. HOOKER *Hist. Irel.* in Holinshed II. 158/1 The daie being spent to small purpose, and the night drawne towards, he incamped.

†**to-'warp**, *v. Obs.* Forms: see WARP. [OE. *toweorpan*, f. TO-^{2} + *weorpan* to throw, WARP *v.* = OFris. *to-*, *tiwerpa*, OS. *tewerpan* (LG. *tewerpan*), OHG. *za-*, *ziwerphan*, *-werfan*, MHG. *ze-*, *zerwerfen*, Ger. *zerwerfen*.] *trans.* To throw about, throw down, overthrow, destroy; also *fig.*

c **888** K. ÆLFRED *Boeth.* xxxv. §4 Þa sceolde he sendan þunras & liȝeta & windas, & toweorpan eall hira ȝeweorc mid. *c* **1000** *Ags. Gosp.* Matt. xxiv. 2 Ne bið her læfed stan uppan stane þe ne beo to-worpen. *c* **1000** ÆLFRIC *Hom.* II.

510 Mennisce handa hit ne mihton towurpan. *c* **1200** ORMIN 14861 þe sæ wass þær Dun till þe grund toworrpenn. *c* **1200** *Trin. Coll. Hom.* 161 Storemes falleð in þe sæ and to-worpeð hit.

to-waste, to-waver, to-wawe: see TO- *pref.*[2]

towayl(e, -aylle, obs. ff. TOWEL.

towch(e, towe, obs. ff. TOUCH, TOUGH, TWO.

towcher, obs. form of TOCHER.

‖**towcok** ('taʊkɒk). [ad. Cantonese *tau-kok* string beans, peas in the pod, f. *tau* bean, pea + *kok* horn, pod.] The Cow-pea, *Vigna* (*Dolichos*) *sinensis*; in India called *chowlee*.

1866 *Treas. Bot.* s.v. *Vigna*, The Chinese.. call the plant Tow-Cok, cook and eat the green pods as we do kidney-beans. When ripe the pods are frequently.. a yard long.

towee, var. TOWHEE, N. Amer. bird.

towel ('taʊəl), *sb.* Forms: see below. [ME. *towaille, -aile*, etc., a. OF. *toaille* (Wace 12th c.), *toaile*, mod.F. *touaille* = Pr. *toalha*, Cat. *tovalla*, Sp. *toalla*, Pg. *toalha*, It. *tovaglia* (whence F., in spec. sense, *tavaïolle*); in med.L. *toacula, toailla, tovalia, toualia*, etc., from the mod. langs.: f. WGer. **þwahljô* (Kluge), OHG. *dwahilla, -ila*, cloth for washing or wiping (MHG. *dwähele, twähele, dwêle*, Ger. dial. *zwehle* napkin), f. OHG. *dwahan, twahan* (OS. *thwahan*, Goth. *þwahan*, OE. *þwéan* to wash, *þwéal* (Goth. *þwahl* washing).]

1. a. A cloth, usually of linen or hemp, for wiping something dry, esp. for wiping the hands, face, or person after washing or bathing. Also formerly more widely, including a table-napkin or other cloth used at meals.

Often with prefix indicating its particular use, as *bath-, dish-, face-, glass-towel*.

α. 3-5 **towaille,** 4 **touwayle, (thoayle, thoyale),** 4-5 **towaile, -ayle,** 5 **tow-, touaylle, towail, -ayl, -ayle (tavayle).**

a **1300** *Floriz & Bl.* 563 þat oþer bringe towaille and bacin For to wasse his honden in. **13..** *Sir Beues* (A.) 3220 On a towaile ȝhe [= she] made knotte riding. **13..** SHOREHAM i. 1387 þo hym wyþ a schete [*marg.* touwayle] ihesus After soper bygerte. *c* **1386** CHAUCER *Monk's T.* 755 And Phebus eek a fair towaille [*v.rr.* towayle, towail, towale, towel] hym broughte To dryen hym with. **1395** *Will of Thornholm* (Comm. Crt. London), Thoayle wt a blak lyst, borthcloth cum vna thoyale accordyngg. *c* **1400** MAUNDEV. (1839) xxiii. 250 Whan þei han eten, þei wypen hire hondes vpon hire skirtes, for þei vse non naperye, ne towaylles. *c* **1435** *Chron. London* (Kingsford 1905) 18 The goode Duk off Gloucetre.. was ffoule mordred at Caleys with ij Tovaylles.. putte aboute his nekke. *c* **1440** *Promp. Parv.* 498/2 Towayl (*H.* towayle or tavayle).. *manitergium*. *c* **1450** *Merlin* 225 The maiden her-silf wosh his visage.. and dried it full softely with a towaile. **1480** *Wardr. Acc. Edw. IV* (1830) 131 Towails playne vj.

β. 3 **towele,** 4-5 **touel,** 4-6 **towelle, -all,** 4-7 **towell,** (5 **toual, towale, towylle,** 6 **touall, towle);** 4- **towel.**

? **1284** Toweles [see 2]. **13..** *Seuyn Sag.* (W.) 3877 Thai set forth water and towell, Herkens now, how if befell! **13..** Touel [see quot. *a* 1300 in γ]. **1378** in *Test. Karl.* (1893) 118, ij lectos, ij dorclaes, ij towels. **1387-8** T. USK *Test. Love* II. ii. (Skeat) l. 62 On his meate borde there shall been borde clothes and towelles many paire. **1407-8** *Durham Acc. Rolls* (Surtees) 607, liiij uln. panni linei emp... pro towales. **1466** *Maldon, Essex, Crt.-Rolls* (Bundle 42, No. 6), Towylles. **1542** Towle [see 2]. **1557** *Lanc. Wills* (Chetham Soc.) I. 71 The best bason and ewer and also the best towall. **15..** in *Laneham's Let.* (1871) Pref. 31 Ane touall off Alifyne. **1609** B. JONSON *Sil. Wom.* IV. v, I will strangle him in this towell. *a* **1658** CLEVELAND *Mary's Spikenard* 31 For a Towel he shall have My hair, such flax as nature gave. **1718** LADY M. W. MONTAGU *Let. to C'tess of Mar* 10 Mar., After dinner, water was brought in a gold basin, and towels of the same kind of the napkins. **1808** *Med. Jrnl.* XIX. 112 His body to be well rubbed by two persons with coarse towels. **1897** MARY KINGSLEY *W. Africa* 563 Wading across to the bank, I wring out my skirts, but what is life without a towel?

γ. 4 **tueil,** 4-5 **tuel, -ell,** 5 **tuayl(e, -ale, tewelle,** 5-6 **tewell,** (8-9 *Sc.* and *north. dial.* **tooel, tool).**

a **1300** *Cursor M.* 15285 (Cott.) Wit a tuell he belted him [*G.* tuel, *F.* touel, *T.* twaile]. *Ibid.* 15299 Wit his tueil efterward þair fete he weped clene. *c* **1450** *Brut* ccxli. 352 þai.. caste þe tewellys aboute þe Dukis nek.. and þan þei drowen her towellis eche wayez. **1494** in *Somerset Medieval Wills* (1901) 323 A Mete cloth and iij tuels. **1496** Tuell, **1504** Tewell [see 2]. **1727** P. WALKER *Life R. Cameron* in *Biog. Presbyt.* (1827) I. 202 He dried his face and hands with a Tool. **1905** *Eng. Dial. Dict.* s.v., *Westmld.* Tooel.

δ. 3-4 **twayle,** 5 **twaylle, twaile,** 6 **twell.**

a **1300** Twayle [see 2]. *a* **1375** *Joseph Arim.* 285 þenne comen two Angeles wiþ twayles white. *a* **1425** Twaile [see quot. *a* 1300 in γ]. **1507** Twell [see 2].

ε. 5 **towaly, twaly, tualy.**

c **1440** *Promp. Parv.* 498/2 Towayl, or towaly (*S.* twaly.., *A.* tuayl or tualy), *manitergium*.

b. Phr. ***to throw*** (***chuck***, or ***toss***) ***in the towel***: to admit defeat. orig. *Boxing*. Cf. SPONGE *sb.*[1] I c.

1915 E. CORRI *30 Yrs. Boxing Ref.* 223 In the nineteenth round Storbeck's seconds 'threw the towel' in literally. **1916** C. J. DENNIS *Moods of Ginger Mick* 132 I've done me limit, an' tossed in the tow'l. **1923** WODEHOUSE *Inimit. Jeeves* xv. 192 He had found the going too hard and had chucked in the towel. **1952** [see DINGO *v.*]. **1979** M. RUSSELL *Touchdown* II. 90 'Don't give up.'.. 'Have no fear... I shan't throw in the towel, I promise you.'

2. Applied to cloths for various other purposes. **a.** *Eccl.* A cloth, either of linen for use at communion, or of silk or other rich material for covering the altar at other times; also, a communion-cloth (see quot. 1737, and quot. 1866 s.v. COMMUNION 8). Cf. F. *tavaïolle*. ? *Obs.*

? **1284** in *Shropsh. Archæol. Soc. Trans.* (1878) I. 358 Item ij. Toweles pro ij. altariis cum apparatu precii xijs. iiij d. *a* **1300** in Hearne *Collect.* 18 Apr. II. 187 Tham that this Cherche, honour with book, with bell, with vestiments, with twayle. **1387** TREVISA *Higden* (Rolls) V. 11 No womman schulde handle þe towayles of þe auȝter. **1474** *Will of Selly* (Somerset Ho.), Howseling towell. **1496** *Croscombe Churchw. Acc.* (Som. Rec. Soc.) 21 A tuell of dyapper. **1504** *Ibid.* 27, ij tewells. **1507** *Ibid.* 29 A twell of dyaper. **1542** in *Archæologia* XLVI. 217 Paid for a new dextclothe & a towle xj d. *c* **1550** in *Labarte's Arts Mid. Ages* ii. (1855) 91 A blest towell for the high altar, of black silk. **1623** *Primer* in *Month* Oct. (1911) 340 If any be to communicate at Mass, the Servitour after the Priest hath taken the Chalice and before he purifieth it, spreadeth a towel or a white vele before them and then sayeth *Confiteor Deo* in their name. **1737** CHALLONER *Cath. Chr. Instr.* (1753) 66 Such of the people as are to communicate,.. taking the Towel, hold it before their Breasts, in such Manner, that, if in communicating, it should happen that any Particle should fall, it may.. be received upon the Towel.

†**b.** A cloth used as a part of dress, e.g. as a head-dress, a girdle, etc. *Obs.*

? *a* **1366** CHAUCER *Rom. Rose* 161 Hir heed y-writhen was, y-wis, Ful grymly with a greet towayle. **1485** CAXTON *Paris & V.* (1868) 80 Mantellys and towellys. **1582** N. LICHEFIELD tr. *Castanheda's Conq. E. Ind.* I. xii. 29 b, The King of Mylynde came.. to our Fleete, apparelled in a Cassocke of Crimson Damaske, lined with greene satten, hauing vpon his head a rich towell. **1615** G. SANDYS *Trav.* 63 Shashes are long towels of Callico wound about their heads. **1634** SIR T. HERBERT *Trav.* 146 The coat.. ingirted with a towell of silke and gold eight or nine yards long.

c. = *sanitary towel* s.v. SANITARY *a.* 3. Also *ellipt.*

1896 *Eng. Illustr. Mag.* Aug. (Advts. Section) 8/2 A sample of the improved 'towel' will be sent free to any lady applying to the Lady Manager. **1907** *Yesterday's Shopping* (1969) 1264 Full-sized towels reduced by pressure, packed in tiny boxes. **1979** *Guardian* 27 Mar. 9/5 A campaign for free sanitary protection through the NHS started in 1973 when the Government imposed VAT on towels and tampons.

3. *slang.* ***oaken towel***, also simply ***towel***, a stick, cudgel (cf. next, 2); ***lead towel***, a bullet.

1739 *Joe Miller's Jests* (1745) 73 The Farmer.. rear'd his Oaken Towel, and.. gave him two.. Drubs on the Shoulder. **1748** SMOLLETT *Rod. Rand.* ii, I shall rub you down with an oaken towel. **1756** TOLDERVY *Hist. 2 Orphans* II. 128 Brandishing his stick [he] cried aloud, 'this towel.. should bastinado the bones of that rascal Tom Throw'. **1812** H. & J. SMITH *Rej. Addr., G. Barnwell* vi, Make Nunky surrender his dibs, Rub his pate with a pair of lead towels. **1815** *Hist. Jn. Decastro* I. 24 Old Crab.. raising his oaken towel gave the door three bangs that shook the garrets.

4. *attrib.* and *Comb.*, as ***towel-coffer, friction, -maker, -room, -warmer; towel-covered*** adj.; **towel-gourd,** a name for *Luffa ægyptiaca* and *L. acutangula*, also called *sponge-gourd* or *washing-gourd*, the fibrous inner layer of the fruit being used in washing like a towel or sponge (cf. LOOFAH); **towel-horse,** a wooden frame or stand on which towels are hung; **towel-pattern** (*Wood-carving*) = *linen-scroll*: see LINEN B. 5; **towel-rack** (see quot.); **towel rail, ring,** a rail or ring on which to hang towels; **towel-roller,** a horizontal roller on which an 'endless' towel (*roller-* or *round-towel*) is hung.

c **1400** *Sc. Troy-bk.* I. 375 Cowpis out brought of golde sa clere, One *towalle burdys arayit & drest. **1891** G. MEREDITH *One of our Conq.* ix, The oaken *towel-coffer. **1916** H. G. WELLS *Mr. Britling sees it Through* I. i. 19 A *towel-covered can of hot water. **1947** *Nation* 22 Feb. 214/1 The crooked towel-covered table. **1898** *Allbutt's Syst. Med.* V. 1031 Spongings.. followed by dry *towel friction. **1872** OLIVER *Elem. Bot.* II. 176 The fibrous inner layer of the pericarp of the *Towel-Gourd.. is used as sponge and gun-wadding. **1833** J. C. LOUDON *Encycl. Cottage, Farm, & Villa Archit.* 349 A *Towel Horse has generally one rail at top... It.. should.. be painted, for the reasons given when speaking of fixed towel rails. **1860** H. F. TOZER in *Vac. Tour.* 386 Hay hanging to dry on large hurdles strongly resembling a gigantic towel-horse. (Cf. **1541** *Aberdeen Regr.* XVII. (Jam.), Ane towall ross of aik worcht vss.) **1878** HUXLEY *Physiogr.* 67 The damp towel on which you have just wiped your wet hands does not stand long on the towel-horse before it becomes dry again. **1591** PERCIVALL *Sp. Dict.*, *Mantelero*, a *towell maker. **1877** KNIGHT *Dict. Mech.*, **Towel-rack*, a frame or rod on which to hang towels to dry. **1833** *Towel rail [see *towel-horse* above]. **1961** *Times* 24 July 13/5 The civilized English custom of having heated towel-rails has not reached the United States. **1895** *Montgomery Ward Catal.* Spring & Summer 126/3 *Towel Ring. Consists of polished hard-wood ring with brass chain and hook. **1977** *Times* 30 July 10/6 Rough towels.. towel rings.. and all manner of taps. **1833** LOUDON *Encycl. Archit.* §609 A *Towel Roller ought to be placed on the back of the kitchen-door of every cottage. *a* **1619** FLETCHER *Wit without M.* IV. v, Allow you but a *towel-room to tipple in. **1884** *Health Exhib. Catal.* 94/2 Hot linen closet, and *towel warmer.

'towel, *v.* [f. prec. sb.]

1. a. *trans.* To apply a towel to; to rub or dry with a towel.

1836-9 DICKENS *Sk. Boz, Ladies' Societies*, The children were yellow-soaped and flannelled, and towelled, till their faces shone again. **1886** D. C. MURRAY *1st Pers. Singular* xix, Zeno.. was towelling himself before the mirror. **1894** A. MORRISON *Mean Streets* 15 Solemn little faces towelled to a polish.

b. *intr.* (with *at*).

1861 DICKENS *Gt. Expect.* xxvi, Letting his head drop into a festoon of towel, and towelling away at his two ears. **1865** —— *Mut. Fr.* I. vi.

c. *absol.* for *refl.* Also with *down, off*.

1972 M. CRICHTON *Terminal Man* IV. ii. 141 One of the girls got out of the pool lithely and began toweling off. **1977** P. MOYES *To kill Coconut* viii. 118 Emmy emerged from the shower, towelling vigorously. **1977** G. FISHER *Villain of Piece* iii. 29, I towelled down, dressed.

2. *slang.* To beat, cudgel, thrash. (Cf. prec. 3.) Also (*Austral.*) with *up*; also *fig.*

1705 J. DUNTON *Life & Errors* (1818) I. ix. 356, I would towel him myself.. if I did not think him an honest man. **1824** in *Spirit Pub. Jrnls.* (1825) 164, I shouldn't have towelled her if she hadn't tempted me to it! **1903** SIR M. G. GERARD *Leaves fr. Diaries* vi. 182 He caught him by the collar and towelled him down with a cutting whip. **1941** BAKER *Dict. Austral. Slang* 78 *Towel up, to*, to beat, thrash. **1951** CUSACK & JAMES *Come in Spinner* 372, I think you deserve the V.C. for the way you towelled Old Mole up. **1973** A. BUZO *Rooted* 42 Gary got his big serve working, I chipped in at the net and we were laughing. Towelled them up in no time.

3. To cover with a towel or towels.

1865 DICKENS *Mut. Fr.* III. iv, I mean to apron it and towel it all over the front.

Hence **'towelled** *ppl. a.*, wrapped in a towel.

1920 T. S. ELIOT *Ara Vus Prec* 23 Doris towelled from the bath Enters padding on broad feet. **1940** G. ARTHUR *Concerning W. S. Churchill* 8 Standing at the edge of a deep swimming pool a junior boy mistook a towelled, stocky figure for a contemporary and playfully pushed him into the water. **1978** C. TOMLINSON *Shaft* 3 The towelled head next.

towel, obs. form of TEWEL.

towelette (taʊə'lɛt). [f. TOWEL *sb.* + -ETTE.] A small towel.

1902 in W. Forrester *Great-Grandmama's Weekly* (1980) iv. 84/1 Artmann's Hygienic towelettes. Superior to any other Sanitary Towels. **1926** *Blackw. Mag.* Apr. 528/1 Drying ourselves on pretty hand-woven towelettes. **1981** *Times* 16 Sept. 9/4 On board, someone opened my milk carton for me and someone else explained the uses of my towelette.

towelling, toweling ('taʊəlɪŋ). [f. TOWEL *sb.* and *v.* + -ING[1].]

I. 1. Linen cloth to be made into towels; material for or of towels.

1583 *Rates of Custome ho.* B vj b, Diaper toweling the peece xxx. s. **1640** in Entick *London* (1766) II. 167 Damask for towelling and napkenning. **1862** *Catal. Internat. Exhib., Brit.* II. No. 3742 Sheetings, towellings, huckabacks. **1880** 'OUIDA' *Moths* II. 19 A dozen yards of bath towelling.

b. A piece of this material, a towel. *nonce-use.*

1845 BROWNING *Flight of Duchess* xi. 15 To wash the hands of her liege In a clean ewer with a fair toweling.

II. 2. Rubbing with, or application of, a towel.

1859 DICKENS *T. Two Cities* II. xi, A correspondingly extra quantity of wine had preceded the [wet] towelling. **1865** —— *Mut. Fr.* I. vi, His head was soon in a basin of water, and out of it again, and staring at her through a storm of towelling. **1911** QUILLER COUCH *Shining Ferry* iv, Her cheeks glowed after a vigorous towelling.

3. *slang.* A beating, drubbing, thrashing.

1851 MAYHEW *Lond. Labour* I. 421/1, I got a towelling, but it did not do me much good. **1906** *Blackw. Mag.* Apr. 446/2 The towelling administered to a dog.. was not pleasant to behold.

towellshell, towelshill, obs. ff. TOLSEL.

'towelry. *nonce-wd.* [f. TOWEL *sb.* + -RY: cf. JEWELRY.] Articles of the towel kind; towels collectively.

1885 R. F. BURTON *Arab. Nts.* I. 201 Then the Wazir.. sent him a suit of the best of his own especial raiment, and napkins and towelry.

†**'towen,** *a. Obs.* [f. TOW *sb.*[1] + -EN[4].] Made of tow, i.e. coarse flax or hemp.

1686 in *Essex Rev.* (1906) XV. 173 Tenn payer of flaxen sheets, fourteen payer of Towen sheets.

†**to-'wend,** *v. Obs.* [OE. *towendan*, f. TO-[2] + *wendan* to turn, WEND.]

1. *trans.* To turn over; to overthrow, demolish; to turn upside down, disturb greatly.

c **893** K. ÆLFRED *Oros.* VI. x. §1 Hi woldon towendon ealle þa ȝesetnessa & ealle þa ȝebodu þe Domitianus hæfde ær ȝeset. *c* **1000** ÆLFRIC *Hom.* I. 46 We ȝehyrdon.. þæt Crist towyrpð þas stowe, and towent ða ȝesetnysse ðe us Moyses tæhte. *c* **1200** *Trin. Coll. Hom.* 191 Mid þusendfeld wrenches þe deuel to-wendeð þe herte. *c* **1205** LAY. 27062 þæ astalden þer flem.. þa rugges to-wenden [*c* 1275 þo torne.. hii þe rugges]. **1225** *Ancr. R.* 324 A wummon þet haueð forloren hir nelde [= needle] oðer a sutare his el, he secheð hine anonrihٰt, & to-went euerich strea uort he beo ifunden.

2. *intr.* **a.** To turn in different directions, disperse, separate. **b.** To go to pieces, break asunder; also *fig.*

c **1175** *Lamb. Hom.* 75 þe twelue apostles.. er heo to-wenden in to al þis middelerd. *c* **1205** LAY. 30235 Duglas þa water wes ihaten þer heo tou-wenden. *c* **1374** CHAUCER *Compl. Mars* 102 His myghty spere as he was wont to fyght He shaketh so that almost it to-wonde Ful hevy was he to walken ouer londe. *c* **1380** *Sir Ferumb.* 2568 Ogier Denys.. smot to sire Mahound þat al to pieces he to-wond & ful doun on þe ground. *a* **1400** *Sir Beues* (E.) 1645 + 27 He smoot þe dore vp wiþ hys ffoot, þat þe dore al towond.

tower (taʊə(r), 'taʊə(r)), *sb.*[1] Forms: α. 1–2, 5–6 torr, 3–4 tor; β. 2–4 tur, 4 ture, (6 *Sc.* tuire); γ. 3–8 tour, 4–7 toure, 9 *Sc.* toor (tur); δ. 3–4 towr, 4–7 towre, (4 towyr, 6 touuer), 6– tower, (8–9 tow'r). [In OE. *torr* masc., ad. L. *turr-is*; in late OE. and early ME. *tūr*, *a* 1300 written *tour*, a. OF. *tor*, *tur* (11th c.), F. *tour* (12th C.) = Pr. *tor*, Sp., Pg., It. *torre*:—L. *turr-em* (*-im*), acc. of *turris* fem. 'tower'. It is doubtful whether the ME. *tor(r* was a survival of the OE. form, since OF. had also *tor*.

(But the Sc. examples in 1 α may perhaps belong to TORE *sb.*[1], and quot. *c* 1400 in 4 to TOR *sb.* 2.)]

I. 1. A building lofty in proportion to the size of its base, either isolated, or forming part of a castle, church, or other edifice, or of the walls of a town.

Often with prefixed word expressing its nature or use, as ***bell-tower, church-tower, gong-tower, Martello tower, sea-tower, watch-tower, water-tower***: see the first element. ***round tower***: see ROUND *a.* 15. ***tower of silence***, the structure on which the Parsees expose their dead (for earlier examples of ***tower of silence*** see SILENCE *sb.* 2 c).

In the Border counties of England and Scotland, 'tower' is often the name of a solitary high fenced house, a tower-house or 'peel-house' (PEEL *sb.*[1] 4, 6), too small to be called a 'castle', e.g. Gilnockie, Goldilands, Smailholm Tower.

α. *c* **897** K. ÆLFRED *Gregory's Past. C.* xi. 64 Ðin nosu is swelc swelce se torr on Libano ðæm munte. *c* **950** *Lindisf. Gosp.* Matt. xxi. 33 Faeder hiorodes seðe..dalf in ðær wintroȝ & ȝetimberde torr [*Ags. Gosp.* stypel]. [*c* **1470** *Golagros & Gaw.* 42 Ane ciete thai se, With torris and turatis, teirfull to tell. **1501** DOUGLAS *Pal. Hon.* III. xvii, Gilt birneist torris, quhilk like to Phebus schone.]

β. *c* **1100–1154** Tur [see 2]. *c* **1200** *Trin. Coll. Hom.* 143 On ure ledene tur, quod interpretatur turris. *c* **1250** *Gen. & Ex.* 661 To make a tur, wel heȝ & strong.

γ. *c* **1290** *S. Eng. Leg.* I. 13/406 A suyþe heiȝ tour of gold and selver. **1297** R. GLOUC. (Rolls) 8303 He ȝeld him vp ..þre toures of þe cite, þat in is warde were. *a* **1300** *Cursor M.* 2230 (Cott.), I rede we bigin a laboure And do we wel and make a toure. *c* **1400** MAUNDEV. (Roxb.) vi. 21 þe toure of Babilon. *Ibid.* ix. 35 A faire kirke with many kirnelles and toures. **1530** LYNDESAY *Test. Papyngo* 633 Adew, fair Snawdoun, with thy touris hie. **1590** SPENSER *F.Q.* III. ix. 35 Which they far off beheld from Trojan toures.

δ. **1375** BARBOUR *Bruce* IX. 451 And syne þe towris euerilkane And vallis gert he tummyll doune. **1382** WYCLIF *Gen.* xi. 4 Comeþ, and make we to vs a citee and a towr, whose heiȝt fulli ateyne vnto heuene. *c* **1440** *Promp. Parv.* 498/2 Towre, *turris*. **1526** TINDALE *Matt.* xxi. 33 Bilt a tower, and lett it out to husbandmen. **1625** BACON *Ess., Building* (Arb.) 550 Those Towers, are not to be of the Height of the Front. **1667** MILTON *P.L.* XII. 44 They cast to build A Citie & Towre, whose top may reach to Heav'n. **1742** GRAY *Eton* 1 Ye distant spires, ye antique towers. **1750** —— *Elegy* 9 From yonder ivy-mantled tow'r The mopeing owl does to the moon complain. **1815** J. SMITH *Panorama Sc. & Art* I. 131 If it be square-topt, it is called a tower. **1849** PARKER *Goth. Archit.* I. iii. (1874) 47 Early in the twelfth century occurred the fall of the tower of Winchester Cathedral. **1853** M. ARNOLD *Scholar Gypsy* iii, And the eye travels down to Oxford's towers. **1910** MRS. YOUNGHUSBAND *Africa & Zanzibar* xxii. 262 Vultures, within one hour of a body being placed in the tower of silence, tear off all flesh from the bones, then the hot tropical sun soon dries and bleaches the bones.

2. a. Such a structure used as a stronghold, fortress, or prison, or built primarily for purposes of defence. (In this sense the name is sometimes extended to include the whole fortress or stronghold of which a 'tower' in sense 1 was the original nucleus.)

Thus the ***Tower of London***, in official designation ***His Majesty's Tower***, and in English History or contextually often simply ***The Tower***, is the entire fortress surrounding the original ***White Tower*** of William Rufus.

c **1100** *O.E. Chron.* an. 1097, þurh þone weall þe hi worhton on butan þone tur [on Lundenne]. *c* **1122** *Ibid.* an. 1101, Se b[iscop] Rannulf..ut of þam ture on Lunden nihtes oðbærst. **1154** *Ibid.* an. 1140, Me læt hire dun on niht of þe tur [at Oxford] mid rapes. *a* **1225** *Ancr. R.* 228 þe tur nis nout asailed, ne þe castel. *c* **1330** R. BRUNNE *Chron.* (1810) 50 Edrik was hanged on þe toure, for his trispas. **1387** TREVISA *Higden* (Rolls) VII. 449 Men myȝte wade bytwene Temsebrugge and þe toure of Londoun. *a* **1400–50** *Alexander* 1296 With trawynns and trebgetes þe towre to assaylle. **1503** WRIOTHESLEY *Chron.* (Camden) I. 5 In Februarie, died Queene Elizabeth at the Towre of London. **1557–75** *Diurn. Occurr.* (Bann. Cl.) 84 Thay war commandit to remayne in waird within the auld tuire quhairin my lord of Murray lugeit. **1613** SHAKS. *Hen. VIII*, v. iii. 89 That forthwith, You be conuaid to th' Tower a Prisoner. **1625** *Crt. & Times Chas. I* (1848) I. 36 A lioness hath whelped in the Tower. **1768** STERNE *Sent. Journ., Hotel at Paris*, The Bastile is but another word for a tower. **1813** SCOTT *Trierm.* II. xvii, She has fair Strath-Clyde and Reged wide, And Carlisle tower and town. *Ibid.* xvi, Carlisle town and tower. **1849** MACAULAY *Hist. Eng.* viii. II. 357 A warrant.. directing the Lieutenant of the Tower to keep them [seven Bishops] in safe custody.

b. In early religious use, often applied to heaven.

a **1240** *Lofsong* in *Cott. Hom.* 207 In syon þe heie tur of heouene. *a* **1300** *Cursor M.* 418 (Cott.) He fordestend tuin creature To serue him in þat hali ture. **13..** *E.E. Allit. P.* A. 965 þou may not enter with-inne hys tor.

3. *fig.* (Cf. 'stronghold', etc.) Freq. in ***tower of strength***. See also IVORY TOWER.

13.. *St. Ambrosius* 793 in Horstm. *Altengl. Leg.* (1878) 20/2 Ambrose..him self was wal and tour, To kepe holi-chirches honour. *c* **1374** CHAUCER *Boeth.* IV. Met. iii. 96 (Camb. MS.) For with inne is Ihydd the strengthe and vigor of men in the secre toure of hir hertes. **1483** CAXTON *Gold. Leg.* 407/1 Thenne she began strongely to assayle the toure of hys conscience. **1549** *Bk. Common Prayer* fol. xv[v], O lorde ..Bee vnto them a tower of strength. **1560** BIBLE (Genev.) *Ps.* cxliv. 2 He is my goodnes and my fortres, my tower and my deliuerer. **1594** SHAKES. *Richard III* v. iii. 12 Besides, the King's name is a Tower of strength. **1605** BACON *Adv. Learn.* I. v. § 11 As if there were sought in knowledge..a tower of state for a proud mind to raise itself upon. **1852** TENNYSON *Ode on Death of Duke of Wellington* 7 O fall'n at length that tower of strength. **1866** MRS. GASKELL *Wives & Daughters* II. xxii. 224 But, my dear Cynthia,—how soon Roger will be back,—a tower of strength. **1909** G. K. CHESTERTON *Orthodoxy* iii. 55 The whole modern world is at war with reason, and the tower already reels. **1956** A. WILSON *Anglo-Saxon Attitudes* II. iii. 394 She's been such a tower of strength all this time. **1970** NEW ENGLISH BIBLE *Prov.* xviii. 10 The name of the Lord is a tower of strength, where the righteous may run for refuge. **1981** P. H. JOHNSON *Bonfire* II. i. 84 He put his arms round Agnes... She thought of him as a 'tower of strength'.

4. *transf.* A lofty pile or material mass.

a **1340** HAMPOLE *Psalter* cl. 4 Orgyns þat is made as a toure of sere whistils. [*c* **1400** *Destr. Troy* 1983 A tempest hom toke on þe torres hegh [of waves].] **1604** E. G.[RIMSTONE] *D'Acosta's Hist. Indies* III. xxvii. 202 There is a place.. where are seene as it were two towers or pikes of a very high elevated rocke, rising out of the middest of the sea. **1840** DICKENS *Barn. Rudge* iv, Sundry towers of buttered Yorkshire cake. **1843** MARRYAT *M. Violet* xli, The Grand Tower, one of the wonders of the Mississippi. It is a stupendous pile of rocks, of a conical form. **1852** THACKERAY *Esmond* I. iii, She had a tower of lace on her head, under which was a bush of black curls. (Cf. 6 b.)

5. In other transferred uses:

a. In ancient and mediæval warfare, a tall movable structure, used in storming a fortified place. Cf. *summer castle*.

c **1440** *Promp. Parv.* 498/2 Towre, made oonly of tymbyr, *fala*. **1483** *Cath. Angl.* 391/1 A Towre of a tree, *fala*. **1552** HULOET, Towre made of tymbre, *fala*. **1665** MANLEY *Grotius's Low C. Warres* 287 The Besiegers erected a great Tower of Wood, after the manner of Antiquity.

†**b.** The 'castle' borne on the back of an elephant. *Obs.*

1553 EDEN *Treat. Newe Ind.* (Arb.) 15 Vpon the pack-saddels, they haue on euery side a little house or towre. [*margin*] The Elephants towre. **1701** W. WOTTON *Hist. Rome, Alexander* ii. 489 They had 700 Elephants, all loaden with Towers. **1762** [see *tower-backed* in 10]. *c* **1820** [implied in TOWERED 1].

c. The gun-turret on an ironclad.

1889 WELCH *Text Bk. Naval Archit.* xiv. 143 The plan of placing the guns in revolving towers or turrets.

d. A railway signal-box. *U.S.*

1900 *Everybody's Mag.* II. 442/2 The tower from which the traffic entering and leaving the Grand Central Station in New York city is directed, is located just outside the station itself. **1910** H. A. FRANCK *Vagabond Journey* 328 A man in the neighbouring tower opened the block, and the diminutive freight screamed by us. **1946** [see *tower house*, sense 10 a below].

e. = PYLON 4.

1930 *Engineering* 9 May 603/2 There are four standard types of tower for the single-circuit lines. **1946** D. C. PEATTIE *Road of Naturalist* iv. 42 The car lamps picked up out of vacancy the marching towers of the power lines. **1963** A. LUBBOCK *Austral. Roundabout* 72 The electric pylons, or towers, as they are called here, stalk up and down great rides cut through the trees, carrying the cable in their upflung arms.

f. = *control tower* s.v. CONTROL *sb.* 5. Also *ellipt.*; *transf.*, the flight-control staff.

1958 'N. SHUTE' *Rainbow & Rose* i. 7 I'll come up to the Tower when we land. **1971** A. DIMENT *Think Inc.* xii. 201 Captain Roberts..asked tower, politely, for permission to taxi. **1977** *Time* 11 Apr. 23/2 The tower ordered KLM to taxi the full length of the runway.

g. *ellipt.* = *tower block*, sense 10 e below.

1970 *Times* 6 July 6/5 The towers, cheerless in their four tones of dun-colour. **1975** M. BRADBURY *History Man* i. 11 Higher on the hill grow the new concrete towers.

6. Applied to various things having the form, figure, or appearance of a tower, or likened to one.

†**a.** *Chess.* The Castle or Rook. *Obs.*

1562 ROWBOTHUM *Play Cheasts* A v, Of the Rooke or Towre. The Towre is named amongest the Spaniards, Portingales, and Italians, *Rocho*. *a* **1649** DRUMM. OF HAWTH. *Fam. Ep.* Wks. (1711) 146 For the towers or castles named rooks, these are the walled towns, which serve for a refuge for the conservation of the kingdom.

b. A very high head-dress worn by women in the reigns of William III and Anne. It was built up in the form of a tower of pasteboard, muslin, lace, and ribbons. Cf. TOUR *sb.* 4. *Hist.*

c **1612** SYLVESTER *Lacrymae Lacrym.* 159 Stript, from Top to Toe, Of giddie Gaudes, Top-gallant Tires and Towers. **1693** DRYDEN *Juvenal* vi. 646 With Curls on Curls, they build her Head before, And mount it with a Formidable Tow'r. [*Note*] This dressing up the Head so high, which we call a Tow'r, was an Ancient way amongst the Romans. **1706, 1894** [? implied in TOWERED 1, TOWERING *vbl. sb.*]. [**1852** THACKERAY *Esmond* II. xv, My Lady of Chelsea in her highest tour, my Lady Viscountess out of black.]

c. Applied to various technical structures and contrivances, now only descriptively: see quots. and cf. *shot-tower*.

1662 MERRETT tr. *Neri's Art of Glass* 243 The Leer (made by Agricola, the third furnace, to anneal and cool the vessels ..) comprehends two parts, the tower and leer. *Ibid.* 365 *Tower* is the Iron on which they rest their Pontee when they scald the Glass. **1688** R. HOLME *Armoury* III. xx. (Roxb.) 228 The Philosophers Tower..is a kind of Tower furnace. .. The Maner of the Tower is four square. **1727–41** CHAMBERS *Cycl.* s.v. *Furnace*. **1857** MILLER *Elem. Chem.* (1862) III. 649 In many works the process of washing with acid is superseded by..a *scrubber*, consisting of a tower, the interior of which is filled with small coke resting upon perforated shelves. **1885** *Athenæum* 21 Feb. 252/1 A concise account of the treatment of iron ores for the blast furnace, a careful examination of the peculiar action of that vast metallurgical tower in all its modified forms.

7. *Astrol.* = HOUSE *sb.*[1] 8, MANSION *sb.* 5 a.

c **1374** CHAUCER *Compl. Mars* 113 Now fleeth Venus in to cilenios toure. **1911** RAMSAY in *Expositor* Mar. 224 The twelve zodiacal stations of the sun were called towers by the Greek astrologers.

II. 8. a. Lofty flight; soaring. (Cf. TOWER *v.* 3.)

1486 *Bk. St. Albans* D iv, Ther is an Hoby. And that hauke is for a yong man. And theys be hawkes of the toure: and ben both Ilurid to be calde and reclaymed. *c* **1518** SKELTON *Magnyf.* II. xv. 926 Torde! man, it is an hawke of the towre. **1575** TURBERV. *Falconrie* 53 She [the hobby] is of the number of those hawkes that are hye fleeing and towre hawkes. **1667** MILTON *P.L.* XI. 185 Nigh in her sight The Bird of Jove, stoopt from his aerie tour, Two Birds of gayest plume before him drove.

b. The vertical ascent of a wounded bird.

1890 *Pall Mall G.* 18 Jan. 2/3 A single goose..bravely struggles onwards, and finally, after a perfectly executed 'tower', falls dead not far from the boat. **1895** J. G. MILLAIS *Breath fr. Veldt* (1899) 82 The outlined figures are intended to represent the tower and drop of a single bird.

III. 9. Phrases. **a.** ***tower and town*** (also ***town and tower***), an alliterative phrase for the inhabited places of a country or region generally. †**b.** ***towers in the air***, visionary projects, 'castles in the air' (see CASTLE *sb.* 11).

a **1300** *Cursor M.* 12983 (Cott.) Al þis werld, bath tur and tun. *c* **1420** *Sir Amadace* (Camden) lxxii, Thenne was he lord of toure and towne. **1599** *Broughton's Let.* ii. 9 Your humours building towers in the ayre,..faine a sounding in your eares. **1813** [see 2]. **1842** WORDSW. *Poet's Dream* viii, O'er town and tower we flew, and fields in May's fresh verdure drest. **1870** TENNYSON *Flower* iv, Thieves..Sow'd it far and wide By every town and tower.

IV. 10. *attrib.* and *Comb.* **a.** Simple attrib. 'of or belonging to a or the tower', as ***tower-bell, -clock, -gate, -gun, -head, -pier, -room, -stair, -top, -ward, -wharf***; 'that is, consists of, has, or contains a tower', as ***tower-distillatory, -furnace, -gateway, -house, -keep, mill, -porch, silo, -steeple***; **b.** objective, as ***tower-keeper, -transporter***; ***tower-bearing, -razing, -supporting, -tearing*** adjs.; **c.** instrumental, locative, etc., as ***tower-backed, -capped, -crested, -crowned, -encircled, -flanked, -full, -studded*** adjs.; **d.** similative, etc., as ***tower-high, -like, -shaped*** adjs.; ***tower-wise*** adv. **e.** Special Combs.: **tower apartment**, an apartment in a tower block, a high-rise flat; **tower-ball**, a game for children; **tower block**, a tall block of flats, a high-rise building, a skyscraper; **tower bolt** = *barrel bolt* s.v. BARREL *sb.* 11; **tower crane** (see quot. 1940); **tower-cress**, the cruciferous plant *Arabis Turrita*; sometimes applied to TOWER MUSTARD, *Turritis glabra*; †**tower-fellow**, a fellow prisoner in the Tower; **tower-fellowship**, a political division of citizens in the states of ancient Greece; **tower hill**, a hill near or on which a tower is built; *spec.* (with caps.) the rising ground by the Tower of London; **tower karst** *Geomorphol.* [tr. G. *turmkarst* (H. von Wissmann 1954, in *Erdkunde* VIII. 122/1)], a type of karst characterized by isolated steep-sided hills; **tower-light**, a window or hole in a tower; **towerman**, one who works in a tower; *spec.* (*U.S.*) (*a*) a railway signalman; (*b*) a look-out for forest fires; **Tower musket** *Hist.*, a tower-proof musket; **tower-proof** *a.*, proved or tested in the arsenal at the Tower of London; also *allusively*; **tower-ring**, a finger-ring bearing an image of a tower; **tower-shell** = *turret-shell* s.v. TURRET *sb.*[1] 5; **tower skull** = *oxycephaly* s.v. OXY- 1; **tower-stamp**, the official stamp or mark on gold and silver articles; hall-mark; † **towers treacle** = TOWER MUSTARD; **tower-wagon**, a wagon with a structure which can be raised and lowered to serve as a platform for repairing overhead wires, etc.; †**tower-window**, each of the turreted lights at the head of a late Gothic or Perpendicular window; **tower-work**, masonry built in the form of towers. Also TOWER MUSTARD, POUND, WEIGHT, -WORT.

1961 *Tower apartment [see MAISONETTE 2]. **1608** SYLVESTER *Du Bartas* II. iv. III. *Schisme* 437 The *Towr-back't Camel, that..on his bunch could have transported yerst Neer a whole Household. **1762** *Judas Macc.* III. 18 The huge Tow'r-back'd Elephants. **1555** EDEN *Decades* 189 The *towrebearynge shoulders of Elephantes. **1592** R. D. *Hypnerotomachia* 7 b, A sound, as if the *tower bell of Saint Iohns Colledge in the famous Vniuersitie of Cambridge had beene rung. **1966** *Atlantic Monthly* Oct. 127 *Tower blocks can be accused of leading to eardrum degeneration, owing to constant use of high-speed elevators. *a* **1974** R. CROSSMAN *Diaries* (1975) I. 82 The jack-block building in Coventry, a fifteen- or sixteen-storey tower block built by a new technique of jacking each storey up after it has been erected. **1982** *Listener* 23/30 Dec. 58/4 Most American film crews refuse to take rooms higher than the second floor of towerblock hotels since this picture. **1911** *Tower bolt [see *barrel bolt* s.v. BARREL *sb.* 11]. **1816** BYRON *Siege of Cor.* i, Yon *tower-capt Acropolis. **1895** A. J. EVANS in *Folk-Lore*

Mar. 44 As soon as the *tower-clock strikes twelve. **1906** *Electr. World* XLVII. 743 An illustrated description of an electrically-operated rotating *tower crane for the Dublin docks. **1940** *Chambers's Techn. Dict.* 856/1 *Tower crane*, a rotatable cantilever pivoted to the top of a steelwork tower, either fixed or carried on rails. **1967** *Listener* 27 July 111/1 A tower crane on our university building site. *a* **1835** MRS. HEMANS *Abencerrage* II. 39 *Tower-crested rocks. **1771** *Gentl. Mag.* Nov. 490/1 At the sight Of distant Bremen's *tower-crown'd height. **1688** R. HOLME *Armoury* III. xx. (Roxb.) 229 This is the form of another *Tower distillatory, but four square in the foundation with a round tower in the midst. **1896** *Spectator* 31 Oct. 586/1 There are other tribes of *tower-dwelling birds. **1730–46** THOMSON *Autumn* 114 Nurse of art, the city reared..her *tower-encircled head. **1709** STRYPE *Ann. Ref.* I. xlv. 457 He and his *Tower-fellows, hearing the bill..should pass. **1847** GROTE *Greece* II. xiii. III. 247 The symmories or *tower-fellowships of Teôs seem to be analogous to the phratries of ancient Athens. **1799** H. GURNEY *Cupid & Psyche* viii. (1800) 18 A vast and *tower-flank'd palace stood. **1598** SYLVESTER *Du Bartas* II. ii. III. *Colonies* 424 Th' ingenious, *Towr-full, and Law-loving Soil. **1688** *Tower furnace [see sense 6c]. *a* **1832** SCOTT *Eve St. John* xxxii, He oped the *tower-gate And he mounted the narrow stair. **1886** WILLIS & CLARK *Cambridge* III. 285 Wykeham's *tower-gateway at New College is in three floors. **1719** D'URFEY *Pills* III. 2 It seiz'd on the *Tow'r Guns. **1767** WESLEY *Jrnl.* 5 Nov., I was surprised..to hear the Tower-guns so plain at above fifty miles distance. **1539** in *Archæologia* XI. 437 Uppon the same *towre hed a saker of brasse of Scottyshe makinge. *c* **1480** WARKW. *Chron.* (Camden) 5 To the *Towre Hylle. **1485** *Rolls of Parlt.* VI. 372/2 The Gardyns upon the Towre hill. **1843** *Penny Cycl.* XXV. 98/1 The chief place of execution was outside the walls [of the Tower of London] on the neighbouring Tower Hill. **1687** A. LOVELL tr. *Thevenot's Trav.* I. 100 A litte *Tower-house, with two or three Rooms. **1797** *Statist. Acc. Scot.* XIX. 602 Tower houses are met with in a ruinous condition. **1946** E. B. THOMPSON *Amer. Daughter* 124 We climbed the little ladder to the railroad tower house. **1954** *Erdkunde* VIII. 122/1 Of the various formations of kegelkarst, two widely differ in appearance from one another... **2.** A river plain, dotted with groups or swarms of limestone towers or castles... This is the *tower karst. **1977** A. HALLAM *Planet Earth* 83/2 Hills with slopes of 70° and more occur, the relief being called tower karst. **1897** WINDLE *Life in Early Brit.* ix. 176 The erection of the rectangular *tower keep, which the Norman used when he was building on a perfectly new site. **1885** MCCOOK *Tenants Old Farm* 135 Easy victims to the vigilant *tower-keeper. **1848** RICKMAN *Archit.* (ed. 5) 220 'Sound-holes'..seems not so appropriate as air-holes or *tower-lights. **1552** HULOET, *Towrelyke, *turreus.* **1625** K. LONG tr. *Barclay's Argenis* IV. xix. 309 Elephants..brought into the Battell with their tower-like carriages. **1729** SAVAGE *Wanderer* IV. 119 He sees yon Tow'r-like Ship the Waves divide. **1893** *Scribner's Mag.* June 718/1 The tower-like building of stone and stucco, octagonal in form, had a forbidding air. **1895** *Tower man [see ROUNDHOUSE *sb.* 4]. **1947** *Sun* (Baltimore) 18 Oct. 7/1 Towermen..serve as the eyes of the fire fighters. **1951** Towerman [see GOLDFISH b]. **1888** *Tower mill [see SMOCKMILL]. **1933** *Times Lit. Suppl.* 14 Dec. 891/1 Even in brick or stone tower-mills the sweeps may be caught in the rear..by a suddenly veering storm. **1979** *Jrnl. R. Soc. Arts* Dec. 3/1 The viewer is taken inside one of the last remaining working tower mills. **1832** A. EARLE *Narr. Residence in N.Z.* (1966) 170 He had with him a beautiful double-barrelled gun, and a very good *Tower musket. **1947** Tower musket [see DANE GUN]. **1880** *Archæol. Cantiana* XIII. 26 Lanfranc's *tower-piers, and a few feet of his crypt walls undoubtedly remain. **1886** WILLIS & CLARK *Cambridge* III. 356 Access to the hall is provided through a *tower-porch. **1673** *Phil. Trans.* VIII. 6072 Powder proved *Tower-proof is a fifth part stronger than any Dutch powder. **1805** T. LINDLEY *Voy. Brazil* 252 Brasil being supplied by the mother country with British tower-proof musquets. **1858** HOGG *Life Shelley* II. 365 Blessed amongst women,..a tower-proof, fire-proof, bomb-proof blue. **1606** SYLVESTER *Du Bartas* II. iv. I. *Tropheis* 401 'Twas the Breach of a *Tower-razing Ram. **1877** W. JONES *Finger-ring* 298 In the same collection is a Jewish '*tower' betrothal ring. *Ibid.*, Another betrothal ring..called 'temple' or 'tower' from the figure of the sacred temple placed on the summit. **1886** WILLIS & CLARK *Cambridge* III. 331 The President is to have certain *tower-rooms. **1897** *Jacob Primmer in Rome* (1903) 319 In this *tower-shaped tomb. **1888** *Cassell's Encycl. Dict.*, *Tower-shell. **1927** HALDANE & HUXLEY *Animal Biol.* xii. 300 One fossil tower-shell stands nearly five feet high. **1959** A. C. HARDY *Open Sea* II. v. 118 The tall slender *Turritella*, or tower-shell, is another common gastropod burrowing just below the surface. **1800** *Hull Advertiser* 17 May 3/3 A pamphlet, just published, price a good *Tower Shilling. **1939** J. R. MCCALMONT *Silo Types & Construction* 2 Silos may be divided roughly into above-ground—*tower or upright—and the below-ground—pit or trench—silo, either of which may be built for temporary or continued use. **1982** *Daily Tel.* 19 Apr. 9/3 Tower silos, standing as they do up to some 60 feet high and painted in various..colours are not particularly attractive features of our rural areas. **1905** *Trans. Ophthalm. Soc.* XXV. 364 (*heading*) Oxycephaly or '*tower skull'. **1918** J. H. PARSONS *Dis. Eye* (ed. 3) xxxiii. 620 Bilateral proptosis occurs in exophthalmic goître..as a result of diminished orbital volume in oxycephaly or 'tower-skull' and leontiasis ossea. **1969** EDINGTON & GILLES *Path. in Tropics* x. 379 Patients with sickle-cell anaemia tend to have a certain type of habitus, with tower-skull, parietal bossing, and long slender, limbs. **1848** THACKERAY *Van. Fair* lxii, The Batavier steamboat left the *Tower stairs laden with a goodly company of English fugitives. **1642** FULLER *Holy & Prof. St.* II. xix. 120 He knows if he sets his mark, (the *Tower-stamp of his credit) on any bad wares, he sets a deeper brand on his own conscience. **1845** CLOUGH *Silver Wedding* xii, That wariest glance would here Faith, Hope and Love, the true Tower-stamp discern. **1610** HOLLAND *Camden's Brit.* (1637) 216 A new Church with..an high spire besides the *Toure steeple. *Ibid.* 468, I saw the towre steeple of a small suppressed Friery. *Ibid.* 290 The *tour-supporting bankes, at Windsore. **1614** SYLVESTER *Bethulia's Rescue* III. 125 *Tower-tearing Mars, Bellona thirsting-bloud. **1840** DICKENS *Old C. Shop* lv, One of these..climbed with her to the *tower-top. **1903** *Daily Chron.* 25 June 4/5 An opportunity of witnessing the coaling of the flagship Majestic by the new Temperley *tower transporter. **1597** GERARDE *Herbal* II. xxii. §3. 213 (*heading*) Towers Mustarde..*Towers Treacle groweth in the west part of Englande vpon dunghils and such like places. **1911** *Daily News* 20 Apr. 1 A collapsible structure similar to a *tower wagon, was blown over by the wind. *c* **1450** *Brut* 423 The persone of the Toure and this ffrere Randulf fillen in debate and stryffe withynne the *Toure ward. *Ibid.* 431 Iohn Mortymere, knyght, brake pryson oute of the Toure of London, and was take ayen vpon the *Toure-wharf. **1593** *Rites of Durham* (Surtees) 43 In this wyndowe, above all, are six little glasened *towre wyndowes. **1581** A. HALL *Iliad* VII. 127 His huge and waightie targe, Which *towerwise so stoode aloft. **1634–5** BRERETON *Trav.* (Chetham Soc.) 94 A little fort..built tower-wise. **1653** H. COGAN tr. *Pinto's Trav.* xxv. (1663) 93 The top of the Platform was bordered with the same stone, cut into great *Tower-work.

tower ('taʊə(r)), *sb.*² Also 5 *Sc.* towar. [f. TOW *v.*¹ + -ER¹.] One who tows or draws with a rope; *esp.* one who tows a boat on a river or canal.

(In quots. 1494 the sense is uncertain; cf. quot. 1494 in TOW *v.*¹ 1, which refers to the same transaction.)

[**1494** *Acc. Ld. High Treas. Scot.* I. 248 For the drawyne of viij treis fra the Sallache to the bote, and to a towar to gid thame,..vs. iiij d. *Ibid.*, Item, gyffyne tyll a towar, for to helpe to bryng doune the cariour fra Lochlomond,..ij s.] **1611** COTGR., *Tireur*, a drawer..tugger, tower. **1795** ANDERSON *Brit. Emb. China* vi. 80 These pieces of wood..rest upon their breasts, and by leaning against them the towers increase the power of their exertions. **1883** M. H. HAYES *Ind. Racing Remin.* 231 The broken ground over which these native towers have to travel. **1887** J. ASHBY STERRY *Lazy Minstrel* (1892) 155 My tow-ers are young and my tow-ers are fair: The one is Eleven, the other Nineteen, The merriest maidens that ever were seen. **1889** J. K. JEROME *Three Men in Boat* ix, A couple of towers walking briskly along.

'tower, *sb.*³ *Sc.* [f. TOW *sb.*² + -ER¹.] A rope-maker, a roper.

15.. *Aberdeen Regr.* (MS.) XXVIII. (Jam.), Towar.

tower, *sb.*⁴: see TOW *v.*⁴

tower (taʊə(r), 'taʊə(r)), *v.* Forms: see the sb. [f. TOWER *sb.*¹]

I. 1. *a. intr.* To rise or extend to a great height like a tower; to rise aloft, stand high.

(In quot. *c* 1400 the sense of *torret* is very uncertain.)

[*c* **1400** *Destr. Troy* 1637 Toures full tore torret aboue, þat were of heght so hoge, as I here fynde.] **1582** STANYHURST *Æneis* I. (Arb.) 31 O wights most blessed, whose wals be thus happelye touring. **1590** SPENSER *F.Q.* II. xii. 30 On th' other side an high rocke toured still. **1610** HOLLAND *Camden's Brit.* (1637) 581 Dudley Castle towreth up upon an hill. **1690** C. NESSE *O. & N. Test.* I. 268 Like pillars of smoke towering upward. **1715–20** POPE *Iliad* II. 565 The king of kings, majestically tall, Tow'rs o'er his armies, and outshines them all. **1834** MRS. SOMERVILLE *Connex. Phys. Sc.* xxvii. (1849) 300 Magnificent trees tower to the height of 150 or 200 feet above the banana, the bamboo. **1863** GEO. ELIOT *Romola* vi, Over every fastness..that towers some huge Frankish fortress. **1885–94** R. BRIDGES *Eros & Psyche, March* xxiv, She saw the evening light In shifting colour to the zenith tower.

b. *fig.* Usually const. *above.*

1776 BOSWELL 11 Apr., in *Johnson*, Does not Gray's poetry, sir, tower above the common mark? **1820** HAZLITT *Lect. Dram. Lit.* 12 He [Shakspeare] towered above his fellows. **1822** —— *Table-t.* Ser. II. iii. (1869) 66 Her voice towered above the whole confused noise of the orchestra. **1869** TROLLOPE *He knew he was Right* xxviii, When she first read the letter..she towered in her passion.

2. *trans.* To raise or uplift to a height; to exalt.

1596 WARNER *Alb. Eng.* XII. lxx. (1612) 295 English Poets Many, Of which are some..that towre their wits too hie. **1645** RUTHERFORD *Trial & Tri. Faith* (1845) 299 The Soul is lifted up and towered like a high building. **1821** CLARE *Vill. Minstr.* I. 75 Where hills tower'd high their crowns. **1849** W. S. MAYO *Kaloolah* vi. (1851) 26 Gigantic trees, which towered their lofty heads to the clouds.

3. *intr.* **a.** *Hawking.* To mount up, as a hawk, so as to be able to swoop down on the quarry: cf. TOWER *sb.*¹ 8. Also *fig.*

1593 SHAKS. *2 Hen. VI*, II. i. 10 My Lord Protectours Hawkes do towre so well. **1605** —— *Macb.* II. iv. 12 A Faulcon towring in her pride of place. **1616** B. JONSON *Epigr.* I. lxxxv, Shee doth instruct men by her gallant flight, That they to knowledge so should toure upright And never stoope, but to strike ignorance. **1878** M. A. BROWN *Nadeschda* 27 Loose thy hawk and let it tower.

b. To soar aloft, as a bird.

1647 N. BACON *Disc. Govt. Eng.* I. xlvii. (1739) 77 The Eagle had cast its Feathers, and could towre no more. *a* **1682** H. BLUNT *Poem addr. to Garth* 14 in *Dispens.* (1709) Pref., So the Young Eagle that his Force would try, Faces the Sun, and tow'rs it to the Sky. **1728** RAMSAY *Lure* 93 See, see! he like a lavrock tours. **1817–18** COBBETT *Resid. U.S.* (1822) 211 The pheasant does not tower, but darts through the trees. **1885–94** R. BRIDGES *Eros & Psyche, Sept.* xvi, He flasht his pens, and sweeping widely round Tower'd to air.

c. To rise vertically, as a bird when wounded.

1799 COLERIDGE *Notebks.* (1957) I. entry 564 Partridges towering after being shot is a certain Proof that they are mortaly wounded. **1812** COL. HAWKER *Diary* (1893) I. 39 With the exception of one which towered, all my birds fell dead to the gun. **1887** [see TOWERING *vbl. sb.*].

†**4.** *fig.* To rise on high, to soar. *Obs.*

1597 DELONEY *Canaans Calam.* (1912) 422 Their mounting minds that towred past their strength. **1641** J. JACKSON *True Evang. T.* II. 113 S. John..towred aloft into the highest mysteries of Divinity. **1643** SIR T. BROWNE *Relig. Med.* II. §8, I have seen a Grammarian towr and plume himself over a single line in Horace. **1748** JOHNSON *Van. Hum. Wishes* 103 Still to new heights his restless wishes tower.

†**5.** *trans.* To soar aloft in or into; to rise to.

1604 DRAYTON *Owle* 149 By Night I towre the Heauen, deuoy'd of feare. *a* **1649** DRUMM. OF HAWTH. *Poems* (1790) 283 He towers those golden bounds He did to sun bequeath. **1667** MILTON *P.L.* VII. 441 Yet oft they quit The Dank, and rising on stiff Pennons, towre The mid Aereal Skie.

†**II. 6.** *trans.* To furnish with a tower or towers.

c **1440** [see TOWERING *vbl. sb.*]. **1450** in *Charters*, etc. *Edinb.* (1871) 71 To..wall, toure, turate, and uther wais to strengthen oure foresaid Burgh. *a* **1548** HALL *Chron.*, *Hen. VIII* 59 This Gardeyn was towred at euery corner.

towerde, -dys, obs. ff. TOWARD, TOWARDS.

towered ('taʊəd, *poet.* 'taʊərɪd), *a.* [f. TOWER *sb.*¹ and *v.* + -ED.]

1. Having a tower or towers; adorned or defended by towers; bearing or surmounted by a tower; raised or rising on high like a tower.

c **1400** *Sege Jerus.* 868 Þis toured toun is tenful to wynne. *c* **1430** *Seven Sag.* (P.) 2842 Who hys thys castel, That hys touryde and kernelde wel? *a* **1552** LELAND *Itin.* II. 67 The Tourrid Steple of the Paroche Chirch. **1632** MILTON *L'Allegro* 117 Towred Cities please us then. **1706** HEARNE *Collect.* 19 Jan. (O.H.S.) I. 165 Cybele..is represented with a Tower'd Head. **1796** W. H. MARSHALL *W. England* II. 208 The towered height of Stourton forms a prominent feature. *c* **1820** S. ROGERS *Italy, Alps* 24 The towered elephant Upheld his trunk. **1832** TENNYSON *Lady of Shalott* I. iv, From the river winding clearly Down to tower'd Camelot. **1909** RIDER HAGGARD *Yellow God* 42 The towered gateway of red brick.

†**2.** Immured in a tower; committed to the Tower of London. (Cf. *prisoned.*) *Obs.*

1716 M. DAVIES *Athen. Brit.* II. 409 The two that turn'd Non-jurors with the t'other five tower'd Bishops. **1750** *Student* (1751) II. 22 The noble Septemvirate of tower'd Prelates.

3. Of a wounded bird: That has 'towered'.

1827 COL. HAWKER *Diary* (1893) I. 320 Besides 4 towered and lost birds.

[**toweret**, 'a little tower', in mod. Dicts., deduced from *towret*: see TURRET.]

towering ('taʊərɪŋ), *vbl. sb.* [f. TOWER *v.* + -ING¹.] The action of the verb TOWER in various senses: *spec.* †**a.** The building of a tower. *Obs. rare*⁻⁰. **b.** Rising, soaring; raising. **c.** See quot. 1887 and TOWER *sb.*¹ 8 b, *v.* 3 c. **d.** *Photog.* See quot. 1891.

c **1440** *Promp. Parv.* 498/2 Towrynge, *turrificacio.* **1646** J. HALL *Poems* (1906) 224 Ambition's towerings do some gallants keep From calmer sleep. **1750** JOHNSON *Rambler* No. 72 ¶5 The hearers either strain their faculties to accompany its towerings, or are left behind in envy and despair. **1887** COUES in *Science* X. 322 The convulsive muscular action which..results in the well-known 'towering' of hard-hit birds. **1891** *Anthony's Photogr. Bull.* IV. 38 How often is it that an otherwise good picture is spoiled by what we might call towering. The top of the building being much narrower than the bottom [etc.]. **1894** *Yellow Bk.* I. 66 Women..gave the best hours of the day to the towering of their coiffures.

'towering, *ppl. a.* [f. TOWER *v.* + -ING².] That towers, in various senses.

1. Rising to a height; standing high; lofty.

1638 SIR T. HERBERT *Trav.* (ed. 2) 193 A spatious Garden, succinct with a great Towring wall of mud. **1697** DRYDEN *Virg. Past.* VII. 91 The towring Ash is fairest in the Woods. *c* **1743** FRANCIS tr. *Hor., Sec. Poem* 46 The cypress, when by storms impell'd,..Low bends the towering head. **1793** *Statist. Acc. Scotl.* VII. 501 The hills are steep and towering. **1833** L. RITCHIE *Wand. by Loire* 21 The girls..with their towering caps of the snowiest muslin. **1859** J. R. GREEN *Lett.* I. (1901) 33 My eye wanders..to the towering dome of the Radcliffe.

b. Of lofty stature; very tall.

1756 JOHNSON *K. of Prussia* Wks. IV. 532 To review this towering regiment was his daily pleasure. **1835** LYTTON *Rienzi* I. iii, The towering form of the smith. **1894** HALL CAINE *Manxman* III. xii, Kate saw him come, a towering dark figure between her and the door.

2. Rising high in flight, as a bird, etc. Also *fig.*

1598 MERES *Pallad. Tamia* II. 285 b, Yong Charles Fitz-Ieffrey, that high touring Falcon, hath..penned the honourable life and death of worthy sir Francis Drake. **1598** DRAYTON *Heroic. Ep.* xix. 179 Vnder thy towring blade haue coucht in fight. *c* **1673** *Roxb. Ball.* (1887) VI. 271 Where towering Larks do soar on high, In consort, making Melody. **1709** PRIOR *To C. Montague* vi, Our Hopes, like tow'ring Falcons, aim At Objects in an airy height. **1765** R. JONES *Fireworks* IV. 128 One rocket on the top of another. When.. thus managed, they are called towering rockets. **1892** GREENER *Breech-Loader* 228 If beaters or keepers are not occupied in picking up, and can look after wounded and towering birds.

3. Rising to a height (*fig.*); exalted; aiming high; ambitious.

1663 BP. PATRICK *Parab. Pilgr.* v. (1687) 18 Others.. teach me to fly aloft in towring speculations. **1702** *Eng. Theophrast.* 4 Nothing less than the writing of a Play can satisfie his towring Ambition. **1781** COWPER *Charity* 536 A bold remark, but which, if well applied, Would humble many a towering poet's pride. **1840** THIRLWALL *Greece* VII. lvi. 179 A man..of towering ambition. **1894** J. KNIGHT *Garrick* iv. 59 No man of towering ability was on the stage.

4. Rising to a high pitch of violence or intensity.

1602 SHAKS. *Ham.* V. ii. 80 The brauery of his griefe did put me Into a Towring passion. **1818** SCOTT *Rob Roy* xviii, I was in a towering passion. **1848** DICKENS *Dombey* liv, The towering fury and intense abhorrence. **1877** BLACK *Green Past.* xxxiii, He came down in a towering rage.

Hence **'toweringly** *adv.*, in a towering manner.

1822 E. Irving *Let.* in Oliphant *Life* (1862) I. vi. 135, I should rise toweringly aloft into the regions of a very noble and sublime character. **1830** *Fraser's Mag.* I. 38 Tall palm-trees, that on the plain stood toweringly. **1885** G. Meredith *Diana of Crossways* xiii, The Hercules of dogs.. toweringly big.

'towerless, *a.* [f. tower *sb.*[1] + -less.] Without a tower; devoid of towers.

c **1820** S. Rogers *Italy, Campagna Florence* 201 Towerless, and left long since, but to the last Braving assault. **1886** Stokes *Irel. & Celtic Ch.* xii. (1888) 238 The earliest Christian churches.. were utterly towerless.

'towerlet. [f. as prec. + -let.] A little tower.

18.. Joanna Baillie (Ogilvie), Our guiding star Now from its towerlet streameth far.

'tower 'mustard. *Herb.* [So named, according to Britten and Holland, from its habit of growth. According to Linnæus, called *Turritis* (Tournefort) as being 'alta et stricta'.] Popular name of a cruciferous plant, *Turritis glabra*, found on banks and cliffs. Called also *towers treacle, towerwort*, and sometimes *tower cress*.

1597 Gerarde *Herbal* II. xxii. 212 Towers Mustarde, of some hath beene taken for a kinde of Cresses. **1731** Miller *Gard. Dict.*, *Turritis*, Tower-Mustard. **1842** C. W. Johnson *Farmer's Cycl.* s.v., *Turritis*, from *turris*, a tower; the foliage is so disposed on the stems as to give them a pyramidal form, and for the same reason the plants are called tower-mustard.

b. Sometimes applied to *Arabis Turrita* (see tower-*cress*); also called bastard tower mustard.

1760 J. Lee *Introd. Bot.* App. 320 Mustard, Bastard Tower, *Arabis*. **1866** *Treas. Bot.* s.v. *Mustard*, Mustard, Tower.. also *Arabis Turrita*. **1874** Gray *Man. Bot.* (ed. 5) 69 *A[rabis] perfoliata*, Lam. (Tower Mustard).

Tower pound. Also 6-8 pound Tower. [So called from the standard pound which was kept in the Tower of London.] A pound weight of 5400 grains (= 11¼ Troy ounces), which was the legal mint pound of England prior to the adoption of the Troy pound of 5760 grains in 1526. So **Tower weight**, weight expressed in terms of the Tower pound.

[**1343** *Close Roll* 17 Edw. III. m. 4 d (P.R.O.), Vne liure de pois de la Tour de Loundres.] **1469** in *Archæologia* XV. 166 For coynage of every lb. of Tour weght of sylver.. iiii s. vi d. **1526** *Proclam.* 5 Nov. (Pat. Roll 18 Hen. VIII. II. m. 2 d. P.R.O.), It is.. determyned.. that the said pounde Towre shalbe no more vsed nor occupied. **1545** *Rates of Customs* d v b, A pounde of Tower wayght wayeth of the Troy .xi. ounces .i. quarter. **1622** Malynes *Anc. Law-Merch.* 292 There hath been vsed from the beginning (in the Mint) both Troy and Tower weight, each of them containing twelue ounces in the pound weight, sauing that the Troy weight is heauier by sixteen penie weight vpon the pound weight: by which Troy weight the merchants bought their gold and siluer abroad, and by the same did deliuer it to the Kings mint, receiuing in counterpeaze but tower weight for Troy, which was the Princes Prerogatiue. **1789** Walter Merrey *Remarks Coinage* 8 The silver penny was about twenty-two grains and a half of Troy-weight, but called a penny-weight Tower. The shilling was twelve of these pennies, and the pound Tower was twenty of these shillings. **1821** J. Q. Adams in C. Davies *Metr. Syst.* (1871) 94 This [silver] penny was the two hundred and fortieth part of the tower pound. **1844** Lingard *Anglo-Sax. Ch.* (1858) II. App. O. 388 The Anglo-Saxon pound is believed to have been that known by the name of the Tower pound; the Norman was the Troy pound, heavier by three-quarters of an ounce than the former.

towers, obs. form of tours.

Tower weight: see Tower pound.

towerwort: see tower mustard.

towery ('taʊərɪ), *a.* [f. tower *sb.*[1] + -y.]

1. Characterized by or having towers; adorned or defended with towers.

1611 Cotgr., *Tourrelé*, Towerie, tower-like, begirt or incompassed with towers. **1672** Dryden *2nd Pt. Conq. Granada* III. iii. 114 The Genius of the place its Lord will meet; And bend its tow'ry forehead to your feet. **17..** Pope *Imit. Spenser* 54 Meandring streams, and Windsor's tow'ry pride. **1834** J. Wilson in *Blackw. Mag.* XXXVI. 842 Crowned with her towery diadem—Queen of the Sea. **1870** Bryant *Iliad* VII. I. 214 Till ye possess the towery city of Troy.

2. Rising to a lofty height; tower-like; towering; also *fig.* aspiring; exalted.

1731 A. Hill *Adv. Poets* xvi. 9 Hence, have all towery Minds, sublimely fir'd, With in-born Strength, to their own Heav'n aspir'd. **1738** H. Brooke tr. *Tasso's Jerus. Del.* II. Poems (1810) 376/1 One step alone 'twixt triumph and defeat, The gulfy ruin and the tow'ry height. **1825** J. Wilson *Poems* II. 114 Long ensigns brightening on the towery mast. **1870** R. R. Coverdale *Poems* 39 'Neath towery trees that lowly bent.

3. *Comb.* **towery-topped** *a.*, having a towery top; topped or crowned with towers.

1602 Carew *Cornwall* II. 121 A towry-topped Castle heere, wide blazeth ouer all.

towgh, -e, towȝ, towh, -he, obs. ff. tough.

towghe, towgher: see toughe, tocher.

towght, obs. form of tought.

towhee ('taʊhiː, 'taʊiː). *U.S.* Also 8 towee, 8-9 towhe. ['From one of its notes' (Newton).] The ground-robin or cheewink of North America, *Pipilo erythrophthalmus*; also ***towhee bird, -finch, -bunting, -goldfinch.*** Also any species of *Pipilo*.

1730 Mortimer in *Phil. Trans.* XXXVI. 430 The Towhe Bird. **1791** W. Bartram *Carolina* 172 The towee birds.. are very numerous. **1859** Bartlett *Dict. Amer.* (ed. 2), *Chewink*, the ground robin... On Long Island it is called the Towhee Goldfinch. **1893** *Scribner's Mag.* June 762/2 He utters his loud 'Towhee', a note so characteristic that it has become one of his names.

† **to-'when,** *interrog. adv. Obs.* [f. to *prep.* + when.] Until what time? How long?

a **1300** *E.E. Psalter* iv. 3 Mennes sones, towhen ofe herte vn-meke? Whi loue yhe fantom, and lighinge seke? *Ibid.* lxxxviii. 45 Towhen, laverd, turnes tou in ende, at laste? Als fire sal bren þi wreth faste?

towher, obs. form of tocher.

† **to-'while,** *conj. adv. Obs.* [f. to *prep.* 7 + while *sb.*, q.v. 2 c.] During the time that, while.

c **950**, *c* **1000**, *c* **1250**, **13..** [see while *sb.* 2 c.] *c* **1330** R. Brunne *Chron. Wace* (Rolls) 4141 To whyle þe kyng & his cosyns I loue loken ar þer lynes.

† **to-'whiles,** *conj. adv. Obs.* Also 4 toquil(i)s, to whils. [f. prec. + *-es* of adverbial genitive: see whiles, whilst.] = prec.; whilst.

13.. *Cursor M.* 4269 (Cott.) Hir luue.. Sco miþed [*Gött.* kithid] it, to-quils [*Gött.* ay quilis] sco moght. *Ibid.* 6264 (Gött.) þe se on ayder side him stod As wallis to quilis þai forth ȝode. **1357** *Lay Folks Catech.* (MS. T.) 139 To whiles that his bodi lai in þe graue The saule with the god-hede went untill hell. *a* **1400** *R. Brunne's Chron. Wace* (Rolls) 2645 þe while [*Petyt MS.* Towhils] þer fader was on lyue For þe royalme gon þey to stryue.

to-whit, to-who(o: see tuwhit, tuwhoo.

† **to-'whither,** *v. Obs.* [ME. *to-hwiðeren*, f. to-[2] + **hwiðeren* (?).] *trans.* To 'whirl in pieces' (Stratm.).

a **1225** *Leg. Kath.* 1964 Ha schal beon tohwiðeret Wið þe hweoles. *Ibid.* 2018 Smit se smertliche herto, þet alle þeos fowr hweoles Tohwiðerin to stucchen. *a* **1225** *Ancr. R.* 362 Loðlease meidenes þe tittes ikoruen of, and to-hwiðered o hweoles, & hefdes bikoruen.

to'willee. *dial.* [See. quot. 1758.] A local name for the Sanderling: cf. curwillet; also, for the Ringed Plover: cf. dulwilly.

1758 Borlase *Hist. Cornw.* 247 Here we have coots, sanderlings, (which, from the noise they make when flying, we call Towillees), sea-larks, sea-pies. **1804** Bewick *Brit. Birds* II. 1 Sanderling, Towillee, or Curwillet. **1880** Rodd *Birds Cornw.* 315/2 *Towillees*, and *Turwillie*, Ringed Plover.

towing ('təʊɪŋ), *vbl. sb.*[1] [f. tow *v.*[1] + -ing[1].]

a. The action of tow *v.*[1]; *esp.* the dragging of a boat or ship by a tow-line; also, the drawing of a fine net behind a boat or other vessel for the capture of marine zoological specimens, and in *pl.* the proceeds of this, the specimens captured.

1494 [see tow *v.*[1] 1]. **1611** [see towage 2]. **1617** Moryson *Itin.* II. 168 Sir Richard Levison,.. with towing, got out the Warspite, the Defiance, the Swiftsure, the Marline. **1725** De Foe *Voy. round World* (1840) 325 By the help of towing and setting as well as they could, they came to a flatter shore. **1857** C. Gribble in *Merc. Marine Mag.* (1858) V. 7 They monopolize the towing in and out. **1887** *Smithsonian Rep.* II. 135 The surface towings he obtained are very rich in interesting forms.

b. *attrib.*, as ***towing-banquette, barge, -bitts, bollard, -boom, bracket, -gear, -vessel***; **towing-bridle** (bridle *sb.* 5 a), a stout chain, cable, or iron rail secured at the ends, with a ***towing-hook*** to which the tow-line is attached; **towing-lights** *sb. pl.*, white lights carried one above another by a vessel which has another or others in tow (*Funk's Stand. Dict.* 1895); **towing-net** = tow-net; **towing-path** = tow-path; **towing-post**: see quot.; **towing-rope** = tow-rope; **towing-timber** = *towing-post*.

1791 *Rep. Navig. Thames & Isis, Estimate* 4 A Loop of the River cut through, a *Towing-Banquete formed, and Water deepened, £90. **1889** Welch *Text Bk. Naval Archit.* xii. 132 Advantage is taken of the hollow *towing bollards.. and the mast.. to utilise these also as uptakes. **1897** G. Grenfell in Sir H. Johnston *Life* (1908) I. xii. 258 [It] had been firmly secured to the after bollards, as well as to the *towing-boom forward. **1959** *Towing bracket [see little man 2]. **1977** *West Briton* 25 Aug. 17/1 (Advt.), All types of caravan repairs undertaken,.. towing brackets supplied and fitted. **1867** Smyth *Sailor's Word-bk.*, **Towing-bridle*, a stout chain, with a hook at each end, for attaching a tow-rope to; also, a large *towing-hook* in the bight of the chain. **1857** Dufferin *Lett. High Lat.* viii. (ed. 3) 205, I began to be afraid that something must have gone wrong with the *towing-gear. **1816** Tuckey *Narr. Exped. R. Zaire* i. (1818) 11 The *towing-net was now.. tolerably successful, taking up from time to time various species of mollusca. **1726** *Lond. Gaz.* No. 6447/7 Using for *Towing or Haleing-Paths. **1795** J. Phillips *Hist. Inland Navig.* Add. 100 The towing path of this canal may be used by occupiers of lands as a bridle-way. **1867** Trollope *Chron. Barset* I. xii. 102 A cottage which stood alone, close to the towing-path of the canal. **1867** Smyth *Sailor's Word-bk.*, **Towing-post*, a substantial timber fixed through the deck of a steam-tug for making the tow-rope fast to. Also, a similar post in canal barges to keep the tow-line up clear of the path. **1838** *Civil Eng. & Arch. Jrnl.* I. 322/1 Whether it was feasible without a *towing-rope to get the barge through the water-way. **1882** E. O'Donovan *Merv Oasis* I. 315 A towing rope was fastened to the top of the mast. **1834** *Oxf. Univ. Mag.* I. 308 The recent introduction of steam *towing-vessels.

towing, *vbl. sb.*[2], [3]: see tow *v.*[3], [4].

† **tow-iren, towyrene,** obs. ff. tew-iron.

1399 *Will W. West* (Comm. Crt. Lond.), Towiren. **1408** *Durham Acc. Roll* in *Eng. Hist. Rev.* XIV. 520 In portagio unius towyrene de forgeo praedicto usque Westaukeland pro emendatione ejusdem, *id.*

towist, variant of toust *Obs.*

towk(e, towker(e: see toque, tuck, tucker.

‖ **towkay** ('taʊkeɪ). [ad. Malay *tauke.*] A Chinese businessman or employer, esp. in Malaysia.

1854 *Jrnl. Indian Archipelago* VIII. 16 Country born Chinese have a club called Sip Gee Seeah; they elect 12 Towkays or trustees. **1900** W. W. Skeat *Malay Magic* v. 253 The Malay *pawang* may squeeze a hundred or perhaps two hundred dollars out of the Chinese *towkay* who comes to mine for tin in Malaya. **1948** *Straits Times* 7 July 4/5 Our lives were probably saved by a Chinese towkay from Karak who used to keep us supplied with fresh fruit and tinned milk. **1966** D. Forbes *Heart of Malaya* iii. 41 Nancy, the fourth daughter of Lee Kwan Bock, the saw-mill *towkay*, was a schoolteacher.

towl (taʊl), *v. dial.* [Imit.] *intr.* To yowl.

1906 Kipling *Puck of Pook's Hill* 283 Dan and Una found a couple of them [*sc.* beagles] towling round the kitchen-garden after the laundry cat. **1930** *Punch* 30 Apr. 478/2 They make reverent overtures to our Siamese Pugsie, who hates them and scurries towling with nerves from their outstretched hands.

towl, towle, towlle, obs. forms of toll.

tow-line ('təʊlaɪn). [f. tow *v.*[1] or *sb.*[4] + line *sb.*[2]] A line, rope, or hawser by which anything is towed; *spec.* in *Whaling*, the whale-line.

1719 De Foe *Crusoe* (1840) II. ix. 204 Taking the end of a tow-line in his hand. **1725** —— *Voy. round World* (1840) 347 The greatest difficulty was for tow-lines to draw the boats by. **1839** Marryat *Phant. Ship* xvii, The boats had cast off the tow-lines. **1881** *Times* 20 June 6/5 The tow-lines of the tugs were made fast to the barque.

towlsell, obs. form of tolsel.

towm(e, var. taum, fishing-line; obs. f. toom.

towmond, towmont, Sc. ff. twelvemonth.

town (taʊn), *sb.* Forms: 1 tuun, 1-4 tūn, (4-5 tounne), 4-5, *Sc.* 6- toun, (4-5 ton, tone), 5-6 toune, (5 townne, 6 toen), 5-7 towne, 5- town, (8-9 *Sc.* toon (= tun)). [OE. *tuun, tūn* m. = OFris., OS., MLG. *tûn* (MDu. *tuun*, Da. *tuin*, LG. *tuun, tūn*), OHG., MHG. *zûn* (Ger. *zaun*); ON. *tūn* neut. (Norw. dial. *tūn* farm-yard, older Da. *tūn*, Sw. dial. *tūn, tōn* hedge, fence):—OTeut. **tûno*[z], *-o*[m], cogn. with Celtic *dûn* in *-dūnum*, OIr. *dûn*, W. *dīn* fortified place, castle, camp. The sense in OHG. was 'fence, hedge', as in Ger. *zaun*; in mod.Du. and LG. it has both the senses 'fence or hedge' and 'enclosed place, garden'. In OE. the sense 'fence, hedge' does not occur, only that of 'enclosed place', as in sense 1, and its developments in senses 2 and 3, in which it was frequently used to render L. *villa*. The modern sense 4 is later than the Norman Conquest, and corresponds to F. *ville* 'town, city', as similarly developed from L. *villa* 'farm, country-house'.]

† **1. a.** An enclosed place or piece of ground, an enclosure; a field, garden, yard, court. *Obs.*

c **725** *Corpus Gloss.* (O.E.T.) 546 *Co[ho]rs*, tuun. *a* **800** *Erfurt Gloss.* 281 *Cors*, tuun. *c* **870** *O.E. Chron.* an 867, His lic lið þær on tune. *c* **950** *Lindisf. Gosp.* Matt. xxvi. 36 Ða cuomon ðe hælend mið him in tun ðe hata gezemani [*Lat.* villam; *Gr.* χωρίον; Wycl. toun; Tind., *Geneva*, 1611, place; Coverd. felde; Cranmer farme place; *Rheims* village]. *c* **1000** *Ags. Gosp.* Mark xv. 21 Simonem cireneum cumende of þam tune [*Lind.* cumende of lond; *Rushw.* cymende of londe; *Lat.* de villa; *Gr.* ἀπ' ἀγροῦ; Wycl. fro the toun; Tind. oute of the felde; Coverd. from the felde; *Gen.*, *Rheims*, 1611, out of the countrey]. —— Luke xiv. 18 Ic bohte ænne tun [*Lind.*, *Rushw.* lond ic bohte; *Lat.* villam emi; *Gr.* ἀγρὸν ἠγόρασα; Wycl. a toun; Tind., Coverd. a ferme; 1611 a piece of ground]. *Ibid.* xv. 15 Ða sende he hine to his tune þæt he heolde his swyn [*Lind.* on lond his; *Lat.* in villam suam; *Gr.* εἰς τοὺς ἀγροὺς αὐτοῦ; Wycl. in to his toun; Tind. to the felde; Coverd. into his felde]. —— John iv. 5 Neah þam tune [*Lat.* juxta prædium; *Gr.* πλησίον τοῦ χωρίου; Wycl. the manere, *gloss* or feeld, *later vers.* the place; Tind. the possession; Coverd. yᵉ pece of londe; *Rheims* the maner; 1611 the parcell of ground]. *c* **1000** *Sax. Leechd.* II. 132 Harewyrt lytelu oftost weaxeþ on tune. *a* **1123** *O.E. Chron.* an. 1114, And þæt ȝehwær on wudan and on tunan ȝecydde. **1388** Wyclif *Matt.* xxii. 5 But thei.. wenten forth, oon in to his toun [1382 vyneȝerd; *Lat.* villam; *Gr.* ἀγρόν; *Ags. G.* tune; Tind. ferme place; Coverd. huszbandrye; 1611 farme], anothir to his marchaundise.

(Cf. also the OE. compounds *tûn-cressa* garden cress, *tún-melde*, *Atriplex hortensis*; *æppel-tún* apple orchard, *cyric-tún* churchyard, *déor-tún* deer-park, *gærs-tún* meadow, *líc-tún* graveyard, *wyrt-tún* vegetable garden.)

† **b.** *spec.* The enclosed land surrounding or belonging to a single dwelling; a farm with its

farmhouse (still *Sc. dial.*); a manor, 'an estate with a village community in villenage upon it under a lord's jurisdiction'; the enclosed land of a village community; sometimes also = parish, when this was coextensive with a manor. *Obs.*

601–4 *Laws Ethelbert* c. 17 Ʒif man in mannes tun ærest ʒeirneþ, vi scillingum ʒebete; se þe æfter irneþ, iii scillingas. **972** *Charter Eadgar* in Birch *Cart. Sax.* III. 586 Þis sind þara feower tuna lond ʒemæra. *a* **1100** *Gerefa* in *Anglia* (1886) IX. 259 And ælcre tilðan timan ðe to tune belimpð. *c* **1200** *Vices & Virt.* 77 Uppe ða chirch-landes, oðer uppe tunes. *c* **1220** *Bestiary* 391 Fox is hire to name.. Ðe coc & te capun ȝe feccheð ofte in ðe tun. *c* **1375** *Sc. Leg. Saints* xxvii. (*Machor*) 93 He gaf of heritable rycht to godis seruice al þat ton In-to fre possessione. *c* **1380** WYCLIF *Serm.* Sel. Wks. I. 22 A man hadde a fermour, as keper of a toun. **1628** COKE *On Litt.* § 1. 5 By the name of a towne, *Villa*, a mannor may passe. *Ibid.* § 193. 125 b, If a matter be alledged *in Parochia*, it shall be intended in Law that it containeth no more Townes then one, vnlesse the party doth shew the contrary. **1785** J. MILL *Diary* (1889) 75 Some hill towns [= farms] had a good deal of corn on the ground to shear.

2. The house or group of houses or buildings upon this enclosed land; the farmstead or homestead on a farm or holding. Now esp. *Sc.*

c **890** tr. *Bæda's Hist.* II. xi. [xiv.] (1890) 140 Þes tun [*villa*] wæs forlæten.. & oðer wæs fore þæm ʒetimbred. *Ibid.* III. xiv. [xvi.] 202 Aslat þa þa tunas ealle ymb þa burʒ onwæʒ. *a* **900** *O.E. Martyrol.* 9 June 92 Þa ongan se tun bernan.. Þa forburnon ealle þara monna hus þa on þæm tune wæron. **1362** LANGL. *P. Pl.* A. x. 134 Barouns and Burgeis and Bonde men of tounes [*MS. U.* towne]. *c* **1400** *Plowman's Tale* III. 1043 Threshing and dyking fro town to town. **1551** ROBINSON tr. *More's Utopia* I. (1895) 57 They whyche plucked downe fermes and townes of husbandrye. *c* **1689** *Depred. Clan Campbell* (1816) 42 Taken out of Achingoul.. be Lochaber men, ten coues... Item, be them out of that toun, 30 sheep and goats. **1814** SCOTT *Wav.* ix, Waverley learned.. from this colloquy that in Scotland a single house was called a *town*. **1815** —— *Guy M.* xxiii, Two or three low thatched houses, placed with their angles to each other, with a great contempt of regularity. This was the farm-steading of Charlie's Hope, or, in the language of the country, 'the town'. **1888** BRYCE *Amer. Commw.* II. xlviii. 226 *note*, In Scotland (where it is pronounced 'toon') it still denotes the farmhouse and buildings.

3. A (small) group or cluster of dwellings or buildings; a village or hamlet with little or no local organization. (Often = L. *vicus*.) Now *dial.*

In var. Eng. dials., *the town* is spec. applied to the hamlet or cluster of houses contiguous to the church; more fully *the church-town*.

c **725** *Corpus Gloss.* (O.E.T.) 557 *Conpetum*, tuun, þrop. *a* **800** *Erfurt Gloss.* 307 *Conpetum*, tuun vel ðrop. *c* **950** *Lindisf. Gosp.* John xxi. 2 Se ðeʒn seðe uæs of Cana ðæm tuune on galilees meʒð. *c* **1000** ÆLFRIC *Hom.* II. 54 ʒifta wæron ʒewordene on anum tune ðe is ʒeciged Chana. *a* **1067** *Charter of Eadweard* in Kemble *Cod. Dipl.* IV. 203, .x. hyden lond on Waltham, and ðe cherche of ðan seluen tune. *c* **1200** ORMIN 7016 Þatt tun wass nemmnedd Beþþ-leæm. *a* **1300** *Cursor M.* 14790 (Cott.) Þat es þe tun of bethleem. *c* **1386** CHAUCER *Prol.* 478 A poure Person of a toun [*v.r.* toune].. Wyd was his parisshe and houses fer a sonder.. With hym ther was a Plowman was his brother. **1387** TREVISA *Higden* (Rolls) II. 39 In Mon [Anglesey] beeþ þre hondred townes [*villas*] þre score and þre, and beeþ acounted for þre candredes, þat beeþ þre hundredes. **1483** *Cath. Angl.* 391/1 A Towne, *pagus, pagulus, pagos grece, villa, villula*. **1508** DUNBAR *Poems* vii. 55 In euery cete, village, and in toune. **1526** TINDALE *John* xi. 1 Lazarus of Bethania the toune of Mary and her sister Martha. **1576** E. WORSELY *Surv. Mannor of Felsted, Essex* 129 (MS.) The highway leading from Felsted towards the town of Leighes. **1731** T. BOSTON *Mem.* vii. (1899) 112 The circumstances of my charge, all in one little town [i.e. the hamlet of Simprin], within a few paces from one end to the other. **1809** MAR. EDGEWORTH *Absentee* ix, He arrived at a village, or, as it was called, a town, which bore the name of Colambre. **1812** BRACKENRIDGE *Views Louisiana* (1814) 119 Amongst the Americans, every assemblage of houses, no matter of how small a number, is denominated a town. **1887** *Pall Mall G.* 19 Aug. 11/1 Wretched villages, misnamed towns, scattered throughout Ireland. **1887** I. R. *Lady's Ranche Life in Montana* 12 We are only a mile from the town (eight houses and an hôtel); but only think, in this barbarous region, being only a mile from railway station, telegraph, and post-office! **1888** BRYCE *Amer. Commw.* II. xlviii. 226 *note*, In parts of eastern England the chief cluster of houses in a parish is still often called 'the town'. **1888** ELWORTHY *W. Somerset Gloss.*, *Town*, a collection of houses... In all parts of the district the villages are called *towns* when the collection of houses is specially referred to.

4. a. In general English use, commonly designating an inhabited place larger and more regularly built than a village, and having more complete and independent local government (esp. one not created a city); applied historically not only to a 'borough', i.e. a corporate town, and a 'city', a town of higher rank, but also to an 'urban district', i.e. a non-corporate town having an 'urban district council' with powers of rating, paving, and sanitation more extensive than those possessed by a parish council or the administrative body (where such exists) of a village. Sometimes also applied to small inhabited places below the rank of an 'urban district' or its equivalent, which are not distinguish-able from villages otherwise, perhaps, than by having a periodical market or fair ('market town'), or by being historically 'towns'.

The distinction between a small town which is not a municipal borough, and a village, is somewhat indefinite; there are also decayed towns, even municipal boroughs, which are surpassed in population by many villages.

1154 *O.E. Chron.* an. 1137. § 3 (Laud MS.) Hi læiden gæildes o þe tunes æure um wile... þa þe uurecce men ne hadden nan more to gyuen, þa ræueden hi & brendon alle the tunes. *c* **1200** ORMIN 8511 Fra land to land, fra tun to tun, Fra wic to wic i tune. *c* **1205** LAY. 14246 Ane burh he arerde muchele & mare.. & for swulche gomen þa tun [Lancaster] hafde þas þreo nomen. *a* **1225** *Juliana* 8, & tuhen him ȝont te tun from strete to strete. *c* **1275** *Passion* 70 in *O.E. Misc.* 39 As he com in-to þe bureh so rydinde þe children of þe tune [Jerusalem] comen syngynde. **1297** R. GLOUC. (Rolls) 5249 Hii come, & londone, & kaunterbury, & oþer tounes nome. **1375** BARBOUR *Bruce* XI. 138 Sum lugit without the townys In tentis and in palȝeowynys. *c* **1400** *Laud Troy Bk.* 7429 Thei dyed thikkere then men dryues gece To chepyng-toun for to selle. *c* **1400** MAUNDEV. (1839) iv. 30 Joppa.. is on of the oldest townes of the world. **1419** *Munim. de Melros* (Bann. Cl.) 502 All þe landis Tenementis and byggynnis.. in þe said Towne of Edynburghe. **1472–3** *Rolls of Parlt.* VI. 33/2 The Chaunceler and Scolers of the Universite in your Toune of Oxonford. **1512** *Act 4 Hen. VIII*, c. 7 § 2 And that in all other Cities, Borowes, and Townes.. the Maires, Bailiffes, or hede Officers, and Wardeyns to haue like Authoritie. And wher noo Wardeyns be, then the hede Officers or Governours of the same Cities, Borowes and Townes to appoynt certeyn persones.. to make serche. *Ibid.* c. 19 § 10 In Hundredes, Townes Corporate & nott corporate, parisshes & all other places. **1552** HULOET, Towne beynge walled, *oppidum*. *Ibid.*, Towne incorporate, *municipium*. **1555** W. WATREMAN *Fardle Facions* 10 Of Tounes, thei made cities, and of villages, Tounes. **1597** in *Maitl. Cl. Misc.* I. 89 Within the toune and citie of Glasgw. *a* **1600** MONTGOMERIE *Misc. Poems* xlviii. 39 Constantinopil .. Eftir his name he callit the citie syn, Becaus he lovit it best of tounis all. **1610** HOLLAND *Camden's Brit.* (1637) 497 This is the chiefe Towne of all this Shire. **1628** COKE *On Litt.* § 171. 115 b, If a Towne be decayed so as no houses remayne, yet it is a Towne in Lawe... It cannot bee a Towne in Law, vnlesse it hath, or in time past hath had a Church and celebration of Diuine Seruice... It appeareth by Littleton, that a Towne is the genus, and a Borough is the species, for .. euery Borough is a Towne, but euery Towne is not a Borough. **1649** BP. GUTHRIE *Mem.* (1702) 80 A Wonder lasts but nine Nights in a Town (as we use to say). **1765** BLACKSTONE *Comm.* I. Introd. iv. 114 The word *town* or *vill* is indeed.. now become a generical term, comprehending under it the several species of cities, boroughs, and common towns. **1809** KENDALL *Trav.* I. ii. 12 A collection of houses joining, or nearly joining each other, is the first requisite in the definition of *town*, though the word be taken in the loosest sense. **1861** M. PATTISON *Ess.* (1889) I. 44 The free towns of Lübeck, Bremen, and Hamburg.

b. Without article, after prepositions and verbs, as ***in, out of, to town, to leave town***, etc.: i.e. the particular town under consideration, or that in or near which the speaker is at the moment; the town with which one has to do, the market-town, the chief town of the district or province, the capital; in England since *c* 1700 *spec.* said of London.

There are earlier uses referring to London, but only as said by persons living there.

c **1250** *Gen. & Ex.* 2311 And quuan he weren ut tune went, Iosep haueð hem after sent. **13..** *Cursor M.* 3346 (Cott.) On morn wit godds beniscon Was mai rebecca lede o ton [*Gött.* of þe tun]. **1377** LANGL. *P. Pl.* B. XIII. 266 Alle Londoun.. liketh wel my wafres... Þere was a carful comune whan no carte come to toune With bake bred fro stretforth. **1389** in *Eng. Gilds* (1870) 5 Be he in toun [London] oþer out of toun. **1431** *Ibid.* 275 If he be in towne [Cambridge] and comyth not. **1450** *Rolls of Parlt.* V. 182/2 The kyng sent for all his Lordes.. thenne beyng in Towne [London]. **1618** BOLTON *Florus* IV. i. (1636) 260 The ambassadours of the Allobroges (at that time, as it hapned, in town [Rome]) were dealt with. **1638** JUNIUS *Paint. Ancients* 122 Strangers.. as soone as they come to Towne [London], enquire for him first of all. **1645** EVELYN *Diary* 31 Oct., We invited all the English and Scotts in towne [Padua] to a feast. **1648** *Commons' Jrnls.* V. 545/1 That a Letter be directed to the Vice Admiral, to desire him to suffer Prince Philip, Brother to the Prince Elector, to come to Town. **1689** in *Acts Parlt. Scotl.* (1875) XII. 60/2 Þat the macers advertise such as are in towne [Edinburgh] That they be present accordingly. **1711** STEELE *Spect.* No. 2 ¶ 1 When he is in Town, he lives in Soho-Square. **1711** HEARNE *Collect.* (O.H.S.) III. 127 Dr. Charlett went out of Town [Oxford] on purpose that he might not be present. **1739** CHESTERF. *Lett.* (1792) II. 122, I shall come to town next Saturday. **1770** FOOTE *Lame Lover* I. Wks. 1799 II. 60 Well known about town. **1791** *Gentl. Mag.* Jan. 1/1 A friend of mine, who was lately in town, saw many of them in the shop-windows. **1815** SIMOND *Tour Gt. Brit.* I. 17 At Richmond.. I set out by myself for town, as London is called *par excellence*. **1825** T. COSNETT *Footman's Direct.* 217 So necessary is it for footmen to know town. **1848** DICKENS *Dombey* xxx, A stately relative.. who was out of town. **1902** R. HICHENS *Londoners* 17, I shall leave town at least by the first of July.

c. *spec.* as distinct from or contrasted with *the country* (COUNTRY 5).

c **1386** CHAUCER *Miller's T.* 194 And for she was of toune [*v.rr.* towne, tounne, town] he profreth meede, For some folk wol ben wonnen for richesse. **1712** LADY M. W. MONTAGU *Let. to W. Montagu* 9 Dec., You say I love the town. **1715** POPE *2nd Ep. Miss Blount* 2 As some fond Virgin, whom her mother's care Drags from the Town to wholesome Country air. **1780** *Mirror* No. 105 ¶ 2, I would beg of those who migrate from the city, not to carry too much of the town with them into the country. **1784** [see COUNTRY 5]. **1909** LLOYD GEORGE in *Daily News* 30 Apr. 8 Land in the town seems to be let by the grain as if it was radium.

d. In ME., and later in ballad poetry, etc., often added after the name of a town, in apposition. *arch.* (Cf. OE. *Rome-burh, Lunden-burh*, etc.)

13.. *Seuyn Sag.* (W.) 551 Whilom a riche burgeis was, And woned her in Rome toun. ? *a* **1700** *Sir Patrick Spence* i. in *Percy Reliques* (1845) 20/1 The king sits in Dumferling toune. ? *a* **1700** *K. John & Abbot* ii. ibid. 167/2 They rode poste.. to fair London toune. **1703** ROWE *Ulysses* Prol. 8 Her husband.. Left her.., to.. battle for a harlot at Troy toun. **1782** COWPER *John Gilpin* i, A trainband captain eke was he Of famous London town. **18..** ROSSETTI (*title*) Troy Town.

5. As a collective sing. **a.** The community of a town in its corporate capacity; the corporation; **b.** The inhabitants of a town, the townspeople; **c.** *spec.* the fashionable society of London (or other leading city thought of); 'society'. *arch.*

c **1330** R. BRUNNE *Chron.* (1810) 334 Þe toþer day on þe morn com þe Brus Roberd, Þe toun wist it beforn, þorgh spies þat þei herd. *c* **1470** HENRY *Wallace* II. 19 So he desirit the toune of Air to se His child with him. **1582** ALLEN *Martyrd. Campion* (1908) 96 All the towne loved him exceedingly. *a* **1616** BEAUMONT *Let. to B. Jonson* 50 Wit able enough to justify the Town For three days past! **1632** MASSINGER & FIELD *Fatal Dowry* IV. i, 'Tis all the town talks. **1665** PEPYS *Diary* 21 June, I find all the town almost going out of town. **1693** DRYDEN *Persius' Sat.* i. 5 That this vast universal Fool, the Town, Shou'd cry up Labeo's Stuff, and cry me down. **1713** SWIFT *Frenzy J. Denny* Wks. 1755 III. I. 144 That vile piece, that's foisted upon the town for a dramatick poem! **1742** POPE *Dunc.* IV. 292 [He], all at once let down, Stunn'd with his giddy Larum half the town. **1849** MACAULAY *Hist. Eng.* iii. I. 405 His Absalom and Achitophel, the greatest satire of modern times, had amazed the town, had made its way.. even into rural districts.

d. *absol.* At Oxford and Cambridge: The civic community or body of citizens or townsmen as distinct from members of the university; esp. in phr. ***town and gown*** (often *attrib.*); cf. GOWN *sb.* 5.

a **1647** PETTE in *Archæologia* XII. 218, I was forced,.. my graces for Bachelor of Arts being passed both in house and town, to abandon the university. **1828** *Sporting Mag.* XXI. 428 Parties of five or six, both 'gown' and 'town', were parading abreast. *a* **1845** HOOD *Lament Toby* xv, Farewell to 'Town!' farewell to 'Gown!' I've quite outgrown the latter. **1853** 'C. BEDE' *Verdant Green* II. iv, The battle of Town and Gown was over. **1861** HUGHES *Tom Brown at Oxf.* xi, I wish .. to disclaim.. all sympathy with town and gown rows. **1912–13** *Kelly's Oxford Directory* 2/2 In 1354 a desperate Gown and Town riot began on St. Scholastica's day, February 10th, and lasted three days, during which 40 students and 60 townsmen lost their lives.

6. *U.S.* A geographical division for local or state government. **a.** A division of a county, which may contain one or more villages or towns (in sense 4); a township; also, the inhabitants of such a division as a corporate body. (Esp. in the New England states.) **b.** A municipal corporation, having its own geographical boundaries (as distinct from a.), considered either in reference to its area or as a body politic.

1808 A. WILSON *Poems & Lit. Prose* (1876) I. 148 The people here make no distinction between town and township, and travellers frequently asked the driver.. 'What town are we now in?' when perhaps we were on the top of a miserable barren mountain. **1809** KENDALL *Trav.* I. ii. 12 In New England.. a town is very commonly described as containing two or three villages. *Ibid.* 13 A town.. in Connecticut, and the other parts of New England, is first a district, or geographical subdivision..; secondly, it is a body politic and corporate. *Ibid.* x. 113 The constitution of the towns appears to be.. a mixture of those of the shire, hundred and parish. **1819** *Boston Centinel* 31 July (Thornton), The crops of hay in the lower towns were in all parts heavy. **1822** Z. HAWLEY *Tour* [*in Ohio*] 33 (ibid.) The timber of these towns is beech.. and black walnut. **1882** W. D. HOWELLS in *Longm. Mag.* I. 42 In New England the 'town' is the township, and there are some 'towns' in which there is no village at all. **1888** BRYCE *Amer. Commw.* II. II. xlviii. 226 The Town is.. a rural, not an urban community. .. Its population is usually small. *Ibid.*, *note*, In New England the word 'town' is the legal and usual one; in the rest of the country 'township'. *Ibid.* 240 The words 'town' and 'township' signify [in Illinois, etc.] a territorial division of the county, incorporated for purposes of local government. **1890** HOSMER *Anglo-Sax. Freed.* 192 Each Massachusetts town sent a representative to a central assembly at Boston. **1906** W. CHURCHILL *Coniston* I. v, The town of Coniston.. was a tract of country about ten miles by ten, the most thickly settled portion of which was the village of Coniston, consisting of twelve houses.

7. *fig.* and *transf.* (from 4). **a.** Something analogous to a town as being the home of many people.

1890 W. J. GORDON *Foundry* 75 The ship is a flying town, self-contained and independent of outside aid. **1898** KIPLING in *Daily News* 7 Nov. 5/2 That which was a line has suddenly become a town on the waters.

b. An assemblage of burrows of prairie-dogs, nests of penguins, etc.

1808 PIKE *Sources Mississ.* II. (1810) 156 *note*, The Wishtonwish of the Indians, prairie dogs of some travellers .. reside on the prairies of Louisiana in towns or villages. **1812** BRACKENRIDGE *Views Louisiana* (1814) 58 The Prairie dog.. lives in burrows, or as they are commonly called towns. **1839** MARRYAT *Phant. Ship* xviii, These [penguins] were in myriads on some parts of the island, which, from the propinquity of their nests.. went by the name of *towns*. **1890** W. P. LETT in *Big Game N. Amer.* 470 Danger occasioned by badger-holes and prairie-dog towns.

8. Phrases. (See also 4 b.) **a.** ***to come*** (†***go***) ***to town***, to make one's appearance, arrive, come in; †to 'come to stay', to become common (*obs.*). Cf. *to come to land* (LAND *sb.*[1] 2 d).

Prob. the original notion was 'come to our village, come to dwell with us, come to the dwellings of men'. In later times associated with the later sense of *town* (4b).

a **1000** *Menologium* (Gr.) 8 Se kalendus cymeð..on þam ylcan dæge us to tune. *c* **1050** *Byrhtferth's Handboc* in *Anglia* VIII. 312/19 Lengten tima..gæð to tune on vii. id'. febr'. *c* **1200** ORMIN 9160 Allse bidell birrþ beon sennd To ȝarrkenn & to greȝȝþenn Onnȝæn hiss Laferrd þær þær he Shall cumenn sket to tune. *a* **1275** *Prov. Ælfred* 534 in *O.E. Misc.* 133 Elde cumið to tune mid fele unkeþe costes. *a* **1300** *Cursor M.* 14277 'Crist', sco said, 'es cummen to tun'. *c* **1475** *Rauf Coilȝear* 349 Folkis..Thankand God..Thair Lord was gane to toun. **1600** *Newe Metamorphosis* (MS.) (Farmer), This first was court-like, now 'tis come to towne; 'Tis common growne with every country clowne. **1851** D. JERROLD *St. Giles* ii. 11 I've been quite in the way of babies to-night,..young master's come to town. **1905** *Daily Chron.* 11 Mar. 4/6 This Thrums sketch proved to delighted Londoners that J. M. Barrie had 'come to town'.

b. ***man about town*** (also formerly ***young fellow, youth, girl about town***), ***woman about town***, one who is constantly seen at public and private assemblies in 'town'; one who is in the round of social functions, fashionable dissipations, etc. (cf. d. (*a*)).

c **1645** HOWELL *Lett.* (1650) II. 94, I was a youth about the Town when he undertook that expedition. **1734** in *15th Rep. R. Comm. Hist. Manuscripts* App. VI. 146 in *Parl. Papers 1897* (C. 8551) LI. 1 Though being what is called an idle man about Town, I generally read all that is writ on both sides. **1749** LADY LUXBOROUGH *Let. to Shenstone* 28 Nov., Miss Jenny Hamilton, a pretty girl about town. **1752** M. W. MONTAGU *Let.* 16 Feb. (1967) III. 6 One of the most disagreable Fellows about Town, as odious in his outside as stupid in his conversation. **1766** GOLDSM. *Vic. W.* xx, I'll show you forty very dull fellows about town that live by it [authorship] in opulence. **1769** CHESTERF. *Let. to Godson* 6 Sept., There are now two sorts of young fellows about Town, who call themselves Bucks and Bloods. **1844** DICKENS *Mart. Chuz.* xxvi, He was quite the man-about-town of the conversation. **1889** W. ROBERTS *Hist. Eng. Bookselling* 121 Wits, men-about-town, and fashionable notabilities. **1927** *Manch. Guardian Weekly* Jan. 75/1 Another surrender to the woman-about-town who wants a different kind of entertainment. **1979** 'S. KEMP' *Goodbye, Pussy* xii. 160 Zoë had been an 'actress'. Actress, model, woman-about-town.

c. ***man*** or ***woman*** (***girl, lady***) ***of the town***: one belonging to the shady or 'fast' side of town life.

a **1700** B. E. *Dict. Cant. Crew, Man o' th' Town*, a Lew'd Spark, or very Debaushe. *a* **1704** T. BROWN *Dial. Dead* Wks. 1730 II. 313, I have been a man of the town..and admitted into the family of the rakehellonians. **1766** GOLDSM. *Vic. W.* xx, The lady was only a woman of the town. **1785** GROSE *Dict. Vulg. T., Man of the town*, a rake, a debauchee. *Ibid.*, *Woman of the town, or..of pleasure*, a prostitute. **1817–18** COBBETT *Resid. U.S.* (1822) 239 Never is there seen in the streets what is called in England, a girl of the town. **1873** G. H. LEWES *Diary* 1 Jan. in *Geo. Eliot Lett.* (1956) V. 357 Trollope came to lunch. Told me of his trouble with Harry wanting to marry a woman of the town. **1886** *Lantern* (New Orleans) 20 Oct. 2/2 Orders were issued to the police to remove all women-of-the-town. **1982** C. CASTLE *Folies Bergère* i. 37 At the back of the stalls..the notorious 'ladies of the town'..plied their trade.

d. ***on the town***: (*a*) in the swing of fashionable life, pleasure, or dissipation; (*b*) getting a living by prostitution, thieving, or the like; cf. *on the streets*; (*c*) chargeable to the parish (*dial.*). So ***to come upon the town***.

1712 STEELE *Spect.* No. 266 ¶2 This Creature is what they call newly come upon the Town. **1727** GAY *Begg. Op.* II. iv, I han't been so long upon the Town. **1819** *Metropolis* I. 213 She had got with her a listening novice on town. *Ibid.* II. 167 We have a man looked up to to-day..in the Gazette in three months, and on the town again, brighter than ever. **1842** EGAN *Capt. Macheath, J. Flashman* (Farmer), Jack long was on the town, a teazer; Could turn his fives to anything, Nap a reader, or filch a ring. **1843** R. J. GRAVES *Syst. Clin. Med.* xxvi. 333 Prostitutes who had been a long time on the town. **1855** THACKERAY *Newcomes* x, Five-and-twenty years ago the young Earl of Kew came upon the town, which speedily rang with the feats of his Lordship.

e. ***town and tower, tower and town***: see TOWER *sb.*[1] 9a.

f. ***to go to town***: to do something energetically, enthusiastically, or without restraint; *spec.* to make a great fuss. Freq. const. *on. colloq.* (orig. *Jazz slang*). See also sense 8a.

1933 [see GET *v.* 70m]. **1940** E. S. GARDNER *Case of Silent Partner* xii. 222 Chocolate creams are one of the fondest things I am of [*sic*]. I was feeling low, and I went to town. **1946** J. B. PRIESTLEY *Bright Day* viii. 252 He surveyed me with mock admiration. 'The only writer who ever made.. Gruman pay him a royalty on the gross... And did we go to town with it, I'll say we did.' **1947** J. BERTRAM *Shadow of War* 238 'Skeleton's' in a bad mood; he's going to town on 'em. **1958** A. HOCKING *Epitaph for Nurse* ix. 159 The local papers naturally went to town over the murder of Sister Biggs. **1960** N. HILLIARD *Maori Girl* II. ix. 128 'It's funny as hell to see girls fight.'..'They're really tough sorts, and boy! do they go to town. And swear! Punching and spitting and pulling hair.' **1972** P. M. HUBBARD *Whisper in Glen* vii. 67 Whoever had painted the thing, he had gone to town on his picture. **1980** *Times Lit. Suppl.* 14 Mar. 290/2 Professor MacAndrew goes to town on this novel, deciphering the code which she believes Henry James to have set up.

9. ***attrib.*** and ***Comb.*** **a.** Simple attrib. passing into adj. use (now usually without hyphen): Of, pertaining to, or characteristic of the town (as distinct from some other place or community, esp. the country); that is or lives in towns or the town; urban.

1468 *Medulla Gram., Comedia*, a toun song. **1560** DAUS tr. *Sleidane's Comm.* 160 The towne wiues, whan they go to here Masse, cary with them bokes of Latin prayers. **1594** HOOKER *Eccl. Pol.* Pref. ii. §3 One of the Towne-Ministers, that saw in what manner the people were bent for the reuocation of Caluine. **1673** *Charac. Coffee-house* (title-p.) The Symptomes of a Town-wit. **1693** J. DUNTON *Athenian Merc.* 14 Nov., The ridiculous Folly of our Town-Sparks who make an Oath their Argument. **1702** STEELE *Funeral* III. i. 44 She has of a sudden left her Dayry, and sets up for a fine Town-Lady. **1710–11** *Examiner* No. 30 Lewdness and intemperance are not of so bad consequences in a town-rake as in a divine. **1753** *World* No. 3 ¶2 According to the town-acceptation of the term. **1794** W. FELTON *Carriages* (1801) II. iii. §2. 35 A neat ornamented, or town coach. **1844** WARDLAW *Lect. Prov.* (1869) II. 16 Town missions and country missions. **1848** MILL *Pol. Econ.* Prel. Rem. (1876) 9 These [agricultural communities of ancient Europe].. were mostly small town-communities. **1848** THACKERAY *Van. Fair* v, He fought the town-boys. **1855** MACAULAY *Hist. Eng.* xiv. III. 493 The difference..between a town divine and a country divine. **1867** H. LATHAM *Black & White* 100 Houses which look like the town-residences of well-to-do gentry. **1887** A. JENKS in *Lippincott's Mag.* Aug. 295 These performances were very attractive to old graduates and town-people. **1897** *Allbutt's Syst. Med.* II. 842 It is safer to take a lower standard for the average town inhabitant.

b. attrib. in sense 'of or belonging to a town as a community or place', as ***town armoury, back, bell, charge, church, clock, close, dike, drummer, father, field, folk, green, herd, loan*** (LOAN *sb.*[2] 2), ***mead, moor, mote*** (MOOT *sb.*[1] 2), ***piper, plate*** (PLATE *sb.* 18), ***pump, relief, seal, stocks, swineherd, wait, watch, wharf***.

1596 SHAKS. *Tam. Shr.* III. ii. 47 An olde rusty sword tane out of the *Towne Armory. **1577** HOLINSHED *Chron.* II. 475/2 All their horsemen issued out of the *towne backe with certayne footemen. **1483** *Cely Papers* (Camden) 137 To be redy in harnesse as sone as the *towne bell rynggyth. **1877** GREEN *Hist. Eng. People* I. 298 Its citizens mustered at the call of the town-bell at Saint Paul's. **1619** *Min. Archdeaconry of Colchester* lf. 104b (MS.), The some of viijd. toward a rate for *towne charge which the Churchwardens of Alresford haue layd out. [**1045** *Will of Thurstan* in Thorpe *Charters* 572 þat [lond]..after here bothere day into þe *tunkirke, and þo men fre.] **1888** P. SCHAFF *Hist. Chr. Ch.* VI. xxvii. 136 He preached both in the Convent and in the town-church. **1779** *Mirror* No. 41 ¶1 He..had been regulating his watch by our *town-clock. **1716** ADDISON *Drummer* I. i, I verily believe I saw him last night in the *Town-close. **1801** *Farmer's Mag.* Jan. 10 The horses, cattle, sheep, and swine..are not to be suffered to go loose within *town-dikes. **1872** C. GIBBON *For the King* i, Bauldy Dodholm, the *town-drummer, at their head. **1892** *Pall Mall G.* 15 June 6/1 At the station the *town-fathers [cf. FATHER *sb.* 10] offered her some refreshments. **1297** R. GLOUC. (Rolls) 1582 þo wende vorþ þe *toun folc. **1907** 'J. HALSHAM' *Lonewood Corner* 33 Town-folk foundered in these drenched wood-paths. **1641** *N. Riding Rec.* 212 A yeoman presented for an encroachment on the *towne-greene by building a barn to the damage of the inhabitants. **1822** GALT *Provost* xxxvii, Tammy Tout, the *town-herd. **1812** W. TENNANT *Anster F.* I. lv, Hobbling in each *town-loan in awkward guise. **1822** GALT *Provost* xlvi, A considerable portion of the *town moor. **1879** GREEN *Read. Eng. Hist.* xiv. 67 The burgesses gathered in *town-mote when the bell swung out from St. Paul's. **1701** *Lond. Gaz.* No. 3729/4 A *Town-plate of about 15l. value will be Run for at the same Place. **1810** CRABBE *Borough* xxi. 171 For *town-relief the grieving man applied, And begg'd with tears, what some with scorn denied. **1594** HOOKER *Eccl. Pol.* Pref. ii. §5 By common consent of their whole Senate, and that under their *Towne-Seale. **1821** SCOTT *Kenilw.* ii, To get your legs made acquainted with the *town-stocks. **1825** —— *Betrothed* vii, He blows like a *town swineherd. *a* **1805** A. CARLYLE *Autobiog.* (1860) 75 His band..consisted of two dancing-school fiddlers and the *town-waits. **1560** ROLLAND *Seven Sag.* 73 Gif I be heir now with the *toun watche found. **1531** *Lett. & Pap. Hen. VIII*, V. 184 Caryng of rubys out of the towne to the *towne wharffis.

c. objective and obj. genitive, as ***town-builder, -taker; town-destroying, -frequenting, -going, -keeping, -loving, -taking*** sbs. and adjs.; see also TOWN-PLANNING; instrumental, etc., as ***town-dotted, -flanked, -girdled, -sick, -stained*** adjs.; locative, similative, etc., as ***town-bred, -cured, -dark, -imprisoned, -killed, -like, -looking, -pent, -spent, -tied, -trained*** adjs.; see also TOWN-BORN, TOWN-DWELLER.

1685 BOWLES *Theocritus' Idyllium* xx. 43 in *Dryden's Misc.* II. 390 How nice these *Town-bred Women are, how vain! **1869** *Routledge's Ev. Boy's Ann.* 396 Smart, active fellows, but thoroughly town-bred. **1859** S. R. STUMBO *Let.* 11 Jan. in L. R. Hafen *Colorado Gold Rush* (1941) 214 The reports you see in the papers..are put in circulation by *town builders for speculative purposes. **1918** D. H. LAWRENCE *New Poems* 26 Gay birds of the *town-dark sea. **1960** R. WILLIAMS *Border Country* 10 It was dark..town dark. **1905** *Daily News* 14 Jan. 4 Painter of sea and shore and *town-flanked river. **1895** *Athenæum* 27 Apr. 530/2 The Danes were a *town-frequenting people. **1812** W. TENNANT *Anster F.* III. xxiv, Fife's *town-girdled shire. **1838** MARY HOWITT *Birds & Fl., Sunshine* i, *Town-imprisoned men. **1899** *Daily News* 23 May 4/6 For *town-keeping people the cart-horse parade was one of the prettiest sights of the day. **1899** *Q. Rev.* Oct. 480 *Town-killed meat is a diminishing element. *c* **1000** *Ælfric's Voc.* in Wr.-Wülcker 127/15 *Comedia*, racu, *tun-lic spæc. **1876** A. PLUMMER tr. *Döllinger's Hippolytus* ii. 73 All that has any townlike appearance relates to Ostia. **1849** J. FORBES *Physic. Holiday* v. (1850) 47 Waldshut is a neater and more *town-looking place than we had yet passed through. **1900** F. W. MAITLAND *Let.* 18 Feb. (1965) 211 The Spaniard of the middle class is a *town-loving animal. **1941** *Mind* L. 396 A statement which no purely town-born, town-bred, town-loving person can..verify. **1649** G. DANIEL *Trinarch., Hen. V* cli, The *Towne-pent Rutters, willingly enlarge Their Quarters. **1840** T. A. TROLLOPE *Summ. Brittany* I. 71 As enchanting a cottage..as *town-sick mortal ever dreamed of. **1654** tr. *Scudery's Curia Pol.* 5 That antient Captaine, which the Greekes stiled the *Towntaker. **1845** E. A. POE in *Broadway Jrnl.* 13 Sept. 155 We poor *town-tied denizens ..can revel in scenes which we may never be able to visit, and snuff up in imagination the incense of the flowers, which only bloom for us through the painter's art. **1849** J. FORBES *Physic. Holiday* i. (1850) 5 That..I may induce some of my town-tied friends to do as I have done.

10. Special combs.: †**town-adjutant**, formerly, a garrison officer, ranking as lieutenant, charged with certain routine duties; cf. TOWN-MAJOR; **town and country planning**, the preparation and construction of plans in accordance with which the development of towns and countryside is to be regulated; cf. TOWN-PLANNING *sb.*; **town ball** *U.S.*, a game resembling baseball; **town belt** *N.Z.*, a belt of public land reserved chiefly for recreational purposes in or round a town; **town-bound** *a.*, (*a*) bound or confined to town; (*b*) townward bound; **town-box**, the town chest; the public funds of a town; **town-bull**, a bull formerly kept in turn by the cow-keepers of a village; hence *fig.* of a man; **town-bushel**, a local standard bushel measure; cf. BUSHEL *sb.*[1] 1; **town car** *U.S.*, a four-door motor car having a passenger compartment which is permanently enclosed and a driver's compartment which is not; **town centre**, a place or a collection of buildings forming a central point in a town (see CENTRE *sb.* 6a); †**town-child**, a child born in the town (where a school is founded, and thus sometimes entitled to be a free scholar); **town clown** *U.S. slang*, a policeman working in a village or small town; **town-council**, the elective deliberative and administrative body of a town: cf. COUNCIL 10; hence **town-councillor**, a member of a town-council; **town-crier**, a public crier; = CRIER 2b; **town-cross**, the market cross of a town; **town-dab** (*local*), the lemon-sole; **town-foot**, the lower end of a town or village; **town gas**, gas manufactured and supplied for domestic or commercial use, based on coal gas; **town-guard**, (*a*) *Sc. Hist.*, the military or quasi-military guard of a town; (*b*) the guard policing a garrison-town; also *attrib.*; **town-head**, the upper end of a town or village; **townhithe** *rare*$^{-1}$, a haven or landing-place in a town; **townhome** *U.S.* = TOWN-HOUSE, TOWN HOUSE 2b; † **town-husband** (*local*): see quot.; **town-life**, life in a town; *spec.* the social life of a town; **town-liver**, one who lives in a town; **town-living**, town-life; also an ecclesiastical benefice in a town (LIVING *vbl. sb.* 5); **town-miss**, a young woman who lives in a town: *spec.* a prostitute; **town-mouse**, *fig.* a dweller in a town, esp. as unfamiliar with country life (in allusion to Æsop's fable); **town-officer**, (*a*) an officer (of excise) posted in a town; (*b*) in New England, a selectman; (*c*) *Sc.* an officer charged with keeping public order (cf. TOWN-MAJOR, *town-guard*); **town-park**: see PARK *sb.* 3a; also *attrib.*; **town-piece** [PIECE *sb.* 13], a token issued by or current in a town; **town-place** (*dial.*): see quots.; **town-plat, town-plot** (*U.S.*), a plan of a township: cf. PLAT *sb.*[3] 2, PLOT *sb.* 3; **town-reeve** (now *Hist.*), the bailiff or steward of a *tún*; **town-row**, the sequence of houses in a town, or of homesteads in a parish or manor; also *fig.* the roll of townsmen: see quots. and cf. HOUSE-ROW; †**town-side**, the land close beside a town; **town-site**, the site of a town; *spec.* in U.S. and Canada, a tract of land set apart by legal authority to be occupied by a town, and (usually) surveyed and laid out with streets, etc.; **town-skip**, a jocular name for a city urchin; **town-taking**, the taking of a town; hence ***town-taking day*** at Hull, the anniversary of the day on which that city was secured for William of Orange; **town-tallow**, English, as distinct from continental tallow; †**town-top**, a whipping-top kept for public use: = *parish-top* (PARISH *sb.* 7); **town trail**, a route through a town for tourists or walkers linking features of interest, which are described and interpreted by explanatory notices, printed leaflets, or a guide; **town-traveller**, a commercial traveller whose operations are confined to the town which is his employer's place of business; **town twinning**, the establishment of regular contacts between two towns in different countries; cf. TWIN *v.*[2] 2; **town-way**, the way to the town; **town-weed**, a name for Dog's Mercury; †**town-widow**, ? a widow supported by public charity; **town-woman**, a woman of the town, a prostitute. See also TOWN BOOK, -CLERK, -GATE, HALL, etc.

1737 *Town-Adjutant [see TOWN-MAJOR]. **1801** *Brit. Mil. Libr.* II. s.v., The Town-Adjutant is an assistant to the Town-Major. **1933** P. ABERCROMBIE (*title*) *Town & country planning. **1941** J. S. HUXLEY in *Times Educ. Suppl.* 6 Dec. 581/2 It is here that adult education, enlightened town and country planning, and deliberate encouragement by the State and local authorities of living art, music, drama and all other branches of cultural life, must be called on to do most of the bridging of the gap. **1972** *Whitaker's Almanack 1973* 1177/2 The Town and Country Planning Act 1971 (consolidating earlier Acts) contains very far-reaching provisions affecting the liberty of an owner of land to develop and use it as he will. **1852** *California Dispatch* 18 Jan. 2/4 A game of '*town ball' which was had on the Plaza during the week, reminded us of other days and other scenes. **1909** *Collier's* 8 May 12/1 In America the corresponding game generally went under the name of 'rounders', and because it was played at the time of town meetings, 'townball'. **1975** E. WIGGINTON *Foxfire 3* 466 We'd go out and play town ball. **1851** E. WARD *Jrnl.* 3 Jan. (1951) 98 We afterwards went on to the *Town Belt and Riccarton. **1889** W. DAVIDSON *Stories N.Z. Life* 61 The native bush which covers a large portion of the 'town belt'. **1858** A. MACMILLAN *Lett.* (1908) 3 Poor *town-bound mechanics and shopmen. **1905** *Westm. Gaz.* 17 Oct. 7/1 There was a breakdown in the Town-bound trams at Balham. **1659** GAUDEN *Tears Ch.* **ij, Upon the confiscation of them to their *Town-box or Exchequer. **1597** SHAKS. *2 Hen. IV*, II. ii. 172 A Kinswoman of my Masters... Euen such Kin, as the Parish Heyfors are to the *Towne-Bull? **1611** COTGR. s.v. *Bannier*, *Taureau bannier*, a common, or town, bull. **1709** *Brit. Apollo* II. No. 55. 2/2 As dull as a Dormouse at hom, but a vary toun Bull abroad. **1647** FULLER *Gd. Th. in Worse T.* (1841) 136 As the *town-bushel is the standard both to measure corn and other bushels by. **1907** *Horseless Age* 16 Oct. 589/3 There will be [from Ford Motor Co.] an enclosed *town car, which is to be an exact copy..of the Renault town car. **1929** *Vanity Fair* (N.Y.) Mar. 89 (*caption*) The Blackhawk, a smaller and lower edition of the Stutz, is represented here by a town car of dignified proportions. **1968** G. N. GEORGANO *Compl. Encycl. Motorcars* 621 *Coupé de ville*,..Some 'de ville' bodies had folding rear quarters as in the landaulette. In America they were more often known as town cars. **1932** T. SHARP *Town & Countryside* x. 203 But even if the naturalistic style could be quite perfectly carried out in the perfect replica of a romantic natural scene, what..is the purpose of such a scene in a sensibly-sized town, when.. genuine countryside [is] accessible within a few minutes' walk of the *town centre. **1966** *Guardian* 10 Sept. 14/1 A recently started town-centre housing scheme. **1980** P. LIVELY *Judgement Day* iii. 26 The street plan of the town centre, an elongated triangle enclosing an open space. **1886** *Dict. Nat. Biog.* VIII. 277/1 Entered at Christ's Hospital, probably as a '*town child' or 'free scholar'. **1927** *Amer. Speech* II. 387/1 The *town clown's badge is called a *tomato can*. **1931** 'D. STIFF' *Milk & Honey Route* i. 20 There should always be some retreat, preferably a thicket, into which the hobos can flee, should they receive an unwelcome visit from the 'town clown', or the law enforcer of the community. **1681** *Acts Parlt. Scotl.* VIII. 411/2 Ane Act of the *Town Council of the Burgh of Dumbartan in favors of the trades therof. **1775** A. BURNABY *Trav.* 75 *note*, Each township is managed by a town-council. **1851**, **1863** [see COUNCIL 10]. **1874** GREEN *Short Hist.* iv. §4. 188 Their merchant-gild.. acted, in fact, pretty much the same part as a town-council of to-day. **1850** J. WILSON *Annals of Hawick* an. 1727, Walter Scott, *town councillor, is degraded as such by the council..in respect of his twice breaking prison, after being convict by the bailies of a riot. **1602** SHAKS. *Ham.* III. ii. 4, I had as liue the *Town-Cryer had spoke my Lines. **1867** TROLLOPE *Chron. Barset* II. lix. 166 Her secret had been published, as it were, by the town-crier. **1836** YARRELL *Brit. Fishes* II. 222 [Lemon, or Smooth Dab] is taken on the Sussex coast, where it is known by the name of *Town-Dab. **1908** F. E. JUNGE *Gas Power* ii. 31 The price for *town gas has been gradually reduced during this period. **1958** *B.S.I. News* Aug. 16 Flexible tubing and connector ends for appliances burning town gas. **1973** C. CALLOW *Power from Sea* iv. 85 The number of people who have been inconvenienced is small compared with the total number converted from town gas to natural gas. **1805** FORSYTH *Beauties Scotl.* I. 107 To raise, for the defence of the city [Edinburgh], a corps of no fewer than 126 men,..which is called the *town-guard. **1811** *Gen. Regul. & Ord. Army* 101 An Adjutant of the Day is to be furnished from the Regiment which gives the Town Guard, or the Commander in Chief's Guard. **1818** SCOTT *Hrt. Midl.* v[i], There was a sentinel upon guard, who, that one town-guard soldier might do his duty.., presented his piece, and desired the foremost of the rioters to stand off. **1905** *Blackw. Mag.* July 100 Not far from the Tolbooth stood the Town Guard House. **1805** G. MCINDOE *Poems & Songs* 62 Some b——h frae the *town head has stown't. **1922** JOYCE *Ulysses* 379 Once her in *townhithe meeting he to her bow had not doffed. **1976** *Washington Post* 19 Apr. C18/2 (Advt.), Rockshire *Townhome w/3 bedrms., 2½ baths, English pub rec.rm., den, show well. **1979** *Arizona Daily Star* 22 July H4/1 Accordingly, when what used to be called 'row houses'—attached houses—became economically desirable, they were at first called 'town houses' and are now in the process of being renamed 'town homes'. **1847–78** HALLIWELL, **Town-husband*, an officer of a parish who collects the moneys from the parents of illegitimate children for the maintenance of the latter. *East.* **1693** *Humours Town* 103 You have none of these in your *Town-life. **1779** *Mirror* No. 58 ¶5 Emilia had acquired a stronger attachment to the pleasures of a town life, than was..right in itself. **1620** E. BLOUNT *Horæ Subs.* 153 Riding, Shooting, ..some *towne-liuers, sometimes make hard shift to practise. **1832** J. J. BLUNT *Sk. Reform. Eng.* iv. 65 Thus it came to pass that *town livings (contrary to all reason) are at present, of all others, the poorest. **1863** E. FITZGERALD *Lett.* (1889) I. 290, I suppose Town-living makes one alive to such a Change. **1749** J. CLELAND *Mem. Woman Pleasure* II. 98, I was not at all out of figure to pass for a modest girl. I had neither the feathers, nor *fumet* of a tawdry *town-miss. **1921** D. H. LAWRENCE *Sea & Sardinia* vi. 245 Two town-misses in fur coats. **1750** *Student* 31 May 190 *Town-mice, he knew, luxurious were. **1857** HUGHES *Tom Brown* II. iii, Here's Arthur, a regular young town-mouse with a natural taste for the woods. **1887** LD. CHURCHILL in *Times* (weekly ed.) 24 June 9/1 What I shall call a town mouse like myself. **1737** J. CHAMBERLAYNE *St. Gt. Brit.* II. (ed. 33) 84 Chief Examiner of *Town-Officers Books for London Brewery. *a***1817** T. DWIGHT *Trav. New Eng.* (1821) I. 243 On the refusal, death, or removal, of a Town-Officer, a meeting is to be holden for..choosing another. **1864** A. MCKAY *Hist. Kilmarnock* (1880) 235 The procession was headed by Mr. Paton, town-officer, on a gallant charger. **1870** *Act 33–4 Vict.* c. 46 §15 Any demesne land, or any holding ordinarily termed '*townparks' adjoining or near to any city or town. **1887** *Act 50–1 Vict.* c. 33 §9 A holding shall not be deemed to constitute a town park, though within the definition of the expression 'Town parks',.. if it is let and used as an ordinary agricultural farm. **1887** in *Pall Mall G.* 24 Mar. 13/2 To secure the just rights of the town park holders. **1805** *Brathwait's Barnabees Jrnl.* Introd. (1818) 42 A Harrington was a *town piece, tradesman's token, or other small coin current in the early part of the seventeenth century. **1787** GROSE *Provinc. Gloss.*, **Town-place*, a farm-yard. *Cornw.* **1867** R. S. HAWKER *Prose Wks.* (1893) 109 There dwelt in scattered villages, or town-places.., the bold and hardy Keltic people. **1880** COUCH *E. Cornw. Words*, *Town*, *Town-place*, applied to the smallest hamlet, and even to a farm-yard. **1656** *Public Rec. Colony of Connecticut* (1850) I. 282 Thos persons that cohabitt in the *towne platte. **1723** *Proprietors' Rec. Waterbury, Connecticut* (1911) 121 To settle the old Town platt Lotts. *a***1817** T. DWIGHT *Trav. New Eng.*, etc. (1821) II. 335 The town-plat is originally distributed into lots, containing from two to ten acres. **1714** in *Hist. Northfield, Mass.* (1875) 134 That the *Town-Plot be stated in the old place, in such form and measure as the Committee can allow it, according to the Court's order. *c***890** tr. *Bæda's Hist.* v. xi. [x.] (1890) 416 þa onfoeng hio se *tunᵹerefa. *c* **1000** *Ags. Gosp.* Luke xvi. 18 Ða herede se hlaford þære unrihtwisness tunᵹerefan. **1861** PEARSON *Early & Mid. Ages Eng.* 100 A few adventurers even sailed to Dorchester, 787 A.D., and slew the town-reeve when he sought to call them to account. **1610** BP. HALL *Apol. Brownists* §52 To bee ranged in the same *Towne-rowes with Iewes, Arrians, Anabaptists. **1825** JAMIESON, *Town-raw*, used to denote the privileges of a Town-ship. *To thraw one's self out o' a toun-raw*, to forfeit the privileges enjoyed in a small community. **1886** *S.W. Linc. Gloss.* s.v. *Town-row*, *By Town-row*, or *by House-row*, was the term for the old plan for keeping men off the parish when work was scarce, by finding them so many days' work at each farm in turn. **1523** FITZHERB. *Husb.* §10 If it be very ranke grounde, as is moche at euery *towne syde, where catel doth resort. **1657** W. COLES *Adam in Eden* cxxxi, The fifth groweth..by hedge sides and path wayes, in fields and town-sides. **1821** *Canad. Courant* 17 Jan. 1/2 There are about fourteen acres cleared for a *Town site but not a single house in a finished state. **1872** RAYMOND *Statist. Mines & Mining* 170 The Silver State Mining Company..have located a town-site—Crystal City..—on the old Salt Lake route. **1878** *N. Amer. Rev.* CXXVII. 445 The improvement of town-sites. **1896** WRENN in *Critic* (U.S.) 31 Oct. 270/1 We have made a plan of Trilby Townsite, Pasco Co., Fl[orid]a. **1837** DICKENS *Pickw.* xxvi, 'Well, young *townskip', said Sam, 'how's mother?' **1788** G. HADLEY *Hist. Kingston-upon-Hull* xxi. 277 Thus by the spirited conduct of the Protestant officers, was Hull preserved, on the 4th of December, 1688; which is still observed as a holiday, under the appellation of *Town Taking Day. **1866** J. J. SLEAHAN *Hist. Hull* (ed. 2) 188. **1912** *Times* 19 Dec. 20/4 To-day's 'Market Letter' quotes—*town tallow, 33s. 6d. per cwt. **1623–33** FLETCHER & SHIRLEY *Night-Walker* I. iii, He..dances like a *town-top, and reels and hobbles. **1670** EVELYN *Sylva* xx. 92 For the Turner, Kyele-pins, great Town-Topps. *a***1780** BLACKSTONE *Note on Shaks.'s Twel. N.* I. iii. 44 To sleep like a town-top. **1973** *Nature* 11 May 105/2 The local College of Education has sponsored the idea of '*town trails' in Leicester. **1980** *Jrnl. R. Soc. Arts* CXXVIII. 303/1 Its 140 pages of practical advice on..town trails, heritage centres and other 'media' are not aimed at the general reader. **1850** DICKENS *D. Copperfield* xi. 114 He was a sort of *town traveller for a number of miscellaneous houses. **1930** A. BENNETT *Imperial Palace* x. 59 A town-traveller in tinned comestibles. **1960** *Sunday Express* 16 Oct. 9/6 *Town twinning between cities of highly developed and under-developed countries. **1981** *Times* 23 Mar. 4/4 The question of Dundee's association with Nablus would be raised with the Scottish Town Twinning Association. **1598** SHAKS. *Merry W.* III. i. 7 *Euans.* Which way haue you look'd..? *Sim...* Euery way but the *Towne-way. **1861** MISS PRATT *Flower. Pl.* V. 3 Perennial or Dog's Mercury... From the growth of the plant in towns and town gardens, it is sometimes called *Town-weed. **1632** BROME *North. Lasse* I. i, [She] has been the *Town-widow these Three years. **1675** WYCHERLEY *Country Wife* II. i, What! you would have her as impudent as yourself?..a mere notorious *town-woman? **1710** ADDISON *Tatler* No. 260 ¶ 11 To regard every Town-Woman as a particular Kind of Siren.

11. Combinations with *town's*, as ***townschildren***, ***townsfolk***, ***town's-hall***, ***town's-piper***; **town's-bairn**, a native of the (or one's own) town (*Sc.*); so **town's-boy**, **town's-fellow**, in similar sense; † **town's husband**, obs. title of a borough official having charge of the accounts, etc.: cf. HUSBAND *sb.* 4; † **town's-like** († **towneslike**) *a.*, townish, townly; **town's-money**, the public funds of a town; **townswoman**, a woman inhabitant of a town; with possessive, a woman of the same town; **Townswomen's Guild**, an urban organization of women, engaging in educational and social activities. See also *town's-book* (Sc. *townis buk*) s.v. TOWN BOOK, *town's-end* s.v. TOWN-END, TOWNSMAN, TOWNSPEOPLE.

1808 J. MAYNE *Siller Gun* III. xvi, M'Ghee, our ain *town's-bairn. **1822** SCOTT *Nigel* iii, He was a kindly Scot himsell, and, what is more, a town's-bairn o' the gude town. **1764** *Mem. G. Psalmanazar* 90 Having acquainted four or five of our clan that were my *townsboys with my design. **1857** GLADSTONE in *Westm. Gaz.* 20 May (1898) 3/3 [Mr. Gladstone gave an address to the assembled pupils in the large lecture-hall, and invented a new phrase by addressing us as] 'fellow townsboys'. **1837** SIR F. PALGRAVE *Merch. & Friar* i. (1844) 23 He found them in the yard, where they were absolutely beset by townsmen, townswomen, and *townschildren. **1906** *Academy* 7 Apr. 328/1 Townschildren and nurses are often woefully ignorant on the subject of edible berries. **1850** ALLINGHAM *Poems, Dream* ii, On they passed,..*Townsfellows all from first to last. **1737** SWIFT *Let. to Richardson* 30 Apr., That the *townsfolks and tenants of the estate round Colrane would be content to double the rent. **1833** HT. MARTINEAU *Berkeley the Banker* I. i, The new banker..could not know so much of the characters of the townsfolks as he who had lived among them. **1866** ROGERS *Agric. & Prices* I. xxvii. 653 Some common market in which the agent for the townsfolk purchased country produce. **1812** J. BIGLAND *Beauties Eng. & Wales* XVI. 412 A large room, now used as a *town's hall. **1757** in *N. & Q.* 7th Ser. VIII. 447/2 James Mihill, *Town's Husband [buried at Beverley]. **1795** *Hull Advertiser* 8 Aug. ibid. 496/1 Wanted by the Corporation of this Town, a proper person for the office of Town's Husband, or Common Officer. **1833** [see HUSBAND *sb.* 4]. **1574** HELLOWES *Gueuara's Fam. Ep.* 296 The good *towneslike craftsman, needes no daughter in lawe that can fril and paint hirselfe. *c* **1600** *Maldon MS. Records* in *Essex Herald* 9 May (1905) 7/5 [One of Cade's charges against the authorities was] spending of *towne's-money against their lawful preacher. **1819** W. TENNANT *Papistry Storm'd* I. (1827) 7 The *town's piper, wi' a blatter. **1684** BUNYAN *Pilgr.* II. 73 And this..is one of my *Towns-Women. **1834** H. MILLER *Scenes & Leg.* xx. (1857) 292 Well-known resorts of his townswomen. **1837** [see *townschildren* above]. **1929** *Times* 26 Nov. 19/4 Lady Cynthia Colville, the president of the *Townswomen's Guild Appeal..spoke of the great need there was in small towns and residential suburbs for the new Townswomen's Guilds, which are to fulfil a role similar to that played by the women's institutes in the rural areas. **1933** *Ludlow Advertiser* 25 Feb. 6/4 The Townswomen's Guild held a whist drive on Monday night in the Guild Room in Broad Street. **1960** J. STROUD *Shorn Lamb* vii. 79 Miss Dashforth stumped the whole area addressing Mothers' Unions, Townswomen's Guilds, Parent-Teacher Associations and so on. **1977** *Belfast Telegraph* 19 Jan. 3/5 Bloomfield Collegiate School—Knock Townswomen's Guild, talk on community relations, 7.45 pm.

Hence (*nonce-wds.*) **'towneen** [with Irish dim. suffix], **tow'nette**, **'townikin** [after G. *städtchen*], diminutives of *town*; **'townhood**, the condition or status of a town.

1893 J. A. BARRY *S. Brown's Bunyip*, etc. 120 An' thin.. Jillibeejee is as ructious a *towneen as is on God's earth. **1839** LADY LYTTON *Cheveley* (ed. 2) II. i. 5 Though not quite a town, it was something more than a village: the French call those mule-like domiciles, between a house and a bandbox, *maisonnettes*, and I don't see why Blichingly should not be called a *townette. **1880** J. B. HARWOOD *Yng. Ld. Penrith* xiii, It would be unreasonable to expect a tiny townette such as I report to engage as the chief of its police a man of tact as well as energy. **1865** E. BURRITT *Walk Land's End* 203 The first centuries of its *townhood.. mellow off under the horizon of the past. **1891** KATE FIELD *Washington* IV. 383/1 At the time of my visit, L—— had just attained the dignity of townhood. **1863** H. MAYHEW *Germ. Life & Mann.* (1864) I. 5 The little village..lying far away on the moors..from which the *townikin..is said to derive its name.

town, *v. rare.* (Only in *pa. pple.* towned.) [f. prec. sb.] *trans.* **a.** To furnish with towns. **b.** To make into or constitute (a community) a town.

1585 R. LANE *Let.* in Hakluyt *Voy.* (1600) III. 254 The continent is of an huge and vnknowen greatnesse, and very well peopled and towned. **1633** P. FLETCHER *Purple Isl.* II. xv, With many a citie grac't, and fairly town'd. **1897** I. O. REICHEL in *Trans. Devon. Assoc.* XXIX. 458 There were reeves of various kinds..the town-reeve in a 'towned' village.

town, obs. form of TUN.

town-adjutant to **-bell**: see TOWN 9, 10.

townage, obs. Sc. var. of TOWNISH.

town book. Also 6 *Sc.* townis buk. A book in which the records of a town are kept.

*a***1547** in J. R. Boyle *Hedon* (1875) App. 72 All suche re[n]talles, presidences, or towne bookes as they had in theire kepinge. **1567** *Reg. Privy Council Scot.* I. 506 The townis bukis, court bukis, and scrollis. **1641** *Rhode Isl. Col. Rec.* (1856) I. 114 Ordered, that each Towne shall provide a Towne Book, wherein they shall Record the Evidences of the Lands by them impropriated. **1765** *Univ. Mag.* XXXVII. 377/1 That this vote be recorded in the town book. **1816** SINGER *Hist. Cards* 41 The Old Town Books of the Suabian and Franconian cities.

'town-born, *a.* Born in a or the town.

1579 LYLY *Euphues* (Arb.) 50 Philautus being a towne borne childe..crept into credit with Don Ferardo one of the chiefe gouernours of the citie. **1674** in *N. & Q.* 9th Ser. IX. 463/1 A free School to teach 20 poor town-born children born in Westminster. **1821** LAMB *Elia* Ser. I. *Old & New Schoolm.*, From the circumstance of my being town-born.

town-bound to **-church**: see TOWN 9, 10.

,town-'clerk. The clerk or secretary to the corporation of a town, who has charge of the records, correspondence, and legal business, the conduct of municipal elections, etc.

1343 *Inq. ad q. d.* 268/18 in *List* (1904) 399 [Si concedamus Thome de Legh de Oxonia] tounclerk. **13..** *S. Eng. Leg.* (MS. Bodl. 779) in Herrig's *Archiv* LXXXII. 419/17 Þey him made toun-clerke.. Alle aȝen his wille. **1433** *Rolls of Parlt.* IV. 476/1 Charged bi the Toun Clerk for the tyme beyng. **1526** TINDALE *Acts* xix. 35 When the toune clarcke [Gr. γραμματεύς] had cessed the people he sayd: Ye men of Ephesus [etc.]. **1631** *High Commission Cases* (Camden) 198 This cause was prosecuted by some of the towne of Stamford, of which the towne clarke was one. **1835** *Act 5 & 6 Will. IV*, c. 76 §58 That the Council of every Borough..

shall appoint a fit Person..to be the Town Clerk of such Borough, who shall hold his Office during Pleasure.

b. = PARISH CLERK. *dial. rare.* Cf. TOWN *sb.* 3.

1597 *Min. Archdeaconry of Essex* lf. 237 (MS.), He willfully deniethe the paiment of the vsuall clerk's wages to father God our towne clerk. **1597–8** *Min. Archdeaconry of Colchester* lf. 186 b (MS.), Great Chishill..Richard Watson ..allegavit that he is towneclerk there. **1879** D. J. HILL *Bryant* 55 [Bryant] being himself at the time, the town-clerk, he was placed in the embarrassing position of having to proclaim his own nuptials.

Hence ˌ**town-ˈclerkship**, the office of town-clerk.

1439 *Coventry Leet Bk.* 192 They ordeyne that Symkyn Birches enjoy and haue off the office off Toun-clerkship terme of hys lyffe. **1521** *Maldon, Essex, Liber B.* lf. 57 b (MS.), The office of towneclerkshipp for this yere followynge. **1817** W. TAYLOR in *Monthly Rev.* LXXXIII. 496 The town-clerk-ship having become vacant.

town-clock to **-councillor**: see TOWN 9, 10.

† **town-cress.** *Obs.* Forms: see TOWN and CRESS. [OE. *túncressa*, f. *tún* garden, TOWN + CRESS.] Garden Cress (*Lepidium sativum*).

a **700** *Epinal Gloss.* (O.E.T.) 676 *Nasturcium*.., tuuncressa. *c* **725** *Corpus Gloss.* 1359 Tuuncressa. *c* **1000** *Sax. Leechd.* II. 22 ȝenim..tun cersan, sio þe self weaxeð, & mon ne sæwð. *c* **1420** *Liber Cocorum* (1862) 42 Take therto Town cresses, and cresses that growene in flode. **1533** ELYOT *Cast. Helth* (1541) 90 Let him eate hartyly small radysshe rootes, townkersis,..or purslane. **1578** LYTE *Dodoens* I. lxiv. 96 The Swines Cresses..is hoate and dry, like to garden or towne Cressis. *Ibid* v. lix. 623. **1615** MARKHAM *Eng. Housew.* II. i. (1668) 30 Take the powder of Town cress dried. **1620** VENNER *Via Recta* vii. 158 Towne-Cresses, or as the vulgar sort doe pronounce, Town-karsse, is more byting in taste then Rocket.

town-crier to **-dike**: see TOWN 9, 10.

towndir, -dire, obs. Sc. forms of TINDER.

town-ditch. Now *Hist.* The ditch or moat surrounding a walled town.

1423 *Coventry Leet Bk.* 48 Poody-Crofte, þe wich lieth from Crow-lane vnto a diche, þat is callyd the town diche in breid. **1568** GRAFTON *Chron.* II. 1349 Ridley and Latimer.. were sone condempned, and after burned in the towne Diche at Oxforde. **1603** HOLLAND *Plutarch's Mor.* 466 At the verie instant there was espied an hare, running crosse over the towne ditch. **1680** C. NESSE *Church. Hist.* 213 Oh that our reformers had cast all Romish reliques into the town-ditch!

town-drummer: see TOWN 9 b.

ˈtown-ˌdweller. One who dwells in a town; a townsman.

1483 *Cely Papers* (Camden) 146 Sarten Town dwellers of Callez hath ben at Bruges. **1550** in Strype *Eccl. Mem.* (1721) II. App. QQ. 142 To take their answers, and the proofs of the said town-dwellers. **1623** MIDDLETON *More Dissemb. Besides Wom.* IV. i, Th' unhous'd race of fortune-tellers May never fail to cheat town-dwellers. **1891** C. JAMES *Rom. Rigmarole* 2 No jaded town-dweller..would grudge the few shillings. **1912** *Times* 19 Oct. 7/3 The ignorance of town-dwellers about the elementary facts of rural economy is astounding.

So ˈ**town-ˌdwelling** *a.*

1899 *Westm. Gaz.* 27 Feb. 2/3 The town-dwelling Westminsterians have beaten the rural Carthusians twice running at football.

towne, obs. form of TOWN, TUN.

townee (ˈtaʊniː, older taʊˈniː), *sb.* and *a.* [f. TOWN *sb.* + -EE.] **A.** *sb.* A townsman, esp. as distinguished from a member of the university (cf. TOWNY *sb.* 2); or (now usu.) as distinguished from a country-dweller (cf. TOWNY *sb.* 1). Freq. pejorative.

1897 *Westm. Gaz.* 13 May 6/3 The 'townees' [at Oxford] had notified their intention of breaking all undecorated windows. **1900** G. SWIFT *Somerley* 69 Mr. Bobber, a Cambridge grocer,..considered that there was one law for the collegian and another for the 'townee'. **1902** *Daily Chron.* 16 Aug. 8/3 Just of as much importance is comfortable foot-gear to the townee as to the dweller in the country. **1929** S. KAYE-SMITH in H. C. Minchin *Legion Bk.* 195 The æsthetic week-ender is like other townees in that he generally fails to realize that the real country-dweller..is a very mass of conventions. **1939** AUDEN in *I Believe* (1940) 18 We frequently admire the 'goodness' of illiterate peasants as compared with the 'badness' of many townees. **1976** J. I. M. STEWART *Memorial Service* xv. 245 Janet as a child had been a townee like myself.

B. *adj.* Of, pertaining to, or characteristic of town-dwellers or the town.

1935 H. H. BASHFORD *Lodgings for Twelve* 110 For the townee, as he called him, and townee pursuits, he had a quite unconcealed if tolerant contempt. **1936** AUDEN *Look, Stranger!* 55 The identical and townee smartness. **1960** W. MILLER *Russians as People* 60 It is all fascinating to the foreigner trying to sniff out 'Russian life', but to the townee Russian it is the shabby side of the familiar. **1972** *Daily Tel.* (Colour Suppl.) 24 Nov. 18/1 The Australians are far and away the most urbanised and townee of all nations.

towneen, townette: see under TOWN *sb.*

town-end. Now *dial.* Also **town's end**. The end of the main street of a town or village; one of the extremities of a town.

c **1440** *Alphabet of Tales* 330 Þe fflawme at had burnyd all þe town-end..sesid. **1591** *Reg. Privy Council Scot.* IV. 625 Quha..raid away with him oute at the toun end of Sanctandrois. **1818** SCOTT *Hrt. Midl.* xxxi[i], She's fast in the stocks at Barkston town-end. **1886** *S.W. Linc. Gloss.* s.v., There's a pinfold at the town-end.

1421 *Coventry Leet Bk.* 30 Ne þat no man..lay no dong at the townsend in no placys, but without the stakes..beyond the Frer gate. **1472** *Paston Lett.* III. 71, I have begonne to felle asshe at the townes ende. **1621** SANDERSON *Serm. 1 Cor. vii. 24* §21 Our idle sturdy rogues, and vagrant towns-end beggars. **1760–72** H. BROOKE *Fool of Qual.* (1809) IV. 55 Yonder church-yard below the town's end.

tow-net (ˈtəʊnɛt), *sb.* [f. TOW *sb.*[4] or *v.*[1] + NET *sb.*[1]] A drag-net or dredge used for the collection of natural specimens. Hence **tow-ˈnet** *v.*, *trans.* to drag with a tow-net; *intr.* to use a tow-net; whence ˈ**tow-netter**, ˈ**tow-netting** *vbl. sb.*

1816 TUCKEY *Narr. Exped. R. Zaire* i. (1818) 9 The tow-net was put overboard, and collected some of these animals. **1883** C. F. HOLDER in *Harper's Mag.* Jan 186/2 Dr. Bennet..captured a specimen in a tow-net. **1891** HERDMAN in *Nature* 23 July 274/1 While townetting during the last few days about the North Cape, we have had some large hauls of Copepoda. **1894** *Q. Rev.* Apr. 367 The direct evidence of tow-netting the upper layers of water with fine silk nets. **1899** *Geogr. Jrnl.* Feb. 153 There are two schools of tow-netters: the old-fashioned method..by which the nets are towed horizontally; and the new method, by which an opening and closing net is let down as vertically as may be, and hauled in open through a given vertical area and then closed. **1902** R. VALENTIN in *Jrnl. R. Inst. Cornw.* XV. 84 No ephyræ were obtained in any of the tow-nettings made in the spring.

towney: see TOWNY *a.* and *sb.*

town-father to **-foot**: see TOWN 9, 10.

townful (ˈtaʊnfʊl). [f. TOWN *sb.* + -FUL.] As many as a town contains or will contain.

1855 MOTLEY *Dutch Rep.* IV. iv. (1866) 617 Had they not slaughtered unarmed human beings by townfuls, at the word of command? **1894** *Westm. Gaz.* 18 June 7/2 There were in the country not only junkers but big townfuls of poorly-paid working people, whose lives depended on a cheap loaf.

ˈ**town-ˌgate**[1]. The gate of a walled town.

1433 *Rolls of Parlt.* IV. 477/1 The kepyng of the Town Yate called the Castell Yate. **1588** SHAKS. *L.L.L.* I. ii. 75 Sampson..carried the Towne-gates on his backe like a Porter. **1799** *Hull Advertiser* 21 Sept. 4/1 Mr. Bray.. protected the town-gate efficaciously with grape.

ˈ**town-ˌgate**[2]. *Sc.* and *north. dial.* Also 6–7 gait(e. [GATE *sb.*[2] 4.] The main street of a town or village.

1587 *Durham Wills* (Surtees) III. 129 Frome the particione of the said barene northward, unto the toune-gaite. **1607** in *N. Riding Rec.* (1883) I. 99 Will. Kidd of Kirby Moorside presented for keeping disorder in the Towne-gate. **1817** *Blackw. Mag.* May 155/1 The straggled houses..with their gable-ends, backs, or corners, turned to the street or town-gate. **1867** *Crim. Chronol. York Castle* 207 The town-gate in Mirfield.

town-green to **-guard**: see TOWN 9, 10.

ˈ**town** ˈ**hall. 1.** A large hall used for the transaction of the public business of a town, the holding of a court of justice, assemblies, entertainments, etc.; the great hall of the town-house or municipal building; now very commonly applied to the whole building. Also *attrib.*

1481–90 *Howard Househ. Bks.* (Roxb.) 460 Item, for pottes that ware brokyn in the towne hall. **1538** LONDON in *Lett. Suppress. Monast.* (Camden) 223 [At Reading] Ther towne hall ys a very small howse, and stondith upon the ryver. **1697** *Lond. Gaz.* No. 3336/3 Colchester, Oct. 28. Yesterday the Mayor..proclaimed the Peace before the Town-Hall and Dutch Bay Hall. **1701** in *Gentl. Mag.* LXXXVIII. II. (1818) 601/2 We inned here at the town-house, the town-hall being over part of it. **1897** R. N. BAIN tr. *Jókai's Pretty Michal* xxii. 172 The clock in the town-hall tower struck eight.

2. *Comb.*: **town-hall clock(s)** = MOSCHATEL.

1900 DICKINSON & PREVOST *Gloss. Dial. Cumberland* (rev. ed.) p. xcv, *Adoxa moschatellina.* Town-hall clock (Carlisle). **1968** F. WARNER *Garland* 13 The red herb-Robert twined a bridge With celandine and town-hall-clocks. **1980** *Country Life* 28 Feb. 589/3 The countryman's name for the four-faced pale green wood-land flower moschatel is..'Town Hall Clocks'.

town-head, -herd: see TOWN 10, 9 b.

† **town-ho.** *Obs.* Also 8 townor. (See quots.)

1791 in *Coll. Mass. Hist. Soc.* (1810) III. 154 The boys, as soon as they can talk, will make use of the common phrases, as *townor*, which is an Indian word, and signifies that they have seen the whale twice. **1851** H. MELVILLE *Whale* II. 78 *Town-ho*,..the ancient whale-cry upon first sighting a whale from the mast-head, still used by whalemen in hunting the famous Gallipagos terrapin.

ˈ**town-house, town house.**

1. a. A municipal building containing the public offices, court-house, and TOWN HALL, and in some continental towns the official residence of the chief magistrate. Cf. F. *hôtel de ville*; Ger. *stadthaus*. In England now commonly called TOWN HALL.

1530 PALSGR. 282/1 Towne house, *pretoire.* **1550** BP. HOOPER *Serm. Jonas* v. 106 Certeyne pictures in the towne house at Basyll. **1579** in W. H. Turner *Sel. Rec. Oxford* (1880) 403 Suche arrowes as the towne howsse nowe hathe. **1610** HOLLAND *Camden's Brit.* (1637) 396 The greater part of the Towne [Buckingham] beareth North, wherein standeth the Towne-house. **1678** *Lond. Gaz.* No. 1287/3 The Burghers of Ghent have been commanded to bring in their Arms to the Town-House. **1701** [see TOWN HALL]. **1756–7** tr. *Keysler's Trav.* (1760) III. 333 Placentia. On the area before the town-house are two bronze equestrian statues. **1765** T. HUTCHINSON *Hist. Mass.* I. iii. 381 A long declaration was read from the balcony..of the town-house. **1773** *Hist. Brit. Dom. in N. Amer.* III. ii. 71 The city-hall, or town-house, is a strong brick building, two stories in heighth. **1857** WHITTIER *Last Walk Autumn* xxi, The painted, shingly town-house where The freeman's vote for Freedom falls. **1896** BARRIE *Sent. Tommy*, If you jest see'd the Thrums townhouse!

b. *U.S.* (*a*) An almshouse, a workhouse. (*b*) A town prison (*Cent. Dict.* 1891).

c **1870** in *Dict. Amer. Eng.* (1944) IV. 2341/2 *Town-house*, an almshouse.—Conn. **1889** FARMER *Americanisms* s.v. *Town, Townhouse*,..in Connecticut, an almshouse. **1889** R. COOKE *Steadfast* 28 Just as soon as the road settled she should 'cart her off to the town-house'.

2. a. (Now usu. *town house.*) A house in a town; a residence in town, as distinguished from a country house.

1771 SMOLLETT *Humph. Cl.* I. 185 He has his town-house, and his country-house, his coach, and his post-chaise. **1825** T. HOOK *Sayings* Ser. II. *Man of Many Fr.* I. 284, I have no other town house to offer. **1862** H. MARRYAT *Year in Sweden* II. 393 The monks possessed a town-house in Söfde. **1886** C. E. PASCOE *London of To-day* xxii. (ed. 3) 211 Where now the maze of little courts and side streets extends to the Thames Embankment, there stood, centuries ago, the town-houses of the bishops, the ambassadors, and the powerful nobles. **1888** SAINTSBURY *Marlborough* x. 203 Tradition.. assigns the fine Georgian house now used as the judge's lodgings [Oxford] as having been built by the Duke for a town house.

b. = *terrace house* s.v. TERRACE *sb.* 7. orig. *U.S.*

Often in multiple units designed in a stylish or adventurous manner.

1965 *Daily Progress* (Charlottesville, Va.) 13 July 13 The City Planning Commission..is to receive a proposed ordinance permitting the development of privately owned town houses. **1968** *Globe & Mail* (Toronto) 17 Feb. 5/3 It would include 1,800 dwellings comprising apartments, maisonettes and townhouses for 5,600 people. **1971** *Rand Daily Mail* (Home Owner) 27 Mar. 7/2 City dwellers are gravitating towards high density living (flat complexes, town houses). **1971** *Ideal Home* Apr. 69/2 Something become apparent is that..the modern terrace, even under the pretty name of 'town house', is not popular. **1977** *Telegraph* (Brisbane) 28 Oct. 49/3 The townhouse is a two-storey 'unit' which features a separate courtyard and more privacy than a home unit. **1977** *Detroit Free Press* 11 Dec. 1-B/2 One east side developer,..would like very much to build a community of townhouses along one of the canals that leads to the Detroit river. **1982** *Habitat Catal.* *1982/83* 28/3 Room 2 has a 'metropolitan' style associated with townhouse living.

town-husband: see TOWN 10.

townie: see TOWNY *a.* and *sb.*

townify (ˈtaʊnɪfaɪ), *v. colloq.* [f. TOWN + -(I)FY.] *trans.* To render town-like, or characteristic of the town. Hence ˈ**townified** *ppl. a.*

1777 MRS. GRANT *Lett. fr. Mount.* (1813) II. ii. 10 You have no notion how townified folks are, in all these little garrisons. **1881** A. STRETTELL in *Macm. Mag.* XLV. 120 This encircling grandeur will prevent it from ever getting a townified air. **1906** *Academy* 15 Dec. 602/1 Besides writing curious little townified poems about green fields, it builds curious little townified cottages in them.

townikin: see under TOWN *sb.*

ˈ**towniness.** *colloq.* [f. TOWNY *a.* + -NESS.] Towny quality or condition.

1881 MISS BRADDON *Asph.* II. 153 Mrs. Turchill was so delighted with Torquay in its increased towniness and shoppiness. **1901** F. W. LAWRENCE *Heart of Empire* ii. 73 There are thus two ideas of towniness: one represented by the number of persons to the acre, and the other by the distance in time and space of the centre from the outer limits of the suburbs.

townish (ˈtaʊnɪʃ), *a.* [f. TOWN *sb.* + -ISH[1].]

† **1.** Of or pertaining to a town; living, situated, or existing in a town; urban. *Obs.*

1412–20 LYDG. *Chron. Troy* I. 1339 To gape & loke, as it wer on a mase; þis townysche folk do so comownly On euery þing þat falleth sodeinly. *a* **1542** WYATT *Sat. J. Poins* 4 A song made of the feldishe mouse: That..Would nedes go se her townish sisters house. **1587** TURBERV. *Trag. T.* (1837) 53 Leave off to leade thy life in lawndes, imbrace thy townish good. **1674** JEAKE *Arith.* (1696) 74 Bakers that dwell in Cities and Towns were allowed 6*s*...which..is still generally allowed to Townish Bakers.

2. Pertaining to or characteristic of the town or town life, esp. as distinguished from the country (in quot. 1500–20, from the court); having the manners or habits of town-dwellers.

1500–20 DUNBAR *Poems* xlii. 39 Ȝe be to townage, be this buke, To be my ladeis presoneir. *Ibid.* lxxv. 247 He wes townysche, peirt, and gukit. **1530** PALSGR. 464 To bringe up an uplandysshe person in better maners or more townysshe condycions. **1600** *Maides Metam.* IV. in Bullen *Old Pl.* (1882) I. 149 As townish damzels lend the hand But send the heart to him aloofe doth stand. **1820** *Blackw. Mag.* VIII. 16 There is a certain townish something about the inhabitants in general.

Hence ˈ**townishly** *adv.*, ˈ**townishness.**

1645 J. BOND *Occasus Occid.* 33 Another Place, Person, or Town-ship, (peradventure) have stood too Townishly upon their Priviledges and Liberties. *a* **1859** DE QUINCEY *Posth.*

Wks. (1891) I. 222 A peculiar style of gossip, of babble, and of miniature intriguing, invests the atmosphere of little 'townishness'.

'town-land. †**a.** OE. *tún-land.* The land forming a *tún* or manor. **b.** In Ireland, A division of land of varying extent; also, a territorial division, a township. **c.** In Scotland, The enclosed or infield land of a farm.

a. 972 in Earle *Land Charters* (1888) 445 Ðis sindon ða lond ȝemæra þæra tun londa ðe into perscoran belimpað. **b. 1658** PETTY in *Calr. S.P, Irel.* (*Advent.*) 362 The survey of every particular townland. **1662** *Ir. Act 14 & 15 Chas. II*, c. 2 (iii). §3 The..number of acres..in each town-land, village, balybo or quarter of land. **1804** MAR. EDGEWORTH *Ennui* v, Two or three cabins gathered together were sufficient to constitute a town, and the land adjoining thereto is called a town-land. **1842** S. C. HALL *Ireland* II. 354 The origin of town-lands..is of great antiquity. **1846** MCCULLOCH *Acc. Brit. Empire* (1854) I. 365 Townlands are sometimes attached to one parish for the assessment of the county taxes, while, with respect to tithes and other ecclesiastical contributions, they are considered as forming part of another. **1873** W. K. SULLIVAN in O'Curry *Anc. Irish* Introd. 98 The modern townland may be looked upon as the representative of all the parcels of land of whatever denomination from the *Baile Biatach* down, which had separate designations. **1892** EMILY LAWLESS *Grania* IV. i. 166 Inishmaan possesses but two townlands, containing six quarters each, with sixteen croggeries to every quarter, and sixteen acres to every croggery. **1903** *Times* 17 Jan. 8/1 Ballycotsey is a townland in the county Tipperary. **c. 1801** *Farmer's Mag.* Nov. 420 The infield, or town-land ..looked to be good.

'townless, *a.* [f. TOWN *sb.* + -LESS.] Having no town or towns; devoid of towns.

a **1400-50** *Alexander* 2288 How tidis it þe [þ]at tounles þi toname is callid? **1601** HOLLAND *Pliny* IV. xii. I. 80 Townlesse, and therfore obscure and of no reckoning. **1846** FORD *Gatherings fr. Spain* 15 This space..appears one townless level. **1884** *Athenæum* 1 Mar. 273/2 The inhabitants of these townless steppes live in carts, each cart containing a family.

townlet ('taʊnlɪt). [f. as prec. + -LET.] A tiny or diminutive town.

a **1552** LELAND *Itin.* V. 94 Oglesfeld and Bradfeld, ij townelettes or villages, long to one paroche chirche. **1610** HOLLAND *Camden's Brit.* II. 32 The coasts are well bespred with prety townlets. **1658** PHILLIPS, *Paston*, a Townlet in Northfolk, giving sirname and residence to an honourable family of this County. **1807** SOUTHEY *Espriella's Lett.* II. 244 One of those townlets in which every thing reminds us of the distance from a metropolis. **1890** *Times* 14 Oct. 4/1 [In Russia] Many townlets are changed by virtue of a local order into villages, and Jews resident in them are expelled.

town-life, -living, etc.: see TOWN 9, 10.

'townling. [f. TOWN *sb.* + -LING[1].]

1. A small town; a townlet.

1887 M. BETHAM-EDWARDS in *Temple Bar Mag.* Apr. 557 So dead-alive this townling of two or three thousand souls. **1892** E. REEVES *Homeward Bound* vi. 165 The rugged, bare mountains that look down on the Gulf of Salerno, and whereon nestle the townlings of Salerno and Amalfi.

2. A town-bred person. Also *attrib.*

1888 DOUGHTY *Arabia Deserta* I. 128 Turns and terms of the herdsmen poets of the desert, which are dark or unknown in any form to the townling Syrians. *Ibid.* 214 He watched to see if the townling were discouraged, in viewing only their empty desert before him.

townly ('taʊnlɪ), *a.* [f. TOWN + -LY[1].] Pertaining to or characteristic of a town; having the manners or habits of town-dwellers; = TOWNISH 2.

1749 FIELDING *Tom Jones* XII. vii, I suppose she is one of your quality folks, one of your townly ladies that we saw last night in the puppet-show. **1822** GALT *Sir A. Wylie* xxiii, I intend to settle my townly affairs. **1895** *Pall Mall G.* 26 Jan. 3/2 Our country manners have grown townly.

Hence **'townliness.**

1832 MRS. F. TROLLOPE *Dom. Mann. Amer.* xxxiii. (1839) 321 They throw off..their airs, and their 'townliness'.

'town-made, *a.* Made or manufactured in a town; spec. in the town of the district. Also as *sb.*

1809 *Edin. Rev.* XIII. 253 This is the very slang of..the lowest of our town-made novels. **1837** DICKENS *Sk. Boz, Dancing Acad.*, [He] bought a pair of the regular seven-and-sixpenny, long-quartered town-mades. **1840** HOOD *Kilmansegg, Marriage* xxv, Town-made joys how dearly they cost. **1853** PERKINS *Haberdashery* (ed. 8) 90 Kid is valuable in proportion to its elasticity. When this quality is united with closeness of texture, the gloves called 'Town made' are so superior to most others of our own manufacture, as to rival the French. **1861** WYNTER *Soc. Bees* 163 Adulteration to which all town-made bread is obnoxious.

'town-'major. *Obs.* or *Hist.* **a.** The major of a town-guard, as formerly in Edinburgh. **b.** The chief executive officer in a garrison-town or fortress. **c.** Applied vaguely to the chief magistrate or administrative officer of a foreign town. **d.** An officer responsible for liaison between troops stationed in a town and the townspeople. (No longer current.)

a. 1676 W. ROW *Contn. Blair's Autobiog.* (1848) 554 Several meetings in Edinburgh were dispersed by Robert Johnston town-major. **1693** *Apol. Clergy Scot.* 29 Town Major of Edenburgh, living in the Parish of Leswade, Major Will. Murray.

b. 1702 *Milit. Dict., Town-Major*, the third Officer in order in a Garrison, and next to the Deputy Governor. He ought to understand the Fortification, and has a particular Charge of the Guards, Rounds, Patrouilles, and Sentinels. **1715** *Lond. Gaz.* No. 5300/5 Robert Dalzell, Esq., to be Town Major thereof [of Portsmouth]. **1737** J. CHAMBERLAYNE *St. Gt. Brit.* II. (ed. 33) 115 (Gibraltar) John Preston, Esq., Town-Major, Mr. Anthony Robinson, Town-Adjutant. **1856** KAYE *Life Sir J. Malcolm* I. iv. 62 The change was beneficial to Malcolm, who was nominated Town-Major of Fort St. George. **1876** VOYLE *Milit. Dict.* (ed. 3) 436/1 *Town-Major*, an officer who regulates the duties of a garrison, such as the detail and supervision of garrison guards, the disposal of prisoners in the garrison guard-room, the roster of officers for garrison duties [etc.].

c. 1748 *Earthquake of Peru* ii. 168 The Town-Major of Callao would not. **1784** T. HUTCHINS *Descr. Louisiana*, etc. 17 The people..sending three deputies to General O'Riley, viz. Messieurs Grandmaison town-major, La Friniere attorney-general, and De Mazant. **1809** A. HENRY *Trav.* 12 After some further delay, in obtaining a passport from the town-major, I dispatched my canoes to Lachine, there to take in their lading. **1864** BURTON *Scot Abr.* II. ii. 159 The town-major, finding them without credentials, or passports, ordered them to be carried to prison.

d. 1917 A. G. EMPEY *Over Top* 312 *Town major*, an officer stationed in a French town or village who is supposed to look after billets, upkeep of roads, and act as interpreter. **1919** A. P. HERBERT *Bomber Gipsy* 19 Town-major jobs that break men's hearts, and billets at the Base.

Hence **town-'majorship.**

1856 KAYE *Life Sir J. Malcolm* I. iv. 62 New arrangements were made for the Town-Majorship of the Fort.

'townman. Forms: see TOWN *sb.*

†**1.** In OE. *túnman* and ME. A villein; a tenant in villenage. *Obs.*

c **1000** ÆLFRIC *Hom.* II. 344 Furseus oncneow sona ða sawle; se wæs his tun-man ær on life. *c* **1000** *Ags. Voc.* in Wr.-Wülcker 333/22 *Uillanus*, tunman. **11..** *Voc.* ibid. 550/14 *Uillanus*, tunmon. **14..** *Metr. Voc.* ibid. 630/3 *Uillicus*, towneman. *c* **1450** *Godstow Reg.* 204, iij. acres liyng in longefurlange vttermost toward the lond of the towne men.

2. A man who lives in a or the town: as contrasted with a countryman, or formerly with a courtier.

1399 LANGL. *Rich. Redeles* II. 41 So trouthe to telle as toune men said, Ffor on þat ȝe merkyd ȝe myssed ten schore. *c* **1475** *Rauf Coilȝear* 523 Thair is mony toun man, to tuggill is full teuch. **1896** N. MUNRO *Lost Pibroch* (1902) 37 A townman would think the world slept, so great was the booming quietness. **1896** *Westm. Gaz.* 17 Apr. 1/3 You are calling upon the townman, the doctor, the lawyer, the shop-keeper, and the artizan, who has his own Local Government to pay for, to pay also for the police, the highways, and the sanitation of his country neighbours.

'town-'meeting. A general assembly of the inhabitants of a town; *spec.* in *U.S.* a legal meeting of the qualified voters of a 'town' for the transaction of public business, having certain powers of local government.

1636 *Salem, Mass., Town Recds.* 16 At a generall Court or towne meeting of Salem held the second of..May a° 1636. **1639** *Boston Town Recds.* 2 July, At the next townes meeting. **1747** SHIRLEY in *Eng. Hist. Rev.* Oct. (1912) 786 The principal cause of the mobbish turn of this town [Boston] is its constitution, by which the management of it is devolved upon the populace, assembled in their town meetings. **1819** JEFFERSON *Autobiog.* Wks. 1859 I. App. 116 The resolutions ..were probably those you mention of the town-meeting of Boston. **1876** BANCROFT *Hist. U.S.* I. xiii. 426 Each town-meeting was a legislative body. **1878** STUBBS *Const. Hist.* III. xx. 414 Those whom their townsmen had chosen in their own town-meeting.

town-moor to **-place:** see TOWN 9, 10.

towne, obs. form of TUN.

town-planning, *sb.* [Orig. with stress on *town*; subsequently more usu. on *planning*.] The preparation and construction of plans in accordance with which the growth and extension of a town is to be regulated, so as to make use of the natural advantages of the site, and to secure the most advantageous conditions of housing and traffic, the convenient situation of public buildings, open spaces, etc. Also *attrib.* So **town-plan** *sb.*, a ground-plan showing the positions of the streets and buildings in the proposed development of a town; **town-plan** *v.*, *intr.* to prepare a plan for the development of a town (whence **town-planned** *ppl. a.*); **town-planner.**

[**1904** T. C. HORSFALL *Improv. Dwellings People* 43 In preparing a rational town-building plan our task will be to avoid these faults. *Ibid.* 56 The preparation of building and town-extension plans.]

1906 (Nov. 6) *Official Rep. Housing Deput. to Prime Minister* 8 Notes on Speeches. [Subject heading.] Town Planning and Village Development Commission. **1907** *Daily Chron.* 3 May 8/4 'The Hampstead Tenants, Limited', began their work of town-planning in earnest yesterday, when the first sod of 'Temple Fortune Farm' (Finchley-road) was cut. **1908** *Westm. Gaz.* 18 Apr. 4/3 Some points of experience..to future town-planners. **1909** *Act 9 Edw. VII*, c. 44 (*title*) An Act to amend the Law relating to the Housing of the Working Classes, to provide for the making of Town Planning schemes [etc.]. *Ibid.* §76 This Act may be cited as the Housing, Town Planning, &c. Act, 1909. **1909** H. I. TRIGGS (*title*) Town Planning, Past, Present, and Possible. **1909** *Daily Chron.* 14 Apr. 6/1 It seems incredible that any town should allow a new suburb to be made without a preliminary 'town plan'. **1909** *Westm. Gaz.* 16 Apr. 12/4 We must learn..at least two lessons before we can hope to 'town plan' successfully. **1909** *Daily Chron.* 14 Sept. 3/3 The town-planned communities of the Continent. **1912** *Daily News* 3 Jan. 4/7 Birmingham will be able to submit to the Local Government Board for approval its first town planning scheme in a completed form. At present the city has secured permission to 'town plan' two or three sites.

town-plat to **-pump:** see TOWN 9, 10.

†**'townred.** *Obs. rare.* In 7 **townredd, town reed.** [f. TOWN *sb.* + -RED.] A township, a cluster of homesteads.

1603 OWEN *Pembrokeshire* (1892) 4 To make a Mappe for that sheere alone, and then he gaue a lardge space to that shere, and placed euerye Townredd farre of from other in distance. *Ibid.* 33 Theire buildinges are Englishe like, in Townreddes and villages, and not in seuerall and lone houses. **1617** *Calr. S.P., Irel.* 153 A late proclamation.. from the Lord Deputy for composing scattered houses into town reeds, and to be so planted..that two or three towns may build together upon the meares and meeting of their several town reeds. **1618** *Ibid.* 231 Every undertaker and native to build in town reedes.

town-reeve to **-row:** see TOWN 9 b, 10.

towns- in comb., as *townsfolk*, etc.: see TOWN 11.

'townscape. [f. TOWN *sb.*, after *landscape*.]

1. A picture or view of a town.

1880 LD. R. GOWER *Figure Painters Holland* 66 It is a landscape, or rather a townscape. **1889** HISSEY *Tour in Phaeton* 263 Some of the quaint townscapes (to invent another word) of our romantic, unspoilt English towns. **1959** *Sunday Times* 18 Jan. 16/8 These townscapes display, in short, the internal contradictions which also mark this painter's portraits of the aged rich. **1962** *Listener* 4 Oct. 515/2 The tranquillity of his land- and town-scapes.

2. The arrangement and overall appearance of the buildings, spaces, and other physical features of a town.

1937 *Evening News* 23 Apr. 10/4, I prefer a townscape with human figures to a landscape with trees. **1939** *Archit. Rev.* LXXXVI. 235/2 That universal Croydon towards which the townscapes of England are tending. **1953** *Ibid.* CXIV. 33 If I were asked to define Townscape I would say that one building is architecture but two buildings is Townscape. For as soon as two buildings are juxtaposed the art of Townscape is released. Such problems as the relationship between the building and the space between the buildings immediately assume importance. **1972** *Oxford Times* 27 Oct. 2/6 Mr John Ashdown, the city's conservation officer, said the monument would add to the townscape and be particularly attractive when seen by people walking up Turl Street. **1983** *Listener* 20 Jan. 27/3 The tall, usurping factor of Aurungzeb's mosque, dominating the townscape that some remember.

Hence **'townscaper,** one who plans townscapes; **'townscaping,** the planning of townscapes.

1949 *Archit. Rev.* CV. 249 Though the townscaper may welcome the contribution of street publicity to the urban scene there is one pitfall he must avoid—impropriety. **1953** *Ibid.* CXIV. 251 The townscaper's box of tricks—enclosure, escape, claustrophobia, surprise, delight, relief. **1959** *New Statesman* 16 May 686/2 All over the unbuilt ground surface of the Churchill Gardens estate there is evidence of an attitude indistinguishable from Townscaping. **1961** *Guardian* 18 Jan. 10/6 This cool new piece of townscaping.

Townsend ('taʊnzɛnd). *Physics.* The name of Sir John *Townsend* (1868–1957), Irish physicist, used *attrib.* with reference to certain phenomena and concepts related to his work on the conduction of electricity through gases, as **Townsend discharge,** a dark, low-current electric discharge in a gas that depends on an external source of ionization for its continuance.

1932 K. K. DARROW *Electr. Phenomena in Gases* ix. 293 The relative importance of the various processes of ionization and electron-expulsion..which figure in the 'Townsend discharge'. **1956** *Nature* 25 Feb. 391/1 The possibility of using the Townsend electron avalanche process in a gas in a stage-by-stage system to give a highly stable electron-multiplication factor. **1968** ROMANOWITZ & PUCKETT *Introd. Electronics* xiv. 563 As the voltage is increased from zero, the dark current (called Townsend current..) increases slowly until the voltage approaches that at which the tube operates with a glow discharge. **1978** J. H. INGOLD in Hirsh & Oskam *Gaseous Electronics* I. ii. 23 At extremely low currents, on the order of micro-amperes and less, the discharge is a Townsend discharge, with little or no visible light emanating from the discharge tube. **1982** *Nature* 28 Oct. 774/1 The main agents of discharges are electrons that participate in Townsend avalanches.

township ('taʊnʃɪp). [OE. *túnscipe*, f. *tún* (see TOWN) + *-scipe*, -SHIP. Cf., for sense, *landscipe*, and Ger. *dorfschaft*. After the OE. period the word was app. disused till 15th c: see sense 2.]

†**1.** In OE., The inhabitants or population of a *tún* or village collectively; the community dwelling in and occupying a *tún* (TOWN *sb.* 1). *Obs.*

c **890** tr. *Bæda's Hist.* v. xi. [x.] (1890) 416 Þa wæs he swiðe eorre; sende þa weord þider & heht ðone tunscipe ealne ofslean, & þone tun forbernan [*orig.* mittens occidit vicanos illos omnes, vicumque incendio consumpsit]. **962-3** *Laws K. Edgar* IV. c. 8 Cyðe hit þonne he ham cyme, and..mid his tunscipes ȝewitnysse on ȝemænre læse ȝebringe. ȝif he swa ne deð ær fif nihtum, cyðan hit þæs tunes men þam hundrodes ealdre. **1154** *O.E. Chron.* an. 1137 §4, ȝif twa men oþer iii coman ridend to an tun, al þe tunscipe fluȝæn fer heom. **1155-8** in *Calr. Charter Rolls* (1912) IV. 183 Homines suos liberos et quietos de..placitis et querelis et portmannesmot et tuncipesmot.

2. a. The inhabitants of a particular manor, parish, or division of a hundred, as a community, or in their corporate capacity. Now chiefly *Hist.*

1444 *Rolls of Parlt.* V. 111/1 [To] assesse well and duly every Tounship withinne the seid Hundredes. **1494** FABYAN *Chron.* VII. 575 (anno 1410) With prouycion y[t] euery towneshyp shuld kepe all poore people of theyr owne dwellers, whiche myght nat labour for theyr lyuynge. **1547** in *E. Anglian* May (1885) 69 Itm solde A[o] primo Ed. sexti Regis &c. by the Towneshippe and Churchewardens [of Beccles] so moche plate as amounteth to the Summe of xl *li.* **1593** SHAKS. *2 Hen. VI*, I. iii. 27 Alas Sir, I am but a poore Petitioner of our whole Towneship. **1628** WITHER *Brit. Rememb.* IV. 203 When halfe the Towneship, and the Hamlets nigh Are met to revell, at some Parish, by. **1817** W. SELWYN *Law Nisi Prius* (ed. 4) II. 773 The court held, that all the subjects of England, of common right, might fish in the sea,..and that therefore a prescription for it as appurtenant to a particular township was void.

b. Applied to the manor, parish, etc. itself, as a territorial division. Now chiefly *Hist.*

1414 *Rolls of Parlt.* IV. 571 The maner and Tounshipe of Chestreton. **1422** tr. *Secreta Secret., Priv. Priv.* 172 He desyrith more grete lordshuppe, othyr lytill rente, than a townshup of londe othyr a grete Some of catele to charlys appertenynge. **1491** *Act 7 Hen. VII*, c. 16 §1 Honours lordshippes townshippes maners londes..and all other hereditamentes. **1523** FITZHERB. *Husb.* §57 That there be no maner of syckenes amonge the cattell in that towneshyp or pasture that thou byest thy catel oute of. **1527** *Plumpton Corr.* (Camden) 227 For the right and intrest of one spring liing within the tewinship of Litle Ribston. **1610** HOLLAND *Camden's Brit.* (1637) 807 Hexham..a manour or Township belonging to the Archbishops of Yorke. **1670** PETTUS *Fodinæ Reg.* 33 All which are in the Township of Skibery Coed. *a* **1677** HALE *Prim. Orig. Man.* II. x. 234 In this Book are entred the Names of the Mannors or inhabited Townships, Boroughs and Cities,..the Number of Plough-Lands that each contains, and the Number of the Inhabitants upon them. **1819** SCOTT *Ivanhoe* xxv, A less orderly and a worse armed force, consisting of the Saxon inhabitants of the neighbouring township.

c. *spec.* Each of the local divisions of, or districts comprised in, a large original parish, each containing a village or small town, usually having its own church (formerly a chapel of the mother church of the original parish, whence such divisions were also known ecclesiastically as *chapelries*).

Township in this sense is chiefly retained in the north of England for the ancient divisions of such original parishes as Crosthwaite, Grasmere, Windermere, and Kendal, e.g. the townships of Borrowdale, Langdale, Rydal, and Ambleside; but it is applied in the Ordnance maps also to the ancient divisions of such original parishes as Cumnor and St. Giles', Camberwell, which for most purposes are now distinct parishes and are usually so called.

1540 *Test. Ebor.* (Surtees) VI. 117 Beinge of the towneshipe of Witley. **1662** *Act 14 Chas. II*, c. 12 §21 That all and every the poore..persons within every Township or Village within the severall Counties aforesaid shall from and after the passing of this Act be maintained..and sett on worke within the several and respective Towneship and Village..and that there shall be yearely chosen and appointed..twoe or more Overseers of the Poore within every of the said Townships or Villages. **1764** BURN *Poor Laws* 111 The head of a township or village is the constable; and there are many townships in a parish wherein there is no churchwarden. **1846** M[c]CULLOCH *Anc. Brit. Empire* (1854) I. 141 In the northern counties, where the parishes sometimes embrace 30 or 40 square miles, the poor laws, the due administration or which must always depend on an intimate knowledge of the situation and character of every one applying for relief, could not be properly carried into effect. To remedy this inconvenience, an act was passed in the 13th of Charles II, permitting townships and villages, though not entire parishes, severally and distinctly to maintain their own poor. Hence townships in the north of England may be regarded as divisions subordinate to parishes; and are, in practice, as distinctly limited as if they were separate parishes. **1891** J. P. EARWAKER *Manch. Constables' Accts.* I. Inrod. 17 The two constables whose proceedings are recorded in the following pages, were appointed for the Township of Manchester alone; but, as that then embraced the whole of the town, they had entire charge of the town. **1906** S. & B. WEBB *Eng. Local Govt.* I. ii. 70 The great parish of Manchester, which extended over an area of quite 54 square miles, included no fewer than thirty semi-independent townships—one of them having, like the whole parish, the name of Manchester.

3. *transf.* Often rendering L. *pagus*, Gr. δῆμος (DEME), and thus applied to independent or self-governing towns or villages of ancient Greece, Italy, and other lands, and sometimes to foreign towns or villages of mediæval or modern times.

1602 FULBECKE *Pandectes* 57 So likewise *Pagi*, towneships, are deriued of the Doricke word *πάγα*, which signifieth a fountaine, and in the Atticall dialect is *πήγη*. **1681** NEVILE *Plato Rediv.* 74 The Swisses consist of Thirteen Soveraignties; some Cities..and some Provinces which have but a Village for their head Township. **1798** W. TAYLOR in *Monthly Mag.* V. 3 Now, the land of Cush (Genesis x. 7,) comprehended the five subdivisions or townships of Seba, Havilah, Sabtha, Raamah, and Sabthechah. **1838** THIRLWALL *Greece* II. xi. 11 The incorporation of several scattered townships in one city, such as took place in Attica. **1841** ELPHINSTONE *Hist. India* I. 39 His internal administration is to be conducted by a chain of civil officers, consisting of lords of single townships or villages, lords of ten towns, lords of 100, and lords of 1000 towns. **1846** GROTE *Greece* II. viii. II. 587 Rescuing the Arcadian townships from their dependence on Sparta. **1872** YEATS *Growth Comm.* 301 An insignificant township named Calcutta. **1905** *Expositor* Feb. 81 A Jebusite township existed around or beside the stronghold Zion. **1908** S. A. COOK *Relig. Anc. Palestine* i. 8 The small townships of Palestine and Syria—the average city was a small fortified site surrounded by dwellings, sometimes with an outer wall.

4. *Sc.* A farm held in joint tenancy.

1813 J. HEDRICK *Agric. Surv. Forfar.* 561 A township is a farm occupied by two or more farmers, in common, or in separate lots, who reside in a straggling hamlet, or village. **1884** MARQ. OF LORNE in *Pall Mall G.* 10 May 1/2 Recommending that the State should prop the fast vanishing feudal tenure of the 'township' of the crofter. **1886** SIR K. MACKENZIE *ibid.* 3 Mar. 11/2 Its Gaelic equivalent 'Baile'..designates a farm held by a number of joint tenants, but it also designates a farm held by an individual tenant... To the Gaelic language, the distinction between farm and township is unknown; and the illusions which seem to hang round this word township would be dispelled if it were realized that it merely means a farm held in joint tenancy by a greater or less number of persons. **1901** *Scotsman* 4 Mar. 7/2 They found..about forty men from the township of Lemreway [in Lewis] outside ready to resist.

5. *U.S.* and *Canada.* A division of a county having certain corporate powers of local administration; the same that in New England is called a town (TOWN *sb.* 6 a).

In the newer states, in which the divisions were laid off by government survey, a township is a division six miles square, and is so called even when still unsettled. The name is similarly used in the western provinces of Canada, from Ontario to British Columbia, and in Eastern Quebec and Prince Edward Island.

1685 PENN *Further Acc. Pennsylv.* 5 We do settle in the way of *Townships* or *Villages*, each of which contains 5000 Acres in square, and at least Ten Families. **1714** S. SEWALL *Diary* 23 Feb., This Court a large Township, of 12 miles square, is granted near Wadchuset. **1775** J. ADAMS in *Fam. Lett.* (1876) 120 The division of our..counties into townships..gives every man an opportunity of showing and improving that education which he received at college or at school. **1779** *Hist. Europe* in *Ann. Reg.* 91 The settlement of Wyoming consisted of eight townships, each containing a square of five miles. **1801** *Farmer's Mag.* Apr. 164 Method of clearing New Land,..as practised in several parts of New Hampshire, particularly in the Township of Dartmouth. **1824** SYD. SMITH *Wks.* (1859) II. 45/2 All the public lands ..are divided into townships of six miles square, by lines running with the cardinal points, and consequently crossing each other at right angles. **1866** J. E. H. SKINNER *After the Storm* I. 85 A 'township' is here a territorial division like a parish with us, and need not necessarily contain any houses. **1871** *Athenæum* 27 May 660 From 20 to 30 feet of pure graphite are stated to exist on the Ottawa river, in the township of Buckingham. **1888** BRYCE *Amer. Commw.* II. II. xl. 91 *note*, A town or township means..generally in the United States, a small rural district, as opposed to a city. It is a community which has not received representative municipal government. **1899** CROSSKILL *Prince Edward Isl.* (1904) 16 The parish lines are but little recognized, the more general sub-division being by lots or townships, of which there are 67 running numerically from west to east. **1912** *Province of Quebec for Brit. Emigr.* 13 The Eastern townships have also a well deserved reputation as a grazing country.

6. a. In Australia and New Zealand, a site laid out prospectively for a town, meanwhile often consisting of a few 'shanties' grouped around a railway station, store, hotel, post office, or the like; a village or hamlet. (Cf. the *town-site* (TOWN *sb.* 10) of U.S. and Canada.)

1802 BARRINGTON *Hist. N.S. Wales* x. 419 The timber of 120 acres was cut down..a township marked out, and some few huts built. **1857** R. B. PAUL *Lett. from Canterbury, N.Z.* iv. 72 Malvern Hills, where Mr Cass thinks there is a site suited for a township. **1861** MRS. MEREDITH *Over the Straits* II. 40 It used to seem to me a strange colonial anomaly to call a very small village a 'township', and a much larger one a 'town'. But the former is the term applied to the lands reserved in various places for future towns. **1890** *Melbourne Argus* 14 June 4/2 Will you come into the township to-night? **1892** A. SUTHERLAND *Elem. Geog. Brit. Col.* xiii. 276 Villages, which are always called 'townships', spring up suddenly round a railway station or beside some country inn. **1911** W. H. KOEBEL *In Maoriland Bush* xviii. 241 Half an hour later the street of the township opens out before the rider. **1977** *N.Z. Herald* 8 Jan. 4-1/5 (Advt.), From Henderson Township take Swanson Rd for 1 mile.

b. In South Africa, an area set aside for non-White occupation.

1934 *Lovedale Sol-fa Leaflet* No. 17.4 When the Bantu Township of Nancefield or Klipspruit (eleven miles West of Johannesburg) was first settled as a Suburb of the Rand Municipality, the late Enoch Sontonga..was a teacher in one of the Methodist Mission Schools. **1946** P. ABRAHAMS *Mine Boy* viii. 98 This side of the township had mostly Coloured people. The other side was where the native people were. **1964** L. NKOSI *Rhythm of Violence* 15 Which black township would you go to? **1971** *Sunday Express* (Johannesburg) 28 Mar. 6/1 The non-Whites..are not going to be satisfied much longer with leading third-rate lives in third-rate townships. **1984** *Observer* 9 Dec. 12/2 The flood [of people] has overflowed the inadequate African townships built by apartheid planners.

†7. The state or condition of a town; also, a jocular title for a town. *Obs. rare.*

1665 SIR T. HERBERT *Trav.* (1677) 193 They..have little or no civility save in Zagathai, where they associate in Township. **1780** *Mirror* No. 105 ¶2 Such people are apt to assume in conversation [a consequence], which, I think, goes beyond the just prerogative of township, and is a very unfair encroachment on the natural rights of their friends.. in the country. **1809** MALKIN *Gil Blas* II. ix. ¶1 Olmédo looks like a..town. I beg its township's pardon, replied the barber.

8. By some 19th c. historical writers, adopted to designate what they consider to have been the simplest form of local or social organization in primitive Old English times.

This modern use of the term does not agree with the OE.; it appears to be founded on a confusion of OE. *tún* and *túnscipe* (sense 1), and the carrying back into early Anglo-Saxon or Teutonic times of the ME. sense 2, 2 b. (See W. J. Ashley *The Anglo-Saxon 'Township'* in *Q. Jrnl. Economics* (Harvard) VIII. Apr. 1894.)

1832 SIR F. PALGRAVE *Eng. Commw.* I. iii. 65 (*marg.* Anglo-Saxon state composed of Townships.) Ascending in the analysis of the Anglo-Saxon State, the first and primary element appears to be the community, which, in England, during the Saxon period, was denominated the Town, or Township. **1853** CREASY *Eng. Const.* iv. 45. **1867** PEARSON *Hist. Eng.* i. 16 The stronger and more warlike tribes secured themselves from surprise in townships or camps,.. fortified with felled timber and a ditch. **1874** STUBBS *Const. Hist.* I. v. §39 The unit of the constitutional machinery, the simplest form of social organisation, is the township, the *villata* or *vicus*. It may represent the original allotment of the smallest subdivision of the free community, or the settlement of the kindred colonising on their own account, or the estate of the great proprietor who has a tribe of dependents. **1881** GREEN *Making of Eng.* iv. 180. **1889** G. E. HOWARD *Local Instit. Hist. U.S.* I. i. 18 In the early records of English history the *tunscipe* or township, appears as the lowest form of self government and the primary division of the state. **1910** J. W. HARPER *Soc. Ideal* xxi. 243 The township is older than the manor..English feudalism destroyed the territorial organisation and reared itself on the ruins of the townships.

9. *attrib.* and *Comb.*, esp. in senses 5, 6: **township bridge, drain, road**, a bridge, etc. made and kept up by the township; **township farm** = sense 4; **township trustee** (*U.S.*), a member of a committee elected to administer the affairs of a township.

1836 *New-Yorker* 30 Apr. 92/1 The vote (by general ticket) for Township Trustees is stated as follows. **1868** *Rep. U.S. Commissioner Agric.* (1869) 43 Harrison County, Ind. —The township trustee of Corydon has paid out to farmers, for loss of sheep by dogs..three hundred and ninety-eight dollars. **1888** BRYCE *Amer. Commw.* II. II. xlviii. 235 *note*, Any county desiring to forsake township organization may do so by a vote of the electors. **1904** *Daily Chron.* 19 Oct. 8/3 A simple and traditional dramatisation of some scene in early English township life. **1910** W. L. MATHIESON *Awakening Scot.* vi. 276 The type of agriculture..is still that of the township farm.

town-side, -site, etc.: see TOWN 10.

townsman (ˈtaʊnzmən). Forms: see TOWN. [f. *town's*, genitive of TOWN + MAN *sb.*[1]]

†1. OE. (*túnesman*). One who lives in a *tún*; a villager, a villein. *Obs.*

962-3 *Laws of Edgar* IV. c. 13 And ic wille, þæt tunesmen and heora hyrdas habban þas ylcan smeaȝunge on minum cucum orfe and on minra þeȝena, ealswa hy habbað on heora aȝenum. **1028-60** *Laws Northumbld. Priests* c. 59 ȝif hwilc tunesman æniȝne pæniȝ forhele oððe forhæbbe, ȝilde se landrica þone pæniȝ and nime ænne oxan æt ðammen.

2. A man who lives in a town or city; a citizen: esp. as distinguished from a countryman, a stranger, a soldier of the garrison, or other such.

1433 in *Hist. Sudbury* (1896) 125 A Supplicacon of the Maior and Tonsmen of Sudbury to the B. of Norwich. **1519** *Coventry Leet Bk.* 666 Iff eny fforener or Townesman fforstall eny Corne within the libertie of this Cetie of Couentre or it com into the markett. **1577** tr. *Bullinger's Decades* (1592) 144 Of the countrie men as well as of the townes-men. **1615** G. SANDYS *Trav.* 6 Here a garrison is kept; supplyed by the townesmen. **1745** *De Foe's Eng. Tradesman* xxvi. (1841) I. 265 She being a good honest townsman's daughter. **1749** *Little Cornard (Suff.) Overseers' Acc.* (MS.), Paid to Sarah Flower by the order of the Townes men that She Laid out. **1863** H. COX *Instit.* III. ix. 727 The whole body of resident trading townsmen.

b. A man of one's own or the same town; a fellow-townsman. Usually after *possessive*. Cf. COUNTRYMAN 2.

1601 A. DENT *Pathway to Heaven* (1617) 18 For me thinks you go too far, you goe beyond your learning in this, that you condemne good neighbours, and good Townes-men. **1715-20** POPE *Iliad* XVIII. 578 There, in the forum swarm a numerous train, The subject of debate, a towns-man slain. **1838** THIRLWALL *Greece* II. xv. 258 A citizen of Abdera advised his townsmen to offer a solemn thanks-giving to the gods.

c. An ordinary citizen or resident of a university town as distinguished from a *gownsman* or member of the university; cf. TOWN *sb.* 5 d.

1768 WILKES *Corr.* (1805) III. 254 Only another proof that the townsmen of Oxford have always hated the university. **1823** LAMB *Elia* Ser. II. *Poor Relations*, The distance between the gownsmen and the townsmen, as they are called..is carried to an excess that [etc.]. **1889** JESSOPP *Coming of Friars* vi. 273 The townsmen under great provocation had seized three of the gownsmen.

3. *New England.* = SELECTMAN.

1656 in T. Dwight *Trav. New Eng.* (1821) I. 343 [In 1656] town's-men [(or select-men) were chosen]. **1696-1715** *Maryland Laws* iv. (1723) 11 Any Action..arising between the Townsmen or Freemen of the said Town. *a* **1817** T. DWIGHT *Trav. New Eng.* (1821) I. 243 At this meeting the inhabitants choose, not exceeding seven men, inhabitants, able, discreet and of good conversation, to be Select-men, or Townsmen, to take care of the order, and prudential affairs of the town.

townspeople (ˈtaʊnzˌpiːp(ə)l). Also 7 **townes people**. [f. as prec. + PEOPLE. Orig. two words; now written as one.] People or inhabitants of a town or towns; townsmen and townswomen; townsfolk. (Usually const. as *pl.*)

1648 CROMWELL *Let.* 25 Nov., And without money the stubborn towns-people will not trust them for the worth of a penny. **1691** in *Somerset & Dorset N. & Q.* June (1905) 263 Many died as also many Townes people of y[e] same distemper. **1833** MARRYAT *P. Simple* xxi, We had no parole, and but little communication with the townspeople. **1849** MACAULAY *Hist. Eng.* v. I. 573 The town's people repaired to the cliffs and gazed long and anxiously. **1872** BAGEHOT *Physics & Pol.* iv. 132 The place was crowded and a whole townspeople looking on.

b. People inhabiting the same town; fellow-townsmen. (Usually after *possessive*.)

1823 *Examiner* 761/1 They are townspeople, we believe, the native place of both being.. Edinburgh. **1870** EMERSON *Soc. & Solit.* iii. 45 Not by his friends or his townspeople or his contemporaries.

town-stocks, townswoman: see TOWN 9, 11.

Townsville (ˈtaʊnzvɪl). The name of a town on the coast of Queensland, Australia, used *attrib.* in **Townsville lucerne, stylo** [abbrev. *Stylosanthes* (see below and STYLO-)] to designate an annual or perennial leguminous plant with trifoliate leaves, *Stylosanthes humilis*, now used as a pasture plant in northern Australia and other tropical regions.

1937 *Jrnl. Council Sci. & Industr. Res.* (Australia) X. 201 The so-called wild or Townsville lucerne.. was introduced accidentally into north Queensland. **1968** *Times* 23 Jan. (Austral. Suppl.) p. xiv/4 Several decades ago a plant, now called Townsville lucerne, drifted ashore from a South American ship at the port of Townsville and took root. **1977** A. V. BOGDAN *Trop. Pasture & Fodder Plants* 402 *Stylosanthes humilis* was known as Townsville lucerne until about 1968–9 when the Queensland Herbage Plant Liaison Committee recommended that the name should be changed to Townsville stylo in order to avoid confusion with species of *Medicago*.

ˈtown-ˈtalk. The common talk or gossip of the people of a town; the subject or matter of such talk or gossip.

1654–5 CROMWELL *Speech to Parl. 22 Jan.* 23 If it be not folly in Me to listen to Town-talk, such things have been proposed. **1667** PEPYS *Diary* 26 Apr., All the town-talk is now-a-days of her extravagancies. **1694** CONGREVE *Double-Dealer* III. i, You'll ruin me if you take such publick Notice of it, it will be a Town-Talk. **1712** SWIFT *Jrnl. to Stella* 26 Mar., The news of the French desiring a cessation of arms .. was but town talk. **1848** THACKERAY *Van. Fair* lv, It was town-talk for at least three days. **1867** AUG. J. E. WILSON *Vashti* xii, Why should she taboo society, and make herself the town-talk?

town-tallow to **-wait:** see TOWN 9, 10.

ˈtown-ˈwall. The wall of a fortified town.

c **1400** *Destr. Troy* 10746 The troiens in toures, & on toun walles, Laidon spies specially. **1480** *Coventry Leet Bk.* 447 Enploye hit to oder reparacions of þe seid town wall. **1548** UDALL, etc. *Erasm. Par. Acts* ix. 36 They.. by nyght let hym downe by a corde of the towne walles, in a basket. **1649** MILTON *Eikon.* viii. Wks. (1847) 294/1 The king much incensed proclaims him traitor before the town walls. **1843** *Penny Cycl.* XXVII. 456/1 The town-wall of Worms.

townward (ˈtaʊnwəd), *adv.* (*a.*) [f. TOWN *sb.* + -WARD.] Towards or in the direction of the town. (Originally *to the townward.*)

1434 *Indenture Fotheringhey* in Dugdale *Monast.* (1846) VI. 1414/2 A dore yn the west side.. to the town-ward. **1633** T. STAFFORD *Pac. Hib.* II. xii. (1821) 362 The Irish.. beat the Spaniards from their ground to the Towneward. **1808** SCOTT *Marm.* III. xxxi, He heard.. The foot-tramp of a flying steed, Come town-ward rushing on. **1846** LONGF. in *Life* (1891) II. 52 A beautiful pile of granite.. looking townward and seaward.

b. *adj.* Going or directed toward the town.

1806 J. GRAHAME *Birds Scot.* 35 Follow his townward steps. **1833** L. RITCHIE *Wand. by Loire* 184 Ditches.. still remain on the townward side. **1864** LONGF. in *Life* (1891) III. 34 Walking.. along the accustomed townward walk,.. I met the East Wind. **1893** *Chicago Advance* 27 July, Evidence of the townward drift of the people.

c. *Comb.*

1870 MORRIS *Earthly Par.* III. IV. 288 In a fair-hung townward-looking bower.

ˈtownwards, *adv.* [-WARDS.] = prec.

1895 P. HEMINGWAY *Out of Egypt* II. 175, I stood watching a vessel in the harbour, that stared townwards with a hundred unblinking eyes. **1908** *Daily Chron.* 15 Feb. 7/5 A West London [cycling] club, recently returning.. townwards, through Brentford.

town-watch to **-woman:** see TOWN 9, 10.

towny (ˈtaʊnɪ), *a.* and *sb. colloq.* Also **-ey, -ie.** Cf. TOWNEE *a.* and *sb.* [f. TOWN *sb.* + -Y.]

A. *adj.* Of, pertaining to, or characteristic of the town; townish.

1837 *New Monthly Mag.* L. 248 His acquired habits were of the town, towny. **1857** E. M. WHITTY *Friends in Bohemia* I. 211 Are you not weary of this towney life? **1908** *Treasury* Feb. 507 A house so towny and stylish, compared with our farm homesteads.

B. *sb.* **1.** A town-brĕd man; *spec.* a Londoner.

1827 P. CUNNINGHAM *N.S. Wales* (ed. 2) II. 227 If we could not say we had committed as many [robberies] as these townies, they would look upon us with contempt. *Ibid.* 230 Many surgeons find that by putting all the old townies into double irons whenever robberies begin to prevail, a cessation soon takes place. **1934** [see BUSHY *sb.*]. **1942** C. BARRETT *On Wallaby* i. 13 A sundowner's life was better than that of the 'townie' who had to work hard for a living and wear clean collars and shirts. **1959** I. & P. OPIE *Lore & Lang. Schoolch.* iv. 62 The 'towney' touches the leaf gingerly. **1972** P. LIVELY *Driftway* vi. 85 He was a real townie, didn't care for walking at all. **1984** *Times* 13 Feb. 2/8 Farmers know and care far more about conservation than meddlesome townies.

2. *U.S. university slang.* A townsman as distinct from a member of the university.

1852 *Deseret News* (Salt Lake City) 7 Aug. 1/1 'O, nothing,' replied the 'towney'. **1853** *Yale Lit. Mag.* XIX. 2 (Thornton) The genus by the German students denominated 'Philistines', by the Cantabs ignominiously called 'Snobs', and which custom here has named 'Townies'. **1869** W. T. WASHBURNE *Fair Harvard* 54 (ibid.) One beholds the conscious 'towney' on his evening promenade.

b. *N. Amer. Circus slang.* A town-dweller, as opp. to a person travelling with a circus or carnival.

1937 [see REUB, RUBE]. **1951** *N.Y. Times Bk. Rev.* 8 Apr. 7/5 A fight [of carnival workers] with the townies. **1971** *Islander* (Victoria, B.C.) 19 Dec. 6/4 Everything had been set up for the show and tickets were being sold when several 'townies' attempted to crash the gate.

3. A fellow-townsman or townswoman. *slang.*

1834 *Knickerbocker* IV. 279 Five or six fellows, whom I knew were friends and 'townies' of his. **1865** *Morn. Star* 18 July, She is a 'towny' (of the same town) of mine, and I want to see her safe home. **1869** *Routledge's Ev. Boy's Ann.* 347 Then you and me's 'towneys' it seems. **1892** STEVENSON & OSBOURNE *Wrecker* xii, A townie of mine was lost down this way, in a coal-ship.

to-wond(e, pa. t. of TO-WEND *v. Obs.*

†**to-worth,** *v. Obs. rare.* [ME. *to-wurðen*, f. TO-[2] + *wurðen*:—OE. *weorðan* to become.] *intr.* To come to nought; to perish.

c **1205** LAY. 20744 For betere us is on londe Mid monscipe to liggen þene we þus here For hungere to-wurðen.

to-wowe, -writhe, -wry: see TO- *pref.*[2] 1.

tow-path (ˈtəʊpɑːθ, -æ-). [f. TOW *v.*[1] + PATH.] A path by the side of a canal or navigable river for use in towing; = *towing-path* (TOWING *vbl. sb.*[1] b).

1788 G. WASHINGTON *Diary* 2 June (1925) III. 361 A tow path on the Maryland side. **1846** WORCESTER, *Tow-path*, a narrow path travelled by horses in dragging boats along a canal. *Baldwin.* **1882** R. MACKENZIE *America* 305 He had begun life on the towpath as a driver of mules. **1910** *Blackw. Mag.* May 634/1 The towpath was knee-deep in water.

tow-pung, ? error or misprint for *tom-pung*, orig. form of PUNG *sb.*[2], q.v., quot. 1851.

towrd, towres, towret, -ette, obs. forms of TOWARD, TOURS, TURRET.

tow-rope (ˈtəʊrəʊp). [f. TOW *v.*[1] + ROPE *sb.*[1]] A rope (hawser, cable, or the like) used in towing.

1743 BULKELEY & CUMMINS *Voy. S. Seas* 119 We called to them to take hold of a Towe-Rope, but they refused. **1801** JEFFERSON *Writ.* (ed. Ford) VIII. 75 You will follow the bark of liberty only by the help of a tow-rope. **1865** DICKENS *Mut. Fr.* III. viii, The tow-rope was slackened by a turn of the stream.

Hence **ˈtow-ˌroping,** in railway-shunting, the drawing of a vehicle by an engine on a parallel line of rails by means of a rope connecting the two.

An illegal practice. See PROPPING *vbl. sb.* 3 for quots.

tow-row (ˈtaʊˈraʊ), *sb.* and *a.* [Reduplicated or extended form of ROW *sb.*[3]; orig. *dial.*]

A. *sb.* An uproar, hubbub, noisy disturbance, din.

1877 *Holderness Gloss., Tow-row*, a confusion, or noisy disturbance. **1886** STEVENSON *Kidnapped* iv, A blinding flash,.. and hard upon the heels of it, a great tow-row of thunder. **1894** CROCKETT *Raiders* (ed. 3) 15 Then.. came a great towrow of laughter. **1894** MAX PEMBERTON *Sea-Wolves* xxii, For a long space they kept up the tow-row and the din.

†**B.** *adj.* Intoxicated (? 'drunk and disorderly'). *slang. Obs.*

1709 STEELE & SWIFT *Tatler* No. 71 ¶8 He that drinks till he stares, is no more Tow-Row, but Honest.

So **tow-row** *v.*, *intr.* (*a*) to make a tow-row; (*b*) *dial.* (see quot. 1854). Hence **tow-rowing** *vbl. sb.*

1840 THACKERAY *Barber Cox* Mar., Directly the tow-rowing began, off went Trumpeter like a thunder-bolt. **1854** MISS BAKER *Northampt. Gloss., Tow-rowing*, cleaning out dirty and disorderly places. 'I've been tow-rowing about all day among the dust'. **1899** MRS. E. KENNARD *Morals Midlands* xxvii. 240 The hounds were tow-rowing all round the covert.

towrpyke, a winding stair: see TURNPIKE.

†**ˈtowry-ˈlowry.** *dial.* (Cf. TIRRA-LIRRA.)

1632 BROME *North. Lasse* I. ii, And then towry, lowry, faith, my noble Governor, and I. **1878** *Cumberld. Gloss., Towry lowry*, all in disorder.

towsell, obs. form of TOLSEL, TOLZEY.

towser (ˈtaʊzə(r)), *sb.* Also 7 **towzer, touzer,** 9 **touser.** [f. TOUSE *v.* + -ER[1]; with senses c, d, e cf. *thumper, whopper*, etc.] One who or that which touses. **a.** (with capital T). A common name for a large dog, such as was used to bait bears or bulls; also *transf.* of a person.

1678 OTWAY *Friendship in F.* IV. i, Fresh Game; that great Towser has started it already. **1681** *Trial S. Colledge* 59 Mr. Char... it was the Pictures of the Tantivies and the Towzer [Roger L'Estrange]. **1681** T. FLATMAN *Heraclitus Ridens* No. 30 (1713) I. 197 *Earn.* What Papers? Did he mean the Towzers, and the Gallows, and the Broom, for which he was so famous? **1682** N. N. (*title*) The Heu and Cry: or, a Relation of the Travels of the Devil and Towzer, Through all the Earthly Territorys, and the Infernal Region. **1684** OTWAY *Atheist* III. i, Never was seen so termagant a Towzer. **1696** tr. *Du Mont's Voy. Levant* 257 Poor Towzer was condemn'd to be Cudgel'd to Death. **1881** A. McLACHLAN in *Mod. Sc. Poets* II. 261 Ahint him Towser wags his tail.

†**b.** The five of trumps in the game of gleek. *Obs.*

1680 COTTON *Compl. Gamester* vi. (ed. 2) 65 The fifth [is called] Towser, the sixth Tumbler, which if in hand Towser is five and Tumbler six, and so double if turn'd up. **1688** R. HOLME *Armoury* III. xvi. (Roxb.) 73/2 Towser, is the fifth of the trumps.

†**c.** A large ship. *Obs.* **d.** A large coarse apron. *dial.* **e.** A rough or energetic person. *dial.*

c. 1690 *Pagan Prince* xxix. 81 Now the Belgians, having lost.. some three or four more of their biggest Towzers, made all the Sail they could to their own Coasts.

d. 1865 R. HUNT *Pop. Rom. W. Eng.* Ser. II. 244 The Touser is a large apron or wrapper to come quite round and keep the under-garments clean. **1882** JAGO *Cornw. Gloss., Touser*, a large coarse apron for kitchen use.

e. 1901 E. PHILLPOTTS *Striking Hours* 222 A wonnerful bowerly maid her was, an' a towser for work, an' 'mazin' even-tempered tu. **1901** R. M. F. WATSON *Closeburn* xiii. 221 A certain big, uncouth, unhallowed 'towser' named Tibbie Murdoch.

Hence **ˈtowser, -zer** *v.* (*nonce-wd.*), *trans.* to worry as a dog does.

c **1680** HICKERINGILL *Hist. Whiggism* I. Wks. 1716 I. 37 If they get a piece of a Text by the end.. they do so tear it, and towze it, and towzer it.. that they lose themselves.

towst, towsy: see TOUST, TOUSY.

towster (ˈtəʊstə(r)). *nonce-wd.* [f. TOW *v.*[1] + -STER.] = TOWER *sb.*[2]

1885 WARREN & CLEVERLY *Wand. 'Beetle'* 24 The towsters came to a halt.

†**towˈtaw,** *v. Obs. rare*[−1]. [f. TOW *sb.*[1] + TAW *v.*[1]] *trans.* To scutch (flax). Cf. TOW *v.*[3]

1649 BLITHE *Eng. Improv. Impr.* (1653) 260 Kilne-drying it, then breaking and towtawing it, then hetchelling and dressing it up.

towtch, obs. form of TOUCH.

towy (ˈtəʊɪ), *a.* [f. TOW *sb.*[1] + -Y.] Like or of the nature of tow.

1601 HOLLAND *Pliny* XIX. i. II. 4 You shall know by the skin or rind thereof if it be loose and readie to depart from the towie substance of the stem. **1673** GREW *Anat. Trunks* I. ii. §30 The Lignous and Towy Parts of all Plants are Tubulary. **1858** *Sat. Rev.* 21 Aug. 184/2 Painted.. with bullet eyes, vermilion cheeks, towy locks, and pudgy limbs. **1881** *Gard. Chron.* XVI. 654/3 Its leaves.. produce a soft towy herbage.

towylle, obs. form of TOWEL.

†**towyth,** obs. erroneous form of THOUGHT.

c **1430** *Hymns Virg.* 121 We be sorry þatt we dede agayn þi wille Or with towyth or with dede.

towze, towzer: see TOUSE, TOWSER.

†**towze-match.** *Obs. rare.* [? f. TOUSE *v.* 4 + MATCH *sb.*[2] 2 b.] 'Match' made of 'toused' or teased hemp or other fibrous material.

1627 CAPT. SMITH *Seaman's Gram.* ii. 13 Okum is old Ropes torne in peeces like Towze Match, or Hurds of Flax. **1630** —— *Trav. & Adv.* v. 8 Over that a strong Searcloth, then over all a good thicknesse of Towze-match well tempered with oyle of Linseed.

tox (tɒks), *sb. Zool.* [ad. Gr. τόξον TOXON[1].] A sponge-spicule having the form of a double curved rod, like a Cupid's bow; = TOXASPIRE.

1909 in *Cent. Dict. Supp.*

†**tox,** *v. Obs.* ? *slang.* Short for *intoxicate*. Hence †**toxed, toxt,** †**ˈtoxing** *ppl. adjs.*

1635 HEYWOOD *Philocothon.* i. 3 When their more sober consciences can Iustifie against their toxed Insolence. *Ibid.* iv. 29 Addicted to strong and toxing drinkes. **1637** —— *Dial.* iv. Wks. 1874 VI. 191 Braines well toxt with wine.

tox-[1], combining form, repr. TOXI- or TOXO-[2] before a vowel. ‖**toxæmia** (tɒkˈsiːmɪə), also anglicized **toxemy** [Gr. αἷμα blood, after *anæmia*, etc.], a morbid condition of the blood caused by a toxin; blood-poisoning; hence **toxæmic** (-ˈiːmɪk) *a.*, pertaining to or affected with toxæmia. **toxalbumin** (-ælˈbjuːmɪn), also **-en,** a poisonous or pathogenic albumin or protein produced by bacteria; a protein toxin; hence **toxalˈbumic** *a.*, pertaining to or caused by a toxalbumin; so **toˈxalbumose,** a poisonous albumose. **ˈtoxamine** (-əmaɪn), a poisonous amine. **toxanæmia** (-əˈniːmɪə), anæmia caused by the action of a poison, usually a ptomaine.

1860 MAYNE *Expos. Lex.*, **Toxæmia*,.. a contaminated state of the blood, as in syphilis; poisoned blood; toxemy. **1881** *Trans. Obstet. Soc. Lond.* XXII. 283 There was a dangerous state of toxæmia. **1876** BRISTOWE *The. & Pract. Med.* (1878) 124 Which so often.. cause *toxæmic symptoms. **1899** *Allbutt's Syst. Med.* VIII. 418 The post-febrile insanities are divisible into two classes—the purely anæmic, and the toxæmic. **1902** *Buck's Handbk. Med. Sc.* V.

33 As the effects of other chemical or *toxalbumic poisons manifest themselves as a psychosis. **1890** *Pall Mall G.* 26 Apr. 6/3 *Toxalbumen is said to be the excretion of a bacillus of diphtheria. **1892** *Pop. Sc. Monthly* XLI. 633 It neutralizes the potent toxalbumin of tetanus in test-tube cultures. **1896** *Allbutt's Syst. Med.* I. 767 Brieger and Fränkel then described a proteid poison which they obtained from cultures of the tetanus bacilli and named toxalbumin. **1902** R. MUIR in *Encycl. Brit.* XXVI. 64/2 Such a powder gives a proteid reaction, and is no doubt largely composed of albumoses, hence the name *toxalbumoses has been applied. **1897** *Allbutt's Syst. Med.* III. 735 Certain specimens of cheese contain a *toxamine, termed by its discoverer, Professor Vaughan, 'tyrotoxicon'. **1891** *Cent. Dict.*, **Toxanemia, Toxanæmia.* **1899** *Syd. Soc. Lex.*, *Toxanæmia, Toxanemia*, anæmia caused by the actions of ptomaines.

tox-[2]: see TOXO-[1].

toxaphene ('tɒksəfiːn). *Chem.* [f. TOX-[1] + *-a-* + *cam)phene* s.v. CAMPH-.] Chlorinated camphene used chiefly as an insecticide for pests of crops and livestock.

1947 *Jrnl. Econ. Entomol.* XL. 79/1 The chlorinated bicyclic terpene, now designated *Toxaphene* is an insecticide developed cooperatively by Hercules Powder Company and University of Delaware entomologists. **1975** *Nature* 9 Oct. 475/2 Over the past ten years toxaphene has been used in the USA in larger quantities than any other insecticide.

toxarch ('tɒksɑːk). *Anc. Gr. Hist.* [ad. Gr. τόξαρχος 'lord of the bow', captain of the archers, f. τόξον bow + -αρχος ruler.] The title of the captain of the city-guard of mercenaries at Athens.

1828 [G. C. LEWIS] tr. *Böckh's Publ. Econ. Athens* I. 278 The public slaves who composed the city-guard..are generally called bow-men (τοξόται), or, from the native country of the majority, Scythians... Their officers had the name of Toxarchs (τόξαρχοι).

toxaspire ('tɒksəspaɪə(r)). *Zool.* [irreg. (for **toxospire*) f. Gr. τόξο-ν bow + σπεῖρα coil, SPIRE.] In sponges, a form of microsclere or flesh-spicule: see quots. Hence **toxa'spiral** *a.*, pertaining to or of the form of a toxaspire.

1887 SOLLAS in *Encycl. Brit.* XXII. 417/2 A turn and a part of a turn of a spiral of somewhat higher pitch than that of a sigmaspire gives the *toxaspire*. **1888** —— in *Challenger Rep.* XXV. p. lxii, *Toxaspire.*—A spiral rod in which the twist a little exceeds a single revolution. The pitch of the spiral is usually great and the spicule consequently appears bow-shaped when viewed laterally.

toxi- (tɒksɪ), combining form arbitrarily repr. TOXIC or TOXIN, in recent scientific words, chiefly pathological. **toxidermic** (-'dɜːmɪk) *a.* [Gr. δέρμα skin], pertaining to skin-disease produced by a poison: cf. *toxicodermitis* in TOXICO-. **to'xiferous** *a.* = *toxophorous* in TOXO-[2]. **toxi'genic** *a.* [-GENIC] = *toxicogenic* adj. s.v. TOXICO-; so **toxige'nicity**, toxigenic property. **toxignomic** (-'gnɒmɪk) *a.* [Gr. γνώμη judgement, opinion], enabling one to diagnose the action of a toxin. ‖**toxi'hæmia** [Gr. αἷμα blood] = *toxæmia*: see TOX-[1]. **toxi-in'fectious, -in'fective** *adjs.*, involving or characterized by infection due to a toxin. ‖**toxiphagus** (-'ɪfəgəs), pl. **-phagi** (-fədʒaɪ) [Gr. -φάγος eating], one who eats poisons: cf. *toxicophagous* in TOXICO-. ‖**toxi'phobia** [-PHOBIA], fear of being poisoned, as a form of insanity or monomania; hence **toxi'phobiac**, one affected with toxiphobia. **toxiphoric** (-'fɒrɪk) *a.* = *toxophoric*: see TOXO-[2]. **toxiresin** (-'rɛzɪn), name of a poisonous substance obtained from digitalis by the action of acids.

1899 *Allbutt's Syst. Med.* VIII. 587 A pilo-sebaceous folliculitis of..microbic or *toxidermic character. **1899** *Syd. Soc. Lex.*, **Toxiferous*, carrying or conveying poison. **1930** J. A. ARKWRIGHT in *Syst. Bacteriol. in Relation to Med.* (Med. Res. Council) I. xi. 344 The new form present may be a variant which makes less growth than a more serviceable strain, or may be less *toxigenic though equally prolific. **1979** *Nature* 8 Feb. 453/1 Toxigenic strains of *E. coli* elaborate two types of toxins. **1929** TOPLEY & WILSON *Princ. Bacteriol. & Immunity* II. xlii. 626 The same association of phenomena, which occurs in the case of virulence, may hold in the case of *toxigenicity. **1977** *Lancet* 19 Mar. 649/2 A half antitoxin Naglar plate was prepared.. for use in toxigenicity testing with specific antiserum. **1890** BILLINGS *Med. Dict.*, **Toxihæmia*, Toxæmia. **1907** *Jrnl. Med. Research* Dec. 352 The statement of Dide, who asserts that there is a diminution in alexin in patients suffering from the '*toxi-infectious' forms of insanity. **1897** *Allbutt's Syst. Med.* III. 749 Microbic agency which sets up *toxi-infective processes. **1875** H. C. WOOD *Therap.* (1879) 377 The *toxiphagi are asserted to be remarkably long-lived people. **1876** C. A. CAMERON in *Dublin Jrnl. Med. Sc.* Feb. 98, I propose to apply the term *toxiphobia to a species of monomania..those labouring under which believe that persistent attempts are being made to poison them. Of the sixty-three *toxiphobiacs, only two were obviously insane. **1902** G. M. STERNBERG in *Science* 24 Oct. 665/1 The atom-groups which..Ehrlich calls the '*toxiphoric side chain'. **1890** BILLINGS *Med. Dict.*, **Toxiresin*, a product of the action of acids upon digitoxin; a powerful cardiac poison. **1899** *Syd. Soc. Lex.*, Toxiresin.

toxic ('tɒksɪk), *a.* (*sb.*) [f. med.L. *toxic-us* poisoned, imbued with poison, f. TOXIC-UM. So F. *toxique* 'poison' (1762 in *Dict. Trévoux*).]

A. *adj.* **1.** Of the nature of a poison; poisonous.

1664 EVELYN *Sylva* 65 The toxic quality was certainly in the liquor.., not in the nature of the wood; which yet he [Pliny] affirms is cur'd of that Venenous quality by driving a brazen wedge into the body of it. **1674** BLOUNT *Glossogr.*, *Toxic*, venemous, poisonous. **1876** T. BRYANT *Pract. Surg.* I. ii. 53 Poisoning..due to the introduction into the torrent of the circulation of toxic substances. **1899** *Allbutt's Syst. Med.* VII. 815 The urine is normally toxic, and incessantly takes from the blood its toxicity.

2. a. Caused or produced by a poison; due to poisoning. ***toxic shock syndrome***, an acute bacterial illness observed esp. in women using tampons, characterized by fever, vomiting, diarrhoea, muscle pain, and some peeling of the skin, and in severe cases followed by shock.

1872 *Contemp. Rev.* XX. 751 Whether it be the toxic condition of the blood. **1874** MAUDSLEY *Respons. in Ment. Dis.* iii. 79 The peculiar disorders of the physical and mental functions..to which he gave the name of Toxic Insanity. **1899** *Allbutt's Syst. Med.* VIII. 310 Toxic insanity depends on poisons either derived from without or generated within the body. **1978** TODD & FISHAUT in *Lancet* 25 Nov. 1117/2 The acute illness we have described and called the toxic-shock syndrome seems to affect older children. **1982** *Brit. Med. Jrnl.* 29 May 1586/1 There is no justification at present for any suggestion that women should avoid using tampons, since the risk of developing toxic shock syndrome is extremely small.

b. Of intoxication, intoxicated, tipsy. *humorous.*

1899 MARY KINGSLEY *W. Afr. Stud.* i. 2 A toxic state where a man can't see the holes through a ladder.

B. *sb.* A toxic substance, a poison.

1890 *Spectator* 6 Dec., M. Pasteur..pointing out..that the lymph is really a 'toxic' or poison, of terrible energy and unknown effects. **1904** *Westm. Gaz.* 15 June 2/1 Alkaloids and toxics, such as chloral, emit the N-rays freely.

toxical ('tɒksɪkəl), *a.* [f. as prec. + -AL[1]: see -ICAL.] Of toxic nature or character.

1607 TOPSELL *Four-f. Beasts* (1658) 199 Goats bloud sod with marrow may be taken against all toxical poison. **1650** CHARLETON *Paradoxes* 65 Why the blood of a Bull is toxicall and poysonous. **1855** WHARTON & STILLÉ *Med. Jurispr.* §496. 378 The production of toxical effects. **1863** *N. Syd. Soc. Year-bk. Med.* 444 Symptoms of the toxical action of the drug. **1884** *Manch. Exam.* 29 Dec. 6/5 Tobacco smoke ..contains a second toxical principle called colidine.

Hence **'toxically** *adv.*, poisonously; in quot., in relation to toxicology.

1887 A. M. BROWN *Anim. Alkal.* 39 This base is toxically interesting.

toxicant ('tɒksɪkənt), *a.* and *sb.* [f. pr. pple. of med.L. *toxicāre* to poison: see -ANT.]

a. *adj.* Acting as a poison; poisonous, toxic. *rare.* **b.** *sb.* A poisonous substance, a poison.

1882 OGILVIE (Annandale), *Toxicant*,..a poison of a stimulating, narcotic, anæsthetic nature, especially such as seriously affects the health when habitually indulged in. *Dr. Richardson.* **1891** *Cent. Dict.*, *Toxicant* adj. **1892** *Illustr. Lond. News* 13 Aug. 211/3 Coffee (that favourite vehicle of the deadlier toxicants in the East). **1951** *Ann. Rev. Plant Physiol.* I. 311 The injury [to vegetation] has economic significance only in 'heavy' smog when..the concentration of the toxicants is raised materially above the usual 'smog' level. **1982** *Nature* 14 Jan. p. xvii/3 The system measures the effect of toxicants on the light output of a special strain of luminescent bacteria.

†**'toxicate**, *ppl. a. Obs.* Also 5 toxicat, 6 tocksicate. [f. med.L. *toxicāt-us*, pa. pple. of L. *toxicāre* to smear with poison: see next.] Charged or infected with poison; poisoned; poisonous.

c **1470** HENRYSON *Mor. Fab.* III. (*Cock & Fox*) xxx, Flatteraris..With fals mening, and mynd maist toxicate. *c* **1475** *Partenay* 1429 The king..With toxicat uenym replete was certain. **1581** J. STUDLEY *Seneca's Hercules Œtæus* 199 b, So yet my wits be tocksicate, although my feare be gone.

†**'toxicate**, *v. Obs.* [f. ppl. stem of med.L. *toxicāre* to poison (in John of Salisbury, *c* 1150), f. L. *toxic-um* poison: see TOXICUM.] *trans.* To poison. Hence †**'toxicating** *vbl. sb.*

1635 HEYWOOD *Hierarch.* VIII. 518 Which Feuer shakes him,..And a strange Megrim toxicates his head. **1653** CHISENHALE *Cath. Hist.* 12 Each morning to bite on Rue, which..secures her against the toxicating of that venomous Basilisk.

toxication (tɒksɪ'keɪʃən). [n. of action f. med.L. *toxicāre*: see prec.] Poisoning: esp. by toxic substances produced by disease-germs.

1821 COLERIDGE in *Blackw. Mag.* X. 243, I..know of no reason, why to these *toxications*, (especially when taken through the skin, and to the cataleptic state produced by them,) we should not attribute the poor wretches' own belief of their guilt. **1860** in MAYNE *Expos. Lex.* **1887** A. M. BROWN *Anim. Alkal.* 127 The patients so affected have all the appearance of toxication, and by the poisonous alkaloids —that is, the vital alkaloids or leucomaines.

toxicity (tɒk'sɪsɪtɪ). [f. TOXIC + -ITY.] Toxic or poisonous quality, esp. in relation to its degree or strength.

1881 *Nature* 3 Nov. 24/2 On the comparative toxicity of different metals, by M. Richet... He named the limit of toxicity the quantity of poison per litre of water, allowing a fish to live more than forty-eight hours. **1881** *Pharmaceut. Jrnl.* 26 Nov. 439/2 Neither would there appear to be any relation between toxicity and chemical function, for although potassium and sodium are nearly allied.., the former is—at least in respect to fish—twenty-four times more poisonous than sodium. **1898** P. MANSON *Trop. Diseases* xvii. 283 The microbes were increased in toxicity to a definite point.

toxico- ('tɒksɪkəʊ), before a vowel **toxic-**, repr. Gr. τοξικόν in sense 'poison' (see TOXICUM), but chiefly used as combining form of TOXIC, in scientific terms, mostly pathological. ‖**toxi'cæmia, -'emia** [Gr. αἷμα blood] = *toxæmia*: see TOX-. ‖**toxicoderma** (-'dɜːmə), **-derma'titis, -der'mitis** [Gr. δέρμα skin: see -ITIS], inflammation of the skin caused by an irritant poison. **toxicogenic** (-'dʒɛnɪk) *a.* [*-genic*: cf. -GEN, -GENY], producing or generating poison. ‖**toxico'hæmia**, also anglicized **-hemy** [Gr. αἷμα blood] = *toxæmia*: see TOX-. ‖**toxico'mania** [MANIA], a morbid craving for poisons. **toxicophagous** (-'ɒfəgəs) *a.* [Gr. -φάγος eating], addicted to eating poisonous substances; so **toxicophagy** (-'ɒfədʒɪ), the habit of eating poisonous substances. **toxicophobia** (-'fəʊbɪə) = *toxiphobia*: see TOXI-. ˌ**toxicotrau'matic** (-trɔː'mætɪk) *a.* [Gr. τραυματικός, f. τραῦμα wound], pertaining to a poisoned wound. See also TOXICODENDRON, TOXICOLOGY, etc.

1857 DUNGLISON *Med. Lex.*, **Toxicæmia*, Toxicohæmia. **1890** BILLINGS *Med. Dict.*, **Toxicoderma* or **Toxicodermatitis*... **Toxicodermitis*, dermatitis caused by a poison. **1899** *Syd. Soc. Lex.*, **Toxicogenic*,..as a toxicogenic micro-organism. **1902** *Buck's Handbk. Med. Sc.* IV. 184 A relatively small number of bacteria are capable of making poisonous products, and to these..the term *toxicogenic* may be applied. **1871** YULE *Marco Polo* III. xxv. (1903) II. 392 *note*, The famous *toxicophagous Sultan Mahmúd Begara (1459-1511). **1899** *Allbutt's Syst. Med.* VI. 657 Oppenheim attributes the latter..to a *toxico-traumatic cause.

‖**Toxicodendron** (ˌtɒksɪkəʊ'dɛndrɒn). *Bot.* [mod.L. (Tournefort, 1700, in sense a), f. Gr. τοξικόν (see TOXICUM) + δένδρον tree.]

a. A former genus, now reckoned as a species of *Rhus* or sumac (*R. Toxicodendron*), a N. American shrub, also called *poison-ivy* (see POISON *sb.* 5 b). **b.** A synonym of *Hyænanche*, a S. African genus of euphorbiaceous trees or shrubs with poisonous fruit, used for killing noxious animals, whence the local names *wolveboon* (i.e. Wolf's-bane) and *hyena-poison*.

1721 W. SHERARD in *Phil. Trans.* XXXI. 147 The Poyson-Tree... Tis a species of Toxicodendron, tho' not nam'd by Dr. Tournefort in his Institutions. **1755** *Gentl. Mag.* Sept. 395/1 Experiments made on staining of linen with the juice of Toxicodendron. **1758** ELLIS in *Phil. Trans.* L. 445 He still insists on it, that these two Toxicodendrons are the same. **1801** MASON *Suppl. to Johnson*, *Toxicodendron*, a North-American plant. **1888** *Nicholson's Dict. Gard.* IV. 63 *Toxicodendron* Syn. *Hyænanche.*

Hence ˌ**toxico'dendric** *a.*, *Chem.* applied to an acid derived from *Rhus Toxicodendron* and other species, subsequently found to be identical with acetic acid; ˌ**toxico'dendrol** [-OL 3], *Chem.* a non-volatile oil constituting the poisonous principle of *Rhus Toxicodendron* and other species.

1865 J. M. MAISCH in *Proc. Amer. Pharm. Assoc.* 172 A new organic acid, for which I propose the name of *Toxicodendric acid.* **1876** DUHRING *Dis. Skin* 325 The poison is an exceedingly volatile acid,—toxicodendric acid. **1898** *U.S. Dept. Agric.*, *Bot.* Bulletin No. 20. 37 The poison is in reality a non-volatile oil. In January, 1895, Dr. Franz Pfaff ..announced this discovery. The oil has since been purified and named toxicodendrol.

'toxicoid, *a.* [f. Gr. τοξικόν (TOXICUM) + -OID.] Resembling poison.

1891 *Cent. Dict.* cites DUNGLISON. **1899** in *Syd. Soc. Lex.*

toxicology (tɒksɪ'kɒlədʒɪ). [= F. *toxicologie* (1812 in Hatz.-Darm.), f. Gr. τοξικόν taken in sense 'poison' (see TOXICUM) and -LOGY.] The science of poisons; that department of pathology or medicine which deals with the nature and effects of poisons. So ˌ**toxico'logical** *a.*, belonging or relating to toxicology (sometimes erron. used for *toxical*). Thence ˌ**toxico'logically** *adv.*, in relation to toxicology; **toxi'cologist**, a person versed in toxicology, one who studies poisons.

1839 *Blackw. Mag.* XLV. 59 To guess whether the *toxicological agent..was a mineral, a vegetable, or an animal poison. **1842** BRANDE *Dict. Sc.*, etc. s.v. *Toxicology*, We have elsewhere..referred to their toxicological history. *c* **1865** J. WYLDE in *Circ. Sc.* I. 320/2 In toxicological analyses. **1882** SPRINGMUHL in *Standard* 23 Mar. 2/2 It differs *toxicologically and constitutionally from pure Aconitine. **1829-32** R. CHRISTISON *Treat. Poison* xiii. (ed. 2) 387 The rule laid down by almost all modern *toxicologists. **1897** *Allbutt's Syst. Med.* II. 876. **1799** HOOPER *Med. Dict.*, **Toxicology*,..a dissertation on poisons. **1853** W. GREGORY *Inorg. Chem.* (ed. 3) 230 The reader is referred to the works on toxicology and legal medicine.

‖**toxicosis** (tɒksɪˈkəʊsɪs). *Path.* Pl. -oses (-ˈəʊsiːz). [mod.L., f. as prec. + -OSIS.] A disease or morbid condition produced by the action of a poison.

1857 DUNGLISON *Med. Lex.*, *Toxicoses*, a family of diseases..caused by the reception of poisons into the system.

‖**ˈtoxicum.** Pl. -a. [L. *toxicum* 'poison', orig. 'poison for arrows', ad. Gr. τοξικὸν φάρμακον poison (φάρμακον) for smearing arrows (τοξικός, -όν, f. τόξα pl. arrows, transf. fr. τόξον bow). Τοξικόν = 'of or pertaining to the bow', and had originally nothing to do with poison. But the effect of using τοξικόν, *toxicum* as short for the Gr. phrase was to transfer the sense 'poison' from φάρμακον to *toxicum*, first as 'poison for arrows' and at length as 'poison' generally, = L. *venēnum*.] Poison: cf. TOXIC *sb.*

1601 HOLLAND *Pliny* XXIX. iv. II. 355 It is generally thought, that for the venome called Toxicum, there is not a better counterpoyson than dogs bloud. **1657** *Physical Dict.*, *Toxicum*, a venom or poyson where with arrows are poysoned. **1669** W. SIMPSON *Hydrol. Chym.* 78 The vital spirits stand amazed as if smitten with a thunder-clap from the uterine toxicum. **1693** tr. *Blancard's Phys. Dict.* (ed. 2), *Toxica*, poysonous Medicaments, wherewith Barbarians use to anoint their Arrows. **1704** in J. HARRIS *Lex. Techn.* I.

toxidermic to **toxi-infective**: see TOXI-.

ˈtoxifer. *Zool.* [ad. mod.L. *Toxifera* (Gray), f. Gr. τόξα arrows (or τόξευμα arrow, dart) + L. *-fer* bearing.] A mollusc of the sub-order *Toxifera*. (Cf. TOXOGLOSSATE.)

1853 J. E. GRAY in *Ann. & Mag. Nat. Hist.* Ser. II. XII. 177 The subulate barbed teeth are implanted by a distinct root into the substance of the tube... The structure and organization of the mouth are so unlike that of the other *Proboscidifera* and *Rostrifera*, where the teeth are placed on a lingual ribbon and used to rasp the food..that I am inclined to form the *Cones* into a third sub-order, which may be called *Toxifera*. **1861** P. P. CARPENTER in *Rep. Smithsonian Instit.* 1860, 193 So far as known, the teeth and proboscis are like those of other Toxifers. **1863** —— in *Proc. Zool. Soc.* 23 June 347 Species belonging to different families of Proboscidifers and Toxifers.

toxin (ˈtɒksɪn). Also *erron.* -ine. [f. TOX-IC + -IN[1].] **a.** A specific poison, usually of an albuminous nature, esp. one produced by a microbe, which causes a particular disease when present in the system of a human or animal body.

1886 E. R. LANKESTER *Advancem. Science* (1890) 168 In other cases the toxin and the vaccin seem almost certainly to be distinct. **1891** *Lancet* 3 Oct. 792 In a few cases..the introduction of the toxines secreted by the bacilli sufficed to set up a commencement of the process in the joints characteristic of rheumatism. **1904** *Brit. Med. Jrnl.* 10 Sept. 557 The union of toxin and antitoxin is dissociable. **1905** G. A. REID *Princ. Heredity* ii. 21 Toxins, extremely complex chemical compounds, are defensive weapons which protect the organisms producing them from their enemies, the phagocytes of the blood and tissues.

b. *attrib.* and *Comb.*

1896 *Allbutt's Syst. Med.* I. 893 In order to produce an immunity all that is required is to render the body toxin-proof. **1902** *Encycl. Brit.* XXVI. 66/2 In the development of toxin-immunity the doses, small at first, are gradually increased. **1903** *Brit. Med. Jrnl.* 4 Apr. 784 No proof is afforded..of a separate toxophore group in the toxin molecule. **1904** *Ibid.* 10 Sept. 576 The chemical interpretation of toxin-antitoxin antagonism. **1910** HISS & ZINSSER *Text-bk. Bacteriol.* xiii. 204 This work..showed that the element of time entered into the toxin-antitoxin reaction, just as it enters into reactions of known chemical nature. **1923** *Daily Mail* 16 Feb. 5/2 Since May in that borough 250 children have been tested and protection has been conferred on 70 by injection of the toxin-anti-toxin mixture. **1951** WHITBY & HYNES *Med. Bacteriol.* (ed. 5) vi. 70 Toxin-antitoxin mixtures become highly toxic if frozen. **1975** E. NNOCHIRI *Med. Microbiol. in Tropics* iii. 43/1 Large visible floccules may be produced following a toxin-antitoxin reaction.

Hence ‖**toxinæmia** (-ˈiːmɪə) [Gr. αἷμα blood], the presence of a toxin in the blood: cf. *toxæmia* (TOX-[1]), *toxicæmia* (TOXICO-).

1900 *Buck's Handbk. Med. Sc.* I. 284 Various toxæmic conditions..and the different toxinæmias induced by the infectious diseases—diphtheria and typhoid or typhus fever.

toxin, rare obs. spelling of TOCSIN.

toxiphagus to **toxiresin**: see TOXI-.

ˈtoxity, abbreviated form of TOXICITY.

1887 A. M. BROWN *Anim. Alkal.* 103 Previous alkaline saturation of the material did not revive its toxity. **1894** *Westm. Gaz.* 11 Oct. 2/1 By multiplying the intensity of the toxity of the bacillus.

‖**toxius** (ˈtɒksɪəs). *Zool.* Pl. toxii (-ɪaɪ). [mod.L., f. Gr. τόξον bow.] A form of sponge-spicule: see quot.

1886 *Proc. Zool. Soc.* 21 Dec. 562 Sponges..Flesh-Spicules... 6. Toxius. Curved in the centre, the two ends in a straight line, thus ⌒.

toxo-[1] (tɒksəʊ), before a vowel tox-, combining form repr. Gr. τόξον bow, in TOXOCAMPID, TOXODON, TOXOLOGY, TOXOPHILITE, etc., q.v.

toxo-[2], used as combining form of TOXIN (cf. TOXI-) or instead of TOXICO-, in recent scientific terms, chiefly of pathology or physiological chemistry. **toxo-inˈfectious** *a.*, involving infection by a toxin: = *toxi-infectious* (TOXI-). **toxoˈpeptone,** (*a*) a poisonous substance, of the nature of a peptone, found in cultures of cholera bacillus (*Cent. Dict. Suppl.*); (*b*) = PEPTOTOXIN. **ˈtoxophil** (-fɪl) *a.* [Gr. -φιλος loving], having affinity for a toxin. **ˈtoxophore** (-fɔə(r)) [ad. G. *toxophor* adj. (P. Ehrlich 1898, in *Deutsch. med. Wochenschr.* 22 Sept. 599/2)], **toxophoric** (-ˈfɒrɪk), **toxophorous** (-ˈɒfərəs) *adjs.* [Gr. -φορος bearing, carrying], poison-bearing; applied to a particular group of atoms in the molecule of a toxin to which its toxic properties are due; also **toxophore** *sb.*, a toxophoric group. **toxophylaxin** (-fɪˈlæksɪn) [Gr. φύλαξ guard, protector], **toxosozin** (-ˈsəʊzɪn) [Gr. σῴζειν to save], names for defensive proteins or antitoxins (see quots.). **toxoprotein** (-ˈprəʊtiːɪn), a toxic protein, or mixture of a toxin and a protein.

1907 *Med. Record* 17 Aug. 279 The original cause of the lack of coagulation may be *toxoinfectious, or due to marked congestion. **1896** *Allbutt's Syst. Med.* I. 526 Scholl, growing the vibrio, in eggs, obtained a *toxo-peptone. **1902** VAUGHAN & NOVY *Cellular Toxins* (ed. 4) 182 The body cells must possess *toxophil side chains. By this we mean that.. there are groups of atoms which may combine with bacterial toxins. **1899** *Toxophore [see HAPTOPHORE]. **1900** *Lancet* 18 Aug. 528/1 The toxophore group of the toxin molecule being much less stable than the haptophore group was much more easily destroyed. **1903** *Brit. Med. Jrnl.* 21 Mar. 654 The other atomic group is toxophore, namely, is the cause of the specific toxic action. **1951** KIRK & OTHMER *Encycl. Chem. Technol.* VII. 121 In World War I, derivatives of trivalent arsenic received considerable attention, the structure —As= being considered a toxophore. **1902** *Brit. Med. Jrnl.* 29 Mar. 785 The toxin molecule..must possess a second group which he [Ehrlich] calls the *toxophoric group. **1904** *Ibid.* 10 Sept. 574 Although the toxophoric group may be similar, the haptophor is dissimilar. **1902** *Encycl. Brit.* XXVI. 65/1 In the molecule of toxin there are at least two chief atom groups—one, the 'haptophorous', by which the toxin molecule is attached to the cell protoplasm; and the other the '*toxophorous', which has a ferment-like action on the living molecule, producing a disturbance which results in the toxic symptoms. **1899** *Syd. Soc. Lex.*, **Toxophylaxin*, a defensive proteid produced in the body of an animal which has acquired immunity for a given infectious disease, and which has the power of rendering inert the toxic products of the pathogenic micro-organisms to which the condition was due. **1896** *Allbutt's Syst. Med.* I. 523 The *toxo-proteins in reality are mixtures of albuminous, proteid, or albuminoid bodies with the true toxins. **1899** *Syd. Soc. Lex.*, **Toxosozin*, a defensive proteid found in the body of a normal animal which has the power of protecting itself to a greater or less degree against micro-organisms and their products.

toxocampid (ˌtɒksəʊˈkæmpɪd), *sb.* and *a.* *Entom.* [ad. mod.L. *Toxocampidæ*, f. *Toxocampa*, f. Gr. τόξον bow + κάμπη caterpillar.] **a.** *sb.* A Noctuine moth of the family *Toxocampidæ*, typified by the genus *Toxocampa*, having bow-shaped marks on the fore wings, e.g. *Toxocampa Pastinum*, the black-neck. **b.** *adj.* Belonging to or having the characters of the family *Toxocampidæ*.

toxocara (tɒksəʊˈkærə). *Vet. Sci.* [mod.L. (C. W. Stiles 1905, in *Bull. Bur. Animal Industry* (U.S. Dept. Agric.) No. 79. 150), f. TOXO-[1] + Gr. κάρα head.] **a.** A nematode worm of the genus of this name, which includes species parasitic in cats and dogs; also in *pl.* sense. **b.** = TOXOCARIASIS.

1940 A. C. CHANDLER *Introd. Parasitol.* (ed. 5) xxii. 388 Toxocara males have a small finger-like process at the tip of the tail. **1962** *Lancet* 6 Jan. 35/1 Duguid has now recorded 28 cases of children with retinal granuloma endophthalmitis due to toxocara. **1968** *New Scientist* 4 Apr. 41/1 The nematode is toxocara, of which there are two important species. **1976** *Milton Keynes Express* 16 July 1/2 Toxocara, a 'rare and horrific' disease caught from dog-dirt, has infected a Bletchley boy.

So **toxoˈcaral** *a.*; **toxocaˈriasis** [-IASIS], infection with *Toxocara* nematodes.

1930 E. C. FAUST *Human Helminthol.* 613/2 (Index), Toxocariasis. **1966** *Arch. Dis. in Childhood* XLI. 222/1 The diagnosis of toxocariasis is essentially a clinical one. **1968** *Brit. Med. Jrnl.* 16 Mar. 677/2 Persistent eosinophilia, hepatomegaly, choroiditis, and pulmonary infiltration are mentioned together or separately as indicating possible toxocaral infection. **1976** *Ibid.* 19 June 1486/2 Of human toxocariasis virtually nothing was known until about 12 years ago. **1981** *Ibid.* 18 July 192/1 A case of arthritis and arthralgia associated with toxocaral infestation.

Toxodon (ˈtɒksədɒn). *Palæont.* [mod.L. (Owen, 1837), f. Gr. τόξον bow + ὀδούς, ὀδοντ- tooth: see quot. 1849.] A genus of large extinct quadrupeds, having strongly curved molar teeth, whose remains are found in Pleistocene deposits in S. America. Hence **ˈtoxodont,** *adj.* belonging to or having the characters of the order *Toxodonta*, typified by this genus; *sb.* a quadruped of this order.

1837 OWEN in *Proc. Geol. Soc.* II. 542 So far as dental characters have weight, the *Toxodon* must be referred to the rodent order. **1839** G. ROBERTS *Dict. Geol.*, *Toxodon*,..a gigantic quadruped, approaching, in character, to the pachydermata. **1849** *Sk. Nat. Hist.*, *Mammalia* III. 115 The molar teeth also were rootless, and curved, whence the name toxodon. **1859** DARWIN *Orig. Spec.* xi. (1878) 294 Remains of Mastodon, Megatherium, Toxodon and other extinct monsters.

ˌtoxoˈglossate, *a.* *Zool.* [f. mod.L. *Toxoglossa* (Troschel, 1848), f. Gr. τόξα arrows, darts + γλῶσσα tongue (not from τοξικόν poison): see -ATE[2] 2.] Having the characters of the *Toxoglossa* of Troschel, a group of gastropod molluscs; the same as Gray's *Toxifera*.

[**1848** TROSCHEL in Wilfmann & Ruthe's *Handbch. d. Zoologie* (ed. 3).] **1853** J. E. GRAY in *Ann. & Mag. Nat. Hist.* Ser. II. XI. 230 [following Troschel] Sub-order *Rostrifera*... Section 2. *Toxoglossa*, lingual membrane with two series of subulate, elongate, often barbed lateral teeth. **1891** *Cent. Dict.* s.v., A toxoglossate gastropod. [**1913** PROF. G. C. BOURNE in *Let.*, I am pretty sure that Troschel compared the teeth to arrows..when he described and classified 3 families as *Toxoglossa*... As a matter of fact all the *Toxoglossa* have a poison-gland, but this was a later discovery.]

toxoid (ˈtɒksɔɪd). [f. TOX(IN (cf. TOX-[1]) + -OID.] A modification or transformation product of a toxin, in which the toxophoric group of atoms is lost, and which has therefore no toxic effect, but retains affinity for the antitoxin. Also *attrib.*

1900 *Lancet* 18 Aug. 528/1 Very sensitive animals such as mice and guinea-pigs might..be easily and rapidly immunised against tetanus by means of toxoids only. **1902** *Brit. Med. Jrnl.* 29 Mar. 785 The modified toxin consists of a molecule with a haptophoric but no toxophoric group and is called 'toxoid'. **1903** *Ibid.* 21 Mar. 654 The toxoids may again be subdivided into three groups, according to their affinity for the antitoxin, which may obviously be either greater (protoxoid), equal (syntoxoid), or less than (epitoxoid) that of the toxin. **1904** *Ibid.* 10 Sept. 577 They were however able to produce toxoid formation in this constituent.

toxology (tɒkˈsɒlədʒɪ). *nonce-wd.* [f. Gr. τόξον bow + -LOGY.] *prop.* The study of the bow, i.e. archery; in quot. humorously used for 'archery'.

1843 *Fraser's Mag.* XXVII. 401 He is reluctant to..run the risk of exposing his well-varnished cab as a pleasing target for the poles of the loitering omnibuses, the drivers of which latter have obtained a well-earned fame for their dexterity in this..department of toxology.

toxon[1] (ˈtɒksɒn). *Zool.* [a. Gr. τόξον bow.] A bow-shaped sponge spicule. Cf. TOX *sb.*

1894 *Jrnl. Marine Zool.* Feb. 40 A second and slender form of spicule, bow-shaped (toxon) can also be made out.

ˈtoxon[2]. *Path. Chem.* [f. TOX(IN + *-on*, -ONE.] (See quots.)

1900 *Lancet* 18 Aug. 528/1 Löffler's diphtheria bacillus produced substances of two kinds—toxins and toxons... The action of the toxons was different from, and weaker than, that of the toxins. **1904** *Brit. Med. Jrnl.* 10 Sept. 567 The diphtheria poison is not a single substance, but consists of two chief components, toxin and toxon.

Hence **ˈtoxonoid,** a modification of a toxon, in which the toxic properties are lost. (Cf. TOXOID.)

1904 *Brit. Med. Jrnl.* 10 Sept. 573 Ehrlich explained the peculiarity that the 'toxon' has acute killing properties, by the assumption of two different kinds of toxon, thus introducing the conception of a new body—the toxonoid.

toxopeptone, toxophil: see TOXO-[2].

toxophilite (tɒkˈsɒfɪlaɪt). [app. f. *Toxophil-us* (imaginary proper name invented by Ascham, and hence title of his book (1545), intended to mean 'lover of the bow' (f. Gr. τόξον bow + φίλος lover), for which the regular Gr. formation would have been *φιλότοξος: see -PHIL, PHILO-) + -ITE[1]: *quasi* 'a follower of Toxophilus'.] A lover or devotee of archery, an archer.

1813 J. C. HOBHOUSE *Journey* (ed. 2) 929 Memorials of the distance to which some of the Sultans, and other distinguished Toxophilites, have shot their arrows. **1845** THACKERAY *Leg. Rhine* viii, His Grace..gives an archery meeting once a year, and prizes for which we toxophilites muster strong. **1868** MISS BRADDON *Dead Sea Fr.* xxi, A triumphant display of his genius as a toxophilite.

b. *attrib.* Of or pertaining to archers or archery.

1794 *Sporting Mag.* III. 206 That the Toxophilite Society shall not exceed the number of one hundred and sixty subscribing members. **1845** THACKERAY *Leg. Rhine* viii, All his new toxophilite friends. **1848** —— *Van. Fair* iii, To wear Lincoln Green toxophilite hats and feathers.

Hence (mostly *nonce-wds.*) **toxophilitic** (-ˈɪtɪk) *a.*, pertaining or relating to archers or archery; **toˈxophilitism, toˈxophilism, toˈxophily,** the practice of, or addiction to, archery.

1887 *All Year Round* 29 Sept. 185 The spirit of *toxophilism is essentially different from..the spirit of the age. **1857** *Chamb. Jrnl.* VII. 141 The *toxophilitic proficiency of William Tell. **1840** T. HOOK in *New Monthly Mag.* LX. 152 Dressed in green, with hats, and feathers, and quivers, and all the paraphernalia of *toxophilitism. **1887** *Field* 16 July 103/1 Amongst the votaries of *toxophily. **1970** M. GILMORE *World Away* 75 Mervyn had become fascinated by toxophily, and he returned with very beautiful equipment for us all. **1983** *N.Z. Listener* 19 Nov. 67

Toxophily,..a very exclusive and fancy word for the shooting of bows and arrows.

toxophore to **toxosozin**: see TOXO-².

toxoplasma (tɒksəʊˈplæzmə). *Zool.* Pl. **-plasmata.** [mod.L. (coined in Fr. by Nicolle & Manceaux 1909, in *Compt. Rend.* CXLVIII. 371), f. TOXO-¹ + PLASMA.] A micro-organism of the genus of this name, which comprises crescentic uninucleate sporozoans that are parasites of vertebrates. Also in pl. sense.

1926 C. M. WENYON *Protozoology* II. II. 1042 Mayer.. discovered a parasite which appeared to be a toxoplasma in the spleen and liver of a bird. *Ibid.*, Though some of the toxoplasmata may be merozoites of hæmogregarines or coccidia, this cannot apply to such an organism as *Toxoplasma gondii.* **1937** *Science* 2 Apr. 336/1 Toxoplasma have been described as the causative agents of various pathologic conditions in birds and mammals, including man. **1962** *Lancet* 6 Jan. 23/2 Only when a woman is initially infected with toxoplasma during pregnancy can she pass the infection to her fœtus. **1973** *Times* 31 Oct. 14/3 It is thought that toxoplasma infection may occasionally lead to abortion, or to some cases of mental abnormality in the child.

Hence **toxoˈplasmic** *a.*; **toxoˈplasmin** [-IN¹], an antigenic preparation of toxoplasma; **ˌtoxoplasˈmosis** [-OSIS], infection with or a disease caused by toxoplasma, which may vary from symptomless to fatal.

1934 *Biol. Abstr.* VIII. 972/2 This is the first observation of incidence of toxoplasmosis in canary birds in Argentina. **1937** *Science* 2 Apr. 337/2 It is not known how toxoplasmic infection is transmitted in nature. **1948** J. K. FRENKEL in *Proc. Soc. Exper. Biol. & Med.* LXVIII. 639/2 The preparation of toxoplasmin, a skin testing antigen made of toxoplasma has been described. **1962** *Lancet* 6 Jan. 23/2 At the end of the third month of pregnancy, all women should be tested by the toxoplasmin skin test, which is cheap and simple. **1971** *Physics Bull.* July 409/2 Recurrent toxoplasmic chorioretinitis, leading to satellite lesions about a scar caused by cysts, presents a serious ocular threat. **1977** *Rolling Stone* 24 Mar. 24/5 Roy Harper, popular British singer and guitarist, almost had to delay a tour of Britain when he caught a rare (in humans), flulike virus called toxoplasmosis while giving mouth to mouth resuscitation to a pregnant sheep.

toxt: see TOX *v.*

toy (tɔɪ), *sb.* Forms: ? 4, 6–7 toye, 6– toy; *Pl.* 6–7 **toyes, toies, 6– toys.** [*Toy* sb. and vb. (formerly *toye*) have been in common use since *c* 1530, when both are given by Palsgr., and used by Skelton and Tindale. But a single instance of *toye* sb., apparently the same word, occurs in Robert of Brunne. It is difficult to conceive how such a word in use *c* 1300 should thus disappear for two centuries, and then should all at once burst into view with a wide sense-development. The etymology is equally problematic, and, in spite of current conjectures, must still be considered unascertained: see Note below.]

I. Abstract senses, meaning action, act, notion, feeling.

†**1.** Amorous sport, dallying, toying; with *pl.*, an act or piece of amorous sport, a light caress.

[**1303** R. BRUNNE *Handl. Synne* 7891 Whedyr hyt be yn a womman handlyng, Or yn any oþer lusty þyng;..Amendeþ ȝow, pur charyte, And makeþ nat a-mys þe toye [*so all MSS.*], þat þe fende of ȝou haue Ioye.] **1565** COOPER *Thesaurus* s.v. *Amo*: *Amatoriæ leuitates*, Louers toyes. **1590** SPENSER *F.Q.* II. vi. 37 A foe of folly and immodest toy. **1594** —— *Epithal.* 365 For greedy pleasure, carelesse of your toyes, Thinks more upon her paradise of joyes, Then what ye do. **1594** WILLOBIE *Avisa* XLVII. iii, These toyes in tyme will make her yielde. **1667** MILTON *P.L.* IX. 1034 So said he, and forbore not glance or toy, Of amorous intent, well understood Of Eve. **1668** ETHEREDGE *She Would if She Could* II. ii, Her toy was such, that every touch Would make a lover madder. **1707** WARD *Hud. Rediv.* II. ii. 8 (Farmer) Kisses, Love-Toys, and am'rous Prattle.

†**2.** A sportive or frisky movement; a piece of fun, amusement, or entertainment; a fantastic act or practice; an antic, a trick. *Obs.*

a **1500** MEDWALL *Nature* I. 786 (Brandl), Though I say yt a praty boy..He maketh me laugh wyth many a toy, The vrchyn ys so mad. *Ibid.* 1001 He that wold lordshyp enioy And playe euer styll the old boy Me semeth he doth but make a toy. **1530** TINDALE *Answ. More* Wks. (1572) 249/1 We heare but voyces with out signification,..& wonder at disguisings & toyes wherof we know no meanyng. *c* **1555** HARPSFIELD *Divorce Hen. VIII* (Camden) 291 Neither was there ever any bearwards Jackanapes that made more pastime and toys to the people, than this. **1561** HOLLYBUSH *Hom. Apoth.* 9 Somtyme croweth he like a cocke, somtyme barketh he like a dogge, and many such foolish toyes vseth he. *c* **1575** *Perfect Bk. Kepinge Sparhawkes* (1886) 15 Lest she get a toye of flinginge her head. **1616** R. C. *Times' Whistle* v. 1948 Are apish tricks and toies, which vse to bring Men in dirision, sportes to breed delight? **1777** *Horæ Subsec.* 437 (E.D.D.) He hath taken a toy to scratch his head, when he is speaking to a gentleman.

3. a. A fantastic or trifling speech or piece of writing; a frivolous or mocking speech; a foolish or idle tale; a funny story or remark, a jest, joke, pun; a light or facetious composition. *arch.*

1542 UDALL *Erasm. Apoph.* I. *Diogenes* §79 Nothyng but a toye, in daliyng with the affinitee and similitude of woordes. **1553** T. WILSON *Rhet.* (1580) A iv, Suche as seeke the greatest praise for writyng of Bookes, should doe beste..to write foolishe toyes, for then the moste parte would best esteme them. **1577** BRETON *Flourish on Fancie* (Grosart) 11/2 Toyes of straung deuise, With stories of olde Robin Hood. **1590** SHAKS. *Mids. N.* v. i. 3, I neuer may beleeue These anticke fables, nor these Fairy toyes. **1621** MOLLE *Camerar. Liv. Libr.* III. xx. 215 They gaue credit to all these foolish toies. **1719** D'URFEY *Pills* (1872) I. 126 Fye George, she crys, these Words are but Toys.

arch. **1821** SCOTT *Kenilw.* xvi, Think of what that arch-knave Shakspeare says—a plague on him, his toys come into my head when I should think of other matters. **1905** R. GARNETT *Shakespeare* 104 She hath heard A little toy of thine, a comedy ('Tis called, I think, The Taming of a Shrew).

b. †(*a*) A light, frivolous, or lively tune. *Obs.* (*b*) A particular turn or phrase of melody in a bird's song: see quot. 1851.

1591 GREENE *Art Conny Catch.* III. (1592) 19 In the time of ceissing betweene the seuerall toyes and fancies hee plaied. **1641** SANDERSON *Serm., Ad Aulam* xiii. (1660) II. 267 One would have a grave Pavane, another a nimbler Galliard, a third some striking toy or Jigg. **1851** MAYHEW *Lond. Labour* (1861) III. 14 There are four-and-twenty changes in a linnet's song... It sings 'toys', as we call them.

†**4. a.** A foolish or idle fancy; a fantastic notion, odd conceit; a whim, crotchet, caprice. *Obs.*

c **1530** H. RHODES *Bk. Nurture* 330 in *Babees Bk.* (1868) 80 Cast not thyne eyes to ne yet fro, as thou werte full of toyes. **1555** W. WATREMAN *Fardle Facions* II. x. 225 This people [Tartarres] hath many supersticious toyes. **1563** B. GOOGE *Eglogs* vii. (Arb.) 59 But yf a toye com in your Brayne, your mynde is altered quyght. **1591** FLORIO *2nd Frutes* 161 Euen as the toy takes me in the head. **1642** ROGERS *Naaman* 98 So deadly doth this conceit and toy of his owne braine worke with him. **1668** R. L'ESTRANGE *Vis. Quev.* (1708) 101 Yet when the Toy took them, they'd make now and then a Sally. **1699** —— *Fables* II. vii. (1715) II. 5 A New Marry'd Couple had a Toy took them in their Heads, so soon as ever the Office was over, to Shrift one another before they came together.

†**b.** *spec.* A foolish or unreasoning dislike or aversion: esp. in phr. ***to take (a) toy*** (in quot. 1612 = to take fright, start, shy) ***at*** something. *Obs.*

a **1593** MARLOWE *Hero & Leander* v. Wks. (Rtldg.) 304/2 [To hear this] Made the well-spoken nymph take such a toy That down she sunk. **1612** *Two Noble K.* v. iv. 79 The hot horse, hot as fire, Took Toy at this. **1647** SANDERSON *Serm., Ad Aulam* xiv. (1660) II. 277 Common friends many times ..take toy at a trifle,..and pick quarrels to desert us. **1697** J. SERGEANT *Solid Philos.* 308 Thence they take a Toy at Metaphysics, and pretend it insuperably hard and mysterious.

II. Concrete senses.

(Sense 5 is also often *abstract*, connecting I and II; the connexion of 10 with the other senses is doubtful.)

5. *gen.* A thing of little or no value or importance, a trifle; a foolish or senseless affair, a piece of nonsense; *pl.* trumpery, rubbish. (In mod. use regarded as *fig.* from next sense.)

1530 PALSGR. 281/2 Toy a tryfell, *truffe, friuolle.* **1538** ELYOT, *Abydena*, trifles, thinges of smalle estimation, wanton toyes, thynges vnseemely for menne to vse. **1587** HARRISON *England* II. vi. (1877) I. 166 To stand vpon such toies would spend much time. **1605** SHAKS. *Macb.* II. iii. 91 From this instant, There's nothing serious in Mortalitie: All is but Toyes. **1631** GOUGE *God's Arrows* I. §29. 44 Of Popish toyes to pacifie God. **1664** H. MORE *Myst. Iniq., Apol.* 554 If they leave not off their animosities and asperities of mind about toys and trifles. **1719** WATTS *Hymn, 'Come, holy Spirit, Heavenly Dove'* ii, Look, how we grovel here below, Find of these earthly Toys. **1848** THACKERAY *Van. Fair* ix, But a title and a coach and four are toys more precious than happiness in Vanity Fair.

6. A material object for children or others to play with (often an imitation of some familiar object); a plaything; also, something contrived for amusement rather than for practical use (esp. in phrase ***a mere toy***). In quot. *a* 1586 ***playing toy***. Now the leading sense, to which the others are referred.

a **1586** SIDNEY *Arcadia* IV. Wks. 1725 II. 771 There was never poor scholar, that having instead of his book some playing toy about him, did more suddenly cast it from him. **1598** BARCKLEY *Felic. Man* (1631) 152 The rattles and toyes which children use to play with. *a* **1656** BP. HALL *Occas. Medit.* (1851) 111 We cry for every toy, even that which may most hurt us. **1672** R. WILD *Poet. Licent.* 29 We all know Popes-head-Alley trades in Toyes, Our Merchants come not thither, but our Boys. **1781** COWPER *Hope* 128 Men deal with life as children with their play, Who first misuse, then cast their toys away. **1881** STEVENSON *Virg. Puerisque, Child's Play* (1905) 157 Lead soldiers, dolls, all toys, in short, are in the same category. **1893** J. A. HODGES *Elem. Photogr.* (1907) 14 The very low-priced sets [of photographic apparatus]..are generally mere toys.

fig. **1893** LIDDON, etc. *Life Pusey* I. xvi. 363 He handles it with the delight that a new mental toy inspires in most men at a certain time of life.

7. a. A small article of little intrinsic value, but prized as an ornament or curiosity; 'a petty commodity' (J.), a knick-knack, trinket, gewgaw; hence (often in allusion to 6) applied to anything small, flimsy, or inferior of its kind (now chiefly *attrib.*: see 12 b).

1596 SHAKS. *Tam. Shr.* IV. iii. 67 Heere is the cap... Why 'tis a cockle or a walnut-shell, A knacke, a toy, a tricke, a babies cap. **1624** CAPT. SMITH *Virginia* I. 3 We presented him with diuers toyes, which he kindly accepted. *c* **1630** HALES *Serm. John* xviii. *36* Rem. (1673) 154 So like one another, that one of them must wear a toy in his cap, that so the spectators may distinguish them. **1711** in *10th Rep. Hist. MSS. Comm.* App. v. 139 A weak town, haveing noe outward works, but a toy of a pallisade before a litle part of the wall. **1712** ARBUTHNOT *John Bull* III. i, Ladies, hung about with toys and trinkets. **1768** *Tom Thumb's Folio* i. 4 His Father was greatly disconcerted at having such a little tiney Toy of a Child. **1888** BLACK *Houseboat* xi, Perched on the top of a hill was a conspicuous toy of a church.

b. Applied technically to small steel articles, as hammers, pincers, buckles, button-hooks, nails, etc. More fully 'steel toys' (? i.e. steel petty things).

1833 J. HOLLAND *Manuf. Metal* II. 319 Heavy Steel Toys. By this not very appropriate description the Birmingham manufacturers refer to a class of articles... To enumerate all the 'toys' of this class would be to transcribe a large list of miscellaneous cheap and useful wares, from a joiner's hammer to a shoemaker's tack. The pincers of the last-named workman, and the edged nippers..in use for breaking up loaf-sugar, are both of them well-known specimens.

c. *Thieves' slang.* A watch; ***toy and tackle***, a watch and chain. Cf. *toy-getter* (see 12 d).

1826 *Sessions Papers* 21 Sept. 546/2 James Boyce..said 'The b—g—r has got no *toy*'; I had no watch. **1877** HORSLEY *Jottings fr. Jail* i. (1887) 17 He was very tricky at getting a poge or a toy, but he would not touch toys because we was afraid of being turned over.

d. *U.S. slang.* A small tin or jar containing opium; the quantity of opium held in such a container.

1934 *Detective Fiction Weekly* 21 Apr. 114/1 *Toy*, small receptacle for opium. **1951** *Suggestions for Teaching Nature & Effects of Narcotics* (U.S. Board of Education) 9 It [*sc.* opium] is usually sold in round tin salve containers, about the size of a five-cent piece, and is known as a 'toy'. **1955** *U.S. Senate Hearings* (1956) VIII. 4161 The containers thereof are known as 'toys' (small jars or like containers). **1961** *Dissent* VIII. 349 Opium itself is often available. However, it is expensive ($15–20 for a *toy*, a ball about the size of a large pea).

8. *fig.* Applied to a person: **a.** (from 5) slightingly or contemptuously; in quot. 1822 affectionately = pet, darling (cf. 7); **b.** (from 6) as being used as a plaything or for sport.

1598 SHAKS. *Merry W.* v. v. 46 Elues, list your names: Silence, you aiery toyes. **1616** B. JONSON *Devil an Ass* IV. vii, I ha' sworne to ha' him by the eares: I feare The toy, wi' not do me right. **1681** DRYDEN *Span. Friar* IV. ii, O, Vertue! Vertue!..That men should leave thee for that Toy, a Woman? **1821** BYRON *Mar. Fal.* I. ii, Thou idle, gilded, and degraded toy. **1822** T. MITCHELL *Aristoph.* II. 171 Why, Xanthias, my toy, Why, what ails the poor boy! **1883** STEPNIAK in *Contemp. Rev.* Sept. 317 A Russian..being a mere toy in the hands of the commonest policeman. **1888** STEVENSON *Black Arrow* 46 This toy..that's not fit for wounds or warfare.

9. Applied to a diminutive breed or variety of animals. **a.** Short for *toy dog*: see 12 c.

1876 *All Year Round* 15 Jan. 377/1 'Toys' repose on velvet cushions. **1877** *Field* 24 Feb. 214/2 In toys no great change has taken place, except that..pugs, Italian greyhounds, and toy terriers are on the decline. **1899** *Pall Mall G.* 3 Oct. 9/1 Ladies' toys were in strong force... Sporting dogs were not numerous. **1903** *Daily Chron.* 25 May 5/2 The 'chiens de luxe', or Toys, are in a roomy and well-warmed 'pavillon' by themselves.

b. Any dwarf variety of tame pigeon.

1855 [see HYACINTH 3 b]. **1909** *Cent. Dict. Suppl.* s.v., The toys resemble the tumblers in general build and are among pigeons what bantams are among fowl.

10. *Sc.* A close cap or head-dress, of linen or wool, with flaps coming down to the shoulders, formerly worn by women of the lower classes in Scotland. ? *Obs.* Also *toy-mutch* (12 d). [In this sense perh. = Du. *tooi* attire, dress: see Note below.]

(The *English* quots. 1611, 1612, are placed here as perh. suggesting the origin; but they may belong to 7.)

[**1611** SHAKS. *Wint. T.* IV. iv. 326 Any Silke, any Thred, any Toyes for your head? **1612** *Two Noble K.* I. iii, On my head no toy But was her pattern.] **1724** RAMSAY *Tea-t. Misc.* (1762) 2 Their toys and mutches were sae clean, They glanced in our ladses' een. **1793** *Statist. Acc. Scot.* IX. 325 The tenants wives wore toys of linen of the coarsest kind, upon their heads, when they went to church, fairs or market. **1816** SCOTT *Old Mort.* xxxix, The face of Alison..now presented itself, enveloped in a 'toy'. **1824** —— *Redgauntlet* Let. iv, An elderly woman, in a grey stuff gown, with a check apron and 'toy'. **1900** H. G. GRAHAM *Soc. Life Scot. in 18th C.* v. vi. (1901) 181 Farmers' wives and daughters with 'toys' or head-covering of coarse linen.

11. *pl.* At Winchester College, a bureau or desk; hence, a cubicle used as a study.

1816 *Hist. Colleges Winchester, Eton & Westminster* 43 Besides his scob, every boy has, in the chamber to which he belongs, another receptacle for his books, with convenience for writing, &c. denominated, in the language of the place, Toys. **1901** *Public School Mag.* VII. 158/1 A series of small compartments, semi-secluded, but answering in their way to private studies. Each of these little dens is known as 'Toys'. **1974** K. CLARK *Another Part of Wood* ii. 74 We all sat in the same large enclosure, round the walls of which were small partitions (known as toyes) like uncomfortable polling booths, with just enough room for two shelves, one to serve as a seat and the other as a desk.

III. 12. *attrib.* and *Comb.* **a.** *attrib.* That is a toy (in sense 6): applied to small models or imitations of ordinary objects used as playthings, as ***toy boat, cannon, dog, engine, horse, house, man, pistol, train, trumpet, woman***, etc.

a **1860** ALB. SMITH *Lond. Med. Stud.* (1861) 13 A stethescope—a curious instrument, something like a sixpenny toy-trumpet with its top knocked off. **1880** MRS. F. D. BRIDGES *Jrnl. Lady's Trav. round World* xviii. (1883) 298 One never quite gets over the impression of being amongst dolls and living in a toy-house..in Japan. **1883**

Toy pistol [see AMORCE]. **1888** HASLUCK *Model Engin. Handybk.* iii. (1900) 24 The most simple form of toy-engine is that illustrated below. **1889** Toy pistol [see AMORCE]. **1897** *Edin. Rev.* Oct. 480 The babies had toy-animals on wheels. **1978** N. FREELING *Night Lords* ii. 11 The bandits..were pathetic imbeciles armed with toy pistols.

b. *transf.* and *fig.* Applied to things of diminutive size, flimsy construction, or petty character, as if intended for sport or diversion rather than serious use.

1821 SCOTT *Kenilw.* xli, You go not to your gew-gaw toy-house yonder; you will sleep to-night in better security. **1855** HT. MARTINEAU *Autobiog.* I. 437 My surprise at the smallness and toy-character of Abbotsford was extreme. **1895** MISS BRADDON in *Westm. Gaz.* 6 Nov. 1/3 A very popular writer may launch three of these toy-pinnaces in a year. **1897** GLADSTONE *E. Crisis* 5 The Concert of Europe included toy-demonstrations, which might be made under the condition that they should not pass into reality. **1909** *Daily Chron.* 19 Feb. 3/2 Ruritana was something more than the first toy-kingdom of our modern stage.

c. Applied to an animal, esp. a dog of a diminutive breed or variety, kept as a pet, e.g. a *toy spaniel* or *terrier*.

1806 M. LEWIS *Jrnl.* 1 July in *Orig. Jrnls. Lewis & Clark Expedition* (1905) V. 178 [Barking squirrels] will generally set and bark at you.., their note being much that of the little toy dogs. **1863** *Sat. Rev.* 28 Mar. 408/1 These very large dogs are not much more useful than the very small ones which are called, with perfect aptness, toy dogs. **1872** B. CLAYTON *Dogs* 20 A Toy Terrier was exhibited which weighed only six ounces. **1889** G. STABLES *Dog Owners' Kennel Comp.* vi. §10. 66 There are several other kinds of Toy Terriers..but I need only mention..the Toy Black and Tan and the Toy Blue or Slate colour.

d. *Comb.*: attrib. (of or for toys), as ***toy-box***, ***-cupboard***, ***-fair***, ***-land***, ***-manufacture***, ***-trade***; objective and obj. gen., as ***toy-maker***, ***-making***, ***-turner***; instrumental, similative, etc., as ***toy-bewitched***, ***-like***, ***-sized*** adjs.; also **toy-block**, one of a set of wooden or papier-mâché blocks, usually with letters or designs, for children to play with; **toy book** *U.S.*, a children's book; **toy-boy** *slang*, a good-looking youth who is 'kept' by an older woman (or occas. man) as a lover; the younger partner of an older woman; **toy-getter** (*Thieves' slang*), a watch-stealer; so ***toy-getting***, †**toy-headed** *a.*, having 'toys' or odd fancies in the head, crotchety; **toy-line** = *toy-railway*; **toy-mutch**, *Sc.* = sense 10; †**toy-pate**, a head full of 'toys', crotchets, or frivolities (cf. *toy-headed*); **toy-railway**, (*a*) a model of a railway, with its engine, train, etc.; (*b*) *pop.*, a small narrow-gauge railway, often orig. constructed for the use of slate-works or the like, but subseq. carrying tourists or other passengers; also *toy-line*; **toy-service**, a church-service at which toys are brought as an offering for sick or poor children; **toy soldier**, a small model of a soldier; also *fig.*; **toy theatre**, a miniature theatre in which the characters are represented by printed pictures mounted on card or wood; also *fig.*; **toy time**, at Winchester College, time allocated for work in toys (see sense 11 above); **toy-woman**, a woman who keeps a toy-shop. See also TOYMAN, -SHOP, -TOWN, -WORT.

1794 COLERIDGE *Relig. Musings* vii, We become An anarchy of Spirits. *Toy-bewitched. **1891** *Cent. Dict.*, **Toy-block*, one of a set of small blocks,..forming a plaything for children. **1801** M. L. WEEMS *Let.* 10 Mar. in E. Skeel *M. L. Weems* (1929) II. 177, I sell the Primers & *toy books wholesale at great discount. **1865** (*title*) Aunt Louisa's Toy Books. **1831** CARLYLE *Sart. Res.* II. vi, He descries lying far below, embosomed among its groves and green natural bulwarks, and all diminished to a *toybox, the fair Town. **1981** *Event* 9 Oct. 29/4 **Toy-boy*, the youthful lover of an ageing woman. **1983** *Financial Times* 31 Mar. 19/4 At the start he is observed as Caesar's toy boy, stripped for the religious ceremony. **1987** *News of the World* 15 Nov. 32/2 At 48 she is like a teenage girl again—raving it up with four different lovers including a toyboy of 27! **1900** *Westm. Gaz.* 11 Dec. 12/1 The season for the ransacking of *toy-cupboards. **1908** *Westm. Gaz.* 29 Oct. 1/2 The order..that there shall be no *toy-fairs in London this Christmas-tide deprives the City of..one of its sights. **1879** *Macmillan's Mag.* Oct. 502/1 The following people used to go in there —*toy-getters (watch-stealers), mags-men [etc.]. **1896** A. MORRISON *Child of the Jago* 102 Dicky knew the small man for a good toy-getter. **1896** A. MORRISON *Child of Jago* xxiv. 239 The gains of the *toy-getting trade were poor, except to the fence. **1633** T. ADAMS *Exp. 2 Peter* ii. 1 It sticks upon the stomach of some *toy-headed professors. **1908** *Daily Chron.* 5 Nov. 7/5 No one realises unless he penetrates into *Toyland how much whimsical humour, how much scientific skill and craftsman's ingenuity are devoted to the invention of the playthings for the festive season. **1818** SCOTT *Hrt. Midl.* i, The gay glancing of the equipage, its diminished and *toy-like appearance at a distance. **1883** *Manch. Exam.* 26 Nov. 5/3 The Swiss lake steamers are.. too toy-like to ensure their passengers against reasonably probable risks. **1878** JENKINSON *Guide N. Wales* 271 Leaving the Cambrian train at Mynffordd Junction, the traveller walks up a path to the *toy line, and enters one of the little carriages. **1859** *Habits of Gd. Society* v. (new ed.) 194 Worth all the amusements which a *toy-maker could dream of. **1858** CARLYLE *Fredk. Gt.* IX. iii. (1872) III. 87 *Toy-manufactures of those simple people. **1742** FORBES *Dominie Depos'd* II. i, The *toy-mutch maun then gae on, Nae mair bare-hair'd. **1693** PENN *Maxims* lx. Wks. 1726 I. 847 He never deals but in substantial Ware, and leaves the rest for the *Toy-Pates (or Shops) of the World. **1892** BADDELEY *Guide N. Wales* (ed. 4) 165 *heading*, Portmadoc to Ffestiniog by the '*Toy' Railway. *Ibid.*, No orthodox tourist visits Wales without taking a turn..on the 'Toy' railway. **190.** *Guide to Lynton, Lynmouth*, etc. Introd. 19 *heading*, Barnstaple to Lynton by the Toy Railway. **1889** *Standard* 1 Feb., '*Toy Services' which are becoming very popular in some of our churches. **1895** CLIVE HOLLAND *Jap. Wife* (ed. 11) 27 *Toy-sized cups of tea. **1850** DICKENS in *Househ. Words* Extra Christmas No. 291/2 The lazy-tongs that used to bear the *toy soldiers. **1922** M. ARLEN *Piracy* III. xi. 232 Poor Hugo..has gone clucking back for to be a toy soldier at Aldershot. **1980** *Listener* 19 June 796/1 A shopful of toy soldiers cast from the same lead mould. **1850** DICKENS in *Househ. Words* Extra Christmas No. 292/1 Out of this delight springs the *toy theatre,..with its familiar proscenium, and..boxes. **1931** A. C. WARD *Found. Eng. Prose* iii. 98 Stevenson loved to play with toy-theatres, and all his novels, with one exception, are reflected through the toy-theatre temperament: life is not in them. **1978** A. & P. MIALL *Victorian Christmas Bk.* 30 The toy theatre..was similar to the kind..still being made by Pollocks of London. The printed figures and scenery were cut out and applied to wooden backings. **1881** W. H. DAVID in C. E. Pascoe *Everyday Life in our Public Schools* 84 The clock marking 7, each junior retires to his 'toys' or bureau, for an hour and a half—during what is known as '*toy-time', when the work of the next morning and the week's composition have to be prepared. **1901** *Public School Mag.* VII. 158/1 Thus we find that from seven o'clock to half-past eight is 'toy-time'. **1757** W. THOMPSON *R.N. Advoc.* 41 Our Sons of War are to be served after our Sons of *Toy-Trade. **1893** A. N. PALMER *Hist. Wrexham* IV. 11, I find mentioned..one *toy-turner. **1827** SCOTT *Diary* 2 Oct., in *Lockhart*, An old lady, who proved a *toy woman in Edinburgh.

[*Note.* Eduard Müller suggested the identity of *toy* with Du. *tooi*, late MDu. *tôi*, 16th c., 'attire, ornament, finery, dress', which suits the form, but hardly the sense (exc. ? in 10 or 7). Others have thought of Du. *tuig* 'harness, horse-trappings', in pl. 'sails, rigging, implements, tools; stuff, lumber, refuse, trash'; in Kilian 1599 *tuygh*, dial. *tuych*, *tugh*, 'arms, implements, armaments, impedimenta, ornaments', = Ger. *zeug* 'apparatus, tools, gear, furniture, stuff, trash, etc.', LG. *tüg*, *tüüg*, MLG. *tûch*, *tûg*. But, if the sense-development shown above is historically correct, it is difficult to see in either of these suggestions, the origin of the English word. It is indeed true that Du. *speeltuig*, Ger. *spielzeug*, and Da. *legetoi*, mean 'play-tool or implement, plaything, toy', and that Sidney in 1586 used 'playing toy', which might conceivably be a rendering of one of these compounds; but this would still leave the earlier English history unexplained.]

toy, *v.* [Goes with TOY *sb.*, q.v.]

1. *intr.* To act idly or without seriousness; to trifle, 'play', deal carelessly (*with* a person or thing); also †to make sport, mock (*obs.*).

a **1529** SKELTON *Bowge of Courte* 290 It was no tyme with him to jape nor toye. **1530** PALSGR. 758/2, I toye, or tryfell with one, I deale nat substancyally with hym, *je me truffe*. **1549–62** STERNHOLD & H. *Ps.* xxxv. 16 Yea abject slaves at me did toy with mocks and cheekes ful stout. **1563** *Homilies* II. *Inform. H. Script.* I. (1859) 373 It is a shame that christian men should be so light headed, to toy as ruffians do with such manner of speeches. **1576** DERING *Expos. Heb.* v. 4–6. Cc iij, They must haue oyle, candels..wine and water,.. trifled and toyed with all. **1653** W. RAMESEY *Astrol. Restored* 19, I fear I do toy in recording these vain Objections. **1868** DIXON *Spir. Wives* I. vii. 75 He toyed with astrology, and had fitful dreams of enjoying the elixir of life. **1888** BRYCE *Amer. Commw.* II. lxxxi. 296 [Class issues] are usually toyed with by both parties alike.

b. So *to toy it*.

1657 J. SERGEANT *Schism Dispach't* 379 Thus Dr. H. toyes it with his Readers. *Ibid.* 574 Let them not toy it now.

2. To sport amorously; to dally, flirt. Usually const. *with*. (Cf. TOY *sb.* 1.)

15.. *Song Bachelor's Life* 7 (Ritson) If he [the married man] be merie and toy with any, His wife will frowne, and words geve manye. **1566** in *Daily News* 10 Sept. (1897) 6/7 That none toy with the maids, on paine of 4d. **1592** SHAKS. *Ven. & Ad.* 106 And for my sake [he] hath learnd to sport, and daunce, To toy, to wanton, dallie, smile, and iest. *c* **1613** MIDDLETON *No Wit like Woman's* v. i, Not toy, nor bill, and imitate house-pigeons. **1727** GAY *Begg. Op.* I. viii, O Polly you might have toy'd and kist. **1811** W. R. SPENCER *Poems* 73 Whilst he and Psyche toy'd together.

fig. **1793** WORDSW. *Descr. Sketches* 52 To where the Alps, ascending white in air, Toy with the Sun, and glitter from afar. **1842** H. ROGERS *Ess.* I. i. 4 He had in early life toyed a little with the muses.

3. To play, sport, amuse oneself; to move sportively, play or frisk about.

1530 PALSGR. 758/2, I toye, I playe with one, *je me joue*. **1590** SPENSER *F.Q.* II. ix. 35 But other some could not abide to toy; All pleasaunce was to them griefe and annoy. **1678** CUDWORTH *Intell. Syst.* I. v. §44. 674 The senseless atoms, playing and toying up and down without any care or thought. **1827** POLLOK *Course T.* v. 1007 The hare, unscared Sported and toyed familiar with his dog. **1836** O. W. HOLMES *Poetry* ii. 18 Pale dreamers, whose fantastic lay Toys with smooth trifles like a child at play. **1848** KINGSLEY *Saint's Trag.* II. iv. 63, I have toyed too long..down the stream of life.

b. *toy with*: to play with (a material object), to handle or finger idly; hence, to work idly or carelessly with or at.

1822 W. IRVING *Braceb. Hall* xxvi. (1845) 121 The gallant general took his station.. at her side, and toyed with her elegantly ornamented work-bag. **1840** DICKENS *Barn. Rudge* lxiv, The fire was seen sporting and toying with the door. **1879** E. GARRETT *House by Works* I. 115 Mrs. Pendlebury looked down, and toyed with her rings.

4. *trans.* (with adv.) To spend or waste in toying; to bring by toying (into or out of some condition).

1575 ABP. PARKER *Corr.* (Parker Soc.) 474, I toy out my time, partly with copying books. **1685** J. SCOTT *Chr. Life* II. 134 So fools and fleers on, till he hath toyed and laughed himself out of all sense of Religion. **1749** JOHNSON *Irene* I. i, He toys his hours away.

toyable ('tɔɪəb(ə)l), *a. nonce-wd.* [f. TOY *v.* + -ABLE.] Fit for toying with.

1922 JOYCE *Ulysses* 213 Phedo's toyable fair hair.

to-yans, to-ȝanes: see TO-GAINS.

toydom ('tɔɪdəm). *nonce-wd.* [f. TOY *sb.* + -DOM.] **a.** The condition of being or resembling a toy. **b.** The realm or domain of toys.

1882 M. A. BARKER in *Macm. Mag.* XLVI. 68/1 The tan sail of a canoe or whiter sheet of a fishing boat..dwarfed into toydom whenever they come near the great war ship. **1905** *Times* 7 Jan. 11/2 At the Crystal Palace..side-shows are numerous, and toydom there is most attractive.

to-year (tə'jɪə(r)), *adv.* Now. *dial.* Forms: see YEAR[1]. [f. TO *prep.* A. 7 + YEAR[1]: cf. *to-day*, *to-night*.] This year.

c **1205** LAY. 8039 Her liggeð to-ȝere Ten þusend of his iferen. *c* **1290** *St. Brendan* 240 in *S. Eng. Leg.* I. 226 Ȝoure ester ȝe schulle holde þer as ȝe dude to-ȝere. *c* **1386** CHAUCER *Wife's Prol.* 168 Yet hadde I leuere wedde no wyf to yeere. *c* **1400** *Gosp. Nicodemus* 966 Of Ioseph..þat ȝe presond to ȝere. **1483** *Cath. Angl.* 391/1 To ȝere, *horno*; *hornus*, *hornotinus*. *a* **1575** R. B. *Appius & Virg.* B j, Man, be mery to yeere. **1623** WEBSTER *Duchess of Malfi* II. i, I have heard of none to year. **1727** GAY *Begg. Op.* I. ii, Betty hath brought more Goods into our Lock to-year than any five of the Gang. **1828** *Craven Gloss.* s.v. *To*, 'We've a famous clip to year', that is, this year. **1882** TENNYSON *Promise of May* I. Poems (1889) 781/2, I reckons they'll hev' a fine cider-crop to-year. **1886** T. HARDY *Mayor of Casterbr.* I. 64 Not but what he's been shook a little to-year about this.

toyel, obs. form of TOOL.

toyer ('tɔɪə(r)). [f. TOY *v.* + -ER[1].] One who toys; a trifler.

a **1713** W. HARRISON *Passion of Sappho* 5 in Nichols *Coll.* (1780) IV. 183 Wanton Cupid, idle toyer. **1814** L. HUNT *Notes Feast Poets* (1815) 51 These toyers in versification.

toyful ('tɔɪfʊl), *a.* Now *rare* or *Obs.* [f. TOY *sb.* + -FUL.] Full of sport or fun; sportive, playful; funny, amusing.

1580 SIDNEY *Let. to Robert S.* 18 Oct., My toyfull Books I will send..by February. *a* **1631** DONNE *Progr. Soul* xlvi, It quickned next a toyfull Ape. **1744** ARMSTRONG *Preserv. Health* II. 290 When Favonius, flush'd with love Toyful and young, in ev'ry breeze descends.

Hence **'toyfulness**.

a **1859** DE QUINCEY *Posth. Wks.* (1893) II. 24 The playfulness and..the toyfulness (if we may invent that word) of childhood.

toy-getter, -headed, etc.: see TOY *sb.* 12 d.

toying ('tɔɪɪŋ), *vbl. sb.* [f. TOY *v.* + -ING[1].] The action of the verb TOY; playing, sporting; trifling, idle or careless dealing (*with* anything), amorous dalliance.

1565–73 COOPER *Thesaurus* s.v. *Arguo*, *Digitorum argutiæ*, toyinges or gesturinges of the fingers: often mouyng. **1580** HOLLYBAND *Treas. Fr. Tong*, *Ragement*, wantonnesse, or toying. **1726** *Adv. Capt. R. Boyle* (1768) 236 After our Toying was over, she told me she was afraid of losing me. **1840** CARLYLE *Heroes* ii. (1872) 67 Toying and coquetting with Truth: this is the sorest sin. **1865** DICKENS *Mut. Fr.* I. xi, Slightly in contrast with this brief airy toying. **1911** W. W. PEYTON in *Contemp. Rev.* Sept. 374 Evil is in toying with imperfection.

'toying, *ppl. a.* [f. as prec. + -ING[2].] That toys; playful, sportive; *esp.* amorously sportive.

a **1566** R. EDWARDES *Damon & Pythias* Prol. 6 Frustrate quite of toying plaies. **1711** STEELE *Spect.* No. 155 ¶4 None of these toying Fools will do any more..to preserve her from Infamy. **1769** G. WHITE *Selborne* xxii. (1853) 93 When the cock has been pursuing the hen in a toying way through the boughs of a tree.

Hence **'toyingly** *adv.*

1731 BAILEY, *Toyingly*, triflingly, wantonly.

toyish ('tɔɪɪʃ), *a.* Now *rare*. [f. TOY *sb.* + -ISH[1].] Having the character of a toy, or addicted to toys (in various senses of the sb.).

1. Trifling, trivial, of no importance, worthless; foolish, senseless, nonsensical.

1574 *Life 70th Abp. Canterb.* Pref. E vj b, The thinges therin described being in part not all so true and in greatest part to to toyishe. **1588** CROWLEY *Delib. Answ.* 48 b, Your ringing of Belles, your burning of lightes in the open day-light, with..many other toyishe diuises. **1653** S. FISHER *Baby Baptism* 7 It's a most Pedantick, toyish and boyish piece of business. **1711** in *10th Rep. Hist. MSS. Comm.* App. v. 119 Mallice..is apt to make any toyish pretence to be her warrant for evil actions. **1850** C. WORDSWORTH *Occas. Serm.* Ser. I. 162 By it we have been secured from the hollow mockery or tedious and toyish ceremonies.

†**b.** Wanting in gravity of style; light, frivolous. ? *Obs.*

1603 G. JOHNSON *Disc. Troub. Eng. Ch. Amsterdam* 135 A copple crowned hatt with a twined band,..Immodest and toyish in a Pastors wife. **1615** MARKHAM *Eng. Housew.* II. i. (1668) 3 Adorn the person, altogether without toyish garnishes, or the gloss of light colours. **1676** MACE *Musick's Mon.* 129 Serabands are of the Shortest Triple-Time: but are more Toyish, and Light.

2. Sportive, playful, frisky, skittish. ? *Obs.*

1577 HARRISON *England* III. vii. (1878) II. 49 The last kind of toiesh curs are named dansers, and those being of a mongrell sort also, are taught & exercised to danse in measure. *c* **1613** ROWLANDS *Paire of Spy-Knaves* 5 From merry drunk, and toyish as an Ape. **1680** O. HEYWOOD *Diaries*, etc. (1883) III. 306 Oh this dodging, toyish, frisking heart kills me.

†**b.** Amorously sportive, wanton, licentious.

1563 *Homilies* II. *Place & Time of Prayer* I. (1859) 341 They rest in wantonness, in toyish talking, in filthy fleshliness.

†**3.** Fantastic, odd, whimsical, queer. *Obs.*

1598 FLORIO, *Humorista*, humorous, fantasticall, toish. **1599** HARSNET *Agst. Darell* 98 Somers had counterfeyted certaine fits and toyish behaviour at M. Brakenburie. **1638** SANDERSON *Serm., Ad Aulam* viii. (1660) II. 158 Some peevish and obstinate, some toyish, fickle, and humorous.

4. Of the nature of, or fit for, a plaything; of a humorous or sportive character, as a writing.

1699 POMFRET *Dies Noviss.* Rem. (1724) 8 Adieu, ye toyish Reeds that once could please My softer lips. **1830** SCOTT *Demonol.* v. 163 They have many light toyish books.

5. Resembling a toy, toy-like; diminutive or flimsy; *spec.* like, or like that of, a 'toy' dog.

1886 *Field* 23 Jan. 113/2 Richmond Puzzle, fourth prize, is at present small and toyish. **1890** *Ibid.* 8 Mar. 355/2 His [a Fox Terrier's] head is now toyish and effeminate.

Hence **'toyishly** *adv.*; **'toyishness.**

1607 MARKHAM *Caval.* II. (1617) 150 He will exercise his lesson with such wantonnesse and apish toyishnesse. **1624** BP. MOUNTAGU *Immed. Addr.* 116 See how toyishly these great Masters play with their owne fancies. **1665** GLANVILL *Scepsis Sci.* Addr. 23 Your Society..will discredit that toyishness of wanton fancy.

toyl, obs. form of TOIL, TOILE[1], TWILL.

toyle, toyll, obs. forms of TOIL, TOOL.

toyless ('tɔɪlɪs), *a.* [f. TOY *sb.* + -LESS.] Destitute of toys; not having any toys.

1898 G. TAYLOR in *Chicago Advance* 13 Jan. 43/3 Telling us of the children's gifts to their toyless little down-town neighbors. **1906** *Blackw. Mag.* Apr. 647/1 My toyless condition was due to anatomical longings.

toym, toyme, obs. forms of TOOM *sb.*[1] and *a.*

toyman ('tɔɪmən). [f. TOY *sb.* + MAN *sb.*[1]] A man who sells toys, or who keeps a toy-shop: formerly, one who sold requisites for sports, trinkets, and fancy goods; latterly, one who makes or sells playthings for children (cf. TOY-SHOP 1, 2).

1707 *Lond. Gaz.* No. 4328/8 Ralph Ayscough, of St. James's Westminster, Toyman. **1710-11** SWIFT *Jrnl.* 7 Jan., I will go to the toyman's here just in Pall Mall, and he sells great hugeous batoons. **1749** FIELDING *Tom Jones* XII. iv, The pocket-book..had cost five and twenty shillings, having been bought of a celebrated toyman. **1758** JOHNSON *Idler* No. 6 ¶5 The toyman will not give his jewels. **1813** SHELLEY *Q. Mab* Notes, Poet. Wks. (1891) 41/1 The jeweller, the toyman, the actor gains fame and wealth by the exercise of his useless and ridiculous art. **1886** C. E. PASCOE *Lond. of To-day* xl. (ed. 3) 347 Those admirable examples of the toyman's craft—whole garrisons of miniature soldiers, artillery, cavalry, and infantry.

toy-mutch, etc.: see TOY *sb.* 12.

toyn, toyne, obs. forms of TONE *sb.*

Toynbeean ('tɔɪnbiːən), *a.* [f. the name of Arnold Joseph *Toynbee* (1889–1975), British historian + -AN.] Of or pertaining to Toynbee, his style, or his theories of the rise and decline of civilizations.

1954 W. K. HANCOCK *Country & Calling* viii. 221 Even when he has attained these two virtues of attachment and justice, the historian still needs a third, which I call *span*. This resembles the Toynbeean quality of remoteness. **1962** *Listener* 8 Feb. 240/1, I would translate your words into Toynbeean English, namely an answer to a challenge. **1966** *New Statesman* 18 Feb. 230/3 A remark..that 'the mature societies of Europe..in numerous ways..responded to the challenge' has the authentic Toynbeean stamp. **1975** *Asian Affairs* LXII. 239, I speak of dominance in the Toynbeean sense of a dominant civilization.

‖**toyon** ('tɔɪɒn). Also tollon. [a. Mexican Sp. *tollon* (toʎon), the native name.] The Californian Holly, *Heteromeles* (*Photinia*) *arbutifolia*, N.O. *Rosaceæ*.

[**1848** BENTHAM *Plantæ Hartweg.* 307 Photinia arbutifolia, *Toyon* incolarum.] **1876** BREWER, etc. *Bot. California* I. 188 *Heteromeles arbutifolia*, Toyon or Tollon. **1884** MILLER *Plant-n.*, Tollon, or Toyon.

†**'toyous,** *a. Obs. rare.* [f. TOY *sb.* + -OUS.]

a. Trifling, ornamental, unessential. **b.** Inclined to toy or flirt, coquettish. Hence **'toyousness.**

1581 MULCASTER *Positions* xxxviii. (1887) 178 Those ouerraught qualities for the toyousnesse therof being misplaced in her, do cause the young woman rather to be toyed with-all..then to be thought verie well of. **1592** WARNER *Alb. Eng.* VII. xxxvi. 157 The faire sweet wittie wench grew toyous in the end.

toy-pate, -railway, etc.: see TOY *sb.* 12.

'toy-shop.

1. A shop for the sale of trinkets, knick-knacks, or small ornamental articles; a fancy shop. *arch.*

1693 W. FREKE *Sel. Ess.* xxxii. 201 Are not these..fitter for a Toy-shop, than a Wise Man's Head? **1711** ADDISON *Spect.* No. 10 ¶6 If they [women] make an Excursion to a Mercer's or a Toy-shop. **1712** *Ibid.* No. 499 ¶5 Ribbons, brocades, embroidery,.. sufficient to have furnished a whole street of toy-shops. **1791** BOSWELL *Johnson* 28 Apr. an. 1778, We stopped again at Wirgman's, the well-known *toy-shop*, ..he sent for me to..help him to choose a pair of silver buckles. **1852** [see 3].

2. A shop for the sale of toys or playthings.

1796 *Boston Directory* 232 Butler, Mary, crockery and toy shop. **1818** SCOTT *Hrt. Midl.* vi, These booths have degenerated into mere toy-shops, where the little loiterers..are..enchanted by the rich display of hobby-horses, babies, and Dutch toys. **1858** LYTTON *What will he do* I. xvi, Lionel could not find in the toyshops of the village a doll good enough. **1886** C. E. PASCOE *Lond. of To-day* xl. (ed. 3) 347 A toy shop, crowded with all sorts of interesting playthings.

3. *attrib.*

1813 *Theatrical Inquisitor* II. 124 Her arms..drop inanimate like the..limbs of a toy-shop harlequin. **1840** DICKENS *Old C. Shop* xxii, Such..as was never before seen or heard of out of a toy-shop window. **1852** THACKERAY *Esmond* III. vi, Esmond found the antechamber crowded with milliners and toyshop women..mercers' men with hangings, and velvets, and brocades.

†**toysome** ('tɔɪsəm), *a. Obs. rare.* [f. TOY *sb.* + -SOME.] Full of 'toys', or having the character of a 'toy'; fantastic, whimsical; inclined to toy, sportive, playful; amorously sportive.

1638 FORD *Fancies* II. i, I have an excellent humour to be pettish, A little toysome. **1659** HOOLE *Comenius' Vis. World* (1777) 178 The fool causeth laughter by his toysome actions. **1719** D'URFEY *Pills* (1872) III. 113 Tom was toysome, Will was sad. **1754** RICHARDSON *Grandison* (1783) VI. 192 As we sat at breakfast, two or three toysome things were said by my Lord (no ape was ever so fond!).

Hence **'toysomeness.**

1697 CREECH tr. *Manilius* Pref. 46 There are so many boldnesses scatter'd thro' his Poem, and so much of Toysomness just by them, that a man may read his Youth in his Writings.

†**'toyson, -e,** obs. ff. *toison*: in quots. short for TOISON D'OR.

a **1505** in Kingsford *Chron. Lond.* (1905) 230 Other honourable personages in Ambassade, as his second Chamberlayn and Knyght of the Toyson. *a* **1548** HALL *Chron., Hen. VIII* 13 b, The lord Bresley, knight of the Toyson. **1601** R. JOHNSON *Kingd. & Commw.* (1603) 244 There is also the order of the Toysone, of which his maiestie is chiefe.

toyte, toit (toit), *v. Sc.* and *north. dial. intr.* To totter, walk feebly or unsteadily.

1787 BURNS *To Auld Mare* xviii, We'll toyte about wi' ane anither. **1871** W. ALEXANDER *Johnny Gibb* xliv, I've toitit aboot wi' you upo' this place naar foorty year noo.

toytown ('tɔɪtaʊn), *sb.* (and *a.*) Also toy-town. [f. TOY *sb.* + TOWN *sb.*] A model of a town used as a plaything; *fig.* a small or insignificant town; also (with capital initial) the name of a town featured in a series of books and radio plays for children by S. G. Hulme Beaman (1887–1932). Also *attrib.* or as *adj.*

1836 [MISS MAITLAND] *Lett. fr. Madras* iv. (1843) 25 Cape Town is just like the Dutch toy-towns. **1864** R. BROWNING *Let.* 22 Aug. in G. R. Hudson *Browning to his American Friends* (1965) 145 A toy-town with boulevards traced through the sand-hills. **1897** 'S. GRAND' *Beth Book* (1898) xxiii. 207 The place..[had] a look of having been..set in order like a toy-town. **1928** S. G. H. BEAMAN *Tales of Toytown* 53 'Did you tell him I am busy?' the Mayor asked, laying down the copy of the *Toytown News* he had been reading. **1941** *Sun* (Baltimore) 27 Nov. 10/7 The demonstration, in the [chemical warfare] school's 'toytown' buildings which simulate actual city conditions, is a regular part of the two-week course at the school. **1964** W. MARKFIELD *To Early Grave* (1965) xi. 191 Platters of marzipan cookies shone with a toytown brilliance. **1971** R. FALKIRK *Chill Factor* iv. 38 Austurvollur Square was still toytown with the little white Lutheran Cathedral. **1972** *Daily Tel.* (Colour Suppl.) 27 Oct. 19/4 The slums of Kingston are horrendous: hovels of cardboard and plywood, tiny packing-case houses like a stricken toytown. **1972** 'S. WOODS' *They love not Poison* vii. 97 She..was..listening to a Toytown play on the Children's Hour. **1973** *Times* 15 Nov. 25/6 The Treasury are also fairly unimpressed by it; they refer to it internally as 'toytown money'. **1979** *Theatre Australia* Apr. 30/1 A *faux naif* toytown set of kitchen cupboard colours clashed dismally with furniture. **1984** *Times* 13 Mar. 17/1 This toytown situation became the occasion for a number of serious-looking people (all men, as it happened) in serious-looking suits to respond in a serious way to the questions of a sombre moderator.

†**'toywort.** *Obs.* [f. TOY *sb.* + WORT.] A local name for the herb Shepherd's purse (*Capsella Bursa-pastoris*), from the resemblance of the capsule to a toy purse.

1597 GERARDE *Herbal* II. xxiii. §2. 215 Sheepheardes purse is called..in the North part of England Toywoort, Pickepurse, and Caseweede. **1657** W. COLES *Adam in Eden* 71.

†**toze, tose** (təʊz), *v.*[1] *Obs.* exc. *dial.* Forms: 3–7 tose, 4–7 toose, 6 tooze (toese), 7–8 toase, (7 toaze), 6– toze. [ME. *tosen* (*a* 1250 in compound *to-tosen*); not recorded in OE.; but the later forms *toase*, etc. indicate an OE. **tásian*, f. verbal root *tás-*:—OTeut. *tais-*, whence also OE. *tǽsan* (:—**taisjan*) to TEASE (q.v. for further relations).] *trans.* To pull asunder; to separate or unravel the fibres of; to comb or card (wool, etc.); = TEASE *v.*[1] 1.

a **1250** [see *to-tose*, TO-[2] 1]. **1346** *Litt. Red Bk. Bristol* (1900) II. 2 Item si fila deficiant in panno vel quod nimis distent quod textores appellant *tosed*. **1390** GOWER *Conf.* I. 17 And what Schep that is full of wulle Upon his back, thei toose and pulle, Whil ther is eny thing to pile. *c* **1400** *Lanfranc's Cirurg.* 41 A good quantite of tow I-tosid. *c* **1440** *Promp. Parv.* 497/2 Toson wulle or other lyke [*v.r.* tosyn or tose wul], *carpo*. **1530** PALSGR. 760/1, I toose wolle, or cotton, or suche lyke, *je force de la laine*, and *je charpis de la laine*. **1567** GOLDING *Ovid's Met.* XIV. 305 What toozing wooll did meene. **1577** NORTHBROOKE *Dicing* (1843) 81 Many..may pick wool, and sow garments, or tose okam. **1615** MARKHAM *Eng. Housew.* II. v. (1668) 123 Toase it every lock by lock. **1622** R. HAWKINS *Voy. S. Sea* (1847) 155 Peeces of a junke or rope, chopped very small,..and after tozed all as oacombe. **1665** HOOKE *Microgr.* 42 The Internal parts..were..as it were, tos'd open like a Lock of Wool. **1725** *Bradley's Fam. Dict.* s.v. *Mixing Colours*, Wool..must be taken out and toas'd over-again: for the first Toasing was to make it receive the Colour or Die; but the second is to..make it fit for Spinning. **1881** MISS JACKSON *Shropsh. Word-bk.* s.v. *Tag*, Snip the end off the tag, an' toze it well as the grace can get among it.

b. *transf.* To pull, pull about. (Cf. TOUSE.)

14.. *Sir Beues* 1952 + 2 (MS. M) That they were in the grene wose, And I shold hem well tose. **1573** TUSSER *Husb.* (1878) 206 For euerie crime, What toesed eares, like baited beares!

c. *fig.* To separate, search out; to analyse; to elicit, 'tease out'.

c **1450** *Cov. Myst.* xlii. (1841) 401 The trewthe fful trewlye he wyl tose, And send ȝow to hevyn or helle. **1611** SHAKS. *Wint. T.* IV. iv. 760 For that I insinuate, or [*printed* at] toaze from thee thy Businesse. **1633** D. R[OGERS] *Treat. Sacram.* II. 44 Doe it more fully, toze your consciences. **1648** JENKYN *Blind Guide* i. 8 The spurious expositions..upon the Scriptures in his tedious tozing of them.

Hence †**tozed, tosed** *ppl. a.*, †**'tozing** *vbl. sb.*; †**'tozer**, a comber or carder (of wool, etc.).

1346 Tosed [see above]. *c* **1440** *Promp. Parv.* 497/2 Tosare, of wulle or other lyke, *carptrix*. Tosynge, of wulle or oþer thyngys, *carptura*. **14..** *Noble Bk. Cookry* (1882) 103 Charge it with the tosed flesshe. **1563-87** FOXE *A. & M.* (1596) 321/1 For euerie sacke of tosed wool, seuen marks. **1632** tr. *Bruel's Praxis Med.* 22 Dippe toosed Wooll herein. **1648** Tozing [see c above]. **1725** Toasing [see above].

toze (təʊz), *v.*[2] *Tin-mining.* Also 9 **toas** (*erron.* **toss**). [Possibly the same word as prec.; but connexion of sense is not certain.

(The spelling *toss* seems due to a bad etymological guess (see quot. 1839) which has passed into dictionaries.)]

trans. To separate tin ore from the gangue or rough ore by stirring the slimes in a kieve, and allowing the heavier particles to settle.

1758 BORLASE *Nat. Hist. Cornw.* 180 The coffer is then emptied the second time, the tin carried again to the keeve, there tozed, skimmed, and packed. **1839** DE LA BECHE *Rep. Geol. Cornw.*, etc. xv. 577 Another let the tin ore fall into it [*sc.* the water] by degrees at the side of the keeve, where it was tozed (tossed), or stirred by the other until the vat was almost full. **1882** JAGO *Cornw. Gloss.*, *Toas*, or *Toze*, to shake or toss the wet tin to and fro in a kieve or vat, with water, to cleanse and dress it.

Hence **'tozing** *vbl. sb.*, the action of thus cleaning the ore; also in comb., as **tozing-tub**, the tub or kieve in which tin ore is tozed. Also **'tozer**: see quot. 1885; (also a Cornish surname).

[**1758** BORLASE *Nat. Hist. Cornw.* 179 The tin-ore is then sifted in a sieve purposely constructed, and if it needs must be sent to be buddled again, then returned to the keeve and worked as before with a shovel, which they call *tozing* the tin.] **1789** J. WILLIAMS *Min. Kingd.* II. 210 They are obliged to take another method to clean it, which is called turloobing, or tozing. *Ibid.* 212 The tozing operation. **1839** URE *Dict. Arts* 1244 The rough is washed in buddles, and in tossing tubs. **1877** KNIGHT *Dict. Mech.* 2603/2 *Tossing*, or *Tozing*, the operation of agitating ore in a kieve; a tub in which it is rotated in water by a stirrer on a vertical axis. **1885** *Black's Guide to Cornw.* (ed. 13) 54 Tozer, the man who tozes, stirs, or washes the crop-tin.

tozie, variant of TOSY.

†**tozy** ('təʊzɪ), *a. Obs.* [app. f. TOZE *v.*[1] + -Y. But cf. TOSY.] Soft like teased wool. Hence †**'toziness**, softness.

1706 PHILLIPS (ed. Kersey), *Tozy*, soft like Wooll. **1727** BAILEY vol. II, *Tozyness*, softness, like tozed Wooll.

absol. **1824** SCOTT *St. Ronan's* xx, I can tell it [a shawl] to be a real *tozie*. *Ibid.*, That tozie now will keep its colour while there is a rag of it left.

†**tphrowh,** *int. Obs. nonce-wd.* An exclamation to arrest or call attention: cf. PROO.

1575 *Gamm. Gurton* I. ii. Aiij, And chad not cryed tphrowh, hoore, shead lept out of his Lees.

†**tprot.** *Obs.* An expression of contempt.

13.. in *Pol. Songs* (Camden) 223 Tprot, Scot, for thi strif! Hang up thyn hachet ant thy knyf.

†**tprw.** *Obs.* Imitation of the sound of a horn.

c **1430** *Pilgr. Lyf. Manhode* II. cxv. (1869) 118 Tprw tprw, j sey, tprw tprw.

tra, Sc. variant of TRAY *sb. Obs.*, affliction.

traas, traass, obs. ff. of TRACE *sb.*[1], TRASS.

‖**tra'bacolo.** Also trabaccolo. [It. *trabacolo*, *-accolo*:—med.L. **trabāculum*, f. L. *trab-em* beam, timber (cf. *tabernāculum*).] An Italian ship of medium size; a small coasting vessel.

1800 E. C. KNIGHT *Let.* 9 Aug. in *Autobiogr.* (1960) 221 Had we sailed, as was first intended, in the imperial [Russian] frigate, we should have been taken by eight trabaccoli, which the French armed on purpose at Pisaro. **1809** CAPT. HOSTE in *Naval Chron.* XXII. 506 A convoy of merchant trabaccolos. **1812** *Examiner* 12 Oct. 648/1 Twelve sail of the enemy's trabaccoloes. **1846** RAIKES *Life Sir J. Brenton* 360 Accompanied by three trabacolos for the purpose of landing the troops. [1866 HOWELLS *Venet. Life* vii, Small coasting vessels (*trabaccoli* at Venice).]

trabal ('treɪbəl, 'træbəl), *a.* [ad. L. *trabāl-is*, f. *trab-s*, *trab-em* beam: see -AL[1].] †**a.** Pertaining to or of the nature of a beam; trabeal. *Obs. rare*-[0]. **b.** *Anat.* Pertaining to the *trabs cerebri* or *corpus callosum* of the brain.

1656 BLOUNT *Glossogr.*, Trabal, of, or belonging to a beame; great or big like a beame. **1889** *Buck's Handbk. Med. Sc.* VIII. 517 *Trabal*..would merely recall the obsolete name for the callosum, *trabs cerebri*. **1899** *Syd. Soc. Lex.*, *Trabal*, pertaining to the *Trabs*; callosal.

‖**trabant** (tra'bant). Also 7 **trabanto, travant,** 7–8 **traband.** [a. Ger. *trabant* a life-guard, an armed attendant, a satellite (also in Astron.), in It. *trabante*, F. *traban*, Boh. *drabanti*; of Turkish (orig. Pers.) origin: see DRABANT.] **1.** In some European countries, a life-guard, an armed attendant, a satellite. Now chiefly *Hist.*

1617 MORYSON *Itin.* III. 188 He [the Emperor] had one hundred for his Guard, (called Trabantoes)... Ten Hascheres and twelue Trabantoes attended each day. *a* **1634** CHAPMAN *Alphonsus* III. F iv b, Six travants well arm'd. **1693** *Lond. Gaz.* No. 2845/2 Thus they went through several stately Rooms, having the Trabands on each side of them. **1762** tr. *Busching's Syst. Geog.* V. 317 The fifty halberdeers and the fifty trabands or horse-guards here being rather instituted for the splendor of the court than the military establishment. **1904** *Daily Chron.* 15 Dec. 1/7 It was announced that the President [of the Hungarian Chamber]..would not appear, and that the guard of 'Trabants' had been removed.

2. *Cytology.* = SATELLITE *sb.* 9.

1926 C. D. DARLINGTON in *Jrnl. Genetics* XVI. 248 A portion thus narrower than the main body of the chromosome seems to require the name of satellite or trabant; such an element, having an attraction for the parent body proportionally less than a larger element, is naturally more subject to external forces, hence the common appearance of flying out. **1967** C. P. SWANSON et al. *Cytogenetics* ii. 26 The region of the chromosome distal to the nucleolar gap is called a trabant or satellite. **1980** *Caryologia* XXXIII. 207 In three individuals we observed different thickness of the intercalary trabant.

‖**trabea** ('treɪbiːə). Pl. **-eæ** (-iːiː). *Rom. Antiq.* [Latin *trabea*.] A toga ornamented with horizontal purple stripes, worn as a state robe by kings, consuls, and other men of rank in ancient Rome.

1600 HOLLAND *Livy* I. 30 Then came Servius abroad in his roiall robe, called *Trabea*. **1702** ADDISON *Dial. Medals* iii. (1726) 160 Our modern Medals are full of Toga's and Tunica's, Trabea's and Paludamentums. *a* **1746** HOLDSWORTH *Rem. Virgil* (1768) 291 The Lituus and Trabea of Romulus and the Ancilia were kept in the Sacrarium of the Salii. **1842** W. SMITH *Dict. Gr. & Rom. Antiq.* s.v. *Toga*, Servius..mentions three kinds of trabeae; one wholly of purple, which was sacred to the gods, another of purple and white, and another of purple and saffron which belonged to augurs. The purple and white trabea was a royal robe.

trabeal ('treɪbiːəl), *a. Arch.* [irreg. f. L. *trab-em* beam, instead of the regular form TRABAL.] Of the nature of a horizontal beam, beam-like.

1862 SIR H. ACLAND in *Macm. Mag.* V. 527 (*Descr. Oxford Museum*) Extending laterally..arise two slender spanners to the [iron] trabeal beam before referred to as sustaining the rafters. **1866** *Athenæum* 18 Aug. 214/2 Trabeal forms prevail.

trabeate ('treɪbiːeɪt), *a. Arch.* [irreg. (for **trabate*), f. L. *trab-s*, *trab-em* beam + -ATE[2], on analogy of TRABEATON, q.v. (L. *trabeātus* meant 'clad in the trabea'.)] = next.

1890 C. H. MOORE *Gothic Archit.* i. 6 *note*, It is not until we scrutinise the joints of masonry that the trabeate principle of its construction is perceived. **1905** *Athenæum* Apr. 441/2 The ordinary house [in Syrian architecture, 85 B.C. to 609 A.D.] was a purely trabeate building... The construction was in cut stone blocks laid without mortar; but the arch..was gradually evolved.

trabeated ('treɪbiːeɪtɪd), *a. Arch.* Also **trabiated.** [f. as prec. + -ED[1].] Constructed with beams; having beams or long squared stones as lintels and entablatures, instead of using the arch; covered with a beam or entablature, as a doorway.

trabeated architecture is opposed to *arcuated*, *arched*, or *vaulted*. ***trabeated ceiling***, a flat ceiling sustained by beams, by which it is divided into compartments, as distinguished from a vaulted ceiling.

1843 *Civil Eng. & Arch. Jrnl.* VI. 96/1 The happy union of the arch and the trabeated systems. **1857** G. J. WIGLEY *Borromeo's Instr. Eccl. Build.* v. 13 Ceiling..(either vaulted or trabiated, according to the proportion of the edifice). **1863** *Sat. Rev.* 21 Mar. 367/1 Strictly it was a propylæum, not an arch, for the opening was trabeated.

trabeation (treɪbiː'eɪʃən). *Arch.* Also 6 **trabiacion.** [irreg. for **trabation*, f. L. *trab-s*, *trab-em* beam: see -ATION.] †**a.** A member resembling a horizontal beam; an entablature. *Obs.* **b.** Construction with horizontal beams or the like, as opposed to arches or vaults; trabeated structure.

1563 SHUTE *Archit.* C j b, This pillor..supported no other..but his owne Trabiacions. **1704** J. HARRIS *Lex. Techn.* I, *Trabeation*, or *Entablature*,..comprehends the Architrave, Frize, and Cornice. **1831** *Fraser's Mag.* IV. 283 To apply to an entire cornice, or even to a whole 'trabeation', those curved forms which have hitherto been exclusively confined to mouldings and lesser details. *a* **1878** SIR G. G. SCOTT *Lect. Archit.* (1879) I. 19 Arcuation plastered over to look like trabeation.

‖**trabecula** (trə'bɛkjʊlə). Pl. **-æ** (-iː). Also **tra'beculum** (-əm), pl. **-a** (-ə); **tra'beculus** (-əs), pl. **-i** (-aɪ); and in anglicized forms **trabecle** ('træbɪk(ə)l), **'trabecule** (-kjuːl). [L. *trabecula*, *trabicula*, dim. of *trabs* beam; the forms in *-um* and *-us* are mod.L. variants.] A structure in an animal or plant resembling a small beam or bar.

spec. **a.** *Anat.* and *Zool.* Each of the plates of bony substance forming the cancellated tissue of a bone; any slender band of tissue extending like a cross-bar across a cavity, as of the heart (*trabeculæ carneæ*), or through the substance of a soft organ, as the spleen or kidney; each of two cartilaginous bars (*trabeculæ cranii*) in front of the pituitary body in the embryo, which coalesce and develop into part of the cranium; each of the calcareous plates connecting the dorsal and ventral walls in echinoderms; each of a pair of appendages on the head in front of the antennæ in certain bird-lice. **b.** *Bot.* A projection extending across the cell-cavity in the ducts of some plants, or across the cavity of the sporangium in mosses and other cryptogams.

1866 *Treas. Bot.*, *Trabecula* (adj. *Trabeculate*), a cross-bar; as in the teeth of many mosses. **1873** T. H. GREEN *Introd. Pathol.* (ed. 2) 137 This tissue, like bone, is made up of trabeculæ and medullary spaces. **1874** COUES *Birds N.W.* 611 Divided..by a cartilaginous trabeculum, which is thrown across from the posterior side to the anterior apex of the base of the pyramid. **1875** SIR W. TURNER in *Encycl. Brit.* I. 853/2 The interior of a bone..is made up of thin delicate plates or bars, or trabecles, which intersect each other at various angles, and form..the spongy or cancellated tissue. **1875** BENNETT & DYER *Sachs' Bot.* II. iv. 413 Both kinds of sporangia [in Isoëtes] are imperfectly segmented by threads of tissue (*Trabeculæ*) which cross from the ventral to the dorsal side. **1890** BILLINGS *Med. Dict.*, *Trabecula cinerea*, soft commissure of the brain.

Hence **tra'becular** *a.*, pertaining to or of the nature of a trabecula; composed of or furnished with trabeculæ; **tra'becularism**, trabecular condition, trabeculation; **tra'beculate, -ated** *adjs.*, furnished with or having trabeculæ; **trabecu'lation**, formation of trabeculæ, trabeculated condition.

1822–34 *Good's Study Med.* (ed. 4) III. 164 A cystic form [of cataract] without pus,..a sil quose and a *trabecular. **1847–9** *Todd's Cycl. Anat.* IV. 773/1 The trabecular tissue consists of..cylindrical fibres. **1891** *Cent. Dict.*, **Trabecularism*, in *anat.*, a coarse reticulation, or cross-barred condition, of any tissue. **1866** *Trabeculate [see TRABECULA]. **1876** tr. *Wagner's Gen. Pathol.* (ed. 6) 359 They..unite by opposite processes into networks, form *trabeculated membranes. **1898** *Allbutt's Syst. Med.* V. 182 Cavities..traversed by tough septa and bridles..are..described as trabeculated. **1900** *Lancet* 5 May 1275/2 *Trabeculation of the bladder. **1904** *Jrnl. R. Microsc. Soc.* Dec. 636.

†**tra'boccant,** *a. Obs. rare.* [ad. It. *traboccante*, pres. pple. of *traboccare* to overflow, superabound.] Superabundant, excessive; preponderant.

1651 HOWELL *Venice* 208 The power of one might not so out-poize and be trabocant that the rest shold be in danger to be blown up. **1654** —— *Parthenop.* Pref. A j b, One could hardly discern which Scale would be traboccant and over-poising.

trabuch (trə'bʊk). *Obs.* or *arch.* Also 7 **trabucche, trabuck.** [a. OF. *trabuc* (Sp. *trabuco*), f. *tra-*, *très-* (:—L. *trans-*, expressing displacement) + OF. *buc* trunk (of the body), bulk, a. WGer. *bûh*, Ger. *bauch* belly.] A mediæval engine of war for throwing great stones against walls, etc.: cf. TREBUCHET.

1610 HOLLAND *Camden's Brit.* I. 400 Of these Mangonells, Patraries, Trabucks..by which..they discharged volies of mighty huge stones..much might heere be said. **1614** CAMDEN *Rem.* 238 Our nation had the practise of most of these, and moreouer of Mangonels, Trabucches, and Bricolles, wherewith they vsed to cast mil-stones. **1890** DOYLE *White Company* xv, The Norman hath a mangonel or a trabuch upon the forecastle.

trabuschette, obs. form of TREBUCHET.

trac (træk). *Basketry.* [Etym. unknown.] In full ***trac border.*** A basketwork border made by taking the remaining length of an upright and weaving it in and out of the following uprights before repeating the process with the next.

1924 C. CRAMPTON *Cane Work* 13 *Back trac*, an additional border worked with the remaining ends of a three-rod plain border. **1959** D. WRIGHT *Baskets & Basketry* ii. 57 A Foot-Border... This is a trac border used for securing stakes to a wooden base with holes in it... Other tracs may also be used. **1964** H. HODGES *Artifacts* x. 146 In the trac border one stake at a time was bent and woven in completely.

‖**tracas** (traka). *Obs.* [Fr., f. *tracasser*: see next.] Bustle, hurry, fuss; embarrassment.

[**1611** COTGR., *Tracas*, much trotting, or hurrying vp and downe; hence also, toyle, trouble, turmoile.] **1656** BLOUNT *Glossogr.* [from Cotgr.], *Tracas*, or *Tracasserie*. **1673** O. WALKER *Educ.* iv. 35 He then desired of the Emperor to be dismissed into his own Countrey, where he might dye in quiet out of the tracas and noise of the World.

‖**tracasserie** (trakasri). [Fr., f. *tracasser* to bustle, worry oneself: see -ERY.] A state of disturbance or annoyance; a turmoil, bother, fuss; an embroilment, petty quarrel. (Chiefly in *pl.*)

1656 [see prec.]. **1658** PHILLIPS, *Tracasserie* (French), a needlesse hurrying, or restlesse travelling up and down. **1715** in P. M. Thornton *Stuart Dynasty* (1890) App. I. 353, I am of your opinion that to avoid tracassaries one should let the different correspondences take their course. **1812** SCOTT *Let. to Miss J. Baillie* 17 Jan., in *Lockhart*, A wonderful man..acquainted with all the intrigues and tracasseries of the cabinets. **1833** T. HOOK *Parson's Dau.* I. vii, Adept as she was in all the tracasseries of flirtation. **1879** MRS. LYNN LINTON in *Life* xvi. (1901) 219 Life seems to me empty of all but tracasseries.

trace (treɪs), *sb.*[1] Forms: 3– **trace**; also 4–5 **tras,** 4–7 **trase,** (4 **traze,** *Sc.* **trass, traiss,** 4–5 **trays,** *Sc.* **traise,** 5 **traas, trayse, (trasche),** 6 *Sc.* **trais).** [a. F. *trace* (12th c. in Godef.) = Pr. *trassa*, It. *traccia* (Sp. *traza* draught, first sketch), vbl. sb. f. OF. *tracier*, F. *tracer*: see TRACE *v.*[1]]

I. †**1. a.** The way or path which anything takes; course, road; esp. in ***to take one's trace***, to make one's way, take one's course, proceed. *Obs.*

a **1300** [see b]. **13..** *K. Alis.* 7759 (Bodl. MS.) Alisaunder & Candace To Chaumber token her trace. **13..** *E.E. Allit. P.* A. 1112 To-warde þe þrone þay trone a tras. *c* **1425** *Cast. Persev.* 1923 in *Macro Plays* 131 Haue don, felaus! & take ȝoure trasche. *c* **1440** *Promp. Parv.* 498/2 Trace, of a wey over a felde, *trames*. *c* **1450** *St. Cuthbert* (Surtees) 3394 To farne agayne he takes his trace. *c* **1470** HENRYSON *Mor. Fab.* IX. (*Wolf & Fox*) xvi, All the trace he [the Cadger] trippit on his tais. **1530** PALSGR. 282/2 Trace, a streyght way, *trace*. **1596** SPENSER *F.Q.* VI. i. 6 Now I begin To tread an endlesse trace, withouten guyde. **1678** CUDWORTH *Intell. Syst.* I. v. §25. 684 The striate particles finding no fit pores or traces for their passage through it. **1768** STERNE *Sent. Journ.* (1778) I. 69, I wanted the traces through which my wishes might find their way to her.

†**b.** *fig.* A course of action or conduct; way of proceeding; 'path', 'way', 'road'; esp. in phrases ***to follow, take, tread the trace.*** *Obs.*

a **1300** *Cursor M.* 25528 Until us þat al to mikel has ben vn-buxs Vnto þi suet trace [*Fairf.* for to folow þi trace]. *c* **1375** *Cato's Mor.* 374 *ibid.* p. 1674 (Fairf. MS.) Gode grante vs grace To folow catouns trace In his teyching. *c* **1375** *Sc. Leg. Saints* xxvi. (*Nycholas*) 43 þus he be-gane to god seke, & held furth ay in þat trace. *c* **1430** *Hymns Virg.* 35, Y took to þe world, & wente from þee, Y folewide þe feend al in his traas. *c* **1586** C'TESS PEMBROKE *Ps.* CXIX. D. iii, From the lyers trace, From falshoods wreathed way, O save me, Lord. **1631** WEEVER *Anc. Fun. Mon.* 67 The rest of the Nobilitie..trode also the same trace. **1652** J. WRIGHT tr. *Camus' Nat. Paradox* VIII. 163 To reduce him into the trace of his Duty and Reason. *a* **1716** SOUTH *Serm.* (1823) III. 252 God, by a secret, unobserved trace of his providence, may cast men under a..seducing ministry.

†**2.** A line, file, or train of persons. *Obs.*

c **1385** CHAUCER *L.G.W.* Prol. 285, I saugh comyng of ladyes Nientene..And after hem coome of wymen swich a traas. **1598** BARRET *Theor. Warres* IV. i. 102 The Sergeant Maiors..haue conducted these Regiments very disorderly, making a long trace, file, or lyne (as it were) of them.

†**3.** A series of steps in dancing; a measure; a dance. *Obs.*

c **1450** *Mankind* ii. 521 in *Macro Plays* 20, I xall make hym to dawnce a-noþer trace! *c* **1460** SIR R. ROS *Belle Dame* 190 Whan he thought tyme to dance with her a trace. **1500–20** DUNBAR *Poems* lxxxi. 26 Thane com the ladyis, danceing in ane trace. **1519** *Interl. Four Elements* (Percy Soc.) 48 Folow all! I wyll lede a trace. **1577** [see TRACING *vbl. sb.*[1] 2].

†**4. a.** *pl.* The series or line of footprints left by an animal; hence in *sing.* a footprint. *Obs.*

13.. *Guy Warw.* (A.) 4732 Of hors traces hy þer seye. *c* **1374** CHAUCER *Boeth.* v. Met. v. 133 (Camb. MS.) Other bestis gladen hemself to diggen hir traas or hir steppis in the Erthe with hir goyngz or with hir feet. **1484** CAXTON *Fables of Æsop* IV. xii, We knowe wel by thy traces that all the beestes whiche haue entryd in to thy hows came not oute ageyne. **1552** HULOET, Trace or steppe, *vestigium*. **1575** TURBERV. *Venerie* 114 In Beasts of pray and rauine as Beare and Bore &c. they are called traces. **1616** SURFL. & MARKH. *Country Farme* 694 There is more regard to bee taken vnto her traces: for the print of the hares foot is sharpe, and fashioned like vnto the point of a knife. **1706** PHILLIPS (ed. Kersey), *Trace* (among *Hunters*), the Footprint of wild Beasts.

fig. **1610** *Crt. & Times Jas. I* (1849) I. 114 One who hath left so good traces and steps wherein to walk.

†**b.** *pl. loosely.* Footsteps. *Obs.*

1613 W. BROWNE *Brit. Past.* I. iv. 294 Till at the last..Ye bend your traces up some shady hill.

5. a. The track made by the passage of any person or thing, whether beaten by feet or indicated in any other way: = TRACK *sb.* 1. ***on one's trace(s)***, in pursuit of one; ***to keep trace of***, to follow the movements of, keep sight of in going.

1375 BARBOUR *Bruce* VI. 553 In his traiss þe hund he set. *Ibid.* 583 þe hund..ay followit þe kyngis trass. *c* **1420** *Anturs of Arth.* v, The king blowe rechas, And folowed fast on þe tras. *c* **1489** CAXTON *Sonnes of Aymon* ix. 238 Men myghte well folow hym bi the trase, by cause of the blode that cam out of his body. **1556** W. TYMMES in Foxe *A. & M.* (1583) 2142/1 A sheepe [= ship] that passeth ouer the waues.., when it is gone by, the trace thereof cannot be found. **1810** SCOTT *Lady of L.* I. vii, Two dogs of black Saint Hubert's breed..Fast on his [the stag's] flying traces came. **1887** BOWEN *Æneid* II. 528 On his traces aflame with murderous stroke, Pyrrhus—behind—the pursuer!

b. *spec.* A beaten path through a wild or unenclosed region, made by the passage of men or beasts; a track, a trail. *U.S.*

1807 WILKINSON in Pike *Sources Mississ.* II. (1810) App. 24 We..took the large Spanish trace for the Arkansaw river. **1808** PIKE *Sources Mississ.* II. (1810) 134 We marched, leaving the Osage trace, which we had hitherto followed. **1817** J. BRADBURY *Trav. Amer.* 65 We..soon fell in with the trace from the Maha village to the monument. **1837** R. M. BIRD *Nick of the Woods* xxiv. II. 247 Leaving the broad buffalo-trace by which he descended the banks. **1904** W. CHURCHILL *Crossing* vii, They were going ahead up the trace towards his mother's.

c. In the West Indies, A grass drive, a lane.

1871 KINGSLEY *At Last* vii, The heat of a cane-field trace is utterly stifling. *Ibid.* xiii, A grass drive, as we should call it in England—a 'trace', as it is called in the West Indies—some sixty feet in width.

6. a. *pl.* Vestiges or marks remaining and indicating the former presence, existence, or action of something; *sing.* a vestige, an indication. Also *to sink without trace*: see SINK *v.* 1 a.

c **1400** MAUNDEV. (1839) vi. 71 Sche mylked hem on the rede stones of marble; so þat the traces may ȝit be sene in the stones alle whyte. **1814** MRS. J. WEST *Alicia de Lacy* III. 2 No trace of inhabitation but the fortified castle or the sacred monastery. **1816** SCOTT *Antiq.* iv, My niece..saw the traces of the ditch at once. **1865** LUBBOCK *Preh. Times* ii. 29 At the end of the coffin were found traces of leather, doubtless the remains of boots. *Mod.* Of the fortifications no trace now remains.

b. A mark or impression left on the face, the mind, etc.

1809 MALKIN *Gil Blas* III. v. ¶ 12 My brain full of joyous traces. **1844** A. B. WELBY *Poems* (1867) 45 Where beauty left so soft a trace. **1848** LYTTON *Harold* I. i, It was on that forehead that time had set its trace.

c. An indication of the presence of a minute amount of some constituent in a compound; a quantity so minute as to be inferred but not actually measured; esp. in *Chem.*; *transf.* a very little. Also in *Meteorol.* (see quot. 1930).

1827 FARADAY *Chem. Manip.* iv. (1842) 99 It burns away completely in a blast-furnace, leaving scarcely a trace of slag. **1838** T. THOMSON *Chem. Org. Bodies* 578 Traces of oxalic acid can be detected. **1859** R. HUNT *Guide Mus. Pract. Geol.* (ed. 2) 209 Its composition is: Gold 48·67, Silver 51·33, Copper, a trace. **1875** DARWIN *Insectiv. Pl.* xvi. 375 The distance was a trace less. **1876** GLADSTONE in *Contemp. Rev.* June 22 Like a chemist who, in a testing analysis,..if he finds something behind so minute as to refuse any quantitative estimate, calls it by the name of 'trace'. **1908** *Observer's Handbk.* (Meteorol. Office) I. 35 Falls [of rain] of less than ·005-inch should be noted in the register by entering the word 'trace'. **1930** *Meteorol. Gloss.* (ed. 2) (Meteorol. Office) 177 The word 'trace' is entered in the daily record sheet when some rain (or other form of precipitation) is known to have fallen and the amount in the gauge is not large enough to be measured. **1974** *Nature* 25 Oct. 694/2 The measurements were made in very light snowfall (which never exceeded a 'trace' in equivalent precipitation rate).

d. *Psychol.* A change in the brain as a result of some mental experience; the physical after-effect *of* such.

1690 LOCKE *Essay Hum. Und.* II. i. 41 The memory of Thoughts, is retained by the impressions that are made on the Brain, and the traces there left after such thinking. *Ibid.* x. 67 There is no reason why the sound of a Pipe should leave traces in their [*sc.* birds'] Brains. **1892** G. F. STOUT *Man. Psychol.* I. I. ii. 76 Mental development would be impossible unless previous experience left behind it persistent after-effects to determine the nature and course of subsequent experience. These after-effects are called.. traces or dispositions. **1927** G. V. ANREP tr. *Pavlov's Conditioned Reflexes* iii. 39 The stimulus this time is not the actual disappearance of an external agent, but the trace left by the action of the agent on the central nervous system after the agent itself has been removed. **1930** W. KÖHLER *Gestalt Psychol.* ix. 232 Learning and those processes the traces of which make reproduction and recognition possible. **1940** *Brit. Jrnl. Psychol.* XXX. 193 This process..works in conjunction with and through the trace-column, the masses of traces, ultimately of a chemical nature, left by past experience. **1978** TARPY & MAYER *Found. Learning & Memory* ii. 22 In trace conditioning, the CS does not impinge directly upon the sense receptors.

e. *Linguistics.* In transformational grammar, a phonetically null element considered to have been left in the position from which another element has been moved by a transformation, and to retain some influence on the resultant sentence.

1975 N. CHOMSKY *Logical Struct. Linguistic Theory* 22 Transformations that move expressions leave a 'trace' in the position from which the item was moved. **1977** *Stud. in Eng. Lit.: Eng. Number* (Tokyo) 95 Traces make it possible to define permissible transformations correctly. **1978** *Language* LIV. 412 S-initial sentential complements are base-generated in topic position.., and are linked to an empty subject position (actually a trace in subject position ..) by a general rule of interpretation.

7. *fig.* A non-material indication or evidence of the presence or existence of something, or of a former event or condition; a sign, mark.

1656 COWLEY *Pind. Odes* I. iii, With Oblivions silent stroke deface Of foregone Ills the very trace. **1696** WHISTON *Th. Earth* II. (1722) 186 There are Traces..of a Tradition that a Comet did appear at the very Beginning of the Deluge. **1710** POPE *Windsor For.* 372 The shady empire shall retain no trace Of war or blood, but in the sylvan chase. **1849** MACAULAY *Hist. Eng.* x. II. 661 In countries where all trace of the limited monarchy of the middle ages had long been effaced. **1850** MCCOSH *Div. Govt.* I. ii. (1874) 36 We discover everywhere in this world traces of design and wisdom. **1909** H. M. GWATKIN *Early Ch. Hist.* xi. 188 There is no trace of any veneration of pictures or images before the fourth century.

8. a. A line or figure drawn; a tracing, drawing, or sketch of an object or of a piece of work; the traced record of a self-recording instrument; in *Fortif.* the ground-plan of a work. (In quot. 1861 app. a tracing-instrument.)

1744 AKENSIDE *Pleas. Imagination* III. 362 Not the sculptur'd gold More faithful keeps the graver's lively trace. **1861** SMILES *Engineers* II. 76 Picked out from the heap were also found his drill,..his trace, his T square,..and his engraving tools. **1879** *Cassell's Techn. Educ.* I. 21 The trace of a work is the plan of its guiding or magistral line. **1895** COL. MAURICE in *United Service Mag.* July 430 He made out both a trace of the work including the interior retrenchment and an exact profile of the ditched parapet. **1898** *Allbutt's Syst. Med.* V. 847 The respiration is an important factor in the blood-pressure, and in the run of the circulation is apparent to everyone who has watched the traces of the kymograph. **1899** BALDOCK *Cromwell* 293 The rampart.. was strong and high, and of regular trace.

b. The luminous line or pattern on the screen of a cathode-ray tube.

1937 G. PARR *Low Voltage Cathode Ray Tube* ii. 28 The effect on the screen is..to break up the line into a series of light and dark patches. **1966** D. BAGLEY *Wyatt's Hurricane* vi. 156 He blinked them open again and stared at the radar screen, following the sweep of the trace as it swept hypnotically round and round. **1975** D. G. FINK *Electronics Engineers' Handbk.* VII. 30 This trace is displayed continuously until erased, so long as the flood beam is maintained in operation.

9. *Geom.* **a.** The track described by a moving point, line, or surface. **b.** The intersection of a line or surface with a surface; *spec.* the intersection of a plane with one of the co-ordinate planes, or with one of the planes of projection. **c.** The projection of a line upon a surface (*Funk's Stand. Dict.* 1895).

1834–47 J. S. MACAULAY *Field Fortif.* (1851) 287 Let AB, Fig. 71, be the horizontal trace of a vertical plane. **1840** LARDNER *Geom.* i. 11 The notion of a mathematical surface may be formed by imagining a mathematical line to move in any manner in space, leaving behind it, as it moves, a trace or track. This trace or track will be a mathematical surface. **1867** THOMSON & TAIT *Nat. Phil.* I. I. §111 When a body rolls and spins on another body, the trace of either on the other is the curved or straight line along which it is successively touched.

†10. *Her.* = TRACT *sb.*[3] 6 (*a*), TRESSURE. *Obs.*

1486 *Bk. St. Albans, Her.* e vij, He berith golde a dowble trace florishyt contrari and a Lyon rampyng of gowles. *Ibid.*, He berith golde a trace triplatit of Siluer.

11. *Math.* The sum of the elements in the principal diagonal of a matrix.

1938 A. A. ALBERT *Mod. Higher Algebra* iv. 80 We call *T(A)* the trace of *A*. **1958** *New Scientist* 10 July 364/2 If A is a matrix it is usual to denote the transpose of A by A′ or A*, and the trace of A by tr A. **1972** *Jrnl. Physics* B. V. 990 Evaluating the constant of proportionality by taking the trace of each side of the result for the particular case of complete recapture.

12. a. *Computers.* The detailed examination of the execution of a program or part of one (usu. to investigate a fault) with the aid of another program that can cause individual instructions, operands, and results to be printed or displayed as they are reached by the first program; the analysis so obtained; also, a trace program. Freq. *attrib.*, as ***trace program, routine.***

1957 M. V. WILKES et al. *Preparation of Programs for Electronic Digital Computer* (ed. 2) 96 A useful error-diagnosis subroutine..prints the function letters of orders as they are executed... The printed sequence of function letters is sometimes known as a trace. **1960** GREGORY & VAN HORN *Automatic Data-Processing Systems* iii. 82 (*caption*) Trace of operations in read-write loop using an index register. *Ibid.* viii. 271 A trace routine is used to observe how the object program..operates while it is being executed. **1966** Trace program [see SNAPSHOT *sb.* 2 b]. **1980** N. RUSHBY in Meek & Heath *Guide to Good Programming Practice* iii. 84 Some debugging compilers provide a trace, which can be used simply to follow the program flow from statement to statement, or can include details of each assignment. **1982** GHEZZI & JAZAYERI *Programming Language Concepts* vii. 221 After the program has terminated, a trace and an indication of the cause of failure can be produced.

b. A request for information to be sought concerning a particular person or thing; an investigation which traces this information (freq. to discover the source of a telephone call).

1974 M. PENOYRE *Breach of Security* i. 4, I might put in a trace to London to see if my Office has got anything on him. **1976** G. SEYMOUR *Glory Boys* iv. 49 Very professional. No possibility of a trace on a call of the length they've been using. **1978** R. LUDLUM *Holcroft Covenant* xxviii. 331 There are men following me... I think it's called a 'trace'. Put out by *you*? **1981** D. BOGGIS *Time to Betray* xxi. 114 He ..got the index number... 'Get me a trace through Yard liaison.'

II. 13. *attrib.* or as *adj.* Present or required only in traces.

1950 *N.Z. Jrnl. Agric.* Sept. 195/1 The control..of peat scours by copper in trace amounts. **1956** *Sun* (Baltimore) 1 May 12/7 The oysters..are loaded with trace minerals. **1962** *Listener* 16 Aug. 243/2 It is the selected drug that is actually the effective agent and not trace amounts of some as yet unrecognized contaminant. **1965** G. J. WILLIAMS *Econ. Geol. N.Z.* vi. 63/2 To place these figures in petro-genetic perspective we must realize that gold is a trace-metal—even where concentrated in a payable reef. **1978** *Sci. Amer.* Dec. 124/1 It is the trace ions (those at least 1,000 times less abundant than hydrogen and helium) that serve to control the nebula thermostatically, maintaining the nebular temperature generally between 5,000 and 15,000 degrees. **1979** *Brit. Med. Jrnl.* 15 Dec. 1529/1 Most trace minerals and other micronutrients required for survival are known.

b. Special Comb.: **trace element**, an element that is present (esp. in the soil) or required only in minute amounts; also *fig.*; **trace fossil** *Palæont.* [tr. G. *spurenfossil* (K. Krejci-Graf 1932, in *Senckenbergiana* XIV. 21)], a fossil that represents the burrowing or similar activity of an animal rather than the animal itself.

1932 *Yale Jrnl. Biol. & Med.* IV. 501 Investigation as to the occurrence and function of '*trace' elements in both plant and animal life is now very active. **1954** R. L. PARKER tr. *Niggli's Rocks & Mineral Deposits* i. 9 Fundamental rock chemistry need consider only comparatively few elements. .. This does not mean that relatively rare elements or even the so-called trace elements lack importance. **1970** *Nature* 17 Oct. 251 Trace element analyses of flint show statistically valid differences between products of major British and European Neolithic flint mines. **1976** *Church Times* 16 July 7/2, I found little that has not been said already by many radical Christian writers. There are trace-elements of Marxism, but hardly more than that. **1956** *Q. Jrnl. Geol. Soc.* CXII. 475 A consideration of the..morphology of the fossil, permits its interpretation as a *trace-fossil resulting from the driving of a system of branching tunnels in the sea-bed sediment. **1974** *Nature* 22 Mar. 328/2 It is generally agreed that the earliest metazoan animals were soft-bodied forms which are rarely preserved but have left tracks, trails and burrows, collectively known as trace fossils.

trace (treɪs), *sb.*[2] Forms: see below. [ME. *trays*, a. OF. *traiz*, *trais*, pl. of *trait* (12th c. in Littré) action of drawing, rope or leather strap by which a draught-beast is harnessed; = It. *tratto*, L. *tractus* draught (*u*-stem), f. *trahĕre* to draw. In Eng. written also *trayse*, *trayce*, *trace*, and treated as collect. pl. and at length (*c* 1400) as a sing. with a new pl. *trasys*, *traces*: cf. TRUCE.]

†1. as *pl.* The pair of ropes, chains, or (subsequently usually) leather straps by which the collar of a draught-animal is connected with the splinter-bar or swingletree. *Obs.*

Usually *collective* like *tongs*, *scissors*, *shears*, *pincers*, etc.; but sometimes a numerical pl., as in quots. 1458, 1481.

4–5 **trais, trays,** 5 **trayse, treyse, trayce,** 5–8 **trace,** 6 **treas,** 7 **tress, traise, traits,** 9 *dial.* **traice.**

13.. *Seuyn Sag.* (W.) 1327 He let him drawe out of the pit ..With trais an two stronge hors. *c* **1350** *Nom. Gall.-Angl.* 884 *Esteles, trays et valuere* [glossed] Hamys, trays, taylerope. *c* **1365–6** *Durham Acc. Rolls* (Surtees) 568 Pro ij paribus de Trays et ij cartrapes; in trays, cartrapes, capistris, et reynes, xviij s. *c* **1386** CHAUCER *Knt.'s T.* 1283 With foure white boles in the trays. **1412–20** LYDG. *Chron. Troy* I. 2209 Ryȝt as an hors out of þe traise at large. **1458** *Nottingham Rec.* II. 368 For treyse and oder ropes. **1480** *Wardr. Acc. Edw. IV* (1830) 123 For v pair trays garnyssht. **1481–90** *Howard Househ. Bks.* (Roxb.) 150 Paid to Iohn Wygge, Ropper, for iij. thrays ij.s. ix.d. **1557** *Lanc. & Chesh. Wills* (1884) 61, iiij payre of treas. *c* **1611** CHAPMAN *Iliad* XXIII. 412 His reins lost, or seat, or with the tress His chariot fail'd him. **1616** SURFL. & MARKH. *Country Farme* 16 Collars, Cart-saddles, Traits, thicke clothes, and other furniture for Horses. *Ibid.* 123 Be carefull that their traise, cart-saddles, collars, bridles, or other parts of their geares, and harnesse, be not torne. **1725** POPE *Odyss.* IV. 861 Twelve young mules, a strong laborious race, New to the plough, unpractis'd in the trace. **1807** A. YOUNG *Agric. Essex* I. 107, 5 pair of plough chain traice.

2. as *sing.* Each of the individual ropes or leather straps mentioned above; in *pl.* = sense 1.

α. *sing.* 5 **trays, -e, trayce, trahys,** 7 **traise, tress,** 9 **traice,** 6– **trace.**

14.. *Voc.* in Wr.-Wülcker 566/26 *Attractorium*, a trayne, *sed melius*, a trays. *Ibid.* 617/7 *Tractorium*, a trays. *c* **1440** *Promp. Parv.* 499/1 Trayce, horsys ha(r)neys, *tenda*. *c* **1475** *Pict. Voc.* in Wr.-Wülcker 811/33 *Hoc retinaculum*, a trayse. **1570** LEVINS *Manip.* 6/44 A Trace for drawing, *traha*, *æ*. **1794** W. FELTON *Carriages* (1801) II. x. 134 A square, bent ring is sewed in the end [of each trace], which, with the trace, forms a loop to hitch round the splinter-bar rolls.

β. *pl.* 5 **tracez, traices,** 5–6 **trasys, -is,** 6 **trasseis,** 6–7 **tresses,** 6– **traces.**

1404 *Durham Acc. Rolls* (Surtees) 397, iiij trasys ij try-syns rapis. **1405–6** *Ibid.* 400 Rec. pro lez tracez del char. **1497** *Naval Acc. Hen. VII* (1896) 95, iij chestes, Anfeld..j, Traices..cxx pair. **1523** FITZHERB. *Husb.* §5 If he go with a hors ploughe, than muste he haue..his hombers or collers, holmes whyted, tresses, swyngletrees, and togwith. **1529** *Act 21 Hen. VIII*, c. 12 §1 Thereof make Cables, Ropes, Halsers, Traces, Halters, and other Tackle. **1569** in *Richmond Wills* (Surtees) 218, vj pair trasis with girthes. **1577** B. GOOGE *Heresbach's Husb.* 11 The smaller sort be these..Traces. **1582** *Shuttleworths' Acc.* (Chetham Soc.) 6 A pare of trasseis vj[d]. **1607** J. CARPENTER *Plaine Mans Plough* 192 Thirdly, the foure Traces or Tresses. **1718** POPE *Iliad* v. 398 His panting steeds..He fix'd with straiten'd traces to the car. **1762** WESLEY *Jrnl.* 30 Mar., The horses pulled till the traces broke. **1841** MISS MITFORD in L'Estrange *Life* (1870) III. viii. 117 About four miles from home one of the traces came undone.

3. *fig.* (from 1 and 2), esp. in phrases; cf. COLLAR *sb.* 8. †***out of trace***, out of proper connexion, out of order. ***into the traces***, into regular work. ***to kick over the traces***: see KICK *v.*[1] 1 c.

c **1518** SKELTON *Magnyf.* 914 All is out of harre And out of trace. **1824** W. IRVING *T. Trav.* I. 203 He was too fond of my genius to force it into the traces. **1843** LYTTON *Last Bar.* I.

iii, Cut thy trace from the cloister, and take thy road to the shop.

4. †**a.** (?) The tug or end-piece of a bell-rope. *Obs.* **b.** *Angling.* A length of gimp or gut of varying fineness attached to the end of the reel line. **c.** *Organ-building.* In the draw-stop action, a rod which connects the draw-stop rod with the trundle, or the trundle with the lever moving the slider; also called *trace-rod.* **d.** *Bot.* The fibro-vascular tissue of a stem, of which the *leaf-trace* is a continuation.

a. 1663 in *Archæol. Æliana* XVII. 126 For two traces for yͤ bellroops 6*d*.

b. 1839 [see MINNOW 3]. **1867** F. FRANCIS *Angling* iv. (1880) 105 A tackle called a trace is used. **1883** *Fisheries Exhib. Catal.* 56 Flights and Traces, Floats for various kinds of fishing.

c. 1852 SEIDEL *Organ* 59 The upper end of the roller.. is connected.. with the end of a short pole called the *trace*. **1876–98** STAINER & BARRETT *Dict. Mus. Terms* s.v. *Organ*, When the stop is pulled out, the arms *aa* draw the trace *b* from right to left. **1881** C. A. EDWARDS *Organs* 90 Another arm communicates with the trace by means of a mortise and pin.

d. 1875, 1877 [see *leaf-trace*, LEAF *sb.*[1] 18]. **1884** BOWER & SCOTT *De Bary's Phaner.* 239 The median bundle of the trace.. as it reaches the four bundles of the leaf-trace of the second node curves to one side, and unites with the lateral bundle of the next lower trace. *Ibid.* 257 Each leaf has three bundles of the trace, one median and two lateral.

5. *attrib.* and *Comb.*: **trace-beaten** *a.*, (of a horse) marked by the beating or friction of the traces; **trace-block**, the splinter-bar or draught-bar; formerly called the *fore-block* or *fore-bar*; **trace-boy**, a trace-horse boy; **trace-buckle**, a large buckle by which the trace is attached to the tug (Knight, 1877); **trace-bundle**, *Bot.*: cf. 4 d above; **trace-chain**, (*a*) a trace of chain, a chain trace; † (*b*) a long chain by which a team is yoked to the plough; = TEAM *sb.* 9; **trace-fastener**, one of a pair of hooks or catches by which the traces are hitched to the draught-bar (Knight, 1877); **trace-galled** *a.*, (of a horse) galled by the friction of the traces; **trace-harness**, harness of trace-horses; **trace-high** *adv.*, to the level of the traces; **trace-hook**, one of the hooks on the draught-bar for attaching the traces (Knight, 1877); **trace-horse**, a horse which draws in traces, as distinct from a shaft-horse; *attrib.* **trace-horse boy**, a boy in charge of a trace-horse; **trace-iron**, one of the upright iron studs round which the traces are looped; **trace-loop** = *trace-ring*; **trace-mate**: see quot.; **trace-ring**, an iron ring fastened to the end of the trace, by which it is attached to the trace-hook; **trace-rod** (*Organ*) = 4 c; **trace-rope**, a trace made of rope; **trace-tug**, a strap supporting the trace; † **trace-wheel** = PULLEY *sb.*[1] 2.

1687 *Lond. Gaz.* No. 2287/8 Stolen.., a brown Mare above 14 hands,..*Traise-beaten on her Ribs. **1707** *Ibid.* No. 4295/4 A brown Gelding.., trace-beaten, most on the further Side. **1900** *Daily News* 12 Nov. 3/4 The firemen.. having attached drag ropes to the *trace blocks, proceeded to drag the carriage to Government House. **1897** *Ibid.* 31 Mar. 7/1 Daily wages..for *trace-boys 2*s.* 6*d.* **1884** BOWER & SCOTT *De Bary's Phaner.* 293 The rapid longitudinal divisions of the bundle-ring always begin..in a young internode, in the position of the single, or of the median *trace-bundle going to the next leaf above. **1844** STEPHENS *Bk. Farm* I. 618 The horse is yoked to the swing-trees by light chains, called **trace-chains*. **1896** *Cosmopolitan* XX. 398/1 The jangling of trace-chains in the quiet, darkening air, as the workmen return from the fields to the barn. **1673** *Lond. Gaz.* No. 783/4 One Iron Grey Nag..a little *trace Galled. **1885** *Wellington Weekly News* 15 Oct. (E.D.D.) Nine sets of breeching and *trace harness. **1899** SOMERVILLE & ROSS *Irish R.M.* ix, Horses that ranged from the cart mare, clipped *trace high, to shaggy and leggy three-year-olds. **1844** STEPHENS *Bk. Farm* III. 1087 In Forfarshire the *trace-horse is harnessed in a different manner. **1907** *Nation* 19 Oct. 79/1 Awaiting the chance of a trace-horse to give our caravan a pull. **1902** *Daily Chron.* 1 July 6/1 One of the horses attached to the fire engine was caught by the *trace-iron on the off side of the cattle-float. **1880** L. WALLACE *Ben-Hur* 208 They termed the two [horses] next the pole yoke-steeds, and those on the right and left outside *trace-mates. **1794** W. FELTON *Carriages* (1801) II. x. §2. 144 The *Trace-Rings are iron square loops sewed in the ends of the traces, a part of which they receive, and loops round the splinter-bar. **1880** E. J. HOPKINS in Grove *Dict. Mus.* (1880) II. 606/1 A **trace-rod*, which spans the distance from the trundle to the end of the soundboard... The trundle partly revolves and moves the trace-rod. **1900** *Daily News* 24 Feb. 6/3 The struggling, terrified horses inextricably mixed the *trace ropes, and the position looked serious. **1794** W. FELTON *Carriages* (1801) II. x. §1. 135 The *trace-tugs are loops for the trace to run through and hang by. **1519** HORMAN *Vulg.* 241 b, There must be made a *trace whele [*tympanum*] to wynd vp stone.

trace (treɪs), *sb.*[3] *Obs.* or *dial.* Forms: 4 **trace,** 5 *pl.* **trasses,** 6 *Sc.* **trase, trais, traiss,** 6 (*Sc.*) 7– *dial.* **trace.** [Possibly an altered form of TRESS *sb.*, with which this largely coincides in sense; but no explanation of the alteration of form presents itself. See also the cognate TRACE *v.*[3]

(The different senses are cited from widely separate localities, so that they can scarcely be considered as a verbal unity, except in their apparent relation to TRESS.)]

†**1.** A tress or plait of hair; = TRESS *sb.* 1. (*s.w. Eng.*) *Obs.* (but cf. TRACE *v.*[3]).

c **1380** *Sir Ferumb.* 5882 Wyþ ȝeȝene graye, and browes bent, And ȝealwe traces, & fayre y-trent. *a* **1400** *Trevisa's Higden* (Rolls) VIII. VII. 63 Þe ȝelew heere of þe womman trasses [*MS. γ.* ȝelou tresses; HIGDEN *trica comæ mulieris flava*] was i-founde hoole and sounde.

†**2.** A flat plait or braid of gold or silver thread, or other material, for trimming a robe, etc. *Sc. Obs.*

1539 *Inv. Roy. Wardr.* (1815) 32 Item, ane nycht gowne of gray dammes with ane walting trais of gold. *Ibid.* 35. [*Ibid.* p. 42 has *tress* of silver; 82 *tres* of gold.] **1543** *Acc. Ld. High Treas. Scot.* VIII. 181 For xx tracis of gold to the cote, weyand thre unce..v li. ij s. **1548** *Ibid.* IX. 149, xxx elnis of trasis to eik ane goun of hirris [= hers] of blak welwote... Item, thre elnis blak welwote to eik this goun. **1549** *Ibid.* 334 Tua unce and ane quarter unce Parice silk to sew the pasmentis and traiss of the said coit.

3. A string of ears of Indian corn plaited together so as to be hung up. (*N. America.*)

1678 *Phil. Trans.* XII. 1066 After 'tis gather'd, it [maize] must, except laid very thin, be presently stripped from the Husks... The common way (which they call Tracing) is to weave the Ears together in long Traces by some parts of the Husk left thereon. **1753** CHAMBERS *Cycl. Supp.* s.v. *Tracing*, These traces of [Indian] corn they hang up within doors,.. and they will..keep good the whole winter.

b. A 'rope' or string of onions. *dial.*

1891 *Hartland (Devon) Gloss.*, *Trace*, a rope of onions. [Cf. *Trecces de cepis* in same sense, in *Tabularia Portus Regii* (Du Cange).] (Cf. also RACE *sb.*[1] 9 b.)

trace (treɪs), *v.*[1] Forms: 4 **trais(e,** 4–7 **trase,** 4– **trace.** [ME. *trace-n*, a. OF. *tracier*, 12th c. (*trasser, traser, traicier*, etc.), F. *trace-r* = Sp. *trazar*, It. *tracciare* to follow by foot, to trace, indicating a pop.L. or Com. Romanic **tractiāre*, f. L. *tractus* a drawing, dragging, trailing, crawling; a train, track, course. The primary meaning of the verb was app. 'to proceed in a line, course, or track'. The early sense-development in OF. and ME. is not very clear, and some of the senses attach themselves immediately to TRACE *sb.*[1] in its sense of 'mark left by anything moving, footprint', itself a derivative of the vb. in its earlier senses.]

I. †**1.** *intr.* To take one's course, make one's way; to proceed, pass, go, travel, tread. Also *fig.*

c **1400** *Rom. Rose* 6745 Yit may he go his breed begging; Fro dore to dore he may go trace, Til he the remenaunt may purchace. ? *a* **1400** *Morte Arth.* 1629 Traise to-warde Troys þe tresone to wyrke. **1503** HAWES *Examp. Virt.* x. viii, No man by yonde this marke may trace. **1513** DOUGLAS *Æneis* VIII. v. 5 The prestis..Gan trasing furth. *a* **1518** SKELTON *Magnyf.* 692 As good to be occupyed as vp and downe to trace And do nothynge. **1598** *Mucedorus* IV. iii. 52 The wood lanes..strawed With violets, cowslips, and swete marigolds For thee to trampel and to trace vpon. **1603** H. CROSSE *Vertues Commw.* (1878) 23 Induce them..to trace in the wholsome path that leadeth to the house of honour. *a* **1688** VILLIERS (Dk. Buckhm.) *Restoration* Wks. (1775) 104 Fall off again,..and every man trace to his house again. **1793** *Minstrel* II. 126 The forest, which she did not chuse to enter, but traced along its edge.

†**2.** *intr.* To pace or step in dancing; to tread a measure; to dance. Also *trans.* (*rare*). *Obs.*

c **1425** LYDG. *Dance of Macabre* in *Bochas*, etc. (1554) 220 b, Death I may not flee, On this daunce with other for to trace. **1445** in *Anglia* XXVIII. 273 Orpheus harpe which trees made trace. **1509** BARCLAY *Shyp of Folys* (1874) II. 290 To hunt to chace: to daunce: to trace: what one is he That beryth face. **1602** HEYWOOD *Woman Killed* Wks. 1874 II. 96 Come, Nick, take you Ioane Miniuer to trace withall. **1697** DAMPIER *Voy.* (1729) I. 541 They traced too and fro promiscuously, often clapping their Hands and singing aloud. **1808** SCOTT *Marm.* v. vii, The king loved well The merry dance, traced fast and light.

†**3.** *trans.* To pass along or over, tread (a path, way, street, etc.). Also *fig. Obs.*

c **1381** CHAUCER *Parl. Foules* 54 Oure present wor[l]dis lyuys space Nys but a maner deth what weye we trace. **1580** SIDNEY *Ps.* VIII. viii, The fish,..And what thing els of waters traceth The unworn paths. **1621** J. REYNOLDS *God's Rev. agst. Murder* I. i. 5 Tracing the street in a neate perfumed boote with iangling spurres. **1650** FULLER *Pisgah* III. xii. 343 The passage..commonly called the dolorous way,..traced with the blessed feet of our Saviour. **1794** BLAKE *Songs Exper., Lit. Girl Found* 8 Arm in arm seven days They traced the desert ways.

fig. **1508** FISHER *7 Penit. Ps.* Prol., Wks. (E.E.T.S.) I. 2 That al tho persones that ententyfely rede or here them may be styred the better to trace the way of eternall salvacion.

†**4.** *trans.* To travel or range over; to go or pass about, around, or through; to tread, traverse.

1430–40 LYDG. *Bochas* VI. iv. (Bodl. MS. 263) lf. 314/2 Fond no loggyng, tracing the contres Saue in kauernys, & in holwe trees. **1577** GRANGE *Golden Aphrod.* G j b, My harte it dothe bothe skippe and ioye to see hir trace the grounde. **1594** MARLOWE & NASHE *Dido* I. i, But hapless I..Do trace these Lybian deserts, all despis'd. **1598** HAKLUYT *Voy.* I. 235 We sayled..with diuers other courses, trauersing and tracing the seas, by reason of sundry and manifolde contrary windes. **1632** LITHGOW *Trav.* IX. 412, I traced the fertile soyles of Carindia. **1807** CRABBE *Par. Reg.* I. 306 He soon arrived, he traced the village green.

II. 5. a. To follow the footprints or traces of; *esp.* to track by the footprints; also with the traces as object; hence, to pursue, to dog.

c **1440** *Pallad. on Husb.* Tab. 39 Been forto trace vnto their dwellyng. **1530** PALSGR. 760/2 It is forbydden to trace hares in snowe tyme. **1559** *Mirr. Mag.*, *Owen Glendour* xxxi, So traste they me among the mountaynes wide. **1605** SHAKS. *Macb.* IV. i. 153 His Wife, his Babes, and all vnfortunate Soules That trace him in his Line. **1632** LITHGOW *Trav.* I. 17 Still left vntold, something there must be seene For them, who trace our feete, with Argus eyne. **1677** W. HUBBARD *Narrative* (1865) II. 124 By the help of the Snow that fell about that Time, [they] were traced till they were overtaken. **1841** ELPHINSTONE *Hist. India* I. 123 Bound to find out the possessor of any stolen property within the township, or to trace him till he has passed the boundary. **1886** C. E. PASCOE *London of To-day* xxi. (ed. 3) 207 We might have traced Thackeray through his wanderings from street to street. *a* **1913** *Mod.* Note the number of the postal order, so that it may be traced if lost.

b. *fig.* To follow, pursue (instructions, example, etc.).

1649 BLITHE *Eng. Improv. Impr.* (1653) 100 Observe my Method, and strictly trace my Instructions. **1745** *Transl. & Paraphr. Sc. Ch.* LII. i, You who the Name of Jesus bear, His holy Footsteps trace.

6. *fig.* To follow the course, development, or history of. Also with the course, etc. as object.

1654 BRAMHALL *Just Vind.* v. (1661) 90 If we trace on this argument a little further, to search out how the Bishop of Rome comes to be Saint Peters heire. **1729** BUTLER *Serm.* Wks. 1874 II. 168 The common virtues, and the common vices of mankind, may be traced up to benevolence, or the want of it. **1766** BLACKSTONE *Comm.* II. xiv. 236 The tracing the inheritance back through the male line of ancestors. **1849** MACAULAY *Hist. Eng.* iv. I. 503 No libel on the government had ever been traced to a Quaker. **1887** *Westm. Rev.* June 309 We have traced the history of Lower Canada down to the year 1839.

b. *intr.* for *pass.* To trace its origin or history; to go *back* in time, to date *back*.

1876 *Rep. Vermont Board Agric.* III. 107 The farmer loses sight of the fact that the character of the calf..may 'trace back', as it is termed, to a remote ancestor. **1886** *Field* 4 Sept. 346/1 The Belvoir Senator and the Brocklesby Harbinger traced directly to the Fitzwilliam. **1889** JACOBS & LANG *Æsop's Fables* 53 The earliest form..cannot trace back earlier than the third..century. **1907** *Daily Chron.* 9 Sept. 3/2 The scare of invasion traces to the Armada of 1588.

7. a. *trans.* To make out and follow (with the eye or mind) the course or line of; to ascertain (the course or line of something).

1703 MAUNDRELL *Journ. Jerus.*, *Euphrates*, etc. (1732) 2 Its Walls, which may be traced all round. **1779** *Mirror* No. 9 ¶3, I..amused myself with tracing in the daughters, those features which, in the mothers and grandmothers, had charmed me so often. **1818** in Tuckey *Narr. Exped. R. Zaire* Introd. 8 The stream of this mysterious river [the Niger] being now traced with certainty from west to east as far as Tombuctoo. **1839** MURCHISON *Silur. Syst.* I. xxxvii. 572 In situations where the boulders may be traced..to their parent rocks. **1856** STANLEY *Sinai & Pal.* i. 19 Often their course can be traced, not by visible water, but a track of moss here, a fringe of rushes there. **1907** *Verney Mem.* I. 2 The form of the ancient manor house may still be traced.

b. To make out (worn or obscure writing); to discern, decipher.

1761 GRAY *Odin* 22 Thrice he traced the runic rhyme. **1792** S. ROGERS *Pleas. Mem.* I. 137 It calls me..to trace The few fond lines that Time may soon efface. **1859** JEPHSON *Brittany* ii. 17 The characters may still be traced on a block of granite.

c. To make a tracing of (a listed item); to derive (a tracing) *from* an index or catalogue; see TRACING *vbl. sb.*[1] 1 b.

1905 *N.Y. State Library Bull.* No. 95. 578 See that every secondary card is traced on one or both main cards. **1914** [see TRACING *vbl. sb.*[1] 1 b]. **1926** *Amer. Speech* II. 93 The catalog cards are 'main entry' cards and 'secondary entry' cards, the latter being 'traced' from the former.

8. a. To discover, find out, or ascertain by investigation; to find out step by step; to search out.

1642 FULLER *Holy & Prof. St.* v. i. 359 God..varieth his ways of dealing with wantons, that they may be at a losse in tracing him. **1697** DRYDEN *Virg. Georg.* II. 699 Happy the Man, who, studying Nature's Laws, Thro' known Effects can trace the secret Cause. **1745** *Transl. & Paraphr. Sc. Ch.* XXII. iv, Tho' him thou can'st not see, nor trace the working of his hands. **1869** TOZER *Highl. Turkey* II. 306 Tracing a connection..where in reality none exists.

b. To discover evidence of the existence or occurrence of; to find traces of.

1697 DRYDEN *Æneid* Ded. (1721) 350 He observes no Method that I can trace, whatever Scaliger the Father, or Heinsius, may have seen. **1782** MISS BURNEY *Cecilia* VIII. ix, The earliest circumstances she could trace were kindnesses received from her. **1856** RUSKIN *Mod. Paint.* III. IV. x. §8 There is a great deal more in your heart, of evil and good, than you ever can trace. *a* **1862** BUCKLE *Civiliz.* (1871) III. v. 367 Black..called it latent heat, because though we conceive it as an idea, we cannot trace it as a fact.

c. *Computers.* To subject (a program) to a trace (TRACE *sb.*[1] 12 a).

1959 M. H. WRUBEL *Primer of Programming for Digital Computers* v. 107 When a program is traced, the machine produces a record of each instruction as it is performed. **1967** KLERER & KORN *Digital Computer User's Handbk.* I. i. 23 The location limits of the program segments to be traced enter as initial parameters to the trace program. **1981** L. A. HILL *Structured Programming in FORTRAN* iii. 73 The program is traced in Table 3-6 with Rule 4 relaxed.

III. 9. *trans.* To mark, make marks upon; *esp.* to mark or ornament with lines, figures, or characters: cf. TRACERY.

a **1400–50** *Alexander* 4914 Þe testre trased full of trones with trimballand wingis þe silloure full of Seraphens. **1523** SKELTON *Garl. Laurel* 395 With diamauntes and rubis there tabers were trasid. **1582** D. INGRAM in Hakluyt *Voy.* (1589) 558 The haire of their heads is shauen in sundry spots, and the rest of their head is traced [? tattooed]. **1832** TENNYSON *Pal. Art* xiii, The deep-set windows, stain'd and traced, Would seem slow-flaming crimson fires From shadow'd grots of arches interlaced. **1858** WHITTIER *Palm-Tree* 24 He holds a palm-leaf scroll in his hands, Traced with the Prophet's wise commands. **1890** *Daily News* 6 Jan. 5/2 Stockings and buckles were richly traced; the pocket was often a blaze of the richest embroidery.

10. To make a plan, diagram, or chart of (something existing or to be constructed); to mark out the course of (a road, etc.) on, or by means of, a plan or map; to mark or set out (the lines of a work or road) on the ground itself. Also *fig.* to devise (a plan of action), map out (a policy).

1374–5, 1399 [implied in *tracing-house, -board*: see TRACING *vbl. sb.*[1] 5]. **1599** PORTER *Angry Wom. Abingd.* (Percy Soc.) 60 When I had doubled my poynt, traste my ground. **1624** LD. KENSINGTON in Ellis *Orig. Lett.* Ser. I. III. 173 What they traced out for the breaking of the match, you follow, pretending to conclude it. *c* **1645** HOWELL *Lett.* (1650) I. 66 The castle [in Milan], by which the citadel of Antwerp was traced. **1669** STAYNRED *Fortification* 6 Tables ..Whereby you may trace out any Fort by help of a Line of Equal Parts. **1696** PHILLIPS (ed. 5), To *Trace*, to draw upon Paper the plane of a Building or Fortification. **1834** L. RITCHIE *Wand. Seine* 120 Rollo's..path, like that of other conquerors, was traced in blood and ashes. **1871** FREEMAN *Norm. Conq.* IV. xviii. 212 The Ermine Street, notwithstanding all the centuries which have passed since it was first traced out and paved, is still distinguished from a yet older track.

11. a. To draw; to draw an outline or figure of; also, to put down in writing, to pen. [So OF. *tracier*.]

1390 GOWER *Conf.* III. 46 Babilla with hire Sones sevene ..With Cernes bothe square and rounde He traceth ofte upon the grounde. *c* **1440** *Promp. Parv.* 499/1 Tracyn, or draw strykys, *protraho*. **1665** BOYLE *Occas. Refl.* v. iii. *heading*, Killing a Crow.., and immediately tracing the ensuing Reflection with a Pen made of one of his Quills. **1712** J. JAMES tr. *Le Blond's Gardening* 96 Then trace upon the Ground the Triangle CDE. **1859** GULLICK & TIMBS *Paint.* 8 The mode of commencing a picture by tracing the outline was followed by the early oil painters. **1888** BURGON *Lives 12 Gd. Men* I. i. 26 These last [annotations] were evidently traced by fingers rendered tremulous by age.

b. To copy (a drawing, plan, etc.) by following the lines of the original drawing on a transparent sheet placed upon it; to make a tracing of.

1762–71 H. WALPOLE *Vertue's Anecd. Paint.* (1786) V. 211 There were an hundred and four heads, hands and feet, traced off from the Cartoons. **1885** 'MRS. ALEXANDER' *At Bay* iii, They practiced duets together, and traced patterns.

IV. †**12.** In phr. ***trace and traverse, trace and rase***, in reference to combatants: sense uncertain: cf. RACE *v.*[3], RASE *v.*[1], and TRAVERSE *v. Obs.*

1470–85 MALORY *Arthur* VI. viii. 194 Thus they ferd two houres or mo trasyng and rasyng eyther other where they myght hytte ony bare place. *Ibid.* VII. iv. 217 They rasshyd to gyders lyke borys tracynge, rasynge and foynynge to the mountenaunce of an houre. *Ibid.* X. xxx. 463 Thus they tracyd and trauercyd and hewe on helmes and hawberkes... And euer sire Tristram tracyd and trauercyd and wente forward hym here and there. **1596** SPENSER *F.Q.* v. viii. 37 Thus long they trast, and trauerst to and fro.

Hence **traced** (treɪst) *ppl. a.*[1], †(*a*) travelled, journeyed: with adverbial qualification (*obs.*); (*b*) outlined, drawn, written; **tracing** *ppl. a.*, that traces or draws lines.

1632 LITHGOW *Trav.* vii. (1906) 293 My life and liberty being deare to me, my long traced feete became more nimble in twelve score paces, then they could follow in eighteene. **1712** J. JAMES tr. *Le Blond's Gardening* 92 The traced Line AB. **1875** SIR T. SEATON *Fret-Cutting* 146 Place the edge of the tool on the traced line. **1884** *Mil. Engineering* (ed. 3) I. II. 21 A sapper should be stationed..to await the arrival of the tracing party. **1907** *Daily Chron.* 24 Jan. 8/1 The spiral ..must be skated boldly,..the knee of the tracing leg rather strongly bent.

†**trace**, *v.*[2] *Obs. rare.* [f. TRACE *sb.*[2]] *trans.* To attach by traces, to harness in traces.

1605 STOW *Ann.* 1432 They [Bayliffs of the Town] presented him with three-score and ten Teeme of horse, all traced to faire new Ploughes. **1656** COWLEY *Pind. Odes, Muse* i, Go, the rich Chariot instantly prepare;..Unruly Phansie with strong Judgment trace, Put in nimble-footed Wit. **1786** BURNS *Inventory* 20 My furr-ahin's a wordy beast, As e'er in tug or tow was trac'd.

trace, *v.*[3] *Obs.* exc. *local.* Forms: 4–5 **trase**, (pa. pple. **trased, trast**), 7– **trace**. [Belongs to TRACE *sb.*[3]; possibly an altered form of TRESS *v.*]

1. *trans.* To plait, twine, interweave, braid. Also with *up*.

13.. *Gaw. & Gr. Knt.* 1739 Þe haȝer stones Trased aboute hir tressour, be twenty in clusteres. *c* **1450** HOLLAND *Howlat* 405 Mony schene scheld With tuscheis of trast silk tichit to the tre. **1613–16** W. BROWNE *Brit. Past.* II. iv. 320 A little lad..Tracing greene rushes for a winter chayre. *Ibid.* 358 As oft as I..Trace the sharpe rushes ends. **1678** [see TRACE *sb.*[3] 3]. **1753** CHAMBERS *Cycl. Supp., Tracing*,..a term used by our planters for the method of preserving the maize... [They] trace it, that is, they leave it in the ear, and weave, or fasten together a great number of ears by the ends of the husks. **1884** *Vermont Agric. Rep.* VIII. 285 The ears thus selected should be 'traced up' and hung away to dry. **1888** ELWORTHY *W. Somerset Word-bk., Trace*, to plait (always) 'I can't only trace dree, but our Jim can trace zix' [plait six strands together]. **1941** *Old Farmer's Almanac* 70 In the early fall the farmers would speak of 'tracing up' the yellow ears of corn to hang from the beams of the woodshed.

2. To plait or braid the hair of the head in tresses; = TRESS *v.* 1.

1832 R. & J. LANDER *Exped. Niger* I. i. 41 Her hair was traced with such extraordinary neatness, that we expressed a wish to examine it more minutely. **1905** *Eng. Dial. Dict.* s.v. (W. Cornwall), She traces her hair every day.

Hence **traced** *ppl. a.*[2]; **'tracing** *vbl. sb.*[2], interweaving, embroidering, braiding; also *attrib.*

c **1450** Trast [see sense 1]. **1549** *Acc. Ld. High Treas. Scot.* IX. 334 Thre score thre elnis trasing silk to the samyn coit. **1681** *Scot. Proclam.* 1 Mar., Silver and gold threde, silver and gold lace, fringes or tracing. **1808–25** JAMIESON s.v., A *traced hat* is a hat bound with gold lace.

trace, obs. erron. form of TRICE *sb.* and *v.*

traceable ('treɪsəb(ə)l), *a.* [f. TRACE *v.*[1] + -ABLE.] Capable of being traced (in various senses of the vb.).

1748 RICHARDSON *Clarissa* (1811) III. ix. 65 Lest we should be traceable by her direction. **1793** RENNELL in *Phil. Trans.* LXXXIII. 184 The gulf stream..is discharged with such velocity, through the Straits of Bahama, that its motion is traceable through the Atlantic, to the Bank of Newfoundland. **1802** PALEY *Nat. Theol.* xxii. (ed. 2) 423 If attraction be..a primordial property of matter, not dependent upon, or traceable to, any other material cause. **1854** W. OSBURN *Mon. Hist. Egypt* II. ii. 55 Fragments on which the remains of hieroglyphics were yet traceable. **1874** CARPENTER *Ment. Phys.* I. viii. (1879) 372 In her family a very characteristic type of handwriting is traceable through five generations.

Hence **tracea'bility**, **'traceableness**, the quality of being traceable; **'traceably** *adv.*, in a manner or degree that can be traced.

1847 WEBSTER, Traceableness. **1855** *Tait's Mag.* XXII. 97 Slightly monotonous, and traceably imitative too, this young melodist yet runs his fingers over the strings with a.. power that instantly make[s] him a marked man. **1875** WHITNEY *Life Lang.* ii. 16 There is, recognizably and traceably, a time when..many of our words came into use. **1891** *Cent. Dict.*, Traceability. **1896** *Law Times* C. 436/2 The doctrine of following trust money depends upon its traceability.

traceless ('treɪslɪs), *a.* [f. TRACE *sb.*[1] + -LESS.]

1. Leaving no trace or track; that cannot be traced; of a surface, that shows no traces or lines.

1651 DAVENANT *Gondibert* II. I. xxiii, Traceless and Swift, and Changing as the Winde. **1789** WOLCOTT (P. Pindar) *Subjects for Painters* xxxv, On traceless copper sees imperial heads. **1889** F. L. OSWALD in *Voice* (N.Y.) 31 Oct., The strangest case of traceless disappearance is perhaps that of the Hungarian poet Petoefi. **1892** J. MATHER *Poems* 68 To traceless nothingness its course has run.

2. *Math.* Having a trace equal to zero.

1966 *Rev. Mod. Physics* XXXVIII. 220/1 To each representation belongs a traceless tensor. **1973** *Nature* 14 Sept. 78/1 A view of the Earth from Polaris, with *W* representing the pole of the traceless part of the nutation tensor. **1979** J. C. POLKINGHORNE *Particle Play* iv. 63 There is a triplet representation of SU(3) which is called the fundamental representation because all other representations..can be constructed by mathematical manipulations on these three fundamental objects. The mathematical operations involved are direct products, symmetrizing, and making traceless.

Hence **'tracelessly** *adv.*, in a traceless manner; without leaving a trace.

1839 BAILEY *Festus* xxix. (1852) 472 May they pass quick and perish tracelessly. **1894** ILLINGWORTH *Personality Hum. & Div.* (1895) Notes 234 Vanishing tracelessly to give place to its successor.

†**'tracent.** *Sc. Obs.* Corruption of F. *treizain* (f. *treize* thirteen), popular name in France for certain heavy *douzains* (silver pieces of 12 deniers tournois) or *grands blancs au soleil* of Louis XI.

These had been issued at 78 to the *marc* instead of 86, and were thus about $\frac{1}{12}$ heavier than the ordinary *douzains*, and passed as worth 13 deniers. (M. Dieudonné, Cabinet de Medailles, Paris, through Mr. G. F. Hill, Brit. Mus.)

1524 *Acts Parlt. Scot.* (1875) XII. 40/2 Forsamekle as sowsis tracentis & karolusis franche monye beand layit wt coper has passage in þis Ralme.

tracer[1] ('treɪsə(r)). [f. TRACE *v.*[1] + -ER[1].] One who or that which traces.

1. One who follows the footprints or track of anything; one who tracks, investigates, or searches out; *spec.* one whose business is the tracing of missing persons, property, parcels, letters, etc.

1552 HULOET, Tracer, *uestigiator*. **1611** FLORIO, *Rintracciatore*, a tracer. Also a sifter out of secrets, a narrow searcher. **1627** HAKEWILL *Apol.* III. i. §5. 152 Plyny..a diligent and curious tracer of the prints of Natures footsteps. **1629** H. BURTON *Truth's Triumph* 210 The timorous..hare ..to deceiue her pursuers or tracers, makes many doubles. **1724** MOFFET *Hesperi-neso-gr.* (1755) 4 To be performed by Some tracer of antiquity. **1866** *Intell. Observ.* No. 56. 99 Some deep-thinking tracer of structural relations. **1888** *Sci. Amer.* 6 Oct. 217/1 Nearly all the great [rail] roads employ a corps of what are known as 'lost car searchers' or 'tracers'. **1902** *Daily Chron.* 18 June 10/7 Furniture (Hire).—Wanted immediately smart man as collector and tracer; must have good knowledge of the hire trade. **1904** *Ibid.* 22 Aug. 4/5 The various postal organisations of sorters, telegraphists, postmen, linemen, tracers, &c.

2. A thing used in tracing; *spec.* **a.** *Anat.* A slender probe used in tracing the course of a nerve or vessel. **b.** In *U.S. railway* or *postal* usage, An inquiry form forwarded from point to point on which the successive movements of a missing car, parcel, or article have to be recorded. **c.** A substance (as a radioactive isotope or a dye) with distinctive properties that is introduced into a system so that its subsequent distribution may be readily followed. Freq. *attrib.*

1882 WILDER & GAGE *Anat. Technol.* 72 The tracer is apparently similar to the 'seeker' of the English anatomists. **1899** *Syd. Soc. Lex.*, *Tracer*, an instrument used in dissection for isolating nerves or vessels by teasing. **1899** *Westm. Gaz.* 17 June 7/2 The 'tracer' had chased the ore into the master-mechanic's possession. **1938** *Encycl. Brit. Bk. of Year* 320/2 The use of deuterium as a tracer in biochemical studies has been important. **1946** *Nature* 12 Oct. 527/1 The attempt..to correlate by radioactive-tracer techniques the localization of heavy metals in the body and their chemotherapeutic activity. **1952** *New Biol.* XIII. 63 One method..involves injecting into such mammals as sheep and rats a very minute dose (called a 'tracer dose') of the isotope. **1960** P. DAUDEL tr. *Eisner's Radioactive Tracers in Chem. & Industry* v. 164 The Russian workers..have investigated the action of modifying agents in the extraction ..of metals..using radioactive tracers. **1962** O. HOCKWIN in A. Pirie *Lens Metabolism Rel. Cataract* 423 We investigated the metabolism of nucleotides and carbohydrates by ion exchange using labelled inorganic phosphate as a tracer. **1963** G. L. PICKARD *Descr. Physical Oceanogr.* vi. 81 Radioactive materials seem attractive as tracers of water movement... A very convenient artificial tracer is the red dye rhodamine-B. **1971** *Physics Bull.* Jan. 22/2 Satellites also have their use in the determination of wind. A tracer moving with the wind and identifiable from the satellite is required; there are two suitable tracers, cloud elements and balloons. **1979** *Sci. Amer.* Apr. 130/1 (Advt.), Using beryllium-7 as a tracer of stratospheric ozone, our scientists found that such ozone is distributed *throughout* high pressure weather systems. **1979** *Nature* 26 July 299/2 Sunspots have long been used as tracers to determine the rotation rate of the Sun.

3. *gen.* One who or that which traces lines or makes tracings; *spec.* **a.** *Mil.* At a siege, one who traces parallels; a member of a tracing party. **b.** One whose work it is to trace copies of drawings or plans. **c.** One whose business is the tracing of patterns for embroidery. **d.** A tool for marking out designs or patterns; also, a chasing or engraving tool. **e.** A stylus for tracing on copying paper; also, the writing instrument of a pantograph or of a self-recording machine. **f.** A mechanical contrivance for making tracings on a larger or smaller scale. **g.** *Ice-cutting*: see quot. 1884.

[**1541** *Aberdeen Regr.* (1844) I. 176 Item, ane traschor, ane stuffin sclyise.] *c* **1790** IMISON *Sch. Art* II. 29 With a little pointed tracer or burnisher go over your strokes which you drew upon the oiled paper, and you shall have the same very neatly and exactly drawn upon the white paper. **1799** G. SMITH *Laboratory* II. 37 Trace the out-line with a brass bodkin, or a tracer, made on purpose, of a piece of wire, of iron or brass. **1812** SHELLEY in Hogg *Life* (1858) II. 150 The tracers of a circle. **1825** J. NICHOLSON *Operat. Mechanic* 317 The frame carrying the dividing-point or tracer, is made to slide on the frame which carries the endless-screw to any distance. **1844** *Civil Eng. & Arch. Jrnl.* VII. 187/1 A solid cone revolving on its axis, during the perpendicular descent of a tracer. **1852** *Trans. Soc. Arts* LVI. 134 The cutters and tracers used together should be of the same size. **1859** F. A. GRIFFITHS *Artill. Man.* (1862) 250 Tracers [of a siege-battery]—1 non-commissioned officer, and 2 privates. **1878** G. B. PRESCOTT *Sp. Telephone* (1879) 297 The lower diagram is what the tracer wrote when the stanza was repeated. **1884** *Cassell's Fam. Mag.* Feb. 188/1 There are.. tracers, or hand-ploughs, to mark out the areas to be cut by grooves [in ice]. **1890** W. J. GORDON *Foundry* 174 At last the film of putty with which the flat plate was spread to show the tracer's progress is scored along every line. The roller is finished. **1908** *Daily Chron.* 12 June 9/6 Tracer for embroidery, female; also cutters wanted. **1911** WEBSTER, *Tracer*,..any of several chasing tools for ornamenting in metal, esp. for making and finishing corners, borders, and the like.

4. a. Bullets or shells whose course is made visible by the trail that they emit during flight; occas. in *sing.* sense. Orig., the trail produced by these.

1910 *Blackw. Mag.* July 6/2 The projectiles of airship guns may possibly give out a jet of flame and a smoke 'tracer' on discharge. **1922** *Encycl. Brit.* XXX. 120/2 For night use, the tracer shows a luminous spark, for day use the tracer gives a smoky trail. **1937** *Times* 16 Apr. 8/6 This was a most spectacular demonstration, the machine-guns using tracer and the new smoke observation projectiles. **1957** P. KEMP *Mine were of Trouble* ix. 173 A minute later bursts of tracer flew over us from high ground on our right. **1967** *Boston Sunday Globe* 23 Apr. 16/4 Helicopter gunships tried to protect the other busy helicopters by circling in pairs, one with a light on to draw a stream of enemy tracers. **1970** L. DEIGHTON *Bomber* xxiii. 335 He was in the nose watching ropes of red and yellow tracer curve towards them and fall away. **1983** 'W. HAGGARD' *Heirloom* xv. 169 He'd seen.. appeals for death..that airman with tracer burning his lungs out.

b. *attrib.* and *Comb.*

1916 'TAFFRAIL' *Pincher Martin* xv. 278 A thin trail of dim light climbed skywards in a curve as a tracer shell hurtled its way through the air. **1918** 'BOYD CABLE' *Air Men o' War* 22 Tracer bullets emit smoke and flame to allow the shooter to follow their flight. **1928** C. F. S. GAMBLE *Story of North Sea Air Station* xii. 179 When about 1,500 feet below the airship, he fired two trays of explosive and tracer ammunition from his Lewis gun into her. **1943** *Sun* (Baltimore) 3 Aug. 4/6 During this exchange of fire, a Japanese plane had managed to get on the tail of Captain Walter's Warhawk. Tracer bullets were flying past him, but none hit. **1944** *Return to Attack* (Army Board, N.Z.) 18/1 The flash and crack of the high-velocity tank guns, the low parabola of the tracer shell.

1969 G. MACBETH *War Quartet* 40 Tracer-filled In open air-space. **1973** M. WOODHOUSE *Blue Bone* xii. 135 A machine-gun stammered and tracer bullets began to draw graceful curves in space. **1976** A. WHITE *Long Silence* vii. 58, I saw a lone fighter come in from the west... Sudden streams of tracer fire came from him.

tracer[2] (ˈtreɪsə(r)). [f. TRACE *sb.*[2] + -ER[1].] A trace-horse; also, a trace-horse boy.

1839 BLACK *Hist. Brechin* ix. 212 He loosed the tracer, leaped on its back..and..went off. **1843** BETHUNE *Sc. Fireside Stor.* 134 The sudden jerk..brought the shaft horse, who was a powerful animal, still nearer to that side of the road, while it made both him and the tracer lower their heads. **1899** J. LUMSDEN *Edin. Poems & Songs* 110 Boot-blackers, news-boys—the smartest we ken! An' their billies, the tracers—Dickie an' Ben.

traceried (ˈtreɪsərɪd), *a.* [f. TRACERY + -ED[2].] Ornamented with or characterized by tracery.

1843 *Civil Eng. & Arch. Jrnl.* VI. 10** Over this traceried wall is a series of clerestory windows of large dimensions. **1849** FREEMAN *Archit.* II. iii. 337 France was the first to produce..traceried windows. **1856** RUSKIN *Mod. Paint.* IV. v. xvi. §26 The narrow meadows and traceried cloisters of the Convent of the Réposoir. **1861** BERESF. HOPE *Eng. Cathedr. 19th C.* ii. 51 In England we are first introduced to complete traceried Gothic in Westminster Abbey.

tracery (ˈtreɪsərɪ). [app. an English formation f. TRACE *v.*[1], or TRACER[1]: see -ERY.]

† **1.** A place for tracing or drawing: cf. *tracing-house* s.v. TRACING *vbl. sb.*[1] 5. *Obs. rare*[−1].

1464 *Rolls of Parlt.* V. 530/1 For the Mansions, Storehouses, Traceries, Voide places for framyng, longyng unto the said Office, within oure Palice of Westm'.

2. *Arch.* The term given to the intersecting rib-work in the upper part of a Gothic window, formed by the elaboration of the mullion, and to the interlaced work of a vault, and that on walls, in panels, and in tabernacle work or screens. (In Fr. *réseau*, *remplissage*.)

In this sense, app. short for *tracery work*, as according to S. Wren 'they (i.e. the masons) called it'; this was perh. connected with sense 1 as work designed in the *tracery* or *tracing-house*, or executed according to tracings thence furnished; but it may have been formed directly from TRACER[1] or from TRACE *v.*[1] senses 9–11; cf. TRACING *vbl. sb.*[1] 3. *Tracery-work* and *tracery* were constantly used by Sir Christopher Wren, and taken from him by Plot and Randle Holme, under whose influence it became generally accepted as the recognized name for this work.

bar-, fan-, flamboyant, geometrical, plate-, wall tracery: see these words. ***stump tracery***: see STUMP *sb.*[1] 19.

1669 WREN *Surv. Salisbury Cath.* in *Parentalia* (1750) 304 The whole Church is vaulted with Chalk between Arches and Cross-springers only,..without Orbs and Tracery, excepting under the Tower, where the Springers divide, and represent a wider Sort of Tracery. *Ibid.*, The Windows are not made too great, nor yet the Light obstructed with many Mullions and Transomes of Tracery-work. **1686** PLOT *Staffordsh.* 360 The tracery in the Stone-work of the West-window..is a curious piece of Art. **1688** R. HOLME *Armoury* III. 112 Trasery is the working of the top part of a Window into several forms and fashions. **1713** WREN in *Parentalia* (1750) 302 The two West-towers..ought certainly to be carried to an equal Height, one Story above the Ridge of the Roof, still continuing the Gothick Manner in the Stone-work, and Tracery. **1750** S. WREN *ibid.* 307 Thus they made their Pillars of a Bundle of little Torus's,..these Torus's split into many small ones, and traversing one another, gave Occasion to the Tracery-work (as they called it) of which this Society were the Inventors. *Ibid.*, A great part of the Outside-ornament of Churches consisted in the Tracery Works of disposing the Mullions of the Windows, for the better fixing in of the Glass. **1820** W. IRVING *Sketch Bk.* II. 5 (Westm. Abb.) The sharp touches of the chisel are gone from the rich tracery of the arches. **1849** MACAULAY *Hist. Eng.* viii. II. 277 Ancient buildings rich with the tracery of the middle ages. **1850** PARKER *Gloss. Archit.* 485 The tympanum..always retains the character of a flat surface or plate of stone pierced with openings. Hence this kind of tracery has been termed plate tracery by Professor Willis. *a* **1878** SIR G. G. SCOTT *Lect. Archit.* (1879) I. 127 The eastern chapels at Winchester, built about 1204..show suggestions of tracery. **1911** R. P. SPIERS in *Encycl. Brit.* XXVII. 115/1 The tracery in windows is usually divided into two sections, plate tracery and rib or bar tracery. *Ibid.* 116/1 The walls and buttresses were all panelled with blank tracery.

3. *transf.* and *fig.* Any delicate interweaving of lines or threads, as in embroidery, carving, etc.; also, an interlacing of boughs or foliage; network, open-work.

1827 HOOD *Mids. Fairies* lix, An elf..Whose coat..was quaintly wrought and overrun With spangled traceries. **1827** KEBLE *Chr. Y.*, *Monday Whitsun Week*, Wild-flower wreaths from side to side Their waving tracery hang. **1841** LEVER *C. O'Malley* lxvii, The thin tracery of the leafless twigs was finely marked.

4. *attrib.* and *Comb.*, as ***tracery bar, glass, head*** (of a window), ***light, -window, -work*** (see 2 above).

1835 R. WILLIS *Archit. Mid. Ages* vi. 53 *note*, The vertical portions below the imposts of the small arches of the lights, are termed *mullions*; the bending and ramifying parts above, I have called *tracery bars*. *Ibid.* 62 Tracery windows of the lancet proportion are great favorites with the Italians. **1886** *Pall Mall G.* 29 Sept. 11/2 The apse has four single-light windows high up in the wall with tracery heads. **1913** EDEN *Anc. Glass* 56 The task of the glass-painter was to fill tracery lights in a way that would harmonise with the glass of the main lights. This he did by making his tracery-glass white and yellow when the lower lights were wholly of that kind.

‖ **trachea** (trəˈkiːə, *often less regularly* ˈtreɪkiːə). Pl. **-eæ**. [med.L. *trāchēa* (Albertus Magnus, *c* 1255) = late L. *trāchīa* (Macrobius, *c* 400), a. Gr. τραχεῖα (fem. of τρᾱχύς rough); short for ἀρτηρία τραχεῖα 'rough artery': see ARTERY 1.]

1. *Anat.* and *Zool.* **a.** The musculo-membranous tube extending from the larynx to the bronchi, and surrounded by gristly (or in birds often bony) rings, which conveys the air to and from the lungs in air-breathing vertebrates; the windpipe.

In early use also in full form (L.) *trachēa artēria*, occas. anglicized as *trache arterie* or *arter trache*, or in one word *trachearteria*, and (from Fr.) *trachiartere*.

c **1400** *Lanfranc's Cirurg.* 153 þouȝ þat trache arterie be peersid..ȝitt he may be heelid wiþ gode medicyns. **1495** *Trevisa's Barth. De P.R.* v. xxiv. (W. de W.) h viij/2 The waye of the brethe, that is callyd Tracheartaria. **1525** tr. *Brunswyke's Surg.* B ij/2 The throte bolle or trachea, ysophagus or meri. **1541** R. COPLAND *Galyen's Terap.* 2 H ij, The vlcere y[t] is in the sharpe artere called tracheia. **1543** TRAHERON *Vigo's Chirurg.* 5 b/2 The Trachea Arteria or wesaunde compouned of gristellye rynges. **1547** BOORDE *Brev. Health* ccxxvi. 77 The longes, the midryffe, the arter trache, the Epigloote. **1548–77** VICARY *Anat.* v. (1888) 44 *Trachia arteria*, that is, the way of the ayre. **1653** URQUHART *Rabelais* II. xviii, Trachiartere or pipe of the lungs. **1693** tr. *Blancard's Phys. Dict.* (ed. 2), *Aspera Arteria*, or *Trachea*, is an Oblong Pipe, consisting of various Cartilages and Membranes. **1713** DERHAM *Phys.-Theol.* IV. vii. 147 Blowing Wind into the Lungs, through the Trachea. **1808** BARCLAY *Muscular Motions* 499 Trachea..should always be pronounced with the *e* long, and not short, as is usually the practice. **1888** ROLLESTON & JACKSON *Anim. Life* 350 The organ of voice..in *Aves* is developed at the junction of the trachea and bronchi, and is known as the syrinx.

attrib. **1878** T. BRYANT *Pract. Surg.* (1879) II. 17 The cartilages and trachea rings. **1898** *Allbutt's Syst. Med.* V. 4 Trachea-bronchitis, or bronchitis of the larger tubes.

b. Each of the tubes, usually opening by stigmata on the surface of the body, which constitute a special form of respiratory organ in insects and other anthropods, conveying air to the blood and tissues generally.

1826 GOOD *Bk. Nat.* (1834) II. 22 The tracheæ, or respiratory organs, are singularly placed at the verge of the tail. **1843** OWEN *Invertebr. Anim.* xix. 251 The smaller Arachnidans breathe by tracheæ exclusively. **1877** HUXLEY *Anat. Inv. Anim.* i. 59 In Arachnida, tracheæ may exist alone, or be accompanied by folded pulmonary sacs.

2. *Bot.* One of the ducts or vessels in the woody tissue of plants, formed from the coalescence of series of cells by disappearance of the partitions between them, formerly supposed to serve for the passage of air; a wood-vessel.

1744 BERKELEY *Siris* §32 By means of air expanded and contracted in the tracheæ or vessels made up of elastic fibres, the sap is propelled through the arterial tubes of a plant. **1753** CHAMBERS *Cycl. Supp.* s.v., Tracheæ, in vegetables, are certain air-vessels. **1813** SIR H. DAVY *Agric. Chem.* (1814) 60 The tracheæ contain fluid matter, which is always thin, watery, and pellucid. **1885** GOODALE *Physiol. Bot.* §271. 84 Ducts, or Tracheæ, are variously marked by pits. **1895** OLIVER tr. *Kerner's Nat. Hist. Plants* I. 276 Formerly the idea was held that these structures [wood-cells and wood-vessels] served for the passage of air, and it was believed that they were analogous to the respiratory organs—the so-called tracheæ—of insects; therefore these wood-vessels were also called 'tracheæ', and the wood-cells 'tracheides'.

tracheal (ˈtreɪkiːəl, trəˈkiːəl), *a.* [ad. mod.L. *trāchēālis*, f. prec.: see -AL[1].]

1. *Anat.* and *Zool.* **a.** Of, pertaining to, or connected with the trachea or windpipe.

tracheal artery: † (*a*) = TRACHEA 1 a (*obs.*); (*b*) each of the small arteries, branches of the inferior thyroid, which supply the trachea.

1710 T. FULLER *Pharm. Extemp.* 271 The Remedy..is convey'd..into the Tracheal Ducts. **1725** *Bradley's Fam. Dict.* s.v. *Spitting of blood*, If it [the Blood] proceeds from the Oesophagum,..or from the Stomach, Lungs, Tracheal Artery, or the Breast. **1849** LYTTON *Caxtons* II. iii, Coughing is either a tracheal, bronchial, pulmonary, or ganglionic affection. **1857** DUNGLISON *Med. Lex.*, *Tracheal Glands*, mucous follicles on the posterior surface of the trachea. **1881** MIVART *Cat* 227 The tracheal cartilages.

b. Pertaining to or of the nature of the tracheæ of insects and other anthropods; connected with tracheæ, as ***tracheal gills***; performed by means of tracheæ, as ***tracheal respiration***. (In quot. 1899 = TRACHEATE *a.*)

1826 KIRBY & SP. *Entomol.* IV. xxxviii. 64 The ramifications of the tracheal tree may be seen without dissection. **1888** ROLLESTON & JACKSON *Anim. Life* 505 (*Insecta*) Respiration is tracheal... Each stigma leads into a single tracheal stem, rarely into several. **1899** *Allbutt's Syst. Med.* VIII. 865 The tracheal order of the Arachnidæ.

2. *Bot.* Of the nature of, or composed of, tracheæ: see prec. 2.

1828 STARK *Elem. Nat. Hist.* II. 454 The Monocotyledonous vegetables have, besides this cellular tissue, porous and tracheal vessels. **1885** GOODALE *Physiol. Bot.* §265. 81 To this class of elements it is difficult to give any satisfactory name... The name Tracheal (or Tracheary),..while it is a significant term when applied to trachea-like bodies (ducts) is a misnomer when applied to an elongated cell wholly free from annular or spiral markings.

trachean (ˈtreɪkiːən, trəˈkiːən), *a.* (*sb.*) *Zool.* [f. TRACHEA + -AN.] Pertaining to or of the nature of a trachea, tracheal; having tracheæ, tracheate. **b.** *sb.* A tracheate arachnid.

1826 KIRBY & SP. *Entomol.* III. xxviii. 21 He has also considered the Trachean and Pulmonary Arachnida as forming one class. *Ibid.* 24 This appears to have had great weight with Lamarck, inducing him to include in his *Arachnida*, not only the Tracheans and Myriapods, but even the apterous Hexapods. **1891** *Cent. Dict.* s.v., Trachean respiration..trachean branchiæ.

trachearian (treɪkiːˈɛərɪən), *a.* (*sb.*) *Zool.* [f. mod.L. *Trāchēāri-a*, neut. pl. + -AN.] Belonging to the order *Trachearia* of arachnids: see TRACHEATE *a.* **b.** *sb.* A tracheate arachnid.

1854 BUSHNAN in *Circ. Sc.* I. *Org. Nat.* 77 The Trachearean Arachnidians..breathe..by means of air-tubes opening upon the surface of the body, by which the air is conveyed to every part of the system.

tracheary (ˈtreɪkiːərɪ), *a.* (*sb.*) [ad. mod.L. *trāchēāri-us*, neut. pl. *-a*: see above.]

1. *Zool.* = prec. **b.** as *sb.* = prec. b.

1835 KIRBY *Hab. & Inst. Anim.* II. xix. 281 Trachearies, or those [Arachnidans] that breathe by spiracles in connection with tracheæ. **1872** LATHAM, *Tracheary*, adj., breathing by means of tracheæ, rather than lungs.

2. *Bot.* = TRACHEAL 2; esp. applied to tissue containing both tracheæ and tracheides.

1885 [see TRACHEAL 2]. **1900** in B. D. JACKSON *Gloss. Bot. Terms.*

tracheate (ˈtreɪkiːeɪt), *a.* (*sb.*) *Zool.* [ad. mod.L. *Trāchēāta*, f. *trāchēa*: see above and -ATE[2] 2.] Furnished with or having tracheæ, as an arthropod; belonging to the group *Tracheata*, in some classifications comprising the insects, myriapods, arachnids, and the genus *Peripatus*, or *spec.* to the order *Tracheata* or *Trachearia* of arachnids, which breathe by tracheæ alone. In quot. 1888[1] = TRACHEAL 1 b. **b.** *sb.* A tracheate arthropod. So **ˈtracheated** *a.*

1877 WOODWARD in *Encycl. Brit.* VI. 654/2 The terrestrial tracheated air-breathing *Scorpionidæ*. **1878** BELL *Gegenbaur's Comp. Anat.* 288 None of these rudiments are retained in any living Tracheate. **1888** ROLLESTON & JACKSON *Anim. Life* 494 (*Arthropoda*) Respiration may be cutaneous..; or branchiate..; or tracheate, and carrying air to all the tissues. *Ibid.* 496 The majority of *Arachnida* are tracheate.

tracheid (ˈtreɪkiː-, trəˈkiːɪd). *Bot.* Also **-ide**. [a. Ger. *tracheïde*, introduced 1863 by Sanio *Bot. Zeitung* 113 'cellulae sive fibrae ligneae tracheïdeae, kurzweg Tracheïdzellen oder Tracheïden': f. TRACHEA + *-ide*, -ID[2].] A vascular cell, with pitted lignified wall, which serves for the conduction of water; a vascular wood-cell.

The wood of the vascular tissue of Gymnosperms and Vascular Cryptogams consists wholly of tracheids.

1875 BENNETT & DYER *Sachs' Bot.* 98 To the Vascular forms belong the ducts and the vascular wood-cells or Tracheïdes. *Ibid.* 99 Vessels with prosenchymatous constituents now form the immediate passage to the vascular wood-cells (Tracheïdes). **1885** GOODALE *Physiol. Bot.* §266. 82 Cells..which are closed throughout..are known as *Tracheids*. **1895** OLIVER tr. *Kerner's Nat. Hist. Plants* I. 276 The walls of the wood-vessels exhibit similar thickenings to those of the wood-cells or tracheides. **1907** D. P. PENHALLOW *Man. N. Amer. Gymnosperms* vi. 88 Such tracheids are invariable features of the ray in all the higher Coniferæ. **1910** J. M. COULTER et al. *Textbk. Bot.* I. iv. 241 Tracheids are single cells thus formed. **1948** [see COLLAPSE *sb.* 4]. **1974** *Sci. Amer.* Apr. 59/1 Tracheids predominate in softwoods, which have no vessel cells or libriform fiber cells.

Hence **tracheidal** (treɪkiːˈaɪd(ə)l, trəˈkiːɪd(ə)l) *a.*, pertaining to or of the nature of a tracheid.

1891 in *Cent. Dict.*

‖ **tracheitis** (treɪkiːˈaɪtɪs). *Path.* Also *erron.* **traˈchitis**. [mod.L., f. TRACHEA + -ITIS.] Inflammation of the trachea.

[**1842** BRANDE *Dict. Sci.*, etc., *Trachitis*, inflammation of the trachea.] **1859** SEMPLE *Diphtheria* 40 A simple tracheitis or even a very mild sporadic affection. **1880** M. MACKENZIE *Dis. Throat & Nose* I. 521 The majority of cases of simple tracheitis scarcely call for any therapeutic measures. **1898** *Allbutt's Syst. Med.* V. 27 The tubular casts of diphtheria and of membranous tracheitis.

trachelate (ˈtrækɪleɪt), *a.* *Entom.* [ad. mod.L. *trachēlāt-us*, f. Gr. τράχηλος neck: see -ATE[2].] Having a neck, or a constriction like a neck: said of the prosternum in certain hymenopterous insects. So **tracheliate** (trəˈkiːlɪeɪt) *a.*, belonging to the division *Trachelia* or *Trachelida* of beetles, which have a neck-like constriction behind the eyes; also **trachelidan** (trəˈkɛlɪdən), *a.* = *tracheliate*; *sb.* a member of the *Trachelida*.

1826 KIRBY & SP. *Entomol.* IV. xlvi. 328 Trachelate... When of itself it forms a neck, the prothorax being represented only by membrane. **1842** BRANDE *Dict. Sci.*, etc., *Trachelidans*, the name of a family of Coleopterous insects, comprising those which have the head supported on a kind of pedicle or neck. **1891** *Cent. Dict.*, Trachelate.. Tracheliate..Trachelidan.

† **trachelipod** (trəˈkɛlɪpɒd), *sb.* and *a.* *Zool. Obs.* [ad. mod.L. *Trachēlipod-a*, neut. pl. (Lamarck), irreg. (for **Trachēlopoda*) f. Gr. τράχηλος neck + πούς, ποδ- foot.] **a.** *sb.* A univalve mollusc of the order *Trachelipoda* in Lamarck's classification, having the foot or locomotive organ attached to the neck. **b.** *adj.* Belonging to or having the

characters of this order. Also †**trachelipodan** (trækɪ'lɪpədən), †**trache'lipodous** *adjs. Obs.*

1835 KIRBY *Hab. & Inst. Anim.* I. ix. 276 The Trachelipods, constituting Lamarck's Third Order of Molluscans. *Ibid.*, The carnivorous, trachelipod Molluscans. **1841** JOHNSTON in *Proc. Berw. Nat. Club* I. No. 9. 263 *Animal* shelled, trachelipode, rarely gasteropode. **1847** ANSTED *Anc. World* xii. 271 The absence of the whole group of Ammonites, and their replacement by a newly introduced genus of carnivorous Trachelipods, animals of lower organization. **1860** MAYNE *Expos. Lex.* 1285 Trachelipodous. **1891** *Cent. Dict.*, Trachelipodan.

trachelo- (trə'kiːləʊ), combining form representing Gr. τράχηλος neck, occurring in modern scientific terms, chiefly of anatomy. **tra,chelo-a'cromial** *a.* and *sb.*, name of a muscle connecting the acromion or extremity of the shoulder-blade with the vertebræ of the neck. **tra,chelo-branchiate** (-'bræŋkɪeɪt) *a. Zool.*, having branchia or gills on the neck, as the division *Trachelobranchia* of gastropod molluscs. **tra,chelo-breg'matic** *a.* [BREGMA], denoting a diameter of the head: see quot. **tra,chelocla'vicular** *a.*, denoting a small muscle occasionally connecting one of the vertebræ of the neck with the clavicle or collar-bone. **tra,chelo'mastoid** *a.* and *sb.*, name of a muscle at the back of the neck, connecting it with the mastoid process of the temporal bone. **tra,chelo-oc'cipital** *a.*, connecting the neck and the occiput: applied to the muscle usually called *complexus* (COMPLEXUS[2]). **tra'cheloplasty** [-PLASTY], **trache'lorrhaphy** [Gr. ῥαφή sewing], *Surg.*, repair or suture of a laceration of the neck of the womb. **tra,chelo'scapular** *a.*, common to the neck and scapular region or shoulder, as the branches of the external jugular vein. **trachelotomy** (trækɪ'lɒtəmɪ) *Surg.* [Gr. τομή cutting], amputation of the neck of the womb.

1891 *Cent. Dict.*, *Trachelo-acromial. **1899** in *Syd. Soc. Lex.* **1891** *Cent. Dict.*, *Trachelobranchiate. **1857** BULLOCK *Cazeaux' Midwif.* 221 The vertical diameter, properly so called, or the *trachelo-bregmatic, traverses the head perpendicularly, passing from the most elevated point of the vertex to the anterior part of the occipital foramen. **1891** *Cent. Dict.*, *Tracheloclavicular. **1899** in *Syd. Soc. Lex.* **1840** G. V. ELLIS *Anat.* 136 The *trachelo-mastoid, the other muscle of prolongation to the longissimus, is situated internal to the transversalis colli. **1891** *Cent. Dict.*, *Trachelo-occipital. **1899** in *Syd. Soc. Lex.* **1890** BILLINGS *Med. Dict.*, **Tracheloplasty*, operation for closure of a laceration of the cervix uteri. **1886** *Brit. Med. Jrnl.* 2 Jan. 1/1 The deep laceration was repaired by *trachelorraphy, five stitches being used. **1891** *Cent. Dict.*, *Trachelo-scapular. **1899** in *Syd. Soc. Lex.* **1890** BILLINGS *Med. Dict.*, **Trachelotomy*, amputation of the cervix uteri.

‖**trachenchyma** (trə'keŋkɪmə). *Bot.* Also anglicized as **tra'chenchym.** [f. TRACHEA + Gr. ἔγχυμα infusion, after PARENCHYMA.] Tracheary tissue: see TRACHEARY 2.

1848 LINDLEY *Introd. Bot.* (ed. 4) I. 21 Vascular tissue, or Trachenchym. **1861** BENTLEY *Man. Bot.* 34 Spiral vessels are sometimes called *Tracheæ* or *Trachenchyma*, from their resemblance to the tracheæ or air-tubes of insects.

tracheo- (trə'kiːəʊ, 'treɪkiːəʊ), used as combining form of TRACHEA, in modern terms of anatomy, zoology, pathology, and surgery. ‖**tracheobranchia** (-'bræŋkɪə), pl. **-æ**, a respiratory organ in certain insect larvæ, combining the characters of a trachea and a branchia or gill. **tracheobronchial** (-'brɒŋkɪəl) *a.*, pertaining to the trachea and the bronchi; also as *sb.* a tracheobronchial muscle (in birds). ‖**tracheobron'chitis**, 'inflammation of the trachea and bronchia' (Dunglison, 1857). **tra'cheocele** (-siːl) [Gr. κήλη tumour], a tumour in or upon the trachea; also loosely applied to goitre or enlargement of the thyroid gland (also called *bronchocele*). **tracheolaryn'gotomy** [LARYNGOTOMY], incision of the trachea and larynx, laryngotracheotomy (see LARYNGO-). **tracheo-œsophageal** (-iːsəʊ'fædʒiːəl) *a.*, pertaining or common to the trachea and the œsophagus. **tra'cheophone** (-fəʊn) [Gr. φωνή voice], *sb.* a member of the *Tracheophonæ* or *Tracheophones*, a group of S. American passerine birds, having the syrinx or vocal organ situated wholly or chiefly in the trachea (cf. *tracheobronchial* above); *adj.* belonging to this group; so **trache'ophonine, trache'ophonous** *adjs.* **tracheophony** (-'ɒfənɪ), 'the sound heard over the trachea on auscultation' (*Syd. Soc. Lex.* 1899). **trache'oscopy** [Gr. -σκοπία, f. σκοπεῖν to view], inspection or examination of the trachea, as with a laryngoscope; so **tracheo'scopic** *a.*, pertaining to tracheoscopy; **trache'oscopist**, one who practises tracheoscopy. See also TRACHEOTOMY, etc.

1877 HUXLEY *Anat. Inv. Anim.* vi. 252 The so-called **Tracheo-branchiæ*..are in no sense branchiæ, but simply take the place of stigmata. **1896** NEWTON *Dict. Birds* 939 One pair of *tracheo-bronchial muscles, arising mostly from the Trachea and attached to one or more of the bronchial semi-rings. *Ibid.*, Two dorsal and one ventral tracheo-bronchials. *Ibid.* 940 According to the position of the sound-producing membranes, three types of Syrinx are distinguishable:—Tracheal, Bronchial and Tracheo-Bronchial. **1828** WEBSTER, **Tracheocele*, an enlargement of the thyroid gland; bronchocele or goiter. *Cyc.* **1880** M. MACKENZIE *Dis. Throat & Nose* I. 561 Tracheocele does not, as a rule, appear to be attended with much danger. **1890** BILLINGS *Med. Dict.*, *Tra'cheocele*, a tumor of the neck containing air and communicating with the trachea. **1909** *Cent. Dict. Suppl.*, *Tracheolaryngotomy. **1897** *Allbutt's Syst. Med.* III. 365 This may lead to a *tracheo-œsophageal or broncho-œsophageal fistula. **1884** *Ibis* July 241 This at once removes it from the *Tracheophones, in which a tenth primary is always present. **1906** *Athenæum* 10 Mar. 304/2 Mr. W. P. Pycraft read a paper on the 'Tracheophone Passeres', which he described as a group differing from all the remaining Passeres in the formation of the syrinx. **1888** NEWTON in *Encycl. Brit.* XXIV. 689 *note*, The *Furnariidæ* of Garrod, consisting of about 8 genera of *Tracheophonine Birds, some of whom build marvellous nests of mud spherical in form. **1896** NEWTON *Dict. Birds* 940 Indications of such a *tracheophonous Syrinx exist in various *Cotingidæ* and *Pittidæ*. **1857** DUNGLISON *Med. Lex.*, **Tracheophony*, Laryngophony. **1880** M. MACKENZIE *Dis. Throat & Nose* I. 519 A *tracheoscopic examination. **1899** *Syd. Soc. Lex.*, *Tracheoscopist. **1880** M. MACKENZIE *Dis. Throat & Nose* I. 502 (*title of section*) *Tracheoscopy. **1904** *Brit. Med. Jrnl.* 10 Sept. 605 Instructions for the practice of laryngoscopy and tracheoscopy.

tracheole ('treɪkiːəʊl). *Entom.* [ad. mod.L. type **trāchĕola*, dim. of TRACHEA: see -OLE.] A small or minute trachea or branch of a trachea (in insects). Hence **tra'cheolar** *a.*, pertaining to a tracheole, or consisting of tracheoles.

1904 *Amer. Nat.* Feb. 134 The tracheæ..pass over into the tracheolar network... The term tracheoles..is used elsewhere in insect histology to designate fine tracheal branches not possessing spiral thickening.

tracheome ('treɪkiːəʊm). *Bot. rare.* [f. TRACHEA + *-ome* as in *rhizome, caulome*, etc.] General term for a wood-vessel (*trachea*), wood-cell (*tracheide*), or other structure of the same class.

1900 B. D. JACKSON *Gloss. Bot. Terms* 273/1 *Tracheome*, stated by Potonié not to be the tracheal, but the hydral system of the bundle, he therefore names it Hydrome.

tracheostomy (treɪkiː'ɒstəmɪ). *Surg.* [f. TRACHEO- + -STOMY.] **a.** The operation of making an opening in the trachea near its upper end, so that the patient can breathe through it; also, the opening so made.

1945 W. V. MULLIN in F. Christopher *Textbk. Surg.* (ed. 4) xix. 774/2 Tracheostomy may be necessary to facilitate the operation. **1961** *Lancet* 7 Oct. 819/2 He spoke of the need for asepsis in managing a tracheostomy, especially during cleaning and replacement of the tube. **1976** *National Observer* (U.S.) 18 Dec. 16/4 Siegel underwent a tracheostomy 2½ months ago. **1977** *Proc. R. Soc. Med.* LXX. 160/1 He was then able to breathe spontaneously and the tracheostomy was allowed to close.

b. tracheostomy tube, a curved tube which can be inserted into the trachea via a tracheostomy.

1961 *Lancet* 7 Oct. 819/2 There was less chance of stenosis of the trachea after removal of the tracheostomy tube. **1977** *Ibid.* 19 Mar. 636/2 Indwelling urinary catheters, endotracheal tubes, and tracheostomy tubes put the patient at special risk.

tracheotomy (treɪkiː'ɒtəmɪ). *Surg.* Also *erron.* **tra'chotomy.** [f. TRACHEO- + -TOMY.] = TRACHEOSTOMY.

1726 QUINCY *Lex. Phys.-Med.*, *Trachotomy*, the same as *Bronchotomy*. **1805** *Med. Jrnl.* XIV. 151 Bronchotomy, or (speaking more correctly) tracheotomy, was now thought of. **1878** T. BRYANT *Pract. Surg.* I. 75 Tracheotomy is one of these means, and deserves trial.

b. *attrib.*, ***tracheotomy instrument***, etc.; **tracheotomy tube**, = *tracheostomy tube*.

1880 M. MACKENZIE *Dis. Throat & Nose* I. 514 *note*, I returned home for my *tracheotomy instruments. **1884** *Health Exhib. Catal.* 104/1 Bronchitis or *Tracheotomy Kettle. **1897** *Allbutt's Syst. Med.* IV. 822 The intubation tube is more comfortably worn than the *tracheotomy tube.

Hence **tracheotome** ('treɪkiːəʊtəʊm), a surgical instrument for performing tracheotomy; **trache'otomist**, one who performs tracheotomy; **trache'otomize** *v.*, *trans.* to perform tracheotomy upon.

1857 DUNGLISON, **Tracheotome*, an instrument of the trocar kind, for opening the trachea. **1890** in BILLINGS *Med. Dict.* **1891** *Cent. Dict.*, *Tracheotomist. **1885** *Science* 27 Feb. 173/2 He [Leo] worked with rabbits, which were *tracheotomized and supplied with pure oxygen.

trachiartere: see TRACHEA.

trachinoid ('trækɪnɔɪd), *a.* and *sb. Ichth.* [f. mod.L. *Trachin-us* (Linnæus, 1758), name of the typical genus + -OID; f. med.L. *trachina*, said in Acts of S. Francis of Paula (1416–1507) to be a local name of a fish (Du Cange).] **a.** *adj.* Resembling, allied to, or having the characters of, the *Trachinidæ* or weevers, a family of spiny-finned fishes. **b.** *sb.* A fish of this family.

[**1774** GOLDSM. *Nat. Hist.* (1862) II. III. i. 295 The Trachinus or Weever.]

trachitis, incorrect form for TRACHEITIS.

trachle, trauchle ('trɑx(ə)l, 'traux(ə)l), *sb. Sc.* [f. next.]

1. A fatiguing or exhausting journey or effort; exhausting struggle or toil.

1823 W. TENNANT *Cdl. Beaton* v. vii. 174 It's een a lang trachle frae the Kirk Wynd in Anster, to the Castle Wynd in St. Andrews. **1840** A. LAING *Wayside Flowers* (1878) 33 A' broken and pined Wi' trachle o' body and trouble o' mind. **1881** P. DUNCAN in *Mod. Scott. Poets* III. 171 Life's trachle's near a close.

2. A person who 'trachles' or gets 'trachled'.

1887 J. SERVICE *Dr. Duguid* xxiii. 157, I have had to ding some useless trauchle out of my gate. **1901** G. DOUGLAS *House w. Green Shutters* 39, I would have thocht the thowless trauchle hadna the smeddum left to interfere. [*Note*] *Trauchle*, a poor trollop who trails about.

trachle, trauchle ('trɑːx(ə)l, 'traux(ə)l), *v. Sc.* [Known from 16th c. Of obscure origin; but bearing a striking resemblance in sense to West Flemish *tragelen*, given by De Bo as a variant of *trakelen*, to go with difficulty, to walk laboriously and heavily; also trans. to drag or trail, as a canal-boat: cf. *tragel* or *trakel* a tow-path. Cf. also Du. *traag*, MDu. *traech* slow, heavy, sluggish; also Sw. dial *traggel* sb., *traggla* v., worry, bother (Rietz).]

1. *trans.* To bedraggle, dishevel; to disorder, injure, or befoul by trampling. (Chiefly in *pa. pple.*)

1549 *Compl. Scot.* vii. 68 Hyr hayr..vas feltrit & trachlit out of ordour, hingand ouer hyr schuldirs. **1825** JAMIESON s.v., A person is said to trauchle corn or grass, when he injures it by treading on it. **1871** W. ALEXANDER *Johnny Gibb* i, We canna hae the beast's maet trachel't amo' their feet.

2. To tire out or fatigue greatly by long walking; to exhaust by over-exertion; *fig.* to distress. (Chiefly in *pa. pple.*)

a **1578** LINDESAY (Pitscottie) *Chron. Scot.* (S.T.S.) I. 274 Thay war voodrous tyrd and foirgeine and trachled gretlie in travell. **1588** J. MELVILL *Diary* (Wodrow Soc.) 263 That night, the Lard..sufferit the [Spanish] souldiours to com a-land..for the maist part young berdles men, sillie, trauchled, and houngered. **1776** C. KEITH *Farmer's Ha'* xxxvi, Quo' they, 'We're trachled unco sair, We've gane twal mile o' yerd and mair'. **1889** BARRIE *Window in Thrums* xx. 189 Ye mauna trachle yersel', mother.

b. *intr.* for *refl.* To tire oneself out; to drudge.

1823 W. TENNANT *Cdl. Beaton* v. vii. 171 I'm a wee forjeskit though, wi' trachlin' sae lang. **1840** A. LAING *Wayside Flowers* (1878) 37 Then why need ye toil on an' trachle sae sair?

Hence **'trachled ('trachlet), 'trauchled** *ppl. a.*; **'trachling, 'trauchling** *vbl. sb.* and *ppl. a.*

1902 *Blackw. Mag.* Sept. 364/2 It's a trauchling game [golf] and I wish I'd never seen it. **1910** *Dundee Advert.* 25 Nov., A scheme..whereby a 'trauchled' working class mother could be relieved of part of her domestic toil.

'trachly, *a. Sc.* [f. prec. sb. or vb. + -Y.]

1825 JAMIESON, *Trachlie*, adj. 1. Always drudging, dirty, and slovenly, *Clydes.* 2. Fatiguing, exhausting, *ibid.*

‖**trachoma** (trə'kəʊmə). *Path.* [mod.L., a. Gr. τράχωμα roughness (Dioscorides), f. τρᾱχύς rough.] An infectious disease of the eyes, characterized by roughness or granulation of the inner surface of the eyelids, often supervening upon purulent ophthalmia; also called *granular lids.* **b.** Also, an affection of the larynx characterized by nodular swellings on the vocal cords (quot. 1880).

1693 tr. *Blancard's Phys. Dict.* (ed. 2), *Trachoma*, a Scab, or Asperity of the inner part of the Eye-lid. **1857** DUNGLISON *Med. Lex.*, *Trachoma*... A roughness of the inner surface of the eyelids. A variety of ophthalmia, of which three kinds have been designated. **1880** M. MACKENZIE *Dis. Throat & Nose* I. 293 This condition has been called *chorditis tuberosa* or *trachoma*. **1904** *Daily Chron.* 18 Oct. 3/4 So prevalent is the disease in Egypt..that a travelling hospital.. has been for some months at work in that country, confining its attention solely to trachoma.

c. *attrib.* **trachoma glands**, a name for the lymph-follicles of the conjunctiva, which increase in number in trachoma.

1873 T. H. GREEN *Introd. Pathol.* (ed. 2) 142 The trachoma glands of the conjunctiva. **1890** BILLINGS *Med. Dict.*, *Bruch, follicles of*, conjunctival lymph-follicles, trachoma glands of Henle.

Hence **tra'chomatous** *a.*, pertaining to, of the nature of, or affected with trachoma.

1891 in *Cent. Dict.* **1900** *Brit. Med. Jrnl.* 12 May *Epit. Curr. Lit.* 74 Trachomatous Pannus cured by intercurrent Erysipelas.

trachomedusan (,treɪkəʊmɪ'djuːsən), *a.* and *sb. Zool.* [f. mod.L. *Trachomedusæ*, pl., f. *tracho-*, var. of TRACHY- + MEDUSA: see -AN.] **a.** *adj.* Belonging to the sub-order *Trachomedusæ* of the order *Trachymedusæ* of Craspedote Hydrozoa. **b.** *sb.* A hydrozoan of this sub-order.

[**1888** ROLLESTON & JACKSON *Anim. Life* 749 The order *Trachymedusæ*..contains Medusæ which possess tentacles with a solid axis... There are two sub-orders, the *Narcomedusæ* and *Trachomedusæ*.] **1907** *Gentl. Mag.* July 97/2 No other known Trachomedusan had gourds on the manubrium.

trachotomy, bad form for TRACHEOTOMY.

trachour, variant of TREACHER *Obs.*, traitor.

trachtscoot, obs. form of TREKSCHUIT.

trachy- (treɪkɪ), combining form, repr. Gr. τραχύ-ς rough, in a few modern scientific terms. **trachy'carpous** *a. Bot.* [Gr. καρπός fruit], rough-fruited. **,trachychro'matic** *a.* [Gr. χρῶμα colour], applied to certain cells in bone-marrow which take a deep stain. **trachy'glossate**, *Zool.* [Gr. γλῶσσα tongue], *a.* belonging to the division *Trachyglossa* of octopod molluscs, having radular teeth upon the tongue; *sb.* a trachyglossate octopod. **,trachyme'dusan**, *Zool.*, *a.* belonging to the order *Trachymedusæ* of Craspedote Hydrozoa; *sb.* a hydrozoan of this order. **trachynemid** (-'niːmɪd), *Zool.* [Gr. νῆμα thread], *a.* belonging to the family *Trachynemidæ* of Craspedote Hydrozoa; *sb.* a hydrozoan of this family. **,trachynote**, a fish of the extinct genus *Trachynōtus*. ‖**trachy'phonia**, *Path.* [mod.L. f. Gr. φωνή voice], roughness or hoarseness of voice. **trachypteroid** (trə'kɪptərɔɪd), *Ichth.* [Gr. πτερόν wing, taken as = fin: see -OID], *a.* resembling or allied to the genus *Trachypterus* or family *Trachypteridæ* of spiny-finned fishes, including the 'king of the salmon', *T. altivelis*; *sb.* a fish of this family. **trachy'spermous** *a.*, *Bot.* [Gr. σπέρμα seed], rough-seeded.

1860 MAYNE *Expos. Lex.*, *Trachycarpus*, having rough fruit,..*trachycarpous. **1900** in B. D. JACKSON *Gloss. Bot. Terms.* **1909** *Cent. Dict. Suppl.*, *Trachychromatic. **1891** *Cent. Dict.*, *Trachyglossate. **1890** *Q. Jrnl. Microsc. Sc.* Feb. 511 No *Trachymedusan has been observed to pass through a hydroid phase. **1888** ROLLESTON & JACKSON *Anim. Life* 751 In the family *Aglauridæ*, the Petasid sub-family *Petachnidæ*, and the *Trachynemid *Pectyllidæ*. **1848** SMART, **Trachynotes*, rough-backed creatures— the generic name of a division of fossil fishes. **1860** MAYNE *Expos. Lex.*, **Trachyphonia*, term for a rough voice. **1891** *Cent. Dict.*, *Trachypteroid. *Ibid.*, *Trachyspermous. **1900** in B. D. JACKSON *Gloss. Bot. Terms.*

b. *Min.* In names of rocks, taken as combining form of TRACHYTE, and denoting an igneous rock or lava intermediate between trachyte and that denoted by the second element, as **trachy'andesite, trachy'basalt, trachy'dolerite, trachy'rhyolite**.

1888 *Cassell's Encycl. Dict.*, Trachybasalt, Trachydolerite. **1897** H. S. WASHINGTON *Jrnl. Geol.* (U.S.) May–June 351 For those intermediate effusive rocks in which the plagioclase occurring along with orthoclase is acid ..the name *trachyandesite*, which is in use in France, will be reserved. *Ibid.*, The intermediate potash-rich rocks..carry basic plagioclase-labradorite to anorthite—along with orthoclase, and such rocks will be called collectively in this paper by the name of *trachydolerite*,..proposed by Abich as far back as 1841. **1909** *Cent. Dict. Suppl.*, Trachyrhyolite.

trachyte ('treɪkaɪt, 'trækaɪt). *Geol.* and *Min.* [a. F. *trachyte* (Haüy); f. Gr. τραχύς rough, or perh. τραχύτης roughness.] A group of volcanic rocks, having a characteristically rough or gritty surface. The name was given by Haüy to certain volcanic rocks from Auvergne, and at first used in a wide sense; now confined to rocks consisting mainly of sanidine (or glassy orthoclase) felspar, as distinguished from oligoclase- and quartz-trachytes, and intermediate forms: see TRACHY- b.

1821 R. JAMESON *Man. Min.* 427 Rocks of extinct and ancient volcanoes... 1. Trachyte. This rock which is of the nature of felspar, is generally porphyritic, the imbedded crystals being most frequently of the glassy kind. **1830** LYELL *Princ. Geol.* I. 386 These isles are formed of brown trachyte..full of crystals of glassy felspar. **1854** MURCHISON *Siluria* xviii. 425 These were, in ancient times, penetrated by granites, porphyries, trachytes, and other eruptive matters. **1876** PAGE *Adv. Text-bk. Geol.* v. 105 The trachytes are rough-grained subcrystalline varieties of felspathic lava. **1911** *Encycl. Brit.* XXVII. 116/2 *Trachyte*.. was long used in a much wider sense..in fact it included quartz-trachytes (now known as liparites and rhyolites) and oligoclase-trachytes, more properly assigned to Andesites.

b. *attrib.*, as *trachyte rock, porphyry*; **trachyte tuff**, a tuff having the composition and structure of trachyte.

1872 C. KING *Mountain. Sierra Nev.* ix. 188 Rounded domes of trachyte rock. **1877** TYLOR in *Nature* 5 July 191/1 In a still larger chulpa [*i.e.* Peruvian burial-tower] there are hewn trachyte blocks as large as twelve feet long [etc.]. **1885** GEIKIE *Text-bk. Geol.* II. II. vii. (ed. 2) 166 Thus we have felsite-tuffs, trachyte-tuffs, basalt-tuffs, pumice-tuffs, porphyrite-tuffs, etc.

trachytic (trə'kɪtɪk), *a.* [f. prec. + -IC: cf. F. *trachytique*.] Consisting, or of the nature, of trachyte; containing, or abounding in, trachyte.

1827 *Edin. Rev.* XLV. 320 Those hills consist of a trachytic formation. **1830** LYELL *Princ. Geol.* I. 396 Where it [felspar] is in great excess lavas are called trachytic; where augite (or pyroxene) predominates, they are called basaltic. **1833–4** J. PHILLIPS in *Encycl. Metrop.* (1845) VI. 767/1 Trachytic porphyry..occurs on the Western shore of the Island of Arran. **1869** PHILLIPS *Vesuv.* viii. 211 Slopes of crumbling tufaceous, pumiceous and trachytic rocks.

trachytoid ('trækɪtɔɪd, 'treɪkɪ-), *a.* [f. as prec. + -OID, after F. *trachytoïde*.] Resembling or allied to trachyte.

1885 GEIKIE *Text-bk. Geol.* II. II. v. (ed. 2) 110 *note*, For this [semi-crystalline] structure the term 'mixed' has been proposed, as being a mixture of the crystalline and amorphous (glassy) structures. It has been designated by Fouqué and Michel-Lévy 'trachytoid', as being typically developed among the trachytes. *Ibid.* vii. 137 Two leading types of structure are recognised by these authors among the eruptive rocks. 1. Granitoid... 2. Trachytoid, distinguished by a more marked contrast between the crystals of the first and second consolidation, the usual presence of an amorphous magma, and the fluxion structure.

tracing ('treɪsɪŋ), *vbl. sb.*[1] [f. TRACE *v.*[1] + -ING[1].] The action of TRACE *v.*[1], or its result.

1. a. The following of traces, tracking; also †*concr. pl.* traces left, tracks (*obs.*).

1523 *Act 14 & 15 Hen. VIII*, c. 10 Diuers persons..by reason of the trasinge in snowe, haue killed and destroied.. the same Hares, by .x.xii. or .xvi. vpon a daye. **1657** THORNLEY tr. *Longus' Daphnis & Chloe* 116 A Wolf pursued me: where are the tracings of a Wolf? **1753** CHAMBERS *Cycl. Supp.*, *Training*, or *Tracing*,..used by our miners to express the tracing up the mineral appearances on the surface of the earth to their head.., and there finding a mine. **1910** M. GASTER in *Encycl. Brit.* XII. 40/1 In various parts of Germany and Austria a special register is kept for the tracing of the genealogy of vagrant and sedentary Gipsy families.

b. The procedure of making a list of all the headings under which a given item occurs in an index or catalogue; an entry in such a list.

1905 *N.Y. State Libr. Bull.* No. 95. 582 Make slip under personal name as in 14*a*, following same method of tracing. **1914** *N.Y. State Libr. School Cataloging Rules* 32 Trace added entries on the back of the main card. Write the tracing for other cards toward what will then be the lower right corner. **1953** R. L. COLLISON *Indexes & Indexing* I. 73 Since revision [of an index]..may sometimes be necessary, it is a good policy to enter 'tracings' of any references made on the main slip. **1978** FOTHERGILL & BUTCHART *Non-Book Materials for Libraries* iv. 191 Then the primary name heading and tracings for added entries and references can be given.

c. The following of the course of the cutting stylus by a reproducing stylus; usu. in ***tracing distortion***, distortion that occurs when the stylus does not describe exactly the same path as the groove owing to its size in relation to the groove.

1942 *Jrnl. Acoustical Soc. Amer.* XIII. 276/1 (*heading*) Tracing distortion in the reproduction of constant amplitude recordings. **1959** *Listener* 26 Mar. 542/1 Turning now to the gramophone record, we find a sound source which suffers from certain well-known inherent defects, among the most important being..tracing distortion. **1961** G. A. BRIGGS *A to Z in Audio* 208 These delicately balanced arms which permit good tracking and tracing at extremely light weights give the best available quality from the finest pickups. **1975** G. J. KING *Audio Handbk.* viii. 192 Incorrect adjustment of the lateral and vertical tracking of the pickup can also aggravate distortion; but that resulting from 'normal' errors is generally less than tracing distortion.

d. *Computers.* The process of performing a trace (TRACE *sb.*[1] 12 a). Also *attrib.*, as ***tracing routine***.

1959 M. H. WRUBEL *Primer of Programming for Digital Computers* v. 107 Tracing is an important technique in testing programs, but it must be used in moderation. **1967** KLERER & KORN *Digital Computer User's Handbk.* I. i. 23 It is possible to build in a tracing structure into any given program. **1969** P. B. JORDAIN *Condensed Computer Encycl.* 539 It is important that the tracing routine leave intact the natural operation of the subject program.

†**2.** The treading of a measure; dancing. *Obs.*

1577 GRANGE *Golden Aphrod.* F iij b, It fell by course N.O. shoulde leade this trace, bycause he knewe it beste, the tracyng of this rounde requyred in the middle thereof a conge. **1596** DAVIES *Orchestra* xiii, No..sight more pleasing to behold, With all their turnes and tracings manifold. **1643** TRAPP *Comm. Gen.* xxix. 22 Of dancing and dalliance, of tracing, and tripping on the toe, we read not.

3. a. Drawing, delineating, marking out; the copying of a drawing, etc., by means of a transparent sheet placed over it.

c **1440** *Promp. Parv.* 499/1 Tracynge, or drawynge for to make an ymage or an other thynge (*K.* to make a pycture or gravynge). **1573** (*title*) A..treatise, wherein is..sett forthe the arte of Limming, which teacheth the order in drawing & tracing of letters, vinets, flowers, armes and Imagery. **1712** J. JAMES tr. *Le Blond's Gardening* 87 The Manner of Tracing, reduced to Twenty Practices. **1815** J. SMITH *Panorama Sc. & Art* II. 728 Tracing against the Light. **1843** *Civil Eng. & Arch. Jrnl.* VI. 236/1 The slow progress of a fresco-painting, from the 'tracing' to the last touch. **1884** *Mil. Engineering* (ed. 3) I. II. 21 The tracing of parallels and approaches is commenced in the dusk of the evening, when sufficiently dark to conceal men from the view of the besieged.

b. *concr.* That which is produced by tracing or drawing; a drawing; *spec.* a copy made by tracing; also, the record of a self-registering instrument.

1811 WELLINGTON in Gurw. *Desp.* (1838) VII. 142 Murray..tells me that he sent after you..a tracing of a large part of Alemtejo. **1857** RUSKIN *Pol. Econ. Art* ii. (1868) 127 Tracings from frescos and other large works are also of great value. **1864** *Lond. Rev.* 27 Aug. 247/2 The Psychonomy of the Hand..is illustrated by tracings from living hands of various endowments. **1866** ROGERS *Agric. & Prices* I. xxvi. 644 A collection of such tracings will be found in the Bodleian Library. **1874** H. H. COLE *Catal. Ind. Art S. Kens. Mus.* 251 The centre [of the embroidered pattern] is occupied by a circular disc of beautiful floral tracing. **1899** *Allbutt's Syst. Med.* VIII. 373 The sphygmographic tracing [in melancholia] usually indicates a feeble systole.

†**4.** A timber used in building; ? a framing timber. *Obs.*

1601 DEACON & WALKER *Answ. to Darel, Catal. D.'s Contradict.* No. 50 The groundsels, the studs, the raysing peeces, the iouystes, the tracings, and all the rest of the timber belonging thereto. **1616** *Nottingham Rec.* (1889) IV. 348 For ouer liggers and trasinges for y[e] same bridge xs.

5. *attrib.* and *Comb.*: **tracing-board**, a board on which a plan, as of a building, is traced; **tracing-braid**, ? narrow braid used in an interlacing design; **tracing-cloth**, smooth transparent linen sized on one side, used for making tracings; **tracing-house**, a house in which the plans of a building are traced; **tracing-instrument**, an instrument for copying any outline or plan on the same or a larger or smaller scale; **tracing-lace**, narrow lace used in an open design; cf. *tracing-braid*; **tracing-linen** = *tracing-cloth*; **tracing-machine** = *tracing-instrument* (*Cent. Dict.* 1891); **tracing-paper**, (*a*) transparent paper for copying drawings, etc. by tracing; (*b*) lithographic transfer paper; **tracing-picket**, a picket used in siege work to mark lines and angles; **tracing-pin**, a peg or pin used to mark out lines on the ground in setting out work; **tracing-point**, (*a*) a point that traces or draws lines; (*b*) in *Fretwork*, a sharp tool used to mark out a design; **tracing-staff**: see quot.; **tracing table**, a table with a translucent top illuminated from underneath; **tracing-thread**, in *Lace-making*, a heavy thread or fillet of fine threads used to form the outline of the pattern; **tracing-wheel**, a toothed wheel or roulette for marking out patterns.

1399 in *York Fabric Rolls* (Surtees) 17 In le loge [mason's work-shop] apud Ebor, in cimiterio, lxix stanexes, j magna kevell, xcvj chisielles ferri.., ij *tracyngbordes. **1906** *Daily Chron.* 4 Oct. 3/4 The jacket was..elaborately braided with silk *tracing-braid. *Ibid.*, The skirt..with a girdle, braided with tracing-braid to match the jacket. **1842–76** GWILT *Encycl. Archit.* Gloss., **Tracing cloth*, a fine white cloth, prepared in a similar way to paper for rendering it transparent. **1873** E. SPON *Workshop Receipts* Ser. I. 6/2 If ink or colour does not run freely on tracing cloth, mix both with a little ox-gall. **1374–5** in Oliver *Exeter Cath.* (1861) 385 Custus nove domus in Calendarhay vocate '*Trasyng hous'. **1581–2** *York Fabric Rolls* (Surtees) 118 For xj daies worke on the leades over the tracinge hows, etc., 10s. 8d. [**1859** *Ibid.* Gloss. 358 *Tracinge-hous*, the place or room used by the draughtsman.] **1877** KNIGHT *Dict. Mech.*, **Tracing-instrument*, an instrument for copying figures on an enlarged or reduced scale. **1901** *Daily News* 13 Feb. 5/1 A very long robe..trimmed with gold lace, some of it what is technically called '*tracing-lace', i.e., arranged in small loops placed alternately hither and thither. **1824** *Mech. Mag.* 31 Jan. 365/2 An excellent method to make *tracing-paper. **1834** *Penny Cycl.* II. 203/2 The design is..copied on very thin transparent paper, called tracing-paper. **1862** *Catal. Internat. Exhib.* II. XIII. 17 To the horizontal arm is fixed the *tracing pencil. **1870** WESSELY *Germ.-Eng. Dict.*, *Absteckpfahl*..*tracing-picket. **1712** J. JAMES tr. *Le Blond's Gardening* 89 Tracing two Portions of a Circle..by means of a small *Tracing-Pin fixed at the End of the Cord. **1815** J. SMITH *Panorama Sc. & Art* II. 728 Where long, straight, or parallel lines occur, the *tracing point may be guided by a ruler. **1712** J. JAMES tr. *Le Blond's Gardening* 84 A **Tracing-Staff*..is a long strait Stick tipt with Iron at the lower End, having the Point triangular..; with this Tracing-Staff you strike out and design all the Figures of a Garden. **1953** A. H. ROBINSON *Elements Cartogr.* v. 82/2 (*caption*) A *tracing table with fluorescent illumination. **1978** *N.Y. Times* 30 Mar. B-21/8 (Advt.), Nuarc lighted tracing table, 5 drawer blueprint files. **1894** J. E. DAVIS *Elem. Mod. Dressmaking* i. 7 Tracing the fitting-lines of the pattern through the doubled lining only..is now almost entirely done by *tracing-wheel. **1969** *Guardian* 30 Sept. 11/2 Singers.. stock everything for dressmaking..hem markers, tracing wheels, fastenings.

tracing, *vbl. sb.*[2]: see TRACE *v.*[3]

(Here perhaps belong quot. 1874 in prec. 3 b, and *tracing-braid*, *-lace* in sense 5.)

track (træk), *sb.* Forms: 5–6 **trak**, 6 **tracke**, 6– **track**. [a. OF. *trac* (1440 in Hatz.-Darm.), *traq*, F. *trac*: ulterior derivation uncertain, but generally thought to be from Teutonic. Diez and Scheler would connect it with MLG. and Du. *treck*, *trek* draught, drawing, pull, line drawn, etc., f. *trecken*, *trekken* to draw, pull, tug, drag, haul (in MDu. rarely *tracken*): see TRACK *v.*[2]

If this be the source, the original sense would appear to have been the line or mark made on the ground by anything hauled or dragged, whence also the mark made or path beaten by the feet of man or beast; the sense-development being parallel to that of TRACE from L. **tractiāre*. It is noticeable that the senses of the verbs *trace* and *track* are sometimes identical; also that *track* and *tract* were often identified in pronunciation and use.]

I. 1. a. The mark, or series of marks, left by the passage of anything; a trail; a wheel-rut; the wake of a ship; a series of footprints; the scent followed by hounds; *spec.* in *Geol.* a series of fossilized footprints of an animal.

1470–85 MALORY *Arthur* x. xiv. 435 Myght I fynde the trak of his hors I shold not fayle to fynde that Knyghte. *c* **1500** *3 Kings' Sons* 30 They came on the trakkys of there enmyes. *c* **1595** CAPT. WYATT *R. Dudley's Voy. W. Ind.* (Hakl. Soc.) 27 Wee discried the track of theire feet in the woodes by the impression of the sandes. **1685** COTTON tr. *Montaigne* (1711) I. xxxviii. 349 Like the Beasts of Chace, who put out the Track at the Entrance into their Den. **1706** PHILLIPS (ed. Kersey), *Track*, a Foot-print, or Foot-step, the rut of a Coach-wheel, the run of a Ship, a Mark that remains of any thing. **1840** DICKENS *Barn. Rudge* viii, The walls and roof..tapestried with the tracks of snails and slugs. **1842** *Act 5 & 6 Vict.* c. 79 §17 Any stage carriage.. the bearing of which on the ground shall be less than 4 ft. 6 in. from the centre of the track of the right or off wheel to the centre of the track of the left or near wheel. **1912** *Return Brit. Museum* 174 A large slab of tracks from the Palaeozoic rocks of the Alleghany Mts.

(*b*) *spec.* in *Particle Physics*, a line marking the path taken by an atomic or sub-atomic particle.

1912 *Proc. R. Soc.* A. LXXXVII. 277 It has now been found possible to photograph the tracks of even the fastest β-particles. **1942** J. D. STRANATHAN *Particles Mod. Physics* i. 43 The ions formed directly by the alpha particle must all have been of very low speed; otherwise the track would not be as narrow and sharply defined. **1955** *Sci. News Let.* 12 Feb. 103/1 When exposed to the special photographic plates, particles from the radioactive samples leave a distinct pattern, known as tracks, on the emulsion. **1973** L. J. TASSIE *Physics Elementary Particles* vi. 50 The forked track, *ab*, in Fig. 23.1 was due to the decay of a heavy neutral particle.. into two charged particles.

†**b.** The pacing of a horse. *Obs.* $rare^{-1}$.

1653 URQUHART *Rabelais* I. xliii, I hear the track [F. *trac*] and beating of the enemies horse feet.

c. *Zool.* The sole of the foot, esp. in birds.

1891 in *Cent. Dict.* **1911** in WEBSTER.

d. A line on the skin made by the repeated injection of an addictive drug. Usu. *pl. slang.*

1964 H. RODRIGUEZ in Larner & Tefferteller *Addict in Street* 34 Tracks are marks,..like a long black streak coming down your arm directly over your vein; that comes from hitting in the same place so much. **1965** *Life* 26 Feb. 86/4 In summer, they [*sc.* addicts] alone wear long sleeves (to cover their 'tracks'—needle marks). **1972** J. MILLS *Report to Commissioner* 104 Whaddya mean, lemme see your tracks? I'm a pros, man, I shoot up in my thighs. **1977** *Rolling Stone* 13 Jan. 14/3 The coroner found four fresh needle marks but no tracks, indicating that Bolan was not a junkie. **1979** R. B. PARKER *Wilderness* i. 10 'Junkie,' he said. The white trooper said, 'Tracks?'.. The black trooper nodded, 'All up and down her right arm.'

†**2.** *fig.* = TRACE *sb.*[1] 6, 7. *Obs.*

1652–62 HEYLIN *Cosmogr.* Introd. (1674) 11/2 Of Sabteca ..I can find no track in any of the Ancient Authors. **1662** J. DAVIES tr. *Olearius' Voy. Ambass.* 219 Now there is no track to be seen of any such thing. *Ibid.* 223 In all this Citie, I found not the least track of Antiquity. **1692** BENTLEY *Boyle Lect.* viii. §8 To consider the Atmosphere and the exterior Frame and Face of the Globe; if we may find any tracks and footsteps of Wisdom in the Constitution of Them. **1694** ADDISON *Story of Calisto* 9 No tracks of heaven's destructive fire remain.

3. A way made or beaten by the feet of men or animals; a path; a rough unmade road.

1643 CROMWELL *Let.* 31 July, We..came to the bottom of a steep hill: we could not well get up but by some tracks. **1675** N. THOMAS in I. Mather *K. Philip's War* (1862) 231 We took notice that an Indian track, newly made, wheeled about from west to South. **1791** MRS. RADCLIFFE *Rom. Forest* i, The road was only a slight track upon the grass. **1832** *Act 2 & 3 Will. IV*, c. 64 Sched. O. 48 The point at which the same [road] meets the mountain track from Dowlais to Quakers Yard. **1883** W. GARDNER in *Science Gossip* May 97 The southern corner is crossed by a mountain track running from Trefriw to Capel Curig.

fig. **1656** COWLEY *To Sir W. Davenant* 36 Thy Fancy like a Flame its way does make, And leave bright Tracks for following Pens to take.

4. a. A line of travel, passage, or motion; the actual course or route followed (which need not be any beaten or visible path, or leave any traces, as the path of a ship, a bird in the air, a comet).

1570–6 LAMBARDE *Peramb. Kent* 287 This place..as also the whole track of their iourney (remaining euer after a greene pathe) the Towne dwellers were wont to shew. **1671** MILTON *P.R.* I. 189 The better to converse With solitude, till far from track of men. **1681** NEVILE *Plato Rediv.* 79 Like Horses who know their Track well enough, without considering East or West, or what business they go about. **1748** *Anson's Voy.* II. x. 240 To give a better idea of the track which they hold in this navigation, I have..laid down the particular route..in..this chart. **1840** R. H. DANA *Bef. Mast* xxxiv. 131 We were just in the track of the tremendous hurricane of 1830. **1853** KANE *Grinnell Exp.* iii. (1856) 24 The ferry-boats and steamers came out of their track to salute us in the bay.

fig. **1565** T. STAPLETON *Fortr. Faith* 126 After the tracke of Caluins trace.

b. The course of a nerve or blood-vessel, or the like; the course of a wound.

1807–26 S. COOPER *First Lines Surg.* (ed. 5) 444 All the surfaces, in contact with each other, and surrounding the track of the wound, become generally so intimately connected together. **1841–71** T. R. JONES *Anim. Kingd.* (ed. 4) 668 The whole track of the intestinal tube, as well as the (so-called) hepatic viscus, is covered internally with vibratile cilia.

c. (?) A long narrow stretch (of light). (But both examples may belong properly to TRACT *sb.*[3]: cf. branch II.)

1693 CONGREVE *To Dryden* in *D.'s Persius* 400 In their room bright Tracks of Light are seen. **1757** GRAY *Bard* 103 In yon bright track, that fires the western skies, They melt, they vanish from my eyes.

d. *Aeronaut.* The projection on the earth's surface of the (actual or intended) course of an aircraft; the representation of this on a chart.

1919 S. F. CARD *Air Navigation* i. 6 The straight line on the map or chart joining the two places will be called the desired track. **1943** REDPATH & COBURN *Air Transport Navigation* viii. 176 Measurement of the line must give us the groundspeed, since track and groundspeed go hand in hand. **1970** TAYLOR & PARMAR *Ground Stud. for Pilots* II. i. 13 Plot in the places carefully on the chart..and join them up, putting the two arrows on the line..to indicate the Track you wish to follow over the Earth's surface.

e. The plane in which the blades of a propeller are intended to rotate.

1920 W. E. PARK *Treat. Airscrews* xii. 206 The relative position of corresponding points in opposite blades..in the side elevation is considered as the 'track' of the blade. **1948** C. E. CHAPEL *Aircraft Power Plants* xv. 323/2 This and the several other methods of field checking the track of the propeller are rough methods only. **1956** W. A. HEFLIN *U.S.A.F. Dict.* 81/2 A blade is said to be *in*, or *out of*, *track*.

f. = LINE *sb.*[2] 19 c.

1931 *Flight* 23 Jan. 73/1 Each fuselage moves along the track to the next [stage]..until at the end of the track the machine is complete. **1979** *Daily Tel.* 3 Aug. 2 The jobs of about 1,000 workers will be affected at British Leyland's Rover saloon car plant..by plans to cut production tracks from three to two. **1981** B. WALSH *Live Bait* ix. 85 Me and Brian work on the track... The assembly line.

g. *U.S. Educ.* = STREAM *sb.* 6 d. Usu. *attrib.*

1959 *Washington Post* 17 May E4/2 The extension of the track system to District junior high and elementary schools ought to benefit most pupils, but the School Board should make certain that Superintendent Carl F. Hansen's 3-track plan for children below the senior high school level is as flexible as possible. **1964** B. FINE *Stretching their Minds* 19 'Acceleration' became fashionable—meaning either old-fashioned 'skipping' or the modern 'multiple-track' plan (in racing terms, a slow track for the average student, a fast track for the superior). **1968** *Economist* 7 Dec. 47/2 It ordered the end of the track system (which divided children according to academic ability, with most Negroes landing inevitably in the lowest track). **1983** *N.Y. Times* 13 Nov. XII. 71/2 There could be different rooms for learners and spurners. If a traditional track system is preferred, there could be a class for those who are on the track and another for those who have derailed.

5. *fig.* **a.** A course of action or conduct; a method of proceeding; 'way', 'path'. ***the beaten track***, the ordinary (*quasi* well-worn) way.

1638 JUNIUS *Paint. Ancients* 242 They..propound unto us the right way, and not one usually beaten track onely. **1658–9** in *Burton's Diary* (1828) IV. 54 You are in a track, and cannot go back or forwards. **1714** LADY M. W. MONTAGU *Lett.* (1887) I. 96 The world never believes it possible for people to act out of the common track. **1742** YOUNG *Nt. Th.* III. 332 To..Pace the Round Eternal?.. To beat and beat The beaten Track? **1785** G. A. BELLAMY *Apology* II. 166 You see me now entered into a new track of life. **1864** SKEAT *Uhland's Poems* 56 Would ye have me wish to wander From the tracks of daily care? **1906** KROPOTKIN *Mem. Rev.* (1908) IV. viii. 254 Austria and Hungary followed in the same track.

b. A train or sequence of events, thoughts, etc.

1681 J. OWEN *Spiritual Mindedness* Wks. 1852 VII. 307 A continual track of fruitless impertinent thoughts about their own concerns. **1693** DRYDEN *Disc. Orig. & Progr. Sat.* Ess. (ed. Ker) II. 29 When he is got into a track of Scripture. **1725** WATTS *Logic* IV. i. §2 In writing the Lives of Men, which is called Biography, some Authors follow the Track of their Years. **1793** BURKE *Corr.* (1844) IV. 199 My pen goes in the track of my thoughts. **1827** R. POLLOK *Course T.* x. *ad fin.*, Thus have I sung beyond thy first request, Rolling my numbers o'er the track of man, The world at dawn, at mid-day, and decline.

6. A path made or laid down for a special purpose; *spec.* **a.** A continuous line of a pair of rails and the space between them, on which railway vehicles travel (commonly called in Great Britain *a* or *the line*, and in some connexions *the rails*). Also used of a single pair of rails, in contrast to a line (which may denote the route and comprise one or more tracks: cf. LINE sb.[2] 26 b). Hence (*U.S.*) with following number, denoting the line served by a particular platform or gate. (Cf. TRACKAGE[2].) Also, an iron path or pair of rails which a carriage in a machine or a gun-chassis traverses. ***off the track***, off the line or rails, derailed; also *fig.*

1805 REES *Cycl.* VI. s.v. *Canal*, Surrey Iron Rail-Way... The width of each track is about 5½ feet, the waggons carry about 3¼ tons each... Crossing rails are used at every passing-place or point where waggons are to pass out of one track of rails into another. *a* **1824** [see RAILWAY 3]. **1860** BARTLETT *Dict. Amer.* (ed. 3), *Track*, the line of a railroad, or rather between the rails. 'A man walking on the track was run over and killed'. **1869** *Bradshaw's Railway Man.* XXI. 390 The length of this line is 94 miles... Of the whole only 33 are 'double track'. **1875** LOWELL *Spenser* Prose Wks. 1890 IV. 277 A series of jolts and jars, proving that the language had run off the track. **1894** *Times* 14 July 7/1 The switch-men [in U.S.]..control the yards, the making up of the trains, and the freedom of the tracks. **1911** *Encycl. Brit.* XXII. 820/2 The Stockton & Darlington railway... This line..was in the first instance laid with a single track. **1955** J. L. AUSTIN *How to do Things with Words* (1962) v. 57 Passengers are warned to cross the track by the bridge only. **1967** [see *double-tracked* s.v. DOUBLE *a.* C. 1]. **1978** R. LUDLUM *Holcroft Covenant* i. 12 He had learned before the announcement that the train for Zurich would leave from track twelve. **1984** *Financial Times* 27 Jan. 2/8 Yesterday, Breton farmers suspended their disruption of rail traffic and removed the barriers they had placed across the tracks in Brittany.

b. A course prepared or laid out for racing, or the like: often in comb., as ***cinder-***, ***race-***, ***racing-***, ***running-track***.

1836 *Spirit of Times* 20 Feb. 5/3 And he will run a match against either, or a sweepstakes with both, one, two, three, or four mile heats, over any good track in East Tennessee. **1851** *Fraser's Mag.* June 657/1 A barouche and four does not differ more from a trottingwaggon..than an English race-course from an American 'track'. **1887** *Field* 20 Aug. 328/2 The six-lap grass track on which the above sports were held. **1912** *Throne* 7 Aug. 228/1 The..Italian sprinter Giongo.. should..be seen frequently on the track at Metropolitan meetings.

c. The distance between a wheel on one side of a vehicle and the corresponding wheel on the other side.

1850 *Western Jrnl.* IV. 96 This distance will, therefore, vary in different sections of the country according to the usual 'track' of wagons. **1910** J. GUNN *Practical Design Motor Cars* viii. 219 The wheel base and wheel track of a motor car require consideration. **1928** [see ROADABILITY]. **1948** J. D. RITTENHOUSE *Amer. Horse-Drawn Vehicles* 1 The term 'track' refers to the extreme width of the vehicle as measured from outside rim of one wheel to the outside of the rim of the opposite wheel, measured at the bottom of the wheel. **1969** *Gloss. Aeronaut. & Astronaut. Terms* (*B.S.I.*) v. 12 *Track*, the distance between the outer points of contact of the port and starboard main undercarriages.

d. Each of the endless bands on certain heavy vehicles, esp. tanks, passing round and driven by wheels and facilitating travel over rough or soft ground. Cf. CATERPILLAR 1 b.

1884 *Patent 269,998* in *Specifications & Drawings* (U.S. Patent Office) 15 Apr. 1384/1 This invention relates to certain improvements in that class of road-engines in which the driving and pilot or guiding wheels are connected by a chain or series of links, which together form an endless track which the wheels traverse in the movement of the engine. **1926** *Encycl. Brit.* Suppl. III. 723/2 The track..was carried all round the tank; this track was driven from the engine through a two-speed gear box. **1931** G. LE Q. MARTEL *In Wake of Tank* 83 The whole of the engine power could be transmitted to the track on the one or the other side of the tank as desired. **1971** *Power Farming* Mar. 13/2 Before the development of the large rubber tyre it was possible to transmit the horse power to the soil only through tracks. **1974** 'W. HAGGARD' *Kinsmen* viii. 82 A simple crane on a pair of tracks was well within his modest competence.

e. (Without article.) The branch of athletics in which a running track is used; track athletics, track events; ***track and field*** (also *attrib.*), athletics in general. orig. *U.S.*

1905 *Outing* XLVI. 490/1 Track and field sport has been working out its own spontaneous solution. **1934** T. V. WILDER *Heaven's My Destination* 66, I was captain of track and basket-ball. **1936** *Nat. Geogr. Mag.* LXIX. 799/2, I progressed the next year to my class squads in football and track. **1964** A. WYKES *Gambling* iv. 102 As for athletics, or 'track and field' sports, there are practically no places where public betting..flourishes to any extent. **1972** *N.Y. Times* 4 June 4/3 The Oregon Track Club is very active in promoting track in the area. **1978** G. A. SHEEHAN *Running & Being* viii. 107 Despite the detailed and accurate statistics of track and field, the scientists consistently underestimate the human body and its potential. **1979** R. JAFFE *Class Reunion* (1980) II. viii. 265 'Do you have a favorite sport?' 'Track.'

f. A ballroom or dance-hall. *U.S. slang.*

1945 L. SHELLY *Hepcats Jive Talk Dict.* 19/2 *Track*, hall for dancing. **1960** WENTWORTH & FLEXNER *Dict. Amer. Slang* 553/2 The Savoy Ballroom in N.Y.C.'s Harlem was widely known as 'The Track' to hepsters. **1965** 'MALCOLM X' *Autobiogr.* xvi. 315, I dig your holding this all-originals scene at the track. **1972** T. KOCHMAN *Rappin' & Stylin' Out* 163 The place where the movement can occur is appropriately termed the 'track', whether the place is a dance hall.., the street.., or, as used figuratively, the life span.

g. A metal or plastic strip designed to carry the sliding fittings from which a curtain is hung, or on which an electric (spot)light may be positioned. Cf. *track lighting* in sense 14 below.

1971 *Guardian* 18 Aug. 9/6 Curtain tracks and pelmets. **1976** *N.Y. Times Mag.* 15 Aug. 47 Installation of the track on the ceiling is tricky, and, in most instances, involves hiding the wires from the ceiling to the light switch. **1979** D. BRIERLEY *Cold War* iv. 39, I checked plugs, sockets..the track for the curtain across the window.

h. *Cricket.* = WICKET 3 c.

1976 J. SNOW *Cricket Rebel* 102 Deliveries..that pitched half way down the track and went through above head high. **1977** *Grimsby Even. Tel.* 31 May 12/6 Fast bowler Robert Herkes again gave a good account of himself and his figures of two for 33 off 16 overs was no mean feat on a track that did not give him a shred of help. **1983** *Daily Tel.* 3 Sept. 12 The commentators—particularly the professional cricketers (active or retired)—use a vocabulary peculiarly their own: the pitch is a 'track', good or bad.

7. *Her.* A longitudinal division of an ordinary or sub-ordinary, or in the representation of certain furs.

1868 CUSSANS *Her.* iii. 53 The Furs Vair, Countervair, Potent, and Counterpotent... They are usually represented as of four rows, heraldically termed Tracks. *Ibid.* iv. (1882) 67 A Bordure or other Ordinary composed of Metal and Colour alternately, is termed Company... If there be two *Tracks*, it is then said to be Counter-Company.

8. [from TRACK *v.*[1]] The action of tracking; the pursuit of a criminal or fugitive.

[**1542–3**: see TRACT *sb.*[3] 10 b.] **1617** *Carte Papers* LXII. 438 The Track shalbee vndertaken within foure and twenty howres, after the goodes have bin stolne,..that the Inhabitants of that place, may have time to put the track forwardes.

9. a. = GROOVE *sb.* 2 c (now *rare* or *Obs.*); hence, a single recorded item (esp. of popular music), which on a long-playing record is a band bounded on both sides by an area of widely-spaced grooves.

1904 S. R. BOTTONE *Talking Machines & Records* 60 We must have some means of controlling or varying the pressure of the stylus of the reproducer on the record, so as to enable it to follow correctly every indentation in the 'track'. **1949** *Playback* Oct.–Nov. 4/2 This took the form of a 10" record with two 'tracks' or 'grooves' impressed on each side. **1956** *Gramophone* Dec. 265/1 None of the tracks lives up to the promise of the star-studded personnel. **1957** [see BAND *sb.*^{2} 9 b]. **1958** *Observer* 28 Dec. 6/7 All the tracks had been released as singles in the era of seventy-eight r.p.m. **1967** A. DIMENT *Dolly Dolly Spy* xii. 160, I wandered over to the juke box and selected a Dylan track for relaxation. **1970** *Honey* June 53/4 Their first LP is so polished. There are some great original tracks. **1980** *Oxford Times* 1 Feb. 23/3 On tracks like 'Rock Music' they seem to want to be a hard rock 'n' roll band... On several other tracks their aim is vague and visionary.

b. *Cinemat.* = *sound track* s.v. SOUND *sb.*^{3} 8 b.

1931 B. BROWN *Talking Pictures* x. 226 To a certain extent surface noise is due to irregularities in the sensitive film used for recording the track. **1976** *Oxf. Compan. Film* 203/1 'Dolbyized' tracks sound 'cleaner' and clearer than ordinary tracks.

c. A lengthwise strip on magnetic tape consisting of a single sequence of signals; more widely, a linear path in any information storage device or medium that accommodates one sequence of signals or corresponds to one head.

Orig. identical with prec. sense.

1947 *Jrnl. Soc. Motion Picture Engineers* XLVIII. 9 A magnetic recording track..on 16-mm film. **1951** *Audio Engin.* Sept. 40/2 The recording medium is an endless polyvinyl-chloride [magnetic] tape with 56 parallel sound tracks spaced at the ordinary rate of four tracks per millimeter. **1951** *Proc. Inst. Electr. Engineers* XCVIII. II. 29/1 As the drum rotates the surface is carried past a fixed magnetic recording and reading head... Many separate tracks can be recorded side by side. **1957** *Practical Wireless* XXXIII. 697/1 Rotation of VR1 should cause it to click in and out as a certain point on the track is passed. **1962** *Times* 5 July 15/6 Some tapes have two tracks, others (in stereo) have four, and a four-track recorder will not produce the best results on a two-track tape. **1969** P. B. JORDAIN *Condensed Computer Encycl.* 305 Data are addressed on a drum by specifying the track number and word number within the drum. **1970** O. DOPPING *Computers & Data Processing* iii. 57 Readers and punches for paper tape can easily be adjusted to different numbers of tracks. **1977** *Time* 4 July 4 (Advt.), There's a film to watch—a recent release—8 tracks of stereo to listen to, free naturally, and plenty of room to stretch out or stroll about. **1983** *Austral. Personal Computer* Aug. 62/1 Files stored on a disk are located by means of a directory set up on a particular grouping of tracks.

10. Phrases. ***in one's tracks***, on the spot where one is at the moment; instantly, immediately. ***on the right track***, having the right idea; heading in the right direction; also ***on the*** (or ***a***) ***wrong track***. ***on the track*** (***of***), in pursuit of; also, having a trace of or clue to. ***to cover*** (***up***) ***a person's tracks***, to conceal or screen his motions or measures. ***to keep track***, to follow or grasp the course, progress, or sequence *of*; to keep account *of*; so ***to lose track of***. ***to make*** (***take***) ***tracks*** (***for***), to make off, to make *for*; to go off quickly (orig. *U.S.*). ***the wrong side of the tracks***, the socially inferior part of town; so ***to cross the tracks*** and similar phrases. ***on the track*** (*Austral.*), tramping from place to place in search of work. ***on track*** (*U.S.*), on course; achieving or doing what is required. ***to comb the tracks***: see COMB *v.*^{1} 4 c. ***to jump the track***: see JUMP *v.* 6 c.

1824 T. D. ARNOLD in M. James *A. Jackson* (1937) 156 He failed to shoot 'Jackson dead in his tracks'. **1835–40** HALIBURTON *Clockm.* (1862) 30 I'd a made him make tracks, I guess. **1843** R. CARLTON *New Purchase* xvii. I. 130 The rifle was fired..and he fell dead in his tracks. **1866** LOWELL *Biglow P.* II. Introd., Poems 1890 II. 189 *In his tracks* for *immediately* has acquired an American accent, and passes where he can for a native. **1871** FARRAR *Witn. Hist.* ii. 49 Not on the false track of myths, artificially elaborated. **1873** J. C. F. JOHNSON *Christmas on Carringa* 19 'Tis Christmas Eve again to day, and I am on 'the track'. **1878** *Masque Poets* 244 Whatever else he lacks, He has the art of covering up his tracks. **1883** GILMOUR *Mongols* (1884) 251 The noise of the two crowds..made it difficult to keep track of what was going on. **1886** EMMA MARSHALL *Tower on Cliff* xii, The men are on the track. **1886** C. M. YONGE *Chantry House* I. xiii. 116 This had done more to convince my father that he was on the right track than the having found him on his knees. **1889** J. K. JEROME *Three Men in Boat* iii. 37 You know we are on a wrong track altogether. We must not think of the things we could do with, but only of the things that we can't do without. **1894** *Outing* (U.S.) XXIII. 387/1 Day after day passes in precisely the same manner.., until one loses all track of the days of the week. **1896** H. LAWSON *While the Billy Boils* 207 I've been knocking round for five years, and the last two years constant on the track, and no show of getting off it unless I go for good. **1902** *Munsey's Mag.* XXVI. 569/1 Theater-goers who have kept close track of the dramatic tastes of New York and London. **1915** A. HUXLEY *Let.* Oct. (1969) 84 These maximal horrors of war are really too unthinkably appalling; but things I trust are on the right track now for health. [**1929** T. SMITH *Stray Lamb* iv. 29 In most commuting towns..there are always two sides of which the tracks serve as a line of demarcation. There is the right side and the wrong side. Translated into terms of modern American idealism, this means, the rich side and the side that hopes to be rich.] **1945** S. LEWIS *C. Timberlane* (1947) xxxiv. 230, I thought at first that she was from the wrong side of the railroad tracks, but she seems to have settled down to being a nice little lady and a good war worker. **1953** 'CADDIE' *Sydney Barmaid* xliv. 255 It would have been impossible for him to maintain the home on a dole ration... He was going on the track. **1954** I. MURDOCH *Under Net* xi. 141 What I saw as I opened the door made me stop dead in my tracks. **1956** W. H. WHYTE *Organization Man* xxi. 269 The boy from Shanty-town was going to have less chance than ever of crossing over the tracks. **1965** E. LAMBERT *Long White Night* 12 His clothes clearly proclaimed him as a man who had been on the track, one of that tattered, aimless, wandering band which the Depression threw up. **1973** *Times* 19 May 6/6 'The Government may fall,' Mr Caulfield reportedly said, complaining: 'Everybody else is on track but you.' **1977** *Listener* 13 Oct. 478/2 Eva Duarte Peron..came from the wrong side of the tracks. **1978** *Detroit Free Press* 16 Apr. F 3 (Advt.), We're looking for a professional who can keep us on track by making contributions that improve efficiency. **1978** *Time* 24 Apr. 20/2 If we can reach a SALT agreement..that will begin to change the whole character of the relationship, put it on the right track again. **1979** B. L. C. JOHNSON *Pakistan* xiii. 199/1 The whole area has something of a 'beyond the tracks' character about it. **1984** *Gainesville* (Florida) *Sun* 3 Apr. 10 B/5 Three weeks ago, Mondale won the Illinois primary and said his comeback was on track.

II. Used by confusion in senses of TRACT *sb.*^{3}

(*Tract* is very commonly pronounced dial. (træk), and some of the senses are identical with those of *track*.)

†**11.** A feature, lineament, trait; = TRACT *sb.*^{3} 7. *Sc. Obs. rare.*

1513 DOUGLAS *Æneis* XII. xiii. 135 And all elike wympillit and cled thir trakis With eddris thrawin, and haris full of snakis. **1808–18** JAMIESON, *Track*, feature, lineament.

12. An extent of land; also, a space of time, a period; also, †a sequence or succession of actions or events (*obs.*); cf. TRACT *sb.*^{3} 1 c, 2, 3.

1687 BURNET *Trav.* iii. (1750) 166 All the Way to Florence this Track of Hills continues, tho' there are several Bottoms. **1760–72** H. BROOKE *Fool of Qual.* (1809) III. 43 Their conquest or seizure of any track of country. **1765** *Museum Rust.* IV. lxii. 268 Very large tracks, of two or three thousand acres. **1796** H. H. HUNTER tr. *St.-Pierre's Stud. Nat.* (1799) I. 132 The track of land inundated was lower than the Ocean. **1835** I. TAYLOR *Spir. Despot.* iii. 91 During a much longer track of time. **1851** *Jrnl. R. Agric. Soc.* XII. I. 127 If a track of dry weather sets in. **1893, 1901** in *Eng. Dial. Dict.* (of weather). **1896** W. B. WILDMAN *Hist. Sherborne* i. 1 A track of country won for England from the West-Welsh.

†**13.** An attraction, enticement; = TRACT *sb.*^{3} 4. *Obs. rare*$^{-1}$.

1673 O. WALKER *Educ.* i. 6 Since we find great tracks and encouragements in the way of pleasure.

III. 14. *attrib.* and *Comb.*, as ***track-chart***, ***-cutting***, ***-side***; in sense 6 a (mainly *U.S.*), ***track-cleaner***, ***construction***, ***elevation***, ***material***; in 6 b or 6 e, ***track athlete***, ***athletics***, ***coach***, ***event***, ***-measuring***, ***meet*** (*U.S.*), ***meeting***, ***-racing*** sb. and adj., ***shirt***, ***shorts***, ***team***; ***track-mounted*** adj.; **track-bed** = BED *sb.* 12 e; **track-brake**, a railway brake which acts by pressure directly against the rail; also, a device consisting of rails with curved ends, kept in position alongside the ordinary rails by springs, which by friction automatically retards a vehicle passing over them by compressing the flanges of the wheels; **track-channeler**, in quarrying, a groove-cutting tool mounted on a rail truck (*Cent. Dict. Suppl.* 1909); **track-chisel**, a plate-layer's hammer with a flat cutting peen (*ibid.*); **track circuit**, an electric circuit formed by the two rails of a railway line, so that the short-circuit produced by the presence of a train can be used to control the signals protecting it; so **track-circuit** *v. trans.*, to equip with or make into a track circuit; **track circuiting** *vbl. sb.*; **track-clearer**, a cross-bar carried immediately in front of the wheels of a locomotive or tram-car to push obstructions off the rails; also, a cow-catcher or snow-sweeper fixed in front of a locomotive; also, a wedge-shaped board fixed at the outer end of the cutter-bar of a reaping machine, which directs the swath to the cutters and leaves a clear track for the next passage of the machine; **track-edge**, the abrupt edge of a millstone furrow; **track-harness** (*U.S.*), light harness for trotting-races (Knight *Dict. Mech.* 1877); **track-hound**, a hound capable of following a track, a sleuth-hound; **track-in**, the movement of a film or television camera towards the subject; **track-iron**, *Golf*: see quot. 1908 and IRON *sb.* 4 e; **track-layer**, (*a*) a man employed in laying or repairing a railway track, a plate-layer; also, a railway truck equipped with machinery for laying rails; (*b*) one who lays the trail in training dogs to track criminals; (*c*) a tractor or other vehicle which travels on endless tracks (sense 6 d above); so **track-laying** *sb.*, (*a*) the laying of railway track; (*b*) in film editing, the putting together of the sound track that is to accompany a picture; **track-laying** *adj.*, (*a*) that lays railway track; (*b*) (of a vehicle) having endless tracks (sense 6 e above); **track-leveller**, a railway truck having heavy projecting wings or shares which can be raised or lowered so as to level the ballast on a railway line as it is drawn along (*Cent. Dict. Suppl.* 1909); **track-lifter**, a wheeled frame or truck with powerful jaws for grasping the rails, and mechanism for getting a lifting purchase against the ground; used in levelling a railway line (Knight *Dict. Mech.* 1877); **track lighting**, lighting in which the lights are fitted on to tracks, allowing variable positioning (see sense 6 g above); **track-line**, the line of a (former) track or path: see quot. 1889; **track-man**, (*a*) a workman employed in the construction or maintenance of a railway or tramway; (*b*) a track athlete; **track-master**, one who is responsible for the inspection and repair of a section of railway track (*Cent. Dict.* 1891); **track-mile**, a mile of 'track' or single line; hence **track-mileage**; **track-rail**, the rail on which the wheels run, as distinct from a guide-rail or the like; **track-raiser**, a jack for lifting sunken rails, a *track-lifter*; **track record**, (*a*) the record performance in a particular athletics event at a particular track; (*b*) the performances achieved by a particular athlete in the past; also *fig.*, known facts about past achievements or behaviour taken as a guide to future performance; **track rod**, a rod that connects the two front wheels of a motor vehicle and transmits the steering action from the steering column to the stub axle of each wheel; **track-scale**, a weigh-bridge for railway vehicles (Knight *Dict. Mech.* 1877); **track-scraper**, a snow-scraper attached to a railway car for clearing the line (*Cent. Dict. Suppl.* 1909); **track-shoe**, (*a*) a track-brake shoe; (*b*) = *running shoe* s.v. RUNNING *vbl. sb.* 17 a; **track-sprinkler**: see quot.; **track suit**, a loose two-piece garment (elasticized at the wrists and ankles) worn by athletes while training and before and after contests; hence **track-suited** *a.*; **track system** *U.S. Educ.* (see sense 4 g above); **track-walker**, a man employed to walk along and examine a certain length of railway track regularly; so **track-walking**; **track-work**, (*a*) the construction of a railway track or line; (*b*) action or use on a racing track. Also TRACKWAY.

1888 *Pall Mall G.* 27 Aug. 14/1 The baseball and *track athletes graduated 34 per cent. of their number... In physical development..the crew men coming first, the baseball players next, and track athletes last. **1890** W. CAMP in *Century Mag.* June 204/2 The..games..generally classed under the term '*track athletics' are walking, running, jumping, bicycling, pole vaulting, throwing of weights, and tug-of-war contests. **1962** *Mod. Railways* Apr. 278/2 The jack, which had been left projecting from the *track bed, did considerable damage to the gear underneath the cars. **1978** W. HJORTSBERG *Falling Angel* xliv. 217, I followed the trackbed of the downtown express, measuring my pace to the spacing of the ties. **1903** *Science Abstracts* VI. §B. 57 The Westinghouse-Newell *track brake... In this an electro-magnet..grips the rail with a pressure which may reach two tons. **1906** *Westm. Gaz.* 29 Oct. 7/2 It seems to Colonel Yorke that the track brake can at its best only be regarded as a supplementary to the wheel brakes. **1911** *Encycl. Brit.* XXV. 76/2 At points the *track circuit is run through a circuit breaker, so that the 'opening' of the points sets the signal for the section. **1931** E. T. MACDERMOT *Hist. G.W.R.* II. 498 Track circuits, whereby the signals protecting an occupied section of line are electrically locked at Danger, were first introduced in August 1907. **1983** *Internat. Railway Jrnl.* May 8/1 The Landskut box controls 125 signals, 83 points and 110 track circuits. **1935** *Economist* 22 June 1419/1 If every mile of line in use were '*track-circuited'..a blunder by a signalman would be impossible; no train could be signalled forward unless the line really was clear. **1931** *Times Lit. Suppl.* 10 Dec. 999/1 Exactly the same argument might be heard to-day against the introduction of *track-circuiting or automatic train control. **1956** *Railway Mag.* Nov. 793/1 Track circuiting at both home and starting signals can be used to give additional safeguards. **1900** *Daily News* 12 Nov. 8/5 With a view to minimising the amount of water used a large number of *track cleaners were employed [on the tramways]. **1877** KNIGHT *Dict. Mech.*, **Track-clearer*, (1) (*Railway.*) (*a*) A cow-catcher... (*b*) A track-sweeper to remove snow. (2) (*Harvesting.*) A triangular frame on the outer end of the cutter-bar of a mowing or reaping machine [etc.]. **1962** A. LURIE *Love & Friendship* x. 199 Hal Humphrey, the *track coach. **1977** J. F. FIXX *Compl. Bk. Running* vii. 85 It has been attributed to..Lauri Pihkala, a pre-World War I Finnish runner, and George W. Orton, at one time Penn State's track coach. **1890** *Goldfields of Victoria* 27 *Track-cutting..enables parties to proceed into the jungle country, which would otherwise be unknown. **1874** KNIGHT *Dict. Mech.* s.v. *Furrow*, The steep edge of the furrow [in a millstone] is called the *track-edge; the more inclined edge is called the feather-edge. **1912** *Times* 29 June 13/1 In the *track events, all of which must be held in the Stadium..there are 95 entries. **1928** *Daily Sketch* 10 Aug. 2/4 There are bound to be fine finishes in the international track events. **1973** C. BONINGTON *Next Horizon* ix. 138 He had always been a brilliant natural athlete, excelling at almost every game and track event in which he took part. **1888** *Century Mag.* May 42/2 Intending to return on the morrow with a good *track hound. **1954** *Encounter* Aug. 53/1 Her abject jealous misery has been..conveyed by the camera's slow *track-in to close-up of her anguished face. **1961** *Listener* 2 Nov. 716/1 A track-in suggests an increase in intensity. **1883** *Standard* 16 Nov. 5/2 He..is ready with..the *track-iron [at golf]. **1908** *Daily Chron.* 3 Aug. 2/4 A collection of 'track' irons, round-headed with concave face, used fifty or sixty years ago to get the ball out of the cart tracks. *a* **1861** T. WINTHROP *Life in Open Air* (1863) 234 'Wanted, experienced *track-layer!' was the word along the files. **1877** KNIGHT *Dict. Mech.*, *Track-layer*, a carriage provided with apparatus for placing the rails in their proper positions..as the machine advances. **1888** *Pall Mall G.* 2 Nov. 7/2 The Provincial tracklayers by a ruse have got a locomotive across the Canadian Pacific Company's line, and are now carrying rails across and laying a new track to the north of that line. **1909** *Lightkeeper* June 14/2 The track-layer..is useful in making 'skid-roads', over which the heavy logs are hauled. **1928** *Daily Express* 19 Sept. 2 Coastguards..acted as track-layers for the open police dog trials. **1934** WEBSTER s.v., The tracklayer is used especially where tractive conditions are poor. **1952** J. W. DAY *New Yeomen of England* viii. 96 In all there are 45 tractors (including 6 track-layers), 4 moto-carts for hauling and odd jobs, and 8 combine harvesters. **1971** *Power Farming* Mar. 13/2 Use of the tracklayer was now mainly restricted to heavy clay soils and industrial duties where its higher costs could still be justified. **1857** R. G. PAYNE *Rep. Condition Railroads Tennessee* 7 The *track-laying is progressng from the southern end of the road. **1884** KNIGHT *Dict. Mech.* Suppl., Track-laying machine. **1900** *Engineering Mag.* XIX. 797/2 Tracklaying by Machinery on the Canadian Pacific Ry. **1920** *Sci. Amer.* 2 Oct. 335 (*caption*) Typical tractors of the wheeled and track-laying species now employed for agricultural and other purposes. **1957** *Times Lit. Suppl.* 27 Dec. 781/3 They resemble (as it says on driving licences) a 'track-laying vehicle steered by its tracks'. **1957** MANVELL & HUNTLEY *Technique Film Music* iv. 178 The four technical branches of film production, i.e., design..photography..sound..and editing (including assembly cutting, track-laying, laboratory liaison, and post-production processes). **1962** A. NISBETT *Technique Sound Studio* xii. 206 Track-laying systems, where a whole series of tracks can be recorded individually on a single broad tape and then scanned together. **1972** *Times* 30 Nov. 18/1 Ceiling mounted spotlights and..*track lighting systems. **1980** D. FRANCIS *Reflex* iii. 41 In the sitting room, white walls..track lighting. **1848** S. ROWE *Peramb. Dartmoor* 47 Greatly similar..are the *Tracklines, or Boundary Banks, which are invariably observed in connexion with aboriginal dwellings and sepulchral remains. **1889** PAGE *Explor. Dartmoor* iii. 43 Oftentimes low banks of earth and stone are observed among the traces of ancient settlements. These are tracklines. **1881** *Chicago Times* 30 Apr., *Track men and mechanics now in employment on the road. **1893** *Labour Commission Gloss.*, *Trackmen*, men who clean the groove of tramway rails with scoops, and when necessary sand or salt the track between the metals. **1901** *Westm. Gaz.* 18 June 8/3 The engineers will..refuse to run trains over a system not properly examined by trackmen. **1972** *N.Y. Times* 4 June 4/2 An illegal water-jump area has impaired the credibility of the three fastest steeplechase performances by American trackmen. **1977** *Evening Gaz.* (Middlesbrough) 11 Jan. 14/2 Teesside Clarion's top trackmen..were among those honoured at their club's annual presentation in the Normanby Hotel last Friday. **1880** P. L. SCLATER *Jacamars & Puff-birds* 75 In 1861 Mr. James M'Leannan, then *track-master of Lion-hill station on the Panama Railway, began to explore the dense tropical forests surrounding his abode. **1904** *Cap & Gown* (Chicago) IX. 215 *Track Meets and Scores, 1903... Second Annual Interscholastic Meet, at Marshall Field. **1976** *Columbus* (Montana) *News* 27 May 1/4 Absarokee and Columbus scored first and second respectively in the Southern C Divisional track meet on May 20. **1909** *Q. Rev.* Oct. 354 The actual *track-mileage of British railways is approximately 53,000 miles. **1977** *Time* 21 Feb. 34/2 He would be inclined to forgo continued development of a mobile U.S. nuclear missile launcher (the MX) if the Soviet Union will abandon deployment of its *track-mounted launcher (the SS-20). **1896** *Daily News* 28 Dec. 5/2 One of the earliest and most notable of *track-racing cyclists. **1877** KNIGHT *Dict. Mech.*, *Track-rail. **1902** *Daily Chron.* 18 Oct. 6/7 The tender for the supply of track rails and other accessories. **1951** *Publ. Amer. Dial. Soc.* XVI. 66 **Track record*, the best time made by a horse over a certain distance on a certain track. **1965** *Life* 15 Jan. 56 A/1 Wilder has had a series of extremely successful pictures... We were betting on his track record that this one would be too. **1972** *Observer* 30 Apr. 12/5 The airlines have over the years had enough confidence in our track record to be perfectly happy about this procedure. **1974** *Spartanburg* (S. Carolina) *Herald* 18 Apr. C2/5 Charles Mathis..set a new track record at Northwestern with a 149'6" in the discus. **1976** *Milton Keynes Express* 25 June 51/3 Houghton Rip..came fourth behind the Irish dog, whose track record was smashed by last year's Derby consolation winner Shamrock Point. **1976** *Time* 20 Dec. 17/1 A lot of the women candidates..have no management track records to be judged on. So they keep being passed over. **1983** *Daily Tel.* 23 Mar. 21 The Trustee Savings Banks, which plan to go public towards the end of next year, badly need to establish a good track record on profits. **1926** *Amer. Speech* I. 686/2 The following list of automobile terms in American and English nomenclature appeared in a 'special' from the Boston News Bureau early in the present year... [American] Tie rod [English] *Track rod. **1930** *Engineering* 12 Sept. 326/3 Each pair of steering pivots is connected by a track rod at right angles to the chassis centre line. **1976** *Flintshire Leader* 10 Dec. 25/10 (Advt.), New springs for Land Rovers and most cars, 1935–70, towing brackets,.. new kingpins, trackrods. **1977** J. F. FIXX *Compl. Bk. Running* x. 121, I bought them all inexpensive track shoes and University of Southern California *track shirts just like Daddy's. **1978** *Detroit Free Press* 5 Mar. A19/1 (Advt.), Juvenile to teen male track shirts, hooded sweatshirts. **1908** *Daily Chron.* 6 May 5/2 Witness admitted that one of the magnetic *track shoes was useless. **1961** WEBSTER, Track shoe. **1970** G. JACKSON *Let.* 28 May in *Soledad Brother* (1971) 261 We're wearing track shoes. **1983** 'J. LE CARRÉ' *Little Drummer Girl* ii. 45 Kids in summer rig and track shoes. **1946** C. MCCULLERS *Member of Wedding* I. 4 She wore a pair of blue *track shorts. **1974** *Index-Jrnl.* (Greenwood, S. Carolina) 23 Apr. 7/6 Smith describes his actions as mild, temporary schizophrenia, or Clark Kent in track shorts. 'When I pole vault..I'm like a complete different person.' **1886** STEVENSON *Kidnapped* i, He..lighted on a big boulder under a birch by the *trackside. **1860** BARTLETT *Dict. Amer.* (ed. 3), **Track-sprinkler*, a contrivance for sprinkling railroad tracks, in order to lay the dust. **1955** R. BANNISTER *First Four Minutes* 46 Not having had the importance of warming up explained to me I did not wear a *track suit. **1980** *Times Lit. Suppl.* 7 Nov. 1258/4 His..wife..memorably fetching in her pink towelling track suit. **1965** R. T. BICKERS *Scent of Mayhem* iv. 42 His sweaty, *track-suited figure. **1907** *St. Nicholas* (N.Y.) XXXIV. 693/2 Hammond has a *track team, but we have n't. **1976** *Billings* (Montana) *Gaz.* 30 June 7-E/1 Aams was also an outstanding performer on the basketball and track teams at East Bay. **1890** GILDERSLEEVE *Ess. & Stud.* 127 The solitary *track-walker, who turns his lantern on every inch of the road. **1905** *Westm. Gaz.* 14 Apr. 6/3 The usual precautions were taken.., including a track-walker at every mile on the line. **1907** *Daily Chron.* 15 July 6/6 The total cost of the *track work from Aldgate to Bow is estimated at about £66,000, which works out at about £11,000 a mile of single track. **1909** *Westm. Gaz.* 23 Feb. 4/2 To encourage young riders to come..and learn the use of their machines for track-work.

track, *v.*[1] [f. TRACK *sb.*: cf. F. *traquer* (*c* 1440) f. *trac.*]

I. 1. a. *trans.* To follow up the track or footsteps of; to trace the course or movements of; to pursue by or as by the track left; with *down*, *out*, *up*, to follow up or trace until found or caught. Also *fig.*

1565 CALFHILL *Answ. Treat. Crosse* 89 Ye may tracke hym by ye foote. **1582** STANYHURST *Æneis* II. (Arb.) 67 Soon fle, they doe track vs. *Ibid.* III. 73 Track owt youre moother. **1590** R. PAYNE *Descr. Irel.* (1841) 8 If you track any stolne goodes into any mans land, he must tracke them from him, or answer them within xl. daies. **1600** HOLLAND *Livy* XXVII. xii. 636 Marcellus tracked him still, and followed him hard at heeles. **1662** J. DAVIES tr. *Olearius' Voy. Ambass.* A iij b, Without which [Maps], it were impossible to track the Travellors through all those remote Countries. **1716** B. CHURCH *Hist. Philip's War* (1867) II. 104 An Indian Souldier..track'd them by the bloud about half a Mile. **1814** WORDSW. *White Doe* VII. 136 The White Doe tracked ..The Lady to her dwelling-place. **1819** SCOTT *Ivanhoe* xxviii, The misfortunes which track my footsteps like slot-hounds. **1834** PRINGLE *Afr. Sk.* viii. 258 The first point was to track the lion to his covert. **1871** R. ELLIS *Catullus* xi. 10 Whether o'er high Alps he afoot ascending Track the long records of a mighty Cæsar. **1874** SYMONDS *Sk. Italy & Gr.* (1898) I. xv. 315 The murderer..was at last tracked down and put to death.

b. To find out and follow (a track, course, etc.).

1681 HICKERINGILL *Vind. Naked Truth* II. i, I am oblieged to Track his Methods. **1799** WORDSW. *Lucy Gray* xii, Then downwards from the steep hill's edge They tracked the footmarks small. **1888** MRS. MCCANN *Poet. Wks.* 70 Through the lonely wilderness brave Howitt tracked his way.

c. *intr.* To follow up a track or trail.

1805 PIKE *Sources Mississ.* (1810) 38 Not knowing how to track, we lost her. **1898** R. POCOCK in *Westm. Gaz.* 12 Sept. 8/2 Henceforth no offer of reward could induce the Indians to continue the hopeless search, and white men cannot track.

d. *intr.* Of the wheels of a vehicle: To run in the same track; hence of a gear-wheel, To be in alinement (*with* another wheel, etc.). Also (*U.S.*) of a horse: to walk with the fore and hind feet placed in the same straight line. Of the feet: to be placed thus.

1826 *Sporting Mag.* XVIII. 390 The wheels had not tracked as they ought. **1838** [see *tracking* vbl. sb. below]. **1857** R. GLISAN *Jrnl. Army Life* (1874) xxvii. 382, I observed..that he does not 'track' (step his hind foot straight after the fore one). **1879** in *Eng. Dial. Dict.* s.v., The machine does not track nicely. **1897** E. HOUGH *Story of Cowboy* 34 His feet, in the vernacular of the range, do not 'track', but cross each other weakly. **1898** H. GRAVES, etc. *Cycling* 10 Next inspect the frame for twists, and see that the wheels 'track'.

e. *intr. Electronics.* Of a tunable circuit or component: to vary in frequency in the same way as another circuit or component, so that the frequency difference between them remains constant.

1932 [implied at TRACKING *vbl. sb.*[1] 3]. **1939** [see PADDER *sb.*[2] 3]. **1948** SLURZBERG & OSTERHELD *Essent. Radio* vi. 271 In order to obtain the maximum fidelity, selectivity, and sensitivity..it is necessary that all the tuning circuits track together over the entire range of the receiver. **1975** D. G. FINK *Electronics Engineers' Handbk.* XIII. 40 The tuned circuits must track across the frequency band, and in the case of the superheterodyne, tracking of the local oscillator is necessary so that a constant frequency difference..is maintained.

f. *trans.* To follow the course of (a distant object) by means of a telescope, radar, or the like.

1950 in WEBSTER Add. **1959** *Listener* 18 June 1057/2 The Jodrell Bank telescope and the smaller one at Bedford, Massachusetts, were tracking the moon. **1966** M. WOODHOUSE *Tree Frog* viii. 64 In order to track it [*sc.* a pilotless plane]..during flight trials..we've had to fit travelling wave reflection amplifiers under the wings. **1971** *Daily Tel.* 20 July 8/8 Every commercial and military aircraft flying over Europe can be tracked by radar. **1976** *Nature* 16 Sept. 216/1 An ITT FW 130 (S20) photomultiplier..was mounted about 40 feet above the ground on a radar dish programmed to track the star.

g. *intr.* To enjoy a rapport or 'get on' *with* another person; to take things in. *U.S.*

1972 *Newsweek* 17 July 22/3 He tracks better with reporters than did his phlegmatic predecessor. **1977** C. MCFADDEN *Serial* (1978) xvi. 38/1 She's practically out of her mind. Like, she isn't even tracking. **1978** J. L. HENSLEY *Killing in Gold* ix. 116 Mom didn't track very well after the second stroke... It didn't mean anything to her any more.

2. a. *trans.* To mark out, trace (a path); to indicate the path or course of; *esp.* to mark out (a path) by repeatedly traversing it; to mark (a way) with tracks; to tread, beat.

1589 [see *tracked* ppl. adj. below]. **1603** DRAYTON *Bar. Wars* I. xxxii, When the straight Course to her Desire was tract [*rimes* act, backt]. *a* **1713** ELLWOOD *Autobiog.* Pref. (1765) 4 But also gain some Direction from the Path so fairly tract out. **1815** ANNE PLUMTRE tr. *Lichtenstein's S. Africa* II. 76 The way was smooth and well tracked. **1869** TOZER *Highl Turkey* I. 36 The Mendere..tracked through all its..windings by the willow-trees on its banks.

b. To make one's way through; to traverse. *to track the dancers*, to go upstairs (*slang*); cf. quots. 1671, 1785 in 3.

1823 SCOTT *Peveril* xxx, His surprise..was increased by the rapidity and ease with which she seemed to track the dusky and decayed mazes of the dilapidated Savoy. **1858** LYTTON *What will he do* III. xvi, Come, my Hebe; track the dancers, that is, go up the stairs. **1871** MACDUFF *Mem. Patmos* xx. 275 When white-winged commerce is tracking..the highway of the nations.

c. *U.S.* To leave a track or trail of footprints upon (a floor); to make a track with (dirt or snow) carried on one's feet. Also, *to track up* (a floor, etc.); to bring *in* (dirt, etc.) on one's feet (also const. preps.). Also *fig.*

1838 C. GILMAN *Recoll. Southern Matron* xviii. 127 Miss Neely, one buckra woman want for track up all de clean floor. **1866** *Harper's Mag.* Jan. 271/2 The snow had been tracked in till it lay pretty thick on the floor. **1869** MRS. STOWE *Oldtown Folks* iii, 'Stand still there!' she called to me ..'and don't come in to track my floor'. **1878** —— *Poganuc P.* i, Sweep out that snow you've tracked in. **1901** MERWIN & WEBSTER *Calumet 'K'* vi. 117 There's going to be a law passed about tracking mud inside the railing. **1915** *Century Mag.* Aug. 496/2 A good live boy..is a drug in the market. There seems to be a general feeling that they track in dirt. **1919** J. REED *Ten Days that shook World* i. 11 The mud underfoot was deep, slippery and clinging, tracked everywhere by heavy boots. **1944** S. BELLOW *Dangling Man* 100 Tracked your mat up. I'm sorry. **1950** M. MEAD *Male & Female* xvi. 338 Floors do not need to be polished so often when there are no children's feet to track them up. **1980** R. HILL *Killing Kindness* ix. 87, I was trying not to track my work into the house too much. **1981** *Farmstead Mag.* Winter 50/2 Birds really use the trees to nest in, and small rabbits revel in tracking up fresh snow.

d. To lay a track on or for (a railway); to furnish with a line of rails. Only in compounds, as ***to double-track***, ***four-track***, ***single-track***. *U.S.*

1874 *Bay State Transp. League, Bill* (Boston, U.S.) 8 It will cost to single track the Massachusetts Central ..$3,000,000. It will cost to double track the same an additional $2,000,000.

3. a. *intr.* To follow a track or path; to make one's way, pass, go, travel. Now *U.S. slang.*

1590 GREENE *Never too late* (1600) 1 Downe the valley gan he tracke, Bagge and bottle at his backe. **1671** [see DANCER 4]. **1676** COLES *Dict.*, *Track*, to go. **1785** GROSE *Dict. Vulg. T.*, *Track*, to go; *track up the dancers*, go up stairs (*cant*). **1843** R. CARLTON *New Purchase* xxvii. 254 I'll track round a little—I wants any how to go over to the post-office. **1868** *Putnam's Mag.* June 670/1 We tracked through the dirty streets till we got to the house. **1897** KIPLING *Captains Courageous* i, 'The West don't suit her. She just tracks around with the boy and her nerves, trying to find out what'll amuse him, I guess'.

b. *Path.* To make a track or path for itself; to find its way.

1903 *Lancet* 18 Apr. 1102/2 The effused blood had tracked down between the coats of the œsophagus into the wall of the stomach. **1905** H. D. ROLLESTON *Dis. Liver* 20 The resulting peritonitis unfortunately is rarely localized, and may then contain gas as well as pus, or track [*mispr.* tract] up from perforation of an inflamed appendix.

c. *Austral.* To keep company *with* (a person of the opposite sex, esp. a woman); ***to track square*** (see quot. 1919).

1916 C. J. DENNIS *Songs of Sentimental Bloke* 51, I swear I'll never track wiv 'er no more. **1919** W. H. DOWNING *Digger Dialects* 50 *Track square*, to pursue an amorous enterprise with honorable intentions. **1926** K. S. PRICHARD *Working Bullocks* 47 Combo's what they call a man tracks round with a gin in the nor'-west. **1933** N. LINDSAY *Saturdee* 239 Who are you trackin' with now? **1949** A. MARSHALL *How Beautiful are thy Feet* 64 He wants me to track square with him. To look at him you'd never think he could talk seriously. **1954** T. A. G. HUNGERFORD *Sowers of Wind* 270, I bet it's that cross-eyed harlot he's been tracking with. **1964** G. JOHNSTON *My Brother Jack* 161 He's been at me for years about how irresponsible I am, and the first time I come back with a girl I'm tracking square with, I get hoisted!

d. Of a stylus or pick-up: to follow the wave-form of a record groove. Also *trans.*, with the record, the groove, or the sound represented as obj.

1929 WILSON & WEBB *Mod. Gramophones* vi. 129 As the needle tracks in the groove it is gradually worn to a chisel point. **1937** *Electronics* Nov. 21/2 The test was stopped when the records had been played 185 times each and the quality had become very bad indeed. The needles still would track the grooves, however, showing that complete breakdown of the walls had not yet occurred. **1950** *Audio Engin.* Aug. 15/2 In ordinary recorded music, the inability of the stylus to track at high groove curvatures leads to objectionable high-frequency distortion. **1957** *Records & Recording* Nov. 20 It is these grooves which must be tracked with absolute accuracy by the pickup needle. **1977** *Gramophone* June 10/2 (Advt.), This cartridge successfully tracks all types of records at forces even lighter than one gram. **1978** *Ibid.* June 128/3 There is a solo flute passage which could only just about be tracked at 1 gram. **1981** *Popular Hi-Fi* Mar. 7/4 The DT1 tracks exceptionally well and retrieves more informations from the grooves.

e. Of a film or television camera, or its operator: to move (esp. *back* or *in*) in relation to the subject being filmed.

1959 *Listener* 30 Apr. 772/1 After we had seen Mac in close-up, the camera suddenly tracked right away. **1960** N. KNEALE *Quatermass II* II. 61 Track in on him fast. Fade in end music. **1961** G. MILLERSON *Technique Television Production* iii. 26 If..he is tracking backwards through an archway at too high an elevation, he might severely injure himself, as more than one cameraman has found. **1962** *Movie* June 5/2 Track into close-up of irrelevant detail; cut to close-up irrelevant detail of new setting; track out and begin sequence. **1975** *Radio Times* 22 May 66/3 Tufano starts a close shot on the broken walls of a bombed house. He then tracks back and pans across the blitzed street.

II. Erroneously used for TRACT *v.*[2]

†**4.** *trans.* To put off, delay; = TRACT *v.*[2] 2.

1524 HEN. VIII in Strype *Eccl. Mem.* (1721) I. App. xiii. 28 By delaies the matier was alwaies tracked, and put over without any fruteful determination.

III. 5. *Comb.* **track-ball** *Computers*, a VDU input device in the form of a small ball that is rotated in a holder to move a cursor on the screen; = *tracker ball* s.v. TRACKER[1] 2.

1969 M. H. MEHR in *Internat. Symposium Man-Machine Systems* V, Positioning to 0·1% of the screen diameter could be accomplished in 3–4 seconds which compares favorably with the published track ball data. **1972** *Acta Crystallogr.* A. XXVIII. S 253/2 The operator can interact with the display by means of a track-ball cursor. **1983** *Austral. Personal Computer* Aug. 60/2 Lisa's engineers are sometimes criticised for selecting the mouse rather than other quick data input devices—notably the trackball, touch-screen and light-pen.

Hence **tracked** (also 6 tract, 7 trackt) *ppl. a.*

1589 NASHE *Anat. Absurd.* Wks. (Grosart) I. 32 The tract path of theyr treacherie. **1653** R. ROBINSON *Christ all* II. (1656) 28 It's a trackt way. Prophets, Apostles..have by their walking made this way smooth and even. **1895** WOOD-MARTIN *Pagan Irel.* 400 Oval pebbles of quartzite, with a score..in the North of Ireland..are styled 'tracked-stones'. **1902** *Daily Record & Mail* 7 Oct. 4 Tracked pathways have long ago given place to good roads.

track, *v.*[2] [app. ad. Du. *trekken* to draw, pull, tug, drag, tow (see TREK), assimilated in form to TRACK *v.*[1]] *trans.* To tow (a vessel), esp. from the bank or tow-path. Also *absol.* Cf. TRACT *v.*[2] 1.

1727 HAMILTON *New Acc. E. Indies* II. xxxiv. 21 They [vessels] come down..before the Stream of the River, but [they] are obliged to track them up again, with Strength of Hand, about 1000 Miles. **1769** FALCONER *Dict. Marine* (1789), *Chemin de halage*, a path on the side of a river, or canal, for horses to track..vessels along the stream. **1817** *Chron.* in *Ann. Reg.* 101/2 The Tug..tracks these vessels between Leith and Grangemouth. **1856** KANE *Arct. Expl.* I. iv. 41 They can generally find room to track their vessels along its solid margin. **1887** J. GIBSON *Gt. Waterfalls* 165 They made their way..through miles of rapids, over which they were tracked, poled, rowed, and portaged.

b. *intr.* To proceed by towing. Said of a boat or of those in it.

1854 MILMAN *Lat. Chr.* IV. v. (1864) II. 304 They tracked in their boats along some of the rivers. **1880** A. E. MOULE *Chinese Stor.* v. 74 Our boat tracked slowly against the stream. **1888** C. D. BELL *Winter on Nile* viii. (1889) 83 You may have to 'track' at a slow pace.

Hence ˈ**tracking** *vbl. sb.*[2] (also *attrib.*) and *ppl. a.*; also ˈ**trackable** *a.*, such as to admit of tracking or towing.

1839 DARWIN *Voy. Nat.* ix. (1879) 178 The party..was divided into two spells, each of which hauled at the tracking line alternately. **1849** E. B. EASTWICK *Dry Leaves* 24 Boats are got up against the stream chiefly by tracking, being towed by the crew. **1853** KANE *Grinnell Exp.* xii. (1856) 88 Enlarging it [a crevice] into a 'trackable' canal. **1873** *Routledge's Yng. Gentl. Mag.* Aug. 524 The channel was too wide to permit of 'tracking', as it is called in Arctic language—that is, towing with ropes along a margin of ice.

track-, stem of TRACK *v.*[2], in comb. (after Du. *trek-* 'draw-, drag-, tow-', similarly used in *trekkoord, -lijn, -schuit*, etc.), as ***track-barge, -line, -path, -road, -rope***; see also TRACK-BOAT.

1795 *Track-barge [see TRACK-BOAT]. **1856** KANE *Arctic Expl.* I. x. 112 Each man had..his own *track-line. **1839** *Civil Eng. & Arch. Jrnl.* II. 221/1 A *track-path to be formed upon the slope of the deep cutting at Laggon. **1828** WEBSTER, **Track-road*, a towing-path. *Cyc.* **1816** TUCKEY *Narr. Exped. R. Zaire* iv. (1818) 143 With the aid of oars, and a *track rope at times, [we] got the boats up. **1864** CARLYLE *Fredk. Gt.* XVII. vii. IV. 589 By oar and track-rope.

trackability (trækəˈbɪlɪtɪ). [f. TRACK *v.*[1] + ABILITY; cf. -BILITY.] The ability of a stylus or cartridge to track adequately (TRACK *v.*[1] 3 d).

1972 ANDERSON & JENRICK in *Jrnl. Audio Engin. Soc.* XX. 162 (*heading*) A practical high-frequency trackability test for phono pickups. **1978** *Gramophone* May 1970/1 Not only does it check trackability, but also the tone-arm resonance over the frequency range of 4–12Hz.

trackage[1] (ˈtrækɪdʒ). [f. TRACK *v.*[2] + -AGE.] The action or process of tracking or towing, or fact of being tracked; towage, haulage.

1820 *Blackw. Mag.* VII. 436 In the Caledonian Canal,..much animal or steam power will be saved, in trackage. **1826** J. ADAMSON *Sk. Inform. Railroads* 39 With such prodigious powers of locomotion and trackage.

ˈ**trackage**[2]. *U.S.* [f. TRACK *sb.*[1] 6 a + -AGE.] The tracks or lines of a railway system collectively. Also *attrib.* **trackage charge**, charge made for the use of a railway line by another company.

1884 *Morning Herald* (Reading, Pa.) 17 Apr., Our general agent has, therefore, advanced this trackage charge. **1888** *Science* 27 July 46/2 The total trackage is twelve miles, the equipment is forty cars. **1894** *Times* 14 July 7/1 Our railroads have about 170,000 miles of trackage and 1,000,000 of *employés*.

ˈ**track-boat.** [f. TRACK- vb.-stem + BOAT *sb.*] A boat which is tracked or towed; a tow-boat. (Originally *Sc.*, rendering Du. *trek-schuit*.)

1632 *Sc. Acts Chas. I* (1870) V. 243/1 Also thair Trakboats, boats, crears, shippes more or lesse..Sall not be arrested. **1795** J. PHILLIPS *Hist. Inland Navig.* 320 The public opening of the..navigation from sea to sea was made by the sailing of a track-barge... In the course of the voyage ..the track-boat passed along..the great aqueduct over the river Kelvin. **1808–18** JAMIESON, *Track-boat*, a boat used on a canal. **1824** in Sidney *Life R. Hill* (1834) 308 Mr. Hill went to Glasgow by the track boat, embarking at Grangemouth. **1908** *Westm. Gaz.* 27 Oct. 6/3 The journey was made by P. and O. steamer to Alexandria (sixteen days), thence in a track boat towed by tugs or horses to Atfeh (forty-eight miles along the Mahmoudieh Canal), thence by Nile steamer 120 miles to Boulac.

track-brake to **-edge**: see TRACK *sb.* 14.

tracked (trækt), *a.* [f. TRACK *sb.* + -ED[2].]

1. Of a vehicle: having endless tracks (TRACK *sb.* 6 d).

1926 *Westm. Gaz.* 26 Jan. 6/2 'Tracked' vehicles, or, as most people would say,..'caterpillar' or roadless tractors. **1950** *Times* 17 Feb. 8/5 With a few bulldozers and grabs and tracked trucks, even the intimidating Snowdonian slate-tips could be put on the road to recovery. **1979** *Daily Tel.* 3 Dec. 3/1 A tracked armoured personnel carrier.

2. Of a hovercraft: confined to a fixed track.

1967 *Jane's Surface Skimmer Systems 1967–68* 52 (*heading*) Tracked air cushion vehicles. **1971** *New Scientist* 24 June 756/1 This time it is the £3·5 million tracked hovercraft project which is coming under attack.

tracker[1] (ˈtrækə(r)). [f. TRACK *v.*[1] + -ER[1].]

1. One who or that which tracks; one skilled in following a track or trail. In quot. *a* 1632, one who follows or walks in a path (*obs.*).

black tracker, an Australian Aboriginal employed by the government to track criminals.

1617 *Carte Papers* LXII. 438 If anie knowne Trackers bee vppon the track, the same tracker vppon reasonable hire of the seuerall tounes, shall followe the track vnto the end. *a* **1632** G. HERBERT *Country Parson* xi. (1652) 51 The Countrey Parson, who is a diligent observer, and tracker of Gods wayes. **1640** BROME *Sparagus Gard.* III. iv, He.. followes pretty feet and insteps like a hare tracker. **1810** SCOTT *Lady of L.* I. iv, The trackers of the deer. **1862** *Melbourne Leader* 5 July, The black trackers could only discover the tracks of six horsemen. **1904** *Blackw. Mag.* Nov. 674/2 The bloodhound is a wonderful tracker.

2. Special Combs.: **tracker ball** *Computers* = *track-ball* s.v. TRACK *v.*[1] 5; **tracker dog**, a dog trained to pick up and follow a scent, esp. a police dog trained to track people; cf. *sniffer dog* s.v. SNIFFER 3 b.

1969 *Advance in Electronics: Proc. 16th Electronics Congr.* 484 The input devices..vary from scheme to scheme but common ones are keyboards, light pens and *tracker balls. **1982** *Internat. Conf. Radar-82* (Inst. Electr. Engineers) 306/1 A Maintrace Section..distributes the radar signals to the displays and an Intertrace Section..generates the video maps and provides interactive keyboard/tracker-ball facilities. **1962** 'J. LE CARRÉ' *Murder of Quality* iv. 51 We've got to rely on laboratories, *tracker dogs and nation-wide searches. **1979** *Sunday Express* 16 Dec. 11 Police with tracker dogs will resume the search to-day for farmer's wife. **1984** *Times* 27 Feb. 8/1 Searching for..explosions with the eagerness of a tracker dog from the bomb squad.

ˈ**tracker**[2]. [f. TRACK *v.*[2]; cf. Du. *trekker*.]

1. One who tracks or tows a vessel; a tower; also, a towing-vessel, a tugboat.

1791–1823 DISRAELI *Cur. Lit.* (1859) II. 143 The severe labour of the trackers, in China, is accompanied with a song. **1817** *Chron.* in *Ann. Reg.* 101/1 A Company in Leith have equipped a powerful steam-vessel, or tracker. **1864** RAWLINSON *Anc. Mon.* II. vii. 174 As there was no room for rowers, trackers were engaged, who dragged the boat along by means of ropes. **1894** *Outing* (U.S.) XXIV. 363/2 We were awakened by the loud cries of the many trackers, making ready to draw the junks through the swift waters.

2. *Organ-building.* A strip or rod of wood forming part of the connexion between the key and the pallet, and exerting a pulling action: cf. STICKER.

1843 *Civil Eng. & Arch. Jrnl.* VI. 108/1 The machinery of the organ is so very extensive, that trackers, if placed in one line, would measure more than 5 miles. **1881** W. E. DICKSON *Organ-Build.* viii. 95 Tracker. A flat riband of pine... Trackers..are now frequently slender round rods. **1887** W. S. PRATT in Gladden *Parish Problems* 435 The keys and stops operate an involved net-work of trackers, slides, rollers, levers, springs, and valves.

b. *attrib.*, as ***tracker-action, -wire, -work***.

1904 *Athenæum* 12 Nov. 666/1 Our author adds that the *tracker action 'is dispensed with'. **1910** *Times* 16 Dec. 13/5 To have the organ taken down with the substitution of pneumatic action for the old 'tracker' action. **1852** SEIDEL *Organ* 64 Below the back end of the keys..the sling of a *tracker-wire is secured. **1878** E. J. HOPKINS in Grove *Dict. Mus.* I. 485/1 If in *tracker-work..the total alteration amounts to no more than one eighth of an inch.

ˈ**tracking**, *vbl. sb.*[1] [f. TRACK *v.*[1] + -ING[1].]

I. 1. The action of TRACK *v.*[1] in various senses. Also *attrib.*

1524 in Strype *Eccl. Mem.* (1721) I. App. xiii. 30 The delaying and tracking of this matier may do moche harme. **1838** *Arcana of Science* 49 The friction arising from the unequal tracking of ordinary carriages is avoided. **1888** in *Times* 13 Oct. 7/6 Testing their [bloodhounds'] tracking powers. **1894** H. NISBET *Bush Girl's Rom.* 49 The tracking down of escaped convicts and bushrangers. **1904** *Westm. Gaz.* 30 Sept. 10/2 The double tracking of the line from coast to coast will be completed in a few years. **1908** *Daily Chron.* 28 Aug. 7/4 Tracking dogs are kept in readiness at certain centres. **1932** *Jrnl. Sci. Instruments* IX. 288 The best tracking conditions are reached by choosing the position of the axis about which the tone arm rotates by the method shown. **1937** *Discovery* Nov. 330/2 The operators of the electron cameras receive their instructions through telephones, so that they can advance or withdraw their cameras (tracking) or swing them sideways (panning) as planned by the producer. **1958** *Listener* 4 Dec. 908/2 The manufacture of the satellite and its instruments, with the associated tracking and computing systems. **1959** *Cambr. Rev.* 24 Oct. 73/1 The technique in this section cuts right across Bazin's distinction between classic Eisenstein montage, and more realistic modern methods of tracking, panning, and so on, on a wide screen. **1969** *Times* 16 July 4/1 The radio tracking instruments spread around the globe for keeping in continuous contact with the spacecraft. **1975** G. J. KING *Audio Handbk.* viii. 184 Tracking ability thus takes account of the compliance, effective tip mass and mechanical resistance.

II. Specific senses. **2.** The formation or occurrence of conducting paths for electricity over the surface of an insulating material.

1931 H. WARREN *Electr. Insulating Materials* III. xix. 239 The surface carbonization, or what is commonly called 'tracking'.., of these materials is their most serious electrical handicap. **1945** *Electronic Engin.* XVII. 600 Moisture..very soon causes..tracking between the connecting tags. **1967** M. CHANDLER *Ceramics in Mod. World* iv. 115 The electrical properties that matter most are high volume and surface resistivity, high puncture strength, and good tracking resistance. **1970** K. BALL *Fiat 600, 600 D Autobook* iii. 34/1 Examine the distributor cap for cracks or signs of carbonisation (tracking).

3. *Electronics.* The maintenance of a constant difference in frequency between two or more connected circuits or components.

1932 *Electronics* Aug. 250/1 (*caption*) Deviation from exact tracking at various intermediate frequencies. **1971** [see PADDER *sb.*[2] 3]. **1975** [see TRACK *v.*[1] 1 e].

4. *U.S. Educ.* = STREAMING *vbl. sb.* f.

1967 *N.Y. Times* 23 June 36 Tracking can be a useful educational device if tests are frequently administered and if movement from one track to another is made easy. **1974** *Florida FL Reporter* XIII. 29/3 School would simplify their task if they could separate those students who want to learn to speak the new dialect from those who do not... This would not be a matter of 'tracking'.

III. 5. Special Combs.: **tracking error**, the error that occurs in gramophone reproduction when the tone-arm is pivoted, so that in general the axis of the cartridge is not in line with the groove; **tracking shot** *Cinemat.* and *Television*, a shot during which the camera tracks (TRACK *v.*[1] 3 e); **tracking snow** *N. Amer.*, snow sufficiently deep to enable hunters to track animals; **tracking station**, an establishment set up to track objects in the sky; **tracking weight**, the weight with which a stylus rests on a gramophone record.

1924 *Gramophone* Sept. 129/2 The '*tracking error'. **1930** *Wireless World* 26 Mar. 340/1 The mean between the highest and lowest deviations..gives a slightly smaller maximum tracking error. **1975** *Gramophone* Jan. 1424/1 Tracking error at all points across the record was within 2° overall. **1940** *Chambers's Technical Dict.* 857/1 *Tracking shot. **1957** MANVELL & HUNTLEY *Technique Film Music* ii. 33 There follows a continuous tracking shot lasting in all for 2 minutes 22 seconds. **1973** D. OSMOND-SMITH tr. *Bettetini's Lang. & Technique of Film* ii. 95 Another narratively effective element is the 'tracking shot'; this consists of moving the whole cine-camera on a mechanical device known as a 'dolly'. **1971** W. HILLEN *Blackwater River* ii. 17 Water running, little hope for *tracking-snow. **1981** *Northeast Woods & Waters* Jan. 12/1 Coos County showed the largest increase (87%) where sportsmen had tracking snow for the entire season. **1963** *Ann. Reg. 1962* 445 The *tracking station in Great Britain held the signal for only a few moments. **1972** *Daily Tel.* 14 Apr. 4/6 The TV signal is received from the Moon..at the Goldstone tracking station in the Mojave Desert. **1978** G. GREENE *Human Factor* IV. i. 197 America maintains a guided missile tracking station and a space tracking station in the Republic. **1962** A. NISBETT *Technique Sound Studio* iv. 87 Recordings played under a *tracking weight of about 1½ oz. were reckoned to have a life of about a dozen playings. **1978** *Lancashire Life* Sept. 131/1 The pick-up arm itself should have an adjustment to enable you to set the correct tracking weight for the cartridge.

tracklement (ˈtræk(ə)lmənt). [Origin obscure. Dorothy Hartley claimed to have invented this word. She also claimed that her use of it in this sense was a *spec.* application of an older word, prob. *dial.*, meaning 'appurtenances, impedimenta', but no evidence of such a word has been found.]

An article of food, *spec.* a jelly, prepared to accompany meat.

1954 D. HARTLEY *Food in England* v. 161 (*heading*) Mutton tracklements and condiment. **1959** *Times* 24 Aug. 11/4 A pleasantly astringent, smokily flavoured jelly as a 'tracklement' with mutton. **1971** R. CONDON *Vertical Smile* (1973) xxxvii. 259 A saddle of lamb..delicate enough to accept only such a tracklement as rowan jelly. **1978** *Observer* 26 Feb. 35/9 Various salads and tracklements are included in the cold table.

trackless (ˈtræklɪs), *a.* [f. TRACK *sb.* + -LESS.] Without a track or path; pathless; not marked by a track; untrodden.

1656 COWLEY *Pind. Odes, Muse* ii, Where Bird..did ne're Row through the trackless Ocean of the Air. **1708** *Brit. Apollo* No. 53. 3/2 A trackless Labyrinth of woe. **1801**

STRUTT *Sports & Past.* Introd. §44 The recesses of a trackless wilderness. **1878** LECKY *Eng. in 18th C.* II. v. 66 The soldiers were easily..bewildered in the trackless mountains.

b. Leaving no track or trace.

1695 BLACKMORE *Pr. Arth.* v. 638 Then thro' the Heavn's their trackless Flight they take. **1864** [implied in TRACKLESSLY]. **1890** 'BOLDREWOOD' *Col. Reformer* (1891) 426 His yacht..could sweep out unchallenged and trackless as the falcon. **1907** C. C. BROWN *China in Leg. & Story* ii. 33 Its gray slabs worn by trackless feet, as the centuries went on.

c. Not running on a track or line of rails, while propelled by electric power from overhead conductors.

1909 *Westm. Gaz.* 22 Sept. 8/1 Leeds is now assured of a system of trackless trams. *Ibid.*, A splendid system of tramways, both trackless and otherwise.

Hence 'tracklessly *adv.*, 'tracklessness.

1847 WEBSTER, Tracklessly, Tracklessness. **1864** LOWELL *Fireside Trav.* 269 The cloud-shadows melted tracklessly toward the hills. **1868** GEO. ELIOT *Sp. Gipsy* I. 83 Shall then pass away Like wind upon the waters, tracklessly.

track-leveller to **-mile**: see TRACK *sb.* 14.

track-line: see TRACK *sb.* 14, and TRACK-.

track-path, -road, -rope: see TRACK-.

track-rail to **-scraper**: see TRACK *sb.* 14.

track-schuyt, -scoot, -scout, -skuit, anglicized forms of TREKSCHUIT.

track-shoe to **-walking**: see TRACK *sb.* 14.

trackster ('trækstə(r)). *U.S.* [f. TRACK *sb.* + -STER.] A track athlete.

1974 *Hartsville* (S. Carolina) *Messenger* 22 Apr. 3A/6 The Hartsville High School Cindermen..won a 67–63 victory over the Hillcrest High tracksters. **1979** *Tucson Mag.* Apr. 70/2 The University of Arizona tracksters host two triangular meets at the Stadium.

trackway ('trækweɪ). [f. TRACK *sb.* + WAY.]

1. A path beaten by the feet of passers, a track; also, an ancient British roadway, a ridgeway.

1818 KIRBY & SP. *Entomol.* II. 98 Gould, speaking of his jet-ant (*F[ormica] fuliginosa*), says that they make several main track-ways, (streets he calls them,) with smaller paths striking off from them, extending sometimes to the distance of forty feet from their nest. **1826** W. A. MILES *Deverel Barrow* 8 The line of hill, south of Maiden-Castle, near Dorchester, where the British trackway runs for many miles. **1848** S. ROWE *Peramb. Dartmoor* 45 Trackways, under which designation those roads, or causeways, which cross the moor in various directions are generally known. **1891** T. HARDY *Tess* xi, They were no longer on hard road, but in a mere trackway.

2. a. A tramway. **b.** A railway (*Funk's Stand. Dict.* 1895).

1858 SIMMONDS *Dict. Trade, Track-way*, a tram-road.

3. [f. TRACK-.] A towing-path.

1873 *Act 36 & 37 Vict.* c. 34 *Preamble*, Any towing path and trackway on the bank of any navigable river.

track-work: see TRACK *sb.* 14.

tract (trækt), *sb.*[1] Also 5–6 tracte. [App. abbreviated from L. *tractātus* TRACTATE; not in any other lang.]

I. †**1.** Literary treatment or discussion. *Obs. rare.*

In some instances difficult to separate from sense 2.

[1432–50: see 2.] **1577** HANMER *Anc. Eccl. Hist.* (1619) 245 It was our part to comprise in few words such things as required a severall tract. **1659** BP. WALTON *Consid. Considered* 14 They do assert and prove the plain contrary, and that not *obiter*, or by the by, but *ex professo*, in full tracts.

2. a. A book or written work treating of some particular topic; a treatise; a written or printed discourse or dissertation: = TRACTATE *sb.* 1. Now *rare* in general sense.

Formerly often applied to what would now be called 'books'.

1432–50 tr. *Higden* (Rolls) II. 257 For cause that a generalle tracte [L. *tractatus generalis*; TREVISA, tretysis ful and general] of the iiij. principalle realmes afore seide.., dothe require a large processe. *Ibid.* III. 219 The philosophres that were diuines..laborede and made tractes of God [L. *de Deo tractaverunt*; TREVISA, þei treted of God]. **1577** HANMER *Anc. Eccl. Hist.* (1663) 84 This present Tract of mine is not made for any ostentation. **1614** RALEIGH *Hist. World* II. (1634) 340 Palastina it selfe is but a Province, as I have noted in the beginning of this Tract. *a***1677** HALE *Prim. Orig. Man.* I. ii. 69 The scope and end of my business in this Tract. **1825** MCCULLOCH *Pol. Econ.* I. 38 In the course of the seventeenth century, a more than usual number of tracts were published on commercial and economical subjects. **1845** —— *Taxation* II. iv. (1854) 183 Mr. Howlett.. has made some statements in his valuable tract on tithe.

b. Applied to a division of a book or literary work, treating of a separate subject or branch. *rare.*

1662 STILLINGFL. *Orig. Sacr.* I. iii. §3 Three books they tell us of, which Zertoost received by Revelation, or rather one book, consisting of three severall tracts, whereof the first [etc.]. **1891** J. E. H. THOMSON *Bks. which influenced our Lord* I. x. 177 The Mishna is divided into six sections, each of these into ten tracts on an average, or sixty-one in all.

3. a. In later use: A short pamphlet on some religious, political, or other topic, suitable for distribution or for purposes of propaganda.

[**1762** *Gentl. Mag.* Nov. 545/2 This little tract affords prescriptions for the soul.] **1806, 1816** [see c]. **1848** THACKERAY *Van. Fair* ix, Whose sister, Lady Emily, wrote those sweet tracts, 'The Sailor's True Binnacle', and 'The Applewoman of Finchley Common'. **1851** KINGSLEY *Let.* in *Life* (1879) I. ix. 237 The barbarians..got into their addle pates that we were emissaries of Mazzini and Co. distributing political tracts. **1866** G. MACDONALD *Ann. Q. Neighb.* xxx, Whether he only distributes tracts with condescending words. **1885** G. MEREDITH *Diana* xviii, Am I really as dull as a tract, my dear? **1911** A. R. BUCKLAND in *Encycl. Brit.* XXVII. 177/2 A tract is understood to be brief and rather argumentative than educational. *Mod.* The British Museum library contains an immense collection of Civil War tracts.

b. ***Tracts for the Times***: the title of a series of pamphlets on theological and ecclesiastical topics (known also as the ***Oxford Tracts***, or simply ***the Tracts***) started by J. H. Newman, and published at Oxford 1833–1841, on the doctrines of which the Tractarian movement was based; also used in *sing.* with small initials, of any literary work put out to meet a particular need of the times.

The earlier of these were, in accordance with their title, brief pamphlets; but some of the later, e.g. that of Pusey on Baptism, were extended treatises, *tracts* in sense 2. The aim of the series was 'to arrest the advance of Liberalism in religious thought, and to revive' what the writers held to be 'the true conception of the relation of the Church of England to the Catholic Church at large' (*Churchman's Guide*). The last Tract, No. 90, by J. H. Newman, 'On Certain Passages in the XXXIX Articles', 'called forth a storm of reprobation; at the instance of Four Tutors, the Heads of the Oxford Colleges pronounced censure upon the author', and at the request of the Bishop of Oxford the publication of the Tracts ceased. In the sequel, many who sympathized with the teaching of the Tracts (including at length Newman himself) seceded to the Church of Rome.

1834 (*title*) Tracts for the Times. By Members of the University of Oxford. **1868** SIR J. T. COLERIDGE *Mem. Keble* xii. (1870) 276 It was Mr. Benson..who gave the authors and favourers of the Tracts the perfectly inoffensive name of Tractarian. **1881** FROUDE *Short Stud.* Ser. IV. (1883) 175 These were the views which we used to hear when the Tracts were first beginning. **1893** LIDDON, etc. *Life Pusey* I. xii. 277 The first Tracts are dated at the beginning of September (1833). They were generally short, several keeping within the suggested limit of four pages: they were chiefly concerned with the constitution, ordinances, and services of the Church. **1927** A. H. MCNEILE *Introd. N.T.* 95 The Tübingen conception of the book [*sc.* the Acts of the Apostles] as a tract for the times mediating between the Judaic and the Pauline factions. **1979** E. H. GOMBRICH *Sense of Order* ii. 41 As a tract for the times the *Seven Lamps* failed to achieve Ruskin's aim of bringing the conditions of the Middle Ages back to industrialized England.

c. *attrib.* and *Comb.*, as (in sense 3) ***tract-distributing*** adj., ***distribution***, ***-led*** adj., ***society***; (in sense 3 b, with capital *T*) ***Tract divine, doctrine, man, movement, system, -writer.***

1760 PRATT in J. Adams *Wks.* (1850) II. 97, I should be very sorry to have the Tract Society dissolved. **1806** W. L. BOWLES *Banwell Hill* II. 360 The tract-led Miss, Who trots to every Bethel club. **1816** 'QUIZ' *Grand Master* VIII. Argt. 18 Let them, if they perceive impiety, Transmit it to the Tract Society. **1841** S. WILBERFORCE *Let.* 30 Mar., in Ashwell *Life* I. vi. 217 You know my dread of the 'Tract' doctrine of Reserve. **1843** *Chr. Lady's Mag.* XX. 211 The opinions of Oxford-tract men..upon the divine efficacy of Sacraments. *Ibid.* 271 The pernicious errors broached.., by the Tract-writers of Oxford. **1846** D. WILSON *Exp. Lect. Col.* II. 20 *note*, The Tract divines add to the three essentials required in the XIXth article a fourth. **1869** W. P. MACKAY *Grace & Truth* (1875) 43 Tract-distributors and pick-pockets. **1882** OGILVIE s.v., In this sense the word is frequently adjectivally used; as, *tract* society,..*tract* distribution, etc. **1893** LIDDON, etc. *Life Pusey* I. xii. 414 It was natural for the Tract-writers to honour the Fathers of the Church.

II. †**4. a.** Negotiation, treating; a treaty. (Cf. TRACTATE *sb.* 2.) **b.** Trade, traffic [cf. Pg. *trato* dealing, trade]. *Obs. rare.*

1501 in *Lett. Rich. III & Hen. VII* (Rolls) I. 135 The kinges majestie had sent to him his seal for tract of pais bytwixt his grace and H. **1502** *Ibid.* 147 A tracte of accorde. **1582** N. LICHEFIELD tr. *Castanheda's Conq. E. Ind.* I. i. 3 They had beene in the Cayro, and understoode there much newes of Ormuse, and of theyr tract had with and into the Indies.

tract, *sb.*[2] *R.C. Ch.* Also 4–5 tracte, 5 tratt. [ad. med.L. TRACTUS, q.v. (In Fr. *trait.*)] An anthem consisting of verses of Scripture, usually from the Psalms, sung instead of the Alleluia in the mass from Septuagesima till Easter Eve.

1387 TREVISA *Higden* (Rolls) VII. 145 When forsoþe it was comen toward þe tracte [L. *Cum autem ad versum tractus ventum fuisset*] in whiche it is songen, *Scitote quoniam Dominus ipse est Deus*. *c***1450** in Aungier *Syon* (1840) 327 From septuagesym in to ester thys tracte *Gaude Maria* schal be songe at lectren. **1483** CAXTON *Gold. Leg.* 412/1 Gelasyus and Gregory added therto collettis and sange to the lessons and gospellys graylles tracte and alleluya. **1483** *Cath. Angl.* 391/1 A Tracte (*A.* A Tratt), *sistema, tractus*. **1546** LANGLEY *Pol. Verg. De Invent.* v. viii. 108b, The Tract Durandus saieth was deuysed by Teleophorus. **1624** DARCIE *Birth of Heresies* xviii. 74 In stead of which Alleluia is sung another song called a tract, with a loud voice, and a protracted note, in a graue kind of Musicke. **1867** C. WALKER *Ritual Reason Why* 155 These were called the *Tract*, from being drawn out (*tractus*) to a mournful cadence. **1877** J. D. CHAMBERS *Div. Worship* 331 The Tract was usually a mournful Psalm, or part of a Psalm.

tract (trækt), *sb.*[3] Also 5–7 tracte, 6 trackte, 6–7 trackt. [ad. L. *tract-us* (*u*-stem), a drawing, dragging, pulling, trailing; a train, track, course, a tract of space or time, course, progress, duration, protraction, f. ppl. stem of *trahĕre* to draw, drag. In certain senses, this word fell together with TRACE *sb.*[1] and TRACK *sb.*, and was sometimes even used in the senses of these words; in others it corresponds with the cognate F. *trait*, OF. *traict*, also *tract*:—L. *tractus.*]

I. †**1. a.** The drawing out, duration, continuance, process, passing, or lapse *of time*; the course *of time*. Cf. L. *tractus temporum*, F. *trait de temps*.

1494 FABYAN *Chron.* III. lvi. 36 This in tracte of tyme made hym welthy. **1575** FENTON *Gold. Ep.* (1577) 6 As tracte of time carryeth with it a lawe of forgetfulnesse of things past. **1651** N. BACON *Disc. Govt. Eng.* II. xxiv. 109 The Seasons now in tract were of short continuance. **1658** ROWLAND *Moufet's Theat. Ins.* 946 We conclude this art.. to be very ancient, and derived to us by long tract of time. **1676** HALE *Contempl.* I. 294 In the tract of long life a man is sure to meet with more sicknesses. *a***1734** NORTH *Exam.* I. ii. §30 (1740) 45 Which being perpetually inculcated, in the Tract of a few Years, created in the People prodigious Resentments.

†**b.** Protraction (of time), deferring, putting off, dilatory proceeding, delay. (Cf. TRACT *v.*[2] 2.)

1503–4 *Act 19 Hen. VII*, c. 28 *Preamble*, By which longe tracte of tyme the seid sueters..shulde be disconforted. **1523** WOLSEY in Fiddes *Life* II. (1726) 76 That no tract or deley bee used therein. **1600** HOLLAND *Livy* XXX. xvi. 751 They sought for nothing else but delaies and tract of time.

c. A space or extent of time, a period. (In later use regarded as *transf.* from 3.)

1494 FABYAN *Chron.* v. cii. 76 Theodebertus..of his.. vncles was greuously warred by longe tracte of tyme. **1524** WOLSEY in Strype *Eccl. Mem.* (1721) I. iv. 53 Considering the tract of time that is requisite. *a***1548** HALL *Chron., Hen. V* 80 This short tyme and smal tract of my mortal life. **1615** G. SANDYS *Trav.* 143 A tract of three hundred sixty and foure yeares. **1799** J. ROBERTSON *Agric. Perth* 169 Waiting for a long tract of serene weather, which may not come. **1850** TENNYSON *In Mem.* xlvi. 9 A lifelong tract of time reveal'd. **1853** MAURICE *Proph. & Kings* iii. 43 Utterly unlike and separated by tracts of time and space. **1865** PALGRAVE *Hymn, 'Thou say'st, Take up thy cross'* iii, Dim tracts of time divide Those golden days from me.

2. The continuance or continued duration *of* some action or state; the course or continuity *of* a narrative, etc.; a continued series. Now *rare* or *Obs.*

1581 SIDNEY *Apol. Poetrie* (Arb.) 65 The whole tract of a Comedy, shoulde be full of delight. **1599** SANDYS *Europæ Spec.* (1632) 178 Yet tract of affliction, much misery, often over-reaching by subtilty of adversaryes, doth finally purge out those grosse-witted humours. **1632** LITHGOW *Trav.* IX. 407 They had wrot the whole tract of his abhominable vices to the Emperour. **1661** FELTHAM *Resolves* II. lviii. 307, I do not remember that we read the name of either Dice or Gaming in the tract of either Scripture. **1679** *Lauderdale Papers* (Camden) 261 A long continued tract of violence and oppressione upon ws. **1732** MACFARLANE *Geneal. Collect.* (1900) 310 He caused Apprehend and Execute at Crief for a train and tract of Depredations Macobertus Strowanus. **1773** ERSKINE *Inst. Law Scotl.* I. i. §47 An uniform tract of decisions of the court of session..is..accounted as part of our customary law. **1858** CARLYLE *Fredk. Gt.* IX. i. (1872) III. 73 Perhaps a sudden tract of good fortune..would have made me too proud.

3. a. A stretch or extent *of* territory, etc.; a space or expanse of land (more rarely, of water, air, etc.); a region, district. Cf. L. *tractus.*

1553 EDEN *Treat. Newe Ind.* (Arb.) 8 The narrowe tracte of the Sea by the coastes of Grouelande. **1610** HOLLAND *Camden's Brit.* (1637) 126 All the Northerne tract of Britaine. **1654** EARL MONM. tr. *Bentivoglio's Warrs Flanders* 73 The Ocean first washing the said two Provinces for a long trackt of ground. **1725** DE FOE *Voy. round World* (1840) 280 This vast tract of land. **1776** TOPLADY *Hymn, 'Rock of ages'* iv, When I soar through tracts unknown. **1814** CHALMERS *Evid. Chr. Revel.* x. 278 Those remote tracts beyond the limits of our astronomy. **1834–5** J. PHILLIPS *Geol.* in *Encycl. Metrop.* VI. 564/2 The great central plateau..is chiefly a granitic and porphyritic tract. **1886** STEVENSON *Kidnapped* 120, I spied a tract of water..which..boiled white all over. *fig.* **1817** CHALMERS *Astron. Disc.* iii. (1852) 88 We do think that this lays open a very interesting tract..of most legitimate and sober-minded speculation. **1902** F. W. H. MYERS *Wordsworth* viii. 90 Large tracts of it [the *Excursion*] have little claim to the name of poetry.

b. *Nat. Hist.*, etc. A region or area of some natural structure, as a mineral formation, or the body of an animal or plant; most commonly one extending longitudinally (cf. 8).

spec. (*a*) *Anat.* The whole extent of an organ or system of organs, as the ***alimentary*** or ***digestive tract***, or a continuous longitudinal structure, such as one strand or division of a nerve-cord; *esp.* applied to particular regions of the brain or spinal cord, as the ***olfactory, optic, pyramidal***, etc. ***tracts***. Cf. *fibre tract* s.v. FIBRE *sb.* 8. (*b*) *Ornith.* A feathered area of the skin of a bird (= PTERYLA), as distinguished from a featherless *space*.

1681 S. PORDAGE tr. *Willis's Remaining Med. Wks.: Treat. No. 4: Anat. of Brain* xiii. 101 Out of the same tract of the oblong Marrow, lesser paths are carried outwardly, here and there, by particular Nerves, arising from the same, within the Skull. **1803** C. BELL *Anat. Human Body* III. I. iii. 115 It [*sc.* the olfactory nerve] takes its origin by three medullary tracts. **1811** PINKERTON *Petralogy* II. 442 This pumice.. commonly lies in long tracts, in the direction of which its vesicles are sometimes lengthened. **1841–71** T. R. JONES *Anim. Kingd.* (ed. 4) 437 The probable existence..of distinct tracts of nervous matter in the composition of the central chain of ganglia. **1867** Feather-tracts [see PTERYLA]. **1879** *St. George's Hosp. Rep.* IX. 127 General congestion of the alimentary tract. **1894** NEWTON *Dict. Birds* s.v. *Pterylosis*, The principal *pterylæ* or feathered tracts are as follows:—(1) Spinal tract... (2) Ventral tract... (3) Neck-tract [etc.]. **1959** W. ANDREW *Textbk. Compar. Histol.* xiv. 566 As one ascends the vertebrate scale, the bundles of white matter or 'tracts' make their appearance running through the gray. **1974** M. C. GERALD *Pharmacol.* x. 189 Ascending nerves transmit sensory impulses up the spinal cord, whereas descending tracts send instructions to effector cells via motor fibers.

attrib. **1899** *Allbutt's Syst. Med.* VI. 535 The tract fibres of each side must be connected with the anterior cornua on both sides. *Ibid.* VII. 79 An instance in which a tract degeneration was established.

c. *U.S.* A plot of land with definite boundaries, esp. one for development; hence, an estate. So ***tract home, house.***

1912 *Oregonian* 20 Oct. IV. 6/2 Trading in farm land last week was devoted chiefly to small tracts. There were, however, several large parcels. **1940** S. L. MCMICHAEL *Selling Real Estate* (rev. ed.) i. 4 An owner who had a tract of land ripe for development would call in a surveyor. **1954** F. L. WRIGHT *Natural House* I. 108 The plan..was for a housing project on a 100 acre tract near Pittsfield. **1963** D. HUGHES *Expendable Man* iii. 72 Raw green tract houses seemed to have taken over the countryside. **1972** Tract home [see REALTY^{2} 4]. **1973** *N.Y. Law Jrnl.* 31 Aug. 1/7 The defendants..were developing a tract with cooperative apartments to be constructed on one part. **1977** *New Yorker* 6 June 99/1 Most of his customers live in tract houses that have tiny bedrooms. **1979** *Tucson* (Arizona) *Citizen* 20 Sept. 1B/1 The Lopezes gave up a nice home on the Northwest Side on an acre lot for a nice house on a cramped lot in one of the tracts that have sprung up in south Tempe during the last two years. **1980** *Times Lit. Suppl.* 19 Sept. 1020/4 An amiable, moderately licentious fellow who readily settles down..in a newly built tract home.

II. †**4.** The action of drawing or pulling (in quots. *fig.*); attraction. *Obs. rare.*

1616 B. JONSON *Devil an Ass* II. ii, He'll ne'r owne mee, But I am taken! the fine tract of it Pulls mee along! **1620** J. PYPER tr. *Hist. Astrea* I. VII. 226 She could feele the tracts of Loue.

†**5.** Drawing, or tracing (of lines). *Obs. rare.*

1677 GILPIN *Demonol.* (1867) 22 Lines and figures are better known from mathematical instruction, than by their bare tract as written in dust. **1688** R. HOLME *Armoury* I. 19/1 The Ordinaries are made, and formed of Lines diversly composed; And according to the divers Tracts and Forms, of those said Lines, they do receive a divers Shape and variation of Names.

III. A material line drawn: = F. *trait* (see TRAIT).

†**6.** *Her.*: (*a*) = TRESSURE; (*b*) = TRACK *sb.* 7.

1486 *Bk. St. Albans, Her.* e vj b, Off tractys in armys. Afore it is sayd of borduris in armys, now it folowith to se of tractis or lynys, and first of a symple tract; and they be calde tractis for as mych as the felde remaynyng of tharmys as wele with in as with owte, & an other lyne is drawyn of an other colowre..to the maner of a shelde. *Ibid.*, He berith asure a playn tract of golde. *Ibid.* e vij, Thys tract is other wyle dowbull as in tharmys of the kyng of Scottelonde. **1610** GUILLIM *Heraldry* I. v. 17 When the Field and the Circumference or Tract about the same,..be both of one metall, colour or furre, then shall you not terme it a bordure. *Ibid.* II. vii. 66, I purpose to present to your view a Three-fold Orle or Tract, which doth include the twofold.

†**7.** A lineament, a feature; = TRAIT 4, 5. *Obs.*

1606 SYLVESTER *Du Bartas* II. iv. I. *Trophies* 1101 Th' admired Tracts of a bewitching Face. **1632** LITHGOW *Trav.* I. 24 Like to the heauenly tract and resemblance of our blessed Sauiour. **1715** tr. *C'tess D'Aunoy's Wks.* 193 His Hair brown, his Tracts all regular, his Teeth fine. **1775** C. JOHNSTON *Pilgrim* 126 To account for some tracts in their national character.

IV. Senses approaching or coinciding with those of TRACK and TRACE.

8. Course, path, way, route; with *of* or possessive, the course or path traversed by a person, animal, or moving object: = TRACK *sb.* 3, 4. Now *rare* or *Obs.*: usually expressed by *track*.

(In quot. 1799, applied to a course or channel for water.)

1555 EDEN *Decades* 255 Vnderstanding..that if I shulde sayle by the way of the northwest wynde, I shulde by a shorter tracte coomme to India [etc.]. **1616** W. FORDE *Serm.* 28 Like a bird in the aire, whose tract the aire closeth. **1665** SIR T. HERBERT *Trav.* (1677) 170 A loose and flying sand,.. accumulated into such heaps as upon any great wind the tract is lost, and passengers (too oft) overwhelmed and stifled. **1726** SHELVOCKE *Voy. round World* 201 In the tract of the Manila ship. **1798** CHARLOTTE SMITH *Yng. Philos.* IV. 279 Perceiving that in the lane was certainly the most beaten tract, I hurried along it. **1799** J. ROBERTSON *Agric. Perth* 302 When the tract for conveying the water has been once made with judgment, it may remain for centuries. **1823** F. COOPER *Pioneers* v, The tract for the sleighs was much more limited. **1843** NICHOLSON *Hist. & Trad. Tales* 196, I..will pursue his tract no longer. **1865** ALEX. SMITH *Summ. Skye* (1880) 143 In Skye one is every now and again coming on the tract of the distinguished travellers.

9. *fig.* Course (of action, etc.); manner of proceeding, way, path: = TRACK *sb.* 5. *rare* or *Obs.*

1566 PAINTER *Pal. Pleas.* I. Pref. 8 The other prescribeth a directe pathe to treade the tracte of this present life. **1581** LAMBARDE *Eiren.* II. ii. (1588) 125 In the Commission of the Peace, they are both conueied vnder this one tracte of speach. **1612** DRAYTON *Poly-olb.* Pref. A j, A Poeme..whose vnusuall tract may perhaps seeme difficult, to the female Sex. **1632** J. FEATLY *Hon. Chast.* 19 Let it suffice that I walke in the vulgar tract, and divide sinne onely into originall and actuall. **1677** HALE *Contempl.* II. 25 In the same path and tract which leads us to Glorifie God, which is our Duty. **1752** HUME *Ess. & Treat.* (1777) II. 23 Any particular thought which breaks in upon the regular tract, or chain of ideas. **1834** H. MILLER *Scenes & Leg.* xxvii. (1857) 394 Men ..who, seeing nothing very knowing in simple honesty, exert their ingenuity in the opposite tract.

10. a. A mark or impression marking the course of a person, animal, or thing; a footprint, trail: = TRACE *sb.*^{1} 4, 5: cf. TRACK *sb.* 1. Now *rare* or *Obs.*; usually expressed by *track*.

a **1547** SURREY *Æneid* II. 920 A blasing sterre, dragging a brand of flame..By a long tract appointing us the way. **1565** JEWEL *Repl. Harding* (1611) 151 There appeared..the very tracts and steps of Christs feet. **1585** HIGINS *Junius' Nomencl.* 390/1 *Orbita*, the trace, tract, or furrow of a cart wheele. **1595** *Blanchardyn* v. B j b, He had not ridden long, but he perceiued the tracktes & footsteps of a horse. **1607** SHAKS. *Timon.* I. i. 50 But flies an Eagle flight..Leauing no Tract behinde. **1632** GUILLIM *Heraldry* III. xiv. (ed. 2) 175 Termes of footing or treading... That of a Fallow Deere [or] Boare is termed Tract or Treading. **1709** DAMPIER *Voy.* III. II. 35, I saw the Tract of an Alligator here. **1807** in Halliwell *Life Shaks.* (1887) II. 143 There was only one waggon tract along the lane. **1857** H. MILLER *Test. Rocks* xi. 435, I was struck..to see how nearly the tract of a small shore crab along the wet sand, resembled them.

†**b.** = TRACK *sb.* 8. *Obs.*

1542–3 *Act 34 & 35 Hen. VIII*, c. 26 §47 If any goodes.. be stolen..thenne upon suite therof hadde and made, the tracte shalbe folowed from Towneshipp to Township.

†**11.** A mark remaining where something has been; an indication, vestige (*lit.* or *fig.*): = TRACE *sb.*^{1} 6. *Obs.*

1583 GOLDING *Calvin on Deut.* clxviii. 1040 Wee shall be handled with such rigour as shall make all them to tremble which see but the tracts thereof. **1610** HOLLAND *Camden's Brit.* (1637) 281 Walles, which, as men may see by their tract, tooke up a mile in circuit. **1615** G. SANDYS *Trav.* 225 But no tract therof [of the Labyrinth] remained in the days of Pliny. **1646** SIR T. BROWNE *Pseud. Ep.* I. x. 37 To obscure the diviner part, and efface all tract of its traduction. **1698** J. CRULL *Muscovy* 57 The Ruins appear now in some places six foot high,..the Tract being quite lost in others.

†**tract,** *v.*^{1} *Obs.* [ad. L. *tractāre* to handle, transact, manage, discuss, treat, freq. of *trahĕre* to draw. Cf. F. *traiter*, OF. *traicter*, rarely *tracter*, to manage, TREAT (Godef.).]

1. *trans.* To negotiate: = TREAT *v.* 1 b.

1508 in *Lett. Rich. III & Hen. VII* (Rolls) I. 451 The l[ove and kindnes] that have been used in the tractinge of our said mariage.

2. To deal with in speech or writing; to discuss or discourse (*trans.*, or *intr.* with *of*): = TREAT *v.* 2, 2 b.

1529 *St. Papers Hen. VIII*, II. 149 Whiche thinge is not to be tracted, or retracted, till the Parliament. **1552** HULOET, Tract or treat of, *tracto*. **1588** A. KING tr. *Canisius' Catech.* 60 The sacraments..haue ane verray highe place in Christiane doctrine, and ar necessarie to be tractit of. **1607** TOPSELL *Four-f. Beasts* (1658) 396 Of all which kinde of traps shall be severally tracted: And first of all those which do catch Mice alive. *a* **1637** B. JONSON tr. *Horace's Art of Poetry* 202 The man, who..Saw many towns and men, and could their manners tract.

3. *trans.* To behave towards: = TREAT *v.* 7.

a **1548** HALL *Chron., Hen. IV* 15 b, The Erle..so gently and familiarly used and tracted the vulgare people. *Ibid.*, *Rich. III* 46 b, Nothinge contented that the erle of Richmonde was in his dominion so vncurteously tracted and entreated.

†**tract,** *v.*^{2} *Obs.* [f. L. *tract-*, ppl. stem of *trahĕre* to draw; cf. *attract, contract, extract*, etc. f. ppl. stem. In some uses associated with TRACE *v.*^{1} and TRACK *v.*^{1} and ^{2}.]

I. 1. *trans.* To draw, pull along, haul, tow. (Superseded by TRACK *v.*^{2})

1523 in *10th Rep. Hist. MSS. Comm.* App. v. 328 All.. goods and marchandis as shalbe labored, tracted, and adventured by ony of the inhabitants of this citie..oute of the haven and porte of the same, into ony where else. **1727** A. HAMILTON *New Acc. E. Ind.* I. xi. 123 To carry a great Number of Men for tracting them up against the Stream, when the Winds are against them. **1769** FALCONER *Dict. Marine* (1789) s.v. *Tract-scout* [= Du. *trekschuit*], It is usually tracted by a horse. **1769** [see *tracting* below].

2. To lengthen out, prolong, protract (time); to spend or waste in delay; to delay, put off.

1527 KNIGHT in Pocock *Rec. Ref.* I. xxviii. 57 The rivers not being alwaye passable he hath of necessity tracted the time. **1529** in Froude *Hist. Eng.* (1856) I. iii. 192 The causes depending..may..be in such wise tracted and delayed, as your subjects suing in the same shall be put to importable charges. **1579–80** NORTH *Plutarch* (1595) 606 He tracted time, & gaue them leisure to prepare to encounter his force. **1647** LILLY *Chr. Astrol.* xlix. 303 By dallying and tracting the time there shall be trouble.

b. *intr.* To be drawn out or prolonged, to continue: in *pres. pple.* protracted, continuous.

1592 [see *tracting* below].

3. *fig.* To draw on, draw out; to induce.

1615 [see *tracting* below].

II. 4. To go or travel along, tread, pursue (a path): = TRACE *v.*^{1} 3. Cf. TRACK *v.*^{1} 3. (In quots. *fig.*)

1579 TWYNE *Phisicke agst. Fort.* II. xxxv. 212 This path is but litle tracted. **1613** MARSTON *Insatiate Countess* I. A ij b, [Death] From whose sterne Caue none tracts a backward path.

5. To pursue or follow up by the footprints or traces; also *fig.*: = TRACE *v.*^{1} 5, TRACK *v.*^{1} 1.

1577 HOLINSHED *Chron.* II. 1007/2 In the ende, they brought him to tract the steppes of lewde demeanor. **1590** SPENSER *F.Q.* II. i. 12 By what meanes may I his footing tract? *Ibid.* vi. 39 As Shepheardes curre..Hath tracted forth some salvage beastes trade [= tread]. **1596** *Ibid.* VI. vii. 3 Well did he tract his steps as he did ryde. **1615** SIR E. HOBY *Curry-combe* To Rdr. 2 Hee that tracts a Fugitiue must take the By-path. **1654** FLECKNOE *Ten Years Trav.* 43 Which false rumours I tracted from the very Fountain.

6. To draw, delineate: = TRACE *v.*^{1} 11.

1611 SPEED *Hist. Gt. Brit.* VI. xviii. (1623) 99 Having seen it [a wall] so tracted in an ancient Chorographicall Chart.

7. *intr.* ? To border *upon*. *rare*$^{-1}$.

1611 SPEED *Theat. Gt. Brit.* xiv. (1614) 27/1 [Of Barkshire] the South neere Kennet doth tract upon Hampshire.

Hence †**'tracting** *vbl. sb.* and *ppl. a.*

1535 *Act 27 Hen. VIII*, c. 3 Without frustrate or wilfull delaye or tractyng of the tyme. **1592** WARNER *Alb. Eng.* VII. xxxvii. (1612) 179, I heard a tracting sound. **1615** J. STEPHENS *Ess. & Char., Huntsman* (1857) 202 The names of Foxe, Hare, and Bucke, be all tracting sillables; sufficient to furnish fifteen meales with long discourse in the adventures of each. Foxe drawes in his exploits done against Cubbes... Hare brings out his encounters [etc.]. **1769** FALCONER *Dict. Marine* (1789), *Tracting*, the act of pulling any vessel..along the stream of a canal or river, by means of a rope.

tractability (træktə'bɪlɪtɪ). [ad. L. *tractābilitās, -āt-*, f. *tractābilis* TRACTABLE: see -BILITY, -ITY.] The quality of being tractable; manageableness, docility.

1531 ELYOT *Gov.* I. xxi, Tractabilitie (which is to be shortly persuaded and meued). **1605** A. WARREN *Poverties Patience* ii, Vaine Perswasion, that deludes Fond Tractability with fallacies. **1778** [W. MARSHALL] *Minutes Agric., Digest* 41 A further proof of their tractability. **1849** LYTTON *Caxtons* I. iii, He, wild man,..not yet civilized into the tractabilities of home.

tractable ('træktəb(ə)l), *a.* [ad. L. *tractābilis*, f. *tractāre*: see TRACT *v.*^{1}, and cf. TREATABLE.]

1. That can be easily managed; docile, compliant, manageable, governable. (Of persons and animals, or their dispositions, etc.)

1502 ATKYNSON tr. *De Imitatione* II. iii. 182 To be conuersaunt with meke, tractable or charitable company. **1548** UDALL, etc. *Erasm. Par. Mark* Pref., The more noble courage and stomacke they be of, the more tractable they are. **1561** T. NORTON *Calvin's Inst.* I. 37 Rather with tractable willingnesse to learn, than with sharpnesse of wit. **1611** BEAUM. & FL. *Knt. Burn. Pestle* II. i, I'm glad the girl Is found so tractable. **1738** BERKELEY *Let.* 11 May, Wks. 1871 IV. 258 You have to do with people of no very easy or tractable spirit. **1832** SCOTT *Woodst.* ii, A large wolf-dog,.. as tractable as he was strong and bold. **1855** PRESCOTT *Philip II*, I. ii. (1857) 24 Philip..found the Aragonese legislature by no means so tractable as the Castilian.

b. Const. *to* with sb. or inf.; in quot. 1651, easily led or persuaded *to* or *to do* something.

1509 BP. FISHER *Funeral Serm. C'tess Richmond* Wks. (E.E.T.S.) I. 291 To god & to the chirche full obedyent & tractable. **1590** GREENE *Never too late* (1600) 82, I..found him not onely guiltie of the crime, but tractable to be reclaimed. *c* **1645** in *Verney Mem.* (1907) I. 428 She is witty & very tractable to please. **1651** BAXTER *Inf. Bapt.* 30 They are silly souls, and tractable to novelty.

†**c.** *transf.* of an action, etc. *Obs.*

c **1609** in *Capt. Smith's Virginia* III. xi. (1624) 89 He had oft brought the Salvages to a tractable trade. **1632** LITHGOW *Trav.* v. 203 Their education to this tractable expedition is admirable.

2. Of things (usually concrete): Easy to manage, deal with, handle, or work; manageable.

1555 EDEN *Decades* 334 This metall [gold] is a body tractable and bryght. **1654** EARL MONM. tr. *Bentivoglio's Warrs Flanders* 57 On which side the ground was more tractable. **1726** LEONI *Alberti's Archit.* I. 27/1 The Nut Tree ..is extremely tractable, and good for most uses. **1898** *Pall Mall Mag.* May 20 She had a small but exquisitely tractable voice. **1900** E. F. SCOTT *Fourth Gosp.* vii. 216 Elements.. not wholly tractable to his method of re-interpretation.

†**3.** That can be handled; palpable, tangible.

1605 WILLET *Hexapla Gen.* 203 These angels had palpable and tractable bodies. **1669** GALE *Crt. Gentiles* I. III. iii. 45 The visible and tractable Mater [matter]. **1694** HOLDER *On Time* i. 16 The other Measures..are of Continued Quantity, Permanent, and Visible, and for the most part Tractable; whereas Time is always Transient,..neither to be seen, nor felt, nor reserved.

†**4.** That one can 'do with' or put up with; tolerable, endurable. *Obs.*

1605 *Tryall Chev.* V. i. in Bullen *O. Pl.* (1884) III. 339 As soone As the cool winds haue fand [= fanned] the burning Sunne And made it tractable for travaylers. **1692** RAY *Disc.* 237 Eternity is the very sting of Hell: take that out, and the Sinner will think it tractable enough.

'tractableness. [f. prec. + -NESS.] The quality of being tractable; tractability.

1561 T. NORTON *Calvin's Inst.* II. 100 Vnlesse he did frame vs to that tractablenesse by his spirit. **1600** SIR W. CORNWALLIS *Ess.* iii. D j b, The tractablenes of his people might keep them in peace. **1726** LEONI *Alberti's Archit.* I. 27/2 None of these [trees] for Tractableness can compare with the Linden. **1860** HOLLAND *Miss Gilbert* v, A gentle sympathetic word would win her into tenderness and tractableness.

'tractably, *adv.* *rare*$^{-0}$. [f. as prec. + -LY^{2}.] In a tractable manner; manageably; with docility.

1611 COTGR., *Tendrement*, tenderly,..gentlely, tractably. **1727** BAILEY vol. II, *Tractably*, after a tractable Manner. Hence in JOHNSON and later Dicts.

† **tractal**, *a.* *Obs.* *rare*$^{-1}$. [? irreg. (for *tractual) f. L. *tractu-s* (see TRACT *sb.*^{3}) + -AL^1.] ? Intended to protract the time. (Cf. TRACT *sb.*^{3} 1 b.)

1632 LITHGOW *Trav.* III. 82 After tractall discourses, and deepe draughts of Leatick, reason failing, sleepe ouercame his sences.

tractarian (træk'tɛərɪən), *sb.* and *a.* [f. TRACT *sb.*^{1} + *-arian*; in 2, after *trinitarian*, etc.]

A. *sb.*

1. A writer, publisher, or distributor of tracts. *nonce-uses.*

(In quot. 1824, referring to the Religious Tract Society.) **1824** *Man of Letters* 15 May 99 The superiority of the vulgar version will be acknowledged, we think, even by the tractarians themselves. **1851** *Illustr. Lond. News* 30 Aug. 270/2 The fanatical tract distributors of London..an itinerant distributor... The Tractarian was silent. **1900** *Speaker* 12 May 170/2 To revive his [James VI's] reputation as a poet or a tractarian.

2. (Freq. with capital initial.) A member of that school of High Churchmen which maintained the doctrines and practices set forth in 'Tracts for the Times' (see TRACT *sb.*^{1} 3 b).

1839 C. BENSON *Disc. Tradit. & Episc.* Pref. 3 The tractarians, that is, the authors, editors, and approvers of the *Tracts for the Times*, are Divines of acknowledged piety, and sincerity, and learning. *Ibid.* 5 The tractarians, if without offence we may so call them. **1841** BP. D. WILSON *Let.* in Bateman *Life* (1860) II. xvi. 188 Her apostasy is like a standard-bearer fainting: and all aggravated by the opposite errors of the Tractarians. **1888** C. A. LANE *Notes Eng. Ch. Hist.* II. VI. xxix. 253 The Tractarians were the extreme wing of the modern 'High Church' party. **1892** F. HALL in *Nation* (N.Y.) 25 Aug. 145/1 Lawless in formation, certainly, is *Tractarian*; and yet it will live in history, to the exclusion of *Tractite*, *Tractuist*, and *Tractator*, all of which have been proposed in its stead.

B. *adj.* **1.** Of or belonging to the Tractarians (A. 2).

1840 I. TAYLOR *Anc. Chr.* (1842) II. 144 *note*, One of the most recent..publications of the Tractarian school. **1841** BP. D. WILSON *Jrnl.* 18 Nov., in Bateman *Life* (1860) II. xvi. 193 Having given my booksellers..orders to send me the Tractarian Controversy publications. *a* **1873** S. WILBERFORCE *Ess.* (1874) II. 262 So strong a Romeward tendency amongst the members of the Tractarian party. **1896** R. PALMER *Fam. & Pers. Mem.* I. xxvii. 397 The 'Tractarian' forces were shattered by the loss of their leader.

2. Distributing tracts. *nonce-use.*

1885 *Athenæum* 11 July 44 [Dr. Lansdell] was soon afterwards arrested for distributing tracts at railway stations... It is not very surprising that a policeman stopped the tractarian traveller.

Hence **Trac'tarianism**, the tenets or principles of the Tractarians, the Tractarian system; adherence to or maintenance of this; **Trac'tarianize** *v.*, *intr.* to teach, maintain, or practice Tractarianism (in **Trac'tarianizing** *vbl. sb.* and *ppl. a.*).

1840 (*title*) Hints to Transcendentalists for working Infidel Designs through *Tractarianism. **1841** BP. D. WILSON in Bateman *Life* (1860) II. xvi. 185 If he had not been imbued for seven years—steeped—in Tractarianism. **1899** BP. STUBBS *Visitation Charges* (1904) 344 What is called the Oxford Movement, the movement represented by the *Tracts for the Times*, Tractarianism as it is still called. **1842** G. S. FABER *Prov. Lett.* (1844) II. 137 More than one young *Tractarianising Cleric. **1880** G. A. SIMCOX in *Macm. Mag.* No. 245. 399 The imputation of tractarianising clung to Wilberforce however he might try to separate himself from the Tractarians.

tractate ('trækteɪt), *sb.* Also 6 *Sc.* tracteit, 6–7 tractat. [ad. L. *tractātus* (*u*-stem) a handling, treatment, discussion, treatise, f. *tractāre*: see TRACT *v.*^{1} Cf. Prov. *tractat*, Sp. *tratado*, It. *trattato*, Fr. *traité*; also Ger. *tractat.*]

1. A book or literary work treating of a particular subject; a treatise.

1474 CAXTON *Chesse* 1 This first chappitre of the first tractate sheweth [etc.]. **1549** *Compl. Scot.* Epist. 6 To present to ȝour nobil grace ane tracteit of the fyrst laubir of my pen. **1641** MILTON *Prel. Episc.* 3 Needlesse tractats stuff't with specious names. **1692** RAY *Disc.* III. ii. (1732) 411 A notable Passage taken out of Plutarch's Tractate. **1877** MORLEY *Crit. Misc.* Ser. II. 270 It was his own sense of the value of Liberty which led to the production of the little tractate. **1883** EDERSHEIM *Life Jesus* (ed. 6) I. 401 In the Rabbinic tractate on the Samaritans.

†**b.** The subject treated of. *Obs.* *rare*$^{-1}$.

1589 NASHE *Anat. Absurd.* 6 When as lust is the tractate of so many leaues, and loue passions the lauish dispence of so much paper.

†**c.** Literary treatment, discussion (*of* a subject).

1586 FERNE *Blaz. Gentrie* Ep. Ded., A matter of it selfe so honorable, namely the tractate and handling of the nobilities and armes of generositie.

†**2.** Negotiation, dealing, transaction. *Obs.*

1618 *Barnevelt's Apol.* F j, By reason of these fiue Regall Embassages, and tractates, it happened, that [etc.]. **1630** *R. Johnson's Kingd. & Commw.* 89 In Paris they dare talke of the Kings mistresses, intermeddle with all tractates of Parliaments and State.

† **'tractate**, *v.* *Obs.* *rare.* [f. L. *tractāre*: see TRACT *v.*^{1}, -ATE^3.] *trans.* To handle, deal with.

1657 TOMLINSON *Renou's Disp.* 669 Things..onely Medicinal..should be tractated by Pharmacopolists alone.

† **trac'tation.** *Obs.* [ad. L. *tractātiōn-em*, n. of action f. *tractāre*: see TRACT *v.*^{1} and -ATION.]

1. The handling or treating of a subject in discourse or writing; literary treatment, discussion.

1570 FOXE *A. & M.* (ed. 2) 22/2 The tractation wherof.. I do refre..to them, that haue more leysure. **1628** BP. HALL *Old Relig.* Ep. Ded. 6 A methode, and manner of Tractation, which might be of vse to plain vnderstandings. **1654** Z. COKE *Logick* 192 Tractation (or Handling) is the meditation of a Theme or matter to be done by Instruments of Art.

b. An instance of this; a passage or work treating of something; a discussion or treatise.

1555 in Foxe *A. & M.* (1563) 974/2 He did ther intreate of the sacrament in that tractation *De cœna domini.* **1577** HARRISON *England* II. v. (1877) I. 116, I might..make a long tractation of the round table. **1669** GALE *Crt. Gentiles* I. I. xi. 60 What I have..in this whole tractation laid down.

2. Conduct towards or dealing with a person or thing; treatment.

1548 *Act 2 & 3 Edw. VI*, c. 23 §2 Sentence for matrymonye, commanding solempnizacion, cohabitacion, consumacion and tractacion as becometh Man and Wyef to have. **1670** MAYNWARING *Vita Sana* i. 22 Irregular and unfit tractation of Infants.

3. Handling, manipulation (in *lit.* sense). *rare.*

1578 BANISTER *Hist. Man* I. 30 The prompt tractation, and handlyng, that now appertaineth to the hand. **1650** BULWER *Anthropomet.* 217 They nourish it much by Art and often tractation.

4. Negotiation, dealing, treaty. *rare*$^{-1}$.

1600 O.E. *Repl. Libel* II. v. 98 Any compact, packe, conspiracy, or tractation to any such purpose. [**1881** *Sat. Rev.* 17 Dec. 743/1 M. Gambetta thought that there might be even with Italy some sort of tractation. One of his hearers called out that this was quite a new word, and M. Gambetta ..replied that he had coined a word, because no existing word expressed the peculiarly delicate arrangement, or approach to an arrangement, which he had in his head.]

5. Use (of a word) in a particular sense. (= L. *tractatio*, Cicero *Part. Or.* v. 17.) *rare*$^{-1}$.

1660 *Author Healing in Church* 26, I have thus done with the General and Theological Tractation of the words.

† **trac'tator.** *Obs.* [a. L. *tractātor*, agent-n. f. *tractāre*: see TRACT *v.*^{1} and -OR 2 c.] One who treats of a subject; the writer of a tractate.

a **1638** MEDE *Wks.* (1672) 386 Justin Martyr, Theophilus Antiochenus, Irenæus, or that it may be another small Tractator or two. **1686** W. HOPKINS tr. *Ratramnus* Dissert. ii. (1688) 25 Phil. Labbe numbers him among the Catholick Tractators, Radbert, Lanfranc, and Guitmund. **1725** tr. *Dupin's Eccl. Hist. 17th C.* I. v. 65 This Name of Treatise was given to it [sermon], because the Holy Scripture was explained in it; and it is upon that account that the Preachers were call'd *Tractators.*

b. *spec.* Any one of the writers of 'Tracts for the Times': see TRACT *sb.*^{1} 3 b.

1842 KINGSLEY in *Life* (1877) I. 81 Talking of the Tractators—so you still like their tone! And so do I. **1844** R. M. BEVERLEY *Ch. Eng. Examined* Pref. (ed. 2) 12 The Oxford tractators..write for this one object, to bring Christians from the Scriptures into tradition.

tracta'torian, *a.* *Ch. Hist.* ? *Obs.* [f. late L. *tractātōri-us* (f. prec.) + -AN.] In ***tractatorian*** or ***tractatory letter***, late L. *epistola tractatoria*, a letter from a synod or council of bishops, so called from L. *tractātus* in the sense of a conference treating of sacred subjects. See Du Cange. Also **'tractatory** *a.* in same sense; *sb.* a tractatory letter.

1672–5 COMBER *Comp. Temple* (1702) 510 St. Augustine, who excommunicated Primianus the Donatist, and sent his Tractatorian letter to all his fellow Bishops to avoid him. *Ibid.* 513 The Tractatorian Epistle, which the Bishops sent in the Name of the Church of Ptolemais to all her sister Churches. **1725** tr. *Dupin's Eccl. Hist. 17th C.* I. v. II. 69 They call'd those Tractatory Letters, by which the Metropolitans invited the Bishops of their Province to Synods... The Excuses of the Bishops who could not come to the Synod were wrote at the Bottom of the Letter which was sent to them, which they call'd Tractory, or Tractatory.

‖ **tractatrix** (træk'teɪtrɪks). Pl. -trices (-trɪsiːz). [L. *tractātrix* (Martial, in sense 1), fem. of *tractātor* shampooer, also one who treats of a subject: see TRACTATOR.]

1. A female shampooer. *rare*$^{-1}$.

1874 M. COLLINS *Frances* II. 117 That stout Miss Susanetta, with her shrill voice, and her hands of the tractatrix, is a strange creature.

2. *Geom.* = TRACTRIX.

1828 in WEBSTER; hence in later Dicts.

tractatule ('træktətjuːl). *rare.* [f. TRACTATE (or L. *tractātus*) + *-ule*, dim. suffix, as in *globule*, *granule*, etc.] A small tractate or treatise.

1892 *Sat. Rev.* 28 May 636/1 The first [volume] contains a much more mixed multitude of tractatules. **1901** N. SMITH in *Fortn. Rev.* Oct. 403 The carnal man cannot help sighing for a tractate—a tractatule even of the tiniest—on English verse, from the Venerable One.

tract-boat, obs. form of TRACK-BOAT.

tracteit, obs. Sc. form of TRACTATE.

‖ **tractellum** (træk'tɛləm). *Biol.* Pl. trac'tella. [mod.L., f. L. *tract-*, ppl. stem of *trahĕre* to draw, after FLAGELLUM: cf. PULSELLUM.] The anterior flagellum of an infusorian, etc., which serves to draw the body after it in swimming. Hence **trac'tellate** *a.* [-ATE^2], furnished with a tractellum.

1880 KENT *Infusoria* I. 429 Among the free-swimming monoflagellate Infusoria.., where the locomotive appendage..fulfils during natation the rôle of a tractellum. **1891** *Cent. Dict.*, *Tractellate.*

† **'tractic.** *Obs.* *rare*$^{-1}$. [irreg. f. L. *tract-āre* (see TRACT *v.*^{1}), ? after *practic.*] = TRACTATE 1.

1651 N. BIGGS *New Disp.* §287 In our Tractick of simple waters.

tractiferous (træk'tɪfərəs), *a.* *nonce-wd.* [irreg. f. TRACT *sb.*^{1} + -(I)FEROUS.] Carrying tracts.

1879 *Yachtsman's Holidays* 52 That curious freak of nature, a tractiferous yachtsman.

tractile ('træktɪl, -aɪl), *a.* *rare.* [ad. late L. *tractil-is*, f. *tract-*, ppl. stem of *trahĕre* to draw: see -IL, -ILE.]

†**1.** Capable of being drawn out to a thread.

1626 BACON *Sylva* §839 The Consistencies of Bodies.. Fragile, Tough, Flexible, Inflexible, Tractile or to be drawne forth in length, Intractile, Porous.

2. That may be drawn, as money from a bank.

1892 STEVENSON & L. OSBOURNE *Wrecker* vii, Eight thousand..was liquid and actually tractile in the bank.

¶**3.** Erron. used for TRACTIVE.

1839 *New Monthly Mag.* LVII. 539 The distinction they have drawn between the tractile capabilities of the horse and the dog.

Hence **tractility** (træk'tɪlɪtɪ), the quality of being tractile; in quot. 1838, *fig.* capacity of being drawn out or protracted.

1713 DERHAM *Phys.-Theol.* v. ix. 350 Silver, whose Ductility and Tractility are very much inferiour to those of Gold. **1838** B. CORNEY *Controversy* 9 His subject possesses tractility.

tracting, *vbl. sb.*: see under TRACT *v.*^{2}

traction ('trækʃən). [ad. med.L. *tractiōnem* (Albertus, *a* 1250), n. of action from *trahĕre*, *tract-um* to draw. So F. *traction*, Sp. *traccion*, Pg. *tracção*, It. *trazione.*]

1. a. The action of drawing or pulling; draught: opposed to ***pulsion*** or pushing, and (in *Dynamics*) to ***pressure***.

force of traction, the force exerted in or required for traction. ***line of traction***, the line along which this force acts. ***angle of traction***, the angle between the line of traction and the surface along which the body is drawn.

1656 tr. *Hobbes' Elem. Philos.* (1839) 343 Motion is distinguished into pulsion and traction. **1837** WHEWELL *Hist. Induct. Sc.* (1857) II. 32 Bodies, on which pressure and traction are exerted. **1843** *Penny Cycl.* XXV. 109/2 When the angle of traction..is 15 or 16 degrees, a horse pulls with good effect... An example of the force of traction exerted by steam. **1868** DUNCAN tr. *Figuier's Insect W.* Introd. 25 The cockchafer..possesses a power of traction equal to more than 14 times its own weight.

b. *Phys.* and *Path.* A drawing or pulling of a part or organ (in an animal or plant) by some vital process, as the contraction of a muscle, or the tension of some adherent part.

1615 CROOKE *Body of Man* 544 In the traction of the first the lid is depressed; in the traction of the latter it is lifted vp. **1669** HOLDER *Speech* 163 The Malleus, being fixed to an extensible Membrane, follows the Traction of the Muscle. **1802** PALEY *Nat. Theol.* xi. (ed. 2) 222 The claws do their office in keeping hold of the support..by the traction of the tendons, in consequence of the attitude which the legs and thighs take by the bird sitting down. **1875** BENNETT & DYER *Sachs' Bot.* 728 The layers which are less turgid and grow more slowly are exposed to a passive traction which promotes their growth. **1876** *Clin. Soc. Trans.* IX. 192 There was..a slight..traction of face to the right side when the patient laughed.

c. A drawing or pulling movement used in massage, etc.: in quot. 1841 applied to the use of metallic tractors (see TRACTOR 1).

1841 *Fraser's Mag.* XXV. 89 The effects produced by traction, or the rubbing of metallic tractors, tipped with little lumps of wax, on the parts affected by pain, are well known. **1887** D. MAGUIRE *Art Massage* iii. (ed. 4) 51 Tractions are movements used on the articulations by pulling one part while holding the other. **1901** *Westm. Gaz.* 28 Nov. 10/2 Traction of the tongue—that is, moving it about in a rhythmical manner—has produced wonderful results in restoring the apparently dead (especially children) to life. Dr. Laborde, of Paris, is the discoverer of the treatment.

d. *fig.* Drawing, attraction, attracting power.

1649 E. REYNOLDS *Hosea* v. 18 Our conversion and sanctification comes from..a supernaturall and omnipotent traction. *a* **1711** KEN *Christophil* Poet. Wks. 1721 I. 425 His Love in Suavities distills, Preventions, Tractions sweet, Devout Christ-hymning Heat. **1883** A. H. WELSH *Eng. Lit.* I. VI. 384 He [Macbeth] feels the resistless traction of fate.

e. *Med.* A sustained pull applied to a part of the body to maintain the positions of fractured bones following reduction of the fracture; the state of being subjected to such a pull; so ***in traction***.

1885 *Boston Med. & Surg. Jrnl.* CXII. 545/1 The high pulleys..were used, as before, for oblique traction from the knee bands. **1939** W. C. CAMPBELL *Operative Orthopedics* ii. 97 The majority of apparatus for either suspension or traction of the upper extremity is extremely cumbersome. **1962** *Lancet* 13 Jan. 61/1 The patient had previously been treated by neck traction and by prolonged physiotherapy, without benefit. **1973** 'D. SHANNON' *Spring of Violence*

(1974) iii. 46 They had one leg in traction. **1981** R. S. H. Browne *Basic Facts in Orthopaedics* 95 Traction is used to overcome painful muscle spasm.

2. *spec.* The drawing of vehicles or loads along a road or track; esp. in reference to the power by which this is done, as ***horse, steam, electric traction***.

1822 Imison *Sc. & Art* I. 27 Dividing the beam..that the point of traction may be as much nearer to the stronger horse. **1826** J. Adamson *Sk. Inform. Rail-Roads* 38 Every change..has..added to our powers of tracktion. **1902** *Daily Chron.* 1 July 4/6 The three stages are horse-traction, steam traction, and electric traction.

b. *transf.* (*a*) A vehicle driven by some special power, as a motor car. *nonce-use.* (*b*) *Stock Exch.* Stocks connected with traction, as tramways, etc.

1896 *Westm. Gaz.* 13 Nov. 5/2 They attended the Court, having ridden in ten miles on the offending traction. **1903** *Daily Chron.* 5 Nov. 8/7 The victory for Tammany early in the session reflected strength in tractions and other municipal utility stocks. **1905** *Ibid.* 4 May 5/7 Prices worked lower. Coalers and tractions showed some strength.

3. Short for *force of traction* (as a measurable quantity); the amount of rolling friction (also ***traction of adhesion***) as measuring this (quot. 1877).

1825 J. Nicholson *Operat. Mechanic* 666 If the speed be increased from six miles an hour to eight, the horses have by no means 1-4th less work to do, supposing the friction a constant quantity, and the traction consequently the same. **1838** *Civil Eng. & Arch. Jrnl.* I. 350/1 A dynamometer, by which the traction might be measured with considerable accuracy. **1877** Knight *Dict. Mech.*, *Traction*, the adhesive friction of a wheel on a rail, a rope on a pulley, etc.

4. *Physical Geogr.* The rolling and bumping of particles along the ground by a stream or the wind.

1914 G. K. Gilbert in *Prof. Papers U.S. Geol. Surv.* No. 86. 15 This second division of current transportation is called by certain French engineers *entraînement* but has received no name in English. Being in need of a succinct title, I translate the French designation..by the word *traction.* **1954** W. D. Thornbury *Princ. Geomorphol.* iii. 48 Traction involves the partial support of the material being transported by the buoyancy of the water or air but consists chiefly of the rolling, pushing, and dragging along of rock particles which are too large to be lifted. **1968** R. W. Fairbridge *Encycl. Geomorphol.* 319/2 Wind carries rock and organic debris by traction, saltation and suspension. **1972** R. J. Small *Study of Landforms* ii. 40 In areas where ..chemical weathering is very active, streams may contain much of their load in solution, and traction, saltation and suspension may be correspondingly small.

5. *attrib.* and *Comb.*, as ***traction company, installation, instrument, movement, power***; **traction aneurism, diverticulum** (see quots.); **traction-gearing**, an inexact name for *friction-gearing* (friction *sb.* 5); **traction-load**, the weight of a locomotive engine or motor car which presses the driving-wheels upon the rail or ground so as to produce the requisite adhesive friction and prevent the wheel from slipping; **traction motor**, an electric motor designed for use in traction; **traction splint** (*Surg.*), a splint with an attachment for pulling upon the limb; **traction-wheel**, a driving-wheel.

1891 *Cent. Dict.*, **Traction-aneurism.* **1899** *Syd. Soc. Lex.*, *T[raction] aneurism*, an aneurism most commonly seen in children, due to traction of the aorta from an incompletely atrophied ductus Botalli. **1897** *Allbutt's Syst. Med.* III. 364 *Traction deverticula generally occur on the anterior wall of the œsophagus. **1899** *Syd. Soc. Lex.*, *T[raction] diverticulum*, a circumscribed sacculation of the œsophagus from the traction of the circum-œsophageal adhesions. **1877** Knight *Dict. Mech.*, **Traction-gearing*, an arrangement for turning a wheel and its shaft by means of friction or adhesion. **1879** *St. George's Hosp. Rep.* IX. 501 On three eyes a *traction instrument was used. **1900** Parshall & Hobart *Electr. Generators* 1. 232 For satisfactory commutation, *traction motors are designed with very high magnetisation at full load. **1950** *Times Rev. Industry* Sept. 25/1 The other two [locomotives] will have single-phase a.c. traction motors of special design. **1969** R. W. Smeaton *Motor Applic. & Maintenance Handbk.* viii. 5 Traction motors are very ruggedly built. **1887** D. Maguire *Art Massage* iv. (ed. 4) 106 Executing..some *traction movements. **1908** *Westm. Gaz.* 13 Feb. 5/2 American machines..are geared so low as to give them a maximum of *traction power at the expense of speed. **1935** *Sun* (Baltimore) 5 Apr. 3/2 The remedy..is use of '*traction splints', devices for automatically pulling ends of broken bones together and holding them. **1976** M. Machlin *Pipeline* xl. 443 He's got a bad break there. You'd better put that leg in a traction splint. **1877** Knight *Dict. Mech.*, **Traction-wheel*, a wheel employed in drawing or impelling a vehicle, as the driving-wheel of a locomotive or traction-engine.

Hence **ˈtractional** *a.*, of or pertaining to traction.

1877 Knight *Dict. Mech.* s.v. *Traction*, The tractional surface of a driving-wheel is the face of its perimeter.

ˈtraction-ˌengine. A steam-engine used for drawing heavy loads along an ordinary road; a road-engine (commonly as distinguished from a *locomotive* or railway-engine).

Also a similar engine used in agricultural work, e.g. for hauling the apparatus for thrashing to the required place, and then (as a stationary engine) driving the thrashing mechanism; or as a stationary engine for hauling a gang of ploughs across a field.

1859 *All Year Round* No. 30. 77, I met a huge lumbering Bonassus of a locomotive..staggering..about Agar-street, Strand. It was called, I believe, a Traction Engine, and will, no doubt, be useful in its generation. **1876** Routledge *Discov.* 19 The idea has been successfully realized in the traction engines lately introduced. **1903** *Motor. Ann.* 202 The law regulating the employment of traction engines on public roads is the Locomotives' Act, 1898.

† **ˈtractioner.** *Obs. rare.* [? f. tract *sb.*^{1} 4, or tract *sb.*^{3}] (?) One to whom a small parcel of land was leased: see quot.

1626 *Direct. to Ld. Deputy* in *S.P.*, *Irel.* CCXLIII. 304 (P.R.O.) That such of the Natives as ought to have leases of certain small Parcells of land in the said Plantacions and are [known] by the name of *Tractioners*, may have the said Leases made unto them at reasonable and moderate rentes.

tractise, obs. var of treatise.

† **ˈTractism.** *Obs.* [f. tract *sb.*^{1} + -ism.] = Tractarianism. So † **ˈTractite** = Tractarian *sb.* (also *attrib.* = Tractarian *a.*).

1834 Whately *Let.* in *Life* (1866) I. 241 Bishop..spoke for four hours, and the Tractites wrote about the removing of candlesticks. **1837** *Ibid.* 390 He perceived with me that the Hampden persecution was the first outbreak of Tractism. **1844** *Ibid.* II. 75 The Tractite path. **1844** in *Daily News* 4 Feb. (1869), I know that many of the opponents of the Tractites and not a few of the supporters expect that a church government would establish and extend Tractism.

† **tractitian** (trækˈtɪʃən). *Obs. nonce-wd.* [f. tract *sb.*^{1}, ? after *politician, practician.*] The writer of a tract or treatise. † **tracˈtitious** *a. Obs. rare*$^{-0}$ (see quot.).

1656 Blount *Glossogr.*, *Tractitious*, that handleth, toucheth or intreats of. **1831** *Fraser's Mag.* III. 483 Such scrubby and execrable treatment as the reverend Tractitian has received from this reviewer of his Principles of Dissent.

† **ˈtractive,** *sb. Sc. Obs.* [f. L. *tract-āre* to treat (cf. tract *v.*^{1}) + -ive.] = tractate 1.

1558 Q. Kennedy (*title*) Ane compendius Tractiue conforme to the Scripturis of almychtie God, ressoun, and authoritie. *a* **1575** *Diurn. Occur.* (Bann. Cl.) 62 The haill lordis past to the tolbuith, and thair proponit ane lang tractive, callit the confessioun of our faith.

tractive (ˈtræktɪv), *a.* [f. L. *tract-*, ppl. stem of *trahĕre* to draw, drag + -ive.] Having the property of drawing or pulling; used for traction.

1615 Crooke *Body of Man* 179 The motion of the expulsiue faculty is one, and that of the tractiue another. **1691** T. H[ale] *Acc. New Invent.* 118 Tractive and Pulsive forces upon swimming Bodies. **1839** *Civil Eng. & Arch. Jrnl.* II. 122/2 The tractive power of the driving wheels is very much reduced. **1859** Smiles *Stephenson* 199 The kind of tractive power to be employed in working the railway. **1894** *Athenæum* 25 Aug. 260/1 This has necessitated much heavier engines to increase the tractive force.

† **b.** *fig.* Attractive, enticing. *Obs. rare*$^{-1}$.

1658 T. Meriton *Love & War* iv. ii, If your own Queen by tractive Operation work effect.

ˈtractless, *a. Obs.* or *arch. rare.* [f. tract *sb.*^{3} 10 + -less.] = trackless.

1628 J. Doughty *Serm. Church-schismes* 14 There want not infinite tractlesse mazes, wherein they can lurke vndiscerned. **1818** *Hervey's Medit.* 190 Ye Fish, that rove through tractless [*earlier edd.* trackless] paths of the sea. **1899** *Westm. Gaz.* 19 Dec. 2/1 In tractless wastes that stretch to Southern Pole, Her restless keel takes its unhindered way.

tractlet (ˈtræktlɪt). [f. tract *sb.*^{1} + -let.] A small tract.

1889 E. Dowson *Let.* 27 Oct. (1967) 112, I have still a soul above tractlets. **1892** *Review of Rev.* 14 Apr. 413/2 This is a neatly-printed little tractlet. **1893** Rickett *Quickening Caliban* xiii, Packets of picture-cards and tractlets. **1895** E. Chester in *Mission. Herald* (Boston, U.S.) Jan. 16 Tens of thousands of our Tamil handbills or tractlets..are scattered through the..Madura district.

† **ˈtractly,** *adv. Obs. rare*$^{-0}$. [f. L. *tract-us* drawn, drawn out, protracted + -ly^2.] See quot.

1552 Huloet, Tractlye or treatablye, or by space or leasure, *tractim.*

tractor (ˈtræktə(r)). [Late or med.L. agent-n. from *trahĕre, tract-um* to draw: see -or.]

1. *pl.* (in full (***Perkins's***) ***metallic tractors***): Name of a device invented by Elisha Perkins, an American physician (died 1799), consisting of a pair of pointed rods of different metals, as brass and steel, which were believed to relieve rheumatic or other pain by being drawn or rubbed over the skin: see Perkinism. *Obs.* exc. *Hist.*

1798 C. C. Langworthy (*title*) A View of the Perkinean Electricity; or, an Inquiry into the Influence of Metallic Tractors. **1801** E. Darwin *Zoon.* (ed. 3) II. 63 With the supposed existence of ghosts or apparitions, witchcraft, vampyrism..and American tractors, such theories..must vanish. **1825** Southey *Lett.* (1856) III. 499 His prayers may cure just as well as tractors or animal magnetism. **1885** Whittier *Pr. Wks.* (1889) II. 314 Jacob Perkins, in drawing out diseases with his metallic tractors, was quite as successful as modern 'faith and mind' doctors.

2. One who or that which draws or pulls something. **a.** In general sense.

1856 Kane *Arct. Expl.* I. 149 His limbs..splendid tractors for the sledge. **1880** *Daily Tel.* 23 Sept., The introduction of the iron road with its steam-horse for tractor.

b. *Surg.* 'An obstetric forceps' (Knight *Dict. Mech.* 1877).

c. A traction-engine; a locomotive engine of any kind used for traction of loaded wagons, artillery, etc., on ordinary roads, or for drawing gang-ploughs; also, 'the frame and steel rope by which a gang of plows is drawn across a field by a traction-engine' (*Cent. Dict.* Supp.). In mod. use (now the usual sense), a rugged, powerful motor vehicle for drawing farm machinery, esp. one with large rear wheels and an elevated driving seat.

1901 *Daily Chron.* 2 Aug. 6/4 These transformers supply the overhead trolley wires, which feed special 'electrical tractors' running along the towing-path, and in these tractors the drivers sit and control operations. **1902** *Ibid.* 29 Oct. 3/4 The County Council has not yet sanctioned the use of the tractor, but it will come before the members for consideration at an early date. **1903** *Motor. Ann.* 253 Rhodesia has appealed to motor manufacturers to supply motor-wagons or tractors for use specially in hilly country. **1905** *Sci. Amer. Suppl.* 4 Nov. 24948/3 At the recent show of the British Royal Agricultural Society great interest was centered in the Scott motor tractor... The motor in this tractor is a 24-horse-power..standard Aster engine. **1910** *Sci. Amer.* 15 Jan. 51/2 American motor tractors used for plowing and threshing usually develop from 12 to 35 horse-power. **1917** *Isle of Ely & Wisbech Advertiser* 28 Nov., This Tractor will operate on any land... It maintains a firm grip without injuring the lightest surfaces. **1932** [see combine *sb.* c]. **1958** *Economist* 11 Jan. 94/2 Antarctica's native inhabitants, on seeing the tractor marks in the snow, may well..ask themselves what will happen next. **1972** R. Adams *Watership Down* xix. 111 Few places are far from human noise—cars, buses, motor-cycles, tractors, lorries.

d. *Aeronaut.* An airscrew mounted at the front of an aircraft so as to exert a pull; an aircraft having this. Usu. *attrib.* (see sense 4 below). Cf. pusher 2 c.

1903 *Work* 18 Apr. 171/1 A screw..working in front and acting as a tractor. **1909** [see kite *sb.* 3 c]. **1914** *Sphere* 7 Mar. 302/3 The Short and Sopwith tractors. **1980** H. F. King *Sopwith Aircraft 1912–20* 20 Concerning the two early Naval Sopwith tractors, it seems worth recording that a demi-official drawing once existed showing just such a machine.

e. The driving section of an articulated lorry.

1926 *Encycl. Brit.* II. 987/2 Another combination for heavy merchandise transportation consisted of a road tractor, which was merely a foreshortened truck chassis, and a semi-trailer. **1951** [see *landing-gear* s.v. landing *vbl. sb.* 8]. **1977** [see prime mover 3]. **1982** *New Scientist* 11 Nov. 339/2 A lorry that has been loaded quite legally will tend to become overloaded on the drive axle (the rear of the two axles on the tractor) if it is gradually unloaded from the rear.

f. The mechanism that draws the paper through a printer.

1970 *U.S. Patent 3,511,354* 2 A switch is operated to reduce the speed of the tractor whenever..an excess of forms queued between the tractor and the stacker is such that a forms jam is imminent. **1983** *Austral. Microcomputer Mag.* Sept. 88/3 The TDS-13 daisy wheel printer handles paper up to 15in wide and has variable tractors and a friction platen to accommodate both continuous forms and sheets.

3. *Geom.* (See quot.)

1867 Cayley *Math. Papers* VII. 73, I use the term 'tractor' to denote a line which meets any given lines. *Ibid.*, Four given lines may be directrices (generating lines) of the same hyperboloid, viz. every tractor of any three of the four lines is then a tractor of all the four lines.

4. *attrib.* and *Comb.*, as (sense 2 c) ***tractor-driver, -station***; ***tractor-drawn, -mounted*** adjs.; (sense 2 d) ***tractor aircraft, airscrew, biplane, machine, monoplane, propeller, screw, seaplane***; **tractorman**, one who drives a farm tractor; **tractor-trailer** *U.S.*, an articulated lorry; cf. *trailer-truck* s.v. trailer *sb.* 9.

1969 K. Munson *Pioneer Aircraft 1903–14* 110/1 A very early British Breguet bore the legend 'B. 3' on the rudder, the prefix letter indicating a tractor aircraft. **1932** *Rep. & Mem. Aeronaut. Res. Committee* No. 1522. 1 The magnitude of the retardation of air flow..has a mean value of 0·05 for a tractor airscrew in front of a medium body. **1912** S. F. Walker *Aviation* iv. 28 In the later form of biplane, known as the tractor biplane, the engine and propeller are placed in front. **1969** K. Munson *Pioneer Aircraft 1903–14* 98/1 Antoinette III was the alternative title of the Ferber IX, a tractor biplane..which was abandoned after only a few trial flights in..1908. **1943** J. S. Huxley *TVA* 43 (*caption*) Terraces, like the one being thrown up by a tractor-drawn grader..retain from 85 to 90 per cent. of the rainfall. **1971** *Power Farming* Mar. 57/1 The machine is tractor-drawn. **1945** H. J. Massingham *Wisdom of Fields* x. 208 The tractor-driver despises the hard work of the older countryman and soon..he will need an elevator to lift him on his seat. **1969** R. Blythe *Akenfield* 17 Most modern farms need..a good tractor-driver or two, as once they needed good ploughmen. **1928** C. F. S. Gamble *Story North Sea Air Station* iv. 67 He was then of the opinion that 'pusher machines' were superior to 'tractor machines'. **1980** H. F. King *Sopwith Aircraft 1912–20* 20 With a tractor aeroplane that was only a little faster than one of his motor-boats..Sopwith could hardly be content. **1946** J. W. Day *Harvest Adventure* xiii. 210 Grover, the head tractorman. **1976** *Northumberland Gaz.* 26 Nov., Farmers appreciate the difficulties faced by shepherds and tractormen, he said. **1960** Tractor monoplane [see monoplane]. **1960** *Farmer & Stockbreeder* 12 Jan. 83/2 Tractor-mounted rotary tiller. **1979** *Internat. Pest Control* Nov./Dec. 139/1 Larger units to fit tractor-mounted spray booms. **1910** R. Ferris *How it Flies* xx. 473 *Tractor propeller*, a propeller placed in front, so that it pulls the machine through the air, instead of pushing, or thrusting it from behind. **1910** C. C. TURNER *Aerial Navigation of To-day* viii. 127 In many monoplanes a single screw in front is used. It *pulls* the machine, and is often called a 'tractor' screw. **1969** K. MUNSON *Pioneer Aircraft 1903–14* 12 A Sopwith tractor seaplane. **1958** *New Statesman* 5 Apr. 423/2 The state is going to sell..some 20 billion roubles worth of farm machinery at present in the garages and parking lots of some 8,000 machine and tractor stations. **1965** M. MICHAEL tr. *J. Myrdal's Report from Chinese Village* (1967) I. 44 We hire one [tractor] from the tractor station at Yenan. **1949** Tractor-trailer [see JACK-KNIFE *v.*]. **1977** D. E. WESTLAKE *Nobody's Perfect* xi. 143 A large tractor-trailer was..trying to back into position.

Hence **tracto'ration**, the use of metallic tractors (see 1): also allusively; **'tractoring** *ppl. a.*, using metallic tractors; **'tractorism** = *tractoration*; **'tractorist**, one who uses metallic tractors; **'tractorize** *v.*, *intr.* to use metallic tractors; *trans.* to get by tractorizing (quot. 1803²); to treat with metallic tractors or similar appliances (quot. 1817); whence **'tractorizing** *vbl. sb.* and *ppl. a.* (All more or less *nonce-wds.* and *Obs.*). Also (in sense 2c) **'tractorcade** [-CADE], a procession of tractors; **'tractored** *ppl. a.*, ploughed or cultivated by tractors; **'tractoring** *vbl. sb.*, activity involving a farm tractor.

1803 (ed. 2) FESSENDEN (*title*) Terrible *Tractoration! A Poetical Petition against Galvanising Trumpery, and the Perkinistic Institution. **1861** O. W. HOLMES *Med. Ess.* Pref. (1891) 9 Homœopathy has not died out so rapidly as Tractoration. **1977** *Detroit Free Press* 11 Dec. 13-A/3 State and local police said there were no reports of traffic problems or arrests as a result of the so-called '*tractorcade'. **1981** *Observer* 22 Nov. 11/1 Towns throughout Northern Ireland will be choked with 'tractorcades' and marches. **1966** AUDEN *About House* 37 A house backed by orderly woods, Facing a *tractored sugar-beet country. **1803** FESSENDEN *Terrible Tractoration* III. xxv, And you'll confound the *tractoring folks By Haygarth's tale. **1949** E. COXHEAD *Wind in West* iii. 69 One [man] got out the tractor... When the tractoring was finished Les..got himself a fork from the byre. **1802–12** BENTHAM *Ration, Judic. Evid.* V. 189 The impostures that..have been seen acted on the spiritual and medical theatres: to exorcism, animal magnetism, and *tractorism. *Ibid.*, The operations..of the magnetist, and *tractorist no less so, in the expulsion of non-existent diseases. **1803** FESSENDEN (*title*) A Poetical Petition against *Tractorising Trumpery, and the Perkinistic Institution. *Ibid.* III. viii, To tractorise away our guineas. **1817** *Monthly Mag.* XLIII. 293 Which cures were performed..by tractorizing them with rusty nails.

tractory ('træktərɪ), *a.* and *sb. rare.* [ad. L. *tractōri-us* of or for drawing, f. *tract-*, ppl. stem of *trahĕre* to draw: see -ORY.]

†**A.** *adj.* Serving for traction; tractive. *Obs.*

1684 tr. *Bonet's Merc. Compit.* x. 368 He shews the various uses of his..tractorie Machine which he invented.

B. *sb.* †**1.** Old name for some part of a plough: see quot. *Obs.*

[**1607** J. CARPENTER *Plaine Mans Plough* xiii. 109 Now..let vs first consider of the Soule, which is that Instrument wherewith being fastened to the Oxen, the Husbandman rippeth vp his land for the Seede.] *Ibid.* xviii. 127 (*heading*) The 5. part of the Soole, is the Tractorie. *Ibid.* xxvii. 160 The Tawe, or that yron Rope which embracing the Beame, assureth it to the Tractory.

†**2.** *Ch. Hist.* = TRACTATORY *sb. Obs.*

1709 J. JOHNSON *Clergym. Vade M.* II. 179 If they cannot come, to write their excuse in the Tractory. **1725** [see TRACTATORY].

3. *Geom.* = TRACTRIX.

1820 G. PEACOCK *Examples Diff. Calc.* I. xxiii. 174 The mechanical tractory of a straight line upon a perfectly smooth plane is an inverted semicycloid. **1853** GLYNN *Power Water* 140 Mr. C. Schiele of Oldham..is the proprietor of this mill, and the curve he has adopted is one discovered by Huygens, in his investigation of the cycloid. It is one of those singular and beautiful curves called 'tractories', and in this case it is produced by drawing the centre point of a radius bar along a straight line, which is the axis of the curve. **1864** WEBSTER, *Tractory, Tractrix*, the curve described on a plane by a heavy point attached to a string, and drawn along by moving the other end of the string.

tractotomy (træk'tɒtəmɪ). *Surg.* [f. TRACT *sb.*³ + -O + -TOMY.] An operation in which certain nerve tracts in the brain are severed or destroyed.

1938 O. SJÖQVIST in *Acta Psychiatrica* (Copenhagen) Suppl. 17. 95 Section of the tract could be performed without accessory lesions or other disadvantages to the patients... The term *trigeminal tractotomy* is proposed for this operation. **1974** R. M. KIRK et al. *Surgery* iv. 61/2 Patients with intractable pain may be helped by division of the posterior nerve roots, spinothalamic tractotomy, and prefrontal leucotomy. **1980** *Daily Tel.* 27 Nov. 3/2 The operations being carried out on the four patients..was a stereo tractotomy, which involved the destruction of brain tissue at points the size of a pinhead by implanting radioactive particles.

‖**tractrix** ('træktrɪks). *Geom.* Pl. 'tractrices (-ɪsi:z). [mod.L. (Huygens) fem. of *tractor*: see TRACTOR, and cf. DIRECTRIX.] A curve such that the intercept on the tangent between its point of contact and a fixed straight line is constant; so called as being traced by the centre of gyration of a rigid rod of which one end is moved along the fixed straight line, or as being the form assumed by an inextensible string which is first laid straight upon a plane surface, and one end of it then drawn in a direction at right angles to that in which the string was laid. Also, one of a class of curves similarly traced, e.g. by movement along a fixed curve.

1727–41 CHAMBERS *Cycl.*, *Tractrix*, in geometry, a curve line, called also *catenaria*. [*Error*: the tractrix is the involute of the catenary, not the catenary itself.] **1843** *Penny Cycl.* XXV. 109/2 *Tractrix*, or *Tractory*, the name given to a curve described by a heavy point attached to a string, the other end of which is moved along a given straight line or curve. **1852** SALMON *Higher Plane Curves* vii. (1879) 289 The involute of the catenary is therefore a curve such that the intercept SN, on its tangent between the point of contact and a fixed right line, is constant. Such a curve is called the tractrix. **1877** B. WILLIAMSON *Int. Calc.* (ed. 2) vii. Ex. 9.

tract-scout, obs. form of TREKSCHUIT.

†**'tracture.** *Obs. rare*⁻¹. [ad. med.L. *tractūra* (Du Cange), f. *tract-*, ppl. stem of *trahĕre* to draw: see -URE.] Drawing, attraction, enticement.

1658 MANTON *Exp. Jude* 6 Wks. 1871 V. 192 The angels being created pure, they had no lust within to incline them; ..there was no evil tracture, no tempter; how could they sin?

‖**tractus** ('træktəs). *R.C. Ch.* [med.L. *tractus*, a spec. use of L. *tractus* 'drawing, drawing out', fr. *trahĕre* to draw; 'quia trahendo, id est tractim, canitur': see Du Cange s.v.] = TRACT *sb.*²

a **1450** MYRC *Festial* 64 Scho layth downe Alleluia and oþyr songys of melody, and takeþe forþe tractus, þat ben songys of mowrnyng, and sykyng, and longyng. **1493** *Festivall* (W. de W. 1515) 5 b. **1854** HELMORE *Pract. Lect. Plain Song* 20 Graduals, Tractuses, Sequences, and Hymns.

tractyse, obs. form of TREATISE.

trad (træd), *sb.* and *a. colloq.* **A.** *sb.* **1.** Short for *traditional jazz*. Also *attrib.*

1956 *Melody Maker* 12 May 8 (*heading*) The great trad battle. **1957** *Observer* 13 Oct. 3/5 Lyttelton, who found 'trad' (traditional jazz) became play-acting and a dead-end, has travelled far from the revival days. **1963** *Times* 4 May 13/3 In an ideal world all 'trad' bands would have a good gritty surface noise built in to give an air of authenticity to their records. **1965** G. MELLY *Owning-Up* xv. 194 In 1960 the Trad boom at its height, and a riot at Beaulieu. **1973** G. BEARE *Snake on Grave* viii. 41 The French like good trad and this was real old stuff out of..old Chicago. It was black men's music. **1979** *Globe & Mail* (Toronto) 14 June 13/6 Molson's Brewery is holding a Canadian Jazz Festival July 21 and 22. Fourteen trad bands will take the stand.

2. Abbrev. of TRADITIONALIST.

1956 *Melody Maker* 12 May 8/4 The 'trads' belong to a strange sort of exclusive society. **1957** S. TRAILL *Concerning Jazz* 11 Those devoted to the older form of the music are referred to by the monstrous and unlovely nickname 'trads', (short for traditionalists). **1960** *Guardian* 11 Jan. 5/2 The ski world is divided to-day between 'trads' and 'modernists'. **1985** *Church Times* 8 Feb. 6/3 A fresh cause for barriers to be raised between the trads and the trendies.

B. *adj.* Abbrev. of TRADITIONAL *a.*

1958 *Spectator* 25 July 133/2 A raucous trad-jazz group struck up 'Basin Street Blues'. **1964** *Harper's Bazaar* Nov. 110/2 For people who like to furnish as trad as possible. **1967** E. GRIERSON *Crime of one's Own* xiii. 108 What's going to happen to dear Dave when even his..dirty books seem tradder than *The Times*' fourth leader? **1974** C. O. BUCHANAN in R. C. D. Jasper *Eucharist Today* ii. 24 The Commission remained resolutely 'trad' until the Liturgical Conference of February 1966. **1981** *N.Y. Times Sunday Mag.* 4 Apr. 90/2 The British fashion press reports London's new look is that of the 'trad English gentleman'.

tradable ('treɪdəb(ə)l), *a.* Also tradeable. [f. TRADE *sb.* or *v.* + -ABLE.] That may be dealt with in the way of trade; marketable.

1599 ESSEX *Let. to Q. Eliz.* 25 June, in Moryson *Itin.* (1617) II. 35 Your good subiects may haue for their mony out of your Maiesties store, that which..may serue for their necessary defence, whereas if once they be tradable, the Rebels will giue such extreme and excessiue prices, that they will neuer bee kept from them. **1702** C. MATHER *Magn. Chr.* I. vi. (1852) 84 One ship..which they fraighted for England with the best part of their tradable estates. **1960** *Farmer & Stockbreeder* 5 Jan. 4/1 For good milling qualities around 25s per cwt, delivered, was the tradeable basis. **1975** *Accountancy* Sept. 32/2 It [*sc.* government spending] signifies a transfer of resources from the tradeable to the non-tradeable sector, which would literally kill the productive section of the economy.

Hence **trad(e)a'bility**.

1979 B. BROWN *Money Hard & Soft on Internat. Currency Markets* 2 A *sine qua non* of currency hardness is free tradability. Residents of the country of issue are permitted to buy and sell a freely tradable currency for foreign exchange. **1983** *Times* 16 Aug. 14/1 The BNOC argument is that Brent crude has a higher 'tradability'.

tradal ('treɪdəl), *a.* [irreg. f. TRADE *sb.* + -AL¹.] Of or pertaining to trade; commercial.

1872 *Lond. & China Telegraph* 4 Mar. 171/1 The true English jealousy with which he has always guarded the port and its tradal interests from outside enemies. **1905** A. STEAD *Gt. Japan* (1906) 392 Bugbears placed in the way of Japan's tradal relations with foreign countries.

traddle, dial. form of TREADLE.

trade (treɪd), *sb.* Forms: 4–6 *Sc.*, 7 trad, 4–7 *Sc.* traid, (5 tradde, 6 traude, trawde, thrade), 7 traide, 5 *Sc.*, 6– trade. [a. MLG. *trade* (*trâ*) fem., track (Schiller & Lubben), LG. *trade* (*traan*:—*traden*) track (Bremisch. Wbch.); also WFlem. *tra* (:—*trade*) walk, march, course (De Bo):—OS. *trada* str. fem. footstep, track = OHG. *trata*, MHG. *trate*, *trat* str. fem. footstep, trace, track, way, passage, f. WGer. ablaut-series *tred-*, *trad-* to TREAD. App. introduced into Eng. in 14th c. from Hanseatic MLG., perh. orig. in nautical lang. for the 'course or track' of a ship; afterwards used in other senses of ME. *trede* TREAD. Cf. also Norw. and Sw. dial. *trad* (Rietz) in similar senses, and see TROD.

In Branch I, senses 1–4 run more or less parallel with the early senses of TREAD *sb.*; in sense 5 differentiation begins, and in branch II the sense-development of *trade*, from *c* 1550, turns sharply away from that of *tread*, which retains its close connexion with TREAD *v.* But in Sc., *tred* continued to represent both *trade* and *tread*: see under TREAD.]

I. †**1. a.** A course, way, path; with *possessive* or *of*, the course trodden by a person, or followed by a ship, etc.; = TREAD *sb.* 3. *common trade*, a public thoroughfare. *Obs.*

c **1375** *Sc. Leg. Saints* xxxviii. (*Adrian*) 629 Sir adryane..bad þame..To þe richt hand þe stere set, & dresse þame to hald þare trad In-to þe sey as þai first had. *c* **1400** *Sc. Trojan War* II. 1725 Dryvand thiddir..and hiddir, That þai mycht hald no certane traid. *c* **1425** WYNTOUN *Cron.* VII. x. 3266 The king..tuke þe se hamewartis his way, Hald-and þare traid fast by Orknay. *a* **1547** SURREY *Æneid* II. 587 A postern ..there was, A common trade to passe through Priams house. **1552** HULOET, Trade, *via.* **1554** *Admiralty Crt., Exam.* 9. 28 Nov., The porte of Groyne standithe and is furthe of the right course and trade towards Cadix. **1561** *Ibid., Exam.* 13. 1 Apr., If the said pilott had followid the trade and course of thother Hamboroughe shippe. **1564** *Ibid., Libels* 35 No. 160 They feared their shippe woulde strike oon grownde yf he kepte that trade.

†**b.** *fig.* Cf. TREAD *sb.* 3 b. *Obs.*

1536 STARKEY *Let. to Cromwell* 24 July, in *England* (1878) p. xliii, You juge me more to be traynyd in phylosophye than in the trade of scripture. **1538** BALE *God's Promises* II, The covenaunt, whych I to Adam made, He regardeth not, but walketh a damnable trade. **1545** ASCHAM *Toxoph.* (Arb.) 98, I trust that you..haue so..noted the nature of it, that you can teache me as it were by a trade or waye how to come to it. **1547** *Homilies* I. *Serm. Gd. Works* III. (1859) 64 The right trade and pathway unto heaven. **1549** COVERDALE, etc. *Erasm. Par. Eph.* vi. 13 b, You shall not be lyke to the common trade of seruauntes. **1613** SHAKS. *Hen. VIII*, v. i. 36 Cromwell..Stands in the gap and Trade of moe Preferments.

†**2. a.** The track or trail of a man or beast; footprints; = TREAD *sb.* 1, 2. *Obs.*

13.. *Guy Warw.* (Caius) 4731 Than loked he aboute vnder the woode shawe: The trade of horse [*Auch.* hors traces] he there sighe. *c* **1470** HENRY *Wallace* v. 136 For thair sloith hund the graith gait till him ȝeid, Off othir trade [*ed.* 1570 tred] scho tuk as than no heid. **1537** *St. Papers Hen. VIII*, V. 97 Diverse of his tenauntes pursewed the trade with a slott hownd. **1590** SPENSER *F.Q.* II. vi. 39 As Shepheardes curre, that..Hath tracted forth some salvage beastes trade. **1591** —— *Tears Muses* 275 The sacred springs ..They trampled haue with their fowle footings trade. **1596** DALRYMPLE tr. *Leslie's Hist. Scot.* (S.T.S.) I. 21 The dog..seases noᵗ afor he find the trad of the fliaris.

†**b.** *transf.* The outer surface of the rim of a wheel, which makes the track or mark on the ground; the TREAD of a wheel. *Obs. rare*⁻⁰.

1556 WITHALS *Dict.* (1568) 18 b/1 *Orbita rotunditas*, a whele trade. *Ibid.*, The vtter parte of the whele, called the trade, *orbis*.

†**3. a.** Course, way, or manner of life; course of action; mode of procedure, method. *Obs.* or *dial.*

1456 SIR G. HAYE *Law Arms* (S.T.S.) 211 It war nocht lyke that thai folowit the trade of oure lord, quhilk in all his accioun was oure instructioun. *a* **1548** HALL *Chron., Hen. IV* 2 Kyng Richarde..was nowe brought to that trade of liuyng that [etc.]. **1549–62** STERNHOLD & H. *Ps.* CXIX. v. i, Instruct me Lord, in the right trade Of thy statutes diuine. **1560** BIBLE (Genev.) *Prov.* xxii. 6 Teache a childe in the trade of his way, and when he is olde, he shal not departe from it. **1567** MAPLET *Gr. Forest* 77 The Cat..is in hir trade and manner of liuing, very shamefast. **1571** *Calr. Carew MSS.* I. 410 Surety to leave their wicked thrade of life, and to fall to other occupation. **1633** BP. HALL *Hard Texts, N.T.* 176 In respect of the trade and course of their life. **1721** STRYPE *Eccl. Mem.* I. lii. 393 Commonly this was the trade: the better benefice, and the cure the more, the seldomer was the Parson or Vicar resident at home. *a* **1825** FORBY *Voc. E. Anglia* s.v., If this is to be the trade.

†**b.** A way or method of attaining an end; a contrivance, expedient. *Obs. rare.*

1572 J. JONES *Bathes of Bath* To Rdr. 1 The arte or trade of maintaining health. *Ibid.* Ep. Ded. 3 But also the Chyrurgians..may fynde a most apte trade of vnderstanding comprehended in few wordes. **1576** FLEMING *Caius' Dogs* (1880) 17 The water Spaniell,..hauing long, rough, and curled heare, not obtayned by extraordinary trades, but giuen by natures appointment.

c. A regular or habitual course of action; a practice or habit of doing something. *Obs.* exc. *dial.*

c **1586** C'TESS PEMBROKE *Ps.* LIX. i, Save me from those Who make a trade of cursed wrong. **1603** SHAKS. *Meas. for M.* III. i. 148 Thy sinn's not accidentall, but a Trade. **1608** —— *Per.* IV. vi. 74 Now prittie one, how long haue you beene at this trade? **1616** R. C. *Times' Whistle* v. 1719 Now let me discourse of drunkennes, Which..is made Even a common ordinary trade. **1652** J. WRIGHT tr. *Camus' Nat. Paradox* VI. 134 Shee had long since forgot the Trade of running away. *a* **1716** BLACKALL *Wks.* (1723) I. 194, I do not make a Trade and Custom of it. **1755** *Man* No. 33. 4 But it now growing a trade in the family to send for *aqua mirabilis*, the master..

forbad his servants to fetch any. *Mod. dial.* He made a trade of going to their house.

†**d.** Used *advb.* in phr. ***to blow trade***, of the wind, to blow in a regular or habitual course, or constantly in the same direction (cf. TRADE-WIND). So, of a ship, ***to run trade*** (rare). *Obs.*

1591–1600 J. JANE in Hakluyt *Voy.* (1600) III. 849 When we were shot in betweene the high lands [in Str. of Magellan], the wind blowing trade, without any inch of sayle, we spooned before the sea. **1670** NARBOROUGH *Jrnl.* in *Acc. Sev. Late Voy.* I. (1694) 84 Neither do I find the Winds to blow Trade; but they are veerable. **1719** DE FOE *Crusoe* 447 The Winds..seemed to be more steadily against us, blowing almost Trade, as we call it, from the East, and E.N.E. [in the China Sea]. **1720** —— *Capt. Singleton* (1906) 198 The winds generally blow trade from the S. and S.S.E. from May to September. **1722** —— *Col. Jack* (1840) 319 We ..kept our course W. by S..., running away, trade, as they call it, into the great gulf of Mexico.

†**4.** Practice; practical exercise, employment, or application. *Obs.*

1575 *Recorde's Gr. Artes* Pref. A v, Apt instrumentes,..if a man coulde applye them to vse, and by teaching of rules, frame them to better trade. *Ibid.* II. Ff j b, To acquainte your minde the better with yᵉ new trade of this rule. **1608** A. TODKILL in *Capt. Smith's Virginia* (1624) 66 The boates trimmed for trade, which..in their Iourney incountred the second Supply.

5. a. The practice of some occupation, business, or profession habitually carried on, esp. when practised as a means of livelihood or gain; a calling; formerly used very widely, including professions; now usually applied to a mercantile occupation and to a skilled handicraft, as distinct from a profession (PROFESSION 6 a), and *spec.* restricted to a skilled handicraft, as distinguished from a professional or mercantile occupation on the one hand, and from unskilled labour on the other. ***in trade***, following a mercantile occupation, *spec.* that of a shop-keeper.

In earliest use not clearly distinguishable from 3; the sense is developed by contextual additions, as *trade* (i.e. practice) *of husbandry*, *of merchandise*, *of fishing*, etc.

1546 *Reg. Mag. Sig. Scot.* 757/2 Except thai be in thair lefull marchandice, traudis and bissynes concerning the wynning of thair leving. **1583** STOCKER *Civ. Warres Lowe C.* I. 22 Againe to sette vppe, and place the accustomed trade of merchandise. **1601** SHAKS. *Jul. C.* I. i. 12 *Mur.* But what Trade art thou? Answer me directly... *Fla.* Thou art a Cobler, art thou? **1601** *Act 43 Eliz.* c. 2 §1 For settinge to worke all such persons..[who] use no ordinarie or dailie trade of lief to get their livinge by. **1638** JUNIUS *Paint. Ancients* 100 His father consulting with his kins-folkes about the trade he should put his sonne to, thought it best to make him a statuarie. **1656** in *Verney Mem.* (1907) II. 91 [If the boy were] to be fitted for a merchant or other trade. **1695** A. TELFAIR *New Confut. Sadd.* (1696) 1 Mackie..who is a Mason [*note* Stonecutter] by Trade, devoted his first Child to the Devil, at his taking of the Mason-Word. **1711** ADDISON *Spect.* No. 47 ¶7 A Neighbour of mine, who is a Haberdasher by Trade. **1737** *Gentl. Mag.* Mar. 189/1 Mr. Will. Potter, of Gainsborough,..By Trade a Butcher. **1798** WORDSW. *Peter Bell* I. 201 A Potter, Sir, he was by trade. **1813** *Sk. Character* (ed. 2) I. 16 He was in trade; and..Miss Aucherly was well aware, his being in trade was an obstacle impossible to be surmounted. **1816** JANE AUSTEN *Emma* II. vii. 118 On the other hand, they were of low origin, in trade, and only moderately genteel. **1828** SCOTT *F.M. Perth* xix, Old Dorothy Glover, as she was called, (for she also took name from the trade she practised). **1856** FROUDE *Hist. Eng.* I. i. 43 No person was allowed to open a trade..unless he had first served his apprenticeship. **1860** LD. DENMAN in *All Year Round* 5 May 83 Every trade..is a business, but every business is not a trade. To answer that description, it must be conducted by buying and selling, which the business of keeping a lunatic asylum is not. **1865** TROLLOPE *Can you forgive Her?* II. xv. 113 There was a little prejudice, because of his being in trade. **1932** LADY DUFF GORDON *Discretions & Indiscretions* v. 60, I could never be presented at Court, because I was in 'trade'. **1953** M. SHARP *Gipsy in Parlour* xii. 125 His father was in trade, and Frederick snubbed him. **1974** 'W. HAGGARD' *Kinsmen* x. 98 When he'd made a great fortune Duncan Gregg had gone up the ladder a little. But not very much, he was still in trade. **1979** A. MCCOWEN *Young Gemini* 53 Living in the Royal Borough of Tunbridge Wells, my father was made to feel over-conscious of being 'in trade'.

b. Anything practised for a livelihood.

1650 BAXTER *Saints' R.* III. xiv. §9 Let men see that you use not the Ministrie only for a trade to live by. **1651** in *Verney Mem.* (1907) I. 482 The multitude of peasants in Savoye which practise the trade of bandittis. **1653** MILTON *Hirelings* Wks. 1851 V. 371 They would not then so many of them, for want of another Trade, make a Trade of thir preaching. **1659** B. HARRIS *Parival's Iron Age* 141 Souldiers desire not an end of War; because they have no other Trade to live. **1693** J. DRYDEN *Juvenal* XIV. 251 A Captain is a very gainful Trade. **1746** FRANCIS tr. *Horace, Epist.* II. i. 167 Unfit for War's tumultuous Trade. **1865** KINGSLEY *Herew.* i, Where learnedst thou so suddenly the trade of preaching? **1878** SIMPSON *Sch. Shaks.* I. 32 Her first venture in the trade which subsequently proved so profitable to her, that of buccaneering.

6. a. ***the trade***: those engaged in the particular business or industry concerned or in question; *spec.* the publishers and booksellers; now more commonly, those engaged in the liquor trade.

1697 DRYDEN *Virg. Past.* IX. 44 A Member of the tuneful trade. **1791** BOSWELL *Johnson* 15 Apr. an. 1778 *note*, As Physicians are called the Faculty,..the Booksellers of London are denominated the Trade. **1837** SIR F. PALGRAVE *Merch. & Friar* Ded. 1 The reluctance with which the 'trade' engage in any work purporting to consist of ancient documents. **1846** H. BRETT *Let.* 17 Oct. in *Licensed Victuallers' Guide & Almanack* (1848) 2, I enclose a copy of the Permit..suggesting that a reprint of it in your Almanack would be highly appreciated by the Trade. **1868** JOYNSON *Metals* 63 Many thousands of tons of 'Bessemer metal'—for the 'trade' are not quite sure whether it is iron or steel. **1868** *Era Almanack* (Advt. Suppl.), Licensed Victuallers' Protection Society, instituted October, 1833, for the protection of the person and property of the licensed vitualler, and for the promotion of the best interests of the trade. **1885** *Cyclist* 19 Aug. 1101/2 Interesting to Cyclists and the Trade. **1885** *Liverpool Echo* 14 Nov., The *Morning Advertiser*,..discussing the action of 'the Trade' in the coming contests, takes a very moderate view. **1886** C. E. PASCOE *Lond. of To-day* xxxix. (ed. 3) 329 Some of the publishing houses of London..are as ready to sell to the general public as to 'the trade'. **1903** *Westm. Gaz.* 7 Mar. 2/2 The House of Commons read a second time yesterday two Bills connected with 'the trade'. The first..was to bring home to the innkeeper his statutory liability to provide food as well as drink.

b. Any one of the corporations of craftsmen (usually seven in number) in a Scottish burgh, each of which formerly elected one or more members of the town-council.

1777 MAYNE *Siller Gun* I. i, Ae Simmer's morning, wi the sun The Seven Trades there Forgather'd. **1781** *Set of the Burgh* (of Hawick), Confirmed by Court of Session, that there presently are, and shall henceforth continue seven Incorporations within the said burgh, vizt.:—Weavers, Tailors, Hammermen, Skinners, Fleshers, Shoemakers, and Baxters, each of which shall..elect two quartermasters for each trade, to continue in office for one year. **1838** W. BELL *Dict. Law Scotl.* s.v. *Burgh, Royal*, In Edinburgh and Glasgow, the convener of trades and the dean of guild are *ex-officio* members of council. **1860** COSMO INNES in Gordon *Hist. Moray* ii. (1882) 23 Do the Bailies and the 'Trades' fill the eye in their fine new Church..?

c. Prostitution. *slang.* [Cf. TRADER 1 b.]

1680 OLDHAM in Rochester *Poems* 122 He Heav'n, one large Seraglio, made, Each Goddess, turn'd a glorious Punk, o' th' Trade, And all that sacred place, Was filled with Bastard Gods, of his own Race! **1937** PARTRIDGE *Dict. Slang* 905/2 *The trade* is prostitution: late C. 18–19. **1962** K. A. PORTER *Ship of Fools* 33 Two inordinately dressed-up young Cuban women, frankly ladies of trade, had been playing cards together in the bar for an hour before the ship sailed.

d. The Submarine Service of the Royal Navy. *slang.*

1916 KIPLING *Sea Warfare* 97 No one knows how the title of 'The Trade' came to be applied to the Submarine Service. **1942** G. HACKFORTH-JONES *One-One-One* xviii. 169, I remember in 1919 listening to and looking at the young submarine captains, most of whom had served their four years of war in the 'Trade'. **1982** A. MELVILLE-ROSS *Trigger* xv. 161 It had been tacitly established in 'The Trade' that you did not mourn friends... The Submarine Service referred to itself as 'The Trade'.

e. The Secret Service. *slang.*

1966 'A. HALL' *9th Directive* xviii. 170 'How long,' I asked her, 'have you been in the trade?'.. 'Three years, on active ops.' **1977** J. GARDNER *Werewolf Trace* x. 87 Heather had that smart plummy voice which spoke of a cut-glass background. The kind of girl the trade enjoyed using: the kind they called a *lady*. **1977** *3rd Rep. R. Comm. Intelligence & Security: Abridged Findings* (Austral.) 4 In the trade, people talk of the 'intelligence cycle'.

II. 7. a. *lit.* Passage to and fro; coming and going; resort. Now *dial.*

1591 SYLVESTER *Du Bartas* I. v. 133 Some [fish] from the Sea..So both the Waters with free Trade frequenting. **1593** SHAKS. *Rich. II*, III. iii. 156 Ile be buryed in the Kings high-way, Some way of common Trade, where Subjects feet May howrely trample on their Soueraignes Head. **1624** DONNE *Devot.* (ed. 2) 154 In Jacobs ladder, they which ascended and descended, and maintained the trade between heaven and earth. **1868** ATKINSON *Cleveland Gloss.* s.v., A vast o' rabbits here, by the trade they make.

†**b.** *fig.* Mutual communication, intercourse, 'commerce', dealings. *Obs.*

1602 SHAKS. *Ham.* III. ii. 346 Haue you any further Trade with vs? **1634** MASSINGER *Very Woman* IV. iii, Long was my travail, long my trade, to win her. *a* **1708** BEVERIDGE *Thes. Theol.* (1710) I. 183 Free trade and commerce for grace and goodness for heaven and happiness.

c. To-do, 'work', fuss, commotion; trouble, difficulty. *dial.*

1854 MISS BAKER *Northampt. Gloss.* s.v., They make such a trade wi' me when I goo to see 'em. **1895** *Westm. Gaz.* 21 Sept. 2/1 What there was in him to make such a trade of, as his wife did, I could not see. **1899** *Leeds Merc., Supp.* 3 June (E.D.D.), They'll hae plenty o' trade on afore they mak' t' business pay.

8. a. Passage or resort for the purpose of commerce; hence, the buying and selling or exchange of commodities for profit; commerce, traffic, trading. †***to beat the trade***, to carry on business (*obs.*). See also FREE TRADE.

1555 EDEN *Decades* 240 The trade of spices which was so commodious and profitable to hym. **1570** J. CAMPION in Hakluyt *Voy.* (1599) II. 114 A safe conduct from the great Turke, for a trade to Chio. **1604** *Hoi. Comm. Jrnl.* I. 218/2 The Mass of the whole Trade of all the Realm is in the Hands of some Two Hundred Persons. **1611** *Reg. Mag. Sig. Scot.* 171/1 Cum privilegio aque de Clyde, mercature lie trafficque et trade ejusdem. **1670** R. COKE *Disc. Trade* 1 Trade is an Art of Getting, Preparing, and Exchanging things Commodious for Humane Necessities and Convenience. *a* **1687** PETTY *Pol. Anat.* (1691) 34 Ann. 1664 ..was the best year of Trade that hath been these many years in Ireland. *a* **1692** POLLEXFEN *Disc. Trade* (1697) 91 The Trade to Swedeland and Denmark having of late Years carried from us great Sums of Money Annually. **1707** HEARNE *Collect.* 12 Nov. (O.H.S.) II. 72 Dr. Davenant..has writ..an Essay upon Ballance of Trade. **1818** SCOTT *Hrt. Midl.* ii, Contraband trade..is not usually looked upon, either by the vulgar or by their betters, in a very heinous point of view. **1835** *Penny Cycl.* III. 309/1 The balance of trade..is the difference between the aggregate amount of a nation's exports or imports, or the balance of the particular account of the nation's trade with another nation. **1889** *Nature* 19 Sept. 492/2 The struggle for the Eastern trade.

†**b.** A trading expedition. *Obs. rare*⁻¹.

1725 DE FOE *Voy. round World* (1840) 356 This new scheme of a trade round the World.

†**c.** A centre of trade, an emporium. *Obs. rare*⁻¹.

1618 in Foster *Eng. Factories Ind.* (1906) I. 27 Surratt will never be a trade unles the Red Sea both supply yᵗ and awe the Guzeratts.

9. With *a* and *pl.* An act of trading, a transaction, a bargain; *spec.* in politics, a private arrangement, a 'deal' or 'job'. Orig. *U.S. slang.*

1829 *Massachusetts Spy* 18 Mar. (Thornton), When the business was completed, there was about an even trade between Mr. A. and Farmer G. **1835–40** HALIBURTON *Clockm.* (1862) 347 Havin' finished that are little trade, squire, there is another small matter I want to talk over with you. **1867** LOWELL *Fitz Adam's Story* in *Heartsease & Rue* (1888) 158 Yet in a bargain he was all men's foe, Would yield no inch of vantage in a trade. **1888** BRYCE *Amer. Commw.* II. III. lxiii. 458 This is a Deal, or Trade, a treaty which terminates hostilities for the time.

(*b*) *spec.* (*N. Amer.*) an exchange of players between two sports clubs or teams.

1913 *Outing* XLII. 133/1 My first big trade was a success. **1968** *Globe & Mail* (Toronto) 10 July 27/5 Riders made another trade, sending Larry De Graw and Bill Cline to Regina Roughriders for Tom Beynon. **1976** *National Observer* (U.S.) 12 June 14/3 The Yankees, who had been spying on Randolph for a year, picked him up last winter in a trade that sent Doc Medich to Pittsburgh for Randolph, Dock Ellis and Ken Brett.

†**10.** A fleet of trading ships under convoy. *Obs.*

1747 *Gentl. Mag.* Nov. 519/1 The signal for the trade to make the best of their way. **1748** *Anson's Voy.* I. ii. 15 This squadron,..and the trade under their convoy,..tided it down the Channel. **1803** NELSON in Nicolas *Disp.* (1845) V. 194 On my arrival at Malta I ordered the Cyclops to proceed with the Trade from thence bound into the Adriatic.

11. a. Stuff, goods, materials, commodities; now *dial.*, usually in depreciatory use: rubbish, trash; in quot. 1697, implements, equipment.

1645 T. WILSON (*title*) Childe's Trade; or the Beginning of the Doctrine of Christ, whereby Babes may have Milk, Children Bread Broken. **1670** NARBOROUGH *Jrnl.* in *Acc. Sev. Late Voy.* I. (1694) 27 These Herbs..for want of which fresh Trade several of my Men were falling into [the Scurvy]. *Ibid.* 58 Green Pease-leaves and such trade. **1697** DRYDEN *Virg. Georg.* III. 535 His house, and household gods, his trade of war, His bow and quiver, and his trusty cur. **1707** MORTIMER *Husb.* (1721) II. 177 They are sown at two Seasons of the Year; in the Spring with other like Kitchen Trade. **1777** *Horæ Subs.* 438 (E.D.D.), I took some trade, which I had of the doctor for my disorder. **1858** SIMMONDS *Dict. Trade, Trade*,..a Derbyshire mining term for refuse or rubbish from a mine. **1875** *Sussex Gloss.*, *Trade*, anything to carry; such as a bag, a dinner-basket, tools or shop-goods. **1889** FARMER *Americanisms* s.v., Medicine is also strangely named *trade* in Rhode Island.

b. A prostitute or pick-up used by a homosexual; a homosexual partner; also, such people collectively. *slang.*

1935, etc. [see *rough trade* s.v. ROUGH *a.* 21 a]. **1941** G. LEGMAN in G. W. Henry *Sex Variants* II. 1177 Trade, generic for male prostitutes to homosexuals, or for heterosexuals to whom homosexuals prostitute themselves. **1968** *Globe & Mail Mag.* (Toronto) 13 Jan. 7/4 If a hustler is not himself homosexual, or maintains the belief that he is not, he is called 'trade'. **1969** *Jeremy* I. III. 23/1 These are men who because they are too old, or unattractive, cannot pick up free 'trade'. **1975** *Daily Tel.* 24 July 3/6 Many of the boys became male prostitutes... They became known as 'rent boys' and were also referred to as 'trade'.

12. Commodities for use in bartering with primitive peoples; also, native produce for barter.

1847 J. PALMER *Jrnl.* 127 The value of fourteen dollars in trade would buy an ordinary horse. **1883** CHESTER in Lovett *J. Chalmers* vii. 239 About £50 worth of trade was distributed to the heads of families. **1884** *Pall Mall Budget* 22 Aug. 9/1 One of these boats has on board the 'trade', as we call the goods by which purchases are effected. **1897** MARY KINGSLEY *W. Africa* 517 Look what a lot of trade he threw away at that funeral of his wife.

13. Abbreviation of TRADE-WIND; chiefly in *pl.*

c **1796** T. TWINING *Trav. Amer.* (1894) 14 The increasing unsteadiness of the wind denoted that we were upon the edge of the 'Trade'. **1806** PINCKARD *Notes W. Ind.* I. xviii. 186 The delay..served but to augment the value of the ever-constant trades. **1853** HERSCHEL *Pop. Lect. Sc.* iv. §19 (1873) 157 The great and permanent system of winds known as the 'trades' and 'anti-trades'. **1857** C. GRIBBLE in *Merc. Marine Mag.* (1858) V. 9 From this I carried a steady Trade, all sail set. **1880** HAUGHTON *Phys. Geog.* iv. 188 The so-called north-east monsoons..are simply the usual Trades of the northern hemisphere. **1899** F. T. BULLEN *Log Sea-waif* 213 The 'south-east trades' being notoriously steady and reliable in the Atlantic, while the north-east trades are often entirely wanting. **1899** 'MARTELLO TOWER' *At School & at Sea* 88 The trade slackened and became fitful.

14. A trade paper or magazine of the entertainment world. orig. and chiefly *U.S.*

1960 G. MARX *Let.* 21 Mar. in *Groucho Lett.* (1967) 270, I assume the trades are shoved under your door each morning. **1969** [see PLANT *sb.*¹ 7 b]. **1978** *Guardian* 11 Dec. 7/2 In Hollywood the two newspapers which report the entertainment industry are known simply as 'the trades'.

III. 15. *attrib.* and *Comb.* **a.** attrib.: in sense 5, 'of or pertaining to a trade or calling', as ***trade-body***, ***-caste***, ***-company*** (COMPANY *sb.* 6), ***-guild***, ***journal***, ***magazine***, ***paper***, ***press***, ***protection***, ***skill***, ***-work***; 'caused by or arising out of one's trade', as ***trade disease, eczema, eruption***; in sense 8, as ***trade advice, agreement, association, attaché, balance, bill, boom, competition, conflict, delegation, depression, fair, figure*** (usu. *pl.*), ***gamble, mart, partnership, product, profit, relation, reverse, rivalry, ship, site, supply supremacy, token*** [TOKEN *sb.* 11], ***town, use, value, wave, word***; in sense 12, 'pertaining to or used for barter', as ***trade bag, blanket, boat, box, calico, chest, gin, glass, goods, gun, stuff***; **b.** instrumental, objective, etc., as ***trade-bound, -destroying, -laden*** adjs.; ***trade-spoiler, -taxer***.

1860 READE *Cloister & H.* lxxxvi, Good *trade advice was to flow from the elders. **1934** WEBSTER, *Trade agreement. **1940** *Economist* 23 Mar. 514/2 Three agreements between the British and Spanish Governments, a Loan Agreement, a Payments Agreement and a Trade Agreement, were signed in Madrid. **1977** *Whitaker's Almanack 1978* 929/1 Portugal has signed a Trade Agreement with EEC. **1909** WEBSTER, *Trade association. **1928** *Britain's Industr. Future* (Liberal Industr. Inquiry) II. viii. §3. 98 Trade Associations are Associations of Traders, Producers, or Employers. **1984** *Economist* 18 Feb. 22 The BBC, IBA and the ITV companies' trade association are all off to Dublin to discuss such an Anglo-Irish deal. **1970** 'D. HALLIDAY' *Dolly & Cookie Bird* vi. 79 The *trade attaché moved a bit nearer. **1980** A. COPPEL *Hastings Conspiracy* xxxvii. 227 He was a trade attaché... He would know with whom to speak to provide a friend of the Soviet Union with friendship. **1907** *Chron. Lond. Mission. Soc.* Oct. 185/1 My mackintosh served as a blanket, and my *trade-bag as a pillow. **1909** WEBSTER, *Trade balance. **1928** *Britain's Industr. Future* (Liberal Industr. Inquiry) I. iii. §4. 26 The increased volume of imports, together with a diminished volume of exports, has made the visible trade balance much less favourable. **1984** *Times* 28 Nov. 13/7 Our trade balance sags under imports of consumer goods. **1892** GRIFFITH tr. *Fouard's St. Peter* 268 *Trades-bodies, political assemblies, and societies for mutual aid. **1925** *Scribner's Mag.* July 59 Nothing in the nature of a '*trade boom' could be discovered. **1928** Trade boom [see *trade cycle*, sense 16 below]. **1897** MARY KINGSLEY *W. Africa* 166 My back is against the *trade box, and behind that is the usual mound of pillows. **1891** E. WESTERMARCK *Hist. Hum. Marr.* (1894) 372 [In India] there is an almost endless number of *trade-castes. **1876** B. MARTIN *Messiah's Kingd.* VI. i. 289 The embittered *trade-conflicts which distinguish our era. **1961** 'J. LE CARRÉ' *Call for Dead* ix. 93 If Blondie was a carrier, it is exceptional.. that he should use a *trade delegation as a staging post. **1978** R. V. JONES *Most Secret War* liii. 520 He had somehow made contact with the Russian Trade Delegation. **1928** *Trade depression [see *trade cycle*, sense 16 below]. **1908** W. JAMES *Mem. & Stud.* (1911) xiii. 322 Priggishness is just like painter's colic or any other *trade-disease. **1899** *Allbutt's Syst. Med.* VIII. 569 A patient suffering from a *trade eczema. *Ibid.* 914 Affections of the Skin produced by Occupations (*Trade Eruptions). **1970** 'D. HALLIDAY' *Dolly & Cookie Bird* iv. 45 One was the commercial attaché.. and the three others were straight from Moscow on a *trade-fair excursion. **1927** *New Republic* 12 Oct. 194/2 The Washington government is alarmed at the growing hostility toward us in Central and South America, which is beginning to be reflected in our *trade figures. **1975** in R. Crossman *Diaries* I. 40 The First Secretary and the Chancellor continued to grapple with the trade figures and to lament the unhappy state of the pound. **1853** LYNCH *Self-Improv.* v. 122 There is much money-getting by *trade-gamble. **1897** MARY KINGSLEY *W. Africa* 664, I give an.. Analysis of Sample of *Trade-Gin. **1881** J. HATTON *New Ceylon* v. 136 The voyage up, with the *trade goods, is done in a canoe. **1874** GREEN *Short Hist.* iv. §1. 163 A wiser instinct of government led Edward to establish *trade-guilds in the towns. **1904** W. M. RAMSAY in *Expositor* July 42 The workers in bronze were one of its numerous trade-guilds. **1873** R. F. BURTON in Lady B. *Life* (1893) II. 20 Those who must often expose themselves.. to Anglo-Ashanti *trade-guns. **1878** *Brooklyn Monthly* Apr. 118/2 The editor of a certain *trade journal in New York. **1910** H. G. WELLS *Hist. Mr. Polly* vii. 218 Every issue of every trade journal has its four or five columns of abridged bankruptcy proceedings. **1981** P. VAN GREENAWAY '*Cassandra*' *Bell* ii. 27 I'm a special features writer for a trade journal—cosmetics. **1897** MARY KINGSLEY *W. Africa* 239 A picturesque series of canoes, fruit and *trade laden. **1907** *Electr. World* XLIX. 674/1 And in other cases space in the *trade magazines has been used as before. **1973** E. MCGIRR *Bardel's Murder* iv. 90 Forrest's desk was.. bare except for a trade magazine. **1904** *Speaker* 9 Apr. 31/2 A *trade-mart should be established. **1903** E. L. SHUMAN *Practical Journalism* 100 Sometimes the easiest line of approach to these coveted posts is through the avenue of the *trade paper or technical journal. **1918** A. BENNETT *Roll-Call* I. ix. 208 It was a chap from the *Builder*, or I wouldn't have seen him. Can't trifle with a trade paper, you know. **1971** *Guardian* 1 July 11/2 The trade papers try to introduce retailers to modern marketing. **1907** *Electr. World* XLIX. 674/1 In some cases the house organ has taken the place of advertising in the *trade press. **1973** 'D. HALLIDAY' *Dolly & Starry Bird* x. 147 She could announce it in the trade press. **1863** FAWCETT *Pol. Econ.* IV. vii. (1876) 626 We have to ascertain whether rates are to be regarded as a deduction from *trade-profits, or whether they are a tax imposed upon the consumers of merchandise. **1883** *Chambers's Encycl.*, **Trade Protection Societies* are associations composed of merchants, tradesmen, and others,.. for the promotion of trade, and for protecting the individual members from losses. **1888** E. BELLAMY *Looking Backwards* xiii. 198 A basis of agreement as to what staples shall be accepted.. for settlement of accounts, being a preliminary to *trade relations. **1897** *Boston* (Mass.) *Jrnl.* 3 Feb. 7/4 British subjects looking for friendly trade-relations. **1874** FORSTER *Dickens* XI. i. (1907) 883 *Trade reverses at Glasgow had checked the success there. **1902** *Q. Rev.* July 243 The bitter *trade-rivalry with France. **1757** DYER *Fleece* II. Poems (1761) 103 The *trade-ship left his streams; the merchant shun'd His desart borders. **1935** *Discovery* Feb. 61/2 Last January there were only 49 deep-sea square-rigged trade ships in the world. **1872** YEATS *Growth Comm.* 301 A *trade site established twenty-one years earlier. **1693** W. FREKE *Art of War* iii. 24 Is your war with a *Trade-state, pen them but in, and stop their Course. **1662** R. MATHEW *Unl. Alch.* §89. 156 That which is *Trade-stuff is fetcht more out of the Firr-tree, then out of the Scurff of Amber. **1888** HASLUCK *Model Engin. Handybk.* (1900) 10 Purchased.. from the usual *trade-supplies. **1910** *Encycl. Brit.* VI. 789/2 Maintenance of *trade-supremacy in the eastern Mediterranean. **1903** *Speaker* 26 Sept. 597/1 The two sections—the 'food-taxers' and the '*trade-taxers'.. can unite in office again. **1889** G. C. WILLIAMSON (*title*) *Trade tokens issued in the seventeenth century. **1933** J. O. MANTON (*title*) Buckinghamshire trade tokens issued in the seventeenth century. **1971** J. R. S. WHITING *Trade Tokens* 11 Broadly speaking I have kept to the strict definition of the term *trade token* (tokens issued for trading purposes, ie as currency). **1657** OWEN *Commun. w. Father*, etc. iii. §3 Wks. 1850 II. 244 According to the *trade use of the word, whence the metaphor is taken. **1891** *Daily News* 15 Apr. 2/5 No doubt the highest point in the *trade-wave has been reached and passed.

16. a. Special combs.: **trade allowance** (see quot. 1858); **trade binding** (see quot. 1971); **trade board**, a council regulating conditions of employment in certain trades; **trade book**, a book published by a commercial publisher and intended for general readership; **trade card**, a tradesman's card bearing his name, the designation of his trade, and place of business; **trade counter**, an area in a shop or business where sales are made only to members of the trade; **trade cumulus**, the cumulus which collects in the trade-wind region in the daytime; the trade-wind cloud; **trade cycle**, a recurring alternation of a period of increased economic activity with one of reduced activity; **trade dinner**, a dinner at which representatives of a trade meet; **trade discount**, a discount allowed by one trader to another, usually one in the same kind of occupation; also *fig.*; **trade dispute**, any dispute between employers and workers, or between different groups of workers, that is connected with the employment or non-employment of any person, with the terms or conditions of employment, or with certain related matters; **trade dollar**, a dollar issued by the U.S.A. for Asiatic trade: see DOLLAR 5; **trade-edition**, (*a*) (see quot. 1849); (*b*) an edition of a book intended for general sale through bookshops, in contrast to special editions or those sold through book clubs or specialist suppliers; **trade effluent**, effluent produced in the course of a trade or industry; any effluent other than domestic sewage; **trade-English**, a pidgin English used in Africa as a medium of communication between English traders and Africans, and between Africans speaking different languages; **trade-fixture**, a fixture put in for trade purposes (which remains the property of the tenant) (*Funk's Stand. Dict.* 1895); **trade gap**, the extent by which a country's imports exceed its exports; cf. *trade surplus* below; **trade-hall** (see quot.); **trade-language**, a language used as a means of communication by people speaking different languages; **trade-last** *U.S.*, a compliment offered in exchange for one that is directed towards the speaker; also, in weakened sense, a compliment, whether reciprocal or not; **trade-master**, one who instructs a class in a trade or handicraft; **trade mission**, a mission sent to another country to promote trade with it; **trade name**, (*a*) a descriptive or fancy name used to designate some proprietary article of trade; (*b*) the name by which an article or substance is known to the trade; (*c*) the name or style under which a business is carried on; **trade-officer**, in a penal institution: = *trade-master*; **trade plate**, a temporary number-plate for an unlicensed vehicle; usu. *pl.*; **trade price**, the price at which the wholesale dealer sells to the retailer; **trade-rat**, a pack rat (lit. and fig.); **trade reduction** = *trade-discount* above; **trade-road**, a trade-route; **trade-room**, a room (in quot., on board ship) devoted to the storage and exchange of trade goods; **trade-route**, a route followed by traders or caravans, or by trading-ships; **trade-sale**, an auction held by and for a particular trade; **trade school**, a school in which handicrafts are taught; **trade secret**, a device or technique used in a particular trade or (*transf.*) occupation and giving an advantage because not generally known; **trade show** *Cinemat.*, a private showing of a new film to the trade, before release; so **trade-show** *v. trans.*; **trade surplus**, the extent by which a country's exports exceed its imports; cf. *trade gap* above; **trade term**, an expression largely confined to a particular trade; **trade test** (see quot.); hence **trade-test** *v.*, to subject to or carry out a trade test; **trade war**, a situation in which governments act aggressively in international markets to promote their own countries' trading interests; **trade waste** = *trade effluent* above; †**trade-way**, (*a*) ? beaten path; passage, thoroughfare; (*b*) the fairway of navigation; **trade-weighted** *a.*, esp. of exchange rates, weighted in relation to the importance of the trade conducted with the various countries included. See also TRADECRAFT, -MARK, UNION, -WIND.

1837 DICKENS *Let.* ? 21 Apr. (1965) I. 250, I want at the usual *trade allowance.. a complete set of the Standard Novels up to this time. **1858** SIMMONDS *Dict. Trade, Trade-allowance, Trade-price*, a wholesale discount, allowed to dealers or retailers on articles to be sold again. **1952** J. B. OLDHAM *English Blind-Stamped Bindings* 3 Copies already bound in what are usually called '*trade bindings'. **1971** L. M. HARROD *Librarians' Gloss.* (ed. 3) 645 *Trade binding.* 1. The binding in which a publisher issues a book... 2. Plain calf or sheep bindings which were used in England by publishers from the fifteenth–eighteenth centuries... Until the nineteenth century, purchasers usually bought books unbound or enclosed in wrappers. **1909** *Daily Chron.* 26 Mar. 6/4 To-day the President of the Board of Trade will introduce the new *Trade Boards Bill, dealing with what are known as 'sweated' trades. **1962** Y. MALKIEL in Householder & Saporta *Probl. Lexicography* 9 Other short word-lists.. include,.. on the *tradebook market, glossaries accompanying contemporary novels and short stories. **1977** *Globe & Mail* (Toronto) 17 May 16/7 Last year 39 percent of the company's sales came from elementary school texts, 7 per cent from university texts and 19 per cent from trade books for the general public. **1927** B. C. LANDAUER (*title*) Early American *trade cards. **1979** *Early Music* Oct. 475/1 The instrument was certainly rebuilt by Taskin in 1783–4, as attested by his two inscriptions, his trade card glued inside the bentside, and his characteristic workmanship throughout. **1977** *Wandsworth Borough News* 7 Oct. 21/3 (Advt.), Young person required by Builders' Merchants in Battersea to assist on *trade counter and learn trade. **1979** P. WAY *Sunrise* vi. 61 David Marriott entered the newspaper building, via the trade-counter door. **1928** *Britain's Industr. Future* (Liberal Industr. Inquiry) v. xxviii. §2. 411 The trade booms.. and trade depressions.. which were so prominent a feature of the pre-war '*trade cycle'. **1976** *Scotsman* 20 Nov. 3/3 The industry was notoriously vulnerable to the trade cycle, and, at present, world supply of shipbuilding capacity was about twice the level of world demand. **1898** G. VAN DE LINDE *Bookkeeping & Other Papers* 414 **Trade Discount*, see 'Cash Discount'. **1901** *Windsor Mag.* Dec. 199/2 Barclay is simply a surly brute, I never liked him, so you can take the usual trade discount off my estimate. **1977** C. RUNDLE *Accountancy for Everyone* vi. 54 The same rate of trade discount must be taken off the return value as was allowed off the original price. **1875** *Act 38 & 39 Vict.* c. 86 §3 An agreement or combination by two or more persons to do or procure to be done any act in contemplation or furtherance of a *trade dispute between employers and workmen shall not be indictable as a conspiracy if such act committed by one person would not be punishable as a crime. **1926** *Brit. Gaz.* 12 May 2/1 No trade dispute has been alleged or shown to exist in any of the unions affected except in the miners' case. **1980** *Illustr. London News* Mar. 19/2 In that case it was held that the interpretation of section 13 was subjective, and that a person was protected provided he honestly thought that his action might help one of the parties to a trade dispute to achieve their objectives, and did it for that reason. **1849** *N. & Q.* 1st Ser. I. 55/2 A custom.. which now passes under the designation of a '*Trade-Edition', the meaning.. being, that the copyright, instead of being the exclusive property of one person, is divided into shares and held by several. **1930** A. HUXLEY *Let.* 8 Mar. (1969) 332 With regard to subsequent unlimited trade editions, I imagine you wouldn't have the organization. **1949** R. CHANDLER *Let.* 3 May (1981) 174 Houghton Mifflin.. want to publish a trade edition collection of my old stories. **1959** L. M. HARROD *Librarians' Gloss.* (ed. 2) 160 *Large paper copy*, or *edition*, an impression of a book printed on larger and better quality paper than the usual trade edition. **1930** *Engineering* 11 July 47/2 (*heading*) *Trade effluents and sewers. **1976** *Eastern Even. News* (Norwich) 9 Dec. 16/6 (Advt.), The post will involve the routine implementation of trade effluent control. **1897** MARY KINGSLEY *W. Africa* 432 That peculiar language, '*trade English'; it is not only used as a means of intercommunication between whites and blacks, but between natives using two distinct languages. *Ibid.* 434, I have a collection of trade English letters and documents, for it is a language that I regard as exceedingly charming. **1961** *Listener* 16 Nov. 816/1 Britain's '*trade gap' narrows during October. **1977** P. JOHNSON *Enemies of Society* v. 55 These fresh supplies of bullion bridged the trade-gap between West and East until western industry was sufficiently developed to mass-produce textiles for export. **1858** SIMMONDS *Dict. Trade*, **Trade-hall*, a meeting-hall, or sale-room in a town, for manufacturers or traders. **1662** OWEN *Animadv. Fiat Lux* Wks. 1851 XIV. 142 [Latin] is the *trade-language of religion among learned men. **1840** Trade language [see CHINOOK]. **1907**, etc. [see MOBILIAN *sb.*]. **1937** M. COVARRUBIAS *Island of Bali* p. xxiii, Malay was the trade language between Balinese and foreigners. **1968** W. J. SAMARIN in J. A. Fishman *Readings Sociol. of Lang.* 661 *Trade language* (*langue de traité*) is usually used for some language not included among the world's majority languages and which is used by some people as a second language in commercial situations. **1891** KIPLING in *Author* July 42 Some day they'll be a Public—not a girl's school swapping *Trade-lasts. **1895** *Inlander* Nov. 61 *Tradelast*, n., compliment. **1920** F. SCOTT FITZGERALD *This Side of Paradise* i. 12 It was based upon some 'trade-lasts' gleaned at dancing-school, to the effect that he was 'awful good-looking'. **1935** H. DAVIS *Honey in Horn* iv. 41 The compliment was pointed enough. Uncle Preston looked pleased but not overwhelmed. He was used to trade-lasts from the ignorant. **1949** M. MEAD *Male & Female* 456, I set myself to collect varieties of little-known folk-customs like trade-lasts. **1975** I. SHAW *Nightwork* v. 57 'While on the subject,' she said, 'let me give you a t.l.' 'What's a t.l.?' '..

T.l. stands for trade last. A compliment. You gave almost the best performance of anyone I've slept with in this town.' **1888** *19th Cent.* Nov. 759 In our prisons the school-master and the *trademaster take the place of the executioner. **1964** S. BELLOW *Herzog* 172 Through a Japanese *trade mission she also met Mr. Nasser and Mr. Sukarno. **1973** *Times* 24 Apr. (São Paulo Suppl.) p. viii/4 The Japanese presence is very real in São Paulo, and on average two trade missions visit the city every week. **1861** in Sebastian *Digest of Cases* 112 So far as the name was used..as a *trade name, the representatives of J. G. Loring were entitled under the Massachusetts Statute (Gen. St. c. 56) to restrain them [etc.]. **1878** SEBASTIAN *Law of Trade Marks* 12 In imitation of trade names..used as such and not as trade marks on goods. **1898** *Patent Office Reports* XV. 134 Goods marked with a trade name (i.e. Brazilian Silver). **1900** HOPKINS *Law unfair Trade* 29 Proper names are not trade marks, and.. there should not be such a thing as a technical trade name. **1904** A. GRIFFITHS *50 Yrs. Public Service* xix. 269 Sometimes *trade officers, such as tailor, shoemaker, or serving mistress, helped themselves to materials from store. **1953** J. WAIN *Hurry on Down* v. 99 The other [formality] was to unscrew the *trade plates which the cars carried in place of the regulation number plates they would have when licensed. **1978** J. FLEMING *Day of Donkey Derby* 110 I've got two sets of number plates, and just for luck, two lots of trade plates. **1805** SCOTT *Let.* 29 Mar. (1932) I. 244 He will of course expect what every author is entitled to—half profits upon the *trade price when an edition shall be disposed of. **1822** —— *Nigel* Introd. Epist., You shall have it at trade price. **1912** R. A. WASON *Friar Tuck* xxiv. 239 Either the pack-rat reformed into a *trade-rat, or else he sold out his claim to a trade-rat. **1948** F. BLAKE *Johnny Christmas* II. 79 Johnny slept that night..disturbed neither by Gitt's snoring nor the scuttle of secretive trade-rats over the packed earth floor. **1970** R. SYMONS *Broken Snare* xxiii. 157 He knew pack rats—trade rats some people called them. They would always make a trade for anything they took. **1852** MRS. GASKELL *Let.* 22 Nov. (1966) 213 Your Uncle Langshaw is to have the *trade reduction of price. **1866** LIVINGSTONE *Last Jrnls.* (1873) I. i. 18 Our course is..in 'wadys', from which, following the *trade-road, we often ascend the heights. **1840** R. H. DANA *Bef. Mast* xiii. 28 The cargo having been entered in due form, we began trading. The *trade-room was fitted up in the steerage. **1873** T. T. COOPER *Mishmee Hills* 33 Calcutta Chamber of Commerce convened a meeting 'for the purpose of discussing the subject of overland *trade-routes with China'. **1876** R. E. LYTTON *Lett.* (1906) II. xiv. 37 The trade-routes have been re-opened. **1791** J. LACKINGTON *Memoirs* xxxi. 230, I purchased very large numbers..at *trade-sales of all sorts, as bankrupt sales, sales of such as had retired from business, [etc.]. **1847** WEBSTER, *Trade-sale*, an auction by and for the trade, especially that of the book-sellers. **1861** *Chambers's Encycl.* II. 230/2 Trade sale. **1910** W. PARKER in *Encycl. Brit.* XI. 352/2 The skins are sold in the trade sale as martens, but as there are many that are of a very dark colour and the majority are almost as silky as the Russian sable, the retail trade has for generations back applied the term of sable to this fur. **1898** *Engineering Mag.* XVI. 133/1 The Proficiency of the *Trade School Plumber. **1906** *Westm. Gaz.* 3 May 12/2 The day trade-schools provided by the Council for the training of boys and girls in certain trades after they leave the elementary schools. **1895** *Atlantic Reporter* XXX. 521/1 (*heading*) Injunction—use of *trade secrets. **1928** R. B. MCKERROW *Introd. Bibliogr.* II. x. 235 Some of the best [facsimiles] are, I believe, produced by a process of lithography, but the details are probably a 'trade secret'. **1942** *R.A.F. Jrnl.* 13 June 36 The chemicals used to produce this foam are a trade secret, so I am not able to tell you what they are. **1978** G. GREENE *Human Factor* II. iii. 82 They have secrets too—trade secrets. **1919** *Biograph* 8 Mar. 3 (Advt.), If you want a film that will pack your house nightly, book The Bride's Awakening... *Trade show will be announced shortly. **1919** *Honey Pot* I. iv. 44 The picture will be trade shown during next February. **1927** G. B. SHAW in *Illustr. London News* 3 Dec. 1004/1 If you have ever been to what is called a 'trade show' and seen all the exhibitors there, [etc.]. **1946** R. CHANDLER *Let.* 30 May (1981) 75 The picture has not even been trade-shown. **1962** N. STREATFEILD *Apple Bough* xv. 214 I'll look out for you at the trade show of the picture. **1984** *Listener* 15 Mar. 8/1 For the other six nights, orchestral works give way to pop, dance.., conferences, trade shows and sport. **1977** *Time* 12 Dec. 18/2 Riding the crest of a gigantic *trade surplus, which last week led to a Japanese Cabinet shake-up.., the yen has risen 22% against the dollar so far this year. **1946** O. JESPERSEN *Mankind, Nation & Individual* 164 Some of these *trade-terms may have originally sprung up as slang. **1977** *Drive* Sept.–Oct. 113/2 He may remember to avoid such obvious trade terms as *hole in the roof* for sunshine roof. **1934** WEBSTER, **Trade test*, a test of proficiency in a given trade, such as plumbing. **1946** *R.A.F. Jrnl.* May 147 Those who were A.C.2s or A.C.1s will be *trade-tested immediately on remustering to their trade. **1960** I. JEFFERIES *Dignity & Purity* vi. 122 Once it had become apparent that I wasn't trade-testing..they [*sc.* the workmen]..did me the favour of answering the questions I..put. **1909** *Cambr. Mod. Hist.* VI. ii. 49 The tariff-war was often the precursor of the *trade-war. **1975** J. DE BRES tr. *Mandel's Late Capitalism* xiv. 472 The use of currency manipulations to gain short-term export advantages threatens to turn into a general trade war. **1902** *Encycl. Brit.* XXXII. 525/1 We may..enumerate some of the principal *trade wastes; these are from dye-works, print works, [etc.]. **1600** SURFLET *Countrie Farme* v. iv. 665 Let them be ditched round about..to cut off the *trade waies of passengers. **1643** *Admir. Crt., Exam.* 58, 1 June, [A ship wrongly anchored in] the trade way. **1976** *Financial Times* 11 Feb., Sterling fell to its lowest level ever against major currencies yesterday, with the Bank of England calculation for its *trade-weighted average depreciation widening to 30·4 per cent from 30·3 per cent. **1984** *Times* 31 Mar. 21/8 Sterling's trade-weighted value against a basket of currencies fell to the lowest for a year yesterday.

b. Combinations with *trades* (pl. or for genitive *trade's*), as **trades-combination** = TRADE UNION; **trades committee**, a committee which regulates conditions of employment in a trade; †**trades-master**, one who has mastered a trade; a master workman (in quot. 1657, as distinct from a journey-man); **tradesperson**, nonce-singular of *tradespeople*. See also TRADESFOLK, TRADESMAN, TRADESPEOPLE, TRADES UNION, TRADESWOMAN.

1910 J. W. HARPER *Soc. Ideal* xxxiii. 272 *Trades-combinations and masters' unions..are stages of progress. They are not final institutions. **1842** COBDEN in Morley *Life* xii. (1902) 43/2, I would rather live under a Dey of Algiers than a *Trades Committee. **1612** R. FENTON *Usury* 96 If he be his *trades-master, he shall not stand in so great need of Gods blessing as other honest men do. **1657** J. WATTS *Dipper Sprinkled* 174 Then to commence Merchant or Trades-master. **1886** E. WARD *Dress Reform Problem* iii. 50 A saving of trouble..both to the *tradesperson and the wearer.

trade (treɪd), *v.* Forms: see prec. [f. prec.]

†**1.** *trans.* To tread (a path); to traverse (the sea); *fig.* to go through, lead (one's life). *Obs.*

1548 H. HARTE (*title*) Godly Newe short treatyse instructyng euery parson howe they shulde trade theyr lyues in yͤ Imytacyon of Vertu and yͤ shewyng of vyce. **1551** RECORDE *Pathw. Knowl.* To Rdr., I will not cease from trauaile the pathe so to trade, that finer wittes maie fashion them selues with such glimsinge dull light. **1556** in S. P. H. Statham *Dover Charters* (1902) 386 All others as tradethe and travaquythe the Narrowe Sease. **1598** SYLVESTER *Du Bartas* II. ii. III. *Colonies* 725 Timber-Trees (Whereof thou buildest Ships and Houses fair To trade the Seas). **1599** NASHE *Lenten Stuffe* (1871) 30 But I have traded them as frequently as the middle walk in Sᵗ Paul's. *a* **1649** DRUMM. OF HAWTH. *Conv. B.J. & W.D.* Wks. (1711) 226 They can hardly be compared together, trading diverse paths.

†**2.** *intr.* To tread, step, walk, go in a course.

1591 SYLVESTER *Du Bartas* I. i. 473 This flowry Mansion where Mankind doth trade. **1618** in Foster *Eng. Factories India* (1906) I. 6 To trad by two at once. **1632** LITHGOW *Trav.* x. 506 These once happy Iles, which long agoe my feet traded ouer. **1642** ROGERS *Naaman* 503 Beware of..self-willednesse in Gods way, but humbly trade with him in it. **1651** HOBBES *Leviath.* II. xxiv. 127 By the labour of trading from one place to another.

†**3.** *trans.* To follow (a course) habitually; to practise; also, to use (something) regularly. *Obs.*

a **1562** G. CAVENDISH *Poems*, etc. (1825) II. 69 You, yong men all, That rageth in youthe and tradyth the courtly lyfe. **1563** FOXE *A. & M.* 851 That no man should speake of the sacramente, but with such wordes, as scripture doth trade, and beare. *c* **1570** in *Redforde's Play Wit & Sc.*, etc. (1848) 103 To those that lerne and trade vertue. **1579–80** NORTH *Plutarch* (1676) 66 Being yet a young man, he devised to trade Merchandize. *a* **1631** DONNE *Aristeas* (1633) 3 The Greeke Language which then was the most traded and vulgar through the whole Universe.

†**4.** To familiarize with the use, practice, or knowledge of something; to accustom or habituate *to* or *to do* something; to train (*up*) *in* or *with* some practice, etc.; to school, exercise. *Obs.*

1553 BECON *Reliques of Rome* (1563) 23 b, Learned scholemaisters to trade vp the Christen youthe in good letters and liberall artes. **1563** B. GOOGE *Eglogs*, etc. (Arb.) 79 Trade thou thy selfe, in seruyng hym aboue. **1570** LEVINS *Manip.* 8/36 To Trade, *tradere, consuefacere.* **1575** *Recorde's Gr. Artes* Pref. A v, This man..dyd trade them to all suche thinges, as eyther were profitable or honest. **1577** BRETON *Toyes Idle Head* (Grosart) 51/1 Desirous..to see Them both in learning traded up. **1603** H. CROSSE *Vertues Commw.* (1878) 51 Being once taught to loath Vice, and traded in wel doing, from the cradle. **1652** GAULE *Magastrom.* 374 He had committed his sonne to a..sorcerer, to be brought up or traded in such arts as were interdicted by the laws.

†**5.** *intr.* **a.** To have dealings; to communicate, converse, have intercourse; to treat, negotiate (*with* a person). *Obs.*

1553 BALE *Vocacyon* 19 b, From that daye..I traded wᵗ myselfe, by all possybylyte to set fourth that doctrine. **1582** N. LICHEFIELD tr. *Castanheda's Conq. E. Ind.* 156 He would come and speake with him and trade for a peace. **1605** SHAKS. *Macb.* III. v. 4 How did you dare To Trade and Trafficke with Macbeth, In Riddles, and Affaires of death. **1638** BRATHWAIT *Barnabees Jrnl.* II. D ij, My Muse with Bacchus so long traded When I walkt, my legs denaid it. **1676** GLANVILL *Seasonable Reflect.* 49 Should Satan send the most malignant spirits of Hell openly and professedly to trade for him.

b. To occupy oneself, be concerned *in* something; to deal, have dealings *in*. *Obs.* exc. as *fig.* from 6 b.

1606 SHAKS. *Ant. & Cl.* II. v. 2 Musicke, moody foode of vs that trade in Loue. **1618** BOLTON *Florus* III. iii. (1636) 173 The Tigurins..trading in robberies, slipt away whither they could. *a* **1661** FULLER *Worthies, Westm.* (1662) II. 241 Hence it was that afterwards he traded so largely in experiments. **1818** SCOTT *Br. Lamm.* xxx[i], In private, however, she traded more deeply in the occult sciences.

6. *intr.* **a.** To resort *to* a place for purposes of trade. Hence, **b.** to engage in or carry on trade (*with* a person, *in* a commodity).

a. **1570** J. CAMPION in Hakluyt *Voy.* (1599) II. 115 Englishmen did trade thither... If we should not trade thither, he should lose so much. **1575** in Tolstoy *1st 40 Yrs. Interc. Eng. & Russia* (1875) 161 Our subiectes trawding theither. **1650** FULLER *Pisgah* I. x. §8 Little of the East-Indies being then known, and less traded to. **1735** JOHNSON *Lobo's Abyssinia, Voy.* iii. 18 Through this [channel] pass almost all the Vessels that Trade to, or from the Red-Sea. **1796** MORSE *Amer. Geog.* I. 524 The people in West Jersey trade to Philadelphia. **1844** H. H. WILSON *Brit. India* I. 565 They traded with profit only to China.

b. **1570** J. CAMPION in Hakluyt *Voy.* (1599) II. 115 In those dayes that we traded in those parts. **1608** R. WIFFIN, etc. in *Capt. Smith's Virginia* (1624) 70 He found the Salvages more readie to fight then trade. **1660** F. BROOKE tr. *Le Blanc's Trav.* 5 They [Dutch merchants] trade there [to Aman] in Cottons. **1718** *Free-thinker* No. 152 ¶2, I began to Trade for my self, in the Year Seventeen Hundred and Four. **1769** COOK *Voy. round World* II. ii. (1773) 311 Those who remained in the canoes traded with our people very fairly. **1776** *Trial of Nundocomar* 68/1, I used..to trade in salt. **1818** SCOTT *Rob Roy* xxxiv, I only trade now as wholesale dealer. **1892** *Photogr. Ann.* II. 671 Robert Cochrane, on behalf of self and partners, Henry Brooks and Edward Gaynor Robinson, trading as Henry Brooks and Co.

c. With sinister implication: To drive a trade *in* (†*with*) something which should not be bought or sold; to traffic *in*.

1663 BP. PATRICK *Parab. Pilgr.* xxi. (1687) 221 That cursed principle I named before, of trading with kindnesses, and putting them out to Use. **1737** *Gentl. Mag.* Mar. 155/2 The Clergy are continually trading in Benefices, wanting to change a worse for a better. **1843** LYTTON *Last Bar.* I. ii, Tradest thou, too, for kisses? **1849** MACAULAY *Hist. Eng.* v. I. 653 The chief justice was fast accumulating a fortune out of the plunder of a higher class of Whigs. He traded largely in pardons. **1853** MAURICE *Proph. & Kings* viii. 133 Trading in religious arts and fears. **1878** VILLARI *Machiavelli* (1898) II. viii. 298 These men traded in war.

d. *to trade on* or *upon*: to make use of for one's own ends; to profit by; to take advantage of.

1884 *Spectator* 4 Oct. 1289/2 All parties in the State repeat, demonstrate, and trade on that unanimity. **1885** CLODD *Myths & Dr.* I. v. 93 They..still trade on the fears and fancies of their fellows. **1907** *Verney Mem.* II. 233 Tom traded on his younger brother's fair fame.

e. *to trade down*: to buy or sell cheaper goods, usually in larger quantities; to sell something and buy a cheaper replacement; similarly *to trade up*. Also *fig.*

1942 *Sun* (Baltimore) 22 July 3/2 Catering to the masses, the fur trade is 'trading down', Green said, offering practical furs..in economical designs. **1959** *Wall St. Jrnl.* 14 Apr. 18/3 Americans have followed the traditional pattern of 'trading up' in foods as well as in other goods and services. **1963** *Guardian* 8 May 7/2 It pays to trade up rather than cater for the masses. **1975** *Times* 14 Mar. (Small Car Suppl.) p. vi/7 The phenomenon of trading up from small to bigger cars is well known... In 1974..as many buyers..traded down as traded up. **1977** *Times* 22 June 23/7 Graduates are being given first crack at the jobs in preference to school-leavers. In other words, companies are trading up. **1982** *Nat. Westminster Bank Q. Rev.* Feb. 3 People..may well 'trade up' at various times by increasing their mortgage in order to move into better property.

†**7.** *trans.* To frequent for purposes of trade; to trade with (a country, etc.). *Obs.*

1585 [see TRADED 3]. *c* **1591** in *Lett. Lit. Men* (Camden) 77 The Companie of Merchauntes tradinge Muskovia havinge bene..preiudiced by the errors. **1598** HAKLUYT *Voy.* I. 458 At the humble sute of the English merchants trading those countreys. **1638** SIR T. HERBERT *Trav.* (ed. 2) 305 Since the Portugalls traded Indya they have shaven their heads. **1707** [see TRADED 3].

†**8.** To carry in the way of trade; *to trade outward*, to export for trade purposes. *Obs. rare*⁻¹.

1638 SIR R. COTTON *Abstr. Rec. Tower* 24 To permit all men bringing in Bullion to Trade outward the value thereof in domesticke Commodities at an abated Custome.

9. a. †To employ (money) in trade (*obs. rare*); to make (anything) the subject of trade, to trade in; to acquire or dispose of by barter (*U.S.*); to buy and sell, to barter, to exchange. *to trade off*: to dispose of by barter; also *fig.*, to give up in exchange for something else, esp. as a compromise.

a **1628** F. GREVIL *Hum. Learn.* cxxvii, Changing, corrupting, trading hope and feare Instead of Vertues. **1660** T. WATSON in Spurgeon *Treas. David* Ps. l. 22 The non-improvement of talents... He had not spent it, only not trading it is sentenced. **1793** in *Mass. Hist. Soc. Coll.* (1810) III. 1 Good crops of corn and rye, which they trade off for spirituous liquors. **1806** T. ASHE *Trav. Amer.* (1808) I. vi. 112 The words *buy* and *sell* are nearly unknown [in Erie, Pennsylvania]; in business nothing is heard but the word *trade.* **1830** GALT *Lawrie T.* II. i, I ain't a-going to trade her. **1834** MAJOR J. DOWNING *Life & Lett.* (Boston, 1835) 39 To see what chance I could find to trade off my ax-handles. **1852** MRS. STOWE *Uncle Tom's C.* xii, Trading negroes from Africa, dear reader, is so horrid!.. But trading them from Kentucky—that's quite another thing! **1863** W. C. BALDWIN *Afr. Hunting* vi. 167 Traded half a dozen large leather sacks from the Maccateese for beads, very cheap; they..are beautifully braided and sewn. **1904** M. HEWLETT *Queen's Quair* I. vi, The peasant women, and girls also, do trade their legs by standing in the lagoon and gathering the leeches that fasten upon them to suck blood. **1917** *Dial. Notes* IV. 402 *Trade,*..also 'to exchange' in general sense... 'Trade places with me.' **1949** F. FERGUSSON *Idea of Theater* i. 21 In the next part of the fight the opponents trade blow for blow. **1951** *N.Y. Herald Tribune* (Paris) 29 Nov. 3 (*heading*) Insults traded in Commons in 20-hour 20-minute session. **1956** S. SEELY *Radio Electronics* xv. 440 Pulse-duration modulation and pulse-position modulation trade bandwidth for an improvement in signal/noise ratio. **1958** L. URIS *Exodus* I. ix. 55 No American Jew would trade places with a Negro or a Mexican. **1972** *Sci. Amer.* June 22/3 Warheads can be traded off for either ABM penetration aids or increased range. **1974** *Times Lit. Suppl.* 8 Mar. 242/5 The bourgeoisie has 'traded off' some of its control to the armed forces acting in their interests. **1978** M. HESSE in Hookway & Pettit *Action & Interpretation* 6 The pragmatic criterion trades these difficulties for others. **1983** *Times* 29 Apr. 8/7 Punches and insults were traded at a rally addressed by..the South African Prime minister. **1984** *Times* 26 Mar. 2/1 Another skinhead leaned from a window and traded insults with seven youths in the street.

b. *spec.* in *N. Amer. Sport.* Of a club or team: to exchange (one of its players) *for* one or more from another club. Also, to exchange (players) between clubs or teams.

1899 *N.Y. Times* 5 Mar. 8/5 There was very little trading of players during the meeting. **1955** *Sports Illustr.* 7 Mar. 38/3 Branch Rickey..traded Southpaw Paul La Palme to the St. Louis Cardinals for Ben Wade, a relief pitcher. **1972** 'E. LATHEN' *Murder without Icing* vi. 62 Nashville wouldn't be forever. I'd be traded sooner or later. And as long as I shoot those goals in, I can get what I want. **1982** *Philadelphia Enquirer* 13 May 1-C/1 The former UCLA star was traded by the Knicks to New Orleans for Jim Barnett and Neal Wala in 1975.

10. ***to trade in***, to give (a used car, etc.) in part payment or exchange *for* a new one. Also *transf.* and *fig.* orig. *U.S.*

1926 G. HUNTING *Vicarion* i. 22 'Don't say you're trying to guard my young innocence, dear,' murmured Carol. 'I traded it in long ago for the new model.' **1955** W. GADDIS *Recognitions* III. ii. 752 You trade in your goddam car, you trade in your goddam wife, and the minute you get used to the goddam thing some bastard puts out a new model. **1973** R. TRAVERS *Murder in Blue Mountains* x. 95 Butler traded in his old black hat for the new one. **1975** D. LODGE *Changing Places* iii. 105 Shall I trade it in for a new one while it's still working? **1977** C. MCCULLOUGH *Thorn Birds* II. vi. 106 Bluey Williams traded in his lovely draft horses and his massive dray for a truck.

11. *intr. Comm.* Of a share: to be bought and sold (*at* a price, etc.).

1976 *Honolulu Star-Bull.* 21 Dec. C-7/1 A 125,000 share block of the stock traded at 17⅛. **1981** *Times* 23 May 19/8 Its shares will start trading on June 1. *Ibid.* 8 June 16/1 The huge discount to net assets at which insurance shares have been trading.

trade, obs. pa. t. of TREAD *v.*

tradeable, var. TRADABLE *a.*

trade bag, -board, etc.: see TRADE *sb.* 15–16.

'tradecraft. [f. TRADE *sb.* + CRAFT *sb.* in various senses.] †**a.** A trade-guild. **b.** Skill or art in connexion with a trade or calling. *spec.* Skill in espionage and intelligence work; cf. TRADE *sb.* 6 e. **c.** The craft or art of trading or dealing.

1810 COMBE *Picturesque* xxv. (1865) 370 And this same Hall their trade-craft found To be a sort of neutral ground. **1866** *Macm. Mag.* Oct. 432 There is tradecraft in literature as well as in painting. **1899** R. WHITEING *5 John St.* xxvi. 258 It is a lesson in tradecraft..to see how the girl holds her own with the dealers. **1961** 'J. LE CARRÉ' *Call for Dead* v. 56 He was suddenly alert... Was it the latent skill of his own tradecraft which informed him? **1979** *Observer* 30 Dec. 7/7 At every juncture of the break-in he made decisions that proved catastrophic, applied 'trade craft' that was ludicrous, and misled his accomplices about matters that were either incriminating to himself or strategic to the break-in's failure.

traded ('treɪdɪd), *ppl. a.* and *a.* [f. TRADE *v.* and *sb.* + -ED.]

I. †**1.** Of a road: Much used or trodden; often traversed; frequented; also *gen.* habitually used.

1570–6 LAMBARDE *Peramb. Kent* (1826) 6 A populous citie, and a well traded highway. **1591** in Hakluyt *Voy.* (1600) III. 488 Heere be many Tygers..they vse the traded wayes. *a* **1631** [see TRADE *v.* 3].

†**2.** Versed, skilled, practised; experienced; conversant, familiar. *Obs.*

1548 GEST *Pr. Masse* in Dugdale *Life* (1840) App. 94 A great clerke and moch traded in auncient wryters. **1589** NASHE *Pref. Greene's Menaphon* (Arb.) 11 Sir Iohn Cheeke, a man of men, supernaturally traded in al tongues. **1606** SHAKS. *Tr. & Cr.* II. ii. 64 Mine eyes and eares, Two traded Pylots 'twixt the dangerous shores Of Will, and Iudgement. **1654** H. L'ESTRANGE *Chas. I* (1655) 17 A gentleman peculiarly qualifyed for and long traded in Sea exploits.

†**3.** Of a place: Frequented or resorted to for the purpose of trading. (Usu. with *well*, etc.) *Obs.*

1585 T. WASHINGTON tr. *Nicholay's Voy.* IV. vii. 118 b, [The] cities of great Persia, wel traded with merchandize. **1610** HOLLAND *Camden's Brit.* I. 450 A proper and fine burrough it is, well traded and pleasantly seated. **1652–62** HEYLIN *Cosmogr.* II. (1682) 94 Hannover,...well built, very strongly fortified, and not meanly traded. **1656** J. CHALONER in D. King *Vale Royall* IV. 30 It [the Isle of Man] is traded with 4. Market-Towns, Castle-Town, Douglas, Peel-Town, and Ramsey. **1707** FUNNELL *Voy.* (1729) 77 The biggest and best traded city in all America.

4. ***traded option***, an option on a stock exchange (see OPTION 4) which can itself be bought and sold.

[**1973** *Business Week* 16 June 78/1 The Chicago Board of Trade's new Options Exchange is drumming up interest in trading options to buy and sell stock—puts and calls.] **1978** *Daily Mail* 11 Mar. 39 In a month, we shall see the opening in Amsterdam and London of markets in traded options, an innovation which took Chicago by storm in April 1973. **1984** *Daily Tel.* 24 Apr. 16/2 Privately Stock Exchange officials are furious that..a major development in the traded options market has been marred by such uncertainty.

II. 5. Having a trade (of such a kind).

1631 T. POWELL *Tom All Trades* (1876) 170 The favour of great traded Merchants. *a* **1656** HALES *Gold. Rem.* I. (1673) 67 To see another man meanly clad, meanly housed, meanly traded.

trade dinner, dollar, etc.: see TRADE *sb.* 16.

†**'trade-ˌfallen**, *a. Obs.* Fallen or broken in trade, bankrupt.

1596 SHAKS. *1 Hen. IV*, IV. ii. 32 Reuolted Tapsters and Ostlers Trade-falne. **1631** HEYWOOD *1st Pt. Fair Maid of W.* I. i, Her father Sold hydes in Somersetshire, and being trade-fallne, Sent her to service. *a* **1632** T. TAYLOR *God's Judgem.* vii. (1642) 111 Many young Shop-keepers.. through Drinking..have suddenly proved Trade-falne.

tradeful ('treɪdfʊl), *a.* [f. TRADE *sb.* + -FUL.] Full of trade; fully occupied or engaged in trading; †full of traffic; also *transf.* indicating busy trade.

1594 SPENSER *Amoretti* xv, Ye tradefull Merchants, that, with weary toyle, Do seeke most pretious things to make your gain. **1598** SYLVESTER *Du Bartas* II. i. IV. *Handie-Crafts* 23 Lo, how our Merchant-vessels to and fro Freely about our tradefull waters go. **1745** WARTON *Pleas. Melanch.* 272 Through the naked street, Once haunt of tradeful merchants, springs the grass. **1845** STOCQUELER *Handbk. Brit. India* (1854) 112 Shops and offices are shut up, or their tradeful hum and bustle all but stagnated.

trade-guild to **-language**: see TRADE 15, 16.

trade-in ('treɪdɪn). [f. vbl. phr. *to trade in* s.v. TRADE *v.* 10.] **1. a.** A transaction in which something is traded in; a part exchange. **b.** An item traded in, esp. a used car; also *fig.* **c.** A sum allowed in return for a trade-in.

1917 *Horseless Carriage* 1 Aug. 28 A used car in a trade-in. **1934** J. O'HARA *Appointment in Samarra* ii. 39 That Studebaker sedan, the black one. The one we took on a trade-in from Doc Lurie. **1945** *Word Study* Dec. 3/1 So useful and practical is English becoming that the time may not be far off when many small nations..may consider some sort of 'trade-in' with their national language for the English language. **1954** P. HIGHSMITH *Blunderer* (1956) xxii. 140 Since he hadn't the money for a brand-new car, Kimmel preferred to keep his ancient one rather than acquire something slightly newer on a trade-in. **1960** V. PACKARD *Waste Makers* xiii. 137 The high trade-in proved to be enormously effective in luring prospects. **1969** F. SARGESON *Joy of Worm* ii. 33 He would sell his machine to Jeremy cheap, and..accept as part of the transaction the trade-in of two push bikes in reasonably good condition. **1970** D. G. ALEXANDER *Retailing in England during Industr. Revol.* v. 143 Refurbished foot-wear which had been received as 'trade-ins' on new foot-wear. **1972** J. BELFRAGE in G. W. Turner *Good Austral. Eng.* vi. 115 Second-hand car dealers who.. beg you to take as-new late models off their hands..for ultra-generous trade-ins on your old bombs. **1980** G. HAMMOND *Reward Game* iv. 46 There's a wee sports car that I took as a trade-in.

2. *attrib.*

1927 *Ladies' Home Jrnl.* Dec. 65/1 Buyers..took prompt advantage of the liberal trade-in allowance on their old equipment. **1929** *Collier's* 12 Jan. 9/2 If more than one third of his..transactions..is represented by trade-in cars. **1946** *Sun* (Baltimore) 27 Jan. 22 (Advt.), No more 'tired power' or expensive engine repair. Extra value at trade-in time. **1958** *Economist* 8 Nov. 535/2 A general move in this direction would shave dealers' profit margins and might affect the trade-in values they could offer. **1974** P. FLOWER *Odd Job* iv. 29 They could get new trade-in jobs on HP... He wouldn't take any more old fridges. **1977** *Cork Examiner* 8 June 14/5 (Advt.), Typewriters all makes, new and secondhand, good trade-in allowance. **1980** *Sunday Express* 24 Aug. 22/1 (Advt.), You could get an exceptional trade-in price for your old car.

tradeless ('treɪdlɪs), *a.* [f. TRADE *sb.* + -LESS.]

1. Without a trade; unskilled in any trade.

1729 YOUNG *Imperium Pelagi* v. xxi, O'er generous Glebe, o'er golden Mines Her beggar'd, famish'd, Tradeless Native roves. **1910** *Blackw. Mag.* Mar. 408/2 The semi-educated and tradeless worker.

2. Without or destitute of trade or commerce.

1840 *Tait's Mag.* VII. 310 The Scotch nobility, in our tradeless days, were not sunk quite so low as the Italian nobility at present. **1897** MARY KINGSLEY *W. Africa* 371 The delta region is tremendously interesting..; but it is tradeless. **1900** H. G. GRAHAM *Soc. Life Scotl. in 18th C.* VII. i. (1901) 233 Consigned to perpetual poverty in some tradeless village.

trade-mark ('treɪdmɑːk), *sb.* [f. TRADE *sb.* + MARK *sb.*[1]] **a.** A mark (secured by legal registration or, in some countries, established by use) used by a manufacturer or trader to distinguish his goods from similar wares of other firms; usually a distinctive device or figure, a fancy name or trade name, or the name of an individual or firm, marked or impressed on the article or upon the package, etc., in or with which it is sold.

[**1571** *Letters Patent to R. Matthews* (in Edmunds *Patent Law* (1897) 885), To make the said haftes called Turky haftes for knyves, and for his marke to haue vpon the blade and hafte of the same knyfes..a halfe Moone.] **1838** MYLNE & CRAIG *Reports of Cases* III. 338 The Court will grant a perpetual injunction against the use, by one tradesman, of the trade marks of another. **1862** *Act 25 & 26 Vict.* c. 88 §1 The Expression 'Trade Mark' shall include any..Name, Signature, Word, Letter, Device [etc.]..lawfully used by any Person to denote any Chattel, or (in Scotland) any Article of Trade [etc.]..to be an Article or Thing of the Manufacture..of such Person, or to be an Article or Thing of any peculiar or particular Description made or sold by such Person. **1880** *Print. Trades Jrnl.* XXXI. 26 The owl is the trade-mark of the firm.

b. *fig.* A distinctive mark or token. Also *attrib.* as *adj.*

1869 'MARK TWAIN' *Innocents Abroad* xxiii. 238 We see other monks looking tranquilly up to heaven, but having no trade-mark. **1873** BROWNING *Red Cott. Nt.-Cap* 947 Trade-mark that stamps each word and deed. **1889** DOYLE *Micah Clarke* 311 The trade mark upon your forehead is especially hard to overlook. **1898** BODLEY *France* II. IV. vi. 406 Opportunists..utilised his name as the trade-mark of their parliamentary group. **1977** *South China Morning Post* (Hong Kong) 13 Apr. 7/2 Jimmy Shtoow'd, to phonetically adopt his trademark drawl, has an unnerving 'look' for interviewers. **1983** *Daily Tel.* 18 Mar. 17/2 Fans need not worry: her trademark French rayon jersey made up at least half the collection.

c. *attrib.*, as ***trade-mark name, registration***.

1901 *Daily Chron.* 2 Dec. 7/1 A belated perambulator.. with the trade-mark name of 'The Prince of Wales'. **1909** *Chem. & Druggist* 20 Feb. 315/2 Invented words should be protected by trade-mark registration; by themselves they cannot be copyrighted.

Hence **'trade-ˌmark** *v.*, *trans.* to affix or imprint a trade-mark upon; **'trade-marked** *ppl. a.*; **'trade-marking** *vbl. sb.*

1904 D. SLADEN *Lovers Japan* x, Bottled beer (made in Japan..and trade-marked with a big dragon). **1906** *Westm. Gaz.* 16 Mar. 5/2 The Bill..provided for the trade-marking of all imported beers. **1936** E. B. WHITE *Let.* 24 Dec. (1976) 146 Your public approval of a trademarked product and your influence can be bought at a price. **1983** P. DEVLIN *All of us There* xi. 133 The old [pub]..with its great copper-banded barrels and old trade-marked mirrors.

trade mart, name, etc.: see TRADE *sb.* 15–16.

tradent ('treɪdənt). *Rom. Law. rare.* [ad. L. *trādens, trādent-*, pr. pple. of *trādĕre* to hand over, deliver.] The person who delivers or hands over any property to another.

1880 MUIRHEAD *Gaius* 580 The conditions upon which it carried the property were that the tradent was owner.

†**tra'dentine**, *a. Obs. nonce-wd.* [f. *tra-* = TRANS- + L. *dent-em* tooth + -INE.] Lying beyond or outside the teeth.

1653 [see CIDENTINE].

trade-off ('treɪdɒf). [f. vbl. phr. *to trade off* s.v. TRADE *v.* 9.] A balance achieved between two desirable but incompatible features; a sacrifice made in one area to obtain benefits in another; a bargain, a compromise.

1961 *Hovering Craft & Hydrofoil* Oct. 32/2 Propulsion system integration allowing trade-offs between the requirements of lift and forward thrust can be achieved in a variety of ways. **1968** *Economist* 21 Sept. 38/1 It may be that the old argument of the 'trade-off' between inflation and unemployment will be superseded. **1970** A. TOFFLER *Future Shock* xx. 425 To provide data on the social and economic costs of various goals, and to show the costs and benefits of proposed trade-offs. **1972** *Sci. Amer.* June 22/3 Although its nominal range of about 2,500 nautical miles is the same as that of the *A-3*, a trade-off between range and payload is always possible. **1975** *New Yorker* 7 Apr. 55/3 Whether it is prudent, let alone safe, for Congress to try for a trade-off between these two priorities—the environment and the economy—remains a question. **1976** *Nature* 27 May 279/2 The alternative strategy of increasing the protein content of cereals would be a difficult task due to the yield/protein content 'trade-off'. **1976** P. R. WHITE *Planning for Public Transport* ii. 48 The household location may be a compromise rather than a trade-off related solely to a place of employment in the central area. **1978** *Jrnl. R. Soc. Arts* CXXVI. 255/1 A quite significant proportion of judgements in life are a trade-off between safety and cost. **1983** *Times* 3 Sept. 7/2 In the long run, there is no trade-off between inflation and unemployment. **1983** *Listener* 8 Dec. 23/3 The trade-off between housing and other objectives of policy has changed.

trader ('treɪdə(r)). [f. TRADE *v.* + -ER[1].]

1. One whose business is trade or commerce, or who is engaged in trading; a dealer or trafficker.

1585 T. WASHINGTON tr. *Nicholay's Voy.* IV. xxv. 140 b, Great traders, with merchandise & ready monie. **1600** E. BLOUNT tr. *Conestaggio* 55 The traders and handie-craftsmen who had not their kinsemen there. **1779–81** JOHNSON *L.P., Milton* Wks. II. 133 Neither traders, nor often gentlemen, thought themselves disgraced by ignorance. **1837** W. IRVING *Capt. Bonneville* II. xx. 40 One of those general gatherings of traders, trappers, and Indians. **1848** J. WILLIAMS *Law Pers. Prop.* II. iv. 108 No farmer, grazier, common labourer, or workman for hire,..shall be deemed as such a trader liable to become bankrupt. **1886** L. O. PIKE *Year Bks. 13 & 14 Edw. III* (Rolls) Introd. 83 Applicable to the servants of traders as well as to the servants of knights.

†**b.** A prostitute. *Obs. slang.*

1682 RADCLIFFE *Poems* 45 Burdellos, T'encourage She-Traders and lusty young Fellows. **1693** *Humours Town* 39, I mean not Common Women, that live by Fornication, publick Traders. **1760** FOOTE *Minor* I. Wks. 1799 I. 247 Tip him an old trader, and give her to the knight.

c. A vessel engaged in trading; a trading ship.

1712 *Lond. Gaz.* No. 5017/2 Ten sail of Irish Traders. **1862** *Catal. Internat. Exhib.* II. XII. 9 A trader for narrow rivers, with new arrangement of rudder. **1887** MRS. DALY *Digging*, etc. *S. Australia* 296 The crews in the pearling schooners and small traders are very short-handed.

†**d.** A tradesman's token (TOKEN *sb.* 10). *Obs.*

1775 R. TWISS *Tour Irel.* (1776) 82 The want of small change [in 1727] was so great, that several persons were obliged to make copper and silver tokens, called *Traders*, which they passed as promissory notes among their work-men, customers, and neighbours.

†**2.** One who is occupied or concerned *in* something; a dealer. *Obs.*

1668 HALE *Pref. Rolle's Abridgm.* a j b, The constant.. course..of these great Traders in Learning, to bring in their several acquests therein..into a common Stock. **1673** [R. LEIGH] *Transp. Reh.* 144 The nonconformists were great traders in Scripture. **1800** COLERIDGE *Piccolom.* I. x, That ancient trader In contraband negociations.

trade-road to **-school**: see TRADE *sb.* 15–16.

trades- in *comb.*: see TRADE *sb.* 16 b.

‖**Tradescantia** (trædɪ'skæntɪə). *Bot.* [mod.L. (Ruppius 1718), f. the name of John Tradescant (the elder), a 17th c. naturalist + -IA[1].] An American genus of perennial herbs (N.O. *Commelynaceæ*) characterized by three-petalled blue, white, pink, or purple ephemeral flowers having six stamens clothed with jointed hairs; spiderwort.

[**1629** PARKINSON *Paradisus* 152 Phalangium Ephemerum virginianum Joannis Tradescant... Tradescant his spider-wort. **1718** RUPPIUS *Flora Jenensis* 55 Tradescantia.] **1766** LEE *Introd. Bot.* App. (1788) 350/2 Spider-wort, Virginian, *Tradescantia*. **1866** *Treas. Bot.* 317 The filaments of the *Tradescantias* have jointed hairs, in which a granular movement is seen under the microscope.

tradesfolk ('treɪdzfəʊk). [f. as next + FOLK.] People in trade; tradespeople: **a.** Artisans; **b.** Shopkeepers.

1760–72 H. BROOKE *Fool of Qual.* (1809) III. 21 This is holiday in the afternoon among us trades-folk. **1885** W. H. WHITE *M. Rutherford's Deliv.* iii, The wine-merchant.. by no means associating with the tradesfolk who displayed their goods in the windows. **1890** POLLARD *Eng. Miracle Plays* Introd. 11 Philosophers, saints, mimes, jugglers, monks, nuns, bishops and tradesfolk have all to play their part.

tradesman ('treɪdzmən). Pl. **-men**. [f. *trade's*, gen. case of TRADE + MAN *sb.*[1]]

1. One who is skilled in and follows one of the industrial arts; an artificer, an artisan, a craftsman. Now *Sc.*, *local* (esp. *rural*) *English*, and *Austral.*

1597 DRAYTON *Heroical Epistles, Edward IV to Shores Wife* 117 The busie lawyer wrangling in his pleas,..The toyling trades-man, and the sweating Clowne. ?*a* **1600** *Robin Hood & Tanner* xxiii, 'What tradesman art thou?' said jolly Robin. **1625** COKE in *Commons Debates* (Camden) 131 The Master of the Ordinance was auntiently a tradesman vntill 37 Henry 8, and then it was conferd on a nobleman. **1657** in *Verney Mem.* (1907) II. 95 [His wish to be bound] apprintice unto some very good traydes-man. **1657** R. LIGON *Barbadoes* (1673) 110 If they be Trades-men, as, Carpenters, Joyners, Masons, Smiths. **1738** SWIFT *Pol. Conversat.* 27 If Things did not break or wear out, how would Tradesmen live? **1825** JAMIESON, *Tradesman*, a name [in Scotland] restricted to a handicraftsman; all who keep shops being..called Merchants. *c* **1880** *Let. to Editor*, *Tradesman* in Australia does not mean a shopkeeper, but the man who works at a trade, i.e. the artisan. **1899** *Times* 25 Jan. 10 At the end of May a deputation of provincial tradesmen (in the Scotch sense) visited London... The carpenters and joiners came to terms with the employers.

2. a. One who is engaged in trade or the sale of commodities; *esp.* a shopkeeper.

1601 DENT *Pathw. Heaven* 71 Couetousnesse..baneth our Gentlemen, it murthereth our Trades-men, it bewitcheth our Merchants. **1622** MALYNES *Anc. Law. Merch.* 92 A Trades-mans shop, and a Merchants ware-house is taken to be publicke and open at the appointed times. **1655** E. TERRY *Voy. E. Ind.* xxvi. 411 There are very many private men..who are Merchants, or Tradesmen that are very rich. **1695** BLACKMORE *Pr. Arth.* IV. 417 The Tradesman quits his Shop. **1717** LADY M. W. MONTAGU *Let. to Abbé Conti* 17 May, Most of the rich Tradesmen were Jews. **1766** FORDYCE *Serm. Yng. Wom.* (1767) I. vii. 294 The daughters of plain tradesmen and honest mechanics. **1885** MISS BRADDON *Wyllard's Weird* I. i. 30 This would give time for the tradesmen to get away from their shops. **1906** *Daily Chron.* 10 Feb. 4/7 'Tradesman', which in the north is used to denote a workman who has learned a trade, while in the south it is made to apply to a man who runs a business.

b. *tradesmen's entrance* (or *door*): a minor or side entrance to a property for use by tradesmen or workmen.

1892 A. W. PINERO *Magistrate* III. i. 113 We're in the scullery, Guv; let's try and find the tradesmen's door. **1904** E. NESBIT *Phoenix & Carpet* vii. 131 At the side of the house ..there is a green gate labelled 'Tradesmen's Entrance'. **1946** 'J. TEY' *Miss Pym Disposes* xiii. 143 'Shouldn't you be going in by the other door?'.. 'I do not take well to tradesmen's entrances.' **1982** M. HINXMAN *Telephone Never Tells* iii. 21 A well-trodden path that wound round to the rear suggested..that the tradesmen's door was a more familiar mode of entry and not only for tradesmen.

c. *tradesman's token* = *trade token* s.v. TRADE *sb.* 15 a. Usu. in *pl.*, *tradesmen's tokens*. Cf. TRADE *sb.* 11.

1660 *CSP Dom.* 6 Oct. (1860) 307 Proposition by Sir Wm. Parkhurst..to meet the necessity for small money, and obviate the inconvenience of tradesmen's tokens. **1757** *Gentl. Mag.* XXVII. IX. 498/2 The best account of the money called Tradesmen's Tokens..is to be drawn from.. Mr Leake's hist. account of English money, London 1745. **1849** J. Y. AKERMAN *Tradesmen's Tokens* p. i, Notwithstanding the dictum of Pinkerton, many persons are yet found who collect Tradesmen's Tokens. **1892** J. ATKINS (*title*) The tradesmen's tokens of the eighteenth century.

Hence '**tradesmanship**, the quality or calling of a tradesman; *transf.* tradesmen collectively. Also *attrib.*

1817 BENTHAM *Parl. Reform* (1818) 52 Say whether Tradesmanship honesty..is not worth all such other honesties put together. **1859** *Sat. Rev.* 10 Dec. 702/1 Tradesmanship in all its proprieties may stand aghast at the revelations of the inner life of a Strand shopkeeper's family.

'**tradesmanlike**, *a.* [f. prec. + -LIKE.] Like, or like that of, a tradesman; characteristic of a tradesman; in quot. 1862, workmanlike, skilful.

1790 *Bystander* 344 A man of tradesmanlike appearance came and knocked at the door. **1862** THORNBURY *Turner* I. 275 Crafty tradesmanlike alterations. **1870** GLADSTONE *Glean.* IV. v. 254 With a tradesmanlike devotion to her peaceful industry.

'**tradespeople**. [f. *trade's*, gen. of TRADE + PEOPLE.] People engaged in trade; tradesmen, and their families and employees; shopkeepers.

1728 VANBRUGH & CIB. *Prov. Husb.* v. ii, Those Trades-people are the troublesomest Creatures! no Words will satisfy them! **1729** FENTON in *Waller's Wks., Observ.* 60/2 No trades-people would trust her for any thing. *a* **1862** BUCKLE *Misc. Wks.* (1872) I. 579 The middle class of trades-people were ignorant and poor.

'**trades,woman**. Pl. **-women**. [f. as prec. + WOMAN.] A woman engaged in trade, or in a particular trade or calling; in quots. 1707, 1778, the wife of a tradesman.

1707 *Reflex. upon Ridicule* II. 212 New-vamped Trades-women, whose Dress and Train, and Furniture and Table, create Envy. **1778** JOHNSON 13 May, in *Boswell*, Trades-women (I mean the wives of tradesmen) in the city. **1889** *Sat. Rev.* 23 Feb. 218/1 The gentle lady must be put off, and the shrewd and thrifty tradeswoman must be put on.

trade 'union, trades 'union. Also (esp. when used *attrib.*) with hyphen. [f. TRADE or pl. *trades* + UNION.] **a.** An association of the workers in any trade or in allied trades for the protection and furtherance of their interests in regard to wages, hours, and conditions of labour, and for the provision, from their common funds, of pecuniary assistance to the members during strikes, sickness, unemployment, old age, etc.

1835 WORDSW. *Postscript* iii. Poet. Wks. (1910) 966 It has no direct bearing upon clubs..nor upon political or trade-unions. **1842** COBDEN in Morley *Life* xii. (1902) 43/2 Nothing can be got by fraternising with trade unions. They are founded upon principles of brutal tyranny and monopoly. **1887** LOWELL *Democr.* 17 But the trade-unions are now debating instead of conspiring. **1896** L. ABBOTT *Chr. & Soc. Probl.* x. 272 The phrase 'trade union' came into existence about the year 1830 and the organization itself came into existence about the same time. **1906** *Westm. Gaz.* 6 Mar. 2/2 A trade union is a quasi-political association, rather than an association for carrying on business.

1831 *Times* 18 Jan. 4/1 There is no doubt that these boys [spinners' apprentices at Haslingden] are kept in countenance by the 'Trades' Union'. **1834** ARNOLD *Let. to Chev. Bunsen* 29 Sept., You have heard..of the Trades' Unions, a fearful engine of mischief, ready to riot or to assassinate. **1868** ROGERS *Pol. Econ.* ix. (1876) 88 The purpose of a trades-union is to keep up the price of labour, and if possible to enhance it. **1878** JEVONS *Prim. Pol. Econ.* 61 A trades-union is a society of men belonging to any one kind of trade, who agree to act together as they are directed by their elected council, and who subscribe money to pay the expenses.

b. *attrib.*; **trade(s) union congress**, (*a*) a national delegate conference of British trade unions, held annually since 1868; (*b*) (with capital initials) the national confederation of British trade unions, originally formed to organize the annual congress.

1831 LADY E. BELGRAVE *Let.* Feb. in G. Huxley *Lady Elizabeth & Grosvenors* (1965) iv. 97 The tremendous Trade Union Club there [in Manchester]... I wish it could be put down and that someone would shoot O'Connell and Cobbett. **1868** F. HARRISON *Let.* 11 Nov. in *Geo. Eliot Lett.* (1956) IV. 483 Since July I have been quite immersed in my Trades-Union work. [**1878** *Chambers's Encycl.* X. 757/1 The Trades' Congress..holds an annual conference in the different leading towns.] **1888** *Encycl. Brit.* XXIII. 501/2 An annual trades union congress is held in some great centre of industry and population..at which delegates from almost all the trade unions in the realm are present. **1895** *Nat. Review* XXVI. 163 The Trade-Union Congress..has made itself a really representative body by adopting the principle of one vote one value. **1911** C. E. PERSONS et al. *Labor Laws & their Enforcement* 115 One of its members, Edward H. Rogers, a trade union leader, made some half-hearted recommendations. **1920** *Times* 11 June 17/2 The majority of trade union leaders..have deserted to the camp of the capitalists. **1926** *Brit. Gaz.* 12 May 1/4 Every man who does his duty by the country and remains at work or returns to work during the present crisis will be protected by the State from loss of trade union benefits. **1926** A. CONAN DOYLE *Hist. Spiritualism* I. xiii. 299 The conduct of conjurers [towards mediums] seems to have been usually determined by a sort of trade union jealousy, as if the results of the medium were some sort of breach of a monopoly. **1926** *Law Rep. Chancery Div.* 540 No trade dispute does or can exist between the Trades Union Congress on the one hand and the Government and the nation on the other. **1927** CARR-SAUNDERS & JONES *Social Struct. England & Wales* 51 Trade-union officials. *Ibid.* 77 Trade-union membership advances in waves. **1936** G. B. SHAW *Millionairess* III. 174 You might as well ask me to pay trade union wages as do all that the inspector wants: I should be out of business in a week. **1941** E. WILSON in *Atlantic Monthly* Apr. 480/2 The trade-union leadership is represented only..by an unscrupulous spellbinder. **1964** T. B. BOTTOMORE *Elites & Society* i. 9 Representatives of new social interests or classes (e.g. trade union leaders). *a* **1974** R. CROSSMAN *Diaries* (1975) I. 335, I am pretty used to Conference now, and being hardened I just opt out of the evening entertainments and the endless trade-union dinners. **1974** P. DICKINSON *Poison Oracle* iv. 100 The hoarse bellowings of an old-style trades union agitator trying to whip an apathetic strike meeting into action. **1975** *Economist* 4 Jan. 75 Mr Gill has been cutting quite a dash since his election as the only communist on the general council of the Trades Union Congress. **1976** *Daily Tel.* 20 July 2/5 When will the British public, 81·5 per cent of whom have no trade union affiliation, realize how rapidly our freedoms are being eroded.

Hence **trade unio'nese** *colloq.*, the style of language supposed to be characteristic of public statements by trade-union officials; **trade(s) 'unionism**, the system, principles, or practice of trade-unions; **trade(s) 'unionist**, a member of a trade-union; also *attrib.*; **trade 'unionize** *v. trans.*, to enrol in a trade union, to form a trade union from among; **trade 'unionized** *ppl. a.*

1927 A. P. HERBERT in *Times* 12 Jan. 13/5 There should be prizes for Essays in the Socialist Language, and polysyllabic Resolutions in *Trade Unionese. **1969** H. E. BATES *Vanished World* xii. 156 Nowadays..we are near-suffocated by tradeunionese, councilese and Americanese, the new extensions of stodge-pudding language that have joined Johnsonese, journalese and politicalese. **1867** *Blackw. Mag.* June 726/2 When Socialism and Communism in all their various forms died out, *Trades-unionism..took their place. **1875** *N. Amer. Rev.* CXX. 215 The theory and possibilities of trades-unionism. **1884** *Pall Mall G.* 10 Sept. 8/2 Although he was both a politician and a trade unionist, he could faithfully say trade unionism had always had his first care and attention. **1888** *Voice* (N.Y.) 14 Nov., China, it seems, is the cradle of tradesunionism, and boycotts are numerous. **1834** *Times* 10 May 5/4 Is it not somewhat unreflecting on the part of *trades' unionists to imagine that they can..set up an opposition monopoly? **1863** FAWCETT *Pol. Econ.* II. ix. (1876) 248 A social terrorism, very analogous to that by which Trades-Unionists so frequently maintain their organizations. **1898** *Westm. Gaz.* 12 Jan. 3/2 Even another self-denying ordinance must be asked of the trade-unionist parent in this good cause. **1960** *Times* 9 Feb. 14/2 (*heading*) Should artists be *trade unionized? **1976** *Carn* Feb. 6/1 Public attention has been diverted from the Bretons to the jailed conscripts who tried to trade-unionise the French army. **1982** *Economist* 17 Apr. 51/3 Buy-outs by employees of bust and heavily *trade-unionised businesses.

trade-way, etc.: see TRADE *sb.* 15, 16.

'**trade-wind**. [f. TRADE *sb.* + WIND *sb.* App. originating in the phrase *to blow trade*: see TRADE *sb.* 3 d. Afterwards often shortened in nautical use to *trade*, in pl. 'the trades': see TRADE *sb.* 13.

The name had in its origin nothing to do with *trade* in the sense 'commerce', or 'passage for the purpose of trading', though the importance of those winds to navigation led 18th c. etymologists (and perhaps even navigators) so to understand the term.]

†**1.** Any wind that 'blows trade', i.e. in a constant course or way; a wind that blows steadily in the same direction. *Obs.* exc. as in 3.

Originally applied to any wind having this character. But as it became gradually known that the only winds of which this is approximately true were the Indian monsoons, and the winds now so called, on each side of the equator in the Atlantic and Pacific Oceans, the name became restricted to these, and at length to the latter (senses 2 and 3). Also *fig.*

1663 COWLEY *To Drake's Ship* iv, The breath of Fame, like an auspicious Gale (The great Trade-wind which ne'er does fail), Shall drive thee round the World. **1666** DRYDEN *Ann. Mirab.* ccciv, But now, the Cape once doubled, fear no more; A constant trade-wind will securely blow And gently lay us on the spicy shore. *a* **1668** DAVENANT *Poems* Wks. (1673) 330 A Pilot, sure of faire Trade-Windes, The Helme in all the Voyage never hands. **1706** PHILLIPS (ed. Kersey), *Trade-Wind*, a Wind that blows regularly at Sea, at certain Seasons of the Year, and serves to promote Trading Voyages. **1726** SHELVOCKE *Voy. round World* 385 Then came on the constant, or what may be call'd the trade wind on this [Pacific] coast [of America] blowing from the W.N.W, except in the night, that it comes about more Northerly. **1735** G. HADLEY in *Phil. Trans.* XXXIX. 61 The same Principle..extends to the Production of the West Trade-Winds without the Tropicks. **1777** COLMAN in Sheridan *Sch. Scand.* Epil. 2, I, who was late so volatile and gay, Like a tradewind must now blow all one way. **1807** CRABBE *Parish Reg.* (1829) 17 But like a trade-wind is the ancient dame, Mild to your wish, and every day the same.

†**2.** Applied to the seasonal winds of the Indian Ocean; = MONSOON 1, 2. *Obs.*

The winter monsoon, from October to April, coincides in direction with the trade-wind of the North Atlantic; the summer monsoon blows in the opposite direction.

[**1634** SIR T. HERBERT *Trav.* 8 Euery houre expecting these Anniuersarie winds, called by the Sea-men and Portugals, *Monzoons*; the property of which wind is to blow constantly one way, sixe moneths, and the other way, the other halfe yeare.] **1650** FULLER *Pisgah* I. vi. §3 Rain,.. like Trade-winds on some seas, came at set seasons. **1687** A. LOVELL tr. *Thevenot's Trav.* III. 1 That Season wherein there is a constant Trade-Wind upon that Sea, begins commonly at the end of October. **1720** DE FOE *Capt. Singleton* (1906) 218 When we came in among the Spice Islands..we had a share of the monsoons, or trade-winds. **1794** SULLIVAN *View Nat.* I. 206 The constant or stated wind usually called the trade wind; and in some parts of the world, the monsoon. **1840** THIRLWALL *Greece* VII. liv. 55 Some weeks were still to come before the trade-winds would set in from the north-east, when they would be perfectly favourable for the voyage.

3. Now *spec.* The wind that blows constantly towards the equator from about the thirtieth parallels, north and south; its main direction in the northern hemisphere being from the north-east, and in the southern hemisphere from the south-east. Cf. ANTI-TRADE.

The N.E. trade is termed in Hawkins' *Voy. Florida c* 1565 (Hakl. Soc.) 25, 46, 'the ordinary breeze' (BREEZE *sb.*[2] 1), the S.E. trade is termed by Linschoten 1583 *general windt*, 'the general wind', after Pg. *vento geral*.

[**1699** DAMPIER *Voy.* II. III. 1 Trade-Winds are such as do blow constantly from one Point, or Quarter of the Compass, and the Region of the World most peculiar to them is from about 30 d. North to 30 d. South of the Equator.] **1712** E.

COOKE *Voy. S. Sea* 446 Getting into the Trade-Winds, our Course was afterwards uniform. **1748** *Anson's Voy.* II. ix. 224 We expected, upon the encreasing our offing from Quibo, to fall in with the regular trade-wind. **1821** R. TURNER *Arts & Sc.* (ed. 18) 17 The trade-winds blow naturally from the N.E. on the north, and from the S.E. on the south of the line, throughout the whole year. **1835** MRS. SOMERVILLE *Connex. Phys. Sc.* xv. (ed. 2) 147 There are many proofs of the existence of the counter currents above the trade winds. **1867** DENISON *Astron. without Math.* 39 The heat of the torrid zone and its velocity of rotation produce the trade winds which blow constantly in the same directions in the same latitudes on the great oceans.

b. *attrib.*, as ***trade-wind region***; **trade-wind cloud**, the trade cumulus (TRADE *sb.* 16).

1860 MAURY *Phys. Geog. Sea* (Low) iv. §255 The hottest place within the trade-wind regions is not at the equator. **1902** *Daily Chron.* 21 Aug. 7/1 As the darkness deepened a dull red reflection was seen in the trade-wind cloud which covered the mountain summit.

tradey, variant of TRADY.

† **'tradiment.** *Obs. rare.* [ad. med.L. *trādimentum* (1190 in Du Cange), f. L. *trādĕre* to hand over, deliver; or a. OF. *trade-*, *tradiment* 'treason' (Godef.).] Treachery, perfidy, treason.

1535 *St. Papers Hen. VIII*, II. 264 The Tholes entred by tradyment into Powers Courte. **1536** *Ibid.* 362 Beyng evicted, and recovered out of our possession by tradyment. **1561** T. HOBY tr. *Castiglione's Courtyer* II. (1577) N j b, If it be true that it is such an abhominable profit and trespace to vse tradiment against a mans very enimy.

trading ('treɪdɪŋ), *vbl. sb.* [f. TRADE *v.* + -ING[1].]

a. The action of the verb TRADE in various senses; *esp.* the carrying on of trade; buying and selling; commerce, trade, traffic. ***trading down, up*** (see quot. 1963 and TRADE *v.* 6 e).

1590 [see b]. **1615** in *Buccleuch MSS.* (Hist. MSS. Comm.) I. 168 Either of us might assist each other in free Trading in those parts. **1645** MILTON *Tetrach.* Wks. 1851 IV. 220 So to serve the commodity of insatiable trading, usury shall be permitted. **1654** *Nicholas Papers* (Camden) II. 82 Hee will stopp all tredding by sea that way. **1799** in Picton *L'pool Munic. Rec.* (1886) II. 219 To prohibit the trading for slaves. **1885** *Athenæum* 5 Sept. 302/1 Successful trading was not at that date quite so important. **1963** *Gloss. Managem. Terms* (Brit. Inst. Managem.) (Typescript), *Trading down*, a seller's practice of handling cheap or low-grade products in order to secure higher volume sales (usually at a low rate of profit with a high stock turn). *Ibid.*, *Trading up*, a seller's practice of handling expensive or high-grade products in order to gain prestige and secure a better class of trade (usually at a high rate of profit with a low stock turn). **1971** *Daily Tel.* 13 Mar. 20/5 This second house is almost certain to be more expensive... Any capital gain on the first home will almost certainly be more than devoured by the additional cost of this 'trading up'. **1976** *Times* 6 Nov. 18/8 When prices increase.. there is a strong tendency to.. buying in smaller quantities or items of poorer quality. This is known in advertising jargon as 'trading down'.

b. *attrib.* and *Comb.*; in sense 'of, pertaining to, or connected with trade', as ***trading course, line, origin***; 'intended for trade or barter', as ***trading articles, cloth, goods***; 'frequented for, employed in, made or done for trading', as ***trading-boat, centre, craft, journey, path, port, -scow, ship, smack, station, tax, vessel, voyage***; **trading account**, an account showing the revenue from sales during a period, the cost of those sales, the stock at the beginning and end of the period, and the resulting gross profit or loss; **trading estate**, an area of land specially developed to accommodate light industry; **trading floor**, the area in a stock exchange where the dealing is done; **trading-house**, a building in which barter was carried on with the Indians in North America; **trading-place**, † (*a*) a place of resort or passage; (*b*) a place frequented for trade; **trading profit**, profit as shown in a trading account; gross profit; **trading-rat** = *trade rat* s.v. TRADE *sb.* 16; **trading stamp** orig. *U.S.*, an adhesive stamp given by a retailer to a customer when he buys goods of a certain value and exchangeable in quantity for goods from the company issuing the stamp.

1920 *Trading account [see *cost account* s.v. COST *sb.*[2] 6]. **1978** J. KELLOCK *Elements of Accounting* x. 174 In the final form, accounts are divided into two sections referred to as the trading account and the profit and loss account. **1738** W. STEPHENS *Jrnl.* 15 June in A. D. Candler *Colonial Rec. State of Georgia* (1906) IV. 156 An Indian *Trading Boat arrived. **1867** J. N. EDWARDS *Shelby* xx. 364 Marmaduke.. hoped to capture a trading-boat, and thus put an immediate quietus on the cotton trade. **1923** 'R. DALY' *Enchanted Island* xv. 154 I'm trying to figure out our chances of being picked up if we stay here. It's not on the track of any regular trading-boats. **1904** *Archæologia Æliana* XXV. II. 255 *note*, The ports and *trading-centres of the Mediterranean. **1672** SIR W. TALBOT *Discov. J. Lederer* 26 Your best Truck is a sort of course *Trading Cloth, of which a yard and a half makes a Matchcoat. **1937** *Ann. Reg. 1936* 8 The Commissioner for the Special Areas of England and Wales.. issued a report... His chief object now, he said, was to establish in the Special Areas what he called '*trading estates' for the purpose of attracting to these areas fresh industries, particularly of the lighter type. **1981** B. HINES *Looks & Smiles* 31 They.. caught a bus out to the Ring Road where a Trading Estate was being developed to attract new industries to the city. **1947** *Encycl. Brit.* XXI. 422/1 As a market place, the *trading floor of the New York Stock exchange affords exactly the same fundamental facilities that a public market does for the housewife. **1971** *Sunday Australian* 8 Aug. 13/9 He also suggested.. greater use of electronic equipment, culminating in the elimination of the current trading floor. **1981** *Times* 19 July 22/1 The trading floor appeared unusally empty. **1984** *Christian Science Monitor* 2 Mar. 10/3 They have to figure out what stocks to buy when the bulls return to the trading floor. **1796** *Saskatchewan Jrnls.* (Hudson's Bay Rec. Soc.) (1967) 73 Sent four men with ten horses to Buckingham House for *trading goods. **1637** in *Mass. Hist. Soc. Coll.* (1863) VI. 215 They say he came from a *trading howse which Plymouth men have at Qunnihticut. **1676** in I. Mather *K. Philip's War* (1862) 99 That the Indian Trading-houses.. be suppressed. **1726** S. PENHALLOW in *New Hampsh. Hist. Soc. Coll.* (1824) I. 21 Trading-houses in several places were hereupon engaged. **1899** H. B. CUSHMAN *Hist. Indians* 478 A trading house for the accommodation of the Chickasaws has been established at the Bluffs. **1775** ADAIR *Amer. Ind.* 395 The ford of the old *trading path, where the enemy now and then passed the river. **1590** GREENE *Never too Late* O iv, Flora did checker all her *trading place. **1755** L. EVANS *Geogr. Ess.* 10 The situation of Indian Villages, trading Places, the Creeks [etc.]. **1883** W. E. HOWE *Country Town* xv. 84, I had never been to Twin Mounds, as there was a post-office and a small trading place several miles nearer. **1719** DE FOE *Crusoe* (1840) II. xii. 251 To put into the first *trading port. **1940** *Economist* 25 May 936/1 A double record of *trading profits and also of true net profits has been kept. **1966** *Daily Tel.* 30 June 1/5 Sears Engineering made trading profits of £2,344,000. **1895** *St. Nicholas* Apr. 501/2, I would like to write an entire paper on the droll ways of certain distinguished members of the Wood-rat, Pack-rat, *Trading-rat, or Bush-rat genus. **1875** 'MARK TWAIN' in *Atlantic Monthly* Feb. 219/2 He ran over the steering-oar of a *trading-scow. **1897** *Catal. Title Entries of Bks.* (Office Reg. Copyright, Libr. of Congr.) No. 326. 21 *Trading stamp book issued by Washington Trading Stamp Company. (Received Sept. 30, 1897.) **1901** *Daily Colonist* (Victoria, B.C.) 30 Oct. 2/4 The city council.. have passed a by-law prohibiting the use of trading stamps or coupons within the municipality. **1933** *Parl. Papers 1932–3* XII. 387 (Cmd. 4385) 12 A trading stamp company sells collecting books and stamps to retailers. **1964** S. BELLOW *Herzog* 121 Postage stamps and trading stamps soaking on the formica counter. **1977** *Times* 10 May 15/1 The Tesco supermarket chain.. has just decided to withdraw from the trading stamp business. **1895** C. M. YONGE *Long Vacation* xviii. 181 He.. set her up at Rockquay with the tobacco-shop. She had chosen that place on account of American *trading-vessels putting in there. **1745** *Roxana* 427 He.. told me, he could help me to a Share in two Ships, one was going a *trading Voyage to the Coast of Africa, and the other a Privateering. **1809** R. LANGFORD *Introd. Trade* 111 The voyage may be.. to several ports, which is called a *trading voyage*.

'trading, *ppl. a.* [f. as prec. + -ING[2].] That trades, in various senses of the verb; *esp.* engaged in trade, commercial.

1690 CHILD *Disc. Trade* (1698) 2 They have in their greatest councils of state and war, trading-merchants that have lived abroad in most parts of the world. **1697** DRYDEN *Virg. Georg.* IV. 20 These rob the trading citizens [bees]. **1711** ADDISON *Spect.* No. 69 ¶1 Factors in the Trading World are what Ambassadors are in the Politick World. **1790** BURKE *Fr. Rev.* 263 A great trading or manufacturing town. **1874** GREEN *Short Hist.* vi. §3. 282 The trading and industrial classes.

Comb. **1727** [DORRINGTON] *Philip Quarll* Pref., Busy Worlds and Trading-Peopled Towns.

† **b.** That trades in or makes a trade of something (e.g. a public office or position). *Obs.*

1787 SIR J. HAWKINS *Johnson* 214 The duke of Newcastle.. gave him [Fielding] a nominal qualification of 100l. a year, and set him up as a trading-justice, in which disreputable station he died. **1796** *Grose's Dict. Vulg. T.* (ed. 3), *Trading Justices*, Broken mechanics, discharged footmen, and other low fellows, smuggled into the commission of the peace, who subsist by fomenting disputes, granting warrants, and other-wise retailing justice. **1812** *Examiner* 30 Nov. 767/1 The Court treated the defendant as a systematic and trading libeller. **1839** LD. BROUGHAM *Statesm. Geo. III*, *Canning* 289 The common herd of trading politicians.

trading post. orig. *U.S.* [f. TRADING *vbl. sb.* + POST *sb.*[3]] **1.** A place occupied for purposes of trade, esp. in a region not fully developed.

1796 in *Coll. Georgia Hist. Soc.* (1916) IX. 15 The land.. has been recommended.. as proper for a trading post. **1837** W. IRVING *Capt. Bonneville* III. xxxiv. 205 Fort Wallah-Wallah is a trading post of the Hudson's Bay Company. **1936** D. MCCOWAN *Animals Canad. Rockies* xxi. 190 The fur trading posts of the far North. **1976** *Sat. Rev.* (U.S.) 30 Oct. 23/1 Lamu—a tiny coral island off the Kenya coast.. once a prosperous trading post of Omani Arabs.

2. One of the posts or positions on the trading floor of a stock exchange, where stocks assigned to that location are bought and sold.

1951 G. L. LEFFLER *Stock Market* xii. 178 There are now 18 active trading posts... The present posts are horse-shoe or U-shaped stations, occupying 100 square feet... A total of 12 clerks can work inside. **1970** *Toronto Daily Star* 24 Sept. 13/1 A bald man in a red jacket leans heavily against a quiet trading post. His eyes are closed. Another sits on a small seat, one of many which can be pulled down from the sides of the trading posts. **1971** *Reader's Digest* (U.S.) Oct. 58/2 Hundreds of brokers were swarming around 17 horseshoe-shaped trading posts to execute the overnight accumulation of orders to sell, sell, sell.

tradish ('treɪdɪʃ), *a. nonce-wd.* [f. TRAD(E *sb.* + -ISH[1].] Of or suggestive of trade or tradesmen.

1803 D. WORDSWORTH *Jrnl.* (1941) I. 243 The houses.. have a tradish look, as if they might have been off-sets from Glasgow.

† **'tradit**, *v. Obs. rare*[−1]. [f. L. *trādit-*, ppl. stem of *trādĕre* to hand over, deliver, f. *trans* across, over + *dare* to give. (Cf. *credit* f. L. *crēdit-*.)] *trans.* To deliver, to communicate.

1657 TOMLINSON *Renou's Disp.* 530 The most usual preparation, is after the manner we have tradited.

† **'traditative**, *a. Obs. rare.* prob. an error for TRADITIVE I.

1657–83 EVELYN *Hist. Relig.* (1850) I. 165 They fancy it very difficult to conceive how this deadly spot [of sin] should adhere so pertinaciously without some traditative emanation, seeing the body does not defile the Soul.

tradition (trəˈdɪʃən), *sb.* Also 4–6 -icion. [a. OF. *tradicion, -iccion* (1292 in Godef.), in 15th c. *tradition*, = Pr. *tradition*, Sp. *tradicion*, It. *tradizione*, ad. L. *trāditio, -ōnem* 'delivery, surrender, handing down, a saying handed down, instruction or doctrine delivered', as in *traditio evangelica, catholica traditio* (Tertullian).]

1. The action of handing over (something material) to another; delivery, transfer. (Chiefly in *Law*.)

1540 in R. G. Marsden *Sel. Pl. Crt. Adm.* (1894) I. 99 The byer.. may entre and take possession of the said shipe goods.. withowte any further tradicion or delyvery. **1601** W. WATSON *Sparing Discov.* 13 In that a Priest is made by tradition of the Chalice, Patten, and Host into his hands. **1658** BRAMHALL *Consecr. Bps.* xi. 225 Then followeth.. lastly the tradition of the Bible into his hands. **1766** BLACKSTONE *Comm.* II. xx. 307 A deed takes effect only from this tradition or delivery. **1773** ERSKINE *Inst. Law Scotl.* II. i. §18 Tradition, which may be defined, the delivery of the possession of a subject by the proprietor, with an intention to transfer the property of it to the receiver. **1774** BP. HALLIFAX *Anal. Rom. Law* (1795) 25 Justinian abolished the distinction, and gave to Tradition, or simple delivery, all the effects of the ancient Mancipation. **1884** *Cath. Dict.* (ed. 2) 626 Handing to the new priest the paten and chalice—an act commonly called the 'tradition of the instruments'.

† **2. a.** A giving up, surrender; betrayal. *Obs.*

1482 *Monk of Evesham* (Arb.) 19 The office and seruice of owr lord ihesu cryste ys tradicion and passion was solenly songe. **1611** W. SCLATER *Key* (1629) 103 By tradition or deliuering them vp to the power of Sathan. **1653** MANTON *Exp. James* i. 13 Wks. 1871 IV. 92 A judicial tradition and delivering them up to the power of Satan and their own vile affections.

b. *spec.* in *Ch. Hist.* Surrender of sacred books in times of persecution: cf. TRADITOR 2.

1840 MILMAN *Hist. Chr.* II. 369 The consecration of a bishop guilty of tradition, was the principal ground on which his election was annulled. *Ibid.* 371 Both denounced their adversaries as guilty of the crime of tradition. **1874** J. H. BLUNT *Dict. Sects* (1886) 128/2 The crime of Tradition was a new one [Diocletian era]. [**1908** C. BIGG *Orig. Chr.* xxxvi. (1909) 484 In Gaul the Donatists themselves allowed that the sin of *traditio* had not occurred.]

3. a. Delivery, *esp.* oral delivery, of information or instruction. Now *rare*.

a **1500** MEDWALL *Nature* 60 Arystotell Whyche hath left in bokys of hys tradycyon How euery thyng by heuynly constellacyon Is brought to effecte. **1575** GASCOIGNE *Making of Verse* in *Steele Gl.*, etc. (Arb.) 33, I couet rather to satisfie you particularly, than to vndertake a generall tradition. **1605** BACON *Adv. Learn.* II. xvi. §1 The expressing or transferring our Knowledge to others.. I will tearme by the general name of Tradition or Deliuerie. **1667** JER. TAYLOR *Dissuas. Popery* II. I. iii. 102 Tradition is any way of delivering a thing, or word to another; and so every doctrine of Christianity is by Tradition. I have deliver'd unto you, saith S. Paul, that Christ died for our sins. **1868** M. PATTISON *Academ. Org.* vii. 327 A national institute for the preservation and tradition of useful knowledge.

† **b.** An ordinance or institution orally delivered.

1382 WYCLIF *Col.* ii. 8 Se ȝe that no man disseyue ȝou by philosofye and veyn fallace.. vp the tradicioun of men, vp elementis of this world, and not vp Crist. **1563** WINȜET *Four Scoir Thre Quest.* §63 Wks. (S.T.S.) I. 115 The Apostill St. Paull commandit in sindry places his traditionis to be keipet. **1565** STAPLETON tr. *Staphylus' Apol.* 153 b, They putt out of S. Paule the worde *Traditions*, and put in his place sometime *Ordinaunces* sometime *Institutions*.

c. ***Tradition of the Creed*** (*Ch. Hist.*): oral instruction upon the Creed given to catechumens.

1888 *Cassell's Encycl. Dict.* s.v., *Tradition of the Creed*,.. the instruction formerly given on certain days to the catechumens upon the Creed at mass. The time and place varied in different Churches. In the Mozarabic Missal it still retains its place before the Epistle on Palm Sunday. At Rome it took place on the Wednesday in Mid-Lent.

4. a. The action of transmitting or 'handing down', or fact of being handed down, from one to another, or from generation to generation; transmission of statements, beliefs, rules, customs, or the like, esp. by word of mouth or by practice without writing. Chiefly in phrase ***by tradition***.

1591 SAVILE *Tacitus' Hist.* (1604) 53 Old songs delivered to them, by tradition, from their fathers. **1625** N. CARPENTER *Geog. Del.* II. xviii. (1635) 282 Some few customes preserued by tradition, not writing. **1626** AILESBURY *Passion Serm.* 3 Punishments which hung over their heads, and, by the tradition of just revenge, upon their children. **1658** PHILLIPS, *Tradition*,.. a bequeathing any Doctrine to posterity from age to age. **1725** DE FOE *Voy. round World* (1840) 191 Rivetted in their minds by tradition from father to son. **1818** HALLAM *Mid. Ages* ix. I. (1819) III. 335 The memory of Greece and Rome would have been feebly preserved by tradition. 1854 MILMAN *Lat. Chr.* IV. iv. (1864) II. 277 Fragments.. tinged with Christian allusion in their later tradition from bard to bard.

b. quasi-personified, usually as a speaker. (Cf. FAME *sb.*[1] 1 b, RUMOUR *sb.* 2 b.)

1658 BAXTER *Saving Faith* 87 Tradition having published it, your labour is to be a great deal the more acceptable for the Authors sake. 1686 AGLIONBY *Painting Illustr.* i. 37 Paintings.. which Tradition affirm'd to be Antienter than the Foundation of Rome. 1797 HT. LEE *Canterb. T., Old Woman's T.* (1799) I. 333 Tradition tells us of numberless miracles performed here! 1863 MARY HOWITT *F. Bremer's Greece* II. xvi. 153 Wolves, so says tradition, first took gold to Delphi.

5. a. That which is thus handed down; a statement, belief, or practice transmitted (esp. orally) from generation to generation.

c 1380 WYCLIF *Wks.* (1880) 392 I-bounden oonly by a posityue lawe or a tradycion þat þai han hem sijlfe made. 1432-50 tr. *Higden* (Rolls) II. 225 Matussale.. lyvenge.. to the grete floode of Noe, and noo longer, after the trewe tradicion. 1599 SHAKS. *Hen. V*, v. i. 76 Go, go,.. will you mocke at an ancient Tradition began vppon an honourable respect? 1704 NELSON *Fest. & Fasts* xiii. (1739) 159 The.. Traditions published under his Name are rejected.. as spurious. 1851 D. WILSON *Preh. Ann.* (1863) II. IV. ii. 234 The traditions associated with these.. monuments. 1872 MORLEY *Voltaire* i. (1886) 4 A collective religious tradition that had lost its virtue. 1878 SIMPSON *Sch. Shaks.* I. 4 Stucley's life has been surrounded with a complete cloud of traditions.

b. More vaguely: A long established and generally accepted custom or method of procedure, having almost the force of a law; an immemorial usage; the body (or any one) of the experiences and usages of any branch or school of art or literature, handed down by predecessors and generally followed. In quot. 1818, an embodiment of an old established custom or institution, a 'relic'.

1593 SHAKS. *Rich. II*, III. ii. 173 Throw away Respect, Tradition, Forme, and Ceremonious dutie. 1818 LADY MORGAN *Autobiog.* (1859) 183 The duke is a tradition of the *grands seigneurs* of the courtly times of France, a tradition fast wearing out. 1865 R. W. DALE *Jew. Temp.* ix. (1877) 89 The glorious traditions of their race seemed against them. 1882 FREEMAN *Amer. Lect.* II. v. 381 The tradition is that a President [of U.S.] may be re-elected once and once only. 1891 *Leeds Mercury* 2 May 6/4 A scheme.. which was contrary to Conservative traditions.

6. *spec.* (*Theol.* and *Eccl.*) **a.** Among the Jews, Any one, or the whole, of an unwritten code of regulations, etc. held to have been received from Moses, and handed down orally from generation to generation and embodied in the MISHNAH.

c 1380 WYCLIF *Sel. Wks.* II. 78 But whi breken ȝe Goddis maundement, for ȝoure veyn tradicioun? 1382 —— *Matt.* xv. 2 Whi thi disciplis ouerpassen, or breken, the tradiciouns [*gloss* or statutis] of elder men [1534 TINDALE, the traditions of the elders]? 1585 ABP. SANDYS *Serm.* i. 11 Vnder the name of doctrine receiued from Moses by word of mouth, without writing, that is to say tradition, the Scribes and Pharisees were able smoothlie to carie away any thing, til Christ recalled all things to the Lawe. 1613 PURCHAS *Pilgrimage* (1614) 170 When two Rabbins (saith their Talmud) maintaine contrary opinions, yet must not men contradict them, because both of them hath his Kabala or Tradition for the same. 1877 C. GEIKIE *Christ* II. xliv. 205 The commands or 'traditions' of the Fathers, handed down from the days of the Great Synagogue, but ascribed with pious exaggeration to the Almighty.

b. In the Christian Church, Any one, or the whole, of a body of teachings transmitted orally from generation to generation since early times; held by Roman Catholics to comprise teaching derived from Christ and the apostles, together with that subsequently communicated to the church by the Holy Spirit, and to be of equal authority with Scripture. Also (as in 4) the transmission of such teaching.

1551 T. WILSON *Logike* (1580) 36 The Churche maie make Lawe, and appointe Tradicions, whatsoeuer thei be. 1562 *Articles of Religion* xxxiv, Whosoever.. doth openly break the traditions and ceremonies of the Church which be not repugnant to the word of God. 1667 MILTON *P.L.* XII. 512 The truth With superstitions and traditions taint. 1704 NELSON *Fest. & Fasts* v. II. (1739) 501 It being the Tradition of the Church. 1737 CHALLONER *Cath. Chr. Instr.* (1753) 213 The Sunday, or the Lord's-Day, which we observe by Apostolical Tradition instead of the Sabbath. 1867 BRANDE & COX *Dict. Sc.*, etc., *Tradition*, in Theology.. is commonly employed to denote any doctrine or alleged fact, delivered or handed down, and received on the faith that the first to whom it was delivered received it from an authentic source.

c. Among Muslims, An account of sayings and doings of Muhammad, not contained in the Koran, but transmitted at first orally, and afterwards recorded; esp. those accepted as authoritative by the Sunnites or orthodox Muslims, but rejected by the Shiites: = SUNNA.

1718 OCKLEY *Hist. Saracens* II. 87 The Muslemans (who intitle themselves Sonnites, that is Observers of the Tradition, and Orthodox). 1727-41 CHAMBERS *Cycl.* s.v. *Sonna*, There are also sectaries among the Mahometans, called Shiites, who reject the traditions of the Sonnites. 1860 GARDNER *Faiths of World, Sonnah*, the Tradition of the Mohammedans, being the authentic record of the sayings and doings of the Prophet... There are six collections of the Sonnite traditions, and four of those of the Schiites.

7. *attrib.* and *Comb.*, as ***tradition-bound***, ***-following***, ***-nourished***, ***-ridden*** adjs.; ***tradition-monger***; **tradition-directed**, *a.*, applied to persons whose behaviour and goals are largely directed by social conventions; cf. *inner-directed* adj. s.v. INNER *a.* (*sb.*[2]) 1 n, *other-directed* adj. s.v. OTHER *adj. pron.* (*sb.*) D. 2.; **Tradition Sunday** (*Ch. Hist.*), a name for Palm Sunday, as the day of 'tradition of the creed' (see 3 c) in some churches.

1719 J. T. PHILIPPS tr. *Thirty-four Confer.* 5 Believing.. the Fables and Reveries of Tradition-mongers, your Poets and Doctors. 1888 *Cassell's Encycl. Dict.* s.v., *Tradition-Sunday.* 1895 *Westm. Gaz.* 17 May 7/2 To think that the tradition-bound Austria-Hungary, of all countries in Europe, should be the first to call a Pole to the post of Foreign Minister! 1901 *Academy* 26 Jan. 81/1 The prosy formula-ridden, tradition-following, go-by-rule eighteenth century. 1901 *Weekly Regr.* 19 Apr. 485/2 The tradition-nourished intellectual life so distinctive of the Catholic Church. 1910 *Westm. Gaz.* 25 June 2/3 Experiments.. for the warning or encouragement of a more crowded and tradition-ridden island. 1950 D. RIESMAN *Lonely Crowd* i. 9 The society of high growth potential develops in its typical members a social character whose conformity is insured by their tendency to follow tradition: these I shall term tradition-directed people and the society in which they live a society dependent on tradition-direction. 1959 *Times* 3 Sept. 13/5 He insists warmly on the importance of establishing three main categories of social character among writers... There are the inner-directed.. the other [*printed* outer]-directed.. and the tradition-directed. 1970 E. FLORES in I. L. HOROWITZ *Masses in Lat. Amer.* ix. 333 In countries ruled by tradition-directed, ignorant landlords,.. it is impossible to apply sophisticated redistributive policies.

tra'dition, *v. rare.* [f. prec. sb.] *trans.* To transmit by tradition; to relate as a tradition.

1640 FULLER *Joseph's Coat, 1 Cor. xi. 23* (1867) 43 Παρέδωκα ὑμῖν... English it as you please, 'I traditioned it unto you'. 1655 —— *Ch. Hist.* VI. iii. 318 The following story is.. traditioned with very much credit amongst our English Catholicks. *a* 1661 —— *Worthies, Somerset.* (1662) III. 20 This I may call a Charitable Curiosity, if true what is traditioned. 1872 *Daily News* 12 Aug., It is traditioned of Mr. Childers that he has been seen in a pea jacket.

So **tra'ditioned** (-ʃənd) *a.* (*rare*), having traditions of a kind or to a degree specified by the prefixed word.

1850 R. SIMPSON *Mem. Worth* iv. 47 The Crawick, a wild traditioned stream pours its waters into the Nith. 1940 W. DE LA MARE *Pleasures & Speculations* 14 One of the most ancient and richly traditioned cities of Denmark.

traditional (trəˈdɪʃənəl), *a.* (*sb.*) [f. TRADITION *sb.* + -AL[1]: cf. F. *traditionnel*, also med.L. *trāditiōnālis* (840) = *trāditōrius* TRADITORY.]

A. *adj.* **1. a.** Belonging to, consisting in, or of the nature of tradition; handed down by or derived from tradition.

a 1600 HOOKER *Eccl. Pol.* VI. v. §7 In sundry traditional writings set down by their great interpreters and scribes. 1641 MILTON *Prel. Episc.* Wks. 1851 III. 78 We esteem his traditionall ware, as lightly as Victor did. 1690 LOCKE *Hum. Und.* IV. xviii. §10 There can be no Evidence that any traditional Revelation is of divine Original, in the Words we receive it, and in the Sense we understand it, so clear, and so certain, as those of the Principles of Reason. 1814 SCOTT *Wav.* lxxii, The traditional records of the respectable and ingenious Mrs. Grant of Laggan. 1911 H. M. R. MURRAY *Erthe upon Erthe* Introd. 23 The popular traditional version of the poem tended to become modified.

b. That is such according to tradition; asserted or related by tradition.

1856 STANLEY *Sinai & Pal.* v. 246 This traditional selection of Gerizim as the scene of the meeting with Melchizedek is further confirmed by all the circumstances of the narrative. 1874 SAYCE *Compar. Philol.* viii. 302 The heirlooms of a traditional past. 1879 S. C. BARTLETT *Egypt to Pal.* xxii. 455 Quarentania, the traditional region of the forty days temptation. 1908 [MISS FOWLER] *Betw. Trent & Ancholme* 19 A traditional 'Rose of Sharon' survives from our great-grandmother's days.

c. Applied to a style of post-war jazz inspired chiefly by the bands of the earliest period of jazz, as opposed to *modern jazz* s.v. MODERN *a.* 3 a. Cf. TRAD *sb.* 1.

1950 *Downbeat* 28 July 10/1 This.. has been the particular gripe of the traditional jazz adherents. 1980 J. WAINWRIGHT *Man of Law* i. 7 A mutual fanaticism for traditional jazz... The small-group combinations beloved of three decades ago.

†**2.** Observant of, bound by tradition. *Obs. rare.*

1594 SHAKS. *Rich. III*, III. i. 45 You are too sencelesse obstinate, my Lord, Too ceremonious, and traditionall... You breake not Sanctuarie, in seizing him. 1644 MILTON *Judgm. Bucer* Wks. 1851 IV. 299 A pervers Age, eager in the reformation of Names and Ceremonies, but in realities as traditional and as ignorant as their forefathers.

†**B.** *sb.* A traditional belief or practice. *rare*⁻¹.

1643 W. GREENHILL *Axe at Root* 13 We stick too much to Mosaicalls, Prelaticalls, and Traditionalls.

Hence **traditionality** (-ˈælɪtɪ), traditional quality or character; a traditional belief or principle.

1834 *New Monthly Mag.* XLI. 455 We may trace a traditionality, perhaps, in the style of representing Falstaff. 1840 CARLYLE *Heroes* vi. (1858) 351 Many a man, doing loud work in the world, stands only on some thin traditionality, conventionality; to him indubitable, to you incredible.

tra'ditionalism. [ad. F. *traditionalisme*, or f. prec. + -ISM.]

1. A system of philosophy which arose in the Roman Church *c* 1840, according to which all human knowledge (or, in a modified form of the system, all knowledge of religious and moral truth) is derived by traditional instruction from an original divine revelation.

[1858 LUPUS (*title*) La Traditionalisme et le Rationalisme examinés.] 1885 W. W. ROBERTS *Pontif. Decrees* Introd. 5 No sound Catholic could hold the opinions on Traditionalism taught at Louvain. 1885 *Cath. Dict.* (ed. 3), *Traditionalism*, a system of philosophy in which intellectual cognition, so far as the human mind is concerned, is reduced to belief in truth communicated by revelation from God, and received by traditional instruction through the medium of language, which was originally itself a supernatural gift. This system is also called *Fideism*, and is a reaction from the extreme of rationalism into an opposite extreme of anti-rationalism. De Bonald (d. 1840) is regarded as its author.

2. Adherence to traditional doctrine or theory; maintenance of, or submission to, the authority of tradition; excessive reverence for tradition: esp. in matters of religion.

1860 THIRLWALL *Rem.* (1877) I. 395 Without this, she would have fallen.. under the blows, not of rationalism, but of traditionalism and superstition. 1869 *Spectator* 24 July 875 A conquest over the slavish legalism of the Pharisee and the timid traditionalism of the pious Jew. 1883 A. ROBERTS *O.T. Revision* ii. 29 Criticism and traditionalism are pitted against each other throughout the entire volume.

tra'ditionalist. [f. TRADITIONAL + -IST.] **a.** An adherent of traditionalism; one who upholds the authority of tradition: = TRADITIONIST 1. Also *attrib.*

1875 E. WHITE *Life in Christ* II. xvi. (1878) 188 If the Pharisaic doctrine of the oral law were the truth.., there was no reason why the Incarnate Wisdom of God should not confirm the doctrine of the traditionalists. 1881 *Nation* (N.Y.) XXXII. 425 The high-handed procedure of the traditionalist leaders. 1881 W. R. SMITH *O. Test. in Jew. Ch.* xi. 326 The superciliousness with which traditionalists declare the labours of the critics to be visionary. 1906 *Edin. Rev.* July 208 To the traditionalist the reformer.. is a profane person.

b. One who plays, appreciates, or supports traditional jazz (see TRADITIONAL *a.* 1 c). Also *attrib.* or as *adj.*

1951 *Jazz Jrnl.* Sept. 15/1 First, the bands... The stars of the Traditionalist show were 'The Saints'. *Ibid.* 15/2 Why did he have to spoil what was otherwise an excellent job of compering by making his usual crack at the traditionalists? 1962 [see MODERNIST 6]. 1983 *New Oxf. Compan. Music* I. 990/1 Parker.. laid his influence on virtually everything and everyone except the dedicated 'traditionalists'.

Hence **traˌditionaˈlistic** *a.*, of or belonging to traditionalists or traditionalism.

1874 tr. *Ueberweg's Hist. Philos.* II. 339 De Bonald (1754-1840) was the chief of the so-called 'traditionalistic' school, the leading dogma of which was the divine creation of language.

tra'ditionalize, *v.* [f. TRADITIONAL *a.* + -IZE.] *trans.* To render traditional; to imbue with or constrain by tradition. Chiefly as **tra'ditionalized** *ppl. a.*, **tra'ditionalizing** *ppl. a.* and *vbl. sb.*

1882 DAVIDSON in *Encycl. Brit.* XIV. 860/2 [Longfellow's visit to Europe] traditionalized his mind.. and rendered him in some measure unfit to feel or express the spirit of American nature and life. 1951 R. FIRTH *Elements of Social Organization* iv. 134 The price system.. may be.. of a highly traditionalized type, with relative inflexibility in rates over long periods, and considerable resistance on the part of producers and consumers to variation in these rates. 1960 C. GEERTZ *Relig. Java* i. 11 The more traditionalized peasants and their proletarianized comrades in the towns. 1976 *World Politics* XXVIII. 250 There may indeed be a traditionalizing role for military rulers in Africa. 1978 *Econ. Devel. & Cultural Change* XXVI. 763 The presence of the petroleum-extraction industry in the desert region surrounding Augila was having the simultaneous effects of modernizing and 'traditionalizing' oasis life. 1982 *Dædalus* Winter 101 What these revolts appear to have in common.. is their class basis and their traditionalizing, but nontraditional, ideologies.

Hence **traˌditionaliˈzation**, the process of making or becoming traditional; adherence to tradition.

1966 A. R. WILLNER *Neotraditional Accommodation to Political Independence* 3 At the microscopic level, the process of traditionalization, as it is described here for Indonesia, involves the increasing influence of indigenous and particularistic rather than modern, rational criteria on the way in which public officials fulfil their prescribed roles. 1977 *Social Problems* XXV. 135 In the Yom-Kippur War, traditionalization emphasized the centrality of the feminine family roles. 1981 R. & M. M. LAROSSA *Transition to Parenthood* i. 24 The practical implications of traditionalization following birth should also not be ignored. 1981 *Stud. in Compar. Internat. Devel.* Fall-Winter 65 The absorption of h.s. immigrants can be described as entailing not modernization, but rather 'traditionalization'.

traditionally (trəˈdɪʃənəlɪ), *adv.* [f. as prec. + -LY[2].] In a traditional manner; by, in the way of, or according to tradition.

1646 SIR T. BROWNE *Pseud. Ep.* I. viii. 31 There are many things concerning the nature of simples, traditionally delivered, and to which I beleeve he gave no assent himselfe. *Ibid.* VII. xviii. 381 If that were true which is traditionally related by Strabo. 1764 GOLDSM. *Hist. Eng. in Lett.* (1772)

I. 211 The common law, which was traditionally delivered to them from their ancestors. **1859** C. Barker *Assoc. Princ.* ii. 37 In an age..when private revenge was traditionally, if not legally, sanctioned. **1901** *Athenæum* 10 Aug. 198/1 The ..effigy..of the maid of Normanton who was traditionally eaten by earwigs.

traditionary (trəˈdɪʃənərɪ), *a.* (*sb.*) [f. TRADITION + -ARY[1]: cf. *additionary*. (In mod.L. *trāditiōnārius*.)]

1. = TRADITIONAL *a.* 1.

1661 Glanvill *Van. Dogm.* 249 Traditionary impositions. *a* **1677** Hale *True Relig.* I. (1684) 2 By Traditionary Transmission of many important Truths.. from Ancestors to their Posterity. **1748** Hartley *Observ. Man* II. iv. 396 The Corrupted Remains of some traditionary Revelation. **1802** Paley *Nat. Theol.* xviii. (ed. 2) 329 What can be the traditionary knowledge of a chicken hatched in an oven? **1857** Livingstone *Trav.* Introd. 1 Our grandfather was intimately acquainted with all the traditionary legends. **1868** Gladstone *Juv. Mundi* ii. (1869) 41 The traditionary, as opposed to the merely mythical, period.

b. = TRADITIONAL *a.* 1 b.

1835 Greswell *Parables* I. 442, I see the vestiges of a traditionary paradise in this dream of the poets. **1840** Hood *Up the Rhine* 314 Some two hundred yards distant stood the mill, in an Arabian waste, as remote from corn as the traditionary Mill of Buccleugh.

c. Characterized by tradition.

1844 Ld. Houghton *Palm Leaves, Burial Ground of Scutari*, 'Tis well to live and lord o'er those By whom his sires were most renown'd, But his fierce heart finds best repose In this traditionary ground.

†**2.** Observant of tradition; = TRADITIONAL *a.* 2.

1613 Purchas *Pilgrimage* III. x. 247 They hate the Persians,..more then they doe the Christians: like as the Traditionary Iew doth the Textuarie, and the Papist the Protestant. **1666** Tillotson *Rule Faith* III. x, Himself and his Traditionary Brethren.

B. *sb.* One who maintains or accepts the authority of tradition; a traditionalist. *rare.*

1727–41 Chambers *Cycl.* s.v., The traditionaries are what we more usually call rabbins, and rabbinists, or talmudists. .. Hillel shone among the traditionaries, and Schammai among the textuaries. **1732** Neal *Hist. Puritans* I. 324 [quotes Strype (see TRADITIONER 1), with *traditionaries*].

Hence **traˈditioˌnarily** *adv.* = TRADITIONALLY.

1804 Mitford *Inquiry* xv. §5 (ed. 2) 347 The antient Welsh airs, which have been transmitted traditionarily by ignorant harpers.

†**traˈditionate**, *a.* *Obs.* *rare*$^{-0}$. [f. TRADITION *sb.* + -ATE[2].] Handed down by tradition, traditional. Hence †**traˈditionately** *adv.* (*obs. rare*$^{-1}$), by tradition, traditionally.

1593 Nashe *Christ's T.* 38 Not all thy seauenty Esdrean Cabalizers, who traditionately from Moyses receiued the Lawes interpretation, could euer rightly teach thee to diuine of the crucified Messias.

traditioner (trəˈdɪʃənə(r)). *rare.* [f. as prec. + -ER[1].] **1.** = TRADITIONIST 1.

1646 J. Gregory *Notes & Observ.* xxv. 122 The Easterne Traditioners meane by this the continuall sadnesse and contristation of heart. **1649** W. Sclater *Comm. Malachy* (1650) 48 The most superstitious Traditioners that ever lived. **1711** Strype *Life Abp. Parker* IV. xxviii. 435 In the Church of the Traditioners there is no other Disciplin than that which hath been maintained by the Antichristian Pope of Rome. **1868** Gladstone *Glean.* (1879) III. 58 We are all of us traditioners in a degree much greater than we think.

2. = TRADITIONIST 2.

c **1882** J. Lucas *Studies Nidderdale* 41 Taken..from the dictation of a female traditioner.

traditionism (trəˈdɪʃənɪz(ə)m). *rare.* [f. as prec. + -ISM.] = TRADITIONALISM 2.

1864 Webster, *Traditionism*, traditionalism. **1896** *Record* 13 Nov. 1127/1 The last reservation borders on traditionism.

traditionist (trəˈdɪʃənɪst). [f. as prec. + -IST.]

1. One who accepts, adheres to, or maintains the authority of, tradition. **a.** *generally.*

1666 Tillotson *Rule Faith* III. x, This fundamental difference about the rule of faith..is fully acknowledged by the traditionists themselves. **1706** Phillips (ed. Kersey), *Traditionist*, one that stands for Tradition. **1872** O. W. Holmes *Poet Breakf.-t.* viii. (1885) 207 The traditionists.. have insisted on eliminating cause and effect from the domain of morals.

b. In Muslim history: see quots. and TRADITION 6 c.

1759 *Universal Hist., Mod.* II. 42 The great schism between the *Sonnites*, or *Traditionists*, that is, those of the Moslems who acknowledge the authority of the *Sonna*, or collection of moral traditions of the sayings and actions of Mohammed, and the *Shiites*, or partisans of Ali. **1847** *Ockley's Saracens* 82 note, Those who consider the caliphs preceding Ali as the rightful successors of Mohammed, are called Sonnites or Traditionists. **1864** *Reader* 30 Apr. 549/3 The language once used by the poets of the Desert, and employed by Mohammed and the traditionists.

c. In Judaism: cf. TRADITION 6 a.

1840 Milman *Hist. Chr.* I. 69 The great schism in the Jewish popular creed, that of the traditionists and anti-traditionists.

2. One who gives vogue to, hands on, or records a tradition; a reporter or relater of traditions.

1759 Pilkington *Rem. Script* v. 15 We are not able to ascertain who the Masorites or Traditionists were, that settled the present Standard of the Hebrew Scriptures. **1789** *Misc.* in *Ann. Reg.* 126/1 Traditionists of grievous tidings and narrators of heart-breaking events. **1841** D'Israeli *Amen. Lit.* (1867) 1 Priests and poets invented, and traditionists expatiated.

So **traˈditionize** *v.*, *intr.* to deal in or give vogue to traditions; to support tradition.

1840 G. S. Faber *Christ's Disc. Capernaum* iv. 101 Ireneus ..against the antiscripturally traditionising Gnostics.

traˈditionless, *a.* *rare.* [f. as prec. + -LESS.] Having no traditions.

1842 J. Wilson *Chr. North* I. 56 A Ruin nameless, traditionless—sole, undisputed property of Oblivion! **1907** *Daily Chron.* 18 June 3/1 A man whose traditions stop short at 1550 is likely to be wrong in so heartily condemning as traditionless..a nation that has gone on for another four centuries with magnificent..energy.

†**traˈditious**, *a.* *Obs.* *rare.* [f. TRADITION: see -OUS. Cf. *seditious*.] = TRADITIONAL 1.

1611 Speed *Theat. Gt. Brit.* (1614) 143/2 How palpably they are carried away by traditious obscurities. **1644** Quarles *Sheph. Oracles* iii, Be not deluded with traditious dreames.

traditive (ˈtrædɪtɪv), *a.* Now *rare.* [app. ad. obs. F. *traditif, -ive* (15th c.) traditional, f. L. *trādit-us*, pa. pple. of *trādĕre* to hand over, deliver: see -IVE.]

1. Characterized by, belonging to, or being transmitted by, tradition; traditional, traditionary.

1611 Cotgr., *Traditif*, traditiue, or of tradition. **1638** Chillingw. *Relig. Prot.* I. ii. §89. 85 If there be any Traditiue Interpretation of Scripture, produce it. **1642** Jer. Taylor *Episc.* (1647) 381 None of the Fathers ever expounded this place of Lay-Elders, so that we have a traditive interpretation of it in prejudice to the pretence of our new office. **1836** Keble *Serm.* viii. Postscr. (1848) 395 The question lay between traditive and private interpretation. **1879** M. Pattison *Milton* xiii. 206 That mysterious combination of traditive with original elements in diction, which Milton and Virgil, alone of poets known to us, have effected.

2. Orally delivered. *rare.*

1849 W. Fitzgerald tr. *Whitaker's Disput.* 553 Paul in this place mentions both traditive and written teaching, and that justly, considering the time.

traditor (ˈtrædɪtə(r)). Also 4 -ore, 5–8 -our. [a. L. *trāditor* deliverer, giver up, betrayer, agent-n. from *trādĕre*: see TRADIT. With *traditour* cf. F. *traditeur* (Froissart). See also TRAITOR.]

†**1.** A betrayer, traitor. *Obs.* in general sense.

c **1375** *Sc. Leg. Saints* xxii. (*Laurentius*) 654 þat man, þat wald tak, & haf Vtheris menis gud with Iniquite, With Iudas traditore suld he be. *c* **1450** *Maitland Cl. Misc.* III. 200 Item ane pharatrum for the sacrament. Item a traditour for the passioun. **1536** in Bolton *Stat. Irel.* (1621) 97 Thomas fitzGerald..who..like a most false disloyal traditour.. rebelled against our soveraigne lord the king. ? **1681** in Somers *Tracts* I. 114 These Traditors of the Gospel have deserted the Plain Paths of Righteousness. **1696** Bp. Compton *Charge* 7 He becomes a Traditor in selling his Duty for a Morsel of Bread. *a* **1711** Ken *Lett.* Wks. (1838) 67 Y[t] they might not have a Latitudinarian Traditour imposed on them, who would betray y[e] baptismall faith. **1819** *Metropolis* I. 14 To our sex, he is a very traditore, and has..planted thorns innumerable in the female breast.

2. *Ch. Hist.* One of those early Christians who in the great persecution under Diocletian, in order to save their own lives, delivered up their sacred books, vessels, etc., or betrayed their fellow-Christians: cf. TRADITION 2 b.

1597 Hooker *Eccl. Pol.* v. lxii. §7 There were in the Church it selfe Traditors, content to deliuer vp the Bookes of God by composition, to the end their owne liues might bee spared. **1634** 'E. Knott' *Charity Maintained* I. vi. §17 Whom they falsly affirmed to haue been ordained Bishop by those who were *Traditours*, or giuers vp of the Bible to the Persecutors to be burned. **1728** H. Herbert tr. *Fleury's Eccl. Hist.* II. 17 The Donatists pretended to prove, that Felix the Bishop of Aptonga was a traditor. **1849** W. Fitzgerald tr. *Whitaker's Disput.* 428 He says..that there was no traditor in that succession from Peter to Anastasius.

attrib. **1877** J. M. Fuller in *Dict. Chr. Biog.* I. 886/2 Exhorting him to cleave to those who had left the traditor-church.

†**3.** One who hands down a tradition. *Obs. rare*$^{-1}$.

1638 Chillingw. *Relig. Prot.* I. iii. §44. 153 *note*, Saving the respect of the Tradition..From whatsoever Traditor it comes.

Hence †**tradiˈtorian** *a.* (*obs. rare*$^{-1}$), †**traditorous** *a.* (*obs. rare*$^{-0}$, implied in †**traditorously** *adv.*), traitorous, treacherous; **ˈtraditorship** (*Ch. Hist.*), the action of a traditor.

a **1734** North *Exam.* III. viii. §42 (1740) 615 The good Ignoramus Sherriff..stood up and maintained the City Rights against those *traditorian Court Slaves. **1536** in Bolton *Stat. Irel.* (1621) 97 Who..rebelled against our soveraigne lord the king, intending most falsly and *traditorously to take the said land of Ireland out of his possession. **1877** J. M. Fuller in *Dict. Chr. Biog.* I. 882/1 Not one present could claim to be free from *traditorship. One had thrown the gospels into the fire, another had offered incense to the gods, a third had delivered up small papers, but kept his codices. *Ibid.* 882/2 The emperor.. subjected the alleged traditorship of Felix to a thorough examination (A.D. 313).

†**ˈtraditory**, *a.* *Obs.* *rare*$^{-1}$. [f. TRADITOR: see -ORY[2]. Cf. med.L. *trāditōrius*, in *trāditōria* (sc. *charta*, etc.), a deed of delivery or investiture: see Du Cange.] = TRADITIONAL 1, TRADITIVE.

a **1653** G. Daniel *Idyll.* iv. 15 What the Ancients Speake From the first Symbole, Traditorie Truth Is soe indeed.

tradle, obs. form of TREADLE.

tradrille, variant (or error for) TREDRILLE.

traduce (trəˈdjuːs), *v.* Also 6 **traduse**. [ad. L. *trādūcĕre* to lead across, transport, transfer, derive; also, to lead along as a spectacle, to bring into disgrace; f. *trans* across + *dūcĕre* to lead.]

†**1.** *trans.* To convey from one place to another; to transport. *Obs.*

1535 *St. Papers Hen. VIII*, VII. 610 The saide Duke of Angolesme shalbe traduced and brought hither into this Realme. **1650** Bulwer *Anthropomet.* 119 Matter is not traduced thorough the Body as it were by stone-gutters. *a* **1677** Hale *Prim. Orig. Man.* II. vii. 183 We have no probable Evidence that any of their Descendents traduced the first Colonies of the American Plantations into America. **1678** Cudworth *Intell. Syst.* I. v. 706 Evil Demons.. exagitating and disturbing the profitable humours,..partly by traducing the noxious into the principal parts.

†**b.** To put into another form or mode of expression, esp. into another language; to translate, render; to alter, modify, reduce. *Obs.* (exc. as an affectation after Fr. *traduire* or L. *trādūcĕre*, or with pun on sense 3; cf. 5).

a **1533** Ld. Berners *Gold Bk. M. Aurel.* (1546) B v b, The auctoures and writers are dispraysed not of them that can traduce and compose werkes. **1552** Huloet s.v. *B*, That whyche they [Grecians] wryte with P. and Ph. is traduced in the Latine in B. **1574** J. Jones (*title*) A Briefe, Excellent and profitable Discourse of the naturall beginning of all growing and liuing things..Collected and tradused aswel forth of the best olde Wryters, as out of the new. **1674** Owen *Vind. Commun. w. God* Wks. 1855 II. 279 Being all of them traduced, and some of them transcribed, from the writings of the Socinians. **1814** Southey in *Q. Rev.* XII. 73 Milton has been traduced into French and overturned into Dutch. **1838** *Blackw. Mag.* XLIV. 615 Count Hypolite writes to us in flowery French, which we will traduce into our own plain English. **1850** Kingsley *Alt. Locke* iii, If ye canna traduce to me a page o' Virgil.

†**c.** To transfer from one use, sense, ownership, or employment to another. *Obs.*

1546 Langley *Pol. Verg. De Invent.* I. xiii. 25 This parte Socrates traduced and applyed from heauenly thinges, to the vse of lyfe. **1619** Sir A. Gorges tr. *Bacon's De Sap. Vet.* 83 In his description the Allegorie may bee applied and traduced to manners. **1632** Lithgow *Trav.* x. 441 An auncient and famous Kingdome,..not long ago traduced to the Castilian King by marriage. **1640** Bp. Hall *Episc.* III. i. 218 It is traduced from that naturall sence, and used to signifie a man of some eminence in place and government.

†**2.** To pass on to offspring, or to posterity; to transmit, esp. by generation. *Obs.*

1568 H. B. tr. *P. Martyr's Comm. Romans* 85 b, To put vs in mynde, that originall sinne is by generation traduced from the parentes into vs. **1606** Bp. Hall *Medit.* I. xxix, Vertue is not traduced in [*Wks.* (1625) by] propagation, nor learning bequeathed by our will, to our heires. **1618** —— *Contempl., N.T.* I. i, It is not in the power of parents to traduce holinesse to their children. **1646** Sir T. Browne *Pseud. Ep.* VI. x. 329 This complexion..is evidently maintained by generation, and by the tincture of the skin as a spermaticall part traduced from father unto son. **1733** Neal *Hist. Purit.* II. 399 The evangelical church.. composing those religious models of Invocation and Thanksgiving, which they have traduced unto us as the Liturgies of St. James, Basil, and Chrysostom.

†**b.** *transf.* To produce as offspring, or in the way of generation; to propagate. (In passive often indistinguishable from 2.) *Obs.*

1599 Davies *Immort. Soul* v. viii, For tho' from Bodies, she [Nature] can Bodies bring, Yet could she never Souls from Souls traduce. *a* **1641** Bp. Mountagu *Acts & Mon.* vii. (1642) 409 There must be a supply of soules for men to be borne,..or soules must be traduced by propagation, as bodies are. *a* **1711** Ken *Hymns Evang.* Poet. Wks. 1721 I. 73 When God traduc'd by His propitious Might, Meal from Meal, Oyl from Oyl, as Light from Light.

†**c.** To derive, deduce, obtain *from* a source. (In passive often indistinguishable from 2.) *Obs.*

1615 J. Wright *Acc. Lady Jane Gray* in *Phenix* (1708) II. 35 Her Religion being traduc'd from the Instructions of her first Parents, and seconded by the learned Admonitions of them of the same Opinion. **1669** Gale *Crt. Gentiles* I. Introd. 3 Contemplations; which he..traduced, originally, ..from the sacred Oracles loged in the Jewish Church. **1709** O. Dykes *Eng. Prov. & Refl.* (ed. 2) 30 A great Part of us, is certainly traduc'd from our Parents.

3. To speak evil of, esp. (now always) falsely or maliciously; to defame, malign, vilify, slander, calumniate, misrepresent; †to blame, censure.

1586–7 *Reg. Privy Council Scot.* IV. 141 To detract, traduce and utter speichis full of dispyte. **1592** *Nobody & Someb.* in Simpson *Sch. Shaks.* (1878) I. 279 Do not traduce the King, hees vertuous. **1593** Abp. Bancroft *Daung. Posit.* II. i. 41 They could not endure to heare her so traduced into all hatred and obloquy. **1602** Marston *Antonio's Rev.* II. ii, My selfe then will traduce his guilt. **1680** Otway *Orphan* III. i. 806 Has he supplanted me by some foul play, Traduc'd my Honour? **1697** Bentley *Phal.* Pref. (1699) 30 What pretense has he for traducing me here, as a proud and insolent man? **1781** Cowper *Expost.* 432 The man that dares traduce, because he can With safety to him-self, is not a man. **1815** Kirby & Sp. *Entomol.* (1828) I. xi. 360 This curious insect so unjustly traduced by a vulgar prejudice.

†**b.** In various obsolete constructions: To state or affirm slanderously (something) *to be* so and

so; to calumniously blame *for*, accuse *of*, charge *with*.

c **1618** MORYSON *Itin.* IV. v. i. (1903) 437 They are confuted, who traduce the English tounge to be like a beggers patched Cloke, which they should rather compayre to a Posey of sweetest flowers. **1630** *R. Johnson's Kingd. & Commw.* 88 Yet are they traduced for many defects. **1632** SIR T. HAWKINS tr. *Mathieu's Unhappy Prosperitie* 49 Those that traduce him of pride. **1643** BAKER *Chron., Eliz.* 59 The Papists everywhere traduced the Queen for cruelty. **1649** MILTON *Eikon.* xvi, The removing of liturgy he traduces to be done only as a thing plausible to the people. **1672** MARVELL *Reh. Transp.* I. 39, I cannot warrant any man who hence took occasion to traduce him of Popery.

†**c.** To expose (to contempt); to bring dishonour upon, dishonour, disgrace. *Obs. rare.*

1605 BACON *Adv. Learn.* I. iii. §3 That which is most traduced to contempt. **1607** TOPSELL *Four-f. Beasts* (1658) 552 Likewise in..many other places of Scripture, whereby God himself must needs be traduced, if there be no Unicorn in the world. *a* **1661** HOLYDAY *Juvenal* 159 By their own ignoble actions they traduce, that is, disgrace their ancestors.

†**4.** To lead astray, mislead, seduce, betray. *Obs.*

a **1625** [see *traduced* below]. **1625** J. ROBINSON *Ess.* vii. Wks. 1851 I. 38 Many make their choice amiss, as.. traduced by some vehement passion of anger, fear, envy, or the like. *a* **1660** *Contemp. Hist. Irel.* (Ir. Archæol. Soc.) I. 286 How those abortiue statists..swarve from theire said first holy principles, traduced to the possitiue opposition therof.

†**5.** To falsify, misrepresent, pervert, turn *into* (something bad). *Obs.*

1643 MILTON *Divorce* II. xii. Wks. 1851 IV. 92 He there cites not the Law of Moses, but the licentious Glosse which traduc't the Law. *a* **1648** LD. HERBERT *Hen. VIII* (1683) 67 Who taking Texts..traduced the Sense thereof. *a* **1674** CLARENDON *Surv. Leviath.* (1676) 200 [It] hath in truth traduced the whole Scheme of Christianity into Burlesque.

Hence (in various senses: see above) **traduced** (trə'djuːst, *poet.* -'djuːsɪd) *ppl. a.*, **tra'ducing** *vbl. sb.* and *ppl. a.* (whence **tra'ducingly** *adv.*).

1601 B. JONSON *Poetaster* v. iii, The malice of traducing tongues. *a* **1625** FLETCHER & MASS. *Laws of Candy* III. ii, I can forget the weakness Of the traduced Souldiers. **1645** MILTON *Tetrach.* Introd., Wks. 1851 IV. 137 The Canon Law..punishes the naming or traducing of any person in the Pulpit. *a* **1711** KEN *Urania* Poet. Wks. 1721 IV. 433 What they all clearly saw We only from traduc'd Sensation draw. **1721** BAILEY, *Traducingly*, slanderously. **1904** *Daily News* 4 May 4/2 His picture of the young Alexander..is less coloured by traducing rumour.

traducement (trə'djuːsmənt). [f. prec. + -MENT.] The, or an, action of traducing; defamation, calumny, slander.

1597 J. KING *On Jonas* (1618) 542 Innocent Christians, after their slanderous and false traducements, carried to their deaths. **1607** SHAKS. *Cor.* I. ix. 22 'Twere a Concealement worse then a Theft, No lesse then a Traducement, To hide your doings. **1839** *John Bull* 19 May, Lady..would have been unjustly immolated..by atrocious traducements there propagated. **1850** BLACKIE *Æschylus* II. 140 For 'gainst the stranger calumny Flows deftly from the tongue, and sweet traducement Costs not a thought.

traducent (trə'djuːsənt), *a. rare.* [ad. L. *trādūcent-em*, pr. pple. of *trādūcĕre* to TRADUCE.] Traducing, slanderous.

1730–6 in BAILEY (folio).

traducer (trə'djuːsə(r)). [f. TRADUCE + -ER[1].] One who traduces.

1. A defamer, slanderer, calumniator.

1614 RALEIGH *Hist. World* II. xxii. (1634) 474 Belike these traducers would commend no actions but of dead Princes. **1779** SHERIDAN *Critic* I. i, You are the greatest traducer of all other authors living. **1868** J. H. BLUNT *Ref. Ch. Eng.* I. 57 In spite of all that was afterwards alleged by Wolsey's enemies and traducers.

†**2.** One who deduces or derives. *Obs. rare.*

1818 in TODD. **1864** WEBSTER cites FULLER.

traducian (trə'djuːsɪən, -'djuːʃ(ɪ)ən), *sb.* and *a.* [ad. late L. *trādūciān-us*, deriv. of *trādux*, *-ducem* a layer or shoot for propagation, also in transferred sense: cf. TRADUCE *v.* 2, 2 b, and -IAN. The sense connects itself with that of the vb., 'to propagate, transmit to posterity'.] **a.** *sb.* (*a*) One who holds that the soul of a child, like the body, is propagated by or inherited from the parents. (*b*) (*less commonly*) One who holds the doctrine of the transmission of original sin from parent to child. **b.** *adj.* Applied to such doctrine or theory.

1727–41 CHAMBERS *Cycl.*, *Traducians, Traduciani*, a name which the Pelagians anciently gave the catholics, because of their teaching that original sin was transmitted from father to children... At present some give the appellation *traduciani* to such as hold that the souls are transmitted to the children by the father. **1864** WEBSTER, *Traducian*, a believer in Traducianism. **1880** H. R. REYNOLDS in *Dict. Chr. Biog.* II. 240 The Ethiopians maintained a vigorous traducian doctrine of the origin of human souls. **1884** W. S. LILLY in *Fortn. Rev.* Jan. 127 The Traducian view—that the soul, like the body, is derived from the parent—has been held by theologians of much repute.

Hence **tra'ducianism**, (*a*) the doctrine of the transmission of the soul from the parents (see a (*a*) above); (*b*) *rarely*, the doctrine of the hereditary transmission of original sin (see a (*b*) above); **tra'ducianist**, a believer in traducianism in either sense; also *attrib.* or *adj.*; whence **traducia'nistic** *a.*, pertaining to traducianists or traducianism.

1848 R. I. WILBERFORCE *Doctr. Incarnation* iii. (1852) 32 This notion was called *Traducianism by the Schoolmen, the system opposed to it being termed Creationism. **1877** SHIELDS *Final Philos.* 199 Tertullian and Gregory of Nyssa had gone to the other extreme of traducianism or the notion of a physical propagation of the soul from parent to child. **1893** *Tablet* 18 Feb. 257 It is not allowable to any loyal Catholic to hold spiritual traducianism or generationism. **1858** J. C. ROBERTSON *Hist. Chr. Ch.* (1875) II. 152 Julian.. declared..that the God of the '*traducianists' (as he styled those who held that sin was derived by inheritance) was not the God of the gospel. **1872** LIDDON *Elem. Relig.* iii. 100 Augustine saw in the Traducianist doctrine an element of materialism. *Ibid.* 102 Of modern Traducianists, Delitzsch among Protestant, and Klee among Roman Catholic writers are perhaps the greatest. **1882–3** *Schaff's Encycl. Relig. Knowl.* III. 2318 He [Tertullian] adopts the *traducianistic view of hereditary sin.

†**tra'ducible**, *a. Obs. rare*$^{-1}$. [f. TRADUCE *v.* + -IBLE: cf. *producible*.] Capable of being 'traduced' or transmitted; transmissible.

a **1677** HALE (J.), Oral tradition..were incompetent without written monuments to derive to us the original laws, because they are of a complex nature, and therefore not orally traducible to so great a distance of ages.

†**tra'duct**, *sb.*[1] *Obs. rare*$^{-1}$. [ad. L. *trāduct-us* sb. (*u*-stem), in same sense, f. *trādūcĕre* to lead across.] A passage, a channel.

1535 STEWART *Cron. Scot.* (Rolls) III. 499 Syne on ane nycht that ilk traduct he brak, Quhair that thair enterit efter at his bak Richt mony sutheron with him that he led.

†**tra'duct**, *ppl. a.* and *sb.*[2] *Obs. rare.* [ad. L. *trāduct-us*, pa. pple. of *trādūcĕre*: see TRADUCE.] **a.** *ppl. a.* (const. as *pa. pple.*) Translated. **b.** *sb.* A translation.

1534 (*title*) Erasmus's Funus, lately traducte into the vulgare Tonge, at the Request of a certayne Gentylman. **1541** R. COPLAND *Galyen's Terap.* 2 A ij, Whiche is the cause wherfore I haue traducte out of latyn in to frenche this fourth boke. *c* **1645** HOWELL *Lett.* II. xlviii, Things translated..lose of their primitive vigor..unless a paraphrasticall version be permitted, and then the traduct may exceed the Originall.

†**tra'duct**, *v. Obs.* [f. L. *trāduct-*, ppl. stem of *trādūcĕre*: see prec.] *trans.* To transmit, esp. by generation; to propagate: = TRADUCE 2, 2 b.

1613 PURCHAS *Pilgrimage* I. v. 24 Although the Soule be not traducted (as they tearme it) and by generation conferred. *a* **1619** FOTHERBY *Atheom.* II. viii. §2 (1622) 281 Our Nature, as it is now depraued in vs, and by the corrupt Conduicts of our sinfull Parents traducted vnto vs. **1657** W. MORICE *Coena quasi Κοινὴ* xxxiii. 306 This uncleannesse is alway diffused and traducted, as legal uncleannesse also was. **1659** H. MORE *Immort. Soul* II. xiii. §6. 256 How this newly-created Soule is infused by God, no man knowes; nor how, if it be traducted from the Parents, both their Soules contribute to the making up a new one.

Hence **tra'ducter, -or,** †(*a*) one who 'traducts'; in quot. 1682 = TRADUCTIONIST (*obs.*); (*b*) a device on the side of a railway carriage that picks up and deposits mail bags while the train is in motion.

1682 H. MORE *Annot. Glanvill's Lux O.* 21 So weak an Illustration is this of what these Traducters would have. **1959** C. J. ALLEN *Mod. Railways* xv. 187 The sacks [of mail] ..are then suspended from hinged traductor arms at the van side. **1970** *Railway Mag.* Oct. 545/2 Post Office Sorting van; has letter sorting racks and some vehicles also have nets and traductor arms. **1978** O. S. NOCK *Gt. Western in Colour* 147/1 Most of these trains had vans fitted with the traductor apparatus for picking up and setting down mails at speed.

traduction (trə'dʌkʃən). [a. OF. *traduction* (13th c. in Hatz.-Darm.), or ad. L. *trāductiōn-em* 'leading across, transference, leading in triumph, public exposure'; in Christ.L. also in sense 3; also, in It. *traduzzione*, F. *traduction* 16th c., in sense of 'translation' into another lang.]

†**1.** Conveyance from one place to another; bringing over, transportation, transference. *Obs.*

?**1501** (*title*) A remembraunce for the traduction of the Princesse Kateryne, doughter to the right high and right myghty Prince the Kinge and Quene of Spayne. **1536** in Strype *Eccl. Mem.* (1721) I. App. lxxvi. 182 Concerning the traduction of the..Duke of Orleans into the realm of England there to bee educated. **1627** HAKEWILL *Apol.* (1630) 233[That] the soule of the Baptist, or Elias, or of one of the Prophets, was by traduction passed into our Saviours bodie. *a* **1677** HALE *Prim. Orig. Man.* II. vii. 198 All the possibility there could be for traduction of the Brutes into America from the known World, could only be by Shipping.

†**b.** ? Course. *Obs. rare*$^{-1}$.

1675 OGILBY *Brit.* Pref. 1 Some following the Natural Traduction of Rivers and Mountains.

†**2.** Translation into another language; *concr.* a translation. *Obs.* or *arch.*

a **1533** LD. BERNERS *Gold. Bk. M. Aurel.* (1546) Bv, I confesse to deserue no merytes for my traduction. **1549** *Compl. Scot.* To Rdr. 10 He that hes the gyft of traductione, compiling or teching, his faculte is..honest. **1663** COWLEY *Pind. Odes* Pref., The verbal Traduction of him into Latin Prose. **1716** M. DAVIES *Athen. Brit.* III. 5 The Jesuit Rapin's Critical Parallels (whereof the English Traduction was so greedily bought up). **1822** SCOTT *Nigel* xxxii, Whilk we do not perceive even in the Latin version of the Septuagint, much less in the English traduction. **1823** BYRON *Juan* XI. xix. *note*, If there be any gem'man so ignorant as to require a traduction.

3. Transmission by generation to offspring or posterity; production, propagation; derivation from ancestry, descent. (Common in 17th c.; now *rare* or *Obs.*)

1593 R. HARVEY *Philad.* 46 The vertues of men are euerlasting, yea and their bodies by traduction are immortall. **1600** O. E. *Repl. Libel* II. iii. 55 Pelagius going about to ouerthrow the traduction of originall sinne in the posteritie of Adam. **1617** HIERON *Wks.* (1620) II. 145 A great question, diuersly disputed to and fro, touching the traduction of the soule. **1640** BP. REYNOLDS *Passions* xxxii. 393 To have Being by Traduction, is, when the soule of the Child is derived from the soule of the Parent, by the meanes of Seed. **1652** N. CULVERWELL *Treat.* I. xi. (1661) 87 The Traduction of the Soul is inconsistent with the Immortality of it. **1875** E. WHITE *Life in Christ* III. xx. (1878) 282 From the first Adam they have received by traduction of being a nature which is animal and perishable.

†**b.** *gen.* Transmission; derivation; handing down, tradition. *Obs.*

1646 SIR T. BROWNE *Pseud. Ep.* I. x. 37 Another Agent, who..proceedeth to obscure the diviner part, and efface all tract of its traduction. **1652** H. L'ESTRANGE *Amer. no Jewes* 50 The generall conflagration of all by fire might easily be conveyed by Sems off-spring, and traduction from Adam. *a* **1677** HALE *Prim. Orig. Man.* II. iii. 150 Arts have their successive invention and perfection and traduction from one People to another. **1727** DE FOE *Syst. Magic* I. i. (1840) 14 His wise dictates..which for so many ages were preserved by oral traduction, and were called the precepts of Noah. **1827** G. S. FABER *Orig. Expiat. Sacr.* 167 That altars and sacrifices were alike independently derived, both to Judaism and to Gentilism, from the common source of primeval Patriarchism: and this traduction he justly deems agreeable to both reason and to history.

†**c.** *transf.* Something transmitted or derived.

1643 SIR T. BROWNE *Relig. Med.* II. §14 God..loves us but for that part which is as it were himself, and the traduction of his Holy Spirit. **1677** GALE *Crt. Gentiles* II. III. 6 Corrupt traductions or broken traditions. **1794** G. WAKEFIELD *Exam. Paine's Age Reason* 49 If no written memorials of the Jewish and Christian dispensations were.. in existence, the present condition of the professors of these systems, as a traduction of believers in a certain system,.. cannot be accounted for.

†**4.** (rendering L. *traductio.*) A rhetorical figure consisting in the repetition of a word (or its derivatives) for some particular effect. *Obs. rare*$^{-1}$.

[**1589** PUTTENHAM *Eng. Poesie* III. xix. (Arb.) 213 Then haue ye a figure which the Latines call *Traductio*, and I the tranlacer: which is when ye turne and tranlace a word into many sundry shapes as the Tailor doth his garment, and after that sort do play with him in your dittie... Here ye see how..this word life is tranlaced into live, liuing, liuely, liuelode.] **1626** BACON *Sylva* §113 The Reports, and Fuges, have an Agreement with the Figure in Rhetorick,..of Repetition, and Traduction. [**1875** E. J. PAYNE *Burke's Sel. Wks.* II. 297 The word is repeated, by the figure called *traductio*, in a contemptuous way.]

5. The action of traducing or defaming; calumny, slander, traducement. *rare.*

1656 BLOUNT *Glossogr.*, *Traduction*, a conveying from one place to another, a translating; a slandering, defaming or traducing. **1793** J. WILLIAMS *Life Ld. Barrymore* 57 But who can restrain the dirty movements of Traduction and Illiberality? **1881** J. NICHOL *Death Themistocles* 17, I left traduction to its perjuries. **1889** *Daily News* 9 Apr. 2/6 The plaintiffs had a right to have their character preserved free of traduction.

6. *Logic* (after *deduction, induction*). Transference or transition from one classification or order of reasoning to another.

1847 JAS. BROUN *Let.* in De Morgan *Formal Logic* App. 332 When, abandoning one scheme of classification, we transfer our knowledge directly to another, we use traduction and traductive syllogism... In political science, what has been predicated by historians of men classed geographically is transferred to men classed according to constitutions of government by traduction. **1855** MISS COBBE *Intuit. Mor.* 76 By a process which modern logicians have happily named 'Traduction' we pass from one order of Reasoning [deductive] to the other [inductive]. **1870** JEVONS *Elem. Logic* xxv. 212 Each conclusion applies to just such an object as each of the premises applies to. To this kind of reasoning the apt name of traduction has been given.

Hence **tra'ductionist**, one who believes in the 'traduction' of the soul (see sense 3 above).

1889 FARRAR *Lives Fathers* I. 232 He [Tertullian] maintains the views of the Traductionists, that the souls of all mankind are derived from Adam.

traductive (trə'dʌktɪv), *a.* [f. L. *trāduct-* ppl. stem (see above) + -IVE.]

1. Having the property of being 'traduced' or transmitted; passing on to another; hereditary; traditional; derivative. Now *rare* or *Obs.*

1657 W. MORICE *Coena quasi Κοινὴ* xxiv. 248 The punishments as wel as privileges are traductive, as in Attainders. **1670** MAYNWARING *Vita Sana* i. 4 Hereditary infirmities, and traductive debilities of Nature. **1741** WARBURTON *Div. Legat.* II. 355 Customs of Men..are all, whether civil or religious, traductive from one another. **1842** ORDERSON *Creol.* Pref., He has..ventured to draw from the sources of his memory traductive events.

2. *Logic.* Involving 'traduction'.

1847 [see TRADUCTION 6].

trady ('treɪdɪ), *a. colloq.* [f. TRADE *sb.* + -Y: cf. *shady*.] Pertaining to or of the nature of trade.

1899 *Cycling* 24 June 481/2 To my mind this worthy minister appears to be taking rather a tradey view of religion. **1901** *Academy* 26 Oct. 375/1 Book-Hunting... There are still possibilities in this least 'tradey' of trades.

tradyment, variant of TRADIMENT *Obs.*

Trafalgar (trəˈfælgə(r), orig. and arch. træfəlˈgɑː(r)). Name of a cape on the S. coast of Spain, famed for a great victory of the British fleet over the combined fleets of France and Spain on 21 Oct. 1805, in which Admiral Nelson was killed. Hence a common element in English names of streets and the like, as Trafalgar Square, London, formerly also of stage-coaches, fabrics, etc.; also, the former name of a large size of printing type: see quots.

1826 *Haberdasher's Guide* 15 Trafalgar Cottons, for working muslins, &c. **1848** THACKERAY *Van. Fair* vii, Whither..is the light four-inside Trafalgar coach carrying us?

1840 *Caslon's Printing Types*, Trafalgar. **1841** SAVAGE *Dict. Printing* 802 Trafalgar. 20 [lines contained in one foot]. *Ibid.* 803 Minion, Brevier, and Trafalgar, may be classed as irregular bodied letters, for they bear no specific regular proportion to any other size. **1888** JACOBI *Printers' Vocab.*, *Trafalgar*, a size of type one size larger than Two-line Double Pica and one size smaller than Canon.

b. Special Comb.: **Trafalgar chair** (see quots. 1934, 1969); **Trafalgar Day**, 21 October, the anniversary of the battle of Trafalgar; **Trafalgar Square** *v. trans. joc.*, to harangue (from the practice of 'soap-box' oratory in such public places).

1822 R. BROWN *Rudiments of Drawing Cabinet & Upholstery Furnit.* (ed. 2) p. xii, Many cabinet-makers, for the sake of notoriety, ridiculously give names to furniture quite inconsistent, such as Trafalgar chairs, Waterloo feet, &c. **1934** M. JOURDAIN *Regency Furnit. 1795–1830* 48/2 The well-known Trafalgar chair..was designed as a light 'parlour' chair, and made normally of beech..with caned seat and loose squab cushion. **1969** J. GLOAG *Short Dict. Furnit.* (rev. ed.) 674 *Trafalgar chair.* Various types of single and elbow chairs, with nautical symbols such as anchors and coiled ropes in the backs, were made after the Battle of Trafalgar in 1805... Apart from the incorporation of such ornament these chairs were usually of the graceful Regency type with sabre legs. **1979** E. CAVE *Blood Bond* I. ii. 22 A Trafalgar chair with a tapestry seat. **1918** A. HUXLEY *Let.* 30 Oct. (1969) 167 On Trafalgar Day this year Cobby made precisely the same remarks about Lord Nelson and Lady Hamilton as last year. **1977** *Navy News* Sept. 24/1 The Exeter Flotilla's Trafalgar Day service will be held in Exeter Cathedral on Sunday, October 23. **1895** A. PINERO *Notorious Mrs Ebbsmith* II. 103, I assure you, dear fellow, I was within three feet of her when she deliberately Trafalgar Squared me. **1944** J. AGATE *Ego 6* 35 But not until I had taken the floor and Trafalgar Square'd K as blisteringly as I could.

†**traffe.** *Obs. rare.* [Cf. OF. *treffe* used in a 14th c. document at Genoa to render It. *traffico* (Hatz.-Darm. s.v. *Trafic*).] Baggage: cf. TRAFFIC *sb.* 4 b.

1566 ADLINGTON *Apuleius* 42 Sodenly the theeves returned home carefull and heavy, bringing no burthens with them, no not so much as traffe or baggage, save onely a maiden.

traffic (ˈtræfɪk), *sb.* Forms: α. 6 traffigo, -ygo. β. 6 trafycke, (*Sc.* trafek, -eque, -eck); 6–7 trafick, -icke, 7–9 trafic. γ. 6 traffyque, -yk(ke, -icc, (*Sc.* traffeck, treffik, trefique), 6–7 trafficke, -ike; 6–8 trafficque, -ique, (*Sc.* traffect), traffick, 6– traffic. [In use soon after 1500, in various forms, cognate with the 15–16th c. F. *trafique* (1441 in Godef.), *trafficque* (fem.), mod.F. *trafic* (m.) (Amyot 1559–74); Prov. *trafec*, *trafey*; Sp. *tráfico*, in 16th c. *tráfago*; Pg. *tráfego*, *tráfico*; It. *tráffico*, also, in 15–16th c. *traffico* (Florio), Venetian (*c* 1500) *traffigo*. The earliest Eng. forms are *traffykke* and *traffigo* (the latter as an alien word); the ordinary forms from 1549 to *c* 1680, *trafficque*, *-ique*, *-icke*, *-ike*, less usually *traf-*, were from the French of the same period; *traffick*, rare before 1600, became frequent in the 17th c. and in the form *traffic* the prevalent one in the 18th c. Some curious Sc. forms occur in the 16th c. The F. *traf(f)ic* was ad. It. *traffico*, which occurs in Pisan documents as early as 1323 (Bonaini, *Statuti inediti della citta di Pisa dal* XII *al* XIV *secolo* (1847) III. 457). OF. had also *trafit*, pl. *-itz* (1440 in Godef. *Compl.*). The sb. appears to have been the noun of action from the verb, It. *trafficare*, Sp. *trafagar*, Cat. *trafegar* to TRAFFIC, the ultimate source and etymology of which present difficulties: see Note below.]

1. a. The transportation of merchandise for the purpose of trade; hence, trade between distant or distinct communities; commerce.

1506 GUYLFORDE *Pilgr.* (Camden) 61 We founde also at Candy .ij. other galyes, Venysyans, ladynge maluesyes, called the galeys of Traffygo. *Ibid.*, We made sayle ayen, and so dyde the other .ij. galeys of Traffigo also in our company. **1549** THOMAS *Hist. Italie* A j b, How commodious the countrey is..to the trafficque of them that liue by merchaundise. **1568** GRAFTON *Chron.* I. 129 That passage and trafficque of Marchaunts was forboden. **1596** SPENSER *F.Q.* VI. xi. 9 Merchants..wount To skim those coastes for bond-men there to buy, And by such trafficke after gaines to hunt. **1596** DALRYMPLE tr. *Leslie's Hist. Scot.* (S.T.S.) I. 38 A citie..to quhilke the frenche men and Spaniȝeards oft because of thair treffik sailed ouir. **1604** E. G[RIMSTONE] *D'Acosta's Hist. Indies* III. xix. 180 The greatest part of the habitation of the coast entertaines all the traffike of Spaine by sea. **1634** SIR T. HERBERT *Trav.* 43 Vessels of Traffique and Warre. **1651** HOWELL *Venice* 83 That the Venetians shold have free and safe trafic into the Pontick Seas. **1719** DE FOE *Crusoe* I. 296 It was not the Way to or from any Part of the World, where the English had any Traffick. **1860** MOTLEY *Netherl.* (1868) I. i. 7 Cadiz,..where the ancient and modern systems of traffic were blending like the mingling of the two oceans.

†**b.** (with *pl.*) A trading voyage or expedition.

a **1548** HALL *Chron.*, *Edw. IV* 241 Thether was one of their common trafficques and ventes of all their Merchaundice. **1598** HAKLUYT (*title*) The Principal Navigations, Voiages, Traffiqves and Discoueries of the English Nation.

2. a. In wider sense: The buying and selling or exchange of goods for profit; bargaining; trade.

1568 GRAFTON *Chron.* I. 4 The honest and simple doings that before tyme had bene vsed..in their exchaunges and trafficques. **1604** R. CAWDREY *Table Alph.*, *Traffique*, bargayning. **1604** E. G[RIMSTONE] *D'Acosta's Hist. Indies* IV. iii. 210 The maner of the Indians trafficke..was to exchange, and give things for things. **1697** EVELYN *Numism.* i. 3 Antient Moneys..first used in Trafick. **1727** W. MATHER *Yng. Man's Comp.* 396 *Traffick* then is the Bartering, Bargaining, or Exchanging of one Man with another. **1786** BURKE *W. Hastings* Wks. 1813 XII. 202 Engaged in a low, clandestine traffick, prohibited by the laws of the Country. **1844** WILSON *Brit. India* III. 128 After a brief interval, Prome again became the seat of industry and traffic.

b. With *a* and *pl.*

1578 T. ELLIS in Hakluyt *Voy.* (1600) III. 40 We did coniecture, that they had either Artificers amongst them, or els a traffike with some other nation. **1604** E. G[RIMSTONE] *D'Acosta's Hist. Indies* V. xxx. 426 Those which made it a trafficke to buy and sell slaves. **1818** SCOTT *Hrt. Midl.* xxxii[i], She..had now, under pretence of a trifling traffic, resumed predatory habits.

c. *fig.*

1505 KILLINGWORTH in *Lett. Rich. III & Hen. VII* (Rolls) II. App. D. 381 As for K[ing] H[enry's] traffykkes they knewe theym wele ynough and better than ye did. **1570** BUCHANAN *Chamæleon* Wks. (1892) 46 The ouersey trafficque of mariage growing cauld. **1633** BP. HALL *Occas. Medit.* (1851) 139 Surely this very traffic of faculties is that, whereby we live;..one man lends a brain; another an arm: one, a tongue; another, a hand. **1697** DRYDEN *Virg. Georg.* IV. 227 The bees have common cities of their own,..beneath one law they live, And with one common stock their traffic drive. **1819** SCOTT *Ivanhoe* xli, I am stout enough to exchange buffets with any who will challenge me to such a traffic.

d. With sinister or evil connotation: Dealing or bargaining in something which should not be made the subject of trade.

1663 BP. PATRICK *Parab. Pilgr.* xxi. (1687) 220 Their courtesies are meer traffique, and they always expect to gain more than they give. **1702** *Eng. Theophrast.* 105 They make a Traffick of Honour, and pay for it with the wind of fair Words. **1790** BURKE *Fr. Rev.* 60 In this political traffick the leaders will be obliged to bow to the ignorance of their followers. **1818** COBBETT *Pol. Reg.* XXXIII. 686 It is notorious, that seats in the House of Commons are an article of traffic. **1880** MRS. FORRESTER *Roy & V.* I. 19 You make the most shameless traffic and barter of yourselves and each other. **1903** *Westm. Gaz.* 31 Dec. 2/3 Fruits of 'the traffic' occupy a prominent place in to-day's Metropolitan police-court reports. *Mod.* The white slave traffic; a traffic in souls and bodies.

e. In phr. ***(as much as) the traffic will bear*** or ***stand*** and varr.: (as much as) the trade or market will tolerate, as much as is economically viable. Also *fig.*

1931 L. STEFFENS *Autobiogr.* V. ii. 853 His wage-earners had their rents raised to all the traffic would bear. **1936** L. C. DOUGLAS *White Banners* vii. 155 We've had all the worry about you that the traffic will stand. **1964** L. DEIGHTON *Funeral in Berlin* xlvii. 294 How much? That's difficult. What do you think the traffic will bear? **1972** *Guardian* 22 May 14/5 The landlord demands a deposit of anywhere from £3 to £150: this is based on what he thinks the traffic will stand. **1976** *Billings* (Montana) *Gaz.* 4 July 2-E/2 The invariable custom is to hire as many deputy superintendents, associate superintendents, assistant superintendents and administrative assistants as the traffic will bear. **1982** T. FITZGIBBON *With Love* I. v. 32 The small neighbourhood shops were..willing to give credit up to a pound, but no more. They knew to a penny what the traffic would bear.

3. *fig.* Intercourse, communication; dealings, business. Now *rare.*

a **1548** HALL *Chron.*, *Edw. IV* 240 The quotidiane entercourse, trafficke and commutacion, which no smal season had ben practised, frequented, & excercised. **1560** DAUS tr. *Sleidane's Comm.* 339 b, That secreat trafficke, that thou haste with infidels. **1592** SHAKS. *Rom. & Jul.* Prol. 12 The fearful passage of their death-mark'd love..Is now the two hours' traffic of our stage. *a* **1628** F. GREVIL *Let. to Hon. Lady* v. Wks. 1870 IV. 285 Shee there vseth the traffique of wit. **1633** T. STAFFORD *Pac. Hib.* I. xv. (1821) 173 The President..returned him no Answer.., utterly refusing any further traffique with him. **1727** DE FOE *Syst. Magic* I. iii. (1840) 62 Perhaps they were not hardened enough at first for the carrying on such a traffick [intercourse with Satan]. **1825** JAMIESON, *Traffeck*, intercourse, familiarity. **1893** STEVENSON *Catriona* xxviii, Our traffic is settled.

†**4.** *transf.* Goods or merchandise in which trade is done; saleable commodities. Also *pl.* (quot. 1604) in same sense. *Obs.*

1555 EDEN *Decades* 157 They bowght them by exchaunge of golde and other of their trafycke. **1560** in Marsden *Sel. Pl. Crt. Admir.* (Selden) II. 119 In which shipps there be any merchaundizes or traffick apperteining to the ennemies. **1604** E. G[RIMSTONE] *D'Acosta's Hist. Indies* IV. xxii. 271 The Cacao..is so much esteemed amongest the Indians (yea and among the Spaniards) that it is one of the richest and the greatest traffickes of new Spaine. *c* **1710** CELIA FIENNES *Diary* (1888) 36 A Considerable ffaire is kept.., ye Traffique mostly hopps. **1716** GAY *Trivia* II. 10 You'll see a draggled damsel, here and there From Billingsgate her fishy traffic bear. **1778** BP. LOWTH *Transl. Isaiah* xxiii. 18 Her traffic and her gain, shall be holy to Jehovah: It shall not be treasured, nor shall it be kept in store.

†**b.** Baggage. *Obs. rare.*

1538 ELYOT, *Impedimenta*, is the caryage and trafyke, that goth with the hooste.

†**c.** A prostitute. Cf. TRADER 1 b. *Obs. rare.*

1591 GREENE *Disc. Coosnage* (1592) 15 These trafickes, these common truls I meane, walke abroad.

d. Worthless stuff, rubbish, trash; also, rascally people; rabble. *dial.*

1828 *Craven Gloss.*, *Traffick*, lumber, trash. 'There wor a deal of oud traffick to sell'... Rabble, low, rascally people, the canaille. **1869** *Lonsdale Gloss.*, *Traffic*, (1) lumber, rubbish. (2) Rabble, low, rascally people.

5. a. The passing to and fro of persons, or of vehicles or vessels, along a road, railway, canal, or other route of transport; also with reference to air travel (usu. prefixed by *air*, and in *Comb.*: see sense 6 below); and *concr.*, the vehicles, etc., collectively.

a **1825** FORBY *Voc. E. Anglia*, *Traffic*,..passing and re-passing on a high road. Ex. 'There is a great deal of traffic on this road'. **1832** HT. MARTINEAU *Weal & Woe* ix, He sauntered along the pier, around which there was no busy traffic. **1886** C. E. PASCOE *London of To-day* xxvi. (ed. 3) 239 The traffic of omnibuses, cabs, carriages, and carts at this point is greater and more confusing than in any other part of London. **1894** SALA *London up to Date* 73 We have long since agreed to call street movement 'traffic'. **1911** E. H. HODGKINSON *Tyranny of Speed* viii. 107 He should hear the traffic coming behind him. **1920** H. B. PRATT *Commercial Airships* vii. 72 Terminal Stations will comprise a landing ground or aerodrome, and will be provided with housing sheds, mooring towers.., with traffic offices, gas generating and storage plant, [etc.]. **1930** W. S. MAUGHAM *Cakes & Ale* ii. 34 There was none of the congested traffic of Jermyn Street. **1935** C. G. BURGE *Compl. Bk. Aviation* 136/1 The cheaper way at intermediate towns or where traffic is light, is to assemble the passengers at a central point, and deal with them at the airport. *Ibid.* 402/2 They were convinced that air traffic would only succeed as a new means of transport if ..international co-operation existed. **1938** [see *traffic control*, sense 6 below]. **1951** R. CAMPBELL *Light on Dark Horse* xvi. 223 The traffic used to collect [in London], like lumber on a river. **1974** J. A. FOSTER in G. P. Howard *Airport Econ. Planning* 5 The data to be collected should not only cover the physical facilities of the airport, but should also indicate the degree of utilization, the volume and composition of traffic, [etc.]. **1982** S. SPENDER *China Diary* 104 There was only one line of traffic in each direction.

b. The amount of business done by a railway, etc., in the transport of passengers and goods; the account of or revenue from this.

1858 [implied in *traffic-return*: see 6]. **1883** *Pall Mall G.* 30 Nov. 5/2 It is obviously advisable that all the railways should adopt the same course, otherwise comparisons of traffic will become even more misleading than they are now. **1885** *Ibid.* 21 Nov. 5/2 Traffics are still decreasing, and this fact is all the more discouraging from the fact that the comparison is with decreased traffics. **1905** *Westm. Gaz.* 28 Sept. 9/1 Satisfaction is again expressed with this week's batch of Home Railway traffics.

c. A railway traffic-rate (RATE *sb.*[1] 6 b).

1899 *Daily News* 14 Mar. 9/1 The Grand Trunk Railway unconditionally withdrew the local traffics of January 6th, and agreed for the present to revert to former rates.

d. *Telecommunications.* The messages, signals, etc., transmitted through a communication system; the flow or volume of such business.

1878 *Telegraphic Jrnl.* VI. 15/2 A monopoly of cable traffic to America. **1889** *Telephone* 15 Oct. 476/2 A Pacific Cable. .. The line..would find traffic enough to pay a fair interest on the investment. **1922** W. F. FRIEDMAN in *Bull. U.S. Signal Office Signal Corps* 1 Oct. 15 In modern military operations, a considerable volume of traffic is available for interception by the enemy. **1935** *Times* 26 Oct. 18/7 These are the busiest hours of the day, during which more than two-thirds of the daily traffic is handled. **1947**, etc. [see ERLANG 2]. **1977** *Times Lit. Suppl.* 25 Feb. 222/5 British Intelligence could decipher German high-grade cipher traffic. **1978** T. ALLBEURY *Lantern Network* iii. 39 He's got his own W/T operator, but sometimes you may have to take his traffic.

6. *attrib.* and *Comb.*, as, in sense 2, ***traffic fellow***, ***instinct***; in 5, ***traffic area***, ***block*** (BLOCK *sb.* 19 a), ***board*** (BOARD *sb.* 8 b), ***congestion***, ***consciousness***, ***-entrance***, ***flow***, ***noise***, ***-privilege***, ***-rate***, ***return*** (RETURN *sb.* 9 c), ***-road***, ***stack***, ***staff***, ***stream***, ***value***; ***traffic-conscious***, ***-free*** adjs.; instrumental, objective, and obj. genitive, as ***traffic-manager***; ***traffic-choked***, ***-congested***, ***-crammed***, ***-furrowed***, ***-laden***, ***-regulating***, ***-thronged*** adjs.; **traffic analysis** *U.S.*, in Cryptography, the obtaining of information through analysis of patterns of communication without the decipherment of individual messages; hence **traffic analyst**; **traffic artery** orig. *U.S.*, a main or arterial road; **traffic circle** orig. and chiefly *U.S.*, a traffic roundabout; **traffic cone**: see CONE *sb.*[1] 9 b; **traffic control**, the regulation of traffic movement through the use of signals or direct commands from authorized persons; a service with this responsibility; in *Aeronaut.*, also as ***air traffic control*** (see AIR *sb.*[1] III. 1); hence **traffic controller**; **traffic cop** *colloq.* (orig. *U.S.*) =

traffic policeman below; **traffic court** orig. *U.S.*, a court of law with jurisdiction over motoring offences; **traffic density**, the number of passengers and of tons of freight carried over any section of a railway in a given period (Webster 1911); **traffic engineer** orig. *U.S.*, one who deals with the design and planning of roads and the control of traffic; hence **traffic engineering**; **traffic island**, a raised or marked area in a road to direct traffic and provide refuge for pedestrians crossing the road; **traffic jam** orig. *U.S.*, a condition in which road traffic cannot proceed freely and comes to a standstill; a stoppage of traffic caused by this, or the vehicles caught in it; also *fig.*; hence **traffic-jammed** *a.*; **traffic lane**, a road carriageway for a single line of moving vehicles; an air or sea route designated as a set course for traffic in order to avoid collisions; **traffic light**, †(*a*) a light used for the guidance of aircraft (*obs. rare*); (*b*) freq. in *pl.*, (one of) a set of lights (usu. red, amber, and green) used for automatic control of road traffic, esp. at junctions; **traffic mile**: see quot.; **traffic offence**, an infringement of the law by the driver of a motor vehicle; **traffic officer** = *traffic policeman* below; **traffic pattern**, (*a*) *Aeronaut.* (see quot. 1956); (*b*) the characteristic distribution of traffic on a route; also *fig.*; **traffic police**, that branch of the police force concerned with road traffic control; hence **traffic policeman**; **traffic-proof** *a.*, of a horse or pony: that can be ridden safely in traffic; so **traffic-proof** *v. trans.*; **traffic sign**, a roadside sign conveying information, warnings, etc., to drivers of motor vehicles; **traffic signal(s** = *traffic light* (*b*) above; **traffic snarl**: see SNARL *sb.*[1] 2 b; **traffic-taker**, a railway official whose business is to compile traffic returns; **traffic ticket** *U.S.*, an official notification of a traffic offence, issued by a traffic warden or the police; **traffic warden**, a person employed to enforce regulations about the parking of motor vehicles and the use of parking meters.

1937 *Hist. Communications Intelligence in U.S.* (Naval Cryptologic Veterans Assoc.) (1982) 29 Information is obtained from communications by..methods short of cryptanalysis, i.e., *traffic analysis. **1979** W. J. HOLMES *Double-Edged Secrets* iii. 18 But until the way was cleared by Rochefort we never discussed the subject of traffic analysis. *Ibid.* Traffic intelligence summaries were produced each day by two *traffic analysts. **1933** *Act 23 & 24 Geo. V* c. 53 §27 It is expedient that the existing *traffic areas under the Road Traffic Act, 1930,..should be varied. **1977** *Chicago Tribune* 2 Oct. XI. B (Advt. Suppl.) 7/4 Washable—great for traffic areas. **1927** *New Masses* June 7/4 In a side street, close to one of the main *traffic arteries of the city of the Angels. **1969** *New Scientist* 13 Mar. 560/1 These additional costs of assimilating a traffic artery into an existing urban area are themselves a massive community burden. **1977** E. V. CUNNINGHAM *One-Penny Orange* (1978) xi. 180 In the twenties..Sunset Boulevard was a quiet carriage road and not the major traffic artery it is today. **1896** *Chambers's Jrnl.* 26 Dec. 822/2 The slow speed and *traffic blocks in crowded streets are apt to tell considerably against electricity. **1904** *Daily Chron.* 17 Feb. 7/2 Traffic blocks are almost unknown. **1905** *Westm. Gaz.* 18 July 8/2 The authority which the Commission recommend to be established is a *Traffic Board. **1977** *Listener* 23 June 809/3 An uneventful march from Speakers' Corner to a rally in Trafalgar Square. No one who took part that day was ever out of sight of one or more of the scores of so-called *traffic cameras that blanket central London and, on these occasions, are connected to the Operations Room [at Scotland Yard]. **1886** *Pall Mall G.* 19 Aug. 3/2 The *traffic-choked streets. **1971** *New Scientist* 1 July 5/1 In traffic-choked cities the slender bike is the fastest means of getting from A to B. **1942** *Policy on Rotary Intersections* (Amer. Assoc. State Highway Officials) 1 The name '*traffic circle' is commonly applied to any intersection design based on the one-way movement of vehicles around a central area. **1970** *Rand Daily Mail* 28 Feb. 7/5 When South Africans say 'traffic circle' for the Englishman's 'roundabout', they give precision to the language. **1934** *Punch* 6 June 634/3 Sir William..urged *traffic-congestion which six-line bridge would bring about in Strand, and reminded his adversaries that old bridge was as much national monument as Cenotaph. **1968** E. A. POWDRILL *Vocab. Land Planning* iii. 55 The case for urban renewal might be based on one or more of the following factors:..traffic congestion, [etc.]. **1948** C. GREATREX in B. Vesey-Fitzgerald *Bk. of Dog* I. 116 The problem of making a dog *traffic-conscious is exceedingly difficult to solve... Far more dogs now possess an inborn instinct of some practical dimension, and as a result show caution and traffic consciousness. **1979** G. N. KNIGHT *Indexing* xiii. 176 An entry such as 'London, its happiness before the invention of Coaches and Chairs' induces a wry smile in our traffic-conscious age. **1936** *Spectator* 10 Jan. 56 The British vice-consulate at Varna, Bulgaria, protests that '*traffic-consciousness' is a horrid word. **1931** *Hansard* (Commons) 6 May 385 Installations of automatic *traffic control signals. **1935** *Discovery* Jan. 2/2 Col. O'Gorman appeals to Science for aid in assessing the improvement due to any change of traffic control, of road layout, or of road code, etc. **1938** *Encycl. Brit. Bk. of Year* 33/1 Increasing volume of traffic forced the development of airport traffic control systems... Experiments in traffic control began almost 20 years ago (using signal lights). **1962** E. SNOW *Other Side of River* (1963) lxxi. 548 How many policemen do you have in New York? Most of ours are for traffic control. **1971** *Flying* Apr. 13/2 With 10 airplanes on the hook in a traffic-control sector that usually has a couple. **1978** L. DEIGHTON *SS-GB* xxiv. 225 The six-ton mobile command-centre—on hand for traffic control during the funeral procession. **1930** *Engineering* 25 July 106/3 Highfield automatic *traffic controller... At present the three-light system appears to be most widely favoured. **1938** *Encycl. Brit. Bk. of Year* 33/1 A glass-enclosed tower is usually provided..to give the traffic controller a full view of the airport and its surroundings. **1963** *Times* 20 Feb. 14/6 As a contrast to her decorative elegance there was the traffic-controller—I hesitate to say policewoman. **1973** *Times* 20 Mar. 8/4 The statement also referred to the month-long strike by French air traffic controllers. **1977** G. MARKSTEIN *Chance Awakening* lxvii. 209 'Some big shot?' asked the RAF squadron leader... 'Guess so,' said the traffic controller. **1908** S. FORD *Side-Stepping with Shorty* xiv. 227 It'll be some time before Langdon'll be pestered anymore by the *traffic cops. *a* **1930** D. H. LAWRENCE *Phoenix II* (1968) 425 One God is relative to another God until he gets into a machine; and then it's a case for the traffic cop! **1961** B. CRUMP *Hang on a Minute, Mate* 23 They..returned to the truck to find a traffic cop standing by it. **1975** R. BUTLER *Where all Girls are Sweeter* vi. 63 There was the usual jam on Putney Bridge... A traffic cop sorted us out. **1919** *Evening Star* (Washington, D.C.) 11 Mar. 24/1 Approval was given last night..to the plan..to establish a *traffic court in this city. **1972** R. HOOD *Sentencing Motoring Offender* v. 105 The remainder [*sc.* motoring offences] would be dealt with at Traffic Courts. **1973** *Times* 17 Oct. 20/3 A traffic court is where a motorist pays to give harmless vent to his frustrations with his car, with traffic jams and wardens, with parking regulations and with authority in general. **1959** P. BULL *I know Face* ix. 164, I arrived at dusk in Casablanca and was driven at breakneck speed to Marrakesh along a *traffic-crammed road, stiff with the results of accidents. **1916** *Proc. 8th Nat. Conf. City Planning* (U.S.) 69 The *Traffic Engineer's duties are along two definite lines. **1959** *Daily Tel.* 8 May 23/3 All the committees were acting independently or their work overlapped. None was able to use the traffic engineers who were being used so effectively in the United States... There seems to be lacking in London the kind of adequately-staffed traffic engineering department which has proved essential in our large cities. **1978** *Jrnl. R. Soc. Arts* CXXVI. 425/1 Increasing the throughput of vehicles on an existing highway..is a field in which traffic engineers have notched up considerable successes as the demand has increased. **1931** *Roads & Streets* Dec. 506/1 A new..occupation has been created in the last few years—that of *traffic engineering. **1959** Traffic engineering [see *traffic engineer* above]. **1970** P. LAURIE *Scotland Yard* ii. 54 They are initiated into the mysteries of traffic engineering. **1886** T. HARDY *Mayor Casterbr.* ix, They..entered..by the back way or *traffic-entrance. **1590** GREENE *Royal Exchange* Ded., Wks. (Grosart) VII. 223 Merchaunts wyth theyr freendes, and *traffique fellowes. **1940** R. S. LAMBERT *Ariel & all his Quality* vi. 146 Broadcasting House..is responsible for a big inward and outward *traffic flow; yet there is nowhere to park a car. **1978** *Dumfries Courier* 20 Oct. 10/3 The traffic operation and parking areas have been designed to ensure maximum traffic flow at all times. **1968** R. K. COX *Retail Site Assessment* xii. 140 The unfortunate word *pedestrianization* means the stopping-up of existing streets..and their conversion into *traffic-free areas for use by pedestrians. **1979** R. PERRY *Bishop's Pawn* viii. 137 Dieter was taken..towards Zurich along..relatively traffic-free roads. **1898** G. MEREDITH *Odes Fr. Hist.* 46 Their *traffic instincts hooded their live wits To issues. **1931** E. E. CUMMINGS *Let.* 7 Jan. (1969) 119 I've just returned from the place de la Concorde..where waited on a *traffic-island for $2\frac{1}{2}$ hours. **1935** L. MACNEICE *Eclogue for Christmas* in *Poems* 16 On all the traffic-islands stand white globes like moons. **1982** 'C. AIRD' *Last Respects* x. 101 The driver negotiated the traffic islands with impatience. **1917** I. CRUMP *Boys' Bk. Policemen* iii. 55 He plunged into the *traffic jam at the next street. **1926** *Sunset* Mar. 38 (*heading*) Traffic jams: how Western cities are trying to reduce congestion on down-town streets. **1939** W. PLOMER *Dorking Thigh* (1945) 20 With a traffic-jam outside (for they turned up in scores). **1957** *Economist* 21 Dec. 1038/1 The Home Universities conference could hardly have chosen a more important subject for discussion last week than the traffic jam of students which piles up every summer when school leavers put in their bids for university places. **1976** *Liverpool Echo* 7 Dec. 1/1 A Buckingham Palace spokesman said she had travelled from Sandhurst and there had been heavy traffic jams. **1964** *Economist* 1 Aug. 476/1 They sit *traffic-jammed in the intractable streets. **1983** *Listener* 1 Sept. 16/1, I was still sitting in my traffic-jammed car five minutes later. **1871** HOWELLS *Wedd. Journ.* (1892) 254 The stream athwart which the ferries sped their swift *traffic-laden shuttles. **1905** KIPLING *Actions & Reactions* (1909) 150 You could not hoist the necessary N.U.C. lights on approaching a *traffic-lane because your electrics had short-circuited. **1937** *Times* 13 Apr. p. x/1 An elaborate Memorandum on the Construction and Lay-out of Roads, covering many subjects, including safety, standard widths, curves, gradients, traffic lanes. **1948** *Jrnl. R. Aeronaut. Soc.* LII. 90 The American omni-directional range which defines ..traffic lanes..between zones of air traffic control at the airports of departure and arrival. **1972** *Daily Tel.* 5 May 3 The Government is taking powers to prosecute masters of British ships caught travelling the wrong way in traffic lanes through the Straits of Dover. **1912** *Traffic-light [see *landing-tower* s.v. LANDING *vbl. sb.* 8]. [**1920** W. P. ENO *Sci. Highway Traffic Regulation* viii. 19 (*heading*) Traffic regulation lights.] **1929** *Sat. Even. Post* 16 Nov. 145/1 T is for Traffic Light, bane of all motorists. **1934** *N. & Q.* 3 Nov. 314/1 These signals somewhat resembled our current traffic lights. **1958** J. CANNAN *And be a Villain* i. 5 Pulling up for the traffic lights at the turning into the High Street. **1973** D. BARNES *See Woman* I. 111 Stryker travelled northbound, cursing the traffic engineer who had planned the traffic-light sequence. **1978** S. WILSON *Dealer's Move* vii. 116 There were road works ahead, with temporary traffic lights. **1862** HELPS *Organiz. Daily Life* 30 A skilful *traffic-manager has been suffered to be too despotic in matters of traffic. **1911** WEBSTER (citing HADLEY), **Traffic mile* is a term designed to furnish an excuse for the erroneous practice of adding together two things (ton miles and passenger miles) which, being of different kinds, cannot properly be added. **1971** 'G. BLACK' *Time for Pirates* vii. 112, I..paused to listen, hearing nothing but *traffic noises. **1960** *Daily Tel.* 29 Jan. 23/4 A 'ticket' system of optional fixed fines for minor *traffic offences. **1981** C. DEXTER *Dead of Jericho* xxxii. 176 Cheque for £6, being the penalty fixed for the traffic offence detailed on the ticket. **1915** *Policeman's Monthly* Oct. 5/1 *Traffic officers in the center of the street are subjected to many hardships. **1971** *Rand Daily Mail* 4 Sept. 5/2 Johannesburg traffic officers will still attend motor accidents in which there is only minor damage. **1956** W. A. HEFLIN *U.S. Air Force Dict.* 531/1 **Traffic pattern*, a pattern in the air above or about an airdrome, which is normally followed under visual conditions either by aircraft prior to touchdown or by aircraft after takeoff. **1968** L. O'DONNELL *Face of Crime* viii. 106 They landed at Kennedy at 8:32.. having been delayed half an hour in the traffic pattern. **1977** *Mod. Railways* Dec. 461/3 These gentlemen cannot both be correct so, for the benefit of those of us who are not familiar with traffic patterns of these routes, would somebody please produce some evidence to prove the point one way or the other? **1977** *Chicago Tribune* 2 Oct. XI. 14/3 But the 'island' arrangement—placing furniture in the middle of a room (if it's large enough), thereby leaving space to walk around it —is a good way to create a traffic pattern. **1978** S. SHELDON *Bloodline* vi. 87 The private Boeing 707-320 was making its final approach to Kennedy Airport, gliding out of the stacked-up traffic pattern. **1906** *Collier's* 20 Jan. 22/3 The effort to find out how it feels to be 'regulated' by the *traffic police of New York. **1959** *New Statesman* 3 Jan. 6/3 He also disliked anything that gave traffic police more discretion or wider powers. **1980** E. LEATHER *Duveen Let.* xi. 134 The Renault..would most certainly receive the attentions of the ever alert Traffic Police. **1917** *Wells Fargo Messenger* Mar. 115/3 The *traffic policeman at Norman is still in doubt as to what it was that went by. **1940** AUDEN *Another Time* 91 Let the traffic policemen wear black cotton gloves. **1980** *Listener* 13 Nov. 653/1 Some of my best friends are traffic policemen. **1971** *Pony* Mar. 347/1 A few months ago I was given the task of *traffic-proofing a pony. **1977** *Horse & Hound* 14 Jan. 40/4 (Advt.), Gelding..Viceless, traffic proof. **1901** *Academy* 22 June 540/1 One sight amazes him ..the effect produced when the *traffic-regulating policeman raises his hand. **1858** SIMMONDS *Dict. Trade*, **Traffic-return*, a periodical statement of the receipts for goods and passengers on a railway line. **1912** *Times* 19 Dec. 16/5 Canadian Pacific Railway shares opened above parity on the satisfactory traffic return. **1915** *Policeman's Monthly* Oct. 5/1 Certain of the cities have given a great deal of thought and attention to *traffic signs and signals. **1936** C. DAY LEWIS *Noah & Waters* 15 Do not be deceived by the two-faced traffic signs. **1973** J. WAINWRIGHT *Devil you Don't* 42 McGuire threaded the Jag. through the city streets. He obeyed every traffic sign. **1917** *Harper's Mag.* June 70/2 The Bostonian, supposedly sesquipedalian of speech, has reduced 'a pedestrian who crosses streets in disregard of *traffic signals' to the compact *jaywalker*. **1934** *Archit. Rev.* LXXV. 184 Traffic signals did not come to Hyde Park Corner until 1932. **1981** 'J. ROSS' *Dark Blue & Dangerous* x. 57 A traffic signal which turned red as he approached it. **1963** L. DEIGHTON *Horse under Water* lii. 219 It's the Seville Traffic Control Zone... If it [*sc.* a plane] gets mixed into that *traffic stack I'm not sure that I'll be able to sort it out. *a* **1930** D. H. LAWRENCE *Last Poems* (1932) 264 The minorities that still see the gleam of life Submit abjectly to the blind mechanical *traffic-streams of..The stone-blind bourgeois, and the stone-blind bolshevist. **1981** H. R. F. KEATING *Go West, Inspector Ghote* xiii. 155 The monster car, slipping easily from one traffic stream to another. **1950** J. D. MACDONALD *Brass Cupcake* iii. 31 Every time you get into that car of yours, you'll get a *traffic ticket. **1979** *Tucson Mag.* Apr. 33/2 The typical suburbanite..never goes downtown except for an occasional Community Center event or a traffic ticket to contest. **1984** *Miami Herald* 6 Apr. 18A/1 The judge's bill suggests that, by putting a thumb print on the traffic ticket, the scofflaw might be more easy to trace. **1959** *Punch* 25 Feb. 274/1 Any supposed similarity of function between the police and the newly-proposed *traffic wardens vanished with the official statement that the wardens 'would help motorists to find parking space'. **1980** J. MCNEIL *Spy Game* xx. 197 It was a Ford, parked by the opposite kerb on..double yellow lines. A traffic warden was ..preparing to write a ticket.

Hence ˈ**trafficful** *a.*, *nonce-wd.*, fully occupied with traffic; ˈ**traffickery**, *nonce-wd.* [-ERY], underhand dealing, intrigue; ˈ**trafficless** *a.*, devoid of traffic.

a **1628** F. GREVIL *Sidney* ix. (1652) 107 Her *traffiquefull, and navigable river. *c* **1810** COLERIDGE in *Lit. Rem.* (1838) III. 387 This indiscreet *traffickery with Romish wares. **1892** *Black & White* Jan. 134/2 Stilled and trafficless streets.

[*Note.* It is clear that the verb and sb. arose in the commerce of the Mediterranean, and in the language of one of the nations by or with whom this was carried on. The earliest uses yet found are *trafficare* and *traffico* in the Pisan *Breve dell' ordine del mare*, cited above, which show both vb. and sb. in full established use in 1325. Etymologists are generally agreed in regarding the word as Romanic, and in seeing in the first element *tra* the regular It. repr. of L. *trans* across. Italian scholars also see in *-ficare* the derivative form of L. *facĕre* to do, make; *transficare* would thus be parallel to *transigĕre* to transact, or engage in transactions. But there are difficulties: see Diez, *traffico*, Körting, *transvicare*, etc. Some have suggested for the word an origin in Arabic, referring it to the verb *taraffaqa*, which sometimes means 'to seek profit'.]

traffic (ˈtræfɪk), *v.* Inflected **trafficked** (-ɪkt), **trafficking**. Forms: see the sb. [ad. OF. *trafiquer* (1441 in Godef. *Compl.*), F. *trafiquer* (1529 in Hatz.-Darm.) = Cat. *trafegar*, Sp. *traficar* (in 16th c. *trafagar*), Pg. *traficar*, *trafeguear*, It. *trafficare* (known in 1325), *traficare* (Florio). As to etymology, see TRAFFIC *sb.* and Note there.]

I. Intransitive senses.

1. To carry on trade, to trade, to buy and sell; to have commercial dealings *with* any one; to bargain or deal *for* a commodity. Sometimes, To resort *to* a place for the purpose of trade: = TRADE *v.* 6 a.

1542 in *10th Rep. Hist. MSS. Comm.* App. v. 410 They that so would bargayn or trafique pertly or oppenly with any such merchauntes. **1555** EDEN *Decades* 317 They do not gladly permitte the Portugales to trafike in theyr kyngedome. **1585** T. WASHINGTON tr. *Nicholay's Voy.* IV. xi. 123 b, Vnto the ports..come to traffick, the merchants of Cambaia. **1613** H. SPELMAN *Relat. Virginia* in *Capt. Smith's Wks.* (Arb.) p. civ, Powhatan..carried our English to their store-house where their corne was, to traffique with them. **1634** SIR T. HERBERT *Trav.* 53 Many Carrauans.. traffiquing to the Portugall[s]. **1716** *Royal Proclam.* 18 Oct. in *Lond. Gaz.* No. 5480/1 Their Factors..should..Traffick, or Adventure into or from the..East-Indies. **1769** COOK *Voy. round World* I. ix. (1773) 93 They trafficked with us for cocoa-nuts and other fruit. **1800** WORDSW. *Brothers* 293 He was..A thriving man, and trafficked on the seas.

b. In a disparaging sense, or said of dealing considered improper: = TRADE *v.* 6 c: cf. prec. 2 d.

c **1657** in *Verney Mem.* (1907) II. 120 [He had made more money] than any man who trafficked in that desperate commodity—rebellion. **1696** PHILLIPS (ed. 5), *Trafic*,..us'd figuratively in an ill Sense, for trading in Simoniacal Contracts, and making an unlawful Gain of Spiritual things. Such a one has long Traffick'd in buying and selling his Countrey. **1853** J. H. NEWMAN *Hist. Sk.* (1873) II. I. ii. 82 He observed that it was somewhat more honourable to destroy idols than to traffic in them. **1854** J. S. C. ABBOTT *Napoleon* (1855) I. iv. 80 Beautiful and dissolute females.. trafficking in their charms.

†**2.** *fig.* To have dealings or intercourse (*with* a person); to carry on negotiations; to be concerned, to busy or exercise oneself (*in* some matter). *Obs.*

1583 GOLDING *Calvin on Deut.* cxxi. 743 But there are meanes to trafique man with man. **1612** T. TAYLOR *Comm. Titus* ii. 13 (1619) 483 Who while they liue in earth, yet traffique and haue their conuersation in heauen. **1656** STANLEY *Hist. Philos.* v. (1701) 173/2 Hermodorus, of whom the Proverb, Hermodorus traffiques in Words. *c* **1721** MRQ. TULLIBARDINE *Let.* 24 Jan., in *10th Rep. Hist. MSS. Comm.* App. I. 126 On no pretence I trafick in any tainting politique. **1882** JAMIESON, *Trafeque*, to hold familiar intercourse. *Banffs.*

b. To have dealings of an illicit or secret character; to deal, intrigue, conspire (*with* some one, *in*, *for*, or *to do* something); to practise. (Cf. 1 b.)

1567 *Reg. Privy Council Scot.* I. 569 Trafficquand with the Papis Nunce. *a* **1649** DRUMM. OF HAWTH. *Hist. Scot.* (1655) 164 He also trafficked by the friends of..the Dowglasses and Humes to perswade them to a Return. **1681**, **1735** [see *trafficking* below]. **1852** MISS YONGE *Cameos* II. ii. 17 Jeanne discovered that he was trafficking with her enemies and tampering with her friends.

3. *dial.* (See 4 b.)

II. Transitive senses.

†**4.** To traverse or frequent for the purpose of trading; to carry on trade in (a place). *Obs.*

1547 *Acts Privy Counc.* (1890) II. 130 The Kynges Majestes subjectes trafeking the seas. **1561** Q. ELIZ. in Hakluyt *Voy.* (1589) 362 Trade of marchandize with your Subiectes, and with other strangers traffiking your Realmes. **1611** W. SCLATER *Key* (1629) 36 Rome,..the seate of the Empire, traffiqued by all Nations.

b. To pass to and fro upon, to frequent (a road, etc.); to traverse. Also *intr.* To pass to and fro, walk or run about. *dial.*

a **1825** FORBY *Voc. E. Anglia*, *Traffic*, to frequent... 'The new road will soon be trafficked'. **1850** MERRYWEATHER *Glimmerings* 52 Some would venture to traffic them in the day, but few would risk such perilous thoroughfares by night. **1877** *N.W. Linc. Gloss.*, *Traffic*, *v.* (1) To walk about without settled purpose. (2) To trespass upon other people's land. *A correspondent writes*, 'Our nurse used to scold us when children for trafficking up and down stairs.'

5. To carry on a trade in, to buy and sell; to dispose of (or †acquire) in the way of trade; to deal in; often with sinister implication; in quot. 1879, to barter *away*. Also *fig.* Now *rare*.

1597 DANIEL *Civ. Wars* VI. xviii, Whil'st wee..Ryot away ..whole Prouinces;..Traffique important Holdes, sell Fortresses. **1598** DALLINGTON *Meth. Trav.* N iv b, *Non patiar mercatores potestatum*, I will suffer none to traffique Offices. *a* **1628** F. GREVIL *Religion* Wks. 1870 I. 272 The world doth build without, our God within; He traffics goodness, and she traffics sin. **1808** *Sporting Mag.* XXXII. 7 An assertion..that his Lordship had trafficked a seat for the Borough of Malton. **1879** *19th Cent.* No. 32. 673 The honour of the proud house of Este was being basely trafficked away. **1893** LANE-POOLE *Aurengzib* xii. 200 The young Prince was suspected of trafficking the Imperial honour with the Marathas.

†**6.** To negotiate (a matter). *Obs. rare.*

a **1649** DRUMM. OF HAWTH. *Hist. Scot.* (1655) 28 He trafficked the return of King James. *Ibid.* 207 Whilst they traffique this Marriage, many false accusations (as Plots laid against his person) are intended one after another at the Court.

Hence **'trafficking** *vbl. sb.* and *ppl. a.*

1570 in Tolstoy *1st 40 Yrs. Interc. Eng. & Russ.* (1875) 103 Kept from traffiquing. **1580** *Nat. Covt. Ref. Princ. Re-exhibited* (1787) 56 Trafficking Papists to be punished. *a* **1649** DRUMM. OF HAWTH. *Hist. Scot.* (1655) 11 The trafficking of a Marriage between Lewis the Daulphine.. with Margaret Daughter to King James. **1681** in *Acts Parlt. Scotl.* (1875) XII. 44/1 They..shall never tolerate priests Jesuits nor traffecking Papists to abide in this Kingdome. **1735** in *Tablet* 19 Mar. (1910) 446/2 Trafficking Papists, I mean such as are continually employed in making Proselytes. **1835** MARRYAT *Pirate* ii, Grief is worth nothing in this trafficking world unless it is paid for. **1863** FROUDE *Hist. Eng.* VIII. viii. 132 Thus the antagonism went on, irritating Elizabeth..into dangerous traffickings with the Bishop of Aquila and his successor. **1903** W. N[EVILLE] *Penal Servitude* xiii. 170 Any officer found guilty of passing a letter out of prison would be liable to instant dismissal, as this comes under what is called 'trafficking'—an unpardonable offence.

trafficable ('træfɪkəb(ə)l), *a.* [f. TRAFFIC *sb.* or *v.* + -ABLE.]

†**1.** Adapted or suitable for traffic or trading. *Obs. rare*$^{-1}$.

a **1603** T. CARTWRIGHT *Confut. Rhem. N.T.* (1618) 469 That being the most traffiqueable and Marchandable Citie of all Asia.

2. That may be bought or sold; marketable.

1649 BP. HALL *Cases Consc.* i. (1654) 4 It is..in some cases a trafiqueable commodity. **1880** A. SOMERVILLE *Autobiog.* 90, I required what may be called trafficable material. **1889** *Sat. Rev.* 19 Oct. 422/1 [They] have been taught..to regard a vote as a commodity, traffickable.

3. Fit or suitable for passage to and fro.

1890 *Goldfields of Victoria* 17 A good trafficable roadway. **1891** *Illustr. Lond. News* 17 Jan. 78/2 The streets are trafficable.

Hence **traffica'bility**, **'trafficableness**, suitability for traffic or passage to and fro.

1899 *Daily News* 16 Nov. 4/5 A paper dealing with.. London's treacherous 'trafficability' was read at the opening meeting of the 146th session of the Society of Arts.

trafficator ('træfɪkeɪtə(r)). [f. TRAFFIC *sb.* + INDIC)ATOR.] A signal arm of a type formerly attached to either side of a motor vehicle, which could be raised and illuminated to indicate the direction in which the vehicle was about to turn; also applied loosely to modern indicators (see INDICATOR 3 g).

1933 *Autocar* 13 Oct. 733/1 (*caption*) The Lucas Trafficator is concealed when not in use. **1935** *Times* 17 Oct. 8/4 The least expensive Morris Eight is the two-seater which sells at £118, or £120 10s. with bumpers and trafficators. **1945** *Autocar Handbk.* (ed. 18) x. 196 The Trafficator arm is generally retained by some positive catch arrangement so long as it lies within its sheath, though other patterns leave the arm free so that it may be pulled out without injury. **1976** J. I. M. STEWART *Memorial Service* x. 167 He had actually flicked up a hand—jerkily, like an old-fashioned 'trafficator' on a car—in greeting. **1982** N. J. CRISP *Brink* i. 28 Jenkins signalled a right turn... The trafficators clicked.

trafficked ('træfɪkt), *ppl. a.* [f. TRAFFIC *v.* (or *sb.*) + -ED.] †**a.** That has trafficked or traded abroad; experienced in traffic (*obs. rare*); cf. *travelled*, *well-read*, *well-spoken*. †**b.** Traversed or explored for traffic or trade (*obs. rare*). **c.** Made the subject of traffic; dealt in as merchandise. **d.** Used for, or beaten or worn by traffic, as a road.

1561 T. HOBY tr. *Castiglione's Courtyer* III. (1577) N v b, I vnderstood by merchaunt men a long time trafficked in that countrey. **1627** MAY *Lucan* VIII. (1631) 364 Let fortune then our sad, and ship wrack'd state Beyond the knowne, and traffiqu'd world translate. **1875** LANIER *Symphony* 234 O trafficked hearts that break in twain. **1909** *Westm. Gaz.* 30 Aug. 2/1 On lightly trafficked roads.

trafficker ('træfɪkə(r)). [f. TRAFFIC *v.* + -ER[1].]

1. One who is engaged in traffic or trade; a trader, merchant, dealer.

1580 *Reg. Privy Council Scot.* III. 327 Divers..honest trafficquers of this cuntrie. **1615** tr. *De Monfart's Surv. E. Indies* 22 They are..great Traffickers. *a* **1727** NEWTON *Observ. Coin* (1730) 10 Traffickers in money will get above 6 per Cent by sending Gold to Spain. **1833** HT. MARTINEAU *Charmed Sea* v, The traffickers were exchanging their goods laboriously. **1863** GEO. ELIOT *Romola* iii, An itinerant trafficker in broken glass and rags.

b. With opprobrious force; cf. TRAFFIC *sb.* 2 d.

a **1785** GLOVER *Athenaid* XIII. Poems (1810) 124/2 Let these to some fell traficker in slaves Be sold. **1839** JAMES *Louis XIV*, IV. 50 These traffickers in poison seem to have been seized with a sort of madness. **1869** *Echo* 28 Aug., Practices familiar to many generations of hardened traffickers in votes.

2. One who carries on an underhand or improper traffic (esp. between other parties); a go-between, a negotiator; an intriguer; a schemer.

1570 in *Calr. Scott. Pap.* (1903) III. 384 Thome Bischop wes ye first trafficquar betuix ye bischop of Ros and ye said Johnne. **1687** *Royal Proclam.* in *Lond. Gaz.* No. 2221/4 For being Papists, Jesuits, or Traffickers, for hearing, or saying of Mass. **1879** FARRAR *St. Paul* I. 561 Lest any should say that he too, like the mass of traffickers around him, did but seek his own gain. **1893** STEVENSON *Catriona* ix. 96 The whole clan of old Jacobite spies and traffickers.

†**traffle**, obs. variant of TAFFEREL, TAFFRAIL.

1805 in Nicolas *Disp. Nelson* (1846) VII. 156 *note*, A Spanish two-decker..waved an English Jack from her traffle.

trafin, -e, obs. forms of TREPHINE.

tragacanth ('trægəkænθ). Also 6 **tragachant**, 7 **tragagant**, 8 **tragant, -anth**; see also ADRAGANT, DRAGANT, DRAGON[2]. [a. F. *tragacante* (16th c.) = It., Sp. *tragacanta*, ad. L. *tragacantha* (Pliny), a. Gr. τραγάκανθα goat's-thorn, tragacanth-shrub, f. τράγος he-goat + ἄκανθα thorn.

The gum was called in L. *tragacanthum* (Celsus), whence Sp., Pg. *tragacanto*.]

1. A 'gum' or mucilaginous substance obtained from several species of *Astragulus* (see 2), by natural exudation or incision, in the form of whitish strings or flakes, only partially soluble in water: see quot. 1875. Used in medicine (chiefly as a vehicle for drugs) and in the industrial arts. Also a similar substance obtained from *Sterculia Tragacantha* of W. Africa. **a.** Commonly called ***gum tragacanth***.

1573 in Feuillerat *Revels Q. Eliz.* (1908) 199 Gum tragachant ii ounces. **1634** J. B[ATE] *Myst. Nat.* 33 With gum tragagant dissolued in faire water. **1643** STEER tr. *Exp. Chyrurg.* xiv. 57 Mixe it with the whites of Egges and Gum Tragacanth. **1714** *Fr. Bk. of Rates* 92 Gum Tragant per 100 Weight 02 10. **1811** A. T. THOMSON *Lond. Disp.* II. (1818) 65 Gum tragacanth is demulcent. **1830** LINDLEY *Nat. Syst. Bot.* 39 The Gum Tragacanth of Sierra Leone is produced by a species of Sterculia. **1875** BENNETT & DYER *Sachs' Bot.* 36 Gum-tragacanth consists of the cells of the pith and medullary rays of *Astragalus creticus*, *A. Tragacantha*, and other species, transformed into mucilage.

b. Called simply ***tragacanth***.

1601 HOLLAND *Pliny* XIII. xxi. I. 398 A pound of Tragacanth is worth thirteen deniers Romane. **1712** tr. *Pomet's Hist. Drugs* I. 181 Traganth or Tragacanth, is a white curl'd Gum made like little Worms. **1875** H. C. WOOD *Therap.* (1879) 577 Tragacanth is used in medicine only in the manufacture of troches and in suspending heavy powders.

†**2.** Any one of several low-growing spiny shrubs of the genus *Astragalus* (N.O. *Leguminosæ*), found in Persia and neighbouring regions, which yield gum tragacanth (see 1). *Obs. rare.*

1601 HOLLAND *Pliny* XIII. xxi. I. 398 The same Iland hath the bush Tragacanth growing in it. **1741** *Compl. Fam.-Piece* II. iii. 373 Columbines, Spireas,..Spanish Broom,.. Tragacantha.

3. *attrib.*

1813 MILBURN *Oriental Comm.* I. 110 Tragacanth gum, or as it is usually called gum dragon. **1836** J. M. GULLY *Magendie's Formul.* (ed. 2) 138 Tragacanth powder. **1876** HARLEY *Royle's Mat. Med.* 633 Tragacanth Bushes..are small, tangled, spiny bushes, resembling stunted varieties of ..furze. **1879** *Sat. Rev.* 8 Nov. 580/1 The tragacanth draught of the ancient Sophists is tolerated.

Hence **traga'canthin** (also contr. **tra'ganthin**), *Chem.*, the essential constituent of tragacanth and other gums: = BASSORIN. (See also quot. 1843.)

1842 BRANDE *Dict. Sc.*, etc. s.v. *Tragacanth*, An analogous kind of gum is found in other plants, and the generic name of *tragacanthin* is sometimes applied to it. **1843** *Penny Cycl.* XXV. 114/1 An artificial substance prepared by boiling starch,..called tragacantin.

tragæ-comedy, obs. form of TRAGI-COMEDY.

tragal ('treɪgəl), *a. Anat.* [f. TRAG-US + -AL[1].] Pertaining to or situated upon the tragus.

1891 in *Cent. Dict.* **1898** J. HUTCHINSON in *Arch. Surg.* IX. No. 36. 378 Those who have abundant vibrissæ very commonly, I believe, have these tragal tufts of hair also.

†**'tragalism.** *Spanish Hist.* [ad. Sp. *tragalismo*, f. *trágala* in '*Trágala, perro!*' ('Swallow it, dog!', where 'it' refers to the Constitution), the refrain of a popular Constitutionalist song.] A designation for the principles of the Spanish Constitutional party of 1820 and succeeding years.

1837 *Q. Rev.* July 68 The bloody tragedy of Spanish Tragalism. **1837** WALTON *Revol. of Spain* II. xii. 325 It was wished..merely to modify the existing plan so as to render it palatable abroad while *tragalism* was enforced at home. [In Smart 1849 *Suppl.*, *Tragalism* (entered with a reference to *Q. Rev.* as above, but no quot.) is explained as 'Goatishness due to high feeding'. This absurd guess, based on a pseudo-etymological reference to Gr. τραγαλισμός ('the eating of dried fruits and sweetmeats', but imagined to be derived from τράγος goat) has been copied (with ingenious variations) in many recent dictionaries.]

†**tra'gediac**, *a. Obs. rare.* [f. L. *tragœdia* TRAGEDY + -AC; an anomalous formation for **tragedic*: cf. It. *tragedico* (Florio) and TRAGEDICAL.] Befitting tragedy; tragic in style.

1782 ELIZ. BLOWER *Geo. Bateman* I. 205 Those ranting tragediac speeches. *Ibid.* III. 117.

†**tra'gedial**, *a. Obs. rare.* [f. as prec. + -AL[1].] Pertaining to tragedy; tragic.

a **1529** SKELTON *Agst. Scottes* 77 Melpomone, O Muse tragediall.

tragedian (trə'dʒiːdɪən). Also 4–5 **tragedyen**, **-ien**, (**tregedien**), 7–8 **tragœdian**. [ME., prob. a. OF. *tragediane* (1372 in Hatz.-Darm.), later and mod.F. *tragédien*, f. *tragédie* TRAGEDY: see -AN.]

1. A dramatist who composes a tragedy or tragedies; a tragic poet or author.

c **1374** CHAUCER *Boeth.* III. pr. vi. 60 (Camb. MS.) A tragedyen [*v.r.* tregedien] þat is to seyn a makere of ditees þat hyhten tragedies. *a* **1631** DONNE *Poems* (1633) 165 Under this curled marble..Sleepe rare Tragedian Shakespeare, sleepe alone. **1671** MILTON *P.R.* IV. 261 What the lofty grave Tragœdians taught In Chorus or Iambic. **1875** SCRIVENER *Lect. Text N. Test.* 6 The dramas of the Greek tragedian Æschylus.

2. A stage-player who performs in tragedy; a tragic actor.

1592 NASHE *P. Penilesse* (ed. 2) 26 b, The Tragedian that represents his person. **1602** SHAKS. *Ham.* II. ii. 342 What Players are they? *Rosin.*... The Tragedians of the City. **1602** MARSTON *Antonio's Rev.* II. iii, I will not swell, like a

Tragedian, in forced passion of affected straines. **1693** DRYDEN *Persius' Sat.* v. 3 The well-lung'd Tragedians Rage. **1711** ADDISON *Spect.* No. 40 *ad fin.*, Mr. Powell..is excellently formed for a Tragœdian. **1870** L'ESTRANGE *Miss Mitford* I. vi. 200 No man can be a perfect tragedian who is not likewise a good actor in the higher branch of comedy.

†**3.** *fig.* A person concerned in a 'tragedy' or dreadful calamity; the victim, or inflicter, of a tragic fate. *Obs.*

1592 WARNER *Alb. Eng.* IX. xlv. (1612) 214 The Tragedies and Tytles too of English Dukes did cease, Which Thomas, Duke of Norffolke, last Tragedian did increase. **1635** R. JOHNSON *Hist. Tom a Lincoln* (1825) 131 The Blacke Knight stayed from his desperate resolution, and from a bloody tragedian became the recoverer of his brothers life.

Hence **tra'gedianess** (*nonce-wd.*), a female tragedian.

1822 *Blackw. Mag.* XII. 657 Was there to be a virtual *non-imprimatur* in force against our songstresses, romance-inditresses, tragedianesses, sonneteeresses?

tra'gedical, *a. rare.* [f. Gr. τραγῳδικ-ός befitting tragedy + -AL[1].] Of the nature, or having the character, of tragedy; tragical.

a **1548** HALL *Chron., Hen. VI* 187b, Thus you haue hearde the..tragedicall hystory of Kynge Henry the sixthe. **1891** W. S. GILBERT *Rosencrantz & Guild.* III, The poor author had hoped to have appalled you with his tragedical end!

‖**tragédie lyrique** (traʒedi lirik). [Fr., lit. 'lyric tragedy'.] A name given to serious French opera of the seventeenth and eighteenth centuries. Cf. *opéra comique* s.v. OPERA 3.

1901 W. F. APTHORP *Opera Past & Present* vi. 117 If the Grand Opera—called *tragédie lyrique* when the libretto conformed to the rules of the classic French *tragédie*—was..a quasi-academic adaptation of the Italian *opera seria* to French taste, the *opéra-comique* may be called the natural growth..of..the Italian *opera buffa.* **1947** A. EINSTEIN *Mus. Romantic Era* xix. 358 In France, there was *tragédie lyrique* and *opéra-comique.* **1976** *Early Music* July 285 In 1966, came a virtually complete recording of Rameau's first and perhaps greatest tragédie-lyrique, *Hippolyte et Aricie.*

‖**tragédienne** (traʒedjɛn). [Fr., fem. of *tragédien* TRAGEDIAN.] A female tragedian or actor of tragedy; a tragic actress.

1851 LONGF. in *Life* (1891) II. 221 We..called on Jenny Lind, and on Mrs. Warner, the tragédienne. **1866** *Standard* 7 Mar. 2/6 On Thursday night Miss Siddons, a young tragedienne..a great-granddaughter of *the* Siddons..made her first appearance..in the character of Juliet.

tragedietta (trədʒiːdɪ'ɛtə). [In form an It. dim. of *tragedia*: see -ETTA: cf. *comedietta*.] A slight or short tragedy; a dramatic sketch of tragic character.

1891 *Pall Mall G.* 19 Oct. 2/3 My 'tragedy'—it is a very little one, a one-act tragedietta. **1902** *Daily Chron.* 2 July 3/1 One of them..might be called a 'tragedietta',..but, as a whole, they may be said to range from comedietta to farce.

†**tra'gedious**, *a. Obs.* [f. L. *tragœdi-a* TRAGEDY + -OUS.] Full of, or having the character of, tragedy; calamitous, tragic.

1494 FABYAN *Chron.* VII. 670 Of whom [Richard III] tedyous it is to me to wryte the tragedyous hystory. **1565** J. HALLE *Hist. Expost.* 25 Most frivolous communications and tragedious doynges. **1616** J. LANE *Cont. Sqr.'s T.* x. 34 His late vncothe dreame was th' oracle of this tragedious schene. **1691** WOOD *Ath. Oxon.* I. 95 A true and most notable history,..in much part tragedious.

Hence †**tra'gediously** *adv.*, in tragic style.

1602 WARNER *Alb. Eng.* XVI. cvi. 414 Our Histories tragediously doe varie hard Euents. **1658** COKAINE *Obstinate Lady* II. ii, The same blade Shall be the instrument, and I receive it Tragediously here on my knees.

tragedist ('trædʒɪdɪst). *rare*$^{-1}$. [f. TRAGEDY + -IST.] A writer of tragedy: = TRAGEDIAN 1.

1823 G. DARLEY in *Lond. Mag.* Dec. 647/2 The *os magna sonans*..is the first great qualification for a tragedist, and this qualification the Author of the Bride's Tragedy most undeniably possesses.

tragedize ('trædʒɪdaɪz), *v.* [f. TRAGEDY + -IZE: cf. *harmon-ize*, etc.]

1. *trans.* To act or perform as a tragedy; *fig.* to do or carry on tragically; in quot. 1593, to treat tragically, subject to a tragic fate.

1593 NASHE *Christ's T.* (1613) 54 Like tragicke Seneca, I should tragedize my selfe, by bleeding to death in the depth of passion. **1599** —— *Lenten Stuffe* 47 The nurse..cowring on the backeside whiles these things were a tragedizing. **1623** [see TRAGEDIZED]. **1734** *Grub St. Jrnl.* 2 May 1/3 As woeful a tragedy as ever was tragedized on the British stage. **1827** *Blackw. Mag.* XXI. 736 This assuredly not less tragical tragedy than any that ever was tragedized by a company of tragedians.

2. *intr.* To perform as a tragedian; *fig.* to act or speak in tragic style.

1756 TOLDERVY *Hist. 2 Orphans* IV. 105 If we do spend this money we can..tragedize for more. **1889** FARRAR *Lives Fathers* II. xiii. 14 Oh air and Oh virtue!—for I will tragedise a little! [tr. GREG. NAZ. *Ep.* v, More tragico exclamabo].

3. *trans.* To convert into a tragedy; to dramatize in tragic form.

1754 D. GARRICK *Let.* 31 July (1831) I. 57 Not like those paltry blasts of art employed in raising storms in a tea-cup, such as tragedizing trivial or even ludicrous situations. **1811** *British Press* 19 Aug., *The Comedy of Errors*, tragedized. *a* **1849** H. COLERIDGE *Ess.* (1851) II. 177 Modern critics, aping the nicety of Athens, which forbade the tragedising of recent history, may think [etc.].

Hence '**tragedized** *ppl. a.*, '**tragedizing** *vbl. sb.*; also ˌ**tragedi'zation**, the action of tragedizing.

1623 COCKERAM, *Tragidized*, killed. **1780** T. FRANCKLIN tr. *Lucian's Works* I. 390 Several of them..fell insensibly into the tragedizing vein. **1796** *Sporting Mag.* VII. 329 The tragedization of Edward the Black Prince. **1813** *Theatrical Inquisitor* II. 182 Ye fair, an *Amateur* before you view, Whose love of tragedising sprung from you.

tragedy ('trædʒɪdɪ). Forms: 4–6 **tragedye**, (4–5 **tregeedie, tregedie**), 4–7 **tragedie**, 5 **-idie**, (**trajedi**), 5–6 **tragedi, -ide**, 6 **tragœdie**, (**trigide, -idy**), 5– **tragedy**. [ME. a. OF. *tregedie, tragedie* (14th c. in Godef.), ad. L. *tragœdia*, a. Gr. τραγῳδία, app. goat-song, f. τράγος goat + ᾠδή ode, song.

As to the reason of the name many theories have been offered, some even disputing the connexion with 'goat'. See L. H. Gray in *Classical Quarterly* VI. 60, and references there given.]

1. A play or other literary work of a serious or sorrowful character, with a fatal or disastrous conclusion: opp. to COMEDY[1] 1. †**a.** In mediæval use: A tale or narrative poem of this character.

c **1374** CHAUCER *Boeth.* II. pr. ii. 23 (Camb. MS.) The cryenges of tragedyes... Tragedye is to seyn, a dite of a prosperite for a tyme þat endith in wrecchydnesse. *c* **1374** —— *Troylus* v. 1786 Go litel booke goo litell my tregeedie. *c* **1386** —— *Monk's Prol.* 83 (Corpus) Or elles tregedys [*v.rr.* -ies, -ise] first wol I telle. *c* **1430** LYDG. *Misericordias* 65 At funeral feestys men synge tragedies With wooful ditees of lamentacioun. **1531** ELYOT *Gov.* I. x, Than shall he, in redyng tragoedies, execrate and abhorre the intollerable life of tyrantes. **1593** CHURCHYARD (*title*) The Earle of Mvrtons Tragedie.

b. Applied to ancient Greek and Latin works: the original (Dorian) being lyric songs, the later (Attic and Latin) dramatic pieces.

c **1430** LYDG. *Min. Poems* (Percy Soc.) 25 The tragidés divers and unkouth Of morall Senec. **1484** CAXTON *Curiall* 11 As seyth Seneke in hys tragedyes, Age cometh to late to peple of smale howses. **1546** LANGLEY *Pol. Verg. De Invent.* I. ix. 17b, As the Alters were kindled with fyre, and the Goate layed on it, the Quire in honor of Bacchus, songe this Meter called a Tragedie. **1579** LODGE *Def. Poetry* (Shaks. Soc.) 24 Tragedies and Comedies..wer inuented..to no other purpose, but to yeelde prayse unto God for a happy haruest, or plentiful yeere. *a* **1637** B. JONSON *Horace's Art of Poetry* 312 Thespis is said to be the first found out The tragedy, and carried it about, Till then unknown, in carts, wherein did ride Those that did sing, and act. **1789** T. TWINING *Aristotle's Treat. Poetry* II. §12. 88 Now, the subjects of the best Tragedies are confined to a few families—to Alcmæon, Oedipus,..and others, the sufferers, or the authors, of some terrible calamity. **1873** SYMONDS *Grk. Poets* ix. 277 His Chorus were attired like Satyrs in goat-skins, to represent the woodland comrades of the god: hence came the name of *Tragedy* or Goat-song.

c. Applied to a modern stage-play.

1538 BALE *Thre Lawes* 1465 Companyons I want to begynne thys tragedye. **1597** SHAKS. (*title*) An excellent conceited Tragedie of Romeo and Iuliet. **1611** —— (*title*) The Tragedie of Cymbeline. **1641** MILTON *Ch. Govt.* II. Pref., Wks. 1851 III. 146 The Apocalyps of Saint Iohn is the majestick image of a high and stately Tragedy,..intermingling her solemn Scenes and Acts with a sevenfold Chorus of halleluja's and harping symphonies. **1703** FARQUHAR *Inconstant* IV. iii, Cry then, handsomely; cry like a queen in a tragedy. **1775** HARRIS *Philos. Arrangem.* Wks. (1841) 316 This excellent tragedy [Macbeth]..is not only admirable as a poem, but is perhaps..one of the most moral pieces existing. **1838–9** HALLAM *Hist. Lit.* III. III. vi. §90. 339 Five of his sixteen plays are tragedies, that is, are concluded in death.

2. That branch of dramatic art which treats of sorrowful or terrible events, in a serious and dignified style: opp. to COMEDY[1] 2. (Sometimes *personified.*)

1412–20 LYDG. *Chron. Troy* II. 852 Tragidie, who so list to knowe, It begynneth in prosperite, And endeth euer in aduersite; And it also doth þe conquest trete Of riche kynges and of lordys grete. **1508** DUNBAR *Lament for Makaris* 59 [Death] That scorpioun fell hes done infek Maister Iohne Clerk, and James Afflek, Fra balat making & trigide. **1598** MERES *Palladis Tamia* 282 Plautus and Seneca are accounted the best for Comedy and Tragedy among the Latines. **1632** MILTON *Penseroso* 97 Som time let Gorgeous Tragedy In Scepter'd Pall com sweeping by. **1757** W. WILKIE *Epigon.* Pref. 5 In Epic poetry, Tragedy, or any other of the higher kinds of poetical composition. **1861** PALEY *Æschylus, Prometh.* (ed. 2) 799 *note*, This use is common in Homer, but rare in tragedy. **1900** W. L. COURTNEY *Idea of Tragedy* 12 Tragedy is always the clash of two powers—necessity without, freedom within.

3. *fig.* An unhappy or fatal event or series of events in real life; a dreadful calamity or disaster. (Cf. COMEDY[1] 4.)

1509 HAWES *Past. Pleas.* xii. (Percy Soc.) 49 His chere is dolorus, As in bewaylyng a woful tragedy. **1535** LAYTON in *Lett. Suppress. Monasteries* (Camden) 76 To tell yowe all this commodie, but for thabbot a tragedie, hit were to long. **1617** MORYSON *Itin.* I. 207 The warre of Hungarie made all those parts full of tragedies and miserie. **1657** TRAPP *Comm. Job* i. 19 Lately at Witney..a scurrilous blasphemous Comedy was by the fall of the room wherein it was acted, turned into a Tragedy, as ending with the deaths of six. **1871** FREEMAN *Norm. Conq.* IV. xx. 572 The turning-point of William's reign, the tragedy of the fate of Waltheof.

†**b.** A doleful or dreadful tale; a passionate complaint. *Obs.*

1565 JEWEL *Def. Apol.* II. xiii. (1611) 255 Iudge thou..how iust causes M. Harding had to mooue these Tragedies. **1594** SPENSER *Amoretti* liv, I waile, and make my woes a Tragedy. **1611** BIBLE *Transl. Pref.* 2 Herevpon they raise vp a tragedie, and wish in their heart the Temple had neuer bene built. **1664** H. MORE *Myst. Iniq., Apol.* 538 Some would raise such Stirres and Tragedies about.

†**c.** With *of* or possessive: Sad story, unhappy fate, misery, misfortune; *esp.* sorrowful end, violent death. *Obs.*

1513 DOUGLAS *Æneis* IV. Prol. 264 Sen I suld thi [Dido's] trigidy endite. *a* **1592** GREENE *Alphonsus* I. Wks. (Rtldg.) 227/1 This sword..should the author be To make an end of this my tragedy. **1598–9** [E. FORDE] *Parismus* I. (1661) 68, I fear he is destroyed by the treachery of that wicked homicide.., who is not contented with his tragedy, but also seeketh my destruction. **1617** MORYSON *Itin.* I. 186 He ceased not to bewaile my misery, and to recount my Tragedy as if it had been the burning of Troy. **1678** MARVELL *Growth Popery* Wks. (Grosart) IV. 412 Men sit by, like idle spectators, and still give money towards their own tragedy. **1738** WESLEY *Psalms* XCI. iv, Thou..shalt look on and see The Wicked's dismal Tragedy.

¶**4.** Misused for TRAGEDIAN 1. *Obs. rare*$^{-1}$.

1460 CAPGRAVE *Chron.* (Rolls) 49 Sophocles and Euripides..were cleped Tragedies. Trajedi is as mech to sey as he that writith eld stories, with ditees hevy and sorowful.

5. *attrib.* and *Comb.*, as ***tragedy-actor, -air, -drum*** (DRUM *sb.*[1] 3), ***-god, -king, -player, -queen, speech, strut, -victim, -writer***; **tragedy-man** the chief tragic actor at a theatre.

1820 W. TOOKE tr. *Lucian* I. 481 Lay aside your proper character and assume that of a *tragedy-actor. **1897** 'A HOPE' *Phroso* v, Her *tragedy-air was quite delightful. **1702** STEELE *Funeral* IV. i. 59 He is a *Tragedy-Drum to one of the Play-Houses. **1820** W. TOOKE tr. *Lucian* I. 505 Properties necessary for the equipment of a *tragedy-god. **1900** *Macm. Mag.* May 50/1 More like a *tragedy-king than a monarch of history. **1821** *Blackw. Mag.* X. 588 The vacant situation of *tragedyman. **1552** HULOET, *Tragedie player, *tragœdus.* **1755** C. CHARKE *Life* 192 Though it was a valuable Gift, but more proper to ornament the Neck of a Country-Housewife, than a *Tragedy-Queen. **1819** [see SAIL *v.*[1] 5b]. **1848** THACKERAY *Van. Fair* xlvi, She bowed me out of the room like a tragedy queen. **1773** GOLDSM. *Stoops to Conq.* v. i, A short *tragedy speech. **1791** PAINE *Rights of Man* (ed. 4) 27 A *tragedy-victim expiring in show, and not the real prisoner of misery. **1552** HULOET, *Tragedie wryter, *tragicus, Sophocles.* *c* **1740** G. WALMSLEY in Hawkins *Johnson* (1787) 39 Johnson is a very good scholar and poet, and, I have great hopes, will turn out a fine tragedy-writer.

tragelaph ('trægɪlæf). Also in L. form **tragelaphus** (trə'gɛləfəs), pl. -i. [ad. L. *tragelaphus*, a. Gr. τραγέλαφος, f. τράγος he-goat + ἔλαφος deer.]

1. (Rendering Gr. τραγέλαφος.) **a.** A name for some foreign species of capriform antelope or other horned beast, vaguely known to the ancients.

1398 TREVISA *Barth. De P.R.* XVIII. ci. (Bodl. MS.), Tragelaphus is icleped Ircoceruus also and haþ þat name tragelaphus of trages þat is a gotte bucke and elephos þat is an herte. *Ibid.*, Tragelaphi..som beþ of þe kinde of þe herte. **1607** TOPSELL *Four-f. Beasts* (1658) 93 Of the first kinde of *Tragelaphus* which may be called a Deer-goat. *Ibid.* 94 There is another kinde..like a Deer..Pliny affirmeth, that they are found about the river Phasis, in Arabia and Arachotæ,..a City of India..which [beast] the Græcians call *Tragelaphos*, and the Germans, *Ein Brandhirse*... The figure of another *Tragelaphus*, or Deer-Goat, expressed by Bellonius..it wanteth a beard, and the hair thereof resembleth an Ibex-Goat..: the horns..like a Goats, but more crooked..which he never loseth. **1656** BLOUNT *Glossogr.*, *Tragelaph* (*tragelaphus*), the great and blackish deere called a stone-buck, deer-goat, or goat-hart. **1774** GOLDSM. *Nat. Hist.* (1862) I. II. v. 327 There is in the forests of Germany, a kind of stag, named by the ancients the *Tragelaphus*, and which the natives call the bran deer, or the brown deer.

b. *Myth.* A fabulous or fictitious beast compounded of a goat and a stag; hence *allusively*.

1644 FEATLY *Levites Scourge* 60 What Chimera's, Tragelaphusses, and Hippocentaurs dost thou talk of? *a* **1670** HACKET *Abp. Williams* II. (1693) 49 Tragelaphi, Satyrs and Griffins, Cocks and Bulls. **1818** R. P. KNIGHT *Anc. Art & Mythol.* §114. 88 Among the principal of these symbols [of Diana] is the deer,..which is sometimes blended into one figure with the goat, so as to form a composite fictitious animal called a Tragelephus. **1898** C. THOMAS *Faust* I. p. lxiv, The 'tragelaph' had to be disposed of!

2. *Zool.* Any antelope of the modern genus *Tragelaphus*, as the S. African boschbok, *T. sylvaticus*, and the W. African harnessed antelope, *T. scriptus*, Speke's Tragelaph, *T. Spekii.*

1888 *Cassell's Encycl. Dict.*, Tragelaphus. **1908** SIR H. H. JOHNSTON *Grenfell & Congo* II. xxxiii. 923 In Tragelaphs the Congo regions are well endowed. **1910** *Contemp. Rev.*, *Suppl.* Nov. 11 Two of these ruffians shot over fifty of the rare antelope called Speke's tragelaph.

So **tragelaphine** (trə'gɛləfaɪn) *a.*, belonging to the group *Tragelaphīnæ* of antelopes, typified by the genus *Tragelaphus*; *sb.* an antelope of this group.

1891 FLOWER & LYDEKKER *Mammals* ix. 345 Tragelaphine Section... Includes large, so-called Bovine, Antelopes now mainly characteristic of the Ethiopian region. **1900** *Nature* 11 Oct. 585/1 If the markings of the Tragelaphines have the significance here attached to them, they should be better developed in the species that live in the bush than in those that frequent the open. **1905** P. C. MITCHELL *Guide Gard. Zool. Soc.* (ed. 3) 43 The Tragelaphine Group (*Tragelaphinæ*) contains mostly large Antelopes with spirally-twisted horns.

† tra,gema'topolist. *Obs. rare*$^{-0}$. [f. Gr. τραγηματοπώλης (Hesychius) + -IST, f. τραγήματ- dried fruit or sweetmeat.] A seller of sweets.
1656 BLOUNT *Glossogr.*, Tragematopolist (tragematopola), he that sells comfits, carawaies and such other ware, made of sugar; a Confectioner. 1658 in PHILLIPS.

trageremics (treɪgə'riːmɪks), *sb. pl.* (const. *sing.*). *Linguistics.* [f. *Trager* (see TRAGER-SMITH), after *phonemics*.] A mock-technical term for the approach to phonemic analysis characteristic of the American linguist George L. Trager. Hence **trage'remic** *a.* (see quot. 1967).
1963 R. I. MCDAVID *Mencken's Amer. Lang.* 249 About 1950 E. Bagby Atwood coined *Trageremics* to designate phonemics according to the specifications of George L. Trager. 1967 —— in *Publ. Amer. Dial. Soc.* XLVII. 4 There does seem to be unnecessary virtuosity in displaying for individual entries the whole range of trageremic differences in the low-front vowel range. *Ibid.* 20 By *trageremic* (a term coined by Atwood) I refer to George Trager's analysis of all English syllable nuclei as composed of nine vowels and three semivowels. 1978 *Amer. Speech* LIII. 171, I mastered Trageremics in the middle 1950s.

Tragerian (treɪ'gɪərɪən), *a.* (*sb.*) *Linguistics.* [f. *Trager* (see next) + -IAN.] Of, pertaining to, or characteristic of the approach to linguistic analysis of George L. Trager. Occas. as *sb.*, an adherent of this method.
1962 R. P. STOCKWELL in *Texas Conf. Probl. Linguistic Analysis in Eng.* 10 The Tragerian pronunciation of *baa* that you wondered about. 1965 *Language* XLI. 168 His phonemics is Tragerian, though he makes tentative use of acoustic distinctive features. 1966 A. A. HILL *Promises & Limitations Newest Type Gram. Analysis* 6 Tragerians always began the description of language with phonemes, and ended it.. with syntax. 1974 *Amer. Speech 1971* XLVI. 126 Since I have usually employed a Tragerian transcription in previous publications on English phonology, it will be adhered to in this paper.

Trager-Smith ('treɪgə 'smɪθ). *Linguistics.* The names of George L. *Trager* (b. 1906) and Henry L. *Smith* (b. 1913), American linguists, co-authors of *An Outline of English Structure* (1951); used *attrib.* with reference to the method of linguistic analysis and phonemic transcription exemplified in this monograph. See also SMITH-TRAGER.
1955 *Language* XXXI. 313 The Trager-Smith phonology .. is the most nearly successful attempt at a statement of the English phonemic system that has yet been made. 1959 WIMSATT & BEARDSLEY in *PMLA* LXXIV. 586 The relation between meter and Trager-Smith linguistics. 1961 *Dissert. Abstr.* XXII. 1990 From the tapes the words were transcribed phonemically according to the Trager-Smith notation. 1962 *Amer. Speech* XXXVII. 154 A Trager-Smith analysis of the Middle English long mid vowels. 1965 A. H. ROBERTS *Statistical Linguistic Analysis of Amer. Eng.* v. 35 The system of notation in the count of French, Carter, and Koenig uses only one character to represent a diphthong, the Trager-Smith system uses two.

traget, -our, -ry: see TREGET, etc.

tragi, pl. of TRAGUS.

tragi- (trædʒɪ), combining form repr. TRAGIC, in a few nonce-words on the model of TRAGI-COMEDY, as ***tragi-catastrophe***, ***-farce***, ***-farcical*** adj. (See also under TRAGI-COMEDY.)
1811 *Henry & Isabella* I. 169 The love of tragi-catastrophe, common to vulgar minds. 1893 *Sat. Rev.* 1 Apr. 342/1 The pitiable tragi-farce of French politics. 1896 *Daily News* 17 Jan. 6/3 The fantastic tragi-farcical experiment.

tragic ('trædʒɪk), *a.* and *sb.* Also 6 -icke, 7-8 -ick. [ad. L. *tragic-us*, a. Gr. τραγικ-ός of or pertaining to tragedy, f. τράγ-ος goat: see -IC; but in sense associated with τραγῳδία TRAGEDY. Cf. F. *tragique*.] **A.** *adj.*

1. a. Of, pertaining, or proper to tragedy as a branch of the drama; of the nature of tragedy; composing, or acting in, tragedy: opp. to COMIC *a.* 1.
1563 *Mirr. Mag., Collingbourne* xv, Witnes theyr Satyr sharpe, and tragicke playes. 1590 SPENSER *F.Q.* III. xii. 3 Yclad in costly garments fit for tragicke Stage. *a* 1637 B. JONSON *Horace's Art Poetry* 122 The comic matter will not be exprest In tragic verse. 1712 ADDISON *Spect.* No. 315 ¶ 10 The ancient Tragick writers. 1788 FITZPATRICK *Prol. Sheridan's 'Critic'*, The tragic Queen to please a tasteless crowd, Has learnt to bellow, rant, and roar so loud. 1827 *Buckham's Theatre Grks.* (ed. 2) Pref. 6 The.. Tragic and Comic metres. 1838 THIRLWALL *Greece* III. xviii. 79 One of these exhibitions commonly followed each tragic performance, and it was always furnished by the tragic poet himself.

† b. ***tragic-comedy***: = TRAGI-COMEDY. *Obs.*
1631 MABBE (*title*) The Spanish Bawd, represented in Celestina: or, The Tragicke-Comedy of Calisto and Melibea. *c* 1650 DENHAM *Old Age* 664 On the world's stage, when our applause grows high For acting here life's tragic-comedy. 1653 H. MORE *Antid. Ath.* II. viii. §3 All might prove but a Tragick-Comedy.

c. Befitting, or having the style of, tragedy: = TRAGICAL 2.
1684 WINSTANLEY *Eng. Worthies, Shaks.* 345 Never any exprest a more lofty and Tragick height. *a* 1718 ROWE (J.), Bid them dress their bloody altars With every circumstance of tragick pomp. 1837 LOCKHART *Scott* xix *note*, Her [Mrs. Siddons'] tragic exclamation to a footboy during a dinner, .. 'You've brought me water, boy, I asked for beer'. 1888 A. K. GREEN *Behind Closed Doors* vi, He wasn't tragic, not a bit of it.

2. Resembling tragedy in respect of its matter; relating to or expressing fatal or dreadful events; connected with or excited by such events; sorrowful, sad, melancholy, gloomy; = TRAGICAL *a.* 1.
1593 SHAKS. *3 Hen. VI*, v. vi. 28 My brest can better brooke thy Daggers point, Then can my eares that Tragicke History. 1667 MILTON *P.L.* IX. 6, I now must change Those Notes to Tragic. 1718 LADY M. W. MONTAGU *Let. to Abbé Conti* 31 July, The tragic story that you are well acquainted with. 1751 JOHNSON *Rambler* No. 156 ¶ 10 That the tragick and comick affections have been moved alternately with equal force. *a* 1780 HARRIS *Philol. Enquiries* Wks. (1841) 430 That pity and terror are the true tragic passions; that they truly bear that name, and are necessarily diffused through every fable truly tragic. 1819 KEATS *Isabella* xxxi, Into her heart a throng Of higher occupants, a richer zest, Came tragic.

3. a. Resembling the action or conclusion of a tragedy; characterized by or involving 'tragedy' in real life; calamitous, disastrous, terrible, fatal. (In quot. 1876, Suffering calamity, extremely unhappy or unfortunate.)
1545 JOYE *Exp. Dan.* viii. 129 b, Noble valeant princes.. haue there bene, which at last.. haue had a miserable tragik ende. 1639 N. N. tr. *Du Bosq's Compl. Woman* II. 80 The Tragick effects of this levity. 1850 CARLYLE *Latter-d. Pamph.* v. (1872) 181 In these tragic days. 1872 YEATS *Growth Comm.* 294 The tragic fate of many bold men. 1876 L. STEPHEN *Eng. Th. 18th Cent.* II. 372 Swift.. is the most tragic figure in our literature. Beside the deep agony of his soul, all other suffering.. is pale and colourless. 1907 *Verney Mem.* I. 98 Throughout his short life to its tragic close.

b. ***tragic flaw*** = HAMARTIA.
1913 L. COOPER *Aristotle on Art of Poetry* ii. 40 For Mary, the tragic flaw of the hero, described as an 'error of judgment', or a 'shortcoming', needs immediate illustration. The single Greek word, *hamartia*, lays the emphasis upon the want of insight within the man, but is elastic enough to mean also the outward fault resulting from it. 1950 W. FARNHAM *Shakespeare's Tragic Frontier* i. 4 In Brutus then, Shakespeare discovered the noble hero with a tragic flaw. By that discovery he made it possible for English tragedy to reach a greatness hitherto attained only by Greek tragedy. 1970 *English Studies* LI. 235 This flaw in the Hegge Pilate .. approximates very closely what is generally meant in dramatic criticism as 'tragic flaw', and the Hegge Pilate may be the first tragic hero in English drama.

4. *Comb.*: (*a*) expressing combination of tragic with some other quality, as ***tragic-comical***, ***-humorous***, ***-ironic***; (*b*) parasynthetic, as ***tragic-fated***.
1839-40 W. IRVING *Wolfert's R., Mountjoy* (1855) 47 Whenever my father looked me in the face, it was with such a tragic-comical leer. 1902 MONKSHOOD & GAMBLE *R. Kipling* 155 Some side scene.. of the great tragic-ironic. 1906 *Daily Chron.* 13 Mar. 3/4 The punishing, in a tragic-humorous manner, of a rascally set of owners. 1908 *Ibid.* 19 Nov. 3/2 At the time of the tragic-fated Struensee.

B. *sb.* **1. a.** A tragic actor: = TRAGEDIAN 2.
1587 *Mirr. Mag., Ferrex* i, Complayne I may with tragiques on y^{e} stage. 1837 THACKERAY *Ravenswing* vi, 'That he is', said Canterfield, the first tragic.

b. A tragic poet or author: = TRAGEDIAN 1.
1594 R. ASHLEY tr. *Loys le Roy* 69 There hath bin a great companie of Tragicks, Comicks [etc.]. *a* 1619 FOTHERBY *Atheom.* II. ii. §5 (1622) 203 Whereof two Tragicks haue giuen vs two notable instances. 1737 SAVAGE *Public Spirit* 7 With lib'ral Light the Tragic charms the Age. 1827 *Buckham's Theatre Grks.* (ed. 2) Pref. 5 To give the student an idea of the manner in which he is expected to read the Tragics.

2. A tragic poem or drama, a tragedy. ? *Obs.*
c 1720 PRIOR *Written in Mezeray's Hist. France* 19 The man in graver tragick known. 17.. *The Link* in Dodsley *Coll. Poems* (1782) IV. 126 In epics and tragics.

3. *fig.* †Tragic fate (*obs.*); a tragic event, a disaster.
1689 KIRKTON *Hist. Ch. Scot.* VIII. (1817) 310 This was her miserable tragick. 1857 CLOUGH *Poems*, etc. (1869) I. 113 Whatever comes of it—pain and grief, suicide and murder, all the tragics you can think of.

4. quasi-*sb.* ***the tragic***: that which is tragic; the tragic side of the drama, or of life; tragic style or manner.
1872 MORLEY *Voltaire* iii. (1886) 132 Sometimes they failed in reaching the tragic, through excessive fear of passing its limits.

tragical ('trædʒɪkəl), *a.* (*sb.*) [f. L. *tragic-us* (see prec.) + -AL^{1}: see -ICAL. In earlier use than *tragic* or F. *tragique*.]

1. Of the nature of, or resembling tragedy in respect of its matter; relating to or expressing fatal or dreadful events; = TRAGIC *a.* 2.
Cf. F. *tragique*, 'tragicall, tragicke,..bloudie, deadlie, dolefull, dismall' (Cotgr.), It. *tragico*, 'tragicall, dismall, deadly' (Florio).
c 1489 CAXTON *Blanchardyn* liv. 213 The vnfortunate report and tragicall tidings. 1596 *Edward III*, v. i. 105 So must my voice be tragicall againe, And I must sing of dolefull accidents. 1641 J. JACKSON *True Evang. T.* I. 43 Eusebius was an eye-witnesse of these things, who tells a most tragicall story hereof. 1828 DUPPA *Trav. Italy*, etc. 150 It represents the tragical fable of Hippolytus.

† 2. Appropriate to or befitting tragedy; having the elevated or dignified style of tragedy; serious and stately; also, affectedly elevated, grandiose, pompous; (of language) grandiloquent, rhetorical, extravagant; (of aspect or manner) grave, formidable; = TRAGIC 1 c. *Obs.* (exc. as involved in 1 or 3).
1548 UDALL, etc. *Erasm. Par. Mark* xii. 78 What with their magnifik and hye titles, and what with their tragicall and masking apparell, as though they had bene almost god almighties peeres. 1565 JEWEL *Def. Apol.* II. xiii. (1611) 255 He.. would thinke these Tragical termes should beare some weight. For sober men seldome vse thus to cry without some cause. 1579 LYLY *Euphues* (Arb.) 137, I would haue tragicall and stately stile shunned. 1591 SHAKS. *1 Hen. VI*, III. i. 125 Why looke you still so sterne, and tragicall? 1673 *Lady's Call.* II. iii. §2 Those tragical furies wherewith some women seem transported.

b. Excited with tragic feeling.
c 1592 MARLOWE *Massacre Paris* II. vi, Though I seem mild and calm, Think not but I am tragical within. 1887 MISS BRADDON *Like & Unlike* i, It will never do for Valentine to surprise us in this tragical mood.

3. = TRAGIC *a.* 3.
1555 EDEN *Decades* 144 The turmoyles and tragicall affayres of the Ocean. 1644 [H. PARKER] *Jus Pop.* 22 The latter part of Neroes tragicall raign. 1716 LADY M. W. MONTAGU *Let. to Lady Rich* 1 Dec., The tragical end of an only son. 1784 P. WRIGHT *New Bk. Martyrs* 797/1, I shall want assistance to help me upon this tragical stage [the scaffold]. 1871 MORLEY *Crit. Misc.* Ser. I. *Condorcet* (1878) 35 A destiny.. as tragical as any in those bloody and most tragical days.

† 4. = TRAGIC *a.* 1. *Obs.*
1589 PUTTENHAM *Eng. Poesie* I. xi. (Arb.) 41 They set forth the dolefull falles of infortunate and afflicted Princes, and were called Poets Tragicall. 1590 SHAKS. *Mids. N.* v. i. 57 A tedious breefe Scene of yong Piramus, And his loue Thisby; very tragicall mirth. *Ibid.* 66, A play there is, my Lord,.. And tragicall.. it is: For Piramus therein doth kill himselfe. 1629 WADSWORTH *Pilgr.* v. 47 They made a Tragicall-Comedy of our voyage, whereby they got much money and honour.

† B. *sb.* A tragical story or strain. *Obs. rare.*
1606 G. W[OODCOCKE] *Hist. Ivstine* XIX. 75 Hauing heard the Tragicall of what was become of them.. they redoubled their griefes. 1621 BRATHWAIT *Nat. Embassie* (1877) 119 Terpnus.. did.. sing on his Lute these wofull tragicalls.

tragicality (trædʒɪ'kælɪtɪ). *rare.* [f. prec. + -ITY.] Tragical quality or style; tragicalness.
1843 CARLYLE *Past & Pr.* III. iii, An air of supreme tragicality.

tragically ('trædʒɪkəlɪ), *adv.* [f. as prec. + -LY^{2}: see -ICALLY.] In a tragical manner or style.

1. With tragic feeling or expression; †in early use, with loud or passionate complaint.
1577 VAUTROUILLIER *Luther on Ep. Gal.* 25 Paul might.. tragically have cried out against them: O ungracious world. *a* 1716 SOUTH *Serm.* (1727) VI. 427 Many complain and cry out very tragically of the Wretchedness of their Hearts. 1781 GIBBON *Decl. & F.* xviii. II. 116 He tragically lamented the cruel murder of Constans. *Mod.* A story very tragically told.

2. With calamitous, disastrous, or fatal issue.
1583 in Hakluyt *Voy.* (1600) III. 154 Our voyage.. ended tragically. 1602 WARNER *Alb. Eng.* Epit. (1612) 384 This king that tragically raigned, being first deposed.. tragically ended. 1693 DRYDEN *Juvenal's Sat.* Ded. (1697) 71 As his Provocations were great, he has reveng'd them tragically. 1885 *Manch. Exam.* 10 July 5/2 Their predictions have been only too tragically fulfilled.

† 3. Grandiloquently, rhetorically. *Obs. rare*$^{-1}$.
1678 CUDWORTH *Intell. Syst.* I. iv. §36. 548 And accordingly is it said of Numenius by him [Proclus], that τρεῖς ἀνυμνήσας θεούς, he did τραγῳδῶν καλεῖν, πάππον, ἔγγονον, ἀπόγονον, having praised the Three Gods, Tragically or Affectedly called them, the Grandfather, the Son, and the Nephew.

'tragicalness. [f. as prec. + -NESS.] Tragical quality.
1667 *Decay Chr. Piety* xiv. ¶ 2 As well in the tragicalness of the event, as the insolence of the undertaking. 1687 BOYLE *Martyrd. Theodora* vi. (1703) 88 A spectacle, whose tragicalness his revenge would make acceptable to him. 1905 A. C. BENSON *Upton Lett.* (1906) 208, I re-read *The Light that failed* for its abundant vitality and tragicalness.

tragicize ('trædʒɪsaɪz), *v. rare.* [f. TRAGIC + -IZE: cf. *criticize*.] *intr.* To speak or write in tragic style, to 'do the tragic'. (Cf. TRAGEDIZE 2.)
1833-40 J. H. NEWMAN *Ch. of Fathers* (1842) 129, I will tragicize a bit.

'tragicly, *adv. rare*$^{-1}$. [f. TRAGIC *a.* + -LY^{2}.] = TRAGICALLY.
1604 STIRLING *Aurora, Elegy* iii. Mj, But I shall sadly sing, too tragickly inclin'd, Some subiect sympathizing with my melancholious mind.

'tragicness. *rare*$^{-1}$. [f. as prec. + -NESS.] = TRAGICALNESS.
1667 WATERHOUSE *Fire Lond.* 124 By the Tragickness of all which, in Battails fought,.. I lost Hundreds of Thousands of Men.

tragico- ('trædʒɪkəʊ), combining form repr. Gr. τραγικός TRAGIC; as in **,tragico-'farcical** *a.*, combining tragic and farcical elements; **,tragico-he,roi-'comic** *a.* (*nonce-wd.*) combining tragic, heroic, and comic elements; **,tragico-hi'storical** *a.*, combining tragic and historical elements. Also, contracted TRAGI-, q.v.

1756 J. WARTON *Ess. Pope* I. iv. 207 Bartolomeo Bocchini ..printed at Venice MDCXLI, a tragico-heroi-comic poem. **1913** E. F. BENSON *Thorley Weir* vi. 206 Tragico-farcical situations. **1919** T. S. ELIOT in *Times Lit. Suppl.* 13 Nov. 637/3 In *Catiline* Jonson conforms, or attempts to conform, to conventions..of tragico-historical drama.

tragi-comedy (ˌtrædʒɪˈkɒmɪdɪ). Also 6 tragy-, 7 trage-, tragœ-; see also COMEDY. [a. F. *tragi-comédie* (1545 in Hatz.-Darm.) = It. *tragi-comedia* (Florio), ad. late L. *tragicōmœdia* (Lactantius *a* 325), syncopated from *tragico-cōmœdia* (Plautus); f. L. *tragicus* tragic + *cōmœdia* comedy.]

1. A play (or, *rarely*, a story) combining the qualities of a tragedy and a comedy, or containing both tragic and comic elements; sometimes *spec.* a play mainly of tragic character, but with a happy ending.

1581 SIDNEY *Apol. Poetrie* (Arb.) 65 The right sportfulnes, is [not] by..mungrell Tragy-comedie obtained. [**1603** HARSNET *Pop. Impost.* xxiii. 150 Our Dæmonopoiia or Devill-fiction is Tragico-Comœdia, a mixture of both as Amphitryo in Plautus is.] **1640** KILLIGREW (*title*) The Prisoners. A Tragæ-Comedy. **1652** C. B. STAPYLTON *Herodian* Advt., He [Herodian] represents ..the Emperors of that Age and their Courts, with Comedies, Tragedies and Tragicomedies. **1664** FLECKNOE (*title*) Love's Kingdom. A Pastoral Trage-Comedy. **1770** LANGHORNE *Plutarch* (1879) I. 178/1 When tragedy took a graver turn, something of the former drollery was still retained, as in that which we call tragi-comedy. **1849** MACAULAY *Hist. Eng.* v. I. 636 Shakspeare had borrowed from Whetstone the plot of the noble tragicomedy of Measure for Measure.

2. *fig.* An event or series of events of mixed tragic and comic character; a combination of pathetic and humorous elements in real life.

1579–80 NORTH *Plutarch* (1676) 619 His acts..may plainly shew, that all that was but a Tragi-comedy ceremoniously ended. *a* **1649** DRUMM. OF HAWTH. *Cypress Grove* Wks. (1711) 126 Every one cometh there to act his part of this tragi-comedy, called life. **1709** STEELE *Tatler* No. 36 ¶5 What heightened the Tragi-Comedy of this Market for Annuities. **1838** LYTTON *Calderon* i, The Tragi-Comedy of Court Intrigue.

Hence ˌ**tragi-coˈmedian**, an actor who performs in tragi-comedy; ˌ**tragi-comediˈetta** (*nonce-wd.*), a slight or sketchy tragi-comedy.

c **1626** MIDDLETON *Mayor of Queenborough* v. i, Comedians, tragedians, tragi-comedians. **1892** *Pall Mall G.* 12 May 3/1 Tragedy is a name not to be taken in vain, least of all by a poet of Mr. Swinburne's calibre. *Tragi-comedietta would have come nearer the mark.

tragi-comic (ˌtrædʒɪˈkɒmɪk), *a.* [f. TRAGI- + COMIC.] Having the character of a tragi-comedy; combining tragic with comic elements.

1683 CAVE *Ecclesiastici, Athanasius* 81 The Tragy-Comick Scene of Arsenius the Meletian Bishop. **1709** *Tatler* No. 68 ¶3 You have a Tragi-comick Genius. **1790** BURKE *Fr. Rev.* 11 In viewing this monstrous tragi-comick scene, the most opposite passions..succeed..each other..; alternate laughter and tears; alternate scorn and horrour. **1831** SOUTHEY in *Q. Rev.* XLIV. 276 A more tragi-comic history could not be imagined. **1840** *New Monthly Mag.* LVIII. 524 Screaming in ecstasy at the tragicomic termination of their attempt.

So ˌ**tragi-ˈcomical** *a.*, of tragi-comic character (hence ˌ**tragi-comiˈcality**, tragi-comic quality, or an instance of this; ˌ**tragi-ˈcomically** *adv.*, in a tragi-comical way). Also ˌ**tragi-ˌcomi-opeˈratical**, **-ˈpastoral** *adjs.* (*nonce-wds.*), combining the qualities of tragi-comedy and opera (or pastoral).

1567 FENTON *Trag. Disc.* xiii. Argt. (1898) 238 A *tragi-comiqual reaport. **1581** SIDNEY *Apol. Poetrie* (Arb.) 43 Some Poesies haue coupled together two or three kindes, as Tragicall and Comicall, wher-vpon is risen, the Tragi-comicall. **1627** (*title*) A Tragi-Comicall History of ovr Times, vnder the borrowed names of Lisander and Calista. *a* **1661** FULLER *Worthies, Leicester.* (1662) II. 129 His tragi-comical life, had a peaceable End. **1878** H. JAMES *Europeans* i, It was extremely clever, and full of a sort of tragicomical power. **1897** *Q. Rev.* Jan. 182 His butterfly *tragicomicalities of romance. **1733** J. BRAMSTON *Man of Taste* 22, I was *tragi-comically got. **1902** SWINBURNE in *Q. Rev.* July 25 The dissolution of a ruined household is.. tragicomically set before us. *c* **1778** PORSON (*title in Daily Chron.* 29 Mar. (1902) 6/7), Out of the Frying-pan into the Fire..a *tragi-comi-operatical farce. **1714** GAY (*title*) The What d'ye call it: A *Tragi-Comi-Pastoral Farce. **1729** HAWKER (*title*) The Wedding: A Tragi-Comi-Pastoral-Farcical Opera..The Overture, by Dr. Pepusch.

‖ˈ**tragion, -ium.** *Herb. Obs.* [L. *tragion*, Gr. τράγιον, f. τράγος he-goat.] A name given by the Greeks to some strong-smelling plant or plants; identified by 16th c. herbalists with *Dictamnus albus* (*D. Fraxinella*, Lyte 343), and *Chenopodium vulvaria* (*Tragium Germanicum*, Lyte 548).

1567 MAPLET *Gr. Forest* 62 Tragion saith Diascorides, onely Crete & Cicilie bringeth forth. **1577** GRANGE *Gold. Aphrod.* F iij, The hearbe *Dictamus*, or Tragion. **1578** LYTE *Dodoens* III. xxi. 343 Of False Dictam... This herbe is called in Greek τράγιον, in Latine *Tragium*: and is the first kind of *Tragium* described by Dioscorides. Some herboristes cal it *Fraxinella*. *Ibid.* v. iv. 549 We do call it in Greeke τράγιον: in Latine *Tragium*, that is to say, Goates herbe. And bycause you shall reade in Dioscorides of two other herbes called *Tragia*, to make some difference betwixt them, we do name this *Tragium Germanicum*: in Frenche, *Blanche putain*: in base Almaigne, Bocxcruyt: some call it *Vuluaria*, by whiche name it is knowen of the Herboristes of this Countrie:..I haue named it in Englishe, The ranke stinking Goate, or stinking Motherwort. **1587** GREENE *Euphues* Wks. (Grosart) VI. 188 The herbe Tragion being once byt with an Aspis neuer groweth. **1706** PHILLIPS (ed. Kersey), *Tragium*, a shrub..whose Leaves in Autumn stink like a Goat; also the Herb white Dittany.

ˌ**tragoˈdrama.** *nonce-wd.* [f. Gr. τραγο-, combining form of τράγος (see TRAGEDY) + DRAMA.] A drama of tragic character.

1793 [see COMODRAMA].

†**traˈgonce.** *Obs. rare*⁻¹. [app. an altered form of *dragonce*, one of the 15–17th c. forms of the plant-name DRAGONS (*Arum Dracunculus*, now *Dracunculus vulgaris*); the variation of *d* and *t* being due to the confusion between *dragontia*, *-cia*, and *taragontia*, *-cia*, and the inclusion by 16th c. herbalists under Δρακοντία, *Dracontia*, or *Dracunculus*, of both Dragons (*Arun Dracunculus*) and Tarragon (*Artemisia Dracunculus*); an inclusion commemorated in the existing botanical names. See etymological note s.v. TARRAGON.] = DRAGONS (or ? TARRAGON).

1575 TURBERV. *Venerie* 43 She purgeth hir with the hearbe called Tragonce.

tragopan (ˈtrægəʊpæn). *Ornith.* [a. L. *tragopān*, Gr. τραγόπāν, name of a reputed bird in Ethiopia (perh. the bearded vulture); f. τράγος goat + Πᾶν Pan; in mod. Ornithology taken as the name of a genus (Cuvier, 1829).] A pheasant of the genus *Ceriornis* (formerly *Tragopan*), characterized by having a pair of erectile fleshy horns on the head; the species are found in India, China, etc.

[**1623** COCKERAM III, *Tragoponadus*, a bird in Ethiope greater then an Eagle, hauing hornes like a Goate. **1706** PHILLIPS (ed. Kersey), Tragopanas.] **1831** GOULD *Birds fr. Himalaya* lxii, The genus Tragopan. **1847** CARPENTER *Zool.* §431 The Tragopans seem to connect the Pheasants with the Turkeys. **1882** *Athenæum* 27 May 671/1 Additions made to the [Zool. Soc.] menagerie during April..: a pair of black-headed tragopans (*Ceriornis melanocephala*);..a male Cabot's tragopan (*Ceriornis Caboti*).

‖**Tragopogon** (ˌtrægəʊˈpəʊgən). *Bot.* [a. Gr. τραγοπώγων (Theophr.), f. τράγο-ς he-goat + πώγων beard.] A genus of Composite plants of which the common wild yellow-flowered English and European species, *T. minor* and *pratensis*, are known as Goat's-beard, and *T. porrifolius* with rose-coloured or purple flowers is cultivated for its esculent root under the name of SALSIFY.

1706 in PHILLIPS (ed Kersey). **1731** [see SALSIFY 1]. **1741** *Compl. Fam.-Piece* II. iii. 376 Products of the Kitchen Garden... Buglos, Borage, Tragopogon. **1830** [see SALSIFY 1].

tragule (ˈtrægjuːl). *Zool.* [ad. mod.L. *Tragulus*, dim. of *tragus*, Gr. τράγος goat.] A quadruped of the genus *Tragulus*, or of the family *Tragulidæ* of ruminants, found in India and Java, resembling small hornless deer; a chevrotain. So ˈ**tragulid**, one of the *Tragulidæ*; ˈ**traguline** *a.*, belonging to the *Tragulina*; also applied to a group of goat-like antelopes including the steenbok, *Nanotragus tragulus*; ˈ**traguloid** *a.*, akin in form to the *Tragulidæ*; *sb.* a member of this group.

1878 BELL tr. *Gegenbaur's Comp. Anat.* 559 This third portion [of the stomach] is wanting in the Tragulidæ and Tylopoda. **1883** *List Anim. Zool. Soc.* 176 Family *Tragulidæ*. Genus *Tragulus* [3 species]. **1891** *Cent. Dict.*, Tragule... Traguline... Traguloid, *a.* **1891** FLOWER & LYDEKKER *Mammals* 307 *Leptomeryx*, from the Miocene of the United States, is regarded as a Traguloid. **1896** tr. *Boas' Text Bk. Zool.* 509 The Tragulids (*Tragulidæ*) form a circumscribed group of small Ruminants without antlers;.. in most respects nearly allied to the Cervidæ.

‖**tragus** (ˈtreɪgəs). *Anat.* Pl. tragi (ˈtreɪdʒaɪ). [Late L., from *tragus*, a. Gr. τράγος he-goat, so named on account of the bunch of hairs which it bears: see quot. 1874.] A prominence on the inner side of the external ear, in front of and partly closing the orifice, opposite to the ANTITRAGUS, and in man usually bearing a tuft of hairs; specially developed in certain bats.

1693 tr. *Blancard's Phys. Dict.* (ed. 2), *Tragus*, the extream Brim of the Ear. **1809** ABERNETHY *Dis. resemb. Syphilis* (1826) 127 Situated on the front of the ear, extending over the tragus. **1874** ROOSA *Dis. Ear* (ed. 2) 19 Rufus of Ephesus, who was the first medical lexicographer, and who lived in the age of Pliny, used the names *helix, lobe, tragus,* and *anti-tragus*, still employed to describe the different parts of the auricle. **1904** *Speaker* 24 Dec. 315/2 The earlet, a curious development of the tragus in insectivorous bats.

traheen (traˈhiːn). *Anglo-Irish.* [ad. Ir. *troighthín* (Dineen), *troighín* (O'Reilly), a little foot or sole, a soleless stocking worn without shoes; dim. of *troigh*, *troighth-* foot (pl. *troighthean*); cf. Gaelic *troidh* foot, pl. *troidhean*.] See quots.

1817 LADY MORGAN *France* (1818) I. 125 *note*, Partial covering of the leg is universal among the peasantry of Ireland, at this day, under the name of 'traheens'. **1836** W. H. MAXWELL *Capt. Blake* II. iii. *note*, *Traheeins* are the legs of Connemara stockings, which case the limbs of the traveller, without cramping his toes.

†**trahent**, *sb.* and *a.* *Obs. rare.* [ad. L. *trahent-em*, pr. pple. of *trahĕre* to draw.]

A. *sb.* App. short for CONTRAHENT, contracting party, or applied to one of the claimants before they enter into a contract.

1537 CROMWELL in Merriman *Life & Lett.* (1902) II. 69 Euery point in the same [letter] bothe touching the title, the demeanors of the trahentes of both parties, And the seruice that may be don be eyther partie.

B. *adj.* Drawing, that draws.

1661 LOVELL *Hist. Anim. & Min.* 518 Potions,..used to evacuate humours, that doe not resist the trahent medicine.

‖ˈ**trahison.** *rare.* [F. *trahison*.] Treason.

1858 KINGSLEY *Red King* 73 Foul mishap and trahison. **1859** G. MEREDITH *R. Feverel* xxxix, She must see the trahison with her eyes.

‖**trahison des clercs** (traizɔ̃ de klɛr). [Fr.] The title of Julien Benda's work *La Trahison des Clercs* (1927), used to denote a compromise of intellectual integrity by writers, artists, and thinkers. Cf. *treason of the clerks* s.v. TREASON *sb.* 1 b.

1935 *New Statesman* 26 Oct. 598/1 Is it one more proof that the intellectual should always advise but never govern? Is it one more case of the *trahison des clercs*? **1952** E. HYAMS *Soil & Civilization* 127 True, there has been some reaction away from this state of mind among a few intellectuals, a kind of uneasy, if wholesome, *trahison des clercs*. **1968** J. M. ZIMAN *Public Knowledge* vi. 123 The aim of Science is understanding, not the accumulation of data and formulae. .. To fail to construct the building, to leave all the bricks lying round in untidy piles, is the *trahison des clercs* of today. **1978** *Listener* 4 May 559/3 Look, they say, terrorism is a phenomenon of our times. Let us..acknowledge that a diplomat..is fair game... I find this *trahison des clercs*.

†ˈ**trahtne**, *v.* *Obs.* [OE. *trahtnian*, f. *traht* text, passage, exposition.] *trans.* To expound.

c **1000** ÆLFRIC *Hom.* I. 510 Hæʒmon trahtnað þis godspell. *Ibid.* II. 278 We woldon ʒefyrn trahtnian be ðam lambe. *a* **1050** *Liber Scintill.* lxv. (1889) 200 Mid were æwfæstum trahtna [*tracta*] be haliʒnysse. *c* **1200** ORMIN 11680 Nimeþþ gom Off þiss þatt here iss trahhtnedd.

trahys, obs. form of TRACE *sb.*²

trahysh, var. TRAISE *v. Obs.*, to betray.

traice, traict, obs. forms of TRAIT, TREAT.

traictise, obs. form of TREATISE.

traid(e, obs. f. TRADE; pa. t. of TRAY *v. Obs.*

traie: see TRAY.

traifoyle, obs. f. TREFOIL.

traik (trek), *sb. Sc.* Also 6 traike, 8 **trake**. [TRAIK *sb.* and *v.* appear together in Sc. soon after 1500. Origin uncertain; with sense 1 cf. Sw. *tråk* 'troublesome task, painfulness, tiresomeness', *tråkig* adj., tiresome, troublesome, wearisome, and the vb. mentioned under TRAIK *v.* It is not clear that sense 2 is the same word, but cf. the vb.]

1. A plague, pestilence; mischief, disaster; also *fig.* of a person, one who is a 'pest' or 'plague'.

1513 DOUGLAS *Æneis* III. ii. 141 Ane cruell pest and traik, ..Fell on our membris with sic infectioun, Was na remeid. *Ibid.* XI. xv. 59 This wench, this vengeabill pest or traike. **1739** A. NICOL *Poems* (1766) 20 The meikle trake come o'er their snouts. **1835** JAMIESON s.v., He that has nae gear will hae nae traik.

2. 'The flesh of sheep that have died of disease or by accident' (Jamieson).

1802 FINDLATER *Agric. Peebles* xiv. 208 The sheep dying of disease are used as flesh meat, under the designation of *traik*. **1815** *Pennecuik's Descr. Tweeddale* Notes 95 The poor,..sluggish Tweeddale shepherd, fed with his dog upon traik (sheep that have died of some disease).

Hence ˈ**traiky** *a.*, weak, worn out, fatigued.

1825 JAMIESON, *Traik, traichie*, weak, in a declining state. **1846** in BROCKETT *N.C. Gloss* (E.D.D.). **1884** J. TAIT in *United Presb. Mag.* 157/2 Sometimes a treaky member of the flock can be utilized as food.

traik (trek), *v. Sc.* Also 6 trake, 6–9 traick. [Goes app. with TRAIK *sb.*, q.v.: origin uncertain, but cf. Sw. *tråka* to rub on, to tug, to drudge, Norw. *traaka* to struggle against, show disinclination to toil or work; to go with difficulty, go slowly, *traakes* to become tired or exhausted, *traakall* adj. unwilling, reluctant.]

1. *intr.* To decline in health, or be in declining health; to become worn out; to break down, collapse. Now *rare*.

1508 [see TRAIKED]. **1535** STEWART *Cron. Scot.* (Rolls) I. 423 Ane seiknes that is into the heid, Without the soner that it get remeid,..The memberis all will rycht sone tyne and traik. **1639** R. BAILLIE *Lett.* 28 Sept., Many of them died; and..the most part of all who remained traicked pitifullie.

1737 Ramsay *Sc. Prov.* xiv. 118 He's the gear that winna traik. 1834 Carlyle in Froude *1st Forty Years* (1882) II. xviii. 451 But for the kindness and helpfulness shown me on all hands I must have traiked.

2. To go idly about, to stroll; to wander, stray, go astray; ***to traik after***, to come after, follow.

1818 Scott *Hrt. Midl.* xxiv, There isna a hussy..that you can bring within your doors, but there will be chields.. coming traiking after them for their destruction. 1825 Jamieson, *Traik*... To wander so as to lose one's self; chiefly applied to the young of poultry, Dumfr. Hence the ..phrase, 'He's nane o' the birds that traik', he can take good care of him-self. 1842 J. Aiton *Domest. Econ.* (1857) 264 In half dozens they are tearing the thatch off the stacks, or they are 'traicking' through the corn-fields, each of them destroying with its feet quite as much as a sheep would eat.

Hence **traiked, traikit,** ('trekɪd, -ɪt) *ppl. a. Sc.* (*a*) wasted; worn out; (*b*) of sheep or cattle: that has died a natural death; cf. braxy; '**traiking** *vbl. sb.*, strolling, wandering, 'walking out'.

1508 Dunbar *Flyting* 118 Bot now, in winter, for purteth thow art traikit. 1562 in Keith *Hist. Scot.* (1734) App. 96 Be the tempestuous Stormis of the Winteris past, the hale Gudis wer sa trakit, smorit and deid, that [etc.]. 1585–6 J. Melville *Let.* in *Wodrow Soc. Misc.* (1844) I. 439 Mr. Andrew has been a sore traicked man since he came home. *a*1598 Rollock *Serm.* Wks. 1849 I. 437 The trakedest bodies that livis, even as gif they wer drawin throw an myre. *c*1680 [F. Sempill] *Banishm. Poverty* 93, I call'd him Turk and traiked tyke. 1825 Jamieson, *Trakit*... 1. Sore fatigued. 2. Wasted, brought into a declining state by being overdriven, starved, or exposed to the inclemency of the weather. 1828 J. Struthers *Hist. Scot.* II. 625 To butcher-meat, except..drowned calves and traiked sheep.. they were total strangers. 1894 Crockett *Raiders* xxxv, His night-hawk traikings and trokings with a dozen hizzies.

trail (treɪl), *sb.*[1] Also 5 **traille, trele,** (6 **treale**), 5–7 **trayle,** 6–8 **traile,** 7 **trayl.** [Known in sense 1 from 14th c.; in other senses only from 15th c. or later. App. f. trail *v.*[1]]

I. Something that trails or hangs trailing.

†**1. a.** The train of a robe or other garment. *Obs.*

13.. *Cursor M.* 28020 (Cott.) Yee leuedis..Thoru your trail bath wide and side, Es not at seke to find your pride. *c*1440 *Promp. Parv.* 499/1 Trayle, or trayne of a clothe, *sirma*. 1688 R. Holme *Armoury* iv. xii. (Roxb.) 503/2 The traile or traine of this great mantle was layd on his left shoulder.

b. A trailing or hanging article of clothing.

1896 Barrie *Sent. Tommy* x, The shrewd blasts cutting through my thin trails of claithes.

c. A long trailing or loose-hanging slender mass of hair, fibres, or the like; 'any thing drawn to length' (J.).

1844 Mrs. Browning *Portrait* iii, Oval cheeks..Which a trail of golden hair Keeps from fading off to air. 1881 Blackmore *Christowell* iii, Running up to him, with her long grape-scissors in her hand, and a trail of bast around her neck.

2. a. A trailing ornament (carved, moulded, or embroidered) in the form of a wreath or spray of leaves or tendrils; a wreathed or foliated ornament.

[Some take this, and esp. 2 b, as belonging to trail *sb.*[2]; prob. the two words tended to run together.]

*a*1423 in *Archæologia* LXI. 171, ij Fiols of on sute of silver and gild, Graven aboute wt a traille of Ive levys. 1454 *Test. Ebor.* (Surtees) II. 175 A couered pece with a trele of roses opon ye couerynge. 1480–81 in Hope *Windsor Castle* (1913) 401 Ac lxii pedum de lez Traillez et Crestes. 1533 *Hampton Crt. Acc.* in E. Law *Hist. Hampton Crt.* (1885) 352 To Robert Skyngke..moulder of Antyke-worke, for a trayle of antyk sett in the great Joull-pece in the Kynges new Hall, conteynyng 71 yards in leyngthe, 8 inches brode, at 16 d. the yard. 1551 Sir J. Williams *Accompte* (Abbotsf. 1836) 52 A riche cope of crymsyn veluet..embrodred all ower with a traile and Fawcions of Venice golde. 1557–8 in Hope *Windsor Castle* (1913) 260 The armes of England and Spaine with the treales to the same. *a*1618 Sylvester *Ode to Astræa* vii, That soft Sattin limme, With blew trayles enameld trimme. 1869 Boutell *Arms & Arm.* v. (1874) 78 A trail of foliage..filled the space between the angular bands.

b. A wreath or spray of (natural) leaves, etc.; a trailing tendril or branch. (Cf. 1 c.)

1598 Drayton *Heroic. Ep.* i. 117 A little Current..Which like a wanton Trayle creepes here and there. 1697 Dryden *Virg. Georg.* iv. 184 The late Narcissus, and the winding Trail Of Bears-foot, Myrtles green, and Ivy pale. 1725 *Bradley's Fam. Dict.* s.v. *Strawberry*, As soon as they shoot forth their Trails, you must take care to cut 'em. 1833 Ht. Martineau *Cinnamon & P.* iii, They had never entangled their feet in trails of the blue convolvulus. *a*1861 T. Woolner *Beautiful Lady, Her Shadow* vii, Nigh clad in trails of tangled eglantine.

c. *attrib.* or as *adj.*

1533 *Hampton Crt. Acc.* in E. Law *Hist. Hampton Crt.* (1885) 352, 71 yardes in length and 8 inches brode, of trayle moldyd worke. 1644 Evelyn *Diary* 1 Apr., Next the streete side..are knotts in trayle or grasse worke. 1649 G. Daniel *Trinarch.* To Rdr. 104 Speed, Cutt in sippetts, Trussell, layd about For a trayle Garnish. 1684 *Lond. Gaz.* No. 1944/4 A Petticoat of Musk coloured Silk,..the Flowers Trail Silver.

II. Something trailed or made by trailing.

†**3.** A sledge [= L. *tragula*]. *Obs.*

1570 Levins *Manip.* 198/43 A Trayle, sledde, *traha*. 1576 in *Ripon Ch. Acts* (Surtees) 379 For a trayle to hym, 12 d. 1588 *Durham Wills* (Surtees) II. 330, ij long lethers, j traile, ij flekes, j nowt heck, 12s. 1600 D. Settle in Hakluyt *Voy.* III. 37 They frank or keepe certaine dogs..which they yoke togither, as we do oxen & horses, to a sled or traile: and so carry their necessaries ouer the yce and snow.

4. A drag-net [= L. *tragula*]. Also *trail-net*: see 17. (Also *fig.*)

1711 W. King tr. *Naude's Ref. Politics* v. 198 The first that made trails, and found out casting-nets to make men captives. 1807 P. Gass *Jrnl.* 29 The fish here are generally pike... What we caught were taken with trails or brush nets.

5. The hinder end of the stock of a gun-carriage, which rests or slides on the ground when the carriage is unlimbered. Cf. train *sb.*[1] 20.

1768 J. Muller *Treat. Artillery* Vocab., *Trail*, is the end of the travelling carriage opposite to the wheels, and upon which the carriage slides, when unlimbered. 1803 Wellington in Gurw. *Desp.* (1837) II. 565 There is no remedy,..excepting to lengthen considerably the trail of the carriage. 1868 *Rep. to Govt. U.S. Munitions War* 95 The gun is mounted on a field-carriage, with trail of the usual form.

6. Anything drawn behind as an appendage; a body or collection *of* things or persons, drawn along by, or following in the wake of, something or some one, or moving steadily along in a lengthened formation so as to suggest this; a train.

1621 Quarles *Argalus & P.* (1678) 85 A rising Sun.. From whence ten thousand trails of gold came down In waving points. 1697 Dryden *Virg. Georg.* i. 504 Seeming Stars..shooting through the Darkness..With..long Trails of Light. 1770 Langhorne *Plutarch* (1851) I. 282/1 Dreadful thunders..mingled with long trails of lightning. 1856 Mrs. Browning *Aur. Leigh* i. 86 From which long trail of chanting priests and girls. 1872 Black *Adv. Phaeton* xx, The wind was apparent in the hurrying trails of cloud.

7. a. A mark left where something has been trailed or has passed along; a trace, track. Also *fig.*

1610 Guillim *Heraldry* ii. vii. (1660) 77 Upton tearmeth it in Latine, *Tractus* which signifieth a Trace, or Traile, because the field is seen both within and without it; and the Traile itselfe is drawn thereupon in a different colour. [See tract *sb.*[3] 6 (*a*).] 1727 Gay *Fables* i. xxiv. 12 A snail,..with slimy trail Crawls o'er the grass. 1817 Moore *Lalla R., Par. & Peri*, But the trail of the serpent is over them all. 1833 Marryat *P. Simple* xxix, I used to watch them [sharks] during the night watch, as their fins, above water, skimmed along, leaving a trail of light behind them. 1856 Mrs. Browning *Aur. Leigh* ii. 21 Brushing a green trail across the lawn With my gown in the dew. 1864 Skeat *Uhland's Poems* 124 The heights were touched with May's fair golden trail. 1899 *Allbutt's Syst. Med.* VIII. 865 In the imperfectly washed, a trail of dirt marks the course of the burrow [of the itch insect].

b. *spec.* in astronomical photography, The line or trace produced by the motion of the image of a star across the plate during exposure.

1889 *Anthony's Photogr. Bull.* II. 185 On developing numerous stars will be found which are invisible to the naked eye. The stars will all leave trails, forming arcs of concentric circles whose center lies near the center of the plate. 1891 *Ibid.* IV. 83 When the plate is developed it will contain a series of lines or trails produced by the light of the star as it crossed the plate.

8. *spec.* The track or other indication, as scent, left by a person or animal, esp. as followed by a huntsman or hound, or by any pursuer. Also *fig.*

1590 Cokaine *Treat. Hunting* D ij b, Take your [otter] houndes to the place..and cast your traylors off vpon the trayle you thinke best. 1602 Shaks. *Ham.* iv. v. 109 How cheerefully on the false Traile they cry, Oh this is Counter you false Danish Dogges. 1607 Topsell *Four-f. Beasts* (1658) 120 The best manner to teach these hounds is to take a live hare, and trail her after you upon the earth;..after-ward set forth your hound near the trail. 1741 *Compl. Fam.-Piece* ii. i. 295 A sure Sign they are upon the Scent; that is, where the Fox hath passed that Night, it is called a Drag or Trail. 1805 Pike *Sources Mississ.* (1810) 38, I was determined..if we came on the trail of elk, to follow them.. in order to kill one. 1806 *Ibid.* 57 My sentinel informed us, that some Indians were coming full speed upon our trail or track. 1827 J. F. Cooper *Prairie* iii, Did you ever run him upon the trail of carrion? 1837 W. Irving *Capt. Bonneville* (1849) 111 Vandenburgh put himself upon their trail, to trace them to their place of concealment. *a*1859 Macaulay *Hist. Eng.* xxiv. (1861) V. 143 The Spanish Ambassador.. followed the trail with such skill and perseverance that he discovered, if not the whole truth, yet enough [etc.]. 1888 P. Lindley in *Times* 16 Oct. 10/5 The hound..took up the stale trail over some rather trying ground without a fault.

b. Something strong-smelling trailed or drawn along the ground to produce a scent for hounds to follow: = drag *sb.* 6 b.

1763 *Brit. Mag.* IV. 553 They ran after a trail drawn by a man on horseback about 10 minutes before the hounds started. 1781 P. Beckford *Hunting* (1802) 85 A cat is as good a trail as any.

9. A path or track worn by the passage of persons travelling in a wild or uninhabited region; a beaten track, a rude path. (Chiefly in *U.S.* and *Canada*; also *N.Z.* and *Austral.*) Cf. *nature trail* s.v. nature *sb.* 15 a.

1807 P. Gass *Jrnl.* 125 We proceeded down the river through dreadful narrows, where the rocks were in some places breast high, and no path or trail of any kind. 1860 J. Burnett *Let.* 15 Mar. in H. F. von Haast *Life & Times Sir Julius von Haast* (1948) viii. 85 Crossed the Alexander stream and struck Mackay's last year's trail. 1875 Temple & Sheldon *Hist. Northfield, Mass.* 50 Indian Paths—which were narrow trails worn by the feet in marching single file —crossed the country in various directions. 1894 C. L. Johnstone *Canada* 81 A trail, as the Canadians call the tracks which do instead of roads. 1939 *WPA Guide to Florida* (1984) i. 117 In Hillsboro River State Park..are overnight cabins, trails, roads, and a museum. 1958 *Tararua* XII. 25 A trail seems to be something narrow and perhaps rather hard to follow—a way marked only by blazes or worn by animals, usually deer. A track seems to be something broader, cut or formed by man. 1968 Mrs. L. B. Johnson *White House Diary* 2 Oct. (1970) 714 A system of urban and rural trails, including the Pacific Coast Trail from Mexico to Canada. 1968 K. Weatherly *Roo Shooter* 47 The ancestors of the roos used this path. It was miles wide and invisible. .. When this country is closely settled and these trails are sealed, the red kangaroos will die out. 1977 *Times* 23 Apr. 12/5 There are well marked trails for independent hikers. *Ibid.* 12/7 The benefit of camping and picnic grounds, walking and hiking trails. 1982 G. M. Fraser *Flashman & Redskins* 161 From Santa Fe to Algodones on the river the trail was dotted that night with emigrant camp-fires.

10. *Geol.* A name for certain mixed glacial or other deposits resting upon older formations.

(So called as app. marking the track of floating ice.)

1866 O. Fisher in *Q. Jrnl. Geol. Soc.* 20 June 555, I have found that cylindrical pits and pipes are generally confined to soluble beds, and that the normal form of the cavities in clays, sands, and gravels is that of troughs or furrows. They are usually filled with materials derived from some neighbouring higher ground... For the sake of a name I shall call the materials which fill these furrows the 'trail'. 1882 Geikie *Text-bk. Geol.* vi. v. ii. §2. 908 A remarkable bed of clay, loam, and gravel ('loess' or 'trail'). 1884 W. G. Smith in *Jrnl. Anthropol. Inst.* XIII. 358 The whole of the 'Palæolithic floor' is..covered with the 'warp and trail' belonging to the last geological period of great cold. 1897 *Archæol. Jrnl.* Dec. 375 Where the flints are buried, in the 'head' or 'rain wash' or 'run o' th' hills' or trail, or whatever we may call the surface accumulation.

11. *Radio* and *Television.* A piece of advance publicity (often an excerpt) broadcast prior to the transmission of a programme. Cf. trail *v.*[1] 4; trailer *sb.* 4 b.

1973 *Listener* 6 Dec. 798/1 Accidentally switching on early ..on Radio 3..I heard..off-putting trails. 1980 *Broadcast* 7 July 24/3 The TV Presentation Department..make hundreds of commercials every year in the form of programme trails.

III. Action of trailing.

12. The action of dragging oneself or something along, or of creeping or crawling; also *dial.*, a tiring walk. *rare.*

*a*1547 Surrey *Æneid* ii. 284 The serpents twine [= twain] with hasted traile they glide To Pallas temple. 1674 N. Fairfax *Bulk & Selv. World* 141 The souls business in the wagon or vehicle of the body is..rather to ride in state than to ride post, ennobling the body by its curious draughts and trails of enlivening sprightlinesses. 1876 *Whitby Gloss.* s.v., 'A lang trail', a tiresome journey.

13. The action of hunting by the trail; chase by the track or scent.

1669 Dryden *Wild Gallant* iii. i, To come upon the spur after a trayl at four in the afternoon to destruction of cold meat and cheese. 1902 O. Wister *Virginian* ix, All winter he had ridden trail, worked at ditches during summer.

14. *Mil.* The act of trailing a rifle, or the position of it when trailed (see trail *v.*[1] 2).

1833 *Regul. Instr. Cavalry* i. 29 The barrel..may be.. examined at the trail. 1847 *Infantry Man.* (1854) 30 *Trail Arms*... Bring it down to the trail on the right side. *Ibid.* 40 b, The short trail must never be used. 1892 Greener *Breech-Loader* 193 At the 'trail', that is, grasped in the right hand, the arm at full length, and the gun horizontal.

15. An act of drawing out, enticing, or befooling. *rare*⁻¹.

1847 [see trail *v.*[1] 3 b].

IV. 16. A woman who trails her dress along the ground; an untidy woman, slattern, slut. *Sc.*

1825 Jamieson, *Trail*, a term of reproach for a dirty woman; as, 'Ye wile trail', you nasty hussy, *Aberd.* 1878 A. Paul *Rand. Writ.* 28 It is a very old saying..that no man should marry a trail, which meant a female who trailed her dress through the gutters. 1901 Trotter *E. Galloway Sk.* 102/2 Come, bring me quick, ye useless trail, The gully knife to sheer the kail.

V. 17. *attrib.* and *Comb.* (some of which may be from trail *v.*[1]), as ***trail-blazer, -blazing*** vbl. sb. and ppl. adj., ***-breaking*** vbl. sb. and ppl. adj., ***-cutter, -herd, -herder, -hunting, -maker, -man, -robbery, -trot***; ***trail-weary*** adj.; see also 2 c; **trail-bar**, a wooden bar for turning the trail of a gun-carriage in pointing the gun; **trail bike** orig. *U.S.*, a motor-cycle designed for use on country tracks rather than on roads; **trail-board**, a carved piece in a ship: see quot.; **trail boss** *U.S.*, a foreman in charge of a cattle-drive; **trail-car** (*U.S.*) = trailer *sb.* 6 a; **trail-cart** (*dial.*): see quots. 1770–1896; **trail-eye** = *trail-plate-eye*; **trail-handspike** = *trail-bar*; **trail head** *N. Amer.*, the beginning of a trail for walkers (occas. also for skiers); an organizational centre at such a place; **trail-hound**, (*a*) [hound *sb.*[1] 4 e] = *trail-blazer* above; (*b*) a small hound bred for the sport of hound trailing; **trail lever**, 'a trailing lever hinged to the spindle-carriage of a spinning-mule' (*Cent. Dict. Supp.*); **trail-net**, a fishing-net that is trailed or drawn along, a drag-net; **Trail of Tears** *U.S.* (see quot. 1930); **trail-plank**, a plank for supporting the trail of a gun-carriage; **trail-plate**, an iron plate attached to the trail of a gun-carriage; hence **trail-plate-eye**, an 'eye' or perforated piece fixed on the trail-plate, used in limbering up; **trail-riding**, motor-cycling with a trail bike; **trail-rope**, a rope used for trailing or drawing something: (*a*)

U.S., a long rope used for tethering animals loosely; (*b*) in a gun-carriage = PROLONGE; (*c*) a rope trailed on the ground to check the speed of a balloon; **trail-scent** = sense 8 b above (cf. TRAIN-SCENT); **trail-spade**, a projection at the lower end of the trail of a gun-carriage; **trailway** *N. Amer.*, a route through rough country cleared and maintained for recreational walking.

1828 J. M. SPEARMAN *Brit. Gunner* (ed. 2) 116 *Trail Bearings. (Cast Iron.) **1969** *Time* 12 Sept. 17 Anyone hoping to escape the..cities for the quiet beauty of our woods, mountains or deserts is in for a rude shock. He is greeted by the rattling snarl of *trail bikes, dune-buggies and the like. **1972** *Fairbanks* (Alaska) *Daily News-Miner* 3 Nov. 23/5 (Advt.), Extended bumper on rear for snowmobile, trail bikes. **1976** *New Motorcycling Monthly* Oct. 4/4 Yamaha, of course, have reincarnated the good old 500cc four-stroke single, but in trail-bike trim. **1908** *Daily Chron.* 19 May 3/2 Mrs. Hubbard's journey..with a small party of '*trail blazers' native to the ways of Labrador. **1937** *Discovery* July p. lix/1 Trail blazers of science. **1972** *Daily Colonist* (Victoria, B.C.) 3 Feb. 8/1 Agriculture Minister Shelford lauded his party as being trailblazers in humanity through fiscal astuteness during the throne speech. **1934** WEBSTER, *Trail blazing. **1957** V. PACKARD *Hidden Persuaders* xxi. 233 *Tide*, the merchandisers' journal, admonished America's merchandisers to pay attention to this trail-blazing development as it might be 'tomorrow's marketing target.' **1968** *Globe & Mail* (Toronto) 3 Feb. 43/3 (Advt.), Acres of wonderful wood for trail blazing and riding. **1971** *Advocate-News* (Barbados) 17 Sept. (Guyana Suppl.) p. iv/3 Volunteers..cleared the last few feet of bush for their historic meeting on top of a hill called Point Jason (after a trail-blazing pioneer who supervises the project). **1973** C. BONINGTON *Next Horizon* xxi. 279 We all agreed that it [*sc.* a climb] was as hard as anything we had ever done, with very little to show for each day's trail-blazing. **1704** J. HARRIS *Lex. Techn.* I, **Traile-board*, in a Ship, is a carved Board on each side of her Beak, reaching from her Main Stem to the Figure, or to the Brackets. **1890** *Stock Grower & Farmer* 21 Jan. 6/3 *Trail bosses bronzed from exposure ..are familiar sights. **1921** [see PILE *v.*[2] 3 c]. **1977** *Daily Mirror* 15 Mar. 24/1 What was the name of the actor who played the trail boss in the TV Western series 'Rawhide'? **1912** L. J. VANCE *Destroying Angel* xviii. 232 'Must I make talk, then?' she demanded. 'If we must, I suppose— you'll have to show the way. My mind's hardly equal to *trail-breaking to-day.' **1965** T. A. SEBEOK in *Language* XLI. 80 In this trailbreaking paper, he [*sc.* Trubetzkoy] reduced the supposed multiplicity of vowel patterns to a small number of symmetrical models. **1971** C. BONINGTON *Annapurna South Face* xiii. 171 Even in descent it took him an hour, and without his trail-breaking from above Martin and Mike Thompson would have had an exhausting time forcing the route from below. **1770–4** A. HUNTER *Georg. Ess.* (1804) II. 370 To bruise out the grain by sledges or *trail carts. **1861** SMILES *Engineers* II. 109 Sledges or trail-carts were also used for the same purpose; but the most common instrument employed was the flail. **1896** CROCKETT *Grey Man* xii, A trail-cart,..a box with shafts like a carriage, but without wheels, mounted on a great brush of branches and twigs, which..scored the ground with a thousand ruts and scratches. **1887** *Pall Mall G.* 30 Mar. 6/1 Large numbers of *trail cattle, driven recklessly into Wyoming in 1881. **1858** *Brit. Colonist* (Victoria, B.C.) 11 Dec. 2/4 The majority of the Lillooet *trail cutters would have remained had it not been grossly mismanaged. **1903** A. ADAMS *Log of Cowboy* vii. 88 Four..strange men..representing themselves as trail cutters. **1958** *Edmonton* (Alberta) *Jrnl.* 24 June 46/1 The trail-cutters work a four-month season in the winter. **1971** *Islander* (Victoria, B.C.) 30 May 12/4 Another satisfactory water supply can be found at the southern end of the beach, just past the *trail head. **1976** *Stillwater* (Montana) *News* 1 July 12/3 Backpackers, fishermen, day hikers, or anyone else using outdoor trails, should sign in on the log book at the trailhead where these are available. **1981** *Nordic Skiing* Jan. 48/2 The Warming Hut on Butternut Lake serves as the trail-head where a skier can..arrange for instruction, rentals, accessories, [etc.]. **1885** *Weekly New Mexican Rev.* 18 June 1/3 The *trail herds in Colfax county must go forward or turn back at once. **1962** G. MACEWAN *Blazing Old Cattle Trail* i. 1 Ever since the Patriarch, Abraham,.. stockmen have been driving trail herds to far places. **1890** *Stock Grower & Farmer* 19 Apr. 3/3 Cattle inspectors of New Mexico were holding up *trail herders for one and one-half cents per head. **1931** *Times Lit. Suppl.* 29 Oct. 839/2 The writer is what in her mountaineering vernacular might be called 'a *trail hound.' **1972** *Shooting Times & Country Mag.* 27 May 27/1 From all this evolved the trail hound, a smaller, lighter type altogether than his near relative, the Fell foxhound. **1978** R. HILL *Pinch of Snuff* vii. 73 She [*sc.* a cat] was born on a Cumberland farm and reckons she's a trail-hound. **1890** NASMITH *Mod. Cotton Spinning Mach.* xi. 206 The traverse of the locking lever prior to locking is gradually lessened as the *trail lever slide L is lowered. **1892** —— *Cotton Spinning* viii. 270 The shoulder R is pulled over the bowl carried at the end of the lever L, called the 'trail' lever, which is hinged to the carriage. **1901** *Wide World Mag.* VIII. 156/2 A couple of the *trail-makers visited the cabin and found the partners there. **1905** *Athenæum* 5 Aug. 183/2 A series of reprints or translations of the narratives of 'Trailmakers', from the earliest times to the close of the eighteenth century. **1858** *Brit. Colonist* (Victoria, B.C.) 27 Dec. 3/2 The man..was no *trail-man but a stranger. **1891** *Harper's Mag.* Nov. 886/2 The trail-men are sent out to cut what in general parlance would be called a path. **1820** JODRELL, **Trailnet*, or *Trawlnet*. **1877** KNIGHT *Dict. Mech.*, *Trail-net*, a net drawn or trailed behind a boat; or by two persons on opposite banks in sweeping a stream. **1930** E. FERBER *Cimarron* 40 Tears came to his own eyes when he spoke of that blot on southern civilization, the *Trail of Tears, in which the Cherokees, a peaceful and home-loving Indian tribe, were torn [1838–9] from the land which a government had given them by sworn treaty, to be sent far away on a march which, from cold, hunger, exposure, and heartbreak, was marked by bleaching bones from Georgia to Oklahoma. **1978** *Peace News* 6 Oct. 7/2 It was named after the many Long Walks since the Andrew Jackson presidency, including walks like the Trail of Tears in which the Indian people were forced to trek vast distances overland as an expansionist government laid claim to their traditional homelands. **1984** *Miami Herald* 6 Apr. 6A/2 Tribal leaders are calling the reunion the most important event for the Cherokee Nation since the Indians were driven from their southern lands in the 1838 'Trail of Tears'. **1859** F. A. GRIFFITHS *Artill. Man.* (1862) 115 One *trail plank... This plank is placed on the ground, so that the trail of a siege carriage may rest on it. **1828** J. M. SPEARMAN *Brit. Gunner* (ed. 2) 17 *Trail-plate Eyes. **1931** C. ALDIN in Hunloke & Aldin *Riding* vi. 105 *Trail riding..gives us a day's riding *with* a picnic, and teaches us where the side tracks and bypaths on a place like Exmoor lead to. **1979** *Daily Tel.* 13 Jan. 8 These tracks..provide great scope for that non-competitive and gentle form of motor-cycling known as trail-riding. **1901** *Wide World Mag.* VIII. 154/2 The territory had been remarkably free from serious crime, and *trail-robberies were unknown. **1826** G. C. SIBLEY *Diary* 15 Mar. in A. B. Hulbert *Southwest on Turquoise Trail* (1933) 162, I have paid away the following sums, since I left Sta. Fee..14 *trail ropes, 14·00. **1851** MAYNE REID *Scalp Hunters* xx, Mules and mustangs, picketed on long trail-ropes. **1899** *Westm. Gaz.* 31 July 10/2 We opened the valve to hasten our descent before reaching it, and at 8.8 our trail-rope touched the ground. **1682** *Lond. Gaz.* No. 1711/8 A *Trail Scent for Hounds. **1781** P. BECKFORD *Hunting* (1802) 85 You say, you should like to see your young hounds run a trail-scent. **1904** *Sci. Amer.* 21 May 402/2 The carriage.. permits of checking the recoil without undue strain.. through a *trail-spade provided with an elastic joint. **1897** *Outing* (U.S.) XXIX. 439/1 From the *trail-start to the death it had been no more than a 15-minutes' run. **1895** KIPLING *2nd Jungle Bk.* 134 They fell into the quick, choppy *trail-trot in and out through the checkers of the moonlight. **1939** *Appalachian Trailway News* July 6/2 The matter of foremost importance was..to obtain the state recognition and interest in the *Trailway project. **1940** *Ibid.* Jan. 20/1 The Appalachian Trail or Trailway is entirely a voluntary amateur project. **1972** E. WIGGINTON *Foxfire Bk.* 276 We'd gone walkin' along th' trailway. **1978** *Globe & Mail* (Toronto) 15 Feb. 1/7 About one-third of the route is already owned by the province and the draft plan calls for the gradual acquisition of a 60-foot-wide 'trailway' from present landowners. **1894** *Outing* (U.S.) XXIV. 398/1 The once *trail-weary emigrant, the ranchman of to-day, does the freighting..from the railroad town.

† **trail**, *sb.*[2] *Obs.* Forms: 5 **treylle**, 5–6 **trayle**, **traile**, 6 **trayll**, **treyle**, 8 **treil**, 7–8 **trail**. [Late ME. *treylle*, *trayle*, app. a. OF. *treille*, *traille* 'a bower or arbour of vine branches sustained by trellis-work' (Littré), also trellis, lattice work grating, grill (for window, door, etc.) = Pr. *treilla*, *trelha*:—L. *trichila*, later also *tricla*, bower, arbour, summerhouse: see also TRELLIS *sb.*[2]]

1. A latticed structure for training climbing plants upon; a trellis.

c **1460** SIR R. ROS *La Belle Dame* 184, I me withdrew.. And set me down aloon, behynd a trayle Ful of leves,..With grene withies y-bounden. **1565** COOPER *Thesaurus* s.v. *Brachium*, *Brachiata vinea*, a vine hauyng longe branches vpon trayles. **1693** EVELYN *De la Quint. Compl. Gard.* I. 132 Muscat-Grapes..ripen not so well when raised upon high Trails. **1727** *Bradley's Fam. Dict.* s.v. *Gardener*, To cut the Trees and Pallisades when there is need of it, as well as the Treils and Arbours.

2. A lattice; a grating; a grill.

1485 CAXTON *Paris & V.* (1868) 64 Or they entred they opened a treylle whyche gaf lyght in to the pryson. *c* **1500** *Melusine* 328 He fonde a grete yron trayll, wherin were closed a hondred men..that the geaunt held for hys prysonners. **1552** ELYOT, *Clatro*..to shutte a wyndowe, specially a lattise window: To close with lattise grates, or treyles.

† **trail**, *sb.*[3] *Obs.* [Aphetic shortening of ENTRAIL, orig. *en'traile*.] Entrails, intestines, collectively; *esp.* those of certain birds, as woodcock and snipe, and fishes, as red mullet, which are cooked and eaten with the rest of the flesh.

1764 SMOLLETT *Trav.* xviii. (1766) I. 291 The thrush is presented with the trail, because the bird feeds on olives. They may as well eat the trail of a sheep, because it feeds on the aromatic herbs of the mountain. **1772** WESLEY *Wks.* (1872) X. 387 Those that are fond of his bowels may put them in again, and swallow them as they would the trail of a wood-cock. **1804** FARLEY *Lond. Art Cookery* 40 Baste them with a little butter, and let the trail drop on the toast. **1827** J. H. H. in Hone *Every-day Bk.* II. 94 Here [in France] they [larks] are always dressed with the trail, like snipes. **1846** SOYER *Cookery* 227 Take the flesh and trails of the woodcocks from the bones.

trail (treɪl), *v.*[1] Forms: 4–7 **traile**, **trayle**, 5 **traylle**, 5–6 **traille**, 6–7 **trale**, 6–8 **trayl**, 6– **trail**. [Occurs soon after 1300; agreeing in form with a late OE. *træȝelian*, *træȝlian*, recorded only in the Prudentius Glosses (*Germania* n.s. XI. 398–9), glossing L. *carpĕre* 'to pluck, snatch, tear away or off', which does not so suit the ME. sense as to make its identity certain. ME. *trayle-n*, *traille*, was app. the same word as ONF. *traille-r* to haul or tow (a boat), 14th c. in Godef., and also as MLG. *treilen*, *tröilen* (1325 in Rügen, 14–15th c. in Brunswick, etc.), MFl. *treylen*, *treilen*, *treelen*, Fl., Du. *treilen*, LG. *treilen*, *treulen*, EFris. *treilen*, *trailen*, all 'to haul or tug (a boat)'. Cf. also LG., Du., Fl. *treil* tow-line; also ONF. *traille* (14th c.), *trele*, *tresle*, mod.Pr. *traillo*, Cat. and Sp. *tralla*, Pg. *tralha*, all meaning 'tow-line' or 'rope'. It is difficult to correlate the German and the Romanic words; but it is generally supposed that all go back to a late L. or Com. Romanic **tragulāre* 'to drag', f. L. *tragula*, meaning (inter alia) a 'drag-net', and a small *traha* or 'sledge', f. L. *trahĕre*, pop.L. **tragĕre* (F. *traire*) to 'draw, drag, haul'. This would also in form give OE. *træȝelian*.

It is somewhat remarkable that while the earliest sense of both the OF. and MLG. words was 'to tow (a boat)', this specific use does not appear in ME., while the chief ME. uses do not appear on the continent. This detracts from the satisfactoriness of the derivation, which is still the best to which the known facts point: cf. also TRAIN *v.*[1], which similarly takes us back to L. *trahĕre*, **tragĕre* with a different suffix.]

I. Primary senses. Transitive.

1. a. To draw behind one; to drag along upon the ground or other surface (esp. something hanging loosely, as a long garment); also, to drag (a person) roughly, to hale; to haul.

c **1375** *Sc. Leg. Saints* xxvi. (*Nycholas*) 690 He hynt þe prioure be þe hare,..& traylyt hyme ful angrely Our al þe floure here & þare. *a* **1380** *Minor Poems fr. Vernon MS.* liii. 356 þei trompe bifore þis traiturs, and traylen hem on tres þorow-out þe Cite. *c* **1489** CAXTON *Sonnes of Aymon* xx. 449 Ye shall see many knyghtes to traylle theyr bowelles thorughe the feeldes. **1530** PALSGR. 760/2 He was trayled upon a hardell thorowe al the towne, *il fust trayné sur vne herce par toute la ville*. *a* **1533** LD. BERNERS *Huon* cxxx. 475 Horses rynnynge abrode traylynge theyr brydels after them. **1623** in Foster *Eng. Factories Ind.* (1908) II. 231 A band of souldiers befor, marching with ther coulers trayled after. **1671** MILTON *Samson* 1402 They shall not trail me through thir streets Like a wild Beast. **1712–14** POPE *Rape Lock* III. 73 What boots..That long behind he trails his pompous robe? **1832** TENNYSON *Lady of Shalott* I. iii, Slide the heavy barges trail'd By slow horses. **1865** DICKENS *Mut. Fr.* I. x, The gentleman has trailed his stick after him.

b. To carry or convey by drawing or dragging, as in a vehicle or ship; sometimes said of something cumbrous figured as if dragged along, = 'drag' used dyslogistically. Also *dial.* to carry (dirt) on the feet into a house.

c **1435** *Torr. Portugal* 1316 They Reysed a gale with a saylle, The Geaunt to lond for to traylle. **1748** H. WALPOLE *Lett. to Mann* (1834) II. 232 The yacht is not big enough to convey all the tables and chairs and conveniences that he trails along with him. *a* **1763** SHENSTONE *Ballad* vi, A coach with a coronet trail'd her to Tweed. **1863** MRS. TOOGOOD *Yorks. Dial.* (MS.), The childer trail a lot o' moock in t' house. **1887** BOWEN *Æneid* III. 325, I, when our homes lay blazing, was trailed o'er sea.

c. To draw (the body or limbs) along wearily or with difficulty in walking, etc., esp. from disablement or exhaustion. So *refl.* to move along slowly and painfully, drag oneself along, crawl.

1562 *Child-Marriages* 138 He..demaundid a tieth goose ..and she wold have gevin him none but one that haltid, and tralid the winge. **1566** BLUNDEVIL *Horsemanship* IV. cix. (1580) 50 b, The Horse will not lift that leg, but traile it nigh the ground. **1740** SOMERVILLE *Hobbinol* II. 404 Her wounded Parts Grov'ling she [a snake] trails along. **1863** W. C. BALDWIN *Afr. Hunting* ix. 413, I have no appetite, and trail my limbs after me as if they did not belong to me. **1908** SIR H. MAXWELL *Guide to Holyrood* 108 He trailed himself, a broken-hearted man, to Falkland Palace.

d. Phr. ***to trail one's coat***, to seek to pick a quarrel; to be provocative in one's conduct. Cf. *to drag his coat-tails, so that some one may tread on them* s.v. COAT-TAIL.

[**1864**: see TRAILER 1.] **1877** C. M. YONGE *Womankind* xxv. 216 Party spirit is equally ready to give offence and to watch for it. It will trail its coat like the Irishman in the fair. **1923** *Daily Mail* 7 Feb. 6 This risk [of war] is greatly increased by the presence of British troops at Constantinople and Chanak. Why should we thus be 'trailing our coats' before the Turks? **1950** D. DIVINE *King of Fassarai* xxxii. 291, I wouldn't put it in a report!.. I don't trail my coat. **1974** *Times* 4 Nov. 15/1 Nobody trails his coat for another election... There is to be no Commons division on the crisis in agriculture. **1980** J. DITTON *Copley's Hunch* I. ii. 35, I was trailing my coat... Trying to get the Luftwaffe to come up and fight.

2. a. *Mil.* orig. To carry (a pike or similar weapon) in the right hand in an oblique position with the head forward and the butt nearly touching the ground; later *spec.* to carry (a lance or rifle) in a horizontal position in the right hand with the arm fully extended downward (as in the British army), or in an oblique position, grasping it just above the balance with the arm extended downward and slightly bent (as in the U.S. army). (Also, formerly, to carry (a pike) reversed, with the pointed head dragging along the ground, as at military funerals: see quot. 1688.) Phr. ***to trail a pike***, to serve as a soldier (*arch.*).

1549 *Compl. Scot.* vii. 70 The eldest of them vas in harnes, traland ane halbert behynd hym. **1565** CHURCHYARD *Chippes* (1575) 58 b, And still I hoept, the warres wold me aduaunce So trayld the piek, and world began a nue. **1622** FLETCHER & MASSINGER *Span. Curate* I. i, How proud.. should I be To trail a pike under your brave command. **1688** R. HOLME *Armoury* III. xix. (Roxb.) 147/2 Trayle your pike, is to take it in the right hand vnder the head and hold it close to your side. In this posture they march. There is an other way of traileing the pike, which is by takeing the but end in the right hand holding it to the side, traileing or drawing the head after vpon the ground. In this posture they march at the funerall of a souldier. **1803** *Regulations for Exercise of Riflemen* 4 *Trail Arms.* The left hand seizes the rifle at the second pipe, the right close over the sight, and trails it on the right side at arm's length. **1825** Scott *Talism.* x, The soldiers wore the downcast..looks, with which they trail their arms at a funeral. **1833** *Regul. Instr. Cavalry* I. 161 The lance is 'trailed' by being carried in the right hand at the balance. **1870** Lowell *Study Wind.* 92 Ben Jonson..trailed a pike in the Low Countries. **1877** *Man. Field Artillery Exerc.* 62 Trail Arms. The Trail. Give the carbine a cant upwards with the right hand, seizing it close behind the back-sight, and bring it to a horizontal position at the full extent of the arm, fingers and thumb round the carbine. **1879** *Martini-Henry Rifle Exerc.* 13 Arms must never be trailed with fixed bayonets.

†**b.** Hence allusively *to trail a pen*, to write, to follow the occupation of a writer. *Obs. nonce-use.*

1680 Dryden *Cæsar Borgia* Prol. 1 The unhappy man who once has trailed a pen Lives not to please himself, but other men.

3. *fig.* or in fig. context, with various implications: e.g. to drag forcibly *to* some course of action; to draw out, lengthen out in time, protract; to utter slowly, drawl; to 'drag *in*' irrelevantly; to subject to dishonour, 'drag in the dust'; to cause (a person) to accompany or follow one, esp. reluctantly; etc.

1604 T. Wright *Passions* I. viii. 31 The sensitive appetite often..traleth and haleth the will to..follow her pleasures. **1648** Crashaw *Music's Duel* 37 [She] Trayles her plaine Ditty in one long-spun note. **1649** Bp. Hall *Cases Consc.* (1650) 396 As for Lyra, who is trayled in here, and cited. **1806** Wordsw. *Ode Intim. Immort.* v, Not in utter nakedness, But trailing clouds of glory do we come From God. **1806** G. Austin *Chironomia* i. 38 The words..should not be trailed nor drawled, nor let to slip out carelessly. **1874** Green *Short Hist.* viii. §3. 479 The policy which had so long trailed English honour at the chariot-wheels of Spain. **1891** E. & D. Gerard *Sens. Plant* III. III. xii. 81 There really is no reason for trailing out the matter longer. **1914** W. Owen *Let.* 24 May (1967) 253 Tofield..is married, and trails a French wife about with him, from Berlitz School to Berlitz School. **1977** 'D. Rutherford' *Return Load* i. 21 Sally..trailing a reluctant Josie, was heading for the exit.

b. To draw as by persuasion or art; to draw on; hence *colloq.* 'to quiz, befool' (Farmer *Slang*).

a **1717** Parnell *Fairy Tale* 158 Then Will, who bears the wispy fire, To trail the swains among the mire. **1748** Richardson *Clarissa* (1811) VII. lxvii. 276, I [was] so long trailed on between hope and doubt. **1847** C. Brontë *J. Eyre* xvii, I..perceived she was (what is vernacularly termed) trailing Mrs. Dent; that is, playing on her ignorance: her trail might be clever, but it was decidedly not good-natured. **1900** Kernahan *Scoundrels & Co.* xxi, To see the Ishmaelites 'trail' a sufferer from 'swelled head' is to undergo inoculation against that fell malady.

4. To give advance notice of (a radio or television programme). Also *transf.* Cf. trail *sb.*[1] 11, trailer *sb.* 4 b.

1941 *B.B.C. Gloss. Broadcasting Terms* 33 *Trail* (*v. trans.*), to draw the attention of listeners to a forthcoming programme or other event of broadcasting importance by means of announcements, recorded excerpts, or other methods calculated to make it widely known. **1942** 'G. Orwell' *Diary* 14 Aug. in *Coll. Essays* (1968) II. 443 Horrabin was broadcasting today... This had been extensively trailed and advertised beforehand. **1960** *Guardian* 8 Nov. 7/2 It remains to me an object of mystery ..why the BBC trailed this programme..as unsuitable for young people. **1976** *Daily Tel.* 20 Dec. 8 Powell blamed newspapers for having ignored his embargo—journalists usually receive copies of his speeches a day or two beforehand—but for years his speeches have been 'trailed' without complaint. **1978** *Times* 7 Aug. 12/5 At least by trailing their message on the envelope the senders have.. reduced wear on my paper knife. **1980** *Musicians Only* 26 Apr. 11/5 Released to trail a three album blockbuster.

II. Intransitive senses.

(But for the doubtful OE. *træglian*, these form the earliest group in Eng. and perh. ought to be branch I.)

5. a. (*intr.* for *pass.* of 1.) To hang down so as to drag along the ground or other surface; to be drawn loosely behind (by a person, animal, or thing in motion).

1303 R. Brunne *Handl. Synne* 3444 What sey ȝe men of ladyys pryde þat gone traylyng ouer syde:..To soule helpe hyt myȝt do bote, þat traylep lowe vndyr þe fote. *c* **1400** *Destr. Troy* 10358 þat so worshipfull a wegh, as þe wight Troilus..Shuld traile as a traytor by the taile of his horse. *c* **1450** *Merlin* xiv. 211 Ther sholde ye se stedes and horse renne Maisterles, their reynes trailynge vndir fote. **1523** Fitzherb. *Husb.* §141 That it [a gate] do not trayle and that the wyndes blowe it not open. **1633** P. Fletcher *Purple Isl.* xii. xvi, His hanging dewlap trail'd along the golden sand. **1823** *Local Act 4 Geo. IV*, c. ii. §98 If any Person..suffer any Timber..carried..upon wheel Carriages, to drag or trail upon the said Bridge or Roads. **1868–70** Morris *Earthly Par.* I. II. 620 The sound Of silken dresses trailing o'er the ground.

b. *Mil.* (*intr.* for *pass.* of 2).

1677 *Lond. Gaz.* No. 1181/2 Amsterdam, March 19. Yesterday was performed the Funerals of the late Lieutenant Admiral de Ruyter, the proceeding was thus: 1. Marched two Companies of Soldiers, their Pikes trailing.

6. To hang down or float loosely from its attachment, as dress, hair, etc.; of a plant: to grow decumbently and stragglingly to a considerable length, so as to rest upon the ground or other support, as a stem or branch of a plant; to 'creep'.

c **1412** Hoccleve *De Reg. Princ.* 466 What help schal he, Wos sleeues encombrous so syde traille, Do to his lord? **1578** Lyte *Dodoens* I. vii. 13 It hath..small braunches.. creping or trayling alongst the ground. **1591** Spenser *Ruines of Time* ii, Her yeolow locks,..About her shoulders careleslie downe trailing. **1687** A. Lovell tr. *Thevenot's Trav.* II. 94 They cover this Table with a large pinked Carpet, which on all sides trails on the ground. **1776** Withering *Brit. Plants* (1796) III. 541 In open sunny situations it [*Prunella*] grows trailing,..but in woods it is upright. **1845** Ford *Handbk. Spain* I. 52 The Spanish horse's tail often trails to the very ground.

7. a. †To walk with long trailing garments (*obs.*); to drag one's limbs, walk slowly or wearily as if dragged along (often, following some person or thing: cf. 5); to move or go in extended order; to creep, crawl, as a serpent or other reptile.

1303 R. Brunne *Handl. Synne* 3440 [see 5]. **13..** *Metr. Hom.* (Vernon MS.) in Herrig's *Archiv* LVII. 303 Ich [the devil] haue longe i-ben þi lord and mad þe traile and [? in] gren In siclatoun and in scarlet. *a* **1400** *Sir Penny* 29 in *Map's Poems* (Camden) 360 He may ger tham trayl syde In gude skarlet and grene. **1513** Douglas *Æneis* v. Prol. 11 Wantoun gallandis to traill in sumptuus wedis. **1608** Topsell *Serpents* (1658) 732 Like the Horned-serpent, so trails this elf on land. **1768** Goldsm. *Good-n. Man* I. i, Nothing diverts me more than one of those fine old dressy things..trailing through a minuet at Almack's. **1864** Lowell *Fireside Trav.* 106 We trailed along, at the rate of four miles an hour. **1868** Kinglake *Crimea* (1877) III. i. 83 The cavalcade which had trailed in his wake. **1905** Sir F. Treves *Other Side Lantern* II. vii. (1906) 73 The camels that trailed away from the city.

b. Of inanimate things: To move along slowly; to drift, glide, or flow slowly (*obs.*); sometimes, to move in the wake of something as if drawn along by it; to form a trail.

1470–85 Malory *Arthur* VII. xxxiv. 267 They..drewe their swerdes, and gafe grete strokes that the blood trayled to the ground. **1650** Fuller *Pisgah* IV. iii. 48 The water issuing thence trailed after them in all their removealls. **1754** J. Love *Cricket* I. 41 The dull Ball trails before the feeble Mace. **1822–34** *Good's Study Med.* (ed. 4) II. 68 Vesicular Erythema:..surface..covered with..minute vesicles.. progressively trailing into the neighbouring sound parts. **1851** Longf. *Gold. Leg.* IV. *Neighboring Nunnery* 59 Through the momentary gloom Of shadows o'er the landscape trailing.

c. Also with *in. U.S.*

1875 *Fur, Fin & Feather* (ed. 3) 112 Light and drink; drop off and trail in. **1907** S. E. White *Arizona Nights* xvi. 234 With exultant cackles of joy they'd trail in, reachin' out like quarter-horses.

8. a. To extend in a straggling line, to straggle.

1600 Hakluyt *Voy.* III. 615 Cape Roxo is a low Cape and trayling to the sea-ward. **1905** J. B. Firth *Highways Derbyshire* vii. 98 The path..sometimes trails across the meadows.

b. *trail off* (fig.): to 'go off' in a careless, casual, or indefinite way *into* something; to tail off.

1845 Dickens *Cricket* iii, The soft-hearted Slowboy trailed off at this juncture into such a deplorable howl..that [etc.]. **1865** —— *Mut. Fr.* II. xvi, Twemlow..trails off into '—actly so'. **1967** W. Styron *Confessions of Nat Turner* I. 32, I heard Hark's voice trail off in something like a stifled laugh, a gurgle of satisfaction. **1982** *Times* 16 June 17/1 The export expansion should trail off substantially this year.

III. Secondary senses, app. from trail *sb.*[1] 2, 8–9.

9. *trans.* To decorate or cover with a trailing pattern or ornament; to adorn in the style of tracery. Const. *with.*

13.. *E.E. Allit. P.* B. 1473 Penitotes, & pynkardines, ay perles bitwene, So trayled & tryfled a traverce wer alle. **1399** Langl. *Rich. Redeles* I. 47 Ypoudride wyth pete þer it be ouȝte, And traylid with troupe, and treste al aboute. *c* **1440** *Promp. Parv.* 499/1 Traylyn, a(s) clopys, *segmento*,..*sirino* [? *sirmo*]. **15..** *Househ. Bk. Earl Northumbld.* (1770) Notes 441, iiij Copes blew Sylk with red Orferes trayled with whitt Braunchis and Flowres. **1596** Spenser *F.Q.* v. v. 2 A Camis light of purple silke..Trayled with ribbands. **1870** Rock *Text. Fabr.* Introd. i. 76 The golden ground is trailed all over with leaf-bearing boughs.

10. a. To follow the trail or track of, to track. Also in *gen.* use, to follow.

1590 Cokaine *Treat. Hunting* D ij b, An otter sometimes wilbe trayled a mile or two before he come to the holt where he lyeth. **1781** P. Beckford *Hunting* (1802) 150 Seeing the hare trailed to her form. **1788** *Gentl. Mag.* LVIII. I. 74/2 General Clarke..after trailing them upon several tracks, at last came up with them. **1880** Harting *Brit. Anim. Extinct* I. 18 In later times the Bear was trailed with boar-hounds. **1910** *Contemp. Rev.* July 33 The ranch-man is away.. trailing horse thieves. **1915** H. L. Wilson *Ruggles of Red Gap* (1917) iv. 79 Think of those two poor fellows trailing you over Paris yesterday trying to save you from yourself. **1925** H. L. Foster *Trop. Tramp Tourists* 70 We trailed the other steamer. We trailed her through the *Boca Chica*... We trailed her past the little forts. **1945** B. Macdonald *Egg & I* (1946) xxiii. 228 Sport and the puppy trailed me everywhere, whining and begging me to explain the smoke and excitement. **1957** 'R. Farre' *Seal Morning* ii. 16 No sooner was she past infancy than Lora [*sc.* a seal] started to waddle after me round the croft and trail me over to the byre.

b. To lag behind (someone or something), in a contest, comparison, etc. Also *intr.*

1957 *Times* 6 Sept. 13/2 Hansen's best work came after he had trailed for the first four rounds. **1961** *Wall St. Jrnl.* 24 Mar. 1/1 The value of contracts for residential building awarded last month trailed February, 1960, by 12%. **1972** *Guardian* 10 Aug. 2/3 The Harris Poll today shows that Senator McGovern now trails President Nixon by 23 points. **1979** *Sci. Amer.* Nov. 56/1 Diabetes mellitus and its complications are now thought to be the third leading cause of death in the U.S., trailing only cardiovascular disease and cancer. **1980** *Times* 3 Nov. 2/1 Most MPs seem to expect Mr Silkin to come third with between 30 to 40 votes and Mr Shore to trail with between 20 and 30. **1983** *Times* 19 Feb. 8/4 A few months ago..she was trailing Mr Daley.

11. a. To mark out (a trail or track); to trace out.

c **1586** C'tess Pembroke *Ps.* LIX. xiii, Abroad they range and hunt apace, Now that, now this, As famine trailes a hungry trace. **1600** Hakluyt *Voy.* (1810) III. 546 By reason there met many wayes traled by the wild beastes, I lost my way. **1891** tr. *Didon's Christ* I. 410 The way of the Kingdom ..is a way trailed with blood.

b. To make trails or tracks in; to make one's way through; see also quot. 1828 (*U.S.*).

1652 Benlowes *Theoph.* XIII. xxvii, The Larks, wing'd travellers, that trail the skie. **1828** Webster, *Trail*... In America, to tread down grass by walking through; to lay flat; as, to trail grass.

12. *intr.* To follow the trail or track of the game.

1741 *Compl. Fam.-Piece* II. i. 306 They will come Trailing along by the River Side. **1810** *Sporting Mag.* XXXV. 194 Mr. Yeatman's hare beagles trailed up to a hare in Pulham Furze. **1880** Shorthouse *J. Inglesant* ii. 41 The hounds came trailing and chanting along by the river side.

IV. 13. *intr.* To fish by trailing a bait from a moving boat; *spec.* to fish from a trailer (see trailer *sb.* 8).

1857 R. Tomes *Amer. in Japan* xiii. 308 Another cluster of fishing-boats..apparently trailing for fish. **1864** Thoreau *Maine W.* iii. 176 My companion trailed for trout as we paddled along.

14. *Billiards.* (See trailing *vbl. sb.* 1 c.)

15. *Cards.* At casino, To play a card that is useless for gaining a point. (Perh. *fig.* from 7.)

1909 in *Cent. Dict. Supp.*

16. *trans. Bowls.* To force (the jack) further up the green with one's bowl.

1908 J. M. Pretsell *Game of Bowls* xi. 194 If a bowl trail the jack through between, and past the line square to the back of, the stationary bowls, it shall score 3. **1923** J. A. Manson *Bowling* 84 The Bowler is required to trail the jack, his own bowl accompanying or 'hugging' it, between the stationary bowls over both of the horizontal lines. **1975** *Oxf. Compan. Sports & Games* 97/2 Occasionally a bowler delivers a bowl which runs on to the jack and stays with it while pushing it a foot or so farther up the green. Basically this is a draw shot delivered with a marginal increase of strength with the object of trailing the jack to a more advantageous position.

†**trail**, *v.*[2] *Obs.* [a. OF. *treillier* to trellis, interweave, from *treille* trail *sb.*[2]] *trans.* To provide with or train upon a trellis.

1398 Trevisa *Barth. De P.R.* XVII. clxxviii. (Bodl. MS.), Vines nedeþ to be trailed to be þe better susteyned.

T rail: see T 3 b.

'trailable, *a. U.S.* and *Austral.* [f. trail *v.*[1] + -able.] Of a boat: that may be towed on a trailer behind a motor vehicle; = trailerable *a.*

1976 *N.Y. Times* 5 Sept. v. 11 As slip and mooring space becomes more difficult to find, the trailable boat represents an alternative—it can be dry sailed from a boatyard or moored at home. **1977** *Herald* (Melbourne) 17 Jan. 19/2 On the Saturday afternoon trailable yachts, Flying Fifteens, Fireballs and International Cadets will compete.

†**'trail,baston.** *Old Law.* Forms: (4 traillebastoun), 4–7 **traile-baston**, 4–5, 7– **trailbaston** (*pl.* 4 **-bastons**); also 4 **traile-**, **traylebastoun**, (4–5 **troille-**, **troyl(e-**, 6 **troyle-bastone**, 8 **trailbaton**); also 4 **trayne-bastoun.** [ME. a. AF. *traille-baston*, f. *traille* imper. of *trailler*, trail *v.*[1] + OF. *baston* stick, cudgel, club, lit. 'one who trails or carries a club or cudgel' (cf. *to trail a pike*).

Cf. for the formation, F. *coupe-bourse*, *coupe-gorge*, *porte-clefs*, *tue-chien*, and Eng. *cut-purse*, *cut-throat*, *pick-pocket*, *turnkey*, *kill-cow*, etc.]

One of a class of violent evil-doers in the reign of Edward I, who, as brigands or hired ruffians, bludgeoned, maltreated, and robbed the king's lieges, during his absence or absorption in foreign wars; also applied to their system of violence, for the suppression of which special justices were instituted in 1304–5; thence contextually applied also to the ordinances issued against them (*ordinatio de trailbastons*), and to the inquisitions, trials, courts, and justices (*justices sur les traylbastouns*, justices *for* or *of* trailbaston), appointed for their suppression. In living use from 1304 to *c* 1390; afterwards only a historical term, often misunderstood.

Evidence of the original application of *traille-baston* to the offenders is chiefly supplied by Anglo-Fr. and Latin writings, difficult to epitomize here. They may be seen in full in E. Foss *Judges of Eng.* vol. III. 28–36 (1851), and F. M. Nichols *Orig. Docmts. illustr. Criminal Law, time of Edw. I*, in *Archæologia* vol. XL (1866). The transference of the name of an offence to the legal process dealing with it, and even to its penalty, is a well-known phenomenon in the history of legal terms. In the 17th c. and later, many guesses were made at the origin of the name; thus the Justices of Trailbaston were fabled to be so called from their 'carrying the staff of justice', and by Coke, 'because they proceeded as speedily as one might draw a staff'.

1304–5 *Ordinance* in Camb. MS. Dd. vii. 6 lf. 61 (13..) Incipiunt Articuli Lincolnie qui dicuntur Traylebastoun. [in Brit. Mus. MS. Hargrave 336 *Les Articles de Traynebastoun.*]..Art. iij. De verberatoribus. De ceux qui sunt baturs e funt les grands bateries el pays, e qui sunt prestz e apparaylleez de estre loweez de tiele chose fayre solum ceo q' hom les vodra loweer ou purparleer, la baterie greyndre ou meyndre. **1305** (April) *Commission* (in Foss III. 31 (docketed)), De transgressionibus nominatis Trailbaston audiendis et terminandis. **1305** *Rolls of Parlt.* I. 178 (*Marginal note*) Ordinatio de trailbastons. *Ibid.* 201/1 Ad petitionem illorum qui steterunt in servicio Regis coram Justiciis de Trailebaston petentium remedium super eo, quod ubi plures homines fuerunt indictati de conspiraciis et aliis transgressionibus [etc.]. **1306** *Ibid.* 218/2 Les Justices qui sont ordenez pur entendre a les busoignes de Traillebaston. *c* **1306** LANGTOFT *Chron.* in *Pol. Songs* (Camden) 319 Trayl-bastouns sunt nomez de cel retenaunce, En fayres et marchez se preferent fere covenaunce, Pur treys souz ou iiij, ou pur la valiaunce, Batre un prodomme ke unk fist nosaunce A cors Cristiene, par nuli temoygnaunce. *c* **1306–7** *Outlaw's Song* ibid. 233 Je lur aprendroy le giw de Traylebastoun, E lur bruseroy l'eschyne e le cropoun, Les bras e les jaunbes, ce serreit resoun, La lange lur tondroy e la bouche ensoun. *c* **1315** LANGTOFT *Chron.* in *Pol. Songs* (Camden) 320 Parmy Engletere gentz de graunz resouns Assignez sunt justizes sur les traylbastouns; Les uns par enquest sunt jugez à prisouns: Li altre alez à fourches à pendre environs. *a* **1328** TRIVET *Chron.* (1845) 404 Hii justitiarii ab hominibus popularibus vocati sunt de Traylebastoun, quod sonat *Trahe baculum.* *c* **1330** R. BRUNNE *Chron.* (1810) 328 Þe kyng herd alle þe fame, þe pleynt of ilka toun, & gaf þam a newe name, & cald þam Traile bastoun... The kyng þorgh þe lond did seke men o resons, & with þe justise þam bond, to site on Trailebastons. **1387** TREVISA *Higden* (Rolls) VIII. 295 Þat ȝere kyng Edward made hard inquisicioun aȝenst evel doers, ..þat manere inquisicioun hiȝte trailebastoun. *c* **1400** *Brut* clxxiii. 195 [He] lete enquere..of alle þe mistakyngus and wrongus done þrouȝ misdoers in Engeland, of alle þe tyme þat he hade bene out of his realme, þat me callede 'Troylebaston'; and ordeynede þerto Iustices. **1494** FABYAN *Chron.* VII. 402. **1611** SPEED *Hist. Gt. Brit.* IX. x. §46 Hee ordained Iustitiars for Trailbaston, who were to enquire of Man-slaughters, Ruffians, Disseisors, Boot-halers, Incendiaries, and other perturbers of the common quiet, and them to punish, by fine, death, and otherwise. *a* **1618** RALEIGH *Prerog. Parl.* (1628) 18 The same yeere the King vsed the Inquisition, called *Traile Baston.* **1754** HUME *Hist. Eng.* (1761) I. xvi. 405 The renewal of the commission of trailbaton. **1851** FOSS *Judges of Engl.* III. 36 Commissions of trailbaston continued to be issued at intervals till the middle of the reign of Richard II, when they finally ceased. **1853** PARKER *Turner's Dom. Archit.* II. i. 23 Strongholds for numerous bands of thieves, or 'trailbastons', as they were called. **1893** F. W. MAITLAND *Memoranda de Parl.* (Rolls) Introd. 53 *note*, This [Ordinatio de trailbastons in 1305] seems to be the first appearance in an official document of the curious word 'trailbaston'. There can be little doubt that it signified a 'club-man', a vagabond with a big stick.

trailed (treɪld), *ppl. a.* [f. TRAIL *v.*[1] + -ED[1].]

1. Drawn behind, dragged along on a surface, etc. (see the verb); *Mil.* carried at the trail, as a pike or rifle; in quot. 1797, made by trailing something.

1653 H. COGAN tr. *Pinto's Trav.* xlii. 169 After them followed forty other Chariots,..full..of..Arms, and trayled colours. **1797** *Encycl. Brit.* (ed. 3) XVI. 112 In different parts of the course of this trailed track, small quantities of meal..should be laid. **1847** *Infantry Man.* (1854) 40*b*, Trailed arms must never be used in field movements. **1865** *Pall Mall G.* 13 May 4 No amount of brushing could make their trailed dresses look quite clean again.

†**2. a.** Decorated with, or constituting, a trailing pattern or ornament. *Obs.*

1490 *Acta Dom. Concil.* (1839) 79 Ane goun of cramasy velvott, upon velvott droppit with gold, and lynit with trail-yeit tweldore. **1552** HULOET, Traylled or purfled, *segmentatus.* **1878** NESBITT *Catal. Glass Vessels S. Kens. Mus.* 119 Pale green glass, with trailed ornament on the under surface.

b. *trailed slip* (Ceramics), a slip used for decorating pottery by applying it through a nozzle or spout.

1957 MANKOWITZ & HAGGAR *Conc. Encycl. Eng. Pott. & Porc.* 15/1 Staffordshire trailed slip posset-pots. *Ibid.* 223/1 They are decorated with 'trailed slip'. **1971** *Country Life* 27 May 1303/1 Trailed slip is the method of pouring out from a cone or can exactly as good cooks decorate birthday cakes with icing sugar. **1974** SAVAGE & NEWMAN *Illustr. Dict. Ceramics* 294 Lead-glazed ware decorated with trailed slip.

3. Publicized in advance. Usu. prefixed by advbs. Cf. TRAIL *v.*[1] 4.

1958 *Spectator* 22 Aug. 247/2 A much-trailed BBC investigation. **1981** *Economist* 20 June 14/1 Ministers at this week's well-trailed cabinet meeting listened to her lectures on the need to cut their spending.

trailer ('treɪlə(r)), *sb.* Also 6 trailor, 6–7 traylor. [f. TRAIL *v.*[1] + -ER[1].]

1. One who trails or drags something.

1808 *Sporting Mag.* XXXII. 134 The trailer indolently drags his stick after him. **1864** *Realm* 13 Apr. 2 Some trailer of coat-tails, looking out for a head to break.

†**2.** One who travels on foot (cf. TRAIL *v.*[1] 7); *esp.* a footpad. *Obs. slang.*

1591 GREENE *Art Conny Catch.* II. (1592) 4 Some base Priggar that..is a Trailer. The Trailer is one that goeth on foot.

3. A hound, or a huntsman, that hunts by the trail; one that follows a trail, a tracker.

1590 COKAINE *Treat. Hunting* B ij, You must chuse out.. two couple to be trailors of an olde Foxe and finders of him. *Ibid.* D ij b [see TRAIL *sb.*[1] 8]. **1859** MARCY *Prairie Trav.* v. 173, I have seen very few white men who were good trailers. **1899** *Scribner's Mag.* XXV. 16/1 The Texas Rangers..were splendid shots, horsemen, and trailers. **1903** *Forest & Stream* 24 Jan. 74/2 Bloodhounds..are not at all superior to the fox-hound as trailers.

4. a. Something that trails, drags along, or hangs draggling; *esp.* a trailing plant or branch (cf. *creeper*); in quot. 1613–39, a trailing decoration. Also *fig.*

1613–39 I. JONES in Leoni *Palladio's Archit.* (1742) II. 45 This single Traylor does well, because of the Distance. **1832** TENNYSON *Eleänore* 38 Many a deep-hued bell-like flower Of fragrant trailers. **1870** LOWELL *Study Wind.* 15 A pair of orioles built on the lowest trailer of a weeping elm. **1880** MISS BIRD *Japan* I. 173 An ocean of trees entangled with a beautiful trailer. **1882** *Garden* 11 Feb. 106/3 Mikania pulverulenta..is a pretty trailer. **1898** J. LONDON *Let.* 6 Dec. (1966) 8 Sent out in this mail, 'trailers' after articles I mailed last September. **1941** H. G. WELLS *You can't be too Careful* III. i. 114, I join with Mrs Richard Tewler in deploring the inaudibility of Mrs Humbelay. If only we could have heard those lost trailers of hers, we might have benefited greatly from her..wisdom. **1952** G. RAVERAT *Period Piece* vi. 112 This remark was..a sort of trailer, which she hoped might lead to more information.

b. orig. in *Cinematogr.* An excerpt of a film, broadcast, etc., used as advance publicity. Also *transf.* and *fig.*

1928 *N.Y. Times* 11 Mar. VIII. 6 *A trailer*, a few hundred feet of film announcing a forthcoming picture. **1930** *Dancing Times* July 360/2 In a 'trailer' advertising the film, it is announced that the producers have aimed more at entertainment than historical accuracy. **1941** *B.B.C. Gloss. Broadcasting Terms* 33 *Trailer*, microphone announcement or short descriptive broadcast, designed to advertise a forthcoming programme or other event of broadcasting importance. **1942** *Punch* 4 Mar. 169/1 The war..has only just started. The trailer will have given you an idea of what it will be like. **1959** *New Statesman* 21 Mar. 403/2 A quasi-newscaster, giving verbal trailers of coming attractions, does not fulfil this function. **1959** *Washington Post* 26 Dec. A19/2 Then some wisenheimer from the agency decided we needed a trailer. **1966** *Listener* 19 May 737/1 Whether there is much point in playing a section of a work, except as a trailer, is another matter. **1971** *Daily Tel.* 28 Jan. 1/1 Mr Barber, Chancellor of the Exchequer, used a lunch-time speech yesterday as a 'trailer' for the White Paper on Public Expenditure..which is to be published this afternoon. **1977** J. AIKEN *Last Movement* i. 9 The evening's sunshine was only a trailer for spring. **1978** *Radio Times* 28 Jan.–3 Feb. 70/1 Once upon a time, in the cinema of my youth, there were trailers—unblushingly commercial attempts to lure in the customers by juxtaposing all the dangerous and sexy bits of the film and overlaying them with the most blatant sales pitch of plots and star appeal.

5. The rear wheel of a front-driven bicycle, or one of the rear wheels of a locomotive, as opposed to the *driver* or driving-wheel; a trailing-wheel.

1884 *Cycl. Tour. Cl. Gaz.* Nov. 341/2 The specimen..has a driving wheel of 36 inches, and a trailer measuring 24 inches. **1895** *Model Steam Engine* 58, 2nd, drivers or driving-wheels; 3rd, trailers or trailing wheels [of a locomotive]. **1906** *Westm. Gaz.* 25 Sept. 7/1 The Atlantic engine..had four driving wheels, two rear wheels which are called trailers, and four wheels in front of the drivers. Only the driving and trailing wheels had brakes.

6. a. A rail or road car designed to be drawn along by a motor vehicle; now usu. an unpowered vehicle towed behind a car or truck, etc.; *spec.* (chiefly *U.S.*) = CARAVAN 4. **b.** A small carriage, usually a light chair on wheels, drawn along behind by a bicycle or tricycle.

1890 *Columbus* (Ohio) *Dispatch* 5 Aug., The line is to start with five motor cars for winter service, with some 'trailers' for excursion business. **1900** *Engineering Mag.* XIX. 737 By the adoption of a steam waggon and trailer, a full load of 5 tons being carried into Manchester twice a day. **1901** *Scotsman* 2 Mar. 12/5 The motor car, or motor car and trailer now so familiar in tramway practice. **1909** *Times* 9 July 3/3 He was in a trailer attached to a motor-tricycle. **1926** *Kansas City* (Missouri) *Star* 11 June, On the Victory highway most any day now one may see the migratory harvesters—a few walking,..more with their families in cars, and a trailer behind, carrying tents, bedding, and cooking utensils. **1931** J. H. STONE *Caravanning & Camping-Out* x. 64 These trailer-caravans are made so exceedingly light..that a low-power motor can draw them with ease. A trailer runs on two wheels or four. **1951** W. FAULKNER *Requiem for Nun* 246 Living now (with now a wife ..and..after that a wife and children) in automobile trailers or G.I. barracks on the outskirts of liberal arts colleges. **1966** *Listener* 9 June 839/3 The first motor-diesel vessel to carry caravans—or, as the Americans call them, trailers—across the ocean is now being designed here in San Francisco. **1976** *New Yorker* 17 May 31/1 The miniature control room of a big white mobile broadcast trailer. **1977** P. WAY *Super-Celeste* I. 44 Family men from Sydney..on a fishing weekend—their wives..in the trailers in the park.

c. *trailer-on-flatcar*, used to denote a system of freight transport whereby trailers (and other unaccompanied road freight vehicles) are carried on railway cars. Cf. PIGGY-BACK *adv. phr.* (*a.*, *sb.*) b(*b*). orig. *U.S.*

1954 [see PIGGY-BACK *adv. phr.* (*a.*, *sb.*) b(*b*)]. **1964** [see *TOFC* s.v. T 6 a]. **1979** *Railway Gaz. Internat.* Aug. 719/2 Piggyback, otherwise known as trailer-on-flatcar (TOFC), has proved to be an area of strong..growth.

7. A kind of self-acting brake consisting of a prop attached to the rear of a vehicle, to catch on the ground and prevent the vehicle from running backwards down an incline; also called a *stopper*.

1877 in KNIGHT *Dict. Mech.*

8. A vessel used about 1800 in mackerel-fishing, having long poles or outriggers on each side, with baited lines about 20 fathoms long fastened to them.

1891 in *Cent. Dict.*

9. *attrib.* and *Comb.*, as (sense 4 b) *trailer film*; (sense 6 a) *trailer-car*, *caravan*, *-coach*, *hitch* [HITCH *sb.* 6], *-wagon*; **trailer camp** *U.S.*, an area where caravans may be temporarily or permanently parked; similarly **trailer court**, **park**; cf. *caravan park*, *site* s.v. CARAVAN *sb.* 4; **trailer home** *U.S.* = *mobile home* s.v. MOBILE *a.* 1 h; also **trailer house**; **trailer tent**, a tent which is attached to and erected on a trailer; **trailer-truck** *U.S.*, an articulated lorry; cf. *tractor-trailer* s.v. TRACTOR 4.

1921 *Outing* Apr. 39/2 (Advt.), Union Trailer Camp... Whether a week-end jaunt or a vacation tour, this outdoor palace makes it a real one... Your car can draw it easily. **1980** M. GORDON *Company of Women* (1981) III. 254 Mothers bringing their children up in trailer camps. **1930** *Motor Body Building* LI. 98/1 There are, of course, already a considerable number of trailer caravans standardised by body builders specialising in this type of vehicle. **1931** [see sense 6 a above]. **1979** W. H. CANAWAY *Solid Gold Buddha* xi. 77 The trailer..served him as living quarters and producer's office... He woke to find the trailer-caravan in darkness. **1939** E. S. GARDNER *D.A. draws Circle* (1941) xiv. 273 How about taking these folks down to the trailer court, Bill? **1979** *Arizona Daily Star* 5 Aug. (Advt. Section) 14/5, 56 space Travel Trailer Court on Wetmore near new shopping center. Can be converted to regular trailer court. **1941** *Electronic Engin.* XIV. 412 The 'trailer' film, interspersed with regular features, has been recognised by a number of manufacturers as a valuable advertising medium. **1953** C. ARMSTRONG *Catch-as-catch-Can* viii. 69 Do you understand how a trailer hitch operates? **1972** D. E. WESTLAKE *Bank Shot* viii. 58 It has a trailer hitch... It doesn't have any wheels. **1940** H. G. WELLS *New World Order* 180 In such large open countries as the United States there has been a considerable development of the mobile home in recent years. People haul a trailer-home behind their cars and become seasonal nomads. **1979** T. GIFFORD *Hollywood Gothic* xxx. 303 He followed her into the neat little trailer home. **1954**, **1969** Trailer house [see MOBILE *a.* 1 h]. **1975** *Budget* (Sugarcreek, Ohio) 20 Mar. 16/2 They move into a trailer house located on his son-in-law, Ben Peachys farm. **1947** *Daily Oklahoman* (Oklahoma City) 21 Sept. D-6/1 The verdict may well point to a bust in the boom enjoyed this year by the nation's tourist camps, hotels, motels, trailer parks,..and restaurants. **1979** *Arizona Daily Star* 5 Aug. B1/6 A talented cook and editor of her trailer-park newsletter, Rosaaen said she knows why so many women like her are working today. **1971** *Rand Daily Mail* 4 Sept. 10/4 The largest selling trailer tent in Scandinavia... Independent suspension,..easy towing and light weight make it easy on your car. **1981** *West Lancs. Even. Gaz.* 25 Apr. 9 (Advt.), Trailer tent. **1958** A. BUDRYS *Edge of Sea* in Aldiss & Harrison *Decade the 1950s* (1976) 54 A long-haul trailer-truck driver. **1976** Trailer-truck [see RIG *sb.*[6] 3 b]. **1904** *Daily Chron.* 12 May 3/3 The Act of 1896..limited the weight of a motor-car to three tons unladen, and of a motor with trailer-wagon to four tons.

'trailer, *v.* [f. the sb.] **1.** *trans.* **a.** To advertise or publicize in advance, esp. by the use of excerpts.

1965 *Observer* 5 Sept. 36/1 French 1964 vintages..are already trailered in some American liquor stores as 'the most heralded vintage of the century'. **1977** *Time Out* 28 Jan.–3 Feb. 5/4 Originally scheduled for broadcast last April and 'trailered' on the air, it has never in fact been run. **1979** *Internat. Jrnl. Sociol. of Law* Feb. 99 The book is reminiscent of a Hollywood film, in the sense of its having been extensively trailered. **1983** *Daily Tel.* 27 Aug. 29/2 *The Winds of War Preview*, excerpts from the series which does not start for another fortnight and has already been heavily trailered.

b. Chiefly *N. Amer.* and *Austral.* To transport on a trailer.

1971 *Islander* (Victoria, B.C.) 31 Jan. 7/2 For most of us, snowmobiling requires that we frequently trailer our machines from where we live to more suitable operating locales. **1976–7** *Sea Spray* (N.Z.) Dec./Jan. 55/3 Cover for a vessel while being trailered may be overlooked. **1977** *Austral. Sailing* Jan. 48/1 (Advt.), A little ship like the Marieholm is easy to trailer. **1984** *Gainesville* (Florida) *Sun* 27 Mar. 6B/1 An end to being trailered, to wearing halters, bridles, bits and saddles.

2. *intr.* **a.** To travel or live in a trailer. **b.** To give advance publicity.

1974 *Listener* 17 Jan. 93/3 [They] give up trailering around and settle back near the old folks. **1975** *Time Out* 22 Aug. 3/3 Trailering with stuff like 'The Leisure Press At Bay'.

Hence **'trailered** *ppl. a.*, towing a trailer, having a trailer (sense 6 a) attached.

1965 'W. HAGGARD' *Hard Sell* ix. 97 The oil came up from Genoa in convoys of trailered lorries.

'trailerable, *a.* Chiefly *N. Amer.* and *Austral.* [f. TRAILER *sb.* 6 + -ABLE.] Of a boat: that may be transported on a trailer attached to a motor vehicle; = TRAILABLE *a.*

1971 *Austral. Sailing* Jan. 6/1 (Advt.), The new standard for small yachts. Eyecatching new trailerable mini ocean racer. **1976–7** *Sea Spray* (N.Z.) Dec./Jan. 112/1 (Advt.), 7m Flybridge trailerable Cruiser. **1980** *Outdoor Life* (U.S.) (Northeast ed.) Oct. 152/3 (Advt.), Boat kits—22 trailerable models.

'trailering, *vbl. sb. N. Amer.* [f. TRAILER *v.* + -ING[1].] The act or practice of travelling with or living in a caravan.

1938 *Amer. Speech* XIII. 196 Trailering..Galahading.. newspapering. **1967** (*title*) Woodall's trailering parks and campgrounds. *Ibid.* 33/1 Along Highway 190 from Oaxaca lies the..colonial village of San Cristobal... A bit of off-beat trailering, well worth the trip. **1973** *Daily Colonist* (Victoria, B.C.) 12 Oct. 25/1 A friend of theirs who had retired to a life of trailering told them of his experiences.

1978 *Sunday Sun-Times* (Chicago) 1 Jan. 122/2 Proper weight distribution is essential to insure safe trailering and should be checked before pulling out of the driveway.

trailerite ('treɪlərait). *N. Amer.* [f. TRAILER *sb.* + -ITE[1].] One who lives in or travels by caravan.

1940 *Capital* (Topeka, Kansas) 28 Jan. 16B/5 Many trailerites, caught unprepared by Florida's worst cold spell. 1977 *Globe & Mail* (Toronto) 7 Mar. 8/7 Your average trailerite has to be a..jack-of-other-trades to get along while prowling the highways and byways.

trailiness ('treɪlɪnɪs). [f. TRAILY + -NESS.] The quality of being 'traily'.

1867 A. J. ELLIS *E.E. Pronunc.* I. iv. 324 [The] frequency [of final *e*'s in German] conveys no feeling of trailiness or weakness, as it does to the mere English reader.

trailing ('treɪlɪŋ), *vbl. sb.* [f. TRAIL *v.*[1] + -ING[1].]

1. The action of TRAIL *v.*[1] in various senses.

a. Dragging along, hanging down as a robe so as to drag, etc.: see the vb.

13.. *Min. Poems fr. Vernon MS.* xlviii. 194 Wher is þat gomen and þat song, þat trayling & þat comelich ȝong, þo haukes and þe houndes? 1377 LANGL. *P. Pl.* B. XII. 242 þe pekok..may nouȝte fleighe heighe; Fro þe traillyng of his taille ouertaken is he sone. 1671 GREW *Anat. Plants* iii. App. §9 In that [shade] all Strawberries delight; and by the trailing of the Plant is well obtain'd. 1865 TYLOR *Early Hist. Man.* iii. 37 The trailing is now done by horses only. 1886 WILLIS & CLARK *Cambridge* I. 579 The trailing of their chains [i.e. of the portcullises in heraldic devices] is as varied in design as that of the stalks and leaves of the roses. 1887 RUSKIN *Præterita* II. 265 The trailings and climbings of deep purple convolvulus.

b. The following of a trail, hunting by the trail.

1742 FIELDING *Jos. Andrews* III. vi, The best hound that ever pursued a hare;..good at trailing. 1902 *St. James' Gaz.* 31 May 20/1 One can understand the absorbing interest of trailing... Every animal leaves a trail. The expert even reads the story of a snake's trail.

†c. *Billiards.* (See quot.) *Obs.*

1775 *Ann. Gaming* viii. 105 What now gives the peculiar advantage to the mace over the cue, is what has been artfully introduced by professed players, under the name of trailing, which is following the ball with the mace to such a convenient distance from the other ball as to make it an easy hazard.

d. A form of bowling played on Scottish greens, the object being to trail or carry the jack into a semicircle drawn beyond two bowls placed three feet apart.

1902 *Encycl. Brit.* XXVI. 329/2 In trailing, two bowls are laid on the turf..and a jack is then deposited equidistant from each bowl... A semicircle is then drawn behind the bowls with a radius of nine feet from the jack. 1923 J. A. MANSON *Bowling* 84 Trailing is the section of the Points game which is most worthy of attention.

e. *Ceramics.* A method of decorating pottery by applying slip or glaze through a nozzle or spout. (See also quots. 1960, 1968.)

1940 B. LEACH *Potter's Bk.* vi. 145 Glazes are applied by dipping, double dipping..dripping, splashing and trailing. 1960 C. WINICK *Dict. Anthropol.* 543/2 *Trailing*, a technique of making broad incised lines in pottery. 1968 J. ARNOLD *Shell Bk. Country Crafts* xix. 241 Glazes are applied in a liquid state, either by immersion or by brush-work; this is called trailing. *a*1977 *Harrison Mayer Ltd. Catal.* 18/2 Slip decoration: trailing, feathering. Slip can be applied by all the usual painting, pouring, trailing and dipping methods.

f. The advance broadcasting of excerpts of films, programmes, etc., as a form of publicity. Cf. TRAIL *v.*[1] 4.

1961 *Listener* 17 Aug. 254/3 The trailing of future programmes by announcement or sampling..now seems to be overdone—especially those repeated alluring snippets of coming films which could equally well be false starts of the next programme. 1978 *Broadcast* 20 Nov. 19/3 Intensive trailing on radio and TV.

2. *concr.* A trailing branch or shoot of a plant, a 'runner'; a trailing part or appendage.

1727 *Bradley's Fam. Dict.* s.v. *Garden*, Strawberries..begin to shoot forth in January... You may cut off their Trailings in March. 1884 *Amer. Meteorol. Jrnl.* I. 8 A heavy, low flying..storm cloud with ragged trailings.

'trailing, *ppl. a.* [f. TRAIL *v.*[1] + -ING[2].]

1. a. That trails (almost always in *intr.* sense); dragging or dragged behind, drifting along, hanging from something, etc.: see TRAIL *v.*[1]

13.. in *Rel. Ant.* II. 15 Ne be þi winpil nevere so jelu ne so stroutende, Ne þi faire tail so long ne so trailende. 1413 *Pilgr. Sowle* IV. xxxvi. (Caxton 1483) 84 A traylyng gowne of twelue yerdes wide solempnly dagged with huge bagge sleues. 1601 MARKHAM *Mary Magd. Lament.* Pref. 70 [She] made a towell of her trayling haires. 1784 COWPER *Task* v. 56 The trailing cloud [of tobacco-smoke] Streams far behind him, scenting all the air. 1858 G. MACDONALD *Phantastes* (1878) II. xix. 109 Walking with a..somewhat trailing and stumbling step.

b. Of a plant, or a branch, stem, or shoot of a plant: see TRAIL *v.*[1] 6. Also in the names of plants with a trailing habit; *trailing arbutus* = *New England mayflower* s.v. NEW ENGLAND b; also *fig.*

1698 *Phil. Trans.* XX. 468 Stalks, round and most commonly upright, not square nor trayling. 1707 MORTIMER *Husb.* (1721) I. 161 The right sort hath long Stalks and trailing Branches. 1784 *Mem. Amer. Acad. Arts & Sci.* I. 413 *Cuscuta*... Trailing Cockspur... Borders of brooks and ditches. 1785 H. MARSHALL *Arbustrum Americanum* 42 Trailing Arbutus..grows naturally upon northern hills, or mountains. 1813 H. MUHLENBERG *Catalogus Plantarum Amer. Septentrionalis* 91 *Salix prostrata.* Trailing willow. *Ibid.* 93 *Juniferus prostrata.* Trailing juniper. 1855 Trailing arbutus [see *New England mayflower* s.v. NEW ENGLAND b]. 1861 *Trans. Illinois Agric. Soc.* IV. 462 We have on the lake shore a beautiful trailing evergreen—the Trailing Juniper. 1877–84 F. E. HULME *Wild Fl.* p. vi, Branches long, very trailing, slender; hooked prickles. 1878 R. T. COOKE *Happy Dodd* 347 A profusion of trailing pine had been stored away in the barn cellar, before frost came. 1899 M. GOING *Field, Forest, & Wayside Flowers* 251 The lycopodiums..under the name of..'club-moss', or 'trailing-evergreen', are familiar to almost every one who has summered in New England. 1939 WODEHOUSE *Uncle Fred in Springtime* i. 18 The male, Barny, was calling me a trailing arbutus..and The Subject was talking about horsewhips. 1979 *United States 1980/81* (Penguin Travel Guides) 633 Among the many woodland trails are no less than 600 varieties of flowering plants—including the trailing yew, unique to this island.

2. In specific technical applications. a. ***trailing wheel***, a wheel to which the motive force is not directly applied (opp. to *driving-wheel*), as one of the hinder wheels of a locomotive, or the rear wheel of a front-driving bicycle. Also applied to parts connected with this, as ***trailing axle***, ***spring***; so ***trailing-weight***, that part of the weight of a locomotive which rests upon the trailing-wheels.

1849–50 WEALE *Dict. Terms*, *Trailing springs*, the springs fixed on the axle-boxes of the trailing wheels of a locomotive engine. *Ibid.*, *Trailing wheels.* 1877 KNIGHT *Dict. Mech.*, *Trailing-axle*, an axle behind the driving-axle in British locomotives. 1904 *Daily Chron.* 2 Feb. 6/6 Two pairs of coupled driving-wheels; then a single pair of trailing-wheels placed behind the fire-box.

b. ***trailing points***, on a railway, points directed away from a coming train (opp. to *facing points*). ***trailing horns*** in a dynamo-electric machine: see quot. 1902.

1889 G. FINDLAY *Eng. Railway* 79 Trailing points..at a distance of 220 yards from the cabin. 1902 SLOANE *Stand. Electr. Dict.*, *Following Horns*, in dynamo-electric machines, the projecting ends of the pole pieces towards which the outer uncovered perimeter of the armature turns... The leading horns are those away from which the armature rotates... Synonym—Trailing Horns. 1909 *Cent. Dict. Supp.* s.v. *Switch*, *Trailing-point switch*, in railroading,.. contrasted with facing-point switch.

c. ***trailing vortex*** (see quot. 1969).

1929 *Proc. R. Soc.* A. CXXIII. 440 The flow behind the screw is the same as if the screw surface formed by the trailing vortices was rigid. 1949 O. G. SUTTON *Sci. of Flight* iv. 112 The trailing vortices actually spring from two wing-tip vortices which, in flight, form just inside the wing tips. 1969 *Gloss. Aeronaut. & Astronaut. Terms (B.S.I.)* IV. 15 *Trailing vortex*, a vortex extending down-stream from the surface of a body.

Hence **'trailingly** *adv.*

1589 FLEMING *Virg. Georg.* IV. 65 Then is their sound heard heauier, and trailingly they hum. 1831 *Blackw. Mag.* XXX. 476 One of them..hangs trailingly along the mossy greensward. 1842 MRS. BROWNING *Grk. Chr. Poets*, etc. 59 Green vine-branches trailingly inclined.

trailing edge. [TRAILING *ppl. a.*]

1. The rear edge of a moving body; *spec.* in *Aeronaut.*, that of a wing or other part of an aircraft.

1909 *Flight* 3 July 390/1 These ribs overlap the rear spar and form a flexible trailing edge. 1934 *Flight* 8 Feb. 123/1 The split trailing edge flaps effect a big reduction in landing speed and length of glide. 1962 [see RIBLET]. 1969 *Daily Tel.* 12 Nov. 14/6 Warning red lights mounted in the interior trailing-edge of the doors come on when a door is opened. 1971 I. G. GASS et al. *Understanding Earth* xix. 263/1 The newly generated crust and its upper mantle is effectively welded to the plate's trailing edge.

2. *Electronics.* The part of a pulse in which the amplitude diminishes.

1945 *Nature* 15 Sept. 319/2 The end or 'trailing edge' [of the pulse] marks the beginning of an invaluable clear period in which the radar echoes..can be received free from the overlaying and interfering effect of the primary signal. 1967 *Electronics* 6 Mar. 160/1 Nearly all of the earlier logic systems were based on trailing-edge triggering, so many engineers consider it normal. 1973 *Sci. Amer.* May 109/2 The trailing edge of the next pulse, the third in the series, causes flip-flop A to change state.

trailless ('treɪllɪs), *a.* [f. TRAIL *sb.*[1] + -LESS.] Having no trails; trackless, pathless.

1884 BAILLIE-GROHMAN in *Century Mag.* XXIX. 195 Vast stretches of..forest..clothe their precipitous slopes..in unbroken and perfectly trailless masses.

†**trail-side**, *a.*[1] *Sc. Obs.* [f. TRAIL *v.*[1] or *sb.*[1] + SIDE *a.*] That is so long as to trail.

1513 DOUGLAS *Æneis* XIII. vi. 18 In robbis lang also, or traill syde goyn.

trailside, *a.*[2] (and *sb.*) [f. TRAIL *sb.*[1] + SIDE *sb.*[1]] Situated at the side of a man-made trail. Occas. as *sb.*, the side of a trail.

1943 F. GARDNER *Philippine Indic Stud.* v. 43 A bamboo letter is fastened in a cleft stick and placed by the trailside. 1980 *Beautiful Brit. Columbia* Summer 33 By now the crowd of hikers has thinned out into an ambling string, leisurely pacing themselves with time to..lie back on a trailside carpet of heather and dwarf spirea. 1981 *Nordic Skiing* Jan. 4/3 These are generally outlined on a board at the touring center, on trail maps, or on trailside signs.

†**trail wind**, app. erron. for *tail-wind*: see TAIL *sb.*[1] 12.

1679 *Admir. Crt. Exam.* 78. 23 Sept., They bore away for Jamaica with a trayl wind.

traily ('treɪlɪ), *a. dial.* and *colloq.* [f. TRAIL *sb.*[1] or *v.*[1] + -Y.] Characterized by trailing; slovenly; lazy; languid: see *Eng. Dial. Dict.*

1851 *Cumberld. Gloss.*, *Traily*, slovenly. 1867 [implied in TRAILINESS]. 1902 *Westm. Gaz.* 23 Jan. 3/1 A muff..with a simple pretty bunch, not the traily extreme effect of the same flowers.

†**trailye, 'trailȝe.** *Sc. Obs.* Also 5 trelȝe, 5–6 treilȝe, 6 treilie. [app. a. OF. *treillis*, var. of *treslis, trelis, treslie, tresli*, 'tissu à maille', network; cf. mod.F. *treillis* glazed calico, also sack-cloth; but the Sc. word was evidently applied to some finer fabric.] A kind of cloth. (See also TRELLIS *sb.*[1]) Also *attrib.*

1490 *Acta Dom. Concil.* (1839) 158/1 Þat James Du..sall ..pay to Dauid Quhitehed..fiue stikkis of trelȝe of sindry hewis. 1495 *Acc. Ld. High Treas. Scot.* I. 226 Item, vj quarteris of quhit treilȝe..to be the King a harnes doublet. 1503 *Ibid.* II. 312 For ane maid doublat of trailȝe to him, vij s. vj d. 1507–8 *Ibid.* IV. 30 For ix½ elne blew trailȝe to be ane couch to the Quene. 1517 *Ibid.* V. 116 Blak trailȝe. 1542 *Inv. Roy. Wardr.* (1815) 92 Ane doublet of blak sating trailye. 1543 *Acc. Ld. High Treas. Scot.* VIII. 232 Fyve quarteris trailȝe to be his grace ane pair of sockis. 1566–7 *Mary's mourning-order at death of Darnley* in Chalmers *Mary* (1818) I. 207 Of treilie buccharem v elle.

train (treɪn), *sb.*[1] Forms: 4–6 trayn, 4–7 trayne, (5 treyne), 5–7 traine, 6–7 *Sc.* tryne, 6– train. [In origin representing two French sbs., *traîne* fem. (OF. also *traïne, trahine*) and *train* masc. (OF. *traïn*, also *trahin*), both held to be vbl. sbs. from *traîner* to drag, draw, etc. (see TRAIN *v.*[1]) and corresponding respectively to It. *traina*, and to Pr. *trahí*, Sp. *tragin* (Diez), It. *traino*. Even in OF., *traïn* and *traïne*, though generally distinct, were sometimes used in the same sense. In English, with the loss of final *e* in pronunciation and its consequent non-significance in spelling, *train* and *traîne* were used indifferently from the 14th c., and in the 17th *train* became the only spelling. On this account, and esp. because senses have arisen in Eng. which have no French prototypes, it is not possible satisfactorily to distinguish two words corresponding to F. *traîne* and *train*. The order here followed is therefore tentative and practical. The F. form, when it exists, is given, and it will be seen that branch II corresponds in the main to F. *traîne*, and branch III to F. *train*. Branches I and IV contain representatives of both F. words.]

I. Nouns of action from F. *traîner* or Eng. TRAIN *v.*[1] in various senses. All *Obs.*

†1. Tarrying, delay. [App. 'a dragging out' of time: cf. TRACT *sb.*[3] 1, 1 b. OF. *traîne, train* 'retard'.] In quots. 1553, *for a train* = for a while, for a little time. *Obs.*

*c*1330 R. BRUNNE *Chron.* (1810) 263 For þe pes to haue, he mad so long a trayne. *Ibid.* 264 Þorgh Edward long trayne Gascoyn is born doun, Non defendes his chayne, but only Bayoun. 1489 CAXTON *Faytes of A.* I. xix. 60 Men holde and kepe the in talkyng as by a long trayne fyndyng alwayes somme controuersies that nede not... But onely for to passe tyme. 1553 *Respublica* v. vii. 1603 Thei wilbe heare soone, byde youe theim here for a traine. *Ibid.* ix. 1665, I leafte people heare for a traine to holde them talke.

†2. a. Course or manner of running (of a horse); a course of riding [F. *train* 'allure']. *Obs.*

1581 A. HALL *Iliad* VIII. 136 His horse he [Jupiter] beates, the ayre they clime, aloft they skimme amaine, Betweene the earth and welkin hie, they tread a iolly trayne. *a*1625 FLETCHER *Woman's Prize* I. iii, A good tough train would break thee all to pieces. 1677 *Lovers Quarrel* 266 in Hazl. *E.P.P.* II. 264 Your choice horses are wild and tough, And little they can skill of their train.

†b. A particular gait of a horse: see quots.

1565 BLUNDEVIL *Horsemanship* I. iii. (1580) Bj b, Their [Turky horses'] trauelling pace is neither amble, racke, nor trot; but a certaine kinde of easie traine. 1607 MARKHAM *Caval.* IV. i. (1617) 5 This shufling and broken incertaine pace,..is neither amble nor trot, but a mixture of both, as taking his time keeping from trotting, and his motion of legges from ambling, and so compound this which is called a Traine or Racking.

†3. *Falconry.* (?) A short flight given to a hawk while being trained. [Not in F.] *Obs.*

1616 [see TRAIN *sb.*[2] 4].

†4. Training, education. [Not in F.] *Obs. rare*$^{-1}$.

1581 MULCASTER *Positions* Ep. Ded. (1887) 3 The generall traine and bringing vp of youth.

II. That which drags or trails, or is trailed.

5. a. An elongated part of a robe or skirt trailing behind on the ground; commonly worn by women of rank or fashion when in full dress, and by sovereigns and high officials on state occasions, and sometimes borne by a page or attendant as *train-bearer*. [OF. *train*, also *trainée*; mod.F. *traîne*.]

*c*1440 *Promp. Parv.* 499/1 Trayle, or trayne of a clothe, *sirma*. *a*1450 in Wr.-Wülcker 564/42 *Appendicium*, a lady trayne *et* a pendaunt of a gyrdyll. *Ibid.* 612/22 *Sirma, i. cauda vestis feminarum*, a trayne. 1457 *Coventry Leet Bk.* 299 Next folowed our seid souerayn lady, & the Duches of Buk[yngham] bere here Treyne. 1577 *F. de L'isle's Leg.* B vj, Would you..wishe that of her who by duetie ought euen to cary vp my trayne I should make my sister in Law? *a* 1600 *Bk. of Precedence* (E.E.T.S.) 26 A Baronesse may haue no trayne borne; but haueing a goune with a trayne, she ought to beare it her selfe. 1617 Moryson *Itin.* III. 168 The ordinary Citizens Wiues haue their gownes made with long traines, which are pinned vp in the house. 1711 Addison *Spect.* No. 42 ¶1 The broad sweeping Train that follows her in all her Motions, and finds constant Employment for a Boy who stands behind her to open and spread it to Advantage. 1791–3 in *Spirit Pub. Jrnls.* (1799) I. 138 He trod on her crape train. 1798 Jane Austen *Northang. Abb.* v, They.. pinned up each other's trains for the dance. 1858 Doran *Crt. Fools* 117 The period [time of Rich. II] when ladies in England first wore trains.

b. The tail or tail-feathers of a bird, esp. when long and trailing, as in the peacock; in *Falconry*, the technical name for the tail of a hawk. †Also formerly, the tail of a quadruped (*obs.*), or of an insect. [Not in F.]

1579 Twyne *Phisicke agst. Fort.* I. xlii. 44 b, Declaryng howe well that byrde [hawk] flue,.. how many feathers of the trayne, and how many of the winges are remaning or lost. 1579 Spenser *Sheph. Cal.* May 281 His tayle he [the fox] clapt betwixt his legs twayne, Lest he should be descried by his trayne. 1591 Shaks. *1 Hen. VI*, III. iii. 7 Let frantike Talbot triumph for a while, And like a Peacock sweepe along his tayle, Wee'le pull his Plumes, and take away his Trayne. 1610 Guillim *Heraldry* III. xv. (1660) 178 The Lyon is one Colour, shaggie brested, with a certain tuft of haire in his traine. 1634 Sir T. Herbert *Trav.* 211 [The dodo's] traine [is] three small plumes. 1639 T. de Gray *Compl. Horsem.* 24 The trayne [of a horse] long, not too thick, and falling to the ground. 1693 J. Clayton *Acc. Virginia* in *Misc. Cur.* (1708) III. 332 Their Turtle-Doves.. the whole Train is longer much than the Tails of our Pidgeons. 1852 R. F. Burton *Falconry Valley Indus* viii. 76 A splendid goshawk,.. with.. a queenly train.

c. The tail of a comet; a luminous trail, such as that following a meteor. [Not in F.]

1602 Marston *Antonio's Rev.* I. iii, A blazing comet shot his threatning traine. 1602 Shaks. *Ham.* I. i. 117 (Qo. 1604) As starres with traines of fier and dewes of blood, Disasters in the sunne. 1663 J. Spencer *Prodigies* (1665) 32 The luminous tail or train of a Comet.. seems to the eye of ignorance the emblem of a flaming sword, or firy rod. 1860 Tyndall *Glac.* I. ii. 17 In falling [it] leaves the light foaming mass.. as a train in the air behind. 1909 Chambers *Story of Comets* 137 The curvature of the train [of Donati's comet, 1858].

6. *poet.* Applied to the current of a river, etc., also to the elongated body of a serpent. [Not in F.]

[*c* 1586 C'tess Pembroke *Ps.* lxxviii. xx, All that rich land, where over Nilus trailes Of his wett robe the slymy seedy train.] 1667 Milton *P.L.* VII. 306 Within those banks, where Rivers now Stream, and perpetual draw thir humid traine. 1695 Blackmore *Pr. Arth.* II. 153 Pure Crystal Rivers through the Meadows flow,.. Their watry Train in Snaky Windings slides. 1727–46 Thomson *Summer* 900 The green serpent.. gathers up his train. *c* 1742 Gray *Ignorance* 4. 1808 Scott *Marm.* III. Introd., Like streamlet.. winding slow its silver train.

†7. Something dragged along the ground to make a scent or trail; a drag; also pieces of carrion or the like laid in a line or trail for luring certain wild beasts, as wolves, foxes, etc. into a trap [so F. *traînée*]. *Obs.*

1575 Turberv. *Venerie* 187 Take a skynne of bacon.. and when it is well broyled.. dippe it and puddle it in this sawce.. and make a trayn therewith, and.. if there be a foxe neare to any place where the trayne is drawne, he will followe it. 1607 Topsell *Four-f. Beasts* (1658) 527 The Hunters in some Countries.. make a train with a Hogs liver sod, cut in pieces and anointed over with hony, and so anointing their shoos with Swines grease, draw after them a dead Cat, which will cause the beast to follow after very speedily. 1727 *Bradley's Fam. Dict.* s.v. *Animal*, For Beasts of Prey, as the Wolf, Fox, Badger, Pole-Cat,.. you must make a Train; and when you come to any of the Places you have so prepared, throw four or five Bits of your Train-Carrion upon it, and of Chickens Guts for smaller Beasts.

8. The (visible) track of an animal. *rare*$^{-1}$. [Cf. OF. *traîne* = trace.]

1908 *N. Hebrides Mag.* Jan. 19 The natives with me saw the train of a turtle on the sand. They thought to capture it, but did not succeed.

III. A suite or sequence of persons or things; a long series.

9. a. A number of persons following or attending on some one, usually a person of rank; a body of attendants, retainers, or followers; a retinue, suite; sometimes, the vehicles conveying the persons and baggage. [F. *train*, OF. *traînée*.]

a 1440 *Sir Degrev.* 1139 The Eorl and he with a trayn To the castel gan fare. 1513 Douglas *Æneis* XIII. viii. 48 Al the chymmys riall rownd abowt Was fyllyt with thar tryne and mekill rowt. 1535 Coverdale *1 Kings* x. 2 She came to Ierusalem with a maruelous greate trayne. 1669 *Lond. Gaz.* No. 333/2 The Venetian Ambassador made his solemn Entry into this City, attended.. by a large Train of Coaches. 1711 Steele *Spect.* No. 113 ¶3 She has ever had a Train of Admirers. 1833 Ht. Martineau *Vanderput & S.* i, The long train of mourners. 1875 Jowett *Plato* (ed. 2) I. 128 A train of listeners followed him.

b. *Mil.* The artillery and other apparatus for battle or siege, with the vehicles conveying them and the men in attendance, following or in readiness to follow an army. [F. *train.*]

1523 Ld. Berners *Froiss.* I. lxxvi. 96 Syr Wyllyam Montagu.. yssued out a horsbacke, and folowed couertly the hynder trayne of the scottes, who had horses so charged with baggage, y^{t} they might scant go any gret pace. 1643 Chas. I *Treaty at Uxbridge* Wks. 1662 II. 527 The said Train of Artillery to be fitted in all points ready to march. 1712 Steele *Spect.* No. 497 ¶2 A blunt honest fellow, who had a command in the train of artillery. 1810 Wellington in Gurw. *Desp.* (1838) VI. 88 They have collected a train of artillery at Salamanca for the siege of Ciudad Rodrigo. 1900 *Daily News* 11 June 4/3 The military expression.. 'our trains', is apt to lead to misunderstanding.. where the troops.. have been actually travelling by railway trains.

†c. The rear of an army or body of soldiers. *Obs. rare.* [F. *train.*]

1598 Barret *Theor. Warres* II. i. 28 How to turne their faces, making front of either flanke or traine. *Ibid.* III. ii. 55 The armed pikes.. shall be.. placed in the front and in traine of the battell.

10. *fig.* A set of attendant things, circumstances, or conditions; a series of consequences; in quot. 1638, something following, a sequel. Often in phr. ***in the train of***, as a sequel to; so ***in its train***.

1570 *Satir. Poems Reform.* xix. 101 That Kingdome sall come to greit ruyne Quhen that deuissioun hes his suit and tryne. 1638 R. Baker tr. *Balzac's Lett.* (vol. II.) 23 For a traine to this first favour I require from you a second. 1721 Berkeley *Prev. Ruin Gt. Brit.* Wks. III. 202 This vice draweth after it a train of evils. 1768 Sterne *Sent. Journ.*, *Passport Paris*, The idea presented itself.. with this in its train. 1833 Ht. Martineau *Brooke Farm* xii, Education came in the train of other good things. 1871 Smiles *Charac.* i. (1876) 9 There is no act, however trivial, but has its train of consequences.

11. A body of persons, animals, vehicles, etc., travelling together in order, esp. in a long line or procession; a succession of persons; *fig.* (chiefly *poet.*) a set or class of persons. [F. *train.*]

1489 Caxton *Faytes of A.* I. xxiii. 70 A longe trayne of men of armes al clos togyder. 1591 Shaks. *1 Hen. VI*, II. ii. 34 Which of this Princely trayne Call ye the Warlike Talbot? 1698 Fryer *Acc. E. India & P.* 291 The best Hawks.. fly in Trains like Wild Geese. 1746 Francis tr. *Horace, Epist.* II. ii. 129 What milder Frenzy goads the rhiming Train? 1829 Scott *Anne of G.* vii, The caravans, or large trains of waggons, by which the internal commerce.. was carried on. 1884 Gilmour *Mongols* 287 Camels, trains of which.. may be seen making their way along the crowded streets.

12. A number of things following one another in time or order; a series or course of actions, events, etc. **a.** A course of action in relation to its manner or purpose; method of procedure; manner of action; way of life; course, drift, or direction of a discourse, argument, etc. Now *rare* or *Obs.* (passing into b). [F. *train.*]

c 1530 (*title*) The ordre or Trayne of Warre, that a prynce or heed Captayne ought to take. 1534 More *Treat. Passion* Wks. 1330/2 They.. corrupte some well mynded menne, before they perceyue the trayne of theyr craftye purpose. 1580 Sidney *Ps.* xv, He that leads of life an uncorrupted traine. *a* 1677 Barrow *Serm.* Wks. 1716 I. 39 God.. by secret methods and undiscernable trains, ordereth all events. 1756 Hume *Hist. Eng.* (1761) II. xxviii. 134 His splendid ostentatious train of life. 1836 *Random Recoll. Ho. Lords* xvi. 388 You never misapprehend the train of his reasoning.

b. In general: A series, succession, sequence (of actions, events, thoughts, or phenomena); a continuous course (of action, reasoning, etc.). Freq. in ***train of thought***.

c 1645 Howell *Lett.* (1650) I. 445 A wife is the best or worst fortune that can betide a man throughout the whole train of his life. 1651 Hobbes *Leviathan* I. iii. 8 By Consequence, or Trayne of Thoughts, I understand that succession of one Thought to another, which is called (to distinguish it from Discourse in words) Mentall Discourse. 1690 Locke *Hum. Und.* II. xiv. §3 A train of Ideas, which constantly succeed one another in his Understanding. 1732 [see tract *sb.*^{3} 2]. 1764 Reid *Inquiry* v. §5 Long and demonstrative trains of reasoning. 1769 Robertson *Chas. V*, I. Wks. 1813 V. 165 A long train of fortunate events. 1770 G. White *Let.* 19 Feb. in *Selborne* (1789) II. iii. 125 Your observation.. struck me so forcibly, that I naturally fell into a train of thought that led me to consider whether the fact was so. 1858 Buckle *Civiliz.* (1871) II. viii. 582 The result of a long train of causes. 1899 W. James *Talks* xv. 190 Our habitual associations of ideas, trains of thought, and sequences of action, might thus be consequences of the succession of currents in our nervous systems. 1912 *Proc. R. Soc.* LXXXVII. 93 The electric disturbance produced by a lightning discharge.. is probably either a solitary wave or a very short train of waves. 1948 *Proc. IRE* XXXVI. 1457/1 A train of reset pulses is applied to the shift register. *a* 1953 E. O'Neill *Hughie* (1959) 34 [*stage direction*] His train of thought interrupted, irritably. 1955 F. O'Connor *Wise Blood* i. 13 Mrs. Hitchcock lost her train of talk. 'I guess you're on your way to visit somebody?' she asked. 1959 F. Astaire *Steps in Time* (1960) i. 6 It is the easiest thing in the world to become discouraged by a well-meant suggestion which may throw you off your original train of thought. 1967 *Electronics* 6 Mar. 130/2 The circuit will oscillate, simultaneously generating a sawtooth wave and pulse train. 1978 *Nature* 4 May 57/1 When the current with one channel present was recorded for a longer time, characteristic trains of short impulses were observed, separated by relatively long intervals when the channel did not conduct.

c. Proper sequence, order, or arrangement for some result; connected order; course, process: in phr. ***in train*** (formerly also ***in a train***, and with defining adj., as ***in (a) good train***).

1528 Gardiner in Pocock *Rec. Ref.* I. xlii. 82 Every-thing in good train and order. 1591 Savile *Tacitus, Agricola* 260 Our men.. were now in traine of winning the fielde. 1690 Locke *Hum. Und.* III. vii. §2 It is not enough that a Man has Ideas clear and distinct.. he must think in train. 1746 W. Horsley *Fool* (1748) II. 23 The Affairs of Europe hereby put in a happy Train. 1842 Macaulay in *Life & Lett.* (1883) II. 114, I am.. desirous to get on with my History, which is.. in a fair train. 1885 'Mrs. Alexander' *At Bay* x, Putting matters in train for the election.

13. a. A line of gunpowder or other combustible substance laid so as to convey fire to a mine or charge for the purpose of exploding it. Also *fig.* [It. *traina* (Florio); F. *traînée.*]

a 1548 Hall *Chron., Hen. VIII* 118 The Frenchmen.. made traynes of gunpouder from strete to strete. 1677 W. Hughes *Man of Sin* I. i. 4 A Mine was made, and Train was laid hereby for blowing up the Gospel it self. 1798 in Nicolas *Nelson's Disp.* (1846) VII. p. clviii, She [a ship] was set on fire by a train. 1839 *Civil Eng. & Arch. Jrnl.* II. 45/1 We were fortunate enough to witness two of these blasting operations... The order for firing the train given... In a few seconds after the ignition of the train, a rumbling sound, like that of.. distant thunder was heard, and the.. whole mass was lifted bodily from its base. 1850 Grote *Greece* II. lxi. VII. 517 He.. had already laid his train.. for revolt. 1855 Macaulay *Hist. Eng.* xxi. IV. 549 The spark had fallen: the train was ready: the explosion was immediate and terrible. After a tumultuous debate [etc.].

b. Pieces of carrion or the like laid in a line or trail for luring certain wild beasts: see sense 7.

14. An extended series of material objects or the like; a row, rank; *esp.* a series of things arranged in a definite order for some purpose; *rarely*, a continuous extent of something.

1610 Holland *Camden's Brit.* (1637) 343 Vpon this shore, lie out with a long traine certaine heapes in manner bankes or rampiers. 1664 Power *Exp. Philos.* I. 43 Being layd of a row or train. 1763 W. Roberts *Nat. Hist. Florida* p. vi, Our more northern colonies.. form one continued train along the whole eastern-side of North-America. 1774 M. Mackenzie *Maritime Surv.* 76 When the Survey has been continued by a Train of stasimetric Triangles. 1863 Lyell *Antiq. Man* xviii. 356 Detached fragments of rock.. in long parallel trains. 1878 Abney *Photogr.* (1881) 280 A train of prisms.. set to the angle of minimum deviation.

15. A set of connected parts of mechanism which actuate one another in series; *spec.* (*a*) the set of wheels and pinions in a clock or watch which turns the hands (***going train***), or that which actuates the striking part (***striking train***); (*b*) a set or pair of rollers used in metal-working; a roll-train.

1797 *Monthly Mag.* III. 464 Thus the progressive motion is communicated to the cotton spindles in the same manner as it is to the different parts of a common time-piece—by a train of wheels. 1831 Brewster *Nat. Magic* xi. (1833) 293 Motions are propagated.. along a great variety of trains of mechanism. 1838 [see going *vbl. sb.* 6]. 1881 [see *roll-train*, roll *sb.*^{1} 18]. 1884 F. J. Britten *Watch & Clockm.* 266 The remarks on the train of a going barrel watch apply equally to the going train of a clock. 1885 C. G. W. Lock *Workshop Receipts* Ser. IV. 307/2 The parts most likely to require repair in the striking trains of clocks.

16. a. A number of railway carriages, vans, or trucks coupled together (usually including the locomotive by which they are drawn). [So F. *train.*] ***armoured train***: see armoured *ppl. a.* 2 a; ***train de luxe***: see luxe 2.

Orig. ***train of carriages***, etc.; now one of the chief uses of the simple word: cf. 22 b.

a 1824 A. Scott *Ess. Rail-roads* in *Trans. Highland Soc.* (1824) VI. 29 By continually shifting the train of waggons at the head and foot of the inclined plane, from the one railway to the other. 1825 in W. Chambers *About Railways* (1865) 6 (Opening of Stockton and Darlington R.) The signal being given, the engine started off with this immense train of carriages. 1830 *Times* 17 Sept., The Northumbrian drawing the splendid train of carriages occupied by the Duke of Wellington... The Northumbrian locomotive engine, which had drawn the train of the Duke of Wellington. 1835 Marryat *Olla Podr.* vi, The trains went on well. 1837 *Cornish's Railway Companion* Title-p., The Company's charges from one station to another;.. time of departure and arrival of each train, etc. 1839 W. Chambers *Tour in Belgium* 73/1 We were speedily carried to the railway terminus, where a train of carriages was in waiting, with its locomotive engine hissing and chafing. 1855 Lynch *Rivulet* LXII. ii, Thus through a distant valley's length Slow seems to glide the train. 1885 Mabel Collins *Prettiest Woman* x, A train left Warsaw early in the morning.

b. Hence, a line of vehicles coupled together.

1883 Gresley *Gloss. Coal-mining, Journey*, a train or set of trams all coupled together.

c. ***to pull a train***: see pull *v.* 11 g.

†17. See quot. *Obs.* [Cf. F. *train*, 'nombre de vibrations qu'un mouvement d'horlogerie produit dans un temps déterminé' (Littré).] (Perhaps not Eng.)

1704 J. Harris *Lex. Techn.* I, *Train*, is the Number of Beats which the Watch maketh in an Hour or any other certain time.

IV. Names of other things (chiefly material) derived from prec. branches.

†18. *Cookery.* A dish consisting of dates, figs, raisins, and almonds strung upon a long thread and covered with batter. *Obs.*

c 1450 *Two Cookery-bks.* 97 Trayne roste. Take Dates and figges.. and þen take grete reysons and blanched almondes, and prik hem thorgh with a nedel into a threde of a mannys length,.. rost the treyne abought the fire in þe spete;.. cast the batur on the treyne as he turneth abought the fire. 14.. *Conuiuium domini de la Grey* ibid. 60 Le .ij. cours.. Halybutte. Plays fryid. Trayne Roste. 14.. *MS. Douce 55* lf. 64.

†19. The carriage of a printing-press. [F. *train.*] (Perh. only French.) *Obs.*

1594 R. Ashley tr. *Loys le Roy* 22 He maketh the train of the presse to roule [etc.].

20. Applied to various material objects that are dragged. **a.** The trail of a gun-carriage: see TRAIL *sb.*[1] 5.

1769 FALCONER *Dict. Marine* (1776) 11, *Crochets deretraite*, the eye-bolts, in the train of a gun-carriage, wherein are hooked the relieving tackles. **1815** [see *train-tackle* in 22c].

b. A rough kind of sledge or sleigh used in Canada for transport. [Cf. F. *traineau.*]

1783 *Quebec Gaz.* 22 May 2/1 No person shall come with traines, carts or other carriages, loaded with hay, straw or wood within the limits of the market-place. **1835** C. F. HOFFMAN *Winter in Far West* I. 210 At last a train [*note*, a rough kind of sled] and a couple of carioles drove up to the door. **1860** BARTLETT *Dict. Amer.*, *Train* (Fr. *traineau*), a peculiar kind of sleigh used for the transportation of merchandise, wood, etc., in Canada.

†**c.** A drag-net, a seine. [F. *traîne.*] *Obs.*

1576 FLEMING tr. *Caius' Dogs* (1880) 14 Such Dogges as serue for fowling... The first kinde of such serue the Hauke, The seconde, the net, or traine. **1609** BIBLE (Douay) *Hab.* i. 15 He drew it in his traine [L. *sagena*], and gathered it into his nette.

†**21.** A rope for dragging a plough or harrow. *local. Obs.*

1798 *Statist. Acc. Scot.* XX. 260 The harrows are drawn side-ways by a train or side rope (like that used in a plough).

V. 22. *attrib.* and *Comb.* **a.** In sense 5, 'Having a train', as ***train-dress, -gown, -petticoat, -skirt***; also **train-bearer**, an attendant who carries the train of a sovereign or other person; also *fig.*; so ***train-bearing*** adj.; **train-tea**, a tea-party on the occasion of a young lady's presentation at court.

1722 *Lond. Gaz.* No. 6084/6 Sir Robert Rich his *Train-bearer sitting over-against him. **1838** Q. VICTORIA *Jrnl.* 28 June, I..went into a robing-room, where I found my eight train-bearers: Lady Caroline Lennox [etc.]. **1871** LOWELL *Pope* Prose Wks. 1890 IV. 56 No poet more often than he makes the second line of the couplet a mere train-bearer to the first. **1848** BUCKLEY *Iliad* 129 The *train-bearing Trojan women. **1792** *Trans. Soc. Arts* X. 199 The principal consumption in this cloth, is in *train-dresses for ladies' wearing. **1831** CARLYLE *Sart. Res.* I. vii, Wives of quality.. have *train-gowns four or five ells in length; which trains there are boys to carry. **1678** *Lond. Gaz.* No. 1287/4 One long *Train petticoat of rich flowred Silk. **1876** T. HARDY *Ethelberta* II. 15 A light muslin *train-skirt. **1897** *Spectator* 16 Jan. 96/1 The '*train-tea' that celebrates the presentation at Court of an English girl in good society.

b. In sense 16, as ***train crash, crew, fare, hand*** (HAND *sb.* 8), ***hostess, journey, -line, -load, ride, -robber, -robbery, -service, -speed, station*** (U.S.), ***-thief, -time, travel, whistle, -wreck, -wrecker, -wrecking, -yard***; also **train-boy**, (*a*) *Coal-mining*: see quot. 1883; (*b*) (*U.S.* and *Canada*), a boy who sells newspapers, etc. on a railway train; **train call** *Theatr.*, (a notice of) the time for touring performers to catch a train to the next tour stop; †**train caller**, a railway official who announces the destinations of departing trains (see quot. 1921) (*obs.*); **train-dispatcher** (*U.S.* and *Canada*), the officer who has charge of the running of trains on a railway; **train-ferry**, a ferry for conveying trains across a piece of water from one railway to another; so ***train-ferriage***; **train-jumper** orig. *U.S.*, one who travels by train without paying the fare; so **train-jumping** *vbl. sb.*; **train master, trainmaster** *U.S.*, a person in charge of a train or trains; *spec.* a railway official responsible for the movement of all trains over a certain stretch of line; **train-mile**, each mile of the aggregate distance run by all the trains on a railway in a given period, as a unit in estimating amount of traffic, working expenses, etc.; so ***train-mileage***; **train-pipe**, a pipe connecting the source of power with the brakes on the cars in a continuous system of brakes on a railway train (also called *brake-pipe*); †**train porter**, a railway official in charge of a train over a single-line section of railway (*obs.*); also *attrib.*; **train-road** = *train-way* (*a*); **train set**, (*a*) a set of trains, tracks, etc., required for a model railway; (*b*) a set of wagons or carriages, sometimes with an engine, coupled together; **train-shed** (*U.S.*), a roof supported by posts forming a shelter for one or more platforms at which trains stop; a roughly built or uninclosed railway station; **train-sheet**, a ruled sheet on which are recorded the movements of every train on a section of railway, according to information telegraphed from the various stations; **train-sickness**, a sickness or nausea to which some persons are subject when travelling by train; so ***train-sick*** adj.; **trainside** *a. U.S.*, at the side of or near a train, taking place next to a train; **train-signal**, a method of signalling from the cars of a train to the engine by a continuous pipe (*Cent. Dict. Suppl.*); **train smash** *Naut. slang*, cooked tinned tomatoes, usu. with bacon; **train-staff**, (*a*) a staff delivered to an engine-driver as authority to travel over a single-line section of railway; (*b*) the staff of employees on a railway train; **train-stop**, (*a*) an automatic apparatus, in connexion with a railway signal, for stopping a train; (*b*) the state of a train's being at a stop; a place at which a train stops; **train ticket**, (*a*) a ticket delivered to an engine-driver as authority to travel over a single-line section of railway; cf. *train staff* (*a*), *staff and ticket* (*system*) s.v. STAFF *sb.*[1] 26; (*b*) a ticket enabling a passenger to travel on a train; **train-way**, (*a*) a temporary line of rails for the conveyance of small loads, as in the course of construction of a railway; (*b*) a platform hinged to a wharf, with a line of rails upon which railway cars or trucks may run to and from a ferry-boat (*U.S.*).

1869 *Atlantic Monthly* July 73/2 [He] prevailed upon me to be his *train-boy. **1883** GRESLEY *Gloss. Coal-mining*, *Train-boy*, a boy who rides upon the *train*, to attend to the rope attachments, etc. **1890** *Opelousas* (Louisiana) *Democrat* 19 Apr. 3/2 A boy who gets a position as train boy for our company must put up a certain amount of money as a guarantee. **1901** *Westm. Gaz.* 21 Feb. 10/2 Scarcely any observer has omitted to complain of the importunities of the train-boy [on American railways], with his merchandise of bananas and candies and chewing gum and dime novels. **1912** C. MACKENZIE *Carnival* (ed. 5) iv. 41 A pal wouldn't let you sleep over the *train-call on a Sunday morning. **1933** P. GODFREY *Back-Stage* xvi. 206 He packs his dress-basket, notes down the time of the train-call from the notice-board by the stage door. **1921** *Dict. Occupational Terms* (1927) §706 **Train caller*; a porter whose only duty is to call out destination of a departing train..; also calls out name of own station on arrival of trains. **1939** *WPA Guide to Florida* (1984) I. 5 Seminole names..were even more plentiful before the railroads interceded in behalf of train callers. **1957** D. DU MAURIER *Scapegoat* x. 133 A *train-crash north of Lyons. **1979** P. THEROUX *Old Patagonian Express* xix. 293, I don't want to be in a train crash. But I have a very bad feeling about this train. **1904** *McClure's Mag.* Apr. 617/1 As for the *train crew, we never had any more trouble with them than if they had been so many sheep. **1976** P. R. WHITE *Planning for Public Transport* viii. 162 If a train is stopped because of a derailment, blockage, etc. between signal boxes..it is necessary for the train crew to protect the trains with emergency lamps. **1881** *Chicago Times* 14 May, John Converse is appointed assistant *train-dispatcher. **1905** J. JOYCE *Let.* 15 Oct. (1966) II. 122, I will send you 100 crowns to pay your *trainfare. **1983** *U.S.A. Today* 19 Apr. 3A/1 In New York, trainfare and bagels were free as 90,000 suburban commuters got their trains back after a six week strike. **1897** *Month* Sept. 281 Behring Strait could be crossed by some powerful system of *train-ferriage. **1900** *Monthly Rev.* I. 41 The present route is across the lake by *train-ferry. **1894** *Westm. Gaz.* 3 Sept. 5/1 Many acts of heroism are reported, especially on the part of *train hands. **1963** *Times* 2 May 16/4 Why don't we have *train hostesses like air hostesses..who visit every carriage and see if we are comfortable and happy? **1971** *N.Z. News* 10 Mar. 5 Train hostesses who serve the needs of passengers on New Zealand Railways' 'Southerner' express trains between Christchurch and Invercargill pose in their distinctive transit red uniforms. **1908** *Daily Chron.* 11 Mar. 9/5 The *train-indicator, a huge framework confronting every passenger when he enters. There are eighteen clock faces, each of which tells the time at which the next train on the various lines departs. **1900** G. SWIFT *Somerley* 94 On our *train-journey home. **1909** WEBSTER, *Train jumper. **1930** *Times Lit. Suppl.* 5 June 482/3 Setting out on his trek across the continent,..as hobo, 'train jumper',..and cook in a Great Lakes freighter. **1965** H. P. TRITTON *Time means Tucker* i. 18, I..silently cursed myself for being fool enough to take on *train-jumping. **1978** *Sunday Mail Color Mag.* (Brisbane) 22 Oct. 6/2 Now, in the early years of this century, train-jumping was an unknown art in Australia. **1882** *Macm. Mag.* XLV. 502 Arrival of the *train-loads of troops. **1894** T. M. COOLEY in *Forum* (N.Y.) Sept. 17 Train-loads of perishable goods were..ruined by delays which the strike had caused. **1880** *News & Press* (Cimarron, New Mexico) 9 Sept. 3/2 Mr. Frank Fulton, *train master on this Division,..gave the following information concerning the damage. **1898** *Engineering Mag.* XVI. 66 Of an American railway..the superintendent..is assisted by a trainmaster, a roadmaster or division engineer,..and a chief dispatcher. **1907** J. W. SCHULTZ *My Life as Indian* xviii. 210 Berry declared that he would do no more freighting to the mines with his bull train; he would either sell it or employ some one as a train-master. **1983** *Mod. Railroads* Apr. 18/1 Along with the yardmaster and trainmaster we observed the handling. **1864** WEBSTER, *Train-mile. **1868** *Q. Rev.* Oct. 300 The working expense per train-mile is 2*s.* 6*d.* **1892** *Daily News* 17 Feb. 2/6 The great industrial lines have run more train-miles, and therefore done more work, during the past half-year. **1868** *Q. Rev.* Oct. 301 A large proportion of the *train-mileage run..is useless, being far in excess of [public] requirements. **1909** *Great Central Railway Report* 6 Aug. 5 The strictest economy has been exercised in train mileage. **1889** FINDLAY *Eng. Railway* 120 While the train is running a continual vacuum is maintained in the *train-pipes. **1859** *Rep. Accidents on Railways 1858* 17 in *Parl. Papers* XXV. 601 The system..of working by means of a *train porter. **1873** *Returns Railways Companies Connections* 11 in *Ibid.* LVII. 765 Single Lines of Railway..Worked under the Train Porter System. **1932** W. FAULKNER *Light in August* vi. 132 Perhaps he remembered suddenly the *train ride and the food. **1980** *Listener* 4 Sept. 296/2 The train ride down the Peninsula is boring: rubber, rubber, grey rubber trees. **1828** WEBSTER, **Train-road*..in mines, a slight rail-way for small loads. **1877** KNIGHT *Dict. Mech.*, *Train-road*, a construction railway; a slight railway for small loads. **1892** GUNTER *Miss Dividends* (1893) 257 An institution.. implacable in its pursuit of *train robbers, highwaymen, and others that raid the precious things the business community intrust to it. **1905** *Daily Chron.* 17 Apr. 4/5 There are two forms of criminal activity in which the United States enjoys an unenviable distinction. One of them is lynching and the other is *train-robbery. *a* **1914** *Mod.* The *train-service to London has been improved. **1939–40** *Army & Navy Stores Catal.* 826/1 This excellent *train set..comprises a No. 1 Special Locomotive..two No. 1 Pullman Coaches..and rails. **1959** G. F. ALLEN *Brit. Railways Today & Tomorrow* vii. 133 The Rosters usually indicate the preceding and succeeding use to which each coach of a train set is to be put. **1980** J. CARTWRIGHT *Horse of Darius* xi. 158 He was playing with his train set... He..passed his days in a world of trains and model airplanes. **1982** WHITEHOUSE & ALLEN *E. Treacy —Railway Photographer* 42 The all-maroon train-set of the northbound 'Flying Scotsman' leaving Copenhagen Tunnel. **1878** F. S. WILLIAMS *Midl. Railw.* 639 The *train setters and their foremen. **1892** *Pall Mall G.* 21 Nov. 7/3 The great iron and glass portal..will constitute the most extensive railway *train-shed in existence [at Philadelphia, U.S.]. **1905** E. M. FORSTER *Where Angels fear to Tread* vi. 163 They crossed the Apennines with a *train-sick child. **1909** *Daily Chron.* 22 July 7/1 Anyone to whom trains give the least sensation of vertigo should sit facing [the engine]. .. Children who are otherwise train-sick will travel fairly well seated thus. **1906** *Westm. Gaz.* 27 Sept. 4/2 Many travellers suffer from *train-sickness. **1932** *Sun* (Baltimore) 21 Sept. 1/6 He [*sc.* F. D. Roosevelt]..jollying *trainside crowds with localized pleasantries. **1940** *Ibid.* 24 July 1/5 In a series of train-side and platform talks..he [*sc.* W. L. Wilkie] lashed out against leading Democratic party machines by name. **1941** *Weekly Tel.* (Sheffield) 13 Sept. 16/1 The boys of the Navy have a lot of slang... They have given the name '*train smash' to a tomato and bacon breakfast. **1978** *Daily Mirror* 19 June 9/1 Train smash is our nickname for tinned tomatoes with bacon. **1901** *Daily Chron.* 1 May 8/7 In these days when *train-speeds in Great Britain are mostly stationary. **1859** *Rep. Accidents on Railways 1858* 17 in *Parl. Papers* XXV. 601 To make the *train staff the means of opening the train-ticket box. **1895** *Funk's Standard Dict.* s.v. *Staff*, Train-staff. **1901** *Daily News* 16 Jan. 5/1 The Isle of Sheppey Light Railway is in single track..and it will be worked on the train-staff and ticket system. **1906** *Westm. Gaz.* 27 Apr. 7/1 The train staff having dealt so promptly with the trouble that the only sign of fire was a little smoke. **1955** W. GADDIS *Recognitions* II. iii. 422 Go to a *train station yourself..or a bus station. **1981** *N.Y. Times Mag.* 21 June 10/3 When was the last time you heard a young, rich-affluent-wealthy type use the phrase *railroad station*? Upper-class use is now *train station*. **1906** *Westm. Gaz.* 27 Feb. 7/2 The *train-stop at the signal-post actuated the continuous brake, and thereby..brought the vehicle to a standstill. *a* **1963** S. PLATH *Ariel* (1965) 43 It is a trainstop, the nurses Undergoing the faucet water. **1977** H. FAST *Immigrants* 10 The food, brought to them at train stops, was a dismal, unchanging diet of cold sausage and stale bread. **1859** *Rep. Accidents on Railways 1858* 17 in *Parl. Papers* XXV. 601 If another engine or train is intended to follow in succession, a *train ticket, stating 'staff following', will be given to the person in charge of the leading train, the staff itself being given to the last. **1941** B. SCHULBERG *What makes Sammy Run?* x. 256 A letter arrived with a train ticket and travelling expenses. **1977** *Lancashire Life* Dec. 60/1 He ..showed early business acumen by taking orders for Wakes Week train tickets, sleeping-out on the doorstep of Thomas Cook's the night before the ticket sale to save others' queueing. **1877** F. M. A. ROE *Army Lett.* (1909) 163 From then on to *train time, Hal was patted and petted and given dainties. **1892** *Pall Mall G.* 15 Mar. 2/1 It was train-time, and I rose to leave him. **1881** *Chicago Times* 17 June, Running a car from a siding on the *train track. **1979** P. THEROUX *Old Patagonian Express* xiii. 200 The difficulties of *train travel in Latin America. **1839** *Civil Eng. & Arch. Jrnl.* II. 46/1 The wagons when loaded..are easily pushed ..down the *trainway to the face of the cliff. **1877** KNIGHT *Dict. Mech.*, *Train-way*, a hinged platform which forms a bridge leading from a wharf to the deck of a ferry-boat. **1927** R. LEHMANN *Dusty Answer* III. i. 128 A far *train-whistle roused her. **1981** V. MEHTA *Vedi* (1982) i. 3, I remember the train whistle. It blew with a rush of steam. **1883** *Manch. Examiner* 28 Nov. 4/6 It is supposed that the would-be *train wreckers were plotting against the Premier's life. **1891** *Boston* (Mass.) *Jrnl.* 26 Oct. 1/6 A train-wrecker caught. **1885** *Manch. Exam.* 10 Jan. 5/1 An unsuccessful attempt at *train-wrecking. **1930** J. DOS PASSOS *42nd Parallel* I. 16 Dumping grounds, *trainyards. **1973** T. PYNCHON *Gravity's Rainbow* I. 171 Out the windows..are a row of bare Army-colored poplars, a canal, a snowy trainyard.

c. In other senses: **train-bolt**, 'a bolt to which the training-tackle of a gun is hooked' (*Cent. Dict.*); †**train-horse**, a horse employed to draw artillery; **train-net** = sense 20c; **train-rope, train-tackle**, a tackle hooked to the trail of a gun-carriage on board ship: see quot.; **train-service** (in sense 9b); **train-shut** *a.*, shut by a train of wheels and pinions; **train-work**, a mechanism consisting of a series of parts (sense 15).

1643 in *13th Rep. Hist. MSS. Comm.* App. I. 131 The county complains that we have not charged the *Train horse according to the letter of the Ordinance. **1710** *Lond. Gaz.* No. 4682/2 Train Horses..employed in drawing forty pieces of Artillery. **1864** *Glasgow Daily Herald* 24 Sept., There is as much damage done with *train nets as with trawl nets. **1887** *Spectator* 3 Sept. 1174 Their *train-services collected and equipped for a campaign. **1632** LITHGOW *Trav.* I. 5 Mine Epitaph shall sound, Of *traine-shut sluces, of the Thespian spring, Where chatring birds, Dodonean trees do sing. **1815** BURNEY *Falconer's Dict. Marine*, **Train-Tackle*,..a combination of pulleys, which is, during action, hooked to an eye-bolt, in the train of the carriage, and to a ring-bolt in the deck... Its use is, to prevent the gun from running out of the port whilst loading. **1867** SMYTH *Sailor's Word-bk.*, Train-tackle. **1876** PREECE & SIVEWRIGHT *Telegraphy* 92 The Morse involves a complicated and expensive *trainwork of mechanism.

†**train**, *sb.*[2] *Obs.* Forms: 4–7 **trayne**, 4–5 **treyne**, **trayn**, 5 *north.* **trane**, 6–7 **traine**, 6–8 **train**. [a. OF. *traïne* guile, deceit, ruse (12th c. in Godef.), n. of action f. OF. *traïr*, (Fr. *trahir*) to betray; cf. *haine* (OF. *haïne*), *saisine*, f. *haïr*, *saisir*. Cf. the

phrases 'withouten train', 'false train', etc. with OF. *sans traine*, *fausse traine*, etc.

In senses 2, 3, and 4 this word appears to be associated with senses 7 and 13 b of TRAIN *sb.*[1]]

1. Without *a* or *pl.*: Treachery, guile, deceit, trickery.

c **1400** *Destr. Troy* 3789 Ulexes..falsest in his fare, and full of disseit, Vndertaker of treyne, of talkyng but litill. *c* **1400** *Non-Cycle Myst. Plays* 7/67 We schal home tell, withouten trayn, Bothe word & werk, how hit was. *c* **1460** *Towneley Myst.* x. 330 Do wa, Ioseph,..Turne home to thi spouse agane, look thou deme in hir no trane, ffor she was neuer ffylde. **1590** SPENSER *F.Q.* I. vi. 41 Thou cursed Miscreaunt, That hast with knightlesse guile, and trecherous train, Faire knighthood fowly shamed. *a* **1600** *Flodden F.* VII. (1664) 70 Trusting his talk was void of trayne.

b. With *a* and *pl.* An act or scheme designed to deceive or entrap, a trick, stratagem, artifice, wile.

c **1330** R. BRUNNE *Chron.* (1810) 295 þe kyng of Almayn[e]..He mad a fals trayn[e]..He sent Edward to say, help him mot he nouht. *a* **1350** *St. Nicholas* 322 in Horstm. *Altengl. Leg.* (1881) 15 Now wote I wele, þou es vntrew..I trow ȝour law be bot a trayne. **1412–20** LYDG. *Chron. Troy* IV. 4904 Dredynge ay þat þese ilke tweyne Be som engyn or conspired treyne To þe Grekes wolden hym be-tray. **1529** RASTELL *Pastyme, Brit.* (1811) 213 Mortymer was, by a trayne, taken in the castell of Notyngham. **1605** SHAKS. *Macb.* IV. iii. 118 Diuellish Macbeth, By many of these traines, hath sought to win me Into his power. **1739** G. OGLE *Gualtherus* 23 An artless Mind, Unpractis'd in the Trains of Womankind. **1767** MICKLE *Concub.* II. xlvi, The Nymph..With wylie Traines the Sonnes of Earth besett.

2. A trap or snare for catching wild animals; also *fig.* (In phrase *to lay a train*, associated with or merged in senses of TRAIN *sb.*[1])

1390 GOWER *Conf.* III. 241 Bot if a king his wille Fro lustes of his fleissh restreigne, Ayein himself he makth a treigne, Into the which if that he slyde, Him were betre go besyde. *c* **1420** ? LYDG. *Assembly of Gods* 773 That no maner trayne nor caltrop theryn wore. **1530** PALSGR. 282/2 Trayne a trappe, *atrappe*. **1624** QUARLES *Sion's Elegies* iii. Poems (1717) 393, I seek my peace, but seek my peace in vain; For every way's a trap: each path's a train. *a* **1630** D. HUME *Hist. Ho. Douglas & Angus* (1644) 30 Fearing..that there was some train laid for them, he turned about to have retired into the Castle. **1697** DRYDEN *Æneid* XI. 1056 Vain Fool and Coward,..Caught in the Train which thou thyself hast laid.

3. Something designed to lure an animal into a trap or snare; a lure, bait, decoy, enticement; also *fig.*

c **1407** LYDG. *Reson & Sens.* 6981 [The tiger] ys deceyved by merours Which the hountys for socours Caste in the waye for a treyne. **14..** *Voc.* in Wr.-Wülcker 566/25 *Attractorium*, a trayne, *sed melius* a trays. **1548** CRANMER *Catech.* 97 b, Thou mayst make no traynes to bring him in to thy snare. **1602** *Hist. Eng.* in *Harl. Misc.* (Malh.) II. 464 The barbarous people..leaving their cattle abroad, as a train, to draw them [the Romans] within danger.

†**4.** A live bird attached to a line, or a lame and disabled bird, given as an enticement to a young hawk during its training. (Sometimes explained as the short flight which the hawk makes in trying to capture this: see TRAIN *sb.*[1] 3.) *Obs.*

1496 *Acc. Ld. High Treas. Scot.* I. 287 Giffin to the man that brocht tua quyk herounis to the King, to make tranys to halkis,..ix s. *Ibid.* 291 Item, for a duke to be a trane to a halk..xij d. **1575** TURBERV. *Falconrie* 117 When a sparow hawke is manned and reclaymed, then give her nine or ten traynes at the least, and when she killeth feede hir up alwayes. **1611** COTGR., *Tome*, a traine with a lame and disarmed Heron, for the making of a young Faulcon. **1616** SURFL. & MARKH. *Country Farme* 709 These flights are called traines, because they only traine or teach a young Hawke how to bestow her wing, and make her selfe victor ouer the prey.

†**train**, *sb.*[3] *Obs.* (exc. in TRAIN-OIL). Forms: 5–6 **trane**, 6 **treine**, 6–7 **trayne**, **traine**, 6– **train**. [In 15–16th c. *trane*, a. MLG. and LG. *trân*, MDu. *traen*, Du. *traan*, whence mod.Ger. *tran*, and Da., Sw. *tran*; all meaning 'oil extracted or made to exude, spec. train-oil'; app. the same word as MLG. *trân*, *trâne*, MDu. *traen*, *trâne*, OHG. *trahan*, OS. **trahan*, pl. *trahni*, OLFrank. pl. *trâni* (Ger. *träne*) 'tear, drop', also gum or resin that exudes from trees, 'lacrymae arborum' (Kilian).] The earlier name of what is now called TRAIN-OIL.

1497 *Maldon, Essex, Burgh-Deeds* Bundle 72 No. 4 Possessiatus de uno barrello olei vocat. trane. **1515** *Sel. Cases Star Chamb.* (Selden) II. 92 The Crafte and misterie of Mercers hath vsed..othir grosse marchaundise as sopp, terre,..pik, Wax,..Trayne. **1545** *Rates of Customs* d j, Woll oyle called trane the tonne iiii li. **1602** CAREW *Cornwall* I. 33 They pack them [pilchards] orderly in hogsheads..which afterwards they presse with great waights, to the end the traine may soke from them into a vessel placed in the ground to receyue it. **1712** A. VAN LEEUWENHOEK in *Phil. Trans.* XXVII. 441 Upon several Parts of these little Membranes, there lay Fat, which..they call the Train. **1766** *Acc. Bks.* in *Ann. Reg.* 283/2 They don't drink train,..but use it in their lamps. **1802** *Trans. Soc. Arts* XX. 212 The cod-oil, or common train, brought from Newfoundland.

b. *attrib.* as ***train-fat***, **-*bottle***. (See TRAIN-OIL.)

1698 *Act 10 Will. III*, c. 14 §7 Any Houses Stages Cook-Rooms Train-Fats or other Conveniencies for fishing there [Newfoundland]. **1707** *Lond. Gaz.* No. 4378/3, 23 Train-Fats burnt;..1568 Hogsheads of Train-Oil destroyed. **1797** CRANTZ in *Encycl. Brit.* (ed. 3) XIV. 610/1 Of the skins of the entrails [of the seal] they [Greenlanders] make their windows..; and they make train bottles of the maw.

train, *v.*[1] Forms: 4–7 **trayne**, (5 **treyne**), 5–7 **trayn**, 6 (*Sc.*), 7 **trane**, 6–7 **traine**, 6– **train**. [ME. a. F. *traîn-er*, in OF. *traïner*, also *trahiner* (11th c. in Hatz.-Darm.); app. a deriv. of L. *trahĕre* (in pop.L. **tragĕre*, whence F. *traire*) to draw, drag; = Pr. *trahinar*; cf. Sp. *trajinar* to convey, '*traginar* to transport by pack-horses' (Minsheu), It. *trainare* 'to traine, to traile, to draggle or draw along the ground' (Florio).

Hatz.-Darm. suppose a sb. **tragina* from **tragere*, formed like *rapina*, *ruina*, fr. *rapĕre*, *ruĕre*, whence the vb. They do not identify this **tragina* with the existing *traine*, which is taken as a new formation from the vb. like *train*, masc.]

I. 1. a. *trans.* To draw or pull along after one; to drag, haul, trail. *Obs.* or *arch.*

c **1450** *Merlin* xviii. 299 He hente hir be the tresses and drough hir toward the horse trailinge..; and so he hath hir trayned and drawen. **1530** PALSGR. 383 To se the body of Hector so trayned by Achilles. **1607** MARKHAM *Caval.* III. i. (1617) 9 This chase or sport we..call a Traine sent, because the sent which the Houndes hunt is trained alongst the fields. **1623** tr. *Favine's Theat. Hon.* VI. iv. 124 To traine the baggadge of the Christian Army there were three score thousand Chariots. **1667** MILTON *P.L.* VI. 553 Behold..the Foe Approaching..; in hollow Cube Training his devilish Enginrie [cannons]. **1831** SCOTT *Ct. Robt.* iii, He cannot be so false of word as to train me to prison under false pretexts.

b. *intr.* (for *pass.*) Of a garment: To hang down, esp. so as to drag or trail. Now *rare*.

1590 SPENSER *F.Q.* II. iii. 27 Below her ham her weed did somewhat trayne. **1702** W. J. tr. *Bruyn's Voy. Levant* xxxi. 117 They let it [the tail] train down till they come to the lower End. **1789** MRS. PIOZZI *Journ. France* I. 184 A full black silk petticoat, sloped just to train a very little on the ground. **1827** [see TRAINING *ppl. a.* 3].

†**2.** *fig.* (*trans.*) **a.** To draw out, lengthen out (in time), protract, spin out; also, to spend, pass (time, one's life); *esp.* to pass slowly or wearily, 'drag on'. Also *intr.* *Obs.*

c **1440** *Promp. Parv.* 499/1 Traynyn, or tranyyn, or longe taryyn (..*S.* or abydyn), *moror, differo*. **1539** [see TRAINING *vbl. sb.* 1]. **1556** J. HEYWOOD *Spider & F.* xcv. 8 To traine the time and tarie you..folli it weare. *a* **1560** BECON *Jewel of Joy* Wks. II. 5 Nether by letters nor yet by report..could we lerne wher you trained your life. **1652** J. WRIGHT tr. *Camus' Nat. Paradox* x. 259 To seek a glorious Death..rather than train so obscure and discontented a Life.

b. To draw *out* in length, to extend; to drawl, utter slowly (a word, phrase, name). *rare.*

1651 CLEVELAND *Smectymnuus* 10 A Name which if 'twere train'd would spread a mile. **1859** G. MEREDITH *R. Feverel* xlii, He trained out the [word] old.

†**c.** To draw after itself, draw *with* it; to involve as a consequence; to bring in its train. *Obs.*

1579 FENTON *Hist. Guicciard.* (1618) 12 If those small forces trained with them so great fortunes. **1619** SIR J. FINETT in *Eng. & Germ.* (Camden) 63 A busynes that is lyke to trayn wyth it a consequence of continuall trouble.

†**d.** To strain the sense of. *Obs. rare*$^{-1}$.

1550 BALE *Eng. Votaries* II. 31 The scriptures he had so trayned with the rules of logycke, that by them he was able to maynteyne all falshede.

†**3.** To draw, lead, conduct, bring. *Obs.*

1549 COVERDALE, etc. *Erasm. Par. Jude* 22 The Hebrues..whom..Iesus trained out of the..bondage of the Egipcians. *c* **1586** C'TESS PEMBROKE *Ps.* CV. xii, His chosen troopes with triumph on he traines. **1642** CHAS. I *Declar.* 12 Aug. 16 Their resort was to the people, whom upon severall occasions they had trained down to Westminster.

II. 4. *fig.* To draw by art or inducement; to draw *on*; to allure, entice, decoy; to lead astray, deceive, take in. *arch.* (The most frequent early sense. ? Influenced by TRAIN *sb.*[2])

1375 BARBOUR *Bruce* XIX. 354 The lord dowglas toward thaim raid;..Thame neir his battell for till trayne. ? *a* **1400** *Morte Arth.* 1683 ȝe do bott trayne us..wyth trofelande wordez. **1412–20** LYDG. *Chron. Troy* III. 1015 His mortall foon þat..him to treyne leide out hoke & laas. **1588** T. HUGHES *Misfort. Arth.* v. i. 88 So did his witte and feature feede that hope, Which falsely trainde me to this wofull hap. **1596** SHAKS. *1 Hen. IV*, v. ii. 21 We did traine him on. *a* **1694** TILLOTSON *Serm.* (1743) I. 237 Being insensibly trained on from one degree of wickedness to another. **1781** *Hist. Eur.* in *Ann. Reg.* 92/1 Being trained into a well-laid ambush. **1899** GOLDW. SMITH *United Kingd.* I. 200 He [Bruce] trained him [Comyn] to a church and stabbed him there.

†**b.** In good or neutral sense: To draw by persuasion; to persuade, induce, convert. *Obs.*

1526 in Strype *Eccl. Mem.* (1721) I. v. 67 The King had hopes to train the Emperor to reason by doulce methods. **1549** COVERDALE, etc. *Erasm. Par. Thess.* 2 Howe easely you were trayned from the supersticion of your forefathers,..vnto the true wurshippe of God. **1612** BREREWOOD *Lang. & Relig.* 154 They have been by little and little brought and trayned to the Greek religion.

III. 5. To treat or manipulate so as to bring to the proper or desired form; *spec.* in *Gardening*, to manage (a plant or branch) so as to cause it to grow in some desired form or direction, esp. against a wall, or upon a trellis or the like.

c **1440** *Pallad. on Husb.* I. 1032 And bowis ore hit trayn So lough and rare, on hem that bees may dwelle. **1688** EVELYN *Diary* 24 Mar., His orangerie and gardens, where the wall fruit trees are most exquisitely nail'd and train'd. **1792** MAR. RIDDELL *Voy. Madeira* 9 The vines are trained and supported by poles. **1837** LOCKHART *Scott* I. ix. 289 A garden..in which Scott delighted to train his flowers and creepers. **1852** O. W. HOLMES *My Aunt* ii, Why will she train that winter curl In such a spring-like way? **1871** [see TRAINED *ppl. a.* 3]. **1888** *Nicholson's Dict. Gard.* s.v. *Training*, Sap flowing most forcibly into branches trained in an upright direction.

6. To subject to discipline and instruction for the purpose of forming the character and developing the powers of, or of making proficient in some occupation. (Also with *up*.)

a. To instruct and discipline generally; to educate, rear, bring up.

1542 UDALL *Erasm. Apoph.* Pref. *** ij b, For teachyng and trainyng young children. **1611** BIBLE *Prov.* xxii. 6 Traine vp a childe in the way he should goe. **1727** GAY *Fables* I. ix, Seek you to train your fav'rite boy? Each caution, ev'ry care employ. **1877** E. R. CONDER *Bas. Faith* iii. 103 This protracted pupilage..is admirably calculated to train and perfect his moral character.

b. To instruct and discipline in or for some particular art, profession, occupation, or practice; to exercise, practise, drill; to make proficient by such instruction and practice (see also TRAINED *ppl. a.*). Const. *in*, *for*, *to*.

1555 W. WATREMAN *Fardle Facions* I. vi. 106 To be trayned, and exercysed in the feictes of warre. **1577–87** HOLINSHED *Chron.* I. 3/1 Bardus..was highlie renoumed..for inuention of dities and musicke, wherein..he trained his people. **1661** in *Verney Mem.* (1907) II. 170 To march, trayne and exercise his company, according to the moderne discipline of warr. *c* **1680** BEVERIDGE *Serm.* (1729) I. 39 Such advocates as had been trained up in the civil law. **1823** SCOTT *Quentin D.* xxxi, To a false tale you will not desire me to train my tongue. **1859** *Musketry Instr.* 92 Bandsmen..fully trained to the use of the rifle. **1869** HUXLEY in *Sci. Opin.* 21 Apr. 464/1 He was thoroughly trained in the physical and chemical science of his day.

c. To discipline and instruct (an animal) so as to make it obedient to orders, or capable of performing tricks; to prepare a race-horse for its work.

1609 *Shuttleworths' Acc.* (Chetham Soc.) 181 Richard Eastwood, for his paynes and his coache, to trayne the horses theirin, xxx[s]. **1660** F. BROOKE tr. *Le Blanc's Trav.* 166 These Lions..are..trained in parkes to hunt others. **1777** PRIESTLEY *Matt. & Spir.* (1782) I. xxii. 286 Dogs..may be trained to catch hares. **1872** J. F. CLARKE *Self-Culture* i. (1880) 33 Animals can be trained by man, but they cannot train themselves. **1894** ASTLEY *50 Years Life* I. 176 The present Robert Sherwood, who now trains at Newmarket.

d. To bring by a course of diet and exercise to the required state of physical efficiency for a race or other athletic feat.

1832 S. AUSTIN tr. *Pückler-Muskau's Tour of German Prince* III. iv. 74, I kept race-horses myself, and had a Newmarket jockey for a time in my service... It amused me greatly to see this fellow 'training' himself. **1835–71** [see TRAINING *vbl. sb.* 2 c]. **1887** STEVENSON *Mem. & Portr.* vi. *Pastoral* 96 A threat of latent anger in the expression, like that of a man trained too fine and harassed with perpetual vigilance.

e. With *adv.* or *compl. adj.*: To bring into a specified condition by or as by athletic training. ***train off***, to throw off by training.

1879 *Spectator* 7 June 720 The beasts, always worn, for that terrible, incessant pulling trains them down almost visibly. **1891** KIPLING *Light that Failed* viii. 165 You're disgracefully out of condition,..pure tallow born of over-feeding. Train it off, Dickie.

7. a. *intr.* for *pass.* To undergo or follow a course of instruction and discipline; in early quots., to go through a course of military drill, to drill.

1605 STOW *Ann.* 1310 The other 3000 citizens..shewed on the Miles end, where they trained all that day. **1685** WOOD *Life* 28 June (O.H.S.) III. 146, 4 loades of muskets, pikes, etc...for the scholars to train with. **1811** BYRON *Hints fr. Horace* 703 The youth who trains to ride, or run a race, Must bear privations. **1906** BEATRICE HARRADEN *Scholar's Dau.* vii, My uncle thought I'd better train to be a doctor.

b. *intr.* With *adv.* To get into some condition by training; as ***train on***, to improve in condition or form by training, to become more proficient; †***train off***, to get out of condition, lose one's vigour or skill, as by over-training; ***train down***, to reduce one's weight with the object of getting fit for an event or feat. Also *fig.*

1767 G. SELWYN *Let.* 29 Dec. in *15th Rep. R. Comm. Hist. Manuscripts* App. VI. 225 in *Parl. Papers 1897* (C. 8551) LI. 1, Lord Beauchamp trains on well, as they say, but *il n' a pas le moyen de plaire*. **1776** E. TOPHAM *Lett. fr. Edinburgh* 98 When they are young they dance extremely well; but afterwards (to speak in the language of the turf) they train off. **1789** *Loiterer* 6 June 7 He *trained on famously* well, and would soon be a very *dashing man*. **1810** *Sporting Mag.* XXXVI. 230 A hard round,..that convinced the judges of boxing that Blake had trained off. **1815** BYRON *Let. to Moore* 10 Jan., It is impossible to read what you have lately done..without seeing that you have trained on tenfold. **1866** MACLAREN *Training* 22 Under it a powerful man dwindles; and this, not from 'training down' as the phrase goes. **1937** *Daily Tel.* 15 Oct. 23/3 He..trained on into a first-rate College oar. **1976** *Horse & Hound* 10 Dec. 48/2 (Advt.), A good sire of fast 2-year-olds that train on.

IV. †**8. a.** *trans.* To pursue by the 'train' or trail; to trace, track. *Obs.*

1583 [see TRAINING *ppl. a.* 2]. **1592** GREENE *Groat's W. Wit* C ij b, They followed and trayned the Foxe and Badger to the hole.

b. *Mining.* (See quots.)

1710 J. HARRIS *Lex. Techn.* II, *Training a Load*, in the Miner's Language, is searching for, and pursuing a Vein of Ore. **1895** *Funk's Standard Dict.*, *Train*, *v.*...5. In mining, to trace, as a lode to its head.

9. *intr.* †**a.** To walk in a person's train or retinue. *Obs. rare*−1. **b.** *train off*: to draw off or away.

1633 P. FLETCHER *Hymen* in *Poet. Misc.* 55 With her a troop of fairest wood-nymphs trains. **1825** T. HOOK *Sayings* Ser. II. *Sutherl.* (Colburn) 27 James gradually trained off from the party. **1833** —— *Widow & Marquess* ii, They [suitors] had trained off, upon finding..that Harriet's boasted fortune was visionary.

c. To associate, ally, or co-operate *with*, (*dial.* also *along of*). *N. Amer. colloq.*

1871 J. HAY *Pike County Ballads* 22 It gravels me like the devil to train Along o' sich fools as you. **1889** *Cent. Dict.* s.v. *train*¹, I don't *train* with that crowd. **1892** 'MARK TWAIN' *Amer. Claimant* i. 5 Have you been training with that ass again? **1907** *Methodist Rev.* Nov. 984 He does not train with the extreme radical theologians. **1935** H. DAVIS *Honey in Horn* i. 4 A couple of bad-acting sons who got drunk, fought and trained around with thieving half-breeds. **1945** 'L. FORD' *Philadelphia Murder Story* ix. 146 She knew as well as I know now—and I don't train with lawyers—that Malone wasn't going to search the house.

10. a. *trans.* To direct, point, or aim (a cannon or other fire-arm, or *transf.* a photographic camera); to bring by horizontal movement to bear (*on*, *upon*, the thing aimed at). Cf. TRAINING *vbl. sb.* 4.

1841 TOTTEN *Naval Text-Bk.* 417 *To train a gun*, to point it forward or abaft the beam. **1870** H. MEADE *New Zealand* 236 A forty-pounder..trained on them during the conference. **1873** *Brit. Q. Rev.* 108 Their 'horizontal range', or the arc over which they could be trained, should be made small. **1889** G. KENNAN in *Century Mag.* May 73/2 We set up the camera and trained it upon a part of the picturesque throng.

b. *intr.*

1891 *Cent. Dict.* s.v., *To train off*, to go off obliquely: said of the flight of a shot.

11. a. *trans.* To convey by a railway train. *rare.*

1886 *Pall Mall G.* 14 July 14/1 Ship it [sewage] to Ireland ..and let Paddy cart or train it away..to his potato patch or cornfield. **1892** *Field* 28 May 783/2 Ship the canoe on to the railway and train it right up the Wye valley.

b. *intr.* To go by train, travel by railway. Also *train it* (*colloq.*).

1856 LD. GRANVILLE *Let.* 12 Feb. in Ld. Fitzmaurice *Life Granville* (1905) I. vii. 163 After acting as godfather, I trained up to town for the Committee of Privileges. **1888** *Pall Mall G.* 2 Apr. 4/2 So exhausted were the men from the effect of the previous day's ride,..that all trained from Winchester to Farnham. **1888** *Harper's Mag.* Nov. 954/2 From Aberdeen to Edinburgh we trained it by easy stages.

12. *intr.* To act sportively, romp, 'carry on'. *U.S. colloq.*

1889 HOWELLS *Hazard New Fort.* II. viii, The girl broke into a fondly approving laugh at his drolling. 'Oh, I guess you love to train!' **1889** FARMER *Americanisms*, *To train*. New England girls use this term to denote acts of romping, or, to employ an English phrase, which seems its exact equivalent, *to train* is 'to carry on'.

†**train**, *v.*² *Obs.* [f. TRAIN *sb.*²; but prob. not always distinguished from TRAIN *v.*¹]

1. *trans.* To lay (a train or snare); to set (a trap). Cf. TRAIN *sb.*² 2.

1412–20 LYDG. *Chron. Troy* IV. 4935 Þat iustly þei may fallen in þe diche Whiche þei han made & for vs y-treyned.

2. *Falconry.* To entice (a hawk) by means of a live bird used as a lure. (Cf. TRAIN *sb.*² 4.)

1575 TURBERV. *Falconrie* 117 Let the quayle wherewithall you trayne hir haue a feather pulled out of each wing and cast off the sparowhawke to hir a farre off.

3. *intr.* Of a hawk: To come to the train or lure.

1579 LYLY *Euphues* (Arb.) 35 The fleetest fish swalloweth the delicatest bait:..the highest soaring Hauke traineth to yᵉ lure.

trainability (treɪnəˈbɪlɪtɪ). [f. TRAINABLE *a.* + -ILITY.] Aptness or capacity for being trained.

1955 G. A. N. LOWNDES *Brit. Educ. System* ii. 40 High trainability is a delicate plant. **1960** *Times* 20 Jan. 9/7 The fine quality of the Northern Ireland labour force, its trainability. **1980** *Observer* 4 May 26/6 If a degree indicates intelligence or trainability.

trainable (ˈtreɪnəb(ə)l), *a.* [f. TRAIN *v.*¹ + -ABLE.] Capable of being trained; amenable to discipline and instruction; educable.

c **1550** (*title*) An Enterlude called Lusty Iuuentus, lyuely describing the frailtie of youth: of natur prone to vyce: by grace and good counsayll traynable to vertue. **1594** CAREW *Huarte's Exam. Wits* iii. (1596) 30 Amongst horses..some there are more trainable than the rest. **1600** HOLLAND *Livy* XXXIX. xl. 1049 This man was by nature so trainable and pliant to all alike, that [etc.]. **1869** *Daily News* 20 Aug., If there were skilled labour, or even trainable labour, to carry it on. **1872** RUSKIN *Fors Clav.* (1896) I. xxii. 442 The horse, the noblest, because trainablest, of wild creatures.

trainage (ˈtreɪnɪdʒ). *rare.* [f. TRAIN *v.*¹ + -AGE: cf. F. *trainage*.] The action of 'training' or drawing along; haulage; conveyance by train.

1611 COTGR., *Trainage*, trainage. **1817** *Mann. & Cust.* in *Ann. Reg.* 479/1 Fortunately (being the necessary conditions for good trainage) it [snow] had fallen on a ground already hardened by the frost. **1890** 'R. BOLDREWOOD' *Col. Reformer* (1891) 42 Men in charge of droves..pursued the old and rugged road, not caring to use the swifter, costlier trainage.

‖**trainante** (trɛnɑ̃t), *a.* Now *rare.* Also **traînante.** [a. F. *traînante* (fem.), f. pres. pple. of *traîner* to drag, as in *voix traînante*, etc.] Of vocal or musical sounds: dragging, drawling.

1818 C. MORGAN *Let.* 16 Sept. in Lady Morgan *Autobiogr.* (1859) 104 The music..possesses here and there fine strains of melody: *per contra*, it is *trainante* often too scientific and old-fashioned in its phrases. **1865** 'OUIDA' *Strathmore* I. x. 170 The tranquil *trainante* tones in which he always spoke his rudest things. **1899** *Westm. Gaz.* 5 Oct. 3/1 Talking in their pleasant, *traînante* tones to and of each other.

ˈ**trainˌband, train-band.** Now *Hist.* [Abbrev. of *trained band*: see TRAINED *ppl. a.* 2.] A trained company of citizen soldiery, organized in London and other parts in the 16th, 17th, and 18th centuries. Also occas. applied to similar forces in other countries, e.g. the French *arrière-ban*.

1630 *R. Johnson's Kingd. & Commw.* 28 In a hard battell there would appeare a great deale of difference betwixt an old beaten souldier..and a man of our traine bands of London. **1654** H. L'ESTRANGE *Chas. I* 19 The Country Captains of the Train-bands were..very unskilfull and rude in the use of their Armes. **1670** COTTON *Espernon* I. II. 56 He commanded that in every Province, the Nobility, and Train-Bands should be ready to march. **1732** POPE *Ep. Bathurst* 214 To town he comes,..And heads the bold Train-bands. **1849** MACAULAY *Hist. Eng.* v. I. 593 The trainbands of Wiltshire had mustered. **1851** HAWTHORNE *Grandfather's Chair* I. iii, Whenever a trainband of Salem was mustered.

b. *attrib.*

1664 D. FLEMING in *Extr. S.P. rel. Friends* II. (1911) 191 The Judges..were met..by all the Trainband horse of this county. **1674** DEAN GRENVILLE in *Surtees Misc.* (1858) 155 His Majestie hath a notorious Sott to his trainband captain. **1782** COWPER *Gilpin* i, A train-band captain eke was he Of famous London town. **1881** BESANT & RICE *Chapl. of Fleet* I. iii, The train-band lieutenant..came swaggering to the inn.

Hence †ˈ**trainˌbanding** (*Obs. nonce-wd.*), raising of, or serving in, a trainband.

1711 E. WARD *Vulgus Brit.* VIII. 95 Watching, Warding, and Trainbanding, Tho' Customs of an ancient Standing.

‖**traineau** (treɪˈnəʊ, ‖trɛno). [F. *traîneau*, in OF. *trahinel*, *traïnel*, deriv. of *traîner*: see TRAIN *v.*¹] A sledge, sleigh; esp. one drawn by one or more horses over snow or ice.

[**1676** LADY CHAWORTH in *12th Rep. Hist. MSS. Comm.* App. v. 34 She hath also great pleasure in one of those sledges which they call *Trainias*, and is pulled up and down the ponds in them every day.] *a* **1715** BURNET *Own Time* (1753) III. iv. 10 He was driving the Princess upon the Snow in a Trainau. **1873** *Forest & Stream* 11 Dec. 273/2 Our traineau, heavily loaded, follows behind.

attrib. **1779** J. MOORE *View Soc. Fr.* (1793) I. 398 Among the winter amusements of this place [Frankfurt], traineau parties may be reckoned.

trained (treɪnd), *a.* [f. TRAIN *sb.*¹ + -ED².]

1. Having a train, as a robe; having a luminous train, as a meteor (quot. 1686).

1588 in *Aston's Manch. Guide* (1804) 25 A traynd gowne lyned wyth chamlett. **1686** GOAD *Celest. Bodies* II. x. 291 Tayl'd and trayn'd Meteors. **1883** 'SYLVIA' *Lady's Guide Dressmaking* 107, 2 trained petticoats. **1905** *Daily Chron.* 13 Nov. 8/1 The average middle-class English woman..should never be tempted to wear a trained skirt out of doors.

†**2.** Attended by a train or retinue. *Obs. rare*−1.

1593 NASHE *Christ's T.* (1613) 4 He sent him not roially trained and accompanied like an Embassador.

trained (treɪnd, *poet.* ˈtreɪnɪd), *ppl. a.* [f. TRAIN *v.*¹ + -ED¹.] In various senses corresponding to those of the verb.

†**1.** Drawn, trailed along, etc.; *fig.* attracted, allured, enticed. *Obs.*

1579 SPENSER *Sheph. Cal.* Oct. 24 Whereto thou list their trayned willes entice.

2. Disciplined; made proficient by discipline.

a. *spec.* Subjected to military discipline and instruction, drilled; esp. in *trained band* = TRAIN-BAND (now *Hist.*); so †*trained man*, *soldier*, a soldier belonging to a trainband (*obs.*).

1570–6 LAMBARDE *Peramb. Kent* (1596) 70 The trained companies only shall resort to the places of their appointed Rendeuous. **1594** SIR H. COCKE in Ellis *Orig. Lett.* Ser. II. III. 175 Havinge..taken a perfect vyewe of all the Trayned Bandes. **1611** BIBLE *Gen.* xiv. 14 Abram..armed his trained seruants. **1617** MORYSON *Itin.* II. 105 To haue six thousand of the trained bands in readines. **1644** PRYNNE & WALKER *Fiennes' Trial* App. 25 Iames Powell of Bristoll, one of the Trained Souldiers of that City [called below Train Soldiers]. **1707** E. CHAMBERLAYNE *Pres. St. Eng.* II. xvi. (ed. 22) 217 Of the standing Militia, or Trained-Bands. **1827** HALLAM *Const. Hist.* (1876) II. ix. 133 The citizens of London mustered their trained bands on holidays.

b. *gen.* Disciplined, instructed, educated; made proficient by discipline and instruction.

1858 HAWTHORNE *Fr. & It. Note-Bks.* (1872) I. 21 The women..have a trained expression that supplies the place of beauty. **1899** *Allbutt's Syst. Med.* VII. 855 To engage a trained hospital nurse. **1910** D. G. HOGARTH in *Encycl. Brit.* I. 248/2 An Art, whose products cannot be confounded with those of any other..by a trained eye.

3. Of a plant: Artificially caused to grow in some desired way; of a woman's figure, made slender or shaped by wearing a corset.

1766 *Compl. Farmer* s.v. *Peach-tree*, Such trees, which are of one year's growth from the budding,..will soon overtake in growth those which are called trained trees. **1786** ABERCROMBIE *Gard. Assist.* 311 Those ready trained, denominated trained trees. **1871** *Figure Training* 90 Slender and elegantly trained figures.

trainee (treɪˈniː). [f. as prec. + -EE.] A person or (formerly) an animal undergoing training: *orig.* correlative to *trainer*. Also *attrib.* or as *adj.*

1841 *Fistiana* 112 An early, light, and nutritive supper would greatly benefit the trainee. **1850** *Fraser's Mag.* XLI. 658 The trainers first double up one of his fore legs, which they bind fast with a cord; this they pull, and thus compel the trainee to come down upon his bent knee. **1861** *Temple Bar Mag.* IV. 58 The trainee is rubbed down dry. **1885** *Daily News* 16 Dec. 6/1 Let her..ask whether she could be admitted as a lady pupil, as a trainee. **1927** *Daily Tel.* 8 Feb. 13/7 The number of new trainees is now so small that a workshop smaller than that which we are now using will suffice. **1932** *Sun* (Baltimore) 19 July 15/6 (*heading*) Trainees at Meade using machine guns. **1942** *Yank* 4 Nov. 11 Basic trainees beat the softball pitching. **1951** *Good Housek. Home Encycl.* 37/1 The majority of nursery training schools do not make any hard-and-fast rule regarding the work which their trainees should take over. **1953** *Manch. Guardian Weekly* 6 Aug. 7/3 A rice paddy..through which trainee squads are sent, as on a Korean patrol. **1956** *B.B.C. Handbk.* 1957 138 Sixteen trainee broadcasters. **1962** *Lancet* 1 Dec. 1156/2 The trainee assistant scheme is on the right lines, but there have been complaints that the scheme has occasionally been abused by trainers who used their trainees as ordinary assistants. **1977** *Grimsby Even. Tel.* 31 May 5/7 Miss Sally Dixon, a trainee nurse, was announced as the hospital's Jubilee representative following a ballot. **1978** *West Lancs. Even. Gaz.* 23 Feb. 17 (Advt.), Vacancies for able young persons as trainees.

Hence **traiˈneeship**, the position of a trainee, a post as a trainee.

1961 *Listener* 14 Dec. 1021/2 Some management traineeship schemes in industry and commerce. **1964** *New Statesman* 13 Nov. 747/1 Bourgeois and ambitious parents ..thrust their sons into low-paid traineeships with prospects of eventual power and wealth. **1966** *Rep. Comm. Inquiry Univ. Oxf.* II. 193 The category 'other' includes general traineeships and postgraduate apprenticeships. **1980** *Nature* 14 Feb. 610/1 The universities hope that the administration can be persuaded to contribute more than $150 million..to provide a national support programme of grants, traineeships and fellowships.

†ˈ**trainel**, *sb. Obs.* Forms: 3–5 **traynelle**, 4 **traynel(e**, 6–7 **trainel**; 6–7 **tranell**, 7 **trannell.** [a. OF. *trainel* (13th c. in Godef.), a trammel or hobble for a horse, a fishing-net (14th c. in Littré).]

(In some cases a graphical confusion between *trainel* and *tramel* seems possible.)

1. Some part of a horse's harness; perh. a hobble or trammel.

1284 *Acc. Exch. K.R.* Bd. 97 No. 3 (P.R.O.) Pro cordis emptis..ad Traynell[is] et Loygnes factis pro eisdem [equis]. *Ibid.* m. 4 Pro loynes et traynellis. *c* **1341** *Durham Acc. Rolls* (Surtees) 541 In Traynels factis pro equis domini Prioris, viij d. In j traynel emp. pro equo Bursarii, iiij d. **1467** *Mann. & Househ. Exp.* (Roxb.) 389 Smythe the sadelere..axsethe for..a new traynelle, viij.d.

2. A drag-net. Also *trainel-net.*

1585 HIGINS *Junius' Nomencl.* 256/1 *Tragula*..*Traineau*, a trainel or drag net. **1601** HOLLAND *Pliny* XVI. viii. I. 461 Much use there is of it [cork]..for flotes to trainels or drag-nets. **1620** J. WILKINSON *Courts Leet* 122 No man ought to fish..but with such Nette or trannell as everie meash shall be two and a halfe inches wide. **1706** PHILLIPS (ed. Kersey), *Trainel-Net*, *Tramel* or *Trammel*, a Drag-Net.

Hence †ˈ**trainel** *v. Obs.*, *intr.* to practise bird-catching with a drag-net (const. *for*).

1530 PALSGR. 586/1, I hoble, I tranell for larkes, *je tremaille*. *Ibid.* 760/2, I tranell for larkes, *je trainelle*. **1676** MARVELL *Mr. Smirke* 37 If a man went out by night on Tranelling, or Bat-fowling.

trainer (ˈtreɪnə(r)). [f. TRAIN *v.*¹ + -ER¹.] One who or that which trains.

1. a. A person who (or thing that) educates or instructs; one who puts a person (or animal) through a course of training and exercise with a view to proficiency in something; an instructor; *spec.* †(*a*) one who trains or drills soldiers, a drill-sergeant (*obs.*); (*b*) one who trains persons or animals for some athletic performance, as a race; *spec.* one who trains race-horses. (Also with *up*.) Also *attrib.*

1598 BARRET *Theor. Warres* I. i. 6 The trayning of men.. done..by such sufficient Trayners. **1659** H. MORE *Immort. Soul* III. xvii. §5. 508 As the basest men are the trainers up of the best sort of Dogs. **1812** *Sporting Mag.* XXXIX. 99 Mr. Price trainer at Newmarket. **1861** PALEY *Æschylus, Agam.* 1599 *note*, Imprisonment and the pangs of hunger are first-rate trainers of the mind for teaching even old age. **1891** S. MOSTYN *Curatica* 45, I took lessons in elocution... I cannot leave this part of my story without pausing to do honour to my trainer.

attrib. **1973** *Philadelphia Inquirer* 7 Oct. 13 (Advt.), Convertible or girls sidewalk bike. Trainer wheels included. **1976** *Milton Keynes Express* 2 July 25/1 (Advt.), Baby walker, babycare bath mat and toddler trainer seat £2, or will sell separately. **1977** *Austral. Sailing* Jan. 46/1 For the very young, the best way into sailing is through a sailing club in a trainer class like the Sabot or Manly Junior.

b. A member of a trainband, esp. when assembled for 'training' or drill; a militiaman. (In later use *U.S.*)

1581–2 *Churchw. Acc. E. Budleigh* (ed. Brushfield) 19 Pd ..for makinge clean of the Caliuers for the trayners, xvjᵈ. **18..** *Mrs. Clavers' Western Clearings* 28 (Bartlett) The gentler sex partake..in the excitement, by running after the trainers. **1860** BARTLETT *Dict. Amer.*, *Trainers*, the militia when assembled for exercise.

c. An aircraft used in training pilots or other aircrew.

1932 AUDEN *Orators* II. 59, 1 Moth trainer fully equipped for advanced training. **1950** *Hansard Commons* 21 Mar. 1771 The introduction of the Prentice as the basic trainer has enabled instrument flying instruction to be improved considerably. **1977** 'J. LE CARRÉ' *Honourable Schoolboy* xvi. 368 A row of single-engined military trainers.

d. A soft running shoe without spikes; a training shoe.

1978 *Guardian* 22 Dec. 9/3 The Poynton Jemmers, a women's morris dance side..are in mufti tonight... But no trainers or pumps: it's clogs or nothing. **1982** *New Society* 4 Mar. 344/2 Skinny teenage boys in the ubiquitous parkas, jeans and trainers. **1983** *Listener* 28 July 19/1 Dr. Garrow is welcome to don trainers and join the ladies I run with on Saturdays.

2. †**a.** One who draws or drags. *Obs.* **b.** A string used in describing a circle. *rare*$^{-1}$.

1648-60 HEXHAM, *Een Sleyper*, a Trainer, or a Dragger. *Een Sleyperesse*, a Traineresse or a Draggeresse. **1854** H. MILLER *Sch. & Schm.* xxi. (1858) 459 There occurred on the ..sand, around decaying tufts of the bent-grass, deeply-marked circles, as if drawn by a pair of compasses or a trainer.

3. A frame upon which plants are trained. *rare*$^{-0}$.

1882 in OGILVIE (Annandale).

4. *Comb.*, as ***trainer-like*** adj.

1836-48 B. D. WALSH *Aristoph., Knights* I. iii, That's a good trainer-like remark.

Hence †**'traineress** [-ESS^1]. *Obs. rare*$^{-0}$.

1648-60 [see 2].

trainful ('treɪnfʊl). [f. TRAIN *sb.*^{1} + -FUL.] As much or as many (goods or passengers) as fill a railway train.

1866 G. O. TREVELYAN in *Macm. Mag.* Mar. 408 At Peschiera, the whole trainful—passengers, guards, and firemen—were forced to alight,..our luggage was opened and emptied. **1885** *19th Cent.* Apr. 635 A trainful of troops.

'train-guard. [f. TRAIN *sb.*^{1}, in various senses + GUARD *sb.*] †**a.** A train of attendants forming a guard. †**b.** A body of men in charge of the train of an army. **c.** The guard of a railway train.

1650 FULLER *Pisgah* IV. v. §32 Pharaohs daughter with her feminine train-guard. **1760** *MS. Audit Office* (Bodl.) 281/125. 7d, Major Oughton and others for the Train Guard at the Battle of Culloden. **1897** *Pall Mall G.* 19 May 4/2 [In Denmark] The all-pervading militarism..of Germany has disappeared; the train-guard is no longer an exaggerated drill-sergeant.

training ('treɪnɪŋ), *vbl. sb.* [f. TRAIN *v.*^{1} + -ING^1.] The action of TRAIN *v.*^{1}, in various senses.

†**1.** Drawing, trailing; drawing out, protracting, etc. *Obs.*

c **1440** *Promp. Parv.* 499/2 Tranyynge, or longe a-bydynge (*S.* trancyynge), *dilacio, mora.* **1539** CROMWELL in Merriman *Life & Lett.* (1902) II. 182 The coldnes on that behalf & traynyng long of the matiers might helpe to conferme the said Counsaillours advises.

2. a. Discipline and instruction directed to the development of powers or formation of character; education, rearing, bringing up; systematic instruction and exercise in some art, profession, or occupation, with a view to proficiency in it; also, of an animal: see quots. 1697, 1874.

1548 UDALL *Erasm. Par. Luke* v. 61 b, In those thynges whiche concerne the bodye,..my trainyng of theim is somewhat with fauour and ientilnesse: but in such matiers as perteine to ye solle, it is a great waie streighter and sharper. **1600** J. PORY tr. *Leo's Africa* III. 148 Schooles..freely bestowed for the training vp of youth. **1697** DRYDEN *Virg. Georg.* III. 321 When once he's broken, feed him full and high..Before his Training keep him poor and low. **1757** FOOTE *Author* I. Wks. 1799 I. 138 He's now in training as a waiter at the Cocoa-tree coffee-house. **1874** CARPENTER *Ment. Phys.* I. i. §24 (1879) 24 The process by which a Horse is taught any unusual performance—as when in 'training' for the Circus or the Stage. **1879** J. T. ROGERS in *Cassell's Techn. Educ.* IV. 53/2 It would be absurd to assign the genius of Mozart to training.

b. *spec.* Military drill; *esp.* in former use, a public meeting or muster at a stated time for drill of militia and volunteer forces; subsequently much used for the periodical camp work of the Territorials.

1578 *Nottingham Rec.* IV. 179 Soldyours trayned with the Kallyver, thys Trayning beyng the 2 of October. **1581** STYWARD (*title*) The Pathwaie to Martiall Discipline, deuided into two Bookes... The Second Booke Entreateth of sundrie proportions and training of Caleeuers. **1598** BARRET *Theor. Warres* I. i. 5 Our countrie Gentlemen and Citizens, who haue the trayning of their shires and townes. **1616** I. T. *ABC of Armes* Avj b, In time of Musters or Traynings. **1748** *Anson's Voy.* III. viii. 375 The training of land troops to the use of their arms. **1845** S. JUDD *Margaret* I. xv, Hash,..at the Spring training, was punished..for disorderly behaviour.

c. The process of developing the bodily vigour and endurance by systematic diet and exercise, so as to fit for some athletic feat; the condition of undergoing this process, or of the resulting physical fitness.

1786 W. COWPER *Let.* 1 May (1981) II. 531 When you come, I shall talk you into training, as the jockeys say, I doubt not that I shall make a nimble and good walker of you in a short time. **1835-6** *Todd's Cycl. Anat.* I. 510/1 By what in England is called training the bulk of the body may be.. rapidly diminished. **1854** DICKENS *Hard T.* I. ii, A professed pugilist; always in training. **1871** L. STEPHEN *Playgr. Eur.* x. (1894) 234, I was in good training.

3. Management (of a plant, etc.) esp. so as to produce the desired form or manner of a growth.

1724 (*title*) A Treatise concerning the Manner of Fallowing of Ground, Raising of Grass-Seeds, and Training of Lint and Hemp. **1871** (*title*) Figure Training. **1888** *Nicholson's Dict. Gard., Training..*, as used in gardening, refers to the management of trees and plants..by regulating their branches to give all a fair amount of space and exposure to light... Also..so as to prevent the sap flowing to any one branch or part..at the expense of another.

4. The action of directing or aiming a fire-arm, etc., esp. by horizontal movement.

1861 *Times* 23 July, The horizontal motion, or training, is effected by turning the shield itself, with the gun, crew, and platform on which they stand. **1870** *Daily News* 1 Feb., Where the fault lies is in bad training of the gun on to the object intended to be aimed at. **1885** *Pall Mall G.* 6 Jan. 2/2 Two [sights] being necessary for correct pointing at certain angles of training.

5. *attrib.* and *Comb.* (chiefly in sense 2), as ***training camp, centre, department, -groom, -ground, -home, -place, prison, programme, session, shoe, -stable, -time***; **training-bank**, a bank constructed to deflect or direct a current (cf. *training-wall* below); **training-bit**, a special kind of bit used in training a vicious horse; **training-college**, a college for training persons for some particular profession; *spec.* a college for training teachers: cf. *training-school* below; **training-day**, a day devoted to training; *spec.* in former use, a stated or legally appointed day for the drilling of militia and volunteer forces; **training-halter**, a form of halter used in training horses: see quot.; **training-level**, a level (LEVEL *sb.* 1) used in training a gun; **training-pendulum**, a form of training-level with a pendulum; **training-post**, a post used in directing a current into a particular channel (cf. *training-bank, -wall*); **training-school**, a school in which pupils are trained for some special profession or occupation; *spec.* (*a*) a school for training teachers, a normal school; (*b*) *N. Amer.*, a vocational institution for juvenile delinquents; **training-ship, -vessel**, a ship on which boys are trained for naval service; **training-wall**, a wall built to direct a current into the desired channel in a river, harbour, etc.

1911 *United Empire* July 489 Two moles and a *training bank are being constructed. **1877** KNIGHT *Dict. Mech.*, **Training-bit*, a wooden gag-bit used when training vicious horses. The cheeks are of iron, and are connected by a rod ..which passes through the wooden mouth-piece, having a head upon one end and a nut on the other. **1894** T. B. ALDRICH *Two Bites at Cherry* 216, I don't fancy he heard a gun fired, unless it went off by accident in some *training-camp for recruits. **1980** *Washington Star* 10 Dec. c6, I felt like a rookie again in training camp. **1926** *Encycl. Brit.* Suppl. III. 819/2 (*heading*) War *training centers. **1962** E. SNOW *Other Side of River* (1963) lxxi. 549 Shanghai and Manchuria have been the biggest training centers for China's modernization. **1829** [**Training College* was in use in Ireland]. **1882** OGILVIE, *Normal school*..a school in which teachers are instructed in the principles of their profession and trained in the practice of it; a training-college. **1884** S. E. DAWSON *Handbk. Canada* 211 A theological training-college for priests. **1901** *Contemp. Rev.* Mar. 361 For years the supply of teachers exceeded the demand; now it is the other way, or soon will be, and that is one of the factors in the training college problem. **1676** WYCHERLEY *Pl. Dealer* II. i, As he passed by my window the last *training-day. **1880** MRS. ROLLINS *New Eng. Bygones* 56 This muster, or 'training-day',..when the militia was drilled in a vacant lot of some fortunate town. **1906** *Rep. Brit. Assoc. Adv. Sci.* 271 To take a course of training in some existing training college or *training department. **1706** S. SEWALL *Diary* 27 May, Col. Noyes invites me to his *Training Dinner. **1816** *Sporting Mag.* XLVIII. 172 The defendant, a *training-groom to the Duke of Dorset. **1644** in *Early Rec. Dedham, Mass.* (1892) III. 102 From the *Trayning ground to the Cart Bridge. **1864** BOWEN *Logic* xiii. 450 To make them [the sciences] only the training-ground, and not the field for the regular employment, of their mental powers. **1871** 'M. LEGRAND' *Camb. Freshm.* xi, Newmarket Heath..is very little changed... The features of this matchless racecourse and training-ground remain pretty much the same. **1877** KNIGHT *Dict. Mech.*, **Training-halter*, a halter made in the same manner as a riding-bridle, with the exception of having short instead of long cheeks, which are provided with rings into which bit-straps may be buckled. **1905** *Westm. Gaz.* 3 Feb. 4/1 To avoid anything approaching institution or *training-home life. **1904** *Daily Chron.* 9 Feb. 3/3 In 1880 the Women's Training Home was established at Clapton and placed under the charge of Emma Booth... She was equal to the task, and well deserved the loving name of the 'Training Home mother'. **1867** SMYTH *Sailor's Word-bk.*, **Training-level*, a gravitating instrument for the same purpose as the training-pendulum. *Ibid.*, **Training-pendulum*, an improved pendulum to facilitate the accurate elevation and depression of guns on board ship. **1884** J. TAIT *Mind in Matter* (1892) 138 A world fitted to be the temporary abode and *training-place of spirits. **1884** *Pall Mall G.* 9 Dec. 12/1 Opening up a deep channel by the use of *training posts and the judicious use of dredging. **1950** *Training prison [see OPEN *a.* 2 d]. **1977** *Herald* (Melbourne) 17 Jan. 2/6 The prisoners were transferred after a security review at country jails following four escapes from Geelong Training Prison in a week last month. **1971** L. B. JOHNSON *Vantage Point* (1972) iv. 81 Our manpower *training programs focused on preparing unskilled men and women for jobs. **1977** *Offshore Engineer* June 36/1 Pilots are selected from employees who show diving aptitude with a full mechanical understanding, and are put through a rigorous training programme. [**1814** *Brit. & For. School Soc., Bye Laws*, The school for children at the Borough Road, and the school for training of schoolmasters.] **1829** *Kildare Place Soc., Rep.*, To draw the attention of the public to these *Training Schools. **1897** GRENFELL & HUNT *New Classical Fragm.*, etc. lxvii. 101 Aurelius Asclepiades.. agrees to hire from Aurelius Theon, the keeper of a training-school, probably at Arsinoe, the services of two dancing-girls. **1905** *First Ann. Rep. N.Y. State Training School for Girls* 4 The Penal Code was amended..so as to authorize the commitment of delinquent girls under the age of sixteen.. to the New York State Training School for Girls. **1978** *Globe & Mail* (Toronto) 11 Jan. 7/3 If training schools are closed, then some group homes will have to have a custodial aspect. **1951** *Sport* 6-12 Apr. 12/2 Most clubs have selected their spot-kicker after careful tests during *training sessions. **1977** J. M. JOHNSON in Douglas & Johnson *Existential Sociol.* viii. 242 A worker in Unit One said she had decided to record her time spent in training sessions on line C of the report. **1905** *Daily Chron.* 28 Apr. 7/5 In the 'danger' passage, between the two *training shafts of the fore barbette. *c* **1860** H. STUART *Seaman's Catech.* 85 These men were never on board a ship before joining the *training ship. **1899** CROCKETT *Kit Kennedy* xxi. 145, I would have placed him [a boy] on a training ship and looked after him there. **1973** *People's Jrnl.* (Inverness) 4 Aug. 20/2 (Advt.), *Training shoes. **1984** *Nutshell* (Gainesville, Florida) Spring 61/1 (Advt.), A remarkable new training shoe designed to take all the wear and tear high-mileage runners can give it. **1894** DOYLE *Mem. S. Holmes* 5 Where the Colonel's *training stable is situated. **1879** MCCARTHY *Own Times* II. xxviii. 349 The campaign had..only been a *training time for us. **1887** *Pall Mall G.* 25 Mar. 5/1 The French torpedo-boats fire bow torpedoes, whereas in our own boats the Whiteheads are shot from a *training-tube. **1908** *Month* Mar. 238 Large *training-vessels. **1883** *Specif. Alnwick & Cornhill Railw.* 43 The *training-walls are to be built of concrete, made of six parts of gravel to one of Portland cement.

training ('treɪnɪŋ), *ppl. a.* [f. as prec. (or from TRAIN *v.*^{2}) + -ING^2.] That trains, in various senses.

†**1.** Drawing; *fig.* attracting, alluring, enticing.

1557 in *Tottell's Misc.* (Arb.) 202 Then finenesse thought by trainyng talke to win that beauty lost. **1567** TURBERV. *Poems* 52 Force not hir traynyng truthlesse eies, but turne thy face away. **1590** C'TESS PEMBROKE *Antonie* 720 Th' enchaunting skilles Of her caelestiall Sp'rite, hir training speache.

†**2.** Tracking, pursuing. *Obs.*

1583 MELBANCKE *Philotimus* F fj, Diana in her trayninge chase delightes.

3. Having a train, trailing. Now *rare.*

1737 SAVAGE *Public Spirit* 7 The Tragic charms the Age; In solemn training Robes she fills the Stage. **1773** N. HOOKE *Rom. Hist.* (1830) I. 6 *note*, Ceres was represented..with a long training robe. **1827** MISS ROBERTS in *Lit. Souvenir* 147 The long training gowns, and flowing head-dresses.

trainless ('treɪnlɪs), *a.* [f. TRAIN *sb.*^{1} + -LESS.]

1. Having no train; devoid of a train (as a robe, a meteor, a peacock).

1868 LOCKYER *Elem. Astron.* xxiv. §305. 132 There was a region in which the meteors appeared trainless,..because they were directly approaching us. **1873** *Daily News* 7 Nov. 5/4 Priests whose trainless gowns showed they belonged to the order of Jesuits. **1904** *Ibid.* 21 Nov. 4 The peacock..that less than a month ago was a dowdy, trainless bird, has grown a 'tail' of bewildering beauty.

2. Devoid of (railway) trains; on which no trains are running.

1859 KINGSLEY *Misc., Agric. Crisis* II. 195 The money will be..surely in a better place than..in repudiated loans and trainless railroads. **1900** *Westm. Gaz.* 25 Aug. 4/3 Only two [railway] systems are now trainless.

'trainman, train man. Also with hyphen. [f. TRAIN *sb.*^{1} (or *v.*^{1}) + MAN *sb.*^{1}]

†**1.** A man belonging to a trainband. *Obs.*

1654 H. L'ESTRANGE *Chas. I* (1655) 106 The Lord Mayor ..and the Sheriffs with a band of Train men, came down and made Proclamation.

2. A railway servant employed on a train; *spec.* (see quot. 1982). orig. *U.S.*

1877 J. D. MCCABE *Hist. Great Riots* 48 These motives have been misunderstood, and..produced the present troubles amongst our trainmen. **1881** *Chicago Times* 30 Apr., All train men..now in employment on the road. **1897** KIPLING *Captains Courageous* 205 Old stories of the railroad that every trainman knows. **1960** [see SHOPMAN 3]. **1964** [see *secondman* s.v. SECOND *a.* 7 a]. **1967** *Guardian* 4 Dec. 1/3 British Rail's intention is to replace them [*sc.* firemen and guards] by a new type of railwayman—a 'trainman'. **1982** *Daily Tel.* 19 June 2/7 The six productivity concessions.. include..the introduction of 'train men' to combine the duties of guards and travelling ticket inspectors.

†**'trainment.** *Obs. rare.* [f. TRAIN *v.*^{1} + -MENT.] An action or process of training.

1571 GOLDING *Calvin on Ps.* xxxii. 4. 119 So far unsufficient were the traynementes wherwith he had bin instructed. **1583** —— *Calvin on Deut.* c. 615 The feast of Tabernacles was a traynment to the people of Israell. **1592** G. HARVEY *Four Lett.* iv. Wks. (Gr.) I. 229 That pretious Trainement is miserably abused, which should be the fountaine of skill.

'train 'oil, 'train-oil. [f. TRAIN *sb.*^{3} + OIL.] Oil obtained by boiling from the blubber of whales, esp. of the right whale; formerly also applied to that obtained from seals, and from various fishes.

c **1553** CHANCELOUR in Hakluyt *Voy.* (1886) III. 40 They haue much oyle which wee call treine oyle. **1591** G. FLETCHER *Russe Commw.* (Hakl. Soc.) 11 An other.. principall commoditie is their trane oyle, drawen out of the seal fish. **1661** LOVELL *Hist. Anim. & Min.* 229 Of the fat [of the tunny] is made Traine-oile for Clothiers. **1712** A. VAN LEEUWENHOEK in *Phil. Trans.* XXVII. 446 The Fat of a Whale,..out of which we boil the Train-Oyl. **1823** J. BADCOCK *Dom. Amusem.* 151 Soft Soap is made of train oil and a little tallow. **1865** PARKMAN *Champlain* ii. (1875) 210 Seeking..the more modest gains of codfish and train-oil.

attrib. **1842** BROWNING *Pied Piper* vii, A drawing the corks of train-oil-flasks. **1865** G. MACDONALD *A. Forbes* 18 Candles or train-oil lamps were burning in most..houses.

† **'train-scent.** *Obs.* Also -sent, -cent: see SCENT *sb.* [f. TRAIN *sb.*^{1} 7 or *v.*^{1} 1 + SCENT *sb.*] Something 'trained' or dragged along the ground to make a scent for hounds to follow (= TRAIN *sb.*^{1} 7); the sport of exercising hounds and horses by means of this (usu. in phr. ***to hunt*** or ***run a train-scent***).

1603 T. M. *Progr. Jas. I*, E iij, There was prouided train-cents, and liue haires in baskets, being carried to the heath, that made excellent sport for his Maiestie. **1638** BROME *Antipodes* I. vi, They hunt trayne-sents with Oxen, and plow with Dogges. **1681** *Lond. Gaz.* No. 1608/4 There will be also a Plate given for Hounds running a Train-scent of four Miles. **1686** N. COX *Gentl. Recreat.* IV. (ed. 2) 93 Be careful to preserve his Speed till the last Train-scent.

† **train soldier.** *Obs. rare.* A soldier belonging to a trainband or the militia, and not forming part of the standing army.

1630 *R. Johnson's Kingd. & Commw.* 329 The Garrison Souldier hath one and twenty shillings a moneth, the traine Souldier nothing. **1644** PRYNNE & WALKER *Fiennes' Trial* App. 25, I William Deane of the City of Bristoll, Baker, lately one of the Traine Souldiers there.

'train-spotter. [TRAIN *sb.*^{1} 16.] One (esp. a small boy) whose hobby is observing trains and recording railway locomotive numbers. Hence **'train-spotting** *vbl. sb.*; **'train-spot** *v. intr.*

1958 *Spectator* 11 July 70/3 A prize of six guineas is offered for a Train Spotters' Anthem. *Ibid.* 1 Aug. 179/1 Many of them must simply spend their time train-spotting. **1959** *Manch. Guardian* 22 July 2/6 British Railways.. announced a ban on train-spotting..on about twelve main-line stations. **1969** *Times* 1 Nov. (Saturday Rev. Suppl.) p. iii/4 A train-spotting recluse, primed with exact information on lines that have rusted into the ground. **1974** P. McCUTCHAN *Coach North* ii. 15 'I reckon you're all past train spotting.'.. The old man didn't look as though he'd ever train spotted. **1978** D. WILLIAMS *Treasure up in Smoke* xiv. 126 The Governor appeared to have graduated from train-spotter to Lord Protector in one short morning.

'trainster. = TRAINMAN 2.

1893 *Daily Graphic* 25 Nov. 18 He worked as trainster on a new railway track some way out of town.

† **'trainy,** *a. Obs. rare*$^{-1}$. [f. TRAIN *sb.*^{3} + -Y.] Having the quality of 'train' or train-oil.

1714 GAY *Trivia* II. 252 And where huge hogsheads sweat with trainy oil; Thy breathing nostril hold.

traipse, trapes (treɪps), *sb. colloq.* and *dial.* Also 9 **trapse.** [Goes with TRAIPSE *v.*, but of later appearance.]

1. An opprobrious name for a woman or girl slovenly in person or habits; 'a dangling slattern'.

1676 *Poor Robin's Intell.* 11–18 Apr. 2/2 A lazy trapes that cares not how late she sits up, nor how long she lies in the morning. **1678** BUTLER *Hud.* III. II. 471 He found the sullen Trapes Possest with th' Devil, Worms, and Claps. *a* **1700** B. E. *Dict. Cant. Crew, Trapes*, a dangling Slattern. **1714** GAY *What d'ye call it* I. i, From Door to Door I'd sooner whine and beg,..Than marry such a Trapes. **1780** H. WALPOLE *Let. to Mason* 31 Aug., There was a trapes of a housekeeper. **1811** *Ora & Juliet* IV. 191 You and your dirty trapes. **1905** *Eng. Dial. Dict.* [cited from Lancash., Yorks. to Essex, Somerset].

2. An act or course of 'traipsing'; a tiresome or disagreeable tramp.

1862 MRS. H. WOOD *Channings* (1866) 471 It's such a toil and a trapes up them two pair of stairs. **1866** MRS. LYNN LINTON *Liz. Lort.* I. xiii. 302 He..asked if the ladies would like to go down the mine?..his lass shouldn't go through such a trapse. **1887** T. HARDY *Woodlanders* xlviii, Leading folk a twelve mile traipse. **1893** COUCH *Delectable Duchy* 196 A brave trapse all the way from Upper Woon.

traipse, trapes (treɪps), *v. colloq.* Also 8–9 *dial.* **trapse,** 9 **traaps; traapess, trapas, trapass, trapess, trapez, trapus, traipass, traipess, traaypess,** etc. [Known *a* 1600. Formerly usu. *trapes*, and evidently related to TRAPE *v.*, but the nature of their relation is not clear. In literary use, the spelling *traipse* and Pope's metrical use show the word as a monosyllable; but many modern dialects have it as two syllables.

If *trappe c* 1400 really belongs to TRAPE *v.*, that would appear to be the earliest word of the group, although *trapes* as vb. would be a deriv. of unusual form; but if not, *trapesing* of 1593 would be the earliest form recorded. The dialect forms *trapass, traipass* strongly recall OF. *trapasser, trapesser, trepasser* (still in Cotgr.), to pass over or beyond (see TRESPASS *v.*), though the senses do not exactly fit.]

1. a. *intr.* To walk in a trailing or untidy way; e.g. to walk or 'trail' through the mud; to walk with the dress trailing or bedraggled; to walk about aimlessly or needlessly. (Usually said of a woman or child.) Also in gen. use, to tramp or trudge, to go about.

1593 [see TRAIPSING *vbl. sb.*]. **1647** in *Verney Mem.* (1907) I. 368 What soever wether comes I must goe trapesing a foote to yᵉ end of yᵉ lane. **1710** SWIFT *Jrnl. to Stella* 13 Dec., I am to go trapesing with Lady Kerry and Mrs. Pratt to see sights all this day. **1710–11** *Ibid.* 2 Mar., I was traipsing to-day with your Mr. Sterne. **1728** (ed. 1) POPE *Dunc.* III. 141 See next two slip-shod Muses traipse along. **1732** SIR C. WOGAN *Let. to Swift* 27 Feb., Ireland is left to trapes in her old draggle-tailed weeds by her own children. **1742** MRS. DELANY in *Life & Corr.* (1861) II. 189 We trapesed all over Babylon garden. **1824** MRS. CAMERON *Pink Tippet* II. 25, I would not go trapsing to school as she does. **1864** MRS. GASKELL *Wives & Dau.* ii, I've been out for these three hours trapesing about the grounds till I'm as tired as can be. **1869** *Punch* 16 Oct. 154/1 Draggletails trapseing along the street. **1884** L. F. ALLEN *New Amer. Farm-Bk.* 313 The frog, traipsing over the dewy fields. **1892** G. H. BILLINGTON in *Times* 1 Jan. 11/3, I only wish the children of the members of the Board..had to traipse a mile and a half to school. **1926** A. HUXLEY *Let.* 4 Mar. (1969) 268, I don't want to spend unnecessarily on traipsing round the continent. **1968** V. S. PRITCHETT *Cab at Door* xii. 238, I traipsed for a year from one paint shop to the next round Paris, selling glue, shellac and, for a hungry period, ostrich feathers and theatre tickets. **1976** *National Observer* (U.S.) 9 Oct. 5/4, I spent one day traipsing after Thomson, but his limousine disappeared at very high speed over a hill and by the time my rented sedan got to the other side he had disappeared. **1978** R. V. JONES *Most Secret War* xix. 159 For days we had to traipse for water down six flights of stairs and hundreds of yards to a stand pipe in the road.

b. To trail along the ground; to hang untidily.

1774 FOOTE *Cozeners* III. Wks. 1799 II. 184 These..skirts of the boy's are so light and genteel..: those we got made in the country trapes and dangle like a parcel of petticoats. **1887** *S. Cheshire Gloss.* s.v., Ah dait [= I doubt] it'll trapes, if yo han it made so long.

2. a. *trans.* To walk or tramp over; to tread, tramp (the fields, streets, etc.). *dial.*

1885 HALL CAINE *Shadow of Crime* xxiii, It's bad weather to trapes the fells. **1901** D. C. MURRAY *Ch. Humanity* v. 80 If you're to begin trapesing the streets again without a farthing in your pocket. **1902** *Monthly Rev.* Aug. 181 I'll gar you trapse the stone-floor bare-fit!

b. To tread (a dance) in a trailing way. *rare.*

1835 *Clouds of Aristophanes* ii. in *Blackw. Mag.* Oct. 526 She's not appearing Drest out Like the rest in filthy guise.. nor trapesing [*printed* trapering] forth a dirty minuet.

c. Causatively: to carry or take about in a trailing way.

1814 H. CAPEL *Let.* July (1955) 53 St. Francis, the tutelary Saint of Brussels who had been previously trapsed round the town with the most astonishing pomp & splendour. *a* **1974** R. CROSSMAN *Diaries* (1976) II. 399 Suddenly I saw a picture of the tiny little woman looking upwards and seeing the soles of the feet of the statues above her as she was traipsed miles and miles around on the red carpet.

Hence **traipsed** *ppl. a.*, trampled, bedraggled.

1884 G. H. BOUGHTON in *Harper's Mag.* Oct. 706/2 The town..looked messy and 'traipsed'. **1887** *S. Cheshire Gloss.* s.v., A woman with dirty garments was called 'a poor, trapes't thing'.

traipsing, trapesing ('treɪpsɪŋ), *vbl. sb.* [f. prec. + -ING^1.] The action of the verb TRAIPSE.

1593 BILSON *Govt. Christ's Ch.* xiv. 296 This t[r]apesing to and fro I impute rather to the rawnesse of your discipline ..This it is to wander in the desert of your owne deuises without the line of Gods worde, or leuell of his Church to direct you. **1800** MAR. EDGEWORTH *Out of Debt* i, Anything's better than trapesing through a shop. **1887** 'H. SMART' *Cleverly Won* vii, If she thought trapesing about with the hounds was the way to get married, she was mistaken. **1895** T. HARDY *Jude* III. ii, The traipsing along to the station, the porter's 'B'your leave!' the screaming of the trains.

'traipsing, 'trapesing, *ppl. a.* [f. as prec. + -ING^2.] That traipses; going about in a slovenly manner.

1760 FOOTE *Minor* I. Wks. 1799 I. 244 One armful of good wholesome British beauty, is worth a ship-load of their trapsing, tawdry trollops. **1773** GOLDSM. *Stoops to Conq.* I. ii, The daughter, a tall trapesing trolloping, talkative may-pole. **1886** HALL CAINE *Son of Hagar* I. vii, Beneath the traipseing feet of the people.

trais, obs. form of TRACE.

† **traise, traish,** *v. Obs.* Forms: α. 4 trais, trayse; *pa. pple.* 4 **traised, traijst, traist, y-treyst,** (**traysted**), 6 *Sc.* **trasit.** β. 4 **traysch,** 5 **trays(s)hen, traisshe, tras(s)he, trahysh;** *pa. pple.* 4 **trayshed, trayscht,** etc. [f. F. *traïss-, trahiss-*, lengthened stem of *trahir* to betray: see TRAY *v.*, and cf. BETRAISE *v.*] *trans.* To betray.

α. *a* **1300** *Cursor M.* 15497 Þou sal be traijst lauerd, to night. *Ibid.* 20042 Ur lauerd crist deied on rode and was traist. **13..** *Guy Warw.* (A.) 2517 He seyd, y-treyst we ben here. **1320–40** *Chron. Eng.* (Ritson) 830 Tho come the traitours..That heden traised Edmond. *c* **1330** R. BRUNNE *Chron.* (1810) 61 Machog, þe Scottes kyng, þat wild þorgh traitourie Haf traised Edward þe kyng. *c* **1350** *Will. Palerne* 2075 Has þat vntrewe treytour traysted me nouþe. *a* **1352** MINOT *Poems* vii. 150 þat daunce with treson was begun, To trais þe bare with sum fals gyn. *a* **1375** *Joseph Arim.* 624, I wol þe nout trayse. **1513** DOUGLAS *Æneis* IX. iv. 8 Drawbriggis befoir the ȝettis vprasit Junct to the wallis, at thai suld nocht be trasit.

β. *c* **1330** R. BRUNNE *Chron. Wace* (Rolls) 5459 Wyst our folk we were þus trayscht [*v.r.* traist], Hit scholde make þem alle abayscht. *c* **1400** *Rom. Rose* 3231 She hath [thee] trasshed, withoute ween. **1412–20** LYDG. *Chron. Troy* IV. 4562 To traisshe her toun þei hild it no repref. *c* **1489** CAXTON *Blanchardyn* xlvi. 178 The good lady thenne hering the cursed and false traytours speke, saw wel that she was trahyshed of all poyntes.

traise, obs. form of TRACE.

† **traisement.** *Obs. rare*$^{-1}$. [a. OF. *traïssement*, f. *trahir*: see TRAISE and -MENT.] Betrayal, treachery.

c **1380** *Sir Ferumb.* 4754 Godes for-bode..þat ich assentede to such a dede, To don hym such traysement.

traish, var. TRAISE *Obs.*; obs. f. TRASH.

traisle, -il, obs. Sc. forms of TRESTLE.

traison, obs. f. TREASON.

traiss, obs. Sc. f. TRACE.

traisse, obs. f. TRASH.

† **traist,** *sb. Sc.* and *north. Obs.* Forms: 4–6 **traiste,** 5 **trayste, treyst, trast,** 5–7 **traist.** [app. a. ON. **trøysti*, **treysti* (mod. Norw. dial. *trøyste* strengthening, strength, firmness), related to ON. *traust* sb., firmness, confidence, security, safety, trust, and to ON. *treysta, trøysta*, TRAIST *v.* Cf. Gothic *trausti* covenant. Cognate with TRUST, TREST, TRIST *sbs.*] Confidence, trust; assurance felt, received, or given.

c **1340** HAMPOLE *Prose Tr.* 18 Puttande all his traiste and his desyre in hym [Ihesu]. *a* **1400** *Relig. Pieces fr. Thornton MS.* (1867) 27 Þat we hafe trayste to com thedyre. *c* **1400** *Apol. Loll.* 96 Sum tyme man is holpun bi treyst þat he haþ in o þing. **1456** SIR G. HAYE *Law Arms* (S.T.S.) 179 He wald geve lytill traist in that sauf condyt. *c* **1500** *Lancelot* 1536 To wer on them In trast of victory. **1513** JAS. IV. *Let.* in Hall *Chron., Hen. VIII* (1548) 30 Bastard Heron..slewe our warden vnder traist of dayes of metyng for iustice. **1596** DALRYMPLE tr. *Leslie's Hist. Scot.* I. (S.T.S.) I. 79 Thair hail traist, and al thair hope was in this opinione. **1678** SIR G. MACKENZIE *Crim. Laws Scot.* I. xi. §16 (1699) 67 Where the Party Slain is under the Traist, Credit, Assurance, and power of the Slayer.

traist, *a.* (*adv.*) *Sc.* and *north.* Forms: 4 **treist, traste, trayste,** 4–5 **traiste, trayst, trast,** 5 **treyst,** 4–7 **traist.** [app. a. ON. *treystr*, pa. pple. of *treysta* (OTeut. **traustjan*) to make firm or strong, used in the sense of ON. *traustr* firm, strong, safe, secure, sure, trusty.]

† **A.** *adj.* **1.** Firm, strong; secure, safe. *Obs.*

a **1300** *Cursor M.* 9883 Þis castel..a-pon þe marche it standes traist, O fede ne dredes it na fraist.

† **2.** Assured, sure, confident, full of trust. *Obs.*

c **1300** *Cursor M.* 17219 (Gött.) Þu mai be ful traist to spede. **1375** BARBOUR *Bruce* IX. 381 Þarfor sekir and trast þai war. *c* **1375** *Sc. Leg. Saints* xxxii. (*Iustin*) 482 Þe feynd þane Wend he traste wes of þe man. *c* **1475** *Rauf Coilȝear* 549 'Be thow traist', said the Coilȝear, 'man, as I am trew, I will not haist me ane fute faster on the way'.

3. Trusty, trustworthy; faithful, true. Now *poet. arch.*

c **1330** R. BRUNNE *Chron.* (1810) 175 Ȝour wille is euer so gode, & ȝour treuth so treist. *c* **1330** —— *Chron. Wace* (Rolls) 8392 Lok þat ȝe be trewe & traist. **1412** in *15th Rep. Hist. MSS. Comm.* App. VIII. 10 Oure traiste and wele belofit cosyng, Schir William of Douglas. *c* **1460** *Towneley Myst.* xxviii. 74, I saide if he nede be-stode to hym shuld none be trastir. *c* **1461** in *Jarrow & Wearmouth* (Surtees) 246, I beseke ȝowe send furth a trayst mane. **1501** DOUGLAS *Pal. Hon.* I. xlix, Constant Lucrece, and traist Penelope. **1535** STEWART *Chron. Scot.* (Rolls) III. 166 Richt nobill men that war bayth traist & trew. **1620** *Reg. Mag. Sig. Scot.* 783/1 Our richt traist cowsing and counsellar Thomas Erle of Kellie. **1919** E. POUND *Quia Pauper Amavi* 11 She has her lover till morn, Till the traist man cry out to warn Them. **1955** —— *Classic Anthol.* I. 21 Shall no one be traist? Mother of Heaven, Shall no one be traist?

B. *adv.* † **a.** Firmly, securely. † **b.** Confidently, assuredly. *Obs.*

c **1470** *Golagros & Gaw.* 292 Trou ye full traist, My hecht sall haldin be for baill or for blis. *Ibid.* 415.

† **traist,** *v. Sc.* and *north. Obs.* Forms: 3–4 **traiste,** 4 **treiste,** 4–5 **trayst(e,** 4–6 **traist, trast.** Pa. t. 4–5 **trast.** [ME. *traist, -en, trayst*, a. ON. (OW.Scand.) *treysta, trøysta* (OTeut. **traustjan*) to make firm, strong, or safe, to give firmness or security to, to confirm; refl. to make oneself secure, safe, or sure, with dat. or *til* to rely upon, trust to; f. *traustr* adj. strong, firm, safe, sure, trusty. Cognate with TRUST *v.*: see also TREST, TRIST.]

1. *trans.* To make secure or safe, to commit in trust; hence *refl.* to commit oneself with security or confidence, to trust, = sense 2.

c **1375** *Cursor M.* 11868 (Fairf.) In quam þat we may traiste vs in. **1456** SIR G. HAYE *Law Arms* (S.T.S.) 179 He wald..nocht traist his persone in it.

2. *intr.* To trust, have confidence, feel assured. (Const. *in, on, of, to,* or *inf.*)

a **1300** *Cursor M.* 7491 He traistes al in his aun hand. *a* **1300** *E.E. Psalter* cxxiv. 1 Þat traisten in Laverd ilk-on. **1340** HAMPOLE *Pr. Consc.* 1366 He may be called witty and wyse, þat..on þis lyfe here traystes noght. **1375** BARBOUR

Bruce v. 531 þe king in hym trastit. *c* **1375** *Sc. Leg. Saints* xxvi. (*Nycholas*) 538 Trastand thru hym to helpyn be. *c* **1460** *Towneley Myst.* xxvii. 47 Thay wold for no tokynyng,.. Trast in that trew. **1530** LYNDESAY *Test. Papyngo* 331 Traistyng to chaip that faitale destanie. **1596** DALRYMPLE tr. *Leslie's Hist. Scot.* x. (S.T.S.) II. 385 Quhilk he mekle trasted in.

b. *trans.* with simple obj. (? *orig.* dative), or clause: To trust, have confidence in.

1375 BARBOUR *Bruce* VII. 179 May I trast the me to valk Till I a litill slepyng tak? *c* **1470** HENRY *Wallace* I. 86 Ressawide he was and trastyt werray trew. **1473-4** *Acc. Ld. High Treas. Scot.* I. 49 It wes trastit the Duc of Glosister suld haue cummyn in. *c* **1500** *Lancelot* 1129, I traist that neuer more was sen No man in feild more knyghtly hyme conten.

c. To expect with confidence.

1518 in *Peebles Burgh Rec.* (1872) 46 The said Johne, traisting trubill in the cuntre.

Hence †**traisting** *vbl. sb.*, trusting, confidence.

a **1340** HAMPOLE *Psalter* lxx. 4 A stabile toure, til þe whilke we sall fle and be sykire in traystynge. **1456** SIR G. HAYE *Law Arms* (S.T.S.) 244 Thair lycht traisting in men that thai knew nocht.

traist, pa. pple. of TRAISE *v. Obs.*; Sc. var. TREST, trestle.

†**'traistful**, *a. Obs.* [f. TRAIST *sb.* + -FUL. Cf. Sw. *tröstful* consolatory.] **a.** Sure, secure. **b.** Trustful, confident. **c.** Inspiring confidence, encouraging, comforting.

13.. *Cursor M.* 29009 (Cott.) Orisun agh for be Buxum, traistful, and priue. **1409** in *Exch. Rolls Scotl.* IV. ccxii, For the mare sikkirnes and traistful keping of..the forsaide thingis. **1533** GAU *Richt Vay* (S.T.S.) 32 He is callit our fader that is to ewerie chrissine man..ane traistful thing. *Ibid.* 45 Thir ar traistful wordis for al chrissine man.

Hence †**'traistfully** *adv.*, surely, confidently.

c **1470** *Golagros & Gaw.* 197, I may refresch yow with folk, to feght gif you nedis, With thretty thousand tald, and traistfully tight.

†**'traistily**, *adv. Obs. rare.* [f. TRAISTY + -LY^2.] Trustfully, with confidence.

The usual variant of *traistly* in Cott. MS. of *Cursor M.*

13.. *Cursor M.* 10569 (Cott.) And siþen traistili [*Gött.* traystli] þe saand þai bade Quar-of þe angel þam bodword made. *Ibid.* 13422, 19950 [see TRAISTLY].

†**'traistly**, *adv. Obs.* [f. TRAIST *a.* + -LY^2.]

a. With feeling of security, securely; with confidence or trust, confidently. **b.** Faithfully, trustily.

a **1300** *Cursor M.* 260 (Cott.) Traistli acountes sal we yeild. *Ibid.* 13422 (Gött.) Þai gun trastli [*Cott.* traistili] trou fra þat dai in vr lauerd iesu. *Ibid.* 19950 (Edin.) Na hope of nan he wil forhu þat wil traistlic [*Cott.* traistili] in him tru. *a* **1340** HAMPOLE *Psalter* lxvii. 1 The prophet traistly couaitis that he wate is at cum. **1375** BARBOUR *Bruce* XVIII. 36 And war thai knyt witte ȝow, ȝe mycht The trastlyar abyde to ficht. *c* **1470** *Golagros & Gaw.* 744 The renkis of the Round Tabill, That has traistly thame tight to governe that gait. *c* **1520** M. NISBET *N. Test. in Scots* Acts ix. 27 In Damasc he did traistlie in the name of Jesu.

†**'traistness.** *Obs.* [f. TRAIST *a.* + -NESS.]

a. Firmness, stability. **b.** Firm confidence, trust. **c.** Faithfulness, trustiness.

a **1300** *Cursor M.* 24054 (Cott.) Moder! traistnes of ur treuth, Do vs to reu al wit þi reuth. *Ibid.* 23645 (Gött.) Þe gode..þir er for traistnes blith and glad. *a* **1340** HAMPOLE *Psalter* cv. 32 Þe traystnes þat he hadde in oþer. **1456** SIR G. HAYE *Law Arms* (S.T.S.) 290 A gude Emperoure..[suld] be full of traistnes and worthynes.

†**traisty**, *a. Obs.* [f. TRAIST *sb.* or ? *a.* + -Y.]

a. Secure, sure. **b.** Faithful, trusty.

13.. *Cursor M.* 59 (Gött.) For quen þu wenis traistiest to be, Þu sal fra hir or scho fra þe. **1513** DOUGLAS *Æneis* v. x. 12 And in his traisty eir thus prevaly He rownis.

trait (treɪ, treɪt). Also 6 traite, 7 traict. [a. F. *trait*, in obs. F. *traict*, *tret*, draught, stroke, touch, line = Pr. *trait* feature:—L. *tractus* drawing, draught: see TRACT *sb.*^{3}

The pronunciation (treɪ), after mod. French, in the 19th c. considered in England the correct one, is becoming less general; in U.S. (treɪt) is the established one.]

†**1.** 'Shot' of any kind, missiles; *orig.* arrows. *Obs. rare.*

c **1477** CAXTON *Jason* 112 Shoting on them arowes & other trait [F. *tirerent sur eulx saietes et aultre trait*].

†**2.** A drawing out; protraction; = TRACT *sb.*^{3} I. *Obs. rare.*

1545 in Leadam *Crt. of Requests* (Selden) 169 Then.. tapper [= to appear] for heryng of the matter without any further traite of tyme.

†**3.** That which is drawn; a line, streak, stripe. *Sc. Obs. rare.*

1561 *Inv. Roy. Wardr.* (1815) 133 Item ane claith of estate of fresit claith of gold and traitis of violet silk partit equalie with violet velvot. [Cf. *below* Drauchtis of violett silk partit equalie with violett velvot.]

4. a. A stroke made with pen or pencil; a short line; a touch (in a picture).

1589 PUTTENHAM *Eng. Poesie* III. i. (Arb.) 150 The skilfull painters [chief praise] is in the good conueyance of his coulours and shadowing traits of his pensill. **1601** HOLLAND *Pliny* XXXV. xi. II. 550 In these [unfinished paintings] a man may (as it were) see what traicts and lineaments remaine to bee done. **1756** J. KENNEDY *Curios. Wilton Ho.* (1786) 45 The Traits are most beautiful, and the Sculpture of the very best Ages. **1823** J. BADCOCK *Dom. Amusem.* 141 The copy.. is correct to a trait.

fig. **1860** WESTCOTT *Introd. Study Gosp.* vi. (1881) 340 The picture which he draws can be completed by traits taken from the other Evangelists. **1863** MARY HOWITT *F. Bremer's Greece* I. vi. 160 Let me now sketch some traits from that grand vision.

†**b.** Something penned; a line, passage, or piece of writing. *Obs.*

1572 ABP. PARKER *Corr.* (Parker Soc.) 414 In reading some words thereof..ye may think he hath mine information, but before God that trait was only of himself.

5. A line or lineament of the face; a feature.

1773 *Life N. Frowde* 52 The ten Thousand lovely Traits, that dwelt in every Feature of her radiant Face. **1809** *Med. Jrnl.* XXI. 329 The latter inherits the general exterior resemblance of his father, or even his shape, characteristic traits, looks, or voice. **1821** SHELLEY *Let.* 15 Aug., Her face is somewhat altered. The traits have become more delicate. **1860** EMERSON *Cond. Life, Behaviour* Wks. (Bohn) II. 385 A man finds room in the few square inches of the face for the traits of all his ancestors.

6. a. A particular feature of mind or character; a distinguishing quality; a characteristic; *spec.* of a culture or social group. Also *attrib.*

1752 H. WALPOLE *Lett. to Mann* 28 Oct., A most sensible trait of the King. **1797** *Monthly Mag.* III. 494 That love of order, which is a remarkable trait in his character. **1803** NELSON in Nicolas *Disp.* (1846) VII. p. ccxxxi, A very excellent young man, and has all the traits for making an excellent seaman and naval officer. **1807** W. IRVING *Salmag.* iii. (1824) 38 Who have no national trait about them but their language. **1859** WRAXALL tr. *R. Houdin* xviii. 258 A pleasing trait of English manners and customs. **1897** GEN. H. PORTER in *Century Mag.* Sept. 744/1 Sheridan now began to exhibit those traits which always made him a tower of strength. **1916** *Amer. Jrnl. Sociol.* Mar. 656 In maize culture as practiced by American farmers we have a fine example of a borrowed culture trait. *Ibid.* 659 The colonists took over all the essential parts of the trait-complex. **1936** R. LINTON *Study of Man* xvi. 280 During this [trial] period both the new trait and the old trait or traits with which it is competing become Alternatives within the total culture complex. *Ibid.* xxii. 397 Every trait is intimately associated with some other trait or traits to form a larger functional unit commonly known as a *trait complex.* **1947** G. MURPHY *Personality* xxi. 506 Most of the trait names that are used represent general action tendencies; and as soon as they are applied to oneself, or..to others, they stimulate a trait psychology in their user. **1976** A. HALEY *Roots* vii. 21 Kunta would always turn and walk away, thus displaying the dignity and self-command that his mother had taught him were the proudest traits of the Mandinka tribe. **1977** R. HOLLAND *Self & Social Context* v. 165 Trait models of professions attempt to list the characteristics of professional activity..as though some essential quality will be revealed by describing and comparing the many examples.

b. Of a thing.

1864 BOWEN *Logic* i. (1870) 7 The Concept refers to all the things whose common or similar attributes or traits it conceives. **1865** LIVINGSTONE *Zambesi* xxiv. 496 This trait was confined to the cool highlands. **1869** TOZER *Highl. Turkey* II. 269 The character of the tales has been altered.., yet..the original traits have..been preserved. **1871** JOWETT *Plato* I. 254 Some lesser traits of the dialogue may be noted.

c. A 'touch' *of* some quality. Now *rare.*

1815 W. H. IRELAND *Scribbleomania* 56 *note*, A poem.. wherein are to be found many traits of exuberant genius. **1830** MOORE *Byron* I. 328 A trait of pathos or high feeling, in comedy, has a peculiar charm. **1835** URE *Phil. Manuf.* 343 Many traits of almost parental kindness on the part of the masters.

7. A stroke: †**a.** of skill or cunning. ***double trait***, a stroke of double dealing. *Obs.*

a **1625** in Gutch *Coll. Cur.* I. 187 You deal with a Nation that hath playd more double Traits..than all the World beside.

b. of wit, sarcasm, pleasantry.

1704 SWIFT *T. Tub* Ded., Embellished with traits of wit so poignant and so apposite. **1781** H. WALPOLE *Let. to H. S. Conway* 16 Sept., In Voltaire's letters are some bitter traits on the King of Prussia. **1859** TENNYSON *Elaine* 320 When he fell From talk of war to traits of pleasantry.

trait, traitee, obs. ff. TREAT *v.*, TREATY.

‖**trait d'union** (trɛ dynjɔ̃). [Fr., lit. 'hyphen'.] A connection between or amongst otherwise unattached characteristics or parties.

1912 J. BUCHAN *Moon Endureth* IV. 127 He had established no *trait d'union* between the intellect..and the senses. **1934** A. TOYNBEE *Study of Hist.* I. II. 190 In the British Empire..this medieval incarnation of political unity [*sc.* the Crown] has latterly acquired a new and unforeseen institutional value as the *trait d'union* between the States Members of the British Commonwealth of Nations. **1959** *Times* 7 Jan. 11/7 M. Moktar Ould Daddah likes to think of his country [*sc.* Mauritania] as a *trait-d'union*, or link, between the Maghreb and West Africa.

traiter, -eres(se, -ere, -eri(e, -erous: see TRAITOR, TRAITRESS, TRAITORY, TRAITOROUS.

‖**traiteur** (trɛtœr). [Fr. agent-n. from *traiter* to TREAT, to supply with food for money.] A keeper of an eating-house (in France, Italy, etc.) who supplies or sends out meals to order.

1751 SMOLLETT *Per. Pic.* xxxix, A party of those young sparks, at the house of a noted traiteur. **1763** —— *Trav.* vi. (1766) I. 86 Your taylor, barber,..hatter, traiteur, and wine-merchant. **1828** [H. BEST] *Italy* 272 Our dinner was sent by the traiteur in a flat oblong basket. **1863** MISS BRADDON *Eleanor's Vict.* iv, I have a cup of coffee and a roll brought me every morning at nine from a *traiteur's* over the way.

traitie, obs. form of TREATY.

traitor ('treɪtə(r)), *sb.* Forms: α. 3 treitre, 5 trai-, traytre. β. 3-4 traitur, traytur, 3-7 traytour, (4-6 -oure), 3-8 traitour, 4-5 -oure, -ur(e, treitour, tretour, 4-6 *Sc.* trature, tratour, 5 tretowre. γ. 4 *Sc.* tratore, 4-5 traytore, 4-8 traytor, 5- traitor. δ. 6 traiter, 6-7 trayter. [a. OF. nom. *traitre* (= Prov. *traire*, F. *traître*):—pop.L. *trā'dītor* for L. '*trāditor* traitor, betrayer; also in acc. form OF. *traitor*, *-ur* (Roland, 11th c.), AF. *-our* (= It. *traditore*, Sp., Pg. *traidor*, Prov. *traidor*, Sard. *traitore*):—L. *trādi'tōrem*, agent-n. f. *trādĕre* to deliver, hand over, f. *trā-* (= *trans*) + *dare* to give, put.]

1. One who betrays any person that trusts him, or any duty entrusted to him; a betrayer. In early use often, and still traditionally, applied to Judas Iscariot.

α. *a* **1225** *Ancr. R.* 194 Heo biswikeð ou, & is ower treitre. *c* **1230** *Hali Meid.* 9 Ha habbeð iricchet te as treitres. **1485** CAXTON *Chas. Gt.* III. ii. 231 To al crysten men thou hast ben traytre.

β, γ. *a* **1300** *Cursor M.* 11530 (Cott.) He was traitur fals in fai. *c* **1375** *Sc. Leg. Saints* vii. (*Jacobus Min.*) 29 þat wekit tratore Iudas. *Ibid.* xii. (*Mathias*) 242 Þo he wyste he suld be traytore. **1377** LANGL. *P. Pl.* B. XIX. 435 Pieres þe plowman .. trauailleth & tulyeth for a tretour also sore As for a trewe tydy man. **1382** WYCLIF *Mark* xiv. 44 The traitour hadde ȝouun to hem a tokene. **1548-9** (Mar.) *Bk. Com. Prayer, Collect St. Matthias*, In the place of the traytor Judas. **1657** TRAPP *Comm. Ezra* vii. 17 Said Christ, even to the very Traytour that did seek and suck his blood. **1867** M. ARNOLD *St. Brandan* iv, It is—Oh, where shall Brandan fly?—The traitor Judas, out of hell!

2. *spec.* One who is false to his allegiance to his sovereign or to the government of his country; one adjudged guilty of treason (including formerly *petit treason*) or of any crime so regarded. Also *fig.* or in extended sense.

Traitor's Gate, the river gate of the Tower of London by which traitors, and state prisoners generally, were committed to the Tower. In quot. 1678 *fig.*

α. **1474** CAXTON *Chesse* II. iv. (1883) 48 Slewe the traytre Goribalde. **1481** —— *Godeffroy* cxvii. 176 Yf ony were vntrew & suche a traytre that wold destroye his countrey.

β, γ. *c* **1290** *S. Eng. Leg.* I. 38/146 'Ey, traytours', quath þe luþere Quen. **1297** R. GLOUC. (Rolls) 10693 In gibet hii were an honge, as to more vilte,..& so hii miȝte lerni traitour to be. *a* **1300** *Cursor M.* 11889 Aha! traiturs..i sale Hing yow bot ye mak me hale. **1375** BARBOUR *Bruce* IV. 19 Maknab, a fals tratour. *c* **1400** *Destr. Troy* 7899 But the triet men of Troy traitur hym cald. **1444** *Rolls of Parlt.* V. 111/2 He to be juged and demed as a Traitour, and suche execution to be don upon his body, as shuld be don uppon a Traitour atteint of hie Treson. **1591** SHAKS. *Two Gent.* IV. iv. 110 Vnlesse I proue false traitor to my selfe. **1606** —— *Tr. & Cr.* v. vi. 5 Turne thy false face thou traytor. **1678** *Yng. Man's Call.* 31 Man enters into the world at traitors gate; born in sin, and conceived in iniquity. **1713** ADDISON *Ct. Tariff* ¶23 He called [him] a lyar [and] a traytor. *a* **1771** GRAY *Dante* 7 If the telling may Beget the Traitour's Infamy. **1821** BYRON *Mar. Fal.* v. i, He is a traitor, and betray'd the state. **1881** BESANT & RICE *Chapl. of Fleet* I. 49 [Did] we not hack the limbs of our traitors, and stick them upon Temple Bar? *Mod.* A traitor in the camp; a traitor to the cause.

δ. **1583** LD. BURLEIGH *Exec. for Treason* (1675) 44 [They] ought to be adjudged Traiters. **1642** in *Verney Mem.* (1907) I. 242 Those thatt told you he was a trayter.

3. *attrib.* or as *adj.* That is a traitor, traitorous.

a **1300** *Cursor M.* 4397 (Cott.) Ne herd yee na wight how Yon traitur juu me wald sceind. *c* **1450** LOVELICH *Grail* lii. 275 A tretour boteler That kyng Marahans sone poysoned. *c* **1470** HENRYSON *Mor. Fab.* IV. ix, This wylie tratour tod On kneis fell. **1593** SHAKS. *Rich. II*, I. i. 102 False Mowbray.. consequently like a Traitor Coward, Sluc'd out his innocent soule through streames of blood. **1700** DRYDEN *Pal. & Arc.* II. 568 Th' assassinating wife, the household fiend, And, far the blackest there, the traitor-friend. **1726** POPE *Odyss.* XXII. 93 He drew his traitor-sword, And like a lion rushed against his lord. **1837** A. TENNENT *Vis. Glencoe* 18 Some traitor spy, Meant to betray thee with a lie. **1887** J. M. FULLER in *Dict. Chr. Biog.* IV. 837/2 Judas the traitor-Apostle.

4. *Comb.*, as ***traitor-led*** adj., ***-like*** adj. and adv., ***traitorwise*** adv.

1594 *Warres Cyrus* 794 Or else Libanio..should die for his so traitorlike reuolt. **1598** in *Archpriest Controv.* (Camden) I. 210 Reputed by our Prince and countrye as trayterwise and disloyal. **1598** ROWLANDS *Betraying Christ*, etc. G ij b, Traitor-led troopes by night did apprehend him. **1721** STRYPE *Eccl. Mem.* III. l. 389 Heavy tidings came.. that the French had won Calais..: for, traitor-like, it was said to be sold and delivered unto them.

†**traitor**, *v. Obs.* [f. prec. sb.] **a.** *trans.* To make (any one) a traitor. **b.** *intr.* To act as a traitor.

16.. LITHGOW (Webster, 1864), But time, it traitors me. *a* **1649** DRUMM. OF HAWTH. *Thyrsis in Dispr. Beauty* Wks. (1711) 23/1 Most woful wretch! whom shining hair and eyes Lead to love's dungeon, traitor'd by a sight. **1656** S. H. *Gold. Law* 5 If it be said, that the King traytor'd such, or as it related to himself only.

traitoress, variant of TRAITRESS.

†**'traitorful**, *a. Obs. rare*$^{-1}$. = TRAITOROUS.

c **1440** *York Myst.* xxxii. 300 Me lathes with my liff, so liffe I to lang. My traitourfull torne he turment my tene.

†**traitorhead.** *Obs. rare*$^{-1}$. In 4 treytorhede. [f. TRAITOR *sb.* + -HEAD.] = next.

1303 R. BRUNNE *Handl. Synne* 4204 Þyr may no man so yware be..þat treytorhede ne wyl hym asayle.

traitorhood (ˈtreɪtərhʊd). [f. as prec. + -HOOD.] The state or condition of a traitor; treachery.

c **1470** HARDING *Chron.* CXXIV. viii. (MS. Arch. Seld. B. 10, lf. 106 b), The Kynge with hoste one Roberte Mowbray Rode Who with the Kynge faughte of his traitourhode. **1871** RUSKIN *Fors Clav.* vi. 11 No more ashamed of Traitorhood, but invoking Traitorhood, as if it covered, instead of constituting, uttermost shame.

traitorism (ˈtreɪtərɪz(ə)m). [f. TRAITOR *sb.* + -ISM.] The practice or principles of a traitor.

1591 *Troub. Raigne K. John* II. (1611) I ij b, But wher fel traitorisme hath residence, There wants no words to set despight on worke. **1661** K. W. *Conf. Charac., Gd. old Cause* (1860) 62 The..most notorious cause of innovation and traitorisme. *a* **1734** NORTH *Exam.* II. v. (1740) 323 The Loyal Clergy of the Church of England at that time [*c* 1680] ..are charged with Traitorism of their Principles. **1888** *Times* (weekly ed.) 29 June 8/1 There was no traitorism in the ranks. **1898** *Columbus* (Ohio) *Dispatch* 5 Jan. 7/1 Charges of conspiracy and traitorism were freely made.

† **ˈtraitorize**, *v. Obs. rare*$^{-1}$. [f. as prec. + -IZE.] *intr.* (with *it*). To act as a traitor, play the traitor.

1656 S. H. *Gold. Law* 11 To Traytorize, Murther, and Thieve it, to bring your ends about.

ˈtraitorling. *nonce-wd.* [f. as prec. + -LING.] A petty or contemptible traitor.

a **1652** BROME *Queen & Concub.* III. x, There was not, But in the Queen, Petruccio, and my self, True Loyaltie in the Court. Away you Traytorling.

† **ˈtraitorly**, *a. Obs.* [f. as prec. + -LY^1.] Having the character of a traitor; traitorous.

a **1586** SIDNEY *Arcadia* III. xxvi. (1912) 506 That coward, and traytorly boy, who slewe my Uncle trayterouslie, and after ranne from me in the plaine field. **1611** SHAKS. *Wint. T.* IV. iv. 821 But what talke we of these Traitorly-Rascals? **1641** PRYNNE *Antip.* 5 An unhappie, if not perfidious Traytorly advice. **1668** ROLLE *Abridgm.*, *Tit. Action sur Case* (G.) pl. 8. 43 You are a Traytorly Rogue, you cheated your Father of all that ever he had.

† **ˈtraitorly**, *adv. Obs.* [f. as prec. + -LY^2.] Like, or in the manner of, a traitor; traitorously.

? *a* **1349** ? HAMPOLE *Wks.* (1895) I. 72 My trewest tresowre sa trayturly taken. **1387** TREVISA *Higden* (Rolls) III. 87 Whanne Ancus was dede, he sente traytourliche Ancus his sones an hontynge. *c* **1450** *Chron. London* (Kingsford 1905) 129 The viscount of Narbon that trayterly slew the duke of Borgoyn. **1535** STEWART *Cron. Scot.* (Rolls) II. 540 Sa tratourlie for to betrais ȝow all.

† **traitoˈrology.** *Obs. nonce-wd.* [f. as prec. + -(O)LOGY, after *martyrology*.] A roll or register of traitors.

1647 VICARS *Just Correction*, etc. *of Scand. Bill* (title-p.) A succinct Traiterologie, in Answer to a lying Martyrologie.

traitorous (ˈtreɪtərəs), *a.* Forms: 4 **treterous, -tourous,** 4–5 **traytrous,** 5–6 **-torouse,** 5–7 **traitrous,** 6 **traytorous, -tourous(e, traterous, -turuse, traytorys, tretrous,** 6–9 **trayter-, traiterous,** 6– **traitorous.** [app. ad. OF. *traitreus, -eux* (*c* 1243 in Godef.), alteration of earlier *traitos, -eus, trahiteus,* conformed to *traitre,* TRAITOR. In Eng. having the appearance of being f. TRAITOR + -OUS.] Having the character of, or characteristic of, a traitor; treacherous; perfidious.

c **1380** *Sir Ferumb.* 5652 France had þo be delyured weel of a ful traytrous man. *c* **1477** CAXTON *Jason* 10 They that.. gyue them vnto these traytrous meuinges may in no manere haue rest daye ne nyght. **1535** COVERDALE *Isa.* lix. 12 Vsinge presumptuous & traytorous ymaginacions. **1568** GRAFTON *Chron.* II. 338 Aduoyde ye false trayterous and vngracious people. **1581** HAMILTON in *Cath. Tractates* (S.T.S.) 84 Maist traturuse tratures aganis thair soueran the Queinis maiestie. **1683** *Brit. Spec.* 170 A traitorous Crew of villanous Phanaticks. **1716** ADDISON *Freeholder* No. 31 ¶10 More of His Friends have lost their Lives in this Rebellion, than of His traiterous Subjects. **1812** G. CHALMERS *Dom. Econ. Gt. Brit.* 429 A spirit of disaffection..followed..by popular disturbances, and traiterous insurrection, affected her quiet, and interrupted her industry. **1871** R. ELLIS *Catullus* v. 12 So we shall not know, nor traitorous eye shall envy.

ˈtraitorously, *adv.* Forms: see prec.: also 4 **traytoures-, traytoursliche, traitoursly,** 5 **traytorsly,** 5–6 **-toursly.** [app. f. TRAITOROUS *a.* + -LY^2, but exemplified somewhat earlier; perhaps after OF. *traitreusement,* var. of *traiteusement* (13–14th c. in Hatz.-Darm.).] In a traitorous or treacherous manner; treacherously.

c **1330** R. BRUNNE *Chron. Wace* (Rolls) 14360 Conan his cosyn þere hym slew Treterously. **1387** TREVISA *Higden* (Rolls) I. 151 Þe firste Amazones were þe wyfes of Gothes, þat took wretche of hire housbondes deþ þat were traytoureslliche i-slawe. **1388** WYCLIF *Ecclus.* xxxii. 19 He that doith tretourousli, schal be sclaundrid ther ynne. **1491** *Act 7 Hen. VII*, c. 15 Certeyn persones..traiterously murdred ..John Mountague late Erle of Sarum. **1512** *Act 4 Hen. VIII*, c. 20 *Preamble*, John Tayler felonsly and traytoursly resetted one Archbold Armestrong. **1601** SHAKS. *All's Well* IV. iii. 339 You that haue so traitorously discouerd the secrets of your army. **1617** MORYSON *Itin.* III. 278 The Prince of Orange..was in the yeere 1584 traiterously slaine. **1792** *Anecd. W. Pitt* I. vi. 152 Those who have traiterously conspired to rob him of his crown. **1867** FREEMAN *Norm. Conq.* I. v. 347 The very enemy with whom he had before traitorously leagued himself.

ˈtraitorousness. [f. as prec. + -NESS.] The quality of being traitorous; treachery.

1571 GOLDING *Calvin on Ps.* xxix. 2. 106 To abuse their highnesse too trayterousnesse. **1592** WYRLEY *Armorie* 136 Which citie yeelded was byth tretrousnes Of their Bishop. **1628** WITHER *Brit. Rememb.* VII. 2221 It is a kind of trait'rousnesse To give them more then due, as well as lesse. **1727** BAILEY vol. II, *Traitorousness,* Treasonableness, Perfidiousness. **1878** SIMPSON *Sch. Shaks.* I. 130 One of the arguments..was the traitorousness of the attempt.

traitorship (ˈtreɪtəʃɪp). [f. TRAITOR *sb.* + -SHIP.] The function or action of a traitor. In quot. 1645, ? the personality of a traitor.

1645 WITHER *Vox Pacif.* 52 Nay, some among you are so void of reason, To buy their Traytorships. **1869** RUSKIN *Crown Wild Olive* iv. (1898) 184 Treasure..which even our traitorship..cannot sully. **1893** *Temple Bar Mag.* XCIX. 2 A sense of traitorship to his own nature.

† **ˈtraitory.** *Obs.* Forms: 4 **traitre, -tere,** 4–5 **-terie,** 4–6 **-tourie,** 4–7 **-torie,** 5–6 **-tory;** 4 **traytrie,** 4–5 **-torye,** 4–6 **-tory, -tery(e,** 5 **-toury, -towrye, -tere,** 5–6 **-torie,** 6 **-tery, -terie;** 4 **traterie, -tourie,** 4–6 **-toury(e,** 5 **-towry, -tory,** 6 **-torie;** 5 **treitorie;** 5 **treytori,** 5–6 **-tory.** [f. TRAITOR + -Y: cf. *ancestry, mastery.*] The conduct or action of a traitor; treachery; treason.

1303 R. BRUNNE *Handl. Synne* 6248 Þou synnest þan wykkedly, And doust þe soule treytory. *c* **1330** —— *Chron. Wace* (Rolls) 9698 Þey ȝede aboute þe court to spye Wher þey myght do þer trayterye. **13..** *K. Alis.* 3983 Thou schalt beo honged and to-drawe,..For thou soche traytory wroughtest! *a* **1375** *Lay Folks Mass Bk.* App. IV. 44 Ȝif he for traytrie weore take. **1375** BARBOUR *Bruce* IV. 22 It wes fer wer þan tratoury For to betreyss sic A persoune. *c* **1380** WYCLIF *Wks.* (1880) 26 In drede of treson of traitre aȝenst god and his lawe. **1390** GOWER *Conf.* III. 334 The king unto his Sone tolde Of Tharse thilke traiterie. **1402** *Pol. Poems* (Rolls) II. 28 Guiltie of traitorie to our realme. *a* **1450** MYRC *Festial* 13 Thre knyghtes also weren enpeched to þe Emperour of traytere. *c* **1450** *Mirour Saluacioun* 111 Of Judas & cosse & the traytourye. *c* **1485** *Digby Myst.* II. 400 He shall repent hys Rebellyous treytory. *c* **1500** KENNEDY *Passion of Christ* 299 Judas last, þat wrocht þe tratory. *c* **1537** *Thersites* (1820) 74 Imagin no tratourye againste your prince. *c* **1550** BALE *K. Johan* (Camden) 61 Never..with owt moch traytery. **1570** LEVINS *Manip.* 106/17 Traytorie, *proditio.* **1571** in *Scot. Poems 16th C.* (1801) II. 280 To commit open tratorie. **1609** SKENE *Reg. Maj.* I. 112 Gif any man be convict of traitorie done to his overlord.

traitoursly, obs. var. TRAITOROUSLY.

† **ˈtraitously**, *adv. Obs.* Also 5 **traytous-,** 6 **trayteous-.** [after OF. *trai-, trayteusement, traitouse-, tra(h)iteusement,* f. *traitos, trayteus* (app. f. stem *trait-* of *trait-eur* + *-eus,* -OUS).] Traitorously.

c **1450** *Brut* cxxiii. 126 (Douce MS.) But þe Erl Godwyne ..falsly & traytously þouȝt to slee þo ij breþerne. **1489** CAXTON *Faytes of A.* IV. viii. 249 The prysoner had other traitously or by som otherwise assaylled whan they were but them two togyder. **1559** *Mirr. Mag., Rich. II* vii, Mine vncle Edmunde..right trayteously arose.

traitress (ˈtreɪtrɪs), **ˈtraitoress.** Forms: 4 **traitores, -eresse,** (6 **-eres),** 4–7 **trayteresse,** (5 **-ures, tratouresse),** 5–6 **traytres(se,** (8 **-ess),** 5–7 **traitresse,** (6–7 **-oresse),** 7– **traitress.** [a. F. *traîtresse* (13th c. in Godef. *Compl.*), fem. of *traître* TRAITOR: see -ESS. In form *traitoress* f. TRAITOR + -ESS.] A female traitor; a traitorous or treacherous woman (or being personified as a woman). Sometimes in an attenuated or playful sense.

c **1369** CHAUCER *Dethe Blaunche* 620 (Fairf. MS.) Fortune ..The trayteresse [*v.r.* traitores] fals and ful of gyle That al behoteth and no thyng halte. *c* **1400** *Rom. Rose* 7391 That false traitouresse untrewe. *c* **1400** *Ywaine & Gaw.* 2587 That sho bitrayed hir lady, Als traytures sal sho haue hyr [= hire], Sho be brent her in this fir. *a* **1450** *Knt. de la Tour* (1906) 73 For a lytel thynge ye haue vndo yow, and haue be to me traitresse. *a* **1536** *Callisto & Melibæa* B iv b, Answere thou traytres how darst be so bold? **1601** SHAKS. *All's Well* I. i. 184 A Traitoresse, and a Deare. **1632** J. HAYWARD *Biondi's Eromena* 34 Mischievous and accursed Traitresse. **1651** tr. *De-las-Coveras' Don Fenise* 276 She saw the trayteresse Fregonde. **1702** ROWE *Tamerl.* IV. i, Death shall free me At once from Infamy and Thee, thou Traytress. *a* **1766** MRS. F. SHERIDAN *Nourjahad* (1767) 103 The traitoresses! they shall pay dearly for thus abusing my indulgence. **1769** BLACKSTONE *Comm.* IV. xiv. 203 If she [the wife] kills such divorced husband, she is a traitress. **1824** LADY GRANVILLE *Lett.* (1894) I. 255 The French Government released the little traitoresses. **1882** STEVENSON *Stud. Men & Bks.* (1905) 236 He [Knox] solemnly proclaims all reigning women to be traitoresses and rebels against God. **1884** TENNYSON *Becket* II. i. 50 *Henry.* Traitress! *Rosamund.* A faithful traitress to thy royal fame.

b. *attrib.* or as *adj. rare.*

1470–85 MALORY *Arthur* I. xxi. 67 Ye are the falsest lady of the world and the most traitresse vnto the kynges person. **1725** POPE *Odyss.* IV. 115 By the dire fury of a traitress wife.

traitrous, traits, traitt, traitur, obs. ff. TRAITOROUS, TRACE *sb.*^{2}, TREAT *v.*, TRAITOR.

Trajanic (treɪˈdʒænɪk), *a.* [f. L. *Trāiān-us* + -IC.] Of or pertaining to the Roman emperor Trajan (A.D. 53–117), esp. to the style of triumphal art associated with him.

1906 *Athenæum* 27 Jan. 113/2 The *extispicium* scene probably represents the nuncupatio votorum before Trajan set out on his Dacian campaign, and is Trajanic in style. **1933** *Times Lit. Suppl.* 9 Nov. 780/3 He finds no sign in either the Trajanic or the Aurelian column of a Court art. **1978** *Antiquaries Jrnl.* LVIII. 82 The Dacian victory is perhaps the most significant of all the triumphal themes in Trajanic art.

traject (ˈtrædʒɛkt), *sb.* [ad. L. *trājectus* a passing over, a place for crossing, f. *trājicĕre, trāicĕre* to throw across, f. *trans* across + *jacĕre* to throw. So F. *trajet, traject* (16th c.).]

1. A way or place of crossing over; *esp.* a place where boats cross a river, strait, or the like; a ferry. Less commonly, a route for crossing a tract of land.

a **1552** LELAND *Itin.* (1907) I. 51 The next *trajectus* from Kingston to the shore of Humbre in Lincolnshir is about a 3 mile to a place caullid Golflete. Yet the communer traject is from Kingeston to Berton apon Humber. **1657** THORNLEY tr. *Longus' Daphnis & Chloe* 39 The Bosphori; the Trajects, or the narrow Seas, swam over by Oxen. **1798** PYE *Naucratia* I. 57 Though his feet the traject often trace. **1810** SCOTT *Let. to Morrit* 9 Aug., in *Lockhart*, He would not again put foot in a boat till he had discovered the shortest possible traject. **1904** *Sci. Amer. Supp.* 5 Mar. 23553/3 As to the new Bagdad line, two different trajects were proposed.

2. The action or an act of crossing over water, land, a chasm, etc.; passage.

1774 PENNANT *Tour Scot. in 1772* 292 Land after a traject of four miles. **1828** A. CLARKE in *Life* xiii. (1840) 458 After a mile's traject [we] were in Lerwick. **1852** MUNDY *Our Antipodes* (1857) 30 We crossed the river by a punt running on a rope. The mode of traject is very inconvenient. **1875** *Wond. Phys. World* I. iv. 129 The only means of traject across these crevasses. **1882** E. O'DONOVAN *Merv Oasis* I. 124 During the whole traject I met with no living things save an enormous black eagle.

b. The action of carrying or conveying across; transport; transference. *rare.*

18.. *Athenæum* (Annandale), At the best, however, this traject was but that of the germ of life, which Sir W. Thomson, in a famous discourse, suggested had been carried to this earth from some other sphere by meteoric agency.

3. = TRAJECTORY *sb.* 1. *rare.*

18.. I. TAYLOR (Webster, 1864), The traject of comets.

traject (trəˈdʒɛkt), *v.* [f. L. *trāject-*, ppl. stem of *trājicĕre*: see prec.]

† **1.** *trans.* To pass across, to cross (a river, sea, etc.). Also *intr. Obs. rare.*

1624 HEYWOOD *Gunaik.* I. 31 She..trajecting many seas ..came at length into Egypt. *Ibid.* v. 231 The river Araxes, which he had late with a mightie host trajected. **1711** in *10th Rep. Hist. MSS. Comm.* App. v. 132 The Prince..would have..marched up by the river to Navan,..and there have trajected. *Ibid.* 169 That induced General de Ginckle..to traject the Shanon.

2. To carry or convey across or over; to transport. † **a.** (something material). *Obs.*

1635 HEYWOOD *Hierarch.* VIII. 510 He would traject them dry-foot through the seas. **1637** —— *Dial.* xvi. Wks. 1874 VI. 236 The ferriman, who from the rivers brim Trajected thee. **1651** C. CARTWRIGHT *Cert. Relig.* I. 30 Him [Christ] we must mastigate, and chew by faith: traject, and convey him into our hearts as nutriment. **1684** T. BURNET *Th. Earth* I. 232 The notion..that the rivers of paradise were trajected out of the other hemisphere into this by subterraneous passages.

b. To transmit (light, shadow, or colour).

1657 TOMLINSON *Renou's Disp.* Pref., Trajecting these lines through the sieve of our Crebrosity. **1661** GLANVILL *Van. Dogm.* 14 The shadow of a horse trajected against a wall. **1672** NEWTON in *Phil. Trans.* VII. 5101 To this way of Compounding Whiteness may be referr'd that other, by Mixing light after it hath been trajected through transparently colour'd substances. **1704** —— *Optics* (1721) 57 A Prism, by which the trajected Light might be refracted either upwards or sideways.

c. To transmit (thought, words, etc.).

a **1711** KEN *Edmund* Poet. Wks. 1721 II. 169 By mutual Thoughts trajected either Soul Began each other sweetly to condole. **1863** COWDEN CLARKE *Shaks. Char.* xiii. 324 She compared him to that dervis who possessed the power of trajecting his soul into the body of any individual that suited his purpose. **1895** MACPHERSON *Ch. & Priory Monymusk* ii. 57 We can account for their name..being even trajected into a longer and more distant period during which they had no existence at all.

trajectile (trəˈdʒɛktɪl, -aɪl), *a.* and *sb. rare.* [ad. mod.L. type **trājectil-is*: see TRAJECT and -IL. As a botanical term a. F. *trajectile* (Littré).]

A. *adj.* Capable of throwing or impelling across.

1838 I. TAYLOR *Home Educ.* 247 A trajectile force, leaping the voids of the universe. **1860** MAURY *Phys. Geog. Sea* (Low) ii. §119 Arising from this difference in the rate of rotation and the trajectile force [of a cannon].

b. *Bot.* (See quot.)

1900 JACKSON *Gloss. Bot. Terms, Trajectile*..when the connective completely separates the anther-cells.

B. *sb.* A body impelled through air or space. (Cf. *projectile.*)

1860 MAURY *Phys. Geog. Sea* (Low) ii. §123 It [a current] should also move in a circle of trajection, or such as would be described by a trajectile moving through the air without resistance and for a great distance.

trajection (trəˈdʒɛkʃən). [ad. L. *trājectiōn-em* a crossing over, transportation, n. of action f. *trājicĕre* to throw or convey across: see TRAJECT.]

1. The action of trajecting or fact of being trajected; a throwing or carrying across; passage through. †**a.** Passage across a river, etc. *Obs.*

1637 HEYWOOD *Dial.* xv. Wks. 1874 VI. 232 My due for thy trajection downe here lay. **1657–83** EVELYN *Hist. Relig.* (1850) I. 144 The spectre at the Rubicon, Caesar hesitating that trajection. **1690** T. BURNET *Th. Earth* II. 88 No long passage or trajection will be requir'd from shore to shore. **1711** in *10th Rep. Hist. MSS. Comm.* App. v. 133 The King observeing the Prince to attempt a trajection [of the Boyne] commanded his army to..face to the enemy.

†**b.** The passing (of anything) through a sieve or the like. *Obs. rare.*

1657 *Physical Dict.*, *Trajection*,..as cheese is strained from the whey. **1657** TOMLINSON *Renou's Disp.* 85 By common trajection..or by a more peculiar colation.

c. Passage or transmission through any medium, or through space.

1652 GAULE *Magastrom.* 254 They might in all parts behold the trajections and motions of the starres. **1661** BOYLE *Cert. Physiol. Ess.* (1669) 166 Such Comets as have by a Trajection through the Ether, for a long time wander'd through the Celestial or Interstellar part of the Universe. **1686** GOAD *Celest. Bodies* II. i. 147 The Trajections and shooting of the Stars. **1713** DERHAM *Phys.-Theol.* VI. v. 365 The Trajection and Distribution of the Blood depends wholly on the Systole of the Heart. **1860** [see TRAJECTILE *sb.*].

d. Transmission (of light, heat, or other form of energy).

1633 T. ADAMS *Exp. 2 Peter* i. 19 Those upon earth that are said to have half a year night; yet are not without some trajection of light. **1661** BOYLE *Spring of Air* II. i. (1682) 21 Supposing light not to be made by a trajection of Atoms through Diaphanous bodies. **1704** NORRIS *Ideal World* II. iii. 189 Vision may be considered..as it signifies the passing or trajection of the rays of light, with all their refractions thro' the several coats and humours of the eye.

e. *fig.*

1888 A. S. WILSON *Lyric Hopeless Love* cxxxvii, Not happiness but purpose drives The dim trajection of our lives. **1905** *Athenæum* 11 Feb. 174/1 His trajection of the ignorance of primitive man on this unknown immensity is very impressive.

†**2.** A perception transmitted to the mind; an impression, a mental image. *Obs.*

1594 *Zepheria* ii, When I empris'd..The siluer lustre of thy brow t' unmask, Though hath my Muse hyperboliz'd trajections: Yet stands it aye deficient to such task. **1646** SIR T. BROWNE *Pseud. Ep.* VII. x. 357 The trajections of such an object [must] more sharpely pierce the martyr'd soul of John, then afterward did the nayls the crucifyed body of Peter.

3. Transposition; metathesis.

1612 BREREWOOD *Lang. & Relig.* 191 Ægypt is by them named..not without some trajection of letters, כתפר for כפתר. **1649** ROBERTS *Clavis Bibl.* 289 Here is a more obscure Trajection or Transposition of the phrases in this verse. **1795** MACKNIGHT *Epist.* (1820) III. 95 The words are placed in the end of the verse by a trajection usual in Paul's writings. **1875** JOWETT *Plato* I. 152 You must suppose him to make a trajection of the word..'truly'. **1895** A. E. HOUSMAN in *Classical Rev.* Oct. 354/1 As a Corpus Poetarum is a work of reference.., there is some disadvantage in admitting even the most certain trajections.

trajectitious (trædʒɛkˈtɪʃəs), *a. rare.* [f. late L. *trājectīcius* that is carried over (sea), f. L. *trāject-*: see TRAJECT *v.* and -ITIOUS[1].] Characterized by trajection or transport over the sea; over-sea, foreign.

1656 BLOUNT *Glossogr.*, *Trajectitious*, belonging to passage; As *trajectitious mony*, is that which is carried over the sea at the peril of the Creditor. **1855** LORENZ tr. *Van der Keessel's Sel. Theses* dlxxiv, In that kind of Exchange which is called local,..mercantile or trajectitious.

trajectory (trəˈdʒɛktərɪ, ˈtrædʒɪktərɪ), *a.* and *sb.* [ad. med. or mod.L. *trājectōri-us* pertaining to trajection (cf. late L. *trājectōrium* a funnel, *c* 400), whence F. *trajectoire* 'casting.. conveying through or over' (Cotgr. 1611); f. L. *trāject-*: see TRAJECT *v.*, and -ORY. The sb. corresponds to L. *trājectōria* (Newton) fem., in F. *trajectoire* sb. (in Cotgr.).]

A. *adj.* **1.** *Physics.* Of or pertaining to that which is thrown or hurled through the air or space.

1668 *Phil. Trans.* III. 807 To explaine that Trajectory rectilinear motion, he subjects the Comet of A. 1652 to a very rigid Calculus. **1851–9** MALLET in *Man. Sci. Enq.* 349 Reach the ground after describing a trajectory path.

2. *Physiol.* Said of a gland into which lymphatic vessels convey their fluids. ? *Obs.*

1747 tr. *Astruc's Fevers* 132 The common receptacles or trajectory glands of several lymphatic vessels.

B. *sb.* **1. a.** *Physics.* The path of any body moving under the action of given forces; by many modern writers restricted to that of a body not known to be moving, like a planet, in a closed curve or orbit; *esp.* the curve described by a projectile in its flight through the air.

Hence loosely used by gun-makers for the height to which a bullet rises above the line of sight, as 'the trajectory of this rifle is one inch in one hundred yards'.

1696 WHISTON *Th. Earth* I. (1722) 8 [This] must change its rectilinear into a curvilinear trajectory. **1704** J. HARRIS *Lex. Techn.* I, *Trajectory, of a Comet*, is the Line which by its Motion it describes. **1726** tr. *Gregory's Astron.* I. i. 73 Kepler, and several Philosophers after him, supposed the Trajectories of Comets to be right Lines. **1728** tr. *Newton's Treat. Syst. World* 142 If this problem was resolved, we should thence have a method of determining the trajectories of Comets to the greatest accuracy. **1795** HUTTON *Math. Dict.* II. 603 *Trajectory*, a term often used generally for the path of any body moving either in a void, or in a medium that resists its motion... Trajectory of a Comet is its path or orbit, or the line it describes in its motion. **1828** J. M. SPEARMAN *Brit. Gunner* (ed. 2) 395 To determine, by theory, the range of a shot, and the form of its trajectory in the air. **1843** MILL *Logic* VI. x. §3 There might be others which, instead of an orbit, describe a trajectory, or a course not returning into itself. **1862** H. SPENCER *First Princ.* II. x. §82 (1875) 252 It is common to assert that the trajectory of a cannon ball is a parabola.

b. *transf.* and *fig.*

1838 *Brit. Critic* XXIII. 1 An examination of..the somewhat eccentric trajectory of his [A. Knox's] thoughts. **1883** LOCKYER in *Times* 8 Dec. 10 We have..got a straight trajectory of the abnormal sunsets from the Seychelles to Brazil. **1883** *Cornh. Mag.* Feb. 217 That majestic spirit passes..through all the upward or downward trajectory between heaven and hell. **1889** BOYD CARPENTER *Perm. Elem. Relig.* Introd. 27 The trajectory of religion must rush away to the infinite beyond.

2. *Geom.* A curve or surface passing through a given set of points, or intersecting each of a given series of curves or surfaces according to a given law, e.g. at a constant angle.

1795 HUTTON *Math. Dict.* II. 603 Newton (Princip. lib. I. prob. 22) proposes to describe a Trajectory that shall pass through five given points. **1816** tr. *Lacroix's Diff. & Int. Calculus* 401 A problem celebrated from the earliest infancy of the Integral Calculus—the problem of Trajectories. Its object is to determine a curve which shall intersect all curves of a given species at a given angle. **1865** B. PRICE *Infin. Calc.* (ed. 2) 606 If the [constant] angle between the two curves is a right angle the trajectory is said to be orthogonal.

3. A projectile, as a bullet. *rare.*

1861 W. H. RUSSELL in *Times* 29 July, As far as I could judge, the men of the regiment were stout and strong material for arresting trajectories.

trajet (‖traʒɛ, ˈtrædʒɪt). [a. F. *trajet*:—L. *traject-us*: see TRAJECT *sb.*]

1. A crossing, passage, 'run across'; = TRAJECT *sb.* 2.

1741 BERKELEY in Fraser *Life* viii. (1871) 268 You may.. come to Bath, and from thence..make a short trajet to our coast. **1825** T. HOOK *Sayings* Ser. II. *Sutherl.* I. 136 During the *trajet* from the Castle Inn at Marlborough. **1885** 'MRS. ALEXANDER' *At Bay* iii, There is an earlier one..by the Dieppe route, but you gain no time, for the *trajet* is longer. **1894** *Field* 1 Dec. 828/1 Made their trajet to Blessington town from Dublin.

2. The course or passage of a nerve or the like.

1849–52 *Todd's Cycl. Anat.* IV. 815/2 The trajet of the nerve is external to that of the internal jugular vein.

trak, trake, obs. forms of TRACK, TRAIK.

Trakehner (trækeɪnə(r)). In sense 2 also **trakehner, trakena, trakener**. [a. Ger., f. the name of the Trakehnen stud.] **1.** A saddle horse belonging to a breed first developed at the Trakehnen stud in east Prussia.

[**1905** W. RIDGEWAY *Origin & Influence Thoroughbred Horse* iv. 472 The extraordinary tractability of the Prussian Trakehnen breed..is a well known feature.] **1926** A. TOPHAM *Chron. Prussian Court* i. 16 The carriages..had been waiting in the shade, each with its four splendid Trakehner horses. **1975** *Islander* (Victoria, B.C.) 13 July 5/1 The Trakehner breed of horses is fairly new in North America, but is famous and long prized in Europe where the breed originated in the areas of Eastern Prussia and Poland. **1980** G. HENSCHEL *Illustr. Guide Horses & Ponies* 155/3 Trakehners often make top-grade show jumpers.

2. A type of fence in the cross-country section of an equestrian three-day event, etc. (see quot. 1973).

1958 S. WILLCOX *Three Days Running* xvii. 174 We made our way up the incline towards a big trakena fence. **1959** R. S. SUMMERHAYS *Encycl. for Horsemen* (rev. ed.) 306/2 *Trakener*, a type of fence used in Cross-country... It is a ditch spanned by rails in the centre. **1973** C. STRATTON *Encycl. Show-Jumping & Combined Training* 271/1 A trakener is a cross-country obstacle made of a 'knife rest' construction, built on a ditch, with a second rail attached to the cross pieces. **1977** *Horse & Hound* 10 June 25/1 Fences 5 (a trakehner over a dry ditch) and 6 (a sloping palisade followed by a bank and ditch) caused most of the trouble across country.

tra-la-la (ˈtrɑːlɑːˈlɑː), *int.* (*sb.*). A vocal utterance forming a musical phrase (usually ascending) expressive of gaiety or joy; also, a cadence or flourish on a horn or similar instrument.

1823 SCOTT *Quentin D.* ix, Lay on the dogs, in the name of the holy St. Hubert!—Ha! ha! tra-la-la-lira-la! **1835** T. MITCHELL *Aristoph.*, *Acharn.* 1099 *note*, If the accent is thrown on the last syllable of this word [τήνελλα], it will approach very closely to modern imitative words of a similar kind: *Tirala! Tirala! Tralalla! Tralalla!* **1886** HISSEY *On Box Seat* 40 The cheery tra-la-la of the guard's horn.

tralatician (træləˈtɪʃən), *a. rare.* [f. L. *trālātīci-us* (see TRALATITIOUS) + -AN.] = TRALATITIOUS 2, 3. So **tralaticiary** (-ˈɪʃərɪ) *a.*

1893 W. PETERSON in *Classical Rev.* Mar. 139/2 That portion of my commentary which represents what I may call the 'tralatician' element,—the ἀναγκαιότατα of textual interpretation. **1900** A. H. J. GREENIDGE in *Eng. Hist. Rev.* July 541 The annual and tralaticiary bill of outlawry which keeps people out of Italy.

†**traˈlation.** *Obs. rare*$^{-1}$. [ad. L. *trālātiōn-em* = *translātiōn-em* a transferring, n. of action of *transferre* to TRANSFER.] The use of a word in a transferred or figurative sense; metaphor.

1620 BP. HALL *Hon. Mar. Clergy* I. §14 According to the broad tralation of his rude Rhemists.

tralaˈtition. *rare*$^{-0}$. [irreg. f. next.] = prec. **1864** in WEBSTER.

tralatitious (trælə'tɪʃəs), *a.* Also 9 -icious. [f. L. *trālātīci-us* usual, customary, common, metaphorical, tropical (f. *trālāt-*, ppl. stem of *transferre* and -ITIOUS[1]).]

1. Characterized by transference; *esp.* of words or phrases, metaphorical, figurative.

1645 TOMBES *Anthropol.* 5, I have planted, Apollo watered; but God gave the increase. Now these things cannot be conceived as tralatitious, for it is said, they were Ministers by whom they believed. **1650** FULLER *Pisgah* IV. vii. 138 Too often guilty of what may be termed tralatitious idolatry, when any thing..is loved, or honoured above, or even with God himself. **1688** R. HOLME *Armoury* III. 253/2 Tralatitious, or Artificiall sentences,..are Borrowed words, ..Termed also a Metaphor, Trope, Parable, or Simile. **1748** HARTLEY *Observ. Man* II. i. 63 A secondary and tralatitious Association. **1880** R. C. CHRISTIE *E. Dolet* 237, I give..both its primary and its second or tralatitious meaning.

†**2.** Passed from hand to hand; common, ordinary, vulgar. *Obs.*

1653 WATERHOUSE *Apol. Learning* 4 By with-drawing those favours..which invigor'd Learning, and nourished men of deserts and worth,..and by appreciating things and persons more tralatitious and vulgar. **1656** BLOUNT *Glossogr.*, *Tralatitious*, transferred or transposed: of the common sort, ordinary, vulgar.

3. Handed down from generation to generation; traditional; also, repeated by one from another, as a statement.

1795 WYTHE *Decis. Virginia* 6 Where an estate of inheritance is acquired not by tralatitious act, as by estoppel, dissesin [etc.]. **1900** MARGOLIOUTH in *Expositor* Aug. 136 The subjects..and expressions are 'tralaticious', borrowed by one generation from another, in so long a series that it is now impossible to name or locate their originator. **1912** SIR W. RAMSAY in *Contemp. Rev.* Mar. 339 Self-satisfied contentment with tralaticious statements, borrowed from good books or teachers..and repeated in book after book.

Hence **tralaˈtitiously** *adv.*, metaphorically.

1657 GAULE *Sap. Justif.* 91 Adams sin was not tropically and tralatitiously, but even litterally and properly, ours. **1669** HOLDER *Elem. Speech* 8 Language..properly..is that of the Tongue... Written Language is tralatitiously so called, because it is made to represent to the Eye the same Letters and Words, which are pronounced.

trale, traleis, obs. ff. TRAIL, TRELLIS.

†**traˈlineate**, *v. Obs. rare.* [f. It. *tralignare* 'to degenerate, to digresse, to growe from kinde' (Florio), repr. a. L. type **tra(ns)līneāre*, f. TRA(NS)- + *līnea* LINE *sb.*[2]: see -ATE[3].] *intr.* To go out of the direct line; to deviate.

1700 DRYDEN *Wife of Bath's T.* 396 If you tralineate from your father's mind, What are you else but of a bastard-kind? **1745** ELIZA HEYWOOD *Female Spect.* No. 16 (1748) III. 193 If sons tralineate from their father's virtues, and each successive race degenerates from the former.

'traliˈra, *int.* (*sb.*) Also redupl. **trallira, trallara.** A kindred vocal utterance to TRA-LA-LA, expressive of light-hearted gaiety.

1801 M. G. LEWIS *Grim White Woman* xix, Trallira! trallara! my old love, adieu! Trallira! trallara! I'll get me a new! **1819** SCOTT *Ivanhoe* xxxiii, Thou art one of those, who, with new French graces and Tra-li-ras, disturb the ancient English bugle notes.

Hence ˌ**tra-li-ˈra** *v.*, *intr.* to sing tra-li-ra.

1862 S. LANIER *Tournament* i. 10 Heart's palfrey caracoled gayly round, Heart tra-li-ra'd merrily; But Brain sat still, with never a sound, So cynical-calm was he.

†**trall**, obs. var. of THRALL *v.*

c **1420** *Chron. Vilod.* 2300 He myȝt not passe ouȝt of þat stede He was ytrallyd in suche aray.

trall, trallace, trallop, obs. ff. TRAWL, TRELLIS, TROLLOP.

†**traˈluce**, *v. Obs.* [ad. L. *trālūc-ēre* to shine across or through. Cf. It. *tralucere* (Florio).] *trans.* To shine through; = TRANSLUCE.

1591 SYLVESTER *Du Bartas* I. ii. 380 The turning Planets influence doth passe..through the glistring Tent Of the traluncing Fiery Element.

†**traˈlucency.** *Obs.* [f. as next: see -ENCY.] = TRANSLUCENCY.

1599 R. LINCHE *Anc. Fict.* F j, The perspicuous and coruscant tralucencie of the sun. **1646** SIR T. BROWNE *Pseud. Ep.* II. i. (1650) 42 The principle and most gemmary affection [of Crystall] is its Tralucency. **1649** G. DANIEL *Trinarch.*, *Hen. V* cxci, Soe the Autumnall Gossamere, well-trimm'd In Dew, retaines an odde Tralucencie.

traˈlucent, *a.* [ad. L. *trālūcēnt-em*, pr. pple. of *trālūcēre*: see TRALUCE. So It. *tralucente* (Florio).] = TRANSLUCENT. Hence †**traˈlucently** *adv. Obs.*

1592 KYD *Sol. & Pers.* II. i, If loue of this my person,.. haue percst through thy tralucent brest. **1597** DRAYTON *Heroic. Ep.*, *Edw. IV to Shore's Wife* Notes 57 Trees, whose gum is Amber, where Flies alighting are oftentimes tralucently imprisoned. **1608** B. JONSON *Masque Beauty*

Wks. (Rtldg.) 548/2 In the centre of the throne was a tralucent pillar, shining with several coloured lights. **1664** POWER *Exp. Philos.* I. 42 They all seem like Fragments of Crystal, or Alum, perfectly Tralucent. **1914** C. MACKENZIE *Sinister St.* II. IV. iv. 932 The benign trees that hung down with tralucent green sprays in the lamplight. **1951** —— *Carnival* (rev. ed.) viii. 81 Her hands were long and white; her lips very crimson and tralucent.

tram, *sb.*[1] Also 4–5 **tramm(e**, **(traimm(e**, **traum(e)**, 4–9 **trame**. [a. F. *trame*, OF. *traime*, *trème*, 12th c. in Godef. *Compl.*, (as in the late sense 1) woof of a web, also *fig.* cunning device or contrivance, machination, plot:—L. *trāma* woof. The literal sense of Fr. and L. appears in Eng. only in a technical use from mod.Fr. in 17th c.; but the fig. sense of 'machination' was adopted already in the 14th c., and app. gave rise to sense 3, which does not occur in French, but seems to belong here.]

I. 1. Woof or weft; *spec.* silk thread consisting of two or more single strands loosely twisted together; used for the weft or cross threads of the best silk goods. Also ***tram silk***.

1679 *Lond. Gaz.* No. 1392/4, 6l. of fine black Worsted, some pounds of Raw trame. **1776–83** JUSTAMOND tr. *Raynal's Hist. Indies* III. 164 The silks of Naples, Sicily and Reggio, whether in organzin or in tram, are all ordinary silks. **1812** J. SMYTH *Pract. Customs* (1821) 214 Tram silk is considered in London as thrown silk, but not as organzine thrown silk. **1868** *Rep. U.S. Commissioner Agric.* (1869) 289 Two or three threads of raw silk twisted loosely two or four times to the inch is tram, shute, or woof. **1911** ALICE DRYDEN *Church Embroidery* 91 For working faces 'tram' silk should be used.

II. Chiefly *north. dial.* and *Sc.* †2. A cunning contrivance or device; a machination, plot, scheme.

13.. *Gaw. & Gr. Knt.* 3 þe tulk þat þe trammes of tresoun þer wroȝt. **1616** J. MAITLAND *Apol. W. Maitl. of Lethington* in *Misc.* (S.H.S., 1904) 187 That plot and trame to tham-selfs and to manie others. **1866** J. E. BROGDEN *Provinc. Words Lincoln.*, *Trame*, 'gillery'.

†3. A mechanical contrivance; a machine, an engine; an implement, instrument, tool; in quot. 13.., tackle or gear of a ship. (Chiefly in *pl.*)

13.. *E.E. Allit. P.* C. 101 Then he tron on þo tres & þay her tramme ruchen. **1375** BARBOUR *Bruce* XVII. 245 He gert engynis and trammys ma [= make]. *a* **1400–50** *Alexander* 127 He toke traimmes him with to tute in þe sternes, Astralabus algate as his arte wald, Quadrentis coruen all of qu[h]yte siluyre full quaynte. *Ibid.* 286 þus as he tuke furth his toylis [= tools] & his trammys schewis. *Ibid.* 1296 Ser Balaan.. Buskes him in breneis with big men of armes, With traumes [*v.r.* trawynns] & with tribochetis þe tild [*v.r.* towre] to assaile. *Ibid.* 1373 Quen he had tiȝt vp þis tram [*v.r.* trame (*i.e.* a siege-tower)] & þis tild rerid.

tram (træm), *sb.*[2] [In sense 1, used in Sc. *c* 1500, and prob. earlier; app. the same word as LG. *traam* 'balk, beam, e.g. of a wheelbarrow or dung-sledge, tram, handle of a barrow or sledge, also a rung or step of a ladder, bar of a chair' (*Brem. Wbch.* 1771), EFris. *trame*, *trâm* beam of wood, rung or step of a ladder, bar of a chair, tram of a wheelbarrow; in MLG. *trame*, *treme*, MDu. *trame* balk or beam, rung of a ladder, etc.; WFlem. *traam*, *trame*.

The specific sense first found in Scotch is 'the tram of a barrow'. The further sense-development presents many difficulties, chiefly from the scarcity of early examples, and the fact that the various senses are from separate localities, so that they cannot be taken as showing any general development. But branch II, in which *tram* is a miners' term for the vehicle for carrying coal or ore (in its development from a hand-barrow, or at least a sledge, to a small 4-wheeled iron wagon) may, on the principle of *pars pro toto*, have arisen out of that of 'barrow-tram' in I. Branch III is more difficult, and is the *crux* of the word. But if it was short for something like 'tram-track', it might have arisen out of II; and if it was applied primarily to the wooden beams or 'rails' laid as wheel tracks, it might conceivably go back to the LG. sense of 'balk' or 'beam': evidence is wanting. From II or III used attributively came *tram-road* (in use in 1800), and the later *tram-way* (in use in 1825); also *tram-carriage* and the modern *tram-car*, known in 1868 and 1873 respectively, and before 1880 shortened in popular English use to *tram*, branch IV, which thus by a circuitous course 'harks back' to a sense akin to branch II.]

I. A shaft of a barrow or cart.

1. a. Each of the two shafts of a cart or wagon, a hand-barrow, or a wheelbarrow, the ends of which in a barrow form the handles. *Sc.*

These shafts are prolongations of the strong side-timbers of the frame or body of the structure: in a hand-barrow these are prolonged both ways, to form shafts or trams both before and behind, by which the two bearers carry the barrow; in a wheelbarrow they are prolonged in one direction to form the shafts, or trams, and in the other to form sockets for the axle of the wheel; in a cart they are prolonged in front to form the strong shafts or trams within which the horse walks, while their ends usually form short projections behind.

1500–20 DUNBAR *Poems* lii. 19, I wald scho war, bayth syd and bak, Weill batteret with ane barrow-tram. **1545** *Acc. Ld. High Treas. Scot.* VIII. 360 Ane pair of sled trammys to be lymmaris to ane of the saiddis falconis [guns]. *a* **1550** Barrow trammis, **1657** Barrow-trams [see BARROW *sb.*[3] 4]. **1766** *State of Proc., D. Macdonald* v. *A. Dk. of Gordon*, Pursuer's Proof 8, Light timber, such as strings and cart trams. **1786** BURNS *Inventory* 31 Ae auld wheelbarrow, mair for token, Ae leg an' baith the trams are broken. **1790** SHIRREFS *Poems* 360 Nor is the naig the worse to draw A wee while in the trams. **1830** GALT *Lawrie T.* IV. viii, I.. sat down on the tram of the wagon. **1833** ALISON *Hist. Europe* (1849) II. vi. §79. 75 Nearly an hour was.. lost, by an accident to one of the trams of the royal carriage.

b. *transf.* In *pl.* The two upright posts of a gallows; also humorously, in *sing.*, a man's leg; particularly, a wooden leg.

a **1670** SPALDING *Troub. Chas. I* (1851) II. 4 Be order, the hangman brak his suord betuixt the crossis of Abirdein, and betuixt the gallowis-tramis standing thair. **1808–18** JAMIESON, *Tram*, in a ludicrous sense, the leg or limb; as *lang trams*, long limbs. **1882** *Ibid.*, Applied also to a person with long ungainly legs, *Clydes.* **1834** M. SCOTT *Cruise Midge* (1863) 48 He began to thunder at the low door with his pillar-like trams. *Ibid.* 206 It must have stumped along for fifty years on a leg of flesh and a tram of wood.

II. A framework, barrow, or the like, on which loads are dragged, carried, or supported.

2. *Coal-mining.* A quadrilateral frame or skeleton truck on which the corves were formerly carried; at first prob. carried like a hand-barrow, then dragged like a sledge, afterwards provided with low wheels on which to run; in some colliery districts applied to the small iron truck which supplies the place of the earlier 'tram' and corve; in others to the part of the 'tub' (on wheels) to which the 'box' is bolted.

1516–17 *Durham Acc. Rolls* (Surtees) 293 Item, ad puteum [pit] de Hett,.. j restis et j cruke de ferro.. ij pykes, ij trammys, et ij shulys. **1585** *Wills & Inv. N.C.* (Surtees) II. 112, j long wayne without wheels, ij yron ax-nailes, and ij yokes, 6s. j cowpe, ij trams, and two ax-trees 2s. 8d. **1708** J. C. *Compl. Collier* (1845) 39 The Wages for the Barrow-Men is.. about twenty pence a Day for each *Tram* (that is to say) for putting so many loaden Corves, as are carried on one Sledge or Tram in one Day to the Pit Shaft. **1789** BRAND *Hist. Newcastle* II. 681 Trams are a kind of sledges on which the coals are brought from the places where they are hewn to the shaft. A tram has four wheels, but a sledge properly so called is drawn by a horse without wheels. **1797** CURR *Coal Viewer* 9 Placing the corf upon a small frame or tram.. and hooking or chaining one tram to another. **1817** FAREY *Derbyshire* III. 439 The Trams.. have stout lower side pieces of wood which project at each end, and are hooped with iron which just meet together and receive the shock when the Trams overtake each other. **1839** URE *Dict. Arts* 982 An improvement.. is to place the basket or corve on a small four-wheeled carriage, called a tram, or to attach wheels to the corve itself. **1841** J. HOLLAND *Hist. Fossil Fuel*, etc. 227 The coals.. were conveyed.. on trams, a narrow framework of wood mounted on four low wheels. **1851** GREENWELL *Coal-trade Terms Northumb. & Durh.* 54 Since the substitution of tubs, the trams have been attached to them. **1867** W. W. SMYTH *Coal & Coal-mining* 149 The northern method was to fill the coals.. into a large basket (corve) of wicker.. and to drag it on a small carriage, or tram, .. to the crane-place on the main road. **1883** GRESLEY *Gloss. Coal Mining* 257 In South Wales *trams* constructed wholly of wrought iron or steel are much used... They have a carrying capacity of 25 cwt. **1888** NICHOLSON *Coal Trade Gloss.*, *Tram*, the term still applies to the part of a tub to which the box is bolted. **1894** *Northumbld. Gloss.* s.v., Trams and tubs are now made in one.

b. *transf.* The one or two lads in charge of a tram; also, the work performed by these.

1856 WHELLAN *Hist. Durham* 94 When a boy 'puts' or drags a load by himself he is designated a tram. **1894** *Northumbld. Gloss.* s.v., Sometimes tram was applied to the two lads in charge of it [the colliery tram]—called a 'tram of lads'. 'Half a tram', the work of one putter where two are engaged on a tram.

3. A quadrilateral frame or bench (like the body of a hand-barrow) supported on four legs or blocks, on which casks or the like stand, or at which an artisan works.

1818 W. MARSHALL *Review* II. 485 (E.D.D.) The cheese-tubs are placed on a small tram or bench. **1884** *S. Worc.* (Upton on Severn) *Gloss.*, *Tram* or *Tramming*, a framework, or a loose arrangement, of stout parallel rails on short legs, or blocks, for supporting casks. **1894** *S.E. Worc. Gloss.*, *Tram*, a strong square frame with four legs on which a wheelwright makes wheels; also a stand for casks.

III. A track of wood, stone, or iron; a tram-road or tramway.

4. A continuous line or track of timber beams or 'rails', or later of stone blocks or slabs, a parallel pair of which lines formed a tramway, originally in or from a mine. Hence, each of the wheel-tracks or 'rails' of a tram-road of an early type, or of a later tramway or railway.

[*a* **1734** NORTH *Life Ld. Keeper North* (1742) 136 The Manner of the Carriage [of coals in Northumberland in 1676] is by laying Rails of Timber, from the Colliery, down to the River, exactly streight and parallel; and bulky Carts are made with four Rowlets fitting these Rails; whereby the Carriage is so easy that one Horse will draw four or five Chaldron of Coals, and is an immense Benefit to the Coal Merchants.] **1826** J. ADAMSON *Sk. Inform. Rail-Roads* 6 The upper flat part [of a rail on a railway], along which the wheel rolls, we may, from its analogy to the old wooden rails, call the tram of the rail. **1834** N. W. CUNDY *Inland Transit* 1 The Manchester and Liverpool railroad, in my opinion, is constructed too narrow both in the trams and the space between them. **1838** SIMMS *Public Works Gt. Brit.* III. 3 He [Mr. Macneill] is laying stone blocks or trams for the wheels to roll upon. **1881** RAYMOND *Mining Gloss.*, *Tram*.. One of the rails of a tramroad or railroad. [See also quot. 1825 in 5, and TRAM-LINE, -ROAD, -WAY.]

5. A road laid with such wooden planks or rails, or with parallel rows of stone slabs or of iron plates or 'rails', for the easier passage of loaded wagons, etc., in a coal-mine or above ground; a tram-road of an early type. (See also Note below.)

[**1825** MACKENZIE *Hist. Northumbld.* I. 146 Square wooden rails laid in two right parallel lines, and firmly pegged down on wooden sleepers. The tops of the rail are plained smooth and round, and sometimes covered with plates of wrought iron. About the year 1786 cast-iron railways were introduced as an improvement upon the tram or wooden rail-way.] **1850** ANSTED *Geol.*, etc. §1117 The loaded waggons, or corves, are conveyed along the tram by lads called putters. **1865** *Pall Mall G.* 27 June 10 Have they not trams in the suburbs of half our Lancashire towns, and is there not a tram on a grand scale for the use of those long ugly *Omnibus Americains* which ply between Paris and Versailles?

IV. Short for *tram-car* or the like.

6. A passenger car on a street tramway; a tram-car.

1879 WEBSTER Suppl., *Tram*, a car on a horse-railroad. *Eng.* **1880** MARY FITZ-GIBBON *Trip to Manitoba* vii. 71 To see if the trams were coming. **1883** G. H. BOUGHTON in *Harper's Mag.* Apr. 702/1 It was so easy to pop into the.. tram. **1884** *Ibid.* Sept. 524/1 Taking the tram to Scheveningen. **1887** *Punch* 12 Mar. 130/2 She is left without a penny to pay for tram or bus. **1902** R. BAGOT *Donna Diana* xiii, The discordant clanging of the gongs of electric trams fall hideously on the ear.

7. An overhead or suspended carrier travelling on a cable.

1905 *Daily Chron.* 23 Sept. 8/1 (Supply of meat at Aldershot) Hoisting gear bears the carcases quickly away for dressing, and when that is done, an overhead carrying line, conveniently referred to as the 'tram', conveys them to the cooling room.

V. 8. *attrib.* and *Comb.*, as ***tram-beam*** (*fig.* in quot.), ***-bell***, ***-boy***, ***-carriage***, ***-conductor***, ***-driver***, ***-fare*** (also *transf.*), ***-horn***, ***horse***, ***-load***, ***-railway***, ***-refuge***, ***ride***, ***-shed***, ***stop***, ***-ticket***, ***-top***, ***-track***, ***-train***, ***-wagon***, ***-wheel***, ***-whistle***, ***-yard***; ***-travelling*** adj.; **tram-man**, a man employed on a tramway, *esp.* a tram-conductor or driver; **tram-rail**, (*a*) a plate-rail: see PLATE *sb.* 8; (*b*) each of the rails of a tramway. See also TRAM-CAR, -LINE, etc.

1879 G. M. HOPKINS *Poems* (1967) 81 Or to-fro tender *trambeams truckle at the eye. **1905** *Daily Chron.* 14 Sept. 3/1 The incessant clanging of the *tram-bell [in Holland]. **1904** J. WELLS *J. H. Wilson* xi. 97 He.. established societies for the *tram-boys [in collieries]. **1868** *Daily News* 22 July, Asking the moderate fee of twopence for its entire journey, the *tram carriage is like a rough omnibus without cushions turned inside out. **1892** ZANGWILL *Bow Mystery* 4 The *tram conductors' bells were.. ringing. **1909** J. R. WARE *Passing Eng.* 249/2 **Tram-fare* (*London Streets*', 1882), twopence. **1922** JOYCE *Ulysses* 696 *Debit*... Tramfare [£.s.d.] 0.0.1. **1978** M. DE LARRABEITI *Rose beyond Thames* 87 He bought.. me a second-hand bike so that I could cycle to school and save the tram fare. **1922** *Blackw. Mag.* Apr. 447/1 The blowing of *tram-horns. **1891** J. L. KIPLING *Beast & Man in India* viii. 206 (*caption*) Bombay *tram-horse wearing horse-cap. **1904** *Daily News* 24 May 12 The crowded *tram-loads along this flowered highway of the West. **1892** ZANGWILL *Bow Mystery* 4 At an early meeting of discontented *tram-men. **1839** URE *Dict. Arts* 982 The rails are called *tram-rails, or plate-rails. **1900** *Westm. Gaz.* 5 Sept. 6/2 The tram rails had been watered in order to lessen friction, and accidents to cyclists are of constant occurrence in the same neighbourhood. **1938** *All England Law Rep. Annotated* I. 339 An illuminated bollard at one end of a *tram refuge had been damaged in an accident. **1919** R. FRY *Let.* 3 Nov. (1972) II. 465 Marseilles is only one and a half hours *tram ride. **1977** *Lancashire Life* Dec. 57/2 One summer's day he changed the routine and took us a tram ride into the country. **1930** R. LEHMANN *Note in Music* I. 19 They arrived at the *tram-stop to find a solid wedge of humanity struggling to get aboard. **1980** P. HARCOURT *Tomorrow's Treason* I. iv. 58 It was a long walk to the nearest tram stop. **1895** G. B. SHAW *Let.* 23 Mar. (1965) I. 504 We .. went to her sister's.. by *tramtop. **1916** JOYCE *Portrait of Artist* ii. 70 He heard the mare's hoofs clattering along the *tramtrack on the Rock Road. **1911** R. FRY *Let.* 15 Apr. (1972) I. 347 A two hours' journey by a *tram-train to the slopes of Mt Olympus. **1894** *Daily News* 5 May 8/5 Of much advantage to the *tram-travelling public of South London. **1824** F. WITTS *Diary* 6 May (1978) 38 The *tram waggons now may be made to travel without horses by steam. **1855** J. R. LEIFCHILD *Cornwall Mines* 150 That the ore may readily fall down to the level below them, whence it is carried in tram-waggons to the shaft. **1825** J. NICHOLSON *Operat. Mechanic* 649 Fig. 644 represents a view of a rolley or *tram-wheel, calculated to move upon a plate railway. **1883** E. F. KNIGHT *Cruise Falcon* (1887) 40 Above the shrill scream of the *tram-whistle rises their shriller Babel. **1909** *London City Mission Mag.* Dec. 241/2 A stableman from an adjacent *tramyard.

(*Note.* The following quot. for *tram* is difficult to place. It has the appearance of belonging to sense 5; but its early date is at variance with this. No part of the road in or near the Bridgegate at Barnard Castle is now known as 'the tram', nor is there any tradition of the former existence of a tramway of any kind there. On the opposite or Yorkshire side of the Tees, the road running southward from the end of the bridge is protected from the river by a heavy stone wall locally known as 'the tram wall'; but this does not seem to answer to the words of the will.

1555 *Will of Ambrose Middleton* in *Wills & Inv. N.C.* (Surtees) II. 37 *note*, To the amendinge of the highewaye or tram, from the weste ende of Bridgegait, in Barnard Castle, 20s.)

Hence **'tramful**, as much or as many as a tram or tram-car will hold; **tramifi'cation** (*nonce-wd.*), the construction of a tramway; **'tramless** *a.*, (*a*) without shafts, as a cart (*dial.*); (*b*) having no trams or tramway facilities.

1905 *Daily News* 20 Sept. 6 The coal came up in little *tramfuls. **1834** *New Monthly Mag.* XL. 372 The whole object of that *tramification is the conveyance of goods—of heavy loads. **1850** A. Maclagan *Cronie O'Mine* Poems (1851) 174 A *tramless cart or a couterless plough. **1904** *Daily Chron.* 29 Mar. 3/6 Tramless Brixton .. the Cars are to be Stopped for Two Months.

tram, *sb.*³ *Mech.* [Short for trammel *sb.*¹]

1. An instrument for describing ellipses; = trammel *sb.*¹ 4.

1884 in Knight *Dict. Mech.* Suppl.

2. The condition of correct adjustment of one part to another (obtained by using the *tram-staff*); used in the phrases ***in tram, out of tram***. Originally used in reference to the adjustment of millstones, thence extended to other mechanical adjustments.

1891 in *Cent. Dict.*; and in later Dicts.

3. *attrib.* and *Comb.*, as **tram-pot**, the step in which the toe of a millstone spindle revolves; **tram-staff**, a straight-edge used by millwrights in adjusting the millstone spindle (*Cent. Dict.* 1891).

1884 Knight *Dict. Mech.* Suppl., *Trampot* (Milling), the seat in which the foot of the spindle is stepped.

tram (træm), *v.*¹ [f. tram *sb.*²]

1. *intr.* To travel by a tramway or on a tram-car (also ***to tram it***). *colloq.* Also (*U.S.*), to drive or operate a tram-car (*Cent. Dict.* 1891).

1826 in *Northumbld. Gloss.* s.v., Liddell, why he from Durham came,.. But home again he'd better tram. **1896** *Westm. Gaz.* 9 Apr. 7/2 The Walworthian has to tram to Greenwich. **1904** E. Nesbit *Phœnix & Carpet* x, They can tram it home.

2. *trans. Mining.* To convey (coal, ore, etc.) by a tram or trams.

1874 J. H. Collins *Metal Mining* (1875) 11 One sees .. the ore and rubbish allowed to accumulate behind the men to a height of several feet before it is trammed back to the shaft. **1887** Raymond *Statist. Mines & Mining* 8 Tramming. **1889** *Eng. Illustr. Mag.* May 572/2 To 'tram' the coal from the working face .. to the sidings where the horses take the waggons. **1893** *Pall Mall G.* 14 Jan. 1/3 In the level below .. only one man was saved, who had been tramming to the shaft the ore which he excavated on previous days.

b. To push (a tram or wagon) to and from the shaft in a mine.

1883 Le Neve Foster in *Encycl. Brit.* XVI. 455/2 (*Mining*) This trolley (which is merely a small platform upon wheels) is pushed (*trammed*) to the shaft; the full kibble is hooked on to the winding-rope and drawn up, whilst an empty kibble is placed upon the trolley and trammed back along the level .. where it is again loaded. *Ibid.*, The motive power for tramming wagons along the levels of metal mines is generally supplied by men or boys.

tram, *v.*² [f. tram *sb.*³] *trans.* and *intr.* To use a tram or tram-staff in adjusting spindles or axles, or in measuring, alining, or the like.

1891 in *Cent. Dict.* (implied in *tramming*); in later Dicts.

tram, in *trim tram*: see trim-tram.

‖**trama** ('treɪmə, 'trɑːmə). *Bot.* [L. *trāma* woof, weft, filling of a web.] The substance between the surfaces of the 'gills' of hymenomycetous fungi. Also called *intralamellar substance, dissepiment*. Hence '**tramal** *a.* (*Cent. Dict.* 1891).

1857 Berkeley *Cryptog. Bot.* §399 In Schizophyllum, the gills split in the direction of their trama. **1874** Cooke *Fungi* 23 In Lactarius and Russula the trama, or inner substance, is vesicular. **1875** Bennett & Dyer *Sachs' Bot.* 250 The substance of the lamella, called the *Trama*.

†'**tramble**, *v. Obs.* [Origin uncertain. Cf. Sw. dial. *tramla, trumla* to fall (Rietz).]

1. *intr.* To roll over and over; to tumble, fall headlong. *rare*⁻¹.

1609 Bible (Douay) *Job* xxx. 14 They haue broken violently vpon me, and are come trambling downe to my miseries [Vulg. *ad meas miserias devoluti sunt*].

2. *trans.* To wash (tin-ore) by agitating it in a trough of water (buddle *sb.*²) with a special shovel called a ***trambling shovel***; to buddle; = toze *v.*²

1671 *Phil. Trans.* VI. 2109 A man .. with a Trambling shovel in his hand to cast up the Ore. *Ibid.* 2110 When this Buddle grows full, we take it up; here distinguishing again the Fore-head from the Middle and Tails; which are trambled over again. **1710** J. Harris *Lex. Techn.* II, *Trambling*, is the Term used in Dressing of Tin-ore, for washing it very clean in Water .. with .. a Trambling-shovel, and in a Frame of Boards, which they call a Buddle.

trambooze: see trampoose.

tram-car ('træmkɑː(r)). [f. tram *sb.*² III. + car.] A public car or carriage running on a tram-way for the conveyance of passengers; called earlier *tramway car*, and already in 1879 simply *tram* (tram *sb.*² 6). *tram-carriage* (tram *sb.*² 8) is cited 1868.

1873 *Engineer* 28 Nov. 353 A trial of Grantham's steam tram car. **1876** *Ibid.* 26 May 400 A heavy vehicle such as an omnibus or a tram car. **1879** *Trans. Soc. Engineers* 195 The Italian tram cars enabled him to see nearly the whole of the city of Turin for .. sixpence. **1883** F. M. Crawford *Dr. Claudius* xiii, The ceaseless ring of the tram-cars stopping every few steps to pick up a passenger. **1905** R. Bagot *Passport* iii, In a quiet and secluded position .. undisturbed by the noise of the tram-cars.

attrib. **1880** *Proc. Inst. Mech. Engin.* 199 The flange of a tramcar wheel.

trame, var. tram *sb.*¹

Traminer (trə'miːnə(r)). [a. Ger., f. *Tramin* (It. *Termeno*), the name of a village in N. Italy.] The name of any of several varieties of vine and grape widely grown in Germany, Alsace, and elsewhere; the white wine with perfumed bouquet produced from this grape. Also *attrib.*

1851 C. Redding *Hist. & Descr. Mod. Wines* (ed. 3) ii. 48 Then there is the *Traminer* with a small berry, sweet, and fond of a marly soil. **1872** Thudichum & Dupré *Treatise on Origin, Nature, & Varieties of Wine* ix. 281 German wines —... Riesling... Forster Traminer. *Ibid.* xvi. 541 There are also some so-called Franconia grapes, which we will describe as white Traminer. **1948** 'J. Tey' *Franchise Affair* xiii. 144 There is a Traminer for dinner. **1960** *Spectator* 13 May 714 Yugoslav traminer came on to the British market during 1959. **1972** *Guardian* 4 May 13/5 The local variety of the Traminer grape called the Savagnin.

[**tramiss.** Misreading of *traunss*, trance.]

'**tram-line.** Also **tramline**. [f. tram *sb.*² 5 or 6 + line *sb.*²: cf. *railway line*.]

1. A tramway; also, a tram-rail.

1886 Hare *Story my Life* (1900) VI. xxiv. 9 We were taken back to the tram-line. **1895** Zangwill *Master* ii. ix, The yellow sand scattered on slippery days along the tram-lines. **1896** *Times* 30 Sept. 7/6 Tenders are to be sent in .. to the tramline's offices. **1905** Visct. Ridley in *Daily Chron.* 21 July 5/5 The Bill dealt with several new tramlines, three of which were uncontested and not very important.

2. *transf.* in *pl.* Either pair of parallel lines bordering the side of a lawn-tennis court, the inner of each pair marking the boundary of the court for singles and the outer for doubles. Occas. *sing.*, one of this pair of lines. *colloq.*

1937 Partridge *Dict. Slang* 906/1 *Tram-lines*, the 4½ ft. wide area on each side of a (doubles) lawn-tennis court: sporting: from ca. 1929. Esp. *down the tram-lines*, i.e. more or less straight along this strip of the court. **1959** *Times* 31 Aug. 12/1 It passed an inch outside the tram-line. **1978** G. Forbes *Handful of Summers* ix. 180 Cliff .. hit a two-hander down Rodney's tramlines.

3. *transf.* and *fig.* Chiefly *pl.*, inflexible, predetermined or restrictive courses of action, principles, etc.

1948 D. Welch *Brave & Cruel* 68, I ran it [*sc.* a nail-brush] up and down his back until I'd made harsh red tramlines. **1955** H. Spring *These Lovers fled Away* iv. 113 One [obstacle] was .. his addiction to social tram-lines. As things had been, they should, in a well-organised world, remain. **1967** *Times Rev. Industry* Oct. 60/2 Tramline thinking .. delays improvement in the quality of the trade union movement itself. **1976** *Listener* 22 July 85/3 The government .. is forced .. more and more on to orthodox, predictable tramlines, and protestations that imagination, vision and radical policy must await more prosperous days. **1979** J. Wainwright *Duty Elsewhere* vii. 28 Most chief constables tend to run on tram-lines... They feel safer.

Hence '**tram-lined** *a.*, furnished with tram-lines.

1924 W. J. Locke *Coming of Amos* xiii. 171 He stepped into the car and .. drove at break-neck speed down the tram-lined hill. **1932** Auden *Orators* iii. 89 Tudor from the tram-lined town.

trammel ('træməl), *sb.*¹ Forms: 5 **tramale, -ell, -elle, (tramaly,** 5–6 **-ely),** 5–6 **tramayle,** (6 *Sc.* **tramalt),** 6–7 **tramell,** 6–8 **-el,** 6–9 **trammell,** 7 **tramaile,** 6– **trammel.** [In sense 1, a. OF. *tramail* (*c* 1220 in Godef. *Compl.*), mod.F. *trémail* a fishing- or fowling-net, with three layers of meshes, = It. *tramaglio*, Sp. *trasmallo*, Pg. *trasmalho*:—late pop.L. *tramaculum* for *tri-, tremaculum* (in Salic Law, Hessels, Cod. 1, xxvii. 20, *tremaclem*, v. rr. *tremalem, tremagilo, tramaculam, trimaclem, tremagolum, tremachlum*, etc.) a kind of fishing-net, generally explained as f. L. *tri-* three + *macula* mesh. In the Romanic langs. the prefix appears to have been taken as = *tra-*, L. *trans.* The history of the other senses here included is difficult: see Note below.]

I. 1. A long narrow fishing-net, set vertically with floats and sinkers; consisting of two 'walls' of large-meshed netting, between which is a net of fine mesh, loosely hung. More fully trammel-net.

The fish enters through the large mesh on one side, drives the fine netting through the large mesh on the other, and is thus trapped in a pocket or bag of the fine netting. Also sometimes applied to other kinds of fishing nets.

1363 [implied in trammeller 1].
c **1440** *Promp. Parv.* 499/1 Tramayle, grete nette for fyschynge (*K.* tramely, *H.*, *P.* tramaly), *tragum*. **14..** *Voc.* in Wr.-Wülcker 617/18 *Tramellum* .. *quoddam genus retis*, .. a tramayle. **1467–8** *Durham Acc. Rolls* (Surtees) 92 Pro j rethe voc. Tramale, xxiiijᵈ. **1558** *Act 1 Eliz.* c. 17 §3 No persone .. shall fishe .. with any maner of Nett, Tramell [etc.], but onely with a Nett or Tramell whereof every Meshe .. shalbee [etc.]. **1633** P. Fletcher *Pisc. Ecl.* v. xiv, Are thy lines broke? or are thy trammels tore? **1787** Best *Angling* (ed. 2) 5 By fishing with trammels or flews in March or April. **1848** C. A. Johns *Week at Lizard* 242 The trammel is a long net, about five feet deep, with a double mesh, one large enough to allow the fish to pass through, the other much smaller. **1883** E. P. Ramsay *Food Fishes N.S. Wales* 33 (Fish. Exhib. Publ.) They are usually taken for market with a Trammel, or Bag-net, set across the stream, or by hook and line.

b. A fowling-net; = trammel-net b.

1530 Palsgr. 282/2 Tramell to catche fysshe or byrdes, *trameau*. **1581** *Act 23 Eliz.* c. 10 §6 To take any Partridges or Feasaunts by night, under any Tramell, Lowbell, Roade-nette or other Engine. **1655** Moufet & Bennet *Health's Impr.* (1746) 173 A Partridge taken in Flight, or a Lark dared with a Hawk, is worth ten taken with Nets, Springs and Trammels. **1895** Quiller Couch *Wand. Heath* 80 He and his mates went out and tilled the trammel.

II. †**2.** A hobble to prevent a horse from straying or kicking; also, a contrivance for teaching a horse to amble, consisting of lines and straps connecting the fore and hind feet on each side, with a strap over the back to which both lines were fastened for support. *Obs.*

c **1550** W. Keth *Tye the Mare, Tom Boy* 35 (Ritson) Yett wer thou much better In trammells to bynd her; A loock and a fetter Befor and behynd her. **1591** Greene *Art Conny Catch.* ii. (1592) 4 Whether they haue horse-locks or no, .. in the night they take him or them away, and are skilfull in the blacke Art, for picking open the tramels or lockes. **1616** Surfl. & Markh. *Country Farme* 133 It is called a Tramell when a Horses neere fore-legge and his neere hinder-legge .. are so fastened together with leathers and cords, that he cannot put forward his fore-legge, but he must perforce hale his hinder-legge after it. **1675** *Lond. Gaz.* No. 1043/4 A .. Nag .. has all his paces, and swellings in his forelegs caused by the tramels. **1766** *Compl. Farmer*, *Tramel*, .. made sometimes of leather, but more usually of ropes, fitted to a horse's legs to regulate his motion, and teach him to amble.

3. *transf.* and *fig.* Anything that hinders or impedes free action; anything that confines, restrains, fetters, or shackles. Chiefly *pl.*

a **1653** G. Daniel *Idyll.* iii. 106 'Tis an easie Chord; ye Flax of Law Makes a soft Trammell. *a* **1680** Butler *Rem.* (1759) I. 266 To put his Wits into a kind of Tramels. **1709** Steele & Swift *Tatler* No. 74 ¶4 The Gentleman is in the true Trammels of Love. **1787** Mme. D'Arblay *Diary* 5 Jan., There seemed to be no opportunity .. of liberating my evenings from official trammels. **1841** D'Israeli *Amen. Lit.* (1867) 462 The destiny of Spenser was .. to wear the silken trammels of noble patrons. **1889** *John Bull* 2 Mar. 148/3 Throughout her career she [Geo. Eliot], for the most part, refused to bind herself by conventional trammels.

4. *Mech.* An instrument for describing ellipses (F. *compas à ellipse*), consisting of a cross with two grooves at right angles, in which slide pins carrying a beam or ruler with a pencil; also applied to the *beam-compass* (beam *sb.*¹ IV). Also *pl.*

So called because the motion of the beam carrying the pencil is trammelled or confined by the restriction of the pins to the grooves.

1725 W. Halfpenny *Sound Building* 7 Make the Tramel .. in the same Form as .. in the Figure. **1780** Ludlam in *Phil. Trans.* LXX. 378 The instrument for drawing ovals upon paper or board .. is much in use among the joiners, and called by them the trammels. **1795** Hutton *Math. Dict.* s.v., All the engines for turning ovals are constructed on the same principles with the Trammels: the only difference is, that in the Trammels the board is at rest, and the pencil moves upon it. **1875** *Carpentry & Join.* 118 We will now add one other method of striking elliptic curves, and describe .. the instrument by which it is done. This is called a trammel. **1884** *Cheshire Gloss.* s.v., In working circular work, a staff of the radius of the circle is a trammel.

III. 5. A series of rings or links, or other device, to bear a crook at different heights over the fire; the whole being suspended from a transverse bar (the crook-tree), built in the chimney, or from a small crane or gallows, the vertical member of which turns in sockets in the jamb and lintel. Now *local Eng.* and *U.S.*

1537 *Bury Wills* (Camden) 130 The tramely yn the chemney, and the racke on the soler. **1630** *Maldon, Essex, Documents* Bundle 217. No. 22 In the little butterye, i iron hooke to hange at the eand of a tramell, 2*d*. **1674** Ray *S. & E.C. Words* 77 A *Trammel*, an iron instrument hanging in the chimney, whereon to hang pots or kettles over the fire. **1866** Whittier *Snowbound* 136 The crane and pendent trammels showed. **1883** *Hampshire Gloss.*, *Trammel*, a hook to hang a boiler on. [An error.] **1889** Lucy Larcom *New Eng. Girlhood* i. 22 We .. sometimes smirched our clean aprons .. against the swinging crane with its sooty pot-hooks and trammels.

IV. †**6.** *pl.* The plaits, braids, or tresses of a woman's hair; in quot. 1594 with play on sense 1.

(Sometimes erroneously explained as a net to confine the hair.)

1589 Greene *Menaphon* (Arb.) 25 She .. wraps affection in the tramels of her haire. **1590** Spenser *F.Q.* ii. ii. 15 Her golden lockes she roundly did uptye In breaded tramels. *Ibid.* iii. ix. 20 Her golden locks, that were in trammells gay Upbounden, did them selves adowne display And raught unto her heeles. **1594** Greene & Lodge *Looking Glasse* G.'s Wks. (Rtldg.) 122/2 For women's locks are trammels of conceit, Which do entangle Love for all his wiles. **1669** A. Browne *Ars Pict.* 86 You may go over the hair, disposing into such forms, folds or tramels, as may become your Picture best. **1673** Jordan *Lond. in Splend.* 12 A long fair Hair, the tramels tyed with small Ribon of all the light Colours.

V. 7. *attrib.* and *Comb.*, as †***trammel-boat*** (? used in fishing with the trammel-net); ***trammel-trick*** [f. trammel *v.*]; **trammel-wheel**, a mechanical device for converting rotary into reciprocal motion, consisting of a wheel with grooves crossing each other, in which slide projections attached to a connecting-rod, so that the rod makes two up-and-down motions for each revolution of the wheel; also a modification of this.

1614 T. GENTLEMAN *Way to Wealth* (1660) 9 The Pinks for barreld Fish, and Trammel boats. **1873** BROWNING *Red Cott. Nt.-cap* 176 Be theirs to drowse Trammeled, and ours to watch the trammel-trick! **1877** KNIGHT *Dict. Mech.*, Trammel-wheel.

[*Note.* French dictionaries have *trémail, tramail*, only in senses 1, 1 b. And indeed the sense-connexion of branches II, III, IV with I, and with each other, is obscure; some of them may perhaps be different words. But the identification of I and II is not confined to English. Du Cange quotes a med.L. statute of Piacenza, in which *tramaiolum* (? read *tramacolum*) is applied to a stick a cubit and a half long, ordered to be fixed to the necks of dogs to prevent them from running into vineyards or other places where they might do mischief; and he identifies this word with It. *tramaglio* and F. *tramail*, and refers to this word as known to be applied not only to a net, but to any kind of shackle or snare (*pedica*). Baretti's Ital. dictionary has *tramaglio* only as 'a trammel or drag-net', but Florio 1611 has it 'a tramell or ensnaring'.]

†**trammel**, *sb.*[2] *Obs.* In 5 tramel, -ale, -aly. [Cf. OF. *tremuie, tremue, tremee* (all 14th c. in Godef.), *trameul, tremouille, tremuë* (Cotgr.), mod.F. *trémie* = Pr. *tremueia*, Cat. *tramuja*, It. *tramoggia*, Sicil. *trimoja*:—L. *trimodia*, a three-peck measure: see Diez, Scheler. Some med.L. and Romanic forms are affected by L. *trem-ĕre* to tremble. In Eng. apparently confounded with TRAMMEL *sb.*[1]] The hopper of a mill.

c **1440** *Promp. Parv.* 246/1 Hopur, of a mylle, or a tramale (*S.* tramel, *a* 1485), *taratantara, farricapsium. Ibid.* 499/1 Tramaly, of a mylle, *idem quod* hopur; *supra*; *et faricapsia.*

'**trammel**, *v.* [f. TRAMMEL *sb.*[1]]

† **1.** *trans.* To bind up (a corpse). *Obs.*

1536 in *Archæol.* XVI. 23 (Funeral Q. Kath.) The Corps must be sered, tramayled, leded, and chested. **1546–7** in Strype *Eccl. Mem.* (1721) II. App. A. 3 (Funeral K. Hen. VIII) Surely bound and trammel'd with cords of silk. *c* **1558** *Leland's Collect.* (1770) V. 308 Whoo [Q. Mary] after her Departuer was..cered, and tramelled in this Manner.

2. *intr.* To use a trammel-net; *trans.* to take (fish or birds) with a trammel-net.

1588–1866 [see TRAMMELLING *vbl. sb.*]. **1846** *Bell's Life* 9 Aug. 7/5 Four men were caught trammelling pheasants.

† **3.** *trans.* To fasten together (the legs of a horse) with trammels (TRAMMEL *sb.*[1] 2); also, to put trammels on (a horse). *Obs.*

1607 MARKHAM *Caval.* IV. ix. (1617) 45, I would haue you in any case..to tramell your horse aboue knee. **1610** —— *Masterp.* II. clix. 468 After you haue tramelled all his foure legges. **1639** T. DE GRAY *Compl. Horsem.* 307 Tramell his fore-feet that he do not lye down.

4. *fig.* To entangle or fasten *up* as in a trammel.

1605 SHAKS. *Macb.* I. vii. 3 If th'Assassination Could trammell vp the Consequence, and catch..Successe. **1819** KEATS *Lamia* II. 52 How to entangle, trammel up, and snare Your soul in mine. **1906** *Hibbert Jrnl.* Jan. 304 Mind is never either mere antecedent or mere consequent. It trammels up its before and hereafter.

5. *fig.* To hinder the free action of; to put restraint upon, fetter, hamper, impede, confine.

1727 POPE *Let. to Gay* 6 Oct., Ill and vicious Habits, of which few or no men escape the infection, who are hackney'd and tramelled in the ways of a court. **1792** A. YOUNG *Trav. France* 236 We are little better than horses in a team, trammelled to follow one another. **1807** E. S. BARRETT *Rising Sun* II. 8 Till he had trammelled himself again with debts. **1865** SWINBURNE *Atalanta* 98 Ripe grasses trammel a travelling foot. **1883** LD. R. GOWER *My Remin.* I. i. 12 Like many great artists, when trammelled with a commission he seemed to lose power.

6. To fasten (a piece of work on the spindle of a lathe) with a clamp. *rare.*

1833 J. HOLLAND *Manuf. Metal* II. vi. 134 The work must be trammelled to the nose of the spindle, by a contrivance called the dog and driver, the former being a sort of clutch, screwed upon the end of the work.

†'**trammelet.** *Obs. rare.* [f. TRAMMEL *sb.*[1] 6 + -ET[1].] *pl.* Braids, tresses: cf. TRAMMEL *sb.*[1] 6.

1654 HERRICK *Descr. Woman* 4 Like Aurora when with pearl she sets Her long discheveld rose-crownd trammelets.

'**trammelled, -eled** (-əld), *ppl. a.* [f. TRAMMEL *sb.*[1] and *v.* + -ED.]

1. †**a.** Of hair: Braided or bound up in trammels.

1609 HEYWOOD *Brit. Troy* v. lxxv, Is her haire browne?.. Browne trameld lockes best grace the brightest hew.

b. (See quot.)

1753 CHAMBERS *Cycl. Supp.* s.v., A horse is said to be tramelled, that has blazes or white marks upon the fore and hind foot of one side;..so called from the resemblance the white foot bears to a half tramel. Cross-trammelled horse, is one that has white marks in two of his feet that stand cross-ways,..as in the far fore-foot, and the near hind-foot.

2. Confined by or as by trammels; fettered, shackled.

1813 SCOTT *Rokeby* v. xxxiii, Harpool clasp'd His knees.. And round the trammelled ruffian clung. **1818** LADY CHARLEVILLE in *Lady Morgan's Autobiog.* (1859) 12 If your book be cut and garbled by those vile inspectors of a trammelled press. **1821** JOANNA BAILLIE *Metr. Leg., Wallace* xvi, Who from their trammell'd country broke.

'**trammeller, -eler.** *rare.* [f. as prec. + -ER[1]. Cf. obs. F. *trameilleur* a kind of boat (Godef.).]

1. ? A fisherman, or a boat, fishing with a trammel.

1363 *Ministers Accts.* Bundle 1028, No. 15, P.R.O. (Rye), Et de xxx. s. receptis de quadam custuma vocata Cristschar' proveniente de piscaria batellorum..de Matheo Samon pro schar' de tramelers iiii. s. *Ibid.*, De consimili custuma..de Roberto Bernhaud pro schars de tramelers xiii. s.

2. A fowler using a trammel-net.

1581 *Act 23 Eliz.* c. 10 §6 This Act shall not..extend to Lowebellers, Tramellers or others, whiche shall unwillinglye happen to take any Partridges. **1618** DALTON *Countrey Just.* 285 To bind trannellers [*sic*] for larkes, that they shall destroy no partridges.

3. One who or that which trammels or restrains.

1864 in WEBSTER; and in later Dicts.

'**trammelling, -eling,** *vbl. sb.* [f. TRAMMEL *v.* + -ING[1].] The action of the verb TRAMMEL in various senses. Also *attrib.* **trammelling-net** = TRAMMEL-NET.

1588 LAMBARDE *Eiren.* IV. iv. 444 If any person..have taken..any Phesants or Partriches..by lowbelling or tramelling. **1616** SURFL. & MARKH. *Country Farme* 133 To be observed in the tramelling of Horses. **1688** R. HOLME *Armoury* III. xxii. (Roxb.) 277/1 A Long Nett, called a Tramelling Nett... The ends are fixed on long poles. **1826** HONE *Every-Day Bk.* I. 952 The larks..at Dunstable..are usually taken..with trammeling nets. **1866** *Daily Tel.* 5 Jan. 5/2 Trawling, shrimping, trammelling..methods deprecated by those who don't happen to practise them.

'**trammellingly,** *adv.* [f. pres. pple. of TRAMMEL *v.* + -LY[2].] In a fettering manner.

1884 J. W. HALES *Notes & Ess. Shaks.* 99 The exuberant growths of fancy cling around them trammellingly.

'**trammel-net.** [f. TRAMMEL *sb.*[1] + NET *sb.*[1]] = TRAMMEL *sb.*[1] 1. Also *attrib.*

1516 in Rogers *Agric. & Prices* III. 564. **1519** HORMAN *Vulg.* 277 b, Caste in the tramell nette ones more [*Inijce everriculum iterato*]. **1552** LYNDESAY *Monarche* 4771 In to thare Tramalt nett thay fangit ane fysche. **1580** HOLLYBAND *Treas. Fr. Tong, Vn Trameau*,..a tramell net. **1657** C. BECK *Univ. Charac.* L vij b, A tramel net or drag. **1787** BEST *Angling* (ed. 2) 63 They set trammel-nets baited, and leave them for whole days and nights, into which the fish enter of their own accord. **1884** *Daily News* 25 Dec. 3/6 A resolution prohibiting trammel-net fishing for salmon.

b. A fowler's net; = TRAMMEL *sb.*[1] 1 b.

1648 HERRICK *Hesper., Country Life* 65 Thy witty wiles to draw, and get The larke into the trammell net. **1669** WORLIDGE *Syst. Agric.* (1681) 252. **1768** PENNANT *Zool.* II. 235 The larker..makes use of a trammel net twenty-seven or twenty-eight feet long and five broad. **1882** BUCKLAND *Notes Anim. Life* 221 They [larks] are taken by thousands on dull nights with trammel nets.

trammer ('træmə(r)). [f. TRAM *sb.*[2] or *v.*[1]]

1. *Coal-mining*, etc. A man or boy who removes the trams of coal, etc. from the workings; a putter.

1839 URE *Dict. Arts* 982 Two persons called trammers are employed to transport the coals. **1878** DAVIES *Slate Quarrying* 117 The trammers..convey the slate blocks from the quarry to the dressers, and..also remove the waste. **1889** *Eng. Illustr. Mag.* May 572/2 Trammers are usually strong youths and prospective colliers. **1905** *Act 5 Edw. VII*, c. 9 §2 Such persons if they are either in charge of working places or are holers, fillers, trammers, or brushers.

2. One who is employed on a tramway; also, a horse used to draw a tram-car.

1889 *Even. News* 7 Oct., The trammers are equally worthy of public sympathy with the dock labourers. **1901** *Daily Chron.* 28 Dec. 9/7 The horses are good trammers, active, and fresh from work, and in good condition.

trammie, trammy ('træmɪ). *colloq.* (esp. *Austral.* and *N.Z.*). [f. TRAM *sb.*[2] + -Y[6], -IE.] A tram-conductor or tram-driver.

c **1926** 'MIXER' *Transport Workers' Song Bk.* 23 Then he slathers up the 'trammies', As the conductor goes through. **1934** L. G. GIBBON *Grey Granite* III. 192 The conductor had seen Alick and caught his arm... The trammie held fast, a squat, buirdly bird with a face like a badly-made barn door. *Ibid.*, That shortened the run, in a minute the Docks, the trammie slowed down at a bend. **1945** F. RYLAND in *Coast to Coast 1944* 166 The soldier sprang wildly to his feet and knocked the trammie in the mouth. **1972** *Guardian* 6 Dec. 13/5 Trammies, truckies and wharfies (Australian for tram and bus conductors and drivers, truck-drivers and dockers). **1979** *Jrnl. Lancs. Dial. Soc.* Jan. 5 At heart I will always be a trammie, for somehow the outlandish humour of those days was born in trams and synonymous with them.

'**tramming,** *vbl. sb.* [f. TRAM *v.*[1] 2 + -ING[1].] Conveyance (of coal, ore, etc.) by a tram or trams.

1875 *Stock Exch. Observer* 9 Feb. 3/1 So much for breaking, tramming and carriage by rail. **1983** *New Scientist* 21 Apr. 162 The next operation is 'tramming', or the actual removal of the ore to the surface using wagons.

trammy: see TRAMMIE.

tramontane (trə'mɒntən, træmɒn'teɪn), *a.* and *sb.* Forms: 4 **tramountayne**, 7 **-mountain**, **-montan**, (6–8 **-ain**, 9 **-aine**), 6– **tramontane**; also in It. forms, 7–9 **tramontana**, 6–8 (*pl.*) **tramontani**; Lat. pl. 7 **tramontanæ**. See also TRANSMONTANE. [ad. It. *tramontana* north wind, pole-star, *tramontani* 'those folkes that dwell beyond the mountaines' Florio (= Sp., Pg. *tramontana* north wind, sunset), whence also Fr. *tramontane* north wind, pole-star, OF. *tramontan(e* sb. and adj. (13th c.) north wind, *tresmontaine* pole-star:—L. *transmontānus* beyond the mountains, f. *trans* across, beyond + *mons, mont-em* mountain: cf. *montān-us* of or belonging to mountains.]

A. *adj.* **1.** Dwelling or situated beyond, or pertaining to the far side of, the mountains (orig. and in reference to Italy, the Alps; in quots. 1806, 1840, referring to other mountains); hence, foreign; in quot. 1662 = occupied by a non-Italian.

1596 NASHE *Saffron-Walden* Wks. (Grosart) III. 131 Were their stuffe by ten millions more Tramontani or Transalpine barbarous than balletry, he would haue prest it vpon Wolfe. *a* **1618** RALEIGH in Gutch *Coll. Cur.* I. 73 Tramontane, as well as Ultramontane Civilians will deem it otherwise. **1662** BARGRAVE *Pope Alex. VII* (1867) 50 The Italians have ever since taken care that St. Peter's chair shall never be a tramontan chair again. **1710** STEELE *Tatler* No. 222 ¶9 As for our Tramontain Lovers..A Man might as well serenade in Greenland as in our Region. **1781** GIBBON *Decl. & F.* xxxi. III. 245 The rustic, or even savage, aspect of those Tramontane warriors, often disguised a simple and merciful disposition. **1806** SCOTT *Let. to G. Ellis* 3 Mar., in *Lockhart*, To undertake your expedition to the tramontane region of Reged this season. **1820** *Edin. Rev.* XXXIV. 185 *note*, The clock in the clock-house built at Westminster in 1288..is usually considered as the earliest recorded instance of a Tramontane clock. **1840** *Blackw. Mag.* XLVII. 245 Our empire in India had waxed so powerful as to attract the envy of the Asiatic tramontane nations. **1884** J. S. BREWER *Reign Hen. VIII*, I. ix. 279 A tramontane ecclesiastic.

b. With the connotation 'uncouth, unpolished, barbarous'. Now *rare.*

1739 CIBBER *Apol.* (1756) I. 233 This I have mention'd to shew not only our Tramontane Taste, but that [etc.]. **1784** COWPER *Task* IV. 533 Virtue is so scarce, That to suppose a scene where she presides Is tramontane, and stumbles all belief. **1796** CHARLOTTE SMITH *Marchmont* IV. 115, I..for a man of fashion had strange tramontane ideas. **1832** *Blackw. Mag.* XXXI. 101, I beg..if these can be your real sentiments, that you will keep them as private as possible. They are totally tramontane in this part of the world.

2. Of the wind: Coming across or from beyond the mountains; *spec.* in reference to Italy, Blowing from beyond the Alps: cf. B. 2.

1705 ADDISON *Italy, Pavia* 27 That Side of the Church.. which faces the Tramontane Wind. **1794** SULLIVAN *View Nat.* IV. 236 Where no tramontane blasts could come from masses of snow. **1869** *Daily News* 10 Dec., I..was exposed to a tramontane wind as bitter as an oration of Mr. Roebuck, in his most sarcastic mood. **1877** A. J. ROSS *Mem. A. Ewing* vi. 63 A fierce tramontane wind usually blowing.

B. *sb.* †**1.** The north pole-star: originally so called in Italy and Provence, because visible beyond the Alps: cf. It. *tramontana* (Florio 1598), OF. *tresmontaine* (*c* 1295 in Godefroy). Also *fig.*

13.. *E.E. Allit. P.* B. 211, I schal telde vp my trone in þe tramountayne. **1604** EDMONDS *Observ. Cæsar's Comm.* 40 Directions, both from the loadstone of reason, and tramontane of experience to shape an easie and successfull course. **1633** DRUMM. OF HAWTH. *Sp. to K. Charles, Jove* 9 The Tramontane which thy faire course directs, Thy Counsels shall approve by their effects.

2. In the Mediterranean and esp. in Italy, The north wind, as coming from beyond the Alps; hence generally, a cold wind from a mountain range. (Now usually in Italian form *tramontana.*)

1615 G. SANDYS *Trav.* I. 38 The boysterous Tramontana ..here [Constantinople] most violently rages. **1664** EVELYN *Sylva* (1776) 316 [Florence and Rome] exposed to the nipping Tramontans (for so they call the Northern winds). **1721** BAILEY, *Tramontane*.., the North Wind. **1773** BRYDONE *Sicily* ii. (1809) 9 This morning..we have gotten a fine brisk tramontane (or North wind). **1794** SULLIVAN *View Nat.* I. 292 The deadening sirrocco wind, which is immediately succeeded by a *tramontana*, the *bise.* **1887** *Pall Mall G.* 21 Mar. 11/2 An excessively cold tramontana is blowing.

3. One who dwells beyond the mountains: orig. applied in Italy to foreigners beyond the Alps; also by these nations to the Italians; hence, a stranger, a foreigner; an outsider, barbarian.

1593 NASHE *Christ's T.* Wks. (Grosart) IV. 184 Let not the Italians call you dulheaded Tramontain. **1622** BACON *Hen. VII* 97 Our Holy Father the Pope likes no Tramontanes [= French] in Italie. **1636** MASSINGER *Gt. Dk. Flor.* II. ii, A happiness Those tramontanes ne'er tasted. **1642** FULLER *Holy & Prof. St.* IV. iii. 251 Yet was it a great labour for a Tramountain to climb over the Alps to S. Peters Chair. **1703** STEELE *Tender Husb.* Epil., Till then forgive your Writers, that can't bear You shou'd such very Tramontanes appear. **1732** FIELDING *Miser* II. iii, Oh! child, you are quite a tramontane; I must bring you to like dear Spadille. **1811** MISS L. M. HAWKINS *C'tess & Gertr.* II. 52 See that horrible tramontane Major Brag who dined here to-day. **1855** MILMAN *Lat. Chr.* XIII. ix. VI. 181 The subtle Italians found themselves circumvented by the steady aggression of the Tramontanes.

†**tramon'tation.** *Obs. nonce-wd.* [n. of action f. It. *tramontare* 'to passe ouer the hils' (Florio), *tramontar del sole* sunset.] Setting (of the sun).

1599 R. LINCHE *Anc. Fict.* Kj, [The sun] vpon his tramontation and discent to the antipodes.

†**tramort.** *Sc. Obs.* [app. f. L. *trā-, trans* beyond + *mors, mortem* death, *mortuus* dead. Cf. It. *tramortire* to fall into a swoon.] A putrefying carcass; a corpse.

1508 DUNBAR *Flyting* 161 Thow Lazarus, thow laithly lene tramort. **15..** —— *Poems* xxvi. 83 Mony stynkand fowll tramort. *Ibid.* xi. 20 Ane vgsum, vglye tramort. **1535** STEWART *Cron. Scot.* (Rolls) III. 117 Bayth pynd and puir like ony peild tramort.

tramosericeous (træməʊsɪˈrɪʃiːəs), *a. Entom.* [f. mod.L. *tramosericeus*, f. L. *trāma* TRAM *sb.*[1]: see SERICEOUS.] Having a satiny lustre, as the elytra of certain beetles.

1826 KIRBY & SP. *Entomol.* IV. xlvi. 284 Tramosericeous (*Tramosericeus*). The splendour of satin. Ex[ample] *Chlamys Bacca, monstrosa*, &c.

tramp (træmp), *sb.*[1] [f. TRAMP *v.*[1]]

1. a. An act of tramping; a heavy or forcible tread, a stamp; hence, an injury to the foot of a horse caused by its setting one foot on another: cf. TREAD *sb.*

1808–18 JAMIESON, *Tramp*.., the act of striking the foot suddenly downwards. **1844** STEPHENS *Bk. Farm* II. 397 [To horses] Tramps are dangerous, besides causing blemishes on the foot,.. they may cause quittor. **1859** *Autobiog. Beggar Boy* 46 Having my right foot severely wounded on the instep, by the tramp of a horse. **1878** BROWNING *Poets Croisic* lxi, As the reed Is crushed beneath its tramp.

b. More fully *axle tramp*. Alternate bouncing of wheels on the same axle.

1935 *Story of Knee Action* (General Motors Corp.) 3 Such erratic wheel movements as 'shimmy' and 'tramp' should be eliminated. **1959** *Motor Manual* (ed. 36) v. 121 Independent rear suspension.. offers the advantages of reduction of unsprung weight and the elimination of axle tramp and patter. **1977** *Drive* Sept.–Oct. 120/2 Banging and jumping from the rear axle.. on fast take-offs from rest or in mid-corner (a condition called 'axle tramp'). **1982** *Motor* 3 July 39/4 Brisk starts are noticeable for their lack of tramp.

2. The measured and continuous tread of a body of persons or animals; hence, the sound of heavy footfalls.

1817 MOORE *Lalla R., Fire-W.* iv, Heard'st thou not the tramp of men Sounding from yonder fearful glen? **1856** AYTOUN *Bothwell* II. iii, Does yet the court-yard ring with tramp Of horses and of men. **1889** QUILLER COUCH *Splendid Spur* (1895) 121 The monotonous tramp-tramp through the slush and mire of the roads. **1891** FARRAR *Darkn. & Dawn* xlvi, The tramp of the changing sentries.. might be to her the echoing footfall of death.

fig. **1870** LOWELL *Among my Bks.* Ser. I. (1873) 186 To feel in her ears the dull tramp of the blood.

3. a. A bout of tramping or journeying on foot; a long, tiring, or toilsome walk or march; a trudge; a walking excursion (*colloq.*).

1786 BURNS *Brigs of Ayr* 188 If haply Knowledge, on a random tramp, Had shor'd them wi' a glimmer of his lamp. **1822** T. BEWICK *Mem.* 138 This [journey] may be regarded as merely one of my 'tramps'. **1845** J. COULTER *Adv. Pacific* x. 120, I continued my tramp round the easternmost part of the island. **1859** JEPHSON *Brittany* xvii. 285, I doubted whether I should be in a condition for a tramp of thirty miles. **1873** TRISTRAM *Moab* ix. 170 Files of hundreds of camels slowly following each other in the weary tramp to Mecca. **1898** J. HUTCHINSON in *Arch. Surg.* IX. No. 34. 104 Much exhausted by a long tramp in hot weather. **1966** *Weekly News* (N.Z.) 3 Aug. 7/4 Two-day tramps from the Milford Hotel up to the Sutherland Falls. **1984** *N.Z. Woman's Weekly* 30 Apr. 121/2 Day tramps are popular.

b. *on (the) tramp*, on one's way from place to place on foot, esp. in search of employment, or wandering as a vagrant.

1760 *Life & Adv. of Cat* 147 An English vagrant, on the common tramp (as they express it). **1813** T. MARTIN *Circle Mech. Arts* 608 When any of them are out of employ, they set out in search of a master, with a sort of Certificate from their last place. This is called going on the tramp. **1866** DORA GREENWELL *Ess.* (1867) 109 Some of the eight are in the army, some in the collieries, some on the tramp. **1888** 'J. S. WINTER' *Bootle's Childr.* iii, Just on tramp she seems to have been.

4. a. A person on the tramp; = TRAMPER 2; one who travels from place to place on foot, in search of employment, or as a vagrant; also, one who follows an itinerant business, as a hawker, etc.

1664 in *Verney Mem.* (1904) II. 204 Thay goo so Lick trampis, so durty, tis a sham to see them. **1790** GROSE *Provinc. Gloss.* (ed. 2), *Tramp*, a tramp; a beggar. *Sussex*. **1808** *Agric. Mag.* III. 43 A certain class of wandering labourers known by the name of tramps. **1828** *Craven Gloss.*, *Tramp*, a pedlar; called also a tramper, an itinerant tinker, or one who travels with any kind of wares. **1842** *Rep. Sanitary Condition Labouring Classes* 357 The houses are stages for the various orders of tramps. **1860** RAMSAY *Remin.* Ser. I. (ed. 7) 157 A wretched woman, who used to traverse the country as a beggar or tramp. **1882–3** *Schaff's Encycl. Relig. Knowl.* II. 910/1 Monks, who.. roamed about in the country, and really were neither more nor less than tramps of the most indolent and impertinent description.

b. *slang* (orig. *U.S.*). A sexually promiscuous woman.

1922 E. O'NEILL *Anna Christie* I. 119 Sure—and another tramp with her. **1936** D. POWELL *Turn, Magic Wheel* I. 60 A wayward, double-crossing, lying little tramp. **1959** 'J. WELCOME' *Stop at Nothing* ii. 28 You can usually tell.. the nice girls from the tramps. **1971** *Sunday Nation* (Nairobi) 11 Apr. 19/2 Even in these permissive times the girl of your age who can't say 'no' can pretty soon earn the title of tramp among her contemporaries. **1979** R. JAFFE *Class Reunion* I. v. 49 Who could blame Richard, so young at prep school, for fooling around with the local tramp?

5. a. In full, *ocean tramp*: A cargo vessel, esp. a steamship, which does not trade regularly between fixed ports, but takes cargoes wherever obtainable and for any port.

c **1880** [Remembered in colloquial use]. **1886** *Shipping Gaz.* 9 July, We think few will deny that the 'ocean tramp' is the product of competition. **1891** M. ROBERTS in *Murray's Mag.* June 795 The pure 'tramp' is not seen to its best advantage in seas whose ports are in connection with England by wire or submarine cable. **1891** [see OCEAN 3 c]. **1893** *Naut. Mag.* Mar. 212. **1900** F. T. BULLEN *Men of Merchant Service* iii. 21 The lowest type of tramp.. is.. built so as to pass Lloyd's surveyor, but without one single item in her equipment that can be dispensed with.

b. *attrib.*, as *tramp steamer, vessel, trade*.

1887 *Shipping Gaz.* 14 Jan., The day of building tramp steamers by means of money raised from single ship companies has passed away—for ever, we hope. **1891** *Pall Mall G.* 21 May 2/1 In many of our tramp boats there is need of great reform in the food supplied to our sailors. **1897** *Daily News* 26 Jan. 3/6 His complaint was against tramp vessels, which were often undermanned. **1902** *Westm. Gaz.* 5 June 4/2 Mr. R——,.. who is largely interested in the 'tramp' trade,.. also young Mr. R——,.. who is also a large tramp owner. **1903** *Ibid.* 2 July 11/3 The volume of tramp shipping is six-sevenths of the whole.. Tramp business cannot exist unless accompanied by cheap and good shipbuilding.

c. An aircraft plying commercially according to demand. Also *attrib.*

1905 KIPLING *Actions & Reactions* (1909) 141 These heavy freighters fly down to Halifax direct... They are the biggest tramps aloft. **1948** *Shell Aviation News* No. 115 8/3 At present the majority of freight charters are on a direct 'out-and-home' basis, but the time is coming when, with the parallel development of the Baltic and heavy duty tramp aeroplanes, 'time charter' will be as commonplace as it is with shipping. **1952** 'J. TEY' *Singing Sands* ix. 130 Most of us fly scheduled routes, but some fly tramps. Take anything anywhere.

6. a. A plate of iron worn under the hollow of the boot to protect it in digging; also the part of the spade, etc., which is pressed upon by the foot. **b.** *Curling.* A piece of spiked iron fastened to the sole of the shoe to give a firm foot-hold on the ice.

1825 JAMIESON, *Tramp*, a plate of iron worn by ditchers below the centre of the foot, for working on their spades. **1830** H. DUNCAN in *Poets Dumfries.* IX. (1910) 266 Gae get you besom, tramps, an' stane, An' join the friendly strife, man. **1844** [see *tramp-pick* in 7]. **1891** KERR *Maggie o' the Moss* 61 (E.D.D.) Wi' tramps on their feet, and besoms in han'. **1894** *Northumbld. Gloss.*, *Tramp*, the part of a spade on which the foot is placed to thrust;.. an iron plate worn by drainers as a guard to the boot in digging.

7. *attrib.* (see also 5 b, c) and *Comb.*, as (in sense 4) *tramp-printer, -scarer, -ward, -woman*; *tramp-like* adj.; **tramp-cell**, a workhouse cell in which vagrants are lodged; **tramp-clog** = sense 6 a; **tramp-cock, tramp-coll** [COLL *sb.*[5]], a heap of hay compressed by treading; **tramp-house**, a lodging-house for tramps; **tramp-master**, a workhouse official charged with the control of the vagrants admitted; **tramp-pick** (*Sc.*), a narrow, pointed pick, with a tread, for breaking up stiff ground; **tramp-rick**, †**-ruck**, a rick or stack of hay compressed by treading.

1905 *Daily Chron.* 22 Sept. 5/6 He was taken back to the workhouse, and placed in a *tramp cell. **1894** *Northumbld. Gloss.*, **Tramp-clog* or *tramp*,.. a piece of iron plate.. used as a guard where the spade is trodden in digging. **1775** *Ann. Reg.* II. 129/2 In these cocks, I allow the hay to remain until .. I judge that it will keep in pretty large *tramp-cocks. **1825** JAMIESON, **Tramp-coll*.., a number of colls or cocks of hay put into one and tramped hard, in order that the hay may be farther dried. *Aberd.* **1850** [C. ROGERS] *Bairnsla Ann.* 42 (E.D.D.) A *tramp-hause. **1899** SIR G. DOUGLAS *Jas. Hogg* 146 In common tramp-houses, a death is.. a god-send. **1904** *Daily Chron.* 29 Oct. 8/3 A *tramp-like personage stands sentinel complacently over a terrific bulldog. **1887** *Leamington Spa Courier* 30 Apr. 5/6 Persons willing to undertake the duties of *Tramp Master at the Workhouse. **1895** *Daily News* 5 Oct. 6/6 He maintained that.. the trampmaster in Salford, had some knowledge of human nature. **1813** G. ROBERTSON *Agric. Surv. Kincardine* vi. 238 The *tramp-pick.. is a kind of lever, of iron, about four feet long, and an inch square in thickness, tapering away at the lower end, and having a small degree of curvature there... It is fitted with a foot step.. on which the work-man presses with his foot. **1844** STEPHENS *Bk. Farm* I. 372 An iron tramp-pick to loosen the subsoil immediately under the mould, and raise the boulder stones... The tramp.. is movable, and may be placed on either side to suit the foot of the workman, where it remains firm at about 16 inches from the point, which gradually tapers. **1895** *Westm. Gaz.* 17 Jan. 8/1 What the.. foreman thought he at once 'spotted' as a *tramp-printer entered the office and asked to be allowed to try his hand at the case. **1799** J. ROBERTSON *Agric. Perth* 220 In making *tramp-ricks, they ought to be secured, by one rope over the top, in the direction of that point from which the most violent winds are expected to blow.., or by two transverse ropes, which is the surest way. **1812** SIR J. SINCLAIR *Syst. Husb. Scot.* I. 396 After it [hay] has been a short time in small cocks, it ought to be put up in what are called tramp ricks. **1588** *Exchequer Rolls Scot.* XXI. 412 For making of 36 dawarkis of hay.. and for wynning and putting of the samyn in *tramp ruckis. **1905** *Blackw. Mag.* Dec. 817/2 The poor animal fulfils his function as a *tramp-scarer. **1906** *Westm. Gaz.* 14 May 12/2 [One] who, disguised as a tramp, has spent days and nights in *tramp-wards, lodging-houses, and shelters. **1902** HARDY *Time's Laughingstocks* (1909) 11 (*poem title*) A *trampwoman's tragedy.

Hence **ˈtrampage**, the habit or condition of a tramp, vagrancy (*U.S.*); **ˈtrampdom**, the 'realm' or sphere of tramps; **ˈtrampess**, a female tramp; **ˈtrampish** *a.*, like or like that of a tramp; **ˈtrampishly** *adv.*, in a trampish manner; **ˈtrampism**, the practice of going on tramp.

1894 *Chicago Advance* 3 May, A menace, a nuisance all along the line of their *trampage. **1897** *Plantation Missionary* (Oberlin, Ohio) Dec., The poor [may be] rescued from pauperism, trampage and crime. **1891** *Contemp. Rev.* Aug. 257 The tramp also finds it convenient to use the highways, but this is not.. common.. for it is on the railroads that *Trampdom thrives as an institution. **1895** *Century Mag.* Oct. 945/1 The love of liquor brings more men and women into trampdom. **1897** RAINE *Welsh Singer* 95 (E.D.D.) She was a *trampess who died in John Powys' barn. **1861** SALA in *Temple Bar Mag.* III. 299 A *trampish woman with a tambourine. **1890** *New York Sun* Feb., The depot policeman was shoving a trampish-looking man out of the place. **1889** *Harper's Mag.* Nov. 831/2 The battered folding-doors *trampishly lean against the walls. **1893** *Columbus* (Ohio) *Dispatch* 5 Sept., The plans will check idiotic processions and *trampism, and men who will not work will get out of the city. **1894** in *Review of Rev.* May 608/2, I make no defense of trampism nor vagabondage.

† **tramp, trampe**, *sb.*[2] *Obs.* Also 7 trempe. [ad. Fr. *trempe* temper of steel (15th c.), f. *tremper* to TEMPER.] Temper of iron or steel. Also *fig.*

1566 PAINTER *Pal. Pleas.* I. 98 b, If you doe euer make any proofe of trial to know of what trampe the arrowes of Loue be. *Ibid.* 166 b, The King of England.. sent him an excellent harness with a sword of the self same tramp. **1581** RICH *Farew.* (Shaks. Soc.) 40 With what trampe bee wee tempered withall. **1581** A. HALL *Iliad* x. 179 His sword.. with point of perfect trampe. **1684** T. GODDARD *Plato's Demon* 40 Both Respect and Obedience too, will break, when bent with too much Rigor and beyond their Trempe.

tramp (træmp), *v.*[1] [ME. *trampe-n* = Ger., LG. *trampen* (whence Da. *trampe*, Swed., Norw. *trampa*) to stamp:—OTeut. **tramp-*, 2nd grade of **tremp*, **tramp*, **trump* to stamp, tread (whence Goth. *ana-trimpan* to tread or press upon, also MHG. *trumpfen* to run, Norw. dial. *trumpa* to knock or push); a nasalized form of OTeut. **trep*, **trap*: see TRAP *sb.*[2]]

1. *intr.* To tread or walk with a firm, heavy, resonant step; to stamp.

1388 WYCLIF *Prov.* vi. 13 He bekeneth with iȝen, he trampith [1382 tramplith, Vulg. *terit pede*] with the foot, he spekith with the fyngur. *a* **1485** *Promp. Parv.* 499/1 (MS. S.) Trampyn [*v.r.* trampelyn], *tero.* **1570** LEVINS *Manip.* 18/40 To Trampe, *strepitare.* **1865** KINGSLEY *Herew.* x, They had passed down the street, tramping and gingling and caracoling. **1877** TALMAGE *Serm.* 23 Hearest thou not the trembling of the ground, as the thunders of the judgment-day are tramping on?

2. *intr.* To tread heavily or with force (*on* or *upon* something); to stamp (*upon*): = TRAMPLE *v.* 3. *to tramp on any one's toes* (*fig.*), to infringe or encroach on his rights or privileges; to 'come down upon' with injurious effect; to take undue advantage of.

1596 DALRYMPLE tr. *Leslie's Hist. Scot.* I. (S.T.S.) 123 Bewar that ȝe neuir trampe thairon [on a grave] with ȝour fute. **1641** *Ferguson's Sc. Prov.* (1785) 30 Tramp on a snail and she'll shoot out her horns. **1776** C. KEITH *Farmer's Ha'* xxxviii, The black cow has nae trampet yet Upo' your taes. **1839** URE *Dict. Arts* 768 [The hides] are then tramped upon by a workman walking repeatedly from one end of the vat to the other. **1862** SHIRLEY *Nugæ Crit.* xi. 477 It secures in practice my right, so long as I do not tramp on my neighbour's toes, to speak and think and act as I choose.

3. a. *trans.* To press or compress by treading; to tread or trample upon.

tramp down, to crush down by heavy or vigorous treading; to suppress, to crush. *tramp under one's foot* or *feet*, to tread or walk heavily upon; *fig.* to treat with contempt.

1533 GAU *Richt Vay* (S.T.S.) 40/4 He suld tramp dwne the heid of the serpent. *Ibid.* 104/17 As the suine trampis the precious peirl onder thair feit. **1565** T. STAPLETON *Fortr. Faith* 86 b, The camamele, the more ye tread it and trampe it, the sweter it smelleth. **1581** N. BURNE *Disput.* in *Cath. Tractates* (S.T.S.) 167 Murther of spiritual magistratis.. be tramping the memoriallis of al religione in guttaris. **1585** JAS. I *Ess. Poesie* (Arb.) 15 They see the painfull Vigneron pull the grapes: First tramping them, and after pressing now The grenest clusters gathered into heapes. **1844** STEPHENS *Bk. Farm* II. 266 A woman is appointed to tramp the straw, [and] spread it regularly over the mow that is forming. **1848** LYTTON *Harold* I. iii, No horse tramps the seeds we have sown for Harold the Earl to reap.

b. To tread (sheets, blankets, etc.) in a tub of soapy water, as part of the process of washing. *Sc.*

1798 *Monthly Mag.* Dec. 438/1 To tramp clothes. **1807** CARR *Caledonian Sk.* (1809) 226 In my way from Hopetounhouse to Linlithgow I saw the process of tramping, that is, of washing. **1842** AITON *Domest. Econ.* (1857) 112 Soak them [blankets, etc.], add to the water in which the linens were washed some soap, and also some of the preparation to produce a strong lather; rub or tramp them, then rinse and dry. **1871** C. GIBBON *Lack of Gold* viii, On washing days, it was tucked up above the knees to 'tramp the claes'.

c. *refl.* Of a horse: To injure itself by setting one foot on another: cf. TRAMP *sb.*[1] 1.

1844 STEPHENS *Bk. Farm* III. 847 The shoes usually worn by stallions are very clumsy, and.. are apt to cause him tramp himself.

d. *to tramp flounders*, to catch flounders by stamping on the wet sand with the bare feet until they rise. *dial.*

1894 CROCKETT *Raiders* (ed. 3) 33, I must.. proceed to the flats and tramp flounders for our breakfast.

4. a. *intr.* To walk; *esp.* to walk steadily or heavily; to trudge; to travel on foot; to go on a walking expedition (*colloq.*); *N.Z. spec.* to walk for long distances in rough country. Also *tramp it*.

1643 in *Verney Mem.* (1904) I. 302 Now the owld man must trampe on foote. **1720** *Humourist* 51 Your Hunters of News, who tramp it half a Score Streets, to know who has got a Wife or a Place. **1818** SCOTT *Br. Lamm.* xxi, My darling boy, whom I would tramp barefooted through the world for. **1820** CLARE *Rural Life* (ed. 3) 91 I've oft meant tramping o'er to see ye. **1840** DICKENS *Barn. Rudge* xlvii, These people, who go tramping about the country. **1862** W. J. STEWART in *Macm. Mag.* May 32 The miner must be prepared to tramp it to that part of the Quesnelle or Cariboo gold-fields. **1935**, etc. [implied in TRAMPING *vbl. sb.*]. **1984** *N.Z. Listener* 28 Apr. 62/1 One of my correspondents tramping with her husband, referred to the 'benched out' track they were following up the hillside.

b. To go about or travel as a tramp. *colloq.*

1846 *Swell's Night Guide* 134/2 *Tramp*, to wander as a beggar. **1891** in *Cent. Dict.* **1898** J. HUTCHINSON in *Arch. Surg.* IX. No. 34. 102 A man..who had tramped from Leeds in July weather, was seized by a fit on his arrival in London. **1909** *Bodleian* Mar. 7/1 I'd rather have tramped it than have gone in for any top-hatted occupation.

5. a. *trans.* To walk through or over with heavy or weary tread; to traverse on foot, *spec.* as a tramp.

a **1774** FERGUSSON *Ode to Bee* 45 Whether they tramp life's thorny way, Or thro' the sunny vineyard stray. *a* **1809** HOLCROFT *Mem.* (1816) I. 23, I and my mother were.. tramping the villages to hawk our pedlary. *a* **1885** in J. Irving *West Scotl. in Hist.* 217 They..tramped the Trongate in pattens and caléche. **1894** HALL CAINE *Manxman* 10 He tramped the island in pursuit of his calling. **1895** P. HEMINGWAY *Out of Egypt* I. v. 55 He determined.. to tramp the streets pretending to look for something to do.

b. To drive into or out of some condition by walking vigorously or steadily. *colloq.*

1853 KANE *Grinnell Exp.* xxvii. (1856) 220 Leaving the deck, where I have been tramping the cold out of my joints, I come below. **1892** *Field* 14 May 732/2 You will tramp your boots and feet into order.

6. a. *intr.* To make a voyage on a tramp steamer; also *trans.* to run (a tramp steamer). *colloq.*

1899 CUTCLIFFE HYNE *Further Adv. Capt. Kettle* viii, He heartily wished himself away back on the steamer, tramping for cargo. *Ibid.* x, You are making a good thing for us out of tramping the 'Parakeet'.

b. To transport goods by road to varying destinations as the load requires.

1959 [implied in TRAMPING *vbl. sb.*]. **1968** in P. G. Hollowell *Lorry Driver* vi. 152 She [*sc.* a lorry driver's wife] didn't like it when I was on tramping... When you're tramping you never know where you're going and when you're coming back.

7. The verb-stem used *advb.*: cf. *bang*, etc.

1796 SCOTT *William & Helen* xlvii, Tramp! tramp! along the land they rode; Splash! splash! along the sea.

Hence **tramped** (træmpt) *ppl. a.*; **tramped pike**, a large rick of hay compressed by tramping: cf. *tramp-cock*, *-rick*, TRAMP *sb.*[1] 7; **'tramping** *vbl. sb.* and *ppl. a.*; **tramping-card**, a certificate issued to a member of a trade organization, entitling him to maintenance while tramping in search of employment; **tramping-drum**, in *leather-dressing*, a revolving chamber in which hides are saturated with oil or dubbing to make them pliable (*Cent. Dict.* 1891); **tramping-machine**: see quot. 1904; **tramping-pestle**, one of the hammers in this machine.

1660 in *Archæologia* XI. 100 *Armorers Tooles.* Small Bickernes, Tramping Stakes, Round stakes, Welting stakes. **1791** MRS. RADCLIFFE *Rom. Forest* vi, They were alarmed.. by the tramping of horses near the abbey. **1828** SCOTT *F.M. Perth* xii, I am not so far to seek for a dwelling, that the same roof should cover me and a tramping princess like that. **1844** STEPHENS *Bk. Farm* III. 970 The large ricks thus formed are named tramped pikes. **1863** W. C. BALDWIN *Afr. Hunting* v. 112, I left..on a tramping tour into the Zulu country. **1878** E. SCHILLER *Eng. Germ. Fr. Technol. Dict.*, Tramping-pestle. **1893** J. MCCARTHY *Red Diamonds* I. 110 The tramping feet of the policemen. **1897** WEBB *Industr. Democracy* I. II. i. 153 And 'out-of-work pay', from the old-fashioned 'tramping card' to the modern 'donation' given when a member loses his employment by the temporary breakdown of machinery. **1904** *Sci. Amer., Supp.* 27 Feb. 23534/3 Tubbing is gradually giving way..to the 'tramping machine'... This machine is adapted from the French apparatus for fulling wool stock. It consists of two wooden hammers, which are moved alternately back and forth or up and down in a suitable receptacle, agitating the skins slowly and constantly,..and developing by friction the necessary heat, thus rendering the pelts soft and pliable. **1935** J. GUTHRIE *Little Country* xxi. 319 The members of the Tem Tramping Club. **1959** A. MCLINTOCK *Descr. Atlas N.Z.* 74 New Zealanders are a people who take full advantage of these open spaces for all manner of recreational activity, including..shooting and fishing, and tramping and mountaineering. **1959** *Times Rev. Industry* June 45/3 Abolition of tramping and conduct of all long-distance movement through..regular trunk services with sufficient terminal arrangements. **1963** *N.Z. Woman's Weekly* 17 June 18/3 [At Jackson Bay] we have the best deer shooting, tramping country and scenery in New Zealand. **1968** P. G. HOLLOWELL *Lorry Driver* iii. 71 Tramping, in contrast to the monotony of trunking, is mainly liked for the variety it affords, both in the types of loads carried, the different parts of the country which are seen, [etc.]. **1975** *N.Z. News* 9 July 5/2 Proper equipment enabled a six-strong tramping party ..to survive near freezing temperatures in the rugged Pouakai Ranges. **1984** *N.Z. Woman's Weekly* 30 Apr. 121/2 Tramping, mountaineering and trout fishing are other attractions in the Nelson Lakes National Park.

†**tramp**, *v.*[2] *Sc. Obs. rare.* Also 7 trampe. [ad. F. *tremper* to soak, steep (trans. and intr.), temper (iron or steel); also to be implicated (in); by metathesis from *_temprer_, ad. L. *temperāre* to temper, qualify, modify: see TEMPER *v.*, TREMP. Cf. TRAMP *sb.*[2]] *trans.* To steep, soak; const. *in*. Also *intr.* for *pass.* Also *fig.*

1568 SKEYNE *The Pest* (1860) 35 Applicand the samin.. vpon the partis pectoralis, with ane lytill scarlote trampit in the decoctioun. **1570** BUCHANAN *Admonitioun* Wks. (1892) 24 Wᵗ..hart..full of fellony toung trampit in dissait. **1597** LOWE *Chirurg.* (1634) 209 Let the end of the pellet or Uvula trampe in it.

tramper ('træmpə(r)). [f. TRAMP *v.*[1] + -ER[1].] One who or that which tramps.

1. a. One who treads heavily, a stamping person. **b.** One who tramples or treads on clothes, etc. in water, as part of the process of washing them; see TRAMP *v.*[1] 3 b. **c.** *pl.* Heavy boots for walking. *Sc.*

a. **1892** *Chamb. Jrnl.* 11 June 372 He is a quiet neighbour —no slammer or tramper.

b. **1725** T. THOMAS in *Portland P.* VI. (Hist. MSS. Comm.) 111 [Here] we had the first sight of the Scotch 'trampers'... These trampers are the women that wash their linen cloth..by putting it into a large tub, in which one or two of them..get in, and instead of making use of hands, trample it with their bare feet.

c. **1790** A. WILSON *Poems & Lit. Prose* (1876) II. 76 Rotten stockings, soleless trampers. **1824** J. WILSON *Noct. Ambr.* Wks. 1856 IV. 181 Hawick rig-and-fur stockins, and Thirlestane trampers a' studded wi' sparables.

2. A person who tramps or travels on foot, a pedestrian; *spec.* a tramp, a vagrant; *N.Z.* a person who walks long distances in rough country for recreation.

1760 in Earwaker *Manch. Constables' Acc.* (1892) III. 119 Pᵈ three Trampers to Scotland. **1772** R. GRAVES *Spir. Quixote* (1783) I. 119 Because Squire Fielding..pretends that Tom Jones was harboured here, we shall be pestered with all the trampers that pass the road. **1818** SCOTT *Hrt. Midl.* xxv[i], D'ye think his honour has naething else to do than to speak wi' ilka idle tramper that comes about the town? **1825** BROCKETT *N.C. Words, Trampers*, beggars, who traverse extensive tracts of country, soliciting from door to door. **1829** E. ELLIOTT *Vill. Patriarch* III. v, Behold the tramper, with his naked toes! **1832** *Boston, Linc.*, etc. *Herald* 31 July 2/1 She never named the tramper woman to me again. **1848** DICKENS *Old C. Shop* xix, Passing numerous groups of gipsies and trampers on the road. **1908** *Sat. Rev.* 30 May 678/2 Tripper or tramper can get as much mountain air and walking as he wants without any Bill. **1960** B. CRUMP *Good Keen Man* 60, I sent my men, who were more likely to lose themselves than find lost trampers, up and down a branch of the stream looking for boot-prints. **1977** G. SCOTT *Hot Pursuit* x. 87 One of the temporary shelters for trampers that are dotted about the New Zealand bush. **1984** *N.Z. Field & Stream* Apr./May 46/3 Wool is excellent for New Zealand conditions, and is widely used by trampers and climbers.

'tram-plate. [f. TRAM *sb.*[2] + PLATE *sb.*] One of the flat or flanged iron plates used in forming early tramways (in mines or above ground), instead of the wooden or stone 'trams' previously used.

1807 *Trans. Soc. Arts* XXV. 87 Improved tram-plates for carriages on rail roads. **1824** T. G. CUMMING *Rail & Tram Roads* 18 We find the flat rail, or tram plate, almost entirely superseded by the edge rail. **1829** *Mechanics' Mag.* XII. 132 The sort of rail employed is that called the edge-rail, in contradistinction to the flat rail or tram-plate. **1838** *Osborne's Guide to the Grand Junction Railway* 7 In the year 1776 Mr. Carr introduced the use of tram-plates in the Duke of Norfolk's colliery at Sheffield. These plates had an upright ledge or flange, from 2½ to 4 inches high, which served to keep the wheels of the trams or waggons on the line. **1851** GREENWELL *Coal-trade Terms Northumb. & Durh.* 16 The tram-plates, or other iron or metal way. **1894** [see PLATE *sb.* 8].

trample ('træmp(ə)l), *sb.* [f. TRAMPLE *v.*] An act or the action of trampling.

1604 *Meeting of Gallants at Ordinarie* (Percy Soc.) 13 They ran..in the middle of the street, with such a violent Trample as if the Diuell had bene Coachman. **1641** MILTON *Reform.* II. ad fin., Under the despightfull controule, the trample and spurne of all the other Damned. **1821** CLARE *Vill. Minstr.* I. 93 Destruction's trample treads them down. **1856** R. A. VAUGHAN *Mystics* XIII. iii. (1860) II. 273 The earth shakes with the trample of a myriad hoofs. **1902** MRS. BARNES GRUNDY *Thames Camp* 143 The elephant is preparing for his final trample [on a man].

trample ('træmp(ə)l), *v.* Also 5 trampel, 6 -pell. [ME. *trampel-en*, *trample-n*, in form a frequentative of TRAMP *v.*[1] (see -LE 3): cf. the analogous MHG., Ger., LG. *trampeln*.]

1. *intr.* To tread or walk heavily; to stamp. (In early use app. not differing in sense from TRAMP *v.*[1])

1382 WYCLIF *Prov.* vi. 13 He tramplith [1388 trampith, Vulg. *terit*] with the foot. **14..** *Beryn* 1350 He trampelid fast with his feet, & al to-tare his ere. *c* **1440** *Promp. Parv.* 499/1 Trampelyn (*S.* trampyn), *tero.* **1530** PALSGR. 760/2 The boyes trampell so over my heed, that I can nat slepe. **1590** SPENSER *F.Q.* I. vii. 37 His stubborne steed..Who under him did trample as the aire, And chauft that any on his backe should sitt. **1600** HAKLUYT *Voy.* III. 320 Certaine others.. gathered their Ananas in the Indians gardens, trampling through them without any descretion. **1891** KIPLING *Light that Failed* x. (1900) 177 The Keneu and the Nilghai were trampling behind him, calling for Dick.

†**b.** *trans.* To tread, traverse; cf. TRAMP *v.*[1] 5; also *intr.* with *on*. *Obs. rare.*

1595 A. FLETCHER in Farr *S.P. Eliz.* (1845) II. 476 Walking rightly, Still trampling vertue's path. **1698** FRYER *Acc. E. India & P.* 128, I was the second Man [that] Trampled on the Top [of the mountain pass].

†**2.** *intr.* To go or travel on foot; = TRAMP *v.*[1] 4; also to go *between*, to act as an intermediary: cf. TRAMPLER b. *Obs. rare.*

1624 GEE *Foot out of Snare* xiii. 83 [He] hath rambled and trampled many miles abroad to bring nothing home. **1631** T. POWELL *Tom All Trades* (1876) 155 They [civil lawyers] admit of few or no Sollicitors, to trample betweene them and the Clyent. So that the Fee comes to them immediately and with the more advantage.

3. *intr.* with *on*, *upon*, *over*. **a.** *lit.* To tread repeatedly upon with heavy or crushing steps. Also in *indirect passive*.

1577 B. GOOGE *Heresbach's Husb.* II. (1586) 64 It delighteth to growe by high waies..and to be trode and trampled on. **1687** A. LOVELL tr. *Thevenot's Trav.* II. 86 For making of Terrasses, they lay..half a foot thick of Earth, but which sinks to far less being trampled and tread upon. **1798** *Monthly Mag.* Dec. 438/1 The Scotch lass..kilts (tucks) her petticoats above her knees and tramples or dances upon the linen, in a tub. **1879** H. PHILLIPS *Notes Coins* 10 A denarius of Julius Caesar bears an elephant trampling upon a snake.

b. *fig.* To treat with contempt; to violate the claims or rights of; to domineer or tyrannize over; †to encroach upon the rights of (*obs.*).

1646 J. HALL *Horæ Vac.* 93 Trample not on the imperfections of any. **1656** EARL MONM. tr. *Boccalini's Advts. fr. Parnass.* I. xxiii. (1674) 26 They should be trampled upon by the most barbarous Nations of the earth. **1692** tr. *Sallust* 152 [They] trample over your Faces magnificently, boasting their chief Pontificates. **1759** JOHNSON *Idler* No. 57 ¶3 Wit tramples upon rules. **1799** NELSON in Nicolas *Disp.* (1845) IV. 82, I am jealous of being trampled upon. **1879** FROUDE *Cæsar* viii. 70 His friends.. were being trampled upon by the populace whom he despised.

4. *trans.* To tread heavily and (esp.) injuriously upon; to crush, break down, or destroy by heavy treading; also ***to trample down***, ***under foot***.

1530 PALSGR. 760/2 Se howe this way is trampelled. **1596** MASCALL *Cattle* 71 To gather vp more cleane, and not for to trample so much vnder their feete. **1611** BIBLE *Matt.* vii. 6 Neither cast yee your pearles before swine: lest they trample them vnder their feet. **1650** TRAPP *Comm. Deut.* xvii. 2 He can as easily blast an oak, as trample a mushrome. **1725** [see TRAMPER 1 b]. **1813** SCOTT *Rokeby* v. xxxiii, Trampling down the dying man. **1833** HT. MARTINEAU *Manch. Strike* i. 11 He would trample us under foot if he could. **1853** WHEWELL *Grotius* III. 290 The lands of neutrals are not to be trampled. **1878** BROWNING *Poets Croisic* xxxvii, As an ox Tramples a flower-bed in a garden.

b. *fig.*

1583 BABINGTON *Commandm.* ii. 97 [If] our heartes were not altogether so hard trampled and beaten as they are. **1603** HOLLAND *Plutarch's Mor.* 982 To insult over Sparta..and at once to tread and trample under foot the high spirit and reputation of that city. **1675** E. WILSON *Spadacrene Dunelmensis* 14 Thus they trample all Learning under foot. **1793** COWPER *Bill Mortality* vii, Who trample order; and the day, Which God asserts His own, Dishonour. **1849** MACAULAY *Hist. Eng.* ii. I. 187 The party which had been vanquished, trampled down, and..annihilated.

5. *trans.* To put *in* or *out* by tramping or stamping; esp. ***to trample out*** (fire); in quot. 1848, to make or cause by trampling.

1573–80 BARET *Alv.* T 344 To tread or trample out: to wring out, *exculco.* **1842** BROWNING *Cristina* vii, The world's honours, in derision, Trampled out the light for ever. **1848** THACKERAY *Van. Fair* xii, I don't want Frederick to trample a hole in my muslin frock. **1858** FROUDE *Hist. Eng.* III. xiii. 113 The security against a spread of the conflagration was to trample it out upon the spot.

trampled ('træmp(ə)ld), *ppl. a.* [f. TRAMPLE *v.* + -ED[1].] Beaten down or crushed by trampling; also *fig.* down-trodden, oppressed.

c **1440** *Promp. Parv.* 499/1 Tramplyd, *tritus.* **1592** *Arden of Feversham* IV. i. 3 The trampled pace Wherein he wount to guide his golden car. *a* **1764** LLOYD tr. *Henriade* Poet. Wks. 1774 II. 223 The trampled Law had lost its ancient force. **1842** TENNYSON *Locksley Hall* 156, I was left a trampled orphan, and a selfish uncle's ward.

trampler ('træmplə(r)). [f. TRAMPLE *v.* + -ER[1].] One who tramples, in various senses.

1580 HOLLYBAND *Treas. Fr. Tong, Trotteur, vn villotier*, a trotter, a trampler. **1611** COTGR., *Fouleur*, a treader (of grapes, &c.), a stamper, or trampler on. **1784** COWPER *Task* VI. 465 Th' injurious trampler upon Nature's law. **1816** BYRON *Ch. Har.* III. xx, The trampler of her vineyards.

†**b.** ? A go-between, intermediary; an attorney. *Obs. Cant.*

1608 MIDDLETON *Trick to Catch Old One* I. iv, [He] has been a trampler of the law, sir; and the devil has a care of his footmen. **1620** MIDDLETON & ROWLEY *World Tost at Tennis* 784 Pity your trampler, sir, your poor solicitor. **1630** J. TAYLOR (Water P.) *Water Cormorant* Wks. III. 13/2 The trampler is in hast, O cleere the way, Takes fees with both hands cause he cannot stay.

'trampling, *vbl. sb.* [f. TRAMPLE *v.* + -ING[1].] The action of the verb TRAMPLE.

c **1440** *Promp. Parv.* 499/1 Trampelynge, *tritura.* **1530** PALSGR. 282/2 Tramplynge with fete, *marchage.* **1577** GOOGE tr. *Heresbach's Husb.* I. 45 Your Meddowes..Let them be kept from..trampling of Cattel. **1693** EVELYN *De la Quint. Compl. Gard.* II. 170 Bringing the Dung..(which cannot be done without much trampling on the Soil). **1828** SCOTT *F.M. Perth* iii, After some..trampling up and down stairs, Dorothy appeared. **1838** THIRLWALL *Greece* II. xv. 286 The universal silence was first broken by the trampling of the invaders, on the leaves with which the face of the woody mountain was thickly strewed.

ˈtrampling, *ppl. a.* [f. TRAMPLE *v.* + -ING[2].] That tramples, in various senses of the verb.

1581 SIDNEY *Astr. & Stella* lxxxiv, My Muse.. Tempers her words to trampling horses feete More oft then to a chamber-melodie. **1608** MIDDLETON *Trick to Catch Old One* IV. v, A just judgment.. upon usury, extortion, and trampling villany! **1697** DRYDEN *Æneid* III. 854 Trampling feet that shake the solid ground. **1839** LONGF. *Wreck of Hesperus* xvi, The sound of the trampling surf On the rocks.

trampoline (ˈtræmpəliːn), *sb.* Also **trampolin** (-ɪn). [f. It. *trampoli* stilts: cf. *trampolare* 'to go on stilts or high startops' (Florio, 1598).] A base of elastic material used as a springboard and landing area in acrobatic exercises and displays; now *spec.* a sheet of canvas, nylon mesh, or the like, held in a frame by springs. Also *attrib.* and *fig.*

1798 *Times* 28 June 7/1 Equestrian Performances with Oranges, Forks, Skipping Rope, Hat, Handkerchief, and a curious Equilibrium with a Hoop and Glass. Wonderful Trampolin Tricks, by Messrs. Smith [etc.]. **1799** *Times* 1 June 3/4 He positively leaps over a large tilted waggon.. and does not make use of a spring board or trampoline. **1833** M. SCOTT *Tom Cringle* xi, [At the Negro Carnival] Then another tumblification of the whole party... Another trampoline. **1928** *Daily Express* 13 June 13 A trampoline act, a wire act.. in fact,.. a complete vaudeville programme. **1930** *Observer* 1 June 21 They perform on the apparatus resembling a spring mattress, which has been dubbed the 'trampoline'. **1938** N. STREATFEILD *Circus is Coming* vii. 109 The things they did when on the trampoline were breath-taking.., shooting up.., then coming down in amazing twists and somersaults. **1960** *Times Lit. Suppl.* 1 July 418/4 [D. H.] Lawrence has been bounced up and down on the trampoline of literary fashion more than most writers. **1961** *U.S. Patents Quarterly* CXXIX. 210/2 As applied to tumbling devices, 'Tram-poline' is completely generic. **1975** *Oxf. Compan. Sports & Games* 1044/2 The trampoline has a steel frame, braced in such a way as to ensure that a landing in the bouncing area.. may be made without fear of hitting any structural members.

Hence **trampolin(e** *v.*, to perform on a trampoline; also *fig.*; **ˈtrampolining** *vbl. sb.*, the practice or sport of performing on a trampoline; **ˈtrampolinist**, a performer on the trampoline. Also **trampolino**: see quot. 1912.

1843 in M. W. Disher *Greatest Show on Earth* (1937) 196 (*in illustration*) Mr. W. T. Twist the Trampolinist.. Astley's Royal Amphitheatre 1843. **1867** H. KINGSLEY *Silcote of Silcotes* xiii, She trampolining away to Hampstead with the children. **1912** ANNE E. GEORGE *Montessori Method* ix. 141 One of the things invented by Séguin to develop the lower limbs.. is the trampolino. This is a kind of swing, having a very wide seat. **1953** *People & Places* (Chicago) Mar. 6/1 (*caption*) When performing the back turn-over or cannonball, a trampolinist attains a tuck or pike position on takeoff. *Ibid.* 6/2 Descended from a centuries-old European circus art, trampolining is one of the newest.. sports to be adopted by the nation's colleges, high schools and private athletic clubs. **1972** *Guardian* 11 Apr. 15/4 Children fenced, trampolined, played volley-ball and football. **1973** *Times* 1 Feb. 16/6 It proved.. difficult.. to trampoline at all except at a speed dictated by gravity. **1978** R. HILL *Pinch of Snuff* xiv. 142 Isn't she.. a trifle overdressed for trampolining? *Ibid.* xiv. 148 Estelle, the teenage trampolinist.

trampoose (træmˈpuːz), *v. U.S. slang.* ? *Obs.* Also **trambooze, -pouse, -pousse(e.** [app. a capricious extension of TRAMP *v.*[1]: cf. *vamoose, vampoose.*] *intr.* To tramp, trudge.

1798 O'KEEFFE *Wild Oats* II. iii, I'd teach 'em to bring a gentleman's son tramboozing about the country. *a* **1818** D. HUMPHREYS *Yankee in Eng.* (Bartlett), Some years ago I landed near to Dover, And seed strange sights, trampoosing England over. **1824** *Blackw. Mag.* XVI. 566 Mr. Moore was 'trampoosing' over America. **1825** J. NEAL *Bro. Jonathan* I. 177 Trampoosing about all night. **1850** PORTER *Tales of South & West* 44 (Bartlett) We trampoused along down the edge of the swamp.

So **tramˈpoose** *sb. rare*, a tramp, a trudge.

1840 J. F. COOPER *Pathfinder* viii, I was with him in one of his trampooses.

trampsoun, -sown, obs. ff. TRANSOM.

tram-road (ˈtræmrəʊd). [f. TRAM *sb.*[2], sense 2 or 4 (more prob. the former) + ROAD.] Orig., in mining districts, a road having 'trams' or beams of wood, lengths of stone, or later, iron plates or 'rails' laid in two parallel lines, to form wheel-tracks for the easier transport of minerals in 'trams' or wagons; hence, generally, a track for vehicles thus made; = RAILWAY *sb.* 1; in parliamentary language, a special track or narrow railroad for wagons or cars, as distinguished from a *tramway* laid down for tram-cars on an ordinary road or street. Also *attrib.*

(The name *tram-road* has been erroneously stated to be derived from the surname of Mr. Benjamin *Outram*, an engineer largely engaged in the construction of tram-roads for traffic, in some parts of the country (see quot. 1800). It is not improbable that, in some locality where tram-roads were a novelty, their name may have been associated in folk-etymology or by pre-scientific etymologers with that of the engineer. Unfortunately, the legend was recorded as a fact by S. Smiles in his *Life of George Stephenson* (1857), p. 59, whence it was quoted and repeated in popular publications, and gained wide currency, although its absurdity, etymologically and otherwise, was clearly pointed out in 1882 by Professor Skeat in his *Dictionary of English Etymology*.)

[Cf. **1793** *Act 33 Geo. III*, c. 96 An Act.. for making.. Rail Ways and Stone Roads from such Canal to several Iron Works and Mines. **1799** *Commons Jrnl.* LIV. 613/1 A Bill for the making of Ways or Roads, usually called Railways or Dram Roads. *Ibid.* 664/1.] **1800** *Agreement* 18 Dec. in J. Lloyd *Old South Wales Iron Works* (1906) 143 The Monmouthshire Canal Company shall.. make a good and sufficient tramroad, according to the plans of Benjamin Outram,.. Engineer, from the Tredegar Iron Works, to join their Canal near Risca Church. **1804** *Act 44 Geo. III*, c. 55 (*title*) An Act for making and maintaining a Railway or Tram-road from the Town of Swansea, into the Parish of Oyster-mouth in the County of Glamorgan. **1818** (*title*) Observations on the Proposed Railway or Tram-road from Stockton to the Collieries, by way of Darlington. **1824** T. G. CUMMING *Rail & Tram Roads* 17 Such is the decided preference given to tram roads, that with the exception of about five miles.. the whole are upon the tram plate principle. **1838** *Civil Eng. & Arch. Jrnl.* I. 328/1 Certain Improvements in the Construction of Railroads and Tramroads to facilitate the ascent and descent of Hills and inclined Planes. **1839** URE *Dict. Arts* 982 The corves descend along the tram-roads. *Ibid.* 994 In the dip-mine a double tram-road is laid. **1843** *Penny Cycl.* XXV. 118/1 Tram-road, a road prepared for the easy transit of trams or waggons, by the insertion, in its surface, of smooth beams of wood, blocks of stone, or plates of iron, as wheel-tracks. **1846** R. RITCHIE *Railways* 12 Several tracks of continuous stone rails, usually termed tram roads, have been constructed. **1852** WIGGINS *Embanking* 63 Good tram-road sleepers may be had at much less money. **1880** DISRAELI *Endym.* lxii, Lancashire with.. its tramroads and its railroads. **1881** YOUNG *Ev. Man his own Mechanic* §1091 The amateur will find his scaffold-boards very handy as a temporary tramroad for his barrow to run over. **1885** *Law Times Rep.* LI. 583/1 The tram-road upon which the steam motor was being driven. **1901** [see TRAMWAY 1 b].

b. *fig.*

1859 A. SEDGWICK in *Darwin's Life & Lett.* (1887) II. 248 After a start in that tram-road of all solid physical truth. **1859** G. MEREDITH *R. Feverel* xxiii, The young man got on the tramroad of his passion, and went ahead.

tramson, obs. form of TRANSOM.

tramway (ˈtræmweɪ). [f. TRAM *sb.*[2] + WAY: cf. TRAM-ROAD, and *railroad, railway.*]

1. A track of parallel rails (originally flat planks of wood, afterwards lengths of stone or plates of iron), forming wheel-tracks for vehicles; a tram-road. **b.** Now *spec.* A track with rails flush with the road surface, laid in a street or road, on which tram-cars are run, for the conveyance of passengers. (For the distinction between *tramway* and *tram-road* in parliamentary language, see quot. 1901.)

1825 E. MACKENZIE *Hist. Northumbld.* I. 147 *note*, From recent experiments.. it has been ascertained that upon an edge-railway one horse can work with a much greater load.. than upon a tram-way. **1830** *Mechanics' Mag.* XIII. 73 (*title*) Stone tramway in the Commercial Road... Tramway.. has been hitherto generally used to designate that description of iron railway in which flat rails or tram-plates level with the ground are employed. **1840** *Penny Cycl.* XX. 33/2 Stone tramways consist of wheel-tracks formed of large blocks of stone, usually granite, the surface of which is made so smooth as to offer very little resistance to the rolling of the wheels. **1846** R. RITCHIE *Railways* 12 Tracks of continuous stone rails... In London.. such tramways for short distances have long been in general use. **1854** W. H. D. LONGSTAFFE *Darlington* 359 Wooden tramways still continued to be used.. to almost our own day. **1861** SMILES *Engineers* II. 201 The adoption of tramways all round the quays. **1862** *Ibid.* III. 88 He [Trevithick] had the wooden tramway taken up in 1808, and a plate-way of cast iron laid down instead. **1882** *Rep. to Ho. Repr. Prec. Met. U.S.* 449 The ore is delivered by cars on a tramway, the descending car drawing up the empty one.

b. **1860** G. F. TRAIN *Observ. Street Railw.* 3, I was surprized to find the progress made [in U.S.] in what the Americans term *Street Railways*, [and] the English *tramways.* **1863** P. BARRY *Dockyard Econ.* 272 So early as 1801, Rennie reported upon the project of an iron rail or tramway between the east and west ends of London. **1864** MUSGRAVE *Ten Days in Fr. Parsonage* I. i. 31 We still travel [more cheaply] on the French tramway. **1883** *Pall Mall G.* 14 Sept. 4/1 The first long electric tramway in the world will be opened to-day in county Antrim... The Portrush electric tramway. **1901** *Standing Orders Ho. Lords, Priv. Bills* 7 In these Orders.. the term 'tramway' means a tramway laid along a street or road; the term 'tramroad' means a tramway laid elsewhere than along a street or road. **1911** *Edin. Rev.* July 52 Tramways pulse and jingle over the old Tournai Causeway.

2. *transf.* A cable or system of cables on which suspended cars travel. *U.S.*

1872 RAYMOND *Statist. Mines & Mining* 318 The tramway consists of two wire cables, each of which is six-tenths of an inch in diameter, extending from the lower adit on the Stevens lode to the base of the hill... All the ore will be sent to the base of the mountain by the tram-way.

3. *attrib.* and *Comb.*, as ***tramway car, company, draught*** (DRAUGHT *sb.* 1), ***driver, man***; **tramway plate**, a plate-rail, = TRAMPLATE; **tramway terms**, the terms on which a municipality is legally able to acquire an existing tramway belonging to a private firm or company: see quot. 1902.

1825 Tramway plate [see PLATE *sb.* 8]. **1872** *Gentl. Mag.* Sept. 359 Asphalte pavements and tramway cars are modern blessings. **1874** *Ibid.* Apr. 454 In the great suburban boulevards the tramway-cars make locomotion alike swift, cheap, nasty, and dangerous. **1877** GEN. C. E. GORDON *Let.* 19 Nov. (in *Pearson's Catal.* (1888) 17), Camels will do well enough for tramway draughts. **1885** *Pall Mall G.* 22 Sept. 11/1 The concession allotted to the so-called tramway steamers [at Venice] is given for five years' time. **1894** *Westm. Gaz.* 6 July 6/2 He had always advocated fair play in dealing with the Tramway Companies. **1897** *Daily News* 7 Apr. 2/2 The tramway men themselves did not desire their hours and wages altered. **1901** D. B. HALL & LD. A. OSBORNE *Sunshine & Surf* i, Down one of whose funnels, they say, two tramway cars can run abreast. **1902** A. CHAMBERLAIN in *Daily Chron.* 12 Dec. 8/7 Right to purchase.. plant.. useful for Post Office purposes on what are commonly known as 'tramway terms'—that is, at its fair market value as plant in use.

Hence **ˈtramway** *v.*, *trans.* to furnish with a tramway; *intr.* to travel by a tramway or tram.

1871 RUSKIN *Fors Clav.* iv. 24 The roads themselves beautifully public-tramwayed perhaps—and with gates set open enough for all men. **1900** *N. Brit. Daily Mail* 13 Feb. 4 Happy the man.. who can exchange the dull prose of walking or of tramwaying for the poetry of motion.. in.. skating.

†**traˈnation.** *Obs. rare.* [n. of action f. L. *trānāre* to swim across: see -TION.] A swimming or passing across, a crossing; also, a passing into another form, a transformation, metamorphosis.

1654 GAYTON *Pleas. Notes* II. v. 52 The Metamorphosis, translation, or rather tranation of Arthur into a Crow. *Ibid.* III. iii. 84 In his Tranation he lookt about, and saw under him (though a farre off) his Lord upon Rosinante, no bigger than a Toad upon a Ducking-stoole. **1664** POWER *Exp. Philos.* III. 159 The Magnetical Fluors.. finding the grain.. of the Stone to lye fit for their Tranation, do channel through to the opposite part of the Stone. **1719** *Glossogr. Angl. Nova*, *Tranation*, a swimming or flying over, a crossing athwart, a piercing.

trance (trɑːns, -æ-), *sb.*[1] Also 4–6 **transe**, 4–7 **traunce**, 5–7 **traunse, trans**, 6 **trawnce**, 6–7 **traunss**. [a. F. *transe* fem., in OF. *transe* m. and f., passage, passage from life to death (*St. Alexis*, 12th c.), great apprehension or dread of coming evil (15th c. in Littré); verbal sb. f. F. *transir* to pass, depart (esp. from life), to die (12th c.), also (later) to benumb or be numbed by fear or cold, ad. L. *transīre* to pass over, cross, f. *trans* across + *īre* to go. (Cf. Sp. *trance* danger, last stage of life, Pg. *trance, transe* a dreadful circumstance; cf. It. *transito* 'a passage or going over; also a trance' Florio).

Palsgrave has 'Traunce a sickenesse, *trance*', and Cotgr. has 'also, a traunce or sowne; a great astonishment, amazement, or appallment', but these senses do not appear in Littré or Godef.; perh. they were Anglo-Fr.; otherwise the chief mod. sense of the Eng. word does not appear in F.]

†**1.** A state of extreme apprehension or dread; a state of doubt or suspense. *Obs.*

c **1374** CHAUCER *Troylus* II. 1257 (1306) Troylus.. That lay, as doth þese loueres, yn a traunce By-twixen hope and derk desesperaunce. **1390** GOWER *Conf.* III. 321 This cherles herte is in a traunce, As he which drad him of vengance. **1412–20** LYDG. *Chron. Troy* IV. 1536 þe verray custom & þe pleyn vsaunce Of þis loveris, hangyng in a trance. *c* **1477** CAXTON *Jason* 46 b, She was in a traunce what she shold saye to her. **1523** LD. BERNERS tr. *Froiss.* I. cccxliii. 542 Thus these maters hanged in a traunce. **1577** GRANGE *Golden Aphrod.* etc. P ij b, In this traunce of troubles my trembling tongue was partly enioyned to silence.

2. An unconscious or insensible condition; a swoon, a faint; in mod. use, a state characterized by a more or less prolonged suspension of consciousness and inertness to stimulus; a cataleptic or hypnotic condition.

c **1386** CHAUCER *Frankl. T.* 353 And longe tyme he lay forth in a traunce. *a* **1533** LD. BERNERS *Huon* lxii. 215 She fell downe in a transe, more lyke to be deed than alyue. **1604** SHAKS. *Oth.* IV. i. Stage direct., [Othello] Falls in a Traunce. **1617** MORYSON *Itin.* I. 249 Most of the night he had lien in a trance. **1715–20** POPE *Iliad* XI. 462 Hector rose, recover'd from the trance. **1821** BYRON *Two Foscari* I. i, Happy to escape to death By the compassionate trance, poor nature's last Resource against the tyranny of pain. **1852** H. ROGERS *Eclipse of Faith* (1864) 296 Paulus thinks that Christ was only in a trance when he seemed to be dead. **1857** DUNGLISON *Dict. Med.* s.v. *Ecstasis*, In catalepsy, there is.. complete suspension of the intellectual faculties. This last condition is in general described as trance. **1861** GEO. ELIOT *Silas M.* vii, When Silas Marner was in that strange trance of his. **1899** *Syd. Soc. Lex.*, *Trance*, catalepsy; ecstasy. The hypnotic state: a prolonged abnormal sleep, in which the vital functions are reduced to a very low ebb, and from which the patients cannot ordinarily be aroused.

3. a. An intermediate state between sleeping and waking; half-conscious or half-awake condition; a stunned or dazed state.

c **1386** CHAUCER *Sompn. T.* 508 The lord sat stille, as he were in a traunce, And in his herte he rolled vp and doun. *c* **1420** ? LYDG. *Assembly of Gods* 15 And as I so lay half in a traunse, Twene slepyng and wakyng he bad me aryse. *Ibid.* 2063 All thys I saw as I lay in a traunce. *c* **1530** LD. BERNERS *Arth. Lyt. Bryt.* (1814) 245 The noble courte.. is all in a traunce, in a maner halfe a slepe. **1549** *Compl. Scot.* xv. 123, I dee daly in ane transe. **1656** W. MONTAGUE *Accompl. Wom.* 17 [They] cannot imagine pensivenesse to be any thing but such a trans, as mad men or sick persons are in. **1757** GRAY *Bard* 13 Glos'ter stood aghast in speechless trance.

b. A state of mental abstraction from external things; absorption, exaltation, rapture, ecstasy.

1434 MISYN *Mending Life* xii. 128 With swetnes of godis lufe as [he] wer rauischyd in trans, meruelusly rauischid. **1594** SPENSER *Amoretti* xxxix, Whylest rapt with joy resembling heavenly madnes, My soule was ravisht quite as in a traunce. **1598** BACON *Sacr. Medit., Impostors*, His.. conuersation towards God is full of passion, of zeale, and of traunssis [*mispr.* tramisses; orig. *plena excessus, et zeli, et extasis*]. **1632** LITHGOW *Trav.* I. 32 This imaginary heauenly trance. **1696** PHILLIPS (ed. 5), *Trance*, an Extasy, a Ravishment or Transportation of the Mind, which puts a Man beside himself. **1756–7** tr. *Keysler's Trav.* (1760) II. 238 The saint is represented lying in a trance. **1817** MOORE *Lalla R., Lt. of Haram* Wks. (1824) 313 As, in a kind of holy trance, She hung above those fragrant treasures.

4. *attrib.* and *Comb.*, as ***trance-coma, faculty, -medium, -mediumship, music, -personality, -sleep, speaker, -state, -subject, -utterance, -writing***; ***trance-bound, -eyed, -like*** adjs.

1860 J. G. WHITTIER *Home Ballads* 90 Shine on us with the light which glowed Upon the trance-bound shepherd's way. **1849** H. MAYO *Truths Pop. Superstit.* v. 82 So are there three degrees of trance-sleep... The middle grade deserves to be called trance-coma. **1957** C. DAY LEWIS *Pegasus* 15 A bright bewildered April, a trance-eyed summer. **1909** W. JAMES *Mem. & Stud.* (1911) viii. 190 All the resources of the automatist, including his or her trance-faculty of telepathy. **1903** F. W. H. MYERS *Hum. Personality* I. 5 The exceptional trance-history of Emmanuel Swedenborg. **1825** J. NEAL *Bro. Jonathan* I. 137 Waking out of a trance-like revery. **1878** EMERSON *Misc. Papers, Fort. Repub.* Wks. (Bohn) III. 389 The trance-mediums.. exasperate the common sense. **1886** H. R. HAWEIS *Christ & Chr., Light of Ages* v. 143 At Delphi.. the priests.. uttered what a modern spiritualist would call *trance-speeches*; they became.. what are known as *trance mediums*. **1870** *Spiritualist* 14 Jan. 37/3 One feature running through the whole range of trance-mediumship, is the fact that the media.. feel symptoms of the death pains of the communicating spirits. **1961** Trance-mediumship [see CONTROL *sb.* 4b]. **1970** *Guardian* 5 June 9/4 The records cover the whole range of Ethiopian music.. through cow milking songs to Moslem trance music. **1890** W. JAMES *Princ. Psychol.* I. viii. 211 The poor passive trance-personality had stuck for weeks in the stagnant dream. **1920** Trance speaker [see AUTOMATIST 2]. **1890** W. JAMES *Princ. Psychol.* II. xxvii. 601 The suggestion-theory may therefore be approved as correct, provided we grant the trance-state as its prerequisite. **1978** *Amer. Speech* LIII. 59 Felicitas Goodman describes behavior in trance states accompanying glossolalia in congregations mostly in Mexico. **1880** Trance-subject [see ASSOCIATE *sb.* 7]. **1890** W. JAMES *Princ. Psychol.* I. x. 394 One curious thing about trance-utterances is their generic similarity in different individuals. **1980** 'S. WOODS' *Weep for Her* 51 So many things are involved... telepathy, clairvoyance, trance utterance, [etc.]. **1911** W. F. BARRETT *Psychical Res.* xv. 218 The group of controls.. manifested themselves also in the trance-writings.

trance, transe (trɑːns, -æ-), *sb.*[2] *Sc.* Also 6–7 **transs**, 6–9 **trans**. [Known from 16th c.: origin obscure. The sense is satisfied by L. *transitus*, which had the concrete sense 'passage, way through', as well as the abstract 'act of passing through or over'. But L. *transitus* could hardly have given Sc. *transs, trans* without passing through French, and the concrete sense is not recorded in OF.] A passage between buildings, or across between two streets; an entry, an alley, a close; also, a passage into, within, or through a house.

1545 in Pennecuik *Blue Blanket* (1756) 34 Lands.. lyand in the burgh of Edinburgh, upon the South-side of the high street thereof, betwixt the trans of the vennel called Hair's-closs, and the trans of the vennel called Borthwick's-closs. **1555** *Burgh Rec. Edinb.* (1871) II. 214 The Freir Wynd heid an ather syde of the trans of the Hie gait. *a* **1578** LINDESAY (Pitscottie) *Chron. Scot.* (S.T.S.) I. 333 Quhilk was left waist of befoir, as transses and throw passagis. **1632** LITHGOW *Trav.* x. 461 Carried.. to the end of a Trance or stone-Gallery. **1659** TORRIANO, *Passaggio*.. a trance from one room to another. *a* **1670** SPALDING *Troub. Chas. I* (1851) II. 327 [He] causit draw his horss out of the stables into the transs. **1826** J. WILSON *Noct. Ambr.* Wks. 1855 I. 156 He had hardly put his hat on a peg in the transe. **1835** HOGG *Tales & Sk.* (1837) V. 222 So proud of 'squiring Lady Jane Gordon down the stairs and along the trance. **1883** *Chamb. Jrnl.* 210 From this single street [of Lerwick] steep lanes or trances lead up to the ridge.

fig. **1632** RUTHERFORD *Lett.* (1862) I. 97 A little sight of that dark trance you must go through ere you come to glory. **1645** —— *Tryal & Tri. Faith* Ded. (1845) 4 Time is but a short trance: we are carried quickly through it.

b. *attrib.* and *Comb.*, as ***trance-door, -window***.

1811 W. AITON *Agric. Surv. Ayrs.* 114 The cattle.. entered by the same door with the family; the one turning to the one hand, by the trans-door to the kitchen, and the other turning the contrary way by the heck-door to the byre or stable. **1880** J. F. S. GORDON *Chron. Keith*, etc. 66 Several juveniles had.. attempted to escape by 'the Trance window' on to the roof of the Weigh House. **1890** J. SERVICE *Thir Notandums* v. 25 At the trance door Provost Painch's fit took the boss.

trance, *sb.*[3] *dial.* Also **traunce**. [f. TRANCE *v.*[2]] ? A skip, a dance; applied ironically, as in 'a fine trance', to a long tedious walk or tramp, a long tiring round.

c **1746** J. COLLIER (Tim Bobbin) *View Lanc. Dial.* Wks. (1862) 40 I've had sitch o' traunce this Morning as eh neer had e' meh live. *a* **1800** PEGGE *Suppl. Grose, Trance*, a tedious journey. Lanc. **1885** *Cheshire Gloss., Traunce*, a tedious journey. 'He led me a fine traunce'.

†**trance,** *sb.*[4] *Obs.* [a. Sp. *trance*, formerly *tranze* danger (see TRANCE *sb.*[1]), the original word in all three quots.] Danger, peril.

1588 PARKE tr. *Mendoza's Hist. China* 356 They were themselues in the same trance and perill [*en el mismo tranze y peligro*], and as nigh their death. *Ibid.* 378 A very good warning vnto all.. to flie from putting themselues into the like trance. **1612** SHELTON *Quix.* I. viii. (1619) 58 This thy Knight, who.. finds himselfe in this dangerous trance [*en este riguroso trance*].

trance (trɑːns, -æ-), *v.*[1] Forms: see TRANCE *sb.*[1] [In sense 1 a. OF. *transir* to pass away, to die: see TRANCE *sb.*[1]; in sense 2 f. TRANCE *sb.*[1]]

†**1.** *intr.* **a.** To 'pass away', to die. **b.** To swoon, faint. **c.** To be in extreme dread, doubt, or suspense. (In some early quotations these senses are difficult to distinguish.) *Obs.*

1340 HAMPOLE *Pr. Consc.* 8158 Þai salle seme, whether þai lyg or stand, Als men in transyng, ay deghand. *a* **1350** *Assumpt. Mary* 325 in Horstm. *Altengl. Leg.* (1881) 116 Þan scho transed þare als fast, And þe saul fra þe body past. **14..** *Tundale's Vis.* 41 As he yn a transynge lay, Hys sowle was in a dredefull way. **1530** PALSGR. 761/2, I trawnce, I fall in a traunce or swounyng, *je me transis*... I feare me.. he wyll dye, for he traunseth often, *je men doute,.. quil mourra, car il se transit souuent*. *c* **1600** BUREL *Pilgr.* in Watson *Coll.* II. 48 Perplexit and vexit Betwixt houp and dispair, Quhyls transing, quhyls pansing, How till eschew the snair. **1632** LITHGOW *Trav.* I. 5, I trancing flye, I fall, I hoarsing scale.

2. *trans.* To throw into a trance or a similar state; †to stupefy; to entrance, enrapture. Chiefly *poet.*

1597–8 BP. HALL *Sat., Defiance to Envie* 33 And trance herself in that sweete extasey. *a* **1619** FLETCHER, etc. *Q. Corinth* II. iii, Why, where am I? How am I traunc'd and moap'd? i' th street—Heaven bless me. **1800** MOORE *Anacreon* xvii, Mingle in his jetty glances Power that awes, and love that trances. **1817** SHELLEY *Rev. Islam* v. xvii, I trod as one tranced in some rapturous vision. **1855** TENNYSON *Maud* II. IV. ii, When I was wont to meet her In the silent woody places.. We stood tranced in long embraces.

fig. **1830** TENNYSON *Mariana* ii, When thickest dark did trance the sky. **1865** J. THOMSON *Sunday up the River* IV. iii, What Sabbath peace doth trance the air! **1876** D. STEVENSON in *Gd. Words* 687 The world was tranced into a slumberous hush.

Hence **'trancing** *vbl. sb.* and *ppl. a.*, entrancing.

1340, 14.. [see sense 1]. **1856** MRS. BROWNING *Aur. Leigh* v. 512 That caressing colour and trancing tone Whereby you're swept away and melted in The sensual element. **1867** F. W. H. MYERS *St. Paul* 52 God with sweet strength, with terror and with trancing Spake in the purple mystery of dawn. **1873** E. BRENNAN *Witch of Nemi*, etc. 146 Let darkness make complete its trancing joy.

trance (trɑːns, -æ-), *v.*[2] *Obs.* exc. *dial.* Forms: 4–9 **traunce**, 6– **trance** (also *dial.* 9 **trawnce**). [Origin and history obscure: see also TROUNCE. (The first quot. is also doubtful in form and sense.)] *intr.* To move about actively or briskly; to prance or skip; in later use applied ironically to moving over the ground with effort or speed; implying more rapidity than *tramp*.

c **1374** CHAUCER *Troilus* III. 641 (690) There was no more to speken [*v. rr.* skipen, schepe] nor to traunce [*MS. Harl.* 3943 taunce]. **1390** GOWER *Conf.* II. 72 He [Achelons] torneth him into a Bole.. The Ground he sporneth and he tranceth, Hise large hornes he avanceth. *a* **1560** ROLLAND *Crt. Venus* I. 192 The younkeir moir wantounlie did trance. *a* **1625** FLETCHER, etc. *Fair Maid Inn* v. i, Traunce the world over You shall never purse up so much gold as when you were in England. **1867** E. WAUGH *Factory Folk* xxii. 195 Thae'rt noan fit to trawnce up an' deawn o' this shap.

tranced (trɑːnst, -æ-, *poet.* 'trɑːnsɪd, -æ-), *ppl. a.* [f. TRANCE *v.*[1] + -ED[1].] In a trance; entranced. Also *fig.*

1605 SHAKS. *Lear* v. iii. 218 There I left him traunst. *a* **1665** SIR K. DIGBY *Priv. Mem.* (1827) 44 A tranced angel. **1808** SCOTT *Marmion* VI. iv, Where oft Devotion's tranced glow Can such a glimpse of heaven bestow. **1820** KEATS *Hyperion* I. 72 A tranced summer-night. **1854** GRACE GREENWOOD *Haps & Mishaps Tour Europe* 62 One of his Madonnas so saintly beautiful in the tranced joy of her divine maternity.

Hence **trancedly** ('trɑːnsɪdlɪ, -æ-), *adv.*

1830 TENNYSON *Arab. Nights* xiii, Then stole I up, and trancedly Gazed on the Persian girl alone. **1855** W. MORRIS in Mackail *Life* (1899) I. 59 The wren sings merrily, But the lark sings trancedly. **1893** *Nat. Observer* 22 July 246/2 To commune trancedly with the woodland spirit.

tranceful ('trɑːnsfʊl, -æ-), *a. rare.* [f. TRANCE *sb.*[1] + -FUL.] Full of trances; entrancing.

a **1883** A. MACLEAN in *Mem.* 120 That witchful, tranceful vision's fled. **1895** J. COOK in *Chicago Advance* 1290/1 Whip-poor-will, Let thy tranceful, tearful tune Charm the listening stars and moon.

†**tranch,** *v. Obs.* Also 6 **traunche**. [a. F. *trancher* to cut: see TRENCH *v.*] *trans.* To carve (a sturgeon or other fish).

1513 *Bk. Keruynge* (W. de Worde) A j b, Traunche that sturgyon. **1688** R. HOLME *Armoury* III. 78 Tranch that Sturgeon. **1840** H. AINSWORTH *Tower Lond.* II. xxxix, In the old terms of his art, he leached the brawn,.. tranched the sturgeon, undertranched the tunny-fish, tamed the crab, and barbed the lobster.

‖**'tranchant,** *a.* Also 6 **tranchaunt**. [= F. *tranchant* (trɑ̃ʃɑ̃) cutting: see TRENCHANT.] Early form of TRENCHANT; also from 18th c. a loan-word from French; esp. in *fig.* sense: = TRENCHANT 2; also of colours, glaring, crude.

a **1529** SKELTON *Agst. Garnesche* III. 138 Your sworde ye swere, I wene, So tranchaunt and so kene. **1776** H. WALPOLE *Let. to W. Mason* 18 Feb., Modest as he is *tranchant* and sly as Montesquieu without being so *recherché*. **1812** *Edin. Rev.* Feb. 475 The Notes are written in a flippant, lively, *tranchant* and assuming style. **1832** L. HUNT *Poems* Pref. 22 Dryden had a tranchant sword, which demanded stoutness in the sheath. **1841** THACKERAY *2nd Funeral Napoleon* iii, The raw *tranchant* colours of the new banners.

tranche (‖trɑ̃ʃ, semi-anglicized as trɑːnʃ), *sb.*[1] [a. F. *tranche*, f. *trancher* to cut: see TRENCH.]

1. A cutting, a cut; a piece cut off, a slice.

c **1500** *Melusine* xi. 43 The said fontayne, where as grett tranchis [*p.* 50 trenchis] or keruyng was made within the harde roche. **1893** P. FITZGERALD in *Month* July 337 Huge baskets.. in which were huge *tranches* of bread.

2. *transf.* and *fig.* Esp. in *Econ.*, *spec.* an instalment of a loan, a quota, a block of bonds or (esp. government) stock.

1930 *Economist* 10 May (Suppl.) 10/1 The first business of the bank will be the arrangement of a loan to raise $300 million... The first *tranche* of the combined loan is expected to be offered about the end of May. **1953** *Ibid.* 15 Aug. 470/2 The gas stock (and a few other tranches, too) remains to be sold. **1962** C. A. R. CROSLAND *Conservative Enemy* v. 83 It is true that, as in Soviet Russia, or any industrial society, the top managerial executives belong to the highest social *tranche* in terms both of income and prestige. **1963** *Ann. Reg. 1962* 477 On 9 May a further tranche, amounting to £300 million, of 5 per cent Treasury Stock 1986–89 was issued at £84½ per cent. **1964** S. BRITTAN *Treasury under Tories* iv. 123 The 'gold tranche' represents the portion of British credit facilities automatically available without conditions. **1966** *Listener* 11 Aug. 206/1 It laid down political conditions which Egypt would have to fulfil in order to get the second *tranche* of the loan. **1973** *Times* 19 Dec. 17/6 To meet the load growth in the meantime, the board says, a 'large tranche of reliable nuclear plant' is required. **1974** *Times* 6 Mar. 15/2 Names have rarely been published except in the cases of the biggest tranches of aid [*sc.* Government aid to private industry]. **1977** *Observer* 3 Apr. 10/2 His second tranche of income-tax cuts. **1978** 'L. BLACK' *Foursome* v. 40 Later, the next tranche of old houses would be knocked down so that the Brickyard Lane estate could be doubled in size. **1980** *Times* 18 Jan. 19/4 Why not approach the institutional or wholesale money market for funds in large tranches rather than continue with the costly exercise of collecting money from a multitude of smaller savers?

3. ‖**tranche de vie** [lit. 'slice of life'], a representation of quotidian existence, *spec.* in literature or painting; also *attrib.*

1934 in WEBSTER. **1957** N. FRYE *Anat. Criticism* 285 This idolatrous form of mimesis is rare, but the thin line of its tradition can be traced from Classical mime writers like Herodas to their *tranche-de-vie* descendants in recent times. **1958** *Spectator* 11 July 52/1 This *tranche de vie* came into my mind while I was talking. **1959** *Times* 1 Sept. 11/7 The static, informal *tranches-de-vie* landscapes of his Antwerp period. **1970** *New Yorker* 12 Dec. 193/1 It is the hand-held camera.. that is designed to deal with the matter of obtaining *tranches de vie*.

‖**tranché** (trɑ̃ʃe), *a.* and *sb.*[2] Also 7–8 **tranche**. [F. *tranché*, pa. pple. of *trancher* to cut, TRENCH *v.*]

A. *adj. Her.* Party per bend: see PARTY *a.* 3.

1661 MORGAN *Sph. Gentry* II. i. 3 Josep[h]s Coat,.. divided as Adams Shield and Checquered with Black and White, or Tranche with averse and different providences. **1704** J. HARRIS *Lex. Techn.* I, *Tranche*, a Word used by the French Armorists... Our English Heralds Blazon it.. per Bend Counterchanged. **1725** COATS *Heraldry, Tranché*, in the French way of Blazon is us'd absolutely, without any addition to denote that honourable Partition which we call Party per Bend Dexter. *c* **1828** BERRY *Encycl. Her.* I. Gloss. **1882** CUSSANS *Handbk. Her.* xxiv. (ed. 3) 316.

B. *sb.* The edge of a coin milled or inscribed, to prevent clipping.

1697 EVELYN *Numism.* vii. 225 The Circumscription about the *Tranché* or Edge.

‖**tranchefer** (trɑ̃ʃfɛr). *Obs.* or *arch. rare.* [F., f. *tranche* vb. imper. cut + *fer* iron.] A name given to a sword.

c **1530** LD. BERNERS *Arth. Lyt. Bryt.* (1814) 208 And Arthur drewe out Clarence, his good sworde;.. also called traunchfer, that is for to say, cutter of yren. **1831** SCOTT *Ct. Robt.* xiii, We will go.. and teach these Easterns how to judge of a knight's sword, by a single blow of my trusty Tranchefer.

‖**tranchet** (trɑ̃ʃɛ). [Fr., f. *trancher* to cut.]

1. (See quot.)

1858 P. L. SIMMONDS *Commercial Dict. Trade Products* 387/2 *Tranchet* (French), a shoemaker's heel knife.

2. *Archæol.* A flint with a chisel-shaped end, found in some mesolithic and neolithic cultures.

1899 R. MUNRO *Prehistoric Scotl.* ix. 332 Among the stone relics are small axes (*tranchets*), precisely similar to those found in the Danish Kjökkenmöddings, knife-flakes, scrapers, &c., but no polished objects. **1926** *Guide to Antiquities of Stone Age* (British Museum) (ed. 3) 150 One of the main flint forms.. is the *tranchet*, or Shell-mound type of axe-head. **1977** G. CLARK *World Prehist.* (ed. 3) v. 214 New forms such as tranchets or miniaturized cleavers.

b. *attrib.* and *Comb.*, designating chisel-shaped implements; **tranchet blow**, (a mark made by) a hard stroke at right angles to the main axis of an implement.

1931 *Antiquity* V. 579 An explanation of the tranchet axe. **1949** *Proc. Prehistoric Soc.* XV. 25 Near the base were also found two rather thick roughly made oval hand-axes with a tranchet blow at one end. **1957** V. G. CHILDE *Dawn Europ. Civilization* (ed. 6) i. 11 Stone tools (including tranchet celts) from high strands on the Norwegian coasts. **1975** J. G. EVANS *Environment Early Man Brit. Isles* v. 103 The chisel-ended, or tranchet, arrowhead, specifically designed for immobilizing birds and other small game.

trancum, variant of TRANKUM *Obs.*

trane, obs. form of TRAIN.

[†**tranect.** *Obs.* Known only in the passage quoted, and prob. only a misreading or misprint of *traiect*, TRAJECT, in It. *traghetto* a ferry.

1596 SHAKS. *Merch. V.* III. iv. 53 Bring them..Vnto the Tranect, to the common Ferrie Which trades to Venice.]

traneen (trəˈniːn). *Irish.* Also **trau-, traw-, thra-, thrawneen.** [Anglicized spelling of Ir. *traithnín, trathnan*, a little stalk of grass (O'Reilly).] The crested dog's-tail grass, *Cynosurus cristatus*. (Often taken as the type of something of little or no value: cf. RUSH *sb.*[1] 2).

[**1808** J. WHITE *Ess. Grasses Irel.* 154 (Britt. and Holl. *Plant-n.*) Trathnin.] **1837** S. LOVER *Rory O'More* ii, You dare n't stand before any one with sich a thraneen as that in your fist. **1839** W. CARLETON *Fardorougha* iii, It's a bargin ..I don't care a trawneen. **1842** S. C. HALL *Ireland* II. 74 She never cared a traneen for him, soul or body, and went off with a richer man. **1884** *Lays & Leg. N. Irel.* 20 Sorra a thrawneen you'll get from us more. **1899** *Blackw. Mag.* Mar. 572 But she'd not a traneen to her fortune.

†ˈ**trangam.** *Obs.* Also 7 **trangame**, 7–8 **-gham, -gum.** [Origin obscure: the first two quots. suggest that it was a fictitious law-term. Obs. after 1719, but recalled by Scott.

In quot. 1712 misquoted by Johnson as *trangram*, which erroneous spelling has been followed by later dictionaries, some of which further associate it with TANGRAM (known only from 1864). Cf. TRANKUM.]

An odd or intricate contrivance of some kind; a knick-knack, a puzzle; a toy, trinket; a gewgaw, trumpery ornament. Applied to anything which the speaker views with contempt.

a **1658** CLEVELAND *Engagement Stated* 21 When neither Arts nor Arms can serve to fight, And wrest a Title from its Law and Right, Must Malice piece the Trangum? and make clear The Scruple? **1672** EACHARD *Hobbs' State Nat.* 21 A Cause is a certain pack or aggregate of trangams, which being all packed up and chorded close together, they may then truly be said in Law to constitute a compleat and essential pack. **1676** WYCHERLEY *Pl. Dealer* III. i, But go, thou Trangame, and carry back those Trangames, Which thou hast stol'n or purloin'd. **1678** MRS. BEHN *Sir P. Fancy* IV. iii, Get you gone, and finefy your knacks and tranghams. **1679** OLDHAM *Sat. Jesuits* iv. (1682) 85 These [pretended sacred relics] are the Fathers Implements, and Tools, Their gawdy Trangums for inveigling Fools. [**1686** GOAD *Celest. Bodies* III. ii. 399 He, who looks upon Architecture and Fortification to be only Trangunims, is a Wise Man.] **1712** ARBUTHNOT *John Bull* III. vi, Hey day, what's here? What a Devil's the meaning of all these Trangams and Gimcracks, Gentlemen? **1719** J. ROBERTS *Spinster* 349 If they should rise from the dead now, and see you dressed up in your painted trangums, and East India rags, while all the poor Spinners hung about you crying for bread and for work. **1820** SCOTT *Abbot* xix, When yon usher..began to inquire what Popish trangam you were wearing... This comes of carrying Popish nick-nackets about you.

†**trangˈdillio.** *Obs. rare.* [Origin unknown: some suggest a mistake for *twangdillio*, f. TWANG.] The twanging sound made by a musical instrument.

a **1704** T. BROWN *Pind. Petit. to Lds. in Counc.* Wks. 1730 I. 62 Even d'Urfey himself, and such merry fellows, That put their whole trust in tunes and trangdillioes, May hang up their harps and themselves on the willows.

trangle (ˈtræŋg(ə)l). *Heraldry.* [a. obs. F. *trangle* (Cotgr. 1611), var. of *tringle*: see TRINGLE.] A diminutive of the fess; a bar or barrulet.

1725 COATS *Heraldry*, *Trangle* is the Diminutive of a Fesse, by us commonly call'd a *Bar*. **1894** PARKER *Gloss. Her.*, *Trangles*,..used by French heralds for bars and barrulets when their number is uneven, instead of *burelles*.

trank[1] (træŋk). *Glove-making.* [? ad. F. *tranche* a cutting.] An oblong piece of kid or other skin from which a glove is to be cut out; also, a glove-shape cut from this, before being sewn.

1862 MRS. H. WOOD *Mrs. Hallib.* I. xxvi, The cutters cut the skins into tranks (the shape of the hand in outline) with the separate thumbs and forgits [= side-pieces of fingers]. **1894** *Times* 17 Aug. 9/4 Glove tranks, with or without the usual accompanying pieces. **1913** T. O. FARDON *Let. to Editor*, Two tranks, 2 thumbs, and 6 fourchettes are required to make a pair of gloves.

trank[2] (træŋk). Also **tranq.** Slang abbrev. of TRANQUILLIZER.

1967 *Wentworth & Flexner's Dict. Amer. Slang* Suppl. 708/2 *Trank*,..a tranquilizer, a pill or capsule containing a tranquilizer. **1973** M. AMIS *Rachel Papers* 196 As late as four fifteen, mother flaked out: either the party had aggravated her sense of intraspecific alienation, or her tranqs, all day neutralized by adrenalin, had hit her together in one clammy punch. **1976** B. BOVA *Multiple Man* xvii. 196 'Y'all got a buzzful of trank in yew, boy.'.. I [was] feeling like my head was numb with Novocain. **1980** A. SKINNER *Mind's Eye* iv. 34 We'll have to go back to slipping tranks into his coffee.

Hence **tranked** (træŋkt) *a.*, drugged by tranquillizers.

1972 M. CRICHTON *Terminal Man* IV. i. 135 He was tranked out of his skull with thorazine. **1974** *Observer* 17 Mar. 34/7 Lulling drugs are prescribed; tots shamble eerily about, tranked.

‖**trankeh, tranky** (ˈtræŋkeɪ, -kɪ). Also 8–9 **trankey.** [a. Pers. *trānkeh*, name in Persian Gulf for a pearl-diver's net, or perh. its adjectival deriv. *trānkī*, applied elliptically to a pearling-boat.] A small undecked vessel used in the pearl-fishery in the Persian Gulf.

1727 A. HAMILTON *New Acc. E. Ind.* I. vii. 57 And then got Trankies (or Barks without Decks) and shipt what belonged to the English for Musskat. *Ibid.* 59 A sufficient Number of small Vessels, called Trankies, for their Transports. **1757** J. H. GROSE *Voy. E. Ind.* 28 Their trankys ..are a kind of uncouth vessels, of seventy to a hundred tons. **1869** *Latest News* 17 Oct., The wind had fallen very light, and the trankies had taken in their sails, and were being impelled along slowly by means of the sweeps.

†ˈ**trankum.** *Obs.* Also **trancum.** [Altered form of TRINKUM, as in the reduplicated *trinkum-trankum*: perh. influenced by TRANGUM. Chiefly used by Scott.] A personal ornament; a trinket.

1819 *Blackw. Mag.* V. 209 I'd be troubled to put on my trancums. **1822** SCOTT *Nigel* xxi, Come, my good boy,.. never mind these trankums. **1824** —— *St. Ronan's* xviii, That shawl must be had for Clara, with the other trankums of muslin and lace, and so forth. **1829** —— *Doom Devorgoil* III. i, I had much ado To get these trankums on.

†**tranˈlace,** *v.* *Obs. rare.* A word app. erroneously altered by Puttenham from *translate* or **tralate*, or the Latin equivalents. Used in one place in the sense 'to transpose'; in another in the sense 'to repeat a word in the shape of its various derivatives or cognates': cf. TRADUCTION 4.

In the latter sense, Day, three years earlier, had used *translate*, which in the sequel is used also by Puttenham himself. Collins app. took the word from Puttenham. So **tranˈlacer**: see quot.

[**1586** A. DAY *Eng. Secretary* II. (1625) 86 By translating of one word into diuers formes, as thus: What manhood call you this, so vnmanly to deale in those actions that especially appertaineth to a man? Here is this word *manhood* translated into *vnmanly* and to *man*.] **1589** PUTTENHAM *Eng. Poesie* II. (Arb.) 124 (End of cancelled pages) The same letters being by me tossed and tranlaced fiue hundreth times. *Ibid.* III. xix. 213 Then haue ye a figure which the Latines call *Traductio*, and I the tranlacer: which is when ye turne and tranlace a word into many sundry shapes as the Tailor doth his garment, and after that sort do play with him in your dittie..Ye see how..this word life is tranlaced into liue, liuing, liuely, liuelode: and in the latter rime this word wit is translated into weete, weene, wotte, witlesse, witty and wise: which come all from one originall. **1617** COLLINS *Def. Bp. Ely* II. vii. 273, I cast mine eyes vpon Theodorets owne texte, not as you trenlace and translate it at pleasure.

trannel, obs. f. TREENAIL; var. TRAINEL *Obs.*

†**trannet, tranet.** *Sc. Obs.* Some piece of horse harness: see quots.

1504 *Acc. Ld. High Treas. Scot.* II. 433 Item to Johne Lethane, sadillar, for..ane trannet, ane molet bit tane for the Quenis stabile. **1506–7** *Ibid.* III. 209 Item, for ane tramtranet for hors to keip thaim fra struiking,..iij s.

tranny, trannie (ˈtrænɪ). Colloq. abbrev. of *transistor radio* s.v. TRANSISTOR *sb.* 3. Also *attrib.*

1969 *Courier-Mail* (Brisbane) 28 Oct. 14/4 Salt and sand have..been eroding the trannie set rather badly. **1969** *Nova* Nov. 144/3 'How do you feel about the Love Generation now?'.. 'Sick to my stomach,' he replied, tuning into *The Archers* on his tranny to get back in touch with decent values. **1976** *Listener* 5 Aug. 152/2 The Controller surely had her tranny in the shed with her. **1978** D. MURPHY *Place Apart* viii. 158 A solitary, yawning customs officer sitting beside a hideously wailing 'trannie'.

†**traˈnont, -ˈoynt,** *v.* *Sc. Obs.* Also 5 **-ount, -ownt.** [Derivation unascertained.] *intr.* To shift one's position; *esp.* to do this rapidly and stealthily; to make a forced march, to steal a march *upon*. Hence †**traˈnonting** *vbl. sb.*

1375 BARBOUR *Bruce* VII. 508 Schir Amery..with sic tranonting..thoucht he suld suppriss þe kyng. *Ibid.* XVIII. 360 Kyng robert..Tranontit [*E.* -ountyt, *Hart* -oynted] swa on hym ane nycht, That, be the morne that it wes day, Cummyn in-till playn feld war thai. *c* **1425** WYNTOUN *Cron.* VIII. xxiv. 3717 Til Anande in tranownttynge þai coyme on þaim in þe dawynge. *c* **1450** HOLLAND *Howlate* 515 Sarazenis..tranoyntit with a trayne apon that trewe knycht. *c* **1470** HENRY *Wallace* VIII. 1564 Apon the morn the ost, but mar awys, Tranountyt north apon a gudlye wys. **1501** DOUGLAS *Pal. Hon.* II. lii, Thir ladyis..Uprais at last, commandand till tranoynt.

tranq, var. TRANK[2].

tranquil (ˈtræŋkwɪl), *a.* Also 7 **tranquill.** [ad. L. *tranquillus* quiet. Cf. F. *tranquille* (1470 in Godefroy *Compl.*).] Free from agitation or disturbance; calm, serene, placid, quiet, peaceful. **a.** Of the mind, or affairs.

1604 SHAKS. *Oth.* III. iii. 348 Farewell the Tranquill minde; farewell Content. **1623** COCKERAM, *Tranquill*, quiet, peaceable. **1755** MRS. DELANY in *Life & Corr.* (1861) III. 328, I thank God all is tranquil again, after many fears and alarms. **1791** MRS. RADCLIFFE *Rom. Forest* i, Adeline appeared more tranquil than she had yet been. **1794** —— *Myst. Udolpho* xliii, She had sat.. watching in tranquil melancholy the gradual effect of evening over the extensive prospect. **1872** HOWELLS *Wedd. Journ.* (1892) 66 They sat down for the tranquiller observance of the wharf.

b. Of the sea, the weather, a landscape, etc.

1748 *Anson's Voy.* I. viii. 83 Relieved by approaching a warmer climate and more tranquil seas. **1807** CRABBE *Library* 52 The treasures of this tranquil scene. **1836** EMERSON *Misc., Nature* Wks. (Bohn) II. 143 In the tranquil landscape..man beholds somewhat as beautiful as his own nature. **1861–75** J. H. BENNET *Winter Medit.* I. v. 122 The ordinary notion of the Mediterranean is that of a blue and tranquil ocean lake.

c. Of things or actions: Steady, regular, even.

1796 KIRWAN *Elem. Min.* (ed. 2) I. 434 Crystallized by tranquil fusion and slow refrigeration. **1827** FARADAY *Chem. Manip.* xiii. (1842) 293 The heating power of the tranquil flame is much economised..by using a jacket. **1886** RUSKIN *Præterita* I. vi. 298 How those winding roads steal with their tranquil slope from height to height.

†**tranˈquille.** *Obs. rare.* [sb. use of F. *tranquille*: see prec. Cf. L. *tranquillum* peace, quietness.] = TRANQUILLITY.

1412–20 LYDG. *Chron. Troy* II. 1084 Þis addre..awakyd Priamus, And..Made him wery to lyuen in tranquille. *Ibid.* 1882 To trouble, allas, þe calm of his tranquille.

tranˈquillify, *v.* *nonce-wd.* [f. L. *tranquill-us* + -(I)FY.] *trans.* = TRANQUILLIZE 1.

1683 E. HOOKER *Pref. Pordage's Mystic Div.* 92 Whom.. the allwise, allmighti and most mercifull God mai..sanctifi, tranquillifi and felicifi.

†**tranˈquillitate,** *v.* *Obs. rare*[−1]. [f. L. *tranquillitāt-em* (see next), or obs. F. *tranquilliter* (Cotgr.): see -ATE[3] 7.] *trans.* = TRANQUILLIZE.

1657 TOMLINSON *Renou's Disp.* 629 Theriack complects all antidotes, which..tranquillitate diseases.

tranquillity (træŋˈkwɪlɪtɪ). Also 4–7 with *y* for *i*, *l* for *ll*, *-te, -tee, -tye, -tie* for *-ty*; 7– (now *U.S.*) **tranquility.** [a. F. *tranquillité* (12th c. in Hatz.-Darm.), ad. L. *tranquillitāt-em*, f. *tranquill-us* TRANQUIL: see -ITY.] The quality or state of being tranquil; freedom from disturbance or agitation; serenity, calmness; quietness, peacefulness. **a.** Of the mind or affairs.

c **1374** CHAUCER *Boeth.* II. pr. iv. 29 (Camb. MS.) By tranquillite [*v.r.* -tee] of thi sowle. **1432–50** tr. *Higden* (Rolls) IV. 29 Lyvenge in peace and tranquillite after that tyme. **1535** COVERDALE *Prov.* xi. 23 The iust laboure for peace and tranquylite. **1610** DONNE *Pseudo-martyr* 17 That Court which is, *forum spirituale*, considers the publique tranquility. **1651** HOBBES *Leviath.* I. vi. 29 There is no such thing as perpetuall Tranquillity of mind, while we live here. **1838** THIRLWALL *Greece* II. xi. 27 A preliminary step toward the restoration of tranquillity. **1866** GEO. ELIOT *F. Holt* i, The tiny birds..hopped about in perfect tranquillity.

b. Of the weather, the elements, etc.

c **1450** tr. *De Imitatione* III. xxvii, Sey to..þe norþen wynde, 'blowe not'; & þere shal be gret tranquillite. **1545** JOYE *Exp. Dan.* Ep. Ded. A ij, Therfore is this tranquilite of the sea for that litle tyme, as a trwce taking in the winter, called the halcions dayes. **1748** *Anson's Voy.* I. viii. 82 We fully expected..to have experienced the celebrated tranquillity of the Pacifick Ocean. **1823** WORDSW. '*A volant Tribe of Bards*', The intense tranquillity Of silent hills, and more than silent sky. *a* **1854** H. REED *Lect. Eng. Lit.* x. (1855) 336 Bearing in..its own deep tranquillity, the reflection of the tranquillity of the heavens.

tranquillityite (træŋˈkwɪlɪtɪaɪt). *Min.* [f. the name of the Sea of *Tranquillity* on the Moon, where the mineral was first collected: see -ITE[1].] A silicate of ferrous iron, titanium, zirconium, and yttrium, $Fe_8(Zr, Y)_2Ti_3Si_3O_{24}$, occurring as dark red laths with a hexagonal crystal structure and found only on the moon.

[**1970** *Sci. Jrnl.* May 23/3 'Tranquilite' is the name Professors Paul Ramdohr and Josef Zaeringer..have given a new mineral they discovered in Moon rock samples collected by *Apollo 11* astronauts.] **1971** J. F. LOVERING et al. in *Proc. 2nd Lunar Sci. Conf.* (*Geochim. & Cosmochim. Acta* Suppl. II) I. 39 Tranquillityite.., a completely new silicate mineral, was first recognized in Apollo 11 basalt rocks as a possible new phase 'A'. **1981** P. H. CADOGAN *Moon* iii. 181 Of all lunar minerals, tranquillityite is perhaps the most important carrier of the naturally radiogenic elements, uranium and thorium.

tranquillization (ˌtræŋkwɪlaɪˈzeɪʃən). [f. next + -ATION.] The action of tranquillizing.

1797 W. TAYLOR in *Monthly Mag.* IV. 335 The conquest of Jerusalem, once accomplished, it would be natural for the Assyrian court to foster its tranquillization. **1850** HT. MARTINEAU *Hist. Peace* II. v. v. 256 How confidently did they..conclude that the tranquillization of Ireland was achieved! **1868** BRIGHT *Sp. Ireland* 14 Mar. (1878) 208, I was satisfied that was not the path of tranquillisation.

tranquillize (ˈtræŋkwɪlaɪz), *v.* Also 8– (now *U.S.*) **-ilize.** [f. TRANQUIL + -IZE, or ad. F. *tranquilliser* (15–16th c. in Hatz.-Darm.).]

1. *trans.* To render tranquil; to calm, soothe.

1623 COCKERAM, *Tranquillize*, to quiet or pacifie. **1748** THOMSON *Cast. Indol.* II. xix, Joys without a name, That, while they rapture, tranquillize the mind. **1782** MISS BURNEY *Cecilia* VIII. ii, Tranquillize, I conjure you, your agitated spirits. **1835** WILLIS *Pencillings* I. iii. 22 It tranquillises the mind as well as the body. **1836** *Gentl. Mag.* Sept. 313/2 He [Lord Stanley] denied that the Bill..would 'tranquillize' Ireland, as it was called. **1860** TYNDALL *Glac.* I. xi. 78 A cigar which he lighted for the purpose tranquillized him.

2. *intr.* To become tranquil or quiet.

1748 RICHARDSON *Clarissa* (1811) V. vii. 79 I'll try, as I ride in my chariot, to tranquillize. **1797** ANNA SEWARD *Lett.* (1811) IV. 396 How much better for England,..that her sons should tranquillize. **1814** BYRON *Corsair* II. iv. 46

'Twas but a moment's peevish hectic past Along his cheek, and tranquillised as fast.

Hence **'tranquillizing**, (*U.S.*) **-ilizing** *vbl. sb.* and *ppl. a.*

1801 SOUTHEY *Thalaba* III. xxiii, The old Man tranquilly Up his curl'd pipe inhales The tranquillizing herb. **1827** E. SUTLEFFE *Ess. Insanity* 13 Extract. Glecomæ constituted my principal remedial source. Its tranquillising effects became immediately operative. **1850** LYNCH *Theo. Trinal* v. 80 Then [I] beheld the tranquillizing moon-rise. **1873** HAMERTON *Intell. Life* I. iii. (1876) 19 The tranquillizing of a sort of uneasiness. **1954** *Proc. N.Y. Acad. Sci.* LIX. 41 Reserpine, like *Rauwolfia*, acts well in combination with other hypotensive drugs. Perhaps because of its peculiar tranquilizing, sedative effect, it smooths the course of the hypotensive response of such drugs. **1955** *Sci. Amer.* Oct. 80/1 The new tranquilizing drugs have introduced a new regime in the management of patients in mental hospitals. **1962** R. CARSON *Silent Spring* ii. 13 When the public protests..it is fed little tranquilizing pills of half truth. **1974** K. CLARK *Another Part of Wood* vi. 223 'Never let the Tories get ye, Kenneth' he [*sc.* Ramsay Macdonald] would say, as Lady Londonderry offered him a Tranquillising pill.

tranquillizer ('træŋkwɪlaɪzə(r)). Also (now *U.S.*) -ilizer. [f. prec. + -ER[1].]

a. One who or that which tranquillizes; *spec.* any of a large class of drugs in widespread use since the 1950s for the reduction of tension or anxiety and the treatment of psychotic states; also *fig.*

1800 F. BURNEY *Jrnl.* 7 Mar. (1973) IV. 402, I find, however, *useful* employment the best tranquiliser, &..I have less of the violent emotions which have hitherto torn me. **1822–56** DE QUINCEY *Confess.* (1862) 241 A tranquilliser of nervous and anomalous sensations. **1824** E. SUTLEFFE *Med. & Surg. Cases* I. 2, I invited the attention of the medical world by introducing this herbaceous tranquillizer [*sc.* ground ivy] to their notice. **1891** T. HARDY *Tess* I, Nightfall..came as a tranquillizer on this March day. **1956** A. HUXLEY *Let.* 21 Jan. (1969) 787 Our impressions of the cutting short of the mescalin experience by this new tranquillizer. **1956, 1957** [see ATARACTIC *a.* b]. **1958** G. GREENE *Our Man in Havana* IV. ii. 176 He found himself taking to truth like a tranquilliser. **1974** *Encycl. Brit. Macropædia* XVIII. 595/1 The antipsychotic tranquillizers act solely on the brain itself, whereas anti-anxiety agents act on the spinal cord as well. **1975** *N.Y. Times* 28 Nov. 37/2 Proposed reforms are only tranquilizers offered in place of the fiscal surgery needed.

b. *attrib.*

1958 *Times* 1 Aug. 7/7 Tranquillizer drugs have cured many animals of the zoo of 'emotional strain and anti-social behaviour'. **1961** *Daily Tel.* 13 Sept. 19/4 Inside the needle is a tranquilliser solution which, when aimed accurately into an unruly dog.., makes the animal docile. **1979** *Globe & Mail* (Toronto) 16 Apr. 9/3 Humane society inspectors arrived and captured the animal with the help of a tranquillizer gun.

‖**tranquillo** (tran'kwillo), *adv.* (*adj.* and *sb.*) *Mus.* [It. *tranquillo* adj. TRANQUIL.] In a tranquil style or tempo; tranquilly. Also *adj.* and *sb.*, (a movement or section) played in a tranquil style or tempo.

1854 *J. Schuberth's Mus. Hand-bk.* (ed. 4), *Tranquillamente, Tranquillo*, calmly, peacefully, tranquil. **1889** GROVE *Dict. Mus.*, *Tranquillo*, an Italian term, meaning 'calmly', 'quietly'. **1905** *Westm. Gaz.* 22 Apr. 12/1 Resting wilt thou Largo play, Presto or Tranquillo? **1939** J. HARRISON *Brahms & his Four Symphonies* x. 204 Brahms changes the..shape of the phrases in a *Tranquillo* section. **1976** *Gramophone* May 1766/3 The 'Rondes printanières' in the first part, together with *tranquillo* woodwind melody that frames them, seems to me to be taken..rather too slow. **1980** *Daily Tel.* 17 Mar. 11/2 The 'Serenade'..by..Gerard Schurmann..tested the acoustics of the hall, the 'presto' and 'tranquillo' being at times almost inaudible from the middle of the hall.

†**tran'quillous**, *a. Obs. rare.* Also 7 *erron.* tranquilious. [f. L. *tranquill-us* TRANQUIL + -OUS.] = TRANQUIL.

1638 HEYWOOD *Rape Lucrece* Wks. 1874 V. 169 He..that may live in tranquillous pleasures. **1656** S. HOLLAND *Zara* (1719) 57 He was no foe to a tranquilious Subsistence.

Hence †**tran'quillousness** (Bailey, 1727, vol. II).

tranquilly ('træŋkwɪlɪ), *adv.* [f. TRANQUIL + -LY[2].] In a tranquil manner; calmly, quietly.

1756 [see EMANATE *v.*]. **1801** [see *tranquillizing*]. **1841** LANE *Arab. Nts.* I. 73 Tranquilly to sit by a mortal enemy. **1847** C. BRONTE *J. Eyre* xi, The reason they rest tranquilly in their graves now. **1851** HAWTHORNE *Snow Image*, etc., *Gt. Stone Face* (1879) 46 More years sped swiftly and tranquilly away.

'tranquilness. *rare.* [f. as prec. + -NESS.] Tranquil condition; = TRANQUILLITY.

1818 in TODD.

trans (trɑːnz, -æ-). *colloq.* Also trans. (with point). [Abbrev.] **1.** = TRANSLATION 2. *U.S.*

c **1877** E. DICKINSON in *Poems* (1955) III. 1055 I dare not write until I hear—Intro without my Trans. **1922** H. CRANE *Let. c* 18 June (1965) 91 *Physique L'Amour*, which I am lately reading in trans. **1955** E. POUND *Section: Rock-Drill* xciv. 97 No full trans Till 1811.

2. = TRANS-CONTINENTAL *sb. Austral.*

1937 E. HILL *Great Australian Loneliness* xxviii. 225 The 'Trans' and its people are a little world sufficient to themselves, a remarkable colony of government servants living in progress and contentment in the desert. **1976** K. THACKERAY *Crownbird* v. 85 The next day they got to Kalgoorlie..and changed onto the 'Trans', a long, streamlined diesel.

3. = TRANSMISSION d.

1954 *Amer. Speech* XXIX. 103 *Trans*,..transmission. **1976** *Billings* (Montana) *Gaz.* 30 June 9-D/5 (Advt.), Plymouth Fury II, 440 high performance, (highway patrol), trans out, $300 firm. **1981** *Pop. Hot Rodding* Feb. 20/3, I own a '68 Datsun pickup and would like to install a 327 Chevy small-block engine with a 350 turbo trans.

trans, obs. form of TRANCE.

trans-, *prefix.* The Latin preposition *trans*, 'across, to or on the farther side of, beyond, over', also used in comb., (1) with verbs, and their derived sbs. and adjs., e.g. *transīre* to go across, *transitio, transitor, transitus, transitīvus, transitōrius*; *transferre* to bear across, transfer, *translātus, translātio, translātor, translātīvus, translātīcius*; (2) with adjs. derived from sbs. (more strictly with sb. + adjectival suffix), as *transfluviālis* beyond the river, transfluvial, *transmarinus* beyond sea, transmarine, *transmontānus* beyond the mountains, tramontane, *translīmitānus* beyond the boundary or frontier; esp. with adjs. in *-ānus*, *-īnus* from names of mountains, rivers, or districts, as *transalpīn-us, transaustrīn-us* (*Auster* south wind), *transdānubiān-us, transpadān-us* (*Padus* Po), *transrhēnān-us* (*Rhēnus* Rhine), *transtiberīn-us, transtigrītān-us*. Before initial *s*, the *s* of *trans-* was generally but not always dropped, as in *tran-spicĕre* to look through, *tran-scendĕre* to transcend, *tran-scrībĕre* to transcribe, *tran-suĕre* to stitch through. In a number of verbs and their derivatives, *trans-* was reduced before a consonant to *trā-*, e.g. *trādĕre* to hand over, *tradūcĕre* to lead across, *trājicĕre* or *trāicĕre* to throw across, *trājectus* a crossing, *trānāre* to swim across.

In med.L. the number of these compounds was increased, and verbs formed also on sbs., as *transaccidentāre* to transpose the accidents, *transubstantiāre* to transmute the substance, *transnoctāre* to pass the night, *transviāre* to change the path or course of. They are also numerous in the modern Romanic languages. Many of the English words came through French; in OF. the inherited form was in *tres-*, as *trespasser* to trespass; the later adapted form is in *trans-*.

In English, *trans-* occurs in compounds representing those already used in Latin, and in others formed analogously from L. elements; also in compounds the second element of which is an English or other non-Latin word. The chief uses are as follows:

1. With the sense 'across, through, over, to or on the other side of, beyond, outside of, from one place, person, thing, or state to another': in verbs and their derivative sbs. and adjs. representing L. compounds, or formed etymologically on Latin elements; e.g. ***transcolate, transcribe, transcript, transcription, transport, transportation.***

2. in verbs, etc. formed on Eng. vbs., adjs., or sbs., as ***transboard, transearth, transfashion, tranship, trans-shape, transtime.***

3. in adjs. and their derivatives, representing L. adjs., or formed analogically on L. words, as *transmarine, transmural*; also on English sbs. or adjs., as *trans-border, -desert, -frontier, -polar.* These may have the sense 'across, crossing', or 'beyond, on the other side of', or both senses, as *trans-oceanic.* Special groups are:

4. in adjs. with the sense 'beyond, surpassing, transcending', as *transhuman, -material, -rational.*

5. a. in adjs., scientific terms (chiefly anatomical), with the sense 'through, across' (the thing denoted by the sb. implied), as ***transabdominal, -antral*** [ANTRUM], ***-capillary, -cervical, -cutaneous, -duodenal, -epithelial, -glottal, -granular, -ovarial, -ovarian, -placental, -pyloric.*** See also TRANSAPICAL, -FRONTAL, -OCULAR, -UTERINE.

1956 *Nature* 18 Feb. 330/2 Although transabdominal puncture of the uterus has been carried out often for therapeutic and experimental reasons without accidents, mere curiosity does not justify the procedure. **1957** *Laryngoscope* LXVII. 566 The degree of orbital tension present in the severe forms of exophthalmos is correlated with the degree of recession obtained by the transantral decompression. **1974** *Nature* 31 May 495/3 Transcapillary and transepithelial water transport. **1963** *Lancet* 19 Jan. 165/2 Transcervical fractures. **1977** *Ibid.* 7 May 983/1 We believe that local warming of the skin and of the capillary blood under the electrode increases Pco$_2$; the transcutaneous Pco$_2$ values are therefore higher than those found in arterial blood. **1908** Transduodenal [see *retro-duodenal* s.v. RETRO- 3. b.]. **1975** H. J. BURHENNE in Najarian & Delaney *Surg. Liver, Pancreas & Biliary Tract* 104 Percutaneous cholangiography will probably be supplanted by transduodenal cannulization. **1974** Transepithelial [see *transcapillary* above]. **1964** J. C. CATFORD in D. Abercombie et al. *Daniel Jones* 31 The trans-glottal air-jets of voice superimpose a periodic fluctuation on the mean air pressure behind the articulatory stricture, resulting in..hiss. **1970** *Language* XLVI. 313 The human..larynx is so constructed that the fundamental frequency of phonation is a function of both the transglottal air pressure drop and the tensions of the laryngeal muscles. **1962** *Science Survey* III. 329 Occasionally the cracks are transcrystalline (trans-granular). **1946** E. A. STEINHAUS *Insect Microbiol.* viii. 439 Transovarial transmission of the virus takes place by the viruses penetrating the walls of the ovary and thence entering the developing ovum. **1971** P. C. C. GARNHAM *Progr. Parasitol.* iii. 34 The tick..may carry over into subsequent generations by transovarial passage. **1954** *Jrnl. Infectious Dis.* XCV. 178/2 The distribution of antibodies in different small age groups of wild birds is further evidence of the transovarian passage of neutralizing antibodies. **1980** *Nature* 7 Feb. 568/2 Another event occurring during oogenesis is trans-ovarian transmission of symbiotic bacteroids..from females to the oocytes. **1902** *Brit. Med. Jrnl.* 17 May 1198/1 Alterations in the transplacental interchanges. **1977** *Lancet* 9 Apr. 795/1 The transplacental leak of fetal red blood-cells. **1905** C. ADDISON *Ellis's Demonstrations of Anat.* (ed. 12) vi. 298 This plane, from its traversing the pyloric end of the stomach, is called the transpyloric. **1977** *Lancet* 28 May 1157/2 The gastric distension..can be relieved by passing an open-ended nasogastric tube, and adequate nutrition maintained by intravenous or continuous transpyloric feeding.

b. In derived advbs.: ***transabdominally, -duodenally, -ovarially, -placentally.***

1962 *Lancet* 8 Dec. 1208/2 A needle passed transabdominally into the liver. **1955** *Radiology* LXIV. 325 When the sphincter of Oddi is sectioned transduodenally, a plastic tube can be inserted into the main pancreatic duct. **1954** *Jrnl. Infectious Dis.* XCV. 168/1 Neutralizing antibodies to western equine encephalitis (WEE) and St. Louis encephalitis (SLE) viruses may be transmitted transovarially. **1979** *Amer. Jrnl. Trop. Med. & Hygiene* XXVIII. 1064 Spores developing in transovarially infected mosquitoes. **1965** *Dorland's Med. Dict.* (ed. 24) s.v. *Listeria*, A septicemic disease which may be transmitted transplacentally in pregnant women.

6. in substantives with the sense 'transverse', as *trans-muscle, trans-stroke.* (*rare.*)

7. a. in geographical adjs., formed on the names of rivers, seas, mountains, territories, etc., with the sense 'situated or lying beyond or on the other side of', as ***trans-Adriatic, -Alleghanian, -Alleghany, -Altaian, -Baikal, -ian, -Cantine*** (the river Cam), ***-Caspian, -Caucasian, -Danubian, -Egyptian, -Euphrat-es (-esian, -ic), -Gangetic*** (Ganges), ***-Grampian, -Indus, -Indine, -Jordan, -ic, -Juran*** (Mt. Jura), ***-Mersey, -Mississippi, -an, -Mosan*** (R. Meuse), ***-Pyrenean, -Severn, -Tiberine*** (also ***-Teverine***, It. *trasteverino*), ***-Trentane*** (R. Trent), ***-Ural, -Volga, -Zambesian***, etc. Also from names of planets, ***Trans-Martian, -Neptunian, -Uranian***, and in humorous nonce-use, as ***trans-bedpost.*** (See also TRANSATLANTIC, TRANS-PACIFIC, TRANSKEI, TRANSLEITHAN.)

1612 DRAYTON *Poly-olb.* viii. 420 The Clees, like louing Twinnes,..that stand Trans-Seuerned, behold fair England tow'rds the rise. *a* **1641** BP. MOUNTAGU *Acts & Mon.* (1642) 144 Satrapaes of the Transeuphratesian Countreyes. **1655** FULLER *Hist. Camb.* (1840) 146 Monks' College..stood on the trans-Cantine side, an anchoret in itself, severed by the river from the rest of the University. **1756** C. LUCAS *Ess. Waters* II. 113 The transmosan territories of Liege. **1797** *Camb. Univ. Calendar* 18 That there cannot be a majority of transtrentane, or men born north of the Trent in the seniority. **1802** RANKEN *Hist. France* III. I. iii. 30 Burgundy Transjurane..now fell under the superiority of Germany. **1814** *Deb. Congress U.S.* 14 Feb. 1422 Even then the trans-Alleganean wilderness was rustling with the preparation of the savage. **1815** J. ADAMS *Wks.* (1856) X. 168 Our trans-Alleghanian States, in patriotism,..are at least equal to any in the Union. **1817** COLEBROOKE in *Trans. Linn. Soc.* XII. 352 Between the cis-gangetic and trans-gangetic regions. **1825** C. D. COLDEN *Mem.* 93 Why should the trans-Allegany States have remained united with those on the Atlantic? **1827** G. S. FABER *Sacr. Calend. Prophecy* (1844) II. 81 The transdanubian and transeuphratic conquests of Trajan. **1831** A. WILSON *Amer. Ornithology* IV. 31 In the trans-Mississippian territories of the United States, the burrowing owl resides. **1836** F. MAHONY *Rel. Father Prout, Barry* (1859) 503 Of an old transtiberine family, he claimed with the *trasteverini* unconditionated pedigree. **1840** MILMAN *Hist. Chr.* I. 177 On the remote border of his transjordanic territory. **1845** S. AUSTIN *Ranke's Hist. Ref.* II. 445 The generals now, under the eyes of the pope, demanded..as security for payment, the Transteverine city. **1854** MILMAN *Lat. Chr.* IV. ix. (1864) II. 424 Leo revenged himself by severing the Transadriatic provinces..from the Roman patriarchate. **1861** J. G. SHEPPARD *Fall Rome* i. 22 Pannonia was nearly equivalent to trans-Danubian Hungary. **1875** *Harper's Mag.* Mar. 572/2 The subdivision ..into the Trans-Alleghany, Valley, Middle, and Tide-water districts. **1876** BLACKIE *Lang. & Lit. Scott. Highl.* 40 The quick sensibilities of trans-Grampian philologers. **1878** GLADSTONE *Prim. Homer* i. §12. 15 Homer..gives an account of the trans-Egyptian Pygmæans. **1888** *Times* 9 Oct. 4/1 These outsiders..will also have to settle peacefully in the Russian Transcaspian. **1898** *Westm. Gaz.* 14 Feb. 2/1 Glimpses of the Jordan valley and the trans-Jordan hills. **1900** MARY C. WILSON *Irene Petrie* xiii. 305 A Campaign in trans-Himalayan lands. **1903** SIR H. H. JOHNSTON in *Times* 17 Feb., A Government Department..dealing with foreign (i.e., trans-Zambesian) labour. **1934** A. TOYNBEE *Study of Hist.* II. 203 Musa had completed the Arab conquest..by occupying the Trans-pyrenaean province of Septimania along the Gallic coast between the Pyrenees and the Rhône.

1852 R. GRANT *Hist. Physic. Astron.* xii. 166 M. Valz, of Marseilles, writing to M. Arago in 1835,..made the following..remarks relative to the probable existence of a Trans-Uranian planet. *Ibid.* 185 On the 2nd September, 1846, he [Mr. Adams] transmitted..an account of his further researches on the Trans-Uranian planet. **1879** *Nature* 27 Mar. 481/2 The Trans-Neptunian Planet.. Observations made at Washington in 1850 of this supposed planet. **1885** CLERKE *Pop. Hist. Astron.* 98 He [Olbers] supposed that both Ceres and Pallas were fragments of a primitive trans-Martian planet.

1864 MISS CORNWALLIS in *Sat. Rev.* XVIII. 463 Pray tell me about the trans-bedpost regions; my whole concern at present is the cis-bedpost—a very narrow domain.

b. in substantives with the sense 'the region beyond' or 'one dwelling beyond or on the other side of', as ***trans-Alleghanian, -Mississippi, -Mississippian.***

1774 J. ADAMS *Dairy* 23 Oct. in *Wks.* (1850) II. 401, I went to the Baptist Church and heard a trans-Alleghanian, a preacher from the back parts of Virginia. **1883** *Century Mag.* Nov. 142/1 If the President was to attempt to reach the Trans-Mississippi at all,..he should move on at once. **1898** *Ibid.* Oct. 844/2 The trans-Mississippians have entered upon no line of rural industry with a more intelligent determination to make it a great success than upon dairying. **1949** BEEBE & CLEGG *U.S. West* 10 Anyone approaching the *matière* of the trans-Mississippi in the nineteenth century as an exploiter of new material is either deluded or an imposter.

8. in geographical adjs., formed as in 7, with the sense 'passing across, crossing', as in ***trans-African, -Algerian, -American, -Andean (-ian, -ine), -Antarctic, -Arabian, -Asiatic, -Australian, -Balkan, -Canada, -Manchurian, -Mersey, -Mongolian, -Pyrenean, -Saharan, -Siberian, -Sierran, -Tasman,*** etc. Many of these occur also in sense 7.

1846 R. FORD *Gatherings from Spain* iv. 31 Newfangled transpyrenean reforms, innovations, and botherations. **1880** *Nature* 4 Mar. 424/2 The future Transalgerian Railway Company. **1884** *Notes on Bks.* (Longman's) 31 May 247 The Transandine exploring and surveying expedition of 1871–2. **1886** *L'pool Courier* 16 Jan., Assisting in opening the trans-Mersey Railway. **1888** *Times* 20 Sept. 3/6 Denham, Clapperton, Barth, and other trans-Saharan travellers. **1898** *Chambers' Jrnl.* I. 543/2, 8000 feet above sea-level, the highest point to which the Trans-Andean railway had been carried. **1901** *Daily Chron.* 13 Nov. 3/3 The reported adoption..of the trans-American route for the conveyance of the Australian mails. **1903** *Ibid.* 17 Mar. 6/6 The project of a Trans-Pyrenean railway is thoroughly practicable. **1907** *Westm. Gaz.* 26 Oct. 16/3 This trans-African voyage of Mr. Savage Landor. **1908** *Busy Man's Mag.* Apr. 95 The Proposed Route of the Trans-Canada Rail-way. **1908** *Edin. Rev.* July 146 The trans-Niger railway, destined to..open up to commerce a magnificent agricultural region. **1916** R. K. WOOD *Tourist's N.W.* 315 A campaign for the improvement and construction of roads which..shall in combination form a trans-Canada motor route. **1933** *Geogr. Jrnl.* LXXXII. 470 Mr. Lincoln Ellsworth..will then make the Transantarctic flight, which is the sole object of the expedition. **1935** E. B. BUCKBEE *Saga of Old Tuolumne* 385 The road survived until the State of California came to look with favour upon its possibilities as a tran-Sierran [*sic*] road. **1938** *Times* 17 Feb. 13/4 The flying-boat Centaurus showed her unsuitability for trans-Tasman traffic. **1950** *Pacific Discovery* Mar.–Apr. 4/1 Did you know that a trans-Sierran highway is now being built in Madera County? **1963** P. DRACKETT *Motor Rallying* iv. 62 The Trans-Canada and Canadian Winter Rallies have not yet reached the lofty eminence of the Safari. **1965** E. MCCOURT *Road across Canada* 199 The Trans-Canada Highway is an engineering, communications, and scenic marvel. **1966** N. MARSH *Black Beech & Honeydew* viii. 175 In..1928 the trans-Tasman steamer sailed..into Cook Strait. **1978** *Times Lit. Suppl.* 25 Aug. 957/4 Shackleton's unsuccessful transantarctic expedition. **1978** J. UPDIKE *Coup* (1979) i. 4 The capital is Istiqlal, renamed in 1960, upon independence, and on prior maps called Caillíéville, in honor of the trans-Saharan traveller of 1828.

9. a. *Chem.* (Also without hyphen as a quasi-adj. Usu. printed in italic.) Designating a compound in which two atoms or groups are situated on opposite sides of some plane passing through the molecule; hence (of a bond or a reaction), characterized by such a relationship.

[1888: see CIS- 3.] **1892** *Jrnl. Chem. Soc.* LXII. 1213 The anhydride of the cis modification invariably melts at a lower temperature than that of the trans form. **1937** *Nature* 3 July 25/1 The trans form of ethylene bromide is considered to be the more 'stable' (preferred) form, even at high temperatures. **1951** C. R. NOLLER *Chem. Carbon Compounds* xvii. 316 It has been proved that *cis*-2-butene is the isomer boiling at 3·73° and *trans*-2-butene is that boiling at 0·96°. **1956** D. J. CRAM in M. S. Newman *Steric Effects in Org. Chem.* vi. 306 The terms *cis* elimination will be used whenever the leaving groups depart from the same side of the incipient double bond, and *trans* elimination when they leave from the opposite side of the incipient double bond. **1972** R. A. JACKSON *Mechanism* i. 7 Bromine adds across an olefinic double bond in a *trans* manner. **1976** *Sci. Amer.* Jan. 124/2 Nearly all peptide bonds are trans and planar, meaning that hydrogen and carbonyl oxygen (CO) are on opposite sides of the bond.

b. *transf.* in Genetics, with reference to the location on different chromosomes of dominant alleles of two or more genes or cistrons.

1941 J. B. S. HALDANE *New Paths in Genetics* i. 17 There are two geometrically isomeric types of rabbit (to use a chemical analogy) heterozygous for recessive white *c* and recessive yellowfat *y*... The trans-rabbit + *y*/*c* + is derived from the crossing of a white-fatted coloured rabbit and a yellow-fatted white. **1957** [see CISTRON]. **1973** R. G. KRUEGER et al. *Introd. Microbiol.* xiii. 385/1 In the diploid the two mutants [*sc.* mutant genes] are said to be trans to one another because they are on different chromosomes.

10. *Biochem.* and *Biol.* In sbs. with the sense 'transfer', as *transacetylase, -amination, -genosis, -methylation, -peptidation* (see as main entries).

11. *Physics.* In adjs. and sbs. with the sense 'having a higher atomic number than; beyond (in the periodic table)'.

1952 *Chem. & Engin. News* 21 Jan. 237/2 The trans-californium elements. **1969** *Nature* 26 Apr. 323/1 Dr Glen Seaborg..was able to proclaim that element 104 is the first of the 'trans-actinide' elements. **1973** *Q. Jrnl. R. Astron. Soc.* XIV. 121 The existence of transbismuth elements in nature.

Pronunciation. In the pronunciation of *trans-* in combination, great diversity prevails locally and individually in cultivated speech. This diversity affects both the vowel *a* and the consonant *s*.

Historically, the *a* is short (æ) as in *man, banns*, and it is so treated in nearly all pronouncing dictionaries. This pronunciation is retained in the north and west of England, in Scotland, in the United States, and by many speakers even in London and its surrounding area. But the general tendency in the London area to substitute for short (æ) before certain consonant groups (as in *chance, branch, demand, chant, pass, fast, ask*) the long vowel (ɑː) or something intermediate between (æ) and (ɑː), also affects *trans-*, so as to make its prevalent pronunciation (trɑːns) in this area, and hence to extend this pronunciation among individuals or groups in other districts. When unstressed, this vowel sinks in some common words or in colloquial utterance to (ə), e.g. in *transfer* vb. (trəns'fɜː(r)).

The *s* of *trans-* is regularly (s) before a breath consonant, as in *'transcolate, trans'change, 'transfer, trans'fer, tran'spire*; also, of course, where *s* coalesces with initial *s* of the second element, as in *transcend, transcribe, transude*. In the South of England many use (trɑːns-) in all *trans-* combinations, irrespective of what consonant or vowel follows. But many, even in the south, use (trɑːnz-) before a liquid, or nasal, or any voiced consonant, and before a vowel, and this is more or less recognized by recent orthoepists. This is specially the case with the word *transact* and its derivatives, where (trɑːn'zækt) appears to be the more prevalent pronunciation. It is to be observed also that the ordinary English school pronunciation of Latin *trans*, as a preposition and in combination, is (trænz) riming with *banns, plans*, and that many classical scholars retain this pronunciation in English in combinations in which the identity of the prefix with Latin *trans* is specially obvious, as in *trans-alpine, trans-danubian, trans-atlantic, trans-Pacific, trans-Jordan, trans-Caspian, trans-Siberian*. In this work (trɑːns-, træns-) is given as the usual form (except in *transact*, etc.); but the alternative (-nz-) is given esp. for words where it has long been recognized (as in *transduce, transgress*, etc.), though in many other words this pronunciation is now also heard.

For the diverse treatment of *a* and *s* in these combinations, cf. Walker, Smart, Ogilvie (Annandale), Cassell's 'Encycl. Dict.', Webster, 'Century Dict.', Funk's 'Standard Dict.', and esp. Schröer *Neuenglisches Sprach-Aussprachwörterbuch*, Heidelberg, 1913, and Michaelis and Jones *A Phonetic Dictionary of the English Language*, Berlin, London, etc. 1913, in which the subject is treated by skilled observers.

transaccidentation (trɑːns,æksɪdɛn'teɪʃən, træns-, -nz-). [ad. Schol. L. *transaccidentātio* (Duns Scotus: the attribution to P. Lombardus in Marbeck is a mistake due to confounding commentary with text); after *transubstantiātio*.] A transmutation of the accidents of the bread and wine in the Eucharist, as distinguished from *transubstantiation*, in which the substance alone is changed.

[*c* **1300** DUNS SCOTUS *Sent.* IV. xi. i. §3 Transitio accidentis in accidens, magis diceretur transaccidentatio, quam transubstantiatio.] **1581** MARBECK *Bk. of Notes* 1101 Long after Boniface the third..did Petrus Lombardus [see above] bring vp these termes of Transmutation, and Transaccidentation. **1861** PEARSON *Early & Mid. Ages Eng.* 443 Such fables really involve a completely different doctrine, which might be called transaccidentation, but which no church has ever yet deliberately set forth. **1874** FISKE *Cosmic Philos.* I. 123 *note*, The schoolman..asserted that the individuality of the bread (its breadness) was exchanged for the individuality of Christ (his humano-divinity)... It was a noumenal, not a phenomenal change: the latter would have been [not transubstantiation, but] 'transaccidentation'.

transacetylase (trɑːnzæ'sɛtɪleɪz, træns-). *Biochem.* [f. TRANS- 10 + ACETYL + -ASE.] Any enzyme that catalyses the transfer of an acetyl group from one molecule to another.

1950 STADTMAN & BARKER in *Jrnl. Biol. Chem.* CLXXXIV. 788 The arsenolytic decomposition of acetyl phosphate by the cell-free extracts of *C[lostridium] kluyveri* can be represented in an analogous way..if it is assumed that the reaction is catalyzed by an acetyl transferring enzyme or trans-acetylase. **1966** *Jrnl. Molecular Biol.* XIX. 576 (*heading*) Transposition of the *lac* region of *Escherichia coli*. II. On the role of thiogalactoside transacetylase in lactose metabolism. **1976** *Ann. Rev. Microbiol.* XXX. 329 To illustrate genetic transfer, Hedges..cites the gene for chloramphenicol transacetylase.

transache'rontic, *a.* [TRANS- 7.] Lying beyond Acheron, a fabled river of the infernal regions; cf. TRANS-STYGIAN.

1854 *Fraser's Mag.* XLIX. 88 His confused and monstrous transacherontic realm of life-after-death.

transact (trɑːn'zækt, træn-, -n's-), *sb.* Now *dial.* Also 9 *Sc.* **-ack, -ac'**. [f. TRANSACT *v.*, or ad. L. *transactum* a thing completed, a transaction.] A transaction.

1659 *New Lords Winding-Sheet* 4 The Transacts of Colonel John Barkstead hath been taken into consideration. **1871** W. ALEXANDER *Johnny Gibb* xli, We sit owre lang gin ance we begin an' clatter aboot our nain transacks. **1887** D. GRANT *Sc. Stories* (1888) 62 The followin' conversation wud tak' place in the coorse o' transac'.

transact (trɑːn'zækt, træn-, -n's-), *v.* [f. L. *transact-*, ppl. stem of *transigĕre* to drive through, accomplish, f. TRANS- + *agĕre* to drive, do, act.]

1. a. *intr.* To carry through negotiations; to have dealings, do business; to treat; also, to manage or settle affairs. Now *rare*.

1584–5 *Reg. Privy Council Scot.* III. 723 Quha..transactit and agreit with Mr. Patrik Gaittis..and be vertew thairof hes obtenit collatioun. **1623** BINGHAM *Xenophon* 79 The Trapezuntines..gaue the Grecians gifts of hospitalitie... They transacted likewise for the next neighbour Colchans. **1658–9** in *Burton's Diary* (1828) IV. 13 The last Parliament would never transact with them as Lords. We were turned out for it. **1683** CAVE *Ecclesiastici, Athanasius* 109 They transact Synodically in separate Assemblies. **1750** JOHNSON *Rambler* No. 74 ⁋1 That..we may secure the love of those with whom we transact. **1872** SYMONDS *Introd. Stud. Dante* 266 Dante denounced the enemies of his country in his Comedy, and refused to transact with them.

b. *fig.* (Usually *dyslogistic*.) To have to do, to compromise.

1888 *Athenæum* 24 Nov. 693/1 The plan..of 'transacting' with political convictions by acquiescence in, if not actually serving, governments the legitimacy of which the politician in his heart..denies. **1890** *Sat. Rev.* 4 Jan. 15/2 In his criticism..he seems to us a little to 'transact' with cant, or even not quite to have cleared his own mind of it. *Ibid.* 15 Nov. 571/1 He does not make the slightest attempt to 'transact' with naturalism or explain away the super-natural.

2. *trans.* To carry through, perform (an action, etc.); to manage (an affair); now *esp.* to carry on, conduct, do (business).

1635 HEYLIN *Sabbath* II. (1636) 190 Provided..that the change be so transacted, that it produce no scandall or confusion in the Church of God. **1649** CROMWELL *Let.* Nov., Whilst these things have been thus transacting [= being transacted] here. **1709** STEELE *Tatler* No. 94 ⁋1 In the Country wherein the Circumstances were transacted. **1751** JOHNSON *Rambler* No. 100 ⁋1 Ignorance of what is transacting among the polite part of Mankind. **1776** ADAM SMITH *W.N.* I. ix. (1869) I. 99 A country fully stocked in proportion to all the business it had to transact. **1817** JAS. MILL *Brit. India* II. IV. v. 211 Affairs of no trivial importance were transacting in the Council. **1883** R. L. STEVENSON *Silverado Squatters* 122 With so strong a helper, the business was speedily transacted. **1950** R. MACAULAY *World my Wilderness* xxii. 158 What careful, crafty affairs had they transacted in the Hall of the Haberdashers? **1970** D. JACOBSON *Rape of Tamar* ii. 14 Gathering together around the king, while he transacts the business of the state.

3. To deal in or with; to traffic in, negotiate about; to handle, treat; to discuss. *arch.*

1654 FULLER *Ephemeris Parl.* (title-p.), Containing the severall Speeches, Cases, and Arguments of Law transacted between his Majesty and both Houses. **1712** ARBUTHNOT *John Bull* II. iv, To have these usurers transact my debts at coffee-houses, and ale-houses; as if I were going to break up shop. **1767** S. PATERSON *Another Trav.* I. 406 Great sums are transacted. **1848** THACKERAY *Van. Fair* xxvi, While these delicacies were being transacted below.

†**4.** To transfer, hand, or take over; to transfer.

[Cf. med.L. *transactāre* = *transferre* (1242 in Du Cange).] **1621** ELSING *Debates Ho. Lords* (Camden) 71 The cause to be brought before us by *habeas corpus cum causa*, or the case to be transacted to the Kinge, and he to determyne yt. **1653** MANTON *Exp. James* i. 13 God's transacting our sin upon Christ is most satisfying to the Spirit. **1889** *Science* 29 Nov. 374 A paper..from which the following passages are transacted.

Hence **tran'sacted** *ppl. a.*, **tran'sacting** *vbl. sb.*

1686 tr. *Chardin's Trav. Persia* 20 In all their Transacting together. **1752** J. LOUTHIAN *Form of Process* (ed. 2) App. 286 For transacted Processes and Decreets, the one Half of what they would have amounted to if extracted. **1854** J. GUTHRIE *Life J. Arminius* Pref. 2 There are other..transacted lives, which not to know..is a loss to the world. **1876** H. K. WOOD *Highw. Salvation* v. 69 There is the direct and personal transacting of a soul with the Saviour.

tran'sact, *ppl. a. rare*[−1]. [ad. L. *transact-us*, pa. pple. of *transigĕre*: see TRANSACT *v.*] Transacted. (Const. as pa. pple.)

1854 SYD. DOBELL *Balder* xxviii, Night by night, when.. that mysterious sorrow is transact Unseen, and there is weeping in the air.

transaction (trɑːn'zækʃən, træn-, -n's-). [ad. L. *transactiōn-em*, n. of action f. *transigĕre*: see prec. Cf. F. *transaction* (13th c. in Godef. *Compl.*).]

1. *Roman* and *Civil Law.* The adjustment of a dispute between parties by mutual concession; compromise; hence *gen.* an arrangement, an agreement, a covenant. Now *Hist.* exc. as in 3 c.

c **1460** *Oseney Reg.* 84 A stryfe..i-stered bytwene thabbot of Eynesham and N. clerke of Karsynton and thabbot of Oseney... In this maner in owr presence, be transaction, to be decidid. **1611** Cotgr., *Transaction*, a transaction, accord, agreement, attonement. **1615** in *Buccleuch MSS.* (Hist. MSS. Comm. 1899) I. 167 [The Spice Trade] is appropriated to the Hollanders as well by right of Conquest as by Transaction. **1631** Massinger *Emperor East* III. iv, In this transaction, Drawn in express and formal terms, I have Given and consigned into your hands..my dear Eudocia! **1786** A. Gib *Sacr. Contempl.* i. 31 A covenant is a transaction between two parties.

2. The action of transacting or fact of being transacted; the carrying on or completion of an action or course of action; †the accomplishment of a result (*obs.*).

1655 *Nicholas Papers* (Camden) II. 286 His carriadge in the transaction of the peace betweene the people of these countryes and Cromwell. **1658** Phillips, *Transaction*, a finishing, or dispatching any businesse. **1782** Miss Burney *Cecilia* III. v, After the transaction of this affair. **1844** L. Woods *Ch. Govt.* ii. 44 Any direction of Christ or..of his apostles respecting the transaction of business in the church.

3. That which is or has been transacted; an affair in course of settlement or already settled; a piece of business; in *pl.* doings, proceedings, dealings. Also *fig.*

1647 Clarendon *Hist. Reb.* I. §18 Discoursing of the Court of France, and the transactions there. *a* **1656** Bp. Hall *Serm. 2 Pet.* i. 10 Wks. 1837 V. 578 In our transactions with men, when we have an honest man's word for a bargain, we think it safe. **1726** Shelvocke *Voy. round World* Contents 1 Our most remarkable transactions there. **1755** Doddridge *Hymn, 'O happy day, that fixed my choice'* iii, 'Tis done; the great transaction's done; I am my Lord's, and He is mine. **1834** L. Ritchie *Wand. by Seine* 192 Every marriage, every baptism, every fête, is a public transaction. **1863** Mary Howitt *F. Bremer's Greece* I. i. 19 Every remarkable transaction obtained its stone-tablet on the Acropolis.

†**b.** A physical operation, action, or process.

1662 South *Serm.* (1697) I. 49 There is not the least transaction of sense and motion in the whole man. **1794** J. Hutton *Philos. Light* 261 Inertia is the law of action and passion by which motion is translated from one body to another..and, in this transaction, the rule observed is the actual weight of the bodies.

c. *Theol.* In reference to the Atonement, 'transaction' has been used in senses ranging from 1 to 3. (In sense 1 chiefly in deprecation.)

1861 Abp. Thomson *Aids to Faith* viii. 351 There is the danger lest the Atonement degenerate into a transaction between a righteous Father on the one side, and a loving Saviour on the other, because in the human transaction from which the analogy is drawn two distinct parties are concerned. **1876** Mozley *Serm.* viii. (1879) 169 Now I have nothing to do here with the mystery of this transaction; the question is the morality of it—how the act of one person can alter God's regards toward another. **1901** Moberly *Atonement & Personality* vii. 138 They seem to make atonement a transaction, historical, final, consummated long ago:—a transaction (I do not ask at this moment between whom; but..) far anterior to, and wholly outside of, the reality of ourselves. **1901** Sanday *Life Christ in rec. Res.* v. ix. (1907) 249 So much at least seems to follow.., that the Scriptures do recognize a mysterious something which, in our imperfect human language, may be described as a 'transaction'.

†**4.** The action of passing or making over a thing from one person, thing, or state to another; transference. *Obs.*

a **1608** Sir F. Vere *Comm.* 69 Her Majesty being in hand with the States to make a transaction from the old treaty to the new. **1613–18** Daniel *Hist. Eng.* (1621) 16 Putting on each others apparel and armes..as if they made transaction of their persons each to other. *c* **1645** Howell *Lett.* (1650) II. II. 20 The transaction of these Provinces which the King of Spaine made as a dowry to the Archduke Albertus. **1691** Sir T. P. Blount *Ess.* v. 127 Did not Commerce..by a continual Motion and Transaction render it [the world] wholesome, and profitable.

†**5.** The action of dealing with or handling a subject; treatment. Cf. transact *v.* 3. *Obs. rare.*

1646 Jer. Taylor *Apol. Liturgy* Pref. §26 Those.. Epistles and Gospels before the Communion..are Scriptures of the choicest, and most profitable transaction.

6. *pl.* The record of its proceedings published by a learned society. Rarely in *sing.* Cf. proceeding *vbl. sb.* 2 c.

1665 (*title*) Philosophical Transactions: Giving some Accompt of the present Undertakings, Studies, and Labours of the Ingenious in many considerable Parts of the World. *Ibid.* I. 75 In the first papers of these Transactions. *a* **1680** Butler *Rem.* (1759) I. 14 They all..Agreed to draw up th' Instrument, And..To print it in the next Transaction. **1805** *Phil. Trans.* XCV. p. iii, To reconsider the papers read before them, and select..such as they should judge most proper for publication in the future Transactions. **1877** A. B. Edwards *Up Nile* Pref. 8 The pages of scientific journals and the transactions of learned societies.

transactional (trɑːnˈzækʃənəl, træn-, -nˈs-), *a.* [f. prec. + -al¹; cf. F. *transactionnel* (Littré).]

a. Of, pertaining to, of the nature of, or involving a transaction; taking place in fact or reality.

1858 Bushnell *Serm. New Life* 94 A relation wholly transactional. **1894** *Thinker* V. 155 The transactional revelation of principles and forces which are essential and eternal.

b. *Theol.*: see transaction 3 c.

1901 Moberly *Atonement & Personality* ix. 218 What the thought of the present day would sum up as the 'transactional' theory of the atonement. **1901** Sanday *Life Christ in rec. Res.* v. ix. (1907) 244 The 'transactional' theory [of the Atonement]. **1905** *Speaker* 4 Feb. 440/2 The Atonement understood in an entirely forensic or 'transactional' sense.

c. *Psychol.* Relating to or involving interpersonal or social communication viewed as transactions of attitude between the participants; *spec.* in ***transactional analysis***, psychotherapeutic analysis based on the attitudes revealed in such transactions (esp. those of parent, adult, and child); abbrev. T.A. (see T 6 a); hence ***transactional analyst.***

1961 E. Berne (*title*) Transactional analysis in psychotherapy. *Ibid.* 12 Transactional analysis, the social aspect of structural analysis, reveals several different types of 'crossed transactions'. **1969** T. A. Harris *I'm OK—You're OK* i. 13 Transactional Analysis is the method of examining this one transaction..and determining which part of the multiple-natured individual is 'coming on'. *Ibid.* 15 Transactional Analysts claim to have found some of these regularities [of language]. **1976** *Listener* 5 Feb. 141/3 Discussing Basil Fawlty in terms of transactional analysis: as to whether, at certain times, Basil was behaving as a parent, or as a child.

Hence **tranˈsactionalist**, one who believes in a theory of social transactions; also *attrib.*; **tranˈsactionally** *adv.*, by means, or by way of a transaction; practically.

1865 Bushnell *Vicar. Sacr.* IV. i. (1868) 452 The object is to give him a lesson transactionally. **1874** —— *Forgiven. & Law* 59 Is it true that God must be gained or tempered transactionally, that is by acts in time, in order to the letting forth of grace upon his enemies? **1972** R. E. Ornstein *Psychol. of Consciousness* ii. 32 (*heading*) The transactionalists. *Ibid.* 37 Some of the most relevant psychological experiments have been performed by Jerome Bruner and by the transactionalist group. **1977** P. Johnson *Enemies of Soc.* xv. 202 Then there is a series of schools, associated with the Americans H. S. Becker and Edwin Lemert, known variously as social-control theorists, social-reaction theorists, transactionalists or labelling theorists.

tranˌsactioˈneer. *nonce-wd.* [f. as prec. + -eer¹.] One who is concerned or has to do with transactions; in quots., with the published 'transactions' of a learned society.

1700 (*title*) The Transactioneer, with some of his Philosophical Fancies; in two Dialogues. [A satire on Sir Hans Sloane and the Philosophical Transactions, by W. King, LL.D.] *Ibid.* Pref. 4, I have no personal Prejudice to the present Transactioneer or any of his Friends. **1700** J. Ray in *Lett. Lit. Men* (Camden) 205 The scurrilous Pamphlet entitled the *Transactioneer*.

transactor (trɑːnˈzæktə(r), træn-, -nˈs-). [a. L. *transactor*, agent-n. f. *transigĕre*: see transact *v.*] One who transacts; a negotiator or intermediary; a manager, conductor, performer, doer.

1611 Cotgr., *Transacteur*, a transactor, dayes-man, accorder. **1653** J. Hall *Paradoxes* 159 He was a great Transactour for the Essex faction. **1660** Milton *Pres. Means* Wks. 1851 V. 457 The transactors of our Affairs with forein Nations. **1863** Kinglake *Crimea* I. i. 7 Not a mere favourite of his sovereign, but the actual transactor of public business.

transalpine (trɑːnsˈælpaɪn, træns-, -nz-), *a.* (*sb.*) [ad. L. *transalpīnus* beyond or across the Alps, f. *trans*, trans- + *alpīnus* Alpine, f. *Alpēs* the Alps.]

A. *adj.* **1.** That is situated beyond the Alps:

a. Originally and usually as viewed from Rome or Italy, i.e. north of the Alps; also, dwelling in or belonging to a region beyond the Alps; also †*transf.* rude, uncultured (*obs.*). Cf. tramontane A. 1, 1 b.

1590 Greene *Orl. Fur.* (1599) 16 Found in the mountaines of Transalpine France. **1656** Earl Monm. tr *Boccalini's Advts. fr. Parnass.* I. xxiii. (1674) 23 Trans-Alpin writers, whose brains are thought to lie in their backs. **1659** Lovelace *Poems* (1864) 225 Where then,..Lies our transalpine barbarous neglect? **1825** C. Butler *Bk. Rom. Cath. Ch.* 120 There certainly are some Transalpine territories in which the Cisalpine opinions on papal power prevail. **1837** Whewell *Hist. Induct. Sc.* (1857) III. 246 The first transalpine garden of this kind arose at Leyden in 1577. **1841** W. Spalding *Italy & It. Isl.* I. 36 The Po is the only Italian river which can be compared with those of transalpine Europe. **1854** Milman *Lat. Chr.* VI. i. (1864) III. 373 Synods of Transalpine prelates, as at Rheims.

b. Beyond the Alps from England, or from Europe generally; Italian.

1624 [Scott] *Votivæ Angliæ* Ded. 3 Those fiery Transalpine, and factious Transmarine English, who haue onely their bodies here, but their harts in Rome and Spaine. **1632** J. Howell in *Biondi's Eromena* b iij, So have I seen Transalpin grafts to grow, And beare rare fruit, remov'd to Thames from Po. **1656** Blount *Glossogr.*, *Transalpine*.., over or beyond the Alpes, forreign, Italian, on the further side of the mountaines. **1718** Rowe *Prol. to Non-Juror* 34 To your Transalpine master's rule resort, And fill an empty abdicated court. **1765** Wilkes *Let. fr. Naples* in *Corr. & Mem.* (1805) II. 200 This is my fourth letter to you since I have been transalpine.

c. Of or pertaining to the party in the Roman Church opposed to the Ultramontanes.

1794 in B. Ward *Dawn Cath. Revival* (1909) II. 63 The doctrine of the Deposing and Dispensing power of the Pope, ..doctrines which have for above a century been distinguished by the names of Ultramontane and Transalpine. **1826** [implied in transalpinely].

2. a. (Passing) across the Alps. *rare.*

1654 H. L'Estrange *Chas. I* (1655) 104 In his Trans-Alpine expedition. **1744** in *10th Rep. Hist. MSS. Comm.* App. I. 282, I hope the K. of Sard[a] will harrass the Fr. and Sp[ds] in their transalpine march.

b. That crosses the Alps, built across the Alps.

1908 *Chambers's Jrnl.* Sept. 647/1 The Simplon is the least steeply graded..of any transalpine railway.

B. *sb.* A native or inhabitant of a country beyond or across the Alps: cf. 1 a and b above. *rare.*

1617 Moryson *Itin.* III. 47 Old Writers..write, that the Diuine Law came from Italy to the Transalpines. **1622** Burton *Descr. Leicester.* 92 Though those Transalpines account vs *Tramontani*, rude and barbarous,..yet may compare either with their olde Dante, Petrarch, or Boccace. **1634** W. Tirwhyt tr. *Balzac's Lett.* (vol. I.) 85 Those wise Transalpines themselves.., who thinke all such to be Scythians who are not Italians.

Hence **transˈalpinely** *adv.* (cf. sense 1 c); †**transˈalpiner** *Obs. rare* = transalpine B.

1826 G. S. Faber *Diffic. Romanism* (1853) 195 *note*, I recollect the practical cisalpine argument of Almain, from the flat judicial contradictoriness of the two *transalpinely infallible Popes, Nicolas III. and John XXII. **1599** Nashe *Lenten Stuffe* Wks. (Grosart) V. 238 As touching butter and cheese, the Hollanders cry By your leaue wee must goe before you, and the *Transalpiners with their lordly Parmasin..shoulder in for the vpper hand as hotly. **1657** Earl Monm. tr. *Paruta's Pol. Disc.* II. ix. 179 That all Transalpiners might be driven out of Italy, was a thing desired..by all Italians.

transame, obs. form of transom.

transˈaminase. *Biochem.* [f. next: see quot. 1940 and -ase.] Any enzyme that brings about transamination.

1940 P. P. Cohen in *Jrnl. Biol. Chem.* CXXXVI. 566 Since the original term *Umaminierung*..has been accepted with the English (and French) equivalent of *transamination* ..it is suggested here that the enzyme (or possibly enzymes) catalyzing the transfer of amino nitrogen be termed *transaminase.* **1970** R. W. McGilvery *Biochem.* xvii. 354 Much of the nitrogen of the amino acids sooner or later appears in the form of glutamate because of the action of transaminases.

transamination (ˌtrɑːnzæmɪˈneɪʃən, ˌtræns-). *Biochem.* [a. F. *transamination* (Schaeffer & Le Breton *L'Action Spécifique des Protides* (1938) 143): see trans- 10, amino-, -ation.] The transfer of an amino group from one organic molecule to another, esp. from an amino-acid to a keto-acid.

1939 *Nature* 8 Apr. 609/1 The reversible transfer of amino groups between aminodicarboxylic acids and α-keto-acids, or 'trans-amination'..is of almost universal occurrence in biological objects. **1946** *Ibid.* 12 Oct. 515/2 Not until it reaches the root cells does the transformation of aspartic acid take place (through deamination, trans-amination, etc.). **1959** A. White et al. *Princ. Biochem.* (ed. 2) xx. 514 In addition to transamination reactions involving L-α-amino acids, transamination of..aldehydes..has also been observed. **1982** T. I. Diamondstone in T. M. Devlin *Textbk. Biochem.* xi. 546 Virtually every protein amino acid undergoes transamination at some point in its metabolic breakdown.

Hence (as back-formations) **transˈaminate** *v. intr.*, to undergo transamination; *trans.*, to deprive of an amino group; to change by transamination; **transˈaminated** *ppl. a.*, **transˈaminating** *ppl. a.* and *vbl. sb.*

1940 *Ann. Rev. Biochem.* IX. 284 The experiments.. disclose the possible operation of the transaminating enzymes within the animal body. **1940** *Jrnl. Biol. Chem.* CXXXVI. 573 Braunstein reports that these amino acids are transaminated to the extent of 17 to 21 per cent. **1955** A. Meister in McElroy & Glass *Amino Acid Metabolism* I. 14 L-Alloisoleucine and its keto analogue..transaminate at somewhat slower rates than L-isoleucine. **1959** A. White et al. *Princ. Biochem.* (ed. 2) xx. 517 The discovery of the transaminating mechanism. **1970** R. W. McGilvery *Biochem.* xvii. 355 Any other amino acid that will transaminate with α-ketoglutarate may be deaminated in the same way. **1972** *Nature* 8 Sept. 101/2 The group..included amino-acids..that are not transaminated or oxidized in myocardium and those..that can be transaminated and used for energy production. **1974** I. B. R. Bowman in K. Elliott et al. *Trypanosomiasis & Leishmaniasis* 268 It is likely that glutamate is trans-aminated to α-oxoglutarate.

†**transˈanimate**, *v. Obs. rare.* [Back-formation from next: see -ate³.] *trans.* To transfer the soul of (a person) from one body to another (also with the soul as obj.): = metempsychose *v.* Hence †**transˈanimated** *ppl. a.*

1608 Bp. J. King *Serm.* 5 Nov. 31 The..strangest μετεμψύχωσις that euer was feigned by Poets, very incarnated, transanimated devils. **1613** Purchas *Pilgrimage* IV. xvii. 376 This Deuill doth transanimate his soule..into a dogge or other beast. **1625** —— *Pilgrims* v. viii. §3. 540 Being metamorphosed and transanimated from men to blockes. *a* **1641** Bp. Mountagu *Acts & Mon.* vii. (1642) 409 According to their beliefe, wicked mens soules be not transanimated at all.

ˌtransaniˈmation. Now *rare.* [ad. med.L. *transanimātiōn-em* (410 in Jerome Epistle 124, 4), f. TRANS- + *anima* soul: see -TION.] Transmigration of the soul; = METEMPSYCHOSIS.

1574 EDEN tr. *Taisner's Bk. Navig.* Ded. (Arb.) p. xlvii, Yf it may be graunted..that the spirites of dead men may reuiue in other (after the opinion and transanimation of Pythagoras). **1612** SELDEN *Illustr. Drayton's Polyolb.* i. 14 This Pythagorean opinion of transanimation (I have like liberty to naturalize that word). **1727** A. HAMILTON *New Acc. E. Ind.* II. liii. 270 They have many Sects among them, but all agree in the Transanimation of Souls.

fig. **1871** EARLE *Philol. Eng. Tongue* vi. 241 As the pronoun passes into the still more subtle conjunction—so also do verbs graduate from particular to general use. Nor does the transanimation stop here.

transˈannular, *a. Chem.* [f. TRANS- 3 + ANNULAR *a.*] Situated, existing, or occurring between non-adjacent atoms forming a ring.

[**1926** DE BARRY BARNETT & MATTHEWS in *Ber. Deut. Chem. Ges.* LIX. 1429 Es dürfte deshalb angezeigt sein, diese besondere Art tautomerer Umwandlungen unter dem allgemeinen Begriff 'Transannular-Tautomerie' zusammenzufassen.] **1926** *Chem. Abstr.* XX. 3003 The name '*trans*-annular tautomerism' is suggested for those cases..where the H migrates across the ring. **1941** *Nature* 21 June 776/1 As the carbon atoms concerned..are components of a cyclic system.., the resulting tautomeric change would be a transannular one and involve the formation of a bridge linkage from C_3 to C_5. **1978** *Further Perspectives Org. Chem.* (CIBA Symposium) 119 This reaction undoubtedly involves fission of the transannular bond.

transapical (trɑːnsˈæpɪkəl, træns-, -ˈeɪpɪkəl), *a. Bot.* [f. TRANS- 5 + L. *apex, apic-em,* APEX *sb.*: see APICAL.] Transverse to the apical axis (of a diatom).

1900 B. D. JACKSON *Gloss. Bot. Terms* 273 *Transapical*,.. at right angles to the apical axis, passing through the centre of the pervalvar (main longitudinal) axis of a Diatom; *transapical Plane*, the plane at right angles to both valvar and apical planes, passing through the pervalvar and transapical axis (O. Mueller).

transaˈquatic, *a. rare.* [f. TRANS- 3: cf. AQUATIC.] Situated across the water or sea; transmarine.

1834 *Oxf. Univ. Mag.* I. 175 A durable connection between the mother country and her transaquatic daughters.

transat (ˈtrɑːnzæt, ˈtræns-). *colloq.* [Abbrev. of TRANSATLANTIC *a., sb.*] A type of large deck-chair (see quot.).

1968 *Daily Tel.* (Colour Suppl.) 29 Nov. 76 (Advt.), A few days flat-out on a 'transat'—a long couch like those on the decks of ocean liners—at the Tahiti beach did the trick. **1978** *N.Y. Times* 30 Mar. C8/1 Along with the regular-sized deck chairs,..there's..a transat..—a chair with an attached foot rest that slides neatly under the seat when you don't need it.

trans-atˈlantal, *a. Anat.* [f. TRANS- 5 + L. *atlas, atlant-em* (see ATLAS *sb.*[1]) + -AL[1].] Transverse to, or crossing the atlas (vertebra).

1893 *Athenæum* 25 Mar. 382/2 Abnormal vertebræ of certain Ranidæ..in which the so-called 'atlas' possessed transverse processes and trans-atlantal nerves.

ˌtransatˈlantic (trɑːns-, træns-, -nz-), *a., sb.* [f. TRANS- + ATLANTIC; cf. F. *transatlantique.*]

1. Passing or extending across the Atlantic Ocean.

1779 WILKES *Corr.* (1805) V. 212 After a long fruitless trans-atlantic voyage. **1892** *Chambers' Encycl.* IX. 403/2 In 1839 Mr. Samuel Cunard..came over to England from Halifax, determined to establish..a line of transatlantic steamships. **1895** *N. Amer. Rev.* Nov. 514 Of the utmost importance to all transatlantic travellers.

2. Situated or resident in, or pertaining to a region beyond the Atlantic; chiefly in European use: = AMERICAN.

1782 JEFFERSON *Writ. & Corr.* (1894) III. 193 To suggest a doubt..whether nature has enlisted herself as a cis- or trans-Atlantic partisan. **1782** SIR W. JONES in *Mem.*, etc. (1804) 217 The sturdy transatlantic yeomanry, will neither be dragooned nor bamboozled out of their liberty. **1807** W. IRVING *Salmag.* xii. (1824) 199 His hat had the true trans-Atlantic declination towards his right ear. **1812** *Gen. Hist.* in *Ann. Reg.* 161/2 The civil war kindled in those regions between the native and transatlantic Spaniards. **1891** *Harper's Weekly* 19 Sept. 705/1 Salem had an aristocracy. The aristocrats were proud of their transatlantic ancestries.

B. *sb.* (absol. use of adj.): One who or that which is across the Atlantic; a native or inhabitant of a transatlantic country; *spec.* an American; also short for 'transatlantic steamer'.

1826 *Blackw. Mag.* Aug. 325/1 The Trans-Atlantics may hope to have some future share of European civilization. **1831** SCOTT *Jrnl.* (1890) II. 402 Count Robert, who is progressing, as the Transatlantics say, at a very slow pace indeed. **1883** *Contemp. Rev.* Aug. 227 A bed in a sleeping-carriage or a berth in a transatlantic. **1892** *Pall Mall G.* 17 Aug. 2/3 Cork, Killarney, and Dublin are this year crowded with transatlantics.

Hence **transatˈlantically** *adv.*, in a transatlantic or American manner; in quot. 1846, across or while crossing the Atlantic; **transatˈlantican, transatlantician** (-ˈɪʃən) = TRANSATLANTIC B.; **transatˈlanticism,** trans-atlantic character, nationality, or behaviour; a transatlantic or American idiom.

1846 *Blackw. Mag.* Apr. 501/1 [He] might, at that moment, be *transatlantically regaling himself at my particular expense. **1885** *Athenæum* 3 Jan. 10/2 She..had what is Transatlantically called 'a good time'. **1908** *Sat. Rev.* 25 July 120/1 It is transatlantically epigrammatic without being transatlantically smart. **1897** *Harper's Mag.* Apr. 724 English attentions to *transatlanticans savor either of patronage or servility. **1839** *Fraser's Mag.* XIX. 467 What has a *Transatlantician to do with European squabbles? **1907** *Daily Chron.* 16 Sept. 4/4 Trans-Atlanticians..are those who cross between New York and Liverpool or Southampton at least once a year. **1858** MOTLEY *Corr.* 6 June, The portentous aspect on the commonest occasions.. which is apt to characterise *transatlanticism. **1895** *Pall Mall G.* 17 Oct. 4/1 The phrase..is only one more trans-Atlanticism.

transˈaudient, *a. nonce-wd.* [f. TRANS- + L. *audient-em* hearing, pr. pple. of *audīre* to hear; after *transparent.*] Permitting the passage of sound; capable of being heard through.

1854 LOWELL *Camb. 30 Yrs. Ago* Prose Wks. 1890 I. 80 Many a proprietor regretted the transaudient properties of canvas, which allowed the frugal public to share in the melody without entering the booth.

transaxle (ˈtrɑːnzæks(ə)l, ˈtræns-). orig. *U.S.* [f. TRANS(MISSION + AXLE[2].] In a motor vehicle: an integral driving axle and differential gear.

1958 *N.Y. Times* 1 June x. 21/4 The engineers call the new system a 'transaxle' or a 'traxle'. **1967** P. H. SMITH in L. Holmes *Odhams New Motor Man.* vi. 160/1 When access is required to the clutch or gearbox on cars having unitary construction of engine and transaxle,..the complete unit must be removed from the vehicle. **1983** *Fortune* 7 Mar. 110/2 Some of the..contracts for high-margin items like engines, transaxles, and sophisticated electronics are going abroad.

trans-ˈbay, *a. U.S.* [f. TRANS- 3 + BAY *sb.*[2]] That crosses a bay, *spec.* San Francisco Bay.

1965 *Newsweek* 19 July 71/1 The most challenging and vital element of all, the Trans-Bay Tube, will be begun next year when a 30-foot-deep trench will be dug across San Francisco Bay. **1966** T. PYNCHON *Crying of Lot 49* v. 130 She tailed him..back..to the trans-bay bus terminal, where he bought a ticket for Oakland. **1975** *New Yorker* 10 Jan. 29/3 Meanwhile, 1,200 commuters are stranded in a BART train in the collapsed trans-bay tube.

transˈboard, *v. rare.* [f. TRANS- 2 + BOARD *v.* 3.] *trans.* To transfer from one ship or vessel into another; to tranship.

1807 J. BARLOW *Columb.* vi. 38 Barks after barks the captured seamen bear, Transboard and lodge thy silent victims there. **1899** *Scribner's Mag.* July 69/1 The boat..for this [postal] service..is equipped with spacious mail-rooms, chutes for transboarding sacks [etc.].

trans-ˈborder, *a.* [f. TRANS- 3 + BORDER *sb.*] Lying or living beyond a (or the) border; occupying territory outside the border; on or from the other side of the border; crossing a border or borders.

1897 L. J. TROTTER *Life J. Nicholson* xv. (1908) 213 Younghusband was speaking about him to a trans-border chief. **1901** *19th Cent.* Apr. 711 Raised in fixed proportion from the transborder and cisborder clans. **1908** *Westm. Gaz.* 6 May 2/2 An Afghan..may be what, on the North-West Frontier, is called a 'Trans-border Pathan'—i.e., one of the independent tribes dwelling between British India and the Ameer of Kabul's territory. **1976** *Globe & Mail* (Toronto) 16 Feb. 9/1 It was detonated..where the DC-8 came to rest after the eight-hour, trans-border ordeal. **1976** *Southern Even. Echo* (Southampton) 1 Nov. 1/2 'We have undertaken hot pursuit operations as a result of trans-border aggression by terrorists,' the communique said. **1980** *Times* 26 Mar. 23/4 Restrictions are imposed by various countries on what is becoming known as 'transborder data flow'.

transbus (ˈtrɑːnzbʌs, ˈtrænz-). *U.S. temporary.* [f. TRANS- (or TRANS(IT *sb.*) + BUS *sb.*[2]] A bus with special design features, including lower floors to give the elderly and disabled easier access.

1973 *Britannica Yearbk. Sci. & Future 1974* 335/1 The three proposals for the so-called Transbus would have several common features, in addition to length... Lower profile, plus further automatic lowering at stops. **1975** *General Motors Transbus* (Gen. Motors Truck & Coach Div.) I. 24 The use of the pantograph entrance on the Transbus allows use of the wheelchair elevator. **1977** *Time* 5 Dec. 34 He expects that the high cost of the trans-buses (as much as $50,000 more than a regular bus) will halt the expansion of the special van service.

transcalent (ˈtrɑːnskələnt, ˈtræns-, trɑːnˈskeɪlənt, træn-), *a.* [f. TRANS- + L. *călent-em*, pr. pple. of *călēre* to be hot, to glow: see CALENT.

Etymologically the pronunciation is '*transcălent*; *tranˈscālent* comes by false analogy with *transˈlūcent* and *tranˈspārent* (in which the vowel is etymologically long).]

Having the property of freely transmitting radiant heat; pervious to heat-rays; diathermanous.

1834 E. TURNER *Elem. Chem.* (ed. 4) 107 Rock salt is remarkably diathermanous or transcalent. **1880** *Contemp. Rev.* Mar. 373 All bodies, so far at least as the heat of the sun is concerned, are more or less transcalent. **1896** *Allbutt's Syst. Med.* I. 269 The air rich in water vapour is less transcalent and translucent than in drier regions.

Hence ˈ**transcalency,** the property of being transcalent; diathermaneity.

1864 in WEBSTER.

transcalescent (-kəˈlɛsənt), *a. rare.* [f. TRANS- + L. *calēscent-em*, pr. pple. of *calēscĕre* to grow hot, to glow; cf. prec., and *fluorescent.*] Properly, Beginning to be transcalent; but in quot. = TRANSCALENT. So ˌ**transcaˈlescence,** the property of being transcalescent.

1850 GROVE *Corr. Phys. Forces* (ed. 2) 42 Bodies..shew a remarkable difference between their transcalescence, or power of transmitting heat, and their transparency... Rock-salt, the most transcalescent body known, may be covered with soot..and yet be found capable of transmitting..heat.

transceiver (trɑːnˈsiːvə(r), træn-). [f. TRANS(MITTER + RE)CEIVER[1].] An instrument combining a radio transmitter and a radio receiver.

1934 *Electronics* Sept. 273/1 The increasing sales of so-called 'transceivers',..usually one or two-tube affairs operating from batteries, is an indication that the early days of radio may be re-enacted. **1952** *Times* 4 Dec. 7/4 Nowhere except on the transceiver network operated from Alice Springs is it possible for the scholars to play an active part by question and answer to their distant teacher. **1977** *Time* 10 Jan. 44/3 Sales of Citizens Band transceivers were boosted dramatically by gutted prices on current 23-channel gear.

transcend (trɑːnˈsɛnd, træn-), *v.* Also 5–6 -send(e, (6 transsend). [ad. L. *tran(s)scend-ĕre* to climb over or beyond, surmount, f. TRANS- + *scand-ĕre* to climb. So OF. *transcender, -scendre* (14th c.).]

†**1.** *trans.* To pass over or go beyond (a physical obstacle or limit); to climb or get over the top of (a wall, mountain, etc.). *Obs.*

1513 BRADSHAW *St. Werburge* II. 1461 That we may transcende this ryuer safe and sure. **1536** BELLENDEN *Cron. Scot.* (1821) I. 251 Gif ony Pichtis transcendit this dike to be punist na les than thay had offendit aganis the majeste of Romanis. **1602** FULBECKE *Pandectes* 4 In harueest he [the sun] transcendeth the other line of the Æquator and so being farre remoued from vs causeth winter. **1615** G. SANDYS *Trav.* IV. 254 Mountaines not to be transcended without much difficulty. **1695** LD. PRESTON *Boeth.* IV. 161, I have nimble Wings which can Transcend the Polar Height.

2. To pass or extend beyond or above (a non-physical limit); to go beyond the limits of (something immaterial); to exceed.

a **1340** HAMPOLE *Psalter* lx. 6 þai ere a day þat contenys and transcendis þe warldis of all generaciouns. **1534** WHITINTON *Tullyes Offices* I. (1540) 45 They without doubt transende the due bonde of measure. **1559** W. CUNNINGHAM *Cosmogr. Glasse* 10 It transsendith the knowledge of man. **1643** BAKER *Chron., Hen. VI* 75 He had transcended his Commission. **1662** STILLINGFL. *Orig. Sacr.* III. i. §5 Infinity transcends our capacity of apprehension. **1713** YOUNG *Last Day* I. 48 'Twill raise thy wonder, but transcend thy praise. **1805** FOSTER *Ess.* IV. iii. 161 A genius almost transcending human nature. **1855** H. SPENCER *Princ. Psychol.* II. xvii. §81 Unable as we are to transcend consciousness. **1875** JOWETT *Plato* (ed. 2) IV. 124 Ideas..derived from external objects as well as transcending them.

b. *Theol.* To be above and independent of: esp. said of the Deity in relation to the universe; see TRANSCENDENCE 1 b.

1898 ILLINGWORTH *Divine Immanence* iii. 71 It is through this power of self-consciousness..that spirit transcends matter. *Ibid.* 72 The divine presence..will be the presence of a spirit, which infinitely transcends the material order, yet sustains and indwells it the while. **1907** —— *Doctr. Trinity* x. 196 On the other hand, we may..think of God as dwelling in the universe, without in any way transcending it. This means pantheism of one kind or another.

†**c.** *intr.* To go beyond, go farther. *Obs. rare*$^{-1}$.

1629 PARKINSON *Paradisi* (1904) 529 Hauing thus furnished you out a Kitchen Garden..let me a little transcend, and..furnish them with some few other herbes.

3. *trans.* To go beyond in some respect, quality, or attribute; to rise above, surpass, excel, exceed.

c **1430** LYDG. *Min. Poems* (Percy Soc.) 8 In sighte transendyng alle erthely creatures. *a* **1529** SKELTON *Dethe Erle Northumbld.* 144 Transendyng far myne homly Muse. **1615** G. SANDYS *Trav.* I. 7 They imitate the Italians, but transcend them in their revenges. **1679** PENN *Addr. Prot.* II. i. (1692) 59 The Roman Church hath chiefly transcended other Societies in these Errors. **1766** FORDYCE *Serm. Yng. Wom.* (1767) I. vi. 222 Thy merits..far transcend them all. **1864** BURTON *Scot Abr.* II. ii. 191 The Poles also..strive to transcend one another in civility. **1866** R. M. FERGUSON *Electr.* (1870) 11 Electro-magnets far transcend permanent magnets in power.

†**4.** *intr.* To ascend, go up, rise; to pass upward or onward. Also *fig. Obs.*

1513 BRADSHAW *St. Werburge* I. 190 Begyn we shall At the Cytee of Chester..And so transcendynge vp towarde Shrewysbury. *a* **1560** ROLLAND *Crt. Venus* II. 604 Bot quhen sic folk abone thair stait transcend. **1596** SIR J. DAVIES *Orchestra* cxii, Shee wheeles about, and ere the daunce doth end, Into her former place shee doth transcend. **1613** HEYWOOD *Silver Age* III. i. Wks. 1874 III. 135 Thy flowers thou canst not spare, thy bosome lend, On which to rest whil'st Phœbus doth transcend.

†**b.** *trans.* To ascend, to mount into. *Obs. rare.*

1601 B. JONSON *Poetaster* v. ii, It will be thought a thing ridiculous..that any poet..should, with decorum, transcend Cæsars chair.

5. *intr.* To be transcendent; to excel. *arch.*

1635 SWAN *Spec. M.* vii. §3 (1643) 344 So one mans knowledge..transcends not seldome above the rest. *a* **1720** SHEFFIELD (Dk. Buckhm.) *Wks.* (1753) I. 260, I see no such distinction, nor wherein Man so transcends, except in arrogance. **1819** SCOTT *Ivanhoe* xxxiii, 'Thou art a mad knave', said the Captain, 'but thy plan transcends!'

†**6.** *trans.* To cause to ascend or rise; to lift, elevate. *Obs. rare.*

1635 HEYWOOD *Hierarch.* VIII. 530 To that People thou a Law hast giv'n, Which from grosse earth transcendeth them to heav'n.

transcendence (trɑːn'sɛndəns, træn-). [ad. med.L. *transcendentia*, f. L. *transcendent-em* TRANSCENDENT: see -ENCE. Cf. F. *transcendance* (18th c.).]

1. The action or fact of transcending, surmounting, or rising above; †ascent, elevation (*obs.*); excelling, surpassing; also, the condition or quality of being transcendent, surpassing eminence or excellence: = TRANSCENDENCY.

1601 SHAKS. *All's Well* II. iii. 40 In a most weake—..And debile minister, great power, great transcendence. **1644** DIGBY *Nat. Soul* x. §7 There is a transcendence from science to science. **1678** *Lively Oracles* II. xix, God, in whom all those qualifications are united, and that in their utmost transcendences. **1744** HARRIS *Three Treat.* III. II. (1765) 215 That very Transcendence is an Argument on its behalf. **1802** ANNA SEWARD *Lett.* (1811) VI. 27 When we reflect that he had been excelled in every separate order of verse, justice may scruple the imputed transcendence. **1876** T. S. EGAN tr. *Heine's Atta Troll*, etc. 43 A temple, whose transcendence Indicates the Almighty's glory. **1907** ILLINGWORTH *Doctr. Trinity* xi. 226 We expect to see Divine action manifested through the operation of general laws, and not through their occasional transcendence.

b. *spec.* Of the Deity: The attribute of being above and independent of the universe; distinguished from *immanence* (see IMMANENT 1).

1848 R. I. WILBERFORCE *Doctr. Incarnation* III. (1852) 32 That Deistic theory of Transcendence, which supposes that the qualities of matter having been bestowed upon it by its Maker, everything has been left to go on by the impulse which was originally bestowed. **1856** R. A. VAUGHAN *Mystics* (1860) I. 214 Not always..able to embrace fully and together these two conceptions of transcendence and of immanence. **1896** *Chicago Advance* 16 Apr. 567/2 We have been accustomed to believe that nature reveals God in his immanence, but that Christ reveals God in his transcendence. **1907** ILLINGWORTH *Doctr. Trinity* x. 197 Divine immanence and divine transcendence are not mutually exclusive, but essentially correlative conceptions.

†**2.** Elevation or extension beyond ordinary limits; exaggeration, hyperbole. *Obs. rare.*

1625 BACON *Ess., Adversitie* (Arb.) 504 This would have done better in Poesy; where Transcendences are more allowed. **1645** MILTON *Tetrach.* Wks. 1851 IV. 234 Why.. should they be such crabbed masorites of the Letter, as not to mollifie a transcendence of literal rigidity?

3. *Math.* The fact of being transcendental: see TRANSCENDENTAL 4.

1902 *Encycl. Brit.* XXXI. 287/2 Lindemann by a similar process proved the transcendence of π.

transcendency (trɑːn'sɛndənsɪ, træn-). [f. as prec.: see -ENCY.] **a.** The condition or quality of being transcendent; excess; surpassing excellency; with *pl.* a transcendent quality.

1615 DAY *Festivals* xii. 341, I speake not against Lawfull Purchasing, it is that Transcendency I strike at, when Men depopulate whole Countries, to people the Land forsooth with Sheepe. **1662** EVELYN *Chalcogr.* Pref., Your modesty do's not permit me to run through all those Transcendencies. **1681** GLANVILL *Sadducismus* II. (1726) 462 The Essential Sanctity and singular Transcendency of the exalted nature of God. **1857** GLADSTONE *Oxf. Ess.* 8 The transcendency of his poetical distinctions has tended to overshadow his other claims and uses. **1886** *Westm. Rev.* Oct. 469 Christ..never reflected on transcendency and immanency.

b. The fact of transcending: = TRANSCENDENCE 1; an instance of this.

1902 W. JAMES *Let.* 14 Dec. (1920) II. 179, I believe that the 'transcendency' of the object will not recover from your treatment. **1907** J. ORR in *Life of Faith* 9 Jan. 26/1 Such deviations from or transcendencies of the natural order we call miracles.

transcendent (trɑːn'sɛndənt, træn-), *a.* and *sb.* Also -**ant.** [ad. L. *transcendent-em*, pr. pple. of *transcend-ĕre* to TRANSCEND. For the spelling with *-ant* cf. F. *transcendant* (14–15th c. in Hatz.-Darm.), also *ascendant, descendant.*]

A. *adj.*

1. Surpassing or excelling others of its kind; going beyond the ordinary limits; pre-eminent; superior or supreme; extraordinary. Also, loosely, Eminently great or good; cf. 'excellent'.

1598 FLORIO, *Trascendente*, transcending, transcendent. **1611** COTGR., *Transcendant*, transcendant, surmounting, surpassing, exceeding. **1611** SPEED *Hist. Gt. Brit.* IX. ii. §64 The Popes transcendent pleasure and power, being the strongest part of the Dukes title to the Crown. *a* **1637** B. JONSON *Goodwife's Ale* in *Athenæum* 1 Oct. (1904), When shall we meete agayne, and have a tast, Of that transcendant Ale we dranke of last? **1649** MILTON *Eikon.* 10 That transcendent Apostle Saint Paul. **1725** POPE *Odyss.* VI. 128 Nausicaa..shone transcendent o'er the beauteous train. **1754** RICHARDSON *Grandison* (1781) III. xxviii. 307 Such transcendant goodness of heart. **1807** CRABBE *Par. Reg.* I. 783 His own transcendent genius found the rest. **1865** SEELEY *Ecce Homo* v. (ed. 8) 48 A person of altogether transcendant greatness. **1878** GLADSTONE *Prim. Homer* vi. §13. 73 Apollo is less transcendent in intellect [than Athenè].

†**b.** With *above, to*: greatly superior to. *Obs.*

1634 RAINBOW *Labour* (1635) 35 Their clothings being by some degrees transcendant to needle worke even wrought with gold. **1634** HABINGTON *Castara* (Arb.) 16 If worth be not transcendant above the title. **1678** CUDWORTH *Intell. Syst.* I. iv. §16. 286 Julian the Emperor..acknowledged besides the Sun, another Incorporeal Deity, transcendent to it. **1713** C'TESS WINCHELSEA *Misc. Poems* 202 If a fluent Vein be shown That's transcendent to our own.

†**2.** Of language: Elevated above ordinary language, lofty. *Obs.*

1631 GOUGE *God's Arrows* III. §15. 212 Those other high transcendent hyperbolicall phrases of the Prophet Isay. *a* **1653** —— *Comm. Heb.* i. 5 (1655) 43 In this sense this high transcendent prophesie (Isa. ix. 6, 7) is to be taken.

†**3.** Of an idea or conception: Transcending comprehension; hence, obscure or abstruse. Cf. METAPHYSICAL 1 b. *Obs.*

1624 GATAKER *Transubst.* 146 These are such transcendent subtilties, if not absurdities, as any metaphysics will afford. **1635** PERSON *Varieties* I. 3 Metaphysicks..medleth with things transcendent and supernaturall. **1646** BP. MAXWELL *Burden Issachar* 31, I confesse, this Divinitie is so transcendent and Metaphysicall, that it exceeds my capacitie.

4. *Philos.* **a.** Applied by the Schoolmen to predicates which by their universal application were considered to transcend the Aristotelian categories or predicaments. See B. 1 a.

[*c* **1300** DUNS SCOTUS *Rep. Par. in Sent.* I. viii. v. §13 Praedicata..quae dicuntur de Deo..sunt praedicata transcendentia..quidquid convenit enti antequam descendat in genera [i.e. the categories] est transcendens.] **1706** PHILLIPS (ed. Kersey), *Transcendent*,..in Logick, surpassing the Predicaments. **1872** LATHAM *Eng. Dict.* s.v. *Transcendental, Transcendent* is used by the scholastics and moderns, as opposed to immanent—meaning transcending the categories.

b. By Kant applied to that which transcends his own list of categories (explained as *a priori* conceptions of the understanding, which it necessarily employs in ordering its experience, but which have no validity outside of experience); hence, transcending or altogether outside experience; not an object of possible experience; unrealizable in human experience. (Distinguished by him from TRANSCENDENTAL 2 b.)

1803 *Edin. Rev.* I. 258 Philosophy..is transcendent when ..it believes that the objects of our senses exist in a manner really known to us. **1815** COLERIDGE *Biog. Lit.* I. xii. (1870) 117 Those flights of lawless speculation, which, abandoned by all distinct consciousness, because transgressing the bounds and purposes of our intellectual faculties, are justly condemned, as transcendent. **1842** BRANDE *Dict. Sc.*, etc., s.v. *Transendental*, Kant..draws a distinction between the *transcendental* and the *transcendent*... The *transcendent*..is that which regards those principles as objectively real to which Kant assigns only a subjective or formal reality, and consequently is by him regarded as beyond the limits of human reason altogether. **1877** E. CAIRD *Philos. Kant* II. x. 422 From the Kantian point of view both the question and the answer are transcendent. For they both involve the doctrine that the world is in space,..apart from its being known as such. *Ibid.* xiv. 523 And this synthesis is transcendent, i.e. it is a synthesis which cannot be represented as a phenomenon, or verified in sensuous experience. **1881** R. ADAMSON *Fichte* v. 112 *note*, For any question or theorem which might pass beyond possible experience, Kant reserved the term transcendent.

5. *Theol.* Of the Deity: In His being, exalted above and distinct from the universe; having transcendence. Distinguished from IMMANENT 1.

Originally often connoting the denial of Divine action or interference in mundane affairs.

1877 D. PATRICK in *Encycl. Brit.* VII. 36/1 (*Deism*) Shaftesbury vigorously protests against the notion of a wholly transcendent God. Morgan more than once expresses a theory that would now be pronounced one of immanence. **1907** ILLINGWORTH *Doctr. Trinity* x. 194 To think of Him [God], in modern phrase, as transcendent, as above and beyond all relative and finite existence. *Ibid.* 195 It is theoretically possible..to conceive of God as simply transcendent, or simply immanent in the world. **1911** R. MACKINTOSH in *Encycl. Brit.* XXVI. 744/1 (*Theism*) God was apt to be thought of [in 18th c.] as purely transcendent, not immanent in the world.

6. *Math.* = TRANSCENDENTAL 4.

1902 *Encycl. Brit.* XXXI. 287/2 Hermite first completely proved the transcendent character of *e* [see E (the letter) 5 a].

B. *sb.* [the adj. used *absol.*]

1. *Philos.* †**a.** A predicate that transcends, or cannot be classed under, any of the Aristotelian categories or predicaments. *Obs.*

Aristotle taught (*Metaph.* x. 2) that *being* and *unity* were neither categories, nor fell under any one category, but could be predicated in all the categories; in *Eth. Nic.* he says the like of *goodness*. Such predicates came to be called by the Schoolmen *transcendentia*, 'transcendents', as transcending the limits of the categories. Their enumeration as six, *Being, Thing, Something, One, True, Good* (found first in a treatise attributed to Thomas Aquinas, but thought by Prantl (*Gesch. der Logik* III. 245) to be subsequent to Duns Scotus), was in regular use down to the time of Kant.

[*c* **1300** DUNS SCOTUS *Op. Oxon. in Sent.* I. viii. iii. §19 Transcendens quodcunque nullum habet genus sub quo contineatur, sed quod ipsum sit commune ad multa inferiora. **13..** in Thomas Aquinas *Opusc.* XLII. ii. (1490) K viij/2 Sunt autem sex transcendentia: videlicet *ens, res, aliquid, vnum, verum, bonum*.] **1581** W. FULKE in *Confer.* III. (1584) Y iij b, It is a transcendent, which is in all predicaments. **1640** G. WATTS tr. *Bacon's Adv. Learn.* III. iv. 143 All Relative and Adventive condicions and Characters of Essences, which we have named Transcendents; as Multitude, Paucity, Identity, Diversity, Possible, Impossible, and such like. **1652** GAULE *Magastrom.* 207 God is a transcendent, and is not under, nor yet within, the predicament of any part of the whole order of nature. **1697** tr. *Burgersdicius his Logic* I. iii. 6 Transcendents, as, Being, Thing, One, True, Good, which by their Community exceed all the degrees of Categories.

b. *transf.* A person or thing that transcends classification.

1591 G. FLETCHER *Russe Commw.* (Hakl. Soc.) 37 In this number the lorde Borris..is not to be reckoned, that is like a transendent,..being the emperours brother in law. **1593** G. HARVEY *New Letter* Wks. (Grosart) I. 267 Hope is a Transcendent, and will not easily be imprisoned, or impounded in any Predicament of auncient or moderne Perfection. **1608** BP. J. KING *Serm.* 5 *Nov.* 23 Both were transcendents not to be placed in the classes or rankes of hitherto experienced or practised wickednesse. **1642** FULLER *Holy & Prof. St.* III. xxiii. 218 Fame falls most short in those Transcendents, which are above her Predicaments; as in Solomons wisdome. **1655** FULLER *Ch. Hist.* VII. i. §37 Here I must set John Dudley Earl of Warwick (as a Transcendent) in a form by himself, being a competent Lawyer (Son to a Judge), known Soldier, and able States man, and acting against the Protector, to all these his capacities.

c. According to the Kantian philosophy: That which is altogether beyond the bounds of human cognition and thought. See A. 4 b.

c **1810** COLERIDGE in *Lit. Rem.* (1838) III. 221 Omnify the disputed point into a transcendant, and you may defy the opponent to lay hold of it. **1825** —— *Aids Refl.* (1848) I. 260 Let X signify a transcendant, that is, a cause beyond our comprehension, and not within the sphere of sensible experience. **1837–8** SIR W. HAMILTON *Logic* xi. (1866) I. 199 The term transcendent,..he [Kant] applied to all pretended knowledge that transcended experience, and was not given in an original principle of the mind.

†**2.** One who or that which transcends or rises high above the ordinary rank of persons or things; a person or thing of great eminence. *Obs.*

1593 G. HARVEY *Pierce's Super.* 18 Were..his lines such transcendentes, as his thoughtes..what an egregious Aretine should we shortly haue. **1612** W. SCLATER *Serm.* 8, I am loth to make them transcendents; yet such, sure, is their authoritie on earth *supra seriem*. **1613** PURCHAS *Pilgrimage* (1614) 175 The Cabalist as a super subtile transcendent, mounteth with all his industrie..from this sensible World unto that other intellectuall. **1679** V. ALSOP *Melius Inquir.* I. i. 73 'The command of a Superior will hallow an erroneous action', as a Transcendent in our Church speaks.

†**3.** That which transcends, surpasses, or excels something else, or things generally. *rare.*

1613 PURCHAS *Pilgrimage* I. ii. 6 A Paradise, faire, shining, delightsome,..a meere transcendent, which eye hath not seene. **1658** COKAINE *Trappolin* III. ii, Your matchless eyes Transcendents of the brightest lightest stars.

†**b.** A transcendent or pre-eminent quality. *Obs.*

1657–83 EVELYN *Hist. Relig.* (1850) I. 76 These are the transcendents and pre-eminences which this admirable heathen attributes to mankind.

†**4.** A 2- or 3-line capital letter such as those put at the beginning of books or chapters. *Obs. rare.*

1602 WILLIS *Stenogr.* A iv b, A Transcendent, is a great Character, which extendeth it selfe further then the distance betweene the lines.

†**5.** *the transcendent*: the ascendancy, the superiority; = ASCENDANT B. 3. *Obs. rare.*

1691 W. NICHOLLS *Answ. Naked Gospel* Pref. C j, His Confidence has generally the transcendent of his Sincerity, which is the common fate of all Hereticks.

6. *Math.* A transcendental expression or function; a non-algebraical function; e.g. log x, sin x, a^x. See TRANSCENDENTAL *a.* 4.

1809 IVORY in *Phil. Trans.* XCIX. 368 They belong to the class of elliptical transcendants. **1816** tr. *Lacroix's Diff. & Int. Calculus* 24 Those functions..not comprehended in the enumeration made in No. 14, are called transcendents. **1887** R. A. ROBERTS *Int. Calculus* I. 3 We might..deduce their properties as we do in the case of the elliptic functions and the higher transcendents.

transcendental (trɑːnsɛn'dɛntəl, træn-), *a.* (*sb.*) [ad. med.L. *transcendentāl-is* (*c* 1365, Wyclif *Materia & Forma* (1902) 242), f. as prec. + *-ālis*, -AL¹. Cf. F. *transcendental* (18th c.), obs. *-el* (16th. c.).]

A. *adj.* **1.** Of transcendent quality or nature; surpassing; excelling; exalted: = TRANSCENDENT *a.* 1.

(In quots. 1790–1868, more or less ironical or sarcastic.)

1701 GREW *Cosm. Sacra* II. viii. 84 The Deity himself, tho' he perceiveth not Pleasure nor Pain..as we do; yet must needs have a Perfect and Transcendental Perception, both of Pleasure, and Pain, and of all other things. **1727** BAILEY vol. II, *Transcendental*, exceeding, going beyond, surpassing. **1790** BURKE *Fr. Rev.* 10 All these considerations ..were below the transcendental dignity of the Revolution Society. **1862** MERIVALE *Rom. Emp.* (1865) VI. xlviii. 59 His [the Emperor's] transcendental being was elevated above the restraints of all inferior existences. **1868** M. PATTISON *Academ. Org.* 6 It related to the transcendental parts of education.

2. *Philos.* **a.** *orig.* in Aristotelian philosophy: Transcending or extending beyond the bounds of any single category; = TRANSCENDENT *a.* 4 a. By 17th c. writers often made synonymous with *metaphysical*.

By Wilkins used with special reference to his own classification of things and notions.

1668 WILKINS *Real Char.* II. i. 25 The most Universal conceptions of Things are usually stiled Transcendental, Metaphysic-all. *Ibid.* xii. 291 The words *sin, fault, trespass, transgression*,.. being compounded with the Transcendental Particle, Diminutive or Augmentative,.. denote a Peccadillo or small fault, or an Enormity or heinous crime. *Ibid.* 318 Those Particles are here stiled Transcendental, which do circumstantiate words in respect of some Metaphysical notion; either by enlarging the acception of them to some more general signification,.. or denoting a relation to some other Predicament or Genus, under which they are not originally placed. **1676** GLANVILL *Ess.* i. 3 So different they [body and spirit] are in all things, that they seem to have nothing but Being, and the Transcendental Attributes of that, in common. **1682** H. MORE *Annot. Glanvil's Lux O.* 177 The Current Doctrine of Metaphysicians, who define Transcendental or Metaphysical Truth to be nothing else but the relation of the Conformity of things to the Theoretical.. Intellect of God. **1710** BERKELEY *Princ. Hum. Knowl.* §118 Those transcendental maxims which influence all the particular sciences. **1734** WATERLAND *Diss. Exist. First Cause* ii. 51 This is that pure, simple, absolute, transcendental Necessity, which the later School-men and Metaphysicians speak of. **1751** JOHNSON *Rambler* No. 131 ¶1 The wish for riches; a wish.. so prevalent, that it may be considered as universal and transcendental. **1807** J. OPIE in *Lect. Paint.* ii. (1848) 270 Learn to see Nature and beauty in the abstract, and rise to general and transcendental truth, which will always be the same.

b. In the philosophy of Kant (1724–1804): Not derived from experience, but concerned with the presuppositions of experience; pertaining to the general theory of the nature of experience or knowledge, *a priori*; critical (see CRITICISM 2 c).

1798 WILLICH *Crit. Philos.* 65 The division of transcendental logic into transcendental analysis and dialectic. *Ibid.* 182 The transcendental is opposed to the empirical. **1801** *Encycl. Brit.* Suppl. II. 355 Kant.. calls all knowledge, of which the object is not furnished by the senses, and which concerns the kind and origin of our ideas, transcendental knowledge. **1803** *Edin. Rev.* Jan. 258 Philosophy.. is transcendental, when.. it investigates the subjective elements, which.. modify the qualities or elements of the object as perceived. **1842** BRANDE *Dict. Sc.* etc., s.v., The transcendental he [Kant] defines to be that which, though it could never be derived from experience, yet is necessarily connected with experience, and which may be shortly expressed as the intellectual form, the matter of which is supplied by sense. **1872** MAHAFFY tr. *Kant's Prolegomena* 243 We must necessarily distinguish two sorts of idealism—transcendental and empirical. By the *transcendental idealism* of all phenomena, I mean the doctrine according to which we regard them all as mere representations, not as things *per se*. **1874** W. WALLACE *Hegel's Logic* §42. 75 That unity of self-consciousness,.. Kant calls transcendental..; and he meant thereby that this unity was only in our minds, and did not attach to the objects apart from our knowledge of them. **1877** E. CAIRD *Philos. Kant* II. v. 289 Transcendental is the word by which we have learnt to distinguish à priori ideas.. so far as they enable us to know objects.

c. Used of any philosophy which resembles Kant's in being based upon the recognition of an *a priori* element in experience.

1829 CARLYLE *Misc.* (1857) II. 74 The Idealist boasts that his Philosophy is Transcendental. **1842** EMERSON *Transcendentalist* Wks. (Bohn) II. 283 It is well known.. that the Idealism of the present day acquired the name of Transcendental, from the use of that term by Immanuel Kant, of Konigsberg. **1872** MINTO *Eng. Prose Lit.* II. ix. 596 German transcendental philosophy. **1878** DOWDEN *Stud. Lit.* 47 The transcendental thinker [holds] that the mind contributes of its own stores ideas or forms of thought not derived from experience.

d. By Schelling 'transcendental philosophy' was used for the philosophy of mind as distinguished from that of nature.

1903 ADAMSON *Developm. Mod. Philos.* I. 265 Philosophy of nature and philosophy of mind or transcendental philosophy are therefore at once parallel and complementary.

3. In uses derived from the philosophical sense: **a.** Beyond the limits of ordinary experience, extraordinary.

1831 CARLYLE *Sart. Res.* II. v. (1858) 87 Sometimes it is even when your anxiety becomes transcendental, that the soul first feels herself able to transcend it. **1837** —— *Fr. Rev.* III. I. i, Very frightful it is when a Nation.. becomes transcendental. **1856** EMERSON *Eng. Traits* Wks. (Bohn) II. 104 This mental materialism makes the value of English transcendental genius. **1863** GEO. ELIOT *Romola* xxxix, That bust of Plato had been long used to look down on conviviality of a more transcendental sort. **1868** NETTLESHIP *Ess. Browning's Poetry* i. 34 Views.. which, while less transcendental.. are perhaps of more practical value.

b. Super-rational, superhuman, supernatural.

1826 SCOTT *Woodst.* xiv, The dexterity with which he threw his transcendental and fanatical notions, like a sort of veil, over the darker visions excited by remorse. **1841** MYERS *Cath. Th.* IV. xvi. 265 A revelation which may justly be termed Transcendental—wholly incapable of being explained, but yet not incapable of being believed. **1850** WHIPPLE *Ess. & Rev.* (ed. 3) I. 228 It [poetry] thus transcends the sphere of the senses, and is, in a measure, transcendental. **1858** KINGSLEY *Lett.* (1878) II. 67 Below all natural phenomena, we come to a transcendental—in plain English, a miraculous ground. **1903** F. W. H. MYERS *Human Personality* I. p. xv, Transcendental vision, or the perception of beings regarded as on another plane of existence.

c. *Vaguely*, Abstract, metaphysical, *a priori*.

1835 I. TAYLOR *Spir. Despot.* v. 212 Abstract and transcendental notions of an intolerant kind. **1840** THACKERAY *Paris Sk.-bk.* xv. (1872) 172 Having watched the Germans with their.. mysterious transcendental talk. **1847** EMERSON *Repr. Men, Plato* Wks. (Bohn) I. 295 If he made transcendental distinctions, he fortified himself by drawing all his illustrations from sources disdained by orators and polite conversers. **1851** CARLYLE *Sterling* I. xv, To such length can transcendental moonshine, cast by some morbidly radiating Coleridge into the chaos of a fermenting life, act magically there. **1853** MAX MÜLLER *Chips* (1880) I. iii. 66 The exhausting atmosphere of transcendental ideas in which they [Hindus] lived. **1856** *N. Brit. Rev.* XXVI. 173 Proofs.. that the most abstract and apparently transcendental truths in physical science will sooner or later add their tribute to supply human wants, and alleviate human sufferings. **1875** JOWETT *Plato* (ed. 2) I. 77 An unmeaning and transcendental conception. **1901** *Edin. Rev.* Apr. 427 He [Mill] rejected all transcendental conceptions.

d. Applied to the movement of thought in New England of which Emerson was the principal figure: see TRANSCENDENTALISM 1 b.

1844 DICKENS *Mart. Chuz.* xxxiv, Two literary ladies present their compliments to the mother of the modern Gracchi... It may be another bond of union.. to observe, that the two L.L.'s are Transcendental. **1887** CABOT *Memoirs of Emerson* I. vii. 249 [In the Boston or New England Transcendentalism] the transcendental was whatever lay beyond the stock notions and traditional beliefs to which adherence was expected because they were generally accepted by sensible persons.

e. ***transcendental meditation***: a method of relaxation and meditation based on the theory and practice of yoga popularized in the West by the Maharishi Mahesh Yogi; abbrev. *TM* (see T 6 a); hence ***transcendental meditator***.

A proprietary term in the U.S.

1966 C. F. LUTES in M. M. Yogi *Sci. of Being & Art of Living* 13 The system on which Maharishi's teaching is based—a simple method of transcendental meditation..—is indeed systematic and produces measurable and predictable results and is therefore scientific. **1973** *Times* 30 June 14/3 Transcendental meditation is becoming popular as a way of coping with the stress of modern life. *Ibid.* 14/5 Transcendental meditators do not like to publicize the possible dangers inherent in mind-bending techniques. **1975** *Physics Bull.* Sept. 397/2 The aim was to measure the breathing rate and lung ventilation of 15 transcendental meditators before, during and after meditation and compare the values with those obtained for 15 non-meditators. **1976** *Official Gaz.* (U.S. Patent Office) 3 Aug. TM77/2 Class 41 —Education and Entertainment. 1,045,673. World Plan Executive Council—United States, Los Angeles, Calif... Transcendental Meditation. **1976** *Early Music* Oct. 467/1 The place of meditation and mantra made familiar to the West by the practitioners of Transcendental Meditation and similar Yoga techniques. **1980** *Times* 27 May 1/8 Transcendental meditation, as taught by the Maharishi's World Government of the Age of Enlightenment.. involves learning the techniques of meditating.

4. *Math.* Not capable of being produced by (a finite number of) the ordinary algebraical operations of addition, multiplication, involution, or their inverse operations; expressible in terms of the variable only in the form of an infinite series.

The typical transcendental functions are sin *x*, e^x, log *x*.

1706 PHILLIPS (ed. Kersey), *Transcendental Curves*,.. are such Curves, as when their Nature or Property comes to be express'd by an Equation, one of the Variable or flowing Quantities there, denotes a Curve or crooked Line. **1811** HUTTON *Course of Mathematics* III. ix. 188 Transcendental or mechanical curves, are such as cannot be.. expressed by a pure algebraical equation. Thus, $y = \log x$, $y = A .\sin x$, .. $y = A^x$, are equations to transcendental curves. **1843** *Penny Cycl.* XXV. 120 The roots of equations of the fifth and higher degrees are.. transcendental: there is no mode of expression except by infinite series. **1879** CAYLEY in *Encycl. Brit.* IX. 818/2 The so-called circular functions.. the exponential function.. the logarithmic function.. are all of them transcendental functions. **1882** GLAISHER *Ibid.* XIV. 773/1 The small group of transcendental functions, consisting only of the circular functions.. sin *x*, cos *x*, &c., .. e^x, and log *x*. **1902** *Encycl. Brit.* XXXI. 287/2 There are numbers.. which cannot be defined by any combination of a finite number of equations with rational integral coefficients. Such numbers are said to be *transcendental*.

B. *sb.* [the adj. used *absol.*] A transcendental conception, term, or quantity.

1668 WILKINS *Real Char.* II. i. 24 The right ordering of these Transcendentals is a business of no small difficulty; because there is so little assistance or help to be had for it in the Common Systems. **1711** HICKES *Two Treat. Chr. Priesth.* (1847) II. 165 Generical terms come so near to the nature of transcendentals, that they are seldom capable of.. exact definition. **1726** SWIFT *Gulliver* II. vii, As to ideas, entities, abstractions, and transcendentals, I could never drive the least conception into their heads. **1843** *Penny Cycl.* XXV. 120 The expression of the old transcendentals as recognised functions, and the writing of them accordingly, as log *x*, sin *x*, cos *x*, &c.

transcendentalism (trɑːnsɛnˈdɛntəlɪz(ə)m, træn-). [f. prec. + -ISM. Cf. F. *transcendantalisme* (Littré).]

1. Transcendental philosophy; a system of this; applied to that taught by Kant and other philosophers; also, to the idealism of Schelling.

1803 *Edin. Rev.* Jan. 265 The theory of transcendentalism may therefore be a better dogmatism than others. **1817** T. L. PEACOCK *Melincourt* III. 40 He has thus discovered the difference between objective and subjective reality and this point of view is transcendentalism. **1851** CARLYLE *Sterling* I. viii. (1872) 46 He was thought to hold.. alone in England, the key of German and other Transcendentalisms. **1866** DK. ARGYLL *Reign Law* ii. (ed. 4) 117 What is transcendentalism but the tendency to trace up all things to the relation in which they stand to abstract Ideas? **1878** DOWDEN *Studies in Lit.* 58 Transcendentalism, seeking the supernatural everywhere, loses sight of it as such.

b. The religio-philosophical teaching of the New England school of thought represented by Emerson and others: see quot. 1911.

1842 EMERSON *Lect., Transcendentalist* Wks. (Bohn) II. 279 What is popularly called Transcendentalism among us, is Idealism. **1876** *N. Amer. Rev.* CXXIII. 468 Boston and its immediate neighborhood.. really made up the kingdom ruled by Transcendentalism. **1887** CABOT *Emerson* I. vii. 248 The Boston or New England Transcendentalism had, as Dr. Hedge says, no very direct connection with the transcendental philosophy of Germany, the philosophy of Kant and his successors. **1911** *Encycl. Brit.* XXVII. 172/2 (*Transcendentalism*) The most famous example of the pseudo-philosophic use of the term is for a movement of thought which was prominent in the New England states from.. 1830 to 1850. Its use originated in the Transcendental Club (1836) founded by Emerson, Frederic Henry Hedge, and others. The movement had several aspects: philosophical, theological, social, economic.

2. Exalted character, thought, or language; also, that which is extravagant, vague, or visionary in philosophy or language; idealism.

1831 CARLYLE *Sart. Res.* I. iii. (1858) 8 If through the high, silent, meditative Transcendentalism of our Friend we detected any practical tendency whatever, it was at most Political. **1837** THACKERAY *Carlyle's Fr. Rev.* Wks. 1900 XIII. 249 It teems with sound, hearty philosophy (besides certain transcendentalisms which we do not pretend to understand). **1859** SMILES *Self-Help* xi. (1860) 287 Nor did the lofty transcendentalism of his books by any means palliate the acted meannesses of his life. **1871** W. H. MILLER *Cult. Pleasure* Pref. (1872) 10 It is time, indeed, that the whole subject of happiness should be dragged down from the regions of transcendentalism.., and be made, if possible, to take its place in the highways and byeways of every-day life.

3. The quality or character of transcendent excellence; transcendency. *rare.*

1840 CARLYLE *Heroes* iii. (1872) 80 Dante and Shakespeare.. dwell apart... In the general feeling of the world, a certain transcendentalism, a glory as of complete perfection, invests these two.

transcendentalist (trɑːnsɛnˈdɛntəlɪst, træn-). [f. as prec. + -IST. Cf. mod.F. *transcendantaliste* (Littré).] An adherent of some form of transcendentalism. Also *attrib.*

1803 *Edin. Rev.* Jan. 267 We will admit to the transcendentalist his solitary noumenon, and its separate functions. **1829** CARLYLE *Misc.* (1857) II. 75 To a Transcendentalist, Matter has an existence, but only as a Phenomenon. **1840** *Boston Q. Rev.* 270 The men who are affected by it [the new movement] are called by their opponents, Transcendentalists. **1876** LOWELL *Among my Bks.* Ser. II. 32 Transcendentalist as he was by nature, so much so as to be in danger of lapsing into an oriental mysticism. **1879** R. H. HUTTON in *W. Bagehot's Lit. Stud.* Pref. Mem. 28 A thorough transcendentalist, by which I mean one who could never doubt that there was a real foundation of the universe distinct from the outward show of its superficial qualities, and that the substance is never exhaustively expressed in these qualities. **1882** *Athenæum* 17 June 767/1 Miss Peabody.. was prominent in the old transcendentalist movement.

Hence **transcendentaˈlistic** *a.*, of, pertaining to, or of the nature of transcendentalism; belonging to or held by transcendentalists.

1892 *Monist* II. 265 If a philosophy denies the existence of transcendentalistic thought-entities or of any such things in themselves, which serve as cement to combine the *disjecta membra* of their world conception, it is generally declared to lead straight on to nihilism.

ˌtranscendenˈtality. *rare.* [f. as prec. + -ITY: cf. Ger. *transcendentalität* (D. Jenisch in *Kant Briefwechsel* 1902, III. 75).] Transcendental quality. (In quot. 1880 *humorous.*)

a **1846** SALISBURY cited in WORCESTER. **1880** W. S. GILBERT *Patience* I. 7 There is a transcendentality of delirium—an acute accentuation of supremest ecstacy.

transcendentalize (trɑːnsɛnˈdɛntəlaɪz, træn-), *v.* [f. as prec. + -IZE.] *trans.* **a.** To render transcendent. **b.** To render transcendental; to idealize. Hence **transcenˈdentalized** *ppl. a.*

1846 MOZLEY *Ess.* (1878) I. 233 The magnanimity, generosity, ardour, and refinement of ordinary virtue were transcendentalised in him. **1866** LIDDON *Bampt. Lect.* viii. (1875) 450 Nor is it to transcendentalize Him into an abstraction which mocks us when we attempt to grasp it as an unsubstantial phantom. **1875** *Contemp. Rev.* Nov. 996 How often even they are found seeking to transcendentalize their own religion, to escape from its old dogmas, and efface its ancient discipline! **1881** *Contemp. Rev.* Mar. 380 Some transcendentalized form of tolerance. **1883** *Century Mag.* XXIX. 200/2 The Venetian gondola, refined, transcendentalized.

transcenˈdentally, *adv.* [f. as prec. + -LY[2].] In a transcendental manner or degree; according to a transcendental system.

1803 *Edin. Rev.* Jan. 277 Of moral duty it may be said, in like manner, that transcendentally it cannot exist. [**1842** MRS. BROWNING *Bk. Poets* Poems 1890 V. 241 Some have discovered that he [Shakspere] individualized, and some that he generalized, and some that he subtilized—almost trans-transcendentally.] **1877** E. CAIRD *Philos. Kant* II. iii. 244 We hold that space and time are transcendentally ideal, i.e. that they have no objective validity.. apart from the constitution of the sensibility through which they are apprehended.

¶ **b.** *erron.* = TRANSCENDENTLY.

1870 *Eng. Mech.* 11 Mar. 636/2 The diamond, so transcendentally beautiful.

‖**transcendentia** (trɑːnsɛnˈdɛnʃɪə, træn-), *sb. pl. Obs. rare*$^{-1}$. [L., neut. pl. of *transcendens* TRANSCENDENT.] Transcendent traits or qualities.

1674 JOSSELYN *Voy. New Eng.* 89 There are certain transcendentia in every creature, which are the indelible characters of God, and which discover God.

transcendently (trɑːnˈsɛndəntlɪ, træn-), *adv.* [f. TRANSCENDENT *a.* + -LY^{2}.] In a transcendent manner or degree; so as to transcend; surpassingly, supremely, pre-eminently.

1623 GOUGE *Serm. Extent God's Provid.* §1 He saith not simply, you are as good; but transcendently, more worth. **1638** SIR T. HERBERT *Trav.* (ed. 2) 85 His genius [is] so transcendently efflated with pride and ambition, that he beholds his equals with disdaine and anger. **1712** ADDISON *Spect.* No. 543 ¶1 It was the work of a Being transcendently wise and powerful. **1871** MORLEY *Crit. Misc., Carlyle* (1904) I. 164 The transcendently firm and clear-eyed intelligence of Goethe. **1907** *Verney Mem.* I. 71 Reserved for some transcendently important occasion.

tranˈscendentness. *rare.* [f. as prec. + -NESS.] The quality or character of being transcendent: = TRANSCENDENCY.

1625 BP. MOUNTAGU *App. Cæsar* viii. 75 Why are you enraged against me, if I cannot attaine the measure of your transcendentnesse, but confesse my disability and imperfection? **1730** [see TRANSCENDINGNESS]. **1874** PUSEY *Lent. Serm.* 308 [S. Paul] piles up words upon words to utter as he may, that which is unutterable; the transcendentness of the might of the grace of God to usward.

†**tranˈscendiary.** *Obs. nonce-wd.* [? irreg. after *incendiary*, f. L. *transcend-ĕre* to TRANSCEND: see -ARY.] A transcendent person or thing; in quot., an eminent quality.

1654 FULLER *Two Serm.* 60 Some grand Vices..infected the transcendiaries of their highest atchievements.

tranˈscendible, *a. rare.* [f. as TRANSCEND + -IBLE.] Capable of being transcended or surmounted.

1684–94 tr. *Plutarch's Mor.* (1874) II. 220 It appears that Romulus slew his brother, because he attempted to leap over a sacred and inaccessible place, and to render it transcendible and profane. **1953** G. M. YOUNG *Victorian Eng.* xx. 118 Such a body of permitted belief as makes the barriers between England and Rome transcendible.

transcending (trɑːnˈsɛndɪŋ, træn-), *ppl. a.* [f. TRANSCEND *v.* + -ING^{2}.] That transcends; surpassing; supereminent; transcendent.

*a***1529** [implied in TRANSCENDINGLY]. **1598** [see TRANSCENDENT A. 1]. **1641** *Vind. Smectymnuus* xiii. 113 A building of that transcending loftiness. **1713** DERHAM *Phys.-Theol.* IV. xii. 216 Man..being endowed with the transcending Faculty of Reason. **1852** MRS. JAMESON *Leg. Madonna* 196 An angel..might well prostrate himself as witness of the transcending miracle.

Hence **tranˈscendingly** *adv.*, transcendently; **tranˈscendingness**, transcendence.

*a***1529** SKELTON *Replyc.* Wks. 1862 II. 232 Excellently enformed and transcendingly sped in moche high connyng. **1730** BAILEY (folio), *Transcendentness*, Transcendingness, Surpassingness. **1817** A. BONAR *Serm.* II. xx. 443 How transcendingly glorious does he appear! **1874** PUSEY *Lent. Serm.* 306 'That the transcendingness of the power', they say, 'may be of God, and not from us'.

transcension (trɑːnˈsɛnʃən, træn-). *rare.* [ad. med.L. *transcensiōn-em* (*c* 380 Jerome Ezech. Homil. XI. 1), n. of action from *transcend-ĕre* (ppl. stem *transcens-*) to TRANSCEND.] A passing beyond or above, transcendence.

*c***1611** CHAPMAN *Hymne to Venus* 487 My muse, affecting first, thy fame to raise; Shall make transcension now, to others praise. **1886** *American* XII. 152 He laid great stress on miracles and all transcensions of law.

†**tranˈscent.** *Obs. rare.* [f. TRANSCEND, after *ascent, descent.*] The act of passing over or crossing.

1621 G. SANDYS *Ovid's Met.* IX. ii. (1626) 177 Nor seekes the smoothest wayes: Nor by declining his transcent delayes.

†**transˈchange,** *v. Obs.* [f. TRANS- 2 + CHANGE *v.*: cf. obs. F. *transchangement* (Cotgr.).] *trans.* To transform; to transmute.

*a***1598** ROLLOCK *Serm.* Wks. 1849 I. 398 Be schining it culd never sa transchange ane creature. *a***1636** FITZ-GEFFRAY *Holy Transport.* (1881) 197 O Tygers into humane shape transchang'd. **1662** J. CHANDLER *Van Helmont's Oriat.* To Rdr., The which colour hath transchanged thee into black darkness; thou being a white and red Virgin.

†**transˈchangeative,** *a. Obs. rare.* [irreg. f. prec. + -ATIVE; cf. *talkative.*] Having the faculty of changing or tendency to change.

1662 J. CHANDLER *Van Helmont's Oriat.* 157 The objects of taste sitting immediately in some body, cannot by reason of their corporeal thickness, form a transchangeative Image. *Ibid.* 244 The transchangeative virtue of the Archeus.

trans-ˈchannel, *a.* [TRANS- 3, 8.] (Passing) across a channel, esp. across the English or Irish Channel; crossing the Channel.

1894 *Westm. Gaz.* 7 June 7/1 Trans-channel cycling. **1901** *Daily Chron.* 6 Sept. 6/2 The Admiralty Pier [at Dover] from which the trans-Channel passenger traffic is now conducted. **1909** *Westm. Gaz.* 12 July 7/1 The monoplane ..would not be ready to make the actual trans-Channel flight.

transchour, obs. form of TRENCHER.

†**transˈclout,** *v. Obs. nonce-wd.* [f. TRANS- 2 + CLOUT *sb.*^{1} 4 b.] *trans.* To transform or disfigure with clouts or mis-shapen clothing.

1647 WARD *Simp. Cobler* 25 Those women..disfigure themselves with such garbes, as not onely dismantles their native lovely lustre, but transclouts them into gant bar-geese.

transˈcode, *v.* [f. TRANS- 2 + CODE *v.*] *trans.* and *intr.* To convert from one form of coded representation to another; to change the code of. Hence **transˈcoding** *vbl. sb.*, the action or result of such conversion.

1962 *Language & Speech* V. 18 A common feature of linguistic and biological information is the ease with which it can be repeatedly transcoded resulting in a multiplicity of codes. *Ibid.*, Print, translation, shorthand and Braille are among many other examples of transcoding. **1965** *Guardian* 24 Mar. 5/6 It is technically possible to 'transcode' from one [television] colour system to another. **1972** *Computers & Humanities* VI. 150 In using either punched-card or paper-tape equipment one has to delegate the transcoding of the special input codes to the computer. **1984** *What Video?* Aug. 5/4 The only course open to you is to have the existing NTSC—standard tape transcoded to UJ—standard PAL 625.

†**ˈtranscolate,** *v. Obs. rare.* [f. ppl. stem of mod.L. **transcōlāre* (after *percōlāre* to PERCOLATE), or obs. F. *transcouler* (Cotgr.) from same source + -ATE^{3}.] *trans.* To cause (liquid) to pass through a porous substance or medium; to strain, filter; = PERCOLATE *v.* 1. Hence †**ˈtranscolating** *ppl. a.*

1615 CROOKE *Body of Man* 416 The vrine is transcolated through the flesh of the kidneis. **1661** LOVELL *Hist. Anim. & Min.* 315 The kidnies..are to draw, seperate, and transcolate whatever is serous and aqueous in the vessels, both veines and arteries. **1684** tr. *Bonet's Merc. Compit.* III. 93 Fortis transcolates the juices through Sand. **1817** PETTIGREW *Mem. Lettsom* III. 303 By transcolation, or by passing through the transcolating pores of all the solids.

†**transcoˈlation.** *Obs.* [f. as prec. + -ATION. Cf. obs. F. *transcoulation* (Cotgr.).] The process of transcolating; straining, filtration; = PERCOLATION a.

1634 T. JOHNSON *Parey's Chirurg.* IX. i. (1678) 216 That solution of Continuity..which is generated by sweating out and transcolation, [termed] Diapedesis. **1662** STILLINGFL. *Orig. Sacr.* III. iv. §6 Meer transcolation may by degrees take away that which the Chymists call the fixed salt. **1702** W. COWPER in *Phil. Trans.* XXIII. 1185 In Bruises when the Blood is extravassated, it goes off either by Transcolation or else causes an Abscess. **1817** [see TRANSCOLATING].

†**transˈcolorate,** *v. Obs. rare.* [f. TRANS- 2 + COLORATE *v.*] = TRANSCOLOUR. Hence †**transˈcolorated** *ppl. a.*, transcoloured.

1823 J. BADCOCK *Dom. Amusem.* 43 The Transcolourated Writing.

transcoloˈration, -colouˈration. Now *rare* or *Obs.* [f. TRANS- + COLORATION.] The action or process of transcolouring; change of colour.

1664 POWER *Exp. Philos.* I. 74 Experiments in the Extraction, Commixtion, and Transcoloration of Tinctures. *c***1790** IMISON *Sch. Art* II. 94 Among the most pleasing as well as surprizing phenomena of nature [are] the transcolourations produced by chemistry. **1827** *Blackw. Mag.* XXI. 781 True, through all transformations, and transfigurations, and transcolorations, to their original.. forms, figures, and colours.

†**transˈcolour,** *v. Obs. rare.* [f. TRANS- 2 + COLOUR *v.*: cf. It. *transcolorare* 'to discolour or chaunge colour' (Florio).] *trans.* To change the colour of; to cause to change colour.

1664 POWER *Exp. Philos.* I. 75 By its acidity is transcoloured into English Beer. **1669** COKAINE *Poems* 47 Do not believe I counterfeit, who think Verses in your praise would transcolour Inke. **1837** C. LOFFT *Self-formation* II. 262, I was never so transcoloured.

transconductance (trɑːnskənˈdʌktəns, træns-, -nz-). *Electronics.* [f. TRANS(FER *sb.* + CONDUCTANCE.] The ratio of the (change in) current at one electrode or terminal of an active device, esp. the output, to the (change in) voltage at another, esp. the input; *spec.* = *mutual conductance* s.v. MUTUAL *a.* 1 f.

1933 K. HENNEY *Radio Engin. Handbk.* viii. 203 The coefficient showing the effect of plate voltage on the grid current has been termed inverse mutual conductance, or the plate-grid transconductance. **1944** *Electronic Engin.* XVI. 318 The transconductance between these two grids is negative. **1950** *Electronics* Feb. 107/1 In push-pull amplifiers, triodes using this type of neutralization compare favorably with pentodes of the same transconductance as wideband amplifiers. **1981** J. C. SPROTT *Introd. Mod. Electronics* vii. 159 At the operating point [of a field effect transistor] the value of the forward transconductance,..and the output resistance,..can be determined.

trans-ˈcondyloid, *a. Surg.* [f. TRANS- 5 + CONDYLE: cf. *condyloid.*] Traversing or cutting across the condyles.

1885 *Buck's Handbk. Med. Sc.* I. 169/2 Hence this [Dr. W. Stokes'] amputation is generally known as the supra-condyloid amputation, that of Carden being known as the trans-condyloid operation. **1899** *Syd. Soc. Lex.*, *Trans-condyloid amputation of thigh.* Carden's operation.

transconˈfessional, *a.* [f. TRANS- 3 + CONFESSIONAL *a.*] Extending across religious denominations; interdenominational.

1975 R. R. WILLIAMS in *Critique of Eucharistic Agreement* i. 11 The agreements we have here are by no means the only trans-confessional agreements of modern times. **1983** *Times Lit. Suppl.* 7 Oct. 1103/1 Edward Schillebeeckx..has been much read beyond the bounds of the Roman Catholic community to which he belongs. He has accepted the title of 'transconfessional' theologian.

transconforˈmation. *Chem.* [f. TRANS- 1 + CONFORMATION.] A change in the conformation of a molecule, esp. a protein; freq. *attrib.*

1954 LUMRY & EYRING in *Jrnl. Physical Chem.* LVIII. 110/1 The bulk of denaturation changes consist of changes in secondary bonds... Such rearrangements of the secondary-bonded structure are defined as changes in conformation... We shall thus speak of transconformation reactions rather than denaturation reactions. **1979** *Nature* 18 Jan. 244/1 Besides the folding of the isolated polypeptide chains, additional transconformation reactions occur after the association of the native quaternary structure has taken place.

transconjugant (trɑːnsˈkɒndʒəgənt, træns-). *Biol.* [f. TRANS- 1 + CONJUG(ATE *v.* + -ANT^{1}.] A plasmid or a bacterial cell which has received genetic material by conjugation with another bacterium.

1974 *Jrnl. Bacteriol.* CXX. 1187/2 Transfer frequencies were calculated from the number of transconjugants formed per donor cell in the mating mixture... (Transconjugants are cells of the recipient strain that have received genetic material by conjugation.) **1977** *Nature* 10 Feb. 560/2 Plasmid transconjugants which combine octopine utilisation of the donor and antibiotic resistance of the recipient grow well on this medium.

trans-ˈconscious, *a. rare*$^{-1}$. [TRANS- 4.] That is beyond or outside of consciousness or cognition.

1865 MASSON *Rec. Brit. Philos.* ii. 96 He recognised the ideas of three supra-sensuous or trans-conscious objects—God, the Soul, and the World.

ˌ**trans-contiˈnental,** *a.* (*sb.*) Also freq. without hyphen. [f. TRANS- 3 + CONTINENTAL. Cf. mod.F. *transcontinental* (Littré).]

A. *adj.* That extends or passes across a continent; also, of or pertaining to the farther side of a continent.

1853 *Harper's Mag.* Feb. 550/2 A company..to construct a trans-continental railroad. **1869** J. A. POOR (*title*) Transcontinental Railway [from Atlantic to Pacific in U.S.]. **1876** J. A. ALLEN *Amer. Bison* (1877) 465 The great trans-continental emigrant route by way of the South Pass. **1883** W. J. SMITH in *19th Cent.* Nov. 841 The transcontinental railway which Queensland is about to construct. **1898** *Westm. Gaz.* 27 Sept. 6/1 Mr. R. L. J——, the well-known Trans-Continental cyclist, arrived safely in Khiva on the 5th inst.

B. *ellipt.* as *sb.* A trans-continental railway, a trans-continental train. Chiefly *Canad.*

1907 *Eye Opener* (Calgary) 18 July 3/3 Dealing with the immense expenditure on the G.T.P. transcontinental. **1920** J. M. GIBBON *Conquering Hero* 147 At Winnipeg the transcontinental was boarded by..a rancher on his way back to the foothills. **1955** *Standard* (Shawinigan Falls, Que.) 12 Jan. 2/2 A rate [for carrying grain] fixed..shortly after the first trans-continental opened for business. **1964** J. CARROLL *Shy Photographer* 6 You heard the one about the squaw on the transcontinental?

†**transˈcorporate,** *v. Obs. rare.* [f. late L. *transcorporāre* (*a* 200 Irenæus): see -ATE^{3}, and cf. med.L. *transcorporātus* (Du Cange).]

1. *trans.* To change into a different body or substance; to transubstantiate.

1570 FOXE *A. & M.* (ed. 2) 1314/1 Not withstandyng that yᵉ substance of bread and wyne was nowe banished out of the Sacrament, and vtterly transcorporated into the substance of Christes very body and bloud: yet was not this body eleuated..nor adored..till the dayes of Pope Honorius the 3.

2. *intr.* To migrate from one body to another; to transmigrate. Hence †**transˈcorporating** *ppl. a.*, holding the doctrine of transmigration.

Cf. TRANSINCORPORATION, and med.L. *transcorporatio.*

1658 SIR T. BROWNE *Hydriot.* iv. 34 The Pythagorians and transcorporating Philosophers, who were to be often buried, held great care of their enterrment.

transˈcortical, *a. Anat.* and *Path.* [TRANS- 5.] Crossing the cortex of the brain; in quot., caused by a lesion involving a cross-section of the cerebral cortex.

1900 *Brit. Med. Jrnl.* 5 May 1104 This phenomenon the author considered analogous to the motor disturbances in the shape of aphasia which has been termed transcortical motor aphasia. **1901** *Lancet* 20 Apr. 1126.

transcreˈate, *v. nonce-wd.* [TRANS- 2.] *trans.* To create by or in the way of transmission.

1834 COLERIDGE in *Lit. Rem.* (1839) IV. 166 Not the qualities merely, but the root of the qualities is trans-created. How else could it be a birth,—a creation?

tranˈscribble, *v. rare.* [f. TRANS- + SCRIBBLE *v.*, after *transcribe.*] *trans.* To transcribe carelessly or hastily. So **tran'scribbler**, a careless or hasty transcriber.

1746 GRAY *Let. to Wharton* in W. Mason *Mem.* (1807) II. 37 He [Aristotle] has suffered vastly from the transcribblers, as all authors of great brevity necessarily must. **1750** COVENTRY *Pompey Litt.* II. xii, He..once in a quarter of a year, took the pains to transcribble a sermon out of various authors. **1821** BYRON *Let. to Moore* 19 Sept., Such licentiousness of Verb and Noun as may tend to 'disparage my parts of speech' by the carelessness of the transcribblers.

transcribe (trɑːn'skraɪb, træn-), *v.* Also 7 transcribe. [ad. L. *transcrībĕre*, f. *trans*, TRANS- + *scrībĕre* to write.]

1. a. *trans.* To make a copy of (something) in writing; to copy out from an original; to write (a copy). Also *absol.*

1552 HULOET, Transcribe, *transcribo.* **1611** COTGR., *Transcrire*, to transcribe, to write or copie out. **1621** ELSING *Debates Ho. Lords* (Camden) 101 He could not tell whether all was transcrybed by his clerke. **1655** *Nicholas Papers* (Camden) II. 238 The enclosed leters..which I have desired your sonne for your beter satisfaction to transscribe. **1732** BERKELEY *Alciphr.* VI. §3 The primitive Christians were careful to transcribe copies of the gospels. **1837** LOCKHART *Scott* I. v. 134 The Writer's Apprentice receives a certain allowance in money for every page he transcribes. **1850** MACAULAY in *Life & Lett.* (1913) II. xii. 266 Tomorrow I shall begin to transcribe again and to polish.

b. Less exactly: To copy or reproduce the matter or statements of (a writing or book) without regard to the wording; to quote, cite. Now *rare.*

a **1633** AUSTIN *Medit.* (1635) 221 A Tradition (which I find not in Abdias, Bishop of Babylon; nor in any of the common Legends that I thinke were almost all transcribed from him). **1646** SIR T. BROWNE *Pseud. Ep.* II. i. 50 Solinus who transcribed Plinie..hath in this point dissented from him. **1676** RAY *Corr.* (1848) 122 All which..makes me suspect he transcribed what he hath out of some writer, either Dutch, French, or Italian. **1726** POPE *Odyss.* V. Notes 285, I have sometimes used Madam Dacier as she has done others, in transcribing some of her Remarks without particularizing them. **1747** WESLEY *Prim. Physick* (1762) p. xviii, A few plain, easy rules. Chiefly transcribed from Dr. Cheyne. **1850** SCORESBY *Cheever's Whalem. Adv.* vi. (1858) 76 Which we have not room to transcribe here.

c. *Biol.* To synthesize a nucleic acid (usu. RNA) using an existing nucleic acid (usu. DNA) as a template, so that the genetic information in the latter is copied. Const. *into* (with the template as obj.), *from*, *off* (with the new acid as obj.).

1962 *Proc. Nat. Acad. Sci.* XLVIII. 544 Only one strand of the DNA is transcribed as functional messenger-RNA. **1973** *Sci. Amer.* Apr. 34/3 Their chromosomes are in a greatly enlarged and uncoiled 'lampbrush' stage where we might be able to see structural details of DNA being transcribed into messenger RNA. **1979** D. R. HOFSTADTER *Gödel, Escher, Bach* xvi. 517 When mRNA is transcribed off of DNA, the transcription process operates via the usual base-pairing. **1981** L. L. MAYS *Genetics* ii. 65 Once RNA is transcribed from DNA, it is cut to its final size, modified in specific ways, and sent to its site of action.

2. a. To write out in other characters, to transliterate; to write out (a shorthand account) in ordinary 'long-hand'; formerly also, to translate or render accurately in another language.

1639 T. C[ARY] (*title*) The Mirrour which Flatters not.. Transcrib'd into English from the French [of La Serre],.. And devoted to the well-disposed Readers. **1669** tr. *Beguinus' Tyroc. Chym.* To Rdr., It becomes every man, about to transcribe, or render the Works of another in his own native Tongue, neither to add any thing of his own, nor to omit of the Author's. **1724** A. COLLINS *Gr. Chr. Relig.* 138 All the books..were transcrib'd, as is usually suppos'd, out of the Hebrew into the Chaldee Character. **1875** RENOUF *Egypt. Gram.* 1 The omitted vowels are conventionally transcribed by the letter *e.* **1877** BROWNING (*title*) The Agamemnon of Æschylus transcribed by Robert Browning.

b. *Mus.* To adapt (a composition) for a voice or instrument other than that for which it was originally written. Also *intr.* for *pass.*

1891 in *Cent. Dict.* **1976** *Gramophone* June 61/1 Vocal ensemble music should transcribe well for brass.

†**3.** *fig.* To copy or imitate (a person, his qualities, actions, etc.); to reproduce. *Obs.*

1647 CRASHAW *Poems* 106 Thou and the lovely hopes that smile in thee Are ta'en out, and transcribed by thy great mother! **1664** EVELYN tr. *Freart's Archit.* Ep. Ded. 5 As many of those Illustrious Persons as by their large and magnificent Structures transcribe your Royal Example. **1709** WATTS *Hymn 'My dear Redeemer'* ii, Such love, and meekness so divine, I would transcribe, and make them mine. *a* **1729** ROGERS (J.), If we imitate their repentance as we transcribe their faults.

†**4.** To attribute or ascribe *to* another by transference. *Obs.*

1561 T. NORTON *Calvin's Inst.* IV. xiv. (1634) 634 *margin*, Sacraments..be meanes whereby faith groweth, yet so that no power proper unto God be transcribed from him unto them. **1610** R. ABBOTT *Old Way* 15 The Papists..who haue transcribed the authority of Religion to mortall Men, to Doctors, and Fathers, and Councels. **1651** C. CARTWRIGHT *Cert. Relig.* II. 34 As he used to transcribe to the Father whatsoever divine power was in him, so the Apostle doth not improperly transferre to the Father that which was Christs most proper work.

5. *Roman Law.* To transfer, assign, make over *to* another; = L. *transcrībere*: cf. TRANSCRIPTION 4.

1880 [see *transcribed* below].

6. a. To make a copy of (a gramophone recording) from a secondary source, not the master recording.

1931 *Gramophone* Dec. 264/1 The Philadelphians have recorded the Fifth Symphony of Beethoven complete on a single 12-in. disc and..thirty-two other discs..have been announced on which existing works..have been 'transcribed'.

b. *Broadcasting.* To record for subsequent reproduction; to broadcast in this form.

1941 W. ABBOT *Handbk. Broadcasting* 245 These are inserted into transcribed programs or into a live program.

Hence **transcribed** (-'skraɪbd) *ppl. a.*; **tran'scribing** *vbl. sb.* and *ppl. a.*

1700 P. LORRAIN in *Pepys' Diary*, etc. (1879) VI. 229 The transcribing of the Appendix. **1709** STEELE *Tatler* No. 19 ¶2 Small Quill-men and Transcribing Clerks. **1880** MUIRHEAD *Gaius* III. §128 A literal obligation is created by transcribed entries; and these are made in two ways,—either from thing to person, or from person to person. **1961** J. UPDIKE in *New Yorker* 17 June 31/1 A transistor radio somewhere in the sand releases in a thin, apologetic gust the closing peal of a transcribed service. **1981** L. L. MAYS *Genetics* ii. 57 Sometimes the transcribed RNA is the final product.

transcriber (trɑːn'skraɪbə(r), træn-). [f. TRANSCRIBE + -ER^1.]

1. One who transcribes; a copyist or copier, as distinct from an original writer.

1610 HOLLAND *Camden's Brit.* (1637), The carelesse negligence of transcribers. **1654** FULLER *Ephemeris* Pref. 3, I..who have no commission to be an Authour, but a Transcriber. **1791** *Gentl. Mag.* Jan. 21/1 The dull transcribers of printed sermons. **1841** D'ISRAELI *Amen. Lit.* (1867) 218 Spurious writings..ascribed by ignorant transcribers to some ancient sage.

2. An item of office equipment on which dictation cannot be recorded, but which replays dictated matter for transcription by an (audio) typist.

1931 *Times* 16 Mar. 1/6 All-electric Dictaphone with Shaver and Transcriber: good condition. **1976** *Southern Even. Echo* (Southampton) 3 Nov. (Advt.), Duties will include shorthand or use of transcriber, typing, correspondence, filing, [etc.].

transcript ('trɑːnskrɪpt, 'træn-), *sb.* (*a.*) Forms: α. 3–4 **transcrit**, (3 **traunscrit**), 5 **transcrite**, (6 **tancrete**). β. 5–7 **transcripte**, (6 **-scrypt**), 5– **transcript.** [a. OF. *transcrit* (AF. also *transescrit*, *transecrit*) copy of a document, etc. (1221 in Godef.):—L. *transcript-um*, sb. use of pa. pples. of F. *transcrire*, and L. *transcrībĕre* to TRANSCRIBE. In 15th c. assimilated to the L. form *transcriptum* (evidenced from *c* 1200, in English use). A worn-down F. form *tancrist*, *tanscrit* (13th c. in Godef.), appears to be represented in 16th c. Eng. by *tancrete* (Skelton): see B.]

A. *sb.* **1. a.** A written copy; also *transf.* a printed reproduction of this; *spec.* in *Law*, a copy of a legal record.

α. *c* **1290** *Beket* 551 in *S. Eng. Leg.* I. 122 Of ower olde lawes transcrit ȝe me take. *Ibid.* 553 Þe king him let a traunscrit take of his custumes echon. **1454** *Rolls of Parlt.* V. 248/1 That a transcrite of this same Act..be sent unto our seid Tresorer. **1522** [see B.].

β. **1467** *Mann. & Househ. Exp. Eng.* (Roxb.) 402 Item, for a transcripte of the offyce of Gorge, ij. s. **1481** *Coventry Leet Bk.* 493 A transcript of which lettre hereaftur ensueth. **1538** FITZHERB. *Just. Peas* 187 The clerke of the petit bagge to certify the transcrypt of every suche offyce. **1611** SPEED *Hist. Gt. Brit.* IX. viii. §54 The Archbishop and other Barons, are so cunningly named in the Popes Transcript, as if [etc.]. **1642** CHAS. I *Answ. Declar. both Ho.* 1 July 36 That which now remains being but a Transcript of a Transcript. **1788** GIBBON *Decl. & F.* xliv. (1869) II. 637 Authentic transcripts were multiplied by the pens of notaries and scribes. **1803** in Gurw. *Wellington's Desp.* (1837) II. 117 *note*, The note that I addressed to him.., a transcript of which is contained in the enclosure. **1875** SCRIVENER *Lect. Text N. Test.* 15 The successive transcripts between the sacred autograph and the document before us.

b. A verbal or close translation or rendering. ? *nonce-use.* Cf. TRANSCRIBE *v.* 2.

1871 BROWNING (*title*) Balaustion's Adventure: including a transcript from Euripides.

2. *transf.* and *fig.* A copy, imitation, reproduction; a representation, rendering, interpretation.

1646 J. GREGORY *Notes & Obs.* Pref. (1650) 1 The Lesser worlds or men are but the Transcripts of the Greater, as Children and Bookes the Copies of themselves. **1647** CLARENDON *Hist. Reb.* I. §53 Some Transcripts of such Expressions..he met with amongst the People. **1657** TRAPP *Comm. Job* iv. 3 Let our lives be a true transcript of our Sermons. **1711** ADDISON *Spect.* No. 166 ¶1 Words are the Transcript of those Ideas which are in the Mind of Man, and ..Writing or Printing are the Transcript of Words. **1781** COWPER *Expost.* 198 They only..Received the transcript of the eternal mind. **1860** WESTCOTT *Introd. Study Gosp.* vii. (ed. 5) 367 The Gospel of St. Mark is essentially a transcript from life. **1869** MCLAREN *Serm.* Ser. II. iii. (1875) 42 The artist that is satisfied with his transcript of his ideal will not grow any more.

3. *Biol.* A length of RNA or DNA which has been transcribed from a DNA or RNA template (respectively).

1961 JACOB & MONOD in *Jrnl. Molecular Biol.* III. 352 The molecular structure of proteins is determined by specific elements, the structural genes. These act by forming a cytoplasmic 'transcript' of themselves, the structural messenger. **1972** *Sci. Amer.* Jan. 33/3 We have uncovered evidence that cancer-causing RNA viruses can produce a DNA transcript of the viral RNA. **1982** *Nature* 13 May 130/2 Transcripts initiated further upstream than postion −675 will yield a protected fragment of $\sim$1,375 nucleotides.

B. *ppl. a.* Transcribed, copied.

c **1450** *Godstow Reg.* 102 A Transcripte charter of philippe Basset I-made to the mynchons of Godestowe. **1522** SKELTON *Why not to Court* 417 It shall be as he wyll Stop at law tancrete, An abstract or a concrete.

†**tran'script**, *v. Obs. rare.* [f. L. *transcript-*, ppl. stem of *transcrībĕre* to TRANSCRIBE.] *trans.* = TRANSCRIBE. Hence †**tran'scripting** *vbl. sb.*

1592 G. HARVEY *Pierce's Super.* Wks. (Grosart) II. 123, I haue lost more labour then the transcripting of this Censure. **1609** *Sir T. Smith's Commw. Eng.* To Rdr. 2 Corruption of coppies, happening..by the often transscripting. **1633** T. STAFFORD *Pac. Hib.* III. xiii. (1821) 625 A Letter from Sir Robert Cecill unto the Lord Deputie, and the same transcripted..unto the President.

transcriptase (trɑːn'skrɪpteɪz, træn-). *Biochem.* [f. TRANSCRIPT(ION + -ASE.] The polymerase responsible for transcription, which catalyses the formation of RNA from a DNA template; ***reverse transcriptase***, the polymerase responsible for reverse transcription, which catalyses the formation of DNA from an RNA template.

1963 SPIEGELMAN & HAYASHI in *Cold Spring Harbor Symp. Quantitative Biol.* XXVIII. 162/1 The transcribing DNA-dependent-RNA-polymerase which produces RNA complements will be referred to as a transcriptase. **1965** *New Scientist* 18 Mar. 713/2 An enzyme exists in cells (called 'RNA polymerase' or sometimes 'transcriptase') which is capable of reading the genic code. **1970** *Nature* 26 Dec. 1255/1 Research..on reverse transcriptases in animal cancer viruses and human cancer cells. **1976** *Ann. Rev. Microbiol.* XXX. 23 Kates & McAuslan..initially demonstrated transcriptase in poxvirus cores isolated from infected cells.

transcription (trɑːn'skrɪpʃən, træn-). [ad. L. *transcriptiōn-em*, n. of action f. *transcrībĕre* to transcribe, or a. F. *transciption* (16th c. in Godef. *Compl.*).]

1. a. The action or process of transcribing or copying. Also *fig.*

1598 FLORIO, *Trascrittione*, a transcription, a writing, or copying out. **1610** HEALEY *St. Aug. Citie of God* 548 The error was committed in the transcription of the copy from Ptolomies library. **1664** H. MORE *Myst. Iniq.* 93 By a diligent comparing of Copies upon every transcription. **1762** J. KENNEDY *Compl. Syst. Astronom. Chronol.* ad fin., Evidence which no transcription can corrupt. *a* **1848** R. W. HAMILTON *Rew. & Punishm.* i. (1853) 43 We might take the Decalogue and trace its transcription upon the soul of man. **1858** J. H. NEWMAN *Hist. Sk.* (1873) III. IV. xi. 416 Manual labour..applied to the transcription and multiplication of books..was a method of instruction.

b. Transliteration.

1869 FARRAR *Fam. Speech* i. (1873) 10 He succeeded in demonstrating the law of transcription, and for the first time reading these names in their proper form. *Ibid.* 24 The transcription into Russian letters.

2. The product of this process; a transcript; a copy.

1650 *Vind. Hammond's Addr.* §88 Besides this transcription, there is but one passage.., to which he thinkes fit to make reply. **1657** RUMSEY *Org. Salutis* Ep. Ded. (1659) 11 Most medicinal Books are usually but bare transcriptions from former Writers. **1696** PHILLIPS (ed. 5), *Transcription*, a Writing copied, or transcribed. **1882–3** *Schaff's Encycl. Relig. Knowl.* I. 116/2 A transcription of the work, made in the beginning of the third century.

3. *Mus.* The arrangement, or (less properly) modification, of a composition for some voice or instrument other than that for which it was originally written; an instance of this, a transcribed piece.

1864 in WEBSTER. **1878** E. J. HOPKINS in Grove *Dict. Mus.* I. 21/1 Variations or adaptations like the popular 'Transcriptions' of the present day. **1885** *Athenæum* 26 Dec. 851/1 To the musicianly ear the term 'transcription' has generally an unpleasant sound, because it frequently bears reference to some uncalled-for distortion of a composer's original idea.

4. *Roman Law.* A transfer, assignment (of a debt or obligation); = L. *transcriptio.*

1677 OWEN *Justif.* Wks. 1851 V. 170 This he [Paul] did by the transcription of both the debts of Onesimus to himself. **1880** MUIRHEAD *Gaius* III. §129 There is transcription from thing to person when, for example, I enter to your debit a sum you already owe me by reason of a purchase, a conduction, or a partnership.

5. a. A gramophone record made from a secondary source, not the master recording.

1931 *Gramophone* Dec. 264/2 'Transcriptions', too, for which our unkind readers used to prefer the phrase 'faked records', are not very popular over here. **1968** *Jazz Monthly* Feb. 4/1 Numerous 'pirate' labels also issuing EPs and LPs, ..tend increasingly to concentrate on air shots and transcriptions from a variety of sources.

b. *Broadcasting.* The recording of a broadcast for subsequent reproduction; a record or broadcast so made. Also *attrib.*

1932 *B.B.C. Year-bk. 1933* 290 The relaying of the Empire station by overseas transmitters cannot for various reasons be assumed to be possible as a regular practice and therefore the recording of programmes on gramophone discs becomes an important subsidiary method of programme circulation... American programmes are already circulated by this method, which is termed 'electrical transcription'. **1936** *Communication* Mar. 5 (*heading*) The growing importance of transcription broadcasting. *Ibid.* 6/2 The transcriptions in every-day use in broadcast stations include both lateral-cut and vertical-cut recordings. **1943** *B.B.C. Year-bk.* 23 An important broadcasting activity little known in this country is the projection overseas, by means of recordings, of the culture and wartime life of Britain... Known collectively as the London Transcription Service, the activity has been undertaken by the BBC for the Empire since the beginning of the war, and for foreign countries for nearly two years. **1956** *B.B.C. Handbk. 1957* 42 English by Radio lessons.. reach an audience of several millions by direct transmission from London, by relays, and by transcription recordings. *Ibid.* 133 Among other transcriptions, the special service for Colonial schools.. proved successful. **1978** *A-Z of BBC* (ed. 2) 225/2 Transcription services are the BBC's channel for selling Radio Programmes to stations overseas.

c. Used *attrib.* to designate equipment used in professional recording or broadcasting transcription, or *gen.* of a standard or type so used.

1936 *Communication* Mar. 8/2 Noise in the output of a transcription equipment is often caused by pickup of the motor vibration. **1943** *Proc. I.R.E.* Feb. 52 (*heading*) The measurement of transcription-turntable speed variation. **1957** *Long Playing Record Library Catal. & Handbk.* 10 The only answer.. is the use of a 'transcription motor', implying a high standard of design and finish and individual care in manufacture. **1962** A. NISBETT *Technique Sound Studio* 271 The large transcription tape decks are normally equipped to play either type. **1965** *Wireless World* Aug. 6 (Advt.), The Goldring-Lenco GL 70 transcription unit with its integrally mounted transcription arm continues to be the first choice of discriminating record lovers with custom-built equipment. **1978** *Lancashire Life* Nov. 110/1 (Advt.), All the illustrated units are complete music centres with Dolby cassette deck-belt driven transcription unit.

6. *Biol.* The process by which genetic information represented by the sequence of nucleotides in the DNA of a cell or virus is copied into molecules of RNA, which are synthesized with the DNA serving as a template; ***reverse transcription***, the reverse process, occurring in some RNA viruses, by which DNA is synthesized from an RNA template.

1961 JACOB & MONOD in *Cold Spring Harbor Symp. Quantitative Biol.* XXVI. 193/1 The second process, which we shall call transcription, allows the gene to perform its physiological function. **1970** *Nature* 27 June 1198/1 For the past twenty years the cardinal tenet of molecular biology has been that the flow or transcription of genetic information from DNA to messenger RNA and then its translation to protein is strictly one way. **1971** [see PROMOTER 1 g]. **1973** *Sci. Amer.* Apr. 34/2 In prokaryotes, which include the many species of bacteria, transcription and translation of messenger RNA occur at the same time and place. **1977** *Nature* 8 Sept. 122/1 Until recently.. most groups studying reverse transcription *in vitro* found the DNA products to be small relative to the size of the RNA templates.

Hence **tran'scriptional** *a.*, of, pertaining to, or of the nature of transcription; **tran'scriptionally** *adv.*, on transcriptional grounds; also, in *Biol.*, in a transcriptional way.

1881 WESTCOTT & HORT *Grk. N.T.* Introd. §29 Transcriptional Probability is not directly.. concerned with the relative excellence of rival readings, but merely with the relative fitness of each for explaining the existence of the others. **1905** J. R. HARRIS in *Expositor* Sept. 166 Traces of such transcriptional errors. **1907** H. S. CRONIN in *Eng. Hist. Rev.* Apr. 294 Both Latin versions must have had some transcriptional history. **1911** K. LAKE *Earlier Ep. St. Paul* 419 The omission is transcriptionally slightly the more probable reading. **1970** *Nature* 29 Aug. 910/1 A similar mechanism controls gene expression at the transcriptional level during bacterial sporulation. **1975** *Ibid.* 5 June 462/2 This transcriptionally active DNA represents r-protein genes. **1981** L. L. MAYS *Genetics* ix. 416 The prokaryotic systems that operate via transcriptional control often utilize different control systems. **1983** *Nature* 23 June 677/1 Transcriptionally active chromatin.

transcriptionist (trɑːn'skrɪpʃənɪst, træn-). *U.S.* [f. TRANSCRIPTION + -IST.] An audio typist.

1977 *Chicago Tribune* 2 Oct. XII. 67/6 (Advt.), 60 wpm typing, plus 1 year experience as a medical transcriptionist, or training in this field qualifies you. **1978** *Detroit Free Press* 16 Apr. F5/5 (Advt.), Medical transcriptionist. For out-patient clinic in university setting. Accurate typing & Medical Terminology necessary.

transcriptitious (trɑːnskrɪp'tɪʃəs, træn-), *a. rare.* [f. L. *transcript-*, ppl. stem of *transcrībĕre* to TRANSCRIBE + -ITIOUS[1]. Cf. late L. *transcriptīcius*, *-ītius* belonging to a transfer or assignment.] Derived from or arising out of transcription; of the nature or character of a transcript.

1655-87 H. MORE *App. Antid.* (1712) 181 That there is no such Idea of God.. as we have describ'd, neither Innate, nor Acquisititious, or Transcriptitious; because it involves in it the Notion of a Spirit. **1802-12** BENTHAM *Ration. Judic. Evid.* (1827) II. 436 Preappointed evidence may be distinguished into original and transcriptitious. *Ibid.* III. 396 Evidence.. termed transcriptitious or transcriptural.

transcriptive (trɑːn'skrɪptɪv, træn-), *a.* [f. as prec. + -IVE; cf. *descriptive*, etc.]

1. Having the quality or habit of transcribing; given, devoted, or tending to transcription.

1646 SIR T. BROWNE *Pseud. Ep.* I. viii. 29 Although excellent and usefull Authors, yet being either transcriptive, or following the common relations of things, their accounts are not to be swallowed at large. *Ibid.* 33 He is to be embraced.. as a transcriptive relator. **1823** BYRON *Let.* in *Eng. Stud.* (1897) XXXIII. 453, I sent to Mrs. S—— a few Scenes more of the drama begun for her transcriptive leisure. **1888** CAVE *Inspir. O. Test.* viii. 455 Transcriptive Inspiration.. moves the writers to write.

2. *Rom. Law.* Transferring obligation: cf. TRANSCRIPTION 4.

1875 POSTE *Gaius* III. §131. 11 Transcriptive entries differ from mere entries of a person as debtor to cash.

Hence **tran'scriptively** *adv. rare*, in a transcriptive manner; by way of transcription.

1646 SIR T. BROWNE *Pseud. Ep.* I. vi. 21 Authors write often dubiously... Not a few transcriptively,.. meerely transcribing almost all they have written.

tran'scriptor. *rare.* [a. L. type *transcriptor, agent-n. from *transcrībĕre* to TRANSCRIBE: cf. rare F. *transcripteur* (Littré).]

†**a.** = TRANSCRIBER 1. *Obs.*

1617 MORYSON *Itin.* II. 29 The Transcriptor fifty three shillings foure pence. **1811** in *2nd Rep. Rec. Irel.* 141 A Transcript of the Process.. lodged with the Transcriptor and Foreign Apposer, previously to passing his Accounts for the year of his Sheriffalty.

b. = TRANSCRIBER 2.

1957 *Practical Wireless* XXXIII. 532/2 Tape transcriptors are also supplied by Collaro. **1958** *Punch* 17 Sept. 366/3 Anita types. You scarcely see The neat transcriptor at her ear. The tape turns confidentially, And no one else can overhear.

tran'scriptural, *a.* [f. L. *transcript-us* transcribed, after *scriptural.*]

= TRANSCRIPTIONAL.

1802-12 BENTHAM *Ration. Judic. Evid.* (1827) III. 223 Chains of written evidence in the form of transcriptural evidence. *Ibid.* V. IX. VI. ii. 516 Whether, provisionally at least, inferior evidence may not be employed..: transcriptural, for instance, instead of original. **1863** WESTCOTT in *Smith's Dict. Bible* II. 517/2 *note*, Two characteristic transcriptural errors occur in the passage.

†**transcrive,** *v. Obs. rare.* [f. TRANS- + SCRIVE *v.* (Cf. F. *transcrīv-*, stem of *transcrire*:—L. *transcrībĕre*.)] = TRANSCRIBE.

1665 in *Maitland Cl. Misc.* (1840) II. 524 For transcryveing a paper in a fine hand sent to London.

trans'crystalline, *a.* [f. TRANS- 5 + CRYSTALLINE *a.*] Of a fracture: passing through individual crystals of a metal rather than following grain boundaries.

1916 H. M. HOWE *Metallogr. Steel & Cast Iron* xxviii. 489 (*caption*) Intergranular and trans-crystalline rupture. **1956** M. C. SMITH *Princ. Physical Metall.* x. 379 The usual fracture of a metal is transcrystalline. **1978** E. LEPA tr. *S. Kocańda's Fatigue Failure Metals* v. 271 The brittle crack propagates.. along cleavage planes, yielding a cleavage transcrystalline fracture, or along the grain boundaries, forming an.. intercrystalline fracture.

trans'cultural, *a.* [f. TRANS- 3, 4 + CULTURAL *a.*] Transcending the limitations or crossing the boundaries of cultures; applicable to more than one culture; cross-cultural; spec. ***transcultural psychiatry***, psychiatry applied to disorders due to migration from one cultural environment to another.

1958 *Internat. Jrnl. Social Psychiatry* III. 245 (*heading*) Some problems of transcultural psychiatry. **1964** I. L. HOROWITZ *New Sociology* 37 Social science is interdisciplinary because social problems are transcultural. **1973** *Observer* (Colour Suppl.) 28 Oct. 34/5 Sailing ships are gone but the sea shanty is still sung: the function is altered but the song remains: the stuff is transcultural. **1976** *Daily Tel.* 27 Apr. 2/8 The congress, on transcultural psychiatry, is being organised by the university and the World Federation for Mental Health. **1978** *Church Times* 3 Feb. 6/5 The resolution of the problem suggested depends on a distinction between meanings which are universal and transcultural and the understanding and expression of those meanings which are limited historically and culturally.

transcultu'ration. [f. TRANS- 3 + CULTURE *sb.* + -ATION.] = ACCULTURATION.

1941 B. MALINOWSKI *Sci. Theory Culture* (1944) ii. 14 Practical problems—such as.. the difficulties of culture contact, and transculturation—problems that legitimately belong to anthropology. **1949** *Psychiatry* XII. 184 This paper.. has shown that the process of transculturation is not really a process of adaptation to a culture but to a political situation. **1970** R. STAVENHAGEN in I. L. Horowitz *Masses in Lat. Amer.* vii. 287 We use the terms 'transculturation' and 'acculturation' interchangeably.

†**trans'cur,** *v. Obs. rare.* [ad. L. *transcurrĕre* to run across. Cf. OF. *transcourir* (12th-15th c. in Godef.).] *trans.* and *intr.* To run across or over; to run or rove to and fro.

1528 LYNDESAY *Dreme* 777 Tygris, Ganges, Ewphrates, and Nyle, Quhilk, in the est, Transcurris mony ane myle. **1626** BACON *Sylva* §720 It is caused by the Fixing of the Minde upon one Object.. whereby it doth not spatiate and transcurre, as it useth.

trans'currence. [f. as next: see -ENCE.]

†**1.** A running or passing over rapidly. *Obs. rare.*

1656 BLOUNT *Glossogr.*, *Transcurrence*.., a running over, a passing over quickly. **1658** in PHILLIPS.

2. *Geol.* The phenomenon of transcurrent faulting.

1971 *Geol. Mag.* CVIII. 40 His [*sc.* S. W. Carey's] concept of megashears is essentially that of transcurrence as defined here. **1979** *Nature* 1 Mar. 12/2 Such transcurrence juxtaposed features whose dissimilarity had instead suggested to many an oceanic gap.

transcurrent (trɑːns'kʌrənt, træns-), *a.* [ad. L. *transcurrent-em*, pr. pple. of *transcurr-ĕre.*]

†**1.** Running or passing across, over, or through.

1608 HIERON *Defence* III. 56 The honoring of a consecrated creature,.. with an honor passant, or transcurrent, from and through it to the Creator. **1664** POWER *Exp. Philos.* III. 169 All the Circles of the Armillary Sphære are really.. inhærent in the Earth, by virtue of the transcurrent Atoms.

2. *Entom.* Extending or running transversely.

1826 KIRBY & SP. *Entomol.* IV. 349 Transcurrent... When a postfrænum is at first adnate to the sides of the postscutellum, and then diverges across the pannel to the base of the wings.

3. *Geol.* Designating or pertaining to a fault which is primarily due to horizontal displacement; *esp.* one of large dimensions and with a nearly vertical inclination; usu. in ***transcurrent fault*** (see quots. 1942[2], 1971).

1942 E. M. ANDERSON *Dynamics of Faulting* i. 1 The term 'Blatt' [used by Suess] will be translated as transcurrent fault. *Ibid.* v. 54 The name Transcurrent Faults has been adopted in this memoir for members of the class which are distinguished by lateral movement, with inclinations which, according to theory, are nearly vertical. **1965** G. J. WILLIAMS *Econ. Geol. N.Z.* i. 2/1 Movement along the Alpine Fault.. is still going on in the form of major clockwise transcurrent movement with a 300 mile shift. **1971** *Geol. Mag.* CVIII. 33 Transcurrent faults are large-scale strike-slip faults which operate between lithosphere plates. **1977** [see *tear-fault* s.v. TEAR *sb.*[2] 4].

†**trans'cursion.** *Obs.* [ad. late L. *transcursiōn-em*, n. of action f. *transcurrĕre* to run across.]

1. The action of running or passing across or through; a going or moving through, transition, penetration; also, a journey or passage through a country, across the sea, etc.

1624 WOTTON *Archit.* in *Reliq.* (1651) 307 Such notes as I have taken in my forraigne transcursions or abodes. **1626** BACON *Sylva* x. Pref., In a Living Creature.. the Sense, and the Affects of any one Part of the Body, instantly make a Transcursion thorowout the whole Body. **1653** H. MORE *Antid. Ath.* II. xii. §17 (1712) 84 To wonder at the transcursion of Comets. **1655** FULLER *Ch. Hist.* x. vi. §6 The transcursion of Italians hither, added much to the discovery of the Papal abominations. **1665** HOOKE *Microgr.* xxxv. 166 To impede, for the greatest part, the transcursion of the Air.

2. *fig.* A running through a subject in discourse.

1641 H. L'ESTRANGE *God's Sabbath* 55 Not to expatiate too farre in collaterall transcursions. **1657** HOWELL *Londinop.* 41 Having made a short transcursion through the Government of the City of London.

3. Passage, lapse (of time).

1622 MABBE tr. *Aleman's Guzman d'Alf.* II. 44 Wisedome is the Daughter of Experience, which is gotten by the transcursion of Time. *Ibid.* 288 Nor was transcursion of time needfull in this case.

†**trans'cursive,** *a. Obs. rare.* [f. L. *transcurs-*, ppl. stem of *transcurr-ĕre* + -IVE.] Characterized by running rapidly over a subject; cursory.

1599 NASHE *Lenten Stuffe* (1871) 8 In this transcursive reportory, without some observant glance, I may not over-pass the gallant beauty of their haven. **1614** JACKSON *Creed* III. To Rdr. 5 b, To sift more of their arguments, then in these short transcursiue disputes I could.

†**trans'cursory,** *a. Obs. rare.* [f. as prec. + -ORY[2]: cf. *cursory*, and late L. *transcursōri-us.*] = prec. Hence †**trans'cursorily** *adv. Obs. rare.*

1727 EARBERY tr. *Burnet's St. Dead* (1728) I. 238, I shall therefore just take a transcursory View of his Arguments. *Ibid.* II. 117, I have transcursorily taken a view of the Doctor's Notions.

transcur'vation. [TRANS- 6.] Transverse or lateral curvature (of the spine).

1822-34 *Good's Study Med.* (ed. 4) III. 263 This species offers us the four following varieties.. γ Lateralis. Tetanic transcurvation.

transdenomi'national, *a.* [f. TRANS- 3 + DENOMINATIONAL *a.*] = TRANSCONFESSIONAL *a.*

1972 *Clergy Rev.* Sept. 658 The first transdenominational church union to take place in Britain in modern times. **1976** *Christian* III. 168 There is a growing hunger for transdenominational eucharistic celebration.

transderi'vational, *a. Transformational Gram.* [f. TRANS- 3 + DERIVATIONAL *a.*] Relating to or involving more than one derivation (see DERIVATION[1] 6 c).

1977 *Language* LIII. 137 One way in which the notion 'superficially optional/obligatory element' could be handled would be by means of a transderivational rule, i.e. a rule referring to another derivation in which the optional element does not occur either in semantic or in superficial representation. **1979** *Trans. Philol. Soc.* 12 In French, by contrast, reflexive deletion is subject to a further transderivational condition.

transdetermi'nation. *Biol.* [f. TRANS- 1 + DETERMINATION.] An alteration of the course of development of an imaginal disc during the culture of *Drosophila* tissue so that it gives rise to a structure that normally develops from a different disc.

1965 E. HADORN in *Genetic Control of Differentiation* (Brookhaven Conf. Rep. BNL-C-44) 157 Since the allotypic organs appear in the offspring of cells which have been first autotypically determined, a change in determination must be postulated. We call this event trans-determination. **1978** *Nature* 2 Feb. 403/2 In general their state of determination (leg, wing, genital, and so on) is conserved during culture, but occasionally a so-called transdetermination occurs whereby a certain type of disk changes to another state of determination.

transdialect (trɑːns'daɪəlɛkt, træns-, -nz-), *v. rare.* [f. TRANS- + DIALECT.] *trans.* To translate from one dialect into another.

1698 C. BOYLE *Bentley's Dissert.* (ed. 2) 52 If some Copyer ..thought that Ocellus's Physics would look better out of Doric, than in it, and therefore transdialected 'em. **1776** BURNEY *Hist. Mus.* I. 331 The poems under the name of Orpheus were written in the Doric dialect, but have since been trans-dialected, or modernised. **1830** J. DOUGLAS *Truths Relig.* (1832) 361 The book of Job appears to be the original Arabic of Job and his friends transdialected and amplified by Moses.

†**trans'dignify,** *v. Obs. rare.* [TRANS- 2.] *trans.* To transfer from one dignity or rank to another.

1655 J. SERGEANT *Schism Disarm'd* 212 The Popes Universal Power must be supposed to be transdignifi'd into a private Patriarchate.

transdisci'plinary, *a.* [f. TRANS- 3 + DISCIPLINARY *a.*] Of or pertaining to more than one discipline or branch of learning; interdisciplinary. So **transdiscipli'narity.**

1972 E. JANTSCH in *OECD: Interdisciplinarity* II. i. 105 The ultimate degree of co-ordination in the education/innovation system,..which may be called *transdisciplinarity*, would..depend on a common axiomatics... The whole education..system would be co-ordinated as a *multi-level, multi-goal* system, embracing a multitude of..interdisciplinary two-level systems, which.. will be modified in the transdisciplinary framework. **1977** R. HOLLAND *Self & Social Context* ix. 267 It is therefore possible to assert three promising criteria for new work: reflexivity, transdisciplinarity and the subversiveness of discovery. **1979** *Nature* 3 May 1/2 A recent workshop jointly sponsored by the American Association for the Advancement of Science and the US Department of Energy has been attempting to lay transdisciplinary foundations for a federally supported research programme on the impact of increasing atmospheric carbon dioxide content.

transdiurnal (trɑːnsdaɪ'ɜːnəl, træns-, -nz-), *a. nonce-wd.* [TRANS- 3.] That is beyond the confines of day.

1848 LOWELL *Fable for Critics* 594 C[arlyle] shows you how every-day matters unite With the dim transdiurnal recesses of night,—While E[merson] in a plain, preternatural way, Makes mysteries matters of mere every day.

transduce (trɑːns'djuːs, træns-, -nz-), *v.* [Back-formation from next.]

1. *trans.* To alter the physical nature or medium of (a signal); to convert variations in (a medium) into corresponding variations in another medium.

1949 L. L. BERANEK *Acoustic Measurements* xiv. 637 The dynamic range of a microphone is the range of levels of input signals which can usefully be transduced by the instrument. It is..limited at high levels by the amount of distortion which can be tolerated in the transduced signal. **1971** *Nature* 19 Feb. 530/2 Rhodopsin, a visual pigment found in vertebrate retinal rods, transduces light into a neural message. **1973** *Sci. Amer.* Sept. 87/1 (Advt.), It transduced a heart's faint signals into a squiggly line that the doctor could compare with those produced by other hearts. **1977** *Listener* 22–29 Dec. 857/4 Carbon granules..to do their delicate work of transducing sound waves into varying electric currents.

2. *Microbiology.* Of a virus: to transfer (genetic material) from one bacterium to another; also used with the first bacterium as obj. Also, to transfer (a genetic characteristic) from one bacterium to another using a virus.

1952 *Jrnl. Bacteriol.* LXIV. 687 *FA* [*sc.* filterable agents] from each of the three LT-7 auxotrophs could transduce the other two. **1965** *Virology* XXVII. 290 (*heading*) Variation in composition of chromosome fragments transduced by phage P22. **1973** R. G. KRUEGER *Introd. Microbiol.* xiv. 404/2 In contrast to the specialized transducing phages, the viruses P1 and P22 can transduce a variety of genes in the bacterial genome. **1977** *Lancet* 9 July 94/2, 47 *gen-r* (ex 8799) was a resistant transductant produced by transducing the gentamicin resistance from strain 75/8799 to propagating strain (PS) 47.

Hence **trans'duced, trans'ducing** *ppl. adjs.*; **trans'ducible** *a.*, susceptible to transduction.

1952 *Jrnl. Bacteriol.* LXIV. 686 All of the transduced cells were still streptomycin resistant. *Ibid.* 687 Several galactose-negative mutants were transducible to galactose-positive by *FA* [*sc.* filterable agent] from their parental wild type. **1952** *Physiol. Rev.* XXXII. 414 The chemical composition of transducing agents has important implications, if they can be regarded as purified genes. **1962** R. GOLDMAN *Ultrasonic Technol.* iii. 67 A transducing crystal must also be mounted in some sort of holder. **1971** G. S. STENT *Molecular Genetics* xiv. 416 Upon closer examination of the clones of transduced bacteria or transductants..it was found..that all the Gal⁺ transductants were either actively lysogenetic.., or were at least immune to infection. **1973** Transducing [see sense 2 above].

transducer (trɑːns'djuːsə(r), træns-, -nz-). [f. L. *transdūcere* to lead across, transfer, f. *trans* TRANS- + *dūcere* to lead: see -ER[1].] Any device by which variations in one physical quantity (e.g. pressure, brightness) are quantitatively converted into variations in another (e.g. voltage, position).

1924 K. S. JOHNSON *Transmission Circuits for Telephonic Communic.* vii. 46 A structure which, when inserted in a circuit, enables this maximum possible power to be absorbed in the receiving circuit is called an ideal transducer. **1948** [see QUANTIZER]. **1957** *New Scientist* 12 Dec. 30/2 The excitation of sensory [nerve] endings, physiological 'transducers' of mechanical changes into electrical signals. **1965** *Wireless World* July 31 (Advt.), Racal Magnetic Transducer..converts rotational movement to a pulse output without physical connection to the shaft under test. **1973** M. WOODHOUSE *Blue Bone* ii. 11 We designed and sold a capacitative transducer head for somebody else's flowmeter. **1976** A. HOPE *Hi-Fi Handbk.* 88 Although we have so far considered only moving coil-moving cone loudspeakers, there are other types of 'transducer' on the market which convert electrical energy into sound in different ways. **1980** *Jrnl. R. Soc. Arts* May 348/2 Huxley and Simmons use extremely fast-acting motors and transducers to record force changes in small fractions of a millisecond.

transductant (trɑːns'dʌktənt, træns-, -nz-). *Microbiology.* [f. TRANSDUCT(ION + -ANT[1].] A cell into which genetic material has been transduced.

1963 *Exper. Cell Res.* XXX. 252 When the histidine-requiring mutants..are crossed by transduction, 1/10⁶ recipient cells become stable *his* + transductants. **1978** *Nature* 1 June 355/2 RNA polymerase was therefore isolated from two transductants, differing only at the *alt* locus.

transduction (trɑːns'dʌkʃən, træns-). [ad. L. *transductiōn-em* (usually *trāductiōnem*), n. of action f. *tra(ns)dūcĕre*: see TRADUCE.]

1. The action of leading or bringing across. *rare.*

1656 BLOUNT *Glossogr.*, *Transduction*, a leading over, a removing from one place to another. *a* **1816** BENTHAM *Offic. Apt. Maximized, Introd. View* (1830) 19 In lieu of *adduction*, as the purpose requires, will be subjoined *abduction, transduction*,..and so forth.

2. The action or process of transducing a signal.

1947 *Jrnl. Acoustical Soc. Amer.* XIX. 307/1 It is rather interesting..that the direct method of electronic transduction, instead of the indirect method of employing a conventional transducer and then amplifying the output with a vacuum tube, has not been developed. **1970** J. EARL *Tuners & Amplifiers* iv. 87 Low impedance pickup cartridges..using the moving-coil principle of transduction. **1975** *Nature* 17 Apr. 625/1 The transduction of light energy into neural signals is mediated in all known visual systems by a common type of visual pigment.

3. *Microbiology.* The transfer of genetic material from one cell to another by a virus or virus-like particle.

1952 ZINDER & LEDERBERG in *Jrnl. Bacteriol.* LXIV. 681 To help the further exposition of our experiments, we shall use the term transduction for genetically unilateral transfer in contrast to the union of equivalent elements in fertilization. **1960** [see F III. 1 l]. **1971** *Nature* 18 June 466/1 It has been suggested that transduction of genes by viruses was an important mechanism in evolution for spreading useful mutations between organisms not formally related. **1977** *Lancet* 9 July 94/2 These were derived by selection of sensitive variants from gentamicin-resistant strains or by transduction of this resistance to sensitive strains.

Hence **trans'ductional** *a.*, of or pertaining to (genetic) transduction.

1956 *Genetics* XLI. 845 (*heading*) Linear inheritance in transductional clones. **1980** *Jrnl. Gen. Microbiol.* CXIX. 51 Transductional analysis revealed that one of the four mutations carried by strain T-693 was responsible for constitutive synthesis of both isoleucine and threonine biosynthetic enzymes.

trans'ductor. *Anat.* [L. agent-n. from *tra(ns)dūcĕre*: see prec.]

‖**1.** That which draws across: applied to a muscle of the great toe.

[**1890** BILLINGS *Med. Dict.*, Transductor hallucis.] **1899** *Syd. Soc. Lex.*, *Transductor*, syn. of *Transversus pedis*.

2. *Electr.* [See quot. 1939.] A reactor (sense 2 a) having a d.c. winding to control the saturation of a core and an a.c. winding whose impedance is thereby changed, so that a small change in direct current produces a large change in alternating current.

1939 U. LAMM in *ASEA Jrnl.* XVI. 71/2 We should like to introduce some explanation of the word 'transductor'... The purpose of this word is actually to express the idea that as regards the mutual action between its two windings the apparatus resembles a transformer whilst, however, at the same time functioning in the A.C. circuit as a reactor or inductor, *i.e.* a conductor. **1975** *IEEE Trans. Nuclear Sci.* XXII. 1277/1 At Fermilab, transductors are used as current measuring devices in the main accelerator quadrupole power supply feedback loop.

transe, obs. form of TRANCE.

†**transearth** (trɑːns'ɜːθ, træns-, -nz-), *v. Obs. rare.* [f. TRANS- 2 + EARTH *sb.* or *v.*] *trans.* To move from one soil to another; to transplant.

1628 FELTHAM *Resolves* II. [I.] xix. 60 Fruites of hotter Countries, trans-earth'd in colder Climates.

trans'earth, *a. Astronautics.* [f. TRANS- 2 + EARTH *sb.*[1]] Of or pertaining to spaceflight or a trajectory towards the earth from the moon or another planet.

1965 *New Scientist* 1 July 12/3 The navigation of the injection into a transearth orbit and the transearth coast are similar to the outward parts of the voyage. **1970** N. ARMSTRONG et al. *First on Moon* xiii. 320 'Now we have only one more thing to worry about.' (She meant transearth injection—the big burn that would let the world know 'Here we come!')

†**transeate** ('trɑːnsiːeɪt, 'træns-), *v. Obs. rare*⁻¹. [erron. f. L. *transe-o* I pass over (as if **transeāre*) + -ATE[3].] *intr.* To pass over or across.

1657 TOMLINSON *Renou's Disp.* 221 The vinous parts of the wine transeating into vinegar.

transect (trɑːn'sɛkt, træn-), *v.* Also 9 **transsect.** [f. TRAN(S- + *sect-*, ppl. stem of L. *secāre* to cut: see SECT *v.*[2]] *trans.* To cut across; to divide by passing across; in *Anat.* to dissect transversely. Hence **tran'sected** *ppl. a.*

1634 SIR T. HERBERT *Trav.* 161 Who with a Sword of a hundred Cubits length, cut off at one blow ten thousand Christians heads, and transected Taurus. **1846** DANA *Zooph.* (1848) 711 The concentric layers in these transsected knobs. **1861** E. T. HOLLAND *Iceland* in *Peaks, Passes*, etc. Ser. II. I. 8 The plain of Thing-vellir..is transected by numerous longitudinal crevasses in the lava. **1888** *Amer. Jrnl. Psychol.* May 488 The transsected sheaths of the tubules. **1890** O. CRAWFURD *Round Calendar in Port.* 178 The river Douro that transects the northern provinces of Portugal from east to west.

So **transection** (trɑːn'sɛkʃən, træn-) [cf. SECTION], the action of transecting; a transverse section.

1899 *Allbutt's Syst. Med.* VI. 518 Transection of the spinal cord above the lumbar enlargement depresses the knee-jerk for a time.

transect ('trɑːnsɛkt, 'træn-), *sb.* [f. the vb.] **a.** A line or a belt of land along which a survey is made of the plant or animal life or some other feature; a survey of this kind.

1905 F. E. CLEMENTS *Research Methods Ecol.* iv. 176 When longer transects are desired, as in the case of forest formations, tapes of 500 or 1,000 meters should be used with eyelets a meter apart. **1939** [see QUADRAT 3]. **1974** *Environmental Conservation* I. 57/2 A second transect in an area of high-centred polygons..exhibited less than 2% differences in total thaw by season's end. **1979** *Rescue News* Dec. 4/2 A transect was plotted from the highest corner of the field to the source of the Gypsey Race. Along this over 20 one-metre square trial holes were dug.

b. *attrib.*, as ***transect count, line, strip.***

1971 *Country Life* 23 Sept. 739/1 The puffin study, involving transect counts of occupied burrows on the island's vertiginous slopes, had been hazardous. **1973** J. J. MCKELVEY *Man against Tsetse* iii. 175 Certain rounds were arranged to follow transect lines according to compass bearings. **1953** SCOTT & FISHER *Thousand Geese* 220 It was not possible to maintain a constant width of transect-strip.

transelement (trɑːns'ɛlɪmənt, træns-), *v.* [ad. med.L. *transelementāre*, f. TRANS- + L. *elementum* ELEMENT.] *trans.* To change or transmute the elements of. Hence **trans'elementing** *vbl. sb.*

1567 JEWEL *Def. Apol. Ch. Eng.* II. 238 For, as he saith, wee are Transelemented, or transnatured, and changed into Christe, euen so,..wee saie, The Breade is Transelemented, or changed into Christes Body. **1583** FOXE *A. & M.* 1379/2 [Chrysostom] hath these same playne words, transelemented, and transformed. **1656** S. HOLLAND *Zara* (1719) 33 For that he remained for a time as one trans-elemented. **1812–29** COLERIDGE in *Lit. Rem.* (1838) III. 94 That the body of our Lord was not transelemented or transnatured by the *pleroma* indwelling, we are positively assured by Scripture. **1855** PUSEY *Doctr. Real Presence* Note Q. 186 The Divine gifts were amnesty of evils, removal of sin, transelementing of nature. **1878** GLADSTONE *Glean.* (1879) III. 264 The old monotheism was (so to speak) transelemented, and caricatured, into the gorgeous but gross and motley religion of the Greek and Italian peninsulas.

So †**transele'mentate** [med.L. *transelementātus*] *ppl. a.*, transelemented; **transele'mentate** *v.* = *transelement*.

1579 FULKE *Heskins' Parl.* 296 The bread & wine are transelementated into the vertue of his flesh & bloud. **1583** FOXE *A. & M.* 1382/1 The bread (sayth [Chrysostom]) is transelementate, and transmuted into an other substaunce then it was before. **1899** W. R. INGE *Chr. Mysticism* vii. 257 *note*, The last-named [Theophylact] goes on to say that 'we are in the same way transelementated into Christ'.

trans,elemen'tation. [n. of action from med.L. *transelementāre*: see above, and quot. 1896.] The action or process of changing the elements of something.

1550 HOOPER *Serm. Jonas* vi. S iij, The transelementacion and alteracion of the breade, no place of yᵉ scripture commaundeth vs to beleue. **1624** F. WHITE *Repl. Fisher* 421 In Transubstantiation the matter is destroyed, and the quantitie and accidents remaine, and in Transelementation the matter remaineth, and the essentiall and accidentall formes are altered. **1654** JER. TAYLOR *Real Pres.* xii. ¶5 The name of Transelementation, which Theophylact did use, seems to approach nearer to signify the propriety of this mysterie, because it signifies a change even of the first elements. **1706** tr. *Dupin's Eccl. Hist. 16th C.* II. v. 53 If any one is offended with the new Term *Transubstantiation*, he will find that the Ancients used the terms *Conversion, Transmutation, Transformation, Transelementation.* **1855** PUSEY *Doctr. Real Presence* Note Q. 223 Through what the transelementation of our nature from mortal to immortal takes place. **1896** R. F. CLARKE in *Month* Feb. 207 A conversion (μεταβολή), a transmutation (μεταποίησις), a transelementation (μεταστοιχείωσις).

†**trans'eminent**, *a. Obs. rare.* [f. TRANS- 4 + EMINENT.] Eminent beyond others; pre-eminent, supereminent. So †**trans'eminency**, pre-eminence; †**trans'eminently** *adv.*, pre-eminently.

1642 *Answ. Observ. agst. King* 19 What State businesses soever are fairely carried,.. redound transeminently and really to the glory of the Crowne. **1660** BURNEY *Κέρδ. Δῶρον* (1661) 3 This is the transeminencie of the Persons, and they have the Illustrious Character of Kings. *Ibid.* 22 Our Soveraign Lord.., who hath Reigned in all ages, in the persons transeminent.

transempirical (ˌtrɑːnsɛmˈpɪrɪkəl, ˌtrænsː-), *a. rare.* [TRANS- 4.] Pertaining to things beyond the range of experiential knowledge; metempirical.

1904 W. JAMES in *Mind* Oct. 465 Whether there be a trans-empirical reality or not. **1906** —— in *Jrnl. Philos., Psychol.*, etc. 20 Dec. 712 A conclusion supposed to flow from the intrinsic absurdity of transempirical objects.

transept (ˈtrɑːnsɛpt, ˈtræn-). Forms: 6 transsept, 7 -scept, 8- transept. [First found in 16th c., ad. med. or mod. (Anglo-) L. **transseptum*, f. TRANS- + SEPTUM, prop. *sæptum* hedge, fence, enclosure, f. *sæpīre* to hedge in, fence in, enclose. (Early history and actual origin unascertained.) Hence mod.F. *transept* (introd. 1828). The Anglo-L. *transeptum* is often used by Leland, and in one instance Englished as *transsept*; but the word was rare before 1700.] The transverse part of a cruciform church considered apart from the nave; also, each of the two subdivisions or arms of this (the ***north*** and ***south transepts***).

1538-42 LELAND *Itin.* (1907) I. II. 131 It stode in the midle of the transeptum of the church. *Ibid.* III. 239 One Sir John Scylley a knight and his wyfe sumtyme dwellyng in that paroche [Crideton] be buried in the north part of the transsept [*ed.* 1711 transept] of this [church]. *Ibid.* 287 In Transepto Eccl. in Merid. parte. *Ibid.* 292 An exceding goodly Chapel in Transepto of Bishop Stillington and King. **1692** WOOD *Ath. Oxon., Fasti* 821 His body was buried in the south Transcept or large south Isle joyning to the Choir of St. Peter's Church in Westminster. **1782** WARTON *Hist. Kiddington* 8 The pediment of the southern Transept is pinnacled, not inelegantly, with a flourished Cross. **1815** J. SMITH *Panorama Sc. & Art* I. 130 The part running north and south is called the cross or transept. **1870** F. R. WILSON *Ch. Lindisf.* 79 The chancel roof,.. like those of the nave and transepts, is open-timbered.

b. *attrib.* and *Comb.*, as ***transept aisle, chapel.***

1890 C. H. MOORE *Gothic Archit.* iii. 160 Where there are no transept aisles.. there are.. no vertical divisions in the façade [end of transept]. **1900** *Yorkshire Archæological Jrnl.* XV. 281 The vaults of the presbytery and transept-chapels.

transeptal (trɑːnˈsɛptəl, træn-), *a.* [f. prec. + -AL[1].] Of, pertaining to, or of the nature of a transept. Hence **tran'septally** *adv.*, in the manner of a transept.

1846 *Ecclesiologist* V. 152 A parclose.. screening off the north transeptal chapel. **1856** *Ibid.* XVII. 88 A spacious narthex with the prescribed chapels.. opening into it transeptally. **1884** *Ch. Times* XXII. 86 Exeter is noteworthy for its transeptal or 'paddle-box' towers. **1886** WILLIS & CLARK *Cambridge* III. 261 The chapel is to the west of the hall, and has a transeptal antechapel.

transepted (ˈtrɑːnsɛptɪd, ˈtræn-), *a. Archæol.* [f. TRANSEPT + -ED[2].] Having chambers resembling transepts; *spec.* designating a type of gallery grave (see quot. 1956).

1939 G. E. DANIEL in *Proc. Prehist. Soc.* V. 143 The present writer defined a type of megalithic burial chamber which was there called the transepted gallery grave. **1956** R. J. C. ATKINSON *Stonehenge* v. 149 The tomb has.. two pairs of chambers opening off its sides, in the manner of transepts in a church; for this reason the type is known technically as a transepted gallery-grave. **1963** [see *gallery grave* s.v. GALLERY *sb.* 12 b].

trans-equa'torial, *a.* [TRANS- 3: cf. *equatorial.*] Situated on the other side of the equator; also crossing the equator.

1900 *Jrnl. R. Geog. Soc.* Apr. 381 The Southern, Australian, or trans-equatorial land of our hemisphere.

transe'ssentiate, *v. rare.* [f. TRANS- 1 + ESSENTIATE *v.*] *trans.* To change from one essence or being into another. Hence **transe'ssentiating** *vbl. sb.* So **transe'ssentiate** *ppl. a.* [ESSENTIATE *ppl. a.*], changed into another essence. (Const. as pa. pple.)

1675 PENN *Eng. Pres. Interests Consid.* Wks. 1782 III. 220 Here is no transessentiating or transubstantiating of being, from people to representative. **1839-52** BAILEY *Festus* xxxv. 554 Curse transessentiate into blessing!

transetorious, -tory, etc., obs. ff. TRANSITORIOUS, TRANSITORY, etc.

transeunce, etc.: see TRANSIENCE, etc.

†**tran'sexion.** *Obs. rare.* [irreg. f. TRANS- + L. *sex-us* SEX + -ION[1], after *connexion*, etc.] Change of sex.

1646 SIR T. BROWNE *Pseud. Ep.* III. xvii. 147 Not only Mankinde, but many other Animals, may suffer this transexion, we will not deny, or hold it at all impossible. *Ibid.* 148 Surely it much impeacheth this iterated transexion of Hares, if that be true which Cardan and other Physitians affirm, that Transmutation of sex is only so in opinion.

transexual, etc.: see TRANSSEXUAL *a.* and *sb.*, etc.

transfashion (trɑːnsˈfæʃən, træns-), *v.* [TRANS- 2.] *trans.* To alter or change the fashion of, to transform.

1601 DEACON & WALKER *Spirits & Divels* 134 He transmuted, transfashioned, transfigured, transformed, or metamorphozed himself into an angel. **1619** W. SCLATER *Exp. 1 Thess.* (1630) 305 To see.. our people so Cameleon-like transfashioned into [etc.]. **1855** PUSEY *Doctr. Real Presence* Note Q. 233 God shall 'transfashion (μετασχηματίσει) our vile bodies, to be made like unto His glorious Body'.

transfeature (trɑːnsˈfiːtjʊə(r), træns-), *v.* [TRANS- 2.] *trans.* To change the features of.

1875 DORA GREENWELL *Liber Hum.* 33 Outward nature itself is transfigured and transfeatured to their view.

transfection (trɑːnsˈfɛkʃən, træns-, -nz-). *Microbiology.* [f. TRANS- or TRANS(FER *sb.* + IN)FECTION.] The introduction of free viral nucleic acid into a cell.

1964 FÖLDES & TRAUTNER in *Zeitschr. für Vererbungslehre* XCV. 61 Infection of cells by the isolated nucleic acid from a virus, resulting in the production of a complete virus will be termed Transfection. **1975** *Nature* 5 June 446/2 The rescue of proviral DNA of Rous sarcoma virus in mammalian cells by 'transfection' to permissive chicken cells. **1980** OLD & PRIMROSE *Princ. Gene Manipulation* i. 7 Transformation of a cell with DNA from a virus is sometimes referred to as transfection.

So **trans'fect** *v. trans.*, to infect (a cell) with free viral nucleic acid; **trans'fected** *ppl. a.* (said of the cell and of the acid).

1964 *Zeitschr. für Vererbungslehre* XCV. 61 For the plating of transfected cells it is essential to use tryptone plates. **1966** *Ann. Rev. Microbiol.* XX. 394 It appears that the genetic basis for the ability to be transformed or transfected is similar. **1974** *Nature* 22 Nov. 319/2 We tried to transfect ΦX-DNA to various bacteria belonging to the *Enterobacteriaceae.* **1983** *Sci. Amer.* Jan. 58/2 Investigators have 'transfected' cultured cells by exposing them to naked foreign DNA.

transfeminate (trɑːnsˈfɛmɪneɪt, træns-), *v. rare.* [f. TRANS- + L. *femina*: cf. EFFEMINATE *v.*] *trans.* See quot. 1656. Hence **trans'feminated** *ppl. a.*

1646 SIR T. BROWNE *Pseud. Ep.* III. xvii. 148 These transfeminated persons were really men at first, although succeeding years produced the manifesto or evidence of their virilities. **1656** BLOUNT *Glossogr., Transfeminate*.., to turn from woman to man, or from one sex to another. **1898** G. MEREDITH *Odes Fr. Hist.* 39 With a breath he blew them out, to beat their wings The way of such transfeminated things.

transfer (ˈtrɑːnsfə(r), ˈtræns-, -nz-), *sb.* [f. TRANSFER *v.*]

1. *Law.* Conveyance from one person to another of property, *spec.* of shares or stock.

1674 *Court Bks. Roy. Afr. Co.* (P.R.O.), [Form of acceptance] I do accept of —— his transfer of £—— abovesaid the day and year abovewritten. **1693** *Act 5 Will. & Mary* c. 7. §47 The Fee for examining.. a Tickett or Tally in order to make a true Assignement or Transfer.. shall.. be One penny. **1694** *Bank of Eng. Charter* 27 July, There shall be constantly kept.. a Register, or Book or Books, wherein all Assignments and Transfers shall be entered. **1727** SWIFT *What passed in Lond.* Wks. 1755 III. I. 189 All the Thursday morning was taken up in private transfers. **1766** BLACKSTONE *Comm.* II. i. 9 The reciprocal transfer of property by sale, grant, or conveyance. **1788** JEFFERSON *Writ.* (1859) II. 367 Observations on the transfer of our domestic debt to foreigners. **1817** JAS. MILL *Brit. India* II. IV. i. 5 The office in which are effected the transfers of the Company's stock and annuities. **1836** J. GILBERT *Chr. Atonem.* vii. (1852) 204 The lowest case of legal transfer is that of a debt.

2. a. *gen.* The act of transferring or fact of being transferred; conveyance or removal from one place, person, etc. to another; transference; transmission.

1785 BURKE *Corr.* (1844) III. 33 To remonstrate against the transfer of an immense sum of public money from the national service. **1811** J. ADAMS *Wks.* (1856) X. 3, I wait with patience for a transfer to another scene. **1843** LYTTON *Last Bar.* I. iii, An amply sufficient cause for the transfer of his allegiance. **1870** JEVONS *Elem. Logic* iv. 32 Equivocal words have become so by a transfer of meaning. **1877** KNIGHT *Dict. Mech.* 1334/2 The third lithographic method is by transfer.. The work is not drawn or engraved upon the stone direct, but is placed there in a completed condition from some source furnishing it. **1907** *Trans. Devon. Assoc.* 50 The transfer of the county See to Exeter.

b. *Naut.* In tacking: The distance traversed at right angles to the line of advance.

1889 *Cent. Dict.* s.v. *Advance* 12, In naval tactics, the distance made by a ship under way, in the direction of her course, after the helm has been put to one side and kept there; opposed to *transfer*, the distance made at right angles to the original course.

c. *Psychol.* (More fully ***transfer of practice, training.***) The carrying over of the effects of training or practice from the learning of one function to the learning of another. Cf. *negative transfer* s.v. NEGATIVE *a.* 8 c; *positive transfer* s.v. POSITIVE *a.* 8 d.

1901 THORNDIKE & WOODWORTH in *Psychol. Rev.* VIII. 386 There is no inner necessity for improvement of one function to improve others closely similar to it, due to a subtle transfer of practice effect. **1924** *Psychol. Rev.* XXXI. 157 There is no evidence for such transfer of training among rats. **1948** E. R. HILGARD *Theories of Learning* ii. 29 The theory proposes that transfer depends upon the presence of identical elements in the original learning and in the new learning which it facilitates. **1970** HALSTEAD & RUCKER in W. Byrne *Molecular Approaches to Learning & Memory* 6 (*heading*) Behavioral modification, née transfer of training.

d. The transference of a worker or player from one location, sphere, sports club, etc., to another; a change of place of employment within an organization.

1895 *Football News* (Nottingham) 2 Nov. 1/6 It is stated that the Forest have offered £70 for Bruce's transfer. **1923** J. D. HACKETT *Labor Terms in Management Engineering* May, *Transfer*, the shifting of a worker from one occupation to another. **1937** [see DOTTED *ppl. a.* 1 c]. **1970** *Times* 13 Oct. 15/3 Trevor Gould.. has been given a free transfer by Coventry City. **1973** J. THOMSON *Death Cap* xiii. 176 'I've been thinking again about putting in for a transfer,' Holbrook said... Finch.. wished now that he could have satisfied the Sergeant over the question of his transfer... A good local policeman meant a lot to a small community.

3. A thing or a person that is transferred; *spec.* writing, drawing, or a design, conveyed from one surface to another in lithography, photography, and the like.

1839 *Trans. Royal Soc.* IV. 133 Twenty-three specimens of photographs, made by Sir John Herschel, accompany this paper.. copies of engravings and drawings, some reverse, or first transfers; and others second transfers or re-reversed pictures. **1864** WEBSTER, *Transfer*.. a soldier removed from one troop, or body of troops, and placed in another. **1877** KNIGHT *Dict. Mech., Transfer*, an impression taken on paper, cloth, etc., and then laid upon an object and caused to adhere thereto by pressure. **1880** *Print. Trades Jrnl.* XXXI. 38 A transfer paper is prepared.., on which the transfer to be preserved is pulled. **1883** *Hardwich's Photogr. Chem.* 311 If a mat surface be desired, the transfer should be stripped from the glass before it is quite dry. **1929** *Daily Express* 7 Nov. 12/4 The prizes will hardly be glittering enough to attract the best 'transfers'. **1970** *Globe & Mail* (Toronto) 26 Sept. 35/6 The Mustangs have six experienced transfers who must be fitted in. **1979** *Arizona Daily Star* 1 Apr. c9/1 The return of 33 lettermen—five senior-college transfers, most of whom will likely start—and 10 junior-college transfers.

4. A means or place of transfer. Chiefly U.S. *spec.* **a.** *U.S. Post Office.* A telegraphic money-order. **b.** On a railway, etc.:

(*a*) A place at which trains or cars are transferred to a ferry for water transport; also, a ferry by which trains or cars are transported. (*b*) A siding connecting tracks at a crossing or on different levels (Webster 1911). (*c*) A transfer-ticket (*Cent. Dict.*). (*d*) The conveyance of passengers and luggage from one railway station to another, when these are not contiguous; hence ***transfer-company***, a company which undertakes such conveyance between stations.

1883 I. M. RITTENHOUSE *Maud* (1939) 187 The sun was just coming up as we crossed the river on the transfer. **1892** S. HALE *Let.* 28 Apr. (1919) 269, I mounted a cable, took a transfer, and went.. out into the suburbs. **1903** A. B. HART *Actual Govt.* 207 In most cities there is a system of free transfers, so that, starting from one suburb, one may often travel for a single fare 5, 10, or 15 miles to another suburb.

c. *Archery.* A sheet to which all scores are transferred from the target-papers.

1909 *Cent. Dict. Suppl.* s.v., The transfers are the official record from which the prize-list is made up.

5. *attrib.* and *Comb.*, as ***transfer agent, -boat, -clerk, -company*** (4 b), ***-deed, -department, -form, list, market, office, payment, price, pricing, -process, rate***; **transfer-book**, a register of transfers of property, esp. that of its shares or stock, kept by a joint-stock company; **transfer case**, (*a*) a case in(to) which materials are transferred; (*b*) *Mech.*, (the housing of) a mechanism for dividing the power between a number of axles in a motor vehicle with two or more driving axles; **transfer chamber**, the chamber in which the material is initially heated in transfer moulding; **transfer-day**, at the Bank of England, a day for the register of transfers of bank-stock; **transfer effect(s)**, the result(s) of transfer of training (see sense 2 c above); **transfer-elevator**, a crane for transferring cargo from one vessel to another; **transfer factor** *Immunol.*, a substance released by antigen-sensitized lymphocytes and capable of transferring the response of delayed hypersensitivity to a non-sensitized cell or individual into which it is introduced; **transfer fee**, (*a*) that charged by a joint-stock company for registering a transfer; (*b*) *Football*, a sum of money paid by one club to another for the transfer of the services of a professional player; **transfer function**, a mathematical function relating the output or response of anything to the input or stimulus; also *transf.*; **transfer-gilding**, in ceramics, transfer of a pattern in gold, as from paper to unglazed ware; **transfer-ink**, ink used in lithography; **transfer-jar**, a jar used in the collection of gases over liquid; **transfer-lathe**: see quot.; **transfer line** *Engin.*, a line of work-stations along which a part is automatically conveyed to be subjected to a sequence of automatic machining operations; **transfer-lithography**: see sense 3; **transfer machine** *Engin.*, a composite machine that performs a series of operations without the intervention of the operator; **transfer mould** *sb.*, the mould cavity in transfer moulding; also (with hyphen) as *v. trans.*, to make by means of transfer moulding; **transfer moulding**, a moulding process used chiefly for thermosetting plastics in which the material is softened in a heated chamber and then forced by a plunger into an adjacent closed, heated mould cavity where it sets; **transfer orbit** *Astronautics*, an orbit that touches two given orbits and therefore provides a trajectory by which a spacecraft can pass from one of them to the other; **transfer-paper**, paper used in making transfers in lithography and other processes; **transfer pot** = *transfer chamber* above; **transfer-press**, in engraving, a transferring machine; **transfer-printing**, a process by which designs are printed on fictile and other ware (so **transfer-printed** adj.); also printing by means of lithography; **transfer RNA** *Molecular Biol.*, RNA that collects particular amino-acids in the cytoplasm of a cell and conveys them to a ribosome, where they are assembled to form part of a polypeptide or protein molecule; **transfer station**, a point at which transfer-tickets are given, and passengers transferred from one car to another (*Cent. Dict. Supp.*); **transfer-table** (*U.S.*), a railway traverse-table; **transfer-ticket**, a ticket entitling a passenger to change from a conveyance to one on another line or route without re-booking or further payment; a through ticket; **transfer-work**, designs made by transferring or transfer-printing.

1869 *Bradshaw's Railway Man.* XXI. 430 All certificates [shall] be signed by both the *transfer agent and register. **1978** A. Maling *Lucky Devil* xix. 103 You are the transfer agent for Lucky Devil Minerals. **1882** *Uncle Rufus & Ma* 52 We ferried over in a *transfer boat. **1888** *Daily News* 10 Dec. 6/8 The transfer boat Maryland was conveying a section of a train from Washington to Boston across the Haarlem River, at midnight. **1694** J. Houghton *Collect. Improv. Husb. & Trade* V. No. 102 (13 July) The Seller goes to the Clerk of the Company..appointed to keep a Book of Alienations, called a *Transferr Book, and there he transferrs the Shares he has sold to the Buyer. **1701** *Lond. Gaz.* No. 3737/4 The Transfer Books of the Bank will be shut up from Monday the 15th Instant to Friday the 10th of October next, in order to a Dividend. **1746** Fielding *True Patriot* No. 10 The cash, transfer books, &c. removed to the tower, from the Bank. **1923** H. A. Maddox *Dict. Stationery* 77 **Transfer Case*, a Binding Case or file for receiving the matter transferred periodically from the live file or loose leaf book. **1949** I. Frazee et al. *Automotive Fundamentals* vi. 378 The transfer case is located behind the transmission. **1970** *Southerly* XXX. 216 Gear box and transfer case and differentials growled a deep throated work song with power to spare. **1983** *Judge of Election Handbk.* (*Board of Election Comm., Chicago*) 11/1 Open the transfer case and check that the official ballot cards are for the proper precinct. **1946** DuBois & Pribble *Plastics Mold Engin.* 353 It is common practice to standardize on the size and design of the *transfer chamber and plunger used with hand molds. **1977** *Times Educ. Suppl.* 21 Oct. 29/5 There has been at least one case of a transfer chamber exploding. **1834** [S. Smith] *Lett. J. Downing* xxvi. (1835) 170 What the Treasury calls contingent drafts, and *transfer checks, and Treasury warrants. **1899** *Westm. Gaz.* 7 Sept. 7/1 It is nothing..for a *transfer clerk to wait for forty-five minutes at the Associated office. **1879** H. T. Williams *Pacific Tourist* 262/1 The *Transfer Company will carry baggage alone for 50 cents. **1909** Eliz. L. Banks *Myst. Fras. Farrington* 159 These trunks had been delivered by a responsible Transfer Company's waggon. **1771** *App. Chron.* in *Ann. Reg.* 209/2 He recollected it was not *transfer-day. **1869** *Bradshaw's Railway Man.* XXI. 63 Certificates must accompany *transfer deeds. **1931** R. Pinter *Educ. Psychol.* xii. 268, I feel sure that actual measurements of the *transfer effects would be very disappointing to me as a teacher. **1955** T. H. Pear *Eng. Soc. Differences* ix. 194 For a time there was a general tendency to be sceptical concerning any claim of transfer-effects. **1963** *Rep. Comm. Inquiry Decimal Curr.* xi. 109 in *Parl. Papers 1962–3* (Cmnd. 2145) XI. 195 Psychologists have advised us that giving an old name to a new currency unit could result in serious 'transfer effect' difficulties. **1977** *Language* LIII. 340 'Transfer effects' may reverse the natural order of the acquisition of a sound or structure. **1884** Knight *Dict. Mech.* Suppl., **Transfer-elevator*, an elevator or crane for hoisting from one vessel into another. **1956** *Jrnl. Exper. Med.* CIV. 328 The above experiments suggest that release of the *transfer factor from sensitive cells may occur under relatively mild circumstances. **1978** J. A. Bellanti *Immunology II* xiii. 333 Attempts to detect antibody in the transfer factor have always been negative, and since its small molecular weight became known, this possibility has been excluded. **1983** *Oxf. Textbk. Med.* I. v. 10/2 Therapy with transfer factor may..find an accepted place in the management of a limited number of clinical situations. **1869** *Bradshaw's Railway Man.* XXI. 63 *Transfer fee, 2*s.* 6*d.* each. **1901** *Football News* (Nottingham) 9 Mar. 6/3 New Brighton offered Everton £135 for my transfer, and Burnley were prepared to pay £200, but neither offer came to anything. Consequently I had to come South out of the reach of transfer fees. **1911** A. Bennett *Card* xii. 296 How are you going to get new blood, with transfer fees as high as they are now? You can't get even an average good player for less than £200. **1976** *Western Mail* (Cardiff) 27 Nov., The three Welsh clubs.. could also release experienced players to Somerton Park on a loan basis, should Newport be able to obtain transfer fees for any of their own professionals. **1948** Brown & Campbell *Princ. Servomechanisms* i. 18 The system behaviour may be represented in terms of *transfer functions *KG* (*jω*), which are complex functions of the frequency variable *ω*. **1963** R. W. Ditchburn *Light* (ed. 2) viii. 304 The transfer function constitutes a better evaluation of the performance of the optical system than a statement of the resolving power. **1971** *Nature* 20 Aug. 564/1 McFarland and Budgell found a transfer function for key pecking by thirsty birds in response to modulations of ambient temperature. **1977** *Gramophone* June 122/1 The speaker converts an electric signal into an acoustic wave and ..may be regarded as a 'black box', with a particular transfer function representing its overall response in terms of sound waves. **1981** D. J. Fisk *Thermal Control of Buildings* i. 9 The transfer function of a room..is not unique but depends on where heat is input..and where its output temperature is measured. **1832** Babbage *Econ. Manuf.* xi. (ed. 3) 78 A single copy might be printed off with *transfer ink. **1827** Faraday *Chem. Manip.* xv. (1842) 322 Capped or *transfer jars are such as, being open above, have a cap cemented upon them, the latter being surmounted by a stop-cock. *Ibid.* xxiv. 627 Fill a transfer jar..with water..over the trough. **1877** Knight *Dict. Mech.*, **Transfer-lathe*, for.. reducing large designs in relief to proportions suitable for coin. **1956** E. Molloy *Automobile Engineer's Ref. Bk.* iii. 210 Only one head is used at the next station. This is at the right of the *transfer line, and is a plunge-cut horizontal milling head for milling the bearing-retaining slots. **1975** *Sci. Amer.* Feb. 25/1 Under mass-production conditions.. the engine block is conveyed automatically along a transfer line. **1951** *People* 3 June 6/7 Still on Spurs' *transfer list at a fee is Cyril Toulouse. **1976** *Star* (Sheffield) 29 Oct. 28/6 Terry Eccles..is on the transfer list at his own request. **1897** *Westm. Gaz.* 5 Apr. 7/3 To the average man the difference between 'lithography' and '*transfer-lithography' matters little. **1951** *Treat. on Milling & Milling Machines* (ed. 4) xvii. 723 In order to reduce handling time, it is often advantageous to perform a number of different machining operations..with a multiple-station automatic machine... Such machines are also known as *transfer machines. **1977** *Sci. Amer.* May 89/1 (Advt.), Transfer machines finish rough castings into complex pieces such as engine blocks. **1970** *Globe & Mail* (Toronto) 25 Sept. B 7/4 Both see what is called the *transfer market—the hundreds of thousands of Canadians who move from one community to another each year—as increasingly important. **1976** *Evening Times* (Glasgow) 1 Dec. 32/2 Partick Thistle could be involved at both ends of the transfer market before the weekend. **1933** *U.S. Patent 1,919,534* 5/1 A device of the class described for *transfer molding an infusibly thermosetting resinous material. **1942** J. Sasso *Plastics for Industr. Use* iii. 36 Figure 13 shows an example of a transfer mold with a transfer plunger entering the transfer well. **1963** H. R. Clauser *Encycl. Engin. Materials* 165/1 Radio and television cabinets weighing up to four pounds have been transfer-molded from phenolic materials. **1971** E. W. Duck *Plastics & Rubbers* iv. 56 Transfer moulds..can be regarded as very crude injection moulds, since they first pre-heat the plastic in the transfer cavity. **1940** J. Delmonte *Plastics in Engin.* xi. 319 The term, *transfer molding, has been used to designate specifically the injection of thermosetting materials. **1963** H. R. Clauser *Encycl. Engin. Materials* 164/1 In the transfer-molding process..the mold is completely closed and under clamping pressure before the material is injected into the mold cavity. This results in little or no flash and accurate control of dimensions. **1693** *Act 5 Will. & Mary* c. 7. §54 The *Transfer Office above mentioned shall bee continued. **1869** *Bradshaw's Railway Man.* XXI. 430 All the stock registered in New York at the transfer office now kept by Duncan, Sherman, and Co., shall also be registered at another office. **1961** W. T. Thomson *Introd. Space Dynamics* iv. 66 Transfer between coplanar circular orbits can be effected by an elliptic orbit with perigee and apogee distances equal to the radii of the respective circles... The cotangential ellipse is known as the Hohmann *transfer orbit. **1964** *Listener* 7 May 748/1 Once the transfer orbit has been entered, the probe will be moving in free fall, and no further thrust need be applied. **1841** *Brit. Pat. 9002* 18 Obtaining several copies of marks by the use of surfaces of *transfer paper. **1858** Simmonds *Dict. Trade*, *Transfer-paper*, prepared paper used by lithographers; thin, unsized paper for taking copies of letters with a copying-press. **1878** Abney *Photogr.* (1881) 171 A piece of transfer paper (which is paper coated with gelatine subsequently rendered insoluble in water by alum or other such body) is placed in water of about 60° C., and softened. **1964** S. M. Miller in I. C. Horowitz *New Sociology* 301 In our country, the redistribution of income takes place to a large extent in *transfer payments of welfare and social assistance. **1973** *Times* 9 June 19/2 A transfer payment is a payment made by the scheme of a former employee to the scheme of the employee's present employer in consideration of which the new employer's scheme takes over the responsibility for benefits in respect of the service with the former employer. **1976** *Hansard* (Canada) 17 Mar. 11881/1 The balance of $22 billion was in the form of transfer payments to persons, provinces and corporations for subsidies, and so on. **1963** H. R. Clauser *Encycl. Engin. Materials* 164/2 When the mold is opened, the small amount of material remaining in the *transfer pot..is removed. **1971** B. Scharf *Engin. & its Lang.* vi. 38 The mould (die) consists of two sections, an upper transfer chamber (transfer pot)..and a lower mould. **1877** Knight *Dict. Mech.*, **Transfer-press*. **1969** J. Argenti *Managem. Techniques* 76 As the complexity and size of the company increases..the task of preparing a budget becomes highly intricate due to such problems as *transfer prices and allocation of central overheads. **1974** *Terminol. Managem. & Financial Accountancy* (Inst. Cost & Managem. Accountants) 17 *Transfer price*, a price related to goods or other benefits transferred from one process or department to another or from one member of a group to another. **1971** D. C. Hague *Managerial Economics* iii. x. 220 The problem of how to price a product as it leaves one department for another—the problem of *transfer pricing—is one that has troubled accountants and managers for many years. **1979** *Abacus* (Sydney) XV. 3 International transfer pricing is concerned with the pricing of goods and services transferred between a company's domestic divisions and foreign subsidiaries or among those foreign subsidiaries themselves. **1869** Lady C. Schreiber *Jrnl.* 15 Sept. (1911) I. 37 We bought a couple of *transfer-printed Wedgwood plates. *Ibid.* 17 Sept. 39, I coveted a small transfer-printed leaf. **1938** *Burlington Mag.* May p. xvii/2 Some rare Liverpool transfer-printed mugs. **1976** *Times* 24 July 9/3 Whieldon plates..and transfer-printed cream-wares. **1865** *Athenæum* 25 Nov. 733/1 *Transfer-printing in pottery. **1905** *Daily Chron.* 24 Aug. 3/2 The single invention in porcelain decoration at our credit in the eighteenth century was transfer-printing. **1877** Knight *Dict. Mech.* 2368/2 Jacob Perkins, of Massachusetts, the inventor of the *transfer-process. **1961** *Ann. Reg. 1960* 402 It was thought a further kind of RNA, called '*Transfer' RNA, might be necessary to link the amino acids into a protein molecule. **1977** *Time* 4 Apr. 39/2 Aaron Klug..first determined the crystalline structure of transfer RNA (tRNA), the molecule that brings amino acids to the ribosome for assembly into protein. **1869** *Bradshaw's Railway Man.* XXI. 198 The negotiations with the South Eastern in reference to a new *transfer station at Waterloo. **1861** *Massachusetts Stat.* 199 §2 *Transfer ticket.

b. Chiefly *Electronics*. Used *attrib.* to designate a ratio of two quantities measured simultaneously at two different points of a circuit or device.

1933 [see mutual *a.* 1 f]. **1943** F. E. Terman *Radio Engineers' Handbk.* iii. 200 The transfer impedance is defined as the ratio of the voltage E_1 applied in mesh 1 to the resulting current I_2 of mesh 2. **1966** *McGraw-Hill Encycl. Sci. & Technol.* III. 429/2 The transfer characteristic *H* of the controller mathematically relates the controller M_1 to its input *E*: $M_1 = HE$. **1975** Havill & Walton *Elem. Electronics* iv. 69 For the particular case of the transistor, the output and transfer characteristics are almost linear over substantial regions of the normal operating range. **1980** J. R. O'Malley *Circuit Analysis* xix. 467 The most popular of these transfer functions are the transfer impedance.., the transfer admittance.., the transfer voltage ratio or voltage gain.., and the transfer current ratio.

transfer (trɑːnsˈfɜː(r), træns-, -nz-), *v.* Also 5–7 -ferre, 7 -ferr. Inflected **transˈferred**, etc. [a. F. *transfér-er* (3rd s. *transfère*) (14th c. in Littré), or its source, L. *transfer-re*, f. trans- + *ferre* to bear, carry, bring.]

1. *trans.* To convey or take from one place, person, etc. to another; to transmit, transport; to give or hand over from one to another.

1382 Wyclif *Ezek.* xlviii. 14 Nether the first fruytis of the lond shuln be transferrid [*gloss* or born ouer, 1388 translatid], for thei ben halewid to the Lord. *c* **1425** *St. Christina* xxxvii. in *Anglia* VIII. 133/35 Þe biggynge of the abbeye was transferred to a better place. *c* **1430** *Art of Nombryng* 9 Put a cifre þer and transferre the article towarde the lift hande. **1516** in *Acts Parlt. Scot.* (1875) XII. 36/2 It is thocht..that þe said governoure..suld transfer himselff to uthir cuntreis. **1624** Godwin *Moses & Aaron* (1641) 158 The moderne Jewes doe transferre the fault upon certaine proselyte Ægyptians who came forth with them. **1655** Stanley *Hist. Philos.* ii. (1701) 73/1 He first transferr'd Natural Philosophy out of Ionia to Athens. **1703** Moxon *Mech. Exerc.* 316 Divide one of these nine equal parts into two equal parts, and transfer that distance to the other eight equal parts. **1771** Goldsm. *Hist. Eng.* II. 357 Campegio.. shortly after transferred the cause before the court of Rome. **1783** Burke *Rep. Affairs Ind.* Wks. XI. 42 If the court of directors should disapprove of his being transferred to Bengal. **1809** R. Langford *Introd. Trade* 86 For transferring £5690 Reduced Stock into the Four per Cents. **1818** in Willis & Clark *Cambridge* (1886) I. 573 Transferring three or four of the trees to another site. **1844** Ld. Brougham *Brit. Const.* vii. (1862) 94 The people's power being transferred to the representative body. **1860** Tyndall *Glac.* i. xxii. 151, I transferred my scrip to his shoulders, and led the way.

b. *fig.* esp. in Sematology: see quots.

1586 A. Day *Eng. Secretary* ii. (1625) 77 *Metaphora*, which is, when a word from the proper or right signification is transferred to another neere vnto the meaning. **1883** Murray *Eng. Dict.* Gen. Explan. p. xxi, As the primitive sense [of words] has been..transferred boldly to figurative and analogical uses.

c. *intr.* for *refl.* or *pass.*

1646 G. Daniel *Upon Virgil* 32 Wks. 1878 I. 22 But Wee ..averre Soules are not lost, or Dye, but doe transfer. **1901** *Daily Chron.* 24 Oct. 3/4 He transferred later to the 19th Hussars, in which regiment he served in the Soudan campaign. **1911** Webster, *Transfer*, to change from one car, line, or the like, to another for continuing one's journey on a transfer.

2. *Law.* To convey or make over (title, right, or property) by deed or legal process.

1598 Florio, s.v. *Trascriuere*, To transfer or giue ouer his right to another. **1651** Hobbes *Leviath.* i. xiv. 67 My right is not transferred, but remaineth till I transferre it by some other Act. **1671** *Court Bks. Roy. African Co.* 19 Dec. (P.R.O.), I do transfer £500 of my subscription in the new joint stock of the Royal Company to the Rt. Hon. George Lord Berkeley. **1694** J. Houghton *Collect. Improv. Husb. & Trade* V. No. 102 [*Form*] 'I A. B. do hereby sell, assign, and transferr unto C. D. Ten Shares in the Joynt-Stock.. with all the present and future Profits thereof'. **1771** *Junius Lett.* lxvii. (1797) II. 235 To this son-in-law..you meant to transfer the..property. **1818** Cruise *Digest* (ed. 2) IV. 65 A grant only transfers what the grantor may lawfully give. **1878** JEVONS *Prim. Pol. Econ.* 14 Sometimes things can be literally handed over, like a watch or a book; sometimes they can be transferred by a written deed.

3. To convey (a drawing or design) from one surface to another, esp. (*a*) to a lithographic stone, to earthenware, glass, etc., by means of transfer-paper; (*b*) to a new back or ground, as an embroidered pattern, etc.

1839 URE *Dict. Arts* 1017 This [roll of flannel] is used as a burnisher, one end of it being rested against the shoulder, and the other end being rubbed upon the paper; by which means it transfers all the engraved traces to the biscuit. **1860** *Ibid.* (ed. 5) III. 501 There are two distinct methods of printing in use for china and earthenware; one is transferred on the bisque..and the other is transferred on the glaze. The first is called 'press printing', and the latter 'bat printing'. **1877** KNIGHT *Dict. Mech.* 2611/2 In engraving, a tracing may be made in pencil and transferred to the ground by running through the plate-press. An impression from a plate or stone may also be transferred to a stone.

Hence **transferred** (-'fɜːd) *ppl. a.*, conveyed from one person, place, sense, etc. to another. ***transferred epithet***, an epithet grammatically qualifying a noun other than (though contextually associated with) the noun to which it literally applies.

1863 H. ALLON *Mem. J. Sherman* 279, 102 members were added in 1839 and 63 in 1840, including transferred members. **1866** A. BAIN *Eng. Comp. & Rhet.* 24 The *Transferred Epithet* is a common figure in Poetry. The shifting of an epithet from its proper subject to some allied subject..is seen in... 'Hence to his *idle bed*.' **1883** MURRAY *Dict.* Gen. Explan. p. xxi, The word was first taken into English..in a figurative, transferred, or specialized use. **1886** J. EBSWORTH *Roxb. Ball.* VI. 165 As a transferred ballad, Dulcina was entered to John White and Thomas Langley, in the Registers of the Stationers' Company. **1947** C. BROOKS *Well Wrought Urn* ix. 159 One can..justify the adjective as a transferred epithet on the model of Vergil's *maestum timorem*. **1958** C. BROOKE-ROSE *Gram. Metaphor* iii. 57, I have not found this transferred epithet in the later texts.

transferable ('trɑːnsfərəb(ə)l, 'træns-, -'fɜː-, -nz-), *a.* [f. prec. + -ABLE: cf. *preferable, referable*. See also TRANSFERRABLE.] Capable of being transferred or legally made over to another; *spec.* of bills, drafts, cheques, etc.: assignable in the course of business from one person to another; negotiable.

1646 SIR T. BROWNE *Pseud. Ep.* VI. iii. 286 If we..fall upon consideration with what incongruity they are transferable unto others. **1711** STEELE *Spect.* No. 149 ¶8 Take him in whom what you like is not transferable to another. **1874** *Act 37 & 38 Vict.* c. 3 §5 The debentures.. shall be transferable by the delivery of such debentures.

(*b*) ***transferable vote***, (in systems of proportional representation) a vote that is transferred to a second or further competing candidate if the candidate for whom it is first cast is eliminated in one of the succession of counts or has more votes than are needed for election; esp. as ***single transferable vote*** (abbrev. *S.T.V.* s.v. S 4a).

1885 W. E. SMITH *Fair Representation* vi. 32 (*heading*) The single transferable vote. **1909** *Westm. Gaz.* 8 Mar. 2/1 The adoption of the single transferable vote system of proportional representation. **1954** B. & R. NORTH tr. *Duverger's Pol. Parties* II. iii. 358 We must distinguish between the result of proportional representation and the consequences of list-voting, which generally coincides with it (except in the transferable Irish vote). **1972** *Guardian* 19 June 10/4 Mr Whitelaw's reintroduction of the single transferable vote in Ulster local government is likely to please minority groups.

Hence **ˌtransferaˈbility**, the quality of being transferable.

1776 ADAM SMITH *W.N.* IV. iii. II. 66 Its easy and safe trans-ferability, its use in paying foreign bills of exchange. **1875** POSTE *Gaius* III. Comm. (ed. 2) 431 The complete transferability of obligations was unknown to jurisprudence. **1893** *Nation* (N.Y.) 25 May 390/1 We shall [in political economy] regard transferability as meaning exchangeability.

transferal: see TRANSFERRAL.

transferase ('trɑːnsfəreɪz, 'træns-, -nz-). *Biochem.* [f. TRANSFER *v.* + -ASE.] Any enzyme that catalyses the transfer of some particular group or molecule from one molecule to another.

1948 *Jrnl. Biol. Chem.* CLXXII. 12 It may be that similar 'transferase' phenomena will be found to be of general occurrence with other types of hydrolases. **1974** [see OXIDOREDUCTASE]. **1981** *Sci. Amer.* June 70/3 In *Penicillium chrysogenum* an acyl transferase then catalyzes the replacement of this side chain by one derived from a utilizable precursor, such as phenylacetic acid.

transferee (trɑːnsfə'riː, træns-, -nz-). Also *erron.* -ferree. [f. TRANSFER *v.* + -EE.]

1. One to whom a transfer is made. (Chiefly in *Law*, as correlative to TRANSFEROR or TRANSFERRER.)

1736 BAILEY (folio) Pref., *Transféree*, the Person to whom any Thing is transferred. **1789-90** A. HAMILTON in *Debates Congress* (1834) II. 2048 The transferable quality of stock.. depends on the idea of complete security to the transferee. **1801** —— *Wks.* (1886) VII. 187 A discrimination between original holders and transferees of the public debt. **1905** *Times* 3 Apr. 8/4 Mr. B. signed a blank transfer as transferee.

2. One who is transferred or removed; e.g. from one position or grade to another.

1892 *Daily News* 27 Oct. 5/5 The children removed under the law from gaols to reformatories in the past year have done fairly well; but, looking to the difficulty in inducing employers to take these transferees into their service, they urge [etc.]. **1899** *Educat. Rev.* XVIII. 27 No disgrace was entailed upon the transferees, who were advanced with the rest of that class at the regular promotion.

transference ('trɑːnsfərəns, 'træns-, -nz-). Also 7-9 *erron.* -ferrence. [ad. L. type **transferentia* (used in med. or mod.L.; e.g. *a* 1541 by Paracelsus), f. *transferent-em*: see next and -ENCE.]

1. a. The action or process of transferring; conveyance from one place, person, or thing to another; transfer.

1760-72 H. BROOKE *Fool of Qual.* (1809) I. 141 The transference was not difficult. **1776** ADAM SMITH *W.N.* v. ii. II. 467 The transference of stock or moveable property. **1791** NEWTE *Tour Eng. & Scot.* 127 In Argyleshire..it became common to convey land, and make other transferences of property in writing. **1827** FARADAY *Chem. Manip.* xv. (1842) 323 Moderately-sized funnels..to assist in the transference of gas into vessels. **1839** *Morn. Herald* 13 June, A transference of power to the moneyed classes. **1875** LUBBOCK *Wild Flowers* i. 8 The transference of the pollen from one flower to another is..effected principally either by the wind or by insects. **1880** SWINBURNE *Stud. Shaks.* 258 A line too apt and exquisite to endure without injury the transference from its original setting. **1885** WATSON & BURBURY *Math. Th. Electr. & Magn.* I. 222 There is a transference, per unit time, of electricity *I* from the extremity *A* to the extremity of *B*.

b. *Psychoanal.* [tr. G. *übertragung*.] The transfer to the analyst by the patient of re-awakened and powerful emotions previously (in childhood) directed at some other person or thing and since repressed or forgotten; the process or state of such a transfer; *loosely*, the emotional aspect of a patient's relationship to the analyst; also *transf.* ***negative transference***: see NEGATIVE *a.* 8c; ***positive transference***: see POSITIVE *a.* 8d.

[**1895** S. FREUD in Breuer & Freud *Studien über Hysterie* iv. 266 Die Uebertragung auf den Arzt geschieht durch falsche Verknüpfung. **1910** tr. *Freud's Orig. & Devel. Psychoanal.* in *Amer. Jrnl. Psychol.* XXI. 215 Every time that we treat a neurotic psychoanalytically, there occurs in him the so-called phenomenon of *transfer* (Uebertragung), that is, he applies to the person of the physician a great amount of tender emotion, often mixed with enmity.] **1911** *Amer. Jrnl. Psychol.* XXII. 434 The reason why the physician is so often the object toward which the transference is made is that the Œdipus complex is almost invariably present in the patient. **1916** C. E. LONG tr. *Jung's Analyt. Psychol.* 245 What has disgusted you in hypnotism is at bottom nothing but the so-called 'transference' to the doctor. **1920** E. JONES *Treatm. Neuroses* 40 He is..reacting not toward the physician, but rather toward the other person who has been brought together ('identified') with the latter in his mind, an occurrence technically known as 'transference'. **1937** A. S. NEILL *That Dreadful School* xi. 155 If you tell a child any vital truth, or if it confides its troubles to you, he or she gets a transference, that is you get all the child's emotions showered on you. **1973** A. JANOV *Primal Scream* xiv. 246 Since I believe that the transference *is* the neurosis, I think that doing anything else with the patient other than helping him to feel his Pain is to render him a disservice.

2. *Sc. Law.* The procedure by which a depending action is transferred from a person deceased to his representative.

1681 STAIR *Inst. Law Scot.* xv. §10. 322 The Decreet will be effectual against all singular Successors, and subsequent Tennents without a new Decreet of Transferrence. **1765-8** ERSKINE *Inst. Law Scot.* IV. i. §60 If the pursuer be dead, it is called a transference *activè*... Where the defender dies, it gets the name of a transference *passivè*. *Ibid.*, Yet a transference cannot proceed against a debtor's apparent heir, till the *annus deliberandi* be expired. **1838** W. BELL *Dict. Law Scot.* 999 Transferences are competent to inferior judges, only when the representatives reside within their jurisdiction, and the principal cause is in dependence before them.

3. *attrib.* and *Comb.*, as (sense 1b) ***transference feeling, situation***; **transference neurosis** *Psychoanal.*, a neurotic stage during transference frequently encountered during analysis and considered beneficial to the therapy; **transference number** *Physical Chem.* (chiefly *U.S.*) = *transport number* s.v. TRANSPORT *sb.* 6.

1964 GOULD & KOLB *Dict. Soc. Sci.* 557/1 Freud's aim in treatment gradually changed..to the interpretation and modification of 'transference feelings' and their underlying unconscious conflicts. **1977** R. HOLLAND *Self & Social Context* iv. 76 The Freudian analyst is prepared to hold the transference feelings, and possible acting out behaviours, long enough for the client to re-experience and go beyond them. **1916** A. A. BRILL *tr. Freud's Three Contributions to Theory of Sex* (ed. 2) iii. 77 Psychoanalysis of the so-called transference neuroses (hysteria and compulsion neurosis) offers us here a reliable insight. **1968** H. RACKER *Transference & Countertransference* i. 15 In the transference neurosis,..the return of the relations to the parents implies the return of the neurotic conflicts with them. **1898** *Jrnl. Chem. Soc.* LXXIV. II. 553 The values were found to be almost independent of the concentration.., the transference numbers for the anions being given by the expressions [etc.]. **1909** [see HITTORF]. **1966** *McGraw-Hill Encycl. Sci. & Technol.* XIV. 18b/2 The two procedures for determining transference numbers by which most of the available data in the literature have been obtained are the Hittorf method and the moving boundary method. **1933** W. GALT *Phyloanalysis* 72 Only this intense transference-situation as it exists socially, however disguised, can account for the extremes of emotional stimulation and response constantly elicited in the process of phyloanalysis upon the slightest, most trivial occasion. **1977** C. STORR *Tales from Psychiatrist's Couch* 41 A probing of his feelings towards me as a mother figure, an exploration of the transference situation.

†**transferent** ('trɑːnsfərənt, 'træns-), *a. Obs. rare.* [ad. L. *transferent-em*, pr. pple. of *transferre* to transfer.] Effecting transference; in reference to sense: tropical, figurative.

1614 RALEIGH *Hist. World* II. vi. §7 Tropicall or transferent, which applies the diuers formes and figures of naturall bodies, to signifie the dignities, fortunes [etc.]..of their Gods, and of men. **1651** C. CARTWRIGHT *Cert. Relig.* I. 46 In a Metaphoricall and transferent sense.

transferential (trɑːnsfə'rɛnʃəl, træns-), *a.* [f. (mod.) L. *transferenti-a* TRANSFERENCE + -AL[1].] Of or pertaining to transference.

1889 G. ALLEN in *Nature* 24 Jan. 290/2 So the Energy of Kinesis is seen to be a mere transferential mode from one kind of separation to another.

transferer ('trɑːnsfərə(r), 'træns-). [f. TRANSFER *v.* or *sb.* + -ER[1].] One who or that which transfers: used sometimes for TRANSFERRER, sometimes in the technical sense of TRANSFEROR.

1807 JOYCE *Sci. Dial.* v. *Pneumatics*, This instrument is called the transferer. **1875** URE *Dict. Arts* III. 620 (Pottery) This impression..is then laid by the transferer [*ed.* 1860 transferrer] upon the ware. **1884** W. H. RIDEING in *Harper's Mag.* May 897/1 That the Bank may be sure that the transferer is the person he represents himself to be. **1906** *Daily News* 12 Jan. 12 Transfer of Labourers [in S. Africa] ..It is provided in the sub-section that 'the transfer..shall be signed by the transferer, the transferee, and the labourer'. **1908** *Daily Chron.* 24 Apr. 11/7 Litho Transferer wanted.

transfeˈrography. [f. TRANSFER *sb.* + -(O)GRAPHY.] (See quot.)

1846 WORCESTER, *Transferography*, the art or act of copying inscriptions from ancient tombs, tablets, etc. *Williams.* **1864** in WEBSTER. Hence in later Dicts.

transferor ('trɑːnsfərɔː(r), 'træns-, -ə(r)). Also *erron.* -ferror. [f. TRANSFER *v.* or *sb.* + -OR.] One who transfers or makes a transfer or conveyance of property, etc. Esp. in legal use, correlative to *transferee*.

1875 POSTE *Gaius* II. (ed. 2) §251 After the transfer of the inheritance the transferror continues heir, the transferree being sometimes quasi heir, sometimes quasi legatee. *Ibid.* Comm. 202 It confers property on the transferee, and discharges the transferor of an obligation. **1876** DIGBY *Real Prop.* iv. §5. 200 The transferee stepping for all purposes into the place of the transferor. **1882** *Act 45 & 46 Vict.* c. 38 §40 The receipt..for any money..discharges the payer or transferor therefrom.

transferotype: see TRANSFERROTYPE.

transˈferrable, *a.* Also 9 -ible. [f. TRANSFER *v.* + -ABLE, on English analogies, as in *transferring, barrable*. *Transferrible* is a hybrid spelling between *transferrable* and analogical L. **transferibilis*. See also TRANSFERABLE.] Capable of being or fit to be transferred.

α. **1660** R. COKE *Power & Subj.* 30 The offices..are alienable, communicable, and transferrable. **1714** *Act 1 Geo. I*, c. 21 §19 That the said Capital or Joint Stock..shall be Assignable and Transferrable or Devisable. **1765** BLACKSTONE *Comm.* I. viii. 328 A new species of money, always ready to be employed in any beneficial undertaking, by means of it's transferrable quality. **1872** O. W. HOLMES *Poet Breakf.-t.* x, Sin was made a transferrable chattel. **1878** ABNEY *Photogr.* xxvi. (1881) 176 Transferrable prints.

β. **1832** LYELL *Princ. Geol.* II. 171 We believe the mean annual temperature of one zone to be transferrible to another. **1875** POSTE *Gaius* II. §21 Similarly transferrible are estates in provincial lands.

Hence **transˈferrableness**, the quality of being transferrable.

1804 W. TAYLOR in *Ann. Rev.* II. 390 In reply to the objection of the transferrableness of machinery.

transferral (trɑːns'fɜːrəl, træns-, -nz-). *erron.* transferal. [f. as prec. + -AL[1]: cf. *conferral*.] The action or fact of transferring; transfer, transference.

a **1790** J. H. BEATTIE *Ess. & Fragments* (1794) III. 295 Instead of reference, preference, commitment..say *referral, preferral*..and the *transferral* of property, instead of the transferring of property. **1863** *Cornh. Mag.* VII. 388 The transferal of Greenwich mean time into sidereal, and vice versâ. **1870** E. MULFORD *Nation* x. 169 All acquisition of territory..is by the United States alone, and the immediate transferal is to the United States. **1875** WHITNEY *Life Lang.* v. 78 The old material of language is constantly suffering extension and transferral to new uses.

transferrer (trɑːns'fɜːrə(r), træns-, -nz-). [f. as prec. + -ER[1]. See also TRANSFERER, -OR.] One who or that which transfers.

1753 HANWAY *Trav.* (1762) II. I. vii. 35 These transfers are made by the personal appearance of the transferrer. **1803** W. TAYLOR in *Ann. Rev.* I. 744 Compelling him to apply only against the immediate transferrer of the bill. **1825** J. NICHOLSON *Operat. Mechanic* 470 The impression when taken off the plate is given to a girl, called a cutter, who cuts it into shapes, and hands the parts to a woman (the transferrer), who puts them on the biscuit. **1860** H. SPENCER *Soc. Organism* in *Westm. Rev.* Jan. 105 A system of vessels which continues ever after to be the transferrer of nutriment. **1862** *Catal. Internat. Exhib.* II. x. 17 This direct transferrer, invented by Mr. George Glover, is now generally used in the gradation of gas-holders for testing meters.

transferrin (trɑːns'fɛrın, træns-, -nz-). *Biochem.* [f. TRANS- + L. *ferr-um* iron + -IN[1].] Any of several beta globulins found in blood serum which bind and transport iron; = *siderophilin* s.v. SIDERO-[1] 2.

1947 HOLMBERG & LAURELL in *Acta Chemica Scandinavica* I. 950 We suggest that the new metal-combining protein (iron-binding component) in serum be called transferrin. **1962** H. HEATH in A. Pirie *Lens Metabolism Rel. Cataract* 364 Ascorbic acid has been shown to be necessary for the transfer of plasma-bound iron, transferrin, into the liver and its incorporation into ferritin. **1971** [see *siderophilin* s.v. SIDERO- 2]. **1977** *Jrnl. R. Soc. Arts* CXXV. 699/1 These transferrin genes show much genetic diversity within herds.

transferring (trɑːns'fɜːrıŋ, træns-, -nz-), *vbl. sb.* [f. TRANSFER *v.* + -ING[1].] The action of the verb TRANSFER; transference.

1573 *Reg. Privy Council Scot.* II. 284 Thai obtenit ane decreit of transfering befoir the Lordis of Counsall and Sessioun. **1651** HOBBES *Govt. & Soc.* ii. §7. 23 Words.. effectuall towards the perfect transferring of his Right. **1688** *Act. Sederunt* 26 July in Fountainhall *Hist. Not.* (Bann. Cl.) 882 After wakenings and transferrings are seen and returned, they need not byde the course of the roll, but may be summarly called and decerned, or debated. **1766** BLACKSTONE *Comm.* II. xxx. 446 If it be a transferring of goods for money, it is called a sale. **1904** D. CUMMING *Lithography* xx. 194 [Zinc and Aluminium] Plates with a fine grain or 'tooth'.. suitable for all classes of transferring and printing.

attrib. **1827** FARADAY *Chem. Manip.* xxiv. (1842) 634 Exhaust the retort.., attach it to a graduated transferring jar.

trans'ferrotype, 'transfero-. *Photog.* [Irreg. f. TRANSFER + -TYPE.] See quot. 1890.

1889 *Anthony's Photogr. Bull.* II. 322 This is not more trouble than the transferrotype process; it was, in fact, my familiarity with the double transfer carbon process which first suggested to me the transferrotype. **1891** *Ibid.* IV. 241 Eastman's transferotype paper answers well for decorating the tiles. **1890** WOODBURY *Dict. Photogr.* 701 *Transferrotype*, a process of transferring bromide prints to any suitable support. [Description follows.] *Ibid.* 702 Warm tones.. may be obtained with transferrotype paper.

†**trans'figurate,** *a.* *Obs. rare.* [ad. L. *transfigūrāt-us*, pa. pple. of *transfigūrāre*: see next.] Transfigured; having its figure or form altered: *spec.* in *Geom.* (see TRANSFIGURED).

1571 DIGGES *Pantom.* IV. Hh ij b, This transfigurate body [Dodecaedron] receiueth an internall Tetraedron, whose solide angles rest in the centers of his trigonall bases. *Ibid.*, Icosaedron within this transfigurate body may be described.

transfigurate (trɑːns'fıgjʊəreıt, træns-), *v.* Now *rare*. Pa. t. and pple. in Sc. 6 **transfigurat.** [f. ppl. stem of L. *transfigūrāre*, f. TRANS- + *figūra* figure.] *trans.* = TRANSFIGURE. Hence **trans'figurating** *ppl. a.*

1432–50 tr. *Higden* (Rolls) II. 211 Thei may thro the permission of God transfigurate similitudes. *a* **1555** RIDLEY *Piteous Lament.* (1556) E iv, This our weake body shall be transfigurated and made lyke vnto christes glorious body. *a* **1560** ROLLAND *Crt. Venus* III. 31 In ane tre scho was transfigurat. **1563** WIN3ET *Four Scoir Thre Quest.* Wks. (S.T.S.) I. 87 Quhen he transfigurat His body afoir His passioun. **1600** F. WALKER *Sp. Mandeville* 145 They can and do so transfigurat themselues. **1819** BYRON *Proph. Dante* IV. 33 High heaven is there Transfused, transfigurated. **1871** MORLEY *Crit. Misc.* Ser. I. *Carlyle* 219 [Carlyle's] epithet.. shoots like a sunbeam on to the matter, throwing a transfigurating light.

transfiguration (ˌtrɑːnsfıgjʊə'reıʃən, ˌtræns-). [ad. L. *transfigūrātiōn-em* (Pliny), n. of action from *transfigūrāre* (see prec.). Cf. F. *transfiguration* (13th c. in Hatz.-Darm.). The specific sense 2 was from its ecclesiastical use the earlier in Eng.]

1. The action of transfiguring or state of being transfigured; metamorphosis.

a **1548** HALL *Chron., Hen. VI* 161 Ihon Cade.. departed secretly in habite disguysed.. but all his metamorphosis or transfiguracion, litle preuailed. **1567** MAPLET *Gr. Forest* 76 He hath so often and so diuers transfiguration in colour. **1569** J. SANFORD tr. *Agrippa's Van. Artes* 69 b, Ouide in his Transfigurations singeth in this sorte. **1607** TOPSELL *Four-f. Beasts* (1658) 361 Of the transfiguration of men into Lions, we shall say more afterward. **1650** BULWER *Anthropomet.* (title-p.), Nations, fashioning and altering their Bodies from the mould intended by Nature; With Figures of those Transfigurations. **1836** EMERSON *Nature, Idealism* Wks. (Bohn) II. 162 This transfiguration which all material objects undergo through the passion of the poet.

2. The change in the appearance of Jesus Christ on the mountain (Matt. xvii. 2; Mark ix. 2, 3).

c **1375** *Sc. Leg. Saints* i. (*Petrus*) 37 Criste.. hym tuk to be hym by In his transfiguracion. **1497** BP. ALCOCK *Mons Perfect.* D iij, This noble transfyguracoun thus shewed to his dyscyples. *a* **1691** BOYLE *Greatn. Mind* I. ii. Wks. 1772 V. 557 How glorious it is in heaven, we may guess by what it was at his transfiguration here on earth. **1856** DOVE *Logic Chr. Faith* v. i. §2. 296 In that sublime spectacle called the transfiguration.

b. *Eccl.* The church festival commemorating this event, observed on the 6th of August.

c **1460** *Brut* cclv. 522 This Calixte instituted & ordeyned þe Feste of Transffiguracion of our Lorde to be halowed on Seynt Sixt day in August. **1510–11** *Rec. St. Mary at Hill* 274 Paid for brede, ale and wyne at þe fest of transfiguracion.

c. A picture or representation of this event.

1712 BLACKMORE *Creation* III. 123 Did.. Raphael's Pencil never chuse to fall? Say, are his Works Transfigurations all? **1753** MRS. DELANY in *Life & Corr.* (1861) III. 209, I have at last put the finishing stroke to the Transfiguration. **1838** EMERSON *Addr., Lit. Ethics* Wks. (Bohn) II. 209 Say to the man of letters, that he cannot paint a Transfiguration.

transfigurative (trɑːns'fıgjʊərətıv, træns-), *a.* *rare.* [f. as TRANSFIGURATE *v.* + -IVE.] Having the quality of transfiguring; that tends to transfigure.

1885 FAIRBAIRN *Catholicism* (1899) II. iv. 76 A splendid example of the power of faith and of the creative and transfigurative force of the religious imagination.

transfigure (trɑːns'fıgjʊə(r), træns-, -'fıgə(r)), *v.* [ad. L. *transfigūrāre* to change the shape of (f. TRANS- + *figūra* form, shape, figure); or a. F. *transfigurer* (12th c. in Hatz.-Darm.).]

1. *trans.* To alter the figure or appearance of; to change in outward appearance; to transform.

a **1300** *Cursor M.* 18497 (Cott.) Þai war transfigurd als tite, Was neuer i-wis snau sa quite. *a* **1340** HAMPOLE *Psalter* xc. 6 When þe fende transfigurs him in aungel of light. *c* **1386** CHAUCER *Knt.'s T.* 247 Venus, if it be thy wil Yow in this gardyn thus to transfigure. **1412–20** LYDG. *Chron. Troy* II. 913 So craftily þei koude hem transfigure, Conformyng hem to þe chaunt[e]plure. *c* **1470** HENRY *Wallace* VI. 91 Thow transfigowryt Wallace out off his weill. **1547** *Bk. Marchauntes* e viij b, Satan.. by cautyle transfigurynge hym into an angell of lyght. **1589** PUTTENHAM *Eng. Poesie* III. xii. (Arb.) 174 Your single wordes may be many waies tranfigured to make the meetre or verse more tunable and melodious. **1607** TOPSELL *Four-f. Beasts* (1658) 193 Wilde-goats are transfigured into many similitudes. **1855** PUSEY *Doctr. Real Presence* Note Q. 230 The Sacraments, which, by the mystery of the sacred prayer, are transfigured into Body and Blood. **1880** MCCARTHY *Own Times* III. xxxii. 49 The mutiny was transfigured into a revolutionary war.

b. In reference to the Transfiguration of Christ.

c **1380** WYCLIF *Sel. Wks.* II. 57 Þis gospel telliþ how þat Crist was transfigurid in si3t of þree apostlis. *c* **1400** MAUNDEV. (1839) x. 114 In þat hille Thabor, oure lord transfigured him before seynt Peter, seynt Iohn & seynt Iame. **1526** TINDALE *Mark* ix. 2 And he was transfigured before them. **1911** J. A. ROBINSON in *Encycl. Brit.* XV. 381/2 They saw Jesus transfigured in a radiance of glory.

c. *intr.* for *refl.* *rare.*

1840 BROWNING *Sordello* II. 214 He no genius rare Transfiguring in fire, or wave, or air, At will.

2. *trans. fig.* (in allusion to the Transfiguration of Christ): To elevate, glorify, idealize, spiritualize.

c **1380** WYCLIF *Sel. Wks.* II. 58 Þus men sein þat transfiguring is turnyng into glorious forme. **1687** BOYLE *Martyrd. Theodora* viii. (1703) 116, I think our notions will then be raised.. and our love and other affections, will be transfigured, as well as our bodies. **1841** MYERS *Cath. Th.* IV. ii. 185 His education becomes devotion, and his morality is transfigured into Religion. **1876** E. MELLOR *Priesth.* i. 15 Temple, priest, and sacrifice were employed and transfigured into glorious spiritual significations. **1879** FARRAR *St. Paul* (1883) 113 [Stephen's] whole being was transfigured by a consciousness which illuminated his very countenance.

†**3.** To transfer by a figure. (A literalism of translation.) *Obs.*

1382 WYCLIF *1 Cor.* iv. 6 This thing I haue transfigurid [Vulg. *transfiguravi*] in to me and in to Apollo; that in vs 3e lerne.

Hence **trans'figured** *ppl. a.* (†in *Geom.* (quots. 1571) applied to a solid in which plane faces are substituted for the original solid angles); **trans'figuring** *vbl. sb.* and *ppl. a.*

c **1380** [see 2]. **1571** DIGGES *Pantom.* IV. Gg i b, This solides inscribed Octaedrons side is triple to the medietie of his contayning transfigured Tetraedrons side. *Ibid.* Gg iij b, A Transfigured Octaedron is a Geometricall Figure incompassed with 14 bases, whereof 8 are equall equiangle Hexagonall playnes, and the other 6 are equall squares. **1678** CUDWORTH *Intell. Syst.* I. v. 805 Bodies.. luciform or lucid, like to our Saviour's then transfigured body. **1717** GARTH tr. *Ovid, Enchantm. Circe* 33 The dow'r desir'd is his transfigur'd friends. **1846** TRENCH *Mirac.* Introd. (1862) 93 Their transforming, transfiguring power. **1880** N. SMYTH *Old Faiths in New Light* iii. (1882) 98 It can shine, a steady and transfiguring light of life, for the world.

trans'figurement. *rare.* [f. prec. + -MENT: cf. OF. *transfigurement* (14th c. in Godef.).] = TRANSFIGURATION.

1865 *Reader* No. 133. 57/1 By sudden transfigurement. **1878** GILDER *Poet & Master* 55 Then did the outer world.. Suffer a sudden strange transfigurement.

transˌfinali'zation. *Theol.* [f. TRANS- 3 + FINALIZATION.] The change in purpose or function undergone by bread and wine at the Eucharist through transubstantiation, expressed in terms of finality or teleology. Cf. TRANSIGNIFICATION.

1965 *Pope Speaks* X. 311 It is not permissible.. to discuss the mystery of transubstantiation without mentioning what the Council of Trent had to say about the marvelous conversion of the whole substance of the bread into the Body and the whole substance of the wine into the Blood of Christ, as if they involve nothing more than 'transignification' or 'transfinalization' as they call it. **1966** *Worship* XL. 337 In the eucharist we ought to be concerned with an interpersonal relationship between Christ and us,.. in which Christ gives himself to man by means of bread and wine which, by this very gift, have undergone a transfinalization and an ontological and therefore radical transignification. **1975** E. L. MASCALL in *Critique Eucharistic Agreement* v. 73 The writers who introduced the notions of transfinalization and transignification were worried that the term 'transubstantiation' as commonly understood suggested a notion both insufficiently dynamic and insufficiently human.

transfinite (trɑːns'faınaıt, træns-), *a.* (*sb.*) *Math.* [f. TRANS- 4 + FINITE.] Beyond or surpassing any finite number or magnitude: see quots. Also, as *sb.*, a transfinite number, etc.

1903 *Nature* 3 Sept. 411/2 To readers unacquainted with [Cantor's] 'Mengenlehre', the introduction of transfinite numbers must appear rather startling. **1907** HOBSON *Funct. Real Variable* 177 Corresponding to a single transfinite cardinal number there is an infinity of transfinite ordinal numbers. **1907** *Athenæum* 14 Sept. 307/2 The simplest conception of a transfinite number may be gathered from the following illustration. A man walks along a road at a uniform pace, and the distance he goes is divided into intervals—$\frac{1}{2}$ mile, $\frac{1}{4}$ mile, $\frac{1}{8}$ mile, and so on. The number of these intervals in the first mile is infinite, but the time taken is finite. We agree to regard the mile as ending with the ωth interval. If the next mile is divided in just the same way, then the intervals regarded as belonging to the same series will be the $(\omega + 1)$th, $(\omega + 2)$th, and so on. These numbers ω, $\omega + 1$, $\omega + 2$, are called by Cantor (who was the first to use them) transfinite ordinal numbers.

transfission (trɑːns'fıʃən, træns-). *Biol.* [f. TRANS- 1 or 6 + FISSION *sb.* 2.] The transverse splitting of a cell or organism as a mode of reproduction; transverse fission.

1891 in *Cent. Dict.*

†**trans'fisticate,** *v.* *Obs.* (*humorous nonce-wd.*) [? f. TRANS- 1 + L. *fistūcare* to ram down or in (cf. FISTUCATE), with allusion to *fist*.] To strike or smash with the fist.

1600 ROWLANDS *Lett. Humours Blood* iv. 64 For though your beard do stand so fine mustated, Perhaps your nose may be transfisticated.

transfix (trɑːns'fıks, træns-), *v.* [f. L. *transfīx-*, ppl. stem of *transfīgĕre*, f. TRANS- + *fīgĕre* to FIX. Cf. OF. *transfixer* (15th c. in Godef.).] *trans.* To pierce through with, or impale upon, a sharp-pointed instrument (also said of the instrument); to fix or fasten by piercing.

1590 SPENSER *F.Q.* I. v. 50 The bold Semiramis, whose sides transfixt With sonnes own blade her fowle reproches spoke. **1626** MASSINGER *Rom. Actor* III. ii, Take A golden arrow to transfix her heart. **1797** MRS. RADCLIFFE *Italian* xxxiii, That monk seemed as if transfixed to the spot. **1802** PALEY *Nat. Theol.* xii. 109 The butcher-bird transfixes its prey upon the spike of a thorn, whilst it picks its bones. **1850** MRS. JAMESON *Leg. Monast. Ord.* (1863) 388 Being absorbed in rapturous devotion, she was transfixed, that is, received the Stigmata. **1875** JOWETT *Plato* (ed. 2) IV. 382 He delights .. to transfix the Eristic Sophist with weapons borrowed from his own armoury.

b. *fig.* To pierce through (esp. with pain, grief, or other emotion); also, to render motionless (with astonishment, horror, etc.).

1649 LOVELACE *Poems* 19 Transfixed Venus stood amas'd. *a* **1711** KEN *Hymnotheo* Poet. Wks. III. 76 Sent by a breaking Heart by Guilt transfix'd. **1791** COWPER *Odyss.* x. 303 His heart transfixt With anguish. **1840** DICKENS *Barn. Rudge* xix, Both of whom were so transfixed at sight of the ladies that.. they.. could do nothing but stare. **1863** GEO. ELIOT *Romola* iv, [He] stood transfixed, with his long dark eyes resting on the unknown man who had addressed him.

Hence **transfixed** (-'fıkst, *poet.* -'fıksıd) *ppl. a.*; *spec.* in *Her.*: see quots. *c* 1828 and 1894; **trans'fixing** *ppl. a.*

1661 BLOUNT *Glossogr.* (ed. 2), *Transfixed*.., sticked or thurst through. *c* **1828** BERRY *Encycl. Her.* I. Gloss., *Transfixed*, pierced through, as a boar's head, &c., transfixed with a spear, &c. **1854** KANE *Grinnell Exp.* xlvi. 429 Then the transfixed and transfixing vessels were both eaten up together by the greedy floes. **1859** SALA *Tw. Round Clock* (1861) 64 Their muskets—prudently divested of the transfixing bayonets. **1894** *Parker's Gloss. Her.* 456 Pierced with an arrow generally means the same as transfixed.

transfi'xation. *rare*[−1]. [f. prec. + -ATION, after *fixation*.] Used for TRANSFIXION (sense b).

1889 *Lancet* 9 Feb. 273/1 Had it [the nævus] been treated by the old method of transfixation and ligature, the infant would not improbably have sunk.

transfixion (trɑːns'fıkʃən, træns-). [f. L. type **transfixiōn-em*, n. of action from *transfīgĕre*, *-fix-* to TRANSFIX: cf. L. *affixiōn-*, *crucifixiōn-*.] The action of transfixing or state of being transfixed.

1609 BP. W. BARLOW *Answ. Nameless Cath.* 335 Hee.. shal finde both an explicit contradiction, and a double transfixion, like that stroake of Phinees.. pearcing with one speech through two at once. **1628** BP. HALL *Serm. Gal.* ii. 20 Wks. 1837 V. 336 Six several times do we find that Christ shed blood; in his Circumcision, in his Agony, in his Crowning, in his Scourging, in his Affixion, in his Transfixion. **1844** *Phrenol. Jrnl.* Oct. 368 The head must have been embalmed, and must have been so before its transfixion.

b. *Surgery.* The process of piercing the limb transversely, and cutting from within outward, in amputation. (Cf. F. *transfixion*, Littré.)

1872 T. Bryant *Pract. Surg.* 1037 In cutting the posterior flap by transfixion..the Surgeon should always support it with his left hand. **1890** Billings *Med. Dict.*, *Transfixion*, a piercing through, as in cutting a flap from within outward. *attrib.* **1883** *Daily News* 19 Feb. 4/8 Perhaps [the murderers] thought transfixion knives nothing worse than an improvement on the admittedly inefficient pikeheads of '48.

transfixture (trɑːnsˈfɪkstjʊə(r), træns-). *rare.* [f. transfix, after fixture.] The condition of being transfixed or fixed to the spot with some feeling.

1886 T. Hardy *Mayor Casterbr.* II. xx. 278 Henchard waited—if that could be called a waiting which was a transfixture. **1955** W. de la Mare *Beginning* 215 In this transfixture, a single commonplace word came sallying nonchalantly up out of his memory.

†**transˈfleet**, *v. Obs. rare*⁻¹. [f. trans- 2 + fleet *v.*¹] *intr.* To float or sail across.

a **1600** *Floddan F.* i. (1664) 2 Before King Henry past the Seas, And ere to France he did transfleet.

transfluence (ˈtrɑːnsfluːəns, ˈtræns-). *Geomorphol.* [ad. G. *transfluenz* (A. Penck *Die Alpen im Eiszeitalter* (1909) III. 804), f. L. *-fluentia* flow: see trans-.] The flow of glacial ice in quantity across a preglacial watershed with consequent severe erosion.

1949 *Scottish Geogr. Mag.* LXV. 123 The ice-flow thus set up across the divides is termed diffluence or transfluence. **1955** *Sci. News* XXXVIII. 55 At the present time transfluence is occurring at the edge of the Greenland ice-cap. **1970** R. J. Small *Study of Landforms* xi. 374 Glacial transfluence is found where the impeded ice cuts out of a valley system not by a lateral distributary but at the very head of the valley.

transfluent (ˈtrɑːnsfluːənt, ˈtræns-), *a.* [ad. L. *transfluent-em*, pr. pple. of *transfluĕre* to flow through.]

a. Flowing across or through; in *Her.* said of a stream represented as flowing through a bridge. *rare.*

c **1828** Berry *Encycl. Her.* I. Gloss., *Transfluent*, an heraldic term, to express water appearing, in a coat, as if running through a bridge. **1847** Parker *Gloss. Her.* 309.

b. *spec.* in *Geomorphol.*, applied to glacial ice undergoing transfluence.

1951 *Trans. Inst. Brit. Geographers* Pub. No. 15, 2 Like Penck he clearly recognised that where a pass was crossed by diffluent or transfluent ice it was markedly eroded by it. **1968** R. W. Fairbridge *Encycl. Geomorphol.* 429/2 Many of the breaches made by transfluent ice involve considerable arrangement of the drainage pattern.

transfluvial (trɑːnsˈfluːvɪəl, træns-), *a.* [ad. post-cl. L. *transfluviāl-is*, f. *trans*, trans- + *fluvi-us* a river: see -al¹.] Situated or dwelling across or beyond a river: in quot. 1806 rendering Heb. *ʿib'ri* 'one from the other side', i.e. from beyond the Jordan or ? the Euphrates.

1806 W. Taylor in *Ann. Rev.* IV. 716 The term Hebrew, which signifies transfluvial,..was applied to the posterity of Abraham, because they came from beyond the Euphrates. **1862** S. Lucas *Secularia* (1863) 92 As the lower curve..was intersected..by the river Avon, it included the transfluvial parishes of St. Mary Redcliffe, Thomas and Temple. **18..** Lowell *Orient. Apol.* v, The sacred rites and laws of his Transfluvial rival.

So **transˈfluvian** *a.*, in same sense.

1848 *Times* 18 Oct. 3/5 His successors were rather kings of Candahar, with some transfluvian provinces, than kings of India in our sense. **1865** *Daily Tel.* 12 Apr. 3 As long as this part of the Mississippi remained to the Confederates all the produce of the transfluvian region was theirs.

transflux (ˈtrɑːnsflʌks, ˈtræns-). *rare*⁻⁰. [f. trans- 1 + L. *flux-us* flowing, flux: cf. *efflux*, etc.] A flowing through, across, or beyond.

1864 in Webster. Hence in later Dicts.

transfluxor (trɑːnsˈflʌksə(r), træns-, -nz-). *Electronics.* [f. trans- 10 + flux *sb.* + -or.] (See quots.)

1955 Rajchman & Lo in *R.C.A. Rev.* XVI. 303 A novel device which is based on the fact that completely new switching and storing functions become possible when two or more apertures are made in the rectangular hysteresis loop cores, thereby creating a number of distinct legs and flux paths in the magnetic circuit. The new device operates by the controlled transfer of flux from leg to leg in the magnetic circuit and was consequently named 'Transfluxor'. **1963** [see laddic]. **1972** G. J. Klir *Introd. Methodol. Switching Circuits* v. 185 Interesting properties are exhibited by a magnetic core which has several holes with windings. This element is called a transfluxor.

transforate (ˈtrɑːnsfəreɪt, ˈtræns-), *v. rare.* [f. ppl. stem of L. *transforāre* to bore or pierce through, f. trans- + *forāre* to bore, pierce.] *trans.* To pierce or bore through, perforate; *spec.* (*Surg.*) to perforate (the skull) in craniotomy.

1727 Bailey vol. II, *Transforate*, to make a hole through. **1775** Ash, *Transforated*, *Transforating*..(not much used).

transforation (trɑːnsfəˈreɪʃən, træns-). [ad. late L. *transforātiōn-em*, f. *transforāre*: see prec.]

†**1.** A seton; a thread or tape drawn through a fold of skin to maintain an issue. *Obs.*

1597 A. M. tr. *Guillemeau's Fr. Chirurg.* cij b/1 The Needle for the Seton, or transforatione. *Ibid.* 39 b/2 All the which [cauteryes] haue but one onlye apertion, or two, and is then called a transforatione or Seton.

2. The action of transforating, as in craniotomy.

1890 Billings *Med. Dict.*, *Transforation*,..repeated perforation of the base of the fœtal skull in craniotomy.

transform (trɑːnsˈfɔːm, træns-, -nz-), *v.* [ad. L. *transformāre*, f. trans- + *formāre* to form, f. *forma* form. Cf. F. *transformer* (14th c. in Godef. *Compl.*), also OF. *tresformer*.]

1. *trans.* To change the form of; to change into another shape or form; to metamorphose.

c **1340** Hampole *Prose Tr.* 15 In transfourmynge of þe saule in þe Godhede. **1382** Wyclif *2 Cor.* iii. 18 Alle we.. ben transformyd into the same ymage. *c* **1400** Maundev. (Roxb.) iv. 11 Of Ypocras daughter transformed from a womman to a dragoun. **1483** Caxton *Cato* b vij b, This catte ..is myn owne daughter the whiche by the plesure and wylle of god hath ben transfourmed in to a catte. **1548** Udall, etc. *Erasm. Par. Mark* i. 5 b, That thynges of muche contrarietie maye easely be transformed, and tourned one into an other. **1590** Shaks. *Com. Err.* iii. ii. 151 And I thinke, if my brest had not beene made of faith, and my heart of steele, she had transform'd me to a Curtull dog, & made me turne i' th wheele. **1660** F. Brooke tr. *Le Blanc's Trav.* 268 When Magicians shall have power to transform a humane body. **1813** Scott *Rokeby* i. xxxi, The victor sees his fairy gold, Transform'd, when won, to drossy mold. **1827** Faraday *Chem. Manip.* xxiv. (1842) 618 Transform several small crystals of sulphate of nickel into a large one. **1853** J. H. Newman *Hist. Sk.* (1873) II. i. ii. 65 To Samarcand..we owe the art of transforming linen into paper.

b. *transf.* To change in character or condition; to alter in function or nature.

1556 J. Heywood *Spider & F.* ii. 5 My whole estate..Is here transformde from myrth to miserie. **1675** Traherne *Chr. Ethics* 270 Love..transformes the most virulent affections into smooth, healing, perfective pleasures. **1796** Morse *Amer. Geog.* I. 306 He transformed an undisciplined body of peasantry into a regular army of soldiers. **1852** H. Rogers *Ecl. Faith* (1853) 16 A volume, which has transformed them from savages into men, and from idolaters into Christians.

c. *Math.* To alter (a figure, expression, etc.) to another differing in form, but equal in quantity or value. More widely, to subject (any mathematical entity) to a transformation (transformation 2 c). Also *absol.*

1743 Emerson *Fluxions* 22 To transform the Fluxion.., assume [etc.]. **1884** tr. *Lotze's Logic* 332 These equations we transform in all sorts of ways by adding on new quantities, by subtracting others, by multiplication and division of the whole. **1885** Watson & Burbury *Math. Th. Electr. & Magn.* I. 155 We now proceed to transform this problem. **1972** M. Kline *Math. Thought* xix. 427 Finding it difficult to evaluate in rectangular coordinates, he transformed to spherical coordinates. **1982** D. M. Schneider et al. *Linear Algebra* v. 181 The function f defined by the equation $f(x) = x^2$. This function transforms a real number into a real number, namely its square.

d. *Physics.* To change (one form of energy) into another, as mechanical energy into electricity, or electric energy into light or heat.

1871 Maxwell *Theory of Heat* (1875) 92 The total energy of any body or system of bodies is a quantity which can neither be increased nor diminished by any mutual action of those bodies, though it may be transformed into any of the forms of which energy is susceptible. **1878** W. Garnett in *Encycl. Brit.* VIII. 208/2 All other forms of energy with which we are acquainted can be transformed into an equivalent amount of heat. **1902** J. Larmor *ibid.* XXVIII. 164/2 There is a certain measurable quantity associated with each type of physical action..numerically identical with a corresponding quantity belonging to the new type into which it is transformed.

e. *Electr.* To change a current in potential, as from high voltage to low voltage, or in type, as from alternating to continuous. ***transform up***, to raise the voltage while decreasing the current. ***transform down***, to lower the voltage while increasing the current.

1883 tr. Hospitalier *Mod. Applications of Electr.* (ed. 2) I. 142 All these apparatus have a common character; they receive electricity and give out electricity, which they transform according to their individual properties. **1888** S. P. Thompson *Dynamo-electr. Mach.* 486 At the generating station the alternating currents of low potential were to be transformed by means of an induction-coil to currents of high potential. **1897** Sloane *Stand. Electr. Dict.* (1902) 547 Such dynamo could transform currents up or down. **1902** S. P. Thompson *Electr. & Magnet.* 502 To transform continuous currents from one voltage to another it is necessary to employ a rotating apparatus, which is virtually a combination of a motor and a generator.

f. *Molecular Biol.* To change (a bacterial cell) into a genetically distinct kind by the introduction into it of DNA from another cell of the same or a closely related species.

1928 *Jrnl. Hygiene* XXVII. 150 An R strain is most readily transformed into the S variety when the killed culture used is of the same serological type as that from which the R strain was derived. **1947** *Jrnl. Exper. Med.* LXXXVI. 449 Repeated attempts both *in vitro* and *in vivo* to transform D39/Int53 to pneumococcus Type III were unsuccessful. **1981** L. L. Mays *Genetics* vi. 274 Pieces of DNA of molecular weight less than $1{\cdot}5 \times 10^7$ daltons cannot transform *Haemophilus influenzae*.

g. *Cytology.* To cause (a eukaryotic cell) to undergo transformation (transformation 3 i).

1959 *Jrnl. Nat. Cancer Inst.* XXIII. 1035 (*heading*) Clonal analysis of variant cell lines transformed to malignant cells in tissue culture. **1982** *Sci. Amer.* Mar. 72/1 Analysis of the DNA of the Rous sarcoma virus has revealed a single gene capable of transforming cells.

2. *intr.* To undergo a change of form or nature; to change.

1597 Beard *Theatre God's Judgem.* (1612) 68 Then did this iolly feast, to fast transforme. **1667** E. King in *Phil. Trans.* II. 427 The Film does onely cover the Maggot, while she is transforming into an Ant. **1717** Addison tr. *Ovid, Transf. Cycnus* 11 His hair transforms to down, his fingers meet In skinny films, and shape his oary feet. **1747** Gould *Eng. Ants* 52 The Female Aurelia's are generally the first which transform, and are those that make their Appearance in the Shape of large Flies. **1827** Hood *Mids. Fairies* lxxxiii, Meanwhile I bade my pitying mates transform Like grasshoppers. **1893** Harkness & Morley *Treat. Theory of Functions* i. 14 If $w = u + iv$ be a one-valued monogenic function of $x + iy$, the systems of orthogonal straight lines $x = a$, $y = b$ transform into systems of orthogonal curves in the w- plane. **1970** Passmore & Robson *Compan. Med. Stud.* II. xxii. 9/2 The function of antigen at the surface of the lymphocyte is to induce it to transform and proliferate into active antibody-producing cells. **1971** *Nature* 26 Nov. 187/1 The larva then transforms to a pupa. **1982** *Suppl. to O.E.D.* III, *Pseudoscalar* sb., a quantity that transforms as a scalar under rotation but changes sign under reflection.

transform (ˈtrɑːnsfɔːm, ˈtræns-, -nz-), *sb.* [f. prec. vb.]

1. *Math.* An expression derived from another by transformation.

1853 Sylvester in *Phil. Trans.* CXLIII. i. 544 *Covariant*, a function which stands in the same relation to the primitive function from which it is derived as any of its linear transforms do to a similarly derived transform of its primitive.

2. *Transformational Gram.* A syntactic structure derived by the application of a transformation.

1955 N. Chomsky *Transformational Analysis* (Ph.D. Dissertation, Univ. Pennsylvania) v. 26 It seems most natural to characterize these sentences in terms of some notation of grammatical transformation, regarding these sentences as transforms of certain sentences which are derived on the level *P* and which do have *P* markers. **1957** —— *Syntactic Structures* (1962) viii. 88 This sentence [*sc.* I found the boy studying in the library] was a transform..of 'I—found studying in the library—the boy'. **1964** R. H. Robins *Gen. Linguistics* vi. 243 The collocational compatibilities..between the particular words of any sentence and its transform are likely to be substantially the same. **1972** R. D. Eagleson in G. W. Turner *Good Austral. Eng.* v. 98 We can see them [*sc.* two versions of a sentence] ..as related to the same underlying structures and as different transforms of it. **1976** *Word 1971* XXVII. 253 There is an embedded sentence corresponding to sentence 7 b, a transform derived from sentence 8 b by a movement of the Aux *haben* ('have').

3. *Geol.* = *transform fault*, sense 4 below.

[**1965** J. T. Wilson in *Nature* 24 July 343/1 A junction where one feature [marking a mobile belt] changes into another is here called a transform.] **1971** *Geol. Mag.* CVIII. 27 It appears that there is a mechanical advantage in overcoming overall transtension by stepped transforms. **1978** *Nature* 16 Feb. 617/1 (*caption*) The three transforms are shown by dashed lines and their possible extensions by dotted lines.

4. *Comb.*: **transform fault** *Geol.*, a transcurrent fault terminating abruptly at both ends, *esp.* one that connects two segments of an oceanic ridge; also, any transcurrent fault associated with two lithospheric plates sliding past one another; hence **transform faulting**.

1965 J. T. Wilson in *Nature* 24 July 343/2 It is proposed that a separate class of horizontal shear faults exists which terminate abruptly at both ends, but which nevertheless may show great displacements... The name transform fault is proposed for the class. **1973** *Ibid.* 10 Aug. 341/2 The boundaries between the rigid plates which make up the Earth's crust are..of three distinct kinds: ridges..; trenches ..; transform faults, along which plates may slip relative to each other. **1976** *Ibid.* 4 Mar. 14/1 There are several transcurrent faults in solid continental rocks which, because they happen to terminate at structural features which 'absorb' their motion, must also be termed 'transform faults' according to Wilson's strict definition. **1980** *Guardian* 20 Nov. 13/4 There are fault boundaries, known as transform faults, along which the plates merely slide past each other. **1971** *Geol. Mag.* CVIII. 27 The sinuous zone of fission as it extends the length of the north and south Atlantic Ocean is necessarily in many places oblique to the direction of spreading. This situation is generally..accommodated by transform faulting.

transformable (trɑːnsˈfɔːməb(ə)l, træns-, -nz-), *a.* [f. as prec. + -able.] That may be transformed; capable of transformation.

1674 Grew *Mixture* iii. §1 All Principles are immutable; as we have above proved; and, therefore, not generable, formable, or transformable. **1870** H. Spencer *Princ. Psychol.* I. vi. §47 (ed. 2) 117 If the psychical force known as effort were transformable into a constant quantity of physical force. **1875** Poste *Gaius* iii. Comm. (ed. 2) 358 An obligation..is always transformable, in the eye of the law, into the payment of a certain sum of money. **1902** J. Larmor in *Encycl. Brit.* XXVIII. 166/2 Constituents.. transformable into each other by chemical or physical action. **1904** *Daily Chron.* 28 Oct. 8/5 Justice..is such a transformable quality, that it is somewhat difficult to define it.

Hence **transformaˈbility**.

1875 POSTE *Gaius* III. Comm. (ed. 2) 358 This transformability of all Objects of obligation into money payments.

trans'formance. *rare.* [f. as prec. + -ANCE: cf. *performance*.] = TRANSFORMATION.
1611 CHAPMAN *May Day* II. iv, Take such a transformance, as you may be sure will keepe you from discouery. **1867** G. GILFILLAN *Night* vii. 220 Small need of such transformance upon thee.

transformant (tra:ns'fɔ:mənt, træns-, -nz-). *Biol.* [f. TRANSFORM *v.* + -ANT[1].] **a.** A transformed bacterium (see TRANSFORM *v.* 1 f). **b.** = *transformed cell* s.v. TRANSFORMED *ppl. a.* b.
1957 *Biochimica & Biophysica Acta* XXVI. 71 The yield of transformants is determined by the prior state of competence of a pneumococcal culture. **1959** *Jrnl. Exper. Med.* CIX. 437 Capsulated transformants producing type II polysaccharide have been obtained by reactions between a number of R mutants of type II pneumococcus. **1971** *New Scientist* 8 Apr. 83/2 Cells selected from a population of transformants by virtue of their resistance to agglutination by concanavalin A, grow to a density expected of untransformed rather than transformed cells. **1980** *Amer. Jrnl. Trop. Med. & Hygiene* XXIX. 1045/1 *(caption)* Transformant clones were plated in duplicate.

†**trans'formate,** *ppl. a. Obs. rare.* [ad. L. *transformāt-us*, pa. pple. of *transformāre* to TRANSFORM.] = TRANSFORMED.
1571 DIGGES *Pantom.* IV. Hh iij b, Then is the superficial capacitie of the transformed Octaedrons Hexagonal playnes, equal to the whole superficies of Tetraedron transformate. *Ibid.* Iij, The lesse semidiameter of the transformate Dodecaedrons trigonall bases.

transformation (tra:nsfɔ:'meɪʃən, træns-, -nz-). [ad. late L. *transformātiōn-em* (Jerome, *a* 400), n. of action from *transformāre* to TRANSFORM. Cf. F. *transformation* (14th c. in Hatz.-Darm.).] The action of transforming or fact of being transformed.

1. a. The action of changing in form, shape, or appearance; metamorphosis.
1432–50 tr. *Higden* (Rolls) II. 209 Monstruous transformaciones of men in to bestes be made..thro charmes of wicches. **1548** UDALL *Erasm. Par. Mark* i. 5 b, Transformacions and naturall chaungynges of thynges. **1555** EDEN *Decades* 43 *margin*, Fables much lyke Ouide his transformations. **1596** SHAKS. *1 Hen. IV*, I. i. 44 Vpon whose dead corpes there was such misuse, Such beastly, shamelesse transformation. **1794** SULLIVAN *View Nat.* I. 112 Matter is capable of many seeming transformations, but no real transmutations have ever been discovered. **1864** BRYCE *Holy Rom. Emp.* xv. 260 No more than a man feels that perpetual transformation by which his body is renewed from year to year.

†**b.** A changed form; a person or thing transformed. *Obs. rare.*
1598 SHAKS. *Merry W.* IV. v. 98 If it should come to the eare of the Court, how I haue beene transformed; and how my transformation hath beene washd, and cudgeld.

c. *Theatr.* More fully *transformation scene*: A mechanical disclosing scene in a pantomime; *spec.* the scene in which the principal performers were transformed in view of the audience into the players of the ensuing harlequinade.
1859 *Punch* 5 Feb. 58/2, I have supped full of gorgeous transformations on which paint, coloured foils, Dutch metal ..have been lavished. **1881** *Playgoer* 1 Jan., A magnificent Transformation, a charming Watteau ballet scene. **1881** G. A. SALA in *Illustr. Lond. News* 1 Jan. 3/2 Two Grand Transformation Scenes. **1885** W. J. LAWRENCE in *The Theatre* Dec. 329 The account of the sixth scene is worthy of quotation, smacking as it does of the modern 'Transformation'. **1885** —— in *Let.*, During the Grimaldi era the term 'transformation scene' referred to that particular juncture of the performance at which the good fairy changed the hero and heroine and their two persecutors in full view of the audience into Harlequin, Columbine, Clown and Pantaloon respectively.

2. *transf.* A complete change in character, condition, etc.
1581 PETTIE *Guazzo's Civ. Conv.* II. (1586) 81 The simple soules not perceiuing that this their transformation or rather deformation, is no more seene than a pose in a mans face. **1602** SHAKS. *Ham.* II. ii. 5 Something haue you heard Of Hamlets transformation: so I call it, Since not th' exterior, nor the inward man Resembles that it was. **1746–7** HERVEY *Medit.* (1818) 59 To behold the prodigious transformation which has taken place on every individual. **1833** ALISON *Hist. Europe* I. i. §60. 104 The transformation of France.. from a feudal Confederacy..to a compact and absolute monarchy. **1900** R. J. DRUMMOND *Apost. Teach. & Christ's Teach.* ix. 347 A regenerative transformation of humanity is practicable.

3. In scientific uses. **a.** *Zool.* Change of form in animal life, as in the successive transformations of insects, etc.; metamorphosis.
1638 MAYNE *Lucian* (1664) 45 A Polypus I have seen, but would gladly learn its transformation from you. **1667** E. KING in *Phil. Trans.* II. 427 The black Speck..cast out of the Maggot in her transformation. **1774** GOLDSM. *Nat. Hist.* (1776) VIII. 7 Of the Transformations of the Caterpillar into its corresponding Butterfly or Moth. **1874** LUBBOCK *Orig. & Met. Ins.* i. 4 Linnæus classed them among the Coleoptera, from which however they differ in their transformations.

b. *Physiol.* and *Path.* Change of form or substance in an organ, tissue, vital fluid, etc.
1834 J. FORBES *Laennec's Dis. Chest* (ed. 4) 587 Interstitial deposition, which..constitutes what is commonly termed transformation of the organ into a cancerous substance. **1843** J. A. SMITH *Product. Farming* (ed. 2) 75 The excrementitious matters of one organ come in contact with another during their passage through the plant or animal, and, in consequence, suffer new transformations. **1860** MAYNE *Expos. Lex.*, *Transformation*, term for a morbid change in a part, consisting in the conversion of its texture into one of a different kind, as of the soft parts into bone or cartilage.

c. *Math.* Change of form without alteration of quantity or value; substitution of one geometrical figure for another of equal magnitude but different form, as of a prism for a cylinder, or of one algebraical expression or equation for another of the same value; †formerly, also, alteration of the form of a solid figure by truncation of the solid angles: cf. TRANSFIGURED, TRANSFORMED. Also, a change of any mathematical entity in accordance with some definite rule or rules; the rules themselves; *spec.* = MAPPING *vbl. sb.* 2.
transformation of co-ordinates, an inaccurate but accepted expression for the substitution of a new set of co-ordinates, involving a transformation of the equation of the locus. Hence, in the case in which the new co-ordinates are measured in a different plane or space, *transformation* is extended to the relation of correspondence between the original and resulting loci, as in projection.
1571 DIGGES *Pantom.* Epist. *ij b, A Discourse Geometricall of the fiue regulare or Platonicall bodyes [with] the manifolde proportions arising by mutuall conference of these solides Inscription, Circumscription or Transformation. **1706** PHILLIPS (ed. Kersey), *Transformation of an Equation*, (in Algebra) the changing of any Equation into one that is more easy. **1882** MINCHIN *Unipl. Kinemat.* 234 It will be convenient to speak of this quantity *K* as a modulus of transformation. **1885** WATSON & BURBURY *Math. Th. Electr. & Magn.* I. 157 The method of transformation used with conjugate functions. **1908** [see LORENTZ]. **1909** *Proc. Section Sci. K. Akad. van Wetenschappen te Amsterdam* XI. 798 A continuous one-one transformation in itself of a singly connected, onesided, closed surface leaves at least one point invariant. **1941** BIRKHOFF & MACLANE *Surv. Mod. Algebra* vi. 128 The 'similarity' transformations of space—those one-one transformations which multiply all distances by a constant factor. **1949** S. LEFSCHETZ *Introd. Topol.* i. 29 If *f* is one to one and bicontinuous (both *f* and its inverse f^{-1} continuous), *f* is said to be a topological transformation or a homeomorphism. **1952** E. T. BELL *Mathematics* vi. 354 The numerical value of f(t) is unaltered when we replace the variable *t* by the linear expression *t* + 1... Thus, the value of the function is invariant under a particular linear transformation. **1958, 1964** [see MAPPING *vbl. sb.* 2]. **1964** [see FOURIER]. **1966** S. BEER *Decision & Control* vi. 109 It is possible to specify a transformation that will map the infinite set of natural numbers on to this other finite set. **1982** D. M. SCHNEIDER et al. *Linear Algebra* v. 181 If *V* and *W* are vector spaces, a function or transformation *T* from *V* into *W* is a rule that associates with every vector *x* in *V* a unique vector in *W*.

d. *Physics.* Change of form of a substance from solid to liquid, from liquid or solid to gaseous, or the reverse; *Chem.* change of chemical composition, as by replacement of one constituent of a compound by another.
1857 MILLER *Elem. Chem.* (1862) III. 67 In order to effect these transformations it is necessary to displace the hydrogen of the acid.

e. Change of energy from one form into another.
1877 W. GARNETT in *Encycl. Brit.* VII. 583/2 The subject of which natural philosophy treats is the transformation of energy, which in all its phases takes place in accordance with two great principles known respectively as the principles of the conservation and the dissipation of energy. **1878** —— *ibid.* VIII. 207/2 If subsequently we allow an equal amount of energy to undergo various intermediate transformations, but to be finally reduced to heat. **1902** *Ibid.* XXIX. 158 In succeeding years [from 1840] he [Joule] published a series of valuable researches on the agency of electricity in transformations of energy.

f. *Electr.* Change of a current into one of different potential, or different type, or both, as by a transformer (TRANSFORMER 2). Also *attrib.*
1884 *Electrical Rev.* 26 July 64 Conditions for arranging a transformation coil, as regards its yield. **1911** *Encycl. Brit.* XXVII. 173/1 Transformers may be distinguished..in accordance with the type of transformation they effect.

g. *Physics.* Change of one element into another, whether artificially induced or by spontaneous decay. Cf. TRANSMUTATION 3 a.
1902 RUTHERFORD in *Phil. Mag.* IV. 395 These changes must be occurring within the atom, and the radioactive elements must be undergoing spontaneous transformation. **1926** R. W. LAWSON tr. *Hevesy & Paneth's Man. Radioactivity* xxi. 150 Similar attempts to influence the velocity of transformation of uranium and radium D, by subjecting them to the action of radiation, have also led to a negative result. **1958** O. R. FRISCH *Nucl. Handbk.* IV. 4 In each unit of time a certain definite fraction of the total number of the atoms present will disintegrate but there is nothing to indicate the moment at which a given atom will undergo the radioactive transformation. **1969** *Times* 12 Mar. 4/8 It is to be assumed that the uranium and thorium in the galaxy were created by the nuclear transformation within densely packed matter at high temperatures.

h. *Molecular Biol.* The genetic alteration of a bacterial cell by the introduction or absorption of extraneous DNA (see TRANSFORM *v.* 1 f).
1928 F. GRIFFITH in *Jrnl. Hygiene* XXVII. 154 Experiments with culture heated at temperatures higher than 60°C. have rarely been successful in causing transformation of type. **1960** *New Biol.* XXXI. 72 The first clear demonstration of transformation was made in 1928 by Griffith, who discovered that an avirulent and normally harmless strain of pneumococcus was changed into a virulent strain when injected into mice together with some virulent pneumococci that had been thoroughly killed by heating. **1970** AMBROSE & EASTY *Cell Biol.* x. 346 Transformation is a very inefficient process but has proved useful for gene mapping in bacteria where a suitable transducing phage is not known. **1980** *Sci. Amer.* Feb. 36/2 In another process, known as transformation, DNA released by cell death or other natural processes simply enters a new cell from the environment by penetrating the cell wall and membrane.

i. *Cytology.* The modification of a eukaryotic (nucleated) cell so that it comes to possess some or all of the characteristics of a cancer cell.
1943 *Jrnl. Nat. Cancer Inst.* IV. 202/1 The cell transformations appeared after a definite latent interval of several weeks following initial exposure to the carcinogen. **1967** *Nature* 8 July 171/2 The concept of contact inhibition has attracted particular interest since the advent of tissue culture investigations on neoplastic transformation. **1982** *Sci. Amer.* Mar. 71/1 Transformation..is due to the action of a gene, which must be expressed continuously to maintain the cancerous state.

j. *Linguistics.* An operation by which one syntactic structure is converted into another by the application of specific rules; a rule converting deep structure to surface structure (see *deep structure* s.v. DEEP *a.* IV c, *surface structure* s.v. SURFACE *sb.* 6 d); the process by which surface structures are generated.
1955 N. CHOMSKY *Transformational Analysis* (Ph.D. Dissertation, Univ. Pennsylvania). 27 A sentence *X* is related to a sentence *Y* if, under some transformation set up for the language, *X* is a transform of *Y* or *Y* is a transform of *X*. **1957** —— *Syntactic Structures* (1962) v. 44 Let us call each such rule a 'grammatical transformation'. **1957** Z. S. HARRIS in *Language* XXXIII. 283 We can proceed to define transformation..based on two structures having the same set of individual co-occurrences. This relation yields unique analyses of certain structures and distinctions which could not be analyzed in ordinary linguistic terms. **1964** *Word* XX. 429 Transformations..may be thought of as manipulations—reordering, combination, addition, deletion —performed on fully formed sentences. **1964** R. H. ROBINS *Gen. Linguistics* vi. 242 Transformation is a method of stating how the structures of many sentences in languages can be generated or explained formally as the result of specific transformations applied to certain basic sentence structures. **1967** D. G. HAYS *Introd. Computational Linguistics* viii. 153 Such a transformation can break down the structure of one sentence and insert all or part of it at a specified place in the structure of the other. **1977** *Canad. Jrnl. Linguistics 1976* XXI. 156 The traditional assumption that transformations do not change meanings.

4. An artificial head of hair worn by women.
1901 *Daily News* 12 Jan. 6/7 Buying toupées, or even 'transformations', as those wigs are called which entirely cover the natural hair. **1903** *Westm. Gaz.* 6 Aug. 3/2 Hairdressers are known to make most of their returns by the producing of these transformations. **1906** *Referee* 9 Dec. 11/4 When he got to the exit door he discovered to his horror that he had dragged off the lady's 'transformation', and it was hanging to his sleeve-link.

5. *attrib.* and *Comb.*: **transformation (playing) card**, a playing card on which the suit signs are incorporated into a design or picture; **transformation-dancer** (*Theatr.*), one who dances successively in several costumes and characters; **transformation-jewel**, a jewel which may be worn in several ways; **transformation product**, *Chem.* a new compound formed by the decomposition or destructive distillation of a complex compound often existing in nature; **transformation scene**: see 1 c.
[**1848** W. A. CHATTO *Facts & Speculations on Origin & Hist. Playing Cards* iv. 260 In 1811 two different packs of caricature cards, imitated..from the picture-cards in Cotta's Almanack, appeared in England... On the wrapper of both packs the inscription is the same: 'Metastasis. Transformation of Playing-cards.'] **1892** *Daily News* 29 Jan. 7/2 She was engaged generally upon the music hall stage... Her peculiar branch was transformation dancing... She was well known as a transformation dancer. **1892** *Pall Mall G.* 17 Mar. 1/3 French jewellers are devoting all their inventive genius to new designs for the setting of these transformation jewels. **1931** H. T. MORLEY *Old & Curious Playing Cards* 152 Transformation cards, 1828. A pack of 52 cards,.. printed from wood blocks. **1960** H. HAYWARD *Antique Coll.* 286/2 *Transformation playing cards*, first issued in London 1808... Making transformation cards from ordinary packs became a fashionable pastime, pen and ink converting cards into designs of topical or personal association. **1966** S. MANN *Collecting Playing Cards* viii. 164 Transformation cards are a rather different case... Their aim is to 'transform' an ordinary pip card into a picture by means of incorporating the pips in their standard positions in a larger overall design.

Hence **transfor'mationist**, (*a*) = TRANSFORMIST 2; (*b*) = TRANSFORMATIONALIST *sb.*
1888 MAX MÜLLER *Nat. Relig.* vi. (1889) 143 We ought to be transformationists and no longer evolutionists. **1962** J. SLEDD in Householder & Saporta *Probl. Lexicogr.* 145 The transformationists..have little interest in pedagogic problems. **1965** *Language* XLI. 124 A Czech study on the structure of German sentences..is contrasted with a study on the same subject by an American transformationist.

transfor'mational, *a.* [f. TRANSFORMATION + -AL[1].] Of or pertaining to transformation; *spec.* in *Linguistics*, of or pertaining to a transformation or transformations (sense 3 j); (more fully ***transformational-generative*** adj.) designating, of, or pertaining to a linguistic model or method of analysis based on the generation of surface structures from underlying structures by transformations; cf. GENERATIVE *a.* 2 b and *TG* s.v. T 6 a.

1894 *Athenæum* 10 Nov. 646/2 The distinction between 'combinational' and 'transformational' theories of experience. **1955** N. CHOMSKY (*title of Ph.D. Dissertation, Univ. Pennsylvania*) Transformational analysis. **1957** —— *Syntactic Structures* (1962) v. 46 Corresponding to the level of phrase structure, a grammar has a sequence of rules of the form $X \rightarrow Y$, and corresponding to lower levels it has a sequence of morphophonemic rules of the same basic form. Linking these two sequences, it has a sequence of transformational rules. *Ibid.* ix. 101 The similarity between active-passive, negation, declarative-interrogative, and other transformational relations would not have come to light if the active-passive relation had been investigated exclusively in terms of such notions as synonymity. **1961** P. H. MATTHEWS in *Archivum Linguisticum* XIII. 196 (*heading*) Transformational grammar. **1963** F. G. LOUNSBURY in J. A. Fishman *Readings Sociol. of Lang.* (1968) 48 One result of transformational analysis . . is to lead linguistics a step closer to a general model for the syntax of language. **1964** R. H. ROBINS *Gen. Linguistics* p. xviii, One of the most striking developments in linguistics in the last few years has been the increasing recognition of the transformational model of linguistic statement. *Ibid.* p. xix, Some transformationalists, as the adherents of transformational-generative grammar are called. **1964** E. A. NIDA *Toward Sci. Transl.* iv. 60 There are some psychological confirmations of transformational theory which seem to have special significance. **1965** *N.Y. Times* 29 Dec. 32 Transformational grammar grew in part from M.I.T. computer experiments to produce mechanical translations of foreign languages. **1966** T. F. MITCHELL in C. E. Bazell *In Memory of J. R. Firth* 354 One cannot help but be puzzled by the refusal of American transformational-generative grammarians to incorporate in their valuable work collocational study of the kind envisaged here. **1966** Y. BAR-HILLEL in *Automatic Transl. of Lang.* (NATO Summer School, Venice, 1962) 7 Transformational grammars seem to have a much better chance of being both adequate and practical. *Ibid.* 12 The fifth aspect of syntactic complexity is, then, transformational history. **1967** [see GENERATIVIST]. **1968** CHOMSKY & HALLE *Sound Pattern Eng.* ii. 15 These observations suggest a general principle for the application of rules of the phonological component, namely, what we shall call the principle of the 'transformational cycle'. **1972** *Language* XLVIII. 442 Arens fails to show . . the essential ideas and assumptions underlying transformational-generative theory. **1973** *Amer. Speech 1969* XLIV. 220 The discussion of Middle English grammar and phonology is based on a transformational-generative view of language. **1973** *Archivum Linguisticum* IV. 35 Presumably, in transformational terms, transitive, intransitive, perfective, imperfective . . are here surface structure categories. **1976** J. HOOPER *Introd. Natural Generative Phonol.* i. 4 The phonological rules . . apply in sequential order. . . Each rule may apply only once, and is assigned a particular place in the sequence or is said to be *ordered* with respect to other rules. The theory with this general form will be referred to as transformational generative phonology. **1977** *Dædalus* Fall 119 The proper division of theoretical labor between rewriting and transformational rules (in particular, how to limit the power of the transformational rules in intuitively reasonable ways) has been a central concern of those who have worked with this conception of grammar. **1980** *Word 1979* XXX. 132 Some degree of exposure to transformational-generative grammar, case grammar and other theoretical approaches is evident in several [Vietnamese] works. **1980** *Canad. Jrnl. Linguistics* XXV. I. 1 The standard theory referred to as transformational generative phonology. **1980** *English World-Wide* I. I. 133 Transformational grammar has shown itself unable to handle the problem of the description of varieties which are as apparent in the 16th and 17th centuries as at the present day.

Hence in *Linguistics*: **transfor'mationalism**, transformational theory; **transfor'mationalist** *sb.*, an adherent of transformational theory; also *attrib.* or as *adj.*; **transfor'mationally** *adv.*, by means of transformation(s), according to transformational rules.

1963 *Amer. Speech* XXXVIII. 240 These attributives can be related transformationally to predications. **1964** E. BACH *Introd. Transformational Gram.* viii. 187 The transformationalists have provided elegant and powerful tools for the description of particular languages. **1969** *Neuphilologische Mitteilungen* LXX. 221 Chomskyan transformationalism rejects a scientific approach for an anti-scientific one. **1973** *Amer. Speech 1970* XLV. 125 A question that challenged the structuralist linguistic theory . . and that seems no more amenable to a transformationalist solution. **1976** *Archivum Linguisticum* VII. 155 It is interestingly novel, however, within the framework of contemporary transformationalism in America. **1977** *Dædalus* Fall 119 If the interrogative sentence 'Are the men here?' is derived transformationally from the phrase structure underlying the declarative sentence 'The men are here', it would seem to imply that a speaker first thinks of the declarative sentence and then transforms it into the interrogative form. **1978** *Language* LIV. 174 Raimo Anttila's 'Revelation as linguistic revolution' . . reads like an extemporaneous sermon on the wickedness of the transformationalists. **1980** *English World-Wide* I. 268 The neglect of the results of earlier scholarship on the part of young linguists, especially of the transformationalist school.

transformative (trɑːnsˈfɔːmətɪv, træns-, -nz-), *a.* [ad. med.L. *transformātīvus* (Albertus Mag. *a* 1280), f. ppl. stem of L. *transformāre* to TRANSFORM: see -ATIVE. Cf. F. *transformatif* (neologism in Littré).]

a. Having the faculty of transforming; fitted or tending to transform.

1671 FLAVEL *Fount. Life* x. 30 The Light of Christ is powerfully Transformative of its Subjects. **1681** —— *Meth. Grace* xxviii. 484 All communion with God is assimilating, and transformative of the soul into his image. **1806** A. KNOX *Rem.* (1844) I. 20 This high, heavenly, transformative Christianity. **1893** J. PULSFORD *Loyalty to Christ* II. 47 The One Divine formative and transformative Form.

b. *Linguistics.* = TRANSFORMATIONAL *a.*, *spec.* in ***transformative-generative*** adj.

1962 P. STREVENS *Papers in Lang.* (1965) v. 73 The three major modern linguistic theories (*i.e.* phoneme-morpheme grammar, transformative-generative grammar, and system-structure grammar). **1965** *Language* XLI. 213 Recent interest taken by transformative-generative linguists in unidirectional transformations and unique derivations.

† **transfor'mator.** *Obs. rare*$^{-1}$. [agent-n., in L. form, from L. *transformāre* to TRANSFORM.] = TRANSFORMER.

1617 COLLINS *Def. Bp. Ely* II. x. 420 No Transformators, no such sauage *Sarcophagi*, as S. Cyrill bends his penne against.

transformed (trɑːnsˈfɔːmd, træns-, -nz-), *ppl. a.* [f. TRANSFORM *v.* + -ED^{1}.]

a. Changed in form or character; in *Math.*, altered in form, but not in value. (In quot. 1413, 'misshapen'.)

In quot. 1571 applied to a solid figure modified by truncation of the solid angles (cf. TRANSFIGURED in same sense).

1413 *Pilgr. Sowle* (Caxton 1483) IV. xxiv. 70 Beres ben brought forthe al fowle and transformyd. **1571** DIGGES *Pantom.* IV. Gg ij, A Transfourmed Cube is a figure geometrical enuironed with 6 equiangle Octogonall and 8 equilater triangular playnes or bases, whose sides are all equall. *Ibid.* Hh ij, A Transformed Dodecaedron. **1743** EMERSON *Fluxions* 29 Proceed thus till the transform'd Fluxion be as simple as possible. **1841** LANE *Arab. Nts.* I. 65 *note*, It was not imagined that this brute was the lost man in a transformed state. **1885** WATSON & BURBURY *Math. Th. Electr. & Magn.* I. 157 By substituting the coordinates . . and placing on corresponding elements the same charges, the transformed system will be in equilibrium. **1904** J. OMAN *Vis. & Author.* III. iii. 190 The first Apostles, the humble, loyal, transformed ambassadors of Christ.

b. ***transformed cell*** (Cytology), a eukaryotic cell which has undergone transformation (TRANSFORMATION 3 i).

1956 *Science* 23 Mar. 503/2 The malignant nature of the transformed cells was demonstrated by the production of sarcomas when the cultures were inoculated into animals of the same strain. **1979** ARMS & CAMP *Biology* xvi. 247 Transformed cells often undergo drastic changes in morphology and metabolism such that they become unresponsive to the normal controls over cell division.

trans'former. [f. as prec. + -ER^{1}.]

1. One who or that which transforms.

1601 DEACON & WALKER *Spirits & Divels* 208 He is no creatour of substances, no transformer of natures. **1765** J. BROWN *Chr. Jrnl.* (1814) 150 Sin, horrid transformer, how hast thou changed our God! **1883** J. D. FULTON *Sam Hobart* 18 The steam locomotive, the material transformer of the world.

2. *Electr.* An apparatus which transforms continuous currents from one voltage to another, or continuous into alternating currents or *vice versa*. (After F. *transformateur* (Hospitalier, 1882).) In mod. use, a static apparatus in which an alternating or pulsating current in one winding induces an alternating current in a second winding, usu. with different values of voltage and current.

1883 tr. HOSPITALIER *Mod. Applications of Electr.* (ed. 2) I. 141 We designate by the term electric transformers apparatus in which electricity is no longer produced directly, but is transformed and changes its properties. **1884** *Electrical Rev.* 26 July 64 The present transformers, those of MM. Goulard and Gibbs, are . . very similar to bobbins. **1886** G. FORBES in *Electrician* 26 Feb. 315 Induction coils used in this way have been called secondary generators or transformers. **1888** S. P. THOMPSON *Dynamo-electric Mach.* 484 For transforming from high pressures to low, several kinds of apparatus are known, namely:— . . Induction-coils, also called for this purpose Secondary Generators, or Transformers, or Converters. **1891** *Times* 28 Sept. 13/6 From the transformer the currents are led to the four collecting rings of the motor, and a continuous current is taken off its commutator. **1911** *Encycl. Brit.* XXVII. 173 A continuous current transformer is an appliance which effects a similar transformation for continuous currents, with the difference that some part of the machine must revolve. **1947** R. LEE *Electronic Transformers & Circuits* vii. 187 Line impedance changes abruptly, and transformers may be necessary for good power transfer. **1955** *Sci. News Let.* 15 Oct. 248/3 A transformer is a device very widely used to increase or lower the voltage of an electric current.

b. *attrib.*, as ***transformer chamber***, ***house***, ***station***. **transformer oil**, a high-grade oil with a low sludge content used to cool and insulate transformers and other electrical equipment.

1888 *Scribner's Mag.* Aug. 196/2 The development of a radically new and very interesting system, known as the secondary or transformer system. **1891** *Pall Mall G.* 12 Sept. 6/2 It furnishes the current for feeding 1,200 glow-lamps, partly fixed to a large frame in the transformer room, partly to a sort of signboard outside the hall. **1894** *Westm. Gaz.* 1 May 7/2 The current is conveyed to Rome on four copper cables. . . Outside the Porta Pia . . it enters a transformer-house, where its pressure is reduced from 5,000 to 2,000 volts. **1904** *Electric Club Jrnl.* I. 228 By transformer oil is meant an oil in which the transformer is completely immersed, forming a homogeneous insulation. **1957** E. B. JONES *Instrument Technol.* III. I. 19 The variable resistance at the transmitter end is immersed in transformer oil which keeps it free from dirt. **1979** *Electr. Rev. Internat.* 7 Dec. 47/3 Transformer oil becomes highly viscous at low temperature.

trans'formerless, *a.* [-LESS.] That does not have a transformer; also, produced without the use of a transformer.

1949 B. GROB *Basic Television* xxii. 498 (*heading*) Transformerless television receiver. **1975** *Physics Bull.* Feb. 81/2 This has been achieved by using a transformerless supply and an aluminium casting for the frame.

trans'forming, *vbl. sb.* [f. as TRANSFORMER + -ING^{1}.] The action of the vb. TRANSFORM; transformation.

1435 MISYN *Fire of Love* 40 Qwhat is lufe bott transfourmynge of desire In to þe þinge lufyd? **1580** HOLLYBAND *Treas. Fr. Tong*, *Transfiguration*, a transforming. **1633** P. FLETCHER *Purple Isl.* VI. lv, With quick and strange transforming. **1883** J. T. BURGESS in *Athenæum* 3 Nov. 569/1 The transforming of the south transept into the vestry.

trans'forming, *ppl. a.* [f. as prec. + -ING^{2}.]

a. That transforms.

a **1653** BINNING *Serm.* (1845) 10 Love is an uniting and transforming thing. **1827** KEBLE *Chr. Y.*, *13th Sunday Trin.* xviii, Our . . Saviour's face . . Bent on us with transforming power. **1842** I. WILLIAMS *Baptistery* I. ix. (1874) 107, I gaz'd Upon the footsteps of transforming time. **1907** W. M. RAMSAY in *Expositor* Jan. 72 The transforming hand of man was applied to it.

b. ***transforming principle*** (Biol.), a substance that genetically transforms bacterial cells (TRANSFORM *v.* 1 f).

1944 *Jrnl. Exper. Med.* LXXIX. 155 If the results of the present study on the chemical nature of the transforming principle are confirmed, then nucleic acids must be regarded as possessing biological specificity the chemical nature of which is as yet undetermined. **1965** PEACOCKE & DRYSDALE *Molecular Basis Heredity* iii. 13 The transforming principle has two properties characteristic of genes, namely, determination of a specific inheritable property and self-reproduction.

Hence **trans'formingly** *adv.*

1865 H. BUSHNELL *Vicar. Sacr.* ii. (1868) 68 He could not so powerfully and transformingly impress the fact. **1874** GEO. ELIOT *Coll. Breakf. P.* 771 That energy Which moves transformingly in root and branch.

transformism (trɑːnsˈfɔːmɪz(ə)m, træns-). [a. F. *transformisme* (Broca, *Congrès d'anthropol.* 1867, p. 401), f. *transformer* to TRANSFORM: see -ISM.]

1. *Biol.* The hypothesis that existing species are the product of the gradual transformation of other forms of living beings (*loosely*, such transformation itself); any form of the doctrine of evolution of species.

1878 BARTLEY tr. *Topinard's Anthrop.* III. i. 527 Direct proofs as to transformism are not wanting. **1880** HUXLEY *Crayfish* vi. 318 We may suppose that crayfishes have resulted from the modification of some other form of living matter; this is what, to borrow a useful word from the French language, is known as . . *transformism.* **1880** *Nature* 27 Jan. 307/1 Degraded plants, affording remarkable specimens of natural transformism. **1883** TYLOR in *Nature* 3 May 8/2 These processes of development, or evolution, or transformism were long ago recognised to no small extent by ethnologists.

2. The doctrine of gradual evolution of moral and social relations: *loosely*, such evolution itself.

1885 *Athenæum* 17 Oct. 510/2 The transformist 'conference' at Paris last year was an eloquent lecture by M. Ch. Letourneau on the evolution of morals. The concluding remarks are as follows: 'In that which relates to education, I am sorry to differ entirely from the principal founder of transformism in morals, H. Spencer'. **1894** *Liberal* 24 Nov. 51/2 A laboratory in which the process of social transformism is carried on.

transformist (trɑːnsˈfɔːmɪst, træns-). [In sense 1, f. TRANSFORM *v.* + -IST; in sense 2, a. F. *transformiste* (Broca, 1867, as in prec.).]

1. One who is occupied in transforming. *humorous nonce-use.*

1799 J. MACGOWAN *Dial. Devils* i. 11 As for the barbers, they are a set of transformists, established wholly by my dexterity.

2. An adherent of transformism. Also *attrib.* or as *adj.*

a **1879** PUSEY in *Athenæum* 19 July 83/1 We think the transformist theories a mere imagination. **1885** [see prec. 2.]. **1890** *Pop. Sc. Monthly* Dec. 257 Agardh . . was a little too earnest a transformist, and believed that certain algæ could become animals.

Hence **transfor'mistic** *a.*, of or pertaining to transformism or transformists.

1887 *Nature* 24 Feb. 389/2 In the chapter on the first appearance of man, the various transformistic theories are passed in review.

† **transformity.** *Obs. nonce-wd.* [f. TRANSFORM, after *conformity*.] The state or condition of being transformed.

1622 T. STOUGHTON *Chr. Sacr.* xiii. 175 The next words are, *But be ye transformed. . .* A plaine opposition betwixt that before, and this now spoken; betwixt that conformitie to this world, and this transformitie.

† **trans'found,** *v. Obs. rare*$^{-1}$. [f. TRANS- 2 + FOUND *v.*^{3}; cf. L. *transfundĕre* to TRANSFUSE.] *trans.* To recast (metal) *into* (some other form).

a **1649** DRUMM. OF HAWTH. *Consid. to Parl.* Wks. (1711) 186 That all bells of steeples . . be taken down and transfounded into pieces of ordnance.

† **'transfretate**, *v. Obs. rare*^−1^. = TRANSFRETE.
1653 URQUHART *Rabelais* II. vi, We transfretate the Sequan at the dilucul and crepuscul.

† **transfre'tation.** *Obs.* [ad. late L. *transfretātiōn-em*, n. of action f. *transfretāre*: see next.] The action of crossing or passing over a strait, channel, or narrow sea.
1612 DAVIES *Why Ireland*, etc. (1747) 69 Since the last transfretation of King Richard the Second. *c* **1645** HOWELL *Lett.* IV. xxiii, She had a rough passage in her transfretation to Dover Castle. **1768** H. WALPOLE *Hist. Doubts* 90 Of this transfretation and Christening, Perkin, in his supposed confession, says not a word. **1782** S. PEGGE *Cur. Misc.* 60 Henry 2. levied numerous subsidies.. for his transfretations (to use a Monkish word) into foreign parts.

† **trans'frete**, *v. Obs.* Also 6 -fret, 7 -freat; *erron.* 6 -freit, 6-7 -freight. [ad. L. *transfretāre*, f. TRANS- + *fretum* a strait, channel; cf. OF. *transfreter* (*a* 1200 in Godef.).]
1. *intr.* To pass over a strait or narrow sea.
c **1540** tr. *Pol. Verg. Eng. Hist.* (Camden) I. 85 The Emperoure Severus.. desierus to procure the destruction of Albinus, transfreted into Fraunce. *a* **1548** HALL *Chron., Hen. IV* 24 Declaryng also that.. he wold transfret and passe the sea himselfe. **1567** DRANT *Horace, Ep.* vi. Dj, Treasure of greater gaine Then all the chaffer that transfretes from Portugal or Spaine. **1606** WARNER *Alb. Eng.* XIV. xci, Hence for Ireland at the least I must transfreat. **1653** WATERHOUSE *Apol. Learn.* 52 The Saxon Merchants.. Arm and Transfreight, and about the year six hundred eighty nine obtain the Rule over us.
2. *trans.* **a.** To convey across a strait or sea. **b.** To cross (a strait or sea).
1594 ? GREENE *Selimus* Wks. (Grosart) XIV. 266 T'await th' arriuall of some ship That might transfreit vs safely vnto Rhodes. **1595** *Locrine* I. i. 108 We.. transfretting the Illirian sea, Arriued on the coasts of Aquitane. **1611** BRATHWAIT *Gold. Fleece, Sonn.* iv. Gjb, With joyfull mirth.. To haue transfreted such a Sea of woes. **1653** URQUHART *Rabelais* I. xxxiii. 151 Have we not.. travelled and toyled enough, in having transfreted and past over the Hircanian sea?

trans'frontal, *a. Anat.* [TRANS- 5.] Crossing the forehead, or the frontal lobe of the brain.
1889 *Buck's Handbk. Med. Sc.* VIII. 152/1 The union of the subfrontal fissure, deeply with the precentral and the three transfrontal fissures.

trans-'frontier, *a.* [TRANS- 3.] Lying, living, or done beyond the frontier of a country.
1877 LD. LYTTON *Lett.* (1906) II. xv. 481 The rudest and most unmanageable transfrontier chieftains. **1909** *Daily Chron.* 22 Jan. 3/4 A personal history of trans-frontier surveys and boundary demarcations.

† **trans'fude**, *v. Obs. rare.* [irreg. f. L. *transfundĕre* (see TRANSFUSE), perf. tense *transfūd-ī*. Cf. *diffude*, *effude*.] *trans.* **a.** To transmit. **b.** To expend lavishly.
1432-50 tr. *Higden* (Rolls) I. 5 Withowte the sollicitude of writers scholde transfude [L. *transfunderet*] to vs the memory of thynges of antiquite. *Ibid.* VII. 153 So that y myȝhte transfude [L. *transfuderim*, v.r. *transfuderem*] my patrimony to youre utilite.

† **'transfuge.** *Obs. rare.* [a. F. *transfuge* (14th c. in Godef. *Compl.*), ad. L. *transfuga*, f. TRANS- + *fug-ĕre* to flee.] A deserter; a fugitive.
1548 *Privy Council Acts* (1890) II. 186 Certein Frenchemen.. demanded by the French King by treaty as transfuges. **1639** SEDGWICK *Milit. Disc.* 78 When a Souldier renounceth his colours, and becomes a transfuge, and runnes to the enemies side. [**1855** LD. STANHOPE *Let. to Ticknor* 12 May in *Misc.* Ser. II. (1872) 18 The protection of deserters and *transfuges* is the invariable rule of every service in the world.]
So † **'transfuger**, in same sense; † **trans'fugious** *a.*, that is a deserter.
1611 SPEED *Hist. Gt. Brit.* IX. xxiv. (1623) 1170 Scotland, the then Refuge of Traiterous transfugers. *Ibid.* 1181 That transfugious Champion.

† **trans'fume**, *v. Obs. rare.* [ad. L. *transfūmā-re*, f. TRANS- + *fūmāre* to smoke, FUME.]
1623 COCKERAM, *Transfume*, to smoake thorow. **1656** in BLOUNT *Glossogr.*

† **trans'fund**, *v. Obs. rare.* [ad. L. *transfund-ĕre*: see next.] *trans.* = next.
1670 H. STUBBE *Plus Ultra* 121 Because this Transfunding of blood hath hitherto been looked on as the primary Invention. *a* **1677** BARROW *Serm.* (1687) I. viii. 97 Speech, that most natural, proper and easie means of.. conveying, and, as it were, transfunding our thoughts and our passions into each other.

transfuse (trɑːns'fjuːz, træns-), *v.* [f. L. *transfūs-*, ppl. stem of *transfund-ĕre*, f. *trans*, TRANS- + *fundĕre* to pour. Cf. F. *transfuser* (17-18th c. in Hatz.-Darm.).]
1. *trans.* To pour (a liquid) from one vessel or receptacle into another.
1601 HOLLAND *Pliny* XXXIII. vi. II. 473 Ever and anon the troubled water ought to be transfused into a vessell of brasse, and clarified therein. **1664** POWER *Exp. Philos.* I. 4 The stings in all Bees are hollow and tubulous.. so that when they prick the flesh, they do also, through that channel, transfuse the poyson into it. **1755** SMOLLETT *Quix.* II. IV. ii. (1803) IV. 141 Transfusing the contents of the bottles into their own bellies. **1829** *Chapters Phys. Sci.* 189 When water or any.. fluid requires to be transfused from one vessel to another.

2. *transf.* and *fig.* To cause to 'flow' from one to another; to transmit; to diffuse into or through something; to cause to permeate; to instil.
c **1425** *St. Mary of Oignies* II. iv. in *Anglia* VIII. 165/15 As in a lighte [He] transfused hym-selfe purgh alle þe body of þe seke. **1594** HOOKER *Eccl. Pol.* I. x. §12 A naturall delight which man hath to transfuse from himselfe into others. **1605** B. JONSON *Volpone* III. v, Where we may so transfuse our wandering souls Out at our lips. **1618** HALES *Gold. Rem.* II. (1673) 9 The sole way of transfusing the principles of Christianity into men. **1709** SACHEVERELL *Serm.* 15 Aug. 4 It's.. Influence is transfus'd thro' several.. Channels. **1877** MISS A. B. EDWARDS *Up Nile* ix. 240 The sun being.. at its highest and the air transfused with light. **1880** E. WHITE *Cert. Relig.* (1881) 17 Their testimony, and teaching, and life, transfuse that certitude into those who receive their word.
3. *Med.*, etc. To transfer (the blood of a person or animal) into the veins of another; to inject (blood or other fluid) into the veins.
1666 *Phil. Trans.* 353 Take up the Carotidal Artery of the Dog or other Animal, whose Bloud is to be transfused into another of the same or a different Kind. **1743** tr. *Heister's Surg.* 305 The Blood of one Animal is transfused into the Veins of another. **1801** *Med. Jrnl.* V. 565 On transfusing red blood into the temporal artery, the animal remained lively and well.
b. To treat (a person) with transfusion of blood (or of some solution).
1897 *Allbutt's Syst. Med.* II. 948 We transfused the patient with saline solution containing sulphates. **1905** ROLLESTON *Dis. Liver* 268 He was transfused but died the same day.
Hence **transfused** (-'fjuːzd, *poet.* -'fjuːzɪd) *ppl. a.*; **trans'fusing** *vbl. sb.* and *ppl. a.*
1652 BENLOWES *Theoph.* v. liv, The Primum Mobile do's seem immense And doth transfused Influence Through all inferiour Orbs.. dispense. **1667** *Phil. Trans.* II. 490 The Conception of that Transfusing design. **1782** A. MONRO *Compar. Anat.* (ed. 3) Introd. 10 Changing their juices by transfusing of new liquors. **1842** LOUDON *Suburban Hort.* 91 They receive from the atmosphere the transfused light on every side. **1903** MORLEY *Gladstone* I. II. iv. 165 The transfusing alchemy of his rather smoky crucible.

transfuser (trɑːns'fjuːzə(r), træns-). *rare.* [f. prec. + -ER^1^.] One who or that which transfuses.
1889 *Nation* (N.Y.) 17 Oct. 319/2 The transfuser of Corean thought.

transfusible (trɑːns'fjuːzɪb(ə)l, træns-), *a. rare.* [f. L. *transfūs-*, ppl. stem (see TRANSFUSE) + -IBLE: cf. *fusible*.] Capable of being transfused.
1661 BOYLE *Style Scriptures* (1675) 156 Expressions.. whose Penetrancy is as little transfusible into any other as the Sun's dazling Brightness.. can be undetractingly Painted. **1826** MISS MITFORD *Village* Ser. III. 267 She could catch even the zest of a repartee, that most evanescent and least transfusible of all things.

transfusion (trɑːns'fjuːʒən, træns-). [ad. L. *transfūsiōn-em*, n. of action from *transfundĕre* to TRANSFUSE. Cf. F. *transfusion* (1307 in Godef. *Compl.*).] The action of transfusing.
1. The action of pouring a liquid from one vessel into another; also *fig.* transference; transmission; translation.
1578 BANISTER *Hist. Man* I. 14 Nerves.. pass through them [bones].. for the transfusion of sense into other partes. *c* **1645** HOWELL *Lett.* (1650) II. II. xlviii. 61 It is with languages as 'tis with liquors which by transfusion use to take wind from one vessel to another. **1700** DRYDEN *Fables* Pref. (1721) 24, I grant that something must be lost in all transfusion, that is, in all translations. *c* **1780** BURNEY in Boswell *Johnson* (1848) 71/2 *note*, He would find the transfusion into another language extremely difficult. **1835** *Fraser's Mag.* XII. 394 Of all poets, Theocritus is perhaps the least susceptible of transfusion. **1850** GROTE *Greece* II. lxviii. VIII. 595 Such persuasion had grown up gradually.., partly by insensible transfusion from others.
2. *Med.*, etc. The process of transferring the blood of a person or animal into the veins of another; the injection of blood or other fluid into the veins.
1643 *Plain English* 21 As if they.. should, of a sudden, receive a Transfusion of Sheeps Blood from the others. **1678** PHILLIPS s.v., Transfusion of the blood is a late Anatomical invention experimented by the Royal Society. **1802** PALEY *Nat. Theol.* xxv. (ed. 2) 484 The experiment of transfusion proves, that the blood of one animal will serve for another. **1877** ROBERTS *Handbk. Med.* (ed. 3) I. 41 In some cases transfusion of blood is demanded, in order to save life and to replace the blood which has been lost.
3. *attrib.* and *Comb.*, as ***transfusion apparatus***, ***plan***; **transfusion cell** (*Bot.*), one of certain cells which remain thin-walled and thus permit the passage of water to the adjacent tissues; so ***transfusion strand***, ***tissue***.
1832 J. BROWN *Lett.* (1907) 25 Give me the latest information about the transfusion plan, specifying the quantities of salt [etc.]. **1875** BENNETT & DYER tr. *Sachs' Bot.* 466 Cells elongated in a direction transverse to the axis of the leaf.. leaving large intercellular spaces (Transfusion-Tissue of Mohl). **1877** KNIGHT *Dict. Mech.* 2613/2 Aveling's Transfusion-Apparatus. **1898** tr. *Strasburger's Text-bk. Bot.* I. i. 112 Special endodermal cells, directly external to the xylem strands, remain unthickened and serve as transfusion cells. *Ibid.* 111 Transfusion strands.
Hence **trans'fusional** *a.*, occurring as a result of or by means of transfusion; **trans'fusionist**, one who advocates or practises the process of transfusion of blood.
1889 *Pop. Sci. Monthly* Apr. 808 The early transfusionists reasoned, in the style of the Christian Scientists, that the blood is the life. **1965** *Endocrinology* LXXVII. 954 (*heading*) Effect of natural and synthetic corticoids on transfusional shock in the rat. **1974** R. ZELEDÓN in K. Elliott et al. *Trypanosomiasis & Leishmaniasis* 70 Besides the normal mechanism of transmission by the insect, two other modes, the transfusional and transplacental, may be epidemiologically important in the maintenance of the disease. **1982** *Jrnl. Pharm. & Pharmacol.* XXXIV. 730 (*heading*) Pyridoxal complexes as potential chelating agents for oral therapy in transfusional iron overload.

transfusive (trɑːns'fjuːsɪv, træns-), *a.* [f. L. *transfūs-*, ppl. stem (see TRANSFUSE) + -IVE. In med.L. *transfūsīvus* (Albertus Magnus, *a* 1280).] Having the quality of or a tendency to transfusion.
1677 W. HUGHES *Man of Sin* II. iv. 72 The Virgin Mary had a transfusive Virginity; which quenched all concupiscence in others towards her. **1850** J. HAMILTON in *Christian Sabbath* (1852) 132 The transfusive good humour which sent every one away with a purpose to come back. **1869** —— *Mem. J. D. Burns* i. 11 The transfusive power of his large and exhaustless vitality.
Hence **trans'fusively** *adv.*, with transfusion.
1635 HEYWOOD *Hierarch.* v. 278 When he his beames transfusiuely shall run Through Mars his Sphere.

transgenosis (trɑːnsdʒɪ'nəʊsɪs, træns-, -nz-). *Genetics.* [f. TRANS- 10 + GEN(E^1^ + -OSIS.] The transfer of genes to an unrelated organism and their subsequent expression.
1973 C. H. DOY et al. in *Proc. Nat. Acad. Sci.* LXX. 723/1 The overall phenomenon of transfer and subsequent expression has been termed transgenosis. **1979** I. H. HERSKOWITZ *Elem. Genetics* xiii. 192 Such transgenosis experiments usually involve either the uptake of naked bacterial DNA or the injection of phage DNA into eukaryotic cells.

trans'global, *a.* [f. TRANS- 3 + GLOBAL *a.*] That travels across or round the world.
1953 [see HOSTESS 2 c]. **1981** *TV Times* 25-31 July 29/3 Prince Charles talks about The Transglobal Expedition.

† **transglu'tition.** *Obs. rare*^−1^. [n. of action from late L. *transglutīre* to gulp down.] The action of swallowing; deglutition. So † **trans'glutting** in same sense.
1541 R. COPLAND *Guydon's Quest. Chirurg.* F iij, The keye of Trachea arteria in the tyme of transgluttynge. **1650** BULWER *Anthropomet.* 118 There are many that drink without the moving of Transglutition.

transgredient (trɑːns'griːdɪənt, træns-, -nz-), *a. rare.* [ad. L. *transgredient-em*, pr. pple. of *transgredī*: see TRANSGRESS *v.*] Transgressing.
a. Violating a law or obligation. **b.** Passing beyond subjective limits; objective.
1837 SYD. SMITH *Wks.* (1850) 608 To paint the other branches of the Church as such slippery transgredient mortals. **1904** *Jrnl. Philos., Psychol. & Sci. Methods* 4 Aug. 426 Pragmatism.. guarantees no objective or social certainty. Its standards are lacking in the essential character of a standard—transgredient reference and verifiability.

transgress ('trɑːnsgrɛs, 'træns-, -nz-), *sb. rare.* ? *Obs.* [ad. L. *transgress-us* a passing over (*u*-stem), f. L. *transgredī*: see next. Cf. OF. *transgres*, 15th c. in Godef. (perh. the immediate source).] Transgression, trespass.
1578 in *Scot. Poems 16th C.* II. 196 There is na sanct may saif your saule Fra the transgres. **1624** HEYWOOD *Gunaik.* II. 73 There be many errors, excesses, and transgresses. *c* **1640** [SHIRLEY] *Capt. Underwit* v. ii, Well, sir, though your transgresse deserve no pardon, Yet I am charitable upon Condition. **1839** READE *Deluge* 112, I heard a Voice that spake within, And said such transgress was a sin.

transgress (trɑːns'grɛs, træns-, -nz-), *v.* Also 6-7 **trans(e)gresse**. [app. a. F. *transgresser* (14th c. in Godef. *Compl.*), f. L. *transgress-*, ppl. stem of *transgredī* to step across, f. *trans* across + *gradī* to step.]
1. a. *trans.* To go beyond the bounds or limits prescribed by (a law, command, etc.); to break, violate, infringe, contravene, trespass against.
1526 *Pilgr. Perf.* (1531) 98 b, So they transgresse & breke the commaundement of god. **1550** CROWLEY *Epigr.* 757 Wyl ye transegresse my lawes? **1560** DAUS tr. *Sleidane's Comm.* 217 That he should suffer for transgressing them-perours commaundement. **1660** *Trial Regic.* 126 That he that knew the Law so well should so much transgress it. **1713** STEELE *Englishman* No. 50. 324 Too great an Inclination one way betrayed him to transgress the Rules of Charity. **1829** SCOTT *Anne of G.* xxii, Other points of etiquette were transgressed in their turn, after the repast was over. **1888** BRYCE *Amer. Commw.* II. xxxvii. 32 Where a statute passed by a State legislature is alleged to transgress the Constitution of the State.
b. *absol.*, or *intr.* (const. *against*): To break a law or command; to trespass, offend, sin.
1526 TINDALE *2 John* 9 Whosoever transgresseth and bydeth not in the doctrine of Christ, hath not God. **1535** COVERDALE *Neh.* i. 8 Yf ye transgresse, then wil I scater you abrode amonge the nacions. **1599** SHAKS. *Much Ado* II. i. 260, I would not marry her, though she were indowed with all that Adam had left him before he transgrest. *a* **1699** LADY HALKETT *Autobiog.* (1875) 12, I did not transgrese against my Mother. **1875** JOWETT *Plato* (ed. 2) V. 50 That the two

states should unite against a third which transgressed, was a great source of security.

†**c.** *trans.* To offend against (a person); to disobey. *Obs. rare.*

*a*1619 FLETCHER *Bonduca* IV. ii, I never Blasphemed 'em, uncle, nor transgrest my parents. *a*1625 —— *Wom. Pleased* III. i, You are too Royal to me; To me that have so foolishly transgress'd you.

2. a. *trans.* (*a*) To go or pass beyond (any limit or bounds).

*a*1619 [see *transgressed* below]. **1641** WILKINS *Math. Magick* II. vi. (1648) 197 He advises that we should not.. transgresse the bounds of nature. **1686** PLOT *Staffordsh.* 322 Nor have these limits of human life been less transgresst by Men..than they have by women. *a*1700 DRYDEN *Ovid's Metam.* XV. *Pythag. Philos.* 669 Hard mouthed coursers.. Apt to run riot, and transgress the goal. **1829** LYTTON *Devereux* I. i, A man never known before to transgress the very slowest of all possible walks.

(*b*) *spec.* in *Geol.* Of the sea: to spread over (the land). Cf. TRANSGRESSION 2.

1909 *Bull. Geol. Soc. Amer.* XX. 479 There are periodic recurrences of extensive emergences of the continents and.. each one is later invaded or transgressed by continental seas. **1978** *Nature* 13 July 131/1 The down faulted and transgressed blocks on Fig. 1 have been numbered to show the sequence and time when the block was first transgressed.

†**b.** *intr.* (*a*) To go beyond limits; to trespass (*on*). (*b*) To digress. *Obs.*

1662 GERBIER *Princ.* 22, I shall not spend time, and transgresse on the Readers patience, concerning the making of Clay, and burning of Bricks. **1689** tr. *Buchanan's De Jure Regni apud Scotos* 14 Let us return from whence we have transgressed.

Hence **transgressed** (-'grɛst) *ppl. a.* (in quot. *a*1619, that has gone beyond ordinary limits, excessive); **trans'gressing** *vbl. sb.* and *ppl. a.*

1535 COVERDALE *Josh.* xxii. 22 Yf this be a transgressynge or trespacynge agaynst the Lorde. **1579** W. WILKINSON *Confut. Familye of Loue* b ij, She shall be guiltles of the transgressing. *a*1619 FOTHERBY *Atheom.* II. ii. §1 (1622) 198 So large.., and transgrest in her proportion. **1651** HOBBES *Govt. & Soc.* xiv. §8. 217 Any one who hath suffered the punishment of the transgressed Law. *a*1812 McLEAN *Comm. Hebr.* (1847) I. 329 The punishment inflicted on his transgressing seed. **1907** *Blackw. Mag.* Feb. 177/1 He brought suits against transgressing shipmasters. **1978** [see above sense 2 a (*b*)].

trans'gressible, *a. rare.* [ad. late and med.-L. *transgressibilis*: see prec. and -BLE.] Capable of being transgressed.

1851 H. L. MANSEL *Proleg. Logica* 100, I..consider the results of my experience as contingent only and transgressible. **1882** in OGILVIE; and in later Dicts.

transgression (trɑːns'grɛʃən, træns-, -nz-). [app. a. F. *transgression* (12th c. in Hatz.-Darm.), ad. L. *transgressiōn-em* a going over; later, a violation, transgression, sin, n. of action from *transgredī* to TRANSGRESS.]

1. a. The action of transgressing or passing beyond the bounds of legality or right; a violation of law, duty, or command; disobedience, trespass, sin.

1426 LYDG. *De Guil. Pilgr.* 1130 Transgressyoun ys for to say A goyyng fro the ryht[e] way, Or shortly, in sentement Brekyng off a comaundement. **1432–50** tr. *Higden* (Rolls) V. 213 Borne in as grete innocency and withowte synne as Adam was afore the transgression. **14..** *Cust. Malton* in *Surtees Misc.* (1888) 60 Alle odyr transgrescyons þt towchys the lordes persons. **1494** FABYAN *Chron.* (1811) 342 Culpable in certayne artycles, towchynge transgressyon agayne the kynge. **1552** ABP. HAMILTON *Catech.* (1884) 27 Dedely synnis quhilke ar transgressionis of Gods commands. **1595** SHAKS. *John* I. i. 256 Heauen lay not my transgression to my charge. **1651** HOBBES *Leviath.* II. xxvi. 148 Punishments ordained beforehand for their transgression. **1722** DE FOE *Relig. Courtsh.* I. ii. (1840) 67 The children shall not be punished for the father's transgression. **1824** L. MURRAY *Eng. Gram.* I. 491 The transgression of this rule makes what are called harsh or forced metaphors.

b. The action of passing over or beyond. (Only as the etymological sense of the word.)

1623 COCKERAM, *Transgression*, a passing or going ouer. **1643** BURROUGHES *Exp. Hosea* (1652) 238 Sin is called by the name of Transgression..that is going beyond their bounds, going over the hedge. **1857** MAURICE *Ep. St. John* iii. 47, I call it transgression; that is, the passing over a boundary which was marked out for me. **1907** ILLINGWORTH *Doctr. Trinity* x. 190 Sin is always transgression, the over-stepping of due bounds, the refusal to be limited.

2. *Geol.* The spread of the sea over the land, as evidenced by the deposition of unconformable marine sediments.

1882 GEIKIE in *Nature* 13 July 242/2 In a section 'Upon Abrasion and Transgression', the author insists upon the paramount influence of the sea as an agent in planing down the surface of the land. **1903** CLAYPOLE in *Amer. Geol.* Aug. 91 The depression in southern Ohio, where the outcrop of the Corniferous limestone and the Corniferous-Hamilton is concealed by the transgression of the shale. **1908**, etc. [see REGRESSION 7]. **1975** J. G. EVANS *Environment Early Man Brit. Isles* iii. 67 Minor changes of sea level and coastal configuration have continued well beyond the main period of marine transgression.

Hence **trans'gressional** *a.*, of or pertaining to transgression; of the nature of a transgression.

1690–1 LD. ROCHESTER *Let.* in Burnet *Own Times* (1823) VI. 284 Forgive this transgressional rapture, and receive my thanks..for your kind letter.

transgressive (trɑːns'grɛsɪv, træns-, -nz-), *a.* [f. L. *transgress-*, ppl. stem (see TRANSGRESS) + -IVE. Cf. late L. *transgressīvus.*]

1. Having the character or quality of transgressing. **a.** Involving transgression; sinful.

1646 SIR T. BROWNE *Pseud. Ep.* I. x. 37 Adam..from the transgressive infirmities of himselfe might have erred alone, as well as the Angels before him. **1797** *Hist.* in *Ann. Reg.* 57/1 The powers assumed..were explicitly termed unconstitutional, and transgressive of the authority lodged in them by the laws.

b. Passing beyond some limit.

1735 H. BROOKE *Univ. Beauty* III. 30 Where the Solar Heat, and searching Air Transgressive, pierce our actuated Sphere.

†**2.** *Music.* ? Not coming in regular sequence; or ? Overlapping (cf. CONJUNCT B. 6). *Obs.*

1760 STILES *Anc. Gk. Mus.* in *Phil. Trans.* LI. 704 Systems were there considered as differing in respect, first, to magnitude; secondly, to genus; thirdly, to the being consonant or dissonant; fourthly, to the being rational or irrational; fifthly, to the being sequent or transgressive.

3. *Geol.* Overlapping: cf. TRANSGRESSION 2. (So Fr. *transgressif* (Littré).)

1854 [implied in TRANSGRESSIVELY]. **1860** MAYNE *Expos. Lex.*, *Transgressivus*,..applied to a couch or bed that becomes deposited on others of different natures and different levels by rising over them, so that it is necessarily more or less inclined: transgressive.

Hence **trans'gressively** *adv.*, in a transgressive manner; *spec.* in *Geol.* †(*a*) unconformably; (*b*) so as to overlap the formation next below it.

1847 WEBSTER, *Transgressively*,..by transgressing. **1854** MURCHISON *Siluria* viii. 169 The Silurian series overlap transgressively or unconformably the edges of the subjacent sandstone. **1879** GEIKIE in *Encycl. Brit.* X. 371/2 Up-raised Lower Silurian rocks, upon the upturned and denuded edges of which the Carboniferous Limestone lies transgressively.

transgressor (trɑːns'grɛsə(r), træns-, -nz-). Also 4–7 -our, 6 -er. [a. AF. *transgressour* = F. *transgresseur* (14th c. in Hatz.-Darm.), a. late L. *transgressōr-em*, agent-n. from *transgredī* to TRANSGRESS.] One who transgresses; a lawbreaker; a sinner.

1377 LANGL. *P. Pl.* B. I. 96 And taken *trangressores* [*v.r.* transgressouris] and tyen hem faste. **1432–50** tr. *Higden* (Rolls) III. 263 He..did chide the transgressores of the lawes. **1463–4** *Rolls of Parlt.* V. 502/2 To committe the transgressours..to the next Gaole. **1526** TINDALE *Jas.* ii. 9 Ye commit synne, and are rebuked off the lawe as transgressours. —— 11 Thou arte a transgresser off the lawe. **1638** *Penit. Conf.* viii. (1657) 235 His Conscience arraigneth him..as a Transgressor. **1667** MILTON *P.L.* XI. 164 Such title should belonge To me transgressour, who for thee ordaind A help, became thy snare. **1875** JOWETT *Plato* (ed. 2) V. 100 Whoever shall transgress the strains by law established is a transgressor of the laws.

transhape, variant of TRANS-SHAPE.

†**transhaw,** *a.* or *adv. Obs. rare.* Meaning and origin uncertain: perh. 'exposed' to the blast, opposed to 'borrow' sheltered from the blast.

1665 D. DUDLEY *Metallum Martis* (1854) 31 How to mend their Natures, by finning or setting the finery, lesse transhaw more borrow, which are terms of art, and by altering and pitching the works. *Ibid.*, If the work be set transhaw and transiring from the blast, the Iron is more coldshare, lesse Fined.

tranship (trɑːn'ʃɪp, træn-), *less commonly* **transship** (trɑːns'ʃɪp, træns-), *v.* [f. TRANS- + SHIP *v.*]

1. *trans.* To transfer from one ship to another; also *transf.*, from one railway train or other conveyance to another. Also *absol.*

1792 LD. MACARTNEY *Jrnl.* in Barrow *Life* (1807) II. 180 All the baggage and presents [were] put on board the large junks, to be transshipped into smaller ones. **1797** —— *Emb. to China* II. i. 4 In order to tranship them. **1802** C. ROBINSON *Adm. Cas.* III. 247 He is not bound..either to tranship or to repair. **1813** WELLINGTON *Let.* 26 June in Gurw. *Desp.* (1839) X. 461, I am afraid it will be necessary to tranship the ordnance &c. into smaller vessels. **1846** ADDISON *On Contracts* II. ii. § 4 (1883) 494 If the vessel becomes disabled..the master is bound to tranship and forward the cargo, if he has the means of transhipment at hand. **1876** CALLIS *Cutlery* 181 It was the practice of German manufacturers..to..transship them without allowing them to land. **1900** *Blackw. Mag.* Oct. 559/1 He didn't give them time to trans-ship enough provisions.

2. *intr.* Of a passenger: To change from one ship or other conveyance to another.

1879 ATCHERLEY *Boërland* 264 At East London..we transhipped into the steamship *African*. **1892** E. REEVES *Homeward Bound* 87 After going a mile or two we stopped, got out, and transhipped into another train. **1892** *Daily News* 18 Oct. 5/6 Passengers going by her had not to transship either at Hong Kong or Shanghai. **1895** RAMSAY *Paul the Trav.* 283 He [Paul] had to transship in Troas.

3. *Comb.* in which '*tranship* is app. = *transhipment*: as **tranship-shed**, a shed at a railway joint station for the transference of goods from one railway to another; **tranship-train**, a train running in connexion with a steamer into which the passengers tranship; **tranship-van**: see quot.

1903 *Westm. Gaz.* 14 Jan. 5/1 We have 'tranship', or road-vans, specially appointed to work on branches and at stations where there is not the heavy traffic. These take goods from a certain starting-point to be delivered at a number of roadside stations. **1903** *Ibid.* 21 Feb. 7/1 Inviting seven English and Scotch companies to co-operate in the matter of a tranship shed at Carlisle. **1904** *Daily News* 22 Oct. 9 When near the new station at Talacre the engine of a heavy tranship train jumped an obstruction... The guard of the disabled tranship hurried Chesterwards.

Hence **tran'shipping** *vbl. sb.* (also *attrib.*).

1801 SIR WM. SCOTT in C. Robinson *Adm. Cas.* III. 259 If he [the master] had not the means of transhipping. **1816** TUCKEY *Narr. Exped. R. Zaire* iii. (1818) 88 The transhipping the stores..being finished. **1840** *Evid. Hull Docks Comm.* 121 The transhipping of them, either by rafts or small vessels. **1892** *Nation* (N.Y.) 1 Sept. 155/1 A better transshipping point.

tran'shipment, trans-'shipment. [f. TRANS- + SHIPMENT, or f. prec. + -MENT.] The action or process of transhipping or changing from one ship or other conveyance to another.

1796 VAUGHAN *Examination* 13 Landing a ship's cargo.. with as few intermediate trans-shipments as possible. **1813** WELLINGTON in Gurw. *Desp.* (1839) XI. 218, I am obliged to go through the details of all the orders for the transhipment. **1846** WARBURTON *Hochelaga* I. 259 The frequent locks and trans-shipment of the cargo must ever be a great embarrassment. **1856** *Farmer's Mag.* Nov. 424 The inconvenience of two transshipments, one at each end of the Erie Canal. **1885** LD. BLACKBURN in *Law Rep. 10 App. Cas.* 419 The cost of transhipment or reshipment, as the case may be. **1899** *Statesman* (Calcutta) 27 Sept., There exists communication by train from Siliguri to Gyabari with one transhipment.

attrib. **1892** *Pall Mall G.* 24 Nov. 2/1, I refer especially to the transhipment trade. **1899** *Westm. Gaz.* 20 Dec. 9/1 Heavy dock charges [etc.] have lost the port the bulk of the transhipment business.

transhi'storical, *a.* [f. TRANS- 4 + HISTORICAL *a.*] (Having significance) that transcends the historical; universal or eternal.

1909 W. R. INGE in *Q. Rev.* Apr. 602 It is not the province of faith to flout scientific knowledge, nor to contaminate the material on which science works by intercalating what M. Le Roy calls 'transhistorical symbols'—myths in fact—which do not become true by being recognised as false, as the new apologetic seems to suggest. **1963** J. A. T. ROBINSON *Honest to God* i. 24 In order to express the 'transhistorical' character of the historical event of Jesus of Nazareth, the New Testament writers used the 'mythological' language of pre-existence, incarnation, [etc.]. **1976** T. EAGLETON *Crit. & Ideology* v. 178 Even where literary science would deem a work to have 'justly' survived, there is no call for materialist embarrassment about the 'metaphysical' quality of such transhistorical status.

transhuman (trɑːns'hjuːmən, træns-, -nz-), *a.* [f. TRANS- 4 + HUMAN; after It. *trasumanar* in Dante.] Beyond the human; superhuman. So **trans'humanate** [It. Dante *trasumanar*, Florio *tra(n)shumanare*], **trans'humanize** *vbs.*, *trans.* to make transhuman; **transhuma'nation** [Florio *tra(n)s(h)umanatione*], a making or becoming transhuman.

1812 CARY *Dante, Parad.* I. 68 Words may not tell of that transhuman change [*orig.* l. 70 trasumanar significar per verba Non si poria]. **1841** GALLENGA *Italy* i. (1848) I. 135 Dante's contact with God was trans-humanating. **1847** *Oxf. to Rome* (ed. 2) 215 A transhumanation takes place. **1872** LOWELL *Dante* Prose Wks. 1890 IV. 168 Souls..transhumanized to the divine abstraction of pure contemplation. **1885** A. J. BUTLER *Parad. of Dante* I. 70 To signify in words transhumanation were impossible. **1892** NORTON *Dante's Parad.* i. 4 Transhumanizing cannot be signified in words. **1936** E. UNDERHILL *Worship* xii. 251 Gazing on the Saints in their manifest humanity, their heroic virtue and 'spiritual persuasiveness', he shares their trans-human experience. **1957** *Economist* 9 Nov. (Suppl.) 12/1 This intensification of life—reaching towards a 'transhuman' level. **1968** S. ROSEN in *PN Rev.* (1979) No. 10. 15/2 We cannot return..to Greek, Jewish, Christian, or any other trans-human gods, whose meaning has been effectively destroyed by the decay of the values they represented.

transhumance (trɑːns'hjuːməns, træns-, -nz-). [a. Fr., f. *transhumer*, ad. Sp. *trashumar* (f. L. *trans* across, over + *humus* ground, soil).] The seasonal transfer of grazing animals to different pastures, often over substantial distances.

1911 M. I. NEWBIGGIN *Mod. Geogr.* vii. 179 The summer drought makes it difficult for even these hardy animals to obtain food, and necessitates in many regions a curious form of nomadism, to which the name of transhumance is given. Transhumance, still well developed in Spain, is the periodic and alternating displacement of flocks and herds between two regions of different climate. **1931** C. F. JONES *South America* 366 Government concessions to permanent ranchers, who do not desire the migrating flocks,..are reducing transhumance. **1954** M. BERESFORD *Lost Villages* vi. 204 Sheep which knew transhumance were not averse to being shepherded a score of miles over to a new pasture. **1975** J. G. EVANS *Environment Early Man Brit. Isles* vi. 133 We do not know to what extent these Bronze Age people were nomadic, or were practising transhumance, or were settled farmers.

Hence **trans'humant** *a.*, migrating between regions with differing climates; of or pertaining to transhumance.

1932 E. H. CARRIER *Water & Grass* 78 The transhumant flocks. **1967** *Listener* 30 Mar. 426/3 The Sarakatsani—transhumant pastoralists of the Balkans. **1976** *Times Lit. Suppl.* 26 Mar. 353/2 The longer transhumant routes from the Pyrenees southwards to Catalonia.

transhy'drogenase. *Biochem.* [f. TRANS- 10 + HYDROGENASE.] Any enzyme which catalyses the transfer of hydrogen from one organic substrate to another. Cf. DEHYDROGENASE.

1952 S. P. COLOWICK et al. in *Jrnl. Biol. Chem.* CXCV. 95 It is shown that the enzyme catalyzes a transfer of electrons (or hydrogen)... The enzyme will therefore be referred to here as 'pyridine nucleotide transhydrogenase'. **1978** *Jrnl. R. Soc. Med.* LXXI. 171 About 60% of insulin entering the liver is inactivated by liver enzymes, such as glutathione insulin transhydrogenase.

transience ('trɑːnsɪəns, 'træns-, -nz-; 'trɑːnʃəns, 'trænʃ-, -nʒ-). Also (in sense 2) **transeunce.** [f. as TRANSIENT: see -ENCE.]

1. The action or fact of soon passing away; also, the condition or state of being transient, transiency.

1745 BROOKE *An Anthem* iv, Here, from time and transience won, Beauty has her charms resign'd. *a* **1822** SHELLEY *Ess. & Lett.* (1852) I. 184 A being..whose 'thoughts wander through eternity', disclaiming alliance with transience and decay. **1849** *Tait's Mag.* XVI. 8 Shadows..glide away, in transience fleet. **1875** JOWETT *Plato* (ed. 2) III. 126 Regarding the transience of pleasure as a proof of its unreality. **1905** *Westm. Gaz.* 22 Apr. 12/3 Any other explanation of the transience of French Protestantism.

2. The state or quality of being 'transient' in sense 2; = TRANSCENDENCE 1 b.

1882–3 *Schaff's Encycl. Relig. Knowl.* I. 370 [Calvinism] emphasizes at once the transience of God beyond, and the immanence of God within, the world. **1906** S. S. LAURIE *Synthetica* I. I. i. 6 The difficulties that arise in connection with the transeunce. **1914** C. D. BROAD *Perception* ii. 105 Leibniz and Lotze would have overlooked the immanence in the whole system,..and fastened on the transeunce within it with respect to its various elements.

transiency ('trɑːnsɪənsɪ, 'træns-, -nz-; 'trɑːnʃənsɪ, 'trænʃ-, -nʒ-). Also (in sense 2 of TRANSIENT *a.*) **transeuncy.** [f. as prec.: see -ENCY.]

1. The quality or condition of being transient; brevity of existence; transitoriness.

1652 GAULE *Magastrom.* 96 How is it possible there should either be any..observation on the artists and art, in a transiency so imperceptible? **1805** W. TAYLOR in Robberds *Mem.* (1843) II. 98 A more eager popularity, like that of the 'Minstrel's Lay', would be symptomatic of transiency. **1812** COLERIDGE in *Lit. Rem.* (1836) I. 381 From their minuteness and transiency not calculated to stiffen or inflate the individual. **1831** *Blackw. Mag.* XXIX. 522 They try to perpetuate the transiency of emotions. **1905** F. YOUNG *Sands of Pleasure* I. v, Vaguely conscious of the transiency and instability of material life. **1942** *Mind* LI. 137 Spinoza's central causal theory refers to the world of adequate knowledge as it is directed to *entia in se*, and its application to transeuncy must be governed by derivation therefrom.

2. A transient thing or being. *rare.*

1866 CARLYLE *Edw. Irving* 318 Poor sickly transiencies that we are, coveting we know not what! **1881** PALGRAVE *Vis. Eng.* 200 On the trivialest transiencies fix'd, or plucking for fruit Dead-sea Apples and ashes of sin, more brute than the brute.

transient ('trɑːnsɪənt, 'træns-, -nz-; 'trɑːnʃənt, 'trænʃ-, -nʒ-), *a.* (*sb.*) Also 7 *erron.* **transeant, -scient;** 7– (chiefly in sense 2) **transeunt.** [f. L. *transiens* (in oblique cases *transeunt-*, whence the form *transeunt*), pr. pple. of L. *transīre*, f. *trans* across + *īre* to go.]

A. *adj.* **1. a.** Passing by or away with time; not durable or permanent; temporary, transitory; *esp.* passing away quickly or soon, brief, momentary, fleeting; *spec.* in *Electr.* (cf. sense B. 3 below).

1607 *Schol. Disc. agst. Antichr.* I. i. 17 Whose parts are transeant and aereall, and presently vanishing. **1612** STURTEVANT *Metallica* v. 56 Instruments and means are said to be Transient, when in respect of their vse, they serue but once. **1659** PEARSON *Creed* (1839) 380 It containeth two distinct parts; one transient, the other permanent. **1662** J. DAVIES tr. *Mandelslo's Trav.* 261 They are transient showers soon over. **1713** BERKELEY *Guardian* No. 70 ¶8 The transient enjoyments of this life. **1813** SIR H. DAVY *Agric. Chem.* (1814) 282 This manure is transient in its effects, and does not last for more than a single crop. **1853** *Proc. Philos. Soc. Glasgow* III. 285 (*heading*) On transient electric currents. **1870** *Phil. Mag.* XXXIX. 428 The galvanometer takes account of the induced transient current as a whole. **1873** HAMERTON *Intell. Life* IV. v. (1875) 166 The few and transient hours that we can call our own. **1962** *Newnes Conc. Encycl. Electr. Engin.* 821/2 The transient current consequent upon the switching-on of a filament lamp. **1969** J. J. SPARKES *Transistor Switching* v. 124 With the pulse steering circuits added..a transient current may flow.

b. ***transient equilibrium*** (*Nuclear Sci.*), the condition in which the half-life of a parent isotope is greater than that of the daughter but comparable to the period of observation, so that after an initial increase the total radioactivity decays with the parent's half-life and the ratio of parent atoms to daughter atoms remains constant.

1912 MAKOWER & GEIGER *Practical Measurement in Radioactivity* viii. 111 The name transient equilibrium has been given to this state of apparent equilibrium, which exists whenever the life of a product is not negligibly short compared with that of the preceding substance which controls the decay. **1961** G. R. CHOPPIN *Exper. Nucl. Chem.* vi. 84 For a parent with a 1 month half life, observation over a few days will seem to be secular equilibrium, whereas observation over a 3 month period will show transient equilibrium.

2. Passing out or operating beyond itself; transitive; opposed to *immanent.* (Often spelt *transeunt* for distinction from sense 1.)

1613 PURCHAS *Pilgrimage* I. i. 4 The workes of God, which are either inward and immanent, or outward and transient. **1625** GILL *Sacr. Philos.* I. 98 You may observe a difference of actions, of which some are immanent, or indwelling in the doer..: some againe are transeunt, or passing from the doer upon that which is done. *a* **1677** HALE *Prim. Orig. Man.* 35 Those two great transeunt or emanant acts or works, the works of Creation and Providence. **1836–7** SIR W. HAMILTON *Metaph.* (1870) II. xxv. 118 An act of the mind going out of itself, in other words, a transeunt act. **1847** DE QUINCEY *Milton v. Southey & Landor* Wks. XII. 177 In metaphysical language, the moral of an epos or a drama should be immanent, not transient. **1890** *Athenæum* 8 Nov. 631/1 Volitionally reactive redintegration with its two stages, immanent and transeunt action. **1903** F. C. S. SCHILLER *Humanism* iv. 64 The impossibility of explaining such transeunt causation compels to the inference that things are not really separate and independent. **1933** *Mind* XLII. 155 The more responsive P*n* is to P*m* the more transeunt action there is between the two. **1942** R. G. COLLINGWOOD *New Leviathan* xx. 140 It [*sc.* the process of ruling] is *transeunt* when that which rules rules something other than itself. **1949** H. W. B. JOSEPH *Lect. Philos. Leibniz* iii. 107 That is the difficulty of transeunt causation—an effect produced in one thing by what is just another.

3. Passing or flowing through; passing from one thing or person to another. Now *rare.*

1619 DENISON *Heav. Banq.* 341 If the worship at our receiuing did determine in the Sacrament, or were transient by it to God. **1644** [H. PARKER] *Jus Pop.* 57 They lurke between scripture and reason, and remain in a kind of transcient posture. **1671** GREW *Anat. Plants* i. (1682) 7 A Filtre to the transient Sap. *a* **1703** BURKITT *On N.T.* 1 Thess. ii. (1818) 16 Hereditary, and..transient from one generation to another. **1847** TENNYSON *Princess* v. 37 Away we stole, and transient in a trice From what was left of faded woman-slough To sheathing splendours..issued in the sun.

4. Passing through a place without staying in it, or staying only for a short time; in quot. 1731 of birds, migratory; *spec.* (*U.S. colloq.*) applied to a guest at a hotel, etc. (often *ellipt.* as *sb.*: see B. 2). Also *transf.*, for transient guests, short-stay.

1685 BAXTER *Paraphr. N.T.*, *Mark* (1701) Introd., Whether this Mark was Bishop of Alexandria, or only a transient Evangelist there a while, is an Historical Controversie. **1713** SWIFT *Cadenus & Vanessa* 768 Love, hitherto a transient guest, Ne'er held possession of his breast. **1731** SIR J. CLERK in *Mem. W. Stukeley* (Surtees) I. 247 There are many transient fowls that come into Britain at certain seasons. **1740** W. DOUGLASS *Disc. Curr. Brit. Plant. Amer.* 3 The Author is not a transient Person, who from Humour or Caprice..may expose the Province. **1788** *Massachusetts Spy* 11 Dec. 3/2 A transient jockey came to the house of Mr. Jonathan Hubbey, and agreed to purchase a horse of him. **1818** H. B. FEARON *Sk. Amer.* 44 Boarding ..is 8 dollars a week, for what is termed 'a transient man'. **1822** MONTGOMERY *Hymn, 'This stone to Thee in faith we lay'* v, But will, indeed, Jehovah deign Here to abide, no transient guest? **1879** F. R. STOCKTON *Rudder Grange* xi. 121 We had no accommodations for them, neither had we any desire for even transient visitors. **1891** *Fur, Fin & Feather* Mar. 185 The transient rate for travelers at the Hilsabeck Hotel in Springfield is $1 a day. **1903** *N.Y. Even. Post* 19 Oct. 3 A 12-story transient hotel. **1906** *Springfield* (Mass.) *Weekly Republican* 9 Aug. 16 They will then rent apartments with or without board to transient and permanent guests. **1942** E. PAUL *Narrow St.* xxii. 175 Would that..some Turk would..rush me to a transient hotel. I am past that age, and never enjoyed a clandestine situation. **1976** *Times* 29 May 1/8 Was placed in transient barracks, a form of solitary confinement. **1981** *Sci. Amer.* Nov. 37/3 More intensive canvassing of places such as pool halls and transient hotels was done in an attempt to include a greater proportion of people who have no permanent address.

5. *Mus.* Introduced in passing, as a note, chord, etc. not belonging to the harmony, or to the key, of the passage; passing.

1801 in BUSBY *Dict. Mus.* **1838** G. F. GRAHAM *Mus. Comp.* 29/2 Passing notes, changing notes, transient notes, etc. **1878** F. TAYLOR in Grove *Dict. Mus.* I. 75/1 A so-called 'auxiliary note' (sometimes 'transient' or 'changing' note).

6. *U.S.* (Esp. of printed matter) occasional, isolated, individual.

1831 *Boston Transcript* 18 Apr. 2/3 We shall use all patrons alike, whether they are annual or transient advertisers. **1841** *Lowell* (Mass.) *Offering* I. 245 The clerk asked her if it was a transient paper. **1857** *Harper's Mag.* Feb. 403/1 The prepayment of postage on transient printed matter has been made compulsory. **1857** *Lawrence* (Kansas) *Republican* 28 May 1 All transient advertisements must be paid for in advance. **1904** *Philadelphia Friends' Intelligencer* 15 Oct. p. ii, For transient advertisements, 5 cents per line.

B. *sb.*

1. A transient thing or being; something passing or transitory, not permanent.

1652 SPARKE *Prim. Devot.* (1663) 279 If we (meanwhile) but rise from graves of sin And transients (which the most are buried in !). **1661** GLANVILL *Van. Dogm.* 81 A kind of stop or arrest, by the benefit of which the Soul might have a glance of the fugitive Transient. *a* **1674** TRAHERNE *Poet. Wks.* (1903) 18. **1860** BOYD *Recr. Country Parson* ii. 27 These gray transients have changed to shivering skeletons.

2. *colloq.* (orig. *U.S.*). A person who passes through a place, or stays in it only for a short time; *spec.* a 'transient guest' at a hotel or boarding-house. Also, a traveller, a tramp, a migrant worker.

1880 MRS. ROLLINS *New Eng. Bygones* (1883) 84 My grandmother held these transients in low esteem. **1893** KATE SANBORN *S. California* 20 On an open, sunny site, and ..frequented by 'transients' and business men of moderate means. **1894** *Outing* (U.S.) XXIV. 260/1 Summer residents, transients, and all, had turned out early. **1941** H. G. WELLS *You can't be too Careful* II. xv. 104 Whenever Doober's had rooms to spare a card was put into the ground floor window, and there would be transients for three or four days. **1946** W. S. MAUGHAM *Then & Now* vi. 33 Piero and the courier were to share a straw mattress in a corridor along with a number of transients only too glad to have a roof over their heads. **1959** M. RENAULT *Charioteer* vi. 114 A respectable tenement full of transients in a time of flux. **1963** C. D. SIMAK *They walked like Men* iii. 17 He was snoring gently and he looked..like a transient who might have wandered in to find a place to sleep. **1978** *Beautiful British Columbia* Winter 17 Transients pile in each winter to work the oil patch as soon as the muskeg freezes.

3. *Physical Sci.* A transient variation in current or voltage, or in any waveform; a transient condition.

1911 C. P. STEINMETZ *Elem. Lect. Electr. Discharges* i. 2 The transient..appears as intermediate between two permanent conditions. **1911** —— in *Jrnl. Franklin Inst.* CLXXII. 41 Transients are not a specifically electrical phenomenon, but occur in any system of forces, where energy storage occurs. **1936** *Physical Rev.* XL. 522/1 Thus Γ is of importance only in determining the initial transients but not the steady rate of absorption. **1947** R. LEE *Electronic Transformers & Circuits* iv. 102 Transients occur when the load is applied..or removed..causing respectively a momentary drop or rise in plate voltage. **1970** V. M. ALBERS *World of Sound* ix. 143 The transients from percussion instruments and a piano are quite severe. **1972** *Nature* 21 Apr. 384/1 Total surface fields of over 100 gammas have been observed when large solar field transients pass the Moon. **1979** *Guardian* 25 Oct. 20/1 Accidental abrupt changes of conditions in reactors—these are called transients.

attrib. **1962** A. NISBETT *Technique Sound Studio* 248 In such [microphone] designs..there are minimal inertial effects and therefore a very good transient response. **1975** G. J. KING *Audio Handbk.* v. 117 A useful signal for transient appraisal is the square wave provided its rise time is significantly smaller than that of the amplifier.

'transiently (see prec.), *adv.* [f. prec. + -LY².] In a transient manner; in passing through; briefly, momentarily; hastily.

1641 R. YOUNGE *Counterpoyson* 398, I have transiently found (in making up the Index) some literall mistakes, points misplaced, &c. **1649** J. H. *Motion to Parl. Adv. Learn.* 25 Some ends which I have transiently..glanced at. **1684** BAXTER *Parish Congreg.* 20 They might occasionally Communicate in our Parishes transiently. **1748** RICHARDSON *Clarissa* VI. xlvi. 69, I thought, transiently thought, that the tea..had an odd taste. **1826** SCOTT *Woodst.* iii, A smile passed transiently over his clouded brow. **1900** *Speaker* 29 Dec. 336/2 Not only transiently, but permanently declining.

'transientness. [f. as prec. + -NESS.] The quality or state of being transient; transience.

1667 *Decay Chr. Piety* x. ¶1 As they resemble the wind in fury.., so they might do also in transientness. **1698** NORRIS *Pract. Disc.* IV. 368 The Pleasure of this Life is..in regard of its Transientness, like the Pleasure of a Dream. **1907** *Edin. Rev.* July 177 Suzanne..could not believe in the transientness of [Gibbon's affections].

transierd: see TRANSIRE *v. Obs.*

transignification (ˌtrɑːnsɪgnɪfɪ'keɪʃən, ˌtræn-). *Theol.* Also **trans-signification.** [f. TRANS- 3 + SIGNIFICATION.] The change in the significance of bread and wine at the Eucharist through transubstantiation, expressed in terms of sacramental symbolism. Cf. TRANSFINALIZATION.

1965, etc. [see TRANSFINALIZATION]. **1968** J. M. POWERS *Eucharistic Theology* iv. 170 It is sometimes proposed that the idea of transsignification is presented as an alternative to the traditional theological idea of transsubstantiation. **1983** M. F. WILES *Faith & Mystery of God* iii. 38 The approach in terms of trans-signification or establishment of new meaning can make the same point in a more constructive way.

trans'iliac, *a. Anat.* [f. TRANS- 5 + L. *īlium*: cf. ILIAC.] Lying across the ilium; extending transversely from one iliac bone to the other.

1891 in *Cent. Dict.*

transilience (trɑːn'sɪlɪəns, træn-). *rare.* [f. as next: see -ENCE.] A leaping from one thing to another, an abrupt transition: *spec.* in *Min.* abrupt transition of one mineral or rock into another.

1657 REEVE *God's Plea* 204 Man may haue..his diffluences, redundances,..and transiliences of speech. **1811** PINKERTON *Petralogy* II. 169 Rocks of black trap, surmounted by porphyry of the same base, the transilience being clear and palpable. **1830** HERSCHEL *Stud. Nat. Phil.* 330 Transferred by contact, or by sudden and violent transilience of the interval of separation..under the form of sparks and flashes.

So † **tran'siliency** [see -ENCY], the quality of being transilient; less correctly = prec. *Obs. rare*⁻¹.

1661 GLANVILL *Van. Dogm.* xii. 114 By an unadvised transiliency leaping from the effect to its remotest cause.

transilient (trɑːn'sɪlɪənt, træn-), *a.* [ad. L. *tran(s)silient-em*, pr. pple. of *tran(s)silīre* to leap across, skip over, omit, f. *trans* across + *salīre* to leap.] Leaping or passing from one thing or condition to another; in *Min.* said of one rock substance passing abruptly into another.

transilient fibres, nerve-fibres passing from one convolution of the brain to another not immediately adjacent (*Syd. Soc. Lex.* 1899).

1811 PINKERTON *Petralogy* I. p. v, The Transilient Rocks, an interesting series, in which one substance.. passes into another, as granite into porphyry, trap into wacken. *Ibid.* 550 British rocks are often anomalous, or transilient, and can scarcely be reduced to precise denominations.

† **transi'lition.** *Obs. rare*⁻¹. [ad. late L. *transilītiōn-em* (Augustine), n. of action f. *transilīre*: see prec.] The action of leaping over or 'skipping'; omission of intermediate numbers.

1582 T. WATSON *Centurie of Loue* lxxx, Founded by transilition or ouer skipping of number by rule and order, as from 1 to 3, 5, 7, and 9. *Ibid.* [see TRANSPOSITION 2].

transilluminate (trɑːnsɪ'l(j)uːmɪneɪt, træns-), *v.* [f. TRANS- + ILLUMINATE *v.*] *trans.* To cause light to pass through; *spec.* in *Med.* to throw a strong light through (an organ or part) to discover the presence or cause of disease. So **transillumi'nation**, the action or process of transilluminating.

1890 *Lancet* 1 Mar. 480/2 It [a tooth] was translucent by electric transillumination, showing that the pulp was living. **1900** *Ibid.* 25 Aug. 617/1 If in a darkened room the electric lamp used for transilluminating the frontal sinus was placed against the thyroid cartilage. **1901** *Ibid.* 11 May 1328/2 Transillumination is often used to find out if the antrum is diseased. **1912** KEITH *Human Body* i. 20 It may have occurred, however, to the onlooker that, since we can transilluminate the human body [*i.e.* with Röntgen-rays], it is no longer necessary to dissect it.

transi'lluminator. [f. prec. + -OR.] **a.** An instrument for examining the conjunctiva and the sclerotic of the eyeball by shining light through them. **b.** An instrument for making visible spots on chromatography plates and electrophoresis gels by shining ultraviolet light through them.

1906 *Ophthalmic Record* XV. 209 (*heading*) Transillumination of the eye in the differential diagnosis of intraocular tumors, with the description of an ocular transilluminator. **1925** B. LANG *Routine Examination of Eye* III. 150 The most important use of the transilluminator is to examine the interior of the globe, particularly in cases of detachment of the retina. **1954** S. DUKE-ELDER *Parsons' Dis. Eye* (ed. 12) vi. 87 For this purpose, special transilluminators may be employed. **1973** *Nature* 16 Feb. 473/2 Both the short-wave and long-wave trans-illuminator ultraviolet lamps were used for detection. **1978** *Ibid.* 17 Aug. 715/2 (*caption*) Gels were stained with ethidium bromide solution and visualised on an ultra-violet transilluminator.

trans-im'pression. *rare*⁻¹. [TRANS- 1.] An impression transferred or taken over (*from* something).

1812–29 COLERIDGE in *Lit. Rem.* (1838) III. 152 The very words, 'conception', 'comprehension', and all in all languages that answer to them, suppose this trans-impression from the mind.

transincorpo'ration. [TRANS- 1.] Passage from one body to another; transmigration of the soul.

1810 W. TAYLOR in *Monthly Mag.* XXX. 47 The doctrine of the trans-incorporation of souls, or of their migration through successive human bodies, was taught.. by a Jewish rabbi. **1843** ROBBERDS *Mem. W. Taylor* II. iv. 305 Its contents are full of curious information, more particularly those on the transincorporation of souls.

transindi'vidual, *a.* [f. TRANS- 4 + INDIVIDUAL *a.*] Not confined to any particular thing or person, more than individual. Cf. TRANSPERSONAL *a.*

1936 *Psychol. Monogr.* XLVII. I. 8 In Scholastic philosophy these realities are regarded as subsisting in the realm of ideas; they are trans-individual. **1938** *Mind* XLVII. 482 The right answer to the question 'What are numerical propositions?' is that they predicate a peculiar kind of trans-individual quality applicable only to groups. **1973** S. HEATH in *Screen* Spring/Summer 105 The transindividual system or code.. of elements and rules underlying and assuring individual messages. **1977** A. SHERIDAN tr. *Lacan's Écrits* iii. 49 Its domain is that of concrete discourse, in so far as this is the field of the transindividual reality of the subject.

trans'insular, *a.* [f. TRANS- 3 + L. *insula* island: cf. *insular*.]

1. Crossing or going across an, or the, island.

1895 *Buffalo Current Hist* (N.Y.) V. 404 When the colony [Newfoundland] would have to work its transinsular railway system. **1900** *Engineering Mag.* XIX. 684 Any trans-insular railroad project is chimerical.

2. *Anat.* Applied to a fissure of the brain that crosses the insula or island of Reil, and divides it into a cephalic and a caudal region.

1889 *Buck's Handbk. Med. Sc.* VIII. 160/1 Normal, human subfissures are.. the transinsular and others crossing the surface of the insula.

‖ **transire** (trɑːns'aɪərɪ, træns-), *sb. Law.* [L. *transīre* to go across, pass over, f. *trans* across + *īre* to go.] A warrant issued by the customhouse, permitting the passage of merchandise.

1599 NASHE *Lenten Stuffe* (1871) 70 They would grant him his coquet, or *Transire*. **1656** in *Misc. Sc. Burgh Rec. Soc.* 30 Receiveing moneys for writeing bills, cocquetts, and transires. **1662** *Order Ho. Com. as to Customs* (1663) 9 A Transire or Let-passe from Port to Port in England. **1750** *Act 23 Geo. II*, c 29 §2 No officer of his Majesty's customs shall sign or grant any cocquet, sufferance, transire, let-pass, warrant, or certificate.. for exporting.. such bar iron. **1888** *Act 51 & 52 Vict.* c. 24 §5 (*a*) Any port.. at which her transire is to be obtained.

† **transire** (trɑːns'aɪə(r), træns-), *v. Obs. rare.* Also 6 **transier.** [irreg. f. L. *transīre* (see prec.), the inf. form being taken instead of the ppl. stem *transit-* (TRANSIT *v.*).] *intr.* To go or pass across; in quot. 1665, ? to lie transversely.

1592 WYRLEY *Armorie* 121 Pretended iorney if they onward hould, Transierd they were, as it was to me tould. **1665** D. DUDLEY *Mettallum Martis* (1854) 31 If the work be set transhaw and transiring from the blast.

trans'ischiac (-'ɪskɪæk), *a. Anat.* [f. TRANS- 5 + L. *ischiac-us*, f. *ischi-um*: see ISCHIUM, and -AC.] Extending transversely from one ischial bone to the other.

1891 in *Cent. Dict.* **1899** in *Syd. Soc. Lex.*

trans-'isthmian, *a.* [f. TRANS- 3 + ISTHMUS: cf. *isthmian*.] Crossing or extending across an isthmus, esp. the Isthmus of Panama.

1885 GROVER CLEVELAND *Ann. Message to Congress U.S.A.* Dec., Our interests in any transisthmian route which may be opened. **1902** *Q. Rev.* Oct. 674 The Key to any possible trans-isthmian canal.

transistor (trɑːn'sɪstə(r), træn-, -n'z-), *sb.* [Blend of TRANSFER *v.* and RESISTOR.]

1. A semiconductor device, usu. having three terminals and two junctions, in which the load current can be made to be proportional to a small input current, so that it is functionally equivalent to a valve but is much smaller and more robust, operates at lower voltages, and consumes less power and produces less heat.

1948 *N.Y. Times* 1 July 46/3 A device called a transistor, which has several applications in radio where a vacuum tube ordinarily is employed, was demonstrated for the first time yesterday. **1948** BARDEEN & BRATTAIN in *Physical Rev.* 15 July 230/1 (*heading*) The transistor, a semi-conductor triode. **1949**, etc. [see *junction transistor* s.v. JUNCTION *sb.* 4]. **1952** *Electronic Engin.* XXIV. 42 Although it is unlikely that the transistor will ultimately displace the electronic valve, there is no doubt that for many electronic applications the transistor.. will be preferred because of its robust and compact form. **1953**, etc. [see *field-effect transistor* s.v. FIELD *sb.* 21]. **1957** *Observer* 1 Sept. 9/7 A novelty now gaining respectability is small-scale radio, with tiny medium-wave sets using printed circuits, and transistors instead of valves. **1962** [see *point contact* s.v. POINT *sb.*¹ B. 14]. **1970** J. EARL *Tuners & Amplifiers* iv. 78 Transistors, particularly the bigger power devices, are regarded as being current-operated... Valves, on the other hand, are often regarded as voltage-operated devices. **1973** *Sci. Amer.* Aug. 48/1 The MOS technology produces transistors of the unipolar type in contradistinction to earlier junction transistors, which are bipolar.

2. *ellipt.* = *transistor radio*, sense 3 below.

1961 *Daily Tel.* 13 July 12/2 Few seaside authorities are likely to risk driving away transistor-addicted visitors to other resorts. **1966** J. BETJEMAN *High & Low* 50 The endless anonymous croak of a cheap transistor Intensifies the loneliness I feel. **1977** *Rep. Comm. Future of Broadcasting* (Cmnd. 6753) iii. 23 Car radios and portable transistors have made radio one of the nation's major daytime diversions.

3. *Comb.*, as (sense 2) ***transistor-addicted*** adj.; **transistor radio**, a small portable radio having transistors and other solid-state devices in place of valves; **transistor set**, a radio or television set having transistors instead of valves; **transistor-transistor logic**, logic in which transistors take the place of many of the coupling resistors; abbrev. *TTL* s.v. T 6a.

1961 Transistor-addicted [see sense 2 above]. **1958** *Spectator* 1 Aug. 167/2 The new miniature transistor radios. **1965** AUDEN *About House* (1966) 15 Nobody I know would like to be buried with.. A transistor radio. **1957** *New Yorker* 13 July 19/1 The kid got one of those compact transistor sets for his birthday, and is absolutely fascinated by it. **1961** *Ann. Reg. 1960* 451 Television became more than ever an intrinsic part of Japanese life, and transistor sets of compact size made its penetration possible everywhere. **1963** Transistor-transistor logic [see TTL s.v. T 6a]. **1977** *McGraw-Hill Yearbk. Sci. & Technol.* 282/2 I²L is transistor-transistor logic (TTL) compatible.

transistorize (trɑːn'sɪstəraɪz, træn-, -n'z-), *v.* [f. prec. + -IZE.] *trans.* To design or make with transistors (rather than valves). Chiefly as **tran'sistorized** *ppl. a.*, employing transistors; also *fig.*

1953 *Sci. News Let.* 7 Feb. 86/1 Because of their ruggedness, 'transistorized' amplifiers should eliminate many an electronic headache under the restless sea. **1959** *Listener* 28 May 930/1 The compactness of transistorized equipment and their small power requirements make them suitable for use in telephone exchanges. **1963** T. D. TOWERS *Transistor T.V. Receivers* viii. 125/1 The line output stage has proved to be the most difficult part of the line time base to transistorise. **1963** *Daily Tel.* 5 Oct. 8/2 What Mr. Wilson has done is to lift the whole nationalisation issue.. out of its traditional context and give it a streamlined, transistorized modern setting. **1972** *Ibid.* 31 July 3/1 Both are powered by a new six cylinder, 2·8 litre twin-cam engine with transistorised ignition and electronic fuel injection. **1976** A. HOPE *Hi-fi Handbk.* 27 When the craze for transistorising everything got under way, in the 1960s, very few true hi-fi enthusiasts would touch a transistor amplifier with a barge pole. **1980** J. GARDNER *Garden of Weapons* II. ii. 132 The screech-boxes looked like.. radio sets. They were in fact transistorised transmitters.

Hence **tran,sistori'zation**, the use of transistors in electronic apparatus.

1957 *Trans. Soc. Instrument Technol.* IX. 41/1 One feels that 'transistorization' is bound to be introduced rapidly, thus reducing cost, weight and power consumption. **1969** *Radio Times* 4 Dec. 68 (Advt.), The Ferguson Colourstar is brilliantly designed for reliability with full transistorisation and modular construction.

transit ('trɑːnsɪt, 'træns-, -nz-), *sb.* Also 5 **trancyte,** 5–7 **transite.** [ad. L. *transit-us* (-*ū* stem), verbal sb. from *transīre* to cross, f. *trans* across + *īre* to go. So It. *transito*, whence Fr. *transit* (17th c.).]

1. a. The action or fact of passing across or through; passage or journey from one place or point to another. Often in phrase ***in transit***, L. *in transitu*.

c **1440** *Gesta Rom.* ii. 12 (Add. MS.) Above oure hede there is a transite of men [*Harl.* passage and goyng of peple]. **1716** M. DAVIES *Athen. Brit.* II. 171 Henry.. of Huntington .., who writ ten Books *Historiæ Anglorum*, from the Transit and Introit of the Saxons hither, to the Year 1153. **1766** W. DIGBY in Jesse *Selwyn & Contemp.* (1843) II. 12, I lay at Gloucester in my transit. **1833** RITCHIE *Wand. Loire* 27 Sometimes.. the transit from Nantes to Orleans takes two months! **1841** CATLIN *N. Amer. Ind.* xlvi. II. 87, I.. made a transit across the prairies. **1853** KANE *Grinnell Exp.* vii. (1856) 50 Of the voyages to Lancaster Sound.. the transit of the middle ice is the essential feature. **1877** BLACK *Green Past.* xxxii, In our rapid transit from place to place.

† **b.** *concr.* A way for passing, a passage.

c **1440** *Promp. Parv.* 499/2 Trancyte, where menn walke, *transitus*.

c. The passage or carriage of persons or goods from one place to another.

1800 COLQUHOUN *Comm. Thames* viii. 259 Property.. stationary on the Quays or in transit on the River. **1855** MACAULAY *Hist. Eng.* xiii. III. 254 While he governed, no prohibition.. impeded the transit of commodities from any part of the island to any other. **1866** ROGERS *Agric. & Prices* I. xx. 504 The cost of carriage. Occasionally.. this is charged in the value given, the transit being.. undertaken frequently by common carriers. **1870** YEATS *Nat. Hist. Comm.* 62 The means of transit are so bad, that much good corn is left to rot upon the ground.

(*b*) *spec.* Public passenger transport; freq. *attrib.* Chiefly *N. Amer.*

1873, etc. [see *rapid-transit* s.v. RAPID *a.* 6]. **1967** *Boston Sunday Globe* 23 Apr. 8/2 Legislature to launch a 10-year, $300 million urban transit program. **1971** *Rand Daily Mail* 27 Mar. 11/1 White bus drivers employed by a transit authority in an unnamed South African city. **1979** *Tucson* (Arizona) *Citizen* 20 Sept. 1 c/3 The Canadian city has good mass transit.

d. *transf.* A place at which a river may be crossed; a crossing. *rare.*

1852 GROTE *Greece* II. lxix. IX. 39 A.. flourishing town, a centre of commerce enriched by the important ford or transit of the river Euphrates close to it.

2. *fig.* (in various senses.) A passing across; a transition or change; *esp.* the passage from this life to the next by death.

1657 W. MORICE *Coena quasi Κοινὴ*, Diat. v. 237 There can be no such transite from one kinde of action to another. **1765** H. WALPOLE *Otranto* iii. (1798) 50 To pray for her happy transit to a better life. **1810** KNOX & JEBB *Corr.* II. 19 The transit from autumn to winter. **1823** SCOTT *Quentin D.* vi, Speak a word of comfort to him ere he make his transit, Trois-Eschelles. **1859** HOLLAND *Gold F.* xv. 182 Old men.. whose work of life is.. done, and who may in peace.. sit down and wait their mysterious transit. **1871** EARLE *Philol. Eng. Tongue* §270 This verb made an early transit to the weak form.

3. *Astrol.* The passage of a planet across some special point or region of the zodiac.

[**1621** BURTON *Anat. Mel.* I. ii. I. iv, If ♄, by his revolution, or *transitus*, shall offend any of those radicall promissors in his geniture.] **1671** SALMON *Syn. Med.* I. xxix. 61 In Directions and Transits three things are to be considered; first the Significator, secondly the Promissor; thirdly the sign and house in which they happen. **1819** J. WILSON *Dict. Astrol.* s.v., The transits of the ☽ are said to cause all the daily passing events of a man's life, as she transits the △, ✱, □, ☍, or ☌, of any particular house.

4. *Astron.* **a.** The passage of an inferior planet (Mercury or Venus) across the sun's disk, or of a satellite or its shadow across the disk of a planet; formerly also applied to an occultation of a star or planet by the moon, or of a star by a planet.

1669 FLAMSTEAD in *Phil. Trans.* IV. 1110 Let me desire those, who have fit.. Instruments, to observe this Transit. **1704** J. HARRIS *Lex. Techn.* I, *Transit*, in *Astronomy*, signifies the passing of any Planet just by or under any Fixt Star; or of the Moon in particular, covering or moving close by any other Planet. **1769** M. CUTLER in *Life*, etc. (1888) I. 20 The 3d of this month happened the Transit of Venus over the sun's disk. **1769** COOK *Voy. r. World* I. xiii. (1773) 137 On Thursday the 1st of June, the Saturday following being the day of the Transit, I dispatched Mr. Gore in the long-boat to Imao. **1829** *Chapters Phys. Sc.* 398 The transits of Mercury and Venus are really eclipses of the sun. **1868** LOCKYER *Guillemin's Heavens* III. II. i. (ed. 3) 478 The value of the Sun's distance at present received has been deduced from the transits of Venus in 1761 and 1769. **1910**

Whitaker's Almanack 88 Only Satellite IV [of Jupiter] will be visible at 2.30 a.m. February 24—Satellite II. being in transit, Satellite III. occulted, and Satellite I. eclipsed.

transf. **1859** in *Merc. Marine Mag.* (1860) VII. 65 The Shoal first seen was in transit with Embleton Island, bearing N.E. ¾E.

b. The passage of a star or other celestial body across the meridian at its culmination.

1812 WOODHOUSE *Astron.* viii. 48 Two successive transits of a star over the meridian. **1834** MRS. SOMERVILLE *Connex. Phys. Sc.* vii. 61 While observing transits of the fixed stars across the meridian at Cayenne.

c. Short for *transit-circle*, *-compass*, *-instrument*, or *-theodolite*: see 5. *colloq.*

1843 *Penny Cycl.* XXV. 122/1 Transit, or Transit Instrument. *Ibid.* 122/2 Such an account of the transit as will enable any one to use it with tolerable success. **1879** NEWCOMB & HOLDEN *Astron.* 74 The meridian transit instrument, or briefly the 'transit'. **1897** *Edin. Rev.* July 66 The institution, furnished only with a transit when he took it in charge.

5. *attrib.* and *Comb.*, usually in relation to the conveyance of goods and passengers, as ***transit-company***, ***-depot***, ***-line***, ***-road***, ***-room***, ***-time***, ***-traffic***, ***-way***; also **transit camp**, a camp for the temporary accommodation of servicemen awaiting posting, refugees, prisoners-of-war, etc.; **transit-circle**, an astronomical instrument consisting of a telescope carrying a large graduated circle, by which the right ascension and declination of a star may be determined by observation of it in transit (sense 4 b); a meridian-circle; **transit-clock**, a clock used in conjunction with a transit-instrument; **transit-compass**, an instrument, resembling a theodolite, used in surveying for the measurement of horizontal angles; **transit-duty**, a duty paid on goods passing through a country; **transit-instrument**, an astronomical telescope mounted on a fixed east-and-west axis, by which the time of the passage of a celestial body across the meridian may be determined; usually applied to one without a circle (cf. *transit-circle*); **transit lounge**, a waiting-room for transit passengers at an airport; **transit man** *N. Amer.*, a surveyor who uses a transit-compass; **transit-pass**, a warrant to pass through a country without payment of duty; **transit passenger**, a passenger making a brief stop at an airport in transit to another destination; **transit-theodolite** = *transit-compass*; **transit-trade**, trade arising out of the passage of foreign goods through a country; **transit visa**, a visa permitting the holder to pass through a country but not to stay there. (See also sense 1 c).

1943 G. GREENE *Ministry of Fear* II. ii. 144 The place was as comfortless as a *transit camp. **1946** E. LINKLATER *Private Angelo* xiii. 151 [He] made his escape..from a transit camp for prisoners of war near Bari. **1956** WALLIS & BLAIR *Thunder Above* (1959) xi. 113 There were 25,000 East German refugees in West Berlin, living in transit camps built to accommodate 13,000. **1980** D. LODGE *How Far can you Go?* i. 7 Purgatory was a kind of penitential transit camp on the way to the gates of Heaven. **1843** *Penny Cycl.* XXV. 133/1 A *transit circle may be made to answer both purposes. **1897** *Edin. Rev.* July 68 In 1851 a new transit circle, of great optical power and enormous mechanical stability, superseded Troughton's master-piece of 1812. **1843** *Penny Cycl.* XXV. 130/1 To have a second clock called a journeyman, which strikes loudly and speaks as it were for the *transit clock. **1845** R. BROWN in *Mem.* ii. (1866) 28 We got into one of the *Transit Company's vans. **1887** MOLONEY *Forestry W. Afr.* 248 The Public Works Department of each Colony offers a ready *transit-depot for such contributions. **1776** ADAM SMITH *W.N.* v. ii. II. 515 In some small states duties..are imposed upon goods carried across the territory..from one foreign country to another. These are in some countries called *transit-duties. **1809** *State Papers* in *Ann. Reg.* 697/1 The transit duties on the goods thus imported or exported. **1812** WOODHOUSE *Astron.* vi. 32 It may be used as a *transit instrument: that is, the presence of a star on the meridian may be ascertained by it. **1894** HARDY *Life's Little Ironies* 179 For South Wessex, the year [*sc.* 1851] formed in many ways an extraordinary chronological frontier or *transit-line, at which there occurred what one might call a precipice in Time. **1962** J. FLEMING *When I grow Rich* iii. 43 After the arrival of the jet, the *transit lounge had filled up with people. **1983** *Jetaway* (Air New Zealand) Sept.–Oct. 28/2 Transit lounge for 500 passengers who are transferring flights or have no need to go through customs. **1973** *Transit man [PACKER[1] 3 c]. **1971** *Islander* (Victoria, B.C.) 8 May 12/1 Harry, a young transit man, had his bed roll next to the Bella Coola trapper. **1889** *Pall Mall Gaz.* 2 Sept. 7/3 Less..than it cost foreigners to bring it to Pakhio under *transit-pass. **1955** E. BOWEN *World of Love* xi. 223 They let the *transit passengers off first. **1972** J. POTTER *Going West* 17 Transit passengers were encouraged to alight for the stopover. **1861** J. NICHOL in *Mem.* (1896) 37 As regular as the *transit-room clock. **1862** *Catal. Internat. Exhib.* II. XIII. 3 A first-rate 6-inch *transit theodolite,..with vertical and horizontal circles. **1948** MARTIN & HYNES *Clin. Endocrinol.* iv. 70 The intestinal *transit-time is decreased with the production of loose stools or frank diarrhœa. **1962** SIMPSON & RICHARDS *Physical Princ. Junction Transistors* vii. 117 When operation at higher frequencies is considered these complexities increase manyfold due chiefly to transit-time effects in the flow of minority carriers. **1974** *Brit. Med. Jrnl.* 19 Jan. 108/2 Constipation is best thought of not in terms of transit-time through the gut ..but rather the type of faeces produced. **1975** D. G. FINK *Electronics Engineers' Handbk.* VII. 27 Transit time is a large factor in considering the upper frequency limitation of electron tubes. **1803** *Edin. Rev.* III. 243 Those..nations whose wealth has been promoted by the *transit trade. **1852** CONYBEARE & H. *St. Paul* (1862) II. xxiii. 329 The Valley of the Nile was the channel of an active transit trade in spices, dyes, jewels, and perfumes. **1903** *Expositor* May 335 Jerusalem had no natural command of the *transit-traffic. **1925** C. CONNOLLY *Let.* May in *Romantic Friendship* (1975) 81, I..had got as far as sending my passport up for some *transit visas. **1979** W. H. CANAWAY *Solid Gold Buddha* xx. 134 Miller went to the Burmese Embassy..and got his transit visa. **1904** *Q. Rev.* Oct. 341 The trade-winds.. contribute greatly to the salubrity and comfort of this *transit-way.

transit ('trɑːnsɪt, 'træns-, -nz-), *v.* [f. L. *transit-*, ppl. stem of *transīre*: see prec. Cf. L. *transitāre*, freq. of *transīre* (instanced in pr. pple. *transitāns* Cic.). In earlier use stressed *trans'ite*.]

1. *intr.* To pass through or over; to pass away.

c **1440** *Gesta Rom.* xc. 415 The porter is the worlde; and right as by the porter so by the worlde we may transite. **1595** CHAPMAN *Ovid's Banq. Sence* (1639) 11 As Intellects themselves transite to each intelligible qualitie. **1775** 'JOEL COLLIER' (Alex. Bicknell) *Mus. Trav.* (ed. 2) 68, I then transited to the gentleman himself. **1797–1803** FOSTER in *Life & Corr.* (1846) I. 173 The comets of the mind; they transit off. **1803** *Ibid.* 196, I have transited into another person. **1852** N. L. WALKER *Life in Spirit* xiii. (1853) 212 One or two transit off from our Divinity Halls annually.

2. *trans.* To pass across or through (something); to traverse, cross. Also *fig.*

1674 JEAKE *Arith.* (1696) 249, I have..transited Decimals and Astronomicals, and shall now apply myself to overlook Logarithmes. **1890** *Pall Mall Gaz.* 10 Mar. 3/1 Another line which would transit Germany, Russia,..Afghanistan, and India.

3. *Astrol.* To pass across (a sign, 'house', or special point, of the zodiac). Also *absol.* or *intr.*

1647 LILLY *Chr. Astrol.* lxvii. 409 When the unfortunate Anareta transits the degree ascending. **1686** GOAD *Celest. Bodies* III. ii. 403 Feavers..do annoy us, when the Heavenly Bodies Transit, or take up Station in such Parts of the Zodiack. **1819** J. WILSON *Dict. Astrol.* s.v. *Transits*, If the lord of the 8th..transit the cusp of the horoscope, it threatens death.

4. *Astron.* To pass across (the disk of a celestial body, the meridian of a place, or the field of view of a telescope). Also *absol.* or *intr.*

In quot. 1686 of the moon, to occult (a star or planet).
1686 GOAD *Celest. Bodies* I. xii. 49 The ☽ transiting ♀ that Night raised the Tides. **1755** B. MARTIN *Mag. Arts & Sc.* I. 45 In the Years 1753, 1786, 1799, in the Month of April, he [Mercury] will transit the Sun's Disk. **1833** HERSCHEL *Astron.* viii. 256 Rendering the planet invisible, unless.. where it transits the sun's disc and appears on it as a black spot. **1870** PROCTOR *Other Worlds* viii. (ed. 2) 184 The markings seen on the third satellite, when transiting Jupiter's disc. **1878** LOCKYER *Stargazing* 354 The value of the divisions of the micrometer screw having been previously determined by allowing an equatorial star to transit.

transitable ('trɑːnsɪtəb(ə)l, 'træns-), *a. rare.* [f. as prec. + -ABLE.] Capable of being passed across or over; affording means of transit.

1843 *Blackw. Mag.* LIV. 660 The river Chagre..is the nearest transitable point to Panama. **1866** RUSKIN in Spielmann *Life* (1900) 50 If you think it at all curable or transit-able, I'll advance her 20 pounds without interest. **1897** *Jrnl. R. Geog. Soc.* July 63 The efforts..made to open a transitable road to [the valley of the Rio Grande de Terraba] from the north..have proven futile.

‖**transi'tarium.** *Obs. rare.* [mod.L., f. TRANSIT *sb.* 4 a; cf. *planetarium*.] An apparatus for illustrating the transit of a planet.

1761 *Brit. Mag.* II. 668 Earl Ferrers..presented to the [Royal] Society..a transitarium invented by his lordship for giving an ocular demonstration of the principles relating to the theory of that planet [Venus].

transi'tation. *rare.* [n. of action f. L. *transitāre*: see TRANSIT *v.* and -ATION.] The action of passing; passage. (In early quots. *humorous*.)

1600–9 ROWLANDS *Knave of Clubs* 37 As on the way I Itinerated, A Rurall person I Obuiated, Interogating times Transitation. **1605** VERSTEGAN *Dec. Intell.* vii. 205. **1915** D. H. LAWRENCE *Rainbow* vii. 187 Containing birth and death, potential with all the noise and transitation of life, the cathedral remained hushed.

'transiter. *rare.* [f. TRANSIT *sb.* or *v.* + -ER[1].] Name for a form of the apparatus usually called a 'recording micrometer', and attached to the eye-end of a transit telescope.

1902 *Science* (U.S.) 2 May 693/2 The actual arrangement in use at the Philadelphia Observatory, called for brevity a 'transiter'... The transiter seemed to furnish all the necessary facilities of motion and of recording, and.. permitted elimination of all errors excepting that of bisection.

transition (trɑːn'sɪʒən, træn-, -'sɪʃən, -'zɪʃən). [ad. L. *transitiōn-em*, n. of action f. *transīre*, *transit-* (see TRANSIT *v.*). Cf. F. *transition* (13–14th c. in Hatz.-Darm.).

(The first and prevailing pronunciation, contrary to the general analogy of words in *-tion*, is app. due (as suggested by Walker) to a desire to avoid the collocation of the two similar (voiceless) sibilants (s) and (ʃ).)]

1. a. A passing or passage from one condition, action, or (rarely) place, to another; change.

1551 GARDINER *Explication, Of Transubstantiation* 123 In the mysterie of Christes person, there is no transition of the deitie into the humanite, or humanite into the deitie. **1621** G. SANDYS *Ovid's Met.* VI. (1626) 109 The vast sky painted with a mightie Bowe: Where, though a thousand seuerall colours shine, No eye their close transition can define. **1751** JOHNSON *Rambler* No. 172 ¶7 A quick transition from poverty to abundance can seldom be made with safety. **1851** HAWTHORNE *Ho. Sev. Gables* xvii, Transition being so facile, what can be any man's inducement to tarry in one spot? **1862** SIR H. HOLLAND *Ess.* i. 1 We are living in an age of transition. **1899** STALKER *Christology of Jesus* v. 186 Death was..only a stage of transition to a higher form of life.

b. *Physics.* A change of an atomic nucleus or an orbital electron from one quantized state to another, with the emission or absorption of radiation of a characteristic wavelength.

1913 *Phil. Mag.* XXVI. 18 We consequently observe an absorption of radiation which is not accompanied by a complete transition between two different stationary states. **1922** tr. *Bohr's Theory of Spectra* III. iv. 118 Emission lines of the X-ray spectra due to transitions between the stationary states corresponding to these energy levels. **1930** *Science* 10 Oct. 376/2 Very little is known about nuclear properties of atoms because of the difficulties inherent in excitation of nuclear transitions in the laboratory. **1962** [see LEVEL *sb.* 3 e]. **1977** *Whitaker's Almanack 1978* 1035/2 By varying the frequency, a detailed analysis of a particular x-ray transition was made.

2. Passage in thought, speech, or writing from one subject to another.

1592 tr. *Junius on Rev.* vii. 1 This first verse is a transition. **1674** MILTON *P.L.* (ed. 2) XII. 5 Heer the Archangel paus'd ..Then with transition sweet new Speech resumes. **1724** WATTS *Logic* IV. ii. vii. §3 Acquaint yourself with all the proper..forms of transition from one part of a discourse to another. **1798** EDGEWORTH *Pract. Educ.* (1811) I. 115 The transition of attention from one subject to another. **1875** JOWETT *Plato* (ed. 2) V. 15 The Timaeus..one of his [Plato's] most finished works, is full of abrupt transitions.

3. *Mus.* †**a.** The passing from one note to another by means of a passing-note (*obs.*). **b.** The passing from one key to another, modulation; *spec.* a passing or brief modulation; also, modulation into a remote key.

1667 C. SIMPSON *Compend. Mus.* 88 A Note is somtimes broken to make a Transition by degrees to some other Concord. These Transitions or Breakings are commonly express'd in Quavers or Crochets. **1877** STAINER *Harmony* xii. §150 A transition is the rapid passing through any key, without remaining sufficiently long in it to establish a modulation. **1889** PROUT *Harmony* x. (ed. 3) 101 Some writers use the term 'Transition', when the modulation is to a remote or unrelated key.

4. The passage from an earlier to a later stage of development or formation. **a.** *Geol.* Formerly *spec.* applied *attrib.* to certain early stratified rocks believed to contain the oldest remains of living organisms; now classified as Silurian: see quot. 1813.

1813 BAKEWELL *Introd. Geol.* (1815) 9 The lowest of the secondary rocks have..been called by the German geologists transition rocks, from the supposition that they were formed when the world was passing from an uninhabitable to a habitable state. **1815** W. PHILLIPS *Outl. Min. & Geol.* (1818) 116 To primitive rocks succeeds another class, which Werner denominates *Transition* rocks. **1823** BUCKLAND *Reliq. Diluv.* 117 It lies in a bed of transition limestone. **1834–5** J. PHILLIPS *Geol.* in *Encycl. Metrop.* VI. 593/2 On the East side of the transition ranges of the Wrekin and Wenlock Edge lies the coalfield of Coalbrook Dale. **1839** MURCHISON *Silur. Syst.* I. xxxiv. 452 It also presents certain beds of transition between the limestone and the Old Red Sandstone. **1855** J. PHILLIPS *Man. Geol.* 104 The two parts connected by a transition band (upper caradoc). **1885** GEIKIE *Text-bk. Geol.* VI. II. ii. §1. 658 Murchison was the first to discover that the so-called 'Transition Rocks' or 'Grauwacke' of early geological literature were capable of subdivision into distinct formations..he gave them the name of Silurian.

b. *Arch.* Change from an earlier style to a later; a style of intermediate or mixed character.

1835 R. WILLIS *Archit. Mid. Ages* i. 9 These may be called Imitation Specimens, to distinguish them from regular Transitions. **1842–76** GWILT *Archit.* Gloss., *Transition*, a term used to denote the passing from one period of a style to another, exhibiting features peculiar to both, some of which have not quite been given up, and some of which were beginning to be introduced. **1874** PARKER *Goth. Archit.* I. iii. 39 The remainder of the eleventh century may be considered as a period of transition.

c. *Philol.* The historical passage of language from one well-defined stage to another; e.g. from Old English or Anglo-Saxon to Middle English; or from Middle English to Modern English; hence applied to the interval occupied by this, and to the intermediate or transitional stage or form of the language during this interval.

1873–4 SWEET *Hist. Eng. Sounds* 160 We have..two periods of transition, one in which *nama* and *name* exist side by side, and another in which final *e* is beginning to drop... The former, commonly called Semi-Saxon.., is characterized by many far-reaching changes. I propose..to call the first the *Transition* period *par excellence*, distinguishing the two, when necessary, as first and second *Transition*, the more important one being generally called simply *Transition* or *Transition-English*. *Ibid.* 38 In the Transition period..we are confronted by [a] curious and apparently inexplicable phenomenon. **1878** MURRAY *Eng. Lang.* in *Encycl. Brit.* VIII. 391/2 Transition Old English, or 'Semi-Saxon' 1120 to 1200... Transition Middle English 1400 to 1485... Many writers carry the Transition Old English down to 1250. *Ibid.* 397/2 The change of the language during the second period of Transition. *Ibid.* 402

Chronological Chart [has] Old English Transition 1123–1200. Middle English Transition, 1400–1485.

5. *Molecular Biol.* The occurrence in a nucleic acid of one purine in place of another, or of one pyramidine in place of another. Cf. TRANSVERSION[1] 3.

1959 E. FREESE in *Proc. Nat. Acad. Sci.* XLV. 630 Each base analogue can induce the transitions.. in both directions (from A–T into G–H and vice versa). **1981** PAI & MARCUS-ROBERTS *Genetics* xv. 477 Substitutions of bases are further classified as transitions or transversions.

6. a. *attrib.*, as ***transition area, belt, form, period, point, region, species, stage, state, zone***, etc.: see also 4a and c. Often equivalent to TRANSITIONAL.

1805–17 R. JAMESON *Char. Min.* (ed. 3) 126 All the crystals that lie between two principal crystals, and form the transition of one into the other, constitute what is called a transition-suite. **1826** KIRBY & SP. *Entomol.* (1828) III. xxix. 161 Groups..connected by certain transition species. **1831** CARLYLE in *Fraser's Mag.* Mar. 144/2 *Don Karlos*, a work of what may be called his transition-period, the turning-point between his earlier and his later period. **1841** J. S. BUCKINGHAM *America* I. 461 Baltimore.. appears from the very first to have been peopled by a race that never had this transition-state to pass through. **1843** R. J. GRAVES *Syst. Clin. Med.* xxvii. 343 The most obstinate form [of the disease] generally selects such transition spots or intermediate tissues. **1853** J. SMITH *Treat. Mus.* 33 Transition or passing notes. **1856** FROUDE *Hist. Eng.* I. ii. 86 Wolsey..holding a middle place between an English statesman and a catholic of the old order, was essentially a transition minister. **1865** TYLOR *Early Hist. Man.* vii. 188 A very good example of this interesting transition work. **1884** J. TAIT *Mind in Matter* (1892) 50 The transition-stages set forth by revolutionists. **1907** E. A. MEARNS *Mammals Mexican Boundary* 135 This station lies in the Transition Zone, the highest peaks extending well into the Canadian or lowest section of the Boreal Zone. **1940** *Chambers's Tech. Dict.* 860/1 *Transition region*, the portion of the axis of a young plant in which the change from root structure to shoot structure occurs. **1950** *Texas Studies in Eng.* XXIX. 254 The transition area (where both [s] and [z] are used), is relatively narrow to the west of Philadelphia. **1957** *Publ. Amer. Dial. Soc.* XXVII. 5 The net effect being to create a transition belt. **1969** J. J. SPARKES *Transistor Switching* i. 15 This results in a narrowing of the collector transition region and a widening of the base region. **1972** H. KURATH *Studies in Area Linguistics* iii. 44 The transition area between the North and the Midland reflects partly the complicated history of the settlement. **1977** *Nature* 14 Apr. 662/1 It is becoming increasingly apparent that FMO interactions are even more important in transition states than they seem to be on inspection of isolated reactant orbitals. **1977** A. HALLAM *Planet Earth* 11/3 Based on its density distribution, the mantle has been divided into three parts: the upper mantle, which extends to a depth of 400km..; the transition zone, which extends from 400 to about 700km..; and the lower mantle. **1978** D. JOY *Railways in Lancashire* 81/1 This view shows the transition period with the new station completed but the old one not yet demolished. **1982** *Amer. Speech* LVII. 293 A discussion of isoglosses and transition belts..underpins Chambers and Trudgill's theory of urban dialects.

b. Special Combs.: **transition element** *Chem.*, †(*a*) any of the nine metallic elements forming group VIII of the periodic table (see quot. 1922); cf. *transitional element* s.v. TRANSITIONAL *a.* c; (*b*) any of a large class of metallic elements making up groups IIIA–VIIA, VIII, and IB of the periodic table (groups 3–11 in the new notation), which are characterized by partly filled *d* orbitals and commonly exhibit variable valency and an ability to form coloured complexes; also extended to include elements having partly filled *f* orbitals (see quots. 1962); **transition fit** *Engin.*, a fit between two mating parts such that, within the specified tolerances, there may be either interference or clearance between them; **transition flow** (see quot. 1969); **transition metal** *Chem.* = *transition element* (*b*) above; **transition probability** *Physics*, the probability of a transition between two given states of a system, *spec.* an atom; **transition temperature** *Physics*, the temperature at which a substance acquires or loses some distinctive property, esp. superconductivity.

1922 E. J. HOLMYARD *Inorganic Chem.* xxx. 530 (*heading*) The 'transition elements'.—Iron, cobalt, nickel; ruthenium, rhodium, palladium; osmium, iridium, platinum. **1953** DE BARRY BARNETT & WILSON *Inorganic Chem.* i. 6 Transition Elements. This term was originally used by Mendeleef for the three triads of elements forming Group VIII of his periodic table.., but this meaning of the term has long since been abandoned. **1962** COTTON & WILKINSON *Adv. Inorganic Chem.* xxiv. 493 The transition elements may be strictly defined as those which, *as elements*, have partly filled *d* or *f* shells. Here we shall adopt a slightly broader definition and include also elements which have partly filled *d* or *f* shells in any of their commonly occurring oxidation states. *Ibid.* 494 The large number of transition elements is subdivided into three main groups: (*a*) the main transition elements or *d*-block elements, (*b*) the lanthanide elements, and (*c*) the actinide elements. **1965** PHILLIPS & WILLIAMS *Inorganic Chem.* I. ii. 52 The valences of the transition and lanthanide elements. **1974** *Encycl. Brit. Macropædia* XVIII. 600/2 The so-called transition elements constitute a group of 56 (the majority of the 105 known elements). **1919** Transition fit [see *interference fit* s.v. INTERFERENCE 6]. **1971** B. SCHARF *Engin. & its Lang.* xi. 111 Transition fits are so designed that either clearance or interference may occur when the mating parts are assembled. Push fits may be tolerance fits. **1969** *Gloss. Aeronaut & Astronaut. Terms* (*B.S.I.*) IV. 11 *Transition flow*, the flow of gases under conditions intermediate between laminar viscous flow and molecular flow. **1942** *Ann. Reg. 1941* 356 Potter.. investigated the resistivity..of pure samples of the transition metals. **1970** *New Scientist* 3 Sept. 457/2 The chemistry of the transition metals..is dominated by their complex compounds. **1926** E. CONDON in *Physical Rev.* XXVIII. 1185 The theory of transition probability which will now be developed is an outgrowth of a picture proposed by Franck. **1942**, etc. [see MARKOV]. **1978** PASACHOFF & KUTNER *University Astron.* xxiv. 598 Even though this transition probability is so very low, there are so many hydrogen atoms in space that enough 21-cm radiation is given off to be detected. **1930** *Sci. Abstr.* XXXIII. 697 In all these cases, at temperatures below the transition temperature, increasing the intensity of the magnetic field to a certain value..causes the super-conductivity to disappear. **1966** C. R. TOTTLE *Sci. Engin. Materials* vi. 127 For the compound Nb_3Sn the transition temperature is as high as 18·2°K. **1982** *Sci. Amer.* May 30/1 Ferroelectric and ferromagnetic transition temperatures.

transitional (trɑːnˈsɪʒənəl, træn-, -ˈsɪʃ-, -ˈzɪʃ-), *a.* (*sb.*) [f. prec. + -AL[1].]

A. *adj.* **a.** Of or pertaining to transition; characterized by or involving transition; intermediate.

c **1810** COLERIDGE in *Lit. Rem.* (1838) III. 262 The Jewish Rabbis..represented the Millennium as the preparative and transitional state to perfect spiritualization. **1859** DARWIN *Orig. Spec.* vi. (1860) 172 By this theory innumerable transitional forms must have existed. **1867** A. J. ELLIS *E.E. Pronunc.* I. i. 30 Shakspere and Milton are transitional between Spenser and Dryden. **1867** FREEMAN *Norm. Conq.* I. i. 3 At a transitional period in the world's developement. **1874** PARKER *Goth. Archit.* I. iii. 58 The arches are transitional, two being round and two pointed.

b. ***transitional case*** in grammar, a case in some languages expressing motion toward.

1890 A. S. GATSCHET *Gram. Klamath Lang.* 484 Transitional case in -na... This locative case-suffix.. corresponds to our *to, toward, into, in.*

c. *Chem.* ***transitional element*** = *transition element* (*a*) s.v. TRANSITION 6b.

1887 C. M. TIDY *Handbk. Mod. Chem.* (ed. 2) ii. 54 In Group VIII. three elements occur. These are termed by Mendeleef 'transitional elements', that is, elements occurring between the even and the odd series of a long period. **1921** J. R. PARTINGTON *Text-bk. Inorganic Chem.* xlviii. 972 The transitional elements.—The eighth group of the Periodic System comprises three sub-groups, with three elements in each, forming the termination of the even series 4, 6, and 8, and connecting the elements of these series with those of the odd series following. For this reason they were called by Mendeléeff the transitional elements.

B. *ellipt.* as *sb.* (in quot. for *transitional cell*: cf. quot. 1904 s.v. MONONUCLEAR).

1904 *Brit. Med. Jrnl.* 10 Sept. 583 They [mononuclear white blood cells] become transformed in the blood (according to Ehrlich) into the transitionals.

Hence **tranˈsitionally** *adv.*, **tranˈsitionalness**.

1874 RUSKIN *Fors Clav.* xliv. 164 This plate of mine, melted down, after being transitionally serviceable to the burglar, will enter again into the same functions among the silver of the world. **1896** *Scot. Leader* 1 Jan. 7 A deep sense of the transitionalness of conclusions which were once thought to be for all time.

transitionary (trɑːnˈsɪʒənərɪ, træn-, -ˈsɪʃ-, -ˈzɪʃ-), *a.* [f. as prec. + -ARY[1].] = TRANSITIONAL.

1685 H. MORE *Paralip. Prophet.* xxi. 181 This third Introductory Vision is a kind of Transitionary Introduction to the Opened Book-Prophecy. **1827** *Examiner* 630/2 The rapid, elastic, transitionary style of this actor. **1858** BUCKLE *Civiliz.* (1864) I. viii. 472 The transitionary state which France began to enter. **1900** *Literature* 14 July 28/1 The Induction..is essentially of a transitionary character.

tranˈsitionist. *rare*[−1]. [f. as prec. + -IST.] One who supports transition; in quot. *attrib.*

1856 E. G. K. BROWNE *Tractarian Movem.* (1861) 438 The advanced guard of the Transitionist party.

†**tranˈsitious,** *a. Obs. rare*[−0]. [f. TRANSITION + -OUS.] Transitional. Hence †**tranˈsitiously** *adv.* (*obs. rare*[−1]), transitionally, by transitions.

1652 URQUHART *Jewel* Wks. (1834) 292 Speeches extending a matter..auxetically, digressively, transitiously.

transitival (trɑːnsɪˈtaɪvəl, træns-, -nz-), *a. Gram. rare.* [f. TRANSITIVE + -AL[1]: cf. *adjectival, genitival*, etc.] = TRANSITIVE 2.

1871 EARLE *Philol. Eng. T.* §270 This was a new and quite different verb, and should have had the transitival use.

transitive (ˈtrɑːnsɪtɪv, ˈtræns-, -nz-), *a.* (*sb.*) [ad. late L. *transitīvus* (Priscian), f. *transit-* (see TRANSIT) + *-īvus*, -IVE; in F. *transitif* (16th c.). With sense 1 cf. OF. *transitif* transient (13th c. in Godef.).]

†**1.** Passing or liable to pass into another condition, changeable, changeful; passing away, transient, transitory. *Obs. rare.*

1560 ROLLAND *Crt. Venus* I. 67 Thair waillit weid..Sa gay it was,..Sa wariant to sicht and transitiue. **1625** BRATHWAIT *Five Senses* 296 What availes it thee now to enjoy the transitive honours of this life? **1845** [implied in TRANSITIVENESS]. **1906** *Springfield* (Mass.) *Weekly Republican* 8 Mar. 6 At present he is in a transitive state.

2. a. *Gram.* Of verbs and their construction: Expressing an action which passes over to an object; taking a direct object to complete the sense.

1571 [implied in TRANSITIVELY a]. **1590** STOCKWOOD *Rules Constr.* 64 A verbe transitiue..is such..as passeth ouer his signification into some other thing, as when I say, 'I loue God'. **1673** O. WALKER *Educ.* 153 Others are transient, when the Agent and Patient are divers, and are expressed by Verbs transitives, as striking, heating [etc.]. **1845** STODDART *Gram.* in *Encycl. Metrop.* (1847) I. 48/1 Verbs transitive and intransitive are, in other words, active and neuter; for the verb active is considered as passing over from the agent to the object, whilst the neuter is considered as not passing over.

b. as *sb.* A transitive verb.

1612 BRINSLEY *Lud. Lit.* 129 That other rule for the Acusatiue after the Verbe, is of Transitiues, whose action passeth into another thing.

3. *Philos.* Passing out of itself; passing over to or affecting something else; operating beyond itself; = TRANSIENT 2. (Opposed to *immanent*.)

1613 PURCHAS *Pilgrimage* I. i. 5 For all the proprieties of God are infinite, as they are immanent in himselfe, yet in their transitiue and forren effectes are stinted and limited to the modell and state of the creature. **1626** BACON *Sylva* §70 Cold is Active and Transitive into Bodies Adjacent, as well as Heat. **1785** REID *Intell. Powers* II. xiv. (1803) I. 306 Logicians distinguish two kinds of operations of the mind; the first kind produces no effect without the mind, the last does. The first they call immanent acts; the second transitive. **1893** FAIRBAIRN *Christ in Mod. Theol.* II. II. iii. 441 It is of the essence of both to be transitive. Love regards an object whose good it desires; righteousness is the conduct which fulfils the desire of love.

4. Characterized by or involving transition, in various senses: that has something passing through it (*obs.*); that itself passes through stages; that forms a transition (real, or in thought) between two stages, positions, or conditions; that is in an intermediate stage or position; transitional; intermediate; transformational. Now *rare* or *Obs.*

1660 JER. TAYLOR *Duct. Dubit.* II. ii. rule vi. §7 An image that is understood to be an image can never be made an idol; or if it can it must be by having the worship of God pass'd thorough it to God;..by being the analogical, the improper, the transitive, the relative (or what shall I call it) object of Divine worship. **1811** PINKERTON *Petralogy* I. 73 This transitive grunstein occurs in the Hartz. **1836** I. TAYLOR *Phys. The. Another Life* xii. (1847) 166 The preparations that are made by any of the transitive species of animals..for their approaching metamorphosis. **1854** F. BAKEWELL *Geol.* 5 The lower portion, resting on the crystalline rocks, being called the transitive series. **1860** MAYNE *Expos. Lex.*, *Transitivus*, applied by Werner to rocks or soils that present ..the vestiges of organised bodies;..as forming the transition of soils from the first class to those of the third, with which they are nearly related: transitive. **1865** GROTE *Plato* I. xvii. 494 The transitive process, above described, represents the successive stages by which every adult mind has been gradually built up from infancy.

5. Of the application of words: Transferred. *rare.* ? *Obs.*

1810 D. STEWART *Philos. Ess.* II. I. i. 226 The greater part of the transitive or derivative applications of words depend on casual and unaccountable caprices of the feelings or of the fancy.

6. *Math.* [ad. G. *transitiv* (S. Lie *Theorie d. Transformationsgruppen* (1888) I. 212).] In the theory of groups: see quots.

1888 *Amer. Jrnl. Math.* X. 297 If..a G_r in *xy* can transform every ordinary point of the plane to every other ordinary point of the plane, the G_r is said to be transitive. **1890** *Cent. Dict.* s.v. *Group*, A group is called doubly, triply, or n times transitive if any set of 2, 3, n elements can be brought to any places. **1902** *Encycl. Brit.* XXIX. 121/1 If it is possible to find an operation S of the group such that O.S is any assigned one of the set of objects, the group is called *transitive* in respect of this set of objects. When this is not possible, the group is called *intransitive* in respect of the set. **1968** [see PRIMITIVE *a.* 5d]. **1971** L. DORNHOFF *Group Representation Theory* A. xxxvi. 215 Nontrivial normal subgroups of primitive permutation groups are transitive.

7. *Math.* and *Logic.* Of a relation: such that if it holds between a first and second item, and also between the second and a third, it necessarily holds between the first and the third.

1856 A. DE MORGAN in *Trans. Cambr. Philos. Soc.* IX. 104 The first is what I shall call *transitiveness*, symbolized in $X-Y-Z = X-Z$; meaning that if *X* stand in the relation denoted by — to *Y*, and *Y* to *Z*, *X* therefore stands in that relation to *Z*. Very many copulæ exist in which this transitive relation is seen. **1870**, etc. [see INTRANSITIVE *a.* 3]. **1903**, etc. [see REFLEXIVE *a.* 7]. **1936** A. J. AYER *Lang., Truth & Logic* iii. 79 As each of these relations is symmetrical.. and also transitive..it follows that the groups of visual and tactual sense-contents which are constituted by means of these relations cannot have any members in common. **1956** E. H. HUTTEN *Lang. Mod. Physics* iv. 143 We take as axiom the statement that the thermal equilibrium is a transitive relation, i.e. if two bodies in thermal equilibrium are in equilibrium with a third body, all three bodies have a common property, that is, the same temperature. **1976** *Nature* 29 Apr. 773/1 Whether or not the young child can make transitive inferences..is still a controversial issue. **1979** GEORGACARAKOS & SMITH *Elem. Formal Logic* ix. 330 Many comparative adjectives provide transitive relations, such as *it is taller than*.

transitively (ˈtrɑːnsɪtɪvlɪ, ˈtræns-, -nz-), *adv.* [f. prec. + -LY[2].] In a transitive manner; in the way of transition. **a.** *Gram.* In a transitive sense or construction; with a direct object.

1571 GOLDING *Calvin on Ps.* vii. 7. 20 The woord might also be taken transityvely for too settle or stablish David in his ryght. *a* **1638** MEDE *Wks.* (1672) 676 To construe the words transitively. **1737** WATERLAND *Doctr. Eucharist* v. 115 Ευλογειν is taken transitively in this very Case by the Apostle.

Mod. Many verbs in English can be used both transitively and intransitively.

b. (See senses 3 and 4 of TRANSITIVE.)

1656 JEANES *Fulness Christ* 32 The divine properties are communicated to the humanity, not transitively, but intransitively. **1660** JER. TAYLOR *Duct. Dubit.* II. ii. rule vi. §4 Vasquez..thinks it lawful to give Divine worship relatively or transitively to a man. **1822** T. TAYLOR *Apuleius* 310 It will always perceive intellectually, without transition, or transitively. **1855** PUSEY *Doctr. Real Presence* Note Q. 257 The bread still remains in its own substance; yet so that the whole proposition should be understood, not as actually, but transitively. 'This is my Body', i.e. passes into the body, or from this becomes the body.

c. *Math.* and *Logic.* (See senses 6 and 7 of TRANSITIVE *a.*)

1889 [see INTRANSITIVE *a.* 4]. **1971** C. W. CURTIS in Powell & Higman *Finite Simple Groups* iii. 139 Any two bases of a root system Δ are conjugate by an element of the Weyl group (i.e., $W(\Delta)$ acts transitively on the set of bases).

'transitiveness. [f. as prec. + -NESS.] The quality or state of being transitive; in quot. 1845, transitoriness.

1845 J. H. NEWMAN *Ess. Developm.* 71 A belief in the transitiveness of worldly goods. **1850** A. DE MORGAN in *Trans. Cambr. Philos. Soc.* (1856) IX. I. 104 The first [copular condition] is what I shall call *transitiveness.* **1903** B. RUSSELL *Princ. Math.* xxvi. 218 Relations may be divided into four classes, according as they do or do not possess either of two attributes, transitiveness and symmetry. **1955** A. N. PRIOR *Formal Logic* III. i. 220 It is as if one presented a study of transitiveness under the guise of a 'logic' of the relation of ancestorhood.

transitivism ('trɑːnsɪtɪvɪz(ə)m, 'trænsـ). *Psychiatry.* [f. TRANSITIVE *a.* (*sb.*) + -ISM.] A mental state or condition in which a patient attributes to others his own experiences and sensations.

1924 A. A. BRILL tr. *Bleuler's Textbk. Psychiatry* ii. 38 The splitting off of parts of a personality in *transitivism* proceeds in a different manner; here the patient's own experiences become detached from him, and are ascribed to another person... Transitivism is an almost common occurrence in schizophrenia. **1960** R. F. C. HULL tr. *Jung's Coll. Wks.* III. 134 The representation of one's own complexes by strange actors in dreams is well known..in psychopathology we know it in the form of 'transitivism'. **1971** *Internat. Jrnl. Psycho-Anal.* LII. 237 The schizophrenic delusion of transitivism, which relates to the loss of ego boundaries, represents a regression of ego development.

transi'tivity. [f. late L. *transitīv-us* TRANSITIVE + -ITY.] = TRANSITIVENESS: see TRANSITIVE 2, 6 and 7.

1891 *Cent. Dict.*, *Transitivity*, the character of being transitive, as a group. **1897** *Monist* Jan. 211 Not only is the relative of correspondence transitive, but it also possesses what may be called antithetic transitivity. **1928** *Mod. Lang. Rev.* Apr. 144 The following chapters [of Jespersen's *Modern English Grammar*] are concerned with..transitivity and predicatives. **1942** J. C. COOLEY *Primer Formal Logic* viii. 339 The generalized postulate for the transitivity of the relation, *older than*, could not be expressed without variables. **1969** J. C. WELLS *E.U.P. Concise Esperanto & Eng. Dict.* 17 Many English verbs are of varying transitivity, since they can be used either transitively or intransitively. **1980** A. J. JONES *Game Theory* iv. 194 To prove the theorem it is only necessary to verify the three defining properties of an equivalence relation... Reflexivity... Symmetry... Transitivity.

transitivize ('trɑːnsɪtɪvaɪz, 'træns-, -nz-), *v. Gram.* [f. TRANSITIVE *a.* + -IZE.] *trans.* To make (a verb) transitive. So **,transiti'vizing** *ppl. a.*; **,transiti'vizer**, an affix that makes a verb transitive.

1964 *Language* XL. 76 With the transitivizing stem formative—cʔi the resulting stem..means 'he sets it down'. **1972** J. L. DILLARD *Black English* iii. 98 Pidgin characteristics, like the *-um* (*-em*) transitivizer. **1978** *Language* LIV. 125 An appropriate transitivizing suffix. **1979** *Trans. Philol. Soc.* 128 The causative **hanjāmaya*- would transitivize a 'joining' that was expressed by *han-gam-*, and thereby allow the past participle *hangmata*- to be used for English 'joined' in both its intransitive and passive sense.

transitorily ('trɑːnsɪtərɪlɪ, 'træns-, -nz-), *adv.* [f. TRANSITORY + -LY².] In a transitory manner; in passing through; temporarily, briefly, transiently.

1611 COTGR., *Casuellement*,.. vncertainly, transitorily. **1612** DONNE *Lett.* (1651) 92, I make account to be in London, transitorily, about the end of August. **1762** KAMES *Elem. Crit.* III. xix. 24 The mind is transitorily amused with the new object. **1847** *Illustr. Lond. News* 10 July 29/1 A flash of lightning now and then illuminated the entire panorama, but too transitorily to catch any of its features. **1899** CAGNEY tr. *Jaksch's Clin. Diagn.* vii. (ed. 4) 394 In acute lead-poisoning..large quantities of albumen are often transitorily present in the urine.

'transitoriness. [f. as prec. + -NESS.] The quality or condition of being transitory.

1590 NASHE *Pasquil's Apol.* I. D ij, In respect of the transitorinesse of worldly kingdoms. **1670** CLARENDON *Contempl. Ps.* Tracts (1727) 685 The vanity of this world, of the unsteadiness and transitoriness of all things in it. **1756** JOHNSON *Let.* 15 Apr. in Boswell, The uncertainty of fortune,..the transitoriness of beauty. **1852** LEWIS *Observ. & Reason. in Pol.* I. 221 Written memorials are distinguished by permanence and solidity, as contrasted with the fugacity and transitoriness of oral tradition. **1899** INGE *Chr. Mysticism* i. 23 We may regard the spiritual world as endless duration opposed to transitoriness.

†transi'torious, *a. Obs.* [f. late L. *transitōri-us* (see next) + -OUS.] = TRANSITORY.

1492 RYMAN *Poems* lxxxv. 1 in *Archiv Stud. neu. Spr.* LXXXIX. 255 This worlde is mutabilite That transitorious is. **1502** ATKYNSON tr. *De Imitatione* I. i. 154 Coruptible ryches, transetorious honours. **1550** BALE *Image Both Ch.* D vj b, Departynge from thys transitoryous lyfe. *a* **1598** ROLLOCK *Wks.* (Wodrow Soc.) II. 4 The creatures of God in themselues are but transitorious shadows.

transitory ('trɑːnsɪtərɪ, 'træns-, -nz-), *a.* (*sb.*) Also 4–5 **transitore**, 4–7 **-itorie**, 5 **-etorie**, **-itoire**, (**trancitorie**), 5–6 **transetory**, **-ytory(e**, **-itorye**, 6 *Sc.* **-itoir**. [ad. F. *transitoire* (12th c. in Godef. *Compl.*), ad. post-Aug.L. *transitōrius* having or allowing a passage through, in Chr.L. transient, passing, f. *transit-*: see TRANSIT *v.* and -ORY².]

1. Having the quality of passing away; not lasting; fleeting, momentary, brief; transient.

c **1374** CHAUCER *Troylus* III. 778 (827) Now yf he wot þat Ioye is transitorie [*v.r.* trancitorie]. *c* **1375** *Sc. Leg. Saints* ii. (*Paulus*) 219 þat eftire þis lyfe transitore Euire-lestand lyfe is me before. **1481** CAXTON *Myrr.* I. iv. 13 This world is not but a vayn thinge and transitoire. **1543–4** *Act 35 Hen. VIII*, c. 1 §6 This Realme, after the Kinges transitorie lief,.. shoulde be destitute of a laufull governour. *a* **1633** AUSTIN *Medit.* (1635) 279 So they are as transitorie as a Shepheards Tent. *Ibid.* 280 Like Things of that transitory nature, they begin to weare away. **1654** H. L'ESTRANGE *Chas. I* (1655) 3 That adventure..gave him also a transitory view of that excellent Lady. **1712** SWIFT *Wonderful Prophecy* (*heading*), This vain and transitory world will shortly be brought to its final dissolution. **1859** KINGSLEY *Misc.* (1860) II. 75 All the Continental Nations look upon our present peace as but transitory, momentary.

†2. Having a passage-way, allowing passage through. *Obs. rare.*

1613 GODWIN *Rom. Antiq.* (1625) 9 It had the name of *Forum Transitorium*, the transitorie Forum, because there was *Transitus, id est*, a way or passage through it into three seuerall market places.

b. Of the nature of a passage or transition; transitional. *rare.*

1592 tr. *Junius on Rev.* xix. 1 This chapter hath..two parts, one transitory or of passage unto the things that follow. **1906** *Rep. Vice-reg. Comm. Poor Law Ref. Ireland* I. 31 The transitory period between the old and new systems.

3. *Law.* ***transitory action***, an action in which the venue might be laid in any county.

1665 EVER *Tryals per Pais* x. 133 The Jurors of one County may finde any transitory thing done in another County. **1708** *Termes de la Ley* 419 An Action of Trespass for Battery, is transitory and not local. **1768** BLACKSTONE *Comm.* III. xxiii. 384 Actions transitory follow the person of the defendant, territorial suits must be discussed in the territorial tribunal. **1848** WHARTON *Law Lex.* 390/1 Personal actions are for the most part transitory, i.e., their cause of action may be supposed to take place anywhere.

†4. (app.) Trifling, of little moment. *Obs.*

1672 DRYDEN *Assignation* II. ii, You may scape with the loss of a Leg, or an Arm, or some such transitory Limb. **1673** —— *Amboyna* II. i, Remember, no transitory sum, three hundred quadruples in your own country gold.

B. *sb.* **†1.** A transitory or fleeting thing. (Chiefly in *pl.*) *Obs.*

1649 ROBERTS *Clavis Bibl.* 367 A comfortable transitory enjoyment of transitories. **1654** WHITLOCK *Zootomia* 15 He that too closely imbraceth Transitories, is much the worse for them. **1665** GLANVILL *Scepsis Sci.* 50 This fleeting Transitory our Life.

†2. a. The transverse limb of the cross-staff (CROSS-STAFF 2). **b.** A transit-instrument. *Obs.*

(In sense a, Bourne has also *transvastory* and *transversary*.)

1574 BOURNE *Regiment for Sea* vi. (1577) 26 To take the heigth of the Sunne, to knowe the Altitude of the Pole aboue the Horizon, doo this... Put the Transitorie [ed. 1580, lf. 29 Transuastorie; ed. 1631, lf. 29 Transuersary] vpon the long staffe, then sette the end of the long staffe close at the corner of your eye [etc.]. [**1578** —— *Treas. Trav.* I. ix. 17 Concernyng the making of a Crosse staffe..you shal make an other short staff, called a Transuastorie, of two foote long, and in the very myddle of it you shall make a square hole.] *Ibid.* x. 18 b, If that the distaunce be further then the Transitorie wyl take, and the wal too shorte: then remoue the Plattes or wynges of the Transitorie to the markes, sixe ynches from both the endes of the Transitorie. **1751** *Phil. Trans.* XLVII. xxii. 159, I had several times seen Venus on the meridian with a three-foot transitory.

transitron ('trɑːnsɪtrɒn, 'træns-). *Electronics.* [f. TRANS(CONDUCTANCE + *-i-* + -TRON.] A pentode in which the suppressor grid is used as the control grid so that the valve exhibits negative transconductance.

1939 C. BRUNETTI in *Proc. IRE* XXVII. 88/2 For the sake of brevity it has been found desirable to provide a name for the retarding-field negative-transconductance device... The name 'Transitron' is suggested. **1945** *Electronic Engin.* XVII. 383 Those devices such as..transitrons, whose negative resistance characteristic can be measured by d.c. tests. **1957** *Practical Wireless* XXXIII. 523/1 The timebase employed in the oscilloscope is of the transitron type.

‖transitu ('trɑːnsɪtjuː, 'træns-), in L. phr. ***in transitu***: see ‖IN 32; also as adj. in ***transitu business***, etc.

1858 HOMANS *Cycl. Comm.* 452/1 The large increase of *transitu* business between the principal southern ports and the markets of Europe. *Ibid.* 453/1 Parties who operate in *transitu* cotton.

†'transiture. *Obs. rare.* [f. L. type **transitūra*: see TRANSIT and -URE.] Passing; passage.

1578 BANISTER *Hist. Man* I. 17 It yeeldeth ample scope.. to the transiture of meate and drinke. *Ibid.* 20 Two Processes..with larger holes for the transiture [*printed* -turie] of the Veyne, and Arterie vnto the Scull.

†'transive, *a. Obs. rare.* [f. *transe*, TRANCE *sb.*¹ + -IVE.] Of the nature of a trance; of or pertaining to a trance.

1609 ARMIN *Maids of More-Cl.* (1880) 103 My mother's fast asleepe, and I awake, am in a transiue maze. **1609** —— *Ital. Taylor* (1880) 149 These transiue apparitions dealt, As madmen in their fits.

†trans'jection. *Obs. rare*⁻⁰. [n. of action f. L. *transjicĕre*, the uncontracted form of *trāicĕre*: see TRAJECT.] = TRAJECTION.

1656 BLOUNT *Glossogr.*, *Transjection*, a casting over, or thorow, an overthrowing.

Transjordanian (,trɑːnsdʒɒ'deɪnɪən, ,træns-, -nz-), *sb.* and *a.* Also (in non-*spec.* senses) **trans-Jordanian.** [f. *Trans-Jordan* (see TRANS- 7), *Transjordan(ia)* (see below) + -IAN, -AN: see JORDANIAN *a.* and *sb.*] **A.** *sb.* A person from beyond the river Jordan (see JORDAN²); also *transf.*; *spec.* (now *Hist.*) a native or inhabitant of Transjordan (Transjordania), a territory east of the Jordan, now part of the Hashemite kingdom of the Jordan. **B.** *adj.* Of or pertaining to the land beyond the Jordan; *spec.* (now *Hist.*) of or pertaining to Transjordan. Cf. *trans-Jordan, -ic* s.v. TRANS- 7.

The emirate of *Transjordan(ia)* was established under British mandate in 1921. The name was retained for the short-lived kingdom (1946–9), now Eastern Jordan.

1920 G. SAINTSBURY *Notes on Cellar-bk.* iv. 52 Gentiles, as it were, or at least trans-Jordanians to the pure Israel of Medoc. **1922** G. BELL *Let.* 18 Dec. (1927) II. xxii. 660 The conquest of Hayil..will bring Ibn Saud into the theatre of trans-Jordanian politics. **1965** M. SPARK *Mandelbaum Gate* iv. 97 He disliked the Lebanese and wished all the Arabs were Palestinian or Transjordanian. **1979** R. THOMAS *Eighth Dwarf* xxvi. 251 The Jews are going to have to fight ..the Syrians and the Egyptians and..the Transjordanians.

Transkei (trɑːns'kaɪ, træns-), *sb.* (*a.*) [f. TRANS- 7 + *Kei*, a river of S. Africa.] An area within Cape Province (formerly Cape Colony), situated across the river Kei which falls into the Indian Ocean, *c* 28° 20′ E., and was from 1847 to 1877 the boundary between Kafirland or Caffraria and Cape Colony. Transkei is now one of two homelands of the Xhosa people (cf. CISKEIAN *a.* and *sb.*), having in 1976 been the first Black homeland to be declared independent by the Republic of South Africa. Also *attrib.* or as *adj.* Hence **Trans'keian,** (*a*) *adj.*, of or pertaining to Transkei; (*b*) *sb.*, a native or inhabitant of the Transkei.

1879 *Whitaker's Almanack* 259/1 The area [of Cape Colony], including Basutoland and Transkei, 222,308 square miles. *Ibid.* 259/2 The Transkeian territories stretch from the Kei to Natal. **1898** *Ibid.* 515 (Cape Colony) The Transkei territories. *Ibid.*, (Principal events) Incorporation of all the Transkeian territories, except part of Pondoland, with the Colony, completed 1885; annexation of Pondoland 1894. **1899** *Daily News* 10 Oct. 7/1 The Pondos and the other Transkei tribes are not absolutely to be relied on. **1911** J. LENNOX *Missions S. Afr.* 81 A question of a much more difficult nature has exercised the Kafrarian and Transkeian Churches. **1974** *Standard Encycl. S. Afr.* X. 564/1 All Transkeian taxpayers over the age of 18 and all other Transkeian citizens over 21..to whom certain disqualifications do not apply are entitled to register as voters. **1976** *Times* 17 Feb. 7/6 The Transkeians want to make independence a success. **1976** *Times* 25 Oct. 13 Tonight the South African flag will be lowered in Umtata and the Transkeian flag will be raised. **1979** J. DRUMMOND *Patriots* ii. 15 The Transkeian labour problem. *Ibid.* iii. 23 Nearly all those who lost their jobs were Transkeians.

trans'lade, *v.* [TRANS- 2.] *trans.* To transfer the lading of one ship or carriage to another. Hence **trans'lading** *vbl. sb.*

1881 *Daily News* 17 Mar. 5/3 A question of transit and the terminal charges for lading, unlading, and translading.

translatable (trɑːns'leɪtəb(ə)l, træns-, -nz-), *a.* [f. TRANSLATE *v.* + -ABLE.] Capable of being translated.

1745 H. WALPOLE *Corr.* (1846) II. 15, I..without having recourse to the Countess's translatable periods, am pleased with his company. **1830** MACKINTOSH *Eth. Philos.* Wks. 1846 I. 88 Modes of expression scarcely translatable into the only technical language in which that mind is wont to think. **1870** EMERSON *Soc. & Solit.* viii. 164 What is really best in any book is translatable.

Hence **translata'bility, trans'latableness.**

1867 LUDLOW *Fleeing to Tarshish* 115 To carry on his cogitations for him, with their accustomed wondrous translatability by the imagination. **1882** *Athenæum* 4 Mar. 278/1 We own to a certain scepticism as to La Fontaine's translatableness. **1911** MUNRO *Fundamentals* 31 The Translatability of Scripture.

†translate, *a.* and *sb. Obs.* Also 7 **-at.** [ad. L. *translāt-us, -a, -um*, pa. pple.: see next.]

A. *adj.* Translated (see next); in quot. 1589, transferred in meaning, metaphorical.

1589 Rider *Bibl. Schol.* Direct. for Rdr., First I place the proper Latine word vnder the figure of 1: then the figuratiue or translate vnder the figure of 2.

B. *sb.* Something translated; a translation. [Cf. L. *translātum* sb., OF. *translat* 13th c.]

1585–6 Earl Leycester *Corr.* (Camden) 467, I sent to the register of the states for the act.., the translate whereof I send your honour hearein. 1619 Carleton in *Eng. & Germ.* (Camden) 85 Divers lettres..I have made transcripts of some, and translats of others. 1655 *Chym. Med. & Chyrurg. Addr., Table*, A Translate of the Eleventh Chapter. 1668 *Lond. Gaz.* No. 254/4 The prohibitions made against the vending or reading any of the late Translates of the New Testament into French. 1803 Collins in Gurwood *Wellington's Desp.* (1837) III. 133 *note*, I..enclose a copy and translate of a note I..received from the Berai Rajah.

translate (trɑːns'leɪt, træns-, -nz-), *v.* Also 4 (*Sc.*), 6 translat, 5–6 traunslate, 6 *Sc.* translait. Pa. t. and pple. **translated**; also 4–6 **translate**, (*pa. pple.*) **translat**. [Prob. first used in *translat(e* pa. pple., ad. L. *translāt-us*, pa. pple. of *transferre* to transfer. The pa. pple. soon became *translat-ed*, and *translate* the verb stem (see -ate suffix³). But the verb may also immediately repr. F. *translater* (12th c. in Godef.). Cf. also med.L. *translātāre* (11th c. in Du Cange).]

I. 1. a. *trans.* To bear, convey, or remove from one person, place or condition to another; to transfer, transport; *spec.* to remove a bishop from one see to another, or a bishop's seat from one place to another, and, in Scotland, a minister from one pastoral charge to another; also, to remove the dead body or remains of a saint, or, by extension, a hero or great man, from one place to another.

a 1300 *Cursor M.* 9162 (Cott.) Helias was in þat siquare, Translated in a golden chiare. *Ibid.* 9220 Þe Iuues now er put o state And þair kingrik translate. *c* 1330 R. Brunne *Chron.* (1810) 208 Þis is þe same Hubert, þat we saw of nam, Þat translate S. Gilbert in þe hous of Sempyngham. *c* 1380 Wyclif *Sel. Wks.* II. 318 We witen þat we ben translatid fro deþ to lyf. 1433 Lydg. *St. Fremund* 819 The Bysshop.. Translatyd hym to Dunstaple. 1432–50 tr. *Higden* (Rolls) II. 77 The seete of the metropolitan of alle Wales, whiche was translate afterwarde to Meneuia. 1517 Torkington *Pilgr.* (1884) 49 Hys body was translat to Rome. 1529 S. Fish *Supplic. Beggars* (Arb.) 13 Then shall not youre.. power, crowne, dignitie..be translated from you. 1579 Lyly *Euphues* (Arb.) 41 Plante and translate the crabbe tree, where..it please you, and it wyll neuer beare sweete Apple. 1613 Purchas *Pilgrimage* (1614) 106 Hee translated the highest seat both of spirituall and Temporall Regiment to Jerusalem. 1625 in Willis & Clark *Cambridge* (1886) II. 445 He translated yᵉ Vestrie. 1651 N. Bacon *Disc. Govt. Eng.* II. xxviii. (1739) 131 This Headship was translated to the King. 1663 Wood *Life* (O.H.S.) I. 472 After he had taken in another class of six there, he translated himself to the house of Arthur Tylliard an apothecary. *c* 1683 Burnet *Orig. Mem.* in *Own Time* (1902) I. Suppl. 67 Morley, made at first bishop of Worcester, and soon after..translated to Winchester. 1794 J. Hutton *Philos. Light*, etc. 47 Heat is translated among bodies in a certain manner, and electricity in another. 1865 *Pall Mall G.* 11 Apr. 4 A discussion has arisen on the question whether the Charterhouse School ought or ought not to be translated into the country. 1869 Freeman *Norm. Conq.* III. xv. §5. 518 The body of Harold, first buried under the cairn by Hastings, was afterwards translated to his own minster at Waltham. 1904 R. Small *Hist. U.P. Congregat.* I. 503 In 1829..the Synod at his own request, and without a vote, refused to translate.

b. To carry or convey to heaven without death; also, in later use, said of the death of the righteous.

1382 Wyclif *Heb.* xi. 5 Bi feith Enok is translatid, that he schulde not se deeth; and he was not founden, for the Lord translatide him. 1387 Trevisa *Higden* (Rolls) II. 213 And so schulde þe body..be translated and chaunged in þe blisse of heuene wiþ oute deienge and deeþ. 1535 Coverdale *Wisd.* iv. 10 He pleased God,..so that where as he lyued amonge synners, he translated him. 1702 *Lond. Gaz.* No. 3809/1 That after a long and happy Enjoyment of this your Earthly Crown, you may be translated to one Immortal. 1798 Coleridge *Fears in Solitude* 121 As if the wretch, Who fell in battle..Passed off to Heaven, translated and not killed. 1848 Mrs. Jameson *Sacr. & Leg. Art* (1850) 331 She was ninety years of age when the Lord translated her. 1904 Jebb in *Proc. Brit. Acad.* 3 Here, and here alone, the Hyperborean land is an Elysium to which mortals are translated without dying.

c. *Med.* To remove the seat of (a disease) from one person, or part of the body, to another. Now *rare* or *Obs.*

1732 Arbuthnot *Aliments* etc. 366 To translate the Morbifick Matter upon the Extremities of the Body. 1754 J. Bartlet *Farriery* (ed. 2) 105 The humours frequently settle, or are translated to the lungs, and other bowels. 1769 E. Bancroft *Guiana* 394 The patient is either relieved, or the disease translated on the extremities. 1826 Southey in *Q. Rev.* XXXIV. 330 He could..cure a carbuncle..by making upon it the sign of a cross, and translate swellings from his pupil's arm to his own.

d. *Physics.* To move (a body) from one point or place to another without rotation: cf. translation 1 f.

e. *Physics. intr.* To undergo translational motion.

1964 *Amer. Jrnl. Physics* XXXII 261/1 If frame β, thus translates rigidly with velocity a as measured in a then frame v translates rigidly with velocity $-v$ as measured in β. 1979 *Sci. Amer.* Jan. 76/2 One is therefore forced to conclude that these deep structures do indeed constitute the lower portions of the continental plates and that they have been translating coherently with the crust for hundreds or even thousands of millions of years.

II. 2. a. *trans.* To turn from one language into another; 'to change into another language retaining the sense' (J.); to render; also, to express in other words, to paraphrase. (The chief current sense.)

a 1300 *Cursor M.* 232 Þis ilk bok it es translate In to Inglis tong to rede. *c* 1350 *Will. Palerne* 167 For he of frensche þis fayre tale ferst dede translate. *c* 1385 Chaucer *L.G.W.* 329 (*Balade*) Thow hast translatid the romauns of the rose. 1477 Earl Rivers (Caxton) *Dictes* 2 It was translated out of latyn in to frenshe. 1589 Puttenham *Eng. Poesie* I. xxxi. (Arb.) 75 Doctour Phaer one that..excellently well translated into English verse Heroicall certaine bookes of Virgils Æneidos. 1689–90 Temple *Ess. Poetry* Wks. 1731 I. 241 The first Change of Poetry was made by translating it into Prose. 1693 Dryden *Disc. Orig. & Progr. Satire* Ess. (ed. Ker) II. 92 'Tis only for a poet to translate a poem. 1776 Johnson 11 Apr., in *Boswell*, Poetry..cannot be translated; and, therefore, it is the poets that preserve languages. 1850 Whipple *Ess. & Rev.* (ed. 3) I. 300 If the phrase, realizing the ideal, were translated into the phrase, actualizing the real, much ambiguity might be avoided. 1874 Green *Short Hist.* vii. §1. 342 Retiring to Hamburg Tyndale translated the Gospels and Epistles.

b. *absol.* To practise translation; to make a version from one language or form of words into another; also *intr.* for *pass.*, of a language, speech, or writing: To bear or admit of translation.

c 1440 *Pallad. on Husb.* I. 735 Yet as myn auctor spak so wold I speke Sith I translate, and looth am from hym breke. 1576 Fleming *Panopl. Epist.* 253 If you translate out of the Latine speach, into the Greeke. 1690 Locke *Hum. Und.* III. iv. §9 This is to translate, and not to define, when we change two words of the same signification one for another. 1731 Fielding *Author's Farce* II. v, The rogue had a trick of translating out of the shops as well as the languages. 1812 Southey *Omniana* II. 30 Claudian throughout would translate better than any of the ancients. 1827 —— *Lett.* (1856) IV. 64 The Welsh, I suspect, is not a language which translates well. 1831 Macaulay *Ess., Johnson* (1887) 194 Sometimes Johnson translated aloud.

†**c.** To use in a metaphorical or transferred sense: see *translated*, quot. 1553, and cf. translate *a.*, translation 4. *Obs.*

d. *Biol.* To use (genetic information in messenger RNA) to determine the amino-acid sequence of a protein during its synthesis; also with the RNA as obj.

1961 *Cold Spring Harbor Symp. Quantitative Biol.* XXVI. 101/2 This finding implied that the information encoded in DNA must somehow be transmitted to the ribosomes where it is translated into the amino acid sequence of a polypeptide chain. 1971 *Nature* 24 Sept. 234/2 Messenger RNAs transcribed in the nuclei of eukaryotic cells have to be transported to the cytoplasm to be translated. 1972 *Sci. Amer.* Jan. 25/2 A length of RNA representing a gene is then translated into a particular protein, a molecule constructed with a 20-letter alphabet, the 20 amino acids. 1977 D. E. Metzler *Biochemistry* xv. 936/2 The ribosome faithfully translates the genetic message, adding amino acids to the peptide chain until a stop codon is reached.

3. *fig.* To interpret, explain; to expound the significance of (conduct, gestures, etc.); also, to express (one thing) in terms of another.

1598 Shaks. *Merry W.* I. iii. 54 He hath studied her will; and translated her will: out of honesty, into English. 1602 —— *Ham.* IV. i. 3 There's matters in these sighes... These profound heaues You must translate. 1850 Mrs. Jameson *Leg. Monast. Ord.* (1863) 55 The emblem has been translated into a fact, or rather into a miracle. 1892 Westcott *Gospel of Life* 58 Right Doctrine is an inexhaustible spring of strength if it be translated into deed. 1903 *Westm. Gaz.* 26 Mar. 1/2 The delightful Norwegian master who..translates the nature of Norway..into music.

III. 4. To change in form, appearance, or substance; to transmute; to transform, alter; *spec.* in industrial use: of a tailor, to renovate, turn, or cut down (a garment); of a cobbler, to make new boots from the remains of (old ones).

c 1386 Chaucer *Clerk's T.* 329 Vnnethe the peple hire knew for hire fairnesse Whan she translated [*v. rr.* transmewed, transformed] was in swich richesse. 1423 Jas. I *King's Q.* viii, How that eche estate As fortune lykith, thame will oft translate. 1487–8 *Rec. St. Mary at Hill* 138 For a man werkyng iij dayes & di. in the house..in translatyng of the steyer and in mendyng of wyndowes. 1536 Bellenden *Cron. Scot.* (1821) II. 72 Quhare he translatit the tempill of Apollo in ane abbay of his ordour. 1543–4 *Act 35 Hen. VIII*, c. 8 No man..shall cutt mynisshe or translate..any barrelles kilderkyns or firkyns. 1575–7 Fenton *Gold. Epist.* (1582) 160 To translate an auncient garment, and reduce him to the present fashion. 1590 Shaks. *Mids. N.* III. i. 122 Blesse thee Bottome, blesse thee; thou art translated. 1621 Burton *Anat. Mel.* I. ii. I. ii. (1628) 40 Nabuchadnezar was really translated into a beast. 1718 J. Fox *Wanderer* 14, I was waiting in Expectation of my own Change, and wondering..what Sort of Being I should be translated to. 1815 *Q. Rev.* Oct. 129 A place near Monmouth-street, where 'they translate old shoes into new ones'. 1905 Preece & Sivewright *Telegr.* viii. 194 Varley introduced repeaters at Amsterdam to translate the English double-current system of working into the Continental single-current system.

5. To re-transmit (a telegraphic message) by means of an automatic repeater.

1855 [implied in translating *station*].

6. To transport with the strength of some feeling; to enrapture, entrance. *arch.*

1643 Sir T. Browne *Relig. Med.* I. §49 That elegant Apostle, which seemed to have a glimpse of Heaven,..was translated out of himself to behold it. 1849 Longf. *Ev.* I. iv. 104 Their souls, with devotion translated, Rose on the ardour of prayer. 1899 Dixon in Mackail *W. Morris* I. 115 There was no train... I was made aware of this by a fearful cry in my ears, and saw Morris 'translated'.

IV. 7. *intr.* Const. *into.* To result in, to be converted into, to manifest itself as.

1975 *Lamp* (Exxon Corporation) Winter 11/2 Any delays in bringing fields into production could quickly translate into lower government revenues and an adverse impact on the balance of payments. 1976 *Sci. Amer.* June 69/1 For maneuvers executed early in a mission this uncertainty translates into an error at the target planet on the order of one kilometer. 1977 *Time* 8 Aug. 42/2 The price of raw coffee could gradually decline to about $1 per lb. on the New York market, which would translate into a retail price somewhere in the $2 range.

Hence **trans'lated** (in quot. 1553, metaphorical: cf. translate *a.*), **trans'lating** *ppl. adjs.*

1553 T. Wilson *Rhet.* (1580) 174 When thei maie haue most apt wordes at hand, yet wil thei of a purpose vse translated words. 1632 Sherwood *Eng. & Fr. Dict.* To Rdr., First the Proper [interpretation]; then, the Translated and Metaphoricall. 1687 T. Brown *Saints in Uproar* Wks. 1730 I. 82 See these translating gentlemen translated to the quarter of lunaticks. 1727 Pope *Macer* 21 In a translated Suit, then tries the Town, With borrow'd Pins, and Patches not her own. 1729 Swift *Direct. Serv.* iv. Wks. (1869) 569 Your wages..spent in translated red-heeled shoes. 1868 Gladstone *Juv. Mundi* ix. (1870) 364 Any deceased or translated hero. 1904 R. Small *Hist. U.P. Congreg.* I. 552 The court came to adjudicate upon a translating call to Mr. Jaffray from Dalry.

translatese (trɑːnsleɪ'tiːz, træns-, -nz-). [f. translat(ion + -ese.] = translationese. Cf. translatorese.

1967 *Listener* 8 June 762/1 He..has couched it in the lukewarm translatese of one of his own more unurgent renderings. 1977 *Times Lit. Suppl.* 25 Feb. 202/1 Paralysing woodenness ('I am concerned to determine'), the dull thud of translatese ('Here is the place to mention Pirandello finally'). 1979 *Studies in Eng. Lit.: Eng. Number* (Tokyo) 228 To the very last his Japanese did not get rid of a 'translatese' completely.

translating (trɑːns'leɪtɪŋ, træns-, -nz-), *vbl. sb.* [f. translate *v.* + -ing¹.] The action of the vb. translate; translation, in various senses.

c 1460 Fortescue *Abs. & Lim. Mon.* xi. (1885) 137 With owt translatynge þeroff to any oþer vse. 1474 *Churchw. Acc. St. Mich., Cornhill* (Camden), Payde for translatyng of the meyres pue. 1535 in *Archæologia* IX. 246 For translating of a gowne of blacke veluette. 1601 R. Johnson *Kingd. & Commw.* (1603) 63 The translating of the Imperiall seate, from Rome to Constantinople. 1683 Burnet tr. *More's Utopia* Pref. 1 The refining and polishing a Language,..the translating of Books into it. 1904 *Q. Rev.* July 7 Translating is a large industry, as any English reviewer of the last ten years can testify.

b. *attrib.*, as ***translating-right***, ***-trade***; **translating-relay** (*Telegr.*): see relay *sb.*¹ 4; **translating-roller**, **-screw** (*Mech.*), a screw which moves a part of a mechanism in relation to the other parts; **translating-station** (*Telegr.*), a station at which an automatic repeater is introduced.

1905 Preece & Sivewright *Telegr.* xi. 235 *Translating relays are required for the intercommunication between stations. 1911 Webster, **Translating-roller* (*Ordnance*) a double-threaded screw for drawing a breech-block longitudinally from its place in the breech. 1891 *Cent. Dict.*, **Translating-screw*,..*spec.*, in breech-loading ordnance, a screw for moving in or out the wedge in the fermeture. 1855 *Patent Office Specif.* No. 314 The instruments are used in pairs at the *translating station. 1894 Sala *London up to Date* 263 The 'Cobbler's Last', that well-known organ of the boot and shoe '*translating' trade.

translation (trɑːns'leɪʃən, træns-, -nz-). [a. OF. *translation* (12th c. in Godef. *Compl.*), or ad. L. *translātiōn-em* a transporting, translation, n. of action f. *translāt-*, ppl. stem of *transferre* to transfer.] The action of translating (or its result).

I. 1. a. Transference; removal or conveyance from one person, place, or condition to another.

spec. The removal of a bishop from one see to another; in the Church of Scotland, the removal of a minister from one charge to another; also, the removal of the body or relics of a saint to another place of interment.

a 1350 *St. Stephen* 211 in Horstm. *Altengl. Leg.* (1881) 30 Of þat ilk translacioun Es named saynt Steuyn inuencioun. *c* 1380 Wyclif *Sel. Wks.* II. 318 Þis translacioun is better þan worldly translacioun of þe pope. 1447 Bokenham *Seyntys* (Roxb.) 30 Of summe relykys to make translacyoun. 1473–4 *Acc. Ld. High Treas. Scot.* I. 52 The translacione of the parliament fra Sanctandros to Edinburgh. 1485 Caxton *St. Wenefr.* 13 Her bones were broughte to thabbay of Shrewsbury, whiche translacion is halowed the 19 day of Septembre. 1597 Hooker *Eccl. Pol.* v. lv. §8 Ascension into heauen, is a plaine locall translation of Christ according to his manhood. 1612 Brerewood *Lang. & Relig.* 12 The translation of the imperial seat to Constantinople. 1635 Swan *Spec. M.* (1670) 198 A fifth [effect of Earthquakes] is the translation of Mountains &c. unto some other places. 1647 N. Bacon *Disc. Govt. Eng.* I. xi. (1739) 22 After the Translation of the Sea from Thetford to Norwich. 1647 Clarendon *Hist. Reb.* I. §188 The necessary forms for the Translation [of Laud from London to Canterbury]. 1777 J. Adams *Wks.* (1854) IX. 470 The rapid translation of property from hand to hand. 1869 Freeman *Norm. Conq.* III. xi. §2. 34 That the Feast of the Translation of Saint Eadward should be kept..on the eve of the day of Saint Calixtus. 1910 in Halsbury *Laws of Eng.* XI. 400 *note*, The fees paid by the late Archbishop Magee on his translation to York amounted to £573 6s.

b. *fig.* of non-material things.

translation of a feast (Eccl.), its transference from the usual date to another, to avoid its clashing with another (movable) feast of superior rank.

c **1530** T. Cox *Rhet.* (1899) 82 Translacion of the faut is, whan he that confesseth his faut, sayeth that he dyd it, moued by the indignacion of the malycyouse dede of an other. **1552** Abp. Hamilton *Catech.* (1884) 8 The translatioun of the sabboth day to the sonday. **1607** Hieron *Wks.* I. 151 Imputation: by which there is a kinde of translation or putting ouer of the beleeuers sinne vnto Christ, and of Christs righteousnesse to the beleeuer. **1681–6** J. Scott *Chr. Life* (1747) III. vii. 153 The very Translation of the Guilts of the People upon them. **1705** Stanhope *Paraphr.* II. 549 A Translation of Punishment and Guilt, from the Person offering to the thing offered.

c. Removal from earth to heaven, *orig.* without death, as the translation of Enoch; but in later use also said *fig.* of the death of the righteous.

1382 Wyclif *Heb.* xi. 5 Enok..bifore translacioun he hadde witnessing for to haue plesid God. **1682** Sir T. Browne *Chr. Mor.* II. §6 Time, Experience, self-Reflexions, and God's mercies, make in some well-temper'd minds a kind of translation before Death. **1727** De Foe *Syst. Magic* I. i. (1840) 12 A glorious example of such faith as was rewarded with an immediate translation of the person [Enoch] into heaven. **1760** G. Whitefield *Let.* 29 Oct. (in *Pearson's Catal.* (1894) 64) Blessed be God for supporting me so well under the news of dear Mr. Polhill's sudden translation. **1878** Gladstone *Prim. Homer* v. 61 The Islands of the Blest, to which Menelaos has a promise of translation on his death.

d. *Med.* Transference of a disease from one person or part of the body to another. Now *rare* or *Obs.*

1665 Boyle *Occas. Refl.* II. xiii. (1848) 140 Madness..by the translation of the Humours into the Brain. **1732** Arbuthnot *Aliments* etc. 368 Translations of Morbific Matter in Acute Distempers. **1857** Dunglison *Dict. Med. Sc.*, *Metastasis*..translation. A change in the seat of a disease; attributed, by the Humorists, to the translation of the morbific matter to a part different from that which it had previously occupied.

e. *Astrol.* (See quots.)

1658 in Phillips. **1706** *Ibid.* (ed. Kersey), *Translation of Light and Nature*, a Phrase us'd by Astrologers, when a light Planet separates from a more weighty one, and presently joyns another more heavy. **1819** J. Wilson *Compl. Dict. Astrol.* 378 Translation of the light and nature of a planet is when a planet separates from one that is slower than itself and overtakes another by conjunction or aspect.

f. *Physics.* Transference of a body, or form of energy, from one point of space to another. ***motion*** or ***movement of translation***: onward movement without (or considered apart from) rotation; sometimes as distinguished from a reciprocating movement as in a wave or vibration.

1715 tr. *Gregory's Astron.* I. (1726) I. 157 The Ratio of the Translations will be compounded of the Ratio of the Differences of the Angular Motions, and of the Ratio of the Distances from the Axis. **1794** J. Hutton *Philos. Light & Heat* 47 We should conclude that the translation of heat, among bodies, is not performed according to the laws observed in that of light. **1854** Moseley *Astron.* viii. (1874) 34 This mass when left to itself will have two motions, one a motion of translation,..the other, a motion..of rotation. **1860** Tyndall *Glac.* I. xxvii. 215 It was, for a time, a mere motion of vibration without any sensible translation. **1878** Huxley *Physiogr.* 171 The motion of the water is a movement of undulation and not of translation. **1884** J. S. Russell (*title*) The Wave of Translation in its Application to the Three Oceans of Water, Air, and Ether.

II. 2. a. The action or process of turning from one language into another; also, the product of this; a version in a different language.

a **1340** Hampole *Psalter* Prol., In þe translacioun i folow þe lettere als mykyll as i may. **1382** Wyclif *N.T.* 595 Thei setten in her translaciouns oneli the names of thre thingis, that is of water, of blood, and of spirit. **1447** Bokenham *Seyntys* Introd. (Roxb.) 4 Thys translacyon..In to oure language. **1535** Coverdale *Bible* Ded., I thought it my dutye..to dedicate this translacyon vnto youre hyghnesse. **1549** (*title*) The Byble in Englyshe, that is the olde and new Testament, after the translacion appoynted to bee read in the Churches. *a* **1568** Ascham *Scholem.* (Arb.) 92 Translation, is easie in the beginning for the scholer. **1581** Pettie *Guazzo's Civ. Conv.* I. (1586) A iij, To present unto you the first sight of this my translation. *c* **1650** Denham *To Sir R. Fanshawe* 10 Nor ought a genius less than his that writ, Attempt translation. **1682** Dryden *Relig. Laici* 242 Various readings and translations. **1805** N. Nicholls *Corr. w. Gray* (1843) 37 Pope's translation of the Iliad stood very high in his estimation. **1837** Lockhart *Scott.* I. iii. 94 His translations in verse from Horace and Virgil were often approved by Dr. Adam. **1874** Green *Short Hist.* vi. §3. 291 He [Caxton] stood between two schools of translation, that of French affectation and English pedantry.

b. *transf.* and *fig.* The expression or rendering of something in another medium or form, e.g. of a painting by an engraving or etching; also *concr.*

1588 Shaks. *L.L.L.* v. ii. 51 Some thousand Verses of a faithfull Louer. A huge translation of hypocrisie, Vildly compiled, profound simplicitie. **1812** R. H. in *Examiner* 30 Nov. 763/2 His translations on copper, to compare them with..verbal translations.., display much of the elegance of Pope. **1829** *Chapters Physical Sc.* xxiv. 308 That correctness of reasoning which..exhibits a faithful translation of the language of facts. **1829** *Examiner* 805/1 Engravers..have here hung up their translations from the works of our landscape and other painters. **1864** *Athenæum* 27 Feb. 305/3 A system of copying which demands two translations,—that of the draughtsman and that of the chromo-lithographer.

c. *Biol.* The process by which genetic information represented by the sequence of nucleotides in messenger RNA gives rise to a definite sequence of amino-acids in the protein or polypeptide that is synthesized.

1963 *Cold Spring Harbor Symp. Quantitative Biol.* XXVIII. 352/1 Polarity mutations affect the RNA to protein translation. **1968** H. Harris *Nucleus & Cytoplasm* iv. 83 In higher cells translation and transcription are not closely coupled. **1970**, **1973** [see transcription 6]. **1977** P. B. & J. S. Medawar *Life Science* xii. 95 This translation of genetic into structural information is irreversible, so there is no known..method by which germinal DNA could be imprinted with information acquired in an organism's own lifetime.

3. a. Transformation, alteration, change; changing or adapting to another use; renovation.

1382 Wyclif *Heb.* vii. 12 Forsothe the presthod translatid, it is nede that and translacioun [1611 change] of lawe be maad. ? *c* **1470** Ashby *Active Policy of Prince* 156 The ruine Of high estates, and translacion, That to vices and outrage dud incline, For the whiche thei suffred mutacion. **1534** More *Treat. Passion* Wks. 1344/1 The translacion of chaunging of it from thynges sensible to thynges intelligible. **1582** in Feuillerat *Revels Q. Eliz.* (1908) 349 Of wages, workemanship, Translations, Attendaunces. **1604** R. Cawdrey *Table Alph.*, *Translation*, altering, chaunging.

b. *spec.* (in workmen's use) The process of 'translating' boots (see translate *v.* 4).

1851 Mayhew *Lond. Labour* (1861) II. 34 Translation..is this—to take a worn, old pair of shoes or boots, and by repairing them make them appear as if left off with hardly any wear. **1865** in Ruskin *Sesame* 90 Her son sat up the whole night to make the 'translations' [of old boots].

†4. *Rhet.* Transference of meaning; metaphor; = tralation. *Obs.*

1538 Elyot, *Metaphora*, a translation of wordes frome their propre sygnifycation. **1553** T. Wilson *Rhet.* (1580) 174 Men vse translation of wordes (called Tropes) for neede sake, when thei can not finde other. **1605** Bacon *Adv. Learn.* I. vii. §17 That excellent use of a metaphor or translation. **1652** Urquhart *Jewel* Wks. (1834) 292 With words diminishing the worth of a thing, tapinotically, periphrastically, by rejection, translation, and other meanes.

III. 5. *Law.* A transfer of property; *spec.* alteration of a bequest by transferring the legacy to another person.

1590 Swinburne *Testaments* 280 Translation of a legacie is a bestowing of the same vpon an other. **1651** Hobbes *Leviath.* I. xiv. 67 All Contract is mutuall translation, or change of Right. **1754** Erskine *Princ. Sc. Law* (1809) 342 If the assignee conveys his right to a third person, it is called a translation. **1875** Poste *Gaius* IV. Comm. (ed. 2) 490 No translation of property is operated by theft.

6. In long distance telegraphy, the automatic retransmission of a message by means of a relay.

1866 F. M. Ferguson *Electr.* (1870) 245 It would be advisable to..resend at the mid-station by translation. **1876** Preece & Sivewright *Telegr.* iv. §113 The circuit can be divided, and the repeating station can work separately..without translation.

IV. 7. *attrib.*, as ***translation element***, ***-equivalent***, ***movement***, ***process***, ***right***, ***theory***, ***work***; **translation loan(-word)** = *loan-translation* s.v. loan *sb.*[1] 5; **translation wave**, an ocean wave with a propelling or forward impulse; a forced wave.

a **1704** T. Brown *Amusem. Ser. & Com.*, *Voy.* ii. Wks. 1709 III. I. 14 He has so mortified himself..that the Translation-Bill may not pass. **1862** H. Spencer *First Princ.* II. v. §56 (1875) 183 What we may call the translation element in Motion. **1963** J. Lyons *Structural Semantics* iv. 70 It may be impossible to find even a 'roughly equivalent' term in another language.., even though we can find satisfactory translation-equivalents for most..of its hyponyms. **1977** *Language* LIII. 295 Thai *khon* and its (near) translation-equivalents in many languages denote 'people'. **1900** E. Björkman *Scand. Loan-Words in M.E.* I. 12 What I should like to call 'translation loan-words'... Thus..*wæpengetæc* 'vote of consent expressed by touching weapons; district governed by such authority'.. distinctively English in form, although..of Scandinavian introduction..*wæpen-* having been put instead of the Scand. *vápn*. **1922** O. Jespersen *Language* xi. 215 (*heading*) Translation-loans. *Ibid.*, Besides direct borrowings we have also indirect borrowings or 'translation loan-words,' words modelled more or less clearly on foreign ones, though consisting of native speech-material. **1958** Translation-loan [see calque]. **1974** R. Quirk *Linguist & Eng. Lang.* vi. 101 We should add here the use of *bower* which is clearly a translation-loan. **1898** P. Manson *Trop. Diseases* i. 5 Slight translation movements of the pigment particles. **1954** Koestler *Invisible Writing* xi. 132 At which stage of the translation-process all these blessings had slipped in, we could not tell. **1967** M. Argyle *Psychol. Interpersonal Behaviour* v. 90 Social interaction..depends on the existence of a learnt store of central translation processes. **1906** *Westm. Gaz.* 15 Oct. 4/2 Their respective delegates have agreed to extend the period during which authors can protect their translation rights. **1936** J. R. Kantor *Objective Psychol. of Gram.* v. 59 No doubt in the translation theory it is these social and cultural factors that have been unnecessarily converted into psychic guides of bodily action. **1978** C. Hookway in Hookway & Pettit *Action & Interpretation* 27 Given the under-determination of translation theory by possible observations, we are invited to conclude that in the field of translation, there is no objective fact of the matter. **1980** *Times Lit. Suppl.* 12 Sept. 992/3 An academic researcher in translation-theory,..one of the very few people in the world..working in this field—had undertaken a questionnaire on the subject and now revealed some of its findings. **1862** Dana *Man. Geol.* iv. 655 The ocean-waves, which the earthquake, if submarine, may produce, have an actual forward impulse, and are, therefore, forced or translation waves. *Ibid.* 729 The sound-wave may be felt before the translation wave, and may travel farther.

translational (trɑːnsˈleɪʃənəl, træns-, -nz-), *a.* [f. prec. + -al[1].] Of or pertaining to translation.

a. Belonging to, or consisting in, translation from one language into another.

1813 E. Henderson *Let.* in *Life* (1859) 119 A translational exhibition of a certain notable portion of the Old Testament. **1869** *Contemp. Rev.* Feb. 134 Mr. Paley's editorial and translational labours. **1907** Salmon *Hum. Element in Gosp.* 244 Many of the variations in our Greek Gospels are simply translational.

b. *Physics.* Consisting in onward motion, as distinct from rotation, vibration, oscillation, etc.

1867 Thomson & Tait *Nat. Phil.* I. I. §107 Imagine this circle to be the inner edge of a fixed ring in space (directionally fixed, that is to say, but having the same translational motion as the earth's centre). **1898** Sir W. Crookes *Addr. Brit. Assoc.* 25 The total energy of both the translational and internal motions of the molecules locked up in quiescent air at ordinary pressure and temperature is about 140,000 foot-pounds in each cubic yard of air.

Hence **transˈlationally** *adv.*, (*a*) as regards language translation; (*b*) as regards, or by means of, translational motion.

1916 M. A. S. Riach *Air-Screws* i. 8 The depth of the cylinder will then represent the distance advanced through translationally by the point, and therefore by the whole air-screw, at each revolution. **1923** C. D. Broad *Sci. Thought* xi. 433 A rotating physical object which is translationally at rest. **1959** *Archivum Linguisticum* XI. 152 It is..no use trying..to measure range of content as the 'number of meanings'..of translationally equivalent words. **1978** J. Dunn in Hookway & Pettit *Action & Interpretation* 172 A translationally adequate science of human meanings must in principle be pragmatically accessible. **1981** C. H. Llewellyn-Smith in J. H. Mulvey *Nature of Matter* iii. 55 If momentum is conserved then the underlying laws must necessarily be translationally invariant.

translationese (trɑːnsˌleɪʃəˈniːz, træns-, -nz-). [f. translation + -ese.] The style of language supposed to be characteristic of (bad) translations; unidiomatic language in a translation; = translatese, translatorese.

1957 R. W. Zandvoort *Handbk. Eng. Gram.* IX. ii. 313 The suffix [*-ese*] may be added in a derogatory sense..to denote a mannered diction or style:..*journalese*, *translationese*. **1961** *Times Lit. Suppl.* 17 Feb. p. iv/5 Translationese in a version from Hebrew is not always easy to detect. **1964** *Listener* 3 Dec. 911/2 The kind of unthinking 'translationese' which has so often..imparted to translated Russian literature a distinctive, somehow 'doughy' style. **1972** C. Day-Lewis in G. W. Knight *Jackson Knight* 11 When I had lapsed into translationese, he never failed to point it out. **1984** *Times* 21 Mar. 17/5 A useless mixture of mushy colloquialisms..and translationese.

†translaˈtitious, *a. Obs.* [f. L. *translātīcius*, *-itius* traditional, customary, metaphorical, f. *translāt-*: see translate *v.* and -itious[1]. Cf. obs. F. *translatice* (Cotgr.).]

1. Characterized by being transmitted, transferred, or carried from one person or place to another.

1611 Cotgr., *Translatice*, translaticious, translatiue; transposed, transferred. **1650** R. Stapylton *Strada's Low C. Warres* v. 138 Religion among Hereticks is not their own, but accidentall and translatitious. **1664** Evelyn *Sylva* I. iv. §8, I have frequently doubted whether it [the Elm-tree] be a pure Indigene or Translatitious. **1692** Washington tr. *Milton's Def. Pop.* vii, A delegated translatitious Majesty we allow, but that Majesty does chiefly and primarily reside in him, you can no more prove, than you can, that Power and Authority does.

2. Transferred in meaning; metaphorical; tralatitious.

1637 J. Williams *Holy Table* 77 The translatitious and borrowed..appellation of that holy utensill. **1673** O. Walker *Educ.* II. i. 228 It appears sometimes under a Metaphor, or some other translatitious expression.

Hence **†translaˈtitiously** *adv.*, traditionally, by custom derived from others.

1666 J. Fraser *Polichron.* (S.H.S.) 2 Translatitiously both in England and Low Countries of Scotland, we, by an inveterat custome derived from thence, doe say as yet Anderson, Jameson, Watson, Williamson, etc.

translative (trɑːnsˈleɪtɪv, træns-, ˈtrɑːnslətɪv, ˈtræns-, -nz-), *a.* [ad. L. *translātīv-us* pertaining to transfer or translation (see translate and -ive); cf. F. *translatif* (14th c.) in legal use.] Involving or of the nature of translation (in various senses).

†1. Involving transference of meaning; metaphorical, tropical. *Obs.*

1589 Puttenham *Eng. Poesie* II. iii. (Arb.) 81 If our feete Poeticall want these qualities it can not be sayd a foote in sence translatiue as here. *Ibid.* III. xviii. 197 Properly..Allegoria is when we do speake in sence translatiue and wrested from the owne signification.

2. Involving transference from one place to another; in *Physics*, of the nature of onward movement without rotation or reciprocation.

a **1682** Sir T. Browne *Wks.* (1835) IV. 370 We may improve their fruits without translative conjunction, that is, by insition of the scion upon his own mother. **1740** Stack in *Phil. Trans.* XLI. 418 It is allowed, that the translative Velocities of its Points cannot be in an inverted Ratio to the Roots of the Distances. **1875** Huxley & Martin *Elem. Biol.* (1877) 27 Watch the Brownian movements; note that they are simply oscillatory—not translative. **1883** *Nature* 15 Mar.

459/1 A screw's motion, which is partly translative along and partly rotative round a polar axis.

3. Tending or serving to translate or render; relating to translation, translational.

1748 RICHARDSON *Clarissa* (1811) VIII. xi. 62 As the translative impulse (pardon a new word..) came upon me. **1819** G. S. FABER *Dispensations* (1823) II. 319 The sense of the Greek translative Diathekè is thus determined by the sense of the Hebrew original Berith. **1882** W. SHARP *Rossetti* iv. 311 Renderings specially admirable for translative excellence and inherent poetic merit.

4. *Law.* Expressing or constituting transference of property, etc.

1875 POSTE *Gaius* II. Comm. (ed. 2) 172 Mancipation.. might be used as a formality..of contract either translative or obligative.

5. *Gram.* (See quot. 1905.)

1896 *Edin. Rev.* Jan. 84 The student [of Finnish] must remember the nominative, partitive,..prolative, translative, essive..and instructive [cases]. **1905** JESPERSEN *Hist. Eng. Lang.* 9 Translative, indicating the state into which anyone or anything passes.

translator (trɑːns'leɪtə(r), træns-, -nz-). Also 4–6 -oure, 4–8 -our, 5 -ore, 6–7 -er. [a. OF. *translator, -our*, F. *-eur* (12th c. in Godef. *Compl.*), or L. *translātor*, agent-n. of *transferre*: see TRANSLATE and -OR.] One who (or that which) translates.

1. a. One who translates or renders from one language into another; the author of a translation.

13.. in Horstm. *Altengl. Leg.* (1878) 25/1101 Of al translatours in to latyn He was flour enditour fyn. *c* **1380** WYCLIF *Sel. Wks.* III. 96 Whiche word þe Ebru translatoure, Aquyla interpretid, 'and þe Lord confermede'. **1413** *Pilgr. Sowle* (Caxton) v. xiv. (1859) 82 The symple and vnsuffisaunt translatore of this litel book. **1509** BARCLAY *Shyp of Folys* (1570) 260 Go Booke,..By thy submission excuse thy Translatour [*rime* honour]. *a* **1680** BUTLER *Rem.* (1759) II. 405 A Translater dyes an Author, like an old Stuff, into a new Colour. **1778** WARTON *Hist. Eng. Poetry* II. Notes 19 Lapus de Castellione, a Florentine civilian, and a great translator from Greek into Latin, about the year 1350. **1837** LOCKHART *Scott* II. iv. 121 Mr. Cary, the translator of Dante.

b. One who renders a painting by engraving, or the like: cf. TRANSLATION 2 b.

1855 *Gentl. Mag.* XLIII. 657/1 Mr. C. Blair Leighton.. lithographer..was one of the earliest translators of water and oil pictures by the chromatic process. **1888** W. P. FRITH *Autobiog.* III. vii. 159 The delightful art of Thomas [Landseer, the engraver], so thoroughly in sympathy with his brother [Edwin, the painter], places the producer in the front rank of the company of translators. **1897** *Daily News* 5 Feb. 8/6 Line engraving and mezzotint—both of them used largely in the service of the 'translators'.

c. *Computers.* A program that translates from one (esp. programming) language into another.

1958 A. J. PERLIS et al. (*title*) Internal translator (IT) a compiler for the 650. **1959** [see LANGUAGE *sb.* 1 d]. **1972** *Computer Jrnl.* XV. 229/1 General parsing algorithms.. used in actual translators are characterised by the use of classes of grammars which are subsets of the class of context free grammars. **1981** POHL & SHAW *Nature of Computation* vi. 193 Language processors, such as translators and interpreters, are called systems programs or systems software because they are normally part of the total computer system presented to a user.

2. a. One who transforms, changes, or alters; *spec.* a cobbler who renovates old shoes.

1594 *Merry Knack* in Hazl. *Dodsley* VI. 566 As long as Jeffrey the translater is Mayor of the town. **1638** BRATHWAIT *Barnabees Jrnl.* A vj, That paltry Patcher is a bald Translater. *a* **1658** CLEVELAND *Gen. Poems* (1677) 23 I'm no Translator, have no vein To turn a Woman young again. **1693** *Humours Town* 77 The Jolly Translator, of Shoes, I mean, not Authors. **1700** T. BROWN *Amusem. Ser. & Com.* 130 The Cobler is Affronted, if you don't call him Mr. Translator. **1851** MAYHEW *Lond. Labour* I. 198/2 I'm a 'translator' by trade. **1886** *Daily News* 15 Oct. 3/6 'Translators', who cunningly metamorphose..old leather almost into new goods.

b. *transf. pl.* A 'translated' pair of shoes. *slang.*

1851 MAYHEW *Lond. Labour* I. 51/2 To wear a pair of second-hand ones [boots], or 'translators' (as they are called), is felt as a bitter degradation.

c. (See quot.)

1884 KNIGHT *Dict. Mech.* Supp., *Translator*,..an instrument whereby one form of energy is converted into another. For instance, the power of a prime motor, say a steam engine, is translated by means of a magneto-electric engine into electricity. **1891** in *Cent. Dict.*

†3. One who transfers or transports. *Obs.*

1545 JOYE *Exp. Dan.* v. I v b, The changer and translator of kyngedoms and tymes. **1630** BRATHWAIT *Eng. Gentlem.* (1641) 53 That translator of the Median Empire to the Persians, victorious Cyrus. *a* **1633** AUSTIN *Medit.* (1635) 94 Constantine the Emperor (whom they make a great Translator of Bones) would not let them rest in their Graves.

4. a. An automatic repeater in long-distance telegraphy. Cf. TRANSLATION 6.

1855 *Patent Office Specif.* No. 314 The use of translators in connection with submarine cables. **1876** PREECE & SIVEWRIGHT *Telegr.* iv. §111 A distance is at last reached where direct working is impossible, and where it becomes necessary..to introduce mechanical repeaters or translators at some intermediate station to bring into play fresh currents.

b. A relay set or station which receives television signals and retransmits them without demodulating them.

1958 *New Scientist* 25 Sept. 898/2 Instead of receiving signals, demodulating them to visual or aural form and then re-transmitting, it just passes on the original signals. The BBC calls it a translator. **1960** *Practical Wireless* XXXVI. 330/2 Tentative plans are being considered for a considerable number of additional TV 'translator' stations of very low power. **1966** *Daily Tel.* 17 Oct. 9/5 TIE may have solved the problem with a television translator powered by sunlight... The translator set on a high point would receive and re-transmit signals to isolated communities.

5. *attrib.* and *Comb.*

1885 *Pall Mall G.* 29 Jan. 4/2 The extraordinary merit of their translator-engravers. **1887** *Ibid.* 28 Sept. 2/2 [He] has fallen into the clutches of a 'translator-traitor' if ever there was one, who has not only corrected no blunder, but added an enormous mass of mistranslations and misprints. **1891** *Ibid.* 8 Dec. 3/1 A little spurt of undignified and vindictive petulance, a new form of translator-treachery.

Hence **trans'latorship**, the function of a translator (in quot. 1786 *humorously* with possessive as a title).

1786 COWPER *Let. to Lady Hesketh* 11 Feb., You must return it [specimen of Homer]..to my translatorship. **1835** *Fraser's Mag.* XII. 53 An aspirant for the honours of translatorship.

translatorese (trɑːns,leɪtə'riːz, træns-, -nz-). [f. TRANSLATOR + -ESE.] = TRANSLATIONESE. Cf. TRANSLATESE.

1915 *Morning Post* 15 Apr. 2/4 The worst 'journalese' is more English than schoolmasters' 'translatorese'. **1967** *Times Lit. Suppl.* 11 May 399/1 There is even a recognizable variant of pidgin English known as 'translatorese'. **1982** I. HAMILTON *Robert Lowell* (1983) xvi. 292 Critics might more damagingly have quoted the limp translatorese that crops up throughout *Imitations*.

translatory (trɑːns'leɪtərɪ, træns-, 'trɑːnslətərɪ, 'træns-, -nz-), *a.* [f. TRANSLATOR: see -ORY².]

†1. Characterized by transferring from one to another. *Obs. rare.*

1727 SWIFT *Art Polit. Lying* ¶6 Wks. 1755 III. I. 117 He divides Political Lyes into several species... The translatory is a lye, that transfers the merit of a man's good action to another who is [etc.].

2. Of or pertaining to physical translation; = TRANSLATIONAL b.

1849 NOAD *Electricity* (ed. 3) 267 The negative tension of an insulated metal is sensibly augmented by giving a translatory motion to the gas which attacks its surface. **1860** TYNDALL *Glac.* II. xxix. 403 Owing to the quicker translatory movement. **1881** —— *Floating Matter of Air* ii. 60 The Bacteria lost their translatory power, fell to the bottom, and left the liquid..clear.

translatress (trɑːns'leɪtrɪs, træns-, -nz-). [f. TRANSLATOR + -ESS.] A female translator.

1638 CHILLINGW. *Relig. Prot.* I. ii. §91. 85 Which Card. Perron and his Translatresse so often translate false. **1759** DILWORTH *Pope* 76 By the French translatress Madam Dacier. **1865** *Even. Standard* 4 Feb., The celebrated French translatress of Darwin's work on the 'Origin of Species'.

trans'latrix. [fem., in L. form, of TRANSLATOR: see -TRIX.] = prec.

1892 *Nation* (N.Y.) 18 Aug. 133/1 The translatrix knows her Greek well enough to do this. **1902** *Speaker* 4 Oct. 19/1 Is it the translatrix or Gregorovius himself who is guilty of [the mistake]?

†**transla'vation.** *Obs. rare*⁻¹. [f. TRANS- 1 + L. *lavātiōnem*, n. of action fr. *lavāre* to wash, LAVE *v.*¹] The action of 'laving' or ladling from one vessel to another.

1601 HOLLAND *Pliny* xxxiv. xviii. II. 519 This translavation ought so long to be continued out of one vessell into another, untill such time as it have done casting any residence downward.

translay (trɑːns'leɪ, træns-), *v. nonce-wd.* [TRANS- 2.] *trans.* To transfer and lay in a new position.

1849 CLOUGH *Easter Day* 14 If not where Joseph laid Him first, why then Where other men Translaid Him after, in some humbler clay.

Transleithan (trɑːns'laɪθən, træns-), *a.* [f. TRANS- 7 + *Leitha*, name of a river.] Beyond the Leitha, a tributary of the Danube, which formed for a short distance the boundary between Hungary and the archduchy of Austria; hence, Magyar or Hungarian, as distinguished from the cis-Leithan provinces of the Austro-Hungarian empire. So **Translei'thanian** *a.*

1870 GLADSTONE *Glean.* IV. v. 201 [Hungary] has attracted to herself the Transleithan Slav population of the South. **1900** *Westm. Gaz.* 5 Jan. 1/3 A sort of tacit understanding that permeates almost all classes of Transleithanian society.

trans'lettering. *nonce-wd.* [f. TRANS- 2 + LETTER *v.* + -ING¹.] = TRANSLITERATION.

1802 W. TAYLOR in *Monthly Mag.* XIII. 12 It may seem strange to fix on a root, which his system of translettering would express by *shiv*.

translimi'tation. *rare.* [f. TRANS- 1 + L. *līmitātiōn-em* fixing of a limit, f. *līmit-em* boundary, limit. Cf. Sp. *translimitacion*.] The sending of troops across the frontier of a foreign state, for the preservation of order, etc.

1845 W. H. KELLY tr. *L. Blanc's Hist. Ten Y.* v. iv. II. 445 All he [Mendizabal] had made up his mind to sanction was the system of *translimitation*, intended solely to deprive Don Carlos of the succours transmitted to him by the northern powers.

transliterate (trɑːns'lɪtəreɪt, træns-, -nz-), *v.* [f. TRANS- 1 + L. *littera* letter, written symbol + -ATE³.] *trans.* To replace (letters or characters of one language) by those of another used to represent the same sounds; to write (a word, etc.) in the characters of another alphabet. Hence **trans'literated** *ppl. a.*

1861 MAX MÜLLER in *Sat. Rev.* 9 Mar. 247/1 Not only proper names, but the technical terms also of the Buddhist creed, had to be preserved in Chinese. They were not to be translated, but to be transliterated. But how was this to be effected with a language which, like Chinese, has no phonetic alphabet? **1861** G. MOORE *Lost Tribes* 158, I transliterate the words into modern Hebrew letters. **1871** EARLE *Philol. Eng. Tongue* §190 To master this alphabet and transliterate passages of English into it. **1884** *American* VII. 378 The transliterated pages and the Devanagari can be kept in sight at the same time.

transliteration (,trɑːnslɪtə'reɪʃən, ,træns-, -nz-). [f. as prec. + -ATION.] The action or process of transliterating; the rendering of the letters or characters of one alphabet in those of another; *concr.* a word or writing thus rendered.

1861 MAX MÜLLER in *Sat. Rev.* 9 Mar. 247/1 Even the Chinese were after a time unable to read—i.e., to pronounce—these random trans-literations. **1861** G. MOORE *Lost Tribes* 257 The transliteration into Hebrew presents a clear sense. **1862** RAWLINSON *Anc. Mon.* I. viii. 215 Too obscure or too illegible for transliteration. **1900** MARGOLIOUTH in *Expositor* Jan. 50 Till the most recent times no scientific method of transliteration had been invented.

transliterator (trɑːns'lɪtəreɪtə(r), træns-, -nz-). [f. as prec. + -OR.] One who transliterates.

1867 ELLIS *E.E. Pron.* I. iii. §4. 191 Sanscrit transliterators. **1895** *Athenæum* 26 Oct. 575/3 Is it the last new idea of the Indian Government transliterator to put a dot under the *t* of Fathpûr, but not under the *h*?

translocalization (trɑːns,ləʊkəlaɪ'zeɪʃən, træns-). *rare*⁻¹. [f. TRANS- 2 + LOCALIZATION.] Translocation, displacement; in quot., in reference to time.

1888 *Amer. Jrnl. Psychol.* May 538 Patients..sometimes cannot repeat the same pseudo-experience twice alike, translocalizations in time being especially common.

translocate ('trɑːnsləʊkeɪt, træns-), *v.* [f. TRANS- + LOCATE. Probably suggested by next, which was used much earlier.]

1. a. *trans.* To remove from one place to another; to displace, dislocate. Esp. in reference to the transfer of wild animals.

a **1832** BENTHAM *Lang.* Wks. 1843 VIII. 325/1 Add, upon the model of *transfer*, and *transfuse*, translocate. **1887** *Amer. Nat.* Oct. 944 The ribs have been translocated from the original position..to the neurapophyses. **1899** *Syd. Soc. Lex.*, *Translocate*, the same as Dislocate. **1971** *Nature* 6 Aug. 374/2 As long ago as 1928 the possibility of translocating rhino from Zululand to other parts of their former range was suggested by the naturalist Herbert Lang. **1980** *Cape Times* 19 Aug. 5/3 The present objective is to translocate as many black rhino as possible to as many of their original areas.

b. *Veg. Physiol.* To subject to translocation.

1911 in WEBSTER. **1931** E. C. MILLER *Plant Physiol.* xii. 696 It appears that the mineral nutrients absorbed by the roots on one side of a plant are, in a large measure, translocated to and used by the trunk, limbs, and leaves directly above them. **1959** *New Scientist* 12 Nov. 931/3 Substances may be translocated through the fungal threads and be accumulated into the fungal tissue which surrounds the root. **1976** *Sci. Amer.* Sept. 124/3 (Advt.), When the proper rate is applied to the weeds' well-grown foliage, the compound is translocated throughout the plant.

2. *Genetics.* To move (a portion of a chromosome) *to* a new position, esp. on a non-homologous chromosome.

1936 *Discovery* Sept. 269/1 In one of the new races the left ends were removed from both the second chromosomes and translocated to a third chromosome. **1949** DARLINGTON & MATHER *Elem. Genetics* v. 102 A piece may be taken out of a chromosome and inserted or translocated wherever else the same or another chromosome may be broken. **1975** *Nature* 3 Jan. 13/3 Genes translocated to positions close to heterochromatin seem in many species to become inactivated.

3. *intr.* To move, change location.

1977 *Lancet* 2 July 15/2 Others..had demonstrable abnormalities of receptor function, such as failure of the receptor hormone complex to translocate to the nucleus.

Hence **translo'cated** *ppl. a.*; **translo'catable** *a.*, able to be translocated.

1930 *Jrnl. Genetics* XXII. 313 Offspring..will then have an excess (triple amount) of genes of the sort present in the proximal portion of the translocated piece. **1975** *Nature* 4 Dec. 384/1 Discrete translocatable elements (transposons) may constitute relatively common genetic units in bacteria. **1976** *Ann. Rev. Microbiol.* XXX. 517 One must also be aware of the prevalence of insertion sequences..and the newly discovered translocatable sequences..discovered in enteric microorganisms. **1980** R. P. WAGNER et al. *Introd. Mod. Genetics* x. 289/2 The two normal chromosomes move to one pole while the two translocated chromosomes go to the other.

translocation (trɑːnsləʊ'keɪʃən, træns-). [f. TRANS- + LOCATION.]

1. a. Removal from one place to another; displacement; dislocation; †transmigration. Esp. in reference to the removal of wild animals.

1624 F. WHITE *Repl. Fisher* 424 Translocation of Christs bodie. **1625** N. CARPENTER *Geog. Del.* II. x. (1635) 174 A seperation was made by translocation of the parts of the Earth. **1665** SIR T. HERBERT *Trav.* (1677) 116 All defending the immortality of the Soul, and the translocation from one into another after death. **1677** CARY *Chronol.* II. i. I. xx. 152 There is..a casual translocation of the Numbers. *a* **1728** WOODWARD *Catal. Eng. Fossils* (1729) II. 4 *margin*, There happen'd certain Translocations at the Deluge. *c* **1814** COLERIDGE in *Lit. Rem.* (1838) III. 80 Translocation is not destruction. **1876** GLADSTONE *Homeric Synchr.* 79 A Revolution involving such extensive change, and such translocation of races. **1877** FOSTER *Phys.* I. ii. §2 (1878) 79 The muscular contraction itself is essentially a translocation of molecules. **1962** *Oryx* VI. 215 By translocation is meant the transfer of wild animals from one area to another. **1969** J. FISHER et al. *Red Bk.* 123/2 Several countries have already used the drug and translocation method to introduce or re-introduce rhinos.

b. *Veg. Physiol.*: see quots.

1887 H. M. WARD tr. *J. von Sachs' Lect. Physiol. Plants* xxi. 347 For starch also is found at places in the tissue where it has neither been originally produced nor is employed, and thus in a condition of translocation towards the places where it is made use of. **1900** B. D. JACKSON *Gloss. Bot. Terms*, *Translocation*..the transference of reserve material from one part to another. **1911** WEBSTER, *Translocation*,..transfer of food materials or products of metabolism from one part to another by osmosis. **1951** *Chambers's Jrnl.* Aug. 457/1 In the case of these perennial weeds with persistent root-stocks the chlorate acts by the method of translocation, working downward, cell by cell, from the sprayed tops to the lowest root-tip. **1976** NOGGLE & FRITZ *Introd. Plant Physiol.* xii. 357 Translocation of sugars in the phloem is through living sieve elements.

2. *Genetics.* A transposition (sense 7), esp. to a position on a non-homologous chromosome; also, a portion of chromosome that is translocated.

1923 *Anat. Rec.* XXIV. 426 (*heading*) The translocation of a section of chromosome-II upon chromosome-III in Drosophila. **1924** [see TRANSPOSITION 7]. **1937** C. D. DARLINGTON *Rec. Adv. Cytol.* (ed. 2) vii. 265 They may also arise with translocation of a segment from one chromosome to another or from one arm of a chromosome to another. **1956** [see ANEUPLOIDY]. **1962** *Lancet* 8 Dec. 1229/2 In all cases diagnosed confidently as having Down's syndrome we have found an excess of material of chromosome no. 21, either as an additional chromosome in the regular trisomic type or as a translocation. **1977** *Nature* 3 Nov. 10/3 It is thought that interaction between the two inverted sequences plays an important part in this translocation.

Hence **translo'cational** *a.*

1930 *Jrnl. Genetics* XXII. 312 (*caption*) Translocational parent. **1965** *Jrnl. Cellular & Compar. Physiol.* LXV. 280/2 There was virtually no translocational movement in the partially rounded individuals.

†trans'luce, *v. Obs. rare.* [ad. L. *translūc-ēre* to shine through, f. TRANS- + *lūcēre* to shine: cf. TRALUCE *v.*] *trans.* To shine through.

1609 J. DAVIES *Holy Roode* (Grosart) 26/1 Let Ioy transluce thy Beauties blandishment.

translucence (trɑːns'l(j)uːsəns, træns-, -nz-). [f. as next: see -ENCE.]

1. The action or fact of shining through.

1826 COLERIDGE *Two Founts* 27 The soul's translucence thro' her crystal shrine! **1830** —— *Lett., to Mrs. Gillman* (1895) 754 What appeared to you a translucence of the love of the good, the true, and the beautiful from within me. **1868** FARRAR *Silence & V.* i. (1875) 18 Nature, which is but the visible translucence of a divine agency working upon material things. **1875** MASSON *Wordsw.*, etc. 123 All the secrets of the earth's interior..are revealed in continuous translucence.

2. Transparency to light: = TRANSLUCENCY.

1755 JOHNSON, *Transparency*, clearness; diaphaneity; translucence; power of transmitting light. **1847–9** *Todd's Cycl. Anat.* IV. 246/2 The epithelium beyond is of excessive delicacy and translucence. **1899** *Allbutt's Syst. Med.* VIII. 592 Having a wax-like translucence.

fig. **1859** I. TAYLOR *Logic in Theol.* 271, I admire the translucence of his character, and its strength.

translucency (trɑːns'l(j)uːsənsɪ, træns-, -nz-). [f. next: see -ENCY: cf. TRALUCENCY.] The quality or condition of being translucent; partial transparency: see quot. 1842. Also *fig.*

1630 J. TAYLOR (Water P.) *Whore* Wks. II. 111/1 So one glance or glimpse of the translucencie of your eyes sun-dazeling corruscancy. **1646** SIR T. BROWNE *Pseud. Ep.* II. i. 52 Ice..its atoms are not concreted into continuity, which doth diminish its translucency. **1831** FARADAY *Exp. Res.* xlvi. 339 Different degrees of colour or translucency. **1842** BRANDE *Dict. Sc.*, etc., *Translucency*, semitransparency. The term is chiefly used in descriptive mineralogy as applied to minerals which admit of a passage of the rays of light, but through which objects cannot be definitely distinguished. **1879** CALDERWOOD *Mind & Br.* 61 A chamber filled with a clear watery fluid, essential for the translucency of the external portion of the eye.

translucent (trɑːns'l(j)uːsənt, træns-, -nz-), *a.* [f. L. *translūcēnt-em*, pres. pple. of *translūcēre* to shine through: see TRANSLUCE, and cf. TRALUCENT.]

†**1.** That shines through; emitting penetrating rays. **b.** In quot. *a* 1652, thoroughly illuminated or luminous. *Obs. rare.*

1596 FITZ-GEFFRAY *Sir F. Drake* (1881) 97 The sunne, That latelie bright translucent splendour shed. *a* **1652** A. WILSON *Jas. I* (1653) 61 She had a translucent passage in the night, through the City of London, by multitudes of Torches. **1791** J. LEARMONT *Poems* 359 The Sun translucent from on high With locks of waving gold salutes the sky.

2. Through which light passes: = TRANSPARENT.

1607 TOPSELL *Four-f. Beasts* (1658) 153 The eye of man is translucent, and containeth in it a horny substance. **1634** MILTON *Comus* 861 Sabrina fair,..sitting Under the glassie, cool, translucent wave. **1725** POPE *Odyss.* I. 180 Replenish'd from the cool, translucent springs. **1847** LEWES *Hist. Philos.* (1867) I. 326 Water, air, and other bodies which are translucent.

fig. **1891** SWINBURNE *Stud. Pr. & Poetry*, *Jrnl. Sir W. Scott* (1894) 23 The translucent treachery of such an impious imposture.

b. Now, more distinctively: Allowing the passage of light, yet diffusing it so as not to render bodies lying beyond clearly visible; semi-transparent.

1784 COWPER *Tiroc.* 120 A pane of thin translucent horn. **1846** GROVE *Corr. Phys. Forces* 29 The glass ceases to be transparent, though remaining translucent. **1851** WOODWARD *Mollusca* I. 66 The shell of the argonaut is thin and translucent. **1905** in *Westm. Gaz.* 17 Mar. 12/1 The windows of this classroom were once transparent, they are now translucent, and if not cleaned very soon will be opaque.

fig. **1843** CARLYLE *Past & Pr.* II. ii, The old centuries melt from opaque to partially translucent, transparent here and there.

Hence **trans'lucently** *adv.*, in a translucent manner or state; so as to be seen through.

1832 LYTTON *Eugene A.* I. i, So translucently pure and soft was her complexion. **1897** *Allbutt's Syst. Med.* III. 82 The skin..is translucently pale and shines like a mirror.

translucid (trɑːns'l(j)uːsɪd, træns-, -nz-), *a.* [ad. L. *translūcid-us* translucent: see prec. and -ID. Cf. F. *translucide* (16th c.).] = TRANSLUCENT 2, and now 2 b.

1626 BACON *Sylva* §872 Which is most easily seen in the Eyes, because they are Translucide. **1651** *Life Father Sarpi* (1676) 18 How infusion by Art makes bark of Trees and Shells and Roots translucid. **1878** MISS J. YOUNG *Ceram. Art* (1879) 51 Porcelain is translucid, and therein differs from pottery, which is opaque.

†**b.** = TRANSLUCENT 1. *Obs. rare*$^{-0}$.

1727 [implied in TRANSLUCIDNESS].

Hence **trans'lucidness** = next.

1727 BAILEY vol. II, *Translucidness*..the Quality of shining through, or permitting Light to shine through.

translucidity (trɑːnsl(j)uː'sɪdɪtɪ, -æ-, -nz-). [ad. F. *translucidité* (16th c. in Hatz.-Darm.): see prec. and -ITY.] The quality or condition of being translucid; translucency.

1694 MOTTEUX *Rabelais* v. 254 The Flickermise flying through the translucidity of the corner'd Gate. **1798** MITCHELL tr. *Karsten's Min. Leskean Mus.* 367 The internal Lustre and the Translucidity are observable. **1855** tr. *Labarte's Arts Mid. Ages* xiv. 413 Owing to its translucidity.

trans'lunar, *a.* [f. as next.]

1. = TRANSLUNARY *a.*

a **1914** N.E.D. s.v. TRANSLUNARY *a.* **1927** W. B. YEATS in *Monthly Criterion* June 292 Being dead, we rise, Dream and so create Translunar Paradise. **1962** F. I. ORDWAY et al. *Basic Astronautics* v. 201 Mechta was instrumented to gather data on cosmic and solar radiations in cis- and translunar space.

2. *Astronautics.* Of or pertaining to space-flight or a trajectory from the earth or another planet towards the moon.

1965 *New Scientist* 1 July 12/2 Corrections will be made several times during the translunar phase..based on measurements made by Earth stations..and..by astronauts. **1969** *Daily Mail* 14 Jan. 1/2 Everybody had built up that burn, and of course it was critical. But so was translunar injection, so was re-entry. **1972** *Daily Tel.* 8 Dec. 1 The correction was the result of a manoeuvre which put Apollo on a trans-lunar trajectory 15 minutes earlier than planned.

translunary ('trɑːnsl(j)uːnərɪ, 'træns-, -nz-), *a.* [f. TRANS- 3 + L. *lūna* moon, after *lunary*.] Lying beyond or above the moon: the opposite of *sublunary*; chiefly *fig.*, etherial, insubstantial, visionary.

1627 DRAYTON *Agincourt*, etc., *To H. Reynolds* 206 Neat Marlow bathed in the Thespian springs Had in him those braue translunary things. **1826** BEDDOES *Let.* Oct., Poems (1851) p. lviii, All my sublunary excursions this summer have been botanical; and my translunary ones..a thought or two for a didactic 'Boem'..on myology. **1892** *Century Mag.* June 183/2 A strayed visitor from some translunary sphere. **1902** AGNES M. CLERKE *Probl. Astrophysics* (1903) 2 The long-divorced sublunary and translunary worlds.

trans'make, *v.* [f. TRANS- 2 + MAKE *v.*, rendering Gr. *μεταποιεῖν*.] *trans.* To make into something different, to refashion. Hence **trans'making** *vbl. sb.*

1844 *Dublin Rev.* Mar. 92 They [the sacramental symbols] are as it were *transmade*, made into a new thing, or, in the apt language of the Catholic dogma, transubstantiated. **1874** PUSEY *Lent. Serm.* 315 Those..whom man could not have changed even by punishing, but the Word transmade, forming and fashioning them after its own will. **1909** D. STONE *Doctr. Eucharist* I. 72 [transl. St. Gregory of Nyssa] That body by the indwelling of God the Word was transmade (*μετεποιήθη*) to the dignity of Godhead.

trans'marginal, *a.* [f. TRANS- 4 + MARGINAL *a.*] Beyond the margin of normal consciousness; subliminal.

1902 W. JAMES *Var. Relig. Exper.* xx. 511 The exploration of the transmarginal field has hardly yet been seriously undertaken. **1915** J. H. TUCKWELL *Relig. & Reality* xi. 220 In the larger transmarginal or subliminal region of consciousness..nothing is ever really forgotten. **1968** W. E. BROEN *Schizophrenia* viii. 201 The level of stimulation necessary to produce the transmarginal inhibition is said to be lower in individuals with weaker..nervous systems. **1973** T. PYNCHON *Gravity's Rainbow* I. 48 Send them over into one of the transmarginal phases, past borders of their waking selves.

†transmarinal, *a. Obs. rare*$^{-1}$. [f. as next + -AL[1].] = TRANSMARINE.

1614 JACKSON *Creed* III. xiii. §11. 137 Hart out of his transmarinall Catechisme, would gladly haue maintained it.

transmarine (trɑːnsmə'riːn, træns-, -nz-), *a.* (*sb.*) [ad. L. *transmarīnus*, f. *trans* across + *mare* sea, after MARINE. Cf. F. *transmarin* (12th c. in Godef.).]

1. That is beyond the sea; born, existing, situated, or found on the other side of the sea; over-sea.

1583 MELBANCKE *Philotimus* Aa j b, An aliaunt, or a transmarine straunger. **1610** T. HIGGONS *Serm. at Pauls Crosse* 3 Mar. (1611) 45 It was borne in transmarine and forraine parts. **1671** F. PHILLIPS *Reg. Necess.* 329 Purchasers of Transmarine Wares and Commodities. **1700** TYRRELL *Hist. Eng.* II. 723 Normandy, and the King's other Transmarine Dominions. **1807** G. CHALMERS *Caledonia* I. I. vi. 193 Contemporary authors..speak of the Scots, as a transmarine people. **1878** *N. Amer. Rev.* CXXVII. 189 If it [India] were the sole transmarine appendage to the crown.

2. Crossing or extending across the sea.

1860 GOSSE *Rom. Nat. Hist.* 84 Species [of birds] which are known to make long transmarine migrations. **1908** *Sci. Amer.* 15 Feb. 106/1 The remarkable transmarine railroad which is under construction from the mainland of Florida to Key West. **1908** F. HARRISON in *Trans. Roy. Hist. Soc.* Ser. III. III. 38 Pitt made all European questions subordinate to his transmarine, world-wide ambitions and schemes.

†**B.** *sb.* One born or dwelling beyond the sea; a native or inhabitant of a transmarine country.

1596 WARNER *Alb. Eng.* XI. lxv. (1602) 280 Perhaps, vnpossible..My loue should equall his, or I a trans-Marine be wrought. **1633** HEYWOOD *Eng. Trav.* II. ii, I am, quoth he, A Trans-marine by birth.

†trans'maritime, *a. Obs. rare*$^{-1}$. [TRANS- 3.] = TRANSMARINE.

1610 BP. CARLETON *Jurisd.* 74 Transmaritim iudgments ought not to be admitted.

transma'terial, *a. rare*$^{-1}$. [TRANS- 4.] Beyond or transcending the material.

1903 *19th Cent.* Apr. 639 He ends by representing it [the subliminal self] as a hyperphysical spirit, whose origin is beyond matter, and whose functions are transmaterial.

transmateri'ation. *rare*$^{-1}$. [f. TRANS- 1 + L. *māteriātiōn-em*: see MATERIATION.] Change of the matter of which a thing consists.

1866 HARPER *Peace thro. Truth* Ser. I. 159 If it be altered it must be either substantially, and that by Transubstantiation, or transformation, or transmateriation, or it must be accidentally.

†'transmeate, *v. Obs. rare*$^{-0}$. [f. ppl. stem of rare L. *transmeāre* to pass across (Pliny), f. *trans* + *meāre* to go, pass.] *trans.* To pass through or across. So **†'transmeable** *a.* [L. *transmeābilis*], that may be crossed, passable, **†'transmeant** *a.* [L. *transmeānt-em* pr. pple.], passing through.

1656 BLOUNT *Glossogr.*, *Transmeable*, to be, or that may be passed over. *Ibid.*, *Transmeate*, to passe or go beyond. **1657** *Physical Dict.*, *Transmea[n]t*, that passeth through the pores of the body, as through the bottom of a sieve. **1727** BAILEY vol. II, Transmeable..Transmeated.

†transmeation (trɑːnsmiː'eɪʃən, træns-). *Obs. rare.* [n. of action from L. *transmeāre*: see prec. and -ATION.] A passing across or over.

1630 LORD *Banians* 52 They did hold, that there was a passage of soules of one creature into another, that this transmeation was of the soules of men into beasts, and of beasts into men. **1658** PHILLIPS, *Transmeation*, a passing through, or beyond.

transmedian (trɑːns'miːdɪən, træns-), *a.* (*sb.*) *Anat.* and *Zool.* [f. TRANS- + L. *medius* middle: cf. MEDIAN.] Passing or situated across the median line of the body; applied to certain muscles in brachiopods. Also as *sb.* a transmedian muscle. Also **trans'medial** *a.*

1876 T. DAVIDSON in *Encycl. Brit.* IV. 193/1 Of the shell or valvular muscles..one pair are transmedians, each member passing across the middle of the reverse side of the shell. *Ibid.*, Transmedial or sliding muscles. **1881** *Cassell's Nat. Hist.* V. 261 The fifth pair of transmedians controls the movements from side to side of the beak or umbonal regions of the shell.

trans'membrane, *a.* [TRANS- 3.] Existing or occurring across a cell membrane.

1961 *Amer. Jrnl. Physiol.* CC. 1252/1 Transmembrane resistance measurements were made by putting a rectangular voltage pulse in series with the microelectrodes. **1974** *Ann. N.Y. Acad. Sci.* CCXXVII. 98 (*heading*) The separation of electrons and protons during electron transfer: the distinction between membrane potentials and transmembrane gradients.

transmental (trɑːns'mɛntəl, træns-), *a.* (*sb.*) *rare.* [f. TRANS- 3 + L. *mens*, *ment-em* mind: cf. *mental*.] Existing beyond the mind; independent of or apart from human thought or perception; as *sb.*, a transmental existence or reality.

1905–6 W. JAMES in R. B. Perry *Thought & Char. W. James* (1935) II. lxxvii. 446 That an idea represents an 'object' may mean that it represents something.. Trans-*mental* altogether, as when it is said to be altogether 'un-knowable'. **1907** *Jrnl. Philos., Psychol. & Sci. Methods* 17 Jan. 45 Should the reply be that some sort of transmental is implied, I would gladly recant, even though Professor James should still insist that the nature of that transmental is irrelevant to all human interests, even the most intellectual.

transmentation (trɑːnsmɛnˈteɪʃən, træns-). *rare.* [f. TRANS- 1 + L. *mens, ment-* mind + -ATION; rendering Gr. μετάνοια afterthought, repentance. Cf. *mentation* and mod. 16th c. L. *transmentātio* (Goclenius in Du Cange).] Change of mind or thinking; mental conversion.

1647 TRAPP *Comm. 2 Cor.* vii. 9 *That ye sorrowed to repentance* Gr. To a transmentation, to a thorow change both of the minde and manners. **1657** REEVE *God's Plea* 63 Where there is μετάνοια, a new braying, or a transmentation. **1835** J. HARRIS *Gt. Teacher* (1837) 181 Repentance, transmentation, a change of mind, was the indispensable condition of enrolment.

†**transmeˈridian,** *a.* (*sb.*) *Obs. rare.* [f. TRANS- 7 + L. *meridiān-us* MERIDIAN.] Beyond the or a meridian. In quot. *absol.* as *sb.*, the region beyond the meridian in the Atlantic which separates the New from the Old World; the Western Hemisphere.

1500–20 DUNBAR *Poems* lxvi. 63 It micht have cuming in schortar quhyll Fra Calzecot and the new-fund Yle, The partis of Transmeridiane; Quhilk to considder is ane pane.

transmeridional (trɑːnsməˈrɪdɪənəl, træns-, -nz-), *a.* [f. TRANS- 3 + MERIDIONAL *a.* 4.] Crossing or traversing the meridian lines; running east and west.

1883 A. WINCHELL *World-Life* II. iii. (1889) 355 How the Mediterranean and Indian Ocean shores came to have general transmeridional trends. **1892** *Chambers' Encycl.* X. 505/2 The Caribbean Sea and the Mediterranean—those great transmeridional depressions.

transmethylation (ˌtrɑːnsmɛθɪˈleɪʃən, ˌtræns-, -nz-). *Chem.* [f. TRANS- 10 + METHYL + -ATION.] The transfer of a methyl group from a molecule of one compound to one of another.

1940 *Jrnl. Biol. Chem.* CXXXIV. 787 It was realized that direct proof of the transfer of the methyl group (transmethylation) was highly desirable. **1976** SMYTHIES & CORBETT *Psychiatry* v. 45 Schizophrenia might result from some disorder of transmethylation.

transmew, transmue (trɑːnsˈmjuː, træns-), *v.* *Obs.* or *arch.* Also 4–5 **-muwe, -mewe,** 5 **-mywe.** [a. F. *transmue-r* (13th c. in Hatz.-Darm.), semi-learned form:—L. *transmūtāre* to change, TRANSMUTE, f. TRANS- + *mūtāre* to change: see MEW *v.*[1]] *trans.* = TRANSMUTE I.

c **1374** CHAUCER *Troylus* IV. 439 (467) Thow most me first transmuwen [*v.r.* transmute] in a ston. *Ibid.* 802 (830) Ioies ..þat now transmuwed ben in cruel wo. *c* **1407** LYDG. *Reson & Sens.* 4323 She to A larke was transmewed. **1512** *Helyas* in Thoms *Prose Rom.* (1828) III. 81 His v. brethren and his sister, which were transmued in to swannes. **1590** SPENSER *F.Q.* I. vii. 35 Men into stones therewith he could transmew, And stones to dust, and dust to nought at all. *a* **1643** W. CARTWRIGHT *Ordinary* v. iv. in Hazl. *Dodsley* XII. 308, I, Robert Moth..do transmue my name to Geffery. **1748** THOMSON *Cast. Indol.* II. xlii, As if transmew'd to stone. **1820** SCOTT *Monast.* xviii, To cast my riding slough, and to transmew myself into some civil form.

†**b.** *intr.* for *pass.* = TRANSMUTE I c. *Obs.*

c **1400** *Rom. Rose* 2526 In siker wise thou hir salewe, Wherwith thi colour wole transmewe. *c* **1407** LYDG. *Reson & Sens.* 303 Dame nature..Alle erthely thing repaireth newe..Eche thinge..Which she seth faylle and transmywe. *a* **1461** —— *Beware Doubleness* 44 Fortune's wheel..Whos cours standeth ever in doute For to transmew.

†**transmigrable,** *a.* *Obs.* *rare*⁻¹. [f. L. *transmigrāre* to TRANSMIGR-ATE + -ABLE.] Capable of transmigration.

1689 G. HARVEY *Curing Dis. by Expect.* xvi. 120 Vegetables..whose fragrant scent is transmigrable with their humidity.

transmigrant (ˈtrɑːnsmɪgrənt, ˈtræns-, -nz-), *a.* and *sb.* [f. L. *transmigrānt-*, ppl. stem of *transmigrāre*: see next.]

A. *adj.* That transmigrates. *rare.*

1654 GAYTON *Pleas. Notes* III. iii. 82 Such an Agonie and maw-Convulsions, that he thought his soule had been transmigrant and Errant from his Body. **1888** *Athenæum* 24 Nov. 695/2 They proceed to tell a secular story of transmigrant souls.

B. *sb.* †**1.** *orig.* One who transmigrates or leaves his own land and dwells in another: including the two notions of 'emigrant' and 'immigrant'.

1622 BACON *Holy War* Wks. 1879 I. 529/1 There are other bands of society, and implicit confederations. That of colonies, or transmigrants, towards their mother nation.

2. In modern use: A person passing through a country or place on his way from the country from which he is an emigrant to that in which he will be an immigrant. Used *spec.* in reference to the Aliens Act of 1905: see quot.

1894 WILLIS in *Rep. Bd. of Trade recent Immigr. fr. E. Europe* 10 The immigrants of [Russian and Polish] nationality formed..in 1892, 64 per cent. of all aliens (not being seamen and not known to be transmigrants) shown.. to have come here from Hamburg. **1905** *Form of Return under Aliens Act*, A. Immigration Ports. Aliens Act, 1905. Transmigrants. That is, alien passengers (other than first-class passengers), who have in their possession prepaid through tickets, and in respect of whom security has been given that they will proceed to places outside the United Kingdom. **1910** *Daily News* 26 Feb. 4/2 Practically no aliens now arrive in this country for the purpose of settling here; they are nearly all transmigrants proceeding via England from the Continent to America.

b. Also said of migratory birds.

3. A soul which transmigrates.

1882 in OGILVIE (Annandale).

†**ˈtransmigrate,** *ppl. a.* *Obs.* *rare*⁻¹. [ad. late L. *transmigrāt-us* (Isidore), pa. pple. of *transmigrāre*: see next.] Transferred, transported; cf. next, 1 b. (Const. as pa. pple.)

1430–40 LYDG. *Bochas* VIII. xx. (MS. Bodl. 263) 393/2 Iherusalem was whilom transmygrat, Ther trewe Prophetis for thei hadde in despiht.

transmigrate (ˈtrɑːnsmɪgreɪt, ˈtræns-, trɑːnsˈmaɪgreɪt, træns-, -nz-), *v.* [f. L. *transmigrāt-*, ppl. stem of (very rare) *transmigrāre*, f. *trans*, TRANS- + *migrāre* to MIGRATE. Cf. mod.F. *transmigrer* (16th c. in Godef.).]

1. *intr.* To remove or pass from one place to another; *esp.* of persons, or a tribe: to move from one place of abode to another, to migrate.

1611 CORYAT *Crudities* 91 The Longobardes..being exceedingly multiplied in their owne country, transmigrated into a bordering Island. **1646** SIR T. BROWNE *Pseud. Ep.* VI. x, This complexion..is evidently maintained by generation, ..the Natives which transmigrate, omit it not without commixture. **1723** *Pres. St. Russia* II. 66 They are transmigrating from one Place to another. *a* **1797** H. WALPOLE *George II* (1847) I. ix. 269 The well affected clans might be induced to transmigrate to those settlements. **1898** *Westm. Gaz.* 1 Apr. 3/1 He found a wider space on the other side, so he transmigrated and slumbered in peace.

b. *trans.* in causal sense: To transfer, transport. (In quots. only in passive.)

1430–40 [see prec.]. **1635** HEYWOOD *Hierarch.* VII. Notes 463 Excellent Spirits..are rather transmigrated from the earth, to reigne with the Powers aboue. **1745** ELIZA HEYWOOD *Female Spect.* No. 11 (1748) II. 216 To try the experiment, Whether, by transferring the blood of one animal into another, the nature of the creature would be transmigrated also.

2. *intr. spec.* Of the soul: To pass after death into another body.

1606 SHAKS. *Ant. & Cl.* II. vii. 51 What manner o thing is your Crocodile?.. It liues by that which nourisheth it, and the Elements once out of it, it Transmigrates. **1616** B. JONSON *Epigr.* cxxxiii. 139 Their spirits transmigrated to a cat. *c* **1645** HOWELL *Lett.* (1650) II. 43, I think my soul would transmigrat into some tree, when she bids this body farewell. **1697** COLLIER *Ess. Mor. Subj.* II. (1709) 174 Methinks I should be loath to Transmigrate into a Child, or lie in a Cradle, with those few Things I have in my Head. **1883** GILMOUR *Mongols* xvii. 202 If souls do not transmigrate, where do they come from at birth, whither do they go at death?

b. *trans.* (causal). To cause to pass: cf. 1 b.

c **1559** R. HALL *Life Bp. Fisher* iii. (1655) 32 Luther's Soul was transmigrated into Henry the eighth. **1681** RYCAUT tr. *Gracian's Critick* 119 The Souls of evil livers, whom God.. had transmigrated into the Bodies of these irrational Creatures. **1876** A. B. GROSART in *Wordsworth's Pr. Wks.* I. Pref. 33 A monkey with a man's soul somehow transmigrated into it.

c. *transf.* and *fig.*

1646 E. G. in M. Ll[uelyn] *Men-Miracles*, etc. A v, While the grosse Bodies of the Poets die, Their Souls doe onely shift. And Poesie Transmigrates, not by chance, or lucke. *a* **1711** KEN *Hymnotheo* Poet. Wks. 1721 III. 186 Desire.. To Love transmigrates when it dies. **1834** HT. MARTINEAU *Moral* IV. 144 The genius of society has before transmigrated through forms as horrid and disgusting as these. **1850** LYNCH *Theo. Trin.* v. 86 Philosophies die or transmigrate.

Hence **ˈtransmigrated, ˈtransmigrating** *ppl. adjs.*

1682 T. FLATMAN *Heraclitus Ridens* No. 55 (1713) II. 98 Whether our Whigs..are not transmigrated Lice, who thrive and increase most in Hospitals and upon poor People? **1693** DRYDEN *Persius' Sat.* VI. 22 Who, in a drunken Dream beheld his Soul The Fifth within the Transmigrating roul. **1728** POPE *Dunc.* III. 49 Who knows how long, thy transmigrating soul Might from Bœotian to Bœotian roll! **1754** FOOTE *Knights* I. Wks. 1799 I. 62 The very abstract of penury! Sir John Cutler, with his transmigrated stockings, was but a type of him. **1898** *Westm. Gaz.* 28 July 2/3 To consider..more mundane matters, such as the number and characters of the transmigrating households.

transmigration (trɑːnsmɪˈgreɪʃən, træns-, -maɪ-, -nz-). [ad. late L. *transmigrātiōn-em* change of country (in Itala 1 Esdr. vi. 16 the Babylonian Captivity), n. of action from *transmigrāre*: see prec. Cf. F. *transmigration* (13th c. in Hatz.-Darm.).]

†**1.** The removal of the Jews into captivity at Babylon; sometimes used for the Captivity. *Obs.*

1297 R. GLOUC. (Rolls) 196 þe vifþe [age] was fram dauid to þe transmigracion Of babiloyne. **1382** WYCLIF *1 Chron.* v. 22 Thei dwelliden for hem unto the transmygracioun. **1430–40** LYDG. *Bochas* IV. iii. (MS. Bodl. 263) 216/2 How God wolde make a transmygracioun Of his kyngdam. **1579** J. STUBBES *Gaping Gulf* B j, The whole people suffered a transmigration irretornable in Assiria. **1609** BIBLE (Douay) *2 Kings* xxv. 27 In the seven and thirteth yeare of the Transmigration.

†**b.** *transf.* The body of transmigrated people; the Jews of the Captivity. *Obs.*

1609 BIBLE (Douay) *Jer.* xxviii. 4 Al the transmigration of Juda, that are entered into Babylon, I wil make to returne. —— *Ezek.* xi. 24 And the spirite..brought me into Chaldee to the transmigration, in a vision in the spirite of God.

2. Passage or removal from one place to another, esp. from one country to another.

1382 WYCLIF *Jer.* xiii. 19 Translatid is al Juda with parfit transmygracioun [1388 passyng ouere]. **1480** CAXTON *Chron. Eng.* III. (1520) 21 b/2 He put Nactanabo the kynge in Ethyopia and many Iewes in transmygracyon. **1534** MORE *Comf. agst. Trib.* III. Wks. 1237/2 Yf my transmigracion into a straunge countrey shoulde be any great griefe vnto me. **1630** T. WESTCOTE *Devon.* 51 Gentlemen's younger sons, who, by means of their travel and transmigration are very well qualified, apt, and fit to manage great and high offices in the republic. **1796** MORSE *Amer. Geog.* II. 419 The modern Italians are in a great measure free from..the transmigration of colonies. **1842** WESTCOTT in *Life* (1903) I. ii. 31 You have heard of my transmigration from Birmingham to Ludlow. **1858** H. W. BEECHER *Life Th.* (1859) 171 Birds in the hour of transmigration feel the impulse of southern lands. **1875** HADDAN in *Dict. Chr. Antiq.* I. 226/1 [According to] the author of the tract *De Translationibus*..the thing prohibited is 'transmigration' (which arises from the bishop himself, from selfish motives), not 'translation' (wherein the will of God and the good of the Church is the ruling cause). **1903** *Ardrossan & Saltcoats Herald* 1 May 2 The great Teutonic, Hungarian, Tartar, and Mongolian transmigrations.

b. *fig.* Of non-material things.

1632 LITHGOW *Trav.* x. 500 Ignoble Gallants..swallow vp the honour of their..Predecessours, with..Gluttony, Lust, and vaine Apparell, making a Transmigration of perpetuity to their present Belly, and Backe. *a* **1711** KEN *Sion* Poet. Wks. 1721 IV. 397 Love instantly rejoin'd Love from the Lover's Mind, To God still am'rous Transmigrations makes. **1824** MISS FERRIER *Inher.* xxxiv, That enviable power of mental transmigration, which placed him..quite beyond the influence of her power.

†**3.** Transition from one state or condition to another; *esp.* passage from this life, by death; also *absol.* death. *Obs.*

1576 FLEMING *Panopl. Epist.* 323 His ioyful estate of heauen, after his transmigration out of the labyrinth of this life. *a* **1631** DONNE *Serm.* lxi. (1640) 613 Enough for thy pilgrimage, enough for thy transmigration, enough for thy eternall habitation. **1675** T. PLUME *Life Bp. Hacket* (1865) 139 His placid departure, with as gentle a transmigration to happiness as..was ever heard of.

¶**b.** Loosely used for *transformation* or *transmutation* (cf. *transmogrification*). *Obs.*

1618 N. FIELD *Amends for Ladies* II. i. in Hazl. *Dodsley* XI. 113 The teeth she had Have made a transmigration into hair: She hath a bigger beard than I. **1643** SIR T. BROWNE *Relig. Med.* I. §39 Those strange and mysticall transmigrations that I have observed in Silkewormes.

4. *spec.* Passage of the soul at death into another body; metempsychosis. Also *fig.*

1594 T. B. *La Primaud. Fr. Acad.* II. 527 This Transmigration of Soules they called Regeneration, because it was vnto them as it were a generation and newe birth. *a* **1625** FLETCHER *Woman's Prize* IV. v, I..know her To be a woman-wolf by transmigration. **1634** SIR T. HERBERT *Trav.* 38 The Bannyans..For they so much detest the slaughter of any creature, though a Louse..Imagining as did Pythagoras, the transmigration of mens soules into other creatures. **1709–10** STEELE *Tatler* No. 134 ¶1 A Discourse on the Transmigration of Men into other Animals. **1892** WESTCOTT *Gospel of Life* 153 The Myths of Plato will shew us how great an attraction this doctrine of transmigration exerts upon the imagination of men.

5. *Path.* The migration or passage of cells through a membrane or the wall of a vessel; the oozing of white blood corpuscles through the unruptured walls of the blood-vessels; diapedesis.

1890 BILLINGS *Med. Dict.*, *Transmigration*, a moving across a limiting membrane or out of a vessel or cavity. **1899** *Syd. Soc. Lex.*, *Transmigration*, the passage of cells or particles through a membranous septum.

Hence **transmiˈgrationism,** the theory or doctrine of transmigration of souls; **transmiˈgrationist,** one who holds this doctrine; also *attrib.* or as *adj.*

1888 F. W. H. MYERS in *Fortn. Rev.* Jan. 103 Is Traducianism conceivable?.. Are we not driven back on some form of *Transmigrationism? **1884** *Chr. Commonwealth* 20 Mar. 545/1 Accessible to the influence of dead and buried Asiatic poetasters and *transmigrationists. **1903** F. W. MYERS *Hum. Personality* II. 267 Both the old traducianist and the old transmigrationist view would thus possess a share of truth.

transmigrative (ˈtrɑːnsmɪgreɪtɪv, ˈtræns-, trɑːnsˈmaɪgrətɪv, træns-, -nz-), *a.* [f. TRANSMIGRATE *v.* + -IVE.] Of, pertaining to, or characterized by transmigration; transmigratory.

1727 D'URFEY *Eng. Stage Italianized* Argt., The Doctor brings the Queen to life by a transmigrative Secret. **1818** G. S. FABER *Horæ Mosaicæ* I. 147 That Adam, and Enoch, and Noah, were alike transmigrative incarnations of him. **1833** —— *Recapit. Apostasy* i. 4 Those preëminent mundane patriarchs who were transmigrative reappearances of one and the same great universal father. **1844** —— *Eight Dissert.* (1845) I. 284.

Hence **transmigratively** *adv.*, by way of transmigration (of the soul).

1818 G. S. FABER *Horæ Mosaicæ* II. 202 He himself was afterwards transmigratively born again in the body of his pontifical Successor Buddas-Addas. **1819** —— *Dispensations* (1823) II. 74 Souls do not perish after death but flit transmigratively from one body to another.

transmigrator ('trɑːnsmɪgreɪtə(r), 'træns-, -nz-). [f. as prec. + -OR.] One who or that which transmigrates; a transmigrant; a transmigrating spirit.

1743 ELLIS *Knowl. Div. Things* ii. 122 Whenever we find a People begin to revive in Literature, it was owing..either to some Transmigrators from those Parts coming and settling among them, or else to their going thither for Instruction. **1837** LYTTON *Athens* II. 63 [Genius] the true spiritual transmigrator—it passes through all shapes, losing identity but not life and kindred to the Great Intelligence which is the Soul of matter.

transmigratory (trɑːns'maɪgrətərɪ, træns-, -nz-), *a.* [f. as prec. + ORY[2]: cf. *migratory*.] Having the quality of transmigrating; of or pertaining to transmigration.

1816 G. S. FABER *Orig. Pagan Idol.* I. 40 Reappearing.. agreeably to the transmigratory system. *Ibid.* II. 80 The latter [Noah] was deemed a transmigratory revival of the former [Adam]. **1871** ALABASTER *Wheel of Law* 90 They are reborn as angels..preparatory to reappearing in their last transmigratory existence as Buddha. **1893** HUXLEY *Evolution & Ethics* 19 That..each human being has his transmigratory representative.

† **trans'migure**, *v. Obs. rare*[−1]. Perversion of TRANSMIGRATE, after *transfigure*, or F. *transmigrer*.

1687 WINSTANLEY *Lives Eng. Poets* 153 The soul of Aristotle was said to have transmigured into Thomas Aquinas.

† **trans'mise**, *v. Obs.* Also 5–6 **-myse**. [In earliest use in pa. pple. *transmised*, app. rendering F. pa. pple. *transmis*, *-mise*; cf. *demise*, *premise*, *promise*.] *trans.* To cause to pass or go; to send; = TRANSMIT.

1480 CAXTON *Ovid's Met.* XIII. vii, Thyder had kynge Priamus transmysed and sent..his sone Polydorus. **1490** —— *Eneydos* xiv. 52 The sonne..shal haue transmysed hys shynynge bemes. **1541** R. COPLAND *Guydon's Quest. Chirurg.* C ij, For the moste parte of the thynges that it [the liver] is composed is flesshely, blody, & therwith ben transmysed dyuers pypes or arteres. **1646** J. HALL *Horæ Vac.* 53 There being an innate desire in every man, to transmise himself unto posterity.

† **trans'miss**, *sb. Obs.* exc. *Hist.* [ad. L. *transmiss-us*, *-um*: see next.] A copy of an Irish Bill returned to the Irish Parliament with the king's approval.

1764 *Jrnl. Irish Ho. Comm.* 11 May, Resolved That no Bill shall pass in this House until a Committee of this House shall compare the Transmiss with the original Heads of a Bill, and report, if any, and what alterations have been made therein, to the House. **1812** in *Rep. Comm. Pub. Rec. Irel.* (1815) 75 Transmisses of Public and Private Acts of Parliament.—The oldest Transmisses we could yet discover, are of the Reign of Henry VIII.

† **trans'miss**, *ppl. a. Obs. rare.* [ad. L. *transmiss-us*, pa. pple. of *transmittĕre* to TRANSMIT.] Transmitted. (Const. as pa. pple.)

1647 H. MORE *Poems* 116 Souls..If they shoot out, be they equally transmisse Around this body? Or but upward start? *Ibid.* 181 Neither Speech nor Language is Where their voice is not transmisse.

† **trans'miss**, *v. Obs. rare.* [f. L. *transmiss-*, ppl. stem of *transmittĕre* to TRANSMIT. It occurs in the pa. pple. *transmiss'd*, app. representing L. *transmissum*. Cf. DISMISS.] = TRANSMIT.

a **1643** W. CARTWRIGHT *Ordinary* III. v, Any reversions yet? nothing transmiss'd?

transmissibility (trɑːnsmɪsɪ'bɪlɪtɪ, træns-, -nz-). [f. next + -ITY. Cf. F. *transmissibilité* (1812 in Hatz.-Darm.).] The quality of being transmissible.

1828 in WEBSTER. **1847–9** *Todd's Cycl. Anat.* IV. 114/1 The associated pus has in reality nothing to do with the transmissibility of the diseases. **1875** BENNETT & DYER *Sachs' Bot.* 826 The hereditary transmissibility of acquired characters exhibits itself in a most marked way when it does not affect the whole of the parent-plant, but only a particular branch. **1894** *Pall Mall G.* 19 Nov. 1/2 He handles the transmissibility question with diffidence.

transmissible (trɑːns'mɪsɪb(ə)l, træns-, -nz-), *a.* [f. L. *transmiss-* (see TRANSMISS *v.*) + -IBLE. Cf. F. *transmissible* (16th c. in Hatz.-Darm.), and L. *remissibilis*, etc.] Capable of being transmitted.

1644 BP. MAXWELL *Prerog. Chr. Kings* v. 59 It is transmissible to his Successor. **1660** BOND *Scut. Reg.* 138 God did declare it transmissible from Adam to the first born. **1798** MALTHUS *Popul.* III. i. (1806) II. 86 Transmissible and contagious disorders. **1869** DK. OF ARGYLL *Primeval Man* II. 39 Some varieties of form are effected..by domestication, and by constant care in the selection of peculiarities transmissible to the young. **1885** SIR E. FRY in *Law Rep. 29 Ch. Div.* 283 The right to a grant of administration is not transmissible.

transmission (trɑːns'mɪʃən, træns-, -nz-). [ad. L. *transmissiōn-em*, n. of action from *transmittĕre* to TRANSMIT. Cf. F. *transmission* (14th c. in Hatz.-Darm.).]

a. The action of transmitting or fact of being transmitted; conveyance from one person or place to another; transference.

1611 FLORIO, *Transmissione*, a transmission. **1626** BACON *Sylva* §2 In the experiment of Transmission of the Sea-water into the Pits, the Water riseth; but in the experiment of transmission of the Water through the Vessels, it falleth. **1759** JOHNSON *Idler* No. 68 ¶2 Alphabetical writing made.. the transmission of events more easy and certain. **1802–3** tr. *Pallas's Trav.* (1812) I. 82 On the transmission of the Black Sea through the Propontis, a great part of its shallow banks consequently became a saline steppe. *a* **1859** DE QUINCEY *Posth. Wks.* (1891) I. 308 One link in the transmission of the Homeric poems.

b. Conveyance or passage through a medium, as of light, heat, sound, etc.; *spec.* in *Radio* and *Television* (see TRANSMIT *v.* 3 b); also, a series of electric signals or electromagnetic waves transmitted, a broadcast.

1704 NEWTON *Opticks* (1721) 238 Their Reflexion or Transmission depends on the constitution of the Air and Water behind the Glass. **1815** J. SMITH *Panorama Sci. & Art* I. 7 Which greatly retards the transmission of the heat. **1834** MRS. SOMERVILLE *Connex. Phys. Sc.* xvii. 147 The transmission of sound as well as light is impeded in passing through an atmosphere of variable density. **1881** SIR W. ARMSTRONG in *Nature* 8 Sept. 449/1 To force a transmission of heat from the fire to the water in the boiler. **1907** *Rep. Brit. Assoc. Adv. Sci.* 731 To determine how many oscillations..take place in a certain wireless transmission. **1921** *Wireless World* IX. 52/2 In Surrey and Kent the transmissions were easily read. **1923** *Radio Times* 5 Oct. 15/2 Transmission from London of Dance Music by Savoy Orpheans. **1929** [see *television transmission* s.v. TELEVISION 3 a]. **1959** *Viewpoint* July 10 A few days before transmission the final camera script will be typed. **1962** A. NISBETT *Technique Sound Studio* v. 99 We have..wide-range hi-fi, demanding not only high-quality transmissions but also a wide dynamic range. **1966** *Listener* 11 Aug. 204/2 *The Black and White Minstrel Show*..has just completed eighty-five transmissions. **1977** *Rep. Comm. Future of Broadcasting* (Cmnd. 6753) ii. 8 The Government..has to regulate the strength of the transmissions to prevent interference with other stations.

c. *Biol.* The transmitting of the peculiar nature, or of some character, of an organism to its descendants; hereditary conveyance.

1871 DARWIN *Desc. Man* II. xviii. II. 297 Equal transmission of ornamental characters to both sexes. **1880** E. R. LANKESTER *Degener.* 13 An organism..inherits, that is to say, is born with—the peculiarities of its parents; this is known as Transmission. **1890** *Sc. Gossip* XXVI. 66 Questions of protective resemblance and hereditary transmission.

d. *Mech.* Transference of motive force from one place to another; *concr.* a device for effecting this; *spec.* short for *transmission-gear* (see e).

1906 *Daily Chron.* 28 June 2/7 There are four large and eleven smaller electric motors driving the transmissions. *Ibid.*, Improvements in devices for preventing accidents with transmissions. **1911** WEBSTER, *Transmission*,..*Horol.* the train of a watch, etc.

e. *attrib.*: **transmission electron microscope**, an electron microscope in which the electrons are detected after they pass through the specimen; *spec.* one in which all parts of the image are formed at the same time; so **transmission electron microscopy**; **transmission-gear**, mechanism for transmitting the power of an engine, etc.; **transmission line**, a conductor or set of conductors designed to carry electricity (esp. on a large scale) or electromagnetic waves with minimum loss and distortion; also *transf.*; **transmission loss**, dissipation of electrical or acoustic power during its passage from one point to another; **transmission print** (see quot. 1960).

1833 BREWSTER *Nat. Magic* ix. 219 The sound will be partly reflected.., and the direction of the transmission wave changed. **1894** *Prospect. Tramway Motor Co.* 2 A transmission gear giving a wide range of continuously varying speed and inversely varying tractive effort. **1894** *Daily News* 3 Nov. 5/3 A large proportion of the sailors paid off there have gladly availed themselves of the transmission scheme. **1901** *Scaffolding* (ed. J. Black) 60 The endeavour to dispense with transmission gear between motor and machine constitutes to-day a recognised principle of construction [in cranes]. **1906** *Westm. Gaz.* 22 Jan. 8/1 The electricity will be conveyed at high pressure to a central spot on the transmission lines. **1908** *Ibid.* 14 Nov. 14/2 Double universal joints to maintain true alignment between the power- and transmission-shafts. **1922** GLAZEBROOK *Dict. Appl. Physics* II. 862/1 The problem of finding the transmission loss due to a piece of apparatus inserted in..a telephone line is the problem of finding out how the current entering the receiving side is altered by the inserted or bridged apparatus. **1934** *Discovery* Dec. 348/1 The transmission loss in steel framing is only one decibel per 1,000 feet, a loss which is acoustically negligible. **1946** *Jrnl. Inst. Electr. Engineers* XCIII. IIIA. 33/1 It has become the common..practice to restrict the term 'wave guide' to devices employing a single hollow conductor, and to reserve the term 'transmission line' to devices employing two conductors. **1960** O. SKILBECK *ABC of Film & TV* 137 *Transmission print*, positive copy of a film intended for T.V. showings. **1968** *Jrnl. Electron Microscopy* XVII. 164/1 Experimental procedures to determine the direction and the sign of the Burgers vector..of a dislocation by means of transmission electron microscopy are described. **1969** *Jrnl. Ultrastructure Res.* XXVII. 403 The resolution of the scanning instrument is an order of magnitude less than that of present transmission electron microscopes. **1970** *New Scientist* 15 Oct. (Suppl.) 13/1 The basic elements in microwave circuits are always some form of transmission lines. **1971** *Sci. Amer.* Apr. 26 The transmission electron microscope is analogous to a conventional light microscope. **1971** *Ibid.* Sept. 235/1 (Advt.), This..guide is..suited for use as an optical transmission line, carrying laser beams in any direction it is bent. **1972** [see *scanning electron microscope* s.v. SCANNING *vbl. sb.* 4]. **1974** *Encycl. Brit. Macropædia* XII. 137/2 Recently, scanning instruments have been used for transmission electron microscopy, with the advantage over the conventional transmission instrument that very low magnification..may be used. **1975** D. G. FINK *Electronics Engineers' Handbk.* XVIII. 67 The transmission loss [of a radio circuit] is usually expressed in decibels. **1976** *Broadcast* 29 Nov. 18/2 Once 'shot' the film has to be 'processed'... A transmission print is achieved several generations later.

Hence **trans'missional** *a.*; **trans'missionist**, one who holds the theory of the hereditary transmission of acquired characters; also *attrib.*

1899 J. A. THOMSON *Sci. Life* xvi. 226 The Lamarckians and Buffonians..believe in the transmission of acquired characters or modifications. They are sometimes, though not elegantly, called 'transmissionists'. **1900** C. LL. MORGAN *Animal Behaviour* iii. §5. 113 It forms a very pretty subject for transmissionists and their critics to quarrel over. *Ibid.* 114 Let us expand the transmissionist position a little further. **1930** *Observer* 4 May 26 Sometimes the music sounded ghostly. There were a few transmissional hiccoughs too.

transmissive (trɑːns'mɪsɪv, træns-, -nz-), *a.* [f. L. *transmiss-* (see TRANSMISS *v.*) + -IVE: cf. L. *remissīvus* remissive.]

1. Having the quality or action of transmitting.

1649 G. DANIEL *Trinarch., Hen. V* ccclxxxvi, Harry (who gave more Of fate in his Transmissive veins, then both Could woke) yet wraps the Infant in that Cloth. **1834** MRS. SOMERVILLE *Connex. Phys. Sc.* xxv. 231 The transmissive power of certain substances having a dark colour exceeds by four or five times that of others perfectly diaphanous. **1903** *Union Mag.* Oct. 437/1 The function of the brain is not 'productive' but 'transmissive' of consciousness.

2. Having the quality of being transmitted.

1700 PRIOR *Carmen Seculare* 164 The Sire [may] inculcate to his Son Transmissive Lessons of the King's Renown. **1775** R. CHANDLER *Trav. Greece* (1825) II. 152 The native quickness of apprehension, which as if transmissive,..is inherited even by the lower classes of the people. **1802–12** BENTHAM *Ration. Judic. Evid.* (1827) I. 68 Modifications of the genus of transmitted or transmissive evidence. **1887** L. P. MERCER *New Birth* (1890) 74 Transmissive dispositions and proclivities to evil, coming down a long line of tainted ancestry.

Hence **trans'missively** *adv.*, by way of transmission; **trans'missiveness**.

1881 SIR W. ARMSTRONG in *Nature* 8 Sept. 451/2 There will be a limit to the distance to which electricity may be profitably conveyed, but within that limit there will be wide scope for its employment transmissively. **1889** *Home Missionary* (N.Y.) Sept. 220 The aim is transmissiveness of the divine motive power.

transmissivity (trɑːnsmɪ'sɪvɪtɪ, træns-, -nz-). *Physics.* [f. TRANSMISSIVE *a.* + -ITY.] The degree to which a medium allows electromagnetic radiation to pass through it.

1913 *Electr. World* LXII. 426/2 The connection between cloudiness and transmissivity. **1928** *Proc. R. Soc.* A. CXXII. 314 The transmissivity of the telescope could then be calculated. **1946** *Nature* 21 Sept. 422/2 The optical efficiency, that is, the sum of the reflectivity and transmissivity, expressed as a percentage of the incident light intensity, is practically 100 for the interference films, owing to the negligible absorption. **1971** *Sci. Amer.* Sept. 89/1 The flux of solar radiation received at the ground is highly variable..because of the variable transmissivity of the atmosphere and the changing degree of cloudiness.

transmissometer (trɑːnsmɪ'sɒmɪtə(r), træns-, -nz-). [f. L. *transmiss-*, ppl. stem of *transmittere* to TRANSMIT *v.* + -OMETER.] An instrument for measuring the degree to which light is transmitted through a medium without absorption.

1955 *Sci. News Let.* 24 Sept. 197/1 Other equipment the Weather Bureau plans to purchase includes:... Ceilometers and transmissometers, instruments that tell cloud ceiling height and visibility. **1966** *McGraw-Hill Encycl. Sci. & Technol.* X. 172/1 Reflectometer. This instrument, also called a transmissometer, combines integrating spheres and barrier-layer cells... The transmittance can be measured by placing a sample of the material in the opening between the two spheres. **1975** *Nature* 3 Apr. 414/2 A volumetric concentration [in the sea] on the order of 0·01–1%, obtained from the acoustic data, enabled us to carry out a first-cut check of acoustic and transmissometer readings.

transmissory (trɑːns'mɪsərɪ, træns-, -nz-), *a. rare.* [f. as prec. + -ORY[2]: cf. *promissory*.] = TRANSMISSIVE 1.

1883 W. A. BUTLER in J. G. Butler *Bible Work* II. 235 Titles [of the Holy Spirit] which impress how truly his function is transmissory of perfections that dwell in Christ.

transmit (trɑːns'mɪt, træns-, -nz-), *v.* [ad. L. *transmittĕre*, f. L. TRANS- + *mittĕre* to send.]

I. 1. a. *trans.* To cause (a thing) to pass, go, or be conveyed to another person, place, or thing; to send across an intervening space; to convey, transfer.

a **1400–50** *Alexander* 4335 Nouthire to toly ne to taunde transmitte we na webbis, To vermylion ne violett ne variant littis. **1544** COVERDALE *Let. to C. Hubert* Wks. (Parker Soc.) II. 509 Take care..that they be transmitted to me with the paper of Cephalæus. **1612** DAVIES *Why Irel.*, etc. (1747) 24 From this time forward untill the 17 year of King John.. there was no army transmitted out of England to finish the Conquest. **1644** MILTON *Areop.* (Arb.) 46 That Eusebian book of Evangelick preparation transmitting our ears through a hoard of heathenish obscenities, to receive the Gospel. **1701** PENN in *Pa. Hist. Soc. Mem.* IX. 77 Hasten in my rents and debts, and transmit them with all possible speed. **1849** MACAULAY *Hist. Eng.* iii. I. 376 The expense of transmitting heavy goods in this way was enormous. **1880** C. R. MARKHAM *Peruv. Bark* iii. 273 They merely transmitted my letter to the Secretary of State, without any recommendation.

b. *intr.* (for *refl.*) To pass to the heirs.

1913 H. GOUDY in *Ess. Legal Hist. of Congr. Hist. Stud.* 208 Where..a delictal action was not strictly penal..it transmitted both actively and passively. *Ibid.* 218 In contracts the right of action almost invariably transmitted both to the heirs of the creditor and against the heirs of the debtor.

2. *fig.* To convey or communicate (usually something immaterial) *to* another or others; to pass on, esp. by inheritance or heredity; to hand down.

1629 BURTON *Truth's Triumph* 91 This word of faith.. wee shall transmit and conuay it, euen vnto posterity. **1651** HOBBES *Leviath.* III. xlii. 267 His Apostles..transmitted the same Spirit by Imposition of hands. **1710** PRIDEAUX *Orig. Tithes* v. 234 The House of Lords..had this power transmitted solely to them exclusive of the House of Commons. **1738** in *Nairne Peerage Evid.* (1874) 42 The said John Nairne..is likewise wholly disabled to take transmit or inherit any real or personal estate. **1828** DUPPA *Trav. Italy*, etc. 84 A glowing diffusion of light, of which Claude's finest pictures transmit but a faint resemblance. **1862** STANLEY *Jew. Ch.* (1877) I. xiii. 248 Samuel..had actually transmitted the office by hereditary succession to his sons. **1910** *Morning Post* 28 June 3/7 Capacity for milk-production, for early maturity [etc.]..are definitely fixed, and definitely transmitted from good sires.

3. *Physics* and *Mech.* To cause (light, heat, sound, etc.) to pass through a medium; also, of a medium, to allow (light, etc.) to pass through; to conduct. Also, to convey (force or movement) from one part of a body, or of mechanism, to another. Also *fig.*

1664 POWER *Exp. Philos.* I. 26 View her with a full light transmitted through a Burning-glass. **1751** JOHNSON *Rambler* No. 156 ¶2 Like light transmitted from room to room. **1795** LD. AUCKLAND *Corr.* (1862) III. 313 Imagination transmits some rays of your comfort at Beckenham to my pensive thoughts. **1831** LARDNER *Pneumatics* iv. 267 It is the nature of a fluid to transmit pressure equally in every direction. **1833** HT. MARTINEAU *Charmed Sea* iv. 54 How..the atmosphere, in its now approaching state, becomes incapable of transmitting sound to any distance. **1842** PARNELL *Chem. Anal.* (1845) 29 Hydrosulphate of ammonia is prepared by transmitting sulphuretted hydrogen gas through solution of ammonia. **1862** *Catal. Internat. Exhib.* II. XII. 2 The motion of the handle on deck is transmitted..by means of a series of shaftings and tooth-wheels. **1866** ROSCOE *Elem. Chem.* (1871) 275 Gold..in thin films, transmits green light. **1878** HUXLEY *Physiogr.* 171 The motion is transmitted from particle to particle, to a great distance.

b. To send out electric signals or electromagnetic waves corresponding to (an image, a programme, etc.).

1877 [see FACSIMILE 3]. **1923** *Radio Times* 28 Sept. 2/1 The first occasion..on which the voice of a public man had been transmitted simultaneously through six wireless stations hundreds of miles apart. **1946** *B.B.C. Year Bk.* 93 A fourth European programme network..allowed four different languages to be transmitted simultaneously. **1969** [see FACSIMILE 3]. **1979** *Financial Times* 18 Sept. (Telecommunications Suppl.) p. vii/2 A related system, generically called teletext, uses the same basic format, but the information is transmitted on spare capacity of the normal television broadcast channels.

II. 4. *Radio.* The infin. used, freq. *attrib.*, in the sense 'transmission'; so ***on transmit***, of a transceiver: in the state of being able to transmit radio signals, with the transmitter switched on; **transmit button, switch**, the button or switch used to activate the transmitter; also *ellipt.*

1968 J. SANGSTER *Touchfeather* xiv. 146 The radio suddenly crackled into life... Marvin flipped the transmit switch. **1973** 'A. HALL' *Tango Briefing* xii. 155, I hit the transmit. *Tango.* She answered straight away. **1976** L. HENDERSON *Major Enquiry* xiv. 89 Keep your personal radio on transmit, don't try to talk but keep the channel open. **1976** K. THACKERAY *Crownbird* vi. 122 He pressed the transmit button. 'Listen carefully.' **1980** *Basildon Recorder* 12 Sept. 1/4 Leaving his personal radio on 'transmit', so officers below could hear what was going on.

Hence **trans'mitted** *ppl. a.*; **trans'mitting** *vbl. sb.* and *ppl. a.*; ***transmitting station***, a building or establishment from which radio or television signals are transmitted.

1681 R. FLEMING *Fulfilling Script.* (1801) I. 430 Study the transmitting of truth and godliness. **1796** KIRWAN *Elem. Min.* (ed. 2) I. 271 By reflected light, blackish brown; but, by transmitted light, yellowish. **1800** HERSCHEL in *Phil. Trans.* XC. 458, I tried the transmitting capacity of the glass, by exposing it with the rough side towards the sun, over one of the transmitting holes of the apparatus. **1869** HADDAN *Apost. Succ.* iii. (1879) 56 The Church..has been held together compactly by the very fact of its transmitted orders. **1876** PREECE & SIVEWRIGHT *Telegraphy* 137 The battery which is connected to..the transmitting portion of the apparatus. **1923** *Radio Times* 28 Sept. 26/3 The 2LO transmitting station. **1977** *Whitaker's Almanack 1978* 759/1 There are two shortwave transmitting and receiving stations in Freetown.

transmit ('trɑːnsmɪt, 'træns-, -nz-), *sb. rare.* [f. prec. vb.; cf. PERMIT *sb.*] An act of transmitting; an order of transmission. Also *attrib.*, as **transmit warrant**, a warrant authorizing transmission.

1672 BP. OF DERRY in *Essex Papers* (Camden) I. 26 That yor Excellcy may not judge me heedles of that transmit to ye King before my leaving Dublin. **1741** W. WILSON *Contn. Def. Reform. Princ. Ch. Scot.* (1769) 407 Their petition could not get the common right of a transmit to the assembly. **1908** *Daily Chron.* 11 May 1/5 The Court signed a transmit warrant for the conveyance of Mrs. Cleary to Claremorris, and she left with the police escort yesterday.

transmittable (trɑːns'mɪtəb(ə)l, træns-, -nz-), *a. rare.* Also less correctly **-ible**. [f. as prec. + -ABLE; cf. ADMITTABLE.] That may be transmitted; transmissible. In quot. 1655, ? capable of being 'thrown' across.

1611 COTGRAVE, *Transmissible*, Transmittable. **1655** MRQ. WORCESTER *Cent. Inv.* §73 A transmittible Gallery over any Ditch or Breach in a Town-wall. **1882** F. DARWIN in *Nature* 20 Apr. 581/2 A heliotropic stimulus is transmittable from one part of an organ to another. **1889** *Pall Mall G.* 1 Aug. 6 A virulent, contagious and transmittable disease.

transmittal (trɑːns'mɪtəl, træns-, -nz-). *rare.* [f. as prec. + -AL[1].] The action of transmitting; transmission.

letter of transmittal, an official letter in which the recipient is informed that certain documents are transferred to his custody. *U.S.*

1724 SWIFT *Drapier's Lett.* vii, The prodigious profit which England receives by the transmittal thither of two thirds of the revenues of this whole Kingdom. **1813** *Brand's Pop. Antiq.* I. Pref. 7 In the transmittal of vulgar rites and popular opinions. **1904** *Athenæum* 18 June 788/1 The letter of transmittal..is dated July 1st, 1899.

trans'mittance. [f. as prec. + -ANCE: cf. *admittance.*]

1. The action of transmitting; transmission. *rare.*

1855 in H. CLARKE *Eng. Dict.*; and in later Dicts.

2. *Physics.* The ratio of the transmitted luminous flux to the incident luminous flux.

1919 *Technologic Papers U.S. Bureau of Standards* No. 119. 10 The transmittance T is defined as the fraction of radiant power transmitted by the first surface which is incident on the second surface. **1960** [see REFLECTANCE]. **1980** *Nature* 29 May 313/1 We had to use a shorter path-length (970 m at Riverside and 750 m at Claremont) because of the poor optical transmittance of the polluted atmosphere at our observation sites.

Hence **trans'mittancy**, the ratio of the transmittance of a solution to that of a similar body of solvent.

1925 *Jrnl. Optical Soc. Amer.* X. 177 (*table*) T_{soll}/T_{sov} = transmittancy. **1936** *Plant Physiol.* XI. 229 The transmittancies were obtained with a Bausch and Lomb visual spectrophotometer. **1959** H. BARNES *Apparatus & Methods Oceanogr.* i. 26 A calibration can then be set up relating transmittancy and concentration from which the concentrations of unknowns may be read when their transmittancies have been determined.

trans'mittant. *rare*[−1]. [irreg. f. TRANSMIT *v.* or L. *transmittĕre* + -ANT. (L. analogy would give **transmittent*).] One who transmits; an official transmitter.

1855 MILMAN *Lat. Chr.* XIV. ii. VI. 406 The transmittants, the sole transmittants, of those graces and blessings which emanate from Christ.

transmitter (trɑːns'mɪtə(r), træns-, -nz-). [f. TRANSMIT *v.* + -ER[1].]

1. a. One who or that which transmits.

1727 SAVAGE *Bastard* 8 He lives to build, not boast a generous Race: No Tenth Transmitter of a foolish Face. **1775** JOHNSON *Tax. no Tyr.* 73 The transmitters of wrong. **1822** *New Monthly Mag.* V. 417 [Not] the inventor, but merely the 'transmitter' of a jest. **1874** L. STEPHEN *Hours in Library* (1892) II. i. 6 The great bulk of mankind are transmitters rather than originators of spiritual force. **1904** *Brit. Med. Jrnl.* 17 Sept. 672 The *stegomyia fasciata* (the transmitter of yellow fever).

b. *spec.* (*a*) That part of a telegraphic or telephonic apparatus by means of which messages are transmitted or dispatched; a transmitting instrument: opposed to RECEIVER 7; (*b*) now *esp.* an apparatus for transmitting radio or television signals.

Also, the part of a stethoscope which transmits the sounds to the ear of the operator (quot. 1901).

1844 *Brit. Patent* 10,257 2, I have an instrument which I denominate a transmitter... If the operator turns a handle fixed to the wheel any number of discharges..may be passed from London to Liverpool. **1859** [see PRINTER 2 a]. **1876** PREECE & SIVEWRIGHT *Telegraphy* 251 The chief faults which are met with in the Transmitter are broken spiral springs and chains, or loose adjusting screws. **1878** G. B. PRESCOTT *Sp. Telephone* (1879) 9 The tone transmitter.. connected by a metallic conductor with the tone receiver.. at the distant station. **1888** *Pall Mall G.* 30 May 11/2 The operator sits watching at his transmitter on the Downs, while another attends in breathless expectation at the instrument in the Haymarket. **1889** PREECE & MAIER *Telephone* 5 The transmitter is the instrument into which the words are spoken. **1898** *Ludgate* Nov. 79 The Marconi Transmitter. **1901** *Munsey's Mag.* XXIV. 522/2 Dr. Schmuetzer placed the stethoscope over his heart,..with the rubber transmitters stuck in his ears. **1902** SLOANE *Electr. Dict.*, *Transmitter*, in general electric phraseology, any instrument which produces signals to be transmitted through a line or circuit... Thus the Morse key in telegraphy or the Blake transmitter in telephony are examples. **1912** *Chambers's Jrnl.* Jan. 60/2, I had got our receiver into 'tune' with the transmitter on board a steamer. **1913** E. C. BENTLEY *Trent's Last Case* ii. 18 Sir James looked at the telephone..and took up the receiver... Presently, as he listened, he..spoke quickly to Mr. Silver over the top of the transmitter. **1934** J. H. REYNER *Television* xvii. 191 It is conceivable that the introduction of some new scanning system may reduce the width of the band needed by a television transmitter providing plenty of detail. **1955** *Radio Times* 22 Apr. 3/2 Unless the listener lives very close to the nearest F.M. transmitter he will need to install a V.H.F. aerial. **1974** G. MARKSTEIN *Cooler* lv. 196 They've all been trained to rig up a wireless transmitter secretly, and send messages under the nose of the Gestapo. **1978** *Sci. Amer.* Mar. 58/2 A typical instrument consists of a handset, containing a transmitter and a receiver, that is connected to the base with an extendable cord.

c. *attrib.*

1876 PREECE & SIVEWRIGHT *Telegraphy* 129 Fig. 90.. contains a plan of the transmitter switch. **1892** *Pall Mall G.* 27 Apr. 7/2 A phonoporic receiver will not be actuated by impulses whose speed is regulated by a transmitter reed tuned to a different note from its own. **1904** *Electr. World & Engin.* 21 May 987 To overcome this difficulty [of being overheard by persons near] a transmitter hood has been patented. This is a metallic box adapted to be fastened upon the transmitter.

d. *Physiol.* = NEUROTRANSMITTER.

1930 *Jrnl. Physiol.* LXX. 142 The only hint as to the chemical nature of the transmitter is provided by the physiological similarity to the action of adrenaline. **1937** J. C. ECCLES in *Physiol. Rev.* XVII. 539 The actual transmission across the intercellular gap of the junctional region must depend upon one or more special factors— which will henceforth be called the synaptic or neuromuscular transmitter. **1954** MARTIN & HYNES *Clinical Endocrinol.* (ed. 2) vii. 168 It has now been shown..that *nor*adrenaline is the sympathetic transmitter-substance. **1970** *Nature* 5 Sept. 1006/2 Enzymes which synthesize transmitter. **1974** *Ibid.* 6 Sept. 14/3 L-Glutamate serves as the neuromuscular transmitter substance of arthropods, taking the place of acetylcholine in vertebrates in this respect.

2. Special Comb.: **transmitter-receiver** = TRANSCEIVER.

1950 *Encycl. Radio & Television* 638/2 *Transmitter-receiver*, assembly comprising a sender and a receiver with provision for changing from send to receive, usually by means of a switching system. **1964** *Discovery* Oct. 23 (Advt.), The BBC 81 mobile VHF transmitter-receiver is so compact that the whole unit can be fitted under the dashboard of almost any vehicle. **1978** R. V. JONES *Most Secret War* xxxvi. 313 He had been parachuted back into France with six radio transmitter-receiver sets for distribution to his sub-agents.

transmittible, var. form of TRANSMITTABLE.

† **trans'modify**, *v. Obs. rare*[−1]. [f. TRANS- 2 + MODIFY.] *trans.* To modify in transmission.

a **1774** TUCKER *Lt. Nat.* (1834) II. 673 Squibs of witticism, stolen and transmodified from the storehouse of philosophy.

transmogrify (trɑːns'mɒgrɪfaɪ, træns-, -nz-), *v. vulgar* or *humorous.* Also 7–9 **-mografy, -mography, -mogriphy,** 8 **-migrafy, -mugrify.** [Origin uncertain: see Note below.] *trans.* To alter or change in form or appearance; to transform, metamorphose (utterly, grotesquely, or strangely).

1656 S. HOLLAND *Zara* vi. (1719) 33 So that he remained for a time as one trans-elemented. [*Note*] Meaning transmografide, or metarmorphosed into a Mandrake. **1671** MRS. BEHN *Amorous Prince* III. iii, I wou'd Love would transmogriphy me to a maid now. **1688** SHADWELL *Sqr. Alsatia* III. i. 39, I know I am Transmography'd; but I am your very Brother, Ned. **1725** *New Cant. Dict.*, *Transmogrify*, or rather *Transmigrafy*. **1728** FIELDING *Love in Sev. Masques* v. iv. 68, I begin to think..that some wicked Enchanters have transmographied my Dulcinea. **1736** tr. *Ruggle's Ignoramus* III. 35 I'll go put on my other Dress, and be transmogrify'd to Dulman. **1751** WARBURTON *Lett.* (1809) 85 The first volume of the Divine Legation..is so transmogrified that you will hardly know it again. **1753** SMOLLETT *Ct. Fathom* xxiv, Thou art so transmographied, and bedaubed, and bedizened. **1786** BURNS *Addr. Unco Guid* v, Social life and Glee sit down,..Till, quite transmugrify'd, they 're grown Debauchery and Drinking. **1844** *Blackw. Mag.* LVI. 777 By proper clipping and pruning..an ingenious editor might transmogriphy these simple epistles into the philippics of Junius. *a* **1888** MARY HOWITT *Autobiog.* (1889) II. 278 It was transmogrified by the addition of two storeys and a flat roof.

b. To astonish utterly, confound. *dial.*

1887 P. M'NEILL *Blawearie* 84 We..made our way here and are quite transmogrified to find everything so outrageously transformed. **1888** *Berks. Gloss.* (E.D.S.), *Transmogrivied*,..surprised, greatly astonished.

[*Note.* If the original form was (as suggested in quot. 1725) *transmigrafy*, this may have been a vulgar or uneducated formation in *-fy* from TRANSMIGURE, or TRANSMIGRATE *vb.* (cf. TRANSMIGRATION 3 b). Apparently, it was originally *persons* that were 'transmografied', or metamorphosed.]

Hence **trans'mogrified, trans'mogrifying** *ppl. adjs.*; also **trans,mogrification** (-fɪ'keɪʃən), the action of transmogrifying, (strange or grotesque) transformation; **trans'mogrifier** (-faɪə(r)), one who transmogrifies.

1661 K. W. *Conf. Charac.*, *Hide-Parke Lady* (1860) 58 It must march at least thrice to the botchers for *transmogrification. **1694** MOTTEUX *Rabelais* v. ii. 6 The

Transmogrification of the Macrobian Children into Swans. *a* **1878** SIR G. G. SCOTT *Recoll.* i. (1879) 47 The Tower.. has undergone strange transmogrifications. *c* **1832** MRS. SHERWOOD in *Life* xxx. (1847) 529 We were led.. over our *transmographied terrace. **1842** BARHAM *Ingol. Leg.* Ser. II. *St. Aloys*, The transmogrified Pagan perform'd his vow. **1676** *Poor Robin's Intell.* 13-20 June 2/1 A notable fewd between a Translator of Shooes and a *Transmogrifier of Garments, that is to say betwixt a Cobler and a Botcher. **1841** *Fraser's Mag.* XXIII. 338 Our modern transmogrifiers and parodists of ancient architecture. **1832** J. P. KENNEDY *Swallow B.* xliii, It [love] is the most *transmogrifying passion. **1904** *Longm. Mag.* Dec. 149 The transmogrifying process is being carried out only too rapidly.

transmontane (trɑːns'mɒnteɪn, træns-, -mɒn'teɪn, -nz-), *a.* [In quot. *c* 1400 a. OF. *transmontane* adj. and sb., altered form of *tramontane*, pole-star, north pole, also *transmontanie* north wind (Godef.); in later use ad. L. *transmontānus*: see TRAMONTANE.]

1. Dwelling or situated beyond, or on the other side of, the mountains; = TRAMONTANE A. 1.

a. From the Italian point of view: North of the Alps.

1727 BAILEY vol. II, *Transmontane*, dwelling or growing beyond the Mountains. **1826** K. DIGBY *Broadst. Hon.* II. *Tancredus* (1846) II. 20 The Britons, English, and other transmontane people. **1857** *Fraser's Mag.* LVI. 503 The proud citizens of Rome witnessed with indignation the influx of a crowd of transmontane artists. **1880** J. NICHOL *Byron* viii. 139 To abandon their transmontane plans, and agree to take up their head-quarters at Pisa.

b. In reference to other mountains, e.g. the Grampians in Scotland, the Rocky Mountains in N. America, the Blue Mountains in New South Wales. Also of traffic, across or over the mountains.

1884 *Science* 22 Feb. 220/1 Keeping back the migration.. in order to monopolize this transmontane commerce. **1890** 'R. BOLDREWOOD' *Col. Reformer* (1891) 124 The transmontane towns. **1897** D. L. LEONARD in *Home Missionary* (N.Y.) Jan. 450 Just now [1842-6] it was that the entire transmontane region was added to the Union. **1900** W. WATT *Aberdeen & Banff* i. 4 The northern or transmontane Picts.

†**2.** ***transmontane star***, also absol. *transmontane*, the north pole-star; = TRAMONTANE B. 1. *Obs.*

c **1400** MAUNDEV. (1839) xvii. 180 In þat lond, ne in many othere beȝonde þat, noman may see the sterre transmontane, ..þat wee clepen the lode-sterre. *Ibid.*, The sterre þat is clept the transmontayne. *Ibid.* 181 Aȝen þat transmontayne is the toþer sterre, þat is clept Antartyke.

Hence †**transmon'tanian** *a. Obs. rare*⁻¹, of or pertaining to the non-Italian section of the Roman Church: cf. TRANSALPINE 1 c.

1624 T. SCOTT *Aphorisms of State* 8 Carion, Auentine, Cuspinianus, and other Transmontanian Writings.

transmorphism (trɑːns'mɔːfɪz(ə)m, træns-). *rare*⁻¹. [f. TRANS- + Gr. μορφή form + -ISM: cf. METAMORPHISM.] Transformation of one thing into another, as in the process of evolution.

1888 SHOREY in *Amer. Jrnl. Philol.* IX. 417 The Democriteans evolve the higher from the lower by the operation of chance... We will.. substitute for the guess of transmorphism the assertion of a metaschematism intentionally devised for ethical ends.

trans'mortal, *a.* Chiefly *poet.* [f. TRANS- 4 + MORTAL *a.*] Beyond what is mortal, immortal.

1932 BLUNDEN *Halfway House* 67 That much I saw without transmortal talk. *a* **1963** C. S. LEWIS *Poems* (1964) 97 Thou art Lord of the unbreathable transmortal air Where mortal thinking fails.

trans'mould, *v.* [f. TRANS- 2 + MOULD *v.*²] *trans.* To mould into another form or shape.

1855 PUSEY *Doctr. Real Presence* Note Q. 218 It seemed good to.. the Maker of all things, to transmould (μετάπλαττειν) the living creature to incorruption. **1860** —— *Min. Proph.* 259 God is all-powerful, and transmouldeth easily the nature of things which are, to what He willeth.

†**trans'mount**, *v. Obs. rare.* [f. TRANS- 2 + MOUNT *v.*] *trans.* To surmount; to pass over or across by mounting.

1600 HOLLAND *Livy* XLIII. xx. 1168 These embassadours having transmounted the top of the hill Scordus. **1601** —— *Pliny* VIII. lviii. I. 233 The wild Asses [never] transmount that hill which divideth Cappadocia from Cilicia.

†**trans'move**, *v. Obs. rare*⁻¹. [In form, f. TRANS- 2 + MOVE *v.*, but in quot., app. mistakenly used for *transmeue*, *-mewe*, *-mywe*, early forms of TRANSMEW, TRANSMUE, and rimed with *love*, *prove*.] *trans.* To transform, transmute, 'transmew'.

1590 SPENSER *F.Q.* III. xi. 43 Saturne.. That to a Centaure did him selfe transmoue.

transmue: see TRANSMEW.

transmundane (trɑːns'mʌndeɪn, træns-, -nz-), *a.* [f. TRANS- 3 + L. *mund-us* world: cf. *mundane*.] That is or lies beyond the world.

1777 J. RICHARDSON *Dict. Persian, Arab.*, etc., Dissert. 29/1 Every ingenious critic may then, like Archimedes of old, require only some transmundane station on which to rear his engines; in order to shake to pieces the reason of man. **1859** G. MEREDITH *R. Feverel* iii, One of the most ancient theories of transmundane dominion and influence on mundane affairs. **1899** W. JAMES *Talks to Teachers on Psychol.* 24 Whatever of transmundane metaphysical insight ..we may carry.

transmural (trɑːns'mjʊərəl, træns-, -nz-), *a.* [f. TRANS- 3 + L. *mūr-us* wall: cf. *mural*.]

1. That is beyond a wall or walls; *spec.* beyond the Roman Wall.

1851 D. WILSON *Preh. Ann.* (1863) II. III. ii. 67 Within the transmural province. **1911** *Edin. Rev.* Apr. 488 With the fourth century this transmural area was lost.

2. *Med.* Existing or occurring across the (entire) wall of an organ or blood vessel.

1951 BURTON & YAMADA in *Jrnl. Appl. Physiol.* IV. 330 It will be convenient.. to call this difference of pressure the transmural pressure. **1968** *Amer. Jrnl. Obstetr. & Gynecol.* CII. 29/2 Hyalinization of vein walls became more patchy and occasionally transmural. **1977** *Lancet* 24/31 Dec. 1331/1 Transmural electrical stimulation of intestinal structures.

'trans-'muscle. [TRANS- 6.] A crossing or transverse muscle.

1836-9 *Todd's Cycl. Anat.* II. 956/2 We have seen similar trans-muscles lying above the membrane.

transmutability (trɑːns,mjuːtə'bɪlɪtɪ, træns-, -nz-). [f. next: see -ITY. Cf. med.L. *transmūtābilitās* (Aquinas, *a* 1274), It. *trasmutabilità* (Florio, 1611), F. *transmutabilité* (*Dict. Acad.*, 1762).] The quality of being transmutable; susceptibility of being changed into something else.

1611 FLORIO, *Trasmutabilita*, transmutability. **1669** W. SIMPSON *Hydrol. Chym.* 60 The transmutability of one salt into another. **1879** tr. *De Quatrefages' Hum. Spec.* 38 A variability which I fully accept, has nothing in common with the transmutability of Lamarck, Geoffroy, and Darwin. **1905** *Speaker* 26 Aug. 499/1 In chemistry.. transmutability has survived merely as a wild and hopeless surmise.

transmutable (trɑːns'mjuːtəb(ə)l, træns-, -nz-), *a.* [ad. med.L. *transmūtābilis* (Albertus Magnus, *a* 1250), f. L. *transmūt-āre* to TRANSMUTE: cf. *mutable*.] Capable of being transmuted or changed into something else.

1460-70 *Bk. Quintessence* I. 14 Oure 5-essencie is þe instrument of alle vertues of þing transmutable if þei be putt in it, encreessynge an hundrid foold her worchingis. **1545** RAYNOLD *Byrth Mankynde* 20 By contynuall circulation of the matter transmutable, she maye brynge her pourpose to passe. **1652** FRENCH *Yorksh. Spa* ii. 6 All Elements are mutually transmutable into one the other. **1731** *Hist. Litteraria* II. 379 Animal Substances are.. more easily transmutable into animal Juices than vegetable. **1879** tr. *De Quatrefages' Hum. Spec.* 39 Lamarck, Geoffroy, Darwin and his school, consider the species not only as variable but as transmutable. **1896** *Buffalo* (U.S.) *Current Hist.* VI. 3 *note*, Professor Dewar and others have shown the X rays to be transmutable into light rays affecting the eye.

†**b.** Liable to change, changeable, mutable.

c **1430** LYDG. *Min. Poems* (Percy Soc.) 197 The world unsuyr, fortune transmutable. **1509** HAWES *Conv. Swearers* v, Worldly rychesse is often transmutable. **1509** —— *Past. Pleas.* xiii. (Percy Soc.) 51 They nothing thynke on fortune variable, Whyche al theyr ryches shal make transmutable.

Hence **trans'mutably** *adv.*, in a transmutable manner; **trans'mutableness**, transmutability.

1666 BOYLE *Orig. Formes & Qual.* I. ii, Some learned modern naturalists have conjectured at the easy transmutableness of water. **1680** —— *Produc. Chem. Princ.* v. 265 The Aristotelian Hypothesis, of the transmutableness of what they call Elements. **1736** BAILEY (folio), *Transmutably*, in a manner capable of being chang'd.

transmutant (trɑːns'mjuːtənt, træns-, -nz-). *Math.* [ad. L. *transmūtānt-em*, pr. pple. of *transmūtāre* to TRANSMUTE.] (See quot.)

1858 CAYLEY *Math. Papers* II. 515 We may say that the function obtained by replacing.. the facients of a covariant or contravariant by the first derived functions of a contravariant or covariant is a Transmutant of the first-mentioned covariant or contravariant.

†**'transmutate**, *ppl. a. Obs.* [ad. L. *transmūtāt-us*, pa. pple. of *transmūtāre* to TRANSMUTE.] Transmuted. (Const. as pa. pple.)

1432-50 tr. *Higden* (Rolls) II. 343 Iupiter.. putte her in a schippe in whom he had a bulle depicte, wherefore poetes feyne Iupiter to be transmutate in to the similitude of a bulle. **1668** BAXTER *Dying Th.* (1850) 156 As if the fiery part of the candle were annihilated or transmutate,.. when the candle goeth out; and were not fire, and in action still.

†**'transmutate**, *v. Obs. rare.* [f. ppl. stem of L. *transmūtāre* to TRANSMUTE: see -ATE³.] *trans.* = TRANSMUTE 1.

1632 VICARS *Æneid* v. 140 Here fortune her faire face first transmutated. **1659** STANLEY *Hist. Philos.* IX. (1687) 550/2 Solid Bodies, whose Elements are four, Fire, Water, Air, Earth; of all which, transmutated, and totally changed, the World consists. **1659** *Ibid.* XI. 763/1 By immixture of some small thing to be transmutated.

transmutation (trɑːnsmjuː'teɪʃən, træns-, -nz-). [a. F. *transmutation* (12th c. Hatz.-Darm.), or ad. late L. *transmūtātiōn-em*, n. of action from *transmūtāre* to change, shift, TRANSMUTE.] The action or process of transmuting or changing; the fact or condition of being transmuted or changed.

1. Change of condition; mutation; sometimes implying alternation or exchange. *Obs.* or *arch.*

c **1380** WYCLIF *Sel. Wks.* II. 297 þus seiþ James, þat at God is not transmutacioun. *c* **1384** CHAUCER *H. Fame* III. 879 Of dyvers transmutacions Of estates and eke of Regions. *c* **1398** —— *Fortune* 1 This wrecched worldes transmutacioun As wele and [*v.r.* or] woo, nowe poure and nowe honour. *c* **1449** PECOCK *Repr.* I. xviii. 107 In lengthe of tyme ful greet transmutacioun and chaunge is alwey maad in and aboute the circumstauncis of politik gouernauncis. *c* **1450** *Mankind* iii. 903 in *Macro Plays* 34 Thynke and remembyr, þe world ys but a wanite, as yt ys prowyd daly by d[i]uerse transmutacyon. **1570** FOXE *A. & M.* (ed. 2) 169/1 Busy you to purchase that palace that euer shal endure in ioy without transmutation. **1851** LONGF. *Gold. Leg.* III. 274 The constant change and transmutation Of action and of contemplation.

2. Change of one thing into another; conversion into something different; alteration, transformation. Also with *a* and *pl.* a case or instance of this.

1398 TREVISA *Barth. De P.R.* XIX. l. (xxxiii. in *Bodl. MS.* lf. 302 b/2), þere may not be passinge transmutacion and chaunginge for þere is defaute of hete & of humoure. **1412-20** LYDG. *Chron. Troy* I. 58 That a sodeyn transmutacioun Was made of amptis to forme of men anon. **1545** RAYNOLD *Byrth Mankynde* 20 When that nature is dysposed to make a transmutation of any matter. **1594** PLAT *Jewell-ho.* III. 65 Alterations, transmutations, & sometimes euen real transubstantiations of white wine into Claret. **1692** BENTLEY *Boyle Lect.* iv. 139 The supposed change of Worms into Flies is no real transmutation. **1725** tr. *Dupin's Eccl. Hist. 17th C.* I. VI. iii. 237 He [Calvin] attacks Transubstantiation. He acknowledges that some of the Ancients made use of the Term Transmutation. **1782** PRIESTLEY *Corrupt. Chr.* II. VI. 7 It is too early.. for.. the transmutation of the bread and wine. **1879** tr. *De Quatrefages' Hum. Spec.* 9 Here.. is no transmutation of force similar to that in a machine worked by electricity or heat. **1896** DK. ARGYLL *Philos. Belief* 69 The inconceivable power of transmutation exerted by that which we call life.

3. *spec.* **a.** *Alch.* The (supposed or alleged) conversion of one element or substance into another, esp. of a baser metal into gold or silver. Hence *allusively*. Also in *Physics*, the (actual) change of one element into another, esp. by irradiation or bombardment (as opposed to spontaneous decay). Cf. TRANSFORMATION 3 g.

1478 *Coventry Leet Bk.* 422 To practise a true and a profitable conclusion in the Cunnying of transmutacion of metals. **1605** TIMME *Quersit.* III. 183 Alchymie.. ordereth and finisheth the transmutations of things. **1750** JOHNSON *Rambler* No. 63 ¶7 Not one appears to have desisted from the task of transmutation, from the conviction of its impossibility. **1812** SIR H. DAVY *Chem. Philos.* 11 The processes supposed to relate to the transmutation of metals, and the elixir of life. **1872** YEATS *Techn. Hist. Comm.* 413 Alchemy, or the transmutation of metals, was virtually the parent of the modern science of chemistry. **1897** *Electrician* 10 Dec. 214/1 Theoretically, if the modern doctrine as to the ultimate constitution of matter be accepted, the transmutation of the elements is a scientific possibility. The fierce atomic bombardments inside a Crookes tube or an electric furnace would seem the most probable of known conditions whereby the operation might be carried on. **1915** K. TORNBERG tr. *Rasch's Electric Arc Phenomena* viii. 184 Since the electrons are ultra-atomic.. the electric arc provides a means for the splitting up of matter, which perhaps makes the synthesis or transmutation of chemical elements not entirely beyond possibility. **1926** R. W. LAWSON tr. *Hevesy & Paneth's Man. Radioactivity* xxi. 147 Up to the present we only know of one method that permits us to resolve the nuclei of the atoms artificially, and thus to achieve.. the transmutation of the elements. **1969** BENNISON & WRIGHT *Geol. Hist. Brit. Isles* i. 5 The rate of 'decay' or transmutation of radioactive minerals. **1974** *Physics Bull.* Dec. 585/2 The process of transmutation ('neutron burning'), as applied for several years now to radioactive waste, where certain isotopes are transmuted to isotopes with shorter half lives or even to stable ones.

b. *Law.* Transfer: usually ***transmutation of possession***, transfer or change of ownership.

1488-9 *Act 4 Hen. VII*, c. 4 An Acte for the passing and transmutacion of landes without Fyne. *Ibid.*, Such persones ..shall nowe lawfully make therof feoffmentes and transmutacion of possession by dede or dedis.. without eny fyne for the said feoffement or transmutacion of possession. **1602** FULBECKE *1st Pt. Parallel* 33 He held that in euery exchaunge there must be a mutuall transmutation of the possession. **1818** CRUISE *Digest* (ed. 2) II. 358, IV. 149. **1876** DIGBY *Real Prop.* vi. 292 In these cases uses are said to be created by a conveyance operating by way of transmutation of possession; that is, they accompany one of the recognised modes of conveying the seisin at common law—feoffment, fine, or recovery.

†**c.** *Rhet.* Transferred use of a word; metonymy. *Obs. rare.*

1553 T. WILSON *Rhet.* 93 Transmutacion helpeth much for varietie, the whiche is when a woorde hath a proper signification of the owne, and beyng referred to an other thyng, hath an other meanyng.

†**d.** = TRANSMIGRATION 4. *Obs. rare*⁻¹.

1594 R. ASHLEY tr. *Loys le Roy* 68 b, The transmutation of soules from bodie to bodie.

†**e.** *Her.* = COUNTERCHANGING. Cf. TRANSMUTED b. *Obs.*

1610 GUILLIM *Heraldry* v. ii. 242 Counter-changing or Transmutation is an Entermixture of seuerall Metals or Colours, both in Field and Charge, occasioned by the apposition of some one or moe lines of partition.

f. *Biol.* Conversion or transformation of one species into another; *spec.* applied to the form of evolution or development propounded by Lamarck (1815-22). Also *attrib.*

1626 BACON *Sylva* §525 The Transmutation of Plants, one into another, is *inter Magnalia Naturæ*: for the Transmutation of Species is, in the vulgar philosophy, pronounced Impossible:.. but seeing there appear some manifest Instances of it, the Opinion of Impossibilitie is to bee rejected. **1691** RAY *Creation* II. (1692) 91 The most that can be inferred from hence is a transmutation of Species. **1722** WOLLASTON *Relig. Nat.* ix. 194 Transmutation of one species into another. **1859** PAGE *Handbk. Geol. Terms, Transmutation*,..a term adopted by Lamarck and his followers to express their hypothetical views of the derivation of existing species from preceding species, by slow and gradual Transmutations of one form of organisation into another form. **1863** LYELL *Antiq. Man* i. 3 Recent modifications of the Lamarckian theory of progressive development and transmutation. **1879** tr. *De Quatrefages' Hum. Spec.* 90 Their ideas may be arranged in two principal groups according as their authors favour a rapid or a gradual transmutation.

g. *Math.* † (*a*) = PERMUTATION 3 b (*obs.*). (*b*) = TRANSFORMATION 3 c (*rare* or *obs.*).

1674 JEAKE *Arith.* (1696) 576 Transmutation..serveth to show what Number of Changes may be made by any Number of..things in their Places or Positions. **1743** EMERSON *Fluxions* I. 53 The 21st and all the following Forms relate to the Transmutation of Fluxions.

4. *attrib.*, as ***transmutation doctrine, theory***; **transmutation glaze**, trade name of a porcelain glaze having a changeable iridescent lustre.

1860 HUXLEY *Lay Serm.* xii. (1870) 306 The so-called 'transmutation' hypothesis considers that all existing species are the result of the modification of pre-existing species, and those of their predecessors, by agencies similar to those which at the present day produce varieties and races. **1876** tr. *Haeckel's Hist. Creat.* I. i. 4 The theory which, through Darwin, has been placed at the head of all our knowledge of nature, is usually called the Doctrine of Filiation, or the Theory of Descent. Others term it the Transmutation Theory. **1904** [see FLAMBÉ *a.* 1].

Hence **transmu'tational** *a.*, of or pertaining to transmutation, esp. in sense 3 f.

1861 WILSON & GEIKIE *Mem. E. Forbes* ii. 41, I can find no room, however, for transmutational ingenuity in writing of Edward Forbes. **1907** *Edin. Rev.* Jan. 31 The crude transmutational theory.

transmu'tationist. [f. prec. + -IST.] One who believes in or advocates a theory of transmutation, esp. that of the transmutation of species in organic nature; a transformist. Also *attrib.*

It might also be, and prob. has been, applied to one believing in the transmutation of metals: an explanation given in Dictionaries from Worcester onward.

1844 *Monthly Rev.* Mar. 384 It is the doctrine of the Transmutationists. **1847** DARWIN in *Life & Lett.* (1887) I. 355 You have introduced several sentences against us Transmutationists. **1850** *Fraser's Mag.* XLII. 368 The author of the *Vestiges*, like the older transmutationists, assumes the mammals of the sea as the ancestors of the mammals of the land. **1866** *Reader* 20 Feb. 153/2 Owen.. pleads..strongly and manfully in favour of the transmutationist doctrine. **1909** *Q. Rev.* Oct. 421 When Darwin first propounded his doctrine of descent..there were few 'transmutationists'.

transmutative (trɑːnsˈmjuːtətɪv, træns-, -nz-), *a.* [ad. med.L. *transmūtātīv-us* (Albertus Magnus *Metaphys.*, *a* 1255), f. L. *transmūtāt-*, ppl. stem of *transmūtāre* to TRANSMUTE: see -IVE.] Having the quality of transmuting; tending to transmute; characterized by transmutation.

1611 SPEED *Hist. Gt. Brit.* IX. vi. (1623) 502 The great Elixar..hath so transmutatiue a faculty, as to make Copper seeme Gold. **1781** *Westm. Mag.* IX. 73 A kind of coagulation which may be called transmutative. **1841** HOR. SMITH *Moneyed Man* III. ii. 50 How little do we mark the effects of Time in ourselves; how suddenly and deeply are we struck by its transmutative touch in others. **1865** GROTE *Plato* I. i. 5 A generative, motive, or transmutative force.

trans'mutatory, *a. rare*⁻¹. [f. ppl. stem of L. *transmūtāre*: see next and -ORY.] = prec.

1616 DONNE *Serm.* (1661) III. 323 Love is..a transmutatory Affection, it changes him that loves, into the very nature of that that he loves.

transmute (trɑːnsˈmjuːt, træns-, -nz-), *v.* Pa. pple. **transmuted**, also 5–6 **transmute**. [ad. L. *transmūtā-re*, f. TRANS- + *mūtāre* to change.

(Occurs first as variant in MSS. of Chaucer's works.)]

1. a. *trans.* To alter or change in nature, properties, appearance, or form; to transform, convert, turn.

14.. *Chaucer's Troylus* IV. 439 (467) (MS. Gg. 4. 27) þu muste me fyrst transmute [*v.r.* transmuwen] in to a ston. [**14..** *Chaucer's Clerk's T.* 329 (Lansd. MS.) Vnneþ þe peple hire knewe for hire faireness Whan sche transemute was in suche rechesse.] **1494** FABYAN *Chron.* VI. clix. 149 The Emperour hauyng compassion of the forenamyd Barnarde, ..transmutyd the sentence of deth vnto perpetuyte of pryson, & losynge of his syght. **1545** RAYNOLD *Byrth Mankynde* 20 Yᵉ lyuer: in whome the iuyce of meat, before of colour white, is transmutyd into red. **1583** MELBANCKE *Philotimus* D div, When Io was transmute of Ioue into an Hefars forme. **1660** SHARROCK *Vegetables* 29 The colour only or some other easily alterable accidents..are transmuted. **1871** TYNDALL *Fragm. Sc.* (1879) I. x. 310 To transmute its energy..into vibratory motion. **1890** *Century Mag.* May 48/2 The tendency of black plumage to become transmuted into white is a familiar..fact in breeding.

b. *Alch.* To change (one substance) into another, esp. a baser metal into gold or silver. Hence *allusively* and *absol.* Also in *Physics*, to change (one element or isotope) *into* another by irradiation or bombardment; to change (one sub-atomic particle) *into* another.

1610 DONNE *Pseudo-martyr* 94 By a new Alchimy, they doe not onely extract spirit out of euery thing, but transmute it all into spirit. *a* **1661** FULLER *Worthies, Worc.* III. (1662) 173 He is said to have transmuted a brass warming-pan (.. onely warming it by the fire, and putting the Elixir thereon) into pure silver. **1750** JOHNSON *Rambler* No. 51 ℙ 11 Some alchymists have obstinately suppressed the art of transmuting metals. **1818** MRS. SHELLEY *Frankenst.* ii. (1865) 51 Metals cannot be transmuted. **1870** M. D. CONWAY *Earthw. Pilgr.* i. 29 You will find the pavements golden only when you can transmute them to gold. **1897** *Electrician* 10 Dec. 214/1 Only the other day we were told how many centuries it would require to 'transmute' a milligram or two of one element into another, in a Crookes tube. **1926** R. W. LAWSON tr. *Hevesy & Paneth's Man. Radioactivity* xxi. 148 This method of transmuting elements is still far from being of any practical importance. **1956** A. H. COMPTON *Atomic Quest* i. 52 The naturally occurring atoms of U-238 and Th-232 can be transmuted into sources of atomic fuel. **1977** *Mod. Railways* Dec. 474/1 Vinyl chloride monomer..leaves by rail for Barry, where it is transmuted into PVC and heavy-duty plastic items. **1979** *McGraw-Hill Yearbk. Sci. & Technol.* 267/2 The pions can produce only a single-charge exchange by transmuting a proton into a neutron. **1981** *Sci. Amer.* Feb. 85/1 Cosmic rays transmute nitrogen 14 in the upper atmosphere into the radioactive isotope carbon 14. **1981** C. H. L. SMITH in J. H. Mulvey *Nature of Matter* iii. 72 In this case, quarks would very occasionally be transmuted into electrons.

c. *intr.* for *pass.* To undergo transmutation; to change or turn *into* something else.

1675 G. R. tr. *Le Grand's Man without Passion* 139 His Strength transmutes into Temerity. **1962** D. G. COGAN in A. Pirie *Lens Metabolism Rel. Cataract* 294 The morgagnian globules..finally transmute into homogeneous milky fluid. **1970** A. ROMER *Radiochem. & Discovery of Isotopes* 127 The radiothorium, transmuting into thorium X.., would gradually disappear. **1978** *Nature* 29 June 707/1 In the weak interaction of radioactivity it has been known for many years that the neutrino turns into an electron or that an up quark transmutes into a down. **1983** *Penthouse* Sept. 169 Do you think capitalism is an eternal system, or will it transmute into something else?

†**2.** *trans.* To remove from one place to another; to transport. [So late L. *transmūtāre*.] *Obs. rare.*

a **1700** *Life & Death Ld. Shaftsbury* in *Harl. Misc.* (1810) V. 372 His malady..that might transmute his soul into that endless happiness, which he had been so long labouring for. **1817** MAR. EDGEWORTH *Ormond* xxx, I was transmuted to Dublin, to be..lodged in Kilmainham.

Hence **trans'muting** *vbl. sb.* and *ppl. a.*

1579 FULKE *Heskins' Parl.* 155 Though we take the word of transuming for changing, turning, transmuting, or transelementing,..yet meane they not chaunge of one substance into another. **1594** PLAT *Jewell-ho.* I. 45 The earth ..by her inwarde heate and transmuting nature..will conuert [etc.]. **1846** TRENCH *Mirac.* i. (1862) 99 An ennobling of the common, and a transmuting of the mean. **1864** MUSGRAVE *Ten Days in Fr. Parsonage* II. v. 150 Efforts ..made to employ public education of the poor as a transmuting power.

transmuted (trɑːnsˈmjuːtɪd, træns-, -nz-), *ppl. a.* [f. prec. + -ED¹.] Changed in form or nature; altered; transformed.

1749 JOHNSON *Van. Hum. Wishes* ad fin., Patience, sov'reign o'er transmuted ill. **1805–6** CARY *Dante's Inf.* XXIX. 35 Who forged transmuted metals by the power Of alchemy. **1871** TYNDALL *Fragm. Sc.* (1879) II. ix. 183 Its matter is for the most part transmuted gas.

†**b.** *Her.* Of a charge on a field of two tinctures: Having the tinctures of the field reversed; = COUNTERCHANGED. *Obs.*

1486 *Bk. St. Albans, Her.* f ij, He berith quarterly Sable and Siluer with a Cheueron of the sayd colowris transmutit. **1572** BOSSEWELL *Armorie* II. 29, I terme these lyons transmuted because ye lyon first placed in ye fielde, is Sable, in Or, and the other is Or, in Sable. *c* **1828** in BERRY *Encycl. Her.* I. Gloss.

transmuter (trɑːnsˈmjuːtə(r), træns-, -nz-). [f. as prec. + -ER¹.] One who or that which transmutes.

1826 SCOTT *Diary* 4 June, in *Lockhart*, The translator of Tasso and Ariosto, and in that capacity a noble transmuter of gold into lead. **1870** LOWELL *My Study Wind.* 254 Chaucer exposes the cheats of the transmuter of metals.

trans'mutive, *a. rare*⁻¹. = TRANSMUTATIVE.

1836 HOR. SMITH *Tin Trump.* (1876) 344 The Chymist, with transmutive art Extracts a poison and a bane.

†**trans'mutress.** *Obs. rare*⁻¹. [f. TRANSMUTER + -ESS.] A feminine transmuter.

1660 tr. *Paracelsus' Archidoxis* I. v. 76 This Tincture is a Transmutress of Bodies to a better State.

trans'mutual, *a. rare*⁻¹. [f. TRANS- 3 + MUTUAL.] Reciprocal, commutual.

1829 COLERIDGE in *Lit. Rem.* (1839) IV. 132 That very discipline, the capability of exercising which in its own specific nature without superinduction of a destructive and transmutual opposite, is the fairest and firmest support of their cause.

transmuwe, -mywe, obs. ff. TRANSMEW.

†**trans'nate**, *v. Obs. rare*⁻⁰. [ad. L. *transnātāre* to swim over.] Hence **transna'tation**, **trans'nation**.

1623 COCKERAM, *Transnate*, to swimme ouer. **1864** WEBSTER, *Transnatation*, the act of swimming across. **1911** *Ibid.*, *Transnation*.

trans'national, *a.* (*sb.*) [f. TRANS- 3, 4 + NATIONAL *a.*] Extending or having interests extending beyond national bounds or frontiers; multinational. Also *ellipt.* as *sb.*, a transnational company.

1921 N. ANGELL *Fruits of Victory* ii. 63 Much of Europe lives by virtue of an international, or more correctly, a trans-national economy. **1941** J. S. HUXLEY *On living in Revolution* (1944) 144 The outstanding case of what we may call a transnational natural region—an industrial area cutting right across national boundaries—is the great concentration of industry in North-Western Europe. **1941** J. MACMURRAY *Challenge to Churches* 59 The Christian religion is the only possible force which can conceivably create the condition of a transnational, non-racial democratic polity. **1956** P. C. JESSUP *Transnational Law* i. 2, I shall use, instead of 'international law', the term 'transnational law' to include all law which regulates actions or events that transcend national frontiers. **1968** *Economist* 13 July 65/2 To these three [*sc.* the ethnocentric, the polycentric, and the geocentric types of multi-national company], Professor Galbraith has added a fourth type, the transnational company, with international stock ownership. **1973** *Reader's Digest* Apr. 167/1 Terrorism ..is 'transnational' in scope—that is, there is a kind of global brotherhood of terrorists who share basic beliefs and techniques. **1977** *Irish Democrat* Mar. 3/5 The Brussels dictators would probably just tolerate a secession provided the transnationals continued to rule the roost economically. **1980** *Telegraph* (Brisbane) 5 Sept. 2/2 Now that multinational has become a dirty word,..multinationals are ..known as transnationals. **1983** *Church Times* 6 May 10/4 It will fall to your lot to assess the transnational corporations ..and see whether in fact they do promote Third World development.

Hence **trans'nationally** *adv.*; **trans'nationalism**.

1921 N. ANGELL *Fruits of Victory* i. 14 Transport and credit, operating trans-nationally. *Ibid.* 300 The old individualist 'trans-nationalism'. **1973** *Listener* 20 Dec. 845 The reality of transnationalism, at any rate in the non-Communist world, simply cannot be denied. **1976** *Times* 13 Feb. 15/6 Surely, a peaceful world needs respect for the rule of law, not only nationally but transnationally.

trans'natural, *a.* [f. TRANS- 4 + NATURAL *sb.*]

†**1.** That is beyond the order of nature; more than natural; supernatural. *Obs.*

1569 SANFORD tr. *Agrippa's Van. Artes* 70 Because they.. are supposed to be aboue nature, therefore they call them transnaturall or Metaphisicke. **1697** J. SERGEANT *Solid Philos.* 248 Great Scholars puzzle their Wits to find out Natural Causes for divers Effects, the true Reason for which is only owing to Trans-natural ones. **1700** —— (*title*) Transnatural Philosophy, or Metaphysicks.

2. Of which the nature is transmuted. *nonce-use.*

1907 E. H. COLERIDGE *C.'s Christabel* 29 The Geraldine of the First Part is a supernatural, of the Second Part a trans-natural being... The idea..of the second Part is.. physiological as well as mythological.

†**trans'naturalize**, *v. Obs. rare*⁻¹. [f. as prec. + -IZE.] *trans.* = next.

1631 BRATHWAIT *Whimzies, Char. Pedlar* 140 He..turnes most impudent dogmaticall quacksalver. What transnaturalized elixers will this mercenarie mountebanke produce to delude the vulgar.

trans'nature, *v.* Now *rare.* [f. TRANS- 2 + NATURE *sb.*] *trans.* To change the nature of.

1567 [see TRANSELEMENT]. **1583** STUBBES *Anat. Abus.* I. (1879) 54 Their curiosity, and nicenes in apparell.. transnatureth them, makinge them weake, tender and infirme. **1627** J. CARTER *Plain Expos.* 72 The Soule, being set as a great Empresse in the bodie of man, hath a Favourite or Minion, to which it hearkeneth, and after which it is carried, yea, is euen so changed, and (as it were) transnatured by it, that if it be heauenly, the Soule is likewise heauenly; if earthly it maketh in like manner, an earthly Soule. **1657** REEVE *God's Plea* 156 Repentance..able to transnature and translate people. **1812–29** [see TRANSELEMENT].

Hence **transnatu'ration**, change of nature. *rare.*

1873 F. HALL *Mod. Eng.* viii. 280 Save by effecting a total transnaturation or stagnation of the human mind, how could a language be prevented from undergoing changes?

trans-Neptunian: see TRANS- 7.

†**transnihi'lation.** *nonce-wd.* [f. TRANS- 1 + L. *nihil* nothing + -ATION.] Transformation (of nothing) into nothings.

1820 COLERIDGE *Lett., Convers.*, etc. I. 29 How and whence did this sterile Nothing split or multiply into plurality? Whence this portentous transnihilation of nothing into Nothings?

transnivean (trɑːnsˈnɪviːən, træns-), *a.* [f. TRANS- 3 + L. *nive-us* snowy (f. *nix, niv-em* snow) + -AN.] Being or living beyond the snows (i.e. in quot. beyond the Himalayas).

1854 HOOKER *Himal. Jrnls.* I. v. 127 Earliest intercourse with the trans-nivean races.

†**trans'nominate**, *v. Obs. rare.* [f. ppl. stem of L. *transnōmināre* to change the name of, name over again: see TRANS- and NOMINATE.] *trans.* To change the name of. Hence †**transnominated** *ppl. a.*

1623 COCKERAM, *Transnominate*, to change one name for another. **1635** HEYWOOD *Hierarch.* VIII. Comm. 523 He also trans-nominated the two moneths of September and October, to Germanicus and Domitian; because in the one he was crowned, and in the other he was borne. **1657** GAULE *Sapient. Justif.* 22 Then seems it so much the more strange ..that so many real effects should proceed from a poorly equivocal and transnominated cause.

† **transnomi'nation.** *Obs.* [ad. late L. *transnōminātiōn-em*, rendering Gr. μετωνυμία metonymy: see TRANS- and NOMINATION. Cf. F. *transnomination* (Littré).] A change of name; *spec.* in *Rhet.* = METONYMY.

1561 T. NORTON *Calvin's Inst.* IV. xiv. 94 When the Apostle exhorteth the Ephesians to remembre that they were forein gestes of the testamentes, .. he saith, that they were not partakers of Circumcision. Whereby he doth (by figure of transnomination) signifie that they were excluded from the promise it self, which had not receiued the signe of the promise. **1675** BROOKS *Gold. Key* Wks. 1867 V. 256 Oh, happy transnomination! Christ's bride being one with himself .. is called, 'the Lord our righteousness'. **1715** KETTLEWELL *Chr. Obedience* 11 An ordinary figure .. which the rhetoricians call a metonomie or transnomination, and that is a transferring of a word, which is the particular name of one thing to express another.

trans'normal, *a.* [f. TRANS- 4 + NORMAL.] Outside the bounds of the normal; beyond or above the normal.

1853 MAX MÜLLER in C. Bunsen *Outl. Philos. Univ. Hist.* (1854) I. 282 Pott adds a fourth class, which he calls *transnormal* or *incorporative*, i.e. the polysynthetic American dialects. **1860** FARRAR *Orig. Lang.* (1865) 53 The 'transnormal' character of these tongues only proves that they are the work of minds incapable of all subtile analysis. **1875** A. W. WARD *Eng. Dram. Lit.* Introd. 23 The distinctive features which already his [Euripides'] quickwitted contemporaries found mirrored in his transnormal productions.

trans'ocean, *a.* [f. TRANS- 3 + OCEAN *sb.*] = TRANS-OCEANIC *a.* 2.

1901 *Daily Record & Mail* 31 Aug. 3 Besides a free trans-ocean passage, passes are issued from Quebec or Montreal to eastern points of the States. **1950** *Travel Topics* Dec. 11 Trans-ocean trips. **1978** J. A. MICHENER *Chesapeake* 102 Steed found it difficult to clarify the difficulties of transocean trading.

trans-oceanic (ˌtrɑːnsəʊʃiː'ænɪk, ˌtræns-, -nz-), *a.* [f. TRANS- + OCEANIC. Cf. F. *transocéanique* (Littré).]

1. Existing or situated beyond the ocean; also *transf.* pertaining to a region beyond the ocean.

1827 *Blackw. Mag.* XXII. 602 Their pristine transoceanic partiality for dram-drinking. **1872** *Daily News* 25 Mar., Then, England .. employed her influence .. in establishing the principle .. of a threepenny rate for European letters, and a sixpenny rate for those intended for trans-oceanic countries. **1899** *Dublin Rev.* Jan. 67 Glimpses of a transoceanic world. **1902** J. LEIGHTON in *Publ. Circ.* 8 Feb. 156/2 This device was .. admired by our transoceanic relatives.

2. Passing or extending across the ocean.

1868 LYELL *Princ. Geol.* (ed. 10) II. III. xli. 420 We probably still remain ignorant of many means of transoceanic migration. **1884** *Q. Rev.* Apr. 453 The most vigilant supervision was exercised over the means of inland and transoceanic transport. **1892** *Times* 2 May 9/2 In 1871 .. the total trans-oceanic emigration from the United Kingdom was 252,435.

trans'ocular, *a.* [f. TRANS- 5 + L. *ocul-us* eye: cf. *ocular.*] Lying across the eye: applied to a longitudinal stripe or colour marking.

1872 COUES *Key N. Amer. Birds* 20 When these [lines] are continuous through the eye, they form a transocular line. **1876** *Proc. Zool. Soc.* 20 June 660 The crown being pure white, with only a transocular line on each side of the head.

transoid ('trɑːnzɔɪd, 'trænz-). *Chem.* [f. TRANS- + -OID.] Designating a compound, group, or structure in which two like atoms lie on opposite sides of a single bond or a line of bonds.

1959 I. L. FINAR *Org. Chem.* (ed. 3) I. xvii. 387 *(caption)* Staggered (transoid). **1965** *Tetrahedron* XXI. 3121 The optical rotatory dispersion of seven other transoid dienes has been determined. **1970** *Nature* 3 Jan. 36/1 Acetylcholine .. in a 'transoid' conformation. **1978** *Ibid.* 29 June 785/1 Bathorhodopsin is a common intermediate between pigments based on two different *cis* isomers and thus must itself contain a 'transoid' chromophore.

transom ('trænsəm). Forms: 5 **traunsum, -som, -sone, trampsoun, -sown, tramson,** 6 **trawnsom,** (**transumpt**), **transume, -same,** 6–7 **-sam,** 6–9 **-sum, -somme,** 7 **-summe,** 6– **transom.** [Late ME. *traunsum, -som*, of obscure history; but app. (as held by Prof. Skeat), a corruption of L. *transtrum*, of which it is the exact equivalent in sense. L. *transtrum* was a derivative of *trans*, or the root *tra-* across, with the instrumental *-trum* = Gr. -τρον, Indo-Eur. *-trom*.

No connecting forms between *transtrum* and *transum* have been found; but perh. the latter was a workmen's corruption, which had assumed this form before it came to be written down: cf. PEDIMENT. (Florio's spelling *transtroms* in 1598 and 1611 can only be taken as his own emendation of the Eng. word after It. *transtri*; he knew also the form *transoms*.)

The obscurity of the history is increased by the fact that senses 5 and 6 and the combination *transom-nail* are known of earlier date than the architectural and naval senses, which being those of L. *transtrum* would etymologically be earlier.]

1. a. In building, etc.: A cross-beam or cross-piece, esp. one spanning an opening to carry a superstructure; a lintel.

1487–8 *Rec. St. Mary at Hill* 137 Item, for v quarteres for traunsones, x d. **1519** HORMAN *Vulg.* 138, I hytte my heed ageynst the soyle or transumpt. **1538** ELYOT, *Transtra*, transoms which do go ouerwhart a house, also the seates [etc.]. **1577** HARRISON *England* II. x, They are inforced for want of stuffe to vse no studdes at all, but onely raysines, groundselles, transomes, and vpright principalles. **1598** FLORIO, *Transtri*, crosse or ouerthwart beames, transtroms [**1611** Transtroms or crosse-beames]. *Ibid.*, *Trasti...* Also a transome or beame going crosse a house [**1611** transoms or crosse beames]. **1667** PRIMATT *City & C. Build.* 63 Suppose a Shop-window to be twenty foot front, .. the Brest-summer will take up twenty six foot of Timber, .. the two Transums for the Stalls eight foot. **1682** WHELER *Journ. Greece* I. 18 [An arch] whose two Lintel-Posts, and Transome, are of three whole Stones. **1879** FARRAR *St. Paul* II. 12 [The Temple of Diana at Ephesus] Its doors .. surmounted by transoms so vast and solid that the aid of miracles was invoked to account for their elevation.

b. The transverse top-beam of a gallows, a swing, or the like; the lintel stone of a trilith.

1615 G. SANDYS *Trav.* 56 Swinging vp and downe, as boyes do in bell-ropes: for which there be gallowses .. of an exceeding height .. by two ioyning ropes that are fastned aboue, they will swing themselues as high as the transome. **1796** MORSE *Amer. Geog.* II. 112 (Stonehenge) The transomes, or over-thwart stones, are quite plain. **1865** LUBBOCK *Preh. Times* v. (1878) 116 Circles of uprights and transoms at Stonehenge.

c. A beam resting across a saw-pit to support the log.

1885 *Cheshire Gloss.*, *Transom*, the cross piece of wood that holds up the log on a saw-pit. A *back-transom* is a spare one always kept under the log for safety. **1888** ELWORTHY *W. Somerset Gloss.*, *Transum*, a cross bearer used by sawyers to support the end of the piece. A spare support thrown across the pit would be also called a transum.

2. a. A horizontal bar of wood or stone across a mullioned window, dividing it in height; also, a cross-bar separating a door from the fan-light above it (Ogilvie, 1882).

1502 *Privy Purse Exp. Eliz. of York* (1830) 25 To John Conewey smyth for foure transoms and xij standardes [of iron for a window]. **1575** LANEHAM *Let.* (1871) 50 Foour great wyndoz a froont, .. euery one a fyue foot wide, az many mo eeuen abooue them, diuided on all parts by a transum and Architraue. **1611** COTGR., *Meneau de fenestre*, the transome, or cross-barre of a window. **1663** GERBIER *Counsel* 19 The middle Transoms of them [windows] above six foot .. since otherwise the middle Transome would be opposite to a mans eye. **1805** *T. West's Antiq. Furness* 365 The wooden mullions and transoms contained in the great [window] were placed there in 1796. **1871** *Athenæum* 29 July 151 The lancet windows of the principal story are long triplets, of ample width, and divided horizontally by broad transoms of sculptured work.

b. Short for *transom window*: A window divided by a transom; also a small window above the lintel of a door. *U.S. colloq.*

1844 KINGLAKE *Eöthen* v. 61 The transom that looks longwise through the street. **1882** *Harper's Mag.* Nov. 893 In trying to climb through the transom into the car he took hold of the guide rope. **1883** *Century Mag.* XXV. 588/2 The dim light that streamed into the room from the transom. **1908** W. CHURCHILL *Mr. Crewe's Career* x, The buzz of talk which he had heard through the closed transom.

3. In technical applications. **†a.** The vane of a cross-staff (CROSS-STAFF 2): see quot. 1696. *Obs.*

1594 BLUNDEVIL *Exerc.* VII. xii. (1597) 322 b, A new kind of crosse staffe, hauing 3 transames or crosses. **1696** PHILLIPS (ed. 5), *Transome*, .. the Vane of a Cross Staff, or Wooden Member, to be set a-cross the cross Staff, having a Socket in it, upon which it slides stiff upon the Square of the Cross Staff, and may be set to any of the Graduations of it.

†b. The transverse member in a cross. *Obs.*

1615 G. SANDYS *Trav.* 184 For it [the Cross of Christ] was framed .. of foure seuerall woods; the foot of Cedar, the bole of Cypresse, the transome of Palme, and the title of Oliue. **1658** SIR T. BROWNE *Gard. Cyrus* i. 96 Some [crosses] being right, and of one single peece without traversion or transome. **1864** R. S. HAWKER *Quest of Sangraal* 33 [The Southern Cross] a Pentacle of stars, whereof two shone for the Transome and three for the Stock.

c. A cross-piece connecting the cheeks of a gun-carriage.

1688 R. HOLME *Armoury* III. xviii. (Roxb.) 138/2 The transomes, are the peeces of wood which hold the cheekes or Limbres togather. **1828** J. M. SPEARMAN *Brit. Gunner* (ed. 2) 114 The 68-pounder carriage has, in addition to the breast transom .., a centre and horizontal one. **1853** STOCQUELER *Milit. Encycl.*, *Transoms*, in artillery, pieces of wood which join the cheeks of gun-carriages. There is but one in a truck-carriage, placed under the trunnion-holes; and four in a wheel-carriage—the trail, the centre, the bed, and the breast-transoms.

d. *Carriage-building.* In a perch-carriage, Each of two cross-timbers (***fore*** and ***hind transom***) framed across the perch, and upon which the springs are fixed.

1794 W. FELTON *Carriages* (1801) I. iii. 46 The fore transom, or fore spring-bar, is the most essential part of the cross framings. It is a strong timber fixed to the perch by means of a hooping-piece. **1877** G. G. THRUPP *Hist. Coaches* ii. 32 The carriage is composed of a transom in front with a perch .. fastened to it.

e. Each of the transverse timbers joining the sides in the frame of a railway carriage bogie-truck.

1891 in *Cent. Dict.* **1907**, etc. [see NOSE *sb.* 14 e].

f. *pl.* On a railway: Cross-timbers laid between (or, formerly, beneath) longitudinal sleepers.

1838 *Civil Eng. & Arch. Jrnl.* I. 341/1 On the Great Western Railway .. the longitudinal sleepers have been laid on transoms and piles. **1872** *Daily News* 15 July, For nearly a mile the transoms have been torn up and smashed, the ballast ploughed up, and the line otherwise injured. **1892** *Pall Mall G.* 23 May 1/3 The 'transoms' are the cross-timbers which hold the longitudinal sleepers at their proper distance apart.

g. The seat of a throne; also, a couch or seat built at the side of a cabin or state-room on board ship.

1847 H. MELVILLE *Omoo* lxxxii. 373, I would find the ship's articles on the cabin transom. **1851** —— *Moby Dick* I. xvi. 91 Seated on the transom was what seemed to me a most uncommon and surprising figure. **1883** F. M. CRAWFORD *Dr. Claudius* vii, The Duke was extended on a transom. *Ibid.* ix, He sat down on the transom. **1896** *Daily News* 19 May 5/2 Each throne has also been furnished with new transomes covered with crimson velvet.

4. *Shipbuilding.* **a.** †A cross-beam in the frame of a ship (*obs.*); *spec.* each of several transverse beams bolted to the stern-post, which support the ends of the decks and determine the breadth of the stern at the buttocks.

1545 ELYOT, *Canonia*, the transomes in a shyppe, whereon the hatches are made. **1584** B. R. tr. *Herodotus* II. xcvi. 94 They vnite and ioyne the plancks together .. binding the same to many transomes that goe both crosse and longe wayes for the strength of the vessell. **1624** SIR W. MONSON *Tracts* (Navy Rec. Soc.) IV. 47 The transom is a timber that lies athwart the stern, and lays out the breadth of the ship at the buttock, which is her breadth from her tuck upwards. **1748** *Anson's Voy.* III. ii. 219 The long boat, which was at this time moored a-stern, was on a sudden canted so high, that it broke the transom of the Commodore's gallery. **1770** COOK *Voy. round World* II. vi. (1773) 398 The 27th and 28th were spent in refitting the ship .., fixing a transom for the tiller, getting stones on board. **1871** BLACKMORE *Maid of Sker* 65 Part of the taffrail was carried away, but the transom and transom-knees stood firm.

b. Short for *transom-frame* (see in 7); hence in *Boat-building*, a board similar in shape and position to a transom-frame: see quot.

1857 P. COLQUHOUN *Comp. to Oarsman's Guide* 28 The stern-post is scarfed on, and upon it comes the transom, that heart-shaped piece of board, found in all cutter-built boats, and secured to the sax-board by transom grips or horizontal knees.

†5. Short for *transom-nail*. *Obs. rare.*

1423 in Rogers *Agric. & Prices* III. 448/4 Hornchurch. Transom. 1 m. @/10. **1427** *Rec. St. Mary at Hill* 65 Also payd for ij ml traunsum, þe ml x d .. xx d. Also pay for iij ml sprigge, þe ml ix d .. xxvij d.

†6. ? A bolster; or part of a bedstead answering the same purpose. *Obs.*

The editor of the *Bury Wills* remarks 'the transome is usually considered to be that part of the bedstead which is between the two head-posts .. but the general association of the word with feather beds would lead us to think the bolster was meant'.

[**1459**: ? implied in TRANSOMER.] **1463** *Bury Wills* (Camden) 23, ij peyre of good shetes, the trampsoun, the costerys of that chambyr. **1479** *Ibid.* 53 A traunson. **1482** MARG. PASTON in *P. Lett.* III. 288 To John Heyth a materas with a traunsom, a peire shetes, a peire blankettes, and a cover-light. **1522** *Bury Wills* (Camden) 115 A ffetherbed, ij trawnsoms, a matras, ij pelowes, iiij payer of schetes. [**1570** LEVINS *Manip.* 161/44 Ye Transome of a bed, *trabula.*]

7. *attrib.* and *Comb.*, as ***transom-shaft, -stone***; ***transom-shaped*** adj. (2 b); **transom-bar**, the cross-bar over a door having a fan-light above it (*U.S.*); † **transom-eyed** *a.*, having a transom or beam (BEAM *sb.*[1] 3 c) in the eye; **transom-frame** (*Shipbuilding*), the aftermost 'square-frame' of a ship, giving shape to and supporting the stern, and bolted to the stern-post; **transom-grip** (*Boat-building*), an angular fastening analogous to a *transom-knee*; **transom-knee** (*Shipbuilding*), each of the curved timbers or angle-irons by which the transoms are fastened to the stern-timbers; **transom-lattice**, a transverse lattice; **transom-lifter**, an apparatus for controlling and fastening the fan-light over a door (*U.S.*); † **transom-nail**, a small size of nail, formerly in use; ? a lath nail; **transom-rib**, a transverse rib; **transom road** (*U.S.*), a railway track on longitudinal sleepers with transoms between them; **transom-stern** (*Shipbuilding*), a vessel's stern formed by or taking its shape from a transom; **transom-window** = 2 b: see quot. 1688.

1909 *Cent. Dict. Supp.*, *Transom-bar. **1601** BP. W. BARLOW *Defence* 67 Thus these *transam-eyed hypocrites can spie small motes in Vs. **1874** THEARLE *Naval Archit.* 85 A deep transverse frame, termed a '*transom frame', situated at the fore ends of the rudder-post, and connected thereto. **1857** *Transom-grip [see 4 b]. **1769** FALCONER *Dict. Marine* (1789), *Courbes d'arcasse*, the *transom-knees, or sleepers. *c* **1850** *Rudim. Navig.* (Weale) 156 *Transom-knees*, knees bolted to the transoms and the side of the ship. **1689** E. HOWARD *Caroloiades* 273 A *transom Lattise did divide that Room. **1359** *Letter-bk. G. London* lf. 83 Item in D. de lathes ij s. iij d. & ob. Item in Ml. & D. de *trasonna(i)l, xviij d. Item in Ml. & D. de Sprig' xv d. **1424** *Hornchurch Account* 2 & 3 Hen. VI. (New Coll. Oxf.), In .Ml. de traunsumnayl emptis pro domo capellani .. x.d. **1835** R. WILLIS *Archit. Mid. Ages* vii. 85 The principal distinction between these [kinds of vaulting] and our own fan vaulting, is the substitution of lozenge-headed compartments in the fans for the English horizontal *transom rib. **1813** SCOTT *Rokeby* v. iv, The moon through *transom-shafts of stone, Which crossed the latticed oriels, shone. **1844** KINGLAKE *Eöthen* v. 60 The *transom-shaped windows suspended over your head. **1770** PENNANT *Zool.* IV. 53 In the interstices between the upright and *transome stones of Stone-henge. **1688** R. HOLME *Armoury* III. 473/2 A *Transome window, hath Cross barrs in it, at the third part of its height. **1837** MARY HOWITT *Rur. Life* III. v. (1862) 264 The state apartments are lofty and spacious, with numerous transom windows.

Hence 'transomed (-səmd) *a.*, divided by or having a transom or transoms; **transomer**, (?) a case or slip for a bolster: cf. sense 6.

1848 B. WEBB *Sk. Cont. Ecclesiol.* 276 The window is *transomed midway. **1876** T. HARDY *Ethelberta* (1890) 3 Lifting his eyes to the mullioned and transomed windows and moulded parapet above him. **1881** *Athenæum* 13 Aug. 216/1 The hall..is lighted by three transomed windows. **1459** *Paston Lett.* I. 480 Canvas in the Warderop and fyne Lynen Clothe of dyvers sortes..ix. berys for fetherbeddys. Item, iiij. *transomers.

† **transon**, *v. Obs. rare.* Also 6 **transsene**. [ad. F. *trançonner*, formerly also *transonner* (14–16th c. in Godef.) to cut into segments or pieces, cut up, carve, variant form of *tronçonner*, f. *tronçon*: see TRUNCHEON *sb.*] *trans.* To carve (an eel).

1513 *Bk. Keruynge* in *Babees Bk.* (1868) 265 Transsene that ele. **1688** R. HOLME *Armoury* III. 78/2 Transon the Eel.

transonance ('trɑːnsəʊnəns, 'træn-). [f. TRANS- + L. *sonānt-em* sounding: see -ANCE.] The passage of the sound produced in one organ (e.g. the heart) through the substance of another (e.g. the lung).

1909 in *Cent. Dict. Supp.*

transonic (trɑːn'sɒnɪk, træn-), *a.* Also **trans-sonic.** [f. TRANS- 3 + SONIC *a.*, after *supersonic, ultrasonic.*] Pertaining to, involving, capable of, or designating speeds close to that of sound, at which some of the flow round a body is supersonic and some subsonic and there are characteristic changes in the behaviour of an aircraft.

1946 *Britannica Bk. of Year* (U.S.) 833/2 *Trans-sonic*, speeds ranging from 550 to 760 m.p.h. **1946** *Jrnl. R. Aeronaut. Soc.* L. 436/1, I propose to say a little about 'supersonic' aerodynamics first, and then to return to the so-called 'transonic' region, which presents the most difficult problem of all. **1948** 'N. SHUTE' *No Highway* xii. 294 The forces on the structure [of an aircraft] were still very much a matter of guesswork in the trans-sonic range. **1966** *New Scientist* 20 Jan. 135/1 A critical phase is reached as the aircraft goes 'transonic'; that is, as it accelerates through the speed band from just below to just above the speed of sound. **1977** *Jrnl. R. Soc. Arts* CXXV. 347/1 Notable examples [of development] since World War II have been jet propulsion, transonic and supersonic aerodynamics, [etc.].

trans'orbital, *a.* [f. TRANS- 5 + ORBIT *sb.*: cf. *orbital.*] Drawn or measured across between the orbits or eye-sockets.

1852 DANA *Crust.* I. 92 Trans-orbital breadth small.

,trans-Pa'cific (,trɑːns-, ,træns-, -nz-), *a.* [TRANS- 7, 8.] **a.** Across or crossing the Pacific Ocean. **b.** On the other side of the Pacific.

1891 *Scribner's Mag.* Sept. 280/2 A newly organized trans-pacific service, running by way of Yokohama to Vancouver. **1897** *Daily News* 30 Jan. 6/1 The proposed 'All-British Trans-Pacific Cable'. **1906** *Athenæum* 17 Feb. 193/3 The Cardinal's Trans-Pacific experiences have accustomed him to such liberties.

transpadane ('trɑːnspədeɪn, 'træns-), *a.* (*sb.*) Also 7 **-an.** [ad. L. *transpadānus* adj. and sb., f. *trans* across + *Padus* the river Po, *padānus* of the Po. Cf. F. *transpadan, -ane* (Littré).] That is beyond the river Po (from Rome); opposed to *cis-padane*. **b.** *sb.* One living north of the Po.

Transpadane Republic, a republic formed by Bonaparte in 1796, consisting of Lombardy and part of Venetia.

1617 MORYSON *Itin.* III. 106 Lombardy of old was part of Gallia Cisalpina, which the River Padus..divides into Cispadan (on this side the Po) and Transpadan (beyond the Po). *Ibid.*, Transpadane..containes the Dukedome of Milan. **1797** BURKE *Regic. Peace* iii. Wks. VIII. 311 Is it to the Cispadane or to the Transpadane republicks..that we address all these pledges? **1896** *Q. Rev.* Oct. 396 The enfranchisement of the Transpadane Gauls. *Ibid.*, So much for Cæsar and his Transpadanes!

trans'palatine, *a.* and *sb.* [TRANS- 5: cf. PALATINE *a.*[2]] **a.** *adj.* Extending transversely across either half of the palate. **b.** *sb.* The transpalatine bone in certain sauropsidan vertebrates.

1891 in *Cent. Dict.* **1893** *British Museum Catalogue, Snakes* I. 71 Maxillary, palatine, and pterygoid movable; transpalatine present. **1899** in *Syd. Soc. Lex.*

trans'palmar, *a. Anat.* [ad. mod.L. *transpalmār-is*, f. TRANS- 5 + L. *palma* PALM *sb.*[2]: cf. *palmar.*] Extending across the palm of the hand, as the ***transpalmar muscle.***

1891 in *Cent. Dict.* **1899** in *Syd. Soc. Lex.*

† **trans'pare**, *v. Obs. rare.* [f. after TRANSPARENT; cf. med.L. *transpārē-re*, f. *trans*, TRANS- 1 + *pārēre* to appear, show oneself; It. *transparere* (Florio, 1598).] *intr.* **a.** To be or become transparent. **b.** To appear or be visible through a transparent medium.

1604 EARL STIRLING *Aurora* lxxiii, Oft haue I wish'd..That th' Alabaster bulwarke might transpare, And that the pillars rarer then they are, Might whiles permit some hapning rayes to passe. *Ibid.* xcix, But through the yce of that vniust disdane, Yet still transpares her picture and my paine. **1661** BLOUNT *Glossogr.* (ed. 2), *Transpare*.., to appear through, to be evident, or clear.

transparence (trɑːns'pɛərəns, træns-, -'pær-). *rare.* [f. as next: see -ENCE, and cf. F. *transparence* (*c* 1400 in Godef. *Compl.*).] = TRANSPARENCY 1.

1594 CAREW *Huarte's Exam. Wits* (1616) 84 That which cannot be read, with oyle is made legible, by yeelding thereto a brightnesse and transparence. **1598** FLORIO, *Trasparenza*, a transparence or through-light. **1619** DRAYTON *Man in Moon* 332 Cleere Amber..Through whose transparence you might easily see The beds of Pearle whereon the Gum did sleepe. **1845** R. W. HAMILTON *Pop. Educ.* x. (ed. 2) 270 Motive may be detected through the transparence of tendency. **1866** J. G. MURPHY *Comm. Exod.* xxiv. 10 Adamantine solidity, transparence, and brilliancy.

† **b.** *transf.* = TRANSPARENCY 2. *Obs.*

1635 HEYWOOD *Hierarch.* IX. 575 The casements standing wide Clearely through that transparence is espy'de This Glutton. **1789** E. DARWIN *Bot. Gard.* IV. 343 O'er her light limbs the dim transparence plays, And the fair form it seems to hide, betrays.

transparency (trɑːns'pɛərənsɪ, træns-, -'pær-, -nz-). [ad. med.L. *transpārēnti-a* (Du Cange), f. *transpārēnt-em*: see next and -ENCY.]

1. a. The quality or condition of being transparent; perviousness to light; diaphaneity, pellucidity.

thermal transparency, perviousness to heat rays; diathermancy; cf. TRANSPARENT 1 b.

1615 H. CROOKE *Body of Man* 556 It is like a thinne and pollished horne of a Lanthorn, not only in transparencie by which meanes it receiueth the light, but also in his substance. **1651–3** JER. TAYLOR *Serm. for Year* I. xviii. 238 His wife may, by seeing the beauties and transparency of that Crystall, dresse her minde and her body by the light of so pure reflexions. **1705** ADDISON *Italy* 26 The Clearness and Transparency of the Stream. **1750** tr. *Leonardus' Mirr. Stones* 36 A stone with a transparency, or a kind of brightness. **1830** HERSCHEL *Stud. Nat. Phil.* 141 Between transparency and opacity there would at first sight appear a direct opposition. **1860** MAURY *Phys. Geog. Sea* (Low) vi. §313 The atmosphere is transparency itself. **1900** *Jrnl. Soc. Dyers* XVI. 7 The particles retain their form and transparency.

fig. **1843** CARLYLE *Past & Pr.* II. i, Written in its child-like transparency. **1866** GEO. ELIOT *F. Holt* v, The transparency of his talk..gave a charm even to his weaknesses.

b. *Linguistics.* The state or quality of being transparent (sense 2 c). With reference to a phonological rule, opp. OPACITY 3 c.

1971 [see OPAQUE *a.* 3 c]. **1975** *Canad. Jrnl. Linguistics* XX. 175 Rules tend to be ordered so as to become maximally transparent, where *transparency* is the opposite of *opacity*. **1981** *Ibid.* XXVI. 73 Transparency of the base word is an important factor in determining speakers' choice of neologism.

c. Of reproduced sound: the state or quality of being transparent (sense 3).

1982 E. GREENFIELD et al. *New Penguin Stereo Record & Cassette Guide* p. ix/2, Disc reproduction continues to offer a marginally greater range of sound and a more subtle inner transparency of detail than the equivalent tape. **1983** *What Hi-Fi?* Dec. 102/3 This £129 speaker offers a high quality of finish and a transparency and accuracy of sound that can compete with models twice the price.

d. The state or quality of transmitting or allowing the passage of sound waves without distortion (see TRANSPARENT *a.* 1 b).

1983 *What Hi-Fi?* Dec. 113/3 The most impressive [feature] was the sheer transparency of the design. **1984** *Gramophone* Mar. 1086/1 The effect (emphasized by the transparency of the CD medium) is of sitting in a small room, very close to the cello and with the lid of the piano wide open.

2. a. That which is transparent; a transparent object or medium.

1591 HARINGTON *Orl. Fur.* III. xvi, To make transparencies to meete in one And so convey the sunne-beames where you will. **1784** COWPER *Task* v. 151 A watery light Gleamed through the clear transparency.

b. *spec.* A picture, print, inscription, or device on some translucent substance, made visible by means of a light behind.

1785 J. WOODFORDE *Diary* 21 June (1926) II. 196 Went to Bunns Gardens... There was tolerable good Music, indifferent singing, some pretty transparencies and tolerable fire Works. **1801** *Sporting Mag.* XIX. 49/1 A transparency, in which a gardener at Hammersmith exhibited a Flower-pot, during the illuminations. **1807** E. ORME (*title*) Essay on Transparent Prints, and on Transparencies in general. **1859** GULLICK & TIMBS *Paint.* 9 A mode of painting 'transparencies' as they would now be called, on linen.

attrib. **1855** W. WILLIAMS (*title*) Transparency painting on linen for decorative purposes.

c. A photograph or picture on glass or other transparent substance, intended to be seen by transmitted light. Also *attrib.*

1866 *Brit. Jrnl. Photogr.* 1 June 264/1 Many of these lantern transparencies had been enlarged from spots of these originals. **1874** CORBET *Venus at Isle of Desolation* 104 (Cassell), I took transparencies of the little photos. he took of my station. **1885** C. G. W. LOCK *Workshop Receipts* Ser. IV. 357/2 A negative or transparency is not fully developed much under 15 minutes. **1892** *Photogr. Ann.* II. 576 Various transparency printing frames. **1897** J. NICOL in *Outing* (U.S.) XXX. 496/2 The transparency plate and negative are placed in the printing frame exactly as in printing on paper. **1965** MRS. L. B. JOHNSON *White House Diary* 9 Feb. (1970) 239 The transparency I have..shows a real John Singleton Copley, of the best early American period. **1969** 'E. LATHEN' *When in Greece* v. 49 He had brought slides..a veritable library of transparencies. **1973** 'H. HOWARD' *Highway to Murder* iv. 46 Like transparencies flashed on a screen I saw pictures of long ago.

† **3.** *Her.* An outline figure, or the shadow of a charge, without the charge itself, painted the same colour as the field, but of a darker tint: = ADUMBRATION 4. *Obs.*

1610 GUILLIM *Heraldry* II. iii. 42 Adumbration or Transparency is a cleere exemption of the substance of the Charge..in such sort, as that there remaineth nothing thereof to be discerned, but the..bare proportion of the outward lineaments thereof. *Ibid.* vii. 65 The Orle..is an Ordinarie composed of a threefold line duplicated, admitting a Transparancie of the field, thorowout the.. space therein enclosed. **1725** COATS *Dict. Her.* s.v. *Adumbration*, Some term such Adumbration, Transparency.

4. A burlesque translation of the German title of address *Durchlaucht*: cf. SERENITY 4.

1844 THACKERAY *B. Lyndon* ix, Hobnobbing..with lovely excellencies, nay, with highnesses and transparencies themselves. *Ibid.*, Pippi..had kept back a note of hand 'her High Transparency' gave us. **1848** —— *Van. Fair* lxii, His Transparency the Duke and his Transparent family..come and occupy the great box in the middle. **1895** *Westm. Gaz.* 7 Feb. 2/1 During the sojourn of grand transparencies beneath your Derbyshire roof.

transparent (trɑːns'pɛərənt, træns-, -'pær-, -nz-), *a.* (*sb.*) Also 5 **-paraunt**, 6–7 **-parant.** [ad. med.L. *transpārēnt-em*, pr. pple. of *transpārēre* (= '*pellūcēre*' Du Cange), f. TRANS- + *pārēre* to appear, be visible. In 15th c. app. stressed *transpa'raunt*, after F. *transparent* (14th c. in Hatz.-Darm.).]

1. a. Having the property of transmitting light, so as to render bodies lying beyond completely visible; that can be seen through; diaphanous.

1413 *Pilgr. Sowle* (Caxton) I. iii. (1859) 4 The erthe seemyd me al clere and transparaunt, soo that I myght see clerely al that was withynne. **1432–50** tr. *Higden* (Rolls) VI. 425 A vesselle made of onichinus, transparente, and polischede by so subtile an arte þat [etc.]. **1588** SHAKS. *L.L.L.* IV. iii. 31 Nor shines the siluer Moone one halfe so bright, Through the transparent bosome of the deepe. **1667** MILTON *P.L.* VII. 265 The Firmament, expanse of liquid, pure, Transparent, Elemental Air. **1712–14** POPE *Rape of Lock* II. 61 Transparent forms, too fine for mortal sight. **1807** Transparent Prints [see TRANSPARENCY 2 b]. **1813** BAKEWELL *Introd. Geol.* (1815) 37 Uncrystallized quartz is seldom transparent, most frequently translucent, but sometimes opaque. **1868** LOCKYER *Elem. Astron.* iii. §23 (1879) 125 Both head and tail [of a comet] are so transparent that all but the faintest stars are easily seen through them.

b. *transf.* Pervious to heat-rays. Hence more widely, allowing the passage of any specified kind of radiation. Also, allowing the passage of sound waves without distortion.

1871 B. STEWART *Heat* (ed. 2) §178 It is probable that no substance is perfectly transparent with respect to heat. **1883** *Illustr. Lond. News* 24 Feb. 203/3 A table of various substances, some of which are opaque to light and transparent to heat, and the reverse. **1947** *Physical Rev.* LXXII. 1114/1 At sufficiently high energies the nucleus begins to be transparent to the bombarding particles. **1962** *Listener* 3 May 770/1 The needles..would be effective only in centimetre wavelengths—to which..the ionosphere is virtually transparent. **1962** A. NISBETT *Technique Sound Studio* ii. 41 Note that rack (as well as table surface) should be made of acoustically transparent mesh. *Ibid.* 269 The rack itself should be transparent to sound. **1974** *Nature* 13 Dec. 613/2 Their seismic data are said to 'reveal a distinct basement ridge' blanketed by acoustically transparent sediments which 'thin subtly near the crest of the buried ridge'. **1976** *Gramophone* Apr. 1682/2 The latter consists of a thin framework carrying two stand-off ribs to give a three-faced appearance when the black, acoustically transparent, stockinette cloth is stretched over it. **1978** *Nature* 21 Sept. 175/1 A container of superfluid ^{4}He whose walls are transparent to neutrons with velocity of 450 ms^{-1}. **1980** *Sci. Amer.* July 56/1 The interstellar medium is highly transparent to gamma rays. **1982** *Nature* 9 Sept. 122/1 The ocean is transparent to sound.

† **c.** That shines through; penetrating, as light.

1593 SHAKS. *2 Hen. VI*, III. i. 353 Like to the glorious Sunnes transparant Beames. **1593** T. WATSON *Tears of Fancie* xxxi, My loues transparent beames and rosy colour.

† **d.** Apparent or visible through something. Cf. TRANSPARE *v.* b. *Obs.*

1609 DANIEL *Civ. Wars* IV. ii, Which, though..Thou ouerlay'st with fayrest colourings; Yet th' vnder-worke, transparent, shewes too plaine. **1712** STEELE *Spect.* No. 490 ¶7 To my fond Eyes she all transparent stood.

† **e.** Admitting the passage of light through interstices. *Obs. rare.*

1617 MORYSON *Itin.* III. 141 Not farre thence is a transparant and pleasant, but little Wood. **1693** CONGREVE in *Dryden's Juvenal* XI. (1697) 280 He, whose thin transparent Rags, declare How much, his tatter'd Fortune wants repair.

2. *fig.* **a.** Frank, open, candid, ingenuous.

1590 SHAKS. *Mids. N.* II. ii. 104 Transparent Helena, nature shewes art, That through thy bosome makes me see thy heart. **1635** R. CAREW in *Lismore Papers* (1888) Ser. II. III. 217 They are very well beloued for their ciuill and transparent carriage towards all sorts. **1878** T. HARDY *Ret. Native* I. iv, An ingenuous, transparent life was disclosed. **1891** E. PEACOCK *N. Brendon* II. 306 She was transparent as the daylight.

b. Easily seen through, recognized, understood, or detected; manifest, evident, obvious, clear. Cf. APPARENT 3.

1592 SHAKS. *Rom. & Jul.* I. ii. 96 Then turne teares to fire: And these who often drown'd could neuer die, Transparent Heretiques be burnt for liers. **1638** CHILLINGW. *Relig. Prot.* I. ii. §150. 111 Your Argument against us, is a transparent fallacy. **1710** STEELE *Tatler* No. 197 ¶5 In Courts, they make transparent Flatterers. **1867** FREEMAN *Norm. Conq.* I. v. 347 A transparent artifice..paralyses them. **1869** J. MARTINEAU *Ess.* II. 178 The fallacy of the remark is transparent. **1879** McCARTHY *Own Times* II. xviii. 37 The transparent sincerity of his purpose.

c. *Linguistics.* Obvious in structure or meaning; that can be extrapolated from surface structure; of a phonological rule: that can be extrapolated from every occurrence of the phenomenon, in which every context implies the rule (opp. OPAQUE *a.* 3 c).

1974 [see OPAQUE *a.* 3 c]. **1975** [see TRANSPARENCY 1 b]. **1977** *Language* LIII. 820 A compound may be highly transparent semantically when it is coined. **1980** *Amer. Speech* LV. 38 The hydronymic element *-kill* and names formed from it are semantically opaque, whereas *creek* and *brook* are transparent. **1981** *Canad. Jrnl. Linguistics* XXVI. 73 They..show no preferences either way if both word boundary and formative boundary derivations are transparent.

3. Of reproduced sound: clear, without tonal distortion, not blurred, with each element distinct.

1950 *Audio Engin.* Sept. 33/2 The sound is then said to be *transparent*..; no *acoustic fog veils* the ensemble, and each instrument stands out with *clarity*.

trans'parently, *adv.* [f. prec. + -LY^{2}.] In a transparent manner or degree; so as to be seen through.

1617 MORYSON *Itin.* III. 81 [Amber] after it is polished, becomes transparantly bright. **1628** tr. *Mathieu's Powerful Favorite* 34 It is so minced and subtile, that falshood may be transparently seene through it. **1667** H. STUBBE in *Phil. Trans.* II. 497 The Sea was black and thick, not transparently blue, as before. **1851** HAWTHORNE *Snow Image*, etc. *Gt. Stone Face* (1879) 39 One enormous pane of glass, so transparently pure. **1861** *Sat. Rev.* 23 Nov. 526 The counter scheme..is much more transparently futile.

trans'parentness. *rare.* [f. as prec. + -NESS.] The quality of being transparent; = TRANSPARENCY 1.

1727 in BAILEY vol. II. **1762** tr. *Busching's Syst. Geog.* VI. 619 The water..besides its perfect transparentness is of a most grateful taste. **1880** *Christy Carew* I. iii. 136 A dull night sky, starless, but with a clear transparentness.

trans'parish, *v. humorous nonce-wd.* [TRANS- 2.] *trans.* To transport beyond the parish.

1819 SYD. SMITH in Lady Holland *Mem.* (1855) II. 187 If it blow before it rains, we shall all be up in the air in the shape of dust, and..transparished we know not where.

† **trans'pass**, *v. Obs. rare.* [= obs. F. *transpasser* 'to passe or goe through, to passe ouer' (Cotgr.), in med.L. *transpassāre* to go beyond (Du Cange), f. TRANS- + F. *passer*, med.L. *passāre* to pass. Cf. also It. *trapassare* 'to passe through, away, or over, to decease, to die' (Florio 1598), 'to passe from life to death' (ibid. 1611). Cf. TRESPASS *v.*]

1. *intr.* To pass away, depart, die.

1592 DANIEL *Descr. Beauty* Wks. (1717) 422 Thy Form and flatter'd Hue, Which shall so soon transpass, Is far more fair than is thy Looking-glass.

2. *intr.* To pass or penetrate across or through; also *trans.* to pass beyond (a boundary or limit).

1626 T. H[AWKINS] *Caussin's Holy Crt.* 176 It is impossible to deceyue God, whose eye..transpasseth through the abysses. **1629** MAXWELL tr. *Herodian* (1635) 320 Had transpassed the banks and bounds of the Roman Empire. **1646** J. GREGORY *Notes & Obs.* 74 The River Hyphasis..he transpassed, and set up Altars on the other side.

† **trans'passable**, *a. Obs. rare.* [f. prec. + -ABLE.] Admitting of being passed through or over; capable of being crossed.

1614 RALEIGH *Hist. World* I. (1634) 98 The navigable River of Tygris..which is everywhere transpassable by boates of great burthen. **1668** CULPEPPER & COLE *Barthol. Anat.* III. vi. 140 The foremore and deeper parts [of the lateral ventricles of the brain] are near to the Mammillary processes, and..they are in some manner transpassable.

† **trans'passage.** *Obs. rare*$^{-1}$. [f. TRANS- 1 + PASSAGE: cf. prec.] Passage over or across.

1603 DANIEL in *Florio's Montaigne* (1632) Pref. Verse, T'applaud his happy setling in our land: And safe transpassage by his studious care Who both of him and us doth merit much.

† **trans'patronize**, *v. Obs. rare*$^{-1}$. [TRANS- 2.] *trans.* To transfer from one to another the patronage of (something).

a **1609** WARNER *Alb. Eng.* IX. *To Sir G. Carey* ii, To transpatronize from him To you mine orphant Muse.

† **trans'pear**, *v. Obs. rare.* Also -peer. [By-form of TRANSPARE, on analogy of *peer*, PEAR *v.*, *appear*, *compear*.] *intr.* To appear or become visible through something; also *fig.* to be apparent.

c **1645** HOWELL *Lett.* VI. lv, Those proofs..are not so clear, as those which break out, and transpeer through the dark clouds of adversity. **1654** Z. COKE *Logick* A ij, By this time then it transpears, That, as Nature needs Grace, so Grace desireth Nature.

transpeciate (trɑːn'spiːʃɪeɪt, træn-), *v.* Now *rare.* [f. TRANS- + L. *speciēs* look, appearance, form, kind, SPECIES + -ATE^{3}.] *trans.* To change into a different form or species; to transform.

1643 SIR T. BROWNE *Relig. Med.* I. §30, I do not credit.. that the Devil hath a power to transpeciate a man into a Horse. **1694** WESTMACOTT *Script. Herb.* (1695) 77 Revived and transpeciated into a quite different and highly useful form. **1721** BAILEY, *Transpeciated*,..changed from one species to another. **1894** G. S. HALL in *Forum* (N.Y.) May 309 There is no better test of educational institutions..than ..how far the lower has been transpeciated into the higher.

Hence **transpeci'ation**, transformation; change from one form or species into another.

1867 MAUDSLEY *Physiol. Mind* 164 Transpeciation is a word used by Sir Thomas Brown which might be found useful at the present day. **1870** —— *Body & Mind* 175 For the exaltation and transpeciation of force and material. **1883** —— *Body & Will* II. iii. 132 First, that there has been what we may call a *nisus* of evolution in nature, and, secondly, that progressive transpeciations of matter have been events of it.

transpecific, var. TRANS-SPECIFIC *a.*

trans'penetrable, *a. rare.* [f. TRANS- 1 + PENETRABLE.] Penetrable from side to side.

1615 JACKSON *Creed* IV. II. vi. §7 The body of the earth (which is not transpenetrable by any light) is directly interposed between the sun and moon.

transpeptidation (ˌtrɑːnspɛptɪ'deɪʃən, ˌtræns-, -nz-). *Biochem.* [f. TRANS- 10 + PEPTIDE + -ATION.] Any reaction in which a peptide bond is broken and the free carboxyl (or amino) group joined to the amino (or carboxyl) group of another molecule so as to form a new peptide bond.

1950 J. S. FRUTON in *Yale Jrnl. Biol. & Med.* XXII. 264 Reactions of this type may be termed 'transpeptidation' or 'transamidation' processes. **1975** *Nature* 10 Apr. 482/2 Various cell-free transpeptidation systems are now known to be sensitive to penicillin.

So **trans'peptidase** [-ASE], any enzyme that catalyses transpeptidation.

1952 C. S. HANES et al. in *Biochem. Jrnl.* LI. 25/1 The enzyme will be referred to as γ-glutamyl transpeptidase. **1981** *Sci. Amer.* June 68/1 The vulnerable enzymes are either transpeptidases (which cross-link one peptide chain of new peptidoglycan to another by displacing a terminal D-alanine) or D-carboxypeptidases (which remove a terminal D-alanine by hydrolysis without cross-linking taking place).

trans,perito'neal, *a. Anat.* [f. TRANS- 5 + L. *peritonēum*: cf. *peritoneal*.] Traversing the peritoneal cavity. Hence **trans,perito'neally** *adv.* So **trans'peritone** *a.*

1891 *Cent. Dict.*, Transperitoneal. **1899** *Syd. Soc. Lex.*, Transperitone. **1900** *Lancet* 18 Aug. 487/1 A case of transperitoneal ligature of the left common iliac artery. **1903** *Ibid.* 6 June 1591/1 The external iliac artery was ligatured transperitoneally just below its origin.

trans'personal, *a.* [f. TRANS- 4 + PERSONAL *a.*] That transcends the personal, transindividual; *spec.* designating a form of psychology or psychotherapy which seeks to combine elements from many esoteric and religious traditions with modern ideas and techniques.

1905–6 W. JAMES in R. B. Perry *Thought & Char. W. James* (1935) II. 445 That an idea represents an 'object' may mean that it represents something either:—1. Trans-*personal*—as when my object is also your object; [etc.]. **1955** *Bull. Atomic Sci.* Apr. 109/1 Science provides the model of a free society of reasonable men co-ordinating themselves voluntarily in the light of a transpersonal standard. **1968** *Jrnl. Humanistic Psychol.* VIII. 77 Transpersonal (or Fourth Force) Psychology is the title given to an emerging force in the psychology field by a group of psychologists and professional men and women..who are interested in those *ultimate* human capacities and potentialities [etc.]. **1972** *Science* 16 June 1203/2 Experiences of ecstasy, mystical union,..and transpersonal knowledge..are simply not treated adequately in conventional scientific approaches. **1980** R. HERINK *Psychotherapy Handbk.* 684 Transpersonal Psychotherapy can be said to have evolved..as the inner or esoteric teachings of all the great spiritual traditions.

transphasor (trɑːns'feɪzə(r), træns-, -nz-). *Electronics.* [f. TRANS(IST)OR *sb.* with PHAS(E inserted.] A semiconductor device in which one light beam can be modulated by another.

1979 MILLER & SMITH in *Optics Communications* XXXI. 101/2 We report the first realisation of an optically bistable device in a semiconductor crystal as well as observation of differential gain both in one beam and, via the modulation of the transmission of one laser beam by a second, in a two beam system. This latter device is analogous to the three terminal transistor and, operating by transferred phase thickness, we term it a 'transphasor'. **1984** *Sunday Times* 18 Mar. 80/1 In a transistor a small electrical current can be used to switch an electrical voltage between a high and a low value... The transphasor does exactly the same thing with laser beams.

transphe'nomenal, *a. Philos.* [f. TRANS- 4 + PHENOMENAL *a.* (*sb.*).] That transcends or goes beyond the phenomenal. Hence **transphe-nome'nality**.

1897 W. M. URBAN *Hist. Princ. Sufficient Reason* vi. 87 The validity of this logical postulate in trans-phenomenal usage. **1904** [see DEREALIZE *v.*]. **1954** W. DESAN *Tragic Finale* ix. 178 Sartre claims that the existence of the external *transphenomenal* being is the condition of my *phenomenal* perception. **1957** H. E. BARNES tr. *Sartre's Being & Nothingness* p. l, The phenomenon of being..is an appeal to being; it requires as phenomenon, a foundation which is transphenomenal. The phenomenon of being requires the transphenomenality of being.

trans,phosphory'lation. *Biochem.* [f. TRANS- 10 + PHOSPHORYLATION.] The transfer of a phosphate group from a molecule of one compound to one of another.

1943 *Jrnl. Biol. Chem.* CXLVIII. 119 Transphosphorylation from adenosine diphosphate to glucose also results in the liberation of 1 acid equivalent. **1970** *McGraw-Hill Yearbk. Sci. & Technol.* 62/2 A transphosphorylation reaction..transfers the phosphate from the hydroxyl of the adjacent nucleotide to the hydroxyl of the pyrimidine sugar, giving a cyclic phosphate.

transpicuous (trɑːn'spɪkjuːəs, træn-), *a.* [f. med. or mod.L. *transpicu-us*, f. L. *transpic-ĕre* to look or see through (f. TRANS- + *specĕre* to look), on analogy of *conspicuous*, *perspicuous*.] That can be seen through; pervious to vision.

1638 WILKINS *New World* I. (1684) 75 Of this Opinion also was *Cæsar la Galla*, whose Words are these, 'The Moon doth there appear Clearest, where she is Transpicuous [*luna est transpicua*], not only through the Superficies, but the Substance also. **1667** MILTON *P.L.* VIII. 141 That light, Sent from her [the earth] through the wide transpicuous aire, To the terrestrial Moon. **1762–71** H. WALPOLE *Vertue's Anecd. Paint.* (1786) IV. 258 Light corridores, and transpicuous arbours through which the sun-beams play. **1910** *Athenæum* 9 Apr. 432/3 A region of mist..no instrument of science can render transpicuous to our eyes.

b. *fig.* Of language, etc.: Plain, clear in meaning; also *gen.* easily perceived or detected; manifest. Cf. TRANSPARENT 2.

1877 PATMORE *Unknown Eros* I. 2 The lonely suns, the mystic hazes and throng'd sparkles bright That..In sweet transpicuous words, shall glow alway. **1896** T. HUTCHINSON in *Academy* 28 Mar. 256/1 Far-reaching and luminous thought..incarnated in language correspondingly grave and transpicuous, or ardent and sublime. **1908** *Month* Jan. 8 Why should we not have new words, so they be musical and their meaning transpicuous?

Hence **tran'spicuously** *adv.*, clearly (in meaning).

1839–52 BAILEY *Festus* xx. 358 To speak transpicuously of things Divine Pertaineth not to nature.

transpierce (trɑːns'pɪəs, træns-), *v.* [a. F. *transpercer*, f. TRANS- + *percer* to pierce. Cf. TRESPERCE.]

1. *trans.* To pierce through from side to side (with the agent or the instrument as subject: cf. PIERCE *v.* 1).

1594 DRAYTON *Idea* i, Then transpierce the Coarse. **1624** HEYWOOD *Gunaik.* III. 160 She snatcht up a sword with which she transpierst her selfe. **1697** DRYDEN *Æneid* II. 68 The sides transpierced return a rattling sound. **1725** POPE *Odyss.* x. 188, I launch'd my spear, and with a sudden wound Transpierc'd his back, and fix'd him to the ground. **1857** DUFFERIN *Lett. High Lat.* xii. (ed. 3) 364 He falls, transpierced by many wounds.

b. *transf.* and *fig.*: esp. said of the effect of emotion, and the action of wind, light, sight, etc.

1598 DRAYTON *Heroic. Ep.*, *C'tess Salisbury to Bl. Prince*, Is that great hart, that did aspire so hie, So soone transpersed with a womans eye? **1601** DANIEL *Civ. Wars* VI. cxiv, Whereof the proofe was such As sharpest pride could not transpearce the same. **1664** EVELYN *Kal. Hort.*, *Mar.* (1729) 197 The sharp Easterly and Northerly Winds transpierce, and dry them up. **1788** GIBBON *Decl. & F.* xlvi. IV. 479 *note*, The eye of Tacitus seems to have transpierced the camp of the Parthians and the walls of the haram. **1841–4** EMERSON *Ess.*, *Spir. Laws* Wks. (Bohn) I. 67 The divine question which searches men, and transpierces every false reputation.

2. To make one's way through; to pass through, penetrate; in quot. 1908, to extend through. *rare.*

1604 W. HARBERT *Poems* (Grosart) 92 If England's loade-starre..Could the firme center's regiment transpearse. **1796** KIRWAN *Elem. Min.* (ed. 2) I. 93 Compound spar... In a porcelain heat, it vitrifies with the crucible, which it transpierces. **1908** *Athenæum* 6 June 701/3 A metal rod.. transpierces the box.

Hence **trans'pierced** *ppl. a.*; **trans'piercing** *vbl. sb.* and *ppl. a.*

1592 DANIEL *Compl. Rosamond* Wks. (1717) 42 Transpiercing Rays of christal pointed Eyes. **1627–77** FELTHAM *Resolves* II. xlv. 247 Such transpiercings as rankle the flesh within. **1838** MRS. BROWNING *Isobel's Child* x, Dear Lord, who spreadest out above Thy loving, transpierced hands.

tran'spinal, *a. Anat.* [ad. mod.L. *transpīnālis*, f. TRANS- + L. *spīna* SPINE.] Of a muscle: Lying between two successive transverse vertebral processes; = INTERTRANSVERSE.

transpirable (trɑːn'spaɪərəb(ə)l, træn-), *a.* [ad. med. or mod.L. *transpīrābilis*, or a. F. *transpirable* (*c* 1560 Paré): see TRANSPIRE and -ABLE.] Admitting of transpiration; capable of being breathed through.

1578 BANISTER *Hist. Man* I. 7 Neither would substance of such, be anything so transpirable as were in that Case expedient. **1611** COTGR., *Transpirable*, transpirable, easie to breath out or through. **1674** R. GODFREY *Inj. & Ab. Physic* 69 So long as we live, our whole Body..is transpirable, and exspirable. **1687** A. LOVELL tr. *Thevenot's Trav.* I. 260 A Bardaque, or Pot, that is Transpirable. **1720** QUINCY tr. *Hodges' Loimologia* 212 The Body must be kept transpirable. **1870** ROLLESTON *Anim. Life* 121 To keep the gill-plates lubricated and transpirable by their secretion.

Hence **transpira'bility**, the quality of being transpirable.
1864–72 WATTS *Dict. Chem.* II. 821 Transpirability of Gases. 1870 ROLLESTON *Anim. Life* 35 The transpirability of the skin.

†**tran'spirately**, *adv. Obs. rare*$^{-1}$. [f. mod.L. **transpīrāt-us*, pa. pple. of *transpīrāre* to TRANSPIRE + -LY².] By or in the way of transpiration.
(But possibly a misprint for *transpiratively*.)
1578 BANISTER *Hist. Man* I. 6b, Those grosse..fumosities (which otherwise by the seamy Commissures, would transpirately euaporate).

transpiration (trɑːnspɪ'reɪʃən, træns-). [ad. med. or mod.L. *transpīrātiōn-em*, n. of action from *transpīrāre* to TRANSPIRE; perh. through F. *transpiration* (1541 in Hatz.-Darm.).] The action or process of transpiring.
1. Exhalation through the skin or surface of the body; formerly, also, evaporation. Also *concr.* matter transpired.
1562 BULLEYN *Bulwark, Dial. Soarnes & Chir.* 16b, Expulsed, or auoided by inuisible transpiracion, which is one of the forces, or benefits of nature. 1605 TIMME *Quersit.* I. xv. 75 Mercury and sulphur doe vanish away by an insensible transpiration. 1707 *Curios. in Husb. & Gard.* 102 A viscous humour,..a plain Transpiration from the Plant. 1718 OZELL tr. *Tournefort's Voy. Levant* I. 131 It supples and mollifies the Skin, thereby facilitating Transpiration. 1826 KIRBY & SP. *Entomol.* IV. xli. 130 The substance secreted appears to be a transpiration through the pores of the body. 1879 G. GLADSTONE in *Cassell's Techn. Educ.* IV. 204/1 The products of transpiration are always of a more or less oily nature. 1898 P. MANSON *Trop. Diseases* xxii. 338 The excessive loss of fluid by cutaneous transpiration creates a powerful thirst.
†**b.** Emanation, effluence. *Obs. rare.*
1652 J. WRIGHT tr. *Camus' Nat. Paradox* x. 248 It is probable that by some kinds of transpiration, or by the means of Spirits, things acted at a distance are conveyed to persons absent, and represented to them in their sleep. 1675 TRAHERNE *Chr. Ethics* 74 A mystery..perhaps founded in a grateful transpiration of spirits from one to the other.
c. *fig.* Outflow (of affection, etc.).
1821–30 LD. COCKBURN *Mem.* 268 Always beloved for the constant transpiration of an affectionate and cheerful heart.
2. *Bot.* The exhalation of watery vapour from the surface of the leaves and other parts of plants, in connexion with the passage of water or sap through the tissues.
1551 TURNER *Herbal* I. Pij, The floures and leues.. whiche.. by ventyng out or transpiration maketh rype and digesteth. 1786 JEFFERSON *Writ.* (1859) II. 56 These leaves having a power of keeping themselves cool by their own transpiration, they impart no heat to the air by contact. 1878 MACNAB *Bot.* iv. (1883) 99 The water that plants give off as watery vapour by transpiration through the stomata.
attrib. 1895 OLIVER tr. *Kerner's Nat. Hist. Plants* I. 276 The bundles of woody cells and vessels..serve as conductors of the transpiration current. *Ibid.* 280 The stomata or transpiration-pores which pierce the epidermis of the leaf.
3. *Physics.* The passage of a gas or liquid under pressure through a capillary tube or porous substance.
1867 HIRST in *Brande & Cox's Dict. Sc.*, etc. s.v., The transpiration of a gas is uninfluenced by the material of which a tube is constructed; it increases with pressure—the greater the density, the shorter the time of transpiration. 1870 ATKINSON tr. *Ganot's Physics* (ed. 4) §132 For the same gas, the rate of transpiration increases, other things being equal, directly as the pressure.
4. The action or fact of something transpiring or becoming indirectly known; also, that which transpires (i.e. in quot. (*erron.*) happens). *rare.*
1802–12 BENTHAM *Ration. Judic. Evid.* (1827) III. 110 Causes of transpiration..disclosure, with or without treachery, on the part of one or more of the co-delinquents. 1908 *Academy* 7 Mar. 529/2, 'I there prosecuted my enquiries and observed for myself what transpired'. The transpirations are disappointing.

†**tran'spirative**, *a. Obs. rare.* [f. ppl. stem of med. or mod.L. *transpīrāre* to TRANSPIRE + -IVE.] Having the quality of transpiring, or a tendency to transpire.
1578 BANISTER *Hist. Man* I. 7 As if it should not haue passage out, after a certaine transpiratiue manner. 1662 J. CHANDLER *Van Helmont's Oriat.* 181 The whole arterial bloud..dispersed by the transpirative evaporation of the Body. 1753 N. TORRIANO *Gangr. Sore Throat* 55 The transpirative Matter,..carried back into the Mass of Humours, corrupts not only the Fluids,..but also the Solids.

transpiratory (trɑːn'spaɪərətən, træn-), *a. rare.* [f. as prec. + -ORY².] = prec.
1855 in H. CLARKE *Eng. Dict.* Hence 1860 in WORCESTER; and in later Dicts.

transpire (trɑːn'spaɪə(r), træn-), *v.* [ad. med. or mod.L. **tran(s)spīrāre* (f. TRANS- + *spīrāre* to breathe), or a. F. *transpirer* (*c* 1560 in Paré).]
1. a. *trans.* To emit or cause to pass in the state of vapour through the walls or surface of a body; *esp.* to give off or discharge (waste matter, etc.) from the body through the skin; of plants: to give off (watery vapour); also, to exhale (an odour); to breathe forth (vapour or fire).
1597 A. M. tr. *Guillemeau's Fr. Chirurg.* 40b/1 When as we desire to transpire, and cause to evaporate, any venomouse vapours. 1647 CRASHAW *Hymn, 'Name of Jesus'*, With wider pores..More freely to transpire That impatient fire. 1664 EVELYN *Sylva* (1776) 29 It transpires the rest of the liquid at the Summites and tops of the branches into the atmosphere. 1774 GOLDSM. *Nat. Hist.* (1862) I. viii. 37 At the [quicksilver] mines near the village of Idra..some in a manner transpiring quicksilver at every pore. 1815 KIRBY & SP. *Entomol.* (1828) I. vi. 201 Aphides that transpire a cottony excretion. 1840 J. BUEL *Farmer's Comp.* 122 Some species transpiring their weight of moisture every twenty-four hours. 1878 MACNAB *Bot.* iv. (1883) 101 For the same reason cut flowers wither. The leaves transpire more fluid than the stem can take up. 1908 A. BENNETT *Old Wives' T.* III. ii, The air was heavy with the natural human odour which young children transpire.
b. To cause (a gas or liquid) to pass through the pores or walls of a vessel.
1864–72 WATTS *Dict. Chem.* II. 820 The volume [of gas] transpired in equal times is inversely as the length of the tube. 1889 ANDERSON in *Nature* 19 Sept., Not only are gases occluded, but they are also transpired under favourable conditions of temperature and pressure.
c. *fig.* To cause to pass like breath. *rare.*
1641 J. JACKSON *True Evang. T.* I. 37 As if Severus had transpired his soule into Maximinus,..he now became the Wolfe, and Leopard.
2. *intr.* Of a body: †To emit vapour or perfume; to give out an exhalation (*obs.*); of the animal body (or a person); to give off moisture through the skin; to perspire (*obs.* exc. as rendering Fr. *transpirer*); now only of plants: to give off watery vapour from the surface of leaves, etc.
1648 HERRICK *Hesper., Appar. of Mistr. Calling him to Elizium* 7 This, that, and ev'ry thicket doth transpire More sweet than storax from the hallowed fire. 1673 O. WALKER *Educ.* 68 Exercises and recreations..such..as may cause the body to transpire plentifully. 1844 KINGLAKE *Eöthen* xviii. (1864) 237, I saw that the Doctor was transpiring profusely. 1878 MACNAB *Bot.* iv. (1883) 102 When the plant is transpiring most rapidly and most water is moving through the stem, the wood cells and vessels are filled with air. 1886 *Jrnl. R. Microsc. Soc.* Oct. 826 If transpiration is suddenly stopped in branches which ordinarily transpire strongly, the leaves fall.
3. a. *intr.* Of a volatile substance: To pass out as vapour through pores (in the human body or any porous substance), to exhale; of a liquid: to escape by evaporation.
1643 DIGBY *Observ. Relig. Med.* (1644) 81 In bodies which have internall principles of Heat and Motion, much continually transpiring out to make roome for the supply of new aliment. 1687 A. LOVELL tr. *Thevenot's Trav.* II. 62 Through these Jars the water transpires and percolates into an earthen Vessel underneath. 1746–7 HERVEY *Medit.* (1818) 161 A fragrance..peculiarly rich and reviving transpires from its opening tufts. 1794 G. ADAMS *Nat. & Exp. Philos.* II. xiii. 17 Moisture can transpire through our skin. 1815 KIRBY & SP. *Entomol.* (1818) I. ii. 29 One of those species [of Aphides] from the skin of which transpires a white cottony secretion. 1889 ANDERSON in *Nature* 19 Sept., Common coal-gas under high pressure transpires through the steel of the containing vessel.
b. *transf.* and *fig.* of non-material things.
1752 A. MURPHY *Gray's-Inn Jrnl.* No. 2 Anxiety and Solicitude, which soon transpire into the Face. 1753 *Ibid.* No. 51 An elegant Way of Thinking, which will be always sure to transpire into their Compositions. 1886 STEVENSON *Dr. Jekyll* ii, The mere radiance of a foul soul that thus transpires through, and transfigures, its clay continent.
†**c.** *trans.* To pass through the pores of. *Obs. rare*$^{-1}$.
1754 MILES in *Phil. Trans.* XLVIII. 526 Occasioned..by warm steams transpiring the earth.
4. a. *fig.* 'To escape from secrecy to notice' (J.); to become known, esp. by obscure channels, or in spite of secrecy being intended; to 'get wind', 'leak out'. Also *impers.*
1741–2 HT. BUTLER *Mem.* (1841) II. 96 Yesterday's quarrel may transpire. 1748 LD. CHESTERFIELD *Let. Dayrolles* 26 Jan., This letter goes to you, in that confidence, which I..place in you. And you will therefore not let one word of it transpire. 1754 RICHARDSON *Grandison* xxxvii. (1781) I. 265 Can he have so many Love-secrets, and yet will he not let them transpire to such a Sister? 1799 *Hull Advertiser* 1 June 2/4 The Hamburgh mail..has just arrived, but no particulars have transpired. 1821 JEFFERSON *Autobiog. & Writ.* (1892) I. 131 What passed between them did not transpire. 1856 FROUDE *Hist. Eng.* II. vii. 143 The conditions of the contract were not allowed to transpire. 1903 G. B. SHAW *Man & Superman* 209 We had hardly recovered from the fruitless irritation of this discovery when it transpired that the officers' mess of our most select regiment included a flogging club presided over by the senior subaltern. 1905 R. BAGOT *Passport* xxx, Not allowing the fact of there being any difficulty..to transpire to Donna Bianca. 1922 W. GERHARDI *Futility* III. vi. 173 It transpired that four regiments composing the division had gone over to the enemy. 1966 D. J. ENRIGHT *Conspirators & Poets* I. 16 But then, to our surprise, it transpires that he doesn't think much of our critics, either. 1982 I. HAMILTON *Robert Lowell* (1983) x. 144 Yaddo, it transpired, had been under FBI surveillance for some time.
¶**b.** Misused for: To occur, happen, take place.
Evidently arising from misunderstanding such a sentence as 'What had transpired during his absence he did not know'.
1775 A. ADAMS *Let.* 31 July in J. & A. Adams *Familiar Lett. Revolution* (1876) 91 There is nothing new transpired since I wrote you last. 1804 *Age of Inquiry* (Hartford, Conn.) 46 When..the reformation transpired in England..almost the whole nation rejoiced. 1810 F. DUDLEY *Amoroso* I. 14 Could short-sighted mortality..foresee events that are about to transpire. 1828 WEBSTER, *Transpire*..3. To happen or come to pass. 1841 W. L. GARRISON in *Life* (1889) III. 16 An event..which we believe transpired eighteen hundred years ago. 1848 DICKENS *Dombey* xxxii, Few changes—hardly any—have transpired among his ship's company. 1858 HAWTHORNE *Fr. & It. Note-bks.* I. 225 Accurate information on whatever subject transpired. 1883 L. OLIPHANT *Altiora Peto* I. 277 His account of what transpired was so utterly unlike what I expected.
¶**c.** Of time: To elapse. *Obs. rare. erron.*
1824 C. WORDSW. *Who wrote Eikon Basilike* 197 The interval of years which had transpired between the conversations and the account of them. 1827 —— *Chas. I* 1 Whether in the interval which has transpired, the convictions at which I had arrived,..have been in any material degree confirmed, shaken, or modified.
Hence **tran'spired** *ppl. a.*, **tran'spiring** *vbl. sb.* and *ppl. a.*
1670 MAYNWARING *Physician's Repos.* 21 A strengthening or transpiring Medicine. 1693 A. VAN LEEUWENHOEK in *Phil. Trans.* XVII. 842 As to the Transpiring Parts of our Bodies. 1725 *Bradley's Fam. Dict.* s.v. *Antimony*, This Diaphoretick alone may be taken..in malignant Fevers, to facilitate the transpiring of the Venom thro' the Pores. 1827 FARADAY *Chem. Manip.* xv. (1842) 345 The transpired matter on the surface of the skin. 1895 OLIVER tr. *Kerner's Nat. Hist. Plants* I. 274 The sap in the transpiring cells becomes more concentrated.

transpirometer (trɑːnspaɪ'rɒmɪtə(r), træns-). [f. TRANSPIRE (or its source) + -OMETER.] An apparatus for recording the amount of watery vapour transpired by a plant.
1904 *Science* 11 Mar. 424/2 An autographic transpirometer,..records..on a drum the transpiration of a plant for a week.

transpiry (trɑːn'spaɪərɪ, træns-). *rare.* [f. TRANSPIRE + -Y, after EXPIRY.] The fact of 'transpiring' or leaking out. In quot. misused for Occurrence.
1884 A. DANIELL *Princ. Physics* Introd. 3 All our arrangements..are subject to the transpiry of facts unknown or unforeseen at the time.

transplace (trɑːns'pleɪs, træns-), *v. rare.* [f. TRANS- + PLACE *v.*] *trans.* To change the place of, transpose; to oust from its position in favour of something else. (Also with the two things as obj.) Hence **trans'placing** *vbl. sb.*
1615 LAWSON *Country Housew. Gard.* (1626) 26 An artificiall transplacing or transposing of a twig, bud, or leafe, commonly called a graft. 1621 AINSWORTH *Annot. Ps.* xlii. 6 The Greeke readeth thus; the salvation of my face and my God; transplacing the Hebrew letters. 1641 WILKINS *Math. Magick* I. xi. (1648) 75 The transplacing of that Obelisk at Rome by Sixtus the first, was done in some few days by five or six hundred men. 1711 J. GREENWOOD *Eng. Gram.* 217 Of Transposition or the transplacing of words and sentences. *c* 1810 COLERIDGE in *Lit. Rem.* (1838) III. 205 'Not so killing but so secret'..transplacing the sentences 'as secret though not so killing'. 1878 VILLARI *Machiavelli* (1898) I. 16 In the 'Decameron' Latin periods already transform and transplace Italian periods.

transplant ('trɑːnsplɑːnt, 'træns-), *sb.* [f. next.]
1. a. That which is transplanted; *spec.* in forestry, a seedling transplanted once or several times; in *Surg.*, etc., an organ, tissue, etc., which has been transplanted into another person or animal.
1756 P. BROWNE *Jamaica* 163 Very few transplants of the kind thrive. 1885 P. MACOWAN *Rep. Cape Town Bot. Gard.* 1884. 9, A box of 25 transplants. 1898 F. WHITMORE in *Atlantic Monthly* Apr. 507/1 There was nothing for it but to sow seeds for transplants. 1913 *Arch. f. Entwicklungsmech. d. Organismen* XXXVII. 254 The homoeoplastic transplants in guinea pigs 5 and 8 were removed for microscopic examination. 1952, 1963 [see *heart transplant* s.v. HEART *sb.* 56]. 1977 J. GILLIS *Killers of Starfish* x. 81 Look a little closer. This hair hat of mine is a transplant... I'm a lot older than Trevor.
fig. 1891 M. DODS *Erasmus*, etc. 81 They do not appear as transplants in the writings of Plato.
b. One who is not native to his place of permanent residence. *U.S.*
1961 M. BEADLE *These Ruins are Inhabited* (1963) v. 73 If she's a good English wife, she doesn't tell him. If she's an American transplant, she does. 1973 T. TOBIN *Lett. G. Ade* 2 The bustling city [of Chicago], which was comprised of numerous rural transplants too busy with the business of living to establish traditions. 1979 *Tucson* (Arizona) *Citizen* 20 Sept. 1B/3 Traffic and the heat are two things the transplants mentioned.
2. The transferring of bacterial organisms from one medium to another for purposes of culture.
1900 *Jrnl. Exper. Med.* (U.S.) 25 Oct. 173 Both micro-organisms failed to survive the exposure, transplants failing to produce a growth on broth and on kidney.
3. *Surg.* An operation in which an organ, tissue, etc., is transplanted from one person or animal to another.
1951 *Sun* (Baltimore) 14 Mar. 34/1 He decided to try a transplant [of a tooth]. 1971 *Daily Tel.* 3 May 1/4 Prof. Christian Barnard..is standing by to carry out his first transplant for two years. 1982 *Sunday Times* 2 Sept. 16/2 It is a type of pneumonia usually found only where there are known causes for a breakdown in the immune system, as in cancer chemotherapy or transplants.
4. *attrib.*
1963 *Guardian* 22 Mar. 1/3 Surgeons at St Bartholomew's Hospital, London, this week carried out the hospital's first kidney transplant operation. 1967 *New Scientist* 7 Dec. 584/3 This [*sc.* the immune reaction] is the problem that

bedevils the whole of transplant surgery. **1968** *Observer* 7 Jan. 1/1 After that we can think about further selection of transplant patients. **1977** P. B. & J. S. MEDAWAR *Life Science* i. 8 The anxious question of whether or when a potential transplant donor..can be regarded as dead.

transplant (trɑːnsˈplɑːnt, træns-), *v.* [ad. post-cl.L. *transplantāre* (Itala, Luc. xvii. 6), f. TRANS- + *plantāre* to PLANT. Cf. F. *transplanter* (16th c.).]

1. *trans.* To remove (a plant) from one place or soil and plant it in another. Also *fig.*

c **1440** *Pallad. on Husb.* III. 504 Transplaunte hem so, & sone up wol they spring. **1555** EDEN *Decades* 135 Transplantyng the roote therof, [he] brought it from wyldenes to a better kynde. **1605** TIMME *Quersit.* I. xvi. 86 They are to be transplanted into home gardens. **1664** EVELYN *Kal. Hort., Aug.* (1729) 213 Transplant such Lettuce as you will have abide all Winter. **1768** STERNE *Sent. Journ.* I. *In the Desobligeant,* The man who first transplanted the grape of Burgundy to the Cape of Good Hope. **1842** TENNYSON *Amphion* x, Methods of transplanting trees.

2. To convey or remove from one place to another; to transport; *esp.* to bring (people, a colony, etc.) from one country to settle in another.

1555 W. WATREMAN *Fardle Facions* Pref. 9 Now gan thei tattempte..to transplante their progenie, and offspring into places unenhabited. **1606** in *Calr. S.P. Irel.* 553 The Grames and others to be transplanted into Ireland were charged with many children. *c* **1630** RISDON *Surv. Devon* §308 (1810) 317 These lands were transplanted into the name of the Poultons. **1769** E. BANCROFT *Guiana* 120 The Bull and the Cow..have been successfully transplanted into Guiana. **1860** PUSEY *Min. Proph.* 43 The policy of transplanting nations..was adopted, as a regular part of Assyrian, Babylonian, and Persian policy. **1899** A. E. GARVIE *Ritschlian Theol.* v. vii. 211 We cannot even transplant ourselves into the religious life of a pious Israelite.

3. *Surg.* To transfer (an organ or portion of tissue) from one part of the body, or from one person or animal, to another.

1786 [see *transplanted* below]. **1906** *Daily Chron.* 22 Sept. 6/7 A..case in which a child..suffering from cretinism, had a portion of its mother's thyroid gland transplanted into its spleen. *Ibid.*, Successful experiments in transplanting the blood vessels of animals. **1909** *Westm. Gaz.* 5 July 6/3 A dachshund, to which the kidneys of a fox-terrier had been transplanted..was apparently in perfect health.

4. *intr.* †**a.** (for *refl.*) To leave one place of abode and settle in another; to emigrate. *Obs.*

1608 [see TRANSPLANTING]. **1655** *Clarke Papers* (Camden) III. 24 The Irish are unwilling to transplant or prove theire qualificacions, but they will bee forc'd to goe and make way for the English planters. **1662** *Jesuits' Reasons* (1675) 130, Why..not..take up your roots and transplant?

b. (for *pass.*) To bear transplanting.

1796 C. MARSHALL *Gardening* xv. (1813) 248 Peas will transplant, and therefore broken rows may be made up. **1817–18** COBBETT *Resid. U.S.* (1822) 302 Persons of advanced age, of settled habits,..do not..'transplant well'. Of all such persons, Farmers transplant worst. **1846** *J. Baxter's Libr. Pract. Agric.* (ed. 4) II. 361 *Transplanting.*—Swedish turnips transplant very well, like the common cabbage; but the true turnip, the white globe or yellow, do not transplant.

Hence **trans'planted** *ppl. a.*

1765 *Museum Rust.* IV. 232 A six-shilling book..on the subject of transplanted lucerne. **1786** J. HUNTER *Treat. Venereal Disease* VII. i. §1 (1810) 586 The transplanted tooth fastened extremely well, and continued so for about a month. **1833** ALISON *Hist. Europe* (1849) I. i. §37. 83 Any transplanted Irishman, found out of his district, might be put to death by the first person who met him.

transplantable (trɑːnsˈplɑːntəb(ə)l, træns-), *a.* [f. prec. + -ABLE.] Capable of being transplanted.

1656 in P. H. Hore *Hist. Wexford* (1911) VI. 508 What popish proprietors of lands Transplantable, do yet remain untransplanted. **1824** MISS MITFORD *Village* Ser. I. (1863) 21 Cabbage-plants and celery, and all transplantable things. **1829** SOUTHEY *Sir T. More* (1831) II. 89 Old forms of government are not transplantable into new countries. **1913** *Jrnl. Exper. Med.* XVII. 482 Much has been added to our knowledge of..tissue grafting in warm blooded animals through the study of the transplantable tumors. **1973** *Nature* 18 May 163/1 These tumours are transplantable and have been transplanted for up to six consecutive passages.

Hence **transplanta'bility**, capability of being transplanted.

1811 W. TAYLOR in *Monthly Mag.* XXXI. 448 The transplantability of the fossils. **1867** T. ARCHER in Macfarlane *Mem.* vii. 185 Some plants are famed for transplantibility. **1913** *Jrnl. Exper. Med.* XVII. 482 (*heading*) Transplantability of tissues to the embryo of foreign species. **1977** *Nature* 6 Jan. 56/1 Increased malignancy of lymphoma cells [was] expressed by serial transplantability and capacity for widespread metastases.

trans'plantar, *a. Anat.* [f. TRANS- 5 + L. *planta* sole: cf. *plantar.*] Lying across the sole of the foot, as a ***transplantar muscle***.

1891 *Cent. Dict.* cites COUES. **1899** in *Syd. Soc. Lex.*

transplantation (trɑːnsplɑːnˈteɪʃən, træns-). [n. of action from TRANSPLANT *v.*: cf. *plantation.* So F. *transplantation* (16th c.).]

I. The action of transplanting.

1. The removing of a plant from one place or soil and planting it in another.

1601 HOLLAND *Pliny* XVII. x. I. 510 Neither need they any remoouing or transplantation at all. **1764** *Museum Rust.* IV. 38 The culture of lucerne by transplantation. **1796** C. MARSHALL *Garden.* xviii. (1813) 296 In all transplantations, it is proper to shorten some of the roots. **1856** DELAMER *Fl. Gard.* (1861) 25 Take them up for division and transplantation every fourth summer at longest.

2. Transference or removal from one place to another; transportation; *esp.* the removal of people from one country and settling of them in another.

1606 in *Calr. S.P., Irel.* 551 The transportation and transplantation of the Grames and other[s]..into the realm of Ireland. **1614** PURCHAS *Pilgrimage* IV. viii. (ed. 2) 385 Those which haue beene here seated by the transplantations of Tamerlane and Ismael..out of other Countries. **1625** GILL *Sacr. Philos.* I. 96 Their foolish thoughts concerning the transplantation of soules. **1633** in Row *Hist. Kirk* (Wodrow Soc.) 360 That all such oaths and subscriptions at ministers entrie or transplantation be discharged. **1720** QUINCY tr. *Hodges' Loimologia* 80 The Transplantation of the Plague from Turkey to Holland. **1882–3** *Schaff's Encycl. Relig. Knowl.* II. 927/2 The Gnostics taught a transplantation of the highest order..into the pleroma.

3. The pretended magical cure of disease by causing it to pass to another person, or to an animal or plant. *Obs.* or *Hist.*

1655 S. BOULTON (*title*) Medicina Magica..containing the general Cures of all Infirmities, by way of Transplantation. **1663** BOYLE *Usef. Exp. Nat. Philos.* II. v. xi. 227 An Example of a most violent pain of the Arme, removed by Transplantation. **1730** BAILEY (folio), *Transplantation* by Approximation (in Nat. Mag.) which is more properly called Approximation, as when a Whitlow is upon a Finger, and is cured by rubbing a Cat's Ear, which is supposed to receive the Pain. **1854–67** C. A. HARRIS *Dict. Med. Terminol.*, *Transplantation,*..a pretended method of curing diseases by making them pass from one person to another.

4. *Surg.* The operation of transferring an organ or a portion of tissue from one part of the body, or from one person or animal, to another.

1813 J. THOMSON *Lect. Inflam.* 239 Besides those examples that are seen in the transplantation of the teeth, it must be confessed that instances of reunion among parts which had been entirely separated are very rare in the human body. **1881** in *Philad. Record* No. 3472. 2 The object aimed at was nothing less than the transplantation of bone. **1890** BILLINGS *Med. Dict.*, *Transplantation,* removal of a portion of living tissue from its normal position, and uniting it with living tissue in another place, in order to repair a defect or lessen deformity. **1909** *Westm. Gaz.* 5 July 6/3 The operation of kidney transplantation.

II. 5. That which has been transplanted; a transplanted company or body.

a **1641** BP. MOUNTAGU *Acts & Mon.* vii. (1642) 467 Salmanassar brought Colonies, and transplantations of mixed people from the countries beyond Euphrates. **1805** W. TAYLOR in *Ann. Rev.* III. 236 He would by propagating and sheltering the new transplantations, have given a vernal ..luxuriance to the appearance of the whole surrounding growth.

transplan'tee. *rare*$^{-1}$. [f. as next + -EE[1] 2.] One who is transplanted.

a **1687** PETTY *Pol. Arith.* iv. (1691) 69 If the Nation who shall be admitted, shall be less able to prejudice and annoy the Transplantees into England than before.

transplanter (trɑːnsˈplɑːntə(r), træns-). [f. TRANSPLANT *v.* + -ER[1].]

1. a. One who transplants. Also *attrib.*

1611 COTGR., *Transplanteur,* a transplanter. **1755** JOHNSON, *Transplanter,* one that transplants. **1827** STEUART *Planter's G.* (1828) 240 The failure and decay of the Top (the great opprobrium of Transplanters) is primarily to be ascribed to the entire want of skill in the preservation of these fibrous roots, on which the Tree mainly depends. **1852** *Meanderings of Mem.* I. 21 So thence uprooted with transplanter care, In other soil it scents another air.

b. *spec.* in *Surg.*, a surgeon who carries out transplant operations.

1970 *Daily Tel.* 15 June 13/2 For Prof. Roy Calne,.. pioneer liver transplanter, there is only one problem: not enough organs are being transplanted. **1971** *Nature* 24 Dec. 440/3 To the transplanter it may well be that if an antibody to a particular antigen can be elicited..certain typing mismatches may be of no consequence. **1977** *Time* 7 Mar. 43 (*caption*) Kidney transplanter Stubenbord with patient Jose Serrano after surgery. **1984** A. SMITH *Mind* v. xv. 299 The needs of the transplanters formed a prime motive for redefining death.

2. An implement or contrivance for transplanting.

1828 WEBSTER, *Transplanter,*..2. a machine for transplanting trees. **1855** DELAMER *Kitch. Gard.* (1861) 16 The transplanter is a tool with handles at one end, and a couple of semicircular blades at the other, which, when closed, form a hollow cylinder. **1909** *Cent. Dict. Suppl.*, *Transplanter,* a horse-power machine used in setting out tobacco or other field plants.

transplanting (trɑːnsˈplɑːntɪŋ, træns-), *vbl. sb.* [f. as prec. + -ING[1].] The action of the vb. TRANSPLANT in various senses.

1608 in *Buccleuch MSS.* (Hist. MSS. Comm.) 77 The natives..will be at no charges in transplanting thither. **1655** FULLER *Ch. Hist.* x. Ded., Plants are much meliorated by transplanting. **1790** PALEY *Horæ Paul.* i. 2 The immediate transplanting of names and circumstances out of one writing into the other. **1883** G. B. GOODE *Fish. Indust. U.S.* 14 (Fish. Exhib. Publ.) The transplanting of fish was practised ..at the close of the last century. **1906** *Daily Chron.* 22 Sept. 6/7 Professor Garré, of Breslau, delivered an interesting lecture on the transplanting of blood vessels and organs.

b. *concr.* That which is transplanted.

1889 *Lancet* 20 Apr. 801/1 Such colonies become so intimately fused with others that not seldom the transplantings from them turn out impure.

c. *attrib.* as ***transplanting machine, wagon,*** etc.

1786 ABERCROMBIE *Gard. Assist.* 172 The transplanting kinds, as cabbage, savoys, broccoli, celery, endive. **1827** STEUART *Planter's G.* (1828) 182 The best and simplest transplanting machine now known. *Ibid.* 223 A cursory idea of my own Transplanting Nurseries. **1877** KNIGHT *Dict. Mech.*, *Transplanting-apparatus,* a machine or truck for removing trees for replanting. **1884** *Ibid.* Suppl., Transplanting Wagon. **1904** R. SMALL *Hist. U.P. Congregat.* I. 19 He was now [in 1841] beyond the transplanting age.

†**trans'plantively**, *adv. Obs. nonce-wd.* [f. an assumed adj. **transplantive* (f. as prec. + -IVE) + -LY[2].] In the way of transplantation.

1606 WARNER *Alb. Eng.* xv. xciv. 376 Her heart to his, his heart to hers, transplantiuely did passe.

tran'splendency. *rare.* [f. as next: see -ENCY.] The quality or condition of being transplendent; supereminent brilliancy or splendour.

1664 H. MORE *Antid. Idolatry* ii. 38 A supernatural and unimitable Transplendency of the Divine Presence. **1915** C. MACKENZIE *Guy & Pauline* 163 The clouds..suddenly melted in a wild transplendency of gold.

tran'splendent, *a. rare.* [f. TRANS- 1 + L. *splendĕnt-em*, pr. pple. of *splendēre* to shine, be bright. Cf. *resplendent.*] Brilliantly translucent; resplendent in the highest degree.

a **1541** WYATT *Compl. Absence of Love* 49 The clere cristall, the bright transplendant glasse. **1622** R. PRESTON *Godly Man's Inquis.* i. 16 Our weakenesse is so great, and his Maiestie on the other side is glorious and transplendent. **1854** J. S. C. ABBOTT *Napoleon* (1855) I. xi. 198 Those energies now so transplendent on the banks of the Mississippi and the Ohio.

Hence **tran'splendently** *adv.*, with surpassing splendour.

1664 H. MORE *Antid. Idolatry* ii. 36 The Divinity..is hypostatically, vitally and transplendently residing in this Humanity of Christ.

trans'pleural, *a. Surg.* [f. TRANS- 5 + L. *pleura*: cf. *pleural.*] Traversing the pleural cavity.

1891 in *Cent. Dict.* **1905** ROLLESTON *Dis. Liver* 149 A transpleural operation, letting out serous fluid from the pleura.

transplu'tonium, *a. Physics.* [f. TRANS- 11 + PLUTONIUM 2 b.] Of a chemical element: having a higher atomic number than plutonium (i.e. 95 or over).

1955 *Physical Rev.* XCIX. 1048/2 It [*sc.* the alpha radiation] was due to a transplutonium element. **1977** *Sci. Amer.* Mar. 29/2 In the absence of fast-neutron reactors..it would be impossible to completely burn the plutonium and its transplutonium derivatives produced by the slow-neutron plants.

trans'polar, *a.* [f. TRANS- 3 + L. *polus* pole + -AR[1]: cf. *polar.*] Crossing the (north) pole or polar region.

1850 SCORESBY *Cheever's Whalem. Adv.* i. (1855) 3 Daring adventures after a north-east or transpolar route to India. **1900** *Scribner's Mag.* Sept. 296/1 That branch which passed by a transpolar migration..from Siberia into Greenland.

transponder (trɑːnˈspɒndə(r), træn-, -nz-). [f. TRANS(MIT *v.* + RES)POND *v.* + -ER[1].] = RESPONDER 2 b.

1945 *Army & Navy Jrnl.* 18 Aug. 1534/4 *Transponder.* The unit in the IFF system which receives the challenge and automatically transmits the reply. **1945** *Electronic Engin.* XVII. 735/3 It became clear that such a 'transponder'.. could set up at any convenient place and would act as a beacon. **1957** [see RESPONDER 2 b]. **1967** R. J. SERLING *President's Plane is Missing* (1968) iii. 55 Henderson pushed the transponder button... The new identifying transponders were hooked to the altimeter. **1974** *Nature* 16 Aug. 558/2 The position of the Archimède was known within 10–200 m, depending on her distance from the nearest of the acoustic transponders. **1983** *Listener* 8 Sept. 6/1 The transponder code ought to have immediately alerted ground controllers.

†**trans'ponent**, *a. Obs. rare*$^{-1}$. [ad. L. *transpōnent-em*, pr. pple. of *transpōnĕre* to TRANSPOSE.] Transposing, transferring: in quot. (*erron.*) = transferred; immanent by communication.

1612 R. SHELDON *Serm. St. Martins* 10 How the attributes, and diuine perfections, of God were transponent in Christ.

trans'ponible, *a. rare*$^{-0}$. [f. L. *transpōn-ere* to transpose + -IBLE.] Capable of being transposed; transposable. So **transponi'bility**.

1891 in *Cent. Dict.* **1902** in *Cassell's Encycl. Dict. Suppl.*

transpontine (trɑːnsˈpɒntaɪn, træns-, -nz-), *a.* [f. TRANS- 3 + L. *pons, pont-em* bridge + -INE[1]. Cf. F. *transpontin* (16th c. in Godef. *Compl.*).]

1. That is across or over a bridge; *spec.* on the other side of the bridges in London, i.e. south of the Thames; *transf.* (from the style of drama in vogue in the 19th century at the 'Surrey-side' theatres), melodramatic, sensational.

1844 ALB. SMITH *Fort. Scatterg. Fam.* ix, It was Monday evening, sacred to the pits and galleries of transpontine theatres. **1860** MRS. P. BYRNE *Undercurrents Overlooked* I. 78 The..Metropolitan theatres, cispontine and transpontine. **1876** C. M. DAVIES *Unorth. Lond.* 130, I was wandering in transpontine London one Sunday morning. **1882** DE WINDT *Equator* 132 Triana, a transpontine suburb [of Seville], is worth a visit in the daytime. **1901** *Scotsman* 9 Apr. 5/4 A new drama strongly seasoned with transpontine flavour.

2. [f. L. *pontus* sea.] That is across the sea; on or from the other side of the ocean, *spec.* the Atlantic, i.e. North American.

1891 R. L. STEVENSON *Let.* Oct. (1923) XXII. 414 The last four chapters of *The Wrecker*!.. Ours is such rude, transpontine business. **1920** *Times Lit. Suppl.* 15 Apr. 232/2 She [*sc.* an American writer] has investigated her subject with typical transpontine enthusiasm. **1922** JOYCE *Ulysses* 416 Thou sawest thy America, thy life-task, and didst charge to cover like the transpontine bison.

transport ('trɑːnspɔːt, 'træns-), *sb.* [f. next. Cf. F. *transport* transfer of rights (1312 in Godef. *Compl.*), med.L. *transportus* (Du Cange) transferment.]

1. a. The action of carrying or conveying a thing or person from one place to another; conveyance.

1611 FLORIO, *Trasporto*, a transportation, a transport. **1621** ELSING *Debates H. Lords* (Camden) 11 The Bill against transport of golde and sylver. **1674** JOSSELYN *Voy. New Eng.* 12 Undertaking the Transport of his Family. **1841** ELPHINSTONE *Hist. India* II. IX. i. 277 Availing himself of the Jamna and Ganges for the transport of his stores and part of his army. **1844** H. H. WILSON *Brit. India* III. III. vi. 251 Sale at prices sufficient to cover the whole cost of transport. **1875** BENNETT & DYER *Sachs' Bot.* 634 The Conducting Tissue for the transport of the formative materials. **1894** *Geol. Mag.* Oct. 470 In the same way the beds at Moel Tryfaen are regarded as examples of glacial transport.

†**b.** *fig.* Transference. *Obs.*

1653 URQUHART *Rabelais* I. ii, Many are now poor wandring beggars.. who are descended of.. great Kings and Emperours, occasioned.. by the transport and revolution of Kingdoms and Empires.

†**c.** Transfer or conveyance of property. *Obs.*

App. the earliest use in English. It is the regular term for 'transfer of shares' in the Minute Books of the East India Company 1624–28.

1456 SIR G. HAYE *Law Arms* (S.T.S.) 133 Men takis landis.. and syne makis transport of thame, and puttis tham in othir menis handis. **1523** LD. BERNERS *Froiss.* I. ccxii. 258 The sayde renounciacion, transportes, sessynge, and leauynge of all the sayde thynges. **1607** (Nov. 13) *E. India Co. Court Bk.* II. 59 (MS.) Notwithstanding the transport made at the last Court of Mr. Bramley's adventure by Agnes Smyth to Mr. Robert Sandie. **1682** SCARLETT *Exchanges* 55 By this Endorsement, he to whom the Bill is sent, is the true and right Possessor of it, and needs no further Assignation, Transport, or any other Title or Right.

†**2.** Transference of a word to a different meaning; metaphor. *Obs. rare.*

1589 PUTTENHAM *Eng. Poesie* III. xvii. (Arb.) 189 To call the top of a tree, or of a hill, the crowne of a tree or of a hill .. because such terme is not applyed naturally to a tree, or to a hill, but is transported from a mans head to a hill or tree, therefore it is called by metaphore, or the figure of transport.

3. The state of being 'carried out of oneself', i.e. out of one's normal mental condition; vehement emotion (now usu. of a pleasurable kind); mental exaltation, rapture, ecstasy. Also with *a* and *pl.*, an instance of this, a fit of joy or rage; sometimes *transf.* an ecstatic utterance.

1658 PHILLIPS, A *Transport*,.. also a sudden trance, or rapture of minde. **1663** BP. PATRICK *Parab. Pilgr.* xiii. (1687) 84 Can you imagine into what transports it will cast your soul to hear the praises of the Creator sung by all his Works? **1686** tr. *Chardin's Trav. Persia* 146 An unheard-of Transport of Fury. *a* **1715** BURNET *Own Times* an. 1660 (1766) I. II. 151 The letter was received with transports of joy. **1796** JANE AUSTEN *Pride & Prej.* l, When the first transports of rage.. were over, he.. returned to all his former indolence. **1854** J. S. C. ABBOTT *Napoleon* (1855) I. xxvi. 413 He was hailed with transport wherever he appeared. **1920** D. H. LAWRENCE *Women in Love* i. 12 She experienced a keen paroxysm, a transport, as if she had made some incredible discovery. **1953** E. JONES *Sigmund Freud* I. xi. 275 A female patient suddenly flinging her arms around his neck in a transport of affection. **1978** A. S. BYATT *Virgin in Garden* xviii. 185 Almost she expected him to rouse himself and roar out transports of self-reproach or self-referring ecstasy, either of which would have embarrassed her profoundly. **1981** A. SCHLEE *Rhine Journey* ix. 111 She had gone on to describe.. the gentle transports she would expect her sensitive nature to endure, the blameless pious raptures.

4. A means of transportation or conveyance; orig. a vessel employed in transporting soldiers, military stores, or convicts; later, the horses, wagons, etc. employed in transporting the ammunition and supplies of an army; = *transport plane*; sometimes including the things so conveyed. Cf. *tape transport* s.v. TAPE *sb.*[1] 4.

1694 [implied in *transport-ship*: see 6]. **1712** E. COOKE *Voy. S. Sea* 140 At Five in the Afternoon, the Transports row'd for the Town of Guayaquil. **1783** JUSTAMOND tr. *Raynal's Hist. Indies* VII. 72 [He] took three thousand men of regular troops or of militia, which he embarked upon twenty-five transports. **1834** NAPIER *Penins. War* XVI. iii. (Rtldg.) II. 341 From the scarcity of transports only 38 guns could be brought to the trenches. **1855** MACAULAY *Hist. Eng.* xiv. III. 411 The Dee was crowded with men of war and transports. **1879** A. FORBES in *Daily News* 13 June 5/5 That all-important element in campaigning, the transport, including in that term the animals, the waggons, and the supplies. **1897** S. L. HINDE *Congo Arabs* 86 One woman and a boy acted as transport. **1900** *Dundee Advertiser* 17 May 4 All our larger transport has arrived without mishap. The men and horses are standing the continuous strain admirably, notwithstanding the heavy roads. **1940** *Times* (Weekly ed.) 7 Aug. 23 German tactics in attacking aerodromes, from the first attempt to divert the fighters to the arrival of low bombers and the landing of parachutists and troop transports are now well known. **1943** C. MILBURN *Diary* 11 Apr. (1979) 174 Forty transports going to supply the Axis were brought down. **1970** *Nature* 15 Aug. 655/2 The project to build a supersonic transport has run into renewed complaints from the environmentalists. **1974** C. RYAN *Bridge too Far* II. i. 79 Transports to carry paratroops and tow-planes to pull the gliders must be diverted from their normal task of supplying the advancing armies and grounded.

5. A transported convict; a person under sentence of transportation. Now *rare.*

1767 *Chron.* in *Ann. Reg.* 58/2 Fourteen transports from Durham.. were put on board.. bound for Virginia. **1777** HOWARD *Prisons Eng.* (1780) 386 The county has for some years.. clothed such transports as were quite indigent. **1817** *2nd Rep. Comm. Police Metrop., Min. Evid.* 392 Have you ever known any instances of returned transports obtaining licences to keep public houses? **1851** D. JERROLD *St. Giles* xix. 199 You don't mean to say.. that you are an escaped transport?

6. *attrib.* and *Comb.*, as ***transport-agent***, ***-carriage***, †***felon***, ***-hoy***, ***-labour***, ***-officer***, ***-service***, ***-wagon***, ***worker***, etc.; †**transport-bill**, †**debenture**, a voucher given for a claim for transport services; †**transport brief, deed**, a transfer-deed; **transport-buoy**, a buoy used for the mooring and warping of vessels; **transport café**, a roadside café for lorry-drivers; **Transport House**, the name of the former headquarters of the Labour Party, used as a synonym for the Labour Party leadership; **transport number** *Physical Chem.*, the proportion of a current flowing through a particular electrolytic solution which can be attributed to the movement of any given ion species; = *transference number* s.v. TRANSFERENCE 3; **transport plane** *Mil.*, an aircraft used for transporting troops, supplies, etc.; **transport-rider** (*South Africa*), a goods carrier; so **transport-riding**, carriage of goods; **transport-ship, -vessel**: see 4.

1897 J. K. LAUGHTON in *Dict. Nat. Biog.* LII. 156/2 He was appointed *transport agent for the expedition to Egypt. **1710** *Lond. Gaz.* No. 4637/3 Lost.., four *Transport-Bills, .. being for two Months Freight each on the Ship *Success*,.. Signed by.. her Majesty's Commissioners for Transportation. **1895** J. BROWN *Pilgr. Fathers* IV. 124 It was conveyed.. by a *transport brief or deed made on the 5th of May 1611. **1793** SMEATON *Edystone L.* §102 The use that was made of *Transport Buoys, in the moving and mooring the king's ships in the Hamoaze. **1938** 'J. CURTIS' *They drive by Night* i. 15 At St. Albans a lorry-driver was sitting hunched up at the counter of a *transport café. **1959** *Manch. Guardian* 29 July 14/3 On the London–Birmingham motorway.. there will be.. two transport cafés, but only one restaurant. **1978** C. A. BERRY *Gentleman of Road* xiii. 130 A welcome stay at the transport café.. on the strength of two cups of tea. **1895** *Daily News* 18 Oct. 5/5 Dr. Hönig's new bicycle *transport-carriages for sick people. **1707** *Lond. Gaz.* No. 4311/3 A *Transport-Debenture for the Year 1697. No. 32. for 965 l. 3 s. 4 d. is lost. **1766** *Chron.* in *Ann. Reg.* 134/2 Three hundred *transport felons.. have been shipped at Blackwall for the plantations. **1937** *New Statesman & Nation* 11 Sept. 364/2 This new orientation fits in exactly with that of the political wing of *Transport House. **1958** *Spectator* 31 Jan. 124/2 On the Labour side, it does not appear as though Transport House is even thinking of coming to grips with reality. *a* **1974** R. CROSSMAN *Diaries* (1975) I. 72 If we as a Cabinet have neglected our relationship with the Parliamentary Party we have equally neglected our relations with Transport House and the Party outside. **1705** *Lond. Gaz.* No. 4167/3 This day came into Kingroad.. two *Transport-Hoys. **1897** M. M. P. MUIR tr. *Lüpke's Elem. Electro-Chem.* I. iii. 43 A Cu ion will pass over two of six spaces, and a SO_4 ion will pass over four in the same time. The quotients $\frac{2}{6}$ = 0·33 and $\frac{4}{6}$ = 0·66 are called by Hittorf the *transport-numbers (die Überführungszahlen) for the kation Cu and the anion SO_4, respectively. **1978** P. W. ATKINS *Physical Chem.* xxv. 843 The following are brief summaries of the three methods used to measure transport numbers of ions and, through them, individual ion conductivities and mobilities. **1917** W. OWEN *Let.* 4 Feb. (1967) 431 It doesn't necessarily mean a job as *Transport Officer straight away. **1945** R. J. OAKES in *Coast to Coast 1944* 99 He had six wounded men to load into the *transport plane. **1977** M. SOKOLINSKI tr. *Merle's Virility Factor* xv. 307 The jeep.. led us straight into the maw of a transport plane that swallowed the truck. **1850** R. G. CUMMING *Hunter's Life S. Afr.* (1902) 10/2 The Dutchman along their road being very unfriendly and inhospitable to the English *transport-riders. **1909** R. CULLUM *Compact* xii. 143 Each waggon has two coloured transport-riders. **1900** HAGGARD *Black Heart* i, *Transport-riding—that is, in carrying goods on ox waggons from Durban or Maritzburg to various points in the interior. **1817** *Parl. Deb.* 584 A resolution then passed for 142,500*l.* for the *transport service. **1694** *Act 5 & 6 Will. & Mary* c. 23 §3 The *Transport Shipps for the Warr of Ireland. **1701** *Lond. Gaz.* No. 3712/3 Several Transport Ships are arrived at Williamstad with Recruits. **1722** DE FOE *Col. Jack* ii, Coming to the common period of that kind of life, I mean to me the transport-ship, or to the gallows. **1700** TYRRELL *Hist. Eng.* II. 795 Fourscore Cogs, a sort of small *Transport-Vessels. **1866** J. LEYLAND *Adventures Far Interior S. Afr.* 11, I travelled by a Dutch *transport waggon. **1936** in N. Rouillard *Matabele Thompson* ii. 46, I found myself at no great distance from a transport waggon, laden with goods intended for a trader in the north. **1903** *Westm. Gaz.* 8 Apr. 5/2 The railwaymen, who are federated with the *transport workers, declining to handle any traffic which had been unloaded by 'free' labourers.

transport (trɑːn'spɔːt, træn-), *v.* [ad. F. *transporter* (14th c. in Hatz.-Darm.), or its source L. *transportāre*, f. *trans* across + *portāre* to carry.]

1. *trans.* To carry, convey, or remove from one place or person to another; to convey across.

Formerly used in general sense: see quots.; now mostly restricted to the conveyance of persons, animals, and things as an organized operation, or with allusion to other senses.

1483 CAXTON *Gold. Leg.* 260 b/1 Where it shalle plese the to enhabyte it transporte me to the. **1490** —— *Eneydos* x. 39 They were separed & transported in-to dyuerse places. **1494** FABYAN *Chron.* VII. ccxxii. 245 Dyuers bysshoppes sees were transported from one place to another; as Selwey to Chechester, Kyrton to Exetoʳ, Wellys to Bathe,.. Dorchester to Lyncolne. *a* **1548** HALL *Chron., Edw. IV* 235 If the Duke of Britayne, would transporte hym into England. **1560** DAUS tr. *Sleidane's Comm.* 284 That he should neither make a brydge nor finde a foorde to transport his armie. **1579** *Galway Arch.* in *10th Rep. Hist. MSS. Comm.* App. v. 430 To tranchporte any manner tymber. **1599** SHAKS. *Hen. V*, II. Prol. 35 The Scene Is now transported (Gentles) to Southampton. **1606** in *Calr. S.P. Irel.* 551 To demise to the said Grames and such other persons as shall be transported.. 120 quarters of land. **1632** LITHGOW *Trav.* x. 457 He made fast the doore, and transported the keyes. **1635** SWAN *Spec. M.* vii. §3 (1643) 323 As a.. Mirrour transporteth the light of the fire, or the sunne against a wall. **1709** STEELE *Tatler* No. 3 ¶6 Mules to transport his Provisions and Ammunition. **1829** SCOTT *Anne of G.* ii, I have no wings to transport me from cliff to cliff. **1853** J. H. NEWMAN *Hist. Sk.* (1873) II. I. ii. 65 This region.. receiving the merchandize of East and North, and transporting it by its rivers. **1856** KANE *Arctic Explor.* II. vi. 75 The dogs are indispensable in.. transporting us to Anoatoh. **1901** [see TRANSPORTABILITY].

b. *fig.* (app. the earliest use.)

c **1374** CHAUCER *Boeth.* III. pr. ix. 65 (Camb. MS.) The errour and folye of mankynde departeth and deuydeth it,.. and transporteth from verray and parfyt good to goodes þat ben false and vnparfyt. *c* **1475** *Partenay* 3739 And in to sorow transport our gladnesse. **1509** HAWES *Past. Pleas.* xxxi. (Percy Soc.) 150 Consyder well that your lusty courage Age of his cours must at the last transporte. **1652** G. COLLIER *Vind. Sabbath* (1656) 45 The Apostolick churches transported the exercises of that day to the Sunday. **1798** FERRIAR *Eng. Historians* 234 They transport our imagination to the scene. **1857** W. SMITH *Thorndale* 547 Man transports himself into nature, endues the great objects or powers of nature with human feelings, human will.

†**c.** To transfer or convey (property). *Obs.*

1523 LD. BERNERS *Froiss.* I. ccxii. 257 All the right that oure sayde brother hath.., he yeldeth and transporteth them to vs perpetually. *Ibid.* 258, 259 [see CESS *v.*[2] 2]. **1607** (July 31) *E. India Co. Court Bk.* II. 44 (MS.) Sir James Deane's letter to the Company that his stock of the 3rd voyage, being £200, be transported over to the account of Andrew Holdip his kinsman. *a* **1649** DRUMM. OF HAWTH. *Hist. Jas. II* Wks. (1711) 24 Transporting lands to themselves and their friends, distributing offices and places of the crown and state.

†**d.** *intr.* for *refl.* To transfer oneself to another place of abode; to emigrate. *Obs.*

c **1540** tr. *Pol. Verg. Eng. Hist.* (Camden No. 29) 143 Six months after that he had transported into Flanders. **1631** WEEVER *Anc. Fun. Mon.* 794 He required him (before he transported) to returne. **1633** T. STAFFORD *Pac. Hib.* II. x. (1821) 338 It shall be lawfull for any of the Inhabitants.. to transport, without any molestation. **1675** tr. *Machiavelli's Prince* viii. (Rtldg.) 56 He transported into Africa.

†**e.** To remove from this world to the next: cf. TRANSLATE *v.* 1 b. *Obs.*

In quot. 1603, a euphemism for 'put to death, kill'. So taken by Schmidt in quot. 1590; but W. Aldis Wright takes it as, in Starveling's language, = 'transform, transfigure', comparing the use of 'translate' in III. i. 122.

[**1590** SHAKS. *Mids. N.* IV. ii. 4 He cannot be heard of. Out of doubt hee is transported.] **1603** —— *Meas. for M.* IV. iii. 72 A creature vnprepar'd, vnmeet for death, And to transport him in the minde he is, Were damnable.

2. *spec.* **a.** *Sc. Ch.* To translate (a minister) from one charge to another.

1637–50 ROW *Hist. Kirk* (Wodrow Soc.) 164 There wes an intention to have had four of the ministers of Edinburgh transported to other places. **1726** *Wodrow Corr.* (1843) III 257 Discharging them to be transported without the consent of the General Assembly, or declared transportable without consent of the people. *a* **1791** GROSE *Otio* (1796) 111 By transported we mean, in Scotland, removed to another parish. **1858** RAMSAY *Remin.* v. (1870) 118 A Seceding minister at Kircaldy. But I hear he expects to be transported soon. **1904** R. SMALL *Hist. U.P. Congregat.* I. 457 It was carried [in] 1830 by a great majority to transport.

b. *Sc. Eccl. Law.* To remove (the site of the church) to a different part of the parish.

1707 *Sc. Act Anne* c. 10 (1824) XI. 433/1 The transporting of Kirks,.. or erecting and building of new kirks, being alwayes with the consent of the heritors of three parts.. at least of the valuation of the parock whereof the kirk is craved to be transported or.. new kirks to be erected and built. **1765–8** ERSKINE *Inst. Law Scot.* I. v. §21 With more ample powers, of.. transporting churches already built to more convenient places. **1838** [see TRANSPORTATION 2 b].

c. To carry away or convey into banishment, as a criminal or a slave; to deport.

1666 *Act 18 & 19 Chas. II*, c. 3 §2 It shall be lawfull to and for the Justices.. to transport or cause to be transported the said Offenders.. into any of his Majestyes Dominions in America. **1667** PEPYS *Diary* 8 Sept., A prisoner being condemned at Salisbury for a small matter.. They were considering to transport him to save his life. **1759** HUME *Hist. Eng.* III. lxi. 326 The rest were sold for slaves and transported to Barbadoes. **1849** MACAULAY *Hist. Eng.* ii. I.

177 It was provided that the offender should not be transported to New England.

3. *fig.* To 'carry away' with the strength of some emotion; to cause to be beside oneself, to put into an ecstasy, to enrapture.

1509 HAWES *Past. Pleas.* xxv. (Percy Soc.) 179 But loke hye his hart to transport. **1596** SPENSER *Hymne Heavenly Beautie* iii, Transported with celestiall desyre Of those faire formes. **1604** E. G[RIMSTONE] tr. *D'Acosta's Hist. Indies* I. xxi. 69 They stood transported with amazement. **1667** MILTON *P.L.* III. 81 Onely begotten Son, seest thou what rage Transports our adversarie? **1712** ADDISON *Hymn*, '*When all thy mercies*', i, Transported with the view, I'm lost In wonder, love, and praise. **1840** DICKENS *Barn. Rudge* lxxi, Transported with the thought that rescue had at length arrived, Emma and Dolly shrieked aloud for help.

transportability (ˌtrɑːnspɔətəˈbɪlɪtɪ, ˌtræns-). [f. next + -ITY.] Capability of being transported; in early quots. referring to translation of ministers (see TRANSPORT *v.* 2 a, TRANSPORTATION 2 a).

1651 *Reg. Comm. Gen. Assembly* 24 Feb. (S.H.S.) III. 538 The motion anent Mr. George his transportabilitie is waved. **1676** ROW *Contn. Blair's Autobiog.* xi. (1848) 344 Mr. Blair supplicated the Presbytery of St Andrews for an act of transportability. **1846** in WORCESTER. **1883** *Century Mag.* July 430/2 The fever's.. transportability was fearfully proven. **1901** *N. Amer. Rev.* Feb. 222 The Transvaal war has shown the transportability.. of the heaviest artillery... The Boers transported their 'Long Tom' as they might have transported a piano.

transportable (trɑːnˈspɔətəb(ə)l, træn-), *a.* and *sb.* [f. TRANSPORT *v.* + -ABLE. Cf. F. *transportable* (1812 in Hatz.-Darm.); mod.L. *transportābilis*.]

A. *adj.* **1. a.** Capable of being transported.

1582 *Reg. Privy Council Scot.* III. 530 In uptaking of the custum of all gudis transportabill furth of this realme. **1642** *Declar. Lords & Comm. to Gen. Assemb. Ch. Scot.* 13 [Soldiers] to be sent presently over to reside amongst them, or declared transportable. **1676** *Phil. Trans.* XI. 680 A Chest of Copper,.. transportable by means of woodden barrs like a Sedan or Chair. **1726** [see TRANSPORT *v.* 2 a]. **1881** J. RUSSELL *Haigs* v. 105 Bringing off whatever was transportable on its own four feet. **1904** R. SMALL *Hist. U.P. Congregat.* II. 1 The Presbytery declared him transportable.

b. *spec.* of computer software: that can be used on more than one kind of machine.

1972 *Rep. Nat. Res. Council Canada* No. 13659 (ERIC Rep. No. 160126) 4 Facilities for producing 'transportable' computer based course materials. **1977** *Proc. Internat. Symp. Computer Aided Seismic Analysis* 121/1 PAL, through its structured logic and easily transportable software, provides a framework which will readily accept modification and expansion. **1983** *Mini-Micro Systems* Feb. 71/3 DEC is encouraging software producers in Europe to make software transportable between countries.

c. Of a computer (see quots. 1983, 1985).

1982 *Byte* Nov. 6 Portable.. refers to a small, transportable computer on which you can touch-type. **1983** *Times* 31 May 20/4 The new breed of portable computers makes some of the older machines.. look immovable by comparison... Once known as portable computers, these machines are now dubbed transportable computers, to distinguish them from smaller machines that are more easily moved. **1985** *Pract. Computing* Jan. 70/3 Although called the Portable, the machine is.. what is more normally termed transportable. That is, it is a mains-powered unit which.. is too heavy to be carried around all the time.

2. Involving or liable to transportation.

1769 BLACKSTONE *Comm.* IV. xvii. 242 The statute.. makes it a felony transportable for seven years. **1815** MISS MITFORD in L'Estrange *Life* (1870) I. 323 It does not.. appear that he ever committed any hangable or transportable offence. **1840** GEN. P. THOMPSON *Exerc.* (1842) V. 371, I remember once discovering that I was living in the commission of transportable offences at the rate of two a-day.

B. *sb.* A transportable television set, computer, etc., *spec.* one which is heavier than a 'portable' appliance.

1959 *Daily Tel.* 27 Aug. 11/3 The transportable [*sc.* a television] is something comparatively new. It has a carrying handle, yet is too heavy to be classed as a lightweight portable. **1971** *Radio Times* 25 Nov. 35 (Advt.), The Deccavision Executive 17" transportable—a black-and-white TV that gives big, bold performance wherever there's a mains point. **1983** *Observer* 19 June 21/1 Although perception of portability differs radically, three categories can be discerned... These are the handhelds, the true portables, and the transportables. **1983** *Austral. Microcomputer Mag.* Nov. 76/1 Despite the provision of a high level of computing power in such recent hand-held portables.., there always should be room for larger transportables.

Hence **tranˈsportableness**, the quality of being transportable; liability to transportation.

1727 in BAILEY vol. II. **1844** P. HARWOOD *Hist. Irish Reb.* 107 Transportableness for life.

†**tranˈsportage.** *Obs.* [f. as prec. + -AGE. Cf. PORTAGE.] = TRANSPORTATION 1, TRANSPORT.

1562 J. SHUTE *Cambini's Turk. Wars* 9 Almost.. oute of hope of any transportage for them. **1600** HOLLAND *Livy* XLIII. xii. 1163 He should give order for their transportage thither. **1631** HEYWOOD *1st Pt. Fair Maid of West* I. i. Wks. 1874 II. 273 Such gold fit for transportage as I have, I'le beare along. **1637** —— *Royall Ship* 12 Vessels.. for the transportage of graine from one province to another.

So **tranˈsportal, tranˈsportance** [see -AL[1], -ANCE: cf. *importance*], transport, conveyance.

1837 DARWIN in *Life & Lett.* (1887) II. 9 Let the powers of transportal be such. **1839** —— *Voy. Nat.* ix. (1879) 187 To explain the transportal of these gigantic masses of rock. **1859** —— *Orig. Spec.* iv. (1866) 104 So as to favour.. the transportal of their pollen from flower to flower. **1893** SIR H. H. HOWORTH *Glacial Nightmare* II. 680 The transportal of drift in directions opposite to the movements of the ice. **1606** SHAKS. *Tr. & Cr.* III. ii. 12 Be thou my Charon, And giue me swift transportance to those fields. *c* **1611** CHAPMAN *Iliad* XVI. Comm. (1857) II. 105 Nor would Homer have any one believe the personal transportance of Sarpedon by Sleep and Death. **1615** BRATHWAIT *Strappado* (1878) 32 There's no fashion knowne, In forraine Courts,.. But by transportance it doth come to thee. **1882** G. MACDONALD *Castle Warlock* xxxi, A doubtful denial of transportance.

†**tranˈsportant,** *a.* *Obs.* *rare*[−1]. [f. as TRANSPORT *v.* + -ANT.] Transporting, ravishing.

1660 H. MORE *Myst. Godl.* VI. v. §5. 227 So rapturous a Joy, and transportant Love.

transportation (trɑːnspɔəˈteɪʃən, træns-). [n. of action f. TRANSPORT *v.* + -ATION. Cf. L. (post-Aug.) *transportātiōn-em* transmigration, and F. *transportation* (1519 in Hatz.-Darm.).]

1. a. The action or process of transporting; conveyance (of things or persons) from one place to another.

Much used in 17th c. down to *c* 1660; afterwards gradually given up for *transport*, prob. to avoid association with penal transportation, sense 2 c.

1540 *Act 32 Hen. VIII*, c. 14 §2 For the fraight transportation conveyaunce or cariage of anny warres. *a* **1600** in Hakluyt *Voy.* III. 174 By reason of the transportation of raw wooll of late dayes more excessiuely then in times past. **1607** HIERON *Wks.* I. 371 Looke how the case stood with their transportation out of Ægypt into Canaan. **1615** G. SANDYS *Trav.* 26 Here is a Ferry for transportation into Asia. *a* **1656** USSHER *Ann.* VI. (1658) 331 Finding no ships there, for his transportation, he divided his army. **1679–88** *Secr. Serv. Moneys Chas. & Jas.* (Camden) 16 To the Bishop of London, for transportac'on of three Chaplains to the Leward Islands.. 60 0 0. **1707** E. CHAMBERLAYNE *Pres. St. Eng.* I. vii. (ed. 22) 63 Upon the Three Articles of Exportation, Transportation or Re-exportation, and Importation, no Kingdom or State in the World can any ways match us. **1827** STEUART *Planter's G.* (1828) 264 It must make the Tree.. more troublesome to be balanced during the transportation. **1855** PRESCOTT *Hist. Philip II*, I. 118 The transportation of the troops was going ..on. **1890** *Wisconsin Hist. Soc. Prospectus*, Upon any gift to the Society, transportation will be cheerfully paid.

b. *Geol.* The movement of land-waste by rivers, ocean-currents, glaciers, wind, etc.

1830 LYELL *Princ. Geol.* I. 81 A geologist, who.. sees the decomposition of rocks, and the transportation of matter by rivers to the sea. **1877** LE CONTE *Elem. Geol.* III. v. (1879) 516 The general direction of the scorings corresponds with that of transportation of the bowlders.

2. *spec.* **a.** *Sc. Ch.* The translation of a minister from one charge to another.

1562 in Row *Hist. Kirk* (Wodrow Soc.) 24 Transportation declared lawfull where there is reason for it. **1663** BLAIR *Autobiog.* ii. (1848) 46 That assembly sets a note upon the act of my transportation. **1717** T. BOSTON in A. Thomson *Life* (1895) 129 In a time wherein there is so little need of transportations.

b. *Sc. Eccl. Law.* ***transportation of a church***, removal of the site of the church to a different part of the parish.

1838 W. BELL *Dict. Law Scot.* s.v. *Transportation of Churches*, The form of applying for transportation is by a summons raised before the Teind Court, concluding for authority to transport, and to have the new church declared the regular parish church.

c. Removal or banishment, as of a criminal to a penal settlement; deportation.

1669 in *10th Rep. Hist. MSS. Comm.* App. v. 95 If.. the said Rice Havard [a condemned felon] doe give in security for his transportacion as before mentioned. **1678** BUTLER *Hud.* III. II. 197 Neither Chains, nor Transportation, Proscription, Sale, nor Confiscation. **1727** GAY *Begg. Op.* I. xiii, Were you sentenc'd to Transportation? **1879** MCCARTHY *Own Times* II. xviii. 33 The sentence of death was changed into one of transportation for life.

3. *transf.* Means of transport or conveyance. *U.S.*

1853 J. L. MCCONNEL *Western Characters* 163 He furnished his own 'transportation', and selected his own encampment. **1861** *Times* 29 July, We captured.. all the enemy's camp equipage and transportation. **1869** T. W. HIGGINSON *Army Life* (1870) 236 There was no transportation to take us. At last, a boat was notified. **1890** *Century Mag.* Feb. 564/1 A lot of miscellaneous transportation, composed of riding horses, ambulances, and other vehicles. **1894** *Outing* (U.S.) XXIV. 234/2 Transportation is furnished for the horses of mounted officers.

b. A ticket or pass for travelling by a public conveyance. *U.S.*

1909 in *Cent. Dict. Suppl.* **1911** in WEBSTER.

†**4.** Transport (of feeling), rapture, ecstasy. *Obs.*

1617 COLLINS *Def. Bp. Ely* II. vii. 286 Not onely in extasie and transportation.. but in the daily forme of prayer. **1660** STANLEY *Hist. Philos.* IX. (1701) 373/1 A soul disturbed with anger or pleasure, or any other unbefitting transportation. **1690** LUTTRELL *Brief Rel.* (1857) II. 68 Which those poor people received with great transportations of joy.

5. *attrib.*, mostly in sense 1, as ***transportation agent, company, money, rate, sentence, system, -wagon***, etc.

1573–4 *Privy Council Acts* (1894) VIII. 212 To aunswer the conduct, transportacion money and wages acording to her Majesties usuall entertainement. **1819** J. A. QUITMAN in J. F. H. Claiborne *Life J. A. Quitman* (1860) I. 36, I went to the agent of a train of transportation-wagons. **1825** in T. L. McKenney *Memoirs* (1846) I. 299, I was appointed transportation agent for the United States at St. Louis. **1844** EMERSON *Lect.*, *Yng. American* Wks. (Bohn) II. 303 The private transportation-shop. **1866** 'MARK TWAIN' *Lett. from Hawaii* (1967) 274 Her transportation wagons will be the freight cars of the Pacific Railroad. **1883** G. B. GOODE *Fish. Indust. U.S.* 67 (Fish. Exhib. Publ.) The construction of refrigerating transportation cars. **1888** BRYCE *Amer. Commw.* II. App. 670 All railroad, canal, and other transportation companies are declared to be common carriers. **1891** *Athenæum* 26 Dec. 862/3 There is not much in it about Siberia,.. and the work is, in fact, one on the Russian transportation system. **1897** P. WARUNG *Tales Old Regime* 148 Her home record was bad, and most likely her transportation-sentence was life.

Hence **transporˈtational** *a.*, of, belonging or pertaining to transportation; **transporˈtationist**, one who favours the transportation of criminals.

1888 J. T. GULICK in *Linn. Soc. Jrnl., Zool.* XX. 230 Transportational segregation, caused by activities in the environment that distribute the organism in different districts. **1840** GEN. P. THOMPSON *Exerc.* (1842) V. 26 On the whole, we seem to have flurried the transportationists.

transportative (trɑːnˈspɔətətɪv, træn-), *a. rare.* [f. TRANSPORT *v.* + -ATIVE, after PORTATIVE.]

1. Adapted or liable to transportation; such as to be carried from place to place, portable.

1643 TRAPP *Comm. Gen.* xxxii. 6 The Ark was transportative, till setled in Solomon's temple. **1657** *Ibid.*, *Job* iv. 19 A tabernacle which hath no foundation, and is transportative. **1680** C. NESSE *Church-Hist.* 151 His ark should be no more transportative, but setled for a long season.

2. Having the quality of transporting.

1886 A. WINCHELL *Walks Geol. Field* 46 The transportative power of the stream had become so abated.

transported (trɑːnˈspɔətɪd, træn-), *ppl. a.* [f. TRANSPORT *v.* + -ED[1].]

1. Conveyed from one place to another.

1693 EVELYN *De la Quint. Compl. Gard.* I. II. x. 26 There is but little to be said.. of Transported Earth,.. it is a Novelty our Age has introduc'd in Gard'ning. **1830** LYELL *Princ. Geol.* I. 193 At the base of such hollow ravines was seen a wide and deep mass of ruins, consisting of transported earth, gravel, rocks, and trees.

b. Compulsorily carried to a distant country.

1728 GAY *Polly* I. (1777) 18 Since he came over [to America] he married a transported slave. **1743** BULKELEY & CUMMINS *Voy. S. Seas* 20 Those Grandees.. in a few Minutes look'd like a Parcel of transported felons. **1890** *Daily News* 18 Sept. 6/1 The transported of 1851 and of 1871 are looked upon as revolutionists who only got what they deserved.

2. 'Carried away' by excitement or vehement emotion; excited beyond self-control; enraptured.

1600 E. BLOUNT tr. *Conestaggio* 247 Troublesome and transported subiects. **1685** BOYLE *Enq. Notion Nat.* v. 173 Like a passionate and transported thing, oppose it,.. with such blind violence. **1746–7** HERVEY *Medit.* (1818) 29 The fondness of thy transported husband. **1874** MOTLEY *Barneveld* I. ii. 177 He had never seen a man so desperate, so transported.

Hence **tranˈsportedly** *adv.*, in a transported manner, in a transport; **tranˈsportedness**.

1652 LOVEDAY tr. *Calprenede's Cassandra* I. 56 [She] *transportedly cryed out [etc.]. **1713** C'TESS WINCHELSEA *Misc. Poems* 27 Assemble here, you watry Race, Transportedly he cries. **1804** J. COLLINS *Scripscrap.* 28 The thief a new Region transportedly hails. *a* **1656** BP. HALL *Rem. Wks.* (1660) 420 Titular respects which those.. can weild without any such taint or suspicion of *transportedness.

transportee (trɑːnspɔəˈtiː, træns-). [f. as next + -EE.] A transported convict.

1883 *Chambers' Encycl.* IX. 518/1 The criminal classes.. heard more about the success than the hardships of the transportees.

transporter (trɑːnˈspɔətə(r), træn-). [f. TRANSPORT *v.* + -ER[1].]

1. One who transports.

1535 *Act 27 Hen. VIII*, c. 14 §1 The said.. Tanners or other person transporter of the same Lether. **1562–3** *Act 5 Eliz.* c. 12 §4 No.. Carrier, Buyer or Transporter of Corne. **1615** G. SANDYS *Trav.* 209 A thing usuall it is betweene Tripoly and Aleppo.. to make tame Doues the speedy transporters of their letters. **1744** J. PATERSON *Comm. Milton's P.L.* 305 The transporter of departed souls into hell. **1906** *Times* 21 Aug. 5/1 The result of the increased number of transporters is that the price of everything has fallen.

2. Any carrying apparatus; *esp.* a device for transporting coal from a quay or from one vessel to another. Also, a vehicle used to transport other vehicles or large pieces of machinery, etc., by road.

transporter-bridge, a bridge over a navigable waterway, high enough not to interfere with navigation, carrying a suspended platform or car which travels from bank to bank and conveys the traffic. So ***transporter car***.

1893 *Westm. Gaz.* 25 July 5/2 Mr. Temperley's ingenious contrivance for coaling rapidly... The 'transporter', as it is called, is made of steel, beam-shaped,.. and fitted with an automatic travelling carriage suspended from the lower flange of the beam. **1894** *Ibid.* 31 July 7/1 The 'B' Fleet has now been coaled with exceptional rapidity and without recourse to the Temperly transporter. **1904** *Ibid.* 2 Sept. 10/2 The Runcorn Transporter Bridge, now being erected, has its towers made wholly of steel. They rise 190 ft. above high-water level. *Ibid.*, The transporter car.. is suspended from the trolly by steel-wire ropes. *a* **1944** K. DOUGLAS

Alamein to Zem Zem (1946) xi. 68 The tanks were to move by transporter. **1976** L. DEIGHTON *Twinkle, twinkle, Little Spy* xxi. 206 In the Sahara there were only Peugeots, and Landrovers, and the smart little cars that came in by transporter.

transporting (trɑːn'spɔətɪŋ, træn-), *vbl. sb.* [f. as prec. + -ING¹.] The action of the verb TRANSPORT; transportation.

1500 in *10th Rep. Hist. MSS. Comm.* App. v. 391 After the transporting of the same to sell the said warres. **1574** in *Maitl. Cl. Misc.* I. 101 Transporting of certane quheit furth of this realme without lycence. **1612** J. MORE in *Buccleuch MSS.* (Hist. MSS. Comm.) I. 125 The transporting of Sir John Ogle's regiment to my Lord Chandos. **1712** J. JAMES tr. *Le Blond's Gardening* 209 Clay is not dear, unless in the Carriage and Transporting of it. **1849** MACAULAY *Hist. Eng.* ix. II. 531 He would be no party to the transporting of the prince into France.

b. *Naut.* (See quot.) Also *attrib.*

c **1850** *Rudim. Navig.* (Weale) 156 *Transporting*, moving a ship from one situation to another by hawsers only. *Ibid.*, *Transporting-blocks*, two snatch-blocks, fitted on each side above the taffrail to admit a hawser, when transporting the ship from one place to another.

c. *Sc.* See TRANSPORT *v.* 2 a, b.

1707 [see TRANSPORT *v.* 2 b]. **1904** R. SMALL *Hist. U.P. Congregat.* I. 446 In September 1825 transporting calls came up to Mr. Ritchie from Dunfermline.. and from the Potterrow. *Ibid.* 469 Mr. M'Gilchrist's mind was not up to the transporting point yet.

tran'sporting, *ppl. a.* [f. as prec. + -ING².] That transports.

1. That removes from one place to another; engaged in transportation.

a **1618** RALEIGH *Apology* 12 That we might have kept our Transporting ships with our men of War. **1830** LYELL *Princ. Geol.* I. 312 The direction and position of their destroying and transporting power. **1834-5** J. PHILLIPS in *Encycl. Metrop.* VI. 705/1 The transporting action of streams. **1886** *Academy* 7 Aug. 82/1 Michael is hurried into the transporting ship which founders with all on board.

2. *fig.* Causing transport, ecstasy, or rapture; ravishing, enchanting.

c **1655** A. SIDNEY *Love* (in *19th Cent.* Jan. (1884) 58), Epicureans allow soe much of it [Love] as conduceth to pleasure, but reject the transporting part. **1707** WATTS *Hymn*, 'My God, the spring of all my joys' iv, My soul would leave this heavy clay At that transporting word. **1796** MRS. INCHBALD *Nature & Art* v, So did Henry survey, with transporting glory, his brother, drest for the first time in canonicals.

Hence **tran'sportingly** *adv.*, in a transporting manner; ravishingly.

1668 H. MORE *Div. Dial.* II. xi. (1713) 121 We see sundry Species of living Creatures this way the most pleasantly and transportingly provided for. *a* **1711** KEN *Hymnotheo* Poet. Wks. 1721 III. 54 [He] felt himself transportingly amaz'd.

transportive (trɑːn'spɔətɪv, træn-), *a. rare.* [f. TRANSPORT *v.* + -IVE.] Having the quality of transporting (*lit.* and *fig.*); tending to transport.

1622 T. ADAMS *Eirenopolis* Wks. 1862 II. 315 It is the voice of transportive fury, 'I cannot moderate my anger'. **1633** —— *Exp. 2 Peter* ii. 19 The running of our own ways, after our transportive fancies. **1899** T. C. CHAMBERLIN in *Jrnl. Geol.* Oct.-Nov. 669 As the declivity increased the cutting and transportive power of the drainage increased.

†**tran'sportment.** *Obs.* [f. as prec. + -MENT. Cf. OF. *transportement* (13-16th c.).]

1. Transportation: = TRANSPORT *sb.* 1. *rare*⁻¹.

a **1619** FLETCHER, etc. *Q. Corinth* IV. i, Are not you he, when your fellow Passengers, Your last transportment being assayl'd by a Galley, Hid your self i' the Cabbin?

2. Vehement emotion, passion; rapture, ecstasy: = TRANSPORT *sb.* 3.

1639 LD. DIGBY, etc. *Lett. conc. Relig.* (1651) 116 When they enveigh against Hereticks; their passions and transportments being at such times greatest. **1652** J. WRIGHT tr. *Camus' Nat. Paradox* XII. 325 To appease the frantick transportments of his Minde. **1686** tr. *Chardin's Coronat. Solyman* 81 Hairbrain'd, and violent actions, and full of a Transportment that truly savour'd of Extravagance.

transposable (trɑːns'pəʊzəb(ə)l, træns-), *a.* Also **transposible.** [f. TRANSPOSE *v.* + -ABLE.] Capable of being transposed; interchangeable. Hence **transposa'bility**.

1835 J. B. ROBERTSON tr. *Schlegel's Philos. of Hist.* I. iii. 95 Instead of the regular art of printing with transposeable letters.. this people [*sc.* the Chinese] make use of a species of lithography, which, to all essential purposes is the same. **1847** A. DE MORGAN *Formal Logic* vi. 122 The whole term is always transposible. **1879** WEBSTER *Suppl.*, Transposable. **1881** ARMSTRONG in *Nature* 8 Sept. 450/2 Heat, electricity and mechanical action, are all equivalent and transposable forms of energy. **1903** A. R. WALLACE *Man's Place in Universe* x. 195 The most important element in protoplasm ..which confers upon it..its extreme mobility and transposibility, is nitrogen.

transposal (trɑːns'pəʊzəl, træns-). *rare.* [f. as prec. + -AL¹; cf. *proposal.*] Transposition.

1695 KENNETT *Par. Antiq.* ix. 106 A transposal from one fraternity to another. **1707** NORRIS *Treat. Humility* iv. 177 A strange turn and transposal of events. **1866** J. G. MURPHY *Comm. Exod.* xx. 17 The transposal of the first two clauses. **1868** MRS. WHITNEY *P. Strong* iii, Like the thing proof-readers put for a sign of a transposal.

trans'pose, *sb.* [f. TRANSPOSE *v.*]

†**1.** = TRANSPOSITION. *Obs. rare.*

1589 PUTTENHAM *Eng. Poesie* II. xii. (Arb.) 121 Of the Anagrame,.. we may terme him, the poesie transposed or in one word a transpose. *Ibid.* 122 This man was very perfit and fortunat in these transposes. **1605** CAMDEN *Rem.* (1637) 175 This transpose of the letters in the name.

2. *Math.* A matrix got from a given matrix by interchanging each row and the corresponding column.

1937 [see SIMILAR *a.* 3 c]. **1939** A. C. AITKEN *Determinants & Matrices* i. 15 The resulting matrix is called the transpose of *A* and is denoted by *A′*. (In the less recent literature the word *conjugate* is used.) **1961** [see HERMITIAN *a.*]. **1978** *Nature* 13 Apr. 605/2 The transpose of the eigenvector matrix of climatic data.

transpose (trɑːns'pəʊz, træns-), *v.* [a. F. *transposer* (14th c. in Hatz.-Darm.), f. TRANS- + *poser* to place: see POSE, COMPOSE.]

†**1.** *trans.* To change (one thing) *to* or *into* another; to transform, transmute, convert. *Obs.*

c **1380** WYCLIF *Sel. Wks.* II. 387 Vertues ben transposid to vices. *c* **1460** *Wisdom* 1005 in *Macro Plays* 68 Gyff a peny in thy lyve, with goode wyll To þe pore, & yt pleysythe Gode more þan mownteynys [*MS.* mowyntenys] in to golde transposyde were; Ande aftir thy dethe, for the dysposyde. **1530** PALSGR. 761/1, I transpose, I chaunge or tourne a thyng... He hath transposed his house quyte newe, *il a transmué*, or *contourné sa mayson tout de nouveau*, or *toute neuue.* **1579-80** NORTH *Plutarch* (1676) 415 To transpose themselves from good Souldiers..to Labourers, Merchants, and Farmers. **1590** SHAKS. *Mids. N.* I. i. 233 Things base and vilde, holding no quantity, Loue can transpose to forme and dignity. **1605** —— *Macb.* IV. iii. 21 That which you are, my thoughts cannot transpose; Angels are bright still, though the brightest fell.

†**2.** To change (a writing or book) *into* another language, style of composition, or mode of expression; to translate; to transfer; to adapt. *Obs.*

1390 GOWER *Conf.* II. 90 The Bible, in which the lawe is closed, Into Latin he [Jerome] hath transposed. **1552** HULOET, Transpose, *transcribo.* **1706** PHILLIPS (ed. Kersey), To *Transpose*,..to turn out of Verse into Prose, to change, or alter the Style. **1858** FABER tr. *Life of Xavier* 256 He spent them in transposing a copious exposition of the Apostle's Creed into Japanese.

†**3.** To change the purport, application, or use of; to apply or use otherwise; to give a different direction to; in bad sense, to corrupt, pervert; to misapply, abuse. *Obs.*

1509 BARCLAY *Shyp Folys* (1570) 106 They frowardly the sentence do transpose, And..By their corrupting and vnlawful glose,..bring to damnable heresie. **1548** GESTE *Pr. Masse* in Dugdale *Life* (1840) App. 101 Can the baptisme water be justly recompted a sacrament when it is transposed to other usage..namely..to christen belles, to washe our clothes withal? **1564** *Brief Exam.* B iv b, They toke..the salarie..consecrated to the Idolles.., and transposed it to finde the Ministers of the Church. **1644** MILTON *Educ.* Wks. (1847) 98/1 Nor should..any private friendship have prevailed with me to..transpose my former thoughts.

4. To remove from one place or time to another; to transfer, shift (*lit.* and *fig.*: now *rare* exc. as in 5); †to transplant (*obs.*); †to convey, conduct (*obs.*).

c **1510** BARCLAY *Mirr. Gd. Manners* (1570) F iv, An olde tree transposed shall finde small auauntage. **1555** in Strype *Eccl. Mem.* (1721) III. App. xlvi. 139 Bisshope Barlo, after he was transposed and..discharged out of the bisshoprick of S^t. Davids. **1578** BANISTER *Hist. Man* v. 77 Many braunches are deriued from this veyne..transposing bloud to euery Membran. **1602** WARNER *Alb. Eng.* Epit. (1612) 389 Thus.. was the Scepter transposed to the House of Lancaster. *a* **1662** HEYLIN *Laud* (1668) 69 Transposing the Communion Table to the East end of the Quire. **1665** MANLEY *Grotius' Low-C. Warres* 671 To transpose his Horsemen, and afterwards his Carriages, into that part of the Sea-Coast. **1742** RICHARDSON *Pamela* III. 215 To.. transpose his Affections to a worthier Object. **1887** RUSKIN *Præterita* II. vii. 243 As I transpose myself back through the forty years of desultory..reading.

5. To alter the order of (a set or series of things), or the position of (a thing) in a series; to put each of (two or more things) in the place of the other or others, to interchange; *esp.* to alter the order of letters in a word or of words in a sentence. (Now the ordinary sense.)

1538 ELYOT, *Metathesis*, where one letter is transposed from one place in a worde into an nother as *Tymber Tymbre.* **1571** GOLDING *Calvin on Ps.* lxxv. 5 Manye because they saw there could no handsom sence be picked out of the words, thoght the order to have bin transposed. **1605** CAMDEN *Rem.* 153 The letters of Elizabetha Regina transposed to signifie that happinesse..O Englands Soveraigne thou hast made vs happy: thus Elizabetha Regina, Angliæ Hera, Beasti. **1612** BRINSLEY *Lud. Lit.* xiv. (1627) 197 This one Verse is turned by transposing the words 104 wayes. **1691-8** NORRIS *Pract. Disc.* (1711) III. 171 Whose Notions..are cross and transposed, that calls Evil Good, and Good Evil. **1706** [see TRANSPOSING]. **1833** J. HOLLAND *Manuf. Metal* II. 289 A common balance..should always be tested in this way:—Let a weight be put in one dish, and balanced by other weights in the other dish; let the weights be then transposed. **1861** PALEY *Æschylus* (ed. 2) *Supplices* 909 *note*, The following four verses Hermann transposes after 927. **1902** SLOANE *Electr. Dict.*, *Transposing*, a method of laying metallic circuits for telephoning. The wires at short intervals are crossed so that alternate sections lie on opposite sides of each other. It is done to avoid induction.

b. *Algebra.* To transfer (a quantity) from one side of an equation to the other, with change of sign.

1810 HUTTON *Course Math.* I. 222 Thus, if $x + 5 = 8$; then transposing 5 gives $x = 8 - 5 = 3$. *c* **1865** in *Circ. Sc.* I. 456/2 The $3x$ is transposed: it is taken from the right and put on the left with changed sign.

†**6.** To discompose, disturb the mental composure of. *Obs. rare.*

1594 KYD *Cornelia* II. 214 Madam, you must not thus transpose your selfe; Wee see your sorrow, but who sorrowes not? **1621** BURTON *Anat. Mel.* II. III. v, Do something or other, let it [grief] not transpose thee.

7. *Mus.* To alter the key of; to put into a different key (in composition, arrangement, or performance).

1609 DOULAND *Ornith. Microl.* 26 To transpose is to remoue a song, or a Key from the proper place. ? **1715** (*title*) Melodies Proper to be Sung To..ye Psalms of David, Figur'd for the Organ, and..the Treble of each Melody Transpos'd for the Flute. **1845** E. HOLMES *Mozart* 30 He transposes *prima vista* the airs he accompanies. **1875** OUSELEY *Mus. Form* 71 At bar 23 the first subject is transposed into the key of E.

Hence **trans'posed** *ppl. a.*, *spec.* in *Math.*, applied to the transpose of a given matrix; **trans'posedly** (-ɪdlɪ) *adv.*

1609 DOULAND *Ornith. Microl.* 16 In transposed Songs. **1683** MOXON *Mech. Exerc.*, *Printing* xxii. ¶ 8 He removes the other Transpos'd Page into the place of the first. **1771** LUCKOMBE *Hist. Print.* 447 If there be more than two Transpos'd Pages in the Sheet. **1858** *Phil. Trans. R. Soc.* CXLVIII. 32 A matrix compounded with the transposed matrix gives rise to a symmetrical matrix. **1889** F. TAYLOR in Grove *Dict. Mus.* IV. 161/2 Transposed editions of songs are frequently published, that the same compositions may be made available for voices of different compass. **1907** M. BÔCHER *Introd. Higher Algebra* ii. 21 Two square matrices.. of which either is obtained from the other by interchanging rows and columns are called conjugate to each other. [*Note*] Sometimes also transposed. **1972** M. KLINE *Math. Thought* xxxiii. 807 The transverse (transposed or conjugate) matrix is defined as the one in which rows and columns are interchanged. **1678** CUDWORTH *Intell. Syst.* I. v. 676 Writing down the..letters of the alphabet transposedly, any how.

transposer (trɑːns'pəʊzə(r), træns-). [f. TRANSPOSE *v.* + -ER¹.] One who transposes: esp. in sense 7.

1882 OGILVIE *Suppl.* s.v., The transposer has written the tune two tones higher. **1894** *Westm. Gaz.* 23 Apr. 1/3 Many great musicians are poor transposers.

transposing (trɑːns'pəʊzɪŋ, træns-), *vbl. sb.* [f. as prec. + -ING¹.] The action of the vb. TRANSPOSE, in various senses.

1550 *Acc. St. Andrew's, Canterb.* (MS.), Item for the transposyng of a cope xviij d. **1559** MORWYNG *Evonym.* 141 By a certain *metempsychosin*, that is a transposinge of the soules or principal vertues. **1574** tr. *Marlorat's Apocalips* 210 b, The cup of his wrath... The transposing of the woorde Cup from his owne proper signification,..is very ryfe in the Scriptures. **1706** A. BEDFORD *Temple Mus.* vii. 156 We hardly meet with a Verse.., but with Transposing would admit of..Rhymes. **1908** *Contemp. Rev.* Apr. 414 There is not much more in it than a transposing of words.

b. *attrib.*: **transposing instrument** (*Mus.*), (*a*) an instrument having a mechanical device for transposing into a different key, as a ***transposing harpsichord, organ, piano***; (*b*) a name for those orchestral instruments the parts for which are written in a different key from that in which they sound.

1840 *Penny Cycl.* XVIII. 142/2 This instrument was called by Mr. Trotter a transposing piano-forte. **1883** W. S. ROCKSTRO in Grove *Dict. Mus.* III. 433/1 In all these Scores, the Parts for the so-called 'Transposing-Instruments' correspond with the separate 'Parts' used in the Orchestra. **1889** A. J. HIPKINS *ibid.* IV. 160/1 Prætorius (A.D. 1619) speaks of transposing clavicymbals (harpsichords) which by shifting the keyboard could be set two notes higher or lower. .. Burney in his musical tour met with two transposing harpsichords; one..at Venice; the other..at Bologna.

transposition (trɑːnspə'zɪʃən, træns-). [prob. a. F. *transposition* (*c* 1560 in Paré), or ad. med.L. *transpositiōn-em* (Du Cange), n. of action from L. *transpōnĕre* (f. TRANS- + *pōnĕre* to place); but, like other nouns in *-position*, associated in F. and Eng. with *transposer*, TRANSPOSE *v.* etc.] The action of transposing, or condition of being transposed; the result of this.

1. a. *gen.* Removal from one position to another; transference.

1538 ELYOT, *Transcribere*, the transposition of a possession from one to an other. **1642** FULLER *Holy & Prof. St.* I. vii. 19 Well may masters consider how easie a transposition it had been for God, to have made him to mount into the saddle that holds the stirrop. **1678** CUDWORTH *Intell. Syst.* I. i. §33. 42 This was the Doctrine of Pythagoras.., that no Real Entity perishes in Corruptions, nor is produced in Generations, but only new Modifications and Transpositions made. **1827** CARLYLE *Misc., Germ. Lit.* (1857) I. 30 A transposition of the critic into the author's point of vision.

†**b.** Translation into another language. *Obs.*

1653 LD. VAUX tr. *Godeau's St. Paul* A ij, To publish this elaborate transposition of your Lordships out of French into English.

2. a. Alteration of order, or interchange of position, esp. of letters in a word, or words in a sentence; metathesis; the result of such action; a word or sentence transposed.

1582 T. WATSON *Centurie of Loue* lxxx, By tables of transilition to decypher any thing that is written by secret transposition of letters. **1630** J. TAYLOR (Water P.) *Life & Death Virg. Mary* Wks. 22/1 For in an Anagram Iskariott is, By letters transposition, Traitor kis. **1675** BAXTER *Cath. Theol.* II. I. 248 Beza..thinks that a transposition of two

Verses hath darkened these Texts. **1727** H. HERBERT tr. *Fleury's Eccl. Hist.* I. 62 There are so many..hyperbatons and transpositions, which render his stile difficult. **1818** SCOTT *Br. Lamm.* xxxiv, The mysterious transposition of the portraits. **1861** PALEY *Æschylus* (ed. 2) *Choeph.* 219 *note*, By the accidental transposition of the verses. **1965** J. J. ROTMAN *Theory of Groups* iii. 35 Of all the permutations, surely the transposition, which merely interchanges two points, is the simplest. **1972** A. G. HOWSON *Handbk. Terms Algebra & Anal.* x. 51 Any permutation can be expressed as a product of transpositions. **1981** *Sci. Amer.* Mar. 19/2 If you are willing to let cycles share members, however, any cycle can be further broken up into 2-cycles (called transpositions, or sometimes swaps).

b. *Math.* The interchange of each row of a matrix with the corresponding column.

1858 A. CAYLEY in *Phil. Trans. R. Soc.* CXLVIII. 31 Two matrices such as $\begin{vmatrix} a, & b \\ c, & d \end{vmatrix}$, $\begin{vmatrix} a, & c \\ b, & d \end{vmatrix}$, are said to be formed one from the other by transposition. **1955** *Geophysics* XX. 300 The transposition of the 'ξ_{12}' matrix was necessary to reveal the trend in the *u*..direction.

3. *Mus.* **a.** Alteration of key; the performance of a piece in a different key from that in which it is written, or the writing of a piece in a different key from the original; also *transf.* a transposed piece. †**b.** Inversion of parts in counterpoint (*obs.*).

1609 DOULAND *Ornith. Microl.* 26 Transposition is the remouing of a Song or a Key from his proper place. **1740** (*title*) Calliope, or English Harmony: a Collection of.. English and Scots Songs,..with the Thorough Bass and Transpositions for the Flute. **1889** F. TAYLOR in Grove *Dict. Mus.* IV. 161/1 In transposition it often happens that a natural has to be represented by a sharp or flat, and *vice versa*.

4. *Algebra.* Transference of a quantity from one side of an equation (or one member of a proportion) to the other.

1664 POWER *Exp. Philos.* II. 130 Here is now four Proportionals, and by any three given, you may strike out [? = hit upon] the fourth, by Conversion, Transposition, and Division of them. **1674** JEAKE *Arith.* (1696) 622 In Transposition of the next Equation..the Signs are accordingly changed. *c* **1865** *Circ. Sc.* I. 456/2 If known and unknown quantities are linked together, separate them by transposition.

5. *Anat.* Abnormal position of the organs of the body, e.g. the heart being on the right side; heterotaxy.

1857 DUNGLISON *Med. Lex.*, *Transposition of the Viscera* ..consists in the viscera being found out of the situations they ordinarily occupy. **1904** *Brit. Med. Jrnl.* 17 Dec. 1643 Heterotaxy, or transposition, the teratogenesis of which is still obscure.

6. *Electr.* An alteration of the relative positions of power lines or telephone lines at intervals along their length, in order to minimize effects of mutual inductance and capacitance.

1911 A. B. SMITH *Mod. Amer. Telephony* xxii. 616 Transpositions are unnecessary when there is but one circuit on a pole line. **1959** K. HENNEY *Radio Engin. Handbk.* (ed. 5) xxviii. 26 In the case of pairs used for high frequencies, the locations of the transpositions must be quite precise. **1975** R. L. FREEMAN *Telecommunication Transmission Handbk.* iv. 164 The dipole type of LP antenna is fed by a balanced transmission line with 180° transpositions at alternate dipole elements.

7. *Genetics.* The transfer of a chromosomal segment to a new position on the same or another chromosome.

1924 *Hereditas* V. 174 In his case of transposition (or translocation) a piece of one of the second chromosomes has been fastened to one of the third chromosomes. **1954** B. P. KAUFMANN in A. Hollaender *Radiation Biol.* I. II. ix. 650 The viable types of intrachromosomal rearrangement include inversions and transpositions. **1978** *Nature* 20 July 211/3 The subsequent transposition of tetracycline resistance from this engineered plasmid must therefore be due to the transposition of the toxin gene.

Hence **transpo'sitional** *a.* (*rare*$^{-1}$), of, pertaining to, or involving transposition.

a **1800** S. PEGGE *Anecd. Eng. Lang.* (1814) 77 The most striking..error in pronunciation among the Londoners.. lies in the transpositional use of the letters *W* and *V*... Thus they always say *Weal*, instead of *veal*.. *Vicked*, for *wicked*.

transpositive (trɑːnsˈpɒzɪtɪv, træns-), *a.* [f. TRANSPOSE *v.*, after *positive*, etc. Cf. F. *transpositif* (18th c.), and rare L. *transpositīva* (Quintil.).] Characterized by or given to transposition.

1783 BLAIR *Lect. Rhet.*, etc. I. vii. 122 The French Language..admits the least of inversion..; But the Italian retains the most of the antient transpositive character. **1869** A. W. POTTS *Lat. Pr. Comp.* (1870) II. ii. 40 The English language..is compelled to obey somewhat rigid rules in the arrangement of the words... The Latin language, on the contrary, is transpositive.

Hence **trans'positively** *adv.*

1946 *Mind* LV. 323 If we accept the premises..that *fa* and ~*fa* severally imply (∃*x*)..then we must accept the consequences..that they do not have contradictories; or, transpositively, if we want our universal propositions to be non-existential..we must repudiate the proposition that *fa* implies (∃*x*)*fx*.

trans'positor. *rare*$^{-1}$. [agent-n. in L. form from *transpōnĕre* (see TRANSPOSE); cf. F. *transpositeur* (1835 Dict. Acad.) and POSITOR.] One who transposes; a transposer.

1824 LANDOR *Imag. Conv.*, *Southey & Porson* 43 We will lay aside the scrip of the transpositor and the pouch of the pursuer.

So **trans'pository** *a.* (*rare*$^{-1}$) = TRANSPOSITIVE.

1837 *Fraser's Mag.* XVI. 478 'Old England', in virtue of this transpository operation, evolves a *Golden Land*.

transposon (trɑːnsˈpəʊzɒn, træns-, -nz-). *Genetics.* [f. TRANSPOS(ITION + -ON^1.] A chromosomal segment that can undergo transposition (sense 7); *spec.* a segment of bacterial DNA that can be translocated *en bloc* between chromosomal, phage, and plasmid DNA in the absence of a complementary sequence in the host DNA.

1974 HEDGES & JACOB in *Molecular & Gen. Genetics* CXXXII. 38 We designate DNA sequences with transposition potential as transposons (units of transposition). **1978** *Nature* 11 May 171/3 The determinants of resistance to at least seven different antibiotics form part of independent structures several kilobase-pairs long, called 'transposons', which can jump between the genomes of bacteria, plasmids and phages of widely different base compositions. **1980** *Sci. Amer.* Sept. 87/3 Some transposons carry genes for traits such as drug resistance that are clearly advantageous to a bacterial host under some circumstances. **1982** *Nature* 21 Oct. 676/1 Transposons, familiar enough in bacteria.., have been identified in..eukaryotic genomes principally because their DNA sequences can crop up at different places.

†**trans'pour**, *v.* *Obs. rare.* [TRANS- 2.] *trans.* To pour from one to another, transfer by pouring.

1585 FETHERSTONE tr. *Calvin on Acts* xv. 9 Faith taketh that of Christ which it transpoureth into vs.

trans'print, *v.* *rare.* [f. TRANS- 2 + PRINT *v.*] *trans.* To reprint from another book, etc. Hence **'transprint** *sb.*, that which is transprinted.

1825 COLERIDGE *Aids Refl.* (1848) I. 337 The celebrated conclusion of the fourth book of Paley's Moral and Political Philosophy, referred to in p. 268,..is here transprinted for the convenience of the Reader. **1827** BENTHAM *Mem. & Corr.* Wks. 1843 X. 577 A transprint of which, in a number of the *Examiner*, is likewise destined to accompany them.

trans'process. *Anat.* [TRANS- 6.] A transverse process of a vertebra; a diapophysis.

1891 *Cent. Dict.* cites COUES.

transprose (trɑːnsˈprəʊz, træns-), *v.* [f. TRANS- 2 + PROSE *sb.* Orig. a nonce-word, to match TRANSVERSE *v.*^{2}, q.v.] *trans.* To turn into prose; to translate or render in prose. (Chiefly humorous.)

1671 VILLIERS (Dk. Buckhm.) *Rehearsal* I. i. (Arb.) 31 *Bayes*... I Transverse it; that is, if it be Prose, put it into Verse, (but that takes up some time); if it be Verse, put it into Prose. *Johns.* Methinks, Mr. Bayes, that putting Verse into Prose should be call'd Transprosing. *Bayes.* By my troth, a very good Notion, and hereafter it shall be so. **1672** MARVELL (*title*) The Rehearsal transpros'd: or, Animadversions upon a late Book, entituled, a Preface, shewing What Grounds there are of Fears and Jealousies of Popery. **1673** [R. LEIGH] *Transp. Reh.* 4 What Miracles men of Art can do by Transversing Prefaces and Transprosing Playes. **1681** DRYDEN *Abs. & Achit.* II. 443 Instinct he follows and no farther knows, For to write verse with him is to transprose. **1710** STEELE *Tatler* No. 194 ¶ 1, I shall transprose it, to use Mr. Bays's Term. **1732** [see TRANSVERSE *v.*^{2}]. **1826** *Museum Criticum* I. 411 Babrius versified them [Æsop's apologues]: various persons, as Mr. Smith says in the Rehearsal, *transprosed* the choliambics of Babrius.

Hence **trans'prosal**, the action of 'transprosing', or something 'transprosed'; **trans'proser**, one who 'transproses' (whence **trans'prosership**); **trans'prosing** *vbl. sb.*

1671 Transprosing [see above]. **1673** *S'too him Bayes* 4 Godsookers you'l spoil all my Transprosal. *Ibid.* 34, I..bid your Transprosership heartily farewell. **1673** *Answ. to 'A Seasonable Disc.'* 19 Has not the judicious Transproser a long Paragraph of the furious temper of these Clergy Men? **1718** J. TRAPP *Æneis* (1735) I. Pref. 81 Tho' the Translating of Poems into Prose is a strange, modern Invention; yet the French Transprosers are so far in the right; because their Language will not bear Verse.

transpro'vincial, *a.* [f. TRANS- 3 + PROVINCIAL *a.*] That crosses a province.

1916 R. K. WOOD *Tourist's N.W.* 316 A trans-provincial highway is building through southern British Columbia from the mountains..to Hope in the Fraser River Valley. **1952** D. F. PUTNAM *Canadian Regions* 338/1 They have not ..been able to get the Ontario Government to construct adequate transprovincial highways.

trans'pulmonary, *a.* [f. TRANS- 5 + L. *pulmo*, *pulmōn-em* lung: cf. *pulmonary.*] Acting or operated through the lungs: said of the respiration in birds, in which the lungs are connected with large air-sacs, into and out of which the air passes through the lungs. ***transpulmonary pressure***, the difference between the pressure in the lungs and that in the intrapleural cavity.

1902 G. B. HOWES in *Rep. Brit. Assoc.* 624 The respiratory process in the bird may be defined as *transpulmonary*. **1957** *Jrnl. Appl. Physiol.* X. 191/1 Measurements of the mechanical properties of the lungs depend on the separation of transpulmonary pressure into separate elastic and flow-resistive components. **1977** *Lancet* 3 Sept. 510/1 When airway collapse does occur, transpulmonary pressure rapidly increases with only a small resultant increase in inspiratory gasflow.

transputer (trɑːnˈspjuːtə(r), træn-, -nzˈ-). *Electronics.* [f. TRANS(ISTOR *sb.* + COM)PUTER.] A chip that incorporates all the functions of a microprocessor, including memory.

1978 I. M. BARRON in D. Aspinall *Microprocessor* VI. 343 The word 'transputer' has been coined to describe the computer on a chip. The word is derived from..'computer' and 'transistor'. **1983** *Times* 2 Nov. 3 Alice [*sc.* Applicative Language Idealized Computer Engine] will incorporate 64 transputers running in parallel, each in itself a 'computer on a chip'. **1984** *Times* 17 Feb. 10/4 The 'transputer' which Inmos, Britain's state-backed chip company, hopes to begin manufacturing in about a year's time,..includes processor, memory and communications on a conventional-sized chip.

†**trans'qualify**, *v.* *Obs. rare*$^{-1}$. [TRANS- 2.] *trans.* To change from one quality to another.

1652 URQUHART *Jewel* Wks. (1834) 223 The fierceness of his foe was in a trice transqualified into the numbness of a pageant.

trans'racial, *a.* [f. TRANS- 3 + RACIAL *a.*] Across or crossing racial boundaries.

1971 *Time* 16 Aug. 46 The Merediths' decision is part of a growing phenomenon known in sociologists' jargon as transracial adoption. **1976** *Indian Jrnl. Social Work* XXXVII. 152/1 The trend..is now moving towards transracial adoptions.

transrational (trɑːnsˈræʃənəl, træns-), *a.* [TRANS- 4.] Going beyond or surpassing what is rational.

1892 R. L. STEVENSON *Let.* in Myers *Human Personality* (1903) I. 302 The transrational felicity of the [dreamed] word..not one [syllable] was in itself significant, and yet the whole expressed to a nicety a voluminous distress of one in a high fever.

trans'real, *a.* [TRANS- 4.] Beyond the real; outside the world of reality.

1901 *Speaker* 3 Aug. 503/2 A foothold in the quicksands of time, 'a jumping-off ground' for his raids into the Transreal.

transreceiver (ˌtrɑːnsrɪˈsiːvə(r), træns-, -nz-). [f. TRANS(MITTER + RECEIVER^1.] = TRANSCEIVER.

1942 *Electronic Engin.* XV. 239/2 Inside the Transreceiver there is a small moving coil mechanism. **1956** 'N. SHUTE' *Beyond Black Stump* ii. 46 David had a radio transreceiver for use with the Flying Doctor service.

†**trans'regionate**, *ppl. a.* *Obs. rare*$^{-1}$. [f. TRANS- + L. *regiōn-em* region + -ATE^2.] Transferred to or inhabiting another region.

1577 HARRISON *England* III. vi. (1878) II. 39 There are some cockescombs..in England, learning it abroad as men transregionate, which make account also of this pastime.

transrhenane (trɑːnsˈriːneɪn, træns-), *a.* [ad. L. *transrhēnānus* adj. and sb., f. *trans* across + *Rhēnus* the Rhine. Cf. F. *transrhénan, -ane* (in Littré).] That is across or beyond the Rhine; hence, German as opposed to Roman or to French.

a **1727** NEWTON *Obs. Dan.* I. v. (1733) 54 Captains of the Transrhenane Franks in the reign of Theodosius. **1830** CROWE *Hist. France* I. 7 A fresh infusion of the ruder spirit of the Transrhenane race came to invigorate the already degenerated Franks of Gaul. **1835** *Fraser's Mag.* XI. 260 The crude chimæras of transcendental and transrhenane philosophy. **1913** *Eng. Hist. Rev.* July 561 The Germans obtained the very rudiments of civilization from the Kelts in their pristine transrhenane home.

transriverine (trɑːnsˈrɪvəraɪn, træns-), *a.* [f. TRANS- 3 + RIVER: cf. *riverine.*] Situated across a (or the) river; transfluvial.

1900 *Athenæum* 22 Dec. 824/2 The town [Birkenhead] was projected at first simply as a residential trans-riverine suburb of Liverpool.

†**transs**, obs. spelling of TRANCE *sb.*

(In the following passage it has been variously taken as TRANCE *sb.*^{1} 3 b, and as *sb.*^{3}: see also Jamieson.)

a **1550** *Christis Kirke Gr.* v, He playt sae schill, and sang sae sweet, Quhyle Towsie tuke a Transs.

transsect: see TRANSECT.

trans-seg'mental, *a.* *Anat.* [f. TRANS- 5 + SEGMENT: cf. *segmental.*] Passing across a segment; extending through one segment of a limb and terminating in another, as a nerve or vessel.

1890 BILLINGS *Nat. Med. Dict.*, *Transsegmental arteries*, those which pass through a region to be distributed beyond.

transsene, variant of TRANSON *v.* *Obs.*

trans-'sensual, *a.* [f. TRANS- 4 + L. *sensu-s* sense: cf. *sensual.*] Lying beyond or transcending the senses.

1807 COLERIDGE in *Lit. Rem.* (1839) IV. 294 Confounding the..effects necessarily predetermined by the precedent causes..with the transsensual ground or actual power.

trans-se'pulchral, *a.* [f. TRANS- 3 + L. *sepulc(h)rum* sepulchre: cf. *sepulchral.*] That is beyond the sepulchre or tomb.

1891 in *Cent. Dict.* **1911** in WEBSTER.

trans'sexual, *a.* and *sb.* Also (A. 1, B.) transexual, (esp. A. 2) **trans-sexual.** [f. TRANS- 3 + SEXUAL *a.*] **A.** *adj.* **1.** Of or pertaining to transsexualism; having physical characteristics of one sex and psychological characteristics of the other.

1957 *Amer. Jrnl. Psychotherapy* XI. 85 Other kinds of secondary experiences might give rise to transsexual tendencies. **1963** A. HERON *Towards Quaker View of Sex* 68 In men..the trans-sexual urge occasionally reaches the point of completely assuming the female role. **1969** *Nature* 2 Aug. 448/2 Cases of transsexual children brought up in unusually close contact with their mothers, who were the dominant members of families in which the fathers were ineffectual characters. **1970** [see *sex change* s.v. SEX *sb.* 5]. **1977** *Proc. R. Soc. Med.* LXX. 792/1 He may sustain sexual relations..by transexual fantasy.

2. Of or pertaining to both sexes. Also, intersexual.

1977 G. MELLY *Rum, Bum & Concertina* viii. 105, I came into her... We made love.., but crossing the trans-sexual barrier didn't convert me overnight. I continued for some years to prefer boys. **1978** *Logophile* VIII. 8/1 The word 'clerk' *sounds* acceptably undiscriminatory and trans-sexual.

B. *sb.* A transsexual person. Also, one whose sex has been changed by surgery.

1957 *Amer. Jrnl. Psychotherapy* XI. 84 Marriage, motherhood, and a husband are a woman's life and he wants that as a fulfillment of his femininity. These persons form the group aptly termed 'transsexuals'. **1966** *New Scientist* 8 Dec. 577/1 Transsexuals..are a..group of individuals 'who have a burning and overwhelming desire to be of the sex opposite to what they are anatomically'. **1971** *Daily Tel.* (Colour Suppl.) 10 Dec. 21/3 Adult transexuals are so resistant that psychological treatment and even aversion therapy is virtually hopeless so far as they are concerned. **1976** *Washington Post* 26 Jan. A2/8 Britain's state-run health service has started a night school for transexuals where men who have changed their sex can learn to face the world as women. **1977** *Times* 18 Aug. 6/2 Dr Renée Richards, aged 42, a trans-sexual who was a man until 1975.

trans'sexualism. Also **trans-sexualism, transexualism.** [f. TRANS- 3 + SEXUALISM.] The state or condition of being transsexual (see TRANSSEXUAL *a.* 1), manifested in an overwhelming desire to belong to the opposite sex.

1953 H. BENJAMIN in *Internat. Jrnl. Sexology* Aug. 12/1 Transvestitism..is the desire of a certain group of men to dress as women, or of women to dress as men. It can be.. overwhelming, even to the point of wanting to belong to the other sex and correct nature's anatomical 'error'. For such cases the term Transsexualism seems appropriate. **1954** *Amer. Jrnl. Psychotheraphy* VIII. 220 Trans-sexualism.. denotes the intense and often obsessive desire to change the entire sexual status including the anatomical structure. **1963** K. WALKER in G. Turtle *Over Sex Border* 11 Transexualism was only defined with any clarity in 1954. **1969** *New Scientist* 24 July 183/1 The very difficult clinical problem of trans-sexualism. **1974** *Adolescence* Spring 71 The increasing rate of transexualism. **1977** E. J. TRIMMER et al. *Visual Dict. Sex* (1978) iii. 46 It is impossible for an ordinary person to be propelled into the condition of transsexualism, as it has nothing to do with free will or voluntary choice.

So **trans'sexualist** *sb.* and *a.* = TRANSSEXUAL *sb.*, *a.* 1.

1954 *Amer. Jrnl. Psychotherapy* VIII. 220 The transsexualist is always a transvestite but not vice-versa... The transsexualist only lives for the day when his hated sex organs can be removed. **1966** *Punch* 28 Dec. 968/1 The transexualist..told us, in a pleasant baritone, how happily married 'she' was—after surgery. **1976** SMYTHIES & CORBETT *Psychiatry* xi. 211 Transexualists believe that a 'mistake' has been made and they really wish to actually become the opposite sex. **1977** A. SHERIDAN tr. *Lacan's Écrits* vi. 209 A trans-sexualist practice, in no way unworthy of being compared with 'perversion'.

transsexu'ality. Also **trans-sexuality, transexuality.** [f. TRANS- 3 + SEXUALITY.] = TRANSSEXUALISM; *loosely*, bisexuality.

1941 O. LEGMAN in G. W. Henry *Sex Variants* II. 1149 *Homosexuality*..is more widely used than any other of the many terms that have been proposed, such as ..*transsexuality*. **1955** J. F. OLIVEN *Sexual Hygiene & Pathol.* xxi. 397 Primary transvestism. *Synonyms*: Idiopathic transvestism... Transsexuality or transsexualism. **1957** *Amer. Jrnl. Psychotherapy* XI. 85 Homosexuality, transsexuality and transvestism. **1973** J. MARKS *Mick Jagger* 142 Jagger's trans-sexuality is just one of the things which makes him qualify as our great hero. **1977** *Lancet* 6 Aug. 261/1 We have investigated 60 patients treated with high doses of methyltestosterone for transsexuality or impotence.

† **trans-'shape, tran'shape,** *sb. Obs.* [f. TRANSSHAPE *v.*] Change of shape; transformation; metamorphosis.

1611 HEYWOOD *Golden Age* IV. i, By our transhapes And guiles of loue. **1613** —— *Silver Age* II. i, But her search He soone deluded in his slye trans-shapes. **1636** —— *Love's Mistr.* I. i, Ile shew thee..What kind of people I commerst withall In my transhape.

trans-shape (trɑːns'ʃeɪp, træns-), † **transhape** (trɑːn'ʃeɪp, træn-), *v.* Now *rare* (? *arch.*). [f. TRANS- + SHAPE *v.*] *trans.* To alter the shape or form of; to transform.

1575 FENTON *Gold. Epist.* (1577) 332 The Oliue and Laurell, into the which were transhaped Lotus and Daphne. **1599** SHAKS. *Much Ado* v. i. 172 Thus did shee an howre together trans-shape thy particular vertues. **1638** HEYWOOD *Rape Lucrece* Wks. 1874 V. 179 Hee's from a toward hopefull Gentleman, Transeshapt to a meere Ballater. **1656** S. HOLLAND *Zara* (1719) 53 Till Soto by degrees was transhaped into a goodly Steed. **1659** *Lady Alimony* II. vi. Eivb, When th' Camel shall Transhape himself into a nimble Wesil,..I shall value you. **1855** SINGLETON *Virgil* I. 45 Or how he told of Tereus' limbs transshaped.

Hence **trans-shaped** (-'ʃeɪpt) *ppl. a.*; **trans-'shaping** *vbl. sb.*

1602 MARSTON *2nd Pt. Ant. & Mel.* IV. i, Rather put on some transhap't cavalier, Some habit of a spitting critick. **1909** tr. *Jusserand's Lit. Hist. Eng.* III. 140 Deeds of sorcery ..: apparitions, evocations, transhapings.

† **trans-'shift,** *v. Obs. rare*$^{-1}$. [TRANS- 2.] *trans.* and *intr.* To shift across or away.

1648 HERRICK *Hesper., Argt.* 9, I sing of times trans-shifting, and I write How roses first came red, and lillies white. *Ibid.*, *On Himselfe*, When monarchies trans-shifted are, and gone, Here shall endure thy vast dominion.

trans-ship, -shipment: see TRANSHIP, -MENT.

trans-Si'berian, *a.* (and *sb.*) [f. TRANS- 8 + SIBERIAN *a.*] That crosses Siberia. Also *ellipt.* as *sb.*, the trans-Siberian railway or express.

1896 *Daily News* 30 Dec. 7/1 The trans-Siberian railway, one of the greatest engineering works of the century. **1911** *Daily Colonist* (Victoria, B.C.) 1 Apr. 14/1 Return from or go to the Coronation via the great Trans-Siberian. **1939** C. ISHERWOOD *Goodbye to Berlin* 278 We'd stop a few days in Warsaw... Then on to Moscow, and take the trans-Siberian. **1964** S. BELLOW *Herzog* 168 She..was repatriated via the Trans-Siberian Railroad. **1974** *Times* 4 Oct. 10/7 The present Trans-Siberian runs for thousands of miles.. almost flush with the Chinese frontier. **1977** *Belfast Tel.* 17 Jan. 8/4 Two days out of Moscow on its seven-day journey to Vladivostock, the Trans-Siberian express was two minutes early.

transsignification, var. TRANSIGNIFICATION.

† **trans-'situate,** *v. Obs. rare.* [TRANS- 2.] *trans.* To shift or alter the situation or position of.

1630 DAVENANT *Cruel Brother* III, He chides Women, for wearing their Halfe-Ruffes, Which pinn'd behind trans-scituates the face.

trans-'solid, *a. rare.* [f. TRANS- 4 + SOLID *a.*] Beyond solid; of a density surpassing solidity.

1898 J. W. POWELL *Truth & Error* v. 43 Geologic facts in a vast system lead to the induction that the centrosphere does not exist in the solid state; if it is metallic the weight reduces it to a trans-solid condition.

trans-sonic, var. TRANSONIC *a.*

trans-spe'cific, *a. Biol.* Also **transpecific.** [f. TRANS- 3 + SPECIFIC *a.*] Passing from one species to another.

1963 E. MAYR *Animal Species & Evolution* xix. 586 The proponents of the synthetic theory maintain that all evolution is due to the accumulation of small genetic changes,..and that the transpecific evolution..is nothing but an extrapolation and magnification of the events that take place within populations and species. **1964** *Discovery* Oct. 29/2 Communication may be trans-specific. This is particularly true of alarm signals.

† **trans-'spirit,** *v. Obs. nonce-wd.* [TRANS- 1.] *trans.* To convey the spirit of (a thing) from one place or person to another.

1652 W. AMES *Saints Security* 33 He is a Christian to purpose, who hath the Bible transpirited into his minde.

† **trans-'spiritualized,** *ppl. a. Obs. rare.* [TRANS- 4.] Spiritualized in a surpassing degree.

1683 E. HOOKER *Pref. Pordage's Mystic Div.* 60 A littl incarnate Cherub..a very highly mystic and transspiritualized Person.

trans-'stellar, *a.* [f. TRANS- 3 + L. *stella* star: cf. *stellar*.] Existing or lying beyond the stars.

1888 J. MARTINEAU *Stud. Relig.* II. III. ii. 270 Transstellar regions. **1893** FR. THOMPSON *Judgm. Heav.* iii. Poems 55 On the far crystalline pale of that transtellar Heaven.

trans-Stygian (-'stɪdʒɪən), *a.* [f. TRANS- 7 + L. *Styx, Styg-em*: cf. *stygian*.] That is on the other side of the Styx; infernal. (Cf. TRANSACHERONTIC.)

1899 R. WALLACE *Geo. Buchanan* v. 91 Despising Pluto and the trans-Stygian penalties.

† **trans-'style,** *v. Obs. rare.* [TRANS- 2.] *trans.* To transform or change the style or title of.

1611 HEYWOOD *Gold. Age* III. i, Archas..by Ioues gift Pelasgia's seate hath wonne, Which after..He hath trans-stil'd Archadia by his name.

trans-sub'jective, *a.* Also **transubjective.** [TRANS- 4.] That transcends or is beyond subjective or individual experience as such.

1887 R. ADAMSON in *Mind* Jan. 127 Pure, mere experience is simply such knowledge as the subject directly has of his own subjective processes. Anything else shows itself on the slightest analysis to contain trans-subjective reference or trans-subjective elements. **1899** JAS. WARD *Naturalism & Agn.* II. 170 The sun as transubjective object is not L's sun or M's sun or N's sun..but rather what is common to them all, neglecting what is peculiar to each. **1902** T. CASE in *Encycl. Brit.* XXX. 668/1 From this epistemology he derives the metaphysical conclusion that the things we know are indeed independent of my consciousness and of yours, taken individually, or, to use a new phrase, are 'trans-subjective'. **1911** JAS. WARD *Realm of Ends* vi. 124 By intersubjective intercourse [men] attain to the trans-subjective or truly objective, both in knowledge and in action.

† **trans-'substancing,** *vbl. sb. Obs. rare*$^{-1}$. [f. TRANS- 2 + SUBSTANCE + -ING[1], repr. med.L. *transubstantiātio*.] = TRANSUBSTANTIATION.

c **1380** WYCLIF *Wks.* (1880) 345 þus power þat prestis han standeþ not in trans-substansinge of þe oste.

transsude, transsume, etc.: see TRANSUDE, TRANSUME, etc.

trans-sy'naptic, *a. Physiol.* Also **transynaptic.** [f. TRANS- 5 + SYNAPTIC *a.*] Involving transmission of a nerve impulse across a synapse. Hence **trans-sy'naptically** *adv.*

1954 PENFIELD & JASPER *Epilepsy & Functional Anat. Human Brain* v. 211 Under deep barbiturate anesthesia.., transynaptic conduction is sufficiently impaired so that spikes recorded beyond a synapse are prolonged by temporal dispersion into slower waves. *Ibid.*, Under light anesthesia..the temporal dispersion of transynaptically conducted spikes may be scarcely detectable. **1974** *Nature* 11 Jan. 112/1 These findings suggest that the rise in T-OH activity elicited by reserpine is mediated trans-synaptically through an increase in ganglionic transmission. **1977** *Proc. R. Soc. Med.* LXX. 671/2 Trans-synaptic regulation and adaptation (both orthograde and retrograde) in the brain.

transtage ('trɑːnsteɪdʒ, 'træn-, -nz-). *Astronaut.* [f. TRANS- + STAGE *sb.*] A final stage of a multistage rocket that can be restarted in order to change the flight path or orbit.

1965 *Daily Progress* (Charlottesville, Va.) 6 May 20 After one 90-minute circuit of the globe in the initial orbit, the transtage was to re-start its engines and swing into an elliptical path. **1975** *Daily Colonist* (Victoria, B.C.) 21 May 1/7 Air force officials said the 'transtage' of the Titan III-C rocket and the two 1,200-pound satellites connected to it began rolling and tumbling out of control.

Transtainer (trɑːns'teɪnə(r), træns-, -nz-). *U.S.* [f. TRANS- + CON)TAINER.] A proprietary name for a mobile gantry crane.

1964 *Official Gaz.* (U.S. Patent Office) 21 July TM 115/1 Pacific Coast Engineering Company, Alameda, Calif... Transtainer. For mobile gantry cranes. First use June 15, 1960. **1969** *Jane's Freight Containers 1968–69* 51 This Transtainer has a 35 foot span and straddles two rows of containers plus a truck roadway. **1977** *Hongkong Standard* 12 Apr. (Business Suppl.) 4/4 This includes a quay crane costing $102 million, four new transtainers valued at $33 million [etc.].

trans'temporal, *a. Anat.* [f. TRANS- 5 + L. *tempora* the temples: cf. TEMPORAL *a.*[2]] Crossing the temples; traversing the temporal lobe of the brain, as 'the transtemporal fissure'.

1889 *Buck's Handbk. Med. Sc.* VIII. 157/1 The crossing of the temporal lobe ventrad of the supertemporal fissure by two transtemporal fissures.

† **transtempo'ration.** *Obs. nonce-wd.* [f. TRANS- + L. *tempus, tempor-* time + -ATION.] Intermission of time, delay.

1651 *Life Father Sarpi* (1676) 59, I would desire the Reader to tolerate a little transtemporation, and digression.

transthoracic, *a. Med.* [f. TRANS- 5 + THORACIC *a.* (*sb.*).] Occurring or carried out through the wall of the thorax or across the thoracic cavity.

1905 J. F. BINNIE *Manual Operative Surg.* III. xii. 429 Close the wound in the diaphragm with sutures introduced by the transthoracic route. **1965** *Dis. Chest* XLVIII. 297/1 Suction aspiration of the lung (transthoracic lung puncture). **1973** *Sci. Amer.* Feb. 11/1 (Advt.), A plug-in module monitors respiration from a set of skin electrodes that detect changes in transthoracic impedance due to respiration.

† **trans'time,** *v. Obs. nonce-wd.* [TRANS- 2.] *trans.* To change as to time.

1647 WARD *Simp. Cobler* (1843) 16 To transplace or transtime a stated Institution of Christ,..is to destroy it.

transubstantial (trɑːnsəb'stænʃəl, træn-), *a.* [f. TRANS- 1 + L. *substantiāl-is*, f. *substantia* SUBSTANCE: cf. CONSUBSTANTIAL.] **a.** Changed or changeable from one substance into another; of or pertaining to transubstantiation. **b.** Made of something beyond substance; non-material, incorporeal.

1567 *Gude & Godlie B.* (S.T.S.) 210 Gif God be transubstanciall In [= into] breid, with *hoc est Corpus Meum.* **1651** BIGGS *New Disp.* ¶ 214 The transubstantial migration of the grapy juice of the papall Sacramentarians. **1892** E. C. STEDMAN in *Century Mag.* Apr. 821/1 The very stuff whereof the Muse fashions her transubstantial garments.

Hence **transub'stantialism**, the theory or doctrine of transubstantiation; **transub'stantialist**, one who holds this doctrine; **transub'stantialize** *v.*, †(*a*) *trans.* to change from one substance to another, to transubstantiate; (*b*) *intr.* to hold or maintain the doctrine of transubstantiation (whence **transub,stantiali'zation**); **transub'stantially** *adv.*, by change of substance, in the way of transubstantiation.

1842 G. S. FABER *Prov. Lett.* (1844) I. 183 The clause, through which Mr. Maitland would charge the Albigenses with acknowledged *Transubstantialism, could never have been uttered by themselves. **1838** —— *Inquiry* 65 It is useful to let a Romanist himself exhibit the blasphemous heresy of the *Transubstantialists in all its naked deformity. **1850** BP.

E. H. Browne *Exp. 39 Articles* XXVIII. i. (1874) 679 If there were no other alternative.. we must perforce acknowledge, that they believed in a carnal presence, and were transubstantialists. For some presence they undoubtedly taught. **1647** TRAPP *Comm. Matt.* iii. 11 [The fire of the Spirit] spiritualizeth and *transubstantializeth us, as it were, into the same image from glory to glory. **1826** G. S. FABER *Diffic. Romanism* (1853) 246 Some.. have rashly charged the Episcopal Church in Scotland with transubstantialising, because the ancient phrase occurs in her eucharistic liturgy. **1846** —— *Lett. Tractar. Secess.* 180 The old phraseology, which Dr. Moehler confidently adduces as proof positive that the Primitive Church transubstantialised from the very beginning. **1826** —— *Diffic. Romanism* (1853) 100 Specimens of such phraseology, by way of demonstrating the *transubstantialisation of the Primitive Church. **1577** tr. *Bullinger's Decades* (1592) 27 To expound the wordes of the Sacrament Sacramentally, and not *Transubstantially. **1579** FULKE *Heskins' Parl.* 428 Basil.. beleeued the bread and wine to be made Christes body and bloud, he meaneth corporally and transubstantially.

ˌ**transubˈstantiate**, *ppl. a. Obs.* or *arch.* Also 5–7 transs-. [ad. med.L. *tran(s)substantiāt-us*, pa. pple. of *tran(s)substantiāre*: see next.] Transubstantiated. (Mostly const. as *pa. pple.*)

c **1450** *Mirour Saluacioun* 1886 Be the preest is brede to ffesshe Transsubstanciate. *a* **1536** TINDALE *Declar. Sacram.* C vij, [They say] the breade and wyne are changed, turned, altered and transsubstancyat in to the very body and bloud of Chryste. **1550** CRANMER *Defence* 30 Yt holdeth, that breade is transubstantiate or tourned into the bodye, and wyne into the bloudde. **1571** FORTESCUE *Forest* 43 Sutche mercilesse and transubstantiate monsters. **1598** DALLINGTON *Meth. Trav.* B iij, He had transubstantiate this fat Fowle into fish. **1678** R. BARCLAY *Apol. Quakers* xiii. §5. 459 The Bread, and.. the Wine.. which they say is Consecrate and Transubstantiate into the very Body of Christ. **1848** KINGSLEY *Saint's Trag.* I. ii. 194 To find the canvas warm with life, and matter A moment transubstantiate to heaven.

transubstantiate (trɑːnsəbˈstænʃɪeɪt, træn-), *v.* Also transs-. [f. ppl. stem of med.L. *tran(s)substantiāre* (Du Cange), f. TRANS- + *substantia* SUBSTANCE. Cf. F. *transsubstantier* (14th c. in Godef. *Compl.*). App. first used in pa. pple.: cf. prec.] *trans.* To change from one substance into another; to transform, transmute.

1584 R. SCOT *Discov. Witchcr.* III. ii. (1886) 45 She [a witch] confesseth that she transubstantiateth hir selfe. **1615** W. LAWSON *Country Housew. Gard.* (1626) 19 The sap.. is consolidated and transubstantiated into the substance of the tree. **1670** PETTUS *Fodinæ Reg.* 44 The Philosophers stone .. which would.. transubstantiate other Metals into.. Gold and Silver. *a* **1711** KEN *Hymns Evang.* Poet. Wks. 1721 I. 98 He Water transubstantiated to Wine. **1870** HUXLEY *Lay Serm.* (1877) 133 A singular inward laboratory, which I possess, will.. convert the dead protoplasm into living protoplasm, and transubstantiate sheep [*i.e.* mutton] into man.

b. *spec.* in *Theol.*: see TRANSUBSTANTIATION 2.

[*c* **1450**: see prec.] **1533** TINDALE *Supper of Lord* B iij, The wyne transsubstanciated into his bloud. **1651** C. CARTWRIGHT *Cert. Relig.* I. 122 After Consecration there is no longer the substance of Bread, but that the Bread is transubstantiated, and turned into the substance of Christs Body. *a* **1774** TUCKER *Lt. Nat.* (1834) II. 483 It is necessary the priest should call down His very body crucified upon the cross into the bread; which must be transubstantiated thereinto, or consubstantiated therewith. *a* **1819** GEO. HILL *Lect. Div.* (1821) III. 362 The practice of partaking in private of a small portion of what the priest has thus transubstantiated.

c. *transf.* and *fig.*

1641 R. BROOKE *Eng. Episc.* 71 So large that no one man .. could sufficiently visit and over-see it except he get the Pope to Transubstantiate him also and so get a Vbiquitarian Body. **1675** OWEN *Author. Script.* Wks. 1851 VIII. 499 A private doctor of the Church of Rome may thus transubstantiate blasphemy into piety. **1759** STERNE *Tr. Shandy* II. ix, Never was a Dr. Slop so beluted, and so transubstantiated. **1884** J. TAIT *Mind in Matter* (1892) 125 Hints are transubstantiated into conceptions.

d. *absol.*

1579 FULKE *Heskins' Parl.* 67 Yᵉ Papistes call consecrating, to change yᵉ substances, or to transubstantiat. **1641** R. BROOKE *Eng. Episc.* II. iii. 74 A Preist can Consecrate, and by Consecration Transubstantiate. **1667** MILTON *P.L.* v. 438 With keen dispatch Of real hunger, and concoctive heate To transubstantiate.

e. *intr.* for *pass.* To become transubstantiated.

1851 W. ANDERSON *Exposure Popery* (1878) 84 If the cake be not genuine in respect of wheaten flour, and if the wine have been made of immature grapes, they will not transubstantiate.

Hence **transubˈstantiated** *ppl. a.*; **transubˈstantiating** *vbl. sb.* and *ppl. a.*

1550 BALE *Apol.* 63 Those *transubstanciated Goddes, were knowne for no Goddes. **1654** JER. TAYLOR *Real Pres.* 47 The spiritual eating of him.. may be done without their Transubstantiated flesh. **1718** J. CHAMBERLAYNE *Relig. Philos.* (1730) I. ii. §5 A metamorphosed or transubstantiated Earth. **1849** SIR J. STEPHEN *Eccl. Biog.* (1850) I. 82 His faltering lips had closed on the transubstantiated elements. **1586** HOOKER *Serm. Justif.*, etc. §11 As *transubstantiating of sacramental elements in the Eucharist. **1800** W. TAYLOR in *Monthly Mag.* X. 319 Scarcely marvellous enough for his *transubstantiating fancy.

transubstantiation (ˌtrɑːnsəbstænʃɪˈeɪʃən, ˌtræn-, -stænsɪˈeɪʃən). Also transs-. [ad. med.L. *tran(s)substantiātio* (in use in the 11th c.), n. of action fr. *tran(s)substantiāre*: see prec. So F. *transsubstantiation* (14th c. in Godef. *Compl.*).

The L. form occurs as a current term, *c* 1070, in St. Peter Damian *Expos. Canonis Missæ* §7 'Quando profertur ipsum pronomen ['Hoc'], nondum est transsubstantiatio'. (Migne *Patrologia* CXLV. 883.)]

1. The changing of one substance into another.

(Often with allusion to sense 2.)

1398 TREVISA *Barth. De P.R.* IX. xxxi. (MS. Add. 27944) lf. 129 þanne þe cene day is day of reconciliacioun, of transubstanciacioun, of consacracioun, and of sacringe, of halewinge of oynement. **1477** NORTON *Ord. Alch.* v. in *Ashm.* (1652) 86 Whereby of Mettalls is made transmutation, Not only in Colour, but transubstantiation. **1574** NEWTON *Health Mag.* 23 Avicen sayeth that fleash is a meate comfortynge the body and of meere transubstantiation and conversion into bloud. **1594** PLAT *Jewell-ho.* III. 65 The Vintners practising.. sometimes euen real transubstantiations, of white wine into Claret. **1651** HOBBES *Leviath.* IV. xlv. 361 The Gentiles.. might excuse their Idolatry, by pretending.. a transubstantiation of their Wood, and Stone into God Almighty. **1768** TUCKER *Lt. Nat.* (1834) I. 286 We look upon.. the change of a substance from one species into another as a transubstantiation. **1872** O. W. HOLMES *Poet Breakf.-t.* xi. 362 It is no longer a wax doll for her, but has undergone a transubstantiation quite as real as that of the Eucharist.

2. The conversion in the Eucharist of the whole substance of the bread into the body and of the wine into the blood of Christ, only the appearances (and other 'accidents') of bread and wine remaining: according to the doctrine of the Roman Church.

Distinguished from *consubstantiation*, in which the elements of the bread and wine are held to coexist with the body and blood of Christ.

1533 TINDALE *Supper of Lord* C iij b, S. Thomas theyr owne doctoure that made theyr transsubstanciacion confessethe that some there were that sayed that Christe dyd fyrste consecrate wyth other wordes, ere he nowe reachyng the bread to his disciple sayed, This is my bodie. *a* **1536** —— *Declar. Sacram.* D iv, As concernyng the transsubstanciatyon I thinke that such a speche was among the olde doctours though they that came after vnderstode them amysse. **1558** BP. WATSON *Sev. Sacram.* viii. 45 The .. church.. did.. well.. when it inuented the worde of *Transubstantiation*, to expresse the olde truthe,.. that the former substaunces of breade and wine be conuerted and chaunged into the body and bloud of Chryste. **1579** FULKE *Heskins' Parl.* 73 Transubstantiation is not so olde as Damascene, neither was it receyued in the Greeke Church, neither is it at this daye. **1635** PAGITT *Christianogr.* 55 The word Transubstantiation is.. first mentioned by Roger Hovenden, who flourished An. 1204. **1664** H. MORE *Myst. Iniq.* xv. 52 That Mysterious conceit of Transsubstantiation and the Idolatry thereon depending. **1678** *Act 30 Chas. II.* Stat. II. §3 Such Peer or Member shall.. audibly repeat this Declaration following. 'I *A. B.* do.. testify and declare, That I do believe that in the Sacrament of the Lord's Supper there is not any Transubstantiation of the Elements of Bread and Wine into the Body and Blood of Christ at or after the Consecration thereof'. **1715** BENTLEY *Serm.* x. 362 By slow degrees Transubstantiation was enacted into an Article of Faith. **1839** KEIGHTLEY *Hist. Eng.* I. 83 As transubstantiation had not yet [11th c.] been established by the papal authority, it.. formed no part of the public system of the Anglo Saxon church. **1901** BP. GORE *Body of Christ* ii. §3. 118 The use.. of the distinction of substance and accidents for the purpose of assisting the doctrine of transubstantiation was already familiar to Berengar,.. he combats the proposed use of it, denying that the accidents can exist apart from their substance or 'subject', or apart from that of which they are attributes. **1901** B. J. KIDD *39 Art.* II. 230–1 It was a crude attempt to secure some real meaning to Our Lord's Words of Institution by the doctrine of a *physical* transubstantiation or change in the material elements. But the Schoolmen now came forward with a subtler defence... Hence the doctrine of a *metaphysical* transubstantiation was adopted [by the Realists].

Hence **transubstantiˈationist**, one who holds the doctrine of transubstantiation. So **transubstantiˈationite, -ˈationalist.**

a **1834** COLERIDGE in *Lit. Rem.* (1839) IV. 192 The Consubstantiationist, or the Transubstantiationist. **1839** J. ROGERS *Antipopopr.* VI. ii. 219 What Bedlam.. contains madmen madder than the mad transubstantiationite? **1884** *N. & Q.* 23 Feb. 149/2 Dr. Samuel Pegge explained it ['please the pigs'] by 'An't please the pyx',.. and so making it equivalent to *Deo volente* in the minds of transubstantiationalists.

transubstantiative (trɑːnsəbˈstænʃ(ɪ)ətɪv, træn-), *a.* [f. as TRANSUBSTANTIATE *v.* + -IVE; cf. CONSUBSTANTIATIVE.] Of the nature of transubstantiation. Hence **transubˈstantiatively** *adv.*, by way of transubstantiation.

1826 G. S. FABER *Diffic. Romanism* (1853) 73 *note*, The fourth Council of Lateran.. determined that the alleged material change in the elements, is not consubstantiative but transubstantiative. *Ibid.* 271 *note*, If, after his ascension, the humanity of Christ had been transubstantiatively changed into his Divinity.

† **transubˈstantiator.** *Obs.* [agent-n. in L. form, from med.L. *transubstantiāre* or TRANSUBSTANTIATE: see -OR. Cf. F. *transsubstantiateur* (16th c. in Godef. *Compl.*).] One who holds the doctrine of transubstantiation; a transubstantialist.

a **1555** RIDLEY *Declar. Lord's Supper* (1556) 53 b, Some amonge the transubstantiators.. walke soe wilely and soe warely betwixte these ij.. opinions. **1624** GATAKER *Transubst.* 82 As these Transubstantiators.. say that the Bread in the Eucharist looseth its owne nature. *a* **1626** W. SCLATER *Exp. Rom. iv.* (1650) 143 Our Transubstantiatours .. delude the simple, perswading the reall presence of Christs body. **1686** H. MORE *Real Pres.* ii. 12 These Transubstantiators have fallen.. into that very absurdity, that they seemed so much to abhor from.

So **transubˈstantiatory** *a.* (*rare*⁻¹), implying or tending to transubstantiation.

1878 E. JENKINS *Haverholme* 184 Transubstantiatory rather, is it not?

transudate (ˈtrɑːnsjuːdət, ˈtræn-), *sb.* [ad. mod.L. *transūdāt-us*, pa. pple. of L. *transūdāre* to TRANSUDE.] A substance transuded: = TRANSUDATION b.

1876 tr. *Wagner's Gen. Pathol.* (ed. 6) 156 Most transudates taken from the cavities of dead bodies contain.. generators of fibrin. **1899** *Allbutt's Syst. Med.* VIII. 500 In nasal catarrh or bronchitis we have.. change of the normal transudate into a morbid exudate.

† **transudate**, *v. Obs. rare.* [f. *transūdāt-*, ppl. stem of mod.L. *transūdāre* to TRANSUDE: see -ATE³.] *intr.* = TRANSUDE.

1684 BOYLE *Porousn. Anim. & Solid Bod.* viii. 128 That Mercury and Aqua fortis being digested together in a Bolthead, may, by rubbing the outside of the Glass, be made visibly and palpably to transudate.

transudation (trɑːnsjuːˈdeɪʃən, træn-). Also 7 transs-. [ad. mod.L. *tran(s)sūdātio*, f. L. *trans* across + *sūdātio* a sweating. Cf. F. *transsudation* (18th c.).] The action or process of transuding; the passing off or oozing out of a liquid through the pores of a substance.

1612 WOODALL *Surg. Mate* Wks. (1653) 274 Transudation is, when in descensory distillation, the essence provoked, sweateth through, and is carried.. into the receiver. **1661** BOYLE *Certain Physiol. Ess.* (1669) 192 The drops.. proceeded not from the transudation of the Liquor within the Glass. **1794** SULLIVAN *View Nat.* I. xiv. 175 It causes transudations, evaporations, exhalations. **1848** CARPENTER *Anim. Phys.* 39 A simple transudation of the watery parts of the blood may take place.. in the dead as in the living body.

attrib. **1899** CAGNEY *Jaksch's Clin. Diagn.* viii. (ed. 4) 418 Transudation fluids may be serous, sanious, or in rare instances, chylous.

b. *concr.* Something which is transuded.

1650 H. BROOKE *Conserv. Health* 183 The more thick Transudation by the Ears. **1707** *Curios. in Husb. & Gard.* 101 The Manna of Calabria, and of Briançon, are only the Transudation of a Humour that breaths out of.. Larch-Trees. **1897** *Allbutt's Syst. Med.* IV. 322 The amount [of proteids] present in the transudations of renal disease are far below those seen in the transudations of cardiac disease.

tranˈsudatory, *a.* [f. ppl. stem of mod.L. *tran(s)sūdāre*: see next and -ORY².] Having the quality of transuding; characterized by transudation.

1752 RANDOLPH *Virtues Bath-Water* 53 It does not.. check the Exhalation of the transudatory Lymph. **1876** *Clin. Soc. Trans.* IX. 142 A cystoid or cicatrix, with their transudatory walls, favours the flow of intra-ocular fluids by exosmose.

transude (trɑːnˈsjuːd, træn-), *v.* Also 7 transsude. [ad. mod.L. *tran(s)sūdāre*, f. *trans* across + *sūdāre* to sweat. Cf. F. *transsuder* (18th c.).]

a. *intr.* To ooze through or out like sweat; to exude through pores (in the human body or anything permeable).

1664 EVELYN *Sylva* 54 From the latter [*Picea*] transsudes a very bright and pellucid Gum. **1744** MITCHELL in *Phil. Trans.* XLIII. 108 In Winter, when they are.. not covered with that greasy Sweat which transudes thro' them in Summer, their Skins feel more coarse. **1784** WEDGWOOD *ibid.* LXXIV. 383 Part of the water transudes through the vessel. **1877** ROBERTS *Handbk. Med.* (ed. 3) I. 31 The vessels become overloaded, and the fluid portion of the blood transudes.

b. *trans.* To ooze through (something) like sweat.

1781 KERR in *Phil. Trans.* LXXI. 378 As the Lac liquifies twist the bag, and when a sufficient quantity has transuded the pores of the cloth, lay it [etc.]. **1814** W. C. WELLS *Ess. Dew* (1866) 110 The pans.. are so porous that they readily permit water to transude them.

c. *trans.* in casual sense: To cause (something) to ooze through.

1861 HULME tr. *Moquin-Tandon* II. IV. i. 214 A fluid which they disgorge or transude from some part of their body. **1877** ROBERTS *Handbk. Med.* (ed. 3) I. 26 The vessels may be so distended as to transude serum.

Hence **tranˈsuded** *ppl. a.*, **tranˈsuding** *vbl. sb.* and *ppl. a.*

1756 NUGENT *Montesquieu's Spir. Laws* (1758) I. XIV. x. 326 After the transuding of the aqueous humour. **1772** *Phil. Trans.* LXII. 467 To let out extravasated or transuding fluids. *c* **1865** *Circ. Sc.* I. 333/1 A very great proportion of the transuded matters does not contribute to the nutrition. **1873** T. H. GREEN *Introd. Pathol.* (ed. 2) 319 The transuded serum usually differs from blood-serum in being of lower specific gravity.

† **tranˈsult**, *v. Obs. rare*⁻⁰. [ad. L. *tran(s)sultāre* to leap over, f. TRANS- + *saltāre* to leap.]

1623 COCKERAM, *Transult*, to leape away. **1656** BLOUNT *Glossogr.*, *Transult*, to leap or jump over, to overleap.

transum, obs. form of TRANSOM.

transume (trɑːn'sjuːm, træn-), *v. Obs.* exc. *Hist.* Also 5-7 **transsume.** [ad. (post-Aug.) L. *tran(s)sūmĕre*, f. *trans* across, over + *sūmĕre* to take, seize; in med.L. *transsumĕre*, *transsumptāre*, to transcribe, make a copy of. Cf. OF. *transumer* (1482 in Godef.).]

1. *trans.* To make an official copy of a (legal) document; = EXEMPLIFY 7. *Obs.* exc. *Hist.*

1482 in Rymer *Foedera* (1711) XII. 165/1 We have Decerned..the said Letters to be Exemplified and Transsumed. **1533** *St. Papers Hen. VIII*, I. 413 That the same Acte may be impressed, transumed, and set up on every churche dore. **1541** *Records of Elgin* (1903) I. 64 Ane transump and instrument transsumit out of Master Androu Cheves prothogall buik. **1545** *Reg. Privy Council Scot.* I. 10 The autentik copy of the said letter of merk autentikly transumyt in the toun of Arkis under the sele of the tabellioun and keparis of the sele of the vecunty of Arkis. **1598** D. WEDDERBURN *Compt Bk.* (S.H.S.) 157 David Ostlar ..restis awin me a Crown for transuming Andro Ostlaris barnis Seasingis. **1693**, **1765-8** [see TRANSUMPT *sb.*]. **1881** S. R. MACPHAIL *Relig. Ho. Pluscardyn* xi. 107 The original bull ..having been produced in court to be transumed.

†**2.** To take from one to another, take over; to transfer, transport. *Obs.*

1483 CAXTON *Pilgr. Sowle* IV. xxix. 76 This word statua, whiche that we transumen in to Englysshe, that is to mene an Image. **1627** W. SCLATER *Exp. 2 Thess.* (1629) 184 Termes properly belonging to time, are yet sometimes transsumed to denote what is pertinent to eternity. **1630** LORD *Relig. Persees* 17 The Angell..bade him close his eyes, and he would transume and rappe him up into that place of glory. **1656** [? J. SERGEANT] tr. *T. White's Peripat. Inst.* 382 Physicians affirm..the Seed of the Man disappears, being transum'd into the Flesh of the Woman.

†**3.** To transmute, change, convert (*into* something else).

1579 FULKE *Heskins' Parl.* 155 The bread and wine are transsumed. *Ibid.*, Though we take the word of transuming for changing, turning, transmuting, or transelementing,.. yet meane they not chaunge of one substance into another. **1652** CRASHAW *Carmen Deo Nostro* Wks. (1904) 249 With a well-bles't bread and wine Transsum'd, and taught to turn divine.

†**b.** *intr.* for *pass.* = TRANSMUTE *v.* 1 c. *Obs. rare.*

1480 CAXTON *Ovid's Met.* xv. iv, They [the four elements] be wont to transume, that one into that other.

¶ Some instances of *transume* in early printed books or modern editions from MS. are mis-readings of *transmue*: see quots. below; and in some of the passages quoted above in senses 2 and 3, *transmue* was possibly the author's word. It is possible that sense 3 originated in this confusion of form between *transume* and *transmue*.

1483 CAXTON *Gold. Leg.* 140/2 He..transumeth the payne perpetuell [*Fr. orig.* le muement de la paine de purgatoyre; *Lat. orig.* poenae purgatoriae..commutatio]..in to payne temporell. **1502** *Ord. Crysten Men* v. vi. (W. de W.) qq iv b, The soule shall be in suche wyse transumed [*Fr. orig.* transmuee] in god. **1543** *Harding's Chron.* CLXXVI. iv, Syr Hugh..was transumed [*rimes* pursued, renewed] In high estate. **1909** ed. of Pecock's *Bk. of Faith* c 1456, p. 157 The siʒt is the principal outward wit, and therfore his name may be transumed [*MS.* (Trin. Coll. Camb.) transmued] in to the name of ech othere outward witt.

transumpt (trɑːn'sʌm(p)t, træn-), *sb.* Also 5-6 *Sc.* **transump**, 5-7 **transsumpt**, 7 **transumt.** [ad. med.L. *tran(s)sumpt-um* transcript (Du Cange), f. ppl. stem of L. *tran(s)sūmĕre* (see prec.). Cf. OF. *transumpt* (15th c. in Godef.).] A copy, transcript; *spec.* a copy of a record, deed, or other legal document; an exemplification. (Chiefly in Sc. legal use from 16th c. to *c* 1870.) Hence, ***action*** or ***decree of transumpt***.

1480 *Acta Dom. Conc.* (1839) 50/1 þe originale letter..or elles ane autentic transump þerof. **1541** [see TRANSUME 1]. *c* **1555** HARPSFIELD *Divorce Hen. VIII* (Camden) 195 The transumpt of the said brief was sent to the King's agents. **1677** GALE *Crt. Gentiles* II. IV. 54 What are the Ten Commandments..but a Transumt,..Abstract or rather extended Copie of the Law of Nature given to man in the beginning? **1693** STAIR *Inst. Law Scot.* (ed. 2) IV. xxxi. §4 Although there be no express obligment to grant Transumpts, yet the Interest in common Evidents, is a sufficient Title to cause them be produced, to be Transumed. **1752** J. LOUTHIAN *Form of Process* (ed. 2) 283 For every Sheet of Decreets of Transumpt..0 14 6 Scots Money. **1755** CARTE *Hist. Eng.* IV. 118 A transumpt or copy was now taken of it. **1765-8** ERSKINE *Inst. Law Scot.* IV. i. §53. 657 An action of transumpt,..is competent to any person who has a partial interest in a writing,..against him in whose custody the writing lies, to exhibit it. *Ibid.*, When a decree of transumpt is questioned upon a ground of falsehood alledged against the writing transumed. **1810** G. CHALMERS *Caledonia* II. III. vi. 274 The citizens of Edinburgh..paid the money on the production of such a transumpt. **1878** DIXON *Hist. Ch. Eng.* I. iii. 151 *note*, An instrument made on a transumpt of the Breve. *Ibid.*, A definition of transumpt, the word lately revived in the State Papers, for a copy made by authority, or an attested copy.

†**b.** A pictorial representation, sketch, or engraving (of a work of art). *Obs. rare*$^{-1}$.

1629 MAXWELL *Herodian* b j *margin*, His [Commodus] naked Statue (as he plaid the Gladiator) is extant at Rome in the Fernesian Palace. See the Transumpt of it in M. G. Sandy's Iournall, p. 271.

†**tran'sumpt**, *ppl. a. Obs.* [ad. L. *transumpt-us*, pa. pple. of *transūmĕre* to TRANSUME.] 'Transumed', transferred, copied. (as *pa. pple.*)

1495 *Trevisa's Barth. De P.R.* II. v. (W. de W.) b iij/2 They [angels] ben lyckened to other thynges that ben take and transumpte of materyall thynges.

transumpt, obs. erron. form of TRANSOM.

†**tran'sumption.** ? *Obs.* Also 5 **transs-.** [ad. late L. *tran(s)sumptiōn-em* (Quintilian), n. of action f. *tran(s)sūmĕre* to TRANSUME. Cf. OF. *transumption* (15th c. in Godef.).]

1. Transcription, copying; a passage copied or taken from any author; a quotation.

1412-20 LYDG. *Chron. Troy* Prol. 264 Veyn[e] fables, whiche of entencioun They han contreved by false transumpcioun, To hyde trouthe falsely vnder cloude. **1451** CAPGRAVE *Life St. Gilbert* 85 All þese transumpciones folowing rehersith our auctour to þis entent, þat men of religion schuld not haue fair condiciones owtward and euel inward,..and soo may men expounne all þe othir transumpciones. *a* **1716** SOUTH *Serm.* (1744) VII. ii. 28 It was not Paul's design, to use these words..by way of citation out of David; but having by a kind of transumption and accommodation borrowed those former words of his.

2. The action of taking over from one to another; transference or translation to another part or place.

1615 CROOKE *Body of Man* 608 The aiery bodie..is nourished by blood brought by the Veines, and that *per Diadosin* that is by Transumption. **1656** E. REYNER *Rules Govt. Tongue* 213 Elijah informed Elisha of such things as should fall out in Israel after this transumption. **1684** tr. *Bonet's Merc. Compit.* VI. 242 A Sinus..out of which, sharp Ichores coming by transumption to the neck of the bladder.

3. *Rhet.* Transfer of terms; metaphor. See also quot. 1553.

c **1449** PECOCK *Repr.* II. xviii. 258 This colour of speche which in rethorick is clepid transsumpcioun. **1553** T. WILSON *Rhet.* (1580) 178 Transumption is, when by degrees wee goe to that, which is to bee shewed. As thus: Suche a one lieth in a darke doungeon, now in speakyng of darkenesse, we vnderstande closenesse, by closenesse, we gather blackenesse, and by blacknesse, we iudge deepenesse. **1624** BARGRAVE *Serm.* 7 Such parabolicall transumptions are to be expounded to the sense, not to the letter. **1677** GALE *Crt. Gentiles* II. IV. 280 The cause of this Transumtion is because we have not a word which properly signifies the stable mansion of Eternitie: wherefore we are forced to transfer, by way of similitude, our temporal words..to Eternitie. [**1880** LEWIS & SHORT *Lat. Dict.*, *Transumptio*, a taking or assuming of one thing for another, transumption, metalepsis, a transl. of μετάληψις, Quint. 8, 6, 37.]

4. *Logic.* In the Aristotelian logic (tr. Gr. μετάληψις), Conversion of a hypothetical proposition into a categorical one.

1628 T. SPENCER *Logick* 293 Aristotle doth call all compound Syllogismes by the name of Hypotheticall, because they inferre the conclusion vpon the supposition of some part thereof: & doth divide them into such as conclude according vnto transumption: and qualitie (that is as Pacius vnderstands it), when the minor is taken out of the maior; as ..If a man, then a living creature. But a man, therefore a living creature. [**1730-6** BAILEY (folio), *Transumptio* (with Schoolmen), a syllogism by concession or agreement, used where a question proposed is transferred to another with this condition, that the proof of this latter shall be admitted for a proof of the former.]

†**tran'sumptive**, *a. Obs.* or *arch.* [ad. L. *transumptīvus* (Quintilian), f. *transumpt-*, ppl. stem of *transūmĕre* to TRANSUME + *-īvus*, -IVE. Cf. OF. *transsumptivement* figuratively (Godef.).] Characterized by transumption; metaphorical.

1597 DRAYTON *Heroic. Epist.*, *Rosamond to Henry II*, Annot., Meander is a riuer in Lycia... Heereupon are intricate turnings by a transumptiue and Metonimicall kind of speech, called Meanders. **1657** W. MORICE *Coena quasi Κοινή* xxvi. 265 Some..apply this text in an accommodate and transumptive sense. **1662** J. CHANDLER *Van Helmont's Oriat.* 153 It was yielded to by a liberty transumptive or of taking one thing for another, without taking heed. [**1876** LOWELL *Among my Bks.* Ser. II. 44 'The form or mode of treatment', he [Dante] says, 'is poetic, fictive, descriptive, digressive, transumptive'.]

transunite (trɑːnsjuː'naɪt, træns-), *v. rare.* [TRANS- I.] *trans.* To unite across a space.

1652 GAULE *Magastrom.* 232 The fourth kind of phrenzie proceeds from Venus; and it doth, by a fervent love, convert and transunite the minde to God.

transuranic (trɑːnsjʊ'rænɪk, træns-, -nz-), *a. Physics.* [f. TRANS- II + URAN(IUM + -IC I b.] Of a chemical element: having a higher atomic number than uranium (i.e. 93 or over), the highest-numbered element to occur naturally in any but trace amounts.

1935 *Proc. R. Soc.* A. CXLIX. 553 Our hypothesis that the 13-minute and 100-minute induced activities of uranium are due to transuranic elements seems to receive further support. **1958** *Times* 29 Aug. 6/3 The..isolation of the transuranic elements. **1976** *Jrnl. R. Soc. Arts* CXXIV. 586/1 Seventy-two of the ninety-two naturally occurring elements are metals. If one includes the man-made transuranic elements the proportion remains about the same.

Also **transu'ranian** (*rare*), **-u'ranium** *adjs.*, in the same sense; also *fig.*

1938 R. W. LAWSON tr. *Hevesy & Paneth's Man. Radioactivity* (ed. 2) xxvi. 289 'Trans-uranium' elements were first prepared by Fermi. **1946** [see AMERICIUM]. **1947** CROWTHER & WHIDDINGTON *Science at War* iii. 129 He [*sc.* Fermi] concluded that he had made new atoms..and supposed that these must be 'trans-uranian' atoms. **1965** C. BROOKE-ROSE in J. Turner *Fourth Ghost Bk.* 181 The rumour spreads..through live material like a transuranian element decaying..into lead. **1971** *Nature* 6 Aug. 366/1 Seaborg..expressed the desire to return to California to resume his research on transuranium elements. **1978** N. FREELING *Night Lords* xxiv. 112 Night is what? A trans-uranium element, perhaps. **1979** *Monitor* (McAllen, Texas) 10 June 11-H/3 A person of almost transuranium energy.

transu'rethral, *a. Surg.* [f. TRANS- 5 + URETHRAL *a.*] Carried out via the urethra. Hence **transu'rethrally** *adv.*

1933 R. HOWARD *Practice of Surgery* (ed. 4) xxxvi. 1266 (*heading*) Transurethral endothermy. **1934** [see RESECTIONIST]. **1951** [see RESECTOSCOPE]. **1972** J. P. MITCHELL *Princ. Transurethral Resection & Haemostasis* xxvii. 227 It is difficult to..photograph the act of resecting transurethrally. **1980** *Brit. Med. Jrnl.* 29 Mar. 937/3 A very reasoned argument in favour of transurethral resection for the majority of benign enlarged prostates.

transuterine (trɑːns'juːtəraɪn, træns-), *a. nonce-wd.* [f. TRANS- 3 + L. *uter-us* womb: cf. *uterine.*] Beyond or outside of the womb.

1830 COLERIDGE *Ch. & St.* (ed. 2) 227 Do not the eyes, ears, lungs of the unborn babe, give notice and furnish proof of a transuterine, visible, audible atmospheric world?

Transvaal (ˌtrɑːns'vɑːl, ˌtræns-, -nz-). [f. TRANS- 7 + *Vaal*, a tributary of the Orange R. in S. Africa.] A former South African republic, now a province of the Republic of South Africa, lying north of the Orange Free State, from which it is separated by the River Vaal.

attrib. **Transvaal daisy**, *Gerbera Jamesonii*, a composite plant, introduced from the Transvaal in 1888.

1901 *Gardener* 12 Jan. 1049/1 The Transvaal Daisy..has been a bright patch for a long time... The large flame-coloured flowers..are a particularly fine sight.

Hence **Trans'vaaler**, a native or inhabitant of the Transvaal; **Trans'vaalian** *a.*, of or belonging to the Transvaal; **Transvaalite** (trɑːns'vɑːlaɪt, træns-, -nz-) *Min.* [-ITE[1] 2], a mineral consisting mainly of black oxide of cobalt, resulting from the alteration of cobalt arsenide, found at a cobalt-mine near Middleburg in the Transvaal.

1887 RIDER HAGGARD *Jess* x, You [are] going to show us *Transvaalers how to do it, eh? **1899** *Daily News* 19 Dec. 3/5 That the position of the Britishers under the *Transvaalian oligarchy would, in the end, become absolutely unbearable. **1890** MACGHIE & CLARK in *Engin. & Mining Jrnl.* (N.Y.) L. 96 *Transvaalite. **1896** in CHESTER *Dict. Min.*

transvalu'ation. [TRANS- I.] An alteration of values; revaluation. So **trans'value** *v. trans.*, to alter the value of, to re-value; **trans'valuer.**

1898 *Contemp. Rev.* May 738 The transvaluation of all values—the reversal of all accepted ideals. **1899** G. B. SHAW in *Sat. Rev.* 13 May (Suppl.) p. iii/1 Nietzsche ..'transvalued' our moral valuations. **1906** *Q. Rev.* Jan. 64 A certain 'transvaluation' of the traditional judgments about the comparative merits of various tendencies in Greek philosophy. **1908** MOZLEY in *Contemp. Rev.* Apr. 425 Christianity..is the real transvaluer of all values. **1911** *Daily News* 20 Oct. 5 On such an island..all moral values would have to be transvalued.

†**'transvasate**, *v. Obs. rare*$^{-1}$. [f. ppl. stem of med.L. *transvāsāre*, f. TRANS- I + L. *vās* vessel. Cf. EXTRAVASATE.] *trans.* = TRANSVASE. So †**transva'sation** [cf. F. *transvasation* (? 16th c. in Godef. *Compl.*)], the action or process of pouring out of one vessel into another.

1601 HOLLAND *Pliny* XXXIV. xviii. II. 519 This transvasation ought so long to be continued out of one vessell into another, untill such time as it have done casting any residence downward. **1673** *Phil. Trans.* VIII. 6022 This Alcalisat odor is lost by transvasation, that salt being thereby steamed away. **1678** CUDWORTH *Intell. Syst.* I. iv. §36. 619 For the Father and Son are not, as they suppose, tranvasated and poured out, one into another, as into an empty vessel; as if the Son filled up the concavity of the Father, and again, the Father that of the Son.

transvase (trɑːns'veɪs, træns-), *v. rare.* [a. F. *transvaser* (12th c. in Hatz.-Darm.), f. TRANS- + L. *vās* vessel.] *trans.* To pour out of one vessel into another. Also *fig.* Hence **trans'vasing** *vbl. sb.*

1839 URE *Dict. Arts* 587 The higher ouvreaux called the lading holes, because they serve for transvasing the liquid glass, are three in number. **1882** *Nature* 23 Feb. 388/1 Errors incident to the collection and the transvasing of the water. **1891** STEVENSON *Lett.* (1901) II. xi. 218 Something better to do than to transvase the work of others.

†**trans'vastory.** *Obs.*, perh. corr. of *transversary*, used by Bourne interchangeably with TRANSITORY B. 2, TRANSVERSARY B. 2.

trans'vectant. *Math.* [f. L. *transvect-*, ppl. stem of *transveh-ĕre* (see next) + -ANT.] An invariant or covariant derived from two binary forms by the operation of transvection.

1876 [see next 2].

transvection (trɑːnsˈvɛkʃən, træns-). [ad. L. *transvectiōn-em*, n. of action from *transveh-ĕre* (*-vect-*), f. *trans* across + *vehĕre* to carry.]

†**1.** The action of carrying or conveying from one place to another; transportation. *Obs.*

1615 CROOKE *Body of Man* 325 The transvection or transportation of aer..to the same Lungs of the infant. **1680** H. MORE *Apocal. Apoc.* 330 The consummate salvation of the Saints, or their transvection into those eternal Mansions of glory. **1682** —— *Annot. Glanvill's Lux O.* xiii. 105 That transposition..is..a transvection of them, rather than pulsion or traction.

2. *Math.* A method used by Clebsch and Gordan for deriving invariants and covariants from a product of two binary forms.

1876 SALMON *Lessons Introd. Mod. Higher Algebra* (ed. 3) xix. 272 If ϕ, ψ be covariants..we can obtain from them the series of covariants $\phi x^{p-k}\ \psi x^{q-k}(\phi\psi)^k$... This operation, in German called *Ueberschiebung*, we shall call transvection, and the covariants generated we shall call transvectants of the two given covariants.

transˈvector. *Math.* [f. TRANS- + VECTOR *sb.*] In *Quaternions*, The sum of a vector and a provector.

1853 SIR W. R. HAMILTON *Quaternions* (1866) 4 If a provector BC be added to a vector AB, the sum is the transvector AC; or in symbols, I..$(B - A) + A = B$; and II..$(C - B) + (B - A) = C - A$.

transˈvenom, *v. rare.* [TRANS- 2.] *trans.* To transform into something poisonous.

a **1667** JER. TAYLOR, Envy..transvenoms the honey of another man's comfort into the poison of asps for its own bosom. **1816** COLERIDGE *Statesman's Man.* 26 That atheistic philosophy, which in France transvenomed the natural thirst of truth into the hydrophobia of a wild and homeless scepticism.

transverbate (trɑːnsˈvɜːbeɪt, træns-), *v. rare.* [f. TRANS- 1 + L. *verb-um* word + -ATE[3]; after *transliterate.*] *trans.* To translate verbally or word for word. So **transverˈbation**, verbal translation.

1885 *Athenæum* 14 Mar. 349/2 (*Philological Society*) Mr. B. Dawson read a paper on the Revised Version of the New Testament... He commended the accuracy of the revisers, but condemned their 'transverbation' of the Greek. **1896–7** H. HAIGH in *Bible Soc. Record* (N.Y.) Jan. 2 If we could take the Hebrew and the Greek and transverbate them it would be comparatively easy.

†**transˈverberate,** *v. Obs. rare.* [ad. ppl. stem of L. *transverberāre*, f. TRANS- 1 + *verberāre* to beat.] *trans.* To strike through.

1623 COCKERAM, *Transuerberate*, to strike thorow. **1640** G. WATTS tr. *Bacon's Adv. Learn.* III. iv. 147 The appetencies of Matter, and the most universall Passions, (which in either Globe are exceeding Potent, and transverberate [L. *transverberant*] the universall nature of things).

So **transverbeˈration**, a striking through.

1881 H. J. COLERIDGE *Life & Lett. St. Teresa* I. 24 The room in which Teresa received her mystical transverberation—the piercing of her heart by a fiery dart.

transversal (trɑːnsˈvɜːsəl, træns-, -nz-), *a.* and *sb.* [ad. med.L. *transversāl-is* (*a* 1255 Albertus Magnus *Animal.* 13. 2. 1): see TRANSVERSE and -AL[1]. Cf. F. *transversal* (16th c. in Hatz.-Darm.).]

A. *adj.* **1.** Lying or passing across; = TRANSVERSE *a.* 1.

c **1440** tr. *Pallad. on Husb.* VI. 179 A double cours of boording..Oon transuersal, another cours directe. **1527** R. THORNE in Hakluyt *Voy.* (1589) 253 One of the transuersall lines. **1541** R. COPLAND *Guydon's Quest. Chirurg.* E iv, Openynge with two transuersall muscles. **1644** DIGBY *Nat. Bodies* xxvi. §5. 236 The hart hath in the ventricles of it, three sortes of fibers:..the third, are transuersall or thwart ones. **1755** *Phil. Trans.* XLIX. 119 Flames, rays, and fiery corruscations, direct and transversal. **1831** FARADAY *Exp. Res.* xlvi. 358 The direct vibration of the luminous body may communicate transversal vibration..to the molecules of the ether. **1908** *Contemp. Rev.* Mar. 369 A scheme for the construction of a transversal line which would link Odessa and Varna.

†**2.** *Genealogy.* Collateral: = TRANSVERSE *a.* 2.

[*a* **1308** DUNS SCOTUS *Sent.* 4. 40. 6 Transversalis.] **1594** PARSONS *Confer. Success.* II. viii. 184 He was of the right discendant lyne of K. John, and the Cardinal was but of the collateral or transuersal lyne. **1907** [? implied in TRANSVERSALLY].

3. *Conch.* = TRANSVERSE *a.* 1 c. (So in F.)

1835–6 *Todd's Cycl. Anat.* I. 710/2 All [shells] that are of greater breadth than length are named transversal.

B. *sb.* †**1.** Something transversal or lying athwart, a transverse line; *fig.* a deviation, digression. *Obs. rare.*

1597 LOWE *Chirurg.* (1634) 256 Three kinds of fibres which are Rights, Obliques, and Transversals. **1620** SHELTON *Quix.* (1746) III. xxvi. 183 On with your Story in a direct Line, and fall not into your Crooks and your Transversals.

2. *Geom.* A line intersecting two or more lines, or a system of lines.

1881 CASEY *Sequel to Euclid* 68 If two parallel lines be intersected by three concurrent transversals, the segments intercepted by the transversals on the parallels are proportional. **1885** EAGLES *Constr. Geom. Plane Curves* 15 Every transversal of a harmonic pencil is divided harmonically in the points in which it intersects the lines of the pencil. **1902** TOWNSEND tr. *Hilbert's Foundat. Geometry* 63 A segment [of a line] joining a vertex of a triangle with a point of the opposite side is called a *transversal*. A transversal divides the given triangle into two others having the same altitude and having bases which lie in the same straight line.

b. *Optics.* The line in which the plane of polarization of a beam of light intersects the wave-front; the transverse plane.

1909 in *Cent. Dict. Suppl.*

3. *Roulette.* A bet placed at the end of any three numbers taking them horizontally. Cf. TRANSVERSE B. 1 h. Also in Fr. form *transversale.*

transversale six, a bet placed on the line, taking in the three numbers above and the three below.

1895 G. MEREDITH *Amazing Marriage* ix, He stated that the number of 17 had won before. Abrane tried the transversal enclosing this favoured number.

‖**transversalis** (trɑːnsvəˈseɪlɪs, træns-). *Anat.* [med. and mod.L.: see prec.] A transverse muscle; one of the muscles, etc., that lie across various parts.

[**1704** J. HARRIS *Lex. Techn.* I, *Transversalis Colli*, is a Muscle of the Neck. **1827** ABERNETHY *Surg. Wks.* I. 292 The internal oblique and *transversalis* muscles.] **1872** HUMPHRY *Myology* 16 Between the external oblique and the transversalis.

transverˈsality. [f. TRANSVERSAL + -ITY.] The condition or state of being transversal.

1850 GREGORY *Reichenbach's Res. Magnet.*, etc. 421 We have placed beyond a doubt, the existence of transversality in the odylic phenomena. **1888** LD. RAYLEIGH in *Encycl. Brit.* XXIV. 450/1 The condition of transversality leads at once to the desired results.

transˈversally, *adv.* [f. as prec. + -LY[2].] In a transversal manner, transversely, athwart.

(In quot. 1641, app. = obliquely.)

1641 WILKINS *Math. Magick* I. xviii. (1707) 77 The several Proportions of Swiftness and Distance in an Arrow shot Vertically, or Horizontally, or Transversally. **1762** tr. *Busching's Syst. Geog.* V. 39 A shield twice longitudinally divided and three times transversally with a scutcheon of pretence. **1907** *Daily Chron.* 19 Jan. 3/1 [In the opinion of some] 'Heredity goes transversally, sideways, not in straight lines'.

transˈversan, *a. Bot.* [f. as TRANSVERSE *a.* + -AN.] (See quot.)

1900 B. D. JACKSON *Gloss. Bot. Terms* 274/1 *Transversan Plane*, that which passes through the centre of a Diatom frustule vertically to the pervalvar axis (O. Mueller).

†**transˈversant,** *a. Obs. rare*[−1]. [f. as TRANSVERSE *v.*[1] + -ANT.] Crossing, transverse.

c **1440** *Pallad. on Husb.* I. 564 But maak this hous wherin they [thrushes] shal abide Light, clene, and playn, with perchis transuersaunt To sitte vppon.

transˈversary, *a.* and *sb.* [ad. L. *transversāri-us* lying across: see TRANSVERSE and -ARY. Cf. F. *transversaire* (Littré).]

†**A.** *adj.* Transverse. *Obs. rare*[−1].

c **1400** *Lanfranc's Cirurg.* 148 Þe wesant..haþ noon [brawnys] transuersarie, þat is to seie goynge ouerþwert, for wiþholdynge is not nedeful to him.

B. *sb.* †**1.** The transverse beam or member of a cross. *Obs. rare*[−1]. [L. *transversarium* crossbeam.]

a **1608** DEE *Relat. Spir.* I. (1659) 185 Neither of the letters in the Transversary of the black Crosse.

2. A cross-piece or vane of a cross-staff. *Hist.*

1594 J. DAVIS *Seaman's Secr.* (1607) 17 Your staffe so ordered, then moue the transversary upon your staffe to and fro as occasion requireth. **1638** OUGHTRED in Rigaud *Corr. Sci. Men* (1841) I. 31 For setting the degrees on the transversary. **1879** A. GEIKIE in *Encycl. Brit.* X. 187/1 The cross-staff was a very simple instrument, consisting of a graduated pole with cross pieces, called transversaries.., also graduated, which were fitted to work on it.

transverse (trɑːnsˈvɜːs, træns-, ˈtrɑːnsvɜs, ˈtræns-, -nz-), *a.* (*sb.*, *adv.*, *prep.*) [ad. L. *transvers-us* turned or directed across, pa. pple. of *transvertĕre*: see TRANSVERT. Cf. F. *transverse* (16th c.).]

A. *adj.* **1. a.** Lying across; situated or lying crosswise or athwart; *esp.* situated or extending across the length of something, *spec.* at right angles (opp. to *longitudinal*). Also const. *to.*

1621 BURTON *Anat. Mel.* I. i. II. iii, *Fibræ* are strings, white and solide, dispersed through the whole member, and are right, oblique, transuerse, all which haue their seuerall vses. *a* **1687** PETTY *Treat. Naval Philos.* I. i, Three perpendicular length-way sections..and..a transverse section of the Hull. **1784** COWPER *Task* I. 561 A kettle slung Between two poles upon a stick transverse. **1815** W. SHEPHERD, etc. *Syst. Educ.* (1822) II. 112 The influence is not exerted in a direction parallel to the wire through which the electricity passes but in a direction transverse to it. **1855** H. SPENCER *Princ. Psychol.* (1872) II. VI. ii. 7 In similar masses of matter which are subject..to the transverse strain, the power of resistance varies. **1870** F. R. WILSON *Ch. Lindisf.* 64 A transverse set of pews in the Chancel.

b. *Her.* Crossing the escutcheon from one side to the opposite one. (Cf. quot. 1610 in D.)

c **1828** BERRY *Encycl. Her.* I. Gloss., Transverse, and Transverse in point, to the dexter and sinister.

c. In a bivalve shell: Of greater breadth than length or height; having the longer diameter transverse to the hinge.

1822 J. PARKINSON *Outl. Oryctol.* 180 A transverse bivalve.

d. In special collocations:

transverse alliteration, in the early verse of some Germanic languages, alliteration of the patterns *abab* or *baab* (the usage of scholars varies somewhat); **transverse artery**, *Anat.* one of the small branches given off at nearly right angles from the basilar; **transverse axis**, (*a*) an axis transverse to the main axis, as in a crystal; (*b*) *Geom.* the axis passing through the foci of a conic section (in an ellipse, the major axis): see AXIS[1] 7; **transverse bone**, *Zool.* in some reptiles, a bone connecting the pterygoid and maxilla; **transverse colon**, *Anat.* (see COLON[1]); **transverse fissure**, *Anat.* (*a*) the cleft below the hemispheres of the brain into which the pia mater extends to form the velum interpositum and choroid plexuses; (*b*) a short transverse cleft on the lower surface of the left lobe of the liver; **transverse flute**: see FLUTE *sb.*[1] 1; (now the usual name when specification is required; see also *cross-flute* s.v. CROSS B, *German flute* s.v. GERMAN *a.*[2] 4, QUERFLÖTE 1, TRAVERSO, etc.); **transverse ligament**, part of the cotyloid ligament; **transverse magnet**, a magnet formed by a combination of bar-magnets so that its poles are at the sides, not at the ends; **transverse magnetism, magnetization**, magnetization at right angles to the length of the bar; **transverse Mercator**, the name of a map projection obtained like the Mercator but with the globe turned through 90 degrees relative to the cylinder, so that the great circle where they meet is a pair of meridians rather than the equator; **transverse muscle**, *Anat.*, any one of various muscles extending across other parts; **transverse myelitis** *Path.*, myelitis which extends across a section of the spinal cord; **transverse process**, a lateral process of a vertebra; **transverse sinus**, a simple network of veins connecting the two inferior petrosal sinuses; **transverse suture**, the suture between the frontal and facial bones; **transverse vein**, *Entom.* any one of the several short veins of the wings of an insect, connecting two longitudinal ones.

1900 O. F. EMERSON in *Jrnl. Eng. & Gmc. Philol.* III. 127 (*heading*) *Transverse alliteration in Teutonic poetry. **1920** R. J. MENNER *Purity* p. lvi, Transverse alliteration—abab —appears in 515 For I se *wel* þat hit is sothe þat alle mannez *wyttez*. **1942** J. C. POPE *Rhythm of Beowulf* 154 Transverse alliteration occurs once with the whole-line pattern bx/ax/ax/bx. **1949** P. F. BAUM in *Mod. Philol.* XLVI. 146 The most interesting of these minor variations is the crossed or transverse alliteration *ab ab*. **1857** DUNGLISON *Med. Lex.* 926/2 *Transverse artery of the face, arises from the temporal, passes transversely across the face..and gives its branches to the different muscles of the cheek. **1704** J. HARRIS *Lex. Techn.* I. s.v. *Latus Transversum*, The longest Diameter in the Ellipsis, which Apollonius calls the *Transverse Axis, or Diameter. **1878** BELL *Gegenbaur's Comp. Anat.* 59 The other connects the sides of the body, and is the transverse axis. **1879** GROVE *Dict. Mus.* I. 536/1 It is held obliquely towards the right side of the player, like the modern *transverse flute. **1959, 1976** [see QUERFLÖTE 1]. **1980** *Early Music* July 313/1 Byzantine musical culture decisively influenced much of the corpus of musical instruments, including..the organ, transverse flute and the bowed instruments. **1840** E. WILSON *Anat. Vade M.* (1842) 101 The *transverse ligament is a strong ligamentous band. **1921** DEETZ & ADAMS *Elem. Map Projection* 104 In latitudes above 60° where the meridional parts of a Mercator projection increase rather rapidly, charts covering considerable area may be constructed..on..a *transverse Mercator, if the locality has predominating north-and-south dimensions. **1969** [see NATIONAL GRID 2]. **1974** *Encycl. Brit. Macropædia* XI. 476/1 Among the variations of cylindrical projections is the Transverse Mercator, in which the axis of the cylinder is parallel to the Equator, a treatment which has advantages in drawing maps that are long in the north-south direction. **1696** PHILLIPS (ed. 5), **Transverse Muscles*, the first pair shew themselves with a Membranous beginning, at the *Transverse Processes of the Vertebra of the Loyns. **1879** *N.Y. Med. Jrnl.* XXX. 387 (*heading*) *Transverse myelitis. **1903** TUBBY & JONES *Mod. Methods in Surg. Paralysis* i. 33 Transverse myelitis in adults is more likely to be confused with the rare condition of poliomyelitis. **1964** J. J. WALSH *Understanding Paraplegia* iii. 16 Approximately 30% of the patients at the National Spinal Injuries Centre develop paraplegia from causes other than injury. Of these a proportion result from infections of various kinds, and are usually grouped under the heading of 'myelitis' or 'transverse myelitis'. **1696** *Transverse process [see *transverse muscle*]. **1840** E. WILSON *Anat. Vade M.* (1842) 8 The transverse processes project one at each side from the laminæ of the vertebra. *Ibid.* 341 The *Transverse sinus passes transversely across the basilar process of the occipital bone. **1741** MONRO *Anat.* (ed. 3) 75 The *Transverse Suture runs quite cross the Face, from the external Canthus of one Orbit to the same Place of the other. **1860** MAYNE *Expos. Lex.*, *Transverse Suture*,..a suture which passes across the face, sinks down into the orbits, joining the bones of the skull to those of the face.

†**2.** Of kindred: Collateral, as between brothers, cousins-german, etc. *Obs. rare.*

1614 SELDEN *Titles Hon.* Pref. B iv, A Monster, that is not like him that got him, nor any other of the ascending or transuerse line. **1651** G. W. tr. *Cowel's Inst.* 154 This Discent ought to be to the next Heirs, Males or Females, in a direct or transverse line. **1660** JER. TAYLOR *Duct. Dubit.* II. iii. rule iii. §9. 401 The Grand Parent of a Family; from whom the direct descendants are for ever to be reckon'd to the Kinred in the strait and proper line: but when once it goes to the transverse and collateral, they not onely have no title to the inheritance, but [etc.].

3. In combination with other adjs. (*Entom.*): **transverse-cubital, -medial** *adjs.* = TRANSVERSO- *cubital, -medial*; **transverse-quadrate** *a.*, quadrate with the transverse diameter the longer.

1840 tr. *Cuvier's Anim. Kingd.* 528 Having the thorax transverse-quadrate.

B. *sb.* [The *adj.* used *absol.*]

1. Something that is transverse: *spec.* †**a.** A cross or transverse part or member. *Obs. rare.* †**b.** *Fortif.* ? = TRAVERSE *sb.* 16. *Obs. rare.* **c.** The transverse axis of a conic section. **d.** See quot.

1867. **e.** A transverse muscle. **f.** *Arch.* (See quot. 1842–76.) **g.** The sprocket axle of a chain-driven motor-car. **h.** *Roulette* = TRANSVERSAL B. 3.

a. *a* **1633** AUSTIN *Medit.* (1635) 108 The Transverse of the Crosse..is held to have bin a peece, much about that length. **1634** BP. HALL *Contempl., N.T.* IV. *Crucifixion*, Having fastened the transverse to the body of that fatal tree.

b. 1704 J. HARRIS *Lex. Techn.* I, *Transverse*, in Fortification, is a little Trench bordered with two Parapets ..which the Besiegers make quite thwart the Moat of the Place, to pass secure from Flank-shot, and to bring the Miners to the Bastions.

c. 1743 EMERSON *Fluxions* 244 Let the Transverse of the Ellipsis = 2*r*, Conjugate = 2*c*.

d. 1867 THOMSON & TAIT *Nat. Phil.* I. I. §120 Mark a line ..along its length, such that it shall be a straight line parallel to the axis... A line drawn from any point of the axis perpendicular to this side line of reference, is called the transverse of the rod at this point.

f. 1842–76 GWILT *Archit.* Gloss. s.v. *Chambranle*, The top of a three-sided chambranle is called the transverse, and the sides ascendants.

g. 1907 *Westm. Gaz.* 22 Nov. 10/1 Their manufactures include live axles of various types and sizes, transverses, change-speed and brake levers [etc.].

h. 1899 *Scribner's Mag.* XXV. 90/1 He placed eight louis on the number nineteen, and 1,200 francs on the line between nineteen and twenty-two, thus playing the 'transverse'.

†**2.** *by transverse* [L. *per transversum*], in a transverse position, crosswise; athwart. *Obs. rare.*

1596 SPENSER *F.Q.* VII. *Mutability* VII. lvi, Nothing doth firme and permanent appeare, But all things tost and turned by transverse.

C. *adv.* In a transverse direction or position; transversely, across, athwart. Now *rare* or *poet.*

1660 R. COKE *Justice Vind.* 41 When they are cut transverse, they are cut to right angles. **1671** MILTON *Samson* 209 These two proportiond ill drove me transverse. **1726** LEONI *Alberti's Archit.* I. 51/2 Beams across from one Wall to the other..are Columns laid transverse. **1798** BLOOMFIELD *Farmer's Boy, Spring* 93 And o'er the whole Giles once transverse again, In earth's moist bosom buries up the grain.

†**D.** *prep.* Across, athwart. *Obs. rare.*

1607 TOPSELL *Four-f. Beasts* (1658) 161 One of them descendeth, and goeth down into the Ditch, and standeth transverse or crosse the same. **1610** GUILLIM *Heraldry* III. xxii. 166 All Fishes being borne Transuerse the Escocheon must in blazon be termed Naiant.

transverse (trɑːns'vɜːs, træns-, -nz-), *v.*[1] Now *rare.* [a. OF. *transverser* (13th c. in Godef.) = med.L. *transvers-āre* (Du Cange) to cross, f. L. *transvers-*, ppl. stem of *transvertĕre*: see TRANSVERT.]

1. *trans.* To pass or lie athwart or across; to cross, traverse. *rare.*

1430–40 LYDG. *Bochas* IX. x. (MS. Bodl. 263) 417/1 Ther shon wer..Richeli transuersed with gold weer. **1545** RAYNOLD *Byrth Mankynde* 7 In Latin: musculi transuersi: Bycause they transuerse or ouerthwart the belly. **1873** MIVART *Elem. Anat.* x. 413 The internal carotid transverses the petrous part of the temporal bone.

†**b.** *fig.* To act or speak in opposition to; to cross, thwart; in *Law* = TRAVERSE *v.* 12. *Obs.*

1387–8 T. USK *Test. Love* I. ii. (Skeat) l. 195, I trowe the strongest and the best that maie bee founde, woll not transuers thy wordes. **1628** SIR S. D'EWES *Jrnl.* (1783) 45 He was presentlie transversed and over-ruled by his flatterers. **1704** J. HARRIS *Lex. Techn.* I. s.v., To transverse an Indictment, is to take Issue upon the chief Matter, and to contradict or deny some Point of it. **1769** R. CUMBERLAND *Brothers* II. ii, That perverse hussey..threatens to transverse all my hopes.

†**c.** *intr. fig.* To go across or athwart; to run counter; to transgress *against*. *Obs. rare.*

1377 LANGL. *P. Pl.* B. XII. 284 Ac trewth þat trespassed neuere, ne transuersed aȝeines his lawe. **1393** *Ibid.* C. IV. 449 And ho so takeþ aȝen treuthe oþer transuerseþ aȝens reson Leaute shal do hym lawe.

2. *trans.* To turn upside down or backwards; to overturn, turn topsy-turvy. Now *rare* or *Obs.*

c **1520** BARCLAY *Jugurth* (1557) 18 As if thei wer belies of ships transversed or turned vp set downe. **1643** HOWELL *Parables on Times* Ep. Ded. 2 These sad confusions which have so unhing'd, distorted, transvers'd, tumbled and dislocated all things. **1738** WHITEFIELD in *Life & Jrnls.* (1756) 50, I could not but transverse the Prodigal's Complaint: How many are ready to perish with hunger, whilst I have enough and to spare. **1859** G. MEREDITH *R. Feverel* xiv, In love, it is said, all stratagems are fair, and many little ladies transverse the axiom by applying it to discover the secrets of their friends.

b. To convert into something different; to alter, transform. (Cf. TRANSVERSE *v.*[2])

1687 PRIOR & MONTAGU (*title*) The Hind and the Panther Transvers'd To the Story of The Country-Mouse and the City-Mouse. *c* **1700** SIR J. MONTAGUE in *N. & Q.* 7th Ser. (1889) VIII. 430/1 Making several essays to transverse.. other parts of the poem. **1702** *Modesty Mistaken* 5 Having transvers'd the two famous Lines of Sir J. Denham to the scandal of Bottled Ale.

Hence **trans'versed** *ppl. a.*, placed crosswise, crossing, transverse.

a **1711** KEN *Hymnotheo* Po. Wks. 1721 III. 85 His heav'nly Banner..Wrought with direct and with transversed Rays.

trans'verse, *v.*[2] [f. TRANS- 2 + VERSE *sb.*; cf. TRANSPROSE. (Orig. as a kind of pun or play on prec.)] *trans.* To turn into verse; to translate or render in verse.

[**1671** VILLIERS (Dk. Buckhm.) *Rehearsal* I. (Arb.) 31, I take a Book in my hand..if there be any Wit in't,..I Transverse it; that is, if it be Prose, put it into Verse.., if it be Verse, put it into Prose.] **1672** [H. STUBBE] *Rosemary & Bayes* 2 To pilfer from other men; and if they write in prose, he doth trans-verse them. **1732** FIELDING *Debauchees* Prol. 10 Old worn-out Jokes..Transvers'd from Prose, perhaps transpros'd from Rhimes. **1881** SAINTSBURY *Dryden* viii. 159 Having taken the fancy to transverse some Arthurian stories.

transversely (trɑːns'vɜːslɪ, træns-, -nz-), *adv.* [f. TRANSVERSE *a.* + -LY[2].] In a transverse manner or direction; across, athwart; crosswise.

1650 BULWER *Anthropomet.* 225 Another membrane, which transversely..doth cover the chink of the Hymen. **1658** SIR T. BROWNE *Gard. Cyrus* i. 96 Not transversly or rectangularly intersected, but in a decussation, after the form of an Andrean or Burgundian cross. **1777** COOK *Voy. Pacific Ocean* II. i. (1784) I. 178 An open end, which represented an ellipse divided transversely. **1822** J. PARKINSON *Outl. Oryctol.* 180 A..transversely oblong bivalve. **1878** W. H. DALL *Later Preh. Man* 16 There are eighteen threads to the inch longitudinally and twenty-four transversely. **1884** BOWER & SCOTT *De Bary's Phaner.* 347 A layer of transversely elongated, partly thick-walled elements.

trans'verseness. *rare.* [f. as prec. + -NESS.] The condition or state of being transverse.

1867 C. J. SMITH *Syn. & Antonyms* s.v. *Across*, Transverseness to a line of movement becomes opposition.

transversion[1] (trɑːns'vɜːʃən, træns-, -nz-). [n. of action fr. L. *transvert-ĕre* to turn across, TRANSVERT; cf. *conversion, inversion*, etc.]

1. The action of turning across or athwart; intersection; a turning into something else, conversion, perversion, transformation; trans-position. *rare.*

1656 BLOUNT *Glossogr.*, *Transversion*, a turning away or crosse, a traversing, or going athwart. **1658** SIR T. BROWNE *Gard. Cyrus* i. 96 Nor shall we take in the mystical Tau, or the Crosse of our blessed Saviour, which having in some descriptions an Empedon or crossing foot-stay, made not one single transversion. **1671** [see next]. **1716–20** *Lett. fr. Mist's Jrnl.* (1722) I. 9 As if they intended a Transversion of Christendom to its first Paganism. **1870** LOWELL *Study Wind.* 331 A transversion common with him.

2. *Logic.* (See quot. 1933.) *Obs.* or *rare.*

1890 E. E. C. JONES *Elements Logic* xix. 143 These may be called *Mixed Eductions*, or *Transversions*. *Ibid.* 148 In Transversion, the most interesting points are that all Inferentials and Alternatives may..be fully and accurately expressed in Categorical form. **1933** C. A. MACE *Princ. Logic* vii. 121 A transversion may be defined as an immediate inference from a proposition of one logical form to another proposition which contains the same 'material content' but is of a different logical form.

3. *Molecular Biol.* The occurrence in a nucleic acid of a purine in place of a pyrimidine or vice versa. Cf. TRANSITION 5.

1959 E. FREESE in *Proc. Nat. Acad. Sci.* XLV. 631 The mutagenic effect of the second kind involves the 'transversion' of a nucleotide pair, in which a purine is replaced by a pyrimidine. **1980** *Nature* 8 May 82/2 All the point mutations are transversions in the second position of each of four codons.

trans'version[2]. [n. of action f. TRANSVERSE *v.*[2]] A turning into verse; *concr.* a metrical version of something.

(Quot. 1671 appears to combine this with prec.)

[**1671** VILLIERS (Dk. Buckhm.) *Rehearsal* I. (Arb.) 31 My first Rule is the Rule of Transversion, or *Regula Duplex*, Changing Verse into Prose, or Prose into verse.] **1796** W. TAYLOR in *Monthly Mag.* I. 404 The following transversion of a passage from Ossian's Carthon, may give an idea of the practicability of such metres in the English tongue. **1898** *Q. Rev.* Jan. 100 Bayes's rules for the composition of plays.. —the rule of transversion for instance.

transversive (trɑːns'vɜːsɪv, træns-, -nz-), *a.* *rare*[−1]. [f. L. *transvers-*: see TRANSVERSE *v.*[1] and -IVE.] Having the effect of crossing or thwarting.

1855 BAILEY *Mystic* 43 The will Of man, so oft transversive of the truth.

transverso- (trɑːns'vɜːsəʊ, træns-), used as combining form of L. *transvers-us* TRANSVERSE (see -o *suffix*), in a few rare scientific terms: **trans,verso-'cubital, trans,verso-'medial** *adjs.*, *Entom.* crossing the cubital, or the medial, cells of the wing, as certain nervures. **trans,verso-'spinal** *a.*, *Anat.* an epithet of several muscles attached to the transverse processes of the vertebræ. **trans,verso-'vertical** *a.*, relating to, or expressing the ratio between, the transverse and vertical dimensions (greatest breadth and greatest height), as the ***transverso-vertical index*** in craniometry.

1857 DUNGLISON *Med. Dict.*, Transverso-spinal. **1891** *Cent. Dict.*, Transversocubital, Transversomedial, Transversovertical.

†**trans'vert**, *v. Obs.* [ad. L. *transvertĕre* to turn across, f. *trans* across + *vertĕre* to turn.] *trans.* To turn across or athwart; to turn *into* something else, transform, convert; to turn about, reverse, overturn.

1432–50 tr. *Higden* (Rolls) II. 191 Somme men hauenge senowes as transuertede and ouercrossede thro alle the body, haue bene of grete myȝhte. *c* **1450** *Craft of Lovers* 419 Why mens langage wol procure and transuert The will of women and virgines innocent? **1552** HULOET s.v. *B*, In composicions, B. is transuerted into these letters C. F. G. P. V. *Ibid.*, Preposterouse, out of order, overthwarth, transuerted. **1608** DOD & CLEAVER *Expos. Prov.* xi–xii. 143 They usually transuert their fauor and iustice, shewing mercy where they should exercise seuerity, and practising cruelty where they should shew mercy. **1651** HOWELL *Venice* 185 To transvert the Keys of Paradise into the Keys of a Prison. *a* **1660** *Contemp. Hist. Irel.* (Ir. Archæol. Soc.) III. 80, I maye lawfully saye, as our Saviour saide unto Saule,..transuertinge onely his name: Vllacke, Vllacke, cur me persequeris?

Hence †**trans'vertible** *a. Obs.*, capable of being transverted.

? **16..** [? SIR T.] BROWNE cited in Webster (1864).

Transverter (trɑːns'vɜːtə(r), træns-, -nz-). *Electr. Engin.* Also **transverter**. [f. TRANS-(FORMER + CON)VERTER.] An apparatus for converting alternating current into high-voltage direct current, and vice versa. (A proprietary name in the U.S.)

1916 *Official Gaz.* (U.S. Patent Office) 16 May 1070/1 *Transverter*... Electric motors, electric generators, and electric-motor generators. **1924** *Glasgow Herald* 17 June 9 The machine..is called a transverter... It both transforms, by raising the pressure and converts into direct current. **1975** *Oxford Times* 5 Dec. 15/4 Mr Geoff Day..spoke.. about a 384MHz amplifier for use with a 23cm transverter.

trans'vesical, *a. Med.* [f. TRANS- 5 + VESICAL *a.*] Passing or performed through the bladder.

1926 YOUNG & DAVIS *Young's Practice of Urol.* I. ii. 52 It is most important to empty the bladder at the end of the test period, to determine from this transvesical urine how much, if any, phthalein has escaped outside the catheters into the bladder. **1976** *Lancet* Dec. 1221/2 An uneventful transvesical prostatectomy was done.

†**trans'vest**, *v. Obs. rare.* [f. TRANS- 1 or 2 + L. *vestīre* to clothe, or Eng. VEST *v.*] *trans.* To clothe in other garments, e.g. those of the opposite sex; to disguise. Cf. TRAVESTY.

1652 J. WRIGHT tr. *Camus' Nat. Paradox* II. 42 How often did shee please her fancy with the imagination of transvesting herself, and by the help of a Man's disguise deceiving the eyes of those that watched her deportments? **1654** tr. *Martini's Conq. China* 199 No Man but some horrid wild Beast, or rather..some Devill transvested in our humane Nature.

transvestic (trɑːns'vɛstɪk, træns-, -nz-), *a.* [f. TRANSVESTISM or TRANSVESTITE *sb.* and *a.*: see -IC.] Of or pertaining to transvestism; transvestite.

1961 in WEBSTER s.v., Patients with transvestic tendencies. **1966** *Internat. Jrnl. Psycho-Anal.* XLVII. 384 (*heading*) The mother's contribution to infantile transvestic behaviour. **1976** *National Observer* (U.S.) 16 Oct. 10/3 Its basic elements are meticulous screening, designed to exclude applicants who are primarily homosexual, transvestic or psychotic.

So **trans'vesticism** (-ɪsɪz(ə)m) (now *rare*) = TRANSVESTISM.

1937 *Times Lit. Suppl.* 27 Feb. 145/2 By his 'transvesticism'..the mother's brother identifies himself with the mother and all she stands for. **1959** *Times* 31 Oct. 8/7 A group of four from the choir are not difficult to name in spite of temporary transvesticism.

transvestism (trɑːns'vɛstɪz(ə)m, træns-, -nz-). [ad. G. *transvestismus*, f. L. *trans* TRANS- + *vestīre* to clothe: see TRANSVEST *v.*, -ISM.] The action of dressing in the clothes of the opposite sex; the condition of having an abnormal desire to dress in the clothes of the opposite sex.

1928 [see EONISM]. **1938** *Spectator* 2 Dec. 962/1 So unimportant is the sexual element that transvestism is common in many dance-forms [in Bali] and produces no feeling of embarrassment. **1959** *Listener* 2 July 31/2 The transvestism which is part of the witch/fairy tradition. **1977** E. J. TRIMMER et al. *Visual Dict. Sex* (1978) xix. 199 The most common cases of transvestism are heterosexual men leading otherwise conventional sex lives.

Hence **trans'vestist** *sb.* and *a.* = TRANSVESTITE *sb.* and *a.*

1944 'M. INNES' *Weight of Evidence* viii. 88 One of those portraits of her in page's costume. She must have been what they call a transvestist nowadays. **1959** P. BULL *I know Face* xi. 197, I played the part of Miss Eve Ashley's mother, and the gentleman dressers at Lime Grove were not unpleased by this transvestist carry-on. **1961** *Guardian* 27 Jan. 8/7, I tired of all those transvestist photographs. **1972** *Daily Tel.* 23 Mar. 8/1 He was a clothes fetishist and eventually a transvestist.

transvestite (trɑːns'vɛstaɪt, træns-, -nz-), *sb.* and *a.* [ad. G. *transvestit*, f. L. *trans* TRANS- + *vestīre* to clothe: see -ITE[1].]

A. *sb.* A person with an abnormal desire to wear the clothes of the opposite sex.

[**1910** M. HIRSCHFELD (*title*) Die Transvestiten.] **1922** J. VAN TESLAAR tr. *Stekel's Bi-sexual Love* ii. 69 Among the transvestites (personifiers) we find the most pronounced examples of marked homosexuality and stressed bi-sexuality. **1937** *Human Biol.* IX. 501 The transvestite must attempt to duplicate the behavior-pattern of his adopted sex. **1964** in W. H. Goodenough *Explorations Cultural*

Anthropol. 490 The *bate*, male transvestites,..excelled women in butchering, tanning, and other domestic tasks. **1976** SMYTHIES & CORBETT *Psychiatry* xi. 211 Transvestites wear the clothing of the opposite sex to obtain sexual gratification.

B. *adj.* Of or pertaining to transvestism or transvestites; of a person: who wears the clothes of the opposite sex.

1925 A. L. KROEBER *Handbk. Indians California* xxxiii. 497 The transvestite sexual perverts recognized by all North American tribes. **1937** *Human Biol.* IX. 501 An almost senile singer, said to be the last person to know the transvestite initiation songs. **1957** *Observer* 29 Dec. 9/1 According to scholarship, the principal boy in our transvestite pantomimes is a Saturnalian hangover. **1971** *Times* 16 Sept. 12/6 He moves as a suburban schoolmaster between the male aggression of his classroom and the frou-frou of his transvestite boudoir.

transvestitism (trɑːns'vɛstɪtɪz(ə)m, træns-, -nz-). [ad. G. *transvestitismus*, f. *transvestit*: see prec., -ISM.] = TRANSVESTISM.

[**1913** M. HIRSCHFELD in *Neurol. Zentralblatt* XXXII. 946 (*heading*) Ein Fall von Transvestitismus bei musikalischem Genie.] **1934** in WEBSTER. **1949** [see MOHAVE]. **1976** *Jrnl. Amer. Psychoanal. Assoc.* XXIV. III. 545 The analysis of a patient with the presenting symptom of transvestitism revealed a prominent set of fantasies of being 'initiated' and taught by a seductive and glamorous woman..in the art of dressing and make-up. **1983** *Financial Times* 4 Oct. 13 If there is a true sub-text to this farcical evening, devoted to voluntary or involuntary transvestitism, it is the satirical reference to psychiatrists' belief that simple things are all the consequence of serious, probably sexual, stimuli.

So **transve'stitic** *a.* = TRANSVESTITE *a.*; **trans'vestitist** *rare* = TRANSVESTITE *sb.*

1936 A. HUXLEY *Eyeless in Gaza* xviii. 233 Beppo giggled. 'Yes, those transvestitists!' he had to admit rapturously. **1977** *Gay News* 24 Mar. 13/1 Thus heterosexual, homosexual..transvestitic, and dozens of other special relationships hold the potential of working well. **1980** *Jrnl. Sex & Marital Therapy* Summer 124 Individuals rarely seek treatment for..transvestitic problems.

†**trans'view**, *v. Obs. rare.* [TRANS- 2.] *trans.* To look through.

1602 J. DAVIES *Mirum in Modum* (Grosart) 9/2 Let vs with Eagles eyes without offence Transview the obscure things that do remaine.

†**trans-'village**, *v. Obs. nonce-wd.* [f. TRANS- 2 + VILLAGE *sb.*] *trans.* To transform or reduce (a town) to the size of a village.

1608 SYLVESTER *Du Bartas* II. iv. IV. *Decay* 242 Their Towns trans-villag'd, the Ten Tribes transported To a far Clime.

†**transvo'lation**. *Obs.* [n. of action from L. *transvolāre* to fly across or over, pass across (in OF. *transvoler*, 14th c.), f. TRANS- + *volāre* to fly.] The action of flying or passing beyond the ordinary limits. (In quots. *fig.*)

1649 JER. TAYLOR *Gt. Exemp.* I. xii. 8 However Jesus had some extraordinary transvolations and acts of emigration beyond the lines of his ordinary conversation, it was but seldom. **1651** —— *Serm. for Year* I. iv. 50 Extraordinary egressions and transvolations beyond the ordinary course of an even piety.

†**trans'volve**, *v. Obs. rare.* [f. TRANS- 1 + L. *volvĕre* to roll. Cf. L. *transvolvĕre* to roll past or by, to unroll.] *trans.* To roll over, overturn.

1644 HOWELL *Eng. Teares* 184 The great Deity of Heaven (who transvolves Kingdomes, and tumbleth down Kings in his Indignation). **1651** —— *Venice* 179 Shall we admit in our free States an Authority, which..pretends to have power to controul, and transvolve the Dominions of others?

†**trans'waft**, *v. Obs. rare.* [f. TRANS- 2 + WAFT *v.*] **a.** *intr.* To float across through air or water. **b.** *trans.* To convey or carry across a river or sea. So †**tran'swaftage** [cf. WAFTAGE], a conveying or floating across.

1624 HEYWOOD *Gunaik.* I. 31 From thence she came to Hæmus, and transwafted thence to a gulfe of Thracia, which by her was called Bosphorus. *Ibid.* IV. 209 In her transwaftage over the flood Evenus. **1635** —— *Hierarch.* III. 128 Because Ioues Trull Europa, he from Sidon into Creet Transwafted, whilest the waue her feet.

trans-'world, *a.* [f. TRANS- 3 + WORLD *sb.*] That travels across the world; world-wide.

1955 R. J. SCHWARTZ *Compl. Dict. Abbrev.* 178/2 *TWA*,.. Trans World Airlines, Inc. **1959** I. & P. OPIE *Lore & Lang. Schoolch.* i. 7 It seems that the schoolchild underground also employs trans-world couriers. **1962** *B.B.C. Handbk.* 50 The BBC Television Service is now looking forward to.. transatlantic and even to trans-world television broadcasting.

trans'written, *ppl. a. nonce-wd.* [TRANS- 2.] Transcribed, or ? translated.

1874 RUSKIN *Fors Clav.* xl, This is an ill written, and worse trans-written, human history, and not by any means 'Word of God'.

Transylvanian (trɑːnsɪl'veɪnɪən, -æ-), *sb.* and *a.* [f. *Transylvania* (see below) + -AN.] **A.** *sb.* A native or inhabitant of Transylvania, formerly the eastern portion of Austria-Hungary, now part of Romania.

1644 MILTON *Areopagitica* 30 Nor is it for nothing that the grave and frugal Transilvanian sends out yearly..their stay'd men, to learn our language and our *theologic* arts. **1757** A. BUTLER *Lives Saints* III. 867/1 The vizir with one hundred and fifty thousand Turks (besides Hungarians, Transylvanians and Tartars) sat down before Vienna. **1927** [see CARTEL *sb.* 3d]. **1976** P. HENISSART *Winter Quarry* xvi. 157 The only smart people in this country [*sc.* Hungary] are the Jews and the Transylvanians.

B. *adj.* Of or pertaining to Transylvania; *spec.* applied to a kind of deep red Turkish rug or carpet frequently found in Transylvanian churches.

1843 *Penny Cycl.* XXV. 165/1 The German universities are frequented by a considerable number of Transylvanian students, especially for divinity. **1875** *Encycl. Brit.* III. 116/1 The Transylvanian Highlands extend over Transylvania..into Moldavia and Wallachia. **1915** *Guide to Collection of Carpets* (Victoria & Albert Museum) ii. 45 It seems probable that these 'Transylvanian' carpets were made in Anatolia. **1929** E. G. METCALFE *Metcalfe Coll. Oriental Rugs* vii. 31 This is an excellent specimen of the finest Transylvanian prayer rugs. **1957** *Encycl. Brit.* XIX. 624/1 (*caption*) So-called 'Transylvanian' rug, Asia Minor, 17th century. **1978** R. WESTALL *Devil on Road* x. 64 The [dog's] collar..had as many studs as a Transylvanian torture-implement.

transynaptic, var. TRANS-SYNAPTIC *a.*

†**trant**, *sb. north. dial. Obs.* [Origin obscure. Identical in form with Du. *trant* 'manner, way, method, kind', in MDu. also 'step, pace'. It is conceivable that from some of these senses there might arise the notion of 'shift, clever or cunning way or course, device, trick' (cf. F. *tour* and Eng. *turn*), but historical links are wanting.]

Cunning action, trickery; a stratagem, a trick (always in an evil sense).

13.. *Gaw. & Gr. Knt.* 1700 Summe fel in þe fute, þer þe fox bade, Traylez ofte a trayteres [? a travers], bi traunt of her wyles. *c* **1400** *Destr. Troy* 12210 For to take hit [Troy] by treason & trantis of hym. *c* **1440** *York Myst.* xxix. 234 þis was a trante of a traytour. *c* **1460** *Towneley Myst.* xvi. 235 Hard I neuer sich a trant that a knafe so slight Shuld com lyke a sant and refe me my right. *Ibid.* xxv. 162, I know his trantes fro top to tayll.

†**trant**, *v.*[1] *Obs. rare*$^{-1}$. [Goes with prec.] *intr.* To practise cunning devices; to employ cunning, craft, trickery, or deception.

13.. *Gaw. & Gr. Knt.* 1707 [The fox] trantes & tornayeez þurȝ mony tene greue.

trant, *v.*[2] *rare.* Now *dial.* Also 6 **traunt**. [app. a back-formation from TRANTER; cf. PEDDLE.] *intr.* To follow the occupation of a tranter. Hence **'tranting** (**'traunting**) *ppl. a.*

1597–8 BP. HALL *Sat.* IV. ii. 145 Who..had some traunting merchant to his sire, That traffick'd both by water and by fire. **1898** T. HARDY *Wessex Poems* 201 Naibour Sweatley..Who tranted and moved people's things.

trant(e, obs. form of TRENTE (at Cards).

tranter ('trɑːntə(r), -æ-). Now *dial.* Also 4–7 **traventer**, 6–7 **trauntor**, **trawnter**, 9 **traunter**. [*Tranter*, *traunter*, *trawnter* known from 1500, app. syncopated from *traventer* (see quot. 1601), in med.(Anglo-)L. *trāvetārius*, of uncertain origin.

A derivation formally possible for med.L. *trāvetārius*, would be that it was a corruption of L. **tra(ns)vectārius*, f. *transvehĕre* to transport, *transvectio* transportation.]

A word having various local uses: chiefly denoting a man who does jobs with his horse and cart; a carrier; a hawker or cadger with horse and cart; a huckster; also, one who buys up things to sell them elsewhere; †in 14–15th c. a tapster: see quots.

[**1233** *Pat. Roll 18 Hen. III*, m. 17 Willelmus de Londonia trauetarius habet literas de conductu car[ucarum] suarum. [(in Calendar p. 32) Safe-conduct until Easter for William de London, the tranter, for his carts.] *Ibid.*, Willelmus de Norhamptona trauetarius Regis habet literas de saluo conductu. **1282** *Welsh Roll* No. 3. m. 2d. (P.R.O.), Accepimus quod trauetarii et alii victualia et alia nobis et fidelibus nostris..in partibus Wallie necessaria ducentes. **1350** *Letter-Bk. F. Lond.* lf. 181 b, Item q' les garsouns des seriauntz..cariage ne pregnont pluis des charettes ne de chivaux q' meister ne soit, et ceo de trauenters et chivaux q' sount allowers. [By Riley *Memorials London* (1868) 256 explained as 'Persons who let out carts on hire.] *a* **1400** *Litt. Red Bk. Bristol* (1900) II. 37 Diuerses trauenters de ceruoise. [*Ibid.* 38 Mettre a vendre ceruoys en trauentrie.]] **1500** *Gloucester Rec.* in *12th Rep. Hist. MSS. Comm.* App. IV. 433 That alle maner of traunters and tapsters sel of the best ale a galon for I d qar. **1562** in Picton *L'pool Munic. Rec.* (1883) I. 79 No..trauntors shall buy any corn until the town be served. **1601** F. TATE *Househ. Ord. Edw. II*, §51 (1876) 35 When he goeth..to make purveiance for poultry, he shal have with him the trauenters, which must be in the same office or some of them; these trauntors names shalbe entred in the warderobe. **1642** *Declar. Lords & Comm.* 31 Dec. 3 The robbing of the common Carriers and Trawnters. **1681** BLOUNT *Glossogr.*, *Tranters*..are those that bring fish from the Sea-side in Wales to the Midland. Elsewhere call'd Ripiers. *a* **1700** B. E. *Dict. Cant. Crew*, *Tranter*, the same as *Crocker*. **1744–50** W. ELLIS *Mod. Husbandm.* IV. II. 103 (E.D.S.) The word traunter I take to mean, strictly, any person that buys wheat in sacks to sell again in sacks. **1801** MASON *Suppl. Johnson*, *Tranters*..Country people, amongst whom alone this word is current, extend its meaning to all those who purchase any kind of provisions in order to sell them again. *c* **1880** *Bedford Dialect.* Mr. So-and-So the corn traunter bought 1500 quarters of wheat yesterday. **1891** T. HARDY *Tess* xvii, One of the family that used to do a good deal of business as tranters over there. **1899** C. K. PAUL *Mem.* 60 He had become a 'tranter', doing odd jobs, haulage of manure, and the like. **1906** SIR F. TREVES *Highways & Byways Dorset* Pref. 8 In this Sleepy Hollow they will find the untroubled life of the past,..will meet the tranter on the leisurely road.

Hence †**'trantery** (in 4 **trauentrie**, 6 **trawntrey**), *Obs.* or ? *dial.*, the occupation of a tranter; retailing of ale, etc.: see also quot. 1670.

1330 *Kenfig Ord.* in Gross *Gild Merch.* (1890) II. 133 [from a 16–17th c. copy] Noe manner of person shall..cutt carne or trawntrey or ostrey hold, unless he be a burgess. *a* **1400** Trauentrie [see above]. **1670** BLOUNT *Law Dict.*, *Trantery*, So in some Mannors they call the Money arising by Amercements of Alesellers and Victuallers, for breaking the Assise of Bread and Ale, as at Luston, and other Mannors in Herefordshire... But why so called *Quære*. **1706** in PHILLIPS (ed. Kersey).

'trantles, †**trantals**, *sb. pl. Sc.* [app. corruption of TRENTALS, taken as a type of trifling ceremonies.] Trifles, trifling or petty articles.

[**1562** A. SCOTT *New Yeir Gift to Q. Mary* 89 Poems (S.T.S.) 4 Thai tyrit God with tryfillis, tvme trentalis, And daisit him with daylie darigeis.] **1697** CLELAND *Poems* 88 Such are baptizing of bells, Hallowing Altars, Kirk and Cells..For to impose gray Gowns, or Mantles, Or any such base Tritle Trantles. **1824** MACTAGGART *Gallovid. Encycl.*, *Trantles*, bits of broken iron; odd things of hardware about a farm-house, same with *trantlums*; there are generally boles or holes about, where broken horse-shoon [etc.] be thrown; these are termed *trantle-boles*. *a* **1903** J. LUMSDEN *Toorle*, etc. 206 A' kind o' trantles they could find They braucht along!

'trantlum, *sb.* (*a.*) *Sc.* Also 8 **trantlin**, **-lim**. [Extension of prec.] A trifle, knick-knack, toy; usually in *pl.*

1768 ROSS *Helenore* I. 32, I came fiercelins in, An' wi' my trantlims made a rattlin dinn. **1776** C. KEITH *Farmer's Ha'* xxix, They finger at the trantlimslang. **1841** W. AITKEN *Poet. Wks.* 67 Your trantlums a' e'en break or burn. **1896** CROCKETT *Cleg Kelly* x, To the curbstane ye gang, wi' a' your traps and trantlums.

b. *attrib.* or as *adj.* Trifling.

1832 RODGER in *Whistlebinkie* (1890) I. 147 Their trantlum gear She couldna bear.

tranylcypromine (ˌtrɑːnaɪl'saɪprəmiːn, -æ-). *Pharm.* [f. *tran*s-2-phen*ylcyclopro*pyl*amine*, the systematic name, f. TRANS- 9a + PHENYL + CYCLO- 2 + PROPYL + AMINE.] A monoamine oxidase inhibitor, $C_9H_{11}N$, used in the treatment of severe depression (usu. in the form of the sulphate).

1959 *Proc. Soc. Exper. Biol. & Med.* CII. 380 (*heading*) Some pharmacological observations on tranylcypromine (SKF *trans*-385). **1964**, **1965** [see PARNATE]. **1976** *Lancet* 27 Nov. 1164/1 Six patients with neurogenic orthostatic hypotension were treated with a chemical preparation of tyramine and tranylcypromine.

trap (træp), *sb.*[1] Forms: 1 **treppe**, **træppe**, 3–5, 7 **trapp**, 4–6 **trappe**, 4– **trap**. [Late (and rare) OE. *treppe*, *træppe* (in *coltetræppe*), ME. *trappe*, *trapp*, agrees in form and sense with rare MDu. *trappe* trap, gin, snare, mod.WFlem. *traap*, *trape* (De Bo), in Kilian, 1599, '*trappe* (old word) mouse-trap, trap'; also with med.L. *trappa*, *trapa*, in Salic Law vii. 10 (MSS. of 8–9th c.), 'trap', OF. *trape* (12th c.), F. *trappe*, Prov. *trapa*, Pg. *trapa*, Sp. *trampa*; cf. also It. *trappola* (dim. of **trappa*); all in sense 'trap, pitfall, gin, snare'. The relations between the Romanic words and the Du. and Fl., and the relation of the latter to MDu. and MLG. *trappe*, *treppe* 'step, stair', are difficult to determine: see *Note* below.]

1. a. A contrivance set for catching game or noxious animals; a gin, snare, pitfall: cf. MAN-TRAP *sb.*, MOUSE-TRAP, RAT-TRAP, SPRING-TRAP.

In the common type, a spring or other device, released by the animal treading upon it, shuts the latter in, or catches hold of some part of it, in this case often killing it.

a **1000** ÆLFRIC *Gloss.* in Wr.-Wülcker 95/13 Ic beswice fuȝelas hwilon mid neton . mid grinum,..mid treppan (*decipula*). *c* **1386** CHAUCER *Prol.* 145 She wolde wepe if that she saw a mous Kaught in a trappe. **1483** *Cath. Angl.* 391/2 A Trapp (*A.* Trape), *decipula*, *pedica*. **1484** CAXTON *Fables of Æsop* I. xviii, The same lyon was take at a grete trappe. **1538** ELYOT, *Decipula*, a grynne [*ed.* 1545 gyn] or trap to take byrdes. **1577** GOOGE tr. *Heresbach's Husb.* 156 b, I would rather counsell you to destroy your Rattes and Mise with Traps. **1597** G. HARVEY *Trimming Nashe* Wks. (Grosart) III. 48 How happie the Rat caught in a trappe, and there dies a living death? **1599** SHAKS. *Hen. V*, I. ii. 177 We haue ..pretty traps to catch the petty theeues. **1611** BIBLE *Jer.* v. 26 They lay waite as hee that setteth snares, they set a trap, they catch men. **1655** MRQ. WORCESTER *Cent. Inv.* §72 It catcheth his hand as a Trap doth a Fox. **1719** DE FOE *Crusoe* I. 171, I set three Traps..and going the next Morning I found them all standing, and yet the Bait eaten and gone. **1791** W. H. MARSHALL *W. England* (1796) II. 256 The Salmon Fishery of the Tavey... At one end of the dam, is a 'weir house' or Trap; on the principle of the vermin trap, whose entrance is outwardly large, but contracted inwardly, so as to..prevent the escape of the animal which has taken it. **1857** TENNYSON *Geraint & Enid* 1571 A sudden sharp and bitter cry, As of a wild thing taken in the trap. **1883** *Fisheries Exhib. Catal.* 252 Fish Traps... Shrimp Trap. Eel Trap. Crab Traps. **19..** *Trade Catal.*, Patent automatic mouse trap. Balloon fly traps. Beetle trap. Patent trap for catching rats, stoats, weasel, rabbits, badger, otter, and other vermin and animals, also..all kinds of birds.

b. *transf.* and *fig.*, and in fig. expressions.

Often applied to anything by which a person is unsuspectingly caught, stopped, or caused to fall; also to anything which attracts by its apparent easiness and proves to be difficult, anything deceptive.

c **1200** ORMIN 12301 He fandeþþ þa to lacchenn þe þurrh trapp off modiȝnesse. *c* **1386** CHAUCER *Frankl. T.* 613 She wende neuere han come in swich a trappe. **1412–20** LYDG. *Chron. Troy* IV. 2659 Ȝif þei myȝt cacche hym in a trappe. **1509** HAWES *Past. Pleas.* xvi. (Percy Soc.) 64 Sodaynly my herte was in a trap By Venus caught. **1611** BIBLE *Rom.* XI. 9 Let their table be made a snare, and a trap, and a stumbling blocke. **1654** BRAMHALL *Just Vind.* iii. (1661) 40 The cruel statute of the Six Articles; which he made.. as a trap to catch the lives of the Poor Protestants. **1765** FORDYCE *Serm. Yng. Wom.* (1767) II. viii. 30 Let her lay traps for admiration. **1879** DIXON *Windsor* I. ii. 15 He resolved to take the Scottish invader in a trap. **1883** E. PENNELL-ELMHIRST *Cream Leicestersh.* 377 Two deep, hidden grips in midfield were nasty traps for blown horses.

c. Popularly applied to a police arrangement for the timing of motorists over a measured distance, in order to secure the conviction of such as exceed the legal speed-limit. Also ***police-trap***.

1906 *Westm. Gaz.* 28 Aug. 4/2 The fear of the traps and the consequent fines is.. an inducement to avoid tours in England... Car owners do not care to take the risks of the traps.

d. A device which allows a pigeon to enter but not to escape from a pigeon loft.

1876 R. FULTON *Illustr. Bk. Pigeons* 274 Let the board, upon which the birds alight (when the trap is closed and admission only to be obtained through the bolting wires) be carried upon a pair of hinges. **1912** W. E. BARKER *Pigeon Racing* i. 5 Others.. swear by a steeply sloping roof.. to compel the birds to drop upon a trap or alighting board. **1961** H. BLUNT *Tackle Pigeon Racing this Way* iii. 30 The trap can be made of stout galvanized wire,.. curved to facilitate use by the birds without injury.

2. a. A movable covering of a pit, or of an opening in a floor, designed to fall when stepped upon; hence applied to any similar door flush with the surface in a floor, ceiling, roof, the top of a cab, or the like: cf. TRAP-DOOR.

13.. *Coer de L.* 4093 Doun ye scholde fallen there, In a pyt syxty fadme deep: Therfore beware,.. At the passing of the trappe, Many on has had ful evyl happe. *c* **1374** CHAUCER *Troylus* III. 692 (741) And with þat word he gan vn-do a trappe, And Troylus he brought In by þe lappe. **1470–85** MALORY *Arthur* XIX. vii. 784 Sir launcelot that no peryl dredde.. trade on a trap and the bord rollyd, and there sir Launcelot felle doune more than ten fadom in to a caue ful of strawe. **1682** DRYDEN *Mac Fl.* 212 Bruce and Longville had a trap prepared, And down they sent the yet declaiming bard. **1800** in S. Rosenfeld *Temples of Thespis* (1978) x. 149 Theatre traps and cutting out bricks. **1838** DICKENS *O. Twist* ix, He.. drew forth.. from some trap in the floor: a small box. **1879** F. W. ROBINSON *Coward Consc.* II. vi, 'All right', said the cabman.. as he closed the trap. **1904** KIPLING in *Windsor Mag.* Jan. 228/2 Pyecroft.. rising like a fairy from a pantomime trap. **1907** H. WALES *The Yoke* xviii, He pushed up the trap with his umbrella: 'Stop at the first jeweller's', he said to the [cab] driver. **1977** S. BRETT *Star Trap* xiii. 142 The stage.. had been equipped with the full complement of trap doors... Downstage were the corner traps, small openings used for the appearance or disappearance of one actor... Then there was the Grave Trap centre stage.. always used for the Gravediggers' scene in Hamlet.

b. The mouth, esp. in phrr.: ***shut your trap!*** be quiet!; ***to keep one's trap shut***, to remain silent. *slang.*

1776 E. GIBBON *Let.* 19 Dec. (1896) I. 298 You may say in general in the family (if any should bark) that you are satisfied with my conduct, and order them to shut their trap. [**1785, 1860**: see *potato-trap* s.v. POTATO *sb.* 7.] **1866** J. T. STATON *Rays fro' Loominary* 90 Shut thy trap, faything. **1899** *Star of Hope* 12 Aug. 1/1 Why in h—— don't those recruits.. keep their traps shut? **1939** A. HUXLEY *After Many a Summer* II. i. 187 If only the rest were silence! But that's the trouble with poets... They will not keep their traps shut, as we say in the Western hemisphere. **1959** J. BRAINE *Vodi* xxiv. 255 'Shut your bloody trap,' Dick said. **1981** M. DUFFY *Gor Saga* II. 48 If Emily should open her great trap and spill the lot she could find herself deep in trouble.

3. a. The pivoted wooden instrument with which the ball is thrown up in the game of TRAP-BALL, q.v.; hence by extension, the game itself.

1591 [implied in TRAPSTICK]. **1598** FLORIO, *Lippa*, a trap or cat, such as children play at. *Ibid.*, *Trappola*... Also a play that children vse called trap. **1637** SHIRLEY *Hyde Park* II. iv. D iv, I have heard you.. in your younger [days] could play at trap well. **1652** J. TAYLOR (Water P.) *Journ. Wales* (1859) 26 The.. laudable games of trapp, catt, stool-ball, racket, etc. **1719** D'URFEY *Pills* III. 162 We merrily Play At Trap. **1801** STRUTT *Sports & Past.* II. iii. §20 The trap.. is generally made in the form of a shoe, the heel part being hollowed out for the reception of the ball; but boys and.. rustics, who cannot readily procure a trap, content themselves with making a round hole in the ground.

b. ***trap (bat) and ball***: = TRAP-BALL.

1825 HONE *Every-day Bk.* I. 430 A game at trap-and-ball. **1868** HUGHES *Tom Brown* (ed. 6) Pref. 11 Playing trap-bat-and-ball. **1877** *Cornh. Mag.* XXXVI. 368 To play trap-and-ball with Robin and Jack.

4. a. A device for suddenly releasing or throwing into the air an object to be shot at, as a pigeon.

1812 *Sporting Mag.* XL. 41 The trap was twenty-one yards from the gun. **1813** *Ibid.* XLI. 84 The parties fired with double-barrelled guns at two pigeons from a trap. **1892** GREENER *Breech Loader* 234 It is wise to shoot pigeons at recognised clubs only.. or experience at the trap may be very dearly bought.

b. In greyhound-racing, the compartment from which a dog is released at the start of a race.

1928 A. R. D. CARDEW *Greyhound Racing* 13 The owner.. is invited.. to attend the draw for trap places 1 to 6, No 1 being the inside trap. *Ibid.* 18 (*caption*) Leaving the starting trap. **1954** R. DAHL *Someone like You* 251 The traps went up and the dogs flew out. **1977** *Listener* 30 June 847/3 The dogs barked in their traps. Then the hare was running.. and the dogs were out.

5. *colloq.* or *slang.* Deceitful practice; trickery; fraud. ***to understand trap***, to know one's own interest; ***to be up to trap***, to be knowing or cunning.

1681 T. FLATMAN *Heraclitus Ridens* No. 5 (1713) I. 30 Well, Brother, I understand Trap. *a* **1734** NORTH *Exam.* III. vii. §63 (1740) 549 Some cunning Persons, that had found out his.. Ignorance of Trap,.. put him in great Fright, telling him he would certainly be hanged. **1785** COWPER *Let. to Lady Hesketh* 15 Dec., He understands book-sellers' trap as well as any man. **1819** *Metropolis* II. 107 A papa too much up to trap to allow his offspring thus to be *had.* **1837** W. IRVING *Capt. Bonneville* II. i. 15 The beaver now being completely 'up to trap', approaches them cautiously. **1842** S. LOVER *Handy Andy* ii, A clever, ready-witted fellow, up to all sorts of trap. **1877** J. HABBERTON *Jericho Road* xix. 170 You needn't come any of your.. moral tricks on me. I'm up to trap. **1902** *Westm. Gaz.* 14 Oct. 2/1 A 'policy' undistinguishable from trap in appearance.

6. One whose business is to 'trap' or catch offenders; a thief-taker; a detective or policeman; a sheriff's officer. Now only *Austral. slang.*

1705 E. WARD *Hud. Rediv.* IV. v. 8 All girt with Chaps, Men, Boys, and Women, Traps Divers, Punks, and Serjeants Yeomen. **1800** *Sporting Mag.* XVI. 26 Send the traps to pull up Bounce and Blunderbuss. **1812** J. H. VAUX *Vocab. Flash Lang.* in *Mem.* (1964) 275 *Traps*, police officers, or runners, are properly so called; but it is common to include constables of any description under this title. **1828** P. CUNNINGHAM *N.S. Wales* (ed. 3) II. 232 While the culprit stood quaking in the dock, surrounded by the traps of office. **1838** DICKENS *O. Twist* xiii, 'Why, the traps have got him, and that's all about it', said the Dodger, sullenly. **1882** T. SHEFFIELD *Story of Settlement* 85 Amusing tales are told of how the excisemen or 'traps' sent to try to obtain evidence of illicit dealing were hoodwinked. **1898** in M. Davitt *Life & Progr. Australia* xxxv. 192 A policeman is a 'Johnny', Or a 'copman' or a 'trap'. **1902** SNAITH *Wayfarers* i, Expecting at every cast of the cards.. to hear the boots of the 'traps' from Bow Street upon the stairs. **1905** *Daily News* 2 Jan. 9 Prisoner.. said he was convicted upon the false evidence of a 'trap'—a Kaffir spy. **1935** L. MANN *Human Drift* xxviii. 185 Suddenly there came a cry 'The traps, look out, the —— traps. The Joes, Joes.' He turned and saw a cordon of mounted and foot-police endeavouring to surround the crowd which scattered away from them. **1945** [see DEMON[2] 1]. **1970** *Sunday Mail Mag.* (Brisbane) 18 Jan. 14/6 After the arrests Derrincourt and Wilson were kept apart. Little did the former know that the latter was telling the traps how William Derrincourt had engineered the whole business.

7. *colloq.* A small carriage on springs; usually, a two-wheeled spring carriage, a gig, a spring-cart. Cf. RATTLETRAP 2.

1806–7 J. BERESFORD *Miseries Hum. Life.* VI. Introd., Bidding a long adieu to Bedlam in the shape of an inn.. and a travelling trap for a sitting room. **1818** in *Illustr. Lond. News* (1884) 4 Oct. 315/3 His 'trap' was at the lodge, and.. he must be off. **1848** THACKERAY *Van. Fair* lxvi, 'Hullo!' said he, 'there's Dob's trap'... The 'trap' in question was a carriage which the Major had bought for six pounds sterling. **1873** M. COLLINS *Squire Silchester* III. xiv. 143 Come with me to the stables. I'll have a trap out and drive to the Rectory. **1902** BUCHAN *Watcher by Threshold* 194 A trap shall be sent for you after dinner.

8. a. A device for preventing the upward escape of noxious gases from a pipe, as a double curve in or U-shaped section of the pipe, in which water stands.

1833 LOUDON *Encycl. Archit.* §464 No smell can penetrate upwards, it being intercepted by the trap and the water into which it dips. **1862** *Catal. Internat. Exhib.* II. x. 46 Traps to prevent effluvia from drains and gulleys. *Ibid.* xxxi. 24 Surface gutter with movable safety covers, sanitary traps. **1884** *Health Exhib. Catal.* 49/2 Water Closet of improved manufacture, ornamental bason and trap. **1892** D trap [see D I. 2].

b. Applied to various contrivances for preventing the passage of steam, water, silt, etc. Also, a ventilation door in a mine.

1877 KNIGHT *Dict. Mech.*, *Steam-trap*, a self-acting device for the discharge of condensed water from steam-engines or steam-pipes. **1900** *Dundee Advertiser* 9 June 8 On the dead levels by the river the drainage water is run through tunnels piercing the embankments, each outlet having a trap or lock to prevent the tide from rushing up to drown the fields. **1900** *Daily News* 14 Feb. 3/2 Here and there [in a coal-mine].. are placed the ventilating doorways, or traps. At each of these sits the little trapper lad alone in the silent gloom. **1911** WEBSTER, *Trap*,.. a device to separate sand and silt from flowing water.

c. *Geol.* An underground rock formation in which an accumulation of oil or gas is trapped; so ***oil trap***.

1920 *Econ. Geol.* XV. 249 Trap structures contain the majority of the important accumulations of oil. **1938** D. HAGER *Pract. Oil Geol.* (ed. 5) iii. 56 Areas of heavily metamorphosed rocks the unfavorable for gas and oil accumulations, unless the oil has migrated to traps in such rocks. **1946** *Nature* 28 Dec. 931/2 In considering the distribution of structures which might act as oil-traps, the field of inquiry may be limited to those geological formations which provide some indication of the presence of oil. **1969** BENNISON & WRIGHT *Geol. Hist. Brit. Isles* xii. 282 Salt-dome structures.. commonly give rise to oil traps, salt being capped by gypsum. **1977** *Offshore Engineer* May 38/1 Seismic evidence suggests thick deeply buried deposits onlapping old ridges which may form hydrocarbon traps.

d. *Radio.* A resonant circuit used as a rejector or acceptor circuit to block or divert signals of a specific frequency, esp. to reduce interference in a receiver tuned to a nearby frequency; = *wave trap* s.v. WAVE *sb.* 10.

1927 B. F. DASHIELL *Pop. Guide to Radio* xii. 236 A properly designed trap should not affect the tuning of the set to any great degree. **1957** *Practical Wireless* XXXIII. 570/1 Should there be any I.F. break-through traps, they should be done [*sc.* aligned] next. **1974** HARVEY & BOHLMAN *Stereo F.M. Radio Handbk.* v. 113 The low-pass filter is followed by a 38 kHz trap.. to remove any residual 38 kHz component.

9. a. A recess in the butt of a musket or rifle, in which accessories are carried.

1844 [implied in *trap-plate*: see 12]. **1891** *Magazine Rifle Firing Exerc., Aiming Drill*, The oil bottle is to be carried in the trap in the butt... Push the thong into the trap,.. press down the end of the thong and close the trap. **1909** *Text-bk. Small Arms* 119 The short Springfield rifle is provided with a butt trap, containing a metal oil-bottle, holding oil at one end and a pull-through at the other.

b. The part of a stake- or trap-net in which the fish are confined.

1859 *Act 22 & 23 Vict.* c. 70 §12 A clear Opening of at least Three Feet in Width in the Traps or Chambers of such Stake Net from the Bottom to the Top thereof.

c. *U.S.* = *trap-net* (see 12).

1888 GOODE *Amer. Fishes* 216 Nets.. similar in many respects to the so-called 'traps' of Seconnet River in Rhode Island. **1891** in *Cent. Dict.*

d. *Golf.* = SAND-TRAP 2. Cf. BUNKER 4 a. Chiefly *U.S.*

1890 H. G. HUTCHINSON *Golf* xiii. 313 That little round trap of a Strath's bunker not three yards nearer you. **1903** J. L. LOW *Concerning Golf* ix. 173 Bunkers.. refuse to be disregarded, and insist on asserting themselves... That little bunker on the seventeenth green at St. Andrews.. that 'trap' bunker at the third green at North Berwick. **1933** F. OUIMET *Game of Golf* xvi. 236 Billy waded into the sand and blasted his ball out of the trap. **1952** B. CERF *Good for Laugh* 173 How many shots did you have in that trap? **1971** 'D. HALLIDAY' *Dolly & Doctor Bird* xv. 215 Wallace Brady.. landed in the long, pale trap in front of the green and stayed there doing explosive shots with a sand-wedge.

10. *Weaving.* A break in the threads of a warp; a faulty place resulting from this in woven cloth.

1871 BURNLEY *Phases Bradford Life* (1872) 197 Ere the loom ceases its motion, what is technically termed 'a trap' has occurred... A large number of 'ends' are broken, and must be tied neatly together again one by one before the work can proceed. **1883** *Gloss. Almondbury & Huddersfield* s.v., A bad place in the cloth is the consequence, and that is also called a trap. **1891** *Labour Commission Gloss.*, *Traps*, also called 'smashes' or 'mashes', are faults in weaving caused by the shuttle becoming *trapped*, which will break out the twist or warp threads for several inches in the width.

11. *Physics.* A site in a crystal lattice which is capable of temporarily immobilizing a moving electron or hole.

1945 *Proc. R. Soc.* A. CLXXXIV. 366 Thermoluminescence and long-period phosphorescence arise from the release of electrons from metastable levels or traps. **1971** *Physics Bull.* Oct. 579/1 Laboratory studies use UV, x ray or corpuscular.. excitation to fill the traps, which are then emptied on heating. **1980** *Cambr. Encycl. Archaeol.* 426/2 In the structure of the crystal lattice of most minerals there are defects or imperfections known as traps.

12. *attrib.* and *Comb.*, as ***trap-bait***, ***-cage***, ***-catch***, ***-chair***, ***-lid***, ***-load***, ***-maker***, ***-mouth***, ***-setter***, ***-setting***, ***-tooth***, ***-way***, ***-window***; ***trap-like*** adj.; **trap-bat**, a bat used in playing trap or trap-ball; also, the game itself; **trap-board**, a perforated board in a Jacquard loom: see quot.; **trap boat** *N. Amer.*, a boat used for fishing with trap-nets; †**trap-bridge**, a drawbridge; **trap-cellar**, the space beneath the trap-doors in the stage of a theatre; **trap-creel**, a basket used for catching lobsters, etc.; **trap-crop**, a crop planted for the purpose of attracting insects or fungus from another crop; †**trap-ditch**, a ditch dug as a pitfall; **trap-fisher**, one who fishes with a trap-net; **trap-gun**, (*a*) (see quot. 1964); (*b*) a shotgun used in trap-shooting; **trap-hatch**, a hatch covered with a trap or trap-door; so **trap-hatchway**; **trap-hole**, a hole closed by a trap-door; also (*pl.*) pits dug in the ground to serve as obstacles to an enemy, *trous-de-loup*; **trap-hook**, a fish-hook fitted with a spring snap, a snap-hook; **trap-house**, a shelter from which clay pigeons are released for trap-shooting; **trap-light**, a light having a device for trapping moths attracted by it; **trap-line**, (*a*) the ensnaring filament in a spider's web; (*b*) *N. Amer.*, a series of hunter's traps; **trap-match**, a trap-shooting match; **trap-nest** orig. *U.S.*, a nesting-box which a hen can enter but cannot leave until released; also as *v. trans.*; hence **trap-nesting** *vbl. sb.*; **trap-net**, a large net for catching fish: see quot. 1877; **trap-pit**, a deep pit in which beasts are trapped; also *fig.*; **trap-plate**, the hinged lid of the trap in a musket or rifle stock (see 9 a); **trap-poacher**, a poacher who traps game; **trap-point**, on railways, a safety-point (POINT *sb.* B. 3 f) which prevents an unauthorized movement of a train or vehicle from a siding on to the main line by derailing it; **trap-seine** (*U.S.*), a kind of trap-net; **trapshoot** *N. Amer.*, a trap-shooting contest or event; **trap-shooter**, **-shot**, one who practises trap-shooting; **trap-shooting**, the sport of shooting pigeons, glass balls, etc., released from a spring trap; **trap-shy** *a.*, of an animal: reluctant to approach a trap; hence **trap-shyness**; **trap-siding**, a siding on a gradient intended to intercept vehicles which break away from an ascending train and to derail them; **trap skiff** *N. Amer.* = *trap boat* above; **trap-tree**, the jack-tree, *Artocarpus integrifolia*, which provides gum for bird-lime; also (*U.S.*) a tree deadened or felled at a time when destructive beetles have entered the bark; **trap-twister**, **-winder**, in *Spinning*, a twisting or winding machine in which the roller or bobbin is stopped by a spring arrangement as soon as the yarn breaks (cf. 10); **trap-valve**: see quot.; **trap-weir** (*U.S.*), a trap-net (*Cent. Dict.* 1891); **trap-yard**, an enclosure into which animals such as horses, sheep, etc. are driven and confined.

1856 Kane *Arct. Expl.* I. xxvii. 356 The foxes seem tired of touching our *trap-baits. **1842** Dickens *Let.* 15 July (1974) III. 271 [I play] some most riotous game at *trap-bat and ball in the Garden with the children. **1849** Lytton *Caxtons* II. i, I wrote home to my father, modestly implying that I was short of cash, that a trap-bat would be acceptable. **1865** *Athenæum* 11 Mar. 351/1 Kites could be flown, trap-bat indulged in. **1900** T. W. Fox *Mech. Weaving* VI. (ed. 2) 143 In or about..1830 William Jennings claimed the invention of a machine to work without hooks... In it a neck cord..passes through a needle eye, through a perforated *trap board, that takes the place of a griffe, and is also threaded through a cross piece at the machine head where a loop is formed upon it, and a piece of twine passed through all the loops in one line, in order to prevent the cords from lifting. **1894** *Rudder* Aug.–Sept. 201/1 She was invited to sail over a course with a fleet of Richibucto's famous *trap boats. **1974** F. Mowat *Boat who wouldn't Float* iv. 38, I was to join the four-man crew of a trap boat. She was a big, broad-beamed skiff powered by a five-horsepower, 'jump-spark' single-cylinder engine. **1585** Higins *Junius' Nomencl.* 390/2 *Pons versatilis*, a draw-bridge: a falling bridg, or a *trap bridge. **1812** *Sporting Mag.* XXXIX. 26 A cage made upon the plan of the gold-finch *trap-cage. **1894** *Youth's Companion* 22 Nov. 562/4 For some weeks past our *trap-catch, both of eels and lobsters, had greatly diminished. *a* **1668** Lassels *Voy. Italy* (1698) II. 106 A chair of revenge, or a *trap-chair for an enemy. **1795** *Statist. Acc. Scot.* XVI. 516 A considerable quantity of lobsters and crabs..are taken, with *trap-creels. **1899** Massee *Plant Diseases* 26 The *trap-crop should consist of some plant readily susceptible to the disease it is intended to catch. **1657** Thornley tr. *Longus' Daphnis & Chloe* 16 Many such *Trap-ditches were digg'd in the fields. **1801** J. Barrow *Travels Interior S. Afr.* I. vi. 360 A *stell-roar* or *trap-gun, set by a Hottentot. **1947** J. Stevenson-Hamilton *Wild Life S. Afr.* xxxv. 307 Crocodiles are sometimes shot by trap guns. **1964** H. L. Peterson *Encycl. Firearms* 323/1 *Trap gun, trip gun.* 'Trap' as here used, has nothing to do with the sport of trapshooting; it refers to devices designed to shoot automatically at men or animals that come into the line of fire. Many of these trap guns are set off by the tripping of a wire or cord. **1976** *Shooting Times & Country Mag.* 16–22 Dec. 47/2 (Advt.), Nikko 5,000-II o/u trapgun. **1980** *Outdoor Life* (U.S.) (Northeast ed.) Oct. 90/2 None of the major arms makers offered specialized trap guns in 16-gauge, but ammo makers did make a special $2\frac{3}{4}$-dram-equivalent $1\frac{1}{8}$oz. 16-gauge load for trap shooting. **1820** Scoresby *Acc. Arctic Reg.* II. 204 The entrance is by a *trap-hatch at the bottom. **1903** J. Conrad & Hueffer *Romance* II. iv, He slipped down the open trap-hatch near the window. **1799** *Hull Advertiser* 28 Dec. 3/2 A labouring man fell through a *trap hatchway at the house of..a baker. **1864** Webster, *Trap-hole. **1883** B. Phillips in *Century Mag.* Apr. 899/1, I discard all *trap-hooks, infernal machines working with springs, as only adapted for the capture of land animals. **1942** *Tee Emm* (Air Ministry) II. 75 We hear that 50 yards is not the best distance between the two *traphouses, if the 'Plus' trap is being used. **1979** G. Hammond *Dead Game* xvi. 206 The local club have put up a tower for high birds [*sc.* clay pigeons]..and built some trap-houses. **1904** *Electr. World* 1 Oct. 563 Instruments..enclosed in a walnut casing with a *trap-lid. **1896** *U.S. Dept. Agric., Cotton Plant, Bulletin* 331 Mally..made extensive experiments with *trap lights for the moths. **1877** A. B. Edwards *Up Nile* xii. 332 Communicate by means of *trap-like openings with vaults below. **1895** *Westm. Gaz.* 29 Nov. 5/1 Pointing to the small trap-like exit under the judge's bench. **1889** H. C. McCook *Amer. Spiders* I. viii. 134 The *trapline of the Labyrinth spider differs..in being composed of several threads instead of a single line. **1926** *Daily Colonist* (Victoria, B.C.) 7 July 3/5 The disappearance of Charles Olson from his trap line on the headwaters of the Parsnip River in Northern British Columbia remains as much a mystery as when it was first reported. **1954** W. Faulkner *Fable* 82 He had no more doubt of where he was than would the old wolf or lynx when he was near a trap-line. **1970** *Islander* (Victoria, B.C.) 10 May 6/1 The men were absent on the trapline and only the women and children were home. **1894** A. Morrison *Mean Streets* 72 Helping with a heavy *trapload of luggage. **1907** *Daily News* 19 Feb. 6 If there were no rats, the *trap-makers of Birmingham would be out of work. **1895** *Outing* (U.S.) XXVII. 67/1 Expert shots assume many attitudes, as may be seen at any important *trap-match. **1894** G. Meredith *Ld. Ormont & Aminta* iv, Eyes bluish-grey..lively to shoot their meaning when the *trap-mouth was active. **1901** G. M. Cowell in *Rep. Marine Agric. Exper. Station 1900* XVI. 97 It was a prime necessity to ascertain the exact record of the eggs produced by each individual. This led to devising the *trap nest. **1908** *Ann. Rep. N.Y. Agric. Exper. Station, Ithaca, 1907* 261 For the poultry-man..who..will trap-nest conscientiously..we think there is a large reward. **1910** W. W. Broomhead *Poultry & Profit* iii. 33, I asked Mr. Tapley if he had his fowls trap-nested. **1960** *Farmer & Stockbreeder* 29 Mar. (Suppl.) 3/1 Three hundred pullets are trapnested ..each year. **1973** *Animal Behaviour* XXI. 98/1 When given access to trapnests the domestic hen has a characteristic behaviour associated with oviposition. **1906** *Reliable Poultry Jrnl.* XIII. 353/1, I read an editorial dealing with this problem of *trap-nesting. **1956** Wilson & Card *Farm Poultry Production* iii. 60 The best way to get complete records is by trap nesting. **1865** *Trap net [see *pound net* s.v. pound *sb.*[2] 6]. **1877** Knight *Dict. Mech.*, *Trap-net*, a fishing-net in which a funnel-shaped piece leads the fish into a pound from which extrication is not easy. **1904** Gallichan *Fishing Spain* 167 Lowering and raising the trap-nets are operations attended with peril. **1652** Benlowes *Theoph.* x. xiii, With dimpled chins, The *trap-pits where a fondling lies. **1849** A. Blackhall *Lays of North* 84 (E.D.D.) Reckless man, who..Revell'd in hell's trap-pit—drinking. **1844** *Regul. & Ord. Army* 106 New brass *trap plate and joint fitted to rifle. **1893** J. Watson *Conf. Poacher* 129 The *trap-poacher is only a casual. **1885** E. B. Ivatts *Railway Managem. at Stations* 555 It is common to speak of a *catch siding* and *catch points*, of a *trap siding* and **trap points*. **1899** *Daily News* 5 July 3/5 A train, travelling from Blackpool to Birmingham, ran into the trap points. Nine coaches were thrown on to an embankment. **1891** *Cent. Dict.*, **Trap-seine*, a trap-net specially adapted to take fish working down an eddy (Rhode Island). **1903** W. Blackwood *Local Veto & Bk.* xvi. 40 The *trap-setters and men-catchers were rapidly hastening the dynasty of Judah to its dissolution. *Ibid.*, What is our licensing system but a process of *trap-setting? **1926** *Daily Colonist* (Victoria, B.C.) 17 July 12/2 Big *Trapshoot at Colwood on Sunday. One of the biggest shoots of years is to be held tomorrow. **1976** *Billings* (Montana) *Gaz.* 18 June 4-D/1 (*heading*) Trapshoot set at Huntley. **1899** Rider Haggard in *Longm. Mag.* July 247 The bruiser, the racing tout, the *trap-shooter and others equally ignoble are all 'sportsmen'. **1892** Greener *Breech Loader* 130 For ordinary *trap shooting a gun is required to shoot as closely as possible at the trap. *Ibid.* 94 Some *trap shots require their guns to carry as many as 6 in. high at forty yards. **1901** *Daily Chron.* 30 Sept. 5/1 He is reputed to be an excellent trap-shot. **1922** *Contemp. Rev.* July 90 After a time the rat grows poison-shy and *trap-shy. **1968** K. Weatherly *Roo Shooter* 39 The rabbits had become trap-shy. **1947** *New Biol.* II. 19 A population which is thus immune to trapping is sometimes called 'trap-shy'. We do not know what *trap-shyness is in terms of rat behaviour, but it is a very real phenomenon. **1885** *Manch. Exam.* 19 Feb. 4/7 The engine left the line at a *trap siding and rolled down an embankment. **1934** *Geogr. Jrnl.* LXXXIV. 44 There were some *trap-skiffs jigging for cod on the shoal. **1969** Trap skiff [see Jack *sb.*[1] 25]. **1868** Browning *Ring & Bk.* I. 1298 In its [the tiger-cat's] silkiness the *trap-teeth joined. **1884** W. S. B. McLaren *Spinning* (ed. 2) 237 Better than any winders for saving waste are *trap twisters where the yarn is not very soft. **1877** Knight *Dict. Mech.*, **Trap-valve*, a valve hinged on one side of its seat, and opening and closing like a shutter or trap-door, a *clack-valve*. **1904** Quiller Couch *Fort Amity* xxiii, Open the *trap-way and show us some light. **1884** W. S. B. McLaren *Spinning* (ed. 2) 237 There are many *trap winders for winding either single threads or two or more together. **1620** Middleton & Rowley *World Tost at Tennis* 456 His eyes look like false lights, cozening *trap-windows. **1836** Marryat *Midsh. Easy* xxxi, A small trap window in the roof. **1906** *Chambers's Jrnl.* 12 May 380/1 There are..two means of capturing these horses... The first is to build a strong *trapyard on their line of retreat, and endeavour to run them into it. **1936** Trap yard [see crush *sb.* 4 c].

[*Note.* The OE. *treppe*, *træppe*, and MFlem. *trappe*, WFlem. *traap*, *trape*, are generally held to be orig. either the same word as MDu. and MLG. *trappe*, 'stair, flight of steps, step', or a derivative of the same verbal stem **trapp-* (the non-nasalized original of **trampan* to tread, LG. *trappen*), for the supposed reason that a 'trap' was originally something laid for a beast to *tread* or step upon, and thus to be either caught by a gin or snare, or precipitated into a deep pit (cf. pitfall). But it is difficult to conceive *trappe*, *treppe* used at once in the general sense 'stair or step', and in the very specific one of 'trap, snare, gin'. It has also to be noticed that it is only in MDu. or rather MFlem. that the word is known in both senses; for in OE. (and Eng. generally, down to 18th c.) *træppe*, *trap* had (like the Romanic *trappa*) only the sense of 'device for catching, gin, snare', while MLG. *trappe*, *treppe*, and thence mod.Ger., and the Scandinavian languages, have only the sense 'stair' or 'step of a stair'. (OHG. has a single instance of *trapa* wk. fem. as a gloss to L. *tenda*, but this rather looks like an adoption or re-adoption from med.L.) The actual relation of these words or senses is thus very obscure.]

† **trap**, *sb.*[2] *Obs.* [Altered form of F. *drap* cloth, covering = Pr. *drap*, Sp. and Pg. *trapo*, It. *drappo*:—med.L. *drappus* cloth (Capit. Charles the Bald *a* 850), of uncertain origin: see Diez, and *Note* below.] A cloth or covering spread over the saddle or harness of a horse (cf. trapper *sb.*[1]); a caparison; a trapping; *transf.* the hangings of a litter. (Usually in *pl.*)

13.. *K. Alis.* 1606 (Bodl. MS.) Þere men miȝ tten quyk yseon Many hors wiþ trappe wryen. *Ibid.* 3416 Many trappe many croupere. **13..** *Coer de L.* 1515 A messanger ther com rydand, Upon a stede whyt so mylke, His trappys wer of tuely sylke. *a* **1400** *Octouian* 954 He bar thre rochys of seluer clere In scheld and trappys. **1513** Douglas *Æneis* XI. xv. 20 Hys rych mantill, of quham the forbreist lappis, Ratling of brycht gold wire, wyth gyltin trappys. **1721** Strype *Eccl. Mem.* III. iv. 36 The Queen [Mary, 1553] in her litter, richly garnished with cloth of gold, with two traps of white damask and cushions.

[*Note.* It is clear that 14th c. *trap* and *trappure* (later trapper *sb.*[1]) correspond to OF. *drap* and *drapure*. The question is how these F. words in *dr-* have *tr-* in Eng. This may have been an Eng. change, due to influence of trap in other senses. But the *trap* form may have existed in Anglo-Fr. or even in Fr. dialects. Du Cange has *trapus* (one example) for med.L. *drappus*; Pg. and Sp. have *trapo* 'clout, rag', formerly 'cloth', also *trapero* (draper), *trapería*, *trapajo*; med.(Anglo-)L. had *trappatura*, the ordinary equivalent of *trappure*, OF. *trappeüre*: see trapper *sb.*[1]]

trap, *sb.*[3] *Sc.* [app. = Du., MFlem. *trap* flight of steps, stair; MDu., early mod.Du. (Kilian) *trappe* step; OFris. *treppe* step of a ladder, etc., EFris. *trappe*, *trap* step (of a stair), also (= *trap-ledder*) ladder with broad flat steps instead of rungs, flight of steps; MLG. *trappe*, *treppe*, *troppe* flight of steps, stair, whence MG. *trappe*, *treppe*, Ger., LG. *treppe* stair; also (from MLG.), Da. *trappe*, Sw. *trappa*, Norw. dial. *trapp*, *tropp* flight of steps, stair. But the Sc. *trap* is by some referred directly to trap *sb.*[1], as if short for *trap-ladder* or *trap-stair*, in sense of a ladder or stair leading up to a trap-door or trap-hole.] A ladder or movable flight of steps leading to a loft or the like.

[**1756** Mrs. Calderwood in *Coltness Collect.* (Maitl. Cl.) 131 When we came to go up stairs to bed, there was a trap, which is the Dutch name for a stair.] **1808** Jamieson, *Trap*, a sort of ladder, a moveable flight of wooden steps. **1858** Simmonds *Dict. Trade*, *Trap*,..a sort of moveable ladder or steps. **1885** A. Munro *Siren Casket* (1889) 136 As you enter'd the door of the house from the street You confronted a trap or a ladder. **1899** J. Colville *Scott. Vernacular* 17 Against its wall stood the trap or ladder leading to the garret.

b. *attrib.* and *Comb.*, as ***trap-like*** adj.; **trap-ladder** [= WFlem. *trap-ladder*, *-leere*, EFlem. (Antwerp) *trapleer*, EFris. *trap-ledder* a ladder with flat steps, a 'pair of steps']; **trap-stair** = *trap*.

1855 Carlyle *Misc.*, *Prinzenraub* (1899) IV. 442 That other little Duke..who had built the biggest bassoon ever heard of; thirty feet high, or so; and was seen playing on it from a *trap-ladder. **1896** J. Lamb *Ann. W. Kilbride* ix. 244 A trap-ladder cost 2*s.* 6*d.* **1897** tr. *Balzac's Cousin Pons* 327 Reached by a short ladder, known among builders as a trap-ladder, there was a kind of garret. **1906** Dk. Argyll *Autobiog. & Mem.* I. ii. 18 Steep, *traplike wooden stairs. **1833** Loudon *Encycl. Archit.* §164 The bottom [of the stair] might either project two double steps..; or a *trap stair, composed of the two lower steps, and made to fold up, might be resorted to. **1837** J. E. Murray *Summer in Pyrenees* II. 245 A little urchin came down a trap-stair at the further end. **1844** Stephens *Bk. Farm* I. 143 It enters from the straw-barn..by means of the stone or wooden trap-stair. **1847** H. Miller *First Impr.* xix. 368 Their terrace-like precipices, that rise over each other step by step—their trap-stairs of trappean rock,—for to this scenic peculiarity the volcanic rocks owe their generic name. **1850** R. Chambers *Burns' Life & Wks.* (1856) I. 145 Almost the only other apartment in the house is a kind of garret-closet, accessible by a narrow trap-stair ascending from the lobby.

† **trap**, *sb.*[4] *Coal Mining*, etc. *Obs.* [History obscure; app. connected with the continental words *trap*, *trappe* step: see prec. (Perh. introduced by foreign miners in 16th c.)] A 'fault' in a seam of coal, also in a mineral vein or in any stratum; an up-throw or down-throw of the stratum (usually ***trap-up*** or ***trap-down***). (Cf. *step-faults* applied to a series of faults in the same direction.)

1719 Strachey in *Phil. Trans.* XXX. 971 As..they are dug near the same Depth, it follows there must be a Trap, or several Traps down, which in all must amount to that Depth between the said Works. **1883** Gresley *Gloss. Coal-Mining*, *Trap-down* [in Bristol Coal-field], a fault which is a down-throw one... *Trap-up*, a fault which is an up-throw one.

Hence **trap** *v.*[3] in ***to trap up*** or ***down***, to be found at a higher or lower level after dislocation by a dike or fault: see quots.; whence **trapping** *vbl. sb.*

1719 Strachey in *Phil. Trans.* XXX. 969 They observe, as they work to the South West, when they meet with a Ridg it Causeth the Coal to trap up, that is..they find it over their heads, when they are thro' the Ridg: but..when they work thro' a ridg to the North East, they say it traps down, that is, they find it under their feet. **1757** Da Costa in *Phil. Trans.* L. 233 The heavings, displacings, trappings, and breaks of the metallic veins. **1811** W. Taylor in *Monthly Mag.* XXXI. 448 Where there is a trapping down of the strata.

trap, *sb.*[5] *Min.* Also 8 **trapp**. [a. Swed. *trapp* (Bergman 1766), so named from the stairlike appearance often presented by the rock, f. *trappa* stair: see trap *sb.*[3]] **a.** A dark-coloured igneous rock more or less columnar in structure: now extended to include all igneous rocks which are neither granitic nor of recent volcanic formation.

[**1794** Sullivan *View Nat.* II. 165 This is what the Swedes call *trapp*, or trapas, from stairs.] **1794** Schmeisser *Syst. Mineral.* I. 184 Trapp... Its name originates from the Swedish language. The term *trapp* describes a stone, which breaks in pieces of a rhomboidal figure, and consequently exhibits..steps like a stair case. **1796** Kirwan *Elem. Min.* (ed. 2) I. 227 Common Trap. Basalt of Werner. **1811** Pinkerton *Petralogy* I. 62 The volcanic eruptions, which are supposed to have produced the mountains of trap. **1863** A. C. Ramsay *Phys. Geog.* ix. (1878) 124 The rocks are pierced by..a white felspathic-looking trap, which has charred the coals at the points of junction. **1872** W. S. Symonds *Rec. Rocks* v. 146 A dyke of trap penetrates the rocks by means of a fissure.

b. *attrib.* and *Comb.*, as ***trap-dike*** (dike *sb.*[1] 9 b), ***-granulite***, ***-porphyry***, ***-rock***, ***-shale***, ***-stone***, ***-tuff***.

1796 KIRWAN *Elem. Min.* (ed. 2) I. 355 Trap Porphyry.. sometimes..abounds..in quartz and felspar. **1811** SIR A. BOSWELL *Poet. Wks.* (1872) 102 Beneath his feet the trap-stone rung. **1813** BAKEWELL *Introd. Geol.* (1815) 118 Rocks in which hornblende forms a predominating ingredient, have been denominated trap rocks. **1821** R. JAMESON *Man. Mineral.* 401 Secondary Trap... The following are the different kinds of these rocks,..Greenstone;..Syenite;..Amygdaloid;..Wacke;..Basalt; and..Trap tuff. **1839** [see INTRUSION 1 b]. **1842** SEDGWICK in *Hudson's Guide Lakes* (1843) 241 Plumbago..has..been found among coal strata near the sides of 'trap dykes'. **1853** in J. Phillips *Man. Geol.* (1855) 102 Roofing-slate,..alternating..with porphyry, trappean conglomerate, trap-shale. **1855** J. PHILLIPS *Man. Geol.* 187 There are no trap dikes in this coal field. **1867** BURTON *Hist. Scot.* (1873) I. ii. 57 It is a small bar of trapstone. **1881** PREVOST in *Knowledge* No. 5. 85 The trap rocks, divisible into two great classes, called diorite and dolerite, contain soda, lime, magnesia, and potash.

†**trap**, *sb.*^{6} *Obs.* [a. OF. *trappe* a baking-tin for tarts (1395 in Godef.).] A kind of dish or pan, app. for baking.

?*c* **1390** *Forme of Cury* in Warner *Antiq. Culin.* 27 Make a crust in a trape. *c* **1420** *Liber Cocorum* (1862) 40 Fyrst make a fole trap.., Pynche hym, cowche hym þy flesshe þerby. *c* **1430** *Two Cookery-bks.* (E.E.T.S.) 54 Sew Trappe.

trap, *sb.*^{7}: see TRAPS, belongings, etc.

trap (træp), *sb.*^{8} *colloq.* (orig. *U.S.*). [Origin unclear. Prob. some slang application of TRAP *sb.*^{1} The explanation in quot. 1938 is unsupported.]

Usu. *pl.* In a jazz or dance band, percussion instruments or devices (e.g. wood-blocks, whistles) used to produce a variety of special effects; these together with the standard jazz or dance band drum-kit.

1903 [see *trap-drummer*, sense b below]. **1925** F. SCOTT FITZGERALD *Great Gatsby* iii. 56 A great number of single girls dancing individualistically or relieving the orchestra for a moment of the burden of the banjo or the traps. **1938** *Oxf. Compan. Music* 948/2 *Traps*,..The origin of the word may be from the nineteenth-century colloquial 'traps' meaning baggage of which the individual in question [*sc.* the trap-drummer] has necessarily a good deal. **1947** J. STEINBECK *Wayward Bus* xvii. 278 It's a rubber drum that you beat with a sponge. It's for the drunks that want to play traps in the orchestra. **1967** *Crescendo* May 26/2 When one packed up after a gig, one simply stuffed the snare drum, stand, pedal and traps—all the bits and pieces were known as 'traps' in those days—inside the open side of the B.D. [*sc.* bass drum]. **1982** B. FANTONI *Stickman* ii. 19 Dance-band drummers, beats me why dames go goofy on them. I played the traps a little myself once.

b. *Comb.* **trap-drum**, (*a*) a drum forming part of a set of traps as opposed to a drum used in an orchestra or military band; (*b*) *pl.* = sense a above; hence **trap-drummer**, a musician who plays the trap-drums; a street musician who plays a drum and other instruments at once.

1924 *Trap-drum [see PLASTERED *ppl. a.* 2]. **1929** T. WOLFE *Look Homeward, Angel* xiv. 180 Mr. Buckner..officiating at the trap drum and tambourine. **1959** W. F. NOLAN *Dark Encounter* in H. Q. Masur *Murder Most Foul* (1973) 125 The sharp, sweet cry of horns could be heard above the rolling trap drums. **1978** *West Africa* 16 Oct. 2042/2 Trap-drums, double-bass, guitar. **1903** *Med. Rec.* (N.Y.) 14 Feb. 268/1 *Trap-drummer's neurosis: a hitherto undescribed occupation-disease... The man's occupation was to beat a drum by the operation of a pedal which is manipulated with the right foot, while with his hands he plays the other drums, triangle, and the various traps. **1926** H. V. MORTON *Nights of London* 168 We entered [the night club]. A trap drummer crouched over his instruments. **1977** *New Yorker* 20 June 93/1 When its complete personnel finally arrived onstage, the Ensemble consisted of two trap drummers.., a reedman who doubled on percussion.., a conga drummer.., a bassist.., and a singing pianist.

trap, *v.*^{1} [ME. *trappen*:—OE. **træppan* in *betræppan*, (*be*)*treppan* (BETRAP), f. *træp*, TRAP *sb.*^{1} Cf. also ATTRAP, ENTRAP (from F.), which may have contributed to the Eng. vb.]

I. Transitive senses.

1. a. To catch in or as in a trap, entrap, ensnare.

[*a* **900** *Kentish Gloss.* 211 (Bosw.-T.) Hio [tr]e[p]te, *inretivit.*] *c* **1460** *Towneley Myst.* xiii. 371 Me thoght with a gyn A fatt shepe he trapt, bot he mayde no dyn. **1530** PALSGR. 761/1, I trappe, I take one by sleyght, or take any beest in a trappe or snare, *je attrappe* and *je trappe*. **1835** W. IRVING *Tour Prairies* xxiii. 211 Three persons are safer than a large number for trapping beaver. **1860** WARTER *Sea-board* II. 39 Wheat-ears, which all shepherds..trap on the Downs.

b. *fig.*

1390 GOWER *Conf.* II. 218 Thus he, whom gold hath overset, Was trapped in his oghne net. *c* **1425** *Cast. Persev.* 2099 in *Macro Plays* 140, & þou, deuyl, with wyckyd wyl, In paradys trappyd us with tresun. **1509** HAWES *Past. Pleas.* xxix. (Percy Soc.) 143 Howe that my hart by Venus was trapt, With a snare of love. **1670** COTTON *Espernon* III. XI. 556 The Duke knowing, that..this was only a device to make him run into some error,..was not easie to be trap'd that way. *a* **1700** DRYDEN tr. *Ovid's Met.* XIII. *Sp. Ajax & Ulysses* 340 With ambush'd arms I trapp'd the foe, or tired with false alarms. **1885–94** R. BRIDGES *Eros & Psyche* July v, They alert with joy to see her trapt, Launch'd forth amain. **1936** *Discovery* Nov. 349/1 Its dust-particle content is..trapped in the volume of liquid. **1952** E. R. JANES *Flower Garden* 49 Cloches were used in conjunction with hotbeds, but their efficacy for forwarding purposes depended chiefly upon their ability to trap solar heat. **1970** L. DEIGHTON *Bomber* xxiii. 342 This cold still air trapped smoke from the furnaces and factories and held it like a grey woollen blanket.

c. *fig.* with ref. to speech: To catch, pull up, or detect in a mis-statement. Also *Sc.* To detect and correct a classmate in an erroneous answer, or to answer a question which he cannot and 'take him down' (TAKE *v.* 80 b (*d*)).

1630 PRYNNE *Anti-Armin.* 136 That contradicts their Doctrine, and traps them in a lye. **1681–6** J. SCOTT *Chr. Life* (1747) III. 601 The Jews having every Day Opportunity of conversing with them, they might have easily trapp'd them in their Relations. **1825** JAMIESON, *To trap*, to correct in saying a lesson at school, so as to have a right to take the place of him who is thus corrected. **1895** CROCKETT *Bog-Myrtle & Peat* 185 He had promptly 'trapped' his way to the head of the class... The operation of 'trapping' was simply performed. When a mistake was made in pronunciation, repetition, or spelling, any pupil further down the class held out his hand,..the 'trapper', providing always that his emendation was accepted, was instantly promoted to the place of the 'trapped'.

2. To furnish with traps; to set (a place) with a trap or traps (in quot. 1908 with arrangements for detecting law-breaking motorists, TRAP *sb.*^{1} 1 c).

1831 J. O. PATTIE *Personal Narr.* 142 We set 40 traps, and ..caught 36 beavers... We concluded..to travel slowly, and in hunters phrase, trap the river clear; that is, take all that could be allured to come to the bait. **1841** CATLIN *N. Amer. Ind.* II. lviii. 251 They assume the right of hunting and trapping the streams and lakes. **1908** *Westm. Gaz.* 8 Dec. 1/1 The owners of motors are not content to take them week by week down the same road, especially when that road is so well 'trapped' as is the highway to the London-by-the-sea. **1940** *Sun* (Baltimore) 2 Feb. 14/7 We plan to trap only a small part of our marshes. **1969** I. KEMP *Brit. G.I. in Vietnam* v. 105, I would usually go flat on the ground in case the door was trapped with a grenade or claymore mine.

3. To furnish (a drain, etc.) with a trap or traps, to prevent the ascent of foul air or gas.

1862 *Catal. Internat. Exhib.* II. x. 46 The drains to be trapped and ventilated. **1881** B. W. RICHARDSON in *Gd. Words* XXII. 55 The chief drain has to be trapped outside the dwelling, a little way before it reaches the common sewer.

4. Chiefly *Mech.* To stop and hold or retain by a trap or contrivance for the purpose; to separate or remove by a trap:

e.g. to stop the shuttle of a loom in the warp; water, air, gas, heat in its passage; esp. anything suspended in water, or condensed from steam or gas, in a pipe.

5. a. *Baseball.* (*a*) To catch (the ball) just after it has hit the ground; (*b*) to hem (a runner) between two fielders.

1892 *Chicago Herald* 16 May 2 Meehan trapped grounders by wholesale. **1912** C. MATHEWSON *Pitching in a Pinch* viii. 181 A Boston batter tapped one to Merkle which I thought he trapped, but Johnstone, the umpire, said he caught it on a fly. **1939** D. E. JESSEE *Baseball* iv. 41 The second baseman will have many opportunities to participate in 'run-down' plays in which a base runner has been 'trapped' between first and second or second and third. **1959** E. ALLEN *Baseball Play & Strategy* v. 105 As a general rule all fly balls are caught... When a runner retreats toward a base with less than two outs, some fly balls may be purposely trapped and two players retired. **1967** R. MERKLE *Concentrated Baseball* 105 On a rundown play between second and third, the trapped runner should be allowed to advance about half the distance toward third base.

b. *Cricket.* To cause (a batsman) to be dismissed leg before wicket.

1919 *Times* 4 July 8/6 The wicket..was nothing like so difficult as made out when once..you had gauged the bowler's spin without being trapped by Trumble's straight one. **1969** *Wisden's Cricketers' Almanack* 679 The use of pads instead of the bat was prevalent with six batsmen trapped leg before in the first innings. **1977** *Sunday Times* 27 Feb. 28/6 Lever broke through in his third over when Sri Lanka batted, trapping Fernando lbw at 16.

c. *Assoc. Football.* To receive and control (the ball), esp. between the foot and the ground.

1950 N. CARDUS *Second Innings* 146 When it [*sc.* the football] was passed to him and it fell at his feet he would 'trap' it and lever it to an inch of where he wanted it. **1976** *Times* 2 Dec. 12/1 The ball was cleared from the United penalty area, Dobson trapped it with his left thigh, and hit it with his right foot, and the ball bounced just in front of Stepney and into the net.

II. Intransitive senses.

6. To practise catching wild animals in traps for their furs; also *gen.* to set traps for game.

a **1807** P. GASS *Jrnl.* 78 Some Frenchmen who were out trapping caught 7 of them [beavers]. **1817** J. BRADBURY *Trav. Amer.* 18 *note*, Soon after he..trapped in company with a hunter named Potts. **1835** W. IRVING *Tour Prairies* xxiii. 210, I should like to come and trap on these waters all winter. **1894** *Times* 10 Dec. 10/2 The provisions of the Ground Game Act had not been observed; tenants were allowed to trap how and when they liked. **1905** D. WALLACE *Lure Labrador Wild* iii. 48 Tom Blake..had trapped at the ..western end of Grand Lake.

7. To use, handle, or work a trap or traps.

a. (also with *it*) To use trap-doors on the stage in a theatrical performance. *nonce-use.*

1886 *Sat. Rev.* 2 Jan. 20/1 Kazrac and the Demon go down and come up trap after trap... They should take a lesson of Mr. Conquest..(we know not whether or not that excellent artist still traps it).

b. To act as a 'trapper' in a coal-mine: see TRAPPER *sb.*^{2} 2.

1842 [see TRAPPING *vbl. sb.*^{2}]. **1900** *Daily News* 14 Feb. 3/2 'How long have you been trapping?' 'Since I come down pit, six months ago.'

c. To handle or work a trap in trap-shooting: see TRAP *sb.*^{1} 4, TRAPPER *sb.*^{2} 3.

trap, *v.*^{2} [f. TRAP *sb.*^{2}] *trans.* To adorn (a horse, mule, or the like) with trappings; to caparison. (Chiefly in *pa. pple.*) Rarely (in 19th c.) said in reference to a man.

13.. [see TRAPPED *ppl. a.*^{2}]. **1375** BARBOUR *Bruce* XIV. 289 The scottis all on fut war then, And thai on stedis trappit weill. *c* **1420** *Brut* 347 A mylke-white stede, sadelled and brydilled, & trapped with white cloth of golde. *Ibid.* 373 Al þe horsses drawyng þe chare were trappid yn blak. *a* **1548** HALL *Chron.*, *Rich. III* 25 b, His horse trapped in blew veluet enbroudered with the naues of cartes burnyng of gold. **1621–3** MIDDLETON & ROWLEY *Changeling* I. i, Call your servants up, And help to trap your horses. **1631** HEYWOOD *Eng. Eliz.* (1641) 63 The Lady Elisabeth..rode in a chariot..drawn with six horses trapt in cloth of silver. **1826** HOR. SMITH *Tor Hill* (1838) I. 29 Dudley hastily trapped himself for the field.

b. *transf.* and *fig.*

c **1412** HOCCLEVE *De Reg. Princ.* 489 Drapers and.. skinners..For suche folk han a special orisoune, That trapped is withe curses..til they be payed for her gere. **1577–87** HOLINSHED *Chron.* (1807) III. 345 One Agnes Daintie a butterwife..being first trapped with butter dishes, was then set on the pillorie. **1590** MARLOWE *2nd Part Tamburl.* I. i, Fair Europe..Trapt with the wealth and riches of the world. **1641** J. JACKSON *True Evang. T.* III. 178 A Prophecy so trapped with the ornaments of speech. **1903** *Daily Chron.* 10 Apr. 5/1 The old mess jacket was a gorgeous affair of innumerable gold buttons, with a gay scarlet waistcoat, also trapped with gold.

trap, *v.*^{3}: see under TRAP *sb.*^{4}

trapan: see TREPAN.

trap-ball (ˈtræpbɔːl). [f. TRAP *sb.*^{1} + BALL *sb.*^{1}] A game in which a ball, placed upon one end (slightly hollowed) of a trap (TRAP *sb.*^{1} 3), is thrown into the air by the batsman striking the other end with his bat, with which he then hits the ball away.

1658 *Churchw. Acc. St. Marg. Westminster* (Nichols 1797) 64 One that played at trap-ball on the Lords day. **1740** CHESTERF. *Lett.* (1792) I. lxxi. 197 You will desire to excell all boys of your age at cricket, or trap-ball, as well as in learning. **1814** *Sporting Mag.* XLIII. 240 A game of trap-ball was played this month on the ice. **1909** *Daily Chron.* 27 Aug. 7/3 An inn..where..trap-ball is played on the lawn... The dictionary already calls it 'an old game'.

attrib. **1845** J. T. SMITH *Bk. Rainy Day* (1861) 18 On the eastern side of the house there was a trap-ball-ground.

b. A ball used in this game. *rare.*

1713 S. SEWALL *Diary* 6 June, Boston..came down a Spit, and clear'd the Leaden throat, by thrusting out a Trap-Ball that stuck there.

ˈ**trap-**ˈ**brilliant.** [app. f. Du. *trap* step (cf. next) + BRILLIANT *sb.*] In diamond-cutting, a form of brilliant in which each of the foundation squares is divided horizontally into two triangular facets at an obtuse angle (when viewed in elevation); also called *step-brilliant*, *split-brilliant*.

1877 KNIGHT *Dict. Mech.* s.v. *Gem-cutting*, There are several varieties of brilliant cuts, known as—Half-brilliant ..Full brilliant..Split or trap-brilliant..Double brilliant or Lisbon cut. **1891** in *Cent. Dict.*

trap-cut. [app. f. Du. *trap* step, stair + CUT *sb.*] A mode of cutting gems, chiefly used with emeralds, rubies, sapphires, etc.; also called *step-cut*, *degree-cut*: see quot. 1877.

1853 O. BYRNE *Artisan's Handbk.* 225 The trap cut, or trapping, as it is called by lapidaries. **1865** EMANUEL *Diamonds* 98 The Trap or Step Cut. This is the most usual, besides being the most advantageous form of cutting emeralds and other coloured stones... There are generally only two or three steps from the table to the girdle. **1877** KNIGHT *Dict. Mech.*, *Trap-cut*, a mode of cutting gems in which the facets consist of parallel planes, nearly rectangular, arranged round the center of the stone.

trap-door (ˈtræpˈdɔə(r)). [f. TRAP *sb.*^{1} + DOOR.]

a. A door, either sliding or moving on hinges, and flush with the surface, in a floor, roof, or ceiling, or in the stage of a theatre.

c **1374** CHAUCER *Troylus* III. 710 (759)'Which weye be ye comen..?' Quod she... 'Here at þis secre trappe dore', quod he. **1489–90** *Rec. St. Mary at Hill* 155 For viij ffoote di. tymber for o trapp dorr. **1579–80** NORTH *Plutarch* (1595) 1092 Aristippus..locked himself..in a litle high chamber with a trappe dore, and set his bed vpon it, and so slept. **1599** SANDYS *Europæ Spec.* (1632) 97 They have their trap doores or pit-falls in darke melancholy chambers. **1704** S. SEWALL *Diary* 12 Sept., Mrs. Tuthill falls through a Trap Door into the cellar. **1774** PENNANT *Tour Scot. in 1772* 93 The trap-door in the floor, contrived for the lowering in of the captives. **1840** DICKENS *Old Curiosity Shop* xxxv, Getting on the roof of the house through the trap-door.

b. *transf.* and *fig.*

1648 GAGE *West Ind.* 82 Never to go to those parts, which were but snares and trap-dores to let down to hell. **1694** MOTTEUX *Rabelais* IV. xxxiv. 136 It no more open'd its Guttural Trap-door. **1860** P. P. CARPENTER in *Rep. Smithsonian Instit. 1859* 206 *note*, The operculum is a horny or shelly appendage to the end of the foot... It may be called ..the trap-door or toe-nail. **1869** J. MARTINEAU *Ess.* II. 94 The trap-door of some hidden paradox.

c. *Mining.* A door in a level for directing the ventilating current; a weather-door.

1851 GREENWELL *Coal-trade Terms Northumb. & Durh.* 54 *Trapper*, a little boy whose employment consists in opening and shutting a trap-door when required. **1883** GRESLEY *Coal Mining Gloss.*, *Trap-door*, a small door, kept locked, fixed in a stopping or bolt, for giving access to firemen and certain others to the return air-ways, dams, or other disused places in a mine. **1886** J. BARROWMAN *Sc. Mining Terms* 68.

d. *Computers.* A method of surreptitiously gaining unauthorized access to data belonging to other users of a computer.

[**1976** D. B. PARKER *Crime by Computer* xii. 112 The Trojan horse had been rolled into the fortified city and fully accepted. In the unsuspecting environment a trap-door in its belly opened, and out popped the soldiers.] **1977** *New Yorker* 29 Aug. 61/1 The nature of a trapdoor is that, while it is known to and usable by a penetrator, it is unrecognized by and unknown to other users of the system—even to the audit-trail mechanism. **1981** *Courier-Mail* (Brisbane) 27 July 5/5 'Trapdoors' allow people sharing a computer to slip into the confidential data streams of other users. **1982** S. F. X. DEAN *Such Pretty Toys* xiv. 191 He just entered the girl's name into the computer.. as some sort of routing key or trapdoor to cut off any trace.

e. *Cryptography.* A piece of secret information that makes it easy to solve an otherwise very difficult code. Freq. *attrib.*

1978 *Communications Assoc. Computing Machinery* XXI. 128 They are called 'trap-door' functions since the inverse functions are in fact easy to compute once certain private 'trap-door' information is known. **1982** BEKER & PIPER *Cipher Syst.* 376 The general name given to this type of function (i.e. for which there does not appear to be a polynomial time algorithm but for which there is one so long as the method of application is known) is a trapdoor function. In our situation it is intended that the genuine receiver should be the only person who knows how to 'open' the trapdoor. **1984** *IEEE Trans. Information Theory* XXX. 595/1 It is this presence of trapdoors that makes some of the attacks on the additive knapsack cryptosystems feasible.

f. *Comb.* **trap-door spider**, one of a group of large spiders, which make a nest in the shape of a tube with a hinged lid which opens and shuts like a trap-door; hence ***trap-door nest***, etc.

1826 KIRBY & SP. *Entomol.* III. xxxiv. 492 The trapdoor or mason spider (*Mygale cœmentaria*). **1864–5** WOOD *Homes without H.* vi. (1868) 116 Of all the burrowing spiders.. none is so admirable an excavator as the Trap-door Spider of Jamaica [*Cteniza*]. **1883** *Pall Mall G.* 29 Dec. 5/1 The trap-door spider is almost the typical natural curiosity of the Riviera. **1897** ANNE PAGE *Afternoon Ride* 58 The.. spider, decoyed out of his well-built trap-door nest.

†**trape**, *v. Obs.* or *dial.* Also ? 5 **trappe.** [Origin obscure. If quot. *c* 1400 belongs here, it may possibly be = MDu. and MLG. *trappen* to tread, trample, in Kilian 'calcare, conculcare pedibus', in EFris. (Doornkaat-Koolman), to set down the foot with force and noise, to tramp.

But this is doubtful, as there is a long gap between 1400 and 1706, and *trape* is not phonetically identical with *trappe*. *Trape* of 1706–49 is moreover preceded 1593–1700 by TRAIPSE *v.*, of which it may have been a mutilated form.]

intr. = TRAIPSE *v.*

[*c* **1400** *Sowdone Bab.* 1802 Fal what so euer by falle, To the Soudon wole they trappe.] **1706** PHILLIPS (ed. Kersey), To *Trape*, to go idly up and down. **1721** in BAILEY. **1749** RICHARDSON *Let.* 4 Aug., in A. Dobson *Fielding* v. (1883) 139 The Lowest of all Fellows, yet in Love with a Young Creature who was traping after him.

b. = TRAIPSE *v.* 1 b.

1875 *Sussex Gloss.* s.v., 'Her gown trapes along the floor'.

trape, erroneous form of TRIPE^2.

trapes, etc.: see TRAIPSE *sb.* and *v.*, etc.

trapezate ('træpɪzeɪt), *a. rare.* [irreg. f. TRAPEZIUM + -ATE^2.] (See quot.)

1826 KIRBY & SP. *Entomol.* IV. xlvi. 264 Trapezate (*Trapezata*), quadrilateral with the four sides unequal, and none of them perfectly parallel.

trapeze (trə'piːz). [a. F. *trapèze* in same senses, ad. L. TRAPEZIUM.]

1. a. An apparatus for gymnastic exercises and feats, consisting of a horizontal cross-bar suspended by two ropes in the manner of a swing.

Prob. orig. applied to a kind in which the ropes formed a *trapezium* (in sense 1 b) with the roof and cross-bar.

1861 *Sat. Rev.* 22 June 635 The ring is neither more nor less likely to cause death than the rope or the *trapèze*. **1865** *Public Opinion* 21 Jan. 81 His performances are of a very extraordinary character; among other things, he holds on to the trapeze by his teeth. **1877** BLACK *Green Past.* xxxvi, Will you.. show the boys how to twist round a trapeze. **1830** *Encycl. Brit.* XI. 350/2 The trapeze consists of a horizontal bar suspended by ropes at a height of 4 or 5 feet from the floor. **1908** *Daily Chron.* 11 June 1/4 At this altitude of two miles above the ground her feet became entangled in the trapeze ropes.

b. *Sailing.* (See quot. 1961.)

1961 F. H. BURGESS *Dict. Sailing* 211 *Trapeze*, in sailing dinghies, a sliding support used by the crew for outboard balancing when they lay up to windward. **1969** *Daily Tel.* 25 Oct. 7/7 The work covers the origins of the trapeze (a means of crew support to help in holding a light dinghy level in a breeze). **1977** *Modern Boating* (Austral.) Jan. 43/3 Try looking at the race with your head upside down sometime when you are.. flat out on the trapeze.

2. a. = TRAPEZIUM. *rare*$^{-0}$.

1864 in WEBSTER: hence in later Dicts.

b. (See quot. 1968); = *trapeze-line*, sense 3 below.

1958 *Spectator* 13 June 761/2 Miss Lee is the only lady member to have adopted the new short skirt.. and none of them has so far ventured upon the trapeze. **1968** J. IRONSIDE *Fashion Alphabet* 30 The trapeze was a wide, stiff full-skirted tent shape stopping at the knees and moulding the figure to a high bust in front while falling free from the shoulders at the back. Trapeze was short for trapezium.. but somehow a circus trapeze seemed to describe it more visually and the fashion magazines showed dresses on, under or in front of them.

3. *Comb.*, as **trapeze artist**, one who performs acrobatics on a trapeze; **trapeze harness** *Sailing* (see quot. 1981); **trapeze-line** [LINE *sb.*^{2} 14 b], a fashion style in which the outline of the garment resembles that of a trapezium (cf. sense 2 b above).

1938 *Amer. Mag.* CXXV. 90 Mother Millette started as a trapeze artist. **1981** W. STRATHERN *Don't look for Me—I'm Dead* iii. 52 The lean and sinewy strength of a trapeze artist. **1946** *Yachts & Yachting* 20 Aug. 383/2 (Advt.), All G.R.P., well equipped boat Needlespar, trolley, cover, certificate, lifting rudder, trapeze harness, ready to race. **1981** B. WEBB *Schult's Sailing Dict.* 297/2 *Trapeze*, gear fitted to fast racing dinghies and some keelboats to enable the crew to put all his weight outboard to windward. The crew wears a trapeze harness or belt with a hook, which he slips into a ring on the lower end of the trapeze wire. **1958** *Vogue* Mar. 119 His [*sc.* Yves St Laurent's] wedge-shaped silhouette—called.. the Trapeze Line—is flared from narrow shoulders to a smooth wide hemline. **1975** 'M. FONTEYN' *Autobiogr.* II. iv. 173 A 'sack' dress,.. a development of Christian Dior's 'Trapeze' line which had been.. worn by so many wrong-shaped ladies.

Hence **tra'pezing**, performance on the trapeze.

1894 G. DU MAURIER *Trilby* I. 70 Fencing and boxing and trapezing seemed to be more in her line. **1905** *Daily Chron.* 6 June 3/1 People who are revivified by trapezings and comic songs have no individuality to be recreated.

†**tra'pezia.** *Obs.* [mod.L. *trapezia*, adj. fem. f. TRAPEZIUM, used absol. for *trapezia figura* trapezial figure or shape.] A quadrilateral figure other than a parallelogram; the 'trapezium' of Euclid, comprising the later trapezium and trapezoid.

1631 DE LA MAIN (*title*) The making, description, and use of a small portable Instrument for the Pocket.. in form of a mixt Trapezia thus called a Horizontall Quadrant. **1693** J. WING *Heptarchia Math.* 64 A Table shewing the Area of Right-line Figures, as Squares, Triangles, and Trapezia's. **1752** A. FLETCHER *Univ. Measurer* I. 98 To reduce a Trapezia *ABCD* to a triangle. **1766** *Compl. Farmer* s.v. *Surveying*, Quadrangular figures.. are either parallelograms or trapesias.

trapezial (trə'piːzɪəl), *a.* [f. mod.L. TRAPEZIUM + -AL^1.]

1. Of or pertaining to a trapezium; having the form of a trapezium, trapeziform.

1681 tr. *Willis' Rem. Med. Wks.* Vocab., *Trapezial*, belonging to a geometrical figure, so called of four sides. **1703** T. N. *City & C. Purchaser* 249 At each corner of the Newel there is a trapezial Half-pace. **1852** DANA *Crust.* I. 312 Their trapezial or quadrate form.

2. *Anat.* Pertaining to the trapezium (in either sense), or to the trapezius muscle.

1891 *Cent. Dict.*, *Trapezial*, in *anat.*, pertaining to the trapezius: as, trapezial fibers or action. **1899** *Syd. Soc. Lex.*, *Trapezial*, pertaining to the *Trapezium* or *Trapezius*.

tra'pezian, *a. Cryst.* [f. as prec. + -AN. Cf. mod.F. *trapézien* (Littré).] Having trapeziform lateral faces in two rows between the two bases, as a crystal of barium sulphate.

1757 tr. *Henckel's Pyritol.* 23 Prismatical, trapezian, or irregular. **1805–17** R. JAMESON *Char. Min.* 203 A crystal is said to be.. Trapezian, when its lateral surfaces consist of trapezia, which lie in two rows, between two bases, as in trapezian heavy-spar... It is a rectangular four-sided table, bevelled on the extremities, where the bevelling planes are trapeziums. **1828** in WEBSTER. Hence in later Dicts.

trapeziform (trə'piːzɪfɔːm), *a.* [f. TRAPEZIUM + -(I)FORM. Cf. F. *trapéziforme* (Littré).] Having the form of a trapezium; quadrilateral with only two sides parallel.

1776 J. LEE *Introd. Bot.* Explan. Terms, *Trapeziforme*, trapeziform. **1817** KIRBY & SP. *Entomol.* (1843) II. 145 The wax-pockets in the hive-bee.. two trapeziform whitish pockets. **1834** MCMURTRIE *Cuvier's Anim. Kingd.* 375 In Mycterus,.. the body is ovoid,.. and the thorax trapeziform. **1868** *Rep. U.S. Commissioner Agric.* (1869) 100 The family Tenebrionidæ consists of insects.. having the thorax square or trapeziform, and as broad behind as the base of the wing-cases (Westwood). **1890** *Cent. Dict.* s.v. *Projection*, *Trapeziform map-projection*, a map-projection in which the space between two meridians and two parallels is represented by a trapezoid [i.e. a trapezium].

trapezihedron, erron. f. TRAPEZOHEDRON.

trapezio- (trə'piːzɪəʊ), used as combining form of TRAPEZIUM in the anatomical sense, as in **trapezio-metacarpal** *a.*, pertaining to the trapezium (bone) and the metacarpus.

1840 E. WILSON *Anat. Vade M.* (1851) 247 The.. trapezio-metacarpal articulation.

trapezist (trə'piːzɪst). [f. TRAPEZE + -IST.] A performer on the trapeze.

1875 T. FROST *Circus Life* x. 179 The first female trapezist appeared. **1888** *Star* 7 June 4/3 You may have heard of my sister Azella, the trapezist? **1893** *Westm. Gaz.* 10 Feb. 9/1 He has been a trapezist, a wire-walker, bar-performer, lifter of weights. **1905** *Ibid.* 11 Sept. 5/1 Aeronaut-trapezist killed.

†**trapezite**, *a. Obs. rare*$^{-1}$. [app. f. TRAPEZIUM + -ITE.] Having the form of a trapezium (in Euclid's sense); trapezial.

1570 BILLINGSLEY *Euclid* x. Def. xi. 232 A figure.. which may be any other rectiline figure, rectangled or not rectangled, triangle, pentagone, trapezite, or what so euer ells.

trapezium (trə'piːzɪəm). Pl. **trapezia, -iums.** [a. mod.L. *trapezium*, ad. Gr. τραπέζιον, dim. of τράπεζα table, in geometry used by Euclid in the general sense (see 1 below), by Proclus (ed. Friedlein, p. 414) in sense 1 b. (The early Latin editions of Euclid 1482–1516 have not *trapezium*, but the Arabic *helmariphe*; *trapezium* is in the Basle ed. of 1546.)

With Euclid (*c* 300 B.C.) τραπέζιον included all quadrilateral figures except the square, rectangle, rhombus, and rhomboid; into the varieties of *trapezia* he did not enter. But Proclus, who wrote Commentaries on the First Book of Euclid's Elements A.D. 450, retained the name τραπέζιον only for quadrilaterals having two sides parallel, subdividing these into the τραπέζιον ἰσοσκελές, *isosceles trapezium*, having the two non-parallel sides (and the angles at their bases) equal, and σκαληνὸν τραπέζιον, *scalene trapezium*, in which these sides and angles are unequal. For quadrilaterals having no sides parallel, Proclus introduced the name τραπεζοειδές TRAPEZOID. This nomenclature is retained in all the continental languages, and was universal in England till late in the 18th century, when the application of the terms was transposed, so that the figure which Proclus and modern geometers of other nations call specifically a *trapezium* (F. *trapèze*, Ger. *trapez*, Du. *trapezium*, It. *trapezio*) became with most English writers a *trapezoid*, and the *trapezoid* of Proclus and other nations a *trapezium*. This changed sense of *trapezoid* is given in Hutton's Mathematical Dictionary, 1795, as 'sometimes' used—he does not say by whom; but he himself unfortunately adopted and used it, and his Dictionary was doubtless the chief agent in its diffusion. Some geometers however continued to use the terms in their original senses, and since *c* 1875 this is the prevalent use.]

1. *Geom.* **a.** Any four-sided plane rectilineal figure that is not a parallelogram; any irregular quadrilateral. (The Euclidean sense.)

[**1551** RECORDE *Pathw. Knowl.* B iv, The fift sorte doth containe all other fashions of foure cornered figures, and ar called of the Grekes *trapezia*.] **1570** BILLINGSLEY *Euclid* I. Def. 34. 6 All other figures of foure sides besides these, are called trapezia, or tables. *Ibid.* 52 A trapesium hauing two sides parallels hath of necessitie the one of them longer then the other. **1660** BARROW *Euclid* I. Def. 33 All other quadrilateral figures besides these are called *Trapezia* or Tables. **1846** POTTS *Euclid* 5. **1862** TODHUNTER *Euclid* 5. **1906** HAMILTON & KETTLE *2nd Geometry Bk.* 39 Some terms for quadrilaterals are variously used by different writers. Here *trapezium* is used for all quadrilaterals that are not parallelograms.

b. *spec.* A quadrilateral having only one pair of its opposite sides parallel. (The specific sense to which the term was restricted by Proclus.)

The specific sense in Eng. in 17th and 18th c., and again the prevalent one in recent use.

[**1570**: see a.] **1698** FRYER *Acc. E. India & P.* 289 Geometrical Figures, like the Trapezium, or Square, in which the opposite sides are parallel. **1706** PHILLIPS (ed. Kersey), *Trapezium* (in *Geom.*) a Quadrilateral, or Square Figure, whose four Sides and Angles are not equal, but two of its Sides are parallel. **1721** BAILEY, *Trapezium*,.. a Quadrilateral Figure in Geometry, whose opposite Sides are parallel to one another. **1788** [see TRAPEZOID *sb.* 1 a]. **1840** LARDNER *Geom.* 72 If the angles at the base of a trapezium be equal, its sides will be equal. **1862** TODHUNTER *Euclid* 5 Some writers propose to restrict the word *trapezium* to a quadrilateral which has two of its sides parallel, and it would be certainly convenient if this restriction were universally adopted. **1882** CASEY *Euclid* 45 A quadrilateral which has one pair of opposite sides parallel is called a *trapezium*. **1903** HALL & STEVENS *School Geom.* 56. **1903** BAKER & BOURNE *Elem. Geom.* 81. **1908** —— *Elem. Mensuration* 48. **1909** GODFREY & SIDDONS *Geom. for Beginners* 77 A quadrilateral which has only one pair of sides parallel is called a trapezium. A trapezium in which the sides that are not parallel are equal is called an *isosceles* trapezium.

c. An irregular quadrilateral having neither pair of opposite sides parallel. (The usual sense in England from *c* 1800 to *c* 1875. Now *rare.* This sense is the one that is standard in the U.S., but in practice *quadrilateral* is used rather than *trapezium.*)

This is the *trapezoid* (τραπεζοειδές) of Proclus: see TRAPEZOID A. 1 a.

1795 HUTTON *Math. Dict.* II. 610/1 *Trapezium*,.. a plane figure contained under four right lines, of which both the opposite pairs are not parallel. When this figure has two of its sides parallel to each other, it is sometimes called a *trapezoid.* **1807** —— *Course Math.* II. 78 Lines are drawn in the fields on the plan, so as to divide them into trapeziums and triangles, the bases and perpendiculars of which are measured on the plan by means of the scale from which it was drawn. **1831** BREWSTER *Optics* xxv. 214 The solid called the icositetrahedron.. is bounded by twenty-four equal and similar trapezia. **1901** T. F. HOLGATE *Elem. Geom.* i. 74 If only two sides of a quadrilateral are parallel, the figure is called a trapezoid. If no two sides of a quadrilateral are parallel, the figure is called a trapezium. **1959** G. & R. C. JAMES *Math. Dict.* 400/2 *Trapezium*, a quadrilateral, none of whose sides are parallel.

2. *Anat.* **a.** A bone of the wrist, articulating with the metacarpal bone of the thumb (so called from its shape); also, the corresponding bone in the lower animals; the first of the distal row of carpal bones. Also *trapezium bone*; Fr. *os trapèze*.

1840 E. WILSON *Anat. Vade M.* (1842) 70 The trapezium is too irregular in form to be compared to any known object. *Ibid.* (1851) 238 Groove in the scaphoid and trapezium bones. **1881** MIVART *Cat* 97 The trapezium is the smallest carpal and the most radial of the distal series.

b. (in full, ***trapezium cerebri.***) A band of nerve-fibres in the *pons Varolii* of the brain.

1890 BILLINGS *Nat. Med. Dict.*, *Trapezium* (*cerebri*), in the pons Varolii a set of transverse fibres situated dorsally from the pyramids. In many animals..these fibres appear on the surface as an irregular quadrilateral area; hence the name.

3. *Astron.* A configuration of stars in the form of a trapezium; *esp.* that in the great nebula of Orion.

1851 NICHOL *Archit. Heav.* 143 All about the trapezium is a mass of stars. **1868** LOCKYER *Elem. Astron.* §354 The constellation Hercules is easily recognised by..the trapezium formed by four of its stars. **1883** *Knowledge* 15 June 357/2 The famous trapezium [in the great nebula in Orion], consisting of four bright stars and two smaller ones.

4. = TRAPEZE 1. *rare.*

1856 *Encycl. Brit.* (ed. 8) XI. 169/2 The triangle and trapezium are two of the most amusing instruments in modern gymnasiums. **1862** A. MACLAREN *Milit. Syst. Gymnastic Exerc.* 92 The trapezium consists of a turned ash bar..suspended by a rope at each end. *Ibid.* 93 The evolutions on the trapezium.

‖**trapezius** (trəˈpiːzɪəs). *Anat.* Pl. **trapezii** (-ɪaɪ). [mod.L. *trapezius* (*musculus*), adj. masc. f. *trapezium*: see prec.] Each of a pair of large flat triangular muscles (together forming the figure of a trapezium) extending over the back of the neck and adjacent parts. Also ***trapezius muscle.***

[**1693** tr. *Blancard's Phys. Dict.* (ed. 2), *Trapesius Musculus*, so called from its Geometric Figure.] **1704** J. HARRIS *Lex. Techn.* I, *T[r]apezius*, is a Muscle of the Shoulderblade, which serves to move it upwards, backwards, and downwards. **1831** R. KNOX *Cloquet's Anat.* 201 Its anterior surface is covered by the subclavius muscle, and the posterior by the trapezius. **1840** G. V. ELLIS *Anat.* 5 The great occipital nerve..perforates the trapezius muscle. **1860** O. W. HOLMES *Elsie V.* iii, The trapezius, lying diamond-shaped over the back and shoulders like a monk's cowl.

trapezohedron (ˌtræpɪzəʊˈhiːdrən, -ˈhɛdrən). *Geom.* and *Cryst.* Pl. **-hedra, -hedrons.** Also 9 **trapezoedron**, *erron.* **trapezihedron.** [f. *trapezo-*, used as combining form of TRAPEZIUM, after *tetrahedron*, etc. Cf. F. *trapezoèdre* (Littré).] A solid figure whose faces are trapeziums or trapezoids; as the icositetrahedron or deltohedron, with 24 faces, and the ***trigonal trapezohedron***, with 6. Hence ˌ**trapezoˈhedral** *a.*, pertaining to or of the form of a trapezohedron.

1816–22 CLEAVELAND *Treat. Min. & Geol.* (ed. 2) I. 361 Another form [in Garnet] is a trapezoedron, or a solid presenting twenty four equal and similar, trapezoidal faces. **1828** WEBSTER, *Trapezihedron*, a solid bounded by twenty-four equal and similar trapeziums. **1847** —— *Trapezohedron.* **1849** DANA *Geol.* xvii. (1850) 628 Garnet in trapezohedral crystals. **1868** —— *Min.* 189 Quartz... Various trapezohedral forms... Many trapezohedrons in other positions. **1895** STORY-MASKELYNE *Crystallogr.* vii. §257 The trigonal trapezohedron. *Ibid.* §273 The trapezohedral tetartohedron. *Ibid.* §274 The trapezohedra that occur on quartz belong to two correlative groups.

trapezoid (ˈtræpɪzɔɪd, trəˈpiːzɔɪd), *sb.* and *a.* [ad. mod.L. *trapezoīdēs*, a. late Gr. τραπεζοειδής, neut. -ές table-like (Proclus 450), f. τράπεζα table: see -OID. Cf. F. *trapézoïde* (1652 in Hatz.-Darm.).]

A. *sb.* **1.** *Geom.* **a.** A quadrilateral figure no two of whose sides are parallel. (Often called by English writers (in 19th c.) TRAPEZIUM.)

This is the sense for which Proclus introduced the term τραπεζοειδές; it is retained in F. *trapézoïde*, Ger. *trapezoïd*, etc. See etymol. note to TRAPEZIUM.

1706 PHILLIPS (ed. Kersey), *Trapezoid*, a Geometrical Figure that has all its four Sides and Angles unequal, and no Sides parallel. **1753** CHAMBERS *Cycl. Supp.*, *Trapezoid*, in geometry, a plane irregular figure, having four sides, no two of which are parallel to each other. **1788** T. TAYLOR *Proclus' Comm.* I. 176 Of non-parallelograms, some have only two parallel sides,..others have none of their sides parallel. And those are called Trapeziums, but these Trapezoids. **1851** R. F. BURTON *Goa* 274 Its shape is a trapezoid, for though quadrilateral, none of its sides are equal or even.

b. With some: A quadrilateral figure having only two sides parallel: = TRAPEZIUM 1 b. Now *U.S.*

A misapplication of the term orig. peculiar to English.

1795 HUTTON *Math. Dict.* II. 611/1 *Trapezoid* sometimes denotes a trapezium that has two of its sides parallel to each other. **1806** —— *Course Math.* I. 291 A Trapezoid, or Trapezium having two Sides Parallel. **1846** POTTS *Euclid* 45 Sometimes an irregular four-sided figure which has two of its sides parallel, is called a trapezoid. **1879** in *Cassell's Techn. Educ.* II. 124 If any two of the sides are parallel to each other the figure is called a trapezoid. **1901** [see TRAPEZIUM 1 c]. **1906** HAMILTON & KETTLE *2nd Geom. Bk.* 39 [Here] *trapezoid* [is used] for quadrilaterals that have one pair of parallel sides. **1925** F. E. SEYMOUR *Plane Geom.* II. 103 If the non-parallel sides of a trapezoid are equal, the trapezoid is called an isosceles trapezoid. **1972** *Whitaker's Almanack 1973* 902/2 Flag [of Kuwait].—Three horizontal stripes of green, white and red, with black trapezoid next to staff. **1975** *Sci. Amer.* Jan. 110/3 The matrix is stretched to a trapezoid, then the artist copies the picture by filling in the trapezoidal cells. **1977** *Monitor* (McAllen, Texas) 6 Jan. E-2/4 The Incas apparently adopted many things from the Mollos, of which the trapezoid is only one.

†**c.** Formerly applied to an irregularly quadrate solid with neither pair of sides parallel. *Obs.*

(Here *-oid* appears to have the same sense as in *ellipsoid*, *paraboloid*.)

1704 J. HARRIS *Lex. Techn.*, *Trapezoid* is a solid irregular Figure, having four Sides not parallel to one another. [The only sense given.] **1795** in HUTTON *Math. Dict.* II. 611/1 [as second sense].

2. *Anat.* A bone of the wrist, the second of the distal row of the carpus: so called from its shape. (Also in L.-Gr. form *trapezoides*; Fr. *trapézoïde*.)

1831 R. KNOX *Cloquet's Anat.* 135 The Trapezoides (*os multangulum minus*), is smaller than the trapezium. **1840** E. WILSON *Anat. Vade M.* (1842) 113 When seen from before, it has a quadrilateral form: it is named trapezoid. **1855** HOLDEN *Hum. Osteol.* (1878) 161 The trapezium and trapezoid form a shallow socket for part of the scaphoid.

B. *adj.* **a.** = TRAPEZOIDAL. (In all the quots. improperly used for TRAPEZIAL.)

1819 G. SAMOUELLE *Entomol. Compend.* 195 Thorax trapezoid, broad behind. **1826** KIRBY & SP. *Entomol.* IV. 264 Trapezoid... Quadrilateral, with two sides unequal and parallel. *Note.* We have departed from the more usual definition of *trapezoid*, 'An irregular figure whose four sides are not parallel', because the above is best suited to forms in insects. **1840** E. WILSON *Anat. Vade M.* (1842) 124 The internal lateral ligament is a broad and trapezoid layer of ligamentous fibres.

b. *Anat.* ***trapezoid body***: = TRAPEZIUM 2 b. ***trapezoid bone***: = A. 2. ***trapezoid ligament*** (F. *ligament trapézoïde*), the CORACO-CLAVICULAR ligament. ***trapezoid line***: see quot. 1890.

1890 BILLINGS *Nat. Med. Dict.* s.v., *T[rapezoid] bone*, second bone of distal row of wrist... *T. line*, a rough ridge for attachment of trapezoid ligament on under surface of clavicle. **1899** *Allbutt's Syst. Med.* VI. 804 Degeneration of the trapezoid body.

trapezoidal (træpɪˈzɔɪdəl), *a.* [f. prec. + -AL[1]: cf. F. *trapézoïdal* (Littré).] **a.** Having the form of a trapezoid; irregularly quadrilateral. Sometimes used for TRAPEZIFORM; this sense is standard in the U.S.

1796 KIRWAN *Elem. Min.* (ed. 2) I. 259 Oriental Garnet.. presenting either 12 rhomboidal planes, or 24 trapezoidal. **1831** R. KNOX *Cloquet's Anat.* 401 Each of these muscles occupies the side of the larynx; it is thin, flat, and of a trapezoidal figure. **1873** M. COLLINS *Squire Silchester* v, An irregular trapezoidal space, where..cattle and sheep are penned. **1955** *Sci. Amer.* Mar. 101/2 The temple has a trapezoidal central pyramid. **1973** *Nature* 21 Sept. 160/1 Trace brightness was modulated by a periodic trapezoidal wave-form.

b. Having trapezoidal faces; trapezohedral.

1796 KIRWAN *Elem. Min.* (ed. 2) I. 36 When a fossil is broken into fragments, the shape of these is..sometimes cubical, rhomboidal, or pyramidal, or trapezoidal. **1805–17** R. JAMESON *Char. Min.* (ed. 3) 201 A Crystal is said to be.. Trapezoidal, when its surface consists of twenty-four equal and similar trapeziums [i.e. trapezoids]... Example, Trapezoidal garnet. **1822** J. PARKINSON *Outl. Oryctol.* 8 Its [coal's] fragments mostly cubical or trapezoidal.

So **trapeˈzoidiform** *a.*

1826 KIRBY & SP. *Entomol.* IV. xlvi. 266 Trapezoidiform. .. Whose horizontal section is trapezoid.

Trapezuntine (træpɪˈzʌntaɪn), *sb.* and *a.* [f. L. *Trapezunt-*, *Trapezus*, Gr. τραπεζόντ-, τραπεζοῦς Trebizond + -INE[1].] **A.** *sb.* A native or inhabitant of the city of Trebizond or Trabzon in north-eastern Turkey.

1900 'ODYSSEUS' *Turkey in Europe* vi. 269 After the conquest of Trebizond in 1461, many noble families migrated from that town to Constantinople, and naturally aspired to the Patriarchate..thus producing another element of discord among the unhappy Greeks, who were now rent by the factions of Trapezuntines and Constantinopolitans. **1956** R. MACAULAY *Towers of Trebizond* viii. 79 We went out to explore, and the first thing we saw in the street was the B.B.C. van taking records, and round it stood a crowd of Trapezuntines staring.

B. *adj.* Of or pertaining to Trebizond, its natives, or inhabitants.

1926 W. MILLER *Trebizond* i. 11 A conspicuous landmark of Trapezuntine history. **1969** A. C. BANDY in *Ibid.* (new ed.) p. ix, The Trapezuntine Empire..continues to interest scholars and students of Greek civilization. **1980** *Times Lit. Suppl.* 4 July 763/5 Trapezuntine princesses married into the Byzantine imperial house and into other Orthodox ruling families.

trapfall (ˈtræpfɔːl). [f. TRAP *sb.*[1] + FALL *sb.*[2]: cf. PITFALL *sb.*] A trap consisting of a trap-door or covering over a pit or cellar arranged so as to give way beneath the feet. Also *fig.*

1596 SPENSER *F.Q.* v. ii. 7 In the same are many trap-fals pight, Through which the rider downe doth fall through oversight. **1610** HEALEY *St. Aug. Citie of God* 373 Avoide these damnable trap-falls of the devill. **1797** HOLCROFT tr. *Stolberg's Trav.* (ed. 2) III. lxxxvi. 132 She is accused of having contrived a trap-fall, in this palace. **1853** *Fraser's Mag.* XLVIII. 347 A manager, who entertains higher notions of his art..than that of a mere snare or trap-fall for audiences.

traphine, obs. form of TREPHINE.

‖**trapiche** (traˈpitʃe). [American Sp. *trapíche*, derivative of L. *trapētum* oil-press.]

1. A mill for crushing the sugar-cane; a sugar-mill; also, a sugar plantation.

1648 GAGE *West Ind.* 179 There was in my time a new Trapiche of Sugar. **1844** BRANTZ MAYER *Mexico* 197 On the east is another huge edifice where the boilers, engines, crushing machines, cooling vats, moulding apartments, etc., constitute the *trapiche* of the hacienda. **1896** *Nat. Geog. Mag.* July 242 The *trapiche* or sugar-cane press of the chief. Here two huge wooden rollers..pressed the cane stalks and large metal vessels received the juice.

2. A rude form of mill for grinding ores.

1881 RAYMOND *Mining Gloss.*, *Trapiche*, a rude grinding machine, composed of two stones, of which the upper is fastened to a long pole.

trapiferous (træˈpɪfərəs), *a.* *Min. rare*$^{-1}$. [f. TRAP *sb.*[5] + -(I)FEROUS.] Containing trap-rock.

1796 KIRWAN *Elem. Min.* (ed. 2) I. 382 Trapiferous Argillite.

'**trapish**, *a.* ? *Obs.* [f. TRAIPSE *sb.* + -ISH[1].] Like a traipse (sense 1); slovenly; slatternly.

1705 ROWE *Biter* II. i, A Couple of the trapishest Creatures I ever saw in Masks. **1706** T. BAKER *Tunbr. Walks* v. i, Always trapish and dirty like an actress at a morning rehearsal. **1762** *Poetry* in *Ann. Reg.* 208 Now monstrous in hoop, now trapish, and walking With your petticoats clung to your knees, like a malkin.

trap-net. see TRAP *sb.*[1] 12.

trappan, obs. form of TREPAN.

trappean (ˈtræpiːən), *a.* *Min.* [f. TRAP *sb.*[5] + *-ean* (L. *-e-us* + -AN): cf. *marmorean*.] Pertaining to, of the nature of, or consisting of trap-rock.

1813 BAKEWELL *Introd. Geol.* (1815) 55 Domes of trappean porphyry. **1855** J. R. LEIFCHILD *Cornwall Mines* 271 A very fertile soil is formed from what is geologically called 'trappean ash', on the trap rocks. **1873** J. GEIKIE *Gt. Ice Age* xvi. 205 The trappean heights..between the valleys of the Clyde and the Irvine.

trapped, trapt (træpt), *ppl. a.*[1] [f. TRAP *v.*[1] and *sb.*[1] + -ED.]

1. Caught in or as in a trap; also, caught in a mistake in class at school (*Sc.*).

c **1440** *Promp. Parv.* 499/2 Trappyd, or be-trappyd and gylyd.., *deceptus, illaqueatus.* **1552** HULOET, Trapped, *irretitus.* **1884** *Pall Mall G.* 8 Aug. 11/2, 3,000 trapped rabbits from this particular warren. **1894** H. NISBET *Bush Girl's Rom.* 93 'What do you want me to do?' asked the trapped gentleman. **1895** CROCKETT *Bog-myrtle & Peat* 185 The trapped boys sometimes rectified matters at the back of the school at the play-hour when fists became a high court of appeal and review.

2. Furnished with a trap or traps, as a drain, etc.

1872 F. ROGERS *Specifications Pract. Archit.* II. ii. 106 To put to the water-closet in the basement-story a strong cast-iron trapped basin. **1892** T. B. F. EMINSON *Epidemic Pneumonia at Scotter* 10 Four..nominally trapped inlets.

trapped (træpt, *poet.* ˈtræpɪd), *ppl. a.*[2] Also 7 **trapt.** [f. TRAP *sb.*[2] and *v.*[2] + -ED.] Protected or adorned with trappings.

13.. *Coer de L.* 3888 Kyng, eerls, barouns, knyghts, and squyers, Ryden ryally on trappyd destrers. **1375** BARBOUR *Bruce* XVI. 185 Trappit horss richt to the feit. *c* **1440** *Promp. Parv.* 499/2 Trappyd, wythe trapure, *faleratus.* **1602** *2nd Pt. Return fr. Parnass.* IV. ii, Mounted on a trapt Palfrey. **1885** B. HARTE *Maruja* iii, Cumbrous vehicles..drawn by gaily trapped mules.

trapped, *ppl. a.*[3] [f. *trap* in TRAP-CUT + -ED.] Of a gem: Cut with the TRAP-CUT.

1875 KNIGHT *Dict. Mech.* 962/2 A thicker stone, trapped in two hights on the front and three on the back.

'**trapper**, *sb.*[1] *Obs.* exc. *Hist.* Forms: 4–6 **trappure**, 5 **trappor**, **-ere**, **trapure**, **-ur**, **-oure**, **-owre**, **-ere**, 5–6 **trappour(e**, **-ar**, 5–7 **traper**, 5–9 **trapper.** [ad. OF. **trapeüre*, **drapeüre*, *drapure* (*a* 1500 in Godef. 'chevaulx couvers de drapures diverses'), also AF. *drapeur* (Stat. 7 Edw. IV in Godef.); = med.(Anglo-)L. *trappātūra* (*a* 1450 in Du Cange): see TRAP *sb.*[2], *v.*[2] With later form cf. *bordure*, *border*, and -ER[2] 3.] A covering put over a horse or other beast of burden, made of metal or leather for purpose of defence, or of cloth for shelter and adornment; trapping; housing.

13.. *Coer de L.* 2262 Ten hundred stedes good and sure King Richard let array in trappure. *c* **1386** CHAUCER *Knt.'s T.* 1641 The scheeldes brighte testeres, and trappures; Gold hewen helmes, hauberkes, Cote Armures. *c* **1400** MAUNDEV. (Roxb.) xxvi. 123 Þai hafe..trappour to þaire hors. **1459** in *Paston Lett.* I. 477, j. pece of skarlot for trappars for horsys. **1463** *Mann. & Househ. Exp.* (Roxb.) 215 To John Wysnacke the same day,..ffor steynynge off my masterys traperys, iij. s. iiij. d. **1470–85** MALORY *Arthur* I. xvi. 58 The swerd..cut thorow the trappere of stele. **1513** DOUGLAS *Æneis* VII. v. 194 Thair brusit trappouris and patrellis reddy boun. *a* **1548** HALL *Chron., Rich. III* 25 b, His horse trapped in blue veluet..which trapper was borne by fotemen from the grounde. **1621** QUARLES *Argalus & P.* (1678) 114 The Trappers seem to hover Like wings..As the horse pranc'd. **1891** *Athenæum* 23 May 670/3 His opinion that the long-shanked spur was for use when the horse was covered with a trapper. **1902** *Jrnl. Archæol. Inst.* Mar. 74 A chain-mail trapper beneath the textile.

fig. **1509** HAWES *Past. Pleas.* xxvii. (Percy Soc.) 132 The good knight Trouth..betrapped fayre and gaye Wyth shyning trappers of curiositie. **1600** SIR W. CORNWALLIS *Ess.* viii. F v, Al these blessings are the trapers of the furniture of Patience.

trapper (ˈtræpə(r)), *sb.*[2] [f. TRAP *v.*[1] and *sb.*[1]]

1. One who sets traps or snares; *spec.* one engaged in trapping wild animals for their furs.

1768 PENNANT *Zool.* II. 338 The trappers..bait the trap with a meal worm..: Ten or a dozen nightingales have been caught in a day. **1827** J. F. COOPER *Prairie* II. i. 7 The hunters and trappers on La Platte. **1840** R. H. DANA *Bef. Mast* xiii. 31 Trappers and hunters..with their valuable skins and furs. **1857** TENNYSON *Enid* 1572 A sudden.. cry, As of a wild thing taken in the trap, Which sees the trapper coming thro' the wood.

attrib. **1851** MAYNE REID *Scalp Hunt.* Pref. 6 My book is a trapper book. **1899** *Daily News* 27 Mar. 8/2 The authors tell us trapper stories and Red Indian tales.

2. A boy stationed to open and shut a trap-door for the passage of trams in a coal-mine. Also ***trapper-boy, -lad.***

1815 *Ann. Philos.* VI. 114 The trappers have seats near their doors, and remain by them all the time the pit is at work. **1845** MRS. NORTON *Child of Isl.* 22 So lives the little Trapper underground: No glittering sunshine streaks the oosy wall. **1892** *Pall Mall G.* 19 Aug. 1/3 Mrs. Keir Hardie ..began life as a trapper boy in a mine. **1900** [trapper lad: see TRAP *sb.*[1] 8 b].

3. One who manages a trap in trap-shooting: cf. TRAP *sb.*[1] 4.

a **1892** *Hurlingham Club Rules for Pigeon Shooting* §6 If, in the opinion of the referee, the shooter is balked by any antagonist or looker-on, or by the trapper,..he may be allowed another bird. **1892** GREENER *Breech-Loader* 246 It is best to take no heed either of bystanders or trappers when going to the mark.

4. *colloq.* A horse which draws a 'trap'.

1883 *Pall Mall G.* 24 Apr. 4/1 The hard-worked 'trapper' ..munches his oats in solitude in many a stable. **1894** ASTLEY 50 *Years Life* I. 57, I..made a journey to Tattersall's, and bought a very clever trapper, a bay mare.

†**ˈtrapper,** *v. Obs. rare.* [f. TRAPPER *sb.*[1]] *trans.* To cover or adorn with trappings. Also *fig.*

1597 G. HARVEY *Trimming T. Nashe* Wks. (Grosart) III. 56 His fierie steedes trapperd in their caparisons. **1620** FELTHAM *Resolves* lxxxiii. 271 To see how Vice goes trapperd [*later edd.* trapped] with rich furniture. **1633** T. SCOT *Highw. God.* 17 As for fear, it's too base an humour to trapper justice.

ˈtrappiness. *colloq.* [f. TRAPPY *a.*[1] + -NESS.] The quality of being 'trappy' or containing traps.

1885 *Field* 26 Dec. 884/1 There were broad pastures and large banks and ditches, innocent of trappiness for the most part, before the riders.

trapping (ˈtræpɪŋ), *vbl. sb.*[1] Chiefly in pl. **trappings.** [f. TRAP *sb.*[2] and *v.*[2] + -ING[1].] A cloth or covering spread over the harness or saddle of a horse or other beast of burden, often gaily ornamented; a caparison.

1398 TREVISA *Barth. De P.R.* XVIII. xli. (Bodl. MS.), The colte is nouȝt..ihiȝt wiþ trappinge and gay harneys. **1553** EDEN *Treat. Newe Ind.* (Arb.) 15 *margin*, The riche trapping of the kinges horse. **1764** HARMER *Observ.* xxv. vi. 283 On a stately steed, with a rich saddle and fine trappings. **1817** MOORE *Lalla R.* (1824) 3 The embroidered trappings of the elephants.

b. *transf.* Chiefly *pl.* 'Ornaments; dress; embellishments; external, superficial, and trifling decoration' (J.). Also *fig.*

1596 NASHE *Saffron Walden* 114 Hee is neuer wont to keep anie man longer than the sute lasteth he brings with him, and then turne him to grasse and get one in newe trappings. **1601** SHAKS. *Twel. N.* v. i. 10 *Duke.* Belong you to the Lady Oliuia, friends? *Clo.* I sir, we are some of her trappings. **1602** —— *Ham.* I. ii. 86 These, but the Trappings, and the Suites of woe. **1685** DRYDEN *Thren. August.* 330 He needs no Trappings of fictitious Fame. **1791** BOSWELL *Johnson* an. 1758 (1906) I. 201 A motto, the usual trapping of periodical papers. **1791** COWPER *Iliad* IV. 167 The stately trapping of some prince. **1859** HELPS *Friends in C.* Ser. II. II. vii. 136 To strip a man of all his trappings of birth, rank, and education.

Hence †**ˈtrappinged** (-ɪŋd) *a.*, adorned with trappings.

1654 GAYTON *Pleas. Notes* IV. xv. 252 What regard would be given to a Praetor without his trapping'd horse, the Gold Chain, and the Cap of maintenance?

trapping (ˈtræpɪŋ), *vbl. sb.*[2] [f. TRAP *v.*[1] + -ING[1].] The action of TRAP *v.*[1] in various senses; catching by or as by a trap, etc.

1398 TREVISA *Barth. De P.R.* v. xi. (Tollem. MS.), þan by trappynge of þe humoure, þat is conten[i]t, he makeþ þe teres falle oute of þe yen [*orig.* per alicationem contenti humoris oculos lacrymari faciunt]. *a* **1533** FRITH *Disput. Purgat.* (1829) 107 To that answereth he neither yea nor nay, for fear of trapping. ?**16..** *Country Gentleman's Vade M.* (Nares), For their art of trapping. **1842** *Rept. Comm. on Employment Children*, The employment..assigned to the youngest children, generally that of 'trapping'. **1867** TROLLOPE *Chron. Barset* I. xxxiii. 286 [He] had his own very strong ideas about the trapping of foxes. **1890** *Lancet* 22 Nov. 1125/2 The defects in drainage arrangement, such as want of proper trappings..were very numerous.

b. *attrib.* and *Comb.*

1837 W. IRVING *Capt. Bonneville* i. (1849) 24 They detach bands..of trappers in various directions, assigning to each a portion of country as a..trapping ground. **1895** FRASER *Whaups of Durley* iii. 36 The trapping lesson, was..the most enjoyable part of the day's work. **1904** GALLICHAN *Fishing Spain* 164 One of these trapping-places [for trout]. **1904** *Westm. Gaz.* 3 Dec. 10/3 The Illicit Diamond Buying Act, said prisoner, was part of a trapping system.

trapping, *vbl. sb.*[3]: see TRAP *sb.*[4]

trapping, *vbl. sb.*[4]: see TRAP-CUT, quot. 1853.

ˈtrapping, *ppl. a.* [f. TRAP *v.*[1] + -ING[2].] That traps or entraps: see TRAP *v.*[1]

a **1548** HALL *Chron., Hen. VII* 22 He allured and enticed with moost flatterynge woordes and trappynge termes, the lady Anne. **1551** T. WILSON *Logike* (1580) 85 b, They are called trappyng argumentes, because fewe that aunswered vnto them, can auoide daunger. **1821** CLARE *Vill. Minstr.* II. 63 Leave, oh leave the murky barn, Ere trapping spiders thee discern.

Trappist (ˈtræpɪst), *sb.*[1] (*a.*) [ad. F. *trappiste*, from *La Trappe*, name of the convent: see below.]

1. a. A monk of the branch of the Cistercian order observing the reformed rule established in 1664 by De Rancé, abbot of La Trappe, in Normandy.

1814 in Brackenridge *Views Louisiana* 288 To make the highest virtue to consist in silence, was reserved for the Trappists. **1870** ROGERS *Hist. Gleanings* II. 24 The..most frivolous profligates have often become the most rigid.. Trappists and Carthusians.

b. *attrib.* or as *adj.* Of or pertaining to this branch of the Cistercian order.

1836 LD. SHREWSBURY in E. Purcell *Life A. P. de Lisle* (1900) I. iv. 69, I..wish..to see a religious establishment on the premises; but I fancy we might have a much more useful one than a Trappist monastery. **1837** J. BINNS *Miseries & Beauties of Ireland* II. xiii. 298 The superintendant of the Trappist Settlement at Mount Melleray. **1847** BUNSEN *Ch. of Future* App. 307 The Count purchased the old Trappist Monastery. **1860** *All the Year Round* No. 74. 560 He intended to enter a Trappist convent. **1871** MORLEY *Crit. Misc.* Ser. I. 28 The Trappist theory of the conditions of virtue.

2. *transf.* A puff-bird of the genus *Monacha*, having inky-black plumage with white about the head; a NUN-BIRD.

1891 in *Cent. Dict.*

ˈtrappist, *sb.*[2] [f. TRAP *sb.*[1] or *v.*[1] + -IST.] A professional trapper (of wild animals).

1880 CARNEGIE *Pract. Trap.* 19 Hares do not offer so large a field for work to the trappist as do rabbits. **1896** *Times* (weekly ed.) 380/4 Russian trappists almost denuded the coast of animals.

Trappistine (ˈtræpɪstɪn, -iːn). [f. TRAPPIST[1] + -INE[3].]

1. A member of an order of nuns affiliated with the Trappists, founded in 1827. Also *attrib.* and as *adj.*

1869 P. G. HAMERTON *Wenderholme* III. xi. 96 He observed a Trappistine silence during the repast. **1884** *Cath. Dict.* 804/1 Mount St. Bernard in Leicestershire and the Trappistine convent of Stapehill in Dorset. **1896** C. K. PAUL tr. *Huysman's En Route* vii. 100 She wandered.. among the Trappistines in Switzerland.

2. A liqueur made by the Trappists. [So in Fr.]

1877 E. S. DALLAS *Kettner's Bk. of Table* 279 Trappistine, distilled by the good fathers of the Grace of God in the Doubs. **1891** in *Cent. Dict.* **1920** G. SAINTSBURY *Notes on Cellar-Book* ix. 138 Benedictine; Trappistine; a certain 'Père Kermann'..and others will occur.

trappoid (ˈtræpɔɪd), *a. Min.* [f. TRAP *sb.*[5] + -OID.] Resembling or allied to trap-rock.

1842 in Phillips *Man. Geol.* (1855) 250 Upon this lies an often trappoid or magnesian conglomerate. **1854** MURCHISON *Siluria* xiii. 334 A reaggregated trappoid breccia. **1889** *Nature* 12 Dec. 140/2 In saucer-like hollows in the solid, tough, trappoid rocks.

trappose (ˈtræpəʊs), *a. Min.* [f. as prec. + -OSE.] Of, pertaining to, or of the nature of trap or trap-rock; trappean. Also **ˈtrappous** *a.* (*rare*—[0]).

1796 KIRWAN *Elem. Min.* (ed. 2) II. 175 Argillaceous Iron Stone... Of this sort also we may reckon the *Trappose Ore used..in Sweden. **1799** —— *Geol. Ess.* 272 The black trappose matter that descends from the summit of the mountain to a torrent at its foot where it forms pillars. **1845** G. H. SMITH in *Encycl. Metrop.* XXIII. 733/2 From Thunder Mountain, Westward, trappose-greenstone is the prevailing rock. **1828** WEBSTER, *Trappous.

trappour, trappure, obs. ff. TRAPPER *sb.*[1]

trappy (ˈtræpɪ), *a.*[1] *colloq.* [f. TRAP *sb.*[1] + -Y.] Of the nature of a trap, 'catchy'; containing a trap or traps.

1882 *Daily Tel.* 13 Nov. 2/5 The fences might have been increased in size, however, without being made 'trappy'. **1883** E. PENNELL-ELMHIRST *Cream Leicestersh.* 56 The jump into the lane is a trappy one. **1888** *Scott. Leader* 5 Apr. 4 Useless, trappy arithmetic, useless frivolities of grammar, the finesse of our exceptional spelling,..must all go if children are to be made more intelligent and observant. **1889** BADEN-POWELL *Pigsticking* 97 The trappy nature of the ground..due to the frequent occurrence of inexplicable holes. **1898** *Engineering Mag.* XVI. 108/1 The earlier engines, with their many cams, springs, gears, and trappy contrivances. **1904** *Daily Chron.* 16 Aug. 7/1 To permit 'trappy' off balls to pass by in such close proximity to his wicket as to make his admirers hold their breath.

ˈtrappy, *a.*[2] *rare.* [f. TRAP *sb.*[5] + -Y.] = TRAPPEAN, TRAPPOSE.

[**1828** WEBSTER, *Trappous*... It ought to be *trappy*.] **1864** in WEBSTER citing WRIGHT. Hence in mod. Dicts.

traps (træps), *sb. pl. colloq.* [A modern word of colloquial origin; app. shortened from *trappings*: see TRAPPING *vbl. sb.*[1] (Some take it as pl. of TRAP *sb.*[1], as referring to the outfit of a trapper.)]

Portable articles for dress, furniture, or use; personal effects; baggage; belongings.

1813 CAPT. R. M. CAIRNES *Let.* 4 Apr. in *Dickson MSS.* (ed. J. H. Leslie, 1910) Ser. III. 866 The rest [of the carriages] is for the Jolly Captain's Shirts and Stockings, &c., besides a mule for his other traps. **1828** *Craven Gloss.*, *Traps*, small tools or implements, always used in the plural number; equivalent to the classical *arma*. **1830** *Chron.* in *Ann. Reg.* 153/2 This was the general signal for getting our 'traps' on the ice. **1831** *John Bull* 7 Aug. 254 No one thought ..that only three days afterwards he would be obliged to pack up his traps and be off. **1833** MARRYAT *P. Simple* xiii, I packed up my traps and went on shore. **1887** J. BALL *Nat. in S. Amer.* 194 To carry some of the traps with which a botanist is usually encumbered.

ˈtrapstick. [f. TRAP *sb.*[1] + STICK *sb.*] A stick used in the game of trap or trap-ball.

1591 PERCIVALL *Sp. Dict.*, *Paleta*, a trapsticke, *Bacillum lusorium*. *a* **1627** MIDDLETON & ROWLEY *Span. Gipsy* II. ii, If my woods, being cut down, can not fill this pocket, cut 'em into trap sticks. **1629** SHIRLEY *Wedding* III. ii, A boy of seven years old beat him with a trap-stick. **1764** T. BRYDGES *Homer Travest.* (1797) I. 272 On high In air he let his trapstick fly. **1862** MARSH *Lect. Eng. Lang.* 40 A mahogany box,..with..several trap sticks projecting through slots in the top of it.

b. *transf.* and *fig.*

1680 *Honest Hodge & Ralph* 14 A meer trap-stick to bang the Phanaticks about. **1714** ADDISON *Spect.* No. 559 ¶6 A foolish Swop between a Couple of thick bandy Legs, and two long Trapsticks that had no Calfs to them. **1796** *Grose's Dict. Vulg. T.*, *Trap Sticks*, thin legs, gambs.

trapunto (trəˈpʊntəʊ). Also **Trapunto.** [a. It., = quilting.] A kind of quilting in which the design alone is padded (see quot. 1967).

1929 *Sewing for Profit* (Woman's Inst. Domestic Arts & Sci., U.S.) 73 Besides the usual kind of quilting..there is the trapunto, or Italian, quilting. **1936** *Home Arts Needlecraft* Jan. 5 (*heading*) Quilting in the Trapunto manner. **1967** E. SHORT *Embroidery & Fabric Collage* ii. 47 In the case of Trapunto, areas of the design are padded where required by splitting the backing and inserting wadding, after which the backing is sewn up again. **1972** *N.Y. Times* 3 Nov. 7/2 (Advt.), Leather-look..coat..with trapunto embroidery. **1979** *Guardian* 25 Apr. 11/8 The needlework designs..used in the country from which the garment hails: embroidery, applique, quilting, trapunto, smocking.

tra-ra (ˈtrɑːrɑː, trɑːˈrɑː), *int.* and *sb.* An imitation of the sound of a horn, or some similar sound. (Cf. TRA-LA-LA.)

1849 tr. *De la M. Fouqué's Sir Elidoc* 23 Hark, forward! hark, forward! Tra-ra, tra-ra! **1900** *Westm. Gaz.* 18 Jan. 4/2 It sounds as if a million kettle-drums were being played—a constant tra-ra-ra-ra, with the boom of the big guns.

tras, trasche, trase, obs. ff. TRACE, TRASH.

‖**trascinando** (traʃiˈnando). *Mus.* [It., pres. pple. of *trascinare* (see next).] (See quots.); = RALLENTANDO.

1876 STAINER & BARRETT *Dict. Mus. Terms* 483/2 *Trascinando (It.)*, dragging, delaying the time. **1947** E. BLOM *Everyman's Dict. Music* 632/2 *Trascinando* (It.), dragging. **1983** *New Oxf. Compan. Music* 1842/1 *Trascinando* (It.), 'dragging', i.e. holding back, *rallentando*.

trascine (traˈsiːn), *v. nonce-wd.* [ad. It. *trascinare* to drag, pull.] *trans.* To carry, to drag.

1922 JOYCE *Ulysses* 48 She trudges,..drags, trascines her load.

†**trase,** *v. Obs. rare.* [Derivation and meaning obscure. It has been suggested to be an early form of TRASH *v.*[1], though the date is against this.]

c **1440** *York Myst.* xxxi. 3 Your tounges fro tretyng of trifillis be trased. *c* **1470** *Golagros & Gaw.* 675 Thair hors.. As trasit in vnquart quakand thai stand.

‖**trasformismo** (trazforˈmizmo). Also Trasformismo. [It.; cf. TRANSFORMISM.] In Italy, a system of shifting political alliances, or of changes of allegiance, to form a stable administration or a workable policy. Cf. OPPORTUNISM.

1925 A. SOLMI *Making of Mod. Italy* vii. 144 The parliamentary phenomena..called *trasformismo*. **1943** C. J. S. SPRIGGE *Devel. Mod. Italy* ii. 57 A struggle between *Trasformismo* and groups which endeavoured to gain power in the name of definite principles. **1957** M. CARLYLE *Mod. Italy* ii. 55 Depretis..with his policy of shuffling and reshuffling of cabinets (*trasformismo*) created the dictatorship of the Cabinet. **1964** *Economist* 27 June 1462/2 This change of heart looked like the wildest sort of *trasformismo*. **1973** P. A. ALLUM *Politics & Society in Post-War Naples* iv. 116 The Piedimonte cobbler was able to fit fascism into his life experience, the classic *trasformismo* of southern boss politics. Before the March on Rome, everyone was socialist, afterwards, they were all fascists.

trash (træʃ), *sb.*[1] Forms: (? 4 trasche), 6 trasshe, traish, trasse, 6–7 trashe, 7 traisse, 6– trash. [With exception of the doubtful instance in 1 b, known only from 16th c.; origin obscure.

Cf. Norw. dial. *trask* lumber, trumpery, trash, baggage (which Falk & Torp refer to *tras* twig, sprig), Icel. *tros* rubbish, fallen leaves and twigs, and Norw. *trase*, Sw. *trasa* rags, tatters.]

1. a. That which is broken, snapped, or lopped off anything in preparing it for use; broken or torn pieces, as twigs, splinters, 'cuttings from a hedge, small wood from a copse' (*E.D.D.*), straw, rags; refuse.

1555 *Bill in Chancery* in *Athenæum* 17 July (1886) 92/2 A carpenter's yarde, wherein he dothe laye his tymber and Trasshe. **1574** Hellowes *Gueuara's Fam. Ep.* (1584) 255 How wil he giue wood to the Hospitall, that warmes himselfe by the trash of straw? **1670** Narborough *Jrnl.* in *Acc. Sev. Late Voy.* I. (1694) 108 The Woods..are so thick with Under-brush, old rotten Trees, and Leaves, and such Trash. **1675** Evelyn *Terra* (1729) 45 If you lay any Fern-brakes, or other Trash about them. *a* **1693** *Urquhart's Rabelais* III. l. 401 They break..to very Trash the woody parcels. **1727** *Bradley's Fam. Dict.* s.v. *Cask*, The Trash, or gross Substance of pressed Grapes. **1763** *Brit. Mag.* IV. 464 The floor being thus prepared,..cover it with wet ground leaves or other tobacco trash. **1867** Baker *Nile Tribut.* ii. 53 Bamboos and reeds, with trash of all kinds, were hurried along the muddy waters.

(*b*) *spec.* in the U.S., domestic refuse, garbage.

1906 H. de B. Parsons *Disposal of Municipal Refuse* iii. 21 Rubbish is discarded trash, composed principally of all kinds of paper, wood, rags, mattresses, bedding, boxes,..tin cans,..bottles,..and the like. **1925** *Amer. City* Jan. 54/2 The collection of garbage and trash may be made by the city with its own organization. **1931** W. G. McAdoo *Crowded Years* i. 12 The abandoned..building... Its steps were littered with trash, and many..windows were broken. **1962** A. Lurie *Love & Friendship* vii. 127 Mother used to get up at five in the morning..to sweep the front porch and carry the trash out. **1977** *New Yorker* 24 Oct. 128/3 Truckloads of trash were taken to the prison dump.

b. An old worn-out shoe. *dial.*

The first quot. fits the sense; but its date, 150 years before any other example of the word, makes its place doubtful.

[*c* **1360** *E.E. Allit. P.* B. 40 Þen þe harlot with haste helded to þe table With rent cokrez at þe kne & his clutte [= clouted] trasches.] *c* **1746** J. Collier (Tim Bobbin) *View Lanc. Dial.* Gloss., *Trash*, unripe fruit; also an over-worn shoe. **1828** *Craven Gloss.* s.v., In the plural *trashes*, a pair of worn-out shoes. **1885** Mrs. Banks *In his own Hand* iv, His week's tramp had..worn his shoes into trashes.

c. Broken ice mixed with water; trash-ice.

1856 Kane *Arct. Expl.* I. xxvi. 342 Warped about one hundred yards into the trash.

†**d.** (?). *Obs.*

? *a* **1550** in *Brand's Pop. Antiq.* (1849) I. 120 For paulme-flowers, cakes, trashes, and for thred on Palme Sonday, viii[d].

2. *spec.* The refuse of sugar-canes after the juice has been expressed; cane-trash, also, the dried leaves and tops of the canes, stripped off while still growing, to allow them to ripen; field-trash.

1707 Sloane *Jamaica* I. p. xlv, It was the custom to burn their Trash, which is the..remainder of the Sugar Canes after the juice is squeezed out. **1790** Castles in *Phil. Trans.* LXXX. 349 Burning the cane trash (or straw of the cane). *Ibid.* 356 The field trash (or the dried leaves and tops of the canes). **1793** J. B. Moreton *W. Ind. Cust.* 47 The [sugar-] canes being cut, and all the trash lopped off. **1842** [see cane *sb.*[1] 10]. **1884** *Macm. Mag.* Nov. 19/2 Just before harvest, when the dead leaves or trash are thick around the canes.

3. a. Anything of little or no worth or value; worthless stuff; rubbish; dross. (Said of things material or immaterial.)

c **1518** Skelton *Magnyf.* 2164 As for his plate of syluer, and suche trasshe. **1604** Shaks. *Oth.* III. iii. 156 Who steales my purse, steales trash. **1612** T. Taylor *Comm. Titus* ii. 14 (1619) 515 What can the Papist say now for his mony-masses, pardons, indulgences, and such trash? **1728** Young *Love Fame* III. 192 Ambition feeds on trash. **1795** Mills in *Phil. Trans.* LXXXVI. 43 The great facility with which the gold might be separated from the trash. **1838** Thackeray *2nd Lect. Fine Arts* Wks. 1900 XIII. 284 Some..new pictures, in the midst of a great quantity of trash. **1852** Mrs. Stowe *Uncle Tom's C.* xix, What poor, mean trash this whole business of human virtue is!

b. *spec.*: see quot.

1749 *Wealth Gt. Britain* 51 There are three kind of mark'd herring among the Dutch;..the last sort are called trash.

c. Worthless notions, talk, or writing; nonsense; 'rubbish', 'stuff'.

1542 Udall *Erasm. Apoph.* E.'s Pref., Like trash & bagguage been those saiynges that are incidente in oracions. **1653** Milton *Hirelings* Wks. 1851 V. 383 Those Theological Disputations..rather perplex and leven pure Doctrin with scholastical Trash. **1737** Fielding *Hist. Register* I. Wks. 1784 III. 319 My Register is not to be fill'd ..with trash for want of news. **1874** Burnand *My time* xxx. 293 Don't let me hear any more of such trash.

†**d.** Contemptuously applied to money or cash; 'dross'. *Obs. slang.*

(Cf. quot. 1604 in 3, which has prob. influenced later use.)

a **1592** Greene *Jas. IV*, III. i, And therefore must I bid him provide trash, for my master is no friend without money. [**1601** Shaks. *Jul. C.* IV. iii. 26 Shall we now, Contaminate our fingers, with base Bribes? And sell..our.. Honors For so much trash, as may be grasped thus?] **1742** Young *Nt. Th.* VI. 218 Drudge, sweat,..for every gain, For vile contaminating trash. **1809** Malkin *Gil Blas* I. viii, Money! said he,..you have a poor opinion of Spanish charity, if you think that people of my stamp have any occasion for such trash upon their travels.

4. A worthless or disreputable person; now, usually, such persons collectively. ***white trash***, the poor white population in the Southern States of America; now also used outside the Southern States of American and in *attrib.* use. Cf. white *a.* 4 a.

1604 Shaks. *Oth.* v. i. 85, I do suspect this Trash To be a party in this Iniurie. **1750** Chesterf. *Lett.* 5 June, Prostitutes, actresses, dancing women, and that sort of trash. **1827** Scott *Chron. Canongate* v, Sheriffs, and bailiffs, and sic thieves and trash of the world. **1831** H. J. Finn *Amer. Comic Ann.* 88 'You be right dere,' observed Sambo, '..else what fur he go more 'mong niggers den de white *trash*?' **1833** F. Kemble *Jrnl.* 6 Jan. (1835) II. 112 The slaves themselves entertain the very highest contempt for white servants, whom they designate as 'poor white trash'. **1863** 'E. Kirke' *My Southern Friends* 55 The poor trash.. scratched a bare subsistence from a sorry patch of beans and collards. **1883** Fiske in *Harper's Mag.* Feb. 423/1 North Carolina was the paradise of the 'white trash'. **1901** W. Churchill *Crisis* I. i. 7, I..put a bullet past his ear, just to let the trash know the sound of it. *Ibid.* II. x. 211 It was not even a wild dream that white-trash Lincoln would be elected. **1932** W. Faulkner *Light in August* xvi. 363 Who told you I am a nigger, you little white trash bastard? **1942** B. Robertson *Red Hills & Cotton* viii. 189 If that was the sort of good-for-nothing trash she was, then she could just leave. **1945** E. Waugh *Brideshead Revisited* I. viii. 180 Who are all this white trash, anyway? **1973** *Sunday Times* 10 June (Colour Suppl.) 51/4 He said that all the Australians were white trash. **1977** J. Didion *Bk. of Common Prayer* IV. i. 158 'Lower that white-trash voice,' Warren said.

5. *attrib.* and *Comb.*, as (see esp. sense 1 a (*b*) above) ***trash basket, -bin, can, collection, collector, compactor, container, pickup, roof; trash-eater, -monger; trash-lined*** adj.; **trash-bag**, (*a*) see quot. 1688; also, old shoes; also, a disreputable or worthless person (*dial.*); (*b*) chiefly *U.S.*, a rubbish bag; **trashman** *N. Amer.* = dustman 1; **trash-house**, a building on a sugar-plantation where the stalks from which the juice has been expressed are stored for fuel; **trash-ice**, broken ice mixed with water (cf. 1 c); **trash-rack**, a rack set in a stream to prevent the passage of floating debris; **trash-reader**, a critical reader of novels and the like for a publisher; **trash-turner**, a metal plate in a sugar-mill, that guides the canes between pairs of rollers (Webster 1911).

1688 R. Holme *Armoury* III. xxii. (Roxb.) 278/1 A *Trash Bagg, of some called an Apron, wherein are seuerall pocketts ..to place the seuerall implyments..which the Angler hath occasion to use. **1792** S. Burdy *Life of Late Rev. Philip Skelton* 161 He had a trash bag, as they call it, in which he kept needles, thread, and such like articles, to put a few stitches, if necessary, in his clothes. **1886** *S.W. Linc. Gloss.* s.v., That son of hern's a regular trashbags. **1887** *S. Cheshire Gloss.*, *Trash-bag*, (1) a person whose boots or clothes are dirty, and generally who is slovenly in dress or habits, (2) in pl. old shoes. **1934** Webster, Trash bag. **1960** *Guardian* 2 Feb. 5/1 The provision..of brown paper 'trash bags' for free issue to picnic parties. **1978** *Sci. Amer.* Feb. 158/3 Some household materials are also suitable: wrapping paper, brown paper bags and plastic trash bags (the kind used to line the inside of garbage cans). **1895** *Dialect Notes* I. 395 **Trash-basket*, waste-paper basket. N.Y. City. **1959** *Listener* 5 Mar. 411/2 The trash basket in his mother's bedroom. **1972** *New Yorker* 26 Aug. 21/3 Trash baskets stood in ranks on the empty sand, like sentinels. **1955** W. Gaddis *Recognitions* I. i. 38 Janet came in a few minutes later to find him sifting through the kitchen *trashbin. **1966** *Punch* 9 Mar. 331/2 How many mushroom enterprises leave the customer with equipment fit only for the trash-bin or the attic? **1976** *Columbus* (Montana) *News* 27 May 1/1 Members of the Columbus High School..have 'bicentennialized' the fire hydrants and trash bins. **1929** *Sci. Amer.* May 445/3 A prominent member of Washington society last winter rolled 25,000 dollars worth of diamonds in a chamois bag and carelessly left the bag on a table where her little son found it and carried it to the *trash can. **1936** W. Stevens *New Caravan* 74 A trash can at the end of the world. **1960** *Times* 14 Sept. 12/7 Our dustbins—sorry, trash cans. **1981** 'P. Mallory' *Killing Matter* xvii. 173 A shaggy dog, working the trash cans. **1967** Mrs. L. B. Johnson *White House Diary* 26 Jan. (1970) 480 One of the Mayors said that his budget for *trash collection and cleaning had tripled in the last two years. **1979** *Arizona Daily Star* 5 Aug. I. 12/3 (Advt.), A continuous city-wide program of trash collection was implemented in 1974. **1967** *Boston Sunday Herald* 26 Mar. I. 34/1, I have a bone to pick with the Dedham *trash collectors. **1973** *Washington Post* 13 Jan. E 16/3 (Advt.), Optional *trash compactors and tub enclosures. **1977** *Chicago Tribune* 2 Oct. XII. 11/7 (Advt.), Kitchen complete with all appliances including disposal and trash compactor. **1968** Mrs. L. B. Johnson *White House Diary* 17 Jan. (1970) 617 We came out loud and strong for one more trash pickup a week..and for more *trash containers. **1712** Steele *Spect.* No. 431 ¶3 Find out some Name for these craving Damsels, ..*Trash-eaters, Oatmeal-chewers, Pipe-champers [etc.]. **1793** J. B. Moreton *W. Ind. Cust.* 48 The canes..are.. spread about the works till they dry, and then..carried to a long large shade, called a *trash-house, where they are piled, as being the only fuel for boiling the sugar. **1864** Webster, **Trash-ice*, crumbled ice mixed with water. **1891** *Cent. Dict.* cites Kane. **1894** J. E. Humphrey in *Pop. Sci. Monthly* XLIV. 496 Placed in *trash-lined bins. **1965** *Amer. Psychologist* Dec. 1014/2 A good idea was translated into banalities about..the friendly postman and *trashman. **1971** *Daily Colonist* (Victoria, B.C.) 9 July 26/7 We used to organize regular expeditions..early on the mornings before the trashman came. **1694** Motteux *Rabelais* V. 236 *Trashmongers and Spanglemakers. **1603** Florio *Montaigne* I. li. (1632) 167 Metonymia, Metaphore, Allegorie, Etimologie, and other such *trashnames of Grammar. **1968** *Trash pickup [see *trash container* above]. **1978** *Detroit Free Press* 16 Apr. (Parade Suppl.) 31/1 You should see Beverley Hills on trash pickup day. **1913** J. B. Bishop *Panama Gateway* v. ii. 3 The entrances [of the penstocks] are closed by cast-iron head-gates and bar-iron *trash-racks. **1757** Smollett *Let.* 12 May in J. Irving *Bk. Dumbarton.* (1879) II. 197 Employed as a *trash reader for the *Critical Review*. **1902** in *Daily Rec. & Mail* 23 Aug. 5 Fine ash and sand rained down..with occasional showers of large stones. Some..were so hot as to set fire to the '*trash' roofs of huts..seven miles from the crater.

b. *attrib.* or as quasi-*adj.*, designating that which is worthless or of poor quality. Chiefly *U.S.*

In quot. 1843 perh. short for trashy *a.* 1.

1843 Dickens *Let.* 7 Aug. (1974) III. 537 We were obliged at the last moment to alter an excellent bill; and the entertainments were very trash. **1940** *Sun* (Baltimore) 23 Jan. 5/1 Flocks of ducks—mostly 'trash' ducks like Black Bay coots and shelducks. **1944** *National Geogr. Mag.* Jan. 27/1 Trash fish and tons of discarded shrimp offal are now valuable in making fertilizer. **1966** 'H. MacDiarmid' *Company I've Kept* xiii. 270 That availability to Yankee trash-culture which has developed apace. **1967** G. Steiner *Lang. & Silence* 103 The serious novel has had to choose topics formerly exploited by trash-fiction. **1971** *Times* 27 Nov. 3/3 The so-called 'trash mail' service, the delivery of unaddressed circulars [by postmen]. **1973** *Daily Colonist* (Victoria, B.C.) 4 Oct. 31/3 Two inventors say they have a great new food product, but the name leaves something to be desired. It's 'trash fish' sausage. **1977** *Amer. N. & Q.* XV. 108/2 The image of Latin America in some German 'trash' novels of the twentieth century. **1979** R. Barnard *Posthumous Papers* xiii. 127 The offspring of shopkeepers, who bribed him with trash food. **1983** *New Yorker* 5 Dec. 160/2 About seven tons of trash fish eventually turned belly-up—Sacramento suckers, hardheads.

Hence **'trashify** *v.*, *trans.* to turn into trash, render trashy; **'trashless** *a.*, free from trash, purified from worthless elements.

1663 Sir G. Mackenzie *Relig. Stoic* 36 Not suffering him to lay over his vitiousness upon Providence, a shift too ordinar amongst such as misunderstand the trashless Doctrine of the reformed Churches. **1831** *Examiner* 132/2 Thus is trash thrice trashified.

trash, *sb.*[2] Now *dial.* [Goes with trash *v.*[1], of which it may be the source, or the vbl. sb.] A cord used to check dogs in breaking or training them; a leash. Also ***trash-cord***.

1611 Markham *Country Content.* I. i. (1615) 15 Your Huntsmans lodging, wherein hee shall also keep his cooples, liams, collars, trashes, boxes. **1830** Scatcherd *Hist. Morley* 195 To 'Trash' signifies to clog, incumber, or impede, and accordingly..the rope tied by sportsmen round the necks of fleet pointers, to..check their speed, is hereabouts called a 'Dog Trash'. **1884** Speedy *Sport* iv. 43 It will be found in many cases necessary to use a trash-cord in breaking dogs. **1899** Dickinson *Cumberld. Gloss.*, *Trash cord*, a long slender rope fastened to the collar of a young pointer (or setter) if headstrong and inclined to run in.

trash (træʃ), *v.*[1] *Obs.* exc. in sense 2. [Of obscure origin; perh. the 15th c. trase is the same word.

As it is a hunting term, a French origin is naturally suspected, but the OF. *trasier*, *trachier* 'to draw a line through, strike out, efface', which agrees in form, does not explain sense 1, though it is app. the origin of sense 2.]

†**1.** *trans.* To check (a hound) by a cord or leash; hence *gen.* to hold back, restrain, retard, encumber, hinder. *Obs.*

1610 Shaks. *Temp.* I. ii. 81 Who t' aduance, and who To trash for ouertopping. *a* **1619** Fletcher *Bonduca* I. i, I fled too, But not so fast;..he trasht me, Nennius. **1646** Hammond *Tracts* 31 Grieving the Spirit of God,..trashing of God in his course of grace. *a* **1660** —— *Serm.* x. Wks. 1683 IV. 534 To incumber and trash us in our violent furious marches. **1837** De Quincey *Revolt of Tartars* Wks. 1862 IV. 145 There was not a chance for them, burdened and 'trashed' as they were, to anticipate so agile a light cavalry as the Cossacks.

2. To efface, obliterate. *western U.S.*

This was prob. a term of the French trappers.

1859 Bartlett *Dict. Amer.*, *To trash a trail*, an expression used at the West, meaning to conceal the direction one has taken by walking in a stream.

trash, *v.*[2] *Obs.* exc. *dial.* [app. f. Norse: cf. Sw. *traska*, Norw. *traske*:—**traðska* in the same sense.]

1. *intr.* To walk or run with exertion and fatigue, esp. through mud or mire.

1607 W. S[mith] *Puritan* IV. i, A guarded Lackey to run befor't, and pyed liueries to come trashing after't. **1608** Middleton *Trick to Catch Old One* I. iv, I still trashed and trotted for other men's causes. **1654** H. L'Estrange *Chas. I* (1655) 59 To trash on foot in the mire on a rainy morning. *a* **1716** South *Serm.* (1744) X. 72 Those that trash through the mire and dirt. **1825** Brockett *N.C. Words*, *Trash*,..to tramp about with fatigue. **1878** *Cumberld. Gloss.*, *Trash*,.. to walk quickly over wet ground. 'Trashan' through thick and thin for a heall day togidder'.

2. *trans.* To fatigue (with walking, running, or exertion); to wear out.

1685 *Life Bp. Jewell* 36 Being naturally of a spare and thin Body, and thus restlesly trashing it out with reading, writing, preaching and travelling, he hastened his death. **1816** Scott *Bl. Dwarf* x, He hasna a four-footed creature but the vicious blood thing he rides on, and that's sair trashed wi' his night wark. **1821** Carlyle *Early Lett.* (1886) II. 5 The fineness of the weather did not prevent the journey from trashing me a good deal. **1911** *Blackw. Mag.* Nov. 605/2 The bullocks will be trashed.

b. *fig.* To labour (a point). [Cf. *thrash*.]

a **1670** Hacket *Abp. Williams* I. (1692) 87 Every Nation know their own way best, to what they are tied, as we know ours. He is a Busie-body that trasheth this in a Pulpit.

Hence **'trashing** *ppl. a.*, fatiguing, wearing out; also **'trash-mire** *dial.*, one who trashes in the mire.

1828 *Craven Gloss.*, *Trash-mire*, a slut. **1861** *Times* 25 Sept., They have had long marches, bivouacs in bad nights, and very trashing work.

trash, *v.*[3] [f. TRASH *sb.*[1]]

1. *trans.* To free from trash or refuse; *spec.* to strip the outer leaves from (growing sugar-canes) so that they may ripen more quickly.

1793 B. EDWARDS *Hist. Brit. Col. W. Ind.* II. v. i. 223 The ancient practice of trashing ratoons (i.e.) stripping them of their outward leaves, being of late..justly exploded. **1902** *Q. Rev.* July 18 White men simply cannot work and 'trash' the cane in tropical Queensland.

2. To treat as trash; hence, to discard as worthless.

1909 in *Cent. Dict. Supp.*

3. a. To vandalize (property or goods), esp. as a means of protest. Occas. *intr.*, to perform such acts of destruction. Also *fig. colloq.* (chiefly *U.S.*).

1970 *Guardian* 14 May 2 On Sunday night a small gang went out to trash but a sudden rainstorm stopped the attack. **1971** *Time* 22 Mar. 26 Backstage at *Comes a Day* he got drunk and trashed his dressing room. **1974** H. L. FOSTER *Ribbin', Jivin', & Playin' Dozens* vi. 266 Students or unauthorized visitors who are physically attacking someone, 'ripping off' school equipment, 'trashing', attempting to burn or blow up a building, or otherwise interfering with instruction or threatening a student or worker with physical harm. **1975** 'S. MARLOWE' *Cawthorn Jrnls.* (1976) xix. 174 The room..had been trashed..by either the patrons..or by the police. **1976** *Globe & Mail* (Toronto) 24 Aug. 29/8 Mine was one of a group of offices trashed at Trinity College in early June. Trashed, not burglarized. Nothing stolen. Art works smashed. Manuscripts and notes left alone, but books soaked in wine or worse. Furniture ripped, ceiling tiles torn. **1984** *New Yorker* 20 Feb. 43/1 They've trashed the laws.

b. To injure seriously, destroy or kill (someone or something). *U.S. colloq.*

1973 W. MCGIVERN *Reprisal* 196 Don't be squeamish... Remember that Jules Levy, a Jew, trashed the pusher who murdered your son. **1977** C. MCFADDEN *Serial* (1978) l. 107/1 Harvey threatened Spenser with grievous bodily harm... 'Whaddaya wanna trash me for?'

c. To reduce or impair the quality of (a work of art, etc.); to expose the worthless nature of (something), to deprecate. *colloq.* (chiefly *U.S.*).

1975 *New Yorker* 12 May 114/2 In Hollywood, the writer is an underling whose work is trashed, or, at best, he's a respected collaborator without final control over how his work is used. **1976** *Time* 5 Apr. 42/2 The presentation is ignorant, cluttered and coarse, and it trashes the sculpture. Works that need to be walked around..can only be seen frontally. **1977** *Saturday Night* (Toronto) May 72/1 With *Ghost Fox*, I thought, Houston would trash all the melodramatic comic-book stuff about Indians with one neat blow. **1981** *London Rev. Bks.* 2–15 July 12/1 She writes..yet another trashing of radical chic. This might be more gripping had she herself not trashed radical chic already.

trash-cord: see TRASH *sb.*[2]

trashed (træʃt), *ppl. a. colloq.* (chiefly *U.S.*). [f. TRASH *v.*[3] 3 + -ED[1].] Bungled, spoiled; ill-treated or injured; run-down. Freq. with advbs.

1926 *Spectator* 22 May 857/1 We don't want any trashed-up peace. **1977** *Sounds* 9 July 30/2 Guthrie was real folk, born (1912) and raised in Oklahoma,..a trashed-on Okie farmer's son when that didn't mean you droned on about being proud of your bigoted ignorance. **1979** *Tucson* (Arizona) *Citizen* 20 Sept. 7B/6 'I've sat through this movie three times.'.. 'In this trashed-out theater? The picture's that good?' 'It's a lousy picture! I can't get my feet unstuck from the floor!!' **1980** *Dirt Bike* Oct. 14/1 Track-N-Trail has just come up with a solution to the age-old problems of mud, cold, rain, and trashed knuckles for you offroaders.

'trasher. [f. TRASH *v.*[3] + -ER.]

1. A person who trashes sugar-cane: see TRASH *v.*[3]

1903 *Daily Chron.* 17 Sept. 6/7 The fierce rays of the torrid sun pouring down on the perspiring trashers of the cane.

2. A vandal or wrecker. Cf. TRASH *v.*[3] 3 a. *colloq.*

1970 *Guardian* 19 Sept. 9/5 The trasher mixes with the non-violent student. **1975** *Time* (Canada ed.) 9 June 8/2 'As a lifelong Tory and ranking member of the legal establishment,' reports Time Canada's Toronto Bureau Chief Robert Lewis, 'Maloney also is not about to pursue his office like a trasher.'

trashery ('træʃərɪ). Also 6 trasshery. [f. TRASH *sb.*[1] + -ERY.] Trash collectively (in various senses); things of the nature of trash or rubbish.

1557 NORTH *Gueuara's Diall Pr.* 367 Water potts, platters, dishes, and other smal trasshery. **1813** SCOTT *Trierm.* II. Interl. iii, Who comes in foreign trashery Of tinkling chain and spur. **1832** in *Examiner* 537/1 It would seem to be time that these trasheries ceased! **1855** *Fraser's Mag.* LI. 201 The ..little Jack-in-the-Green..is hardly to be discovered amongst the florid trashery in which he is involved.

trashify, trashless: see TRASH *sb.*[1]

trashily, trashiness: see TRASHY.

'trashing, *vbl. sb.* [f. TRASH *v.*[3] + -ING[1].]

1. The action of TRASH *v.*[3] 1.

1847 *Simmonds' Col. Mag.* Mar. 295 Plant-canes require at least four weedings and trashings before they are fit to shift for themselves. **1897** *Daily News* 23 June 15/3 In Northern Queensland..the white farmer and his family do most of the work themselves, except at 'trashing' time, when Kanakas are employed.

2. The action of TRASH *v.*[3] 3 a; vandalism or an instance of this. *colloq.* (chiefly *U.S.*).

1970 *N.Y. Times* 29 Apr. 40/1 The new breed of campus revolutionaries..are now turning to what they call 'trashing'—the setting of fires, hurling of rocks, smashing of windows. **1971** *Publishers' Weekly* 4 Oct. 24/1 Student riots and trashings of college stores. **1973** D. MARTIN *Tracts against Times* v. 47 The 'trashing' activities which damaged all property within a half-mile radius of the University of Wisconsin. **1979** *Listener* 3 May 614/2 'Trashing', the destruction of buildings and property, became commonplace.

†**trash-nail.** *Obs.* Also 6 **trashe, traishe nayle.** [Derivation and specific sense uncertain. (Cf. *traverse nail* in TRAVERSE *sb.* 23.)] Some kind of nail (used app. in fixing up the stage or scenery for revels).

1556–7 in Swayne *Sarum Churchw. Acc.* (1896) 102 Trashe nayles, ij d. **1578** in Feuillerat *Revels Q. Eliz.* (1908) 308 Trashe nayle xiiii[d]. **1584** *Ibid.* 369 Threed, fire, candles, traishe nayle etc. **1620** THOMAS *Lat. Dict.*, *Clavi vmbellati*, ..Trash nailes.

trashtrie ('traʃtrɪ). *Sc.* [perh. a perversion of **trashry, trashery*: cf. *deviltry*.] = TRASHERY.

1786 BURNS *Twa Dogs* 63 Yet ev'n the ha' folk fill their pechan, Wi' sauce, ragouts, and such like trashtrie. **1896** J. SKELTON *Summers & Wint. at Balmawhapple* I. 161 Pope, and Swift,..feckless bodies wi' their fushionless English trashtrie.

trashy ('træʃɪ), *a.* [f. TRASH *sb.*[1] + -Y.]

1. Of the nature of trash; rubbishy; worthless.

a **1620** J. DYKE *Sel. Serm.* (1640) 286 Such slovenly meate, such trashy meat, such bitter meat. **1693** G. POOLEY in *Phil. Trans.* XVII. 675 The..sparry, stony, and trashy parts rise up to the top. **1868** *Athenæum* 14 Mar. 397/2 Trashy words set to trashy music. **1871** CARLYLE in *Mrs. C.'s Lett.* (1883) I. 14 Reading the trashiest heap of novels.

2. Encumbered with trash, that is, with the withered growth of the previous season. *U.S.*

1905–6 *Trade Catalogue* (Cent. Dict. Supp.), The high curve of the beam prevents fouling in trashy land.

3. Of people: worthless, disreputable. *colloq.*

1862 'E. KIRKE' *Among Pines* vii. 167 He regarded the white man as altogether too 'trashy' to be treated with much ceremony. **1898** B. KIRKBY *Lakeland Words* 148 Of bad habits sairy man. Dick, Ah's flait he's nobbut trashy. **1931** H. NICOLSON *Diary* 31 Dec. (1966) 100, I am thought trashy and a little mad. I have been reckless and arrogant. **1935** [see *piney-woods cracker* s.v. PINEY WOOD]. **1977** *Detroit Free Press* 11 Dec. 13-C/1, I honestly couldn't believe such things happened except in low class trashy families.

Hence **'trashily** *adv.*; **'trashiness.**

1836 J. BROWN *Lett.* (1907) 34, I have been..feeling miscellaneously and therefore trashily. **1857** *Sat. Rev.* 10 Jan. 37/2 A work of uniform trashiness. **1880** VERN. LEE *Stud. Italy* II. ii. 26 A grand thought..mixed and amalgamated with trashiness.

Traskite ('træskaɪt). *Ch. Hist.* Also 7 **Thraskite, Threskite.** [f. *Trask*, a surname + -ITE[1].] A follower of John Trask, who *c* 1617 began to advocate certain Jewish ceremonies, including the observance of the seventh-day Sabbath; now represented by the Seventh-day Baptists. Also †**'Traskist** *Obs.*

1618 T. ADAMS *Bad Leaven* Wks. 1861 II. 343 There is a fourth leaven,..the mixing of law with gospel... This leaven might well..have moulded away, if there had not been a late generation of Thraskites to devour it as bread. **1631** WEEVER *Anc. Fun. Mon.* 54 Precisians, Disciplinarians, Iudaicall Thraskists. **1631** R. H. *Arraignm. Whole Creature* x. §1. 78 Our Iudaizing Threskites. **1634** (Apr. 1) *Order Commiss. Eccles. Courts*, [To take measures for the suppression of] Brownists, Anabaptists, Arians, Traskists, Familists [etc.]. **1661** BLOUNT *Glossogr.* (ed. 2), *Thraskites*, are the followers of John Thraske. **1694** E. CHAMBERLAYNE *Pres. St. Eng.* III. (ed. 18) 377 Traskists, now called Seventh-day-men, who keep the Jewish Sabboth. **1874** BLUNT *Dict. Sects*, Traskites.

†**trason**, *v.* *Venery. Obs.* Also 5 **tresone.** [Etymology obscure: the first part seems to be OF. *tras-, tres-*:—L. *trans* across, as in *trespass*.] *intr.* Of a roe: To cross or double before the hounds. Hence †**'trasoning** *vbl. sb.*

1486 *Bk. St. Albans, Hunting* e ij b, When ye hunt at the Roo, then shall ye say thoore He crosses and tresones yowre howndys byfoore. **1575** TURBERV. *Venerie* xlv. 143 His [the roe's] crossings and doublings before the houndes are called Trasonings. **1688** R. HOLME *Armoury* II. 189/1. *a* **1700** B. E. *Dict. Cant. Crew*, *Trasoning* [printed *Trajoning*], when a Roe crosses and doubles. **1847–78** HALLIWELL, Trasenings.

trason, -oun, etc., obs. ff. TREASON, etc.

trass (trɑːs, -æ-). Also 8 **traas, traass.** [a. Du. *tras*, Ger. *trasz*, earlier *te'rras, ti'ras*.] = TARRAS.

[**1793** SMEATON *Edystone L.* §201 Tarras. [*Note*] This substance, when prepared for use, is by the Dutch called *Tras*, from which our appellation of *Tarras* undoubtedly originates.] **1796** KIRWAN *Elem. Min.* (ed. 2) I. 354 Often mistaken for volcanic traass. **1811** PINKERTON *Petralogy* II. 427 The trass of the environs of Andernach, on the left bank of the Rhine, is a kind of puzzolana formed of small fragments of pumice, and several species of lavas... Trass is transported by water as far as Dort, to be reduced to powder in stamping mills worked by the wind... The Dutch also supply England with trass. **1838** *Civil. Eng. & Arch. Jrnl.* I. 412/2 Tarras, or trass, is a bluish black cellular trap or lava, quarried at Andernach on the Rhine, into millstones. **1862** G. P. SCROPE *Volcanos* (ed. 2) 178 Both puzzolana and trass, when mixed up with lime, set readily under water.

trass, trasse, obs. ff. TRACE, TRASH *sb.*[1], TRUSS.

trassel, obs. form of TRESTLE.

trassene, error for *transsene*: see TRANSON *v.*

trasshe, obs. f. TRASH, TRAISE *v. Obs.*, to betray.

trast, var. TRAIST *Obs.*; obs. f. TREST.

trat (træt). *local.* [Origin unascertained. Cf. TROT *sb.*[1] 6 and *v.* 5.] Also **trat-line**, a name on the east coast of England for a line having baited hooks hung along its length, laid near the water's edge, and fastened down at each end, to catch fish when the tide flows over it; a set line.

1894 *Daily News* 26 Apr. 6/5 At Deal..the catches of two boats consisted of nearly 700 fine whiting as well as codfish and dabs. These were taken on rods and 'trat' lines. **1905** in *Eng. Dial. Dict.* (from Yorkshire).

trat, earlier northern form of TROT *sb.*[2]

traterie, -erous: see TRAITORY, TRAITOROUS.

tratore, -orie, -ory, -our, -ouresse, -oury: see TRAITOR, TRAITORY, TRAITRESS.

tra-trip, variant of TREY-TRIP *Obs.*

tratt, trat (træt), colloq. abbrev. of TRATTORIA.

1969 R. AIRTH *Snatch!* xv. 149 We stopped off at a little trat Bruno knew of..and had a last one. **1969** *Queen* 17–30 Sept. 18/3 Luigi..who served you dinner in last week's trendy tratt. **1970** *Guardian* 6 Mar. 9/5, I have been thinking about trattorias. Mostly I mean the white-tiled tratts of SW 1, 3, and 7.

†**trattle**, *sb.*[1] Chiefly *Sc. Obs.* Also 6 (*pl.*) **tratlis, trattillis, tratilis, trattils, tratelles.** [n. of action from TRATTLE *v.*: cf. *tattle, prattle* as sbs.] Idle tales or talk; gossip; chatter.

1513 DOUGLAS *Æneis* VIII. Prol. 83 Off tratlis and tragedeis the text of all talk is. *a* **1592** GREENE *Jas. IV*, I. iii, But leave this trattle, and tell me what news. **1597** JAS. I *Demonol.* II. iv, Like old womens trattles about the fire.

trattle ('træt(ə)l), **trottle** ('trɒt(ə)l), *sb.*[2] *local.* Also 6–7 **tret(t)le**, 6, 9 **truttle.** [Origin obscure: usually held to be related to TREDDLE.] *pl.* The rounded droppings of sheep, hares, rabbits, etc.

1547 BOORDE *Brev. Health* cxii. 42 b, If the egestion.. doth loke like shepes tretles, there is abundance of coler adusted. **1598** FLORIO, *Tronzoli*, the dung or truttles of any cattle, as of sheepe. **1600** SURFLET *Countrie Farme* II. xii. 217 Break three or fower trottles of a goate or sheepe. **1639** T. DE GRAY *Compl. Horsem.* 62 His doung..hee putteth forth with round and hard trattles. *a* **1825** FORBY *Voc. E. Anglia*, *Trattles*,..the small pellets of the dung of sheep, hares, rabbits, &c. **1865** COCKAYNE in *Sax. Leechd.* II. Gloss. s.v. *Tyrdelu*, Called sheeps tredles in Somerset, trattles in Suffolk. **1877** *N.W. Linc. Gloss.*, *Trottles*, the dung of sheep, lambs, or rabbits. **1886** *S.W. Linc. Gloss.*, *Treddles, Truddles, Truttles.*

†**'trattle**, *v.* Chiefly *Sc. Obs.* Forms: 5 **tratyll, -el, -ill, tratle**, 6 **trattil, -ill, -yll**, 6, 8 **trattle**; also *pres. pple.* 5 **tratlyng**, 5–6 *Sc.* **tratland**, *pres. pple.* and *gerund* 6–7 **tratling**; *pa. t.* 6 *Sc.* **tratlit.** [app. related in some way to TATTLE, but actually found earlier, and not in the sense 'stammer', in which *tattle* was first used. Probably echoic.] *intr.* and *trans.* To talk idly; to chatter, gossip.

a **1400** [see TRATTLING *vbl. sb.*]. *c* **1425** WYNTOUN *Cron.* VII. x. 3454 Ye rawe [= rave], & tratelys [*v.r.* tratlys] all foly. **1508** KENNEDIE *Flyting w. Dunbar* 313 Sen thow on me thus, lymmer, leis and trattillis. *a* **1555** BP. GARDINER in Foxe *A. & M.* (1563) 751 Ouer grosse opinions, to enter into your learned head, whatsoeuer the vnlearned woulde trattle. **1568** GRAFTON *Chron.* II. 107 He..vsed to trattle and talke more than ynough. *a* **1592** GREENE *Jas. IV* Induct., Many circumstances too long to trattle on now. *a* **1800** *Earl Richard* v. in Child *Ballads* (1885) III. 152/1 Better..Than thou canst keep thy clattering toung, That trattles in thy head.

†**'trattler.** Chiefly *Sc. Obs.* In 5–6 **tratlar**, 6 **-or**, 7 **-er.** [f. TRATTLE *v.* + -ER[1].] One who 'trattles'; an idle talker, chatterer, gossip.

1456 SIR G. HAYE *Law Arms* (S.T.S.) 78 The tane is a grete tratlar, the tothir a still herkenare. **1500–20** DUNBAR *Poems* xli. 10 Be ȝe ane lear, that is werst of all, Be ȝe ane tratlar, that I hald als ewill. **1599** JAS. I *Βασιλ. Δωρον* (1603) 100 Where yee finde a tratler, away with him. **1670** RAY *Prov.* 260 A tratler is worse then a thief.

†**'trattling**, *vbl. sb. Obs.* [f. TRATTLE *v.* + -ING[1].] The action of the verb TRATTLE; idle talking or chattering; gossiping.

a **1400** *Cursor M.* 27824 (Cott. Galba) Couatyse es ane euil syn... Of þis cumes tratilling of tresoune. *c* **1460** *How Gd. Wife taught Daughter* 17 (MS. St. John's, Camb.) Nocht oyss [= use] of tratlyng in the toune. **1570** *Satir. Poems Ref.* xxiii. 115 Thocht Lethingtoun with tratling he do trane thame. **1603** *Proph. of Waldhaue* (Bann. Cl.) 34 This taile that I tell you,..It is a tratling but trueth, the suth the to say.

†**'trattling**, *ppl. a. Obs.* [f. as prec. + -ING[2].] That 'trattles'; chattering, tattling, gossiping.

1500–20 DUNBAR *Poems* xviii. 39 Thair tratling tungis that all furth temiss. **1559** AYLMER *Harborowe* P j b, The tratling Scot shal knocke out your chestes botoms. *a* **1585** POLWART

Flyting w. Montgomerie 129 Ȝet, tratling truiker, truth to tell [etc.].

trattoria (trato'ria, træ'tɔːriːə). Pl. **-ias**, ‖**-ie**. [a. It., f. *trattore* host, f. *trattare* to treat.] **a.** In Italy, an eating house, a takeaway, a restaurant. **b.** Outside Italy, a restaurant serving Italian food.

1832 W. GELL *Pompeiana* I. iv. 49 A trattoria and coffee-house. **1873** 'OUIDA' *Pascarel* I. II. iv. 169 Then he would pass methodically across the piazza to his favourite trattoriâ. **1922** [see FETTUCCINE]. **1955** E. POUND *Section: Rock-Drill* xci. 74 'Dodici Apostoli' (trattoria). **1966** *Punch* 20 July 112/1 The High Street sees a new Restaurant, a new Trattoria or a new Bistro opening every week. **1971** 'A. BURGESS' *MF* ix. 101 The Great Giro..was piling cold plates together like a *trattoria* waiter. **1973** *Times* 25 Aug. 12/7 An insipid stew (*veau Berichonne*), with tough meat, that one would get in lesser known London trattorie. **1975** FELTON & FOWLER *Best, Worst & most Unusual* 216 Pizzas of all shapes and varieties are served in restaurants and trattorias throughout Italy.

trature, -uruse, obs. ff. TRAITOR, TRAITOROUS.

trau, var. THROW *sb.*[1] *Obs.*; obs. f. TROW *v.*

trauail(e, -aill(e, obs. ff. TRAVAIL, TRAVEL.

trauchle, variant of TRACHLE *sb.* and *v. Sc.*

traue, obs. form of TROW *v.*

traueil, -el, -eilous, -elous, obs. ff. TRAVAIL, TRAVEL, TRAVAILOUS.

traught, traul, obs. ff. TROUGH, TRAWL.

traulism ('trɔːlɪz(ə)m). *rare.* Also in L. form **traulismus.** [ad. Gr. τραυλισμ-ός, f. τραυλίζειν to lisp, τραυλός adj. lisping, mispronouncing letters.] A stammering, stuttering.

[**1589** R. HARVEY *Pl. Perc.* A ij, And so foorth following the Traulila-lilismus, as farre as Will Solnes stuttring pronunciation may stumble ouer at a breath.] **1678** PHILLIPS (ed. 4), *Traulismus*,..a stammering repetition of the first syllable, or letter of a word, as *Tu-Tu-Tullius.* **1680** DALGARNO *Deaf & Dumb Man's Tutor* 128 Childish and ridiculous Traulisms. *a* **1800** S. PEGGE *Anecd. Eng. Lang.* (1803) 93 A stammering kind of syllable, rhetorically called a Traulismus. **1893** *Westm. Gaz.* 6 Oct. 2/1 A professor of elocution who has caught a trick of stammering from those whom he has cured of traulism.

trauma ('trɔːmə, 'traʊmə). Pl. **traumas, traumata.** [a. Gr. τραῦμα wound.]

1. *Path.* A wound, or external bodily injury in general; also the condition caused by this; traumatism.

1693 tr. *Blancard's Phys. Dict.* (ed. 2), *Trauma*,..a wound from an external cause. **1706** PHILLIPS (ed. Kersey), *Trauma*, a Wound. **1899** *Allbutt's Syst. Med.* VI. 855 *Trauma* may lead to compression in one or other of the following ways.

2. a. *Psychoanal.* and *Psychiatry.* A psychic injury, esp. one caused by emotional shock the memory of which is repressed and remains unhealed; an internal injury, esp. to the brain, which may result in a behavioural disorder of organic origin. Also, the state or condition so caused.

1894 W. JAMES in *Psychol. Rev.* I. 199 Certain reminiscences of the shock fall into the subliminal consciousness, where they can only be discovered in 'hypnoid' states. If left there, they act as permanent 'psychic *traumata*', thorns in the spirit, so to speak. **1895** *Pop. Sci. Monthly* July 386 We have named this psychical trauma, a morbid nervous condition. **1896** *Brain* XIX. 402 The author thought that the painful area on the thigh increased in size with the accession of fresh 'psychical traumas'. **1927** BRYAN & STRACHEY tr. *Abraham's Sel. Papers* i. 47 He [*sc.* Freud] assigns a secondary rôle to sexual traumas in youth and assumes the presence of an abnormal psychosexual constitution. **1927** HENDERSON & GILLESPIE *Textbk. Psychiatry* iii. 56 Trauma may produce mental symptoms in one of two ways. Either it causes structural injury to the brain, or it causes emotional disturbances... In the first instance the mental reaction is of the organic type..in the second the result is usually a psychoneurosis. **1941** S. H. KRAINES *Therapy of Neuroses & Psychoses* xv. 343 Simple trauma to the brain does not produce psychotic symptoms. **1950** *Brit. Jrnl. Psychol.* June 235 Complexes can be regarded as 'dissociated partial psyches'..the dissociation being produced by traumata, moral conflicts, etc. **1954** W. MAYER-GROSS et al. *Clin. Psychiatry* x. 398 Mental disease due to brain trauma is only rarely a cause of admission to mental hospital. **1967** H. P. LAUGHLIN *Neuroses* iv. 184 The specific trauma or event is not the *raison d'etre*, the cause of the depression. **1980** *Daily Tel.* 6 Dec. 12/3 Among the many shops and houses which advertise 'Counselling' (i.e., fortune-telling), I came across a hand-written notice which said 'Traumas Treated'.

b. In general and *fig.* use.

1977 H. GREENE *FSO-1* x. 96 We know the trauma you suffered..but you've gone about it all wrong. **1977** *Mod. Railways* Dec. 486/2 Because of the trauma in the American rapid transit vehicle business—caused largely by the dilution of the market by the aerospace companies and the absence of long runs of standard designs—only two firms had put in tenders. **1978** S. BRILL *Teamsters* vi. 248 Much of that trauma had come not from the real damage Dorfman had done but from the way the press had misstated or exaggerated it. **1981** *Daily Tel.* 30 Oct. 1/1 This is a sensible deal. It will mean that we do not have to go through the trauma of possible strike action.

traumatic (trɔː'mætɪk, traʊ'mætɪk), *a.* and *sb.* [ad. late L. *traumatic-us*, ad. Gr. τραυματικός of or pertaining to a wound or wounds, f. τραῦμα, -ματ- wound. Cf. F. *traumatique* (16th c. in Godef. *Compl.*).]

A. *adj.* **1.** Of, pertaining to, or caused by a wound, abrasion, or external injury, as ***traumatic erysipelas, insanity, idiocy***; †formerly, used for the cure of wounds, vulnerary, as a ***traumatic balsam, herb.***

1656 BLOUNT *Glossogr.*, *Traumatick*, belonging to wounds or to the cure of wounds, vulnerary. **1676** WISEMAN *Chirurg. Treat.* I. iv. 29 Nature..was assisted the while by Traumatick Decoctions, &c. as in such cases is usual. **1835–6** *Todd's Cycl. Anat.* I. 163/1 Inflammation traumatic or idiopathic. **1869** G. LAWSON *Dis. Eye* (1874) 152 Traumatic Cataract, or cataract the result of an injury to the eye. **1913** *Times* 11 Aug. 13/3 Prof. V. Soubbotitch.. presented his military experiences of traumatic aneurysms.

2. a. *Psychoanal.* and *Psychiatry.* Of, pertaining to, or caused by a psychic wound or emotional shock, esp. leading to or causing behavioural disturbance.

1889 T. SAVILL tr. *Charcot's Clin. Lect. Dis. Nervous Syst.* III. 388 The existence of traumatic psychosis [*psychose traumatique*] adds still more to the gravity of the prognosis. **1909** A. A. BRILL tr. *Freud's Sel. Papers Hysteria* i. 1 It is quite evident that in 'traumatic' hysteria it is the accident which evokes the syndrome. **1929** *Times Lit. Suppl.* 4 July 528/2 The Freudian traumatic theory. **1941** S. H. KRAINES *Therapy of Neuroses & Psychoses* xv. 352 In the traumatic psychoses, damaged brain tissue is irreparable. **1979** A. STORR *Art of Psychotherapy* x. 94 Women who react to traumatic events with depression are generally contending with a variety of difficulties.

b. In general use: distressing, emotionally disturbing.

1962 A. HUXLEY *Let.* 17 June (1969) 935 Memories of traumatic events in childhood. **1965** M. NAYLOR *Your Money* ix. 54 You will only have sacrificed one-seventh of your original capital. This is depressing enough, of course, but it is a good deal less traumatic than losing half. **1973** *Howard Jrnl.* XIII. 287 It was felt by some that this would ..make leaving prison at the end of the sentence less traumatic. **1977** E. HEATH *Travels* viii. 167 Whatever the outcome, the impact on the United States of the decade of war in Vietnam was traumatic. **1984** *Daily Tel.* 2 Feb. 2/3 We see manufacturing industry only feebly recovering from the traumatic experience of the last five years.

3. *Bot.* ***traumatic acid***, a plant hormone that is found in damaged tissue in some plants and promotes its repair; dodec-2-ene-1,12-dioic acid, $HOOC(CH_2)_8CH{:}CHCOOH$.

1939 J. ENGLISH et al. in *Science* 6 Oct. 329/2 It would seem appropriate and convenient to refer to this substance as 'traumatic acid'. **1966** R. M. DEVLIN *Plant Physiol.* xvii. 427 The effect of traumatic acid on inducing cells to divide does not appear to be general. **1971** J. Z. YOUNG *Introd. Study Man* xii. 160 In plants..injured cells release a.. traumatic acid.

†**B.** *sb.* A vulnerary agent or remedy. *Obs.*

1683 SALMON *Doron Med.* I. 18 A very good Traumatick and Vulnerary. **1694** —— *Bate's Dispens.* (1713) 496/2 An excellent traumatick and vulnerary.

Hence **trau'matically** *adv.*

1866 A. FLINT *Princ. Med.* (1880) 143 Chronic pleuritis may be produced traumatically. **1897** *Allbutt's Syst. Med.* IV. 771 It [tonsillitis] may occur traumatically. **1972** D. BLOODWORTH *Any Number can Play* viii. 56 His patriotic and anti-communist postures are almost traumatically compulsive. **1976** *Listener* 11 Nov. 615/1 A view of life, of being, that would lead me ineluctably into false hopes and traumatically real disappointments.

traumaticin (trɔː'mætɪsɪn). Also **-ine.** [f. as prec. + -IN[1].] (See quots.)

1857 DUNGLISON *Med. Lex.*, *Traumaticine*, a name given by Eulenberg to a solution of gutta-percha in chloroform, which is applied externally in various chronic cutaneous diseases. **1890** in BILLINGS *Nat. Med. Dict.* **1896** LYMAN in *Voice* (N.Y.) 9 Apr. 7/3 Another delicate, neutral, and durable dressing, termed traumaticin.

traumatism ('trɔːmətɪz(ə)m, 'traʊ-). [f. Gr. τραῦμα, τραυματ- wound + -ISM. Cf. F. *traumatisme.*]

1. *Path.* The action of a wound or external injury in producing a morbid condition; the condition so produced.

1857 DUNGLISON *Med. Lex.*, *Traumatism*,..the condition of the organism occasioned by a grave wound. **1876** DUHRING *Dis. Skin* 526 Anæsthesia may also result from traumatism. **1899** *Q. Rev.* July 274 Such [diseases] as are the consequence of inorganic poisons or traumatisms.

2. *Psychol.* and *Psychiatry.* A morbid condition of the psyche resulting from repression to the unconscious of emotional wounds or shock which are unacceptable to the conscious mind. Also *loosely* in general use, a shock or unpleasantly startling experience.

1898 H. ELLIS in *Alienist & Neurologist* XIX. 610 They may be said to have shown conclusively, what has already been more or less hesitantly suggested by others, that the most typical hysteria is really a 'psychic traumatism'. **1926** J. I. SUTTIE tr. *Ferenczi's Theory & Technique Psycho-Anal.* 77 A certain amount of infantile sexual experience (that is to say, a little 'sexual traumatism'). **1973** D. MATIAS tr. C. Metz in *Screen* Spring/Summer 51 The actor gave the impression of reciting a sparse and laconic text which cut across the preceding silence producing a minor aesthetic traumatism for the spectator.

traumatize ('trɔːmətaɪz, 'traʊ-), *v.* [f. as prec. + -IZE.]

1. *trans.* To inflict a wound upon, to wound (as in a surgical operation).

1903 *Therapeutic Gaz.* Feb. 100/1 In spite of the general insensibility the orifices retain their sensibility, the patient struggling when they are traumatized, though he will preserve no recollection of this. **1929** *Jrnl. Amer. Med. Assoc.* 13 July 116/2 The white bands disappeared promptly when care was taken not to traumatize the fold of skin with the orangewood stick. **1954** S. DUKE-ELDER *Parson's Dis. Eye* (ed. 12) xxii. 361 In this way they may be severely traumatized; and at the same time the wave of pressure, striking the retina and choroid, may do considerable damage.

2. To inflict an emotional wound or shock upon; to impair or damage psychologically. Also *fig.*

1949 M. MEAD *Male & Female* xvi. 336 Two bitter little rivals may otherwise spend hours quarrelling and traumatizing each other. **1958** *Spectator* 28 Feb. 255/1 A Roman Catholic lad who traumatised me by telling me that God was always about. **1965** *New Statesman* 17 Dec. 960/2 In the intervening period, 34 people were killed..1,032 were injured... The event has traumatised California. **1970** A. TOFFLER *Future Shock* x. 194 The year 2000 is closer to us in time than the great depression, yet the world's economists, traumatized by that historic disaster, remain frozen in the attitudes of the past. **1974** *Sci. Amer.* Aug. 56/2 For children who come from environments in which the capacity of the family to function has been most severely traumatized by such destructive forces as poverty, ill health and discrimination, the consequences for the child are seen [etc.]. **1979** P. THEROUX *Old Patagonian Express* (1980) xiii. 264 The passengers were either asleep or sitting silently, traumatized by the heat.

Hence **traumati'zation**; **'traumatized, 'traumatizing** *ppl. adjs.*

1935 *Proc. Soc. Exper. Biol. & Med.* XXXII. 1249 If profound and fatal shock is to be obtained in the intact dog by traumatization, the severity of tissue injury must be very much greater than is required to induce shock symptoms in the equally healthy and vigorous animal lacking adrenal glands. **1935** *Amer. Jrnl. Physiol.* CXI. 430 Such traumatized animals lacking adrenals die within 24 hours or less. **1949** M. MEAD *Male & Female* v. 118 Two inexperienced adolescents had a first sex-affair..and became traumatized by their own clumsiness. **1950** E. H. ERIKSON *Childhood & Society* (1951) i. 37 The condition started with such damage, or at least with momentary traumatization. **1966** *Lancet* 31 Dec. 1464/1 Fat from traumatised adipose tissue can on occasion enter the circulation and produce fat-embolisation. **1971** K. MILLETT *Sexual Politics* (1972) II. iv. 180 We perceive that the traumatizing circumstance of being born black in a white racist society invests skin color with symbolic value. **1977** M. SOKOLINSKY tr. *Merle's Virility Factor* xvi. 330 There is an excess of love..an instinct that, in women, is no longer stifled by the traumatizing sense of her social inferiority. **1979** *Daily Tel.* 31 Oct. 15/2 Thousands of traumatised survivors of the Pol Pot horrors were starving and dying. **1979** *Nature* 13 Dec. 727/1 It was important to ascertain whether our surgical procedure led to any transient denervation or traumatisation of synapses made by the soleus nerve.

traumato- (trɔːmətəʊ), repr. Gr. τραυματο-, combining form of τραῦμα wound, in a few rare scientific terms, chiefly mod.Lat. ‖**,traumatocace** (-'ɒkəsiː) [Gr. κάκη badness], traumatic gangrene. ‖**,traumato'comium** [Gr. κομεῖν to tend], a hospital for the wounded. **trauma'tology**, the scientific description of wounds.; in mod. use, the branch of medicine concerned with the treatment of wounds and serious injuries and with the disabilities they cause; hence **trauma'tologist**, a specialist in this. ‖**,traumato'nesis** (-'niːsɪs) [Gr. νῆσις spinning], suture of wounds. ‖**,traumato'pnœa** (-'pniːə) [-πνοια breathing], the passage of air through a wound in the thorax during respiration. ‖**,traumato'pyra** [πῦρ fire, fever-heat], traumatic fever. ‖**,traumatosa'prosis** [σαπρόειν to putrefy], traumatic gangrene.

1890 BILLINGS *Nat. Med. Dict.*, **Traumatocace*, traumatic gangrene. **1899** *Syd. Soc. Lex.*, *Traumatocace*, synonym of Hospital gangrene. **1857** DUNGLISON *Med. Lex.*, *Traumato-comium. **1935** *Dorland's Med. Dict.* (ed. 17) 1427/2 *Traumatologist. **1948** *Excerpta Medica Section IX* II. 944 Traumatologists must devote themselves not only to special treatment, but also to the prevention of injuries. **1981** *Sci. Digest* Aug. 52 'Half a million out of eighty million accident cases a year need Shock Trauma's services,' says one veteran traumatologist. **1899** *Syd. Soc. Lex.*, *Traumatology. **1948** *Excerpta Medica Section IX* II. 944 The necessity for special traumatology is caused by the progress of civilization. **1964** *Acta Universitatis Carolinae Medica Suppl.* XIX. 296 Modern scientific experiences and results of research of many teams offer more and more effective and better means to traumatology and raise the standard of its work. **1977** *Lancet* 30 Apr. 961/2 A national institute of traumatology in the United Kingdom cannot be put off any longer. **1980** R. OWEN et al. (*title*) Scientific foundations of orthopaedics and traumatology. **1890** BILLINGS *Nat. Med. Dict.*, *Traumatonesis. **1879** *St. George's Hosp. Rep.* IX. 245 No *traumatopnœa, no emphysema, no hæmoptysis. **1854–67** C. A. HARRIS *Dict. Med. Terminol.*, *Traumatopyra. **1860** MAYNE *Expos. Lex.*, **Traumatosaprosis*,..term for putrescence of a wound.

traumatol ('trɔːmətɒl). [f. Gr. τραῦμα, τραυματ- wound + -OL.] Trade-name of an iodoorthocresol, a reddish powder used as a dressing for wounds.

1899 *Syd. Soc. Lex.*, *Traumatol*,.. prepared by the action of iodine on oxytoluene.

traumatropism (trɔːˈmætrəʊpɪz(ə)m). *Biol.* Also **traumatotropism**. [Short for **traumatotropism*, f. Gr. τραῦμα wound, after *geotropism*, *heliotropism*, etc.] A peculiar growth or curvature of an organism (esp. a plant) resulting from a wound. **traumaˈtropic** *a.*, of, pertaining to, or of the nature of traumatropism.

1898 R. BEER in *Nat. Science* June 390 The latent period ..can be greatly extended both in geotropism..and in traumatropism. *Ibid.*, It [a seedling of *Lupinus albus*] at once executed a traumatropic curvature. **1965** BELL & COOMBE tr. *Strasburger's Textbk. Bot.* 380 Galvanotropism, traumatotropism and thermotropism..are possibly only special forms of chemotropism.

traunce, -nse, obs. ff. TRANCE.

traunch, trauncher, traunchfer, traunslate, obs. ff. TRANCH, TRENCHER, TRANCHEFER, TRANSLATE.

traunt, traunter, -or: see TRANT, TRANTER.

trauþ(e, trauthe, obs. ff. TROTH.

trautonium (traʊˈtəʊnɪəm). [f. the name of Friedrich *Trautwein* (1888–1956), German scientist and inventor of the instrument, after EUPHONIUM.] An electronic musical instrument, capable of producing notes of any pitch.

1931 *Electronics* July 18/2 The 'Trautonium' is a recent development at the Radio Research section of the Berlin Academy of Music... Paul Hindemith..is himself an excellent Trautonium player and has written music specially for it. **1936** *Discovery* July 224/2 The Trautonium, due to Dr. Trautwein and developed at the Charlottenburg Music High School (Conservatoire), where it so interested Hindemith that he not only wrote for it but even himself learnt to play it. **1959** *Chambers's Encycl.* V. 131/2 Instruments such as the theremin and the trautonium derive music directly from the tuned circuits in oscillation and have no mechanical vibrator except the diaphragm in the loudspeaker. **1978** P. GRIFFITHS *Conc. Hist. Mod. Music* viii. 111 Hindemith wrote a concertino for trautonium and orchestra in 1931.

trauyl(l, etc., obs. ff. TRAVAIL, TRAVEL, etc.

‖**travado** (trəˈvɑːdəʊ). *Obs.* Also 8 **travat**. [Portuguese *travados* a kind of whirlwind, pl. of *travado*, pa. pple. of *travar* to twine, twist.] A sudden violent storm of wind and rain with thunder and lightning; a tornado.

[**1625** PURCHAS *Pilgrims* II. VII. ii. §6. 952 Very foule weather there with Thunder and Lightning, (which the Portugals call *Trauados*).] **1686** GOAD *Celest. Bodies* I. i. 2 Those Dire Tempests..known amongst us by the names of Spouts, Huracans, Tornados, Travados. **1770** J. R. FORSTER tr. *Kalm's Trav. N. Amer.* (1772) II. 63 A peculiar kind of storm called a Travat or Travado, happened to-day. **1867** SMYTH *Sailor's Word-bk.*, *Travado*, or *Travat*, a heavy squall, with sudden gusts of wind, lightning, and rain, on the coast of North America; like the African tornado.

travail (ˈtræveɪl, -eɪl), *sb.*[1] Forms: (*v* before 1600 usually written *u*, in Sc. often *w*). *α.* 3–7 **trauail**, **-ayl**, 4–6 **-ayll**, **-aille**, **-ale**, 4–7 **-aill**, **-aile**, **-ayle**, 5–6 **-aylle**; 4 **travail**, 4–7 **-aill**, **-aile**, **-ayle**, 5 **-all(e**, 5–6 **-ayll**, **-ale**; *Sc.* 4–5 **trawaill**, **-wailȝe**, **-aile**, **-ayle**, (5 **trewaill**), 4–6 **trawayll**. *β.* **traueylle**, 4–7 **-ell**, **-el**, 5 **-eyle**, 6 **-eill**, **-ille**, **-yll**; 5 **travelle**, 5–7 **travell**, 5–8 **travel**, (7 **travil**); 5–6 *Sc.* **trawel**, **-ell**. [a. OF. *travail* suffering or painful effort, trouble (12th c. in Godef. *Compl.*) = Prov. *trebalh*, Sp. *trabajo*, Pg. *trabalho*, It. *travaglio*; vbl. sb. from *travailler*, etc.: see TRAVAIL *v.* OF. and Pr. had also fem. forms *travaille*, *trebalha*, labour, fatigue.

(As to the diverse sense-development in Fr. and in Eng. see TRAVAIL *v.*)]

I. 1. Bodily or mental labour or toil, especially of a painful or oppressive nature; exertion; trouble; hardship; suffering. *arch.*

α. *c* **1250** *O. Kent. Serm.* in *O.E. Misc.* 33 Clepe þo werkmen and yeld hem here trauail. *c* **1290** *S. Eng. Leg.* I. 61/247 [H]is trauail nis no þe lasse. *a* **1300** *Cursor M.* 9703 (Cott.) Qua wil for þes his trauaill [*v.r.* trauayl] spend. *Ibid.* 20942 Was nan sua mikel trauael mad. **13..** *Ibid.* 12765 (Gött.) Ferli þaim toght hu he might last, Wid sua grete trauale [*other MSS.* travaile] and fast. *c* **1375** *Sc. Leg. Saints* ii. (*Paulus*) 911 He tholit trawal ful gret. *c* **1386** CHAUCER *Frankl. T.* 889, I wol nat taken a peny of thee For al my craft ne noght for my trauaille [*v.rr.* -ayle, -aile]. **1390** GOWER *Conf.* III. 231 And lusti youthe his thonk deserveth Upon the travail which he doth. **1422** tr. *Secreta Secret.*, *Priv. Priv.* 152 His modyr that..with grete trauaill hym norishid. *Ibid.* 158 Ne be not al tymys in trauaille and in thoghtis. *c* **1470** HENRY *Wallace* VI. 672 We may thaim wyne, and mak bot lycht trawaill. **1549** CROWLEY *Last Trumpet* 268 Then holde thy selfe therwyth contente, As wyth the wage of thy travayle. **1570** *Satir. Poems Reform.* xvii. 13 Betuix gude and euill markand our trauaill [*rimes* saill, fraill]. **1596** DALRYMPLE tr. *Leslie's Hist. Scot.* I. (S.T.S.) I. 78 The diligens,..Industrie, and trauale of this Thanaus. **1597** HOOKER *Eccl. Pol.* v. lii. §1 With care and trauaile to preserue this Article from..sinister construction. **1621** ELSING *Debates Ho. Lords* (Camden) App. 146 For which my paines and travaill they gave me two pesses a manne. **1660** JER. TAYLOR *Worthy Commun.* Introd. 1 Faint and sick with travaile and fear. **1826** E. IRVING *Babylon* I. II. 64 The common everyday travail of men in trade and handicrafts. **1867** F. FRANCIS *Angling* xiv. (1880) 489 Ah, what travail have I not endured in the pursuit of May fly hooks.

β. **13..** *Cursor M.* 89 (Cott.) Quat bote is to sette traueil [*v.rr.* -ail, -ayle, -aile] On thyng þat may not auail. [**1375** (MS. 1487) BARBOUR *Bruce* VII. 45 We haf tynt þis trauell [*rime* avale].] **1382** WYCLIF *Gen.* xxxi. 42 Myn affliccioun and the traueil of myn hondis the Lord bihelde. *c* **1400** *Rule St. Benet* 1855 For vnto trauel wor we born, And al our elders vs be-forn. *c* **1450** *Merlin* ii. 26 He that ought doth for a gode man, lesith not his traueyle. **1530** PALSGR. 282/2 Traveyle, labour, *trauayl*. **1535** STEWART *Cron. Scot.* (Rolls) II. 191 This Conranus..Greit travell dalie did vpoun him tak. **1570** *Ane Tragedie* 32 in *Satir. Poems Reform.* x. 83 He to serue vs na traueil did spair. **1577** NORTHBROOKE *Dicing* (1843) 56 As Iob sayeth, a man is borne to trauel as the sparkes flee vpward. **1642** ROGERS *Naaman* To Rdr. §1 A great peece of my travell in these Lectures. *a* **1770** JORTIN *Serm.* (1771) I. iv. 67 He wrought with labor and travel night and day. **1774** PENNANT *Tour Scot. in 1772* 225 After some travel [we] found the inside.

†**2.** With *a* and *pl.* A piece of bodily or mental labour; a work, a task; in *pl.* labours.

c **1350** *Will. Palerne* 4712 þi tenful trauayles þow hast for me suffred. **1390** GOWER *Conf.* III. 133 Thei hadde a gret travail on honde. **1494** FABYAN *Chron.* VI. cxlix. 135 His manyfolde trauayllys, susteynyd for the weale of the realme. **1568** GRAFTON *Chron.* II. 10 One that much desyred to eschew the trauayles of Martiall affayres. *c* **1620** FLETCHER & MASSINGER *Trag. Barnavelt* v. i, Heaven direct And prosper theis your charitable traviles. **1690** PENN *Rise & Progr. Quakers* vi. (1834) 80 O it is a travail, a spiritual travail! **1724** A. COLLINS *Gr. Chr. Relig.* Pref. 21 He that seeketh her early shall have no great travels.

†**3.** The outcome, product, or result of toil or labour; a (finished) 'work'; *esp.* a literary work.

1563 SHUTE *Archit.* Fij b, I submyt my trauel, vnto allother..of like well wylling affection, wherwith I do offer this my poore atemptes and smal trauailes. **1597** MORLEY *Introd. Mus.* 183 The publication..of those neuer enough praised trauailes of master Waterhouse. **1624** WOTTON *Archit.* I. ad fin., I will conclude the first Part of my present Travel. The second remaineth concerning Ornaments.

4. The labour and pain of child-birth. Phr. ***in travail*** (Fr. *en travail*). Now chiefly *fig.*

1297 R. GLOUC. (Rolls) 237 Vor in trauail of his beringe is moder was verst ded. *c* **1300** *St. Margarete* 283 Eni womman ..in trauail of childe. **1512** *Helyas* in Thoms *Prose Rom.* (1828) III. 27 In great paine and travaille of bodye she childed .vi. sonnes and a faire doughter. **1535** COVERDALE *Ps.* xlvii[i]. 6 Feare came there vpon them, & sorowe as vpon a woman in hir trauayle. **1599** B. JONSON *Cynthia's Rev.* v. x, Doe you not see how his legs are in trauaile with a measure? **1611** BIBLE *John* xvi. 21 A woman, when shee is in trauaile, hath sorrow, because her houre is come. **1650** BULWER *Anthropomet.* 180 His wife dying after travel of a daughter. **1754–64** SMELLIE *Midwif.* II. 70 She felt all the Praeludia of an imminent travail. **1825** J. NEAL *Bro. Jonathan* III. 448 In the time of her travail. **1837** CARLYLE *Fr. Rev.* III. VI. vii, What a distracted City;..the Hour clearly in travail,—child not to be named till born! **1897** T. HARDY *Well-Beloved* II. xiii, Between the travail of the sea without, and the travail of the woman within.

†**5.** *transf.* The eclipse of a heavenly body. Cf. LABOUR *sb.* 7. *Obs. rare.*

1601 HOLLAND *Pliny* II. xii. I. 9 Seeing these things, and the paineful ordinarie travels (since that this tearme is now taken up) of the starres. [**1627** HAKEWILL *Apol.* x. (1630) 82 Eclipses of the Sun and Moone, in which they are commonly thought to suffer, and to be as it were in travell during that time.] **1640** BP. REYNOLDS *Passions* i. 2 No eye gazeth on the Moone, but in her Travell.

†**6.** *transf.* The straining movement of a vessel in rough seas. (Cf. LABOUR *v.* 17.) *Obs. rare*$^{-1}$.

1687 A. LOVELL tr. *Thevenot's Trav.* II. 10 If the Vessel made but the least Travel, they thought themselves lost.

II. 7. Journeying, a journey.

For this and the senses derived from it, see TRAVEL *sb.*, the spelling under which these senses are now differentiated from the preceding.

III. 8. *attrib.* and *Comb.*, as **travail-pain**, **-pang**, pain or pang of child-birth (also *fig.*).

1814 SCOTT *Ld. of Isles* IV. xxvii, Thou heard'st a wretched female plain In agony of travail-pain. **1827** KEBLE *Chr. Y.*, *4th Sund. Trinity*, The travail pangs of earth must last Till her appointed hour. **1860** PUSEY *Min. Proph.* 86 The travail-pangs are violent, sudden, irresistible.

†**travail, -aile**, *sb.*[2] *Obs.* [= F. *travail*, pl. *travails* (1467–8, *traval* in Godef. *Compl.*, in same sense). Cf. Cotgr., '*Travail*:..also the frame whereinto Farriers put vnrulie horses, when they shooe or dresse them.' Derivation disputed: by some referred to L. *trepālium* (see TRAVAIL *v.*), by others to L. **trabāculum*, or other deriv. of *trabs*, *trabem* beam, thing made of beams or timbers.] A kind of quadrangular frame in which restive horses are secured in order to be shod. Cf. TRAVE *sb.* 2.

1594 NASHE *Unfort. Trav.* Wks. (Grosart) V. 141 The trauaile wherein smithes put wilde horses when they shoo them. **1753** CHAMBERS *Cycl. Supp.*, *Travail*, in the manege. See the article Travice... This in some of the remoter parts of England goes by the name of a *break*; and is called in French *Travail*. **1771** *Misc.* in *Ann. Reg.* 177/2 *Trabale* is derived from *trabs*, from whence, as I conjecture, proceeds the word *travail* (*travise*), which..denotes that machine in which Farriers confine mettlesome and vicious horses in order to shoe them.

‖**travail, -aille** (travɑj), *sb.*[3] [App. the same as F. *travail*, which in Canada (pronounced *travày*) is applied to the space between the two shafts of a vehicle in which the horse runs (cf. TRAVE *sb.* 1 b); this may well be originally the same word as prec., and ult. from L. *trabs*, *trabem* beam. *Travaux* is a false plural, found in books, for *travails*.] See quotations, and cf. TRAVOIS.

1801 A. HENRY *Jrnl.* 13 Oct. in E. Coues *New Light on Greater Northwest* (1897) I. iv. 190 Chamanau arrived from the hills, bringing his deceased wife on a travaille to be buried here. **1865** MILTON & CHEADLE *N.W. Passage by Land* 171 A *travaille* is an Indian contrivance, consisting of two poles fastened together at an acute angle, with crossbars between. The point of the angle rests upon the back of the dog or horse, the diverging ends of the poles drag along the ground, and the baggage is put on to the crossbars. The Indians use these contrivances instead of carts. **1889** *Century Mag.* Jan. 339/2 In a month 'Richard's himself again', ready to fly over the grassy sward with his savage master or to drag the *travaux* and pack the buxom squaw. **1891** *Cent. Dict.*, *Travail*, A means of transportation, commonly used by North American Indians... Also called *travois*, *travee*.

travail (ˈtrævəl, -eɪl), *v.* Forms: *α.* 3–5 **trauaille**, 3–7 **-aile**, (4– **-alle**), 4–6 **-aill**, **-ayle**, **-ayll(e**, **-ale**, **-all**, 4–7 **-ail**, 6 **-al**. 4–5 **travaylle**, 4–6 **-aille**, 4–7 **-ayle**, **-aile**, 5 **-ale**, 5–6 **-aill**, 5– **travail**; 4–5 *Sc.* **trawayll**, **-ale**, 5 **-aill**. *β.* 4–5 **traueil(e**, **-eyll(e**, 4–6 **-eyle**, **-ele**, 5–7 **-elle**, **-el**, 6–7 **-ell**; 4–7 **travele**, 5 **-eylle**, 5–6 **-eille**, **-eyl(e**, 5–7 **-ell**, 5–9 **travel**. [ME. *travaill-en*, *-vaylle*, *-vaile*, *-veyle*, *-veile*, etc. (usually with *u*, or Sc. *w*, for *v*), a. OF. *travaillier*, *-vailler*, *-veillier*, *-veiller*, mod.F. *travailler* = Prov. *trebalhar* (also Pg. *trabalhar*, Sp. *trabajar*, It. *travagliare*); held by Romanic scholars generally to represent a late pop.L. or Com. Rom. **trepāliāre*, deriv. of *trepālium* (A.D. 582 in Du Cange), an instrument or engine of torture (prob. f. L. *trēs*, *tria* three + *pālus* stake, being so named from its structure). The etymological sense was thus 'to put to torture, torment', passing at an early stage into those of 'afflict, vex, trouble, harass, weary'. Through the refl. sense 'to trouble, afflict, or weary oneself', came the intrans. 'to toil, work hard, labour'. Thence also (as is generally thought) the verbal sbs. OF. *travail* m. and *travaille* f., ME. *travail*, *-aile*: see TRAVAIL *sb.*[1]

The sense-development has not followed the same course in French and in English. Thus English has not developed the simple sense 'work', for which the OE. word has lived on. On the other hand, French has not evolved the sense 'journey' = F. *voyager*, which appeared early in Anglo-Fr., and has become the main sense in English, and is differentiated by the spelling TRAVEL, while the more original senses, so far as they continue in use, retain the earlier spelling *travail*.]

I. 1. *trans.* To torment, distress, harass, afflict, vex, trouble; to weary, tire. *Obs.* or *arch.*

1303 R. BRUNNE *Handl. Synne* 6035 þe fende yn-to hym was lope, And traueyled hym þre dayys with pyne. **1382** WYCLIF *Deut.* viii. 16 After that he trauelde thee and strengthide [1388 turmentid thee, and preuede], at the eende he hadde mercy of thee. **1387** TREVISA *Higden* (Rolls) IV. 473 Preostes schulde be worshipped to fore oþer men, and nouȝt i-travalled and i-greeved. **1483** CAXTON *Gold. Leg.* 192 b/1 They were wery and sore traueyled by the waye which was longe. *c* **1489** —— *Sonnes of Aymon* iii. 70 For their strengthe, they trayueylle us moche. **1568** GRAFTON *Chron.* II. 252 He came thether in such haste, that hys horse and men were sore traueyled. **1627** *Lisander & Cal.* III. 39 Apt words to expresse the griefes, wherwith..we begin to be travelled. **1695** LD. PRESTON *Boeth.* Pref. 11 We are travelled with Uneasiness and Inquietude amidst our largest Enjoyments. **1816** SCOTT *Old Mort.* iv, I jalouse he wad hae liked to hae ridden by, but his horse..was ower sair travailed. **1832** [see TRAVAILED 1].

†**b.** *refl.* To put oneself to trouble, to weary or exert onself, to labour or work hard: = Fr. *se travailler*, passing into the intr. sense 2. *Obs.*

a **1300** *Cursor M.* 22775 (Edin.) þai..trauaild [*v.rr.* -ailed, -alid, -ailed] þaim on al wis To paien him in his seruis. *c* **1374** CHAUCER *Boeth.* III. pr. xi. 76 (Camb. MS.) Euery beest trauaylith hym to deffende and kepe the sauacion of hys lyf. **1556** *Aurelio & Isab.* (1608) I v, Whoo lovethe not, travaillethe not him selfe. **1581** PETTIE *Guazzo's Civ. Conv.* II. (1586) 99 To exercise and trauaile himselfe in gouerning his subiects with iustice.

†**c.** *trans.* To put to work, cause to work; to exert, employ, bring into action. *Obs.*

1390 GOWER *Conf.* II. 16 And if he wolde have holde him stille And nothing spoke, he scholde have failed: Bot for he hath his word travailed And dorste speke, his love he spedde. **1577** B. GOOGE *Heresbach's Husb.* III. (1586) 118 b, To trauell them [mares] moderately, will doe them rather good then harme. **1596** DANETT tr. *Comines* (1614) 328 The poore man that trauelleth and toileth his body to get foode. **1610** FLETCHER *Faithf. Sheph.* v. i, Let the floud..give remedy To greedy thirst, and travel not the tree That hangs with wanton clusters. **1630** EARL OF CORK in *Lismore Papers* (1888) Ser. II. III. 163, I haue with all affectionate zeale traveled my thoughts and stirred vp my best observacions [etc.].

†**d.** To shake, stir, 'work' (a thing) about.

c **1440** *Pallad. on Husb.* XI. 403 Seuen curnels of a pynappul do In oon sester of wyn that is impure And trauayle hit a tyme to and fro And aftir suffre hit to reste go. *c* **1440** *Anc. Cookery* in *Househ. Ord.* (1790) 455 Alway travaile hit wel over the fyre.

†**e.** *trans.* To labour at, to perform (some work, duty, or service). *Obs. rare*$^{-1}$.

1569 *Reg. Privy Council Scot.* I. 673 The Precheouris and utheris travelling the charge of ministerie within the kirk.

2. *intr.* (for *refl.*; cf. 1 b). To exert oneself, labour, toil, work hard. *arch.*

c **1250** *O. E. Kent. Serm.* in *O.E. Misc.* 34 þos laste on ure habbeþ i-trauailed. **1303** R. Brunne *Handl. Synne* 10408 Y prey þe.. To trauayle so moche for me. **13..** *E.E. Allit. P.* A. 549 þenne þe fyrst bygonne to pleny & sayden þat þay hade travayled sore. **1423** Jas. I *Kingis Q.* lxx, As Tantalus I trauaile ay but-les. **1484** Caxton *Fables of Æsop* vi. xvii, Who trauaylleth wel, he hath euer brede ynough for to ete. **1577** Googe *Heresbach's Husb.* 13 b, That he be not.. vnable to trauayle for age. **1615** W. Lawson *Orch. & Gard.* (1623) 2 Such a Gardner as will conscionably, quietly and patiently, trauell in your Orchard. **1878** B. Taylor *Deukalion* i. ii. 22, I travail for my children.

fig. **1883** Stevenson *Silverado Sq.* v. (1886) 76 Even in its gentlest moods the salt sea travails, moaning among the weeds or lisping on the sand.

b. Const. *about, for, in* (some matter), *to do* something. *arch.*

c **1290** *S. Eng. Leg.* I. 82/29 ȝwat neode is it for to trauailli ferrore me to lede? *Ibid.* 350/161 þou trauailest, he seide, a-boute nouȝt. *a* **1325** *Prose Psalter* xlviii[i]. 8 For þe pris of his raunsoun he shal trauail wyþ-outen ende. **1375** Barbour *Bruce* ix. 165 Thai had no-thing for to et, Bot gif thai trauailit it to get. *c* **1400** Maundev. (Roxb.) ix. 33 þis folk.. trauailez noȝt aboute tillyng of land. *c* **1489** Caxton *Blanchardyn* vi. 26 In vayne he traueylled for to require her from him. **1559** Bp. Scot in Strype *Ann. Ref.* (1709) I. App. vii. 18, I shall nede to travell in provinge of the same. **1560** Daus tr. *Sleidane's Comm.* 240 He wyll sende Ambassadours, whiche shall trauell for peace. **1612** T. Taylor *Comm. Titus* i. 7 (1619) 158 Trauell not too much to be rich. **1678** Wanley *Wond. Lit. World* v. i. §93. 467/2 He travelled exceedingly for establishing the Peace of Christendom. **1704** Swift *T. Tub* Introd., I have been prevailed on.. to travel in a compleat and laborious dissertation. **1897** W. Beatty *Secretar* xxv. 213 Gif the meenisters uprightly travelled to punish vice.

†**c.** To work as a student, to study (*in* a subject or author). *Obs.*

1551–1742 [see travailed 2]. **1570** T. Wilson *Demosthenes* Ded. 2 Maister Cheeke, hauing traueyled in Demosthenes as much as any one of them all.

3. Of a woman: To suffer the pains of childbirth; to be in labour. Also *fig.*

a **1300** [see travailing *vbl. sb.*]. **1388** Wyclif *Rom.* viii. 22 And we witen, that ech creature sorewith, and trauelith with peyne [1382 childith] til ȝit. **1470–85** Malory *Arthur* viii. i. 273 She byganne to trauaille fast of her child. **1565** *Reg. Privy Council Scot.* I. 396 The Countes of Buchane, quha than wes travelland with chyld. **1634** Sir T. Herbert *Trav.* 14 Flowres which only Dame Nature trauels with. **1658** T. Wall *God's Revenge agst. Enemies Ch.* 56 Travelling with the pangs of a false zeal, they fall in labour of a monstrous Reformation. **1730** T. Boston *Mem.* App. 28, I have long travailed in pain about it. **1827** Scott *Surg. Dau.* viii, Her son, for whom she had travailed and sorrowed. **1860** Pusey *Min. Proph.* 455 God's word.. contains its own fulfilment in itself, and travaileth until it come to pass.

†**4.** Of a ship: To 'labour', to roll or pitch heavily and right itself with difficulty. *Obs. rare.*

a **1340** Hampole *Psalter* ix. 34 þi haly kirke.. trauailand as a ship in gret stormes. **1390** Gower *Conf.* III. 296 The yonge king makth mochel wo So forto se the Schip travaile.

II. †**5.** To journey, etc.: see travel *v.*, under which spelling these senses are now differentiated from the preceding.

travailed ('trævəld, -eɪld), *ppl. a.* [f. prec. + -ed^{1}.]

1. Wearied in body or mind; troubled; harassed. *Obs.* or *arch.*

c **1420** *Prov.* in *Rel. Ant.* I. 233 Wele traveled wymen or wele traveled horsses were never good. *c* **1540** tr. *Pol. Verg. Eng. Hist.* (Camden) I. 79 Agricola issuinge owte of his tentes succored and refresshed his traveled soldiers. **1644** Milton *Educ.* Wks. 1738 I. 140 Composing their travail'd spirits with the solemn and divine harmonies. **1832** L. Hunt *Poems* 255 Could my spirit.. Slip from my travailled flesh.

†**2.** Experienced, versed, or learned (*in* a subject, etc.), as the result of working at it. (Cf. *well-read.*)

1551 T. Wilson *Logike* (1580) A iij b, Your grace [Edw. VI].. little needeth any helpe.., beeyng so well trauailed bothe in the Greke and in the Latine. **1647** Torshell *Design* 18 Daniel was a man.. much travelled in Revelations. **1742** Fielding *Jos. Andrews* ii. ix, I am not much travelled in the history of modern times.

3. That is or has been in travail or child-bed.

1842 R. S. Hawker *Cornish Ballads*, etc. (1908) 130 A cottage bed, for there A travailed woman lay.

'travailer. *Obs.* or *arch.* Also 4–5 -our. [ME. *travailour*, a. OF. *travailleor* one who harasses (*a* 1300 in Godef.), one who labours or travails (13th c.), agent-noun from *travaillier*: see travail *v.* and -er^{2} 3.] One who travails or labours; †one who torments or harasses.

1377 Langl. *P. Pl.* B. xiii. 239 Alle trewe trauaillours and tilieres of þe erthe. *c* **1430** *Pilgr. Lyf Manhode* ii. lxvii. (1869) 101 He ne is but a turmentour and a trauailour of folk. **1548** Udall *Erasm. Par. Luke* xx. 155 Earnest trauaillers for yͤ peoples behouf and profite. **1598** Stow *Surv.* 479 By profession busie Bees, and trauellers for their liuing in the Hiue of this common welth. **1611** Speed *Hist. Gt. Brit.* ix. vi. §107 Thomas Talbot an exact trauailer in genealogies.

b. A woman in labour.

1388 Wyclif *2 Kings* xix. 3 Sones camen til to the child-beryng, and the traueler of childe hath not strengthis.

'travailing, *vbl. sb. arch.* [f. travail *v.* + -ing^{1}.] The action of the vb. travail; labouring, toiling; labour of child-bearing; distress, fatigue, etc.

a **1300** *Cursor M.* 3487 (Cott.) In trauelling [*v.rr.* trauayling, -alyng].. Ful herd it was þair moderpain. **1362** Langl. *P. Pl.* A. vii. 235 With techinge or with tilynge or trauaylynge of hondes. *c* **1440** *Alphabet of Tales* 402 He wiste not at sho was with childe to sho was evyn at travellyng. **1571** Digges *Pantom.* ii. vi. M iij b, No small ease and discharge of laborsom trauayling. **1859** J. Thomson *Cast. Indol.* i, Long years of restless travailing.

'travailing, *ppl. a.* [f. as prec. + -ing^{2}.] That travails.

1. Labouring, toiling, hard-working. *Obs.* or *arch.*

a **1340** Hampole *Psalter* viii. 7 þa ere trauailand men gastly in haly kirke. **1456** Sir G. Haye *Law Arms* (S.T.S.) 3 [To] put this travailland warld in pes and rest. **1579** Fenton *Guicciard.* (1618) 2 He was possessed with a mind trauelling, busie, & ambitious.

2. Of a woman: Suffering the pains of childbirth; in labour. Also *fig.*

c **1386** Chaucer *Knt.'s T.* 1225 A womman trauaillynge was hire biforn. **1535** Coverdale *Isa.* xlii. 14, I will crie like a trauelinge woman. **1641** Milton *Reorfin.* ii. Wks. 1851 III. 69 Let her cast her Abortive Spawne without the danger of this travailling and throbbing Kingdome. **1657** Trapp *Comm. Esther* vii. 8 The pains of a travelling woman.

†**3.** Tormenting, harassing. *Obs.*

1398 Trevisa *Barth. De P.R.* xvi. xlviii. (Bodl. MS.), þe same stone [jet] boþe blacke and ȝelow strengþeþ aȝens fantasies and aȝens.. trauailinge fendes bi nyȝt.

travailler: see trevally^{1}.

'travailous, *a. Obs.* or *arch.* Forms: 4 trau-, traveilous, (trauyliouse), 4–5 trauelous, 4–6 trauailous, 5 trauaillous, traueyllous, (travelos), 6 trauaylous, 4–6, 9 travailous. [a. OF. *travaillos, traveilleus, -ous* toilsome (12th c. in Godef.), f. *travail* travail *sb.*^{1}: see -ous.] Full of or characterized by 'travail' or hard labour; toilsome; laborious; wearisome.

c **1340** Hampole *Prose Tr.* 29 Lya [Leah] es als mekill at say as trauyliouse, and betakyns actyfe lyfe. *c* **1380** Wyclif *Sel. Wks.* III. 273 þe opyn meke and pore and traveilouse lif of Crist. **1382** —— *Exod.* vi. 6, Y the Lord, that schal lede ȝow out of the traveilous prisoun of Egipciens. **1565** Stapleton tr. *Bede's Hist. Ch. Eng.* 21 To take any more such trauaylous iourneis. **1888** Doughty *Arabia Deserta* I. 59 Better his mother had been barren, than that her womb should have borne such a sorry travailous life.

Hence †**'travailously** *adv. Obs. rare.*

c **1380** Wyclif *Wks.* (1880) 439 þei moten lyue, trewely, trauelously & perelously. **1382** —— *Bible, Pref. Epist. St. Jerome* i, Plato to.. thilk brynk of Itali,.. ful traueilousli ȝede. **1382** —— *Wisd.* xv. 7 The crockere, the nesshe erthe threstende, trauailously [Vulg. *laboriose*], maketh to oure vses eche vessel.

†**'travailsome,** *a. Obs.* [f. travail *sb.*^{1} + -some.] Laborious; wearisome; toilsome.

1549 Chaloner *Erasm. on Folly* O iv b, A travailsome and carefull life. **1577** tr. *Bullinger's Decades* (1592) 911 Ashamed.. of their trauelsome idlenesse. **1617** J. Moore *Mappe Mans Mort.* ii. vi. 137 Certaine sorrow, vncertaine pleasure, trauelsome labour, fearefull rest.

travaise, obs. form of traverse.

†**travale** (trə'vɑːl, trə'vɑːleɪ). *Obs.* [Origin obscure.] In tambourine playing, a roll or drone-effect produced by drawing the wetted thumb over the parchment in a circular direction.

1798 *Monthly Mag.* Feb. 136/1 Terms and characters necessary to be understood by the performer on the tamburino; such as the single travale, the double travale, the flamps. **1876** Stainer & Barrett *Dict. Mus. Terms* s.v. *Tambourine*, To make the 'Travale'.. draw your wetted thumb in a circular direction over the skin. The 'double-travale' is twice as quick.

travale, -alla, all(e)y: see trevally$^{1, 2}$.

travant, variant of trabant.

travarse, -as, -ass, obs. ff. traverse.

travat, variant of travado, trevat.

'travated, *a.* [Formed after It. *travata*, F. *travée* (Cotgr.), 'a bay of joists, the space between two beams' (Phillips 1706), f. L. type **trabāt-us*: cf. trabeated.] 'Noting a ceiling divided into a series of traves, or transverse bays' (Webster 1911).

†**travature.** *Obs. rare*$^{-1}$. [ad. It. *travatura* (f. as prec. + *-ura*, -ure), 'a frame or ioyning togither of beames of timber' (Florio).] A joist.

1730 A. Gordon *Maffei's Amphith.* 327 The Modilions which are prominent inwardly.. are hollowed cross-ways, and adapted for receiving the Travatures.

‖**travaux préparatoires** (travo preparatwar), *sb. pl. Law.* [Fr., lit. 'preparatory works'.] Drafts, records of discussions, etc., pertaining to legislation or a treaty under consideration (see quot. 1980).

1935 *Harvard Law Rev.* Feb. 562 French courts exhibited the tendency to limit recourse to *travaux preparatoires.* **1957** H. F. Jolowicz *Roman Foundations Mod. Law* ii. 16 No text appears to deal with *travaux préparatoires*, but it is in accordance with the civilian tradition that resort to drafts, speeches in Parliament, and similar evidence is usually allowed more widely on the Continent than in England. **1962** *Listener* 15 Mar. 456/1, I am thinking about our rule which excludes the so-called *travaux preparatoires*; that is to say, statements made in negotiation, prior to the treaty, which might throw light on its meaning. **1980** *Oxf. Compan. Law* 1231/1 *Travaux préparatoires*, materials used in the preparation of, and having formative effect on, the ultimately adopted form of an agreement, or legislation, or an international treaty. Such materials include, in the domestic sphere, reports, proposals and technical advice, in the legislative sphere, Select Committee or Royal Commission or other reports, academic studies, Green Papers, White Papers, and the like, and in the international sphere reports of expert committees, discussions and proposals, drafts, and the like.

trave, *sb. Obs.* exc. *dial.* [In sense 1, a. OF. *trave* beam: cf. It. *trave* beam:—L. *trabem*, acc. of *trabs* beam. Its application in sense 2 is difficult; but cf. F. *entrave* clog, fetter, shackle, hindrance, restraint.]

1. A (timber or wooden) beam.

1395 in *Archæologia* XXIV. 313 Pro cariagio de ij traves pro justes de hospicio. **1574** *Richmond Wills* (Surtees) 251, ix hogesheads in the buttrie with the gantrees and traves there. *a* **1701** Maundrell *Journ. Jerus.* 2 Mar. (1721) 7 For its Ceiling only some rude traves laid athwart it. *Ibid.* 28 Apr. (1732) 125 The Ceilings and Traves are.. richly Painted.

b. *dial.* ? One of the shafts of a cart, or the shafts collectively. Also *attrib.*

1823 E. Moor *Suffolk Words* s.v., Horses harnessed ready for work, are said to be 'in the trave'—or, 'in the traves'. **1905** *Eng. Dial. Dict.* s.v., In phr. *to be in the trave*, of horses: to be harnessed ready for work.

2. A frame or enclosure of bars in which a restive horse is placed to be shod: cf. travail *sb.*^{2}

c **1386** Chaucer *Miller's T.* 96 She sproong as a colt doth in the traue. **1483** *Cath. Angl.* 391/2 Trave for to scho horse jn, *ferratorium, ergasterium.* **1613** R. Cawdrey *Table Alph.* (ed. 3), *Traue*, a place to shoe wilde horses in. **1656** Blount *Glossogr.*, *Trave* (from the Fr. Travée, i. a bay of buildings), a trevise or little roome made purposely to shoo unbroken horses in. **1706** Phillips (ed. Kersey), *Trave, Travel*, or *Travise*, a Place enclosed with Rails, to shooe an unruly Horse in. **1847–78** Halliwell, *Trave*, a frame into which farriers put unruly horses.

†**b.** *pl.* See quot. 1706. *Obs. rare*$^{-0}$.

1706 Phillips (ed. Kersey), *Traves*, a kind of Shackles for a Horse that is taught to amble, or pace. **1726** in *Dict. Rust.* (ed. 3).

trave, dial. var. thrave, threave.

traveis, obs. form of traverse, travis^{1}.

travel ('trævəl), *sb.* Forms: α. 4 travall, *Sc.* trawaile, -ale, 4–5 *Sc.* trawaill, trauaille, 4–7 -aile, 5 *Sc.* trawal, 5–7 trau-, travayle, 5–8 travail, 6 trauaylle, -eile, travaill, *Sc.* travale, 6–7 -aile. β. 5 *Sc.* trawel(l, 5–7 trauel(l, travell, (6 trauyll), 5– travel, (9 *Sc.* traivel). [orig. the same word as travail *sb.*^{1}, in a specialized sense and form; the latter due to shifting of stress.]

†**1.** Labour, toil; suffering, trouble; labour of child-birth, etc.: see travail *sb.*^{1} 1–6.

2. a. The action of travelling or journeying.

α. *c* **1375** *Sc. Leg. Saints* xxv. (*Julian*) 9 þe trawalouris.. for trawale ware wery. *c* **1400** Maundev. (Roxb.) viii. 28 þe way es comoun and wele ynogh knawen with all men þat vsez trauaile. *c* **1460** *Towneley Myst.* xiv. 94 That I may haue som beyldyng by, In my trauayll. **1500–20** Dunbar *Poems* lxxxv. 36 Way stricht, cler dicht, to wilsome wicht, That irke bene in travale. **1561** T. Hoby tr. *Castiglione's Courtyer* i. (1577) E j b, After a yeares trauayle abrode. **1660** Blount *Boscobel* i. (1680) 49 His feet.. much galled with travail.

β. **1375** (MS. 1487) Barbour *Bruce* iv. 664 My twa sonnys with ȝow sall I Send to tak with ȝow trawell [*rime* fale]. *a* **1533** Ld. Berners *Huon* xxii. 65 Huon was wery of trauyll. *a* **1550** *Freiris of Berwik* 65 in *Dunbar's Poems* (S.T.S.) 287, I pray grit God him speid Him haill and sound in-to his travell. **1584** B. R. tr. *Herodotus* i. 33 The way is short, & the trauell easye. **1650** in *Verney Mem.* (1907) I. 464 The wayes are everywhere unsafe for travell. **1768** Sterne *Sent. Journ.* (1775) I. 72 (*The Rose*) The advantage of travel.. was by seeing a great deal both of men and manners. **1897** *Westm. Gaz.* 11 Aug. 2/3 Continental travel is looking up. By travel we mean quick and comfortable travel.

b. With *a* and *pl.* An act of travelling; a journey. Now only in *pl.*, except *dial.*

1559 W. Cunningham *Cosmogr. Glasse* Pref. A v b, His eloquence, prudence,.. and other like vertues.. insued of hys peregrinations, and travails. **1610** Day *Festivals* iii. (1615) 56 He made (as it were) foure Trauailes. *a* **1700** Dryden *Theodore & Hon.* 57 His travels ended at his country seat. **1753** C. Gist *Jrnls.* (1893) 84, I was unwilling he should undertake such a travel. **1821** Clare *Vill. Minstr.* II. 182 In mortal wisdom, thou'st already ran A circled travel of eternity. **1836** H. Coleridge *North. Worthies* (1852) I. 6 Soon after we find him on his travels in Italy. **1883** Cleland *Inchbracken* iv. 28 Ye've had a sore travel. *a* **1905** in *Eng. Dial. Dict.* s.v., (Westmoreland) Es ya wad see in a day's travel.

c. *pl.* (*ellipt.*) 'Account of occurrences and observations of a journey into foreign parts' (J.).

[**1591** (*title*) The Rare Trauailes of Iob Hortop.] **1706** Phillips (ed. Kersey), *Travels*, Journeys, Voyages; or a

Book giving a particular Account of such Voyages. **1710** *Tatler* No. 254 ¶1 There are no Books which I more delight in than in Travels. **1817** Malthus *Popul.* (ed. 5) II. III. viii. 387 Some very intelligent Travels..written in 1810. **1841** Elphinstone *Hist. India* I. 255 We possess the travels of a native of that country in India in the fourth century. *Mod.* He took Gulliver's Travels with him on his journey.

d. *transf.* Passage of anything in its course or path, or over a distance; movement.

1742 Young *Nt. Th.* IV. 713 [A comet] revisits earth, From the long travel of a thousand years. **1888** *Encycl. Brit.* XXIII. 701/2 The more the variety of characters is multiplied, the more 'travel' of the compositor's hand over the cases is necessary for picking them up. **1898** *Allbutt's Syst. Med.* V. 843 Cardiomotive force is equal to the output of the heart plus the resistance to the travel of the blood in the vascular system.

e. Passage over; traffic. *rare.*

1830 Hood *Haunted H.* I. xviii, Each walk as green as is the mantled pool For want of human travel.

3. A single movement of some part of mechanism, as a piston, slide-valve, etc.; also, the distance through which it moves; length of stroke.

1841 *Civil Eng. & Arch. Jrnl.* IV. 251/2 To find..the travel of the valve corresponding to the travel..of the piston substitute. **1883** *Times* 8 Feb., A thin copper rod moved slowly backwards and forwards over them, with a travel of about 2 in. **1892** Greener *Breech-Loader* 32 When the gun is fired the 'travel' of the mainspring is utilised as an automatically acting trigger. **1904** *Westm. Gaz.* 2 May 9/3 The incoming of 'three colour [printing] at one travel of paper'.

4. Capacity or force of movement.

1816 Scott *Antiq.* xxx, The breaker was never able to bring her under command. She has more travel than any bitch I ever knew. **1844** Stephens *Bk. Farm* II. 625 A dog of high travel..will drive [sheep] hither and thither. **1892** *Daily News* 31 Dec. 3/4 A crew of men in the boat kept her rocking rapidly from side to side to give her more force and travel.

5. *attrib.* and *Comb.*, as ***travel article, bag, -book, film, literature, -monger, permit, poster, ticket, time, voucher, warrant***; objective, as ***travel editor, -reader, -writer; travel-loving, -minded*** adjs.; instrumental, as ***travel-broken, -disordered, -soiled, -spent, -stained, -tainted, -tattered, -tired, -toiled, -wearied, -weary, -worn*** adjs.; **travel agency**, a firm which makes arrangements for the transport, accommodation, etc., of travellers, and which acts as an agent for tour-operators (see TOUR *sb.* 12); **travel agent**, one who owns or works for a travel agency; **travel allowance**, (*a*) the amount of money given to a traveller to cover the expenses of a journey; (*b*) under the Exchange Control Bill, the maximum amount of money travellers were allowed to take out of the U.K. during the period 1946–80; **travel brochure**, a booklet advertising travel and describing the features and amenities of holiday resorts or other places of travel; **travel bug** *colloq.*, a strong urge to travel (cf. BUG *sb.*[2] 3 a); **travel bureau** = *travel agency* above; **travel document**, a document required for travel; *spec.* a document allowing foreign travel, held by one not entitled to a passport; **travel folder** = *travel brochure* above; **travel sickness**, nausea induced by the motion of a vehicle; carsickness; hence **travel-sick** *a.* affected by travel sickness; **travel trailer** *U.S.*, a variety of caravan.

1927 *World Travel* Oct. 39/2 (Advt.), Imperial Airways. Daily Services Between London Cologne Brussels Paris... Book through any *Travel Agency or direct with the Company. **1975** B. Bainbridge *Sweet William* iii. 79 He was going to get brochures from a travel agency. He thought they should all go to Spain. [**1902** *Encycl. Brit.* XXVII. 227/2 Cook, Thomas (1808–1892), travelling agent, was born at Melbourne in Derbyshire.] **1925** *Times* 1 May 2/2 (Advt.), Write to-day for your copy of 'Economy Tours to America', to..leading *Travel agents. **1980** S. Brett *Dead Side of Mike* vi. 61 Toby Root played a travel agent. **1937** *Travel allowance [see SECOND *a.* 6 b]. **1951** *Ann. Reg. 1950* IV. 453 The basic annual travel allowances were increased in December to £100 for adults. **1978** A. Waugh *Best Wine Last* xviii. 237 In 1947..the meagre travel allowance was again reduced. **1895** *Westm. Gaz.* 23 Apr. 7/1 A literary man who writes *travel articles in the Anglo-American magazines. **1939–40** *Army & Navy Stores Catal.* 875/2 Popular *travel bag, with..passport pocket. **1968** L. Deighton *Only when I Larf* i. 9 Umbrella in one hand, travel bag in the other, he marched off. **1843** Dickens *Let.* 2 Nov. (1974) III. 591 The *travel-book, if to be done at all, would cost me very little trouble. **1878** Browning *La Saisiaz* 60 That rare nook..touched on by no travel-book. **1953** P. Scott *Alien Sky* I. vi. 75 A plan I have to issue highly coloured *travel brochures with a photo of myself on an elephant. **1972** F. Warner *Maquettes* 42 A copy-writer for the travel brochures. **1856** Kane *Arct. Expl.* II. xx. 205 The condition of my own *travel-broken animals. **1976** P. Cave *High Flying Birds* i. 13 The *travel bug. Ants in your suitcase. **1930** E. Waugh *Labels* iii. 51 Their speech is rich with the words of the *travel bureau's advertising manager. **1966** A. K. Train *Spoken like Frenchman* 94 (*heading*) At a travel bureau. **1840** Dickens *Old C. Shop* xlvi, Dusty shoes, and *travel-disordered dress. **1963** *Listener* 14 Feb. 281/2 Soblen, provided with an Israeli *travel document valid for travel to any country except Israel, left by air. **1980** E. Behr *Getting Even* xiv. 166 He was not to volunteer information about the man's travel documents. **1910** *Bradshaw's Railway Guide* Apr. 1054/2 'Clonsilla' En Pension... Recommended by *Travel Editor of 'Queen'. **1977** *Chicago Tribune* 2 Oct. IV. 19/5 Travel Editor Holt was born and reared in West Virginia. **1922** *Travel film [see SCENIC *sb.* 2]. **1978** A. Waugh *Best Wine Last* ix. 107 Marrakesh has been a subject of many articles and travel films. **1955** W. Gaddis *Recognitions* II. v. 488 A tour from a *travel folder. **1980** D. Bloodworth *Trapdoor* xii. 68 The secluded Kahala Hilton with its sun-swept beach..could have been torn straight out of a travel folder. **1934** *Travel literature [see *courtesy card* s.v. COURTESY *sb.* 12]. **1955** E. Blunden *Addresses on General Subjects* 285 It is an example of the prolific travel-literature of England. **1932** *Travel-minded [see MINDED *ppl. a.* 4 c]. **1962** *John o' London's* 1 Mar. 202/1 Everyone these days is travel-minded. **1768** Baretti *Mann. & Cust. Italy* II. 324 Credit your *travel-mongers about the character of the Italians. **1942** M. Cable *Gobi Desert* 245 It was no longer he who issued the *travel permits and received official visits. **1978** T. Willis *Buckingham Palace Connection* v. 96 The British Vice-Consul..had promised to get her the necessary travel permit. **1958** *Times Lit. Suppl.* 10 Jan. 22/5 This is no excuse for a *travel-poster jacket and flamboyant title. **1979** R. Jeffries *Murder begets Murder* xv. 91 Sun from dawn to dusk just like the travel posters had promised. **1959** *Times* 13 July 9/1 Some of the children will be *travel-sick. **1978** *Times* 30 Dec. 4/4, I felt travel sick as we were driving along the lane. **1900** Dorland *Med. Dict.* 710/2 **Travel-sickness.* .. Same as *Car-sickness.* **1941** W. Graham *Night Journey* xx. 246, I was talking to your husband on the problem of travel sickness. **1979** R. Perry *Bishop's Pawn* i. 15, I was going to swallow a handful of travel sickness pills. **1810** Scott *Lady of L.* III. xxi, Panting and *travel-soiled he stood. **1847** Mary Howitt *Ballads* 194 Neither to the other told How they were *travel-spent. **1840** Dickens *Old C. Shop* xliv, Her *travel-stained dress. **1597** Shaks. *2 Hen. IV*, IV. iii. 40 *Trauell-tainted as I am. **1753** Smollett *Ct. Fathom* (1784) 52/1 Our hero travel-tainted, lay sunk in the arms of profound repose. **1949** Dylan Thomas *Let.* 1 Dec. (1966) 341, I must..hurry everything up, as visas, *travel-tickets, etc., cannot be too easy to procure. **1980** *Daily Tel.* 26 Jan. 17/3 Auckland..is not the place to buy travel tickets, as there is a 10 per cent tax on them there. **1887** J. Ashby Sterry *Lazy Minstrel* (1892) 218 Fast our *travel-time has sped. **1946** Travel time [see *flying time* s.v. FLYING *vbl. sb.* 3]. **1976** P. R. White *Planning for Public Transport* viii. 160 Over routes of about 200 to 250 m..total travel times by air and rail are similar. **1822** Byron *Werner* I. i. 475 A poor sick man, *Travel-tired. **1821** Scott *Kenilw.* xxiv, Horses or light carriages to meet them, and bring them up without being *travel-toiled. **1961** *Mobile Home Jrnl.* Dec. 21/1 Harold Martin..is now the proud owner of a twenty-seven foot Yellowstone *travel trailer... The twenty-seven foot model is the largest in the Yellowstone line of travel trailers. **1978** *Sunday Sun-Times* (Chicago) 1 Jan. 122/1 Travel trailers are of two types: The conventional, rectangular-shaped unit constructed of aluminum or molded fiberglass over wall studs, and the fifth-wheel trailer. **1964** L. Deighton *Funeral in Berlin* iii. 21 The *travel vouchers and tickets are ordered. **1978** P. Bryers *Cat Trapper* xxviii. 180 His travel vouchers were made out for the motel at Kishinev. **1952** 'R. West' *Meaning of Treason* (ed. 2) I. vii. 156 A *travel warrant issued by the Ministry of Labour. **1919** W. de la Mare *Flora* 40 Noonday to night the enigma of thine eyes Frets with desire their *travel-wearied brain. **1927** W. B. Yeats *October Blast* 22 Cease to remember the delights of youth, travel-wearied aged man. **1856** E. FitzGerald *Salamán* (1909) 47 Kurd..*Travel-weary, Fain would go to sleep. **1837** W. Irving *Capt. Bonneville* I. v. 100 Both men and horses were..much *travel-worn. **1765** Sterne *Tr. Shandy* VII. iv, A *travel-writer would say, 'it would not be amiss to give some account of it'. **1949** C. Graves *Ireland Revisited* viii. 125 Every travel-writer and poet who has visited the Lakes of Killarney has made some attempt to do justice to their loveliness. **1972** W. Garner *Ditto, Brother Rat!* xi. 80 A guest! A famous travel writer.

travel ('træv(ə)l), *v.* Forms: see prec. [orig. the same word as TRAVAIL *v.*; cf. prec. Derivatives, as *travelled, -er, -ing*, etc. are usually spelt with *ll* in Gr. Britain, with single *l* in America.]

†**1.** To torment, distress; to suffer affliction; to labour, toil; to suffer the pains of parturition; etc.: see TRAVAIL *v.* 1–4.

2. a. *intr.* To make a journey; to go from one place to another; to journey. Also *fig.*

α. *c* **1290** *S. Eng. Leg.* I. 25/61 For ȝe þus i-trauailede beoth fram so ferre londe..Ich eov nelle greui nouȝt. *c* **1330** R. Brunne *Chron.* (1810) 3 He was of grete elde, & myght not trauaile. **1413** *Pilgr. Sowle* (Caxton) I. i. (1859) 1, I had longe tyme trauayled toward the holy Cyte of Ierusalem. **1548–9** (Mar.) *Bk. Com. Prayer, Litany*, To preserue all that trauayle by lande or by water. **1590** Spenser *F.Q.* I. ii. 28 Long time they thus together traveiled. **1603** Shaks. *Meas. for M.* I. iii. 14 He supposes me trauaild to Poland. **1691** Norris *Pract. Disc.* 94 Why should we..quit the Road.., if we may safely travail in it? **1714** Gay *Sheph. Week* Proeme, Other Poet travailing in this plain Highway of Pastoral.

β. *c* **1375** *Sc. Leg. Saints* xxxi. (*Eugenia*) 326 Sen scho mycht nocht trawel hym til. *c* **1410** *Sir Cleges* 16 To men, that traveld in londe of ware. **1483** *Cath. Angl.* 391/2 To Travelle, *itinerare.* *a* **1550** *Freiris of Berwik* 39 in *Dunbar's Poems* (S.T.S.) 286 For he wes awld, and micht nocht wele travell. **1594** Nashe *Unfort. Trav.* 68 He is no bodie that hath not traueld. **1600** Shaks. *A.Y.L.* I. iii. 111 What danger will it be to vs,..to trauell forth so farre? **1697** Dryden *Virg. Georg.* IV. 147 A thirsty Train That long have travell'd thro' a Desart Plain. **1768** Sterne *Sent. Journ.* (1775) I. 15 (*Desobligeant*) An Englishman does not travel to see Englishmen. **1855** Paley *Æschylus* Pref. (1861) 28 They have..pointed out the path in which succeeding editors should travel. **1901** W. R. H. Trowbridge *Lett. Mother to Eliz.* iv. 13 [They] travelled down from London in a special Pullman attached to the Bristol express.

b. *to travel it*: to make a journey; *esp.* to go on foot.

1768 Sterne *Sent. Journ.* (1775) II. 135 (*Moulines*) To travel it through the Bourbonnois. **1903** *Speaker* 19 Dec. 293/1 Laird, I just travel't it.

c. *spec.* of a Methodist preacher: To go round a circuit. (Cf. quot. 1791 s.v. CIRCUIT 6.)

1789 [see TRAVELLING *ppl. a.* b]. **1791** Hampson *Mem. J. Wesley* III. 84 Every preacher was considered, when admitted to travel, as a member of conference. **1885** *Minutes Wesleyan Confer.* 8 The above have travelled two years. **1913** *Daily News* 17 July 4 On leaving Didsbury College he ..afterwards 'travelled', as the Methodists say, in the Brentford and Twickenham circuits.

d. To journey from place to place as a commercial traveller (TRAVELLER 3). Const. *in* the commodity for which the traveller solicits orders, and *for* the concern for which a commercial traveller works.

1830 Lamb *Let. to Wordsworth* 22 Jan., A rider in his youth, travelling for shops. **1841** Thackeray in *Fraser's Mag.* Sept. 330/2 I've got a place—a tip-top place..to travel in the West of England in oil and spermaceti. **1872** Geo. Eliot *Middlem.* III. VI. lx. 336, I travelled for 'em, sir, in a gentlemanly way—at a high salary. **1898** *Westm. Gaz.* 2 May 5/2 One lady 'travels in balloons', it was said, meaning not that she soared aloft, but that she vended toy-balloons to drapers and others. **1906** B'ness von Hutten *What bec. Pam* 70 Mr. Bingle travelled in whisky. *Ibid.* 71 A gentleman who travelled in hygienic flannels. **1906** *Blackw. Mag.* Apr. 541/1 The Sophist who in ancient times 'travelled' in sophistry as our bagmen 'travel' in soap. **1922** Joyce *Ulysses* 111, I travelled for cork lino. **1964** 'J. Melville' *Murderers' Houses* ii. 46 He travels for Associated Boxes. It's the big firm on the London Road.

e. Of an animal: To walk or run; *spec.* of deer, to move on while browsing.

1877 C. Hallock *Sportsman's Gaz.* 88 If the deer is 'travelling', as it is called, one has to walk much faster. **1907** J. H. Patterson *Man-Eaters of Tsavo* xxii. 249 [The lion] was travelling leisurely, and I was delighted to find that I was gaining on him fast.

f. ***to travel light***: to travel with little luggage. Also *fig.*

1921 E. O'Neill *Emperor Jones* i. 166, I travels light when I wants to move fast. **1931** 'Grey Owl' *Men of Last Frontier* 13 As he has also to break his own trail, he travels light, taking only a sheet of canvas for a windbreak and one blanket. **1954** I. Murdoch *Under Net* xviii. 252, I just couldn't help making money, and I don't want that. I want to travel light. **1977** *Time* 19 Dec. 18/2 West German terrorists are especially difficult to fathom because ideologically they travel light.

3. a. *transf.* To move, go; to pass from one point or place to another; to proceed, advance; to wander; *esp.* in mod. scientific use, to pass, to be transmitted.

1662 Evelyn *Chalcogr.* 29 Sculpture..travell'd and came to Rome. **1781** Cowper *Expost.* 582 Thy thunders travel over earth and seas. **1839** G. Bird *Nat. Philos.* 129 Sound travels through different bodies with very different degrees of velocity. **1843** R. J. Graves *Syst. Clin. Med.* xxx. 400 Pains commencing in particular parts of the body, and travelling back towards the spine. **1878** Huxley *Physiogr.* 117 The earthquake-wave, as it travels along, causes the ground to rise and fall. **1911** E. Rutherford in *Encycl. Brit.* XXII. 794/1 In an electric field, the positive ions travel to the negative electrode and vice versa.

b. *fig.* of some action figured as movement. ***to travel out of the record***: see RECORD *sb.* 4 c.

1600 Shaks. *A.Y.L.* III. ii. 326 Time trauels in diuers paces, with diuers persons. **1606** —— *Tr. & Cr.* III. iii. 154 Honour trauels in a straight so narrow, Where one but goes a breast. **1664** Marvell *Corr.* Wks. (Grosart) II. 181 His Royal Highness who hath travelled thorough all hearts. **1818** Scott *Hrt. Midl.* xxii, I must remind the learned gentleman that he is travelling out of the case before us. **1874** Whyte Melville *Uncle J.* viii, It seems that we are travelling out of the record.

c. Of a piece of mechanism: To move, or be capable of being moved, along a fixed course. (Cf. prec. sb. 3.)

1815 Scott *Guy M.* lvii, A large iron ring, which travelled upon the bar we have described. **1867** Smyth *Sailor's Word-bk.*, *Travel*, [as] a thimble, block, &c., to run along on beams or ropes. **1892** *Photogr. Ann.* II, The top travels, so as to bring the case over another groove at the back.

d. *colloq.* To bear transportation.

1852 *Beck's Florist* Dec. 271 They do not..make good plants for exhibition, as they travel badly. **1887** J. B. Sheppard *Lit. Cantuarienses* (Rolls) I. Introd. 81 The monks knowing that so small a wine would not travel,.. always sold it on the spot.

e. To move on, esp. with speed. *colloq.* or *slang.*

1884 *Reports Provinc.* (E.D.D.), 'How he travels', said of a dog, running very fast. **1894** *Outing* (U.S.) XXIV. 473/1 The yachts were kept traveling from start to finish. **1911** G. Stratton-Porter *Harvester* v. 74 Betsey..wants to meander along the road with a loaded wagon... Betsey, you must travel! *a* **1914** *Mod.* That car is travelling, and no mistake! *Mod. U.S.* Keep traveling (= clear out, go on or away). **1970** M. Kenyon *100,000 Welcomes* xxi. 178 Mercy, the lorry's travelling. Foot down.

4. a. *trans.* (or with advb. accus.) To journey through (a country, district, space, etc.); to pass over, traverse (a road, etc.); to follow (a course or path).

†*to travel the road*, to practise highway robbery; cf. ROAD *sb.* 5 b.

1303 R. Brunne *Handl. Synne* 1952 Þarfore, y am come to þys cyte, And haue trauayled many a iurne. **1526** *Pilgr. Perf.* (W. de W. 1531) 8 Foure thynges be necessary to be.. obserued of all them that entendeth to trauayle the same [journey]. **1578** Lyte *Dodoens* VI. iii. 659 Peter Belon..hath much haunted and trauayled the Ilande of Crete. **1644** Evelyn *Diary* 4 Nov., From hence we travell a plain and pleasant champain to Viterbo. **1682** Hickeringill *Black Non-Conf.* xvi, The Apostles that had the gift of Tongues travelled all Nations. **1706–7** Farquhar *Beaux Strat.* IV. ii, There's a great deal of address and good manners in robbing a lady; I am the most a gentle-man..that ever travelled the road. 1823 F. CLISSOLD *Ascent Mt. Blanc* 21 Our path..now became far less dangerous than that we had just travelled. 1885 *Act 48 & 49 Vict.* c. 57 §1 The senior judge..who actually travels that circuit. 1894 *Outing* (U.S.) XXIV. 366/2 The path was well traveled.

b. *fig.* or in *fig.* context.

1612 T. JAMES *Corrupt. Script.* To Rdr., Hauing now..fully trauelled this vast wilderness of Sin. 1779 *Mirror* No. 16 ¶7 His brethren, travelling the same road, and subject to the like calamities with himself. 1784 COWPER *Task* III. 156 Some..travel nature up To the sharp peak of her sublimest height. 1822 SCOTT *Pirate* xviii, I have travelled books as well as seas in my day.

c. To traverse, cover (a specified distance).

1660 BLOUNT *Boscobel* III. (1680) 31 He passed through more dangers than he travailed miles. 1660 F. BROOKE tr. *Le Blanc's Trav.* 12 Having travelled five and forty dayes travail from Macharib. 1804 W. TENNANT *Indian Recreat.* II. 70 Their number is..greater than that of the miles you travel.

5. a. To cause to journey, to drive or lead from one place to another. Also *fig.*

1598 HAKLUYT *Voy.* I. 479 Their horses are but smal, but very swift and hard, they trauell them vnshod both winter and Sommer. 1607 TOPSELL *Four-f. Beasts* (1658) 242 In ancient time, if horses were to be travelled through snow, they made them boots of sackcloth to wear in their journey. 1784 R. BAGE *Barham Downs* I. 170 His masters..having travelled him through forty pages of Cornelius Nepos, advanced him to the dignity of Cæsar's commentaries. 1864 *Pall Mall G.* 4 Sept. 10/2 Graziers..stated that they prefer travelling their animals on foot distances of fifty, sixty, and seventy miles rather than exposing them to the cruelties exercised on them by the railway companies. 1891 *Melbourne Argus* 9 May 10/6 It would be advisable..not..to travel any stock at present.

b. *Theatr.* To take (costumes, equipment, etc.) with one from place to place.

1930 E. WALLACE *Lady of Ascot* i. 15 She had sapphire rings and clips..of an incredible value, and she 'travelled' them, as they say in theatrical circles. 1966 'J. HACKSTON' *Father clears Out* 123 The taller of these two guests travelled a broken concertina with him.

c. *Publishing.* To take (books) from place to place in order to promote and sell them. Cf. sense 2 d.

1937 V. WOOLF *Let.* 10 Feb. (1980) VI. 106 We're taking Tuesday off at Rodmell to travel our books in Sussex. 1977 B. COLLOMS *Victorian Country Parsons* xi. 219 [George Routledge] liked to travel his own books in the north country so that he could keep in touch with book-sellers.

travellable, travelable ('trævələb(ə)l), *a.* [f. TRAVEL *v.* + -ABLE.] Capable of being travelled over; adapted to travelling.

1602 CAREW *Cornwall* I. 53 b, The Westerne [roads] are better travaileable, as lesse subiect to these discommodities. *c* 1815 REES *Cycl.* s.v. *Road*, A line which is travellable at any season. 1858 BRIGHT *Sp. India* 24 June (1876) 22 More travelable roads than are to be found in the whole of India. 1886 HISSEY *On Box Seat* 125 The Government should keep the old main roads..in decent travellable order.

travel(l)ator: see TRAVOLATOR.

travelled, traveled ('trævəld), *ppl. a.* [f. TRAVEL *v.* + -ED[1].]

1. That has travelled, esp. to distant countries; experienced in travel. Also with adv. as ***far-travelled***. Also *transf.*

1413 *Pilgr. Sowle* (Caxton 1483) IV. xxxiii. 81 Auncyen trauayled men that ben experte in dedes of armes. 1525 LD. BERNERS *Froiss.* II. clxviii. 469 A well trauelled knight and well knowen. 1613 SHAKS. *Hen. VIII*, I. iii. 19 The reformation of our trauel'd Gallants. 1711 ADDISON *Spect.* No. 45 ¶3 One of these Travelled Ladies. 1780 *Mirror* No. 97 ¶18 Nothing can be more grotesque than her travelled language. 1821 BYRON *Juan* IV. lxxxviii, You Have got a travell'd air. 1966 *Listener* 11 Aug. 210/1 Synge, already a travelled man when Yeats suggested to him that he'd find the Aran Islands more to his liking than Paris was a foreigner in his own country. 1978 G. GREENE *Human Factor* II. i. 51 We need travelled gentlemen like you to deal with foreign affairs.

2. a. *Geol.* Of blocks, boulders, etc.: Transported to a distance from their original site, as by glacial action; erratic.

1830 LYELL *Princ. Geol.* I. 175 That the position..of a great portion of these travelled materials should now appear most irregular [etc.]. 1833 —— *Elem. Geol.* xi. (1874) 146 The multitude of 'travelled' blocks and striated rocks. 1842 SEDGWICK in *Hudson's Guide Lakes* (1843) 196 The travelled bowlders of Shap granite. 1880 A. R. WALLACE *Isl. Life* vii. 106 The phenomenon of travelled or perched blocks is also a common one in all glacier countries.

b. Of earth or soil: That is not *in situ*; that has been brought to, or deposited in, the place where it is; made up, artificial. *Sc.*

1802 PLAYFAIR *Illustr. Hutton. Th.* 197, I am not sure whether this earth is travelled or not. 1805 FORSYTH *Beauties Scotl.* I. 16 The whole ground..is formed, not of natural, but of what builders term travelled earth. 1816 SCOTT *Antiq.* xxiii, It's travell'd earth that,..it howks sae eithly. 1839 D. D. BLACK *Hist. Brechin* xi. (1867) 253 Travelled or artifical earth has repeatedly been found.

3. Of a road, etc.: Frequented by travellers.

1845 J. C. FRÉMONT *Rep. Exploring Expedition* 163 [To Fort Hall] along the travelled road from the town of Westport..is 1,323 miles. 1869 *Bradshaw's Railway Man.* XXI. 433 The travelled route through this country crosses formidable ranges of mountains. 1882 B. HARTE *Flip* ii, It came..with voices in the travelled roads and trails.

4. ***travelled blood*** (see quots.).

1962 'J. LE CARRÉ' *Murder of Quality* iii. 41 There's a lot of what we call travelled blood..that's to say, blood spurted from an open artery. 1981 *Event* 9–15 Oct. 29/4 *Travelled blood*... A pathologist's description of blood that has spurted from a severed artery.

traveller, traveler ('trævələ(r)). Forms: 4 **travaillour, 4–6 travellour, -eiler**, etc. (see TRAVEL *v.*); 6– **traveller**, 9– (*chiefly U.S.*) **traveler**. [agent-noun f. TRAVEL *v.*: see -ER[2], and cf. TRAVAILER.] One who or that which travels.

1. a. A person who is travelling or going from place to place, or along a road or path; one who is on a journey; a wayfarer; a passenger.

c 1375 *Sc. Leg. Saints* xxv. (*Julian*) 20 Sic hope in-to sancte Iulyane þe traualouris þane had tane. *c* 1475 *Rauf Coilȝear* 82 Fyre, drink, nor meit, Nor nane vther eismentis for trauellouris behufe. 1552 ABP. HAMILTON *Catech.* (1884) 51 Certane travelars will nocht begin thair jornay on the satterday. *a* 1591 H. SMITH *Serm.* (1637) 327 A traveller passeth from towne unto towne, untill he come to his Inne. 1715–20 POPE *Iliad* XVI. 316 As wasps, provok'd by children in their play,..In swarms the guiltless traveller engage. 1828 WEBSTER, Traveler. 1843 MIALL in *Nonconf.* III. 429 The traveler, however, had a Scotch tongue in his head. 1886 C. E. PASCOE *London of To-day* xx. (ed. 3) 203 The 'Royal Forest Hotel' offers many attractions as a traveller's rest. 1889 'L. CARROLL' *Sylvie & Bruno Concl.* (ed. 2) Pref. 10 As to such words as 'traveler', I hold the correct principle to be, to double the consonant when the accent falls on that syllable: otherwise, to leave it single.

fig. 1387 TREVISA *Higden* (Rolls) I. 7 Among oþere noble trauaillours of þe þre pathes. 1631 T. POWELL *Tom All Trades* Title-p., An old Travailer in the sea of Experience. 1804 WORDSW. '*She was a phantom*' iii, A Traveller between life and death.

b. = TRAMP *sb.*[1] 4 (now *dial.*); a gypsy; *spec.* in Australia: see quot. 1896. Also, a travelling showman.

1763 *Gentl. Mag.* Sept. 461/2 Mrs. Jewel..was robbed..in the middle of the day by some Irish travellers. 1825 JAMIESON, *Traveller*, a beggar. 1851 MAYHEW *Lond. Labour* I. 243/2 There are many individuals in lodging-houses who are not regular patterers or professional vagrants, being rather, as they term themselves, 'travellers' (or tramps). 1868 M. CLARKE in *Australasian* 5 Sept. 305/3, I remember at one station, situated on the main road for 'travellers', that the unhappy cook was 'put on the fire' by a crowd of these gentry. 1891 'F. W. CAREW' *No.* 747 ii. 18 A little commercial transaction—known among 'travellers' as 'trucking'. 1896 *Australasian* 8 Aug. 249/2 (Morris) These travellers lead an aimless life, wandering from station to station, hardly ever asking for and never hoping to get any work. 1904 A. GRIFFITHS *50 Y. Public Service* xxiii. 347 These 'travellers' or 'foreigners' as they were styled locally, were responsible for a great part of the serious crime of the neighbourhood. 1906 *Gentl. Mag.* July 17 In some parts of the Midlands the tramp is generally known as the traveller. 1945 [see PASSAGE *sb.* 1 e]. 1967 *New Scientist* 7 Dec. 582/3 The question is whether or not gypsies (who call themselves Travellers) are members 'of the Romany race'. 1971 *New Society* 1 July 18/2 Scotland's 2,000-odd itinerant tinkers—or, as they prefer to be called 'travellers'... Some claim descent from the roving Irish tinsmiths or Scottish outlaws, others from the true romany gypsies.

c. *transf.* A sermon delivered by a preacher in various places on different occasions. *colloq.*

1892 *Pall Mall G.* 10 May 6/2 This sermon..was what is known amongst students as a 'traveller'. 1904 J. WELLS *Life J. H. Wilson* xxii. 205 His sermon on this subject was one of his 'travellers'.

2. a. *spec.* One who travels abroad; one who journeys or has journeyed through foreign countries or strange places.

1556 ROBINSON tr. *More's Utop., P. Giles to Buslyde* (1895) p. xcvi, The very famous and renowmed trauailer Vlysses. 1600 SHAKS. *A. Y. L.* II. iv. 18 When I was at home I was in a better place, but Trauellers must be content. 1610 —— *Temp.* III. iii. 26 Trauellers nere did lye, Though fooles at home condemne 'em. 1667 SPRAT *Hist. R. Soc.* 411 Cæsar..had Conquer'd more Countries than most Travailers have seen. 1718 LADY M. W. MONTAGU *Let. to C'tess Mar* 10 Mar., We travellers are in very hard circumstances... If we tell anything new, we are laughed at as fabulous. 1834 L. RITCHIE *Wand. by Seine* 94 Some readers will think we are drawing our traveller's bow with a vengeance. 1885 *Encycl. Brit.* XIX. 404/1 Marco Polo (*c* 1254–1324) the Venetian, the most famous perhaps of all travellers. 1890 *Chambers' Encycl.* VI. 669/1 David Livingstone, missionary and traveller, was born at Blantyre..1813. 1913 MAURICE BARING *Lost Diaries* xvii. 177 The doctor..scoffed at the idea of the sea serpent, which, he said, was a travellers' tale.

b. ***to play*** (also, slang, ***to tip***) ***the traveller***: 'to tell wonderful stories, to romance' (Grose); hence, with ***upon***, to deceive, befool, impose upon: in allusion to the mendacious or incredible character ascribed to 'traveller's tales'.

1739 BP. HERRING in *J. Duncombe's Lett.* (1773) II. 133, I am a little afraid, if I should be particular in my description, you would think I am playing the traveller upon you; but indeed I will stick religiously to truth. 1762 SMOLLETT *Sir L. Greaves* vi, Aha! do'st thou tip me the traveller, my boy? 1796 in *Grose's Dict. Vulg. T.* (ed. 3).

3. *spec.* (in full, ***commercial traveller***: see COMMERCIAL 6): An agent employed by a commercial firm to travel from place to place showing samples of goods and soliciting custom.

1790 J. WEDGWOOD *Let.* 13 July (1965) 328 Such distinguished favours cannot but make a deep impression on my mind. Nor will they be forgotten by the travellers. 1800 *Hull Advertiser* 19 July 2/4 That capital Inn..many years established as a Travellers' House. 1819 *Hermit in London* II. 186 Common bag-men styled travellers of the house of Messrs. So-and-So. 1830 N. S. WHEATON *Jrnl.* 497 At the Inn..I found a number of commercial travellers. 1851 MAYHEW *Lond. Labour* I. 381/2 Some tallymen who keep shops have 'travellers' in their employ, some of whom have salaries, while others receive a percentage upon all payments. 1894 *Times* 22 Jan. 13/4 Carpet travellers are now all out on their journeys, but are not sending in as many orders as could be wished.

4. a. A horse, or other beast of burden or draught, a vehicle, etc., that travels or goes along (fast, well, etc.). Cf. TRAVEL *v.* 3 e. **b.** Applied to birds making a long flight, or migrating.

1660 F. BROOKE tr. *Le Blanc's Trav.* 26 Dalascian Asses..are good travellers,..they will go thirty miles a day with-out any wearinesse. 1874 J. W. LONG *Amer. Wild-fowl* i. 21 Frequently in spring continuous shooting may be had at 'travellers',..i.e., ducks making long flights, often migrating. 1889 *Pall Mall G.* 21 Aug. 2/1 He stands 16 hands high, and looks every inch a traveller.

5. a. A piece of mechanism constructed to 'travel', run, or slide along a support; as a travelling crane, an overhead truck, a movable bridge bearing a crab for lifting and transporting heavy objects from one part to another of an engineering workshop or shed, a travelling or moving platform, etc.

1828 A. SHERBURNE *Mem.* iii. 61 He and other officers contrived to haul the men ashore... He fixed a traveller on the rope, by which he first went ashore, so that he could not wash off. 1842 *Civil Eng. & Arch. Jrnl.* V. 359/1 The 'traveller'..was moved forward from the other end of the dam. 1866 *Cycl. Usef. Arts* I. 2/2 Four pairs of balks.., where travellers are attached for holding the carcasses. 1896 *Allbutt's Syst. Med.* I. 369 The current is then increased by sliding the traveller of the rheostat from its maximum to a lower value. 1898 *Engineering Mag.* XVI. 80 A traveller, or portable platform,..is hoisted out, run across, and raised to the proper level, forming a level gangway..for the transit of passengers and goods from one platform to the other.

b. *Naut.* An iron ring or thimble running freely on a rope, rod, spar; in quot. 1882, a rope on which such a ring slides; also, a rope or rod along which a yard may slide.

1762–9 FALCONER *Shipwr.* II. 258 Some, travellers up the weather-back-stays send. 1790 *Naval Chron.* XXIV. 50 The hauling rope of the traveller got foul. 1840 R. H. DANA *Bef. Mast* Gloss., *Traveller*, an iron ring, fitted so as to slip up and down a rope. 1882 NARES *Seamanship* (ed. 6) 135 In sending the royal yard down..a weather top-gallant backstay can be used for a traveller. 1883 KELLY in *Harper's Mag.* Aug. 449/2 A jib,..hooked to a ring, called a traveller, ..is hauled out to the bowsprit by a tackle.

c. In ring-spinning, a metal ring or loop used to guide the yarn in winding it on the spindle.

1853 URE *Dict. Arts* II. 832 Messrs. Sharp,..of Manchester, exhibited a throstle spinning frame on the 'ring and traveller' principle. 1877 KNIGHT *Dict. Mech.* 1944/1 As the spindles revolve, the thread passing through the traveler revolves it rapidly, and the horizontal bar ascending and descending alternately winds the yarn regularly upon the spools. 1884 W. S. B. McLAREN *Spinning* (ed. 2) 167 The traveller..is to wind the yarn on to the bobbin and to affect the drag... By reducing the size of the traveller the drag can be made exceedingly slight.

d. *Theatr.* The mechanism for flying fairies, angels, ghosts, etc. above the stage.

1859 SALA *Gaslight & D.* ii. 21 You may see the wires or 'travellers', used by 'flying fairies'.

e. *Angling.* A tackle which permits the bait to travel or move down the swim. Also *attrib.*

1867 F. FRANCIS *Angling* i. (1880) 49 This kind of fishing, which is called 'traveller' fishing (the float being the traveller). *Ibid.* iv. (1883) 42 Barbel are taken with the traveller in the Nottingham fashion.

f. A craftsman's tool used for measuring circumferences, esp. of wheels (see quots.).

1879–81 G. F. JACKSON *Shropshire Word-Bk.* 454 *Trindle*, a disc used by blacksmiths for measuring the circumference of wheels—a 'traveller'. 1923 G. STURT *Wheelwright's Shop* xxiii. 122 The new tyre..had to be measured, as also had the wheel it was meant for. Blacksmiths kept a special implement for this purpose—a 'traveller' or 'tyre-runner'. The traveller was a thin circular disk of iron, six or seven inches across, which the smith would hold out, waist-high, at right angles to himself, and run round wheel and tyre in turn. 1969 G. E. EVANS *Farm & Village* xiv. 148, I cut the band to the exact circumference of the stone. I find this with a device I made... It's called a *traveller*... It's a metal wheel. I roll this round the stone and count the revolutions. .. (This device works on the same principle as the measuring wheel used by the old road surveyors—a trundle wheel or way-wiser.) 1976 *National Observer* (U.S.) 10 July 9/1 'This here is called a traveler,' he says..displaying a round, flat device used to measure the perimeter of a wagon wheel... 'You won't find too many of them left.'

6. A suitcase, trunk, or travelling bag. Chiefly *U.S.*

1895 *Montgomery Ward Catal.* Spring & Summer 564/3 Canvas Traveler... Large square box made of the best basswood, covered with extra heavy duck... A most handsome ladies' trunk. 1965 *Harper's Bazaar* Dec. 89/1 Cosmetic traveller lined with silk for girls who are on the go all day. 1983 *Country Life* 1 Dec. 1677 (Advt.), Travel-bag—this great, waterproof traveller holds three leakproof bottles.

7. *attrib.* and *Comb.*, as ***traveller fishing***, ***float*** (see 5 e), ***monk***, ***vocation***; ***traveller-like*** adj.

1832 J. P. KENNEDY *Swallow B.* ix, I have not been idle in my traveller-vocation. 1847 W. CORY *Lett. & Jrnls.* (1897) 47, I felt more lively and traveller-like than I had before. 1907 T. C. MIDDLETON *Geog. Knowl. Time Discov. Amer.* 6 Cosmas Indicopleustes—the traveler-monk of Egypt [*c* 500–547].

b. Combinations with *traveller's*: **traveller's cheque** orig. *U.S.*, a cheque for one of several specified amounts of money, which can be cashed at a bank in most countries, or used in payment for goods, on the holder's endorsement against his original signature; also written ***travellers(') cheque***; **traveller's joy**, a name (given by Gerarde) for the wild shrub *Clematis Vitalba*, from its trailing over and adorning hedges by the wayside; **traveller's palm, traveller's tree**, names for certain trees which yield water or sap sought after by travellers to allay thirst, as *Ravenala madagascariensis* (*Urania speciosa*), N.O. *Musaceæ*, a palm-like tree of Madagascar whose hollow leaf-sheaths contain a store of water.

1891 (*title no. 24775 in Library of Congress copyright registration bk.*) American Express Company, *Travelers Cheque. Ten Dollars. **1894** *N.Y. Tribune* 11 July 5/2 The American Express Company's travellers' checks are of great assistance to tourists abroad. **1907** M. ROLLINS *Money & Investments* 218 Express companies have made a speciality of issuing 'travellers' cheques'. **1922** F. SCOTT FITZGERALD *Beautiful & Damned* II. i. 150 On his dressing-table were spread a number of articles..their tickets to California, the book of traveller's checks. **1957** D. DU MAURIER *Scapegoat* iii. 32 Twenty-five pounds of travellers' cheques still uncashed. **1969** *Times* 15 Nov. 7/7 The counterfeiting of travellers cheques. **1981** 'E. LATHEN' *Going for Gold* iii. 29, I assume these foreign traveler's checks work like American Express? **1597** GERARDE *Herbal* II. cccxi. 739 Decking and adorning waies and hedges, where people trauell, and thereupon I haue named it the *Traueilers Ioie. **1678** PHILLIPS (ed. 4), *Travailours-joy*, a sort of Herb called in Latin *Clematis*. **1776** WITHERING *Brit. Plants* (1796) II. 500 Traveller's-joy. Great Wild Climber. Virgin's Bower. Honesty. Hedges and shady places, in calcareous soil. **1885** LADY BRASSEY *The Trades* 177 We also saw [in Venezuela] many specimens of the *travellers' palm, each leaf of which ..yields, when cut by the thirsty traveller, from half a pint to a pint of water. **1857** GOSSE *Omphalos* vii. 148 One of the stateliest of plants,—the *Traveller's Tree (*Urania speciosa*). **1883** *Encycl. Brit.* XV. 170/1 The traveller's-tree (*Urania speciosa*), with its graceful crown of plantain-like leaves.. supplying a quantity of pure cool water.

Hence 'travelleress (*rare*), a female traveller; **travellership** *rare*, in various *nonce* usages.

1820 KEBLE in Coleridge *Mem.* (1869) I. 99 A little sickliness now and then..on the part of some of my fellow-travelleresses. **1886** *Sat. Rev.* 21 Aug. 253/1 A much more common figure is the merely wrong-headed and cantankerous traveller—and particularly travelleress. **1920** JOYCE *Let.* 20 Aug. (1966) III. 17 Giorgio has been offered a position here in an American Trust Agency which would develop into a secretaryship and travellership for same. **1961** *Times* 24 June 9/6 We left early..accompanied in somewhat distant travellership by an austerely demeanoured delegation from Communist China.

travelling, traveling ('trævəlɪŋ), *vbl. sb.* [f. TRAVEL *v.* + -ING[1].] **a.** The action of the verb TRAVEL; journeying.

1375 BARBOUR *Bruce* II. 283 Sen þai come owt off trawelling. **1382** WYCLIF *Jer.* xxix. 18 Wery trauailing to alle rewmes. *a* **1568** ASCHAM *Scholem.* (Arb.) 72 Disposed to prayse traueling, as a great commendacion. **1669** R. MONTAGU in *Buccleuch MSS.* (Hist. MSS. Comm.) I. 458 There has been so much snow that..there is no travelling for the post. **1738** CHESTERF. *Common Sense* No. 93 ¶10 Travelling is, unquestionably, a very proper part of the education of our youth. **1847** HELPS *Friends in C.* I. vii. 112 Travelling is a great trial of people's ability to live together. **1875** URE *Dict. Arts* II. 538 The gas is said to bear travelling through this length of pipe very well.

b. *attrib.* = of travelling, as ***travelling accomplishment, charge, companion, day, expenses, movement, pace, pay, power, propensity***; esp. in sense 'used, or adapted to be used, for or in travelling', or 'carried or taken with one when travelling', as ***travelling album, arms, bag, baroscope, box, cap, carriage, case, chariot, chest, cloak, clock, commission, cup, dress, equipage, kitchen, pistol, rug, suit, trunk***; **travelling-cabinet**, a small chest of drawers secured by outer doors so as to be safely portable on a journey: much used in 17th c. (*Cent. Dict.*); **travelling-carriage**, a strong carriage used for travelling before railways were introduced; **travelling-couvert** [F. *couvert* = COVER *sb.*[1] 7], 'a set of table utensils..made to pack closely, for use in traveling' (*Cent. Dict.*); **travelling fellowship, scholarship**, a fellowship or scholarship given to enable the holder to travel for purposes of study or research; **travelling road**, *Mining* (see quot. 1883).

1748 RICHARDSON *Clarissa* Wks. 1883 V. 495 A price that is often paid for *travelling accomplishments. **1709** HEARNE *Collect.* 7 Mar. (O.H.S.) II. 174 Whose hand and signet I have in my *traveling Album. **1689** in *Acts Parlt. Scotl.* (1875) XII. 52/1 To make use of horses and ordinary *travelling armes in the countrey. **1838** C. GILMAN *Recoll. Southern Matron* ii. 18 He..called the little boy who held the *travelling bag a 'black-faced nigger'. **1862** *Catal. Internat. Exhib., Brit.* II. No. 6932 Dressing cases, travelling bags, and despatch boxes. **1669** BOYLE *Contn. New Exp.* xxii, The making of portable or *travelling baroscopes. **1835** WILLIS *Pencillings* I. vii. 43 The *travelling-books caution against sleeping in the carriage while passing these marshes. **1726** SWIFT *Gulliver* II. v, Glumdalclitch setting down my *travelling box, I went out of it to walk. **1790** *Pennsylvania Packet* 2 Jan. 4/2 (Advt.), Trimmings..for Gentlemens *Travelling Caps. **1859** JEPHSON *Britanny* i, 1, [I] pull my travelling-cap over my eyes. **1798** S. LEE *Canterb. T., Yng. Lady's T.* II. 385 [He] purchased a *travelling-carriage. **1744** H. PUREFOY *Let.* 26 Feb. (1931) I. 119, I desire you will send mee an allarum to pull up together with a *Travelling Case. **1895** *Montgomery Ward Catal.* Spring & Summer 257/2 Ladies' and men's toilet and traveling cases. **1984** A. PRICE *Sion Crossing* iv. 48 He walked meekly to the nearest bench..tucking his travelling case beside him. **1618** in J. Charnock *Hist. Mar. Arch.* (1801) II. 236 For *travelling charges to solicit for money. **1852** DICKENS *Bleak Ho.* xii, The *travelling chariot rolls on to the house. **1854** E. B. BROWNING *Plea for Ragged Schools of London* I If she shakes a *travelling cloak, Down our Appian roll the scudi. **1944** A. CLARKE *Coll. Plays* (1963) 245 A figure appears, tall and handsome, in travelling cloak with tricornered hat. **1860** C. M. YONGE *Hopes & Fears* II. xii. 236 Phœbe was strongly tempted to answer, but the little *travelling clock struck. **1902** R. BAGOT *Donna Diana* ix, A travelling clock on the writing-table. **1726** SWIFT *Gulliver* II. iv, It was always in my *travelling closet. **1813** COL. HAWKER *Diary* (1893) I. 67 The *travelling companion who was bundled into the mail. **1844** LOUISA S. COSTELLO *Béarn & Pyrenees* II. 88 In its snow-cold water I dipped my *travelling-cup. **1856** BONAR *Hymn, 'I heard the voice of Jesus say'* iii, In that light of life I'll walk Till *travelling days are done. **1815** J. MAYNE *Jrnl.* Feb. (1909) xii. 282 We ran off, the instant we arrived, in our *travelling dresses, were in the theatre at eight o'clock. **1844** J. T. HEWLETT *Parsons & W.* xxiv, While Madeline was changing her travelling-dress. **1793** J. WOODFORDE *Diary* 23 Oct. (1929) IV. 75 *Travelling Expenses..amounted in the whole—78.19.7. **1797** F. REYNOLDS *The Will* III. i, Suppose I try to get our travelling-expences out of him? **1907** G. B. SHAW *John Bull's Other Island* I. 13 An advance on his salary—for travelling expenses. **1977** D. FRANCIS *Risk* xvii. 230 He'd invented travelling expenses to the races for horses which..had never left the yard. **1789** *J. Lewis' Mem. Dk. Glocester* 87 *note*, [Dr. Radcliffe] also founded two *travelling Fellowships for young Physicians. **1782** J. ADAMS *Diary* 26 July, I had on my *travelling gloves. **1825** J. NICHOLSON *Operat. Mechanic* 423 The rack..for regulating the *travelling-movement of the spinning or any other machine, on a rope-walk. **1815** *Chron.* in *Ann. Reg.* 57 Going over Uxbridge-common, at a regular *travelling pace. **1692** LUTTRELL *Brief Rel.* (1857) II. 401 On Friday next the persons belonging to the train for the descent enter into *travailling pay. **1782** MISS BURNEY *Cecilia* x. ii, My *travelling pistols were already charged. **1875** URE *Dict. Arts* II. 538 As to storage and *travelling power, Mr. Hastings..reports favourably. **1883** GRESLEY *Gloss. Coalmining*, **Travelling road*, an underground passage..used expressly..for men to travel along to and from their working places. **1911** *Act 1 & 2 Geo. V*, c. 50 §49 A person shall not..travel or work in any travelling road or working place which is not so made secure. **1911** *Daily Colonist* (Victoria, B.C.) 23 Apr. 18/3 (Advt.), Lost—*Travelling rug and overcoat, between Empress Hotel and the outer wharf. **1977** C. MCCULLOUGH *Thorn Birds* iii. 66 The big tartan traveling rugs all the suitcases bore on their outsides. **1911** R. BROOKE *Let.* 1 Mar. (1968) 282 Benians, of John's, is staying in Munich a week on his way round the world on one of these Kivet Kahn *Travelling scholarships. **1967** E. LEMARCHAND *Death of Old Girl* i. 13 I'm certainly going to mention the art department's successes, especially Miss Cartmell's travelling scholarship. **1867** AUG. J. E. WILSON *Vashti* xxvii, Elsie was waiting to clothe me in my *travelling-suit. **1779** *Mirror* No. 17 ¶13 A draw-bridge, which..exactly resembled the lid of a *travelling-trunk. **1854** *Rep. Trans. Pennsylvania State Agric. Soc.* 97 Their very handsome riding saddle and russet traveling trunk. **1981** *Christian Sci. Monitor* (Midwestern ed.) 12 Feb. B4 A 'traveling trunk' program, in which the institute sends out to schools actual trunks of touchable Texas gear.

'travelling, traveling, *ppl. a.* [f. as prec. + -ING[2].]

1. a. That travels, or goes from place to place; journeying, itinerant; moving; also *fig.*

1375 BARBOUR *Bruce* VII. 241 'A travalland man, dame', said he, 'þat traualys heir throu þe cuntre'. *c* **1420** *Anturs of Arth.* li, These ij traueling men truly vppe thay take. **1495** *Act 11 Hen. VII*, c. 2 §2 None other calling himself a Souldeour Shipman or travelyngman. **1605** SHAKS. *Macb.* II. iv. 7 By th' Clock 'tis Day, And yet darke Night strangles the trauailing Lampe. **1619–20** *Archdeaconry of Essex Minutes* lf. 241 (MS.) A travelinge or Wayfaringe woman. **1715** HEARNE *Collect.* (O.H.S.) V. 80 The two travelling Physitians, that are to be Dr. Radcliffe's Fellows of University College. **1827** MACKENZIE *Hist. Newcastle* II. 723 *note*, Fire-engines,..there is a travelling tank attached. **1837** H. EARLE in *Rep. Sel. Comm. Railw. Commun.* 60 For the purpose of having a travelling post-office, that they could sort the letters as they went on. **1867** F. FRANCIS *Angling* i. (1883) 12 Stream fishing..with a travelling or tripping bait, with or without a float. **1890** 'R. BOLDREWOOD' *Col. Reformer* (1891) 254 Great hordes of travelling sheep laid waste a portion of the run.

b. *spec.* of a Methodist preacher: see TRAVEL *v.* 2 c.

1775 F. ASHBURY *Jrnl.* 6 Nov. (1821) I. 124 At this meeting we admitted F. P. T. F. and J. H—y as travelling preachers. **1789** WESLEY *Wks.* (1872) IV. 464, I had much satisfaction in this Conference;..conversing with between forty and fifty travelling Preachers. **1825** *Mem. Isab. Wilson* 169 She came to reside..under the same roof as the Travelling Preachers near Wetherby. **1874** E. EGGLESTON *Circuit Rider* xxvii. 252 The incessant activity of a traveling preacher's life.

c. Of plants: Creeping, or spreading by horizontal growth of the rootstock.

1842 LOUDON *Suburban Hort.* 569 A new plantation may be made every six or seven years, or oftener,..if their travelling roots should grow out of bounds. **1885** *Pall Mall G.* 11 Feb. 5/1 To the number of curious plants,..a new specimen has lately been added which is described as the travelling plant. It is said to be of the lily of the valley species ..and has a root formed of knots, by which it annually advances about an inch..from the place where the plant was first rooted.

d. *Mech.* Constructed to 'travel' or move in a fixed course, either in a circuit or to and fro, as a crane, a platform or side-walk, etc.

1834–47 J. S. MACAULAY *Field Fortif.* (1851) 70 To permit of a gun on a travelling carriage..being fired over the parapet. **1835** URE *Philos. Manuf.* 216 A novel mechanism adapted to the travelling-comb called the gill. **1862** *Catal. Internat. Exhib.* II. x. 21 Travelling Crane, the traversing motion being worked from the crab. **1873** *Iron* 5 July 23/3 Spier's Travelling Sidewalk. **1900** *Engineering Mag.* XIX. 701 At the Paris *Exposition*... The traveling sidewalk..is here carried out on a far larger scale than ever before attempted... It forms a continuous connection between the main portions of the exposition.

e. Physics. ***travelling wave***, a wave in which the nodes and antinodes travel (cf. *standing wave* s.v. STANDING *ppl. a.* 11 e); freq. *attrib.*, as ***travelling wave tube***, an electron tube in which a guided electromagnetic wave is amplified by interaction with a beam of electrons travelling at about the same velocity.

1908 C. P. STEINMETZ *Gen. Lect. Electr. Engin.* 273 Where a traveling wave is reflected, the combination of the reflected wave and the incoming wave produces a standing wave or oscillation, that is, a wave in which the voltage maxima and the zero points or nodes have fixed positions on the line. **1946** *Wireless World* Nov. 371/3 The travelling wave tube.. consists..of..a long and straight helix of wire supported in an evacuated glass envelope containing also an electron gun for producing an electron beam and a collector. **1963** G. TROUP *Masers & Lasers* (ed. 2) v. 66 For the travelling wave maser, the gain coefficient..is [etc.]. **1967** *Oceanogr. & Marine Biol.* V. 25 A travelling wave is an essential feature of surge phenomena in the North Sea. **1974** Traveling-wave tube [see PLASMA 6].

2. Special collocations. ***travelling exhibition***; **travelling circus**, (*a*) a circus which travels from place to place giving performances; (*b*) *Mil. slang*: in the war of 1914–18, a mobile military unit; a squadron of aeroplanes (cf. CIRCUS 2 d); also *fig.*; **travelling library**, a library which is transported from place to place and serves remote rural communities, hospitals, etc.; a mobile library; **travelling salesman** = TRAVELLER, TRAVELER 3; **travelling salesman problem** *Math.*, the problem of determining the shortest route that passes through each of a set of given points once only and returns to the starting point; **travelling stock** *Austral.* and *N.Z.*, livestock which is driven from place to place; freq. in Comb., as ***travelling stock road, route***; **travelling stock reserve**, land decreed as stock-routes; cf. *stock-route* s.v. STOCK *sb.*[1] 63.

1883 *Harper's Mag.* June 137/1 The travelling circus.. had journeyed on and left her. **1917** [see CIRCUS 2 d]. **1919** F. A. MCKENNA *Battery A—103rd Field Artillery in France* 36 Field Marshal Von Hindenburg's troops, nicknamed by the Yanks, 'The Traveling Circus', composed of the famous Prussian Guards and picked Turkish storm troops, were reported in the sector opposite. **1946** *Happy Landings* (Air Ministry) July 1/1 Among the latest exhibits added to the Directorate's 'travelling circus' are components from a Sabre engine. **1974** G. MITCHELL *Javelin for Jonah* xi. 137 He had been with a travelling circus for some time, but they dismissed him. **1937** *Discovery* Aug. 236/1 A travelling exhibition which will penetrate into the remotest country districts. **1977** J. R. L. ANDERSON *Death in City* vi. 87 Bringing 'Pictures to the People' in the form of travelling exhibitions. **1910** A. E. BOSTWICK *Amer. Public Library* 108 Traveling libraries are simply collections of books sent to communities, associations, or individuals for circulation. **1960** *Library Assoc. Rec.* Aug. 262/2 *Travelling Library*, a vehicle of small size..shelved or otherwise equipped to provide a rural service to villages and isolated farms and houses. **1982** H. INNES *Black Tide* v. i. 220 The *Mabinogion*. .. She'd got it from the travelling library. **1885** *South Florida Sentinel* (Orlando) 1 July 3/3 The popular traveling salesman..will leave in a few days. **1954** *Jrnl. Operations Res. Soc. Amer.* II. 393 Little is known about the traveling-salesman problem. **1960** G. A. W. BOEHM *New World Math.* 114 Equally exasperating is the traveling salesman problem, with which a good many mathematicians have wrestled unsuccessfully for more than twenty years. **1978** I. B. SINGER *Shosha* v. 105 Baskets and boxes accumulated from the time Zelig was a traveling salesman. **1979** PAGE & WILSON *Introd. Computational Combinatorics* iv. 79 These are very interesting paths and circuits as they can be generalised into the well-known 'travelling salesman' problem. **1891** R. WALLACE *Rural Econ. Austral. & N.Z.* xxvi. 364 Should the land [of a sheep station] be mountainous or a travelling-stock road pass through it, the numbers [of employees] require to be increased. **1930** L. G. D. ACLAND *Early Canterbury Runs* 1st Ser. viii. 196 There was a travelling stock reserve there, and it was in the hut belonging to it that the man was murdered. **1977** C. MCCULLOUGH *Thorn Birds* vi. 120 There was an official Travelling Stock Route or TSR winding its way near the Barwon River.

travelogue ('trævəlɒg). orig. *U.S.* [f. TRAVEL *sb.* + -LOGUE, after MONOLOGUE *sb.*] An (illustrated) lecture about places and experiences encountered in the course of travel; hence a film, broadcast, book, etc., about travel; a travel documentary.

1903 *Daily Chron.* 16 Apr. 6/7 Mr. Burton Holmes, an American entertainer new to London, delivered last evening the first of a series of 'Travelogues'. **1921** *Glasgow Herald* 7 Nov. 10 The..Travelogue film, 'With Allenby in Palestine and Lawrence in Arabia'. **1927** H. E. FOSDICK *Pilgrimage to Palestine* p. vii, Some [books] are simply travelogues in which the successive experiences of the traveler furnish the strand for the narrative. **1931** [see SPONSOR *v.* 2]. **1932** [see DOCUMENTARY *a.* 4]. **1935** R. MACAULAY *Personal Pleasures* 67 Dido and her court feasted Æneas and his warriors, and after supper listened to his mournful travelogue. **1956** S. ERTZ *Charmed Circle* 78 Reality lay wholly within the boundaries of the United States, and..what she saw in Europe was a sort of illustrated travelogue. **1976** A. DAVIS *Television* 119 There were zoo programmes and the travelogues of Armand and Michaela Denis. **1983** *Listener* 20 Jan. 27/2 It is part travelogue, part autobiography.

traventer: see TRANTER.

traversa: see TRAVERSO.

traversable (ˈtrævəsəb(ə)l), *a.* [f. TRAVERSE *v.* + -ABLE.]

1. Capable of being traversed or crossed.

a **1656** USSHER *Ann.* vi. (1658) 218 Darius commanded it to be made all level, that it might be made the more traverseable for his horse. **1768** TUCKER *Lt. Nat.* (1834) I. 8 The land of philosophy..partly..traversable only by the speculative. **1812** *Examiner* 31 Aug. 557/2 Every quarter of the traversible globe. **1859** TENNENT *Ceylon* II. VII. ii. 121 Roads..open and traversable at all seasons.

2. *Law.* Capable of being traversed or formally denied.

1534 *Star Chamb. Cases* (Selden) II. 323 Eny other thyng, being materyall or trauersable, and not before aunswered confessed, avoyded, or trauersed, is true. **1588** W. LAMBARDE *Eiren.* IV. v. (1602) 473 It neither contained the place where, nor the person to whome the lether was sold, both which be materiall and trauersable. **1620** J. WILKINSON *Courts Leet* 110 A presentment made by fewer than by xii is traversable. **1726** AYLIFFE *Parergon* 70 The Bishops Certificate..is not Peremptory but Traversable. **1884** SIR H. COTTON in *Law Times Rep.* LI. 535/2 Returns such as this..have not generally been traversed..but it does not..follow that they are not traversable.

3. Capable of being traced continuously, as a geometrical figure.

1905 J. C. WILSON *Traversing Geometr. Figures* I. §29. 43 Resolution of a figure into a minimum of figures traversable in one traverse.

traversal (trəˈvɜːsəl, ˈtrævəsəl). [f. TRAVERSE *v.* + -AL.] = TRAVERSE *sb.* 2.

1909 in WEBSTER. **1936** [see *line frequency* s.v. LINE *sb.*² 32]. **1955** J. A. WHEELER in W. Pauli *Niels Bohr* 171 The increase of α in the traversal of the fission barrier will be of the order of unity. **1982** *Times* 22 Oct. 10/5 As he began on Wednesday the traversal of all Beethoven's sonatas..it was piercingly evident that here was someone who does far more than play the piano. **1984** *Observer* 15 Jan. 49/8 Speed—the traversal of the maximum space in the minimum time—was a disturbing obsession.

†**traversant**, *a.* *Obs. rare.* [a. F. *traversant*, pr. pple. of *traverser* to cross: see -ANT.] Thwarting; unfavourable, inauspicious; = next.

14.. *MS. Cantab. Ff. I. 6* lf. 137 (Halliw.) Thou hast a dominacioun traversaunt, Wythowte numbre doyst thou greeve.

traversary (ˈtrævəsərɪ), *a.* *Astrol.* [By-form of TRANSVERSARY, after L. *trāversus* = *transversus*.] Lying across, crossing; unfavourable, inauspicious.

1851 K. H. DIGBY *Compitum* V. 2 Where men enter into the orbit which astrologers style a traversary planet. **1871** —— *Ouranogaia* XII. 3 But all the earth feels not its dulcet ray. For traversary planets round us roll.

traverse (ˈtrævəs, trəˈvɜːs), *sb.* Forms: 3–7 trauers, 4–8 travers, (4, 6 trau-, traverce, 5 traverss, 5–6 trau-, travarse), 5–7 trauerse, 5– traverse. Also β. 5 travas, -vass, 5–6 trevass, 5–7 trauas; 5 trauest, trevesse, 5–6 traves, 5–8 treves, 6 traues, 6–7 travess, traveis, trau-, travesse; 5–7 travis, 6 trevis, trevys, 6–7 trauyce, traviss, 6–8 travice, 7 trauis, -ise. See also TRAVIS, TREVIS. [Represents two OF. sbs., *travers* masc. (11th c.), and *traverse* fem. (12th c.), which, through the loss or misuse of final *e*, have fallen together in Eng. F. *travers* (dial. *travais, travars, travé*, in Prov. *travers*, Cat. *traves*, Pg. *traves* = It. *traverso*) is:—pop.L. *trāversum*, for L. *transversum*, neuter of *transversus*, TRANSVERSE *a.* F. *traverse* (Prov. *traversa*, Cat., Pg. *travessa*, It. *traversa*) is, according to Hatz.-Darm., chiefly from *traverser* TRAVERSE *v.*, but in some uses it appears to represent a late L. *trāversa* sb. fem. from pa. pple. of *transvertĕre* to TRANSVERT. From the falling together of these words under the current form *traverse*, and the rise in English of many new senses, it is not possible to distinguish the senses which belong etymologically to F. *travers* from those which belong to F. *traverse*.]

I. The action of TRAVERSE *v.* in a local sense.

1. The act of passing through a gate, or crossing a river, bridge, or other place forming a boundary (*obs.*): represented in quots. only by the sense, A toll paid on crossing the bounding-line of a town or lordship; = PASSAGE 5. *Obs.* exc. *Hist.*

Also called *toll traverse*: see TOLL *sb.*¹ 2 g.

[**1284** *Chanc. Inq. P.M. Edw. I* 40/6 (Norf.) (P.R.O.) De quadam consuetudine que vocatur travers et valet per annum 3s. **1292** BRITTON I. xx. §1 Soit ausi enquis, quels del counté cleyment..de aver lestage..ou travers, ou toluen. [*Note, Traverse*, a toll paid for passing through the limits of a town or lordship.] **1347** *Inq. P.M. Edw. III*, File 86 (Norfolk Inq.) Est apud Brandone quedam custuma vocata 'travers' que est parcella manerii de Thefford.] **1598** KITCHIN *Courts Leet* (1675) 208 To have toll Travers is good. **1636, 1670** [see TOLL *sb.*¹ 2 g]. **1754** T. GARDNER *Hist. Dunwich*, etc. 134 *note*, Robert FitzRogers had customary Travers for Passage through Blythburgh and Walberswick. **1852** *Hull Shipping Dues Act* 2209 Certain tolls called..Toll Traverse. **1911** [see TOLL *sb.*¹ 2 g].

2. The action of traversing, passing across, or going through (a region, etc.); passage, crossing: orig. from side to side, but soon also from end to end, or in any course. Also *fig.* [= OF. *travers*, F. *traverse*.]

1599 MARSTON *Sco. Villanie* II. vi. 199 Thinkst thou that I..will once vouchsafe to trip A Pauins traverse? **1642** ROGERS *Naaman* 89 He led them a traverse of fourty yeares. **1658** PHILLIPS, Advt., Some Critticks perhaps will expect the names of Authours in the traverse of this Worke to be often set down. **1725** DE FOE *Voy. round World* (1840) 314 They were one-and-twenty days in this traverse. **1806** PIKE *Sources Mississ.* (1810) 67 In making a traverse of the lake, some of my men had their ears, some their noses, and their chins frozen. **1808** *Ibid.* II. 189, I determined to attempt the traverse of the mountain. **1902** *Speaker* 2 Aug. 485/1 He completed his traverse of Persia from north to south. **1904** P. FOUNTAIN *Gt. North-West* vii. 61 When a bay or inlet is come to, the crew [of the canoe]..like to strike straight across from headland to headland. In the technical language of the voyageurs this is termed making a traverse. **1907** G. D. ABRAHAM *Complete Mountaineer* 476 *Traverse*... Also used to define a climb up one side of a peak and down the other.

3. *Surveying.* A single line of survey carried across a region or through a narrow strip of country, by measuring the lengths and azimuths of a connected series of straight lines; used either where there is no general trigonometrical survey, or in filling up the details of one. Also, a tract of country so surveyed.

1804 M. LEWIS in *Orig. Jrnls. Lewis & Clark Exped.* (1905) VI. 232 A Circumferentor..has also been employed in taking the traverse of the river. **1881** GEIKIE in *Nature* 6 Jan. 224/2 In about three months the traverses for the construction of the map were completed. *Ibid.* 225/1 The geological structure of different traverses of the country. **1887** *Encycl. Brit.* XXII. 706/1 In Indian Survey..the traverses are executed in minor circuits following the periphery of each village and in major circuits comprising groups of several villages. **1900** H. M. WILSON *Topogr. Survey.* x. 195 Traverses made in connection with topographic mapping are of several degrees of accuracy.

4. The traversing or continuous tracing of a geometrical figure or part of one: see TRAVERSE *v.* 2 b.

1905 J. C. WILSON *Traversing Geometr. Figures* I. §2. 6 A traverse must exhaust the point at which it ends: for if any path from it were left untraversed, the traverse would leave the point by the path, and so it would not be the point at which the traverse ends. *Ibid.* §9. 16 If the first traverse is a single path, that will be the characteristic of the whole traverse chosen.

†**5.** *Fencing.* The action or an act of traversing: see TRAVERSE *v.* 5, 15. Also *fig.* *Obs.*

1547 HOOPER *Declar. Christ* xii. L vij, Marke the trauyce and pley betwene the law of God, and the conscience of Paule. **1599** G. SILVER *Paradoxes Defence* 61–2 This Cob was a great quareller..and..was sure by the cunning of his Trauerse, not to be hurt by anie man: for at anie time finding himselfe ouermatched would suddenly turne his backe and runne away... And this..was called Cobs Trauerse. **1599** MARSTON *Sco. Villanie* III. ii. 225 Each gallant he doth meete He fronts him with a trauerse in the streete. **1706** FARQUHAR *Recruit. Officer* III. ii, [Direction] Plume and Brazen fight a traverse or two about the stage.

6. *Mountaineering.* An act of traversing or making one's way in a horizontal direction across the face of a mountain or rock (see TRAVERSE *v.* 21); also *concr.* a place where a traverse is made.

1893 C. WILSON *Mountaineering* vi. 88 Short traverses are often difficult; you ascend a gully..as far as possible; and, when progress by that avenue is..barred, a traverse is undertaken to the left or the right. *Ibid.* 90 We eventually accomplished the ascent by a long traverse which led round a corner and on to broken rocks. **1897** O. G. JONES *Rock-climbing* 113 Three o'clock found us still working westwards on the traverse. **1900** DENT *Mountaineering* 438 *Traverse*, sometimes used substantively to denote a surface of rock, snow, or ice that has to be crossed horizontally.

II. Senses denoting (or connected with) non-physical action (opposition, thwarting, or the like).

7. Something that crosses, thwarts, or obstructs; opposition; an obstacle, impediment; a trouble, vexation; a mishap; misfortune, adversity; *pl.* crosses. Now *rare.* [OF. *travers*.]

1390 GOWER *Conf.* III. 384 His nature is so divers, That it hath evere som travers Or of to moche or of to lite. **1530** LYNDESAY *Test. Papyngo* 402 Quhate trauers, troubyll, and calamitie Haith bene in courte within thir houndreth ȝeris! **1654** H. L'ESTRANGE *Chas. I* (1655) 2 In the very nick of time (a strange traverse of Providence) dyes Pope Gregory, whose death put all to a stand. **1670** COTTON *Espernon* I. I. 34 He could not overcome those traverses, and difficulties, that his Majesties enemies still strew'd in his way. **1703** PENN in *Pa. Hist. Soc. Mem.* IX. 252 It is my lot to meet with traverses and disappointments. **1814** WORDSW. *Excursion* III. ad. fin., Like traverses and toils Must he again encounter. **1900** MORLEY *Cromwell* iii. 48 In days of fierce duress, of endless traverses and toils.

8. *Law.* The traversing or formal denial in pleading of some matter of fact alleged by the other side; also, a plea consisting of this; also, ? a case in which a traverse is pleaded.

1429 in *Calr. Doc. rel. Scot.* (1888) 405 For declaracion of traverss made or to be made be assise. **1459** *Rolls of Parlt.* V. 371/1 Jugement [was] yeven for the Kyng, in the said traverse. **1542–3** *Act 34 & 35 Hen. VIII*, c. 5 §15 Vntill the saide office be lawfully vndone by trauers or otherwyse. **1647** N. BACON *Disc. Govt. Eng.* I. xxiii. (1739) 41 That King put a Judge to death, for sentencing one to suffer death upon the Coroner's record, without allowing the Delinquent liberty of Traverse. **1780** BURKE *Sp. Econ. Reform* Wks. III. 247 His plea or traverse may be allowed as an answer to a charge, when a charge is made. **1824** H. J. STEPHEN *Pleading* 215 It is laid down as a rule that a traverse must not be taken upon matter of law. **1911** ODGERS *Comm. Law Eng.* V. xvii. II. 1214 The contradiction in terms of an allegation in the preceding pleading is technically known as a 'traverse'.

transf. **1575** LANEHAM *Let.* (1871) 17 If the dog in pleadyng woould pluk the bear by the throte, the bear with trauers woould claw him again by the skalp. *a* **1662** HEYLIN *Laud* II. 261 There was no Traverse to be made to this Dilemma. **1877** MORLEY *Crit. Misc.* Ser. II. 293 It is enough to meet them by a direct traverse, throwing the burden of proof upon them.

†**9.** A dispute, controversy. *at, in traverse*: in debate, in dispute. *Obs.*

c **1410** LYDG. *Life our Lady* in *MS. Soc. Antiq. 134* lf. 18 (Halliw.) Whanne they were at travers of thise thre, Everiche holdynge his opinioun. *c* **1448** in *Rec. City Norwich* (1906) 345 The pryour of Norwich that tyme being in travers with the said meir and comonalte. *c* **1490** *Paston Lett.* III. 366 The matier depending in travers bitwixt the saide parties. **1524** in J. H. Glover *Kingsthorpiana* (1883) 64 The forseid land and growns now in traves. **1553** GRIMALDE *Cicero's Offices* I. (1558) 27 If there bee a trauers in lawe: you shall rather defende your kinsman and frende than your neighbour. **1611** SPEED *Hist. Gt. Brit.* IX. xxiv. §279 The LL. Generals..would heare of no composition but for the Merchants ships onely, which whilest it was in trauise to and fro [etc.]. **1651** HOWELL *Venice* 2 These traverses twixt Saint Peter and Saint Mark could never shake Venice in the main of the Roman Religion.

†**10. a.** ? = PASSAGE *sb.* 13 c. *Obs.*

1599 DALLAM in *Early Voy. Levant* (Hakl. Soc.) 25 The firste day of maye we saw there greatest traverses or sportes that they have in all the yeare. **1604** E. G[RIMSTONE] *D'Acosta's Hist. Indies* IV. xxxix. 315 The fooleries, trickes, traverses, and pleasant sportes they make when they are taught. **1643** J. M. *Soveraigne Salve* 11 The malignant traverses of our Calumniators.

†**b.** ? A passage from a discourse or writing. *Obs.*

1608 PANKE *Fall of Babel* 56 He must needes meane by their own trauises out of him that Christ both spake and meant the bread when he said this is my body.

III. Senses denoting way across, crossing, way, path, track, course.

11. a. A passage by which one may traverse or cross; a way, pass; a crossing.

a **1678** MARVELL *Poems, Appleton Ho.* 17 The field In whose new traverse seemeth wrought A camp of battle newly fought. **1773** MRS. GRANT *Lett. fr. Mount.* (1807) I. viii. 66, I have got cold in these meadowy traverses. **1805** PIKE *Sources Mississ.* (1810) 22 The storm..burst upon us, in the Traverse, while making to Point de Sable. **1892** W. PIKE *North. Canada* 25 We put out..to paddle across the open traverse to the first of a group of islands.

b. *Arch.* (See quot.)

1842–76 GWILT *Encycl. Archit.* Gloss., *Traverse*, a gallery or loft of communication in a church or other large building.

12. *Naut.* **a.** The zigzag track of a vessel sailing against the wind; with *a* and *pl.*, each of the runs made by a ship in tacking.

1594 J. DAVIS *Seaman's Secr.* (1607) 46 A Travers is the varietie of the ships motion vpon euery alteration of Corses. **1644** MANWAYRING *Sea-Mans Dict.* 109 We call the way of the Ship (in respect of the points whereon we saile, and the Angles which the Ship makes in going to, and againe) the travers of the Ship. **1676** WOOD *Jrnl.* in *Acc. Sev. Late Voy.* I. (1694) 156 Courses *per* Traverse; true Course Protracted, with all impediments allowed, is North 43 d. **1762** *Gentl. Mag.* Mar. 99/1 This distance..may be increased tenfold by traverses which vessels must..make on such occasions. **1834** *Nat. Philos.* III. *Navig.* I. ii. §17 (Usef. Knowl. Soc.) She will be found one mile to the west of that place at the end of the traverse, for the total amount of westings exceeds the eastings by one mile.

β. **1669** STURMY *Mariner's Mag.* II. 46 Agreeing so well with his Travisses at Sea. *Ibid.* II. v. 64 [see *traverse-scale*].

b. = *traverse-board*: see 23. ? *Obs.*

1627 CAPT. SMITH *Seaman's Gram.* ii. 11 Vpon the Bittacle is also the Trauas, which is a little round boord full of holes..vpon which..they keepe an account, how many glasses they steare vpon euery point.

c. *transf.* Each lap, length, or *pli* of a zigzag ascending road.

1731 *Gentl. Mag.* Nov. 488/1 The Descent..is now firm, smooth and gradual, by 17 Traverses. **1775** JOHNSON *West. Islands* Wks. X. 353 We mounted by a military road cut in traverses.

IV. Concrete senses denoting something placed or extending across.

In these the popular forms *traves, -is*, etc., were very frequent: cf. TRAVIS, TREVIS.

13. a. A curtain or screen placed crosswise, or drawn across a room, hall, or theatre; also, a partition of wood, a screen of lattice-work, or the like. *Obs.* exc. *Hist.*

c **1374** CHAUCER *Troylus* III. 625 (674) Here after soone The voyde dronke, and trauers [*v.r.* traueres] drawe anoon. *c* **1386** —— *Merch. T.* 573 Men drynken and the trauers [*v.r.* trauys] drawe anon. **1474** in *Househ. Ord.* (1790) 28 We will that our sayd sonne in this chamber and for all nighte lyerye to be sette, the traverse drawne anone upon eight of the clocke. **1589** PUTTENHAM *Eng. Poesie* I. xvii. (Arb.) 51 The floore..had in it sundrie little diuisions by curteins as trauerses to serue for seueral roomes where they might..change their garments. **1605** B. JONSON *Volpone* V. iii. [Stage direct.] Volpone peeps from behinde a trauerse. **1700** FLOYER *Hot & Cold Bath.* I. iii. 55 Parted in the middle by a Travers of Wood. **1870** ROCK *Text. Fabr.* Introd. vii. 143 At top of and all along the travers ran the minstrel-gallery.

β. **1423** JAS. I *Kingis Q.* lxxxii, Ryght ouerthwert the chamber was there drawe A trevesse thin and quhite. *c* **1440** *Promp. Parv.* 499/2 Trauas, *transversum.* **1480** *Wardr. Acc. Edw. IV* (1830) 126 For making of ij travasses of grene sarsinett..iij s. **1488** *Acc. Ld. High Treas. Scot.* I. 100 For vij elne of tartar to a trevass. **1503** *Ibid.* II. 203 For xvj elne taffeti to be ane trevis to the Kingis bed. **1547** *Test. Ebor.* (Surtees) VI. 263 One traves for hir chamber of grene sarcenett and reide. **1613** BEAUMONT *Masque Inner T.* Argt., The fabricke was a mountaine with two descents, and severed with two travesses.

b. *fig.*

1609 DANIEL *Civ. Wars* VIII. lxxxviii, He drawes a Trauerse 'twixt his greeuances. **1655** FULLER *Ornithol.* (1867) 261 It is the hanging of such Curtains and Traverses before our Deeds which keep up our Reputation.

14. A small compartment shut off or enclosed by a curtain or screen in a church, house, etc.; a closet. *arch.*

1494 FABYAN *Chron.* VII. 473 Vpon a Saterdaye, the .xiiii. daye of the moneth of Octobre, both kynges beynge in .ii. trauersys, and in one chapell at Caleys, a masse was said before them. **1527** in Fiddes *Wolsey* (1726) II. 201 To the high alter wheare on the south side was ordeyned a goodlie travers for my Lord Cardinal. **1602** SEGAR *Hon. Mil. & Civ.* IV. xxii. 240 All Viscountesses may haue their gownes borne vp by a man... Also they may haue a Trauerse in their owne houses. **1633** DELL in *Ceremon. Coronat. Jas. I* (1685) 15 A little Traverse is to be made on the South side of the Altar.., for the King to..disrobe himself. **1902** *Westm. Gaz.* 11 Aug. 5/2 The King [Edward VII] went into his traverse and was there disrobed of his Imperial Mantle or Robe of State. *Ibid.*, In St. Edward's Chapel 'traverses', or dressing-rooms, had been curtained off for the use of the King and Queen.

β. **1526** *St. Papers Hen. VIII*, I. 172 Aftyr his first Masse was done, I wente unto hym, withyn his travesse. **1536** WRIOTHESLEY *Chron.* (Camden) I. 46 The King..then went into the traves that was made for him at the alters end. **1559** *Fabyan's Chron.* an. 1554. 562*/2 She [Q. Mary] went into a traueis [STRYPE traverse] made on the right side, and he into an other on the left side. **1593** in Hardman *Prayer-Bk.* (1890) 71 Her Majestie [Q. Elizabeth] entered her travess. **1605** *Ibid.* 157 Travase.

†**15.** A bar or barrier across anything; in quot. 1759 = BAR *sb.*[1] 15. *Obs.*

1575 CHURCHYARD *Chippes* (1817) 152 With baskets big, and things to serue the turne A crosse the streete, a trauers made there was. **1654** H. L'ESTRANGE *Chas. I* (1655) 137 The Communion Table..to be placed at the East end,.. with..a woodden traverse of railes before it, to keep Profanation off. **1700** FLOYER *Hot & Cold Bath.* I. iii. (1706) 58 [Baptisteries] were parted in the middle by a Travers of Wood. **1759** ADM. HOLMES in *Naval Chron.* July (1810) XXIV. 117 The Dublin and Medway got over the traverse [in the River St. Lawrence].

16. *Fortif.* A barrier or barricade thrown across an approach, the line of fire, etc. as a defence; *spec.* (*pl.*) parapets of earth raised at intervals across the terreplein of a rampart or the covered way of a fortress, to prevent its being enfiladed [= OF. *traverse.*]; a pair of right-angled bends in a trench for protection against enfilading fire.

1599 HAKLUYT *Voy.* II. 81 The captaine caused to make the traverses upon the wall whereas the breach was. **1602** LD. MOUNTJOY *Let.* in Moryson *Itin.* (1617) II. 213 The enemy having raised from mountaine to mountaine, from wood to wood, and from bogge to bogge long Traverses, with huge and high Flanckers of great stones, mingled with Turffe. **1700** RYCAUT *Hist. Turks* III. 112 The Defendants ..sprang a Mine under the Ruins of the Ravelin; which threw so much Earth into the Traverses of the Enemy, as buried many of their Labourers. **1767** STERNE *Tr. Shandy* IX. xxvi. 115 Uncle Toby..got his wound before the gate of St. Nicolas, in one of the traverses of the trench. **1802** C. JAMES *New Mil. Dict.* s.v. *Trenches*, On the angles or sides of the trench, there are lodgments or epaulements, in form of traverses, the better to hinder the sallies of the garrison. **1882** E. O'DONOVAN *Merv Oasis* II. xxxiii. 68 Opposite each gate was a large traverse, to protect it from artillery fire. *a* **1917** E. A. MACKINTOSH *War, the Liberator* (1918) 136 As MacTaggart turned back at the corner of the traverse he felt strangely comforted by the sight of MacRae. **1957** P. KEMP *Mine were of Trouble* iv. 76 It struck me that the trenches were very badly constructed, being..dug almost in a straight line instead of with traverses. **1971** S. HILL *Strange Meeting* ii. 139 The men had been getting their mid-day meal in this traverse when the bomb had landed in the middle of them.

β. **1598** BARRET *Theor. Warres* v. i. 125 The parts of a Bulwarke are the Trauesses or flankers. **1622** F. MARKHAM *Bk. War* IV. iii. 132 Lading and carrying the earth in barrels, baskets, and wheele barrows, by which are framed the Trauesses or flankers of the Bulwarke.

17. A natural structure forming a transverse partition, as the diaphragm; anything lying transversely or across. [= F. *traverse.*]

1604 T. WRIGHT *Passions* VI. 311 No man..can satisfie those demaunds..whether it [the Emmet] hath a Lyver, or no..whether a traverse or midriffe. **1657** THORNLEY tr. *Longus' Daphnis & Chloe* 136 His resolution was to imagine pleasure on this side the traverse.

18. Anything laid or fixed athwart or across; a cross-piece; a cross-beam in a timber roof; a transom; the transverse member in a cross; each of the rungs of a ladder (in quot. *fig.*), etc. [= F. *traverse.*]

1708 J. CHAMBERLAYNE *St. Gt. Brit.* II. III. x. (1737) 429 The Traverse or Cross of the Sword being of Silver over Gilt, is in Length seventeen Inches and a Half. **1727-41** CHAMBERS *Cycl.*, *Traverse* is particularly used for a piece of wood or iron placed transversely, to strengthen and fortify another: such are those used in gates, windows, etc. **1730** A. GORDON *Maffei's Amphith.* 295 Two round Holes in the Stone of the Threshold,..and two others correspondent with them, in the Traverse above. **1766** ENTICK *London* IV. 197 Upon that ball was a cross, 15 feet high, whose travers measured six feet. **1793** BURKE *Conduct Minority* Wks. VII. 285 To make every man..cautious how he makes himself one of the traverses of a ladder, to help such a man..to climb up to the highest authority. **1838** *Civil Eng. & Arch. Jrnl.* I. 198/1 The cast iron rail can be fixed to the blocks or bearers with the patent vertical ties, chairs, and traverses, or in any of the usual ways.

19. *Card-making.* A transverse section of a cardboard.

1837 WHITTOCK, etc. *Bk. Trades* (1842) 100 The boards are first cut into slips, or, as they are termed, traverses, containing five cards each.

†**20.** The reverse side of a coin or medal. *Obs.*

1622 PEACHAM *Compl. Gent.* xii. (1634) 119 *As*..was worth a halfe-penny farthing. And it is discerned by this figure I. with the head or prowe of a Ship on the traverse; and Janus bifrons on the forepart.

¶**21.** *Her.* Stated to denote a bearing resembling a pile or a chevron turned sideways.

(But app. an error due to mistaking TRAVERSE *a.* 2, 2 b, for a sb.; Guillim, cited for this use, has the word only as adj.)

c **1828** BERRY *Encycl. Her.* I. Gloss., *Traverse*, sometimes termed a *doublet*, and, in French, *embrassé droit*, is a bearing, according to Guillim, resembling the cheveron, which issues from two angles of one side of the escocheon, and meets in a point about the middle of the other side.

V. Phrases and Combinations.

†**22.** Phrases. **a.** ***at, in, on travers, traverse***, crossways, sideways, transversely; in flank; with a side glance, askance. *Obs.* (Cf. A-TRAVERS.) [OF. *à, en travers.*] See also 9.

c **1330** R. BRUNNE *Chron. Wace* (Rolls) 13394 Þe seriauntz & þe archers..were set..To kepe þe Romayns at trauers. *c* **1450** *Merlin* 262 He turned the heed in trauers, and made semblant as he hadde hym not herde. *Ibid.* 425 He loked proudly on trauerse. **1586** FERNE *Blaz. Gentrie* 29 Great peeces of tymber or logges of woode..set in trauerse ouer some passage, bridge or gate. **1659** LEAK *Waterwks.* 14 They must be soldered a travers above the great Pipes. **1678** MOXON *Mech. Exerc.* iv. 66 Joyners work as well upon the Traverse..as with the Grain of the wood.

†**b.** ***through the travers***, lit. rendering of F. *par le travers*, through the transverse extent, through the breadth, across. *Obs.*

c **1489** CAXTON *Sonnes of Aymon* xxviii. 576 [He] went.. thrugh the travers of the wodes wel the space of viii dayes.

23. *attrib.* and *Comb.* (sometimes of the verb-stem), as ***traverse-rag*** (see 13), ***-sailing*** (see 12); **traverse-board, travis-board**, *Naut.* a circular board marked with the points of the compass, and having holes and pegs by which to indicate the course of the ship (cf. 12); **traverse-book, travis-book**, a log-book; **traverse-circle**, a circular or segmental track on which a gun-carriage is turned to point the gun in any required direction; **traverse-drill**, a drill in which the boring tool has at the required depth a lateral motion; also, a drill in which the drill-stock is adjustable laterally on the bed; **traverse jury**, a jury empanelled to adjudicate on an appeal from another jury: see sense 8 and TRAVERSE *v.* 12; **traverse line**, a line in a traverse-survey; **traverse-man**, one who makes the traverses (sense 3) in a topographical survey; **traverse-map**, a rough map, the main points on which have been determined by traversing: see TRAVERSE *v.* 7; †**traverse-nail**, a kind or size of nail used in making partitions; **traverse-point**, the highest point of a mountain-pass; **traverse-saw**: see quot.; **traverse-scale, travis-**: see quot.; **traverse-survey**, a survey made for the purpose of locating the features of a country along a narrow strip, as for a canal, a railway, or a boundary line, as distinct from a general trigonometrical survey of the whole country; **traverse-warp machine**, a bobbin-net machine in which the warp traverses instead of the carriages.

a **1625** *Nomenclator Navalis* (MS. Harl. 2301), **Trauers bord* is a board which they keepe in the Steeridg hauing the 32 pointes of the Compasse marked in it with little holes on every pointe like a Noddy-bord. **1626** CAPT. SMITH *Accid. Yng. Seamen* 11 The trauas boord. **1704** J. HARRIS *Lex. Techn.* I, *Traverse-Board*..upon it, by moving of a little Peg from Hole to Hole, the Steers-man keeps an account how many Glasses (that is, half Hours) the Ship Steers upon any Point. **1867** SMYTH *Sailor's Word-bk.*, *Traverse-board.* *a* **1679** SIR J. MOORE *Syst. Math.* (1681) I. 271 This account ruff taken off the Log-board, ought to be entred into a Book called a *Traverse Book or Log Book. **1727-41** CHAMBERS *Cycl.* s.v. *Log*, They are entered into the log-book, or traverse-book, ruled and columned just as the log-board is. **1877** KNIGHT *Dict. Mech.*, **Traverse-circle*,..a circular track on which the chassis traverse-wheels of a barbette carriage, mounted with a center or rear pintle, run while the gun is being pointed. **1864** WEBSTER, **Traverse-drill*, 1. a machine-tool for feeding a drill into the work. (*Local U.S.*) 2. A cotter-drill. (*Eng.*) **1877** KNIGHT *Dict. Mech.*, *Traverse-drill.* **1823** *Rep. Sel. Comm. Sewers Metrop.* 15 We have never had any *traverse juries in the Tower Hamlets sewers within my recollection. **1900** H. M. WILSON *Topogr. Survey.* x. 195 *Traverse lines may be run in conjunction with a trigonometric survey to fill in the details. *Ibid.* 202 The *traverseman having set up and oriented his plane table. **1901** *Year-bk. U.S. Dept. Agric.* 121 When there are [no] accurate county maps it is almost impossible to carry on the soil survey except through the co-operation of State institutions which will undertake to make a *traverse map. *c* **1350** in Hope *Windsor Castle* (1913) 165 In xxx[ml] *Traversnail emptis pro parietibus camerarum canonicorum. **1358-60** *Ibid.* 216 In..lx mill. clavorum vocatorum travers. **1886** RUSKIN *Præterita* I. ix. 304 This main pass of Jura..reaches its *traverse-point very nearly under the highest summit of that part of the chain. **1700** CONGREVE *Way of World* v. i, Dining behind a *traverse rag in a shop no bigger than a bird-cage. **1787** A. CLARKE in *Life* (1840) App. 154 After much *traverse sailing, occasioned by the wind being almost directly opposite, we came to anchor. **1843** *Penny Cycl.* XXV. 169/2 Traverse sailing..is merely the sailing on different points of the compass, for short distances, in succession. **1877** KNIGHT *Dict. Mech.*, **Traverse-saw*, a cross-cutting saw which moves on ways across the piece. **1669** STURMY *Mariner's Mag.* II. 46 A Portable most useful *Travis-Scale. *Ibid.* II. v. 64 The Travis-Scale... An Instrument the most easie, ready, and necessary..for the working of Travises, and correcting your dead Reckoning. **1896** MARKHAM in *Geog. Jrnl.* VII. 187 [He] set out to explore the river Madre de Dios... He was supplied with compass, sextant, and chronometer, and corrected his *traverse-survey by daily observations of the sun. **1839** URE *Dict. Arts*, etc. 733 There are six different systems of bobbin-net machines. 1. Heathcoak's patent machine. 2. Brown's *traverse warp [etc.].

traverse ('trævəs, trə'vɜːs), *a. rare.* Also 5, 7 **travers**, 7 **treverse**. [a. OF. *travers* (also in Cotgr. 1611):—late pop.L. and med.L. *trāversus*:—L. *transversus*: see TRANSVERSE *a.*]

1. Lying, passing, or extending across; cross, transverse.

1426 LYDG. *De Guil. Pilgr.* 6999 Ouer my shuldere she yt [the scrip] caste And be-gan to bookele yt faste I travers wyse. **1598** STOW *Surv.* xl. (1603) 410 The oversight and profites of a Crosse ferrie, or trauerse ferrie ouer the Thames ..before that any bridge was builded. **1625** PURCHAS *Pilgrims* II. VII. vi. 1122 The treverse wind..is so forcible.. that it raiseth great heapes of sand. **1634** in *Archæologia* XXXV. 197 In the kitchen... A travers barre for the chimney. **1703** MAUNDRELL *Journ. Jerus.* (1721) 112 The traverse part of the Cross. **1894** *Westm. Gaz.* 9 May 4/2 The explosions at the Waltham Cordite Factory..the strong traverse walls being blown to pieces.

†**2.** Slanting; oblique. *Obs.*

1609 HOLLAND *Amm. Marcell.* 412 With grim lookes and traverse cast of eye. **1610** GUILLIM *Heraldry* I. viii. 34 A Gusset..is formed of a Trauerse line drawne either from the Dexter or Sinister Chiefe point..tending to the Honour point, and descending from thence..to the extreme base parts of the Escocheon. *a* **1649** DRUMM. OF HAWTH. *Fam. Ep.* Wks. (1711) 146 The deviser of this [chess] would represent unto us a game of state..the bishops..should be ..grave men, who by oblique, traverse and mystical ways.. should effectuate their master's designs and safety.

b. *Her.* ***parted per pile traverse***: said of the shield when divided by oblique transverse lines forming the figure of a pile (PILE *sb.*[1] 4) turned sideways.

1638 GUILLIM *Heraldry* v. i. (ed. 3) 365 He beareth parted per pyle traverse, Argent, and Gules. **1704** J. HARRIS *Lex. Techn.* I. s.v., There is also a Partition of an Eschucheon used in Heraldry of this Figure, which they call Parted per Pile [*printed* Pale] Traverse, Argent and Gules.

traverse ('trævəs, trə'vɜːs), *v.* Forms: 4-7 **trauerse**, (4 *Sc.* **trawers**), 5-7 **trauers, travers**, (6 **trauarse, trauerce**), 6- **traverse**. Pa. t. and pple. **traversed**: formerly often **traverst**. Also *β.* 5 **trauess**, 6 *Sc.* **trevess, treviss, treveiss**, 6-7 **traues, -ves**; 4-5 **trauys**, 5 **trauiss**, 6 **trauice**, 6-7 **trauise**, 7 **traviss**; 6-7 (9 *dial.*) **travish**; 6 **trauas, -ase, -aise**, 6-8 **travas**. [a. F. *traverser* (11th c.) to cross, thwart, f. *travers* TRAVERSE *sb.* or *a.* Cf. Prov. *traversar*, Sp. *travesar*, Cat. *-essar*, It. *traversare*:—late pop.L. *trāversāre* for *transversāre*, in late L. to cross, throw across, f. *trāversus* = *transversus*, pa. pple. of *transvertĕre* to turn across: see TRANSVERT *v.* The *β*-forms are popular corruptions, due to phonetic weakening of second syllable: cf. the Sp. and Cat. forms. The vb. is now often stressed on the 2nd syllable in British and American English, and this has influenced the pronunciation of its derivative forms.

I. To run across or through; to cross.

For intransitive uses related to these, see branch IV.

1. *trans.* †**a.** To run (something) through *with* a weapon; to pierce, stab (*obs.*); **b.** to pass through as a weapon, to penetrate, pierce. Now *rare.*

c **1400** *Laud Troy Bk.* 5841 With a spere he him trauersed. **1513** DOUGLAS *Æneis* x. viii. 98 The schaft..throw the bordour of the scheyld swa persyt, Quhill fynaly in sum deyll it traversyt, And hurt a part of Turnus big body. **1613** R. CAWDREY *Table Alph.* (ed. 3), *Trauerse*, strike, or thrust through. **1846** BRITTAN tr. *Malgaigne's Man. Oper. Surg.* 410 The needles..traverse the intestine on the opposite side. **1878** BROWNING *La Saisiaz* 356 While I watch it [torture] traversing the human heart.

c. To cross (a thing) with a line, stripe, bar, barrier, or anything that intersects. In *passive*, To be crossed *with* lines, etc. Now *rare.*

c **1420** *Anturs of Arth.* 354 (Thornton MS.) In paulle purede with pane, fulle precyously dyghte, Trofelyte and trauerste wythe trewloues in trete. *a* **1548** HALL *Chron.*, *Hen. VIII*, 6 b, Twoo long gouenes of yelowe satin, trauarsed with white satin. **1600** DYMMOK *Ireland* (1843) 45 The rebells traversed the same [entrance] with a barricado with doble flancks. **1748** *Anson's Voy.* II. vi. 196 They traversed the streets with barricadoes. *a* **1810** TANNAHILL *Poems* (1846) 37 His chequered robes excited their surprise, Richly travers'd with various glowing dyes.

†**d.** To get across (a horse); to mount, bestride.

1438 *Bk. Alexander Gt.* (Bann. Cl.) 101 Bot he had nocht this counsale than, Trauersit his hors as michty man, He turnit nocht abasitly.

e. *Her.* To place across or crosswise (on the shield).

1610 BOLTON *Elem. Armories* 21 Three parallel Arrowes trauersed barre-ways.

2. a. To cross (a mountain, river, sea) in travelling; now *esp.* to pass or journey across, over, or through; to pass through (a region) from side to side, or from end to end; also, to pass through (a space or solid body), as rays of light, etc.

In quot. 1708, to pass the fingers across.

c **1489** CAXTON *Sonnes of Aymon* iii. 105 Every man wente to hys countrey not the ryght waye but traversynge the mountaynes. **1590** GREENE *Mourn. Garm.* (1616) 4 What Experience Vlisses got by trauersing strange Countries. **1667** MILTON *P.L.* IX. 66 Thrice the Equinoctial Line He circl'd; four times cross'd the Carr of Night From Pole to Pole, traversing each Colure. **1708** J. PHILIPS *Cyder* Poems (1778) 111 Blind British bards with volant touch Traverse loquacious strings. **1748** *Anson's Voy.* Introd. Civb, The Manila ships are the only ones which have ever traversed this vast ocean. **1839** G. BIRD *Nat. Phil.* 264 Currents of positive electricity will traverse the wire. **1868** LYELL *Princ. Geol.* (ed. 10) II. III. xxxix. 355 The jaguar traverses with ease the largest streams. **1880** C. R. MARKHAM *Peruv. Bark* 49 They traversed the valley of Chinchao.

β. *a* **1533** LD. BERNERS *Huon* xxxv. 111 Thou dydest swym in yᵉ see, & trauesyd yᵉ grete waues. **1585** T. WASHINGTON tr. *Nicholay's Voy.* II. xi. 45 b, Trauishing this goulph, a Northerly wynde came full in the face of vs.

b. To trace (a geometrical figure, or part of one) continuously without lifting the pen or pencil. Also *intr.* or *absol.*

1905 J. C. WILSON *Traversing Geometr. Figures* I. §1. 5 To traverse in a figure, or in a part of it, is to trace a path along its lines, no line being traced twice over, ending at a point at which no path in the figure, or the given part of it, remains untraced. *Ibid.* §9. 16 Rules for traversing figures which can be exhausted by a single traverse.

3. *fig.* (and in *fig.* context). To 'go through' (life, time, or anything figured as an extended space or region); to read through or consider thoroughly (a subject, treatise, etc.).

c **1477** CAXTON *Jason* 4 Their lyf was trauersid in contynnuelle bewailing. **1573** TUSSER *Husb.* (1878) 137 Timelie to trauerse the thing that thou triue. *a* **1716** SOUTH *Serm.* (1744) X. 186 Traversing those several Scriptures, which these men alledge in the behalf of their opinion. **1823** SCOTT *Quentin D.* iv, Such were the thoughts which hastily traversed the mind of young Durward. **1874** GREEN *Short Hist.* vii. §6. 398 It was in the years which we are traversing that England became firmly Protestant.

β. **1590** NASHE *Pasquil's Apol.* I. Aiv, M. Bucer, Peter Martyr, and..the B. of Sarisburie, haue trauast our Church with as graue a gate as he. **1606** S. GARDINER *Bk. Angling* To Rdr., After thou hast but cursorily trauised this Treatise. **1616** W. FORDE *Serm.* 4 We will, by Gods assistance.. travish the same ground we have began to tread.

4. Of a thing: To lie, be situated, extend, stretch, or 'run' across (something); to cross, intersect.

1481 CAXTON *Myrr.* II. iii. 68 Thise two flodes [Tygris & Eufrates] trauerse many grete contrees. **1682** SIR H. PIERS *Descr. Westmeath* in *Collect. de Rebus Hibern.* I. 65 The lintel that traverseth the head of the door is of one entire stone. **1683** *Brit. Spec.* 145 The Romans gave them their help to build another Wall of Stone,..traversing the Island in a direct line from East to West. **1748** *Anson's Voy.* II. iii. 142 The country in the neighbourhood was so..traversed with mountains. **1829** I. TAYLOR *Enthus.* viii. 204 The dead solitudes of sand, traversed..by the Nile. **1835** W. IRVING *Tour Prairies* xviii. 155 Deeply worn footpaths..traversing the country. **1851** RICHARDSON *Geol.* viii. 270 Canals that everywhere traverse bone..called Haversian.

5. To go to and fro over or along; to cross and recross. ***to traverse one's ground***, to move from side to side, in fencing or fighting.

1590 SPENSER *F.Q.* II. viii. 35 So both attonce him charge ..With hideous strokes.. That forced him his ground to traverse wyde. **1595** *Locrine* I. Prol. 5 A mightie Lion, ruler of the woods,..Traverst the groues. **1625** K. LONG tr. *Barclay's Argenis* IV. xiii. 283 He..traversed his ground, came on, and gave backe, tyring his Enemy with change of play. **1829** SCOTT *Anne of G.* xxv, The Duke traversed the apartment with unequal steps, in much agitation. **1878** C. STANFORD *Symb. Christ* v. 142 The spirit of evil traversing the earth to tempt the members of Christ's flock.

β. **1577** HARRISON *England* II. xiv. (1877) I. 265 To meet with his enimie in the plaine field..where he may trauaise his ground. **1592** WYRLEY *Armorie, Capitall de Buz* 152 Trauasing Fraunce vp and downe at pleasure. **1613** SIR E. HOBY *Countersnarle* 27 Thus doth this Spider-Catcher travaise his ground, with a goodly flourish.

†**6.** *Carpentry.* To plane (wood) across the grain. *Obs.*

1678 [see TRAVERSING *vbl. sb.*]. **1703** T. N. *City & C. Purchaser 268 Traverse*, A Term in Joynery, signifying to plain a Board, (or the like) across the Grain.

7. *Surveying.* To determine the positions of points on the earth's surface by measuring the lengths and azimuths of a connected series of straight lines; to make or execute a traverse (TRAVERSE *sb.* 3) of (a region); to delimit (an area) by thus determining the position of points on its boundaries; to trace the course of (a road, river, etc.) in this way.

1874 C. C. KING *Map & Plan Drawing* 69 The next operation is that of tracing, or, it is technically called, 'traversing', any roads that may intersect the area, or if none be present, a line passing through that portion which contains the largest number of natural or artificial peculiarities. **1900** H. M. WILSON *Topogr. Survey* x. 195 Their topography is most easily obtained by means of traversing. **1908** H. LYONS *Cadastral Surv. Egypt* 211 The province..was divided up into sections..which approximated to districts, and these large blocks were traversed with care, the work being done by the more efficient of the staff who also traversed the villages lying on the boundary.

II. To turn, move, or bring (a thing) across.

8. a. *trans.* To alter the position of (a gun, etc.) laterally, so as to take aim. Also *absol.*

1628 DIGBY *Voy. Medit.* (1868) 78 His men..were seene busie traversing their gunnes vpon the Eagle. **1688** R. HOLME *Armoury* III. xviii. (Roxb.) 140/2 The laying or remoueing of a peece of Ordinance till it come to lie with the marke, is termed traversing of the peece. **1727–41** CHAMBERS *Cycl.*, *Traverse*, in gunnery, signifies to turn or point a piece of ordnance..upon her platform. **1859** F. A. GRIFFITHS *Artill. Man.* (1862) 196 No. 3..traverses with the handspike. **1899** *Westm. Gaz.* 30 Nov. 4/2 The gun can be traversed—that is, the direction of its aim laterally can be varied—by means of a wooden handspike.

β. **1622** R. HAWKINS *Voy. S. Sea* (1847) 195 An English gunner..being travesing of a peece in the bowe, to make his shott, had his head carryed away with the first or second shott made out of our shippe. **1627** CAPT. SMITH *Seaman's Gram.* xiv. 65 To trauas a Peece is to turne her which way you will vpon her Platforme. **1644** NYE *Gunnery* II. (1670) 2 There you may best observe, as the Peece is travissing, when you are in a direct line with the Mark. **1704** J. HARRIS *Lex. Techn.* I, *Travas*, a Term in Gunnery.

b. *intr.* To carry a gun so that it points at the head or body of another sportsman.

1886 *Badminton Libr., Shooting* (1895) 177 Many men who shoot a great deal 'traverse' habitually, and the habit once acquired is most difficult to eradicate.

†**9.** To turn away, to divert; *fig.* to pervert. *Obs. rare.*

1623 SIR E. DIGBY *Sp.* in Rushw. *Hist. Coll.* (1659) I. 132 For the Recovery of the Patrimony belonging to the King of Bohemia, now almost traversed from him, and in the possession of a powerful Enemy. **1689** OWEN *True Nat. Gosp. Ch.* x. Wks. 1855 XVI. 183 It is the mystery of iniquity that hath traversed these things into..a posture unintelligible to spiritual wisdom.

10. To carry in a trailing manner; to trail. *dial.*

1814 W. NICHOLSON *Peacock* III. 22 So ha'e I seen.. mystic knighthood o' the apron; Wi' empty pride, in monkish gown, Travish a Bible thro' the town. **1824** MACTAGGART *Gallovid. Encycl.*, *Travish*, to carry after a trailing manner.

III. To direct oneself or act against.

11. a. *trans.* To act against, to go counter to; to cross, thwart, oppose.

c **1400** *Gosp. Nicodemus* 1301 (Galba MS.) He has me tenid and trauerst [**14..** *v.r.* trauyst] ay in all þe werkes I haue wroght. **14..** *Beryn* 3411 We submit vs all..nevir for to travers o word þat þow seyst. **1548** UDALL *Erasm. Par. Luke* xii. 119 The vnluckie ende of trauersing the lawe. **1652** NEEDHAM tr. *Selden's Mare Cl.* 2 Here..the difficultie ceased not, becaus som did travers the execution of the sentence. **1712** ARBUTHNOT *John Bull* IV. iii, He resolved to traverse this new project. **1771** LUCKOMBE *Hist. Print.* 274 To inclose a whole sentence between Parentheses..is traversing the intention of Parentheses. **1855** MACAULAY *Hist. Eng.* xvii. IV. 75 Berwick had sent Maxwell to watch their motions and to traverse their designs.

β. **14..** [see a]. *c* **1460** *Towneley Myst.* xxv. 153 That trature trauesses vs all-way. *c* **1480** *Kyng & Hermit* 87 in Hazl. *E.P.P.* I. 17 When that they were travyst [? travayst] And of herborow were abayst.

†**b.** *intr.* To go (*against*), go counter. *Obs. rare.*

1377 LANGL. *P. Pl.* B. XII. 284 Trewth þat trespassed neuere ne transuersed [*v.r.* trauersed] aȝeines his lawe. **1393** *Ibid.* C. IV. 449 Ho so takeþ aȝen treuthe oþer transuerseþ [*v.r.* trauerseth] aȝens reson.

12. a. *trans. Law.* To contradict formally (a matter of fact alleged in the previous pleading); to deny at law; *spec.* in phr. ***to traverse an indictment***, to deny or take issue upon an indictment; ***to traverse an office***, to deny or impeach the validity of an inquest of office. Also *absol.*

[**1292** BRITTON II. xxvi. §2 Et autres plusours excepcions ..porra le tenaunt traverser, et dire, qu il ne fust unques seisi.] *a* **1325** *MS. Rawl. B. 520* lf. 96 b, þer me ne mai noȝt vochen warant out of þe lignage bote onliche trauersen þe Entree. **1467** in *Eng. Gilds* (1870) 394 To travers the seid presentements or accusement for his acquitalle. **1553** T. WILSON *Rhet.* 47 In traversyng a cause before a judge. **1588** LAMBARDE *Eiren.* IV. xiii. 542 To Trauerse an Enditement.. is to take issue vpon the chiefe matter therof, which is none other..then..to deny the point of the Enditement. **1647** N. BACON *Disc. Govt. Eng.* I. xxxvi. (1739) 54 In the answer of the Defendant, he either traversed the matter in fact, or confessed and justified, or confessed and submitted. **1791** HAMPSON *Mem. J. Wesley* II. 33 If they were disappointed at the quarter sessions,..they traversed and appealed to the upper courts. **1823** *Rep. Sel. Comm. Sewers Metrop.* 17 In all cases where the presentment of the jury is traversed,..that traverse must be tried by another jury, to be summoned by the sheriff, which is called a traverse jury. **1911** ODGERS *Comm. Law Eng.* V. xvii. II. 1214 Allegations of fact alone should be traversed, and these he must not traverse 'evasively, but answer the point of substance'.

†**b.** To affirm, by way of contradicting a charge or allegation. *Obs.*

1491 *Act 7 Hen. VII*, c. 2 §4 Yf..any man will travers that the seid Warrant is not the dede of hym that is named. **1654** FULLER *Two Serm.* 16 What will it benefit a Lamb to traverse his innocence in the pawes of a Lyon?

†**13.** To dispute; to discuss. *Obs.*

c **1440** *Partonope* 1772 Eche man did travers Others witte. **1503** HAWES *Examp. Virt.* xxviii, Longe, haue they trauerst ..Whiche of them sholde haue the preemynence. **1549** COVERDALE, etc. *Erasm. Par. 1 Cor.* 16 The matter..muste bee trauersed before the commen officers. **1589** NASHE *Anat. Absurd.* Epist. ¶iij, Amongst other talke which was generally traversed amongst us. **1599** —— *Lenten Stuffe* (1871) 29, I could run ten quires of paper out of breath, in further traversing her rights and dignities.

IV. Intransitive sense allied to I and II.

These do not appear in Fr., in which *traverser* is always transitive. But in Eng. they sometimes appear earlier than the transitive senses to which they are specially allied.

14. a. *intr.* To move, pass, or go across; to cross, cross over; (of a ship) to tack. (Cf. 2 and 5.)

1375 BARBOUR *Bruce* XVII. 532 So lang thai raid distroyande swa, As thai trauersit to and fra. **1517** TORKINGTON *Pilgr.* (1884) 6 We traversed owt of that Ryver into a nother lytell Ryver. **1677** W. HUBBARD *Narrative* Pref., Purchase wrote much, Hacluyt traversed farr. **1782** ELIZ. BLOWER *Geo. Bateman* II. 124 For some minutes he traversed backwards and forwards from the window to the door. **1897** *Scotsman* 14 May 6/1 The railway would so seriously injure the scenery of the valley and lake along which it would traverse.

β. **1438** *Bk. Alexander Gt.* (Bann. Cl.) 85 Daucline.. Trauissit challange for to maik. **1568** *Satir. Poems Reform.* xlvi. 53 Steir be the compas..Syne treveiss still, and lay abowt. *a* **1578** LINDESAY (Pitscottie) *Chron. Scot.* (S.T.S.) I. 213 Thair was tuo schipis..trevessing wpe and doune the firth. **1591** LYLY *Endym.* III. iii, We will trauice. Will you goe, sir? **1892** QUILLER COUCH *Three Ships*, etc. 179 Not a tint did he work, but kept travishing back and forth.

b. *fig.*

1566 PAINTER *Pal. Pleas.* I. 90 This miserable louer, trauersing in seuerall mindes,..chaunged his mynde a thousand times in an hower. **1645** MILTON *Tetrach.* Wks. 1738 I. 250 That it does not traverse from the Closet of Conscience to the Courts of Civil or Canon Law. **1747** *Mem. Nutrebian Crt.* I. 203 We shall traverse back to some particulars of her education. **1824** GALT *Rothelan* II. xiii, His thoughts tossed and traversed like the inconstant clouds.

†**c.** In dancing: see quot. 1616. *Obs.*

1584 B. R. tr. *Herodotus* II. 86 Many [women] trauise & daunce minionly. **1616** BULLOKAR *Eng. Expos.*, *Trauerse*, to march vp and downe or to moue the feete with proportion, as in dancing.

15. To move from side to side; to dodge (cf. 5); in quot. 1635 *trans.* to drive by 'traversing'. *Obs.* or *arch.*

1470–85 MALORY *Arthur* X. xxx. 463 Thus they tracyd and trauercyd and hewe on helmes and hawberkes. *a* **1548** HALL *Chron., Hen. V*, 50 Thus this battaile continued iii long houres, some strake, some defended, some foyned, some trauersed, some kylled, some toke prisoners. **1598** SHAKS. *Merry W.* II. iii. 25 To see thee fight, to see thee foigne, to see thee trauerse. **1635** EARL STRAFFORD *Lett. & Disp.* (1739) I. 478 He shall be a very artificial Fencer..that traverseth me forth of my Ground. **1823** SCOTT *Quentin D.* xiv, To harass his antagonist, by traversing on all sides, with a suddenness of motion and rapidity of attack. **1858** MORRIS *Def. Guenevere* 13 The fight began,..Ever Sir Launcelot kept him on the right, And traversed warily.

†**16.** To digress. *Obs. rare.*

1530 PALSGR. 761/2, I traverse, I go from one mater to an other... Nowe you leave the purpose and begyn to traverse.

17. To come or fall across each other; to cross. (Cf. 4.)

1669 STURMY *Mariner's Mag.* I. ii. 17 It bloweth a storm —furle the Sail fast, and fasten the Yards, that they may not travers and gall.

18. To run freely in its proper socket, ring, channel, or course (as a rope); to turn or move freely from side to side on a traverse-circle (as a gun); to turn about on a pivot (as the needle of the compass). (Cf. 8.)

1829 MARRYAT *F. Mildmay* xxiii, Sharp frosts..obliged us to pour boiling water into the sheaves of the blocks to thaw them, and allow the ropes to traverse. **1832** *Nat. Philos.* II. *Magnetism* iii. §91. 22 (Usef. Knowl. Soc.) In moving..towards the position which it thus tends to assume, the needle of the compass is said to traverse. **1849** CUPPLES *Green Hand* iv, The tiller-ropes cheeping as they traversed. **1851** *Ord. & Regul. R. Engineers* §19. 94 Iron Traversing Platforms..so constructed, that..they may be made to traverse in any direction. **1856** KANE *Arct. Expl.* I. x. 113 It traversed freely by a ring on a loop or bridle. **1863** *Possibilities of Creation* 175 Let the head..have no power of traversing upon the atlas, and..that..spinal column.. become as stiff as an iron bar, and..poor humanity would be completely crippled.

19. a. *Falconry.* To move from side to side, to wriggle, as a hawk. **b.** *Manège.* To advance obliquely, as a horse: see quot. 1753.

1486 *Bk. St. Albans, Hawking* a vij, Ye shall knawe it whan she trauersith withe hir bodi. **1544** BETHAM *Precepts War* I. cxi. Fvb, To take vp his horse with the spurres, that he may praunse, trauerse, and flyng wyth the heeles. **1610** GUILLIM *Heraldry* III. xx. (1660) 223 She [a Hawk] putteth over, when she removeth her meat from her Gorge, into her Bowels, by traversing with her body, but chiefly with her Neck, as a Crane..doth. **1753** CHAMBERS *Cycl. Supp.* s.v., A horse is said to traverse, when he cuts his tread cross-wise; throwing his croupe to one side, and his head to another. **1884** E. L. ANDERSON *Mod. Horsemanship* II. xii. 119 *Traversing* is the movement in which the horse passes to either side..upon two paths, the forehand following one, the hind-quarters, slightly retired, the other.

20. To advance or ascend in a zigzag line. (Cf. TRAVERSE *sb.* 12 c.)

1773 Johnson *Let. to Mrs. Thrale* 6 Sept., Our way now lay over the mountains, which are not to be passed by climbing them directly, but by traversing.

21. *Mountaineering.* To make one's way in a horizontal or transverse direction across the face of a mountain or rock. (See TRAVERSE *sb.* 6.)

1893 C. Wilson *Mountaineering* vi. 88 To traverse for some distance on steep snow or grass. *Ibid.* Gloss., *Traverse*, ..(*a.*) to cross a mountain slope horizontally. **1897** O. G. Jones *Rock-climbing* 123 At the foot we joined up again and traversed round to the 'sheep walk'. *Ibid.* 269 The climber hangs by his hands,..and traverses across the face by sheer strength of his arms.

V. From TRAVERSE *sb.*

22. *trans.* To furnish or fortify with a traverse or traverses (see TRAVERSE *sb.* 16). *rare.*

1828 J. M. Spearman *Brit. Gunner* (ed. 2) 360 Of 170 shells, filled with powder, that were fired at the work when traversed, 58 took effect;..the effect on the traverses was considerable, and they were much ruined.

†**traverse**, *adv.* (*prep.*) *Obs.* Also 5–7 **travers.** [Sometimes app. aphetic for A-TRAVERS *adv.* = F. *à travers*; sometimes advb. use of TRAVERSE *a.*] Across; crosswise; athwart; transversely.

c **1450** Lovelich *Grail* liii. 211 Into A wast lawnde he happede there..and thus travers he Rod tyl Myd Nyht. **1525** Ld. Berners *Froiss.* II. xli. 128 The erle..caused..hyghe trees to be hewen downe, and layde trauers one ouer another. **1640** Howell *Dodona's Gr.* (1645) 2 A square of 550 miles travers. **1725** *Bradley's Fam. Dict.* s.v. *Willow*, Let them be copp'd Traverse, and not Obliquely, at one foot or somewhat more from the Ground.

b. *traverse to*, *of*, right across; = B.

1548 Patten *Exped. Scotl.* G vij, The furrowes laye trauers to their course. **1654** H. L'Estrange *Chas. I* (1655) 68 Coming counter and travers of our Canon, they received the greater losse.

B. *prep.* Across. (Cf. A-TRAVERS *prep.*)

a **1548** Hall *Chron., Hen. VIII*, 3 After them came sir Thomas Brandon..clothed in tissue..and traverse his body, a greate Bauderike of Gold. **1610** Holland *Camden's Brit., Scot.* II. 25 Hardly one by one can passe up, and that ..by Grees or steps cut out aslope travers the rock.

traversed ('trævəst, trə'vɜːst), *ppl. a.* Also 6–7 **trauerst.** [f. TRAVERSE *v.* + -ED[1].]

1. Placed or laid across; crossed; transverse.

1607 Shaks. *Timon* v. iv. 7 [We] Haue wander'd with our trauerst Armes, and breathd Our sufferance vainly. **1621** Lodge *Summary Du Bartas* I. 286 The Stomake..closeth it selfe on euery side, by meanes of the trauersed fibers.

2. Passed or travelled over; traced continuously; penetrated, pierced.

1599 T. M[oufet] *Silkwormes* 61 Lifelesse in midway of their trauerst round. **1878** Browning *La Saisiaz* 357 Traversed heart must tell its story uncommented on. **1905** J. C. Wilson *Traversing Geometr. Figures* I. §4. 10 If *B* was intermediate, the traversed lines at *B* are even in number.

3. Of a horse: see quots. Cf. TRAVERSE *v.* 19 b.

1611 Cotgr., *Travat*, a horse which is trauersed; viz. hath two white feet on the right, or left side. **1678** in Phillips (ed. 4). **1720** W. Gibson *Dict. Horses* i. 5 Those which are cross-traversed, having the Fore-foot on the Near Side, and Hinder Foot on the Far Side, or [vice versa] White.

4. *Her.* See quot., and cf. TRAVERSE *a.* 2, 2 b.

c **1828** Berry *Encycl. Her.* I. Gloss., *Traversed*, (French, *contourné*) turned to the sinister side of the shield.

traversely ('trævəslı, trə'vɜːslı), *adv. rare.* [f. TRAVERSE *a.* + -LY[2].] Crosswise; transversely.

1656 [?J. Sergeant] tr. *T. White's Peripat. Inst.* 151 Being carry'd traversly by some motion of the Aire, 't is call'd a Gliding Star. **1738** Wheler in *Phil. Trans.* XLI. 100, I tied ..at the End of the larger Arm, a Piece of Stick traversly. **1826** Kirby & Sp. *Entomol.* III. xxxv. 606 They [elytra] may ..help them in flying traversely and before the wind.

traverser ('trævəsə(r), trə'vɜːsə(r)). Also 7 **traueser.** [f. TRAVERSE *v.* + -ER[1].] One who or that which traverses.

1. A person or thing that crosses or passes over.

1613 M. Ridley *Magn. Bodies* 1 The two trauesers about the Sunne, called Venus and Mercury. **1830** Howitt *Seasons* (1837) 3 A dismal time for the traversers of wide and open heaths.

†**2.** = TRAVERSE *sb.* 16. *Obs. rare.*

1645 Slingsby *Diary* (1836) 159 Ye town..was made a kind of Garison wth some traversers and light works built about it.

3. *Law.* One who traverses a plea.

1812 *Examiner* 21 Sept. 607/1 The traverser was prevented from hanging himself. **1886** Dowden *Shelley* (1887) I. vi. 240 The charge of Chief Justice Downes made clear the case against the traverser.

4. On a railway: A platform, moving laterally on wheels, by which trucks or carriages may be shifted from one set of rails to another parallel to it.

1851 T. Dunn in *Pract. Mechanic's Jrnl.* III. 258, I was the first person who invented a traverser. **1878** F. S. Williams *Midl. Railw.* 643 The truck is now clear, and.. will be run on to the 'traverser', and..drawn sideways on to the next line of rails.

'**traverse-,table.** [f. TRAVERSE *sb.* 12.]

1. *Naut.* A table from which the difference of latitude and departure corresponding to any given course and distance may be ascertained.

1669 Sturmy *Mariner's Mag.* iv. i. 141 By the Traverse-Table..you may find the Difference of Latitude and departure from the Meridian. **1706** Phillips (ed. Kersey), *Traverse-Table*, a Paper on which are set down the Traverses, or Various Courses of the Ship, with the Points of the Compass. **1828** J. H. Moore *Pract. Navig.* (ed. 20) 178 The variation is 11° 52′ E., and must be allowed..in all courses steered, or bearings taken by the compass, before they can be put in the Traverse Table. **1839** *Civil Eng. & Arch. Jrnl.* II. 352/1 He also shows how his traverse tables may be applied in setting out railway curves. **1843** *Penny Cycl.* XXV. 169/2 The traverse table is a table of double entry, into which, going with the angle of the course and the distance run, we find in two columns the corresponding departure, and length of the side called difference of latitude.

2. On a railway: = TRAVERSER 4. *U.S.*

1864 Webster, *Traverse-table*, (Railways), a platform with one or more tracks, and arranged to move laterally on wheels, for shifting cars, etc.; a traverser. **1877** in Knight *Dict. Mech.*

†'**traverse-ways**, *adv. Obs.* [f. as next + -WAYS.] = next.

1610 Guillim *Heraldry* II. vi. (1611) 61 A Canton parted trauerswaies whether it be from the dexter corner, or from the sinister, doth make two base squires.

'**traverse-,wise**, *adv.* [f. TRAVERSE *a.* or *sb.* + -WISE.] Crosswise.

1697 Dampier *Voy.* (1729) I. 336 The Beams or Bamboes ..are fasten'd traverse-wise to the Outlayers on each side.

traversible, variant of TRAVERSABLE.

traversing ('trævəsıŋ, trə'vɜːsıŋ), *vbl. sb.* [f. TRAVERSE *v.* + -ING[1].] The action of the verb TRAVERSE, in various senses.

1589 Nashe *Martins Months M.* To Rdr., This our young masters Father..then was lept from the Bellfree, vp into the Chauncel of the Church..and vnder tooke the trauersing of greater matters. *a* **1642** Sir W. Monson *Naval Tracts* III. (1704) 344/1 They [cannon] are..better in Traversing and Mounting. **1678** Moxon *Mech. Exerc.* iv. 65 This way of Cross-Grain'd working, is, by Workmen called Traversing. **1690** Leybourn *Curs. Math.* 641 Let these two Examples suffice for Traversing both by Protraction, Calculation, and by the Traverse Table. **1851** Sir F. Palgrave *Norm. & Eng.* I. 487 Amongst the marchings and traversings of the Northmen. **1883** *Contemp. Rev.* June 883 Forty years' laborious traversing of record offices and corporate archives. **1886** *Badminton Libr., Shooting* (1895) 177 The..system of 'traversing'..cannot be too strongly deprecated. **1887** *Encycl. Brit.* XXII. 705/2 (*Surveying*) Traversing is a combination of linear and angular measures in equal proportion. **1895** *Westm. Gaz.* 25 Nov. 4/3 The 'traversing' or drawing sideways of the new bridge so that it would occupy..the place where the up line had formerly stood. **1905** J. C. Wilson *Traversing Geometr. Figures* 1 On the continuous description or traversing of Geometrical Figures.

b. *attrib.* and *Comb.*

1825 J. Nicholson *Operat. Mechanic* 407 The alternate traversing motion is produced on the same principle as that applied to Baker's horizontal mangle. **1841** *Civil. Eng. & Arch. Jrnl.* IV. 318/1 What is..termed the 'taking-up' or 'traversing motion' of the plank during..sawing. **1888** Rutley *Rock-Forming Min.* 18 Mechanical traversing arrangements..are rather an encumbrance than an advantage.

traversing ('trævəsıŋ, trə'vɜːsıŋ), *ppl. a.* [f. as prec. + -ING[2].] That traverses; crossing, transverse.

1561 Eden *Arte Nauig.* III. ix. 73 See also that the markes whiche you make in the yarde [= cross-staff], be trauersyng lines. **1771** Luckombe *Hist. Print.* 476 In distributing of Musical Notes,..care ought to be taken to save the edges of the traversing lines from battering. **1865** Gillespie *Argt. Being & Attrib. God* III. ii. (1910) 93 Other lines, some of them..traversing lines, besides the main line of life.

b. In specific collocations: see quots.

traversing jury, a traverse jury (see TRAVERSE *sb.* 23).

1823 *Rep. Sel. Comm. Sewers Metrop.* 17 A traversing jury. **1828** Spearman *Brit. Gunner* (ed. 2) 63 The guns are mounted on traversing platforms, and, in that case, fire over the epaulement. **1829** Marryat *F. Mildmay* xvii, The traversing beam of a steamboat. **1877** Knight *Dict. Mech.*, *Traversing-jack*, *a.* A jack used for engines or carriages upon the rails. *b.* A lifting-apparatus, the standard of which has a movement on its bed, enabling it to be applied to different parts of an object or used for shifting objects horizontally without moving the bed. *Ibid.*, *Traversing-pulley*, a pulley so arranged as to traverse upon a rope or rod. **1878** F. S. Williams *Midl. Railw.* 664 Sidings and traversing tables will be laid between all these various shops, and also through them, so that there will always be more than one way by which trollies or trains can get in and out. **1884** C. G. W. Lock *Workshop Receipts* Ser. III. 294/1 The traversing mandril should be made of the very finest steel. **1887** D. A. Low *Machine Draw.* (1892) 96 The lever..for turning the horizontal screw of a traversing screw jack.

traversion (trə'vɜːʃən). *rare.* [f. TRAVERSE *v.* on the type of a L. **tra(ns)versiōnem*: cf. TRANSVERSION.]

1. †**a.** The action of traversing or moving sideways in fencing: cf. TRAVERSE *v.* 5, 15 (*obs.*). **b.** The action of traversing a geometrical figure.

1637 Nabbes *Microcosm.* II. i. C ij b, I was..bred up in Mars his Fencing-schoole: where I..learn't..Time, motion and action; progression, reversion, and traversion; blowes thrusts, falses [etc.]. **1905** *Westm. Gaz.* 30 Sept. 2/2 The general principles underlying this continuous traversion of figures, complete or incomplete.

†**2.** ? The transverse member of a cross. *Obs.*

1658 Sir T. Browne *Gard. Cyrus* i. 96 Some [crosses] being..of one single peece without traversion or transome.

traverso (trə'vɜːsəʊ). *Mus.* Also **traversa.** [a. It.] = *transverse flute* s.v. TRANSVERSE *a.* 1 d.

[**1776** J. Hawkins *Gen. Hist. Sci. & Pract. Mus.* II. iv. iv. 452 It seems that the invention of the traverse flute is not to be attributed either to the Germans or the Helvetians.] **1801** Busby *Dict. Mus.* s.v. *Traversa*, (Ital.) a German flute. **1884** Grove *Dict. Mus.* IV. 163/1 *Traverso*, (Ger. *Querflöte*), the present form of flute, held *square* or *across* (*à travers*) the performer... In Bach's scores it is called Flauto traverso, Traverso, and Traversiere. **1932** C. S. Terry *Bach's Orchestra* iv. 79 Bach's treatment of the traverso has peculiar interest. **1938** *Oxf. Compan. Mus.* 949/1 *Traversa, traverso* (It.); traversière (Fr.); Traversflöte (Ger.). **1979** *Early Music* July 357/1 Open and forked fingerings..are basically the same on oboe and traverso.

†'**travers-'tile.** *Obs.* [Origin of name obscure; in quot. 1703 referred to obs. F. '*travers* crosse, crosse-wise, thwart, ouerthwart, ill-placed, out of order' (Cotgr.).] See quots.

1703 T. N. *City & C. Purchaser* 273 Travers. These Tyles are (by our common Bricklayers) call'd Travis, or Travas Tyles; but I suppose it should rather be Travers Tyles; for the word *Travers* is perfect French, signifying Irregularity; these..Travers Tyles are..irregular plain Tyles, viz. Such as have the Pin-holes broken out, or one of the lower Corners broken off. **1725** *Bradley's Fam. Dict.* s.v. *Tiles, Travers*, which they lay with the broken Ends upwards upon Rafters where pinn'd Tyles cannot hang. **1727–41** Chambers *Cycl.* s.v. *Tyle*, Traverse Tyles.

travertine, -in ('trævətın). Also **trevertine.** [ad. It. *travertino*, older *tivertino* 'a kind of stone to build withall' (Florio):—L. *tiburtīnus* TIBURTINE. Cf. F. *travertin*, in Cotgr. *trevertin.*] A white or light-coloured concretionary limestone, usually hard and semi-crystalline, deposited from water holding lime in solution; also called ***travertine stone***; quarried in Italy for building. A less solid porous form is known as *calcareous tufa.*

[**1555** Eden *Decades* 340 And [silver] is often tymes founde in an other stone lyke vnto Treuertino or in Treuertino it selfe.] **1797** Holcroft tr. *Stolberg's Trav.* III. lxxxviii. 455 They are..of the travertine stone. **1868** Lyell *Princ. Geol.* (ed. 10) II. III. xlvii. 544 Encrusted with a calcareous cement resembling travertin. **1875** Merivale *Gen. Hist. Rome* lxxix. (1877) 669 The travertine, or limestone of Tivoli,..was used to a great extent to cover the plain brickwork. **1878** Huxley *Physiogr.* 122 At the falls of the Anio, the travertine has formed bed after bed to the thickness of four or five hundred feet.

b. *attrib.* Of, composed of, or of the nature of travertine.

1797 [see above]. **1842** *Civil Eng. & Arch. Jrnl.* V. 171/2 The Italian fresco workers..sometimes used puzzolano mixed with Trevertine lime. **1909** *Eng. Rev.* Feb. 585 Sanger found these travertine mounds in every stage of development.

traves, -ess(e, obs. forms of TRAVERSE.

†**travested**, *pa. pple. Obs.* [An earlier formation than *travestied* pa. pple. of TRAVESTY *v.*; prob. intended as the repr. of It. *travestito*, F. *travesti*, on analogy of *vested*, *invested*, etc.] Disguised; travestied.

1656 Blount *Glossogr.*, *Travested*, disguised or shifted in apparel; And metaphorically it may be applyed to any thing that is translated out of one language into another. **1687** Montague & Prior *Hind & P. Transv.* Pref. A iij, Homer has been Burlesque'd, and Virgil Travested without suffering any thing in their Reputation from that Buffoonry. **1725** Bentley *Rem. Collins' Disc. Freethink.* liv. III. 12, I see poor Lucan Travested, not apparel'd in his Roman Toga, but under the cruel Sheers of an English Tailor. **1752** Warburton *Serm. Ps. cxliv. 3* Wks. 1788 V. 30 To make God..the..inspector into human actions, is..returning him to the people, travested to the mortal size of local godship.

†**travesteere**, *v. Obs. rare.* [= F. *travestir*, It. *travestire*: cf. Du. *travesteeren* (Keupers, 1901), Ger. *travestieren.*] *trans.* To travesty.

1672 Marvell *Reh. Transp.* I. 44 Who by a perverse Wit and Representation might travesteere the Scripture. **1673** [R. Leigh] *Transp. Reh.* 144 He..makes conscience of using scripture..yet he makes none of travesteering it. **1675** V. Alsop *Anti-Sozzo* III. ii. 132 They who first taught this.. Age to Travesteere serious matters.

travestier ('trævıstıə(r)). [f. TRAVESTY *v.* + -ER[1].] One who travesties.

1883 Ebsworth in *Roxb. Ballads* IV. 161 *note*, A solemn travestier of many old Songs (and Dramas). **1901** E. Yardley in *N. & Q.* 9th Ser. VII. 161/2 Anthony Hamilton ..travestier of the 'Arabian Nights'.

'**travestiment.** *rare.* [f. TRAVESTY *v.* + -MENT.] An act of travestying; the wearing the dress of the opposite sex; a travesty.

1832 *Examiner* 373/2 Miss E. Tree is to add to the amusements of Whit-Monday by playing *Romeo.* Though we do not advocate travestiements, we wish her success. **1892** *Graphic* 24 Dec. 778/3 The sight of these travestiments overcame the antique Spartan simplicity of the British toilettes.

'**travestize**, *v. rare.* [f. TRAVESTY + -IZE; cf. *botany*, *botanize.*] *intr.* To practise travesty.

1847 *Tait's Mag.* XIV. 811 You are travestising.

travesty ('trævıstı), *ppl. a.* and *sb.* Also 7–8, 20– **-ti**, 7–9 **-tie.** [Originally a. F. *travesti*, fem.

travestie, pa. pple. of (*se*) *travestir* (Montaigne *a* 1592), 'to disguise him, or take on another man's habit' (Cotgr.), ad. It. *travestire* to disguise (Florio), f. *tra-* = TRANS- + It., L. *vestire* to clothe. The adoption from It. in 16th c. accounts for the retention of *s* in Fr., as opposed to *vêtir*, *revêtir*. Made known in England in the title of Scarron's *Le Virgile Travesty en vers burlesques* (= Vergil travestied in burlesque verses), 1648, whence occasionally in other connexions, and at length as a sb., used first in Scarron's sense, and later in the etymological one.]

A. *ppl. a.* **1.** Dressed so as to be made ridiculous; burlesqued. (Const. as pa. pple.) *Obs.* or only as F.

c **1662** DAVENANT *Play House to Let* I. i, What think you Of Romances travesti..Burlesque and Travesti? These are hard words, And may be French, but not Law-French. **1664** COTTON (*title*) Scarronides: or, Virgile Travestie. A Mock-Poem. Being the First Book of Virgils Æneis in English, Burlésque. **1672** J. PHILLIPS (*title*) Maronides, or Virgil Travestie: Being a New Paraphrase upon the Fifth Book of Virgils Æneids in Burlesque Verse. **1673** O. WALKER *Educ.* II. iii. 245 Virgil we have seen publickly, and even the holy Writings we heard to have been, travesty. *a* **1774** TUCKER *Lt. Nat.* (1834) II. 130 One may laugh heartily at Virgil travestie, without either despising Cotton, or abating one's admiration of Virgil.

B. *sb.* **1.** A literary composition which aims at exciting laughter by burlesque and ludicrous treatment of a serious work; literary composition of this kind; hence, a grotesque or debased imitation or likeness; a caricature.

1674 BUTLER *Hud.* I. III. Annot. 196 This Vickars.. translated Virgils Æneides into as horrible Travesty in earnest, as the French Scaroon did in Burlesque. **1751** WARBURTON *Note Pope's Dunc.* II. 268 Accusing him..on a mere report from Edm. Curl, that he was Author of a Travestie on the first Psalm. **1789** BELSHAM *Ess.* II. xxxvi. 300 It..has sometimes the effect of a ludicrous travesti of the Odyssey. **1846** WRIGHT *Ess. Mid. Ages* I. v. 178 Those romances were but barbarous travesties of the original stories. **1871** FARRAR *Witn. Hist.* ii. 73 The vulgar travesty of a miracle alleged to have been wrought by a coarse soldier.

2. a. Chiefly *Theatr.* In etymological sense: An alteration of dress or appearance; a disguise. *Spec.* (dressing in) the attire of the opposite sex. Freq. (*en*) *travesti*.

The phr. *en travesti*(*e*), which is not recorded in Fr., represents a misinterpretation of the F. pa. pple. as a sb.

1732 SIR C. WOGAN *Let. to Swift* 27 Feb., My design was to have travelled..*incognito*... But all my art and travestie was vain. **1823** BYRON *Juan* V. lxxiv, 'At least', said Juan, 'sure I may inquire The cause of this odd travesty?' **1850** THACKERAY *Pendennis* II. x. 102 He went into the pit, and saw..that eminent buffo actor, Tom Horseman, dressed as a woman. Horseman's travestie seemed to him a horrid and hideous degradation. **1957** G. B. L. WILSON *Dict. Ballet* 212 *Petipa*, Marie S... Her husband created for her a dance, *The Little Moujik*, in which she appeared en travesti. **1959** *Times* 3 Nov. 15/5 Defrance's troupe leaders and the girls in *travesti* receiving their last-minute counsels remain unaffectedly convincing. **1975** *New Yorker* 12 May 131/1 Nero, Otho, Tamerlane, and Julius Caesar will still have to be played by women *en travesti* or by countertenors. **1980** *Daily Tel.* 15 Dec. 10/1 Shapely young women have been showing off their legs *en travesti* since they were allowed on the English stage.

b. *Comb.* **travesty role**, a role designed to be played by a performer of the sex opposite to that of the character represented.

1958 *Listener* 5 June 955/3 Michel Sénéchal handled the *travesti* role of Platée with tact and sang the difficult music in an accomplished style. **1978** *Times* 23 Aug. 11/4 At the Coliseum Dennis Wicks makes the most of his travesty role.

travesty ('trævɪstɪ), *v.* [f. F. *travesti* pa. pple.: see prec. App. first used in the pa. pple. *travestied* = F. *travesti* or It. *travestito*. The simple vb. has not been found until after 1700. Cf. the history of TRAVESTED.]

1. *trans.* To alter in dress or appearance; to disguise by such alteration.

1686 F. SPENCE tr. *Varillas' Ho. Medicis* 408 He slunk out of Rome thus ridiculously travesty'd. **1754** WARBURTON *Bolingbroke's Philos.* ii. 73 Old Naturalism thus travestied under the name of Religion, his Lordship bestows..on his own dear Country. **1827** SCOTT *Napoleon* Introd. ix. II. 305 Processions entered.., travestied in priestly garments. **1853** FELTON *Fam. Lett.* ix. (1865) 70 About ten courses of meat, so mixed, blended, and travestied with seasonings and vegetables, that it would puzzle a Philadelphia lawyer to tell what any of them is made of.

2. To turn into ridicule by grotesque parody or imitation; to caricature, burlesque.

1673 BP. WARD *Apol. Myst. Gosp.* 42 Are the Mysteries of this Gospel..to be travestied or turned into Burlesque or Macaronique? **1756** J. WARTON *Ess. Pope* I. 57 One would imagine that John Dennis..had been here attempting to travesty this description of the restoration of Eurydice to life. **1874** MAHAFFY *Soc. Life Greece* vii. 197 The comic poets..travestied known characters so as to make them hardly recognisable. **1888** BURGON *Lives 12 Gd. Men* II. vi. 87 The true version of a story which..has been grossly travestied in the repetition.

Hence **'travestied** (-tɪd) *ppl. a.*

1864 *Ess. Social Subjects* 186 A reason which barely represents half your motives to yourself is sure to enter the other mind in such travestied guise as to convey nothing as you intend it. **1891** S. C. SCRIVENER *Our Fields & Cities* 68 Teaching the older histories from a travestied standpoint.

traveys, travice, obs. ff. TRAVERSE, TRAVIS.

travis[1], **trevis** ('trævɪs, 'trɛvɪs). Forms: α. 5 traveys, 6 traveis, 8 travice; β. 6 trevys, 9 trevis. [A variant of TRAVERSE *sb.* in sense of OF. *travers* (= 'travail, machine pour ferrer' in Godef., who cites 'Ung travers a ferrer chevaulx' from a document of 1472), ad. L. *traversum*.

In Eng. the word has undergone the same popular deformation as TRAVERSE *sb.* and *v.*, and is now identified in form with next, of which indeed in the Eng. Dial. Dict. it is treated as a sense.]

A framework or railed enclosure in which restive horses are put to be shod; a smith's shoeing shed; = TRAVE *sb.* 2.

α. **14..** *Voc.* in Wr.-Wülcker 617/19 *Tramerium*, traveys, *ergasterium idem est.* **1583** *Burgh Rec. Edinb.* (1882) IV. 287 To sett vp ane traveis of tymmer for shoing of horsis besyde his smiddy. **1727** BAILEY vol. II, *Travice*, a small Inclosure ..consisting of four Pillars or Posts, kept together by cross Poles, for keeping in and holding unruly Horses in the time of Shoeing, or any other Operation. **1905** in *Eng. Dial. Dict.* s.v. *Traverse*, recorded from Cheshire, E. Anglia, Sussex.

β. **1530** PALSGR. 283/1 Trevys to shoe a wylde horse in, *trauayl a cheual.* **1831** YOUATT *Horse* xxii. (1847) 430 The trevis is a machine indispensible in every continental forge.

travis[2], **trevis** ('trævɪs, 'trɛvɪs). Also 8 treves, 8–9 travisse, 9 trevesse, -vis, -ise, -iss, travis, -ise, -iss; *Sc. dial.* traivis, triviss, -ess, trivage; *Eng. dial.* travvis, travase, trivitch. [dial. var. of TRAVERSE *sb.* q.v.

Similar forms occur as obs. or dial., variants in senses for which TRAVERSE is the current form; but in the following senses the altered forms are alone in use.]

1. A wooden partition 4½ to 6 feet high, separating two stalls in a stable. (See TRAVERSE *sb.*, branch IV, of which this is a specific sense.)

1818 SCOTT *Hrt. Midl.* xxv[i], Beyond the 'treviss', which formed one side of the stall, stood a cow. **1826** —— *Woodst.* i, Stakes and trevisses of rough-hewn timber..seemed to intimate that the hallowed precincts had been..made the quarters of a troop of horse. **1827** HOGG in *Blackw. Mag.* XXI. 69 As I was suppering the horses the night..behold I looks up, and there's my auld master standing leaning against the trivage. **1833** LOUDON *Encycl. Archit.* § 1070 The trevises to be 6 feet high at the front posts, and 4 feet and a half high at the hind posts. *Ibid.* § 1103 The back posts of the trivesses to be made of oak 6 inches square. **1844** STEPHENS *Bk. Farm* I. 125 The hind posts of travises should be of solid wood rounded in front.

2. A horse's stall in a stable.

(Bears the same relation to 1 as TRAVERSE *sb.* 14 to 13.)

1756 MRS. CALDERWOOD in *Coltness Collect.* (Maitl. Cl.) 152 There were fifty-eight treveses in one end [of the stables]. **1859** J. BROWN *Rab & Fr.* (1862) 33 He [Rab] lay in the treviss wi' the mear, and wadna come oot. **1884** J. PURVES in *Gd. Words* Nov. 766/2 The horses crunching their food and rattling their halter-chains in the treviss. **1896** J. LUMSDEN *Battle of Dunbar*, etc. 13 Her neibor in the nearer triviss The maist redoubted naig alive is!

3. Comb. *travis-* or *trevis-board*, *-boarding* (in a stable).

1833 LOUDON *Encycl. Archit.* §1070 1½-inch trevise-boards to be mortised into the hind post, which must be set 8 feet from the front wall. *Ibid.* § 1103 The trivess boarding to be 7 feet high in front, and 8 feet at the back end.

travis, -ish, -iss, obs. forms of TRAVERSE.

travise, -ish, -iss, obs. or dial. ff. TRAVIS.

travisher ('trævɪʃə(r)). [Origin uncertain: *travish* is recorded as a dial. form of *traverse* (*Eng. Dial. Dict.*).] A carpenter's shave used for the final smoothing of chair seats.

1929 *Architects' Jrnl.* LXIX. 138/1 The travisher was invented—a spokeshave with a curved cutting iron, to be used, after the adze, in making the seat more comfortable. **1953** A. JOBSON *Household & Country Crafts* xx. 182 Of the four remaining tools, the top two are travishers, for finishing off the elm seats after adzing. **1968** J. ARNOLD *Shell Bk. Country Crafts* 133 Smoothing off follows with a succession of shavers:—the travisher, the smoothing-off iron and a devil.

‖**travois, -voise** (træ'vɔɪ, -'vɔɪz), *sb. North Amer.* Also †travoi, try-voy, etc. (which represent an older form). [Corruptions of TRAVAIL *sb.*[3], pronounced in Canada *travày* (tra'vaɪ), and by Métis of the Red River, Assiniboine, etc., *travòy* (tra'vɔɪ), pl. *travòys*. This has been perverted by writers into an assumed F. *travois*, pl. *travois*, and this again englished as *travois*, *-voise*, pl. *-voises*. A form nearer to the original is preserved in the lumbermen's TRAVOY; see TRAVOY *sb.*

For the facts of the history we are indebted to Judge Prudhomme of St. Boniface, Winnipeg, through the good offices of Prof. Moyse of Montreal, and Prof. Rivard of Quebec.]

The North American Indian means of transport, = TRAVAIL[3]. Also *attrib.*

1847 K. CARSON in W. F. Cody *Wild West* (1888) 349 The Tlamaths..prevented his body from falling into our hands by drawing it away on a travoi. **1879** J. G. BOURKE *Diary* VIII. 847 (MS.), [He] says he will stick with the column if he has to be hauled on a travois. **1885** *Boston* (Mass.) *Jrnl.* 31 Jan. 6/8 The pony..dragging that primitive Indian carriage, the travoise. **1892** J. RALPH in *Harper's Mag.* Mar. 508/2 On the plains they will have horses dragging travoises, dogs with travoises. **1896** G. B. GRINNELL *Story of Indian* ix. 156 Three vehicles were known to the primitive Indian —the travois in the south and the sledge in the north for land travel, and the canoe wherever there were water ways. **1899** *Daily News* 12 Jan. 6/1 Groups of silent men with bows and quivers at their backs, of women riding or leading patient pack ponies that dragged their travois. **1926** C. S. WALGAMOTT *Reminisc. Early Days* 26/2 George..found.. five head of horses with two riders the other three horses dragging either lodge poles or try-voy, possibly both. **1959** E. TUNIS *Indians* 86/1 Those Indians trained their dogs to help with the transport job by carrying packs or by dragging tent poles and small travois on which burdens could be lashed. **1974** J. A. MICHENER *Centennial* iv. 149 The travois, that primitive but functional invention for hauling goods, was constructed always from two poles used otherwise to support the tipi.

attrib. **1894** *Outing* (U.S.) XXIV. 448/2 An old travois pole which some squaw had discarded.

Travolator ('trævəleɪtə(r)). orig. *U.S.* Also with small initial, and **travelator**, **travellator**. [f. TRAVEL *v.*, after ESCALATOR.] The proprietary name of a moving pavement designed for use at railway stations, airports, shopping centres, etc. (see quot. 1955).

1955 *Sci. News Let.* 8 Oct. 232/3 A moving sidewalk with cleated escalator treads had been developed by the Otis Elevator Company... Designers foresee use of the moving platform, called 'Trav-o-lator', for such congested areas as airports, subway stations, [etc.]. **1957** *Country Life* 13 June 1186/3 Travolators..represent an improvement on the moving-staircase principle, since they will possess a flat surface along which the passengers can walk while they are moving. **1957** *Economist* 28 Sept. 1043/1 Two 300 foot 'travelators'—stepless escalators that carry pedestrians along slight gradients—are expected to be in operation at the Bank underground station in London towards the end of next year. **1958** *Trade Marks Jrnl.* 26 Feb. 196/1 *Trav-o-lator*..Passenger-carrying conveyors (machines). Otis Elevator Company..260, Eleventh Avenue, New York.. United States of America; Merchants and manufacturers. **1959** *Official Gaz.* (U.S. Patent Office) 19 May TM98 Otis Elevator Company, New York, N.Y. Filed Nov. 28, 1958. *Trav-o-lator.* For Endless Conveyors. First use July 28, 1955. **1959** *Archit. Rev.* CXXVI. 321 Victorian Street, which is a rather dead shopping area, receives wedges of new shops, with rear servicing, on both sides of the travellator system. **1967** 'W. HAGGARD' *Conspirators* iv. 40 He bought a ticket from the coin-machine, going down to the train on the travolator. He didn't walk but let it carry him. **1967** *New Scientist* 19 Oct. 180/3 Whether all the oceans are continually in movement, like giant travolators. **1977** B. COCKS *Mid-Victorian Masterpiece* xx. 195 Members found that even without a travelator they could reach the Chamber within the six minutes allowed before the lobby doors are locked for a division. **1980** [see TERMINAL *sb.* 5 a].

travoy (trə'vɔɪ), *sb.* [A broad vocalization of *travày*, Canadian pronunc. of French *travail*: see TRAVOIS, -VOISE *sb.* So called from its analogy to the Indian *travày* or *travail.*] In *lumbering*, a sledge used in dragging logs; one end of the log rests on the sledge and the other trails on the ground.

1878 *Lumberman's Gaz.* 2 Feb. 87 The haul at the former camp is too long to use travoys. *Ibid.* 9 Feb., The 'travoy' is kept busy on short hauls.

attrib. **1901** *Munsey's Mag.* XXV. 387/1 These 'travoy-roads'—the name comes from the French *travois*—have to be cleared by the 'swampers'. *Ibid.* 387/2 While the travoy road is in the process of construction.

Hence **tra'voy** *v. trans.* and *intr.*, to use a travoy, to haul (logs) by means of a travoy; whence **tra'voying** *vbl. sb.*

1878 *Lumberman's Gaz.* 2 Feb. 86 Travoying can be carried on to good advantage. *Ibid.* 87 Those who have short enough hauls to travoy are not much more than paying expenses. **1901** *Munsey's Mag.* XXV. 386/1 Second, it must be 'travoyed' from a hundred yards to a mile; third, it is hauled on sleighs as far as fifteen or sixteen miles; fourth, it is driven down a river, and I have known drives three hundred miles in length.

traw, trawe: see THROW *sb.*[1], TRAVE *sb.*, TROW *v.*, TRUE.

trawaile, -al, -el, -ell, etc., obs. Sc. spellings of TRAVAIL, TRAVEL.

trawethe, obs. f. TROTH.

trawl (trɔːl), *sb.* Also 7 trall, (troul, 8–9 trowl). [Origin and age obscure. If quot. 1481–90 belongs here, *trawelle* might be related to rare MDu. *traghel* drag-net (in *Teuthonista* 1475), referred by Verwijs and Verdam ult. to L. *tragula* drag-net. But the MS. reading is indistinct, and some would read *tramelle* (TRAMMEL *sb.*[1] 1).

Apart from quot. 1481–90, the vb. appears earlier than the sb., and may be its source, but is no less obscure in origin. The forms *troul*, *trowl* were perh. due to confusion with *trowl*, TROLL, another fishing term.]

I. 1. A strong net or bag dragged along the bottom of fishing-banks; a drag-net; = TRAWL-NET 1; esp. that now often distinguished as the *beam-trawl*, described in its modern form in quot. 1880. Also applied to a similar smaller drag-net used for the scientific investigation of the sea-bottom, dredging for deep-sea organisms, etc.

[**1481–90** *Howard Househ. Bks.* (Roxb.) 192 My lorde Rekened with his netter and he had sent home to stoke a dragge of viij fadam yᵉ fadam xij d... Item a trawelle (?) of vij fadam, the Fadam vj d.] **1759** B. MARTIN *Nat. Hist. Eng.* I. *Isle of Wight* 120 Tho' the Method of using Trawls, which of late Years has prevailed, is no small Diminution of their Plenty, it being found by Experience to destroy the Spawn. **1763** ELLIS in *Phil. Trans.* LIII. 419 The Animal..was taken in a trawl in 72 fathoms water. **1834** [see TRAWL-NET 1]. **1877** W. THOMSON *Voy. Challenger* I. i. 17 A portion of a huge Pyrosoma..was brought up in the trawl. **1880** *Chamber's Encycl.* IX. 524 The *Trawl*, or *Beam-trawl*..is a triangular purse-shaped net, about 70 feet long, usually having a breadth of about 40 feet at the mouth, and gradually diminishing to 4 or 5 feet at the commencement of the *cod*, or smaller end.., which is about 10 feet long, and of nearly uniform breadth. The upper part of the mouth is secured to a wooden beam about 40 feet long, which keeps the net open; this beam is supported on two upright iron frames, known as the *trawl-heads* or *irons*. The under side of the net..is made with a deeply-curved margin attached to the ground-rope, the whole length of it in contact with the ground... Two stout ropes..are fastened, one to the front of each of the trawl-heads, the other ends united to form a bridle, to which is shackled a warp 150 fathoms long. By this warp the trawl is towed. *Ibid.* 525 A kind of trawl called the pole-trawl..is now used only in the south of Ireland. It is much less effective than the beam-trawl. **1884** *Science* IV. 225/2 American appliances for deep-sea investigation.—Trawls and Tangles. *Ibid.* 226/2 The method of attaching the bridle in the Challenger trawl was similar to that afterwards adopted for the Blake trawl. **1887** E. J. MATHER *Nor'ard of Dogger* ix. (1889) 114 The cry of the watch on deck, 'Haul here! haul the trawl! all haul! all haul!' roused me at 5 a.m.

2. †**a.** (?) The action of trawling, or (?) a trawling-ground. *rare. Obs.*

1630 in *Descr. of Thames* (1758) 76 No Trawler to work in Tilbury Hope after Michaelmas, with any Manner of Net under four Inches for Plaice all the Net over. And no Trawler To come upon any Trawl with any other Net at any Time of the Year.

b. *fig.* An act of 'trawling' in order to find a person or persons (esp. a new employee) from among a larger population.

1971 *Daily Tel.* 2 Mar. 3/3 A 'trawl' is being made among civil servants to find a suitable man and an appointment is expected within two months. **1980** C. MOORHEAD *Fortune's Hostages* v. 97 The generals..rounded up 4,000 suspected leftists. They did very well in the trawl. **1984** *Times* 5 Apr. 1/8, I am going to make a serious trawl through the profession and see if I can find circuit judges whom I can safely appoint.

II. 3. *U.S.* Applied to a buoyed line used in sea-fishing, having numerous short lines with baited hooks attached at intervals: see quot. 1864; a trawl-line. Cf. also *trawl-anchor*, *-buoy*, *-roller* in 4.

to set, shoot, or ***throw a trawl***, to place a baited trawl-line in position for fishing; ***to strip a trawl***, to examine a trawl-line in position and remove the fish caught.

(The connexion of this with sense 1 is doubtful.)

1864 WEBSTER, *Trawl*,..a long line, sometimes extending a mile or more, having short lines with baited hooks attached to it, used for catching certain fish, as cod, mackerel, and the like. *Ibid.* s.v. *Trawl-line*, It is used in deep-sea fishing, and is over-hauled every hour or so by men in small boats, who remove the fish (*strip the trawl*) and rebait the hooks. **1897** KIPLING *Captains Courageous* 75, I helped bait up trawl ashore 'fore I could well walk.

III. 4. *attrib.* and *Comb.*, as ***trawl-boat***, ***-fish***, ***-fisherman***, ***-fishing***, ***-hawse***, ***-smack***, ***-twine***; **trawl-anchor**, a small anchor for a trawl-line (*Cent. Dict.* 1891); **trawl-beam**, the beam which holds open the mouth of a trawl-net; **trawl-buoy**, a buoy for buoying up a trawl-line; **trawl-head** (see quots.); **trawl-keg**, a keg-buoy used in connexion with a trawl-line (*Cent. Dict.*); **trawl-line**: see sense 3; **trawl-man**, one trained to use a trawl or drag-net; one who fishes with a trawl-net (in either sense); **trawl-master**, the master of a trawler: see TRAWLER 2; **trawl-roller**: see quot.; **trawl-warp**, the warp or rope of a trawl-net; **trawl-wings** *sb. pl.*, towing-nets attached one to each side of a small beam-trawl for the collection of free-swimming animals. See also TRAWL-NET.

1904 KIPLING in *Windsor Mag.* Jan. 226/2 At no time could we see the trawler, though we heard the click of her windlass, the jar of her *trawl-beam. **1799** *Naval Chron.* I. 344 A mast for his *trawl boat. **1636** *Maldon, Essex, Borough Deeds* Bundle 110, lf. 4 Re[ceived] for the groundage of a boate that brought *trall fish, 2*d.* **1865** *Daily Tel.* 5 Jan. 5/1, 80,000 tons of 'trawl-fish' alone..are sent to the metropolis in [a year]. **1886** *York Herald* 10 Aug. 7/5 There was a good supply of trawl fish at to-day's market, brought in by cutters. **1907** *Q. Rev.* Jan. 163 Out of 600 bottles more than 54 per cent. were returned by *trawl-fishermen. **1895** *Daily News* 16 Apr. 5/2 The new law enacted by the Danish Government prohibiting the carrying of *trawl fishing-gear within the territorial waters of Iceland. **1904** *Daily Chron.* 24 Oct. 5/2 One shot..went straight through the mizzen-mast, and passed through the casing and the trawl-fishing board. **1904** *Blackw. Mag.* Dec. 730 The swirl of the water beneath the *trawl-hawse. **1858** LEWES *Sea-side Stud.* 277 Along the edge of the wide opening is a stout wooden beam, to the ends of which are fastened the *trawl heads, namely, thick flat semicircular bands of iron. **1880** [see sense 1]. **1883** *Fisheries Exhib. Catal.* 48 Improved Trawl-heads, capable of clearing with safety submarine cable and similar obstacles. **1867** G. E. CLARK *Seven Years of Sailor's Life* 308 The old mother fish, full of spawn, are snaked on, to their miles of *trawl line. **1883** *Standard* 13 Sept. 5/4 The 'bultow' is..a set line, called in some places a 'trawl line'. **1775** FALCK *Day's Diving Vessel* 25 An experienced *trawlman, accustomed to sweeping [dragging the sea-bottom]. **1864** [see TRAWL-NET 2]. **1902** *Scotsman* 3 Jan. 7/6 In Aberdeen, the headquarters of trawling, *trawlmasters ought to be more careful than anywhere else. **1877** KNIGHT *Dict. Mech.*, **Trawl-roller*, a roller having a number of grooves cut in its periphery, and attached to the side of the wherry or dory, and over which the trawls are drawn into the boat. **1895** *Daily News* 20 May 7/6 The *trawl smack Hilda also came in with a hand gone. **1864** WEBSTER, **Trawl-warp*, a rope passing through a block, used in managing or dragging a trawl-net. **1887** E. J. MATHER *Nor'ard of Dogger* (1888) 158 Our skipper..run out some eight-inch trawl-warp over each bow. **1884** *Science* IV. 227/2 Fig. 3. The *trawl-wings attached to the beam-trawl in use.

trawl (trɔːl), *v.* (Also 8 **trowl**, 9 **troll.**) [Goes with TRAWL *sb.* q.v.: cf. MDu. *traghelen* to drag, f. *traghel.*]

1. a. *intr.* To fish with a net the edge of which is dragged along the bottom of the sea to catch the fish living there, esp. flat-fish; to fish with a trawl-net or in a trawler.

1561 EDEN *Arte Nauig.* Pref. ℂ iv b, Certayne Fyshermen that go a trawlyng for fyshe in catches or mongers. **1630** in *Descr. Thames* (1758) 77 No Trawler that..doth use to Trawl to take Soal, Chates, Plaice or Thorn-back. **1778** *Eng. Gazetter* (ed. 2) s.v. *Rye*, All the rest of the year they trowl for soles, plaise,..brills, &c. **1822** W. ROBINSON in J. A. Heraud *Voy. & Mem. Midshipm.* v. (1837) 91 We managed to trawl several times in going over these banks. **1866** *Daily Tel.* 16 Jan. 7/4 To think that..Columbus, in his most famous voyage of discovery, commanded a craft no bigger than the lugger in which the Brighton fisherman goes out trawling!

b. To drag or dredge: cf. DRAG *v.* 7 b.

1861 *Stockton Times* 15 Nov., The body was being trawled for on Saturday.

c. *trans.* To fish over (a ground) with a trawl-net; in quots. *fig.*

1906 *Academy* 10 Feb. 136/1 Mr. Macmichael has trawled every source of information. **1979** 'J. LE CARRÉ' *Smiley's People* (1980) xix. 234 Kirov dutifully trawls the émigrés, but without result. **1984** *Observer* 8 Apr. 32/6 We trawled Britain, the United States, Australia and South Africa for a chief executive.

2. *intr.* To drag a seine-net behind and about a shoal of herring, etc., in order to drive, enclose, and catch them. (Also *trans.* with the net as obj.: see quots.)

1864 *Glasgow Daily Herald* 24 Sept., Trawling went on in this loch without much objection till the trawlers went into the narrow waters above Otter Spit. If trawling was to be allowed inshore they would trawl out. **1880** *Chambers's Encycl.* IX. 525/1 The term trawling is commonly, although incorrectly, employed in Scotland to designate a particular mode of herring-fishing, which, however, is only seine-net fishing..on the principle of encircling shoals of fish, as has been practised in pilchard-fishing on the south coast of England from time immemorial. **1887** *Fisheries U.S.* Sect. v. II. 306 The net used for driving is 200 fathoms long, 8 fathoms deep, with meshes 6 inches square, made of 9-yarn rope... The net is trawled behind and about the herd [of seals] so as to drive them into the fiord and keep them there. Sometimes they rush under or over the net.

3. *trans.* To catch or take with a trawl or trawl-net. Hence **trawled** (trɔːld) *ppl. a.*

1864 *Glasgow Daily Herald* 24 Sept., I have seen the curers anxious to get the trawled herring. **1864** *Rep. Sea Fisheries Comm.* (1865) II. 1188/1, I believe I got the second shot of trawled fish that was ever fished in this country. **1883** *Fisheries Exhib. Catal.* (ed. 4) 175 Swatching and Trolling Old Hoods [seals]. **1890** *Philos. Mag.* Ser. v. Aug. 199 A specimen of Triassic conglomerate trawled seven miles south of the Deadman headland. **1906** *Daily Chron.* 15 Oct. 6/2 The steam trawler Herbert Ingram has landed at Boston a Royal sturgeon, which weighed 20 st... It was trawled up in the North Sea.

¶**4.** Often confounded with *trowl*, TROLL *v.* (q.v.).

The following quot. appears to be the earliest instance of this confusion.

1701 *Cowel's Interpr.* s.v. *Trawlermen*, Hence to trowle or trawle with a Trowling-line for Pikes.

trawler (ˈtrɔːlə(r)). [f. TRAWL *v.* + -ER[1].]

1. One who trawls; one who fishes (*a*) *orig.* with a trawl or trawl-net; (*b*) in W. of Scotl., etc. as in TRAWL *v.* 2; (*c*) in *U.S.* with a trawl-line.

1599 [implied in *trawler boat*: see 3]. **1630** [see TRAWL *sb.* 2, *v.* 1]. **1652** *Order Council of State* May 31–June 10 in *First Du. War* (Navy Rec. Soc.) I. 258 The Council did not intend ..that fishermen..trawlers and others..should be stayed. **1864** *Glasgow Daily Herald* 24 Sept., If trawling recommences all will become trawlers. *Ibid.*, The trawlers have damaged my nets, and stolen some of them, too.

2. A vessel employed in fishing with a trawl-net; now applied to a STEAM-TRAWLER.

1847 WEBSTER, *Trawler*, a fishing vessel which trails or drags a net behind it. (*Eng.*) **1848** *Life in Normandy* (1863) II. xiii. 254 When I was in a trawler we always studied the run of the tide..and ran as clear before it as we could. **1881** *Times* 21 Dec. 4/4 An action of salvage for services rendered by the owners, masters, and crews of the steam trawler Restless Wave, and the smacks Urgent and Harry Sinclair, to the iron ship Culzean. **1887** E. J. MATHER *Nor'ard of Dogger* ix. (1889) 114 The modern plan of fitting the trawlers with steam-capstans had not come..into vogue.

3. *attrib.* and *Comb.*, as ***trawler-boat***, ***-fleet***; **trawler-man**: see quots.

1599 *Admir. Crt. Exam.* 34, Jan. 31, There came.. Thomas Segar with his *trawler boat. **1909** *Daily Chron.* 28 Dec. 1/4 The Picton Castle, a steam trawler belonging to the Castle *trawler fleet..has been capsized in the River Douro. **1633** *Stow's Surv. London* 19 Fishermen..stiled by the name of T[r]inckermen,..Hebbermen, Petermen, *Trawlermen, &c., that have lived (in precedent times) by very unlawfull fishing on this River. **1701** *Cowell's Interpr.*, Trawlermen. **1839–40** [see HEBBERMAN]. **1934** *Sun* (Baltimore) 8 Oct. 7/5 Trawlermen of Hampton, Phoebus, Portsmouth and nearby harbors are planning a union. **1958** *Times* 9 Oct. 11/6 The distant water trawlermen..are doing work that for its hazards, long hours, and gruelling conditions would be difficult to compare with any job ashore. **1976** 'W. TREVOR' *Children of Dynmouth* i. 9 A few boys became trawler-men, but life was easier and richer at the fish-packing station. **1984** *Times* 20 Feb. 1/4 As the son of a trawlerman..he wanted to see the very highest level of safety of people crewing vessels of all kinds.

trawley, variant of TROLLEY.

trawling (ˈtrɔːlɪŋ), *vbl. sb.* [f. TRAWL *v.* + -ING[1].] Fishing with a trawl-net or beam-trawl; also, the action of TRAWL *v.* in other applications. Also *attrib.* as ***trawling apparatus***, ***sloop***, ***smack***, etc.

1561, **1689** [see TRAWL *v.* 1, TRINKING]. **1823** BYRON *Juan* XIII. cvi. *note*, Even net fishing, trawling, &c., are more humane and useful—but angling! **1858** LEWES *Sea-side Stud.* 276, I got initiated into the art and mystery of trawling, having made friends with a fisherman, master of a Trawler. **1864** *Glasgow Daily Herald* 24 Sept., When trawling was going on it took down the price of the herring. .. If the trawling commences again they may stop the drift-nets altogether, for they would get no fish. **1860** *Daily News* 20 Mar., A large number of trawling-sloops have been caught at sea, and much anxiety is felt for their safety. **1883** *Fisheries Exhib. Catal.* 7 Trawling Apparatus for Smacks and Yachts. **1887** E. J. MATHER *Nor'ard of Dogger* (1888) 114 Aboard a trawling-smack in one of the Yarmouth fleets. **1889** *Act 52 & 53 Vict.* c. 23 §6 It shall not be lawful to use the method of fishing known as beam trawling or otter trawling within three miles of low water mark of any part of the coast of Scotland.

trawl-net. [f. TRAWL *sb.* or *v.* + NET *sb.*[1]]

1. A fishing-net used in trawling; *esp.* = TRAWL *sb.* 1.

1696 *Phil. Trans.* XIX. 350 Here [Lincolnshire] are also good plenty of large Soals, taken in Troul-Nets, the Smacks being under Sail trailing them along. **1769** PENNANT *Zool.* III. 190 They [soles] are usually taken in the trawl-net; they keep much at the bottom. **1834** *Tait's Mag.* I. 125/2 The trawl-net scrapes along the ground; and as the flat fish breed in the channel, it appears that much injury and destruction has been done to the young fry when the trawl has been used near the shore. **1880** *Chambers's Encycl.* IX. 525/1 Smaller trawl-nets than those above described are used in bays and estuaries.

2. *Sc.* and *U.S.* Applied (erroneously) to a kind of seine-net used to surround and enclose shoals of herring and other fish.

1855 *Zoologist* XIII. 4670 The trawl-nets in Loch Fine. **1864** *Glasgow Daily Herald* 24 Sept., I think the trawl men might be content if they were allowed to use their trawl nets inshore without taking them into deep water.

¶ See also TROLLNET, with quot. 1558.

trawnter, obs. form of TRANTER.

trawt, obs. pa. pple. of TROW *v.*

trawth(e, trawþe, obs. forms of TROTH.

Traxcavator (ˈtrækskəveɪtə(r)). Orig. *U.S.* Also **traxcavator**. [Blend of TRACK *sb.*, TRACTOR, and EXCAVATOR.] The proprietary name of a type of mechanical excavator which moves on endless steel bands or tracks (see quot. 1940).

1940 *Official Gaz.* (U.S. Patent Office) 30 Apr. 1035/2 *Traxcavator.* For excavating, grading and loading machinery—namely high shovels, tractor shovels, tractor loaders, bull-dozers, graders, and the like. Claims use since Jan. 22, 1940. **1952** *Law Rep. Queen's Bench Div.* II. 608 A traxcavator, a tracked vehicle with a speed of $2\frac{1}{2}$ miles an hour turned this corner and stopped. **1956** *Trade Marks Jrnl.* 22 Feb. 181/2 *Traxcavator*... Machines for mechanical handling. Caterpillar Tractor Co..; 800, Davis Street, San Leandro, State of California, United States of America; manufacturers. **1968** *Industrial Tribunals Reports* III. 176 The material was excavated by mechanical diggers and a traxcavator. **1977** *N.Z. Herald* 5 Jan. 2–17/10 (Advt.), Morton Brown Asphalt Ltd., paving Auckland's carparks, drives, etc since 1948. Own traxcavators, graders, rollers and pavers.

†**tray**, *sb.*[1] *Obs.* Forms: 1 **treȝa**, 2 **treȝe**, 3 **treiȝe**, 3–4 **treie**, 4 **trei**, **treye**, **trai**, **traie**, 4–5 **trey**, **tray**, 5 **trye**, 5–6 **traye**, 6 *Sc.* **tra**. [OE. *treȝa* (wk. masc.) trouble, pain = ON. *tregi* (wk. masc.), Goth. *trigô* (wk. fem.):—OTeut. **treȝ-on-*, *-ôn-*, f. **treȝ-*: see TRAY *v.*[1]] Pain, grief, affliction, trouble, vexation; esp. in alliterative phr. ***tray and teen***, ***teen and tray***.

c **700** *Cædmon's Gen.* 2274 (Gr.) Ic fleah wean,..treȝan and teonan. *a* **1000** *Boeth. Metr.* v. 42 Forðæm þa tweȝen treȝan teoð tosomne. *c* **1020** *Rule St. Benet* iv. (Logeman) 20/10 Treȝan debemus, ȝedonne dæde ȝeþyldelice ah forþyldian. *a* **1200** *Moral Ode* 371 Þer is blisse abuten treȝe [*v.r.* treiȝe]. *a* **1240** *Ureisun* 61 in *Cott. Hom.* 193 Muruhðe moniuold wið -ute teone and treie. **1357** *Lay Folks Catech.* 26 With-outen travaile or trey [*v.r.* tray] or passyng of tyme. *c* **1450** *Life St. Cuthbert* (Surtees) 112 Tene and tray of tormentoures. **1560** ROLLAND *Seven Sages* 17 Sum gettis plesure, vthers gettis tray and tene.

tray (treɪ), *sb.*[2] Forms: 1 ***trieȝ**, **triȝ**, 4–7 **trey**, (*pl.* 4 **treyes**), 6 **treie**, **traie**, (7 **trea**), 4– **tray** (*pl.* 4 -es, 4– -s). [OE. **trieȝ*, *tríȝ* = ON. **trøy*, OSw. (Dalecarl.) *trø̄* a corn-measure of definite capacity:—OTeut. **traujo*^{m}. For the form-history cf. HAY *sb.*[1], formerly (3–7) *hey*, OE. *híȝ*, ON. **høy*, *hey*, OSw. *hø̄*:—OTeut. **haujo*^{m}. The base *trau-* is in ablaut-relation with *treu-*, whence Goth. *triu*, OE. *treow* TREE, so that the primary sense may have been 'wooden (vessel)'.

It is remarkable that the word should appear so rarely in OE. and should be so common later. See on the etymol. Holthausen *Indog. Forsch.* XIX. 294, E. Lidén *ibid.* XVIII. 413.]

1. a. A utensil of the form of a flat board with a raised rim, or of a shallow box without a lid, made of wood, metal, or other material, of various sizes and shapes (round, oval, quadrilateral with rounded corners, etc.); now used for carrying plates, dishes, cups and other vessels, cards, etc., for containing and exhibiting small articles, as jewellery, natural history specimens, etc., and for various other purposes, as in mining, photography, chemistry, or other arts and sciences. (Often with defining word expressing its purpose, as *bread-tray*, *card-tray*, *tea-tray*, etc.: see these words.) Formerly more widely applied to shallow open vessels generally. In 13-14th c., app. also, as in OSwedish, name of a measure of capacity.

10.. *Læceboc* in *Sax. Leechd.* II. 340 Nim þæt reade ryden, do on triʒ, hæt þonne stanas swiþe hate, leʒe on þæt triʒ innan. **1270** in *Sel. Cas. Law Merchant* (Selden Soc.) I. 7 Detinuerunt ei quinque marcas et quinque solidos.. pro xj. treys [h]ordei sibi venditis. **1317** *Ibid.* 105 Cum simul emissent xx. treys carbonis maris. **13..** *Coer de L.* 1490 Bye us vessel gret plente, Dysschys, cuppys, and sawsers, Bolles, treyes, and platers. **1374** *Acc. John de Sleford* (Acc. Exch. K.R. 397/10, P.R.O.), Pro iiij trays de ligno precii pecie .iij. d. *c* **1475-1500** *Inv.* in Noakes *Worcester Mon.* (1866) 173 In duobus vasis de navo factis, vocatis trayes. **1494** FABYAN *Chron.* IV. lxix. 48, xii. Cophyns or Treys full of Erth he bare away vpon his shulders. **1553** EDEN *Treat. Newe Ind.* (Arb.) 18 They.. haue theyr meate in great disshes or treys of copper. **1608** TOPSELL *Serpents* (1658) 659 Of a.. healthy stock of Hornets.. they have gathered three or four trays or baskets full of combes. **1639** HORN & ROB. *Gate Lang. Unl.* xl. §434 Implements of a kitchin are.. a trivet, a grater, treas, boles, water pitchers, platters. **1674** tr. *Scheffer's Lapland* 93 A kind of trey made of birch. **1848** THACKERAY *Van. Fair* vi, Sambo came into the room.. with.. a note on a tray. **1884** KNIGHT *Dict. Mech.* Supp. 893/1 *Thomson Battery* (Electricity), a modification of Menotti's battery, in which a copper tray replaces the copper plate, and contains the sulphate of copper crystals, and the superstratum of wet sawdust upon which rests the zinc element. **1885** R. BUCHANAN *Annan Water* vii, He soon returned carrying the tray, with teapot, cups, and saucers, [etc.].

(*b*) *spec.* a tray of food brought to one not able or not wishing to eat at table; hence (*loosely*), a light snack.

1914 L. S. WOOLF *Wise Virgins* xiv. 296 I'll ask them to bring you up a tray. What would you like? A little beef-tea and fish—or chicken? **1939** E. F. BENSON *Trouble for Lucia* ix. 199 My maid would bring me a tray instead of dinner. **1951** L. HELLMAN *Autumn Garden* II. ii. 88 You have had no dinner? I have made a tray for you. **1982** J. S. BORTHWICK *Case of Hook-Billed Kites* (1983) xxiv. 72 Mrs. Brent and Miss Fellows had had trays in their room.

b. In other uses: †(*a*) A mason's hod or vessel for mortar (*obs.*); (*b*) A butcher's tray: see quot. 1665; (*c*) A pig's trough.

1350-1 *MS. Acc. Exchequer K.R.* Bundle 492. 27 (P.R.O.) Pro vj trayes emptis pro mortero imponendo iij s. **1573** TUSSER *Husb.* (1878) 37 A lath hammer, trowel, a hod, or a traie. **1573-80** BARET *Alv.* T 353 A Treie, or such hollowe vessell.. that Laborers carrie morter in to serue Tilers, or Plasterers. **1611** COTGR., *Oiseau*.. also, a Hodd; the Tray wherein Masons, &c., carrie their Mortar. **1665** HOOKE *Microgr.* xlvi. 197 Those hollow Trayes, in which Butchers carry meat. **1714** GAY *Sheph. Week, Friday* 65 No more her care shall fill the hollow tray, To fat the guzzling hogs with floods of whey.

c. *Ordnance.* See quot.

1911 WEBSTER, *Tray*.. a flat or curved piece of metal used to hold ammunition or any part of the mechanism of a gun; specif., in heavy cannon, a brass or steel part (called also *plugtray*) of the breech mechanism hinged on the rear.

d. = SAND-BOX 2 e.

1938 F. MACCUNN *Cats* ii. 33 The tray, or pan, should have a low side all round it; put it in a dark corner—not close to the cat's bed. **1948** P. M. SODERBERG *Cat Breeding* 178 Once the use of the tray has been taught in the house it is an excellent plan to encourage the kitten to go outdoors. **1969** 'A. GILBERT' *Missing from Home* vii. 103 You really can't have a cat in the flat, there's no outlet, and I think.. a tray is unhygienic. I don't care how often it's changed.

e. *Austral.* The part of a truck on which goods are carried.

1960 'N. SHUTE' *Trustee from Toolroom* v. 100 The semi-trailer stood by the aircraft with the sausage-like component on the tray swathed in hessian. **1980** P. DAVIS *Australians on Road* xiv. 125/2 Ford management conceived the idea of producing a vehicle which could be said to be an essential part of farm equipment, yet was still comfortable enough for the farmer to take his wife out for an evening in town. The result was a passenger-type cab, married to an enclosed load tray; it was called the coupé utility, later corrupted to 'ute'.

2. *dial.* A hurdle.

1829 [J. R. BEST] *Pers. & Lit. Mem.* 256 The hurdles or trays as we [in Lincolnshire] call them, in which the sheep are to be penned. **1832** *Stamford Mercury* 27 Jan. 2/5, 4 dozen of fence trays. **1851** *Jrnl. R. Agric. Soc.* XII. II. 402 The field.. should be partitioned by 'trays' (or hurdles).

3. Part of the life-guard used on tram-cars and similar vehicles, a flat grid on which obstructions are picked up.

1910 (April) *Board of Trade Mem., Tramways* [etc.] *on Public Roads.* (4) (*c*) The tray of the guard should be provided with a spring so as to hold the front edge down to the surface of the roadway when the tray is dropped. **1913** E. T. RUTHVEN-MURRAY *Let.*, If the car strikes anything on the track, the gate is pushed backwards and releases a 'trigger' (a catch sustaining the tray) which allows the tray to fall so that it slides along on the road and scoops up the obstruction.

4. *attrib.* and *Comb.*, as ***tray-board***, ***-load***, ***-man***, ***-monger***; ***tray-like*** adj.; **tray-battery** *Electr.* (see quot.); **tray-buggy** (*U.S.*), a buggy having a flat tray-like body; **tray-cloth**, a cloth or napkin placed upon a tray on which dishes, etc. are carried; **tray-galley**, in printing, a tray to which the type is transferred from the composing-stick; **tray lunch(eon)**, lunch served on a tray; a light lunch; **traymobile** *Austral.* and *N.Z.* [-MOBILE], a small wheeled table or stand on which food, etc., may be transported; a tea-trolley; **tray-sheet**, a sheet of sheet-iron to be made into a tray; **tray stand**, a small table on which to rest a tray; **tray supper**, supper served on a tray; a light supper; **tray top**, (*a*) a rimmed table top which can be removed and used separately as a tray; (*b*) *Austral.* a truck with a pick-up body.

1884 KNIGHT *Dict. Mech.* Suppl., **Tray Battery* (*Electricity*), one in which the tray forms one of the elements of the combination. **1875** SIR T. SEATON *Fret Cutting* 42 The *tray-board should be five-eighths of an inch. **1890** 'R. BOLDREWOOD' *Miner's Right* xviii, A quiet horse and a light *tray buggy. **1889** *Cent. Dict.*, *Tray-cloth. *c* **1909** D. H. LAWRENCE *Collier's Friday Night* (1934) iii. 59 Beatrice Wyld sits in the armchair, and Nellie Lambert on the sofa, the latter doing drawn-thread work on a white tray-cloth. **1971** *Islander* (Victoria, B.C.) 25 Dec. 5/2 The very best cups and saucers.. were set on a hemstitched linen traycloth in a large, round wicker tray. **1897** *Westm. Gaz.* 25 Jan. 2/1 The poor fellow was borne to his rest on the shoulders of his friends, in a shallow, open *tray-coffin, the dead young face lying among flowers. **1896** T. L. DE VINNE *Moxon's Mech. Exerc., Printing* 407 The long *tray-galley of wood. **1906** R. WHITEING *Ring in New* 115 A small cabinet of *tray-like drawers. **1908** H. WALES *Old Allegiance* i. 13 When the servant had disappeared with the last *tray-load [of supper things]. **1970** V. CANNING *Great Affair* iv. 58 The steward .. served our *tray lunches. **1936** P. BOTTOME *Level Crossing* xvi. 193 After what Nelly called a '*tray luncheon', she suggested showing Deidre the house. **1948** V. PALMER *Golconda* xx. 169 Her attention was on the *traymobile the girl had wheeled in beside her. She began to pour out the tea. **1965** G. MCINNES *Road to Gundagai* v. 79 Against the vacant wall is the 'dumb waiter' or 'traymobile' on which food and crockery come in from the kitchen. **1764** *Poll Knts. of Shire Chelmsford 13th & 14th Dec. 1763*, Robert Dolphin *Traymonger. **1891** *Daily News* 9 Nov. 2/6 *Tray sheets for stamping purposes. **1844** T. WEBSTER *Encycl. Domestic Econ.* 241 A *tray-stand.. formed of two frames and girth to fold up. **1895** *Army & Navy Co-op. Soc. Price List* 15 Sept. 311 Cairo Tray Stand. **1825** H. WILSON *Mem.* I. 43 Amy gave us merely a *tray-supper, in one corner of the drawing-room. **1933** H. EDWARDS *All Night at Mr. Stanyhurst's* 23 Me and you were going to the play, and coming home to a tray supper. **1962** M. CARLETON *Dread Sunset* (1963) ii. 36 Her own tray suppers looked deceptively simple. **1934** WEBSTER, *Tray-top table. **1951** *Catal. Exhibit, South Bank Exhib., Festival of Britain* 144/1 Occasional table with removable tray top. **1969** *Northern Territory News* (Darwin) *Focus '69* 97/3 It is a relief for the semi or tray top crews when they reach Alice—and the bitumen of the Stuart Highway. **1979** *Truck & Bus Transportation* (N.S.W.) Sept. 46/1 The general cartage fleet comprises.. three Albions with tray-top bodies.

Hence **'traylet** (*nonce-wd.*), a diminutive tray.

1825 *Blackw. Mag.* XVII. 222 A small napkin-covered traylet, containing a cold sheep's head.

†**tray**, *sb.*[3] *Obs. rare.* [app. f. TRAY *v.*[2]] Deceit, stratagem, ambush, trick.

c **1430** *Syr Gener.* (Roxb.) 7150 That we wer homward, I you pray, For euer I drede me of som fals tray. *c* **1440** *York Myst.* xxix. 60 Oure knyghtis þai are furth wente To take hym with a traye.

tray, *sb.*[4] *Venery.* Also **trez.** [The same word as TREY three, in dice, cards, etc.; re-spelt after BAY *sb.*[6] Believed to go back in oral use to 18th c. at least.] The third branch of a stag's horn. Also ***tray antler***, ***tray tine***.

1812 LD. GRAVES *Let.* (June 2) *to Ld. Ebrington in ref. to Stag-hunting Establmt. of Devon* (Exeter 1814) 14 His brow, bay, and tray antlers are termed his Rights. **1838** SCROPE *Art Deer-stalking* 2,3 The stag's brow, bay and tray antlers are called his rights... A warrantable stag has brow, bay and tray, and two points on the tops of both horns. *Note.* I have taken my nomenclature from the Devonshire Hunt, as the best authority. It has been founded considerably above a century. **1863** KINGSLEY *Water-Bab.* ii. 62 You may know.. what his rights mean, if he has them, brow, bay, tray, and points. **1884** JEFFERIES *Red Deer* iv, Close to the head a point springs from the beam and is curved upwards; this is called the brow point. Just over it a second starts,.. this is called the bay. There is then an interval, till some way up the beam, or main stem, a third—the tray—appears. **1893** LYDEKKER *Horns & Hoofs* 269 The third the trez, tray, or royal tine. *Ibid.* 320 [The elk's] antlers.. rise from the sides of the skull by a narrow beam.. without either brow, bez, or trez-tine.

†**tray**, *v.*[1] *Obs.* Forms: 1 **treʒian**, 3 **treʒe**; *pa. t.* 3 traied, 4 traid; *pa. pple.* 3 treyde, 4 trayed. [OE. *treʒian* (wk.), = OS. *tregan* (strong vb.) to rue, ON. *trega* (str.) to grieve:—OTeut. **treʒ-*: cf. TRAY *sb.*[1]] *trans.* To pain, grieve, trouble, vex, afflict.

a **1000** *Eadwine's Cant. Psalter* iii. 1 Drihten to hwi ʒemanifalde synt þa þe treʒiaꝺ oððe swencaꝺ me [*qui tribulant me*]. **1104** *O.E. Chron.* (Laud MS.), Eall þis wæs God mid to gremienne and þas arme leode mid to treʒienne. *c* **1250** *Gen. & Ex.* 3975 Quaꝺ balaam, 'for ðu treʒest me; Had ic an swerd, ic sluʒe ðe'. *a* **1300** *E.E. Psalter* v. 12 Out-put þam þar þai sal be, Lauerd for þai traied þe. **13..** *K. Alis.* 3046 (Bodl. MS.) Ich am so trayed þat neeʒ ich wepe!

†**tray**, *v.*[2] *Obs.* Forms: 3-5 **traye**, (3 **trayʒe**), 3-6 **traie**, 4-6 **tray** (4 **trai**, 4-5 **treie**). [ad. OF. *traïr* (Roland 11th c.), F. *trahir* to betray:—late pop.L. **tradīre*, for L. *trādĕre* to deliver over, f. *tra-* (TRANS-) + *dare* to give.] *trans.* To betray.

c **1275** *Passion our Lord* 194 in *O.E. Misc.* 42 Mid þine valse cosse þu trayest monnes sune. *a* **1300** *Cursor M.* 15277 (Cott.) þat i ha luued, he sal me trai [*Fairf.* tray]. **1377** LANGL. *P. Pl.* B. III. 123 Truste of hire tresore treieth ful manye. *c* **1400** *Laud Troy Bk.* 18053 Thei swore bothe to traye the toun. **1559** *Mirr. Mag.* (1563) F iv, [To] punysh such as had my brother trayed. **1568** T. HOWELL *Newe Sonets* (1879) 117 A canckred poyson.. Full closely coucht in pleasant bayte, with that poore soule to tray.

tray, *v.*[3]: see TREY, TRAY *v.*

†**tray**, *int. Obs.* [Exclamatory use of OF. *trai*, *tray*, pa. pple. of *traïr* to betray: see Godef. *Compl.*] Betrayed! Treachery! Treason!

c **1440** LOVELICH *Merlin* xiv. 14130 And evere he cride: 'Tray, tray, tray!' **1600-1** in *Hatfield Papers* (Hist. MSS. Comm.) XI. 46 But Orrell.. did run and leap in the forefront with Sir Christopher Blount and Mr. Busshell, their weapons drawn, crying, 'Saw, Saw, Saw, Saw, tray, tray'.

tray, obs. form of TREY, TROW *v.*

trayce, obs. form of TRACE *sb.*[2]

†**trayer.** *Obs. rare.* Also 5 **trayhour**, 6 **trayhor**, **trayor.** [ME. a. OF. *traieor*, *traior*, *trayeur*, nom. *traierre*, *trayeres* (*de vin*, etc.) (13th c. in Godef.), f. *trai-re* to draw (:—L. *trahĕre*): see -OR.] A drawer; a tapster.

1473 *Rolls of Parlt.* VI. 96/2 Henry Fylongley, late Yoman trayer of our Celer. **1485** *Ibid.* 379/2 James Ederich, Yeoman Trayhour of oure Seller. **1526** in *Househ. Ord.* (1790) 234 That noe Hoggesheads be meddled with by the Trayhor untill that the said Groome-Grobber hath perused the same.. whether it be drawne out as much as it ought to be, or not. **1596** SIR J. CÆSAR *Crt. Requests* (1597) 159 Tho. More, gromme Trayor of the Kings Celler.

trayfle, -folde, -fole, obs. ff. TREFLE *sb.*, TREFOIL.

trayful ('treɪfʊl). [f. TRAY *sb.*[2] + -FUL.] As much as a tray will hold.

1634-5 BRERETON *Trav.* (Chetham Soc.) 22 The kine give twenty seven great trease-full of milk. **1838** [MISS MAITLAND] *Lett. fr. Madras* (1843) 193 The Zemindar sent a very polite message with a tray-full of oranges. **1883** *Century Mag.* XXVI. 53 He has smashed a trayful of crockery. **1896** YOUNGHUSBAND *Hrt. Continent* vii. 170 Fruit is brought before you in huge trayfuls.

trayish, variant of TRAISE *v. Obs.*, to betray.

trayl(e, trayll(e, obs. forms of TRAIL.

traylles, obs. form of TRELLIS.

†**'trayment.** *Obs. rare*[—0]. [f. TRAY *v.*[2] + -MENT; or a. OF. *traiement* (13th c. in Godef.).] Betrayal.

1468 *Medulla Gram.* (in *Cath. Angl.* 30 *note*,) Prodicio, a trayment.

trayn-, trays-, trayt-: see TRAI-.

†**trayne.** *Obs. rare*[—1]. [Etymology obscure; perh. an error for *tayner*.] A fox's burrow or earth.

c **1400** MAUNDEV. (1839) xxvi. 267 In the time of Antecrist, a fox schall make there his trayne [*Roxb.* den; Fr. *vn vopil ferra sa taignere*], and mynen an hole, where kyng Alisandre leet make the ʒates.

trayor, var. TRAYER *Obs.*

trays(e, obs. ff. TRACE.

trayse: see TREY.

trayse, traysch, etc., var. TRAISE, TRAISH.

trayson, -oun, etc., obs. ff. TREASON.

trayte, -tee, -tye, obs. ff. TREAT, TREATY.

†**'traythly**, *adv. Obs. rare.* Etymology and meaning obscure.

13.. *E.E. Allit. P.* B. 907 For we schal tyne þis toun & trayþely disstrye. *Ibid.* 1137 & entyses hym to tene more trayþly þen euer In Iuda.

traytice, -yse, var. TRETIS *a. Obs.*

tray-trip, var. TREY-TRIP *Obs.*

traywe, obs. f. TROW *v.*

traze, obs. form of TRACE *sb.*[1]

trea, obs. form of TRAY *sb.*², TREY.

† **treacher** ('trɛtʃə(r)). *Obs.* Forms: 3 trichor, 3–5 -our, 4 trychor, (tryschor), 5 trychour, -eour, -eur, 6 trycher; 4 trechur, trecchour, 4–6 (8) trechour, 5 -ure; 6 trechor, (trachour, treitcheoure), 6–7 trecher, 6–8 treacher, -our, 8 -or. [a. OF. *trecheor*, *-eur*, *tricheor*, *-eur* (12th c. in Godef.), F. *tricheur*, agent-n. (see -ER², -OR) fr. OF. *trechier*, *tricher* to cheat, trick: see TRECHE, TRICH *v.* (Cf. Prov. *trichaire*, *trichador*, It. *trecchiero*.]

A deceiver, a cheat; one who deceives by trickery; *sometimes*, a traitor.

c **1290** *S. Eng. Leg.* I. 332/326 Þov art symon Magus, godes trichor. *Ibid.* 348/104 Askebert he was i-cleoped, a strong trichour, alas! ? *a* **1366** CHAUCER *Rom. Rose* 197 That is she that makith trechoures. **1481** CAXTON *Godeffroy* lxxx. 127 He was a trychour. **1513** DOUGLAS *Æneis* VIII. Prol. 97 Sum trachour [*v.r.* treitcheoure] crynis the cunȝe, and kepis corn stakis. **1591** SPENSER *M. Hubberd* 1255 Those same treachours vile. **1613** *Answ. Uncasing of Machivil's Instr.* G j b, If to Countrie thou hast a trechers heart. **1713** CROXALL *Orig. Canto Spenser* xxxv. (1714) 24 But smiling on the Treachour stood aloof. **1767** MICKLE *Concub.* I. xxxvii, The hungrie Trout the glitteraund Treachor eyes.

b. *attrib.* or as *adj.* Cheating, treacherous.

c **1400** *Rom. Rose* 6308 Forsothe I am a fals traitour God iugged me for a theef trichour. **1422** tr. *Secreta Secret., Priv. Priv.* 235 Whoso hath the neke ful shorte he is voucheous, deceyuant, and trechure. **1508** DUNBAR *Flyting* 55 The trechour tung hes tane ane heland strynd.

† **'treacherer.** *Obs.* Forms: 6 trecherer, tretcherer, 7 treacherer. [app. f. TREACHER-Y + -ER¹: cf. *fripper-y*, *-er*, *adulter-y*, *-er*.] = prec. (In quot. 1592 with pun on *treasurer*.)

1571 FORTESCUE *Forest* 104 b, The ribaulde and the gracelesse tretcherer. **1592** *Declar. Causes Gt. Troubles agst. Realm Eng.* 60 The Lord Trecherer I trust can giue her maiestie and the realme good accomptes of them. **1601** W. WATSON *Imp. Consid. Sec. Priests* (1675) 77 Stanley is a treacherer.

† **'treacherize**, *v.* *Obs. rare.* [f. TREACHER or TREACHERY + -IZE.] *intr.* To act in a treacherous manner; to play the deceiver or traitor. Hence † **'treacherizing** *vbl. sb.*

1656 S. H. *Gold. Law* 4 Do they not by this render themselves Traytors, as contrary to trust, duty, and engagement, to trecherize it? *Ibid.* 10 Is not this to..go on in your Trecherizings, in hope of revenge and advancement?

† **'treacherly**, *adv.* *Obs. rare*⁻¹. [f. TREACHER + -LY².] = TREACHEROUSLY.

c **1394** *P. Pl. Crede* 475 Y pray þe, þou me telle More of þise tryflers, how trechurly þei libbeþ?

treacherous ('trɛtʃərəs), *a.* Forms: 4 tricherous, -ows; 4–7 trecherous, (4–5 -us, 5 -owse, treccherous, 6 trechrous, 7 tretcherous), 6– treacherous, (6 -ouse). [a. OF. *trecher-*, *tricheros*, *-us*, *-eus* (12th c. in Godef.), f. *trecheur*, *tricheur* TREACHER: see -OUS.]

1. Of persons, their attributes or actions: Characterized by treachery; deceiving, perfidious, false; disloyal, traitorous.

c **1330** R. BRUNNE *Chron. Wace* (Rolls) 16519 Þe tricherous Saxons—þeyr tricherye vs euere mones. **1387** TREVISA *Higden* (Rolls) I. 357 Þe men beeþ variable and vnstedefast, trecherous and gileful. **1483** *Cath. Angl.* 392/1 Trecherus, *vbi* fals (*A.*). **1570** LEVINS *Manip.* 226/34 Treacherouse, *proditorius*. **1611** SHAKS. *Cymb.* IV. ii. 317 To write, and read, Be henceforth treacherous. **1644** EVELYN *Diary* 17 Nov., After a true tretcherous Italian guise. **1725** DE FOE *Voy. round World* (1840) 91 As fierce cruel treacherous and merciless a crew of human devils as any I have met with. **1897** MARY KINGSLEY *W. Africa* 329 A treacherous, thievish, murderous cannibal.

2. *fig.* Of things: Deceptive, untrustworthy, unreliable; of ground, ice, etc., unstable, insecure.

1610 B. JONSON *Alch.* II. iii, O, yes, but I forgot. I haue.. One o' the treacherou'st memories, I doe thinke, Of all mankind. **1709** POPE *Ess. Crit.* 492 The treach'rous colours the fair art betray, And all the bright creation fades away. **1806–7** J. BERESFORD *Miseries Hum. Life* (1826) II. v, The ice proving treacherous. **1855** MACAULAY *Hist. Eng.* xiii. III. 335 Up steep crags, and over treacherous morasses, he moved as easily [etc.]. **1860** TYNDALL *Glac.* I. xv. 102 Over other [crevasses] a thin and treacherous roof was thrown. **1901** ALLDRIDGE *Sherbro* xxvi. 288 We scrambled over a treacherous-looking bamboo bridge.

'treacherously, *adv.* [f. prec. + -LY².] In a treacherous manner; by or with treachery.

a **1340** HAMPOLE *Psalter* xiii. 5 With þaire tongis tricherously þai wroght. **1596** SPENSER *F.Q.* v. vi. 26 A Spaniell wayting carefully Least any should betray his Lady treacherously. **1678** WANLEY *Wond. Lit. World* v. ii. §6. 469/1 Gratian..was treacherously murdered. **1860** TYNDALL *Glac.* I. xi. 69, I stepped..upon a block of granite ..; it treacherously turned under me.

treacherousness ('trɛtʃərəsnɪs). [f. as prec. + -NESS.] The quality of being treacherous.

1610 BP. HALL *Apol. Brownists* xxiii, If you could..wash your hands of vnnaturall impietie, and trecherousnesse. **1647** BOYLE *Let. to Hartlib* 8 Apr., Wks. 1772 I. p. xxxix, The treacherousness of my memory. **1865** *Ice-Caves of France* etc. 76 [He] had..experienced the treacherousness of this slope of ice.

treachery ('trɛtʃərɪ). Forms: 3–4 tricherie, -eri, trycherye, (3 tricheriȝe), 3–5 tricherye, (4 trichcherye, tricchori, 5 triccherry(e, trichory, 6 tritcherie); 4–7 trecherie, -ery, (4 -eri, -ori, trecchery, -eri, trecchry, 4–5 treccherie, 5 trechory, -ury, tretcherye, 6 -erie, 5–6 trecherye), 6– treachery, (7 treacherie). [a. OF. *trecherie*, *tricherie* (12th c. in Godef.), F. *tricherie* treachery, f. *tricher* to cheat + *-erie*, -ERY. See TREACHER.] Deceit, cheating, perfidy; violation of faith or betrayal of trust; perfidious conduct.

a **1225** *Ancr. R.* 202 Þe Vox of ȝiscunge haueð þeos hweolpes: Tricherie & Gile, Þeofðe, Reflac [etc.]. *c* **1300** *Havelok* 2988 Hwou he woren with wronge ledde..with trecherie. **1422** tr. *Secreta Secret., Priv. Priv.* 231 Dysposyd to trechury and othyr ill tecchis. **1474** CAXTON *Chesse* III. iii. (1883) 94 To make amendes to them that by theyr tricherye they haue endomaged. **1596** SPENSER *F.Q.* v. iv. 46 But Talus usde, in times of jeopardy, To keepe a nightly watch for dread of treachery. **1599** DALLAM in *Early Voy. Levant* (Hakl. Soc.) 55 We doubted that some tritcherie would hapen unto us. **1611** COTGR., *Tricherie*, (whence, as it seemes, our trecherie) cousenage, deceit, a cheating, a beguiling. **1748** *Anson's Voy.* II. vi. 191 In case of any misconduct or treachery, he threatened..that the Pilots should be instantly shot. **1866** LIVINGSTONE *Last Jrnls.* (1873) I. x. 258 Treachery was suspected.

fig. **1896** *Allbutt's Syst. Med.* I. 268 Presenting some resemblance in climate to the Riviera, it [S. California] shares some of its drawbacks, treachery amongst them.

b. *esp.* The deception of perfidy of a traitor; treason against a sovereign, lord, or master.

a **1300** *Cursor M.* 18882 (Cott.) It most nu nede þe writte be fulfild..O iudas and his trecheri [*Gött.* trechori]. **13..** *Gaw. & Gr. Knt.* 4 Þe tulk þat þe trammes of tresoun þer wroȝt, Watz tried for his tricherie. *a* **1425** *Cursor M.* 15476 (Trin.) Bettur..to haue bene deed..þen wiþ a kissyng on þis wise His lord done triccherye [*v.r.* tresun]. **1570** LEVINS *Manip.* 106/18 Traytorie, *proditio*. Treachery, *idem*. **1651** N. BACON *Dist. Govt. Eng.* II. xl. 98 They preferred the good of their Countrey above all; accounting trechery against it.. to be a crime of great concernment. **1706** PHILLIPS (ed. Kersey), *Treachery*, Unfaithfulness, Disloyalty. **1911** G. MILLIGAN in *Encycl. Brit.* XV. 536/1 In ecclesiastical legend ..Judas Iscariot is generally treated as the very incarnation of treachery.

c. With *a* and *pl.* An instance of this, an act of perfidy or treason.

a **1300** *Cursor M.* 3870 (Cott.) Laban said, 'frend, ful blethli.' Bot þar he did a trecheri. *c* **1300** *Havelok* 443 He þouthe a ful strong trecherie. A trayson, and a felony,..forto make. **1586** J. HOOKER *Hist. Irel.* in *Holinshed* II. 142/1 They..revolve, as dogs to their vomits, so they to their treasons and treacheries. **1651** *Nicholas Papers* (Camden) I. 235 Hee that discovered to mee a trechery intended by one Tickell against mee in Irelond. **1726** LEONI *Alberti's Archit.* I. 66/1 Angles jutting out from..the Wall,..for treacheries, and for the safer throwing their Darts..are of some advantage to the Enemy. **1847** HELPS *Friends in C.* Ser. I. viii. 151 You hear a child reprimanded about a point of dress, or some trivial thing, as if it had committed a treachery.

d. *transf.* A substance that treacherously gives way under the feet.

1870 LOWELL *Wks.* (1890) III. 277 Slumping clumsily about in the mealy treachery. **1886** G. ALLEN *Kalee's Shrine* xiii. 142 The intervening belt [of mud] was one huge waste expanse of liquid treachery.

† **treachet.** *Obs.* A name for the lob-worm.

1787 BEST *Angling* (ed. 2) 16 The Lob-worm, Dew-worm, Garden-worm, Twatchel, or Treachet.

† **treachetour.** *Obs.* [? f. TRECHET *v.* + -OUR; or perh. a scribal or printer's error for **treacherour*, TREACHERER.] A deceiver, a traitor.

1590 SPENSER *F.Q.* II. x. 51 The king was by a Treachetour Disguised slaine, ere any thereof thought. **1596** *Ibid.* VI. viii. 7 Ye caytiue treachetours vntrew.

treacle ('triːk(ə)l), *sb.* Forms: α. 4–6 tryacle, 4–7 triacle, 5 tryacall, -cul, -kylle, -kell, 6 tri-, tryakle, tryackill, 7 triackle, -akcle; β. 5 tracle, treakill, -ylle, 6 treakil, 6–7 treakle, 4– treacle; γ. *dial.* 9 threeakle, traycle, etc., *Sc.* trykle. [ME. *try'acle*, *tri'acle*, a. OF. *triacle* (*a* 1200 in Godef. *Compl.*, s.v. *Theriaque*), beside *tiriacle* (1460), *teracle* (15th c.): = Prov. *triacla*, Sp., It. *triaca*, Pg. *triaga*, popular forms for Pr. *tiriaca*, Sp. *teriaca*, Pg. *theriaga*, It. *teriaca*, repr. a pop. late L. **triaca* for *thēriaca*:—Gr. θηριακή antidote against a venomous bite: see THERIAC, THERIACLE. The sense development in Eng. has proceeded further than in the Romanic langs.]

I. Original sense: chiefly *Obs.*

† **1. a.** *Old Pharm.* A medicinal compound, orig. a kind of salve, composed of many ingredients, formerly in repute as an alexipharmic against and antidote to venomous bites, poisons generally, and malignant diseases. Cf. THERIAC, THERIACLE. *Obs.*

As to its alleged composition, see THERIACLE.

1340 *Ayenb.* 17 Vor-zoþe he is ine grat peril to huam alle triacle went in to uenym. *c* **1386** CHAUCER *Pard. Prol.* 28, I almoost haue caught a Cardynacle By corpus bones but I haue triacle [*v.r.* treacle]. **1390** *Earl Derby's Exp.* (Camden) 12 Pro factura unius pixidis de argento pro treacle imponendo. *a* **1400** HYLTON *Scala Perf.* (W. de W. 1494) III. xix, This oynement is precyous..for it is tryacle made of venym to destroy venym. *c* **1425** *St. Mary of Oignies* I. ix. in *Anglia* VIII. 143 Hee..ȝaf hym firste tryacul, þat hee myghte þe more priuely bringe in after venym. **1483** *Cath. Angl.* 392/1 Treakylle (*A.* Tryakylle), *tiriaca*. **1535** COVERDALE *Jer.* viii. 22, I am heuy and abashed, for there is no more Triacle at Galaad. **1545** J. HEYWOOD *Four P.P.* Plays (1905) 46 Richer is one box of this triacle Than all thy relics that do no miracle. **1628** WITHER *Brit. Rememb.* II. 315 A sixth of Cordials and Elixars prates; And some of Treacles, and of Mithridates. *a* **1658** CLEVELAND *Wks.* (1687) 18 Do study Salve and Triacle. **1693** SIR T. P. BLOUNT *Nat. Hist.* 348 The chief Use of Vipers is for the making of Treacle. **1804** *Med. Jrnl.* XII. 139 His anti-venereal treacle, well-known for curing the venereal disease, rheumatism, scurvy, old-standing sores.

† **b.** *transf.* Anything to which alexipharmic or antidotal virtue is ascribed; a sovereign remedy.

1544 PHAER *Regim. Lyfe* (1560) L viij b, A nut is called the triacle of fish, shaled and sugred with a litle rose water. **1563** HYLL *Art Garden.* (1593) 75 Hearb grace..may well be kept for fiue yeares, and the leaues dryed, for all poysons, and a peculiar Triacle for the poor. **1727** *Bradley's Fam. Dict.* s.v. *Garlick*, To eat Garlick fasting is the Treacle of the Country People in the time of a Plague.

† **c.** In the names of particular kinds, with various qualifications, indicating place of origin, etc.; as ***treacle of Andromachus*** = VENICE TREACLE; ***treacle of Genoa***, ***treacle of Flanders***, ***London treacle***, ***Roman treacle***.

1479 J. PASTON in *P. Lett.* III. 259 Send me by the next man that comyth fro London ij pottys of tryacle of Jenne, —they shall cost xvjd. **1545** *Rates of Customs* c vj b, Tryacle of flaunders the barrell xx s. Tryacle of Jeane the pounde iiii d. **1586** *Ibid.* F j, Treacle of Flaunders the barrel xl.s. **1651** WITTIE tr. *Primrose's Pop. Err.* I. vii. 25 That ancient, and in all ages well approved Triacle of Andromachus, as also the Mithridate of Damocrates. *a* **1668** LASSELS *Voy. Italy* (1670) II. 213 The Apothecaries shop, where a Lay brother makes excellent Roman Treacle. *c* **1720** W. GIBSON *Farrier's Dispens.* v. III. (1734) 147 *London Treacle*... This seems to have been designed as a Succedaneum for the Mithridate, or Venice Treacle, and is that which the Country Apothecaries sell the Farriers under the general Name of Treacle, which many of the latter distinguish from the common Molossus-Treacle, by calling it, The Doctor's, or the Apothecaries Treacle. **1753** J. BARTLET *Gentl. Farrier* iii. 27 Genoa treacle twelve ounces, oil of anniseed one ounce.

2. *fig.* *Obs.* or *arch.*

a **1310** in Wright *Lyric P.* v. 26 Trewe triacle y-told with tonges in trone. **1340** *Ayenb.* 144 Þe oþer..hatte þe yefþ of pite. Þet is propreliche a dyau and a triacle a-ye alle kueadnesse, and nameliche aye þet uenim of zenne of enuie. *c* **1430** LYDG. *Min. Poems* (Percy Soc.) 236 The name of Jhesu! Geyn goostly venyms, holsomest tryacle. **1529** MORE *Dyaloge* IV. Wks. 273/2 Nowe tourne they the tryacle of holye scrypture quite into poyson. **1573** G. HARVEY *Letter-bk.* (Camden) 22 Let me understand a part how your London triacle hath wrouht against your Cambridg poisun. **1635** QUARLES *Embl.* v. xi. 42 Thou art the treacle that must make me sound. **1641** MILTON *Ch. Govt.* II. Concl., Wks. 1851 III. 178 With the sovran treacle of sound doctrine..to fortifie their hearts against her Hierarchy. [**1883** J. PARKER *Tyne Ch.* 267 Where is the triacle, the treacle, the balm, that drops its sacred healing on the soul's leprosy?]

† **3.** Entering into the names of plants formerly reputed to have medicinal virtues, as ***churl's t.***, Garlic (*Allium sativum*); ***countryman's t.***, (*a*) Garlic; (*b*) Rue (*Ruta graveolens*); (*c*) Great Valerian (*V. officinalis*); ***English t.***, Water Germander (*Teucrium Scordium*); ***poor man's t.***, (*a*) Garlic; (*b*) Hedge Garlic (*Alliaria officinalis*). *Obs.*

1398 TREVISA *Barth. De P.R.* XVII. x. (Tollem. MS.), Tame garlek..was not with oute cause clepid triacle of cherles [orig. *tiriacum rusticorum*]. **1538** TURNER *Libellus*, *Chamedrys*,..anglice Germander aut englysshe tryacle dicitur. **1548** —— *Names of Herbes*, *Camedrys*,..in englishe Germander or englishe Triacle. **1551** [see ENGLISH *a.* 2 b]. **1578** LYTE *Dodoens* v. lxxi. 638 Garlyke..is good against all venome & poyson... Therefore Galen..called it poore mens Treacle. **1597** GERARDE *Herbal* App., Churles Treacle is *Allium*. **1611** COTGR., *Ail*, Garlicke, poore-mans Treacle. *Ibid.*, *Trissage*, Germaunder, English Treacle. **1661** J. CHILDREY *Brit. Baconica* 23 The Country men in Cornwall are great eaters of Garlick for healths sake, whence they call it there, the Country mans Treacle. **1745–7** T. SHORT *Med. Brit.* (ed. 2) 246 Rue..or the Country Man's Treacle. *Ibid.* 295 It [*Valeriana officinalis*] is called the Countryman's Treacle. **1866** *Treas. Bot.*, *Countryman's treacle*, an old name for *Ruta graveolens*.

II. 4. a. The uncrystallized syrup produced in the process of refining sugar; also sometimes extended to the uncrystallizable syrup that drains from raw sugar; = MOLASSES 1. (See Note there.)

1694 WESTMACOT *Script. Herb.* (1695) 6 Good store of Molossus or common Treacle to sweeten it. **1727–41** CHAMBERS *Cycl.* s.v. *Sugar*, Sugar of syrop, or treacle... There are three kinds of syrops that run from sugar... The Dutch and German refiners first taught the islanders how to turn their treacle into sugar. **1731** [see MOLASSES 1]. **1789** MRS. PIOZZI *Journ. France* I. 84 Few of us could return..to ..a roll and treacle. **1838** DICKENS *Nich. Nick.* viii, They have the brimstone and treacle..in the way of medicine. **1873** F. HALL *Mod. Eng.* 128 *note*, The very marked distinction between *molasses* and *treacle* is commonly ignored in America, where the latter is seldom heard. **1902** GREENOUGH & KITTREDGE *Words* 267 'Treacle' is applied indifferently to the 'spume of sugar', to 'maple syrup', and to 'molasses'.

b. An inspissated saccharine juice obtained from various trees and plants: see quots.

1731–3 P. SHAW *Chem. Lect.* x. (1755) 193 A Kind of Treacle from Malt might be procured in cheap Years, for the Service of the Vinegar-maker, the Brewer, and the Distiller. **1753** CHAMBERS *Cycl. Supp.* s.v., Dr. Shaw, in his Essay on Distillery, has endeavoured to bring into use several sorts of Treacles, which..would serve..for the distillation of spirits, or the making of potable liquors. These are the inspissated juices or decoctions of vegetables:

Such as the sweet juice of the birch, or sycamore. **1839** DARWIN *Voy. Nat.* xii. (1879) 256 Palm..Valuable on account of a sort of treacle made from the sap. **1902** [see 4].

c. *fig.* Something sweet or clogging; *esp.* complimentary laudation, blandishment; cf. BUTTER I f.

1771 SMOLLETT *Humph. Cl.* 13 July, He began to sweeten the natural acidity of his discourse with the treacle of compliment and commendation. **1819** KEATS *Let.* 23 Aug., in Rossetti *Life* (1887) 146, I equally dislike the favour of the public, with the love of a woman; they are both a cloying treacle to the wings of independence. **1860** READE *Cloister & H.* lxxv, 'Oh, you nasty, cross old wretch!' screamed Catherine, passing in a moment from treacle to sharpest vinegar.

III. 5. *attrib.* and *Comb.*: in sense 1, as ***treacle-box, -monger, plaster, -pot, tap***; sense 4, as ***treacle-pad*** (see quot.), ***phrase, -pot, pud(ding, toffee, -well***; ***treacle-like*** adj.; **treacle ale, beer,** a light ale or beer brewed from treacle and water; **Treacle Bible,** a collectors' name for any of the English versions or editions of the Bible having 'triacle' or 'treacle' where others have 'balm', as in Jer. viii. 22, etc.; **treacle-butter-cake,** see quot.; **treacle-carrier, treacle-conner,** contemptuous terms for an itinerant quack doctor or medical practitioner; **treacle-moon,** contemptuous for *honey-moon*; **treacle-parkin** = PARKIN; **treacle-posset,** a hot drink made of cider or milk and treacle; **treacle sleep** *colloq.*, a deep, unbroken sleep; **treacle-vinegar, treacle-water,** a cordial distilled with a spirituous menstruum from Venice treacle, with other drugs and simples. See also TREACLE CLOVER, MUSTARD.

a **1833** A. PICKEN in *Casquet of Lit.* (1896) V. 195/2 Ye shall taste my wife's *treacle ale. **1806** *Naval Chron.* XV. 264 The liquor to which he was most partial was *treacle beer. **1899** *B. Quaritch's Rough List* No. 193. 40 Cranmer's Bible..1569... This is also a *Treacle Bible. **1457** *Will of Poole* (Somerset Ho.), A siluer *triacle boxe. **1828** *Craven Gloss.*, **Treacle-butter-cake*, oat cake spread over with treacle. **1621** MOLLE *Camerar. Liv. Libr.* III. xii. 187 These Mounte-banks, *Triacle-carriers, and such other Dog-leaches. **1706** BAYNARD in Sir J. Floyer *Hot & Cold Bath.* II. 227 One of the Tribe of *Treacle-conners..whether Apothecary or Physician, I can't tell. **1871** GARROD *Mat. Med.* (ed. 3) 329 Tar is a reddish-black, *treacle-like liquid. **1411** *Close Roll 12 Hen. IV*, m. 7d, Henricus Kirtone ..*Treacle-monger. **1815** BYRON *Let. to Moore* 2 Feb., The *treacle-moon is over, and I am awake and find myself married. **1906** *Daily Chron.* 5 Nov. 6/6 Once more the old '*treacle-pad trick' has been employed by burglars. Part of the window is smeared with treacle, which is then covered with a sheet of thick brown paper. **1626** *Art. agst. Dk. Buckhm.* in Rushw. *Hist. Coll.* (1659) I. 352 Strange effects to follow upon the applying of a *Treacle plaister. **1739** E. SMITH *Compl. Housewife* (ed. 9) 319 Those who can't afford mountain-whey, may drink *treacle-posset. **1876** BRISTOWE *The. & Pract. Med.* (1878) 627 Frequent sipping of warm milk, barley-water, gruel, or 'treacle posset'. **1466** SIR J. PASTON in *P. Lett.* II. 293, I send yow..iij. *tracle pottes of Geane. **1769** J. BERRIDGE *Wks.* (1864) 444 Like children, always wanting the treacle-pot. **1974** I. MURDOCH *Sacred & Profane Love Machine* 314 What about some *treacle pud, it's awfully good here. **1861** MRS. BEETON *Bk. Househ. Managem.* 688 *Rolled *treacle pudding*..suet crust..treacle ..grated ginger. **1841** CARLYLE in Froude *Life in Lond.* viii. (1884) I. 210, I fell first into sluggish torpor, then into *treacle-sleep, and so lay sound as a stone. **1973** 'H. HOWARD' *Highway to Murder* x. 117, I slept a treacle sleep from nine p.m. until the alarm clock went off..next morning. *a* **1500** *Piers of Fullham* 228 in Hazl. *E.P.P.* II. 10 Yn tyme therfore tye up yowr *tryacle tappe; Let not to long thy fawset renne. **1885** R. HOLLAND *Gloss. Words County of Chester* 367 **Traycle toffy*, *s.*, sometimes called *toffy sticks*, a very favourite sweetmeat amongst Cheshire school children. **1924** 'R. CROMPTON' *William—the Fourth* viii. 124 William was..deeply engrossed in his treacle toffee. **1983** 'A. T. ELLIS' *Other Side of Fire* xx. 133 Think what fun it will be ..parkin and treacle toffee. **1727–41** CHAMBERS *Cycl.* s.v. *Theriaca*, Treacle water, and *treacle vinegar are found good preservatives against putrid air. **1727–41** CHAMBERS *Cycl.* s.v. *Water*, *Treacle-Water..is directed..to be made of green walnuts, rue, carduus, marigold, baum, butter-bur-roots, burdock, angelica, master-wort, water-germander, Venice-treacle, mithridate, canary-vinegar, and lemon-juice, steeped and distilled... A more simple treacle-water, made from venice treacle, with an equal quantity of brandy and vinegar. **1865** 'L. CARROLL' *Alice's Adventures in Wonderland* vii. 107 The Dormouse..said, 'It was a *treacle-well.' **1909** *Blackw. Mag.* May 605/1 A University College varies its facial expression about as frequently as the Sphinx and about as violently as a treacle-well.

'treacle, *v.* [f. prec. sb.]

† **1.** *trans.* To make into a 'treacle'; to give the qualities of a 'treacle' to. *Obs. rare*$^{-1}$.

c **1500** BOLLARD tr. *Godfredus on Palladius*, To make a vyne treaclede.

2. a. To smear or spread with treacle; to dose with (brimstone and) treacle; to sweeten or render palatable with treacle (also *fig.*).

1838 DICKENS *Nich. Nick.* viii, A long row of boys waiting ..to be treacled. **1873** *Daily News* 11 Nov. 5/4 The pill may be treacled with apparent concessions. **1906** *Daily Chron.* 28 Mar. 1/7 'Treacle' thieves..treacled the window.., broke the glass with a brick, and stole eight trays of jewellery. *Mod.* We treacle the trunks of trees, in order to attract moths.

b. To catch (moths) by attracting them with treacle or the like spread on trees. Also *intr.*

1905 *Daily Chron.* 29 June 8/1 Country rambles with long-handled nets and cool summer night trips, 'treacling' moths. **1915** H. G. WELLS *Boon* iv. 124 Going round with the lantern when one is treacling for moths. **1941** —— *You can't be too Careful* III. xxii. 218 As moth hunters treacle for moths.

3. *intr.* To flow as treacle, to trickle. *humorous nonce-use.*

1899 'A. HOPE' *King's Mirror* xxiii, I could almost see the words treacling from his thick lips. **1966** J. BETJEMAN *High & Low* 25 *In blest Bethesda's limpid pool* Comes treacling out of Sunday School.

Hence **treacled** ('triːk(ə)ld) *ppl. a.*, smeared with treacle; **treacling** *vbl. sb.*

1895 *Daily News* 11 Oct. 7/3 The thieves..smashed the window, having previously placed some treacled paper upon it to deaden the sound. **1903** *Daily Chron.* 10 June 7/2 There were barely enough flies to make a decent show on the treacled paper which constitutes his advertisement. **1913** *Daily Citizen* Oct. 4/2 The catching of insects by this method of treacling requires great experience before it is successful.

†,**treacle 'clover.** *Herb. Obs.* A name given by the herbalists to more than one leguminous plant; esp. to *Psoralea bituminosa*, a native of the Mediterranean and Levantine region.

1562 TURNER *Herbal* II. 158b, The sede and the leaues of triacle clauer, dronken in water, help the pleuresye. **1578** LYTE *Dodoens* IV. xli. 500–1 Of the right Trefoyle, or Treacle Clauer... The flowers grow from the sides of the stalkes vpon long stemmes,..of a deepe blew or skye colour. **1579** LANGHAM *Gard. Health* (1633) 148 Treacle, or garden Clauer..prouoketh vrine and termes, and cleanseth the matrix. **1884** MILLER *Plant-n.*, Treacle Clover, *Psoralea bituminosa*.

,**treacle 'mustard.** A name applied by 16th c. herbalists to the plant *Thlaspi arvense* on account of its supposed medicinal virtue; by later writers applied to *Clypeola Jonthlaspi*, and to *Erysimum cheiranthoides*.

1548 TURNER *Names of Herbs* 79 *Thlaspi*..may be named in englishe dysh-mustard, or triacle Mustard, or Boures Mustard. **1562** —— *Herbal* II. 152. **1597** GERARDE *Herbal* II. xix. 205 Treacle Mustarde hath long broade leaues. **1712** tr. *Pomet's Hist. Drugs* I. 4. **1760** J. LEE *Introd. Bot.* App. 330 Treacle Mustard, *Thlaspi*. *Ibid.*, Treacle Mustard, *Clypeola*. **1856** GRAY *Man. Bot.* (1860) 35 *Erysimum*, Treacle Mustard. **1882** G. ALLEN *Colours Flowers* ii. 43 In treacle-mustard (Erysimum), the yellow is very pale, and the petals often become almost white.

†**'treacler.** *Obs. rare*$^{-1}$. [f. TREACLE *sb.* + -ER[1].] ? A vessel to contain 'treacle' of Genoa, or the like.

1415 *Will of Ld. Scrope* in *Promp. Parv.* 500 *note*, Tracleere argenteum et deauratum cum costis de birall.

treacle wormseed: see WORMSEED.

treacly ('triːklı), *a.* [f. TREACLE *sb.* + -Y.] Resembling treacle in quality or appearance; having the sweetness or sticky consistence of treacle; also *fig.* characterized by excessive sweetness: cloyingly sweet; sugared, honeyed.

1733 SHAW *Chem. Lect.* xi. (1755) 218 A proper, or rich, syrupy, or treacly Substance. **1800** W. TAYLOR in *Monthly Mag.* X. 317 It bestows..even on novelty of thought, a flat featureless mien, an insipid treacly sameness,..very unfavourable to impression. **1837** T. HOOD in *Mem.* (1860) I. 159 Whose book..although so treacley..does not please the natives. **1866** R. M. FERGUSON *Electr.* (1870) 243 India-rubber..some specimens of it having become treacly. **1930** J. B. PRIESTLEY *Angel Pavement* iv. 176 The organ was shaking out cascades of treacly sound. **1947** AUDEN *Age of Anxiety* (1948) i. 26 A doomed Sodom dancing its heart out To treacly tunes. **1980** S. BRETT *Dead Side of Mike* xiii. 143 Treacly, undistinguished music.

Hence **'treacliness,** treacly quality or condition.

1884 *Nature* 22 May 89/1 The property of viscosity or treaclyness possessed more or less by all fluids is the general influence conducive to steadiness.

treact, treactise, obs. ff. TREAT, TREATISE.

tread (trɛd), *sb.* Forms: 3 (*pl.*) **treden, treoden;** 5 **trede, tredd,** (5–7 *Sc.*) **tred;** 6 *Sc.* **treade,** 9 *n. dial.* **treed,** *s.e. dial.* **trade,** 6– **tread.** [Early ME. *trede* (pl. *treden*), f. stem of OE. *tredan* to TREAD. Cognate with MDu. *trēde* m. and f., MLG. *trēde*, *tret* m., MHG. *trit*, Ger. *tritt* step, footstep, path, etc.; cf. also, from same root, TRADE, between which and *tread* in their earlier senses there is a close parallelism; see also TROD.]

I. 1. A footprint; the mark made in treading. *rare.*

a **1225** *Ancr. R.* 380 [He] scheaweð in ham his owene treden þet me trodde him in ham. *Ibid.*, Auh þe dunes underuoð þe treden [*v.r.* (MS. Titus 120) trodes] of him suluen. *c* **1230** *Hali Meid.* 15 He[e] seð þe folhen hire treoden. Meiden gan as heo dude. **1727** *Bradley's Fam. Dict.* s.v. *Animal*, An Otter's Tread is almost like that of a Badger, saving that his Toes..are longer one than another.

† **2.** A line of footsteps; the track or trail left by the steps or passage of a man or animal: = TRADE *sb.* 2. *Obs.*

c **1400** *Laud Troy Bk.* 1006 When he was comen to that stede, Ther he saw the schepes trede. **1513** DOUGLAS *Æneis* VIII. iv. 67 And, that thar tred suld na way be persaue, Onto his cave ay bakwartis by the talis To turn thair futsteppis he thaim harlis and tralis. **1570** *Satir. Poems Reform.* x. 340 Sum saw him weill, and followit his hors tred. **1570** *Henry's Wallace* v. 136 For thair sloith hund the graith gait till him ȝeid, Off othir tred [*c* 1470 trade] scho tuk as than no heid. **1727–41** CHAMBERS *Cycl.*, *Piste*, in the manage, the track or tread, which a horse makes upon the ground he goes over. **1815** SCOTT *Guy M.* xxiii, He passed a solitary house, towards which the horseman..had apparently turned up, for his horse's tread was evident in that direction. **1820** —— *Monast.* xxxiv, I tracked the knight's horse-tread as far as near to the ford.

† **3. a.** A trodden or beaten way, a path, a track. *Obs.* exc. **b.** *fig.* path or way (of life or action).

14.. *Bone Flor.* 1882 Sche fonde a tredd and forthe ys gon ..To a noonre. **1628** FELTHAM *Resolves* II. [I.] xiii. 35 We wander in the tread of seuerall paths. *a* **1711** KEN *Psyche* Poet. Wks. 1721 IV. 229 When Jesus journy'd too and fro, ..The Female Vot'ries by you lead [= led] Still follow'd his instructive Tread. *a* **1862** BUCKLE *Civiliz.* (1869) III. iii. 132 Conditions which determine the tread and destiny of nations.

† **c.** Those who are on the ordinary way; the common 'run' of passers. Cf. TRADE *sb.* 1 b. *Obs.*

1615 CHAPMAN *Odyss.* XVII. 748 That the bread, Which now he begg'd amongst the common tread.

4. a. The action or an act of treading or trampling; a step.

c **1400** *Laud Troy Bk.* 13440 Thei drow him fro her hors tred. **1640** R. CHAMBERLAIN *Pref. Verses* in Brome *Antipodes*, On th' Antipodes..tis thus, Their feet do tread against the tread of us. **1671** FLAVEL *Fount. Life* v. 12 The least Tread awry may ingulph us in the Bogs of Error. **1733** W. ELLIS *Chiltern & Vale Farm.* 15 The tread of the Sheep makes this Ground turn before the Plow in a clotty Substance. **1812** J. WILSON *Isle of Palms* II. 379 Thy noiseless tread..Fell soft as snow on snow. **1823** J. F. COOPER *Pioneers* xxxviii, Louisa was startled by the low, cracking, but cautious treads, of some one approaching through the bushes. **1840** DICKENS *Old C. Shop* i, That incessant tread of feet wearing the rough stones smooth and glossy. **1843** J. SMITH *Forest Trees* 64 He gives a tread with his foot to render it firm. **1878** M. A. BROWN *Nadeschda* 18 She followed with her ears his tread.

b. Manner of treading; hence, style of walking.

1609 *Old Meg of Herefordsh.* (1816) 10 Howe doe you like this Morris-daunce of Hereford-shire?.. Haue they not the right footing? the true tread? **1727** POPE *Lament. Glumdalclitch* 67 How wast thou wont to walk with cautious tread. **1812** BYRON *Ch. Har.* I. lxxiv, The ground, with cautious tread, is traversed o'er. **1840** R. S. HAWKER *Cornish Ball.*, etc. (1908) 89 Pause and move onward with obedient tread. **1850** MRS. BROWNING *Dead Pan* xi, Where O Juno, is the glory Of thy regal look and tread? **1881** LADY HERBERT *Edith* 7 She had the tread of an Empress.

c. *transf.* The quality or kind of the thing trodden upon; the sensation produced by treading on something (considered as an attribute of the thing). *rare.*

1819 KEATS *Lamia* 181 A sloping green of mossy tread.

II. 5. Course or manner of action; way of acting; *esp.* a habitual course; practice, custom; = TRADE *sb.* 3, 3 c. Chiefly *Sc.*

Tred is still the ordinary Sc. dial. word in all these senses = TRADE *sb.*, senses 3–9.

1562 *Reg. Privy Council Scot.* I. 212 Gif the tred wer nocht samekle usit be the inhabitantis of this realme. *a* **1572** KNOX *Hist. Ref.* Wks. 1846 I. 410 Quhat tred and ordour of doctrine thay have keipitt. **1572** *Satir. Poems Reform.* xxxiv. 10, I doe espy The Scottisch tred and nauchtie fassioun To be so bad. **1579** *Reg. Privy Council Scot.* III. 146 Following the bludie treade quhilk they and thair foirbearis of the same name had used of befoir. **1817** G. CHALMERS *Churchyard's Chips* Pref. 14 Three years..he saw the Emperor's wars: then homeward drew, as was his wonted tread. *Mod. Sc.* Ye mauna mak a tred o' gangin' there.

6. Regular occupation or business: = TRADE *sb.* 5. *Sc.*

1584 *Reg. Privy Council Scot.* III. 706 That na honest merchand..may peciablie travell nor use tred. **1588** *Ibid.* IV. 303 His Majesteis..subjectis ar havelie opprest and the tred of fisheing..gritlie impedit. **1596** *Sc. Acts Jas. VI* (1816) IV. 100/1 The following of ane lauchfull tred. **1603** *Reg. Mag. Sig. Scot.* 513/2 Cum libertate exercendi *the tred and traffique of merchandrice*. **1657** *Scott. Convention Rec.* III. 440 The whole tread only competent to merchandis of free burrowis. *Mod. Sc.* What's the man's tred? This weather is bad for tred. The tred o' the toon.

7. Coming and going; resort; intercourse; also, fuss, work; = TRADE *sb.* 7 a, 7 b, 7 c. *Sc. rare.*

1567 *Reg. Privy Council Scot.* I. 510 Having dalie and continewall tred with the inhabitantis. **1591** *Ibid.* IV. 627 Not onlie sall thair tred in thai pairtis be cutt of, bot a cruell wear salbe denunceit aganis his majestie. *Mod. Sc.* What a tred aboot getting them off!

III. 8. a. *Farriery.* A bruise or wound of the coronet of a horse's foot, caused by setting one foot upon the other, or by over-reaching.

1661 LOVELL *Hist. Anim. & Min.* 62 The skinne wrapped about a horse's foot, that hath a tread, helpeth the same. **1754** BARTLET *Farriery* xxxix. (ed. 2) 313 A quittor..arises often from treads and bruises. **1846** J. BAXTER *Libr. Pract. Agric.* (ed. 5) I. 451 Quittor..a severe tread, which the horse accidentally inflicts upon itself in its endeavours to avoid falling upon its sides. **1894** *Northumbld. Gloss.* s.v. *Treed*, When a horse has injured himself by setting one foot on another he is said to have 'getten a treed'.

b. An act of treadling or pedalling a machine.

1680 MOXON *Mech. Exerc.* x. 188 Keeping exact time in Treads,..the Workman gives a quick Tread upon the Treddle. **1790** A. WILSON *Poems & Lit. Prose* (1876) II. 243 Whene'er the smooth tread I apply My shopmates deplore how I've sped.

9. a. The action of the male bird in coition. **b.** The cicatricula or chalaza of an egg; = TREADLE *sb.* 3.

a. **1674** N. FAIRFAX *Bulk & Selv. World* 124 An egg,..a thing that sprang from the impetus of the tread,..to be what 'tis, after laid by the Hen. **1725** *Bradley's Fam. Dict.* II. P ij b/2 A Hen..will lay Eggs without the Tread of the Cock, but these Eggs..are good for nothing to hatch. **1765** *Treat. Dom. Pigeons* 23 She will squat, and readily receive his tread, by which she is rendered prolific.

b. **1593** SOUTHWELL *St. Peter's Compl.* 51 Kill bad Chickins in the tread. **1647** *Husbandman's Plea agst. Tithes* 40 Whether the Cocks tread.. be in every egge. **1796** MRS. GLASSE *Cookery* xx. 311 Strain off your eggs from the treads. **1871** HUXLEY *Anat. Vertebr. Anim.* (1882) 9 A patch of primary tissue;..the so-called *cicatricula*, or 'tread', which is observable in the new-laid egg, is of this nature.

10. Various technical senses.

a. The flat under side of the foot or of a shoe, which comes into contact with the ground in treading; the sole. **b.** A wheel track, a rut (*dial.*); the transverse distance between the two wheels of a cart or other vehicle; also, the width between the pedals of a bicycle or tricycle; the outer surface of a wheel, tire, or sledge runner; *spec.* the thick moulded surface of a pneumatic tyre, which runs in contact with the ground (as opp. to the sidewalls); cf. RETREAD *sb.* 1; also, the rail surface on which the wheel bears. **c.** A shaped plate of iron worn under the hollow of the shoe to protect it in digging; a tramp. **d.** *Shipbuilding*: see quot. *c* 1850. **e.** The projecting foot-rest or step of a stilt (*Cassell's Encycl. Dict.* 1888). **f.** The upper side of the bed of a lathe between the headstock and back-centre (Knight *Dict. Mech.* 1877).

a. *c* **1720** W. GIBSON *Farrier's Guide* I. v. (1738) 76 The.. Plantaris, or Muscle of the Soal or Tread. **1898** J. HUTCHINSON in *Arch. Surg.* IX. No. 36. 337 The symptom ..was pain under the tread of his left foot.

b. **1735-6** PEGGE *Kenticisms, Tread*, a wheel-tread, rut, tract [i.e. track]. **1765** *Museum Rust.* IV. lix. 248 It would be less material what breadth the wheels themselves were of, so that their tread be flat. *Ibid.* 249 If carts were to have the distance of their [wheels] either equal to the greatest or least tread of the waggons, it would generally help to preserve and commode the roads. **1797** J. CURR *Coal Viewer* 25 Plain turn plates. Used for going round a turn. The trod or tread of these [tram-]plates are 4 inches broad. **1844** STEPHENS *Bk. Farm* III. 1163 This standard..has..been fixed at 4 feet 4 inches between the tread of the wheels. **1875** *Sussex Gloss.* s.v. *Trades*, 'You will never get your carriage down that laine, for it can't take the trades'. **1887** BURY & HILLIER *Cycling* 346 To keep 'the tread' of the machines, i.e. the width from pedal to pedal as narrow as possible. **1897** *Cycl. Tour. Cl. Gaz.* Sept. 399 A large hob-nail..in the middle of the tread [of a pneumatic tire]. **1902** C. L. FREESTON in A. C. Harmsworth *Motors & Motor-Driving* 237 *The Collier* ..this type is provided with an unusually stout tread. **1913** *Sci. Amer.* 11 Jan. 53/1 The tread is made up independently of the tire by laying up narrow strips of rubber..in such a way that the center of the tread is thicker than the edges. **1929** *Rubber & Tyre Rev.* Jan. 148/1 On pneumatic tyres for buses an average of 6,000 miles per ⅛ in. tread thickness can be safely assumed. **1964** *Amer. Speech* XXXIX. 275 *Tread, n.*, the outer, final component of the assembled tire. It is made up of the cap which contacts the road surface and the sidewall. **1982** M. RUSSELL *Rainblast* iv. 28 People come along fast... The treads find they've a little extra to do.

c. **1842** LOUDON *Suburban Hort.* 133 To save the shoes of the operator, a plate of iron about two inches broad, with leather straps, called a tread, is tied to his shoe.

d. *c* **1850** *Rudim. Navig.* (Weale) 156 *Tread of the keel*, the whole length of the keel upon a straight line.

11. a. The horizontal upper surface of a step in a stair; also, the width of this from front to back; also, each of the rungs of a ladder.

1712 J. JAMES tr. *Le Blond's Gardening* 125 Each Step may have 15 or 16 Inches Tread, to five or six Inches Rise. **1791** SMEATON *Edystone L.* (1793) §88 There was but one flat or tread of a step above the center of the house. **1833** LOUDON *Encycl. Archit.* §239 One inch and a quarter oak treads with rounded nosings. **1838** *Civil Eng. & Arch. Jrnl.* I. 268/1 Ladders were of..rude construction..formed of two uprights with nailed treads or rounds on the face. **1884** *Health Exhib. Catal.* 49/1 Terra Cotta steps, with patent silicon treads. **1884** F. T. HODGSON *Stair-building* 12 Wall strings are the supporters of the ends of the treads and risers.

b. *Fortif.* A terrace at the back of a parapet, on which the defenders stand to fire over the parapet.

1834-47 J. S. MACAULAY *Field Fortif.* (1851) 3 The tread of the banquette..is made 3 feet wide, when the parapet is to be defended by a single rank. **1853** STOCQUELER *Milit. Encycl., Tread*, of a banquette, the upper and flat surface on which the soldier stands whilst firing over the parapet.

c. *Geomorphol.* The approximately horizontal part of each of the step-like parts of a glacial stairway or similar landform.

1904 [see STAIRWAY b]. **1930** F. E. MATTHES *Geol. Hist. Yosemite Valley* 95/2 Rock structure, or, more broadly, rock resistance,..determines in large measure at what points in a given canyon the individual sills and treads shall develop. **1954** *Jrnl. Glaciol.* II. 421 Fig. 2..shows a *roche moutonnée* of step-like form... The contrast between the smoothed upper tread and the irregular 'plucked' riser can be seen. **1968** R. W. FAIRBRIDGE *Encycl. Geomorphol.* 467/1 Where the overdeepened treads are undrained, there are rock-cut depressions or partly moraine-dammed pools... They are known as paternoster lakes.

IV. 12. *attrib.* and *Comb.*, as (sense 4) *tread-mire*; (sense 10 b) *tread cover, rubber, surface*; † **tread-behind**, a doubling; an evasion, artifice, shift; **tread-board**, the tread of a step = sense 11; also, each of the steps in a treadmill; † **tread-fowl**, the male bird; cf. 9 a; **tread plate**, (*a*) a footplate or runner which forms or protects the step on a vehicle; (*b*) (see quot. 1967); **tread-road** (*dial.*): see quot.; cf. *tread-way*; **treadsman** = TREADER; † **treadsole**, a door-sill; **tread-steps**, carriage-steps with flat treads; **tread-trap** *Archæol.*, a wooden device for trapping an animal by the foot; † **tread-way**, a roadway, thoroughfare. See also TREADMILL, TREAD-WHEEL.

1844 S. NAYLOR *Reynard the Fox* 20 His tricks and traps and *tread-behinds. **1908** *Westm. Gaz.* 16 Nov. 5/3 As regards the round and square *tread covers their imperviousness to cutting by flints [etc.]. *c* **1386** CHAUCER *Monk's Prol.* 57 Thou woldest han been a *tredefowel aright. **1888** G. M. HOPKINS *Poems* (1967) 105 Stanches, starches Squadroned masks and manmarks *treadmire toil there Footfretted in it. **1949** *Automobile & Carriage Builders' Jrnl.* CIV. 59 (*heading*) P-G-P aluminium *tread-plate. **1967** *Gloss. Sanitation Terms* (*B.S.I.*) 57 *Tread plate.* 1. Glazed ceramic, or other hard wearing, edging to the floor finish adjacent to the channel of a urinal. 2. Glazed ceramic, or other hard wearing, non-slip footrests on each side of a squatting W.C. pan. **1894** *Northumbld. Gloss.*, **Treed-road*, a beaten path. **1909** *Westm. Gaz.* 1 June 4/2 The rubber used in their non-skid is not ordinary '*tread' rubber. **1519** HORMAN *Vulg.* 237 The iewest..that the *tredisman.. brouseth out of the grapis. *c* **1546** JOYE in Bp. Gardiner *Declar.* 14 The *tredsole or groundsole whereupon..the dore is turned and returned. **1837** W. B. ADAMS *Carriages* 87 *Tread Steps, for the coachman to mount by. **1896** *Godey's Mag.* Apr. 347/1 The *tread surface of the canvas tube was covered with two or three layers of the sheet rubber. **1952** J. G. D. CLARK *Prehist. Europe* ii. 51 A type of *tread-trap ..appearing for the first time in the Late Bronze Age.. symbolizes the part still played by trapping in the closing stages of European prehistory. **1630** T. WESTCOTE *Devon.* II. xxiii. (1845) 187 For whose more christian-like burial there is (in a spacious large *tread-way near the place of execution) a plot of ground enclosed with strong stone walls.

Hence **'treaded** *a.* [-ED²], of a tyre: having or furnished with a moulded tread; **treadless** *a.* [-LESS], having no tread or treads (esp. of tyres).

1906 *Westm. Gaz.* 6 Mar. 4/2 The substitution of single pneumatic tyres for the present double-treaded ones. **1968** A. DIMENT *Great Spy Race* x. 186 The treadless tyres teetered on tiptoe across the road. **1973** 'D. RUTHERFORD' *Kick Start* vi. 139 The bike canting at a steep angle, we were holding on to the road surface by the treaded edge of the competition tyre. **1974** *Observer* 3 Nov. (Colour Suppl.) 27/2 Wearing treadless shoes, [we] were let into a dusty attic with a forged key. Another prisoner followed us, replacing anything we might move.

tread (trɛd), *v.* Pa. t. trod (trɒd), *arch.* trode (trəʊd). Pa. pple. trodden ('trɒd(ə)n), trod (trɒd). Forms: see below. [OE. *tredan* (pa. t. *træd*, pl. *trǣdon*, pa. pple. *treden*); ME. *treden* (*trad*, *trêden*, *treden*); a Common Teut. strong vb., = OFris. *treda* (*trad*, *tred*, *trêd-*, *treden*), OS. *tredan* (*trad*, *trâd-un*, *treden*); MDu., MLG. *trēden*, Du., LG. *trēden*, OHG. *tretan* (*trat*, *trâtun*; *gi-tretan*), MHG., Ger. *treten*; Da. *træde*, Sw. *träda*, Norw. *treda*; OTeut. **tređ-*; **trađ-*, pl. **trǣđ-*; *tređ-*, of which a weak grade *truđ-* gave Goth. *trudan* (**trap*, **trêdum*, *trudans*), and ON. *troða* (*trað*, *trǫðum*; *troðinn*). Not certainly known outside Teutonic. In the 14th c. (in Hampole *a* 1340), either under Norse influence, or by assimilation to vbs. of Class IV (*brecan*, *bræc*, *brocen*), the pa. pple. *troden* (later *trodden*, *trode*, *trod*) began to be substituted for the original *treden*, although the latter in its shortened form *tred(e*, *tread* survived with some to the 17th c., and is still in dialect use. In the end of the 14th c. *troden* is found in the pl. of the pa. t., and from the 16th c. *trode*, *trod* also in the sing. Ormin has a weak pa. pple. *trededd* for *treden*, and a weak pa. t. *tredide*, *tredde* appears in the later Wyclifite version. Cf. OE. *treddian*, OHG. *trettôn*, ON. *treðja*, OTeut. type **tradjan*, perh. orig. intensive, but subseq. mixed up with the primary strong vb.]

A. Illustration of Forms.

1. *Inf.* and *Pres. stem.* 1 tredan, (trædan), 3-4 treden, 3-5 trede, (4 tredde), 4-7 tred, (5 tredyn, tradde), 6-8 treade, 6- tread. *Inflexions* 1 trædað, trides, trideð, 4 tredeth, 6 treddis.

a **700** *Beowulf* 1965 Ȝewat him þa se hearda..sæ-wong tredan. *a* **800** *Riddles* viii. 1 þonne ic hrusan trede. *Ibid.* viii. 5 Trædað bearonæssas. *Ibid.* lxxxi. 24 Hio..grundbedd trideð. *c* **825** *Vesp. Psalter* xc. 13 Ðu..trides leon & dracan. *a* **1000** *Ags. Ps.* (Th.) lv[i]. 1 Miltsa me, Drihten, forðon me man tredeð. *c* **1200** ORMIN 11946 Godess þeowwess gan onn himm & tredenn himm wiþþ fote. *a* **1340** HAMPOLE *Psalter* vii. 5 þe enmy..tred [*conculcet*] in erth my lyf. *c* **1386** CHAUCER *Knt.'s T.* 2160 The harde stoon..on which we trede and goon. **1388** WYCLIF *Rom.* xvi. 20 God of pees tredde Sathanas vndur ȝoure feet. *c* **1440** Tradde [see B. 11]. **1523** FITZHERB. *Husb.* §21 Let hym beware, that he trede not to moche vppon the corne. **1535** COVERDALE *Job* xl. 7 Treade all the vngodly vnder thy fete. **1567** *Gude & Godlie B.* (S.T.S.) 108 Thow sall..tred on the cruell Cocketrice. **1567** *Sc. Acts Jas. VI* (1814) III. 41 þame þat treddis hairis in þe snaw. **1570** LEVINS *Manip.* 206/1 To Treade, go, *gressus ponere*. **1583** BABINGTON *Commandm.* viii. (1590) 354 Vntoothsome is that trueth euer, that treadeth downe my liking. **1596** SPENSER *F.Q.* VI. ix. 27 Which..under foot doth tread The mightie ones [*rime* dread].

2. *Pa. t.* α. 1 træd, 2-5 trad; 3-5 tradd, 4-5 trade, 5 tradde. β. 6 *Sc.* tred, (8 tread). γ. 6-9 trode, 6- trod (6 trodd). δ. *pl.* 1 trǣdon, 4 trêden, (treeden), 4-5 trōden, 5 trāden, trād, 6 trood, 4-9 trode, 6- trod. ε. (*weak conj.*) 4 treddede, *pl.* trediden, tredden, 5 treyde, 20 treaded (only in phr. *treaded water*: see sense 7).

α. *a* **700** *Beowulf* 1882 Beowulf þanan..græs-moldan træd. *c* **1200** ORMIN 2561 Forr ȝho tradd deofell unnderrfot. **1388** WYCLIF *Ecclus.* xxiv. 11 Y trad bi vertu on the neckis of all excelent men. **1470-85** MALORY *Arthur* XIX. iv. 778 His hors..trade his [own] guttes..vnder his feet. **1481** CAXTON *Reynard* xxxix. (Arb.) 105 The wulf trade forth to the foxe in grete wrath. **1484** —— *Fables of Æsop* II. xx, The oxe.. thradde and thrested her [the frog] with his fote. *c* **1489** —— *Blanchardyn* xxiv. 89 The grasse wher vpon he trad.

β. **1560** ROLLAND *Seven Sages* 37 With feit [scho] it tred. **1737** WHISTON *Josephus, Antiq.* II. ix. §7 Moses..tread upon it with his feet.

γ. **1535** COVERDALE *2 Kings* xiv. 9 A wylde beest..ran ouer yᵉ hawthorne and trode it downe. [So *2 Chron.* xxv. 18.] **1600** HEYWOOD *2nd Pt. Edw. IV*, II. iv. Wks. 1874 I. 139 Pity that ere awry she trod her shoe. **1738** GRAY *Tasso* 15 Against the stream the waves secure he trod. **1823** BYRON *Juan* VI. cxi, The way in which he trode. **1823** SCOTT *Quentin D.* xxvi, One of the bravest and most noble gentle-men that ever trode a court.

δ. ? *a* **1300** *Debate of Body & Soul* 423 Ther alle þe fendes fet it trode [*rime* brode]. **1377** LANGL. *P. Pl.* B. XI. 347 Some [birds] troden hir makes and on trees bredden [C. XIV. 166 And some treden..and on trees bredden]. **1382** WYCLIF *2 Kings* ix. 33 The hors houes that treden [**1388** to tredden] hyre. *c* **1420** *Chron. Vilod.* 2940, & nyst neuer where þey wenton ny trede. **1483** CAXTON *Gold. Leg.* 173 b/2 They trad the corne in the feldes doun. **1526** TINDALE *Luke* xii. 1 In so moche that they trood won another. **1535** COVERDALE *2 Kings* vii. 17 The people trode [WYCL. trade] vpon him, so that he dyed. *a* **1604** HANMER *Chron. Irel.* (1633) 33 The Irish..trode not upon Scottish soile. **1715-20** POPE *Iliad* XV. 412 The wondering crowds the downward level trod. **1850** HAWTHORNE *Scarlet L.* Introd. (1879) 16 Trode the unworn street.

ε. (*weak conj.*) **1388** WYCLIF *2 Kings* xiv. 9 The beestis.. passiden, and treddeden [*v.r.* tretedden] doun the cardue. —— *Luke* xii. 1 So that thei treden [*v.rr.* treeden, traden, trediden; 1382 troden] ech on othir. **1432-50** tr. *Higden* (Rolls) VII. 9 His feete..with whom he treyde [L. *pulsaverat*] the tumbe of blissede Odo. **1944** *Stars & Stripes* (London ed.) 1 May 3 While Huie and four crewmen clambered into the liferaft, three others treaded water for three hours before succeeding in blowing up another raft by lung power. **1947** H. E. BATES *Purple Plain* x. 113 He treaded water for a moment or two. **1974** J. IRVING *158-Pound Marriage* viii. 193 He said nothing; he treaded water.

3. *Pa. pple.* α. 1-3 treden, 3-4 i-trede, y-tredde, 6 tredden, tredd(e, 6-7 *Sc.* tred, 7 tread. β. 4-7 troden, (4 troddun), 6- trodden; 4 i-trode, 4-9 trode, (7 troad(e), 5- trod. γ. (*weak conj.*) 3 (*Orm.*) trēdedd.

α. *a* **900** tr. *Bæda's Hist.* III. xvi. [xxii.] (1890) 224 Utworpen..&.fotum treden[e] & in eorðan ȝehwyrfde wæron. *c* **1315** SHOREHAM *Poems* i. 821 Namore ne greueþ hyt ihesus þane sonne [? stone] itrede in felþe. *c* **1410** *Master of Game* (MS. Digby 182) xxiv, If ye se it [the lair] gret and brode and wele ytredde. **1509** BARCLAY *Shyp of Folys* (1570) 208 They under foote are tred. *c* **1520** M. NISBET *N. Test. in Scots, Rev.* xiv. 20 The lake was treddin [**1388** WYCLIF, troddun] without the citee. **1549** COVERDALE, etc. *Erasm. Par. Rom.* 31 Lye they on the grounde and are tredde vnderfoote. **1580** SIDNEY *Ps.* XXXI. vi, Like a broken pott, in myer tredd. **1600** HAMILTON *Facile Traictise* Ded., Brocht in contempt and tred vnderfut. **1608** TOPSELL *Serpents* (1658) 619 The Water-nep..which under-foot is tread [*rime* bed]. **1687** A. LOVELL tr. *Thevenot's Trav.* II. 86 Being trampled and tread upon.

β. *a* **1340** HAMPOLE *Psalter* xvii. 42 þai sall be troden vndire my luf. *c* **1350** *Will. Palerne* 3402 Wit here horse troden. **1600** HOLLAND *Camden's Brit.* (1637) 821 The Percies with it troden under foot. **1614** T. ADAMS in Spurgeon *Treas. Dav.* Ps. xiii. 5 Are trodden down by the poor.

1387 TREVISA *Higden* (Rolls) V. 379 Hym semede þat he [a cross] was nouȝt worþy to be trode [CAXTON, trede] wiþ his feet. *Ibid.* VIII. 113 His baner was i-trode in þe fen. **1607** TOPSELL *Hist. Four-f. Beasts* (1658) 234 Hens do lay egges being not troad by a Cock. **1614** EARL STIRLING *Domes-Day* III. lxxx, Their empty channels may be troad on dry. **1621** BP. MOUNTAGU *Diatribæ* 359 To haue..trod vnder foot the Law of God. **1725** POPE *Odyss.* v. 124 By mighty Jove's command..have I trod this pleasing land. **1774** BEATTIE *Minstr.* II. vi, Which heretofore his foot had never trode.

γ. *c* **1200** ORMIN 5728 Beo trededd dun.

B. Signification.

1. a. *trans.* To step upon; to pace or walk on (the ground, etc.); to walk in (a place); hence, to go about in (a place, etc.).

a **700** *Beowulf* [see A. 1]. **1362** LANGL. *P. Pl.* A. x. 101 Selden Moseþ þe Marbelston þat men ofte treden. **1382** WYCLIF *Deut.* xi. 24 Eche place that ȝoure foot tredith, shal be ȝour. **1591** *Troub. Raigne K. John* (1611) 26 Treading my Confines with thy armed troupes. **1594** ? GREENE *Selimus* Wks. (Grosart) XIV. 212 Then let our winged coursers tread the winde. **1697** DRYDEN *Virg. Georg.* III. 543 He who treads the bleak Meotian Strand. **1729** G. ADAMS tr. *Sophocles, Oedip. Colon.* I. v. II. 102 The Goddesses.. whose Ground you have trod. **1802** WORDSW. *Sonn. 'Here, on our native soil'*, 'Tis joy enough and pride For one hour's perfect bliss, to tread the grass Of England once again. **1823** CHALMERS *Serm.* I. 397 As hardy adventurers as ever trode the desert in quest of novelty. **1837** W. IRVING *Capt. Bonneville* II. 53 The trapper stands..and gazes upon a promised land which his feet are never to tread.

b. Phrases. *to tread the stage* (*the boards*), to act upon the stage, to follow the profession of an actor (also *fig.* to write stage-plays). *to tread* †*clay, this earth, shoe-leather*, to be alive, to live; *to tread the deck*, to be on board ship, be a sailor; *to tread the ground*, to walk.

1691 G. LANGBAINE *Acc. Eng. Dram. Poets* 465 Shakespear by him reviv'd now treads the Stage. **1700** DRYDEN *Flower & Leaf* 182 Methought she trod the ground with greater grace. **1711** STEELE *Spect.* No. 22 ¶2 One that never trod the Stage before. **1748** *Anson's Voy.* II. xiii. 274 As skilful seamen as ever trod a deck. **1789** BURNS *To Dr.*

Blacklock x, She is a dainty chuckie, As e'er tread clay. **1825** SCOTT *Talism.* xxiv, The steeds..chafed on the bit, and trod the ground more proudly. **1828** J. T. SMITH *Bk. Rainy Day* (1861) 255 A better man never trod shoe-leather. **1858** LYTTON *What will he do* I. viii, She had never then trod the boards. **1868** FREEMAN *Norm. Conq.* II. viii. 164 No man that ever trod this earth was ever endowed with greater natural gifts.

2. a. To step or walk upon or along; to follow, pursue (a path, track, or road); also *fig.*

a **700** *Beowulf* 1353 On weres wæstmum wræc-lastas træd. **1551** RECORDE *Pathw. Knowl.* To Rdr., I will not cease.. treading the paths of labour. **1697** DRYDEN *Virg. Georg.* IV. 517 The downward track he treads. **1754** CHATHAM *Lett. Nephew* vi. 40 Those who have trod the paths of the world before them. **1841** JAMES *Brigand* xix, I never forget a path I have once trodden. **1884** W. H. WHITE *Mark Rutherford's Deliverance* viii. (1892) 111 Yet he treads his path undisturbed.

b. †*to tread a person's steps* (*fig.*), to walk in the steps of, follow the example of (*obs.*); *to tread back one's steps* (*fig.*), to retrace one's steps (now *rare* or *obs.*).

1579 W. WILKINSON *Confut. Familye of Loue* 100 To.. tread the steppes of Gods sonne. **1641** J. JACKSON *True Evang. T.* II. 117 S. Philip..was fastened to the Crosse, and stoned to death, treading the steps both of his Master, and of Stephen. *a* **1704** T. BROWN *Ess. on Women* Wks. 1711 IV. 152 They tread the Steps of their Parents, meerly by instinct. **1752** FOOTE *Taste* Ded. (ed. 4) 6 In the following Sheets her Steps have been trode with an undeviating Simplicity. **1777** PRIESTLEY *Matt. & Spir.* (1782) I. i. 7 The philosophical part of the world [may] tread back their steps. **1831** D. E. WILLIAMS *Life & Corr. Sir T. Lawrence* I. 243 We must tread back our steps.

†**c.** *to tread the feet of*, to trace the footprints of. *Sc. Obs. rare.*

1596 DALRYMPLE tr. *Leslie's Hist. Scot.* VI. (S.T.S.) I. 350 To schue thrie suofte horses backward, that..the persewer ..mycht not find how to tred the horses fute rycht.

d. *to tread a measure,* †*a dance*, etc., to go through a dance in a rhythmic or stately manner; to go through in dancing; so *to tread a march. arch.* and *poet.*

1577 GRANGE *Golden Aphrod.* M ij b, After these came Silenus..treadyng the hornpype. **1580** H. GIFFORD *Gilloflowers* (Grosart) 118 Thrice happy is their chaunce, That never knew to treade the lover's daunce. **1590** GREENE *Orl. Fur.* Wks. (Rtldg.) 90/1 That did but Venus tread a dainty step. **1592** SHAKS. *Ven. & Ad.* 1148 Teaching decrepit age to tread the measures. **1808** SCOTT *Marm.* V. xii, 'Now tread we a measure!' said young Lochinvar. **1810** —— *Lady of L.* II. vii, The proud march which victors tread. **1859** JEPHSON *Brittany* iii. 30 The favoured one who should tread a measure with her Imperial Majesty.

3. a. *intr.* To walk, go, pace; to set down the feet in walking; to step. Also said of the foot.

In quot. *c* 897 rendering L. *terere* of the Vulgate.

c **897** K. ÆLFRED *Gregory's Past. C.* xlvii. 357 Aworpen mon..bicneð mid ðæm eaʒum, & trit mid ðæm fet, & spricð mid ðæm fingre. *a* **1400–50** *Alexander* 1515 All þe brade stretis..þar he trede sulde. **1481** CAXTON *Reynard* xxxix. (Arb.) 105 The wulf trade forth to the foxe in grete wrath. **1535** COVERDALE *Deut.* xi. 24 All the places that the soles of youre fete treade vpon, shalbe yours. —— *Ezek.* xliii. 19 Yᵉ Leuites that..treade before me to do me seruyce. **1599** SHAKS. *Hen. V*, IV. vii. 149 As arrant a villaine and a Iacke sawce, as euer his blacke shoo trodd vpon Gods ground. **1601** —— *Jul. C.* I. i. 29 As proper men as euer trod vpon Neats Leather. **1632** LITHGOW *Trav.* I. 22, I haue trod foure seuerall times from end to end of it. **1748** THOMSON *Cast. Indol.* II. xxxv, An honest sober beast, that..full softly trode. **1816** BYRON *Prisoner of Chillon* xi, Avoiding only, as I trod, My brothers' graves without a sod. **1860** TYNDALL *Glac.* I. xxi. 149, I crossed the glacier, treading with the utmost caution along the combs of ice.

b. *intr.* In phrases, esp. in fig. sense. *to tread on air*, to walk buoyantly or jubilantly; cf. *to walk upon air* s.v. WALK *v.*¹ 5 l; *to tread on eggs, on delicate ground, on thin ice*: see the sbs.

1481 CAXTON *Reynard* xliii. (Arb.) 118 Eueriche of them tredeth in the foxes path and seketh his hole. **1580** SIDNEY *Ps.* xxv. vi, He doth..teach the humble how to tread. **1668** DENHAM *Prudence* Poems 147 Sense, her Vassal, in her footsteps treads. **1694** F. BRAGGE *Disc. Parables* xi. 381 Misery, and shame, and repentance, always tread close at the heels of wickedness. **1709** POPE *Ess. Crit.* 625 Fools rush in where Angels fear to tread [*rime* dead]. *a* **1734** NORTH *Lives* (1826) I. 266 He had his jury to deal with, and if he did not tread upon eggs, they would conclude sinistrously. **1796** R. M. ROCHE *Children of Abbey* I. viii. 154 Such were the ideas of the innocent and romantic Amanda; ideas, which made her seem to tread on air. *a* **1817** JANE AUSTEN *Northanger Abbey* (1818) II. xi. 223 If Wednesday should ever come!.. It came—it was fine— and Catherine trod on air. **1817** JAS. MILL *Brit. India* II. v. vi. 560 On the principal ground, however, the parliament..trode nearly blindfold. **1839** T. MITCHELL *Aristoph., Frogs* 452 *note*, Was the author treading upon still more delicate ground than the Scholiast has imagined? **1874** W. MELVILLE *Uncle J.* xxii, Leaving the gaol..Mr. Lexley seemed to tread on air.

4. a. *intr.* To step *on* (something in one's way); to put the foot down *upon* accidentally or intentionally, esp. so as to press upon.

c **1384** [see b]. *c* **1489** CAXTON *Blanchardyn* xiv. 49 His courser..tradd vpon one of his armes. **1561** T. NORTON *Calvin's Inst.* III. 274 He will come..to thinke it vnlawfull.. to treade vpon a strawe lying a crosse. **1603** SHAKS. *Meas. for M.* III. i. 79 The poore Beetles that we treade upon. *c* **1643** LD. HERBERT *Autobiog.* (1824) 180 Finding my bare feet hurt by the stones I trod on. **1852** MRS. STOWE *Uncle Tom's C.* xx, A body can't set their foot down without treading on 'em. **1887** BOWEN *Æneid* II. 380 When a traveller..Treads on a snake unseen.

b. Phrase. *to tread on any one's heels* or *toes* (also *fig.*); see the sbs.

c **1384** CHAUCER *H. Fame* III. 1063 Tho behynde begunne vp lepe And clamben vp on other fast..And troden [*v.r.* treden] fast on other heles. **1638** JUNIUS *Paint. Ancients* 15 To come so neere as to tread upon their heeles. **1710** ADDISON *Tatler* No. 250 ¶11 If asking Pardon is an Attonement for treading upon ones Toes? **1711** STEELE *Spect.* No. 153 ¶1 The Cocking young Fellow who treads upon the Toes of his Elders. **1868, 1879** [see TOE *sb.* 5 i]. **1896** SIR W. WALROND in *Libr. Mag.* Dec. 504 If they legislated too much they were bound to tread on somebody's toes.

c. *to tread on the gas*: see GAS *sb.*²

5. *trans.* †**a.** To step or walk with pressure on (something) esp. so as to crush, beat down, injure, or destroy it; to trample. *Obs.* (exc. as in b.)

c **825** [see A. 1]. *a* **900** Fotum treden [see A. 3]. *a* **1000** *Ags. Ps.* (Th.) xc. 113 þu..miht..bealde nu basiliscan tredan. *a* **1340** HAMPOLE *Psalter* xxiv. 1 Wha sa ligges þare in, þe deuel tredis him. **1387** [see A. 3 β]. **1535** COVERDALE *Luke* xii. 1 There were gathered together an innumerable multitude of people, in so much that they trode one another. **1573–80** BARET *Alv.* V 23 Treade a worme on the taile, and it turneth againe. **1656** B. HARRIS *Parival's Iron Age* (1659) 145 He was found amongst the dead, so trodden, and tumbled..that he was hard to be known. **1712** tr. *Pomet's Hist. Drugs* I. 160 To make 'em tight..they imploy Men to tread them [raisins] with their Feet.

b. With adverbial extension, as *to tread down, under foot, in the mire, to the ground, to pieces*, etc.; *to tread to death*, to kill by trampling.

c **1200** ORMIN 2248 Alle þa þatt tredenn dun & cwenkenn All þatt tatt iss onnʒæness Godd. *c* **1290** *S. Eng. Leg.* I. 206/207 þe deoulene ornen opon hem and treden heom to þe grounde. **14..** *Sir Beues* 1195 (MS. M.) He..tredith hym vnder his fete In the dirte. **1523** LD. BERNERS *Froiss.* I. ccccxxii. 739 In the thicke of the prease, they..were troden vnder fote to dethe. **1556** OLDE *Antichrist* 99 b, The B. of Rome..is not ashamed to treade yᵉ Lordes anointed neckes under his abominable feet. **1652** C. B. STAPYLTON *Herodian* xix. 159 Some he kils and some he treads to Jelly. **1678** BUNYAN *Pilgr.* I. 79 He thought he should be..troden down like mire in the Streets. **1726** SWIFT *Gulliver* II. viii, Being trod to death like a frog or a young puppy. **1823** SCOTT *Quentin D.* xvi, The wild boar of the forest, which treadeth down with his hoofs, and rendeth with his tusks.

c. *fig.* To crush, to oppress; to treat with contemptuous cruelty.

1526 *Pilgr. Perf.* (W. de W. 1531) 21 Tredynge vnder fote & vtterly despysynge all worldly pleasure & payne. **1652** in W. M. Williams *Ann. Founders' Co.* (1867) 32 For manie years extreamly trodden and kept under foote by the power and will of the Master. **1766** GOLDSM. *Vic. W.* xxix, The luxuriant great ones of the world shall no more tread us to the earth. **1775** S. J. PRATT *Liberal Opin.* xlviii. (1783) II. 66 In the city, the spirit of humanity is too often trod under feet by the spirit of trade. **1857** HOLLAND *Bay Path* xxix, Her memory..trodden under feet by malice, prejudice, and superstition. **1889** GRETTON *Memory's Harkb.* 163 In his early days the masses were a good deal trodden down.

d. *intr.* for *pass.* To be trampled *down.*

1837 CARLYLE *Fr. Rev.* III. II. i, The Gironde..has trodden on it, and yet not trodden it down... It is a well-spring, as we said, this black-spot; and will not tread down.

6. *intr.* To trample *on* or *upon.* Also *fig.*

c **1000** *Ags. Gosp.* Luke x. 19 Ic sealde eow anweald to tredenne ofer næddran & snacan. *c* **1330** *Amis & Amil.* 2096 He..trad [*MS.* drad] on him in the slough. **1382** WYCLIF *Luke* x. 19, I haue ȝouun to ȝou power of defoulinge, [*gloss*] othir tredinge, on serpents, and scorpiouns. *c* **1450** tr. *De Imitatione* III. xiv. 82 þat al men mowe goo over þee, and trede vppon the as vppon myre of the streete. **1590** MARLOWE *2nd Pt. Tamburl.* III. ii, Tread upon his neck, And treble all his father's slaveries. **1596** DALRYMPLE tr. *Leslie's Hist. Scot.* IV. (S.T.S.) I. 225 The sygne of the croce..vpon the ground, quhairthrouche feit mychte haue occasione to tred or tramp thairvpon. **1683** *Col. Rec. Pennsylv.* I. 79 James Kilner Trode upon him on board the Ship. **1733** FIELDING *Quix. in Eng.* II. i, Each man rises to admiration by treading on mankind. **1818** SCOTT *Rob Roy* xxxix, A hatred as intense..as if my foot trode on your neck. **1884** PAE *Eustace* 79 Was he a worm to be trod on thus without turning?

7. *trans.* To press (something) downwards with the foot or feet treadling or pedalling.

to tread water, in swimming, to move the feet as in walking upstairs, while the body is kept erect and the head above water; also *fig.*, to withhold oneself from progressive action, to 'mark time'.

1680 MOXON *Mech. Exerc.* xii. 209 The nearer the Fore-end of the Treddle you Tread, the easier you bring down the Pole. *Ibid.*, Tread the Treddle nimbly down. **1800** *Hull Advertiser* 15 Nov. 4/3, I always raised myself by treading water. **1853** KANE *Grinnell Exp.* xxxviii. (1856) 343 Seal breast-high, were treading water with their horizontal tails. **1942** J. LEES-MILNE *Ancestral Voices* (1975) 46 Although they miscalculated in assuming that the campaign would be over before last winter, they have been treading water since then, and merely keeping up their line. **1967** *Guardian* 24 May 9 In the absence of the Secretary-General, the UN delegations were treading water. **1980** N. MARSH *Photo-Finish* vi. 180, I am really..treading water until the police arrive.

8. a. Of the male bird: To copulate with (the hen). Also *absol.*

a **1250** *Owl & Night.* 501 Sone so þu hauest itrede Ne myht þu leng a word iqueþe. **1377** [see A. 2 δ]. *c* **1386** CHAUCER *Nun's Pr. T.* 358 (Ellesm.) He..fethered Pertelote twenty tyme And trad [**14..** *Lansd. MS.* trade hire] as ofte. **1599** T. M[OUFET] *Silkwormes* 24 Before the hardie Cocke Beganne to tread, or brooding henne to clocke. **1614** MARKHAM *Cheap Husb.* (1623) 143 If your Henne be trodden with a carryon Crow, or Rooke,..it is mortall and incurable. *a* **1687** COTTON tr. *Martial* III. lviii. (1689) 59 I' th' Yards are seen, Cocks treading Rhodian Hens. **1721** BRADLEY *Philos. Acc. Wks. Nat.* 78 It is common for Cock Pheasants to tread the Hens of common Poultry. **1774** GOLDSM. *Nat. Hist.* (1776) V. 165 It matters not much whether she be trodden by the cock or no; she will continue to lay. **1910** A. PLATT tr. *Aristotle's De Generatione* III. viii. 751 When once the hens have been trodden, they all continue to have eggs almost without intermission.

b. *absol.* Of birds: To copulate.

1486 *Bk. St. Albans, Hawking* a ij, We shall say that they [Hawks] trede. *a* **1659** OSBORN *Queries* Wks. (1673) 612, I my Self have seen both Swallowes and Hobbies build and tread upon their first Appearance. **1774** G. WHITE *Selborne* 28 Sept., The fact that I would advance is, that swifts tread, or copulate, on the wing.

†**c.** *trans.* with *out*: To engender, beget (offspring). *Obs. rare*⁻¹.

1594 LYLY *Moth. Bomb.* I. i, As your Worship being wise begot a foole, so he being a foole may tread out a wise man.

9. a. *trans.* To thresh (corn) by trampling it on a threshing-floor: said of the oxen, etc. or of one using them; also with *out.* **b.** To press out the juice of (grapes) by trampling them in a vat. **c.** To tramp (clothes) in washing; see TRAMP *v.*¹ 3 c.

1382 WYCLIF *Deut.* xxv. 4 Thow shalt not bynde the mouth of the oxe tredinge thi fruytis in the flore. —— *Isa.* xvi. 10 Wyn in the presse he shal not trede, that to treden was wont; the vois of the trederes I toc awey. **1446** LYDG. *Two Nightingale Poems* ii. 155 It is [I], quod he, that trade it al alone. Withouten felawe I gan the wyne out-presse. **1577** B. GOOGE *Heresbach's Husb.* 42 b, Corne..in some place they..lyke to tread it out with Oxen. **1792** A. YOUNG *Trav. France* 31 This universal one of treading out the corn, with which all the towns and villages in Languedoc are now alive. **1801** *Farmer's Mag.* Aug. 313, I was long, and greatly prejudised against treading wheat. **1848** CLOUGH *Bothie* ii, The clothes that they trod in the wash-tub. **1871** B. TAYLOR *Faust* (1875) II. I. ii. 20 Who wine desires, let him the ripe grapes tread.

10. To make or form by the action of the feet in walking; *esp.* to beat (a path or track). Const. *out.*

c **1410** Wele ytredde [see A. 3 α]. **1552** HULOET, Tread out, *exculco, as.* **1563** *Homilies* II. *Rogation Week* IV. (1640) 235 The ancient terris of the fields, that old men beforetime with great paines did tread out. **1580** LYLY *Euphues* (Arb.) 450 Hee that diggeth the garden, is to be considered, though he cannot treade the knottes. **1856** FROUDE *Hist. Eng.* I. i. 51 Paths trodden by the footsteps of ages. **1860** TENNYSON *Sea Dreams* 117 But she with her strong feet up the steep hill Trod out a path. **1865** VISCT. MILTON & CHEADLE *N.-W. Passage by Land* viii. (1867) 114 A track would require to be trodden out with snow-shoes to enable the dogs to travel.

11. *Horticulture.* To beat down and consolidate (soil) by treading; also with plants, etc. as object.

c **1440** *Pallad. on Husb.* II. 256 Sette hem depe..And tradde hem fast aboue. **1693** EVELYN *De la Quint. Compl. Gard.* II. 149 The first layer being thus compleated..the Gard'ner proceeds to lay the second, third, &c. beating them with the back of his Fork, or else treading them with his Feet. **1842** LOUDON *Suburban Hort.* 661 The ground should be previously trodden or rolled. **1845** *Florist's Jrnl.* 31 The whole should be gently trod with the feet.

12. *intr.* Of land (*tread loose*, hence ellipt. *tread*): To yield or give to the tread (? as after frost). *dial.*

1847 *Jrnl. R. Agric. Soc.* VIII. I. 73 When the soil treads loose in the spring, it is very important to use the heavy roller, or some other means of consolidating the soil. **1891** MALDEN *Tillage* 49 When once the land 'treads' the horses are best in the furrow. *Ibid.* Gloss. s.v., Land is said to tread when it puddles or poaches under the feet of the horses employed upon it.

13. a. *trans.* With advbs.: To get or put into or out of some position or condition by treading; *esp.* to put *out* (fire) by treading. (See also 5 b, c.)

to tread up (partridges), to flush them by walking up to the covey (? in contrast to the practice of using dogs).

1600 W. WATSON *Decacordon* (1602) 3 The fire..would breake out (if not troade out in time) of it selfe. *c* **1682** J. COLLINS *Salt & Fishery* 121 The Meat is..pack'd or trodden into Cask..with Salt betwixt every Lane or Lay. **1697** DRYDEN *Virg. Georg.* II. 314 Trample with thy Feet, and tread it in. *a* **1745** SWIFT *Direct. Servants* iii, Throw the [candle] snuff on the floor, and then tread it out, to prevent stinking. **1756** MRS. CALDERWOOD in *Coltness Collect.* (Maitl. Cl.) 118 One of them asked..would I have my toes trode off? 'Is your toes trode off?' said I. **1808** COL. HAWKER *Diary* (1893) I. 13, I trod up the whole covey. **1847** W. C. L. MARTIN *Ox* 168/1 Buried deep..with quick lime, and covered up with earth closely trodden down. **1849** MACAULAY *Hist. Eng.* I. I. 149 The flame of civil war..was trodden out before it had time to spread. **1888** J. INGLIS *Tent Life in Tigerland* 8 The cattle had trod down all the dried leaves.

b. *to tread one's shoe awry* (*the shoe, one's foot, amiss*, etc.), to fall from chastity. See also AWRY A. 2 c. ? *Obs.* So *to tread one's shoes straight*, to conduct oneself circumspectly, to walk warily (*dial.*).

c **1422** HOCCLEVE *Min. Poems* xxiv. 66 No womman..But swich oon as hath trode hir shoo amis. **1520–1662** [see AWRY A. 2 c]. **1616** R. C. *Times' Whistle* VI. 2541 Due pennance thou deservst to doe For tredding thus awry thy slippery shoe. **1642** J. EATON *Honey-c. Free Justif.* 110 If she chance to tread her foot a little awry. **1870** E. PEACOCK *Ralf Skirl.* I. 112 They mun tread their shoes very straight or there'll be a row with our Squire.

Hence **ˈtreading** *ppl. a.*

1562 J. HEYWOOD *Prov. & Epigr.* (1867) 214 There be mo treadyng cockes then one.

treader (ˈtrɛdə(r)). [f. TREAD *v.* + -ER¹.]

1. One who or that which treads, in various senses.

1382 WYCLIF *Amos* ix. 13 The erer shal cacche the reper, and treder of grape the man sendynge seed. **1538** ELYOT, *Lenobates*, a treader of grapes. **1599** T. M[OUFET]

Silkwormes 33 Hence, sparrow treaders liue out scarce a year. **1601** R. JOHNSON *Kingd. & Commw.* (1603) 123 The Gothes and Vandales, the verie treaders downe of the Roman Empire. **1760** LAW *Spir. Prayer* II. 112 The seed of the woman, the treader on the serpent's head. **1826** SCOTT *Woodst.* xiv, A treader of mortar, or a bearer of a hod. **1869** *Pall Mall G.* 15 Nov. 3 More grapes were now thrown in, and again the treaders set to work. **1887** *Suppl. to Jamieson*, *Tredder*, a cock-bird, but generally applied to a [domestic] cock.

†**b.** See quot. *Obs.*

1552 ELYOT, *Anteambulo*,..the vssher or treader that goeth before his maister.

c. One who is on the treadmill. *rare.*

1824 SYD. SMITH *Wks.* (1859) II. 35/2 A treader, untried by a jury of his countrymen,..striving against the law of gravity.

2. = TREADLE *sb.* 2. *rare.*

1747 *Gentl. Mag.* Jan. 16/1 A wheel, to which motion was given by the foot by means of a treadle or treader.

3. = TREAD *sb.* 11.

1881 YOUNG *Every Man his own Mechanic* §1321 If a garden step or any other step with a treader of stone is required to be made.

treading ('trɛdɪŋ), *vbl. sb.* [-ING¹.]

1. The action of the verb TREAD in various senses.

c **1410** *Master of Game* (MS. Digby 182) xxiv, Ye may Jugge..an herte chaseable..by þe tredynge of þe grasse. **1523** FITZHERB. *Husb.* §128 Well hardened with caryage and treading vpon. **1615** W. V[ALLANS] *Hon. Prentice* 33 A flat Marble stone..much defaced with treading, and neere worne out. **1709–10** STEELE *Tatler* No. 126 ¶4 He heard.. the Treading of one who approach'd. **1842** LOUDON *Suburban Hort.* 660 To press the soil on it firmly by treading.

b. *plural.*

c **1440** *Promp. Parv.* 501/1 Tredyngys, wythe the foote. **1535** COVERDALE *Song Sol.* vii. 1 O how pleasaunt are thy treadinges with thy shues. **1634** SIR T. HERBERT *Trav.* 20 The women..equall if not exceed the men in their more laborious treadings [in dancing]. **1760–72** H. BROOKE *Fool of Qual.* (1809) III. 89, I heard secret treadings and mutterings. **1865** *Englishm. Mag.* Feb. 147 With treadings slow and whisperings low Men sadly count the slain.

2. *concr.* Anything made by treading; *spec.* the footprint of a boar. See also COCK-TREADING.

1573, 1655 [see COCK-TREADING]. **1575** TURBERV. *Venerie* 237 The footyng or print is called..of a Bore, the tracke or the Treading. **1731–3** TULL *Horse-Hoeing Husb.* xx. 295 Their [horses'] Treadings are cut so small by the Coulters, that the Earth is not kept from dissolving.

3. *attrib.* **treading-mill** = TREADMILL; **treading-room**, a room in which the materials of porcelain are kneaded together by treading.

1535 COVERDALE *Isa.* xli. 15, I wil make the a treadinge cart & a new flale, yᵗ thou mayest throsshe & grynde the mountaynes. **1675** COTTON *Scoffer Scoft* 54 [Jove did] transform himself into a Swan, to try The treading way of Letchery. **1752** *Gentl. Mag.* Aug. 348 The next (on the ground floor) is the slip and treading rooms. **1830** SOUTHEY in *Q. Rev.* XLIII. 50 Road-making..which serves in those islands in place of the treading-mill.

treadle ('trɛd(ə)l), *sb.* Forms: 1 tredel; 5 tredel, -yl, -ylle, 6–9 treddle, (8 -el), 7 tredle, (treedle), 8–9 treadel, 6– treadle; *β.* 7 trydle, triddle (also 9 *dial.*); *γ.* 7 tradle, 9 *dial.* traddle. [f. TREAD *v.* + -LE 1.]

†**1.** A step or stair. *Obs. rare*⁻⁰.

a **1000** *Ælfric's Voc.* in Wr.-Wülcker 117/6 *Bases*, tredelas, *uel* stæpas. *c* **1440** *Promp. Parv.* 501/1 Tredyl, or [*v.r.* of] grece, *gradus*, *pedalis*. *c* **1490** *Ibid.* 209/1 (MSS. K. & H.) Grece, or tredyl, *P.* or steyre, *gradus*. **1847–78** HALLIWELL, *Treddle*, the step of a stair, etc.

2. a. A lever worked by the foot in machines and mechanical contrivances, usually to produce reciprocating (as orig. in the loom) or rotary motion.

14.. *Voc.* in Wr.-Wülcker 592/33 *Liciatorium*, a tredel. *Ibid.* 614/14 *Subpedium*, a tredel. **1483** *Cath. Angl.* 392/1 A Tredylle of ye lummys, *suppodium*. **1573–80** BARET *Alv.* T 347 The Treadle of a weauers loome, *insile*. **1608** TOPSELL *Serpents* (1658) 785 Consider the strange trydles of their Looms. **1667** in Pettus *Fodinæ Reg.* (1670) 35 Large Smelting Bellows with Beams, Frames, Swords, Triddles. **1680** MOXON *Mech. Exerc.* x. 183 Of the Treddle and Cross-Treddle. **1688** R. HOLME *Armoury* III. xxi. (Roxb.) 252/1 By the riseing and falling of the Tradles, these play vp and down. **1806** W. TAYLOR in *Ann. Rev.* IV. 772 Until the method of lifting it by treadels, or foot-staves. **1831** G. R. PORTER *Silk Manuf.* 215 Treadles on which the weaver presses his feet alternately. *Mod.* A sewing-machine worked by treadles.

b. A pedal of a bicycle or the like.

1887 MISS E. P. THOMPSON in *Monthly Packet* Jan. 88 My feet are unapt to move without the treadles under them. **1895** H. C. BEECHING *Poems, Going down hill on a bicycle* v, When the wheels scarce crawl, My feet to the treadles fall.

c. On a railway: see quot.

1904 *Westm. Gaz.* 15 Nov. 10/1 There is an electric treadle just outside Shepherd's Bush Station which is operated by a brush fixed to the rear car of the train; and this operates on the block signal.

3. a. = TREAD *sb.* 9b. Now *dial.*

1658 SIR T. BROWNE *Pseud. Ep.* III. xxviii. (ed. 4) 225 The Grando or tredle are but the poles and establishing particles of the tender membrans. **1713** DERHAM *Phys.-Theol.* VII. iv. 391 At each end of the Egg is a Treddle, so called, because it was formerly thought to be the Sperm of the Cock. **1747** MRS. GLASSE *Cookery* vii. 70 The Treadels of the Eggs. **1794** G. ADAMS *Nat. & Exp. Philos.* I. v. 180 The chicken contained in embryo, in..the treadle of the egg.

†**b.** See quots. (Cf. TREAD *v.* 8, *sb.* 9.) *Obs.*

1638 FORD *Fancies* III. iii, Whore, bitch-fox, treedle, fa la la la! [**1847–78** HALLIWELL, *Treddle*, a whore.]

4. *attrib.* and *Comb.*, as ***treadle-board, -cord, -crank, -lever, -wire***; worked by a treadle or treadles, as ***treadle-brake, -grindstone, -loom, -machine, -wheel***; also ***treadle-shaking*** adj.; **treadle mat**, a mat or casing which activates a mechanism when stepped on or otherwise depressed.

1881 YOUNG *Every Man his own Mechanic* §550 Fastened to this shaft is the *treadle-board. **1903** *Westm. Gaz.* 20 Oct. 10/1 By slow degrees, we got the present serviceable *treadle brake that acts on the whole 'bus. **1766** *Compl. Farmer* s.v. *Flax*, The sword or upright timber-rod which turns the wheel by the *treadle-crank. **1902** MARSHALL *Metal Tools* 72 For larger tools..a *treadle grindstone..will be found more convenient. **1839** URE *Dict. Arts* 269 A platform, which is raised up by a *treddle lever. **1882** FLOYER *Unexpl. Baluchistan* 45 The manufacturers sit in holes in their gardens before their rather clumsy *treadle-looms. **1937** *Times* 13 Apr. p. xvi/4 Pneumatic *treadle mats cover the steps so that the doors when released by the driver may be automatically opened by passengers standing on the steps. **1966** *Electronics Weekly* 16 Mar. 3/1 The passage of the wheels over a treadle mat causes the light to change to red. **1893** A. S. ECCLES *Sciatica* 7 Working a *treadle sewing-machine for some hours. **1812** W. TENNANT *Anster F.* II. xxvi, Their *treadle-shaking feet now scour apace Through Gallow town. **1680** MOXON *Mech. Exerc.* x. 188 The *Treddle Wheel is used for small work only. **1880** CARNEGIE *Pract. Trap.* vi. 41 The *treadle wire itself may be flattened.

treadle ('trɛd(ə)l), *v.* [f. TREADLE *sb.*]

1. *intr.* To work a treadle; to move the feet as if doing this; also, of a cyclist: to make one's way by treadling or pedalling one's cycle: also *trans.* with *way*. Hence **'treadling** *vbl. sb.*

1891 T. HARDY *Tess* xxxv, In the strenuousness of his concentration he treadled fitfully on the floor. **1891** *Daily News* 7 Sept. 6/3 Two or three of these persecutor-cyclists were quietly treadling about the town as early as eight in the morning. **1896** *Ibid.* 25 July 8/1 We treadled our way swiftly through the..streets. **1912** *Ibid.* 21 Mar. 5 A little weakness which makes it difficult to do much treadling.

2. *trans.* To operate (a machine) by working a treadle.

1906 H. BEGBIE *Priest* xvi, You'd be in Queer Street, treadling a sewing-machine for eighteen pence a day.

Hence **'treadler**, one who treadles.

treadler's cramp, cramp of the legs affecting persons engaged in working treadle-machines.

1891 *Lancet* 14 Feb. 410/1 Medical Society of London... A case of Treadler's Cramp. **1899** *Allbutt's Syst. Med.* VIII. 15 The lameness and the 'treadler's cramp' appeared simultaneously.

treadled ('trɛd(ə)ld), *a.* [f. TREADLE *sb.* + -ED².] Having or furnished with a treadle or tread.

1877 BLACKMORE *Erema* xxxv, With his treddled heel scraping the shoulder of his shining spade. **1894** —— *Perlycross* 24 Nor linger for a moment at the treddled stile.

treadmill ('trɛdmɪl), *sb.* [f. TREAD *v.* + MILL *sb.*¹] A horizontal cylinder made to revolve by the weight of persons treading on boards arranged as equidistant steps around its periphery. Formerly in use as an instrument of prison discipline.

1822 (*title*) Description of the Tread Mill invented by Mr. William Cubitt of Ipswich, for the Employment of Prisoners. **1824** SYD. SMITH *Wks.* (1859) II. 36/1 The labour of the tread-mill is irksome, dull, monotonous, and disgusting to the last degree. **1836** GEN. P. THOMPSON *Exerc.* (1842) IV. 107 Religious observances of other people ..forced upon us with a faggot or a treadmill. **1886** J. K. JEROME *Idle Thoughts* xii. 139 Too much getting up and down stairs..puts one unpleasantly in mind of the tread-mill.

transf. and *fig.* **1827** SCOTT *Chron. Canongate* i, A kind of mental tread-mill, where you are perpetually climbing, but can never rise an inch. **1862** H. AÏDE *Carr of Carrlyon* I. 262 A return to the treadmill of London society. **1897** G. ALLEN *Typewriter Girl* xv, The squirrel who turns the unceasing treadmill of his cage. **1905** LYALL *Life Mrq. Dufferin* II. v. 173 He found himself again on the official treadmill.

attrib. **1849** E. B. EASTWICK *Dry Leaves* 5 There is no winding or sloping here... No! all is fair treadmill work. **1885** C. HARRISON in *Harper's Mag.* Mar. 548/1 Back again at the tread-mill round of business.

Hence **'treadmill** *v.*, *intr.* to labour on or as on the treadmill; **'treadmiller**, a person who is 'on the treadmill' (*fig.*), esp. one who follows a dull and arduous working life.

1899 *Westm. Gaz.* 18 Nov. 3/2 My feet..slipped on the pedal till I was treadmilling clumsily with the middle instead of the ball of the foot. **1902** *Messenger* (N.S.W.) 5 Dec. 253 The..prison discipline of past days, in which tread-milling was the only work prisoners were permitted to do. **1923** D. H. LAWRENCE *Kangaroo* viii. 164 Better a 'wicked creature' any day, than a mechanical tread-miller of a careerist. **1956** H. GOLD *Man who was not with It* (1965) viii. 66, I even thought of..that shy treadmiller Joy.

'tread-ˌsoftly. [f. imper. of TREAD *v.* + SOFTLY.] A name for a herbaceous perennial stinging plant (*Jatropha urens var. stimulosa*) of the southern United States; the spurge-nettle.

1814 PURSH *Flora Amer. Septentr.* II. 602 *Jatropha stimulosa*..is a very injurious weed.., as it ruins the Negroes' feet when they tread upon it; from which it is known by the name of *Tread-softly*. **1884** in MILLER *Plant-n.*

'tread-wheel, *sb.* [f. TREAD *v.* + WHEEL *sb.*] A wheel rotated by the treading of persons or animals to give motion to machinery, to pump, or raise water, etc.; *esp.* a wheel turned by the weight of a person or animal walking forward on the inside of its periphery; also, = TREADMILL.

c **1573** *Lansdowne MS. 101*, lf. 81 The Trade Whele where uppon men or horse stondyth. **1629** *Patent Specif.* (1856) No. 48. 1 An engine..which goeth downe to the bottome.. of the Worke where it is to be used either by a Treadwheele meanes, hands [etc.]. **1660** R. D'ACRES *Art Water-drawing* 12 Certain great hollow wheels, hanging perpendicularly, in which men tread (called by some tread-wheels) not unlike unto a dog in a spit-wheel. **1799** *Specif. Hardie's Patent* No. 2300 The steps..serve for the men to mount upon or dismount from the tread wheel. **1822** *Gentl. Mag.* July 9 A party of prisoners..working one of the Tread-wheels of the Discipline Mill, invented by Mr. Cubitt. **1839** I. TAYLOR *Anc. Chr.* I. iii. 362 Ascetics..wasting themselves to skeletons on the treadwheel of their devout taskwork.

Hence **'tread-wheel** *v.*, *trans.* to inflict the discipline of the treadmill upon; whence **'tread-wheeling** *vbl. sb.*

1831 *Lincoln Herald* 7 Oct. 4 Let these officials moderate their..fines, and treadwheeling.

†**treaf**, *a. Obs. dial.* Also 7 trefe. [Etymology unknown.] Peevish, bad-tempered.

1601 DENT *Pathw. Heaven* 389 Though her yoong suckling crie all night, and be exceeding treafe and waiward. **1627** J. CARTER *Plain Expos.* 16 They are pronounced blessed, not who are treafe, and teachie, irefull and snappish,..but the meeke who..submit themselues vnder the mightie hand of God. **1659** GAUDEN *Slight Healers* (1660) 34 To quiet the Trefe and Wayward people. **1691** RAY *S. & E.C. Words* (E.D.S.), *Treaf*, peevish, froward, pettish, very apt to be angry. Hence **1787** in GROSE *Provinc. Gloss.*

treager, variant of TREGAR.

†**treague** (triːg). *Obs.* [ad. med.L. *tregua, treuga, treugua* (*c* 1220 in Du Cange), = It. and Sp. *tregua*, Pr. *tregua, trega*, Pg. *tregoa*, ad. Goth. *triggwa* treaty, covenant, f. *triggws* true, sure. In OF. *trive, treve*, F. *trève*: see also TREVE, TRUCE. (For form cf. LEAGUE.)] A truce.

1590 SPENSER *F.Q.* II. ii. 33 Which to confirme, and fast to bind their league, After their weary sweat and bloody toile, She them besought, during their quiet treague, Into her lodging to repaire a while. *a* **1660** *Contemp. Hist. Irel.* (Ir. Archæol. Soc.) II. 174 A trumpeter..desiringe a treague or cessation of armes for a peremptorie time.

treaky, var. *traiky* (see under TRAIK *sb.*).

treand, treangell, -gle, obs. ff. TREND, TRIANGLE.

treas, treasance: see TRACE *sb.*², TRESANCE *Obs.*

treason ('triːz(ə)n), *sb.* Forms: 3–4 **treison**, 5–6 **treyson**; 3–5 (*Sc.* -6) **trayson, -one**, 4 (*Sc.* -6) **-oun**, 6 *Sc.* **-oune**; 4 (*Sc.* 6) **traison**, 4–6 **-oun**; 3–5 **tresun, -oun**, 3–7 **-on**, 4–5 **-une, -oune, -one**, 5 **-own**; 4 **tressun**, 5 **-on**, 5–6 **-one**, 6 *Sc.* **-oun**; 5– **treason**, (5 **-oune**, 5–7 **-oun**, *Sc.* 5–6 **treson**, 6 **-oun, -oune**, 7 **treassoune**). [a. AFr. *treysoun, tresun, treson, -oun*, = OF. *traïson* (11th c.), in mod.F. *trahison* = Pr. *traicio*, Cat. *traició*, Sp. *traición*, Pg. *traição*:—L. *trāditiōn-em*, n. of action from L. *trādĕre*, OF. *traïr*, F. *trahir* to deliver up, betray: see TRAY *v.*², TRAISE *v.*]

1. a. The action of betraying; betrayal of the trust undertaken by or reposed in any one; breach of faith, treacherous action, treachery.

a **1225** *Ancr. R.* 56 Dauid..dude..treison and monsleiht on his treowe kniht Vrie, hire louerd. *a* **1240** *Wohunge* in *Cott. Hom.* 279 Barabas a þeof þat wið tresun..hefde a mon cwelled. **1297** R. GLOUC. (Rolls) 2337 Vor hii..in trayson were cointe þat hii ssolde þen king sle. *a* **1300** *Cursor M.* 3882 (Cott.) Qui has þou don me sli tresum? *a* **1340** HAMPOLE *Psalter* ix. 29 Whas mouth is ful of weriynge & bitternes & treson. **13..** *K. Alis.* 1362 (Bodl. MS.) And he þat þe traisoun dede Was fore hakked in þat stede. *c* **1400** *Song Roland* 176 For men dred tresson wher they it finden, And thought on tresson þer trist was neuer. *c* **1400** MAUNDEV. (Roxb.) xi. 43 He had done treyson, when he slogh Vry. *a* **1450** *Knt. de la Tour* lxxiv. (1906) 96 It is treson whanne a man trustithe in her [his wife] and she discouered his counsaile. **1596** SHAKS. *Merch V.* III. ii. 27 Vpon the racke Bassanio, then confesse What treason there is mingled with your loue. **1611** SIR W. MURE *Misc. Poems* i. 15 By subtil slight, or treassoune, To siege, and sack the Rampier of my ressoun. **1825** SCOTT *Talism.* i, From whom I should demand security, did I not know that treason seldom dwells with courage.

b. ***treason of the clerks*** = TRAHISON DES CLERCS.

1940 W. EMPSON *Gathering Storm* 34 Treason of the clerks, boys, curtains that descend, Lights becoming darks, boys, waiting for the end. **1970** C. C. O'BRIEN *Camus* iii. 61 The proposition that failure to take an anti-communist stand constituted 'the treason of the clerks' of which Benda spoke. **1979** *Guardian* 6 June 14/7 Ex-King's men will be revealed as those whose bogus liberalism led them to 'the treason of the clerks'.

2. *Law.*

In old English law treason was either *high treason*, an offence against the king's majesty or the safety of the commonwealth, or *petit* or *petty treason*, an offence committed against a subject. Petit treason is now punished only as murder, and high treason is usually styled simply *treason*. Many acts of high treason are now treated as *treason felony*.

[**1292** BRITTON I. ix. §1 Tresun est en chescun damage qe hom fet a escient ou procure de fere a cely a qi hom se fet ami. Et poet estre treysoun graunt et petit.]

a. ***high treason*** or ***treason*** proper: Violation by a subject of his allegiance to his sovereign or to the state.

Defined 1350-51 by Act 25 Edw. III, Stat. 5, c. 2, as compassing or imagining the king's death, or that of his wife or eldest son, violating the wife of the king or of the heir apparent, or the king's eldest daughter being unmarried, levying war in the king's dominions, adhering to the king's enemies in his dominions, or aiding them in or out of the realm, or killing the chancellor or the judges in the execution of their offices. In 1795 the offence was extended to actual or contemplated use of force to make the king change his counsels, or to intimidate either or both of the Houses of Parliament (but from 1848, see also *treason-felony*: sense 4 b below). As a result of the Treason Act (1945), the procedure for murder was applied to treason cases.

[**1292** BRITTON I. ix. §2 Graunt tresoun est a compasser nostre mort, ou de nous desheriter de noster reaume, ou de fauser noster seal, ou de contrefere nostre monee ou de retoundre.] **1303** R. BRUNNE *Handl. Synne* 10258 Yn no þyng wote y more tresun, Þan brynge þy lorde to hys felun. **1473** WARKW. *Chron.* (Camden) 5 The Lorde Hungerforde was.. behedede for hye treasoune. **1593** SHAKS. *Rich. II*, III. iii. 93 Tell Bullingbrooke.. That euery stride he makes vpon my Land, Is dangerous Treason. *a* **1612** HARINGTON *Epigr.* IV. 5 Treason doth never prosper, what's the reason? For if it prosper, none dare call it Treason. **1660** *Trial Regic.* 31 To stand Mute in High-Treason, is all one, as to Confess the Fact. **1781** GIBBON *Decl. & F.* xvii. II. 60 A fatal maxim.. that in the case of treason, which included every offence that the subtlety of lawyers could derive from an hostile intention towards the prince or republic, all privileges were suspended. **1814** SCOTT *Wav.* xli, The charge brought against you of aiding and abetting high treason. **1902** *Westm. Gaz.* 12 June 10/1 At present there is only one species of treason—that known as high treason, by way of contradistinction to petty treason. **1907** *Verney Mem.* I. 34 Sir Robert Whittingham was attainted of treason. **1911** W. B. ODGERS & ODGERS *Comm. Law Eng.* I. 145 Writing treasonable words is, no doubt a more deliberate act than merely uttering them. But.. if the writings be not published, they do not constitute an overt act of treason.

b. ***petit*** or ***petty treason***, treason against a subject; *spec.* the murder of one to whom the murderer owes allegiance, as of a master by his servant, a husband by his wife, etc. Now only *Hist.*

[**1351-2** *Rolls of Parlt.* II. 239/1 Il y ad autre manere de Treison, c'est assaver quant un Servant tue son Mestre.] **1496** *Ibid.* VI. 513/1 An Acte to make some Offences Petty Treason. **1580** G. HARVEY *Let. to Spenser* iv. Wks. (Grosart) I. 103 Reputing it Petty Treason to reuolt there-fro. **1625** MASSINGER *New Way* III. ii, How! strike a Justice of Peace! 'Tis petty treason. **1763** *Brit. Mag.* IV. 273 Mary Head,.. who was convicted at Chester assizes of petit treason, in killing her husband.. was burnt. **1777** *Chron.* in *Ann. Reg.* 183/2 Joseph Armstrong was tried for petty treason, in poisoning his master's lady. **1828** *Act 9 Geo. IV*, c. 31 §2 Every Offence, which before a Commencement of this Act would have amounted to Petit Treason, shall be deemed to be Murder only.

c. ***constructive treason***, action which though not actually or overtly coming under any of the acts specified in the Statute of Treason, was declared by law to be treason and punishable as such. ***misprision of treason***: see MISPRISION.

a **1714**, **1769** [see CONSTRUCTIVE *a.* 4 b]. **1882** LECKY *Eng. in 18th C.* xiii. III. 522 The charge [against Lord George Gordon] was what is termed by lawyers 'constructive treason'. It rested upon the assertion that the agitation which he had created and led was the originating cause of the outrages that had taken place.

d. In exclamatory use (in sense 1 a or 2 a). Cf. TRAY *interj.*

1388 WYCLIF *2 Chron.* xxiii. 13 Sche to-rente hir clothis, and seide, Tresouns! tresouns! [**1539** BIBLE (Great), treason, treason.] **1470-85** MALORY *Arthur* IV. iii. 121 They herd a grete noyse and many cryed treson, treson. Alass, said kynge Arthur, we ben bitrayed. *a* **1491** J. ROSS *Hist. Reg. Angl.* (1716) 218 Sæpius se proditum clamans & dicens, Treson, Treson, Treson. **1593** SHAKS. *Rich. II*, V. ii. 72 Treason, foule Treason, Villaine, Traitor, Slaue. **1602** —— *Ham.* V. ii. 334 *Ham.* Then venome to thy worke. (*Hurts the King.*) *All.* Treason, treason.

†**3.** With *a* and *pl.* An act of treason, in prec. senses; also, a species of treason. Also *fig.*

c **1330** R. BRUNNE *Chron. Wace* (Rolls) 7128 In casteles he sette garnysons ffor þe drede of oþer traysons. *c* **1330** —— *Chron.* (1810) 172 His traitour ert þou now, þou did him a tresoun. **1474** CAXTON *Chesse* III. iii. (1883) 95 In assemblyng the peple thus to gyder they make moo traysons in the cytees than they make good alyances. **1593** SHAKS. *Rich. II*, III. ii. 51 His Treasons will sit blushing in his face. **1605** M. SUTCLIFFE *Brief Exam.* 2 Manifold rebellions and treasons against their princes. *a* **1709** ATKYNS *Parl. & Pol. Tracts* (1734) 23 By this means Men will be discouraged from discovering Treasons. **1708** *Termes de la Ley* 450 Petit Treason is a Treason of a lower degree; as if a Servant kill his Master, a Wife her Husband.

4. *attrib.* and *Comb.*, *as* ***treason-charge***, ***court***, ***-law***, ***-monger***, ***-plot***, ***-tavern***, ***trial***, ***-worker***; ***treason-canting***, ***-hatching***, ***-haunted*** adjs.

1682 *Dryden's Medall* To Author 26 All their *Treason-canting Priests. **1900** *Echo* 9 Jan. 2/7, I.. was then discharged on the high *treason charge. **1900** *Daily News* 12 Nov. 5/2 At to-day's sitting of the *Treason Court, Mr. Schroeder.. was released on bail. **1659** *Burton's Diary* (1828) III. 437 Her custom was.. to come into the dining-room to him in her *treason-gown, (as I called it,) I telling him, that when she had that gown on, he should allow her to say anything. **1745** AYRE *Life Pope* II. 85 The sacred Character of a lurking, *treason-hatching Jesuit. **1871** J. HAY *Pike County Ball.* (1880) 110 Its stealthy echoes pour Through *treason-haunted regions. **1810** *Edin. Rev.* XVI. 105 The principles of *treason-law. **1746** M. HUGHES *Jrnl. Late Reb.* 5 Among all these *Treason-mongers, old Gordon, the Laird of Glenbucket is a notable Instance of Loyalty. **1839** LD. BROUGHAM *Statesm. Geo. III, Gibbs* 127 A rabble-leader or a treason-monger, a libeller or a blasphemer. **1640** YORKE *Union Hon.* 174 That bloody and damnable *treason-plot. **1681** DRYDEN *Abs. & Achit.* II. 459 Og from a *treason-tavern rolling home. **1930** *Economist* 6 Dec. 1054/2 *Treason trials are the grand elixir of revolutionary régimes; and for years the Soviet Government, like competent theatrical producers, have managed to stage a series of such performances in almost uninterrupted succession. **1979** A. MELVILLE-ROSS *Two Faces of Nemesis* viii. 47 Treason trials don't help the national image. **1553** in *Howell's St. Trials*, (1809) I. 788 Then shall there be men loving themselves, covetous, proud, disobedient to parents, *treason-workers.

b. **'treason-'felony**, an offence, formerly included among acts of treason, which by subsequent legislation has been removed from these, and is not punishable with death. So **'treason-'felon**, one convicted of treason-felony.

Defined (though not so named) by the Crown and Government Security Act, 11 & 12 Vict. c. 12 (1848) by which treasons not directed at the person of the Sovereign were mitigated to felonies, punishable with penal servitude for life, or for a term of not less than five years.

1865 *Annual Register* 252 The Attorney General said that the Act of Parliament respecting treason-felony created several offences and these were of three descriptions. **1865** *Times* 29 Nov. 10/2 Counsel for the prisoner was taken by surprise in finding bills for treason-felony instead of high-treason sent up to the grand jury. **1881** R. F. LITTLEDALE in *Academy* 29 Jan. 75 The experiences of a treason-felon. **1892** *Daily News* 26 Feb. 3/1 Out of the 23 treason-felony prisoners confined in British prisons during the last ten years, one had become insane.

'treason, *v. rare.* Forms: see prec.; also 4-5 **traysen**, **trassen**. [f. prec. Cf. OF. *traisonner* to betray.] *trans.* To betray; to act treasonably towards.

13.. *K. Alis.* 723 Thy fadir hastow tresond here! *c* **1330** R. BRUNNE *Chron.* (1810) 105 þei wer fulle wele knowen, þat wild haf tresond him. *c* **1374** CHAUCER *Troylus* IV. 410 (438) To traysen [*v.r.* trassen] a wight þat trewe is vn-to me. **1890** L. LEWIS *Proving of Gennad* xv. 104 Ere morning, thou shalt know who treasons thee.

treasonable ('triːz(ə)nəb(ə)l), *a.* [f. TREASON *sb.* + -ABLE.] Of the nature of treason; characteristic of or involving treason; perfidious, treacherous. (Orig. *Sc.*)

1375 BARBOUR *Bruce* v. 550 þis tratour ay Had in his thocht.. How he mycht best bring till ending þis tresonabill vndirtaking. *c* **1470** HENRY *Wallace* XI. 829 Be this tresonabill concord Schyr Jhon suld be off all the Lennox lord. **1546** *Reg. Privy Council Scot.* I. 32 The tressonabill slauchter of umquhile David Cardinale Archbischop. **1596** DALRYMPLE tr. *Leslie's Hist. Scot.* x. (S.T.S.) II. 402 Thir trasonable trahitouris. **1634** *Documents agst. Prynne* (Camden) 27 In a most infamous, daungerous, and treasonable waye. **1675** tr. *Camden's Hist. Eliz.* an. 1601. 625 The Earl of Essex.. had accused him as an Instigatour of him to this treasonable Attempt. **1741** RICHARDSON *Pamela* (1824) I. 110 So, Pamela, we have seized, it seems, your treasonable papers? **1818** HALLAM *Mid. Ages* viii. III. (1819) III. 233 Their participation in a treasonable conspiracy being manifest. **1855** MACAULAY *Hist. Eng.* xvii. IV. 18 The treasonable packet had been found in his bosom.

Hence **'treasonableness**, treasonable quality or character.

1679 *Jenison's Popish Plot* Pref. 8 Treasonableness in point of Loyalty. **1727** in BAILEY vol. II.

treasonably ('triːz(ə)nəblı), *adv.* [f. prec. + -LY^{2}.] In a treasonable manner. (Orig. *Sc.*)

c **1375** *Sc. Leg. Saints* xxvi. (*Nycholas*) 786 þat cristine man tuk in hy þe ymag þare tresonably. *c* **1470** HENRY *Wallace* VII. 914 Syne held it lang, quhill tratouris tresonably Causit his dede. **1549** *Compl. Scot.* viii. 72 Tha deserue as grite reproche as tha hed sellit traisonablye the realme to there enemeis. **1660** *Trial Regic.* 17 Did Maliciously, Treasonably, and Feloniously.. condemn our late Soveraign Lord King Charls the First. **1839** JAMES *Louis XIV*, III. 18 The government of Mazarin.. was treasonably assailed. **1884** *Manch. Exam.* 14 May 5/2 It was said that French military plans had been treasonably revealed.

treaso'nette. *nonce-wd.* [f. TREASON *sb.* + -ETTE.] A small or petty act of treason.

1824 LADY GRANVILLE *Lett.* (1894) I. 254 The absurdity of hunting out these treasonettes with such severity.

treason-felony: see TREASON 4 b.

† **'treasonful**, *a. Obs. rare.* [f. as prec. + -FUL.] Full of treason; treasonous; treacherous.

13.. *Cursor M.* 13960 (Cott.) þe Iues.. wit þair mani tressunful red, þai soght ihesu at do to ded. **1650** TRAPP *Comm. Num.* xvi. 14 They add rebellion to sin, and justifie their treasonful practices.

† **'treasonish**, *a. Obs. rare.* [f. as prec. + -ISH^{1}.] Of the nature of treason; somewhat treasonable.

1672 EACHARD *Hobbes State Nat.* 98 Is not this very pragmatical and somewhat treasonish? **1681** T. FLATMAN *Heraclitus Ridens* No. 26 (1713) I. 169 Is not endeavouring to subvert it [monarchy] something like Treasonish?

'treasonist. *nonce-wd.* [f. as prec. + -IST.] One who practises or is concerned in treason.

1796 COLERIDGE *Lett.* (1895) 179 Interesting to you, virtuous high-treasonist, and your friends the democrats.

† **'treasonless**, *a. Obs. rare*$^{-1}$. [f. as prec. + -LESS.] Without or free from treason.

1591 *Troub. Raigne K. John* xii. 84, I plead not guiltie, treasonles and free.

treasonous ('triːz(ə)nəs), *a.* [f. as prec. + -OUS.] Full of or abounding in treason; characterized by treason or treachery; treasonable.

c **1450** [implied in TREASONOUSLY]. **1593** NASHE *Christ's T.* Wks. (Grosart) IV. 196 Bannings, cursings, secrete murmurings, out-rage, murder, iniustice, all which are high treasonous trespasses against God. **1605** SHAKS. *Macb.* II. iii. 138 Against the vndivulg'd pretence, I fight Of Treasonous Mallice. **1784** *New Spectator* No. 18. 3 To prohibit such and such pieces, that were blasphemous, libellous, or treasonous. **1875** W. WARBURTON *Edw. III*, i. 21 That he had trepanned the Earl of Kent into a treasonous conspiracy.

Hence **'treasonously** *adv.*, in a treasonous manner.

c **1450** *Mirour Saluacioun* 2757 And Jhū crist with Judas kissis he tresovnously. **1821** MILMAN *Fortune* 181 Steep'd treasonously in great Pompey's gore.

† **'treasonry.** *Obs. rare*$^{-1}$. [f. as prec. + -RY.] Treasonable practice or action.

a **1600** *Sang Outlaw Murray* 110 in Scott *Minstr. Scott. Bord.*, I am right rad of treasonrie.

† **'treasony.** *Obs. rare*$^{-1}$. [f. as prec. + -Y.] = TREASON.

16.. *Young Waters* xiv. in Child *Ballads* IV. (1886) 344 It is tauld me the day, sir knight, Ye've done me treasonie.

treasurable ('trɛʒərəb(ə)l), *a. rare.* [f. TREASURE *v.* + -ABLE.] Fit or worthy to be treasured; valuable; precious.

1607 NORDEN *Surv. Dial.* v. 242 Many treasureable blessings lie hid from slouthfull men. **1811** *Henry & Isabella* II. 195 The treasurable object, for whom they were going to stake their existence. **1886** *Athenæum* 28 Aug. 265/3 His verses are a treasurable document to the literary student.

Hence **'treasurableness**, treasurable quality.

1898 *Weekly Reg.* 28 May 700 The.. treasurableness of small and lovable things.

treasure ('trɛʒ(j)ʊə(r), -ə(r)), *sb.* Forms: 2-6 **tresor**, 3-6 **-ur**, **-our**, 4-6 **-ore**, **-oure**, 5 **-owre**, **-er**, 5-6 **-ure**, 5 **treysour**, **treasoure**, 5-6 **-our**, 6 **-or**, 6- **treasure**. (Also 4-5 **trissor**, 4-6 **tressour**, 7 **treassour**; 4 **thresur**, 5-6 **-our**, **-oure**, 6 **threasour**, **-ure**.) [In 12th c. *tresor*, a. OF. *tresor* (11th c. in Littré):—pop.L. of Gaul **trēsaur-us* for cl.L. *thēsaur-us* (whence Pr. *thesaur*, OCat. *tesor*, Sp., It. *tesoro*, Pg. *thesouro*), a. Gr. θησαυρός treasure. Cf. the Sc. THESAUR.]

1. a. Wealth or riches stored or accumulated, esp. in the form of precious metals; gold or silver coin; hence in general, money, riches, wealth. Usually *collective*, without article or plural.

1154 *O.E. Chron.* an. 1137 (Laud MS.), He hadde ʒet his tresor ac he to deld it & scatered sotlice. *a* **1225** *Ancr. R.* 150 þe þet bereð tresor openliche in one weie þet is al ful of þeoues. *c* **1325** *Poem Times Edw. II* 321 in *Pol. Songs* (Camden) 338 Thurfte him noht seke tresor so fer. **13..** *Cursor M.* 16534 (Gött.) He kest þaim dune apon þe grund, threti penis þar fell. Bot þe Iuus.. þe thresur [*v.r.* tresur] forsok þai noght. *Ibid.* 24807 (Cott.) Wit trissor [*Edin.* tresori] son his scipp was tift. **1480** CAXTON *Chron. Eng.* IV. (1520) 31/2 Linus and.. Cletus.. were made to mynyster the treasoure of the chyrche to the people. **1597** J. PAYNE *Royal Exch.* 44 Where a mans threasure ys there is his hart. **1599** MASSINGER, etc. *Old Law* I. i, To fly my severe country; To turn all into treasure. **1686** tr. *Chardin's Trav. Persia* 71 A Man that.. look'd upon five or six of those Pieces to be a great Treasure. **1695** LOCKE *Further Consid. Value Money* 23 Gold is Treasure as well as Silver, because it decays not in keeping, and never sinks much in its value. **1750** tr. *Leonardus' Mirr. Stones* 50 Some stones.. preserve and increase treasure; others cure diseases. **1821** BYRON *Mar. Fal.* V. i, Goods, and jewels, and all kinds of treasure.

b. *pl.* in same sense.

c **1330** R. BRUNNE *Chron.* (1810) 98 Now is Henry.. lord of mykelle þing, & riche man of tresours. ? *a* **1366** CHAUCER *Rom. Rose* 184 To take and yeve right nought ageyne, And gret tresouris up to leyne. **1474** CAXTON *Chesse* III. iv. (1883) 108 The resseyuours of the tresours royall. **1596** RALEIGH *Discov. Gviana* 9 Greate Cities, Townes, Temples, and threasures. **1838** *Murray's Hand Bk. N. Germ.* 45/1 The treasures of the once celebrated bank of Amsterdam.. were kept in the vaults below the building. **1857** RUSKIN *Pol. Econ. Art* 4 The last coin out of all their treasures.

c. *fig.*

1382 WYCLIF *Luke* xviii. 22 Sille thou alle.. and ʒyue to pore men, and thou schalt haue tresour in heuene. **1753** CHALLONER *Cath. Chr. Instr.* 128 The Treasure of the Church.. are the Merits and Satisfactions of Christ and his Saints.

†**d.** A store or stock *of* anything valuable. *Obs.*

1382 WYCLIF *Jer.* xli. 8 Wee han tresor in the feld, of whete, and of barly, and of oile, and of hony. **1604** E. G[RIMSTONE] *D'Acosta's Hist. Indies* IV. v. 217 The Creator hath furnished the Weast Indies with so great a treasure of silver. **1707** *Curios. in Husb. & Gard.* 55 A Treasure of central Fire, that manifests itself by the Vents of the Vulcanos.

†**e.** = TREASURE-TROVE. *Obs. rare.*

1602 FULBECKE *1st Pt. Parall.* 16 A treasure properly is, when money or things of good value haue lyen from time out of minde hidden in the ground, so that no man now hath propertie in it.

f. ***treasure found***: see TREASURE-TROVE b.

2. *transf.* and *fig.* Anything valued and preserved as precious; also of a person, a 'jewel', 'gem' (*colloq.*); also as an affectionate term of address.

c **1200** *Vices & Virt.* 135 þat derworðe tresor, þat is, ðe hali gast. *a* **1340** HAMPOLE *Psalter* xxv. 11, I am rych in gostly tresoure. *c* **1530** H. RHODES *Bk. Nurture* in *Babees Bk.* (1868) 83 A seruaunt to suffer in anger, to his mayster is a treasure. **1611** SIR W. MURE *Misc. Poems* i. 79 To losse ane Infinit and endles treassour. **1663** BP. PATRICK *Parab. Pilgr.* xxxii. (1687) 393 A faithful friend is a strong defence: and he that hath found such an one, hath found a Treasure. **1791** BOSWELL *Johnson* 16 May an. 1778, Let me then comfort myself with the large treasure of Johnson's conversation which I have preserved. **1810** LADY GRANVILLE *Lett.* (1894) I. 18 My month nurse, a treasure, and the most respectable of dames. **1844** A. B. WELBY *Poems* (1867) 97 Our treasures are this little boy, contentment, peace, and health. **1907** *Verney Mem.* II. 60 The fine house and its treasures. **1920** 'K. MANSFIELD' *Let.* 31 Oct. (1977) 194 But, my treasure, my life is ours. You know it. **1967** N. FREELING *Strike Out* 40 Next week, treasure, we're going to make a cruise... Go and buy yourself some clothes.

†**3.** A treasury; a treasure-house, a treasure-chest. *Obs. rare.*

[**1382** WYCLIF *1 Kings* xv. 18 Al the siluer and gold, that lafte in the tresours [*v.r.* tresories] of the hows of the Lord.] **1426** LYDG. *De Guil. Pilgr.* 8837 She tooke [hem] ful lowly .. And in hyr tresour vp hem layde. *c* **1475** *Pict. Voc.* in Wr.-Wülcker 782/5 *Hoc gazophilacium*, a tresure. **1550** CROWLEY *Epigr.* 185 Why can you neuer finde a time of leasure To se where the treasure will finde them workinge? **1596** DALRYMPLE tr. *Leslie's Hist. Scot.* x. (S.T.S.) II. 350 In the Quinȝehous or in the Kingis tresour.

4. *attrib.* and *Comb.*, as ***treasure-box***, ***-chamber***, ***-chest***, ***-coffer***, ***-digger***, ***-galleon***, ***-giver***, ***hoard***, ***-hunter***, ***-hutch***, ***-keeper***, ***-room***, ***-seeker***, ***-ship***, ***-store***, ***-vault***, etc.; ***treasure-baited***, ***-bearing***, ***-laden*** adjs; **treasure-city**, a city in which supplies were stored; **treasure-flower**, local name of a South African composite flowering plant of the genus *Gazania*, esp. the species *G. Pavonia*, the peacock treasure-flower; **treasure-hunt**; a hunt for treasure; freq. *fig.* and *transf.*, a game in which hidden objects are searched for, often by following a trail of clues; **Treasure State** *U.S. slang*, the State of Montana; **treasure-wheat**: see quot. See also TREASURE-HOUSE, -TROVE.

1876 *Treasure-box [see *powder keg* s.v. POWDER *sb.*[1] 5 b]. **1887** I. R. *Lady's Ranche Life Montana* 130 The robbers then rifled the treasure-box, and rode off delighted with their booty. *a* **1547** in J. R. Boyle *Hedon* (1895) App. 80 Foure keys belonging the *tresasor [*sic*] chambere. **1823** SCOTT *Quentin D.* xxiii, Having carefully locked his treasure-chamber, the wealthy Fleming next conveyed his guest to the parlour. **1849** THACKERAY *Pendennis* xxiii[i], [She] had quite a little museum of locks of hair in her *treasure-chest. **1895** *Daily News* 23 Nov. 7/1 The treasure chests [for the Ashanti war] consist of heavy iron safes filled with specie .. packed at the Bank of England. **1611** BIBLE *Exod.* i. 11 And they built for Pharaoh *treasure-cities, Pithom and Raamses. **1610** HOLLAND *Camden's Brit.* (1637) 106 Roman mony .. in *treasure coffers. **1866** *Treas. Bot.*, *Treasure-flower, *Gazania*. **1898** G. MEREDITH *Odes Fr. Hist.* 51 Seen like some rare *treasure-galleon, Hull down, with masts against the Western hues. **1899** KIPLING *Stalky* vi, Three months ago he was commanding a *treasure-guard—a cart full of rupees to pay troops with—five thousand rupees in silver. **1913** J. VAIZEY *College Girl* xii. 166, I was thinking .. of a *treasure hunt! .. lots of presents, stowed away in odd corners. **1919** E. H. JONES *Road to En-Dor* (1920) vi. 58 A treasure-hunt has a glamour of its own. **1939** T. S. ELIOT *Family Reunion* II. ii. 110 You have a long journey... Think of it as like a children's treasure hunt. **1977** M. GREEN *Children of Sun* 22 One of those Twenties' treasure hunts, in which people drove .. across all England, in search of some otherwise unprocurable item. **1851** H. MELVILLE *Moby Dick* II. xxxvi. 241 He proceeds very heedfully, like a *treasure-hunter in some old house, sounding the walls to find where the gold is masoned in. **1898** *Folk-Lore* IX. 17 At Sidon, the so-called Alexander Sarcophagus was found by a treasure-hunter. **1983** S. VIZINCZEY *Innocent Millionaire* xiii. 111 Maybe I was meant to be a treasure-hunter. **1862** H. MARRYAT *Year in Sweden* II. 409 The great secret of *treasure-hunting is to hold your tongue. **1531** *Pilgr. Perf.* (W. de W.) 178 b, Graunt me lady .. (o holy *tresour huche of God) one halfe farthinge to cast in to thy laude & prayse. **1567** *Trial Treas.* A ij b, One with *treasure lack his life framed. **1880** *Archæol. Cantiana* XIII. 455 It may have been a strong *treasure-room. **1890** J. G. FRAZER *Golden Bough* II. iv. 367 The *treasure-seeker places the rod on the ground after sundown, and when it rests directly over treasure, the rod begins to move as if it were alive. **1982** 'C. AIRD' *Last Respects* viii. 81 There are treasure-seekers, Inspector, who would .. not care that they were destroying priceless marine archaeology. **1900** H. BARBIE *In Mod. Spain* 25 Many of her *treasure-ships may have found their way to English ports. **1934** M. H. WESEEN *Dict. Amer. Slang* 412 *Treasure State, Montana. **1976** *Billings* (Montana) *Gaz.* 20 June 6-c/1 A solid century of mining has failed to put much of a dent in the state's gold, silver, copper and coal reserves. So the slogan, 'Treasure State', which used to grace Montana license plates, is still appropriate. **1892** EARLE *Deeds Beowulf* 160 The grand *treasure-sword had been left behind. **1871** B. TAYLOR *Faust* (1875) II. III. 196, I hunted on the *treasure-trail. **1813** SCOTT *Rokeby* VI. iv, 'To Rokeby *treasure-vaults!' they quaffed, And shouted loud and wildly laughed. **1590** *Acts Privy Counc.* (1899) XIX. 117 Certaine wheats (called the *threasour wheats) belonging to everie church within that Island [Jersey]. [Cf. **1682** WARBURTON *Hist. Guernsey* (1822) 66 The trésors, which are certain rents anciently given for the repairs .. to the churches .. but have .. been employed to uses merely secular.]

'treasure, *v.* [f. TREASURE *sb.* In Wyclif rendering *thēsaurizāre* of the Vulgate.]

1. *trans.* To put away or lay aside (anything of value) for preservation, security, or future use; to hoard or store up. Often ***to treasure up***.

1382 WYCLIF *Isa.* xxxix. 6 Alle thingus .. that ben in thin hous, and that thi fadris han tresored. —— *Baruch* iii. 16 Wher ben the princes .. that siluer tresoren and gold? **1712–14** POPE *Rape Lock* v. 114 Some thought it mounted to the Lunar sphere, Since all things lost on earth are treasured there. **1769** COOK *Voy. round World* II. i. (1773) 281 Taking a Cheshire cheese from a locker, where it had been carefully treasured up for this occasion. **1821** SHELLEY *Ginevra* 131 As if the future and the past were all Treasured i' the instant.

†**b.** *absol.* To lay up treasure. (A literalism of translation.) *Obs. rare.*

1382 WYCLIF *Ecclus.* iii. 5 As he that tresoreth, so and he that wrshepith his moder.

2. *fig.* To keep in store, lay up (e.g. in the mind, in memory).

1382 WYCLIF *Jas.* v. 3 ȝe han tressourid to ȝou wrath in the laste dayes. **1482** *Monk of Evesham* (Arb.) 61 The whyche .. tresur to hem .. the wrathe of owre sauyur ihesu cryste. **1631** GOUGE *God's Arrows* II. §12. 148 God doth sometimes treasure up the sinnes of predecessours. **1741** WATTS *Improv. Mind* I. xvi. §3 To acquire and treasure up a large store of ideas and notions. **1826** DISRAELI *Viv. Grey* v. xi, The ladies would treasure their energies for the impending ball. **1887** BOWEN *Æneid* III. 436 [I] Bid thee again and again in thy memory treasure the theme.

†**3.** To furnish or endow with treasures; to supply with treasure, to enrich. *Obs. rare.*

c **1600** SHAKS. *Sonn.* vi, Treasure thou some place, With beauties treasure. **1630** J. TAYLOR (Water P.) *Mem. Monarchs* II. Wks. II. 287/1 By a heauy taxe the King was treasur'd.

4. To hold or keep as precious; to cherish, prize.

1907 *Verney Mem.* II. 403 Treasured as his most precious possessions. **1911** J. A. MACCULLOCH *Relig. Anc. Celts* xiv. 221 A feather was left at each house and carefully treasured.

Hence **treasured** ('trɛʒəd) *ppl. a.*, stored, hoarded up, highly valued; **'treasuring** *vbl. sb.*

1602 *Archpriest Controv.* (Camden) I. 232 Every baker or brewer, for stewarding and treasuringe, must, by this newe device, be made equall with you. **1675** BROOKS *Gold. Key* Wks. 1867 V. 136 Wrath to come is treasured-up wrath. **1715–20** POPE *Iliad* VI. 359 The Phrygian queen to her rich wardrobe went, Where treasur'd odours breath'd a costly scent. **1856** KANE *Arct. Expl.* I. xxxi. 434 To give him a grating of our treasured potatoes.

'treasure-,house. A house, building, or chamber in which treasure is kept; a treasury.

c **1475** *Pict. Voc.* in Wr.-Wülcker 804/29 *Hoc gazafilacium*, a treserhouse. **1486** *Lichfield Gild Ord.* 24 We will and ordeyne that the one parte of the Indentures hereoff made, .. remayne in the treasure-house of the seid cathedrall church. **1494** *Acc. Ld. High Treas. Scot.* I. 241 To put in the copburd in the Tressourhous. **1573–80** BARET *Alv.* T 351 The place where treasure is kept, a treasure house, *aerarium*. **1910** *Soc. Antiq. O. Sarum Excavation Fund* 5 In 1181–2 £9 1[s] were spent on the treasure-house within the tower.

b. *fig.*

1552 LATIMER *Serm.* (1584) 302 b, The poore mans treasure house is his labour and trauayle. **1596** SHAKS. *Merch. V.* II. ix. 34 Why then to thee thou Siluer treasure house. **1890** 'R. BOLDREWOOD' *Col. Reformer* (1891) 135 Intellectual and artistic treasure houses. **1895** *Educat. Rev.* Oct. 223 The key which unlocks the treasure-house of literature.

treasureless ('trɛʒəlɪs), *a.* [f. TREASURE *sb.* + -LESS.] Without treasure or treasures.

1598 SYLVESTER *Du Bartas* II. i. III. *Furies* 809 Our fields are flock-lesse, treasure-lesse our Towns. **1868** G. MACDONALD *Seabd. Par.* xii, Man goeth treasureless to his grave.

treasurer ('trɛʒərə(r)). Forms: 3–6 tresourer, -urer, 4–7 -orer, (4 -orere, -oriere, -erour, -urrer, 5 -oreere, -owrere, *Sc.* -orair, 6 -ourar, trezerer); 5–7 thres-, 6–7 threasorer, -urer, -ourer; 6 treasorer, 6–7 -ourer, 6- treasurer. [In 13–14th c. *tresorer*, *-ourer*, a. ONF. and AF. *tresorer* = OF. *tresorier*, f. *tresor* TREASURE, after late L. *thēsaurārius* (whence Pr. *thesaurier*, Sp. *tesorero*, Pg. *thesoureiro*, It. *tesoriere*, OSc. THESAURER): see TREASURE and -ER[2].]

1. One who has officially the charge of treasure; originally, a person entrusted with the receipt, care, and disbursement of the revenues of a king, noble, or other dignitary, of a state, city, or church; now, one who is responsible for the funds of a public body, or of any corporation, association, society, or club.

treasurer of a cathedral: see quot. 1701.

c **1290** *Edmund Conf.* 394 in *S. Eng. Leg.* I. 442 At salesburi .. prouendes of churches he hadde, and was tresurer [*v.r.* tresourer]. **1382** WYCLIF *Rom.* xvi. 23 Erastus tresorer, or kepere, of the cite, greetith ȝou wel. **1419** in *Surtees Misc.* (1888) 14 Maister Thomas Haxey, Tresorer of the Cathedrale Kirk of Seint Peter of York. **1607** COWELL *Interpr.*, *Treasurer*... Most corporations through the kingdome, haue an officer of this name, that receiueth their rents, and disburseth their common expences. **1670** COVEL in *Early Voy. Levant* (Hakl. Soc.) 119 The two new Treasurers of the Turkey Company. **1701** *Cowell's Interpr.*, *Treasurer in Cathedral Churches*, a Dignitary who was to take charge of the Vestments, Plate, Jewels, Reliques, and other Treasure belonging to the said Church. **1806** *Med. Jrnl.* XV. 357 The treasurer of each hospital must annually verify upon oath his accounts. **1913** *Kelly's Oxford Direct.* 148/2 Ashmolean Natural History Society, .. G. C. Druce .., treasurer.

b. ***Lord High Treasurer of England***, ***of Great Britain***, also called *Treasurer*, *Lord Treasurer*, *High Treasurer*, *Treasurer of the Exchequer*, formerly, the third great officer of the Crown, controlling the revenues of the sovereign.

The office was put into commission several times in the 17th c., and definitely in the reign of George I, its duties subsequently being discharged by five Lords of the Treasury: see TREASURY 3.

[**1292** BRITTON I. xix. §10 Solom la discrecioun des Thresorers et des Barouns de nos Eschekers.] *c* **1330** R. BRUNNE *Chron.* (1810) 280 To Berwik cam þe kynge eschekere, .. Walter of Admundesham he was Tresorere. **1556** *Chron. Gr. Friars* (Camden) 71 Item the xj. day of October was made .. the lord trezerer markes of Wynchester. **1562** in Feuillerat *Revels Q. Eliz.* (1908) 115 To the Threasourer and Chamberlaines of our Exchequier greeting. **1589** *Hay any Work* 27 Our L. high Chancellor, high Treasurer, and high Steward of Englande. **1607** COWELL *Interpr.* s.v., The Treasurer of England, who is a Lord by his office .. vnder whose charge and gouernment is all the Princes wealth contained in the Exchequer. **1631** WEEVER *Anc. Fun. Mon.* 524–5 Lord Treasurers Remembrancer .. maketh Proces against all Sheriffes .. and Bayliffes, for their accounts. **1711** SWIFT *Jrnl. to Stella* 10 Apr., They talk of great promotions to be made: that Mr. Hardy is to be Lord-Treasurer. **1863** H. COX *Instit.* III. vii. 682 In earlier times, the Treasurer acted personally at the Exchequer.

c. ***Lord High Treasurer of Scotland*** (in Scotch, †***Lord*** (***High***) ***Thesaurer***), formerly, the officer having charge of the receipt and disbursement of the revenues of the kingdom, whose duty it was to examine and pass the accounts of the sheriffs and others concerned in levying the revenues, to receive resignations of lands, etc. In 1663 he was declared President of the Court of Exchequer.

1473–89, **1685–1708** [see THESAURER]. **1877** *Accounts Ld. High Treasurer of Scotland* I. Pref. 13–14 In 1424 James I .. assigned two newly created offices, the Comptroller and the Treasurer. *Ibid.* 26 The earliest appointment of a Treasurer which remains on record is a letter under the Privy Seal 25 June 1526. *Ibid.* 34 None of these [accounts] are of earlier date than fifty years after the institution of the office; the earliest being of the year 1473–4.

d. *United States.* An officer of the Treasury Department, who receives and keeps the moneys, disbursing them only upon warrants drawn by the Secretary of the Treasury and duly recorded and countersigned; also an officer having the same function in each State.

1790 HAMILTON *Wks.* (1886) VII. 52 The treasurer of the United States shall be the receiver of all payments for sales at the general land-office. **1821** J. Q. ADAMS in C. Davies *Metr. Syst.* III. (1871) 255 The weights were to be stamped .. in figures denominating their weight, and to be kept by the public treasurer. **1879** *Constit. California* Art. v. §17 (in Bryce *Amer. Commw.* (1889) I. 695) A Secretary of State, a Controller, a Treasurer, an Attorney-General, and a Surveyor-General shall be elected at the same time and places.

e. In other official designations.

a **1505** in Kingsford *Chron. Lond.* (1905) 230 The Maister of his Requestes, and his Tresorer generall. **1533** WRIOTHESLEY *Chron.* (Camden) I. 18 Mr. Treasorer and Mr. Controwler of the Kinges howse. **1552** in *Vicary's Anat.* (1888) App. ii. 118 The Thresourer of y[e] Kinges maiesties Chambre. **1601** F. TATE *Househ. Ord. Edw. II* (1876) 6 The thresorer of the warderobe. **1607** COWELL *Interpr.* s.v., Then is there a Treasurer of the kings houshold .. Treasurer of the Nauie, or Treasurer of the warres .. Treasurer of the Kings chamber .. Treasurer of the Chauncerie .. Treasurer of the Kings Wardrobe. **1613** *Voy. to Guiana* in *Harl. Misc.* (Malh.) III. 210 A treasurer-general for the plantations shall be resident in London. **1781** GIBBON *Decl. & F.* xvii. II. 54 The extraordinary title of *count of the sacred largesses*, was bestowed on the treasurer-general of the revenue.

2. *fig.* One who or that which is entrusted with the keeping of anything precious or valuable.

a **1300** *Cursor M.* 24672 (Edin.) To faintis was ti faiþe ne fere For þi þu was his tresorer [*Cott.* tresurrer]. **1340** *Ayenb.* 231 Þe drede of god is þe tresoriere þet þet tresor of madenhod lokeþ. *a* **1586** SIDNEY *Arcadia* I. (1622) 9 Knowing .. that I shall finde your eares faithfull treasurers. **1671** BARROW *Serm. Ps. cxii. 9* Wks. 1687 I. 444 Rich men are indeed but the treasurers, the stewards, the caterers of God for the rest of men. **1831** SCOTT *Cast. Dang.* viii, The secrets of which thou seemest to be a too faithful treasurer. **1856** EMERSON *Eng. Traits*, *Aristocr.* Wks. (Bohn) II. 84 These lords are the treasurers and librarians of mankind.

3. [f. TREASURE *v.* + -ER[1].] One who treasures or hoards up; a hoarder, preserver, keeper *of* something precious.

1597 J. PAYNE *Royal Exch.* 31 The wch noble vertu ought to be desirable to Lords, ladies, and the greatest Threasurers in the world. **1613** in *Crt. & Times of Jas. I* (1848) I. 247, I am a bad treasurer-up of names. **1631** B. JONSON *Underwoods*, *Epit. M. Drayton*, When thy ruins shall disclaim To be the treasurer of his name.

treasurership ('trɛʒərəʃɪp). [f. prec. + -SHIP.] The office of treasurer.

1483 in *Lett. Rich. III & Hen. VII* (Rolls) I. 15 Thoffice of tresorership of Calais. **1529** *Act 21 Hen. VIII*, c. 13. §31 Noo Deanery, Archdeaconry, Chauncellershippe, Tresourershippe, Chauntershippe, or Prebende in any Cathedrall or Collegyall Churche. *a* **1635** NAUNTON *Fragm. Reg.* (Arb.) 55 Then did the Queen .. give him her assistance, and advanced him to the Treasurership. **1709** STRYPE *Ann. Ref.* I. xlv. 456 Being preferred .. to a prebend of Winchester, and the treasurership of Sarum. **1886** DOBLE in *Hearne's Collect.* (O.H.S.) II. 456 He held the Treasurership of the Navy.

treasuress (ˈtrɛʒərɪs). [In 15th c. *tresoresse* for *tresoreresse*, f. *tresorer*, TREASURER: see -ESS. Cf. OF. fem. *tresorière*.] A female treasurer.

c 1450 in Aungier *Syon* (1840) 287 The priores..schal depute a..suster experte in temporal rewle and gouernaunce for to assiste the tresouresses. *Ibid.* 292 The treseres and undertreseres. **1491** CAXTON *Vitas Patr.* (W. de W. 1495) I. cxxxviii. 151 The Tresoresse & moder of Orphanes. **1598** YONG *Diana* II. 57 One of my approoued friends, and treasouresse of my secrets. **a 1688** DK. BUCKHM. *Instalm.* Wks. 1705 II. 84 A throng of Ladies, that did press To pay their Duty to the Treasuress. **1863** FABER *De Montfort's True Devotion Virg.* 12 He has made her the treasuress of all that His Father has given Him.

treasure-trove (ˌtrɛʒəˈtrəʊv, ˈtrɛʒəˌtrəʊv). [Orig. two words, in AF. *tresor trové* = L. *thesaurus inventus*, in 15th c. rendered in Eng. *tresoure founden, founde, found*; in 16th c. with the Fr. form anglicized *treasure trovey, trove, trouve*.] *lit.* *treasure found* (see b), i.e. anything of the nature of treasure which any one finds; *spec.* in *English Law*: Treasure (gold or silver, money, plate, or bullion) found hidden in the ground or other place, the owner of which is unknown.

In original use a merely descriptive phrase, of general application. But from an early period a distinction arose; treasure which had been lost (and not claimed), or voluntarily abandoned (of which the amount was naturally small and inconsiderable) was allowed to be kept by the first finder; while that which had been (certainly or presumably) hidden, was claimed by the Crown. This practically included all ancient treasure, and to this the name *treasure trove* was specifically restricted. To encourage the giving up of such treasure, when found, and to prevent the destruction of valuable antiquities, the Crown may award things found or their value to the finder. (For full discussion, see Wm. Martin in *Law Quart. Rev.* (1904) XX. 27.)

[**a 1190** GLANVILL *De Leg. et Consuet. Angl.* XIV. ii, Placitum de occultatione inventi thesauri fraudulosa. **1292** BRITTON I. ii. §18 Et ausi apent a lour office de enquere de viel tresor trové en terre. **1348** *Year-bk. 22 Edw. III, Easter* (in Statham *Abridgement* (? 1491) h ij), Thesaurum inuentum competit domino meo regi et non domino libertatis. *Ibid., Mich.* h ij b, Punysshement pur treasoure troue pris et emporte de were de meere. **1443–4** *Year-bk. 22 Hen. VI, Mich. (ibid.* g viij), Cestuy a qui le proprete est auera tresoure troue. **1527** RASTELL *Expos. Terminorum, Tresour troue* est quant ascun money ou argent plate ou bolion est troue ascun leu et nul conust a quele properte est, doncques le properte de ceo apperteynt al roy et ceo est dit tresour troue [see 1567 below].]

1550 *Acts Privy Counc.* N.S. (1891) III. 14 To go with certein persons that have offred to finde treasure trovey. **1567** *Expos. Terms Law* (1579) 180 b/2 Treasure founde is when any money, gold, or siluer, plate, or bolion, is found in any place, & no man knoweth to whom the property is, then the property thereof belongeth to the queene, and that is called treasure troue, that is to say treasure found. **1572** WOGAN in T. Wright *Q. Eliz. & Times* (1838) I. 442 One of the parties charged with the saide threasure trove. **1591** SYLVESTER *Du Bartas* I. v. 737 As wroth, that men upon his right should rove, Or theevish hands usurp his Treasar-trove. **c 1634** COKE *Inst.* III. 132. **1765** BLACKSTONE *Comm.* I. viii. 295. **1776** ADAM SMITH *W.N.* II. i. (1869) I. 282 Treasure-trove was in those times considered as no contemptible part of the revenue of the greatest sovereigns in Europe. **1904** W. MARTIN in *Law Q. Rev.* XX. 32 From the present-day point of view..we may say that if the discovered treasure has not been hidden..it is not specifically treasure trove.

attrib. **1868** G. STEPHENS *Runic Mon.* II. 515 They have been continually sent to the melting-pot, thanks to the old Treasure-trove law.

fig. **c 1700** PRIOR *Dial. Dead* Poems (1907) 227 Substances, Identity, Diversity, and fifty other glorious Tresor-trouves, to which you [Locke], the Master of the Soil, have the only right and Property. **1864** TENNYSON *Aylmer's Field* 515 There the manorial lord too curiously Raking in that millennial touchwood-dust Found for himself a bitter treasure-trove.

†**b.** Rendered **treasure found**. *Obs.*

1467–8 *Rolls of Parlt.* V. 583/1 Deodandes, Tresoure founden, and also all maner Goodes, Catelles and forfaitures. **1482** *Ibid.* VI. 205/1 Wrekke of the See, Tresour founde, and all such Issues, Fynes and amerciamentes. **1567** [see above]. **1651** G. W. tr. *Cowel's Inst.* 66 There is a propriety gained by finding, as in case of Treasure found,.. by Treasure we mean an ancient hoarding of Money or other Mettall. **1670** BLOUNT *Law Dict.* s.v. *Treasure-trove*, The punishment for concealing Treasure found is imprisonment and fine. [**1887** *Act 50 & 51 Vict.* c. 71 §36 A coroner shall continue as heretofore to have jurisdiction to inquire of treasure that is found, who were the finders, and who is suspected thereof.]

†ˈ**treasurous**, *a. Obs. rare.* [f. TREASURE *sb.* + -OUS: cf. *traitorous, treasonous*.] Full of or of the nature of treasure; precious.

c 1611 CHAPMAN *Iliad* To Rdr. 123 They fail'd to search his deep and treasurous heart. **1616** —— *Homer's Hymns, To Earth* 29 Goddesse full of grace, And treasurous Angell t' all the humane Race.

treasury (ˈtrɛʒərɪ), *sb.* Forms: 3–5 tresorye, 3–6 -orie, 4–5 -oury(e, 4–6 -ory, 5 -owrye, -owri, 7 -ury; 5 tresurry, -ie, tressurry; 5–6 thresory(e; 5–7 treasorie, 6 -ory, -urye, 6–7 -urie, 6– treasury. [ME. a. OF. *tresorie* (11th c. in Godef.), f. OF. *tresor*, TREASURE (after med.L. *thesauria*: see THESAURY) + *ie*, -Y.]

1. A room or building in which precious or valuable objects are preserved, *esp.* a place or receptacle for money or valuables (now *Hist.*); *transf.* the funds or revenue of a state or of a public or private corporation.

c 1290 *Beket* 2151 in *S. Eng. Leg.* I. 168 þis luþere kniȝtes wenden a-non to is tresorie. **c 1380** WYCLIF *Serm.* Sel. Wks. II. 211 Jesus biheld how þe puple caste moneye into þis tresorie. **1464** *Coventry Leet Bk.* 327 þe remembrances of sich libertes as perteyned to Cheylesmore weron yn the Tresory of the Duch[y] of Lancastre. **1560** DAUS tr. *Sleidane's Comm.* 360 Mony..taken out of the common treasorie for the war. **1660** F. BROOKE tr. *Le Blanc's Trav.* 221 Gold..of her own proper treasury, and not her husbands. **1780** HARRIS *Philol. Enq.* Wks. (1841) 484 There was no more left in his treasury than forty-seven pieces of silver, and one of gold. **1840** THACKERAY *Barber Cox* July, Lady de Sudley thought a fête at Beulah Spa..might bring a little money into its treasury. **1849** ROCK *Ch. of Fathers* I. v. (1903) I. 287 In the treasury of the Cathedral at Aix-la-Chapelle there is a fine, whole, uncut chasuble.

2. *fig.* A repository of 'treasures'; a thesaurus; a 'treasure-house', 'storehouse'.

c 1384 CHAUCER *H. Fame* II. 16 In the tresorye hyt shette Of my brayn. **1535** COVERDALE *Job* xxxviii. 22 Wentest thou euer in to the treasuries off the snowe, or hast thou sene yᵉ secrete places of the hale? **1673** *True Worship God* 61 The abundance of Divine Knowledg contained in the rich Treasury of Gods Word. **1772** PRIESTLEY *Inst. Relig.* (1782) I. Ded. 6 Value the scriptures, as a treasury of divine knowledge. **1861** PALGRAVE (*title*) The Golden Treasury of English Songs. **1879** P. BROOKS *Influence Jesus* iv. 209 Almost all men appropriate out of the great treasury of the language certain words which they make their own.

3. a. The department of state which controls the collection, management, and expenditure of the public revenue; *spec.* that of the United Kingdom; also that of the United States.

In the United Kingdom, the office of Lord High Treasurer is now discharged by the Board of Lords Commissioners, the First Lord of the Treasury (who is now always the Prime Minister), the Chancellor of the Exchequer, and junior Lords not more than five in number, who act as party whips. The actual head of the department is the Chancellor of the Exchequer, who is assisted in his duties by the Financial Secretary in the House of Commons, and by the Permanent Secretary and his staff in the Treasury.

All money raised by taxation or otherwise accruing to the Government is paid into the Consolidated Fund, the Exchequer account at the Bank of England. Money cannot be paid out of this account without requisitions and orders from the Treasury, authorized by votes of the House of Commons, and sanctioned by the Comptroller and Auditor General.

c 1383 in *Eng. Hist. Rev.* Oct. (1911) 742 Neiþir prelatis neiþir preestis..shulden han seculer officis, þat is chauncerie, tresorie, priuy seal, & oþere siche seculer officis in þe chekir. **1642, 1711, 1739, 1893** [see LORD *sb.* 11]. **1695** in *Calr. Treas. Pap.* I. Pref. 17 The King was graciously pleased to bestow on mee the place of Secretary to the Treasury. **1769** *Junius Lett.* xii. (1770) 58 With this precedent..every county in England, under the auspices of the treasury, may be represented as completely as the county of Middlesex. **1787** *Constit. U.S.* Art. i. §9 No money shall be drawn from the Treasury, but in consequence of appropriations made by law. **1827** HALLAM *Const. Hist.* (1876) III. xv. 112 They saw Godolphin..still in the treasury. **1849** MACAULAY *Hist. Eng.* iii. I. 309 The lord treasurer..had eight thousand a year, and, when the treasury was in commission, the junior lords had sixteen hundred a year each. **1888** BRYCE *Amer. Commw.* I. xvii. (1889) I. 172 In the United States the Secretary of the Treasury sends annually to Congress a report containing a statement of the national income and expenditure. **1911** MAITLAND *Const. Hist.* 409 Nothing whatever can be done which involves the expenditure of public money without the consent of the Treasury.

b. The building where the Treasury Commissioners transact business; formerly also ***Treasury Office***.

1706 PHILLIPS (ed. Kersey), *Treasury*,..also the Treasury-Office. **1815** WRAXALL *Hist. Mem.* (1904) 483 The daily Newspapers..represented Lord Shelburne.. advancing under cover of the night, to blow up the Treasury. **1879** *Whitaker's Almanac* 302/2 Government Offices..Admiralty, Horse Guards, Treasury, War Office.

c. *pl.* Treasury bills.

1922 *Daily Tel.* 12 June 2/1 New secondhand Treasuries were dealt in at 2¼ per cent. **1930** *Daily Express* 6 Oct. 14/4 The banks bought short-dated Treasuries at 2 per cent.

4. *Theatrical slang.* The weekly payment of a company of actors.

1885 *Diary of Actress* 132 The engagement turned out as I feared, no money. They said Treasury would be at night, but there was nothing. **1885** J. K. JEROME *On the Stage* 159 On Saturday, we came to the theatre at twelve for treasury. The Captain was not there... He would be back by the evening..and treasury would take place after the performance. **1892** *Daily News* 8 Nov. 5/1 We must never lose sight of the fact that he had to provide 'treasury' at the week's end.

†**5.** = TREASURE *sb.* 1. *Obs.*

1297 R. GLOUC. (Rolls) 7832 He het dele ek poueremen Muche of is tresorie. *Ibid.* 8431 þis cristinemen so wel astored nere Of armes ne of tresorie. **13..** [see TREASURE *sb.* 1]. **c 1440** *Alphabet of Tales* 196 þe bisshop askid hym if he had fon any tresurrie. **1593** SHAKS. *2 Hen. VI*, I. iii. 134 Thy sumptuous Buildings, and thy Wiues Attyre Haue cost a masse of publique Treasurie. **1609** DANIEL *Civ. Wars* VIII. xlv, As he, who hauing found great Treasury. **1672** CAVE *Prim. Chr.* III. ii. (1673) 254 To impart the Treasuries of the Gospel.

6. *attrib.* and *Comb.*, as ***treasury board, certificate, -chamber, -chest, -door, office, -vault***; **treasury-bench**, the front bench on the right hand of the Speaker in the House of Commons, occupied by the Prime Minister (the first Lord of the Treasury), and other members of the Government; **treasury-bill**, an instrument of credit, usually drawn for 3 or 6 months, issued by authority of Parliament to the highest bidder, when money is temporarily needed by the Commissioners of the Treasury; **treasury-bond**, an exchequer bond; **treasury chest fund** (now *Hist.*), a banking account not exceeding £1,000,000 from which advances are made for the public service at distant stations, accounted for and repaid by the departments concerned; **Treasury Department**, in the U.S. government, the finance department under the Secretary of the Treasury; **treasury lord**, one of the commissioners of the Treasury; **treasury letter**, a 'whip' issued by the government to its supporters in parliament; **treasury minute**, an administrative regulation for any department under the Treasury; **treasury note**, (*a*) chiefly *U.S.*, a demand note issued by the Treasury Department, receivable as legal tender for all debts; = *currency note* s.v. CURRENCY 6; (*b*) = *treasury letter*; **treasury tag** = *India tag* s.v. INDIA 6; formerly consisting of a length of lace with a blunt pin at one end which was secured through a socket at the other; **treasury-warrant**, a warrant or voucher issued by the Treasury for any sum disbursed by the exchequer.

1775 F. E. BOSCAWEN *Let.* 28 June in C. Aspinall-Oglander *Admiral's Widow* (1942) 64 Our cruel patriots.. would willingly wade through blood, provided it led to the *Treasury Bench. **1785** *Rolliad* (1790) 10 While on the Treasury-Bench you, Pitt, recline. **1882** W. CORY *Mod. Eng. Hist.* II. 482 The House of Commons [in 1835] did not show any wish to make the Prime Minister sit on its own Treasury Bench. **1797** *Hist. Europe* in *Ann. Reg.* 198/1 If the advances on *treasury bills had been paid off when required. **1912** *Standard* 20 Sept. 7/4 The offering by rival quarters of lines of Treasury bills cannot be helpful to Chinese credit. **1855** *London as it is to-day* vii, The *Treasury Board holds its meetings here. **1858** SIMMONDS *Dict. Trade*, **Treasury bond*, a species of exchequer-bill. **1791** *Ann. Congress* (1849) III. 1071 *Treasury certificates issued in exchange for loan office settlement certificates. **1852** GROTE *Greece* II. lxxviii. X. 265 Thebes was commemorating her recent victory by the erection of a *treasury-chamber, and the dedication of pious offerings at Delphi. **1877** *Act 40 & 41 Vict.* c. 45 §3 An account..showing the receipts and payments of the *Treasury Chest Fund, distinguishing those of the several Treasury chests. *Ibid.*, The Treasury may employ the Treasury Chest Fund to make temporary advances for any public service..to be repaid out of money appropriated by Parliament to such service. **1896** *Westm. Gaz.* 11 June 5/2 There was not a precedent for paying the expense of a military expedition out of the Treasury chest without such expedition having previously been sanctioned by Parliament. **1878** T. L. CUYLER *Pointed Papers* 54 A plain, coarsely-clad man..is seated in the *treasury-court of the Temple at Jerusalem. **1784** *Jrnls. Congress* 7 May, To revise the institution of the *treasury department. **1789** *Ann. Congress* 19 May (1834) I. 385 Mr. Madison moved..that there shall be a Treasury Department. **1892** A. B. HART *Form. of Union* 144 In establishing the Treasury Department a strong effort was made to create a Secretary of the Treasury as an agent of Congress. **1663** BP. HOPKINS *Serm. Vanity* (1685) 87 A seal set upon the *Treasury-door which none can break or violate. **1866** FELTON *Anc. & Mod. Gr.* II. II. iii. 298 He became a receiver of the public revenues, and acquired the name of *treasury-eater. **1778** H. WALPOLE *Last Jrnls.* II. 299 Not content with the usual *Treasury letters, Lord North issued a second batch, signed by himself, earnestly pressing attendance. **1756** in S. M. Hamilton *Lett. to Washington* (1898) I. 202 Who is hereby required to pay the same in *Treasury Notes, to be emmitted by Virtue of the said Act of Assembly. **1812** *Act of Congress* 20 June, Treasury notes shall be every where received in payment of all duties and taxes laid by the authority of the United States. **1815** *Deb. in Congress* 8 Dec. (1854) 1626 Having thus absorbed a portion of the Treasury note debt..the Secretary of the Treasury proceeded to assign funds for the payment of the Treasury notes. **1820** *Kaleidoscope* 25 July 30/1 Or (summoned by a Treasury-note) Night after night to sit and vote. **1899** *Westm. Gaz.* 24 Jan. 2/3 'Treasury Notes' are recognised by the student of our political history as the earliest form of Parliamentary 'Whips'. **1903** PORRITT *Unref. Ho. Comm.* I. xxv. 509 The circulars issued by the administration to its supporters became known as treasury notes in the reign of George III. **1923** A. HUXLEY *Antic Hay* iii. 50 It was with reluctance that Gumbril parted from his Treasury notes. **1974** *Encycl. Brit. Micropædia* X. 103/2 *Treasury note*, government security, usually marketable, with maturity ranging from one to five years. **1812** *Sporting Mag.* XXXIX. 177 The danger I should be exposed to..if I disclosed their instructions, or the *Treasury-Orders. **1912, 1963** *Treasury tag [see *India tag* s.v. INDIA 6]. **1975** 'M. SINCLAIR' *Long Time Sleeping* iv. 48 A little tray of pins, paperclips and little bits of coloured string known as Treasury tags. **1661** WOOD *Life* 1 Apr. (O.H.S.) I. 389 They conveyed themselves thro the cellar dore next to the *treasury-vault, locked it, and one of them put the key into his pocket. **1834** MACAULAY *Ess., Thackeray's Hist. Chatham* (1887) 319 Legge, the Chancellor of the Exchequer, refused to sign the *Treasury warrants which were necessary to give effect to the treaties. **1863** H. COX *Instit.* III. vii. 681 The Treasury warrant authorized the drawing an order upon the Tellers of the Exchequer.

Hence **'treasury** *v.* (*nonce-wd.*), in *pass.* to be honoured by the Treasury.

1855 DICKENS *Dorrit* xxxiii, He was.. Treasuried, Barred and Bishoped, as much as he would.

'treasuryship. [f. prec. + -SHIP.] = TREASURERSHIP.

1700 TYRRELL *Hist. Eng.* II. 889 The King..required him to give an Account of his Treasuryship. **1876** BANCROFT *Hist. U.S.* III. xii. 179 George Grenville..took the treasuryship of the navy. **1903** *Daily Chron.* 30 July 3/6 The treasuryship of the connexional funds.

treat (triːt), *sb.*[1] Forms: 4–6 **trete**, (5 **trett, treet, treyte**), 5–6 (9 *Sc.*) **tret**, 6 *Sc.* **treit**, 6–7 **treate**, (7 **trait, trayte**), 6– **treat**. [In branch I, f. TREAT *v.*; in II. from F. *trait*, or other derivative of the same stem.]

I. Senses arising out of TREAT *v.*

†**1.** The action or an act of treating, or discussing terms; parley, negotiation; agreement; treaty.

1375 BARBOUR *Bruce* x. 125 Schir alexander of Argill.. send tretis to þe king, And com his man but tarying. *Ibid.* XI. 35 [He] tald quhat tretis he had maid, And quhat day he thame [the English] gevyn had. *c* **1380** WYCLIF *Serm.* Sel. Wks. II. 248 In þis failen many men in tretes and acordis makynge. **1412–20** LYDG. *Chron. Troy* I. 2222 With-out assaut þe castel were y-ȝolde;..in swyche case longe trete were in veyne. **1448** *Paston Lett.* I. 75 That comynycasyon and trete schold be had betwyxt hys counsayle and myne. **1529** *Registr. Aberdon.* (Maitl. Cl.) I. 396 We þe saidis prowest bailȝeis consall and communite riplie auisit..be lang tret conuening togidder. **1590** SPENSER *F.Q.* III. viii. 16 [He] Bad that same boaster,.. To leave to him that lady for excheat, Or bide him batteill without further treat.

†**2.** An entreaty, a beseeching. *Obs.*

1601 WEEVER *Mirr. Mart.* D iv, The King..Then vowes, prayes, treates; vowes, treates, and prayers vaine, From prayers, treates, and vowes he doth refraine. **1632** VICARS *Æneid* IV. 105 But none of all her treats or bitter teares Remove his thoughts. *a* **1660** *Contemp. Hist. Irel.* (Ir. Archæol. Soc.) II. 133 By word of mouth [he] made faire promises mingled with many treates.

†**3. a.** = TREATMENT 1; an instance of this. *Obs.*

1671 BUTLER *Ode to Du-Val* iii, France..That serves the ruder Northern Nations With Methods of Address and Treat. **1702** C. MATHER *Magn. Chr.* II. iv. (1852) 123 Those harsher and harder treats, which he sometimes had from the frowardness of not a few. *a* **1711** KEN *Hymnotheo* Wks. 1721 III. 286 All..Who had from him receiv'd injurious Treat.

†**b.** Treatment of guests or visitors; reception, entertainment. *Obs.*

1689 *Andros Tracts* I. 107 After a very unkind Treat, we humbly prayed his Excellency [etc.]. **1698** VANBRUGH *Æsop* II. i, I don't know how I shall return your friendly treat. *c* **1710** CELIA FIENNES *Diary* (1888) 148 Mr. Wm. Allen.. gave me a very civil treate, being an acquaintance of my Brother.

4. *concr.* An entertainment of food and drink, esp. one given without expense to the recipient; a feast, refection, collation. *Obs.* or merged in b.

1651 EVELYN *Char. Eng.* (1659) 32 They drink their crowned Cups roundly,..daunce after the Fiddle, kiss freely, and tearm it an honourable Treat. **1705** LUTTRELL *Brief Rel.* (1857) V. 536 According to the late acts, no money is to be spent or treats made upon account of elections. **1725** DE FOE *Voy. round World* (1840) 260 A very handsome table, covered with a cold treat of roasted mutton and beef. **1736** DRAKE *Eboracum* I. viii. 379 He performed all the exercises and gave the usual treat for the degree of doctor in divinity. **1819** WORDSW. *Waggoner* II. 46 Our treat shall be a friendly bowl.

b. Hence, An entertainment of any kind given gratuitously, esp. to children; a pleasure party or the like.

1683 KENNETT tr. *Erasm. on Folly* 156 For a concluding Treat you expect a formal epilogue. **1791** BURKE *App. Whigs* Wks. VI. 131 The Bastile could inspire no horrours into them. This was a treat for their betters. **1841** THACKERAY *Gt. Hoggarty Diamond* ii, I had promised a dozen of them a treat down the river. **1885** *L'pool Daily Post* 23 Apr. 5/2 Vanloads of happy urchins, bent on enjoying their Sunday school treat.

c. The action of treating or entertaining; one's part or turn to treat; an invitation to eat or drink.

1690 CROWNE *Eng. Friar* v. Wks. 1874 IV. 120 The bride is my kinswoman, so the treat to-night is mine, and I invite all this good company. **1888** LIGHTHALL *Yng. Seigneur* 135 'Shut up, Potdevin!' said the only man who understood English, fearful lest the second treat should go astray.

d. *to stand treat*: to bear the expense of a treat.

1837 MARRYAT *Dog-fiend* lv, Neither she nor the corporal would stand treat. **1841** THACKERAY *Gt. Hoggarty Diamond* ix, We had a very merry party at Vauxhall, Gus insisting on standing treat. **1885** 'MRS. ALEXANDER' *Valerie's Fate* i, That stingy old thing..would not go into a cake-shop, though I offered to stand treat.

5. a. Something highly enjoyable; a great pleasure, delight, or gratification. Also rarely applied to a person as an emotional expression of commendation (quot. 1825). *colloq.*

1770 J. WEDGWOOD *Let.* 13 Oct. (1965) 98 Your stay here ..was a most agreeable treat to us and all your friends in this part of the world. [**1802** PALEY *Nat. Theol.* xix. (ed. 2) 373 Carrion is a treat to dogs, ravens, vultures, fish.] **1805** E. DAYES *Wks.* 127 Here the admirer of nature will receive a high treat, from..woods, sinking into deep glens [etc.]. **1823** JEFFERSON *Writ.* (1830) IV. 385 Her 'Few Days in Athens'..has been a treat to me of the highest order. **1825** LADY GRANVILLE *Lett.* (1894) II. 13 Lord Dudley is a treat, and deserves his cutlets for the admirable despatch he wrote. **1880** MCCARTHY *Own Times* III. xxx. 4 His speeches were an intellectual treat. **1887–9** T. A. TROLLOPE *What I remember* II. 267 The excursion..was another-guess sort of treat. **1901** ALLDRIDGE *Sherbro* xxiii. 237 An open shed-kitchen, so clean that it was quite a treat to look at it.

b. *a treat* (*advb.* and *adj.*): so as to gratify highly; extremely well; also (*gen.* or *ironically*) extremely, excessively. *colloq.*

1898 [see DUKE *sb.* 7]. **1899** *Daily News* 8 May 4/2 This air makes yer liver work a fair treat. **1910** *Ibid.* 24 Dec. 4 I've begun with a white-washing job. It pays out my arms a treat. **1942** *R.A.F. Jrnl.* 18 Apr. 10 We..set light to a..dump of Iraqi petrol which went up a fair treat. **1959** A. SILLITOE *Loneliness of Long-Distance Runner* iii. 185 The sports ground looked a treat: with big tea-tents all round and flags flying. **1960** *Guardian* 23 Dec. 7/2 He had a stroke..but he's come on a treat. **1984** *New Yorker* 17 Sept. 56/1, I knew this floor had life left in it... It's come up a treat.

II. Various obsolete or dialectal senses, not directly from the verb.

†**6.** In phr. *on* (*in*) *treat*, (*a*) ? at full length; in a series; (*b*) ? continuously, uninterruptedly, at length, at leisure. *Obs.* [Cf. OF. *à trait* 'lentement, posément, a loisir' (Godef.).]

? *a* **1400** *Morte Arth.* 3655 The marynerse..Towyne trvsselle one trete, trvssene vpe sailes. *c* **1450** MYRC *Par. Priest* 1174 Hath þy herte be wroth or gret When goddes serues was drawe on tret? *c* **1460** *Towneley Myst.* xxx. 130, For wysely he spekys on trete.

†**7.** *Med.* A plaster or ointment spread on a cloth. *Obs.* [? Aphetic for ENTRETE, OF. *entrait* adhesive plaster.]

c **1400** *Lanfranc's Cirurg.* 132 Take .iiij. partis of rosyn, & þe .v part of wex, & drawe abrood þat treet on a cloop, & leie it on þe wounde. *a* **1450** *Stockh. Med. MS.* 87 For to make trete þat ys callyd playster of plombe. *Ibid.* 111 A tret for iche wound sanatyf. **1483** *Cath. Angl.* 393/1 Trett, *tractura, emplastrum.* **1562** TURNER *Herbal* II. 30 b, Wyth a cerote or treat made of waxe. **1639** T. DE GRAY *Compl. Horsem.* 304 This is a most soveraign treate or salve.

†**8.** = TREATISE *sb.* 1, b, c. *Obs.* [? A curtailed form of *tretis*, TREATISE, the *-is* being taken as pl. suffix. But cf. also F. *traité* treatise.]

c **1400** tr. *Secreta Secret., Gov. Lordsh.* 87 We shhall determyn after by a short trete, of propertez & vertuz of herbes. *c* **1440** *Promp. Parv.* 502/2 Trete (*H.*, *P.* tretye or tretyce, *A.* tretyng), *tractatus.* *c* **1450** HOLLAND *Howlat* 307 At the forsaid trist quhar the trete tellis. *c* **1485** *Digby Myst.* IV. 3 Rede this treyte. **1536** BELLENDEN *Cron. Scotland* (1821) I. p. liv, To schaw the auld maneris of Scottis..under ane compendius treit. **1548** GEST *Pr. Masse* in H. G. Dugdale *Life* (1840) App. 72 Thys matteir..I have chosen ..too entreate upon, in respecte ye treate therof is.. avaylable and nedeful. *a* **1555** PHILPOT *Exam. & Writ.* (Parker Soc.) 340 Let us proceed unto another treate of Florebell's.

†**9.** = TRACE *sb.*[2] 1, 2: chiefly in *pl.* traces. *Obs. rare.* [a. F. *traits*, earlier *traiz*, *trais*, whence Eng. *trays*, TRACE (taken as sing., with pl. *traces*).]

1611 COTGR., *Traict*,..a team-trace, or trait; the cord or chaine that runs betweene the horses, etc. **1613** MARKHAM *Eng. Husbandman* I. I. viii. (1635) 45 The Treates by which the Horses draw, being strong cords made of the best Hempe. **1620** —— *Farew. Husb.* II. xiii. (1668) 61 To the big end of this harrow you shall fix a strong rope with a swingle-tree with Treats, Coller, and Harness. [*c* **1880** ELWORTHY *Let. to Editor*, Traces of rope, by which horses drag the plough. Still called *traites* in Dorsetsh. to distinguish from chain-traces.]

†**10.** A feature, lineament: = TRACT *sb.*[3] 7; cf. TRAIT 4. *Obs.*

1721 RAMSAY *Tea-t. Misc.*, *O'er Bogie* iii, There a' the beauties do combine Of colour, treats and air.

11. *attrib.* †**treat net**, some kind of fishing net; ? a drag-net (*obs.*).

1584 in *Descr. of Thames* (1758) 63 Treat Nets, Peter Nets, must be two Inches large in the Meish.

treat, treet, *sb.*[2] Now *dial.* Also 7 **treate**, 9 **trait, -e**; (in sense 2) 3–4 **trait**, 3–5 **tret, treyt**, 5–7 **trayt**, 7 **treate, trete.** [Origin uncertain; perh. F. *trait*, *traite* pa. pple. drawn, withdrawn, extracted: but no sense 'bran' appears in F.]

1. The second of the three qualities of bran removed by bolting from wheaten meal.

(Halliwell has '*Trait*, the coarser meal, *Cornw.*'; but this is not given in any of the Cornwall Glossaries.)

1641 BEST *Farm. Bks.* (Surtees) 105 In every bushell of meale that commeth from the mill there is very neare a pecke of chizell drossed out; which, hereaboutes, is called *treate*, in the South-country, *branne*. **1829** BROCKETT *N.C. Words, Bye-bootings*, or *Sharps*, the finest kind of bran; the second in quality being called *Treet*, and the worst *Chizzel*. **1894** *Northumbld. Gloss.*, *Treet*, the second quality of bran. The finest quality is called 'sharps' and the coarsest 'chizzel'. *a* **1905** SARAH HEWETT *MS. Collect.* (*Devon*) in *Eng. Dial. Dict.* s.v. *Trait(e*, Near Barnstaple I heard a farmer's wife say—'Yu ant atuked the traite out fine enough; there's a gude dayle o' the cuse bran long wi' this yer' [You haven't taken the treat out fine enough; there's a good deal of the coarse bran along with this here].

†**2.** Here app. belongs the denomination **bread of trete** (AF. *pain de trayte*, med. (Anglo-)L. *panis de trete, treit*), also simply *trayt*, the second lowest and cheapest quality of bread specified in the Statute of Bread and Ale, 51 Hen. III, 1266; the name remained in use down to the 15th c.

Also discussed by the legal antiquaries of the 17th c. and later (in many cases with erroneous guesses: e.g. in Blount *Law Dict.* 1670, Phillips (ed. Kersey) 1706, Jamieson *Sc. Dict.* s.v. *Trayt*, etc.).

The Statute of 1266 specified three (or four) varieties of bread of fine flour, of which the standard form was the *wastel* (OF. *gastel*, F. *gâteau*), and three qualities of inferior bread, viz. bread of whole wheat, bread of trete, and bread of any kind of grain; the farthing loaf of trete was to weigh twice the weight of wastel, on account of the bran left in it.

1266 *Act 51 Henry III, Stat. Bread & Ale*, Quando quarterium frumenti venditur pro xij. d. tunc panis quadrantis de Wastello..ponderabit sex libras & sexdecim solidos..Panis vero de trait [*v.r.* tret] ponderabit duos Wastellos. *c* **1290** FLETA II. ix. §1 [*quoting prec.*] Panis de Treyt. *a* **1325** (Eng. tr.) *MS. Rawl. B. 520* lf. 43 b, Of al hol bred þe furþingwort sal weie a Coket ant an half. Bred of trait sal weie tuuei wasteles. Bred of alle kunne corne sal weie tuuei cokettes. **14..** *Ipswich Domesday* in *Blk. Bk. Adm.* II. 175 Summe [bakers] maken wastel, ferst coket, and trayt all oonly; and summe symnel and trayt. **1420** *Marescalcia Prioris* in *Durham Acc. Rolls* (Surtees) 359 Non panem album nec tret, non pondera. **1425** *Ibid.* 371 Panis albus ob' minus þer iij s. & panis de tret. **14..** *Iter Camerarii* c. 9 in *Acts Parl. Scot.* (1844) I. App. iv. 697 Tercio quod non panificant quodlibet genus panis ut lex burgi requirit, videlicet quachetum, wastellum, Symnellum, panem alsamyn, purum panem, et panem mixtum de treyt. **1609** SKENE *Chalmerlane Air* ix. in *Reg. Maj.* 150 b, Baksters sould be challenged that..4 They make not all kindes of bread, as law requyres; that is ane fage, symmell, wastell, pure cleane breade, mixed breade, and bread of trayt. **1607** COWELL *Interpr.* s.v., *Breade of treate*, anno 51 H. 3, Statute of breade, &c., what it signifieth, I cannot learne. *Ibid.* s.v. *Cocket*, In the statutes of bread and ale, made anno 51 H. 3 ..you have mention of bread coket, wastell bread, bread of trete, and bread of common wheate. **1674** JEAKE *Arith.* (1696) 74 Bread of Treet seems to be Houshold-Bread of the best Wheat unravelled, or ravelled through the coursest Boultel. **1863** *Chambers' Bk. Days* 15 Jan. I. 119/2 *Trete bread*, or *bread of trete*,..made of wheat meal once bolted, or from which the fine flour at one sifting had been removed. This was also known as 'bis' or brown bread, and probably owed its name to..bran being so largely its constituent.

treat (triːt), *v.* Forms: 3–6 **trete**, 4–5 **treete**, 4–6 **tret**, (5 **treite, trette, treatte**), 5–6 **trayte, traict(e**, *Sc.* **trait**, 5–7 **treate**, 5–8 *Sc.* **treit**, (6 **treact, traite**, *Sc.* **traitt**), 6– **treat**. *Pa. t.* and *pple.* **treated** (4–6 **treted(e**, etc.); also *contr.* 5 **trete**, 6 *Sc.* **treit, trett**, 6–7 *Sc.* **treat**, 6– *Sc.* and *n. dial.* **tret**. [a. OF. *tretier*, *traitier* (12th c. in Godef.), F. *traiter*:—L. *tractāre* to drag, frequentative (intensive) of *trahĕre* to draw, pa. pple. *tractus*; cf. Pr. *tractar*, Sp. *tratar*, It. *trattare*.

The chronological order of senses in Eng. does not agree with that of L. *tractāre* or even of F. *traiter*. Senses 5 and 7 come nearest to the primary notion of *tractāre*.]

1. a. *intr.* To deal or carry on negotiations (*with* another) with a view to settling terms; to discuss terms of settlement; to bargain, negotiate.

1297 R. GLOUC. (Rolls) 10383 Þe verste day of octobre þis conseil bigan, Vor to trety of is lond þer was mani a man. *c* **1375** *Sc. Leg. Saints* xi. (*Symon & Judas*) 178 Or ellis ger þi fays be Rycht wondir fayne to tret with þe. **1390** GOWER *Conf.* I. 250 And aftir that of Mariage Thei trete and axen of hir wille. *c* **1430** LYDG. *Min. Poems* (Percy Soc.) 150 Begyn no trouble whan men trete of pees. **1568** GRAFTON *Chron.* II. 302 They treated for a peace betweene the two kinges, but nothing came to effect. **1617** MORYSON *Itin.* I. 195, I.. was forced to treat with unknowne Merchants for taking money upon exchange. **1647** SPRIGGE *Anglia Rediv.* III. ii. (1854) 140 The governor beat a parley, desiring to treat. **1795** LD. AUCKLAND *Corr.* (1862) III. 353 My private opinion has ever been, that it is right in war to treat at all times. **1838–42** ARNOLD *Hist. Rome* III. xlv. 306 They began to treat with Marcellus for the surrender of Syracuse. **1895** *Times* 16 Jan. 14/2 The railway company..served upon Lord Gerard a notice to treat for certain land.

†**b.** *trans.* To handle or discuss (an affair) with a view to settlement; to negotiate, arrange, plan; rarely in bad sense, to plot (quot. 1622). In early use also with *obj. cl. Obs.*

1357 *Lay Folks Catech.* (T.) 46 Oure fadir the Ercebishop ..Has treted and ordayned for commune profet, Thurgh the consaile of his clergie, That ilkane that vndir him has kepynge of saules,..Teche and preche. **1375** BARBOUR *Bruce* IV. 177 Quhen þis cunnand þus tretit wes. **1406** *Rolls of Parlt.* V. 417/1 Come for to trete Pees or Trieues. **1485** CAXTON *Paris & V.* 52 He trayted that she sholde haue of two barons that one. **1533** *Acc. Ld. High Treas. Scot.* VI. 154 Passing to the Newcastell to treit the peace. **1622** MABBE tr. *Aleman's Guzman d'Alf.* II. 154 Which of vs two treats falsehood, which intends diceit? **1658** BRAMHALL *Consecr. Bps.* v. 133 That these things should be treated, and concluded, and executed all at one meeting. *a* **1715** BURNET *Own Time* an. 1673 (1823) II. 30 He was treating a marriage with the archduchess.

c. With advb. extension: To bring or get (into or out of some position or condition) by negotiation.

1414 *26 Pol. Poems* xiii. 139 While ȝe trete, ay þey gete. Ȝe trete ȝoure self out of ȝoure riȝt. *c* **1440** LOVELICH *Merlin* 6554 A gret partye of the lond they hadden j-treted jnto here hond. **1681** *Moores Baffled* 3 They..advanced to besiege Tanger, but were violently repulsed, say some; others say, fairly treated off by the Portuguezes. **1882** SCHOULER *Hist. U.S.* II. 111 Eaton..indulged in some indiscreet reflections upon the administration for treating out himself and Hamet.

2. a. *intr.* To deal with some matter in speech or writing; to discourse. (In quot. 1509 *transf.* of pictorial representation.) Const. *of*, formerly also *on, upon*.

c **1374** CHAUCER *Troylus* I. 686 (742) Man maketh ofte a yerde With which þe makere is hym self beten In sondry maneres as þis wyse treten. **1382** WYCLIF *1 Kings* IV. 33 [Solomon] tretyde of the beestis, and foulis. **1390** GOWER *Conf.* II. 215 To trete upon the cas of love,..I finde write a wonder thing. **1509** HAWES *Past. Pleas.* IV. (Percy Soc.) 17

The hall was hanged, .. With cloth of arras .. That treated well of a ful noble story. 1579 FULKE *Heskins' Parl.* 527 The Sixtieth Chapter treateth vpon this text. 1652 NEEDHAM tr. *Selden's Mare Cl.* 150 Objections .. brought out of Writers treating of other matters. 1676 MOXON *Print Lett.* 3 The Roman Capitals have .. been treated of. 1681 tr. *Belon's Myst. Physick* Introd. 46 The Author of this Discourse .. having already .. sufficiently .. treated on that point. 1732 BERKELEY *Alciphr.* I. §3 Certain writings of our divines that treat of grace. 1766 GOLDSM. *Vic. W.* xx, What subject did you treat upon? *a* 1873 DEUTSCH *Rem.* (1874) 173 This book .. treating of a most abstruse subject.

b. *trans.* To deal with (a subject) in speech or writing; to discuss. In mod. use often with mixture of sense 10: to deal with in the way of literary art.

c 1325 *Song of Yesterday* 155 in *E.E.P.* (1862) 137 Ensaumple here of i wol ȝou trete. *c* 1380 WYCLIF *Last Age of Chirche* p. xxiii, Aftir þe opynioun of hem þat trete þis matir. 1382 —— *Mark* ix. 32 What tretiden ȝe in the weie? *c* 1425 *Craft of Nombrynge* (E.E.T.S.) 3 þis boke tretys þe Craft of Nombryng. 1523 LD. BERNERS *Froiss.* I. i. 1, I syr John Froissart, wyll treat and recorde an hystory of great louage and preyse. 1590 in Fuller *Ch. Hist.* (1655) IX. vii. §27 That he [Thos. Cartwright] with others in some .. Conference .. or .. Assembly .. did treat, and dispute .. these six Articles. 1734 tr. *Rollin's Anc. Hist.* (1827) I. Pref. 2, I have already treated them at some length. 1860 TYNDALL *Glac.* I. xii. 86 Questions which shall be treated under their proper heads. *Mod.* I wonder how he will treat the subject.

†3. a. To entreat, beseech, request (*trans.* and *absol.*); in quot. 1500–20, to get by entreaty. *Obs.*

c 1375 *Sc. Leg. Saints* xliv. (*Lucy*) 16 Hir modyr .. Scho tretyt with hire for to ga. *c* 1400 *Sowdone Bab.* 1923 Thus thay treted him to and fro; At the laste he sayde, he wolde. *c* 1470 *Golagros & Gaw.* 1047, I trete for na favour. *Ibid.* 1066 Schir Gawyne tretit the knight to turn his entent. 1500–20 DUNBAR *Poems* xvi. 14 Giftis fra sum ma na man treit. 1515 BARCLAY *Egloges* iv. (1570) Dj/2 To treate a tiran it is but thing in vayne. 1601 [see TREAT *sb.*[1] 2]. 1630 J. TAYLOR (Water P.) *Laugh & be Fat* Wks. II. 74/2 He from thy labour treats thee to giue o're.

†b. *trans.* To speak to, address. *Obs. rare.*

c 1400 *Destr. Troy* 5309 Then Teutra þo triet men tretid o þis wise:—'Ye worshipfull weghes, well be you euer'. *Ibid.* 12844 Tretis hom truly all with tried wordes.

†4. To deal with, apply oneself to, work at, carry on, manage (something). *Obs.*

1375 BARBOUR *Bruce* I. 35 Off þaim I thynk þis buk to ma; Now god gyff grace þat I may swa Tret It, and bryng It till endyng. *c* 1450 tr. *De Imitatione* III. iii. 67 Write my wordes in þin herte, and trete hem diligently. 1500–20 DUNBAR *Poems* xx. 42 With all thy hart treit bissines and cure. 1562 WINȜET *Cert. Tractatis* ii. Wks. (S.T.S.) I. 21 He intendit to offer the signe onelie, and ȝe, to treit the veritie self of the sacrifice off the Kirk.

†5. To handle (in literal sense); in quot. 1607, ? to operate upon. *Obs. rare.*

1382 WYCLIF *Col.* ii. 22 Nether ȝe schulen touche, nether taste, nether trete with hondis tho thingis. *c* 1440 *Pallad. on Husb.* I. 75 Loke yf hit be glewy, tough to trete. 1485 CAXTON *Chas. Gt.* iii. 35 In especyall were ordeyned xij persones .. whych shold treate & see the relyques. 1607 MARKHAM *Caval.* I. xix. (1617) 83 Those barbarous .. Horsemen, which with distempered hands, rough brackes, or t[w]ownd snaffles, doe treate and breake their horses mouthes.

†6. To manage, rule, govern (a person); to lead, induce (*to* some course of action); *refl.* to conduct oneself, behave. *Obs.*

1387 TREVISA *Higden* (Rolls) VII. 335 þis Lanfrank tretede [*MS.* tredede] and bylad kyng William conquerour by an holy craft, nouȝt wiþ grym chidynge. 1425 *Paston Lett.* I. 21 The seyd priour and his brether, and I also, willen gladdely in these matieres by treted by yow. 1436 *Rolls of Parlt.* IV. 501/2 The more sufficient that men be of liflode .. þe more unlikly they are .. to be treated or moeved to perjurie. 1496 *Dives & Paup.* (W. de W.) I. xlii. 82/1 We may not treaten god ne put hym to no lawes. *a* 1550 in *Dunbar's Poems* (S.T.S.) 309/34 Treit weill thy self, and stand content.

7. a. To deal with, behave or act towards (a person, animal, etc.) in some specified way; to 'use' (well, ill, properly, reverently, etc.).

c 1374 CHAUCER *Troylus* v. 134 And þat ye me wolde as youre broþer trete. 1375 BARBOUR *Bruce* I. 222 Alas! þat folk, þat euir wes fre, .. War tretyt þan sa wykkytly, þat þar fays þar Iugis war. *c* 1450 *St. Cuthbert* (Surtees) 552 Sho walde haue trete him all a mys. 1572 *Satir. Poems Reform.* xxx. 79 Thy houshald trim and treit weill, thay confest. 1632 LITHGOW *Trav.* VII. 332 There are many Turkish and Moorish slaues, very rudely treat. 1711 STEELE *Spect.* No. 53 ¶2 That Mahometan Custom .. of treating Women as if they had no Souls. 1746 FRANCIS tr. *Horace, Epist.* I. ii. 15 Paris treats this Counsel with Disdain. 1816 J. WILSON *City of Plague* I. iv. 299 Treat his grey hairs with reverence. *c* 1850 *Arab. Nts.* 604 The caliph .. spoke to the young man, whom he had seen treat his mare so ill.

†b. *intr.* To deal *with* in a specified way. *Obs.*

c 1400 *Rule St. Benet* 441 þai þat wil hir lare despise .. With þam aw hir for to trete With preson & with penance grete. 1707 *Curios. in Husb. & Gard.* 242 He treats with Aristotle, as one might do with Moses.

c. *trans.* To consider or regard in a particular aspect and deal with accordingly. (Often with *as.*)

1456 SIR G. HAYE *Law Arms* (S.T.S.) 122 Gif thare be ony thing .. possible to be done, he sall nocht trait it to be impossible. 1844 THIRLWALL *Greece* VIII. lxii. 147 The loss of so many captives was treated as a happy riddance. 1868 M. PATTISON *Academ. Org.* ii. 35 The clergy are often treated as obstacles to the diffusion of knowledge. 1886 *Law Times* LXXXII. 94/1 Rules of judicial discretion .. are not to be treated as hard and fast rules that can never be broken.

d. Colloq. phr. *to treat 'em rough*, to manhandle (people, etc.), to treat harshly or aggressively. As a motto: see quot. 1918. Also (hyphened) as *attrib. phr.* Chiefly *U.S.*

1918 W. H. ALLEN *Stories of Americans in World War* 162 The men in the tank service have chosen 'Treat 'Em Rough' as their slogan, and a huge black cat as the emblem and mascot. Any cat that looks black enough and fierce enough is apt to be kidnapped and adopted by some tank battalion. 1930 *Amer. Speech* VI. 83, I never have the same girl twice; I take 'em young and treat 'em rough. 1962 *Times* 6 July 15/4 A treat-'em-rough warden of the old school.

†8. *spec.* To deal kindly with; to show kindness or respect to; to indulge, favour; to honour. *Obs.*

c 1440 *Alphabet of Tales* 128 þe thrid confessur hard hym mekelie & spak frendlie vnto hym, & tretid hym. 1500–20 DUNBAR *Poems* lxxvii. 60 Hir for to treit thai sett thair haill ingyne. 1549 *Compl. Scot.* xi. 92 He vil tret, cheris, and promes grit reches til ony of ȝou that vil adhere til hym. 1556 LAUDER *Tractate* 27 To ponysche Vice, and treit virtew. 1581 *Satir. Poems Reform.* xliii. 134 Gif he did gud, God wald he sould be tret. 1596 DALRYMPLE tr. *Leslie's Hist. Scot.* II. (S.T.S.) I. 136 He mekle delyted in hunting .. he trett mekle the seikeris of wylde beistes.

9. a. To entertain, esp. with food and drink; to show hospitality to; to regale, feast, esp. at one's own expense, by way of kindness or compliment, or *spec.* of bribery, as at an election (see TREATING *vbl. sb.* 5).

1500–20 DUNBAR *Poems* lxxxii. 64 Thairfoir strangeris and leigis treit, Tak nocht ouer meikle for thair meit. *a* 1578 LINDESAY (Pitscottie) *Chron. Scot.* xx. (S.T.S.) I. 91 Schir patrick gray satt downe to his denner and the erle treatit him and maid him guid cheir. 1644 EVELYN *Diary* 27 Feb., At an inn in this village is an host who treats all the greate persons in princely lodgings .. but they pay well for it. 1682 LUTTRELL *Brief Rel.* (1857) I. 162 The Morocco ambassadors attendants were treated yesterday by sir Thomas Boles, in Graies Inn. 1695 PRIOR *Prol. in Westminster Sch.* 16 Our generous scenes are for pure love repeated, And if you are not pleas'd, at least you're treated. 1709 STEELE *Tatler* No. 95 ¶1 She had been searching her Closet for something very good to treat such an old Friend as I was. 1839 THACKERAY *Fatal Boots* Feb., They gave me plenty of cakes and barley-sugar .. I'd no need to spend my own money, for they would insist upon treating me. 1848 —— *Vanity Fair* xxxvi, Rebecca .. ordered a bottle of sherry and a bread cake .. to treat the enemy's lawyers.

b. *to treat* (a person, etc.) *†with* or *to*: To entertain with (food or drink, or any enjoyment or gratification); also *fig.* (sometimes *ironically*).

a 1550 in *Dunbar's Poems* (S.T.S.) 308/6 Sa mony ar thair ladeis treitis With triumphand amowres balleitis, And dois thair bewteis pryiss so he. 1662 J. DAVIES tr. *Olearius' Voy. Ambass.* 168 Some of the Caravan had been so treated with Aquavitæ, that being all dead asleep [etc.]. 1711 BUDGELL *Spect.* No. 161 ¶3 The Squire .. treats the whole Company .. with a Hogshead of Ale. 1712 ARBUTHNOT *John Bull* III. viii, I treated the Lawyers, their wives, and daughters, with fiddles, hautboys, drums, and trumpets. 1735 JOHNSON *Lobo's Abyssinia, Descr.* xiv. 134 He treated us with the most opprobrious Language. 1852 THACKERAY *Esmond* III. iii, I treated her to the fiddles twice. 1897 'TIVOLI' (H. W. Bleakley) *Short Innings* xiv, Dick had treated himself to two ices and a strawberry squash.

c. *absol.* or *intr.* To give, or bear the expense of, a treat or entertainment; to stand treat.

1710 SWIFT *Jrnl. to Stella* 11 Oct., I dined to-day with Dr. Garth and Mr. Addison, at the Devil Tavern, by Temple Bar, and Garth treated. 1720 PRIOR *Prol. to Orphan* 6 Our generous scenes for friendship we repeat; And if we don't delight, at least we treat. 1771 SMOLLETT *Humph. Cl.* 23 June, The ladies treat with tea in their turns.

10. *trans.* To deal with in the way of art (literary, pictorial, musical, etc.); to handle or represent artistically, esp. in a specified manner or style.

1695 DRYDEN *Observ. Art Paint.* Wks. 1822 XVII. 493 Zeuxis and Polygnotus .. treated .. their subjects in their pictures as Homer did in his poetry. 1762–71 H. WALPOLE *Vertue's Anecd. Paint.* (1786) II. 134 Familiar subjects .. treated with great lustre and fullness of colouring. 1848 MRS. JAMESON *Sacr. & Leg. Art* (1850) 318 The life of St. Stephen .. has been treated in mural frescoes. 1889 PARRY in Grove *Dict. Mus.* IV. 27/1 The choral part [of Beethoven's 9th Symphony] .. treats the theme in the form of variations apportioned to the several verses of the poem.

11. To deal with in order to some particular result. **a.** To deal with or operate upon (a disease or affection, a part of the body, or a person) in order to relieve or cure. Const. *with* a remedy or remedial process, *for* a disease, etc.

1781 *Med. Jrnl.* Mar. 150 The second class [of symptoms] are to be treated in the manner just now directed. *Ibid.* June 427 Seven patients in this disorder treated with mercury. 1797 *Encycl. Brit.* (ed. 3) XI. 347/1 A new-born infant, instead of being treated with syrups, oils, etc., ought to be allowed to suck the mother's milk. *Ibid.* 352/1 Cutaneous eruptions have been successfully treated with electrization. 1800 *Misc. Tracts in Asiat. Ann. Reg.* 327/2 The most adviseable method of treating the bite of a serpent. 1843 R. J. GRAVES *Syst. Clin. Med.* xxviii. 359 We were treating the woman for the pains I have .. alluded to. 1875 JOWETT *Plato* (ed. 2) I. 12 If his eyes are to be cured, his head must be treated. 1912 *Times* 19 Oct. 8/2 Making the necessary allocation of the insured persons to the doctors who will treat them.

b. To subject to chemical or other physical action; to act upon *with* some agent.

1816 ACCUM *Chem. Tests* (1818) 66 To treat the mineral water with the re-agents. 1845 MCCULLOCH *Taxation* (1852) 334 Potato-starch when treated with sulphuric acid becomes sugar. 1903 *Times* 7 Mar. 7/5 These roads .. should .. be treated with a steam roller.

Hence **'treated** *ppl. a.* in various senses of the vb.

1710 STEELE *Tatler* No. 195 ¶5 Three Times in Four the treated Persons have been Males. 1893 *Outing* (U.S.) XXII. 113/2 A glossy black substance, .. which I concluded was highly treated asphaltum. 1897 *Daily News* 5 July 3/3 They were similar in all respects, except that one was made of 'treated' timber and the other of ordinary timber. 1905 *Daily Chron.* 10 Feb. 8/3 It is in shades that these treated metals are most effective.

treata'bility. [f. TREATABLE *a.*: see -BILITY.] The quality of being treatable; responsiveness to medical or psychotherapeutic treatment.

1957 *Rep. Committee on Homosexual Offences* v. 32 in *Parl. Papers 1956–57* (Cmnd. 247) XIV. 85 The question of treatability. 1959 B. WOOTTON *Social Sci. & Social Pathol.* viii. 241 If treatability is taken as the test of responsibility, it follows that those who cannot or will not be treated must be regarded as liable to punishment. 1976 *Economist* 21 Aug. 18 The importance of treatability as a criterion. 1982 *Daily Tel.* 29 Oct. 18/6 The inclusion of 'treatability' among criteria for admission.

treatable ('triːtəb(ə)l), *a.* Forms: 4–7 tretable, (5 treteable, tretabill, -ylle, 6 -yl), 5– treatable. [ME. *tretable*, a. F. *traitable* (13th c. in Godef.):—L. *tractābilem*: see TRACTABLE. In some senses f. TREAT *v.* + -ABLE.]

1. a. Easily handled or dealt with; tractable, manageable, docile; open to appeal or argument, 'easy to be entreated', affable. (Of persons, etc. or their attributes.) *Obs.* or *arch.*

1303 R. BRUNNE *Handl. Synne* 1992 Makayre ioyed þat þey were .. so tretable; He þankeþ God þat he haþ founde So mylde wymmen yn wedlak bounde. *c* 1386 CHAUCER *Pars. T.* ¶584 Man is a quik þing by nature and tretable to goodnesse. 1496 *Dives & Paup.* (W. de W.) x. v. 376/2 Yf he be meke & tretable, gyue hym [horse] a smothe brydel. 1578 *Chr. Prayers in Priv. Prayers* (Parker Soc.) 489 Thou .. art treatable and mild, .. thou shewest mercy unto thousands. 1667 *Decay Chr. Piety* xvii. ¶10 Suffer themselves to cool into a treatable temper. 1711 SHAFTESB. *Charac.* II. ii. (1737) I. 238 Those arts, by which the people were render'd more treatable in a way of reason and understanding. 1888 DOUGHTY *Arabia Deserta* I. 583 Nasr .. had showed himself more treatable since the others' departure.

b. Of things: Tractable; yielding to treatment, as a disease; flexible or ductile, as a metal. *Obs.* exc. in *Med.*

1340 *Ayenb.* 94 God .. huanne he nhesseþ þe herte, and makeþ zuete and tretable, ase wex ymered, and ase land guod and agrayþed. *Ibid.* 167 Gold .. þe more hit is ine uere: þe more hit is clene and clyer and tretable. *c* 1425 tr. *Arderne's Treat. Fistula* 27 Considere þe lech bisily, þe wounde .. if it be wele tretable and with-out hardnes. 1543 TRAHERON *Vigo's Chirurg.* II. xi. 45 Yf the canker be tretable in the begynnynge, .. and in suche parte of the bodye, that it maye seme possible to be rooted uppe. 1974 E. AMBLER *Dr. Frigo* II. 141 Muscular dystrophy .. is to some extent treatable and controllable. 1978 *Bull. Amer. Acad. Arts & Sci.* Feb. 29 Heart disease and strokes are related to .. potentially treatable but undetected hypertension.

†c. Of or in reference to actions, etc.: Gentle, easy, moderate, deliberate, not violent. *Obs.*

c 1430 *Stans Puer* 78 in *Babees Bk.* (1868) 31 Be soft in mesure, not hasti, but treteable. 1597 HOOKER *Eccl. Pol.* v. xlvi. §1 Somewhat there is why a vertuous minde should rather wish to depart this world with a kinde of treatable dissolution, then to bee suddainely cut off. 1612 T. TAYLOR *Comm. Titus* ii. 15 (1619) 536 Doctrine may be ponderous and waightie, where the speach is calme and treatable, stil waters often runne the deepest. 1690 TEMPLE *Misc.* II. *Gard. Epicurus* Wks. 1731 I. 182 In France, and the Low-Countries .. the Heats or the Colds, and Changes of Seasons, are less treatable than they are with us.

†d. Of utterance: Deliberate; distinct, clear, intelligible. *Obs.*

1450–1530 *Myrr. our Ladye* 55 To abyde vpon the tretable sayng of theyre seruyce, be yt neuer so werysom. 1561 BP. PARKHURST *Injunct.* A iv, Whether the parsons .. doth reade the common seruice with a lowde, distinct, and treatable voyce. 1632 G. HERBERT *Country Parson* vi, [The parson's] voyce is humble, his words treatable and slow. 1641 MILTON *Ch. Govt.* II. Pref., Wks. 1851 III. 147 All these things with a solid and treatable smoothnesse to paint out and describe.

†2. Capable of being handled or touched, tangible; exposed to touch. *Obs. rare.*

1382 WYCLIF *Heb.* xii. 18 Ȝe han not come to the tretable fyer [1388 the fier able to be touchid], and able to come to. 1541 R. COPLAND *Guydon's Quest. Chirurg.* Hij, What woundes of the bely are moste peryllous and moste dyfficyle to heale? .. They in the myddes of the bely bycause the partyes there ben more treatable.

3. Capable of being or proper to be treated or dealt with.

1570 LEVINS *Manip.* 2/42 There be many other [adjs.] in *able*, deriued of Englishe verbes, .. as .. Treatable, worthy or able to be treated upon. 1657 J. SERGEANT *Schism Dispach't* 614 More liable to the rigour of Martiall law and treatable as a greater enemy. 1741 WARBURTON *Div. Legat.* II. 44 Treatable by the common Rules of Art. 1833 LAMB *Elia* Ser. II. *Barrenness Imag. Faculty*, From the moment that Sancho loses his reverence, Don Quixote is become a—treatable lunatic.

Hence **'treatableness**, the quality of being treatable; †in quots., tractability, docility; clearness of utterance; mildness of disposition.

1526 *Pilgr. Perf.* (W. de W. 1531) 144 b, In dede iustyce, in workes mercy, in maners discyplyne & tretablenes. 1546 LANGLEY *Pol. Verg. De Invent.* I. x. 21 To .. furnysh it with Elegance of termes & picked wordes: .. to vtter it with comely gesture .. for the conuenient treatablenesse thereof, doth teache and plainly declare the thing. 1700 RYCAUT

Hist. Turks III. 410 He commended the Wisdom of the present Vizier, his Humanity and Treatableness.

treatably ('triːtəblɪ), *adv.* [f. TREATABLE + -LY².] In a treatable manner; †in quots., deliberately, distinctly, with clear utterance; without haste or violence, gently, easily, moderately.

1450–1530 *Myrr. our Ladye* 53 To vse theyr tongue to say yt tretably and dystynctely, wythout faylyng or ouerskyppnge of worde or sylable. **1527** ANDREW *Brunswyke's Distyll. Waters* b iij b, Than make fyre vnder it that it may droppe treatably as yf you wolde tell the clock. **1612** BRINSLEY *Lud. Lit.* 151 You are to vtter each word leasurely and treatably; pronouncing euery part of it, so as euery one may write.. as fast as you speake. **1693** SLARE in *Phil. Trans.* XVII. 906 In the space of a Minute I have made Twelve Respirations, (when I was very sedate, and drew in my Breath very treatably).

†**'treatance.** *Obs. rare*⁻¹. [f. TREAT *v.* + -ANCE.] = TREATMENT I.

1644 [H. PARKER] *Jus Pop.* 54 Tis not sufficient to say, such a Nation was slavishly treated, they must prove, that there was cleer Law for that Treatance.

treatee (triː'tiː). *rare.* [f. as prec. + -EE.] One who is treated or entertained: see TREAT *v.* 9.

1841 J. T. HEWLETT *Parish Clerk* III. 71 The interpretation of which was left to the treatees. **1884** STOCKTON in *Century Mag.* XXVIII. 588 Each took a cigar with that careless yet deferential manner which always distinguishes the treatee from the treator.

treater ('triːtə(r)). Forms: 5 *Sc.* **treyter**, 6 *Sc.* **tretar**, 7, 9 **treator**, 6– **treater.** [In sense 1, a. OF. *traiteor*, *traiteur* ambassador (1275 in Godef.); in other senses, f. TREAT *v.* + -ER¹.] One who treats, in any sense of the verb.

1. One who negotiates terms of settlement; a negotiator.

1489 *Barbour's Bruce* x. 125 Schir alexander of Argill.. send tretis [*Edinb. MS.* treyteris] to þe king, And com his man but tarying. **1550** *Reg. Privy Council Scot.* I. 91 Subscrivit be the commissaris, tretaris of the pece betuix France and Ingland. **1644** *Pr. Rupert's Jrnl.* 20 Nov. in *Eng. Hist. Rev.* (1898) XIII. 738 Treaters came with 27 propositions. *a* **1656** USSHER *Ann.* VI. (1658) 368 And he instead of a treator, played the traitor with them. **1859** W. CHADWICK *Life De Foe* vi. 324 A misunderstanding among the treaters or negotiators. **1885** H. C. MCCOOK *Tenants Old Farm* ii. (1888) 13 A pedigree ante-dating William Penn,.. his treaties and his aboriginal treators.

2. One who treats of or writes upon a subject.

1594 BLUNDEVIL *Exerc.* (1636) A iij b, Modern Writers, and Treaters of that Art. **1892** A. C. DEANE *Frivolous Verses, Eng. Lit. Tripos* v, Here we possess highly-competent treaters, Ready to deal with all authors of note.

3. One who gives a treat, or stands treat; an entertainer, feaster.

1692 E. WALKER tr. *Epictetus' Mor.* lvii, You may, 'tis true, your Appetite appease, But not your Company, nor Treater please. **1884** [see TREATEE]. **1906** *Daily Chron.* 19 June 6/3 Any hospitality which is likely to secure to the treater the goodwill of the treated, which has reference to some election,.. is 'corrupt treating'.

treating ('triːtɪŋ), *vbl. sb.* [f. TREAT *v.* + -ING¹.] The action of the verb TREAT.

1. Negotiation of terms.

1375 BARBOUR *Bruce* XIV. 8 He send and had treting With the erischry of Irland. *c* **1440** *Jacob's Well* 207 Be tretyng or counscylyng þei myȝte haue sped bettere. **1525** LD. BERNERS *Froiss.* II. cxix. [cxv.] 341 We be in treatynge togyther.., wherfore we wolde gladly make an exchaunge with certayne prisoners. **1638** R. BAKER tr. *Balzac's Lett.* (vol. II) 147 If in treating together, we should not sometimes violate the laws of our Art, [etc.].

2. Discoursing, discussion.

c **1450** tr. *De Imitatione* I. x. 10 Tretyng and talking of seculer dedes,.. lettiþ muche. **1720** WATERLAND *Eight Serm.* 114, I was once inclinable to defer the Treating of it some time longer.

3. Behaviour towards a person, etc.; usage.

1549 *Compl. Scotl.* viii. 74 Al the gude treittyng that scottis men gettis in ingland changis in ane vile seruitude. **1588** A. KING tr. *Canisius' Catech.* 36 Irreverent traicting of yᵉ name of god.

†**4.** Entreaty, beseeching. *Obs.*

1595 DANIEL *Civ. Wars* II. lxxxix, With earnest 'treating she procur'd her Passe To come to him.

5. Regaling, feasting, entertaining; *spec.* the action of providing a person (wholly or partly at one's own expense) with food or drink at a parliamentary or other election in order to obtain (or in return for) his vote; bribery or corruption by feasting (illegal in Great Britain since 1854 by 17 & 18 Vict. c. 102, §4).

1709 STEELE *Tatler* No. 73 ¶ 14 An evil and pernicious Custom has of late.. prevailed at the Election of Aldermen, by treating at Taverns and Alehouses, thereby engaging many unwarily to give their Votes. **1842** *Act 5 & 6 Vict.* c. 102 (*title*) An Act for the better Discovery and Prevention of Bribery and Treating at the Election of Members of Parliament. **1863** H. COX *Instit.* I. viii. 116 Treating.. invalidates the vote of an elector treated.

6. *attrib.* †**treating-house**, a house of entertainment or refreshment, an eating-house (*obs.*).

1680 in *Verney Mem.* (1907) II. 369 Eate a Tart at the treating house by Knightsbridge. **1704** *Gentl. Instr.* III. (1713) 353 His first jaunt is to a Treating-house.

'treating, *ppl. a.* [f. as prec. + -ING².] That treats, in any sense of the verb; in quot., negotiating, discussing terms.

1820 A. RANKEN *Hist. France* VIII. I. iv. 95 The principal treating powers agreed to employ their endeavours in terminating the war.

treatise ('triːtɪs, -ɪz), *sb.* Forms: 4–5 **tretis, -ys, -ice,** (4 **-es, -esse, -yss, -ies,** 5 **-ise, -yce**), 4–6 **tretyse,** (5 **treetise, -ys**); 5 **treatis,** 5–6 **-ys(e, -yce,** 6 **-es, -esse, -ice, -ize,** 6– **treatise.** β. 6 **tractise, -yse; traictise, treactise.** [a. AF. *tretiz* masc. (one instance *c* 1250 in Godef.) representing an OF. **traitëiz*, f. *traitier*, F. *traiter*, TREAT *v.* The forms *tract-*, *traict-*, *treact-* were 16th c. 'etymological' spellings after L.]

1. a. A book or writing which treats of some particular subject; commonly (in mod. use always), one containing a formal or methodical discussion or exposition of the principles of the subject; formerly more widely used for a literary work in general: see also b, c.

13.. *Cast. Love* Introd., Her byginnet a tretys.. þat bisschop Grosteyȝt made, ywis. *a* **1375** *Lay Folks Mass Bk.* App. IV. 1 Her techeþ þys tretys þenne Hou mon scholde here hys masse. *c* **1391** CHAUCER *Astrol.* Prol. 1 To lerne the tretis of the astrelabie. *c* **1400** *Cursor M.* 27548 (Cott. Galba) Here will I tell a schort tretice Made of þe seuyn dedly vice. **1422** tr. *Secreta Secret., Priv. Priv.* 236 Here endyth the tretyse of Physnomye, and begynnynge the tretyce of gouernance of helthe. **1493** *Dives & Paup.* (Colophon) Here endith a compendiouse treetise dyalogue of Diues & paup. **1526** TINDALE *Luke* i. 1 For as moche as many have taken in hond to compyle a treates off thoo thynges which are surely knowen amonge vs. —— *Acts* i. 1 In my fyrst treatise (Deare frende Theophilus) I have written off all that Jesus began to do and teache. *c* **1530** *Crt. of Love* iv, That she, my lady, of her worthinesse, Accept in gree this little short treatesse. **1530** BAYNTON in *Palsgr.* Introd. 14 Whiche compendious tractyse.. Whiche brefe traictise. **1542** UDALL *Erasm. Apoph.* E.'s Pref., This present treactise. **1588** *Marprel. Epist.* (Arb.) 27 In my next treatize, I shal proue the matter to be cleare. **1633** in *Verney Mem.* (1907) I. 76, I remember 'tis a letter, noe treatise, I have in hand. **1741–3** WESLEY *Extract of Jrnl.* (1749) 15 Turretin's history.. (a dry, heavy, barren treatise). **1869** FARRAR *Fam. Speech* iv. (1873) 107 You will see it stated in many modern treatises.

†**b.** A story, tale, narrative (spoken or written).

c **1374** CHAUCER *Troylus* IV. 642 (670) The whiche tale a-noon right as Criseyde Had herd, she.. Ful bysily to Iuppiter by-soughte Yeue hym myschaunce þat þis tretis broughte. **1580** LYLY *Euphues* (Arb.) 226 To rehearse an olde treatise of an auncient Hermitte [etc.]. **1605** SHAKS. *Macb.* V. v. 12 The time ha's beene.. my Fell of haire Would at a dismall Treatise rowze, and stirre.

†**c.** A descriptive treatment, description, account (*of* something). *Obs.*

1570–6 LAMBARDE *Peramb. Kent* (1826) 151, I will here conclude the treatise of Dover. **1601** DOLMAN *La Primaud. Fr. Acad.* (1618) III. 686 The circles of the sphere,.. the treatise whereof I refer to you.

†**2. a.** Negotiation, treating, discussion of terms; arrangement of terms. *Obs.*

c **1374** CHAUCER *Troylus* IV. 36 (64) Whan Calkas knew þis tretys sholde holde In Consistorie a-mong þe Grekes soone. **1375** BARBOUR *Bruce* XIX. 145 The scottis messingeres thar he fand Of pese and rest to haf tretise. The kyng wist schir yngerame ves vise. *c* **1440** *Partonope* 1336 Better.. to dye Than in tretyse trust her curtesy. **1470–85** MALORY *Arthur* XX. xix. 831, I shalle sende a messager vnto my lord Arthur a treatyce for to take, for better is pees than allwayes warre. **1529** RASTELL *Pastyme, Hist. Brit.* (1811) 216 By the treatyse of the Countess of Henaude.. a meane was made for a truse. *a* **1641** BP. MOUNTAGU *Acts & Mon.* iv. (1642) 253 Antony and Octavius were reconciled;.. both ready and willing to yeeld to treatise, as standing in feare, the one of the other.

†**b.** A treaty; = TREATY *sb.* 3 a, b. *Obs.*

1460 CAPGRAVE *Chron.* (Rolls) 216 Thanne [1354] was the town [Oxford] put under interdict.. tyl a tretys was mad thus. *c* **1475** *Harl. Contin. Higden* (Rolls) VIII. 442 A tretys was made at Brugges. **1489** *Barbour's Bruce* XX. 47 (Edinb. MS.) And monymentis and lettrys ser, That thai off Ingland that tyme had,.. In-till that tretyss wp thai gaff. **1530** PALSGR. 282/2 Treatyse bytwene two princes, *traicte, trete.* **1544** A. COPE *Scipio & Hannibal* 133 b, Also graunted in that treatise of peace.

†**3.** (?) An entreaty; = TREAT *sb.*¹ 2, TREATY 4. (But the quots. may possibly belong to sense 2.)

1470–85 MALORY *Arthur* IV. xxv. 153 They asked herborow, but the man of the courtelage wold not lodge them for no treatyce that they coude treate. *Ibid.* VI. xv. 207 Syr launcelot leue that swerd behynde the, or thou wil dye for it. I leue it not sayd syr launcelot for no treatys.

4. *Comb.*, as **treatise poem**, a didactic poem of the eighteenth century.

1936 C. S. LEWIS *Allegory of Love* VI. i. 233 In our Augustan period we find a form which has not yet been named and which is only less dominant than satire. I mean the long Treatise Poem (if I may risk the invention of a name where one is badly needed) as practised by Thompson, Armstrong, Young, Akenside, Cowper, and the like. **1980** *Times Lit. Suppl.* 1 Aug. 863/3 The eighteenth-century treatise-poem of Akenside and the rest.

Hence †**'treatise** *v.*, *trans.* to make a treatise on, to treat or write of; †**'treatising**, writing of a treatise, treatment of a subject.

1502 *Ord. Crysten Men* (W. de W. 1506) v. vii. 413 Yᵉ dampnacyon of the body that hath ben the meane of synne hath ben fyrst treatysed. **1605** HIERON *Short Dialogue* 15 Some.. will.. distast this your froothy and wordy treatising.

†**'treatiser.** *Obs.* Also 7 **-our, -or.** [f. prec. sb. or vb. + -ER¹.] The writer of a treatise.

1604 HIERON *Wks.* I. 518, I remember a saying of S. Hieromes; 'I know.. that I otherwise esteeme of the apostles then of other treatisers'. **1610** BP. HALL *Apol. Brownists* lv. 136 The poysoned workes of Origen, and other dangerous Treatisours. **1637** C. DOW *Answ. H. Burton* 169 Answering a Popish treatisor. **1646** R. BAILLIE *Anabaptism* (1647) 178 Unto those Arguments.. the Treatiser adds nothing considerable.

†**treatly, tretely,** *adv.* *Obs.* [f. TREAT *sb.*¹ + -LY².] = TREATABLY; deliberately.

c **1435** *Chron. London* (Kingsford 1905) 21 Holdyng the Scrowe in his hande.. dystynctely and tretely he redde yt ouer.

treatment ('triːtmənt). Also 6 **trait-**, *Sc.* **treit-**. [f. TREAT *v.* + -MENT. Cf. F. *traitement* (1255 in Hatz.-Darm.).]

1. Conduct, behaviour; action or behaviour towards a person, etc.; usage. (Const. *of* the person, etc. who is the object of the action.)

c **1560** A. SCOTT *Poems* (S.T.S.) iv. 46 Sic treitment is a trane To cleive thair quaver caice. **1585** Q. ELIZ. in *Four C. Eng. Lett.* (1880) 29 My ambassador writes so muche of your honorable traitment of him. **1647** CLARENDON *Hist. Reb.* I. §49 This kind of Treatment was so ill suited to the Duke's great Spirit. **1719** DE FOE *Crusoe* I. 38 The generous Treatment the Captain gave me, I can never enough remember. **1809–10** COLERIDGE *Friend* (1865) 85 Had Luther been himself a prince, he could not have desired better treatment. **1907** *Verney Mem.* I. 280 Edmund complains of the treatment of the army by the treasurer.

2. Entertainment, feasting; an entertainment, banquet (= TREAT *sb.*¹ 4). *Obs.* exc. *dial.*

a **1656** USSHER *Ann.* VI. (1658) 437 As to the treatments of the guests, sometimes 1000, otherwhiles 1500 tables were most richly spread. **1715** tr. *C'tess D'Anois' Wks.* 452 He gave her Treatments, with enchanted Balls, and Comedies every Evening. **1725** POPE *Odyss.* XIV. 71 Accept such treatment as a swain affords.

3. Management in the application of remedies; medical or surgical application or service.

1744 BERKELEY *Siris* §95 Many are even rendered incurable by the treatment of inconsiderate physicians. **1781** *Med. Jrnl.* Feb. 98 The third part.. relates to the pathology and treatment of disorders of the nerves. **1797** *Encycl. Brit.* (ed. 3) XI. 352/1 If this treatment prove very disagreeable to the patient. **1863** AITKEN *Pract. Med.* (1866) II. 65 Treatment is chiefly conducted by diet and by medicines. **1875** H. C. WOOD *Therap.* (1879) 380 Arsenic has long been used.. as a remedy in the treatment of cutaneous diseases.

4. Subjection to the action of a chemical agent.

1828 WEBSTER s.v., The treatment of substances in chemical experiments.

5. a. Action or manner of dealing with something in literature or art; literary or artistic handling, esp. in reference to style.

1856 *Sat. Rev.* II. 322 The mode of treatment adopted by the Rouman balladists. **1879** H. PHILLIPS *Notes Coins* 8 The boldness of design and power displayed in the treatment of their subjects. **1889** PARRY in Grove *Dict. Mus.* IV. 20/2 The last movement [of Mozart's 'Jupiter' Symphony], with its elaborate fugal treatment, has a vigorous austerity.

b. *Cinemat.* A preparatory version of a screenplay, including descriptions of sets and of the camerawork required.

1928 L. NORTH *Parasites* i. 33 We always make treatments of our stories—it's a sort of synopsis suggestin' what to use an' what to put in the discard. **1938** A. HUXLEY *Let.* 18 Nov. (1969) 437 I've done a fair amount of work: a 'treatment', as they call it in the jargon of the films, of the life of Mme Curie for Garbo. **1959** HALAS & MANVELL *Technique Film Animation* 342 *Treatment*, preliminary stage to writing script. Assembling ideas and situations for the film in hand. **1981** L. DEIGHTON *XPD* xxix. 240 We asked the FO to request a copy of the treatment... They would have got a copy of the script too.

c. ***the full treatment***, the most elaborate manner of dealing with a subject, 'the works', esp. in phr. ***to give*** (or ***get***) ***the full treatment***. Also (often less emphatically) without *full*. *colloq.*

1950 E. HEMINGWAY *Across River* xxiv. 170 We'll give breakfast the full treatment. **1958** *Sunday Express* 9 Nov. 17/4 In *No Concern of Mine* it gets the full treatment in a first act which is brilliantly contrived. **1959** *Listener* 4 June 999/2 This programme was admirably free from the piety or boost which seems to be unavoidable when some celebrities are given the treatment. **1967** MRS. L. B. JOHNSON *White House Diary* 25 June (1970) 539 She seemed impressed with the kitchen when we took her through. Betty gave her the full treatment about the washer and dryer and disposal. **1973** R. HILL *Ruling Passion* I. iii. 26 I'm really getting the treatment, thought Pascoe. What does he expect from me?

6. Discussion of terms of settlement; negotiation. *rare.*

1828 SIR W. NAPIER *Penins. War* III. i. (Rtldg.) I. 116 The stipulations of a treatment between the juntas.

7. (rendering F. *traitement*, sense 5 in Littré.) Salary, emolument. *nonce-use.*

1852 *Fraser's Mag.* XLV. 170 The Professorship.. is a very desirable appointment... Its 'annual treatments' (to borrow a delicate Gallicism) amount to four hundred a-year.

8. *attrib.*, as ***treatment plant, room, tank.***

1963 A. LUBBOCK *Austral. Roundabout* 114 These were the trucks which transport the ore from the mine to the treatment plant. **1975** *Petroleum Rev.* XXIX. 315/1 A treatment plant for the removal of impurities. **1961** I. FLEMING *Thunderball* iv. 43 It was a white cubicle treatment-room like all the others. **1977** J. A. KOTARBA in Douglas & Johnson *Existential Sociol.* ix. 259 These conversations occurred in the waiting room, double occupance treatment rooms..and occasionally over coffee. **1900** *Westm. Gaz.* 2 May 9/3 Four extra cyanide treatment tanks [for gold ore].

treator, variant of TREATER.

treatrip(pe, variant of TREY-TRIP *Obs.*

†**'treature.** *Obs. rare*⁻¹. [f. TREAT *v.* + -URE.] = TREATMENT 1.

1494 FABYAN *Chron.* VI. ccvi. 219 [Canute] sayde, 'All erthly kynges may knowe..that none is worthy to haue the name of a kynge but he that hath all thynges subiecte to his hestes, as here is shewed, by worchynge of his treature by this water'.

treaty ('triːtɪ), *sb.* Forms: 4-5 **tretee**, 4-6 **trete, trety**, 5 **treetee, tretie, -ye, (tretty); traitee, -ie, -ye, traytee, -ye, (traytte, -ye**, 6 *Sc.* **treittie)**, 5-7 **treatye**, 6 **-ee**, 6-7 **-ie**, 6- **treaty**. [ME. *trete, tretee*, a. AF. *treté*, OF. *traité, traitié*, ppl. sb. of *traiter* TREAT *v.*, and:—L. *tractātum* TRACTATE.]

†**1. a.** The treating of a subject in speech or writing; (literary) treatment; discussion. *Obs.*

1382 WYCLIF *Ezra* Prol. 32 But that to short tretee I come [L. *sed ut ad compendium veniam*]. **1483** CAXTON *Cato* 3 The second partye pryncipal is the trayttye and alle the maner of this present book. **1552** HULOET, Treaty of any thyng, *dissertatio.* **1570-6** LAMBARDE *Peramb. Kent* (1826) 87 It followeth..that.. I handle such particular places..as are mentioned in hystorie: in which treatie, I will observe this order. **1619** J. DYKE *Caveat Archippus* 10 That a full Treatie of the particulars..should come within..one houres discourse. *a* **1663** BP. SANDERSON in Spurgeon *Treas. Dav.* Ps. xix. 13 Such a presumptuous sin as we are now in treaty of.

†**b.** A work in which some subject is treated of; a treatise, dissertation; in early use, a story, narrative, written account (= TREATISE 1, b, c).

c **1400** tr. *Secreta Secret., Gov. Lordsh.* 90 The tretee folwand in þe whilk we sall determyn of singuleryte. *c* **1470** HENRY *Wallace* VII. 901 As witnes weill in to the schort tretty Eftir the Bruce, quha redis in that story. **1508** DUNBAR *Gold. Targe* heading, Here begynnys ane littil tretie intitulit the goldyn targe compilit be Maister Wilyam Dunbar. **1585** T. WASHINGTON tr. *Nicholay's Voy.* I. xv. 16 Villegaignon in his treaty which he hath made of the warres of Malta. **1646** SIR T. BROWNE *Pseud. Ep.* II. iv. 80 Sir Kenelme Digby in his excellent Treaty of bodies. *a* **1715** BURNET *Own Time* an. 1672 (1823) I. 567 In some sermons, and in some printed treaties, they charged the judges with corruption.

2. The treating of matters with a view to settlement; discussion of terms, conference, negotiations. Now *rare* or *Obs.* exc. in phr. ***in treaty***.

c **1386** CHAUCER *Frankl. T.* 491 At after soper fille they in tretee [*v.r.* trete]. *c* **1450** *Brut* 491 þe Frensh men..labored to haue A traitie with þe King of Englond. *c* **1470** HENRY *Wallace* VII. 1267 Dunde thai gat sone be a schort trete. *c* **1500** *Melusine* xx. 113 In long treatee lyeth somtyme grete falshed. **1560** DAUS tr. *Sleidane's Comm.* 159 After a long treatie, albeit they coulde not throughlye agree, yet a trewce was made. **1615** G. SANDYS *Trav.* 234 A litle boate with a flag of treatie..to agree for the redemption of captiues. **1625** in Foster *Eng. Factories Ind.* (1909) III. 57 This was but yett in treatie. **1683** *Pennsylv. Archives* I. 70, I was in Treaty about your yea and nay going for an Oath. **1788** FRANKLIN *Autobiog.* Wks. 1840 I. 163 The treaty was conducted very orderly. **1881** MRS. L. B. WALFORD *D. Netherby* x, It appears he is in treaty for a place in the North.

3. †**a.** A settlement or arrangement arrived at by treating or negotiation; an agreement, covenant, compact, contract. *Obs.* exc. as in b and in phr. ***private treaty***: see PRIVATE *a.* 7 f.

1427 *Rolls of Parlt.* IV. 318/2 My Lady of Gloucestre so be pourveyde fore be way of traitee or in other wise. **1469** *Plumpton Corr.* (Camden) 23 Sir John Malevera gave me a chalenge for him, & said he was outlawd under my trety: I told him I treted never; I bare your message to him. **1552** HULOET, Treaty or agreement, *pactio.* **1753** JOHNSON *Let. to J. Warton* 8 Mar., in *Boswell*, For descriptions of life, there is now a treaty almost made with an authour and an authouress.

b. *spec.* A contract between two or more states, relating to peace, truce, alliance, commerce, or other international relation; also, the document embodying such contract, in modern usage formally signed by plenipotentiaries appointed by the government of each state. (Now the prevailing sense.)

1430-31 *Rolls of Parlt.* IV. 371/2 In ye Tretee of ye Pees, made nought longe agoo. **1545** ELYOT, *Fœdus*.., a treatie of peace, or league betwene princes. **1622** BACON *Hen. VII*, Wks. 1879 I. 760/1 A peace was concluded..being in effect rather a bargain than a treaty. **1671** EVELYN *Corr.* 31 Aug., The..height of the Warr.. to the conclusion of it in the Treaty at Breda, 1667. **1776** ADAM SMITH *W.N.* IV. i. (1869) II. 24 By advantageous treaties of commerce, particular privileges were procured in some foreign state for the goods and merchants of the country. **1841** HAYDN *Dict. Dates* s.v., The first formal and written treaty made in England with any foreign nation was entered into at Kingston between Henry III and the dauphin of France..11 Sept. 1217. **1874** BANCROFT *Footpr. Time* viii. 195 A treaty of alliance with France. **1888** T. E. HOLLAND in *Encycl. Brit.* XXIII. 530/2 A treaty is a contract between two or more states. The term 'tractatus', and its derivatives..began to be commonly employed, in lieu of the older technical terms 'conventio publica', or 'foedus', from the end of the 17th century. In the language of modern diplomacy the term 'treaty' is restricted to the more important international agreements, especially to those which are the work of a congress, while agreements dealing with subordinate questions are described by the more general term 'convention'.

†**4.** Entreaty, persuasion, request. *Obs.*

c **1450** *Mirour Saluacioun* 3972 A wise womman..whilk turned the prince ire to pece thorgh hire tretee. *c* **1470** *Golagros & Gaw.* 1083 For ony trety may tyde..I wil noght turn myn entent. *c* **1470** HENRYSON *Mor. Fab.* II. (*Town & C. Mouse*) xxiv, With fair tretie yit scho gart hir ryse And to the burde thay went. **1606** SHAKS. *Ant. & Cl.* III. xi. 62 Now I must To the young man send humble Treaties, dodge And palter in the shifts of lownes. **1649** DAVENANT *Love & Hon.* II. i, The gentle Treaties, Sir, of love are fit For hours more happy.

†**5.** Treatment, usage; behaviour. *Obs. rare.*

1630 B. JONSON *New Inn* I. i, *Host.* They call me Goodstock. *Lov.* Sir, and you confess it, Both in your language, treaty, and your bearing. **1654** tr. *Martini's Conq. China* 118 To partake of his sweet treaty, rather than of his cruelty. *Ibid.* 217 They were to expect no better Treaty from this Tyrants hands.

6. *attrib.* and *Comb.*, as ***treaty-ally, -breaker, -money, -right, skill, -stipulation***; ***treaty-breaking, -making*** sbs. and adjs.; ***treaty-bound, -sealed*** adjs.; **treaty coast, shore**, a coast on or along which some foreign nation has certain rights guaranteed by treaty; **treaty Indian** *N. Amer.* (now chiefly *Canad.*), an Indian whose tribe or band has signed a treaty with the Government, a ward of the Government; **treaty-port**, a port opened to foreign commerce by a treaty (esp. applied to certain ports in China, Japan, and Korea, in relation to commerce with European nations); **Treaty stone**, the stone on which the Treaty of Limerick (3 Oct. 1691) was reputedly signed (see quot. 1866).

1904 *Daily Chron.* 1 Feb. 5/1 It would ill beseem King Edward, the *treaty-ally of the Mikado, to pay a visit to the Tsar. **1908** *Westm. Gaz.* 29 Feb. 3/1 The French are *treaty-bound to keep the open door. **1706** PRIOR *Ode to Queen* xx, Thus the Royal *Treaty-Breaker said. **1723** BLACKMORE *Alfred* x. 359 At his Tribunal let them be arraign'd Who *Treaty-breaking Principles maintain'd. **1909** *Daily Chron.* 7 July 3/1 Any delay in that grant would have led to an accusation of treaty-breaking. **1899** *Westm. Gaz.* 26 June 7/1 The whole *treaty coast is in a most excited state. **1876** R. I. DODGE *Black Hills* 139 Every year since the treaty was signed has witnessed more or less pillage, depredation, and murder, by the *treaty Indians. **1936** B. BROOKER *Think of Earth* I. v. 59 He wore the shoddy black clothes, moccasins and red neckerchief which the Treaty Indians of the neighbourhood had affected years before. **1973** 'M. CAMPBELL' *Halfbreed* ii. 18 Grandma Dubuque was a treaty Indian woman. *c* **1500** *Melusine* xxviii. 214 For to fulfyll..that he had promysed at *traytee makynge of the peas. **1856** KANE *Arct. Expl.* I. xvii. 210 They did not return: I had read enough of treaty-makings not to expect them too confidently. **1796** WASHINGTON *Let. to U.S. Ho. Repr.* 30 Mar., The *treaty-making power. **1763** SCRAFTON *Indostan* iii. (1770) 102 Demanded security for the payment of the remainder of the *treaty-money. **1933** *Beaver* June 53 Upon the arrival of the Indian agent, the payment of the treaty money is usually first proceeded with. **1956** H. S. M. KEMP *Northern Trader* (1957) iii. 35 Had he been on the books as an Indian, he would have been considered a ward of the Government, drawn his Treaty Money and supplies, [etc.]. **1863** *Times* 24 Nov. 9/6 (*heading*) The Yang-tze-Kiang and the new *Treaty Ports. **1881** J. HATTON *New Ceylon* iv. 114 With the treaty ports of China and with Hong Kong we exchange annually upwards of twenty million pounds' worth of goods. **1901** *Westm. Gaz.* 4 Jan. 2/2 The extinction of the rights clearly possessed by France on the *Treaty Shore [of Newfoundland]. **1742** BLAIR *Grave* 500 Now vain their *Treaty-Skill! Death scorns to treat. **1842** J. P. LAWSON *Gazetteer of Ireland* 602/2 It is said by tradition that this famous document was signed by both parties on a large stone near Thomond Bridge,..which is locally designated the **Treaty Stone.* **1866** M. LENIHAN *Limerick* xxxiv. 271 The treaty is said to have been signed..near the Red Gate... Tradition does not admit that it was signed on what has been called the 'Treaty Stone', which has occupied a place on the North side of Thomond Bridge for many years, and which was originally a stone, used by country people for getting on horses when leaving town. **1922** JOYCE *Ulysses* 324 Remember Limerick and the broken treatystone. **1977** *Irish Democrat* Mar. 6/3 In the breach of death my Donal fell and he sleeps near the Treaty Stone.

Hence (*nonce-wds.*) **'treaty** *v.*, *intr.* to make a treaty; *trans.* (with advb. extension), to bring or get (into some specified condition) by a treaty; **'treatyist**, one who frames or is bound by a treaty; **'treatyless** *a.*, having no treaty.

1862 CARLYLE *Fredk. Gt.* XIV. ii. (1873) V. 152 In spite of treatyings innumerable. **1888** *Glasgow Even. Citizen* 3 Sept. 2/5 China must feel..irritated in having her people 'treatied' out of America and our Colonies. **1888** *Voice* (N.Y.) 26 Apr., A yearly addition of 150,000,000,000,000 of young codfish to vex future treatyists. **1892** *Nation* (N.Y.) 25 Aug. 137/3 There the negotiations hang, leaving these two high-protection countries in almost as helpless and ridiculous a plight as unhappy and treatyless England.

†**treave,** obs. var. THRAVE, THREAVE *sb.* and *v.*

1768 *Case of Jeffry Ruffle* 2 When cut down, the whole ought to be put into treaves of an equal size, and every tenth treave set out for the tythes. *Ibid.*, He tythed it at the times he gathered in his corn for treaving or loading, by separating and setting out every tenth sheaf.

†**trebant,** obs. variant of TRABANT.

1712 *Lond. Gaz.* No. 4967/1 His Majesty [at Vienna].. was on Horseback, preceded..by the Trebants, who are a sort of Yeomen of the Guards.

trebget, -got, obs. forms of TREBUCHET.

treble ('trɛb(ə)l), *sb.* Forms: see next. [a. OF. *treble*, sb. use of TREBLE *a.*]

I. 1. Anything threefold; a sum or quantity three times as great as another; the product of a sum or magnitude multiplied by three.

[**1324-5** *Rolls of Parlt.* I. 416/1 Que amounteront a treble & quatreble de lour coustages.] *c* **1430** *Art Nombryng* xi. (E.E.T.S.) 17 Thow most trebille the digit, and that triplat is to be put vnder the 3rd next figure towarde the right honde, And the vnder-trebille vnder the trebille. **1463** *Rolls of Parlt.* V. 502/2 Forfeiture..of the treble of his seid wages. **1475** *Ibid.* VI. 121/2 Uppon peyn of forfeiture of the treble of somoche as he so hath receyved or taken. **1799** WILSON in *Phil. Trans.* LXXXIX. 302 The equation of the halves, or quarters, or doubles, trebles, &c. of those functions.

2. In technical and elliptical uses. **a.** A triple barrier; an obstacle consisting of three successive fences.

1569 STOCKER tr. *Diod. Sic.* III. xi. 120/2 Hys Campe which he with a treble of wood and earth fortified. **1895** *Daily News* 1 May 7/5 The fences..On one side of the ring ..are arranged in a 'treble', just far enough apart to give room between for a horse to pull himself together for each effort.

b. *Paper-making* and *Printing.* A frame on which hand-made paper or printed sheets are hung to dry.

1727-41 CHAMBERS *Cycl.* s.v. *Paper*, Carried up into the loft, and hung six or seven sheets together upon lines fastened to a thing called a Tribble, each tribble containing thirty lines ten or twelve foot long. **1766** C. LEADBETTER *Royal Gauger* II. xiv. (ed. 6) 371 The Sheets of Paper, taken from between the Felts, are laid one upon the other till the next Day and then are hung up, on Lines called Trebles, in the Drying-House. **1896** *Daily News* 23 Mar. 8/4 If time be no object, the sheets are hung on 'trebles' (the towel-horse is the domestic equivalent) in an ordinary room.

c. A kind of step-dance; the measure of or music for this. *dial.*

1805 G. MCINDOE *Poems* 18 We'll sen' for fiddling Alic, and the piper he'll play treple. **1895** D. D. DIXON *Whittingham Vale* v. 67 A variety of step-dancing such as the 'treble', the single and double 'shuffle', the 'cut' [etc.].

d. *Whist.* A game (at short whist) in which one side scores five and the other none, counting three points to the winners.

1870 HARDY & WARE *Mod. Hoyle* 30 If one side scores five while the adversaries have made not one point, the winning side makes a treble. **1876** A. C. WALKER *Correct Card* (1880) Gloss., *Treble*, scoring five before your adversary scores one.

e. *pl.* A quality or grade of small coal.

1901 *Scotsman* 15 Oct. 4/8 There are four bush washers.. one for trebles.

f. A method of crocheting in which three loops of thread are carried on the hook; also a line or chain of crochet work done by this method.

1872 *Young Englishwoman* Oct. 555/1 *Crochet rosette*..3rd row:..work 11 treble on each chain scallop. **1882** CAULFEILD & SAWARD *Dict. Needlework* 127/2 s.v. *Crochet, Treble Stitch, Raised.*— Work three rows of Ribbed Stitch. Fourth row—work 2 Ribbed Stitches, and make a Treble for next, putting the hook into the stitch underneath it of the first row, work 2 Trebles in this way [etc.]. *c* **1900** THÉRÈSE DE DILLMONT *Encycl. Needlework, Crochet* 304 Trebles are little columns or bars made of loops or stitches... They are of different kinds; the half or short treble, the plain or ordinary treble [etc.].

g. *Racing.* (*a*) A total of three races won by the same horse; (*b*) a bet on three horses to win the respective races in which they are entered (the usual sense).

1924 C. HAWTREY *Truth at Last* xix. 226 Many [*sc.* starting-price bookmakers] have further altered that rule, now limiting the odds to 50 to 1 for the double event, and 100 to 1 for treble. **1931** *Daily Express* 21 Sept. 15/4 Peacock wound up a fine week in Scotland, where Nevett landed a treble for him on Saturday. **1951** [see ACCUMULATOR 4]. **1964** A. WYKES *Gambling* viii. 194 (*caption*) The bettor has staked a total of 27s. 6d. on his four chosen horses with 11 separate bets of 2s. 6d.—the bets consisting of six 'doubles', four 'trebles', and an 'accumulator' bet. **1981** P. INCHBALD *Tondo for Short* vi. 70 Cigars, liqueurs, brandy—has he won a big treble or something?

h. *Darts.* A throw into the narrow space between the two middle circles on a dartboard, worth three times the single score for the sector in which the dart lands; the space itself.

1936 [see DOUBLE *sb.* 3 s]. **1981** R. LEWIS *Seek for Justice* ii. 53 The first dart flicked into the treble twenty. It was followed by a second... The microphone boomed:..'Can he nail a third treble?..He's done it'.

i. *Assoc. Football.* The winning of three national or international competitions by one football club during a season.

1959 *Listener* 19 Feb. 331/1 The treble of League, Cup, and European Cup seemed to be at least a possibility. **1977** *News of World* 17 Apr. 21/2 That would make me unique, the only player who has done the double and treble.

j. A drink of spirits of three times the standard measure.

1968 J. F. STRAKER *SIN & Johnny Inch* 131 Sinclair poured yet another whisky. Like the others, it came well up the glass. A good treble, Johnny reckoned. **1979** M. BABSON *So soon done For* ii. 12 Crispin poured drinks for himself and Kay. Jeremy, he noted, had given himself a treble.

3. One of three things or persons that are exact counterparts. *nonce-use* after DOUBLE *sb.* 2 b.

1898 *Westm. Gaz.* 29 June 1/2 There are many 'doubles' in the House of Commons. There seem..to be in that assembly at least two groups of trebles.

II. 4. *Music.* The highest part in harmonized musical composition; the soprano part. Cf.

TREBLE *a.* 2. [The musical use is supposed to have arisen from the fact that in early contrapuntal music the chief melody or *cantus firmus* was given to the tenor (TENOR *sb.* 4 a), the voice parts added above being the *discantus* or alto, and the *treble* (? third part) or soprano; but the history is somewhat obscure, esp. as *triplex*, *triplus* meant 'threefold' and not 'third', and in OF. *treble* was applied to a trio.]

c **1330** R. BRUNNE *Chron. Wace* (Rolls) 11263 Þo clerkes þat best couþe synge, Wyþ treble, mene, & burdoun. *c* **1430** LYDG. *Min. Poems* (Percy Soc.) 54 Thi [nasal] organys so hihe begynne to syng ther messe, With treble meene and tenor discordyng as I gesse. **1500–20** DUNBAR *Poems* xxxii. 19 All to small To sic ane tribbill to hald ane bace. **1567** *Trial Treas.* B iv, I will sing the trouble with all my harte. **1626** BACON *Sylva* §109 In one of the lower Strings of a Lute, there soundeth not the Sound of the Treble,..but only the Sound of the Base. **1782** BURNEY *Hist. Music* (1789) II. v. 456 The third and Triplum the highest or treble, of which term this was the origin. **1884** H. C. DEACON in Grove *Dict. Mus.* IV. 165 *Treble*..has been said to be a corruption of Triplum, a third part superadded to the Altus and Bassus. *fig.* **1532** MORE *Confut. Tindale* II. i. 95 His false translacyon wyth theyr farther false construccion, they thought sholde be the basse and the tenour wheruppon they wold synge the trouble wyth mych false descant. **1577** B. GOOGE *Heresbach's Husb.* III. (1586) 112 The grasiers trade the treble and the tillers occupation the base. **1638–56** COWLEY *Davideis* I. 458 Water and Air he for the Tenor chose, Earth made the Base, the Treble Flame arose. **1892** *Daily News* 16 Sept. 3/3 The dark tone of the ground..acts as bass to the treble of the silk.

5. a. A treble voice; also, a singer having a treble voice; one who sings the treble part.

?*c* **1475** *Sqr. lowe Degre* 782 Than shall ye go to your evensong, With tenours and trebles among. **1658** MARVELL *Poems, Music's Empire* 10 And Virgin Trebles wed the manly Base. **1719** D'URFEY *Pills* (1872) I. 7 The ravishing trebles delight every ear. **1801** STRUTT *Sports & Past.* IV. i. 254 Two celebrated trebles;..who occasionally made twenty shillings a day by ballad-singing.

b. *transf.* A high-pitched or shrill voice, sound, or note.

1600 SHAKS. *A.Y.L.* II. vii. 162 His bigge manly voice, Turning againe toward childish trebble, pipes And whistles in his sound. **1647** H. MORE *Poems, Cupid's Conflict* vi, How well agreed the Brooks low muttering Base, With the birds trebbles. **1827** DISRAELI *Viv. Grey* VI. iii, 'So please your Serene Highness, I am here!' answered a very thin treble. **1855** TENNYSON *Brook* 40, I chatter over stony ways, In little sharps and trebles.

6. The string of treble pitch in a musical instrument; also, the chanter of a bagpipe.

1562 J. HEYWOOD *Prov. & Epigr.* (1867) 186 Which string ..wouldst thou..harpe on? Not the base.., Nor the treble. **1623** LISLE *Ælfric on O. & N. Test.* Ded. xxxviii, What sports they now deuise With Treble and Drone, and Bonfiers, and Bels. **1682** DRYDEN *MacFl.* 46 At thy well-sharpened thumb,..The treble squeaks for fear, the basses roar.

†**7. a.** A musical instrument of treble pitch, as a violin. *Obs.*

1634 *MS. Archd. Oxon, Berks.* c. 74 lf. 230 He plaied uppon a trebble in the house of Francis Iennings uppon a Sondaie. **1670** EACHARD *Cont. Clergy* 62 People..presently phansi'd the Moon, Mercury, and Venus to be a kind of violins or trebles to Jupiter and Saturn. **1710** in E. W. Dunbar *Soc. Life in Moray* (1865) 15, I can play on the Treble and Gambo, Viol, &c.

b. = *treble bell*: see TREBLE *a.* 2 b.

1598–9 in Swayne *Sarum Churchw. Acc.* (1896) 147, ij newe gudgins for yᵉ Treble and nailes, 3*s.* 6*d.* **1652–3** *Ibid.* 227 The Sexton shall ring the Treable at 5 a Clocke in the Morning. *a* **1658** FORD, etc. *Witch Edmonton* II. i, Double Bells!.. Trebles: buy me Trebles, all Trebles: for our purpose is to be in the Altitudes.

8. *attrib.* and *Comb.*, as **treble bob**: BOB *sb.*⁵; **treble-ringer**, the ringer of the treble bell in a peal.

1872 Treble bob royal [see BOB *sb.*⁵]. **1899** *Westm. Gaz.* 31 Oct. 10/1 For sixty-seven years..Bunce was the treble ringer.

treble ('trɛb(ə)l), *a.* and *adv.* Also 4–8 trebble, 6 -il; 5 trebel, -yl(le, -ille, -ull, 6 treabell, 6–7 -ble, 7 *Sc.* treeble; 5 tribull, 5–6 *Sc.* trib(b)ill, 5–7 trible, 7–8 (9 *dial.*) tribble; 5 tryble, -ylle; (6 trouble). [a. OF. *treble*, *trebble*, *treuble*, etc. (12th c. in Godef.):—pop.L. *triplus* for L. *triplex*. See also prec.]

A. *adj.* **1. a.** Consisting of three members, things, or sets combined; threefold; made of three thicknesses or layers of material; = TRIPLE *a.* 1.

c **1374** CHAUCER *Boeth.* IV. metr. vii. 115 (Camb. MS.) He drowh cerberus the hownd of helle by his treble cheyne. **1413** *Pilgr. Sowle* (Caxton) I. xxv. (1859) 30 Byndyng with double and treble boundes. *a* **1673** J. CARYL in Spurgeon *Treas. Dav.* Ps. cxl. 3 Serpents are..said to have a treble tongue, because, moving their tongue so fast, they seem to have three tongues. **1697** DRYDEN *Æneid* x. 1112 Thro' treble Plates it went Of solid Brass. **1781** GIBBON *Decl. & F.* xviii. II. 107 A treble inclosure of brick walls was defended by a deep ditch. **1832** R. & J. LANDER *Exped. Niger* II. xii. 183 They had formed themselves into a large treble circle. **1907** C. HILL-TOUT *Brit. N. Amer., Far West* vii. 130 A kind of shirt of double or treble elk-hide.

b. Of actions, conditions, etc.: Of threefold character or application; existing or occurring in three ways or relations; of three kinds.

1390 GOWER *Conf.* III. 159 Thus thei worchen treble sinne, That ben flatours aboute a king. *c* **1450** *Mirour Saluacioun* 1529 The feend thoght crist to tempt be treble vice. **1571** GOLDING *Calvin on Ps.* lx. 6 The greate men were dubble and trebble traytours. **1694** F. BRAGGE *Disc. Parables* vii. 238 It would be a double and treble charity; 'twould provide for the happiness of both body and soul. **1818** SCOTT *Br. Lamm.* xii, It was attended with a treble difficulty. **1886** F. HARRISON *Choice Bks.* iii. 49 Every part and episode has its double and treble meaning.

c. Three times as much or as many; of three times the number or amount; triple.

1423 *Rolls of Parlt.* IV. 257/2 Uppon peine de inprisonement..and trible dammages to the partie greved. **1489** *Barbour's Bruce* XVIII. 30 (Edin. MS.) Schir Eduard.. said, that he suld fecht that day, Thouch tribill and quatribill war thai. **1563** W. COTHE in *15th Rep. Hist. MSS. Comm.* App. II. 32 It is not treble the company we have here, that is able to defend it. **1664** M. FELL in *Extr. S.P. rel. Friends* II. (1911) 187 People had theire goods distreaned trible the vallue of their fines. **1788** JEFFERSON *Writ.* (1859) II. 526 It sells..for treble the price of common whale oil. **1835** URE *Philos. Manuf.* 156 The roller A, moving with a treble surface velocity.

(*b*) *spec.* of a drink of spirits: constituting three times the standard measure.

1964 L. DEIGHTON *Funeral in Berlin* xxiii. 126 He.. ordered three treble brandies. **1977** 'J. D. WHITE' *Salzburg Affair* xvi. 137 Hendryks..raised an urgent hand for the waiter. 'A treble scotch.'

2. *Mus.* Of, pertaining to, or suited to the highest part in harmonized musical composition.

treble voice: a voice ranging from about middle C to a twelfth or two octaves above it; a soprano voice. *treble clef*: the G clef when placed (as usually) upon the second line of the stave.

c **1440** *Promp. Parv.* 501/1 Treblesonge (*K.* treble of orgene songe, *S.* trebyl songe), *precentus*. *Ibid.*, Trebyl syngare. **1530** PALSGR. 286/1 Wayte treble, *bussine*. **1674** PLAYFORD *Skill Mus.* 43 Increasing of the Voice in the Treble Part..doth oftentimes become harsh. **1678** PHILLIPS (ed. 4), *Treble*, the highest part in Musick, called in Latin *Altus*. **1801** BUSBY *Dict. Mus.* Introd. 23 The Treble-cliff is used for the first or shrillest class, both of voice and instruments. **1876** STAINER & BARRETT *Dict. Mus. Terms* (1898) s.v., The treble or soprano voice is the most flexible of all vocal registers.

b. Hence in the names of musical instruments (or strings) of the highest pitch. Cf. *bass*, *tenor*.

treble bell: the smallest bell of a peal.

1530 PALSGR. 282/2 Treble stryng of an instrument, *chanterelle*. **1595–6** in Swayne *Sarum Churchw. Acc.* (1896) 145 A Rope for yᵉ Treabell bell, 2*s.* 5*d.* **1597** SHAKS. *2 Hen. IV*, III. ii. 351 The Case of a Treble Hoeboy was a Mansion for him. **1674** PLAYFORD *Skill Mus.* 109 The Treble-Violin is a cheerful and spritely Instrument. **1872** ELLACOMBE *Ch. Bells Devon*, etc. 235 In 1718, two treble bells were added to the peal of S. Bride's.

c. High-pitched; high or sharp in tone; shrill.

1562 J. HEYWOOD *Prov. & Epigr.* (1867) 110 In hir treble voyce, she fell so to cacklyng. **1602** MARSTON *Ant. & Mel.* III. Wks. 1856 I. 35 What trebble minikin squeaks here? **1727** GAY *Fables* xlvi. 15 A village cur,..Imagined that his treble throat Was blest with music's sweetest note. **1860** GEO. ELIOT *Mill on Fl.* III. vi, Bob spoke with a sharp and rather treble volubility.

†**d.** ? Upper. *Obs. rare.*

1551 *Gray's N. Y. Gift* iii. in Furniv. *Ball. fr. MSS.* I. 418 Yet at this presence—ye shall vnderstand—The papest be Ranke, and on the treble hand: Som cornfford the have; I cannott tell howe.

3. Special collocations. ***treble agent***, a spy who works for three countries, his superiors in each being informed of his service to the other, but usu. with actual allegiance only to one. ***treble bar***, ***treble gold stripe***, collectors' names for various moths: see quots. ***treble block***: see quot. ***treble chance***, a form of football pool in which various points are awarded for a draw, an away win, and a home win. ***treble hook***, a fish-hook consisting of three single hooks fastened back to back. †***treble letter***, a letter consisting of three sheets formerly charged triple postage (*obs.*). ***treble lock***, a lock operating by three turns of the key. ***treble star***, three stars so near (really or visually) as not to be separately visible without a telescope. †***treble time*** (*obs.*), triple time. ***treble X***, a brand or strength of beer. See also in 2.

1967 *Punch* 11 Oct. 542/1 A list of our *treble agents in Bulgaria. **1978** W. WINGATE *Bloodbath* i. 12 He wants out. Reckons he's earned it as a double, or treble, agent. **1832** RENNIE *Conspect. Butterfl. & Moths* 201 The Tawny *Treble Bar (*Argyromiges trifasciella*, Curtis)..Wings.. with three somewhat straight, equidistant, brown bands. **1867** SMYTH *Sailor's Word-bk.*, **Treble-block*, one fitted with three sheaves or rollers. **1951** 'M. INNES' *Operation Pax* II. iv. 64 'Heard what was last week's *treble chance?' he asked. 'Ninety-eight thousand.' **1972** M. JONES *Life on Dole* II. i. 102 Luck..seems as evasive as the treble-chance. **1832** RENNIE *Conspect. Butterfl. & Moths* 201 The *Treble Gold Stripe (*Argyromiges tristigella*, Stephens). Wings..tawny-brown, with a straight silvery-golden band before, and a second in the middle. **1895** *Outing* (U.S.) XXVII. 222/2 Attached to each line were a sinker and a *treble hook, i.e., three hooks soldered together at such angles that when a fish has once gorged the thing, disgorgement is almost an impossibility. **1753** *Scots Mag.* July 328/2 The rates of double letters, are always double; of *treble letters, treble. **1805** *Act 45 Geo. III*, c. 11 §1 For every single letter one penny; for every double letter twopence; for every treble letter or other letter under an ounce in weight three-pence. **1661** BAXTER *Mor. Prognost.* II. xxi. 50 There shall be a *Treble-Lock upon the Door of the Ministry. **1782** HERSCHEL in *Phil. Trans.* LXXII. 100 The beautiful *treble star in Monoceros's right fore-foot. **1686** PLOT *Staffordsh.* ix. 371 Seven bells rung together in peal... Their number excludes them, from ever being brought, either into common or *treble-time. **1856** GEO. ELIOT in *Westm. Rev.* Jan. 5 German ennui must be something as superlative as Barclay's *treble X. **1858** C. M. YONGE *Christmas Mummers* vii. 95 They began to sing at the next house as loud as if they thought they should get..more than three times treble XXX ale! **1880** E. W. HAMILTON *Diary* 7 Dec. (1972) I. 85 The Irish 'soup' (as Mr. Gladstone terms it) is 'thickening' and becoming what the brewers would call 'Treble X'.

B. *adv.* **1.** In three ranks or rows, threefold; to three times the extent; three times over; trebly.

13.. *K. Alis.* 6696 In hire mouth buth teth treble set. **1552** HULOET, Treble, *tripliciter*. **1563** A. NEVELL in B. Googe *Eglogs*, etc. (Arb.) 87 All these conclude him blest.. And trible blest agayne. **1622** FLETCHER *Beggar's Bush* v. i, And I'll deserve it treble. **1675** WOOD *Life* 18 Sept. (O.H.S.) II. 322 Piers was double or treble paid by Dr. Fell. **1708** *Constit. Watermen's Co.* lvii, Every person offending therein, shall forfeit..treble as much as he or they respectively shall demand.

2. In a high-pitched tone; shrilly.

1811 [implied in *treble-skirling*: see C. 2].

C. Combinations.

1. The adj. in combination. **a.** with sbs., as **treble-coursing**, the division of an air-current in a mine into three courses or channels; **treble-seam** (*Cricket slang*), a leathern cricket-ball stitched with three seams; **treble-tree**, an arrangement of swingle-trees for three horses abreast.

1897 *Globe* 9 July 1/5 The old bowler..declared there was a lot of human nature in a *treble-seam. **1877** KNIGHT *Dict. Mech.*, **Treble-tree*, a whiffletree for three horses. An equalizer.

b. Parasynthetic combs. forming adjs., as ***treble-barrelled***, ***-breathed***, ***-caped***, ***-headed***, ***-mailed***, ***-piled***, ***-rampired***, ***-seated***, ***-sinewed***; **treble-voiced**, having a treble or soprano voice.

1784 *New Spectator* No. 1. 4 The ladies have assumed the *treble-caped great coat and belt. **1805** *Med. Jrnl.* XIV. 92 How our *treble-headed Pithon is to be augmented and increased. **1876** GEO. ELIOT *Dan. Der.* xxxvi, Gnawed by a double, a treble-headed grief. **1611** COTGR., *Tremaillé*, *treble-mailed. **1821** SCOTT *Kenilw.* xxiv, Velvet, single, double, *treble-piled. **1649** G. DANIEL *Trinarch., Hen. IV*, cxvii, As the wings of long-lost Day Breakes *treble-Rampierd Clouds. **1808** BENTHAM *Sc. Reform* 36 The permanent substitution of *treble-seated..to single-seated judicature. **1606** SHAKS. *Ant. & Cl.* III. xiii. 178, I will be *trebble-sinewed, hearted, breath'd. **1552** HULOET, *Treble voyced, or shyll tuned, *acutus, a, um*.

c. With sbs., forming adjectives or attributive phrases, as ***treble-cylinder***, ***treble-shovel***; **treble-bite**, **treble-wedge-fast**, systems of breech-action in hand guns.

1892 GREENER *Breech-Loader* 22 With an efficient holding-down bolt, engaging with it as in the *treble-bite breech-action. **1877** KNIGHT *Dict. Mech.*, **Treble-cylinder Steam-engine*, an engine having a pair of large cylinders for the continuation of the expansion, one at each side of the small cylinder. *Ibid.*, **Treble-Shovel Plow*, one having three shares. A form of cultivator. **1881** GREENER *Gun* 174 Our patent *treble-wedge-fast action, with either hammerless or back-action locks and low hammers.

2. The adv. in comb. **a.** with pples., forming adjectives, as ***treble-brandished***, ***-damned***, ***-refined***, ***-ribbed***, ***-riveted***, ***-twisted***, etc.; **treble-dated**, living three times as long (as man); (in sense B. 2) ***treble-skirling***. **b.** with vbs., as ***treble-man***, ***-shot***.

1877 TENNYSON *Harold* I. i, Yon grimly-glaring, *treble-brandish'd scourge. **1824** COLERIDGE *Lett., to J. Gillman* (1895) 730 If he be not a *treble-damned liar. **1601** SHAKS. *Phœnix & T.* 17 Thou *treble-dated crow,..'Mongst our mourners shalt thou go. **1805** PIKE *Sources Mississ.* (1810) 51 We were obliged to take on but one sled at a time and *treble man it. **1694** SALMON *Bate's Dispens.* II. vi. (1713) 604/2 With its equal Weight of *trebble-refined Sugar. **1896** *Daily News* 14 Nov. 6/6 Besides deed-boxes, there were other receptacles..some *treble-ribbed with iron or copper. **1662** GERBIER *Princ.* 18 Casements *treble riveted, to keep out Wind and Rain. **1874** THEARLE *Naval Archit.* 131 For treble-riveted butt straps, nineteen diameters in breadth are required by Lloyd's. **1884** H. COLLINGWOOD *Under Meteor Flag* 74 Request Mr. Flinn to *treble-shot his larboard broadside. **1811** W. TENNANT *Anster Concert* xiii, High o'er the tenor sounded shrill The *treble-skirling women. **1867** BAKER *Nile Tribut.* ii. (1872) 32 A powerful hook, fitted upon *treble-twisted wire.

treble ('trɛb(ə)l), *v.* [f. prec. Cf. OF. *trebler* (13th c. in Godef.).]

1. *trans.* To make three times as many or as great; to increase threefold; to muliply by three.

a **1325** *MS. Rawl.* B. 520 lf. 32 ȝif þe contreie..ne ansuuerez noȝt..þe peine sal ben itrebbled. *c* **1430** *Art of Nombryng* xi. (E.E.T.S.) 17 Thow most trebille the digit. **1596** SHAKS. *Merch. V.* III. ii. 302 Double sixe thousand, and then treble that. **1666** SANCROFT *Lex Ignea* 28 His Insolence doubles and trebles the Vexation. **1720** *Lond. Gaz.* No. 5833/2 Which trebles the Duty..payable by the Exporter. **1885** DUNCKLEY in *Manch. Exam.* 20 July 6/1 During the present century the population has just about trebled itself.

b. To fold in three thicknesses; to make in three layers.

1598 HAKLUYT *Voy.* I. 62 Caparisons for their horses made of leather artificially doubled or trebled vpon their bodies. **1638** SIR T. HERBERT *Trav.* (ed. 2) 316 A Cambolin of pure lawn..trebled on and about their naked shoulders.

c. To be three times as many or as much as.

1615 G. SANDYS *Trav.* 115 Madein, A coyne of siluer that trebles the Asper for value. **1842** BORROW *Bible in Spain*

xxxiv. (Pelh. Libr.) 250 A body of the Carlists, .. whose numbers more than trebled his own.

2. *intr.* (for *refl.*) To grow to three times the number, amount, or size; to become threefold.

1625 FLETCHER *Noble Gent.* II. i, Now I see your Fathers honours Trebling upon you. **1797–8** WELLINGTON in Owen *Desp.* (1877) 777 It has more than trebled since the peace of '83. **1815** SIMOND *Tour Gt. Brit.* I. 170 The rent of land has trebled in the last fifty years. **1882** PEBODY *Eng. Journalism* xix. 145 Mr. Levy reduced the price of the paper... The circulation doubled, trebled, quadrupled.

†**3.** *intr.* To emit a high-pitched or shrill sound; also, to sing the treble part to (const. *upon*) the lower parts or plain-song in a harmonized composition (in quots. *fig.*). *Obs.*

c **1425** *Cast. Persev.* 1900 in *Macro Plays* 134, I here trumpys trebelen al of tene. *a* **1591** H. SMITH *Wks.* (1866) I. 458 A nightingale .. when she is in a pleasant vein, quavers and capers, and trebles upon it. **1606** S. GARDINER *Bk. Angling* 103 The singster of Israel hath .. giuen vs the Notes wee must alwayes treble vppon.

†**b.** *trans.* To utter in a high-pitched or shrill tone. *Obs. rare*$^{-1}$.

1616 CHAPMAN *Homer's Hymn to Hermes* 645 He outrageously (when I accus'd him) trebled his reply.

Hence '**trebled** *ppl. a.*, made treble, threefold.

?*c* **1400** LYDG. *Æsop's Fab.* i. 23 With trebled [*v.r.* treble] laudis yeve to the trynité. **1653** R. SANDERS *Physiogn., Moles*, etc. 38 Divide the trebled number into two. *a* **1711** KEN *Preparatives* Wks. 1721 IV. 43 While I by trebled Zeal and Tears Strive to retrieve my careless Years.

†'**treblefold**, *a.* and *adv. Obs.* [f. TREBLE + -FOLD.] **a.** *adj.* Three times as great or numerous; threefold. **b.** *adv.* Three times as much, thrice over.

1387–8 T. USK *Test. Love* I. iii. (Skeat) l. 152 Treble folde so mokell muste I suffer, ere tyme come of myne ease. **1561** T. HOBY tr. *Castiglione's Courtyer* I. (1577) C vij, They speake accompanying euery worde with certaine treblefolde sighes. **1587** Q. ELIZ. in H. Campbell *Love Lett. Mary Q. Scots* App. (1824) 62 God reward thee trebblefold in the double for the most troublesome charge so well discharged.

'**trebleness**. *rare.* [f. TREBLE *a.* + -NESS.]

†**1.** Treble quality (of sounds); high pitch.

1626 BACON *Sylva* §183 The Just and Measured Proportion of the Aire Percussed, towards the Basenesse or Treblenesse of Tones, is one of the greatest Secrets in the Contemplation of Sounds.

2. The quality of being threefold.

1888 in *Cassell's Encycl. Dict.*

†**trebler**, a treble-singer: see TRIBLER.

treblett, erron. form of TRIBLET.

trebling ('trɛblɪŋ), *vbl. sb.* [f. TREBLE *v.* + -ING[1].] The action of the verb TREBLE.

1. Increasing threefold; multiplication by three.

1591 PERCIVALL *Sp. Dict.*, *Trasdobladura*, trebling, *triplicatio.* **1694** *Phil. Trans.* XVIII. 70 The doubling, trebling, quadrupling, &c. of Rations is performed by squaring, cubing, biquadrating, &c. of the terms.

2. *Naut.* See quots.

1856 KANE *Arct. Expl.* I. xxxi. 423 The outside trebling or oak sheathing. **1867** SMYTH *Sailor's Word-bk.*, *Trebling*, planking thrice around a whaler's bows in order the more effectually to withstand the pressure of the ice.

trebly ('trɛblɪ), *adv.* [f. TREBLE *a.* + -LY[2].]

1. In a threefold degree or manner; triply.

1590 SPENSER *F.Q.* I. xi. 22 Trebly augmented was his furious mood. **1629** WADSWORTH *Pilgr.* v. 47 She was left destitute, the .. Iesuites being trebly paid. **1697** DRYDEN *Æneid* x. 1113 Linnen trebly rowl'd. **1814** SCOTT *Ld. of Isles* III. vii, Wicket and gate were trebly barr'd, By beam and bolt and chain. **1850** TENNYSON *In Mem.* cii. 16 This hath made them trebly dear.

†**2.** In a treble or high-pitched tone. *Obs. rare*$^{-1}$.

1679 in *Verney Mem.* (1907) II. 330 A Mercy, w[ch] makes mee merrily & Trebly sing, Gaudiamus and Haleluia.

trebuchet ('trɛbəʃɛt, ‖trebyʃɛ). Forms: α. 4 trepejette, trepget, 4–5 -eget, 5 trepgett(e, trip-, trypgette, 6 trepegett, -gete, trepa-; β. 4–5 tri-, tre-, treybochet; 5 trebget (*err.* -got); 6 trabu-, 7 trebuschet, (8–9 trebucket), 8– trebuchet. [In I, a. OF. *trebuchet*, also *trebuket*, *-busket*, *trabuchet* (12th c. in Godef.) siege-engine, bird-trap, mod.F. *trébuchet* trap, balance (= Prov. *trabuquet*, Sp. *trabuquete*, It. *trabocchetto*, med.L. *trā-*, *trēbuchētum*, Du Cange), f. OF. *tre-*, *tres-*, *trabucher* (11th c.) to overturn, overthrow, stumble, fall, in med.L. *trābuchāre*: see TRABUCH. The early α-forms (trɛpɛ'dʒɛt, etc.) are imitations of OF. *trebuchet* (trɛbu'tʃɛt). The word was obsolete in the 16th c.; from 18th c. historical and antiquarian. Sense 3 is from mod.Fr. In II, an application, in England, of med.L. *trēbuchētum* (see above), to the device known popularly from *c* 1200 as *cuck-stool*, *cucking-stool*. The Latin form remained app. as a legal term, rendered *trebuchet* in 17th c. by the legal antiquaries.

Cf. **1611** COTGR., *Trebuchet*, a pitfall for birds; a pit, with a trap doore, for wild beasts; also, a paire of gold weights; also, an old-fashioned Engine of wood, from which great, and battering stones were most violently throwne.]

I. 1. A mediæval military engine for casting heavy missiles. *Hist.*

Described as consisting of a pivoted lever with a sling at one extremity, which was strained back against a heavy counterpoise, and then suddenly released. Cf. CATAPULT *sb.* 1.

[**1224** *Close Roll 8 Hen. III*, m. 4 Facias usque Doura maeremium ad trubechetum nostrum faciendum. —— *9 Hen. III*, m. 24, viij. Roellas ereas quas fieri fecistis at trubechettum nostrum. **1377** *Rolls of Parlt.* III. 10/2 Un trebuchet outre ascun mesure qe l'en avoit unqes veeu.]

α. **13..** *Coer de L.* 5227 With trepeiettes they slungen alsoo. **1388** WYCLIF *1 Macc.* vi. 20 Thei maden arblastis, [*gloss*] ether trepeiettis, that is, an instrument for to caste schaftis, and stoonys. *c* **1400** [see MANGONEL]. *c* **1420** *Brut* 428 The Kynge .. leid therto his grete Gounnys, Trepgettis and Engenys, and bete adowne the wallis. **1520** *Caxton's Chron. Eng.* VII. 145/1 Gonnes, Engynnes, and trypgettes [**1482** trip-]. **1599** THYNNE *Animadv.* (1875) 41 'Trepegett' yo[u] expounde 'a Ramme to batter walles'. But the trepegete was the same that the mogonell. [**1896** *Eng. Hist. Rev.* Apr. 357 Eustace the monk was taken, and Stephen of Winchelsea .. gave him his choice of having his head cut off on the trapget or the bulwarks [rather of being hurled from the trapget or having his head cut off on the bulwarks].]

β. *a* **1400–50** *Alexander* 1296 With traumes & with tribochetis þe tild to asaile. *c* **1400** *Siege of Troy* 838 in *Archiv neu. Spr.* LXXII. 33 An hundrid gynnys þer were vpset, Of Maungeneles and Treybochet. *c* **1440** *Promp. Parv.* 501/1 Trebget, for werre (*S.* trepgette), *trabucetum.* **1795** SOUTHEY *Joan of Arc* VIII. 198 Who kneeling by the trebuchet, Charged its long sling with death. **1825** SCOTT *Betrothed* viii, 'Well driven, trebuchet—well flown, quarrel!' cried the monk. **1885** C. W. C. OMAN *Art of War* 57 The feeble siege-artillery of the day, perrieres, catapults, trebuchets, and so forth.

†**2.** A trap or gin to catch small birds or beasts. *Obs. rare.* (So in Fr. from 14th c.)

1362 LANGL. *P. Pl.* A. XII. 86 þou tomblest wiþ a trepget ȝif þou my tras folwe. *c* **1440** *Promp. Parv.* 501/1 Trebget [*pr.* -got], sly instrument to take brydys or beestys (*S.* trepgette), *tendicule.*

3. A small delicately poised balance or pair of scales; an assay balance; a tilting scale. (So Fr.)

1550 *Reg. Mag. Sig. Scot.* 105/1 Par de lie trabuschettis 15 sol. **1613** BP. FORBES *Comm. Rev.* xviii. §6. 191 It is a hard thing to fall into the hands of the Lord: before whom all Nations are but as the droppe of a Bucket, or as the dust of a Trebuschet. **1871** M. C. LEA *Photogr.* 420 The French pattern of 'trebuchet', or tilting scale, now largely manufactured here. **1877** KNIGHT *Dict. Mech.*, *Trebucket.*

II. 4. An instrument of punishment, = CUCKING-STOOL, q.v.

[*c* **1200** *Chron. of Jocelin de Brakelond* (Camden) 38 Levaverunt homines de Illegga quoddam trebuchet, ad faciendam justiciam pro falsis mensuris panis vel bladi mensurandi. ?**1266–7** *Judicium Pillorie* in *Stat. Realm* (1870) I. 201/1 Paciatur judicium corporis, scilicet, Pistor Collistrigium, et Braciatrix trebuchetum vel castigatorium. *c* **1440** *Promp. Parv.* 107/1 Cukstole, for flyterys, .. *turbuscetum, cadurca.* **1500** *Ortus Vocab.*, *Terbichetum*, a cok-stole.] *c* **1640** J. SMYTH *Hundred of Berkeley* (1885) 143 Cucking stool and other Judicials, Collistrigia et trebuchets. **1667** E. CHAMBERLAYNE *Pres. St. Eng.* I. (1684) 48 Scolding women are to be set in a Trebuchet, commonly called a Cuckingstool .. placed over some deep water into which they are let down and plunged under water thrice. **1769** BLACKSTONE *Comm.* IV. xiii. 169 A common scold, .. if convicted, shall be sentenced to be placed in a certain engine of correction called the trebucket, castigatory, or cucking stool. **1867** *Cornh. Mag.* Jan. 38 A homely provision made for the punishment of mere bad language in the bridle and trebuchet or ducking-stool.

†**trebuke**, variant of TRABUCH.

c **1482** J. KAY tr. *Caoursin's Siege of Rhodes* (1870) ¶ 11 A man of Greece, .. counseyled the Lord Mayster and the Rhodyans to make and ordeygne an engyne called Trebuke lyke a slynge, which was grete hye and myghty, and casted grete and many stones into the hoste of the Turkes.

†**trebuler**, *a. Obs.* [f. *Trēbula*, name of a place: cf. *Trēbulāna vina* (Pliny).] ? Of Trebula.

1606 S. GARDINER *Bk. Angling* ix. 158 The trebuler sort [of vines] that are thrust to the wall, that neuer growe high, or ouerdreepe others little.

trebuttar, obs. form of TRIBUTARY.

trecche: see TRECHE *v.*

treccher, -erie, -erous, -our, etc., obs. forms of TREACHER, -EROUS, -ERY, etc.

†**trecentene**, *a. Obs. rare*$^{-0}$. [f. L. *trecentēnī* three hundred each.] (See quotation.)

1656 BLOUNT *Glossogr.*, *Trecentene*, pertaining to three hundred.

‖**trecento** (tre'tʃɛnto). [It., lit. 'three hundred', short for *mil trecento* 1300; cf. CINQUECENTO.] The fourteenth century (13..), as a period of Italian art, architecture, etc.; also *attrib.*

1841 W. SPALDING *Italy & It. Isl.* II. 215 The vigour and expressiveness of the *trecento.* **1873** 'OUIDA' *Pascarèl* I. 9 The beautiful *trecento* windows were filled with eager faces. **1878** VILLARI *Machiavelli* (1898) I. III. viii. 149 The literature of the Trecento may be considered as exclusively Tuscan. **1899** *Westm. Gaz.* 17 Mar. 3/1 They treat .. of the *trecento* painters, of Giovanni Bellini and the early Venetians.

Hence **tre'centist**, ‖**trecen'tista** (It., pl. -isti), an Italian artist, author, etc., of the 14th c.

1821 BYRON *Juan* III. lxxxvi, In Italy he'd ape the 'Trecentisti'. **1883** C. C. PERKINS *Ital. Sculpt.* Introd. 23 The character of his work is so different from that of any other Italian trecentist.

‖**treche, trich**, *v. Obs.* Also 3 tricche, 5 trecche. [a. OF. *trichier*, *trechier* (3rd s. pres. *triche*, *treche*), to deceive, cheat, in Picard *trikier*, (*trike*), mod.F. *tricher*, Prov. *trichar*, *triquar*, It. *treccare.* Ulterior origin uncertain: supposed by Diez to be from a German dialect (cf. also Mackel *Germ. elemente in franz.* 104); but others think from a late L. **triccāre* for L. *trīcārī* to trifle, shuffle, play tricks, f. *trīcæ* trifles, quirks, wiles, tricks (see Storm in *Romania* V. 172).

For the family of words belonging to this vb. see TREACHER to TREACHERY, also TRICHARD, and (more remotely) TRICK and its derivatives.]

trans. To deceive, cheat, betray, play false with.

c **1230** *Hali Meid.* 9 Nu þu sest þat ha habbeð itricchet te as treitres. *a* **1327** *Pol. Songs* (Camden) 69 Richard, thah thou be ever trichard, trichen shalt thou never more. *c* **1425** *Cast. Persev.* 253 in *Macro Plays* 84 þese iij are nobyl, trewly I trowe, Mankynde to tenyn, & trecchyn a tyde.

treche, var. TRESCHE *Obs.*

trecher, -erous, -ery, etc., obs. ff. TREACHER, -EROUS, -ERY.

†**trechet**, *v. Obs. rare.* [deriv. of TRECHE *v.* (perh. error for *trecher*).] *trans.* To deceive, cheat, play false with. Hence †**trechetting** *vbl. sb.* (See also TREACHETOUR.)

c **1330** R. BRUNNE *Chron.* (1810) 313 þe[i] sent ageyn & said to kyng, 'it was no haunte Of certeyn sette & laid, to trechet þer conaunte. *Ibid.* 164 Whan he with trechettyng bi nyght away so ran. Wenes he our men Inglisse for to tretcher [*MS.* trecther] so?

trechmannite ('trɛkmənaɪt). *Min.* [? f. surname *Trechmann* + -ITE[1].] A rare mineral occurring in red rhombohedral crystals in the dolomite of the Binnenthal. It is prob. a sulpharsenite of silver.

1909 in *Cent. Dict. Suppl.*

trechometer (trɛ'kɒmɪtə(r)). [a. F. *trechomètre*, f. Gr. τρέχ-ειν to run: see -METER.] An instrument which records the distance run by a vehicle.

1858 SIMMONDS *Dict. Trade*, *Trechometer*, a French machine for reckoning distances, specially adapted for vehicles.

trechor, -our, -ory, -ur, -ure, -ury: see TREACHER, TREACHERY.

trechoure, obs. f. TRESSURE.

treck- in *treckschuit*, etc.: see TREK-.

trecker: see TRIGGER.

trecther, scribal error for *tretcher* (cf. TREACHER): see TRECHET *v.*

tred, obs. f. TREAD.

tredding: see TRADING *vbl. sb.* (quot. 1654).

treddle ('trɛd(ə)l). Now *dial.* Forms: α. 1 tyrdel, 5 -dyl, 6 -dell, -dle, tirdil, turdyll, 6–7 terdle, 7 tir-, turdle; β. 5 tredel(e, triddil, tridel, trydelle, 7–9 truddle, 6– treddle; γ. 6 treatle. See also TRATTLE *sb.*[2] [ME. *tyrdyl*, etc. (whence by metathesis *tridil*, *treddle*), = OE. *tyrdel*, dim. of *tord*, TURD: see -EL *suffix*[1].] A pellet of sheep's or goat's dung: usually in *pl.*

α. *c* **1000** *Sax. Leechd.* II. 72 ȝenim gate tyrdlu. *Ibid.* 214 Haran tyrdlu. *c* **1440** *Promp. Parv.* 494/2 Tyrdyl, schepys donge. **1530** PALSGR. 281/2 Tyrdell. *Ibid.* 284/1 Turdyll shepes donge, *fient de brebis.* **1552** HULOET, Tyrdles of gootes or shepe, *rudus, eris.* **1563** HYLL *Art Garden.* (1593) 107 If you take the seeds of euery colour of Gilliflours and put them altogither into a thin small reed, or terdle of a sheep or goat. **1647** HEXHAM I, Sheeps dung or tirdles. **1671** SKINNER *Etymol. Ling. Angl.*, The Treddles *vel* Truddles, q.d. Turdles.

β. *c* **1410** *Master of Game* xi. (1904) 40 Men clepen þe steppes or þe marckes of þe Otere .. and his fumes tredeles or spraintes. **14..** *MS. Lincoln Med.* lf. 291 (Halliw.) The triddils of an hare. **1483** *Cath. Angl.* 393/2 A Trydelle, *ruder.* **1577** B. GOOGE *Heresbach's Husb.* II. (1586) 55 b, Taking a Treddle of Sheepe, or Goates doung. **1601** HOLLAND *Pliny* XIX. xii. II. 33 The round treddles of a Goat. **1736** W. ELLIS *New Exper. Husb.* 25 Price for the neat Treddle, clear of all Hay, Straw, Flaff, or other Mixture. **1905** in *Eng. Dial. Dict.* from Lincoln, Herts, Kent, Surrey.

treddle, variant of TREADLE.

treddling ('trɛdlɪŋ), *sb. dial.* In 5 tirdelyng; 9 also (*pl.*) trid(d)lings, treddlins. [f. TREDDLE + -ING[1].] Treddles of sheep, etc. in the mass.

c **1440** LYDG. *Hors, Shepe & G.* 381 Of the sheepe .. To the lond gret profite doth his tirdelyng [*v.r.* tyrtelyng]. **1828** *Craven Gloss.*, *Tridlins*, excrement of sheeps. **1869** *Lonsdale Gloss.*, Treddlin's, Triddlin's. **1876** *Whitby Gloss.*, Triddlings.

†'**tredecile**, *a.* or *sb. Astrol. Obs.* Also -il. [ad. mod.L. *tredecīl-is*, f. L. *trēs* three + *dec-em* ten;

cf. *quartile, sextile*.] Denoting an aspect, introduced by Kepler, in which the planets are $\frac{3}{10}$ of a circle, i.e. 108°, apart. Cf. DECILE.

1647 LILLY *Chr. Astrol.* iii. 32 Of late one Kepler, a learned man, hath added some new ones as follow..A Tredecile..consisting of 108 degrees. **1674** JEAKE *Arith.* (1696) 11 Aspects... Sesquiquintil or Tredecil. **1727–41** CHAMBERS *Cycl., Aspect*, To the five ancient aspects, the modern writers have added several more; as decile,.. tridecile,..[etc.]. **1819** J. WILSON *Compl. Dict. Astrol.* 101 The new aspects invented by Kepler are mostly produced by sub-dividing the others... The Tredecile, of 108°, is a quintile and half, or three deciles... Those arising from a division of the Δ or ✱ by 5 were [thought by Kepler to be] good; thus..the tredecile, being a quintile and a half, is good.

†**tre'decuple**, *a. Obs. rare.* [f. L. *tredecim* thirteen, after *decuple*.] Thirteen times as great.

1570 BILLINGSLEY *Euclid* XVI. xxix. 453 To proue that an octohedron geuen, is tredecuple sesquialter to a trilater equilater pyramis inscribed in it.

tredel, obs. form of TREADLE, TREDDLE.

tredge, obs. form of TRUDGE.

tredrille, tredille (trɛ'drɪl, -'dɪl). Also 8 tresdille, 9 tradrille. [f. QUADRILLE by substitution of *tre-* three for *qua(d-*.] A card-game played by three persons, usually with thirty cards.

1764 H. WALPOLE *Let. to Earl Hertford* 8 June, Lady Albemarle was at tredille. **1767** LADY MARY COKE *Jrnl.* 2 May, The Duchess, Lady Blunt and I play'd at tresdille. **1769** *Ibid.* 15 June, I play'd at tredrille..with Madame de Viry and a French Officer for a shilling a fish. **1816** SINGER *Hist. Cards* 266 *Tredrille*, a modification of Quadrille which might be played by three persons... It was considered as very inferior to the game Quadrille played by four. **1821** LAMB *Elia* Ser. I. *Mrs. Battle's Opinions on Whist*, To explain to me how far it [ombre] agreed with, and in what points it would be found to differ from, tradrille. **1825** MRS. SHERWOOD *Bitter Sweet* II. 5 A hand at tredille or three-handed whist. **1860** T. L. PEACOCK *Gryll Gr.* xxiii, Quadrille is played with forty cards: tredrille usually with thirty: sometimes, as in Pope's Ombre, with twenty seven.

tree (triː), *sb.* Forms: see below. [OE. *tréow, tríow*, OE., ME. *tréo*, etc. = OFris. *trê* (NFris. *trê, træ̂*), OS. *trio, treo, trew-* (MDu. in comb. *-tere, -tære*, Kilian); ON. *tré* (Da. *træ*, Sw. *trä* timber, *träd* tree); Goth. *triu*, gen. *triw-is* wood (wanting in OHG. and now also obsolete in LG. and Du.):—OTeut. **trewo-*, cognate with Skr. *dru* tree, wood, *'dāru* wood, log, and with Gr. δρῦς oak, δόρυ spear; OSlav. *drievo* (from *dervo*) tree, wood, *drŭva* pl. wood, Russ. *'derevo, dre'vo* tree, wood, Serb. *drvo* tree, *drva* wood, Czech *drva*, Pol. *drwa* wood; Lith. *dervà* pine-wood; also with OIr. *daur*, Welsh *derwen* oak. The modern Eng. *tree* is a regular repr. of OE. *tréo*, ME. *treo*; *trē* is the form in the Bestiary of *c* 1220; but the final prevalence of this over the other ME. forms *treow, trew, trow, trau*, was prob. assisted by its coincidence with Norse *tré*; *trē, tree* are the northern forms from *Cursor Mundi* onward. For form-history cf. KNEE.]

A. Illustration of Forms and Inflexions.

1. *Sing. nom.* 1 triow, (*late*) tryw, 1–2 treow, treu, (1) 3 trew, (1)–4 treo, 3–6 tre, 3– tree; 4 (*Kent.* trau, tra(u)w); trough; 5 *Sc.* trey, 6–7 trie. *dat.* 1 treowe, tréo, 2 treuwe, trewe, 4 trow(e, trauwe. [The development of OE. nom. acc. sing. was OTeut. **trewoᵐ*, *trewa, trew, tréu, tréo*, then with *w* from oblique cases (*trewes, treowes*, etc.), *tréow*, (*triow*).]

c **890** tr. *Bæda's Hist.* II. xi. [xiv.] (1890) 138 He..of treo [*v.r.* treowe] cirican ʒetimbrode. *c* **897** K. ÆLFRED *Gregory's Past. C.* xlv. 338 Ælc triow [*v.r.* treow] man sceal ceorfan. *c* **1000** *Ags. Gosp.* Matt. iii. 10 Ælc treow [*MS. B.* tryw, *Lind.* treu] þe godne wæstm ne bringð. *c* **1200** *Vices & Virt.* 27 Ðe treu of paradise. *c* **1200** *Trin. Coll. Hom.* 107 Of coren of eorðe, and of treuwe. *c* **1220** *Bestiary* 674 Ðus fel adam ðurȝ a tre, Vre firste fader, ðat fele we. *c* **1250** *Gen. & Ex.* 3301 A funden trew ðor-inne dede Moyses. *a* **1300** *Cursor M.* 657 (Cott.) þis tree ys done in my friþe. **1340** *Ayenb.* 28 Ne in gerse, ne in busse, ne in trauwe. *Ibid.* 95 þet trau of lyue. *Ibid.* 202 þys traw wext and profiteþ. **13..** *K. Alis.* 6829 Alle tho That scholde with him to the trough go. **1393** LANGL. *P. Pl.* C. XXI. 200 Yf þei touchede þe treo and of þe frut eten. *c* **1530** R. HILLES *Common-Pl. Bk.* (1858) 140 Sone crokyth the tre that crokyed wyll be. **1535** STEWART *Cron. Scot.* (Rolls) II. 687 With the speir that wes of suir trie, He hit the king richt in at the e. **1573** TUSSER *Husb.* (1878) 109 Let Iuie be killed, Else tree will be spilled. *a* **1584** MONTGOMERIE *Ch. & Slae* 341 The trie sa hich of growth.

2. *Pl. nom.* α. 1 trēo, treow, triowu, treowu, -a, 1–2 treowe; 2 treowen, 2–4 treon, 3–6 trēn, 4 (troen), trene, 4–7 (-9 *dial.*) treen, 5 trenne, 5–6 treene. β. 2 treos, 2–3 (*Orm.*) trewwes, 2, 4 trewes, 2–5 tres, 3 troues, 3–4 trouwes, 3–5 treus, 4 trews, trowes, traues, trawes, 4–6 treis, 5 trese, 6 treys, *Sc.* treyis, 6–7 tries, 4– trees. [The development of OE. nom. acc. pl. was WGer. *trewu, tréu, tréo*; then again with *w* (from oblique cases), *tréow, treowu (-a)*. The pl. *tréo* occurs in Vesp. Ps. and Lind. Gosp.]

c **825** *Vesp. Ps.* cxlviii. 9 Treo westemberu and alle cederbeamas. *c* **890** tr. *Bæda's Hist.* I. (1890) 26 Hit is weliȝ þis ealond on wæstmum & on treowum. *c* **897** K. ÆLFRED *Gregory's Past. C.* xl. 292 Sumu treowu he watrade. *a* **1000** *Epist. Alex. ad Aristot.* in Cockayne *Narrat.* 27 Eac þær wæron oþre treow. *Ibid.* 28 Ða halȝan triow-swiðe wepen. *c* **1000** ÆLFRIC *Hom.* II. 588 Deorwurðe stanas, oþþe treowa. *c* **1175** *Lamb. Hom.* 5 Heo stiȝen uppe on þe godes cunnes treowe. *Ibid.* 41 He him sceawede heȝe treon. *c* **1200** ORMIN Introd. 13 Full gode treos inoȝhe. *Ibid.* 15468 Off gresess, & off tres. *c* **1200** *Trin. Coll. Hom.* 25 Gres and trowen. *Ibid.* 37 Hwile uppen trewes. *c* **1250** *Gen. & Ex.* 3305 Then [*i.e.* ten] and sexti palme tren. *c* **1275** LAY. 511 Alle hi solde hongie vppe heȝe troues. *a* **1300** *Cursor M.* 545 (Cott.) It groues tres [*Fairf.* trees] and gress. **13..** *Ibid.* 651 (Gött.) Of treis..here es gode wone. ? *a* **1300** *XI Pains of Hell* 33 þer beoþ bernynde treon. *a* **1325** *MS. Rawl. B. 520* lf. 32 b, þis statut ne portenez noȝt to oþere grete troen. *a* **1325** *Prose Psalter* xcv[i]. 12 þan shul alle þe trews of þe wodes gladen. **13..** *K. Alis.* 6763 þou shalt fynde trowes two. **1340** *Ayenb.* 25 þe greatte traues. *Ibid.* 95 Uol of guode trawes. **1387** TREVISA *Higden* (Rolls) III. 445 Where þou knowe nouȝt þe treen [*v.r.* tren]. *a* **1400** *Pistill of Susan* 90 Turtils troned on trene. *c* **1400** Trees [see B. 1]. *c* **1400** *Ywaine & Gaw.* 2965 He loked in bitwix the trese. **1422** tr. *Secreta Secret., Priv. Priv.* 239 With lewys of trenne. *Ibid.* 243 The humours of tren and herbis. *c* **1430** LYDG. *Min. Poems* (Percy Soc.) 17 Twoo grene treene there grewe uprighte. *a* **1450** MYRC *Festial* i. 3 Treus and herbys. **1562–3** in Willis & Clark *Cambridge* (1886) II. 568, x greate tries at xxviijᵈ the trie. **1563** *Mirr. Mag.* Induct. 2 With blustring blastes had al ybared the treen. **1565** *Satir. Poems Reform.* i. 45 Wynter windes..that doth I-bayre the tren. **1570** *Ibid.* xv. 50 All greinis and plesand treis [*rime* eyis]. **1596** DALRYMPLE tr. *Leslie's Hist. Scot.* VII. (S.T.S.) II. 17 Aple tries, and orchardis. **1600** FAIRFAX *Tasso* III. lxxv, The shadie tops of shaking treene. **1635, 1771, 1861** Trees [see B. 1]. **1843** E. JONES *Poems, Sens. & Event* 38 Vast interbranching treen.

B. Signification.

1. a. A perennial plant having a self-supporting woody main stem or *trunk* (which usually develops woody branches at some distance from the ground), and growing to a considerable height and size. (Usually distinguished from a *bush* or *shrub* by size and manner of growth; but cf. b.)

c **825**, *c* **890**, *c* **897** [see A. 2]. *c* **1000** ÆLFRIC *Gen.* iii. 6 þæt treow wæs god to etanne. *c* **1175** *Lamb. Hom.* 109 Iliche þan treo þe bereð lef and blosman. *c* **1290** *St. Brendan* 41 in *S. Eng. Leg.* I. 221 Of treon and herbes, þikke i-novȝ. **1377** LANGL. *P. Pl.* B. xv. 327 A forest..ful of faire trees. **1398** TREVISA *Barth. De P.R.* XVII. i. (Tollem. MS.), A tre haþ ..þe rynde, bowes, twigges, leues, blosmes, floures and frute. *c* **1400** *Destr. Troy* 12467 Trees thurgh tempestes tynde hade þere leues. **1481** CAXTON *Reynard* xii. (Arb.) 28 He brake a rodde of a tree. *c* **1530** R. HILLES *Common-Pl. Bk.* (1858) 140 Hyt ys a febyll tre thet fallyth at the fyrst strok. **1600** FAIRFAX *Tasso* VII. i, Through forrests thicke among the shadie treene. **1635** LAUD *Diary* 1 Dec., Many elm leaves yet upon the trees. **1771** *Junius Lett.* lvii. (1820) 298 He or his deputy were authorised to cut down..trees. **1861** BENTLEY *Man. Bot.* 540 Cunoniaceæ... Nearly allied to Saxifragaceæ, but differing from them in being trees or shrubs.

b. Extended to include bushes or shrubs of erect growth and having a single stem; and even some perennial herbaceous plants which grow to a great height, as the banana and plantain.

c **1340-** [see ROSE-TREE]. *c* **1532** [see GOOSEBERRY 7]. **1640** [see PLANTAIN² 4]. **1649** [see CURRANT 4]. **1697** [see BANANA 1]. **1765** [see RASPBERRY 6]. **1855** BROWNING *Women & Roses* i, I dream of a red-rose tree. **1858** HOGG *Veg. Kingd.* 790 As a food, the Plantain is wholesome and agreeable. A tree generally contains three or four clusters.

c. Applied *fig.* or allusively to a person.

1594 SHAKS. *Rich. III*, III. vii. 167 The Royall Tree hath left vs Royall Fruit. **1807** WORDSW. *Force of Prayer* xiii, He was a tree that stood alone, And proudly did its branches wave.

d. = CHRISTMAS-TREE.

[**1838** H. MARTINEAU *Retrospect* III. 182, I was present at the introduction into the new country of..the German Christmas-tree... The tree was the top of a young fir, planted in a tub.] **1851** E. RUSKIN *Let.* 28 Dec. in M. Lutyens *Effie in Venice* (1965) II. 236 They wanted me to come in the evening when the tree was lighted to see the presents all divided. **1945** N. MITFORD *Pursuit of Love* iii. 23 We got back late for the tree... Uncle Matthew..was struggling into his Father Christmas clothes! **1979** M. MCCARTHY *Cannibals & Missionaries* I. 19 Distribution of presents..and the darned crèche and parish-house tree to set up.

2. The substance of the trunk and boughs of a tree; wood (esp. as a material of which things are made); timber. *Obs.* or *arch.*

to go between the bark and the tree: see BARK *sb.*¹ 6.

c **890** tr. *Bæda's Hist.* II. xi. [xiv.] (1890) 138 He þær hræde ʒeweorce of treo ciricean ʒetimbrode. *c* **1122** *O.E. Chron.* an. 626 (Laud MS.) þær he ær her ʒetimbrian cyrican of treowe. *c* **1290** *S. Eng. Leg.* I. 91/154 In one cheste of treo. ? *c* **1366** in Arnolde *Chron.* (1811) 138 Affixed wᵗ nayles of irne or of tree. *c* **1440** *Partonope* 407 A brygge of stone and not of tree. *c* **1500** *Whole Prophecie of Scotland* 1603 (in Murray *Thomas of Erceldoune* Introd. p. xxxv), At Aberladie he shall light With hempen halters and hors of tree. **1531** ELYOT *Gov.* III. xvii, Eatyng his meate in a disshe of tree. **1638** JUNIUS *Paint. Ancients* 124 A horse made of maple tree. **1896** KIPLING *Seven Seas, Sea-Wife* iv, To ride the horse of tree [a ship].

3. A piece of wood; a stem or branch of a tree, or a portion of one, either in its natural state, or more usually (now always) shaped for some purpose. **a.** A pole, post, stake, beam, wooden bar, etc.; *esp.* (now only) one forming part of some structure, as a vehicle, plough, ship, etc.; usually as the second element in combinations, as AXLE-TREE, CHESS-TREE, CROSS-TREE, DOOR-TREE, DRAUGHT-TREE, ROOF-TREE, SWINGLE-TREE, etc.

971 *Blickl. Hom.* 187 Ond þa æfter þon het Neron ʒewyrcean mycelne tor of treowum & of mycclum beamum. *c* **1200** ORMIN 15835 þatt temmple þatt wass wrohht Off trewwess & off staness. *a* **1300** *Cursor M.* 12399 (Cott.) þe knaue þat þis timber fett..ouer scort he broght a tre. **1375** BARBOUR *Bruce* XIII. 238 Schetis..Thai festnyt in steid of baneris Apon lang treis and on speris. **1523** FITZHERB. *Husb.* §3 The ploughe-beame is the longe tree aboue. *Ibid.* §4 The sharbeame is the tre vnderneth, wherevpon the share is set. **1642** in J. Watson *Jedburgh Abbey* (1894) 85 Thrie scoir singill tries, threttie double tries, two hundred daills to be scaffolding and centtries. **1787** *MS. Deed*, Such trees and pipes as are now laid for conveying water from the said spring. **1848** KINGSLEY *Night Bird* 4 All night I heard a singing bird Upon the topmast tree. **1887** *Suppl. to Jamieson* s.v., A straight piece of rough timber used as a pole, lever, prop, or stay, is called a *tree*; as, a dyer's-*tree*, a raising-*tree* or lever for moving a mill-stone.

b. A stick, *esp.* a staff, cudgel: cf. PLANT *sb.*¹ 1 b. *Obs.* exc. *Sc.*

c **893** K. ÆLFRED *Oros.* IV. i. §6 Hie namon treowu, & sloȝon on oþerne ende moniȝe scearpe isene næȝlas. *c* **1205** LAY. 25978 His fur he beten agon & muchele treowen læide on. *a* **1225** *Ancr. R.* 402 'Louerd', cweð heo to Elie,.. 'lo! ich geder two treon'. **14..** *Emaré* 365 She was wax lene as a tre. *c* **1470** HENRY *Wallace* II. 97 A huntyn staff in till his hand he bar; Thar with he smat on Willȝham Wallace thair. Bot for his tre litill sonȝhe he maid. **1588** *Reg. Privy Council Scot.* Ser. I. IV. 270 The said Robert Lekky..maliciouslie straik and dang thame with rungis and treis. *c* **1680** *Songs of Scotl.* (1893) 43, I am a puir silly auld man, And hirplin' ower a tree. **17..** *Gude Wallace* x. in Aytoun *Ballads Scot.* (1858) I. 56 He's gane to the West-muir wood, And there he pull'd a trusty tree.

4. a. The cross on which Christ was crucified, the holy rood. *arch.* and *poet.*

a **1000** *Rood* 25 (Gr.) Hwæðre ic..beheold hreowceariȝ hælendes treow. *c* **1275** *On Serving Christ* 30 in *O.E. Misc.* 91 As he for monkunnes neodes don wes on þe treo. **1382** WYCLIF *Acts* v. 30 The God of oure fadris reyside Jhesu, whom ȝe slowen, hangynge in a tree [TINDALE, and hanged on tree]. —— *1 Pet.* ii. 24 He..suffride, [*gloss*] or bar, oure synnes in his body on the tree. **1460** CAPGRAVE *Chron.* (Rolls) 106 A nayle, with whech oure Lord was nayled to the tre. **1596** R. COTTON *Armor of Proofe* xiv, Christ,..who did our sinnes and foes to tree fast binde. **1635** PAGITT *Christianogr.* III. (1636) 52 Helena the Empresse found the Crosse, and adored the King, but not the Tree. **1707** WATTS *Hymn*, '*Alas! and did my Saviour bleed?*' iii, Was it for crimes that I had done He groan'd upon the tree? **1820** T. KELLY *Hymn*, '*We sing the praise of Him who died*' ii, He bears our sins upon the tree.

b. A gallows. Also † ***dry tree, Tyburn tree***.

c **1425** *Cast. Persev.* 177 in *Macro Plays* 82 Pyncecras, Parys, & longe Pygmayne, And euery toun in Trage, euyn to þe dreye tre. **1500–20** DUNBAR *Poems* xvii. 28 Sum..nevir fra taking can hald thair hand, Quhill he be tit vp to ane tre. *a* **1533** LD. BERNERS *Huon* xviii. 49 Not lettynge for fere of any deth, though it be to go to the dry tre. **1535** COVERDALE *Esther* vi. 4 To hange Mardocheus on ye tre yᵗ he had prepared for him. **1609** B. JONSON *Masque of Queens* ad init., From the dungeon, from the tree That they die on, here are we [witches]! *a* **1704** T. BROWN *Satire on Quack* Wks. 1730 I. 62 Though it was thy luck to cheat the fatal tree. **1818** SCOTT *Hrt. Midl.* iv, The area of the Grassmarket..in the centre of which arose the fatal tree, tall, black, and ominous, from which dangled the deadly halter. **1847** KINGSLEY *Outlaw* x, And when I'm taen and hangit,..ye'll steal me frae the tree.

5. a. The wooden shaft of a spear, handle of an implement, etc.; hence, a spear, lance (in phr. ***to break a tree***). Now *dial.*

? *a* **1366** CHAUCER *Rom. Rose* 948 Ten brode arowis hilde he there,.. But iren was ther noon ne stelle, For al was golde, ..Outake the fetheres & the tree. *c* **1400** *Laud Troy-Bk.* 12697 He was wounded with a spere..Hede & tre lefft bothe In him. *a* **1600** MONTGOMERIE *Misc. Poems* xlix. 24 We dout not bot they [thy knights] dar..be bold to brek a tre. **1611** COTGR., *Abrier d'Arbeleste*, the tree of a Crossebow. **1765** *Museum Rust.* III. 240 The person should have a spade.. about four inches broad, and eighteen inches long in the bit, ..with a tree in it of three feet six inches long. **1881** *Leicester Gloss., Tree*, a wooden handle or stail.

†**b.** A wooden structure; applied *poet.* or *rhet.* to a ship; in quot. 1513 to the wooden horse at the siege of Troy. *Obs.*

1382 WYCLIF *Wisd.* xiv. 1 Another thenkende to seilen,.. the tree berende hym. **1513** DOUGLAS *Æneis* II. i. 60 In this tree ar Grekis closit. **1535** COVERDALE *Wisd.* x. 4 Whan yᵉ water destroyed yᵉ whole worlde, wyszdome preserued the righteous thorow a poore tre. **1594** MARLOWE & NASHE *Dido* IV. iv, Here's Aeneas' tackling, oars, and sails... Oh, cursed tree, hadst thou but wit or sense, To measure how I prize Aeneas' love.

c. A wooden vessel; barrel, cask, 'the wood'. *Sc.*

1513 *Acc. Ld. High Treas. Scot.* IV. 487 Item to hir in aile, full to seywart xxiiij last and a barrell,..ilk barrell contenand xij gallonis, price of the galloune xx d; summa of the last with the tree..xiij li. viij s. **1532** *Ibid.* VI. 156, xij ½ barrellis of aill, ilk barrell contenand v gallonis... Item, for xij treis to put the samyn intill, for ilk tree xviij d. **1656** TUCKER *Rep. Revenues Scot.* (Bann. Cl.) 10 The Scots use noe certaine vessells, but such as by a generall terme they call Trees,..some holding more or lesse gallons the tree. *a* **1814** RAMSAY *Scotl. & Scotsmen in 18th C.* viii. (1888) II. 78 The scourging a nine-gallon tree..consisted in drawing the spigot of a barrel of ale, and never quitting it..till it was drunk out.

d. The framework of a saddle: = SADDLE-TREE, q.v. for earlier quots.

1535 STEWART *Cron. Scot.* (Rolls) III. 300 Ane hors he fand..Without saidill, curpall, tre, or brydill. **1591** GREENE *Art Conny Catch.* II. (1592) 5 His sadle is made without any tree. **1665** SIR T. HERBERT *Trav.* (1677) 314 Saddles of the better sort are usually of Velvet; . . the trees are curiously painted. **1737** BRACKEN *Farriery Impr.* (1756) I. 328 If the Saddle be too narrow in the Tree. **1862** *Catal. Internat. Exhib., Brit.* II. No. 4721 Elliptical spring-seat saddle, and tree showing action of spring.

e. A block upon which a boot is shaped or stretched: = *boot-tree* (BOOT *sb.*³ 8).

1541 *Knaresborough Wills* (Surtees) I. 35, ij paire of boytte treys. **1596** NASHE *Saffron Walden* 17 Rayse thy conceipt on the trees, or . . new corke it at the heeles, before it should thus walke bare-foote. **1766** [see *boot-tree*, BOOT *sb.*³ 8]. **1839** THACKERAY *Fatal Boots* Nov., As I was polishing on the trees a pair of boots. **1891** KIPLING *Light that Failed* viii, As Dick . . busied himself among the former's boots and trees.

6. Something resembling a tree with its branches. **a.** A diagram or table of a family, indicating its original ancestor as the root, and the various branches of descendants; in full, ***family*** or ***genealogical tree***. Also *fig.* a family, race, stock. (*b*) ***Porphyrian tree*** (*Logic*): see PORPHYRIAN.

1297 R. GLOUC. (Rolls) 7255 þo smot uerst þis tre aȝen to is kunde more [*i.e.* natural root]. *a* **1300** *Cursor M.* 1625 (Cott.) Bot first a tre, . . I sal sette hire [*v.r.* here] of adam kin. **1693** STEPNEY in *Dryden's Juvenal* viii. 11 Vain are their Hopes, who fancy to inherit By Trees of Pedigrees, or Fame, or Merit. **1762–71** H. WALPOLE *Vertue's Anecd. Paint.* (1786) V. 305 Two genealogic trees. **1825** T. HOOK *Sayings* Ser. II. *Doubts & F.* v, A more honourable tree does not flourish in the archives of heraldry than ours. **1858** M. ARNOLD *Merope* 865 So dies the last shoot of our royal tree!

b. Any structure or figure, natural or artificial, of branched form.

spec. (*a*) (tr. *arbor* in med.L. phrases). An arborescent mass of crystals forming from a solution, as of silver (DIANA'S *tree*), of lead (SATURN'S *tree*), etc. (*b*) Applied to the spinal nervous system, consisting of the spinal cord and the nerves branching out from it. More widely, any branching system of vessels or organs in the body. (*c*) A branched respiratory organ in Holothurians. (*d*) A worked design of tree-like form. (*e*) *Math.* A figure or diagram consisting of branching lines; (also in *Linguistics*, etc.) a set of items that can be represented by such a diagram. (*f*) *Oil Industry* (see quot. 1954); cf. CHRISTMAS-TREE 2, quot. 1930.

1706– [see DIANA 2]. **1843** R. J. GRAVES *Syst. Clin. Med.* xxx. 396 A certain portion of the extreme branches of the nervous tree. **1844** Lead-tree [see LEAD *sb.*¹ 12]. **1857** CAYLEY *Math. Papers* (1890) III. 242 On the Theory of the analytical Forms called Trees. **1865–8** WATTS *Dict. Chem.* III. 478 By the electro-chemical action of zinc in a solution of acetate of lead, it is deposited in an arborescent form, known under the name of *Saturn's Tree*. **1870** ROLLESTON *Anim. Life* Introd. 145 In the Holothurioidea these coeca take a great development, and are known as the 'lungs' or 'respiratory trees'. *Ibid.* 149 The left respiratory tree. **1879** *Unif. Reg.* in *Navy List* July (1882) 497/1 Tree of trimming braid at top of back. **1881**, etc. [see ROOT *sb.*¹ 14c]. **1930** T. S. ELIOT tr. *St.-J. Perse's Anabasis* 59 You shall see me for long time unspeaking under the female tree of my veins. **1952** [see CAVITATION 2]. **1954** *Time* 11 Jan. 3/2 (Advt.), These *trees of steel*, with their long *metal roots* extending thousands of feet into the earth, are actually assemblies of valves and fittings which control the flow of oil from reservoirs. Oilmen call them 'trees' or 'Christmas trees' because of the many unusual patterns and designs obtained when this wellhead equipment is put together to control wells of various kinds, varying pressures, and unique producing characteristics. **1958** W. H. BURGE in *Information & Control* I. 183 The tree used is a hierarchical network with a finite number of points arranged in levels. **1959** *Nuovo Cimento* Suppl. XIII. 499 The restriction on the number of symbols that can be rewritten in a single rule guarantees that given a terminal string . . it will be possible to discover the associated tree or trees. **1972** *Computers & Humanities* VII. 5 With the use of a light gun the linguist can select from alternative expansions in phrase structure trees. **1973** C. W. GEAR *Introd. Computer Sci.* vii. 294 If it is necessary to trace through a tree in order frequently, it is worth storing the trace path. **1976** *Canad. Jrnl. Linguistics* XXI. 129 The psychological reality of aspects of deep structure and surface structure trees is open to interpretation in several respects. **1976** *Offshore Engineer* Mar. 6/3 Shell Expro is going ahead with subsea completion of a stepout well on the Brent field this summer and will be using one of the most sophisticated underwater trees in the world. . . The tree is described as 'wet, diverless', and flowline connection can be carried out from a rig or a drillship. **1977** *Lancet* 4 June 1187/1 Angiography has made it possible to assess with reasonable confidence the state of the cerebral vascular tree. **1977** *Ibid.* 6 Aug. 278/1 After cholecystectomy for gallstones, it is not unusual for a stone to be left behind in the biliary tree. **1978** *Nature* 24 Aug. 745/1 The amount of work involved in searching a tree of moves is B^D, where *B* (the branching factor) is the average number of alternatives throughout the tree, and *D* is the depth of search.

7. a. Phrases. ***at the top of the tree***, in the highest position: see TOP *sb.*¹ 14. ***up a tree*** (*colloq.*, orig. *U.S.*), debarred from escape, like a hunted animal driven to take refuge in a tree; entrapped; in an awkward position, in a difficulty or 'fix'. ***money*** (etc.) ***does not grow on trees*** (orig. *U.S.*): money (etc.) is not easily obtainable; ***out of*** (***one's***) ***tree*** (U.S. slang) (see quot. 1971). ***one cannot see the wood for the trees***: see WOOD *sb.*

1669 'POOR ROBIN' *Almanack* sig. B8, Minc'd Pyes do not grow upon every tree, But search the Ovens for them, and there they be. **1750** W. CHANCELLOR *Diary* Nov. in *Pennsylvania Mag. Hist. & Biogr.* (1968) XCII. 471 Africa, where tis so falsly said, that Gold grows on the Trees. **1774** FOOTE *Cozeners* I. (1778) 16 Master Moses is an absolute Proteus; in every elegance, at the top of the tree. **1782–** [see TOP *sb.*¹ 14]. **1787** *Amer. Museum* II. 383 When the new government is established, 'money will grow upon the trees'. **1825** J. NEAL *Bro. Jonathan* II. 103 If I didn't—I'm up a tree—that's a fact. **1833** F. MARRYAT *Peter Simple* in *Metropolitan Mag.* Aug. 302/2 Clothes don't grow upon trees in ould Ireland. **1839** THACKERAY *Major Gahagan* v, I had her in my power—up a tree, as the Americans say. **1857** HUGHES *Tom Brown* I. vii, 'What a pull', said he, 'that it's lie-in-bed, for I shall be as lame as a tree, I think'. **1932** W. MCFEE *Harbourmaster* xxi. 371 Can I make money? Does it grow on trees out there? **1964** J. AIKEN *Black Hearts in Battersea* (1965) iv. 51 You'll be wanting it yourself come dinner-time. Sausages don't grow on trees in London. **1966** *Current Slang* (Univ. S. Dakota) Fall 6 *Tree*, n., mind, esp. in the expression 'drive one out of one's tree.' . . She drives me right out of my tree. **1971** E. E. LANDY *Underground Dict.* 143 *Out of one's tree*, expression meaning (1) be thinking, talking or acting in an irrational way—e.g. *You are talking out of your tree* or (2) be in an unfamiliar place. **1976** N. THORNBURG *Cutter & Bone* ii. 45 'We is duh [= the] loanees.' 'You're out of your tree.' **1977** 'S. WOODS' *Thief or Two* 118, I don't imagine these things [*sc.* jewels] grow on trees.

b. Phrases with *of*. ***tree of Buddha***, or ***of wisdom*** = BO-TREE. ***tree of chastity*** = AGNUS CASTUS (*Treas. Bot.*); also called *chaste-tree* (CHASTE *a.* 9). ***tree of Diana***: see DIANA 2, and cf. 6 b (*a*) above. ***tree of heaven*** = AILANTHUS. ***tree of Jesse***: see JESSE¹. ***tree of knowledge***, (*a*) loosely used as = next; (*b*) a figurative or symbolic expression for knowledge in general, comprising all its 'branches'. ***tree of the knowledge of good and evil***: see Gen. ii. 9, etc. ***tree of liberty***, a tree (or a pole) planted in celebration of a revolution or victory securing liberty (chiefly in reference to the French Revolution); also *fig.* ***tree of life***, (*a*) a tree symbolic of life or immortality, esp. that in the narrative of the garden of Eden (Gen. ii. 9, etc.); also *fig.*; (*b*) a shrub of the genus *Thuya*; = ARBOR VITÆ 1; (*c*) *Anat.* = ARBOR VITÆ 2; (*d*) a schematized representation of a tree or shrub used as an artistic motif, esp. in oriental work; freq. *attrib.* ***tree of mercy***, in mediæval legend, the allegorical tree which yielded the oil of mercy, and was at length to bear Christ for the healing of mankind. ***tree of Paradise***, the plantain (*Musa paradisiaca*). ***tree of Porphyry*** (*Logic*): = PORPHYRIAN *tree*. ***tree of the universe***, the mythical ash-tree or *Yggdrasil* of Scandinavian mythology. ***tree of wisdom*** = ***tree of Buddha***.

c **1820** *Philos. Recreat.* 131 A curious Chemical Experiment, called the Tree of *Diana. *Note*, This is the modern silver tree. **1849** [see DIANA 2]. **1845** Tree of *heaven [see AILANTHUS]. **1898** *Daily News* 31 May 5/3 Some handsome specimens of tropical trees—the tree of heaven and the tulip tree. **1535** COVERDALE *Gen.* ii. 9 The tre of life in the myddest of the garden, and the tre of *knowlege of good and euell. **1848** LOWELL *Fable for Critics* 766 Their backs he salutes With the whole tree of knowledge torn up by the roots. **1765** *Universal Mag.* XXXVII. 376/2 (*Amer.*) Known by the name of the Tree of *Liberty ever since the memorable 14th of August. **1837** CARLYLE *Fr. Rev.* II. I. xii, A Tree of Liberty sixty feet high; and Phrygian Cap on it, of size enormous. **1890** LECKY *Hist. Eng.* xxvii. VII. 207 Trees of liberty had been planted in Antrim, and bonfires lit in consequence of French victories. **1382** WYCLIF *Gen.* ii. 9 The tree of *lijf in the mydle of paradys. **1599** DAVIES *Immort. Soul* XXXI. vii. (1714) 109 But Truth, which is eternal, feeds the Mind; The Tree of Life, which will not let her die. **1712** J. PETIVER in *Phil. Trans.* XXVII. 423 American Tree of Life. **1760** J. LEE *Introd. Bot.* App. 317 Tree of Life, *Thuya*. **1880** G. C. M. BIRDWOOD *Industrial Arts India* 336 The tree of life represented on modern Yarkand rugs is always a pomegranate tree. **1913** R. C. MACLAGAN *Our Ancestors* viii. 121 There was another locality for the Tree of Life. **1931** A. U. DILLEY *Oriental Rugs & Carpets* Pl. 57 (*caption*) Beluchistan Prayer Rug with Rectangular Niche and Tree of Life. **1960** B. SNOOK *Eng. Historical Embroidery* 81 Hangings worked in polychrome, . . with flowing stems or a Persian 'Tree of Life' rising from a ground of grass-grown mole hills. **1972** *Islander* (Victoria, B.C.) 28 May 5/2 A most recently finished piece [of weaving] is done in the universal tree-of-life symbol. **1977** *Times* 25 June 2/3 A Kashan silk Tree of Life rug . . made £3,000. *c* **1375** *Canticum de Creatione* 620 in Horstmann *Altengl. Leg.* (1878) 132 And to þe tre of *mercy blyf Where out renneþ oyle of lyf His angel wil doun sende. *Ibid.* 695 To haue mercy on Adam, . . And hem senden his angel fro hy To ȝeuen hem of þe tre of mercy Oyle, to helen him wyth. **1567** MAPLET *Gr. Forest* 63 The tree of *Paradise saith Cardane, is of short life, for the second yeare his bodie drieth vp and waxeth barraine: It beareth fruit like a cluster of Grapes, but in bignesse of an Apple. **1910** *Encycl. Brit.* IV. 739/1 The sacred Bo tree or tree of *wisdom.

8. *attrib.* or as *adj.* (in sense 2). Made or formed of 'tree', wooden: = TREEN *a.* 1. *Obs.* exc. *dial.*

c **1375** *Cursor M.* 12389 (Fairf.) Tree [*v. rr.* treen, trein] beddis coude he make. *Ibid.* 21048 Of tree wandis golde he wroȝt. **1402–3** *Durham Acc. Rolls* (Surtees) 217, j stane-trogh et j tre trogh. **1480** CAXTON *Chron. Eng.* IV. (1520) 37/1 In olde tyme the consecracyon . . was made in tree vessell. **1587–8** *Burgh Rec. Edinb.* (1882) IV. 515 To caus mak ane pair of tree buits. **1599** *Lanc. Wills* (Chetham Soc.) III. 10 All other tree vessell whatsoever. **1640** R. BAILLIE *Canterb. Self-Convict.* 77 Their very tree-shoone. **1750** in *Cloud of Witnesses* (1778) App. 361 A cripple with a tree leg. **1881** *Leicester Gloss.* s.v., A 'tree leg' is a wooden leg.

9. *attrib.* and *Comb.* **a.** General attrib. (= 'of a tree or trees'), as ***tree-avenue***, ***-bark***, ***-belt***, ***-bole***, ***-bough***, ***-branch***, ***-crop***, ***-foliage***, ***-foot***, ***-fork***, ***-fruit***, ***-group***, ***-growth***, ***-life***, ***-lore***, ***-nursery***, ***-root***, ***-seed***, ***-shadow***, ***-soul***, ***-stem***, ***-stump***, ***-trunk***, ***-twig***, etc. **b.** Objective and obj. gen., as ***tree-enchanter***, ***-fancier***, ***-feller***, ***-lopper***, ***-planter***; ***tree-boring***, ***-chopping***, ***-climbing***, ***-daubing***, ***-felling***, ***-growing***, ***-haunting***, ***-inhabiting***, ***-lopping***, ***-loving***, ***-planting***, ***-shadowing***, ***-smearing*** sbs. and adjs. **c.** Instrumental, as ***tree-arched***, ***-bordered***, ***-bound***, ***-clad***, ***-covered***, ***-crowned***, ***-dotted***, ***-fringed***, ***-garnished***, ***-girt***, ***-grown***, ***-hung***, ***-lined***, ***-planted***, ***-scattered***, ***-screened***, ***-set***, ***-shaded***, ***-shadowed***, ***-skirted***, ***-surrounded***, ***-tangled***, ***-wrapt***, etc. adjs. **d.** Locative, as ***tree-dweller***; ***tree-dwelling***, ***-feeding***, ***-living***. **e.** Similative, etc., as ***tree-great***, ***-like*** adjs.

c **1857** J. R. LOWELL *Power of Sound* in *Uncoll. Poems* (1950) 123 A parson's son, through *tree-arched country ways, I rode. **1936** W. FAULKNER *Absalom, Absalom!* ix. 365 They walked up the rutted tree-arched drive. **1910** HADDON *Races of Man* 74 Men still wear the *tree-bark loincloth and the women a tree-bark wrapper. **1962** E. SNOW *Other Side of River* (1963) lxvi. 502 Another *tree belt had been more than half planted over a length of 720 miles. **1886** HARDY *Mayor of Casterbridge* I. iv. 49 From the centre of each side of this *tree-bound square ran avenues. **1951** L. MACNEICE tr. *Goethe's Faust* II. 202 Through a great plain Peneios freely takes His bush-bound, tree-bound course through quiet lakes. **1836–48** B. D. WALSH *Aristoph., Clouds* I. iv, Fly to the tops of the *tree-clad mountains! **1943** J. S. HUXLEY *TVA* 102 An unusual line of TVA research concerns the development of so-called *tree-crops. **1958** *Times* 22 Aug. 12/4 Tree-crops, small fruits, grains, seeds, and livestock are the main farming interests. **1894** *Pop. Sci. Monthly* June 69 Such is the name of the *tree-dweller. **1908** SIR H. JOHNSTON *Grenfell & Congo* II. xxi. 507 These *tree-dwelling Pygmies. **1865** KINGSLEY *Herew.* xxx, Swaffham, Quy, and Waterbeach, and the rest of the *tree-embowered hamlets which fringed the fen. **1788** COWPER *Mrs. Throckmorton's Bullfinch* xi, The *tree-enchanter Orpheus. **1853** *Zoologist* II. 4035 Instances of *tree-feeding species. **1759** *Crit. Rev.* Sept. 178 Why, for example, should we be so complaisant to the French, as to use their terms of *carcasse*, . . *abbattement* . ., and *coup de main*; when we can say *fire-ball*, . . **tree-felling*, . . and *bold stroke*? **1849** J. FORBES *Physic. Holiday* i, They . . indulge in farming, gardening, tree-felling. **1855** KINGSLEY *Heroes* III. (1868) 32 Round the *tree-foot was coiled the dragon. **1922** JOYCE *Ulysses* 191 A runaway in blighted *treeforks from hue and cry. **1946** DYLAN THOMAS *Deaths & Entrances* 22 A she bird sleeping . . Within the nested treefork. **1704** J. PITTS *Acc. Mohammetans* 66 They have but little *Tree-Fruit. **1946** *Nature* 2 Nov. 605/1, I presented the fundamental and elementary culture of the Mediterranean based on a combination of cereal agriculture and tree-fruit crops. **1970** D. WATERFIELD *Continental Waterboy* i. 8 A family could make a living off ten acres by growing tree-fruits. **1601** WEEVER *Mirr. Mart.* E vij, *Tree-garnisht Cambriaes loftie mountaines. **1812** W. TENNANT *Anster F.* II. xxxiv, All the *tree-girt country-seats. **1904** SPENCER & GILLEN *North. Tribes Central Australia* xvii. 527 A visit to the *tree grave. **1600** FAIRFAX *Tasso* XI. xxxvii, With dreadfull hornes of iron tought *tree-great. **1846** J. G. WHITTIER *Poems* (1849) 321 Ghosts of old Beliefs still flit and moan . . O'er *tree-grown barrow and gray ring of stone. **1978** *Detroit Free Press* 5 Mar. (Parade Suppl.) 15/3 Tree-grown cherries . . demand years of tender care. **1917** *Amer. Forestry* XXIV. 732 (*caption*) Comparison of 43 years of rainfall and *tree growth. **1956** *Nature* 21 Jan. 124/1 The variety and abundance of insect life as a whole rapidly fall off beyond the limits of tree-growth. **1871** DARWIN *Desc. Man* II. xvi. (1890) 489 *Tree-haunting birds. **1927** J. ELDER *Thomasina Toddy* xii. 118 Leafy backwaters, sunny fields, and *tree-hung banks to suit all tastes. **1981** *Sunday Express* 11 Oct. (Colour Suppl.) 23/2 There is a little, tree-hung, irregular village square with an island of greenery at its hub. **1898** *Saga-Bk. Viking Club* Jan. 122 The *tree-life of Western Greenland. **1630** *R. Johnson's Kingd. & Commw.* 7 The hollow trunckes of most *tree-like canes being full of water. **1776** WITHERING *Brit. Plants* (1796) II. 316 Stem tree-like. **1910** *Bradshaw's Railway Guide* Apr. 1123 (Advt.), The smartest bijou hotel in London. . . Situate in wide *tree-lined thoroughfare. **1978** R. LUDLUM *Holcroft Covenant* xi. 130 He . . drove rapidly through the peaceful, tree-lined suburban area. **1844** MRS. BROWNING *Lost Bower* iii, A little wood . . As it climbeth . . Sideway from the *tree-locked valley. **1589** FLEMING *Virg. Bucol. & Georg.* 3 The *treelopper . . Shall chaunt and sing. **1885–94** R. BRIDGES *Eros & Psyche, Aug.* xiv, The great hill-haunting and *tree-loving Pan. **1905** A. R. WALLACE *Life* II. 153 The gardens, the greenhouses, the *tree-nursery. **1864** H. WOODWARD in *Intell. Observer* V. 181 Piece of a Vase ornamented with a *tree pattern. **1879** C. M. YONGE *Magnum Bonum* III. xl. 904 The broad *tree-planted streets of the old Quaker city. **1962** E. SNOW *Other Side of River* (1963) lxx. 539 Strolling down a tree-planted street of new apartment houses I chose one to enter. **1825** COBBETT *Rur. Rides* (1885) II. 227 Experienced *tree-planters. **1872, 1902** *Tree-planting [see ARBOR DAY]. *a* **1974** R. CROSSMAN *Diaries* (1975) I. 67 Today I was busy with Pritchett about tree-planting on the bends of the Cherwell between Upper Prescote and Prescote. **1980** P. LIVELY *Judgement Day* vii. 90 He . . had refused to contribute to the Tree Planting Fund. *c* **1440** *Alphabet of Tales* 48 He sett hym down at a *tre-rute in þe son to comfurth hym. **1951** *Tree-scattered [see *river-winding* s.v. RIVER *sb.*¹ 5 g]. **1923** KIPLING *Irish Guards in Great War* II. 163 A close and blind land of woods, copses, farms, mills and *tree-screened roads. **1870** MORRIS *Earthly Par.* III. IV. 385 Like to a *tree-set garden. **1909** *Westm. Gaz.* 20 Oct. 4/1 Matthew Arnold's *tree-shaded grave lies to the south-east of the church. **1958** O. CAROE *Pathans* xvii. 285 A place he loved, covered with green turf, tree-shaded beside the broad stream. **1954** J. R. R. TOLKIEN *Fellowship of Ring* I. iii. 87 As silent as *tree shadows. **1952** S. SPENDER *Learning Laughter* ix. 117 Ben Shemen is a charming, *tree-shadowed place. **1912** E. POUND *Ripostes* 37 In streams and *tree-shadowing Forests on hill slopes. **1854** H. MILLER *Sch. & Schm.* xxiii. (1858) 499 A *tree-skirted glade. **1871** KINGSLEY *At Last* xi, We were aware, between the *tree-stems, of a green misty gulf. **1857** T. MOORE *Handbk. Brit. Ferns* (ed. 3) 56 A decaying mossy *tree-stump. **1915** W. B. YEATS *Reveries over Childhood & Youth* ii. 16 Next to Merville where I lived, was another *tree-surrounded house. **1925** A. HUXLEY *Those Barren Leaves* II. v. 125 Round as a fruit, *tree-tangled, shines The moon. **1894** H. NISBET *Bush Girl's Rom.* 200 There..sat the chief ..with his back against a *tree-trunk. **1914** MUNRO *Prehist. Britain* viii. 185 Only two or three..tree-trunk coffins have been found in Britain. **1886** W. B. YEATS *Mosada* 3 Whose dwelling was a *tree-wrapt island.

10. Special Combs. **a.** in names of plants, usually denoting species or varieties that grow to the stature or in the form of a tree, sometimes those that grow on trees; as ***tree amaranthus, cabbage, carnation,*** CELANDINE, ***crane's-bill, fuchsia,*** HOUSE-LEEK, MALLOW, ***melon,*** MIGNONETTE, ONION, ***pea,*** POPPY, PRIMROSE, ***rhododendron,*** TOMATO, VIOLET, WILLOW, WORMWOOD; **tree aloe,** *Aloë dichotoma*; **tree azalea,** *Azalea* (*Rhododendron*) *arborescens*; **tree-beard,** (*a*) *Tillandsia usneoides*; (*b*) the lichen *Usnea barbata*; **tree-box,** any of several larger varieties of the common box, *Buxus sempervirens*; **tree cactus,** a tall-growing cactus, as the saguaro; **tree-climber** = LIANA, LIANE; cf. TREE-CREEPER 2; **tree clover,** *Melilotus alba*; **tree cotton,** *Gossypium arboreum*; **tree cranberry** = CRANBERRY-*tree*; **tree-daisy** = OLEARIA; **tree-fuchsia,** a shrub or small tree, *Fuchsia excorticata*, native to New Zealand and bearing pendent reddish-purple flowers with blue pollen; cf. KONINI; **tree germander,** *Teucrium fruticans* (Miller *Plant-n.*); **tree golden-rod** = GOLDEN-ROD *tree*; **tree-hair**: see quots.; **tree heath,** *Erica arborea*; **tree lily,** (*a*) a plant of the genus *Vellozia* (N.O. *Amaryllidaceæ*), comprising arborescent species found in Brazil and S. Africa, with lily-like flowers; (*b*) a name for the genus *Dracæna* (N.O. *Liliaceæ*); **tree lotus,** the nettle-tree, *Celtis australis*; = LOTE-TREE a; **tree lucerne** (see quot. 1965); **tree lungwort,** (*a*) a lichen, *Sticta pulmonaria*, = LUNGWORT 5; (*b*) a boraginaceous plant, *Mertensia virginica* (cf. LUNGWORT 3 b); **tree lupine,** *Lupinus arboreus* of California; **tree medick**: see quot.; **tree nettle** = NETTLE-TREE 2; **tree onion**: see ONION 2; **tree orchid, orchis,** an orchid growing on trees, as those of the genus *Epidendrum*; **tree pæony, peony** = MOUTAN; **tree poke,** *Phytolacca dioica*; **tree purslane** = PURSLANE-*tree* (*b*); **tree sorrel,** *Rumex Lunaria*; **tree-tobacco**: see quot. (See also TREE-CREEPER 2, -FERN, -MOSS, -TREFOIL.)

1786 ABERCROMBIE *Gard. Assist.* 115 India pink, mignonette,..*tree-amaranthus. **1884** MILLER *Plant-n.*, *Azalea arborescens*, Smooth Azalea, *Tree Azalea. **1861** BENTLEY *Man. Bot.* 675 *Tillandsia usneoides* is commonly called *Tree-beard or Old Man's Beard, from the..mass of dark coloured fibres, which hang from the trees in South America. **1731** P. MILLER *Gardeners Dict.* s.v. Buxus. All the Varieties of the *Tree or large Box are proper to intermix in Clumps of Ever-greens. **1785** G. WASHINGTON *Jrnl.* 13 Apr. (1925) II. 360, 12 Horse Chestnut Trees..and an equal number of cuttings of the Tree Box. **1858** J. A. WARDER *Hedges & Evergreens* II. 240 Where a moderate or low hedge is needed,..nothing can be better than the Tree-box. **1829** *Glover's Hist. Derby* I. 199 The ten-thousand-headed cabbage, or *tree cabbage. **1864** J. A. GRANT *Walk across Afr.* 339 A *tree-climber (*Landolphia florida*?) lay with its trunk winding like a huge snake. **1884** *De Candolle's Orig. Cultiv. Plants* 406 Upper Egypt,..where we know the *tree-cotton to be wild. **1868** B. J. LOSSING *Hudson* 35 Here and there among the rocks..the *tree-cranberry appeared. **1712** J. PETIVER in *Phil. Trans.* XXVII. 420 Hermans round-leaved Cape *Tree Cranes-bill. **1926** *Tree-daisy [see *daisy-tree* s.v. DAISY 7]. **1958** COCKAYNE & TURNER *Trees N.Z.* (ed. 4) 142 Weeping tree daisy..common in Central Otago. **1906** LAING & BLACKWELL *Plants N.Z.* 294 (*heading*) Fuchsia excorticata (the *tree fuchsia). **1910** L. COCKAYNE *N.Z. Plants* iii. 29 The tree-fuchsia..offers a transition to the scrambling habit. **1970** *S. Afr. Panorama* Feb. 35/3 Below the platform a minute sunbird with iridescent blue plumage hovered before the crimson blooms of a tree-fuchsia. **1597** GERARDE *Herbal* II. cciii. 532 Of *Tree Germander. **1866** *Treas. Bot.* 1161 **Tree-hair*, a name sometimes given to the dark wiry pendulous entangled masses of a lichen, *Cornicularia jubata*,..not uncommon on trees in sub-alpine woods. *Ibid.* 1197 The species [of *Usnea*] ..are often called Tree Moss or Tree Hair. **1777** HUNTER in *Phil. Trans.* LXVIII. 40 The *erica arborea* or *Tree-heath, a native of Spain and Portugal. **1907** *Gentl. Mag.* July 98/2 The big tree-heaths begin about 9500 ft. **1891** *Cent. Dict.* s.v. *Vellozia*, *Tree-lily. **1933** *Bulletin* (Sydney) 14 June 25/1 *Tree lucerne is very hardy and easily grown from seed. **1965** *Austral. Encycl.* V. 383/1 The white-flowered tagasaste of Teneriffe (*Cytisus proliferus*), which is a very large broom, is often known in Australia as tree lucerne, a name strictly applicable to the yellow-flowered bush *Medicago arborea.* **1981** *Southern Horticulture* (N.Z.) Spring 53/1 Weather conditions could influence the situation, as too could the presence of tree lucerne near-by. **1597** GERARDE *Herbal* III. clix. 1377 *Lichen arborum*, **Tree Lungwoort.* **1882** *Garden* 3 June 381/1 The *Tree Lupine..bears a profusion of yellow flowers. **1884** MILLER *Plant-n.*, *Medicago arborea*, Moon-Trefoil, *Tree-Medick. **1905** *Daily Graphic* 16 Jan. 4/4 The mummy-apple, a delicate *tree-melon. **1811** W. T. AITON *Hortus Kewensis* (ed. 2) III. 315 Chinese *Tree Pæony. Moutan. Nat[ive] of China. **1842** J. AITON *Domest. Econ.* (1857) 287 The laburnums,..the dwarf almond on the verge of the walks, and the tree-peony. **1880** [see MOUTAN]. **1962** I. MURDOCH *Unofficial Rose* I. 44 The more intense evening light against a long bed of yuccas and tree peonies. **1980** R. GROUNDS *Private Life Plants* xxiii. 133 As many as 3,000 flowers have been counted on a tree peony. **1884** *Leisure Hour* Feb. 84/1 The *tree-pea, a shrub bearing pods very similar to those familiar to us all. **1882** *Garden* 22 July 73/3 The *tree Purslane..is a loose, rambling plant. **1848** tr. *Hoffmeister's Trav. Ceylon*, etc., iv. 181 A forest of magnificent *Tree-Rhododendrons. **1753** CHAMBERS *Cycl. Supp.* s.v. *Sorrel*, The roundish-leaved *tree-sorrel. **1895** *Daily News* 28 Aug. 5/4 A very undesirable weed from the Argentine is spreading in the Canary Islands. This is the *Tree-tobacco... It is a troublesome pest in New South Wales and Victoria, where it is regarded as poisonous to cattle and horses.

b. in names of animals living in or on or frequenting trees, as ***tree-ant, -bee, -beetle, -boa, -chafer,*** -CUCKOO, ***-falcon,*** -KANGAROO, ***-leech, -linnet*** (Sc. ***-lintie***), ***-monkey, -partridge,*** -PIPIT, -SHRIKE, ***-slug,*** -SQUIRREL, -SWALLOW, -SWIFT, -WASP; **tree-asp,** a venomous serpent of the genus *Dendraspis*; **tree-bear** (*U.S. local*), a name for the racoon; **tree-bug,** any one of various hemipterous insects which feed upon the juices of trees and shrubs; **tree-butterfly,** a butterfly that lives among trees, as those of the S. African genus *Charaxes*; **tree-cat,** (*a*) a viverrine animal of the genus *Paradoxurus*, a palm-cat; (*b*) = *tree-fox*; **tree-crab,** a species of land-crab, *Birgus latro*, also called *palm-crab* (see PALM *sb.*[1] 7); **tree-cricket,** a cricket of the genus *Œcanthus*; **tree-crow,** (*a*) any one of various Oriental birds intermediate between crows and jays, as the genera *Crypsirhina, Dendrocitta*, etc.; (*b*) ***wattled tree-crow,*** a crow of the sub-family *Glaucopinæ*, a wattle-crow; **tree-dove,** any one of numerous arboreal species of pigeon of India, Australia, etc., belonging or allied to the genus *Macropygia*; **tree-duck,** a duck of the genus *Dendrocygna* or an allied genus; **tree-finch** = TREE SPARROW a; **tree-fish**: see quot.; **tree-fly,** a fly of the family *Xylophagidæ*; **tree-fox**: see quot.; **tree-hoopoe,** a bird of the genus *Irrisor*, a wood-hoopoe; **tree-hopper,** any one of various homopterous insects which live on trees; sometimes *spec.* the cicada; **tree-lark** = *tree-pipit*; **tree-lizard,** a lizard of the group *Dendrosaura*; **tree-lobster** = *tree-crab*; **tree-louse,** an aphis, a plant-louse; **tree-martin,** (*a*) an Australian bird, *Petrochelidon nigricans* (Morris *Austral Eng.*); (*b*) a S. American bird, *Progne tapera*; **tree-mouse,** (*a*) any species of mouse of arboreal habits; (*b*) see quot. 1897; **tree-oyster,** an oyster found upon the roots of the mangrove; **tree-pie,** a tree-crow of the genus *Dendrocitta*, found in India, China, and neighbouring countries; **tree-pigeon,** any one of various arboreal pigeons inhabiting Asia, Africa, and Australia; **tree-porcupine,** any porcupine of the subfamily *Sphingurinæ*, inhabiting America and the West Indies, living in trees, and having prehensile tails; **tree-rat,** an arboreal rodent, as those of the West Indian genera *Capromys* and *Plagiodon*; **tree-runner,** a brightly coloured Australian nuthatch of the genus *Neositta*, esp. *N. chrysoptera*; **tree-serpent, tree-snake,** any snake of arboreal habits, as those of the families *Dendrophidæ* and *Dipsadidæ* (both non-venomous); **tree-shrew,** an insectivorous animal of the genus *Tupaia*, a squirrel-shrew; **tree-spider,** any of many spiders that live on the trunks or branches of trees; **tree squirrel,** an arboreal squirrel, distinguished from a ground squirrel; **tree-tiger,** a name for the leopard (*Cent. Dict.*); **tree-warbler,** a bird of the genus *Hypolais* (sometimes reckoned as a subgenus of *Sylvia*). (See also TREE-CREEPER 1, -FROG, -GOOSE, -SPARROW, -TOAD, -WORM.)

1899 F. V. KIRBY *Sport E. C. Africa* xv. 163 A colony of those terrible insects, the red *tree-ants. **1891** *Cent. Dict.*, *Tree-bear. **1902** *Westm. Gaz.* 31 May 2/1 Joe produced from the recesses of his loose blouse a baby tree-bear and a handful of gum leaves. **1693** *Phil. Trans.* XVII. 612 He admires the..Contrivance of the Honeycomb, and particularly the *Tree-Bee. **1747** BAKER *ibid.* XLIV. 578 The *Tree-Beetle, or blind Beetle, vulgarly in Norfolk called the Dor. **1842** LOUDON *Suburban Hort.* 108 Besides the above-mentioned Ichneumonidæ, ants, field or *tree bugs, and many sorts of spiders, contribute..to the extirpation of various insects. **1869** R. TRIMEN in *The Cape & its People* (ed. R. Noble) 99 One of these *tree-butterflies, massive of thorax and broad and rigid of wing. **1885** HORNADAY *2 Yrs. in Jungle* vii. 70 It proved to be a *tree-cat (*Paradoxurus musanga*). **1894** LYDEKKER *Royal Nat. Hist.* I. 457 The palm-civets, tree-cats, or toddy-cats, as they are indifferently called. **1704** PETIVER *Gazophyl.* II. xix, The great Brown-*Tree-Chaffer. **1816** KIRBY & SP. *Entomol.* xxiii. (1818) II. 321 The less savage but equally destructive tree-chafers (*Melolonthæ*). **1859** RIPLEY & DANA *Amer. Cycl.* VI. 63/1 They form the genus *œcanthus*, and are called *tree or climbing crickets. **1879** E. P. WRIGHT *Anim. Life* 246 Of the *Tree Crows we can only mention—The Benteot (*Crypsirhina varia*) of Java. **1872** COUES *N. Amer. Birds* 45 The crural feathers are..sometimes long and flowing, as in ..our *tree-cuckoos. **1824** STEPHENS in Shaw *Gen. Zool.* XII. II. 98 *Tree Duck..inhabits the West India islands and the adjacent continent... It is said to make a whistling ..noise, and to build its nest in trees. **1668** CHARLETON *Onomast.* 66 *Falco Arborarius*,..the *tree-Falcon. **1783** LATHAM *Synopsis Birds* III. 252 *Tree Finch..is observed always to build on trees, and not in buildings like the House Sparrow. **1888** GOODE *Amer. Fishes* 263 *Sebastichthys serriceps*,..known as the '*Tree-fish', an appellation originating with the Portuguese..and without obvious application. **1834** *Chambers's Edin. Jrnl.* III. 357/3 Much wood..during warm and summer months, raining down great store of *tree-flies. **1904** P. FOUNTAIN *Gt. North-West* x. 104 The *tree-fox, or tree-cat, of the trappers..is *Mustela pennanti*, often called the fish-marten. **1873** *Cassell's Bk. Birds* III. 15 The *Tree Hoopoes (*Irrisor*) inhabit the forests of Africa... [They] pass their lives exclusively upon trees. **1836–9** *Todd's Cycl. Anat.* II. 868/2 The..*tree-hoppers.. approach to the *Terebrantia.* **1850** GOSSE *Rivers of Bible* (1878) 286 Probably tree-hoppers, *cicadæ*, are meant. **1900** POLLOK & THOM *Sports Burma* II. 40 The *tree-leeches, so plentiful in forests..in Lower Burma, are a sad drawback to the pleasures of sport. **1844** *Zoologist* II. 508 Chaffinch, '*Tree-lintie'. **1797** *Monthly Mag.* III. 454/2 Bonnet.. applied himself..to collecting..his experiments and observations concerning the *tree-louse and the worm. **1893** *Outing* (U.S.) XXII. 109/2 Swarms of *tree-monkeys congregate in chattering throngs. **1897** BLANCHAN *Bird Neighbors* 84 White-breasted Nuthatch (*Sitta carolinensis*). .. Called also *Tree-mouse. **1904** *Q. Rev.* Oct. 472 The tree-mice and the veldt-rats. **1767** ELLIS in *Phil. Trans.* LVII. 432 The *Tree Oyster, and the Slipper Barnicle. **1901** *Daily Chron.* 28 Sept. 5/2 Proposal for increasing and improving the cultivation of tree-oysters. **1864** J. A. GRANT *Walk across Afr.* 93 The..*tree-partridge resembles the painted one of India, has yellow legs, beautiful plumage, and weighs about a pound. **1895** LYDEKKER *Royal Nat. Hist.* IV. 413 The common tree-partridge (*A*[*rboricola*] *torqueolus*) ranging to an elevation of fourteen thousand feet. **1871** KINGSLEY *At Last* v, The *Tree Porcupine, or Coendou,.. climbs trees after leaves, and swings about like the monkeys. **1885** HORNADAY *2 Yrs. in Jungle* xv. 171 Two *tree-rats (*Mus rufescens*) used to come into my hut from the jungle. **1901** A. J. CAMPBELL *Nests & Eggs Austral. Birds* I. 337 The true home of the Orange-winged Sittella or *Tree Runner is Eastern Australia. **1964** A. L. THOMSON *New Dict. Birds* 545/2 The so-called 'treerunners' or 'sitellas' are widely distributed in Australia. **1731** MEDLEY *Kolben's Cape G. Hope* II. 163 The *Tree-Serpent is so call'd on account of her being seen mostly in trees. **1893** LYDEKKER *Royal Nat. Hist.* I. 312 With the *tree-shrews, or tupaias, we come to the first family of the true Insectivores. **1866–8** OWEN *Vertebr. Anim.* (L.), Some nocturnal *tree-snakes have a prolonged snout. **1904** W. H. HUDSON *Green Mansions* ii. 33 The shaft reveals a tangle of shining silver threads—the web of some large *tree-spider. **1910** W. DE LA MARE *Three Mulla-Mulgars* iii. 45 They sat and ate..with scorpions and speckled tree-spiders watching them. **1934** A. RUSSELL *Tramp-Royal in Wild Austral.* xxxviii. 249 So strong and thickly-woven are the webs of the Central Australian tree or orchid spider that small birds are often caught in them. **1822** J. WOODS *Two Years' Residence Eng. Prairie* 193 *Tree-squirrels are of two or more sorts, and are eaten here. **1872** *Routledge's Every Boy's Ann.* 614/1 Dennis climbs like a tree squirrel. **1968** *Ecol. Monogr.* XXXVIII. 31 (*title*) The adaptive nature of social organisation in the genus of tree squirrels *Tamiasciurus.* **1881** SEEBOHM *Brit. Mus. Catal. Birds* V. 78 The Icterine *Tree-Warbler breeds in Central and Northern Europe, from the Atlantic to the Ural Mountains, extending northwards as far as the Arctic circle.

c. Other Special Combs.: **tree-agate,** a variety of agate with dendritic or tree-like markings (cf. MOSS-*agate*); **tree-box,** a frame used to protect a young tree; **tree-bridge,** †(*a*) a wooden bridge (*obs.*); (*b*) a bridge formed by a fallen tree; **tree-burial,** the custom, among some peoples, of disposing of dead bodies by placing them in hollow trunks, or among the branches, of trees; **tree-calf** (*Bookbinding*): see quots.; **tree-claim** (*U.S.*), a 'claim' or piece of land allotted with the proviso that it shall become the property of the occupier after a fixed term on condition of his planting a certain proportion of it with trees; **tree-climber,** a person or animal that climbs a tree or trees; *spec.* (*a*) = TREE-CREEPER 1; (*b*) a fish, the ANABAS or climbing perch; **tree-clipper** (*local*), the common tree-creeper (*Certhia familiaris*); **tree-coffin,** a prehistoric coffin made of a hollow tree-trunk; †**tree-cop** (*obs.*) = TREE-TOP; **tree-coral,** a branching coral; **tree-coupling,** in a vehicle, a piece connecting a 'single-tree' or singletree and a double-tree; †**tree-crop** (*obs.*) = TREE-TOP; **tree-cult, -cultus** = *tree-worship*; **tree-deity** = *tree-god*; **tree-diagram** = sense 6 b (*e*); **tree-digger**: see quot.; **tree doctor** = *tree surgeon* below; **tree-drum,** a drum made from the trunk of a tree; **tree farm** orig. and chiefly *U.S.*, an area of forest managed in a way that ensures the regular production of timber; hence **tree farmer, farming**; **tree-feeder,** an animal that feeds on the foliage of trees or the insects living on leaves or bark; **tree-god,** a divinity supposed to inhabit a tree, or a tree that is an object of worship; so **tree-goddess**; †**tree-honey** (*obs.*), a sweet juice or gum exuding from certain trees; **tree-house,** (*a*) a house built in a tree (as by the natives of New Guinea) for security against enemies; (*b*) a child's playhouse (sense 2 a) built in a tree; **tree-**

iron: see quot.; † **tree-jobber** (*obs.*) [JOBBER 1], a woodpecker; **tree-legged** *a.* (*obs.* or *dial.*), wooden-legged; **tree-lifter**: see quot.; **tree-limit**, the line beyond which trees do not grow, with reference to either altitude or latitude; cf. *tree-line* (*a*); **tree-line**, (*a*) the line or level on a mountain above which no trees grow (cf. *snow-line*); (*b*) a row of trees; the edge of a wood; **tree-maker**, a maker of saddle-trees; **tree-man**, one of a race of men living in trees; **tree-marble**, **-marbling** (*Bookbinding*), marbling or staining in a tree-like branching pattern (cf. *tree-calf*); **tree-marking**, a tree-like or branched marking on the body of a person struck by lightning; **tree-milk**, a milky juice used for food, obtained from a tree or tree-like plant, as those called COW-TREE, or the COW-PLANT of Sri Lanka; **tree-nest**, a nest built in a tree, in contrast to one built at ground level; **tree-nymph**, a nymph supposed to inhabit a tree; **tree-oil** = TUNG-*oil*; **tree-path**, the track of an arboreal animal; **tree-people**, in fantasy or fiction: (*a*) persons that live in trees; (*b*) animated trees; **tree preservation order**, an order prohibiting the felling or removal of a tree or group of trees; **tree-protector**, a contrivance for protecting the bark of a tree from injury by destructive insects, etc. (Knight *Dict. Mech.* 1877); **tree-pruner**, an implement for pruning trees; so **tree-pruning** (also *transf.*, the removal of branches from a tree diagram); **tree-remover**, an apparatus for transplanting trees (Knight, 1877); **tree-ring**, an annual growth ring in the trunk of a tree; hence **tree-ring analysis, dating** = DENDROCHRONOLOGY; **tree-road** = *tree-path* above; **tree-rune**, one of a set of runes or alphabetic characters of branched or tree-like form; **tree-scraper**, an implement for scraping moss, dead bark, etc. from trees (Knight, 1877); **tree search**, a search in which a situation or entity is represented by a tree diagram, e.g. to facilitate efficient searching; **tree-spirit**, a spirit believed to inhabit a tree (cf. *tree-god, tree-nymph*); † **tree-stone**, a precious stone having tree-like markings (cf. *tree-agate*); **tree stool**, the stump of a fallen tree as preserved in a peat bog; **tree structure**, a structure in which there are successive branchings or subdivisions; cf. *tree diagram* above; **tree surgeon**, a practitioner of tree surgery; **tree surgery**, the pruning, repair, and preservative treatment of ornamental trees, first professionally organized by John Davey (1846–1923), American landscape architect; † **tree-turned** *a.* (*obs.*), turned or changed into a tree; **tree-village**, a village consisting of *tree-houses*; **tree-wax**, any kind of wax produced from a tree, as Chinese wax, Japan wax; **tree-wool**, a woolly substance obtained from a tree, as pine-wool (PINE *sb.*[2] 7); † **tree-work** (*obs.*), work in wood, carpentry; so † **tree-worker**, a carpenter; **tree-worship**, worship rendered to trees or to the spirits supposed to inhabit them; so **tree-worshipper**, **tree-worshipping**.

1876 'MARK TWAIN' *Tom Sawyer* ii. 27 [Tom] sat down on the *tree-box discouraged. **1896** J. C. HARRIS *Sister Jane* 157 Whittling away with his pocket-knife on the tree-box, against which he was leaning. **1596** DALRYMPLE tr. *Leslie's Hist. Scot.* v. (S.T.S.) I. 276 Thay..casting doune the *trie brig,..erected a fayre stane brig. **1805** T. E. WHITE *Jrnl.* 20 July (1904) 26, I..cross'd the creek on a tree bridge an came through the woods. **1839–52** BAILEY *Festus* xxvi. 446 To dare the broken tree-bridge across the stream. **1901** *Proc. Zool. Soc.* 2 Apr. 309 In the States of Patalung and Singgora ..the Siamese practise a form of *tree-burial. **1879** *Cassell's Techn. Educ.* IV. 89 A third style of ornamentation is called *tree-calf. **1895** ZAEHNSDORF *Bookbinding* 28 Tree Calf.—Bright brown calf stained with acids in conventional imitation of the branches of a tree. **1890** L. C. D'OYLE *Notches* 44, I filed on the north-west quarter of 10 as a 'homestead', and the north-east quarter as a '*tree-claim'. **1879** JEFFERIES *Wild Life in S. Co.* 175 If you sit down on the elm butt..and watch quietly, before long the little *tree-climber will come. **1885** C. F. HOLDER *Marvels Anim. Life* 36 The tree-climber (*Anabas scandens*) one of which he had ..captured. **1885** SWAINSON *Prov. Names Birds* 57 Tree Creeper..*Tree clipper (Oxon). **1877** GREENWELL *Brit. Barrows* 32 *note*, Stowborough, Dorsetshire, where a body was discovered in 1767, in a *tree-coffin. *c* **1425** *St. Christina* x. in *Anglia* VIII. 123/21 She was constreyned to flee into *tree-coppys or touris, or in to oþere summe hygh þinges. **1871** *Harper's Mag.* June 28 On the confines of this channel may be seen in clear water a perfect forest of coral—*tree-coral, we call it, on account of its great size. **1915** E. R. LANKESTER *Diversions Naturalist* 11 Great tree-coral of these waters—the Paragorgia. **1877** KNIGHT *Dict. Mech.*, **Tree-coupling*, a piece uniting a single to a double tree. **14..** *Childh. Jesus* 644 in Horstm. *Altengl. Leg.* (1878) 120 Alle þe chyldron..In to þe *tree-croppe hem toke. **1560** ROLLAND *Seven Sages* 66 The hird was sair feirit..That the tre crop he suld gar turne dounwart. **1905** CLODD *Animism* xiv. 74 In such customs and beliefs..are the materials of the manifold *tree-cults. **1871** TYLOR *Prim. Culture* xv. II. 202 The whole *tree-cultus of the world must by no means be thrown indiscriminately into the one category. **1911** *Encycl. Brit.* XXVII. 237/1 The powers of the *tree-deities. **1965** N. CHOMSKY *Aspects of Theory of Syntax* i. 14 A *tree-diagram of a sentence. **1978** *Language* LIV. 15 In a tree diagram, only the configuration of nodes matters, not the length of branches and sub-branches. **1877** KNIGHT *Dict. Mech.*, **Tree-digger*, a kind of double plow employed in nurseries for cutting off the roots of trees which have been planted in rows. **1776** tr. *Béardé de l'Abbaye's Ess. in Agriculture* vi. 37 There was a person, who assumed the title of *Tree doctor. **1908** *Harper's Weekly* 5 Dec. 15/1 The services of the tree doctor are needed. **1976** 'M. ALBRAND' *Taste of Terror* xx. 115 The tree doctor..took a look at the willow. **1849** CUPPLES *Green Hand* xvii, I could make out the hollow booming of the African *tree-drum. **1941** *N.Y. Times Mag.* 9 Nov. 13/2 Instead of reseeding sketchily over immense areas, the industry is laying out '*tree farms'. **1973** P. A. WHITNEY *Snowfire* xii. 231 He told me..about the controlled growth..on a tree farm. **1984** *New Yorker* 23 Jan. 78/3 Tree farms [in China] have also begun to experience problems with theft. **1942** *Jrnl. Forestry* XL. 596/2 *Tree farmers..should be eligible for the same.. treatment as other farmers. *Ibid.*, *Tree farming appears to be off to a good start. **1962** Tree-farming [see *clear-fell* s.v. CLEAR *a.* D. 3]. **1973** P. A. WHITNEY *Snowfire* ii. 21 Julian had gone into tree farming. **1914** *Chambers's Jrnl.* Jan. 75/1 A species of rhinoceros..was particularly a *tree-feeder. **1953** N. TINBERGEN *Herring Gull's World* vii. 66 Great Tits ..being tree-feeders, they do not peck at the ground. **1905** W. E. GEIL *Yankee in Pigmy Land* v. 66 Their *tree-god, hideous and ridiculous. **1911** S. A. COOKE in *Encycl. Brit.* XXVII. 237/2 *note*, An African tree-god with priests and 'wives'. **1895** A. J. EVANS in *Folk-Lore* Mar. 21 A *Tree-Goddess akin to the Dryads of old. **1626** BACON *Sylva* §848 It seemeth that there was, in old time, *Tree-Honey, as well as Bee-Honey. **1867** J. C. PATTESON in C. M. Yonge *Life J. C. Patteson* (1874) II. xi. 275, I am high and dry, and have ..a broad ladder—up to my house. The Mahaga lads and I call it my *tree-house. **1901** *Wide World Mag.* VI. 518/1 A New Guinea tree-house. **1908** *Daily Chron.* 19 Mar. 6/6 A large store of ammunition in the shape of heavy stones is kept in the tree-houses, and is dropped with skill and discrimination upon the heads of..raiders. **1949** A. WILSON *Wrong Set* 128 Go see if she's in the Tree House... It's a kind of funny old place she and Hamish made when they were kids. **1979** R. JAFFE *Class Reunion* I. iv. 40 She couldn't go up in the tree house anymore. **1877** KNIGHT *Dict. Mech.*, **Tree-irons*, the irons connecting single to double trees, or the latter to the tongue of the vehicle. Also the hooks or clips by which the traces are attached. **1601** HOLLAND *Pliny* x. xxix, There be no wood-pecks or *tree-jobbers. **1832** BALLANTINE in *Whistlebinkie* (1890) I. 177 Ilk *tree-legged man, ilk club-taed laddie. **1844** G. GREENWOOD (*title*) The *Tree-lifter; or, a new method of transplanting Forest Trees. **1934** *Discovery* June 167/1 They extend well above the local *tree-limit. **1953** D. BANNERMAN *Birds Brit. Isles* I. 209 The typical Swedish race..and the west European race ..have a very wide distribution on the continent of Europe, where their combined range extends north to the tree-limit. **1893** *Outing* Aug. 346/1 We struck the *tree-line again in the immense ravine between them. **1903** KIPLING *Five Nations* 53, I camped above the tree-line—drifted snow and naked boulders. **1905** *Westm. Gaz.* 2 Sept. 2/3 Now we are high up, above the tree-line. **1936** F. CLUNE *Roaming round Darling* xiv. 123 The trail..wended down the Barwon, branching off at the various blazed tree-lines to the numerous creeks where they settled. **1977** D. HARSENT *Dreams of Dead* 23 In single file the women left the treeline, a flicker at the corner of his eye. **1828** *Sporting Mag.* XXIII. 103 In making saddles..the trees of them are occasionally leaded by a *tree-maker. **1904** *Edin. Rev.* Apr. 348 The horrible little *tree-men discovered by Stanley. **1885** C. G. W. LOCK *Workshop Receipts* Ser. IV. 266/1 Marbling on leather is produced by small drops of colouring liquids, drawn..into veins, and spread into fantastic forms resembling foliage—hence often called '*tree-marble'. **1900** *Lancet* 27 Oct. 1199/2 There was numbness in both legs and *tree-marking on the left breast. **1924** J. A. THOMSON *Sci. Old & New* x. 55 A..Tineid caterpillar, found in the *tree-nest of one of the Termites. **1953** D. A. BANNERMAN *Birds Brit. Isles* I. 16 These tree-nests [of crows] are often most conspicuous. **1831** KEIGHTLEY *Mythol. Gr. & It.* I. xvi. 206 The *Tree-nymphs (Hamadryades), who were born and died with the trees. **1897** J. L. ALLEN *Choir Invisible* xv. 227 The grass-path or the *tree-path of the cougar. **1954** J. R. R. TOLKIEN *Fellowship of Ring* II. vi. 355 That was the custom of the Elves of Lórien, to dwell in the trees... Therefore they were called the Galadrim, the *Tree-people. **1964** *Listener* 24 Dec. 1003/1, I think an intelligent plant would be large and virtually immobile; the tree-people in Olaf Stapledon's *Star Maker* might just qualify. [**1943** *Act 6 & 7 Geo. VI* c. 29 §8 If it appears to any interim development authority that it is expedient..to make provision for the preservation of trees or woodlands..they may..make an order (in this section referred to as an 'interim preservation order') with respect to such trees.] **1947** L. SILKIN in *Hansard* (Commons) 22 Apr. 779 One hundred and six *tree preservation orders have been submitted for my approval. **1976** *Leicester Mercury* 16 July, A tree preservation order has been made by the Harborough District Council to protect trees in and around the grounds of Little Bowden Rectory. **1887** *Illustr. Catal. Garden Furniture* (J. B. Brown & Son) 83 The 'standard' *tree pruners. **1933** R. TUVE *Seasons & Months* iv. 160 February-by-the-fire has been crowded out by putting an extra *tree-pruning picture into the series. **1966** *Math. Linguistics & Automatic Translation* (Harvard Univ. Computation Lab. Rep. No. NSF-17) IV-1 (*heading*) A proposal rule of tree-pruning. **1976** J. S. GRUBER *Lexical Structures in Syntax & Semantics* II. iii. 365 We will have the following four derived trees... Each of these will undergo tree-pruning. **1919** A. E. DOUGLASS *Climatic Cycles & Tree-growth* iii. 23 The plan of using *tree-rings for the general purpose of a check on astronomical and meteorological phenomena was first formulated in 1901. **1982** *Nature* 6 May 28/1 Others have sought an explanation of..variations in tree rings. **1946** F. E. ZEUNER *Dating Past* i. 6 *Tree-ring analysis is based on a well-known structural feature of wood, namely the annual growth-rings. **1977** *Times* 20 July 13/4 Tree-ring analysis —or..dendrochronology—can..help to date..old paintings on oak panel. **1946** F. E. ZEUNER *Dating Past* 11 The scope of *tree-ring dating is extending rapidly. **1895** KIPLING *Second Jungle Bk.* 218 When he tired of ground-going he threw up his hands monkey-fashion to the nearest creeper,..he would follow a *tree-road till his mood changed. **1863** J. M. MITCHELL *Mesehowe* 49 The six *tree Runes form the word *Arrier*. **1901** *Trans. Yorksh. Dial. Soc.* May 82 An inscription in the cryptic characters, sometimes called 'tree-runes'. **1970** O. DOPPING *Computers & Data Processing* xxii. 362 *Tree search and heuristic programming cover a wide field of problems and are in principle well suited for automatic computation. **1980** *Daily Tel.* 26 May 10/6 In a complex game, a computer normally moves after conducting a 'tree search' of all possible moves, a process which if unlimited by time, would take billions of years. **1871** TYLOR *Prim. Cult.* I. xi. 430 The belief in *tree-spirits, and the practice of tree-worship. **1897** *Daily News* 1 May 8/1 Our Jack-in-the-Green was originally the human embodiment of the tree spirit. **1698** J. FRYER *Acc. E. India & P.* 215 *Tree-stones. Stones with the lively Representation or Form of a Tree thereon. **1898** *Geogr. Jrnl.* XI. 431 The deeply submerged peats and *tree-stools indicated..that the post-glacial recovery brought the land-level almost to normal pre-glacial conditions. **1975** J. G. EVANS *Environment Early Man Brit. Isles* vi. 140 Peat now covers these hills, but..they..were once forested as is shown by the presence of tree stools at the base of the peat. **1965** N. CHOMSKY *Aspects of Theory of Syntax* i. 12 The most obvious formal property of utterances is their bracketing into constituents of various types, that is, the '*tree structure' associated with them. **1971** *Computers & Humanities* V. 292 Special language facilities in the fields of list processing, string processing, tree structure operations. **1983** *Austral. Microcomputer Mag.* Aug. 51/2 WangNet's cable topology is a duplicated tree structure. **1908** *Harper's Weekly* 5 Dec. 15/1 The attention given by the *tree surgeon to the aged and decaying historical trees of the country..is equal to that given a wealthy invalid by his physician. **1978** *Cornish Guardian* 27 Apr. 19/1 (Advt.), Tree Surgeons. Fully qualified and insured for all felling, planting, pruning and repair work. **1902** J. DAVEY *Tree Doctor* 14 Learn to do your own *tree surgery, or direct it personally. **1973** *Country Life* 7 June 1706/3 (Advt.), Southern Tree Surgery Company (Consultants and Tree Surgeons). **1605** SYLVESTER *Urania* lx, That sacred *Tree-turn'd Lady.. From whose pure locks your still-green Laurels grow. **1901** *Field* 27 Apr. 572/2 Another *tree village.., where I saw three houses erected on one tree. **1857** MILLER *Elem. Chem.* (1862) III. 267 The *tree wax of Japan consists of pure palmitin. **1870** ROCK *Text. Fabr.* i. (1876) 5 Embroidered with gold and *tree-wool. *c* **1205** LAY. 22899 Ich con of *treo-wrekes [= -werkes: *c* **1275** treo-workes] wunder feole craftes. **1382** WYCLIF *Isa.* xliv. 12 The crafti man *tree werkere. **1860** E. S. POOLE in *Smith's Dict. Bible* I. 95/2 (*Arabia*), The stone-worship, *tree-worship, &c., of various tribes. **1840** THORPE *Anc. Laws* II. 249 We forbid..*tree worshipings [*OE.* treowwurþunga].

tree, *v.* [f. prec. sb.]

† **1.** *intr.* with *it*: To grow into a tree, attain the size of a tree. *Obs. rare*$^{-1}$.

1650 FULLER *Pisgah* II. x. 210 Authors have affirmed that hyssope doth tree it in Judea.

b. *intr.* To take a tree-like or branching form, as a deposit from a solution under the influence of an electric current.

1884 *Science* 17 Oct. 392/1 It will not prevent treeing.. which is one of the most serious defects of the Faure battery.

2. *trans.* To drive into or up a tree; to cause to take refuge in a tree, as a hunted animal, or a man pursued by a wild beast. (In quot. 1854 *refl.* = 3.) Also *fig.* to put into a difficulty or 'fix' (cf. *up a tree*, prec. 7).

a **1700** B. E. *Dict. Cant. Crew*, *Tree the Martern*, Dislodge him. **1834** [S. SMITH] *Lett. J. Downing* xxxii. (1835) 220 It wasn't long afore he tree'd a rakoon. **1854** THOREAU *Walden* xii. (1863) 250 Some small squirrel which has treed itself for security. **1859** H. KINGSLEY *G. Hamlyn* v, It's no use,..you are treed, and you can't help yourself. If I give information you swing.

b. *Fox-hunting*: see quot.

1781 P. BECKFORD *Hunting* (1803) 214 In some countries ..they have a method of treeing him. [*Note*] The intention of it is, to make the hounds more eager, and to let in the tail hounds. The fox is thrown across the branch of a tree, and the hounds are suffered to bay at him for some minutes before he is thrown amongst them.

3. *intr.* To climb up or perch upon a tree; *esp.* to take refuge in a tree from a hunter or pursuer.

a **1700** B. E. *Dict. Cant. Crew*, *A Martern Treeth*, Lodgeth. **1834** J. HALL *Kentucky* II. 191 The raccoon.. when the tree fell..was completely surrounded by his enemies, who took care to prevent him from again 'treeing'. **1866** *Reader* 3 Nov. 908 In America everything seems to 'tree' or perch—quail, grouse, snipes, and, lastly, foxes. **1902** P. FOUNTAIN *Mts. & Forests S. Amer.* v. 129 Then the hunter must tree for his life.

4. *trans.* To plant with trees. (Mostly in *pa. pple.*; cf. TREED 1.)

1891 'ANNIE THOMAS' *That Affair* II. ix. 144 A secluded spot, well treed and shrubbed in.

5. Technical senses. **a.** To furnish with an (axle-)tree. **b.** To stretch or shape upon a tree, as a boot or saddle: see prec. 5 e, d. **c.** To fit (a spade, pick, etc.) with a wooden handle. **d.** To provide with supporting timbers or beams, as the roof of a coal-mine.

1765 *Museum Rust.* IV. lix. 250 The edges of new wheels wear off much faster than the edges of old ones; and if treed a small matter wider, or narrower, the impediment is greatly encreased. **1856** *Chamb. Jrnl.* V. 26/2 A Wellington boot beautifully 'treed' and polished. **1864** STRAUSS *Eng. Workshops* 94 The holes for the nails and rivets are then punched out, and the tool [a shovel] is finally treed up. **1887** P. MCNEILL *Blawearie* 76 To warn the men to have their wall-faces all cleared up, and their roofs well treed.

Hence **'treeing** *vbl. sb.*

1884 [see 1 b]. **1885** NEWHALL in *Harper's Mag.* Jan. 286/2 Wax finishes are so generally used for men's shoes that 'treeing' and 'dressing' with gum and blacking..are important. **1902** *Daily Chron.* 28 July 3/3 The American grouse differs essentially..from the British variety. All the different kinds frequently perch on trees; in fact..this habit of 'treeing' is characteristic of the breed.

treeangle, obs. form of TRIANGLE.

'tree-ˌcreeper.

1. A name for various birds which creep on the trunks and branches of trees; *esp.* the common European *Certhia familiaris*, or other species of the family *Certhiidæ*; also, a bird of the South American family *Dendrocolaptidæ*. Cf. CREEPER 3.

1814 *Sporting Mag.* XLIV. 184 A tree-creeper, one of our smallest birds. **1815** KIRBY & SP. *Entomol.* ix. (1818) I. 290 In America, the tree-creeper is furnished with a box at the end of a long pole to entice it to build in gardens, which it is ..particularly useful in clearing from noxious insects. **1869** G. ROOPER *Flood, Field & F.* (1874) 208 The pretty lady-like tree-creeper ran like a mouse up the tree. **1871** DARWIN *Desc. Man* II. xvi. 206 An Australian tree-creeper (*Climacteris erythrops*).

2. A plant that creeps or climbs upon trees (cf. CREEPER 4); *spec.* the African rubber-plant, *Landolphia florida*.

1887 MOLONEY *Forestry W. Afr.* 94 The plant that produces it [india-rubber] is the giant tree-creeper (*Landolphia florida*?), covering the highest trees and growing principally on those near rivers or streams.

treed (triːd), *ppl. a.* [f. TREE *sb.* or *v.* + -ED.]

1. Planted or covered with trees; wooded.

1860 *All Year Round* No. 43. 403 Treed slopes high above the sea. **1909** *Blackw. Mag.* May 677/1 A little treed enclosure.

2. Driven to take refuge in a tree, as a hunted animal, or a man pursued by wild beasts.

1891 *Tablet* 25 Apr. 660 Like a tree'd squirrel. **1894** *Times* 30 Mar. 14/1 He was alone and treed on a bitter cold night, with the lions..regularly patrolling the environs. **1902** *Outing* (U.S.) June 298/1 Old hunters throw the light of a torch upon a treed raccoon.

3. Decorated with a tree-like pattern: *treed calf* = *tree-calf* (TREE *sb.* 10c).

1892 J. H. BADLEY in *Pall Mall G.* 5 Oct. 2/1 A copy of ..'Self-made Men' in treed calf.

tree-fern. A fern with an upright stem, growing to the size and form of a tree; as those of the genera *Cyathea* and *Alsophila*, found in tropical regions, and in Australia and New Zealand.

1846 J. L. STOKES *Discov. Australia* I. viii. 251 The tree-fern..forms a canopy that perfectly excludes the piercing rays of even an Australian sun. **1871** KINGSLEY *At Last* xi, Calling a halt..to look at some fresh curiosity; now a tree-fern, now a climbing fern. **1886** A. WINCHELL *Walks Geol. Field* 150 Much of the coal-vegetation was of the nature of ferns,—some of them tree-ferns.

tree-frog. Any frog of arboreal habits; often loosely used for *tree-toad*.

1738 MORTIMER in *Phil. Trans.* XL. 348, 71. *Rana viridis arborea*. The green Tree Frog. These Frogs are always found sticking to the under Sides of Leaves of Trees, and other Plants. **1802** BINGLEY *Anim. Biog.* (1813) II. 389 *Hylæ*, or *Tree-Frogs*,..are generally smaller than Frogs, and more elegant in all their proportions. **1849** CUPPLES *Green Hand* xv, At times the tree-frogs broke out in a loud clicking chirrup. **1860** GOSSE *Rom. Nat. Hist.* 28 Then there come.. sounds like the snoring of an oppressed sleeper,..or..the groaning..of a ship's timbers in a heavy gale... These are produced by great tree-frogs.

treeful ('triːfʊl), *sb. rare.* [f. TREE *sb.* + -FUL 2.] A quantity or number that fills or crowds a tree (in quot. 1910, a Christmas tree).

1837 *Blackw. Mag.* XLI. 418 All awoke..to the sound of a falling fountain, and a treeful of birds. **1910** *Daily News* 28 Dec. 6 A treeful of toys.

treeful ('triːfʊl), *a. rare.* [f. TREE *sb.* + -FUL 1.] Full of trees; abounding in trees.

1855 BAILEY *Mystic, Spir. Leg.* 83 Woods And treeful tracts. **1889** HISSEY *Tour in Phaeton* 205 A level, green, and treeful country.

'tree-goose. *Obs.* exc. *Hist.* A name for the barnacle-goose, formerly believed to be produced from a tree, in the form of the barnacle (cirriped): see BARNACLE *sb.*[2] 1.

1597 GERARDE *Herbal* III. clxvii. 1391 Foules whom we call Barnakles,..and in Lancashire tree Geese. **1622** DRAYTON *Poly-olb.* xxvii. 304 Those..trees..send from their stocky bough, A soft and sappy Gum, from which those Tree-geese grow, Call'd Barnacles by vs. **1655** H. MORE *Antid. Ath.* App. xiii. §5 He also adds a story of another sort of Tree-geese which he gathered in their shells from an old rotten tree upon the shore of our English Coast. **1768** PENNANT *Zool.* II. 452 These are the birds that..were believed to be generated out of wood, or rather a species of shell..often found sticking to the bottoms of ships,..and were called Tree-geese. **1835** *Penny Cycl.* IV. 312/2.

treehood ('triːhʊd). *rare.* [f. TREE *sb.*, after *manhood*, etc.] The state of a (full-grown) tree.

1847 H. MILLER *First Impr.* ix. 154 The saplings..have expanded into the dignity of full-grown treehood. *Ibid.* xvi. 292 Solid mid-aged treehood.

treeify ('triːɪfaɪ), *v. nonce-wd.* [f. as prec. + -(I)FY.] *trans.* To make or change into a tree.

1848 LOWELL *Fable for Critics* 31 Daphne—before she was happily treeified.

treeiness ('triːɪnɪs). *rare.* [f. TREEY + -NESS.] The state or quality of being 'treey'.

1904 *Academy* 27 Feb. 228/2 The suggestion of the leafage would give a sense of roundness and what one may call 'tree-iness'.

treeless ('triːlɪs), *a.* [f. TREE *sb.* + -LESS.] Destitute of trees; containing no trees.

1794 W. B. STEVENS *Jrnl.* 19 Nov. (1965) II. 205 On your Tree-less Coast indeed You can have no falling leaves to warn you of the approach of Winter. **1814** WORDSW. *Excurs.* II. 337 A quiet treeless nook. **1841** *Civil Eng. & Arch. Jrnl.* IV. 266/2 Another hundred years may see the United States a treeless country. **1873** J. GEIKIE *Gt. Ice Age* xxiv. 322 A bare and treeless state must have preceded the age of forests.

Hence **'treelessness.**

1869 LADY BARKER *Station Life N. Zealand* iv. (1874) 25 The utter treelessness of the vast Canterbury Plains. **1884** *Macm. Mag.* Nov. 18/2 A diminished rainfall warned the planters that treelessness means rainlessness.

treelet ('triːlɪt). *rare.* [f. as prec. + -LET.] A little tree; a young tree, a sapling.

1874 W. CORY *Lett. & Jrnls.* (1897) 372 A dozen dead treelets.

So **'treeling** [-LING[1]].

1847 *Man in Moon* Feb. 103 These same treelings have an odd notion of coming out strong the first fine day in spring. **1883** O. W. HOLMES in *53rd Cincinnati School Rep.* 99, I should delight in seeing you a treeling.

'tree-moss a. Any moss or moss-like plant that grows on trees; applied esp. to certain lichens. **b.** A moss-like plant of branched form like a miniature tree, as club-moss (*Lycopodium*).

1611 FLORIO, *Musco*,..greene tree mosse. **1681** GREW *Musæum* II. III. iv. 235 The Creeping Tree Mosse of America. **1766** J. BARTRAM *Jrnl.* 27 Jan., in Stork *Acc. E. Florida* 54 We encamped..on a bed of long tree-moss, to preserve us from the..damp ground. **1866** *Treas. Bot.* 1197 The species [of *Usnea*]..are often called Tree Moss or Tree Hair. **1884** MILLER *Plant-n.*, Tree, or Beard, Moss, a name applied to various Lichens of the genera *Usnea*, *Ramalina*, *Cornicularia*, &c.; also to *Lycopodium Selago*. **1897–8** BRITTON & BROWN *Amer. Flora* Index, *Tree Moss* [= The Fir Club-moss, *Lycopodium Selago*; The Cypress Spurge, *Euphorbia Cyparissias*].

treen ('triːən, triːn), *a.* (*sb.*) Forms: 1 **treowen, triwen, trywen**, 4–6 **trene, treyn**, 4–7 **trein, treene**, 5 **tren, trenne**, 6 **treine, treyne**, (**treing, tryen**, 7 **tryne**), 4– **treen.** [OE. *tréowen*, etc., f. *tréow*, TREE + -EN[4]: cf. Goth. *triweins* wooden.]

A. *adj.* **1.** Made of 'tree' (TREE *sb.* 2); wooden. *Obs.* exc. *dial.*

c **1000** *Sax. Leechd.* II. 180 ȝetrifula on treowenum mortere. *c* **1000** ÆLFRIC *Voc.* in Wr.-Wülcker 125 *Coturnus*, triwen sceo. *a* **1300** *Cursor M.* 12389 (Cott.) For plogh and haru..Treen beddes for to make. **1375** BARBOUR *Bruce* x. 361 Of hempyn rapis ledderis ma, With treyn steppis bundin. **1422** tr. *Secreta Secret.*, *Priv. Priv.* 177 Ettynge of a tren dysshe. **1533** BELLENDEN *Livy* v. xviii. (S.T.S.) II. 210 Þe way þat ledis fra þe trene brig oure tiber. **1563–83** FOXE *A. & M.* 259/2 Some go on treen shoes or Pattins, some bare-footed. **1749** *Ann. of Banff* (New Spald. Cl.) I. 129 By 2 dales [= deals] for mending Treen-mare [MARE[1] 2b] for the soldiers, £1. 14*s.* **1888** *Athenæum* 14 July 68 A treen paten of ancient date.

†**2.** Of or belonging to a tree or trees; in quot. 1670, obtained or made from trees. *Obs. rare.*

1340–70 *Alex. & Dind.* 351 Wiþ trene bowus [L. *frondibus arborum*] we ben on þe body keuered. **1387** TREVISA *Higden* (Rolls) VIII. 237 A book also greet as a psawter, wiþ trene leves, i-wrete in Grew, Hebrew, and Latyn. **1545** *Records of Elgin* (New Spald. Cl.) I. 85 The trein corce [cross] anent the Gray freris vynd. **1590** SPENSER *F.Q.* I. ii. 39 So left her, where she now is turnd to treen mould. **1670** EVELYN *Sylva* xvi. §7. (ed. 2) 75 That a large Tract of the World almost altogether subsist on these Treen Liquors; Especially, that of the Date.

B. as *sb.* = WOODWARE, esp. when regarded as antiques. Const. as *pl.*

1927 H. V. MORTON *In Search of England* i. 7 'Before people used pewter for plates and tankards,' he explained, 'wooden trenchers, drinking cups and bowls—called 'treen' —were used by everyone.' **1949** E. H. PINTO *Treen* 3 The small useful woodware of to-day is the treen of to-morrow. .. The turnery side of treen-making is much more alive than most people realise. **1971** *Canadian Antiques Collector* Apr. 22/1 Articles ranging from ladles to snuff boxes, candlesticks to combs, may be included in the group known as treen. **1980** *Daily Tel.* 26 Feb. 13/3 Hand-turned treen are a joy to look at and a great pleasure to use. **1981** *Rescue News* Mar. 2/6 The site has also yielded a great deal of domestic material, including a rich collection of pottery, pewter and treen.

treen, treene, obs. or dial. pl. of TREE.

treenail, trenail ('triːneɪl, 'trɛn(ə)l), *sb.* Forms: 3–5 **trenayl(e**, 6 **treenale**, 7 **trey naile, treenaile, tre-naile, tree-nell**, 8 **treenel, trenel**, 7– **treenail, trenail**; β. 7–9 **trennel, trunnel**, (7–8 **trunel**, 8 **trundle**), 9 **trennail.** [f. TREE *sb.* + NAIL *sb.*

Some confusion seems to have existed between this word and TRUNDLE (small wheel or roller); cf. the *trun-* forms, and *trundles* in sense 'cylindrical pins or staves forming teeth of lantern-wheel'.]

A cylindrical pin of hard wood used in fastening timbers together, esp. in shipbuilding and other work where the materials are exposed to the action of water.

1295 *Exch. Accts.* Bundle 5. No. 21 (P.R.O.) [Accts. of building a galley at Lyme.] In loco ij. operariorum per ij. septimanas qui perforaverunt Galeam et imposuerunt trenayl..iiij. sol. In iij. miliariis de trenayl emptis vj. sol. et. ix. den. **1495** *Naval Acc. Hen. VII* (1896) 164 C di Tre nayles xij[d]. [**1561–3** in Rogers *Agric. & Prices* (1882) III. 414/2–4 Tree nails, 6 *m.* 30 inch @ *c* 2/6... 15 *m* 16 inch @ *c* 1/4... 6 *c* 24 inch @ 2/-.] **1571** *Wills & Inv. N.C.* (Surtees) I. 361, iij houndrethe treenales viij[d]. **1627** CAPT. SMITH *Seaman's Gram.* ii. 4 The other parts of those plankes are made fast with good Tree-nailes and Trunnions of well seasoned timber. **1691** T. H[ALE] *Acc. New Invent.* 118 Trenails. **1861** SMILES *Engineers* II. 39 *note*, Holes being bored through every piece of stone, one course was further bound to another by oak trenails. **1862** M. HOPKINS *Hawaii* 98 The English seamen seizing some wooden treenails, struck the natives with them. **1864** *Daily Tel.* 30 July, The line was opened in 1854, and the chairs were then secured to the sleepers by Ransome's trenails.

β. *c* **1635** CAPT. N. BOTELER *Dial. Sea Services* (1685), Trennels. **1691** T. H[ALE] *Acc. New Invent.* 22 The fastening of our Plank we perform with wooden Trunnels. **1711** W. SUTHERLAND *Shipbuild. Assist.* 39 The Plank.. fasten'd to the Timbers..with Trennels or Pins of Wood. **1769** *Nat. Hist.* in *Ann. Reg.* 100 *note*, Great square logs of pine, laid one upon another, and pinned together with oak trunels. **1776** G. SEMPLE *Building in Water* 95 These Belts are to be..pinned with Oak Trundles of about ¾ Inch Diameter. **1828** CUNNINGHAM *N.S. Wales* 67 Cargoes consisting of wool, skins,..trennails, and hides.

b. *attrib.*

1497 *Naval Acc. Hen. VII* (1896) 313, ij lode of Trenayle wode. **1863** P. BARRY *Dockyard Econ.* 110 Seventeenth in order stand the trenail-houses. For the year the expenditure in these houses was £4,411 11*s.* 10½*d.* **1867** SMYTH *Sailor's Word-bk.*, *Tree-nail wedge*, a cross is cut in the tree-nail end, and wedges driven in, caulked.

Hence **'treenail** *v.*, *trans.* to fasten or secure (timbers) with treenails. (Chiefly in *pa. pple.*)

1627 CAPT. SMITH *Seaman's Gram.* ii. 14 All the plankes to be treenailed to the beames. **1633** T. JAMES *Voy.* 76 She was ready to be boulted and trenneld. **1793** SMEATON *Edystone L.* §38 The balks, in all their intersections with each other, trenailed together. **1834** *Gentl. Mag.* CIV. I. 94/2 The timber head of a vessel,..built chiefly of oak timber, with some elm and fir, clinker built, and trunnelled.

treescape ('triːskeɪp). [f. TREE *sb.*, after *landscape*: see SCAPE *sb.*[3]] A landscape or scene consisting of or abounding in trees; a painting or drawing of such.

1885 'G. STABLES' *Cruise 'Wanderer'* xi. (1886) 105 The treescapes, the wood and water peeps, are fine just before you reach Darlington. **1896** *J. Bamber & Co.'s Catal.* May 30/1 Treescape, Etching by F. E. Weirotter, with stream and figures. **1950** *Archit. Rev.* CVIII. 53 (*caption*) A lovely, casual treescape at Marsh Lock..another fine treescape at Cookham Dean. **1960** *Guardian* 15 July 7/1 The tree-scape seen from inside appears to be part of the walls. **1969** B. PATTEN *Notes to Hurrying Man* 62 Above tree-scapes the fawn smells black Smoke drifting. **1978** *Times* 5 June 12/8 This particular polished granite..has a very high reflectivity, and will tend to mirror the treescape of Euston Square.

treeship ('triːʃɪp). *rare.* [f. as prec. + -SHIP.] The condition of being a tree; existence as a tree.

1791 COWPER *Yardley Oak* 61 Through all the stages..Of treeship—first a seedling,..Then twig; then sapling [etc.]. **1849** H. MILLER *Footpr. Creat.* xiv. (1874) 246.

'tree ˌsparrow. Name for two distinct birds: **a.** *Passer montanus*, a species of sparrow, widely distributed in Europe and Asia, and found locally in Britain. **b.** *Spizella monticola*, a bird (not of the sparrow family) common in N. America.

1770 PENNANT *Zool.* IV. 17 Tree Sparrow. Mountain Sparrow. Common near Lincoln,..conversant among trees, but does not frequent houses. **1831** A. WILSON *Amer. Ornithol.* II. 252 *Fringilla Arborea*. Tree sparrow. The tree sparrow is six inches and a half long, and nine and a half in extent. **1889** *Science-Gossip* (U.S.) XXV. 145 As I neared a clump of cedars..a host of tree sparrows fluttered about me. .. These lively birds come to us from Canada in October and stay until April. **1897** *Times* 5 Jan. 5/4 The tree sparrow ..is, in these islands, an exceedingly local..bird.

treet, treete, treetee, treetise, obs. ff. TREAT, TREATY, TREATISE.

'tree-toad. Any toad of arboreal habits, esp. those of the family *Hylidæ*, found chiefly in tropical America: often erroneously called *tree-frogs*.

1778 J. CARVER *Trav.* (1794) 253 Among the reptiles of North America there is a species of the toad, termed the tree toad, which is nearly of the same shape as the common sort, but smaller and with longer claws. **1855** KINGSLEY *Westw. Ho* xxi, When the sun went down, tree-toads came out.

'tree-top, tree top.

a. The top of a tree; the uppermost branches of a tree.

1530 PALSGR. 233/1 Housetoppe or treetoppe. **1620** MIDDLETON *Chaste Maid* III. iii, Perch at tree-top, And shake the golden fruit into hir lap. **1796** *Mother Goose's Melody* 15 Hush-a-by, baby On the tree top, When the wind blows the cradle will rock. **1821** CLARE *Vill. Minstr.*, etc. (1823) I. 73 The sun each tree top mounted o'er. **1904** R. BRIDGES *Demeter* 318 As the light clouds fly O'er the tree-tops high.

b. *attrib.* passing into *adj.* Of or pertaining to tree-tops; in the tops of trees. Also *fig.*

1896 R. L. STEVENSON *In South Seas* III. iii. 246 The folk of the town streamed by us intermittingly... In the first grey of the morning, and again late in the afternoon, these would straggle past about their tree-top business..and vanish from the face of earth. **1945** *New Yorker* 10 Feb. 23/3 Bombers went to critical missions, at tree-top level. **1961** *Sunday Express* 26 Feb. 5/3 A tree-top hotel..in the Aberdare Mountains. **1977** *Daily Mail* 24 Sept. 15/6 One man with a few machines can run a dawn-to-dusk radio station. Britain's few fugitive tree-top pirates do the same on the odd Sunday afternoon. **1979** P. NIESEWAND *Member of Club* xxi. 165 Colonel Winter heard the jets flash over; just above tree-top height.

ˌtree-ˈtrefoil. Forms: 6 tretrifoly, 6–7 -ie, 7 tree-trifolie, tre-trifoly, (trettifollie); 8–9 **tree trefoil.** The shrub *Medicago arborea*, also called *tree-medick* (TREE *sb.* 10 a); the *κύτισος*, *cytisus* of the ancients.

Not the genus *Cytisus* (L.) of botanists, nor the 'Cytisus' of florists (*Genista racemosa*).

1552 ELYOT, *Cytisus*, an herbe which is good to geue to cattell agaynst the rotte, some call it tretrifolie. **1601** HOLLAND *Pliny* XVI. xxiv. I. 471 The Elme, and the Tree-trifolie, are full of small and little braunches. **1657** S. PURCHAS *Pol. Flying-Ins.* I. xv. 94 Tre-trifoly with yellow knops. **1861** MISS PRATT *Flower. Pl.* II. 92 The Moon Trefoil, or Tree Trefoil (*Medicago arborea*).

treeward (ˈtriːwəd), *a. nonce-wd.* [f. TREE *sb.* + -WARD.] Toward a tree or trees. So **ˈtreewards** *adv.*

1854 *Tait's Mag.* XXI. 307 Birds are winging Treewards. **1869** *Routledge's Ev. Boy's Ann.* 584, I took care to be on the treeward side of the amputation.

treewe, obs. form of TRUE.

†**ˈtree-worm.** *Obs.* [f. TREE *sb.* + WORM *sb.*] The teredo or ship-worm.

1398 [see TEREDO 1]. **1398** TREVISA *Barth. De P.R.* XVIII. cxvi. (Bodl. MS.), A ful tender tre worme þat hatte teredo ..& is fulle nasche in kinde & ȝitte he þorleþ moste harde treen. **1483** *Cath. Angl.* 393/1 A Tre worme, *teredo*.

treey (ˈtriːɪ), *a. rare.* [f. as prec. + -Y.] Abounding in trees; well wooded.

1852 CLOUGH *Poems*, etc. (1869) I. 179 A sort of wide, tolerably rich, and treey upper valley. **1883** *Standard* 28 Dec. 5 There still linger treey tracks as wild as that 'savage wood'.

‖**tref** (trɛv). *Wales.* [W., hamlet, home, town.] A social unit that was once traditional in Wales, consisting of a hamlet or homestead or the community occupying it (see quot. 1889).

1841 A. OWEN tr. *Anc. Laws & Institutes of Wales* 1004/2 *Trev, a vill*:—A territorial division of land containing four gavaels or 256 erws. **1889** H. LEWIS *Anc. Laws Wales* I. iii. 57 In modern Welsh 'trev' means a village or town, in ancient times it is said to have meant a single house or homestead... In..laws we have a frequent use of trev in a sense having reference to the land of the joint family, that is to their settlement and group of dwellings. **1895** *Wales* July 304/2 There was a good deal of feasting amongst the hillside *trefs*. **1900** RHYS & BRYNMOR-JONES *Welsh People* vi. 218 We now turn to consider briefly the law relating to property in or possession of land... The cymwd was thus divided: Four *erwau* in every *tyðyn* (homestead),..four *gafaelion* in every *tref* (vill or township). **1968** [see GWELY].

‖**trefa, trifa** (ˈtreɪfə, ˈtraɪfə). *Jewish Ritual.* Also **trephah, tripha(h, (tryfer), trayf, treff, treife, trifah,** etc. [repr. Heb. *ṭ^e rēphâ*, Rabbin. *ṭ^e rēphâ*, lit. 'that which is torn', flesh of an animal torn (or pounced upon fatally) by a wild beast (Lev. xvii. 15); f. *ṭāraf* to tear, rend. In later use the word passed into the extended sense now used.] Flesh meat forbidden to be eaten by Jews because the animal has not been slaughtered in the manner prescribed by the Law; also *trefa meat*. Opposed to KOSHER. Chiefly *attrib.* or as *adj.*, not prepared according to the Law, applied to any food. Also *transf.*

1837 *Brit. & Foreign Rev.* V. 424 The Jews call..*treff* all that is prohibited to be used as food. **1851** MAYHEW *Lond. Labour* II. 120 Not being particular about eating 'tryfer,' —that is, meat which has been killed by a Christian. **1868** *Standard* 15 Dec. 6 The defendant..pleaded..that meat killed and sold by a person not so licensed, was not 'kosher' meat, but 'trefa', and..unlawful to be eaten by Jews. **1892** ZANGWILL *Childr. Ghetto* I. 88 Even pious people eat *tripha* cheese and butter. *Ibid.* I. 173 We decided that the fowl was tripha and could not be eaten. *Ibid.* III. 39 Their money is *kosher*; they are *tripha*. **1906** *Jewish Encycl.* XII. 109 s.v. *Ṭerefah*, 'Terefah' in a broader sense includes also a regularly but unskilfully killed animal, in contradistinction to *Nebelah*. **1907** I. ZANGWILL *Ghetto Comedies* 68 The *tripha* meat cooked in Simon's mess-tin. **1911** *Daily News* 11 Feb. 4 The Shechita Board notifies the Jewish public that the meat killed and sold under the supervision of the second rabbi is trifa—prohibited to be eaten by Jews. **1961** A. W. MOSS *Valiant Crusade* vi. 81 If more than one cut is necessary..the carcase is rejected as 'Trifah', i.e. unfit for Jewish..food. **1966** H. KEMELMAN *Saturday the Rabbi went Hungry* (1967) xix. 115 When a utensil becomes tref, the way you cleanse it is to bury it in the earth. **1975** G. MEIR *My Life* i. 5 He served in the Russian army for another thirteen years, and never once..did he touch *treife* (non-kosher) food. **1978** I. B. SINGER *Shosha* ix. 168 To me he's as *trayf* as pork.

trefallow, trefe, var. TRIFALLOW, TREAF.

trefele, obs. f. TRIFLE.

trefet, -ett, obs. ff. TRIVET.

‖**treffend** (ˈtrɛfənt), *a.* [Ger.] Apposite, fitting, pertinent.

1850 S. AUSTIN *Let.* 21 Jan. in J. Ross *Three Generations* (1888) I. 244 It is perfectly and thoroughly *treffend*. **1900** W. JAMES *Let.* 13 Mar. (1920) II. 119 His surface thoughts..of a scientific order, were extraordinarily *treffend* and clearly expressed.

treffle, treffoyle: see TREFLE *sb.*, TREFOIL.

trefid: see TRIFID *a.* b.

trefine, obs. form of TREPHINE.

trefle (ˈtrɛf(ə)l), *sb.* Also 6 **trayfle,** 9 **treffle.** [a. F. *trèfle* (16th c. *treffle*, 1314 *tresfle*, in Hatz.-Darm.):—pop. L. **trifolum* for cl. L. *trifolium*.]

†**1.** = TREFOIL 1. *Obs.*

1510 STANBRIDGE *Vocab.* (W. de W.) D ij b, *Trifolium*, trefle grasse. **1527** ANDREW *Brunswyke's Distyll. Waters* K j, Trayfles, Trifolium in latyn.

2. *Mil.* A mine having three chambers: see quots.

1756 MANNINGHAM *Compl. Treat. Mines* 104–5 [contains full description and figures]. **1853** STOCQUELER *Milit. Encycl.*, *Trefle* (*Trefoil*), a term used in mining, from the similarity of the figure to trefoil. The simple trefle has only two lodgments; the double trefle, four; and the triple one, six. **1877** KNIGHT *Dict. Mech.*, *Trefle* (*Fortification*), a mine with three chambers, like a trefoil.

3. A figure or arrangement like that of a triple leaf: = TREFOIL 3.

1877 COUES & ALLEN *N. Amer. Rod.* 151 Anterior lower molar of 5 to 8 prisms, of which the anterior forms an irregular treffle. **1889** *Pall Mall G.* 3 Jan. 4/1 The placing of the Maxim gun underneath the orchestra,..pointing across the ballroom... Around it was a trefle of harness and carbines.

‖**treflé, treflee** (trɛˈfleɪ, -ˈiː), *a. Her.* Also 9 **trefflee.** [F. *tréflé* having the form of a trefoil.] Adorned with trefoils: either along one edge, as a ***bend treflé***, or at the end of each arm, as a ***cross treflé*** (in the latter case = BOTONÉ). So **ˈtrefled, ˈtreffled** *a.* (*Cent. Dict.* 1891).

1725 COATS *New Dict. Her.*, *Trefleé*, a *Cross Treeflé*, is that whose Arms end in three Semicircles each representing the Trefoil or three-leav'd Grass. **1864** BOUTELL *Hist. & Pop. Her.* xix. §5 (ed. 3) 314 A bend treflée vert. **1882** CUSSANS *Handbk. Her.* viii. 130 *Treflé*, ensigned with Trefoils. The Arms of Saxony, borne by the Prince of Wales, afford an example of a *Bend treflé*. **1892** *Jrnl. Cork Hist. Soc.* May 85 The special pattern of the cross is trefflee or trefoil.

trefoil (ˈtriːfɔɪl, ˈtrɛfɔɪl), *sb.* (*a.*) Forms: α. 5–7 **trifolie,** 5 **tryfolye,** 5–6 **-foly,** 6 **-folly,** 6–7 (9 *arch.*) **trifoly.** β. 5 **treyfoyle,** (**iij.foill**), 6 **treifoile; traif-, treff-,** (**terf-, treef-**), **tryfoyle;** 6–7 **tri-, tre-, -foil(e, -foyl(e,** 7 **trey-,** (**tree-**) **foile,** 5– **trefoil.** γ. 5 **trey-, trayfole,** (6 **-folde**), 6–7 **trifole,** 7 **trifol, tre-fole.** See also TREFLE *sb.* [The α-forms appear to be directly ad. L. *trifolium*, f. *tri-* three + *folium* leaf, whence Sp. *trifolio*, It. *trifoglio*; the β-forms, from AF. *trifoil* (*c* 1265 in Wr.-Wülcker 556/33): cf. late OF. *trefeuil*, *-feul* (15th c. in Godef.), Pr. *trefueil*. The Fr. form *trèfle* represents a late L. **trifolum*: cf. the γ-forms.]

1. A plant of the genus *Trifolium*, having triple or trifoliate leaves; a clover: commonly applied to species or varieties other (esp. smaller) than those cultivated under the name of 'clover'; often to the yellow-flowered *T. minus*, and also to the similar *Medicago lupulina*.

α. *a* **1450** *Stockh. Med. MS.* II. 666 in *Anglia* XVIII. 323 Of trifolie ȝif þou take þe jows. **1562** TURNER *Herbal* II. 5 Ye lefe [of Fenegreke] is lyke vnto trifoly. **1657** S. PURCHAS *Pol. Flying-Ins.* I. xv. 94 Another kinde of Trifoly with long red blossomes. **1840** BROWNING *Sordello* III. 2 Braid moon-fern now with mystic trifoly.

β. *c* **1400** *Three Kings Cologne* 92 þe leuys be liche treyfoyles. *c* **1440** *Pallad. on Husb.* I. 701 For wonte of gresse, on trefoil let hem byte. **1552** HULOET, Trifoyle herbe, *trifolium*. **1577** B. GOOGE *Heresbach's Husb.* I. 45 The best hearbe for Pasture or Meddowe, is the Trefoyle or Clauer. **1601** CHESTER *Love's Mart.* (1878) 82 Sweete trefoile, Weed-wind, the wholesome Wormewood..Stone hearts tongue, Blessed thistle, and Sea Trifoly. **1610** GUILLIM *Heraldry* III. x. (1660) 146 The Treefoile is accounted the Husbandmans Almanack, because when it shutteth in the leaves it foretelleth raine. **1765** *Museum Rust.* IV. 120 Those useful grasses, the clovers and trefoils. **1815** ELPHINSTONE *Acc. Caubul* (1842) I. 387 They first soil them [horses] with trefoil, and then give them lucerne. **1830** *Withering's Brit. Plants* (ed. 7) III. 854 *note*, [St. Patrick] plucking a Trefoil, and thereby illustrating the mystery of the Trinity in Unity. *Ibid.*, Hence originated the custom of wearing the Shamrock, (a bunch of Trefoil) on the anniversary of that Saint [Patrick].

γ. [*c* **1420** Trayfole: see 3.] **1580** LYLY *Euphues* (Arb.) 376 As salfe..as sleeping in the grasse Trifole, where..no serpent..dare venture. **1670** EVELYN *Sylva* (ed. 2) 3 The Tre-fole or Clover.

†**b.** *gen.* Any plant with trifoliate leaves, as wood-sorrel. *Obs. rare*$^{-1}$.

c **1425** tr. *Arderne's Treat. Fistula* 68 Panis cuculi alleluya, i. wodsour, is a treyfole growyng vnder buschez..a ful sour herbe.

c. With defining words, applied to particular species of *Trifolium*, or to plants of other genera having triple leaves, or otherwise resembling trefoil.

bird's-foot trefoil, a book-name for *Lotus corniculatus* and other species. **bitumen** or **bituminous trefoil,** *Psoralea bituminosa*, a S. European evergreen shrub. **bog trefoil,** *Menyanthes trifoliata*. **hare's-foot trefoil,** *Trifolium arvense*. **honeysuckle trefoil,** a former name for the white and red clovers (*Trifolium repens* and *T. pratense*). **hop trefoil:** see HOP *sb.*[1] 4 b. **meadow trefoil, purple trefoil,** *T. pratense*, also the wild *T. medium*. †**sea trefoil (trifoly),** a name given by Turner to *Astragalus Glaux*. **shrub trefoil,** the same as TREE-TREFOIL; formerly also identified with *Cytisus*, and by some applied to Yellow Jasmine; also to the Shrubby Trefoil of N. America. **shrubby trefoil,** in Gerarde, app. the same as prec.; now the N. American hop-tree, *Ptelea trifoliata*; sometimes vaguely applied to other shrubby plants with trifoliate leaves. †**sour trefoil,** an old name for wood-sorrel. **strawberry-bearing** or **strawberry-headed trefoil,** the strawberry clover, *Trifolium fragiferum*. **sweet trefoil:** see quot. 1884. **thorny trefoil,** a thorny shrub of the genus *Fagonia*, esp. *F. cretica*. **water trefoil,** *Menyanthes trifoliata*. **white trefoil,** white or Dutch clover. **yellow trefoil,** any yellow-flowered species of *Trifolium*, as *T. procumbens*; also *Medicago lupulina*. **zigzag trefoil,** *Trifolium medium*. See also BEAN-TREFOIL, HEART *t.*, MARSH *t.*, MELILOT *t.*, MILK-*t.*, MOON-*t.*, SNAIL *t.*, TICK *t.*, TREE-TREFOIL.

1760 J. LEE *Introd. Bot.* App. 330 *Bird's foot Trefoil, *Lotus*. **1833** [see BIRD'S-FOOT 2]. **1658** ROWLAND *Moufet's Theat. Ins.* 1063 Take seed of *bituminous Trifoly. **1884** MILLER *Plant-n.*, *Psoralea bituminosa*, Bitumen Trefoil. *Ibid.*, *Menyanthes trifoliata*,..*Bog-Trefoil,..Marsh Trefoil, Water Trefoil. **1867** BABINGTON *Man. Brit. Bot.* (ed. 6) 85 *T*[*rifolium*] *arvense*..*Hare's-foot Trefoil. **1763** *Museum Rust.* I. 27 The sweet white-flowered, or *honeysuckle trefoil. **1796** [see HONEYSUCKLE 8]. **1707** MORTIMER *Husb.* (1721) I. 41 The Yellow *Hop Trefoil. **1855-** [see HOP *sb.*[1] 4 b]. **1578** LYTE *Dodoens* IV. xxxvi. 495 *Medow Trefoyle, or Common Trefoyle. **1785** MARTYN *Rousseau's Bot.* xxv. (1794) 367 *Purple Trefoil. Honeysuckle Trefoil, or Red Clover. **1548** TURNER *Names of Herbes* 40 *Glaux*..may be called in englishe *sea Trifoly. **1597** GERARDE *Herbal* III. xiv. 1128 Of the *shrub Trefoile, ..most do call it *Cytisus*, but we had rather name it *Trifolium fruticans*. **1640** PARKINSON *Theat. Bot.* 1466 Shrub Trefoile or the ordinary yellow Iasmine. **1771** J. R. FORSTER *Flora Amer. Septentr.* 6 Ptelea trifoliata. Shrub trefoil. Virginia. **1597** GERARDE *Herbal* III. xi. 1122 The first kinde of *Cytisus* or *Shrubbie Trefoile. *Ibid.* xiv. 1129. **1866** *Treas. Bot.* 936 *P*[*telea*] *trifoliata*, the Shrubby Trefoil of North America, is frequently grown in shrubberies. **1884** SARGENT *Rep. Forests N. Amer.* 31 Hop tree. Shrubby Trefoil. Wafer Ash. **1578** LYTE *Dodoens* IV. xliii. 503 This herbe is called..in English Wood-sorel,..*Sower Trifoly. **1796** WITHERING *Brit. Plants* (ed. 3) II. 430 *Oxalis Acetosella*..Wood Sorrel..Sour Trefoil. **1796** H. HUNTER tr. *St.-Pierre's Stud. Nat.* (1799) I. 10 One species..bears.. it's seeds aggregated into the form of a strawberry, from which it derives the botanic name of *trifolium fragiferum*, the *strawberry-bearing trefoil. **1884** MILLER *Plant-n.*, *Melilotus cœrulea*, *Sweet Trefoil. **1760** J. LEE *Introd. Bot.* App. 330 *Thorny Trefoil, of Candia, *Fagonia*. **1860** MAYNE *Expos. Lex.*, *Marsh Trefoil*, **Water Trefoil*, common names for the *Menyanthes trifoliata*, or buckbean. **1785** MARTYN *Rousseau's Bot.* xxv. (1794) 367 *White Trefoil, commonly called Dutch clover, has a creeping perennial stem... The *Yellow Trefoil, cultivated under this name, or that of Nonesuch. **1870** MORRIS *Earthly Par.* III. IV. 191 Some from amidst the daisies gleaned The yellow trefoil. **1796** WITHERING *Brit. Plants* (ed. 3) III. 651 *Zigzag Trefoil,..*Tr. medium*. **1843** *Penny Cycl.* XXV. 211/1 [*T. medium*] can be recognised by its zigzag stem, from which.. it is sometimes called Zigzag Trefoil.

†**2.** A set or rosette of three leaves; the first three leaves of a young plant. *Obs. rare*$^{-1}$.

c **1440** *Pallad. on Husb.* III. 623 To make hem [mustard and colewort] hoor as frost..Let grounden glaȝ go syfte on hem aboute, When theyr trefoyl or quaterfoyl is owte.

3. An ornamental figure representing or resembling a trifoliate leaf; *spec.* in *Arch.* an ornament with an opening divided by cusps so as to present or suggest the figure of a three-lobed leaf. (Cf. CINQUEFOIL, QUATREFOIL.)

1418 *E.E. Wills* (1882) 36 Wroght wit mapil leues and fret of .iij.foill. *c* **1420** *Anturs of Arth.* 510 (Thornton MS.) Trayfolede with trayfoles, and trewluffes by-twene. **1536** in *Antiq. Sarisb.* (1771) 198 Four Basons,..with Trifoils within pounced and chased in the midst with a Falcon of Gold. *a* **1548** HALL *Chron., Hen. VIII* 207 A cote of greate riches, in braides of golde laied lose on Russet Veluet and set with Traifoyles, full of pearle and stone. **1551** SIR J. WILLIAMS *Accompte* (Abbotsf. Cl.) 76 Another paier of candelstickes chased withe trayfoldes. **1842–76** GWILT *Encycl. Archit.* Gloss., *Trefoil*, in Gothic architecture, an ornament consisting of three cusps in a circle. **1863** SIR G. G. SCOTT *Glean. Westm. Abb.* (ed. 2) 38 The tracery is not only in circles, but in quatrefoils and trefoils.

b. *Her.* A bearing conventionally representing a clover-leaf with its stalk; resembling a small cross with rounded leaves or lobes in place of the three upper arms.

1562 LEIGH *Armorie* 172 b, He bearethe Or, a Treffoyle, doble, slepped vert. **1622** PEACHAM *Compl. Gentl.* xvi. (1634) 206 Hee beareth Argent: a Cheveron Azure between 3 Treyfoiles Vert. The Treyfoile is the Herald of the Spring and the first grasse that appeareth; hereupon it was the Embleme of Hope. *c* **1828** BERRY *Encycl. Her.* I. Gloss., *Trefoil*, or Three-leaved Grass. This bearing often occurs in coat-armour.

4. *fig.* A set of three closely united.

1826 SCOTT *Mal. Malagr.* i. 48 One leaf of the holy Trefoil —one distinct and component part of the United Kingdoms. **1827** CARLYLE *Germ. Rom.* IV. 47 Among the children.. Wilhelm noticed Felix; the other two were the Angels of last night. The friendly trefoil came running towards him.

5. as *adj.* Three-leaved; consisting of three leaflets or lobes; having the figure of a trefoil or clover leaf; furnished with such figures.

1752 H. WALPOLE *Lett.* (1845) II. 440 A beautiful tomb, all in our trefoil taste. **1785** MARTYN *Rousseau's Bot.* xxv. (1794) 350 They are ternate, trefoil, or three-leaved. **1874** PARKER *Goth. Archit.* I. iv. 151 Small trefoil arches.. between the corbels.

6. *attrib.* and *Comb.*, as ***trefoil head, juice, leaf, seed; trefoil-headed, -like, -purpled*** adjs.; ***trefoil-wise*** adv.; **trefoil burnet, trefoil green,** moths of which the larvæ feed on trefoil.

1825 OWEN & BLAKEWAY *Hist. Shrewsbury* II. 88 Six narrow pointed arches,..decorated with *trefoil heads. **1874** PARKER *Goth. Archit.* I. iv. 134 A window of two *trefoil-headed openings. **1619** SIR A. GORGES tr. *Bacon's De Sap. Vet.* 30 The Goate..doth greedily aspire To haue the *trifol iuyce passe downe her throate. **1758** MRS. DELANY in *Life & Corr.* (1861) III. 504 The receipt for tooth-ache is, 'Little *trefoil leaves, primrose leaves and yarrow pounded'. **1911** *Encycl. Brit.* XX. 399/2 The wood-sorrel, a small stemless plant with radical *trefoil-like leaves. **1782** J. SCOTT *Elegy* iii, The fragrant *trefoil-purpled field. **1765** *Museum Rust.* IV. 79 *Trefoil-seed, 2 d. per pound. **1727-41** CHAMBERS *Cycl.* s.v. *Mistletoe*, Its flowers grow by three and three, *trefoil-wise. **1889** *Q. Jrnl. Geol. Soc.* Feb. 64 Groups of three globulites massed trefoilwise.

trefoiled (ˈtriːfɔɪld, ˈtrɛ-), *a.* [f. prec. + -ED[2].]

1. (Chiefly *Arch.*) Ornamented with a trefoil or trefoils; formed as a trefoil (sense 3).

c **1420** [see prec. 3]. **1815** J. SMITH *Panorama Sc. & Art* I. 154 The [window] heads being arched, are trefoiled or cinquefoiled. **1849** RUSKIN *Sev. Lamps* iv. §27. 117 The wall in the trefoiled lights is curved. **1874** PARKER *Goth. Archit.* I. iv. 144 [Early English] Doorways are generally pointed or trefoiled.

2. Composed of, or having leaves composed of, three leaflets, trifoliate; *transf.* three-lobed.

1854 S. THOMSON *Wild Fl.* III. (ed. 4) 200 Trefoiled plants. **1892** M. STOKES *Six Months in Apennines* 19 Bursting from its trefoiled shell.

treˈfoliated, *pa. pple.* or *a.* Bad formation for TRIFOLIATED (after TREFOIL): = prec.

1835 R. WILLIS *Archit. Mid. Ages* v. 47 A quatrefoil, each of whose foils is trefoliated with an entire trefoil. **1900** *Daily News* 17 Mar. 4/6 On each section of the trefoliated leaves a blood-red spot was distinctly visible.

† **ˈtrefoot.** *Obs.* Also 6 treifoote, 7 trifoote, treefot. [f. L. *tres*, or OF. *treis* three + FOOT. Cf. OE. *trefet*, TRIVET.] A three-footed object; a tripod; a trivet.

1559 W. BAVAND tr. *Montanus' Comm. Weale* VII. i. 133 b, Thales..vnto whome..his..countreie men gaue the Golden treifoote whiche the Fisshermen had drawne vp. **1630** J. TAYLOR (Water P.) *Wks.* II. A a j, Euery man is not borne to make a Monument for the Cuckoo; to send a Trifoote home alone. **1634** T. JOHNSON tr. *Parey's Chirurg.* XXVII. ii. (1678) 664 A Kettle, set upon a Treefot. **1651** FRENCH *Distill.* i. 3 A Kettle, or a Pot set upon a Trefoot.

[**trefte,** misreading of *treste*: see TRESS *v.*]

trefues, obs. f. *treves*: see TREVE, TRUCE.

treg, variant of TRIG *v.*[4], to fill full, cram.

† **ˈtregar.** *Obs.* In 7 treager, -s. [Corruption of *Treguier*, name of a place in Brittany. Cf. DOWLAS, LOCKRAM, POLDAVY.] A linen fabric made at Treguier; a kind of lockram.

1642 *Rates of Merchandizes* 72 (*Rates Inwards*) Lockerams ..Treager, grest and narrow or common dowlasse, the piece containing 106 ells £5.00.00. **1674** JEAKE *Arith.* (1696) 65 In 1 Piece of Lockram called Treagers, 106 Ells. **1721** C. KING *Brit. Merch.* I. 290 Thred Bruges, 22 Dozen. Tregar, 306 Pieces. Verdigrease, 327 lib.

tregedie, obs. form of TRAGEDY.

† **treˈget,** *sb. Obs.* Also *Sc.* 4 tryget, 6 traget, trigit, (?troget). [a. OF. *tresgiet, treget* (12th c. in Godef.) enchantment, magic, vbl. sb. of *tresgeter*: see TREGETOUR.] Jugglery; trickery, deceit.

a **1300** *Cursor M.* 8675 (Cott.) Sco..stal mi liuand child a-wai; Bot i kneu wel be light o dai O þis treget [*v.r.* tresun] sco had me don. *c* **1375** *Sc. Leg. Saints* x. (*Mathou*) 98 Þat gere fele men wene þat þai Throw tryget are goddis verray. *c* **1400** *Rom. Rose* 6267 Sith they cowde not perceyve His treget, and his cruelte. *Ibid.* 6825 By my treget I gadre & threste The gret tresour into my cheste. **1513** DOUGLAS *Æneis* IV. Prol. 247 Of thi trigittis [*ed.* **1553** tragetis] quhat toung can tell the trible?

b. *attrib.* or as *adj.* Juggling, deceitful.

1519 HORMAN *Vulg.* 280 b, A iugler with his treget [*pr.* troget] castis deceueth mens syght.

† **treget,** *v. Obs. rare.* [a. OF. *tre(s)geter*: see next.] *intr.* To practise juggling tricks. Hence † **tregetting** *vbl. sb.*

c **1440** *Promp. Parv.* 501/1 Tregettyn, *prestigior, pancracio. Ibid.* 501/2 Tregettynge, *mimatus, prestigium.*

ˈtregetour. *arch.* Also 4 tregetowr, -ettur, trigettur, tri-, trygetoure, 4-5 tregetoure, -itour, -e, trigetour, 4-6 tregettour, 5 -etur, -ettowre, (trageotour), 6 try-, tragetour, treageter, trogeter, -ettar. [a. OF. *tre(s)geteo(u)r* (12th c. in Godef.) a juggler, mountebank, agent-n. of *tre(s)geter* to cast across or to and fro:—L. type **tra(ns)jectāre*, f. TRANS- + *jactāre* to throw, cast: see TRAJECT. Cf. It. *tragettatore* juggler; and, for sense, CAST *sb.* 24, CASTER I.] One who works magic or plays tricks by sleight of hand; a conjurer; a juggler; hence, a trickster, a deceiver.

a **1300** *Cursor M.* 12247 (Cott.) A tregetur [*v. rr.* trigettur, tregit-, tregettour] i hope he be, Or elles godds self es he. **1340** HAMPOLE *Pr. Consc.* 4213 Als negremanciens and tregettours, Wiches and false enchauntours. *c* **1380** *Antecrist* in Todd *3 Treat. Wyclif* 128 Wiþ tregetours & tomblers, wiþ gestours & japeres. *c* **1520** *Treat. Galaunt* 106 in Furniv. *Ballads* I. 449 For trygetours & tryflours that tauernes haunte. **1533** tr. *Erasmus' Com. Crede* 65 b, These persons do make Christe a iuglere or a trogeter and a wonderfull deceiuer. **1609** HOLLAND *Amm. Marcell.* XXIII. v. 223 A dauncing Tregetour..was acting and counterfeiting certaine gestures that were commonly and usually taken up. **1819** SCOTT *Ivanhoe* xliii, The sewer thought I was dressed to bear a part in the tregetour's mummery. **1843** LYTTON *Last Bar.* I. ii, The more sombre *Tregetour*..promised to cut off and refix the head of a sad-faced little boy.

† **ˈtregetry.** *Obs.* Also tregetrie, -re, tregettrie, -rye. [a. OF. *tre(s)geterie* (Godef.) enchantment, magic: see prec. and -ERY, -RY.] Juggling; deception, trickery.

c **1380** WYCLIF *Sel. Wks.* III. 410 Elles mot þei putt tregettrye and falsenes in Crist. *c* **1400** *Destr. Troy* 1624 Soche soteltie þai soght to solas hom with; The tables, the top, tregetre also. **14..** *Beryn* 2774 The wiche been so perfite of Nygramance, And of þe arte of apparence, and of tregetrie.

trehala (trɪˈhɑːlə). Also tricala. [ad. Turkish *tīqālah*, native name.] The substance of the cocoons of a coleopterous insect, *Larinus maculatus*, found in Asia Minor; also called ***trehala-manna***, *Turkish* or *Syrian manna.*

1862 WATTS *Gmelin's Handbk. Chem.* XV. 300 When pulverised trehala manna is treated with boiling alcohol, trehalose sometimes crystallises from the extract on cooling. **1868** — *Dict. Chem.* V. 878 *Trehala* or *tricala*, a substance imported from Persia, and consisting of the hollow cocoons of a coleopterous insect (*Larinus maculatus*). The larva of this insect eats the branches of *Echinops persica*, for the sake of the sugar, starch, and gum contained in them, and afterwards voids these substances to form its cocoon... Trehala has a sweetish taste, swells up in water, and is converted into a thick mucilaginous paste.

Hence **trehalose** (ˈtriːhələʊs, triːˈhɑːləʊs), *Chem.*, a white crystalline sugar, $C_{12}H_{22}O_{11} \cdot 2H_2O$, obtained by Berthelot in 1857 from trehala.

1862 MILLER *Elem. Chem.* (ed. 2) III. 73 The most important of these [varieties] is the common sugar, furnished by the sugar cane,..related to which are some others of small importance, viz. trehalose, melezitose, and melitose. **1865-8** WATTS *Dict. Chem.* III. 1068 *Mycose* or *trehalose.* $C_{12}H_{22}O_{11}$... Berthelot..obtained from trehala-manna..a sugar which he called trehalose, and at first regarded as different from mycose; but on further examination he was led to infer that the two are identical.

trehalase (trɪˈhɑːleɪz). *Biochem.* [ad. F. *tréhalase* (E. Bourquelot 1893, in *Bull. de la Soc. mycologique de France* IX. 194): see TREHALA and -ASE.] An enzyme which catalyses the hydrolysis of trehalose to two molecules of glucose.

1893 *Jrnl. Chem. Soc.* LXIV. 451 The author proposes to call the special ferment trehalase. **1926** WAKSMAN & DAVISON *Enzymes* x. 182 Trehalase has been demonstrated in the intestinal secretions of certain animals (horse, cattle), certain fishes, in malt, in various fungi, in yeasts and in certain bacteria. **1977** *Lancet* 5 Nov. 982/2 Sucrase, trehalase and lactase activities were absent.

trei, treie: see TRAY, TRY.

treid, obs. f. *tried*, pa. t. and pple. of TRY *v.*

treifoile, obs. f. TREFOIL.

treigntalle, obs. f. TRENTAL.

treil, var. TRAIL *sb.*[2] *Obs.*

† **ˈtreilȝe,** var. of TRAILYE *Sc.* a kind of cloth. Cf. also TREILLIS. This is perh. the meaning of *treilȝeis* in the following quot., which Ruddiman referred to F. *étrilles* currycombs, L. *strigulæ, strigiles* scrapers.

1513 DOUGLAS *Æneis* XII. ii. 92 Thar [stedis] lokrand manis and thar crestis hie Dressys wyth treilȝeis and camis honestlye.

treillage (ˈtreɪlɪdʒ, ‖trɛjaʒ). Also 7 treilliage, 8 treilage. [a. F. *treillage* (16th c. in Hatz.-Darm.), f. *treille*, TRAIL *sb.*[2] + *-age*, -AGE.]

1. Lattice-work; a framework upon which vines or ornamental plants are trained; a trellis.

1698 W. KING tr. *Sorbière's Journ. Lond.* 28 At St. James's Park there were no Pavillions nor decoration of Treilliage and Flowers. **1712** ADDISON *Spect.* No. 477 ¶1 There are as many kinds of Gardening as of Poetry:..Contrivers of Bowers and Grotto's, Treillages and Cascades, are Romance Writers. **1830** GREVILLE *Mem. Geo. IV* 20 Apr. (1875) I. 335 A walk under a treillage of vines. **1907** *Edin. Rev.* Jan. 151 The garden is laid out with treillage and grass plot.

b. *attrib.*

1803 REPTON *Landscape Gard.* (1805) 104 Advantage may be taken of treillage ornaments to admit light. **1835** *Fraser's Mag.* XII. 524 Several vines trained over treillage-work.

2. A lattice or grill in a room.

1836 T. HOOK *G. Gurney* (new ed.) 35, I was placed in the manager's box, allotted the seat of honour behind the treillage.

Hence **treillaged** *a.*, trellised.

1810 SHELLEY *Zastrozzi* iv, Their treillaged ornaments were silvered by the clear moonlight.

treille (treɪl). [a. F. *treille* (trɛj) trellis, lattice:—L. *trichila* trellis for a vine: see TRAIL *sb.*[2]] **a.** *Her.* = TRELLIS *sb.*[2] 1 d.

1780 EDMONDSON *Heraldry* II. Gloss., *Trillise*, or *Treille*, a lattice. It differs from a fret in..that the pieces which compose it are not interlaced..but lie strait upon the under-most pieces, fixed with nails. **1889** ELVIN *Dict. Her.*, Treille, or Trillise.

b. *Lace-making.* See quot. 1882.

1865 F. B. PALLISER *Hist. Lace* vii. 119 The thick 'treille' and scanty flowers of the old laces [in West Flanders]. **1882** CAULFEILD & SAWARD *Dict. Needlewk.* 500/2 *Treille*, one of the names by which the Réseau Grounds of Pillow and Needle Laces are distinguished from the Toile or pattern. The value of many laces is decided by the thickness or fineness of the thread used in the Treille, and the number of Twists given to the Bobbins when making it.

‖**treillis** (ˈtrɛljiː, treji). Also (3 Anglo-L. treyliz), 8 trellis. [mod.F. *treillis*. Orig. the same word as TRELLIS, OF. *treliz*, L. **trilīcium*, f. *trilīx, -līcem*, the original sense of which it closely preserves. See TRELLIS.] A stout or coarse kind of cloth; in later use, buckram, sacking ('toile grossière pour sacs, vêtements de travail', Hatz.-Darm.; see also Littré s.v. senses 5, 6). See also TRAILYE.

[*c* **1250** *Faringdon Compotus* (MS. Barl. 49[2] lf. 6), Vna ulna canabi Valet. .ij. den. ob... Vna ulna buretell' Valet vnum den... Vna ulna treyliz Valet .iij. den.] **1706** PHILLIPS (ed. Kersey), *Trellis*,..also Cloth, otherwise call'd Buckram. **1714** *Fr. Bk. of Rates* 80 Treillis of Germany, per Piece of 10 Ells. **1858** SIMMONDS *Dict. Trade*, *Treillis*, a kind of coarse quilted linen, imported into France.

trein, -e, treing, obs. ff. TREEN *a.*

treinke, var. TRINK *sb.*[1] *Obs.*

treip, obs. Sc. f. TRIP.

treische, var. TRESCHE *Obs.*

treison, obs. f. TREASON.

treist, var. TRAIST *Obs.*; obs. Sc. f. TREST.

treit, obs. Sc. f. TREAT.

treitcheoure, var. TREACHER *Obs.*

treitour, -tre, obs. ff. TRAITOR.

trei trippe, var. TREY-TRIP *Obs.*

treittie, obs. Sc. f. TREATY.

trek (trɛk), *sb.* Orig. *S. Afr.* [a. Cape Du. *trek* = Du. *trek* draw, pull, tug, march, f. *trekken*, TREK *v.*]

1. a. *S. Afr.* In travelling by ox-wagon, a stage of a journey between one stopping-place and the next; hence, a journey or expedition made in this way; also, journeying or travel by ox-wagon.

(Cf. *trek-tow* occurring in 1834.)

1849 E. E. NAPIER *Excurs. S. Africa* II. 1 First day's 'trek' in lower Albany. **1863** W. C. BALDWIN *Afr. Hunting* vii. 233, I joined Swartz..and went with him to Letloche, about fourteen days' trek. **1906** *Harper's Mag.* June 30/2 Distances in Africa are not reckoned by miles, but by treks or days.

(*b*) Now in gen. use elsewhere, a long journey or expedition, esp. one overland involving considerable physical effort.

1941 I. L. IDRIESS *Great Boomerang* i. 6 Risky treks against hazards different from those of the general Australian bush. **1968** R. M. PATTERSON *Finlay's River* 168 There they made camp, cached their canoe and load, and sorted out what they wanted to take for their next overland trek—this time a hunting trip. **1972** D. CRAIG *Double Take* i. 8 The trekking lesson always ended like this... The other members of the trek looked at Brian.

b. *S. Afr.* An organized migration or expedition by ox-wagon.

1890 *Times* (weekly ed.) 28 Feb. 17/3 The proclamation of President Kruger forbidding the formation of a 'trek' to enter Mashonaland. **1901** *Scotsman* 8 Mar. 6/2 There had been a Boer trek into German South-west Africa, but it was only on a small scale. **1901** *Daily Chron.* 30 May 3/2 The men above-mentioned, or their sons,..led the great trek of 1836-9.

c. *transf.* and *fig.*

1895 J. G. MILLAIS *Breath fr. Veldt* v. 102 A big troop of guinea-fowls..following each other in their afternoon trek to the water. *Ibid.* vi. 123 From the sun-parched wilderness of Africa to art criticism is a big trek. **1902** CORNISH *Naturalist Thames* 67 The first [birds] to begin the 'trek' down the river are the early broods of water-wagtails.

2. *attrib.* and *Comb.*, as ***trek-cattle, -ox***; **trek Boer,** (*a*) a Boer who moved his family and grazing stock from place to place; (*b*) = VOORTREKKER; also, a participant in a later migration of Afrikaners; **trek-bok,** *pl.* **bokke(n),** an antelope, esp. a springbok, in a migrating herd; **trek-cart,** a light cart used by (boy) scouts for transporting stores, etc.; **trek chain** = TREK-TOW; **trek-farmer** = *trek Boer* (*a*) above; **trek fever,** an insatiable longing for travelling or wandering in the veld; **trek-net** = SEINE *sb.*[1]; hence **trek-netter; trek path,** a right of way across the land of another farmer; **trek-rope** =

TREK-TOW; **trek sheep**, sheep driven or carried a long way for pasturage.

1835 A. STEEDMAN *Wanderings S. Afr.* II. III. iii. 53 The next day we met a *Trek Boor, with his cattle. 1847 in C. Pettman *Africanderisms* (1913) 513 All the most intelligent of the *Trek Boers* whom I have seen, look forward with dread to the course the Government are pursuing. 1882 C. DU VAL *With Show through Southern Afr.* I. 106 Abolition of slavery was the primary cause of the movement of these 'trek Boers'. 1929 D. REITZ *Commando* xxiv. 281 We moved north through country thinly occupied by Nomad Boers (Trek Boers), who spend their lives going from one well to another with their flocks. 1941 C. W. DE KIEWIET *Hist. S. Afr.* 17 When the Trekboers entered it with their flocks and tented wagons, they left the current of European life. 1981 *Times Lit. Suppl.* 13 Feb. 159/2 The Afrikaner remains, according to Lambley, the atavistic, insular, racially arrogant *trekboer*. 1824 *S. Afr. Jrnl.* I. 72 On the approach of the *Trek-Bokken or migrating spring-boks, the grazier makes up his mind to look for pasturage elsewhere. 1827 G. THOMPSON *Trav. & Adv. S. Afr.* II. vi. 274 The destructive flocks of *trek-bokken*, or migratory springboks, pressed by the long droughts, occasionally inundate the northern parts of the Colony. 1896 H. A. BRYDEN *Tales S. Afr.* ix. 215, I have passed across these plains through a herd of trek-bokken.. three or four miles broad. 1966 E. PALMER *Plains of Camdeboo* ix. 157 The springbuck migrations..are something we shall never see again. Colonists called them 'trekbokke' or 'travellingbuck'. 1928 R. A. KNOX *Footsteps at Lock* v. 43 The bigger boys had gone.. with the *trek-cart to bring our stores over. 1977 *Drive* Jan.–Feb. 15/2 Boy scouts' trek-cart needed. 1900 *Daily News* 6 Apr. 3/1 The local supply of *trek cattle..from the farms of the Boers. 1878 H. A. ROCHE *On Trek in Transvaal* 332 Our oxen were free, walking off a yard or two with our *tree-disselboom* and *trek-chain. 1972 *Farmer's Weekly* (S. Afr.) 21 Apr. (Advt.), Chain traces 55c each; Trek chains R1.55. 1912 *East London Daily Dispatch* 1 May 5 (Pettman), The desirability of amending the railway tariff for trek-sheep to enable *trek farmers to avail themselves of the railway. 1966 E. PALMER *Plains of Camdeboo* vii. 128 The mountain bush had housed the first trek-farmers in hard and stormy weather. 1980 FIRST & SCOTT *Olive Schreiner* i. 28 Boer trek-farmers moved away from British control. 1897 J. P. FITZPATRICK *Outspan* 3 When..this instinct awakens,..it becomes a madness, and they call it *trek-fever. 1943 D. REITZ *No Outspan* viii. 106 Gauko-Otawi, the 'Rustplaats' or resting place of the Trekkers. Here it was that in 1878 they had built a church, their trek-fever temporarily stilled. 1913 W. W. THOMPSON *Sea Fisheries Cape Colony* ii. 46 The seine, or '*trek-net', has from the very earliest period of the European occupation of the country been the type of net generally adopted. 1970 *Cape Argus* 24 Dec. 2 They had cast trek nets in the surf. 1956 J. L. B. SMITH *Old Fourlegs* i. 9, I..lived with the coastal *trek-netters. 1850 CUMMING *Hunter's Life S. Afr.* (ed. 2) I. 220, I purchased..several excellent horses and *trek-oxen. 1906 *Harper's Mag.* June 29/1 The northernmost limit of the trek-ox in Africa. 1934 WEBSTER, *Trekpath. 1936 *Cape Argus* 18 Mar. 13 The trek-path controversy has led many men to fence their farms. 1955 L. G. GREEN *Karoo* xii. 142 A trek path is a definite route which a farmer is entitled to follow when leading his sheep to new pastures. 1883 *Cornh. Mag.* Mar. 293 The oxen loosened from the *trek rope. 1912 *Trek sheep [see *trek-farmer* above].

trek (trɛk), *v.* Orig. *S. Afr.* [a. Du. *trekk-en* to draw, pull, tug, tow, march, travel; MDu., MLG., MHG. *trecken*, OWFris. *trekka*; orig. an intensive derivative of MDu., MLG. *trēken*, MHG. *trechen*, OHG. *trechan* to draw.]

1. a. *intr.* To make a journey by ox-wagon; hence, to travel, migrate; also, to go, proceed; to go away, depart (*slang*). Also *transf.* of wild animals. *S. Afr.*

1850 R. G. CUMMING *Hunter's Life S. Afr.* (1902) 12/2 [The elephants] turned their faces to the north-east, and trekked or migrated from their ancestral jungles to lands unknown. *Ibid.* 74/2 At dawn of day, we inspanned, and trekked about five hours in a north-easterly course. 1863 W. C. BALDWIN *Afr. Hunting* vi. 154 The wagons had been quietly treking along over an immense open country. 1891 *Spectator* 25 Apr. 583/2 A large body of them [Boers]—five thousand, it is said—therefore resolved to 'trek' into Mashonaland and establish a Republic upon the great plateau. 1895 J. G. MILLAIS *Breath fr. Veldt* ii. 25 The springbuck..were beginning to trek backwards and forwards uneasily.

(*b*) Hence generally in extended use: to travel, esp. arduously, to make one's way. Freq. trivially.

1911 C. E. W. BEAN *'Dreadnought' of Darling* xxxviii. 342 When the police first saw them they were trekking through the scrub. 1912 *Standard* 20 Sept. 7/1 He [the King] met the whole of the Third Division, who were trekking to their rest camps from their overnight bivouac. 1943 *Sun* (Baltimore) 11 June 13/2 The hungry pilot trekking over the tundra should beware of the liver of the Polar bear. 1955 [see TREKKING *vbl. sb.*]. 1976 *Oadby & Wigston* (Leics.) *Advertiser* 26 Nov. 7/6, I was surprised as I trekked from shop to shop how much prices varied. 1977 C. MCCULLOUGH *Thorn Birds* xvii. 438 It would mean trekking down to the kitchen again, and..no one appreciates the patter of my little feet.

b. *trans.* To cover (ground, a distance) by 'trekking'. *S. Afr.*

1890 SIR F. YOUNG *Winter Tour S. Africa* 118 The ground which I have myself treked.

2. *trans.* To draw or drag (a vehicle): said of oxen and other beasts of draught. Also *absol.*

1863 W. C. BALDWIN *Afr. Hunting* vi. 152 My oxen could not possibly trek my wagon through the heavy sands in their present condition. *Ibid.* viii. 309 We ultimately got the ox tied up to the wagon-wheel,..inspanned him next morning, and he treks well. 1893 H. M. DOUGHTY *Wherry in Wendish L.* 53 A farm horse..which trekked us for four or five miles.

'trekker. [f. TREK *v.* + -ER[1].] **a.** In *S.Afr.* contexts: one who 'treks'.

1851 R. GRAY *Jrnl. Bishop's Visitation Tour through Cape Colony in 1850* 27 Only a few of the latest trekkers have a friendly feeling towards the English government. 1891 *Times* 13 May 5/3 The committee of trekkers are having a copy taken..of the original documentary treaty. 1905 *Ibid.* 4 Sept. 6/1 A score of trekkers [of the British Association] started in the morning in mule wagons for Kimberley. 1973 *Sunday Times* (Johannesburg) 9 Dec., Many Coloureds.. trekked to..the Cape Flats, but unlike other trekkers before them there was no promised land.

b. A person travelling a long distance, esp. on foot; *spec.* a rambler or hiker. Cf. *pony-trekker* s.v. PONY *sb.* 7 b.

1932 *Sun* (Baltimore) 7 Jan. 2/5 The main body of the small army marching from Pennsylvania..is not expected until late tonight... The trekkers..found no difficulty in obtaining admission to the gallery. 1939 R. GODDEN *Black Narcissus* iv. 39 It isn't even on the route that the trekkers take. 1968 *Punch* 14 Aug. 234/2 The Association has 'on call' about seventy ponies—for sixty trekkers, six experienced guides, and a few spares. 1977 *Times Lit. Suppl.* 13 May 595/2 It will just about go into the side pocket of your rucksack, and no intelligent trekker should go off to Gurung country without one. 1984 *Times* 18 Feb. 14/1 In their hearts trekkers are all pilgrims.

trekkie ('trɛkɪ). [f. TREK *sb.* + -IE.]

1. *S. Afr.* A small group of trekkers.

1888 J. BIRD tr. *D. P. Bezuidenhout's Narrative* in *Annals of Natal* I. 367 Five men were first sent forward to seek a road to the Drakensberg... A small 'trekkie' (party of emigrants) had preceded us. 1953 J. COLLIN-SMITH *Locusts & Wild Honey* I. i. 10 It was a bright autumn morning when we had inspanned the sixteen oxen, and the wagon wheels had turned, and the little trekkie had started away.

2. Also **Trekkie.** An admirer of the U.S. science fiction television programme *Star Trek*; hence, a space-traveller; one interested (trivially) in space travel.

In S. Africa the form *trekker* is also used for this sense.

1976 *New Yorker* 16 Feb. 39 (*caption*) Of course, I didn't know George was a Trekkie when I married him. 1977 *Time* 15 Aug. 50/2 Berry admits that his first trekkies would not know where they might emerge or if they would ever get back. 1978 *Sunday Sun* (Brisbane) 17 Sept. 45/3 Fans—called Trekkies—still number in their tens of thousands. 1981 *Space World* Aug.–Sept. 6/3 Many of the [L-5] society's other members were considered space Trekkies more interested in social experimentation than in technology. 1983 *Oxf. Univ. Press (N.Y.) Spring Catal.* 27 The audience for science fiction now runs the gamut from the high school 'trekkie' to the serious literary scholar.

'trekking, *vbl. sb.* and *ppl. a.* [f. TREK *v.* + -ING[1], [2].] Going on a 'trek' (see TREK *sb.*); *spec.* = *pony-trekking* s.v. PONY *sb.* 7 b.

1850 R. G. CUMMING *Hunter's Life S. Afr.* (1902) 28/2 We ..came upon an immense, compact herd of several thousand 'trekking' springboks. 1858 SIMMONDS *Dict. Trade*, *Trekking*, a colonial term in the Cape colony, for departing or leaving to settle in another country. 1901 *Scotsman* 7 Mar., Heavy rains made trekking almost impossible. 1942 ZUCKERMAN & BERNAL in S. Zuckerman *From Apes to Warlords* (1978) vii. 143 The situation in Hull has been somewhat obscured..by the occurrence of trekking, which was made possible by the availability of road transport. 1955 *Times* 22 July 9/6 About 35,000 came last year, and more are expected this summer... They come to fish and shoot or to trek in the mountains. 'Only the English like trekking,' one agent said. 1962 *Times* 21 Apr. 11/3 There is also a list of trekking and riding holiday centres which have been awarded a certificate of approval. 1968 *Punch* 14 Aug. 234/3 While some of the ponies probably would be kept in any case..the majority are now kept principally for the revenue from the trekking. 1972 [see TREK *sb.* 1 a]. 1976 *Horse & Hound* 3 Dec. 42/4 His book is well illustrated and there are some useful appendices, though that claiming to list a brief selection of trekking centres in fact is so brief as to be almost comic. 1984 *Times* 18 Feb. 14/1 Trekking has an aura which is irresistible to the romantic.

‖**trekschuit, treck-** ('trɛkskɔɪt, ‖-sxœyt). Forms: α. 7 draggescutte; 7–9 track-, 7–8 -scoute, 8 -skuit, 8 (9) -scoot, 8–9 -s(c)huyt, (8 trachtscoot, tract-scout); β. 8–9 treck-, 8 -schuyte, -scuit, -scoit, -scute, -scoot, 8–9 -schuit, 9 -schuyt, -shwytt, -shut, 8 trekschuyt, 9 trekschuit. (Cf. forms of SCHUIT, SCOUT *sb.*[3], SHOUT *sb.*[1]) [Du. *trekschuit*, formerly -*schuyt*, f. *trek* sb. or *trek*- vb.-stem of *trekken* to draw, pull, tug + *schuit*, MDu. *schûte* = MLG., LG. *schûte* boat, barge:—OTeut. **skûtô*, ME. *schûte*, ON. *skúta*: see SCHUIT and SHOUT *sb.*[1]] A canal- or river-boat drawn by horses, carrying passengers and goods, as in common use in Holland; a track-boat.

1696 *Caldwell Papers* (Maitl. Cl.) I. 174, 13 June. I went to Bruxelles in a Draggescutte. *Ibid.* 176 July 1st. I went in the Trackscoute fra y[re] to Bruges. 1711 ADDISON *Spect.* No. 130 ¶4 As the Trekschuyt, or Hackney-boat, which carries Passengers from Leyden to Amsterdam, was putting off [etc.]. 1737 G. SMITH *Curious Relat.* I. i. 99 We took our Lodgings at the first Inn..where the Treckscutes landed. 1756 MRS. CALDERWOOD in *Coltness Collect.* (Maitl. Cl.) 131 There is no treck-scoot goes from Helvest. 1769 *De Foe's Tour Gt. Brit.* III. 278 We should then travel with as much Safety, Certainty, and Dispatch, as in the Trachtscoots in Holland and Flanders. 1769 FALCONER *Dict. Marine* (1789), *Tract-scout*, a vessel employed to carry goods or passengers up and down the rivers or canals. 1772 *Tour Holland*, etc. 26 On Monday evening we went in the treckschuyte to Leyden. 1783 WESLEY *Jrnl.* 16 June, We set out in a track-skuit for the Hague. 1796 MORSE *Amer. Geog.* II. 335 Covered boats, called treckscuits, which are dragged along the canals by horses. 1816 SOUTHEY *Poet's Pilgr.* I. 26 Beside the busy wharf the Trekschuit rides. 1846 THACKERAY *Cornhill to Cairo* xv, Harmlessly as if we had been in a Dutch trackschuyt. 1893 STEVENSON *Catriona* xxii. 262, I.. arranged..to send on my chests by track-scoot to an address I had in Leyden. 1902 *Westm. Gaz.* 17 Nov. 3/2 It is a change from the tearing of motor-cars to note the slow progress of the *trekschuit*.

‖**trek-tow** ('trɛktəʊ). *S. Africa.* Also **tracktoe, trektou(w).** [Cape Du., f. Du. *trek* sb. or vb.-stem (see TREK) + *touw* rope, cord, tow.] The central chain or cable of twisted hide attached to a wagon-pole, to which the yokes of the oxen are fastened.

1822 W. J. BURCHELL *Trav. Interior S. Afr.* I. 151 The trektouw (draw rope or trace), is a long rope made of twisted thongs of raw hide, made fast by a hook to the staple at the end of the pole, and having iron rings attached to it at proper distances, into which rings the yokes are hooked. 1834 PRINGLE *Afr. Sk.* ii. 141 A strong central trace (trektow), formed of twisted thongs of bullock's or buffalo's hide. 1835 A. SMITH *Diary* 8 June (1940) II. 60 In this river the crocodile abounds; one carried off and swallowed a tracktoe belonging to a trader. [*Note*] Trek-touw, or draught rope. 1850 R. G. CUMMING *Hunter's Life S. Afr.* (ed. 2) I. 24 The waggon is steered by a pole, called the dissel-boom, to the end of which is fastened the trektow, a stout rope formed of raw buffalo-hide. 1939 S. CLOETE *Watch for Dawn* ii. 26 As the wagon topped the rise they trotted down with slack trek-tous. 1972 A. SCHOLEFIELD *Wild Dog Running* 214, I didn't know how many had been in the pride but two bullocks had been killed where they stood. A third had been dragged some yards from the *trektou*, the strong leather thong around his neck snapped like cotton.

trelapse, -er, variant of TRILAPSE, -ER.

trele, obs. form of TRAIL *sb.*[2]

treles, -ez, obs. forms of TRELLIS.

†**trellis,** *sb.*[1] *Obs.*: see TREILLIS.

trellis ('trɛlɪs), *sb.*[2] Forms: 5–6 trelis, -ys, -es(e, 5 -ez, tril(l)es, 5–6 traylles, 6 treliss, -ies, trallace, treylles, trellesse, 7 trellize, treillis, 7–9 trellice, 8 trellies, 6– trellis. *Pl.* 5–6 trelis, -iz; 6 trelesez, treyl(le)sys, trellisses, 7 -izes; 9 -ises. *β. Sc.* 5 terlys, 6 trelies, traleis, tarlies, traylles, treylles, treilȝeis, (trailzeys), tirleise, -lis, tyrleis, 6–7 tirleis, -lies, 7 tirlace, 8 -lass, -less. [ME. a. OF. *treliz*, *-is*, fem. *trelice* (orig. adj.):—late pop. L. **trilīci-us*, f. L. *trilīx*, *-līcem* (in Isidore nom. *trilīcis*) = Gr. τρίμιτος, having three threads in the warp, f. L. *tri-* three + *līcium* a thread of the warp; said of strong woven fabrics (cf. TREILLIS). OF. had also a rarer form *tresliz*, showing an early confusion of the prefix with OF. *tres-*:—L. *trans-*: so Pr. *treslitz*, It. *traliccio*, med.L. *trans-*, *trās-*, *trālīcium*, a stout woven fabric. The application of the word to things woven of iron wire, gold, withes, etc. app. brought the sense into contact with OF. *treille*, Pr. *treilla*, *trelha*, med.L. *trelia*, *trillia*, etc. (see TRAIL *sb.*[2]), and resulted in the later F. form *treillis* and the later signification 'lattice, grille'. Some of the 16th c. Scottish forms are difficult to distinguish from the pl. of *treilȝe*, TRAILYE.]

1. a. A structure of light bars of wood or metal crossing each other at intervals and fastened where they cross, with open square spaces between; used as a screen in window openings or the like; a window, gate, screen, etc. so constructed; a lattice; a grating. Now *rare.*

*a*1400–50 Treles [implied in TRELLIS *v.* 1]. 1422 Trelys [see *trellis-window* in 3]. *c*1440 *Promp. Parv.* 501/2 Trelys, of a wyndow, or oþer lyke (or grate..), *cancellus.* 1450–1 *Durham Acc. Rolls* (Surtees) 240 Et in ij Trelis emp. pro fenestra cove, vij d. 1498–9 *Ibid.* 101 Pro iij fenistris voc. trelez pro Scaccario Cellerarii et le Sethynghous. 1513–14 *Ibid.* 663 Pro ij trelesez ad ustrinum, vj d. 1531–2 *Durham Househ. Bk.* (Surtees) 74 Et Roberto Kyrver pro factura le treylsys 8 d. 1532–3 *Ibid.* 163 Pro factura le trellyesys. 1535 COVERDALE *Judg.* v. 28 His mother..cried piteously thorow the trallace. —— *Prov.* vii. 6 Out of the wyndowe of my house I loked thorow the trelies. 1549 *Aberdeen Regr.* (1844) I. 271 Conuikit..for the strublance of Duncane Freser and ryving of his tirleise of his vyndok. 1553–4 *Burgh Rec. Edinb.* (1871) II. 285 Payit for ane tyrleis of irne to the portell of the counsal hous dure. 1582–8 *Hist. James VI* (1825) 46 Upoun the wyndo thairof, he..cuttit a small hole of the blak cloth that coverit the traleis. 1634 SIR T. HERBERT *Trav.* 49 The Windowes [at Gombroon]..in stead of Glasse vse wooden trellizes or casements. 1641 R. BAILLIE *Lett.* (Bann. Cl.) I. 316 (*Trial of Strafford*) At the back of the throne, there was two roomes on the two sydes; in the one did Duke de Vanden ..and other French nobles sitt; in the other, the King, the Queen [etc.]; the tirlies, that made them to be secret, the King brake doun with his own hands; so they satt in the eye of all. 1768 STERNE *Sent. Journ.* (1775) II. 86 (*Passport, Hotel Paris*) The bird..attempting his deliverance, and thrusting his head through the trellis, pressed his breast against it, as if impatient. 1886 SHELDON *Flaubert's Salammbô* 21 Darting..glances through the golden trellises into the silent apartments.

†**b.** An enclosure of lattice-work, a grating.

*c*1500 *Melusine* lii. 329 Whan they that were in the traylles of yron herd it. 1555–6 *Burgh Rec. Edinb.* (1871) II. 364 Item, coft vij jestis to be ane tirleis to the deid banis at the south kirk dur. *Ibid.*, Item to Hennislie to cast the deid banis in the west tirleis iij s. **1593** *Rites of Durham* (Surtees 1903) 37 Y^e highte of ye said trellesse was striken full of iron pikes ..to thentent y^t none should clyme ouer it.

c. Short for *trellis-door* or *-gate*: see 3. *Sc.*

?*c* **1800** *State, Fraser of Fraserfield* 194 (Jam.) At or near the westmost pole—there is a tirlass, at which a single person may enter.

d. *Her.* The figure of a trellis used as a charge. ***in trellis***, with the pieces of which the charge is composed crossing and nailed at the joints, not interlacing.

1823 SCOTT *Quentin D.* xxxiii, Sable, a musion passant Or, oppressed with a trellis gules, cloué of the second. **1882** CUSSANS *Her.* vii. (ed. 3) 120 Portcullis: An iron gate formed of bars armed at the base, and bolted in trellis. **1889** [see TRELLISED 2 b].

e. Short for *trellis stitch*: see 3.

1912 L. F. PESEL *Stitches from Old Eng. Embroideries* 19 (*caption*) Trellis with cross-stitch couching. **1921** A. G. I. CHRISTIE *Samplers & Stitches* v. 57 Trellis is used for solid fillings.

2. A similar framework used as a support upon which fruit-trees or climbing plants are trained.

1513 DOUGLAS *Æneis* XII. Prol. 100 The wyne grapis ȝing Endlang the treilȝeis [ed. **1553** trailzeys] dyd on twystis hing. **1725** *Bradley's Fam. Dict.* s.v. *Pomegranate*, He must ..take Care to plash all the Branches..against a Trellis made on purpose. **1766** *Compl. Farmer* s.v., Some persons.. erect trellises against their walls, extending from the inside of one pier to the nearest inside of the next. **1818** SHELLEY *Let. to Mrs. Shelley* 20 Aug., The vines are..trailed on low trellisses of reeds. **1850** *Beck's Florist* Feb. 59, I always fix the trellis on the pot at the time of potting.

fig. **1861** S. WILBERFORCE *Let.* in *Life* (1881) II. xiii. 454 The earthly love becomes the trellice, up which the heavenly love creeps. **1894** H. DRUMMOND *Ascent Man* 193 Language formed the trellis on which Mind climbed upward.

3. *attrib.* and *Comb.*, as ***trellis-border, -door, -frame, -gate, -grating, -hut, -lace, -pattern; trellis-covered, -shaded, -woven*** adjs.; **trellis stitch**, in embroidery or knitting, an arrangement of stitches between parallel lines to give a lattice effect; **trellis-window**, a window furnished with a trellis; see also quot. 1913. See also TRELLIS-WORK.

1897 *Daily News* 12 Apr. 7/7 A pair of beakers, with baskets and sprays of flowers in *trellis borders. **1867** LADY HERBERT *Cradle L.* i. 14 The ladies..were conducted by black eunuchs through *trellis-covered walks. **1756** MRS. CALDERWOOD in *Coltness Collect.* (Maitl. Cl.) 219 They's chapells!..and a fine dressed-up Virgin in every one of them, and a *tirless door to let her be seen! **1897** R. N. BAIN tr. *Jókai's Pretty Michal* xxxii. 251 At the stroke of two, she was already in the shop below, the trellis-door of which, leading to the street, was closed. **1766** *Compl. Farmer* s.v. *Trellis*, For peach, nectarine, and apricot trees..the squares of the *trellis frame should not exceed three or four inches. **1697** in *Mem. Alloa* (1874) 66 To put on a *tirlace gate, with lock and key thereto. **1825** JAMIESON (1882), *Tirless-yett*, a turnstile. **1876** B. CHAMPNEYS in Willis & Clark *Cambridge* (1886) III. 238 *Trellis gratings fitted with adjustable valves. **1825** HONE *Every-day Bk.* I. 289 This saint lived in a *trellis hut. **1874** H. H. COLE *Catal. Ind. Art S. Kens. Mus.* 173 Bracelet. *Trellis pattern of plain and green glass beads. **1921** A. G. I. CHRISTIE *Samplers & Stitches* v. 57 The thread for working *Trellis stitch should be untwisted for the best effect to be gained. **1974** *Guardian* 26 Jan. 15/2 Trellis, moss and blackberry stitch by which..Aran mothers recognise their drowned sons. **1422** *Searchers Verdicts* in *Surtees Misc.* (1888) 16 The *trelys wyndowe at the somer hall. *a* **1651** CALDERWOOD *Hist. Kirk* (1843) II. 11 So Bothwellhauche shott at him with a hacquebutt, through a tirleis window. **1913** EDEN *Anc. Glass* 51 The branches of the tree or vine seemed to run in and out of a trellis, a circumstance which has given name to such windows—trellis windows. **1751** G. WEST *Education* xvii, Labyrinths involv'd and *trellice-woven bow'rs.

trellis ('trɛlɪs), *v.* Forms: see prec. [Almost always in pa. pple. *trellised* ('trɛlɪst), f. prec. + -ED. Cf. F. *treillisé* (14th c. in Godef. *Compl.*).]

1. *trans.* To furnish with a trellis or with lattice-work; to enclose in a trellis or grating.

a **1400-50** *Alexander* 3343 Þe thrid [step] of a Topas a-tyred & trelest & grauen. *c* **1470** HENRY *Wallace* XI. 197 A fell lyoun..With in a barrace,..Terlyst in yrn. **1593** *Rites of Durham* (Surtees 1903) 37 Aboue ye said dor, it was like-waies trellessed almoste to ye hight of ye valt aboue. **1634** SIR T. HERBERT *Trav.* 61 Windowes trellized very curiously. **1816** GALT *Life B. West* 92 Near a pile of ruins fringed and trellissed with ivy. **1883** 'VERNON LEE' in *Mag. Art* Nov. 3/1 Two villages, with..paved lanes trellised with grapes.

fig. **1873** E. BRENNAN *Witch of Nemi* etc. 224 Some love that trelliseth the heart.

2. *intr.* To make a trellis. *rare.*

c **1520** *Mem. Ripon* (Surtees) III. 202 Will'mo Caruer trelyssyng et carvyng per j diem, 6*d.*

3. *trans.* To train (a plant) upon a trellis; to support on or as on a trellis. Also *fig.*

1818 SHELLEY *Jrnl.* 26 Mar., The vines..are trellissed upon..stakes. **1849** RUSKIN *Sev. Lamps* iv. §34. 125 The living flowers..which..the French and Italian peasantry often trellis with exquisite taste about their casements. **1873** E. BRENNAN *Witch of Nemi* 5 A virgin round the summers of whose years Love trellissed joys to warp consuming fears.

trellised ('trɛlɪst), *ppl. a.* [f. TRELLIS *sb.*² or *v.* + -ED.]

1. Furnished with a trellis or trellis-work; formed of trellis-work; trained upon a trellis.

1472 *Durham Acc. Rolls* (Surtees) 94 Pro iiij Trillest-wyndous empt. pro coquina. **1513** DOUGLAS *Æneis* III. iii. 10 The full mone..In throw the tirlist wyndo schane by nycht. **1656** BLOUNT *Glossogr.*, *Trellised*, crosse-barred, latticed, grated, with wood. **1814** SOUTHEY *Roderick* XVI. 28 Their trelliced vines. **1844** LEVER *T. Burke* xxvii, The trellised walls covered with honeysuckles and wild roses. **1889** S. LANGDON *Appeal to Serpent* ii. 42 Assisting the tendrils of a beautiful passion-flower to grasp the next highest bar of a trellised arch.

2. a. Shaped or arranged like a trellis; having a pattern or markings resembling a trellis.

1664 POWER *Exp. Philos.* I. 5 The Common Fly..The like foraminulous perforations or trelliced eyes are in all Flyes. **1822** J. PARKINSON *Outl. Oryctol.* 40 Ramifications.. disposed in a trellised form. **1828** TYTLER *Hist. Scot.* (1864) I. 320 [The armour of David earl of Huntingdon] is of the species called by the contemporary Norman writers the 'trellissed', and consists of a cloth coat, or vest,..intersected by broad straps of leather, laid on so as to cross each other, but to leave intervening squares of the cloth, in the middle of which is a round knob or stud of steel. **1835-6** *Todd's Cycl. Anat.* I. 712/1 These *striæ*, ridges and furrows, may cross one another, and the shell is then trellised. *a* **1873** LYTTON *Ken. Chillingly* II. ix, Its..trellised [wall-]paper.

b. *Her.* = LATTICED 2 c.

1889 ELVIN *Dict. Her.*, *Treille* or *Trillise*, a Lattice, or Trellis, a pattern resembling fretty, but always nailed at each intersection; also termed Trellised cloué. **1894** in *Parker's Gloss. Her.* 586.

c. *Physical Geogr.* Of a drainage pattern: resembling the pattern of a vine growing on a trellis, with tributaries flowing in a direction approximately at right angles to the stream they join and bends in the main stream being approximately right-angled.

1895 *Monogr. Nat. Geogr. Soc.* No. I. vi. 186 (*caption*) On the head waters of Bluestone River..the branches are adjusted to tilted hard and soft beds, forming an example of 'trellised' drainage. **1937** WOOLDRIDGE & MORGAN *Physical Basis Geogr.* xiv. 192 In all such cases, whether the network of major valleys is rectangular or rhomboidal, the drainage plan may be described as 'trellised'. **1970** R. J. SMALL *Study of Landforms* vii. 227 The weaker strata are gradually eroded to form strike vales, separated by cuestas associated with the more resistant rocks, and are occupied by tributary streams which, with the passage of time, form an increasingly dominant component of the trellised pattern.

trellising ('trɛlɪsɪŋ), *vbl. sb.* [f. TRELLIS *v.* + -ING¹.]

1. The action of TRELLIS *v.*; the making of, or furnishing with, a trellis.

1474-5 *Durham Acc. Rolls* (Surtees) 95 Operantibus circa le trilessyng et facturam..fenestrarum.

2. *concr.* Trellis-work, a trellis.

1860 *All Year Round* No. 41. 341 A gallery, latticed like a dairy window, behind which birdcage trellising women were admitted. **1913** MRS. WHARTON *Custom of Country* I. ix, Under the leafless trellising of a wistaria arbour.

'trellis-work. [f. TRELLIS *sb.*² + WORK *sb.*] Wood or metal work consisting of light cross-bars; = TRELLIS *sb.*² 1. Hence, anything resembling this in structure or pattern. Also *attrib.*

1712 J. JAMES tr. *Le Blond's Gardening* 74 Cabinets of Trellis-work altogether plain. **1739** GRAY *Let. to West* 21 Nov., Trellis-works covered with vines. **1814** WORDSW. *White Doe* IV. 49 Shades Of trellis-work in long arcades. **1822-34** *Good's Study Med.* (ed. 4) IV. 99 The corpus spongiosum as well as the corpora cavernosa [of the penis] are divided into cells or trellis-work by an infinite number of fine membranous plates. **1878** STUBBS *Const. Hist.* III. xviii. 214 The two kings met, with a grating of trellis-work between them, on the bridge of Pecquigny. **1898** *Westm. Gaz.* 10 Mar. 3/2 A very charming blouse..is that with a trellis-work. **1898** *Daily News* 5 Sept. 5/1 The tomb..was whitewashed all over and surrounded by a trelliswork fence. **1908** [MISS FOWLER] *Betw. Trent & Ancholme* 10 A Clematis Montana, surrounding the trellis-work frame.

Tremadoc (trɪ'mædɒk). *Geol.* The name of a village in Gwynedd, N. Wales, used *attrib.* to designate a series of Tremadocian rocks (see next) about 300 metres thick that form the top of the Harlech Dome and comprise mudstones, shales, and slates; also, more widely, = next.

1847 A. SEDGWICK in *Q. Jrnl. Geol. Soc.* III. 145 The anomalous position of the Tremadoc rocks,..and the dislocation of the beds above noticed along the Merioneth coast, were probably all produced by the same set of disturbing forces. *Ibid.* 157 The Festiniog or the Tremadoc group. **1882** A. GEIKIE *Text-bk. Geol.* 655, 12 species of lamellibranchs from the Tremadoc beds of Ramsay Island and St. David's. **1885** C. LYELL *Student's Elem. Geol.* (ed. 4) xxviii. 448 Mr. Callaway has shown that the Shineton shale of Shropshire is of Lower Tremadoc age. *Ibid.*, *Orthoceras sericeum* and *Cyrtoceras præcox* are of the Upper Tremadocs. **1938** A. K. WELLS *Outl. Hist. Geol.* iii. 20 The graptolites.. had made their first appearance in Tremadoc (Upper Cambrian) times. **1970** R. M. BLACK *Elements Palaeont.* xiv. 222 Primitive pterobranchs are found in rocks of Tremadoc age. **1974** *Encycl. Brit. Micropædia* X. 108/3 Important Tremadoc sequences are..known from Australia.

Tremadocian (trɛmə'dɒkɪən), *a. Geol.* [f. prec. + -IAN.] Of, pertaining to, or designating a stratigraphic series typified by the Tremadoc beds, orig. placed in the Upper Cambrian but now sometimes regarded as Lower Ordovician. Also *absol.*

1910 W. G. FEARNSIDES in Monckton & Herries *Geol. in Field* xxxii. 795 Across the denuded edges of Tremadocian and Olenidian rocks rest the basal members of the great Arenig series. **1927** *Q. Jrnl. Geol. Soc.* LXXXVIII. 145 The order of that succession is applicable in all its detail to the type-area of the Tremadocian in the western parts of Wales. **1950** DAVID & BROWN *Geol. Commonw. Austral.* I. iii. 135 By Tremadocian time graptolites had begun to make their appearance in Victoria. **1974** *Nature* 18 Oct. 575/1 None of the formal papers included any discussion of the boundaries of the Ordovician, most speakers making it clear whether they regarded the Tremadocian as Cambrian (as in English usage) or Ordovician.

trematode ('trɛmətəʊd), *a.* and *sb. Zool.* [ad. mod.L. *Trĕmatōda* neut. pl., a. Gr. τρηματώδης having holes, perforated, f. τρῆμα hole, orifice.]

A. *adj.* Belonging to the class or order *Trematoda* or *Trematoidea* of parasitic worms, found in the bodies of various animals, having a flattish or cylindrical form, with skin often perforated by pores, and usually furnished with adhesive suckers; the flukes (FLUKE *sb.*¹ 2) are typical examples.

In Cuvier's classification the *Trematoda* constituted the second family of parenchymatous entozoa, containing besides the flukes some animals not now reckoned as trematodes.

1836-9 *Todd's Cycl. Anat.* II. 121/1 The Trematode Order..includes only two species infesting the human body. **1864** *Reader* 3 Dec. 712/1 He had discovered upon the angel-fish (*Squatina angelus*) a trematode worm of very singular organization, which will constitute a new genus. **1867** J. HOGG *Microsc.* II. iii. 567 One of the most remarkable of the Trematode helminths is Bilharzia haematobia of Cobbold. **1876** *Beneden's Anim. Parasites* Introd., Cestode and trematode worms.

B. *sb.* A trematode worm.

1859 [see BILHARZIA, BILHARZIA]. **1876** tr. *Wagner's Gen. Pathol.* 120 Trematodes are parasitic solitary flat-worms with inarticulate leaf-shaped bodies. **1877** [see BILHARZIA, BILHARZIA]. **1904** *Brit. Med. Jrnl.* 17 Sept. 663 Sections of a minute adult trematode. **1905** *Q. Rev.* Apr. 488 The pearls in our fresh water mussel were formed by the larvae of a fluke (a trematode). **1962** J. D. SMYTH *Introd. Animal Parasitol.* xiii. 138 The great majority of digenetic trematodes are inhabitants of the vertebrate alimentary canal or its associated organs.

So **'trematoid** *a.* and *sb.*

1882 OGILVIE (Annandale), Trematode, Trematoid, *a.* **1891** *Cent. Dict.*, Trematoid, *a.* and *n.*

†**'tremblable,** *a. Obs. rare.* [f. TREMBLE *v.* + -ABLE; cf. OF. *tremblable* (Godef.).] Fitted to cause trembling or fear; **a.** Demanding reverential fear; **b.** Causing dread or horror; dreadful.

1560 DAUS tr. *Sleidane's Comm.* 318 That the Canon of the Masse..be spoken softlye, to the intente those tremblable misteries maye retaine theyr auncient dignities. **1609** G. BENSON *Serm.*, etc. 72 Which is tremblable and monstrous, there be some, who, when God smites them, they fly vnto a witch or an Inchauntresse, and call for succour. **1651** R. WITTIE tr. *Primrose's Pop. Err.* II. vi. 93 In this Country the Consumption is an evill so ordinary and tremblable.

tremblant ('trɛmblənt), *a.* [f. TREMBLE *v.* + -ANT¹.] Of an ornament, jewel, etc.: incorporating springs or fine projecting wires which tremble or vibrate when affected by movement.

1970 *Times* 26 Mar. 12 A very fine diamond tremblant brooch in the shape of a five-petalled flower brought the same price. **1973** *Country Life* 13 Dec. (Suppl.) 32*b* A late 18th Century diamond head ornament, the sunburst tremblant. **1979** *Ibid.* 3 May (Suppl.) 56/1 A mid Victorian ruby and diamond tremblant spray brooch.

tremble ('trɛmb(ə)l), *sb.* Forms: see the verb. [f. TREMBLE *v.*]

1. An act or the action of trembling; a fit or state of trembling; a tremor; a vibration.

1609 BIBLE (Douay) *2 Esdras* xv. 37 They shal shake..and tremble shal take them. **1677** *Phil. Trans.* XII. 836 (According to him) Sound may be caused by the tremble of solid bodies without the presence of gross Air. **1719**, **1760-72** [see b]. **1775** ASH, *Tremble* (s. *colloquial*, from the verb), a tremor. **1848** DICKENS *Dombey* xxvii, A terrible tremble crept over her whole frame. **1884** T. WOOLNER *Silenus* I. II. 21 Sitting beside the reeds He saw a tremble shivering thro' their leaves. **1894** 'IAN MACLAREN' *Bonnie Brier Bush, Cunning Sp. Drumtochty* (1895) 185 He micht gie a bit trimmil.

b. In colloq. phrases ***(all) in, all of a tremble, on*** or ***upon the tremble***, trembling, esp. with agitation or excitement.

1719 MISS HOWE in *Lett. C'tess Suffolk* (1824) I. 39 Mama has invited me to stay here,..which put me in such a tremble that I am hardly recovered. **1760-72** H. BROOKE *Fool of Qual.* (1809) II. 151, I am already all of a tremble. **1800** LAMB *Let. to Manning*, I am still on the tremble, for I do not know where we could go. **1818** COLERIDGE in *Lit. Rem.* (1836) I. 206 Why should I be in such a tremble all the while he talked? **1830** *Chron.* in *Ann. Reg.* 35/2 He seemed all of a totter and tremble.

c. Tremulousness or unsteadiness (of the voice) caused by emotion.

1779 *Mirror* No. 54 ¶ 13 There is a melting tremble in her voice, which..is inimitably beautiful and affecting. **1848** DICKENS *Dombey* xxxiii, A deep impassioned earnestness.. that made the very tremble in her voice a part of her firmness.

2. *pl.* ***the trembles***: Any disease or condition characterized by an involuntary shaking, as ague or palsy (esp. in sheep); the tremor due to mercurialism, delirium tremens, etc.; the 'shakes'; in N. Amer., milk-sickness (MILK *sb.* 10).

1812 J. WALKER *Ess. Nat. Hist.* 525 Ovis in pascuis montosis morbo obnoxia est, hactenus insanabili,..the Trembles. **1848** A. S. TAYLOR *Poisons* xxxiii. 561 The disease produced by the use of the flesh or milk of animals fed in these districts, is known under the name of milk-sickness, or *trembles*. **1860** MAYNE *Expos. Lex.*, *Trembles*, a popular term for the disorder mercurial tremor. **1864** HAWTHORNE *S. Felton* (1883) 321 A hardness of hearing, and a dimness of sight, and the trembles. **1865** DICKENS *Mut. Fr.* IV. viii, What are popularly called 'the trembles' being in full force upon him. **1887** *Buck's Handbk. Med. Sc.* V. 9/1 The flesh of an animal suffering from trembles.. would also produce the disease [milk-sickness].

3. The American aspen, *Populus tremuloides*.

1749 in *Rep. Comm. Ho. Comm.* II. 246/2 (Hudson's Bay Co.) The Beavers chiefest Food is, the Poplar or Tremble. **1770** J. R. FORSTER tr. *Kalm's Trav. N. Amer.* (1772) II. 356 They likewise make use of those which grow on the asp-tree or tremble.

†**tremble**, *a. Obs. rare*$^{-1}$. [ad. L. *tremulus*, after next.] Trembling.

1568 TURNER *Herbal* III. 81 To be geuen.. vnto them that haue the palsey, or any num or tremble member.

tremble ('trɛmb(ə)l), *v.* Forms: *α.* 4–5 **tremle, -el, -yl,** (4 **trenle,** *Sc.* **tremal**), 5 **-ylle, -ul, trymmel,** 5–6 *Sc.* **tri-, trymle,** 6 *Sc.* **trimm-, trymm-, -le, -yll,** etc., **trumle,** 9 *Sc.* **trimmil;** *β.* 4–6 **trem-,** (**trim-, trym-**), **-bel, -byl,** etc., (6 **trumbill**), 4– **tremble.** [a. F. *trembler* (11th c. in Godef. *Compl.*):—pop. and med.L. *tremulāre* (Du Cange), by which the early *tremel*, *-le*, *-yl* form may have been influenced, f. L. *tremul-us* tremulous, f. *tremĕre* to tremble, quake, shake. Cf. Prov. *tremblar*, Sp. *temblar*, It. *tremolare*.]

1. *intr.* Of persons (less commonly of animals), or of the body or a limb: To shake involuntarily as with fear or other emotion, cold, or weakness; to quake, quiver, shiver.

1303 R. BRUNNE *Handl. Synne* 9390 Hys herte began to tremle and colde. **13..** *St. Cristofer* 629 in Horstm. *Altengl. Leg.* (1881) 461 For ferde he tremlide ylka bone. *c* **1375** *Sc. Leg. Saints* xvi. (*Magdalena*) 877 He tremaland, as he mocht. *Ibid.* xxxiii. (*George*) 257 Fast tremeland. **1412–20** LYDG. *Chron. Troy* III. 5425, I.. þat.. Fele myn hond boþe tremble and quake. **1413** *Pilgr. Sowle* (Caxton 1483) I. xv. 11, I tremble as doth a leef vpon a tree. *c* **1475** *Rauf Coilȝear* 458 Trewlie that tenefull [a tiger] was trimland than. **1514** BARCLAY *Cyt. & Uplondyshm.* (Percy Soc.) 6 We tremble naked, and dye almost for colde. **1598** SYLVESTER *Du Bartas* II. i. III. *Furies* 204 At every word they trimbléd then for aw. *a* **1668** DAVENANT *Siege* II. i, I tremble like a tender Lamb, In a cold Winter night. **1681** FLAVEL *Meth. Grace* ix. 192 The bird that has been delivered out of the tallons of the hawk, trembles afterward at the noise of his bells. **1797** MRS. RADCLIFFE *Italian* i, He trembled with anxiety. **1820** W. IRVING *Sketch Bk.* I. 51, I felt Leslie's hand tremble on my arm. *a* **1850** ROSSETTI *Dante & Circ.* I. (1874) 94 Gives me full oft a fear that trembleth: So that I call on Death. *Ibid.* 167 Ah! Ballad, unto thy dear offices I do commend my soul, thus trembling.

b. *fig.* and *rhet.* To be affected with dread or apprehension, or with any feeling that is accompanied by trembling. Const. *at*, *for*, *to do* something.

c **1400** *Apol. Loll.* 55 W[h]o is þe formar and original cause .. of þis þus gret iuel, I drede ungly to sey, tremel and quake. **1552** LYNDESAY *Monarche* 6018, I trimyll tyll heir tell The terribyll Turmentyng of hell. **1562** WINȜET *Last Blast* Wks. (S.T.S.) I. 40 We exhorte ȝow.. to feir and trimble at the feirfull exemplis of deid. **1717** LADY M. W. MONTAGU *Let. to C'tess Bristol* 1 Apr., The Grand Signior, with all his absolute power, trembles at a janissary's frown. **1766** GRAY *Kingsgate* 6 Earl Goodwin trembled for his neighbouring sand. **1778** COWPER *Hymn*, '*What various hindrances we meet*' iii, Satan trembles when he sees The weakest saint upon his knees. **1815** SHELLEY *Dæmon* 282 While human tongues Tremble to speak. **1911** MARET *Anthropol.* ii. 43 Then man presumably killed game.. on top of the Wealden dome, how many years ago one trembles to think.

2. Of things: To be agitated or affected with vibratory motion; to shake, quake, quiver.

c **1374** CHAUCER *Boeth.* I. met. i. 1 (Camb. MS.) The slake skyn tremblyth of myn emptyd body. *c* **1375** *Cursor M.* 24413 (Fairf.) þe erþ be-gan to tremble & quake. **1484** CAXTON *Fables of Æsop* IV. xiv, Whan the toune is taken.. the Country aboute.. ouȝt to tremble and shake. **1555** EDEN *Decades* 322 The poynt of the needle styll respected the northe.. sauynge that it sumwhat trembeled and declyned a lyttle. **1697** DRYDEN *Æneid* x. 418 They run their ships aground: the vessels knock,.. and tremble with the shock. **1827** CARLYLE *Misc.*, *Richter* (1869) 20 Then began the Aeolian Harp of the Creation to tremble and to sound. **1908** [MISS FOWLER] *Betw. Trent & Ancholme* 39 A little Harebell trembling in the breeze.

b. Said of the tremulous or vibratory motion or effect of light, sound, speech, etc.

c **1400** [see TREMBLING *vbl. sb.*]. *c* **1440** *Partonope* 5790 Wyth voys tremelyng. *a* **1628**, **1634** [see TREMBLING *ppl. a.*]. **1708** POPE *Ode St. Cecilia* 17 In broken air, trembling, the wild music floats. *Ibid.* 114 Yet ev'n in death.. Eurydice still trembled on his tongue. **1737** —— *Imit. Hor.* II. vi. 189 Tell how the Moon-beam trembling falls. **1821** SHELLEY *Epipsych.* 548 Where the pebble-paven shore.. Trembles and sparkles as with ecstasy. **1842** TENNYSON *Vision of Sin* 17 Low voluptuous music winding trembled.

c. *fig.*

1819 SHELLEY *Fragm.*, *Questions* 8 A dream, Part of which comes true, and part Beats and trembles in the heart. *a* **1862** BUCKLE *Civiliz.* (1869) III. iii. 121 The liberties of Scotland .. were trembling in the balance.

†**3.** *trans.* To regard with trembling or dread; to tremble at. (Cf. L. *tremĕre*.) *Obs. rare.*

1382 WYCLIF *Isa.* lxvi. 2 To whom.. shall I beholde, but to my porelet [Vulg. *pauperculum*] and contrit in spirit, and tremblende [*trementem*] my wrdis? **1450–1530** *Myrr. our Ladye* 185 Thy mother, whome the companyes of helles tremel and drede. **1565** T. STAPLETON *Fortr. Faith* 104 That whiche.. the deuil, aboue al thinges, trembleth.

4. To cause to tremble or shake.

1591 SPENSER *Virg. Gnat* 616 Either Scipion.. To whom the ruin'd walls of Carthage vow'd, Trembling their forces, sound their praises lowd. **1649** G. DANIEL *Trinarch.*, *Hen. V*, xxv, The Palsey of the common Earth, Trembles my Quill. **1651** W. DURHAM *Maran-atha* (1652) 11 It was much that a prisoner should so soon tremble his Judge. **1746** TANSUR *New Mus. Gram.* 23 A Shake, or Trilloe,.. is to shake, tremble, or warble your Voice, or Instrument. **1818** KEATS *Endym.* I. 468 Thou art as a dove Trembling its closed eyes. **1850** MRS. BROWNING *Woman's Shortcomings* ii, She trembles her fan.

5. *intr.* To pass tremulously. Chiefly *poet.*

1730–46 THOMSON *Autumn* 151 Soon as the morning trembles o'er the sky And unperceived unfolds the spreading day. **1795** COLERIDGE *Eolian Harp* 46 Organic Harps.. That tremble into thought. *a* **1817** T. DWIGHT *Trav. New Eng.* etc. (1821) II. 413 With a snail-like progress .. we trembled through this part of our way. **1842** TENNYSON *Talking Oak* 161 A teardrop trembled from its source. **1864** LOWELL *Fireside Trav.* 295 On the dial of time the shadow has not yet trembled over the line that marks the beginning of the first century.

6. *trans.* ***tremble out***: To utter tremulously or falteringly.

1868 ADAH I. MENKEN *Infelicia* 35 And trembling out prayers, and waiting to die.

Hence '**trembled** *ppl. a.*, made to tremble.

1819 KEATS *Ode to Psyche* 11 The whispering roof Of leaves and trembled blossoms.

tremblement ('trɛmb(ə)lmənt). [a. F. *tremblement* (15th c. in Godef.), f. *trembler* to TREMBLE: see -MENT.]

1. The action or condition of trembling (*lit.* and *fig.*); vibration, agitation; also, an instance of this, a tremor.

1677 GALE *Crt. Gentiles* II. IV. 147 It is.. vapors within the bowels of the earth, raised up by subterraneous fires that cause Earthquakes and Tremblements. **1844** MRS. BROWNING *Lost Bower* iv, The wood.. Thrills in leafy tremblement. **1867** JEAN INGELOW *Christ's Resurrect.* xvii, The waiting world doth quake with mortal tremblement.

2. A cause of trembling; a terror. *rare.*

1677 GALE *Crt. Gentiles* II. IV. 131 Some read it thus, 'Ephraim was a tremblement to him that heard him', i.e. so long as he kept close to God he was formidable to al his enemies. **1895** *Daily News* 27 May 8/3 Italian villains, pirate marquises, 'and almost every possible tremblement'—fierce wars and faithful loves—do moralise his song.

‖**3.** *Mus.* (trɑ̃bləmɑ̃) = SHAKE *sb.*[1] 5, TRILL *sb.*[2] 1 b.

[**1883** GROVE *Dict. Music* III. 479 Shake or trill (Fr. *trille*, formerly *tremblement*).] **1884** F. NIECKS *Conc. Dict. Mus. Terms* s.v., *Tremblement* (Fr.), a shake. **1893** E. DANNREUTHER *Mus. Ornamentation* I. xiv. 100 In the Méthode the tremblements are generally marked [*sign given*]. **1915** A. DOLMETSCH *Interpret. of Music of 17th & 18th Centuries* iv. 163 The 'Tremblement et Pincé' is a shake with a Turn as termination. **1946** E. BLOM *Everyman's Dict. Music* 482/1 *Tremblement appuyé* = prepared shake. **1978** *Early Music* Oct. 517/2, I have left aside certain details, for example, whether the *tremblement* is to be played slowly at first and increasing in speed, or is to be trilled equally throughout.

trembler ('trɛmblə(r)). [f. TREMBLE *v.* + -ER[1]: cf. F. *trembleur*.] One who or that which trembles.

1. One who trembles, esp. with fear; a timorous or terrified person.

1552 HULOET, Trembler, *tremulus*, *i.* *a* **1660** HAMMOND *Serm. Matt.* xi. 30 Wks. 1684 IV. 479 Those base submissions, that the covetous Mammonist or cowardly trembler drudges under. **1770** GOLDSM. *Des. Vill.* 199 Well had the boding tremblers learned to trace The day's disasters in his morning face. **1878** SEELEY *Stein* II. 531 A frightened trembler and maker of obeisances.

†**2.** A name given to those whose devotional exercises were accompanied by trembling, quaking, or shaking; *spec.* a Quaker. *Obs.* or *Hist.*

[**1678** R. BARCLAY *Apol. Quakers* xi. §8 (1736) 359 Sometimes the Power of God will break forth;.. every individual will be strongly exercised, as in a Day of Battle; and there-by Trembling and a Motion of Body will be upon most, if not upon all:.. And from this, the Name of Quakers, i.e. Tremblers, was first Reproachfully cast upon us.] **1689** R. WARE *Foxes & Firebrands* III. 198 These Sectaries.. be as follows: 1 Independents.. 17 Quakers, or Tremblers. **1706** E. WARD *Hud. Rediv.* xv. 21 Of these quaint primitive Dissemblers, In old queen Bess's Days call'd Tremblers. *a* **1741** CHALKLEY *Wks.* (1766) 101, I was one called a Quaker, or Trembler. **1820** tr. *Trav. Cosmo III* (1821) 447 The sect of the Tremblers or Quakers was begun by James Naylor.

3. *transf.* Applied to **a.** a fish which gives an electric shock, as the electric eel of Africa; **b.** a bird or other animal which keeps up a shaking motion of the tail or body.

1832 LYELL *Princ. Geol.* II. 106 The trembler, or *Silurus electricus* [belongs] to the rivers of Africa. **1867** SCLATER & SALVIN *Exotic Ornithol.* Pl. x, *Cinclocerthia ruficauda*, (Red-tailed Trembler). **1911** WEBSTER, *Trembler*, any of certain West Indian birds of the genera *Cinclocerthia* and *Rhamphocinclus*, of the family *Mimidæ*.

4. *Electr.* A vibrating spring blade which alternately makes and breaks the circuit in an induction coil. Also, such a blade used as a make-and-break sensitive to physical disturbance.

1877 *Telegr. Jrnl.* 15 Nov. 280/1 M. Trouvé, Paris, has made some improvements in the contact-breaker or trembler of induction coils. *Ibid.*, Vibrating stem of the trembler. **1903** *Motor. Ann.* 80 Troubles.. caused through the petrol, float-jet, or tremblers not having been understood by the motorist. **1907** *Daily News* 10 Apr. 6 Next the trembler in the coil stuck, and the engine stopped. **1943** N. BALCHIN *Small Back Room* xv. 185 It was the terminals I had to get wires on to, not the trembler. **1958** A. B. HARTLEY *Unexploded Bomb* ii. 13 When the bomb struck its target.. the shock caused the trembler to function and electrically to ignite the flash-pellet in the base of the fuze. **1973** J. DRUMMOND *Bang! Bang!* xii. 26 A Banx is an anti-personnel device... Set it for time-fuse, or a trigger-action, even a trembler. **1978** R. JANSSON *News Caper* 8, I held the control column rock steady, as if it were a bomb with a trembler fuse.

5. *attrib.* (in sense 4), as ***trembler-blade***, ***-coil***; **trembler-bell**, an electric bell rung by a hammer attached to a trembler; also called ***trembling bell***.

1884 in *Jrnl. Franklin Inst.* (1886) CXXI. Supp. 69 Audible signals are given.. on board the locomotive by a *trembler bell. **1905** PREECE & SIVEWRIGHT *Telegraphy* (new ed.) 254 There are many forms of these trembler bells, but the principle in all is alike. **1904** in *Westm. Gaz.* 28 May 5/3 The *trembler blade which governs the spark, and is in its turn controlled by the movement of the motor. **1908** *Ibid.* 6 Feb. 4/2 The ignition is effected by high-tension magneto and accumulator with *trembler-coil and self-starting switch.

‖**trembleuse** (trɑ̃blœz), *a.* or *sb. attrib.* [F., fem. of *trembleur* trembler; cf. Littré, '*Trembleuse*, tasse retenue dans sa soucoupe par une sorte de galerie'.] In ***trembleuse cup***, a cup having a saucer with a 'well', into which it fits so as to be kept from falling off. Also as *sb. absol.*

1869 C. SCHREIBER *Jrnl.* 17 June (1911) I. 13 A pair of Trembleuses and Stands, ruby glass, with white Smalto inside.. £7. **1883** *Daily News* 26 June 3/1 Sale of.. china.. a gros bleu trembleuse cup and saucer, exotic birds, 95*l.* **1893** *Auction Catal. Porcelain Cassiobury Park* 5 Old Sèvres Porcelain. 20. A Trembleuse Cup, Cover and Saucer. **1894** *Times* 16 June 7/6 A trembleuse cup and saucer, with landscape and trophies in medallions on white and gold ground.

trembling ('trɛmblɪŋ), *vbl. sb.* [f. TREMBLE *v.* + -ING[1].] The action of the verb TREMBLE in various senses; in quot. 1902, *spec.* ague in sheep (see TREMBLE *sb.* 2).

1303 R. BRUNNE *Handl. Synne* 4912 Ȝyf he lerne gylerye Fals wurde and feynt trenlyng [*v.r.* tremlynge]. **1382** WYCLIF *Eph.* vi. 5 Seruauntis, obeysche ȝe to fleishly lordis with drede and tremblyng, in symplenesse of ȝoure herte, as to Crist. *c* **1400** *Song Roland* 54 Trymlinge of tabers And tymbring soft. *c* **1440** *Promp. Parv.* 501/2 Tremelynge, or qwakynge, *tremor*. **1526** *Pilgr. Perf.* (W. de W. 1531) 112 b, Transformynge our gesture or countenaunce, as in tremblynge. **1647** H. MORE *Song of Soul* II. App. iv, All my spirits move with pleasant trembeling. **1693** LUTTRELL *Brief Rel.* (1857) III. 25 A ship from Jamaica brings that the earth there had some tremblings again. **1809–10** COLERIDGE *Friend* (1865) 2 At the sound of the word trembling came upon me. **1902** N. MUNRO in *Blackw. Mag.* Nov. 602/2 Sheep has been lost by the trembling.

b. *attrib.*, as ***trembling fit***; †**trembling-stop**, a tremolo organ-stop.

1659 LEAK *Waterwks.* 34 The Systemes and Measures of the Organ Pipes,.. also of the manner of the Registers,.. the Trembling stop, &c. **1856** KANE *Arct. Explor.* I. xvi. 191 Men.. were seized with trembling-fits and short breath.

'**trembling**, *ppl. a.* [f. as prec. + -ING[2].]

a. That trembles, in various senses of the verb.

a **1400–50** *Alexander* 4914 (Ashm. MS.) Þe testre trased full of trones with trimballand wingis. **1526** *Pilgr. Perf.* (W. de W. 1531) 257 With tremblynge herte and holy fere, thynkyng hym selfe vnworthy to touche that moost holy body. *c* **1614** SIR W. MURE *Dido & Æneas* I. 269 A contrare blast Doth force his saile against the trembling mast. *a* **1628** SIR J. BEAUMONT *Bosworth F.* 66 Which like a twinkling Star, with trembling Light Sends radiant Lustre through the darksome Air. **1634** SIR T. HERBERT *Trav.* 207 The lookers on incessantly warble out soft trembling Musique. **1797** MRS. RADCLIFFE *Italian* xi, It was delivered in.. low and trembling accents. **1877** FROUDE *Short Stud.* (1883) IV. I. x. 122 [He] let in the trembling wretches who had been shut out.

b. *transf.* Characterized or accompanied by trembling.

c **1430** LYDG. *Min. Poems*, *Pater Noster*, Atwyxe dred and tremblyng reuerence Astoned I am. **1613** SHAKS. *Hen. VIII*, I. ii. 95 Sixt part of each? A trembling contribution. **1794** BLAKE *Songs Exper.*, *Little Boy Lost* 10 In trembling zeal he seized his hair. **1818** SCOTT *Br. Lamm.* xxxv, To the butler's trembling entreaties.. he at first returned no answer.

c. In specific applications: **trembling aixies** or **exies** (cf. ACCESS *sb.* 10), the ague (*Sc.*); **trembling beef**, some dish of boiled beef (? *obs.*); cf. *trembling-piece*; **trembling bog**, bog-land formed over water or soft mud, which shakes at every tread, a quaking bog; so ***trembling prairie***, in Louisiana, U.S.A.; **trembling-chair**: see quot.; **trembling eel**, the gymnotus; **trembling-grass**, quaking-grass (*Briza media*); **trembling-ill**, the ague in sheep (*Sc.*); **trembling palsy**, paralysis characterized by trembling of the extremities or the head (*Syd. Soc. Lex.*, 1899); **trembling-piece** [F. *pièce tremblante*], a joint of beef so interlarded with fat as to quiver; **trembling-poplar**, the Aspen,

Populus tremula, also the N. American *P. tremuloides*.

1808–18 JAMIESON, *Trembling Fevers*, the ague, Ang. *Trembling Aixes [*ed.* **1825** Exies]. **1818** SCOTT *Br. Lamm.* xi, The cookmaid in the trembling exies. **1806** A. HUNTER *Culina* (ed. 3) 238 *Trembling Beef. Take a brisket of beef, and boil it gently [etc.]. **1697** DRYDEN *Virg. Georg.* III. 653 He lives on standing Lakes, and *trembling Bogs. **1899** *Syd. Soc. Lex.*, **Trembling chair*, a vibrating chair used in the treatment of paralysis. **1807** JOYCE *Sci. Dialogues* xvi. (1846) 397 (*Electricity*) In Firmin's 'Natural History of Surinam' is some account of the *trembling eel. **1853** G. JOHNSTON *Bot. E. Bord.* 216 *Briza media*, *Trembling-grass: Quaking-grass. **1833** WILSON *Fr. & Eng. Dict.* s.v. *Tremblant*, *Trembling-piece. **1731** P. MILLER *Gardeners Dict.* s.v. Populus. The *Trembling Poplar, or Aspen-Tree. **1861** MISS PRATT *Flower. Pl.* V. 120 (Aspen, or **Trembling Poplar*) . . is a middle-sized tree.

tremblingly (ˈtrɛmblɪŋlɪ), *adv.* [f. prec. + -LY².] In a trembling manner; tremulously; with trembling; so as to tremble.

1552 HULOET, Tremblyngly, *trepidanter.* **1581** A. HALL *Iliad* x. 183 He stoode so tremblingly, That one full wel might heare his teeth togither so to shake. **1617** COLLINS *Def. Bp. Ely* I. i. 95 Tremblingly we referre them to the heauenly censure. **1733** POPE *Ess. Man* I. 11 Or touch, so tremblingly alive all o'er, To smart, and agonize at ev'ry pore? **1771** MME. D'ARBLAY *Early Diary* 3 July, That . . agonizing sensibility which is tremblingly alive to each emotion of sorrow. **1818** C. R. MATURIN *Women* I. ii. 40 Ignorant of music as a science, but 'tremblingly alive' to its influence, he listened. **1863** W. PHILLIPS *Speeches* viii. 217 Tremblingly anxious to save Garrison's life.

ˈtremblingness. *rare*⁻⁰. [f. as prec. + -NESS.] The state of trembling; tremulousness.

1727 BAILEY vol. II, *Tremulousness*, tremblingness.

tremblor (ˈtrɛmblɔː(r)). orig. and chiefly *U.S.* [Alteration of Sp. *temblor* shudder, (in Amer. Sp.) earthquake, influenced by Eng. TREMBLER.] An earthquake or earth tremor.

1913 C. C. GOODWIN *As I remember Them* 193 He . . received the sobriquet of 'Earthquake' Stewart, because of the theory that he put out, that the tremblors in California were caused . . by . . electrical disturbances in the air and in the earth near the surface. **1925** *N.Y. Times* 1 July 2/2 Dr. U. S. Grant . . does not agree with Prof. Goode that the same tremblors shook Montana and California. **1926** *Daily Colonist* (Victoria, B.C.) 1 July 1/5 Today's shocks occurred in areas more than 100 miles removed from the lower coast line, where tremblors were felt yesterday. **1977** *Chicago Tribune* 2 Oct. 1. 10/5 Californians, long accustomed to earthquake jitters, have become concerned over a rapid-fire series of minor tremblors along a 20-miles stretch of the mysterious San Andreas Fault.

trembly (ˈtrɛmblɪ), *a. colloq.* [f. TREMBLE *v.* or *sb.* + -Y¹.] Full of trembling; tremulous.

1848 LOWELL *Fable for Critics* (1865) 223 A single anemone trembly and rathe. **1848** DICKENS *Dombey* i, So trembly and shaky from head to foot. **1879** O. W. HOLMES *Archbishop & Gil Blas* 21 Is your voice a little trembly?

† **ˈtremebund**, *a. Sc. Obs.* [ad. L. *tremebundus* trembling, f. *tremĕre* to tremble.] Inclined to tremble; timorous, timid.

c **1560** A. SCOTT *Poems* (S.T.S.) xxvi. 56 Thay [women] . . ar of nature tremebund.

† **tremeˈfaction.** *Obs. rare.* [ad. late L. *tremefactiōn-em*, n. of action f. *tremefacĕre* to cause to tremble.] Shaking, trembling. So † **tremefacting** *ppl. a.*, that shakes or trembles.

1597 A. M. tr. *Guillemeau's Fr. Chirurg.* 28/2 The Chyrurgiane must, without anye tremefactione, vse the same [lancet]. **1599** —— tr. *Gabelhouer's Bk. Physicke* 197/2 The braynes of a Hare . . will præuent the tremefactione both of handes and feete. *Ibid.* 207/2 Croockede, and tremefactinge Ioynctes.

tremefy (ˈtrɛmɪfaɪ), *v. rare*⁻¹. [ad. L. *tremefacĕre* (see prec.), with -FY, prop. repr. L. *-ficāre*: cf. *satisfy*.] *trans.* To cause to tremble.

1832 J. WILSON in *Blackw. Mag.* XXXI. 424 A nod that tremefies Olympus.

tremel, obs. form of TREMBLE.

‖ **Tremella** (trɪˈmɛlə). *Bot.* [mod.L. (Dillenius 1741), dim. from *tremulus*, *-ula* shaking, shivering.] A genus of amorphous hymenomycetous fungi consisting of tremulous gelatinous substance, typical of the N.O. *Tremellaceæ* or *Tremellineæ*, most species of which grow on decayed wood, but a few on the ground.

Tremella auricula is known as Earth-jelly, *T. albida* as Fairy Bullet. *T. mesenterica* is conspicuous in dead hedges in winter from its orange tint.

1760 J. LEE *Introd. Bot.* Table i, Tremella, Cryptogamia, Algæ. **1778** LIGHTFOOT *Flora Scot.* II. 901 *Tremella purpurea* . . . Little red-knobb'd Tremella. **1786** THOMPSON in *Phil. Trans.* LXXVII. 124 Any thing resembling tremella or that kind of green matter, or water moss, which forms upon the bottom and sides of the vessel.

Hence **tremellaceous** (trɛməˈleɪʃəs) *a. Bot.*, pertaining to the *Tremellaceæ* or *Tremellineæ*; **treˈmelliform** *a. Bot.*, of the form of the thallus in *Tremella* (Webster, 1911); **treˈmellin** *Chem.* [cf. F. *trémelline* (Littré)], (see quot. 1868); **ˈtremelline** *a. Bot.*, pertaining to the genus *Tremella* or N.O. *Tremellineæ* (*Funk's Stand. Dict.*, 1895); **tremeˈllineous** *a. Bot.* = *tremellaceous*; **ˈtremelloid** *a. Bot.*, resembling *Tremella* in form or substance; **ˈtremellose** *a. Bot.*, shaking, like *Tremella*, tremulous.

1860 MAYNE *Expos. Lex.*, *Tremellin. **1868** WATTS *Dict. Chem.* V. 878 *Tr[emella] mesenterica* was found by Brandes to contain, in the dry state, . . 5 pts. of a peculiar crystallisable resinous body, called tremellin. **1860** MAYNE *Expos. Lex.*, *Tremelloides*, . . applied to a lichen, the membranous, delicate, and almost transparent expansions of which resemble those of the *Tremella*: *tremelloid. **1874** COOKE *Fungi* 72 Anomalous as it may at first sight appear to include these tremelloid forms with the dust-like fungi. **1887** W. PHILLIPS *Brit. Discomycetes* 333 *Calloria luteo-rubella* . . . Somewhat tremelloid. *Ibid.* 22 *Leotia lubrica* . . . Gregarious, somewhat cæspitose, *tremellose. *Ibid.* 420 *Tremellose*, shaking like jelly, of a jelly-like consistence.

† **treˈmend**, *a. Obs. rare.* [ad. L. *tremend-us*: see next.] = TREMENDOUS.

1581 MARBECK *Bk. Notes* 346 Earthquakes, Thunderings and Lightenings, be tokens and tastes of Gods most treme[n]d and dreadfull power. **1650** TRAPP *Comm. Deut.* x. 8 That sacred and tremend function of the ministery.

tremendous (trɪˈmɛndəs), *a.* Also 7–8 tremenduous; *dial.* and non-standard **tremenj(i)ous, treminjous**, etc. [f. L. *tremend-us* 'that is to be trembled at, fearful, dreadful, frightful, terrible', gerundive of *tremĕre* to tremble, tremble at: see -OUS. The by-form in *-uous* was shaped after adjs. from L. adjs. in *-uus*, as *conspicuous*.]

1. a. Such as to excite trembling, or awe; awful; 'dreadful; horrible; astonishingly terrible' (J.).

1632 LITHGOW *Trav.* x. 460 Hee, after many tremenduous threatnings, commanded the Scriuan to draw vp a Warrant. **1657–83** EVELYN *Hist. Relig.* viii. (1850) II. 17 Not blaspheming the tremendous name of God. **1661** BLOUNT *Glossogr.* (ed. 2), *Tremendous* . . , greatly to be feared. **1689** T. PLUNKET *Char. Gd. Commander* 44 But the tremenduos Tetragrammaton Will not, not always be a looker on. **1742** YOUNG *Nt. Th.* IV. 9 Black-boding man Receives, not suffers death's tremenduous blow. **1796** J. MOSER *Hermit of Caucasus* I. 166 Rocks, torrents, and all the variety of tremenduous scenery. **1803** JANE PORTER *Thaddeus* ix, The air . . was rendered livid and tremendous by long spires of fire. **1871** MACDUFF *Mem. Patmos* xi. 147 The Day, the Great day . . of His wrath . . . Now, to what does this tremendous description refer?

b. *absol.* That which is tremendous. *nonce-use.*

1742 YOUNG *Nt. Th.* v. 691 What heart of flesh Would trifle with tremendous? dare extremes? Yawn o'er the fate of infinite?

2. a. Hyperbolically, or as a mere intensive: Such as to excite wonder on account of its magnitude or violence; astounding; extraordinarily great; immense. (Cf. the similar use of *awful*, *frightful*, *terrible*, etc.) Also as quasi-*adv. colloq.*

1812 SOUTHEY *Ess.* (1832) I. 111 During the last forty years, a tremendous change has been going on. **1835** [see LATHERING *vbl. sb.*]. **1845** FORD *Handbk. Spain* I. 16 They . . drive at a tremendous pace. **1866** G. MACDONALD *Ann. Q. Neighb.* vi, A tremendous splash reached my ears from the pond. **1882** FLOYER *Unexpl. Baluchistan* 91 He . . evidently determined to smother his feelings in a tremendous dinner. **1886** R. D. BLACKMORE *Springhaven* in *Harper's Mag.* Oct. 755/1 Makes us pay tremenjious for 'most everything. **1888** KIPLING *Phantom 'Rickshaw* 92 Then ten men with bows and arrows ran down that valley, chasing twenty men with bows and arrows, and the row was tremenjus. **1892** 'Q' *I saw Three Ships* v. 97 'Ay, naybours all,' broke in Farmer Tresidder . . . 'I shudn' wonder if ye was to see me trottin' to Parlyment House in a gilded coach . . I be so tremenjous rich.' **1901** M. FRANKLIN *My Brilliant Career* xvii. 150, I thought them straps couldn't break only onder a tremenjous strain. *Ibid.* xix. 162 'How are you enjoying yourself?' . . 'Treminjous intoirely, sor.' **1952** M. ALLINGHAM *Tiger in Smoke* ii. 39 'Was it fun?' 'Tremenjous.' **1977** E. W. HILDICK *Loop* vii. 37 She had 'tremenjous powers of seeing the future'.

b. Extraordinary in respect of some quality indicated in context. *slang.*

1831 *Ch. Patronage Reporter* Jan. 26 Owing . . latterly to the tremendous state of the weather. **1847** HELPS *Friends in C.* I. vii. 117 Over-managing people . . are tremendous to live with. **1866** GEO. ELIOT *F. Holt* ii, This young Debarry is a tremendous fellow at the classics.

tremendously (trɪˈmɛndəslɪ), *adv.* [f. prec. + -LY².] In a tremendous manner or degree; dreadfully; hence *colloq.* as a hyperbolical intensive: Exceedingly, extremely, excessively, very greatly.

1680 BAXTER *Cath. Commun.* (1684) 36 And Peter oft, and once tremendously . . rebuk't by Christ. **1731** BAILEY, *Tremendously*, dreadingly. **1776** PENNANT *Zool.* (ed. 4) I. 177 White Owl: This species . . will often scream most tremendously. **1817** SOUTHEY *Ess.* (1832) II. 43 The game was of the same kind, though the stake differed tremendously in magnitude. **1863** W. C. BALDWIN *Afr. Hunting* ix. 394 If he should have gone, I shall have some tremendously hard work for nothing. **1904** *Yorks. Post* 9 Sept. 4/3 How tremendously costly a thing naval 'supremacy' has become.

tremendousness (trɪˈmɛndəsnɪs). [f. as prec. + -NESS.] The quality of being tremendous.

1727 BAILEY vol. II, *Tremendousness*, . . tremendous Quality, Worthiness to be feared or dreaded. **1851** H. MELVILLE *Whale* xli, The pre-eminent tremendousness of the great Sperm Whale. **1894** *Chicago Advance* 3 May, It is good . . to recognize the tremendousness of death. **1906** *19th Cent.* June 974 Æschylus overpowers us with his tremendousness.

‖ **tremendum** (trɛˈmɛndəm). [Shortened from MYSTERIUM TREMENDUM.] The overwhelming awe which can be part of religious experience.

1923 J. W. HARVEY tr. *Otto's Idea of Holy* iv. 12 (*heading*) The analysis of 'tremendum'. *Ibid.* 16 The elements which unfold as the 'tremendum' develops. **1930** A. G. HEBERT tr. *Brilioth's Eucharistic Faith & Practice* ii. 65 It is an expression for the awfulness of the holy, the *tremendum*, which belongs to all deep religion. **1950** [see NUMINOSUM]. **1960** R. F. C. HULL tr. *Jung's Coll. Wks.* III. 260 The originally chaotic or frightening impression is replaced by the picture, which, as it were, covers it up. The *tremendum* is . . made harmless and familiar.

‖ **tremie** (tremi). *Engin.* [F. *trémie*, OF. *tremuie*, *-uye* (mill-)hopper (*c* 1300 in Godef. *Compl.*) = It. *tramoggia*:—L. *trimodia* a three-peck measure, f. *tri-* three + *modius* peck.] A movable tube, widening at its upper end into a hopper, for depositing concrete under water.

1905 *Engineering Rec.* (N.Y.) 14 Jan. 53 Up to a height of 6 ft. below low water level, the concrete was deposited under water by means of a tremie. **1911** *Min. Proc. Inst. Civ. Engin.* CLXXXV. 9 The deposition of concrete . . by means of tremies operated from scows.

tremissis (trɪˈmɪsɪs). Also erron. **tremis(s.** Pl. **tremisses.** [late L., gen. sing. of *trēmis*, f. *trēs* three, after *sēmis* half an as: cf. SEMIS¹.] A late Roman or early Byzantine gold coin, the third part of a solidus; a Merovingian or other imitation of this.

1706 PHILLIPS (ed. Kersey), *Tremissis*, or *Golden Triens*, a Roman Gold Coin worth five Shillings Sterling. **1756** NUGENT *Montesquieu's Spir. Laws* (1758) II. XXII. ii. 72 The sou of two tremisses [F. *deux tremisses*] answered to an ox of twelve months. **1952** *Antiquity* XXVI. 77 All the coins from Sutton Hoo are tremisses (thirds of solidi). **1962** H. R. LOYN *Anglo-Saxon England* ii. 74 The *solidus* (or sou) was . . essentially . . the imperial coin reformed by Constantine; more frequent in Gaul was the *tremissis* (or *triens*), the third part of a sou. **1976** *Anglo-Saxon England* V. 176 Small Merovingian gold tremisses . . had been penetrating the south-east of England. *Ibid.* 177 There is considerable circumstantial evidence for the equation of a Merovingian tremissis with an Anglo-Saxon gold shilling. **1983** *Times* 6 Apr. 16/4 The discovery of a remarkable Visigothic *tremiss* minted in gold in Southern Gaul in AD 455–475, in the final levels of one site excavated in late 1982, shows that some form of 'urban' life continued until nearly the end of the fifth century.

tremle, obs. form of TREMBLE.

‖ **tremocˈtopus.** *Zool.* [mod.L., f. Gr. τρῆμα hole, pore + OCTOPUS.] A subgenus of Octopus having two large aquiferous pores on the back of the head.

1851 WOODWARD *Mollusca* I. 65 Between the branchiæ are two rows of brown or violet spots, like the pigment cells of the tremoctopus. **1878** BELL *Gegenbaur's Comp. Anat.* 327 Sometimes over a few of the arms only (4 in Tremoctopus), or over them all.

tremogram (ˈtrɛməgræm). [f. Gr. τρέμειν to tremble, quiver + -GRAM.] **a.** A tracing recording involuntary muscular motion. **b.** An irregularity characterizing a person's handwriting: see quot. 1907. So **ˈtremograph** [-GRAPH], an instrument for recording involuntary muscular tremor.

1899 *Syd. Soc. Lex.*, *Tremogram*, the tracing of tremor made by means of the Tremograph. **1904** G. S. HALL *Adolescence* I. iii. 145 The tremograph, a thimble attached to a pivoted lever moving freely in all directions, showed that children could not hold the index-finger still for half a minute. **1907** P. FRAZER in *Jrnl. Franklin Inst.* Apr. 268 The curious marginal irregularities which accompany and seem to a certain degree to characterize the handwriting of each writer, which I have called 'tremograms'.

‖ **tremolando** (tremoˈlando). *Mus.* Also **tremulando.** [It., pr. pple. of *tremolare* to shake, quaver, warble (Florio).] **a.** *adj.* (or *attrib.*) Tremulous, shaking. **b.** *adv.* In a tremulous or quivering manner; with a tremolo; used to indicate that a note or passage is to be thus rendered. **c.** *ellipt.* as *sb.* = TREMOLO 1, 2.

1852 SEIDEL *Organ* 24 Another absurd . . contrivance is the tremulando, a register which . . was to indicate the sobbing, sighing, and trembling of men. **1854** J. SCHUBERT *Mus. Hand-bk.* (ed. 4), *Tremolant*, a stop in german organs producing a tremolando effect. **1876–98** STAINER & BARRETT *Dict. Mus. Terms*, *Tremolando*, . . (1) A chord or note played or bowed with great rapidity so as to produce a quivering effect. (2) Vibration of the voice in singing, arising from nervousness or a bad production; or used for the purpose of producing a special effect. *Ibid.*, *Tremolant*, . . a fan-wheel by rotating in front of the wind chest causes a *tremolando*. **1887** *Athenæum* 26 Nov. 720/1 The violins accompany *tremolando* in descending thirds.

tremolant (ˈtrɛmələnt). [a. G. *tremolant*, ad. It. *tremolante*, TREMULANT.] = TREMOLO 2.

1854 [see prec.]. **1876–98** STAINER & BARRETT *Dict. Mus. Terms*, *Tremolant*, or *Tremulant*, an organ and harmonium stop which causes the air as it proceeds to the pipes or reeds to pass through a valve having a moveable top . . . The up and down movement of the top of the valve gives a vibratory movement to the air which similarly affects the sound produced.

tremolist ('trɛməlɪst). [f. TREMOLO + -IST.] One who uses the tremolo.

1927 *Proc. Musical Assoc. 1926–7* 18 The soprano tremolist is no longer tolerated. **1952** B. ULANOV *Hist. Jazz in Amer.* (1958) vi. 63 The first boogie-woogie crew, who must have influenced the second wave of C-major tremolists, the famous Chicagoans.

tremolite ('trɛməlaɪt). *Min.* [Named 1796, f. *Tremola*, in Switzerland, where found + -ITE[1].] A white or grey (sometimes transparent) variety of AMPHIBOLE, composed of magnesia and lime, with little or no iron, occurring in fibrous masses or thin-bladed crystals. Also called *grammatite*.

1799 KIRWAN *Geol. Ess.* 219 Not far from St. Gothard, it is found mixed with tremolite, and stratified. **1807** T. THOMSON *Chem.* (ed. 3) II. 476 *Tremolite*..is a compound of silica and lime, or perhaps rather carbonate of lime. **1834–5** J. PHILLIPS *Geol.* in *Encycl. Metrop.* VI. 563/1 That [*sc.* marble] of Glen Tilt, characterized by its accompanying tremolites, lies in a quartzose mica slate. **1849** DANA *Geol.* xvii. (1850) 631 Acicular crystals of white hornblende or tremolite.

Hence **tremo'litic** *a.*, of the nature of, or containing tremolite, as ***tremolitic marble***.

1879 DANA *Man. Geol.* (ed. 3) 70 Granular Limestone.. Varieties.—a. Statuary Marble;..Tremolitic; contains bladed crystallizations of..tremolite.

‖**tremolo** ('tremolo, anglicized 'trɛmələʊ). *Mus.* In 8 tremola; also 9 tremulo. [It. *tremolo* adj. trembling, shaking, quavering:—L. *tremul-us* TREMULOUS.]

1. A tremulous or vibrating effect produced on certain musical instruments or in the human voice in singing, esp. to express intensity of emotion: cf. VIBRATO.

[**1724** *Short Explic. For. Wds. in Mus. Bks.*, *Tremola*, to Tremble, a particular Grace in Musick.] **1801** BUSBY *Dict. Mus.*, *Tremolo*, *Tremolante*, or *Tremente*, a word intimating that the notes are to be drawn out with a tremulous motion. **1865** MISS BRADDON *Sir Jasper* xvii, The trickling arpeggios and treble tremulos of a modern nocturne were all-sufficient. **1884** H. C. DEACON in Grove *Dict. Mus.* IV. 166/2 The instrumental tremolo is more nearly allied to the vocal vibrato. Indeed, what is called 'vibrato' on bowed instruments is what would be 'tremolo' in vocal music.

attrib. **1896** *Godey's Mag.* Feb. 195/1 Some cheap melodramatic stuff with *tremolo* shudders in the orchestra.

b. *transf.* and *fig.*

1877 LOCKHART *Mine is Thine* xviii, Her back still turned and a tremolo in her voice. **1897** *Daily News* 23 Nov. 6/2 He [a writer] executes so many tremolos and elaborate modulations on his theme.

2. A mechanical contrivance in an organ by which such an effect is produced; a tremulant. Also ***tremolo stop***.

1867 AUG. J. E. WILSON *Vashti* xi, The..overwhelming pathos of the tones affected Dr. Grey much as the tremolo stop in some organ-overture in a dimly-lighted cathedral. **1869** M. J. MATTHEWS in *Eng. Mech.* 31 Dec. 385/3 A sixth is the 'tremolo', the least valuable of the lot.

tremor ('trɛmə(r), 'triːmə(r)), *sb.* Also 4–9 -our, 5 -oure. [ME. *tremour*, a. OF. *tremor*, *-our* fear, terror (13th c. in Godef.), also a trembling or quivering (15th c.):—L. *tremor*, *-ōrem*, f. *tremĕre* to tremble. In 17th c. reintroduced in L. form *tremor*.]

†**1.** Terror. *Obs.*

c **1374** CHAUCER *Troylus* v. 255 Swich a tremor [*v.r.* tremour] fele a-boute his herte That of þe feer his body sholde quake. **1490** CAXTON *Eneydos* xv. 60 To solace and dysporte thy self euermore wyth the thondre and weddrynges, for to gyue unto vs tremoure and feere. *Ibid.* xxii. 81 Horrible dremes & cruel, comen to-fore her in hir mynde that tormente her in tremoure merueyllous.

2. Involuntary agitation of the body or limbs, resulting from physical infirmity or from fear or other strong emotion; trembling: see quot. 1866.

[**1611** SHAKS. *Wint. T.* I. ii. 110, I haue *Tremor Cordis* on me: my heart daunces.] **1615** CROOKE *Body of Man* 401 The disease called Tremor, or the shaking palsie. **1762–71** H. WALPOLE *Vertue's Anecd. Paint.* (1786) IV. 154 His lips are contracted by tremor. **1807** *Med. Jrnl.* XVII. 428 An approach to syncope, accompanied with more or less of universal tremor, and spasmodic twitchings, are said to have occurred. **1866** A. FLINT *Princ. Med.* (1880) 815 Tremor, that is, alternate contraction and relaxation of muscles in rapid succession, is a symptom of certain lesions of the nervous centres.

b. With *a* and *pl.* An instance of this; a fit of trembling.

1616 BULLOKAR *Eng. Expos.*, *Tremour*, a trembling. **1731** ARBUTHNOT *Aliments* v. (1735) 146 By its styptick and stimulating Quality it [tea] affects the Nerves..occasioning Tremors. **1813** J. THOMSON *Lect. Inflam.* 97 A tremor of the hands is often lessened or removed, for a while, by a dram, or some strong wine. **1871** R. ELLIS *Catullus* lxiv. 305 To a tremor of age their gray infirmity rocking.

c. *fig.* A nervous thrill caused by emotion or excitement; also, a state of tremulous agitation or excitement.

1754 RICHARDSON *Grandison* IV. vii. 51 He ceased speaking. I was in tremors. **1814** SCOTT *Ld. of Isles* VI. ii, The tremors that unbidden rise. **1838** DICKENS *Nich. Nick.* xxviii, He went about all day in a tremor of delight. **1866** G. MACDONALD *Ann. Q. Neighb.* xii, [She] drew herself up very haughtily..to hide her tremor.

3. A tremulous or vibratory movement caused by some external impulse; a vibration, shaking, quivering. ***earth-tremor***, an earthquake.

1635 HEYWOOD *Hierarch.* IX. 570 One of these Tremors lasted forty dayes, When six and twenty tow'rs and castles fell. **1656** BLOUNT *Glossogr.*, *Tremor*, quaking, trembling, shaking, great fear, also an earthquake. **1728** PEMBERTON *Newton's Philos.* 270 Motion consequent upon the tremors of the air, excited by the vibrations of sonorous bodies. **1830** LYELL *Princ. Geol.* I. 324 All countries are liable to slight tremors..when some great crisis of subterranean movement agitates an adjoining volcanic region. **1853** KANE *Grinnell Exp.* xxix. (1856) 250 The peculiar tremor of a cotton-factory. **1878** HUXLEY *Physiogr.* 187 Waves or tremors may be propagated in all directions through the solid ground.

4. A tremble or quaver in the voice; a tremulous sound or note.

1797 MRS. RADCLIFFE *Italian* ii, The tremor of his voice.. heightened its eloquence. **1838** LYTTON *Calderon* ii, There seemed a touch of true feeling in the tremour of his rich sweet voice. **1866** G. MACDONALD *Ann. Q. Neighb.* xxxi, There was a tremor in the old lady's voice more of disappointment and hurt than of anger.

5. *attrib.*, as **tremor disk**, the telescopic image of a star, as apparently enlarged by the vibration of the telescope and of the atmosphere; **tremor storm**, a prolonged series of earth-tremors.

1889 MILNE in *Nature* 31 Oct. 658/1 At certain seasons tremor storms are very marked. **1905** H. F. NEWALL in *Athenæum* 29 Apr. 534/1 On the general design of spectrographs for equatorials of large aperture, considered from the point of view of 'tremor discs'.

Hence **'tremorful** *a. dial.*, **'tremorous** *a. rare*, full of tremor; tremulous.

1901 'ZACK' *Tales Dunstable Weir* 39 'I'll not go nigh the maid', Martin cried, sort of tremorful. **1907** F. THOMPSON *New Poems, Orient Ode* 28 The tremorous nurse of joy.

tremor ('trɛmə(r)), *v.* [f. the sb.] *intr.* To be agitated by a tremor or tremors; to shake or tremble.

1921 *Chambers's Jrnl.* XI. 858/1 The ship tremored, vibrated like mad. *Ibid.* 860/2 Her voice had tremor'd.. with urgency. **1926** M. WALSH *Key above Door* x. 113 His strong, big jowl was..tremoring with the chill. **1928** —— *While Rivers Run* vi. 68 His car was purring and tremoring. **1963** A. SMITH *Throw out Two Hands* xvi. 162 They [*sc.* zebras] went by in droves, and the earth tremored beneath them.

tremorine ('trɛməriːn). *Pharm.* [f. TREMOR *sb.* + -INE[5].] A crystalline compound, 1,4-dipyrrolidino-2-butyne, $C_{12}H_{20}N_2$, capable of inducing the symptoms of Parkinsonism and used in research into this disease.

1956 G. M. EVERETT in *Federation Proc.* XV. 420/2 'Tremorine', when given in doses of 5–20 mg/kg by all routes, produces a marked sustained tremor. **1970**, **1972** [see OXOTREMORINE]. **1976** *Nature* 15 July 221/2 Tremorine, which is oxidised *in vivo* to oxotremorine by mammals, showed only slight activity against ticks.

tremorless ('trɛməlɪs), *a.* [f. TREMOR *sb.* + -LESS.] Without tremor or excitement; untrembling, unshaken. Also *fig.*

1869 *Contemp. Rev.* XI. 43 A suicide, whose words, written just before he committed the act, prove his lucid and tremorless sanity. **1882** *Fraser's Mag.* XXV. 415 An albatross blown along by its outstretched tremorless wings. **1898** R. PRIMROSE in *Brit. Weekly* 6 Oct. 411/1 Brave men.. with tremorless souls the worst can face.

Hence **'tremorlessly** *adv.*, without tremor; without a ripple.

1890 CLARK RUSSELL *Ocean Trag.* III. xxxii. 187 The sea ..tremorlessly circling the island.

†**tremp,** *v. Obs. rare.* [a. F. *tremp-er*: see TRAMP *v.*[2]] *trans.* To mix, temper.

1480 CAXTON *Ovid's Met.* x. vii, She gaf hym a dranke, tremped wt herbes & wyne.

trempe, var. TRAMP *sb.*[2], temper. *Obs.*

tremulant ('trɛmjʊlənt), *a.* and *sb.* Also erron. -ent. [ad. *tremulānt-em*, pr. pple. of late L. *tremulāre* to TREMBLE; in B. 2 repr. It. *tremolante* in same sense.]

A. *adj.* Tremulous; trembling.

1837 CARLYLE *Fr. Rev.* I. v. ii, Hapless De Brézé; doomed to survive long ages, in men's memory, in this faint way, with tremulent white rod. **1884** *Pall Mall G.* 8 July 4/2 The Queen of the Opera can sing clean and firm, and with a touch of tremulant emotion, only just when and where it is wanted. **1899** *Allbutt's Syst. Med.* VI. 516 The muscular contractions which execute willed movements are themselves found..to be often slightly tremulant.

B. *sb. Mus.* **1.** = TREMOLO 2.

1862 *Catal. Internat. Exhib., Brit.* II. No. 3411, 9. Tremulant to swell. **1876** HILES *Catech. Organ* iii. (1878) 20 A Tremulant is a contrivance that gives to the tone of any department of an Organ to which it may be applied, a waving, or undulating effect. **1903** *Westm. Gaz.* 26 Mar. 8/1 The largest organ in the world is being built..for the St. Louis Exhibition of 1904... There are to be ninety-nine mechanical appliances, thirty-six couplers, five tremulants, and forty-eight adjustable pistons.

2. = TREMOLO 1.

1884 *Pall Mall G.* 30 Apr. 4/1 We strongly recommend Mesdames Durand and Laterner to subdue the tremulant in their voices.

tremulate ('trɛmjʊleɪt), *v. rare.* [f. late L. *tremulāre* to tremble (Quicherat *Addenda*): see -ATE[3] 5, 6.]

1. *intr.* To tremble, vibrate; to palpitate, quiver.

1749 ABP. RHYS *Tour Spain & Port.* (1760) 92 Tender Limbs, that tremulate and wanton in the air. **1768** [W. DONALDSON] *Life Sir B. Sapskull* I. xiv. 137 His heart flutter'd! and the whole man was tremulating with affection! **1813** T. BUSBY *Lucretius* II. IV. Comm. 34 The auditory nerve tremulates, and the brain is agitated.

2. *trans.* To cause to tremble or vibrate.

1764 GRAINGER *Sugar Cane* III. 205 The faint breeze oft flags on listless wings, Nor tremulates the cocos airiest arch. **1813** T. BUSBY *Lucretius* I. III. Comm. 8 No musician is provided..to tremulate the strings. *Ibid.* II. VI. Comm. 8 [The winds] tremulate whatever substances they encounter.

Hence **'tremulated, 'tremulating** *ppl. adjs.*

1813 T. BUSBY *Lucretius* I. II. 467 Those colours which.. Impress the tremulating nerves of sight. *Ibid.* II. IV. Comm. 27 Certain pulsations communicated to the air, by the tremulating organs of the voice. *Ibid.* 28 Substituting for his philosophy of vocal atoms, that of a tremulated medium.

tremulation (trɛmjʊ'leɪʃən). [n. of action f. TREMULATE: see -ATION.] The action or condition of trembling; an instance of this, a trembling.

1651 WITTIE *Primrose's Pop Err.* III. xiii. 173 Hence do palsies, tremulations, and other evils arise. **1665** HOOKE *Microgr.* lviii. 219, I have often taken notice of the tremulation of the Trees and Bushes. **1718** *Entertainer* No. 9. 67 Before most violent Eruptions of Mount Etna,..they feel Convulsions and Tremulations in the Earth thereabout. **1880** H. A. A. NICHOLLS in *Nature* 19 Feb. 373/2 The resistance to the volcanic force was too small to cause much tremulation.

tremulous ('trɛmjʊləs), *a.* [f. L. *tremul-us* trembling, quivering, shaking (f. *trem-ĕre* to tremble, shake) + -OUS.]

1. Of persons, their limbs, etc.: Characterized or affected by trembling or quivering from nervous agitation or weakness, of mental or physical origin; hence, fearful, timorous.

1611 SPEED *Hist. Gt. Brit.* IX. viii. (1623) 569 The Monkes [being] very tremulous to enter matter of new intrications. **1667** *Decay Chr. Piety* xi. 310 The tender tremulous Christian, 'tis easie to discern how much he must be distracted and amaz'd by them. **1714** R. FIDDES *Pract. Disc.* I. 310, I shall appear to be of an abject and tremulous spirit. **1784** COWPER *Task* II. 729 His voice unstrung Grew tremulous. **1897** R. HICHENS *Londoners* (1902) 101 She gained the purple drawing-room on rather tremulous feet.

b. Said of writing, a line, or the like, done by a tremulous hand; hence, finely wavy.

2. Of things: Characterized by trembling or vibration; vibratory; easily caused to vibrate or tremble.

1616 CHAPMAN *Homer's Hymns, To Mother of Gods* 4 That doth with Cymball sounds, delight her life; and tremulous diuisions of the Fife. **1664** POWER *Exp. Philos.* I. 21 In my long Telescope I can some days see a tremulous Motion and Agitation of rowling fumes, and strong Atoms in the air. **1774** GOLDSM. *Nat. Hist.* (1776) VI. 265 A tremulous motion which this animal [torpedo] is found to possess. **1815** J. SMITH *Panorama Sc. & Art* II. 497 Gelatine, or jelly,..has a soft tremulous consistence. **1860** FARRAR *Orig. Lang.* i. 6 The tremulous ripple on the surface of the sea.

b. Ready to vibrate in response *to* some influence; also *fig.* tremblingly sensitive or responsive.

1794 G. ADAMS *Nat. & Exp. Philos.* IV. xlix. 349 Columns of marble or porphyry are tremulous to thunder explosions, and to certain tones of an organ. **1867** H. MACMILLAN *Bible Teach.* i. (1870) 3 He is tremulous..to all the influences of the hour and scene.

†**3.** Affecting the organs of taste with a trembling or quivering sensation. *Obs. rare.*

1675 GREW *Disc. Tasts Plants* i. §15 Tasts are either Still, as usually; or may be called Tremulous, as the Heat produced by *Pyrethrum*. **1707** *Curios. in Husb. & Gard.* 39 Grew..finds in Plants sixteen sorts of Tastes... 16. Tremulous, as the Root of wild Pellitory.

4. Characterized by use of the tremolo in singing. (*nonce-use.*)

1884 *Pall Mall G.* 26 July 4/1 He quivered and shook himself all to pieces with the tremulous fever now so fashionable. **1887** *Daily News* 25 July 4/8 The tremulous vocalists one after the other failed to win popular favour.

tremulously ('trɛmjʊləslɪ), *adv.* [f. prec. + -LY[2].] In a tremulous manner; tremblingly.

1730–6 BAILEY (folio), *Tremulously*, with trembling, tremblingly. **1757** W. WILKIE *Epigon.* v. 127 Their lofty spires..O'er the pale ashes tremulously glow. **1811** SHELLEY *Let.* in Dowden *Life* (1886) I. iv. 167 Once I was tremulously alive to tones and scenes. **1886** *Manch. Exam.* 9 Jan. 5/1 The great Protestant and industrial interests stand tremulously on the watch.

tremulousness ('trɛmjʊləsnɪs). [f. as prec. + -NESS.] The state or quality of being tremulous.

1727 BAILEY vol. II, *Tremulousness*, tremblingness. **1755** JOHNSON, *Trill*, quaver; tremulousness of musick. **1817** J. EVANS *Excurs. Windsor*, etc. 74 His whole manner evidently marked by a nervous tremulousness. **1857** H. SPENCER in *Fraser's Mag.* Oct. 401/2 This tremulousness of voice is very effectively used by some vocalists.

tremyl, -ylle, obs. forms of TREMBLE.

tren, trenail: see TREE, TREEN, TREENAIL.

trench (trɛn(t)ʃ), *sb.* Also 4–7 trenche, (6 trenshe, *Sc.* treinch, trinch, -e, trynsch(e, trinsch(e, 7 trintch). See also TRANCHE. [a. OF. *trenche* (1288 in Godef.), later OF. and mod.F. *tranche*, an act of cutting, a cut, a gash; a ditch or trench; a slice, etc., verbal sb. from OF. *trenchier*, F. *trancher* to cut, TRENCH *v.* See also TRANCHE. Many of the Eng. senses, wanting or obs. in mod.F., are supplied by *tranchée*.]

†**1.** A path or track cut through a wood or forest; an alley; a hollow walk. *Obs.*

c 1386 CHAUCER *Sqr.'s T.* 384 And in a trench [*v.r.* trenche] forth in the park gooth she. *c* 1420 LYDG. *Thebes* I. in *Chaucer's Wks.* (1561) 358/2 As thei rengen the trenches by and by Thei heard a noise. 1575 TURBERV. *Venerie* 98 By this word Trench is vnderstoode euery small way, not so commonly vsed... So is there also a difference betweene a Trench and a path. For trenches as I say, be wayes and walkes in a woode or Forest.

2. a. A long and narrow hollow cut out of the ground, a cutting; a ditch, fosse; a deep furrow. Also *fig.*

1489 CAXTON *Faytes of A.* I. ix. 23 To lepen ouer trenchis or dyches. 1553 EDEN *Treat. Newe Ind.* (Arb.) 13 They moued neare vnto the trenche or ditche of the castell. 1677 YARRANTON *Eng. Improv.* 192 The River Dee must be carried in a large Cut or Trench through the lands..as far as Flint Castle, and then dropt by a large Cut, into the Deep Water below the Brewhouse. 1782 MISS BURNEY *Cecilia* VII. vi, How deep a trench of real misery do you sink, in order to raise this pile of fancied happiness! 1842 TENNYSON *Audley Court* 41 Be shot for sixpence in a battle-field, And shovell'd up into some bloody trench. 1911 J. WARD *Roman Era in Brit.* viii. 140 A single trench disclosed broken pottery and charcoal.

b. An elongated channel in the sea-bed; *spec.* one of the very long ones, several kilometres deep, that run parallel to the edge of a continent or an island arc and are believed to mark subduction zones.

1936 *Amer. Jrnl. Sci.* CCXXXI. 401 Recent discoveries of many valley-like trenches that interrupt the outer steeper slopes ('continental slopes') of continental shelves are truly startling. 1948 F. P. SHEPARD *Submarine Geol.* xi. 283 A series of deep trenches skirt the Pacific. 1963 G. L. PICKARD *Descriptive Physical Oceanogr.* ii. 10 The greatest depths in the oceans occur in these trenches. 1972, etc. [see SUBDUCTION 6]. 1975 *Offshore Engineer* Sept. 60/1 The Norwegian trench is a pitfall that has always tempered Norway's oil future. Crossing it is beyond the current state of pipeline technology. 1977 A. HALLAM *Planet Earth* 94 The island arcs and ocean trenches that border the northwest and southeast Pacific.

3. *Mil.* An excavation of the kind described in sense 2 a, the earth from which is thrown up in front as a parapet, serving either to cover or to oppose the advance of a besieging force. Chiefly in *plural*. **a.** More particularly applied to the ditch or excavation.

c 1500 *Three Kings Sons* 42 That ther might be made grete trenches, that ther might be grete nombre of people hid theryn. 1513 DOUGLAS *Æneis* XI. xvii. 104 Thai..delvys trynschis all the wallis about. *a* 1548 HALL *Chron., Hen. V*, 74 b, They without made mynes, cast trenches and shot gunnes dayly at the walles. 1623 MASSINGER *Bondman* II. i, There are trenches too..In which to stand all night to the knees in water In gallants breeds the tooth-ache. 1879 *Cassell's Techn. Educ.* II. 103/2 When this excavation is behind the mound it is called a trench.

b. *pl.* Including both the excavation and the mound or embankment: see quot. 1828. ***to mount, relieve the trenches***: see quot. 1706. ***to open trenches***: see OPEN *v.* 4 b, quot. 1853.

1585 T. WASHINGTON tr. *Nicholay's Voy.* I. xvii. 20 [They] did in the meane space diligently aduaunce their trenches and approaches for planting of their ordinance. 1607 SHAKS. *Cor.* I. vi. 12, I saw our party to their Trenches driuen. *a* 1674 CLARENDON *Hist. Reb.* XIII. §22 Cromwell knew them too well to fear them..when there were no Trenches..to keep him from them. 1706 PHILLIPS (ed. Kersey) s.v., Trenches are Works..either cut into the Ground..or else raised above it when rocky, with Bavins, Wool-packs, Bags or Baskets filled with Earth. *Ibid.*, *To Mount the Trenches*, is to go upon Duty in them. *To Relieve the Trenches*, is to relieve those that have been upon Duty there. 1777 WATSON *Philip II* (1839) 95 By the advice of Dragut he resolved to extend his trenches and batteries, on the side next to the town. 1828 J. M. SPEARMAN *Brit. Gunner* (ed. 2) 397 Trenches. A general term for all the approaches at a siege. 1848 LYTTON *Harold* VII. iii, On the other side of the trenches were marching against them their own countrymen.

†**c.** Sometimes more particularly applied to the rampart, mound, or embankment. *Obs.*

1536 BELLENDEN *Cron. Scot.* (1821) I. 160 To bring treis to fill the fowseis,..otheris maid sindry instrumentis to breke down thair trinschis. 1560 DAUS tr. *Sleidane's Comm.* 259 To bring yᵉ pionners to cast down their trenches. 1617 MORYSON *Itin.* II. 169 It was resolued that the ditches.. should bee deepned, and the trenches highthned. 1678 tr. *Gaya's Art of War* II. 113 A Trench, a casting up of Earth by way of Parapet, with a Ditch or Foss on the side of the Enemy. 1693 in *Macfarlane's Geog. Collect.* (S.H.S.) II. 218 Ane ruinous tour surrounded with ane trintch of stone and earth. 1726 LEONI *Alberti's Archit.* II. 100/1 Severus threw up a trench a hundred and twenty two miles long.

d. *fig.* or *transf.*

1601 R. JOHNSON *Kingd. & Commw.* (1603) 23 The sea, which to the inhabitants is a deep trench against hostile inuasions. 1677 GILPIN *Demonol.* (1867) 299 A soul that is within the trenches of present peace. 1723 MANDEVILLE *Fab. Bees* (1725) I. 66 Seducers..don't make their Attacks at Noon-day, but cut their Trenches at Night. 1970 G. JACKSON *Let.* 23 Mar. in *Soledad Brother* (1971) 188 I've been living in the trenches where it's understood that it's us against them, hide and seek. 1977 *Rolling Stone* 24 Mar. 13/2 He has been in the trenches too long not to be a master at mixing sincerity with evasiveness.

4. *transf.* Something resembling a trench. **a.** A cut, scar, furrow, or deep wrinkle in the face.

1588 SHAKS. *Tit. A.* V. ii. 23 Witnesse these Trenches made by griefe and care. 1823 SCOTT *Quentin D.* vii, 'Thou name ladies' love, with such a trench in thy visage!' said Guthrie. 1830 GODWIN *Cloudesley* II. xii. 185 Without trench or wrinkle, in his honest countenance.

b. *Anat.* and *Zool.* A cavity, pit, fossa.

1615 CROOKE *Body of Man* 392 That cauity which is commonly called..the Trench or Spoone of the heart. 1631 WIDDOWES *Nat. Philos.* 62 From the trench of the veynes hang downeward white, narrow veynes. 1634 T. JOHNSON tr. *Parey's Chirurg.* III. i. (1678) 54 The trench of the heart which..the Latines [called] *scrobiculus cordis*. 1846 DANA *Zooph.* (1848) 257 Bottom of trench convoluto-porous. *Ibid.* Gloss., *Trench* (Fossa), a meandering cell in the Meandrine Corals.

†**5.** A slice. Cf. TRANCHE. *Obs. rare.*

1558 WARDE tr. *Alexis' Secr.* (1559) 70 Take..sixe Lemons cut in trenches.

†**6.** A trencher. *Obs. rare.*

(Perh. only in pl. *trenches* for *trenchers*.)

1602 in *Collect. Archæol.* (1863) II. 105 Pottes and cruses xxx..Trenches viij dossen.

†**7.** = TRENCHEFIL, TRANCHEFIL (in both senses).

a. 1611 COTGR., *Trenchefile*,..the trench, or trenching of a Crossebow string; that part thereof whereinto the neb of the arrow entreth.

b. 1607 TOPSELL *Four-f. Beasts* (1658) 251 The Indians were wont to use no bridles..but only..putting a long round trench through his [the horse's] mouth, to the edge whereof they fasten the rains, wherewithall they guide the beast. 1614 MARKHAM *Cheap Husb.* I. ii. (1668) 16 Now and then drawing the trench to and fro in his Mouth. 1639 T. DE GRAY *Compl. Horsem.* 345 Tye it to his snaffle, trench, or bit. *c* 1720 W. GIBSON *Farrier's Dispens.* IX. iii. (1734) 201.

†**8.** A griping or colic in the horse; also, a kind of worm infesting the horse. [= F. *tranchée*; cf. Cotgr., '*Trenchée*.., a fretting, wringing, or griping in the bellie..; the wormes, or bellie-ache.'] *Obs.*

1578 LYTE *Dodoens* II. lxxiv. 246 It cureth the trenches or gryping payne in the small of the bellie or bowels. 1587 MASCALL *Govt. Cattle, Horses* (1596) 133.

9. *ellipt.* for *trench-coat*, see sense 10 below.

1972 *New Yorker* 14 Oct. 1 (Advt.), Bonwit's velvet rain trench plays matinees and evenings. 1974 [see MIDI-]. 1978 *N.Y. Times* 30 Mar. A9/3 (Advt.), Three styles for sizes 8 to 16. Double breasted trench for reg. and petite.

10. *attrib.* and *Comb.*, as ***trench-cutting, -digger, -digging, -fighting, -guard, kit, life, light, -lines, raid, raiding, rifle, strafing, system, war, -work***; ***trench-encircled, -like, -stale, trench-to-trench*** adjs.; **trench boot**, (usu. in *pl.*) combined boot and leggings; **trench-brace**, an extensible screw-brace or strut used to prevent the caving in of the side walls or to support the sheet-piling of a trench; **trench-cart** *Mil.*, a narrow hand-cart on which ammunition can be carried through the trenches; **trench-cavalier** *Mil.*, a high parapet constructed by the besiegers upon the glacis to command and enfilade the covered way of the fortress; **trench-coat**, a waterproofed overcoat worn by officers in the trenches; a long, belted raincoat for civilian use; hence **trench-coated** *adj.*; **trench-drain, trench-elm**: see quots.; **trench fever**, an epidemic louse-borne rickettsial disease that was common among soldiers in the war of 1914–18, causing splenomegaly and recurrent fever; **trench foot, feet**, a painful condition of the feet caused by prolonged immersion in cold water or mud, marked by swelling, blistering, and some degree of necrosis; **trench-kitchen** *Mil.*, a field-kitchen where the fire is made in a small trench; **trench-knife**, a knife with a double-edged blade, orig. used in trench raids; **trenchman**, a labourer who opens trenches for pipe-laying; †**trench-master**, an officer in charge of the construction of trenches; **trench mortar**, a small mortar designed to propel bombs from a front trench into enemy trenches; hence as *v. trans.*; **trench mouth**, Vincent's angina of the mouth (see VINCENT[2]); **trenchoscope** = next; **trench-periscope**, a kind of tube-and-mirror apparatus used in trench warfare (see quot. 1918 for *trenchscope* below); cf. prec. and PERISCOPE 3; **trench-planting**: see quot. 1905; **trench-rat**, the brown or Norway rat, *Rattus norvegicus*; **trenchscope** = *trench periscope* above; cf. also *trenchoscope* above; †**trench-sergeant**, cf. *trench-master*; **trench warfare**, hostilities carried on by means of or in trenches; also *fig.*, a protracted dispute or conflict in which the parties seek to maintain their entrenched positions while launching persistent attacks upon their opponents; cf. *trench war* above. See also TRENCH-PLOUGH.

1933 J. BUCHAN *Prince of Captivity* II. i. 132 He wore a tattered trench waterproof and..ancient *trench-boots. 1973 *Country Gentlemen's Mag.* Mar. 184/2 Officer's brown leather calf length trench boots..practically new. 1877 KNIGHT *Dict. Mech.*, *Trench-cart. 1834–47 J. S. MACAULAY *Field Fortif.* (1851) 234 A return is then made to the trench, and the whole of the end of each is converted into a *trench cavalier. 1853 STOCQUELER *Milit. Encycl.* 254/2 At the angle of the glacis, high breastworks, called trench cavaliers, are formed, to allow a plunging fire..to be directed into the covered-way. 1916 W. OWEN *Let.* 16 Aug. (1967) 405 My poor troops were wet to the bone. (But I had my *Trench Coat.) 1918 E. FERBER in *Best Short Stories of 1917* 209 Jo Hertz, in one of those pinch-waist belted suits and a trench coat..was a sight for mirth or pity. 1944 M. LASKI *Love on Supertax* xi. 107, I got a job in a trench-coat factory in Manchester. 1978 W. F. BUCKLEY *Stained Glass* xi. 109 A young man dressed in an old army trenchcoat walked slowly out, dragging his wooden leg like a ball and chain. 1941 N. ALLEY *I Witness* xxxv. 296, I compensated my desire with the wishful thought that I'd be running across his familiar *trench-coated figure some time later. 1980 *Listener* 29 May 697/3 A trench-coated Micawberish librarian. 1876 'OUIDA' *Winter City* vi, Palestrina often saw its lord..plan *trench-cuttings to arrest the winter-swollen brooks. 1770 LANGHORNE *Plutarch* (1851) II. 1045/2 Making excursions to harass the *trench-diggers. 1846 *J. Baxter's Libr. Pract. Agric.* (ed. 4) I. 153, I have often had fine crops [of carrots] upon poor soils by *trench-digging the land to the depth of twenty inches. 1805 R. W. DICKSON *Pract. Agric.* II. 923 *Trench Drain.—A deep ditch, or drain, which meets the trenches for the purpose of taking the water away speedily after the irrigation is performed. 1676 M. COOK *Forest-trees* xi. 50 The best sort [of Elm] is that which..shoots with a shoot not much less than a Sallow when it is lopped: it is called by some the *Trench-Elm, by others the Marsh-Elm. 1915 *Lancet* 25 Sept. 734/1 The case of a twice-inoculated soldier suffering from *trench fever, whose case was diagnosed as pyrexia. 1917 G. S. GORDON *Let.* 22 May (1943) 77 He says I've got what they call vaguely 'Trench' Fever. 1933 J. BUCHAN *Prince of Captivity* I. iii. 85 Blown-up, buried, dysentery, trench-fever, and most varieties of wounds. 1976 *West Lancs. Even. Gaz.* 13 Dec. 7/1 After convalescing in England from trench fever, he successfully applied for a commission. 1881 W. CORY *Lett. & Jrnls.* (1897) 468 A few bits of *trench-fighting. 1915 *Lancet* 17 Apr. 812/2 The term *trench-foot appears to us to be the most suitable for a condition which has practically only been met with in those who have had to remain for long periods in the trenches. 1916 W. S. CHURCHILL *Let.* 6 Jan. in M. Gilbert *Winston S. Churchill* (1972) III. Compan. II. 1359, I wish you wd write for me a brief description of your 'trench feet routine'. *a* 1918 W. OWEN *Poems* (1920) 23 But never..fever, trench-foot, shock, Untrapped the wretch. And death seemed still withheld. 1940 *War Illustr.* 12 Jan. 603/1 Though the men had plenty of food all were suffering from exposure and trench feet when they landed at a South Coast port. 1969 [see *immersion foot* s.v. IMMERSION 5]. *a* 1976 A. CHRISTIE *Autobiogr.* (1977) V. ii. 239 Half our patients seemed to be trench feet cases. 1982 *Times* 31 May 5/3 There have been cases of exposure and trench foot. 1903 O. CAUSTON in *Cornh. Mag.* Feb. 202 The long white *trench-graves on the summit move one more, perhaps, than any others in South Africa. 1849 JAS. GRANT *Kirkaldy of Gr.* xxviii, He drove the *trench-guards down the Lawn-market in disorder. 1914 *War Illustr.* 19 Dec. 416/1 He inspected their *trench kit of goatskins and strawbags. 1900 *Westm. Gaz.* 19 Jan. 2/1 The *trench kitchen is more generally used in South Africa. 1926 *Scribner's Mag.* Aug. 194/2 A Boche lad I killed with me *trench-knife. 1979 R. BLYTHE *View in Winter* iv. 188, I had a trench knife in one hand and a pistol in the other. 1917 W. OWEN *Let.* 15 Aug. (1967) 484 Nothing like his [*sc.* Sassoon's] *trench life sketches has ever been written. 1977 A. WILSON *Strange Ride of R. Kipling* vii. 298 What he [*sc.* Kipling] saw of trench life..horrified him. 1918 G. FRANKAU *Judgement of Valhalla* 18 Downwards, and on, where *trench-lights shone—For *we*, we might not rest. 1908 *Blackw. Mag.* Apr. 502/1 A treble tier of *trench lines. 1577–87 HOLINSHED *Chron.* III. 1133/2 Edward Chamberleine esquier capteine of the pioners, sir Richard Leigh *trenchmaster. 1617 MORYSON *Itin.* II. 148 Captain Josias Bodley, Trench-Master. 1915 D. O. BARNETT *Let.* 19 May 143 In the afternoon we had a *trench-mortar duel with the Allymans. 1973 M. WOODHOUSE *Blue Bone* xii. 129 What looked like a three-foot metal pipe with a rectangular base... 'Five-centimeter trench mortar,' said Yancy. 1920 *Chambers's Jrnl.* 20 Mar. 254/1 He shelled it; he *trench-mortared it, he raided it. 1918 *Evening Mail* 1 May 3/4 We have *trench mouth, just as we have trench feet. Otherwise known as ulcero-membranous stomatitis, or Vincent's disease. 1946 J. LEES-MILNE *Diary* 1 Jan. (1983) 3 Went to the dentist who said it *is* trench mouth that I am suffering from. 1981 G. PRIESTLAND *Priestland's Progress* 8 Chris Rees had to take to his bed with a rare attack of trench mouth. 1915 *Morning Post* 11 Feb. 3/5 The Adams *trenchoscope is the latest periscope for use in the trenches. 1915 *Trench-periscope [see *hyposcope* s.v. HYPO- II]. 1830 *Planting* 35 (Libr. Usef. Knowl.) Slit-planting..holing or pitting..*trench-planting..furrow-planting. 1905 *Terms Forestry* (U.S. Dep. Agric., Bulletin lxi.), *Trench planting*, a method of planting on dry ground, in which the seeds or young trees are set in trenches. *Syn.*: pit planting. 1917 A. G. EMPEY *Over Top* 313 **Trench raid*, several men detailed to go over the top at night and shake hands with the Germans, and, if possible, persuade some of them to be prisoners. 1961 W. VAUGHAN-THOMAS *Anzio* i. 5 A struggle in the mud, complete with duck-boards, trench-raids and patrols in no-man's-land. 1974 A. PRICE *Other Paths to Glory* II. viii. 213 It's a sawn-off Lee Enfield... Used for *trench raiding... The trench rifle had been Jarras's newest toy. 1916 G. FRANKAU *Guns* 22 The *trench-rats patter And nibble among the rations. 1917 A. G. EMPEY *Over Top* 308 There are three things in this world that Tommy loves: a slacker, a German, and a trench-rat. 1974 *Trench rifle [see *trench raiding* above]. 1918 E. S. FARROW *Dict. Mil. Terms* 629 **Trenchscope*, a simple periscope, used in the trenches (permitting a safe view to the front), consisting of parallel mirrors in a long wooden box, both set 45° to the long axis of the box. 1755 *Mem. Capt. P. Drake* II. iii. 73 He would make me *Trench-Sergeant... In this Duty I was to attend in the Trenches twice a Day,..to have under my Command a Detachment of thirty unarmed Men..to gather the Pick-axes, Shovels, Wheel-Barrows, etc. that should be left or scattered by the Workmen. 1915 KIPLING *France at War* v. 55 One understood after a while the nightmare that lays hold of *trench-stale men. 1931 *Times Lit. Suppl.* 22 Oct.

822/1 The squadron was required to assist the hard-pressed infantry by..'*trench strafing'. **1918** E. S. FARROW *Dict. Mil. Terms* 629 **Trench system*, all the field-works included in a defense zone. **1923** KIPLING *Irish Guards in Gt. War* I. 227 Some half-wiped-out German trench-systems. **1975** P. FUSSELL *Gt. War & Mod. Memory* ii. 36 From the winter of 1914 until the spring of 1918 the trench system was fixed. **1923** KIPLING *Irish Guards in Gt. War* II. 143 There are certain analogies between *trench-to-trench attack and 'soccer'. *Ibid.* I. 20 The *trench-war was solidifying itself. **1918** F. M. FORD *Let.* 6 Jan. (1965) 86, I could do a very good one [novel] about *trench warfare. **1973** *Times* 7 Dec. 18/3 In industry we have had continuing trench warfare deriving from low pay, and authoritarian and remote management. **1978** F. MACLEAN *Take Nine Spies* iv. 125 He had fought at Dixemude..before settling down later that winter [in 1914] to the horrors of trench warfare. **1980** R. BARNARD *Death in Cold Climate* vii. 69 Sterile trench-warfare with colleagues over matters of principle. **1884** *Mil. Engineering* (ed. 3) I. II. 29 Fig. 1..represents this arrangement in a parallel executed by common *trench-work, and Fig. 2 in one constructed by flying trench-work.

trench (trɛn(t)ʃ), *v.* Forms: see the sb. [a. OF. *trenchier* (11th c. in Godef. *Compl.*), F. *trancher* to cut, hew, slice, etc. = Prov. *trencar, trinquar*, Catal. *trencar*, Sp., Pg. *trincar*; cf. It. *trinciare*. These Romanic forms are held to represent a popular L. **trincāre*, altered from L. *truncāre* to cut or lop off, f. *truncus* the trunk of a tree: cf. TRUNCHEON. Our sense 1 is directly from OF. Senses 3–5 are either immediately from TRENCH *sb.* or largely influenced by it. Senses 6–8 are not in French; they prob. arose as figures from the action of extending military trenches so as to reach or touch the place besieged.]

I. To cut, make a cutting.

1. *trans.* To cut; to divide by cutting, slice, cut in pieces; to sever by cutting, cut off; to cut into, make a cut in; to cut *one's way*. Also *absol.*

1483 CAXTON *Gold. Leg.* 104b/2 Thomas is as moche to saye as..double or trenchyd and heuen. **1485** —— *Chas. Gt.* II. x. 63 [He] gaf hym a stroke vpon his helme so sharply that he trenched moo than vc maylles. *c* **1510** BARCLAY *Mirr. Gd. Manners* (1570) Bj, Though the toth [of a serpent] trencheth, the tayle beareth poyson. **1513** DOUGLAS *Æneis* VI. iv. 32 Enee hym self..to the, Proserpyne, A ȝeld kow all to trynschit. *c* **1520** BARCLAY *Jugurth* (1557) 9 To bringe vnto him the heed of Hiempsal trenched from the body. **1725** POPE *Odyss.* x. 615 Draw thy falchion, and on every side Trench the black earth a cubit long and wide. **1856** BRYANT *Two Graves* 43 Trench the strong hard mould with the spade. **1867** FROUDE *Short Stud.* (ed. 2) 167 They are trenching their way thro' the weak place in the Pentateuch.

†**b.** To cut or carve *in* or *into* a surface. *Obs.*

1591 SHAKS. *Two Gent.* III. ii. 7 This weake impresse of Loue, is as a figure Trenched in ice. **1665** J. WEBB *Stone-Heng* (1725) 148 Inscriptions cut or trencht in one of the Stones. —— 150 Those..had Epigraphs trencht into the Craggs.

†**c.** To make (a cut, gash, or wound) *in* or *into* something. *Obs. rare.*

1592 SHAKS. *Ven. & Ad.* 1052 The wide wound, that the boare had trencht In his soft flanke. **1610** FLETCHER *Faithf. Sheph.* IV. ii, The wound by cruel knife Trencht into him.

2. To cut or make a cutting through a ridge or raised surface. The object of the vb. may be (*a*) the cutting made, (*b*) the ridge or surface cut through.

1601 R. JOHNSON *Kingd. & Commw.* (1603) 50 For the ease of pilgrims..iournieng between Cair and Mecha, she began to trench a water course alongst the way. **1865** GEIKIE *Scen. & Geol. Scot.* ix. 238 The ridge is deeply trenched with gullies and narrow glens. *Ibid.* x. 285 If then the chain of the Sidlaws once ran unbroken to the south-west..how could the Tay trench it? **1881** GEIKIE in *Nature* 3 Nov. 1/1 In the general denudation of the country, deep valleys have been trenched through it.

b. *fig.* (with the surface cut or furrowed as *obj.*)

1624 QUARLES *Job* xi. 50 Thy Hand hath trenched my cheekes with water-furrowes. **1787** BURNS *To Haggis* iii, His knife see rustic Labour dight,..Trenching your gushing entrails bright, Like ony ditch. **1840** R. H. HORNE *Gregory VII*, IV. i, Oft have I marked a deep awe trench his face. **1868** NETTLESHIP *Browning* iii. 95 A mouth..trenched on either side by early pronounced lines.

c. *Naut.* ***to trench the ballast***: see quots.

1627 CAPT. SMITH *Seaman's Gram.* vii. 33 To finde a leake, they trench the Ballast, that is, to diuide it. **1867** SMYTH *Sailor's Word-bk.*, *Trench the ballast*, to divide the ballast in a ship's hold to get at a leak, or to trim and stow it.

d. ***to trench beaver***: to cut their dam, so as to catch the beavers.

(Cf. **1830** *Gardens & Menag. Zool. Soc.* I. 167 When the sheet of water they inhabit is merely kept up by a dam, they are..taken up by letting off the water, and leaving their huts completely dry.)

1822–34 *Good's Study Med.* (ed. 4) IV. 80 A young Chipewyan had separated from the rest of his band for the purpose of trenching beaver.

II. From TRENCH *sb.*; to do something to, with, or by a trench.

3. To cut a trench or trenches in (the ground).

1530 PALSGR. 761/2, I trench the grounde, *je trenche*.. They have trenched a large myle and more. **1541** *Act 33 Hen. VIII* c. 35 The place..so broken dygged or trenched. **1870** N. F. HELE *Aldeburgh* iv. 25 We trenched the tumulus in a radiate manner, from the centre towards the circumference. **1872** G. DOWKER in *Archæol. Cantiana* VIII. 8 We subsequently trenched the surface of the platform.

b. *spec.* in *Agric.* and *Hort.* To make a series of trenches in digging or ploughing (a piece of ground), so as to bring the lower soil to the surface. ***to trench up***, to lay (land) in trenches and ridges alternately (cf. RIDGE *v.* 2); ***to trench down***, to bury (soil or weeds) in trenching. Also *absol.*

1573 TUSSER *Husb.* (1878) 83 Thy garden plot latelie well trenched and muckt. **1649** in *Archæologia* X. 432 A musk-milion ground trenched, manured, and very well ordered. **1763** MILLS *Pract. Husb.* IV. 68 This may..be prevented by ..trenching the ground up in ridges. **1793** *Trans. Soc. Arts* (ed. 2) V. 11, I trenched up the whole to the depth of eighteen inches. **1798** NICOL *Scotch Forcing Gard.* (ed. 2) 202 Trench three spits deep, by which the bottom and top are reversed, and the middle remains in the middle. **1799** J. ROBERTSON *Agric. Perth* App. 491 Many farmers were wont to trench down the low moss, and to cover it furrow deep, with clay taken out of the trench. *Mod.* The garden ought to be trenched.

c. *intr.* or *absol.* To dig a trench or trenches.

1786 in J. Lloyd *Old S. Wales Iron Works* (1906) 34 Free power..to bore, dig, delve, and trench in, upon, or under the said..Parcel of land. **1833** HT. MARTINEAU *Tale of Tyne* i, Walter was..busy trenching in his garden. **1882** *Garden* 30 Dec. 577/1 Trench deeply..and as early in the winter as possible. *Ibid.*, When trenching..use half decayed manure.

†**d.** *intr.* Of a torrent: To cut its way. *Obs.*

1613–16 W. BROWNE *Brit. Past.* II. i, As all the floods (Down trenching from small groves and greater woods) The vast insatiate Sea doth still devoure.

4. *trans.* To furnish with, set, or place in a trench. †**a.** To divert (a river) by means of a trench. *Obs. rare*$^{-1}$.

1596 SHAKS. *1 Hen. IV*, III. i. 112 A little Charge will trench him [the Trent] here, And on this North side winne this Cape of Land, And then he runnes straight and euen.

b. To set or plant in a trench.

1678 R. L'ESTRANGE *Seneca's Mor.*, *Epist.* ix. (1696) 515 This would not have been..if you had Trenched them and Water'd them. *Mod.* Celery is usually trenched.

c. To bury in a trench.

1870 *Standard* 14 Dec., They detail squads of their soldiers to trench their fallen comrades.

d. To drain (land) by means of open trenches or ditches; to ditch.

1811 T. DAVIS *Agric. Wilts* App. 261 *Trenching or Guttering Land*, draining it with open drains. **1875** [implied in TRENCHER[2] 2].

5. *Mil.* To surround or fortify with a trench; to cast a trench *about*, *around* (a post, army, town, etc.); to entrench; also, to confine by means of a trench (*rare*, ? *obs.*).

a **1548** HALL *Chron.*, *Hen. V* 65b, The Frenchmen diched, trenched and paled their lodgynges for feare of after clappes. *Ibid.*, *Hen. VI* 165b, The place which they had trenched, dytched, and fortefied with ordenaunce. *Ibid.*, *Edw. IV* 220b, The duke of Somerset..trenched his campe rounde about of suche an altitude, and so strongly. **1667** MILTON *P.L.* I. 677 Bands Of Pioners with Spade and Pickaxe arm'd Forerun the Royal Camp, to trench a Field, Or cast a Rampart. **1715–20** POPE *Iliad* xx. 175 A mound Of earth congested, wall'd, and trench'd around. **1827** KEBLE *Chr. Y.*, *10th Sund. Trin.* v, Now foes shall trench thee round, And lay thee even with earth. **1899** [see *trenched* below].

b. *fig.* To entrench.

1601 ? MARSTON *Pasquil & Kath.* I. 113 Trench your selfe within the peoples loue. **1624** GEE *Foot out of Snare* 46 Trenching themselues in the Mines of their Labyrinths at home, or masking in their gold and siluer abroad. **1624** MASSINGER *Renegado* II. iv, A hermit in a desert, trenched with prayers. **1759** MASON *Caractacus* 52, I spy'd their helms 'Mid brakes and boughs trench'd in the heath below. **1838** CHALMERS *Wks.* XII. 81 One who..was..trenched among what he thought the speculations of orthodoxy.

†**c.** *intr.* To cast trenches, in siege works; in quot. 1623, to make one's way by trenching (*fig.*). ***to trench at***: to lay siege to by means of trenches.

1582–8 *Hist. Jas. VI* (1804) 231 The pyoneris hade trinchett in the castell hill of Edinburgh, and erectit a braid sconce to hyde thame. **1623** B. JONSON *Time Vind.* Wks. (Rtldg.) 636/1 The boy with buttons, and the basket-wench, To vent their wares into my works do trench! **1742** YOUNG *Nt. Th.* VI. 21 Like pow'rful armies trenching at a town, By slow, and silent, but resistless sap.

III. †**6.** *intr.* ***to trench to*** (***unto***): To extend in effect to; to extend so as to affect or touch. (Cf. TOUCH *v.* 20.) *Obs.*

1612 BACON *Ess.*, *Judicature* (Arb.) 458 The thing deduced to Iudgement, may bee *meum et tuum*, when the reason and consequence thereof may trench to point of estate. *a* **1625** SIR H. FINCH *Law* (1636) 83 In law it is said the demise of the King, and a gift unto the King, without saying more, trencheth to his successors. **1628** COKE *On Litt.* 209b, Because the money at the beginning trenched to the Feoffee in manner as a dutie. **1633** T. NASH *Quaternio* 234 If a man shall suborne two witnesses to depose a thing which trencheth to the life of a third person.

†**b.** *intr.* To extend or stretch (to a distance or in some direction); to trend. *Obs. rare.*

1720 DE FOE *Capt. Singleton* viii. (1840) 133 The land trenched away to the west. **1775** ROMANS *Florida* App. 12 The shore is pretty bold too, except at the two ends, where the bars of said two rivers trench off a great way. *Ibid.* 19 From Hobé inlet we find the coast trenching about S 20 E or nearly SSE for about 3½ leagues.

7. †**a.** ***to trench into*** (***unto***): To 'cut' into, to enter into so as to affect or concern intimately. *Obs.*

1621 ELSING *Debates Ho. Lords* (Camden) 59 This trencheth deeper unto us then we all conceave. A delinquent is brought before us, and, before yt was determined, resumed into the Kinges hands. **1622** MISSELDEN *Free Trade* (ed. 2) 131 It..is a matter that trencheth into the Supreme power and dignity of the King, and is peculiar to Him alone. **1641** W. HAKEWIL *Libertie of Subject* 91 A thing which trencheth as deeply into the privat interest of the Subject as the laying of Impositions.

b. ***to trench on*** or ***upon***: To encroach or infringe (however slightly) *on* or *upon* a region which is the domain of another. †***to trench too near, too nigh***, = to come dangerously near infringing upon (*obs.*).

1622 MABBE tr. *Aleman's Guzman d'Alf.* II. 15 The King ..being desirous to know, if any man of worth had presumed so farre to trench vpon what he had done. **1627** E. F. *Hist. Edw. II* (1680) 59 Nor may you trench too near your Soveraigns actions. **1629** N. CARPENTER *Achitophel* II. (1640) 78 [It] seems to me to trench too farre on Gods Prerogative. **1647** N. BACON *Disc. Govt. Eng.* I. xl. 98 They would not allow their secular affairs to trench too nigh that days devotion. **1649** G. DANIEL *Trinarch.*, *Rich. II* ccc, But least my running Tent may Trench vpon Another's feild, I fixe my Pole downe here. **1799** J. ROBERTSON *Agric. Perth* 553 This scheme..may seem to trench on the liberty of individuals. **1865** MERIVALE *Rom. Emp.* VIII. lxiv. 116 He trenches a little on the night,..but no one finds the time long. **1866** MRS. H. WOOD *St. Martin's Eve* xiii, Though I squandered my own property, I have not trenched on yours.

c. in vaguer use, To come in thought, speech, or action close *upon* (something); to border closely *upon*, to verge *upon*; to approach *towards*; hence, to have a bearing *upon* or reference to (something).

1635 HEYLIN *Sabbath* I. (1636) 190 Some..have trenched too neere upon the Rabbins, in binding men to nice and scrupulous observances. *a* **1639** W. WHATELEY *Prototypes* III. xxxix. (1640) 24 He did trench a little too neare upon an untruth. **1643** BAKER *Chron.*, *Hen. VI* 5 Knowing how far they trenched upon the Dukes destruction, and her own. **1691** *Case of Exeter Coll.* Pref. Aijb, Insignificant suggestions that trench nothing at all on the merits of the Cause. **1746** FIELDING *True Patriot* No. 23 They hold them [other persons and things] of no consequence,..unless they trench somewhat towards their own order or calling. **1841** D'ISRAELI *Amen. Lit.* (1867) 355 Some unlucky jest, trenching on treason, flew from the lips of the unguarded jester. **1876** C. M. DAVIES *Unorth. Lond.* 20 The opinions of this school—where they trench most closely on orthodoxy.

†**d.** *trans.* To trench or encroach upon. *Obs.*

1626 B. JONSON *Staple of N.* v. vi, Who did? I? I trench the liberty o' the subiects?

Hence **'trenched, 'trenching** *ppl. adjs.*

1589 PUTTENHAM *Eng. Poesie* II. xi. (Arb.) 107 With sharpe Trenching blade of bright steele. **1596** SHAKS. *1 Hen. IV*, I. i. 7 No more shall trenching Warre channell her fields. **1605** —— *Macb.* III. iv. 27 Safe in a ditch he bides, With twenty trenched gashes on his head. **1763** MILLS *Pract. Husb.* IV. 322 Whatever..might afterward press down the trenched earth. **1899** *Daily News* 14 Dec. 5/5 The Highlanders formed up to renew the attack on the trenched kopje.

trenchancy ('trɛn(t)ʃənsɪ). [f. next: see -ANCY.] The quality of being trenchant, 'sharp', or 'cutting'; incisiveness; causticity.

1866 *London Rev.* 24 Nov. 568 Expected..to accept bitterness and passion for satire and trenchancy. **1877** MORLEY *Crit. Misc.* Ser. II. 390 Trenchancy whether in speaker or writer is a most effective tone for a large public. **1892** STEVENSON *Across the Plains* 203 With the same trenchancy of contrast.

trenchant ('trɛn(t)ʃənt), *a.* (*sb.*) Also 4–5 **trenchaunt**, (5 **-aunte**), **-ande**, (5 *Sc.* **trensand**, 6 **trenchand**, 7 **trencheant**, **trinchante**); see also TRANCHANT. [a. OF. *trenchant* (mod.F. *tranchant*), pr. pple. of †*trenchier*, *trancher* to cut: see TRENCH *v.* and -ANT.]

1. Cutting, adapted for cutting; having a keen edge, sharp; †sharp-pointed (*obs.*). *arch.* and *poet.*

c **1330** R. BRUNNE *Chron. Wace* (Rolls) 4414 Nemny on þe heued he smot; Hit was trenchaunt, ouer fer hit bot. *c* **1380** *Sir Ferumb.* 537 Ich hem wolde wel conquere wiþ my swerd trenchaunt. *c* **1400** MAUNDEV. (1839) v. 47 This monstre.. hadde ij hornes trenchant on his forhede. *c* **1470** HENRY *Wallace* IV. 662 The trensand blaid to-persyt euirydeill. *c* **1477** CAXTON *Jason* 8b, Jason smote another Centaure in the nekke with a trenchaunt arowe. **1590** SPENSER *F.Q.* I. i. 17 He..with his trenchand blade her boldly kept From turning backe. **1663** BUTLER *Hud.* I. I. 359 The trenchant Blade, Toledo trusty, For want of fighting was grown rusty. *a* **1774** GOLDSM. *Surv. Exp. Philos.* (1776) I. 236 The thin or trenchant end [of the wedge] is applied to the timber to be cleft, and the thick end struck upon by an hammer. **1830** TENNYSON '*Clear-headed friend*' ii, Nor martyr-flames, nor trenchant swords Can do away that ancient lie.

b. *Zool.* Of a tooth, bill, etc.: Having a cutting edge; sectorial.

1831 McMURTRIE *Cuvier's Anim. Kingd.* II. 136 In a fourth tribe [of fishes], the teeth are trenchant. It comprises two genera, *Boops* and *Oblada*. **1835–6** *Todd's Cycl. Anat.* I. 312/2 Trenchant bills which are..flattened horizontally. **1881** MIVART *Cat* 29 The lower molar..having a more completely trenchant form than any other tooth.

c. *transf.*, or in *fig.* or *allusive* use.

1603 HOLLAND *Plutarch's Mor.* 30 Whose blood..now Trenchant Mars hath shed. **1809** W. IRVING *Knickerb.* VI. viii. (1849) 369 Pursuing its trenchant course, it severed off a deep coat pocket. **1851** GLADSTONE *Glean.* VI. lix. 39 Must it not be dangerous to place weapons so keen and trenchant in the hands of raw recruits? **1865** *Trav. by 'Umbra'* 10 Carve the impalpable and viewless air with thy trenchant paper knife. **1871** FREEMAN *Hist. Ess.* Ser. I. v. 117 The biographer of Edward [III], Mr. Longman, cannot wield the trenchant weapons of Lord Brougham.

2. *fig.* esp. of language: Incisive; vigorous and clear; effective, energetic.

a **1325** [implied in TRENCHANTLY]. **1663** BUTLER *Hud.* I. III. 882 Their Swords Were sharp and trencheant, not their Words. **1824** MISS MITFORD *Village* Ser. I. (1863) 208 Some trenchant repartee, that cuts off the poor answer's head like a razor. **1842** —— in L' Estrange *Life* (1870) III. ix. 159 The most trenchant and violent writer of the 'Times'. **1877** OWEN *Wellesley's Desp.* p. xxxvi, For all these evils.. Wellesley devised prompt and trenchant remedies, most unpalatable to his employers.

3. *transf.* and *fig.* Sharply defined or outlined; clear-cut; distinct.

1849 RUSKIN *Sev. Lamps* iii. §14. 78 The use of the dark mass characterises, generally, a trenchant style of design. **1852** DANA *Crust.* II. 745 This subtribe has trenchant limits. **1873** H. ROGERS *Orig. Bible* ii. 78 The line of demarcation is seemingly most sharp and trenchant.

¶**4.** *erron.* Capable of being cut.

1824 LAMB *Elia* Ser. II. *Blakesmoor in H——shire*, What herald shall go about to strip me of an idea? Is it trenchant to their swords?

†**B.** *sb.* One who or that which cuts or severs; a cutter, a divider. *Obs. rare*$^{-1}$.

a **1660** *Contemp. Hist. Irel.* (Ir. Archæol. Soc.) I. 133 A turne-coate of lawfull confederacie, a trinchante of holy union, a scandall and reproofe of all Christian pietie.

†**b.** ***esquire trenchant***, an esquire carver; cf. ESQUIRE *sb.*[1] 1 c and 5, quot. 1797. *Obs.*

1563 RANDOLPH in *Calr. Scott. Pap.* II. 3 A longe yonge man..one of her graces esquire trenchantes. [Cf. **1611** COTGR., *Trenchant, Escuyer,..valet trenchant*, a Caruer.]

trenchantly (ˈtrɛn(t)ʃəntlɪ), *adv.* [f. prec. + -LY².] In a trenchant manner; 'cuttingly', incisively; sharply and effectively; definitely; so as to go to the root of a matter.

a **1325** *MS. Rawl. B.* 520 lf. 61 b, Him bi-houez to seggen trenchauntliche þat he is bastard. **1870** R. B. BROUGH *Marston Lynch* xiii. 116 He is trenchantly severe on better painters than himself. **1873** HAMERTON *Intell. Life* VII. iii. (1875) 241 The educations of the two sexes were so trenchantly separated that neither had access to the knowledge of the other. **1877** LE CONTE *Elem. Geol.* iii. (1879) 161 Groups of species confined within certain areas differing from other groups, sometimes overlapping them, sometimes trenchantly separated. **1896** W. C. SIDGWICK in *Times* 11 Dec. 10/6, I hope the 'roughness of my methods' only means that I dealt trenchantly with his theories.

So **ˈtrenchantness**, the quality of being trenchant.

1892 *Temple Bar Mag.* Oct. 289 She..says so, with a trenchantness which brings up a little cloud of disappointed surprise.

†**trenchefil, tranchefil.** *Obs. rare.* [a. F. *tranchefil* (Cotgr. *trenchefile*), f. *tranche*, imper. of *trancher* to cut + *fil* thread.]

1. In a double-stringed cross-bow, the part by which the two strings were united and into which the neb or tip of the bolt was set in shooting; the material of which this was made. Cf. TRENCH *sb.* 7 and quot. 1611 there.

1369–1372 *Exch. Acc. K.R.* Bundle 178 No. 16 m. 4 (P.R.O.) Patricio Byker artillario Regis..lxiiij lb. fili pro cordis balistarum lij lb. trussyngthred lj. lb. di. trenchefyll.

2. Part of a bridle: according to Cotgrave, 'a snaffle, or the mouth of a snaffle, or watering Bit'.

1730–6 BAILEY (folio), *Bitt* (with Horsemen) in general signifies the whole Machine of a Bridle, as the Bit-mouth, the Branches, the Curb, the sevil Holes, the Tranchefil, and the Cross-chains. **1753** CHAMBERS *Cycl. Supp.*, *Tranchefile*, in the manege, the cross chain of a bridle that runs along the bit-mouth, from one branch to the other.

†**ˈtrenchepain.** *Obs. rare*$^{-1}$. [f. F. *tranche* vb. imperative, cut + *pain* bread.] A bread-cutter; an attendant who cut the bread at table.

a **1400** *Sir Perc.* 513 Bot thanne spak syr Gawayne, Was the kynges trenchepayne.

trencher[1] (ˈtrɛn(t)ʃə(r)). Forms: 4–5 trencheour, -chour, 4 -chur, 4–6 -chor, 5 -chowre, trenschowre, -shoure, ? 4, 5– trencher, (6 *Sc.* trunsch(e)our, -owr, -zour), 7 trentcher. [a. AF. *trenchour* = ONF. *trencheor* (1206 in Godef.), *tren-*, *trancheur*, = OF. *tranchouoir* (14th c. in Littré), *trencheoir* (Cotgr.), mod.F. *tranchoir*, f. †*trenchier*, *trancher* to cut, TRENCH *v.*, with suffix *-oir*, representing L. *-ātorium*. Godef. exemplifies the word in senses corresp. to both our branches I. and II.]

I. †**1.** A cutting or slicing instrument; a knife.

c **1330** R. BRUNNE *Chron.* (1810) 166 Fulle broþely & brim he kept vp a trencheour, & kast it at Statin,..His nese & his ine he carfe at misauentoure. *c* **1400** *Songs Costume* (Percy Soc.) 50 My baselard hath a trencher kene, Fayr as rasour scharp and schene. *c* **1410** *Master of Game* (MS. Digby 182) xxxiii, With a sharpe trenshoure kut as thyk as he canne þe flessh a doune to þe necke bone. *c* **1440** *Promp. Parv.* 501/2 Trenchowre, knyfe. **1553** *Acc. Ld. High Treas. Scotl.* X. 204 For ane cais to put sylver trunscheouris in of my lord governoures.

II. 2. A flat piece of wood, square or circular, on which meat was served and cut up; a plate or platter of wood, metal, or earthenware. *arch.* and *Hist.*

c **1308** *Song Times* in *Pol. Songs* (Camden) 204 A row3 bare trenchur, other a crust. **1360–70** *Durham Acc. Rolls* (Surtees) 175 In j pare de Trenchours pro priore, xij s. **1505** in *Exch. Rolls Scotl.* XII. 673, xxiiij poter dischis, xxiiij saw[s]aris, xij trunzouris. **1529** *Reg. Mag. Sig. Scot.* (1883) 177 A half galloun, a quart..a dische, a salsar and a trunscheour, extending to 1¾ stanis of puder. **1547** *Bk. Marchauntes* b ij, Thei mak them kisse a trenchor or a small platter of gold, siluer, or lead: which thei name the platine. **1573–80** BARET *Alv.* T 357 A Trencher to eate meate on,.. A broad trencher..A round trencher. **1624** CAPT. SMITH *Virginia* III. ii. 48 They imagined the world to be flat and round, like a trencher. **1696** PHILLIPS (ed. 5), *Trencher*, a square, thin Plate of Wood, for People to cut their Meat upon. **1801** MAR. EDGEWORTH *Angelina* ii, The first dinner which she ate on wooden trenchers delighted her. **1895** LYON *Chron. Finchampstead* 90 A very ancient oak table which had round places scooped out in it to receive a trencher or wooden basin for each person who dined at it.

†**3.** A slice of bread used instead of a plate or platter. *Obs.*

c **1380** WYCLIF *Serm.* Sel. Wks. I. 115 Siche whelpis shulden ete trenchours of lordis. **1392** *Earl Derby's Exp.* (Camden) 218 In pane pro trenchors, v duc. di. *c* **1430** *Two Cookery-bks.* 41 Take whyte Brede, & kytte to trenchours. **1490** CAXTON *Eneydos* xxxiv. 121 They sette hemselfe atte dyner, & made trenchers of brede for to putte theyr mete vpon. **1513** DOUGLAS *Æneis* VII. iii. 26 Ne spair thai nocht at last..Their fatale four nukit trunschowris for to eit.

4. a. A trencher and that which it bears; a supply of food; cf. TABLE 6 c. *arch.*

1576 FLEMING *Panopl. Epist.* 238 What benefites are obteined, by the sweate of other mennes labours, and also by the fatte crumbes of other mennes trenchers. **1612** DEKKER *If it be not good* Wks. 1873 III. 280 Waite on the Priors Trencher soberly. **1659** W. BROUGH *Schism* 535 These new rabbis..are chaplains extraordinary to the trencher. **1667** L. STUCLEY *Gospel-Glass* xxii. (1670) 224 We have..brought our Children to live upon others trenchers. **1820** W. IRVING *Sketch Bk.*, *Spectre Bridegroom*, Even the poor relations paused for a moment from the indefatigable labours of the trencher.

b. In proverbial phrases, chiefly of obvious meaning. ***to lick the trencher***, to toady; to play the parasite. ***trim as a trencher***: see quot. 1542.

1542 UDALL *Erasm. Apophth.* II. 246 b, Fillyng vp as trymme as a trencher yᵉ space that stood voide. **1589** PUTTENHAM *Eng. Poesie* III. xxv. (Arb.) 307 To speake faire to a mans face, and foule behinde his backe, to set him at his trencher and yet sit on his skirts. **1602** [see LICK *v.* 1 b]. **1649** BP. HALL *Cases Consc.* III. iii. (1654) 189 Carve you for your selfe and looke to your owne trencher. **1692** WASHINGTON tr. *Milton's Def. Pop.* viii. M.'s Wks. 1851 VIII. 185 You were there a few years ago, and began to lick a Cardinal's Trencher. **1852** THACKERAY *Esmond* II. xv, He will be at Roncq time enough to lick my Lord Duke's trenchers at supper.

5. *transf.* A flat board, circular or otherwise.

c **1511** *1st Eng. Bk. Amer.* (Arb.) Introd. 28/1 That Lande is so full of sande yat they muste goo vpon brode trenchers that they falle not & synke. **1669** BOYLE *Contn. New Exp.* I. xli. (1682) 144 In the midst of the fixed Trencher (as we call a piece of solid wood shap'd like a Milstone). **1710** J. CLARKE *Rohault's Nat. Phil.* (1729) I. 61 Water in a Pail is made to ascend up a Trunk, such as they shoot with, open at both Ends, and one End fixed in a Hole in a Trencher which exactly fits the whole Superficies; upon depressing the Trencher, the Water is forced up. **1825** SCOTT *Talism.* vi, At the barriers, when swords are blunted at point and edge, and spears are tipped with trenchers of wood, instead of steel pikes. **1889** *Harper's Mag.* Jan. 238/2 He next binds his [beaver] trap to a flat stone 'about the size of a teakettle', opens the jaws, and arranges the 'trencher', as the pan is called, pressure on which springs the trap.

b. Applied to a butcher's 'tray'.

1903 F. MARKHAM *Recoll. Town Boy Westminster* 97 The butcher had his long trencher in which he carried his meat about.

6. *spec.* = TRENCHER-CAP.

1834 [implied in *trencherless*: see below]. **1848** THACKERAY *Bk. Snobs* xiv, [The Master of a College's] crawler would have no objection to carry his trencher. **1862** MRS. H. WOOD *Channings* i, The boys began to file out, putting on their trenchers, as they clattered down the steps. **1906** *Daily Chron.* 26 Sept. 5/6 The girl students..in their red gowns and trenchers adorned with a red tassel.

7. *attrib.* and *Comb.* **a.** simple attrib., as ***trencher-basket***, ***-food***, ***-house***, ***-room***, ***-side***; in sense 4, or in allusion to presence or entertainment at the table of a patron, as ***trencher-analect***, ***-art***, ***-attendant***, ***-buffoon***, ***-companion***, ***-critic***, ***-fury***, ***-hero***, ***-knight***, ***-labourer***, ***-law***, ***-mate***, ***-philosopher***, ***-poetry***, ***-rascal***, ***-saint***, ***-schoolmaster***, ***-service***, ***-slave***, ***-squire***, ***-waiter***. **b.** objective, etc., as ***trencher-carrier***, ***-licker*** (see 4 b), ***-maker***, ***-making***, ***-scraper***, ***-shifter***; also ***trencher-like*** adj. **c.** Special Combs.: **trencher-beard**, a beard resembling a trencher, i.e. large, flat, and square or round; †**trencher-bread**, bread made of unbolted flour for use as trenchers (sense 3); *Obs.* exc. *Hist.*; **trencher-coat**, in gilding: see quotation; **trencher-fed** *a.*, of fox-hounds: kept and fed by the several owners or members of the hunt, as distinguished from a pack that is kept in the hunt kennels; †**trencher-fee**, scraps of food given in alms; †**trencher-knife**, a pantry knife for cutting bread into 'trenchers'; †**trencher-loaf**, cf. *trencher-bread*; **trencher-plate**, a plate shaped like or used as a trencher; *spec.* in *Ceramics*, a flat earthenware plate with a narrow rim; also (*collective*) plate or precious metal of which trenchers were made; **trencher-salt**, **-salt-cellar**, a small salt-cellar placed near a guest's trencher at table; **trencher table**, a table at which members of domestic staff were seated at meal times; **trencher-time**, dinner-time, meal-time. See also TRENCHER-CAP, -CHAPLAIN, etc.

a **1643** W. CARTWRIGHT *Ordinary* III. v, No gleanings, James? No *trencher-analects? *a* **1661** HOLYDAY *Juvenal* (1673) 64 No man to rarer *trencher-art aspir'd. **1592** NASHE *Four Lett. Confut.* Wks. (Grosart) II. 224 Your *trenchor attendant..intends to tickle vp a Treatise of the barly kurnell, which you set in your garden. **1630** *Maldon, Essex, Documents* Bundle 217 No. 22, 1 *trentcher basket 6d. *a* **1668** DAVENANT *News fr. Plymouth* Wks. (1673) 3 Her Parent With a soure brow, and *Trencher Beard. *c* **1460** J. RUSSELL *Bk. Nurture* 56 *Trencher bred iiij. dayes [old] is convenyent & agreable. **1882** F. MICHEL *Crit. Inquiry into Scottish Lang.* iii. 54 [Edinburgh] citizens had four different kinds of wheaten bread: the finest called *manchet*, the second *cheat* or *trencher* bread. **1974** Trencher-bread [see JUMBAL, JUMBLE]. **1596** NASHE *Saffron Walden* Wks. (Grosart) III. 143 He was to make a iourney to London..to haue his blue coate (being destitute of euer another *trencher-carrier) credit him vp, though it were thrid bare. **1847–78** HALLIWELL, **Trencher-cloak*, a kind of cloak worn formerly by servants and apprentices. **1839** URE *Dict. Arts* 613 Coat of assiette; *trencher coat. This is the composition on which the gold is to be laid. **1816** SCOTT *Old Mort.* iii[i], The *ci-devant* laird, once his patron, but now glad to be his *trencher-companion. **1598** BP. HALL *Sat.* IV. iv. 23 Neuer haue I Salerne rimes profest To be some Ladies *trencher-criticke guest. **1887** A. E. PEASE (*title*) The Cleveland Hounds as a *Trencher-Fed Pack. **1892** *Daily Tel.* 27 Aug., The oldest pack of regular, as distinguished from trencher-fed foxhounds. **1641** BROME *Jov. Crew* III. Wks. 1873 III. 396 Dainty *Trencher-Fees, from a Gentleman's house; Such as the Serving-men themselves, sometimes, Would have been glad of. **1642** H. MORE *Song of Soul* I. II. lxxx, Our mind cannot attend our *trencher-food. **1641** MILTON *Ch. Govt.* II. Wks. 1851 III. 149 A work..like that which flows at wast from..the *trencher fury of a riming parasite. **1607** G. WILKINS *Miseries Enforced Marr.* v. I iv, You knaue Slaue—*trencher-groome. Who is your maister? **1792** WOLCOTT (P. Pindar) *Churchwarden* iv. Wks. 1812 III. 111 The *Trencher Heroes hate All Obstacles that keep them from the plate. **1691** *Case of Exeter Coll.* 18 A little Room in the Colledge, called the *Trencher-house. **1392–3** *Earl Derby's Exp.* (Camden) 195 Clerico panetrie per manus eiusdem, pro j *trenchurknyff per ipsum empto. **1459** *Paston Lett.* I. 488 Item, j. trencher knyfe. **1588** SHAKS. *L.L.L.* v. ii. 464 Some mumble-newes, some *trencher-knight. **1654** WHITLOCK *Zootomia* 506 This *Trencher-labourer will not drink with that Divine. **1597–8** BP. HALL *Sat.* IV. iv. 21 When splenish morsels cram the gaping Maw, Withouten diets care, or *trencher-law. **1812** W. TENNANT *Anster F.* IV. i, A *trencher-licker in Apollo's court. **1727** *Bradley's Fam. Dict.* s.v. *Blowing of Flower*, To shade it.. with a *Trencher-like Board, or some other Device. *c* **1460** J. RUSSELL *Bk. Nurture* 197, viij. louys bred with iij. or iiij. *trenchere lovis. **1588** in Lyon *Chron. Finchampstead* (1895) 212 James Redinge of Fynchamsted in the County of Barkes *Trenchermaker. **1733** W. ELLIS *Chiltern & Vale Farm.* 98 The Trencher-maker is..cautious of getting the Sap out of this Wood. **1815** SCOTT *Guy M.* vii, The art of *trencher-making, of manufacturing horn-spoons, and the whole mystery of the tinker. **1597** HOOKER *Eccl. Pol.* v. ii. §2 These *trencher-mates..frame to themselues a way more pleasant. **1605** BACON *Adv. Learn.* I. iii. §9 Those *Trencher Philosophers, which, in the later age of the Romane State, were vsually in the houses of great persons. **1580** HOLLYBAND *Treas. Fr. Tong*, *Vne Assiette & trencheoir*, a *trencher plate. **1625** in Rymer *Fœdera* (1726) XVIII. 239/1 Sixe Trencher Plates of Goulde with Armes. **1641** in Rushw. *Hist. Coll.* III. (1692) I. 281 For the relieving the present Necessity of Money, a Proportion of Plate should be melted for Coyn; and that the same shall be Trencher-Plate, and Dish-Plate. **1597–8** BP. HALL *Sat.* I. i. 13 Such hunger-starven *trencher-poetrie. **1610** B. JONSON *Alch.* I. i, Away, you *trencher-raskall. **1691** *Case of Exeter Coll.* 8 And then she went to the *Trencher Room. **1649** G. DANIEL *Trinarch., Hen. V*, lix, These *Trencher-Sᵗˢ; full-paunch't Boetians. **1614** TOMKIS *Albumazar* v. i. K j b, *Alb.* Shall I haue nothing? *Ron.* No, not a siluer spoone. *Fur.* Nor couer of a *Trencher-salt. **1625** in Rymer *Fœdera* (1726) XVIII. 238/2 A Trencher Salte of Golde in Forme of a Castle. **1967** *Times* 24 Feb. 14/6 The most unusual objects in a silver sale at Sotheby's yesterday were two miniature trencher salts, 1½in. diameter and weighing only to 10 dwt. by George Middleton, 1864. **1970** *Canad. Antiques Collector* Mar. 23/1 Salt cellars were made in many shapes, starting with plain, round or oblong, so-called trencher salts in the early 1700's. **1681** *Lond. Gaz.* No. 1614/4 Two Silver *Trencher-Saltsellers, being marked within side S.W.E. **1609** SIR E. HOBY *Let. to T. H*[*iggons*] 23 The multiplicitie of Schools, needlesse Lecturers, and *trencher Schoole-masters. **1650** WELDON *Crt. Jas. I* (1651) 34 He had starved, had not a *Trencher-scraper, sometime his servant..releived him with scraps. **1594** NASHE *Unfort. Trav.* Wks. (Grosart) V. 27 My state, you are not ignorant, depends on *trencher seruice. **1829** SCOTT *Ho. Aspen* II. ii, Here's much to do about an old crazy *trencher-shifter. **1571** GOLDING *Calvin on Ps.* To Rdr. 9 There bee also certein *trencher-slaves, of whom David complaineth. **1617** MORYSON *Itin.* III. 113 The English were neuer more idle,..neuer more base..trencher slaues, then in that age, wherein great men keept open houses for all commers. **1706** J. DUNTON *Life & Err.* (1818) II. xiii. 485 Thou art a *Trencher-snake, a swallow-guest. **1628** SHIRLEY *Witty Fair One* I. iii, How now, my officious *trencher-squire? **1692** R. L'ESTRANGE *Fables* xxxiv, Trencher-Squires, that spend their time in Hopping from One Great man's Table to Anothers. **1968** *Canad. Antiques Collector* June 9/1 Dinner..was served on two tables. One was at floor level—the '*trencher' table—where the steward, the curate, the governess and members of the staff were seated. **1977** D. E. WESTLAKE *Nobody's Perfect* II. iii. 110 Ratty pieces of living-room furniture..and an old trencher table. **1846** LANDOR *Exam. Shaks.* Wks. II. 280/1 Did he discourse at all at *trencher-time? **1638** FORD *Lady's Trial* II. ii, In your girl's days, you fell, forsooth, In love, and married..A *trencher-waiter.

Hence **'trencherful**, as much as a trencher will hold; **'trencherless** *a.*, without a trencher (in quot. a trencher-cap).

1660 PEPYS *Diary* 16 Feb., We went to the Sun Taverne in expectation of a dinner, where we had sent us only *trencherfulls of meat. **1883** GILMOUR *Mongols* xxi. 266 A trencherful of hard sour masses of material. **1834** *Blackw. Mag.* XXXVI. 779 Pozzlethwayte was..cravat-less, hat-less, *trencher-less, and, alas! wig-less.

trencher[2] ('trɛn(t)ʃə(r)). [f. TRENCH *v.* + -ER[1].] One who trenches.

†**1.** One who carves; a carver. *Obs. rare.*

a **1625** FLETCHER *Noble Gent.* III. i, I was not born, I take it, for a trencher, Nor to espouse my mistress' dairy-maid.

2. One who cuts or digs trenches; one who trenches ground.

1871 BLACKIE *Four Phases* i. 83 The trencher of the moral soil, not the planter of the seed. **1875** W. ALEXANDER *Sk. Life among Ain Folk* 188 A 'tramp' to save the sole of his boot while operating as trencher or drainer. **1875** tr. *Comte de Paris' Civ. War Amer.* I. 397 All these works were executed by the soldiers, who showed themselves excellent trenchers.

'trencher-cap. [f. TRENCHER[1] + CAP *sb.*[1]] A popular name for the academic or college cap, 'in shape thought to resemble an inverted trencher with a basin upon it' (Farmer and Henley); a 'mortar-board'. Also *transf.* one who wears a college cap, a collegian: cf. CATERCAP.

1721 AMHERST *Terræ Fil.* xxxv. (1754) 186 Neither do I find that these trencher-caps are more polite to their own dear countrymen, than they are to foreigners. **1796** *Grose's Dict. Vulg. Tongue* (ed. 3), *Trencher Cap*, the square cap worn by the collegians, at the universities of Oxford and Cambridge. **1811** *Chron.* in *Ann. Reg.* 74/1 His Royal Highness..was covered, during the whole time of his sitting .., by a trencher cap, with a gold tassel. **1861** HUGHES *Tom Brown at Oxf.* i, I walked about two inches taller in my trencher cap after it.

†**'trencher-,chaplain.** *Obs.* A chaplain who eats at a patron's table; a domestic chaplain. *contemptuous.*

1589 *Hay any Work* 37, I doe disdaine to deale with a contemptible trencher chaplaine. **1610** BOYS *Expos. Domin. Ep.*, etc. Wks. (1630) 511 It is the fashion of parasites and trencher-Chaplaines to flatter, or at the least humour great men at their table. **1676** MARVELL *Mr. Smirke* Wks. (Grosart) IV. 15 It savors of the liquorishness of a trencher-chaplain, little concerned in the 'curâ animarum'.

†**'trencher-fly.** *Obs.* [f. TRENCHER[1] + FLY *sb.*[1], as a creature that infests the table.] A parasite.

1590 GREENE *Never too Late* Wks. (Grosart) VIII. 165 Fed vppon with Trencher flies, eaten aliue with flatterers. **1603** H. CROSSE *Vertues Commw.* (1878) 29 He shall not want trencher-flies, clawbackes, and Sycophants. **1692** R. L'ESTRANGE *Fables* No. 337. I. 294 To try, which of 'em were Friends, and which, only Trencher-Flies, and Spungers.

'trencher-friend. ? *Obs.* A parasite; a toady.

1590 GREENE *Never too Late* Wks. (Grosart) VIII. 130 Flattering Gnatos, that only are time pleasers and trencher friends. **1607** SHAKS. *Timon* III. vi. 106 You Fooles of Fortune, Trencher-friends, Time Flyes, Cap and knee-Slaues. **1681** W. ROBERTSON *Phraseol. Gen.* (1693) 647 A Trencher friend; *amicus mensæ*. **1763** C. JOHNSTON *Reverie* II. 243 He gathered all his old pot-companions and trencher-friends about him, and fell to carousing as usual.

†**'trenchering.** *Obs. rare.* [f. TRENCHER[1] + -ING[1].]

1. *vbl. sb.* Devotion to the trencher; eating; feasting.

1594 HARINGTON *Nugæ Ant.* (1804) I. 170 Some men who love gameing,..some men who love wine, and some who love trencheringe.

2. Trenchers collectively.

1610 SHAKS. *Temp.* II. ii. 187 No more dams I'le make for fish,..Nor scrape trenchering, nor wash dish.

'trencher-man. [f. as prec. + MAN *sb.*[1]]

†**1.** A cook or caterer. *Obs. rare.*

a **1586** SIDNEY *Arcadia* I. iv. (1912) 29 He had alreadie bene more fed to his liking, then hee could bee by the skilfullest trencher-men of Media.

2. A feeder; an eater; usually qualified, as *good*, *stout*, *valiant*, etc., one who plays a good knife and fork; one who has a hearty appetite.

1590 GREENE *Never too Late* Wks. (Grosart) VIII. 199 Mullidor tried himselfe so tall a trencher man, that his mother perceiued by his drift he would not die for loue. **1596** SHAKS. *Much Ado* I. i. 51 He's a very valiant Trencher-man, hee hath an excellent stomacke. **1663** DAVENANT *Siege* II. i, You Are a rare Trencher-man. **1694** MOTTEUX *Rabelais* v. Prol., Dry and hungry Souls, Pot and Trenchermen. **1805** *Sporting Mag.* XXVI. 52 One or two distinguished trencher-men. **1880** R. S. WATSON *Vis. Wazan* xii. 226 As much as would serve a valiant trencher-man in England for half a week.

3. One who frequents a patron's table; a parasite, dependent, hanger-on.

1599 NASHE *Lenten Stuffe* Ep. Ded., A dismall world for trenchermen, when theyr maisters bond shal not be so good as theirs. **1643** WITHER *Campo Musæ* 40 By these virtues, from a trencher-man A Princes Minion, riseth, now and than. **1849** THACKERAY *Pendennis* xx, Everybody knew old Pen, regular old trencher-man at Gaunt House, notorious old bore, regular old fogey.

So **'trencher-,woman.**

1891 T. HARDY *Tess* xxxiv, To be sure, 'a was always a good trencher-woman, as her face showed.

'trenchful. [f. TRENCH *sb.* + -FUL.] As many or as much as a trench holds or will hold.

1900 *Blackw. Mag.* July 125/2 The Commandant of the trenchful of Boers. **1901** 'LINESMAN' *Words Eyewitness* vii. (1902) 151 Behind them again the advanced guard of a trenchful of curious private soldiers.

trenching ('trɛn(t)ʃɪŋ), *vbl. sb.* [f. TRENCH *v.* + -ING[1].] **a.** The action of the verb TRENCH, in its various senses.

1543-4 *Act 35 Hen. VIII*, c. 10 Any digging trenching or breakinge of suche Grounde. **1632** SANDERSON *Serm.* (1657) I. 372 Sufficient to acquit..the Constitutions from that trenching upon Christian liberty, wherewith they are charged. **1799** J. ROBERTSON *Agric. Perth* 278 The trenching of land in the open fields..is not so expensive as is generally supposed. **1899** *Westm. Gaz.* 20 Nov. 7/3 Commandant Cronje had marked each step of his advance on the town by elaborate trenching.

b. *attrib.* and *Comb.*, as ***trenching-fork***, ***-knife***, ***-plough***, ***-spade***, ***-system***, ***-tool***; **trenching-plane**, a grooving-plane.

1875 *Encycl. Brit.* I. 335/2 To have those patches of ground..which are missed in ploughing, gone over with the *trenching-fork. *c* **1510** *Kalender of Sheph.* E v, A great bochery, where as Yreful men and women were thorowe persyd with *trenchyng knyues. **1859** F. S. COOPER *Ironmongers' Catal.* 134 *Trenching Plane. **1669** WORLIDGE *Syst. Agric.* (1681) 231 The *Trenching-Plough or Coulter is a certain Instrument used in Meadow or Pasture-ground, to cut out the sides of Trenches, Carriages, or Drains. **1733** W. ELLIS *Chiltern & Vale Farm.* 326 The Trenching Plough, is either a Wheel or Foot-plough. **1866** *Harper's Mag.* Oct. 636/1 Rough-boarded warehouses crammed with ..gun-carriages,..*trenching spades, and axes. **1904** *Daily News* 18 Aug. 8/1 Parties of soldiers..were going about the field with trenching spades burying the dead. **1779** in *9th Rep. R. Comm. Hist. MSS.* App. III. 148 in *Parl. Papers 1910* (Cd. 5038) XXXV. 675 A large quantity of *trenching tools, etc., had been put on board. **1809** A. HENRY *Trav. & Adventures Canada* xv. 130 The most common way of taking the beaver is that of breaking up its house, which is done with trenching-tools. **1979** R. BLYTHE *View in Winter* iv. 172 They was now shellin' like anything... I got my trenchin'-tool out. **1780** A. YOUNG *Tour Irel.* I. 17 Great quantities of potatoes planted in the *trenching way.

'trenchless, *a.* [f. TRENCH *sb.* + -LESS.] Applied to pipe-laying and draining machinery, etc., that dispenses with the cutting of a trench.

1969 [see PIPE-LAYER]. **1971** *Power Farming* Mar. 60/1 This is a dual-purpose trenchless drainer. **1979** *Daily Tel.* 31 Dec. 15/5 There is the so-called trenchless machine which, in one operation, can lay the pipe without any soil being removed.

'trenchlet. *rare.* [f. TRENCH *sb.* + -LET.] A small or miniature trench.

1787 W. MARSHALL *Norfolk* II. 362 The trenchlets were shoveled, and the banks smoothed. **1793** —— *W. England* (1796) II. 348 By running parallel trenchlets along the face of the slope.

[**trenchman,** app. a misreading of *treuchman*, var. TRUCHMAN, an interpreter, DRAGOMAN.

1632 LITHGOW *Trav.* x. 460, I pleaded for a Trench-man, [it] being against their Law, to accuse or condemne a Stranger, without a sufficient Interpreter. **1666** *Despaut. Gram. Instit.* VII. (Jam.), *Interpres*, an interpreter or Trench-man. **1867** SMYTH *Sailor's Word-bk.*, *Trugman*..also called *trench-man*. **1879** BODDAM-WHETHAM *Roraima* 147 A strong active young fellow..acted as our trenchman.]

†**'trenchment.** *Obs. rare.* [f. TRENCH *v.* + -MENT, or aphetic for *entrenchment*.] A work formed by trenching; an entrenchment.

1604 E. GRIMSTONE *Hist. Siege Ostend* 214 The trenchments being finished, the besieged resolued to bandon the olde rampere. **1700** RYCAUT *Hist. Turks* III. 117 So many Trenchments, Retrenchments, and Palisadoes.. that it was almost impossible for the Enemy to advance ten Paces.

trenchmore ('trɛn(t)ʃmɔə(r)), *sb. Hist.* Also 6 -mour, -moore, 7 -moor. [Origin uncertain. Perhaps a place- or family-name.] An old English country dance, of a lively or boisterous nature; also, the air to which it was danced.

1551-2 in Feuillerat *Revels Edw. VI* (1914) 79 Thre garmentes of sarsenett..for them that daunsed trenchemore. **1579** GOSSON *Sch. Abuse* (Arb.) 33 Paris led the shaking of sheetes with Domitia, and Mnester [led] the Trenchmour, with Messalina. **1597** DELONEY *Gentle Craft* (1912) 154 Like one dancing the trench more he stampt up and downe the yard, holding his hips in his hands. **1611** BARREY *Ram Alley* III. i, Ile make him daunce a trenchmoor to my sword. *a* **1654** SELDEN *Table T.*, *King of Engl.* (1689) 28 In King Charles's time, there has been nothing but Trench-more [*mispr.* Fr——] and the Cushion Dance, *omnium gatherum*, tolly, polly, hoite come toite. **1776** SIR J. HAWKINS *Hist. Mus.* IV. IV. i. 392 In the..Rehearsal, the Earth, Sun, and Moon are made to dance the Hey to the tune of Trenchmore.

†**b.** quasi-*adv.* In a frisky, lively, or boisterous manner. *Obs.*

1577 STANYHURST *Descr. Irel.* in *Holinshed* II. 16/1 They beeset a diuine as well, as for..an ape to strike trenchmoore in a paire of buskins and a doublet. **1605** *Lond. Prodigal* I. ii, I' faith and thy tongue trips trenchmore. **1636** W. SAMPSON *Vow-Breaker* II. i. D ij b, We had a Wedding to day, and the young fry tickle trench-more.

Hence **'trenchmore** *v. nonce-wd.*, *intr.* to dance the trenchmore.

1598 MARSTON *Pygmal.* ii. 145 He doth curtsie, and.. Trenchmore with Apes, play musick to an Owle.

trench-plough, -plow ('trɛn(t)ʃplaʊ), *v.* [f. TRENCH *sb.* or *v.* + PLOUGH *v.*] *trans.* and *intr.* To plough to the depth of two furrows, bringing the lower soil to the surface; to turn a second furrow-slice on the top of the first, by following in the same furrow with a plough set much deeper.

1731-3 TULL *Horse-hoeing Husb.* xix. 274 We Trench-plow where the Land will allow it. **1764** *Museum Rust.* III. xciv. 378 When I trench-plough a field, I go as deep with the second plough as four good horses and strong cattle can well draw. **1844** STEPHENS *Bk. Farm* I. 664, I trench-ploughed a field of 25 acres.

Hence **'trench-plough** *sb.*, a plough designed or adjusted for trench-ploughing; also used for trench-making in warfare; **'trench-ploughing** *vbl. sb.*, the action of the verb.

1763 *Museum Rust.* I. 343 If..the land had a trench-ploughing, it would be of great advantage. **1805** R. W. DICKSON *Pract. Agric.* I. 11 The Trench-Plough, which is so contrived as to turn up the ground to a great depth. **1844** STEPHENS *Bk. Farm* I. 499 A conduit..was built and covered with land stones obtained from the field by trench-ploughing. **1918** E. S. FARROW *Dict. Mil. Terms*, *Trench-plough*, a kind of plough for opening land to a greater depth than that of common furrows; a plough used in trench making.

trend (trɛnd), *sb.* [f. next.]

1. A rounded bend or circuit of a stream. *dial.*

c **1630** RISDON *Surv. Devon* §253 (1810) 261 In the trend of Touridge,..stands Meeth. *a* **1874** MADOX-BROWN *Dwale Bluth* I. iv. (1876) I. 87 We'd dew best ter palch along ter th' trend i th' holler hinder.

2. Wool (partly cleaned) wound in tops for spinning: cf. next, 2 b. *dial.*

1858 SIMMONDS *Dict. Trade*, *Trend*, clean wool.

3. *Naut.* **a.** That part of the shank of an anchor where it thickens towards the crown.

1794 *Rigging & Seamanship* I. 79 Several parts of the anchor are governed by the size of the trend, which is marked on the shank at the same distance from the inside of the throat as the arm measures..to the extremity of the bill. **1867** SMYTH *Sailor's Word-bk.*, *Trend of an Anchor*, the lower end of the shank, where it thickens towards the arms, usually at one-third from the crown.

b. The angle between the direction of the anchor-cable and that of the ship's keel.

1879 in WEBSTER Suppl.

4. a. The way something trends or bends away; the general direction which a stream or current, a coast, mountain-range, valley, stratum, etc. tends to take.

1777 *Horæ Subsecivæ* 438 (E.D.D.). **1803** W. TAYLOR in *Ann. Rev.* I. 438 Tracing the course of streams, or the trend of coasts. **1854** MURCHISON *Siluria* xii. 305 The trend and character of the marine currents. **1872** C. KING *Mountain. Sierra Nev.* i. 2 Numerous ridges..having a general north-east trend. **1876** A. H. GREEN *Phys. Geol.* (1877) 316 As we recede..along the trend of a belt of shale.

b. *fig.* The general course, tendency, or drift (of action, thought, etc.). Now freq. with qualifying word and without const.

1884 *Chr. Commw.* 12 June 823/2 The trend of the thought and action of the churches is..towards the consecration of every department of life. **1902** G. W. E. RUSSELL *Londoner's Log-Book* xiv. 243 Beyond doubt, Bounderley's local popularity is waning. The 'trend' is pointing in another direction. **1912** LADY BURGHCLERE *Life Jas., 1st Dk. Ormonde* I. xii. 377 The general trend of affairs in Munster. **1928** *Granta* 3 Feb. 240 Show me a play that's Russian with a psycho-symbolical trend. **1930** M. A. MAGEE (*title*) Materials for the study of business trends in location of the women's clothing industry. **1967** SINGHA & MASSEY *Indian Dances* i. 38 This can be regarded as a healthy trend since it has aroused a consciousness of the dance.

c. *spec.* in *Educ.* (See quots.)

1960 *Where?* III. 18/1 '*Trend*', *the*, jargon for the increasing tendency of pupils to stay at school beyond the compulsory school-leaving age. **1962** A. SAMPSON *Anatomy of Britain* xii. 185 Since the war more children are staying on voluntarily than had been expected..(the phenomenon known to schoolteachers as 'Trend'). **1969** H. PERKIN *Key Profession* v. 208 The 'trend', that is, the growing demand on the part of the young and their parents for higher education expressed in the tendency to stay on at school beyond the statutory leaving age.

5. *Geol.* A geological formation which is a source of oil or gas. Cf. sense 4 a.

1939 *Bull. Amer. Assoc. Petroleum Geologists* XXIII. 860 The Jackson trend continued to lead in the number of discoveries with 16 new [oil] fields. **1977** *Time* 5 Dec. 59/1 In Louisiana, the 'trend' (main potential gas-producing formation) lies four miles beneath the green bayous and sugar-cane fields.

6. Special Comb.: **trend analysis**, analysis of (esp. statistical) data in order to detect or study any trend represented in them; **trend line**, a line indicating the general course or tendency of something (as a geographical feature or a set of points on a graph); **trend-spotter**, one who observes (or seeks to predict) the changing tide of fashion, in dress, ideas, etc.; **trend surface**, a mathematically defined surface computed as a best fit to the sampled values of some parameter over an area of interest; so ***trend surface analysis***.

1934 M. SASULY *Trend Analysis of Statistics* i. 6 The primary purpose of this book is to derive formulas and computation schedules that will simplify..practical trend analysis. **1964** M. ARGYLE *Psychol. & Social Probl.* xv. 183

For purposes of trend analysis it is not particularly interesting to know how particular people have changed, since this confuses developmental with historical trends—we want to compare groups of people today with equivalent groups at a previous date. **1971** *Jrnl. Gen. Psychol.* LXXXIV. 107 Trend analysis showed that performance under steady illumination did not vary over wavelength. **1912** *Q. Rev.* Apr. 532 The trend-lines of mountain systems are the results..of something more than a lateral pressure. **1930** M. EZEKIEL *Method of Correlation Analysis* xvi. 239 The residuals from the final trend line might be again plotted against the other curves, to see if any further changes were necessary. **1959** *Listener* 2 Apr. 581/2 The almost level trend-line of coal production. **1965** G. J. WILLIAMS *Econ. Geol. N.Z.* iii. 30/2 The lateral displacements are as much as 95 ft from the trend-line of the lode. **1976** *National Observer* (U.S.) 6 Nov., If you slow growth, it means that the trend line for the production of automobiles, refrigerators, houses, and so forth will begin to taper down. **1965** *Punch* 21 Apr. 570/2 As trend-spotters will have spotted, the sweet-and-twenty blonde, who was last year selling us Scotch, shirts and motor-cars from the hoardings is increasingly yielding place to little winsome children. **1980** *Times Lit. Suppl.* 21 Nov. 1316/4, I don't deny that ideology can be adopted as a fashionable mode, but ideas, real ideas, do not make their appearance and disappearance merely to satisfy the shaping whims of trend-spotters; and to pretend that they do is to become a trend-spotter yourself. **1956** R. L. MILLER in *Jrnl. Geol.* LXIV. 425 The problem of defining and analyzing contemporary environments of sedimentation is approached from the point of view of mapping 'trend surfaces'. **1959** *Jrnl. Geophysical Res.* LXIV. 823 Trend surface analysis is a procedure for separating the relatively large-scale systematic changes in mapped data from essentially non-systematic small-scale variations due to local effects. **1978** B. CHAPMAN *Clarke's Analytical Archaeol.* (ed. 2) x. 455 (*caption*) The location of the cultural assemblages in the Central Plains which have been analysed by trend-surface analysis.

trend, *v.* Also 7 treand, trent, 8–9 *dial.* trind. Pa. t. and pple. trended; also 4 *pa. t.* trent, trend(e, *pa. pple.* trent, i-, y-trent, 6 *pa. pple.* trend. [ME. *trenden*, OE. *trendan* (rare):—OTeut. **trandjan*, f. ablaut series **trend*: **trand*: **trund*, which appears also in OE. *trinde* round lump, ball, OFris. *trind, trund*, NFris. *trind*, MLG. *trint, trent, trunt* adjs. round, MLG. *trent* ring, circumference, boundary, Du. *trent* circumference, *omtrent* around, about; also Da., Sw. *trind* round. Ulterior relations obscure: cf. Falk and Torp. See also TRENDLE, TRINDLE, TRUNDLE.]

†**1.** *intr.* To turn round, revolve, rotate, roll; to turn or roll oneself about; also *fig.* *Obs.*

a **1000** *MS. Cott. Faust. A.* x. in *Anglia* I. 285 Se æppel næfre þæs feorr ne trenddeð, he cyð, hwanon he com. [*c* **1000** in Napier *O.E. Glosses* 5 *Teretes, i. rotundos*, sintrendende [*v.r.* sintredende], sinhwyrfende.] **13..** *Guy Warw.* (A.) 314 He went and trent [*Caius MS.* He wende, he trende] his bed opon, So man þat is wo bigon. **1398** [see TRENDING *vbl. sb.* 1]. **14..** *Beryn* 2038 The trowth woll be previd, how so men evir trend. **1654** VILVAINE *Epit. Ess.* I. 32 The whol frame doth round in her orb trend.

†**2.** *trans.* To cause (a thing) to turn round; to turn or roll (anything); to twist, plait, curl; *fig.* to revolve in one's mind. *Obs.* (exc. as in b).

c **1315** SHOREHAM vii. 78 A myȝt..þat halt vp þerþe and sterren bryȝte Aboute itrent. *c* **1374** CHAUCER *Boeth.* III. met. xi. 79 (Camb. MS.) Lat hym rollen and trenden with-Inne hym self the Lyht of his inward syhte. *c* **1380** *Sir Ferumb.* 5881 Wyþ eȝene graye, and browes bent, And ȝealwe traces, & fayre y-trent. **1594** WILLOBIE *Avisa* (1880) 87 The Spindle that you see me driue, Hath fyld the spill so often trend. **1613–16** W. BROWNE *Brit. Past.* II. iii, Not farre beneath i'th valley as she trends Her siluer streame.

b. To wind (wool, partly cleaned) into tops for spinning. *dial.* (Cf. TRENDLE *sb.* 5.)

1777 [see *trended*]. **1794** *Young's Ann. Agric.* XXVI. 454 Herefordshire is the only county that I know which continues the practice of trinding (or winding the wool in tops, ready sorted in some degree for fine drapers). **1828** WEBSTER, *Trend, v.t.*, in rural economy, to free wool from its filth. (*Local.*)

†**3.** *intr.* To make a circuit, travel around or about the edge of a region or piece of land; to skirt, coast (*about, along*). *Obs.*

1580 in Hakluyt *Voy.* (1599) I. 437 You shall trend about the very Northerne and most Easterly point of all Asia. **1615** G. SANDYS *Trav.* 137 The maine Desarts: which all this while we had trented along, and now were to passe through. **1622** R. HAWKINS *Voy. S. Sea* (1847) 179 Trending about the cape, wee haled in east north-east, to fetch the bay of Atacames.

†**b.** More vaguely: To turn or direct one's course. *Obs.*

1618 in Foster *Eng. Factories India* (1906) 11 Their provisions trend from Mosambique to the Mulluccas. **1647** [see TRENDING *vbl. sb.* 2 b]. **1846** LANDOR *Imag. Conv.* Wks. I. 87/1 The religion of blood, like the beasts of prey, will continue to trend northward.

†**c.** *trans.* To coast along, skirt; to make the circuit of, to round (a point of land). *Obs.*

1600 HAKLUYT *Voy.* III. 206 We trended the said land about 9. or 10. leagues, hoping to finde some good harborough. **1602** CAREW *Cornwall* II. 98 b, From thence trending Penlee poynt, you discouer Kings Sand and Causam Bay.

4. *intr.* To turn off in a specified direction; to tend to take a direction or course expressed by the context; to run, stretch, incline, bend (in some direction), as a river, current, coast-line, mountain-range, territory, stratum, etc.

1598 HAKLUYT *Voy.* I. 104 The riuer of..Volga..issueth from the North part of Bulgaria..and so trending along Southward disimboqueth into a certain lake. **1610** HOLLAND *Camden's Brit.* I. 766 The shore treandeth out more and more. **1635** *Voy. Foxe & James to N.W.* (Hakl. Soc.) II. 354, I see the land trent to the Southward. **1779** FORREST *Voy. N. Guinea* 194 From the island of Ebus, the coast trends to the northward. **1860** MAURY *Phys. Geog. Sea* ii. §116 In its course to the north, the Gulf Stream gradually trends more and more to the eastward. **1876** GREEN *Stray Stud.* 290 Their path lay along the coast trending round to the west. **1892** STEVENSON *Across the Plains* 232 The rail-road trended to the right.

b. *fig.* To turn in some direction, to have a general tendency (as a discussion, events, etc.).

1863 G. A. LAWRENCE *Border & Bast.* xiii. 243 In which direction do the sympathies and interests of the Border States actually trend? **1886** DOWDEN *Shelley* I. iv. 164 The discussion..trended away from theology in the direction of politics. **1901** B. MEAKIN *Land of Moors* xx. 407 The Land of the Moors, which, as things trend to-day, must in time form part of her [France's] colony.

c. *trans.* in casual sense: To turn or bend the course of in a particular direction. *rare.*

1840 *Civil Eng. & Arch. Jrnl.* III. 109/1 Laying the several courses perpendicular to the face of the arch..and trending them to the abutments in an angle dependent on the given obliquity.

Hence **'trended** (*dial.* **trinded**) *ppl. a.* (*spec.* of wool: see 2 b), **'trending** *ppl. a.*; also **'trender** (*dial.*), one employed in winding (cleaned) wool.

1777 *Horæ Subsecivæ* 438 (E.D.D.) Trinded wool, wool winded and fastned together with the 'rind of a tree'. **1794** [see TRENDING *vbl. sb.* 1 b]. **1805** LUCCOCK *Nat. Wool* 300 From the trended fleece of Herefordshire about one tenth of its weight is taken of coarse and inferior locks. **1828** WEBSTER, *Trender*, one whose business is to free wool from its filth. (*Local.*) **1856** J. MARTINEAU *Ess.*, etc. (1891) IV. 44 No treaty..can trace a boundary-line any more than a mountain-chain or trending coast can keep out the Almighty Maker of them both. **1968** D. L. CLARKE *Analytical Archaeol.* VI. v. 274 Once again we have six trending variables, each with three crude attitudes.

†**trende**, *a.* *Obs. rare*$^{-1}$. Perhaps 'rounded, circular'.

c **1400** *Sowdone Bab.* 940 O Thow, rede Marz Armypotente, That in the trende baye hase made þy trone.

Trendelenburg (trɛn'dɛlənbɜːg). *Med.* Also (*erron.*) -**berg.** The name of Friedrich *Trendelenburg* (1844–1924), German surgeon, used in the possessive and *attrib.* to designate certain phenomena observed and medical procedures invented by him, as **Trendelenburg('s) position**, an operating position in which the patient lies supine on a tilted table or bed with the pelvis higher than the head; **Trendelenburg('s) test**, (*a*) a test for disorders of the hip joint or gluteus muscles in which the patient stands on one leg and raises the other, a dropping of the pelvis on the unsupported side being a positive sign (***Trendelenburg's sign***); (*b*) a test for varicose veins in which the leg is raised to drain it of blood and then quickly lowered, immediate and rapid distention of the leg veins indicating valve incompetence.

1892 KEEN & WHITE *Amer. Text-bk. Surg.* II. III. viii. 948 The further manipulations within the pelvis will be much facilitated by the elevation of the pelvis.., the position being known as Trendelenburg's position. **1907** *Practitioner* Aug. 288 The abdomen is opened with patient in the extreme Trendelenburg position. **1912** A. H. TUBBY *Deformities* (ed. 2) I. III. ix. 586 Trendelenburg's sign is this: If the patient stands on the affected limb and flexes the hip of the second side..the pelvis slips downwards on the sound side. **1923** JONES & LOVETT *Orthopedic Surg.* xxvii. 556 The so-called Trendelenburg sign..is very characteristic and explains a good deal of the curious gait. **1930** H. BAILEY *Demonstrations of Physical Signs in Clin. Surg.* (ed. 2) xxi. 214 Trendelenburg's test is not diagnostic of congenital hip disease. **1967** G. M. WYBURN et al. *Conc. Anat.* vi. 170/2 With paralysis of gluteus medius or minimus the pelvis drops on the unsupported side when standing on the affected limb (Trendelenberg's sign). **1974** J. D. MAYNARD in R. M. Kirk et al. *Surgery* xi. 239 Trendelenburg test... Confirmation of retrograde flow in the superficial veins is carried out. **1975** *Year Bk. Ear, Nose & Throat* 116 The patient is placed in the 8-degree reversed Trendelenburg position.

trendily ('trɛndɪlɪ), *adv.* [f. TRENDY *a.* + -LY[2].] In a fashionable or 'trendy' manner; modishly. Also in *Comb.* with *ppl. adjs.*

1967 *Guardian* 24 Apr. 4/4 A trendily dressed couple. **1971** *Rolling Stone* 24 June 3/1, I passed a trendily-attired Mendelsohn in front of Bullock's Westwood. **1974** *Listener* 21 Nov. 685/1 His young, trendily radical mistress. **1980** S. BRETT *Dead Side of Mike* ix. 101 A trendily-dressed blonde teenager of thirty-seven.

'trendiness. [f. TRENDY *a.* + -NESS.] The uncritical following of fashionable modes of thought, dress, etc.; the quality of being trendy.

1966 *Guardian* 11 Oct. 6/2 Trendiness seemed worse than going to the common hordes. **1968** *Listener* 26 Dec. 871/2 Its breathless combination of trendiness and self-righteousness. Admittedly, *How It Is* is not alone in turning civil rights, say, into a fashion; and fashion..into a tyranny. **1972** J. MCCLURE *Caterpillar Cop* iii. 42 The homes..were modest bungalows succumbing..to an ill-becoming trendiness; bright colours had been painted over the exterior woodwork. **1974** *Economist* 5 Jan. 13/1 As a result of yesterday's trendinesses, we have now created in the developed world an unfortunate excess of both birth control devices and anti-pollution controls. **1982** S. RADLEY *Talent for Destruction* x. 70 Indeed he is! A very popular Rector, I put it down to the fact that he's not trendy. Trendiness doesn't do in a parish like Breckham Market.

trending ('trɛndɪŋ), *vbl. sb.* Also 8 **trinding.** [f. TREND *v.* + -ING[1].] The action of TREND *v.*

†**1.** Turning round, revolution, rotation. *Obs.*

1398 TREVISA *Barth. De P.R.* IX. i. (Tollem. MS.), Meuynge haþ cause firste and principally of trendynge [1535 trendlynge] aboute of heuen. *Ibid.* XI. x, Of his longe trendynge [1535 trendlynge] aboute comeþ his roundnesse.

b. The winding of wool in a top: see TREND *v.* 2 b. *dial.*

1794 *Young's Ann. Agric.* XXVI. 455 [I] send you, by Drew, a trinded top of wool..with the locks left out of it at trinding.

2. The fact or manner of turning, bending away, or taking a general (specified) direction, as a coastline, etc.; general direction, trend.

1600 HAKLUYT *Voy.* III. A ij, For the space of fiue thousand leagues..considering the trending of the land. **1697** DRYDEN *Æneid* VII. 200 The Coasts and Trendings of the Crooked Shore. **1770** COOK *Voy. round World* III. i. (1773) 484 This point..may be known by the trending of the coast, which is north on the one side, and south-west on the other. **1823** SCORESBY *Jrnl. Whale Fish.* 472 Trending differs from bearing, inasmuch as it is..the direction of a coast or line of ice in regard to itself; whereas the bearing usually refers to the direction of an object, in regard to the place of an observer. **1863** KINGLAKE *Crimea* II. xvi. 222 The trending away of the hills leaves a hollow or recess.

†**b.** The action of continuing a course. *Obs.*

1647 G. TOOKE *Belides* 30 As a streame descending From his faire heads to sea, becomes in trending More puissant.

trendle ('trɛnd(ə)l), *sb.* Forms: 1–5 **trendel**, 4–6 **-il**, 5 **-ill, -yl, -ull, (trenle)**, 5–6 **trendell(e, -yll**, 7 **-al**, 4– **trendle.** [OE. *trendel* circle, ring, coronet, disk, orb, circus, = MLG. *trendel* round disk, MHG. *trendel, trindel* ball, circle, whence (acc. to Falk and Torp) OSw. *trindhel* circle, Sw. dial. *trinnel*:—OTeut. **trendilo-*, f. root of TREND *v.* See also TRINDLE, TRUNDLE.]

†**1.** A circle, a ring, a coronet; a circular disk, orb; a ball, globe. *Obs.*

a **900** *O.E. Chron.* an. 806 An wunderlic trendel [*mirabilis corona*] wearð ateowed abutan ðare sunnan. *a* **1000** *Ags. Manual Astron.* in *Sax. Leechd.* III. 242 Ðaes monan trendel is symle ȝehal. *c* **1000** ÆLFRIC *Hom.* (Th.) II. 606 Seo lichamlice edwist, þæt is þære sunnan trendel. *c* **1050** *Byrhtferth's Handboc* in *Anglia* VIII. 333 Brevis [virgula] [i.e. ˘] ys anes trendles dæl þus licgende. **1388** WYCLIF *Isa.* xxix. 3, Y schal cumpasse as a round trendil [1382 a bal; *Vulg.* sphæram] in thi cumpasse,..and Y schal sette engynes in to thi bisegyng.

2. A wheel: = TRINDLE *sb.* 1, TRUNDLE *sb.* 1, 2. *Obs.* exc. *dial.*

1324 *Acc. Exch., K. R.* Bd. 165 No. 1. m. 4 (P.R.O.) Pro xxviij snekkes cum xxviij stapulis ad tenendum trendles ligni pro springaldis tendendis. *c* **1400** *Destr. Troy* 453 Hir Ene as a trendull turned full rounde, First on hir fader, for feare þat she hade. *c* **1440** *Promp. Parv.* 502/1 Trendyl, *troclea.* **1538** ELYOT, *Spiræ*, thynges whyche doo tourne and wynde in dyuers cerkles lyke a trendell... Also a cake made like a trendell. **1570** LEVINS *Manip.* 126/26 A Trendil, *rota.* **1887** *Suppl. to Jamieson, Trendle, trindle, trenle, trinle, trunle*, the wheel of a barrow, also the wooden portion of the wheel; a small wooden wheel such as is used for a trundle-bed.

†**3.** A suspended hoop or wheel on which tapers were fixed, forming a chandelier, used in churches on certain occasions before the Reformation. *Obs.*

1423 *Will Hodesole* (Somerset Ho.), Lego ad mantenendum le trendil ibidem. **1452** in *Berks., Bucks. & Oxon. Archæol. Jrnl.* Oct. (1903) 78 At ye makyng of ye Est[er] tapur & ye trendull we spendyd iiij. d. **1476** *Croscombe Churchw. Acc.* (Som. Rec. Soc.) 57 Item for a rope for the Trendell..ix^d^. **1502–3** in Kerry *Hist. St. Lawrence, Reading* (1883) 53 It. payed to John Turner for makyng of the Trendyll ij s...for corde to the same Trendyll, vj d...for tymber to make þe trendyll whele..for a bolte and a swevyll to the trendyll, ij d. **1524** *Churchw. Acc. St. Giles, Reading* 22 For makyng of the trendell xviij^d^.

4. A vessel of flat rounded form; a round or oval tub used for various purposes; a circular trough or tray used by bakers. *dial.*

1493 *Yatton Churchw. Acc.* (Som. Rec. Soc.) 119 Thes be perselles that longyth to the Cherche howse..ix barellys..xxj trendyllys..ij trowys. **1516** *Ibid.* 135 Payd for hopyng a trendelle of ye churche..iij^d^. **1669** WORLIDGE *Syst. Agric.* (1681) 323 A *Trendle*, a flat Vessel, by some called a Kiver. **1847–78** HALLIWELL, *Trendle*,..a brewer's cooler. *West.* **1874** T. HARDY *Far fr. Madding Crowd* II. iii. 39 A clock with a face as big as a baking-trendle.

5. A bundle of (partly cleaned) wool 'trended' or wound up (see TREND *v.* 2 b). *dial.*

1805 LUCCOCK *Nat. Wool* 298 Sworn winders..are engaged to strip off the coarse part of the fleece and to wind up only the better kind of wool; to tie about half a dozen fleeces together, and to ticket the weight of each bundle, or as it is there called trendle.

6. Applied to various round or rounded objects (the identity of which cannot always be ascertained).

14.. *Voc.* in Wr.-Wülcker 571/19 *Catantrum*, a trendell. *Ibid.* 586/29 *Giraculum*, a trendel. *c* **1468** *Medulla Gram.* (*MS. Harl.* 1738, lf. 39/2), *Insubulus*, a websters trendyl. [*Insubuli* is rendered *web-beamas* in Wr.-Wülcker 188/4.] **1542** UDALL *Erasm. Apoph.* 29 A maiden..did..cast vp and receiue again one after another twelf trendles or roundles. **1766** *Compl. Farmer, Trendle*, any thing that turns round. **1887** *Suppl. to Jamieson, Trendle*,..a wooden roller on which a heavy block is moved along.

† **trendle**, *v. Obs.* Forms: see prec.; also 3 treondlin. [f. prec. Cf. also TRINDLE, TRUNDLE.]

1. *trans.* To cause to roll or revolve; to roll: = TRUNDLE *v.* 1 a.

[*a* **1000** *Boeth. Metr.* v. 17 Atrendlod of ðæm torre.] **1382** WYCLIF *Judg.* vii. 13 Y saw3 a sweuen, and it seemed to me, as a loof of barlich..to be trendlid and into the tentis of Madyan to goo doun. *c* **1420** *Liber. Cocorum* (1862) 45 Take white pese,..Put hom in pot..Trendel hom in platere and pyke hom clene. *c* **1440** *Promp. Parv.* 502/1 Trendelyn a rownd thynge (*A.* trendlyn as with a rownde thynge), *trocleo, volvo.* **1552** HULOET, Trendle a ball, *proijcere pilam.* **1570** LEVINS *Manip.* 65/29 To Trendle, *rotare.*

2. *intr.* To roll, revolve: = TRUNDLE *v.* 1 b.

a **1225** *Leg. Kath.* 2361, & te riche lefdis Letten teares treondlin. *a* **1250** *Owl & Night.* 135 þeyh appel trendli from þe treo. *c* **1400** *Laud Troy Bk.* 5954 Sche turnes & trendeles as doth a bal. *c* **1450** *Guy Warw.* (C.) 3712 He smote the sowdan with hys sworde, That the hedde trendyld on þe borde. **1495** *Trevisa's Barth. De P.R.* IX. i. (W. de W.) y ij/1 A thynge that trenlyth [*Bodl. MS.* trendeþ] rounde abowte chaungyth not place towchynge all the hole. **1598** YONG *Diana* 300 A certaine thing like a round ball..that ran trendling in the meadow before vs.

Hence † **'trendling** *vbl. sb.* and *ppl. a.*

1495 *Trevisa's Barth. De P.R.* IX. i. (W. de W.) y ij/1 Some meuynge that is chaungynge of place is trenlynge [*Bodl. MS.* trendinge] and rounde wynded abowte. *a* **1577** GASCOIGNE *Flowers, Fruites of Warre* xliv, A tickell treasure, like a trendlynge ball.

† **'trendled**, *a. Obs.* [f. prec. + -ED[1].] Rounded.

c **1220** *Bestiary* 737 Panter is an wilde der... He is blac.. Mið wite spottes sapen [shapen] al Wit [white] and trendled als a wel [wheel].

trendle tayle: see TRUNDLE-.

'trend-setter. [f. TREND *sb.* + SETTER *sb.*[1]] One who or that which establishes trends in dress, thought, etc.

1960 *Guardian* 17 Mar. 4/3 Powerful trend-setters, outstanding personalities. *Ibid.* 7 Dec. 6/3 The magazines ..are the chief trend-setters. **1966** *Listener* 2 June 814/1 The music and aesthetics of modern Italy's musical trend-setter, Casella. **1973** *Times* 24 Apr. 10/2 His big shouldered jackets are important trendsetters. **1979** D. HURD *End to Promises* ii. 26 My strongest feeling was satisfaction that the experts, the know-alls, and the trend-setters had been confounded.

Hence (as back-formation) **'trend-set** *v. intr.*; **'trend-setting** *ppl. a.*

1960 *House & Garden* Oct. 172 The big news from..those trend-setting couturiers. **1965** *Punch* 7 July 34/3 That hairstyle, do you think it will trend-set? **1971** M. LEE *Dying for Fun* v. 42 Pollie Potter, dress designer, had been trendsetting now for two years. **1976** *Times* 26 Aug. 13/2 The trend-setting intellectuals of our day.

trendy ('trɛndɪ), *a.* and *sb.* [f. TREND *sb.* + -Y[1].]

A. *adj.* Fashionable, up to date, following the latest trend. (Sometimes dismissively.)

1962 *Punch* 7 Nov. 654/3, I saw the headline 'The Trendiest Twin Set'. **1965** *Sun* 20 May 7/6 The BBC's Debussy film..must have been the first to use the screen credit 'Art Nouveau Consultant'... This is trying to be trendy: what's wrong with art-adviser? **1972** *Lancet* 20 May 1104/1 Pathobiology (a trendy name for general pathology) seems to be a fashionable subject in the United States. **1977** B. PYM *Quartet in Autumn* viii. 74 That was how it had always been and how it would go on in spite of trendy clergy trying to introduce so-called up-to-date forms of worship. **1982** *Chicago Sun-Times* 11 Nov. 88 (*heading*) Bargains still available in trendy neighborhoods.

B. *sb.* One who follows the latest trends or fashions.

1968 J. FLEMING *Kill or Cure* xi. 143 She was well in with what is now called the Chelsea set.., there are trendies and *personae non gratae* amongst them. **1971** *New Scientist* 26 Aug. 450/1 Amphetamine..to the young trendy..provides a means of staying awake all night. **1974** *Courier-Mail* (*Brisbane*) 30 Mar. 8/3 Some of us have fought all our lives to be trendies. **1982** *Listener* 16 Dec. 20/2 The 'trendies'' concern for the individual seems to relate more to his place in society than to his soul.

'trendyism. [f. prec. + -ISM.] = TRENDINESS.

1977 *Spare Rib* July 4/1 The coy use of Christian names ..reminds me of the clubby, in-group atmosphere of competitive trendyism I found so depressing at the last WLM conference. **1981** *Observer* (Colour Suppl.) 13 Dec. 66/1 An encroaching tide of trendyism.

trendyl, -yll, trendyll bed, obs. ff. TRENDLE, TRUNDLE-BED.

trene, obs. f. THRENE, TREEN; var. TRINE *v.*[2]

trenefald, var. THRINFALD *Obs.*, threefold.

trenel, trenite, obs. ff. TREENAIL, TRINITY.

trenke, var. TRINK *sb.*[1] *Obs.*, kind of net.

† **trenket.** *Obs.* Also 5-6 **trynket.** [a. OF. (Picard) *trenquet*, OF. *trenchet*, f. *trenquer*, *trencher* to cut: see TRENCH *v.*] A knife; *spec.* a shoemaker's knife.

c **1440** *Promp. Parv.* 502/1 Trenket, sowtarys knyfe, *anxorium.* **1483** *Cath. Angl.* 392/1 A Trenket, *ansorium.* **1486** *Bk. St. Albans* f vij, A Trynket of Corueseris [= Shoemakers]. **1530** PALSGR. 283/1 Trynket a cordwayners toole. **1547** SALESBURY *Welsh Dict.*, *Tranket kyllell krydd*, Trenket. [Cf. **1611** COTGR., *Trenchet de cordoüannier*, a Shoo-makers cutting-knife.]

trenlace, trenle: see TRANLACE, TRENDLE.

trenne, trennel: see TREE, TREEN, TREENAIL.

trensh-man, error for *treush-man*, TRUCHMAN.

† **trent.** *Obs.* [a. F. *trente* thirty, or ? abbreviation of *trental.*] = TRENTAL.

1389 in *Eng. Gilds* (1870) 8 On þe morwe to seie a trent of masses atte same ffreres.

trent, obs. f., also pa. t. and pple., of TREND *v.*

trental ('trɛntəl). Also 4-5 (9 *Hist.*) trentale, 4-6 -alle, 5 -ayl, -el, -elle, (trintal), 5-7 trentall, (6 treigntalle). [ad. med.(eccl.)L. *trentāle* (12th c. in Du Cange), f. pop.L. **trenta, *trinta* (:—L. *trīgintā*, whence F. *trente* thirty) + *-āl-is, -āle*, -AL[1]. So OF. *trentel* (12th c. in Godef.).]

1. A set of thirty requiem masses, said on the same day or on different days; also, the payment made for this. *arch.* and *Hist.*

13.. *Minor Poems fr. Vernon MS.* xxxiv. *heading*, Þe Pope trental. *Ibid.* lf. 303 Here bygunnet þe guldene trental þat ou3te be loued swyþe wel. [Cf. xxxiv. 126 Let sei þeos Masses bi 3oure hestes Wiþ-Inne þe vtaues of þe ffestes.] *c* **1386** CHAUCER *Sompn. T.* 16 Trentals seyde he, delieuren fro penaunce Hir freendes soules. *c* **1420** *Anturs of Arth.* 218 Were thritty trentales done, By-twene vnder and none. **1487** *Paston Lett.* III. 463 Every weke folowing unto my monthes mynde oon trentall, and iij. trentalles at my monthes mynde. **1530** LYNDESAY *Test. Papyngo* 695 With gret blys, bury we sall 3our bonis, Syne trentalls twenty trattyll all at onis. **1531** *Wills & Inv. N.C.* (Surtees 1908) 127 Three treigntalles of masse. **1593** BELL *Motives Romish Faith* (1605) 24 For which Masses, Diriges, and Trentals, huge summes of money are giuen daily. **1694** MOTTEUX *Rabelais* (1737) V. 221 Obits, Trentals, and Services for the Dead. **1813** SCOTT *Rokeby* v. xxvii, Let mass be said, and trentals read. **1881** BRIDGETT *Hist. Holy Eucharist* II. xi. 150 St. Gregory's Trental..consisted of ten different masses three times repeated... According to..others they were said in thirty consecutive days, and even by thirty priests in one day.

† **b.** *transf.* A set or series of thirty. *Obs. rare.*

1508 KENNEDIE *Flyting w. Dunbar* 319 Thow says for thame few psaltris, psalmis, or creidis. Bot geris me tell thair trentalis of misdeidis. **1586** P. WYOT *Diary* Oct. in Chanter *Sk. Lit. Hist. Barnstaple* (1866) 92 On St. Luke's day this yere there was a trental of sermons at Pylton.

† **c.** *loosely.* An elegy or dirge. *Obs.*

1648 HERRICK *Hesper.*, *Dirge upon Death of B. Stuart*, Soft silence let us have, While we this Trentall sing about thy grave. *Ibid.*, *To Julia*, Deare Julia, thou shalt have A trentall sung by virgins o're thy grave.

2. Used as = MONTH'S MIND, the commemoration service on the thirtieth day after burial. *arch.*

1659 H. L'ESTRANGE *Alliance Div. Off.* 302 The thirtieth [day] (called therefore..in old English the Months-mind, in after times the Trental). **1860** READE *Cloister & H.* ci, The convent will keep his trentals, but will feast, not fast.

3. *attrib.* and *Comb.*

1471 in *Somerset Medieval Wills* (1901) 222 Item, to Sir John Cerne to say a trentall mass for me, 2s. 6d. **1591** *Troub. Raigne K. John* (1611) 60 The arch prowd titled Priest of Italy,..Is busied now with trentall obsequies,..To ease their soules in painefull purgatorie.

‖ **trente.** Also 7-8 **trante.** [F. *trente* (trɑ̃t):—Com. Romanic **trinta, *trenta*, for L. *trīgintā* thirty.]

† **1.** *Cards.* ? A combination of cards counting thirty, or the score gained by them. *Obs.*

1706 MRS. CENTLIVRE *Basset-Table* IV, I have lost a Trante and Leva, my ill fortune has not forsook me yet.

2. trente et quarante (‖ trɑ̃tekarɑ̃t), in 7 erron. **trante a courante** [F. = thirty and forty], another name for the game of *rouge-et-noir* (in which thirty and forty are respectively winning and losing numbers).

1671 LADY MARY BERTIE in *12th Rep. Hist. MSS. Comm.* App. v. 22 Wee play sometimes at trante a courante. **1764** H. WALPOLE *Let. to Earl Hertford* 25 Nov., Hazard, *Quinze*, and *Trente-et-Quarante.* **1848** THACKERAY *Van. Fair* lxiii, A room for *trente-et-quarante* and roulette. **1892** F. WICKS *Veiled Hand* xviii, He would have one look at the *trente et quarante* table.

trentillment, obs. var. TRINKLEMENT.

Trentine ('trɛntaɪn), *a.* [f. *Trent* (see def.) + -INE[1].] Belonging to Trent, a city of the Tyrol; *spec.* pertaining to the Council of Trent (1542-52, 1562-3): = TRIDENTINE. So † **'Trentish** *a.* in same sense; † **'Trentist**, an adherent of the doctrines of the Council of Trent.

1601 BP. W. BARLOW *Defence* 148 The Trentish Conuenticle confesseth, that it was no sacrament in the olde testament. *Ibid.* 149 Neither was it, say the Trentistes, a sacrament before Christes resurrection. **1675** J. SMITH *Chr. Relig. Appeal* I. 52 The Trentish Anathema would fall heavy upon me. **1826** C. BUTLER *Vind. Bk. Rom. Cath. Ch.* 108 The decree of the Trentine doctors which declared the attendances of Catholics at the Protestant services to be unlawful. **1851** GALLENGA *Italy* 149 Bands of armed peasants from the Trentine valleys had come to Milan.

Trenton ('trɛntən). *Geol.* A name given (*attrib.*, or *ellipt.* as *sb.*) to a limestone formation exemplified at Trenton Falls, New York, and hence to the group or series of Lower Silurian rocks to which it belongs.

1854 MURCHISON *Siluria* xvi. 413 From the 'Potsdam sandstone'..up to the slates and arenaceous schists over lying the Trenton limestone, the group so composed represents the Lower Silurian. **1873** DAWSON *Earth & Man* iv. 59 The Trenton. **1885** LYELL *Elem. Geol.* (ed. 4) 445 The Hudson River Group, and the Trenton Limestone, agree palæontologically with the Caradoc or Bala Group.

trenyte, -tie, obs. forms of TRINITY.

treo, obs. form of TREE.

† **treouse**, *v. Obs.* [OE. *treowsian*, *trywsian*, early ME. *treosi-en*, *tr(e)ousi-en*, f. *treow* troth, faith.] **a.** *refl.* and *intr.* To pledge oneself, give assurance, engage. (Only OE.) **b.** *trans.* To prove to be true. **c.** *intr.* To rely *on.*

a **901** *Laws of K. Ælfred* c. 19 Gyf he hine trywsian wylle ..ðæt he mot. *a* **1000** *O.E. Chron.* an. 972, Him comon onȝean .vi. cyningas and ealle wið [hine] trywsodon [*v.r.* ȝetreowsodon] ðat hi woldon [etc.]. *c* **1205** LAY. 8315 And þu hit nult ileuen..Ich hit wulle trousien. —— 8489 þas weord ich wulle þe treosien þurh mine tirfulne god. —— 9308 þe king him treousede on, For he wes swa æht mon.

treouþe, obs. form of TRUTH.

treowe, treowthe, obs. ff. TRUE, TRUTH.

trepan (trɪ'pæn), *sb.*[1] Forms: 5-7 **trepane**, 5-6 **trapane**, 6 **trappan(e**, 7-8 **trapan**, 6- **trepan.** [a. F. *trépan* (also †*trapan*) a borer, surgical crown-saw (14th c.), ad. med.L. *trepanum* (Du Cange) a crown-saw, ad. Gr. τρύπανον a borer.]

1. A surgical instrument in the form of a crown-saw, for cutting out small pieces of bone, esp. from the skull.

c **1400** *Lanfranc's Cirurg.* 127 þis schal be þe foorme of a trepane wiþ þe whiche þe brayn scolle schal be trepaned wiþ. **1525** tr. *Jerome of Brunswick's Surg.* xxxiv. Hj/2 If the bone be stronge, bore ther throughe many holes with the trappane. **1676** WISEMAN *Chirurg. Treat.* v. ix. 393, I began to work with the Trepan, which I much prefer before a Trephine, it being an Instrument which doth its work lightly, and cutteth the Bone equally. *a* **1715** BURNET *Own Time* an. 1660 (1766) I. 146 The operation of the trepan and the cure was counted one of the greatest performances of surgery at that time. **1846** BRITTAN tr. *Malgaigne's Man. Oper. Surg.* 166 The trepan is applied to the cranium, sternum, and to the tibia, in cases of sequestrum. The scapula has also been trepanned, the os coccyx, the inferior maxilla, &c.

† **2.** A military engine formerly used in sieges: ? for boring holes in walls. *Obs.*

1584 HUDSON *Du Bartas' Judith* III. 107 And there th' Inginers haue the Trepan drest, And reared vp the Ramme for battry best. **1608** SYLVESTER *Du Bartas* II. iv. IV. *Decay* 994 There-under (safe) the Ram with yron horn,..The boistrous Trepane, and steel Pick-ax play Their parts apace, not idle night nor day. **1610** W. FOLKINGHAM *Art of Survey* I. xiii. 45 Engines..Militarie; as Battering-Rams,.. Trepanes.

3. A boring instrument for sinking shafts. (Usually treated as F., *trépan.*)

1877 KNIGHT *Dict. Mech.*, *Trepan*..2. (French.) A workman's name for the steel at the foot of a boring rod. **1903** *Illustr. Lond. News* 10 Oct. 528 The great boring instrument or trêpan, rises and falls with a regular motion. **1903** *Daily Chron.* 22 Oct. 3/5 An 18 ft. shaft has reached a depth of nearly 1,100 ft., the small trépan having gone much further down.

4. *attrib.*, as **trepan hole**, a hole made in a bone by a trepan; **trepan saw**, a saw of the form of a trepan, a crown-saw.

1839 URE *Dict. Arts* 148 *A* is a pulley... It has the crown or trepan saw *a* fixed to it. **1899** *Allbutt's Syst. Med.* VII. 239 A piece of metal tubing..is screwed into the trepan hole.

trepan, trapan (trə'pæn), *sb.*[2] *Obs.* or *arch.* Also 7-8 **trapan, (trappan).** [A word of obscure and low origin, prob. originally a term of thieves' or rogues' slang. According to the known evidence, originally applied to a *person* in sense 1 below (quots. 1641, 1653). Thence arose the verb describing the action of such persons, TREPAN *v.*[2], found in various constructions 1656-62. Hence, finally, a second use of the sb. as a name of the action, 1665, sense 2 here. The earlier spelling of the sb. was *trapan*, probably formed in some way from TRAP *sb.*[1] or *v.*[1] The change to *trepan*, seen first in the vb., may have been due to association with TREPAN *v.*[1] (a much earlier and well known word), of which TREPAN *v.*[2] may have been supposed to be some sort of fig. application.

No F. *trapan* or *trapaner* in this sense is recognized by Littré, Hatz.-Darm., Cotgrave, Godefroy. Nor is there any reason to connect *trapan* with OProv. *trapon* 'sorte de piège', nor with It. *trapanare* = TREPAN *v.*[1]]

1. A person who entraps or decoys others into actions or positions which may be to his advantage and to their ruin or loss. Also applied to an animal (quot. 1686).

1641 T. JORDAN *Walks of Islington* II. ii. (1657) D ij b, If we had known you had been a Trapan, you should ne'r have been admitted into our company. **1653** (*title*) The Total Rout, or a Brief Discovery Of a Pack of Knaves and Drabs, intituled Pimps, Panders, Hectors, Trapans, Nappers,

Mobs, and Spanners. 1686 J. DUNTON *Lett. fr. New-Eng.* (1867) 35 In colour he [alligator] is of a dark brown, which makes him the more imperceptable when he lies as a Trapan in the Waters. *a* 1734 NORTH *Exam.* I. ii. (1740) 119 He was a Rogue, and a manifest Trapan of the Earl's. 1855 MACAULAY *Hist. Eng.* xvii. IV. 32 Old associates who had once thought him a man of.. spotless honour,.. hinted their suspicions that he had been from the beginning a spy and a trepan.

2. [f. TREPAN *v.*^{2}] The action of entrapping; a stratagem, trick; a trap or snare.

1665 *Surv. Aff. Netherl.* 131 So the Muscovite likely, upon a Trepan upon him, to be none of their mildest Foes, hath Engrossed the Comerce of the Caspian Sea. *c* 1668 *Roxb. Ball.* (1891) VII. 380 Beware of Trappans: Maids, look to your Hits. 1671 SOUTH *Serm., Worldly Wisdom* (1715) 341 There being a Snare, and a Trapan almost in every Word we hear. 1684 EARL ROSCOM. *Ess. Transl. Verse* 16 But what a thoughtless Animal is Man, (How very Active in his own Trepan!) 1823 SCOTT *Peveril* xlii, Aware, by experience, how many trepans, as they were then termed, were used betwixt two contending factions.

tre'pan, *v.*^{1} Forms: see TREPAN *sb.*^{1} [f. TREPAN *sb.*^{1}, or F. *trépaner* (14th c. in transl. of Lanfranc).] **a.** *trans.* To operate upon with a trepan; to saw through with a trepan, as a bone of the skull. Also *absol.*

c 1400 *Lanfranc's Cirurg.* 127 [see TREPAN *sb.*^{1} 1]. *Ibid.* 133 þanne I stoppe þe sijk mannes eeris, þat he mowe not heere þe soun of þe yren þat trepaniþ. 1597 A. M. tr. *Guillemeau's Fr. Chirurg.* 10 b/1 We trepane or open the sculle. 1666–7 PEPYS *Diary* 28 Jan., Prince Rupert is.. so bad, that he do now yield to be trepanned. 1751 *Affect. Narr. of Wager* 145 The poor Surgeon.. could.. trapan a broken Scull. 1846 [see TREPAN *sb.*^{1} 1]. 1899 *Allbutt's Syst. Med.* VII. 240 If the skull be trepanned during the condition of acute cerebral compression, the pulsation may be visibly increased.

b. In brush-making: see *trepanning*, quot. 1877, *trepanned*, quot. 1891.

c. *Engin.* To cut an annular groove or hole in (something) by means of a crown saw or other tool; to make (a hole) thus, the core being removed as a solid piece.

1909 in *Cent. Dict.* Suppl. 1919 A. G. ROBSON *Engin. Machine Tools & Processes* ix. 195 With the cutters at hand it was impossible to get a feed greater than 1/200 inch per revolution when trepanning steel from the solid without breaking the cutter. 1953 G. S. SCHALLER *Engin. Manufacturing Methods* xiii. 221 The solid forging is trepanned instead of being bored in the conventional manner. 1970 I. BRADLEY *Myford ML10 Lathe Man.* xi. 64 The smaller holes are best bored, but large holes can be trepanned in order to save a useful piece of material.

Hence **trepanned** (-'pænd) *ppl. a.*, **tre'panning** *vbl. sb.* and *ppl. a.*: **trepanning-elevator**, see quot. 1877, and cf. ELEVATOR 2.

c 1400 *Lanfranc's Cirurg.* 127 þis manere trepanynge suffiseþ to þee. 1597 A. M. tr. *Guillemeau's Fr. Chirurg.* 14 b/2 The edges of the trepannede perforatione beinge verye sharpe. 1759 ADAM SMITH *Mor. Sent.* I. II. iii. 72 A trophy.. of saws for cutting the bones, of trepanning instruments.. would be absurd. 1877 KNIGHT *Dict. Mech.*, *Trepanning. (Brush-making.)* The tufts or bristles are drawn into the holes in the stock by means of wire inserted through holes in the edge, which are then plugged. *Ibid.*, *Trepanning-elevator*, a lever for raising the portion of bone detached by the trephine. 1880 M. P. BALE *Woodworking Machinery* xvii. 168 A Mr. Murdock, in 1810, took out a patent for an improved machine for forming wooden or stone pipes. For boring wood he employed a hollow cylinder, fitted at its extremity with a circular trepanning saw. 1891 *Cent. Dict.*, *Trepanned brush*, a drawn brush having the holes for the bristles drilled partially through the stock to meet lateral holes drilled from the edge or end. The tufts of bristles are drawn into these holes by strong silk or thread passing through the laterals. 1949 W. S. CHURCHILL *2nd World War* II. II. xviii. 319 Trepanning consisted of making a hole in the bomb casing in order to deal with the explosive contents. 1974 *Sci. Amer.* Jan. 36/2 In trepanning a hollow cathode shaped according to the specified pattern lifts parts of complex shape and uniform thickness from a metal slab.

trepan, trapan (trə'pæn), *v.*^{2} *Obs.* or *arch.* Also 7 trappan, trepane. [f. TREPAN, TRAPAN *sb.*^{2}, q.v.] *trans.* To catch in a trap; to entrap, ensnare, beguile.

1656 BLOUNT *Glossogr.*, To *Trepan*, or rather *trappan* (from the Ital. *Trappare* or *trappolare*, i. to entrap, ensnare, or catch in a gin) in the modern acception of the word, it signifies to cheat or entrap [etc.]. 1658 SLINGSBY *Diary* (1836) 431, I see that I am trepan'd by these two fellows. 1664 BUTLER *Hud.* II. III. 617 Some by the Nose with fumes trappan 'em, As Dunstan did the Devil's Grandamm [= Grannam]. 1745 *De Foe's Eng. Tradesman* (1841) II. xxxvi. 87 To lie upon the catch to trepan his neighbour. 1827 SCOTT *Surg. Dau.* vi, That he should have trepanned the friend who had reposed his whole confidence in him. 1894 CROCKETT *Raiders* 38 Fellows who would.. trepan a lass from the Cumberland shore, or slit the throat of a Dumfries burgher.

b. To lure, inveigle (*into* or *to* a place, course of action, etc., *to do* something, etc.).

a 1661 FULLER *Worthies* (1662) II. 2 Some Setters trapanned him.. to hear Masse. 1678 DRYDEN *Limberham* I. i, Hast thou trepan'd me into a Tabernacle of the Godly? 1700 S. L. tr. *Fryke's Voy. E. Ind.* 227 These Men trapan that sort of People to go a Voyage that commonly proves their Destruction. *a* 1715 BURNET *Own Time* (1766) II. 18 To make use of him to trepan a man to his ruin. 1829 SCOTT *Rob Roy* Introd., James Mohr Drummond was secretly applied to to trepan Stewart to the sea-coast, and bring him over to Britain. 1838–9 HALLAM *Hist. Lit.* III. III. vii. §7. 353 Pallavicino having been trepanned into the power of the Pope, lost his head at Avignon.

c. To do (any one) *out of* (a thing) by craft or guile; to cheat or beguile *out of*; to swindle.

1662 J. DAVIES tr. *Olearius' Voy. Ambass.* 163 Ten of those Rogues had trapann'd him out of 500. Crowns. 1725 DE FOE *Voy. round World* (1840) 12 The Spanish Captain.. greatly enraged.. at being.. trepanned out of his ship. 1832 AUSTIN *Jurispr.* (1879) II. xxxvi. 629 Trepanned out of their interests by that ridiculous juggling.

Hence **trepanned** (-'pænd) *ppl. a.*; **tre'panning** *vbl. sb.* and *ppl. a.*; whence **tre'panningly** *adv.*, by cheating or strategy (Bailey, 1731).

1670 WALTON *Lives, Hooker* 222 A slander which this Age calls Trepanning. 1682 in *Lond. Gaz.* No. 1714/5 That.. Insinuating and Trapaning Association. 1701 GREW *Cosm. Sacra* 189 Some may think of Jael, that.. she was no better than a Trapanning Hussy. 1702 C. MATHER *Magn. Chr.* III. II. v. (1852) 384 Pursevants employed for the trepanning and entrapping of them. 1824 GALT *Rothelan* I. II. xii. 259 The fate of the trapanned page. 1826 W. E. ANDREWS *Exam. Fox's Cal. Protestant Saints* 94 Trepanning questions about the power of the pope and the queen in spirituals were put to him.

trepanation (trɛpə'neɪʃən). [f. TREPAN *v.*^{1} + -ATION; cf. F. *trépanation* (14th c. in tr. of Lanfranc).] The operation of trepanning; perforation of a bone, esp. of the skull, by a trepan.

c 1400 *Lanfranc's Cirurg.* 126 & þese, in as myche as touchinge trepanacioun, worchiþ best. 1597 A. M. tr. *Guillemeau's Fr. Chirurg.* 56 b/2 Opinione of Avicenna touchinge trepanatione. 1882 *Athenæum* 16 Dec. 817/2 Numerous cases of surgical and posthumous trepanation.

‖**trepang** (triː'pæŋ). Also 8 **tripam**, 9 **tripang**, **trepong**. [Malay *trīpang* (Yule). The early form *tripam* was app. from Fr.] A marine animal, an echinoderm (*Holothuria edulis*), called also *sea-cucumber*, *sea-slug*, *sea-swallow*, or *bêche-de-mer*, eaten as a luxury by the Chinese.

1783 JUSTAMOND tr. *Raynal's Hist. Indies* I. 277 [Celebes] furnishes.. tripam, a species of mushroom, which increases in value in proportion to the roundness of it's form, and the blackness of it's colour. 1793 J. TRAPP *Rochon's Voy. Madagascar*, etc. 390 The tripam is a little spungy plant without root, and like a mushroom... It grows in great profusion in the island of Celebes. 1802 CAPT. ELMORE in *Naval Chron.* VIII. 380 Sea swallow (called beach de mar by the Portuguese, and trepong by the Malays). 1836 *Penny Cycl.* V. 188/2 The tripang swala, or sea-slug. 1879 WRIGHT *Anim. Life* 572 So far as we know, but one species is used for food. This, the Trepang of the Chinese (*Holothuria edulis*), is found in the Indian Ocean.

b. *attrib.* and *Comb.*, as ***trepang-fisher***, ***-fishery***.

1846 J. L. STOKES *Discov. Australia* I. vii. 211 These lighter coloured people are Malays, captured from the Trepang fishers. 1878 P. L. SIMMONDS *Commerc. Prod. Sea* I. ix. 105 The trepang fishery of the Pacific and Eastern Seas. 1904 HOWITT *Native Tribes S.E. Australia* i. 26 The trepang fishers.. are the Bugis, a Malayan people, who form the principal nation of the Island of Celebes.

tre'panger. [f. TREPANG + -ER^1.] A trepang-fisher.

1912 A. SEARCY *By Flood & Field* xlviii. 302 Our confrere then informed us that as soon as the famous hunter gained his liberty he had purchased a ketch, fitted her up with the requirements of a trepanger, and sailed away. 1934 *Bulletin* (Sydney) 14 Mar. 33/1 The trepangers with their long, sharp iron spears will soon be working the Rowley Shoals.

† **trepanize,** *v. Obs. rare.* [f. TREPAN *v.*^{1} + -IZE.] = TREPAN *v.*^{1}

1601 HOLLAND *Pliny* XVII. xxvii. I. 545 Even their bones also use to be trepanized and bored through as well as ours. 1684 *Contempl. St. Man* I. v. (1699) 47 Some have been cured by tripanizing the Scull, or drawing Bones from it.

tre'panned, *ppl. a.*^{1} and ^{2}: see TREPAN *v.*^{1} and ^{2}.

trepanner^1 (trɪ'pænə(r)). [f. TREPAN *v.*^{1} + -ER^1.]

1. One who operates with a trepan.

1727 in BAILEY vol. II. 1775 in ASH; and in later Dicts.

2. *spec.* in *Coal Mining* (see quot. 1967).

1956 ATKINSON & WHITE in D. L. Linton *Sheffield* 269 Intensive efforts are being made to replace the hand-loading of coal.. by mechanical power-loaders and.. considerable success is being achieved with.. Gloster Getters, Trepanners,.. and Huwood Slicers. 1967 *Gloss. Mining Terms (B.S.I.)* VIII. 27 *Trepanner*, a longwall power loader, usually double ended, the main cutting element of which is a trepanning wheel. 1971 [see PLOUGH, PLOW *sb.*^{1} 5 i]. 1974 P. WRIGHT *Lang. Brit. Industry* xiv. 145 He may.. hear.. shearer and trepanner for types of coal-cutters.

tre'panner^2. *arch.* Also 7–8 tra-. [f. TREPAN *v.*^{2} + -ER^1.] One who trepans; an entrapper, decoy, swindler.

1658–9 in *Burton's Diary* (1828) IV. 157 There came several trepanners from Whitehall, it pleased God to keep us upright. *a* 1709 ATKYNS *Parl. & Pol. Tracts* (1734) 339 This Trapanning proves.. that the Trapanner did bear a Spight and Malice against the Person trapanned. 1818 SCOTT *Rob Roy* xxxiv, The turmoils which the political trepanner.. is.. putting into motion.

trepanning, *vbl. sb.*^{1} and ^{2}, *ppl. a.*^{1} and ^{2}: see TREPAN *v.*^{1} and ^{2}.

trepas, -pase, -passe, obs. ff. TRESPASS.
See esp. TRESPASS *v.*

trepeget, -eiette, trepget, obs. ff. TREBUCHET.

trepett, var. TRIPPET *Obs.*

trephine (trɪ'faɪn, -'fiːn), *sb.* Forms: 7 **trafine**, **trafin**, **trefine**, **traphine**, 8– **trephine**. [Orig. *trafine*, according to the inventor f. L. *trēs fīnēs* three ends (see quot. 1628), app. formed with reference to *trapan*, TREPAN *sb.*^{1} (to which the later form *trephine* shows a nearer approach). F. *tréphine* is from Eng.]

1. a. An improved form of trepan, with a transverse handle, and a removable or adjustable sharp steel centre-pin which is fixed upon the bone to steady the movement in operating.

1628 WOODALL *Viaticum* Wks. (1639) 313 The Trafine.. an Instrument of my owne composing,.. although it may be said to be a derivative or Epitomy of or from the Trapan.. I thought fit to put the name of a Trafine upon it (*a tribus finibus*) from the three ends thereof. 1656 RIDGLEY *Pract. Physic* 172 Raise it with a Trepan, or a Trefine. 1767 GOOCH *Treat. Wounds* I. 304 That kind of trepan, called the *trephine*, is now in general use,.. it is more commodious than the other. 1855 H. SPENCER *Princ. Psychol.* (1873) I. I. iv. 70 When by means of a trephine, the depressed portion of bone is cut out, the brain.. at once resumes its duties.

transf. 1854 BADHAM *Halieut.* 441 The patient may plunge and writhe, but the operation of trephine goes on, and soon .. does the lamprey push his tongue through the bony plates of the skull, and draw it back, with a sample of brains adhering.

b. *attrib.*, as ***trephine hole***, ***opening***, ***saw*** (cf. TREPAN *sb.*^{1} 4).

1877 KNIGHT *Dict. Mech.*, *Trephine-saw*, a crown-saw; a cylindrical saw with a serrated end, to make a circular kerf by the rotation of the saw. 1878 T. BRYANT *Pract. Surg.* I. 220 The trephine opening was filled in by a tough membrane. 1891 W. H. WHITE in *Jrnl. Physiol.* XII. 247 The same sized trephine hole was made in the skull.

2. = *trephination* s.v. TREPHINE *v.*

1958 F. G. SLAUGHTER *Daybreak* I. ii. 13 A patient should be more than a chart number.. even to a neuro-surgeon performing a preliminary trephine. 1976 *Lancet* 9 Oct. 769/2 Bone-marrow aspirate and trephine confirmed acute myeloid leukæmia.

tre'phine (see prec.), *v.* [f. prec.] *trans.* To operate upon with a trephine. Also *absol.*

1804 ABERNETHY *Surg. Obs.* 174 Which opinions would induce us to trephine in cases of slight depression [of bone in fractured skull]. 1860 O. W. HOLMES *Elsie V.* xxvi, He was trephined at Greenwich Hospital. 1892 'G. TRAVERS' *Mona Maclean* (1893) III. 102 A fractured skull came in.. and I waited to see them trephine. 1899 *Allbutt's Syst. Med.* VI. 293 The sinus is then exposed by trephining the mastoid.

Hence **trephined** (-'faɪnd, -'fiːnd) *ppl. a.*, **tre'phining** *vbl. sb.* (also *attrib.*); also **trephi'nation**, the operation of trephining.

1862 *Catal. Internat. Exhib., Brit.* II. No. 3552 Trephining Instruments. 1874 ROOSA *Dis. Ear* 425 Many cases of trephination of the mastoid. 1886 *Athenæum* 24 Apr. 557/2 A skull.. which exhibits a remarkable instance of post-mortem trephining. 1891 *Ibid.* 19 Sept. 390/3 Amulets from portions of the trephined skulls.

trepid ('trɛpɪd), *a. rare.* [ad. L. *trepid-us* scared, alarmed.] Trembling; agitated; fearful.

1650 W. BROUGH *Sacr. Princ.* (1659) 421 Trembling, and chilness and confusion in the powers of action.. a stupid, trepid, troubled motion. 1675 tr. *Machiavelli's Prince* vi. (Rtldg.) 39 The defence is so trepid and faint. 1760–72 H. BROOKE *Fool of Qual.* (1809) IV. 25 [He] presented his trepid hand to conduct the fair.. to her carriage. 1859 THACKERAY *Virgin.* lxx, The poor little trepid creature, panting and helpless under the great eyes.

Hence **'trepidly** *adv.*, **'trepidness**.

1727 BAILEY vol. II, *Trepidness*, Trepidity, Fearfulness. 1911 *Daily News* 13 Nov. 4 With a show of boldness, but really trepidly and distrustfully.

'trepidant, *a. rare.* [ad. L. *trepidānt-em*, pr. pple. of *trepidāre* to TREPIDATE.] Trepidating, trembling with fear or agitation.

1891 [see ABASIA]. 1892 *Black & White* 2 July 2/2 In either party are many trepidant hopes and fears. 1907 F. THOMPSON *Sel. Poems* 50 Its keys are at the cincture hung of God, Its gates are trepidant to His nod.

Hence **'trepidancy**, the quality of trepidating.

1845 POE *Tales, Fall of Ho. Usher*, Futile struggles to overcome an habitual trepidancy.

† **'trepidat, -ate,** *a. Obs. rare.* [ad. L. *trepidāt-us*, pa. pple. of *trepidāre*: see next.] Agitated, disturbed. (Cf. TREPIDATION 3.)

1605 S. DOVE *Confut. Atheism* 19 The celestiall spheres in continuall volubilitye.. their diurnall or daylye course from the East to the West, their retrograde and vyolent motion from the West to the East, their trepidat motion from the South to the North.

trepidate ('trɛpɪdeɪt), *v. rare.* [f. ppl. stem of L. *trepidāre* to hurry, bustle, be agitated or alarmed. Cf. OF. *trepider* (14th c. in Godef.).] *intr.* To tremble with fear or agitation; also simply, †To shake, be agitated (*obs.*).

1623 COCKERAM, *Trepidate*, to tremble for feare. 1653 R. G. tr. *Bacon's Hist. Winds* 364 Let the eighteenth Motion be the Motion of Trepidation, to which (as is understood by Astronomers) we give no great credit... In which bodies being not altogether well placed.. doe trepidate or agitate continually. *a* 1774 TUCKER *Lt. Nat.* (1834) II. 126 Vanity.. insinuates among our pores,.. trepidates through the nerves,.. and runs throughout the whole constitution. 1854

Fraser's Mag. L. 355 A thing which causes our mind to trepidate with quaking fear.

Hence **'trepidating** *ppl. a.*

a **1774** TUCKER *Lt. Nat.* (1834) II. 620 A calm and steady alertness..never anxious nor trepidating. **1866** J. B. ROSE tr. *Ovid's Met.* 202 The flush of pain And panting breath, and trepidating vein.

trepidation (trɛpɪˈdeɪʃən). [ad. L. *trepidātiōn-em*, n. of action fr. *trepidāre*: see prec. Cf. F. *trépidation* (15th c.).]

1. Tremulous agitation; confused hurry or alarm; confusion; flurry; perturbation.

1607-12 BACON *Ess., Of Seditions & Troub.* (Arb.) 414 There vseth to be more trepidacion in Courtes vponn the breaking out of troubles then were fitt. *a* **1639** WOTTON *Election Dk. Venice* in *Reliq.* (1651) 176 The success of that great day, in such trepidation of the State made every man meritorious. **1780** JOHNSON *Let. to Mrs. Thrale* 9 June, They did their work at leisure..without trepidation, as men lawfully employed. **1796** MME. D'ARBLAY *Camilla* I. 323 Miss Margland..in equal trepidation from anger and from fear. **1879** M. ARNOLD *Mixed Ess., Geo. Sand* 318, I found a large party assembled. I entered with some trepidation.

2. Tremulous, vibratory, or reciprocating movement; vibration; oscillation, rocking; an instance of this; also, involuntary trembling of the limbs, as in paralytic affections; tremor.

1605 BACON *Adv. Learn.* II. ii. §8 Massiue bodies..haue certaine trepidations and wauerings, before they fixe and settle. **1696** J. EDWARDS *Demonstr. Exist. & Provid. God* I. p. xii, Earth-quakes and trepidations of the earth. **1750** JOHNSON *Rambler* No. 1 ¶13 My impatience..will not suffer me to attend any longer the trepidations of the balance. **1822-34** *Good's Study Med.* (ed. 4) III. 227 A considerable degree of trepidation reached occasionally to her finger's end. **1837** WHEWELL *Hist. Induct. Sc.* (1857) II. 240 The trepidation of the body struck perpetually generates a new sound. **1899** *Syd. Soc. Lex., Trepidation*, a rhythmic movement of the foot in certain forms of paraplegia and in epilepsy.

3. *Astron.* A libration of the eighth (or ninth) sphere, added to the system of Ptolemy by the Arab astronomer Thabet ben Korrah, *c* 950, in order to account for certain phenomena, esp. precession, really due to motion of the earth's axis.

a **1631** DONNE *Valedict.* Poems (1633) 193 Moving of th' earth brings harmes and feares, Men reckon what it did and meant, But trepidation of the spheares, Though greater farre, is innocent. **1653** [see TREPIDATE *v.*]. **1667** MILTON *P.L.* III. 483 They pass the Planets seven, and pass the fixt, And that Crystalline Sphear whose ballance weighs The Trepidation talkt, and that first mov'd. **1670** EACHARD *Cont. Clergy* 52 Up presently to the primum-mobile, and the trepidation of the firmament. **1834** *Penny Cycl.* II. 532/2 Thabet ben Korrah..about A.D. 950..revived an old notion ..(not mentioned by Ptolemy, but by Theon [A.D. 385]) of a variation in the position of the ecliptic, which has been called a *trepidation*.

trepidatory (trɪˈpɪdətərɪ), *a.* [f. as prec. + -ORY[2].] Of, pertaining to, or characterized by trepidation or tremor.

1881 G. F. RODWELL in *Knowledge* 16 Dec. 130/2 The most severe shock lasted for 70 seconds, and combined oscillatory, trepidatory, and rotatory movement. **1890** W. O'BRIEN *When we were Boys* 191 'You are joking', he said, in the trepidatory tone of one who had just heard the last Trumpet was about to sound.

trepidity (trɪˈpɪdɪtɪ). [f. L. *trepid-us* TREPID + -ITY.] Agitation, alarm, fearfulness.

1721 BAILEY, *Trepidity*, trembling, fearfulness. **1807** W. TAYLOR in *Ann. Rev.* V. 193 Pecuniary cowardice is far viler than animal trepidity. **1898** *Westm. Gaz.* 7 Sept. 7/1 It was with some trepidity that..one looked out of the window.

treponema (trɛpəʊˈniːmə). *Biol.* and *Med.* Pl. **-'nemata.** Also anglicized as **'treponeme.** [mod.L. (coined in Ger. by F. Schaudinn 1905, in *Deutsch. med. Wochenschr.* 26 Oct. 1728/1), f. Gr. τρέπ-ειν to turn + νῆμα thread.] An anærobic spirochæte of the genus of this name, the members of which are parasitic or pathogenic in man and warm-blooded animals and include those causing syphilis and yaws.

1908 [see *spirochæte* s.v. SPIRO-]. **1922** *Nature* 20 May 667/2 Existence of the treponeme in the cytoplasm of the nerve cells of the cerebral cortex. **1949** M. A. JENNINGS in H. W. Florey et al. *Antibiotics* II. xxxi. 1011 In a patient with concurrent typhoid fever the treponemata disappeared but the typhoid infection ran its usual course. **1970** *New Scientist* 19 Mar. 543/1 Late in the disease, dormant treponemes persist in some instances in lymph nodes and other tissues. **1981** *Brit. Med. Jrnl.* 18 Apr. 1312/1 Walt Disney's serried ranks of gonococci and treponemes.

Hence **trepo'nemal** *a.*, of, pertaining to, or caused by treponemes; **treponema'tosis** (pl. **-oses**), infection with, or a disease caused by, treponemes.

1913 CASTELLANI & CHALMERS *Man. Trop. Med.* (ed. 2) xliv. 1191 These drugs seem to act in frambœsia more quickly and powerfully than in any other spirochætal and treponemal condition. **1927** *Jrnl. Laboratory & Clin. Med.* XII. 670 In this paper we are using the term 'treponematosis' to include syphilis and the condition called yaws. **1970** *New Scientist* 19 Mar. 543/1 Venereal syphilis of adults is rare in tropical regions where the endemic treponematoses, yaws and pinta, prevail. *Ibid.*, The results of a quarter of a century's experience with penicillin in the treatment of treponemal disease, notably syphilis, are now available. **1980** *Nature* 7 Feb. 573/2 Treponemal infection in irradiated mice.

treponemicidal (ˌtrɛpəniːmɪˈsaɪdəl), *a.* [f. prec. + -I- + -CID(E + -AL.] Of, pertaining to, or causing the destruction of treponemata.

1933 J. E. MOORE *Mod. Treatment of Syphilis* xxvi. 382 In early meningeal neurosyphilis..the desideratum of treatment is treponemicidal effect applied as powerfully as possible. **1970** *New Scientist* 19 Mar. 543/1, 2·4 mega-units of long acting benzathine penicillin can maintain a treponemicidal blood and tissue level for three weeks or more.

‖**très** (trɛ), *adv. colloq.* [Fr.: see TRES-.] With English adjs.: very. Usu. with reference to a fashionable or modishly superior quality, freq. as *très snob*, very 'posh'.

[**1815** F. BURNEY *Let.* 10 July (1980) VIII. 285 He is *très* what those on the other side the question call *exalté*.] **1819** KEATS *Let.* 3 Jan. (1931) I. 292 A full, true, and très particular account of Miss M's ten Suitors. **1939** 'N. BLAKE' *Smiler with Knife* iv. 63 It's a sort of county club. Très snob. Très cad. On the Thames. **1959** A. SINCLAIR *Breaking of Bumbo* v. 74 The continental millionaires, who thought it *très snob* to bring out their young in the last society in Europe. **1968** A. DIMENT *Gt. Spy Race* viii. 126 *Très, très* sexy. It was fairly obvious..which section of 'trad' spy-craft Mrs Omega was going to test. **1976** *Publishers Weekly* 8 Mar. 67/2 The picture on the cover, a *très* cool modern kid who doesn't look a bit like the novel's hero. **1978** J. SHERWOOD *Limericks of Lachasse* xii. 140 Students..who were of good family and *très snob*.

tres, obs. f. *trees*, pl. of TREE; obs. f. TRESS.

†**tres-**, a. F. *très* (trɛ) adv. 'very':—L. *trans* beyond; formerly in occasional Eng. use prefixed to adjs., properly French (or identical in form with French), as *treschristien* [= mod.F. *chrétien* Christian], *tresgrand* (very great), *tresnoble*, *trespuissant*, *tres-royal*; sometimes to English adjs., as *tres-sacred*, *tres-splendent*. Hence rarely in derived sb., as *trespuissance*.

1572 *Satir. Poems Reform.* xxxviii. 19 Thy style was *Treschristien, maist Cristen King. **1605** BROUGHTON *Corrupt. Handl. Relig.* 104 The trespas is doubtles *tres-grand. **1587** FLEMING *Contn. Holinshed* III. 1977/1 Of this *tresnoble and *trespuissant monarch, I find these few verses. **1577-87** HOLINSHED *Chron.* I. 181/1 The *tres-puissance of Cnute, the amplenesse of his dominions. **1647** WARD *Simp. Cobler* 57 *Tres-Royall Sir, I once againe beseech you. **1600** W. WATSON *Decacordon* (1602) 49 The same *tres-sacred bodie..was both dead and buried. **1648** *Petit. East. Assoc.* 12 To behold..our *Tres-splendent Crown carried into a desolate Wardrope.

tre'saiel, tre'sayle. *Obs.* exc. *Hist.* Forms: 5-6 **tresaill**, 6 **tresaioul**, 7-8 **tresaile**, 8 **tresail**, 6-9 **tresayle**. [AF., formed after BESAIEL; cf. F. *trisaïeul* (16th c. in Godef. *Compl.*), f. *tri-*, TRI- + *aïeul* grandfather, AIEL.] A grandfather's grandfather; a great-great-grandfather.

1491 *Ordin. Yarmouth* in H. Swinden *Gt. Yarm.* (1772) 135 King Henry tresaill of our sovereigne lord the kyng that now is. **1550** J. COKE *Eng. & Fr. Heralds* §35. (1877) 66 His [Charlmayne's] tresaioul, named Pepyn. **1607** COWELL *Interpr., Cosenage*.., is a writ, that lyeth where the tresaile (that is, *tritavus*, the father of the besaile, or of the great grandfather) is seysed in his demesn as of fee, at the day of his death, of certaine lands or tenements, and dyeth: and then a straunger entreth and abateth. **1768** BLACKSTONE *Comm.* III. x. 186 If it mounts one degree higher, to the tresayle or grandfather's grandfather,..the writ is called a writ of cosinage, or *de consanguineo*.

b. *writ of tresayle*: see quot.

1772 *Jacob's Law Dict.* (ed. 9), *Tresayle*, the name of a writ, to be sued, on ouster, by abatement, on the death of the grandfather's grandfather; now obsolete. **1848** in WHARTON *Law Lex.*

†**tresance.** *Obs.* Also 5 **-auns**, **-aunce**, 5-6 **-awnce**, **-ens(e**, 6 **treasance**. [ad. med.L. *tre-, trisantia*, of uncertain meaning, but app. the covered passage round a cloister: see Du Cange, ed. 1887. Etymology obscure: perh. *tres-* = L. *trans-*.]

1. A passage in or through a house; a corridor.

1428 in Heath *Grocers' Comp.* (1869) 6 The seide parlore and the tresance lattizid, glazid, and selyd. [**1429-30** in Hope *Windsor Castle* (1913) 395 Pro factura ostii de la tresaunt in capella.] *c* **1440** *Promp. Parv.* 502/1 Tresawnce, in a howse.., *transitus*. *c* **1475** *Crabhouse Reg.* (1889) 58 The tresense fro the chawmbur dore to the halle dore. **1519** HORMAN *Vulg.* 291 b, I mette hym in a tresawnce: where one of the bothe muste go backe. **1579** TWYNE *Phisicke agst. Fort.* I. cxviii. 148 His other Gallerie and large Treasance. [**1851** TURNER *Dom. Archit.* I. v. 233 (Roll of 35 Hen. III) Wainscote also the tresance [*tresancia*] between the hall and the aforesaid bed-chamber.]

2. ? A window; ? a lattice or screen.

1510 STANBRIDGE *Vocab.* (W. de W.) B j b, *Transcenna*, a tresens. [**1525** est fenestra in summitate domus.] **1530** PALSGR. 282/2 Tresens drawen over an estates chambre, *ciel*.

†**tresche.** *Obs.* Also **treische**, **treche**. [a. OF. *tresce*, *tresche* a dance, merry gathering (12th c. in Godef.); cf. It. *tresca* 'a kind of Antike or merrie dance' (Florio); 'a country-dance' (Baretti).] A dance, revel, merry-making.

tresche of giants, a popular name of prehistoric stone-circles. Cf. CAROL *sb.* 4.

c **1290** *S. Eng. Leg.* I. 88/65 Huy sounguen ofte..and treches [*v.r.* tresches] huy gonne lede. **1297** R. GLOUC. (Rolls) 1221 þe kinges neueu & þe erles neueu of kent..In þat noble tresche [*v.rr.* treische; companye; reuel] strif bigonne arere. *Ibid.* 3062 þat was þe treche of geans, vor a quointe worc it is Of stones al wiþ art ymad, In þe world such non is..þus was stonheng uerst ymad, þat men al day ysep. *Ibid.* 7067 Roberd þis noble duc as he wende ouer-lond A wel vair maide as him þo3te in a tresche [*v.rr* one treche: a strete] he vond.

trese, obs. f. *trees*, pl. of TREE.

†**trese'mayns.** *Obs.* [= OF. *treis* (*trois*) *semaines* three weeks.] The space of three weeks.

1545 in Leadam *Crt. of Requests* (Selden) 168 The tenauntes..shall brynge afor theym at Westminster the tresemayns of Ester next commyng all suche auncient Courte Rolles and Recordes.

‖**tresette** (‖treˈsɛtte, treɪˈsɛt). Also **trisette**, **trissett**, **tresset**. [Ital. *tresette*, f. *tre* three, *sette* seven, F. *tré-sept*.] An Italian card-game for four persons, played with a pack of 40 cards (the 8, 9, and 10 of each suit being excluded), in which the 3 and 7 are the winning cards.

1785 C'TESS ROSENBERG *Ess.* II. 109 A priest who used to come every day to make up my father's party at trisette. **1858** MISS BRIGHTWELL *Life Linnæus* 172 Mostly played at the Swedish game of trissett. **1902** tr. *Ct. Kielmansegge's Diary* 57 We were home by dinner-time, and spent that evening..at Richmond, playing a game of tresset amongst ourselves. **1903** *Review of Rev.* Aug. 250/2 He liked..to sit down..to a four-cornered card game of tresette.

†**tres'get.** *Obs. rare*[-1]. [a. OF. *tresgiet*, *tresget* act of throwing across, darting (12th c. in Godefroy), n. of action fr. *tre(s)geter*: cf. TREGET.] Casting of darts.

13.. *K. Alis.* 7383 (Bodl. MS.) Wel hij fi3tten on þe pleyn Wiþ tresget [*v.r.* target] wiþ reremeyn.

†**tresgressor.** *Obs. rare*[-1]. Altered form of TRANSGRESSOR, with F. *tres-* = L. *trans-*, as in *trespass*.

1549 *Compl. Scot.* xiv. 118 Ane tresgressor that hed committit cryme.

‖**tresillo** (treˈsiʎo). [Sp., factitious dim. of *tres* three.] A Spanish card-game; = OMBRE.

1829 W. IRVING in *Life & Lett.* (1864) II. 403 The countess comes up to the Alhambra with a little party to play at Tresillo. **1878** H. H. GIBBS *Ombre* 4 The game [Ombre] is now played in Spain under the name of *Tresillo*, meaning a threesome game.

tresle, obs. form of TRESTLE.

†**tresmoun'tain**, *a.* *Obs. rare*[-1]. [a. OF. *tresmontaine* polestar (13th c. in Godef.), with *tres-* = *tras-*, *trans-*: see TRA-, TRANSMONTANE.] = TRANSMONTANE 2; cf. TRAMONTANE B. 1.

c **1430** *Pilgr. Lyf Manhode* IV. xxiii. (1869) 189 Summe j drawe to þe pitee of þe ryal magestee of god,..summe ooþere to þe sterre tresmountayne.

tresnoble: see TRES-.

treson, **tresor**, **-our**, obs. ff. TREASON, TREASURE.

trespass (ˈtrɛspəs), *sb.* Forms: 3-7 **trespas**, (4-5 **trispas**, **trispase**), 4-6 **trespace**, 4-7 **trespasse**, (5 **truspas**, **trespaas**, 6 **tresspas**, **treaspas**), 7- **trespass**. *β.* 4 **trepas**, **-pase**, *pl.* **-pasis**. [ME. *trespas*, a. OF. *trespas* passing across, passage, transgression of an order or law, offence, vbl. sb. fr. *trespasser*, mod.F. *trépasser* to pass away, die: see TRESPASS *v.* The legal application of the words seems specially English.]

1. A transgression; a breach of law or duty; an offence, sin, wrong; a fault.

c **1290** *S. Eng. Leg.* I. 23/152 He [St. Dunstan]..for-3af hem [his servants] heore trespas..And a-soylede hem of heore sunnes. *c* **1330** R. BRUNNE *Chron.* (1810) 171 þei did a foule trespas, it was vnsemly þing. **1382** WYCLIF *Matt.* vi. 14 3if 3ee shulen for3eue to men her synnys, and 3oure heuenly fadir shal for3eue to 3ou 3oure trespassis. *a* **1425** *Cursor M.* 822 (Trin.) Furst shulde he bie dere þat trespace [*rime* grace]. *c* **1440** *Alphabet of Tales* 502 In þat mene while ..it [a soul] mot hafe done suche penance for þe truspas at it had done, at it mot hafe bene delyverd fro payn. **1526** TINDALE *Matt.* vi. 12 [see TRESPASS *v.* 3 b]. *Ibid.* 14 And [= if] ye wyll not forgeve men there trespasses, no more shall youre father forgeve your treaspases. **1611** SHAKS. *Wint. T.* I. ii. 265 Be plainer with me, let me know my Trespas. **1687** A. LOVELL tr. *Thevenot's Trav.* II. 179, I lookt upon it as a Trespass against human prudence, to run the hazard a second time of being hindered to go into the Indies. **1768** BLACKSTONE *Comm.* III. xii. 208 Trespass, in it's largest and most extensive sense, signifies any transgression or offence against the law of nature, of society, or of the country in which we live. **1831** SCOTT *Ct. Robt.* v, My head..is at your imperial command, prompt to pay for the unbecoming trespass of my tongue.

2. *Law.* In a wide sense, Any violation or transgression of the law; *spec.* one not amounting to treason, felony, or misprision of either.

c **1290** *Beket* 462 in *S. Eng. Leg.* I. 119 It nas neuere lawe ne ri3t, double dom to take For o trespas. *c* **1330** R. BRUNNE *Chron.* (1810) 50 Edrik was hanged on þe toure, for his trispas. **1421** *Coventry Leet Bk.* 24 Noo Osteler bake no maner of bred in hur houses, nodur mannys bred ne horse-bred, to sell, up the payne of vj s. viij d. at every trespas.

1428 *Surtees Misc.* (1888) 5 His trespas of forgeyng and utteryng of fals osmunds and castyng of fals tyn. **1472–5** *Rolls of Parlt.* VI. 157/1 Trespasses doon with force and armes ayenst your peas. **1553** T. WILSON *Rhet.* 49 Sometimes a man is accused of felonye, and yet he proueth his offence to be but a trespace. **1651** G. W. tr. *Cowel's Inst.* 211 The word Trespasse..comprehends every violation of the Law. But our discreet Lawyers call only private crimes Trespasses, and make distinctions even amongst these. **1895** POLLOCK & MAITLAND *Hist. Eng. Law* II. viii. §3. II. 510 Trespass (*transgressio*) is the most general term that there is; it will cover all or almost all wrongful acts and defaults. Every felony, says Bracton, is a trespass, though every trespass is not a felony. In a narrower sense therefore *trespass* is used [in 13th c.] as a contrast to *felony*.

β. c **1308** in *Pol. Songs* (Camden) 197 Of feloni hi ne taketh hede, Al thilk trepas is a-go.

3. *Law. spec.* Any actionable wrong committed against the person or property of another; also short for *action of trespass*.

a. ***trespass to person.***

13.. *Cursor M.* 29391 (Cott. Galba) Of him þat dose a light trispase To prest or clerk vnwitandly. **1444** *Coventry Leet-Bk.* 203 In satisfaccion of the trespas doon to hym the tyme þat he was beeton. **1767** COMYNS *Digest* V. 534 Trespass to the Person may be by Menace, Assault, Battery or *Mayhem*. **1822** HAMMOND *Comyns' Digest* VII. 495 A throws a squib among the people at a market, it lights near B who throws it from him, C does the same, and it strikes D and puts out his eye: D has trespass *vi et armis* against A. **1876** POLLOCK *Leading Cases done into Eng.* 17 And now 'gainst Shepherd, for loss of eye, Question is, whether trespass will lie.

b. ***trespass to goods.***

1590 SWINBURNE *Testaments* 183 If the testator make diuerse executors, and do bequeath to the one of them the residue of his goodes;..if the other executor enter thereunto, hee is subiect to an action of trespasse. **1768** BLACKSTONE *Comm.* III. 257 He may bring an action of trespass for taking away his goods. **1863** H. COX *Instit.* II. ix. 523 Another remedy for the unlawful taking of goods is by action of trespass, to recover damages for the loss of goods. **1909** HOLDSWORTH *Hist. Eng. Law* III. 271 The place of appeal was taken by the semi-criminal action of trespass *de bonis asportatis*. **1913** *Laws Eng.* (ed. Halsbury) XXVII. 865 The gist of an action of trespass is an unlawful taking or removing or damaging of a personal chattel.

c. ***trespass to land.*** A wrongful entry upon the lands of another, with damage (however inconsiderable) to his real property.

c **1455** *Forest Lawis* c. 21 in *Acts Parl. Scot.* (1844) I. 692 Of trespas in forest of Baron. [**1472–3** *Rolls of Parlt.* VI. 43/2 Noo persone nor persones, which have taken any..profittes of any of the premisses, or have entred and doon trespas.] **1768** BLACKSTONE *Comm.* III. xii. 209 In the limited and confined sense..it signifies no more than an entry on another man's ground without a lawful authority, and doing some damage, however inconsiderable, to his real property. .. Every unwarrantable entry on another's soil the law entitles a trespass by breaking his close. **1818** CRUISE *Digest* (ed. 2) IV. 319 If a person grants a piece of ground in the middle of his estate; he at the same time impliedly grants a way to it, and the grantee may pass over the land of the grantor..without being guilty of a trespass.

d. ***trespass on the case,*** a form of action now obsolete in which the damage complained of is a result not immediate, but consequential of an unlawful act. So called from the L. name of the writs (***brevia de transgressione super casum***) under which it was brought; also the name of the writ itself.

1429 *Rolls of Parlt.* IV. 346/1 Speciall actions of dette or trespasse uppon her cas. **1641** *Termes de la Ley* 257 If not that it bee a trespasse upon the case, and then the words *Vi et armis* are left out, and in lieu thereof the writ shal say in the end thereof, *Contra pacem*. **1768** [see CASE *sb.*[1] 6 e]. **1875** POSTE *Gaius* III. Comm. (ed. 2) 473 What was done by the introduction of the action of Trespass on the Case, was exactly analogous to what the praetors did. **1888** F. POLLOCK in *Encycl. Brit.* XXIII. 454 In the 16th century, a special form of 'trespass on the case' became, under the name of *assumpsit*, the common and normal method of enforcing contracts not made by deed, and remained so till the middle of the present century.

4. A passing beyond some limit. Now generally associated with TRESPASS *v.* 4. *rare.*

16.. *Jolly Pinder of Wakefield* ii. in Child *Ballads* (1888) III. 131 There is neither knight or squire..Dare make a trespasse to the town of Wakefield. **1681** tr. *Belon's Myst. Physick* 46 Some small Trespasses beyond the Rules of Physick. **1798** CHARLOTTE SMITH *Yng. Philos.* I. 49 He was frequently involved in scrapes for harmless frolics and trespasses out of bounds.

5. An encroachment, intrusion *on* or *upon*: cf. TRESPASS *v.* 5.

1769 GOLDSM. *Hist. Rome* (1786) II. 23 Mankind are ever most offended at any trespass on ceremony. **1799** JEFFERSON *Writ.* (1859) IV. 287, I know the extent of this trespass on your tranquillity. **1805** *Med. Jrnl.* XIV. 575 Would not a publication of this kind be a species of trespass on the board of health, lately instituted in Ireland? **1830** GLADSTONE in Morley *Life* (1903) I. App. 639 One trespass more I must make on your patience.

6. *attrib.* and *Comb.*, as ***trespass act, -board*** (BOARD *sb.* 2 b), ***-fine, money, -offering*** (cf. SIN-OFFERING); ***trespass-chiding*** adj.

1906 F. S. OLIVER *A. Hamilton* II. iii. 121 By this victory he smashed the *Trespass Act. **1908** *Nation* 21 Nov. 299/1 These writers have a disregard of all *trespass-boards. **1847** TENNYSON *Princ.* v. 36 Boys that slink From ferule and the *trespass-chiding eye. **1611** BIBLE *2 Kings* xii. 16 The *trespasse money, and sinne money was not brought into the house of the Lord. **1535** COVERDALE *Lev.* v. 15 Yf a soule trespace..he shal brynge his *trespaceofferinge vnto the Lorde. **1845** KITTO *Cycl. Bibl. Lit.* s.v. *Adultery*, Bringing a trespass offering (a ram) to the door of the tabernacle, to be offered in his behalf by the priest.

'trespass, *v.* Forms: 4–6 **trespas, -pace, -passe,** (4–5 **trispas,** 6 **treaspas**), 6– **trespass.** *β.* 4–6 **trepasse,** 6 **-pase.** [f. TRESPASS *sb.*; or a. OF. *trespasser* to pass beyond or across, mod.F. *trépasser* to pass away, die, Pr. *tras-, tres-, trapassar*, Sp. *traspasar*, It. *trapassare*, med.L. *transpassare* to pass beyond, f. L. *trans* beyond (F. *très*) + *passare*, etc. to PASS. (The chief sense in Eng. attaches itself rather to the Eng. sb. than to the Fr. verb.)]

1. *intr.* To commit a transgression or offence; to transgress, offend; to sin. Also *fig.*

1303 R. BRUNNE *Handl. Synne* 4250 He..þat may, and wyl nat, here hys messe,..he trespasyþ more yn þe lay. **13..** *Seuyn Sag.* (W.) 3921, I trispast namare than did he. **1382** WYCLIF *Sel. Wks.* III. 514 Summe prelatis þat trespaceden. **1387** TREVISA *Higden* (Rolls) V. 153 He had i-trespassed. *c* **1430** *Syr Tryam.* 1062 Yf he had trespaste oght. **1591** SPENSER *Virg. Gnat* 365 Not vnto him that neuer hath trespast, But punishment is due to the offender. **1797** MRS. RADCLIFFE *Italian* ix, Father Schedoni would be the last among us so to trespass. **1805** WORDSW. *Waggoner* I. 112, I trespassed lately worse than ever.

β. c **1400** *Lanfranc's Cirurg.* 98 (Add. MS.) 3if þat þe blode trepasse [*Ashm. MS.* trespace] onlye in qualyte, amende hym.

b. Const. *against* (†*to, unto, for*).

1303 R. BRUNNE *Handl. Synne* 1217 Þou hast trespast apertly A3ens þys comaundment so hy. ? *a* **1366** CHAUCER *Rom. Rose* 1036 Who so durste to hir trespace, Or til hir folk, in werk or dede. *c* **1380** *Antecrist* in Todd *3 Treat. Wyclif* (1851) 135 He preied for3yveness of his Fadre for hem þat trespassedd for hym. *c* **1386** CHAUCER *Melib.* ¶911 Ye haue mysborn yow and trespassed vn-to me. **1426** *Paston Lett.* I. 26, I have nought trespassed ageyn noon of these iij. **1523** FITZHERB. *Husb.* §168 To forgyue them that haue trespaced to the. **1770** BURKE *Pres. Discont.* Wks. II. 341 He trespasses against his duty who sleeps upon his watch. **1845** M. PATTISON *Ess.* (1889) I. 22 He would not..trespass against the law and the canons.

†**2.** *trans.* with the matter of the trespass as object: To do (something wrong); to commit. *Obs.*

1375 BARBOUR *Bruce* XI. 553 For he thoucht that he suld amend That he trespassit had. **14..** *Eng. Fragm. Med. Service-Bks.* 8 To for3eue alle maner of men and women þat þey haue trespased to the. *Ibid.* 9 Alle þe sennes that i haue trespased a3ens the wilful passioun of oure lord. **1542** UDALL *Erasm. Apoph.* 229 b, The offense euen of it self was hainous & besides that, trespaced in the emperours owne doughter. **1591** SPENSER *Virg. Gnat* 448 The faults which life hath trespassed. **1631** MAY tr. *Barclay's Mirr. Mindes* I. 25 It begins to censure with much rigour, the trespassed errours of the same.

†**3. a.** To transgress, violate (a law, etc.) *Obs.* [So in OFr.]

1483 CAXTON *G. de la Tour* d vij b, She had trespaced his commaundement. *a* **1536** TINDALE *Pathway* Wks. (1573) 385/2 To punish vs if we trespasse the law and good order. **1613** DANIEL *Hist. Eng.* I. (1650) 223, I must not so much trespasse Vertue, as to overpasse one memorable particular.

β. **1523** LD. BERNERS *Froiss.* I. ccxxxiii. 323 These lordes and knightes..durst nat trepase the popes commaundement.

†**b.** To offend against, wrong, violate (a person). *Obs.*

1427 in *10th Rep. Hist. MSS. Comm.* App. v. 294 If ony man shal trespasse or ly by ony nurishe or apprentise. **1523** LD. BERNERS *Froiss.* I. cclxxx. 420 They had greatly trespassed the prince, wherof than they repented them, but than they coulde not remedy it. **1526** TINDALE *Matt.* vi. 12 And forgeve vs oure treaspases, even as we forgeve them which treaspas vs. **1556** J. HEYWOOD *Spider & F.* xix. 7 At the least thou hast trespassed me.

4. *Law. intr.* To commit a trespass (see TRESPASS *sb.* 2); *spec.* to enter unlawfully on the land of another, or on that which is the property or right of another. Const. *on, upon.*

c **1455** *Forest Lawis* c. 21 in *Acts Parl. Scot.* (1844) I. 692 Item gif a fre man hapyn to trespas [orig. *delinquat*] in þe forest of ony baroun to quham þe king be fre charter has granted a forest... All þat is fundin with him trespassand in þe forest. **1590, 1651** [implied in TRESPASSER 2; cf. also sense 5]. *a* **1718** PRIOR *Epitaph* 20 Each Virtue kept it's proper Bound, Nor Trespass'd on the other's Ground. **1755** JOHNSON, *Trespass*, 2. to enter unlawfully on another's ground. **1843** PRESCOTT *Mexico* (1850) I. vi. 160 The lad answered, 'It was the king's wood, and he would punish him with death if he trespassed there.' **1844** in Ashbee *Last Rec. Cotswold Commun.* (1904) 37 Pd. Wm. Hands for.. preventing Cattle from Trespassing on the Corn 4 weeks. 4 s. **1858** LYTTON *What will he do* III. viii, I trust we are not trespassing. **1880** *Chambers' Encycl.* IX. 535/1 If he is.. trespassing with intent to catch or kill game, he may in some cases be apprehended and given into custody... If..A.'s cattle trespass on B's land, B can impound them.

fig. **1818** KEATS *Endymion* IV. 870 No pearl Will trespass down these cheeks.

5. *intr. fig.* with *on* or *upon*: To make an improper or uninvited inroad on (a person's time, attention, patience, etc.); to intrude on or upon the rights or domain of; to encroach on, infringe.

1652 URQUHART *Jewel* 274, I am afraid that I have trespassed a little upon the patience of the Reader. **1663** *Flagellum or O. Cromwell* (ed. 2) 5 Herein he trespassed upon that respect and lenity due and usual to Children of his Birth and quality. **1724** DE FOE *Mem. Cavalier* (1840) 231 We made bold..to trespass upon the country for a few horses. **1803** *Med. Jrnl.* IX. 53 Fearing that I have already trespassed on the limits of your Journal. *a* **1881** A. BARRATT *Phys. Metempiric* (1883) 206 Science is on those occasions trespassing on Metempiric, and is talking about things of which it cannot possibly know anything.

†**6.** *intr.* (in form **trepass.**) To pass beyond this life; to die. Also *trans.* in ***to trepass this life.*** ***trepassed,*** deceased. (The only sense in which this vb. is preserved in mod.F.) *Obs. rare.*

14.. [implied in TRESPASSEMENT]. **1523** LD. BERNERS *Froiss.* I. xx. 29 As soone as I am trepassed out of this worlde. *Ibid.*, Soone after thys, noble Robert de Bruse, Kyng of Scotland, trepassed out of this vncertayne worlde. *Ibid.* ccxxix. 305 To gyue ayde and helpe, and to recomforte his cosyn, the wyfe of therle Charles trepassed. *a* **1533** —— *Huon* vii. 17 It is .vii. yere syns he trepasyd thys lyfe.

Hence **'trespassed, 'trespassing** *ppl. adjs.*

1631 Trespassed [see sense 2]. **1731–3** TULL *Horse-Hoeing Husb.* xix. 277 A very good Crop (except part of it, which being eaten by the trespassing Sheep..was somewhat blighted). **1788** D. GILSON *Serm. Pract. Subj.* xiv. (1807) 265 One trespassing Egyptian might thrust him away. **1824** G. C. RENOUARD *Ceylon* in *Encycl. Metrop.* (1845) XVI. 445/2 As all trespassing beasts are forfeited, the poor natives who live in the neighbourhood of plantations, are often deterred from rearing cattle.

†**'trespassable,** *a. Obs. rare.* Also 5 **trepassable.** [f. as TRESPASS *v.* + -ABLE; in sense 1 a. OF. *trespassable* that may be crossed (12th c.).]

1. That may be passed through or crossed.

c **1400** MAUNDEV. (1839) xvii. 182 All the parties of see & of lond han here appositees habitables or trepassables.

2. Subject or liable to an action of trespass.

1681 DEGGE *Parson's Counsellor* (ed. 3) 169 The Parson may have an Action of Trespas against any body that shall do any Trespassable act in the Church, or Church-yard.

'trespassage. *rare.* [f. TRESPASS *v.* + -AGE.] A trespassing, a trespass.

1874 W. BRUCE *Hebrew Odes* 74 Is there any God like the Lord above Who passeth over trespassage?

†**'trespassant,** *a. Obs. rare.* [a. AF. *trespassant*, pr. pple. of *trespasser*: see TRESPASS *v.* and -ANT.] That trespasses.

1587 HARRISON *England* II. xi. (1877) I. 226, I would wish the partie trespassant, to be made bond or slaues vnto those that receiued the iniurie.

†**tre'spassement.** *Obs. rare.* [a. OF. *trespassement* (12th c. in Godef.), F. *trépassement*: see TRESPASS *v.* and -MENT.] A passing away (from life); departure, decease.

14.. in *Wars Eng. in France* (1864) II. 523 Incontynent aftir his [Henry V's] trespasement..Johne, duc of Bedforde ..was made regente. **1475** *Bk. Noblesse* (Roxb.) 41 Frome the second yere of his reigne..into the day of his trespassement the space of .vij. yere.

trespasser ('trɛspəsə(r)). Forms: 4–5 **trespasour,** 4–6 **-passour, -oure,** 5 **-pasor, -owre, -passor,** 5–6 **-pacer,** 6 **-passar,** 6– **trespasser.** [ME. a. AF. *trespassour* = OF. *trespasseor*, agent-n. of *trespasser* to TRESPASS.] One who trespasses.

1. A transgressor, a law-breaker; a wrong-doer, sinner, offender.

[**1292** BRITTON I. xxi. §11 Touz trespassours encountre la forme de nos estatuz.] **1362** LANGL. *P. Pl.* A. I. 94 And take trespassours and tei3en hem faste. **1387** TREVISA *Higden* (Rolls) VII. 117 Of þe whiche statut þe firste trespasour was þe erle. **1450–1530** *Myrr. our Ladye* 75 And forgyue vs oure trespasses, as we forgyue oure trespassoures. **1535** COVERDALE *Josh.* vii. *heading*, The trespacer is stoned vnto death. **1648** *Petit. East. Assoc.* 26 We see no reason, why.. our Trespassers be our Judges. **1742** J. GLAS *Lord's Supper* v. vi. 234 The Trespasser humbles himself to confess his Fault.

2. *Law.* One who commits a trespass; *esp.* one who trespasses on the lands of another.

c **1455** *Forest Lawis* c. 22 in *Acts Parl. Scot.* (1844) I. 692 Item gif ony wylde best be fundyn dede or wondyt and þe trespassour be nocht fundyn, at þe next mut þar aw to be inquisicioun made. **1590** SWINBURNE *Testaments* 237 Whosoeuer as a meere trespasser, entereth into the goods of the testator. **1651** G. W. tr. *Cowel's Inst.* 231 The party following them [stray beasts], and endeavouring to keep them from committing Damages, is no Trespasser. **1700** TYRRELL *Hist. Eng.* II. 1108 Concerning Trespassers in Parks. **1837** DICKENS *Pickw.* xix, Remind me to have a board done about trespassers, and spring guns, and all that sort of thing, to keep the common people out. **1895** POLLOCK & MAITLAND *Hist. Eng. Law* II. 166 The man who has bought or hired goods from a trespasser, how has he broken the king's peace and why should he be sent to gaol?

fig. **1702** NORTH *Let.* 6 Dec., in *Lives* (1890) III. App. 247 If I am too much a trespasser on your better time.

†**3.** *Rhet. lit.* 'That which oversteps or passes beyond'; hyperbaton. *Obs. rare*⁻¹.

1589 PUTTENHAM *Eng. Poesie* III. xii. (Arb.) 180 To all their speaches which wrought by disorder the Greekes gaue a general name (*Hiperbaton*) as much to say as the (*trespasser*).

trespassing ('trɛspəsɪŋ), *vbl. sb.* [f. TRESPASS *v.* + -ING[1].] The action of the verb TRESPASS.

a **1340** HAMPOLE *Psalter* c. 4 Doand trispasyngis i hatid [*Vulg.* facientes preuaricaciones odiui]. **1388** WYCLIF *Rom.* iv. 15 Where is no lawe, there is no trespas, nethir is trespassyng. **1561** T. NORTON *Calvin's Inst.* III. 266 They winking at their own trespassings. **1852** CHR. ROSSETTI *Poems* (1904) 148/2, I..weep for my trespassing. **1886** *Pall Mall G.* 7 Oct. 4/2 Trespassing, in English law..is distinctly not a criminal offence; the trespasser cannot be 'given into custody', as the notice-boards have it.

'trespassory, *a.* [f. TRESPASS *sb.* + -ORY².] Pertaining to or of the nature of a trespass.
1888 POLLOCK & WRIGHT *Possession in Comm. Law* 131 Possession originally obtained by consent cannot become trespassory.

†**tre'sperce**, *v. Obs. rare*⁻¹. [a. OF. *trespercier* (12th c. in Godef.), f. *tres*:—L. *trans*, TRANS- + *percier* to PIERCE.] *trans.* To pierce through, transpierce.
1483 CAXTON *G. de la Tour* K iij, A suerde shold tresperce her sowle and her herte.

trespuissance, -ant: see TRES-.

tress (trɛs), *sb.* Forms: *pl.* 3 tressene, 4- **tresses**, (5 **-is, trissis**); *sing.* 4-6 **tresse**, (6 *Sc.* tres), 6- **tress.** See also TRACE *sb.*³ [a. F. *tresse*, in OF. *tresce* a plait or braid of hair (12th c. in Littré, etc.) = Pr. *tressa, treza*, It. *treccia*, beside the vb. F. *tresser*, OF. *trecier*, It. *trecciare* 'to plaite, to tie..vp in tresses, as womens haires are' (Florio). In Sc. and some Eng. dialects this appears also in the forms *trais(s* and *trace*: see TRACE *sb.*³, *v.*³ The OF., Pr., and It. sbs. point to a late L. or Romanic *tricia, trecia*, which appears in med.L.: see Du Cange.
For the derivation, Diez favours a form **trichea* (or **trichia*) f. Gr. τρίχα threefold, taking the primary sense to be 'a triple plait'. Hatz.-Darm. take *tresse* as vbl. sb. from the vb. *tresser*.]

1. A plait or braid of the hair of the head, usually of a woman: cf. TRACE *sb.*³ 1.
13.. *Seuyn Sag.* (W.) 478 With both honden here yaulew here Out of the tresses sche hit tere. *c* **1386** CHAUCER *Knt.'s T.* 191 Hir yelow heer was broyded in a tresse Bihynde hir bak, a yerde longe I gesse. *a* **1400-50** *Alexander* 3450 Hire hede vn-helid was on hiȝe & hild all in trissis. *c* **1440** *Promp. Parv.* 502/1 Tresse, of heere, *trica.* **1530** PALSGR. 282/2 Tresse of heer, *tresse.* **1581** PETTIE *Guazzo's Civ. Conv.* III. (1586) 136 b, Certain women, whereof one had her tresses crossed in such sort vpon her head, that they made the likenesse of two hearts bound together. **1590** SPENSER *F.Q.* II. ix. 19 Her yellow golden heare Was trimly woven and in tresses wrought. **1613** R. CAWDREY *Table Alph.* (ed. 3), *Tresses*, lockes of hayre broyded vp. **1717** LADY M. W. MONTAGU *Let. to Lady Rich* 1 Apr., Their beautiful hair [was] divided into many tresses, hanging on their shoulders. **1777** ROBERTSON *Hist. Amer.* I. II. 92 Their black hair..was bound in tresses around their heads. **1793** EARL MACARTNEY *Jrnl. Emb. China* 4 Aug., [Their hair] is platted in a tress, and falls down the back.

b. (By extension) A long lock of hair (esp. that of a woman), without any sense of its being plaited or braided; mostly in pl. *tresses.* (The usual current sense.)
c **1290** *S. Eng. Leg.* I. 325/82 Heo droȝ of hire tressene and caste a-wei. *c* **1384** CHAUCER *H. Fame* I. 230 A queynt array As she had ben an hunteresse With wynde blowynge vpon hir tresse. *c* **1450** *Merlin* xviii. 298 She was all discheuelee in her heer, and Taurus hir heilde be the tresses and drough hir after his horse. **1595** WEEVER *Epigr.* IV. xxii. (1599) E vj, Rose-checkt Adonis with his amber tresses. **1696** PHILLIPS (ed. 5), *Tresses*, said of the Hair, when it hangs down in dishevell'd Locks. **1717** POPE *Sappho to Phaon* 85 Nor braids of gold the varied tresses bind, That fly disorder'd with the wanton wind. **1824** W. IRVING *T. Trav.* I. I. vi. 75 Her long dishevelled tresses hanging to the ground. **1871** R. ELLIS *Catullus* lxvi. 47 What shall a weak tress do, when powers so mighty resist not?

c. *transf.* and *fig.* (and in fig. context). Applied to long leafy shoots or tendrils, rays of the sun, etc.
1423 JAS. I *Kingis Q.* i, In Aquary, Cinthia the clere Rynsid hir tressis. **1598** SYLVESTER *Du Bartas* II. i. IV. *Handicrafts* 139 Somtimes the Plane, somtimes the Vine they shear, Choosing their fairest tresses. *c* **1620** Z. BOYD *Zion's Flowers* (1855) 145 My sonnes..will by the tresses snatch The fittest time. **1641** J. TRAPPE *Theol. Theol.* v. 205 The radiant tresses of the sun. **1810** T. L. PEACOCK *Genius of Thames* 65 The weeping willow droops to lave Its leafy tresses in the wave. **1875** TRISTRAM *Moab* ii. 29 Luxuriant tresses of maiden-hair fern.

d. (*Our*) *Lady's tresses*: see LADY'S TRACES.

†**2.** A flat plait or braid (of interwoven threads, fibres, hairs, rushes, straw, etc.) Cf. TRACE *sb.*³ 2, 3. *Obs.*
1491 CAXTON *Vitas Patr.* (W. de W. 1495) I. xxxvi. 38 b/2 Saynt Anthonye made a tresse for to make a lytyll basket. **1542** *Inv. Roy. Wardrobe* (1815) 82 Ane cott of variand taffatie with ane small walting tres of gold [cf. 1539, p. 32 trais of gold]. **1550** *Acc. Ld. High Treas. Scot.* IX. 455 Item, xvj elnis tressis put on the saittis of the saidis chiris.

†**3.** *Her.* = TRESSURE 2. Cf. TRACE *sb.*¹ 10. *Obs. rare.*
1577 HOLINSHED *Chron.* I. *Hist. Scot.* 358/2 They beare in their armes the Lion and Lillyes, wyth the tresse in fourme and fashion as the King of Scotlande beareth hys.

4. *attrib.* and *Comb.*, as ***tress-lifting, -like, -shorn, -topped*** adjs.
1819 KEATS *Lamia* I. 207 Down through *tress-lifting waves the Nereids fair Wind into Thetis' bower. **1647** R. STAPYLTON *Juvenal* xv. 277 Th'orphane..Whose *tresse-like haire, and eyes still dropping pearle. **1845** KITTO *Cycl. Bibl. Lit.* s.v. *Babylon*, It bears spreading and ever-green branches,..adorned with long tress-like tendrils. **1866** J. B. ROSE tr. *Ovid's Met.* VIII. 234 And matrons Eveninan, *tresses-shorn. **1871** BROWNING *Balaust.* 1323 Past the pines *Tress-topped.

Hence **'tressful** *a.*, full of or fully furnished with tresses; **'tressless** *a.*, having no tresses; **'tresslet**, a little tress.
1606 SYLVESTER *Du Bartas* II. iv. III. *Magnif.* 734 Pharo's faire daughter..Was queintly dressing of her *Tress-full head Which round about her to the ground did spread. **1865** CARLYLE *Fredk. Gt.* XX. iii. (1873) IX. 51 The Bernburg Officers, tragically *tressless in their hats. **1882** J. WALKER *Scotch Poems* 136 A glossy *tresslet of her lint-white hair.

tress, *v.* Now *rare* exc. in *pa. pple.* Also 4 **tresce.** [ME. a. F. *tresser*, OF. *trecier* (12th c. in Littré) = Pr. *tressar, trezar*, It. *trecciare* to arrange in a tress, braid, plait; goes with TRESS *sb.*
The OF. form *trecier* indicates a late L. type **triciāre*, f. *tricia, trecia* (or **trichia*): see TRESS *sb.*]

1. *trans.* To arrange (hair) in tresses.
? *a* **1366** CHAUCER *Rom. Rose* 569 And with a riche golde treasour Her hedde was tressed queintly. **1390** GOWER *Conf.* III. 255 And hou hir yelwe her was tresced And hire atire so wel adresced. *c* **1440** *Promp. Parv.* 502/1 Tressyn heere, *trico.* **1623** tr. *Favine's Theat. Hon.* II. iv. 78 The Sicambrians were observed by their yellow haire, tressed and knit in cordons. **1827** ROBERTS *Voy. Centr. Amer.* 29 The hair was worn long and tressed behind with a cord. **1867** *Morn. Star* 19 Sept., Neither sex wears any covering on the head, preferring to tress..that with which nature has provided them.

b. To arrange or dispose (threads, etc.) in braids.
1862 [see *tressing* below]. **1904** *Westm. Gaz.* 24 May 1/3 The tiny fingers threw the bobbins swiftly from side to side, moved the pins on the pricked paper pattern, tressed the lace that had to be finished before eventide.

2. *intr.* Of the hair: To fall in tresses; to admit of being arranged in tresses.
1867 *Morn. Star* 19 Sept., The hair of the Abyssinians is ..sufficiently long to tress well.

Hence **'tressing** *vbl. sb.*
c **1425** *St. Mary of Oignies* I. i. in *Anglia* VIII. 135/34 Tressynge & tiftynge of here. **1862** *Catal. Internat. Exhib., Brit.* II. No. 4542, Skilful tressing, and most careful workmanship and finish, in which the exhibitor endeavoured not to be surpassed by any of his fellow competitors.

tress, obs. form of TRACE *sb.*², TREST *sb.*²

-tress, ending of feminines of agent-nouns in *-ter, -tor*, etc., usually short for *-ter-ess, -tor-ess*: as in *actress, auditress, huntress, mistress, seamstress, songstress, traitress, vintress*: see -ESS¹.

tres-'sacred, most sacred: see TRES-.

‖**tresseau** (trɛso). [Fr.:—OF. *tressel*, deriv. of *tresse* TRESS.] Applied to a vine, of which the grapes grow in a much elongated cluster. Also *attrib.*
1763 MILLS *Pract. Husb.* IV. 381 If some plants of the tresseau, whose fruit never ripens easily, are mixed with the pineaus, it is..because our forefathers..judged it necessary to add these tresseaus. *Ibid.* 382 A reasonable proportion of the tresseau grape should always be planted with the others in sandy soils.

tressed (trɛst, *poet.* 'trɛsɪd), *ppl. a.* and *a.* [f. TRESS *sb.* and *v.* + -ED.]

1. Of the hair: Arranged in tresses; braided.
c **1386** CHAUCER *Wife's Prol.* 344 Ye wommen shul apparaille yow..noght in tressed [*v.rr* trussede, tressede] heer and gay perree. **1500-20** DUNBAR *Poems* xlvi. 77 Hir goldin tressit hairis redomyt. **1579** SPENSER *Sheph. Cal.* Apr. 12 He plongd in payne his tressed locks dooth teare. **1612** tr. *Benvenuto's Passenger* II. 573 In two faire eyes, or in the tressed lockes.

2. Having or furnished with tresses; often as the second element in a parasynthetic compound, as ***gold-tressed.***
13.. *K. Alis.* 5393 (Bodl. MS.), Hij weren..tressed in þe nekkes as a woman. **1412-20** LYDG. *Chron. Troy* IV. 2645 Firy Titan, gold-tressed in his spere. **1601** WEEVER *Mirr. Mart.* Cviij, A Comet..Bearded, or trest, or stretching forth his taile. **1623-4** MILTON *Paraphr. Ps. cxxxvi.* 30 He..caus'd the Golden-tressed Sun All the day long his cours to run. **1758** *Poetry in Ann. Reg.* 413 The silver tressed Summer's gone. **1830** TENNYSON *Recoll. Arab. Nts.* xiii, A brow of pearl Tressed with redolent ebony.

tressel, -il, etc.: see TRESTLE.

tressilate ('trɛsɪleɪt), *v. rare.* [ad. F. *tressaillir* to thrill, tremble, f. *tres*-:—L. TRANS- + *saillir* to jump.] *intr.* To start with sudden agitation, as with a thrill of surprise, joy, etc.
1889 D. C. MURRAY *Danger. Catspaw* xiv, The ladies tressilated deliciously. The crime began to take an air of romance.

tresson, -oun, -un, obs. forms of TREASON.

tres-splendent, *a.*, 'most' or 'very illustrious': see TRES-.

tressure ('trɛs(j)ʊə(r), 'trɛʃə(r)). Forms: α. 4-6 tressour, (5 -owre, tresour, -ewyr, treasour, trissoure, 7 tresseur); β. 5 tressur, trussure, 6 treasure, 5- tressure; γ. 5 trechoure. [ME. *tressour* represents OF. *tresseor, -eour*, also *tressoir, tressoer* (13th c.):—L. **triciātōrium*: see -OUR; ME. *tressure* = OF. *tressure, -eure* (12-13th c.): see -URE; f. F. *tresse* TRESS.]

†**1.** A ribbon or band worn round the head; a net with which a woman's tresses are confined; a head-dress; also, app., the arrangement of her hair in tresses, her *chevelure. Obs.*
a **1310** in Wright *Lyric P.* xxxvii. 105 The ryche ledies in huere bour, That wereden gold on huere tressour. **13..** *Gaw. & Gr. Knt.* 1739 Þe hazer stones Trased aboute hir tressour, be twenty in clusteres. ? *a* **1366** [see TRESS *v.* 1]. *c* **1420** *Metr. Life St. Kath.* (Halliw.) 11 Maxent..bad anon hys turmentours Do hange hur be hur tresourys. *c* **1425** *Voc.* in Wr.-Wülcker 656/17 *Hoc tricatorium*, tressure. *c* **1475** *Pict. Voc.* ibid. 792/18 *Hec tricatura*, a tresewyr. **1483** *Cath. Angl.* 392/2 A Tressowre, *trica, tricatura. Ibid.* 394/1 A Trissoure of A woman hedde, *cincinnus*,..*trica, tricatura, cincinnaculus.*

2. *Her.* A diminutive of the orle (ORLE 1 a), consisting of a narrow band of one-quarter the width of the bordure; usually borne counterfleury, or double and fleury counter-fleury, as in the arms of Scotland. Formerly also called *trace* (TRACE *sb.*¹ 10), *tract* (TRACT *sb.*³ 6 (*a*)).
a **1440** *Sir Degrev.* 635 Hure botenus was toore, Anamelede with azoure; With topyes and trechoure Overtrasyd. *Ibid.* 1031 He beres in cheef of azour, Engrelyd with a satur, With doubule tressour. **1572** BOSSEWELL *Armorie* II. 41 b, Without mention made of anye tracte, or Tressour Counter-florie. **1592** WYRLEY *Armorie, Ld. Chandos* 77 Two Ermin Lions passant crowned gold, With Scottish treasure. **1611** COTGR., *Trescheur*, a Tracke, or Tresseur (in Blason). **1704** J. HARRIS *Lex. Techn.* I, *Tressure*, a term in Heraldry for an Orle when it is flowered; and if there be two of them, it is called a double Tressure. **1707** E. CHAMBERLAYNE *St. Gt. Brit.* II. ii. (ed. 22) 90 In the second place, Or, within a Double Tressure, Counter-flower'd Lys, Gules, a Lyon Rampant of the Second, for the Royal Arms of Scotland. **1808** SCOTT *Marm.* IV. vii, The double tressure might you see, First by Achaius borne. **1857** J. PATERSON *Hist. Regality Musselburgh* 180 Three crescents within a double tressure.

3. *Numism.* An ornamental enclosure, circular or of several arches, containing the type or distinctive device, found on many gold and silver coins of former centuries.
1745 M. FOLKES *Eng. Silver Coins* 16 He..omitted the double tressure surrounding the head upon the former groats. **1817** RUDING *Annals Coinage* III. 400 In a double tressure of ten arches with trefoils in the outer angles, the English Lion [etc.]. **1841** HAWKINS *Silver Coins* (1876) 206 Edward III. 1327 to 1377... The Groats were struck at London or York: the type has the bust of the king, front face, within a double tressure of nine arches. **1898** G. B. RAWLINGS *Brit. Coinage* 39 Gold florin of Edw. III... *Rev.* A short ornate beaded cross, enclosed by a tressure of four arches, with a lion in each angle.

Hence **'tressured** *a.*, provided with (in quot. *loosely*, borne upon) a tressure.
1805 SCOTT *Last Minstr.* IV. viii, The tressured fleur-de-luce he [Thirlestane] claims To wreathe his shield.

tressy ('trɛsɪ), *a.* [f. TRESS *sb.* + -Y.] Resembling, characterized by, or adorned with tresses.
1614 SYLVESTER *Bethulia's Rescue* III. 230 Like two Popplars which..their tressie Tops doe hide Amid the Clouds. **1795** COLERIDGE *Lewti* 10 Pendent boughs of tressy yew. *a* **1845** HOOD *Ruth* iv, Her hat, with shady brim, Made her tressy forehead dim.

†**trest**, *sb.*¹ *Obs.* Forms: 4-5 treste, 4-6 **trest.** [A parallel form to TRAIST *sb.*, TRIST *sb.*, TRUST *sb.* It may in some instances be a variant of *traist* (which is probable at least for the 16th c. Scotch use); but is viewed by Morsbach as a variant of *trist.*] Confidence, assurance, trust.
a **1300** *Floriz & Bl.* 408 Al mi trest is þe upon. **1422** tr. *Secreta Secret., Priv. Priv.* xl. 198 Iosue..by the grete treste that he had in god, comanded the Sone and the mone. **1570** *Satir. Poems Reform.* xxiv. 48 To hing, As tratouris sould, for schuitting vnder trest. *a* **1600** MONTGOMERIE *Misc. Poems* xxx. 23 Sen he took me vnder trest.

trest (trɛst), *sb.*² Now only *Sc.* and *dial.* Forms: α. 4-6 **treste**, 6 *Sc.* **treist**, 5- **trest.** β. 5 *Sc.* **trast**, 6 *Sc.* **traist.** γ. 5 **tryste**, 5-6 **tryst**, 6 **trist.** δ. 6 **triss**, 6-9 **tress.** [a. OF. *treste*, var. of *traste*, orig. *trastre, trestre* (12-13th c. in Godef.):—L. *transtrum*, **trāstrum* cross-beam, transom; cf. obs. It. *trasto*, pl. *trasti* the benches of a galley, transoms (Florio), which has also lost the second *r.*]

1. = TRESTLE 1.
13.. *Seuyn Sag.* (W.) 3874 The kinges dener wele was grayd; Thai set trestes and bordes on layd. **13..** *E.E. Allit. P.* B. 832 Þe trestes tylt to þe woȝe & þe table boþe. **1432** *Test. Ebor.* (Surtees) II. 22, j met bord wᵗ j pare trystes. *c* **1470** HENRY *Wallace* x. 40 Thai..Past our the bryg; Wallace gert wrychtis call, Hewyt trastis: wndyd the passage all. **1501** DOUGLAS *Pal. Hon.* III. lxx, Traists, formis, and benkis, war poleist plane. **1565** in Hay Fleming *Reform. Scotl.* (1910) 610 Ane aikin burd standand on treistis. **1627** MAY *Lucan* x. 133 High tresses golden tables bore. **1665** J. FRASER *Polichron.* (S.H.S.) 197 The trests and supporters of the oaken table. **1825** SCOTT *Betrothed* xiv, When the boards and tresses on which the viands had been served were withdrawn. **1886** J. BARROWMAN *Sc. Mining Terms*, *Tress*, a trestle; the fulcrum for the lever used in boring.

†**b.** A rest used with a harquebus or other fire-arm: = TRESTLE 4 a. *Obs.*

1513 *Acc. Ld. High Treas. Scot.* IV. 527, ij cartis with gwnstainis,.. the cran with the traistis for the gwn. 1515 *Ibid.* V. 15 Four gret eschin treis to mak trestis for hacbuschis. 1543–4 *Ibid.* VIII. 248 For fraucht of thre boittis witht the said artalʒe, having tressis,.. and other necessaris convenient thairfore.

2. A tripod; a three-legged stool: = TRESTLE 2. Now *dial.*, and variously used.

1483 *Cath. Angl.* 393/2 A Tryste (*A.* A Tristylle), *tripos, tristula.* 1513 DOUGLAS *Æneis* III. vi. 11 God Apollois divinationis, Vnder his trestis and burdis at Delphos schene. 1547–64 BAULDWIN *Mor. Philos.* (Palfr.) 10 Certaine fishers found a golden treste or triuet, on which was written 'sapienti', that is, Giue this to a wise man. *a* 1800 PEGGE *Suppl. Grose, Trest*, a strong large stool. Lanc. 1882 *Lanc. Gloss., Trest*, a strong bench; a butcher's block [cf. sense 1].

† **trest**, *a. Obs.* [A parallel form to TRAIST *a.*, TRIST *a.*[1]: cf. TREST *sb.*[1] and next.]

1. Firm, strong: = TRAIST *a.* 1.

c 1470 *Golagros & Gaw.* 526 He.. Turnit to ane hie toure, that tight wes full trest.

2. Confident, sure: = TRAIST *a.* 2.

a 1300 *Cursor M.* 17219 Þou mai be ful trest to spede.

3. Trusty, faithful: = TRAIST *a.* 3.

c 1560 A. SCOTT *Poems* (S.T.S.) ix. 28 Ane constant hairt bayth trest & trew. 1566 *Inv. Roy. Wardrobe* (1815) 177 Service done.. be our trest cousing Johnne now erle of Mar. 1584 HUDSON *Du Bartas' Judith* v. 134 So shall you finde me,.. as faithfull, secret, trest, and trew.

Hence † **'trestly** *adv. Obs.*, confidently.

a 1568 in *Bannatyne Poems* (Hunter. Cl.) 213 Thair is nocht faithfulnes fundin in to this erd; Now is nocht thre may trestly trow in the ferd.

† **trest**, *v. Obs.* Forms: 3 treste(n, 5–6 trest; also 4 *pa. t.* treste. [A parallel form to TRAIST *v.*, TRIST *v.*, TRUST *v.*

Morsbach considers it a phonetic variant of *trist*. But in the northern and Sc. examples it may be merely a variant spelling of *traist*, perh. under English influence.]

1. *refl.* To commit oneself securely, to trust (*in*, *of*, *on*): cf. TRAIST *v.* 1.

a 1250 *Prov. Ælfred* 505 in *O.E. Misc.* 132 On him þu maist þe tresten. 1422 tr. *Secreta Secret., Priv. Priv.* xl. 198 That neuer he shold hym treste of the helpe of his god.. This kynge Ezechie hym trested in god.

2. *intr.* To trust (*of*, *to*, or with *inf.*): = TRAIST *v.* 2.

c 1275 LAY. 17941 For sealde he aswint þat to him seolue trested. 13.. *Sir Beues* (A.) 3520 Meche a [= he] treste to Arondel. *c* 1400 *Apol. Loll.* 66 Wan þe man trestiþ of þis absolucoun, wening him siker.. & mendiþ not. 1405 in *Roy. & Hist. Lett. Hen. IV* (Rolls) 159 Treste ʒe nought to no Leutenaunt. *c* 1425 *XI Pains of Hell* 347 in *O.E. Misc.* 221 Y pray ʒou seris trest wele hereto. *c* 1560 A. SCOTT *Poems* (S.T.S.) xxii. 17 Ay tresting for to speid.

b. *trans.* with simple obj. (? *orig.* dative), or clause: = TRAIST *v.* 2 b.

c 1275 LAY. 2351 Ac he nam one hired man þat wel he treste con. 1500–20 DUNBAR *Poems* xiii. 11 Is na man thair that trestis ane vther. *c* 1560 A. SCOTT *Poems* (S.T.S.) xxx. 8 Trest weill this taill is trew. 1570 *Satir. Poems Reform.* xvii. 183 He may, I trest, set vs at rest.

trest, obs. form of TRYST.

trestle ('trɛs(ə)l), *sb.* Forms: α. 4–5 trestele, 4–6 -el, -ell(e, -ill(e, 5 -iel, -ul, 5–6 -yll(e, 6 -il, -yl, 4– trestle; 4–6 tresselle, 6–8 -ell, 7 -il, -al, (tresle), 5–9 tressel, 7–9 tressle; (6 *Sc.* traisle, 7 threstle, 8 trassel). β. 5–6 trystell(e, 6 -el, tristell, -il, -ill(e, tristle, trys(s)elle, trisselle. γ. 5 trostyle, 6 -ell, trustyll, 7–8 trussell, 7–9 -el, (8 trusle), 8–9 trussle, 9 trustle. [ME. *trestel*, a. OF. *trestel* (12th c. in Hatz.-Darm., mod.F. *tréteau*) a transom, beam:—pop.L. **transtellum*, dim. of *transtrum* beam: see -LE 2 and cf. TREST *sb.*[2] Pop.L. **transtellum* would normally have given OF. *trastel*, but cf. *treste*, TREST *sb.*[2] from *transtrum*.]

1. A support for something, consisting of a short horizontal beam or bar with diverging legs, usually two at each end; *esp.* one of a pair or set used to support a board so as to form a table.

13.. *Coer de L.* 102 They sette tresteles, & layde a borde. *c* 1400 *Brut* clxxxvii. 206 Þis Piers of Gauaston.. went into þe Kyngus tresorie.. and toke þe table of golde, wiþ þe tresteles of þe same, and meny oþere riche gewelles. 1495 *Naval Acc. Hen. VII* (1896) 196 Mete tables in the Captayns Caban and.. Trystelles for the same. 1522 in *Archæologia* XXV. 457 A tabill & the trostells. 1525 LD. BERNERS *Froiss.* II. clvii. [cliii.] 434 These burgesses sette downe the lytter on two trestels. 1543 *Ludlow Churchw. Acc.* (Camden) 15 Payde for makynge of the tryselle.. ij d. 1572 in Feuillerat *Revels Q. Eliz.* (1908) 165 Tables and tressells. 1688 R. HOLME *Armoury* IV. xii. (Roxb.) 502/1 Then was the Body.. set on a Tressell between two crosses, and couered with a large purple veluett pall. 1703 T. N. *City & C. Purchaser* 3 Horses, or Trussels,.. to lay the Poles.. on whilst they are boring. 1743 in H. S. Wyndham *Ann. Cov. Gard. Theatre* (1906) II. 312 A Mountebank's stage and tressells. 1792 A. YOUNG *Trav. France* 217 In Italian inns.. the bedstead is usually four forms, like trussels, set together. *a* 1800 PEGGE *Suppl. Grose, Trussell*, a stand for a barrel. Kent. 1806–7 J. BERESFORD *Miseries Hum. Life* XVIII. 195 The proverbial obstinacy of the pig rather increases than diminishes when he is laid on the tressel for execution. 1838 DICKENS *O. Twist* v, An unfinished coffin on black tressels. 1861 WRIGHT *Ess. Archæol.* II. xiv. 41 The Anglo-Saxon table was formed merely by placing a board upon trestles at the time of eating.

† **2.** A three-legged stool or seat; a tripod. *Obs.*

c 1440 *Promp. Parv.* 503/1 Trostyle, *tristellus*, Kylw. *et* Dicc. *tripos*, Comm. 1552 HULOET, Trestle, *tripus*,.. whych hath thre fete. 1561 T. NORTON *Calvin's Inst.* IV. 151 These be the answers, of the Holy see, these be yᵉ Oracles of the Apostolike trestle. *Margin*, Apollo among yᵉ Heathen gaue.. Prophecies at a threefooted boord or trestle. 1570 LEVINS *Manip.* 126/28 A Tristil, *tripes.* 1656 BLOUNT *Glossogr.*, *Trestle* (*tripus*), a three footed-stool, or any thing with three feet, a trevet. 1658 in PHILLIPS.

b. A three-legged frame or stand for a support; a tripod. Now *dial.*

1790 ROY in *Phil. Trans.* LXXX. 165 We made shift, by the help of a long beam, and a moveable trestle by way of fulcrum for it to rest upon, to get the instrument up to the top if its own proper scaffold. 1795 *Ibid.* LXXXV. 435 The plank and bar were supported on five of the tressels, or tripods, belonging to the Royal Society. 1828 *Craven Gloss.*, *Tressel*, a frame to support a scaffold, made of three feet.

3. *Her.* A low stool or bench used as a bearing: usually represented with three legs.

1610 GUILLIM *Heraldry* IV. ix. (1611) 213 He beareth gules, a fesse Humet, or, betweene three trestles argent... This charge.. is of some.. taken.. for a Table. 1894 *Parker's Gloss. Her., Tressel*, a three-legged frame to support a table, borne chiefly by branches of one family.

4. In various specific uses. † **a.** A support or rest for a harquebus or other early fire-arm (see REST *sb.*[1] 11 a): = TREST *sb.*[2] 1 b. *Obs.* **b.** A framework consisting of upright (or more or less inclined) pieces with diagonal braces, used to support a bridge or other elevated structure. **c.** and **d.** See quots. **e.** One of the timber props or shores used to support a ship while being built. † **f.** A stand or frame for candles or tapers burning in religious worship. *Obs.* **g.** = TRESTLE-TREE (*Century Dict.*).

a. 1497 *Naval Acc. Hen. VII* (1896) 95 Trestelles for hakbusses.

b. 1796 MORSE *Amer. Geog.* I. 438 [A bridge] 160 feet long and 22 feet wide, supported by two wooden trussels, and two stone pillars. 1811 WELLINGTON in Gurw. *Desp.* (1838) VIII. 351 A certain quantity of timber for the construction of a pile engine and of a Trustle. 1861 SMILES *Engineers* II. 183 The centres spanning the whole width of the arch were composed of eight ribs each, formed in one piece, resting upon the same number of solid wedges, supported by inclined tressels placed upon longitudinal bearers, firmly fixed to the offsets of the piers and abutments. 1900 *Jrnl. Sch. Geog.* (U.S.) Apr. 135 There is not a difficult grade or an embankment or trestle of any importance between New York and Buffalo.

c. 1823 NICHOLSON *Pract. Build.* IV. 231 Trussels, four-legged stools for ripping and cross-cutting timber upon. 1882 YOUNG *Ev. Man Own Mech.* §517 A trestle, or sawing-stool.

d. 1839 URE *Dict. Arts*, etc. 378 The horse or trestle consists of a strong wooden frame... Upon the middle of this.. two uprights and a strong cross beam, for supporting the thick plank upon which the skins are worked. 1875 *Ure's Dict. Arts* III. 93 A high *trussel* is frequently used, across which the leather is thrown, after undergoing any of the processes.

e. 1860 LONGF. *Wayside Inn* I. *Build. Long Serpent* xvi, Then they launched her from the tressels, In the ship-yard by the sea.

f. 1523 *Will R. Broster* (Somerset Ho.), ij s to make a Trisell to brenne at Masse. 1546 *Ludlow Churchw. Acc.* (Camden) 26 Payde for a trisselle and holy candelles.

5. *transf.* and *fig.*: esp. (*pl.*) applied to the legs.

1610 B. JONSON *Alch.* IV. iii, He lookes in that deepe ruffe, like a head in a platter Seru'd in by a short cloake vpon two tressils. *c* 1620 T. ROBINSON *Mary Magd.* 232 Or rather cast a due-deuoted glaunce Vpon the marble tressels vnder plac't: But then her douelike feete themselues aduance. *Ibid.* 1471 Happy wert thou to touch yᵉ tressells bare Of thy beloued, heau'nly paramour. 1649 G. DANIEL *Trinarch., Hen. IV*, ccxciii, The Bishop wᵗʰ his Colleague Arundel, Were the first Tressells vnto Henrie's Throne. 1650 B. *Discolliminium* 16, I must not cut off her.. legs.., and set her upon Tressels.

6. *attrib.* and *Comb.*: **trestle-bed**, a portable or movable bed supported upon trestles, as used in a hospital tent, etc.; **trestle-board**, a board laid upon trestles to form a table; **trestle-bridge**, a bridge supported upon trestles or trestlework (see 4 b); † **trestle-candle**: cf. 4 f; **trestle-post**: cf. 4 b; **trestle-table**, a table made of a movable board or boards laid upon trestles; **trestlework**, a framework composed of a series of trestles (of wood or iron) fastened together, for supporting a bridge or viaduct, esp. on a railway.

1870 DISRAELI *Lothair* lx, Princesses.. might be seen by the *tressel beds. 1856 C. W. MOORE (*title*) New Masonic *Trestle-Board, adapted to the work and lectures as practised in the Lodges.. of Knights Templars in the United States of America. 1867 BRANDE & COX *Dict. Sc.*, etc., s.v., Two or more [trestles] are used for carrying a bridge, called a *trestle bridge. 1889 G. FINDLAY *Eng. Railway* 62 A temporary trestle bridge was erected. 1559 *Ludlow Churchw. Acc.* (Camden) 90 For ij li... of *tryssille candelle. 1799 A. YOUNG *Agric. Lincoln.* 74 He has.. conducted the water to a very large wheel, in troughs, upon *trussle-posts 20 feet high. 1891 *Cent. Dict.*, *Trestle-table. 1905 *Macm. Mag.* Nov. 4 A small white bell-tent,.. at its door a long trestle-table was set out with a bench on either side. 1861 W. H. RUSSELL in *Times* 10 July, The road led to a cypress swamp, over which the engines bustled.. at a perilous rate along a high *trestlework.

Hence **'trestle** *v. trans.*, to place upon trestles; **trestled** ('trɛs(ə)ld) *a.*, provided with or supported upon trestles; **'trestlewise** *adv.*, in the manner of a trestle (in quot., ? upon trestles); **'trestling**, a structure of trestles, trestlework.

1879 *Daily News* 7 Apr. 3/3 Having disembarked and '*tressled' their boats, the two crews returned to Putney. 1885 B. HARTE *Maruja* v, The black *tresselled bed. 1434 *E.E. Wills* (1882) 102 A litil tabel peynted *trestelwise. 1887 *N. York Tribune* 20 May (Cent.), *Trestling.

trestle-tree. *Naut.* Forms: see TRESTLE. [f. TRESTLE *sb.* + TREE *sb.* 3 a.] *pl.* Two strong pieces of timber fixed horizontally fore-and-aft on opposite sides of a mast-head, to support the cross-trees, the top, and the fid of the mast above.

a 1625 *Nomenclator Navalis* (Harl. MS. 2301) *Tressel-trees*, are ioyned to the Cross-trees and doe lie crosse each other, and serue to the same vse, theie differ onlie that the Tressel trees ar those wᶜʰ goe Long-ships, the other thwart ships. 1626 CAPT. SMITH *Accid. Yng. Seamen* 12 The trussell trees or crosse trees. 1804 A. DUNCAN *Mariner's Chron.* Pref. 16 Certain timbers fixed upon the hounds and cheeks of the masts, and called the trestle trees, and cross-trees. *c* 1860 H. STUART *Seaman's Catech.* 76 The trussle-trees.. are usually made of oak. 1911 E. GOSSE *Poems, Ships on Sea* iii, Less steadfast, o'er the trackless wave I strayed, And follow still their vanishing trestle-trees.

tresun, obs. form of TREASON.

tret (trɛt), *sb. Comm. Obs.* exc. *Hist.* [Known *c* 1500; origin and history obscure.

Generally conjectured either to be identical with OF. and AF. *tret*, variant of *trait* act of drawing, draught, etc. (see TRAIT), or to represent OF. *traite* 'a draught.. a transportation, vent outward, shipping ouer; and an Imposition vpon commodities exported, or so transported' (Cotgr.): cf. It. *tratta* 'permission or priuilege to transport from out any country any merchandice.. also that custome that is paid for things carried out' (Florio); see also med.L. *tracta* in Du Cange. These senses of the Fr., It., and med.L. words do not satisfactorily explain the commercial use of *tret* in Eng.; but it is possible that the term may have originated in connexion with a single class of commodities or of transactions, and have been extended by 1670 to others. See Du Cange s.v. *tracta*; also Skeat *s.v.*, and E. Weekley in *Trans. Philol. Soc.* June 1909. Cf. also CLOFF, DRAFT 1, DRAUGHT 13.]

An allowance of 4 lb. in 104 lb. (= $\frac{1}{26}$) on goods sold by weight after the deduction for tare.

The reason or ground of the allowance was apparently forgotten already in the 17th c., and has been variously given since: see quots.

a 1500 in *Arnolde's Chron.* 47/2 Your said suppliant shulde be rebated for the tare of euery of the said xij bales iiij ll. and for the cloff of euery off the said xij bales ij ll. Som. lxxij ll. and for the tret of yᵉ same peper cxxxvij ll. 1670 BLOUNT *Law Dict.* s.v. *Tare and Tret*, The other [Tret] is a consideration allowed in the weight for wast, in emptying and reselling the Goods. 1674 *Lond. Gaz.* No. 892/4, 59 Bails at fifteen pence, and 17 Sacks at sixteen pence a pound, with Tret and Tare as Custom. 1674 JEAKE *Arith.* (1696) 82 There is an Overweight allowed by Merchants called Tret, which is 4 lb. upon every Hundred of 112 lb. 1678 PHILLIPS (ed. 4), *Tret*, a certain allowance that is made by Merchants, before a Commodity is garbled from its refuse [1706 ed. Kersey adds] as Dust, Moats, &c., which is always 4 in every 104 Pounds. 1711 STEELE *Spect.* No. 136 ¶7 There is my little Merchant,.. there's my Man for Loss and Gain, there's Tare and Tret. *a* 1850 J. GRAY *Introd. Arith.* (ed. 100) 58 What is the value of 12 bales of pepper.. tare 3 lb. per bale, allowing also tret and cloff? 1882 BITHELL *Counting-ho. Dict., Tret*, an allowance made for wear, damage, or deterioration in goods during transit from one place to another.

† **tret**, *a. Obs. rare*[−1]. [App. a shortened form of TRETIS.] = TRETIS. (Cf. TRETY *a.*)

c 1470 HENRY *Wallace* IX. 1928 Braid breyst and heych, with sturdy crag and gret; His lyppys round, his noys was squar and tret [*ed.* 1570 treit].

tret, tretabill, -ble, tretar, obs. ff. TREAT, TREATABLE, TREATER.

tretcherer, -ous, -ye: see TREACHER, -OUS, -Y.

trete, obs. f. TREAT, TREATY.

treteable, obs. f. TREATABLE.

tretee, tretes, -esse, obs. ff. TREATY, TREATISE.

treterous, obs. f. TRAITOROUS.

tretice, -is(e, tretie, obs. ff. TREATISE, TREATY.

† **tretis**, *a. Obs.* Forms: 4 tretys, 5 tretis, -ise, -ez, traytice, -yse. [a. OF. *traitis*, *tretis* slender, graceful, well-built (12th c. in Godef.):—pop.L. type **tractīcius* drawn-out, slender, f. *tract-us*, pa. pple. of *trahĕre* to draw: see -ITIOUS[1].] Well-proportioned, neat, graceful, handsome.

? *a* 1366 CHAUCER *Rom. Rose* 932 That other bowe was.. Tretys and long, of good fasoun. *c* 1380 *Sir Ferumb.* 5883 Hure vysage was fair & tretys. *c* 1386 CHAUCER *Prol.* 152 Hire nose tretys [*Hengwrt* tretez, *Camb.* tretis], hir eyen greye as glas. 1490 CAXTON *Eneydos* xxix. 112 Her forehed brod and highe ynoughe, the browes traytice and broun. *Ibid.*, The necke [of Dydo].. longe ynoughe.. and traytyse on the backe syde.

tretour, (-owre), -ourous, obs. ff. TRAITOR, TRAITOROUS.

tretrifolie, -y, trettifollie, obs. ff. TREE-TREFOIL.

tre-trip, var. TREY-TRIP *Obs.*

trett(e, tretty, obs. ff. TREAT, TREATY.

trettle, obs. f. TRATTLE *sb.*[2]

†**'trety**, *a. Obs. rare*$^{-1}$. = TRETIS *a.*
c **1450** *St. Cuthbert* (Surtees) 7362 He had a lange trety face.

trety, -ye, obs. ff. TREATY.

tretys, obs. f. TREATISE; var. TRETIS *Obs.*

treu, obs. f. TREE, TROW, TRUE.

treuage, treuandise, treuant, treuce, treuchman: see TREWAGE, TRUANDISE, TRUANT, TRUCE, TRUCHMAN.

treuges, treuis, treugth, obs. ff. TRUCE, TRUTH.

treukour, obs. Sc. f. TRUCKER.

treuliche, -ly, obs. ff. TRULY.

treumph, obs. Sc. f. TRIUMPH.

†**treunt**, *v. Obs. rare.* [Etymol. obscure: has some likeness to TRANONT.] *intr.* ? To depart.
? *a* **1400** *Morte Arth.* 1976 Trussene fulle traystely, and treunt there-aftyre. *Ibid.* 2017 This traytour has treunt this tresone to wyrche! He has the cete forsett appone sere halfez. *Ibid.* 3900 Than the traytoure treuntede the Tyseday thar-aftyre, Trynnys in with a trayne tresone to wirke.

treus, obs. pl. of TREE; obs. f. TRUCE.

treush-man, obs. f. TRUCHMAN.

treut, treuth(e, treuþ(e, obs. ff. TRUTH.

treuwes, treux, treuys, obs. ff. TRUCE.

†**trevally**[1]. *Obs.* or *dial.* Forms: 7 trevall, (travailler), travalley, 7–8 travally, 7, 9 *dial.* trevally. [perh. a corruption of REVEILLE.]
1. A signal made by beating the drum; also attrib., ***trevally-beat***. Also *transf.*
1645 R. SYMONDS *Diary Civ. War* (Camden) 224 When the trevall was beate, and they lett downe their bridge for their scouts. **1675** CROWNE *Country Wit* II. i, Beat a Travalley on the drums of their ears. **1685** B. RINGROSE *Bucaniers Amer.* II. IV. 10 We heard..a small arm discharged, and after that a drum beating a Travailler. **1688** R. HOLME *Armoury* III. xix. (Roxb.) 154/2 The seuerall Beates or points of warre are these..14 A Revally, or Trevally, and ruvalley. **1698** FRYER *Acc. E. India & P.* 144 The next Morning I..Landed presently after Travally-Beat. **1798** O'KEEFFE *Highland Reel* I. ii, Your rattan would be the drumstick of the corps, to beat the travally on my back—row-dy-dow!
2. A disturbance, a noisy 'to-do'.
1819 *St. Patrick* I. 162 (Jam.) Gin ye could airt me tae ane o' them [runnigates], we wad let you see a fine trevallie. **1866** KENNEDY *Irish Celts* 19 (E.D.D.) There was such a thravally ruz..about it. **1881** *Cumberland Gloss.*, *Trevally*, disturbance, quarrelling.

‖**tre'vally**[2]. Also -valley, -valli, -valla, travalley, -vale. [Supposed to be an alteration of CAVALLY.] A name applied in Australasia to several sea-fishes, mostly of the family *Carangidæ* or Horse-Mackerels.
Six species of *Caranx*, *Neptonemus*, and *Teuthis*, to which the name is applied, are enumerated by Morris *Austral English.*
1883 E. P. RAMSAY *Food-Fishes N.S. Wales* 20 The white trevally, *Caranx georgianus*,..on the New South Wales coast..seldom..weighing over $1\frac{1}{2}$ to 2 lbs., is found on the shores of Queensland of a much greater size. **1883** *Fisheries Exhib. Catal.* (ed. 4) 184 The Collection also contains..the ..'Trevalley'. **1886** SHERRIN *Fishes of New Zeal.* 99 Dr. Hector says: 'The trevalli is the arara of the Maoris, or the trevalli or cavalli of the fishermen... The fish known as trevalli in the Dunedin district is a different fish.' **1890** *Victorian Statutes, Fisheries Act*, Schedule 2, Travale.

trevass, obs. form of TRAVERSE, TRAVIS *sb.*

†**trevat** ('trɛvət). *Obs.* Also travat, trivet, trevette (*Cent. Dict.* 1891). [Derivation unascertained.] An instrument with a sharp blade formerly used for cutting the loops which form the pile of velvet, Wilton carpets, etc., when hand-woven.
1831 G. R. PORTER *Silk Manuf.* 279 Running a sharp instrument called a trevat along the groove of the wire. **1844** G. DODD *Textile Manuf.* vi. 203 A cutting instrument called a trevat..severing the pile threads. **1864** *Q. Rev.* July 31 These rows of loops are afterwards cut through by an instrument now called a 'trevat', and thus the peculiar surface of velvet is given. **1877** KNIGHT *Dict. Mech.*, Trivet. **1888** *Encycl. Brit.* XXIV. 467/1 Along this groove a cutting knife called a trivet is run to cut the loops. **1914** (Apr. 21) *Let. fr. Tomkinson & Adam, Kidderminster*, The word, as we understand it here, is spelt 'Travat', and [the specimen] is so labelled in the Museum; but the knife has been out of use so many years that only men who are 80 years of age or thereabouts remember anything of it.

†**treve.** *Obs. rare.* Also 5 trieue (for trieve), 6 trefue (for trefve). [a. F. *trêve*, OF. also *trive* (12th c. in Godef. *Compl.*), *trieve* (*c* 1275), also *truive*, *trueve*, *true*; = Pr. *treva*, *treg(u)a*, Sp., It. *tregua*, med.L. *tregua*, *treuga*, *treugua*, Com. Romanic type **treuwa* (Darmesteter), from Germanic. In OF. often, in Eng. always, in pl. *treves* (cf. *unes triuwes*, Froissart). Ultimately the same word as TRUCE (ME. *trewes* pl. of *trewe*), q.v. for its further etymology.] = TRUCE.
1406 *Rolls Parlt.* V. 417 Come for to trete Pees or Trieues. **1410** in *Proc. Privy Council* (1834) I. 325 That ferme pees other longe and goode trieues..may be accordede and stablisshede. **1523** (Dec. 18) SAMPSON & JERNINGHAM *Let. to Wolsey* (MS. Cott. Vesp. C. II. 228: See *St. Papers Henry VIII*, VI. 211), The Frence men requiryd treves for v or vi monethis... The Lord Chauncelier enteryd in to the communication off a peace or treves... Iff the King our mastre might know thEmperour determinid to a peace or treves... He nevyr wold enclyne or gyue hering to owthir peace or treves. **1550** NICOLLS *Thucyd.* 132 b, The Beotians made trefues for tenne dayes onely. *Ibid.* 134 b, Wyllynge to compryse the..Corinthyans in the trefues of tenne dayes.

†**tre'veer**, *v. Obs. rare.* [? ad. F. *trevirer* for *chavirer* to capsize, upset, f. *tre-* = TRANS- + *virer* to whirl, roll.] *trans.* ? To upset.
1636–7 *Admir. Crt. Exam.* 115. 24 Jan., Six butts of the articulate shipp's ladinge..were by reason the said shipps giveing waie in foule weather treveered, and one of them was quite out and the other aboute one third out.

treveiss, obs. form of TRAVERSE *v.*, TRAVIS.

treverse, obs. f. TRAVERSE *a.*

trevertine, var. TRAVERTINE.

treves, -ess(e, obs. ff. TRAVERSE, TRAVIS.

trevet, obs. f. TRIVET.

trevice: see TRAVIS[1].

Trevira (trə'vɪərə). Also **trevira**. The proprietary name of a type of artificial fibre or the fabric made from it (see quots.).
1959 *Official Gaz.* (U.S. Patent Office) 24 Nov. TM160/1 Trevira. Owner of German Reg...dated Mar. 21, 1956.. For table linen and bed linen; net, lace, woven and mesh fabrics; textile ribbons, textile trimmings; carpets and rugs; mats; curtains; flags; and felt. **1960** *Trade Marks Jrnl.* 21 Dec. 1650/2 *Trevira*... All goods included in Class 24. Farbwerke Hoechst Aktiengesellschaft Vormals Meister Lucius & Brüning..45, Brüningstrasse, Frankfurt-am-Main—Hoechst, Germany; Manufacturers and Merchants. **1964** *Which?* Aug. 253/3 *Polyester*... Brand names: *Dacron* (USA), *Tergal* (France), *Terlenka* (Holland), *Terylene*, *Trevira* (W. Germany). **1967** *Daily Tel.* 30 Oct. 11/3 Now there's another new test-tube fibre name to memorize... Trevira will pop into Britain's fashion shops from December. **1972** *Guardian* 22 Aug. 9/2 Trevira/rayon shirt. **1977** *N.Z. Herald* 5 Jan. 2-18/3 (Advt.), Lincoln Fabrics... Plain and fancy crimps and treviras.

trevis, -iss, obs. ff. TRAVERSE, TRAVIS.

trevit, obs. f. TRIVET.

trevorite ('trɛvəraɪt). *Min.* [f. the name of T. G. *Trevor* (1865–1958), South African geologist and mining official + -ITE[1].] A black, magnetic, isometric oxide of nickel and ferric iron, $NiFe_2O_4$, belonging to the spinel group.
1921 A. F. CROSSE in *Jrnl. Chem., Metallurgical & Mining Soc. S. Afr.* XXI. 126/2 One of the most interesting mineralogical discoveries..in the Transvaal..is an extraordinarily rich nickel ore... This ore is as far as I am able to judge a new and undescribed mineral... I should like to call it 'Trevorite' after Major T. G. Trevor, Mining Inspector for the Pretoria District. **1976** *Mineral. Abstr.* XXVII. 252/2 Microprobe analyses of grains of ferroan trevorite from a serpentine massif in south-western China reported Ni 3·4-8·8% but no Ti.

†**trew**, *v. Sc. Obs.* [f. *trew*, obs. sing. of *trewes*, TRUCE.] *trans.* To protect by a truce.
c **1425** WYNTOUN *Cron.* VII. viii. 1654 Þe lordis of Northumbyrlande Askyt trewis at þe Kynge..Tyl þe fest of þe Trynyte He grantyde thaim trewit for to be.

trew, obs. f. TREE, TROW *v.*, TRUCE, TRUE.

†**'trewage, 'truage.** *Obs.* Forms: 3–6 truage, treuage, 4 truwage, 4–5 trowage, 4–6 trewage, 4–7 trouage, 5 triwage, trywage. [a. OF. *treuage* (12th c. in Godef.) tribute, f. OF. *trëu*, *trëu* (Roland, 11th c.):—L. *tribūt-um* TRIBUTE + -AGE.] Tribute.
c **1275** LAY. 7189 Romleode Com to þissere þeode, And setten truage in þisse lond [*c* 1205 and sette ȝeld a þisse londe]. *Ibid.* 25044 Nou axeþ þorh cunde truage of þis londe. *c* **1330** R. BRUNNE *Chron.* (1810) 7 Grete treuage þei toke of þis lond here. *c* **1400** tr. *Secreta Secret., Gov. Lordsh.* 57 þerfore trowages and þe kynges rentys encresys. *c* **1440** *Generydes* 1792 Defende your lande that it pay noo trewage. **1525** LD. BERNERS *Froiss.* II. xl. 125 When he hath wonne a countrey..he desyreth nothynge but truage. **1530** PALSGR. 283/1 Truage, trybute, *treuaige*. **1593** NASHE *Christ's T.* (1613) 104 Our God..asketh no other treuage at our handes for giuing, but asking and thanksgiuing. **1661** MORGAN *Sph. Gentry* II. viii. 102 At Rome hastily will I be: not to give you Truage but to have Truage of you.
b. Toll, custom; payment for some privilege.
c **1380** *Sir Ferumb.* 1731 'Ȝe mote furst', quaþ þe Sarazyn, 'syþþe ȝe þyder fondeþ, For þe truwage make fyn þat to þis brigge longeþ'. **14..** *Cov. Corp. Christi Pl.* i. 524 Nor also aleond stranger throȝ my realme pas, But the[y] for there truage do pay markis fyve. **1596** WARNER *Alb. Eng.* x. lx, For their Charters did they offer..to undergo all Truage, Taxe and Charge. **1657** HOWELL *Londinop.* 49 Wooll Key, where was used to be the Trouage of Woolls.
¶ Misused for 'homage'.
1592 NASHE *P. Penilesse* (ed. 2) 31 As he should stoop to doo him truage, he might seaze vpon his throat and stifle him.
Hence †**'trewager** *Obs.*, one subject to tribute, a tributary. (Cf. *homager.*)
c **1330** R. BRUNNE *Chron.* (1810) 45 Þe folk wild not suffre to be treuwageres.

trewaill, trewbut(e, trewcht, obs. Sc. ff. TRAVAIL, TRIBUTE, TRUTH.

trewand, -ant, -andise, etc., obs. ff. TRUANT, TRUANDISE *Obs.*

trewce, obs. form of TRUCE.

†**trewe.** *Obs. rare.* [a. OF. *trëu*, older *trëud* (Roland, 11th c.): see TREWAGE.] Tribute. ***bring to trewe***, to subject to tribute, make tributary.
c **1330** R. BRUNNE *Chron. Wace* (Rolls) 4600 Al my conqueste preise y nought, Bot þe Bretons to trewe be brought. *Ibid.* 11921 To aske hym trewe, hit is for nought.

trewe, trewell, obs. ff. TRUCE, TRUE, TROWEL.

†**tre'werne.** *Obs.* [prob. from a place or personal name.] A wagon or truck of some kind.
1667 in Pettus *Fodinæ Reg.* xxv. (1670) 38 One great Trewerne with Iron wheels to carry out deads belonging to the Addits.

trewes, trewice, -is, obs. ff. TRUCE.

treweth(e, trewht, obs. ff. TRUTH.

trewit, obs. f. TRIVET.

trewker, obs. Sc. f. TRUCKER.

trewliche, -lie, obs. ff. TRULY.

trewmph, obs. Sc. f. TRIUMPH.

trews (truːz), *sb. pl.* Also 6 trewis, (8–9 truis). [ad. Irish *trius*, Gael. *triubhas*, sb. sing., ad. Eng. TROUSE (singular, with pl. *trouses*), but from the final (sound of) *s* treated as a plural, with no singular in use: cf. *drawers*, *breeches*.]
a. Close-fitting trousers, or breeches combined with stockings, formerly worn by Irishmen and Scottish Highlanders, and still by certain Scottish regiments.
a **1568** MONTGOMERIE *Misc. Poems* liv. 3 Smoir cunary takin trewis breikles McBradȝan. [**1581** A. TROLLOPE *Let.* 12 Sept. in *Cal. St. Papers, Irel.* 1574–85, 318 They had ech of them a hatt, a lether jerken, a payre of hosen, which they called trowes, and a payre of broges.] *a* **1653** Z. BOYD *Zion's Flowers* (1855) Introd. 19 Content to weare the Irish trews. **1728** RAMSAY *Tea-t. Misc.*, *Highland Laddie* ii, I'd take young Donald without trews, With bonnet blew, and belted plaidy. [**1746** *Act 19–20 Geo. II*, c. 39 §17 The Plaid, Philibeg, or little Kilt, Trowse, Shoulder Belts, or whatsoever of what peculiarly belongs to the Highland Garb.] **1771** PENNANT *Tour Scot. in 1769* (1794) 210 The truis were worn by the gentry, and were breeches and stockings made of one piece. **1790** BURNS *On Battle of Sheriffmuir* iii, Had you seen the philibegs, And skyrin tartan trews, man. **1808** SCOTT *Marm.* v. v, The chequer'd trews, and belted plaid. **1834** PLANCHÉ *Brit. Costume* 338. **1860** KNIGHT *Pop. Hist. Eng.* VI. viii. 134 *note*, Prince Charles Edward is painted as wearing the truis, the breeches and stockings in one piece, or hose pantaloon. **1911** C. F. ATKINSON in *Encycl. Brit.* XXVII. 585/1 Highland regiments wear tartan kilt..; Lowland regiments (also Scottish Rifles, Highland Light Infantry, and all mounted officers) tartan trews.
b. Trousers in general (tartan or otherwise), including close-fitting trousers worn by women.
1847 H. S. RIDDELL *Poems* 19 When I brought ben your clase, Sae beaten with the weather, And gae the trews a wee bit touch, Out flew goud guinea frae ae pouch. **1883** F. SUTHERLAND *Sunny Mem. Morayland* 57 The soor-moo'd limmer wears the trews. **1917** N. MUNRO *Poetry* (1931) III. 51 His body unadorned by Highland raiment, Trammelled, for glorious hours, in Saxon trews. **1931** E. LINKLATER *Juan in America* II. iv. 94 His Tyrolean costume made evident that even his knees were comely—strong, round, and rosy under their brief leather trews. **1958** *Woman's Own* 5 Mar. 16/3 They make a handsome pair, when she's wearing a blouse with matching tapered trews in printed wool. **1959** H. HOBSON *Mission House Murder* i. 5 She was wearing tartan trews, a black cashmere sweater and a short red duffle-coat.
Hence **'trewsman**, one who wears trews; a Highlander.
1819 SCOTT *Leg. Montrose* iv, We have a wheen canny trewsmen here.

trews, trewse, trewyce, -ys, obs. ff. TRUCE.

trewþ(e, trewthe, obs. forms of TRUTH.

trey (treɪ), *sb.* Forms: 4–7 treye, 6– tray, 7 trye, 5– trey. [a. OF. and AF. *treis*, *trei*, F. *trois*, dial. *tray* = Prov. *treis*, nom. *trei*, Sp. *tres*, It. *tre*:—L. *trēs* three.]
1. The three at dice or cards. **a.** *Dice.* That side of the die that is marked with three pips or spots; a throw which turns up this side.
c **1386** CHAUCER *Pard. T.* 325 Seuene is my chaunce, and thyn is cynk and treye [*Corpus*, *Lansd.* fyue and þre]. *c* **1450** *Bk. of Brome* 17 Ȝowr cast wosse sysse and dobyll trey. **1588** SHAKS. *L.L.L.* v. ii. 232 *Qu.* Hony, and Milke, and Suger: there is three. *Ber.* Nay then two treyes,..Methegline, Wort, and Malmsey; well runne dice: There's halfe a dozen

sweets. **1668** DRYDEN *Evening's Love* III. i, Two sixes and a trey wins it. **1772** FOOTE *Nabob* II. Wks. 1799 II. 301 Tray, ace, or two deuces. **1910** *Nation* 1 Jan. 566/1 There's luck under the deuce but none under the tray.

b. *Cards.* That card of any suit which is marked with three spots. *rare.*

1680 COTTON *Compl. Gamester* xv. (ed. 2) 93 The best Putt-Cards are first the Trey, next the Deuce. **1816** SINGER *Hist. Cards* 195 The trey presents us with the separation of a lover and his mistress. **1896** J. K. BANGS *House-boat on Styx* v, I do not know a trey of diamonds from a silver salver.

†**c.** In proverbial phrase ***ere you can say trey-ace*** (see 3), of which *treis, trayse* appears to be a contracted form. *Obs.*

1390 GOWER *Conf.* I. 142 Al sodeinliche, as who seith treis, Wher that he stod in his Paleis, He tok him fro the mennes sihte. *c* **1400** *Laud Troy Bk.* 8917 A man schuld not so sone say 'trayse', As he fel ded & held his payse. *a* **1553** UDALL *Royster D.* III. iii. (Arb.) 48 Bydde them high apace. *M. Mery.* I wyll be here with them ere ye can say trey ace.

2. *slang.* The number three, in various connexions; a set of three; a threepenny piece; *spec.* in the U.S., a three-dollar packet of a narcotic.

[**1859** HOTTEN *Dict. Slang* 204 *Tray saltee*, threepence.. tre soldi.] **1887** J. W. HORSLEY *Jottings from Jail* i. 3 And he who 'does a tray' (serves three months' imprisonment) therein, borrows his word from our Gallican neighbours. **1896** VIZETELLY tr. *Zola's Rome* 372 Stake their luck on a cardinal, just as they nurse a 'trey' in the lottery. **1897** MARSHALL *Pomes* 71 (Farmer) And the magistrate..left but very little doubt That the moons she'd have to do would be a tray. **1907** *Daily Chron.* 26 July 4/7 One easily sees why it [threepence] is a 'tray'. **1944** D. BURLEY in A. Dundes *Mother Wit* (1973) 214 A deuce or tray of haircuts ago. **1960** 'A. BURGESS' *Doctor is Sick* xiii. 98 'I know all about you. You did a tray on the moor.'.. 'It wasn't a tray..it was only a stretch.' **1967** [see *nickel bag* s.v. NICKEL *sb.* 3 a]. **1972** J. MILLS *Report to Commissioner* 98 She wants to buy two treys, $3 bags of heroin. He says he has treys, but wants $3.50 for them. **1977** *National Times* (Austral.) 17 Jan. 11/3 Service of the kind just described is as rare these days as finding a trey in the Christmas pudding.

3. *Comb.* **trey-ace**, a throw that turns up trey with one die and ace with the other; so **trey-deuce**; **trey-bit** (freq. **tray-bit**) *Austral.* and *N.Z. slang* (now *Hist.*), a three-penny piece; also ***trey-piece***; **trey-point** = sense 1; †**trey-table**, a dicing-table; †**trey-trace**, (?).

a **1553** *Trey ace [see 1 c]. **1725** LD. STANHOPE in *C'tess Suffolk's Lett.* (1824) I. 186 Wishing you all imaginable success at Trey-ace, Commerce, or whatever else may be the prevailing diversion. **1898** *Bulletin* (Sydney) 1 Oct. 14, 3d. a '*traybit'. **1901** *Bulletin Reciter* (Sydney) 181 Den I socked me bit upon 'er—Ev'ry tray-bit I could bring. **1937** F. SARGESON in *Tomorrow* 17 Mar. 310/2, I upend them to collect the tray bits. **1953** A. UPFIELD *Murder must Wait* xviii. 162 I'll bet my job against a trey bit you're right. **1977** *Sunday Sun* (Brisbane) 1 May 16 When it comes to unique competitions the people of outback Winton reckon they're the full quid—and you can bet your last zac or traybit on it! **1680** COTTON *Compl. Gamester* xxxiii. *Hazzard* (ed. 2) 122 Five [has] but two chances, Trey Ace and two Deuces, or *Trey Deuce and Quater Ace. **1899** *Bulletin* (Sydney) 14 Jan. (Red Page), We have here [*sc.* in Tauranga, N.Z.].. slang words for..3d.—*thrum, half-tiz, tray*, or **tray-piece*. **1657** C. BECK *Univ. Char.* L vij b, A *tray point on a die. **1646** EVELYN *Mem.* (1857) I. 249 There is also a bowling-place, a tavern, and a *trey-table. **1575** R. B. *Appius & Virg.* Bj, With hey tricke, how trowle, trey trip, and *trey trace.

trey, tray, *v.* [app. f. TREY *sb.*] app. To divide or deal (a pack of cards) into three heaps in order to separate the suits (in the order of which new cards are or were packed), before shuffling in the usual way.

(This is the explanation given by the majority of those who answered a query as to this word in the *Pall Mall Gazette* of 5 Jan. 1914. Two of these, Mr. R. H. Macaulay, M.A., and Mr. C. B. Lacey, both resident in India in 1888, remember the word as there used in this sense. Several other explanations were suggested, e.g. that *tray* was for F. *trier* to pick out.)

1888 *Times* 15 Feb. 8/2 The new packs were opened, and were 'trayed' and shuffled in the usual way. Dr. Sanders had one of the packs cut to him, and proceeded to deal. He turned up the Knave of Clubs, and on sorting his hand found that he had the other 12 trumps.

trey, obs. Sc. f. TREE.

trey, treye: see TRAY.

treybochet, obs. f. TREBUCHET.

treyfoile, -fole, -foyle, obs. ff. TREFOIL.

†**treygo'bet.** *Obs.* [Evidently, *trey go bet* = three go better: cf. *hey-go-bet* (HEY 3); but origin unknown.] Name of an old game at dice.

1426 LYDG. *De Guil. Pilgr.* 11623 Pleye at the ches, pley at the tablys, At treygobet & tregetrye, In karyyng & in Iogolory. *c* **1554** *Interlude of Youth* C iij, Syr I can teache you to play at the dice..The Treygobet and the hasarde also. **1587** M. GROVE *Pelops & Hipp.* (1878) 117 On bench with clownes whole peny vp, at trey gobet to play.

treylle, var. TRAIL *sb.*[2] *Obs.*

treylles, treylsys: see TRELLIS.

treyn, treyne: see TRAIN, TREEN *a.*, TRINE *v.*[2], [3].

trey-sail, obs. f. TRYSAIL.

treyse, obs. f. TRACE *sb.*[2]

treyson, -oun, obs. ff. TREASON.

treyst (y-treyst), pa. pple. of TRAISE *v. Obs.* to betray; var. TRAIST *Obs.*

treyte, treyter, obs. f. TREAT *sb.*, TREATER.

treytori, -ory, var. TRAITORY.

†**trey-trip.** *Obs.* Also 6–7 trea-, 7 tray-, trei-, tre-, tra-. [app. f. TREY *sb.* + TRIP *v.* (?).] A game at dice, or with dice, in which success probably depended on the casting of a trey or three.

1564–78 BULLEYN *Dial. agst. Pest.* (1888) 94 He is plaiyng at the trea trippe with our hoste sonne. **1575** [see *trey-trace*, TREY *sb.* 3]. **1588** *Marprel. Epist.* (Arb.) 38 Because the gamesters..wan all his monie at trey trip. **1602** in *Sir R. Cecil's Corr.* x. (1766) 127 There is great danger of being taken sleepers at tray-trip, if the King sweep suddenly. **1617** *Machiavell's Dogge* B j b, But leauing Cardes, let's goe to dice awhile, To Passage, Treitrippe, Hazarde or Mumchaunce... And trippe without a Treye makes had I wist To sitte and mourne among the sleepers ranke. **1636** DAVENANT *Wits* Wks. (1673) 195 My Watch are playing above at Treatrip For some Suffolk Cheese. **1639** MAYNE *City Match* II. iv, Find himself business at tre-trip i'th'hall. **1660** TATHAM *Rump* IV. i, It seems he plays better at tratrip with thee then thy husband Ireton did.

treyumphe, obs. f. TRIUMPH.

treyvette, obs. f. TRIVET.

trez, var. TRAY *sb.*[4]

trezerer, obs. f. TREASURER.

tri- (traɪ, *occas.* trɪ), *prefix*, a. L. *tri-* and Gr. τρι-, combining form of *trēs*, τρεῖς three, τρίς thrice.

The *i*, etymologically short in Greek and Latin, was in Latin sometimes lengthened, esp. in numerals (*trīcēnī, trīgintā*, etc.). In Eng. it is now usually long and diphthongal (aɪ), except in derivatives before two consonants, as *triple, triptych*, also in *trilogy, trimeter*. In scientific books *tri-* is often represented by the numeral, as *3-bracteate*, 3-carbon.

I. Forming adjs. (and derived sbs. and advbs.) with the senses:

1. Having, characterized by, or consisting of (*rarely*, belonging or relating to) three (of the things denoted by the second element).

a. In comb. with adjs. derived from sbs. (usually L. or Gr.), or less commonly with the sb. without adjectival termination. **triac'nodal** *Geom.*, having three acnodes or conjugate points (see CONJUGATE *a.* 6 a). **'triact, tri'actinal, tri'actine** *Zool.* [Gr. ἀκτίς, ἀκτῖν- ray], having three rays: said of a sponge-spicule. **trialate** (traɪ'eɪlət), *Nat. Hist.* [L. *āla* wing], three-winged (*Cent. Dict.* 1891). **tria'llelic** *Genetics*, having three different alleles of a gene. **tri'annulate** *Zool.* [L. *annulus* ring], having or consisting of three rings. **tri'anthous** *Bot.* [Gr. ἄνθος flower], having three flowers. **tri'arctic** (see quot.). **tri'arcuated** [L. *arcu-s* bow, ARCH], three-arched. **tri'areal**, comprising or divided into three areas. **tri'axon, -'onian, -onid** [Gr. ἄξων axis], of sponge-spicules: having three axes; = TRIAXIAL. **tri'basilar** *Anat.*, designating a bone formed by union of three bones at the base of the skull. **tri'blastic** *Zool.* [Gr. βλαστός germ], having three layers (epiblast, mesoblast, hypoblast) in the blastoderm of the embryo. **tri'bracteate** *Bot.*, having three bracts; so **tri'bracteolate**, having three bracteoles or minute bracts. **tri'carinate, -ated** *Nat. Hist.* [L. *carīna* keel], having three keels or ridges. **tricar'pellary, tri'carpellate** *Bot.*, consisting of or having three carpels. **tri'carpellite** [ad. mod.L. *Tricarpellītēs*], a fossil tricarpellary nut-like fruit, found in the London Clay. **tri'carpous** *Bot.* [Gr. καρπός fruit], 'bearing three fruits or three carpels' (*Syd. Soc. Lex.* 1899). **tri'caudal, tri'caudate** [L. *cauda* tail], having three tails or tail-like processes, as the *retrahens auris* or *tricaudālis* muscle, or the hind margin of the posterior wings in some *Lepidoptera*. **tri'cellular**, having or consisting of three cells. **tri'central**, having three centres; so †**tricen'treity**, the fact or attribute of having three centres. **trice'phalic, tri'cephalous** [Gr. τρικέφαλος, f. κεφαλή head], having three heads, three-headed. **trico'lumnar**, having three columns; arranged in or occupying three columns of print. **triconti'nental**, embracing three continents. **tricornigerous** (traɪkɔː'nɪdʒərəs) [late L. *tricorniger*, f. *cornu* horn: see -GEROUS], **tri'cornute, tri'cornuted**, three-horned; having three horn-like processes. **tricoryphean** (-kɒrɪ'fiːən) [Gr. κορυφή peak], having three peaks. **tri'costate** [COSTATE], three-ribbed. **tricoty'ledonous** *Bot.*, having three cotyledons. **tricru'nodal** *Geom.*, having three crunodes. **tri'crural** [L. *crūs, crūr-* leg], three-legged; consisting of three branches radiating from a common centre. **tridi'ametral**, having three diameters. **tri'digitate**, (*a*) *Zool.* having three digits (fingers or toes); (*b*) *Bot.* digitate with three leaflets, ternate; so **tri'digital, tri'digitated**. **tridynamous** (traɪ'dɪnəməs) *Bot.* [after DIDYNAMOUS, TETRADYNAMOUS], having six stamens of which three are longer than the others. **triele'mentary**, composed of three elements. **tri'fasciated** *Zool.* [L. *fascia* band], having or marked with three bands. **tri'faucian** [L. *trifaux* (Vergil *Æn.* vi. 417), f. *faucēs* throat], having three throats. **trifilar** (traɪ'faɪlə(r)) [L. *fīlum* thread], consisting of three threads. †**tri'fistulary** [L. *fistula* pipe], having three pipes or tubes. **triflagellate** (traɪ'flædʒələt) *Biol.*, having three flagella, as an infusorian. **tri'floral, tri'florous** *Bot.* [L. *flōs, flōr-* flower], bearing three flowers (on one stem); three-flowered. **tri'foveolate, -ated** *Entom.*, having three foveolæ or shallow pits. **tri'functional** *Chem.*, having three functional groups in the molecule; hence **tri'functionally** *adv.* **tri'gastric** *Anat.* [after DIGASTRIC], having three bellies, as a muscle. **trige'neric** *Gram.* [GENERIC], of three genders. **tri'glandular** *Bot.* [mod.L. *glandula* (GLANDULE), dim. of *glans* acorn], 'having three nuts or nutlets in one involucre' (*Cent. Dict.* 1891). **tri'guttulate** *Nat. Hist.* [GUTTULATE], having three spots like small drops. **trihemeral** (traɪ'hɛmərəl) [Gr. τριήμερος, f. ἡμέρα day], lasting three days. **trihilate** (traɪ'haɪleɪt) *Bot.* [HILUM]: see quot. **trihypo'static**, existing in three 'hypostases' or 'persons': see HYPOSTASIS 5 (*b*). **'trijugate, 'trijugous** *Bot.* [L. *jugum* yoke; cf. *trijugus* triple], having three pairs of leaflets: said of a pinnate leaf. **tri'labiate** *Nat. Hist.* [L. *labi-um* lip], three-lipped. **trila'mellar, tri'lamellated, tri'laminar, tri'laminate** *Nat. Hist.* and *Cytology* [LAMELLA, LAMINA], having or consisting of three layers. **tri'lophodont** *a. Zool.* [Gr. λόφος ridge + ὀδούς, ὀδοντ- tooth], having molar teeth with three transverse ridges, as the genus *Trilophodon* of mastodons. **trilophous** ('trɪləʊfəs) [Gr. λόφος crest], having three rays forked, as a sponge-spicule. **tri'luminar, tri'luminous** [L. *lūmen* light], 'having three lights' (Bailey, 1727). **tri'mastigate** *Biol.* [Gr. μάστιξ, -ιγ- whip] = *triflagellate*. **tri'membral**, 'having, or consisting of, three members' (Webster, 1864). **tri'muscular**, furnished with three muscles. **trinoctial** (traɪ'nɒkʃəl) [L. *nox, noct-* night], belonging to or lasting three nights. **tri'nucleate** *Biol.*, having three nuclei. **tri'nucleotide** *Biochem.*, an oligonucleotide in which the number of nucleotides is three. **tri'ocular** [L. *oculus* eye], having three eyes. **trio'perculate** *Nat. Hist.*, having three opercula (see OPERCULUM). **trior'thogonal** *Geom.* [ORTHOGONAL], pertaining to or consisting of three systems of lines or surfaces, each intersecting the other two at right angles. **tri'ovulate** *Bot.*, having three ovules. **tri'paleolate** *Bot.*: see quot. **tri'papillated** *Zool.*, having three papillæ. **tripa'rental** *a. Microbiology*, involving or resulting from the infection of a bacterium by three different bacteriophages at the same time. **tri'paschal** [PASCHAL], including three passovers. **triphasic** (traɪ'feɪzɪk), having or exhibiting three phases. **triphy'letic** [Gr. φυλετικ-ός, f. φυλέτης tribesman, φυλή tribe]: see quot. **tri'polar**, having or characterized by three poles. **tripros'thomerous** *Comp. Anat.* [f. *prosthomere*, f. Gr. πρόσθεν forwards + μέρος part], consisting of three prosthomeres, i.e. somites which, with their parapodia, have passed forwards from the thorax. **triprostyle** (traɪ'prɒstaɪl) [PROSTYLE], of an ancient temple: having a portico with three pillars in front (also said of the portico). **tri'punctal** [med.L. *tripunctālis* (Wyclif), L. *punct-um* point: cf. PUNCTAL], occupying three points in space. **tri'punctate** [L. *punct-um* point], marked with three points or dots. **tri'pupillate** *Entom.* [cf. PUPILLATE], having three 'pupils' or included spots, as an ocellated spot on an insect's wing. **tripy'ramidal** *Cryst.*, characterized by three types of pyramid: applied to a class of the hexagonal system. **triqua'drantal** *Geom.*, formed by three quadrants, as a spherical triangle. **trirec'tangular**, having three right angles, as a spherical triangle (Worcester, 1860). **trirhombo'hedral** *Cryst.*, characterized by three types of rhombohedron: applied to a class of the hexagonal system. **trisceptral** (traɪˈsɛptrəl), having, or pertaining to, three sceptres. **tri'sensory**, pertaining to or affecting three of the senses. **tri'sepalous** *Bot.*, having or consisting of three sepals. **tri'septate**, having three septa or partitions. **tri'serial** (whence **tri'serially** *adv.*), **tri'seriate**, arranged in three series or rows. **tri'setose** *Entom.*, bearing three setæ or bristles (*Cent. Dict.* 1891). **tri'sinuate, tri'sinuated**, having three sinuses or inward curves, as the margin of an insect's wing. **tri'spermous** *Bot.* [Gr. σπέρμα seed], containing three seeds. **tri'spinose, tri'spinous** *Nat. Hist.*, having three spines. **trisplanchnic** (traɪˈsplæŋknɪk) *Anat.* [Gr. σπλάγχνα viscera], applied to the sympathetic nerve, as having connexions with the viscera of the three great cavities (cranial, thoracic, abdominal) of the body. **trisporic** (traɪˈspɒrɪk), **trisporous** (traɪˈspɔərəs) *Bot.*, having or consisting of three spores. **tristachyous** (traɪˈstækɪəs) *Bot.* [Gr. στάχυς ear of corn, spike], having three spikes. **tristig'matic, tri'stigmatose** *Bot.*, having three stigmas. **tri'stylous** *Bot.*, having three styles. **tri'verbal** [L. *verb-um* word], consisting of three words. **tri'verbial** [f. L. *tria verba* three words]: see quot. **tri'vertebral** *Anat.*, consisting of three vertebræ united. **tri'virgate** *Zool.* [L. *virga* twig, rod, stripe], marked with three streaks or stripes. **trivo'luminous**, consisting of three volumes; composing a work in three volumes. **tri'zomal** *Geom.* [Gr. ζῶμα girdle], applied to a curve having an equation of the form √U + √V + √W = 0: cf. POLYZOME, and *tetrazomal* s.v. TETRA-.

b. With Eng. sbs. (without adj. ending); chiefly nonce-wds. instead of the usual formations in *three-*: as ***tri-church, -county, -letter, -party, -phase, state***.

c. Occas. with sb. + -ED[2] (instead of the usual *three- . . ed*): as ***tri-bladed, -breakered, -cornered, -faced, -legged, -membered, -pointed, -sceptred, -shaped, -zoned***.

1873 SALMON *Higher Plane Curves* 245 The quartic is a *triacnodal curve composed of a trigonoid figure within the triangle and of the three vertices as acnodes. **1886** LENDENFELD in *Proc. Zool. Soc.* 560 The calcareous triaxon spicules have only three rays—*triact. [**1886** *Proc. Zool. Soc.* 21 Dec. 563 *Triactina*, with three rays.] **1891** *Cent. Dict.*, *Triactinal. **1887** SOLLAS in *Encycl. Brit.* XXII. 416 (Fig. 12) *c*, triod (triaxon *triactine). **1944** S. S. ATWOOD in *Proc. Nat. Acad. Sci.* XXX. 70 Because suitable terms to describe multiple alleles in autotetraploids would facilitate the discussion, the following new terminology is suggested and will be used in this paper: . . *Triallelic. **1975** *Nature* 24 July 310/2 Triallelic plants . . cannot be obtained by any normal form of inheritance and their appearance is strong evidence for the occurrence of an unusual genetic transfer process. **1901** *Proc. Zool. Soc.* 5 Mar. 197 The sixth [segment] is *triannulate. **1891** *Cent. Dict.*, *Trianthous. **1883** A. R. WALLACE in *Nature* 22 Mar. 482/2 Heilprin . . seeks to show that the Neoarctic and Palæarctic should form one region, for which he proposes . . '*Triarctic Region', or the region of the three northern continents. **1822** J. PARKINSON *Outl. Oryctol.* 264 A series of *triarcuated, imbricating, transverse slips. **1897** *Allbutt's Syst. Med.* II. 142 Gresswell, under the names '*triareal' and 'pentareal', has described certain peculiarities of the tongue. **1886** *Triaxon [see *triact*]. **1887** *Amer. Nat.* Oct. 938 A *triaxonian star with five or six rays. **1911** *Encycl. Brit.* XXV. 729/1 Sponges with a skeleton composed of siliceous spicules, . . either *triaxonid and hexactinellid in form, or derivable from the triaxonid . . type. **1878** BARTLEY tr. *Topinard's Anthrop.* v. 173 Cretinism, according to [Virchow] is due to the synostosis of the *tri-basilar bone—that is to say, of the spheno-basilar suture, and the suture of the body of the anterior sphenoid and the posterior sphenoid. **1890** H. M. STANLEY *Darkest Africa* II. xxi. 22 *Tri-bladed and four-bladed knives were shown to me. **1901** *Science* 6 Dec. 891/2 A possible basis for a division of the '*triblastic' animals into two parallel but independent series. **1870** HOOKER *Stud. Flora* 305 Flowers . . in 1- or more-flowered *3-bracteate spikelets. *Ibid.* 321 Flowers . . minutely *3-bracteolate. **1834** MEDWIN *Angler in Wales* I. 258 Along the *tri-breakered sea-shore. **1897** *Proc. Zool. Soc.* 2 Feb. 198 Dorsal scales very strongly *tricarinate. **1802** SHAW *Gen. Zool.* III. 54 *Tricarinated Tortoise. **1872** OLIVER *Elem. Bot.* II. 253 A *tricarpellary pistil. **1900** B. D. JACKSON *Gloss. Bot. Terms*, *Tricarpellate. [**1859** PAGE *Handbk. Geol. Terms*, **Tricarpellites* . ., fossil nut-like fruits from the London clay, so called from their consisting of three carpels or seed-cells.] **1882** OGILVIE, Tricarpellite. **1891** *Cent. Dict.*, *Tricarpous. **1860** MAYNE *Expos. Lex.*, *Tricaudalis*, having three tails; three-tailed: *tricaudal. **1891** *Cent. Dict.*, *Tricaudate. *Ibid.*, *Tricellular. **1900** in B. D. JACKSON *Gloss. Bot. Terms.* **1642** H. MORE *Song of Soul* II. iii. II. vi, The second way that makes the soul *tricentrall. *Ibid.* I. viii, The *Tricentreity Of humane souls. **1913** *19th Cent.* Aug. 284 The dual monarchy is not only bicephalic . . but . . *tricephalic. **1891** *Cent. Dict.*, *Tricephalous. **1907** *Daily News* 13 Mar. 2 The *Tri-Church Conference of the Congregational, United Brethren, and Methodist Protestant Churches of the United States. **1865** *Pall Mall G.* 15 June 9 The *tricolumnar 'Historicus' favours the *Times* at his usual length with a letter. **1892** *Athenæum* 4 June 725/1 Fifty-six pages of index, mostly tricolumnar. **1962** M. HARDWICK *Sherlock Holmes Compan.* 199 Watson's astonishing statement about his *tri-continental experience of women. **1966** *Economist* 22 Jan. 299/1 The tricontinental conference held in Havana . . will increase the prestige of Dr Castro. **1819** KEATS *Let. to G. & Georgiana Keats* 13 Mar., The black badger with *tri-cornered hat. **1903** *Bradford Antiq.* July 348 Tricornered bits of wood. **1727** BAILEY vol. II, **Tricornigerous* . ., bearing or having three Horns. **1891** *Cent. Dict.* cites WESTWOOD for *Tricornute. **1816** G. S. FABER *Orig. Pagan Idol.* II. 502 The Mount of Olives; which he adopted as the local *tricoryphèan Meru or Ida of his apostasy. **1861** BENTLEY *Man. Bot.* (1870) 146 If a ribbed leaf has 3 ribs . . it is said to be 3-ribbed or *tricostate. **1828** BRANDE in *Lancet* 14 June 323/1 Containing three [cotyledons], *tricotyled[on]ous. **1974** *News & Courier* (Charleston, S. Carolina) 19 Apr. 6-A/1 A municipal scramble for federal recreation funds is under way in the *tri-county. **1978** *Detroit Free Press* 5 Mar. 13/2 These centers cater to some 150,000 deaf adults in the tri-county area. **1873** SALMON *Higher Plane Curves* 245 If the ellipse cuts each side in two real points, then the quartic is *tricrunodal. **1873** HOOKER tr. *Le Maout's Bot.* 915 The macrospores are marked on one hemisphere with a *tricrural line. **1891** *Cent. Dict.*, *Tridiametral, . . *Tridigitate. **1881** *Tridigital [see BIDIGITATE]. **1900** B. D. JACKSON *Gloss. Bot. Terms*, *Tridigitate*, . . thrice digitate, ternate. **1811** SHAW *Gen. Zool.* VIII. 105 *Tridigitated Kingfisher . . is a native of New Holland; . . the legs and feet red, with three toes only. **1866** ODLING *Anim. Chem.* 25 Comparing *tri-elementary bodies of this kind with tri-elementary mineral substances. **1835** BURNES *Trav. Bokhara* (ed. 2) II. 162 The great *trifaced idol of Elephanta. **1777** PENNANT *Zool.* (ed. 4) IV. 75 Tellina . . *Trifasciated, with a very brittle shell. **1802** SHAW *Gen. Zool.* III. 542 Trifasciated Snake. **1716** M. DAVIES *Athen. Brit.* II. To Rdr. 41 Those reviving Hydra's and Triceptick or *Trifaucian Cerberus's have been often and are still daily baffl'd and defeated. **1903** *Nature* 5 Feb. 334/1 An inertia table . . in which an aluminium ring was supported by a *trifilar suspension. **1646** SIR T. BROWNE *Pseud. Ep.* III. xii. 132 Nor will the solitude of the Phænix allow this denomination, for many there are of that species, and whose *trifistulary bill and crany we have beheld our selves. **1891** *Cent. Dict.*, *Triflagellate . . *Trifoveolate. **1860** WORCESTER, *Trifloral. **1771** J. R. FORSTER *Flora Amer. Septentr.* 25 Ranunculus abortivus . . *triflorous. **1861** HAGEN *Synopsis Neuroptera N. Amer.* 193 Each side with a fuscous, *trifoveolated stripe. **1929** W. H. CAROTHERS in *Jrnl. Amer. Chem. Soc.* LI. 2550 Among compounds having more than one functional group, those of the type x—R—y may be called bifunctional, R″x₃, *trifunctional, etc. **1975** *Nature* 10 Apr. 482/2 An essential feature is that some of these amino acids are trifunctional. **1941** *Jrnl. Amer. Chem. Soc.* LXIII. 3085/2 (*caption*) Schematic representation of a *trifunctionally branched three-dimensional polymer molecule. **1676** *Phil. Trans.* XI. 770 He makes an ingenious supposition of a *trigastrick muscle. **1880** EARLE *Philol. Eng. Tongue* §420 The old adjective had . . even a double set of *trigeneric inflections. **1887** W. PHILLIPS *Brit. Discomycetes* 27 Sporidia 8, narrowly fusiform, bi- or *tri-guttulate. **1840** G. S. FABER *Prim. Doctr. Regen.* II. vi. 140 You were thrice plunged into the Water, . . symbolically exhibiting the *trihemeral continuance of Christ in the sepulchre. **1866** *Treas. Bot.*, **Trihilate*, having three apertures, as some sorts of pollen grains. **1862** NEALE *Hymns East. Ch.* 32 Three co-eternal, co-enthroned, . . *Tri-hypostatic Essence. **1880** GRAY *Struct. Bot.* (ed. 6) 417/2 Pinnate leaves are unijugate, with a single pair of leaflets, bijugate, with two pairs, *trijugate, with three pairs [etc.]. **1819** *Pantologia*, **Trijugous leaf*, . . a pinnate leaf with three pairs of leaflets. **1856–8** W. CLARK *Van der Hoeven's Zool.* I. 192 Body anteriorly obtuse, . . Mouth *trilabiate. **1900** B. D. JACKSON *Gloss. Bot. Terms*, *Trilamellar. **1822** J. PARKINSON *Outl. Oryctol.* 186 One [tooth of the shell] . . slightly *trilamellated. **1889** *Cent. Dict.*, *Trilaminar. **1971** *New Scientist* 1 Apr. 24/1 (*caption*) Electron micrographs of mitochondrial membranes reveal a trilaminar or railway track appearance. **1977** *Jrnl. Protozool.* XXIV. 18/1 The trilaminar construction of the ciliate cortex. **1882** SLADEN in *Jrnl. Linn. Soc.* XVI. 243 The spinelets are . . regularly *trilaminate. **1844** TUPPER *Crock of G.* ii, A ricketty triangular and *trilegged table. **1902** *Westm. Gaz.* 6 Aug. 6/1 A new telegraphic code has been invented . . known as Baldrey's *Tri-Letter Code. . . Every word in any language is represented by three letters only. **1909** *Cent. Dict.* Supp., *Trilophous. **1891** *Cent. Dict.*, *Trimastigate. **1626** PRYNNE *Perpet. Regen. Man's Est.* 331 A threefold and *trimembred objection. **1875** C. C. BLAKE *Zool.* 108 The larynx is *trimuscular. **1623** COCKERAM, **Trinoctial*, belonging to three nights. **1880** MUIRHEAD *Gaius* Digest 623 *Manus*, . . avoidance of it by trinoctial interruption. **1887** W. PHILLIPS *Brit. Discomycetes* 254 Sporidia . . *3-nucleate or pseudo-septate. **1918** *Jrnl. Chem. Soc.* CXIV. I. 48 The simultaneous liberation of the *trinucleotide, triphosphonucleic acid, and the mononucleotide, uridine-phosphoric acid, indicates that the three constituent mononucleotides in triphosphonucleic acid must be combined in a different manner from the uridine-phosphoric acid in the parent molecule of yeast-nucleic acid. **1974** *Nature* 25 Oct. 734/2 The two RNAs are known to contain an identical trinucleotide at their 5′ terminal. **1844** TUPPER *Heart* iv, Men . . being neither naturally monocular nor *triocular. **1900** B. D. JACKSON *Gloss. Bot. Terms*, *Tri-operculate. **1891** *Cent. Dict.*, *Triovulate. **1866** *Treas. Bot.* 1172 **Tripaleolate*, consisting of three pales or paleæ, as the flower of a bamboo. **1891** *Cent. Dict.* cites H. ALLEN for *Tripapillated. **1951** *Cold Spring Harbor Symp. Quantitative Biol.* XVI. 471/2 Important information about genetic recombination comes from experiments in which the frequency of *triparental recombination is measured. **1961** *Genetics* XLVI. 1314 Occurrence of triparental recombinants between two Hfr and one F^- has been demonstrated in *E. coli* $^{K-12}$. **1976** *Ann. Rev. Microbiol.* XXX. 517 Nonconjugative plasmid transfer by such triparental matings may occur under ideal laboratory conditions. **1907** *Daily Chron.* 11 Mar. 4/4 The great danger ahead of Australia is . . her *tri-party system of government, which places parties in office that do not command the confidence of the country. **1883** SCHAFF *Hist. Chr. Church* (ed. 2) I. §16. 130 Three theories [of the length of Christ's public ministry], . . designated as bipaschal, *tripaschal, and quadripaschal schemes, according to the number of Passovers. **1900** *Engineering Mag.* XIX. 778/2 The Central Station of the '*Tri-Phase' Company at Asnières, Seine . . which will furnish tri-phase currents to Paris. **1901** *Buck's Handbk. Med. Sc.* III. 105 In the frog's heart the variation shown by the capillary electrometer is diphasic. For the human heart the later work seems to show a *triphasic current. **1900** B. D. JACKSON *Gloss. Bot. Terms*, **Triphyletic*, . . used of hybrids containing the blended strains of three species. **1605** SYLVESTER *Du Bartas* II. iii. III. *Lawe* 487 'Gainst the *tri-pointed wrathfull violence Of the drad dart. **1865** MANSFIELD *Salts* 33 The general idea of a *tripolar compound, the simplest form of which is supposed to be water. **1894** BATESON *Variation* xvi. 430 Tripolar division of nucleus in embryonic tissue of Trout. **1902** E. R. LANKESTER in *Encycl. Brit.* XXV. 700 Arthropoda—Hexapoda. Head shown by its early development to be *triprosthomerous. **1841** *Civil Eng. & Arch. Jrnl.* IV. 118/2 Only the portico part of the temple (a Corinthian hexastyle, *triprostyle) advanced into the enclosed area in front. **1897** DZIEWICKI *Wyclif's De Logica* III. Introd. 23 If the Equator consist of *tripunctal atoms, it cannot be a circle. **1841** *Penny Cycl.* XX. 74/2. **1872** NICHOLSON *Palæont.* 491 Oval or elliptical *tripunctate areoles. **1826** KIRBY & SP. *Entomol.* IV. xlvi. 287 An ocellus is called bipupillate, *tripupillate, etc., when there are two, three, etc. of these spots. **1896** C. W. CROCKETT *Elem. Plane & Sph. Trigon.* 126 A *triquadrantal triangle has three sides each equal to a quadrant. *Ibid.*, A *tri-rectangular triangle is also triquadrantal. *a* **1886** FERGUSON *Ogham Inscript.* (1887) 153 This symbol in a bi-sceptral form traverses the crescent; in a *tri-sceptral form, the other emblem. **1792** J. BARLOW *Conspir. Kings* 78 The *tri-sceptred prince, of Austrian mould. . . Theresa's son. **1894** *Trisensory [see BISENSORY *a.*]. **1895** *Edin. Rev.* Jan. 108 A 'trisensory hallucination', 'visual', 'auditory', and 'tactile'. **1903** F. W. H. MYERS *Human Personality* I. 254. **1830** LINDLEY *Nat. Syst. Bot.* 286 *Tri-sepalous calyx. **1874** COOKE *Fungi* 27 The spores . . at first unilocular, but afterwards *triseptate. **1860** WORCESTER, **Triserial*, **Triseriate* (Bot.), in three rows, one below another. *Gray.* **1866** *Treas. Bot.* 1174 *Triserial*, in three rows. **1891** *Cent. Dict.*, **Triserially*, in three series; so as to be triserial. **1613** HEYWOOD *Silver Age* III. Wks. 1874 III. 156 The triple-headed dogge . . Hels *tri-shap't porter. **1891** *Cent. Dict.*, *Trisinuate. **1849** JOHNSTON in *Proc. Berw. Nat. Club* II. No. 7. 366 The frontal margin *trisinuated. **1760** J. LEE *Introd. Bot.* II. (1765) 159 *Rhamnus*, with a *trispermous Fruit. **1819** G. SAMOUELLE *Entomol. Compend.* 93 Interior antennæ with the first joint of the peduncle *trispinose. **1828** STARK *Elem. Nat. Hist.* II. 162 Thorax granulated, carinated, *trispinous. **1826** KIRBY & SP. *Entomol.* IV. xxxvii. 4 Called the great sympathetic, the intercostal, or *trisplanchnic nerves. **1857** DUNGLISON *Med. Lex.*, *Trisplanchnic Nerve*. . . Great sympathetic, Inter-costal, Ganglionic or vertebral nerve. **1866** *Treas. Bot.* 1174 *Trisporic. **1891** *Cent. Dict.*, *Trisporous. *Ibid.*, *Tristachyous. **1963** *Times* 15 Jan. 9/6 A *tri-state transportation committee is carrying out a survey . . of New York, New Jersey, and Connecticut. **1983** *Listener* 22 Sept. 5/2 The attractions of the US market—and the New York tri-state area in particular—have been appreciated for a long time. **1891** *Cent. Dict.*, *Tristigmatic . . *Tristigmatose. **1900** B. D. JACKSON *Gloss. Bot. Terms*, Tristigmatic. **1891** *Cent. Dict.*, *Tristylous. **1900** in B. D. JACKSON *Gloss. Bot. Terms.* **1817** JAS. MILL *Brit. India* I. II. vi. 279 The *tri-verbal phrase, and the triliteral syllable. **1768** BLACKSTONE *Comm.* III. xxvi. 424 In the Roman calendar there were in the whole year but twenty eight judicial or *triverbial days allowed to the praetor for hearing causes [*note*, Otherwise called *dies fasti, in quibus licebat praetori fari tria verba, do, dico, addico*]. **1871** HUXLEY *Anat. Vertebr. Anim.* viii. 341 The last cervical and the anterior dorsal vertebræ [in *Glyptodon*] are ankylosed together into a single '*tri-vertebral' bone. **1863** *Ibis* Jan. 15 *Acc[ipiter] nisoides* . . closely resembles the preceding one, *A. nisus*, but is smaller, with *trivirgate throat. **1857** READE *Course of True Love* 191 Paper is not absolutely valueless, whatever the *trivoluminous may think. **1892** *Athenæum* 31 Dec. 914/2 In tri-voluminous fiction. **1867** CAYLEY *Math. Papers* VI. 485 On the *Trizomal Curve and the Tetrazomal Curve. **1840** R. HORNE *Gregory VII*, v. iv. (ed. 2) 100 *Tri-zoned Jove's star-set eternity.

2. a. Triply; three times; in three ways, directions, etc. **tri'curvate**, 'curved in three directions, as a sponge-spicule' (*Funk's Stand. Dict.*). **'triequal**, consituting three that are equal. **trigo'neutic** *a.* [Gr. γονεύειν to generate], producing three broods in a year, as certain insects (cf. *trivoltine* in 4 b); so **trigo'neutism**. **tri'larcenous**, three times convicted of larceny. **tri'quadrifid** *Bot.* [QUADRIFID], having three lobes each deeply divided into four segments. **tri'quinate** *Bot.* [QUINATE], having three lobes each divided into five. **'trisonant** [L. *sonānt-em* sounding], sounding in three ways; in quot. *loosely*, comprising three classes of vocal sounds. **trisquare** (ˈtraɪskwɛə(r)), 'three-square; having three equally wide plane faces' (*Cent. Dict. Suppl.* 1909). **tri'tactic** *Geom.* [L. *tact-*, ppl. stem of *tangĕre* to touch: cf. TACTIC *a.*[2]], having or involving three coincident points of contact. Also TRITERNATE. **b.** *spec.* in *Cryst.* denoting forms having three ranges of facets, the number in each range being expressed by the second element: as **tri-dodeca'hedral** (12), **tri-hexa'hedral** (6), **tri-octa'hedral** (8); also **tri-rhom'boidal**, having eighteen faces occupying the positions of those of three different rhomboids.

1805–17 R. JAMESON *Char. Min.* (ed. 3) 205 *Tri-dodecahedral red silver-ore . . a six-sided prism, acuminated on the extremities with three planes, and truncated on all the edges. **1839** BAILEY *Festus* v. (1848) 44 Injustice, hate, uncharitableness, *Triequal reign round earth, a Trinity of Hell. **1805–17** R. JAMESON *Char. Min.* 204 *Trihexahedral, . . when [the crystal's] surface consists of three . . ranges of planes, disposed six and six above each other. . . Tri-hexahedral nitrate of potash . .; a six-sided prism, acuminated on both extremities with six planes. **1823** SYD. SMITH *Botany Bay* Wks. (1850) 369 The man of three juries, who has three times appeared at the Bailey, *trilarcenous.

1805–17 R. JAMESON *Char. Min.* 205 *Tri-octahedral sulphat of lead,..a four-sided pyramid,..the edges of the common base truncated, the angles on it very deeply bevelled, the bevelling planes set on the lateral edges, and the bevelling edges again deeply truncated, so that the crystal..consists of three rows of planes, of which each row contains eight planes. **1833** HOOKER *J. E. Smith's Eng. Flora* V. I. 113 The upper leaves..are *tri-quadrifid. **1891** *Cent. Dict.*, *Triquinate. **1805–17** R. JAMESON *Char. Min.* 202 *Tri-rhomboidal; this, in the Wernerian Crystallography, is a double six-sided pyramid, with alternately broad and narrow lateral planes,..and..acuminated on the extremities with three planes, which are set on the smaller lateral planes. Example, Tri-rhomboidal calcareous-spar. **1876** DOUSE *Grimm's L.* xlvii. 97 The priority of any one of the known *tri-sonant systems over the others is untenable.

3. In combination with an adj. (usu. in *-ly*) derived from a sb. denoting a period of time: Comprising three ——, lasting three ——, occurring or appearing every three (days, etc.); also (*loosely*) occurring three times (a day, etc.); those in *-ly* are also used as advbs. = every three (days, etc.) or three times a (day, etc.): as ***tridaily***; ***tri'horal*** [L. *hora* hour]. See also TRIMONTHLY, -WEEKLY; TRIANNUAL, -DIURNAL, etc.

1887 *Science* IX. 79 The system of *tridaily [meteorological] observations. **1860** WORCESTER cites LD. ELLESMERE for *Trihoral.

II. 4. Forming sbs., with the senses:

a. Something consisting of or equivalent to three (of the things denoted by the second element); a triple ——. ‖**tria'chænium** (irreg. **-akenium**) *Bot.* [mod.L: see ACHENE], a fruit composed of three achenes. **'triaster** *Biol.* [Gr. ἀστήρ star: cf. DIASTER], a figure bearing some resemblance to three conjoined stars, resulting from a tripolar division of a nucleus. †**tricube** *Math. Obs.*, the third power of a cube, a ninth power. †**tridia'pason** *Mus. Obs.* [DIAPASON 1], an interval of three octaves, a twenty-second. †**trifluctu'ation** *Obs.* [L. *fluctus* wave]: see quot. **trihemi'obol** [Gr. τριημιωβόλιον], an ancient Greek coin of the value of 1½ obols. **tri'junction**, a junction or union of three. †**tri'million**, the third power of a million; also (quot. 1707) a thousand thousand millions, i.e. a billion (= TRILLION in both senses: cf. etymology of BILLION). **,trimillio'naire** [after *millionaire*], a person possessed of three millions of money (pounds, dollars, francs, etc.). **'tripair** *Math.*, a set of three pairs. †**tri'papalty** [PAPALTY], a period during which there were three rival popes. †**tri'quadrate** *Math. Obs.* [QUADRATE *sb.*[1] 1 b], the third power of a square, a sixth power. **tristigm** ('traɪstɪm) *Geom.* [Gr. στίγμα prick, point], a system of three points with the straight lines connecting them (*Cent. Dict. Suppl.* 1909).

b. Something having, or related in some way to, three (of the things denoted or indicated by the second element). **'tri-axle**, a trailer or articulated lorry with three (rear) axles. **tricephal** (traɪ'sɛfəl) [Gr. τρικέφαλος adj., f. κεφαλή head: see *tricephalic* in I. 1 a], a three-headed figure or image of a deity. ‖**tri'orchis** [mod.L., f. Gr. ὄρχις testicle; cf. τριόρχης]: see quot. 1857. **'triplane**, an aeroplane with three supporting planes; also *attrib.* **triqua'ternion** *Math.*, an expression of the form $q_1 + \omega q_2 + \mu q_3$, where q_1, q_2, q_3, are quaternions, and ω and μ are commutative with quaternions. **,trisacramen-'tarian**, one who recognizes three and only three sacraments. **tri'voltin(e)** [Ital. *volta* turn, time], a silkworm of a breed which yields three cocoons in a year.

c. Something (denoted by the second element) having three of some characteristic part, or related to three things. **tri-car** (**-machine, -mobile, -motor-car**), a motor-car with three wheels; a motor tricycle with a seat for a person or a carrier for luggage in front. **tri'ceptor** *Phys. Chem.* [L. *-ceptor* = *captor* taker], an intermediary body having three haptophorous groups. **tri'coaster**, a combination of a three-speed gear with a 'coaster' brake on a cycle. **'tri-mix**, a breathing mixture for deep-sea divers composed of nitrogen, helium, and oxygen. †**tri-plu'rality**, a plurality in which three benefices are held at once. **tri'pyramid** *Cryst.*, a triangular pyramid, as a form in certain calcareous spars. **tri-schism** (*nonce-wd.*), schism of three parties. **tri-spear** (*nonce-wd.*), a trident.

1882 OGILVIE, *Triachenium, triakenium. **1900** B. D. JACKSON *Gloss. Bot. Terms*, Triachænium. **1894** BATESON *Variation* I. xvi. 431 *note*, A case of the presence of *triasters in two bilaterally symmetrical tracts of the blastoderm of Loligo. **1909** J. W. JENKINSON *Experim. Embryology* 30 Triaster, a tripolar figure with three spindles. **1971** M. TAK *Truck Talk* 173 **Triaxle*, a semi with three rear axles and consequently a greater weight-carrying allowance. **1978** *Detroit Free Press* 16 Apr. F 8/1 (Advt.), Trailer: 1967 Ravens 29' dump on 34' frame, tri-axle with air-lift. **1981** *Daily Tel.* 10 Dec. 9 (*caption*) A..38-tonne tri-axle lorry. **1903** *Motor* 6 May 279/1 (*heading*) The new Rex '*Tricar'. **1904** *Sat. Rev.* 20 Feb. 228/1 The development of the tri-car is especially important. *Ibid.*, There is a great future for the useful tri-car. **1906** *Westm. Gaz.* 21 Aug. 4/2 Experience is going to show that the final form of the tri-car for delivery purposes will be of a very different pattern. **1888** RHŶS *Hibbert Lect.* i. 81 *note*, The wide distribution of the *tricephal has induced M. Mowat to declare for the improbable hypothesis, that it was..but the Roman Janus..naturalized in Gaul. **1902** VAUGHAN & NOVY *Cellular Toxins* (ed. 4) 132 The intermediary body [usually an] 'amboceptor',..may be a *triceptor, quadriceptor, etc. **1908** *Daily Chron.* 21 Nov. 9/4 He made use of the Sturmey-Archer *Tri-coaster, which is the three-speed gear in association with a foot-acted brake. **1674** JEAKE *Arith.* (1696) 273 Some to shorten..the long Names of..Higher Powers..call..ϕϕ a Bicube, ϕϕϕ a *Tricube &c. **1811** BUSBY *Dict. Mus.* (ed. 3), *Tri-Diapason. **1646** SIR T. BROWNE *Pseud. Ep.* VII. xvii. 377 *Τρικυμία*..is a concurrence of three waves in one, whence arose the proverb, τρικυμία κακῶν, or a *trifluctuation of evils. **1887** B. V. HEAD *Hist. Numorum* 336 There are also *trihemiobols..of later style, for the Pegasus on the obverse has pointed wings. **1887** *Athenæum* 29 Jan. 164/2 To have the *trijunction of Tibet, India, and Burma focussed within the four corners of a map. **1707** *Curios. in Husb. & Gard.* 155 These ten Thousand Willows..will produce each of them likewise a hundred more. Thus we have a Million; then a hundred Millions: next come the Tens of Bimillions; then the *Trimillions. **1806** [see TRILLION]. **1848** *Tait's Mag.* XV. 646 A *tri-millionaire buys it for a deer-forest. **1976** *Jrnl. Appl. Physiol.* XL. 605/2 Each subject..breathed either air or a mixture of 36% helium, 21% oxygen, and 43% nitrogen (*tri-mix) during cycles of immersed work. **1981** *New Scientist* 12 Feb. 390 Last week a team of divers ..broke the world record for a simulated dive, experiencing pressures equivalent to those 686 metres beneath the sea surface... Part of the secret of the test's success was that the divers breathed a recently developed gas mixture, called trimix. **1905** *Westm. Gaz.* 28 Dec. 7/3 Returning home in a *tri-motor-car. **1650** H. MORE *Observ.* in *Enthus. Tri.*, etc. (1656) 92 If you have not a sleight of Art to Metamorphize your selves into *Triorchises. **1857** DUNGLISON *Med. Lex.*, *Triorchis*, one who has three testicles. **1878** CAYLEY *Math. Papers* X. 450 We have thus..a system of..63 hexpairs; and selecting at pleasure any three pairs out of the same hexpair, we have a system of (63 × 20 =) 1260 *tripairs. **1651** N. BACON *Disc. Govt. Eng.* II. xvii. (1739) 89 During the *Tripapalty much money had been levied..to serve for the recovery of the Popedom to one of an English interest. **1908** *Times* 3 Oct. 6/3 Experiments with a *triplane machine. **1909** *Westm. Gaz.* 4 Mar. 4/2 In machines of the biplane and triplane types. **1909** Triplane [see QUADRUPLANE]. **1920** *Glasgow Herald* 10 July 5 The Pullman triplanes of the British Company carry 18 people. **1977** J. CLEARY *High Road to China* ii. 47 'What did you fly?'..'Albatros D's and Fokker Triplanes. I was with von Richthofen.' **1425** *Rolls of Parlt.* IV. 290/2 That mony a Parsone..have pluralite, and somme *tripluralite. [**1753** CHAMBERS *Cycl. Supp.*, **Tripyramides*,..the name of a genus of spars... The bodies of this genus are spars, composed of single pyramids, each of three sides,..affixed by their bases to some solid body.] **1828** WEBSTER, Tripyramid. **1674** JEAKE *Arith.* (1696) 273 Some..call ʒʒ a Biquadrate, ʒʒʒ a *Triquadrate. **1902** G. COMBEBIAC cited in *Cent. Dict. Supp.* for *Triquaternion. **1727–41** CHAMBERS *Cycl.*, **Trisacramentarians*,..a sect.. who admit of three sacraments, and no more... There have been several trisacramentarians among the protestants, who allowed of baptism, the eucharist, and absolution, as sacraments. **1896** J. H. WYLIE *Hist. Eng. Hen. IV*, III. 388 Instead of schism, *tri-schism, which threatened to become centi-schism. **1887** MORRIS *Odyss.* v. 292 His hand the *tri-spear grasping. **1888** *Trivoltin [see BIVOLTINE *a.*].

III. 5. In Chemical nomenclature, in the names of compounds and derivatives, with general sense 'three', 'three times'.

a. Prefixed to names of compounds of elements, radicals, or groups, names of salts, etc., to signify three atoms, groups, or equivalents of these elements or radicals in combination with another element or radical; e.g. **tribromide**, a compound of 3 atoms of bromine with another element or radical, as ***tribromide of boron***; **trisulphate**, a compound of three SO_4 groups with a metal or radical (or in earlier nomenclature of three SO_3 groups with a basic oxide). So **trichloride, -cyanide, -fluoride, -hydride, -iodide, -oxide, -sulphide** (*-sulphuret*); **-carbonate, -chlorate, -cyanate, -hydrate, -phosphate, -thionate**, etc. Also in names of some organic compounds, referring to their composition, as TRIAMIDE, TRIAMINE, and the compound ethers or esters of glycerin with acids, as TRIACETIN, **tri-butyrin, -palmitin, -stearin**, etc.; **tri'terpane**, a terpane with the formula $C_{30}H_{60}$, analogous to the triterpenes; **tri'terpene**, any of the group of terpenes of formula $C_{30}H_{48}$, found in plant gums and resins; also, a triterpenoid; **tri'terpenoid**, a triterpene or a derivative of one. See also TRIACETATE, TRISILICATE.

In early nomenclature, *tri-* or *tris-* prefixed to the name of a salt meant 3 molecules not of the acid, but of the base; thus $3PbO.C_4H_5O_3$ was called *tris-* or *tri-acetate of lead*; similarly B_3O was called *trioxide of* any element B.

1826 HENRY *Elem. Chem.* I. 591 Tri-phosphate of lime. **1850** DAUBENY *Atomic Theory* (ed. 2) 112 When the number of proportionals of base is 2, the prefix *di* or *dis* is adopted; when 3, *tris*; when four, *tetrakis*...*tri*silicate of iron, 3 of base to 1 of silicic acid. *Ibid.* 338 The gaseous trifluoride of boron, which contains no hydrogen. **1856** FOWNES *Chem.* (ed. 6) 607 Three compounds of stearic acid with glycerin.. which M. Berthelot distinguishes as monostearin, bistearin, and tristearin. **1863–72** WATTS *Dict. Chem.* I. 895 The metals which form trichlorides are antimony, arsenic, bismuth, gold, molybdenum, thallium, vanadium, and probably indium. **1866** ROSCOE *Elem. Chem.* xvi. 142 Arsenic unites with chlorine, bromine, and iodine, to form arsenic trichloride, tribromide, and triiodide. *Ibid.* xxiv. 207 Metallic antimony occurs native, but its chief ore is the trisulphide. **1880** ROSCOE & SCHORLEMMER *Chem.* II. ii. 319 Antimony Trifluoride, SbF_3, is obtained as a dense snow-white mass, by distilling antimony with mercury fluoride. **1902** F. J. POND tr. *Heusler's Chem. Terpenes* 432 Several well characterized compounds which occur in elemi-resin belong to the class of triterpenes. **1932** *Chem. Abstr.* XXVI. 3244 (*heading*) Contribution to the accurate determination of the empirical formulas of several triterpenes and triterpenoids. **1945** Triterpene [see ISOPRENOID *a.* and *sb.*]. **1965** *Proc. Nat. Acad. Sci.* LIV. 1406 We wish to report now the isolation and identification of..a C_{30}-pentacyclic triterpane from the branched-cyclic alkane fraction of the Green River Shale. **1978** Triterpene [see STEVIOSIDE]. **1978** *Nature* 16 Mar. 217/1 Polycyclic triterpenoids are found in petroleum and their presence was at first taken as evidence of non-marine contribution, as they had been detected in the lipid extract of ferns. **1981** *Jrnl. Chromatogr. Sci.* XIX. 156/1 This study deals with the apparent effect that maturation has on the relative concentration of individual triterpanes [*etc.*].

b. Prefixed to adjs., or to sbs. used attrib., in the names or descriptions of acids, alcohols, compound ethers or esters, oxides, salts, etc.; e.g. ***trisodic*** or ***trisodium***, (a salt) containing 3 atoms of sodium; ***triethylic*** or ***triethyl*** (a compound) containing 3 ethyl groups; ***triethylene***, containing three non-contiguous ethylene radicals in the molecule. So ***trihydric*** or ***trihydrogen***, ***tricalcic*** or ***tricalcium***, ***triargentic*** or ***tri-silver***, ***tricarbon***, ***trichloric***, ***trimethylic*** or ***trimethyl***, ***triplumbic***, ***trithionic***, ***triacetic***, etc.

1866 ODLING *Anim. Chem.* 108 We meet with still less oxidised tricarbon molecules. **1869** ROSCOE *Elem. Chem.* xv. 154 The three atoms of hydrogen in trihydrogen phosphate may be replaced by three different metals. **1873** WATTS *Fownes' Chem.* 340 A trisodic orthophosphate, sometimes called subphosphate. *Ibid.* 451 Triplumbic tetroxide, or Red lead. **1888** MUIR & MORLEY *Watts' Dict. Chem.* I. 99 Alcohols are classed as monohydric, dihydric, trihydric.. according to the number of hydroxyl-groups which they contain. **1920** *Jrnl. Chem. Soc.* CXVII. 1090 (*heading*) Triethylene tri- and tetra-sulphides. **1953**, etc. [see *thiotepa* s.v. THIO- 1]. **1962** H. BURN *Drugs, Med. & Man* xix. 193 Tri-ethylene melamine..is used in the textile industry... It is now widely used in the treatment of Hodgkin's disease.

c. Prefixed to the names of elements or radicals, or their combining forms (as *azo-*, *bromo-*, *chloro-*, *hydro-*, *hydroxy-*, *iodo-*, *nitro-*, *oxy-*, *sulpho-*, *thio-*: see these) entering into the name of a compound, to signify that three atoms or groups of the element or radical are present, or are substituted for hydrogen, in the substance designated by the rest of the name: as ***tri,bromo'benzene***, $C_6H_3Br_3$, in which three of the hydrogen atoms of benzene, C_6H_6, are replaced by three bromine atoms; so ***trimethylbenzene***, $C_6H_3(CH_3)_3$; ***tri,ethyl-'carbinol***, $C(C_2H_5)_3OH$; ***tri'methylamine***, $N(CH_3)_3$; ***trichlorhydrin***, $C_3H_5Cl_3$; so ***tribrom-hydrin***, etc. Combinations of this kind are formed when wanted, and are unlimited in number: only a few are mentioned in this work: see TRIBROM-, TRICHLOR-, etc. Illustrated below are: **tributyl phosphate**, an oily liquid, $(C_4H_9O)_3PO$, that is a solvent used as a plasticizer and in the solvent-extraction of nuclear fuels; **tri'cresyl phosphate** [CRESYL], a colourless liquid, $(CH_3C_6H_4O)_3PO$, used as a fuel additive, plasticizer, and fire retardant; **,trietha'nolamine** [ETHANOLAMINE], an oily alkaline liquid alcohol, $(HOCH_2CH_2)_3N$, used as a solvent and a stabilizer; **trihydro'calcite** *Min.* [ad. Russ. *trigidrokal'tsit"* (P. N. Chirvinsky 1906, in *Ezhegodnik" po Geol. i Mineral. Rosii* VIII. 241/1)], a trihydrate of calcium carbonate, $CaCO_3.3H_2O$, the natural occurrence of which is uncertain; **,triiodo'thyronine** *Biochem.* [THYRONINE], a thyroid hormone similar to thyroxine (tetraiodothyronine) but having greater potency; $HO{\cdot}C_6H_3I{\cdot}O{\cdot}C_6H_2I_2{\cdot}CH_2CH(NH_2)COOH$.

1930 *Brit. Patent* 330,228 1/2 The excess of alcohol and later the tributyl phosphate are distilled off in vacuo. **1957** *Financial Times Ann. Rev. Brit. Industry* 69/1 The concentrate is dissolved in nitric acid..where it is extracted with tributyl phosphate, producing uranium. **1882** *Jrnl. Chem. Soc.* XLII. 839 The authors have thus obtained triphenyl, tri-β-naphthyl and tricresyl phosphate from the corresponding phenols. **1959** *Economist* 10 Jan. 153 (Advt.), The Ignition Control Additive based on tricresyl phosphate ..was developed..to overcome serious problems of power loss and rough running. **1962** *Punch* 15 Aug. 218/3 Tricresyl phosphate was a chemical similar to triorthocresyl phosphate. **1897** *Jrnl. Chem. Soc.* LXXII. 314 (*heading*) Triethanolamine (trihydroxytriethylamine). **1939** *Jrnl. R. Aeronaut. Soc.* XLIII. 617 Strips of brass sheet were.. immersed respectively in pure glycol, commercial glycol and commercial glycol treated with triethanolamine phosphate. **1976** *New Yorker* 8 Mar. 67/1 (Advt.), Its mild 'heavy-molecular' triethanolamine-base formulation is chemically balanced to remove surface dirt and makeup without penetrating and robbing the sub-layers of the skin. **1910** *Mineral. Mag.* XV. 432 Tri-hydrocalcite... Hydrated calcium carbonate, $CaCO_3.3H_2O$, occurring as a mould-like encrustation on chalk-marl near Nova-Alexandria. **1928**, etc. Trihydrocalcite [see *pentahydrocalcite* s.v. PENTA-]. **1952** *Lancet* 1 Mar. 439/1 (*heading*) The identification of 3:5:3'-L-triiodothyronine in human plasma. **1975** *Jrnl. Endocrinol.* LXIV. 573 In the present culture system the thyroid hormones (tri-iodothyronine and thyroxine) inhibited the action of PTH.

d. In verbs and their pples. derived from sbs. as in a, as **tribrominated, trichlorinated,** in which three hydrogen atoms have been replaced by atoms of bromine or chlorine; **trihydrated,** containing three molecules of water.

1857 MILLER *Elem. Chem.* III. 47 Trichlorinated Dutch Liquid. **1868** Trihydrated: see TRIHYDRATE.

IV. 6. Forming verbs (and derivatives), as TRI-FALLOW, TRISECT, TRISECTION, q.v.

triable ('traɪəb(ə)l), *a.*[1] [a. AF. *triable*, f. as TRY *v.* + -ABLE.] That may be tried.

1. *Law.* Capable of being tried in a court of law; liable to judicial trial. Also *transf.*

a. Of a cause or offence.

1429 *Rolls of Parlt.* IV. 346/1 What issue triable be enquest.. happethe to be taken.. that hit be tried be enquest of the corps of the saide Shire. **1495** *Act 11 Hen. VII*, c. 21 Plees.. triable by any Jury or Inquest. **1600** TATE in Gutch *Coll. Cur.* I. 8, I hold all appeals triable in the King's Bench lawfull. **1770** BURKE *Pres. Discont.* Wks. II. 339 A direct simple issue.. triable by plain men. **1865** NICHOLS *Britton* II. 161 *note*, A writ of right, triable by battle or great assise.

b. Of a person.

1554 *St. Trials, Sir N. Throchmorton* (1730) I. 76/1 The Partie triable.. shall finde himselfe in much worse case, than before when those cruell Lawes stoode in force. **1577–87** HOLINSHED *Chron.* III. 1113/2 The principall and accessaries in felonie and murther be triable and punishable by the common law. **1697** tr. *C'tess D'Aunoy's Trav.* (1706) 243 All that belong to the Inquisition being not subject to or tryable by any other Jurisdiction. **1757** J. LIND *Lett. Navy* ii. 99 All persons are triable by court martials. **1883** *Sat. Rev.* 10 Feb. 170/2 Englishmen are now triable for all kinds of misdemeanours and crimes.. in the High Court at Allahabad.

2. That may be ascertained, tested, or proved.

1612 STURTEVANT *Metallica* (1854) 27 A triable Inuention is an inuention whose worth and goodnesse cannot certainly appeare before trialls and experiments. **1626** DONNE *Serm.* xxi. (1640) 202 The matter is matter of faith.. considerable, and triable by reason. **1660** BOYLE *New Exp. Phys. Mech.* i. 28 In our above-mentioned first Experiment, and.. others tryable in our Engine. **1706** BAYNARD in Sir J. Floyer *Hot & Cold Bath.* II. 210 She had tried all things triable.

Hence **'triableness.**

1847 in WEBSTER.

†**'triable,** *a.*[2] *Obs. nonce-wd.* [f. TRI- + -ABLE.] Divisible into three.

1647 WARD *Simp. Cobler* 55 Whatsoever is duable or triable, is fryable.

triac ('traɪæk). *Electronics.* [f. TRI(ODE *a.* and *sb.* + *A.C.* s.v. A III.] A three-electrode semiconductor device that will conduct in either direction when triggered by a positive or negative signal at the gate electrode.

1964 E. K. HOWELL in *IEEE Internat. Convention Record* XII. IX. 86/2 To simplify the control of AC power, a completely new silicon semiconductor has been developed. 'Triac' is a generic term coined for this *triode AC* switch. **1975** *Hi-Fi Answers* Feb. 78/2 The light pulses from the led are picked up by a photo-conductive cell, and applied to the ..triggering circuit of the triac. **1981** *Computer-Aided Design* Jan. 7/1 During the past two decades the application of triacs and thyristors in the control of power and machines with complex feedback arrangements has rapidly replaced the use of their conventional counterparts in almost all sectors of industry and public services.

triacad (*Anc. Greek History*): see TRIAKAD.

triacanthoid (traɪə'kænθɔɪd), *a.* and *sb. Ichth.* [f. mod.L. *Triacanthus*, generic name (f. Gr. τρι-, TRI- + ἄκανθα spine) + -OID.] **a.** *adj.* Belonging to or having the characters of the family *Triacanthidæ* of plectognath fishes, typified by the genus *Triacanthus*. **b.** *sb.* A fish of this family.

1891 in *Cent. Dict.*

triacetate (traɪ'æsɪteɪt). *Chem.* [f. TRI- + ACETATE.] †**a.** A compound in which an acetate group is combined with three atoms or molecules of a base. *Obs.*

1860 SCOFFERN *Orr's Circle of Sciences, Chem.* (new ed.) 467 The most important is the tris or triacetate [of lead].

b. A compound containing three acetate groups in the molecule; *spec.* cellulose triacetate, in which acetate groups replace hydrogen atoms in (notionally) all three hydroxyl groups in each constituent glucose molecule; a man-made fibre made from this.

1895 C. F. CROSS et al. *Cellulose* I. 35 Heated at 180° in a sealed tube, in the proportion by weight of 1 of cellulose to 6 of the anhydride, the cellulose is converted into the triacetate. **1921** *Jrnl. Soc. Chem. Industry* 31 Jan. 8T/2 If the ratio of chlorine to sulphur dioxide be nearer to unity then the product is mainly cellulose triacetate. **1956** W. J. ROFF *Fibres, Plastics, & Rubbers* 25 A method of preparing fully acetylated triacetate possessing exceptionally good electrical properties. **1960** *Which?* Jan. 19/1 Triacetate is very similar to ordinary acetate, but not so soft to handle; it will take permanent pleats and creases. **1978** *Lancashire Life* Mar. 113/3 Each item can be bought separately—the triacetate and nylon shirt at about £13.50.

triacetic: see TRI- 5 b and ACETIC.

triacetin (traɪ'æsɪtɪn). *Chem.* [f. TRI- 5 a + ACET(IC + -IN[1] (the termination of the compound ethers of glycerin: see ACETIN).] Glyceryl triacetate, $C_3H_5(OC_2H_3O)_3$, the compound ether or ester of glycerin or glycerol, $C_3H_5(OH)_3$, and acetic acid, $C_2H_4O_2$, the three H atoms of the OH groups in glycerol being replaced by three acetyl groups, C_2H_3O; also called *acetic triglyceride*; a colourless liquid boiling at 258–259°C.; it is found in the oil of the seeds of the spindle-tree.

1858 FOWNES *Elem. Chem.* (ed. 7) 504 Berthelot has pointed out three classes of compounds which glycerin is capable of forming... With acetic acid, for instance, it forms three combinations.. monacetin, diacetin, and triacetin.

triachænium: see TRI- 4 a.

triacid (traɪ'æsɪd), *sb.* and *a.* [f. TRI- + ACID *a.* and *sb.*] **A.** *sb.* [partial tr. G. *triacidlösung* 'three-acid solution'.] A biological stain consisting of methyl green, orange G, and acid fuchsin. Also *attrib.*

1896 A. B. LEE *Microtomist's Vade-Mecum* (ed. 4) xviii. 223 Ehrlich's Triacid Mixture.—According to a custom which, I believe, originated with Ehrlich himself, and which would, perhaps, be better honoured in the breach than the observance, the name of Triacid ('Triacidlösung') has been given to a mixture of the same three dyes as in the Ehrlich-Biondi mixture, but in such proportions that the 'acid' colours therein have a larger share assigned to them. **1899** [see POLYCHROMATIC a. 2]. **1929** SLIDER & DOWNEY in C. E. McClung *Handbk. Microsc. Technique* vii. 248 The triacid stain is used for five minutes. *Ibid.*, Triacid contains methyl green, orange G and acid fuchsin. **1976** P. COLLARD *Devel. of Microbiol.* v. 54 In 1880 he [*sc.* P. Ehrlich] published an account of his famous tri-acid stain for the differential staining of leucocytes.

B. *adj.* Of a triglyceride: containing three different acid radicals in the molecule.

1945 CHEN & DAUBERT in *Jrnl. Amer. Chem. Soc.* LXVII. 1256/1 'Triacid triglycerides' is used in this report to describe those triglycerides consisting of three different fatty acids. **1977** *Appl. Spectrosc.* XXXI. 122/1 Seven diacid and five triacid saturated triglycerides have been investigated by infrared spectroscopy.

triacle, obs. form of TREACLE.

triacnodal: see TRI- 1.

triacontad (traɪə'kɒntæd). [ad. Gr. τριᾱκοντάς, -αδ-, f. τριάκοντα thirty.] The number thirty, or a set of thirty. So **triacontaëterid** (-ɛ'tɪərɪd) [ad. Gr. τριακονταετηρίς, -ιδ, f. τριακονταετής adj. of or for thirty years], a period of thirty years, or a festival recurring every thirty years; **triacontahedral** (-'hiːdrəl, -'hɛdrəl) *a.* [Gr. ἕδρα base, side], contained by thirty faces, esp. by thirty rhombs, as a crystal; **tria'contarchy** (triak-) *Anc. Gr. Hist.* [ad. Gr. τριακονταρχία, f. ἀρχή rule], the rule of the Thirty at Athens (see THIRTY A. 1 c); **triaconter** (traɪə'kɒntə(r)) [ad. Gr. τριακοντήρης], an ancient Greek galley with thirty oars.

1621 BP. MOUNTAGU *Diatribæ* 258 Their Ogdoades, Duodecads, *Triacontads,.. and all the Æones, blasphemous speculations. **1839** *Fraser's Mag.* XX. 202 The *Triacontaëterid of the pillar of Rosetta—the grand period of the Panegyres, or festivals of the gods, which returned each thirty years. *Ibid.* 328 The great triacontaëterid or panegyry of the resurrection. **1805–17** R. JAMESON *Char. Min.* (ed. 3) 201 A Crystal is said to be.. *Triacontahedral when its surface consists of thirty rhombs. **1852** GROTE *Greece* II. lxxii. IX. 259 Isokrates, who speaks with indignant horror of these Dekarchies,.. denounces those features which they had in common with the *Triakontarchy at Athens. **1859** RAWLINSON *Herodotus* IV. cxlviii. III. 124 Theras.. took ship, and sailed, with three *triaconters, to join the descendants of Membliarus. *Note*, Triaconters were vessels of 30 oars, 15 on each side.

triact, -actinal, -actine: see TRI- 1.

triactor (traɪ'æktə(r)). *Canad.* [TRI- 4 c.] A form of betting on race-horses (see quot. 1979); freq. *attrib.*

1976 *Telegraph-Jrnl.* (St. John, New Brunswick) 23 Aug. 12/2 *Charlottetown*—Two big triactor payoffs.. highlighted a 10-dash harness racing card here Saturday. **1979** *Beautiful Brit. Columbia* Winter 36 The triactor bettor.. had to name the first three finishers, in order, in the last race each day and lived in hopes of making up to $1,000 for his $2 bet. **1984** E. WRIGHT *Smoke Detector* iv. 124 It is sometimes nearly as helpful if you know which horse *can't* win a race... It helps with the triactor, anyway.

triad ('traɪæd). Also 6–7 **-ade.** [f. L. *triad-*, stem of *trias*, a. Gr. τριάς, τριαδ-, a group of three. Cf. F. *triade* (1564 in Hatz.-Darm.).]

1. a. A group or set of three (persons, things, words, attributes, etc.); three collectively or in connexion.

1546 *St. Papers Hen. VIII*, XI. 341 Two thynges I noted in thEmperour, diligent heryngе of me, and good wordys; yf deadis shal nowe folowe accordingely, the triade shall be perfecte. **1614** T. ADAMS *Divell's Banket* 28 Sometimes they daunce in Triades, by threes. *a* **1774** TUCKER *Lt. Nat.* (1834) II. 228 Descend, celestial Graces, sacred Triad. **1862** MERIVALE *Rom. Emp.* VI. liii. 128 The triad of matricides, Nero, Orestes, Alcmæon. **1898** J. T. FOWLER *Durham Cath.* 49 Three triads of Lancet windows.

b. The number three (in Pythagorean philosophy).

1660 STANLEY *Hist. Philos.* IX. (1701) 381/1 The Triad is the first number, actually odd, and the first perfect number, and middle, and proportion. **1875** JOWETT *Plato* (ed. 2) I. 485 The triad or number three is uneven.

2. Specific uses. **a.** Applied to the Trinity. [repr. Gr. τριάς trinity, used by Theophilus of Antioch and Clement of Alexandria, *a* 200.]

1661 BP. G. RUST *Origen & Opin.* 19 There is nothing in that blessed Triad he describes which can be called Creature. **1721** BAILEY, *Triad*.. the Trinity. **1806** T. MAURICE *Fall of Mogul* I. ii, Divine, ineffable, eternal triad! **1909** H. B. SWETE *Holy Spirit in N.T.* II. i. 124 [What] He [Jesus] had taught concerning these Three Persons by presenting Them as at once a Triad and a Unity.

b. A group of three associated or correlated deities, beings, or powers.

a **1746** HOLDSWORTH *Rem. Virgil* (1768) 83 Virgil.. means the great Triad of deities first received all over the East. **1813** PRICHARD *Phys. Hist. Man* vii. §6. 394 We see the attributes of the three persons of the Triad, united in one figure, which represents the supreme Deity, holding conjoined the characters of Creator, Preserver, and Destroyer. **1907** ILLINGWORTH *Doctr. Trinity* vii. 130 The many artificially arranged triads,.. like that of Brahma, Siva, and Vishnu in India.

c. In Welsh literature: A form of composition characterized by an arrangement of subjects or statements in groups of three.

[**1611** SPEED *Hist. Gt. Brit.* VI. liv. §12. 189 The Booke *Triades* mentioned by the Author of the Reformed History of Great Britaine. **1809** W. BLAKE in *Compl. Writings* (1972) 560 Three Ancient Britons overthrowing the Army of armed Romans.. From the Welch Triades.] **1838** [see AFANC]. **1852** MISS YONGE *Cameos* (1877) I. xxxii. 274 Instructions were still oral, and for convenience of memory were drawn up in triads, or verses of three. **1868** SKENE *Four Anc. Bks. Wales* I. 28 As early as the date of the Black Book of Caermarthen some of the Welsh traditions appear under the form of short triads, and that MS. contains a fragment of what were probably the earliest—the Triads of the Horses.

d. *Mus.* A chord of three notes, consisting of a given note with the third and fifth above it; e.g. a common chord (without the octave).

The third may be *major* or *minor*, the fifth *perfect*, *augmented*, or *diminished*; hence the triad is described by these adjs. accordingly.

1801 in BUSBY *Dict. Mus.* **1881** BROADHOUSE *Mus. Acoustics* xv. 320 There are within the octave only three triads or chords of three notes which are consonant. **1889** PROUT *Harmony* viii. §181 A chord.. containing a major third and an augmented fifth.. is called an augmented triad.

e. *Chem.* A trivalent element or radical, i.e. one which combines with three atoms of hydrogen or other monovalent element or radical.

1865 *Reader* 1 Apr. 372/2 The family of triatomic atoms or triads, consisting of nitrogen and its analogues, gold and boron. **1865–8** WATTS *Dict. Chem.* III. 964 There are four triad metals properly so called, namely, aluminium, thallium, indium, and gold. **1868** FOWNES *Elem. Chem.* (ed. 10) 252 Each element is connected with others by a number of lines, or connecting bonds, corresponding to its degree of equivalence; a monad being connected.. by only one such bond, a triad by three.

f. *Biol.* (*a*) A group of three cells, e.g. spores. (*b*) A tertiary unit of organization consisting of an aggregate of dyads: cf. DYAD 2 b. Also *attrib.*, as *triad-deme*: see DEME *sb.*[2] 2.

1876 tr. *Schützenberger's Ferment.* 52 The two spores connected together have only one plane surface, the triads have two. **1883** [see DEME *sb.*[2] 2].

g. *Pros.* A group of three lines having different rhythms.

1885 [see DYAD 2 c].

h. *Math.* (*a*) A set of three things, esp. in *Geom.* of three points. (*b*) In Quaternions, An indeterminate product of three vectors.

1850 CAYLEY *Math. Papers* I. 481 Forming with seven letters.. a system of seven triads containing every possible duad. **1885** LEUDESDORF *Cremona's Proj. Geom.* 37 If the triad *ABC* be projected from *S* upon s_1 (giving $A_1B_1C_1$), and the triad *A'B'C'* be projected from *S* upon s_2 (giving $A_2B_2C_2$); then the triads $A_1B_1C_1$ and $A_2B_2C_2$ will be in perspective.

i. *Cryst.* ***triad axis***, an axis of trigonal symmetry.

1909 in *Cent. Dict. Supp.*

j. *Path.* A group of three symptoms or signs.

1899 E. LANG in T. L. Stedman *20th Cent. Pract.* XVIII. 267 Since the work of Hutchinson, who looked upon a keratitis parenchymatosa in conjunction with a frequently observed deafness and anomaly of the incisors as an expression of hereditary syphilis (Hutchinson's triad), affections of the cornea are numbered among the most frequently occurring manifestations of syphilis. **1908**, etc. [see HUTCHINSON]. **1909** G. DOCK in Osler & McCrae *Syst. Med.* VI. xvii. 439 The early idea that the disease [*sc.* exophthalmic goitre] was characterized by a 'triad' of symptoms gives way slowly. **1948** [see TRIDIONE]. **1954** D. NABARRO *Congenital Syphilis* ii. 14 He pointed out that interstitial keratitis and notched incisor teeth were frequently associated with 8th nerve deafness—the three signs being known as the Hutchinsonian triad. **1982** *Sci. Amer.* Aug. 82/2 The classic triad of the inflammatory reaction is redness, warmth and swelling.

3. ***Triad Society.*** [tr. Chinese *San Ho Hui*, lit. 'three unite society', i.e. 'triple union society', according to Giles meaning 'the union of Heaven, Earth, and Man'.] A secret Chinese society, formed in the reign of Yung Chêng, 1723–36, with the alleged purpose of ousting the Manchu dynasty; later having a large membership in Southern China and various foreign countries. Hence ***Triads*** = members of the Triad Society; also, secret societies, freq. of a criminal character, into which the Triad Society has become divided, and which flourish among overseas Chinese. Also in *sing.* Freq. *attrib.*

1821 W. MILNE *Acc. Triad Society* in *Trans. Royal Asiatic Soc.* (1827) I. 240 The name..seems..to be the *San hŏ hwuy*, i.e. 'The Society of the Three united, or the Triad Society'. **1836** SIR J. DAVIS *Chinese* xi. II. 15 The *San-hŏ-hoey*, or Triad Society... The name seems to imply that when Heaven, Earth, and Man combine to favour them, they shall succeed in subverting the present Tartar dynasty. **1848** S. W. WILLIAMS *Middle Kingd.* I. viii. 395 The English government of Hongkong, enacted in 1845, that any Chinese living in that colony who was ascertained to belong to the Triad Society, should be declared guilty of felony, be imprisoned for three years, and after branding expelled the colony. **1900** *Daily News* 13 Nov. 9/3 The programme of the Triads. **1907** *Daily Chron.* 28 May 1/7 A rebellion has broken out in Kwantung. About 30,000 persons, headed by the Triad Secret Society, have risen. **1960** D. WHITEHEAD *Journey into Crime* (1961) 27 Triad gangs poured into the streets..and fought the police. **1962** M. & G. GORDON *Journey with Stranger* (1963) xxiv. 139 The Triads, those secret criminal societies that sought to monopolize every kind of racket. **1975** D. BLOODWORTH *Clients of Omega* vii. 64 A rival society buried your body, it seems. The 18-K Triad. **1976** *Spectator* 14 Feb. 3/2 Chinese Triad gangs made their mark in London by kicking to death a man in a Soho gambling club. **1976** *Daily Colonist* (Victoria, B.C.) 2 Mar. 3/1 A heroin smuggling racket that may be linked with the world-wide Chinese secret society known as Triad. **1977** *Hongkong Standard* 14 Apr. 5/1 As far as triad influence in these committees was concerned, Mr Lam admitted his department had received complaints in the past. **1978** *Daily Tel.* 3 Apr. 3/3 Yard chiefs concerned about the increasing violence between rival triads..have ordered a further big crackdown.

triadelphous (traɪə'dɛlfəs), *a. Bot.* [f. TRI- + Gr. ἀδελφός brother + -OUS, after DIADELPHOUS.] Of stamens: United by the filaments into three bundles. Of a plant: Having the stamens so united.

1830 LINDLEY *Nat. Syst. Bot.* 87 Stamens [of the Pea tribe]..either distinct or monadelphous, or diadelphous; very seldom triadelphous. **1896** HENSLOW *Wild Flowers* 18 In the St. John's worts, they [the filaments] are grouped into clusters..of three or five. These are therefore triadelphous and pentadelphous.

triadic (traɪ'ædɪk), *a.* (*sb.*) [f. TRIAD + -IC.] Of, pertaining to, or constituting a triad; consisting of triads.

1788 T. TAYLOR *Proclus* I. 123 We shall find a line [to be] monadic; but a superficies dyadic, and a solid body triadic. **1839** BAILEY *Festus* viii. (1848) 95 Nature's great Triadic principle, in all things seen. **1850** CAYLEY *Math. Papers* I. 481 On the triadic arrangements of seven and fifteen things.

b. ***triadic canon*** (*Gr. Ch.*): a hymn (CANON *sb.*[1] 7 b) in honour of the Trinity.

1862 NEALE *Hymns East. Ch.* 160 It would be impossible without wearying the reader, to translate the whole of the Triadic Canons.

c. *Chem.* That is a triad; trivalent.

1882 in OGILVIE (Annandale).

d. *Anc. Pros.* (*a*) Containing three different metres or rhythms. (*b*) Composed of groups of systems, each of which contains three unlike systems.

1891 in *Cent. Dict.*

e. Of or belonging to the Welsh Triads.

1849 T. STEPHENS *Lit. Kymry* 447 The Triadic form is frequently seen in the poems of Aneurin, and Llywarch Hen. **1906** C. SQUIRE *Mythol. Anc. Brit.* v. 52 We learn.. that the battle of Camlan was one of the 'Three Frivolous Battles of Britain',..and that the usual 'Three' alone escaped from it, though Arthur himself is, in spite of the triadic convention, added as a fourth.

B. *sb. Math.* In Quaternions, A sum of products of three vectors.

So **tri'adical** *a.*, = *triadic*; **tri'adically** *adv.*, according to triads, in the manner of a triad (in quot. 1860, in sense 2 c: cf. e above).

1837 WHEWELL *Hist. Induct. Sc.* (1857) I. 223 The intellectual gods produce all things triadically. **1860** J. J. THOMAS *Brit. Antiq.* 214 The gallant Cymro triadically repeated..several englynion. **1890** *Dublin Rev.* Jan. 60 *note*, A transcript of an old Triadical commentary.

triadism ('traɪədɪz(ə)m). [f. as prec. + -ISM.] Method, system, or principle of triads; arrangement in groups of three; threefold constitution.

1846 T. W. JENKYN *Baxter's Wks.* Pref. Ess. 50 The method which Baxter adopted for systematizing the doctrines of Theology may be called Triadism. [Cf. TRICHOTOMIZE.] **1909** A. R. COLQUHOUN in *Q. Rev.* Apr. 672 The suggestion that triadism should supersede dualism as the basis of the [Habsburg] monarchy supposes the erection of a third (i.e. a Slav) State.

triadist ('traɪədɪst). [f. as prec. + -IST.]

1. A composer of triads (see TRIAD 2 c). *Welsh Lit.*

1868 T. NICHOLAS *Pedigree Eng. People* 197 *note*, Caer-Llion, as the seat of King Arthur, obtains from the Triadist pre-eminence even superior to the two Municipia, London and York.

2. *pl.* Members of the Triad Society (see TRIAD 3). *rare.*

1855 *North-China Herald* 17 Mar. 132/2 The Triadists, who so recently held Shanghae.

triæne (traɪ'iːn, 'traɪiːn). *Zool.* [ad. Gr. τρίαινα trident.] A kind of sponge-spicule.

Variously described as 'a rhabdus having at one end three prongs or "cladi" diverging at equal angles', and 'a tetraxon spicule with 1 long and 3 equal shorter tangential rays'.

1887 SOLLAS in *Encycl. Brit.* XXII. 417/1 (*Sponges*) A particular case of the cladose rhabdus,..of the most frequent occurrence, is the triæne.

Hence **triænostrongyle** (traɪiːnəʊ'strɒndʒɪl) [Gr. στρογγύλος rounded], a triæne in which the main arm is blunt at the end; **tri'ænostyle** (-staɪl) [Gr. στῦλος pillar, STYLE], one in which it is sharp; **tri'ænotyle** (-taɪl) [Gr. τύλη cushion], one in which it is blunt and rounded.

1909 in *Cent. Dict. Supp.*

triage ('traɪɪdʒ; in sense 2 also ‖ trijaʒ, 'triːɑːʒ). [a. F. *triage* (14th c. in Hatz.-Darm.), n. of action f. *trier* to pick, cull: see TRY *v.* and -AGE.]

1. The action of assorting according to quality. Also *attrib.*; hence *concr.* (see quots.)

1727–41 CHAMBERS *Cycl.* s.v. *Wool*, Each fleece consists of wool of divers qualities, and degrees of fineness, which the dealers therein take care to separate... If the triage, or separation be well made, in 15 bales there will be [etc.]. **1825** *Gentl. Mag.* XCV. I. 216/1 These [pickers] sort the [Coffee] berries into three classes; 'best quality', 'middling', and the third of all the bad broken berries..is called 'triage coffee'. **1880** *Spons' Encycl. Manuf.* I. 705 The broken beans [of coffee], or 'triage', must also be separated by hand from the dust. **1880** *Daily News* 28 Oct. 3/8 Coffee.—..Costa Rica;.. Triage 59*s.* 6*d.*

2. a. The assignment of degrees of urgency to wounds or illnesses in order to decide the order or suitability of treatment. Freq. *attrib.* Hence (*rare*) as *v. trans.* (see quot. 1977).

1930 F. A. POTTLE *Stretchers* 222 A special triage officer at once surveys the patients to determine the urgency of their injuries. **1945** *Jrnl. R. Army Med. Corps* LXXXIV. 125 The word 'triage', literally 'assessment according to quality', has recently been adopted to describe the process. **1973** *Parade* 18 Feb. 8/1 Chicago's Michael Reese Hospital ..has instituted a 'triage', or selection system, whereby incoming patients are evaluated by an RN as to their degree of urgency, and sent to the appropriate area. **1973** N. MEYER *Target Practice* viii. 95 And presto, we were all second-lieutenant navy doctors. For six months I worked in *triage* there, operating sometimes around the clock. **1975** *Observer* 11 May 6/7 Hundreds of 'borderline' cases have been at the mercy all this week of 'triage' panels trying to sort out patients desperately in need of care. **1976** *Lancet* 15 Nov. 1061/1 Triage at an early stage can label the patient with coma as surgical or medical. **1977** M. HERR *Dispatches* 82 He was so bad that the doctor triaged him, passed him over to treat the ones that..could still be saved. **1978** *Tucson Mag.* Dec. 55/1 An extremely efficient triage nurse, an RN, greets new arrivals and determines the severity of the problem.

b. *transf.*

1974 *Time* 11 Nov. 80 In the West, there is increasing talk of triage, a commonsense if callous concept that teaches that when resources are scarce, they must be used where they will do most good. **1975** *Globe & Mail* (Toronto) 3 Nov. 7/2 The concept should now be applied to countries crippled by food shortages, famine and over-population. 'The triage discussions now seek to classify nations into those what do not need help, those that are capable of responding to help and those "broken back" states that are in such difficulty that they cannot be helped,' says Mr Hopper. **1979** *Guardian* 18 Oct. 5/8 There is [*sc.* in New York] an unofficial 'triage' system in which teachers and school administrators concentrate their limited resources on helping those students who seem to be capable of succeeding.

triagonal (traɪ'ægənəl), *a.* [Erroneous formation for TRIGONAL, after *tetragonal*, *pentagonal*, etc.; cf. TRIALOGUE.] Triangular.

1665 HOOKE *Micrographia* 158 Piggs-hair (A) is somewhat *triagonal*, and seems to have neither pith nor pore. **1794** A. THOMAS *Newfoundland Jrnl.* (1968) 121 Its shape is Triagonal and it measures Three Hundred and Fifty Miles in length. **1822** SCOTT *Pirate* xv. *note*, They change ranks, and place themselves in a triagonal figure. **1879** *Proc. U.S. Nat. Museum* II. 270 Ostracionts with triagonal, tetragonal, or pentagonal carapaces.

triakad, triacad ('traɪəkæd). *Anc. Gr. Hist.* [ad. Gr. τριᾱκάς, -αδ-, the number thirty (also as below): cf. TRIACONTAD.] 'At Athens, a political division of the φυλή containing thirty families; at Sparta, either 30 families ($\frac{1}{10}$ of an oba), or 10 families ($\frac{1}{30}$ of an oba)' (Liddell and Scott). Cf. OBE.

1846 GROTE *Greece* II. viii. II. 602 Herodotus tells us that Lycurgus established the military subdivisions peculiar to Sparta—the Enômoties, the Triākads, and the Syssitia. **1868** SMITH *Smaller Dict. Grk. & Rom. Antiq.* (ed. 7) 389/1.

triakis- ('traɪəkɪs), repr. Gr. τριάκις thrice; used in combination in *Geom.* and *Cryst.* in **ˌtriakisˌicosa'hedron**, **ˌtriakisˌocta'hedron**, **ˌtri-akisˌtetra'hedron** (pl. in all cases **-hedra**), names of solids derived respectively from the icosahedron, octahedron, and tetrahedron by erecting a triangular pyramid on each face, thus multiplying the original number of faces by three. (In *Geom.* specially applied to those forms in which the pyramids are of such altitude as to make all the solid angles regular.) Hence in derived adjs., as **ˌtriakisˌocta'hedrid**.

1878 GURNEY *Crystallogr.* 89 The form..called the triakisoctahedron. **1895** STORY-MASKELYNE *Crystallogr.* vii. §174. 199 The triakisoctahedron or octahedrid pyramidion ..the more acute the pyramidion the more nearly it approximates in aspect to a rhomb-dodecahedron. *Ibid.* §187. 220 Triakisoctahedrid forms met with in combination. *Ibid.* §189. 224 The triakistetrahedra..(tetrahedrid pyramidia).

triakontarchy: see TRIACONTARCHY.

trial ('traɪəl), *sb.*[1] Also 6 *Sc.* triel, 6–7 *Sc.* tryel(l, 6–7 tri-, tryall, 7–8 (9 *dial.*) tryal. [= AF. *trial*, *triel*, f. *trier* to TRY, instanced in 16th c., but prob. earlier: see -AL[1]. Cf. Du Cange s.v. *triallum*.] The action or fact of trying or being tried, in various senses of TRY *v.*

(The senses are here arranged not according to the chronological order of the quotations cited, but in accordance with the sense-development seen in TRY *v.* and TRIABLE.)

1. *Law.* The examination and determination of a cause by a judicial tribunal; determination of the guilt or innocence of an accused person by a court.

Hence to ***bring*** (a person or cause) ***to trial***; to ***put*** (a person) ***on his trial***, to ***stand*** (***one's***) ***trial***, etc.; also ***trial by the country***, ***by jury***, ***by proviso***, etc.: see these words.

a **1577** SIR T. SMITH *Commw. Eng.* (1633) 189 The clarke asketh him how he will be tried and telleth him he must say, by God and the countrie, for these be the words formall of his triall after inditement. **1651** HOBBES *Leviath.* II. xxvi. 146 In the ordinary trialls of Right, Twelve men of the common People, are the Judges. **1712** ARBUTHNOT *John Bull* App. iii, So Jack resolved; but he had done more wisely to have put himself upon the trial of his country. **1838** THIRLWALL *Greece* IV. 73 He was brought to trial.. Theramenes, lately his intimate friend, became his accuser. **1885** *Manch. Exam.* 10 July 5/1 In this case the parties were first put upon their trial. **1911** *Act 1 & 2 Geo. V*, c. 6 §9 (1) Any sheriff or his lawful deputy before whom a writ of inquiry or a writ of trial is executed.

b. The determination of a person's guilt or innocence, or the righteousness of his cause, by a combat between the accuser and accused (***trial by battle***, ***by*** (***single***) ***combat***, ***by wager of battle***, ***by the sword***); 'a combat decisive of the merits of a cause' (Schmidt); see also *trial by* ORDEAL. These methods of trial are now abolished; but expressions originally referring to them are still in fig. use. Thus, war is often spoken of as a 'trial by battle' with God for judge.

1593 SHAKS. *Rich. II*, I. i. 81 Ile answer thee in any faire degree, Or Chiualrous designe of knightly triall. **1595** —— *John* II. i. 286 Those soules That to their euerlasting residence, Before the dew of euening fall, shall fleete In dread-full triall of our kingdomes King. *Ibid.* 342 England thou hast not sau'd one drop of blood In this hot triall more then we of France. **1600** —— *A.Y.L.* I. ii. 199 Let your faire eies, and gentle wishes go with mee to my triall. **1617** [see COMBAT *sb.* 1]. **1641** [see BATTLE *sb.* 2]. **1738** GLOVER *Leonidas* III. 564 By single combat were the tryal vain. **1819** *Act 59 Geo. III*, c. 46 Whereas..the Trial by Battel in any Suit, is a Mode of Trial unfit to be used; and it is expedient that the same should be wholly abolished..be it..enacted, That..in any Writ of Right now depending, or which may here-after be..commenced, the Tenant shall not be received to wage Battel, nor shall Issue be joined nor Trial be had by Battel. **1868** G. PRYME *Autobiog. Recoll.* vii. (1870) an. 1818. 133.

(*b*) ***trial by television*** or ***the media***, subjection of a public figure under some cloud to discussion of his case on television or in the media, usu. in such a way as to imply his guilt.

1960 J. FREEMAN in *New Statesman* 15 Oct. 556/1 A group of Labour MPs had..written to *The Times* complaining that my questions to Mr. Foulkes, in the BBC programme *Panorama*, about specific..allegations of malpractice in his union amounted to public trial by television. **1968** *Punch* 6 Mar. 327/1 Urged to stop 'trial by television', the Postmaster-General..said..he himself had no power over the content of programmes. **1979** *Broadcast* 4 June 10/1 There have been predictable references to 'trial by the media', 'trial by television'.

2. a. The action of testing or putting to the proof the fitness, truth, strength, or other quality of anything; test, probation. Applied *spec.* in *pl.* to a boat's trial run (see sense 13 a below).

1526 *Pilgr. Perf.* (W. de W. 1531) 108 The tryall of our fayth, & examinacyon or proue of our hope. **1548** UDALL, etc., *Erasm. Par. Mark* viii. 53 b, Nowe maketh he a triall howe much his disciples haue profited ghostly. **1600** J. PORY tr. *Leo's Africa* IX. 339 The most certaine triall of these horses is when they can ouertake the beast called Lant or the

Ostrich in a race. **1604** E. G[RIMSTONE] *D'Acosta's Hist. Indies* IV. vi. 221 The triall of mettall by fire. **1695** WOODWARD *Nat. Hist. Earth* I. (1723) 23 They answer all Chymical Tryals in like Manner as the Sea-Shells do. **1903** *Motor. Ann.* 145 The Automobile Club..held a series of practical and official brake trials in Welbeck Park. **1921** *Daily Colonist* (Victoria, B.C.) 25 Mar. 17/2 On Friday the Traveller was taken out for her trials... Slight trouble arose in the main bearings and the vessel returned to the dock for adjustments. **1969** F. MOWAT *Boat who would not Float* (1970) vii. 70 Seamen refer to the first tentative voyage of a newly commissioned ship as her trials.

b. The fact or condition of being tried by suffering or temptation; probation. †In quot. *c* 1550, temptation (*obs.*). (Cf. 9.)

c **1550** CHEKE *Matt.* xxvi. 41 Can ie not watch oon hour with me, watch and prai yt ie enter not into trial. **1644** MILTON *Areop.* (Arb.) 45 That which purifies us is triall. **1755** YOUNG *Centaur* i. Wks. 1757 IV. 108 Is not this stretching out our boldness even beyond the day of tryal? **1871** MACDUFF *Mem. Patmos* vi. 71 The hour of trial—the testing hour of suffering arrived.

c. A contest designed to test the capabilities of motor-cyclists or (formerly) car-drivers and their vehicles, in which riding or driving takes place over long distances or rough terrain. Freq. in *pl.* Cf. *reliability trial* s.v. RELIABILITY 3.

1926 [see SCRAMBLE *sb.* 2b]. **1935** *Encycl. Sports* 429/1 Among the more famous English trials that have been run for many years are the London-Edinburgh run, the London-Exeter run, the London-Land's End Trial and the London-Gloucester Run. **1950** *Oxf. Jun. Encycl.* IX. 328/2 The famous Scott Trial in Yorkshire was the first of such rough-riding fixtures [in motor-cycling contests]. **1963** P. DRACKETT *Motor Rallying* i. 10 The Thousand Miles Trial of 1903 went several steps nearer to the rally as we know it to-day, with road sections and timed hill-climbs. **1976** *Southern Even. Echo* (Southampton) 3 Nov., Trials enthusiasts will be out in force in Hampshire this weekend to watch the Hood Trophies and Perce Simon Trials—two major events in the British motor cycle calendar.

†**3.** Inquiry or investigation in order to ascertain something; examination, elucidation. *to take* (*get*) *trial*, to make inquiry. *Sc. Obs.*

1557–72 *Diurnal Occur.* (Bann. Cl.) 72 Ane conventioun ordanit to convene in Sanctandrois for taking tryell of the matter aboue writtin. **1575** in *Maitl. Cl. Misc.* I. 126 To be diligent for gaitting of tryall of the deid barne that wes cassin furth in Foresteris wynd. *a* **1657** SIR W. MURE *Ps.* cxxxix. 3 My pathes, my lying doun thou eyest, And narrow tryall takes.

4. a. Action, method, or treatment adopted in order to ascertain the result; investigation by means of experience; experiment. *rule of trial and error*: see POSITION 3. *trial and error*, (*a*) also in non-mathematical contexts, the process of succeeding by repeated trying with or without improvement of method by learning from failures; (*b*) *spec.* in *Psychol.*, with reference to the theory that a primitive form of learning results, over a series of trials, from erroneous random responses to a problem being replaced by the correct response, rather than from insight. Freq. (with hyphens) *attrib.*

1570 LEVINS *Manip.* 13/14 A Tryall, *experimentum.* **1608** BACON *Comment. Sol.* Wks. 1868 IV. 63 A collection of phainomena, of surgery, destillations, minerall tryalls. **1726** LEONI *Alberti's Archit.* II. 106/1 In what season it is best to make these tryals has not been..declared. **1806** HUTTON *Course Math.* I. 256 They may be all readily solved by the following easy rule of Double Position, sometimes called Trial-and-Error. **1812** WOODHOUSE *Astron.* xxxix. 387 Astronomers have sought, by the indirect methods of trial and conjecture, to avoid them. **1894** C. L. MORGAN *Introd. Compar. Psychol.* xiv. 241 Such a proceeding can be completely explained in terms of sense-experience. The process was throughout one of trial and error. **1898** E. L. THORNDIKE in *Psychol. Rev. Monogr. Suppl.* II. VIII. 105 If the method of trial and error, with accidental success, be the method of acquiring associations among the animals, the slow progress of primitive man..becomes suggestive. **1900** C. L. MORGAN *Animal Behaviour* iv. 139 The method of varied trial and error with the utilization of chance success, is a lengthy and somewhat clumsy process; but it suffices. **1907** *Verney Mem.* I. 536 He will have some alders set in the wet places..for a trial. **1940** HILGARD & MARQUIS *Conditioning & Learning* x. 252/2 The behavior of animals in the trial and error situation yields evidence of more intelligent behavior than is implied in the simple process of stamping in correct responses and stamping out wrong ones. **1951** PARSONS & SHILS *Toward Gen. Theory of Action* II. ii. 129 Invention may be..trial-and-error learning. **1957** J. S. HUXLEY *Relig. without Revelation* ix. 230 Scientific hypotheses..are better organisations for coping with our experience of physical phenomena than are trial-and-error methods. **1962** *Listener* 15 Nov. 796/1 There had been fitful, trial-and-error attempts to create a National Assembly. **1967** M. DOBB *Capitalism, Devel. & Planning* v. 242 In the Lange trial-and-error process..it was variable prices (accounting prices) that were fixed by the top-level authorities. **1972** *New Yorker* 26 Aug. 32/1 The American psychologist Edward L. Thorndike..is credited with the first rigorous investigation of trial-and-error, or instrumental, learning.

†**b.** The result ascertained by testing; effect; efficacy. (Cf. PROOF *sb.* 7.) *Obs. rare.*

1559 MORWYNG *Evonym.* 30 They giue it to drinke against the fittes of the falling sycknes with maruellous tryall.

†**5.** *transf.* Evidence, proof. *Obs.*

1532 FRITH *Let.* Wks. (1573) 81/1 Whan can be more triall of a fayththfull hart, then to adventure not onely to ayde and succour by the meanes of other,..but also personally to visite the poore oppressed? **1577** HARRISON *England* II. vi. (1877) I. 153, I will not saie..if I should, I could easilie bring my triall. *a* **1586** *Satir. Poems Reform.* xxxvi. 86 Thow.. gave gud tryell of thy lytill treuth. *a* **1670** SPALDING *Troub. Chas. I* (1851) II. 33 Thir newis turned to nothing, for there wes no tryel found that sic materis were trew.

6. a. A testing of qualifications, attainments, or progress; examination.

spec. the examination prescribed by Presbyteries for the licensing of preachers or the ordination of ministers; also, in Scotland, the public probation of a Lord of Session; (*pl.*) at Eton College, Harrow, and other schools, the terminal examination; at Oxford and Cambridge, short for *trial eights* (see 13).

1672 *Mem. J. Fraser* in *Sel. Biog.* (Wodrow Soc.) II. 309 After trial of my gifts and conversation by several exercises and pieces of trial..they agreed to trust me in the name of Christ with the dispensation of the Gospel. **1706** *Act 6 Anne* c. II. Art. xix, No writer to the signet [shall] be capable to be admitted a lord of the session unless he undergo a private and publick tryal on the civil law. **1708** J. CHAMBERLAYNE *St. Gt. Brit.* (1710) 425 The Manner of Admission into this Society [*sc.* the Faculty of Advocates] is..sometimes, tho' rarely, by a Trial in the Scots Law. **1710** T. HALYBURTON *Mem.* ii. (1824) 238, I underwent the other parts of my private trials and on May 1, 1700 was ordained at Ceres. **1815** SCOTT *Guy M.* xix, He went to stand trial for his license as a preacher. **1847** in Hare *Story my Life* (1896) I. 223 We are busy at our Trial, which we do with our masters in form. **1849** HARPER *E. Erskine* i. 11 Mr. Erskine was after the usual trials licensed by the Presbytery of Kirkcaldy. **1905** VACHELL *The Hill* ix, If we put our backs—and heads—into Trials, we can easily get a remove. **1908** G. D. LAW in Boston *Acc. Life* 84 *note*, The trials of a probationer about to be ordained were similar to those of a divinity student applying for licence. **1908** *Westm. Gaz.* 7 Oct. 12/1 The ceremony..which every Scottish judge has to 'pass', is called his 'trials'.

b. *Sport.* A match held to select players for a major team; esp. in *Rugby Football.* Cf. *trial match*, sense 13.

a **1914** J. E. RAPHAEL *Mod. Rugby Football* (1918) 249 E. W. Baker played for the South and in other important trials. **1921** E. H. D. SEWELL *Rugby Football* 337 He was nominated to play on the wing in the third Trial. **1950** [see SIGNING *vbl. sb.* 1b]. **1978** *Rugby World* Apr. 5/2 Jeeps was the man who instigated the new system of trials which operated this season, involving games between England's regions and divisions.

c. A contest in which horses, dogs, etc., are put through various tests and assessed on their performance.

1942 R. B. KELLEY *Animal Breeding* xvi. 145 The second kind of trial endeavours to set out a course during which the dog is required to perform the tasks of everyday life. **1946** M. C. SELF *Horseman's Encycl.* 196 Working hunter trials. Jumps 4 feet to 4 feet 6 inches. On special course. Details of course to be withheld until one hour before class. **1960** J. STROUD *Shorn Lamb* xv. 175, I was..flitting round the suburbs like a sheepdog at a Trial. **1974** *Encycl. Brit. Micropædia* I. 723/3 The park [at Badminton] is also well-known for its horse trials.

†**7.** The fact of undergoing or experiencing; experience. *to have* (or *make*) *trial of*, to experience. *Obs.*

1600 J. PORY tr. *Leo's Africa* v. 257 Whereof I my selfe haue had often triall. **1631** WEEVER *Anc. Fun. Mon.* 512 Henries command was a Law; of which Cromwell had a triall. **1656** EARL MONM. tr. *Boccalini's Advts. fr. Parnass.* I. xxiii. (1674) 26 Tyrants, by whom they made trial of the most deplorable miseries. **1657** —— tr. *Paruta's Pol. Disc.* 72 Even Augustus himself made trial of many Insurrections in Spain, Germany, and in the Eastern parts. **1687** A. LOVELL tr. *Thevenot's Trav.* I. 178 We had a tryal then of these Panniers, and for my part I was much at my ease.

8. An attempt to do something; an endeavour, effort. (In quot. 1614, an attempt to gain.)

1614 RALEIGH *Hist. World* v. iii. §11 [He] went to a greater enterprise; euen to fight in tryall of the Empire. **1638** SIR T. HERBERT *Trav.* (ed. 2) 72 Ecbar is poysoned;..after foureteene dayes violent torment and trialls to expell the poyson, yeelds up his ghost. **1720** SWIFT *Fates Clergymen* Wks. 1755 II. II. 24 But this I confess is a trial too dangerous often to engage in. **1793** SMEATON *Edystone L.* §98, I proposed to make a trial for landing if the weather should suit. **1853** LYNCH *Self-Improv.* i. 6 If you take away trial, you get rid of failure, but of success too. **1860** TYNDALL *Glac.* I. xviii. 128 He said he would make the trial.

9. That which puts one to the test; *esp.* a painful test of one's endurance, patience, or faith; hence, affliction, trouble, misfortune. (Cf. 2b.)

1754 RICHARDSON *Grandison* (1781) III. i. 9 How would such a creature..have behaved under such tryals? **1831** SCOTT *Cast. Dang.* xiv, Trials by which the most generous affections may be soured. **1838** DICKENS *Nich. Nick.* iv, All people have their trials. **1865** —— *Mut. Fr.* I. iv, Lavinia has not known the trial that Bella has known. **1885** 'MRS. ALEXANDER' *At Bay* ix, Her life has been a very trying one. .. I trust its trials will soon be over.

10. a. Something that serves as a sample or proof of a manufacture or material, or of the skill of a maker or operator, the progress of an operation, etc.; *spec.* in *Pottery manuf.* a piece of clay or the like by which the progress of the firing process may be judged; a trial-piece.

1608 R. WIFFIN etc., in *Capt. Smith's Wks.* (Arb.) 128 Capt. N. being dispatched with the tryals of pitch, tarre, glasse, frankincense, and sope ashes, with that [= what] clapbord and wainscot could bee provided. **1609** ? N. POWELL *ibid.* 154 Wee..produced a triall of glasse; made a well..re-couered our Church [etc.]. **1825** J. NICHOLSON *Operat. Mechanic* 469 In different parts of the oven..rings of Egyptian black clay are placed, as trials, by which an experienced fireman can tell how much longer the process must be carried on. **1870** J. ROSKELL in *Eng. Mech.* 18 Feb. 548/2 If the Copper is intended for rolling purposes, then a large sample termed a trial is taken.

†**b.** See quot. *Obs. rare.*

1611 COTGR., *Languette*,..the tryall, or cocke of a ballance.

c. Short for *trial-ball, trial-gallop.*

1884 *Illustr. Lond. News* 1 Nov. 410/3 Three guineas for a 'lose' (besides four guineas for every private 'trial'). **1897** 'TIVOLI' (Bleakley) *Short Innings* vi, 'That was a trial!' he explained. 'It was the second ball!' cried Tuckett.

11. A sieve or sifting screen. Now *dial.*

1825 J. NICHOLSON *Operat. Mechanic* 446 The spout.. receives the bark from the stones, and conveys it into the tryal..which tryal is wired, to shift or dress the bark as it descends from the stones. **1885** *Cheshire Gloss.*, *Trial*, a coarse sieve in a winnowing machine.

12. Phrases. ***on trial*** (sense 2), on the basis or condition of being tried, as *to take* a person or thing ***on trial***, to take subject to the condition of being satisfactory when tried. ***to be on*** (***his, her,*** or ***its***) ***trial*** (2, 6), to be in a state of probation until it is seen how he or it will succeed or work. See also *to put* a person *on his trial*; *to bring to trial*; *to stand* (*one's*) *trial*, *trial by television* (*media*) in sense 1.

1741 WESLEY *Wks.* (1872) I. 301 The others were put upon trial again. **1889** JESSOPP *Coming of Friars* iii. 133 During the thirteenth century they [the monks] were, so to speak, upon their trial. **1904** H. PAUL *Hist. Eng.* I. 409 Speaking at the Trinity House on the 9th of June [1855], Prince Albert declared that Constitutional government was on its trial, and urged the duty of placing more confidence in the Ministers of the Crown. [But Pr. Albert's words, as given in *Illustr. Lond. News* 16 June, 1855, and other newspapers, were 'Gentlemen, our Constitutional Government is undergoing a heavy trial' [etc.]. See also Th. Martin *Life of Pr. Consort* (1874–9).] *Mod.* I will take the maid for a month on trial. You may have the dust-extractor three days on trial.

13. *attrib.* and *Comb.* Of or pertaining to trial; made, done, used, or taken for or as a trial: as ***trial animal, -chord, -correction, day, -examination, -feat, -fire, flight, -ground, heat*** (HEAT *sb.* 10), ***-hole, -hour, -impression, lot, marriage, match*** (Cricket), ***night, number, -ordeal, -pan, parlour, pit, plot, race, separation*** [SEPARATION 3], ***stone, time, -working, -yard***; also *pl.*, as ***trials cap, man, secretary***; also **trial balance**, in book-keeping by double entry, an addition of the whole of the entries on each side of the ledger, when the sum of the debits ought to balance the sum of the credits; † **trial ball** *Cricket*, a practice ball which a bowler was formerly allowed to bowl before beginning his first over (*obs.*); **trial balloon** = BALLON D'ESSAI; **trial bar**, 'a cuboid used by turners for testing the inclination of planes' (*Cent. Dict. Suppl.* 1909); **trial bit**, an adjustable bit for measuring a horse's mouth (Knight *Dict. Mech.* 1877); **trial-book**, a book in which a cashier enters sums paid and received so as at any time to take out a trial balance of cash in hand; **trial-bred** *a.*, of a dog: bred to compete in trials (TRIAL *sb.*[1] 6c); **trial case** = *trial sight*; **trial cock** (see quot.); **trial court**, a court before which trials take place in the first instance; distinguished from an appeal court; **trial eight**, *Boat-racing*, an eight-oared boat's provisional crew, from among whom some members of the final eight may be chosen; **trial glasses** (*pl.*), a set of graduated glasses for ascertaining the requirements of defective vision; **trial-jar** (see quot.); **trial judge, t. justice**: cf. *trial court*; **trial jury**, a petty jury, distinguished from a grand jury (Webster, 1911); **trial lawyer**, a lawyer practising in a trial court; **trial-list**, the register of causes or prisoners to be tried; the calendar (*Cassell's Encycl. Dict.* 1888); **trial-piece**, something made or taken as a specimen; *spec.* a coin or the like struck as a test of the die, or as a specimen of the design; **trial plate**, in assaying coin (see quot.); **trial proof**, a proof taken from a plate during the process of engraving to show its state; **trial run**, a preliminary trip given to a new vessel or vehicle, to test its performance; freq. *transf.* or *fig.*; **trial sight** (see quot.); **trial (spectacle) frame**, an adjustable frame with revolving graduated fittings to hold *trial glasses* (q.v.); **trial square**, a try-square (Knight *Dict. Mech.* 1877); **trial trench** *Archæol.*, an exploratory trench dug on a site; hence ***trial-trench*** vb. intr.; **trial-trip**, a trip taken to test the speed and other qualities of a vessel, etc.,

1905 *Brit. Med. Jrnl.* 27 May 1141 The dose which the *trial animals stood will set up serious symptoms in the infected ones. **1838** *Trial Balance [see *balance-sheet* s.v. BALANCE *sb.* 22]. **1910** *Encycl. Brit.* IV. 227/1 *A trial balance* is thus no very adequate safeguard against fraud. **1978** *Detroit Free Press* 5 Mar. c 16/5 (Advt.), Local Co. needs a mature individual for full-charge bookkeeping thru trial balance. **1830** in R. S. Holmes *Hist. Yorks. County Cricket* (1904) 25 It is usual for a bowler, before he commences, to bowl a *trial ball at one of his colleagues. **1870** *Times* 1 Sept. 10/4 The former [bowler] preluded his successes..with three trial balls. **1939** *Sun* (Baltimore) 21 Apr. 3/4 Congressional moves to bar alliance members from relief funds are in the '*trial balloon' stage. ? **1949** Q. HOWE in W.

Safire *New Lang. Politics* (1968) 454/1 He [*sc.* Theodore Roosevelt] also originated the 'trial-balloon' technique and gave favored correspondents 'off-the-record' statements that they attributed to 'authoritative sources'. If the statement caught on, Roosevelt would make it his own. If it fell flat, he would drop it. *a* **1974** R. CROSSMAN *Diaries* (1976) II. 590 Since I'd been wanting to launch a trial balloon on this subject, I aired my views at length. **1890** *Times* 11 July 13/5 Witness drew his attention to the figures in the cashier's *trial-book, and asked how he accounted for them. **1948** J. A. REID in B. Vesey-Fitzgerald *Bk. Dog* 749 The '*trial-bred' collie. **1960** *Farmer & Stockbreeder* 9 Feb. 91/3 Many collies lie down almost instinctively and, among trial-bred dogs, getting them to stay on their feet is far more difficult. **1901** *Daily Chron.* 23 Nov. 9/5 A '*Trials' cap is eagerly sought after, and the inclusion of 'Old Blues' robs other men of their chance. **1889** BRINSMEAD *Hist. Pianoforte* 187 The *trial-chord, when struck, should produce a rapid beat or series of undulations of sound. **1825** J. NICHOLSON *Operat. Mechanic* 167 *Trial or gauge cocks..to ascertain the height of the water in the boiler. **1867–77** G. F. CHAMBERS *Astron.* I. xi. 129 Applying this..to the eclipses in the form of a *trial-correction. **1890** *U.S. Rep.* (Supreme Court) CXXXVII. 347 On review in this court, the rulings of the *trial court were sustained. **1907** *Westm. Gaz.* 4 Apr. 2/1 The new law permits the Government to appeal from certain judgments of the trial Court. **1593** SHAKS. *2 Hen. VI*, III. i. 114 That Doyt that ere I wrested from the King..Be brought against me at my *Tryall day. **1873** C. C. KNOLLYS *Oxf. Univ. Challenge Races* p. iii, The crews of the *Trial and University Eights. **1900** W. E. SHERWOOD *Oxford Rowing* 63 In 1858..considerable alterations were made..the most important perhaps being the establishment of the Trial Eight Race. **1878** STUBBS *Lect. Med. & Mod. Hist.* (1886) 157 [The Crusades] were the *trial-feat of the young world. **1598** SHAKS. *Merry W.* v. v. 88 With *Triall-fire touch me his finger end. **1909** F. ASH *Trip to Mars* xii. 89, I only took my *trial flight in it yesterday! **1891** *Cent. Dict.*, *Trial glasses. **1895** *Arnold & Sons' Catal. Surg. Instrum.* 125 Spectacle Frame, plain, for Trial Glasses. **1878** URE *Dict. Arts* IV. 323 The Mont Cenis tunnel formed the greatest *trial-ground ever brought to the attention of inventors and makers of either rock-drills or air-compressors. **1909** *West. Gaz.* 29 May 9/4 Arrangements have been made for aeroplane flights..at Wembley, where an excellent stretch of suitable trial-ground exists. **1894** A. ROBERTSON *Nuggets*, etc. 212 He turned from side to side, apparently looking for a digger's *trial-hole that would suit his purpose. **1907** SIR W. M. RAMSAY in *Expositor* Sept. 203 The terms of our firman permitted..the making of trial-holes. **1847** MARY HOWITT *Ballads*, etc. 317 In this, the fiercest *trial-hour, My doubting soul sustain! **1879** H. PHILLIPS *Addit. Notes Coins* 1 There are also leaden *trial-impressions of the dies. **1877** KNIGHT *Dict. Mech.*, **Trial-jar*, a tall glass vessel used for containing liquids to be tested by the hydrometer. **1892** *U.S. Rep.* (Supreme Court) CXLI. 562 The conclusion of the *trial judge was that the second claim of the reissue was an enlargement of the single claim of the original patent. **1884** *Pacific Reporter* IV. 255 A *trial jury in this territory is a body of 12 men, possessing the requisite qualifications, duly summoned, and sworn to well and truly try the questions of fact submitted to them by the court, and a true verdict render according to the law and the evidence. **1929** R. R. MORTON *What Negro Thinks* 146 His practice is seldom that of a *trial lawyer, but rather as an adjuster of cases and an adviser in civil processes. **1983** 'E. LATHEN' *Green grow Dollars* vi. 48 She..had steered Wisconsin Seedsmen into the arms of the right trial lawyer. **1908** *Westm. Gaz.* 11 June 2/1 They..gave orders for *trial lots [of soft wire-rods]. **1897** *Outing* (U.S.) XXIX. 485/1 The result is a lot of fast *trial-machines, all of one general family. **1905** *Daily Chron.* 1 July 6/4 Both crews are awarded their distinctive medals, and every member may wear the 'Trials' cap—the white flannel cap with the crossed oars. The '*Trials' man is out of the ruck. **1906** E. C. PARSONS *Family* vii. 142 **Trial*-marriage is a variety of time-marriage, it being distinctly agreed that the relationship may be dissolved by either man or woman at any time. **1930** *New Statesman* 27 Dec. 355/2 The Bishops of Miss Dunbar's Church recently gave an episcopal blessing to birth control, one prominent clergyman approving trial marriage. **1977** *Time* 4 Apr. 11/2 For the moment, the Liberals and Labour are only committed to keep their trial marriage going until the end of this parliamentary session in November. **1833** NYREN *Yng. Cricketer's Tutor* 58 The whole country round would flock to see one of their *trial matches. **1825** P. EGAN *Life of Actor* vii. 253 Our hero received a letter, offering him a **trial night* in Hamlet. **1904** W. D. ADAMS *Dict. Drama* I. 187/2 At last in 1817 he was granted, through the influence of friends, a trial-night at Covent Garden. **1884** F. J. BRITTEN *Watch & Clockm.* 273 The Greenwich method of arriving at the *trial number. **1874** RAYMOND *Statist. Mines & Mining* 500 Inasmuch as the samples of ore were not large in quantity, they commenced making small *trial-pans. **1555** BRADFORD *Let.* in Foxe *A. & M.* (1570) 1834/2 You are in the schole-house and *triall parlour of the Lord. **1663** *Inscr. Simon's Petit. Crown*, Thomas Simon most humbly prays your Majesty to compare this his *tryall piece with the Dutch [etc.]. **1830** [E. HAWKINS] *Anglo-French Coinage* 64, I cannot consider this as current money, neither does it exactly come under the description of a trial piece. **1859** *Edin. Rev.* CIX. 377 Cicero attempted to make words, and his trial-pieces were very neat..struck of good metal. **1904** *Westm. Gaz.* 11 July 10/2 Some interesting trial-pieces..executed in true fresco on a suitable ground before beginning to paint on the wall. **1905** D. MACKENZIE *Let.* in *Observer* (1962) 11 Feb. 11/3 The many preliminary *trial-pits sunk in the early years of the excavation. **1966** Trial pit [see *soil survey* s.v. SOIL *sb.*[1] 10]. **1883** *Encycl. Brit.* XVI. 484/1 Pieces cut from *trial plates of standard fineness,..being assayed against the coins under examination. **1906** *Westm. Gaz.* 20 Aug. 3/1 The county [Gloucestersh.] happens to be one which affords a great variety of experiment owing to the variety of its soils... Hence the advent of the *trial plots. **1891** *Cent. Dict.*, *Trial proof. **1900** *Westm. Gaz.* 8 Nov. 1/3 These rare mezzotints are all in trial proof state. **1903** *Daily Chron.* 3 Aug. 3/3 The prints exist in a far less 'restricted' number than he imagines, and are not by any means chiefly trial-proofs. **1847** *Illustr. Lond. News* 10 July 23/2 The first day is to be occupied with the *trial races. **1903** *Trans. Inst. Naval Archit.* XLV. 295 Some twenty *trial runs..were made under various conditions as to speed. **1909** *Chambers's Jrnl.* 25 Sept. 675/1 The first great trial-run of a number of motor-cars. **1949** *Sun* (Baltimore) 22 July 1/2 The House rejected the proposal for a 'trial run' of the Brannan farm program for a period of two years. **1962** *Rep. Comm. Broadcasting 1960* 4 in *Parl. Papers 1961–2* (Cmnd. 1753) IX. 259 Two trial runs of local sound broadcasting were arranged for us. **1974** D. SEAMAN *Bomb that could Lip Read* xviii. 177 The government desperately wants the new [Irish] Assembly to have a peaceful trial run. **1968** *Listener* 4 Oct. 439/2 We are telling our friends that he's not around because we've agreed to a *trial separation. **1978** M. TRIPP *Wife-Smuggler* ii. 20 When I suggested..a trial separation she said..I didn't have the guts to make a clean break. **1884** KNIGHT *Dict. Mech.* Supp., **Trial Sight* (Optical), an oculist's case of trial lenses, etc., for testing sight. *Ibid.* 903/2 A *trial spectacle frame, with double grooves to each eye, graduated to 180°... Used for finding the axis of imperfect vision in astigmatism or cylindrical cornea. **1877** W. R. COOPER *Egypt. Obelisks* xxii. (1878) 126 A *trial stone for every idle Greek or ignorant tourist to cut his initials upon. *c* **1841** ARNOLD in Stanley *Life* (1845) II. x. 300 The first seventy years of the eighteenth century,..the abused *trial time of modern Europe. **1860** PUSEY *Min. Proph.* 79 It was a long trial-time, in which they were taught entire dependance upon God. **1947** *E. African Ann. 1946–7* 67/2 Once *trial trenches had been cut, it became obvious that the site was even more important than we had at first believed. **1980** *Rescue News* Sept. 2/3 In the first small trial trench was found a rim of Saxo-Norman pottery. **1954** M. BERESFORD *Lost Villages* App. III. 416 The position of each house is clearly visible, thus precluding the need to *trial-trench to find structures. **1858** SIMMONDS *Dict. Trade*, **Trial-trip*, an experimental trip. **1902** ELIZ. L. BANKS *Newspaper Girl* 211, I wouldn't let any reporter take the trial trip, anyway. **1905** A. R. WALLACE *Life* II. 182 The house being used for prospecting purposes and *trial-workings.

b. *attrib.* in *pl.* (cf. sense 2 c above), as ***trials bike, rider, riding***, etc.

1969 *Daily Tel.* 25 Oct. 8/8 Quite a few leading trials riders are farmers... Light-weight two-stroke machines are now favoured for trials work. **1976** Trials enthusiast [see sense 2 c above]. **1976** *Southern Even. Echo* (Southampton) 10 Nov. 21/1 The cream of British trials riders left their native Yorkshire and came south to compete in rain and mud in the National Perce Simon and Hoad Trophy Trials. **1976** *Norwich Mercury* 19 Nov. 12/1 Trials riding is the cheapest form of motor cycle sport. **1977** *West Briton* 25 Aug. 10/3 The new trials bike group..have raised half the £180 for their trials machine by a sponsored walk.

†**trial**, *sb.*[2] *Obs. rare.* In 5 **tryall**. [App. an ignorant combination of TRI- + -AL[1].] A group or set of three, a triad. (In the second quot. confusedly used for each one of the three.)

? *a* **1500** *Chester Pl.* i. 7, I am the tryall of the trynitie that neuer shall be twynninge. *Ibid.* 17 These three tryalls in a Trone and true Trynitie Be grounded in my godhead, exalted by my exellence.

'**trial**, *a. Gram.* [f. L. *tri-*, stem of *trēs*, *tria* three + -AL[1], after *dual*.] Applied to a 'number' or inflected form denoting three, in some languages of New Guinea and Polynesia; = TRINAL *a.* 3.

1886 J. INGLIS *In New Hebrides* ix. 99 There are four numbers in the personal pronouns [used by the Aneityumese], the singular, the dual, the trial, and the plural; as *I, we two, we three,* and *we all.* **1911** *Bible in World* July 206/2 The Kiwai language is one of the most difficult in New Guinea... The verb..distinguishes singular, dual, trial (3) and plural number both in the subject and object.

trial ('traɪəl), *v.* [f. TRIAL *sb.*[1]] *trans.* To submit (something, esp. a new product) to a test or trial; to test.

1981 M. H. ASTON in Lewis & Tagg *Computers in Educ.* 385 Several distribution models are already being trialled in the United Kingdom. **1982** *Internat. Conf. Road Traffic Signalling* (IEE Conf. Ser. CCVII.) 123/1 The radar was briefly trialled in two road situations, a T-junction and a straight section of road. **1982** *ICL News* Mar. 2/5 The 2946 [computer] was successfully trialled on the weekend of February 19. **1984** *Proc. Conf. NATO Advisory Group Aerospace Res. & Devel.* CCCXLIV. xiv. 1 Field trials models weighing 17kg..have been..extensively trialled in field conditions.

trialate: see TRI- 1.

trialism ('traɪəlɪz(ə)m). [f. TRIAL *a.* + -ISM, after *dualism*.]

1. The doctrine of the threefold constitution of man, as body, soul, and spirit, or other three separate essences.

1891 in *Cent. Dict.*

2. A union of three states or countries.

1908 *Westm. Gaz.* 16 Jan. 2/1 The substitution of a Trialism, consisting of Austria, Hungary, and Bohemia,..for the present Dualism. **1911** *Q. Rev.* July 260 There has been revived in Austria the idea of 'trialism', that is to say, the amalgamation of all the Servo-Croatian countries of the Monarchy into a unit, which, with the German States and Hungary, would form a kind of federal empire.

trialist ('traɪəlɪst), *sb.*[1] [f. as prec. + -IST.] One who advocates or follows trialism (sense 2); used *spec.* with reference to a proposed German–Magyar–Slav state. Also *attrib.*

1931 J. A. R. MARRIOTT *Europe 1815–1923* 429 On one detail of their programme the 'Trialists', as they began to be called, were not unanimous. **1935** H. A. L. FISHER *Hist. Europe* III. xxviii. 1097 Would it not be possible..to substitute for the dual monarchy, resting on the dominion of the Magyars and the Germans, a trialist state founded on the equal fellowship of Slav, Magyar, and German? **1980** *Times Lit. Suppl.* 4 Jan. 22/2 *The Southern Slav Question* builds up to a plea for a modified 'trialist' state of Austrian, Hungarian and Slav units.

'**trialist**, *sb.*[2] Also **triallist**. [f. TRIAL *sb.*[1] + -IST.]

1. One involved in a judicial trial (TRIAL *sb.* 1).

1967 *Guardian* 17 Nov. 11/1 Letter from trialists' relatives. The 'Guardian' received..a copy of a letter addressed to the Prime Minister by the relatives of the 50 Greeks whose trial begins in Salonika today. **1979** J. DRUMMOND *Patriots* vii. 48 The Treason Trialists were acquitted.

2. a. One who takes part in a preliminary match or contest, with a view to being selected for a major team. Cf. TRIAL *sb.*[1] 6 b.

1960 D. STOREY *This Sporting Life* I. ii. 37, I took this to mean he was watching me, though there were four other trialists in the team. **1961** *Listener* 19 Oct. 628/1 The contestants [*sc.* bridge-players] are all international trialists. **1971** *Daily Tel.* 15 Sept. 12 An Olympic trialist, who was training in the same pool. **1977** *Western Morning News* 1 Sept. 10/7 Richmond include..Dave Whibley, their England triallist full-back.

b. One who takes part in a contest or competition, esp. a motor-cycle trial (TRIAL *sb.*[1] 2 c).

1961 *Times* 5 Oct. 4/5 The American motor cycle trialist. **1971** *Daily Tel.* 18 Oct. 22/8 Griffiths, this season's leading time trialist, covered the [cycle] course in 5hr 54min 14sec. **1980** *Observer* (Colour Suppl.) 12 Oct. 54 (*heading*) Alan Road reports on the bumpy world of the triallist. **1982** *Daily Tel.* 24 Nov. 3 The future of two top Welsh international sheep dog trialists hangs in the balance after an allegation that they tried to influence the selection of a competition judge.

c. One who takes part in clinical tests or trials of new drugs, etc.

1977 *Lancet* 17 Sept. 595/2 The conditions of a trial can be adjusted so that only the most dramatic results emerge with the statisticians' stamp of approval, though trials conducted under such harsh discipline would yield neutral results more often than not and triallists would fade away through frustration. **1983** *Glaxo Group News* Mar. 1/1 The..programme, attended by nearly 800 doctor-delegates (mainly triallists and specialists in infectious diseases) from more than 30 countries, included 83 presentations.

triality (traɪ'ælɪtɪ). *rare.* [f. as TRIALISM, after *duality*, *plurality*.]

†**1.** The holding of three benefices at once. *Obs.*

a **1529** SKELTON *Col. Cloute* 564 Of tryalytes, And of tot quottes, They commune lyke sottes. **1536** *Act 28 Hen. VIII*, c. 16 §4 Pluralities, unions, trialities, appropriacions..And other bulles, breves, and faculties. **1587** HARRISON *England* II. ii. (1877) I. 63 So plentifullie gat he by his perquisits, as elections, procurations, appeales, preuentions, pluralities, tot quots, trialities [etc.]. **1637** BASTWICK *Litany* II. 9 The Pope selleth nonresidences, pluralityes, trialityes, totquots, the Prelats doe the same.

2. The condition or quality of being threefold.

1872 DORAN *Mem. Gt. Towns* xiii. (1878) 294 Dr. Wigan ..not only wrote on the Duality of the Mind, but on the Triality (if we may coin a word), the threefold excellence, of the Brighton atmosphere.

triallelic: see TRI- 1 a.

trialogue ('traɪəlɒg). [Erroneous formation on supposed analogy of *dialogue*, the first syllable of this being mistaken for the prefix DI-[2] = two. Cf. med.L. *trialogus* (Wyclif).] A dialogue or colloquy between three persons.

1532 MORE *Confut. Tindale* Wks. 431/2 As though it wer a dyalogue, or rather a tryalogue betwene himself, the messenger and me. **1691** WOOD *Ath. Oxon.* I. 21 Trialogue between Tho. Bilney, Hugh Latimer, and W. Repps. **1721** D'URFEY *Two Queens Brentford* v. i, This Epilogue..is a Trialogue, and to be perform'd between Sol, Rain, and Boreas. **1900** G. W. E. RUSSELL *Conf. Bks. & Men* 150 A trialogue, called 'A contention between a wife, a widow, and a maid'.

triamcinolone (traɪəm'sɪnələʊn). *Pharm.* [f. *triamcin-* (etym. unkn.) + PREDNIS(OLONE.] A synthetic glucocorticoid which resembles prednisolone in its effects but is a more potent anti-inflammatory agent; 9α-fluoro-16α-hydroxyprednisolone, $C_{21}H_{27}O_6F$.

1957 *Jrnl. Amer. Med. Assoc.* 7 Dec. 1821/1 The purpose of this clinical study was to evaluate the anti-inflammatory and antipruritic properties of a new steroid compound, Aristocort diacetate (also known as triamcinolone diacetate). **1961** *Lancet* 12 Aug. 347/2 Some children with nephrosis do not respond to high doses of prednisolone, but they do respond to 'equivalent' doses of triamcinolone. **1979** *Nature* 13 Dec. 736/2 The gluco-corticoids dexamethasone, triamcinolone,..stimulated interferon production more than 20-fold.

triamide ('traɪəmaɪd). *Chem.* [f. TRI- 5 a + AMIDE.] A compound in which the three acid hydroxyls (OH) of a tribasic acid are replaced by three amidogen groups (NH_2): the hydrogen of the amidogen groups may be replaced by metals or by one or more monovalent radicals; e.g. citramide, $C_3H_4(OH)(CO.NH_2)_3$, the triamide of citric acid, $C_3H_4(OH)(CO.OH)_3$; cyanuramide or melamine, $C_3N_3(NH_2)_3$, the triamide of cyanuric acid, $C_3N_3(OH)_3$. For the earlier view of the structure of triamides, see quot. 1863–72.

1862 MILLER *Elem. Chem.* (ed. 2) III. 427 As an instance of a *secondary triamide*, phenylcitramide may be given. **1863–72** WATTS *Dict. Chem.* I. 173 *Primary Triamides.*—They represent 3 molecules of ammonia, in which 3 atoms of hydrogen are replaced by a triatomic acid-radicle:—Phosphamide.. $N^3.(PO)'''.H_6$. **1866** ODLING *Anim. Chem.* 19 $C_3N_3(H_2N)_3$ Cyanuric triamide.

triamine ('traɪəmaɪn). *Chem.* [f. TRI- 5a + AMINE.] A carbon compound containing three amidogen or amino-groups (NH_2), but excluding the amides, in which the amidogen may be viewed as replacing acid hydroxyl groups; the hydrogen of the amidogen groups may be replaced by one or more monovalent radicals: see also quot. 1868.

1868 FOWNES *Elem. Chem.* (ed. 10) 882 Triamines. These are bases derived from..three molecules of ammonia.. N_3H_9, by substitution of..trivalent alcohol-radicals for a part or the whole of the hydrogen. A portion of the hydrogen may at the same time be replaced by univalent alcohol-radicals. **1887** TIDY *Mod. Chem.* (ed. 2) 758 Aniline red is a salt of base *rosaniline*, $C_{20}H_{19}N_3$. This..is a triamine.

trian ('traɪən), *a. Her.* [app. f. L. *trēs*, *tria* three + -AN.] In *trian aspect*: see quot.: cf. THREE-QUARTERED b.

c **1828** BERRY *Encycl. Her.* I. Gloss., *Trian-aspect*, showing three-fourth parts of the body, as an eagle, &c. in a trian-aspect: it is what painters term three-quartered.

‖**Triandria** (traɪ'ændrɪə). *Bot.* [mod.L. (Linnæus 1735), f. mod.L. *triandr-us*, f. Gr. τρεῖς three + ἀνήρ, ἀνδρ- man, male, taken as = stamen: see -ANDROUS.] The third class in the Linnæan Sexual System, comprising plants having hermaphrodite flowers with three stamens not cohering; also an order in some classes, comprising plants with three stamens. So **tri'ander** (*rare*), a triandrous plant; **tri'andrian, tri'andrious**, and (usually) **tri'androus** *adjs.*, having three stamens; belonging to the class (or order) *Triandria*.

1828 WEBSTER, **Triander*. **1748** LINNÆUS *Hortus Upsaliensis* Classis iii. 13 *Triandria. **1760** J. LEE *Introd. Bot.* II. xxiii. (1788) 139 Of the twentieth Class, *Gynandria* ..Order II, *Triandria*, comprehending such Plants as have three Stamina. **1828** WEBSTER, **Triandrian*. **1786** ABERCROMBIE *Gard. Assist.*, *Arrangem.* 35 Willow tree.. Common white leaved... *Triandrious, white barked. **1830** LINDLEY *Nat. Syst. Bot.* 261 [Irideæ] differ from Amaryllideæ..in being *triandrous. **1870** HOOKER *Stud. Flora* 430 Hierochloe... Holy Grass..upper flower 2-sexual 2-androus; 2 lower male, 3-androus.

triangle ('traɪæŋg(ə)l, traɪ'æŋg(ə)l), *sb.* Also 5 tri-, tryangyl, 5-7 tryangle, 6 triangil, tryanghel, 6-7 triangill; 5-6 treangle, 6 treeangle, treangell. [a. F. *triangle* (13th c. in Godef. *Compl.*), or ad. its source, L. *triangulum*, sb. neut. from *triangulus* adj. three-cornered, f. *tri-*, TRI- + *angulus* ANGLE.]

1. *Geom.*, etc. A figure (usually, a plane rectilineal figure) having three angles and three sides.

In *mod. Geom.* a triangle is regarded as a system of three points not collinear, together with the three straight lines joining them; or as a system of three straight lines each intersecting the two others at different points.

circular triangle, a plane triangle formed by three intersecting circular arcs. ***spherical triangle***, a triangle formed by three arcs upon the surface of a sphere: see SPHERICAL. ***triangle of forces***, the theorem in statics that if three forces in one plane, acting at one point, be in equilibrium, three straight lines in that plane parallel to their directions will form a triangle whose sides are proportional to their magnitudes.

1398 TREVISA *Barth. De P.R.* XVII. cviii. (Tollem. MS.), Some [nuts] ben distinguid in þe cop as it were with þe schap of a triangle [orig. *per formam trianguli*]. *c* **1400** *Lanfranc's Cirurg.* 258 þe nose is maad of .ij. boones in þe maner of a triangle in þis manner. ΔΔ. **1551** RECORDE *Pathw. Knowl.* I. Defin., A triangle is nothinge els to say, but a figure of three corners. **1560** DAUS tr. *Sleidane's Comm.* 451 Betwyxt Caleis, Arde and Grauelyn, Townes..set as it were a treangle. **1646** SIR T. BROWNE *Pseud. Ep.* 25 In every triangle, two sides which soever be taken are greater then the side remaining. **1781** GIBBON *Decl. & F.* xvii. II. 3 The figure of the imperial city [Constantinople] may be represented under that of an unequal triangle. **1885** LEUDESDORF *Cremona's Proj. Geom.* 145 A series of theorems ..relating to the inscribed pentagon, quadrangle, and triangle..a series of correlative theorems relating to the circumscribed pentagon, quadrilateral, and triangle.

b. A figure of this form used symbolically (e.g. an equilateral triangle as a symbol of the Trinity), or in magic or necromancy. In *Her.* a figure of this form as a bearing; ***in triangle***, said of three or more bearings arranged in the form of a triangle.

1584 R. SCOT *Discov. Witchcr.* XV. ii. (1886) 322 He is a lier, except he be brought into a triangle, and there he speaketh divinelie. **1766** PORNY *Heraldry* (1787) 175 Azure, three Trouts fretty in Triangle Argent. **1810** SOUTHEY *Kehama* XIX. viii, The sacred Triangle..Holding the Emblem which no tongue may tell. *c* **1828** BERRY *Encycl. Her.* I. Gloss., *Triangle*, this sometimes occurs as a bearing in coat-armour. See Cross of Triangles, or twelve triangles in cross. **1864** BOUTELL *Her. Hist. & Pop.* xix. §5. (ed. 3) 311 A nail in every point thereof, in triangle. **1894** *Parker's Gloss. Her.* s.v., Charges may be described as *fretted in triangle*, e.g. in the arms of Troutbeck (under *Salmon*)... The insignia of the Isle of Man are sometimes blazoned as *flexed in triangle*.

c. *fig.* A group or set of three, a triad. Esp. a love-relationship in which one member of a married couple is involved with a third party; freq. as ***eternal triangle***.

1621 T. WILLIAMSON tr. *Goulart's Wise Vieillard* 129 In this sacred triangle is included the renouncing of our selues. **1659** WHITING (*title*) Old Jacob's Altar, newly repaired; or, the Saints Triangle of Dangers, Deliverances, and Duties. **1907** *Daily Chron.* 5 Dec. 3/4 Mrs. Dudeney's novel..deals with the eternal triangle, which, in this case, consists of two men and one woman. **1913** KIPLING *Diversity of Creatures* (1917) 358 The couples had rearranged themselves or were re-crystallizing in fresh triangles. **1919** G. B. SHAW in F. Harris *Contemp. Portraits* 2nd Ser. 332 For the modern drama, with its eternal triangle and so forth, he claims nothing, but that it proves adultery to be the dullest of subjects. **1938** H. G. WELLS *Apropos of Dolores* iv. 162 He was much more substantial than in the days of our romantic triangle. **1955** H. KURNITZ *Invasion of Privacy* (1956) vi. 48 The details of the story, the way the husband and wife first met..the other woman in the triangle. **1963** A. HERON *Towards Quaker View of Sex* iv. 39 Most examples of the 'eternal triangle' are produced by boredom and primitive misconduct. **1979** J. PHILIPS *Why Murder?* (1980) II. ii. 90 A husband, a wife, a lover—the classic triangle.

d. ***North Atlantic Triangle***: a name given to the tripartite alliance between Great Britain, Canada, and the United States.

1945 J. B. BREBNER (*title*) North Atlantic Triangle. **1957** H. HEATON in L. B. Pearson *Where do we go from Here?* 2 Canada was one of the three points in 'the North Atlantic Triangle'—the others were Great Britain and the United States. **1978** J. HUTCHESON *Dominance & Dependency* i. 12 The nationalistic position..has been complicated by Canada's location in the North Atlantic Triangle.

2. Something having the form of a triangle; any three-cornered body, object, or space.

a **1618** SYLVESTER *Mem. Mortalitie* II. lx, Th' Earth cannot fill thy heart's unequall Angles, Thy heart's a Triangle, the earth's a Round. **1788** GIBBON *Decl. & F.* l. (1846) V. 2 The Arabian peninsula may be conceived as a triangle of spacious but irregular dimensions. **1791** NEWTE *Tour Eng. & Scot.* 120 The present fort, which is a triangle, has two bastions. **1843** CARLYLE *Past & Pr.* II. i, In what wig and black triangle dost thou walk abroad? **1847** MRS. A. KERR tr. *Ranke's Hist. Servia* i. 13 The Servians..in the first half of the 14th century..formed the strongest power of the Illyrian triangle. **1895** R. W. CHAMBERS *King in Yellow, Demoiselle D'Ys* i, A long wavering triangle of water-fowl drifted southward over our heads.

(*b*) ***the Bermuda*** or ***Devil's Triangle***: a name given to an area of sea between Bermuda and Florida credited with a high number of unexplained disappearances of boats and aircraft; hence used allusively; ***the golden triangle***, an area at the meeting-point of Burma, Laos, and Thailand, where much opium is grown.

1964 V. GADDIS in *Argosy* Feb. 28 (*heading*) The deadly Bermuda triangle. *Ibid.* 116/2 Draw a line from Florida to Bermuda, another from Bermuda to Puerto Rico, and a third back to Florida through the Bahamas. Within this area, known as the 'Bermuda Triangle', most of the vanishments have occurred. **1973** *Bangkok Post* 22 Apr. 1 Both the opium and the morphine base almost certainly originated in the so-called 'golden triangle' where the opium poppy grows in abundance. **1975** *Collier's Encycl. Year Bk.* *1976* 161 The Atlantic region known as the Bermuda, or Devil's, Triangle. **1978** *Times* 23 Jan. 2/6 The increasing importance of South-East Asia's 'golden triangle' as a source of narcotics. **1979** A. PRICE *Tomorrow's Ghost* vi. 99 [She] had stepped out for a breath of fresh air..and she hadn't been seen again... She had turned a quiet piece of English countryside into a Bermuda Triangle. **1983** *Times* 12 Feb. 4/8 Drugs from the Golden Triangle were in heavy demand in Europe before 1979.

spec. * *natural objects.*

b. *Palmistry.* A triangular figure made by three of the lines of the hand: see quot. 1653.

c **1460** METHAM *Wks.* (E.E.T.S.) 86 A tryangyl that ys off one length, evyn on alle partys..betokynnyth bodyly strengh and bold off herte. *Ibid.*, The fyrste lyne ys the fyrst parte off the tryangyl, and yt gothe aboute the hylle of the thombe. **1653** R. SANDERS *Physiogn.* 58 This Triangle is made in the hand by three Lines, that of Life, the middle natural Line, and that of the Head.

c. *Astron.* The constellation *Triangulum*, north of *Aries*, characterized by three stars in the positions of the angular points of an isosceles triangle.

Also, *Triangulum minus*, the Lesser Triangle, a constellation immediately south of this, introduced by Hevelius in 1690, but now disused; *Triangulum australe*, the Southern Triangle, a modern constellation near the South Pole.

1551 RECORDE *Cast. Knowl.* (1556) 265 By hir [Andromeda's] lefte foot is ther a small constellation.. commonly called the Triangle. **1868** LOCKYER *Guillemin's Heavens* (ed. 3) 334 The Altar and the Southern Triangle, which lie along the Milky Way in looking towards the pole.

d. *Anat.* Applied, with defining words, to the triangular areas bounded by certain muscles: as ***triangles of the neck, anterior*** (subdivided into the ***submaxillary triangle*** and the ***superior*** and ***inferior carotid triangles***) and ***posterior*** (subdivided into the ***occipital*** and ***subclavian triangles***); ***triangle of Petit***, above the crest of the ilium; ***Scarpa's tr.***, in the upper part of the thigh.

1846 BRITTAN tr. *Malgaigne's Man. Oper. Surg.* 147 The inferior triangle of the popliteal space is bounded on each side by the heads of the gastrocnemius. **1876** *Clin. Soc. Trans.* IX. 41, I removed all the enlarged glands in front of the sterno-mastoid, and thus cleared the anterior triangle of the neck. **1897** *Allbutt's Syst. Med.* IV. 418 [An abscess] may open superficially in the loin through the triangle of Petit.

e. *Entom.* A triangular marking or space on an insect's wing.

1832 [see 4]. **1891** *Cent. Dict.*, *Triangle*... In *entom.* a large three-sided cell found in the wings of many dragonflies.. often called the *discoidal* triangle, to distinguish it from the *internal* triangle, which adjoins it on the inner side, and the *anal* triangle, which lies close to the anal border of the wing.

f. A species of box-fish of triangular form, as *Ostracion trigonum*.

** *artificial objects.*

g. A small ornament or piece of jewellery of a triangular form.

1528 *Will of W. Mores* (Somerset Ho.), A triangill of siluer and gilte. **1529** *Will of Leigh* (ibid.), My corsse gurdell wt the Treeangle of flowres of silver and golde. **1531** *Rec. St. Mary at Hill* 48 A demysent [girdle] with..a pendantte a treangell of selver and gelt. **1632** J. HAYWARD tr. *Biondi's Eromena* 120 This Iewell..a triangle of three rich diamonds, each angle..enriched with a great pearle.

†**h.** *Eccl.* A stand or frame on which copes were hung up. *Obs.*

1532 in *Archæol. Cant.* (1872) VIII. 124 Item a treangle for copys, a presse [*Editor's Note*, a crane or stand for hanging copes]. **1538** in *Archæologia* XLIII. 226, ij chestes and the tryangle for the same ornaments to be hengyd. **1849** ROCK *Ch. of Fathers* II. vi. 43 [A doubtful statement].

†**i.** (More fully ***triangle virginal***), an early kind of keyboard stringed instrument. *Obs.*

[**1661** PEPYS *Diary* 14 June, I sent to my house by my Lord's order his shipp and triangle virginall.] **1662-3** *Ibid.* 18 Mar., This day my tryangle which was put in tune yesterday, did please me very well.

j. A musical instrument of percussion, consisting of a steel rod bent into a triangular form, but open at one corner; it is struck with a small straight steel rod. Also *transf.* = TRIANGLER.

1801 in BUSBY *Dict. Mus.* **1811** LADY GRANVILLE *Lett.* (1894) I. 21 We play upon the..guitar, triangle, and castagnettes. **1878** F. HUEFFER in Grove *Dict. Mus.* I. 28/1 He is said to have accepted the appointment of supernumerary triangle at the Gymnase. **1913** *Times* 14 May 8/5 The only percussion (even the usual drums are excluded) consists of triangle and cymbals.

k. Name for a kind of large tripod composed of three poles or spars joined at the top, bearing a pulley for hoisting heavy weights, or for weighing: see also quot. 1867.

1699 EVELYN *Kal. Hort.* (ed. 9) 63 If the Tree be too ponderous to be lifted perpendicular by the Hand alone, by applying a Triangle and Pully..draw out the Tree. **1707** MORTIMER *Husb.* (1721) I. 187 Set up three Poles (like unto a Triangle wherewith they usually weigh heavy Ware) spreading at the Bottom. **1867** SMYTH *Sailor's Word-bk.*, *Triangle*,..a machine formed by spars for lifting weights, water-casks, &c. Also, a stage hung round a mast, to scrape, paint, or grease it. **1873** in *5th Rep. Dep. Kpr. Irel.* 26 The Records were lowered through the aperture in the centre of the floor by means of a rope, supported by a triangle raised over the opening.

l. *Mil.* (Usually *pl.*) A tripod, orig. formed of three halberds stuck in the ground and joined at the top, to which soldiers were formerly bound to be flogged; a structure resembling this.

[**1796** GROSE *Dict. Vulg. T.* s.v. *Halbert*, Soldiers of the infantry, when flogged, being commonly tied to three halberts, set up in a triangle, with a fourth fastened across them.] **1847** in WEBSTER. **1853** STOCQUELER *Milit. Encycl.*, *Triangles*, a wooden instrument consisting of three poles so fastened at top that they may spread at bottom in a triangular form... An iron bar, breast high, goes across one side of the triangle. The triangles were used in some regiments for..inflicting military punishments. **1871** G. LAWRENCE *Anteros* i. (1872) 11 He was unsparing both of his tongue and of the lash—the triangles were an honoured institution in those days. **1897** P. WARUNG *Tales Old Regime* 29 Already, at Molong [Australia], there is one military-post and a triangles, and at Wellington Valley there is another military-post and another triangles.

m. *Pottery.* A triangular piece of baked ware, with points projecting from the angles, placed between pieces of biscuit ware to prevent their adhering to each other when baking.

1877 in KNIGHT *Dict. Mech.*

n. *Angling.* A set of three hooks fastened together so that their barbs are at the angular points of a triangle.

1867 F. FRANCIS *Angling* iv. (1880) 116, I had used a single flight of small brazed triangles. **1904** GALLICHAN *Fishing Spain* 145 The flying triangles are to blame. It is not often that one loses a fish hooked on the tail triangle.

o. A drawing-instrument in the form of a right-angled triangle of wood, vulcanite, etc.; a set square.

1877 KNIGHT *Dict. Mech.*, *Triangle*... A three-cornered straight-edge,..for drawing parallel, perpendicular, or diagonal lines. It has one right angle, the two others being each of 45°, or one of 30° and the other of 60°.

p. A triangular warning sign placed on the road to mark the presence of a broken-down vehicle or vehicles.

1969 B. WEIL *Dossier IX* ii. 8 There's your red break-down triangle... They're obligatory in France. **1971** H. PACY *Road Accidents* i. 33 Utilize the special warning triangles larger trucks carry for this purpose. **1977** 'J. FRASER' *Hearts Ease* ii. 12 Superintendent Bill Aveyard braked his car when he saw the flashing torches and warning triangles at the side of the road.

3. Collectors' name for certain moths. See also 4.

1832 RENNIE *Conspect. Butterfl. & Moths* 55 The Triangle (*Gr*[*aphiphora*] *Triangulum*, Ochsenheimer) appears the end of July. *Ibid.* 164 The Triangle (*P*[*seudotamia*] *trigonana*, Stephens). Near London.

4. *Comb.*, as (sense 1 c) ***triangle drama***; (sense 2 j) ***triangle-player***; ***triangle-marked*** adj.; **triangle inequality** *Math.*, the statement that the modulus of the sum of two quantities is less than or equal to the sum of their moduli; (so called from the analogy with the distances between the vertices of a triangle); **triangle moth**, *Limacodes asellus*; **triangle-ways** *adv.* (*rare*) = TRIANGLEWISE.

1931 E. A. ROBERTSON *Four Frightened People* i. 22 Just another triangle drama. **1961** *Times* 13 May 5/2 In an all too successful attempt to turn Shakespeare's tragedy into a conventional triangle-drama, Rossini's librettist, Berio, built up Rodrigo. **1941** BIRKHOFF & MACLANE *Survey Mod. Algebra* vii. 183 In any Euclidian vector space, length has the following properties:..$|\xi + \eta| \leq |\xi| + |\eta|$ (the triangle inequality). **1972** M. KLINE *Math. Thought* xlvi. 1083 Schwarz's inequality and the triangle inequality are proved for the norm. **1832** RENNIE *Conspect. Butterfl. & Moths* 228 The Triangle-marked Purple (*G[racillaria] purpurea*, Haworth). Wings..purple, with a three-cornered central halfband... The Triangle-marked Red (*G. stigmatella*, Stephens)... The Triangle Marked Buff (*G. ochracea*, Haworth). **1906** J. JOYCE *Let.* 4 Oct. (1966) II. 170 AE ought now to write some..dreamy thing about a..Triangle-player. **1971** D. E. WESTLAKE *I gave at Office* 24 Arnold dropped an occasional word in, like the triangle player at the Philharmonic. **1689** *Lond. Gaz.* No. 2485/4, 16 silver Trencher-Plates;..marked with a Cypher triangle-ways.

†**triangle**, *a.* *Obs.* [ad. L. *triangulus*, f. TRI- + *angulus* corner.] Having three angles; three-cornered, triangular. Also quasi-*adv.* In the form of a triangle, triangularly.

1474 CAXTON *Chesse* 136 In one of the corners was made a tour treangle as a shelde. **1525** tr. *Jerome of Brunswick's Surg.* B ij/1 The bony part [of the nose] hath .ij. tryangle bonis. *a* **1548** HALL *Chron., Edw. IV*, 201 b, Three hilles, not in equal distaunce,..but liyng in maner although not fully triangle. **1660** BLOOME *Archit.* Aj, *Gutta*, are drops sometime round, sometime in Triangle fashion. **1661** [see TRIANGLE *sb.* 2 i]. **1803** SHAW *Gen. Zool.* IV. II. 444 Triangle Sparus [a fish]. Mentioned by Cepede from Commerson: native of the Indian seas.

Comb. **1655** MRQ. WORCESTER *Cent. Inv.* §69 A little triangle scrued Key. *Ibid.* §71 A Key perfectly square,..no heavier then the triangle-scrued Key.

triangle, *v.* *rare.* [f. TRIANGLE *sb.*]

†**1.** *intr.* ? To lie or extend in the form of a triangle. *Obs.*

1595 *Aberdeen Regr.* (1848) II. 129 The said wmquhill Mr Androis yard dyk ascendis south eist..triangling throw an[d] athort the hedis of the yardis of the said vmquhill Badie.

2. *trans.* To flog at the triangles (*sb.* 2 l).

1879 L. WINGFIELD *Lords of Strogue* III. iv. 110 His henchman had been well triangled..to extort evidence against his master.

triangled ('traɪæŋg(ə)ld, traɪ'æŋg(ə)ld), *a.* Forms: see TRIANGLE *sb.*; also 5 **triangulit**, 6–7 **-uled**. [f. as prec. + -ED; cf. L. *triangulāt-us*.]

†**1.** Three-cornered, triangular. *Obs.*

1486 *Bk. St. Albans, Her.* e v, Euery body triangulit is moore of lengthe then of brede and naamly conyt. *a* **1505** in Kingsford *Chron. Lond.* (1905) 250 A Cupbourde of 6 stages height, beyng Tryangled. **1570** BILLINGSLEY *Euclid* XI. def. x. 314 If the base of a Pyramis be a triangle, then is it called a triangled Pyramis. **1613** ZOUCH *Dove* 24 Triangl'd Sicily. **1688** R. HOLME *Armoury* III. 293/2 There are Round, Square, Triangled,..many cornered,..Pies.

†**b.** *Arith.* = TRIANGULAR 2 b. *Obs. rare*$^{-1}$.

1603 HOLLAND *Plutarch's Mor.* 796 It [the number of nine] standeth of two triangled numbers, to wit, a senarie and a ternarie.

2. Arranged in a triangle; situated at the angular points of a triangle. ? *Obs.*

1610 GUILLIM *Heraldry* III. xxiii. (1611) 167 Fishes are borne..Imbowed, extended, endorsed..fretted and triangled. **1632** LITHGOW *Trav.* IV. 135 In one of these triangled points..standeth the Pallace of the Great Turke.

3. *Her.* Divided into triangles by crossing lines.

c **1828** BERRY *Encycl. Her.* I. Gloss., *Triangled* and *Trianglée*, formed into triangles, as indentings point in point.

triangler ('traɪæŋglə(r)). [f. as prec. + -ER[1].] A performer on the triangle in a musical band.

1840 *New Monthly Mag.* LX. 79 Mr. Gamut not knowing where to find another professional triangler. *a* **1868** M. J. HIGGINS *Ess.* (1875) 251 His grandson, who had lately been elevated to the post of triangler in the band of the Duke of York's school.

† **'triangle,wise**, *adv.* *Obs.* [f. TRIANGLE *sb.* or *a.* + -WISE.] In the manner or form of a triangle; triangularly.

1523 FITZHERB. *Husb.* §4 Somme plowes haue a bende of yron tryanglewise, sette there as the plough eare shulde be. **1597** A. M. tr. *Guillemeau's Fr. Chirurg.* 18 b/1 When as we cutte the skinne, we must doe it triangle wyse. **1670** NARBOROUGH *Jrnl.* in *Acc. Sev. Late Voy.* I. (1694) 62 They lie Triangle-wise one of another.

† **tri'anglify**, *v.* *Obs. nonce-wd.* [f. as prec. + -[I]FY.] *trans.* To make into or arrange in a triangle or triangles.

1589 FLEMING *Virg. Georg.* III. 49 Vnder Septentrio (or Charles waine, seuen stars trianglifide).

App. an erroneous rendering of *septem subjecta trioni* (Verg. *Georg.* iii. 381), *trioni* being dat. of *trio* plough-ox: see SEPTENTRION.

triangulable (traɪ'æŋgjʊləb(ə)l), *a.* *Math.* [f. TRIANGUL(ATE *v.* + -ABLE.] Of a topological space: capable of undergoing triangulation (sense 2 b).

1940 *Proc. Nat. Acad. Sci.* XXVI. 359 *Triangulable manifold*, a topological manifold which can be subdivided into the cells of a complex. **1975** I. STEWART *Concepts Mod. Math.* xii. 184 We know that *S* is triangulable, so there exists a map on *S* (with triangular faces).

triangular (traɪ'æŋgjʊlə(r)), *a.* (*sb.*) Also 6–7 -er, -are, (7 triangler). [ad. late L. *triangulār-is*: see TRIANGLE and -AR[1]. Cf. OF. *triang(u)lier* (13th c. in Godef.).]

1. a. Having, or arranged in, the form of a triangle; contained by three sides and angles; three-cornered, three-sided.

1541 R. COPLAND *Guydon's Quest. Chirurg.* E iv, The bony substaunce [of the nose] hath two trianguler bones wherwith the brydge is reysed vp. **1590** SPENSER *F.Q.* II. ix. 22 The frame thereof seemd partly circulare, And part triangulare. **1644** EVELYN *Diary* 3 Feb., A triangular brick building. **1776** WITHERING *Brit. Plants* (1796) II. 375 *Populus*... Leaves nearly triangular, toothed and angular. **1825** SCOTT *Talism.* i, His triangular shield suspended round his neck.

b. Situated at the angular points of a triangle. (In quots. quasi-*adv.*) ? *Obs.*

1622 DRAYTON *Poly-olb.* xxii. 1152 Three..hils that stand Triangler. **1707** MORTIMER *Husb.* (1721) II. 74, 3 or 4 quarter Stakes set triangular or quadrangular.

c. Having three edges, as a prism or pyramid; three-edged, trihedral, triquetrous.

1644 DIGBY *Nat. Bodies* xxix. §1. 257 Those..cunning in Optikes..by refractions..make all sortes of colours out of pure light: as we see..in..triangular glasses, or prismes. **1665** SIR T. HERBERT *Trav.* (1677) 384 Other strange Fish we had..some were globous, others triangular. **1727–41** CHAMBERS *Cycl.* s.v. *Pyramid*, The pyramid is said to be triangular, quadrangular, &c. as the base is triangular, quadrangular, &c. **1807** HUTTON *Course Math.* II. 262 To find the Number of Balls in a Triangular Pile. **1852** MRS. STOWE *Uncle Tom's C.* vi, The small, sharp, triangular beech-nuts lay scattered thickly on the ground. **1873** E. SPON *Workshop Receipts* Ser. I. 330/2 Triangular glovers' needles for sewing up skins.

d. Contained by triangles, as a solid figure; of which the faces are triangles. *rare.*

1805–17 R. JAMESON *Char. Min.* (ed. 3) 144 Triangular Dodecahedron..consists of two six-sided pyramids, joined base to base.

2. a. Pertaining or relating to a triangle: as ***triangular compasses***, a kind of compasses with three legs, used for taking off triangles; ***triangular co-ordinates*** (*Geom.*), a kind of trilinear co-ordinates. ***triangular quadrant***: see quot. 1706.

1701 MOXON *Math. Instr.* 21 Triangular Compasses, containing 3 Legs or Feet, to take off at once any Triangle used on Maps, Globes, etc. **1706** PHILLIPS (ed. Kersey), *Triangular Quadrant*, is a Sector with a loose Piece to make it an Equilateral Triangle; having the Calendar graduated on it, with the Sun's Place, Declination, &c. It is an Instrument of great Use in the Arts of Dialling, Navigation, and Surveying. **1807** T. YOUNG *Lect. Nat. Philos.*, etc. I. x. 102 Triangular compasses are sometimes used for laying down a triangle equal to a given triangle.

b. Arith. ***triangular numbers*** (also *ellipt.* as sb. pl. ***triangulars***), the first series of POLYGONAL numbers (1, 3, 6, 10, 15, 21, etc.), obtained by continued summation of the natural numbers 1, 2, 3, 4, 5, 6, etc.: see quot. 1837.

1706 W. JONES *Syn. Palmar. Matheseos* 165 In a Rank of Triangulars their Sums are called Triangulars or Figurates of the 3d Order. **1796** HUTTON *Math. Dict.* I. 468/2 The triangular numbers 1, 3, 6, 10, 15, &c. **1806** —— *Course Math.* (1810) I. 214 The sides or faces in either the triangular or square piles, are called arithmetical triangles; and the numbers..in these, are called triangular numbers. **1837** BABBAGE *Bridgew. Treat.* 37 They are called triangular numbers because a number of points corresponding to any term can always be placed in the form of a triangle.

3. *fig.* Relating to or taking place between three persons or parties, three-sided; also, constituting a triad or set of three, threefold, triple; *spec.* with reference to the 'eternal triangle' (see TRIANGLE *sb.* 1 c).

1812 JEFFERSON *Writ.* (1830) IV. 175 The triangular war must be an idea of the Anglomen and malcontents. **1816** T. L. PEACOCK *Headlong Hall* xv, Avarice, luxury, and disease constitute the triangular harmony of the life of man. **1871** W. WHITE *Jrnls.* (1898) 244 We had an interesting triangular talk. **1880** HARDY *Fellow-Townsmen* in *New Q. Mag.* Apr. 357 The triangular situation—himself—his wife—Lucy Savile—was the one clear thing. **1908** *Times* 9 July 15/5 [The Australians] were unable to take part in the suggested triangular contest in this country next year. *a* **1914** *Mod.* In these elections there will be several triangular contests. **1914** W. L. GEORGE *Dramatic Actualities* 39 The difficulties of matrimony, triangular or other, financial or monetary entanglements. **1968** S. HYNES *Edwardian Turn of Mind* vi. 181 The hero [is] involved in a triangular situation that Shaw took from his own amatory experience. **1976** *Southern Even. Echo* (Southampton) 13 Nov. 13/7 The Mid-Hants (Southampton) girls' netball teams had a successful time in a triangular tournament against Derbyshire and Berkshire at Reading. **1977** *Gay News* 24 Mar. 24/4 Husband, wife and female lodger involved in a triangular relationship.

4. *Comb.*: **a.** parasynthetic, as ***triangular-bodied, -headed, -leaved, -pointed, -spotted***; also ***triangular-wise*** adv. **b.** *Bot.* in combination with other adjs. of form, as ***triangular-cordate, -crenate, -dentate, -hastate, -ovate, -rhomboid, -subulate***. **c. triangular trade**, a multilateral system of trading in which a country pays for its imports from one country by its exports to another; *spec.* (Hist.) in the slave trade (see quots.).

1707 MORTIMER *Husb.* (1721) I. 189 Placing another Row at the Ends where the forked Sticks meet Triangular-wise. **1731** MILLER *Gard. Dict.* s.v. *Aloe*, The upright triangular-leav'd viscous Aloe. **1768** PARSONS in *Phil. Trans.* LVIII. 194 The triangular-headed Cameleons. **1804** SHAW *Gen. Zool.* V. 420 Triangular-bodied, unarmed Trunk-Fish. **1823–5** SIR J. E. SMITH *Eng. Flora* (1828) II. 9 Mercury Goose-foot. Leaves triangular-arrow-shaped, entire. **1870** HOOKER *Stud. Flora* 264 Scrophularia nodosa..leaves ovate or triangular-cordate. **1887** W. PHILLIPS *Brit. Discomycetes* 99 Margin triangular-dentate. **1934** C. M. MACINNES *England & Slavery* iii. 39 After the Restoration a great triangular trade developed between England, the West Coast of Africa and the West Indies or the continental colonies. **1948** T. S. ASHTON *Industrial Revolution 1760–1830* ii. 47 Cloth, firearms, hardware, and trinkets were sent to Africa and exchanged for slaves, who were shipped to the West Indies to pay for the luxuries and raw material which constituted the final cargo in this disreputable, triangular trade. **1971** C. & D. PLIMMER *Damn'd Master* ii. 26 With the profits from the sale of the slaves in the West Indies they bought sugar..which, back in Europe, they sold for a second profit with which in turn they bought more goods... This became known as the triangular trade.

triangularity (traɪæŋgju:'lærɪtɪ). [f. as prec. + -ITY; cf. med.L. *triangulāritās* (Duns Scotus, *a* 1308: prob. older).] The quality of being triangular; triangular form.

a **1688** CUDWORTH *Immut. Mor.* (1731) 14 Things are White by Whiteness, and Black by Blackness, Triangular by Triangularity, and Round by Rotundity. *a* **1751** BOLINGBROKE *Ess., Hum. Knowl.* v. Wks. 1754 III. 436 We say, for instance, not only that certain figures are triangular, but we discourse of triangularity. **1788** T. TAYLOR *Proclus' Comm.* I. 48 Its triangularity would be essential, supposing every species of triangles but the isosceles extinct. **1805** R. P. KNIGHT *On Taste* I. iii. (ed. 2) 38 It partook..of the qualities of the immutable idea of triangularity.

tri'angularly, *adv.* [f. as prec. + -LY[2].] **a.** In a triangular way; in the form or manner of a triangle.

1604 T. WRIGHT *Passions* v. 221 The heart..of man triangularly respecteth the blessed Trinitie, every corner a Person, and the solide substance your common Essence. **1610** NORDEN *Spec. Brit., Cornw.* (1728) 70, 3 whyte stones sett triangulerly as pillers supportinge another stone. **1681** GREW *Museum* III. I. v. 307 A Spar with Crystals Triangularly pointed. **1702** W. J. *Bruyn's Voy. Levant* xxxiv. 134 This Town is Triangularly built.

b. *fig.* As three parties to a transaction (cf. TRIANGULAR 3).

1890 KIPLING in *Pioneer Mail* 15 Jan. 92/3 We nodded triangularly in all good will and swore eternal friendship. **1892** *Sat. Rev.* 31 Dec. 758/2 The Russian refusal to negotiate 'triangularly' with England and China.

† **tri'angulary**, *a.* *Obs.* [f. as TRIANGULAR: see -ARY[2].] = TRIANGULAR 1.

1622 MABBE tr. *Aleman's Guzman d'Alf.* II. 191 A kinde of triangulary sayle. **1653** URQUHART tr. *Rabelais* I. xliv. 197 Lifting up in the upper part of the scul the two triangularie bones called sincipital.

triangulate (traɪ'æŋgjʊlət), *a.* (*sb.*) [ad. med.L. *triangulāt-us* triangular (Albertus Magnus, *a* 1255), f. L. *triangul-um* TRIANGLE: see -ATE[2]; but possibly pa. pple. of med.L. **triangulāre* vb.]

1. Having three angles, triangular; in later use only in *Nat. Hist.*, applied to parts or structures of triangular form.

1611 HOPTON *Speculum Topogr.* II. ii. 187 Be it round, square, triangulate, or multiangulate. **1819** G. SAMOUELLE *Entomol. Compend.* 166 Antennæ with the three last joints forming an oblong triangulate mass. **1852** DANA *Crust.* I. 307 A few species have a somewhat triangulate and subrostrate form.

2. Made up or composed of triangles. (In later use in *Nat. Hist.*) †Also as *sb.* a figure made up of triangles (*obs.*).

1610 HOPTON *Baculum Geodæt.* VI. xiv. 135 The sides of a tryangulate are more by 2, then the tryangles whereof he is made. **1611** —— *Speculum Topogr.* I. ii. 7 Of Triangulates. A Triangulate is a mixt figure composed of Triangles, and may be resolued into the same againe. **1766** *Compl. Farmer* s.v. *Surveying*, Right-lined figures..are either triangles or triangulate, that is, such as are compounded of, and resolvable into triangles.

3. *Nat. Hist.* Marked with triangles; having triangular markings.

1891 *Cent. Dict.* s.v., A triangulate bar is generally formed of triangles with their bases together..; it is a form of ornamentation common on the wings of *Lepidoptera*.

Hence **tri'angulately** *adv.*, in a triangulate manner; triangularly; so as to form triangles.

1852 DANA *Crust.* I. 428 Carpus triangulately dilated at inner margin. **1891** *Cent. Dict.* s.v., A margin or surface marked triangulately with black.

triangulate (traɪ'æŋgjʊleɪt), *v.* [f. L. *triangul-um* + -ATE[3], or f. ppl. stem of med.L. **triangulāre*: cf. also F. *trianguler*.]

1. *trans.* *Surveying* (also *transf.*, as in *Astron.*). To measure and map out (a region or territory) by tracing a series or network of triangles from a baseline and measuring their sides and angles; to determine (e.g. a distance or altitude) in this way. Also *absol.*

1833 HERSCHEL *Astron.* iv. 157 We may, as upon the earth, triangulate, by measuring..their [the stars'] angular distances from each other. **1855** F. GALTON in *Cambr. Ess.* 93 A running survey of a new country is best made by triangulating as much as is practicable. **1891** *Cent. Dict.* s.v., To triangulate the height of a mountain.

fig. **1860** O. W. HOLMES *Elsie V.* xix, A sagacious person, ..who has triangulated a race, that is taken three or more observations from the several standing-places of three different generations.

b. *gen.* or *allusively.* To mark out into triangles.

1853 KANE *Grinnell Exp.* xxvi. (1856) 212 The entire plain is triangulated with ice-barricades. **1879** J. TIMBS in *Cassell's Techn. Educ.* IV. 343/2 The system of wires.. stretching across the sky-line of great thoroughfares, and visibly triangulating the metropolis in every direction.

2. To divide or convert into triangles.

1864 WEBSTER, *Triangulate*..2. To make triangular. **1901** C. W. BROWN in *Cycl. Tour. Cl. Gaz.* July 298/2 A plan which completely triangulates the four-sided figure of the frame and converts it into two distinct triangles.

Hence **tri'angulating** *vbl. sb.* and *ppl. a.*

1861 WILSON & GEIKIE *Mem. E. Forbes* x. 280 He was ready and eager to avail himself of a triangulating cruise with Lieutenant Spratt. *Ibid.* 290 Messrs. Spratt and Forbes proceeded to make the triangulating observations.

triangulated (traɪ'æŋgjʊleɪtɪd), *ppl. a.* and *a.* [f. as prec. adj. or vb. + -ED.]

1. a. = TRIANGULATE *a.* 1. **b.** Formed into a triangle. **c.** Converted or divided into triangles; composed of triangles.

1610 HOPTON *Baculum Geodæt.* II. i. 18 If right lined, whether a Tryangle or Tryangulated? **1752** J. HILL *Hist. Anim.* 286 The triangulated Ostracion. **1897** *Westm. Gaz.* 6 Dec. 9/1 A [bicycle] frame..worthy of attention is that known as the 'triangulated', designed by Mr. C. W. Brown for ladies' machines.

2. Measured or mapped out by means of triangles, as in surveying. (In quot. 1894 *fig.*)

1894 *Thinker* VI. 344 There may be a vast terra incognita lying back of the triangulated regions of consciousness. **1969** G. C. DICKINSON *Maps & Air Photographs* ii. 40 From about 1750 onwards a few of the better cartographers had begun to accept the need, for accuracy's sake, of providing a full triangulated framework for their county maps.

triangulation (traɪæŋgjʊ'leɪʃən). [ad. med.L. *triangulātiōn-em* (Abelard, *a* 1142), n. of action from **triangulāre* to TRIANGULATE. So F. *triangulation* (1835 in *Dict. Acad.*).] The action or process of triangulating.

1. The tracing and measurement of a series or network of triangles in order to survey and map out a territory or region, *spec.* by measuring the angles and one side of each triangle (cf. TRILATERATION). Freq. *attrib.*, as ***triangulation point*** (also *fig.*).

1818 *Blackw. Mag.* III. 463 The English triangulation, begun by General Roy. **1826** T. DRUMMOND in *Phil. Trans.* CXVI. II. 334 Slieve Snaght, the highest hill of Innishowen, ..forms an important point in the triangulation, which connects the North of Ireland with the western islands of Scotland. **1863** A. C. RAMSAY *Phys. Geog.* xxxi. (1878) 550 The triangulation of Scotland for the Ordnance Survey. **1864** J. HUNT tr. *Vogt's Lect. Man* Index, Triangulation of the skull.

attrib. **1923** *Geogr. Rev.* XIII. 465 The recent remarking of the Meades Ranch Station calls attention to the unique importance of this triangulation point. **1947** A. R. HINKS *Maps & Survey* (ed. 5) ix. 172 The methods of trigonometrical survey..divide themselves into the following sections: 1. Determination of mean sea level... 9. Transference of the triangulation points to the plane-table sheets. **1977** *Times Lit. Suppl.* 22 Apr. 494/1 Dispassionate yet sensitive, his *Lenz*..deservedly became the triangulation-point for a whole generation.

2. a. Division of a rectilinear figure into triangles.

1891 *Cent. Dict., Triangulation,* 1. A making triangular; formation into triangles.

b. *Math.* (See quot. 1956); also, the result of such a process.

1940 *Proc. Nat. Acad. Sci.* XXVI. 360 This result is but one of the implications of a triangulation. **1956** E. M. PATTERSON *Topology* v. 89 Triangulation..is the process of dividing up a [topological] space into pieces which are homeomorphic with the interior of a triangle or its analogues in other dimensions. **1974** *McGraw-Hill Yearbk. Sci. & Technol.* 412/2 These developments [in topology] were highlighted by the solutions in 1969 of the annulus conjecture..and of the triangulation problem for manifolds. **1977** *Sci. Amer.* Oct. 113/1 A triangulation that represents a minimal five-chromatic map cannot have any vertices with fewer than five neighbors.

triangulato- (traɪæŋgjʊ'leɪtəʊ), used as combining form of med. or mod.L. *triangulātus*, TRIANGULATE *a.*, in terms of *Nat. Hist.* denoting a combination of this with another form, as ***triangulato-'excavate, -'ovate, -sub'ovate*** adjs.

1849 DANA *Geol.* App. I. (1850) 714 Very broad triangulato-ovate. **1852** —— *Crust.* I. 630 This segment is deeply triangulato-excavate posteriorly.

tri'angulator. [a. mod.L. *triangulātor* (Pontanus, *a* 1500), agent-n. from **triangulāre* to TRIANGULATE.] One who triangulates. Also, an instrument used in triangulation.

1891 in *Cent. Dict.* **1933** *Geogr. Jrnl.* LXXXII. 444 Norway, Poland, Romania, and the United States are the most active triangulators. **1938** *Ibid.* XCII. 434 In this exhibition there were also shown..a radial triangulator.

triangulo- (traɪ'æŋgjʊləʊ), used as combining form of L. *triangulum* TRIANGLE, in **triangulo-pyramidal, triangulo-triangular** *adjs.*, applied to certain series of figurate numbers: see quots., and cf. PYRAMIDAL 4, TRIANGULAR 2 b.

[**1646** F. VIETA *Opera* 294 In prima adfectione per unitatis crementum, in secunda per numeros triangulos, in tertia per numeros pyramidales, in quarta per numeros triangulo-triangulos, in quinta per numeros triangulo-pyramidales.] **1715** *Phil. Trans.* XXIX. 183 A series of Fractions..whose Numerator is a given Number and Denominators are triangular or pyramidal or triangulo-triangular Numbers, &c. **1785** HUTTON *Math. Tables* 7 The several orders of figurate numbers, which he [Vieta] calls triangular, pyramidal, triangulo-triangular, triangulo-pyramidal.

tri'anguloid, *a. rare.* [f. L. *triangul-um* TRIANGLE + -OID.] Resembling a triangle; of somewhat triangular form.

18.. H. SPENCER (O.), A trianguloid space.

† **triannual** (traɪ'ænjuːəl), *a. Obs. rare.* [f. TRI- 3 + ANNUAL.] Occurring every three years; lasting for three years; = TRIENNIAL.

1640 *Par. Acc. St. Barth. by Exchange* in *Archæologia* XLV. 78 Pd. the ringers for joy of the tryannual Parliament, o. 2. 6. **1656** EARL MONM. tr. *Boccalini's Advts. fr. Parnass.* I. lxix. 133 He was deputed a Triannual President of the Isle of Negrapont.

¶ **b.** Occurring thrice a year.

1901 *Daily Chron.* 8 June 5/2 The ladies..we learn..will hold 'tri-annual invitation meetings'... That, we suppose, means an invitation once in four months.

triannulate: see TRI- 1.

triantelope (traɪ'æntɪləʊp). *Australia.* Also **triantulope.** Popular corruption of TARANTULA, applied to a large spider of the genus *Voconia.*

1846 C. P. HODGSON *Remin. Australia* 173 The tarantulas, or 'triantelopes' as the men call them, are large, ugly spiders. **1909** *Daily Chron.* 13 Apr. 4/7 What is a 'triantelope'?.. Originally it was the children's..way of saying tarantula, but people generally came to adopt it.

trianthous: see TRI- 1.

tri'apsal, *a.* [f. TRI- + L. *aps-is, apsid-em* APSE + -AL[1].] Having three apses. Also **tri'apsidal.**

1849 FREEMAN *Archit.* I. viii. 191 A vestige of the triapsal termination of the basilicas. **1875** —— *Venice* (1881) 131 The arrangement of the triapsidal basilica. **1883** *Mag. of Art* June 338/2 It is triapsal, the transepts as well as the choir ending in a semi-circle. **1898** J. T. FOWLER *Durham Cathedr.* 22 The original triapsidal east end.

triarch ('traɪɑːk), *sb.* [f. TRI- + *-arch* in *tetrarch*: cf. Gr. τρίαρχος chief ruler, and next.]

1. The ruler of one of three divisions of a country or territory.

1886 J. BURY in *Jrnl. Hellenic Stud.* VII. 314 These three lords were called the *terzieri* (*tierciers*) of Negroponte. Hopf calls them *Dreiherrn*, and we may call them *triarchs. Ibid.* 321 William laid claim..to the north of Euboia, calling himself a triarch.

2. In Fourier's social organization: A ruler of the third (ascending) rank.

1848 *Tait's Mag.* XV. 706 There will be duarchs for four phalanx, triarchs for 12, tetrarchs for 48, and so on until the douzarch reigns over a million.

Hence **'triarchate**, *rare*[−1] [cf. *patriarchate*], an association of three rulers.

1881 HARTSHORNE *Glance 20th C.* 15 Then, the triarchate; is it not surprising? Pope, Patriarch, and Primate of Canterbury! Roman, Greek, and Anglican, united at last!

triarch ('traɪɑːk), *a. Bot.* [f. TRI- + Gr. ἀρχή beginning, origin.] Arising from three points of origin, as the woody tissue of a root: cf. DIARCH.

1884 BOWER & SCOTT *De Bary's Phaner.* 354 As a rule the xylem-plates are diarch in Lupinus varius,..triarch in Pisum sativum,..tetrarch in Phaseolus. *Ibid.* 363 Triarch and tetrarch bundles sometimes occur in thick roots of species which are usually diarch. **1895** [see TETRARCH *a.*].

† **'triarchist.** *Obs. rare*[−1]. [f. TRI- + Gr. ἀρχή beginning + -IST.] One who maintains the existence of three original principles of being.

1678 CUDWORTH *Intell. Syst.* I. iv. §13. 216 Plutarch was both a Triarchist and a Ditheist,—an assertor of Three Principles, but of Two Gods.

triarchy ('traɪəkɪ). [f. TRI- + Gr. -αρχία government, or ad. Gr. τριαρχία triumvirate.]

1. The government or jurisdiction of a triarch; one of three divisions of a country ruled by triarchs.

1601 HOLLAND *Pliny* v. xviii. I. 101 There lye betweene and about these cities, certaine Royalties called Triarchies, containing every one of them as much as an whole countrey.

2. Government by three rulers or powers jointly; three persons associated in government, a triumvirate. Cf. TETRARCHY 2.

1656 BLOUNT *Glossogr., Triarchie (triarchia)*, a government, where three are in like authority. **1658** in PHILLIPS. **1859** *Morn. Star* 28 Apr. 4/3 The Emperor of the French..proposed to the Queen that the pentarchy of the five Powers should be put an end to, and a triarchy of France, England, and Russia, be established in its stead. **1892** *Nation* (N.Y.) 20 Oct. 305/3 He proposed to establish a sort of triarchy, which was to consist of the Emperor of Austria and the King of Prussia..and a sovereign to be chosen periodically by and from the heads of the smaller principalities.

3. A group of three districts or divisions of a country each under its own ruler.

1660 HOWELL *Parly Beasts* 143 [The rational soul] dividing her Empire into a Triarchy,..governs by three Viceroys, the three Faculties. **1799** S. TURNER *Anglo-Sax.* I. II. x. 355 The island, though nominally under an hexarchy, was fast verging into a triarchy. **1888** *Voice* (N.Y.) 27 Dec., Three ambitious little kingdoms..Greece, Servia and Bulgaria. This triarchy cannot long endure; one must take the lead, with the prospect of absorbing the others.

triarctic to **triareal**: see TRI- 1.

† **tri'arian**, *a.* (*sb.*) *Obs.* [f. L. *triāri-ī* (see TRIARY) + -AN.] Consisting of *triarii* (see TRIARY); also *allusively.* **b.** *sb.* (*pl.*) The *triarii.*

1642 *View of Print. Book int. Observat.* 39 The Triarian legion, in which they put their last and chiefest strength. **1658** PHILLIPS, Triarians. **1663** COWLEY *Ode Restor. Chas. II* xi, Let our weak Days lead up the Van; Let the brave Second and Triarian-Band, Firm against all impression stand. **1715** M. DAVIES *Athen. Brit.* I. 65 His best Veteran and Triarian, Regular Troops.

,triar'ticulate, *a.* [f. TRI- 1 + L. *articulus* joint + -ATE[2].] Three-jointed.

1826 KIRBY & SP. *Entomol.* III. 518 Flies..with triarticulate antennæ. **1875** C. C. BLAKE *Zool.* 296 The Colopoda ..—The feet are very short,..indistinctly triarticulate.

† **'triary.** *Obs.* Pl. triaries. [ad. L. *triāri-ī*, sb. pl. (see below), f. *trēs, tri-* three.] *pl.* (also *collect. sing.*) The *triarii*, or soldiers of the third line in the ancient Roman army. Also *fig.* or *allusively.*

1533 BELLENDEN *Livy* IV. ix. (S.T.S.) II. 79 Seand þe Inemyis sett ernistlie to wyn þe tentis, he Ischit on þare richt hand with ane feirss cumpany of triaris. **1589** IVE *Du Bellay's Instr. Warres* 76 Naming..the Souldiers of the fyrst battaile *Hastaries*; those of the second *Princes*, and those of the third *Triaries.* **1663** COWLEY *Ess. in Verse & Prose, Danger Procrast.*, If I should draw upon you all my forces out of Seneca and Plutarch upon this subject, I should overwhelm you, but I leave those as Triary for your next charge. **1679** V. ALSOP *Mel. Inquir.* II. viii. 368 This is the last retreat of these Gentlemen; hither they retire as to their Triary and strong reserves.

trias ('traɪæs). [a. late L. *trias*, a. Gr. τριάς the number three: see TRIAD. In 2, a. Ger. *Trias.*]

1. The number three; a set of three, a triad.

1610 BOLTON *Elem. Armories* 182 One is onely best: next to that the Trias, Ternio, or number three, and so the rest of the Odde to Fifteen. **1635** HEYWOOD *Hierarch.* II. 68 Sometimes, what's proper vnto Man alone, Is giuen to this Trias, three in One: As, when we attribute vnto him Wings. **1728** H. HERBERT tr. *Fleury's Eccl. Hist.* I. 250 This is the first time that we meet in the ancients with the word *Trias*, or Trinity in this sense. **1864** *Daily Tel.* 9 Sept., A people with whom drinking, smoking, and spitting are the Trias of social bliss.

2. *Geol.* (Usu. with capital initial.) Name for the series of strata lying immediately beneath the Jurassic and above the Permian; so called because divisible, where typically developed (as in Germany), into three groups (*Keuper, Muschelkalk*, and *Bunter Sandstein*); represented in Britain by the Upper New Red Sandstone and associated formations.

1841 MURCHISON, etc. in *Proc. Geol. Soc. Lond.* (1842) III. 403 The Trias of German geologists. **1842** SEDGWICK in *Hudson's Guide Lakes* (1843) 204 In France and Germany the series of rocks..admits of a triple division (called 'Trias', or the 'Triassic system'). **1876** PAGE *Adv. Text-Bk. Geol.* xvi. 289 The reason for regarding the Trias as mesozoic. **1912** *Return Brit. Museum* 169 A slab of Rhynchocephalian and other footprints from the Trias of Storeton, Cheshire.

attrib. and *Comb.* **1855** J. PHILLIPS *Man. Geol.* 248 Bands of red and blue trias-like sandstones and clays. **1867** W. W. SMYTH *Coal & Coal-mining* 240 Reaching coal beneath the Permian and Trias formations.

Triassic (traɪ'æsɪk), *a. Geol.* [f. TRIAS + -IC.] Of or belonging to the Trias; ***Triassic system*** = TRIAS 2.

1841 SIR P. G. EGERTON in *Proc. Geol. Soc. Lond* (1842) III. (*title of paper*) A Notice on the Occurrence of Triassic Fishes in British Strata. **1868** LYELL *Princ. Geol.* (ed. 10) II. III. xlix. 592 A long narrow island..composed partly of granite and partly of triassic sandstone. **1889** *Science-Gossip* XXV. 122/2 The Triassic and Permian formations show a time of 'great physical disturbance,..volcanic eruptions discharging vast beds..of lava and layers of volcanic ash'.

triaster: see TRI- 4 a.

triathlon (traɪ'æθlən). [f. Gr. τρι- TRI- + ἄθλον contest, after *decathlon*, etc.] An athletic or sporting contest composed of three different events.

1973 *Daily Tel.* 21 July 14 A new event..called the 'Triathlon'. In this all four members of a team have to demonstrate their prowess in clay pigeon shooting, fly fishing and riding a handy hunter-course over jumps. **1981** *Austin* (Texas) *Amer.-Statesman* 28 Mar. (Time Out section) 8 The Triathlon consists of a 2·5 mile surf swim, followed by a 112-mile bike race, followed by a full marathon. **1983** *Times* 26 Feb. 22/1 The word 'triathlon' is the label that has been attached to the so-called 'Iron Man contests' which.. basically consist of a swim in the open sea, a long cycle ride of up to 100 miles and then a marathon run.

triatic (traɪ'ætɪk), *a. Naut.* [Origin obscure; app. f. TRI- three.] In ***triatic stay***: see quots.

1841 DANA *Seaman's Man., Triatic Stay*, a rope secured at each end to the heads of the fore and main masts, with thimbles spliced into its bight, to hook the stay tackles to. **1867** SMYTH *Sailor's Word-bk.* [as in Dana, with this addition] This term applies also to the jumper-stay, extending in schooners from the mainmast-head to the foremast-head, clearing the end of the fore gaff. **1895** *Funk's Stand. Dict.* s.v., *Triatic stay* (*Naut.*), a device consisting of two pendants attached respectively to the foremast-head and mainmast-head, and having thimbles spliced to the other ends, to which the third part, or span, is attached, as are also the stay-tackles; used principally for hoisting boats in and out of a vessel.

triatomic (traɪə'tɒmɪk), *a. Chem.* [f. TRI- + ATOM *sb.* + -IC.] **a.** Having three atoms in the molecule. †**b.** = TRIVALENT. *Obs.* **c.** Containing three hydroxyl groups (OH); = TRIHYDRIC *a.*[1]

1862 MILLER *Elem. Chem.* (ed. 2) III. 53 To the triatomic group [of elements] belong nitrogen, phosphorus, arsenic, antimony, bismuth, and gold. **1863-72** WATTS *Dict. Chem.* I. 464 To classify them [primary hydrides and chlorides] in four principal groups, thus: Monatomic, Diatomic, Triatomic, Tetratomic. **1872** *Ibid.* VI. 237 Nitrogen, which combines with 3 atoms of hydrogen, is triatomic, triadic, or trivalent. **1882** ROSCOE *Elem. Chem.* xxxv. 320 The possible number of derivatives of the triatomic alcohols is much larger than that of either of the preceding classes. **1894** *Times* 18 Aug. 10/3 No doubt the passage of.. the diatomic form of the substance to the triatomic form.. takes place with evolution of heat. **1903** *Edin. Rev.* Oct. 393 It [radium] can ozonise oxygen—that is, condense it by rendering its molecules tri-atomic.

triatomid (traɪ'ætəmɪd), *a.* (*sb.*) [f. mod.L. family name *Triatomidæ*, f. generic name *Triatoma* (F. L. Laporte 1832, in *Mag. Zool.* II. IX. 11), f. TRI- + Gr. τέμνειν to cut, in allusion to the antennæ of the insects: see -ID[3].] Of or pertaining to the family Triatomidæ, now usually included in the family Reduviidæ. Also as *sb.*, a blood-sucking assassin bug of the family Triatomidæ, which includes several vectors of disease.

1955 *Sci. News Let.* 29 Oct. 280/1 The blood-suckers are triatomid bugs and are known to carry the germs from animals, such as opossums, to man. **1961** E. R. & G. A. NOBLE *Parasitol.* xv. 726 Some triatomids.. obtain meals by tapping the blood-engorged bodies of other arthropods. **1971** P. C. C. GARNHAM *Progress in Parasitology* iii. 30 In the State of São Paulo.. the writer saw typical dwellings in which the incidence of the infection was 19 per cent in the dogs, 16 per cent in the cats, and nearly 100 per cent in the triatomid bugs. **1974** F. PIFANO in K. Elliott et al. *Trypanosomiasis & Leishmaniasis* 77 The source of food of the triatomids captured in the palm trees was investigated with the precipitin test.

triatomine (traɪ'ætəmiːn), *a.* (*sb.*) [f. mod.L. subfamily name *Triatominæ* (see prec. and -INE[1]).] = TRIATOMID *a.* (*sb.*), when the group is considered as a subfamily of the family Reduviidæ.

1962 GORDON & LAVOIPIERRE *Entomol. for Students of Med.* xxxix. 237 Triatomine bugs are almost entirely American in distribution. **1974** *Nature* 29 Nov. 392/2 The triatomine bugs.. are medically important as vectors of Chagas' disease in the Americas. **1978** *Ibid.* 27 Apr. 820/2 The second type (type II) was found in acute and chronic cases of Chagas' disease, cats, house mice, rats and guinea pigs, from houses infested by the domiciliated triatomine *Panstrongylus megistus*. **1979** *Pharmacol. & Therapeutics* VII. 86 *T. rangeli* is a non-pathogenic trypanosome with a wide range of hosts which is also transmitted by triatomine vectors.

tri'axal, *a.* [f. TRI- 1 + L. *axis* AXIS + -AL[1].] = TRIAXIAL *a.*

1891 *Cent. Dict.* s.v., Triaxal coördinates.

tri'axial, *a.* [f. TRI- 1 + L. *axi-s* AXIS + -AL[1].] Having three axes: said in *Geom.* of co-ordinates; in *Zool.* of sponge-spicules. Also, occurring or responding in three mutually perpendicular directions.

1886 *Proc. Zool. Soc.* 21 Dec. 581 A regular triaxial network is formed. **1896** DK. ARGYLL *Philos. Belief* 110 The intercalation of triaxial spiculae, at the proper intervals or interspaces. **1924** J. G. A. SKERL tr. *A. Wegener's Origin of Continents & Oceans* xiii. 202 In his latest work Helmert infers, from the distribution of the force of gravity on the earth's surface, that the earth is a triaxial ellipsoid. **1951** *Engineering* 14 Dec. 746/2 A state of triaxial stress, according to its severity, suppresses deformation by shear and makes cleavage more probable. **1975** *Nature* 31 Jan. 327/2 A single range triaxial fluxgate magnetometer capable of measuring fields up to 10 gauss along each orthogonal axis. **1978** *Sci. Amer.* Jan. 48/2 The criterion of triaxial motion meant that a ball-and-socket arrangement would be the best means of achieving a mechanical interlock between components.

Hence ˌ**triaxi'ality**, triaxial nature; **tri'axially** *adv.*

1970 *Nature* 14 Mar. 1008/2 Because of triaxiality the Moon theoretically has three free oscillations with periods of about 1, 40 and 800 months in the directions of its axes. **1972** *Physics Bull.* Nov. 669/1 There are clearly cases when the micromode of fracture is dependent on triaxiality of stress and very sensitive to temperature or strain rate. **1982** *Sci. Amer.* May 116c/1 (Advt.), By means of a triaxially stabilized altitude control system, it.. directs the solar panels towards the sun.

tri-axle: see TRI- 4 b.

triaxon, triaxonian: see TRI- 1.

triazine (traɪ'æzaɪn). *Chem.* [f. TRI- 5 a + AZ(OTE + -INE[5].] A general term, invented by Widman (1888), for compounds the molecules of which contain a cyclic group consisting of three carbon and three nitrogen atoms.

These may be arranged in three ways: (*a*) the consecutive or vicinal form, also called *osotriazine*; (*b*) the unsymmetrical; (*c*) the symmetrical, also called *cyanidine*: thus

(1) $N\left\langle\begin{matrix}N.C\\N.C\end{matrix}\right\rangle C$, (2) $N\left\langle\begin{matrix}N.C\\C.C\end{matrix}\right\rangle N$, (3) $N\left\langle\begin{matrix}C.N\\C.N\end{matrix}\right\rangle C$,

1894 *Jrnl. Chem. Soc.* LXVI. I. 57 New Triazole and Triazine Derivatives. **1900** SMITH *Richter's Org. Chem.* II. 604 Alkyl- and phenyl-derivatives of symmetrical triazine or cyanidine are obtained.

triazo- (traɪ'æzəʊ). *Chem.* [f. TRI- 5 c + AZO-.] A formative of the names of compounds containing three atoms of nitrogen arranged in a ring, thus $-N\left\langle\begin{matrix}N\\ \ddot{N}\end{matrix}\right.$, as ***triazobenzene***, $C_6H_5N\left\langle\begin{matrix}N\\ \ddot{N}\end{matrix}\right.$. It has also been used somewhat differently, as in ***triazo-acetic acid***, $N_2\left\langle\begin{matrix}CH(CO_2H).N_2\\CH(CO_2H).N_2\end{matrix}\right\rangle CH(CO_2H)$. Also *attrib.* as in ***triazo compounds, derivatives***, etc.

1896 *Jrnl. Chem. Soc.* LXX. I. 338 Ethylic diazoacetate.. with concentrated alkali, triazoacetic acid. **1901** *Ibid.* LXXX. I. 104 Preparation of Azoimides (Triazo-compounds).. p-*Triazobromobenzene* forms crystals melting at 20°. **1910** DESCH & LAPWORTH in *Chem. Soc. Ann. Reps.* VII. 124 Substances containing the triazo-group, N_3.

triazole (traɪ'æzəʊl). *Chem.* Also -ol. [f. TRI- 5 a + AZ(OTE + *-ole* (= *oleum* oil).]

a. A general term for compounds the molecules of which contain a cyclic group consisting of three nitrogen and two carbon atoms. The ring may be arranged in two ways, $.N\left\langle\begin{matrix}C.N\\C.\dot{N}\end{matrix}\right.$ and $N\left\langle\begin{matrix}C.C\\N.\dot{N}\end{matrix}\right.$.

b. A compound having the formula $C_2H_3N_3$ and containing a triazole ring with two double bindings. Five isomers are possible, and are variously named; e.g. *triazole, osotriazole, isotriazole*.

1888 MUIR & MORLEY *Watts' Dict. Chem.* I. 423 Triazol. A name given to the hypothetical $C_2H_3N_3$. **1894** [see TRIAZINE]. **1900** SMITH *Richter's Org. Chem.* (ed. 3) II. 512 Triazole, $C_2H_3N_3$, melting at 121° and boiling at 260°, is obtained from formamide and formhydrazide.

tribade ('trɪbəd, ‖tribad). [a. F. *tribade* (16th c.), or ad. its source L. *tribas, -ad-*, Gr. τριβάς, τριβαδ-, f. τρίβειν to rub.] A woman who engages in sexual activity with other women; a Lesbian. Also *attrib.*

1601 B. JONSON *Forest* x. *Præludium*, Light Venus.. with thy tribade trine, invent new sports. **1890** H. H. ELLIS *Criminal* iii. § 7. 106 Such emblems are common among pæderasts and tribades.

Hence '**tribadism**, (*a*) the activity of a tribade; (*b*) *spec.* in modern use (see quot. 1965); '**tribady** = TRIBADISM (*a*).

1811-19 *Woods and Pirie v. Gordon* (*Index Catal. Libr. Surgeon-General's Office U.S.A.* XIV. 752), Lady C. G... who had charged them with the practice of tribadism. **1864** tr. *Caspar's Forensic Med.* (N. Syd. Soc.) III. 335 Tribadism. Even in the Old Testament there is distinct allusion to this form of sexual aberration. **1882** PAYNE *1001 Nights* II. 156. **1909** *Cent. Dict. Suppl.*, Tribady. **1965** *New Statesman* 26 Mar. 492/3 The first [technique of lesbian intercourse], known as 'tribadism', consists in one woman lying on top of the other and simulating the movements of heterosexual intercourse in such a way as to stimulate the clitoris of each. **1970** G. GREER *Female Eunuch* 293 The prevalence of tribadism as the principal lesbian mode of lovemaking argues the relative unimportance of the masculine fantasy.

tribal ('traɪbəl), *a.* (and *sb.*) [f. L. *trib-us* TRIBE + -AL[1]: hence mod.F. *tribal* (Littré).]

1. **a.** Of or pertaining to a tribe or tribes; characteristic of a tribe.

1632 LITHGOW *Trav.* VI. 296 They are.. of colour Tauny, boasting much of their triball Antiquity. **1740** WARBURTON *Div. Legat.* v. iii. ¶40 Even the tribal Sceptre was established long after the death of Jacob. **1849** STEPHENS *Bk. Farm* (1891) III. 409 The white face has been well described as the 'tribal badge' of the Hereford [ox]. **1906** PETRIE *Relig. Anc. Egypt.* viii. 58 Of these some are probably tribal gods.

b. Characterized by the tendency to form groups or by strong group loyalty.

1951 H. ARENDT *Burden of Our Time* II. viii. 227 Tribal nationalism always insists that its own people is surrounded by 'a world of enemies', 'one against all'. **1970** G. GREER *Female Eunuch* 182 In the tribal teenage situation there are some boys with whom one does not go out. **1977** *Time* 10 Oct. 113/1 A Jew in this rural, tribal and fiercely Christian heartland [*sc.* Savannah, Georgia] is a wanderer indeed.

c. As *sb.*, a member of a tribal community (usu. in *pl.*). Chiefly *Indian English.*

1958 *New India: Progress through Democracy* III. vi. 378 Illiteracy is almost universal among tribal peoples... Tribals are being trained as teachers. **1964** *Economist* 18 Apr. 261/1 More are arriving daily, among them Christian and Buddhist tribals. **1971** *Illustr. Weekly India* 25 Apr. 42/2 An elaborate welfare scheme.. reached both the settlers and the tribals. **1973** *Country Life* 14 June 1715/2 A ceremonial bag of five tigers slain by tribals in Nagaland in 1964. **1979** *South China Morning Post* 28 Dec. 3/1 Teams of mountain tribals are to join the search for three Singapore Air Force Skyhawks which disappeared over the northern Philippines eight days ago.

2. Special collocations: ***tribal council***, the organ of internal self-government of a recognized U.S. Indian tribe, since the Indian Reorganization Act of 1934; ***tribal mark***, a scar resulting from the traditional or ritual cutting of the face practised among certain African tribes; hence ***tribal marking***; also ***tribal scar, scarring***; ***tribal territory***, an administrative division of the Northwest Frontier Province of Pakistan (formerly of India).

1948 *Salt Lake Tribune* 17 Dec. 16/5 Other tribal council members, speaking in Navajo.., agreed with Mr. Akeah. **1976** *Billings* (Montana) *Gaz.* 5 July 1-D/4 The Northern Cheyenne Tribal Council has launched a drive for redesignation of the air quality level on the south-eastern Montana reservation. **1980** *New Age* (U.S.) Oct. 5/1 Through CERT and the tribal councils, thousands of acres of traditional tribal land have been turned over to mining companies searching for uranium and coal. **1897** M. H. KINGSLEY *Trav. in W. Afr.* xxiii. 530 The cicatrices are sometimes tribal marks, but sometimes decorative. **1965** W. SOYINKA *Road* 73 Are you sure you know who I mean? Sort of tall but a little on the short side. Tribal marks, but beginning to wear off. **1925** W. D. HAMBLY *Hist. Tattooing & its Significance* iii. 176 Are there among the accounts of tribal markings any present-day accounts or ancient legends, which reveal that these marks have.. an important social significance? **1973** 'A. HALL' *Tango Briefing* xx. 251 The carved teakwood statuette.. was obviously a god, wide nosed and with tribal markings on the forehead. **1977** P. RAYMOND *Matter of Assassination* iii. 23 An expressionless Negro face marked with tribal scars across the cheeks. **1982** D. WILTSE *Wedding Guest* ii. 33 The ritual scars.. had been worked.. into her cheeks with a needle... The tribal scarring had been outlawed for thirty years. **1908** *Imperial Gazetteer India* XIX. 166 In tribal territory, besides the tribes already alluded to, the Torwāl and Garhwī reside in the higher ranges of Swāt. **1951** KHAN & STARK *Young Pakistan* xxiv. 199 In the far north, an observer standing on the high mountains can in fact look down on five different lands—Afghanistan.. and Pakistan (Tribal territory) in the south west. **1974** *Encycl. Brit. Macropædia* XIII. 256/2 Between the settled districts to the south and the Afghan border is the tribal territory, whose inhabitants enjoy a large measure of independence.

Hence **tribally** ('traɪbəlɪ) *adv.*, as a tribe; in the manner of, or in relation to a tribe.

1890 *Science* 27 June 383/2 It is probable that Professor Putnam is not justified in concluding that the people of the two sections were tribally identical. **1908** F. SPENCE *Chr. Reunion* vii. 109 *note*, The election (federally or tribally) of the elders of the Ecclesia by its members.

tribalism ('traɪbəlɪz(ə)m). [f. TRIBAL + -ISM.]

a. The condition of existing as a separate tribe or tribes; tribal system, organization, or relations.

1886 *Edin. Rev.* Apr. 443 No national life, much less civilisation, was possible under the system of Celtic tribalism. **1893** GOLDW. SMITH *Ess.* 176 National churches have lapsed into something very like tribalism in this respect [about war]. **1898** *Weekly Reg.* 29 Oct. 561 Those who have set the maxims of Christ above those of narrow tribalism.

b. Loyalty to a particular tribe or group of which one is a member.

1955 *Times* 30 Aug. 9/7 If a stable parliamentary democracy is to be introduced one stable political party, avoiding if possible the extremes of tribalism and anti-tribalism, would seem necessary. **1969** *Busara* (Nairobi) II. II. 56 According to Reinhold Niebuhr, 'the chief source of man's inhumanity to man seems to be the tribal limits of his sense of obligation to the other man'. In *tribalism* Niebuhr includes race, language, religion, class and culture as important traits. **1976** *Drum* (E. Afr. ed.) Apr. 3/1 Tribalism? Isn't it true that in some firms about 75 per cent of the employees come from one tribe—depending, of course, on which tribe the bosses come from. **1978** *Times Lit. Suppl.* 1 Dec. 1390/5 His call for a fusion or integration of cultures is one that commits him to the course of liberal tolerance, and sets him against closed systems of thought such as Marxism and tribalism.

tribalist, *sb.* (and *a.*) [f. TRIBAL *a.* + -IST.]

a. A tribesman. *rare.*

1888 in *Cassell's Encycl. Dict.*

b. An advocate or practitioner of tribalism (sense b). Also *attrib.* or as *adj.* (cf. next).

1960 *Times* 29 Sept. (Nigeria Suppl.) p. iv/4 Opponents have accused him of being a tribalist. **1970** J. D. CAUTE *Fanon* vi. 70 The Nationalist Parties drove the political opposition into retrograde, tribalist forms.

tribalistic (traɪbə'lɪstɪk), *a.* [f. TRIBAL *a.* + -ISTIC.] = TRIBAL *a.* 1 a, b. Also, characterized by tribalism. Cf. TRIBALIST b.

1961 in WEBSTER. **1976** *Daily Sketch* (Ibadan) 26 Oct. 1/2 They.. recommended that Nigeria's future President should not be arrogant, tribalistic but should be consistent. **1980** in S. Terkel *Amer. Dreams* 320 It [*sc.* a cocktail party] was a tribalistic ritual. I was the meat on the altar.

tribalize ('traɪbəlaɪz), *v.* [f. as prec. + -IZE.] *trans.* To render tribal, to unite on a tribal basis; to imbue with tribal loyalty. So '**tribalized** *ppl. a.*; ˌ**tribali'zation**.

1927 *Other Lands* Jan. 59/2 The United Free Church worked more among the tribalized communities. **1959** *Times Lit. Suppl.* 6 Mar. 127/5 There are still many who share Mary Kingsley's predilection for 'tribalized' peoples. **1964** M. McLuhan *Understanding Media* (1967) xxiv. 249 The war had fraternalized and tribalized us. **1984** *Times* 16 Oct. 14/6 The main effect [in Poland] has been the tribalization of politics..the bike boys, the punks..the hippies..the tough and the meek.

tribasic (traɪ'beɪsɪk), *a. Chem.* [f. Gr. τρι-, TRI- + βάσ-ις base + -IC.] Having three bases.

1. Of an acid: Having the property of exchanging three atoms of hydrogen for three of potassium or sodium, and thus forming a salt; e.g. phosphoric acid, H_3PO_4, which reacts with sodium hydroxide, NaOH, forming trisodium phosphate, Na_3PO_4. Of a salt: Containing three molecules of the basic oxide; e.g. tribasic lead acetate.

In the first half of the 19th c., the acid oxide was considered to be the acid itself (not as now when *acid* means the compound of this oxide with water), and *tribasic acid* was applied to an oxide which united with three equivalents of base to form a salt: hence the name.

1837 Graham in *Phil. Trans.* 62 A new nomenclature of these salts..I offer for consideration..Tribasic phosphate of water..(3 HO, PO_5). Tribasic phosphate of water and soda..(NaO, 2 HO, PO_5). Tribasic phosphate of soda and water..(2 NaO, HO, PO_5). Tribasic phosphate of soda..(3 NaO, PO_5). **1849** D. Campbell *Inorg. Chem.* 317 Salts which are isomorphous with the salts of tribasic phosphoric acid. **1862** Miller *Elem. Chem.* (ed. 2) III. 255 The..synthetic experiments of Berthelot..have shown that the ordinary varieties of natural fats and oils, are the tribasic ethers of the triatomic alcohol glycerin. **1875** *Ure's Dict. Arts* (ed. 7) III. 863 *Phosphates of Soda*... The principal are the normal tribasic phosphate, the well-known rhombic phosphate [etc.]. **1899** Cagney *Jaksch's Clin. Diagn.* vii. (ed. 4) 378 Being a tribasic acid, it forms three classes of salts—acid, neutral, and basic.

†**2.** Of an element: = TRIATOMIC b. *Obs.*

1862 Miller *Elem. Chem.* (ed. 2) III. 52 Triatomic or Tribasic elements, each atom of which is in combination equivalent to H_3 or three atoms of hydrogen. **1880** Cleminshaw *Wurtz' Atom. The.* 204 Nitrogen has been represented as a tribasic element derived from the type of three condensed molecules of hydrogen.

tribasilar: see TRI- 1.

tribbill, tribble, obs. var. TREBLE.

tribbler: see TRIBLER.

tribe (traɪb), *sb.* Forms: α. 3 (*pl.*) tribuz, 4–6 tribu, (*pl.* -us), 5 trybu-s. β. 4–6 trybe, (7 *Sc.* tryb), 4– tribe. [In earliest form, ME. *tribu*, a. OF. *tribu*, Sp., Pg. *tribu*, It. *tribù*, *tribo*, a. L. *tribus* (*u*-stem); but as the OF. has not been found in the sing. before 14th c. the ME. *tribuz* of 1250 may directly represent L. *tribūs* pl. The later *tribe* may have been f. L. *tribus* on the usual pattern of derivatives from L. sbs. in *-us*.

L. *tribus* is usually explained from *tri-* three and the verbal root *bhu, bu, fu* to be. It is thought by some to be cognate with Welsh *tref* town or inhabited place.

The earliest known application of *tribus* was to the three divisions of the early people of Rome (attributed by some to the separate Latin, Sabine, and Etruscan elements); thence it was transferred to render the Greek φυλή, and so to the Greek application of the latter to the tribes of Israel. This, from its biblical use, was the earliest use in English, the original Roman use not appearing till the 16th c.]

1. a. A group of persons forming a community and claiming descent from a common ancestor; *spec.* each of the twelve divisions of the people of Israel, claiming descent from the twelve sons of Jacob.

ten tribes, the tribes of Israel which revolted from the House of David, leaving only Judah and Benjamin to the kingdom of Judah. Their history after their deportation by Shalmaneser is lost, and they are often referred to as the ***lost tribes***, whose identification in remote regions has been a matter of frequent speculation.

α. *c* **1250** *Gen. & Ex.* 3813 Ðoȝ he wenen ðat god sal taken Of ðo .xii. tribuz summe mo. *c* **1449** Pecock *Repr.* II. vi. (Rolls) 173 In her tribu or kinred..as in the hous of Miche... The Tribu of Dan. **1481** Caxton *Godeffroy* clxxi. 253 Whan the .x lygnages or trybus departed fro the heyer of Salamon And helde them to Ieroboam. **1526** *Pilgr. Perf.* (W. de W. 1531) 24 b, Shall syt in trones..& iudge the xii tribus of Israel. **1531** Elyot *Gov.* I. ii, Wherfore ix partes of them which they called Tribus forsoke hym, and elected Hieroboaz..to be theyr kynge.

β. *c* **1380** Wyclif *Wks.* (1880) 365 Þe trybe or kynrede of leuy. **1390** Gower *Conf.* III. 279 Of whom..The tribes [*v.r.* tribus] tuelve of Irahel Engendred were. **1480** Caxton *Chron. Eng.* III. (1520) 20 b/2 The dukes were euer of the trybe of Iuda. **1535** Coverdale *Ps.* lxxvii. 67 He refused the tabernacle of Ioseph, and chose not the trybe of Ephraim. **1671** Milton *Samson* 1540 An Ebrew, as I guess, and of our Tribe. **1715–20** Pope *Iliad* II. 431 In tribes and nations to divide thy train. **1819** Scott *Ivanhoe* xxxvi, Where dwelt a Jewish Rabbi of his tribe. **1866** *Smith's Smaller Dict. Bible* (1907) 487/1 Samaria retained its dignity as the capital of the ten tribes... In B.C. 721, Samaria was taken,..and the kingdom of the ten tribes was put an end to. *Ibid.* 487/2 Since the deportation of the ten tribes by Shalmaneser. **1910** *Encycl. Brit.* I. 315/1 A circumstance which led Bernier to speculate on the Kashmiris representing the lost tribes of Israel.

b. A particular race of recognized ancestry; a family.

c **1400** Maundev. (1839) viii. 67 With his wyf Eue..he gatt Seth; of whiche tribe, þat is to seye, kynrede, Ihesu Crist was born. **1617** Sir R. Winwood *Let.* 29 July, in *10th Rep. Hist. MSS. Comm.* App. I. 102 The howse of Austria for many yeares together interchangebly hath maried in their owne trybe. **1623** Cockeram, *Tribe*, a kindred. **1667** Milton *P.L.* XII. 23 And dwell Long time in peace by Families and Tribes Under paternal rule. **1719** Watts *Hymn*, '*Jesus shall reign*' vii, In Him the tribes of Adam boast More blessings than their father lost. **1838** Lytton *Alice* I. vi, To what tribe of Camerons do you belong?

2. a. *Roman Hist.* One of the traditional three political divisions or patrician orders of ancient Rome in early times (see quot. 1842); later, one of the 30 political divisions of the Roman people instituted by Servius Tullius, and in B.C. 241 increased to 35.

1533 Bellenden *Livy* I. xvii. (S.T.S.) I. 96 Þe toun of rome was dividit..in sindri partis, and euery ane of þir partis war callit tribis, be thirllage of tribute þat þai aucht to pay to þe king..þir tribus pertenit na thing to þe distribucioun and nowmer of centuries. **1560** Daus tr. *Sleidane's Comm.* 412 Themperor..abrogateth all the tribes, and restoreth the same state of the common weale. **1600** Holland *Livy* I. xliii. 31 b, Having divided the citie into foure Wards, according to the quarters and hils; those parts which were inhabited, he [Servius Tullius] called Tribes, of the word Tribute (as I suppose). **1611** B. Jonson *Catiline* II. i, I ha' been writing all this night..unto all the tribes And centuries for their voices, to help Catiline In his election. **1842** *Smith's Dict. Grk. & Rom. Antiq.* 994/1 The three ancient Romulian tribes, the Ramnes, Tities, and Luceres,..to which the patricians alone belonged, must be distinguished from the thirty plebeian tribes of Servius Tullius. **1902** W. M. Ramsay in *Expositor* Jan. 25 Citizenship necessarily implied membership of one of the tribes of which the city was composed.

b. *Grecian Hist.* Rendering the Greek φυλή.

1697 Potter *Antiq. Greece* I. ix. (1837) 57 Cecrops..divided them [the Athenians] into four φυλαί, or tribes; each tribe he subdivided into three parts. **1842** *Smith's Dict. Grk. & Rom. Antiq.* 990/2 In the earliest times of Greek history mention is made of people being divided into tribes and clans. *Ibid.* 991/2 Of the Dorian race there were originally three tribes. *Ibid.* 993/1 [At Athens] the Tribes or Phylae were divided..each into three φρατρίαι (a term equivalent to fraternities). *Ibid.* 993/2 Solon..abolished the old tribes, and created ten new ones, according to a geographical division of Attica.

c. *Irish Hist.* ***tribes of Galway***: the families or communities of persons having the same surname.

1834 *Encycl. Brit.* (ed. 7) X. 306/1 After..1270, it [Galway] became the residence of a number of enterprising settlers... Of these settlers, the principal families, fourteen in number, are still known by the name of the Tribes of Galway... These families became so closely connected by intermarriages, that dispensations are frequently requisite for the canonical legality of marriages among them at present. **1898** *Westm. Gaz.* 10 Oct. 2/1 A day at least must be given to Galway—the 'City of the Tribes'.

d. A division of some other nation or people.

1693 Tate *Juvenal* xv. 194 [Teach] stragling Mountainers, for publick Good, To Rank in Tribes, and quit the savage Wood. **1784** Cowper *Task* v. 222 When man was multiplied and spread abroad In tribes and clans. **1788** Gibbon *Decl. & F.* xlii. (1869) II. 554 The nation was divided into two powerful and hostile tribes.

†**e.** A division of territory allotted to a family or company. *Obs. rare.*

1643 Baker *Chron., Jas. I* 158 Now they began to divide the Country [Bermudas] into Tribes and the Tribes into Shares.

3. A race of people; frequently applied to a group of primitive people, esp. a primary aggregation, under a chief or headman.

1596 Shaks. *Merch. V.* I. iii. 111 For suffrance is the badge of all our Tribe. **1604** —— *Oth.* III. iii. 175 Good Heauen, the Soules of all my Tribe defend From Iealousie. *Ibid.* v. ii. 349 Of one, whose hand (Like the base Indean) threw a Pearle away Richer then all his Tribe. **1745** ? Randall *Hymn*, '*Behold, the mountain of the Lord*' iv, Him shall the tribes of earth obey, Him all the hosts of heaven. **1823** J. Marshall *Const. Opin.* (1839) 273 Territory..occupied by numerous and warlike tribes of Indians. **1835** Thirlwall *Greece* I. iv. 113 The Ionians were a Hellenic tribe, who took forcible possession of Attica and a part of Peloponnesus. **1836** W. Irving *Astoria* I. xiii. 214 Engaged in trading expeditions..among the tribes of the Missouri. **1875** Maine *Hist. Inst.* iii. 65 The tribes themselves, and all subdivisions of them, are conceived by the men who compose them as descended from a single male ancestor. *Ibid.* 69 In some cases the Tribe can hardly be otherwise described than as the group of men subject to some one chieftain.

4. a. A class of persons; a fraternity, set, lot. Now often *contemptuous.*

c **1600** Shaks. *Sonn.* cvii, Ile liue in this poore rime, While he insults ore dull and speachlesse tribes. *a* **1684** Earl Roscom. *Prol. to Dk. York at Edin.* 2 Folly and vice are easy to describe, The common subjects of our scribbling tribe. **1712** Addison *Spect.* No. 529 ¶6 There is another Tribe of Persons who are Retainers to the Learned World... I mean the Players or Actors of both Sexes. **1719** Swift *To Yng. Clergym.* Wks. 1755 II. II. 4 Professors..in most arts and sciences are generally the worst qualified to explain their meanings to those, who are not of their tribe. **1796** Burke *Reg. Peace* ii. Wks. VIII. 218 The tribe of vulgar politicians are the lowest of our species. **1843** Ruskin *Arrows of Chace* (1880) I. 18 Dr. Waagen is a most favourable specimen of the tribe of critics. **1850** J. H. Newman *Diffic. Anglic.* I. xii. (1891) I. 388 Perish sooner a whole tribe of Cranmers, Ridleys, Latimers, and Jewels!

b. ***tribe of Ben***, a name applied to themselves by literary associates and disciples of Ben Jonson in his later life. ('*Sealed*' appears to refer to Rev. vii. 3–8.)

a **1637** B. Jonson *Underwoods* lxv. (*title*) An epistle, answering to one that asked to be sealed of the Tribe of Ben. *Ibid.* 78 Now stand, and then, Sir, you are Sealed of the Tribe of Ben. **1911** Sir A. W. Ward in *Encycl. Brit.* XV. 505/1 At the festive meetings where he ruled the roast among the younger authors whose pride it was to be 'sealed of the tribe of Ben'.

c. A gang of criminals or delinquents. Also, in recent use, a group of hippies or other drop-outs.

1914 Jackson & Hellyer *Vocab. Criminal Slang* 85 *Tribe*, used principally by yeggs and begging bums, though current, too, amongst grafters who operate in cliques. A gang; a class. **1955** D. W. Maurer in *Publ. Amer. Dial. Soc.* xxiv. 83 In general, [pickpocketing] mobs are also known as *tribes*. **1968** *Guardian* 29 Apr. 7/5 The fifteen hundred 'Tribes' of San Francisco..beg their food and sleep where they can. **1973** R. C. Dennis *Sweat of Fear* vii. 44 A room with wall-to-wall mattresses. Sprawled about were a half-dozen members of the tribe.

5. a. *Nat. Hist.* A group in the classification of plants, animals, etc., usually forming a subdivision of an order, and containing a number of genera; sometimes used as superior and sometimes as inferior to a family; also, loosely, any group or series of animals.

1640 Parkinson (*title*) Theatrum Botanicum: the Theater of Plants..Distributed into sundry Classes or Tribes, for the more easie knowledge of the many Herbes [etc.]. **1667** Milton *P.L.* XI. 279 O flours..Who now shall reare ye to the Sun, or ranke Your Tribes? **1672** Grew *Idea Philos. Hist. Plants* §2 We commonly say, *Centaurium Majus and Minus, Chelidonium Majus and Minus*,..which yet are distinct Species, and of very different Tribes. **1766** *Compl. Farmer* s.v. *Vegetable*, Vegetables, according to the analyses made of them by chemistry, are distinguishable into two grand tribes, the acid and the alkaline. **1774** Goldsm. *Nat. Hist.* (1776) III. 256 This tribe of the cat kind with spotted skins and a long tail. **1832** Ht. Martineau *Life in Wilds* v, A tribe of birds whose habit is to unite in flocks. **1880** Gray *Struct. Bot.* ix. § 1. (ed. 6) 326 *Tribe* has been for a generation or two..established in both kingdoms, as a grade inferior to order and superior to genus.

b. A class, group, kind, or sort of things.

1731 in *10th Rep. Hist. MSS. Comm.* App. I. 269 The slimy tribe of Snails and Worms. **1744** Berkeley *Siris* §87 The whole tribe of chronical diseases. **1776** G. Campbell *Philos. Rhet.* I. v. (1801) I. 114 Under it I include these three tribes: experience, analogy and testimony. **1822–34** *Good's Study Med.* (ed. 4) I. 446 The same tribe of medicines will generally be found useful in the third variety. **1844** Stephens *Bk. Farm* II. 678 It is..a member of the harrow tribe of implements.

6. A number or company of persons or animals; a 'troop'; in *pl.*, large numbers, 'flocks'.

1711 Pope *Temp. Fame* 356 Then came the smallest tribe I yet had seen, Plain was their dress, and modest was their mien. **1820** Scoresby *Acc. Arctic Reg.* II. 209 The same tribe of whales were seen in the latitude of 78°. **1833** Ht. Martineau *Brooke Farm* i, There were tribes of children in most of the cottages. **1909** *Blackw. Mag.* Feb. 160/2, I could fancy her..writing lengthy epistles to a tribe of nieces.

7. a. *attrib.* and *Comb.*, as ***tribe-book***, ***-chief***, ***-chieftainship***, ***-guest***, ***-land***, ***-league***, ***-man***, ***-mark***, ***-name***, ***-territory***; ***tribe-invited***, ***-like*** adjs.

1893 P. White *Hist. Clare* 12 He must have used..the *tribe-books then in existence. **1864** Bryce *Holy Rom. Emp.* xii. (1889) 189 The first barbarian kings had been *tribe chiefs. *Ibid.* Supp. Ch. 424 The German kingdom..was then passing from primitive *tribe-chieftainship into a feudal monarchy. **1746** P. Francis tr. *Horace, Ep.* I. xiii. 17 A *Tribe-invited Guest Carries his Cap and Slippers to a Feast. **1872** E. W. Robertson *Hist. Ess., Rome* 248 The *tribe-land, in early times, was probably divided into local districts corresponding with the Centuries of the tribe. **1899** Baring-Gould *Bk. West* II. 102 The old tribeland or principality of Gallewick was reduced in the Middle Ages to a Manor. **1864** Bryce *Holy Rom. Emp.* viii. (1889) 116 The five or six great tribes or *tribe-leagues which composed the German nation. **1859** R. F. Burton *Centr. Afr.* in *Jrnl. Geog. Soc.* XXIX. 90 If he suspect that it belongs to a fellow *tribeman. **1884** W. Wright *Empire Hittites* 129 The scratchy *tribe-marks of the Bedawin. **1886** Conder *Syrian Stone-Lore* ix. (1896) 323 *note*, The *tribe-names of Arabia may be best explained by the early linguistic condition in which the abstract and the comparative were unknown. **1876** tr. *Keil & Delitzsch's Ezekiel* II. 384 Every *tribe-territory shall stretch from the Jordan to the Mediterranean.

b. Combinations with *tribe's*, as TRIBESMAN, q.v.; ***tribesfolk***, ***tribespeople***, ***tribeswoman***.

1888 Doughty *Arabia Deserta* I. viii. 222 There is no Beduwy so impious that will chide and bite at such, his own *tribesfolk. **1888** in *Jrnl. Anthrop. Inst.* Aug. (1889) 90 He sent me a list of a number of the *tribespeople. **1853** Hickie tr. *Aristoph.* (1872) II. 404, I come with water to rescue my fellow *tribes-women being on fire. **1899** W. Canton in *Expositor* Feb. 130 There were tribeswomen who were hospitable enough to welcome the young mother.

tribe, *v. rare.* [f. prec. sb. Cf. *to class*, *to group*.] *trans.* To classify in tribes; also, to group or place in the same tribe *with*.

1696 Bp. Nicolson *Eng. Hist. Libr.* i. 19 Our Fowl, Fish, and Quadrupeds are well Trib'd by Mr. Willughby and Mr. Ray. **1838** [see *tribed* below]. **1852** *Meanderings of Memory* I. 104 Her nature may with thine be tribed.

Hence **tribed** (traɪbd) *ppl. a.*, divided into tribes.

1838 S. Bellamy *Betrayal* 65 Trib'd Decapolis Ye need not seek.

ˈ**tribeless**, *a.* [f. TRIBE *sb.* + -LESS.] Belonging to no tribe.

1819 SHELLEY *Prometh. Unb.* III. iv, Man Equal, unclassed, tribeless, and nationless. **1875** POSTE *Gaius* I. Comm. (ed. 2) 126 The tribeless man (*aerarius*) forfeited his vote and became incapable of military service.

tribelet (ˈtraɪblɪt). [f. as prec. + -LET.] A small tribe.

1855 BAILEY *Spir. Leg.* in *Mystic*, etc. 69 The hill Altäic named the almighty god, By Tchudic tribelets of the age of mounds. **1873** DIXON *Two Queens* II. VII. iv. 25 An Irish tribelet, who had swept across the land. **1899** OLIVE SCHREINER in *Fortn. Rev.* July 1 They were split up into endless tribelets.

tribeship (ˈtraɪbʃɪp). [f. as prec. + -SHIP.] The condition or position of being a tribe; the members of a tribe collectively, or their territory. ***free tribeship, sceptre t.***, the position of being a free tribe or the 'sceptre-tribe'.

1782 J. BROWN *Comp. View Nat. & Rev. Relig.* IV. i. 291 The Sceptre Tribeship, or power of Supreme Government ..is now long ago departed. **1840** J. WILSON *Our Israelitish Origin* vi. (1865) 69 The greater part of the tribeship of Judah lay South of Jerusalem. **1862** W. BARNES in *Macm. Mag.* Mar. 412/1 Trial by Jury seems..to have been practised by the Celtic people..in their times of free tribeship.

tribesman (ˈtraɪbzmən). [f. *tribe's*, genitive of TRIBE *sb.* + MAN *sb.*[1] (Cf. *clansman.*)] **a.** A man belonging to a tribe; a member of a tribe. Chiefly *pl.* **b.** With possessive, a man of one's own tribe, a fellow-tribesman.

1798 SOUTHEY *Rose* 28 For her Her tribes-men sigh'd in vain. **1837** WHEELWRIGHT tr. *Aristoph.* II. 117 Why spare our stones, my fellow tribesmen? **1883** *Standard* No. 18465. 5/2 To make a meal off the grasshopper with the tribesmen of the Sierra Nevada. **1893** ELIZA R. SUTHERLAND in Barrows *Parl. Relig.* I. 635 An animal dying of itself may not be eaten by a tribesman, but might be sold to a stranger. **1905** *Times* 13 Sept. 3/3 A patrol..has been fired on by Tebetekentzy tribesmen.

tribill, trible, var. TRIBUL, TRIBULE.

tribit, obs. form of TRIBUTE.

tri-bladed, -blastic: see TRI- 1 c, a.

†**tribler, tribbler**, app. obs. for ***trebler**, a treble-singer.

1539 *Wills & Inv. N.C.* (Surtees 1908) 162 To Robte Belryngar xij d. To everye on of the Tribulars xx d. **1546** *Yorks. Chantry Surv.* (Surtees) II. 361, vj choresteriez, vj tribblers, one orgayne player. *Ibid.*, The vj triblers for ther yerlie stipend lij[s] vj[d].

triblet (ˈtrɪblɪt). Also 8 **triboulet**, 9 **treblett, tribolet.** [= F. *triboulet* in the sense 'wooden cylinder used by goldsmiths for rounding articles' (Littré); of uncertain origin: see Littré.] A cylindrical rod or mandrel used for forging nuts, rings, tubes, etc., or for drawing lead-pipe. Also *attrib.*: ***triblet tubes***, thin tubes which slide one upon the other, as in a telescope.

1611 COTGR., *Triboulet*, a Triblet; the toole whereon Goldsmiths and Clockmakers put Rings, and little wheeles, when they file, or otherwise worke, them. **1736** AINSWORTH *Lat. Dict.* I, A triblet, or triboulet (goldsmith's tool for making rings). **1778** NAIRNE in *Phil. Trans.* LXVIII. 854 In the uppermost room stood a large iron triblet, of about three feet in height. **1853** URE *Dict. Arts* I. 724 A mandril,.. which consists of a long rod of iron, having a short steel treblett on its end. **1877** KNIGHT *Dict. Mech.* s.v., The nut having been cut from the bar, the hole is punched and enlarged by the triblet. **1895** *Model Steam Engine* 95 Triblet drawn tube (i.e., tube made by drawing a steel mandrel through the inside as well as drawing the outside through a hole).

tribo- (ˈtraɪbəʊ, ˈtrɪbəʊ), comb. form repr. Gr. τρίβος rubbing, as ˌ**triboelecˈtricity** [ad. F. *triboélectricité* (O. D. Chwolson *Traité de Physique* (1913) IV. I. ii. 268)], electricity generated by friction; so **triboeˈlectric** *a.*, **-eˈlectrically** *adv.*; ˌ**triboelectrifiˈcation**, the production of triboelectricity; ˌ**tribonucleˈation** (see quot. 1967); ˈ**tribophysics**, the physics of friction; hence **triboˈphysical** *a.*; **tribosphenic** (-ˈsfiːnɪk) *a. Palæont.* [Gr. σφήν wedge] (see quots. 1936, 1975[2]); ˌ**triboˌthermolumiˈnescence**, thermoluminescence produced in a material as a result of friction.

1917 *Nature* 27 Dec. 337/1 The research provides an explanation of the well-known readiness with which materials change their tribo-electric character. **1967** W. R. HARPER *Contact & Frictional Electrification* v. 77 The notorious difficulty of performing triboelectric experiments in damp weather proclaims the importance of adsorbed water. *Ibid.*, Glass cleaned with alkalis became triboelectrically ⊕ve with respect to metals. **1972** *Sci. Amer.* Mar. 54/3 Yarns, plastic films, paper and kindred materials moving at high speeds inevitably lead to triboelectric troubles. **1979** *Adv. Colloid & Interface Sci.* XI. 64 The roles of tribo-electricity in everyday life and in industry are numerous both as a nuisance and hazard and as a phenomenon to be exploited. **1938** G. P. HARNWELL *Princ. Electr. & Magn.* i. 1 The production of electrification by the frictional process of rubbing is known as triboelectrification. **1967** W. R. HARPER *Contact & Frictional Electrification* v. 85 The loosely bound ions are available to diffuse to another surface brought into contact with the one under consideration, and might be important..for triboelectrification. **1967** *Brit. Jrnl. Appl. Physics* XVIII. 641 If a solid body such as a stirrer rod is rubbed against the inner wall of a vessel containing either a supersaturated solution of a salt or a supercooled liquid, the nucleation of crystals is likely to occur at the point of contact. This phenomenon is known as tribonucleation ('nucleation by rubbing'). **1974** *Nature* 20 Dec. 696/1 One mechanism for the production of micronuclei in man, tribonucleation, has been suggested by Ikels. **1977** *Jrnl. Catalysis* L. 542/1 The catalyst produced by the tribophysical procedure is more active longer than the conventional one. **1950** *Engineering* 17 Mar. 303/3 The new Division of Tribophysics has developed from a section which, during the war, evolved some interesting theories regarding the fundamental nature of friction and lubrication. **1976** *Sci. Amer.* Apr. 30/2 Sanders, who is chief research scientist in the Tribophysics Division, heads a group that is engaged in studying the reactivity of metallic surfaces, relying mainly on electron microscopy. **1936** G. G. SIMPSON in *Dental Cosmos* LXXVIII. 797/1 At this stage the upper molar is implanted by two external and one internal root, the latter generally largest, and the lower molars are implanted by two sub-equal roots, one beneath the trigonid and one beneath the talonid... In order to have a single word..by which this type of molar dentition can be unequivocably..designated, I propose to call it 'tribosphenic'. **1975** *Nature* 31 July 402/1 Therian mammals with tribosphenic molars were probably in existence at the beginning of the Cretaceous. *Ibid.*, Tribosphenic molars have an additional cusp on the upper molars (protocone) which fits into a basin (talonid) on the matching lower molar. **1930** NYSWANDER & COHN in *Physical Rev.* XXXVI. 1257 The term tribothermoluminescence has been given to the phenomenon under consideration which involves the process of grinding followed by application of heat. **1971** *Nature* 23 July 257/2 Thermoluminescence (TL) of fossil bones and of various kinds of recent biological material has been reported by Jasińska and Niewiadomski, who suggest that such materials could be used for dating purposes, but draw attention to difficulties which arise due to tribothermoluminescence (TTL, which is thermoluminescence derived from the mechanical energy of grinding).

tribochet, obs. form of TREBUCHET.

tribology (traɪˈbɒlədʒɪ). [f. TRIBO- + -OLOGY.] The branch of science and technology concerned with interacting surfaces in relative motion and with associated matters (as friction, wear, lubrication, and the design of bearings).

Mr. H. P. Jost (see quot. 1968), chairman of a working group of 'lubrication engineers', corresponded with me in 1965 about the need for a new term and accepted *tribology*, a word suggested by Mr. C. G. Hardie of Magdalen College. —R.W.B.

1966 (Feb.) *Lubrication (Tribology)* (Dept. Educ. & Sci.) 4 Tribology is defined as follows: Tribology is the science and technology of interacting surfaces in relative motion and of the practices related thereto. **1968** H. P. JOST in *New Scientist* 8 Feb. 292 After consultation with the English Dictionary Department of the Oxford University Press—the publishers of the *Oxford Dictionary*—we chose the term 'tribology'. **1969** *Sunday Times* 30 Nov. 30/2 Two chairs of tribology have been established, one at Leeds and another at Salford. **1975** *Sci. Amer.* July 50/3 This field of study is known, more commonly in Britain than in the U.S., as tribology. **1980** *Canada Weekly* 19 Nov. 4/1 As Canada's main centre of expertise on tribology..the..laboratory examines the problem of wear and failure of rails and wheels.

Hence **triboˈlogical** *a.*, of or pertaining to tribology; **triˈbologist**, an expert or specialist in tribology.

1966 *New Scientist* 19 May 423/1 They suggested that the Institution of Mechanical Engineers should organize 'professional institution activities in the tribological sphere'. **1969** *Lubrication Engin.* Feb. 88/3 (*heading*) Dr. Finkin named chief tribologist. **1973** *Nature* 6 Apr. 361/3 The tribological problems the centre has tackled have ranged from making gas bearings to designing window hinges for high rise flats. **1974** *Globe & Mail* (Toronto) 18 Apr. 45/2 Tribologists believe they can save Canadians several hundred million dollars a year. **1977** *Engin. Materials & Design* Aug. 35/2 This compound layer has excellent tribological properties under dry running as well as lubricated conditions.

triboluminescence (ˌtrɪbəʊl(j)uːmɪˈnɛsəns). [f. Gr. τρίβος rubbing + LUMINESCENCE.] The quality of emitting light under friction or violent pressure.

1889 *Philos. Mag.* Sept. 151 According to the mode of excitation I distinguish Photo-, Electro-, Chemi-, and Tribo-luminescence. **1899** *Nature* 27 Apr. 618/1 The name tribo-luminescence has been applied by E. Wiedemann to an emission of light not due to rise of temperature which occurs on crushing certain substances. *Ibid.* 619/1 Crystals of saccharin which, when freshly prepared, flash brilliantly on crushing,..after a few weeks' preservation show no appreciable triboluminescence.

Hence **triboluміˈnescent** *a.*, exhibiting triboluminescence.

1904 W. G. LEVISON in *Science* 27 May 827/2 A zinc-blende from Utah..was the most intense tribo-luminescent substance..yet investigated.

tribometer (traɪˈbɒmɪtə(r)). [ad. F. *tribomètre*, f. as prec. + *-mètre*, -METER.] An instrument for estimating sliding friction.

a **1774** GOLDSM. *Surv. Exp. Philos.* (1776) I. 293 He [Muschenbrook] calls it a Tribometre, a name compounded ungrammatically enough, but it means a measurer of friction. **1870** C. DRAPER in *Eng. Mech.* 28 Jan. 478/3 This apparatus [a loaded beam of wood] is called a *tribometer.* **1877** KNIGHT *Dict. Mech.*, *Tribometer*, an apparatus resembling a sled, used in estimating the friction of rubbing surfaces.

tribophosphorescent (ˌtrɪbəʊfɒsfəˈrɛsənt), *a.* [f. as prec. + PHOSPHORESCENT.] = TRIBOLUMINESCENT. So **triboˈphosphoroscope**, an instrument for examining triboluminescence.

1904 W. G. LEVISON in *Science* 27 May 826/1 Note on a Tribophosphoroscope, and the Duration and Spectrum of Tribophosphorescent Light.

tribowne, obs. Sc. form of TRIBUNE *sb.*[1]

tribrach[1] (ˈtraɪbræk, ˈtrɪb-). *Prosody.* In 6 **tribracchus**, 8 **tribrachus**, 8–9 **-ys**; 7 **tribrack.** [ad. L. *tribrachys*, a. Gr. τρίβραχυς, f. TRI- + βραχύς short. Cf. F. *tribraque* (Littré).] A metrical foot consisting of three short syllables.

1589 PUTTENHAM *Eng. Poesie* II. xiii. (Arb.) 133 For your foote tribracchus of all three short, ye haue very few trissillables. **1602** T. CAMPION *Art Eng. Poesie* iv. 11 We may vse a Spondee or Iambick and sometime a Tribrack or Dactile. **1706** PHILLIPS (ed. Kersey), *Tribrachus*, or *Tribrachys*, (Gr.) a Foot in Greek and Latin Verse, consisting of three short Syllables; as Populus. **1827** TATE *Grk. Metres* in *Theat. Grks.* (ed. 2) 436 Of all the resolved feet, the Tribrach in Trochaic verse with its ictus on the first syllable..is most readily recognised by the ear as equivalent to the Trochee. **1885** GOODELL in *Trans. Amer. Philol. Assoc.* XVI. 88 The plain tribrach is frequent in every one's reading.

Hence **tribrachic** (traɪˈbrækɪk) *a.*, consisting of three short syllables; also, composed of tribrachs.

1852 J. S. BLACKIE *Pronunciation of Greek* 43 The tendency to the ineffective tribrachic and even proceleusmatic accent in the termination of our polysyllables. **1866** BLACKIE *Homer & Iliad* I. 401 If the range of pure tribrachic measure, or of tribrachs intermingled with trochees, appears much wider in our song-books than in volumes of poetry written to be read.

tribrach[2] (ˈtraɪbræk). [f. TRI- + Gr. βραχίων arm.] A figure or object having three arms or branches; *spec.* a prehistoric flint implement of this form. So **tribrachial** (traɪˈbreɪkɪəl) *a.*, having three arms or branches.

1873 A. WAY in *Archæol. Jrnl.* XXX. 28 The implement ..is of a form that may be designated tribrachial, having three branches radiating from the centre. *Ibid.* 31 The unique tribrachial implement. *Ibid.*, The flint tribrach was presented..by the late Dr. Martin in 1853, with other objects from Ventnor. **1897** SIR. J. EVANS *Anc. Stone Implem. Gt. Brit.* iv. 78 A singular instrument chipped out of flint, like three celts conjoined.., so as to form a sort of tribrach.

tribracteate, etc.: see TRI- 1.

tribrom-, tribromo- (traɪˈbrəʊm(əʊ)). *Chem.* [f. TRI- 5 c + BROM(O-.] A formative signifying that three atoms of bromine are substituted for hydrogen in the substance designated by the rest of the name; e.g. *tribromobenzene*: see TRI- 5 c.

1852 ANDERSON in *Q. Jrnl. Chem. Soc.* IV. 117 The yellow precipitate thus obtained is the hydrobromate of tribromocodeine. **1900** SMITH *Richter's Org. Chem.* II. 92 Aniline, acted upon by..bromine, yields..Tribromaniline.

tribromhydrin (traɪbrəʊmˈhaɪdrɪn). *Chem.* [f. TRI- 5 a + *bromhydr(ic* + -IN[1] (termination of the compound ethers of glycerin: see ACETIN).] Glyceryl tribromide, $C_3H_5Br_3$, a haloid ester or compound ether of glycerin or glycerol, $C_3H_5(OH)_3$, in which the three OH groups are replaced by bromine atoms.

1862 MILLER *Elem. Chem.* (1869) III. 326 Glycerin forms with hydrobromic acid compounds analogous to those which it yields with hydrochloric acid, such as *monobromhydrin* ($C_3H_7BrO_2$), *dibromhydrin* ($C_3H_6Br_2O$), and *tribromhydrin* ($C_3H_5Br_3$). **1899** SMITH *Richter's Org. Chem.* I. 474 Tribromhydrin fuses at 16°, and boils at 220°.

tribromide: see TRI- 5 a and BROMIDE.

tribual (ˈtrɪbjuːəl), *a.* [f. L. *tribu-s* TRIBE + -AL[1]: cf. *gradu-al*, *manu-al*. (L. had in this sense *tribuārius*.)] Of, belonging or pertaining to a tribe; tribal.

1650 FULLER *Pisgah* II. x. 207 The first tribuall defection to idolatry Dan was guilty of. *a* **1661** —— *Worthies, Leicester.* (1662) II. 126 The Tribual Lisping of the Ephramites. **1817** G. S. FABER *Eight Dissert.* (1845) I. 229 We are apt to fancy, that this extraordinary people have no tribual distinctions among themselves. **1822–34** *Good's Study Med.* (ed. 4) IV. 268 It would..have been a much greater improvement..to have employed hydrops as a generic, instead of hydropes as a tribual or family name. **1881** BENTHAM in *Jrnl. Linn. Soc.* XVIII. 287 Observations on the most important tribual and subtribual characters.

Hence ˈ**tribually** *adv.*, by tribes, tribally.

1817 G. S. FABER *Eight Dissert.* (1845) II. 181 Here, apparently, they were first tribually planted, when Nimrod and his baffled Cuthim migrated from Babel to Ashur.

†ˈ**tribul**, *v.* Chiefly *Sc. Obs.* Forms: 4–6 **trible**, **tribul(e**, 6 **tribull**, **-bill**, **-bil**. [a. OF. *triboler*, *-bouler*, *-buler*, etc. (12th c. in Godef.), ad. L. *trībulāre* to press, oppress, afflict: see

TRIBULATION.] *trans.* To bring tribulation upon; to distress, harass, afflict.

a **1325** *Prose Psalter* xxxviii[i]. 9 Man for-soþe in likenes passeþ; ac in vayn he hys tribled [*v.r.* sturblyd]. **1375** BARBOUR *Bruce* IV. 58 It wes gret pite for to heir Folk till be tribulit on þis maneir. **1456–70** in *Acts Parlt. Scot.* (1875) XII. 20/2 Part of ewyl myndit personis..wrangis and tribulis ws and our pwr tenentis. **1563** WINȜET *Wks.* (S.T.S.) II. 28 Men of corruptit mynd,..tribuland thair wit about quæstions and stryfe of wordis. **1572** EARL ARGYLE *Let.* in *Munim. Irvine* (1890) I. 60 Quhatsomevir persone or personis..sall attempt to tribull, molest, harme or injure the foirsaidis provest, baillzies [etc.].

Hence †'**tribular** *Sc. Obs.*, one who distresses or afflicts; †'**tribulness** *Sc. Obs.* = TRIBULE; †'**tribulous** *a. Sc. Obs.*, full of tribulation.

1574 *Reg. Privy Council Scot.* II. 395 The saidis declarit tratouris,..and *tribularis of the commoun weill. *c* **1375** *Sc. Leg. Saints* xxiv. (*Alexis*) 327, & neuir for ony *tribulnes Spak he Il..mare ore les. **1563** WINȜET *Four Scoir Thre Quest.* To Rdr., Wks. (S.T.S.) I. 51 That quhilk the Prophete spak..apperis in thir our *tribulus dayis almaist fullelie complete.

tribulage ('trɪbjʊlɪdʒ). *local.* Now *Hist.* [ad. med.L. *tribulāgium* (*trubl-*), f. *tribulum* threshing-sledge (in med.L. app. some other crushing-machine): see -AGE.] A species of poll-tax formerly levied on each tin-miner in some of the stannaries: see quots. Cf. TRIBULARY.

[**1296–7** *Ministers' Accts. 24–5 Edw. I* (*Bailiff's Accts. Edmund of Cornw.*) (P.R.O.), *Perquisita stagnariorum.* Idem reddit compotum de cxj solidis vij denariis de minutis amerciamentis Nigre More hoc anno et de vj solidis de Trublagio hoc anno. **1338** —— *12 Edw. III* 816/11 De x solidis iij denariis de quadam consuetudine vocata Tribulagium videlicet de quolibet homine operante cum tribula, obolum.] **1537** *Let. Hen. VIII* in Rymer *Foedera* (1712) XIV. 581/1 Concedimus eidem Johanni Greynfeld Tribulagium nostrum, sive consuetudinem vocatam le Tribulage, infra Hundreda nostra de Penwyth et Kerr. **1906** G. R. LEWIS in *Victoria County Hist., Cornwall* I. 537/1 Tribulage, a poll tax levied in Blackmore at the rate of ½*d.*, and in Penwith and Kerrier at ¼*d.*..for each labouring tinner. *Ibid.* 538 *note*, The Civil War brought with it the final extinction of tribulage, dublet, and the fine of tin. **1908** —— *Stannaries* v. 140 The tax known as 'tribulage', or 'shovel money', which represents the only attempt at a capitation tax in the Cornish stannaries, was paid in two stannaries only, Penwith and Kerrier, and, after 1342, Blackmore. *Ibid.* 141 The record of tribulage payments is necessarily incomplete from the fact that the duty was collected and paid to the receiver by the head bailiff, and often included in their accounts with the perquisites of the stannary courts.

†'**tribulance.** *Obs. rare.* [a. OF. *tribulance* (*a* 1300 in Godef.), f. *tribuler*, ad. L. *trībulāre*: see TRIBULATION and -ANCE.] Tribulation.

1560 ROLLAND *Crt. Venus* II. 531 Greit tribulance, or famine accidentaill.

tribular ('trɪbjʊlə(r)), *a. rare*⁻⁰. [f. L. *tribūl-is* one of the same tribe with another + -AR.] Tribal.

1864 in WEBSTER; whence in later Dicts.

tribular: see TRIBLER.

†'**tribulary.** *Obs. rare*⁻¹. [f. as TRIBULAGE + -ARY.] = TRIBULAGE.

1467–8 *Rolls of Parlt.* V. 610/2 Thoffice of Baillyf of oure Stannarie of Penwith and Kerye..togeder with alle þe tribularye within oure said Stannarie commyng.

†'**tribulate,** *ppl. a. Obs. rare.* In 6 *Sc.* tribulat. [ad. L. *tribulāt-us*, pa. pple. of *trībulāre*: see next.] Tribulated. (Const. as *pa. pple.*)

1560 ROLLAND *Crt. Venus* III. 32 [Q]uhen he on sey be storme was tribulat.

tribulate ('trɪbjʊleɪt), *v.* [f. L. *trībulāt-*, ppl. stem of *trībulāre*; or perh. from TRIBULATION, q.v.] *trans.* To afflict; to oppress; to trouble greatly.

a **1637** N. FERRAR *110 Consid.* (1638) 122 If such a one be needy, tribulated, and afflicted, it is because it so pleaseth God. **1829** LANDOR *Imag. Conv.*, *Cdl. Albani & Picture-Dealers* Wks. 1846 II. 7/2 The Pontifical Chancery and the Ruota Criminale would never tribulate gallant men in this guise. **1845** CARLYLE *Cromwell* IX. (1871) IV. 136 Otherwise tribulated by subaltern authorities. **1885** S. COX *Expositions* I. xxiii. 306 'He will tribulate them that tribulate you', says St. Paul to the Thessalonians.

'**tribulated,** *ppl. a.* [f. L. *trībulāt-us* pa. pple. of *trībulāre* (see next) + -ED¹.] Subjected to tribulation, afflicted.

1682 DEWSBURY *Gen. Epist.* 6, I dearly beseech you..that you Watch over the Tender and Tribulated ones. *a* **1715** NELSON *T. à Kempis' Chr. Exerc.* III. xvi. 140 The Comforter of the afflicted and Tribulated. **1858** CARLYLE *Fredk. Gt.* v. ii. (1872) II. 67 Friedrich's Sister, Father, Mother, were tribulated, almost heartbroken.

tribulation (trɪbjʊ'leɪʃən). *arch.* Also 4–6 try-, -cion, etc. [a. OF. *tribulacion* (12th c. in Godef. *Compl.*), ad. Chr.L. *trībulātiōn-em* (Itala *a* 200, etc.), n. of action from L. *trībulāre* to press, oppress, afflict, f. *trībul-um* a threshing-sledge, app. f. *trī-*, var. stem of *ter-ĕre*, *trīvi*, *trītum* to rub, grind + *-bulum*, forming names of instruments.]

1. A condition of great affliction, oppression, or misery; 'persecution; distress; vexation; disturbance of life' (J.).

c **1330** R. BRUNNE *Chron.* (1810) 206 He lyued in wo & strife, & in tribulacioun. *c* **1374** CHAUCER *Troylus* v. 988 Myn herte is now in tribulacion. **1382** WYCLIF *Matt.* xxiv. 21 Thanne schal be greet tribulacioun. *c* **1440** *Gesta Rom.* viii. 22 (Harl. MS.) To þis Cite is a þorny wey and a sharp, *scil.* penaunce and tribulacion in erþe. **1534** MORE *Comf. agst. Trib.* I. Wks. 1158/1 Tribulacion is euery such thing as troubleth and greueth a man either in bodye or mynde. **1667** MILTON *P.L.* XI. 63 Tri'd in sharp tribulation, and refin'd By Faith and faithful works. **1696** PHILLIPS (ed. 5), *Tribulation*, Affliction, Misery; generally spoken of that which a Christian takes in good part, as being inflicted by the hand of God. **1862** *Sat. Rev.* 8 Feb. 141 The sufferers..are sustained in their tribulation by the proud consciousness that they are assisting to uphold a great national principle.

b. With *a* and *pl.* An affliction.

a **1225** *Ancr. R.* 402 None wateres, þet beoð worldliche temptaciuns ne tribulaciuns..ne muwen þeos luue acwenchen. *a* **1450** *Knt. de la Tour* (1906) 75 Many tribulacions and euylls. **1526** *Pilgr. Perf.* (W. de W. 1531) 11 b, Yᵉ paynes, aduersitees, tribulacyons..& all other labours & besynesses of this worlde. **1667** MILTON *P.L.* III. 336 The just shall..after all thir tribulations long See golden days.

†**c.** One who or that which causes trouble. (In quot., app. a cant name for a gang of disturbers.)

1613 SHAKS. *Hen. VIII*, V. iv. 65 These are the youths that thunder at a Playhouse..that no Audience but the tribulation of Tower Hill, or the Limbes of Limehouse, their deare Brothers, are able to endure.

†**2.** The condition of being held in pawn or pledge. *Obs. slang.*

1663 DRYDEN *Wild Gallant* I. ii, Sirrah, Boy, fetch my Suit with the Gold Lace at Sleeves from Tribulation. **1764** *Low Life* (ed. 3) 15 Pawnbrokers..busy in altering the Dates of Cloaths under Tribulation.

†**tribule.** *Sc. Obs.* Also trible, -ill, -il. [f. as TRIBUL *v.*] Tribulation, distress, affliction.

1513 DOUGLAS *Æneis* IV. Prol. 247 Of thi trigittis quhat toung can tell the trible [*v.r.* tribill]? **1549** *Compl. Scot.* ix. 75 Afflictione ande tribil. **1563** WINȜET *Four Scoir Thre Quest.* To Rdr., Wks. (S.T.S.) I. 49 Thai suffer in this lyfe ..that be diuers tribulis thai mot enter..in the lyfe eternall. *Ibid.* 63 For na trible of tyme nor tyrannie of man.

tribuloid ('trɪbjʊlɔɪd), *a. Bot.* [f. mod.L. *Tribulus* + -OID.] (See quot.)

1900 B. D. JACKSON *Gloss. Bot. Terms*, *Tribuloid* (εἶδος, resemblance), like the fruit of *Tribulus*, beset with sharp bristles, echinate (Heinig).

‖**Tribuna** (tri'buna). *Obs.* [It. and med.L. *tribūna*, f. L. *tribūnus* TRIBUNE *sb.*¹] An octagonal saloon in the Galleria degli Uffizi at Florence containing many famous paintings and statues.

1644 EVELYN *Diary* 20 Nov., The quire, roofe and paintings in the Tribuna are excellent. **1756–7** tr. *Keysler's Trav.* (1760) II. 19 That admirable chamber called *la Tribuna*, or *l'Octogone*, which name it derives from its octangular figure... On entering the tribuna, the eye is immediately struck with six marble statues standing in the center, among which is that famous statue, called the Venus de Medicis.

tribunal (traɪ-, trɪ'bjuːnəl), *sb.* (*a.*) Also 6 try-, 6–7 -all. [ad. L. *tribūnāl*, *-āle* sb. neut., a tribunal, judgement seat, f. *tribūn-us* TRIBUNE *sb.*¹: see -AL¹. Cf. F. *tribunal* (13th c. in Hatz.-Darm.), perh. the immediate source; also Sp., Pg. *tribunal*, It. *tribunale*.

By Spenser stressed *tribu'nal* as in French.]

A. *sb.* **1.** Originally, A raised semicircular or square platform in a Roman basilica, on which the seats of the magistrates were placed; a dais; a raised throne or chair of state; a judgement seat (also *fig.*).

1526 *Pilgr. Perf.* (W. de W. 1531) 212 We all shall stande before the tribunall of god. **1590** SPENSER *F.Q.* III. v. 53 And crowne your heades with heavenly coronall, Such as the Angels weare before Gods tribunall. **1642** in *10th Rep. Hist. MSS. Comm.* App. IV. 429 Making 2 Tribunalles or seates for the judges at the last assizes. **1702** ECHARD *Eccl. Hist.* (1710) 612 They will be both read in the day of Judgment, before the Tribunal of Jesus Christ. **1833** CRUSE *Eusebius* v. i. 170 Those around the tribunal cried out against him.

2. a. A court of justice; a judicial assembly.

1590 SPENSER *F.Q.* II. ix. 53 Painted faire..with picturals Of Magistrates, of courts, of tribunals. **1610** HOLLAND *Camden's Brit.* (1637) 177 The Tribunals, or Courts of Justice in England. **1667** MILTON *P.L.* III. 326 When thou ..shalt..from thee send The..Arch-Angels to proclaime Thy dread Tribunal. **1687** T. BROWN *Saints in Uproar* Wks. 1730 I. 82, I am forced to appeal to your impartial tribunal. **1835** ALISON *Hist. Europe* (1847) IV. xiv. 137 On the 14th October [1793] the Queen was brought before the Revolutionary Tribunal. **1867** FREEMAN *Norm. Conq.* I. vi. 574 The judgement of a competent tribunal is always worth something.

b. *fig.* Place of judgement or decision; judicial authority.

1635 QUARLES *Embl.* II. xiii. 49 Go up, my soul, into the tribunal of thy conscience. **1734** tr. *Rollin's Anc. Hist.* (1827) I. 153 The field of battle is a tribunal without partiality and cabal. **1817** BENTHAM *Parl. Reform* Introd. 222 By the tribunal of public opinion it ought to be taken as and for confessional evidence. **1875** WHITNEY *Life Lang.* viii. 150 Our recognition of the community as final tribunal which decides whether anything shall be language or not.

c. Any of various local boards of officials empowered to settle disputes, esp. between an individual and a government department, to adjudicate on fair rents, exemption from military service, etc.; ***industrial tribunal***, a board arbitrating in disputes arising out of employment, such as complaints of unfair dismissal. Also (in full ***tribunal of inquiry***), a board set up by the government to investigate some matter of public concern.

1916 *Act 5 & 6 Geo. V* c. 104 §2 An application may be made at any time before the appointed date to the Local Tribunal established under this Act..for a certificate of exemption from the provisions of this Act. **1921** (*title of Act*) Tribunals of inquiry (evidence) act. **1932** L. GOLDING *Magnolia Street* II. iv. 321 The Baritone, at least, managed to convince tribunal after tribunal that it would be a mistake to put him into khaki. **1945** [see RENT *sb.*¹ 4 c]. **1949** *Britannica Bk. of Year* 309/2 Public interest was focused upon the judicial tribunal set up, under the chairmanship of Mr. Justice Lynskey, to inquire into allegations of corrupt practices involving several ministers and public servants. **1962** L. GOLDING *Dict. Local Govt.* 158 A Committee..was set up to consider..the constitution and working of administrative tribunals, particularly those dealing with the compulsory purchase of land. **1971** *Mod. Law Rev.* XXXIV. 657 The industrial tribunal may only recommend reinstatement. *Ibid.*, The tribunals may award.. compensation. **1974** M. MEACHER *Scrounging on Welfare* iii. 38 In 1971 the Supplementary Benefits Commission reported 153 cases to a Tribunal under Section 12/1.

†**3.** = TRIBUNE *sb.*² 1, 2. *Obs.*

1644 EVELYN *Diary* 7 Nov., [In Rome] the..Churches of St. Cosmo and Damiano,..a pretty odd fabriq, with a Tribunal, or Tholus within, wrought all of Mosaic. *Ibid.* 12 Nov., The tribunal of the high altar is of exquisite worke. **1694** *Ibid.* 5 Oct., Placing columns on pilasters at the East tribunal [of St. Paul's]. **1722** J. RICHARDSON *Statues, etc. Italy* 319 The Tribunal, or *Mezzo Cupola* of Dominichino. **1797** *Encycl. Brit.* (ed. 3) VII. 300/2 The..Venus of Medici ..stands in a room called the Tribunal [*Tribuna*].

B. *attrib.* or as *adj.*

1. Pertaining to, of the nature of, or authorized by a tribunal.

1554–5 BRADFORD *Let.* 16 Feb. in Coverdale *Lett. Martyrs* (1564) 471 A thing wherof I doute not to answer..before the tribunal seat of Iesus Christ. **1560** ROLLAND *Crt. Venus* II. 1020 Or Rhamnusia in hir sait Tribunall. **1610** *Histrio-m.* VI. 91 Affliction is the perfect way That leads to Joves tribunall dignity. **1645** MILTON *Tetrach.* Wks. 1851 IV. 216 A law to suffer a kind of tribunall adultery. **1708** PRIOR *Mice* 37 When we meet at God's tribunal throne.

†**2.** Of or pertaining to a tribune. *Obs. rare.*

1577 HANMER *Anc. Eccl. Hist.* (1663) 21 A sign being given from the tribunal seat. **1577–87** HOLINSHED *Chron.* I. 34/1 Narcissus went vp vnto the tribunall throne of Plautius, to declare the cause of his comming. **1670** *Narr. Long Parl.* in Somers *Tracts* (1748) I. 32 Persons..of a tribunal Spirit and Temper.

Hence **tri'bunalled** *a.*, having or seated on a tribunal; †**tri'bunalship** = TRIBUNESHIP.

1654 R. CODRINGTON tr. *Iustine* XIII. 213 The chief Tribunalship of the Camp was given to Seleuchus. **1852** *Meanderings of Memory* I. 32 Tribunalled judge, he weds the weaker cause, Holds sternly up as he lays down the laws.

†**tribunary,** *a. Obs. rare.* [f. TRIBUNE *sb.*¹ + -ARY. Cf. OF. *tribunaire* (14th c. in Godef.).] Of or pertaining to tribunes; tribunitian, tribunitial.

1612 W. SHUTE *Fougasse's Venice* i. 8 Now the Tribunarie Gouernment..shall be rightly termed Infancie.

tribunate ('trɪbjuːnət). [ad. L. *tribūnāt-us*, f. *tribūnus* TRIBUNE *sb.*¹: see -ATE¹. Cf. F. *tribunat*.]

1. The office of tribune; tribuneship; government by tribunes.

1546 LANGLEY *Pol. Verg. De Invent.* II. iii. 38 b, During that office [dictatorship] all other magistrates were abrogated except the Tribunate or Prouostship of the commons. **1603** HOLLAND *Plutarch's Mor.* 877 The Tribunate was an empeachment, inhibition, and restraint of a magistracie, rather than a magistracie it selfe. **1746** MELMOTH tr. *Pliny's Lett.* VII. xxii. (1748) II. 410, I so strongly pressed you to confer the Tribunate upon my friend. **1869** SEELEY *Lect. & Ess.* ii. 35 The great Roman Revolution which began with the tribunate of Gracchus and ended with the battle of Actium.

2. *French Hist.* A representative body of legislators established under the constitution of the year 8 of the Revolutionary calendar (1800–1).

[**1804** *Ann. Rev.* II. 85/2 Our author was present at a sitting of the tribunat, in the Palais Royal.] **1827** SCOTT *Napoleon* XV, A Tribunate of one hundred deputies. **1861** M. ARNOLD *Pop. Educ. France* 136 Both in the Tribunate and in the Legislative Body his measure encountered strenuous resistance. **1905** *Edin. Rev.* July 90 Benjamin Constant and nineteen others were turned out of the Tribunate.

attrib. **1802** in *Spirit Pub. Jrnls.* VI. 394 [Bonaparte] planted the hedges with *legislative* and *tribunate* shrubs, and apparently gave them a good root in the earth.

tribune ('trɪbjuːn, 'traɪ-), *sb.*¹ Also 4 *Sc.* tribone, -owne, trybone, 5 -bun(e, 7–8 tribun. [ad. L. *tribūnus*, lit. 'head of a tribe', f. *tribu-s* TRIBE; cf. F. *tribun* (13th c. in Hatz.-Darm.).]

1. A title designating one of several officers in the Roman administration; *spec.* **a.** ***tribune of the people*** (L. *tribūnus plebis*), one of two (later five, then ten) officers appointed to protect the interests and rights of the plebeians from the patricians. **b.** ***military tribune*** (L. *tribūnus mīlitāris*), one of six officers of a legion, each being in command for two months of the year.

c **1375** *Sc. Leg. Saints* xxii. (*Laurentius*) 171 þane was þare a mychtty tribowne. *Ibid.* xxxiii. (*George*) 22 Quhare he wes mad..a trybone. & þu sal wit, a tribone is he þat [of] þe thred-part of a cyte or of a cunctre kepare is; & a tribone is als I-wise þat trybut gadris to þe king..& he his tribune als, þu kene, to quham ansueris a thousand men. **1387** TREVISA *Higden* (Rolls) II. 273 After consuls, tribunes plebis and dictatores rulede the comounte anon to Iulius Cesar his tyme. **1456** SIR G. HAYE *Law Arms* (S.T.S.) 45 Ane othir maner of officiaris..callit trybunys. **1533** BELLENDEN *Livy* IV. iii. (S.T.S.) II. 61 The ȝere iijᶜx. fra þe first fundatioun of rome was þe first tyme þan ony tribunis militare war create with power consulare. **1678** R. L'ESTRANGE *Seneca's Mor.* I. xv. (1696) 77 He that is a Tribune, would be a Prætor. **1741** MIDDLETON *Cicero* I. Pref. 36 A new order of Magistrates, of their own body, called Tribuns. **1838–42** ARNOLD *Hist. Rome* I. viii. 139 The tribune's power of protection enabled him to interpose in defence of the unfortunate. **1879** FROUDE *Cæsar* iv. 37 He forced his way steadily upwards..to the rank of military tribune.

2. *transf.* and *fig.* **a.** An officer holding some position analogous to that of a Roman tribune; a judge; a protector of the rights of the people; a popular leader, a demagogue.

1587 HARRISON *England* II. v. (1877) I. 109 The cheefe or high tribune of the excheker is of custome called lord cheefe baron. *a* **1660** *Contemp. Hist. Irel.* (Ir. Archæol. Soc.) II. 147 Himself alone with his fewe Conatian tribunes..will disannull all this. **1756** NUGENT *Gr. Tour, Italy* III. 78 Venice was originally a democratical state, under consuls and tribunes... The Tribunes were succeeded by the Doges. **1853** MACAULAY *Biogr., Atterbury* (1860) 13 By the body of the clergy he was regarded as the ablest and most intrepid Tribune that had ever defended their rights. **1882** W. CORY *Mod. Eng. Hist.* II. 283 Mr. Cobbett..took his seat on the Treasury Bench. To have a tribune of the people sitting between Ministers..would be a hindrance to business.

b. (With capital initial.) The title of a British weekly journal, founded in 1937, advocating radical left-wing policies: used *attrib.* with reference to this type of socialism, esp. as ***Tribune group***, a group of Labour MPs sharing these views.

1952 *Ann. Reg. 1951* I. ii. 33 *One Way Only*, a *Tribune* pamphlet published on 9 July. **1968** *Times* 9 July 9/6 The trade unionists who are moving against the Government are not, as the *Tribune* group supposes, moving to the left. *a* **1974** R. CROSSMAN *Diaries* (1975) I. 562 They were really completely answered by Raymond Fletcher, a left-winger from the Tribune group. **1975** *Times* 16 July 14/7 Those who regarded themselves as the keepers of the socialist conscience—the Tribune group. **1976** A. PRICE *War Game* I. viii. 165 Not even the Tribune Group will be able to complain about the high cost of security. **1976** [see TRIBUNISM]. **1977** *Times Lit. Suppl.* 3 June 685/1 Orwell..was a Tribune-style socialist (egalitarian, libertarian).

Hence †**tri'bunian** *a. Obs. rare*, of or pertaining to a tribune. Also **'Tribunism**, socialist policies of the type advocated by the *Tribune*; **'Tribunite**, a member of the Tribune group (freq. *attrib.*).

a **1693** *Urquhart's Rabelais* III. xxxix. 328, I give out Sentence in his favour, unto whom hath befallen the best Chance by Dice; Judiciary, Tribunian, Pretorial, what comes first. **1970** *Times* 18 Nov. 12 Frank Allaun, the Tribunite M.P. *Ibid.* 7 Dec. 2 The second day took in a debate led by..Mr. Stan Orme, the redoubtable Tribunite, and Mr. Neil McBride. **1976** *Times* 15 Mar. 13/2 The influx of new MPs..has probably weakened Tribunism rather than reinforced it. But a new generation of Tribune men is beginning to assert its influence. **1977** *Listener* 28 July 125/2, I do not believe that the Tribunite view..goes by default. **1981** *Times* 22 June 2/7 Neither have Tribunites north of the border made any open moves to become involved.

tribune ('trɪbjuːn, 'traɪ-), *sb.*² Also 7 tribun. [a. F. *tribune* (1409 in Godef. *Compl.*), ad. It. and med.L. *tribūna* (914 in Du Cange), taking the place of L. *tribūnāle* TRIBUNAL.]

1. = TRIBUNA.

1645 EVELYN *Diary* 27 Feb., The edifice without is Gotiq, but very glorious within, especialy the roofe, and one tribune well painted. *a* **1668** LASSELS *Voy. Italy* (1670) II. 103 There are divers other pictures in that vaulted Tribun in Mosaick worke. **1843** *Penny Cycl.* XXVI. 249/2 The apartment of the Imperial Gallery at Florence, which is called the Tribune (Tribuna).

2. The semicircular or polygonal apse of a basilica or basilican church, usually domed or vaulted.

a **1771** GRAY *Archit. Gothica* Wks. 1843 V. 332 The difference between the body and ailes of the choir at Peterborough, with the east side of the transept, and the semicircular tribune which finishes the same choir. **1794** W. HUTCHINSON *Hist. Cumberld.* I. 155 *note*, Warwick church, remarkable for its tribune or rounded east end. **1841** W. SPALDING *Italy & It. Isl.* III. 157 The length of the church, from the principal entrance to the end of the tribune, is 601 feet. **1874** PARKER *Goth. Archit.* Gloss. 329 *Tribune*, the semicircular space at one end of the Basilica, for the judges. In Churches copied from the Basilicas it was retained as the apse.

3. A raised platform or dais; a rostrum; a pulpit; the throne or stall of a bishop.

1762–71 H. WALPOLE *Vertue's Anecd. Paint.* (1786) III. 61 A large inscription over the tribune at the end of the hall. **1790** BURKE *Fr. Rev.* 46 Any of the discoursers in our pulpits, or on your tribune;..Dr. Price, or..the Abbé S[i]eyes. **1842–76** GWILT *Archit.* Gloss. s.v. *Apsis*, The bishop's throne being raised by steps above the ordinary stalls..was sometimes called *exhedra*, and in later times *tribune*. **1850** W. IRVING *Mahomet* xiv. (1853) 87 A pulpit or tribune..to which he ascended by three steps. **1866** GEO. ELIOT *F. Holt* xxiv, Mr. Lyon was seated on the school tribune or dais at his particular round table. **1885** WOODROW WILSON *Congress. Govt.* ii. 127 Members [of the French Chamber of Deputies] do not speak from their seats..but from the 'tribune'..a box-like stand,..resembling those narrow, quaintly-fashioned pulpits..still to be seen in some of the oldest of our American churches.

4. A raised and seated area or gallery, esp. in a church; also applied to stands at continental race meetings (F. *tribune*).

1865 *Pall Mall G.* 13 June 5 Last year..it was easy to move about from the saddling-ring to the tribunes, to get places in the latter to sit down, and to promenade in front of the tribunes, with plenty of elbow-room. **1865** *Times* 1 Aug. 7/4 There were not more than 45 or 50 ladies in the 'tribunes'—the low galleries on the side of the hall are so called. **1870** DISRAELI *Lothair* lxvi, The church was crowded; not a chair or tribune vacant. **1883** *Mag. Art* June 338/2 The unfamiliar storey is known as a tribune, and runs immediately above the nave at the point usually occupied by the triforium. It is a lofty gallery. **1891** *Winchester Word-Bk., Tribunes*, large pews in ante-chapel reserved for ladies. (Obs.) **1904** PRINCESS RADZIWILL *Recoll.* ix. 160, I never left the tribune from which ladies were allowed to hear the debates.

'tribune, *v.* [f. TRIBUNE *sb.*¹] †**a.** *trans.* To regulate or control by tribunal authority. *Obs. rare*⁻¹. **b.** *intr.* To play the tribune (*Funk's Standard Dict.* 1895).

1647 WARD *Simp. Cobler* (1843) 52 These Essentialls, must not be Ephorized or Tribuned by..a few mens discretion.

tribuneship ('trɪbjuːnʃɪp, 'traɪ-). [f. TRIBUNE *sb.*¹ + -SHIP.] The office of a Roman or other tribune; the term of this office. Also *transf.*

1541 PAYNEL *Catiline* li. 74 b, The senate decreed, that Metellus shuld leaue vp his trybuneshyp and Cesar his pretorshyp. **1603** HOLLAND *Plutarch's Mor.* 877 This Tribuneship having taken originally the first beginning from the common people, is great and mighty in regard that it is popular. **1636** E. DACRES tr. *Machiavel's Disc. Livy* I. xiii. 72 The accustomed Religion help'd well..for the restitution of the Tribunship to the Nobility. **1756** WARD in *Phil. Trans.* XLIX. 699 The year 50, which answers to the ninth tribuneship of Claudius. **1842** W. C. TAYLOR *Anc. Hist.* xv. §6 (ed. 3) 440 Becoming a candidate for the tribuneship,..[he] was elected without much opposition. **1849** MACAULAY *Hist. Eng.* vi. II. 41 The crimes which had disgraced the stormy tribuneship of Shaftesbury.

tribunitial, -icial (trɪbjuː'nɪʃəl), *a.* [f. L. *tribūnīci-us* + -AL¹. Cf. OF. *tribunicial* (14th c. in Godef.).] Of or pertaining to a Roman tribune; tribunitian. Also *transf.*

1598 GRENEWEY *Tacitus' Ann.* III. xii. (1622) 81 Tiberius ..sent letters to the Senate, requesting the Tribuniciall authority for Drusus. **1621** JAS. I *Answ. to Petit. Comm.* in Rushw. *Hist. Coll.* (1659) I. 46 If you would give as good ear to them, as you do to some Tribunitial Orators among you. **1783** BLAIR *Lect. Rhet.* (1813) I. xiii. 295 Those terrible tribunitial harangues, by which he inflamed..the citizens of Rome. **1858** BUSHNELL *Nat. & Supernat.* xii. (1864) 380 Reason may be allowed to have a tribunitial veto against it. **1885** G. SALMON in *Academy* 5 Dec. 368/1 The tribunicial power was conferred on Trajan in the month of October.

tribunitian, -ician (trɪbjuː'nɪʃən), *a.* [f. as prec. + -AN. Cf. F. *tribunicien* (14th c. in Hatz.-Darm.).] Of, belonging, or pertaining to a Roman tribune, or the office of tribune.

1533 BELLENDEN *Livy* III. iv. (S.T.S.) I. 255 Þis auctorite tribuniciane was devisit to þe vniuersall proffitt and supporte of þe ciete. **1598** GRENEWEY *Tacitus' Ann.* VI. iv. (1622) 126 By a Tribunitian law it was brought vnto halfe one in the hundred; and in the end Vsury was wholly forbidden. **1730** A. GORDON *Maffei's Amphith.* 342 The Tribunitian *Viatores* had places. **1842** DE QUINCEY *Pagan Oracles* Wks. 1858 VIII. 180 The very same reason which had obliged Augustus not to suppress..the tribunitian office. **1891** FARRAR *Darkn. & Dawn* lx, He would exercise his ancient tribunician privilege, and veto a decree of condemnation.

b. *transf.* and *fig.* Having the power of veto like the Roman tribunes; popularly appointed; demagogic; factious.

1637 HEYLIN *Answ. to Burton* 80 Mass. Prinne is of a factious Tribunitian spirit. **1783** *Town & Country Mag.* 19 He must..exercise a tribunitian power of..preventing the exhibition of what the nominal physician prescribes. **1846** LANDOR *To J. Forster* Wks. II. 675 Steadfast Cromwell's tribunitian throne. **1854** MILMAN *Lat. Chr.* VII. i. (1864) IV. 21 The tribunitian fury of ecclesiastical demagogues. **1888** *Pall Mall G.* 20 Jan. 2/2 The association would be..a great associated tribune of the people, with more than tribunitian powers.

†**tribu'nitious**, *a. Obs. rare.* [f. as prec. + -OUS.] Factious or violent, after the manner attributed to the Roman tribunes; = TRIBUNITIAN b.

1600 HOLLAND *Livy* XXXIV. ii. 853 Yours will the blame bee, if yee have brought women now to raise and stirre up tribunitious seditions. **1625** BACON *Ess., Counsell* (Arb.) 87 Let them not come in Multitudes, or in a Tribunitious Manner.

tri'bunitive, *a. rare.* [irreg. f. L. *tribūnus* TRIBUNE *sb.*¹, by false analogy with such words as *unitive, punitive*, etc.] Of or pertaining to a tribune or popular champion.

1856 GOLDW. SMITH in *Oxford Ess.* 310 Whatever democratic or tribunitive spirit it might have.., would not be corrupted by evil communications with hereditary despotisms.

tributable ('trɪbjuːtəb(ə)l), *a.* [f. TRIBUTE *sb.* + -ABLE.] Liable to pay tribute; subject to tribute.

1830 W. TAYLOR *Hist. Surv. Germ. Poetry* II. 126 He ought not be waited on for nothing, To whom so many heads are tributable.

tributary ('trɪbjuːtərɪ), *a.* and *sb.* [ad. L. *tribūtāri-us*: see next and -ARY¹. Cf. F. *tributaire* (12th c. in Godef. *Compl.*).]

A. *adj.* **1. a.** Paying tribute; subject to imposts.

1382 WYCLIF *1 Macc.* xiii. 39 ȝif eny other thing was tributarye [*gloss*] or bounden to tribute, in Jerusalem, nowe be it not tributarie. **1422** tr. *Secreta Secret., Priv. Priv.* xxxiii. 185 Al..by-came lyeges and Subiectes tributarijs by grete othis for ham and hare kyngedomes and lordshuppes. **1494** FABYAN *Chron.* II. xlviii. 31 At those dayes a great parte of yᵉ worlde was trybutary to Rome. **1570–6** LAMBARDE *Peramb. Kent* (1826) p. xii, These therefore were by Iulius Cæsar subdued to the Romane Empire, and their countrie made a tributarie Province. **1665** DRYDEN *Ind. Emp.* I. ii, This Charles is some poor Tributary Lord. **1786** BURKE *W. Hastings* III. III. xxviii. Wks. XI. 460 As far independent as a tributary prince could be. **1845** STOCQUELER *Handbk. Brit. India* (1854) 9 Many states, hitherto independent, were compelled to become tributary to the Company.

b. *fig.*

c **1412** HOCCLEVE *De Reg. Princ.* 89 Þat fretynge aduersarie Myn hert[e] made to hym tributarie. **1577** HELLOWES *Gueuara's Chron.* 232 Traiane did vse to say, that Rome was more tributarie then any place of the world: for that they could not eate, but if it were giuen them from other kingdomes. **1796** BURNEY *Mem. Metastasio* II. 218 Productions..for which they used to be tributary to the industry of other nations.

2. *transf.* and *fig.* Furnishing subsidiary supplies or aid; subsidiary, auxiliary, contributory; also said of a stream or river which flows into another.

1611 SHAKS. *Cymb.* IV. ii. 37 Th'emperious Seas breeds Monsters; for the Dish, Poore Tributary Riuers, as sweet Fish. **1764** GOLDSM. *Trav.* 49 For me your tributary stores combine. **1823** C. B. VIGNOLES *Observations upon Floridas* 56 The Choctawhatchie river, and all its tributary streams discharge into the eastern end of this bay. **1860** TYNDALL *Glac.* I. vii. 57, I climbed up among the tributary glaciers. **1878** HUXLEY *Physiogr.* 5 With reference therefore to the rivers tributary to the Thames. **1899** *Allbutt's Syst. Med.* VI. 651 The neuralgia may affect the whole of the tributary nerves of the plexus.

3. Paid or offered as tribute; of the nature of tribute; contributory.

1588 SHAKS. *Tit. A.* I. i. 159 Loe at this Tombe my tributarie teares, I render. **1632** LITHGOW *Trav.* II. 55 They pay a yearly tributary pension vnto the great Turke. **1771** *Poetry* in *Ann. Reg.* 206 Immortal fame Shall grace with tributary praise thy name. **1780** COWPER *Table Talk* 112 Many a dunce, whose fingers itch to write, Adds, as he can, his tributary mite. **1814** SCOTT *Ld. of Isles* I. i, Each minstrel's tributary lay Paid homage to the festal day.

4. Of which one bears the cost; expensive.

1632 LITHGOW *Trav.* I. 9 The chargeable expences of a tributary iourney. *Ibid.* III. 114 This tributary, tedious, and sumptuous peregrination.

B. *sb.* (Absolute use of the adj. So in Fr.)

1. One who pays tribute. Also *fig.*

[*c* **1375** *Sc. Leg. Saints* xii. (*Mathias*) 123 With trybvtaris he fled þane to þe towne of Ierusaleme.] **1432–50** tr. *Higden* (Rolls) I. 275 For Sicambri were tributaryes to thempyre of Rome vn to the tyme of Valentinian. **1535** COVERDALE *1 Macc.* i. 4 He..subdued yᵉ londes and people with their prynces, so that they became tributaries vnto him. **1612** DAVIES *Why Ireland*, etc. (1787) 10 The Irish Lords did only promise to become tributaries to King Henry the Second. And such as pay only tribute..are not properly subjects but sovereigns. *a* **1704** T. BROWN *Alsop's St. Conform.* Wks. 1711 IV. 119 Living a constant Tributary to those Vermin the Bailiffs. **1866** ROGERS *Agric. & Prices* I. xx. 509 A tributary and vassal to the English monarch.

2. *transf.* and *fig.* One who or that which furnishes subsidiary supplies or aid.

a. *spec.* A stream contributing its flow to a larger stream or lake; an affluent, feeder.

(Not in TODD 1818, WEBSTER 1828, or CRAIG 1849.)

1822 W. H. SIMMONS *Notices of East Florida* iii. 29 [The] appearance [of bonnet leaf]..indicates from a distance, the influx of some tributary of the main stream. **1836** W. IRVING *Astoria* III. 261 A fortified post and port..commanding the trade of that river and its tributaries. **1846** MᶜCULLOCH *Acc. Brit. Empire* (1854) I. 35 The Medway can hardly be called a tributary of the Thames; but..it falls into the æstuary of the latter. **1866** M. ARNOLD *Thyrsis* xi, What sedged brooks are Thames's tributaries. **1897** MARY KINGSLEY *W. Africa* 354 Two new rivers..both of which he surmised were tributaries of the Congo.

b. Of other things.

1859 CORNWALLIS *Panorama New World* I. 137 At the foot of this terraced hill was the necropolis, and near it its tributary, the Bendigo Hospital. **1859** GEO. ELIOT *A. Bede* ii, The lower sphere might be said, at a rough guess, to be thirteen times larger than the upper, which naturally performed the function of a mere satellite and tributary. **1870** EMERSON *Soc. & Solit., Bks.* Wks. (Bohn) III. 84 The great metropolitan English speech, the sea which receives tributaries from every region under heaven.

Hence **'tributarily** *adv.*, **'tributariness**.

1727 BAILEY Vol. II, *Tributariness*, the Condition or State of those that pay Tribute. **1847** WEBSTER, *Tributarily*, adv. in a tributary manner.

tribute ('trɪbjuːt), *sb.* Also 4 trebute, tribuyt, -uit, -it, 4–6 tribut, trybut, -e, 5 *Sc.* trewbut, -e. [ad. L. *tribūtum*, neut. of *tribūtus*, pa. pple. of *tribu-ĕre* to assign, give, pay. Cf. F. *tribut* (15th c. in Hatz.-Darm.), and the semi-popular and inherited OF. forms *trebus* (14th c. in Godef. *Compl.*) and *trèu*: see TREW.]

1. a. A tax or impost paid by one prince or state to another in acknowledgement of submission or as the price of peace, security, and protection; rent or homage paid in money or an equivalent by a subject to his sovereign or a vassal to his lord.

1340–70 *Alex. & Dind.* 710 þei..taken of ȝou tribit þat traie is to paie, Of ȝoure offringus alle ofte in þe ȝere. *?a* **1400** *Morte Arth.* 114 With-owttyne more trouflyng the trebute we aske, That Julius Cesar wane wyth his jentille knyghttes! **1490** CAXTON *Eneydos* xxxi. 117 They of Athenes muste sende eueri yere for a trybute to the kynge Mynos of Crete ..seuen men and seuen wymen. **1560** DAUS tr. *Sleidane's Comm.* 41 b, Germany is muche impouerished with warres .. and with tributes. **1610** SHAKS. *Temp.* I. ii. 113 He.. Confederates..with King of Naples To giue him Annuall tribute, doe him homage. **1781** GIBBON *Decl. & F.* xvii. (1869) I. 470 A large portion of the tribute was paid in money. **1843** *Penny Cycl.* XXVII. 503/2 Edgar..liberat[ed] the Welsh from the payment of the tax of gold and silver on condition of an annual tribute of three hundred wolves. **1872** FREEMAN *Gen. Sketch* xii. §14 (1874) 225 The successes of the Turks were largely owing to their taking a tribute of children from their Christian subjects.

b. Hence contextually, The obligation or necessity of paying this; the condition of being tributary, as ***to lay a tribute on***. ***under, †on tribute***: under obligation to pay tribute (also *fig.*: cf. 2).

1377 LANGL. *P. Pl.* B. xix. 37 Wonyeth þere none But vnder tribut & taillage as tykes & cherles. *c* **1470** HENRY *Wallace* v. 589 Still scho duelt on trewbute in the toune, And purchest had king Eduuardis protectioune. **1535** COVERDALE *Prov.* xii. 24 A diligent hande shal beare rule, but the ydle shal be vnder tribute. **1609** BIBLE (Douay) *ibid.*, The hand..which is slothful, shal serve under tributes. **1662** BP. HOPKINS *Serm. 1 Pet.* ii. 13 (1685) 4 If a fast did only lay a tribute upon our eyes. **1793** R. HALL *Apol. Freed. Press* iv. 50 His imperial fancy has laid all nature under tribute.

2. *transf.* and *fig.* **a.** Something paid or contributed as by a subordinate to a superior; an offering or gift rendered as a duty, or as an acknowledgement of affection or esteem.

1585 T. WASHINGTON tr. *Nicholay's Voy.* IV. xxvii. 145 b, The euils..wherof by the tribute of death, they were deliuered. **1665** SIR T. HERBERT *Trav.* (1677) 39 His Father ..having paid Nature her last Tribute..the year before. **1671** MILTON *P.R.* III. 258 From his side two rivers flow'd, ..Then meeting joyn'd thir tribute to the Sea. **1750** GRAY *Elegy* 80 Some frail memorial..Implores the passing tribute of a sigh. **1806** *Med. Jrnl.* XV. 318 The committee..also declare, that they cannot conclude their report, without returning a just tribute of acknowledgement to the illustrious author of this discovery, Dr. Jenner. **1850** *Syd. Smith's Wks.* I. 8/1 *note*, I cannot read the name of Malthus without adding my tribute of affection for the memory of one of the best men that ever lived. **1860** HOOK *Lives Abps.* I. vi. 323 To the merits of Grimbald no higher tribute could have been paid.

b. A praiseworthy thing attributable *to*, a testimony *to*.

Often (as by Fowler in quot. 1926) regarded as an incorrect use.

1926 in H. W. Fowler *Dict. Mod. Eng. Usage* 662/2 The debate on the whole was a tribute to the good taste and good form of the House of Commons. **1937** W. H. S. SMITH *Let.* 3 May in *Young Man's Country* (1977) ii. 69 Are the Guildford's using their old Coronation Robes? If so, it's a tribute to Lady G.'s figure. **1961** *New Statesman* 8 Feb. 198/1 Perhaps..the gusty vigour of the heroes of the period from Grant to McKinley is a tribute to the American character.

3. In *Mining* (originally in the tin-mining of Cornwall; now in general use). **a.** The proportion of the value of the ore raised, paid by the miners to the owners or lessors of the land or their representatives.

1778 PRYCE *Min. Cornub.* 330/1 *Tribute*, [called] a *Cope* [in] North of England, a consideration or share of the produce of a Mine either in money or kind..paid by the Takers or Tributors to the original Adventurers or owners, for the liberty granted to the Takers of enjoying the Mine, or a part thereof, called a Pitch, for a limited time. **1886** *N. Zealand Herald* 1 June 6/7 Tributes were let to several parties, whose contributions to the company during the year amounted to £153 19s. 6d. The receipts showed calls to be £1573 4s., tributers £153 19s. 6d., sundries (such as crushing, interest, and overdraft) £47 9s. 6d.: total, £1774 13s. **1911** C. BOYD in *United Empire* July 393 The Tributor is a small goldminer..paying tribute on his holding.

b. The proportion of ore raised or its value, paid to the miners by the owners of the mine or land, in payment of their labour.

1832 BABBAGE *Econ. Manuf.* xxvi. (ed. 3) 252 *Tribute*, which is payment for raising and dressing the ore, by means of a certain part of its value when rendered merchantable. **1855** J. R. LEIFCHILD *Cornwall Mines* 143 The ores so raised are sold every week, and the miner immediately receives his tribute or per centage for which he agreed to work. **1865** R. HUNT *Pop. Rom. W. Eng.* Ser. I. (1871) 90 The inducements of very high 'tribute' were held out to the miners.

c. Hence, ***to work on tribute***, or ***on the tribute system***, to work on the plan of paying or receiving certain proportions of the produce.

1869 R. M. BALLANTYNE *Deep Down* xxviii. 359 When a man works on 'tribute' he receives so many shillings for every twenty shillings' worth of ore that he raises during the month. **1875** *Melbourne Spectator* 12 June 63/2 The company pleaded that the mine was let on tribute. **1877** RAYMOND *Statist. Mines & Mining* 85 The Wyoming and Pittsburgh are worked on tribute. **1885** *Money Market Rev.* 29 Aug. (Cassell), Some twelve men are now working old dump, concentrating on tribute.

d. Work performed in excavating and dressing the ore, as distinguished from *tut-work*, which consists in sinking shafts, driving of adits, and similar preparatory operations.

1839 *Penny Cycl.* XV. 246/1 The dead work is denominated 'tutwork', and the raising of ores 'tribute'. *Ibid.*, The mode of payment adopted in tutwork and tribute is entirely different: in the former case..the miner..is paid at so much per fathom..; in the latter case..the miner receives a certain percentage on the actual value [of the ore], being paid at the rate of so many shillings in the pound upon that value.

4. *attrib.* and *Comb.*, as ***tribute-bribe, -coin, -gatherer, -offer, -payer, -payment, -piece, -quittance, -river, -roll***; in sense 3, as ***tribute-man, -pitch*** (PITCH *sb.*[2] 12), ***system, -taker, work***; ***tribute-bearing, -paying*** adjs.; **tribute-children**, children surrendered as tribute; **tribute rice** *Chinese Hist.*, a grain tax paid in kind. See also TRIBUTE-MONEY.

a **1661** HOLYDAY *Juvenal* (1673) 21 Yet in his life Paid *tribute-bribes to his own conscious wife. **1603** KNOLLES *Hist. Turks* (1638) 332 Far the greatest part of these *tribute children, taken from their Christian parents,..hee caused to be dispersed into euery city and country of his dominion in Asia. **1630** *R. Johnson's Kingd. & Commw.* 510 *margin*, The *Iemoglans*, or tribute-children. **1582** N.T. (Rhem.) *Matt.* xxii. 19 Shew me the *tribute coine. And they offred him a penie. **1552** HULOET, *Trybute gatherer, *telo*. **1649** MILTON *Eikon.* iv, They had stoned his tribute-gatherer. **1839** DE LA BECHE *Rep. Geol. Cornw.*, etc. xv. 503 It seems they worked in different parties..like the *tribute-men of the mines. *a* **1586** SIDNEY *Arcadia* II. xvii, Fair streames..let the *tribute-offer of my teares unto you, procure your stay a while with me. **1552** HULOET, *Trybute payer, *stipendarius*, ..*tributarius*. **1598** HAKLUYT *Voy.* I. 60 From what countrey soeuer tribute payers, or ambassadours come vnto him. **1860** J. CAIRNS *Mem. J. Brown* vi. 186 The true Christian doctrine of civil obedience and *tribute paying. **1592** KYD *Sp. Trag.* I. iii, Is our embassadour dispatcht for Spaine?.. And *tribute paiment gone along with him? **1610** HOLLAND *Camden's Brit.* (1637) 101 Whether these *tribute-pieces were coined by the Romans..I may not easily affirme. **1778** PRYCE *Min. Cornub.* 189 A *Tribute-Pitch consists of a few fathoms in length on the course of the Lode [in a Copper Mine]. **1865** R. HUNT *Pop. Rom. W. Eng.* Ser. I. (1871) 105 She was promised no end of good luck.. and Jan the best luck in tribute-pitches. **1853** *North-China Herald* 26 Mar. 134/4 (*heading*) Destruction of the Che Hien's House and *tribute rice. **1959** P. FLEMING *Siege at Peking* v. 61 Tungchow, whose prosperity depended on its status as an entrepot for tribute-rice brought by canal from the interior, had economic as well as ideological motives for disliking the railway. **1819** SHELLEY *Prometh. Unb.* III. iii, Indus and its *tribute rivers. **1605** SYLVESTER *Du Bartas* II. iii. IV. *Captaines* 119 A thousand Streamlings that ne'er saw the Sun, With *tribute silver to his service run. **1872** R. B. SMYTH *Mining Statist.* 83 There does not appear any very good reason why prospecting ventures should not, as a rule, be established on the *tribute system. **1883** *Encycl. Brit.* XVI. 449/2 The third method is that which is known as the tribute system. The miner working on tribute..gives the mining company all the ore he extracts at a certain proportion of its value, after he has paid all the cost of breaking it, hoisting it to the surface, and dressing it. **1778** PRYCE *Min. Cornub.* 189 A *Tribute-Taker, as well as every other Miner in a Bal, obliges himself and partners to lend a hand gratis at the capstan whenever required. **1874** J. H. COLLINS *Metal Mining* 127 What are the advantages and disadvantages of the different forms of 'tut work' as compared with '*tribute work'?

tribute ('trɪbjuːt), *v.* [f. prec. sb.]

†1. *intr.* To yield tribute; *trans.* to pay as tribute. *Obs. rare.*

c **1440** *Pallad. on Husb.* IV. 555 But hem I sette in wel pastyned londe, And they tributed with felicite. **1570** LEVINS *Manip.* 196/26 To Tribute, *tribuere*. **1654** WHITLOCK *Zootomia* 302 Amorous Trifler, that spendeth.. his Afternoones in discourse with Paint, or Lust, tributing most precious Minutes, to the Scepter of a Fanne.

2. *Mining. trans.* and *intr.* To work on tribute. Hence **'tributed** *ppl. a.*; **'tributing** *vbl. sb.* and *ppl. a.*

1855 J. R. LEIFCHILD *Cornwall Mines* 143 Tributing..is a business requiring keen judgment and close application. *Ibid.* 152 Dolcoath miners,..tut-working and tributing, to send up copper for coinage, for tea-urns, for tea-kettles, and for trinkets. **1909** *Westm. Gaz.* 29 Dec. 10/4 All the tributing parties, owing to their being unable to earn a living, threw up their contracts. **1912** *Times* 19 Dec. 19/1 From all of the tributed properties they were receiving revenue.

'tribute-,money. Money paid in tribute.

1526 TINDALE *Matt.* xxii. 19 Let me se the tribute money. And they toke hym a peny. **1706** ARBUTHNOT *Serm.* Misc. Wks. 1751 II. 185 Let down your Nets; and you may fetch your Tribute-Money out of your Fishes. **1814** SCOTT *Wav.* xv, Paying the arrears of tribute money. **1881** W. W. NEWTON *Childr. Serm.* xii. 67 The tribute money was about one shilling and threepence.

tributer: see TRIBUTOR.

tributor, tributer ('trɪbjutə(r)). Also (5 -ir), 5–6 -our, 6 tribitour. [f. TRIBUTE *v.* (or ? *sb.*) + -OR, -OUR (after agent-nouns from L. or F.), and -ER[1] (on English analogies). Cf. rare late L. *tribūtor* one who gives.]

†1. One who pays tribute. Also *fig. Obs.*

1483 *Cath. Angl.* 393/2 A Tributir, *tributarius*. **1534** WHITINTON *Tullyes Offices* III. (1540) 152 That the cytes that Lucius Scylla made fre..shulde be tributers agayne. **1547** BOORDE *Introd. Knowl.* xxiv. (1870) 181, I am a Venesien..For part of my possession, I am come tributor to the Turke. **1588** PARKE tr. *Mendoza's Hist. China* 60 The prouince of Santon 3. millions and 700. thousand tributers. **1596** FITZ-GEFFRAY *Sir F. Drake* (1881) 70 The mighty Silver-river..His tributorie sandes to him reveal'd; Nor sdained it to be a tribitour, Vnto the Oceans mightie Emperour. *a* **1648** LD. HERBERT *Hen. VIII* (1683) 435.

†2. A giver, bestower. *Obs. rare*[−1].

a **1548** HALL *Chron., Hen. V* 50 b, Almightie God geuer & tributor of this glorious victory.

3. *Mining.* A miner who works 'on tribute': see TRIBUTE *sb.* 3 c.

1778 PRYCE *Min. Cornub.* 188 The Tributor..has several persons concerned with him. *Ibid.* 330/1 [see TRIBUTE *sb.* 3 a]. **1855** J. R. LEIFCHILD *Cornwall Mines* 147 The ore sold for £182:2:2, and, as the tribute was 7*s.* 6*d.* in the pound, the share for the tributers was £68:5:9. **1875** *Melbourne Spectator* 29 May 46/1 A fight between the few Europeans employed on the works and the Chinese tributers. **1877** *Encycl. Brit.* VI. 218/1 Capitalists, landowners, inventors, Cornish tributers..are all brought under the stimulating influence of self-interest. **1886, 1911** [see TRIBUTE *sb.* 3 a]. **1902** *Daily Record* 1 Oct. 4 The concessions by the late Boer Government..have got into hands so grasping that their excessive terms to tributors for water-rights and power have kept a large area of these fields fallow.

tributorian (trɪbju'tɔərɪən), *a. rare.* [f. late L. *tribūtōri-us* TRIBUTORY + -AN.] Of or pertaining to tribute or payment.

1880 MUIRHEAD *Gaius* IV. §72 There is the tributorian action against a father or owner, whose son or slave has with his father's or owner's knowledge invested his *peculium* in merchandise.

†tribu'torious, *a. rare.* [f. as prec. + -OUS.]

1727 BAILEY vol. II, *Tributorious*, pertaining to Distribution.

†'tributory, *a.* and *sb. Obs.* [ad. (jurid.) L. *tribūtōrius* of or concerning payment, f. *tribūtor*, agent-n. from *tribu-ĕre* to bestow, give, pay: cf. *contributory*. Superseded by the nominal derivative TRIBUTARY.]

A. *adj.* Paying tribute; = TRIBUTARY *a.* 1.

c **1460** FORTESCUE *Abs. & Lim. Mon.* iii. (1885) 115 The peple..sought helpe of the Romayns, to whom thai hade be tributori. **1530** PALSGR. 283/1 Trybutorie, *tributayre*. **1585** T. WASHINGTON tr. *Nicholay's Voy.* III. xiii. 95 [They] are not tributorie in any gabels or money taxes. **1596** [see TRIBUTOR 1]. **1615** G. SANDYS *Trav.* 219 My father..that rich country tributory made.

B. *sb.* = TRIBUTARY *sb.* 1.

1585 T. WASHINGTON tr. *Nicholay's Voy.* II. vii. 37 They became tributories vntoo the prince of the Turkes. [But cf. I. ix. 12 A newe Kyng, vnto whom they..rendred them selues as his tributaries.]

tributyl phosphate: see TRI- 5 c.

tributyrin (traɪ'bjuːtɪrɪn). *Chem.* [f. TRI- 5 a + BUTYRIN.] Glycerol tributyrate, $C_{15}H_{26}O_6$, the compound ether or ester of glycerin and butyric acid: cf. TRIACETIN: a colourless oily liquid, boiling at 285°C., the characteristic constituent of butter-fat.

1855 *Q. Jrnl. Chem. Soc.* VII. 282. **1863–72** WATTS *Dict. Chem.* I. 697 Tributyrin..is a neutral, oily liquid, with an odour analogous to that of [monobutyrin and dibutyrin], and a pungent taste, with irritating aftertaste.

tricalcic (traɪ'kælsɪk), also **tri'calcium,** *a. Chem.* [f. TRI- 5 b + CALCIC, CALCIUM.] Applied to a salt containing three atoms of calcium; e.g. ***tricalcic*** or ***tricalcium phosphate***, $Ca_3(PO_4)_2$, a salt of calcium and orthophosphoric acid, H_3PO_4.

1871 VALENTIN *Pract. Chem.* 147 Hydric disodic phosphate gives a bulky white precipitate of tricalcic phosphate. **1876** HARLEY *Royle's Mat. Med.* 61 The ashes of bones..consist chiefly of tricalcic phosphate. **1911** *Jrnl. Chem. Soc.* C. II. 396 Action of a solution of Sodium hydroxide on Tricalcium phosphate.

tricapsular (traɪ'kæpsjʊlə(r)), *a. Nat. Hist.* [f. TRI- + L. *capsula* CAPSULE + -AR.] Having three capsules.

1694 *Phil. Trans.* XVIII. 278 Tricapsular Seed-vessels. **1760** J. LEE *Introd. Bot.* II. xxix. (1765) 145 In *Aconitum* some are tricapsular, and others quinquecapsular.

tri-car to **tricaudate**: see TRI- 4 c, 1 a.

tricarballylic (ˌtraɪkɑːbə'lɪlɪk), *a. Chem.* [f. TRI- + *carballylic acid* s.v. CARB-.] ***tricarballylic acid***: a crystalline tribasic acid found in immature beets and produced synthetically; propane-1,2,3-tricarboxylic acid, HOOC·CH $(CH_2COOH)_2$.

1865 M. SIMPSON in *Jrnl. Chem. Soc.* XVIII. 334 This body has been named by Kekule carballylic acid... I propose..in order to avoid confusion, to call it *tri*-carballylic acid. *Ibid.* 335, I have prepared and analysed several of the salts and ethers of tri-carballylic acid. **1950** I. L. FINAR *Org. Chem.* xvii. 348 Tricarballylic esters have been used as plasticisers. **1980** *Polish Jrnl. Chem.* LIV. 1681

In the course of biological studies on new potential anticonvulsants, a number of substituted tricarballylic acids . . were synthesized.

tricarbon ('traɪˌkɑːbən), *a. Chem.* [f. TRI- 5 b + CARBON *sb.*] Containing or derived from three atoms of carbon, as the ***tricarbon series*** of hydrocarbons.

1866 [see TRI- 5 b]. **1866** ROSCOE *Elem. Chem.* xxvii. 239 Whilst CH_4 is the type of the mono-carbon series, C_2H_6 is that of the di-carbon series, and similarly, C_3H_8 that of the tri-carbon series. *Ibid.* xxx. 273 Tricarbon Series: Propyl alcohol C_3H_8O.

tricarboxylic (ˌtraɪkɑːbɒk'sɪlɪk), *a. Biochem.* [f. TRI- + CARBOXYL + -IC.] ***tricarboxylic acid***: any acid with three carboxyl groups in each molecule; ***tricarboxylic acid cycle***, the Krebs cycle (see KREBS).

1894 PERKIN & KIPPING *Org. Chem.* I. xiii. 246 Citric acid is tricarboxylic acid, and . . forms three classes of salts. **1938** G. H. RICHTER *Textbk. Org. Chem.* xvi. 302 Aconitic acid is an example of an unsaturated tricarboxylic acid. **1945** *Jrnl. Biol. Chem.* CLXI. 413 (*heading*) Fatty acid oxidation and the Krebs tricarboxylic acid cycle. **1947** *Ibid.* CLXXI. 446 Tricarboxylic acids may be formed in plants by a process involving the addition of CO_2 to an α-ketoglutarate. **1950** [see KREBS]. **1974** B. A. NEWTON in K. Elliott et al. *Trypanosomiasis & Leishmaniasis* (Ciba Symp. No. 20) 299 Some of the changes which occur during the development of T. cruzi, such as the activity of the tricarboxylic acid cycle enzymes . ., may only be quantitative changes. **1982** M. S. OLSON in T. M. Devlin *Textbk. Biochem.* vi. 278 Various investigators defined many of the enzymes and di- and tricarboxylic acid intermediates in this pathway, but it was Krebs who pieced together these components in his formulation of the 'Krebs cycle'.

tricchery, -ori, obs. forms of TREACHERY.

† **trice**, *sb.*[1] *Obs. rare.* Also 5 tryys, -st, -ste. [a. MDu. *trîse*, *trijs*, Du. *trijs* windlass, pulley, hoisting-block = MLG. *trîsse*, *trîtse* tackle, hoisting-rope (whence also Da. *tridse*, *trisse*, Sw. *trissa* sheave, pulley, Ger. *trieze* crane, pulley). Cf. TRICE *v.*] A pulley or windlass.

1357–8 *Ely Sacr. Rolls* (1907) II. 178 In j trice empt. de Domino Priore 6s 8d. *c* **1440** *Promp. Parv.* 503/1 Tryyste, wyndas [*v.rr.* tryys, tryyst], *machina, carchesia.* **1462–3** *Norwich Sacr. Roll* (MS.), Pro le trice ad trahendum plumbum, xx d. In fune et hawuseris pro le trice, iij s. ix d.

trice (traɪs), *sb.*[2] Forms: 5–6 **tryse**, 6 **tryce**, 6–7 **trise**, 6– **trice**. [Found first in phrase *at a trice*, app. originally 'at one pull or tug, at one effort', *trice* being app. verbal sb. from TRICE *v.*; soon passing into the sense 'at once, immediately, in a moment, instantly', whence in later use the simple sb. comes to be equal to 'instant, moment'. Cf. the sense-development of Fr. †*à un coup*, *à coup*, †*tout à un coup*, *tout d'un coup*, orig. 'at a stroke', hence 'at once, immediately, instantly'.

The later phrase *in a trice* recalls the Sp. *en un tris* instantly, orig. 'in a crack' (CRACK *sb.* 2), from *tris* the noise made by cracking or breaking of glass; but the Eng. phrase 'at a trice' appears too early for Spanish influence. Rather are the English, French, and Spanish phrases parallels expressing suddenness of action.]

1. † **a.** ***at a trice***, *lit.* at a single pluck or pull; hence, in an instant; instantly, forthwith; without delay. *Obs.*

c **1440** *Ipomydon* 392 The howndis . . Pluckid downe dere all at a tryse. *a* **1530** HEYWOOD *Love* (1534) B iv, At dore were this trull was, I was at a tryce. **1540** PALSGR. *Acolastus* N j b, Open the dores at ones, or at a tryce. **1603** HARSNET *Pop. Impost.* 59 They made sure to have a Devil readie at a trice. *a* **1635** NAUNTON *Fragm. Reg.* (Arb.) 49 True it is, He had gotten the Queens eare at a trice.

† **b.** ***with a trice*** in same sense. *Obs.*

1515 BARCLAY *Egloges* iii. (1570) B vj/2 Sometime thy bedfelowe is colder then is yse, To him then he draweth thy cloathes with a trice. *a* **1566** R. EDWARDES *Damon & Pithias* (1571) H j, Now Pithias kneele downe, . . And with a trise thy head from thy shoulders I wyll conuay. **1577** NORTHBROOKE *Dicing* (1843) 129 The gaine gotten by this playe at dyce, when all is gotten with a trice ouer the thumbe, without anye traficke or loane. **1625** *Gonsalvio's Sp. Inquis.* 140 Immediatly after this confession thus by them made, they broke their necks with a trice.

c. ***in a trice*** († ***on a trice***) in same sense.

1508 SKELTON *P. Sparowe* 1131 To tell you what conceyte I had than in a tryce, The matter were to nyse. **1553** BECON *Reliques of Rome* (1563) 266 The Aungells . . maye as a man would say in a trise go downe vnto them. **1577–87** HOLINSHED *Chron.* II. 31/1 Suddenlie . . in a trice it skippeth to the top of the rocke. **1610** SHAKS. *Temp.* v. i. 238 On a trice, . . Euen in a dreame, were we diuided from them. **1699** LD. TARBUT in *Pepys' Diary*, etc. (1879) VI. 195 In a trice, from words they came to blows. **1782** COWPER *Gilpin* xxx, In a trice the turnpike-men Their gates wide open threw. **1847** C. BRONTË *J. Eyre* xx, I'll make you decent in a trice. **1872** BLACK *Adv. Phaeton* ix, A fire is lit in a trice.

† **2.** One single attempt or act; the time taken for this; an instant or moment; a very brief period. *Obs.*

1579 TOMSON *Calvin's Serm. Tim.* 899/2 Wee shall marueile howe the deuill coulde so deceiue vs at the first trice. **1589** R. HARVEY *Pl. Perc.* (1590) 5 Stand by a trice, but looke you depart not the court. **1597–8** BP. HALL *Sat.* IV. vii. 57 The whiles the likerous priest spits euery trice. **1605** SHAKS. *Lear.* I. i. 219 That she . . should in this trice of time Commit a thing so monstrous. *a* **1618** RALEIGH *Advice of Son* (1651) 8 Nothing would be so much esteemed as a short trice of time, which now by days, and moneths, and years, is most lavishly misspent. **1668** WILKINS *Real Char.* 186 By Time . . Instant, Moment, Trice, Nick.

† **trice**, *sb.*[3] *Obs.* Origin and meaning obscure.

(Variously conjectured to be a variant or erroneous form of TRACE *sb.*[1] in sense 'way, course (of action)', or of TRIST, TRYST.)

c **1460** G. ASHBY *Dicta Philos.* 598 A kynge sholde not sett hym selfe in myche price, Ner his counseil haue of hym gouernance, Ne ofte use huntyng, keping wele his trice, Ner take any newe way by ignorance. [*L.* Decet regem non multum appreciare seipsum, nec gubernari suo consilio, nec vti frequenter venacione, nec incedere semita quam ignorat.]

trice (traɪs), *v.* Also 4–7 **tryce**, **trise**, 5–6 **tryse**; 8–9 *erron.* **trace**. [a. MDu. *trîsen*, Du. *trijsen* to hoist = MLG. *trîssen*, *trîtsen*, whence also Da. *trisse*, Ger. *triezen* to hoist. Ulterior history obscure.]

† **1.** *trans.* To pull; to pluck, snatch, draw with a sudden action; rarely, to carry off (as plunder). ***to trice*** one ***out of*** a thing, to do one out of it by sudden force. *Obs.*

c **1386** CHAUCER *Monk's T.* 535 By god out of his sete I wol hym trice [*v.rr.* tryce, trise]. **1421–2** HOCCLEVE *Dial.* 208 in *Min. Poems* 117 Whan that deathe shall men from hence trice. **1446** LYDG. *Nightingale Poems* i. 336 Deth wyll you trise, ye wot not how ne whenne. *c* **1450** LOVELICH *Grail* xiii. 20 In the tyme Of the chas, Alle Tholomes harneis Itrised was. **1500–25** in *Thoms' Anecd.* (Camden) 31 Sir William . . makes no more adoe but trices him up, and throwes him into the Thames. **1540** PALSGR. *Acolastus* Argt. C j, After he was left naked and triced away from al his goodes, or bereued of al that euer he had. **1600** W. WATSON *Decacordon* (1602) 103 Vntill they might get him triced out of their way. **1611** SPEED *Hist. Gt. Brit.* IX. viii. §38 Thus to be triced out of that which so vehemently . . he tooke care to see effected. **1618** BOLTON *Florus* (1636) 106 Wee neverthelesse had tryced him out of most of her Townes and Countries.

2. To pull or haul with a rope; *spec.* (*Naut.*) usually with *up*, to haul or hoist up and secure with a rope or lashing, to lash up.

? *a* **1400** *Morte Arth.* 832 They trisene vpe þaire saillez, And rowes ouer the ryche see. **1579–80** NORTH *Plutarch* (1676) 401 They threw him down a Rope from the wall, which he tyed about his middle, and so was triced up by it. **1622** R. HAWKINS *Voy. S. Sea* (1847) 105 We cast a snare about his neck and so tryced him into the ship. **1627** CAPT. SMITH *Seaman's Gram.* iv. 18 Ropes fast triced together with handspikes. *Ibid.* v. 22 Bunt lines is . . a small rope . . to trice or draw vp the Bunt of the saile. **1688** R. HOLME *Armoury* III. xv. (Roxb.) 34/2 They trise vp the anchor from the Hawse to the top of the fore-castle. **1836** MARRYAT *Midsh. Easy* x. 28 All the wet sails were also spread on the booms or triced up in the rigging. **1907** *Macm. Mag.* Feb. 316 Aft there, two of you, . . and trice the ladder up.

Hence **'tricing** *vbl. sb.*; also *attrib.* as ***tricing-batten***, ***-line***, ***-rope***: see quots.

1404 *Durham Acc. Rolls* (Surtees) 397, iiij trasys ij trysyng rapis. **1627** CAPT. SMITH *Seaman's Gram.* I. viii. 36 For slinging the yards, bousing or trising. **1769** FALCONER *Dict. Marine* (1776), *Tracing-Line* [ed. **1815** *Tricing-Line*], . . a small cord . . used to hoist up any object to a higher station. . . Such are the tracing-lines of the awnings, and those of the yard tackles. **1804** A. B. in *Naval Chron.* XII. 381 [He] cut one of the tricing lines of the netting. **1836** E. HOWARD *R. Reefer* xlv, My tricing-up to the truck. *c* **1850** *Rudim. Navig.* (Weale) 156 *Tricing battens*, . . to which the sailors trice-up the middle of their hammocks out of the headway. **1909** *Athenæum* 30 Mar. 339/2 The tricing-up of a refractory midshipman to the mast-head.

-trice, *suffix*, a. F. *-trice*, ad. L. *-trīx*, *-trīce-m*, or It. *-trice*; in Latin forming feminines to agent-nouns in *-tor*. In Eng. formerly used in many words, as in *corruptrice*, *directrice*, *genetrice*, *imperatrice*, *mediatrice*, *oratrice*, *salvatrice*, *victrice*, also (from *deserter*) *desertrice*. Modern Eng. prefers the form -TRIX from the L. nominative, esp. in legal and learned words; but, in others, generally substitutes the compound suffix -TRESS.

Tricel ('traɪsɛl). Also **tricel**. [f. TRI- (in *triacetate*) + CEL(LULOSE *sb.*] A proprietary name for a man-made fibre made from cellulose triacetate, and for material made from this.

1954 *Trade Marks Jrnl.* 22 Dec. 1300/2 *Tricel* . . Raw or partly prepared artificial fibrous textile materials not being yarns or threads. British Celanese Limited, Celanese House . ., London W.1; manufacturers. **1956** *Official Gaz.* (U.S. Patent Office) 20 Nov. 88/1 *Tricel* . . For staple fibres made wholly or partially of cellulose derivatives. **1965** *Guardian* 31 Mar. 13/2 The two fabrics looked identical, but 'Tricel' had got something that the other hadn't got—easy-care properties. **1969** W. J. BURLEY *Death in Willow Pattern* i. 13 Susan . . put on a simple short-sleeved Tricel dress. **1977** *Lancashire Life* Feb. 22/2 A top cup of cotton embroidered nylon tricel.

tricellular: see TRI- 1 a.

tricenary (traɪ'siːnərɪ), *a.* and *sb.* Also 5 *erron.* **tricenn-**. [ad. L. *trīcēnāri-us* of, pertaining to, or consisting of thirty, f. *trīcēnī* thirty each.]

A. *adj.* Of or pertaining to thirty; containing, or lasting, thirty days. ? *Obs.*

1655 STANLEY *Hist. Philos.* III. (1701) 75/2 After Solon's time, the Civil year . . consisted of Months, . . alternately of twenty nine, and thirty days, at Athens, though divers places of Greece . . did not for a long time after part with their tricenary Months. **1671** H. M. tr. *Erasm. Colloq.* 389 Tricenary and yearly Masses.

B. *sb. R.C. Ch.* [med.L. *tricēnārium*, Du Cange.] A series of masses said on thirty consecutive days: cf. TRENTAL.

1482 *Monk of Evesham* (Arb.) 94 That sche schulde orden to be seyde for me. v. tricennarijs of messys. **1911** A. M. BUCHANAN tr. *Contempl. Life* xxi. 101 Numerous anniversary Masses are said, and the suffrages for the dead are increased by tricenaries, during which Masses are offered on thirty consecutive days.

So **trice'narious** *a.* (*rare*⁻⁰) = *tricenary* adj.

(In some mod. Dicts. misspelt **tricennarious**, and confused in form and sense with TRICENNIAL.)

1656 BLOUNT *Glossogr.*, *Tricenarious*, of or belonging to thirty. [**1836** SMART, *Tricennial*, belonging to the number thirty; *Tricennarious* is less used. **1882** OGILVIE (Annandale), *Tricennarious*, tricennial; belonging to the term of thirty years.]

† **tri'cennal.** *Obs.* [ad. med.(Anglo-)L. *trīcennāle*, in form neuter of L. *trīcennālis* of or belonging to thirty years, f. *triciēs* thirty times + *annus* year, but app. erroneously used for a tricenary or trental.] = TRICENARY B.

1537 tr. *Latimer's 2nd Serm. bef. Convoc.* E ij, Your forefathers sawe somwhat whiche made this constitution, against the venalitie and sale of Masses, that vnder peine of suspending, no priest shuld sell his sayinge of tricennals, or annals. [**1707** FLEETWOOD *Chron. Prec.* (1745) 109 Tricennalia were called Trentals from Trigintalia, and in English, a months-mind, because the service lasted a month or 30 days, in which they said so many masses.]

tri'cennial, *a. rare*⁻⁰. [f. L. *trīcenni-um* period of thirty years (f. *triciēs* thirty times + *annus* year) + -AL[1].] Of or belonging to thirty years.

1656 BLOUNT *Glossogr.*, *Tricennial*, of thirty or thrice ten years. **1731** BAILEY, *Tricennial*, belonging to the Term of 30 Years. **1864** WEBSTER, *Tricennial*, of, pertaining to, or consisting of, thirty years; occurring once in every thirty years.

tricentenary (traɪ'sɛntɪnərɪ, -sɛn'tiːnərɪ), *a.* and *sb.* [f. TRI- + CENTENARY: cf. L. *trecentēnī* three hundred each.] = TERCENTENARY.

1846 WORCESTER, *Tricentenary*, a period or space of three hundred years. *Ec[lectic] Rev[iew].* **1882** OGILVIE (Annandale), *Tricentenary*, *n.* 1. That which consists of or comprehends three hundred; the space of three hundred years. 2. The commemoration of any event which occurred three hundred years before, as the birth of a great man; as, Shakspere's *tricentenary*. Called also *Tercentenary*. *Tricentenary*, *a.*, relating to or consisting of three hundred; relating to three hundred years; as, a *tricentenary* celebration. Called also *Tercentenary*.

So **tricente'narian**, a person 300 years old.

1889 *Academy* 20 July 34/3 Perhaps the interior of the Antarctic continent may yield a crop of tricentenarians, since, according to Herodotus, the most wonderful things are generally found at the extremities of the earth.

tricentennial (traɪsɛn'tɛnɪəl), *a.* and *sb. rare.* [f. TRI- + L. *centenni-um* a space of a hundred years + -AL[1]: cf. prec.] = TERCENTENNIAL.

1882–3 *Schaff's Encycl. Relig. Knowl.* II. 1051/2 The great national Luther tri-centennial of 1817. **1893** *Cycl. Rev. Current Hist.* (U.S.) III. 311 The tricentennial exercises were held in the exposition building.

tricentral to **tricephalous**: see TRI- 1 a, 4 b.

triceps ('traɪsɛps), *a.* and *sb.* [a. L. *triceps*, *tricipit-em* three-headed, f. TRI- + *-cep-s*, *-cipit-*, deriv. form of *cap-ut* head. Cf. F. *triceps* (16th c.).]

A. *adj.* Three-headed (in quot. 1577 *loosely*, consisting of three heads); *spec.* of a muscle: Having three heads or points of origin (see B).

1577 GRANGE *Golden Aphrod.*, etc. R ij b, The Triceps head of Cerberus. **1804** ABERNETHY *Surg. Obs.* 99 An agitation of fluid was felt beneath the triceps muscle in the inside of the arm. **1881** MIVART *Cat* 96 A rough process or 'tuberosity', into which the triceps muscle is inserted.

B. *sb.* A triceps muscle; *spec.* that of the thigh (*triceps extensor cruris*, *t. femoralis*) and that of the upper arm (*t. extensor cubiti*, *t. humeralis*).

1704 J. HARRIS *Lex. Techn.* I, *Triceps*, is a Muscle of the Thigh, so called from its three Heads or Beginnings. **1846** BRITTAN tr. *Malgaigne's Man. Oper. Surg.* 211 The brachial [artery] . . between the biceps and the internal portion of the triceps. **1860** O. W HOLMES *Elsie V.* iii. (1887) 33 The triceps . . furnishes the *calf* of the upper arm.

Hence † **tri'ceptic** *a.* (*nonce-wd.*) [irreg. for TRICIPITAL], three-headed.

1716 M. DAVIES *Athen. Brit.* II. To Rdr. 41 Those . . Triceptick or Trifaucian Cerberus's.

triceptor: see TRI- 4 c.

‖ **triceratops** (traɪ'sɛrətɒps). *Palæont.* [mod.L., f. Gr. τρικέρατ-ος three-horned + ὤψ face.] A genus of gigantic predentate dinosaurs of the family *Ceratopsidæ*, having a strong nasal horn, besides two large pointed horns above the eyes; found in the Laramie beds of the United States.

1892 *Pall Mall G.* 22 Mar. 7/1 In the same neighbourhood also has been discovered recently another reptilian monster called the triceratops, which had an enormous bony frill around the back of its neck . . measuring six feet across . . . The animal, though tremendously massive, was only thirty feet long. **1910** *Spectator* 21 May 838/2 The oddest is the gigantic triceratops, the three-horned herbivorous dinosaur.

tricesail, variant of TRYSAIL.

tricesimo-secundo: see -MO.

trich, variant of TRECHE *v. Obs.*, to cheat.

trichæsthesia to **trichauxis**: see TRICHO-[1].

† **'trichard**. *Obs.* [a. OF. *trichart*, mod.Norm. dial. *trichard*, f. *trichier*, *trechier*, TRECHE *v.*] A deceiver, a cheat.

a **1327** *Pol. Songs* (Camden) 69 Richard, thah thou be ever trichard, trichen shalt thou never more.

trichechine ('trɪkɪkaɪn), *a.* and *sb. Zool.* [f. mod.L. *Trichech-us* (Artedi 1705–35; f. Gr. θρίξ, stem τριχ- hair + ἔχ-ειν to have; applied to the manatee 'quia solus inter pisces fere hirsutus est'); name (now disused) of a genus including the manatee and walrus: see -INE[1].]

a. *adj.* Belonging to or having the characters of the family *Trichechidæ* or walruses. **b.** *sb.* An animal of this family, a walrus. So **trichechodont** (trɪ'kɛkəʊdɒnt) [Gr. ὀδούς, ὀδοντ- tooth] *a.*, characterized by molar teeth like those of the manatee, with cusps confluent into two or more transverse crests; *sb.* an animal having such molar teeth; **'trichechoid** *a.* and *sb.* = *trichechine*.

[**1842** BRANDE *Dict. Sci.*, etc., Trichechus.] **1887** COPE *Orig. Fittest* vii. 249 Many of the Tapirodonts have the Trichecodont type of mandibular teeth. *Ibid.* 255 Trichecodonts.—The Mastodons and Elephants form a most complete series between this form and the Bunodonts. **1888** *Cassell's Encycl. Dict.*, Trichechine. **1891** *Cent. Dict.*, Trichechoid.

tricherie, -erous, obs. ff. TREACHERY, -EROUS.

trichi ('trɪtʃɪ). *colloq.* or *slang*. Also **trichy**, and with capital initial. Short for TRICHINOPOLI (cigar).

1877 R. F. BURTON *Sind Revisited* I. i. 7 We smoked, generally Manilla cheroots, now supplanted by foul Dindigals and fetid 'Trichies'. **1886** YULE & BURNELL *Hobson-Jobson*, *Trichies* or *Tritchies*, the familiar name of the cheroots made at Trichinopoly; long, and rudely made, with a straw inserted at the end for the mouth. **1889** *Blackw. Mag.* Aug. 238, I had smoked a trichy whilst lazily watching the fleecy clouds.

‖ **trichiasis** (trɪkɪ'eɪsɪs, trɪ'kaɪəsɪs). *Path.* [Late L., a. Gr. τριχίασις (Galen), f. τριχιᾶν to be hairy.]

a. Introversion of the eye-lashes; also, growth of an extra row of eye-lashes beneath the normal ones. **b.** A disease in which small filamentous bodies are passed in the urine: = PILIMICTION. **c.** A disease of the breasts in suckling women, in which the nipples crack into fine fissures.

1661 LOVELL *Hist. Anim. & Min.* 340 The trichiasis, when haires grow under the natural, and prick the eye. **1693** tr. *Blancard's Phys. Dict.* (ed. 2), *Trichiasis*,..hairy Urine, such as by reason of pituitous Humours Hairs seem to swim in. **1706** PHILLIPS (ed. Kersey), *Trichiasis*, or *Trichosis*, a growing of much Hair: Also a fault in the Eye-lids when there is a double row of Hairs. **1839–47** *Todd's Cycl. Anat.* III. 82/2 One of the operations for trichiasis is to extirpate the roots of the eye-lashes. **1857** DUNGLISON *Med. Lex.*, *Trichiasis*... This name has been given.. 1. To a disease of the kidneys or bladder, in which filamentous substances, resembling hairs, are passed in the urine... 2. To a painful swelling of the breasts, in child-bed women, when the milk is excreted with difficulty. **1878** T. BRYANT *Pract. Surg.* I. 312 The hair bulbs may become displaced, causing the eyelashes to be misdirected—'trichiasis'.

‖ **trichidium** (trɪ'kɪdɪəm). *Bot.* Pl. **-ia**. [mod.L., f. Gr. θρίξ, τριχ- hair: cf. ANTHERIDIUM.] A simple or branched hair-like body which supports the spores in certain fungi, as *Geaster*.

1842 BRANDE *Dict. Sci.*, etc., *Trichidium*, a netted filamentous organ..in which the spores of some kinds of fungi are included. **1866** *Treas. Bot.*, *Trichidium*, a hair which bears the spores of such fungals as *Geastrum*.

‖ **trichina** ('trɪkɪnə, trɪ'kaɪnə). *Zool.* Pl. **-æ**. Also in anglicized form (or from Fr.) **trichine**. [mod.L. *Trichina* (whence F. *trichine*), f. Gr. τρίχινος adj. 'of hair', f. θρίξ, τριχ- hair.] A genus of minute parasitic nematoid worms; *esp.* the species *T. spiralis*, which infests man and various animals, the adult inhabiting the intestinal tract, and the larvæ migrating to and becoming encysted in the muscular tissue, causing TRICHINOSIS.

1835 *Trans. Zool. Soc.* I. 323, I have seen in..the diseased muscle, groups of minute oblong vesicles..these may..be germs of the *Trichina*. **1858** COPLAND *Dict. Pract. Med.* III. 1399 The *Trichina* having found a resting place, a cyst closely adhering to the tissues is formed round it. **1875** tr. *von Ziemssen's Cycl. Med.* III. 651 To exterminate the rat is to exterminate trichinæ.

attrib. **1857** tr. *Küchenmeister's Anim. & Veg. Parasites* (Syd. Soc.) I. 351 The spot to which it reached during the trichina-life. [**1865** *Even. Standard* 12 Dec. 5/2 The trichine disease continues its ravages at Hadersleben.] **1897** *Allbutt's Syst. Med.* II. 1051 Examination of the rats of different countries proves the extreme liability of this rodent to trichina infection. **1901** *Mem. & Lett. Sir J. Paget* iii. 58 Epidemics of this trichina-fever.

Hence **'trichinal** *a.*, of or pertaining to the trichina (in quot. 1857 *spec.* the larva); **tri'chinatous** *a.* erroneous formation for TRICHINOUS; ‖ **trichiniasis** (trɪkɪ'naɪəsɪs) [mod.L.: cf. *elephantiasis*] = TRICHINOSIS; **'trichinid**, a worm of the family *Trichinidæ*; **trichiniferous** (trɪkɪ'nɪfərəs) *a.* [-FEROUS], containing or conveying trichinæ; **trichinize** ('trɪkɪnaɪz) *v.*, *trans.* to infect with trichinæ (hence ˌ**trichini'zation**, **'trichinized** *ppl. a.*); **trichinoid** ('trɪkɪnɔɪd) *a.*, resembling or allied to *Trichina*.

1857 tr. *Küchenmeister's Anim. & Veg. Parasites* (Syd. Soc.) I. 346 It is almost impossible to determine during the *Trichinal existence, to which of the two sexes the mature animal would belong. **1885** A. W. BLYTH in *Leisure Hour* Jan. 25/2 This ham..was discovered to be swarming with..trichinal cysts. **1870** NICHOLSON *Man. Zool.* xxvi. I. 152 If ..a portion of *trichinatous muscle be eaten by a warm-blooded vertebrate, and so introduced into the alimentary canal, an immediate development of young Trichinae is the result. **1854–67** C. A. HARRIS *Dict. Med. Terminol.* s.v. *Trichina*, The disease..called *Trichiniasis or Trichina disease. **1871** SIR T. WATSON *Lect. Princ. & Pract. Physic* (ed. 5) II. 636 Within a month after the dinner 20 of these persons had died of, and more than 80 were then suffering from, 'trichiniasis'. **1869** E. A. PARKES *Pract. Hygiene* (ed. 3) 195 The eating of raw *trichiniferous pork is the chief cause of the propagation of the entozoon to man. **1864** *N. Syd. Soc. Year-bk. Med.* 175 Experiments with picro-nitrate of potash on *trichinised rabbits. **1866** *Standard* 19 Feb., The cat and the dog were both trichinised experimentally.

trichinelliasis (trɪkɪnɛ'laɪəsɪs). *Med.* [f. mod.L. *Trichinella*, generic name superseding TRICHINA (f. L. *-ella*: see -EL[2]) + -IASIS.] = TRICHINOSIS.

1907 *Allbutt's Syst. Med.* (ed. 2) II. II. 914 The girl had evidently died, not of enteric fever as was supposed, but of trichinelliasis. **1930** E. C. FAUST *Human Helminthol.* xxiii. 327 The disease trichinelliasis or, more familiarly, trichinosis, may be divided into three stages. **1977** SCHMIDT & ROBERTS *Foundations of Parasitol.* xxiii. 424/2 *Trichinella spiralis* is the only species in the family..and is responsible for the disease variously known as trichinosis, trichiniasis, or trichinelliasis.

Also **trichine'llosis** [-OSIS], in the same sense.

1958 *Excerpta Medica* IV. 479, 209 wild rats..and 21 domestic rats..were examined for trichinellosis. **1965** *Jrnl. Amer. Med. Assoc.* 13 Sept. 182/1 So-called meat inspection ..provides no mechanism for detection of trichinellosis. **1971** P. C. C. GARNHAM *Progress in Parasitol.* v. 64 In the Mau Mau emergency the youth went wild on Mount Kenya, ignoring the ancient tribal taboo regarding the consumption of the flesh of certain animals and devoured uncooked wild pig: a severe outbreak of trichinellosis, with many deaths, was the result.

Trichinopoli (trɪtʃɪ'nɒpəlɪ). Also **-poly**. Name of a district and city in the state of Tamil Nadu (formerly in the Madras Presidency) in S. India; used *attrib.*, as ***Trichinopoli chain, cigar, work***; also *absol.* = *Trichinopoli cigar* (*colloq.* abbreviated to TRICHI).

1863 *Reliquary* Oct. 68 It [an Irish brooch] has also an attached silver chain, of that peculiar construction known as Trichinopoly-work. **1879** *Encycl. Brit.* IX. 163/2 Round plaited gold chains of fine wire, such as are still made by the filigree workers of India, and known as Trichinopoly chains. **1887** DOYLE *Stud. Scarlet* I. iii, He..smoked a Trichinopoly cigar. *Ibid.* I. iv, Such an ash as is only made by a Trichinopoly.

trichinoscope ('trɪkɪnəʊ-, trɪ'kaɪnəʊskəʊp). [f. TRICHINA + -SCOPE.] An instrument for examining meat in order to detect the presence of trichinæ (*Cent. Dict.* 1891).

trichinosis (trɪkɪ'nəʊsɪs). *Path.* [mod.L., f. TRICHIN-A + -OSIS.] A disease caused by the introduction of trichinæ into the alimentary canal, and the migration of their embryos or larvæ into the muscular tissue; characterized by digestive disturbance, slight fever, swelling, pain, and lameness in the muscles, etc. Also *attrib.*

1866 *Daily Tel.* 18 Jan. 5/2 Learned professors have declared that a large proportion of the flesh of swine sold in the markets of Berlin..is poisoned by a dreadful distemper called trichinosis—by myriads of trichinæ. *Ibid.*, A congress of *savants* and medical men to confer on the great trichinosis question. **1890** B. A. WHITELEGGE *Hygiene & Public Health* ix. 211 Trichinosis in man is generally due to the consumption of the imperfectly cooked flesh of a pig suffering from the disease.

Hence **trichinosed** ('trɪkɪnəʊzd) *ppl. a.*, infected with trichinosis, or with trichinæ; **trichinotic** (-'ɒtɪk) *a.*, pertaining or relating to trichinosis.

1881 *Daily News* 3 Feb., The rejection by Italy and Germany of whole cargoes of American trichinosed bacon has glutted with it the French market. **1889** *Lancet* 4 May 901/2 The very long duration of the disease is a slight argument also against the trichinotic view.

trichinous ('trɪkɪnəs), *a.* [f. TRICHINA + -OUS.] Infested with trichinæ; affected with, or of the nature of, trichinosis.

1857 tr. *Küchenmeister's Anim. & Veg. Parasites* (Syd. Soc.) I. 353 In pigeons fed with trichinous mole's flesh, Herbst found many free Trichinæ. **1866** *Reader* 10 Feb. 154/3 The town of Hadersleben in the Hartz was the scene of a terrible outbreak of a trichinous disease, resulting in the death of some eighty people.

trichite ('trɪkaɪt, 'traɪ-), *sb.* [f. Gr. θρίξ, τριχ- hair + -ITE[1]; in *Min.*, a. Ger. *trichit* (Zirkel, 1867).]

1. *Min.* A name for very minute dark-coloured hair-like bodies occurring in the substance of some vitreous rocks.

1868 DANA *Min.* (ed. 5) 805 The name *Trichite*..is applied by Zirkel..to microscopic capillary forms, often curved, bent, or zigzag,..opaque and black or reddish-brown, of undetermined nature, which he detected in some ..glassy..volcanic rocks. **1879** RUTLEY *Study Rocks* x. 162 Trichites..are minute elongated bodies resembling small hairs or fibres.

2. *Zool.* A name for extremely fine siliceous fibres found in certain sponge-spicules, or for such spicules themselves: see quot. 1887. Also *attrib.*

1887 SOLLAS in *Encycl. Brit.* XXII. 418/1 (*Sponges*) A curious group of flesh spicules are the *trichites*. In this group silica..forms within the scleroblast a sheaf of immeasurably fine fibrillæ or trichites... The trichite sheaf may be regarded as a fibrillated spicule. **1890** *Cassell's Nat. Hist.* VI. 322 In other forms, the trichites grow radiately outward.., and becoming thickened with age, produce a trichite-stellate, or, if they are very numerous, a trichite-globate or globate spicule.

3. *Bot.* (See quot.)

1900 B. D. JACKSON *Gloss. Bot. Terms* 275 *Trichite*, a needle-shaped crystal of amylose in starch grains, stated to form the latter by aggregation (A. Meyer).

Hence **trichitic** (-'ɪtɪk) *a.*, pertaining to or of the nature of a trichite, or containing trichites.

1879 RUTLEY *Stud. Rocks* x. 170 Minute granules and trichitic bodies.

† **'trichite**, *a. Obs. rare.* [f. as prec.] Characterized by very fine fracture, so as to resemble or suggest hairs or fine filaments.

1764 PLATT in *Phil. Trans.* LIV. 41 The shells of the trichite kind. *Ibid.*, *note*, The more debased sort breaks in a hairy trichite manner.

trichiurid (trɪkɪ'jʊərɪd). *Ichthyol.* [f. mod.L. *Trichiūridæ* pl. (see -ID[3]), f. *Trichiūrus*, properly *Trichūrus*, generic name, f. Gr. θρίξ, τριχ- hair + οὐρά tail.] A fish of the family *Trichiuridæ* (the hair-tails), typified by the genus *Trichiurus*, characterized by a ribbon-like body and a long filament at the end of the tail. Also **trichiure**. So **trichi'uriform**, **trichi'uroid** *adjs.*, having the form of the fishes of this genus or family.

[**1774** GOLDSM. *Nat. Hist.* (1862) II. III. i. 294 Trichurus.] **1819** *Pantologia*, *Trichiurus*, Trichiure... 1. *T. lepturus*, Silver-trichiure. **1854** BADHAM *Halieut.* 407. **1865** *Athenæum* 20 May 688/1 A new form of Trichiuroid Fishes. **1891** *Cent. Dict.*, Trichiuriform. **1895** *Funk's Standard Dict.*, Trichiurid.

trichlor-, trichloro- (traɪ'klɔər(əʊ)). *Chem.* [f. TRI- 5 c + CHLOR(O-.] A formative analogous to TRIBROM(O-, expressing the substitution of three atoms of chlorine for hydrogen, as in ***trichlorobenzene***, $C_6H_3Cl_3$; so ***trichloracetic acid***, $CCl_3.CO_2H$, etc. Also **triˌchloro-**, ˌ**trichloracet'aldehyde** = CHLORAL.

1845 HOFMANN in *Mem. & Proc. Chem. Soc.* II. 286 Trichloraniline..$C_{12}H_4Cl_3N$..procured..by the direct action of chlorine on aniline or the chlorinated base. **1876** HARLEY *Royle's Mat. Med.* 339 The aldehyde thus formed is immediately attacked by the chlorine and converted into hydrochloric acid and trichloraldehyde or chloral. **1912** THORPE *Dict. Appl. Chem.* II. 44 Chloroform, *Trichloromethane* $CHCl_3$..was discovered by Liebig in 1831. **1921** J. S. CHAMBERLAIN *Textbk. Org. Chem.* 226 The tri-chlor acet-aldehyde then reacts with an alkali present yielding chloroform. **1964** N. G. CLARK *Mod. Org. Chem.* x. 189 Acetaldehyde..may be chlorinated to chloral (trichloroacetaldehyde..), an important intermediate in the manufacture of 'D.D.T.'.

tri'chlorate, tri'chloride: see TRI- 5 a.

trichlorhydrin (traɪklɔə'haɪdrɪn). *Chem.* [f. TRI- 5 a + *chlorhydr(ic* + -IN[1] (termination of the compound ethers of glycerin: see TRIACETIN).] Glyceryl trichloride, $C_3H_5Cl_3$, a haloid ester or compound ether of glycerin or glycerol, $C_3H_5(OH)_3$, in which the three OH groups are replaced by chlorine atoms.

1862 MILLER *Elem. Chem.* III. 281 Trichlorhydrin..is a neutral liquid, insoluble in water.

trichloroethylene (traɪˌklɔərəʊ'ɛθɪliːn). *Chem.* Also **trichlorethylene**. [f. TRI- + CHLORO-[2] + *ethylene* s.v. ETHYL.] A liquid organochlorine compound, C_2HCl_3, used as a solvent, analgesic, and anæsthetic. Cf. TRILENE.

1889 G. M'GOWAN tr. *Bernthsen's Text-bk. Org. Chem.* 60 (*table*) C_2HCl_3, Tri-chloro-ethylene. **1930** *Engineering* 26 Dec. 814/2 The use of chemical cleaners, such as petrol.. and trichlorethylene, is more effective. **1955** *Ann. Reg.* *1954* 411 Midwives should be allowed..to use a new pain-relieving vapour called trichlorethylene B.P. **1976** *National Observer* (U.S.) 17 July 2/3 The Food and Drug Administration said it will ban use of a chemical once used in decaffeinated coffees and some beers. The chemical, trichloroethylene, has been found to cause liver cancer in mice.

tricho-[1] (trɪkəʊ, traɪkəʊ), before a vowel **trich-** (trɪk, traɪk), ad. Gr. τριχο-, τριχ-, combining stem of θρίξ hair, in many terms of botany, zoology, etc. ||trichæs'thesia *Path.* [mod.L., f. Gr. αἴσθησις feeling], a form of paræsthesia consisting in a sensation as of a hair on the skin. ||trichangia (-'ændʒɪə) *sb. pl.* [f. Gr. ἀγγεῖον vessel], the capillary blood-vessels; hence ||tri,changiec'tasia, -'ectasis *Path.* [f. Gr. ἔκτασις extension], dilatation of the capillaries. ||tricha'trophia *Path.* [see ATROPHY], atrophy of the hair-bulbs, causing brittleness of the hair. ||tri'chauxis [f. Gr. αὔξη, αὔξησις increase], excessive growth of hair. ||trichobac'teria, (*a*) the filamentous or thread-like bacteria; (*b*) bacteria which possess flagella (Dorland *Med. Dict.* 1900–13). 'trichoblast *Bot.* [Gr. βλαστός germ, taken as = cell], name for certain special cells or idioblasts resembling hairs. ||trichobranchia (-'bræŋkɪə) *Zool.* [BRANCHIA], (in pl. -æ), name for the gills, set with filaments, of certain decapod crustaceans; hence tricho'branchial *a.*, pertaining to or of the nature of such gills; tricho'branchiate *a.*, having or characterized by such gills. tricho'carpous *a. Bot.* [Gr. καρπός fruit], having hairy fruit (*Cent. Dict.* 1891). ||trichocephalus (-'sɛfələs) *Zool.* [mod.L. (Goeze, 1782), f. Gr. κεφαλή head], a genus of parasitic nematoid worms, having the head filamentous; hence tricho'cephalid, a worm of the family *Trichocephalidæ*, typified by this genus; tricho'cephaloid *a.*, resembling or akin to the genus *Trichocephalus*. ||tricho'clasia, -'oclasis [Gr. κλάσις fracture], brittleness of the hair. ||trichocryp'tosis [Gr. κρυπτός concealed], disease of the hair-follicles. 'trichocyst (-sɪst) *Zool.* [CYST: named by Allman 1855], one of a number of minute rod-like bodies, each containing a coiled protrusible filament, found in the cuticle of many *Infusoria*, resembling the thread-cells of cœlenterates; hence tricho'cystic *a.* (*Cent. Dict.* 1891). ||trichodectes (-'dɛktiːz) [Gr. δέκτης receiver, beggar], a genus of insects parasitic on quadrupeds; *T. lotus* is the dog-louse; *T. sphærocephalus*, the red-headed sheep-louse. tricho'dontid *Ichthyol.*, a fish of the family *Trichodontidæ* [mod.L., f. *Trichodon* (Tilesius, 1811), f. Gr. ὀδούς, ὀδοντ- tooth], a sand-fish; so tricho'dontoid *a.*, akin to the sand-fishes. 'trichogen (-dʒɛn) [-GEN], a hypodermal cell, in insects and other arthropods, from which a hair arises. tri'chogenous *a.*, producing, or promoting the growth of, hair. tricho'glossine *a.*, *Ornith.* [Gr. γλῶσσα tongue], belonging to the subfamily *Trichoglossinæ* or brush-tongued parakeets, of which *Trichoglossus Swainsonii* (Swainson's lory) is a well-known Australian example. 'trichogyne (-dʒaɪn) *Bot.* [Gr. γυνή woman], a hair-like process forming the receptive part of the female reproductive organ or procarp in certain algæ and fungi; hence trichogynial (-'dʒɪnɪəl), trichogynic (-'dʒɪnɪk) *adjs.* tricho'maniac *nonce-wd.*, a hair fetishist. trichomonad (-'mɒnæd) *Zool.* [MONAD 4], an infusorian of the genus *Trichomonas*, characterized by several flagella and hair-like processes; some species are parasitic in man and other animals. tricho'monal *a.*, of, pertaining to, or caused by trichomonads. tricho'mycterine, -'mycteroid *adjs.*, *Ichthyol.* [Gr. μυκτήρ nostril], belonging respectively to the subfamily *Trichomycterinæ* and the family *Trichomycteridæ* (or *Pygidiidæ*) of fishes (cat-fishes), found in S. American rivers (*Cent. Dict.*); also as *sbs.* tricho'notid *Ichthyol.* [Gr. νῶτος back; from the long hair-like dorsal ray of the species *Trichonotus setigerus*], a fish of the family *Trichonotidæ*; so tricho'notoid *a.* and *sb.* tricho'pathic *a.* [Gr. πάθος suffering], relating to diseases of the hair; so tri'chopathy [-PATHY], treatment of diseases of the hair. trichophocine (-'fəʊsaɪn) *a.*, *Zool.* [Gr. φώκη seal], belonging to the subfamily *Trichophocinæ* or hair-seals (*Cent. Dict.*). 'trichophore (-fɔə(r)) [Gr. -φόρος bearing], (*a*) *Bot.* (see quot. 1860: ? *obs.*); (*b*) *Bot.* the structure which bears the trichogyne in florideous algæ; (*c*) *Zool.* one of several projections of the integument in certain annelids, from which spring bundles of setæ or bristles; tricho'phoric (-'fɒrɪk) *a.*, pertaining to or of the nature of a trichophore; tri'chophorous *a.*, bearing hairs or hair-like bodies; of the nature of a trichophore. tri'chopter *Entom.* [Gr. πτέρον wing], a member of the group *Trichoptera* of neuropterous insects, characterized by specially hairy wings; a caddis-fly; so tri'chopteran *a.* = *trichopterous*; *sb.* = *trichopter*; tri'chopterist, one who studies the *Trichoptera*; tri'chopterous *a.*, belonging to or having the characters of the *Trichoptera*, hairy-winged. trichopterygid (-'ptɛrɪdʒɪd) *Entom.* [Gr. πτέρυξ wing], *sb.* a member of the family *Trichopterygidæ* of clavicorn beetles, having the wings fringed with hairs, and comprising the smallest beetles known; *adj.* belonging to or having the characters of this family; so tricho'pterygoid *a.* trichoptile (trɪ'kɒptɪl) *Ornith.* [Gr. πτίλον down], a hair-like prolongation of the sheath of a growing feather, forming part of the downy covering of the young of certain birds; hence tri'choptilar *a.*, pertaining to or of the nature of a trichoptile. ||tricho'rrhœa [Gr. -ροια flowing], falling off of the hair. ||trichoschisis (-'ɒskɪsɪs) [Gr. σχίσις splitting], splitting of the hair. tricho'somatous *a.*, *Zool.* [Gr. σῶμα body], belonging to the division *Trichosomata* of flagellate *Infusoria*. ||,trichospo'rangium, pl. -ia (also anglicized tri'chosporange) *Bot.*, Thuret's term for the multilocular sporangium of certain fucoid algæ, which appears to consist of jointed hairs (distinguished from OOSPORANGIUM); hence trichospo'rangial *a.* 'trichospore *Bot.*, a spore or conidium borne upon a filamentous stalk, in certain fungi. tricho'stomatous *a.*, *Zool.* [Gr. στόμα mouth], belonging to the order *Trichostomata* of *Protozoa*, having the mouth and pharynx provided with vibratile membranes and cilia, by the movements of which particles of food are drawn in. tricho'thallic *a.*, *Bot.* (see quots.). ,trichotillo'mania [ad. F. *trichotillomanie* (H. Hallopeau 1889, in *Ann. de Dermatol. et Syphilol.* X. 441), f. Gr. τίλλεσθαι to pull out (hair)], a compulsive desire to pull out one's hair; hence ,trichotillo'maniac, a person with this.

1902 *Nature* 7 Aug. 360/1 On a new form of tactile sensibility, *trichesthesia, by MM. N. Vaschide and P. Rousseau. 1857 DUNGLISON *Med. Lex.*, *Trichangia ..*Trichangiectasia. 1890 BILLINGS *Nat. Med. Dict.*, *Trichangiectasis..*Trichatrophia..*Trichauxis. 1882 VINES *Sachs' Bot.* 85 These cells..present the appearance, when the petiole is broken across..of tough, slender hairs projecting out of the tissue. For idioblasts of this kind I [Sachs] propose the term *Trichoblast, in order to express their resemblance to many epidermal trichomes. 1878 *Proc. Zool. Soc.* 4 June 776 They..may be called '*trichobranchiæ', in contradistinction to the lamellar gills or 'phyllobranchiæ', which are met with in a large number of other Crustacea. 1891 *Cent. Dict.*, *Trichobranchial. 1878 *Proc. Zool. Soc.* 4 June 777 Among the *trichobranchiate Podophthalmia, the Euphausidæ possess no other than podobranchiæ. 1880 E. R. LANKESTER in *Nature* 12 Feb. 355/2 Crayfishes..differ from prawns..in being 'trichobranchiate' in place of 'phyllobranchiate'. 1819 *Pantologia*, *Trichocephalus, a genus of the class vermes. 1846 *Proc. Amer. Phil. Soc.* IV. 232 He had found the tricocephalus in the human cœcum after death. 1897 *Allbutt's Syst. Med.* II. 1048 Found in association with a high degree of trichocephalus infection. 1895 *Funk's Standard Dict.*, *Trichoclasia..*Trichoclasis. 1890 BILLINGS *Nat. Med. Dict.*, *Tricho-cryptoses. 1900–13 DORLAND *Med. Dict.*, Trichocryptosis. 1859 J. R. GREENE *Man. Anim. Kingd.*, *Protozoa* 66 In the cortical layer of Bursaria, certain peculiar fusiform bodies or '*trichocysts' have been detected, and from these Prof. Allman states that he has observed the emission of minute filaments [resembling] the urticating organs of the fresh-water polype. 1880 KENT *Infusoria* I. 249 A sheaf-shaped fascicle of rod-like trichocysts. 1876 tr. *Beneden's Anim. Parasites* 71 The *trichodectes of the dog has lately attracted the especial notice of naturalists. 1898 PACKARD *Text-bk. Entomol.* 188 Each of these pores communicates with a hair-forming hypodermal cell, called by Graber a **trichogen*. 1853 E. WILSON *Healthy Skin* (ed. 4) Index, *Trichogenous remedies. 1879 A. R. WALLACE *Australas.* iii. 59 The *Trichoglossidæ, or brush-tongued Lories. 1875 BENNETT & DYER *Sachs' Bot.* 212 The term *Trichogyne is given to a long thin hair-like hyaline sac, which serves as a receptive organ, and springs from a structure..called the Trichophore. The latter is a body usually consisting of several cells. 1877 HUXLEY *Anat. Inv. Anim.* Introd. 29 The protoplasmic body of the trichogyne, which unites with the spermatozooids, does not undergo division itself. 1882 VINES *Sachs' Bot.* 238. 1900 B. D. JACKSON *Gloss. Bot. Terms*, **Trichogynial*, relating to a trichogyne. 1891 *Cent. Dict.*, *Trichogynic. 1949 R. GRAVES *Common Asphodel* 303 From descriptions in his poems it is clear that the first thing that he [*sc.* Milton] saw in a woman was not her bright love-darting eye (as it was to practically all his contemporaries), but her hair. He was, in fact, a *trichomaniac. 1861 HULME tr. *Moquin-Tandon* II. VII. 407 The *Trichomonads..form irregular masses with the particles of thickened mucus. 1889 J. M. DUNCAN *Clin. Lect. Dis. Wom.* xxii. (ed. 4) 179 At one time it was supposed that the discovery of trichomonads, or a leptothrix, or a vibrio, would decide whether it was venereal or not. 1948 *Jrnl. Amer. Med. Assoc.* 18 Sept. 231/2 The diagnosis and treatment of *trichomonal vaginitis may not always be as simple as depicted. 1970 G. GREER *Female Eunuch* 259 Cases of incurable trichomonal infection are all due to a combination of fear, superstition and doctors' sloppiness. 1891 *Cent. Dict.*, *Trichopathic. 1900–13 in DORLAND *Med. Dict.* 1860 MAYNE *Expos. Lex.*, **Trichopathy*, a term proposed..for the system of treating diseased affections of the hair. *Ibid.*, *Trichophorus*... Name by Nees von Esenbeck for the filamentous base of mushrooms, when the filaments, by their agglutination, form a kind of membrane: a *trichophore. 1875 [see *trichogyne*]. 1877 HUXLEY *Anat. Inv. Anim.* v. 229 Stiff hair-like appendages..developed within diverticula of the integument, or trichophores, in which their bases always remain enclosed. 1882 VINES *Sachs' Bot.* 238 In the true Florideæ..a lateral row of cells bears at its apex a closed hair-like prolongation, the trichogyne, and is hence termed the *Trichophore*. 1891 *Cent. Dict.*, *Trichophoric. 1892 *Jrnl. Linn. Soc., Bot.* XXIX. 74 Not unfrequently this trichophoric apparatus consists of three cells—two basal trichophoric cells and the trichogyne. 1864 WEBSTER, *Trichopter. 1826 KIRBY & SP. *Entomol.* IV. xlvii. 379 The existence..of the collar in the *Trichoptera. 1835 KIRBY *Hab. & Inst. Anim.* II. xx. 318 The *Trichoptera* (Caseworm-flies) have four hairy membranous wings. 1842 BRANDE *Dict. Sci., Art*, etc., *Trichopterans. 1897 *Naturalist* 115 Neuropterists and *trichopterists have commenced..as lepidopterists. 1816 KIRBY & SP. *Entomol.* (1818) II. xxi. 243 *Phryganea grandis*..is a *trichopterous insect. 1826 *Ibid.* IV. xlvii. 375 There is no tendency in the saw-flies towards a Trichopterous type. 1891 *Cent. Dict.*, *Trichopterygid. 1895 *Funk's Standard Dict.*, *Trichopterygoid. 1900 *Ibis* Oct. 665 The actual feather-sheath makes its appearance, pushing before it its *trichoptilar appendage, which has now become abraded. *Ibid.* 654, I shall term these thread-like structures *trichoptiles. 1860 MAYNE *Expos. Lex.*, *Trichorrhœa. 1857 DUNGLISON *Med. Lex.*, *Trichoschisis. 1891 *Cent. Dict.*, *Trichosporange. 1900 in B. D. JACKSON *Gloss. Bot. Terms.* 1887 *Trans. Roy. Soc. Edin.* XXXII. 591 The *trichosporangial form [of fruit of *Ectocarpus*] is well known. 1857 BERKELEY *Cryptog. Bot.* §67. 88 The two organs called Oosporangia and *Trichosporangia by Thuret. 1909 *Cent. Dict. Suppl.*, *Trichostomatous. 1890 *Athenæum* 29 Nov. 743/1 The formation of the plantlets by *trichothallic gemmation from the tufts of..hairs..on the old thallus of *P*[*unctaria*] *plantaginea* and *P. latifolia*. 1900 B. D. JACKSON *Gloss. Bot. Terms*, *Trichothallic*..when the shoot ends in one or more multicellular hairs or tufts of such. 1905 *Rep. Soc. for Study of Dis. in Children* V. 28 (*heading*) A case of *trichotillomania. 1980 *Brit. Med. Jrnl.* 29 Mar. 881/2 The loss is patchy and must be distinguished from.. trichotillomania, in which the child pulls out his or her hair and may eat it. 1962 *Woman* 26 May 9 (*heading*) Don't be a *trichotillomaniac! That is, in simple terms, someone who tears out hair!

tricho-[2] (trɪkəʊ, traɪkəʊ), combining form repr. Gr. τρίχα, τριχῇ in three, triply: used in a few more or less technical words. These are modern, formed on the analogy of Gr. compounds in διχο-, DICHO-. (Gr. compounds in τριχο- are only from θρίξ, τριχ- hair: see prec.) **trichocladose** (trɪ'kɒklədəʊs) *a. Zool.* [Gr. κλάδος shoot], having triple or trifurcate *cladi* or secondary rays, as a sponge-spicule. **trichotriæne** (-traɪ'iːn) *Zool.*, in sponge-spicules, a triæne of which each of the three *cladi* is trifurcate. See also TRICHOTOMIC, etc.

1887 SOLLAS in *Encycl. Brit.* XXII. 416 (Fig. 13) (*Sponges*) *p*, amphitriæne (this is trichocladose). *Ibid.* 423/2 Canal system diplodal. Spicules trichotriænes.

trichodal (trɪ'kəʊdəl), *a. Zool.* [f. Gr. τριχώδης hair-like (f. θρίξ, τριχ- hair: see -ODE[1]) + -AL[1].] Extremely thin: applied to a sponge-spicule.

1888 SOLLAS in *Challenger Rep.* XXV. p. lviii, Both the rhabdus and the style may..be..immeasurably thin (trichodal, τριχώδης, hair-like).

trichoid ('trɪkɔɪd), *a. rare.* [ad. Gr. τριχοειδής (applied by Galen to the capillary blood-vessels), f. θρίξ, τριχ- hair + εἶδος form: see -OID.] Resembling hair or a hair; hairlike; capillary.

1854–67 C. A. HARRIS *Dict. Med. Terminol.*, *Trichoid*, resembling a hair.

tri'chology. [f. Gr. θρίξ, τριχ- hair: see -OLOGY.] The study of the structure, functions, and diseases of the hair. Hence **tricho'logical** *a.*, pertaining to or engaged in trichology; **tri'chologist**, one who is versed in trichology.

1860 MAYNE *Expos. Lex.*, *Trichology*, term for the doctrine of the hair. 1887 *Standard* 28 Oct. 5/3 The Elements of Trichological Science. *Ibid.*, The Trichologists study the physiology and the diseases of the hair. 1895 J. J. RAVEN *Hist. Suffolk* 253 Something may be discoverable by craniology, trichology, odontology. 1913 *Daily News* 4 Oct. 9 The study of the hair is becoming a science with a national institute of its own—the National Institute of Trichologists.

||**trichoma** (trɪ'kəʊmə). Pl. **tri'chomata.** [mod.L., a. Gr. τρίχωμα a growth of hair, f. τριχοῦν to cover with hair.]

1. *Path.* A disease of the hair: = PLICA 1.

1799 HOOPER *Med. Dict.*, *Trichōma*, a disease of the hair. See *Plica polonica*. 1857 DUNGLISON *Med. Lex.*, *Trichoma*, Capillamentum, Plica.

2. *Bot.* Each of the filaments composing the thallus in algæ of the order *Nostochineæ*.

1866 *Treas. Bot.*, *Trichoma*, the filamentous thallus of algals, as *Conferva*. 1879 W. G. FARLOW *Marine Algæ* (1881) 11 In..the Nostochineæ, the cells are..attached to one another in the form of filaments, to which the name of *trichomata* is given.

Hence (from sense 1) **tri'chomaphyte** (-faɪt) [Gr. φυτόν plant], a cryptogamic growth formerly supposed to cause trichoma; **tri-'chomatose** *a.*, affected with trichoma.

1857 in DUNGLISON *Med. Lex.*

||**Trichomanes** (trɪ'kɒmɒniːz). *Bot.* [L. (Pliny), a. Gr. τριχομανές a kind of fern (cf. τριχομανία a mania or passion for long hair).] A genus of

ferns, having filamentous outgrowths from the margins of the fronds; the bristle-ferns.

1562 TURNER *Herbal* II. 157 b, Trichomanes (that is our English Maydens heare). **1706** PHILLIPS (ed. Kersey), *Trichomanes*, the Herb Maiden-hair or Goldilocks. **1757** PARSONS in *Phil. Trans.* L. 401 We see the leaves of ferns of several kinds, polypodium, tricomanes, and other capillary plants. **1885** LADY BRASSEY *The Trades* 234 Such ferns as trichomanes, hymenophyllums, and many others growing in the greatest luxuriance.

Hence **tri'chomanoid** *a.*, resembling or akin to the ferns of this genus.

1900 in B. D. JACKSON *Gloss. Bot. Terms.*

trichome ('trɪ-, 'traɪkəʊm). [ad. Gr. τρίχωμα (see TRICHOMA); cf. CAULOME.] **1.** *Bot.* The general name for any outgrowth of the epidermis or superficial tissue of a plant, as hairs, scales, prickles, etc.

1875 BENNETT & DYER tr. *Sachs' Bot.* 129 We may term all appendages of other parts which originate as outgrowths of epidermis-cells, whatever their form and function, Hairs (Trichomes). Thus the so-called paleæ and sporangia of Ferns are trichomes. **1876** *Encycl. Brit.* IV. 90/1 Hairs, scales, prickles, &c.,..all have been embraced under the general name *trichome*.

2. *Ent.* In myrmecophilous insects, a tuft of hairs near a gland producing a secretion attractive to ants.

1911 E. JACOBSON in *Tijdschr. Ent.* LIV. 177 The bug possesses a very curious tuft of yellow hair (a trichome) which apparently secretes some substance with a flavour agreeable to the ants. **1923** W. M. WHEELER *Social Life among Insects* v. 227 The trichomes surround the openings of singular glands, the aromatic, volatile secretions of which ..are licked off by the ants. **1971** E. O. WILSON *Insect Societies* (1972) xx. 390/2 The *Cremastocheilus* adults are furnished with tufts of golden hairs ('trichomes') at the anterior and posterior corners of the thorax.

trichomoniasis (ˌtrɪkəʊmə'naɪəsɪs). *Med.* and *Vet. Sci.* [f. mod.L. *Trichomonas*, generic name (coined in Fr. as *Trico-monas* by A. Donné 1836, in *Compt. Rend.* III. 386), f. TRICHO-[1] + -MONAS: see -IASIS.] Infection with trichomonads, which in humans is often symptomless; *esp.* (*a*) a venereal disease of women caused by *Trichomonas vaginalis*, in which there are vaginal irritation and a discharge; (*b*) a venereal disease of cattle caused by *T. fœtus*, characterized by abortion, pyometra, and sometimes sterility.

1915 *N.Y. Med. Jrnl.* CI. 886/2 (*heading*) Clinical and experimental trichomoniasis of the intestine. **1972** *Daily Colonist* (Victoria, B.C.) 19 May 2/2 Another common cause of persistent or recurrent discharge is a parasitic infection called trichomoniasis. **1980** *Trop. Med. & Hygiene News* Dec. 25 Investigations on trichinellosis, hydatid disease and trichomoniasis.

trichophyte ('trɪkəfaɪt). Chiefly in mod.L. form **tri'chophyton.** [f. Gr. θρίξ, τριχ- hair + φυτόν plant.] A genus of minute fungi, parasitic on the skin; esp. the species *Trichophyton tonsurans*, which produces ringworm.

1862 H. MACMILLAN in *Macm. Mag.* Oct. 463/1 Another variety of tric[h]ophyton or hair-plant which luxuriates on the beard. **1876** DUHRING *Dis. Skin* 70 The trichophyton, giving rise to three affections, tinea circinata, tinea tonsurans, and tinea sycosis. **1898** P. MANSON *Trop. Diseases* xxxvii. 579 Itching rings, or segments of rings, of trichophyton infection. **1899** *Allbutt's Syst. Med.* VIII. 779 Conglomerative pustular perifolliculitis..due to one of the trichophyton fungi. *Ibid.* 855 Sabouraud thinks it probable that the trichophytes, or some of them, may exist independently as saprophytes.

Hence **trichophytic** (-'fɪtɪk) *a.*, of or pertaining to a trichophyte; **trichophy'tosis**: see quot. 1890.

1890 BILLINGS *Med. Dict.*, *Trichophytosis*, disease of the skin produced by the tric[h]ophyton fungus. **1899** *Allbutt's Syst. Med.* VIII. 854 It is rare to find the same species of large-spored fungus in any two cases of trichophytic ringworm. *Ibid.* 863 Lesions of trichophytic appearance. *Ibid.*, Lesions having the circinate form..characteristic of trichophytosis.

trichoplax ('trɪkəʊplæks). [mod.L. (F. E. Schulze 1883, in *Zool. Anzeiger* VI. 92), f. TRICHO-[2] + Gr. πλάξ plate.] A minute marine animal with a body formed of three layers of cells, formerly included in the genus of this name but now usually considered to be a modified form of a hydrozoan planula.

1897 PARKER & HASWELL *Text-bk. Zool.* I. iv. 220 Trichoplax is a compressed plate-like body of irregular and extremely variable shape, but circular in the resting condition. **1940** L. H. HYMAN *Invertebrates* iv. 243 *Trichoplax* and *Tetroplax* were found actually to be modified planulae of Hydroidea.

trichor, -our, -ory: see TREACHER, TREACHERY.

trichord ('traɪkɔːd), *sb.* and *a.* [ad. Gr. τρίχορδος three-stringed, f. τρι-, TRI- three + χορδή string, CHORD.] **a.** *sb.* A musical instrument of three strings; a three-stringed lyre or lute. **b.** *adj.* Having three strings to each note: applied to a pianoforte in which most of the keys have three strings each.

1776 BURNEY *Hist. Mus.* I. 211 Though so ancient and honourable an origin has been assigned to the Dichord and Trichord. **1866** MRS. RIDDELL *Race for Wealth* xxiii, One of Collard's Repetition Trichord grand pianos.

‖**trichosis** (trɪ'kəʊsɪs). *Path.* [med. or mod.L., a. Gr. τρίχωσις growth of hair (f. τριχοῦν 'to cover with hair', in pass. 'to be hairy').]

a. = TRICHIASIS a. **b.** = TRICHOMA I.

1693 tr. *Blancard's Phys. Dict.* (ed. 2), *Trichosis*, the same with *Trichiasis*. **1706** PHILLIPS (ed. Kersey), *Trichiasis*, or *Trichosis*, a growing of much Hair. **1890** BILLINGS *Med. Dict.*, *Trichosis*, disease of the hair, plica.

trichothecin (trɪkəʊ-, traɪkəʊ'θiːkɪn). *Biochem.* [f. mod.L. *Trichothec-ium*, name of a genus of fungi (H. F. Link 1809, in *Mag. d. Ges. Naturforschender Freunde zu Berlin* III. 18), f. TRICHO-[1] + THECIUM: see -IN[1].] A crystalline trichothecene, $C_{15}H_{19}O_3{\cdot}O{\cdot}CO{\cdot}C_3H_5$, that is an ester of butenoic acid produced by the fungus *Trichothecium roseum* and is toxic to some other fungi.

1948 FREEMAN & MORRISON in *Nature* 3 July 30/1 Antagonistic activity to other fungi by *Trichothecium roseum* Link..has been reported... The name 'trichothecin' is suggested for the active substance. **1981** COLE & COX *Handbk. Toxic Fungal Metabolites* v. 152 Examples of trichothecenes that do not contain a carbonyl function at C-8 are T-2 toxin,..and trichothecin.

Hence **tricho'thecene**, any of a class of sesquiterpenoids based on a tetracyclic ring system $C_{15}H_{22}O_2$.

1971 *Analytical Biochem.* XLIII. 327 The trichothecenes are a family of closely related tetracyclic sesquiterpenoid metabolites of various strains of *Fusarium*, *Trichoderma*, *Trichothecium*, *Myrothecium*, and other species of imperfect fungi commonly found in soil, and on grains and other foods and feeds. **1978** *Experientia* XXXIV. 1333/1 Samples from 2 lots of corn in France suspected of causing infertility, hyperestrogenic signs and feed refusal in swine were analyzed for zearalenone and trichothecenes. **1982** *Daily Tel.* 24 Mar. 18 Trichothecene toxins should be seen as the murderous successors to mustard gas.

trichotomic (trɪkəʊ-, traɪkəʊ'tɒmɪk), *a.* [f. Gr. τρίχα triply + -τομ-ος cut + -IC, after DICHOTOMIC.] = TRICHOTOMOUS.

1873 WAGNER tr. *Teuffel's Hist. Rom. Lit.* I. 442 A certain fondness of trichotomic composition. **1880** *Athenæum* 25 Dec. 851/3 To construct..the whole sum of human knowledge on the plan of a trichotomic system of self-division. **1882–3** *Schaff's Encycl. Relig. Knowl.* III. 2394/1 The trichotomic view [of human nature] is found in the New Testament.

trichotomism (trɪ-, traɪ'kɒtəmɪz(ə)m). [f. as prec. + -ISM: cf. DICHOTOMISM.] A trichotomous system; trichotomy.

1912 W. GEMMEL *Diamond Sutra* 17 *note*, In later ages.. trichotomism was taught as to the nature of all Buddhas.

trichotomist[1] (trɪ-, traɪ'kɒtəmɪst). *nonce-wd.* [f. Gr. *τριχοτόμος adj. hair-cutting (implied in τριχοτομεῖν to cut the hair) + -IST.] A hair-cutter.

1875 R. F. BURTON *Gorilla L.* (1876) I. 205 Whatever absurdity in hair may be demanded by the trichotomists and philopogons of Europe, I can at once supply it to any extent from Africa.

trichotomize (trɪ-, traɪ'kɒtəmaɪz), *v.* [f. as next + -IZE: cf. DICHOTOMIZE.] *trans.* To divide into three parts; to arrange or classify in three divisions, or in groups of three. Also *absol.* Hence **tri'chotomist**[2], one who trichotomizes or practises trichotomy.

1651 *Fuller's Abel Rediv.*, *Colet* (1867) I. 121 The latter [sayings, etc.] he intended to trichotomize, or reduce unto ternaries. **1681** BAXTER *Councels Yng. Men* Catal. *j, Shewing that Trinity in Unity is imprinted on the whole Creation, and that Trichotomising is the just distribution in Naturals and Morals. **1846** T. W. JENKYN *Baxter's Wks.* Pref. Ess. 50.

trichotomous (trɪ-, traɪ'kɒtəməs), *a.* [f. Gr. τρίχα triply + -τομ-ος cut + -OUS; cf. DICHOTOMOUS.]

1. *Bot.* Dividing into three branches; so branched that each successive axis divides into three.

1800 *Misc. Tr.* in *Asiatic Ann. Reg.* 273/2 Peduncles axillary,..trichotomous. **1806** GALPINE *Brit. Bot.* §29 Aira. .. Culm almost naked: pan[icle] spreading trichotomous. **1880** S. YOSINO in Sir E. J. Reed *Japan* II. 44 *note*, Its stem and branches are trichotomous.

2. Making three divisions, classes, or categories; involving or of the nature of trichotomy.

1855 N. LINDLEY *Introd. Jurisprudence* App. 85 The passages cited..are all against the trichotomous and in favour of the dichotomous division of *culpa*. **1899** ROBERTSON in *Expositor* May 351 A trichotomous psychology.

Hence **tri'chotomously** *adv.*

1830 LINDLEY *Nat. Syst. Bot.* 204 Flowers in regular cymes, branched bi- or trichotomously. **1853** ROYLE *Mat. Med.* (ed. 2) 444 Panicles short, trichotomously divided.

trichotomy (trɪ-, traɪ'kɒtəmɪ). [f. Gr. τρίχα triply + -τομία cutting: after DICHOTOMY.] Division into three; arrangement or classification in three divisions, classes, or categories.

1610 HEALEY *St. Aug. Citie of God* 303 This Trichotomy or triple division doth not contradict the other Dichotomy. **1734** J. KIRKBY tr. *Barrow's Math. Lect.* viii. 119 His [Aristotle's] trichotomy..into Hypotheses, Definitions, and Axioms. **1836–7** SIR W. HAMILTON *Metaph.* xli. (1870) II. 416 It remained..for Kant to establish..the decisive trichotomy of the mental powers. **1868** *Contemp. Rev.* VII. 598 Popular theology is rather founded on the dichotomy of man into body and soul, than on the Christian trichotomy of body, soul, and spirit.

trichroic (traɪ'krəʊɪk), *a.* [f. Gr. τρίχρο-ος, τρίχρους three-coloured + -IC: cf. DICHROIC.] Having or showing three colours; *spec.* of crystals, exhibiting three different colours when viewed in three different directions.

1881 S. P. THOMPSON in *Nature* 15 Sept. 465/2 Di- or trichroic absorption is a general property of all coloured crystals other than those of the cubical system. **1888** RUTLEY *Rock-Forming Min.* 100 Such crystals are said to be trichroic.

trichroism ('traɪkrəʊɪz(ə)m). [f. as prec. + -ISM. Cf. F. *trichroïsme*.] The property of being trichroic: *spec.* **a.** *Cryst.*: see prec.

1847 WEBSTER cites Dana. **1860** in MAYNE *Expos. Lex.* **1865–8** WATTS *Dict. Chem.* III. 670 Some biaxial crystals exhibit trichroïsm; thus certain Brazilian topazes of a yellowish rose tint in the direction of the median line, are violet when viewed along the complementary line, and yellowish white perpendicular to the plane of the axes. **1881** S. P. THOMPSON in *Nature* 15 Sept. 465/2 Crystals in which the electric conductivity differs in three different directions will exhibit trichroism.

b. *Nat. Hist.* The occurrence of three different colorations in three varieties of a species, as in certain birds and insects.

1899 SHARP in *Cambr. Nat. Hist.* VI. vi. 351 *H[eliconius] erato* exhibits the very rare condition of trichroism, the hind wings being either red, blue, or green.

trichromasy (traɪ'krəʊməsɪ). *Ophthalm.* Also -chromacy. [f. TRI- + Gr. χρῶμα colour: see -Y[3].] Colour vision in which three pure colours, in different combinations, are required to match all the colours that can be perceived (as in normal vision).

1911 *Amer. Jrnl. Psychol.* XXII. 371 Guttmann.. identifies color-weakness with anomalous trichromacy. **1923** *Proc. R. Soc.* CII. 359 Trichromasy, in my experience, seems to approach monochromasy directly without passing through dichromasy as an intermediate stage. **1973** (see PROTANOMALY]. **1980** *Nature* 27 Mar. 306/1 Our trichromacy has a 'blue' channel that is about 100 times less sensitive than the 'red' and 'green' channels.

trichromat (traɪ'krəʊmæt). *Ophthalm.* Also †**-ate.** [f. TRICHROMAT(IC *a.*] An individual with trichromasy, esp. an anomalous form of it.

1906 *Arch. Ophthalm. & Otol.* XXXV. 27 A thorough study was made of only two normal and two abnormal trichromates. **1925** M. COLLINS *Colour-Blindness* i. 14 It is customary to divide these anomalous trichromates into.. deuteranomalous trichromates..and protanomalous trichromates. **1940** *Nature* 17 Aug. 226/2 It might happen that a building matched its background for the normal person, yet, for the anomalous trichromat, the two would be distinct. **1978** J. PARR *Introd. Ophthalm.* iii. 69/2 The normal individual requires a minimum of three primaries and is said to be a trichromat.

trichromatic (traɪkrəʊ'mætɪk), *a.* [f. Gr. τρι-, TRI- + χρωματικός CHROMATIC; Gr. has τριχρώματος.] Having, showing, or pertaining to three colours; trichroic: *spec.* **a.** *Optics.* Having or relating to the three fundamental colour-sensations (red, green, violet) of normal vision. **b.** Applied to lithographic printing in three colours; also to a photographic process by which the natural colours are reproduced by super-position or combination of photographs taken in three different-coloured lights.

1891 in *Cent. Dict.* [in sense a]. **1896** C. G. ZANDER *Photo-trichromatic Printing* Pref., Trichromatic printing does not make the headway it deserves. *Ibid.* 36 The Young-Helmholtz theory of trichromatic vision. **1900** *Westm. Gaz.* 14 Nov. 2/1 'A Handbook of Photography in Colours'..by Messrs. Thomas Bolas, Alexander Tallent, and Edgar Senior. The curious will find every phase of trichromatic photography expounded. **1904** *Daily News* 17 Aug. 5 Trichromatic Toy-Books... I noticed the other day that a large toy-book..was done entirely by the three-colour process—literally three printings in all.

So **tri'chromatism**, the quality of being trichromatic; *spec.* (*a*) = TRICHROISM b; (*b*) combination of three different colours, as in painting or colour-photography; (*c*) = TRICHROMASY; **tri'chromatist**, one who uses (only) three different colours or pigments.

1854 *Blackw. Mag.* LXXVI. 330 With the unsparing use of these three unmitigated colours only.. decorators..should style themselves Trichromatists [not Polychromatists]. **1895** *Funk's Stand. Dict.*, Trichromatism. **1910** M. GREENWOOD *Physiol. Special Senses* 239/1 (Index), Trichromatism. **1925** M. COLLINS *Colour-Blindness* i. 13 Nagel rejects the term colour-weakness as being too wide, and prefers the term anomalous trichromatism. **1946** [see PROTANOMALY]. **1956** *Jrnl. Optical*

Soc. Amer. XLVI. 1075/1 The commonest form of aberrant color vision, namely anomalous trichromatism.

trichrome (ˈtraɪkrəʊm), *a.* [f. TRI- + Gr. χρῶμα colour.] = TRICHROMATIC *a.*; *spec.* applied to a stain and method of staining in which different kinds of tissue are stained in one or other of three different colours.

1918 H. CROY *How Motion Pictures are Made* xiii. 289 To show the trichrome pictures a special projecting-machine was needed. **1929** *Jrnl. Technical Methods* XII. 83 Sections intended for the trichrome stain—Hæmalum, Erythrosin-Saffron, should previously undergo a collodionisation. **1931** *Museum Jrnl.* XXII. 213 The artist had at his disposal monochrome, bichrome and trichrome decorations of pleasing though simple geometric designs. **1938** *Amer. Jrnl. Path.* XIV. 237 Trichrome methods are rapidly replacing the ancient hematoxylin-eosin technique so largely used in pathology. **1939** *Times* 10 Mar. 17/6 A number of trichrome jars of varying shapes. **1975** *Nature* 6 Nov. 71/2 Material for histological examination was fixed in neutral formal saline, embedded in wax and sections were stained with haemalum and eosin or Masson's trichrome stain.

trichromic (traɪˈkrəʊmɪk), *a.* [f. Gr. τρι-, TRI- + χρῶμα colour + -IC: cf. DICHROMIC.] Three-coloured, three-colour; = TRICHROMATIC.

In quot. 1900 applied to abnormal vision in which only three different colours are perceived.

1881 LE CONTE *Sight* 63 Herschel regarded normal vision as trichromic. **1897** *Daily News* 6 Jan. 3/3 By the method of trichromic photography..the colours of natural objects were shown. **1900** EDRIDGE-GREEN in *Lancet* 4 Aug. 323/1 A person whose colour vision is trichromic may see a spectrum of the same length as the normal-sighted, but he sees only three colours—red, green, and violet.

trichronous (ˈtraɪkrəʊnəs), *a. Anc. Pros.* [f. Gr. τρίχρον-ος, of three times or measures (f. τρι-, TRI- + χρόνος time) + -OUS.] Containing or consisting of three times or *moræ*; having the duration of three short syllables: = TRISEMIC.

1889 *Cent. Dict.* s.v. *Dichronous*, A dichronous long (that is, an ordinary long, equal to two shorts, distinguished from a trichronous or other protracted long).

trichur, variant of TREACHER *Obs.*

Trichuris (trɪˈkjʊərɪs). *Zool.* and *Med.* Also trichuris. Pl. **Trichurides** (-ɪdiːz). [mod.L., f. Gr. τριχ-, θρίξ hair + οὐρά tail.] A nematode worm of the genus of this name, which comprises filamentous worms (whipworms) several centimetres long that are intestinal parasites of man and higher animals.

[**1799** *Mem. Med. Soc. London* V. 226 It is now five years since I first discovered a new species of worm..but it was not till lately that I found that the same worm was first mentioned by Roederer, in the year 1760... By him it was first called Trichuris, and under that name I have described it.] **1807** *Edin. Med. & Physical Dict.* II, s.v. *Worms*, Dr. Hooper has seen upwards of twenty trichurides in some fæces of a child of six years old. **1929** E. R. STITT *Diagnostics & Treatm. Tropical Dis.* (ed. 5) xlii. 517 Of the cosmopolitan round worms *Ascaris* and *Trichuris* are the most common. **1951** P. KOURÍ in R. B. H. Gradwohl et al. *Clin. Tropical Med.* xxxvii. 842 A great number of Trichuris were found attached to the prolapsed and congested [rectal] mucosa. **1962** [see ASCARIS]. **1977** SCHMIDT & ROBERTS *Foundations Parasitol.* xxiii. 421/1 (*caption*) A male *Trichuris*. Note the slender anterior end and the stout posterior end.

Hence **trichuˈriasis** [-IASIS], infection with such worms, which in man may be inapparent but can cause diarrhœa and other symptoms.

1921 *Amer. Jrnl. Tropical Med.* I. 375 (*heading*) The treatment of trichuriasis with leche de higueron. **1970** PASSMORE & ROBSON *Compan. Med. Stud.* II. xix. 29/2 All these species [of worms] are cosmopolitan, though ascariasis and trichuriasis are probably less common in Britain than they used to be. **1981** M. CHEESBROUGH *Med. Lab. Man. Tropical Countries* I. xxi. 266/1 The laboratory diagnosis of trichuriasis is by finding the characteristic eggs in stool specimens.

tricipital (traɪˈsɪpɪtəl), *a. rare*$^{-0}$. [f. L. *triceps, -cipit-em* + -AL[1].] = TRICEPS A.

1891 in *Cent. Dict.*

tricircular (traɪˈsɜːkjʊlə(r)), *a. Geom.* [f. TRI- 1, 2 + CIRCULAR.] **a.** Referred to three fixed circles: said of a system of co-ordinates. **b.** Passing three times through each of the circular points at infinity: said of a curve.

1876 CAYLEY *Math. Papers* IX. 562 The sextic is a tricircular sextic having the three points *A, B, C* for foci.

trick (trɪk), *sb.* Forms: 5-6 trik, *pl.* trikkes, 6-7 tricke, 6- trick, (7 trike). [In sense 1, a. OF. *trique*, Picard and Norman form of *triche* deceit, treachery, cheating, Norm. dial. *trique* trick (Moisy), going with, and prob. verbal sb. from, *trikier*, Norm.-Picard form of *trichier, trechier, trecier* to deceive, cheat, mod.F. *tricher* = Prov. *trichar, triquar*, It. *triccare* to cheat; cf. also TRECHE *v.*, TREACHER, etc. Both sb. and vb. have in Eng. had developments of signification unknown to F. *triche* and *tricher*.

The origin of the Romanic word is disputed. It was held by Diez to be of German origin; he compared Du. *trek* 'drawing, pull', which has also the sense 'trick, cunning'. But most Romanic scholars refer it to a late L. or Com. Rom. **triccāre*, alteration of *tricāre, tricārī*, 'to trifle, play tricks', f. *tricæ* 'trifles, toys', also 'subterfuges, quirks, wiles, tricks': see Storm in *Romania* V. 172, Ulrich in *Zeitschr. f. Rom. Phil.* IX. 566.]

I. 1. a. A crafty or fraudulent device of a mean or base kind; an artifice to deceive or cheat; a stratagem, ruse, wile; esp. in phrase ***to play* (*show*) *one a trick, to put a trick*** or ***tricks upon***: see PLAY *v.* 9, PUT *v.*[1] 23 d, and cf. sense 2.

c **1412** HOCCLEVE *De Reg. Princ.* 2286 Of suche vnknyghtly trikkes he nat roghte. **1560** ROLLAND *Seven Sag.* 82 Quha can excuse..Sic ane fals trik sa trymlie playit to him? **1570** LEVINS *Manip.* 120/23 A Trick, *facinus.* **1588** GREENE *Pandosto* (1607) 4 Vnder the shape of a friend to shew him the tricke of a foe. **1622** in Foster *Eng. Factories Ind.* (1908) II. 138 [Watching their opportunity] to put a tricke uppon us. **1649** JER. TAYLOR *Gt. Exemp.* II. Ad Sect. xii. 54 Let every man..deale with justice, noblenesse, and sincerity.. without trickes and stratagems. **1707** J. STEVENS tr. *Quevedo's Com. Wks.* (1709) 350 Such..Sayings..As for Instance,..do not put Tricks upon Travellers. *c* **1740** CAREY *God save the King* ii, Frustrate their knavish tricks! **1790** BURKE *Fr. Rev.* 150 Ashamed, as of a silly deceitful trick. **1842** TENNYSON *Lady Clare* 73 Play me no tricks. **1867** FREEMAN *Norm. Conq.* I. v. 347 He was again at his old tricks [*O.E. Chron.* an. 1003 his ealdan wrenceas]. **1888** BRYCE *Amer. Commw.* II. lviii. 404 Public opinion, deterring even bad men from the tricks to which they are prone.

b. Without article: Trickery, fraud. *rare.*

1833 NYREN *Yng. Cricketer's Tutor* 78 His word was not always to be depended on..he would now and then shuffle, and resort to trick.

c. An illusory or deceptive appearance; a semblance, sham. ? *arch.* or *Obs.*

1592 KYD *Sp. Trag.* III. xii, Art thou not sometimes mad? Is there no trickes that comes before thine eies? **1781** COWPER *Conversation* 782 And all her love of God..A trick upon the canvass, painted flame. **1856** WHITTIER *Panorama* 207 In this poor trick of paint You see the semblance, incomplete and faint, Of the two-fronted Future.

d. ***trick of*** (or *o'*) (***the***) ***loop***, a cheating game; = FAST AND LOOSE a, ***strap-game*** s.v. STRAP *sb.* 18. Also *fig. Anglo-Irish.*

1886 M. B. BUCKLEY *Diary of Tour in Amer.* 16 The thimble-rigger and trick-o'-loop man are nowhere to be found. **1907** J. M. SYNGE *Playboy of Western World* III. 57 And he after bringing bankrupt ruin on the roulette man, and the trick-o'-the-loop man. **1922** JOYCE *Ulysses* 318 Norman W. Tupper bouncing in with his peashooter just in time to be late after she [*sc.* his wife] doing the trick of the loop with officer Taylor. **1974** *Listener* 21 Feb. 239/1 Their cities were..crowded..with pilgrims, curiosity-mongers, refugees from justice and trick-of-the-loop men [in medieval Ireland].

2. a. A freakish or mischievous act; a roguish prank; a frolic; a piece of roguery or foolery; a hoax, practical joke.

1590 SHAKS. *Com. Err.* I. ii. 80 Or I shall breake that merrie sconce of yours That stands on tricks, when I am vndispos'd. **1605** *Tryall Chev.* v. ii. in Bullen *O. Pl.* III. 346 That's a tricke..to mocke an Ape. **1687** A. LOVELL tr. *Thevenot's Trav.* I. 61 These Buffoons are always playing some foolish Tricks amongst themselves to make him laugh. **1796** MME. D'ARBLAY *Camilla* III. 252 If any one plays their tricks upon me, they shall pay for their fun. **1846** MRS. CARLYLE *Lett.* (1883) I. 367 Fortune has played me such a cruel trick this day. **1888** *Pall Mall G.* 10 Oct. 4/1 If they were more numerous they could afford to play tricks.

b. A capricious, foolish, or stupid act; a thing done without full thought or consideration. Usually *contemptuous* or *depreciative.*

1591 SHAKS. *Two Gent.* IV. iv. 43 Did'st thou euer see me doe such a tricke? **1598** —— *Merry W.* II. ii. 117 That were a tricke indeed! **1603** —— *Meas. for M.* II. ii. 121 Proud man, Drest in a little briefe authoritie..Plaies such phantastique tricks before high heauen As makes the Angels weepe. **1693** CONGREVE *Old Bach.* IV. v, I hope you don't mean to forsake it; that will be but a kind of a mongrel cur's trick. **1829** CARLYLE *Misc.* (1857) II. 115 It were but a fool's trick to die for conscience.

c. ***trick or treat***, a traditional formula used at Hallowe'en by children who call on houses threatening to play a trick unless given a treat or present; also as *sb.*, this practice. Hence ***trick-or-treating*** vbl. sb. and ppl. adj. orig. and chiefly *U.S.*

1947 *Amer. Home* Oct. 150/2 The household larder needs to be well stocked on October 31, because, from dusk on, the doorbell rings, bright eyes peer through crazy-looking masks, and childish voices in ghostlike tones squeal, croak, or whisper, 'Trick or Treat!' **1950** *Sun* (Baltimore) 31 Oct. 12/1 So let the kids go out tonight and have a grand time with their masquerading and trick-or-treating. **1954** *Ibid.* 22 Oct. 18/4 Now that the 'Trick or Treat' season is upon us, let us hope that thoughtful parents will discourage the practice. **1968** MRS. L. B. JOHNSON *White House Diary* 31 Oct. (1970) 731 He and his mother had stopped by the office on their way to 'trick or treating' at some friends' houses. **1973** M. CROWELL *Greener Pastures* 64 Trick-or-treat begins at Grandma Latimer's down the road in the little green house. **1974** *New Yorker* 25 Feb. 112/2 Like a horde of trick-or-treating children who have suddenly been turned middle-aged and paunchy by a wicked witch. **1982** *Daily Tel.* 29 Oct. 3/1 A tradition of allowing children out on Halloween 'trick-or-treat' expeditions.

3. A clever or adroit expedient, device, or contrivance; a 'dexterous artifice' (J.); a 'dodge'. ***bag of tricks***: see BAG *sb.* 18.

1573 TUSSER *Husb.* (1878) 123 Gather the lowest, and leauing the top, Shall teach thee a trick, for to double thy crop. **1588** SHAKS. *L.L.L.* v. ii. 466 Som Dick That.. knowes the trick To make my Lady laugh. **1618** BOLTON *Florus* (1636) 76 There also, the Carthaginians vented another new trick of their trade. **1638** JUNIUS *Paint. Ancients* 307 This was a meere tricke of the Painter. **1752** HUME *Ess. & Treat.* (1777) I. 107 (*Eloquence*) The moderns..reject with disdain all those rhetorical tricks. **1815** JANE AUSTEN *Emma* xvi, Making..a trick of what ought to be simple. **1896** *Boston* (Mass.) *Jrnl.* 21 Nov. 7/3 The novelist..knows the tricks of his trade.

4. The art, knack, or faculty of doing something skilfully or successfully. ? *arch.*

1611 SHAKS. *Cymb.* III. iii. 86 Nature prompts them In simple and lowe things, to Prince it, much Beyond the tricke of others. **1667** PEPYS *Diary* 5 Apr., Several that had got ground..for charity, to build sheds on, had got the trick presently to sell that for 60*l.* which did not cost them 20*l.* **1825** SCOTT *Talism.* xxvii, Thou art even matchless at the trick of the sword. **1897** KIPLING *Captains Courageous* ii, Thet was right smart fer a passenger. There's more trick to it in a sea-way.

5. a. A feat of dexterity or skill, intended to surprise or amuse; a piece of jugglery or legerdemain.

1606 SHAKS. *Tr. & Cr.* v. ii. 24 A iugling tricke, to be secretly open. **1697** DRYDEN *Æneid* Ded., Ess. (ed. Ker) II. 201 Like Merry-Andrew on the low rope, copying lubberly the same tricks which his master is so dexterously performing on the high. **1738** SWIFT *Pol. Conversat.* 56 You have more Tricks than a Dancing Bear. **1848** THACKERAY *Lett.* 28 July, The wizard..asked them..if they didn't like a trick he had just performed.

b. A robbery, theft; chiefly in phr. ***to turn a trick***, to commit a successful robbery or theft. *U.S. slang.*

1865 *Leaves from Diary of Celebrated Burglar & Pickpocket* xxvii. 94/2 Directly he had done the trick he 'namased' with his booty. **1904** 'No. 1500' *Life in Sing Sing* 254/1 *Trick*, a theft. *Ibid.* 258/1 *Turning a trick*, accomplishing a theft. **1904** H. HAPGOOD *Autobiogr. of Thief* v. 104, I am hounded for the old trick; and the detectives are looking everywhere for these negotiable bonds. **1926** *Flynn's* 30 Jan. 843/1 Ewing was a thief, who..had settled in Chicago... He did not ply his trade here, but after 'turning a trick' outside of the city, would return to Chicago to plan the next excursion into the country. **1935** *Jrnl. Abnormal Psychol.* XXX. 365 *Trick, go on a*, to commit a robbery. **1956** [see SCORE *sb.* 15 c]. **1979** D. MACKENZIE *Raven settles Score* 70 Campbell's claim was that he hadn't turned a trick in a year but the money had to be coming in from somewhere.

c. In Negro folk-magic or hoodoo: a spell cast on a person; an object used to 'conjure' a person or put him under a spell. Cf. *trick-doctor*, sense 14 below.

1893 [see *door-stone* s.v. DOOR 8]. **1895** A. M. BACON in A. Dundes *Mother Wit* (1973) 367/1 Either after or before the cure of the patient is well under way, the doctor will make an effort to find the 'trick' or 'conjure' and to identify the miscreant who has caused the trouble. **1962** [see ROOT *sb.*[1] 3 c]. **1966** D. J. CROWLEY *I could talk Old-Story Good* ii. 17 Stories about the return of spirits, murder or curing through obeah, love-potions, 'tricks' (aggressive magic) and 'guards' (protective charms) are all traditional in theme. **1977** J. DILLARD *Lexicon Black Eng.* vii. 119 The conjure doctor.. is involved in the performance of *tricks.* To *trick* the victim is the frequently recorded phrase.

6. *concr.* †**a.** Something devised or contrived; a clever contrivance or invention. *Obs. rare.*

a **1548** HALL *Chron., Hen. V* 48 b, Sence that tyme, they haue imagined caltrappes, harowes and other newe trickes. **1601** B. JONSON *Ev. Man in his Hum.* (Qo.) II. iii, This brasse varnish being washt off, and three or foure other tricks [*Fol.* patches] sublated.

b. A trifling ornament or toy; a trinket, bauble, knick-knack; hence *pl.*, small and trifling articles; 'traps', personal belongings or effects (*U.S.*).

a **1553** C. BANSLEY *Treatise* xviii. (Percy Soc.) 6 Take hede ..Least youre wives raymente, and galante trickes doo make youre thryfte full bare. **1596** SHAKS. *Tam. Shr.* IV. iii. 67 A knacke, a toy, a tricke, a babies cap. **1599** HAKLUYT *Voy.* II. I. 64 The women of this countrey weare aboue an hundreth tricks and trifles about them. **1821** SCOTT *Kenilw.* xvii, These court tricks, and gambols..are the tricks and trinkets that bring fair fortunes to farthings. **1877** C. HALLOCK *Sportsman's Gaz.* 640 Camp 'tricks' should be kept in their places, not thrown helterskelter, or left lying where last used. **1894** MARY J. JAQUES *Texan Ranch Life* xxvi. 258 There was no need to pack our 'tricks' for England, we were assured, since we should never return to Texas; to say nothing about sailing. *a* **1904** A. ADAMS *Log Cowboy* xiii, After I get a shave..and buy what few tricks I need.

c. Applied playfully to a small or amusing person, animal, or child. *U.S.* and *Austral. colloq.*

1887 *Century Mag.* May 113/1 We uns played tergether w'en we wuz little tricks. **1890** *Stock Grower & Farmer* (Las Vegas) 29 Mar. 7/1 Down in the Panhandle..I used to ride a little trick named Dandy. **1907** H. B. WRIGHT *Shepherd of Hills* iv. 39 She ain't had no mother since she was a little trick. **1941** BAKER *Dict. Austral. Slang* 78 *Trick*, an amusing person or child, esp. the latter. **1945** S. LEWIS *Cass Timberlane* xxiv. 156 'What kind of a girl he marry?' 'Cute little trick, bright's dollar.' **1951** H. GILES *Harbin's Ridge* ii. 7 She was a little trick of a person. **1963** *Sunday Mail* (Brisbane) 10 Mar. 19/1 My wife was mystified when somebody in Brisbane described our daughter Sally, who is nearly five, as a 'trick'.

II. 7. A particular habit, way, or mode of acting; a characteristic quality, trait, practice, or custom. (Usually, a bad or unpleasant habit.) Phr. ***at*** or (now more usually) ***up to one's*** (***old***) ***tricks***, misbehaving or plotting mischief in one's characteristic way.

1576 FLEMING *Panopl. Epist.* 244 It is not my propertie to be enuious against other (which is a tricke incident to a great number). **1581** PETTIE *Guazzo's Civ. Conv.* III. (1586) 129 A maide of ripe yeeres, who is hardlie brought to..leaue her olde ill tricks, if she haue taken anie. **1596** SHAKS. *1 Hen. IV*, v. ii. 11 The Foxe, Who ne're so tame, so cherisht, and lock'd vp, Will haue a wilde tricke of his Ancestors. **1650** FULLER *Pisgah* II. xii. 251 The lazy trick of the wild Irish.. who to save pains, burn the straw, so to part the grain from it. **1688** PENTON *Guard. Instr.* (1897) 23 The danger in great Schools of..learning ill Tricks. **1709** STEELE *Tatler* No. 8 ¶5 My Valet de Chambre knows my University-Trick of reading there [in Bed]. **1754** EARL CHATHAM *Lett. Nephew* v. (1804) 35 The trick of laughing frivolously is by all means to be avoided. **1791** SIR J. REYNOLDS in Boswell *Johnson* an. 1739 (1848) 42/1 Those motions or tricks of Dr. Johnson are improperly called convulsions. **1823** SCOTT *St. Ronan's Well* II. i. 15 Aweel, I trust he is not at his auld tricks again, goodwife? **1863** H. E. P. SPOFFORD *Amber Gods* 206 'You are at your old tricks again!' said he. **1884** *Cassell's Fam. Mag.* Mar. 220/2 The Wey..has a trick of overflowing its banks. **1898** G. B. SHAW *Man of Destiny* 181 What do you mean? Eh? Are you at your tricks again? Do you think I dont know what these papers contain? **1935** *Time* 7 Jan. 55/1 She and Dill are soon up to their old tricks.

8. a. A habit or fashion of dress. Also *fig. arch.*

1543 BECON *Nosegay* E iij, Some tyme we followe the fasshyon of the Frenche men. Another time we wil haue a tricke of the Spanyyardes. **1564–78** BULLEYN *Dial. agst. Pest.* (1888) 17 Fine knottes vppon his girdle after Frances trickes. **1760** C. JOHNSTON *Chrysal* (1822) III. 147 He threw himself at her feet in all the trick of woe. **1874** R. W. BUCHANAN *Poet. Wks.* III. 150 In the very trick of woe he clad His features.

b. A characteristic expression (of the face or voice); a peculiar feature; a distinguishing trait.

1595 SHAKS. *John* I. i. 85 He hath a tricke of Cordelions face. **1605** —— *Lear* IV. vi. 108 The tricke of that voyce, I do well remember: Is't not the king? **1847** LYTTON *Lucretia* II. iv, He detected..even the trick of his walk. **1881** BESANT & RICE *Chapl. of Fleet* II. i, An old-fashioned bearing and trick of speech.

c. The mode of working a piece of mechanism, etc.; the system upon which a thing is constructed.

1663 BP. PATRICK *Parab. Pilgr.* xx. (1687) 203 If you will have so much patience, I will discover to you the trick of it, and shew you by what mechanical powers this liveless Engine..is stirred. **1819** SHELLEY *Cenci* v. iv. 6 He frowned, as if to frown had been the trick Of his machinery. **1888** J. PAYN *Myst. Mirbridge* xxi, No one who did not know the trick of it could have opened yonder safe.

9. a. *Naut.* The time allotted to a man on duty at the helm; a spell; a turn; esp. in ***to take*** or ***stand one's trick (at the wheel***, etc.). Also *transf.*

1669 STURMY *Mariner's Mag.* IV. i. 138 Seamen when their trike or turn have been out, and the Log hove. **1769** FALCONER *Dict. Marine* (1789) s.v. *Spell*, The spells..to steer the ship; which..is generally called the *trick*. **1835** MARRYAT *Jac. Faithf.* xviii, His duty is to take his trick at the wheel. **1892** M. GIBBS in *Science* 19 Aug. 99 The male [robin], who shares the duties of sitting, when going to take his trick, almost invariably flies..in the same path. **1912** [see *trick-duty* in 14].

b. *U.S. slang.* A term of service on a ship. Also, a term in prison.

1933 *Amer. Speech* VIII. III. 32/2 *Trick*, a prison term. **1939** *Sun* (Baltimore) 28 Jan. 20/6 After serving a few tricks in the penitentiary they might turn State's evidence. **1942** *Ibid.* 19 Mar. 15/1 He reenlisted as a corporal, a rank he held at the end of his former trick. **1975** J. GORES *Hammett* i. 16 He got caught..and did a little trick at Quentin.

10. a. An instance of the sexual act or any of its variations; usu. *spec.* a prostitute's session with a client. Esp. ***to turn a trick***, to perform a sexual act with a casual partner, usu. for money. *slang* (orig. and chiefly *U.S.*).

In quot. 1926 the context concerns repeated sexual acts.

1926 C. VAN VECHTEN *Nigger Heaven* 252, I said, Now, daddy, do you know any more tricks? **1946** MEZZROW & WOLFE *Really the Blues* 30 'Turning a trick' was how they described one session with a john. **1956** B. HOLIDAY *Lady sings Blues* (1973) iii. 30, I had decided I was through turning tricks as a call girl. **1962** A. LURIE *Love & Friendship* xv. 300 Twenty-four dollars a time. That's pretty cheap for a girl like you... In New York, with the right connections, I bet you could get at least a hundred a trick. **1974** *Telegraph* (Brisbane) 16 July 14/2 She said in June: 'I'm lucky if I turn five to 10 tricks a week now.' **1975** J. F. BURKE *Death Trick* ii. 20 It was a true lovers' tryst, not a trick. **1977** *Time* 28 Nov. 45/1 Some of the young prostitutes live at home and turn tricks merely for pocket money.

b. A casual sexual partner; usu. *spec.* a prostitute's client. *slang* (orig. and chiefly *U.S.*).

1925 in Odum & Johnson *Negro & his Songs* 189 Lawd, I went to my woman's do' Jes' lak I been doin' befo'; She says, 'I got my all-night trick, baby, An' you can't git in.' **1931** B. L. REITMAN *Second Oldest Profession* viii. 118 Lillian has four children. Billy, her man, is a fourth-rate taxi-driver pimp. Billy goes out and gets 'tricks', and she takes care of them in the home where her children are. **1968** B. TURNER *Sex Trap* xv. 148, I doubt there's one trick in twenty who isn't a married man. **1973** [see JOHN 1 f]. **1979** *Globe & Mail* (Toronto) 2 July 10/1 Young male prostitutes vie for tricks, the street name for a client.

III. 11. *Her.* A sketch in pen and ink of a coat of arms; ***in trick***, sketched in pen and ink. (Perhaps a different word: see TRICK *v.*)

1572 BOSSEWELL *Armorie* II. 30 b, The tricke of this cote I toke, as I found it paynted on a Table, in a parishe churche of Nottingham. **1610** BOLTON *Elem. Armories* 87 Drawing the blacke lines, which giue the shape,..lastly they sometime call it a Trick. **1792** *Gentl. Mag.* Jan. 21/1 A large manuscript collection of arms in trick, done in the reign of Elizabeth. **1890** DILLON in *Archæologia* LII. 130 The flags are only shown in trick with the heraldic tinctures noted. **1908** *Let. of Richmond Herald of Arms* (MS.), Not a painting of the Coat of Arms, but a trick, i.e. a pen and ink sketch with all the heraldic colours marked on it.

IV. 12. *Card-playing.* The cards (usually four) played, and won or 'taken' in one round, collectively; hence ***to take a*** or ***the trick***. ***odd trick***: see ODD *a.* 1.

In quots. 1599, 1602, a hand of cards (*obs.*): in other early quots. with a play upon other senses.

1599 MASSINGER, etc. *Old Law* III. i, Here's a trick of discarded cards, of us! **1602** HEYWOOD *Woman Kill'd* Wks. 1874 II. 123 Many a deale I haue lost, the more's your shame. You haue seru'd me a bad tricke. **1607** TOURNEUR *Rev. Trag.* III. iv, Wee'll get thee out by a trick... You know a trick is commonly foure Cardes. **1611** COTGR., *Mornifle*,.. a tricke at Cards. **1622** MABBE tr. *Aleman's Guzman d'Alf.* I. 1 Leauing..to others..to play out that tricke of Cards for mee. *a* **1658** CLEVELAND *Smectymnuus* 21 A Murnival of Knaves Pack'd in a Trick. **1688** R. HOLME *Armoury* III. xvi. (Roxb.) 73/2 A Trick, is as many cards as is won at one laying downe either at the game of Whisk or Picket. **1778** C. JONES *Hoyle's Games Impr.* 51 (*Whist*) The Odds then is 2 to 1 in Favour of B's winning of a Trick. **1837** DICKENS *Pickw.* vi, Impossible to have made another trick. *a* **1839** PRAED *Poems* (1864) II. 63 Well—four by honours, and the trick!

V. Phrases and Combinations.

13. Phrases. **a.** ***a trick worth two of that***, a much better plan or expedient (cf. 3). **b.** ***to do the trick***, to accomplish one's purpose, do what is wanted; also (chiefly *U.S.*) ***to turn the trick***. **c.** ***to miss a trick***, to fail to take advantage of an opportunity or notice something important; esp. ***he*** (or ***she***) ***never misses*** (***does not miss***, etc.) ***a trick*** (see MISS *v.*[1] 5 d). *colloq.* (orig. *U.S.*). **d.** ***how's*** (less freq. ***how are***) ***tricks?*** how are things? how are you getting on? *colloq.* (orig. *U.S.*).

a. 1596 SHAKS. *1 Hen. IV*, II. i. 41 Nay soft I pray ye, I know a trick worth two of that. **1654** H. L'ESTRANGE *Chas. I* (1655) 65 Old Sir John Savil found a trick worth two of that, he had a project would bring in double that mony. **1773** GRAVES *Spir. Quixote* III. xv, I was thunder-struck..; but she said, 'she knew a trick worth two of that'. **1855** THACKERAY *Newcomes* i, Best be off to bed, my boy—ho, ho! No, no. We know a trick worth two of that. 'We won't go home till morning, till daylight does appear.'

b. 1812 J. H. VAUX *Flash Dict.*, Do the Trick. **1823** EGAN *Grose's Dict. Vulg. T.*, *Do the trick*, to accomplish any robbery, or other business successfully;..a man who has imprudently involved himself in some great misfortune, from which there is little hope of extrication, is declared by his friends..to have done the trick for himself. [**1872** TROLLOPE *Eustace Diamonds* (1873) II. xxxvii. 134 Then the boy was done with and was carried away. She had played that card and had turned her trick.] **1872** *Punch* 9 Nov. 196/1 Pail of whitewash and box o' paints will do the trick. **1895** G. MEREDITH *Amazing Marriage* xv, I've brought him safe;..He'll do the trick today. **1933** *Sun* (Baltimore) 20 Apr. 10/3 It is our hope and prayer that Mr. Farley may turn the trick. We should be glad to see any administrator make a go of the postal service. **1942** *R.A.F. Jrnl.* 3 Oct. 24 But it was the Old Man who really turned the trick. **1960** I. WALLACH *Absence of Cello* 230 It takes many years to live without a deliberate confusion about anyone's wants, including our own. Some people never turn the trick. **1976** *Springfield* (Mass.) *Daily News* 22 Apr. 39/2 A couple of American college products turned the trick for the Whalers. North Dakota graduate Alan Hangsleben and New Hampshire alumnus Cap Raeder shared the hero's role in the triumph.

c. [*a* **1916** H. JAMES *Sense of Past* (1917) IV. iii. 266 It was ..for him to have kept it as..she preferred it. He had begun so..and how..came it therefore that he now repeatedly missed that trick?] **1922** S. LEWIS *Babbitt* xix. 241 'I'll bet.. you were a bad old egg when you were a kid!' 'Well, I wasn't so slow!' 'I bet you weren't! I'll bet you didn't miss many tricks!' **1943** N. COWARD *Middle East Diary* (1944) 11 He is a highly intelligent man and doesn't miss a trick... He had clear, alert views on the most diverse subjects. **1957** 'J. WYNDHAM' *Midwich Cuckoos* xii. 99 He went on, with a puzzled frown on his brow as he realised that somewhere he had missed a trick; something had been kept from him. **1962** *Oxford Times* 28 Dec. 15/2 Peter Butterworth and Joe Black are pantomime professionals who never miss a trick. **1965** *Harper's Bazaar* Feb. 66/1 Fenwicks..never misses a trick when it comes to picking up a new accessory idea. **1965** *Weekly News* (Auckland, N.Z.) 10 Mar. 49/1 The fact that the Wellington [boxing] association could match three Auckland fledgling professionals with three unknown Australians and make a profit points to someone else missing a trick. **1967** 'E. LATHEN' *Murder against Grain* iv. 32 You have to hand it to them. Those boys haven't missed a trick. **1967** O. NORTON *Now lying Dead* vi. 109 He never missed a trick. **1973** S. B. JACKMAN *Guns covered with Flowers* viii. 131 Clever chap... Doesn't miss a trick.

d. 1915 J. LONDON *Jacket* xiii. 149 'How's tricks?' I asked finally. **1924** W. HOLTBY *Crowded Street* i. 21 'Well, Mrs. H., how's tricks?' His wife flushed slightly at the vulgarity of his phrase. **1934** D. RUNYON in *Collier's* 24 Nov. 8/4 Meyer Marmalade and I are glad to see her looking so well, and we ask her how are tricks. **1959** 'A. FRASER' *High Tension* ix. 91 'Well,' he greeted me, 'how's tricks?' **1980** N. MARSH *Photo-Finish* ii. 36 'Giddy,' said Les Smith. 'How's tricks, then, Bert?'

14. *attrib.* and *Comb.* (chiefly in sense 5): Of, pertaining to, or of the nature of a trick or tricks, as ***trick change***, ***-dealer***, ***fall***, ***-flying***, ***-rider***, ***-riding***, ***-shower*** (SHOWER *sb.*[2]), ***-work***, ***-writing***; ***trick-leap***, ***-ride*** vbs.; in senses 9 and 12, ***trick-duty*** (see quot.), ***-making***, ***-score***, ***-taking***; skilled in or trained to perform tricks (sense 5), as ***trick-animal***, ***-dog***, ***-donkey***, ***-horse***, ***-pony***; made or used for performing tricks, as ***trick-bag***, ***-chair***, ***-cycle***, ***-dagger***, ***-property***, ***-staircase***, ***-sword***, ***-wig***; also **trick-cycling**, (*a*) the action or process of riding a trick-cycle; (*b*) *humorously*, psychiatry (cf. *trick-cyclist* (*b*) below); **trick-cyclist**, (*a*) one who rides a trick-cycle; (*b*) humorous alteration of PSYCHIATRIST; **trick-doctor**, ? a Negro sorcerer; **trick-film**, a film using trick photography; **trick-line** *Theatr.*, a strong fine line used in pantomime transformations; so **trick-scene**, a transformation scene; **trick photography**, photography using montage and other technical devices to create visual illusions; **trick picture** = *trick-film* above; **trick question**, a question designed to elicit more information than it appears to on the surface, or to trick the respondent into giving a wrong answer; **trick shot**, (*a*) in golf, etc.: a particularly clever or devious shot; (*b*) a camera shot made by means of trick photography; **trick wheel**, an auxiliary steering wheel on a ship.

1884 *World* 3 Dec. 16/2 The original stud from which the renowned breed of *trick-animals, pink-eyed and piebald, has sprung. **1910** *Nation* 22 Jan. 665/1 A hocus-pocus loaf out of a conjuror's *trick-bag. **1904** *Daily Chron.* 23 Aug. 3/2 It is of a piece with..the murder of Ithocles in an 'engine', otherwise *trick-chair. **1896** *Westm. Gaz.* 8 Jan. 2/3 Quick changes—'*trick changes' is perhaps more technical a term— were accomplished with remarkable ingenuity. **1901** *Wide World Mag.* VIII. 140/1 An open space here afforded room for a little figure-skating, or rather *trick-cycling. **1951** G. FRANKAU *Oliver Trenton* xvi. 139, I picked it up from one of our surgeons, who's rather keen on trick-cycling. **1966** G. B. MAIR *Kisses from Satan* vii. 79 Don't try and sell that stuff about trickcycling to someone with rheumatism and gall stones. **1897** *Nat. Police Gaz.* 26 May 14/4 That noted *trick cyclist, Lee Richardson, left London for America on Saturday. **1903** *Daily Chron.* 20 May 8/3 A young trick-cyclist..met with a fatal accident to-day while practising looping the loop. **1930** H. WOLFE *Uncelestial City* III. 112 A trick-cyclist gravely reassembling The features of the ectoplasmic dead. **1971** P. SCOTT *Towers of Silence* v. iii. 345 That's why the trick-cyclist wallah insists on coming. **1977** *Listener* 31 Mar. 414/3 Is neurotic, inadequate, unhappy..is up in Harley Street being sorted out by a trick cyclist. **1889** P. A. BRUCE *Plant. Negro* 116 The *trick doctor..employs the arts of the Obeah practitioners ..with the arts of the Myal. **1886** C. SCOTT *Sheep-Farming* 204 A well-trained and experienced collie excels in sagacity all others of the dog family. His was not the intelligence of the *trick dog. **1881** *Chequered Career* 120 If you don't pay us our accounts, we will collar your *trick-donkey. **1912** *Boston Transcript* 24 July 7/3 Company reduces the time for those who do *trick duty [refers to telephone exchange; a night trick is 7 hours' duty between 10 p.m. and 7 a.m.]. **1912** F. A. TALBOT *Moving Pictures* xix. 207 The achievements of Mélies and Paul set a very high standard of excellence in trick pictures. Their popularity precipitated a '*trick film' fever. The market became flooded with so-called magic pictures. **1914** *Chambers's Jrnl.* 6 June 429/2 A certain number of these craft [*sc.* aeroplanes] are kept..for ..*trick-flying, &c. **1932** E. WALLACE *When Gangs came to London* xxii. 198 You used to do trick flying. **1861** *Windsor Express* 5 Oct., The well-known American Circus..45 *trick and ring horses. **1922** JOYCE *Ulysses* 428 Bloom *trickleaps to the curbstone. **1908** *Westm. Gaz.* 4 Jan. 14/1 All aces are valuable as honours in a 'trump' game, as well as in their *trick-making capacity. **1913** *Technical World* XIX. 464 It merely accomplishes what is known as '*trick photography'. **1928** R. KNOX *Footsteps at Lock* xxiv. 238 His cousin was fond of trick photography. **1984** *Listener* 2 Feb. 37/3 He achieved the crucial transformation scenes without the help of trick photography on cutaways. **1912** *Trick picture [see *trick film* above]. **1908** *Daily Chron.* 31 Dec. 4/4 Special masks for the grotesques and '*trick' properties will often break into a couple of hundred pounds. **1939** R. STOUT *Red Threads* xv, in *Mystery Bk.* 516, I could easily ask you some *trick questions that would put sweat on your brow. **1954** N. TOMALIN in J. Philip et al. *Best of Granta* (1967) II. 139 He plugs away at trick questions..like: 'You *did* say you were giving the money to Dr Barnardo's didn't you sir?' **1978** P. NIESEWAND *Underground Connection* 86 The journalists..filed out... He had not expected any trick questions, and none came. **1887** *Bicycl. News* 10 Sept. 371/2 Probably Maltby will be matched against Temple..to *trick-ride. **1902** *Billboard* 31 May 18/1 (Advt.), The motor wonders Arthur Stone and Joe Judge pace Frank Armstrong (who knows no fear as a *trick rider). **1976** *National Observer* (U.S.) 24 July 18/4 Keitel calmly saying, 'Hi, Joy,' to a trick rider flashing past slung from the side of her horse. **1885** *Cyclist* 19 Aug. 1088/2 He entertained the spectators with a *trick-riding performance. **1929** *Trick-score [see OVERTRICK]. **1938** J. CULBERTSON *Contract Bridge for Beginners* vii. 71 A three-bid in no-trumps will produce a trick-score of 100 points. **1924** C. J. TOLLEY *Mod. Golfer* 229 He tried to recover by the aid of a *trick shot. **1926** *Daily Colonist* (Victoria, B.C.) 20 Jan. 11/3 He told me that Joe Kirkwood, the marvelous trick-shot golfer had just given an exhibition. **1933** *Jrnl. Soc. Motion Picture Engineers* XX. 319 If the subject should contain more than the usual number of so-called 'trick' shots..the shooting time will easily run from 125 to 150 hours. **1981** *Sunday Times* 23 Aug. 54 At an exhibition they expect you to play about 10 frames [of snooker] and then to do some trick shots like hitting a ball into someone's handkerchief. **1983** J. GARDNER *Elephants in Attic* xii. 110 My one experience of the film world had been devising trick shots for Alexander Korda. **1677** *Descr. Diamond Mines* in *Misc. Cur.* (1708) III. 255 Light Women-Dancers, and *Trick-Shewers. **1899** *Daily News* 9 Jan. 6/6 The King..rolls head over heels down a '*trick' staircase. **1901** A. DUNN *Bridge* 52 A sequence of cards equal for *trick-taking purposes, such as king, queen, knave. **1936** E. CULBERTSON *Contract Bridge Complete* xxxvii. 398 The low cards in long and short suits have their own trick-taking power. **1977** *Jrnl. Playing-Card Soc.* May 23 Reversis is historically important as the earliest known negative complex trick-taking game. **1942** *Sun* (Baltimore) 18 June 8/4 Men were stationed at the '*trick wheel'—an auxiliary wheel situated deep inside the ship, where it was operated by hand. **1972** L. M. HARRIS *Introd. Deepwater Floating Drilling Operations* 244 The emergency steering wheel and trick wheel. **1888** *Pall Mall G.* 1 Sept. 3/1 A *trick wig, with the hanging hair..on a spring piece that allows this fringe to turn over back or down over the forehead. **1876**

'OUIDA' *Winter City* vi, The little Meissonier pictures were clever, if they were mere *trick-work and told no story. **1894** *Westm. Gaz.* 5 July 8/1 Article-writing is to a great extent *trick-writing. To 'catch on' they must dogmatise in pointed commonplace.

trick (trɪk), *v.* [In branch I not found till late in the 16th c.; app. f. TRICK *sb.* (The date of appearance is too late to refer it directly to Norman-Picard F. *trikier, triquer.*) Branches II and III are a little earlier, and may perh. be of different origin; the last is especially difficult to connect with the primary sense of the verb. Cf. sense 11 of the sb.]

I. 1. a. *trans.* To deceive by a trick; to cheat. (In quot. 1630 with word-play on *trick* and *trump* at cards.)

1595, 1606 [see TRICKING *vbl. sb.* 1, TRICKER 1]. **1630** B. JONSON *New Inn* I. i, When she [Fortune] is pleas'd to trick or tromp mankind, Some may be coats, as in the cards; but, then, Some must be knaves. **1706** E. WARD *Wooden World Diss.* (1708) 94 However he tricks his Captain in other Things, his Plate and Dishes are every Day forth coming. **1802** MAR. EDGEWORTH *Moral T.* (1816) I. xiii. 104 To trick a gauger was thought an excellent joke. **1852** THACKERAY *Esmond* I. vii, He was often tricked about horses, which he pretended to know better than any jockey. **1884** W. C. SMITH *Kildrostan* I. ii. 235 'Tis plain I have been tricked and overreached.

b. To cheat *out of*; to deprive *of* by trickery.

1698 FRYER *Acc. E. India & P.* Contents p. vii, Syddy Jore trick'd out of his Life by Bullul Caun. **1727** GAY *Begg. Op.* I. ii, She tricks us of our money. **1888** BRYCE *Amer. Commw.* III. lxxxi. 66 His belief that he who makes the wealth of the country is tricked out of his proper share in its prosperity.

c. To beguile *into*; to induce *into* by trickery.

1706 E. WARD *Wooden World Diss.* (1708) 88 The Tide-waiter, voluntarily trick'd into a Game at All fours. **1801** CHARLOTTE SMITH *Lett. Solit. Wand.* II. 240 Her contempt of one who could so basely contrive to trick her into his power. **1874** GREEN *Short Hist.* ix. §3. 625 To trick them into approval of a war with Holland.

d. *absol.* or *intr.* To practise trickery, to cheat.

a **1700** DRYDEN *To Mr. Granville* 23 Thus they jog on, still tricking, never thriving. **1701** PENN in *Pennsylv. Hist. Soc. Mem.* IX. 73 If in the least he tricks, use him accordingly. **1909** *Nation* 2 Oct. 11/2 To the ignorant and superstitious everything tricks and deludes.

e. To put a spell on (a person), 'conjure'. Cf. TRICK *sb.* 5c. *U.S. dial.* (esp. in the speech of *U.S. Blacks*).

1829 *Virginia Lit. Museum* 25 Nov. 384 And, amongst the degraded and ignorant part of our own population, the notion of '*tricking*' or bewitching is universally..received. **1895** L. HERRON in A. Dundes *Mother Wit* (1973) 360/2 The conjure doctor's business was of two kinds: to conjure, or 'trick', a person, and to cure people already conjured. **1970** H. M. HYATT *Hoodoo-Conjuration-Witchcraft-Rootwork* I. 688 Well, if a man is got de skill upon 'im tuh make a man do 'jes whut he want 'im to do without *hurtin*' 'im, dat's *trickin*' a man. **1977** [see TRICK *sb.* 5c].

2. To get or effect by trickery or cheating. *rare.*

1662 in *Verney Mem.* (1907) II. 178 London is a Theife will trick your purse as well as mine. **1895** G. S. STREET *Introd. to Congreve's Comedies* 25 The trick..of a tricked marriage is common in Congreve.

3. a. *intr.* To play tricks *with*; to trifle *with*.

1881 STEVENSON *Virg. Puerisque*, etc. (1895) 162 We may trick with the word life..until we are weary of tricking. **1913** *Daily News* 23 Sept. 5 The fireman was 'tricking' with girls on the platform.

b. To have casual sexual intercourse, esp. for money; chiefly const. *with*. Cf. TRICK *sb.* 10 a, b. *U.S. slang.*

1965 C. BROWN *Manchild in Promised Land* (1966) vi. 163 Since her mother was laying so many cats, why shouldn't she be tricking. **1967** C. HIMES *Black on Black* (1973) 133 He was trying to get his old lady, Tang, to go down into Central Park and trick with some white man so they could eat. **1973** J. WAMBAUGH *Blue Knight* xii. 207 He tricked with a whore the night before in the Orchid Hotel. **1978** A. MALING *Lucky Devil* xxix. 154 'You *know* him?' I asked. 'We've tricked,' he replied.

†**4.** *trans.* To sophisticate or adulterate (wine, etc.). *Obs. rare.*

1594 PLAT *Jewell-ho.* III. 66 This makes the Vintners to tricke or compasse all their naturall wines, if they bee a little hard, with Bastarde to make them sweeter. **1662** [see TRICKING *vbl. sb.* 1].

II. 5. a. *trans.* To dress, array, attire; to deck, prank; to adorn (usually with the notion of artifice). Const. *with, in.* Also *intr.* with *it.* Also *fig.*

? *a* **1500** *Mylner of Abyngton* 457 in Hazl. *E.P.P.* III. 117 The wenche she was full proper and nyce,..For she coulde tricke it point device. *a* **1553** C. BANSLEY *Treat.* xii. (Percy Soc.) 5 Sponge up youre vysage, olde bounsynge trotte, and tricke it wyth the beste, Tyll you tricke and trotte youre selfe, to the devyls trounsynge neste. *a* **1592** GREENE *George-a-Greene* Wks. (Rtldg.) 266/2 Some peasants trick'd in yeoman's weeds. **1632** MILTON *Penseroso* 123 Till civil-suited Morn appeer, Not trickt and frounc't..But Cherchef't in a comly Cloud. **1759** MASON *Caractacus* Poems 1830 II. 138 His clemency,..trick'd and varnish'd by your glossing pen-men. **1873** BROWNING *Red Cott. Nt.-cap* III. 408 The late death chamber, tricked with trappings still. **1890** R. BRIDGES *Shorter Poems* II. 1 What musical array Tricks her sweet syllables.

b. Often strengthened with *up, off, out.*

c **1533** LATIMER *Let.* in Foxe *A. & M.* (1563) 1316/1 A poore purgatory. So poore y^t it should not be able to fede so fatte, and tricke vp so many idell and slouthful lubbers. *c* **1590** GREENE *Fr. Bacon* x. 38, I cannot trick it up with poesies. **1622** BACON *Hen. VII* 27 That the King..to blinde the eyes of simple men had tricked up a Boy in the likenesse of Edward Plantagenet. **1727** GAY *Begg. Op.* III. v, To trick out young Ladies, upon their going into Keeping. **1821** *Examiner* 19/2 She was well tutored and tricked off for the occasion. **1822** SCOTT *Fam. Lett.* 18 Feb., I must trick out my dwellings with something fantastical. **1878** E. JENKINS *Haverholme* 153 Tricking out tables to look like altars.

c. *transf.* To dress *up*, to prepare (food). *rare.*

1824 W. IRVING *T. Trav.* I. 10 A slight repast had therefore been tricked up from the residue of dinner.

†**6.** To arrange, adjust, trim. Often in phrase *to trick and trim.* Cf. TRIG *v.*[4] *Obs.*

1552 ELYOT s.v. *Caesaries, Repexa caesaries*, a busshe twise or thrise kemed and tricked. **1570** LEVINS *Manip.* 120/33 To trick, or trim, *concinnare.* **1579–80** NORTH *Plutarch* (1676) 624 Being not of authority..to take the stern in hand, and govern the ship, he took himself to tricking the sails. **1639** S. DU VERGER tr. *Camus' Admir. Events* 206 He consumed so much time..in tricking and trimming his head. **1770** M. BRUCE *Elegy* viii, On the green furze..The linnet sits, and tricks his glossy plumes. **1810** SOUTHEY *Kehama* VIII. ii, No human hand hath trick'd that mane From which he [the steed] shakes the morning dew.

III. 7. To sketch or draw in outline; to delineate or trace the outline of (*obs.*); *spec.* in *Her.*, to draw (a coat of arms) in outline, the tinctures being denoted by initial letters (*o, a, s,* etc.) or by signs. Also with *out.*

(In many passages incorrectly used or confused with sense 5.)

1545 ELYOT, *Adumbro*..some do suppose that it signifieth, to trycke a thynge, or drawe it grossely, as paynters doo at the begynnyng. **1562** LEIGH *Armorie* (1597) 106 This cote I had in the Monasterie of Saint Katherins besides the Towne of Rone, which for the rarenes therof I tricked. **1594** CAREW *Huarte's Exam. Wits* viii. (1596) 111 The boy..with his pen can tricke a horse to the life. **1657** WOOD *Life* 14 Aug. (O.H.S.) I. 223 He..tricked out with his pen the ichnography of the church and cloyster and buildings adjoyning. **1859** *Symonds' Diary* (Camden) Introd. 14 The..shields of arms recorded in the MS. are ..'tricked',..thus necessitating a description of the bearings. **1908** H. HALL *Formula Bk.* I. 123 The feature of these instruments [Chancery Warrants]..being the technical description of the arms which are usually tricked on the original.

IV. 8. *trick and tie* (*trick* app. = to take one's turn at something; cf. TRICK *sb.* 9), to be equal or even *with* someone or something; chiefly as *adj.* (sometimes hyphened); occas. as *sb.*

1825 C. M. WESTMACOTT *Eng. Spy* I. 241 Trick and tie you know is fair play. **1829** P. EGAN *Boxiana* 2nd Ser. II. 132 The Grecian, in order to make 'trick and tie' with his opponent, put his best foot foremost, and pursued him. **1883** W. H. COPE *Gloss. Hampshire Words & Phr.* 96 *Trick-and-tie*.., equal to each other. **1890** BARRÈRE & LELAND *Dict. Slang* II. 374/1 *Trick and tie* (sport). To be *trick and tie*, or touch and go, is to be equal in a race, or other athletic performance. **1905** *Eng. Dial. Dict.* VI. 234/1 [Wiltshire] 'I'll keep trick-and-tie wi' un', will keep even or level with him, in mowing or standing pots of beer or anything else.

†**trick**, *a.*[1] and *adv. Obs.* [In use from *c* 1530 to 1630, very common from *c* 1550 to 1600. Origin obscure: it does not seem to be connected in sense with TRICK *sb.* or *v.* On the other hand its two senses correspond closely to senses 2 and 3 of TRIG *a.*[1] The latter was at that time only northern; midland and southern speakers may have associated it with the known sb. and vb. *trick*, and adopted it in this form. Often alliteratively coupled with *trim.*]

A. *adj.* **1.** Smart, adroit, clever, nimble, 'neat'. *rare.* Cf. TRIG *a.*[1] 2.

(Quot. 1545 may belong to sense 2.)

1542 [implied in TRICKLY *adv.*] **1545** ASCHAM *Toxoph.* (Arb.) 28 Two bowes..whereof the one is quicke of cast, tricke and trimme both for pleasure and profyte: the other is a lugge slowe of cast, folowing the string. ? *a* **1550** *Schole Ho. Women* 100 in Hazl. *E.P.P.* IV. 109 So tricke a way they haue to kisse With open mouth and rowling eyes. **15..** *Six Ballads w. Burdens* (Percy Soc.) 8 Say-well in wordes is proper and trycke. **1589** WARNER *Alb. Eng.* VI. xxx. (1612) 147 Trimmest fidling on the trickest kit. **1593** LODGE *Phillis*, etc. (Hunter. Cl.) 71 Sweet chaines of honny speech, Deliuered by a trick Herculean tongue Able to tice all eares.

2. Trim, neat, handsome, in form or feature; smart, 'fine', ornate in dress. Cf. TRIG *a.*[1] 3, 3b.

c **1530** REDFORDE *Play Wit & Sc.* (1848) 1 See That all thynges be cleane and trycke abowte ye. **1533** J. HEYWOOD *Play of Weather* Plays (1905) 123 As dearly my youth I might have sold As the trickest and fairest of you all. *a* **1548** HALL *Chron., Hen. VIII* 70 A tricke waggon, on the which sat a ladie richely appareled. *a* **1553** C. BANSLEY *Treat.* xxiv. (Percy Soc.) 7 Lustye wylfull wyll wyll..cause the tryckeste of you all, to synge a carefull songe. **1570** LEVINS *Manip.* 120/40 Trick, *nitidus, concinnus.* **1581** A. HALL *Iliad* II. 39 Bryseis his tricke and gallant trull. *a* **1586** SIDNEY *Arcadia* III. (1629) 390 A neighbour mine..That maried had a tricke and bonny lasse. **1630** W. FREAKE *Doctrines Jesuits* 43 Gay Gownes..wherewith hee can make her both tricke and trimme.

B. *adv.* **1.** Cleverly, 'neatly', 'finely'.

1564–78 BULLEYN *Dial. agst. Pest.* (1888) 94 He plaieth tricke vpon the Gitterne. **1584** PEELE *Arraignm. Paris* I. i, But tell me, wench [Flora], hast done't so trick indeed? [i.e. deck'd the earth with parti-colour'd flowers].

2. Neatly, smartly, elegantly, 'trigly'.

1594 GREENE & LODGE *Looking-Glasse* G.'s Wks. (Rtldg.) 122/2 Unless you coy it trick and trim. **1615** BRATHWAIT *Strappado* (1878) 190 A sumptuous graue, Which garnisht is without full tricke and trim. *a* **1658** CLEVELAND *Myrtle-Grove* 50 Her gamesome Hair..in wild Rings ran trick about the air.

trick, *a.*[2] *U.S. colloq.* [f. the sb.] = TRICKY *a.* 2; liable to give way unexpectedly, defective, unreliable.

1961 in WEBSTER. **1968** *Punch* 21 Feb. 256/2 He would have been out there himself, he said, only he had this trick knee, had it since he was a kid, gave him hell. **1977** *Time* 8 Aug. 14/1 Private Citizen Henry Kissinger has a trick back like millions of other Americans. **1977** *Hot Car* Oct. 42/1 Best upholstery went to Sandy Ventriglin for her work on a very trick Viva.

tricked (trɪkt), *ppl. a.* Also 7 **trickt.** [f. TRICK *v.* + -ED[1].] **a.** Done or made by trickery. **b.** Artfully decked or adorned; dressed up.

1549 COVERDALE, etc. *Erasm. Par. Jas.* 35 Not in subtill reasonynges..or tricked fyne termes of eloquence. *a* **1619** FLETCHER, etc. *Knt. Malta* I. i, Thou trickt up toy. **1837** LYTTON *E. Maltrav.* III. iii, Affected, tricked-out, well-dressed children. **1868** SWINBURNE *Blake* 69 A special colour or savour which redeems the offences of a tricked and tinselled style. **1869** BLACKMORE *Lorna D.* xxi, This pretty youth, so tricked and slender, seemed nothing but a doll to me. **1895** [see TRICK *v.* 2].

tricker[1] (ˈtrɪkə(r)). [f. TRICK *v.* + -ER[1].]

1. One who plays tricks or practises trickery; a cheat, deceiver, trickster; also, one who plays a trick or prank.

1562 J. HEYWOOD *Prov. & Epigr.* (1867) 107 This tricke ..Brought to this tricker nother muse nor mase. **1606** *Choice, Chance*, etc. (1881) 7 Leaue tricks to trickers. *a* **1734** NORTH *Lives* (1826) II. 418 All the various species of politicians and trickers. *a* **1849** H. COLERIDGE *Ess.* (1851) II. 135 These trickers unwittingly speak truth.

†**2.** One who tricks out, decks, or artfully adorns.

a **1553** C. BANSLEY *Treat.* xxx. (Percy Soc.) 8 A wanton tricker..Wyth a double fardyngale and a caped cassoc, moche lyke a players gowne. **1567** *Triall Treas.* (1850) 24 She hath an amiable face; A tricker, a trimmer, in faith that she is, The goddess of wealth, prosperitie and bliss. **1600** KEMP *Nine Daies Wond.* i. A iij, Caualiero Kemp..onely tricker of your Trill-lilles, and best bel-shangles betweene Sion and mount Surrey.

3. One who tricks a coat of arms.

1586 FERNE *Blaz. Gentrie* To Gentl. Inner Temple, I did alwaies abhor the nude title and bare skill of a Blazoner, things common to each painter and tricker of armes. **1688** R. HOLME *Armoury* I. 2/2 Every Painter, Tricker, or a meer Blazoner of Arms, will not serve to make..an absolute Herauld.

†**4.** Some tool used by burglars. *Obs. rare.*

1592 GREENE *Art Conny catch.* II. D iij, He [the curber] hath his trickers, which are engines of Iron so cunningly wrought, that he wil cut a barre of Iron in two with them.

ˈ**tricker**[2], early and dial. form of TRIGGER *sb.*[1] (q.v.). Hence **tricker-firelock**, a hand fire-arm of the middle of the 17th c., discharged by pulling a trigger; **tricker-lock**, name in the 17th c. for a gun-lock furnished with a trigger, whether a ***match tricker-lock***, or a ***wheel tricker-lock***.

1629 *Schedule* in Meyrick *Antient Armour* (1824) III. 100 For a match tricker-lock compleat..1s. For a handle or guard of a tricker..vid. For furnishing and setting of a tricker lock in place of a feare lock, with a handle, tricker, and tricker pynnes. iis. vid. **1824** MEYRICK *ibid.* 88 The tricker-lock, I conceive, to be that furnished with a hair-trigger, as it is now called. **1855** *Jrnl. Brit. Archæol. Assoc.* XI. 255 Mr. G. Wright exhibited..a fine example of the lock of a Tricker firelock,..exhumed..from the battle-field of Worcester [1651]. The rising piece above the pan is furrowed, to facilitate the production of the sparks from the pyrites or flint.

trickeration (trɪkəˈreɪʃən). *U.S. Blacks.* [f. TRICKER(Y + -ATION.] A trick or stratagem (see also quots. 1940, 1970).

1940 *Music Makers* May 37/3 *Trickeration*, struttin' your stuff, muggin' lightly and politely. **1946** MEZZROW & WOLFE *Really the Blues* ix. 138 History was laying some trickeration on us. **1951** L. HUGHES *Montage of Dream Deferred* 18, I believe my old lady's pregnant again! Fate must have some kind of trickeration to populate the cullud nation! **1970** C. MAJOR *Dict. Afro-Amer. Slang* 116 *Trickeration*, to show off.

trickery (ˈtrɪkərɪ). [f. TRICK *sb.* + -ERY.] The practice of tricks; deceitful conduct or practice; deception, artifice; imposture.

1800 PARR *Spital Serm.* Wks. 1828 II. 394 Good sense without the trickeries of art, good language without the trappings of rhetoric. **1824** MISS MITFORD in L'Estrange *Life* (1870) II. ix. 174 He has a great deal of real sensibility, mixed with some trickery. **1825** T. HOOK *Sayings* Ser. II. *Man of Many Fr.* (Colburn) 91 Versed in all the experimental trickeries of science. **1881** JOWETT *Thucyd.* I. 118 We rely not upon management or trickery, but upon our own hearts and hands.

ˈ**trickful**, *a. rare.* [f. TRICK *sb.* + -FUL.] Full of tricks; tricky. Hence ˈ**trickfully** *adv.*

1775 S. J. PRATT *Liberal Opin.* xlviii. (1783) II. 17, I was ..as thoughtless, and as trickful as the best, or rather—the worst of them. *c* **1790** MRS. LARPENT in *19th Cent.* Aug. (1913) 312 Mrs. Siddons..acted well, Kemble stiffly, trickfully, yet in one sense sensibly!

†ˈ**trickify**, *v. Obs. rare.* [f. TRICK *v.* or TRICKY *a.*: see -FY (cf. *beautify, prettify*).] *trans.* To trick, deck, adorn: = TRICK *v.* 5.

1678 E. COOKE *Naked Breasts & Shoulders* 56 They could better imploy their time, than in so adorning and trickifying their Bodies.

trickily ('trɪkɪlɪ), *adv.* [f. TRICKY *a.* + -LY[2].] In a tricky manner.

1895 *Treas. Relig. Thoughts* (N.Y.) Oct. 459/1 Actually enforcing laws trickily made to be evaded. **1899** H. M. GREY *Moorish Captivity* iii. 34 The current twirled very trickily through the narrow channel between the reefs.

trickiness ('trɪkɪnɪs). [f. as prec. + -NESS.] The quality of being tricky; deceitfulness; also intricacy, complexity.

1723 *Caldwell Papers* (Maitl. Cl.) I. 250 Allowing a child's prevaricating, and laughing at its little trickiness and cunning. **1868** *Morn. Star* 19 June, A good deal of trickiness in the matter of petitions has lately been discovered. **1885** *Spectator* 8 Aug. 1041/1 Even the brilliance of his literary expression is beginning to be suspected of trickiness. **1894** BARING-GOULD *Kitty Alone* III. 56 Her simple mind..with no trickiness or dissimulation in it.

tricking ('trɪkɪŋ), *vbl. sb.* [f. TRICK *v.* + -ING[1].] The action of TRICK *v.*

1. The action of cheating, deceiving, or beguiling; trickery, deceit; in quot. 1662, †the sophistication of wine (*obs.*).

1595 *Enquiry Tripe-wife* (1881) 145 Your valorous assaults against The Tricking of the Tripe-wife. **1662** CHARLETON *Myst. Vintners* (1675) 203 The Transmutation or Sophistication of Wines, which they call Trickings or Compassings. **1799** W. GILPIN *Serm.* I. ix, [The world] will shew you, that tricking, and deceit of various kinds, are very consistent with christianity. **1810** W. WILSON *Hist. Dissent. Ch.* III. 46 The disingenuous arts of craft and tricking.

2. Dressing up, decking out, ornamentation (in quot. 1598 *concr.*).

1549 COVERDALE, etc. *Erasm. Par. Eph.* Prol. Cij, Men fynely broughte vp in trickynge of termes and tounges. **1598** SHAKS. *Merry W.* IV. iv. 79 Go get vs properties And tricking for our Fayries. **1695** BP. J. SAGE *Article* Wks. 1844 I. 371 So much needless ostentation, so much odd external tricking about it.

3. Sketching or drawing in outline; *spec. Her.* the delineation of armorial bearings in black and white: see TRICK *v.* 7.

1562 LEIGH *Armorie* ad fin., The olde order in trickyng of all maner of Armes, is to vse one letter for one word. O. Or. Yelowe [etc.]. **1864** *Lond. & Middlesex Archæol. Soc. Trans.* II. 58 The authority for this engraving is a tricking in a volume at the College of Arms.

'tricking, *ppl. a.* [f. as prec. + -ING[2].] That tricks; cheating, deceiving; using trickery.

1697 DRYDEN *Virgil, Life* (1721) I. 71 The Craft and Tricking part of Life, with which Homer abounds. **1790** BURKE *Fr. Rev.* Wks. V. 302 The degenerate fondness for tricking short-cuts, and little fallacious facilities. **1815** SCOTT *Guy M.* xlvii, All the world knows him to be sordid, mean, tricking, and I suspect him to be worse.

Hence **'trickingly** *adv.*, so as to cheat, artfully.

1833 *Fraser's Mag.* VII. 244 The small portion of notice which you condescend to bestow on Mr. Lytton Bulwer in the Magazine of this month, so trickingly put to the well-known ritornella of 'Whiston and Ditton'.

trickish ('trɪkɪʃ), *a.* [f. TRICK *sb.* + -ISH[1].]

1. Characterized by or given to tricks or trickery; rather tricky, crafty, or cunning.

1705 STANHOPE *Paraphr.* II. 391 The little trickish Arts of Dissimulation. **1760** J. ADAMS *Diary* 18 Dec., His habitual trickish, lying, cheating disposition. **1879** MCCARTHY *Own Times* II. xviii. 19 The somewhat cunning and trickish agitation which O'Connell had set going.

2. = TRICKY 2; TICKLISH *a.* 5.

1900 C. LEE *Cynthia* v. 72 Terr'ble trickish work. **1907** *Black Cat* June 24 It was trickish work handling a canoe among those pounding logs and frequent dead-heads.

Hence **'trickishly** *adv.*, **'trickishness.**

1788 V. KNOX *Winter Even.* xxxiv. (1790) I. 291 That odium, which..has branded the whole tribe with charges of duplicity..and trickishness. **1824** *Examiner* 57/1 Religion, trickishly wedded to Priestcraft. **1897** SARAH GRAND *Beth Bk.* xxii, It was another instance of the trickishness of her memory.

trickle ('trɪk(ə)l), *sb.*[1] [f. TRICKLE *v.*] **1.** A falling or flowing drop; a tear; a small quantity of liquid; a small fitful stream.

1580 HOLLYBAND *Treas. Fr. Tong, Pleur*, a teare, a trickle. So **1611** in COTGRAVE. **1730–6** BAILEY (folio), *Trickle*, a drop. **1855** BROWNING *Another Way of Love* iii, Delicious as trickles Of wine poured at mass-time. **1857** MRS. GATTY *Parab. fr. Nat.* Ser. II. (1868) 12 The waterfall..was reduced to a miserable trickle. **1897** 'A. HOPE' *Phroso* ix, Vlacho's blood began to curl in a meandering trickle from beneath the curtain.

fig. **1853** C. BRONTË *Villette* viii, No flow, only a hesitating trickle of language. **1895** BARING-GOULD *Noémi* v, But it [money] comes in in trickles and goes out in floods. **1897** MARY KINGSLEY *W. Africa* 637 It will only serve to bring down the little trickle of native trade.

2. Special Comb.: **trickle charger** *Electr.*, a device for charging a storage battery at a low rate over a long period; hence **trickle-charge** *sb.* (in quot., *attrib.*) and *v. trans.*; **trickle-charged** *ppl. a.*; **trickle-charging** *vbl. sb.*; **trickle irrigation** (see quot. 1969); hence (as back-formation) **trickle-irrigate** *v. trans.*

1959 *Times* 11 Sept. 7/4 It is ideal for trickle-charge operation. **1974** *Undercurrents* July–Aug. 3/3 This..produced a few hundred milliamps at about 10 volts in a fair breeze—enough to trickle-charge a small battery. **1938** *Proc. Physical Soc.* L. 422 The driving, demultiplying, and amplifying circuits were operated by trickle-charged batteries. **1927** *Observer* 24 July 4/5 A fool-proof set..is provided with a 'trickle charger' for keeping the filament battery up to strength. **1977** *Film & Television Technician* Mar. 11/3 Complete with its internal rechargeable batteries and a built-in trickle charger, the D34 weighs in at only 12 lbs. **1960** E. L. DELMAR-MORGAN *Cruising Yacht Equipment & Navigation* xvi. 175 This 'trickle charging' is..harmful for the type of batteries used in yachts. **1971** *World Bk. Sci. Ann. 1972* 255 Vast areas in the Negev Desert of Israel are now trickle-irrigated. **1969** *Gloss. for Landscape Work* (*B.S.I.*) v. 13 *Trickle irrigation*, a method of supplying water by means of a restricted, controlled flow to the surface of a growing medium (usually at discrete points, one to each plant). **1975** *N.Z. Jrnl. Agric.* Sept. 43/1 The research workers..are hopeful that trickle irrigation, by maintaining even soil moisture, will give some help.

'trickle, *sb.*[2] Variant of *triddle*, TREDDLE. Cf. also dial. *tricklings* in *Eng. Dial. Dict.*

1598 FLORIO, *Cacarelle*, the trickles or dung of sheepe, goates, rats or conies. **1639** O. WOOD *Alph. Bk. Secrets* 23 Sheepes trickles.

† **'trickle,** *a. Obs. rare.* [f. TRICK *sb.* or *v.* + -LE 1 (as in *brittle*), but apparently influenced by TICKLE *a.*] Tricky, treacherous; ticklish; requiring caution; = TRICKY *a.* 2.

1579 SPENSER *Sheph. Cal.* July 14 In humble dales is footing fast, The trode is not so trickle [*v.r.* tickle]. **1594** WILLOBIE *Avisa* (1880) 136 Such trickle trades procure a suddaine fall.

Hence † **'trickleness.** *Obs. rare*[−1].

a **1618** J. DAVIES *Wittes Pilgr.* (Grosart) 45/2 O Time..That neuer mou'st, but dost my Sences moue To mind thy flight, and this lifes tricklenesse.

trickle ('trɪk(ə)l), *v.* Forms: 4–6 **trekel,** (4 *Sc.* **trygle,** 4–5 **trikle, trekil,** 6 *Sc.* **trigle, -il),** 5 **trikel, -il, -trekyl, -ll,** 5–6 **trickil, -el, -ell,** 6 **tryckel,** (**triccle, trycle,** 7 **truckle**), 6– **trickle:** see also TRINKLE *v.*[1] [History doubtful. In the first Chaucer passage (sense 1) one MS. out of seven, the Lansdowne, has *strikle*, which is taken by Prof. Skeat as the original form (the initial *s* being lost after a prec. word in *-s*, e.g. *teres*), and this as a freq. or dim. of ME. *striken* to strike (the reading of two of the Chaucer MSS.) occurring twice elsewhere in sense 'flow' ('ase strem that striketh stille', 'strikeð a stream ut of þæt stanene þruh'), OE. *strícan* to strike, also to go, move, run. As to form and sense, this is possible; but no other ME. examples of *strikle* are known, so that the evidence is scanty.

(Cf. however MHG. *strîchen* to strike, also to move, travel, wander, and Ger. *streichen*, said of a ship as 'das Schiff streicht durch die Wellen'.)]

1. *intr.* **a.** Originally said of tears: To flow or fall in successive drops.

c **1375** *Sc. Leg. Saints* xxii. (*Laurentius*) 278 þane laurence handis one hym lad With t[r]ygland terys. *c* **1386** CHAUCER *Prioress' T.* 222 Hise salte teeris trikled [*v.rr.* trekelede, stryked, striked, strikled] doun as reyn. —— *Sompn. T.* 156 With many a teare triklyng [*v.rr.* trynkelynge, trillyng] on my cheke. *a* **1400–50** *Alexander* 4974 þar trekild doun of þa teres of iemmes [gems], Boyland out of þe barke bawme & mirre. **1513** DOUGLAS *Æneis* IV. vi. 66 (ed. 1553) Be al thir teris trigilland [*ed. Small* tringling] ouer my face. *Ibid.* VI. xi. 14 The teris trigling [*ed. Small* thringling] ouer his chekis ran. **1548** UDALL *Erasm. Par. Luke* vii. 74 The fete of Iesus beeyng well washed with teres tryclyng down from hir yies. **1565** GOLDING *Ovid's Met.* I. (1593) 12 The bitter teares did trickle downe their cheeke. **1702** POPE *Sappho* 200 And silent tears fall trickling from my eyes. **1843** LEVER *J. Hinton* xi, Tears of..joy trickled slowly down her cheeks.

b. Of other liquids; rarely of powders or granulated substances. Also, to flow in a very scanty and halting stream.

1526 *Pilgr. Perf.* (W. de W. 1531) 249 b, Yssued out blode & water..lyke droppes tricclyng downe to the grounde. **1610** HOLLAND *Camden's Brit.* (1637) 583 From his spring heads Trent trickleth downe. **1683** WARE *Hunting of Romish Fox* v. 87 The Blood..ran thrô the crevises of the Crown of Thorns, and truckled down the Face of this Image. **1725** DE FOE *Voy. round World* (1840) 261 The hill or gullet where the water trickled down from the rocks. **1866** G. MACDONALD *Ann. Q. Neighb.* iii, The flour was trickling down out of two wooden spouts. **1871** L. STEPHEN *Playgr. Eur.* (1894) x. 241 A small glacier trickles into the desolate valley.

c. *transf.* and *fig.* Also used facetiously for 'to make one's way, go'. Cf. OOZE *v.*[1] 2 c.

1628 [see TRICKLING *vbl. sb.*] **1728** POPE *Dunc.* III. 201 Fluent nonsense trickles from his tongue. **1758** JOHNSON *Idler* No. 7 ¶4 The rivulets of intelligence which are continually trickling. **1899** *Allbutt's Syst. Med.* VIII. 5 What can be more wonderful than to see a man's thoughts trickling from the end of his pen at the rate of nearly a word a second! **1901** *Scotsman* 11 Mar. 9/1 Then another thousand rupees came trickling in. **1912** R. BROOKE *Let.* Feb. (1968) 357, I wrote to *her*, about her perhaps trickling down to Rugby. **1936** WODEHOUSE *Laughing Gas* iii. 32 In these circs, it seemed to me that the best way of passing the time would be to trickle over to the table where the drinks were and brace myself with one or two. **1961** —— *Service with Smile* (1962) vii. 100 He headed for the lake. I trickled after him. **1983** *Country Life* 5 May 1194/3 Trickling through morning traffic..it [*sc.* a car] showed its docility by contentedly running in fifth.

2. *intr.* To emit falling or flowing drops; to drip or run (*with* tears, blood, etc.); to shed tears.

c **1400** *Destr. Troy* 8058 Yf the ton ee with teres trickell on hir chekes. **1582** STANYHURST *Æneis* I. (Arb.) 32 Fast he stood: and trickling dyd speake. **1611** BIBLE *Lam.* iii. 49 Mine eye trickleth downe and ceaseth not. **1865** DICKENS *Mut. Fr.* III. ix, His hand was trickling down with blood.

3. a. *trans.* To emit or give forth in successive drops or a thin fitful stream; also, to cause to trickle; to pour drop by drop, or in a fitful stream.

1602 MARSTON *Antonio's Rev.* V. v, The vaines..Trickling fresh goare about my fist. **1671** WOODHEAD *St. Teresa* I. xxii. 147 We behold him..trickling blood. **1746–7** HERVEY *Medit.* (1818) 186 Ye gushing Fountains, that trickle potable silver through the matted grass. **1854** DICKENS *Hard T.* II. i, The mills..oozed and trickled it [oil]. **1863** READE *Hard Cash* xxi, With adroit and tender hands they..trickled stimulants down her throat. **1878** T. L. CUYLER *Pointed Papers* 144 He knows every wound that trickles its silent drops from the bleeding spirit.

b. *fig.* with *off* or *out*: To let go one by one.

1657 REEVE *God's Plea* 26 Thus doth the voluptuous man measure out his time, trickle out his hours. **1907** *Blackw. Mag.* July 36/2 The company commanders begin to trickle off their men.

c. *Sport.* To cause (a ball) to travel slowly over the ground, esp. in golf. Also ***to trickle a putt.*** Also *absol.*

1902 *Daily Chron.* 20 Aug. 7/3 He can..trickle the ball away to fine-leg with a delicate turn of the wrist. **1903** *Westm. Gaz.* 6 Feb. 3/2 If you bolt at the hole, you will not need to make the same allowance for incline as if you trickled. **1927** *Daily Tel.* 14 Mar. 13/1 'I will trickle the..putt up to the hole.'..It certainly was a trickle..for the ball stopped five feet short of the hole.

4. *Comb.*: **trickle-down** *a.*, of or based on the theory that economic benefits to particular groups will inevitably be passed on to those less well off; also *transf.* as *sb.*, a filtering down (of money or ideas). orig. and chiefly *U.S.*

[**1931** W. ROGERS in *Tulsa Daily World* 12 July IV. 7/3 What about the old Boys here on the home grounds? Well maybe this thing will eventually reach him in some beneficial way. Lord knows what way it may trickle down to him some day.] **1944** *Antioch Rev.* Summer 192 In agriculture, as in business, they are devotees of the trickle-down philosophy. **1949** H. S. TRUMAN in *Sun* (Baltimore) 6 Jan. 6/1 We have rejected the discredited theory that the fortunes of the nation should be in the hands of a privileged few. We have abandoned the 'trickle-down' concept of national prosperity. **1954** *Sun* (Baltimore) 13 Feb. (B ed.) 2/1 The Administration has already offered us a trickle-down tax program. Now, we are presented with a trickle-down housing program. **1962** C. WALSH *From Utopia to Nightmare* i. 18 There has been a trickle-down [of ideas] and permeation. **1971** *Publishers' Weekly* 6 Dec. 17/2 It is to be hoped that textbook writers come in contact with frontier thinkers or their writings and translate some of the results into educational materials. This is known as the 'trickle-down' process. **1977** *Time* 16 May 38/2 It's classic trickle-down economics. **1980** *Jrnl. R. Soc. Arts* July 508/2 The theory that if you build the industrial capability and increase the GNP of the country there will be a trickle-down to people at subsistence level. **1981** PLATE & DARVI *Secret Police* ii. 42 If the sovereign himself is corrupt or family and relatives are corrupt, there can be a trickle-down effect into the ranks. **1984** *New Yorker* 16 Apr. 82/2 To Fink this often sounded suspiciously like Republican trickle-down economics.

trickless ('trɪklɪs), *a.* [f. TRICK *sb.* + -LESS.] Possessing no tricks (*spec.* in *Cards*).

1927 *Observer* 29 May 25 If he finds his partner trickless, he must go down enormously. **1977** *Times* 17 June 12/1 Anyone who regularly makes preemptive opening bids on hands which are trickless in defence has only himself to blame.

'tricklet. [f. TRICKLE *sb.* + -LET (or -ET[1]).] A small or minute trickle; a minute streamlet.

1880 *Daily Tel.* 28 Oct., Merely the result of tricklets of perspiration. **1886** RUSKIN *Præterita* I. ix. 292 A tricklet here at the bottom of a crag. **1888** R. L. STEVENSON in *Scribner's Mag.* Oct. 511/1 A tricklet of a stream divides them.

trickling ('trɪklɪŋ), *vbl. sb.* [f. TRICKLE *v.* + -ING[1].] **a.** The action of the verb TRICKLE; also *concr.* that which trickles.

1628 GAULE *Pract. The.* (1629) 34 The slow tricklings of his Mercie;..the full streame of outward blessings. **1814** BYRON *Lara* II. xvii, The tides [of blood]..In feebler, not less fatal tricklings flow. **1863** BARING-GOULD *Iceland* 134 Shale..wet with tricklings from the rock overhead.

b. trickling filter = *percolating filter* s.v. PERCOLATING *vbl. sb.*

1903 W. J. DIBDIN *Purification of Sewage & Water* (ed. 3) p. xv, I think it is quite practicable to deal with Leeds sewage on trickling filters without antecedent septic treatment. **1976** *Ann. Rev. Microbiol.* XXX. 266 Bacterial and viral aerosols are generated..and bacteria have been detected at least 0·8 mile from a trickling filter.

'trickling, *ppl. a.* [f. as prec. + -ING[2].] That trickles: see the verb.

c **1375** [see TRICKLE *v.* 1 a]. **1513** DOUGLAS *Æneis* XIII. iv. 23 With habundans of mony trigland teir Wetand thar brestis. **1557** in *Tottell's Misc.* (Arb.) 215 Not euery tricklyng teare doth argue inward paine. *c* **1586** C'TESS PEMBROKE *Ps.* LXXVIII. vii, The trickling springs to such huge rivers grew. **1665** SIR T. HERBERT *Trav.* (1677) 181 Rivers..which after a long trickling race..disembogue themselves into the Caspian. **1791** COWPER *Iliad* IV. 170 Stained with thy trickling blood. **1848** EDMESTON *Sacr. Poetry* (1868) 202 Dry the trickling tear.

† **'trickly,** *a.*[1] *Obs. rare.* [f. TRICK *a.*[1] + -LY[1]: cf. *goodly, sickly, weakly*.] Smart-looking, showy.

1573 TUSSER *Husb.* (1878) 164 Though trickly to see to, be gallant to wiue, Yet comely and wise is the huswife to thriue.

trickly ('trɪklɪ), *a.*[2] *rare.* [f. TRICKLE *sb.* or *v.* + -Y.] Characterized by trickling.

1876 MISS BROUGHTON *Joan* II. x, Her boots no longer rattle, nor do cold and trickly rills race down the nape of her neck. **1910** *Westm. Gaz.* 12 Mar. 15/2 The heron is ever on the look-out to use his long neck for a quick blow and trickly gulp.

† **'trickly**, *adv. Obs.* [f. TRICK *a.*[1] + -LY[2].]

a. Cleverly. **b.** Neatly, smartly, trigly, finely.

1542 UDALL *Erasm. Apoph.* 108 Feactely & trickely representing..a certain lasciuious playe. **1581** A. HALL *Iliad* III. 58 The place was trickly decked vp. **1592** GREENE *Groat's W. Wit* (1617) 21 The olde womans daughter was trickly attyred. **1599** MINSHEU, *Limadamente*, exquisitly, trickly. **1608** H. CLAPHAM *Errour Left Hand* 103 In shadowie plots, the Vipers, Monkscowle groes, Which with his yellowe flower full trickly shoes.

† **'trick-madam.** *Obs.* [a. F. *trique-madame* (1545 in Hatz.-Darm.), of uncertain origin.] An old name of one or more species of Stonecrop, formerly used in salads; called also PRICK-MADAM and TRIP-MADAM.

According to Lyte, Prick-madam was the plant now called *Sedum reflexum*, and Wild Prick-madam, *S. album*; according to Littré, *trique madame* in France is 'l'orpin blanc', or 'trique blanche', ? *Sedum album*; according to Eugène Rolland *Flore populaire* VI. 108–110, *trique-madame* is in France applied indiscriminately to *Sedum acre* and *S. album*, but it is doubtful if the name was ever applied in England to the former (Biting Stonecrop or Wall Pepper).

1600 SURFLET *Countrie Farme* II. xvi. 223 Tricke-madam doth nothing feare the cold. *Ibid.* II. lx. 397 Steepe the seedes for a certaine time in the iuice of trick-madame. **1699** EVELYN *Acetaria* 70 Trick-madame..is cooling and moist. **1725** *Bradley's Fam. Dict.* s.v. *Sallet*, The Cimes and Tops of Trick-Madam, when young and tender, drest as Purslain, is a frequent Ingredient in our cold Sallet.

trickment ('trɪkmənt). *rare.* [f. TRICK *v.* + -MENT.] Decoration, adornment.

In earliest use app. heraldic ornament; cf. HATCHMENT.

a **1619** FLETCHER, etc. *Knt. of Malta* IV. ii, A new tomb, new trickments too. *a* **1619** —— *Mad Lover* V. iv, No tombe shall hold thee But these two armes, no Trickments but my teares. *a* **1843** SOUTHEY in *Fraser's Mag.* (1868) LXXVIII. 106 Other poets,..forced their verses with far-fetched conceits and tawdry trickments of art.

† **'trickness.** *Obs. rare.* [f. TRICK *a.*[1] + -NESS.] The condition or quality of being 'trick'; neatness, smartness, or trigness of attire.

1600 ABP. ABBOT *Exp. Jonah* 593 He saw some as proud, and glad of their tricknesse, as Ionas was of his shadow.

trickology (trɪ'kɒlədʒɪ). *nonce-wd.* [f. TRICK *sb.* + -OLOGY.] The science of trickery. Hence **tri'ckologist**, a trickster.

1723 (*title*) Trickology, or a Letter of Advice to a Student of Medicine. *Ibid.* 4 Trickology, which a Greek would name *Technology*, a Part by far more witty and lucrative than all the other five. *Ibid.* 20 A serious Sense of Religion..shall never make a good Trickologist.

tricksical, tricksily: see under TRICKSY *a.*

tricksiness ('trɪksɪnɪs). [f. TRICKSY *a.* + -NESS.] The quality or condition of being tricksy.

1. Artful smartness of apparel. *rare.*

a **1553** C. BANSLEY *Treat.* xix. (Percy S.) 6 Loke well, ye men, to your wives trycksynes, whyche is to shamefull wyde.

2. Playfulness, sprightliness; mischievousness.

1846 D. JERROLD *Chron. Clovernook* Wks. 1864 IV. 439 The tricksiness of an extravagant spirit. **1871** G. MEREDITH *H. Richmond* II. 21 Pride in their physical prowess, their dexterity, ingenuity, and tricksiness, and their purity of blood. **1876** GEO. ELIOT *Dan. Der.* I. vii, There was none of the latent fun and tricksiness which had always pierced in her greeting of Rex.

3. Deceptiveness, trickiness.

1888 J. T. WALKER *Reason. Chr.* 2 The Judge points out ..its tricksiness and capacity for self deception.

† **'tricksing**, *ppl. a. Obs. rare.* [as if f. a vb. **tricks* + -ING[2]; cf. TRICKSY *v.* and TRICKING.] Tricking, cheating, treacherous.

1681 COTTON *Wond. Peak* (ed. 4) 45 Some of which hanging tablets [stones], as he still Made further progress up the tricksing hill, He found so loose, they threatned as he went To sweep him off and be his Monument.

tricksome ('trɪksəm), *a.* [f. TRICK *sb.* or *v.* + -SOME.]

1. Given to playing tricks; = TRICKY *a.* I.

1648 *Church-lands not to be sold* 48 The Pope had made.. the necessity,..that he might fleece the Clergy; which that just Councel well weighing,..made him finde some other tricksom way, to salve his necessity. **1761** *Antiq.* in *Ann. Reg.* 169/2 The Dracs, supposed to be malicious, or at least tricksome demons. **1821** *New Monthly Mag.* III. 555/2 Mr. Kemble was often artificial; but all his art was employed on those passages where Mr. Kean is merely tricksome. **1858** LYTTON *What will he do?* X. v, I have been a tricksome shifty vagrant.

2. Playful, sportive, frolicsome.

1815 J. SCOTT *Vis. Paris* (ed. 2) I. ii. 17 Some ladies..their flowing shawls..and tricksome gait, bade our young gentlemen prepare their compliments in a new language. **1824** *Examiner* 107/2 A tricksome youth full of mischievous merriment. **1832** L. HUNT *Poems, To J. H.* 27 My tricksome Puck. **1870** F. JACOX *Rec. Recluse* I. xii. 249 [He] has pictured Handel with..his delicacies and tricksome graces.

b. Of music.

1820 L. HUNT *Indicator* No. 60 (1822) II. 60 The most tricksome harmonies and accompaniments of Mozart and Beethoven. **1822** *Examiner* 266/1 The situations are often too serious, and the devotion too solemn, to allow of tricksome passages.

trickster ('trɪkstə(r)). [f. TRICK *sb.* or *v.* + -STER.] One who practises trickery; a rogue, cheat, knave.

1711 *Medley* No. 39 The other..was such a Lubbard Trickster, so awkward at Mischief, that he deserv'd only to be laugh'd at. **1741** RICHARDSON *Pamela* II. 260 Tho' I have won the Game, I hope, Sirs, I am no Trickster. **1844** DISRAELI *Coningsby* IX. vi, The Whigs were known to be feeble; they were looked upon as tricksters. **1879** MCCARTHY *Own Times* II. xviii. 2 Diplomatists..commissioned to act as tricksters. **1879** DIXON *Windsor* II. xvi. 171 The woman whom he knew to be a trickster.

attrib. **1889** *Voice* (N.Y.) 7 Mar., The bad faith so frequently shown by trickster party leadership.

Hence **'trickstering**, the action of a trickster (also *attrib.*); **'trickstress**, a female trickster.

1821 SCOTT *Kenilw.* xxxvi, I like not this lady's tampering and *trickstering with this same Edmund Tressilian. **1883** *Times* 12 July 10 Due to political trickstering directed against Mr. Bradlaugh. **1889** J. J. THOMAS *Froudacity* 77 Since the trickstering days of Governor Irving. **1870** E. H. PEMBER *Trag. Lesbos* viii. 119 Nay, young *trickstress, nay!

tricksy ('trɪksɪ), *a.* Also 6–7 tricksie, -sey, trickesie, trixsie, trixy. [app. f. *tricks*, pl. of TRICK *sb.* + -Y, with the natural meaning 'given to, distinguished by, or abounding in tricks'.]

1. Artfully trimmed or decked; spruce, smart, fine.

1552 LATIMER *Serm., John xv. 12* (1572) 153 Let them go as tricksie as they wil in this world, yet for all that they be foule and filthy inough before God. **1577** KENDALL *Flowers Epigr.* 19 b, Thou wandrest trixsie trimsie fine, with crispt and curled heare. **1589** FLEMING *Virg. Georg.* III. 51 When he is new become againe, Hauing cast off his skin, and tricksie trim with youth afresh. **1598** FLORIO, *Immarzapanato*, become or made fine,..sweete, or daintie, ..trickesie, and trim as a marchpane. **1631** *Celestina* VII. 88 To see every thing so trimme and tricksie about you. *a* **1820** J. R. DRAKE *Culprit Fay* iv. (1835) 12 Their little minim forms arrayed In the tricksy pomp of fairy pride! **1852** D. G. MITCHELL *Dream Life* 150 The tricksy panoply that he has wrought out of the mettle of his classics.

2. Full of or given to tricks or pranks; playful, sportive; mischievous, capricious, whimsical.

1596 SHAKS. *Merch. V.* III. v. 74, I doe know A many fooles..Garnisht like him, that for a tricksie word Defie the matter. **1598** MARSTON *Sco. Villanie* II. Prol., Tricksey tales of speaking Cornish dawes. **1604** DEKKER *Honest Wh.* I. xi. Wks. 1873 II. 63 [Stage-direction] Enter Candido like a Prentise. *Wife.* Why how now mad-man, what in your tricksi-coats? **1610** SHAKS. *Temp.* V. i. 226 *Ariel.* Sir, all this seruice Haue I done.. *Prospero.* My tricksey Spirit. **1831** CARLYLE *Sart. Res.* I. iv, A rich, idiomatic diction, picturesque allusions, fiery poetic emphasis, or quaint tricksy turns. **1871** R. ELLIS *Catullus* ii. 5 My lady..Bends her splendour awhile to tricksy frolic. **1895** CROCKETT *Love Idylls* (1901) 125 The tricksy maid clapped her hands and laughed merrily.

3. Full of tricks or deception; tricky, crafty, cunning, cheating.

1766 GOLDSM. *Vic. W.* xxvi, I still continued tricksy and cunning, and was poor, without the consolation of being honest. **1809–10** COLERIDGE *Friend* (ed. 3) I. 25 The tricksy humilities of the ambitious candidates for the favorable suffrages of the judicious public. **1856** R. A. VAUGHAN *Mystics* (1860) I. 241 Willoughby had to tell of the escapades of tricksy trout.

4. That is apt to play tricks upon one; that needs cautious handling: = TRICKY *a.* 2, TICKLISH.

1835 WILLIS *Pencillings* I. xxi. 146 The second and third stories are ornamented with tricksy-looking iron balconies. **1862** *Morn. Star* 21 May, Kidderminster is a tricksy borough. Its people have a knack of taking their own way. **1900** H. SUTCLIFF *Shameless Wayne* i, A lass is tricksy handling ut sich times.

Hence **'tricksical** *a.*, inclined to be tricksy or to play tricks; **'tricksily** *adv.*, in a tricksy or sportive manner.

1866 ALGER *Solit. Nat. & Man* III. 163 The heathen deities,..that once tricksily danced over the classic landscapes. **1889** *Pall Mall G.* 28 May 3 Imagination is, indeed, a tricksical jade.

† **'tricksy**, *v. Obs. rare.* In 6 trixie. [f. prec.] *trans.* To make 'tricksy' or spruce.

1598 FLORIO, *Nimfarsi*, to trim, to smug, to trixie, to decke or spruce himselfe vp as a nimphe.

trick-track: see TRIC-TRAC.

tricky ('trɪkɪ), *a.* [f. TRICK *sb.* + -Y.] Characterized by or full of tricks.

1. a. Given to the practice of crafty or deceitful tricks; characterized by trickery.

1786 BURNS *To Auld Mare* v, Tho' ye was trickie, slee, an' funnie, Ye ne'er was donsie. **1812** WALKER in P. Graham *Agric. Surv. Stirling* 401 A minister..paid in kind from the small tricky heritors, who are imposing upon him grain of the worst quality. **1831–54** LD. COCKBURN *Jrnl.* ii. (1874) 113 As Lord President he was tricky. **1868** E. EDWARDS *Ralegh* I. ii. 27 Very characteristic..of the tricky and tortuous policy of Elizabeth's government.

b. Skilled in performing clever tricks or dodges.

1887 *Daily News* 19 May 3/3 It had gained many prizes, and was what he might call a tricky dog. **1890** L. C. D'OYLE *Notches* 63, I used to be what they call a 'tricky' hunter. **1901** *Essex Weekly News* 29 Mar. 8/3 His partner..was the trickiest forward on the field.

2. Having the deceptive character of a trick; containing unexpected difficulties; needing cautious action or handling; risky, catchy, ticklish. *colloq.*

1868 C. L. EASTLAKE *Hints Househ. Taste* vii. 176 Chromo-lithography..accustoms the eye to easily rendered and therefore *tricky* effects of colour which falsify rather than illustrate nature. **1887** SAINTSBURY *Hist. Elizab. Lit.* iv. (1890) 111 One of the tricky things called echo sonnets. **1887** *L'pool Daily Post* 14 Feb. 5/7 Accompanying certain recitations with music, which at first appeared a rather tricky experiment. **1891** KIPLING *Light that Failed* i, Revolvers are tricky things for young hands to deal with.

triclad ('traɪklæd, 'trɪklæd), *a.* and *sb. Zool.* [ad. mod.L. *Triclada*, neut. pl., f. TRI- + Gr. κλάδος branch.] **a.** *adj.* Belonging to the division *Triclada* or *Tricladida* of turbellarian worms, having a main intestine with three branches. **b.** *sb.* A worm of this division. (Cf. POLYCLAD.)

1888 ROLLESTON & JACKSON *Anim. Life* 579 Bundles of dorso-ventral muscle-fibres, &c. in *Nemertea* and Triclad *Turbellaria*. *Ibid.* 672 Transverse fission has been observed in the Triclads *Planaria subtentaculata*..and *Polycœlis cornuta*. **1909** J. W. JENKINSON *Experim. Embryol.* 273 The reunion of separated blastomeres in Triclads.

† **'triclasite.** *Min. Obs.* [ad. Ger. *triclasit* (Hausmann 1808), f. Gr. τρι-, TRI- + κλάσ-ις breaking, fracture + -ITE[1].] Obsolete synonym of FAHLUNITE.

1835 *Encycl. Brit.* (ed. 7) XII. 37/1 Triclasite. Specific Gravity 2·61 to 2·66. **1850** ANSTED *Elem. Geol., Min.* etc. §401 Fahlunite, Triklasite, Hydrous silicate of alumina with magnesia, oxide of iron, and oxide of manganese. **1868** DANA *Min.* (ed. 5) 485 The name triclasite alludes to three cleavages, and is therefore bad, as they are not cleavages of the species, but in part of the original iolite.

tri'clavian. [f. TRI- + L. *clāvus* nail + -IAN.] One who holds that only three nails were used at the crucifixion of Christ. Hence **tri'clavianism**.

1838 G. S. FABER *Inquiry* 398 The author of the Noble Lesson, whom I suppose to have been a Triclavian, mentions the five wounds. *Ibid.* 397 Pope Innocent III finally and infallibly determined, that four nails were used, and that the Roman soldier pierced the right side of Christ; a decision, which of course stamped the brand of heresy upon Triclavianism.

triclinate ('traɪ-, 'trɪklɪneɪt), *a. Cryst.* [f. TRI- + L. *clīnāt-us* inclined.] = TRICLINIC.

1837 DANA *Min.* 40 On examining the figure of anorthite ..we..have no reason for a doubt, that this crystal is triclinate. **1849** —— *Geol.* App. II. (1850) 732 Cleavage oblique, probably indicating triclinate crystallization.

† **tricline.** *Obs.* Also 5 -yne. [ad. L. *triclīnium*: see below: cf. OF. *triclin*, 14th c., *tricline*, 15th c.] = TRICLINIUM.

c **1440** *Pallad. on Husb.* I. 391 And half as high thyn chamber & tricline [*v.r.* -clyne] Thou make, as hit is mesure long by lyne. **1492** RYMAN *Poems* xii. 9 in *Archiv Stud. neu. Spr.* LXXXIX. 181 O floure of all virginitie..O triclyne of the trinitie.

triclinial (traɪ'klɪnɪəl), *a.* [f. TRICLINI-UM + -AL[1].] Pertaining to a triclinium. So **tri'clini-arch** [ad. L. *triclīniarchēs*, Gr. *τρικλῑνιάρχης: cf. ARCHITRICLINE], the president of a feast; † **tri'cliniary** *a.* [ad. L. *triclīniāris*] = *triclinial.*

1874 I. TAYLOR *Etruscan Researches* iii. 47 The couches on which the corpses repose have a *triclinial arrangement. **1656** BLOUNT *Glossogr.*, **Tricliniarck* (*tricliniarches*), the master of the dining chamber or room, the huicher. **1892** *Harper's Mag.* Dec. 131/1 There is no need thus to punish your tricliniarch. **1646** SIR T. BROWNE *Pseud. Ep.* V. vi. 243 From this *Tricliniary disposure, we may illustrate that obscure expression of Seneca. **1695** J. EDWARDS *Perfect. Script.* 133 This was their posture..on their tricliniary beds.

triclinic (traɪ'klɪnɪk), *a. Cryst.* [f. Gr. τρι-, TRI- + κλῑν-ειν to incline, lean, slope + -IC.] Applied to that system of crystalline forms in which the three axes are unequal and obliquely inclined (also called *anorthic*, *tetartoprismatic*, or *doubly oblique*); belonging to this system.

1854 DANA *Min.* Introd. (ed. 4) 29 In the Triclinic System, the three axes are unequal, and all the intersections are oblique. **1869** ROSCOE *Elem. Chem.* (1871) 267 Copper sulphate..crystallizes in large blue crystals belonging to the triclinic system. **1897** GEIKIE *Anc. Volcanoes Gt. Brit.* I. 27 The bottom of the flow was thickly crowded with triclinic felspars and augites.

‖ **triclinium** (traɪ'klɪnɪəm, trɪ'klaɪnɪəm). *Roman Antiq.* Pl. -ia. [L. *triclīnium*, a. Gr. τρικλίνιον, dim. of τρίκλῑνος, as sb. a dining-room with three couches, f. κλίνη couch, bed.] A couch, running round three sides of a table, on which to recline at meals; a table-couch; also, a room for eating in; a dining-room.

1646 SIR T. BROWNE *Pseud. Ep.* VII. xviii. 381 Fishponds, Gardens, Tricliniums. **1797** S. LYSONS *Rom. Antiq. Woodchester* 17 These [apartments] occupy the situation assigned by Vitruvius for the *triclinia* of the spring and autumn. **1848** MRS. JAMESON *Sacr. & Leg. Art* (1850) 106 In the Triclinium of the old palace of the Lateran.

triclino'hedric, *a. Cryst.* [f. as TRICLINIC + Gr. ἕδρα base.] = TRICLINIC. So **triclino'hedral** *a.*

1837 DANA *Min.* 15 Oblique Rhomboidal Prism... It.. forms the class *Triclinata*... *Note.* Triclinohedral of Naumann. **1882** OGILVIE (Annandale), Triclinohedric.

tricoaster: see TRI- 4 c.

tricoccous (traɪˈkɒkəs), *a. Bot.* [f. TRI- + COCCUS + -OUS.] Of a fruit: Composed of three *cocci* or carpels; also of a plant, having a fruit of this kind. Also **triˈcoccose** *a.*

1697 *Phil. Trans.* XIX. 396 Tricoccos Shrubs called Widdow-Wayles. **1703** J. PETIVER *ibid.* XXIII. 1458 The Berry is perfectly tricoccose. **1707** SLOANE *Jamaica* I. 124 A tricoccous, rough seed-vessel. **1845** LINDLEY *Sch. Bot.* vii. (1858) 114 The fruit of this order is tricoccous; that is, it consists of 3 carpels.

tricolic (traɪˈkəʊlɪk), *a. Gr. Pros.* [f. Gr. τρίκωλος (f. τρι-, TRI- + κῶλον limb, clause) + -IC.] Consisting of three cola: see COLON[2] 1. So **triˈcolon**, a period consisting of three cola.

1706 PHILLIPS (ed. Kersey), *Tricolon*,.. a Stanza, or Staff of three Verses. **1891** *Cent. Dict.*, Tricolic.

tricolorous (traɪˈkʌlərəs), *a.* [f. late L. *tricolor, -ōr-em* (see next) + -OUS.] = next, A.

1891 in *Cent. Dict.*

tricolour, tricolor (ˈtraɪˌkʌlə(r), ˈtrɪkələ(r)), *a.* and *sb.* [ad. late L. *tricolor, -ōrem* adj. (Priscian *c* 500), and F. *tricolore* adj. (often in phr. *drapeau tricolore*: see A. 2, B. 2).]

A. *adj.* Having three colours; three-coloured.

1. *Nat. Hist.*, esp. in reference to a black, white, and tan dog.

1866 *Treas. Bot.*, *Tricolor*, consisting of three colours. **1900** in B. D. JACKSON *Gloss. Bot. Terms.* **1922** R. LEIGHTON *Compl. Bk. Dog* viii. 113 At Cruft's in 1913 an especially nice tricolour puppy named Jason was placed high above Lerwick Jarl. **1971** F. HAMILTON *World Encycl. Dogs* 103 The coat is smooth and short and the colors are tricolor, black, tan and white.

2. Of a flag, cockade, etc.; esp. of the national flags of France, Italy, and Mexico: see B. 2.

1815 SOUTHEY in *Q. Rev.* July 482 (tr. *Napoleon*) Tear down those colours which the nation has proscribed; mount the tri-colour cockade. **1832** tr. *Sismondi's Ital. Rep.* xvi. 362 The French general Baraguai d'Hilliers entered the city.. and planted.. the tricolour banner on St. Mark. **1860** W. G. CLARK in *Vac. Tour.* 56 [They] made haste to take all the tricolor flags from their windows. **1886** *Pall Mall G.* 3 July 8/2 Many.. supporters had also donned tricolour rosettes.

3. a. Employing or pertaining to the use of the three primary colours. Cf. THREE-COLOUR *a.*

1898 A. C. AUSTIN (*title*) Practical half-tone and tri-color engraving. **1909** *Chambers's Jrnl.* 27 Mar. 268/1 A remarkable new development.. promises to revolutionise the art of printing in photogravure. The process is three-colour; and.. the results.. are far in advance of anything that has yet been attempted in tricolour printing. **1937** J. S. MERTLE *Photolithography & Offset Printing* 101 Three-color photography proper is based on the photographic separation of the colored original into three primary color-record (separation) negatives, which are obtained by exposing three separate color-sensitive plates through what are termed 'tri-color' filters. *Ibid.* 103 Tri-color images. **1968** *Gloss. Terms Offset Lithogr. Printing* (*B.S.I.*) 17 *Tricolour filter*, a colour filter that transmits a primary band of the spectrum, i.e., red, green or blue.

b. *gen.* Three-coloured.

1979 *Washington Post* 20 Oct. F7/2 Even the large sculptures are hard to find among the visual chaos—amid blaring tricolor trashcans, telephone booths, [etc.]. **1983** *Christian Sci. Monitor* 14 Nov. B12/1 Almost anything Chinese— whether Tang Dynasty tricolor jars, Ming molded gourds, or cheap jade trinkets—can be bought in Hong Kong.

B. *sb.* (Not so used in French.)

1. *Gardening* (in form **tricolor**). Short for *Amarantus tricolor*, a species of amaranth from China, cultivated for its brightly coloured leaves, compounded of green, yellow, and red.

1786 ABERCROMBIE *Gard. Assist.* 239 Fine balsams, cockscombs, tricolors, etc.

2. a. A tricolour flag, cockade, etc.; *esp.* the national flag of France adopted at the Revolution, consisting of equal vertical stripes of blue, white, and red.

1797 *Political Censor* Mar. 84 To strut and hector over the poor fallen *Tricolor*, and to call on your readers to 'unite under their *own flag*'.. entitles you to but very little praise. **1798** SCOTT *War-song* viii, If ever breath of British gale Shall fan the tri-color [*rime* shore]. **1815** BYRON *On the Star of 'the Legion of Honour'* iv, A rainbow.. Of three bright colours. *Note*, The tri-colour. **1832** MARRYAT *N. Forster* xli, The French tricolour hardly had time to blow clear. **1837** CARLYLE *Fr. Rev.* I. v. v, Red and Blue, our old Paris colours: these, once based on a ground of constitutional White, are the famed Tricolor,—which (if Prophecy err not) 'will go round the world'. **1847** DISRAELI *Tancred* IV. ii, The flag of England has beaten even the tricolour. **1855** W. MORRIS in Mackail *Life* (1899) I. 82 The Russian tricolour, horizontal stripes of blue, red, and white. **1870** *Daily News* 1 Dec., An unpretending house.. has a sentry at the gate, and a North German tricolour displayed above the garden wall.

b. The green, white, and orange Irish Republican flag.

1969 *Listener* 28 Aug. 268/2 The tricolour had been raised in Bogside once before. **1977** *Belfast Tel.* 22 Feb. 5/5 No Irish tricolours were displayed.

3. A black, white, and tan dog.

1905 J. WATSON *Dog Bk.* lxvi. 724 The tricolour has been neglected in the fashion for black and tans. **1971** F. HAMILTON *World Encycl. Dogs* 97 Two tricolors can produce a pure golden-sable.

4. A combination of the three primary colours.

1978 *SLR Camera* Dec. 88/3 In theory, the yellow, magenta-red, and cyan-blue tricolour forming the image of the slide should each perfectly reflect two-thirds of the spectrum of white light.

tricoloured, -colored (ˈtraɪˌkʌləd), *a.* (Often with hyphen.) [f. TRI- + COLOURED, after prec., simulating a parasynthetic compound, as *three-coloured.*] = prec. A.

1795 *St. Papers* in *Ann. Reg.* 234/2 That tri-coloured standard [of 1789, when the red and blue of Paris were added to the white of the French King]. **1797** S. & HT. LEE *Canterb. T.*, *Frenchm. T.* (1799) I. 234 Each wore a tri-coloured ribbond in his hat. **1806** A. DUNCAN *Nelson* 98 The tri-colored cockade.. caught his eye. **1840** MACAULAY *Ess.*, *Ranke* (1887) 592 The tricoloured flag floated on the top of the Castle of St. Angelo. **1913** F. T. BARTON *Toy Dogs* ix. 41 The Ruby and Tri-coloured, or Prince Charles Spaniels, have a separate classification.

tricolumnar: see TRI- 1.

‖**tricon** (trikɔ̃). *Cards.* [F. *tricon*: origin unknown; perh. jocularly f. L. *tri-* three + *con-*, CON-, together.] In certain card games, as Commerce: see quots.

1798 *Sporting Mag.* XII. 142 The tricon is three tens, three nines, three fours, or any three cards of the same rank. **1850** *Bohn's Hand-Bk. Games* 329 At this game [Commerce] are three parts: 1st, That which takes place of all others, called the tricon, or three cards of the same denomination, similar to pair-royal at Cribbage.

triconodont (traɪˈkəʊnədɒnt), *a. Zool.* [f. TRI- + Gr. κῶνος cone + ὀδοντ- tooth: cf. CONODONT.] Having molar teeth with three conical cusps, as the extinct genus *Triconodon* or family *Triconodontidæ* of mammals (supposed to be marsupials); also said of such teeth. So **tricono'dontid**, an animal of this family; **tricono'dontoid** *a.*, belonging to or having the characters of this family; *sb.* = *triconodontid*; **tri'conodonty**, the condition of being triconodont.

1881 *Q. Jrnl. Geog. Soc.* XXXVII. 378 The fourth premolar of *Triacanthodon* approaches the triconodont or true molar type. **1895** *Funk's Standard Dict.*, Triconodontid, Triconodontoid. **1897** *Amer. Nat.* Dec. 998 The triconodont crown.. was predominant in the Lower Jurassic period. *Ibid.* 999 Both the 'haplodont' and 'triconodont' crowns are seen to-day among the Cetacea. **1899** *Proc. Zool. Soc.* 2 May 571 The famous theory of the gradual complication, of triconodonty and trituberculy, is an untenable hypothesis.

ˌtriconso'nantal, *a.* [f. TRI- + CONSONANTAL.] Consisting of or containing three consonants: said chiefly of the radical words of the Semitic languages. Hence **triconso'nantalism**, triconsonantal formation. So **triconso'nantic** *a.*

1863 *Smith's Bible Dict.* III. 1539/1 It is more than probable that the triconsonantal has been evolved out of a biconsonantal root. *Ibid.*, The bisyllabism [of the Hebrew verb] is in reality triconsonantalism, the vowels not forming any part of the essence of the root. **1869** FARRAR *Fam. Speech* iii. (1873) 88 The root of the Semitic verb is always triliteral, or rather triconsonantic.

tricontinental: see TRI- 1 a.

tricorn (ˈtraɪkɔːn), *a.* and *sb.* Also (as or after Fr.) tricorne. [ad. F. *tricorne* or L. *tricornis* three-horned, f. *tri-*, TRI- + L. *cornū* horn.]

A. *adj.* Three-horned; having three horns or horn-like projections; *spec.* applied to a cocked hat with the brim turned up on three sides.

1844 HOBLYN *Dict. Med. Terms*, *Tricorne*,.. a term applied to each lateral ventricle of the brain, from its three-horned shape. **1864** M. J. HIGGINS *Ess.* (1875) 201 With their tricorn hats they looked very much like Knaves of Spades. **1883** A. WALLIS in *N. & Q.* 6th Ser. VIII. 363/1 A white bob-wig surmounted by a tricorne hat completes the ordinary costume of a gentleman living in the second Georgian period. **1909** *Daily Graphic* LXXX. 13/1 An ermine tricorne hat.

B. *sb.*

1. An (imaginary) creature with three horns.

1760 *Impostors Detected* III. viii. II. 78 These creatures were distinguished.. by a lump on their heads,.. supported by three small protuberances; from whence they were called Tri-corns. **1823** [see BICORN]. **1895** F. E. HULME *Nat. Hist. Lore & Leg.* 147 What can have.. suggested the idea of such a very unpleasant tricorn, it is impossible to say.

2. A tricorn hat: see A.

1876 G. MEREDITH *Beauch. Career* ii, A shocking bad, bald, brown-rubbed old *tricorne*. **1903** J. CONRAD & HUEFFER *Romance* v. i, He wore a large and shadowy tricorn.

So †**tri'cornous** *a.* (*obs. rare*[−0]), three-horned.

1656 in BLOUNT *Glossogr.*

tri-cornered, -cornigerous, -cornute, etc.: see TRI- 1 c, 1.

tricorporal (traɪˈkɔːpərəl), *a.* [f. TRI- + L. *corpus, corpor-* body + -AL[1]: cf. *corporal.*] Having three bodies; three-bodied. So **tri'corporate, tri'corporated** *adjs.* in same sense, *spec.* in *Her.*: see quots.; also **tri'corporous** *a.* (*rare*[−0]).

1730–6 BAILEY (folio), **Tricorporal*, that hath three bodies. **1822** T. TAYLOR *Apuleius* III. 59 Coequal to the destruction of the tricorporal Geryon, or the three-headed Cerberus. **1731** BAILEY vol. II, **Tricorporate, Tricorporous*, that hath three bodies. *c* **1828** BERRY *Encycl. Her.* I. Gloss., *Tricorporate* is said when the bodies of three beasts are represented issuing from the dexter, sinister, and base points of the escocheon, and meeting conjoined to one head in the centre point. **1572** BOSSEWELL *Armorie* II. 42 *Tricorporated. **1610** GUILLIM *Heraldry* III. xv. (1611) 141 A Tricorporated Lion issuing out of the three corners of the Escocheon all meeting vnder one head. **1727** BAILEY vol. II, **Tricorporous*.

tricoryphean, -costate: see TRI- 1.

'tricosane, tri-'icosane. *Chem.* [f. Gr. τρία three + εἴκοσι twenty + -ANE.] A hydrocarbon belonging to the paraffin series, containing 23 atoms of carbon.

1894 MUIR & MORLEY *Watts' Dict. Chem.* IV. 793 *n*-Tri-icosane $C_{23}H_{48}$ (melting point 48°C.)... Obtained also by fractional distillation of paraffin oil from brown coal... Glittering plates. **1902** *Jrnl. Chem. Soc.* LXXXII. I. 734 Pennsylvania Petroleum.. furnished a small proportion of a solid tricosane, $C_{23}H_{48}$, which melts at 45°.

†**tricot**[1]. *Obs. rare*[−1]. [Allied to OF. *tricotage* chicanery, trickery (Godef. *Compl.*), *tricotement* chicane (*c* 1400 in Godef.), *tricoterie* 'cousenage, cheating, trecherie, deceit, in the following of a suit, etc.' (Cotgr.), which imply a vb. **tricoter* to cozen, cheat, and perh. a sb. **tricot*; but these do not appear in this sense, unless they are fig. uses of *tricoter* to knit, *tricot* knitting.] Trickery, fraud.

c **1430** *Pilgr. Lyf Manhode* III. xxvi. (1869) 150 The oother hand.. is cleped.. tricot.. and disceyuaunce.

‖**tricot**[2] (triko). [F. *tricot* knitting, knitted work, f. *tricoter* to knit; of uncertain origin.]

a. (*a*) Knitting; knitted work or fabric; a woollen fabric, knitted by hand, or by machinery in imitation of hand-knitting; (*b*) the name of a woollen fabric (see quot. 1904); (*c*) a pair of close-fitting knitted tights; (*d*) short for *tricot-stitch.*

1859 L. WRAXALL tr. *Robert-Houdin's Mem.* II. ix. 259 And the whole [false stomach] being concealed beneath a flesh-colour *tricot*, appeared to form part of his body. **1872** BROWNING *Fifine* iii, The human beauty.. Tricot fines down if fat, padding plumps up if lean. **1882** CAULFEILD & SAWARD *Dict. Needlework* 128/2 Make a Foundation chain.. and work a row of Tricot. **1893** A. ZIMMERN tr. *Blümner's Home Life Anc. Grks.* xii. 440 The costume and the tricots, as well as the grotesque masks, are worthy of notice. **1898** *Daily News* 5 Mar. 6/4 A mourning walking dress in woollen tricot. **1904** *Woollen Draper's Terms* in *Tailor & Cutter* 4 Aug. 480/1 *Tricots*, a woollen fabric, with diagonals running straight across the piece, and something like cassimere handle. **1926** *Spectator* 6 Feb. 219/1 Let us hope that the odious 'tricot', or tights, which create, by emphasizing, indecency have disappeared for ever—at any rate in Paris [music-halls].

b. *attrib.*, as ***tricot-stitch, -work.***

1880 *B'ham Weekly Post* 2 Oct. 1/5, I have an interminable piece of trico work in hand, which has been my resource for several years. **1882** CAULFEILD & SAWARD *Dict. Needlework* 128/1 *Tricot stitch*... The easiest of crochet stitches, but only suitable for straight work; it is usually worked with Berlin or fleecy wool, and a wooden hook, and is suitable for couvrepieds, counterpanes, muffatees, mufflers, and other warm articles.

†**tricotee**, *sb. Obs.* Also 7 trick-a-tee, 8 tricotez. [a. F. *tricotets*, also *tricotée* (Lamonnoye in Littré), f. *tricoter* to dance in a lively manner: origin uncertain.] A lively kind of old dance. Hence †**tricotee** *v.* (with *it*), to dance this. *Obs.*

1659 *Lady Alimony* I. ii. A iij b, A Monkey dancing his Trick-a-tee on a Rope. **1664** COTTON *Scarron.* IV. (1741) 120 Poor Dido.. tho' oppressed with Woe and Care, cut Capers, and Tricotee'd it barefoot. **1667** FLECKNOE *Damoiselles à la Mode* IV. ii. 80 The dancing Bears shall dance the Tricotees with him for a wager. *a* **1701** SEDLEY *Grumbler* II. i, Will you have a minuet, Sir?.. What then? (here he names half a dozen dances) The trocanny, tricotez, rigadon?

‖**tricoteuse** (trikɔtœz). Also Tricoteuse. [Fr.]

1. A woman who knits; applied *spec.* to women who, during the French Revolution, sat and knitted at meetings of the Convention or at guillotinings. Also *transf.*

1830 HAZLITT *Life of Napoleon Buonaparte* I. vi. 284 It was this [popular fury] that inspired the Furies of the Guillotine, and sat and smiled in the galleries of the Convention with the *tricoteuses* of Robespierre! *a* **1886** M. B. CHESNUT in C. V. Woodward *M. Chesnut's Civil War* (1981) viii. 183 Jenny Barron, Jenny Cooper and Mary Hammy have gone to have their photographs taken as 'Tricoteuses', each armed with their knitting. **1905** BARONESS ORCZY *Scarlet Pimpernel* i. 8 The old hags, 'tricotteuses' [*sic*] as they were called, who sat there and knitted, while head after head fell beneath the knife. **1940** M. DICKENS *Mariana* viii. 309 The eyes of the *tricoteuses* nearly came out of their heads, and the less hardened of them dropped a stitch. **1961** *Guardian* 19 Apr. 10/6 Is it fair that the Conservative Women's Conference should..be thought of as..a collection of elegant Tricoteuses? **1972** R. QUILTY *Tenth Session* I. 66 The inner circle around the victim, the eager *tricoteuses* who always collected at any drama on the streets. **1973** *Listener* 22 Nov. 727 The wife of the production manager..sits sourly knitting on set like a *tricoteuse* at the guillotine.

2. *Antiques.* (See quot. 1960.)

1960 H. HAYWARD *Antique Coll.* 287/2 *Tricoteuse* (Fr.), a term probably of 19th-cent. origin, applied to a small work-table surrounded by a gallery, part of which can be lowered to contain sewing materials. **1973** *Country Life* 30 Aug. (Suppl.) 72/2 Mahogany Tricoteuse with black line inlay. English, circa 1810.

Tricotine ('trɪkətiːn). Also tricotine. [f. TRICOT[2] + -INE[4].] A worsted fabric with a double twill.

A proprietary term in the U.S.

1914 *Official Gaz.* (U.S. Patent Office) 27 Oct. 1236/2 'Tricotine'... Woolen, Worsted, Silk, Mohair and Cotton Piece Goods and Piece Goods Made of a Combination of Two or More of Those Fibers. **1920** G. BELL *Let.* 10 Oct. (1927) II. xviii. 502 I've got bills for tricotine and things which Elsa kindly bought for me. **1921** *Daily Colonist* (Victoria, B.C.) 5 Oct. 8/6 Smartly fashioned dresses..of Tricotine and Serge, comprise this special offering. **1930** *Daily Express* 6 Oct. 6/1 (Advt.), Smart in every sense of the word in a tricotine finished faced-cloth.

tricotyledonous: see TRI- 1.

Tricouni (traɪ'kuːnɪ). Also tricouni. [Swiss trade name, app. f. TRI- + CO- + UNI-.] The proprietary name for a kind of climbing-boot nail with a serrated edge. (Now *disused.*)

1914 O. ECKSTEIN in *Climbers' Club Jrnl.* Mar. 77 (*title*) The Tricouni Nail. *Ibid.*, A new nail, bearing the above name, has lately been invented by a Swiss climber, Mr. F. Genecand; it is intended for nailing boots used on mountains. **1920** G. W. YOUNG *Mountain Craft* ii. 82 An even better nail appears to be the lately invented Tricouni nail. **1934** *Trade Marks Jrnl.* 3 Oct. 1276/1 Tricouni... Boot and shoe nails; and cleats and calks; all of ordinary metal. Tricouni S.A..., Geneva, Switzerland; manufacturers. **1946** J. E. Q. BARFORD *Climbing in Britain* ii. 20 Tricounis are better on snow and ice because the sharp edges bite in well. **1957** J. MASTERS *Far, Far the Mountain Peak* 143 They had spent those eight hours hanging by fingertips and tricounis over the Bowl. **1972** M. WOODHOUSE *Mama Doll* ii. 4 Boots nailed with what..are..called tricounis.

tri-county, tricresyl phosphate: see TRI- 1 b, 5 c.

tricquet, variant of TRIQUET *Obs.*

tricrotic (traɪ'krɒtɪk), *a. Physiol.* [f. TRI-, after DICROTIC; cf. Gr. τρίκροτος rowed with triple stroke, as a trireme.] Of the pulse or a sphygmographic tracing: Having or showing three undulations for each beat of the heart. ***tricrotic wave***, the third of such undulations. So **'tricrotism**, tricrotic condition; **'tricrotous** *a.* = *tricrotic.*

1876 tr. *Wagner's Gen. Pathol.* (ed. 6) 630 The pulse of aged persons is tricrotic. **1877** ROBERTS *Handbk. Med.* (ed. 3) II. 21 This form of pulsation is sometimes called tricrotous. **1890** BILLINGS, *Tricrotic wave*, the third curve of the sphygmogram. **1891** *Cent. Dict.*, Tricrotism. **1913** DORLAND *Med. Dict.* s.v. *Pulse, Tricrotic pulse*, one that is marked by three abnormally distinct sphygmographic waves to the pulse-beat.

tricrunodal, -crural: see TRI- 1.

tric-trac ('trɪk'træk). Also 7- trick-track. [a. F. *tric-trac*, †*trique-trac* (16th c. in Littré; cf. also *jeux de triquetactz*, Godef. *Compl.*); so called from the clicking sound made by the pieces in playing the game: F. *tric-trac*, an echoic word (15th c.), applied to various clicking noises.] An old variety of backgammon: = TICK-TACK *sb.* 2.

[**1653** URQUHART *Rabelais* II. vii. 41 The trictrac of the knocking Friars.] **1687** SEDLEY *Bellamira* IV. i, I lost three sets at back-gammon, and a tout at trick-track. **1690** R. DAVIES *Jrnl.* (Camden) 78, I taught them to play grand tric-trac. **1788** *Gentl. Mag.* Dec. 1071/1 One of the kinds of trictrac used in Europe. **1852** THACKERAY *Esmond* I. iv, He loved to play at cards and tric-trac with him. **1897** DOWDEN *Fr. Lit.* v. i. 336 The destiny of nations is satirically viewed as a vulgar game of trick-track.

attrib. **1800** MAR. EDGEWORTH *Belinda* xxx, There's Mrs. Delacour leading Miss Portman off into the trictrac cabinet. **1819** LAMB *Let. to Miss Wordsworth* 25 Nov., In the trick-track board, where the hits are figured.

tricube, tricurvate: see TRI- 4 a, 2.

tricuspid (traɪ'kʌspɪd), *a.* (*sb.*) [ad. L. *tricuspis, -cuspid-em* three-pointed, f. *tri-*, TRI- + *cuspis* point: cf. F. *tricuspide* (Littré).] Having three cusps or points. **a. tricuspid valve** or **valves** (*Anat.*): the valve consisting of three triangular segments (or, as otherwise regarded, the set of three triangular valves) which guards the opening from the right auricle into the right ventricle of the heart. Also *absol.* or as *sb.*; hence *attrib.*, as ***tricuspid murmur, obstruction, opening, regurgitation***, etc.

1670 *Phil. Trans.* V. 2097 We did also observe two Ventricles with the tricuspid [and] sigmoid-valves. **1834** J. FORBES *Laennec's Dis. Chest* (ed. 4) 547 In hypertrophy of the right ventricle..the thickening..is always a little greater in the vicinity of the tricuspid valves. **1872** HUXLEY *Physiol.* ii. 36 On the right side there are..three of these broad pointed membranes, whence the whole apparatus is called the tricuspid valve. **1877** ROBERTS *Handbk. Med.* (ed. 3) II. 10 Said to accompany tricuspid obstruction. *Ibid.* 43 Tricuspid Regurgitation. **1898** *Allbutt's Syst. Med.* V. 786 Valvular incompetence..at the tricuspid opening. *Ibid.* 869 We may notice occasionally..a tricuspid systolic murmur.

b. Of various structures, as a tooth, leaf, etc.: also *absol.* or as *sb.* a tricuspid tooth.

1849 *Florist* 212 There is something very striking..about their tricuspid petals, and quaint, lively markings. **1856** WOODWARD *Mollusca* III. 449 The central teeth are.. tricuspid in Loligo. **1881** J. ANDERSON *Scot. in Early Chr. T.* iii. 130 In the West Highland crosses they are..terminated by a peculiar conventional, tricuspid leaf.

So **tri'cuspidal, tri'cuspidate, tri'cuspidated** *adjs.* in same sense.

1822-34 *Good's Study Med.* (ed. 4) I. 520 The *tricuspidal valve, with the..sigmoid valve of the pulmonary artery.. never exhibit bony deposits. **1852** SALMON *Higher Plane Curves* vi. (1879) 253 The quartic is tricuspidal. **1752** J. HILL *Hist. Anim.* 11 The Brachionus, with..a *tricuspidate tail. **1881** BAKER in *Jrnl. Linn. Soc.* XVIII. 280 Stigma capitate, obscurely tricuspidate. **1822** J. PARKINSON *Outl. Oryctol.* 197 An inequivalved..shell; *tricuspidated at the base. *Ibid.* 275 Teeth of cartilaginous fishes..triangular, conical, single pointed, tricuspidated, tridentated.

tri'cussate, *a. Bot.* [irreg. f. DECUSSATE, with substitution of TRI- for *de-*.] (See quot.)

1900 B. D. JACKSON *Gloss. Bot. Terms*, *Tricussate*, used for whorls of three leaves each, the leaves of each whorl alternating with those above and below.

tricyanate, tricyanide: see TRI- 5 a.

tricycle ('traɪsɪk(ə)l), *sb.* [a. F. *tricycle*, used in sense 1 in 1827; in sense 2 in *Dict. Acad.* 1878; f. TRI- + Gr. κύκλος circle, wheel: cf. BICYCLE.]

†**1.** A three-wheeled coach or omnibus drawn by two horses, formerly used in Paris. *Obs.*

1828 *Chron.* in *Ann. Reg.* 185/1 Tricycles.—Christmas-day was rendered memorable to the Parisians by the starting of this new species of carriage... The tricycle is a kind of coach, mounted on three wheels; it is drawn by two horses only.

2. a. A velocipede with three wheels (now usually one in front and one on each side behind), driven by treadles actuated by the feet, or (***motor tricycle***) by a small motor attached.

1868 *London Society* Nov. 411 The tricycle, or three-wheeled Velocipede, is easier to guide and safer to use than the bicycle. **1881** *Philad. Record* No. 3459. 2 M. Trouve riding at ease through the streets of Paris upon a tricycle driven by stored-up electricity. **1896** Motor tricycle [see MOTOR A. 5]. **1902** *Encycl. Brit.* XXVII. 325 As far back as 1883 or 1884 the whole of Europe had been covered by women on tricycles.

attrib. and *Comb.* **1885** *Graphic* 21 Feb. 186/1 An Englishman..tricycle-riding the country. **1896** *Daily News* 28 May 3/2 Infantry bring up a tricycle Maxim gun.

b. A three-wheeled motorized invalid carriage.

1974 *Guardian* 26 Mar. 32/4 Disabled drivers' tricycles should be replaced with modified production cars. **1976** *Times* 24 July 1/7 Invalid tricycles are to be phased out... The existing 21,265 tricycle drivers will be able to keep their vehicles until they wear out.

c. An aeroplane with a three-wheeled undercarriage.

1942 *Tee Emm* (Air Ministry) II. 95 The pilot..strikes the sea at the normal three-point landing attitude (slow landing attitude for tricycles).

3. *Comb.* **tricycle undercarriage** *Aeronaut.*, a three-wheeled undercarriage; also **tricycle landing-gear**.

1938 *Sun* (Baltimore) 26 Sept. 13/5 The 'tri-safety' tricycle landing gear, with a nose wheel under the pilot's cockpit. **1960** *Economist* 31 Dec. 1382/2 Development of the tricycle landing gear has been the greatest single factor in making a flier out of a businessman. **1937** *Flight* 18 Nov. 483/1 (*heading*) Simplified control system for all-metal pusher with tricycle undercarriage. **1966** D. FRANCIS *Flying Finish* x. 129 The bump from the tricycle undercarriage as we touched down. **1976** *Official Programme Farnborough Internat. Exhib.* 28 The aircraft has a fixed tricycle undercarriage.

Hence **'tricycle** *v.*, *intr.* to ride a tricycle (whence **'tricycling** *vbl. sb.* and *ppl. a.*); **'tricycler, 'tricyclist**, one who rides a tricycle; **tri'cycular** *a.* [irreg. after *vehicular*; cf. BICYCULAR], pertaining to tricycles.

1883 *Sat. Rev.* 28 July 107/2 The modern heroine..rides, boats, *tricycles, and plays lawn-tennis. **1902** *19th Cent.* Nov. 764, I was tricycling homeward one evening. **1881** *Daily News* 18 July 5/5 Some member of Parliament should take the matter up, so as to relieve the steam *tricyclers from the restriction. **1888** J. & E. R. PENNELL *Sent. Journ.* 180 A meeting of tricyclers was not an every-day occurrence in their town. **1882** *Standard* 15 May 2/8 *Tricycling divisions of bicycle clubs. **1882** RICHARDSON in *Gd. Words* 177 Mr. Browning called my attention to tricycling as a healthful recreation. **1878** *Prospectus Bicycle Touring Club*, Any amateur Bicyclist or *Tricyclist—lady or gentleman—is eligible for election to the Bicycle Touring Club. **1887** *Times* 9 Apr. 5/5 The tricyclists were formed into the main column. **1870** *Belgravia* Feb. 444 The latest contrivance in that way comes more under the *tricycular head.

tricyclic (traɪ'sɪklɪk, -'saɪklɪk), *a.* (*sb.*) [f. Gr. τρι-, TRI- + κύκλος circle + -IC.]

1. *Bot.* Arranged in three whorls.

1900 in B. D. JACKSON *Gloss. Bot. Terms.*

2. *Chem.* **a.** Of a carbon compound: Having three rings or closed chains of atoms in its structural formula; e.g. phenanthrene. (Ger. *tricyklisch.*)

1891 *Jrnl. Chem. Soc.* LX. 1258 The two best known tricyclic compounds, anthracene and phenanthrene.

b. *spec.* in *Pharm.*, designating or pertaining to a group of antidepressant drugs based upon a molecular structure of three fused rings; also as *sb.*

1966 *Internat. Jrnl. Neuropharmacol.* V. 299 (*heading*) Association between biochemical and behavioral actions of tricyclic antidepressants. **1972** *Daily Tel.* 4 Mar. 32/3 He said pregnant women should steer clear of all drugs if possible, particularly drugs known as tricyclic anti-depressants. **1973** *Sci. Amer.* Sept. 121/2 The chemical structures of these two classes of antidepressants—the monamine oxidase inhibitors and the tricyclics—are quite different. **1980** J. WAINWRIGHT *Man of Law* i. 18, I suggested..a good tricyclic antidepressant.

‖**Tridacna** (traɪ-, trɪ'dæknə). *Zool.* [mod.L. (Da Costa 1776), f. Gr. τρίδακν-ος eaten at three bites, f. τρι-, TRI- + δάκν-ειν to bite.] A genus of bivalve molluscs, including the *Tridacna gigas* or Giant Clam, the largest bivalve shell known. Also *attrib.*

1776 DA COSTA *Conchol.* 294 A Tridacna, the Bason Conch or Clamp. **1860** WRAXALL *Life in Sea* xiv. 299 The giant Tridacna, which is five feet broad, forms entire submarine banks. **1904** *Athenæum* 24 Sept. 419/1 In graves at Rubiana were found rings of tridacna shell and other objects of the same material carved in a fretwork design.

So †**tridacnan** *a. Obs. rare*[−0].

1623 COCKERAM, *Tridacnan*, any thing that is so big that must be cut in three pieces, or morsels, ere it can be eat.

tridactyl (traɪ'dæktɪl), *a.* Also -yle. [ad. Gr. τριδάκτυλ-ος, f. τρι-, TRI- + δάκτυλος finger, digit.] Having three fingers or toes.

1812 SHAW *Gen. Zool.* VIII. 104 Tridactyle Kingfisher. **1822** J. PARKINSON *Outl. Oryctol.* 321 The feet of this animal were tridactyle. **1877** LE CONTE *Elem. Geol.* I. (1879) 431 Only three functional toes on the hind foot, which therefore formed a tridactyl track. **1912** *Return Brit. Museum* 179 A tridactyl Reptilian foot-print.

tri'dactylous, *a.* [f. as prec. + -OUS.]

1. = prec.

1828 in WEBSTER. **1851** MANTELL *Petrifact.* i. §3. 65 The foot-tracks are, for the most part, tridactylous (three-toed). **1856-8** W. CLARK *Van der Hoeven's Zool.* II. 379 Feet tridactylous, palmate, with hallux none.

†**2.** *Chem.* Applied to a compound of an atom of one element with 3 atoms of another, as SO_3. *Obs.*

1865 MANSFIELD *Salts* 483 The simple molecule Sn... does not imitate the molecule Sb. in forming tridactylous compounds either with O. or with H.

tridaily: see TRI- 3.

triddil, triddle: see TREADLE, TREDDLE.

‖**tride** (‖trid, traɪd), *a.* ? *Obs.* [F. *tride* 'terme de manège, vif, serré' (Littré), a. Eng. *tread* in sense 'gait, pace'.] (See quots.)

1727 BAILEY vol. II, *Tride* (with Horsemen), short and swift. *Tride-pace*, is a going of short and thick Motions, tho' united and uneasy. *Tride-career*, a fast Gallop that has its Times and Motions short and nimble. To work Tride.. upon Volts, is to mark his Time with his Haunches short and ready. [Also in later Dicts. and Cyclopædias.]

tride, obs. f. *tried*, pa. t. and pple. of TRY *v.*

tridecane ('traɪdɪkeɪn). *Chem.* [f. Gr. τρία three + δέκα ten + -ANE.] A colourless liquid hydrocarbon of the paraffin series, containing 13 atoms of carbon; its melting point is −6°C. and boiling point 234°C.

1894 MUIR & MORLEY *Watts' Dict. Chem.* IV. 793 Tridecane, $C_{13}H_{28}$. **1902** *Jrnl. Chem. Soc.* LXXXII. I. 733 Hydrocarbons in Pennsylvania Petroleum... Tridecane [etc.].

So **tridecyl** ('traɪdɪsɪl) [-YL], the radical ($C_{13}H_{27}$) contained in tridecane. Hence **tride'cylic** *a.* in ***tridecylic acid***, $C_{13}H_{26}O_2$; also called **tride'coic** or **trideca'toic acid**.

1868 WATTS *Dict. Chem.* V. 880 Tridecyl. **1880** *Jrnl. Chem. Soc.* XXXVIII. 34 Tridecylic, Pentadecoic, [etc.] Acids..The discovery of tridecoic and pentadecoic acids makes the list of fatty acids complete as far as stearic acid. **1913** THORPE *Dict. App. Chem.* (ed. 2) V. 529 Tridecatoic or Tridecylic Acid..crystallises in thin plates; m.p. 40·5°.

†**tride'cennary**, *a. Obs. rare*[−1]. [An irregular formation from L. *tredecim* thirteen.] Intended to mean: Of or pertaining to the number thirteen.

(By the form, it ought to mean 'Of thirteen years'.)

1783 ROBERTSON *Hist. Amer.* (ed. 4) III. 385 Computed.. first by what he calls a tridecennary progression of days from one to thirteen,..and then by a septenary progression of days from one to seven, making in all twenty.

ˌ**trideci'lateral**, *a. rare.* [irreg. f. L. *tredecim* thirteen + LATERAL.] Thirteen-sided.

1882 VINES *Sachs' Bot.* 205 The shoot itself may be said to be tri-, quadri-, quinqui-, octo-, trideci-lateral, &c.

tridecile, tridel: see TREDECILE, TREDDLE.

trident ('traɪdənt), *sb.* (*a.*) [ad. L. *tridens, trident-em*, f. *tri-* three + *dens, dent-em* tooth. Cf. F. *trident* (13-14th c. in Godef. *Compl.*).]

1. An instrument or weapon with three prongs. *esp.* **a.** A three-pronged fish-spear or sceptre as the attribute of the sea-god Poseidon or Neptune, also figured as borne by Britannia.

1599 NASHE *Lenten Stuffe* (1871) 18 In the swing of his trident he constituted two lord admirals ouer the whole navy of England. **1607** SHAKS. *Cor.* III. i. 256 He would not flatter Neptune for his Trident, Or Ioue, for's power to Thunder. **1612** DEKKER *Lond. Triumph.* Wks. 1873 III. 241 In his hand he holds a siluer Trident, or Three-forked Mace. **1697** DRYDEN *Æneid* I. 208 The God himself with ready trident stands, And opes the deep, and spreads the moving sands. **1849** JAMES *Woodman* vii, Some serrated at the edges like Neptune's trident. **1898** RAWLINGS *Brit. Coinage* 113 In 1797 we have the first English regal copper penny... Britannia seated to right, the union shield at her side, a palm branch in her right hand and a trident in her left.

b. A three-pronged spear used by the *retiarius* in ancient Roman gladiatorial combats.

1693 STEPNEY in Dryden *Juvenal* viii. (1697) 209 As Retiarius he Attacks his Foe; First waves his Trident ready for the throw, Next casts his Net. **1891** FARRAR *Darkn. & Dawn* xxxix, He flung down net and dagger and trident, and, retreating to the barrier, stood there with folded arms.

c. *fig.* or in *fig.* context.

1638 R. BAKER tr. *Balzac's Lett.* (vol. II.) 202 The Syllogisme, which by the saying of a Grecian is the Trident and Mace of Philosophie, is in your Writings all painted and perfumed. **1698** CONGREVE *Birth of Muse* 109 To Worlds remote, she [Britannia] wide extends her Reign, And wields the Trident of the stormy Main. **1804** A. DUNCAN (*title*) The British Trident; or, Register of Naval Actions. **1812** WELLESLEY *Parl. Deb.* 30 Nov., To concede the points.. would be to throw into her hands the trident of the main.

d. (With capital initial.) (*a*) The name of a type of U.S. nuclear-powered submarine designed to carry ballistic missiles; (*b*) a type of submarine-launched ballistic missile designed to be carried by a Trident submarine. Cf. *ULMS* s.v. U II. 5 a.

1972 *N.Y. Times* 17 May 25/2 The Navy's projected new nuclear submarine and missile, known until now as Ulms, has been renamed the Trident. **1975** *Bull. Atomic Scientists* (Chicago) XXXI. IV. 13 Trident—A proposed super-quiet, highly maneuverable sub designed to fire very long-range missiles. **1978** *Collier's Encycl. Year Bk.* 1977 102 A new submarine-launched ballistic missile.., the Trident, entered the flight test phase January 18. **1986** *Daily Tel.* 17 Nov. 16/1 Mrs Thatcher has returned from Camp David with the assurances she sought over Trident.

2. *transf.* Applied to something resembling a trident in shape or configuration, as a three-pronged fork, a piece of land with three promontories.

1730 SWIFT *Let. to Gay* 10 Nov., Tell her Grace, that the ill management of forks is not to be help'd when they are only bidential..her Grace hath cost me thirty pounds to provide Tridents for fear of offending her. **1869** TOZER *Highl. Turkey* I. 101 The two other peninsulas, which form the trident of Chalcidice.

3. *Geom.* Name of a plane cubic curve of a form suggesting a three-pronged weapon; also ***trident curve***. Also called *Cartesian parabola* (PARABOLA b).

1710 J. HARRIS *Lex. Techn.* II, *Trident* is a Name given by Sir Is. Newton to that kind of Parabola, by which D'Cartes constructed Equations of six Dimensions. **1795** HUTTON *Math. Dict.* II. 191 Cartesian Parabola..$xy = ax^3 + bx^2 + cx + d$..being Newton's 66th species of lines of the 3d order, and called by him a *Trident*. **1864** CAYLEY *Math. Papers* V. 364 The Trident Curve.

4. *attrib.* and *Comb.*, as ***trident-bearer, -swayer, tooth***; ***trident-armed, -bearing, -shaped*** adjs.

1866 J. CONINGTON *Æneid* I. 226 He, *trident-armed, each dull weight heaves. **1749** G. WEST *Odes Pindar* I. Antistr. v, Invocating oft the name Of the *Trident-bearing God. Strait the *Trident-bearer came. **1871** KINGSLEY *At Last* xiv, A curious *trident-shaped stand..on the horns of which garlands of flowers are hung as offerings. **1904** C. LANIER *Sonn.* in *Daily Chron.* 21 Apr. 3/2 *Trident-swayer of emotion's trembling sea! **1901** G. MEREDITH tr. *Iliad, Reading of Life* 128 The God drives deep his *trident teeth.

B. as *adj.* Having three prongs or forks; tridental. Also *fig.*

1589 GREENE *Menaphon* (Arb.) 24 Neptune..with his trident mace. **1648** EARL WESTMORELAND *Otia Sacra* (1879) 97 A Trident mischeif that doth wound, Requires a Treble Patience to afford Relief. **1864** [see 3 above]. **1910** *Expositor* Aug. 139 He is represented..hurling the trident lightning and with a huge club.

tridental (traɪ'dɛntəl), *a.*[1] [f. as prec. + -AL[1].]

†**1.** Bearing a trident. *Obs. rare.*

1635 QUARLES *Embl.* I. ii. iv, The white-mouth'd Water now usurpes the Shore, And scornes the pow'r of her trydentall Guide.

2. Of, pertaining to, or of the nature of a trident; three-pronged, trifurcate.

1648 GAGE *West Ind.* vii. 20 Catching one with a tridentall iron Fork. **1791** COWPER *Iliad* v. 458 The bold Son of Amphytrion with tridental shaft Her bosom pierced. **1843** R. H. HORNE *Orion* III. iii. 166 Now had Poseidon with tridental spear Torn up the smitten sea. **1892** *Graphic* 28 May 637/2 These picturesque tridental bays have contributed backgrounds to many of the artist's pictures.

tri'dental, *a.*[2] *rare*⁻⁰. = TRIDENTINE. Hence **tri'dentally** *adv.*, in accordance with the Tridentine decrees.

1842 G. S. FABER *Prov. Lett.* (1844) II. 49 A very possible advance, from the fourth century, to the yet more fully instructed, because tridentally instructed, sixteenth.

tridentate (traɪ'dɛntət), *a.* [f. TRI- + L. *dentāt-us* toothed: see -ATE[2] 2.] **1.** *Bot.* and *Zool.* Having three teeth or tooth-like processes; three-pronged, three-pointed.

1760 J. LEE *Introd. Bot.* II. xxii. (1765) 124 Corolla.. either..tridentate; or quinquedentate. **1852** DANA *Crust.* I. 662 The only species..have the front of the carapax deeply tridentate. **1856-8** W. CLARK *Van der Hoeven's Zool.* I. 313 Tarsi with tridentate claws.

2. *Chem.* Of a ligand: forming three separate bonds (usu. but not necessarily with the same central atom). Of a molecule or complex: formed by such a ligand.

1925 *Jrnl. Chem. Soc.* CXXVII. 2030 Werner also identified groups capable of treble attachment to metallic atoms, such tridentate residues containing three fused chelate groups. **1966** PHILLIPS & WILLIAMS *Inorg. Chem.* II. xxvii. 347 The cyclopentadienyl and benzene ligands are best regarded as tridentate and their transition-metal complexes are strongly stabilized in the sandwich symmetry only.

So †**tri'dentated** *a. Obs.* = sense 1 above.

1752 J. HILL *Hist. Anim.* 35 The grey Fly..with tridentated marks on the abdomen. **1822** J. PARKINSON *Outl. Oryctol.* 275 Numerous teeth of cartilaginous fishes.. triangular,..tricuspidated, tridentated.

tridented, *a.* [f. as TRIDENT + -ED.]

1. (traɪ'dɛntɪd). Three-toothed, three-pronged; = TRIDENTATE.

1620 QUARLES *Jonah* Sect. vi. Fij, Neptune..Held his tridented Mace vpon the South. **1816** *Encycl. Perthensis* V. 639/2 The pappus [is] monophyllous and tridented.

2. ('traɪdəntɪd). Having or furnished with a trident.

1624 QUARLES *Sion's Elegies* iii. 12 Tridented Neptune. **1866** J. B. ROSE tr. *Ovid's Met.* VIII. 236 Unto Neptune tridented I prayed.

†**tri'dentifer.** *Obs. rare.* [a. L. *tridentifer*, f. as TRIDENT + *-fer* bearing.] He who bears a trident; the wielder of the trident; Neptune.

1600 TOURNEUR *Transf. Metamorph.* xl, Is that great gift Tridentifer presents, To make faire passage for his foule intents?

So **triden'tiferous** *a.*, trident-bearing.

1656 in BLOUNT *Glossogr.* **1727** in BAILEY vol. II.

Tridentine ('trɪdəntaɪn, traɪ'dɛntaɪn), *a.* and *sb.* [ad. med.L. *Tridentīn-us*, f. *Tridentum* the city of Trent.] **A.** *adj.* Of or pertaining to the city of Trent in Tyrol, or to the Council of the Roman Catholic Church held there (1545-63).

1561 BARLOW in H. N. Birt *Eliz. Relig. Settlement* x. (1908) 424 Thomas Stapleton and Edward Goddeshalfe..as it is bruited were the last summer at Tridentine Council. *a* **1711** KEN *Hymnarium* Poet. Wks. 1721 II. 134 The Faith Nicene he spake exact, But when to that the Tridentine he tack'd, This a new Gospel is. **1849** SIR J. STEPHEN *Eccl. Biogr.* (1850) I. 475 The most promising quarrel which had arisen in the Church since the close of the Tridentine Council. **1901** BP. GORE *Body of Christ* iv. §4 (1907) 257 When they [Protestants] rejected the Tridentine doctrine of the Melchizedekian priesthood.

B. *sb.* One who accepts and conforms to the decrees of the Council of Trent; an orthodox Roman Catholic.

a **1836** R. H. FROUDE *Rem.* (1838) I. 434 [In answer to the statement that] the Romanists were Schismatics in England, but Catholics abroad, [Froude replied] No, they are wretched Tridentines every where. *a* **1882** *Dublin Rev.* (Ogilvie), Anglicans have styled Catholics of the present day Tridentines.

So **'Tridentize** *v. rare, intr.* to conform to the Tridentine decrees.

1826 G. S. FABER *Diffic. Romanism* (1853) 110 [It] is evident to common sense, and will readily be admitted by the tridentising Romanist.

ˌtride'rivative. *Chem. rare.* [TRI- 5 c.] A derivative containing three substituted atoms of radicals of the same kind; a tri-substitution product.

1875 *Jrnl. Chem. Soc.* XXVIII. 567 Contributions to our knowledge of the Connection between the Bi- and Tri-derivatives of Benzene. **1891** *Cent. Dict.* s.v., Trichloracetic acid is a triderivative of acetic acid.

tridge, dial. and obs. form of TRUDGE *v.*

tridiametral, -diapason, -digital, etc.: see TRI- 1, 4 a.

tri-dimensional (traɪdɪ'mɛnʃənəl, -daɪ-), *a.* [f. TRI- 1 a + DIMENSIONAL.] Having or exhibiting three dimensions, as a solid body.

1858 *Q. Jrnl. Math.* II. 182 An analogous method of transformation is applicable to tridimensional space. **1875** CAYLEY in *Phil. Trans.* CLXV. 678 Theorem C, in the particular case of tridimensional space. **1894** *Nation* (N.Y.) 23 Aug. 145/1 The tridimensional graphs of Wislicenus. **1906** *Athenæum* 19 May 612/3 An ingenious series of star charts..which when looked at through red and green spectacles exhibit the stars as appearing in tri-dimensional space.

Hence **tridimensio'nality**, the condition or quality of being of three dimensions (in quot. 1894 loosely used); also **tridi'mensionally** *adv.*

1894 *Nation* (N.Y.) 13 Sept. 192/2 There are three fundamental color-sensations..; but there is nothing corresponding to this tri-dimensionality in the vibrations themselves. **1901** TITCHENER *Exper. Psychol.* I. ix. 138 The two figures will approach each other, and at last will overlap. .. At the moment of complete overlapping, the cone stands out with an almost startling tridimensionality. **1919** R. T. BROWNE *Mystery of Space* vii. 240 Trace out the biologic development of each mental faculty..and it will be found that..the nature of each of these has been to express itself tridimensionally. **1956** H. READ *Art of Sculpture* v. 102 One of the most striking developments in our time has been in the direction of linear sculpture, another apparent contradiction of terms that can be justified in so far as the lines are used tridimensionally to indicate volume.

triding: see TRITHING.

Tridione (traɪ'daɪəʊn). *Pharm.* [f. TRI- + -DIONE.] A proprietary name for an analgesic agent (also called *troxidone*).

1944 RICHARDS & EVERETT in *Federation Proc.* III. 39/2 Preliminary clinical investigations have shown that Tridione is an effective analgesic. **1948** *Official Gaz.* (U.S. Patent Office) 24 Feb. 607/1 *Tridione*... For anticonvulsant intended for use in treatment of the petit mal triad and other convulsive disorders. **1948** *Trade Marks Jrnl.* 25 Feb. 141/2 *Tridione*... Therapeutic compounds being alkyl derivatives of diketo oxazolidine. Abbott Laboratories.., City of North Chicago,..manufacturers. **1974** M. C. GERALD *Pharmacol.* xi. 212 Trimethadione (Tridione) was originally synthesized as an aspirin substitute; however, its lack of dependable analgesia caused it to be rapidly discarded for this purpose. **1979** R. JAFFE *Class Reunion* I. ix. 95 Time to get to the pharmacy.., fill her prescriptions for Dilantin and Tridione.

tridiurnal (traɪdaɪ'ɜːnəl), *a.* [f. TRI- 3 + DIURNAL.] **a.** Comprising three days.

1828 J. STERLING *Ess.*, etc. (1848) II. 45 Various minor periods,..monthly, weekly, tridiurnal, and daily.

b. Occurring three times a day.

1884 *Athenæum* 10 May 602/1 He..commenced to make tridiurnal meteorological observations and to issue a daily weather report.

tri-dodecahedral: see TRI- 2 b.

‖**tri-do'minium.** [In form mod.L., f. TRI- + L. *dominium* lordship, rule, DOMINION.] The joint rule of three powers or states: applied to the former rule of Gt. Britain, Germany, and the United States in Samoa, and of Great Britain, Greece, and Turkey in Cyprus.

1899 *Westm. Gaz.* 1 Mar. 2/3 Herr von Bülow..is reported to have said with regard to Samoa that the Tri-dominium had failed. **1900** *Edin. Rev.* Apr. 499 The break up of the unworkable tridominium..has been satisfactory to all parties. **1955** *Times* 25 July 7/7 The second scheme is, broadly, that the island should be turned into some form of 'tri-dominium' with, perhaps, a British Governor and one Greek and one Turkish deputy Governor, and with all three national flags flying over Government House. **1958** *Times* 20 June 11/2 The next stage may be independence, condominium, or even the perpetuation of tridominium, but it can scarcely be absorption by either Greece or Turkey.

tridrachm ('traɪdræm). *Gr. Antiq.* [ad. Gr. τρίδραχμον, f. τρι-, TRI- + δραχμή DRACHM.] A silver coin of ancient Greece, of the value of three drachms: see DRACHM 1.

1771 RAPER in *Phil. Trans.* LXI. 469 Their larger Coins above the Drachm were, the Didrachm, the Tridrachm, and the Tetradrachm. **1827** ROBINSON *Archæol. Græca* V. xxvi. (ed. 2) 550, 3 dr[achmæ] or tridrachm, 1/11¼. **1842** *Smith's Dict. Grk. & Rom. Antiq.* s.v. *Drachma*, Among those [silver coins] now preserved, the tetradrachm is commonly found; but we possess no specimens of the tridrachm, and only a few of the didrachm.

triduan ('traɪdjuːən), *a.* Also 7 **-ane.** [ad. L. *trīduān-us*, f. *trīduum*: see below and -AN.] Lasting for three days (in quot. 1600 *transf.*); also, occurring every third day.

1597 J. KING *On Jonas* (1618) 299 The triduan rest of Christ in the graue, must bee vnderstood by the figure *synecdoche*, a part put for the whole. **1600** W. WATSON *Decacordon* (1602) 48 To raise a triduane Lazarus from death to life againe. **1658** PHILLIPS, *Triduan*, (Lat.) continuing three dayes. **1755** JOHNSON, *Triduan*, 1. Lasting three days. 2. Happening every third day.

‖**triduo** ('traɪdjuːəʊ). *R. C. Ch.* [It. and Sp. *triduo*:—L. *trīduum*: see below.] A three days' prayer or festal celebration.

1848 MANNING *Jrnl.* in *Life* (1895) I. xix. 402 Then was sung the *Veni Creator* (a triduo for the Roman State at this time). **1869** *Life of Marg. M. Hallahan* (1870) 473 We are meditating a great Triduo to our Holy Mother. **1871** *Echo* 28 Feb., The Cardinal Vicar is at present occupied in getting up triduos for the tercentenary of the Battle of Lepanto.

‖**triduum** ('traɪdjuːəm). [L. *trīduum*, prop. neut. of **trīduus* adj. (sc. *spatium*), f. *tri-*, TRI- + *diēs* day.] **a.** A period of three days; *esp.* in *R. C. Ch.* the last three days of Lent. **b.** = TRIDUO.

1873 G. M. HOPKINS *Jrnl.* 9 Feb. (1959) 230 Began a triduum. **1883** SCHAFF *Hist. Church* II. XI. lxxi. 525 The mysterious triduum between the crucifixion and the resurrection. **1885** *Pall Mall G.* 7 Nov. 7/2 Yesterday there commenced at the Church of the Servite Fathers..a Triduum to celebrate an event of interest in the early history of our Royal family. **1910** *Universe* 3 June 9/1 A solemn Triduum in honour of the feast of Corpus Christi was preached in St. Mary's Cathedral, Edinburgh.

tridymite (ˈtrɪdɪmaɪt). *Min.* [ad. Ger. *tridymit* (vom Rath 1866), f. Gr. τρίδυμος threefold, f. τρι-, TRI- + -δυμ-ος, as in δίδυμος twin; named in allusion to its compound forms consisting of three individual crystals.] A crystallized form of silica, occurring in small hexagonal tables, found in trachyte and other igneous rocks.

1868 DANA *Min.* (ed. 5) 805 Tridymite occurs in small hexagonal tables, colorless and transparent, which are usually compound, and mostly of three individuals. **1888** RUTLEY *Rock-Forming Min.* 130 Tridymite is essentially a volcanic mineral.

tridynamous: see TRI- 1.

trie, trielie, early forms of TRY *a.*, TRYLY.

trie, obs. form of TREE, TRY *v.*

tried (traɪd), *ppl. a.* [f. TRY *v.* + -ED[1].]

1. Separated from the dross or refuse; of metals: purified, refined; of fat: rendered, clarified; of an egg-yolk: separated from the white; of flour, etc.: sifted, bolted, fine. Mostly *Obs.*

tried out, said of a whale the blubber of which has been cut off, melted down, and run into casks.

13.. *K. Alis.* 828 (Bodl. MS.) Riche rede Itried golde. **13..** *Coer de L.* 6342 Tryyd sylvyr and tresore fyn. **1382** WYCLIF *Ex.* xvi. 31 The taast of it as of tryed floure with hony. *c* **1430** *Two Cookery-bks.* 51 Take fayre y-tryid ȝolkys Raw, & Sugre, an pouder Gyngere. **1611** COTGR., *Argerite*, the (Siluer-coloured) foame of tried lead. **1627** CAPT. SMITH *Seaman's Gram.* xv. 75 Legs of Mutton..with tried sewet or butter. **1639** T. DE GRAY *Compl. Horsem.* 304 Take..of old tryed hogs grease one pound.

†**2. a.** Chosen, select, choice; excellent. *Obs.*

13.. *E.E. Allit. P.* B. 1317 He trussed hem in his tresorye in a tryed place. **1362** LANGL. *P. Pl.* A. I. 126 Treuþe is tresour triedest on eorþe. *c* **1400** *Destr. Troy* 1840 Fro Priam, full prist,..That in Troy truly is a triet kyng. *Ibid.* 10842 A tryet ost Of grekes..were gedrit. **1581** A. HALL *Iliad* v. 97 Dame Iuno of the tryed horsse in hand doth take the raynes.

†**b.** As *sb.* Distinguished one. *Obs.*

c **1400** *Destr. Troy* 13791 To the toumbe of þat tried truly ho yode.

3. a. Proved or tested by experience or examination.

c **1412** HOCCLEVE *De Reg. Princ.* 2097 Deth hath but smal consideracioun Vnto þe vertuous,..No more..Than to a vicious maistir losel tried. *c* **1440** *Promp. Parv.* 502/2 Tryyd, ..*probatus, examinatus.* **1508** KENNEDIE *Flyting w. Dunbar* 513 Cankrit Caym, tryit trowane, Tutiuillus. **1583** STUBBES *Anat. Abus.* II. (1882) 100 Choose foorth certeine persons of a tried conuersation. **1604** G[RIMSTONE] *D'Acosta's Hist. Indies* II. vii. 95 It is approoved by many tryed experiences. **1724** DE FOE *Mem. Cavalier* (1840) 277 He [was] an old tried soldier. **1760** R. BROWN *Compl. Farmer* II. 17 My design is ..to promote tried experiments. **1841** W. SPALDING *Italy* III. 82 Public men of tried abilities.

b. Phr. ***tried and true***, proved reliable by experience.

1954 W. FAULKNER *Fable* 352 His enslavement to the demonic progeny of his own mechanical curiosity, from which he will emancipate himself by that one ancient tried-and-true method by which slaves have always freed themselves: by inculcating their masters with the slaves' own vices. **1967** *Listener* 6 Apr. 474/3 Miss Aukin had had the good sense to use the tried and true concealment gambit by which eventually two young officers, bent on cuckolding a greengrocer, were compelled to hide in the same grandfather clock. **1979** *Tucson Mag.* Apr. 47/1 A beautifully made 'period' movie, written and directed by tried-and-true Michael Crichton.

Hence †**'triedly** *adv. Obs.*, in a tried manner; choicely; experiencedly.

c **1400** *Destr. Troy* 3054 Hir tethe þat tryetly were set, Alse qwyte & qwem as any qwalle bon. *Ibid.* 10583 þai tild vp a toure, triedly wroght. **14..** *Langland's P. Pl.* B. Prol. 14, I seigh a toure on a toft trielich [*MS. O.* triedliche] ymaked. **1549** COVERDALE, etc. *Erasm. Par. 1 Peter* iv. 12 That thing ..whyche wente long ago before in the triedly proued prophetes. **1557** *Tottell's Misc.* (Arb.) 141 So triedly did he treade..That fortune found no place to geue him once a check.

triedral, obs. variant of TRIHEDRAL.

tri-elementary: see TRI- 1.

triene (ˈtraiːn). *Chem.* [f. TRI- + -ENE.] Any organic compound containing three double bonds between carbon atoms.

1917 *Chem. Abstr.* XI. 3031 These hydrocarbons give exaltations greater than those of the aromatic series: with the trienes the difference is proportionally greater than with the dienes. **1936** [see *diene value* s.v. DIENE b]. **1976** *Nature* 22 Apr. 726/2 We recorded the laser Raman spectrum of vitamin D_3 (in CCl_4), which has a conjugated triene structure.

†**tri'ennal,** *a.* and *sb. Obs. rare.* Also 4 tri-, tryenal(e, -ennal(e, -el, trinel. [ad. med.L. *triennāl-e* (sc. *officium*), neuter of *triennālis* of three years: cf. F. *triennal* (16th c.).]

A. *adj.* = TRIENNIAL. *rare*$^{-0}$.

1611 COTGR., *Triennal*, triennall, of three yeares.

B. *sb.* A dispensation or indulgence for three years. (In 14th c. a disyllable = ˈ*trīnal.*)

1362 LANGL. *P. Pl.* A. VIII. 157 [I] diuinede þat Dowel Indulgence passede, Bienals and Trienals and Busschopes lettres. *Ibid.* 166 Bote trustene to Trienals [B. VII. 170 triennales; C. x. 330 triennels] treuly me þinkeþ Is not so syker for þe soule sertes, as do-wel. *c* **1380** WYCLIF *Sel. Wks.* III. 400 Biggynge of beneficis, of indulgensis and trinels, pardouns, and veyne privilegies.

triennial (traɪˈɛnɪəl), *a.* and *sb.* Also 7 **tryenniall, triennuall,** 8 **trienial.** [f. L. *trienni-s* of three years, *trienni-um* a space of three years (f. *tri-*, TRI- + *annus* year) + -AL[1]. Cf. prec.]

A. *adj.* **1.** Existing or lasting for three years, three-years'; changed every three years.

Triennial Act (*Eng. Hist.*), an act of 1640, limiting the duration of parliament to three years; also the name given to an act of 1694, following an earlier one of Charles II, providing against any longer intermissions of parliament than three years. Cf. sense 2.

1640 *Jrnls. Ho. Comm.* II. 83 Amendments..to the Bill of Triennial Parliaments. **1643** PRYNNE *Sov. Power of Parl.* II. 25 The Admiralls Patents (which anciently were..but annuall or Triennuall at most). *c* **1645** HOWELL *Lett.* (1650) I. 70 My friends, whom I so much long to see after this triennial separation. **1701** *Lond. Gaz.* No. 3756/9 Whenever the Dissolution of this Present..Parliament shall happen, either by Virtue of the Trienial Act, or Prerogative Royal. **1807** HORSLEY *Serm.* (1812) II. 316 We, in the writings of the evangelists have a complete summary of his [Christ's] triennial preaching. **1863** H. COX *Instit.* I. vi. 35 The Triennial Act of William III limited the duration of Parliament to three years at the furthest.

2. Recurring every three years.

1642 HOWELL *For. Trav.* (Arb.) 77 If these Lights grow dim, there is a Trienniall Snuffer for them. **1663** BLAIR *Autobiog.* v. (1848) 77 Primate Usher's triennial visitation. **1782** T. WARTON *Hist. Kiddington* 8 To the bishop for Procurations, on account of his triennial visitation. **1821** MISS MITFORD in L'Estrange *Life* (1870) II. vi. 140 We have been very gay..with our triennial theatricals. **1872** YEATS *Growth Comm.* 182 There was a triennial change of officers.

B. *sb.* **1.** A period of three years; a triennium.

1661 *Sir H. Vane's Politics* 13 During our Principality, which breathed out many Triennials. **1892** *Min. Nat. Counc. Congr. Ch.* (U.S.) 143 No other triennial in the history of the society has a tithe of the work in the way of.. printed appeals.

2. An event recurring every three years; *spec.* the visitation of his diocese by a bishop every three years.

1640 *Archdeaconry of Essex Minutes* 29 July (MS.) We were this day inhibited for the Bp's. of London's tryenniall, by Gilson. **1724** BP. DOWNES in *Nicolson's Epist. Corr.* 576 The expence of the Triennial may leave your pocket empty.

Hence **trienni'ality** [cf. F. *triennalité*], the condition of being triennial.

1806 W. TAYLOR in *Ann. Rev.* IV. 240 The parliament.. produced fewer great men during its trienniality, than since the prolongation. **1817** BENTHAM *Parl. Reform* Introd. (1818) 283 Moderate reform insists at stopping at the stage indicated by the word trienniality.

triennially (traɪˈɛnɪəlɪ), *adv.* [f. TRIENNIAL *a.* + -LY[2].] Every three years; once in three years.

1689 in *6th Coll. Papers rel. Pres. Juncture* 25 The Parliament to be chosen Triennially, and to meet Annually. **1727** BAILEY vol. II, Triennially. **1806** W. TAYLOR in *Ann. Rev.* IV. 714 It appears that the tithe ought to be levied triennially. **1881** *Chamb. Jrnl.* No. 914. 419/1 The gorgeous festival given..triennially at the Crystal Palace.

†**'trienniated,** *a. Obs. rare.* [f. L. *trienni-um* (see below) + -ATE + -ED.] Made triennial. (In quot., as the second element of a compound.)

1661 *Sir H. Vane's Politics* 8 By obliging sundry eminent Chieftans of our long-trienniated Assembly.

‖**triennium** (traɪˈɛnɪəm). [L., prop. neuter of **triennius* adj. (sc. *spatium*), f. *tri-*, TRI- + *ann-us* year.] A space or period of three years.

1847 BUNSEN *Church of Future* v. 119 The first theological examination follows upon the academical triennium. **1876** BOURNE *Life Locke* I. ii. 52 He adopted the less usual course of shortening his triennium by two terms. **1894** *Nation* (N.Y.) 14 June 444/1 Just home from his triennium in Germany.

‖**triens** (ˈtraɪɛnz). Pl. **trientes** (traɪˈɛntiːz). [L., = third part.] The third part of anything; *spec.* in *Rom. Antiq.* a copper coin worth one-third of the as; also in later times, a gold coin, one-third of the aureus: cf. next.

1601 HOLLAND *Pliny* XXXIV. xiii. II. 513 The Servilij.. have among them a certaine peece of brasse coine called a Triens (*i.* the third part of a Romane Asse) which they doe keepe and feed with silver and gold... I will set downe..the verie words of old Messala: The house (quoth he) of the Servilij hath a certaine sacred Trient. **1693** tr. *Blancard's Phys. Dict.* (ed. 2), *Triens*, the third part of a physical Pound. **1706** PHILLIPS (ed. Kersey), *Triens* (Lat.), the third part of the Roman Pound, or Coin call'd *As*, weighing four Ounces: Or the third of any entire Thing divisible into twelve Parts.

†**trient.** *Obs.* [ad. L. *triens, trient-em* third part.] **a.** The ancient Roman copper coin called *triens*: see prec. **b.** An angle of 120°, comprising one-third of the circumference of a circle; in *Astrol.* = TRINE B. 2 (also *adj.* = TRINE A. 2).

1563 HYLL *Art Garden.* (1593) 24 When they are asunder 120 degrees, which is called a triangle, Trygon, or Trient aspect. **1601** [see TRIENS]. **1657** TOMLINSON *Renou's Disp.* 160* Three ounces..or at most a trient, that is four ounces. **1657** *Physical Dict.*, *Trient*, a third part. **1673** WALLIS in Rigaud *Corr. Sci. Men* (1841) II. 570 If the angle be more than a trient, and less than two trients, whose subtendant.. I suppose to be the chord of a trient increased by one of the arches.

†**tri'ental,** *a.* and *sb. Obs. rare.* [ad. L. *trientālis* f. *triens, trient-em*: see TRIENT and -AL[1].]

A. *adj.* Pertaining to or constituting a third part (e.g. ⅓ of a foot in length, of a pound in weight, etc.).

1656 BLOUNT *Glossogr.*, *Triental* (*trientalis*), of or being four inches broad or ounces in weight. **1891** *Cent. Dict.*, *Triental*, *a.* of the value of a triens; of or pertaining to the triens, or third part.

B. *sb.* An ancient Roman drinking-vessel containing one-third of a *sextarius*.

1656 BLOUNT *Glossogr.*, *Triental* (Lat.), a vessel containing the third part of *Sextarius*, half our Pint. **1789** MADAN tr. *Persius* iii. (1795) 91 But a trembling comes on whilst at his wine, and the warm triental He shakes out of his hands.

triequal: see TRI- 2.

trier (ˈtraɪə(r)). Forms: 4-5 **triour,** 5 **tryoure,** 6 **trior, tryar,** 7 **triar,** 6- **trier, tryer;** in senses 2 and 4, also 6-8 **triour,** 7 **tryor,** 8-9 **trior.** [f. TRY *v.* + -ER[1]; in the early form *triour*, a. AF. **triour* (-OUR) in legal use. Cf. F. *trieur*.]

1. One who examines and determines a cause or question; one who examines judicially; a judge.

c **1330** R. BRUNNE *Chron.* (1810) 250 þe triours alle þat caste, & put þer saw tille on. **1472** *Coventry Leet Bk.* 382 These persons folowyng be ordeyned & chosen to be triours within þis Cite to determyn variances betwixt parties within þis Cite as touchyng metes & bondes & Gutters & such oþer. *a* **1586** SIDNEY *Arcadia* III. Wks. 1724 II. 693 The almighty powers, whom I invoke as triers of mine innocency, and witnesses of my well-meaning. **1645** *Ordinance* in Neal *Hist. Purit.* (1736) III. 293 That certain persons be appointed Triers..to determine the validity of Elections. **1650-60** *Free Parl.-Letany* iii, From Vow-breakers & King-tryers—Libera nos, Domine! **1809** JEFFERSON *Writings* (1830) IV. 128 The testimony..is the more grateful, as proceeding from eye-witnesses and observers, from triers of the vicinage. **1821** SCOTT *Kenilw.* xi, To get old Gaffer Pinnie-winks, the trier of witches,..to comprehend Wayland Smith. **1821-30** LD. COCKBURN *Mem.* ii. (1874) 101 A dexterous and practical trier of ordinary cases. **1885** DIXON *Hist. Ch. Eng.* III. 377 The bishop himself was to be the chief trier.

2. *pl.* Two persons appointed by a court of law to determine whether a challenge made to the panel of jurors, or to any of them, is well founded.

[*a* **1377** *Rolls of Parlt.* II. 400/1 Sur quele chose furent esleuz Triours par la Court, qe disoient qe le Viscounte fust eidaunt et bien voillant a la partie du dit Evesqe.] **1511** in W. H. Turner *Sel. Rec. Oxford* (1880) 4 He commawnded the ij tryarse in the King's name to tell Hullys parte owt of the dore [of the gildhall]. *c* **1570** *Pride & Lowl.* (1841) 18 Ye shall have triers two or three, That shall judge of their [jurymen's] indifferencie. **1665** EVER *Tryals per Pais* ix. 128 When any challenge is made to the Polls, two tryors shall be appointed by the Court, and if they try one indifferent, and he be sworn, then he and the two tryors shall try another. **1768** BLACKSTONE *Comm.* III. xxiii. 363. **1863** H. COX *Instit.* II. iii. 354 Two triers appointed by the Court.

3. *Hist. pl.* A committee appointed by the King to determine to which court petitions should be referred, and if necessary, to report them to the parliament. The practice was disused in 1886.

[**1332** *Rolls of Parlt.* II. 68/1. **1485** *Ibid.* VI. 268/1 Et sount assignez Triours des Petitions de Gascoigne, et d'autres Terres et Paiis de par dela, et des Isles [names follow].] **1844** T. E. MAY *Treat. Parl.* xix. 301 Receivers and triers of petitions were appointed... The triers were committees of prelates, peers, and judges [etc.]... By them the petitions were examined... The functions of receivers and triers of petitions have long since given way to the immediate authority of Parliament at large. **1878** STUBBS *Const. Hist.* §757 III. xx. 452 As soon as the opening speech of the chancellor was ended, the names of the receivers and triers of petitions were read by the clerk of the crown. The receivers were clerks or masters in chancery; the triers were selected by the king from the list of the lords spiritual, the lords temporal, and the justices. [**1886** *Jrnls. Ho. Lords* CXVIII. 19/2 Les Triours des Petitions, etc. as in 1485.]

4. *pl.* Members of the House of Lords sitting as a jury at the trial of a peer for treason or felony. In full, ***Lords triers.***

1539 *Act 31 Hen. VIII*, c. 10. §9 Peres that shalbe called hereafter to be triours of suche treasons. **1596** WARNER *Alb. Eng.* x. lvi. (1612) 246 These Noble Tryers, iustly then examining the Cause. **1676** C. HATTON in *Hatton Corr.* (Camden) 134 Ther were 31 Lords tryers present. **1794** BURKE *Rep. Lords' Jrnls.* Wks. 1842 II. 607 A course of precedents, in a legal court, composed of a peer for judge, and peers for triers. **1831** MACKINTOSH *Hist. Eng.* II. vii. 198 Queen Anne and her brother Rochford were tried..before the duke of Norfolk,..assisted by twenty-six 'lords triers', who in some degree performed the functions of jurors in this tribunal. **1849** MACAULAY *Hist. Eng.* vi. II. 39 The high steward was sole judge of the law; and the lords triers formed merely a jury to pronounce on the question of fact. Jeffreys was appointed high steward. **1855** *Ibid.* xviii. IV. 158 The Lords insisted that every peer should be entitled to be a Trier. The Commons were with difficulty induced to consent that the number of Triers should never be less than thirty six.

5. *Church Hist.* One of a body of commissioners appointed in 1654 'for the approbation of all public preachers and lecturers before their admission to benefices'. Also *transf.*

1655 *Clarke Pap.* (Camden) III. 53 His Highnesse..left Mr. Cordwell, the minister, to bee concluded by the Tryers of London. **1657** [see EJECTOR 1]. **1664** BUTLER *Hud.* II. II. 813 And do they not as Triers sit To judge what Officers are fit? *a* **1691** BAXTER in *Reliq.* (1696) 72. **1691** WOOD *Ath. Oxon.* I. 861 Afterwards he enjoyed two livings successively without examination by the Tryers. **1808** W. WILSON *Hist. Dissent. Ch.* I. 471 The Commissioners were in all thirty-eight..and were commonly known by the name of Tryers. **1862** VAUGHAN *Nonconformity* 186 The number of ministers ejected by the Triers was considerable.

6. An umpire in sports or games. Now *dial.*

1607 MARKHAM *Caval.* III. (1617) 79 These Tryers are certaine indifferent Gentlemen, chosen by both the parties that make the match, who are to see that there be faire play, and that the Articles be fully performed on both parties. **1747** J. RELPH *Poems* 16 At spworts, if I was trier. **1826** *Sporting Mag.* XVIII. 321 A trier, or stickler as he is commonly called, is an umpire. **1888** ELWORTHY *W. Somerset Word-bk.*, *Trier*, the umpire at a wrestling, cudgel-playing, or any other match.

7. One who or that which tests or proves something; a power; a tester or test.

a **1483** *Liber Niger Edw. IV* in *Househ. Ord.* (1790) 75 This seyde sergeaunt, or the yoman tryoure, or the groome tryoure,..dayly to be redye in the hall. **1538** ELYOT, *Spectatores*, beholders, triers of money. *a* **1541** WYATT *Poet. Wks.* (1861) 169 Of good and bad the tryers are these twain. **1552** HULOET, Tryers, *comprobatores.* **1607** SHAKS. *Cor.* IV. i. 4 You were vs'd To say, Extreamities was the trier of spirits. **1610** BP. CARLETON *Jurisd.* Pref., When it was examined by vnskilfull and deceitfull triars,..taking vpon them to be triars of truth. **1712** BUDGELL *Spect.* No. 307 ¶7 There should be certain Triers or Examiners..to inspect the Genius of every particular Boy. **1760** *Cautions to Officers of Army* 162 There was formerly in the Army, particularly in Queen Ann's Time, a Sett of Officers in most Corps, who were called Provers, or Tryers; these upon a young Officer's joining the Regiment,..without any Cause picked a Quarrel with him: when, if the young Man acquitted himself with Honour, and escaped with Life, he passed the Rest of his Time quietly enough. **1796** CAPT. BOWEN in *Naval Chron.* XXIII. 368, I ordered one gun to be fired, as a trier of her intention. **1817–18** COBBETT *Resid. U.S.* (1822) 98 They are the best of triers. Whatever they prefer is sure to be the richest thing within their reach. **1869** SPURGEON *Treas. Dav.* Ps. lxxiii. 21 God is frequently called..the Trier of the hearts and reins.

8. One who (or that which) tries out or separates (metal, honey, grain, oil, etc.) from impurities.

1523 LD. BERNERS *Froiss.* I. ccccii. 699 They set but lytell by the manassyng of a sonne of a tryer of hony. *a* **1637** B. JONSON *Eupheme's Mind* vii, Disdaining any tryer, 'Tis got where it can try the fire. **1725** *Phil. Trans.* XXXIII. 262 The Triers, that open them [whales] when dead,..never observed any Grass, Fish, or any other Sort of Food in the right or Whalebone Whale. **1869** *Lonsdale Gloss.*, *Trier*, a corn-screen.

†**9. a.** One who finds *out* or tries to find out by search or examination. *Obs.*

1547–64 BAULDWIN *Mor. Philos.* (Palfr.) 65 Law is the finder & trier out of truth. **1563** FOXE *A. & M.* 1297/1 Mayster Thomas Bilney..a trier out of Sathans subtleties.

b. *spec.* (See quot.)

1778 *Eng. Gazetteer* (ed. 2) s.v. *Youle*, Youle, York, E. Rid... Here are a sort of people, called triers, who with a long piece of iron search into the soft boggy ground hereabouts for subterraneous trees.

10. One who tries or attempts to do something; in *Cricket slang*, a player who perseveres in trying to win.

1891 in *Cent. Dict.* **1897** *Daily News* 28 July 11/5 He trusted they would remember that even when the eleven did badly they were always tryers. **1903** *Daily Chron.* 24 Feb. 3/2 Mr. Bernard Capes may be described, in the language of the cricket-field, as 'a great try-er'. **1927** C. A. WILSON *Empire's Junior Partner* 227 There are many opportunities to acquire land on easy terms, very many farmers' trading concerns which are ready to back a 'trier'. **1942** *Tee Emm* (Air Ministry) II. 133 One day his Instructor said 'That chap's a trier' and sent him to a Squadron. **1955** *Times* 10 June 4/7 Pritchett has always been a real trier, and his game has looked more mature since his return from the United States.

11. a. Something devised to try or test quality. **b.** Something that is trying or difficult, or that tries one's patience or mettle.

1797 *Encycl. Brit.* (ed. 3) VIII. 238/1 Though the common powder-triers may show powder to be better than it really is, they can never make it appear to be worse than it is. **1893** *Field* 11 Feb. 187/2 The district being a trier, many and various were the mishaps. **1901** *U.S. Dept. Agric., Year-bk.* 237 These samples are drawn by means of a 'trier', or clover-seed sampler, which is thrust through the bag, allowing the seed to run out at the open end of the trier.

12. ***trier on***, one who 'tries on' garments in order to test the fit; *spec.* an assistant to a clothier or dressmaker who helps customers to try on garments, or who displays their style by wearing them (= MODEL *sb.* 11 b).

1895 *Blackw. Mag.* Apr. 557 The girl bethought herself of the 'tryer-on' [*cf. above* 'a young woman, discharging in perfection her function of wearing clothes so skilfully as to tempt buyers with them']. **1900** *Westm. Gaz.* 12 Jan. 5/3 The 'tryers-on'..had spent nearly four hours in hard work.

trierarch ('traɪərɑːk). *Gr. Hist.* Also 7 -arck, 9 -arc. [ad. L. *triērarch-us*, or its Gr. source τριήραρχος, -άρχης, f. τριήρης trireme + -αρχος ruling, ruler. Cf. F. *triérarque* (Oresme, 14th c.).] **a.** The commander of a trireme. **b.** A citizen who, singly or in conjunction with others, was charged with the duty of fitting out a trireme or galley for the public service.

1656 BLOUNT *Glossogr.*, *Trierarck*.., the mr. of a Ship or Galley. **1697** POTTER *Antiq. Greece* I. xxvi. (1715) 158 The Trierarchs, and Overseers of the Navy. **1734** tr. *Rollin's Anc. Hist.* XIII. vii. (1827) V. 290 The..Trierarchs..were appointed to fit out the galleys in time of war.

trierarchal ('traɪərɑːkəl), *a.* [f. as prec. + -AL[1].] Of or pertaining to a trierarch or trierarchs. So **trie'rarchic, -ical** *adjs.* [Gr. τριηραρχικός].

1837 WHEELWRIGHT tr. *Aristophanes* II. 127 The city had been full of martial tumult and trierarchal clamour. **1853** GROTE *Greece* II. lxxxvii. XI. 381 Demosthenes belonged to a trierarchic family. **1865** FELTON *Anc. & Mod. Gr.* I. II. xii. 502 The fitting out of war-ships, called the trierarchic liturgy. **1891** *Athenæum* 25 July 128/1 The law of Periander in 357 B.C...placing 1,200 citizens in the trierarchical symmories.

trierarchy ('traɪərɑːkɪ). [ad. Gr. τριηραρχία, f. τριήραρχος TRIERARCH.] The position or office of a trierarch; the equipment and maintenance of a trireme or other vessel, as a public service or 'liturgy'; the system by which a fleet was thus maintained. **b.** 'The trierarchs collectively' (Ogilvie, 1882).

1837 BULWER *Athens* II. 462 Extraordinary liturgies—such as the Trierarchy or equipment of ships which entailed also the obligation of personal service on those by whom the triremes were fitted out. **1839** THIRLWALL *Greece* VI. xlv. 51 The citizens who were liable to the charges of the trierarchy. **1850** GROTE *Greece* II. lv. VII. 47 As a rich young man, also, choregy and trierarchy became incumbent upon him. **1869** A. W. WARD tr. *Curtius' Hist. Greece* II. III. iii. 477 The trierarchy, i.e. the obligation incumbent upon the citizens to make the ships belonging to the state ready for sea, to hire crews, etc.

Triestine (triː'ɛstiːn), *sb.* and *a.* [f. *Trieste*, name of a city and province in north-eastern Italy + -INE[1].] **A.** *sb.* A native or inhabitant of Trieste. **B.** *adj.* Of Trieste or its inhabitants.

1905 J. JOYCE *Let.* 12 July (1966) II. 93 Nora can speak about thirty words of Triestine dialect. *Ibid.* 24 Sept. (1966) II. 112 Two little Triestines went into a hall-way and laughed till they beat each other. **1921** *Contemp. Rev.* July 46 Sig. Scaramanga, was a Triestine, and therefore an ex-Austrian subject. **1975** 'D. RUTHERFORD' *Mystery Tour* iv. 69 Maria, his homely and chubby Triestine wife.

triet, obs. form of TRIED.

trieteric (traɪɪ'tɛrɪk), *a.* and *sb. Antiq.* [ad. Gr. τριετηρικός, L. *trietēricus*, f. τριετηρίς a festival celebrated every third, i.e. alternate, year, f. τρι- three + ἔτος year.]

A. *adj.* Taking place every alternate year, as the festivals of Bacchus and other divinities.

1656 BLOUNT *Glossogr.*, *Trieterick*.., that is every third year. **1847** LEITCH tr. *C. O. Müller's Anc. Art* §390 The Mænads at the trieteric festival on Mount Parnassus thought they descried the satyrs and heard their music. **1852** GROTE *Greece* II. lxxv. IX. 477 *note*, The Isthmian games were trietêric, that is celebrated in every alternate year. **1911** *Athenæum* 15 Apr. 493/3 Dr. Farnell has..a theory of 'trieteric' agricultural rites.

B. *sb.* (also *pl.*) A festival, esp. of Bacchus, celebrated every alternate year.

1592 R. D. *Hypnerotomachia* 90 b, As in the daunce called Thiasus, in the trieteric [*pr.* -ie; *orig.* Trieterici] of Bacchus. **1627** MAY *Lucan* v. 86 To whome in mixed sacrifice The Theban wiues at Delphos solemnize Their trieterickes.

So †**trie'terical, trie'terican** *adjs. Obs.* = A.

1646 J. GREGORY *Notes & Obs.* xxi. 106 The trietericall sports,..that is the mysteries of Bacchus. **1775** ASH *Suppl.*, *Trieterican*, belonging to the trieterica.

triethanolamine, triethylene: see TRI- 5 c, b.

triethyl (traɪ'ɛθɪl). *Chem.* [f. TRI- 5 + ETHYL.] **a.** A formative denoting the presence of three ethyl groups, C_2H_5, in a compound, as **,triethyl'bismuthine**, $Bi(C_2H_5)_3$, **triethyl phosphine**, $P(C_2H_5)_3$; see also *triethylamine* below. **b.** *spec.* denoting the substitution of three ethyl groups for three hydrogen atoms in the substance designated by the rest of the name; e.g. **,triethyl'benzene**, $C_6H_3(C_2H_5)_3$, in which three ethyl groups take the place of three H atoms in benzene, C_6H_6; so **,triethyl'methane**, $CH(C_2H_5)_3$ from methane, CH_4; **,triethyl-'carbinol**, $C(C_2H_5)_3OH$; **,triethyl'urea**, $CONH(C_2H_5)N(C_2H_5)_2$. Also used attrib., as ***triethyl phosphate***, $(C_2H_5)_3PO_4$.

1858 FOWNES *Elem. Chem.* (ed. 7) 615 Triethylstibine $SbAe_3$. **1868** WATTS *Dict. Chem.* V. 880 Triethylglycerin or Triethylin..is a liquid having a pleasant ethereal odour. **1889** MUIR & MORLEY *Watts' Dict. Chem.* II. 506 Triethyl-phosphine... Colourless mobile liquid. Its odour is very penetrating but not disagreeable.

Hence **triethylamine** (traɪ'ɛθɪləmaɪn), the tertiary amine of ethyl, $N(C_2H_5)_3$, in which the three hydrogen atoms of ammonia, NH_3, are replaced by three ethyl groups; formerly also called ***triethyl ammonia*** and ***triethylia***; **trie'thylic** *a.* = triethyl *attrib.*

1850 DAUBENY *Atom. The.* viii. (ed. 2) 242 Triethylamine, consisting of 3 atoms of ethyle replacing 3 of hydrogen. **1857** MILLER *Elem. Chem.* III. 211 Triethylia..is also a soluble, volatile, and powerful base. **1858** FOWNES *Elem. Chem.* (ed. 7) 595 Triethylamine, Triethyl-ammonia...is a colourless, powerfully-alkaline liquid, boiling at 91°C. **1873** FOWNES *Chem.* 587 Triethylic borate is formed by the action of boron trichloride on alcohol.

trieues, -eux, -ewis, obs. ff. TREVE, TRUCE.

triexoctoedron, var. TRI-HEXOCTAHEDRON.

tri-faced: see TRI- 1 c.

trifacial (traɪ'feɪʃəl), *a. Anat.* [f. TRI- + FACIAL.] A name for the fifth pair of cranial nerves (also called TRIGEMINAL), which divide into three branches supplying the face and some adjacent parts. Also *transf.* pertaining to or affecting the trifacial nerves.

1840 G. ELLIS *Anat.* 82 Branches of..the first, second, or third divisions of the fifth or trifacial nerve. **1842** E. WILSON *Anat. Vade M.* (ed. 2) 407 The Trifacial Nerve is analogous to the spinal nerves in its origin by two roots. **1863** J. DEAN *Gray Subst. Medulla Obl.* etc. II. i, I have not been able to discover any connection between these columns and the trifacial or auditory roots. **1899** *Allbutt's Syst. Med.* VI. 662 A carious tooth may set up a trifacial neuralgia.

†**'tri,fallow**, *v. Obs.* Also 8 try-, tre-; see also THRY-FALLOW. [app. altered from the earlier *three-*, *thry-fallow*, after TWIFALLOW, or under the influence of TRI- prefix as in *tri-weekly*, *triennial*, etc.] *trans.* To plough (land) a third time in the course of its lying fallow. Also *absol.*

[**1573, 1641**: see THRY-FALLOW]. **1610** W. FOLKINGHAM *Art of Survey* I. ii. 43 Orders and seasons for fallowing, twifallowing, trifallowing and seed-furre. **1681** WORLIDGE *Dict. Rust.* s.v. *Fallow*, Thus may you fallow, twifallow, and trifallow; that is once, twice, or thrice plough it before the seed-time. **1707** MORTIMER *Husb.* (1721) I. 53 About the latter end of July or beginning of August, is the time of Try-fallowing, or last plowing before they sow their Rye or Wheat. **1766** *Complete Farmer*, *To Trefallow*, to plough land the third time before sowing.

trifarious (traɪ'fɛərɪəs), *a. rare.* [f. L. *trifāri-us* (compared by some with Gr. τριφάσιος in same sense) + -OUS.]

1. Of three sorts; facing three ways.

1656 BLOUNT *Glossogr.*, *Trifareous* (*trifarius*), of three manner of wayes. *c* **1800** BP. MILNER in Husenbeth *Life* (1862) 39 No longer prate on huge Briareus, On monstrous triple bodied Geryon; For I have seen a real trifarious Protesting—Catholic—Presbyterian!

2. *Bot.* Arranged in three rows.

1846 WORCESTER, *Trifarious*,..in three rows. **1857** BERKELEY *Cryptog. Bot.* §565 Leaves trifarious, the third row smaller than the others.

trifasciated, -faucian: see TRI- 1.

trifecta (traɪ'fɛktə). *N. Amer.*, *Austral.*, and *N.Z.* [f. TRI- + PER)FECTA.] (See quot. 1977.) Also *fig.*

1974 *Daily News* (N.Y.) 6 Feb. 46 The money that is bet on gimmick races like the trifecta is placed in a separate pool from the straight win, place, and show wagering. **1975** *Cleveland* (Ohio) *Plain Dealer* 6 Apr. 13-C/1 Before acting on the request for trifecta wagering..the ORC must advertise in affected counties 30 days before the hearing. **1977** *Daily Colonist* (Victoria, B.C.) 26 Nov. 32/1 To win the trifecta, a bettor must select the first, second and third place horses in order. **1979** *Sunday Mail* (Brisbane) 19 Aug. 6/5 A new bride on Thursday, a $50,000 win in the New South Wales lotteries on Friday and a winning day at the races on Saturday. That's last week's trifecta for Sydney's biggest bookmaker. **1984** *N.Z. Truth* 23 May 6 The T.A.B. is accepting trifecta and quinella on this feature event which is also the 1st leg of the Double and Treble.

†**'triferous**, *a. Obs. rare.* [f. L. *trifer* (f. TRI- + -*fer* bearing) + -OUS.] Thrice-bearing; bearing fruit or flowers thrice a year.

1656 BLOUNT *Glossogr.*, *Triferous* (*trifer*), that brings forth fruit thrice a year. *a* **1682** SIR T. BROWNE *Tracts* 70 Some are biferous and triferous which bear twice or thrice in the year.

trifet, obs. form of TRIVET.

triffid ('trɪfɪd). Also Triffid. [f. TRI-, prob. after TRIFID *a.*, as the plant was supported on 'three bluntly-tapered projections extending from the lower part' of the body.] In the science-fiction novel *The Day of the Triffids*, by John Wyndham (1903–69), one of a race of menacing plants, possessed of locomotor ability and a poisonous sting, which threaten to overrun the world. Hence used allusively of vigorous plants, or *transf.* of anything invasive or rapid in development.

1951 'J. WYNDHAM' *Day of Triffids* ii. 46 A catchy little name originating in some newspaper office as a handy label for an oddity—but destined one day to be associated with pain, fear and misery—*triffid*. *Ibid.* 54 He had also established that the infertility rate of triffid seeds was something like ninety-five per cent. **1965** *New Scientist* 11 Mar. 619/3 Ninety per cent of British households have television..and neither bindweed, triffids, nor dragon's teeth grew more rapidly than the angular aerial. **1972** S. HUGHES in M. Bygrave et al. *Time Out's Bk. of London* ix. 90/1 The south is sprouting with tall dark buildings like triffids. **1977** *Times* 10 Feb. 5/2 Roots and suckers started appearing all over our gardens... They were like 'Triffids'. **1978** R. H. LEWIS *Antiquarian Bks.* iv. 86 Books 'taking over' in Triffid style is a common experience.

Hence **tri'ffidian** *a.*; **'triffid-like** *a.* and quasi-*adv.*

1951 'J. WYNDHAM' *Day of Triffids* ii. 49 It was assumed ..that their characteristic of suddenly losing their immobility and rattling a rapid tattoo against the main stem was some strange form of triffidian amatory exuberance. **1971** *Daily Tel.* 16 Jan. 10/6 This cactus had run wild and, Triffid-like, had taken over thousands of square miles of good agricultural land. **1971** *New Scientist* 9 Sept. 589/3 Even the departure of four million..inhabitants..did not appear to check the spread of the Triffid-like condition.

†**triff-traff.** *Obs.* In 6 **tryfetrafe.** [app. a reduplicated form of TRAFFE baggage: cf. *trish-trash*, redupl. from *trash*. But it may also be associated with *riff-raff*.] Trumpery, trash, rubbish; = RIFF-RAFF[1] 2.

1547 *Bk. Marchauntes* bjb, Of brotherhodes, inuentions, tradicions, deceptions, lawes and wythout nombre of such tryfetrafe, wherby they can meruelously well drawe money to them.

trifid ('traɪfɪd), *a.* (and *sb.*) [ad. L. *trifid-us*, f. *tri-*, TRI- + *fid-*, stem of *findĕre* to split.]

a. Split or divided into three by deep clefts or notches; three-cleft; *esp.* in *Bot.* and *Zool.*

1753 CHAMBERS *Cycl. Supp.* s.v. *Leaf.* **1760** J. LEE *Introd. Bot.* II. ix. (1765) 93 Such as have Trifid Corollæ. **1769** PENNANT *Brit. Zool.* III. 320 The tail is naturally bifid, but in many is trifid. **1872** MIVART *Elem. Anat.* ii. 50 In the Howling Monkeys we find a trifid spine. **1895** *Pop. Sci. Monthly* Sept. 692 As far back as 1800 Pliny Moody had observed trifid markings upon sandstones.

b. *gen.* Divided into three parts, or of the nature of such division; tripartite. *rare.*

1871 EARLE *Philol. Eng. Tongue* viii. 417 In that chapter the third section assumed a trifid form. **1902** *Sat. Rev.* 6 Dec. 711/1 The old trifid division of mammals.

c. Also **tref(f)id.** Designating a type of antique spoon (see quot. 1977). Also *absol.* as *sb.*

1892 C. J. JACKSON in *Archaeologia* LIII. I. 138 The stem of this [Puritan] spoon is as wide as that of the trifid-ended form which immediately succeeded it. **1911** —— *Hist. Eng. Plate* II. xvii. 521 The earliest *Trifid Spoon* known to the author is one bearing the Dublin hallmarks for 1663. **1927** N. GASK *Old Silver Spoons of England* ix. 96 (*heading*) Lobed-ends, variously called Trifids, Trefoils, Split-ends or Pieds-de-Biche. **1932** *Antique Collector* Nov. 394/1 The Trifid type of handle, introduced with the Restoration, appears to have been evolved in turn from the Puritan. **1952** G. E. P. HOW *Eng. & Scottish Silver Spoons* I. II. xiv. 325 The Trefid Spoon, in its fully-developed form, was apparently introduced to London from the Continent at the Restoration of the Monarchy. **1956** G. TAYLOR *Silver* v. 111 The so-called Puritan spoon seems to be the starting-point for more decorative developments. The plain square end was hammered out into a thin leaf-shaped blade which is most commonly notched on either side of the pointed end to form a simple trefoil... Such spoons are therefore described as 'trefid' (or 'trifid')... Larger trefid spoons with the same characteristics, but a much longer stem, are found. **1974** [see RAT-TAIL 3b]. **1977** FLEMING & HONOUR *Penguin Dict. Decorative Arts* 802/1 *Trifid* or *Trefid spoon*, a C17 English type of spoon with a flat handle widening towards the end which is divided into three parts by deep notches.

trifilar to **triflagellate:** see TRI- 1.

trifle ('traɪf(ə)l), *sb.* Forms: *α.* 3–5 **trufle,** (3–4 **truyfle**), 4 **trufel, truffle,** (**trewful**), 4–5 **truful,** 5 **-fulle, truffulle, truffille.** *β.* 4 **trofle, trofil,** 4–5 **trofel,** (5 **trowful**). *γ.* 4 **tryffel,** 4–5 **trifil(e, -ful,** (4 **tryuol, trefle,** 4– 5 **-fele**), 4–6 **tryfel, -fyl, -fle,** 4–7 (8 *Sc.*) **triffle,** 5 **tryfil, trifelle, triffol,** 5–6 **tryfell(e,** 6 **-fille, -full(e, -fyll(e,** (**tryefull**), **trifill, -fulle, triffelle, triffill(e,** 7 **triffel, tryffel, -le,** 4– **trifle.** [ME. *trufle*, etc., a. OF. *trufle* (13th c. in Godef.), *treufle*, *truffle* (1370), parallel forms of *trufe*, *truffe*, 'moquerie, tromperie' (1265 in Godef.), = It. *truffa*, 'a cozening, cheating, conicatching' (Florio), Pr., obs. Sp. and Pg. *trufa*, 'a gibe, a iesting or ieering' (Minsheu); of uncertain origin. The phonology of the word in English presents difficulties; but *trufle*, with *ü*, would give later *tryfle*, *triffle*; and *u* sometimes varied dialectally with *o*, as in the ME. *trofel*. The short *ĭ* indicated by *ff* in *tryffel*, *triffol*, *triffle*, appears from the 14th to the 18th c.; but *trifle* with single *f* is ambiguous, and does not show when *trĭfle* became *trīfle*.

For the ulterior etymology, Diez was inclined to identify F. *truffe*, *trufle* with *truffe*, Pr. *trufa* (Littré), a TRUFFLE, a subterranean edible fungus. But it is app. only in F. (and Prov.) that the two words have the same form, and no connexion of sense has been ascertained: see TRUFFLE.]

†**1.** A false or idle tale, told (*a*) to deceive, cheat, or befool, (*b*) to divert or amuse; a lying story, a fable, a fiction; a jest or joke; a foolish, trivial, or nonsensical saying. *Obs.*

The shades of sense cannot always be distinguished.

α. *a* **1225** *Ancr. R.* 106 þeos ant oðre trufles þet he bitrufleð monie men mide. **1297** R. GLOUC. (Rolls) 8613 Wanne me sede him of suche wondres..to trufle [*v.rr.* trifle, tryffel] he it wende. **1340** *Ayenb.* 58 þe bourdes and þe trufles uol of uelþe and of leazinges. **1390** GOWER *Conf.* III. 344 Mi Sone, unto the trouthe wende..And lete all othre truffles [*v.rr.* trifles, triffles] be. **1393** LANGL. *P. Pl.* C. XXI. 151 Hit is trufle [*v.rr.* tryfle, triful, trewful] þat þou tellest. *c* **1440** *York Myst.* v. 125 Allas! þat I.. trowed þe trufuls þat þou me saide. *Ibid.* xxxi. 300 But telle vs nowe some truffillis betwene vs twoo. **1483** *Cath. Angl.* 395/2 Truffillis, *nuge*, *gerra*.

β. **13..** *Cursor M.* 253 (Cott.) To wast þair liif, in trofel and truandis. *Ibid.* 27623 (Cott. Galba) Of pride cumes.. sang of trofils [*Cott.* truful] or lesing. **1340** HAMPOLE *Pr. Consc.* 183 Many has lykyng trofels to here. *c* **1400** *Rule St. Benet* 1735 Tales of trofils þai sal non tel.

γ. **1303** R. BRUNNE *Handl. Synne* 5031 þys yche tale ys no tryfyl, For hyt ys wryte yn þe bybyl. **13..** *Gaw. & Gr. Knt.* 108 Talkkande bifore þe hyȝe table of trifles ful hende. **1377** LANGL. *P. Pl.* B. XVIII. 147 It is but a trufle [*v.rr.* tryfule, truyfle] þat þow tellest. *c* **1380** WYCLIF *Wks.* (1880) 442 Iapis & gabbingis or oþere tryuolis. *c* **1440** *Generydes* 4664 These are butt triffolys and delayes. **14..** *Voc.* in Wr.-Wülcker 617/42 *Trufa*, a trefele. *c* **1440** *Promp. Parv.* 502/2 Tryfle, *trufa*. *c* **1518** SKELTON *Magnyf.* 1142, I am yet as full of game As euer I was, and as full of tryfyls [*rime* nyfyls]. **1548** UDALL, etc. *Erasm. Par. Matt.* xv. 67 The Phariseis teache and obserue supersticiously these folysh tryfles. **1681** W. ROBERTSON *Phraseol. Gen.* (1693) 1258 Nifles and trifles; vain tales of Robin Hood; *aniles fabulæ*.

2. a. Hence, A matter of little value or importance; 'a thing of no moment' (J.); a trivial, paltry, or insignificant affair.

c **1290** *S. Eng. Leg.* I. 412/345 þare-fore mot ech holi man ..tuyrne is herte to some truyfle. **1340** *Ayenb.* 142 þer treteþ he of his greate quereles hueruore alle oþre niedes him þingþ trufles. *c* **1380** WYCLIF *Sel. Wks.* II. 185 Worldli goodis, fame of þe world, and oþer trifilis. **1513** MORE *Rich. III* (1883) 48 Leneth mi lord thi master so muche to such trifles? **1585** *Reg. Privy Council Scot.* IV. 32 The materis..wer bot triffillis in respect of uthiris of greitar importance. **1604** SHAKS. *Oth.* III. iii. 322 Trifles light as ayre, Are to the iealious, confirmations strong As proofes of holy Writ. **1706** E. WARD *Wooden World Diss.* (1708) 33 He's a mighty exact Man about Trifles. **1758** JOHNSON *Idler* No. 23 ¶7 There is scarcely any man without some favourite trifle which he values above greater attainments. **1833** HT. MARTINEAU *Brooke Farm* ix. 110 Some trifles went wrong in the cottage. **1882** PEBODY *Eng. Journalism* xxii. 176 A Society journal, dealing..with the trifles of the day.

b. Without article. *rare.*

1768 TUCKER *Lt. Nat.* (1834) I. 219 The advantage of virtue over vice and trifle does not lie in the very act, but in the consequences. *Ibid.* 620 As well in matters of trifle as of moment.

†**c.** *transf.* A worthless person; a trifler. *Obs.*

c **1475** *Pict. Voc.* in Wr.-Wülcker 806/21 *Hic nugigerulus*, a trifelle. *a* **1623** FLETCHER *Love's Cure* III. iv, *Syav.* Pray wear these trifles. *Clara*... You are a trifle, wear your self, sir, out. **1675** TRAHERNE *Chr. Ethics* 392 You will look as like a trifle, a knave, or a fool, as one of them; and be as very a mad man. *a* **1716** SOUTH *Serm.* (1744) XI. 18 It shews him to be a fop, a trifle and a mere picture.

3. *concr.* A small article of little intrinsic value; a toy, trinket, bauble, knick-knack.

1375 *Will of Eliz. Lister* (Somerset Ho.), A goun et vnum triffle sȝelf egged. *a* **1400–50** *Alexander* 1894 þe trufils þat ȝe to me sent, þe herne-pan, þe hand-ball, þe hatt made of twiggis. **1530** PALSGR. 283/1 Tryfell, a knacke, *friuolle*. **1630** *R. Johnson's Kingd. & Commw.* 196 Divers sorts of Linnen-cloth, with innumerable other small trifles. **1719** DE FOE *Crusoe* I. 44 To purchase..for Trifles, such as Beads, Toys, Knives, Scissars, Hatchets, Bits of Glass, and the like; not only Gold Dust,..Elephants Teeth, &c. but Negroes. **1756** MRS. CALDERWOOD in *Coltness Collect.* (Maitl. Cl.) 148 If you buy a triffle..then they are very civill. **1912** *Daily Graphic* 31 Dec. 13/2 These elegant trifles [hat-pins] are made in a variety of graceful designs.

4. A literary work, piece of music, etc., light or trivial in style; a slight or facetious composition; a bagatelle. Often used in meiosis.

1579 LYLY *Euphues* (Arb.) 106 If Lucilla reade this trifle, shee will straight proclaime Euphues for a traytour. **1665** BOYLE *Occas. Refl., Disc. Occas. Medit.* (1848) 1 The Trifles of this kind, your Commands make me trouble you with. *a* **1704** T. BROWN *1st Sat. Persius* 66 Read his trifles, and scarce in one line You'll find him guilty of the least design. **1751** EARL OF ORRERY *Remarks Swift* vi. (1752) 47 Poems to Stella, and trifles to Dr. Sheridan, fill up a great part of that period. **1837** KEITH *Bot. Lex.* 2 Anacreon, in one of his little trifles in honour of drinking, makes the very trees of the forest drink. **1884** W. C. SMITH *Kildrostan* 47 A little song —A trifle..Which I had writ for Mairi once to sing.

5. a. A small sum of money, or a sum treated as of no moment; a slight 'consideration'.

c **1595** CAPT. WYATT *R. Dudley's Voy. W. Ind.* (Hakl. Soc.) 39 The Captaine præsentinge him with a trifle from our Generall, hee [etc.]. **1615** G. SANDYS *Trav.* 116 Giving a trifle for oile, about midnight we departed. **1746** FRANCIS tr. *Hor. Sat.* II. iii. 214 'What will it cost? Nay, hold!'—'A very trifle.'—'Sir, I will be told.'—'Three pence.' **1762–71** H. WALPOLE *Vertue's Anecd. Paint.* (1786) II. 157 Some not suiting the places, were brought back, and sold for a trifle after the death of my father. **1818** SCOTT *Let.* 30 Apr. in Lockhart *Life* (1837) IV. iv. 138, I could bet a trifle the doors, &c. will arrive the very day I set out.

b. An insignificant quantity or amount.

1722 DE FOE *Plague* (1884) 132 Here is fifty thousand.., within a Trifle. **1911** BEVERIDGE *North Uist.* v. 63 Nor can it ever have afforded more than a mere trifle of arable soil.

c. ***a trifle*** (advb.): To a trifling or slight extent; in a small degree, a little; somewhat, rather.

1859 READE *Love me Little* xi, The bank itself was small and grave and a trifle dingy. **1860** G. MEREDITH *E. Harrington* xi, The chairman welcomed them a trifle snubbingly. **1887** JESSOPP *Arcady* vii. 214 Jehu is a trifle below middle height. **1892** *Speaker* 3 Sept. 291/2 We may inquire, perhaps, if it be not a trifle arrogant.

6. †**a.** A dish composed of cream boiled with various ingredients. *Obs.* **b.** A light confection of sponge-cake or the like, esp. flavoured with wine or spirit, and served with custard and whipped cream.

1598 FLORIO, *Mantiglia*, a kinde of clouted creame called a foole or a trifle in English. **1688** R. HOLME *Armoury* III. 85/1 *Triffel*, is Cream boiled with Sugar, Mace and Cinnamon. **1736** BAILEY *Househ. Dict.* 571 To make a Trifle. Boil a quart of cream,..sweeten it,..put to it two spoonfuls of rennet; let it stand till it comes like cheese. **1755** H. GLASSE *Art of Cookery* (ed. 5) xvi. 285 Trifle. Cover.. your Dish..with Naples Biscuits..Mackeroons..and Ratafia Cakes..wet them..with Sack, then make a good boiled Custard..pour over it..then put a Syllabub over that. **1781** COWPER *Let.* 18 Feb., There is some froth, and here and there a bit of sweetmeat, which seems to entitle it justly to the name of a certain dish the ladies call a trifle. **1836–9** DICKENS *Sk. Boz*, *Bloomsbury Christening*, There were fowls, and tongue, and trifle, and sweets, and lobster salad. **1860** O. W. HOLMES *Elsie V.* vii. (1891) 110 That most wonderful object of domestic art called trifle,..with its charming confusion of cream and cake and almonds and jam and jelly and wine and cinnamon and froth.

7. Name for a kind of pewter of medium hardness; in *pl.* also, articles made of this.

1610–11 [implied in TRIFLER 3]. **1612–13** in Welch *Hist. Pewterers' Co.* (1902) II. 61 Att wch tyme was Syzed by them theis seuerall parcells of Tryffles as followe vizt: Great duble bells wth peper boxes & baules... The greate beak^{r}..Middle beake^{r}..Smale beake^{r}..The great beere bowle... The large wrought Cupps..[etc.]. **1668–9** *Ibid.* 140 It is..agreed.. that..every person that taketh Hollow-ware of any workman & returneth not him for the same ½ plate mettle and ½ London Trifles, shall pay unto such workman for want of plate mettle after the rate of 3^{s} 6^{d} per Cent and deliver him good London Trifles. **1839** URE *Dict. Arts* 952 The English tradesmen distinguish three sorts, which they call plate, trifle, and ley pewter; the first and hardest being used for plates and dishes; the second for beer-pots; and the third for larger wine measures. **1875** KNIGHT *Dict. Mech.* 1677/1 To regulate the quality..a button of pure tin weighing 182 grains was employed; a similar button of plate-pewter would weigh 183½ grains; of trifle, 185½ grains; and of ley, 198½ grains.

8. a. *attrib.* or as *adj.* Trifling.

1607 TOPSELL *Four-f. Beasts* 170 This is no trumpery tale, nor trifle toy.

b. *Comb.*, as ***trifle-bearer***, ***-dish***, ***-monger***, ***-worship***; **trifle-pewter** = sense 7; **trifle-ring**, 'a ring having some hidden mechanism or play of parts, as a gimmel-ring, puzzle-ring, or one composed of three or more hoops working on pivots' (*Cent. Dict.*).

1561 WITHERS tr. *Calvin's Treat. Relics* Aij, Certaine *trifle bearers, who..did exercise a most vilainous and filthy kynd of cariyng hyther, and thether reliques of martyrs. **1859** LANG *Wand. India* 107 The soup..was served up in a *trifle-dish which had formed part of a dessert service belonging to the 9th Lancers. **1819** *Hermit in London* III. 81 These selfish *trifle-mongers. **1875** KNIGHT *Dict. Mech.* 1677/1 The *trifle-pewter has, tin 83; antimony 17; with a good deal of lead occasionally. *a* **1860** J. A. ALEXANDER *Gosp. Jesus Christ* xv. (1861) 203 The exchange of spiritual life for ..factitious morals and a senseless *trifle-worship.

Hence (*nonce-wds.*) **'trifledom**, the realm of trifles; **triflet** ('traɪflɪt), a small trifle (in sense 4).

1895 *Daily News* 8 Nov. 3/2 A skit upon the Haymarket piece..described..as 'A Trilby Triflet'. **1903** *Westm. Gaz.* 22 Sept. 2/3 Twin synonyms of frolic mild,..Are ye from Trifledom exiled?

trifle ('traɪf(ə)l), *v.*[1] Forms: (3 **bitrufle(n)**, 4 **treoflen, trufly, trofel, -le, trofulle,** 5 **trufylle, tryfulle, trefele, troufle, tryffle, trifel, -ful,** 5–6 **tryfle,** 6 **tryffel, tryfell, -fyll, -ful, trifyll,** (7 **triffle**), 6– **trifle.** [ME. a. OF. *truffle-r*, *truiffle-r*, parallel form of *truffer*, *trufer*, *trupher* (13th c. in Godef.) to make sport of, deceive, jeer or laugh at, = It. *truffare* 'to cozen, to cheate, to coniecatch' (Florio): cf. *truffe*, *trufle*, *truffle* mockery, cheating: see TRIFLE *sb.*]

†**1.** *trans.* To cheat, delude, befool; to mock. ***trifle out***, to dismiss with mockery. *Obs. rare.*

[Cf. *a* **1225** Bitrufle: see TRIFLE *sb.* 1 *a.* *c* **1290** *S. Eng. Leg.* I. 412/323 Wel bi-trufleth he þat folk.] *a* **1450** MYRC *Festial* 194 Symon Magvs..trifuld þe pepull to holde hym an holy man. **1523** LD. BERNERS *Froiss.* I. cc. 237 Than the comons of the cite beganne to saye, howe dothe our bysshop tryfle and mocke vs. **1533** TINDALE *Supper Lord* Eijb, To tryful out ye trouth wyth tauntes and mockes, as More doth.

2. †**a.** *intr.* To say what is untrue, to jest in order to cheat, mock, amuse, or make sport. *Obs.*

c **1305** *St. Dunstan* 74 in *E.E.P.* (1862) 36 Treoflinge heo smot her and þer. **1340** *Ayenb.* 214 Naȝt uor to iangli, uor to lheȝȝe, ne uorto trufly. *c* **1430** *Chev. Assigne* 48 He was trewe of his feyth & loth for to tryfulle. *c* **1440** *Promp. Parv.* 502/2 Tryflon, or iapyn (*K.* trifelyn,..*P.* tryfflyn), *trufo*, *ludifico*. **1483** *Cath. Angl.* 395/1 To Trufylle, *nugari*,..*neniari*, *trufare*. **1538** ELYOT, *Ineptio*.., to tryfle. **1551** ROBINSON tr. *More's Utop.* I. (1895) 98 The vyle bonde-men skoffynge and tryfelynge amonge them selfes. **1573–80** BARET *Alv.* T. 366 To trifle, to do, or speake a thing vnmeete for the purpose, *inepto*. **1602** SHAKS. *Ham.* II. i. 112, I feare he did but trifle, And meant to wracke thee.

b. ***trifle with***: To treat with a lack of seriousness or respect; to 'play' or dally with.

1523 LD. BERNERS *Froiss.* I. ccccix. 712 Sirs, methynke the frenchmen do but tryfell with me, and with the countre of Flaunders. **1530** PALSGR. 562/1, I gest, I bourde or tryfyll with one, *je bourde*. **1605** SHAKS. *Lear* IV. vi. 34 Why I do trifle thus with his dispaire, Is done to cure it. **1670** COTTON *Espernon* I. III. 133 At last the Duke nettled to see himself so pursu'd, and trifled withal by his Enemy, commanded [etc.]. **1769** *Junius Lett.* xxxv. (1820) 168 This is not a time to trifle with your fortune. **1794** MRS. RADCLIFFE *Myst. Udolpho* xii, I let him see that I was not to be trifled with. **1852** MRS. SMYTHIES *Bride Elect* xliii, He shall not trifle with your affections. **1869** FREEMAN *Norm. Conq.* III. xii. 253 Trifling with what ought to be solemn engagements.

†**c.** So ***trifle it.*** *Obs.*

1563 FOXE *A. & M.* 1190/1 Bradford desired my lord Chauncelor not to trifle it, saying that he wondred his honoure woulde make solemne oths (made to God) trifles in that sorte. **1657** J. SERGEANT *Schism Dispach't* 577 You have broke the Unity of the former church (and not of the court onely, as you trifle it) which you were in.

3. *intr.* To toy, play (*with* a material object); to handle or finger a thing idly; to fiddle, fidget *with*.

c **1460** J. RUSSELL *Bk. Nurture* 287 Put not youre hands in youre hosen..nor pikynge, nor trifelynge ne shrukkynge. **1530** PALSGR. 549/1, I fydell, I tryfle with my handes, *je fretille mes mayns.* **1618** M. BARET *Horsemanship* I. 75 If when he standeth..he coueteth to goe backe, or trifle with his body or feete, then [etc.]. **1715** POPE *2nd Ep. Miss Blount* 17 O'er cold coffee trifle with the spoon. **1842** TENNYSON *Will Waterpr.* xxix, Silent gentlemen, That trifle with the cruet. **1865** DICKENS *Mut. Fr.* I. ii, He trifles quite ferociously with his dessert-knife.

b. *trans.* To play with. *rare.*

1817 KEATS *Endym.* IV. 210 Young Bacchus stood, Trifling his ivy-dart.

4. *intr.* To dally, loiter; to spend time idly or frivolously; to waste time.

?*a* **1400** *Morte Arth.* 2932, I red thowe trette of a trewe, and trofle no lengere. **1560** DAUS tr. *Sleidane's Comm.* 114 b, He trifleth and dalieth thus with doubtfull wordes. **1638** SIR T. HERBERT *Trav.* (ed. 2) 133 Let us now triffle no longer, but view the City. **16..** EVELYN *Diary* 21 Oct. an. 1632 Whiles I was now trifling at home I saw London. **1751** JOHNSON *Rambler* No. 153 ⁋5 While I was thus trifling in uncertainty. **1856** OLMSTED *Slave States* 91 They must have 'trifled' a great deal, or they would have accomplished more than they had.

†**5.** *trans.* To pass or spend (time) frivolously or idly; to waste (time). *Obs.* exc. as in b.

1586 J. HOOKER *Hist. Irel.* in Holinshed II. 157/2 He still lingered and trifled the time and came not. **1596** SHAKS. *Merch. V.* IV. i. 298 We trifle time, I pray thee pursue sentence. **1611** HEYWOOD *Gold. Age* IV. i. Wks. 1874 III. 66 Wee haue trifled the night till bed-time. **1697** CONGREVE *Mourn. Bride* II. vii, I haue not leisure to reflect, or know, Or trifle time in thinking. **1742** R. BLAIR *Grave* 572 Fain would he trifle time with idle talk.

b. esp. with *away*, †*off*, to fritter away idly. †With *forth*, *out*, to defer or put off idly.

1532 HERVET *Xenophon's Househ.* 59 b, His worke men and laborers.. tryfyll away the day. *Ibid.*, His folke..trifle forth the time. **1609** HOLLAND *Amm. Marcell.* 305 He a long while trifled out the time. **1613** SHAKS. *Hen. VIII*, V. iii. 179 Come Lords, we trifle time away. **1657** J. WATTS *Dipper Sprinkled* 86 Trifle away paper with needless repetitions. **1774** *Trinket* 172 *Une affaire de cœur*, is at best a silly business, yet mighty necessary to trifle off that trifle, life. **1818** SCOTT *Hrt. Midl.* vi[i], Why do you trifle away time in making a gallows?—that dyester's pole is good enough for the homicide.

†**6.** To make a trifle of; to render trivial or insignificant. *Obs. rare*$^{-1}$.

1605 SHAKS. *Macb.* II. iv. 4 This sore Night Hath trifled former knowings.

7. *intr.* To act (or speak) in an idle or frivolous way, esp. in serious circumstances.

1736 BUTLER *Anal.* II. v. Wks. 1874 I. 207 A person rashly trifling upon a precipice. **1779** *Mirror* No. 60 One of the most important lessons to be learned in life, is that of being able to trifle upon occasion. **1815** SCOTT *Guy M.* xviii, I cannot help trifling, Matilda, though my heart is sad enough. **1867** AUG. J. E. WILSON *Vashti* xxviii, 'Oh, Salome! you have trifled.' 'No, sir. Take that back. I never stoop to trifling; and the curse of my life has been my almost fatal earnestness of purpose'.

8. *trans.* To utter or pass in a trifling manner.

1822 LAMB *Elia* Ser. I. *Old Actors*, She used him for her sport..to trifle a leisure sentence or two with. **1825** C. M. WESTMACOTT *Eng. Spy* I. 226 Trifles a little badinage.

ˈtrifle, *v.*[2] *dial.* [Eng. Dial. Dict. suggests deriv. from OE. *trifulian*, *tribulian*, *ȝetrifulian*, ad. L. *trībulāre* to thresh, bruise, pound, grind, f. *trībulum* threshing-sledge; this seems probable, though no examples are known between the 11th and 17th c., and the sense is not exactly identical.] *trans.* To beat or trample down (standing corn or grass).

[*c* **1000** ÆLFRIC *Voc.* in Wr.-Wülcker 114/26 *Pilurus*, *uel pistor*, se þe pilaþ, *uel* tribulaþ.] *c* **1000** *Sax. Leechd.* II. 150/3 Eft withier rinde ȝebærn to ahsan do eced to trifula swiðe. *Ibid.* 186/10 Menge eall togædere & trifoliȝe. *c* **1050** *Gloss.* in Wr.-Wülcker 423/25 *In tritura*, in trifelunge. **1641** BEST *Farm. Bks.* (Surtees) 54 A mower..may mowe (with as much ease) amongst ranke barley as other, if it stande streight, and bee not trifled, neyther with the winde, nor with cattle-feete. **1846** BROCKETT *N.C. Words* (ed. 3), *Trifled-corn*, corn that has fallen down, in single ears, mixed with standing corn. **1893–4** *Northumbld. Gloss.*, *Trifled*, beaten down with wind or rain; applied to grass or grain.

trifler (ˈtraɪflə(r)). Forms: (4 troiflard), triffler(e, -our, triflere, 4–6 trifeler, 4–7 tryfler, 5 trufeler, truffilere, tryfflare, tryfelare, -fulere, -fuller, (-pheler), trifulere, 6 tryfelar, -fullar, 6–7 triffel(l)er, tryf(f)eler, 6– trifler. [a. OF. *trufleor*, *-eour*, *-eur*, nom. *trufflere* (beside *trufeor*, *truffeur*, etc., all 13th c.) liar, cheat, trifler, agent-n. from *truffer*, *truffler*: see TRIFLE *v.*[1] and -ER[2]. Also with other suffixes: see -ER[1].] One who trifles.

1. A teller of feigned or idle stories, one not to be believed or taken seriously; a jester, a joker; a nonsensical speaker; a worthless fellow.

1382 WYCLIF *Wisd.* ii. 16 As trifleres [**1388** triffleris, *marg.* trifeleris; that is, men of no vertu; L. *nugaces*] wee ben eymed of hym. *c* **1394** *P. Pl. Crede* 475 Telle More of þise tryflers hou trechurly þei libbeþ? *Ibid.* 742 Y miȝt tymen þo troiflardes to toilen wiþ þe erþe, Tylyen & trewliche lyven & her flech tempren! **1399** LANGL. *Rich. Redeles* III. 118 þe tale of a triffloür. *c* **1420** ? LYDG. *Assembly of Gods* 685 Tregetours, tryphelers, feyners of tales. *c* **1425** *Voc.* in Wr.-Wülcker 651/11 *Hic nugator*, trifulere. *c* **1440** *Promp. Parv.* 502/2 Tryfelar.., *trufator*, *nugax.* **1483** *Cath. Angl.* 395/1 A Trufeler (*A.* Truffilere), *gerro*,..*nugifer*, *nugigerulus.* **1519** HORMAN *Vulg.* 77 Thys felowe is a tryfullar, leude, of no truste, or reputacion. *a* **1533** LD. BERNERS *Gold. Bk. M. Aurel.* (1546) Ii v, Gamners and trifelers, and such other iuglers. **1576** FLEMING *Panopl. Epist.* 399 Then Poggius the babbler, the trifler, the railer.

2. One who is not serious or earnest in what he does; one who wastes his time on trivialities; a frivolous person.

1607–12 BACON *Ess.*, *Beauty* (Arb.) 210 A man cannot tell whether Appelles or Albert Durere were the more trifler. **1710** PALMER *Proverbs* 244 Many a one will prove but a trifler in Latin or Greek, who in his mother-tongue might have appear'd to advantage. **1756** JOHNSON in W. Payne *Game of Draughts* Ded., Triflers may find or make any thing a trifle. **1781** COWPER *Charity* 355 The solemn trifler with his boasted skill. **1818** SCOTT *Br. Lamm.* xxxiii, At present, I have no leisure for the disputes of triflers. **1833** MACAULAY *Ess.*, *War Succession Spain* (1887) 280 Harley, we believe, was a solemn trifler,—St. John a brilliant knave. **1872** MORLEY *Voltaire* i. (1886) 4 Erudition figures him as shallow and a trifler.

3. One who works in the kind of pewter called 'trifle' (see TRIFLE *sb.* 7).

1610–11 in Welch *Hist. Pewterers' Co.* (1902) II. 56 It was ordered..that..the tryflers shall have for ther ware as they do delyver to the company..mettall and money and vppon the complaynt of any of those tryflers wch ar not so payed it is ordered that they shall have *x d.* a pound for ther mettall and also to be fynd. **1612–13** *Ibid.* 61 A meeteinge..of certen tryffeleres for the Syzeinge of wares. **1614–15** *Ibid.* 68 Triffelers.

†**triflery.** *Obs. rare*$^{-1}$. In 4 triphilrie. [a. AF. **truflerie* = OF. *truferie* (13th c.), f. *truffer*, *trufler*: see TRIFLE *v.*[1] and -RY.] False, feigned, vain, or idle speech or action.

13.. *Cursor M.* 10131 (Gött.) þis bok es of na triphilrie [*Cott.* ribodi; *Fairf.* iapery; *Trin.* iaperie], Bot of godd and vr leudy.

trifling (ˈtraɪflɪŋ), *vbl. sb.* [f. TRIFLE *v.*[1] + -ING[1].] The action of the verb TRIFLE; jesting or frivolous talk; fooling; idle, foolish, or frivolous conduct or practice; frivolous delay or waste of time; †also *concr.* (*pl.*) trumpery (quot. *c* 1540).

1382 WYCLIF *Wisd.* iv. 12 Forsothe the priue desceyuyng of trifling [L. *fascinatio nugacitatis*] derkneth goode thingus. ?*a* **1400** *Morte Arth.* 114 With-owttyne more trouflynge the trebute we aske. *c* **1460** [see TRIFLE *v.*[1] 3]. **1530** PALSGR. 283/1 Tryflynges, scoffynges, *fredaines.* *c* **1540** HEYWOOD *Four P.P.* A iv b, Euery pedler In euery trifull must be a medler Specially in womens triflynges, Those vse we chiefly aboue all thynges. **1586** J. HOOKER *Hist. Irel.* in Holinshed II. 163/1 He returned his answer by a letter..vsing therein nothing but triflings and delaies. *a* **1694** TILLOTSON *Serm.* (1742) III. 345 What a frivolous contention, what a trifling in serious matters. **1768** CHESTERF. *Let. to Godson* 15 Sept., Wit if you have any, and..agreable trifling or *badinage.* **1840** KINGSLEY *Lett.* (1878) I. 50 You are not bigoted by the solemn trifling of the schools. **1873** M. ARNOLD *Lit. & Dogma* (1876) p. xi, All other religious discussion is idle trifling. **1885** *Manch. Exam.* 4 May 5/2 Speeches..marked by a good deal of brilliant trifling.

ˈtrifling, *ppl. a.* [f. as prec. + -ING[2].]

†**1.** Cheating, befooling, false, feigning. *Obs.*

?*a* **1400** *Morte Arth.* 1683 ȝe do bott trayne vs to daye wyth trofelande wordez! **1547** *Bk. Marchantes* e vj, Was there no suche folysh fayned triflyng deceite in England. *a* **1548** HALL *Chron.*, *Hen. IV* 17 The kyng gaue many friuolus and trifelyng aunswers. **1560** DAUS tr. *Sleidane's Comm.* 37 b, So trifelynge & wicked a doctrine should haue bene dispised of all men.

2. Behaving idly or frivolously; not serious; frivolous; foolish.

1535 COVERDALE *1 Tim.* v. 13 Not onely are they ydell but also tryflinge & busybodies speakynge thinges which are not comly. **1659** *Gentl. Calling* (1696) 92 Shall more and baser be sought out, every the triflingest and vilest Entertainment? **1703** ROWE *Ulyss.* IV. i, Oh trifling, idle Talker. **1709** STEELE *Tatler* No. 109 ⁋ 4 The trifling Way the Women have in spending their Time, and gratifying only their Eyes and Ears. **1885** *Athenæum* 23 May 661/1 The perverse intrusion of trifling thoughts at agonizing moments.

3. Of little moment or value; paltry, trumpery; insignificant, petty.

1538 STARKEY *England* I. iii. 94 Delycate wynys, fyne clothys,..and a thousand such tryfelyng thyngys. **1645** EVELYN *Diary* 25 Jan., The worke of 10 years study for a trifling reward. **1659** *Gentl. Calling* (1660) 139 [One] that for every the triflingest injury expects..to be avenged seventy and seven fold. **1722** DE FOE *Plague* (1754) 8 Those were trifling Things to what followed immediately after. **1814** *Rep. Comm. Publ. Rec. Irel.* (1815) 75 To receive some trifling sum by way of Fee. **1869** FREEMAN *Norm. Conq.* III. xi. 66 The danger..was comparatively trifling.

ˈtriflingly, *adv.* [f. prec. + -LY[2].] In a trifling manner or degree.

1547–64 BAULDWIN *Mor. Philos.* (Palfr.) 126 See that thou swearest not..falsely & vntruely, or vainely & triflingly. **1601** DEACON & WALKER *Answ. to Darel* 123 You deale too triflinglie with your ignorant Reader. **1759** GOLDSM. *Pol. Learn.* ii, When philosophy became abstruse, or triflingly minute. **1763** WILKES *Corr.* (1805) I. 173 However triflingly this affair may have been talked of, it is, in reality, of very serious and general consequence. **1865** G. MEREDITH *Rhoda Fleming* vi, He had winced triflingly at one or two expressions.

ˈtriflingness. [f. as prec. + -NESS.] The quality of being trifling; triviality, pettiness.

1581 SIDNEY *Apol. Poetrie* (Arb.) 71 The triflingnes of this discourse, is much too much enlarged. **1752** CARTE *Hist. Eng.* III. 507 Ross and his colleagues shewed the triflingness of this excuse. **1821** *J. Smith's Sel. Disc.* Pref. 10 A profitable companion; nothing of vanity and triflingness in him. **1912** *19th Cent.* No. 1023 The triflingness of free negro agricultural labour.

trifloral, triflorous: see TRI- 1.

†**triflous**, *a. Obs. rare.* Also 6 **tryfelous**, **triflelous**. [app. f. TRIFLE *sb.* + -OUS: cf. OF. *trufous* (13th c.).] Trifling; insignificant, trivial; frivolous.

1509 BP. FISHER *Fun. Serm. C'tess Richmond* Wks. (E.E.T.S.) I. 291 Tryfelous thynges that were lytell to be regarded. **1535** —— *Ways Perfect Relig.* ibid. 384 How light, & howe triflelous a thing it is. **1662** J. CHANDLER *Van Helmont's Oriat.* 43 It is a Childish and triflous thing. *Ibid.* 340 These races of vapours out of the Stomack, are triflous.

trifluctuation: see TRI- 4.

trifluoperazine (ˌtraɪfluːəʊˈpɛrəziːn). *Pharm.* [f. TRI- 5 + FLUO- + PI)PERAZINE.] A phenothiazine derivative used as a tranquillizer and anti-emetic (usu. administered as the hydrochloride); 10-[3-(4-methylpiperazin-1-yl)propyl]-2-trifluoromethylphenothiazine, $C_{21}H_{24}F_3N_3S$.

1958 *Amer. Jrnl. Psychiatry* CXIV. 747 (*heading*) Triflupromazine and trifluoperazine: two new tranquilizers. *Ibid.* 747/2 The chlorine atom of the phenothiazine nucleus has been replaced by carbon trifluoride... This differentiates..trifluoperazine from prochlorperazine. **1965** [see STELAZINE]. **1977** *Lancet* 15 Oct. 816/2 A 65-year-old woman had been taking 'Parstelin' tablets (tranylcypromine 10 mg, trifluoperazine 1 mg), one three times daily for a depressive illness for 4 years. **1984** *Brit. Med. Jrnl.* 8 Sept. 612/1 He was diagnosed as having an anxiety neurosis and was prescribed trifluoperazine together with orphenadrine.

triˈfluor-, triˈfluoro-. *Chem.* [f. TRI- 5 + FLUOR(O-.] A formative analogous to TRICHLOR(O-, expressing the substitution of 3 atoms of fluorine for hydrogen, as in ***trifluoromethane*** or ***fluoroform***, CHF_3, from methane, CH_4; so ***trifluorethylene***, $CF_2{:}CHF$, from ethylene, $CH_2{:}CH_2$.

1899 *Jrnl. Chem. Soc.* LXXVI. I. 197 Trifluorotoluene ($C_6H_5.CF_3$) is not decomposed at high temperatures, and not attacked by water, alkalis.

trifocal (traɪˈfəʊkəl), *a.* and *sb.* [f. TRI- + FOCAL *a.*] **A.** *adj.* †**a.** (See quot.) *Obs.*

1826 J. I. HAWKINS in *Repertory Patent Inventions* III. 386 When three pairs [of glasses] are worn in one frame..which I denominate trifocal spectacles, the opening should be a circle of one inch diameter.

b. Of a lens: having three parts with different focal lengths. Of spectacles: having such lenses.

1921 *Amer. Jrnl. Ophthalmol.* IV. 406/2 The writer does not claim that every presbyope should have a pair of trifocal spectacles. **1928** W. S. DUKE-ELDER *Pract. Refraction* xxiii. 343 For some purposes tri-focal lenses are advocated. **1969** K. VONNEGUT *Slaughterhouse-Five* v. 93 She was wearing tri-focal lenses in harlequin frames.

B. *sb.* A trifocal lens; usu. *pl.*, trifocal spectacles.

1899 J. THORINGTON *Refraction* xi. 283 Trifocals.—Occasionally, a patient is not content with bifocals, but will demand a focal point somewhere between infinity and his working distance. **1946** BERENS & ZUCKERMAN *Diagnostic Examination of Eye* I. xii. 319 (*caption*) Double-segment panoptik trifocal for sculptors. **1962** L. S. SASIENI *Optical Dispensing* vii. 172 Where the gardener does not need a distance correction, the best combination may be reading and weak intermediate. A trifocal is the obvious alternative. **1973** R. HAYES *Hungarian Game* xxiv. 147 He was a pallid man with eyes that were weirdly distorted by trifocals.

trifoil, -fol(e: see TREFOIL.

trifold (ˈtraɪfəʊld), *a. rare.* [f. TRI- + -FOLD: cf. BIFOLD.] Threefold, triple.

1579 LYLY *Euphues* (Arb.) 142 Ther is amongst men a trifold kinde of life, Actiue..Speculatiue... The third is..a lewde lyfe, and idle and vaine life. **1867** J. B. ROSE tr. *Virgil's Æneid* 228 The trifold janitor Of Stygian Orcus. **1900** G. H. KINGSLEY *Sport & Trav.* 416 The trifold affection existing between the three.

trifoliate (traɪˈfəʊlɪət), *a.* [f. TRI- + L. *foliātus* leaved: cf. *trifolium* TREFOIL.] Three-leaved; *esp.* in *Bot.* consisting of three leaflets, as a compound leaf; also of a plant, having such leaves; *transf.* having the form of such a leaf.

1753 CHAMBERS *Cycl. Supp.* s.v. *Leaf.* **1756** ELLIS in *Phil. Trans.* XLIX. 867 The pinnated one called by the gardeners the poison ash, did not strike so deep a black as the other two trifoliate ones. **1845** LINDLEY *Sch. Bot.* v. (1858) 56 Leaves stalked, trifoliate; leaflets toothed. **1897** *Allbutt's Syst. Med.* III. 148 The pelvic brim [in some cases of osteomalacia] assumes a trifoliate form.

Also **triˈfoliated** *a.*, (*a*) *Bot.* = prec.; (*b*) *Arch.* Having or consisting of trefoils: see TREFOIL *sb.* 3.

1698 J. PETIVER in *Phil. Trans.* XX. 315 The Leaves of this are many times only trifoliated. **1733** MILLER *Gard. Dict.*

(ed. 2) s.v. *Leaves*, A Trifoliated Leaf, is a digitated Leaf, consisting of three Fingers, as the Trefoil. **1850** INKERSLEY *Styles Archit. France* 309 The Clerestory window-archway ..is divided into three pointed trifoliated lights. **1863** WALBRAN *Mem. Fountains Abbey* (Surtees) 147 A trifoliated canopy.

trifolie, variant of *trifoly*: see TREFOIL.

trifoliolate (traɪˈfəʊlɪələt), *a. Bot.* [f. TRI- + med.L. *foliolum* leaflet, dim. of L. *folium* leaf: see -ATE².] Consisting of three leaflets, or having leaves of this form; trifoliate. (Abbrev. *3-foliolate.*)

1828 in WEBSTER. **1868** LOSSING *Hudson* 35 The bright trifoliolate oxalis, or wood-sorrel. **1870** HOOKER *Stud. Flora* 242 Leaves alternate 3-foliolate.

‖**Trifolium** (trɪˈfəʊlɪəm, traɪ-). *Bot.* [L. *trifolium* (Pliny), f. *tri-*, TRI- + *folium* leaf. Cf. TREFOIL.] A large genus of leguminous plants, with trifoliate leaves, and flowers mostly in close heads; including many valuable fodder-plants, known as *clovers* or *trefoils*: *spec.* in recent agricultural use, applied to the species *T. incarnatum*.

[*c* **1000** ÆLFRIC *Voc.* in Wr.-Wülcker 133/22 *Trifolium* geaces sure, *uel* þrilefe. *c* **1625** *Names of Plants* ibid. 556/33 *Trifolium*, [F.] trifoil, [Eng.] wite clouere.] **1541** R. COPLAND *Galyen's Terap.* 2 F iij, Verbascum soden, and leaues of trifolium. **1596** LODGE *Marg. Amer.* 23 The fortunate husband, well trained to yoake and plough, learned of trifolium who lifteth up her leaves against tempest. **1885** *Manch. Exam.* 16 June 5/1 A large quantity of trifolium..has grown with immense rapidity.

attrib. **1900** *Westm. Gaz.* 15 Mar. 10/1 Several varieties of the great *trifolium* family lay claim to the honour of being the true 'St. Patrick's Cross'.

trifoly, trifoote: see TREFOIL, TREFOOT.

triforial (traɪˈfɔːrɪəl), *a.* [f. next + -AL¹.] Of, pertaining to, or constituting a triforium.

1848 B. WEBB *Cont. Ecclesiol.* 45 Each of these arches is situated below a blank triforial arcade of two arches. **1854** J. L. PETIT *Archit. Stud. France* 37 The triforial arches of Amiens and Evreux. **1861** BERESF. HOPE *Eng. Cathedr. 19th C.* vi. 217 Previously to its reappearance in Germany, the triforial gallery had made good its position elsewhere.

‖**triforium** (traɪˈfɔːrɪəm). *Arch.* Pl. -ia. [med.(Anglo-)L., found first in Gervase of Canterbury, *c* 1185; then, from him, in Battely's ed. of Somner *Antiquities of Canterbury*, 1703. In these, referring only to Canterbury Cathedral; in current English use, and in reference to cathedrals generally, only since 1800. Mentioned by Viollet-le-Duc, *Dict. d'Architecture* 1868, as introduced into architectural nomenclature by the English archæologists. Etymology unknown: see Note below.] A gallery or arcade in the wall over the arches at the sides of the nave and choir, and sometimes of the transepts, in some large churches. Originally applied to that in Canterbury Cathedral; in the nineteenth century extended as a general term.

[*c* **1185** GERVASE (of Canterbury) *Tract. de Combust. et Repar. Cant. Eccl.* Wks. (Rolls) I. 13 Hic murus chorum circuiens in circinatione illa piliariorum in capite ecclesiæ in unum conveniebat. Supra quem murum via erat quæ triforium appellatur, et fenestræ superiores.] **1703** N. BATTELY *Somner's Antiq. Canterb.* II. I. iv. 16 The former Quire had but one Triforium, now there are two round the Quire, and one in each side Isle of the Quire. *Ibid.*, A multitude of Marble Pillars..placed about the double Triforium, one above the other. **1726** J. DART *Hist. Canterb. Cath.* 8. **1774** GOSTLING *Walk Canterbury* 150 Above these large windows is a walk which Mr. Battely calls a triforium. **1815** J. SMITH *Panorama Sc. & Art* I. 155 Another.. distinction of these arches, in large buildings, is the absence of the triforium or gallery. **1833** DALLAWAY *Disc. Archit. Eng.*, etc. 95 Above them [pointed arches] are the triforia, continued through every part. **1848** *Builder* 8 July 328/2 A discourse was..delivered by Prof. Willis, on the triforium of ancient churches... The only ancient work in which such a term could be found..was a history of Canterbury (by Gervase), in which it occurred in three places... He [Willis] verily believed that the modern term was a clumsy latinization of 'thoroughfarium'. **1868** A. K. H. BOYD *Less. Mid. Age* 368 The nave [at Norwich], of fourteen bays, vaulted in stone, and with the heavy round arches of the triforium as large as those below, makes the choir, of four bays, ending in a pentagon, seem small in comparison. **1874** PARKER *Goth. Archit.* Gloss. 329 *Triforium*, or *Blind-story*, the middle story of a large church, over the pier-arches and under the clere-story windows.

attrib. **1835** R. WILLIS *Archit. Mid. Ages* vii. 87, *ff* is the clerestory string, and *gg* the triforium string. *Ibid.* ix. 137 *note*, The clerestory wall is recessed back over the triforium gallery. **1835** WHEWELL *German Churches* (1842) 103 These intermediate vaulting shafts spring from the triforium tablet. [*Note.*] The running tablet or cornice below the triforium. **1905** BOND *Goth. Archit.* 519 The term *triforium* ..is often used, not of the arcade, but of the space at the back of the arcade. So that it means sometimes the triforium arcade, sometimes the triforium chamber.

[*Note.* On the face of it, *triforium* looks like a normal L. formation (cf. *tricennium*, *triennium*, *trifinium*, *trifurcium*) from *tri-* three or thrice + *fores* 'a door of two leaves' = 'something consisting of or containing three doors'. Hence it has been explained as referring to a gallery or arcade with triple openings, as found at Amiens and in some other cathedrals; but this is not the case in Canterbury cathedral, to which alone the term was applied down to 1800, so that the explanation is not consistent with the facts. Others have suggested formation from L. *forāre* to bore, pierce, with *tri-* for F. *tres*, L. *trans*. Various other conjectures have been offered (see e.g. *N. & Q.* series 2, vol. IV. 269, 320, 371, 481, 522; V. 57, etc.); but none of them are satisfactory. The word itself may have been erroneously formed or misapplied by Gervase: see also med.L. *triforium* in the sense 'border, ornamental bordering' in Du Cange.]

triform (ˈtraɪfɔːm), *a.* [ad. L. *triformis*, f. *tri-* + *forma* FORM: cf. F. *triforme* (15th c. in Godef.), perh. the source in quot. *c* 1450.]

1. Having a triple form; combining three different forms; formed or composed in three parts.

c **1450** *Mirour Saluacioun* 683 This temple of Salomon had on it pynacles thre Be whilk the triforme Auriole of marye takened may be. **1660** STANLEY *Hist. Philos.* IX. (1701) 379/2 Something which hath beginning, middle and end. To such a form and nature they attributed the number Three, saying, That whatsoever hath a middle is triform. **1678** CUDWORTH *Intell. Syst.* I. v. 673 Centaurs, and Scyllas, and Chimæras,..mixtly boviform and hominiform, biform and triform animals. **1805–17** R. JAMESON *Char. Min.* (ed. 3) 202 A crystal is said to be..Bi-form, tri-form, when it contains a combination of two or three remarkable forms.

2. Existing or appearing in three different forms.

1623 COCKERAM, *Triforme*, hauing three formes or fashions. **1667** MILTON *P.L.* III. 730 The neighbouring Moon..With borrowd light her countenance triform Hence fills and empties. **1678** CUDWORTH *Intell. Syst.* I. iv. §17. 304 Damascius..tells us..that Orpheus introduced τρίμορφον θεὸν, a Triform Deity. **1684** T. BURNET *Th. Earth* I. 164 This epistle..taught that the heavens and the earth had chang'd their form, and would do so again..; so as the same world would be triform in success of time. **1742** tr. *Algarotti on 'Newton's Theory'* II. 161 Her triform Goddess we before admired. **1847** LEITCH tr. *C. O. Müller's Anc. Art* §206 In the representation of the tri-form Hecate. **1867–77** G. F. CHAMBERS *Astron.* I. xii. 136, I [Galileo] have observed the most distant planet [Saturn] to be tri-form. **1879** H. W. WARREN *Recr. Astron.* viii. 169 Huyghens..solved the problem of the triform appearance of Saturn.

3. *erron.* Triangular.

1621 J. TAYLOR (Water P.) *Superbiæ Flagellum* Wks. 34/2 That heights, depths, bredths, triforme, square, oval, round, And rules Geometricall in beards are found.

So ˈ**triformed** (-fɔːmd), **triˈformous** *adjs.* in same senses; **triˈformity** (*rare*⁻⁰) [late L. *triformitās* (Claudian)], the quality of being triform.

1644 DIGBY *Nat. Bodies* xxiii. §8. 212 That which is most watry, is fittest to fabricate the body..of the *triformed plant. *a* **1662** HEYLIN *Land* (1668) 368 Governed by a Tryformed Presbytery of Pastors, Elders, and Deacons. *a* **1739** JARVIS *Quix.* I. IV. xliii. (1885) 242 O thou triformed luminary, bring me sweet tidings of her! **1816** G. S. FABER *Orig. Pagan Idol.* I. 413 She [Sphinx] was likewise triformed, blending together in one figure a lion, a virgin, and a bird. **1727** BAILEY vol. II, **Triformity*, the having three Forms or Shapes. **1841** WILKINSON *Mann. Egypt.* Ser. II. I. xii. 232 The idea entertained by the Pagan Egyptians of a '*triformous Deity',..who assumed different names according to the triad under which he was represented.

triˈformol. [f. TRI- 5 + *form*(*aldehyde*) (see FORM-) + -OL.] A commercial name of paraformaldehyde (see PARA- 2), used as an antiseptic.

1907 WOOD *U.S.A. Dispens.* 1604 *Paraformaldehyde, Triformol*..may be considered as a polymerized formaldehyde.

triforoid (ˈtraɪfərɔɪd), *a.* (*sb.*) *Zool.* [f. mod.L. *Triforis* (f. TRI- + *foris* door, opening) + -OID.] Belonging to or having the characters of the family *Triforidæ* of gastropods, typified by the genus *Triforis*. **b.** *sb.* A gastropod of this family.

1891 in *Cent. Dict.*

trifoveolate, -foveolated: see TRI- I.

trifunctional, -ally: see TRI- I a.

trifurcate (traɪˈfɜːkət), *a.* [f. L. *trifurc-us* three-forked, f. *tri-*, TRI- + *furca* FORK + -ATE². Cf. mod.F. *trifurqué* (Littré), *trifourche* (Cotgr.), also F. *trifurcation* (Bonnet).] Divided into three branches like the prongs of a fork; three-forked, three-pronged, trichotomous. Also *fig.* So **triˈfurcal** *a.* (*rare*⁻¹); ˈ**trifurcate** *v.*, *intr.* to divide or branch into three; ˈ**trifurcated** *a.* = *trifurcate* adj.; also, having some part, as a fin, trifurcated, as the ***trifurcated blenny*** or ***hake***; ˈ**trifurcating** *vbl. sb.*, in ***trifurcating box*** (see quot. 1940); **trifurˈcation**, division into three branches, or the point at which this takes place; †**triˈfurcous** *a. Obs. rare*⁻⁰ = *trifurcate* adj.

1716 M. DAVIES *Athen. Brit.* III. *Suppl. Diss. Drama* 8 Whether he took himself to be affronted..and consequently that he deserv'd such *Trifurcal Repartees. **1811–31** BENTHAM *Logic* App., Wks. 1843 VIII. 291/2 Instead of bifurcate, two-pronged, suppose the plan of division, for example, *trifurcate, three-pronged. **1866** R. M. FERGUSON *Electr.* (1870) 97 Occasionally when darting between the clouds and the earth, it breaks up near the latter into two or three forks, and [lightning] is then called bifurcate or trifurcate. **1887** SOLLAS in *Encycl. Brit.* XXII. 417/1 (*Sponges*) The arms of a triæne may bifurcate..or they may *trifurcate. **1894** *Geol. Mag.* Oct. 438 The primary ribs of the Australian fossil..trifurcate more regularly. **1727** BAILEY vol. II, **Trifurcated*,..three-forked. **1769** PENNANT *Zool.* III. 131 A very singular trifurcated spine. **1836–9** *Todd's Cycl. Anat.* II. 933/2 The antenna on one side..was trifurcated. **1922** *B.I. Handbk.* (Brit. Insulated & Helsby Cables Ltd.) (ed. 3) 447 (Index), *Trifurcating boxes. **1940** *Chambers's Techn. Dict.* 864/2 *Trifurcating box*, a cable dividing box for enclosing the joints between a three-arc or triple concentric cable and three single-core cables or conductor terminals. **1884** M. MACKENZIE *Dis. Throat & Nose* II. 224 In two cases there was *trifurcation of the trachea. **1656** BLOUNT *Glossogr.*, **Trifurcous*,..three-forked.

trig (trɪg), *sb.*¹ [Goes with TRIG *v.*¹; the vb. being app. the source of the sb.]

1. A wedge or block placed under a wheel or cask to prevent it from rolling; hence in a mine, a bar used as a brake for the wheel of a tram; also *U.S.*, a brake-shoe, a skid; in extended use applied to any material, as hay or gravel, laid on a slide to check the motion of a sledge going over it. In quot. 1647 *fig.* Cf. TRIGGER *sb.*²

Its fig. use in quot. 1647 points to an earlier literal use: see also TRIG *v.*¹

1647 R. STAPYLTON *Juvenal* xvi. 62 Nor is his suite in danger to be stopt, Or with the trigges of long demurrers propt. **1830** SEBA SMITH *Major J. Downing* (1860) 72 I've seen the wheels chocked with a little trig not bigger than a cat's head. **1858** SIMMONDS *Dict. Trade*, *Trig*, a wedge or block to prop up a cask, or to stop a wheel. **1883** GRESLEY *Gloss. Coal Mining*, *Trig*, a sprag used for stopping or putting the brake on trams, wagons, &c. **1886** J. BARROWMAN *Sc. Mining Terms* 68 *Trig*, a piece of wood laid in front of a waggon wheel to stop its motion.

†**2.** *Thieves' slang.* See quot. *Obs.* (perh. a different word, or ? belonging to TRIG *sb.*²)

1812 J. H. VAUX *Flash Dict.*, *Trig*, a bit of stick, paper, &c., placed by thieves in the keyhole of..the door of a house, which they suspect to be uninhabited; if the trig remains unmoved the following day, it is a proof that no person sleeps in the house. This..is called trigging the jigger.

trig, *sb.*² Now *dial.* and in workmen's speech. Also 7 trigg. [Goes with TRIG *v.*², of obscure origin.] A line traced, cut, or marked out on the ground, as a boundary or centre line, a guide for a cutting, etc.; the line or score at which a player at bowls, quoits, curling, etc. stands, or from which runners start in a race; hence ***to foot*** or ***toe the trig*** (see TOE *v.* 2); also *dial.* a shallow trench, gutter, or small ditch, a narrow path or track (*Eng. Dial. Dict.*).

1648 DAVENANT *Long Vac. in Lond.* 98 Now Alderman in field does stand, With foot on Trig, a Quoit in hand. **1688** R. HOLME *Armoury* III. xvi. (Roxb.) 70/1 The Trigg is the place or mark on which the players are to set one foot, or foot the Trigg, when they deliuer their Bowles. **1796** *Grose's Dict. Vulg. T.* (ed. 3), *Trig*, the point at which schoolboys stand to shoot their marbles at taw; also the spot whence bowlers deliver the bowl. **1843** *Civil Eng. & Arch. Jrnl.* VI. 22/1 He is also..to preserve the centre or trig line, especially in curves. **1893–4** *Northumbld. Gloss.*, *Trig*, the starting line in a race, which may be either a stretched cord, a stick, a post, or an imaginary boundary. **1895** *E. Anglia Gloss.*, *Trig*, (2) The mark from which a ball is delivered.

trig, *sb.*³ *dial.* or *colloq.* [f. TRIG *v.*³] A trot, a hurried walk; a tramp on foot, a trip.

1884 HOLLAND *Cheshire Gloss.* (E.D.S.) s.v., He's allus uppo th' trig (always in a hurry). **1888** *Blackw. Mag.* Sept. 392 The goings on of himself and his comrade on the 'great trig' in the wilds of the Scotch Highlands.

attrib. Ibid. 396 Nothing remained but to declare the 'trig' field season at an end.

trig (trɪg), *a.*¹ (*sb.*⁴) Forms: 2–7 trigg, 6 (*Sc.*) tryg, 7 trigge, 5– trig. [a. ON. *tryggr* faithful, trusty, trustworthy, secure (Norw., Sw. *trygg*, Da. *tryg* secure, safe, sure); = Gothic *triggws* true, faithful: see TRUE. Orig. northern Eng. and Sc.; in general literary use in 19th c.]

(The sense development between 1200 and 1500 is not very clear, and the order of senses given is mainly chronological; perhaps sense 4 ought to stand before 3. Cf. the note to TRIM *a.*, which is to a great extent applicable also to TRIG.)

I. 1. True, faithful; trustworthy, trusty. Now only *north. dial.*

c **1200** ORMIN 6177 Þin laferrd birrþ þe buhsumm beon & hold & trigg & trowwe. **1818** T. THOMPSON *Canny Newcassel* in Midford, etc. *Coll. Songs* (1819) 8 For Geordy aw'd dee,—for my loyalty's trig. **1829** BROCKETT *N.C. Words*, *Trig*, true, faithful. **1893–4** *Northumb. Gloss.*, *Trig*, neat, spruce, true, reliable.

II. †**2.** Active, nimble, brisk, sprightly, alert. *Sc.*

c **1470** HENRYSON *Mor. Fab.* VII. (*Lion & Mouse*) i, Ane trip of myis..Richt tait and trig, all dansand in ane gyis. **1513** DOUGLAS *Æneis* XII. Prol. 184 Litill lammis Full tait and trig socht bletand to thar dammis. **1724** RAMSAY *Eagle & Robin* 23 A tunefull Robin trig and ȝung.

3. Trim or tight in person, shape, or appearance; of a place, Neat, tidy, in good order. Chiefly *Sc.* and *dial.*

1513 DOUGLAS *Æneis* IX. x. 89 The beste sal be full tydy, tryg, and wycht. **1697** R. PEIRCE *Bath Mem.* I. iv. 71 Her.. Foot and Leg [were] as shapely, strong, and trigge. *Ibid.* vi. 107, I, by chance, met her trigg and lusty, in the Market-Street. **1816** SCOTT *Antiq.* xxiv, And it's like some o' them will be sent back to fling the earth into the hole, and mak a' things trig again. **1821** GALT *Ayrsh. Legatees* x, The wonted ornaments of every trig change-house kitchen. **1824** SCOTT

St. Ronan's xxviii, A damsel so trig and neat that some said she was too handsome for the service of a bachelor divine. **1837** R. NICOLL *Poems* (1843) 126 My Sandie was the triggest lad That ever made a lassie glad. **1889** *Scribner's Mag.* Aug. 168/1 Bait is a dirty substitute for the trig fly.

b. Trim or neat in dress; smartly-dressed; spruce, smart, well-dressed.

1725 RAMSAY *Gentle Sheph.* I. ii, Few gang trigger to the kirk or fair. **1821** CLARE *Vill. Minstr.*, etc. II. 96 Trig as new pins, and tight's the day was long. **1825** BROCKETT *N.C. Words*, *Trig*, neat, trim; or rather tricked out, or what is called fine. **1873** HOWELLS *Chance Acquaint.* iv, The trig corporal, with the little visorless cap worn so jauntily. **1884** *Century Mag.* XXVIII. 541 The stylish gait and air of the trig little body who wore them. **1893** 'J. S. WINTER' *Aunt Johnnie* II. 181 She really looked very smart and trig and jaunty.

4. In good physical condition; strong, sound, well; also, firm, steady; in quot. *a* 1722, *advb.*

1704 LOCKE *Let. to Churchill* 27 June, in Fox Bourne *Life* (1876) II. 546, I hope..that I may congratulate your safe return, strong and trig as you were before. *a* **1722** LISLE *Husb.* (1757) 270 A man will keep so much the greater awe over [oxen when ploughing], and will make them go trig. **1847–78** HALLIWELL, *Trig*, (5) well in health. *West.* (6) sound and firm. *Dorset.* **1858** *Brit. Q. Rev.* LVI. 548 Those noble [Greek and Roman] youths..sitting on the bare backs of their chargers, and guiding them with their hands;..they do not sit badly considering they have not the advantages..of pig's skin and stirrups to keep them square and trig. **1890** AMELIA E. BARR *Olivia* xvii. 351, I wish I was in mid-ocean all trig and tight. Then I would enjoy such a passion of wind.

5. Prim, precise, exact; in depreciative use: Cut and dried, smug. *rare.*

1793 J. PEARSON *Political Dict.* 38 Trig and demure, the [girl] comes back. **1832** J. P. KENNEDY *Swallow B.* viii, A certain trig and quaint appearance given by his tight dark-colored small-clothes. **1868** TUCKERMAN *Collector* 74 A trig nurse, with Saxon ringlets, dragging a petulant urchin. **1872** H. W. BEECHER in *Chr. World Pulpit* II. 341 Our system of trig and prig theology. **1876** BLACKIE *Songs Relig. & Life* 137 A little man, smooth, and close-shaven, very trig, and smug.

6. Full, distended, stuffed to the utmost, 'tight'. *north. dial.*

1811 WILLAN *W. Riding Gloss.* (E.D.S.), *Trig*,..full, distended. **1825** BROCKETT *N.C. Words*, *Trig* a., full. **1905** in *Eng. Dial. Dict.* from Cumbld., Yorksh., Lincolnsh. *Ibid.* (N. Lincoln), 'Thoo mon't shuv no moore i'to that bag, it's oher trig noo'.

†**B.** *sb.*[4] A trim, spruce fellow; a dandy, a coxcomb. *Obs.*

1610 B. JONSON *Alch.* IV. vii, You are a Pimpe, and a Trig, And an Amadis de Gaule, or a Don Quixote.

Hence **'trigly** *adv.*, **'trigness.**

1728 RAMSAY *Lure* 40 What fowl is that,..that stands sae trigly on your hand? **1821** GALT *Ann. Parish* ii. 29 The lassies, who had been at Nanse Banks's school, were always well spoken of..for..the trigness of their houses, when they were..married. **1853** KANE *Grinnell Exp.* ii. (1856) 18 Their spars had no man-of-war trigness. **1896** J. TWEEDDALE *Moff* i. 14 Fields were subdivided by trigly cut hedges.

trig, *a.*[2] and *sb.*[5] Colloq. abbrev. of TRIGONOMETRICAL *a.*, TRIGONOMETRY. Freq. as ***trig point, station.***

1862 *McLean Papers* (MS.) XX. 87 Mr Swainson informs me that the Trig Station pulled down was not one erected by him. **1895** W. C. GORE in *Inlander* Nov. 65 Trig. n., trigonometry. **1924** P. MARKS *Plastic Age* 36 Kane announced the textbook, and when Hugh caught the word 'trigonometry' he actually thrilled with joy. He had had trig in high school. **1926** J. DEVANNY *Lenore Divine* xx. 184 They reached the trig station at the top, two thousand five hundred feet above sea-level. **1936** H. S. L. WINTERBOTHAM *Key to Maps* iii. 28 On the ordnance maps and plans you will find..little triangles with dots inside... Each one represents a place fixed by careful instrumental measurement, and the sum total represents the skeleton.. upon which all our maps depend... 'Trig. Points', represented by the triangles, control the map in plan, 'Bench-marks' in height. **1959** J. BRAINE *Vodi* vi. 92 I've not done those trig. problems. **1968** G. R. CRONE *Maps & their Makers* xi. 143 Transference of the trig. points to the sheets issued to the plane tablers. **1976** J. LEE *Ninth Man* i. 48 Andy flunked trig for the second time (damn higher mathematics, anyway). **1981** *Times Lit. Suppl.* 22 May 577/1 Surveyors had to be trained [for Ordnance Survey mapmaking]; trig-points and bench-marks established.

trig, *v.*[1] Inflected **trigged, -ing.** [Etymology uncertain: perhaps ad. ON. *tryggja*, ODa. *trygge* to make firm or secure, from *tryggr* firm, sure, true.

This derivation fairly suits the sense; the difficulty being that *to trig* (in this sense) is not a northern or Sc. word, but is at home in dialects south of the Thames, which makes a Norse origin unlikely.]

1. *trans.* To make firm or fast; to prevent from moving; *esp.* to apply a wedge, block, or the like, to (a wheel) in order to stop or retard its motion.

1591 PERCIVALL *Sp. Dict.*, *Calzar*, to shoo. *Calceare*, to trig a wheele [*mod.Sp. Dict.*, *calzar*, to shoe..to stop a wheel]. **1651** CARTWRIGHT *Poems* (Nares), Times wheels are trig'd, and brib'd to make a stand. *a* **1661** HOLYDAY *Juvenal* (1673) 155 With free Chariot, fat Damasippus hurries; he, (He! even the consul) triggs the wheel. **1726** *Dict. Rust.* (ed. 3) s.v. *Trigger*, An Iron to Trig or Stay a Wheel. **1802** in *Spirit Pub. Jrnls.* VI. 235 Our friend Haterius should be trigged like a cart-wheel on an inclined plane. **1830** SEBA SMITH *Major J. Downing* (1860) 72 They make pesky bad work, trigging the wheels of Government. **1845** S. JUDD *Margaret* III. (1871) 397, I stand ready to trig the wheels in all the steep places.

2. To support or shore up with a wedge; to wedge up; to prop. Often with *up.*

1711 W. SUTHERLAND *Shipbuild. Assist.* 26 Shores, which ought to be placed on Timber Foundations, called Sholes, and well nog'd or trig'd. **1883** BARING-GOULD *J. Herring* xiv, She made him raise the hearthstone, and trig it up with a piece of granite. **1899** —— *Bk. West* xvii, To prevent the springs being broken..the axle-trees had been 'trigged up' below with blocks of wood.

†**3.** *Thieves' slang.* See TRIG *sb.*[1] 2. *Obs.*

Hence **'trigging** *vbl. sb.*

1667 FLAVEL *Saint Indeed* (1754) 148 The wheels being oiled with delight, run nimbly, and have often need of trigging. **1682** —— *Fear* vi. 78 Our thoughts run nimbly.. like oyled wheels, and have need of trigging.

trig, *v.*[2] *dial.* Inflected **trigged, -ing.** [Goes with TRIG *sb.*[2]: origin of both obscure.

(As Du. *trekker* has become in Eng. *trigger*, it is conceivable that Du. *trekken* 'to draw a line' might become *trig*; but nothing corroborative of such an origin has been found.)]

trans. To make a score on (the ground) for a player at bowls, quoits, etc., to stand at; also, to mark out (ground) with a line or shallow trench. ***trig out***, to mark out or trace, as a boundary line. Also *absol.*

1706 PHILLIPS (ed. Kersey), *Trig*,..to set a mark to stand at, in playing at Nine-pins. **1727** BAILEY vol. II, *Trigged*, having a Mark set to stand in playing at Nine Pins. **1843** [implied in TRIGGER *sb.*[2]]. **1881** MISS JACKSON *Shropsh. Word-bk.*, *Trig*,..to make shallow furrows, or trigs, as between seed-beds for onions, carrots, etc.—'I trigged the ground afore I put the seed in'. **1893** H. PEASE *Borderland Stud.* 36 Gravely he consulted with his 'marrow' (mate) who 'trigged' for him.., carefully noted the indicated line. *a* **1905** *MS. Gloss.* (Warwick) in *Eng. Dial. Dict.* s.v. *Trig* v.[1], Plots of ground let for building are trigged out, i.e. the boundaries are marked by cutting a small trench in them. **1914** H. F. RUTTER (M. Inst. C.E.) in *Let.*, I have been asked scores of times by a ganger [over navvies] 'Could you come and trig out the centre line for us, Sir?'

trig, *v.*[3] Now *dial.* Also 6 **trigge**, 7 **trigg**; infl. **trigg-.** [Origin unknown.] *intr.* To trot; to walk quickly or briskly; to trip; also *to trig it*; *spec.* (*slang*) see quot. 1796; also *trans.* or with advb. acc., as in ***to trig the country***, to tramp; ***to trig*** (a distance).

1599 NASHE *Lenten Stuff* 49 Away to the landes ende they trigge. **1647** TRAPP *Comm. 2 Thess.* i. 3 How oft are we sitting down on earth,..till affliction call to us, as the angel to Elijah, 'Up, thou hast a great way to go', and then we trigg. *a* **1652** A. WILSON *Inconstant Lady* II. i, Hee triggs it to Romilia's. *a* **1680** T. GOODWIN *Blessed State* xii. Wks. 1703 V. III. 83 His Servant..(who must presently, without more ado, trig and Foot it after his Master). **1700** T. BROWN *Amusem. Ser. & Com.* 66 She..Trig'd away Hand in Hand with the Gentleman. **1796** *Grose's Dict. Vulg. T.* (ed. 3), *To trig it*, to play truant. *a* **1825** FORBY *Voc. E. Anglia*, *Trig*, to trot gently; or trip as a child does after its nurse. 'They trigged off together'. **1872** HARTLEY *Yorksh. Ditties* Ser. II. 72 Mony a mile he had to trig One sweltin' summer day. **1891** B. GREGORY in *Wesl. Meth. Mag.* 56 A travelling tailor, having 'trigged the country' in search of work as far as 'Newrak'.

trig, *v.*[4] Now *dial.* Infl. **trigg-.** [f. TRIG *a.*[1] 3, 6; with both senses cf. TIGHT *v.*[3]]

I. 1. *trans.* To make trig or trim, to trim, to make tidy or neat; now often, to dress smartly or finely. ***trig out***, to dress or deck out. Chiefly *Sc.* and *north. dial.* Hence **'trigging** *vbl. sb.*, the action of the verb; *concr.* finery.

1696 *Song*, '*This is no my ain House*' i, Sin' ho claimed my daddy's place I downa bide the triggin o't. **1724** RAMSAY '*This is no my ain house*' i, Mine ain house I'll like to guide, And please me with the trigging o't. **1793** RITSON *N. Garland* (1809) 71 He rigg'd and trigg'd, and rid away. **1877** R. W. THOM *Jock o' Knowe* 54 Beauty..shines divine when seen Trigged oot in love and charity. **1896** KIPLING *Seven Seas, Rhyme Three Sealers* 62 He has rigged and trigged her with paint and spar. **1897** W. BEATTY *Secretar* xxx. 243 (Fifeshire) She had gotten me into her room to see that I was trigged out as I should be.

II. 2. *trans.* To fill full, to stuff, cram. (Cf. to fill 'tight'.)

1660 H. MORE *Myst. Godl.* IV. iii. 105 By how much more a mans skin is full treg'd with flesh, blood and natural Spirits. **1771** SMOLLETT *Humph. Cl.* 15 May, O Molly! the sarvants at Bath..lite the candle at both ends. Here's nothing but ginketting, and wasting, and thieving, and tricking, and trigging. **1790** GROSE *Provinc. Gloss.* (ed. 2) Supp., *Trig thy kite*, fill thy belly. **1825** BROCKETT *N.C. Words*, *Trig*, to fill, to stuff. **1828** *Craven Gloss.* s.v., 'He's trigg'd his hamper;' that is, he has filled his belly. **1905** in *E. Dial. Dict.* from Cumbld., Westmld., Durham, Yorksh.

trigamist ('trɪgəmɪst). [f. as TRIGAMY + -IST.] † One who has been married three times (*obs.*); now, one who has three wives or husbands at the same time. Cf. BIGAMIST. Also *attrib.*

1656 BLOUNT *Glossogr.*, *Trigamist*,..he that hath had three wives. **1854** *Tait's Mag.* XXI. 316 We could have spared..the memorials of the trigamist Doctor. **1895** *Daily Tel.* 28 Nov. 7/2 Collis being already a bigamist or trigamist. **1899** RODWAY *Guiana Wilds* 266 The Church would not permit me to baptize a trigamist, and the chief would not part with either of his wives.

trigamous ('trɪgəməs), *a.* [f. Gr. τρίγαμ-ος thrice married (f. τρι- + γάμος wedding) + -OUS.]

1. Characterized by, involving, or living in trigamy.

1886 *Pall Mall G.* 25 Jan. 4 'The Man with Three Wives' never lives in the trigamous state. **1900** P. F. WILLERT in *Eng. Hist. Rev.* July 590 Bigamous and trigamous marriages. **1908** *Daily Chron.* 22 Jan. 5/5 All three combine to avenge the treachery of the trigamous husband.

2. *Bot.* Having male, female, and hermaphrodite flowers in the same head. (Cf. POLYGAMOUS 3.)

1842 BRANDE *Dict. Sc.*, etc., *Trigamous*,..containing three sorts of flowers in the same flower-head; that is to say, males, females, and hermaphrodites. **1900** in B. D. JACKSON *Gloss. Bot. Terms.*

trigamy ('trɪgəmɪ). [ad. late L. *trigamia*, a. Gr. (eccl.) τριγαμία, f. τρίγαμος: see prec. So F. *trigamie* (Littré).]

1. *Eccl. Law.* Marriage for the third time after the death of former wives or husbands. ? *Obs.*

1615 G. SANDYS *Trav.* 82 For them [priests] it is lawfull to marry: but bigamy is forbidden them, and trigamy detested in the Laity. **1727–41** CHAMBERS *Cycl.*, *Trigamy*, a third marriage; or the state of a person who has been married three times... In the ancient church, trigamy was only allowed to such as had no children by their former marriages.

2. The state of having three wives or husbands at the same time; the crime of contracting a third marriage while two previous spouses are alive.

a **1634** COKE *On Litt.* III. xxvii. (1648) 88 The difference between Bygamy, or Trigamy, &c. and Polygamy. **1706** PHILLIPS (ed. Kersey), *Trigamy*, (Gr.) the having three Husbands or three Wives at once. **1884** *Chr. World* 16 Oct. 795/5 A woman 30 years of age was charged with trigamy, all three husbands being still alive.

trigastric: see TRI- 1.

trigeminal (traɪ'dʒɛmɪnəl), *a.* (*sb.*) *Anat.* [f. L. *trigemin-us* born three at a birth (see below) + -AL[1].] A name for the fifth pair of cranial nerves, from their dividing into three branches: also called TRIFACIAL. Also *absol.* as *sb.*

1830 R. KNOX *Béclard's Anat.* 349 The nerves of the arteries belong either to the sympathetic nerves, or to the spinal and trigeminal nerves. **1872** HUXLEY *Physiol.* xi. 264 Each nerve of the fifth pair is very large..and, having three chief divisions, is often called trigeminal. **1899** *Allbutt's Syst. Med.* VI. 744 Such pain follows the distribution of peripheral branches of the trigeminal.

b. Pertaining to, occurring in, or affecting the trigeminal nerve.

1874 GARROD & BAXTER *Mat. Med.* (1880) 22 In cases of intercostal and trigeminal neuralgia. **1899** *Allbutt's Syst. Med.* VII. 354 The trigeminal anæsthesia affects either the whole of the region..or only that supplied by special divisions.

tri'geminous, *a.* [f. as prec. + -OUS.]

1. (See quots.) *rare.*

1656 BLOUNT *Glossogr.*, *Trigeminous* (*trigeminus*), three-fold, three at a birth. **1658** PHILLIPS, *Trigeminous*, (Lat.) three brought forth at a birth; also treble, or threefold.

2. *Anat.* = TRIGEMINAL.

1891 in *Cent. Dict.*

3. *Bot.* = *trijugate* (see TRI- 1).

1900 in B. D. JACKSON *Gloss. Bot. Terms.*

‖**trigeminus** (traɪ'dʒɛmɪnəs). *Anat.* [L. *trigeminus* born three at a birth, f. TRI- + L. *gemin-us* born at the same birth.]

†**1.** A former name for the complexus muscle (COMPLEXUS[2]). *Obs.*

[**1704** J. HARRIS *Lex. Techn.* I, *Complexus*, a Muscle of the Head, serving to move it backwards. It is also called *Trigeminum*, because it hath plainly a three-fold beginning, and seems to be compounded of 3 Muscles.] **1706** PHILLIPS (ed. Kersey), Trigeminus or Trigeminum.

2. The trigeminal nerve. Also *attrib.*

1875 tr. *von Ziemssen's Cycl. Med.* II. 574 Neuralgia in the branches of the trigeminus nerve. **1899** *Allbutt's Syst. Med.* VII. 354 Tactile sensibility may be impaired in the region of the trigeminus on the side of the lesion.

[† **trigen,** app. an error of some kind for *triger*, TRIGGER *sb.*[2], appearing first in 1659; whence in Phillips *New World of Words* 1678, and in many subsequent Dictionaries.

1659 HOOLE tr. *Comenius' Visible World* lxxxv. 175 He.. stoppeth the wheel with a trigen [*sufflamine*] in a steep descent. **1678** PHILLIPS (ed. 4), *Trigen*, a kind of Pole whereby a Coach or Waggon is stopped from going too fast down a Hill. **1688** R. HOLME *Armoury* III. 339/2. **1847–78** HALLIWELL, *Trigen*, a skidpan for a wheel.]

trigeneric: see TRI- 1.

trigenic (traɪ'dʒɛnɪk), *a.* [app. f. TRI- 5 b + Gr. γένος kind + -IC: the acid was so named by Liebig and Wöhler, 1846, regarding it as the product of *three kinds* of substances, cyanic acid, aldehyde, and ammonia.] **1.** *Chem.* In ***trigenic acid***, $NH{:}2(CO.NH){:}CH.CH_3$, also called ethylidene (or ethidene) biuret, as being biuret, $NH{:}2(CO.NH_2)$, in which two atoms of H are replaced by ethylidene, $CH.CH_3$; it crystallizes in small prisms, slightly soluble in water.

1868 WATTS *Dict. Chem.* V. 883. **1882** *Jrnl. Chem. Soc.* XLII. 168.

2. *Genetics.* [Cf. GENIC *a.*] Involving or controlled by three genes.

1941 [see POLYGENIC *a.* 3]. **1979** *Experientia* XXXV. 172/2 The trigenic ratios have been reported here for the first time for the above-mentioned characters.

trigentale, -all, obs. forms of TRIGINTAL.

† **triger,** corruption of *chigger*, CHIGOE.

1782 P. H. BRUCE *Mem.* 426 Trigers..get through the soles of peoples feet and lodge between the skin and the flesh.

trigesimal (traɪˈdʒɛsɪməl), *a. rare.* [f. L. *trigēsim-us* thirtieth + -AL[1].] † **a.** Thirtieth. *Obs.* **b.** *loosely.* Consisting of thirty (i.e. in quot., days).

1637 SALTONSTALL *Eusebius' Constantine* 141 The trigesimall yeare of his raigne. **1839** *Fraser's Mag.* Aug. 203/1 The upper part may originally have been a crescent, implying monthly... The figure thus connects itself with the monthly trigesimal period.

trigetour, -ettur, var. TREGETOUR *Obs.*

trigger (ˈtrɪgə(r)), *sb.*[1] Forms: α. 7–8 (9 *dial.*) **tricker,** (7 **trycker**); β. 8 **triger,** 7– **trigger.** [In form *tricker*, ad. Du. *trekker* a trigger, f. *trekken* to pull: see TREK. The form *trigger* occurs in 1660, but *tricker* remained the usual form down to *c* 1750, and is still in dialect use from Scotland to the English Midlands.]

1. A movable catch or lever the pulling or pressing of which releases a detent or spring, and sets some force or mechanism in action, *e.g.* springs a trap.

1621 MARKHAM *Prev. Hunger* 39 Hard by this loope [of the net] shall there be fastened..a little broad thin trycker, made sharpe and equall at both ends. *Ibid.* 40 The loope and the tricker. **1735** *Phil. Trans.* XXXIX. 84 That Tricker has a Pin. **1764** *Museum Rust.* III. lxv. 298 The triggers to throw the rake behind the roots. **1853** SIR H. DOUGLAS *Milit. Bridges* vi. (ed. 3) 301 The ram was worked by hand-ropes (fig. 8) attached to the fall, which is a much quicker way than by the trigger and drop. **1885** C. G. W. LOCK *Workshop Receipts* Ser. IV. 428/2 (Photography) A trigger is provided for releasing the shutter. **1913** E. T. RUTHVEN-MURRAY *Let.* 30 Dec., If the tram-car strikes anything on the track, the gate is pushed backwards and releases a 'trigger' (in this case a catch sustaining the tray) which allows the tray to fall so that it glides along on the road and scoops up the obstruction.

2. *spec.* **a.** A small steel catch which, on being 'drawn', 'pulled', or pressed by the finger, releases the hammer of a gun-lock. Hence *to pull trigger*, to fire a gun (*at, on*).

α. **1622** F. MARKHAM *Bk. War* I. ix. 35 Let the Cocks and Trickers be nimble to goe and come. **1660** BOYLE *New Exp. Phys. Mech.* xiv. 89 We took a Pistol.., and..ty'd to the Tricker one end of a string. *Ibid.* 100 The Trigger was pull'd. **1759** ADAM SMITH *Mor. Sent.* II. iii. (1781) 161 Each of them draws the tricker of a gun. **1828** MOIR *Mansie Wauch* xii, It was an act of desperation to draw the tricker.

β. **1660** [see α]. **1688** CAPT. J. S. *Art of War* 17 Your musquet being levelled breast high with your fingers upon the trigger. **1753** HANWAY *Trav.* (1762) II. I. xi. 58 We could not pull the trigers of their muskets. **1868** *Rep. to Govt. U.S. Munitions War* 24 The trigger is pulled, *h* is drawn down and the spring, released, darts the needle through the guide into the cartridge, the blunt end of the needle sharply striking the fulminate and thus igniting the charge. **1888** 'R. BOLDREWOOD' *Robbery under Arms* xlix, Not once or twice..you've pulled trigger on me.

b. A lever or snib in a cross-bow the pulling or pressing of which releases the string.

1681 GREW *Musæum* I. v. iii. 113 Just as when a Cross-Bow is let off by pulling down the Tricker. **1688** R. HOLME *Armoury* III. xvi. (Roxb.) 77/1 The string is..lett fly by a Tricker or button. **1846** GREENER *Sc. Gunnery* 12 It remained thus until the trigger of the cross-bow suggested a contrivance to convey, with equal certainty and greater rapidity, the burning match to the pan.

3. In *fig.* and *allusive* uses. ***in the drawing of a trigger***, in a moment, instantaneously. ***quick on the trigger***, quick to act in response to a suggestion, to take advantage of a situation, or the like.

1706 FARQUHAR *Recruit. Officer* I. i, This is the cap of honour, it dubs a man a gentleman in the drawing of a tricker. **1808** M. L. WEEMS *Let.* 22 Apr. in E. E. F. Skeel *M. L. Weems: Works & Ways* (1929) II. 377, I trust that all your Aids will be quick on the trigger. **1842** C. M. KIRKLAND *Forest Life* II. xlvii. 223 'Pretty quick on the trigger!' muttered Uncle William. **1871** TYNDALL *Fragm. Sc.* (1879) II. ii. 12 Prayer is the trigger which liberates the Divine power. **1887** G. H. DARWIN in *Leisure Hour* May 354/2 The attraction of the moon or the variation in atmospheric pressure pulls the trigger. **1905** *Daily Chron.* 16 Feb. 4/5 A born musical leader, fertile in ideas, quick on the trigger. **1946** *Lancet* 19 Jan. 97/1 A theory of the nervous initiation of contraction—the trigger without which voluntary muscle remains inert. **1961** M. LASKI *Ecstasy* ii. 16 Of the circumstances in which they found themselves when ecstasy took place, they identified certain objects, events, and ideas as standing in some kind of a causal relationship to their ecstatic experiences. These objects, events, and ideas I am calling *triggers*. **1977** J. L. HARPER *Population Biol. of Plants* 64 Triggers to development which predict a changing environment will generally be more efficient than those that are themselves the changed conditions.

4. *Electronics.* **a.** A trigger circuit or trigger tube.

1945 *Electronic Engin.* XVII. 329/1 The charging circuit producing the used forward stroke operates continuously even through the flyback period when the trigger is conducting. **1946** [see FLIP-FLOP *sb.* e]. **1962**, etc. [see SCHMITT]. **1969** J. J. SPARKES *Transistor Switching* v. 126 The reasons should be understood for always using a negative-going trigger to drive *npn* transistors off rather than a positive one to drive them into the conducting state. **1981** J. C. SPROTT *Introd. Mod. Electronics* x. 239 The Schmitt trigger is useful..for generating square waves from a sinusoidal input.

b. A momentary signal or change in signal level that causes a change of state in a trigger tube or other device.

1948 *Gloss. Computer Terms* (Mass. Inst. Technol. Servomechanisms Lab. Rep. R-138) 11 *Trigger.* See *trigger pulse.* **1953** *Electronic Engin.* XXV. 143/1 A trigger derived from the phantastron is used to initiate the multivibrator circuit. **1979** M. M. MANO *Digital Logic & Computer Design* vi. 210 Asynchronous flip-flops..require an input trigger defined by a change of signal level... Clocked flip-flops are triggered by pulses.

5. A fission bomb built into a fusion bomb in order to initiate the fusion reaction.

1955 *Times* 13 Aug. 5/4 It was a question of arranging the proper conditions, and there was no reason why fusion energy should not be obtained without the use of a fission bomb as 'the trigger'. **1969** *Listener* 5 June 773/3 It's necessary to have a trigger made of an ordinary fission bomb, and there is good evidence that this must consist of fissile uranium or uranium-235 and not fissile plutonium. **1982** *New Scientist* 2 Sept. 642/1 The X-rays produced by the triggers are absorbed and re-emitted by an ellipsoidal casing of ^{238}U, and the fraction which is re-emitted inwards goes on to strike the main bulk of the thermonuclear fuel.

6. *attrib.* and *Comb.*, as ***trigger-action, -catch, -detent, effect, -guard*** (GUARD *sb.* 16 d), ***-jig*** (JIG *sb.*[1] 6), ***-line, -plate, -pull, -pulling, question, -string, switch, -touch, word; trigger-pulling*** adj.; **trigger area,** *Phys.* and *Path.*, a sensitive area of the body, irritation of which causes some special effect in another part (so *trigger point*); **trigger-block,** a piece of mechanism in a steam-engine, which automatically allows the steam-valve to close when a certain speed is attained; **trigger circuit** *Electronics*, a circuit that behaves like a trigger tube; also, a circuit for producing a trigger pulse; **trigger finger,** (*a*) the forefinger of the right hand, with which the trigger of a fire-arm is pulled; (*b*) *Path.* an affection of a finger (see quot. 1890); **trigger-fish,** a fish of the family Balistidæ; so called because the large first ray of the dorsal fin is depressed by depression of the second, like the hammer of a gun-lock by the trigger; **trigger-hair,** *Zool.* a fine hair or filament at the mouth of a thread-cell in some cœlenterates, which operates like a trigger in emission of the stinging-hair; **trigger-happy** *a. colloq.* [-HAPPY], over-ready to shoot at anything at any time or on slight provocation; also *transf.* and *fig.*; hence **trigger-happiness; trigger man** *slang* (chiefly *U.S.*), a gunman; a hired thug or bodyguard; also *fig.*; **trigger-plant,** a plant of the genus *Candollea* (formerly *Stylidium*), characterized by the two stamens being united with the style into a highly irritable column; **trigger-point,** (*a*) *Phys.* and *Path.* (cf. *trigger area* above); (*b*) *U.S.*, a price level at which price controls are imposed or re-imposed; **trigger price** *U.S.*, a minimum selling price for steel imported into the U.S., such that any steel imports below that price incur investigation to ensure that dumping is not taking place; **trigger pulse** *Electronics*, a pulse that acts as a trigger (sense 4 b above); **trigger tube** *Electronics*, a vacuum tube that has two operating states and changes rapidly from one to the other in response to a momentary application of, or change in, a signal. See also *tricker-firelock, tricker-lock* (TRICKER[2]).

1915 W. M. BAYLISS *Princ. Gen. Physiol.* x. 304 The difference between what is sometimes called '*trigger action' and catalysis. *Ibid.*, Supersaturated solutions are cases of 'trigger action'. They remain indefinitely as such until infected with a crystal, and then the rate of crystallisation is independent of the amount of crystals added. **1950** A. HUXLEY *Lett.* (1969) 623 Trivial acts of selfishness and wantonness may release, as though by a kind of trigger action, a huge avalanche of tragic destiny. **1891** *Cent. Dict.*, *Trigger area. **1900** DORLAND *Med. Dict.* (1913), *Trigger area*, an area stimulation or irritation of which may cause physiologic or pathologic changes in another area. **1893** D. K. CLARK *Steam Engine* III. 58 A square *trigger-block..slides vertically through..the catch-block. **1861** FAIRBAIRN *Iron* 123 The movement of the roller *o* causes the shoulder of the rod P to get under the point of the *trigger-catch *u*; the valve is by these means kept closed till the whole force of the blow is struck. **1868** *Rep. to Govt. U.S. Munitions War* 24 The small lock-tube is drawn back, pulling with it..the needle-bolt, till the shoulder *a* is caught behind the trigger-catch. **1938** *Rev. Sci. Instruments* IX. 223/1 Another *trigger circuit which has inherent possibilities as a counting circuit is shown in Fig. 2. **1951**, **1962** [see BISTABLE *a.*]. **1974** A. VAN DER ZIEL *Introd. Electronics* xi. 262 (*caption*) Transistor monostable circuit with trigger circuit. **1881** GREENER *Gun* 470 The *trigger-comb arrangement is very ingenious, and is such that the barrels may be fired simultaneously or in quick succession, by adjusting a small screw. **1868** *Rep. to Govt. U.S. Munitions War* 24 The needle-bolt, and with it the needle, is held back by the shoulder *a*, catching against the *trigger-detent *h*. **1931** *Prof. Papers Inst. Post Office Electr. Engineers* No. 136. 19 The adjustments were such as to avoid definitely the '*trigger' effect. **1949** M. MEAD *Male & Female* x. 218 In the..patterning of a woman's sexual receptivity now one part of the body, now another,..may be sensitive enough to develop a trigger effect. **1829** W. H. MAXWELL *Stories of Waterloo* I. 223 Removing Mr. Clinch's *trigger-finger. **1890** BILLINGS *Med. Dict.*, *Trigger finger*, sudden arrest of the movement of extension (or, less frequently, of flexion) of one of the fingers, until a special effort is made, when the movement is completed with a snap or jerk. **1849** H. MELVILLE *Mardi* I. xlviii. 131 The rank and file of the *Trigger-fish—so called from their quaint dorsal fins being set in their backs with a conical curve, as if at half-cock. **1882** OGILVIE, Trigger-fish. **1884** *Longm. Mag.* Mar. 529 Trigger-fish and trunk-fish. **1908** *Westm. Gaz.* 3 Oct. 6/1 It penetrates into the body of the oyster in the expectation of its host being broken up and eaten by the trigger-fish. **1859** *Musketry Instr.* 38 To see that every man holds his rifle firmly with the left hand;..that the fingers of the right hand are behind the *trigger guard. **1868** *Rep. to Govt. U.S. Munitions of War* 51 The breech-block..works vertically in the shoe, being depressed or elevated by a hinged lever, fitting with a catch, over the trigger-guard. **1945** C. BURNEY *Dungeon Democracy* III. 82 There was much *trigger-happiness, men shooting each other, shooting themselves and shooting into thin air. **1970** *Daily Tel.* 23 Mar. 16 The trigger-happiness with which workers are now ready and eager to enforce their fantastically increased claims by industrial action..leaves Britain with the choice between being ruined by runaway inflation or by a series of disastrous strikes. **1978** N. FREELING *Night Lords* xxi. 95 Suddenly she said 'Have you killed people?'.. I thought it the usual accusation of trigger-happiness. **1943** F. J. BELL *Condition Red* 190 Yes, they missed us, and the *G* hereby absolves whoever it was along that section of coast that got a little *trigger-happy early one December morning. **1946** *Archit. Rev.* CI. 47/1 On the Acropolis itself a group of trigger-happy gendarmerie lounged with an assumed nonchalance by the lower entrance. **1957** *Time* 2 Sept. 19/1 Some trigger-happy U.S. radio commentators..helped confuse it further by proclaiming that Syria was already Russia's newest satellite. **1971** H. WILSON *Labour Govt.* xxxvi. 937 It was fairly clear that the main issues now were relief and the avoidance of atrocities, which, if they occurred, would be most likely to be caused by trigger-happy young soldiers. **1974** F. WARNER *Meeting Ends* I. ii. 7 If only you knew how trigger-happy he is when he gets a dialling tone. **1984** *Miami Herald* 6 Apr. 12 A/2 We have a president who is trigger-happy and who commits troops for impossible missions. **1795** R. DODD *Rep. Hartlepool* 16 The seaman, standing with the *trigger-line in his hand, at a sufficient distance from the gun's recoil. **1930** *Amer. Mercury* Dec. 458/2 **Trigger man*, an assassin; a body guard. 'He's trigger man for Big Tony.' **1934** *Sun* (Baltimore) 22 Aug. 13/1, I was the triggerman in both hold-ups. **1954** 'N. BLAKE' *Whisper in Gloom* iii. 42 A graceful, self-possessed, cat-like walk..the tread of the trigger-man. **1974** *Times* 2 May 6/5 P[resident]. .. You feel that really the trigger man was really Colson on this thing? D[ean] No... He was just in the chain. **1977** *Hongkong Standard* 12 Apr. 9/3 He was said to be a senior triggerman—an overseer of 'hit men'—for reputed mob boss Anthony 'Big Tuna' Accardo. **1981** W. SAFIRE in *N.Y. Times Mag.* 1 Mar. 9/3 The triggerman of this slim but explosive volume is described on the cover as 'formerly professor of Romance languages and literatures at Harvard University, where he is now emeritus professor'. **1884** MILLER *Plant-n.*, *Trigger-plant, *Stylidium graminifolium* and other species. **1860** *All Year Round* No. 71. 500 The stock is divided into..lock-side, head, small, trigger-guard, *trigger-plate, trigger [etc.]. **1891** *Cent. Dict.*, *Trigger point. **1900** in DORLAND *Med. Dict.* (1913). **1952** *N.Y. Times* (Late City Ed.) 12 Aug. 32/6 The federation estimates that at the beginning of suspension the average of current prices was 69.39 per cent of their 1951 highs, which meant that they could rise a little more than 15 per cent before reaching the so-called 'trigger-point'. **1979** H. KISSINGER *White House Years* ix. 330, I had to learn an entire vocabulary of international trade, such as 'export subsidy techniques' as well as the arcane complexity of 'trigger points' (at which restraints would go into effect). **1978** *Business Week* 23 Jan. 25/2 (*heading*) Steel *trigger-prices start sowing discord. *Ibid.* 26/3 Jack Meyer, assistant director of the Council on Wage & Price Stability, which devised the trigger-price system. **1981** *Economist* 24 Jan. 88/1 The renewal of trigger prices last October coincided with a recovery in demand for, eg, tubes for the oil and gas industry, plates and girders for process plant and construction. **1892** GREENER *Breech-Loader* 187 Gentlemen ..should state exactly what weight the *trigger pulls are desired. **1906** *Sub Target Rifle* 13 For practice in *trigger-pulling it is of great advantage. **1924** J. A. THOMSON *Sci. Old & New* xix. 105 A current of air is necessary as the trigger-pulling stimulus. **1946** *Radar: Summary Rep. & Harp Project* (U.S. Nat. Defense Comm., Div. 14) 144/2 **Trigger pulse*, a pulse which starts a cycle of operations. **1956** *IRE Trans. Electronic Computers* V. 124/1 For trigger pulses of a few mμsec duration there will be little or no interference between the trigger pulse and the change of voltage at the cathodes of the EFP-60's. **1981** J. D. LENK *Handbk. Digital Electronics* ii. 84 The circuit changes state only when both the input pulse and a clock pulse are present simultaneously. (The clock pulse is also known as a gate pulse or trigger pulse.) **1927** J. ADAMS *Errors in School* 213 In external written examinations, where..the clever pupil..is led astray by expecting a question, and then treating one of the questions actually set as the one he expected. These '*trigger questions', as they may be called, set off the candidate on the wrong track. **1973** T. PYNCHON *Gravity's Rainbow* (1975) I. 147 Hyperkinetically, waiting only the right trigger-question to start blithering 200 words a minute about their special, terrible endowments. **1892** *Photogr. Ann.* II. 885 The exposure is made by pneumatic or *trigger release. **1952** 'J. WYNDHAM' in *Galaxy Sci. Fiction* July 72/1 He brought the cutter up, and pressed the *trigger-switch. **1894** *Electrician* 15 June 188/1 Zehnder's *trigger tube. **1939** H. J. REICH *Theory & Applications of Electron Tubes* vii. 208 A single pentode may also be used as a trigger tube. **1978** R. V. JONES *Most Secret War* viii. 69 My first step was to take the electronic trigger tube down to my former colleagues at the Admiralty Research Laboratory, to get them to evaluate its performance. **1975** *Listener* 17 July 74/1 Those of us who work in radio..rely on *trigger words, Pavlovian clichés which become a kind of bogus mental shorthand.

Hence **'triggerless** *a.*, without a trigger.

18.. ? BROWNING *Miniature* iv. (in *The Sibyl* (Rugby Sch.) 1 Apr. 1893), Arquebuses and pistols triggerless.

trigger ('trɪgə(r)), *sb.*[2] [f. TRIG *v.*[1] + -ER[1].]

1. A device or appliance to retard or stop the motion of a vehicle descending a slope. Now *dial.*

1591 PERCIVALL *Sp. Dict.*, *Estornija de carro*, the trigger of a cart, *sufflamen.* **1611** COTGR., *Enrayer vne rouë*, to stay, or hold a wheele backe with a Trigger. *Enrayoir*.. a Trigger, the staffe thats put before a cart-wheele, to keepe it from ouer-throwing, or ouer-hastie going. **1631** ANCHORAN *Comenius' Gate Tongues* 88 To the wheeles are put triggers [L. *sufflamina*, F. *les enrayoirs*]. **1648** HEXHAM *Dutch Dict.*, *Radt-sperre*.., that which is put into the Wheele, lest the Cart be overthrowne, or a Trigger [*ed.* 1678 trigger]... *Rede, ofte Wagen-span*, the Trigger of a Wheele to stay it. *a* **1661** HOLYDAY *Juvenal* (1673) 282 The souldier..has not his estate worn-out with such delay, like a waggon-wheell with the trigger that stops it. **1681** W. ROBERTSON *Phraseol. Gen.* 1246/2 A Trigger to stay a Cart wheel up hill, *sufflamen.* **1888** ELWORTHY *W. Som. Word-bk.*, *Trigger*, anything used to trig or block. 'Here! thick gurt stone 'll do vor a trigger.'

fig. *a* **1661** HOLYDAY *Juvenal* xvi. (1673) 279 Their means ne're, without fruit, Are gaul'd with the long trigger of a suit.

b. See quot.

1893 *Wilts. Gloss.*, *Trigger*, the rod let down to 'trig up' the shafts of a cart.

2. *Ship-building.* A support holding the dog-shore in position; also *transf.* the dog-shore itself.

1867 in SMYTH *Sailor's Word-bk.* **1877** KNIGHT *Dict. Mech.*, *Trigger*... A piece of wood placed under a dog-shore to hold it up until the time for launching. **1896** *Strand Mag.* XII. 324/2 This obstacle, known variously as the 'trigger', 'dagger', or 'dog-shore', is usually a short length of hard-wood interposed—in a sloping direction, and in such a way as to promptly yield to a smart downward blow—between fixed projections on the side of the standing ways and of the sliding ways. **1899** *Daily News* 16 Jan. 7/3 The last blocks had been knocked away and the Oceanic was held in place only by a 'trigger' on each side. These huge triggers of cast steel..work in hydraulic pistons, and fit into slots of the sliding ways. **1900** *Engineering Mag.* XIX. 681 From these triggers, dog shores, bearing only about one-quarter of an inch outside of the fulcrum, extend up against the keel.

'trigger, *sb.*[3] [f. TRIG *v.*[2] or *sb.*[2] + -ER[1].] **a.** See quot. 1843. **b.** = TRIG *sb.*[2]

1843 HARDY in *Proc. Berw. Nat. Club* II. No. 11. 56 Two men, named triggers, must see that when the race for the succeeding cast of the bowl has concluded, the straw is exactly between the feet of the party whose turn it is to dismiss the bowl. **1891** H. JOHNSTON *Kilmallie* xix. II. 110 (*Curling*) The second, third, and fourth players, on each side, footed the trigger, and sent their stones hurtling along the as yet unpolished ice towards the goal.

trigger ('trɪgə(r)), *v.* [f. TRIGGER *sb.*[1]] **1.** *trans.* To act as a 'trigger' (sense 3) for, causing another event (esp. a chain reaction) to occur; to stimulate or 'set off'; to activate, to bring about; to spark *off* (an idea, etc.). Also *lit.*, to pull (depress, etc.) the trigger of (a gun or other device).

1930 R. CAMPBELL *Adamastor* 94 When life is triggered by a hair And stands upon the peak of death. **1938** *Sun* (Baltimore) 18 Apr. 8/5 Denmark, whose people thrive on thrift, milk, bacon and eggs, and never need 'triggering' into activity by shot-in-the-arm spendings of borrowed billions. **1948** *Sat. Even. Post* 20 Mar. 39/3 There is certainly no lack of evidence that the typical glaucoma patient has a nervous temperament and that emotional episodes will increase the pressure within the eyeball and even trigger off acute attacks. **1949** *Sun* (Baltimore) 26 Sept. 4/1 The strike..was triggered by two rival AFL unions. **1950** *Ibid.* 21 July 14/3 A system by which the powers are prepared but lie dormant until triggered into action by specific congressional action is the ideal. **1958** W. J. H. SPROTT *Human Groups* 163 May it not be that a crowd is 'triggered off' by people whose 'thresholds of mob-involvement'..are low? **1958** *Spectator* 19 Sept. 379/1 But as a space-veteran who once triggered a ray-gun with Flash Gordon, let me advise you to read on. **1958** *Listener* 23 Oct. 648/2 Artists like Joan Mitchell, Al Leslie..have all been triggered by de Kooning's example. **1959** *Ibid.* 18 June 1083/2 Sir Faithful Fortescue..whose loyalties were so finely triggered that he rode across from Parliament side to Royalist. **1968** J. D. MCCAWLEY in Bach & Harms *Universals in Linguistic Theory* 168 Chomsky..in effect asserts that all lexical insertion takes place in the base component unless triggered by other transformations. **1972** *Amateur Photographer* 12 Jan. 42/2 (*caption*) Recently there have been a number of flash meters on the market which, when placed at the subject position read out the correct f/stop to use when the flash is triggered. **1973** C. BONINGTON *Next Horizon* xiii. 190 We tiptoed up the snow, hardly daring to talk, as if the resonance of our voices might trigger off an avalanche. **1977** *New Yorker* 5 Sept. 80/3 Before I improvise, I just listen, and that triggers me. **1978** S. SHELDON *Bloodline* xlii. 361 His eyes were fixed on the ribbon that the girl was wearing around her neck. It triggered a memory. **1978** *New York* 3 Apr. 10/1 The Israeli invasion of Lebanon and the mass murder that triggered it have nearly obliterated from the public consciousness the killing of Egyptian editor Yousef el-Sebai. **1981** *Times* 5 May 15/7 The fact that no danger signals were triggered during the growth of Norton Warburg has alarmed the City.

2. *Electronics.* **a.** To initiate a change of state or a cycle of behaviour in (a device).

1937 *Proc. Cambr. Philos. Soc.* XXXIII. 551 In order that it may be used in a scale-of-two counter, it is necessary to provide some simple means of triggering the circuit, that is to say changing from one stable state to the other. **1945** *Electronic Engin.* XVII. 473 A differential circuit and pulse generator which triggers a thyratron. **1967** *Electronics* 6 Mar. 160/1 A d-c flip-flop is triggered by the leading edge and clamped until the pulse is removed. **1974** A. VAN DER ZIEL *Introd. Electronics* xi. 262 A monostable multivibrator is a circuit that goes through a complete wave form when triggered.

b. *intr.* Of an electronic device: to change state in response to a momentarily applied signal.

1933 *P.O. Electr. Engineers' Jrnl.* XXVI. 63/2 A tube is now manufactured capable of 'triggering' both 'on' and 'off'. **1967** [see SCHMITT].

Hence **'triggered** *ppl. a.*, furnished with or activated by a trigger; **'triggering** *vbl. sb.* (freq. *attrib.*) and *ppl. a.*

1944 *Electronic Engin.* XVI. 380 The harmonics generated in the circuit provide standard frequencies..for..high speed triggering etc. **1945** *Electronic Industries* Sept. 226 *Triggered spark gap*, a fixed spark gap in which the discharge passes between two electrodes and is struck (started) by a subsidiary electrode, the trigger, to which low power pulses are applied at regular intervals from a pulse amplifier, thus closing the switch. **1958** K. AMIS *I like it Here* xii. 152 The sight of it at this moment must have had some triggering effect on Bowen's alimentary canal. **1962** *Listener* 3 May 770/2 This would involve installing a 'triggering' device in the vehicle. **1967** *Ibid.* 30 Nov. 694/1 The triggered responses which might deter me..no longer apply. **1972** *Language* XLVIII. 299 Identity-of-reference deletions involve two coreferential NP's, a vanishing NP and a triggering NP. I propose that the rule of deletion.. superimpose the vanishing NP over the triggering NP, keeping both NP nodes. **1977** J. L. HARPER *Population Biol. Plants* xviii. 520 Most of these annuals have a precisely triggered transition from the vegetative to reproductive phase depending on photo-period. **1977** SAVAGE & RUMBAUGH in D. M. Rumbaugh *Language Learning by Chimpanzee* xvi. 289 Hockett..defined communication as an act by which one individual 'triggered' the behavior of another ('triggering' in this sense implies that the energy expended during the output of a communicative pattern is unrelated to the energy of the response).

triggerable ('trɪgərəb(ə)l), *a.* [f. TRIGGER *v.* + -ABLE.] Susceptible to triggering.

1964 *Anesthesiology* XXV. 200/1 You will need both triggerable and automatic respirators. **1973** *New England Jrnl. Med.* 4 Oct. 735/1 If such triggerable foci, in which spontaneous activity can be either initiated or terminated by the appropriately timed arrival of a propagated impulse, exist in depressed areas of the heart they might well serve to initiate or sustain fibrillation.

trigide, trigil, obs. ff. TRAGEDY, TRICKLE.

trigintal (traɪ'dʒɪntəl). Now only *Hist.* Also 5-6 **-gen-**. [ad. med.L. *trīgintāle*, f. L. *trīgintā* thirty: see -AL[1].] = TRENTAL. Also *attrib.*

1491 *Cartular. S. Nicholai Aberdon.* (New Spald. Cl.) I. 257 Ye Songe mess with note on ye morne yereftire at Sanct nicholess alter, and trigental of saidis messis in ye oulk follouinge. **1530** in *N. & Q.* 9th Ser. VI. 414/1 An hole trigintall of masses to be saide in the churche where I shalbe buryed. **1726** AYLIFFE *Parergon* 190 Trentals or Trigintals were also a number of Masses, to the Tale of Thirty,.. instituted (as pretended by St. Gregory). **1898** A. F. LEACH *Beverley Act Bk.* I. p. lxxx, The annuals, trigintals..with legacies and Lenten tithes are worth 20 marks.

trigin'tennial, *a. rare*[−1]. [f. L. *trīgintā* thirty + *-enni-um* (f. *ann-us* year) + -AL[1].] Taking place once in thirty years.

1894 *Yale News* (New Haven, Conn.) 29 June, About twenty-five members of the class were present at their trigintennial reunion.

triginti'sextuple. *rare*[−1]. [f. L. *trīgintā* thirty + **sextuplex*, f. *sextus* sixth, as in *duplex*, *triplex*, etc.] The product obtained by multiplying a given quantity by 36.

1690 LEYBOURN *Curs. Math.* 349 If any Root be Multiplied by 6 the Product shall be the Root of the Trigintisextuple.

trigit, variant of TREGET, *Obs.*

‖**trigla** ('trɪglə). *Ichth.* [mod.L. *trigla* (Linn. 1758), a. Gr. τρίγλη, -λα, the red mullet, whence also It. *triglia* ('triʎʎa).] A genus of fishes, family *Triglidæ*, the gurnards; any species of this genus.

1752 J. HILL *Hist. Anim.* 265 The red Smoothheaded Trigla, without any beards. The King of the Mullets. *Ibid.* 267 The red Trigla.. The Red Gurnard. The French call it Marrude. **1854** BUSHNAN in *Circ. Sc.* (1865) I. 294/2 The trigla utters a grunting sound when it is taken out of the water.

triglandular: see TRI- 1.

trigle, obs. Sc. form of TRICKLE.

triglochid (traɪ'gləʊkɪd), *a. rare.* [f. Gr. τριγλώχῑς, -ῑν- (f. τρι-, TRI- + γλωχίς, γλωχίν point of an arrow) + -ID[2].] Having three points; tricuspid. Also **tri'glochin** *a.*

1760 J. LEE *Introd. Bot.* III. xviii. (1765) 213 *Triglochid*, three pointed. **1836-9** *Todd's Cycl. Anat.* I. 581/1 This valve ..receives the name of the..triglochin valve.

trigloid ('trɪglɔɪd), *a.* and *sb. Ichth.* [f. Gr. τρίγλη TRIGLA + -OID.] **a.** *adj.* Belonging or akin to the group *Trigloidea* or family *Triglidæ* of fishes, typified by the genus TRIGLA. **b.** *sb.* A fish of this group or family. Also **'triglid.**

1888 *Proc. U.S. Nat. Museum* XI. 577 He especially instanced the Triglids and Dactylopterids as two groups which exhibit great diversities. *Ibid.* 588 The Trigloid, Cottoid, Gobioid, and Lophioid families... To even still greater a degree are the Agonoids, the Trigloids, and Dactylopteroids divergent.

triglot ('traɪglɒt), *a.* and *sb.* [f. Gr. τρι-, TRI- + γλῶττα tongue, after *polyglot.*] **a.** *adj.* Of a book or writing: In three languages. **b.** *sb.* A book, esp. a Bible, in three languages.

1882-3 *Schaff's Encycl. Relig. Knowl.* III. 1864 A Samaritan Pentateuch Triglot,..Hebrew..Samaritan.. Arabic. **1890** (*title*) The Triglot Bible. Comprising the Holy Scriptures of the Old and New Testament in the Original Tongues, the Septuagint, the Syriac (of the New Testament) and the Vulgate Versions, in parallel columns. **1901** H. BROWNE (*title*) Triglot Dictionary of Scriptural Representative Words in Hebrew, Greek, and English.

trigly: see under TRIG *a.*[1]

triglyceride (traɪ'glɪsəraɪd). *Chem.* [f. TRI- 5 (irregularly used) + GLYCERIDE.] A compound in which three acid radicals are united by oxygen to glyceryl; i.e. they replace the three H atoms of the OH groups in glycerin or glycerol, $C_3H_5(OH)_3$; e.g. stearin is called the triglyceride of stearic acid.

1860 DEBUS in *Q. Jrnl. Chem. Soc.* XII. 243. **1895** LEWKOWITSCH *Benedikt's Oils, Fats, Waxes* 46 Glycerol.. deporting itself like a trihydric base, is able to combine with three radicles of fatty acids... The resulting compounds are called 'triglycerides'. **1912** THORPE *Dict. App. Chem.* (ed. 2) I. 577 The glycerides of butter fat contain butyric, caproic, caprylic, capric, lauric, myristic, palmitic, stearic, and oleic acids, as triglycerides.

triglyph ('traɪglɪf). *Arch.* Also *erron.* 7-9 **tryglyph**, 7 **triglife, -iphe**, 8-9 **trigliph**. Formerly in L. form **triglyphus**, pl. **-i**. [ad. L. *triglyphus* (Vitr.), a. Gr. τρίγλυφ-ος thrice-grooved, f. τρι-, TRI- + γλυφή carving. So F. *triglyphe* (1545 in Hatz.-Darm.).] A member or ornament in the Doric order, consisting of a block or tablet with three vertical grooves or glyphs (strictly, two whole grooves, and a half-groove on each side), repeated at regular intervals along the frieze, usually one over each column, and one or two (see DITRIGLYPH 2) between every two columns.

1563 SHUTE *Archit.* C iij b, The Canalicoli, standing vpright within the Triglyphi... Bitwixte the .2. Triglyphos, you shall set Methopa. **1624** WOTTON *Archit.* in *Reliq.* (1651) 230 A sober garnishment..of Triglyphs and Metopes alwayes in the Frize. **1704** J. HARRIS *Lex. Techn.* I, *Triglyph*..is a Member of the Frize of the Dorick Order. **1797** HOLCROFT tr. *Stolberg's Trav.* (ed. 2) III. xc. 528 A triglyph..was nine feet and a half high. **1823** P. NICHOLSON *Pract. Build.* 467 The architrave and trigliph, representing the beams and joists [of a primitive building]. **1871** B. TAYLOR *Faust* (1875) II. I. vii. 76 The pillared shaft, the triglyph even rings, I think, indeed, the whole bright temple sings.

Hence **'triglyphal** *a.* = *triglyphic* (*a*); **triglyphed** (-glɪft) *a.*, furnished or adorned with triglyphs; in quot. 1880 as *pa. pple.*, ? carved in the manner of a triglyph; **tri'glyphic**, **tri'glyphical** (*rare*[−0]) *adjs.*, (*a*) pertaining to or of the nature of a triglyph; (*b*) 'containing three sets of characters or sculptures' (Webster, citing Gliddon).

1890 MARQUAND in *Amer. Jrnl. Archæol.* VI. 54 The Egyptian scotia..is replaced in the Greek entablature by the *triglyphal frieze. **1837** *Penny Cycl.* VII. 217/2 The plain capital composed of merely an echinus and abacus, and a *triglyphed frieze, enable us to pronounce at once that the order is the Doric. **1849** FREEMAN *Archit.* II. ii. 110 Some Sicilian examples exhibit the triglyphed frieze. **1880** F. W. PERCIVAL in *Academy* 4 Sept. 173 The hair..represented in long parallel tresses distinctly triglyphed in the rock. **1847** WEBSTER, **Triglyphic*, **Triglyphical*. **1866** RUSKIN *Crown Wild Olive* App. (1898) 219 They attack Brandenburg, under its Triglyphic protector.

trigness: see under TRIG *a.*[1]

trigon ('traɪgɒn). Also 7 **trygon**, 7-8 **trigone**. [ad. L. *trigōn-um*, ad. Gr. τρίγων-ον triangle, neuter of τρίγωνος, f. τρι-, TRI- + -γων-ος -angled, -cornered.]

1. A figure having three angles and three sides; a triangle.

1600 FAIRFAX *Tasso* II. li, Let Ismen with his squares and trigons war. *a* **1628** SIR J. BEAUMONT *Bosworth F.* 346 When the Cranes direct their Flight on high,..they in a Trigon fly. **1694** MOTTEUX *Rabelais* IV. Prol. (1737) 78 An equilateral Trigone. **1806** HUTTON *Course Math.* I. 272 An Equilateral Triangle is also a Regular Figure of three sides..being also called a Trigon. **1859** F. A. GRIFFITHS *Artil. Man.* (1862) 333 Trigon..Heptagon..Octagon.

2. *Astrol.* **a.** A set of three signs of the zodiac, distant 120° from each other, as if at the angles of an equilateral triangle; = TRIPLICITY 3. (Also *fig.* or *allusively*.) **b.** The aspect of two planets distant 120° from each other; = TRINE *sb.* 2.

1563 [see TRIENT]. **1589** WARNER *Alb. Eng.* VI. xxxi. (1612) 158 She Euen at the firie Trigon shall your chiefe Ascendant be. **1593** G. HARVEY *Pierce's Super.* 100 His zeale to God, and the Church, was an aery Triplicity: and his deuotion to his Prince, and the State, a fiery Trigon. **1597** SHAKS. *2 Hen. IV*, II. iv. 288. *a* **1633** AUSTIN *Medit.* (1635) 7 If the Astronomers hold there was a great Trigon of Constellations at his [Christ's] Birth: I am sure here is a great Trigon of Trigons, at his Conception. **1644** LILLY *Eng. Proph. Merlin* (title-p.) The beginning, and end of the Watry Trygon: An entrance of the fiery Triplicity. **1664** BUTLER *Hud.* II. III. 905 Some..Affirm the Trigons chopp'd and chang'd, The wat'ry with the fiery rang'd. **1704** HEARNE *Duct. Hist.* (1714) I. 23 Saturn and Jupiter..having run through all the four Trigons, meet again, according to Kepler, at the end of 800 Years. **1819** JAS. WILSON *Compl. Dict. Astrol.* s.v. *Triplicity*, The first trigon is composed of ♈, ♌, and ♐, and is therefore called the fiery triplicity.

3. †**a.** A triangular instrument used in surveying; also, one used in dialling. *Obs.*

1590 J. BLAGRAVE *Baculum Familliare* (title-p.) A Booke of the making and vse of a Staffe, newly inuented by the Author, called the Familiar Staffe,..which..staffe..readily performeth all the seuerall vses of the Crosse staffe, the Quadrate, the Circle, the Quadrante, the Gunners Quadrante, the Trigon, [etc.]. **1704** J. HARRIS *Lex. Techn.* I. s.v., In Dyaling there is sometimes used an Instrument of a Triangular Form, which is called, a Trigon.

†**b.** A triangular fort. *Obs.*

1688 R. HOLME *Armoury* III. xvi. (Roxb.) 98/1 A Trigon, a figure of a fort with three corners.

c. An ancient lyre or harp of triangular form.

1727-41 CHAMBERS *Cycl.* s.v., The trigon was a kind of triangular lyre, invented by Ibycus. **1776** HAWKINS *Hist. Mus.* I. II. ix. 247 The Trigon..was..struck either with a quill, or beaten with little rods. **1879** STAINER *Music of Bible* 11 Attempts to shew that the *kinnor* was a trigon, or three-cornered harp.

4. *Zool.* A bivalve of the genus *Trigonia.*

1835 KIRBY *Hab. & Inst. Anim.* I. viii. 263 The Trigons, nearly related to the cockle, are mostly fossils.

5. Name of an ancient game at ball (Gr. τρίγων, L. *trigōn* ('lusum trigonem', Hor. *Sat.* I. vi. 126)).

1842 W. SMITH *Dict. Gr. & Rom. Antiq.* 761/2 The most favourite game at ball seems to have been the trigon or *pila trigonalis*,..played at by three persons, who stood in the form of a triangle.

6. *Comp. Anat.* The triangle formed by the three cusps of the upper molars in primitive mammals.

1897 H. F. OSBORN in *Amer. Nat.* Dec. 1002 Our studies among the Mesozoic mammals have left no doubt that the upper and lower triangles, or 'trigon' and 'trigonid', were derived from the reptilian protocone by the addition of lateral cusps... The 'trigon' was essentially a cutting apparatus, so perfect that many mammals retained it without further evolution.

trigonal ('trɪgənəl), *a.* (*sb.*) [ad. L. *trigōnāl-is*, f. *trigōn-um*: see prec. and -AL[1].]

A. *adj.* **1. a.** Of, pertaining or relating to, a trigon or triangle; of the form of a triangle, having three angles, triangular. (In q. 1570 = TRIANGULAR 2 b.)

trigonal co-ordinates (*Geom.*), a system of co-ordinates related in a particular way to trilinear co-ordinates, invented by S. Levi in 1876.

1570 BILLINGSLEY *Euclid* VII. def. x. 186, 6 in diuers respectes is a lineall number..and also a trigonall or trianguler number. **1571** DIGGES *Pantom.* IV. def. viii. Tj b, When any equiangle triangle..is..described within a circle..[its] sides are called the trigonal..Cordes of that circle. **1849** FREEMAN *Archit.* II. v. 170 A fine lofty pile, with..three trigonalapses. **1891** *Cent. Dict.* s.v., A linear equation in trigonal coördinates of the first class represents a cubic [curve].

b. *Geom.* and *Cryst.* Applied to a solid figure with triangular faces, or having some other relation to a triangle. Also, Having a relation to three angles: as ***trigonal quoin***, a solid angle contained by three plane angles; ***trigonal symmetry***, the symmetry of a figure or body which coincides with its original position after rotation about an axis through an angle of 120° or 240°.

1878 GURNEY *Crystallogr.* 38 If three symmetral planes and no more intersect in the same straight line, it is called an axis of trigonal symmetry. **1891** *Cent. Dict.* s.v. *Trisoctahedron*, The trigonal trisoctahedron has each face an isosceles triangle. **1895** STORY-MASKELYNE *Crystallogr.* iv. §79. 98 A plane figure may..be symmetrical with regard to a point within it as a pole of symmetry... Where n = 2, or = 3, 4, or 6, the symmetry may be defined as being *diagonal, trigonal, tetragonal*, or *hexagonal. Ibid.* vii. §180. 211 The trigonal dodecahedron,..a tetrahedron with a three-faced pyramid on each of its faces. *Ibid.* §257. 302 The trigonal trapezohedron..has trapezoids for its faces, which meet in two trigonal quoins.

c. *Chem.* Characterized by three orbitals lying in a plane and directed to the corners of an equilateral triangle.

1939 L. PAULING *Nature Chem. Bond* 429/2 (Index), Trigonal bond orbitals. **1961** A. STREITWIESER *Molecular Orbital Theory* i. 20 Linear combinations of *s*- and two of the *p*-orbitals result in three trigonal sp^2-orbitals. **1979** B. M. GIMARC *Molecular Struct. & Bonding* iv. 79 These complexes are mainly trigonal bipyramidal..in structure with the bonds to the axial ligands..being slightly longer than those to the equatorial ligands.

2. Triangular in section, triquetrous: now *esp.* in *Zool.* and *Bot.*

1571 DIGGES *Pantom.* IV. xi. Yiij b, The solide of Tetraedron may..be parted into 4 equal Trigonal Pyramides. *a* **1728** WOODWARD *Nat. Hist. Fossils* (1729) I. 158 Spar of a yellow Hue, shot into numerous trigonal pointed Shoots. **1753** CHAMBERS *Cycl. Supp.* s.v. *Leaf, Trigonal Leaf*, one much like the triquetrous, only that..the several faces are each hollowed in form of channels. *Ibid., Lilium*, the lilly..The pistil..finally becomes an oblong and trigonal fruit. **1854** WOODWARD *Mollusca* II. 225 Shell impunctate, oblong, or trigonal. **1895** W. M. MACPHERSON *Monymusk* v. 76 A plain roundheaded door with a trigonal hood.

3. *Astrol.* Relating to, or of the nature of, a trigon (in either sense): see prec. 2.

1603 SIR C. HEYDON *Jud. Astrol.* xxi. 470 All trigonall aspects doe accord. **1635** SWAN *Spec. M.* v. §2 (1643) 105 The Trigonall revolution..of the Planets [cf. TRIGON 2 quot. 1704].

†**4.** Of or pertaining to a trigon (TRIGON 3 a). Also as *sb.* short for *trigonal instrument. Obs. rare.*

1593 FALE *Dialling* 39 Your Diall being made, and the Stile placed therein: take your Trigonall Instrument, and set it upon the Stile, so that the whole Diameter thereof may stand plaine upon the edge or upper part, the centre A, of your Instrument... Then fasten a thread at the uppermost end of your Trigonall in every line of the signes so y^t you may direct downeward by the centre A, to the plat of your Diall: and..then moving the Trigonall on the right hand, so that the thread may be stretched on the left hand, make there likewise a prick upon the plat.

B. *sb.* **1.** See A. 4.

2. *Anat.* = TRIGONE, TRIGONUM 2 (*Cent. Dict.*).

Hence **'trigonally** *adv.*, (*a*) triangularly (*rare*⁻⁰); (*b*) *Chem.*, in a trigonal manner.

1891 *Cent. Dict.* **1962** P. J. & B. DURRANT *Introd. Adv. Inorganic Chem.* xviii. 590 (*heading*) Compounds in which the carbon atom is trigonally hybridised. **1982** *Nature* 25 Feb. 658/1 The borates, where trigonally and tetrahedrally bonded atoms may occur.

trigonate ('trɪgənət), *a. Zool.* [f. as prec. + -ATE[2].] = prec. adj. 1 and 2.

1815 STEPHENS in Shaw *Gen. Zool.* IX. I. 226 Female without the white trigonate spot beneath the chin. **1828** STARK *Elem. Nat. Hist.* II. 203 *A*[*mmothea*] *Caroliniensis*,..back with three trigonate tubercles.

trigone (trɪ'gəʊn, 'traɪgəʊn). *Anat.* [a. F. *trigone* (trigɔn), ad. L. *trigōn-um* TRIGON.] The triangular area at the base of the urinary bladder, between the openings of the ureters and urethra.

1835-6 *Todd's Cycl. Anat.* I. 385/1 The posterior part of the trigone is thinner than the anterior. **1876** GROSS *Dis. Bladder* 137 The usual seat of villous tumor is the trigone. **1898** P. MANSON *Trop. Diseases* xxxii. 503 In the trigone of the bladder, there are..patches of inflammatory thickening.

trigone, obs. form of TRIGON.

trigonel ('trɪgənɛl). *rare*⁻¹. [ad. F. *trigonelle*, or mod.L. *Trigonella* (Linnæus, 1737), dim. of L. *trigōna*, fem. of *trigōn-us* adj., a. Gr. τρίγωνος (see TRIGON); so called from the triangular appearance of the flowers.] A plant of the genus *Trigonella*, N.O. *Leguminosæ*.

1884 *De Candolle's Orig. Cultivated Pl.* 112 Trigonel, or Fenugreek—*Trigonella fœnum-græcum.*

Hence **trigo'nelline** *Chem.* [f. mod.L. *Trigōnell-a* + -INE[5]], an alkaloid occurring in the seeds of fenugreek, in hempseed, and in peas, and prepared artificially from nicotinic acid.

1886 *Jrnl. Chem. Soc.* L. 85, Jahn's *Trigonelline*, $C_7H_7NO_2 + H_2O$, crystallises in colourless, flat prisms, of feeble saline taste; it is readily soluble in water.

trigonellite (trɪgə'nɛlaɪt). *Palæont.* [ad. mod.L. *Trigōnellītēs* (given as a generic name), f. mod.L. *Trigōnella*: see prec. and -ITE[1] 2 a.] A fossil of triangular form and shelly consistence, found in the Kimmeridge clay; 'probably the operculum of a cephalopod' (Lyell).

[**1748** J. HILL *Hist. Fossils* 646 That kind [of Cockle] call'd by authors Trigonella... This kind..approaches to a triangular figure.] **1831** MURCHISON in Phillips *Man. Geol.* (1855) 301 Hard, compact, not oolitic, containing brachyphyllum, ferns, and trigonellites. **1851** WOODWARD *Mollusca* I. 80 They were described in 1811, by Parkinson, who called them trigonellites. **1885** LYELL *Elem. Geol.* xx. (1885) 295.

trigoneutic, -goneutism: see TRI- 2.

‖**trigonia** (traɪ'gəʊnɪə). *Conch.* [mod.L. generic name, f. as TRIGON + -IA[1].] A genus of bivalve molluscs having a shell of triangular form.

1837 *Encycl. Brit.* (ed. 7) XV. 343/1 The trigonia now forms along with castalia, the small family of Trigonées. **1851** WOODWARD *Mollusca* I. 11 The cockle and trigonia have the foot bent, enabling them to make short leaps. **1883** *Fisheries Exhib. Catal.* (ed. 4) 176 Collection of Trigonias..exhibited by Dr. J. C. Cox, F.L.S. of Sydney.

Hence **trigoniacean** (traɪgəʊnɪ'eɪʃ(ɪ)ən), (*a*) *adj.* belonging to the group *Trigoniacea* of bivalve molluscs, typified by the genus *Trigonia*; (*b*) *sb.* a mollusc of this group.

In recent Dicts.

trigonic (traɪ'gɒnɪk), *a. rare.* [ad. Gr. τριγωνικός triangular, f. τρίγωνος: see TRIGON and -IC.] Of or pertaining to a trigon or triangle.

trigonic co-ordinates (*Geom.*), a system of co-ordinates invented by W. Walton in 1868, determining a point in a plane by the angles subtended at the point by the sides of a fixed triangle.

1788 T. TAYLOR *Proclus* I. 54 The soul from material triangles or circles, forms in herself the trigonic, or circular species.

So †**tri'gonical** *a. rare*, = TRIGONAL 3.

1644 LILLY *Merlinus Angl.* To Rdr. Ajb, The Government of the World by the seven Planetary Angels under the severall Trygonicall Revolutions of Saturne and Iupiter.

trigonid ('trɪgənɪd). *Comp. Anat.* [f. TRIGON + -ID (arbitrarily used).] The triangle of cusps of the lower molar teeth in primitive mammals.

1897 [see TRIGON 6].

trigonitis (trɪ-, traɪgəʊ'naɪtɪs). *Med.* [f. TRIGON(E + -ITIS.] Inflammation of the trigone of the bladder.

1900 in DORLAND *Med. Dict.* **1912** R. GUITERAS *Urology* II. lxiii. 508 Gonorrhea of the neck of the bladder, trigonitis, is not uncommon. **1974** J. D. MAYNARD in R. M. Kirk et al. *Surgery* viii. 178/1 In young women, urethral trauma from intercourse commonly leads to recurrent attacks of urethritis and trigonitis.

trigono- ('trɪgənəʊ, trɪ'gəʊnəʊ), combining form repr. Gr. τρίγωνο-ς adj. three-cornered, triangular, neut. τρίγωνον as sb. a triangle; used in several scientific terms. **trigono'cephale, -'cephalous** *adjs.*, *Zool.* [Gr. κεφαλή head], having a triangular head, as a serpent of the genus *Trigonocephalus*; so **trigonoce'phalic** *a. Anthrop.*, having a malformation of the skull, caused by premature closing of the medio-frontal suture, in which the sides are flat and converge to an apex in front; **trigono'cephaly**, the condition of being trigonocephalic. **trigonocerous** (-'ɒsərəs) *a.*, *Zool.* [Gr. κέρας horn], having horns of triangular section. **trigono'cuneate** *a.* [L. *cune-us* wedge], triangularly wedge-shaped. **tri'gonodont** *a.*, *Comp. Anat.* [Gr. ὀδούς, ὀδοντ- tooth], having the primitive cusps of the molar teeth arranged in a triangle. **tri'gonotype**, *Geom.* [Gr. τύπος figure, image, TYPE], name for a trigonal trapezohedron (*Cent. Dict.* 1891).

1865 *Morn. Star* 13 Mar., A *trigonocephale black serpent, brought over in 1842, is alive. **1878** BARTLEY tr. *Topinard's Anthrop.* v. 176 **Trigonocephalic*, skull triangular at the top anteriorly, supposed to be owing to the medio-frontal synostosis. *Ibid.* Index, *Trigonocephaly. **1904** DUCKWORTH *Morphol. & Anthropol.* x. 253 A skull which viewed from above presents a peaked or rostrated appearance and has been described as triangular or trigonocephalic. **1848** SMART, **Trigonocerous*, having three-angled horns,—applied to a species of fossil stag. **1864** in WEBSTER. **1822** J. PARKINSON *Outl. Oryctol.* 224 *Trigono-cuneate, rather smooth on the upper part, longitudinally sulcated. **1897** H. F. OSBORN in *Amer. Nat.* Dec. 1002 '*Trigonodont' is most appropriate because the first step in molar morphology is to identify the primitive triangle.

trigonoid ('trɪgənɔɪd), *a.* and *sb. Geom.* [ad. Gr. τριγωνοειδής of triangular form: see TRIGON and -OID.] **a.** *adj.* Resembling a triangle; approximately triangular. **b.** *sb.* A plane figure contained by three circular arcs of equal radius meeting at angles; a species of curvilinear triangle. So **trigo'noidal** *a.*, (*a*) *Nat. Hist.* = *trigonoid* adj.; (*b*) *Geom.* 'like a trigonoid' (*Cent. Dict.* 1891).

1822 J. PARKINSON *Outl. Oryctol.* 217 Subcordated, trigonoidal. **1873** SALMON *Higher Plane Curves* 245 The quartic is a triacnodal curve composed of a trigonoid figure within the triangle and of the three vertices as acnodes.

trigonometer[1] (trɪgə'nɒmɪtə(r)). [f. TRIGONOMETRY, on analogy of *chronometer, thermometer*: see -METER.] A name given to various trigonometrical instruments.

1767 J. FERGUSON *Tables & Tracts* (1771) 80 Mr. Mungo Murray..contrived a very useful instrument..which he calls The Armillary Trigonometer. **1796** HUTTON *Math. Dict., Armillary Trigonometer*, an instrument..consisting of five semicircles..so divided and graduated, as to serve for expeditiously resolving many problems in astronomy, dialling, and spherical trigonometry. **1828** *Amer. Jrnl. Sc.* XIV. 270 A trigonometer..which may be conveniently carried in the pocket. **1860** in *Abridgm. Specif. Patents Optical*, etc. *Instr.* (1875) 345 An improved mathematical or plotting instrument [denominated by the inventor] a protracting trigonometer.

trigo'nometer[2]. [f. TRIGONOMETRY, on analogy of *geometer*, and the like.] A person versed in trigonometry; *spec.* one engaged in a trigonometrical survey.

a **1852** MACGILLIVRAY *Nat. Hist. Dee Side & Braemar* (1855) 92 We arrived at the centre of the broad top..seating ourselves on the base of the pyramidal cairn of the Trigonometers. **1902** *Westm. Gaz.* 10 Nov. 12/2 Kabru is..higher than Aconcagua—its height is,..according to the trigonometers, above 24,000 ft.

trigonometric (,trɪgənəʊ'mɛtrɪk), *a.* [f. TRIGONOMETRY + -IC: perh. through F. *trigonométrique* (1762 in *Dict. Acad.*).] = next.

1811 PINKERTON *Petral.* I. 184 The mountains, on which their trigonometric operations had conducted them. **1862** C. P. SMYTH *Three Cities in Russia* II. 186 The trigonometric operations require the observer..to be for long periods under canvass.

trigonometrical (,trɪgənəʊ'mɛtrɪkəl), *a.* [f. TRIGONOMETRY or mod.L. *trigonometria* + -IC

+ -AL[1]; after *geometrical*, etc.] Of, pertaining to, or performed by trigonometry.

trigonometrical functions, those functions of an angle, or of an abstract quantity, used in trigonometry, viz. the sine, tangent, secant, etc.: see TRIGONOMETRY. ***trigonometrical point, station***, a reference point on high ground, usu. marked by a small pyramidal structure, used in triangulation. ***trigonometrical survey***, a survey of a country or region performed by triangulation and trigonometrical calculation.

1666 [implied in TRIGONOMETRICALLY]. **1690** LEYBOURN *Curs. Math.* 552 To find the Altitude..by Trigonometrical Calculation. **1706** W. JONES *Syn. Palmar. Matheseos* 278 Any three..being given, the other three may be found by Trigonometrical Calculation. **1758** MURDOCH in *Phil. Trans.* L. 543 A table of the trigonometrical analogies. **1801** CAPT. W. MADGE (*title*) Account of the Operations carried on for accomplishing a Trigonometrical Survey of England and Wales, 1797. **1807** HUTTON *Course Math.* (1811) II. 3 A Trigonometrical Canon is a table showing the length of the sine, tangent, and secant, to every degree and minute of the quadrant, with respect to the radius, which is expressed by unity or 1. **1860** TYNDALL *Glac.* I. xi. 69 A pyramid of stones used as a trigonometrical station by Professor Forbes. **1886** T. P. WHITE *Ordnance Survey of U.K.* iv. 68 In very many cases the old trigonometrical points were again observed to or from. **1949** T. W. BIRCH *Maps* vi. 56 The *trigonometrical points* or *stations* determined by theodolite are accurately plotted on the plane-table sheet.

ˌtrigonoˈmetrically, *adv.* [f. prec. + -LY[2].] In a trigonometrical manner; by means, or by the method, of trigonometry.

1666 COLLINS in Rigaud *Corr. Sci. Men* (1841) I. 115 Problems that seem easy trigonometrically, but not so analytically. **1751** J. STUART in *Lett. Lit. Men* (Camden) 382 An exact Map of all the Province of Attica trigonometrically surveyed. **1859** R. F. BURTON *Centr. Afr.* in *Jrnl. Geog. Soc.* XXIX. 8 Such as cannot be ascended should be measured trigonometrically.

trigonometrician (trɪgənɒmɪˈtrɪʃən). [f. TRIGONOMETRIC: see -ICIAN.] = TRIGONOMETER[2]. So **trigoˈnometrist**.

1884 *Manch. Exam.* 4 Oct. 5/4 The base-line of the trigonometrician admits of fresh refinements in precision. **1900** *Athenæum* 18 Aug. 223/3 The autobiographer became a trigonometrician, and astronomer at large.

trigonometry (trɪgəˈnɒmɪtrɪ). [ad. mod.L. *trigōnometria* (B. Pitiscus 1595), f. Gr. τρίγωνο-ν triangle + -μετρία measurement. So Fr. *trigonométrie* (1629 in Hatz.-Darm.).] That branch of mathematics which deals with the measurement of the sides and angles of triangles, particularly with certain functions of their angles or of angles in general (the SINE, COSINE, TANGENT, COTANGENT, SECANT, and COSECANT), and hence with these functions as applied to abstract quantities; thus including the theory of triangles, of angles, and of (elementary) singly periodic functions.

Trigonometry comprises ***plane trigonometry***, which treats of plane triangles and angles, and ***spherical trigonometry***, which treats of spherical ones, i.e. those described on the surface of a sphere.

[**1595** B. PITISCUS (*title*) Trigonometria: sive De Solvtione Triangvlorvm Tractatus breuis & perspicuus.] **1614** (*title*) Trigonometry: or The Doctrine of Triangles. First written in Latine, by B. Pitiscus.., and now Translated into English, by Ra. Handson. **1631** R. NORWOOD (*title*) Trigonometrie. Or, The Doctrine of Triangles: Divided into Two Bookes: The first shewing the mensuration of Right lined Triangles: The second of Sphericall. **1738** *Gentl. Mag.* Jan. 13/1 A few Calculations by Trigonometry. **1816** PLAYFAIR *Nat. Phil.* II. 13 It often happens..that the stars must be observed when they are not on the meridian, and their positions..must then be derived from spherical trigonometry. **1854** KINGSLEY *Alexandria* i. 31 For the purpose of working out this theory he [Hipparchus] required a science of trigonometry plane and spherical: and this he accordingly seems to have invented.

‖**trigonon** (trɪˈgəʊnɒn). *Antiq.* [a. Gr. τρίγωνον triangle, a musical instrument of this form.] = TRIGON 3 c.

1727–41 CHAMBERS *Cycl.*, *Trigon, trigonon*,..a musical instrument, used among the ancients. **1847** LEITCH tr. *C. O. Müller's Anc. Art* §425. 505 A concert of female players on the flute, the cithern and the trigonon. **1864** ENGEL *Mus. Anc. Nat.* 195 The trigonon ought..more properly to be classed with the lyre than with the harp.

trigonous (ˈtrɪgənəs), *a. Nat. Hist.* [f. Gr. τρίγων-ος (see TRIGON) + -OUS.] = TRIGONAL 2.

[**1760–88** J. LEE *Introd. Bot.* Gloss., *Trigonus caulis*, a three-sided stalk.] **1821** W. P. C. BARTON *Flora N. Amer.* I. 114 Capsule truncate, trigonous. **1828** STARK *Elem. Nat. Hist.* I. 259 *Dendrocolaptes*,..Bill depressed and trigonous at the base. **1870** HOOKER *Stud. Flora* 245 Convolvulus arvensis..seeds 4, obtusely 3-gonous.

‖**trigonum** (trɪˈgəʊnəm). [L., ad. Gr. τρίγωνον triangle: see TRIGON.]

1. *Antiq.* A musical instrument: = TRIGON 3 c.

1727–41 CHAMBERS *Cycl.* s.v. *Music*, Of stringed instruments we hear of the lyra or cithara, the psalterium, trigonum, sambuca [etc.]. **1801** BUSBY *Dict. Mus.*, *Trigonum*, or *Triangular Harp*, an instrument supposed to have been of Phrygian invention. *Ibid.*, From Sophocles we learn, that a certain musician..was so admirable a performer on the Trigonum,..that [etc.].

2. *Anat.* = TRIGONE.

1879 *St. George's Hosp. Rep.* IX. 322 The walls of the bladder were slightly hypertrophied, and there was a small ulcer on the left half of the trigonum.

†**trigony** (ˈtrɪgənɪ). *Obs. rare*[−1]. [ad. Gr. τριγονία third generation, f. τρι-, TRI- + γόν-ος, γονή offspring, family, generation.] Threefold generation or production.

1660 HOWELL *Parly Beasts* 140 Man is that great Amphybium in whom lye Three distinct Souls by way of trigony.

trigram (ˈtraɪgræm). [f. Gr. τρι-, TRI- + γράμμα, -ατ-, line, letter, or γραμμή stroke, line.] **a.** An inscription of three letters; also, = TRIGRAPH (Webster 1864); *spec.* in *Psychol.*, a (nonsense) word of three letters used in the study of learning or memory (see esp. quot. 1960). **b.** A figure or character formed of three strokes; also *spec.*, a figure traditionally used in the Chinese philosophy of the I Ching for the purposes of divination. **c.** *Geom.*, etc. A set of three lines; *spec.* the figure formed by three straight lines in one plane not intersecting in the same point; also more generally, any figure composed of three elements.

1606 BIRNIE *Kirk-Buriall* (1833) 17 Inscryving their tombes with a trigram of D.M.S. **1801** J. HAGER *Babylon. Inscr.* 54 What connexion is there between the first trigram, or three united strokes, to represent heaven, and..the second trigram,..three broken ones, to represent the earth? **1877** J. LEGGE in *Encycl. Brit.* VI. 263/2 The *Yih King*..the rudiments of which are assigned to Fuh-hsi in the 30th century B.C. Those rudiments, however, are merely the 8 trigrams and 64 diagrams, composed of a whole and a broken line. **1882** *Athenæum* 2 Sept. 297/1 The hexagrams ..are composed each of a double trigram... The trigrams consist of three lines one above the other. **1897–8** *Ann. Rep. Bur. Amer. Ethnol.* 842 The swastika itself merely represents two super-posed trigrams. **1923** J. P. BRUCE *Chu Hsi & his Masters* vi. 127 The Grand Terminus..produced the two elementary Forms. These two Forms produced the four Symbols, which, again, produced the eight Trigrams. The eight Trigrams served to determine the good and evil issues of events. **1957**, **1965** [see I CHING]. **1960** E. J. ARCHER in *Psychol. Monogr.* LXXIV. x. 1/2 This study is a re-evaluation of the meaningfulness of all possible three-letter combinations of the Roman alphabet of the form consonant-vowel-consonant... It is herewith proposed to call these combinations 'trigrams', and in view of their form to further specify them as 'CVC trigrams'. **1970** *Jrnl. General Psychol.* LXXXIII. 214 The study..assumes that an object elicits a given number of mediating responses with which a CVC trigram can be associated. **1973** *Jrnl. Genetic Psychol.* CXXIII. 15 Correct recognitions of trigrams on test trials. **1974** *Sci. Amer.* Jan. 108/2 There are two ancient ways of displaying the eight trigrams in a circle.

So **trigraˈmmatic**, **triˈgrammic** *adjs.*, consisting of three letters (= TRILITERAL) or sets of letters; **triˈgrammatism** = TRILITERALISM.

1824 T. YOUNG in *Suppl. Encycl. Brit.* IV. 43/1 The 'trilinguar' or rather trigrammatic Stone of Rosetta. **1839** DONALDSON *New Cratylus* §70 (1850) 107 Their apparent [Semitic] trigrammatism, their etymological disintegration, and the tertiary condition in which their oldest remains are found, must be referred to the constant intermixtures, re-unions [etc.]. **1846** WORCESTER, *Trigrammic*, containing three letters. *Thomson.* **1847** WEBSTER, *Trigrammatic*, containing three sets of characters or letters. *Gliddon.*

trigraph (ˈtraɪgrɑːf, -æ-). [f. Gr. τρι-, TRI- + γραφή writing, drawing.] A combination of three letters denoting a simple sound, as *eau* in F. *beau*, *sch* in Ger. *schaf*.

1836 in SMART; hence in later Dicts.

trigraphy (ˈtrɪgrəfɪ). *Geom.* [f. after HOMOGRAPHY: see TRI-.] A group of three sets of points or lines having a relation analogous to that of *homography* between two (see HOMOGRAPHY 1); that branch of geometry which deals with such relations. Hence **trigraphic** (traɪˈgræfɪk) *a.*, pertaining to trigraphy.

1895 J. W. RUSSELL in *Proc. Lond. Math. Soc.* XXVI. 446 (*title*) Applications of Trigraphy... Trigraphic ranges... A trigraphy projects into a homographic trigraphy. *Ibid.* 448 Given the trigraphic relation, to construct the vague points. *Ibid.* 450 Trigraphic Pencils. *Ibid.* 452 Trigraphic Properties of a Quadric Surface.

triguttulate: see TRI- 1.

‖**Trigynia** (traɪˈdʒɪnɪə). *Bot.* [mod.L. (Linnæus), f. TRI- + Gr. γυνή woman, taken as = female organ, pistil.] An order in many classes of the Linnæan System, comprising plants having three pistils. Hence **ˈtrigyn**, a plant of the order *Trigynia*; **triˈgynian**, **triˈgynious** *adjs.*, of or belonging to the order *Trigynia*; **trigynous** (ˈtrɪdʒɪnəs) *a.*, having three pistils.

[**1748** LINNÆUS *Hortus Upsaliensis* 23 Trigynia.] **1760** J. LEE *Introd. Bot.* II. viii. (1765) 92 *Trigynia*, comprehending such Plants as have three Styles. **1775** ASH, *Trigynous*, having three pistils. **1806** GALPINE *Brit. Bot.* 64 Hypericum... Fl[owers] trigynous. **1828** WEBSTER, Trigyn ..Trigynian. **1846** WORCESTER cites LINDLEY for *Trigyn.* **1860** MAYNE *Expos. Lex.*, *Trigynius, a, um*...*Bot*... trigynious.

trihedral (traɪˈhiːdrəl, -ˈhɛdrəl), *a.* (*sb.*) *Geom.*, *Cryst.*, *Nat. Hist.*, etc. Also **triedral**. [f. Gr. τρι-, TRI- + ἕδρα base + -AL[1].] Of a solid figure or body: Having three sides or faces (in addition to the base or ends); bounded laterally by three surfaces; triangular in section. ***trihedral angle*** or ***quoin***, a solid angle formed by three surfaces meeting at a point.

1789 A. CRAWFORD in *Med. Commun.* II. 355 Obtuse trihedral pyramids. **1812** SIR H. DAVY *Chem. Philos.* 125 Thus 6 particles may compose an octoedron or triedral prism. **1839–47** *Todd's Cycl. Anat.* III. 267/2 The inferior molars are..divided into two triedral portions. **1878** GURNEY *Crystallogr.* 85 The trihedral quoins of the rhombic dodecahedron. **1880** HUXLEY *Crayfish* iii. 116 Each of these joints is trihedral, the outer face being convex; the inner, flat; and the upper concave.

B. *sb. Geom.* A trihedral figure; the figure determined by three planes meeting at a point (*Cent. Dict. Suppl.* 1909). Also **triˈhedron**.

1828 WEBSTER, *Trihedron*, a figure having three equal sides. **1860** WORCESTER cites DAVIES.

trihemeral, -hemiobol: see TRI- 1, 4 a.

trihemimer (ˈtraɪhiːˌmɪmə(r)). *Anc. Pros.* Usually in Lat. form **triheˈmimeris** (also **trie-**). [ad. mod.L. *trihēmimeris*, ad. Gr. type *τριημιμερής consisting of three halves, f. τρι- + ἡμι- half + μέρ-ος part: cf. HEPHTHEMIMER, PENTHEMIMER.] A group or catalectic colon of three half-feet; esp. as constituting the first part of a hexameter, preceding the cæsura. Hence **triheˈmimeral** *a.*, applied to a cæsura occurring in the middle of the second foot.

1704 J. HARRIS *Lex. Techn.* I, *Triemimeris*, is a Branch of the Cæsura of a Latine Verse, when after the first Foot of the Verse there remains an odd Syllable, which helps to make the next Foot. **1871** *Public Sch. Lat. Gram.* (1876) 529 The next best form is obtained by uniting with the hephthemimeral cæsura the trihemimeral, in the middle of the second foot. *Ibid.* 550 In both verses the rhythm is helped by the trihemimeris.

trihemitone (traɪˈhɛmɪtəʊn). *Mus.* ? *Obs.* [ad. Gr. τριημιτόνιον, f. τρι-, TRI- + ἡμιτόνιον HEMITONE.] An interval of three semitones, or a tone and a semitone; a minor third; esp. that used in the ancient Greek (Pythagorean) scale.

1694 W. HOLDER *Harmony* (1731) 61, I would..call the greater Third (as the Greeks do) *Ditone*,..and the Third Minor, *Trihemitone*.., as consisting of three half-Tones, (or rather of a Tone and half a Tone). **1746** *Phil. Trans.* XLIV. 268 The Trihemitone of the Ancients falls short of the third Minor by a Comma. **1753** CHAMBERS *Cycl. Supp.* s.v. *Interval*, Trihemitone of the Greek Scale, or deficient third Minor, 32/27,..Third Minor, 6/5,..Trihemitone Major, 4096/3375.

tri-hexahedral: see TRI- 2 b.

†**tri-hexoctaˈhedron**. *Geom. Obs.* In 8 triexocto-. [f. TRI- 2 + HEXOCTAHEDRON.] A solid figure having 18 (= 3 times 6) square and 8 triangular faces.

1765 KIRBY *Perspective made Easy* (ed. 3) 45.

trihilate: see TRI- 1.

trihybrid (traɪˈhaɪbrɪd), *a.* [f. TRI- + HYBRID *sb.* and *a.*] **1.** *Genetics.* Of or pertaining to a hybrid that is heterozygous with respect to three independent genes.

1918 *Genetics* III. 591 The undepleted litters in our trihybrid ratio show a suggestive order or arrangement of frequencies.

2. Involving or pertaining to a descent from three different races or types that interbred.

1941 TINDALE & BIRDSELL in *Records S. Austral. Museum* VII. I. 6 The Australian aboriginal no longer may be considered as a pure race of unusual homogeneity, but a well-blended group of at least dihybrid and probably trihybrid origin. **1969** A. A. ABBIE *Original Australians* xi. 215 My own observation on Aborigines in many parts of Australia have not disclosed the physical differences the 'trihybrid theory' demands. **1979** *Nature* 15 Nov. 298/2 In spite of an earlier model postulating a trihybrid origin, a theory favouring a homogeneous colonising stock had gained some acceptance.

trihydrate (traɪˈhaɪdrət). *Chem.* [f. TRI- 5 a + HYDRATE.] A compound containing three molecules of water combined with an element or radical or with another compound; also, a compound containing three hydroxyl groups, OH, united to an element or radical; e.g. ***bismuth trihydrate***, which may be regarded as Bi_2O_3, $3H_2O$ or as $Bi(OH)_3$. So **trihydrated** *a.*, combined with three molecules of water.

1854 SCOFFERN in *Orr's Circ. Sc.*, *Chem.* 374 A crystallized trihydrate of phosphoric acid results. **1868** WATTS *Dict. Chem.* IV. 83 Nitrates..Copper also forms a trihydrated salt, $Cu''N^2O^6.3H^2O$. **1873** —— *Fownes' Chem.* (ed. 11) 391 The trihydrate is the ordinary gelatinous precipitate obtained by treating solutions of aluminium salts. **1888** MUIR & MORLEY *Watts' Dict. Chem.* I. 145 Aluminium.. Trihydrate... Occurs native, in hexagonal fibrous crystals, as *gibbsite*, and *hydrargyllite*.

trihydric (traɪˈhaɪdrɪk), *a.*[1] *Chem.* [f. TRI- 5 + Gr. ὕδωρ water + -IC.] Containing three hydroxyl groups, OH; thus glycerin or glycerol, $C_3H_5(OH)_3$, is a trihydric alcohol; pyrogallic acid or pyrogallol, $C_6H_3(OH)_3$, is a trihydric phenol.

1866 FRANKLAND *Lect. Notes* 269 Relations of Glycerin to the Trihydric Acids, Glyceric Acid,..and Tartronic Acid. **1881** FRANKLAND & JAPP *Lect. Notes* (ed. 3) II. 105 Trihydric Alcohols. Glycerin..series. These alcohols contain three semimolecules of hydroxyl. **1900** SMITH *Richter's Org. Chem.* (ed. 3) II. 140 The phenols, like the alcohols, are distinguished as mono-, di-, and trihydric, according to the number of hydroxyl groups which have entered.

trihydric, *a.*[2] *Chem.* = TRIHYDROGEN (which is now preferred).

1866 ROSCOE *Elem. Chem.* xv. 136 The three atoms of hydrogen in trihydric [*ed.* 1869 trihydrogen] phosphate may be replaced by three different metals. **1887** TIDY *Modern Chem.* (ed. 2) 163.

trihydro- (traɪˈhaɪdrəʊ). *Chem.* [f. TRI- 5 + Gr. ὑδρο-, combining form of ὕδωρ water: see HYDRO-.] A formative denoting that the compound contains the elements of three molecules of water, H_2O, united to the substance designated by the rest of the name; e.g. ***trihydrostrychnine***, $C_{21}H_{28}N_2O_5$, which differs from strychnine, $C_{21}H_{22}N_2O_2$, by $3H_2O$.

1879 *Jrnl. Chem. Soc.* XXXVI. 387 Another basic substance was obtained, *trihydrostrychnine.*

trihydrocalcite: see TRI- 5 c.

triˈhydrogen, *a. Chem.* [TRI- 5 b.] Containing 3 atoms of hydrogen in combination, as ***trihydrogen phosphate***, H_3PO_2.

1869 [see TRIHYDRIC *a.*[2]].

trihydrol (traɪˈhaɪdrɒl). *Chem. Obs.* exc. *Hist.* [f. TRI- + HYDROL.] A supposed trimer of water, $(H_2O)_3$, formerly thought to be present especially in ice.

1900 [see HYDROL 2]. **1932** *Proc. Nat. Acad. Sci.* XVIII. 136 (*heading*) The physiological effect of trihydrol in water. **1957** [see HYDROL 2]. **1972** H. S. FRANK in F. Franks *Water* I. xiv. 531 Many of the detailed models..have been overtaken by events and are now of hardly more than historical interest. Perhaps the classic example of such obsolescence is found in the theory put forward in 1900.. representing water as a mixture of monohydrol (monomeric, steamlike), dihydrol (dimeric, intrinsically liquid), and trihydrol (trimeric, icelike) molecules.

trihypostatic to **trijunction:** see TRI- 1, 4.

tri-icosane: see TRICOSANE.

tri-iod-, tri-iodo-. [TRI- 5 c.] A formative analogous to TRIBROM(O-, TRICHLOR(O-, expressing the substitution of three atoms of iodine for hydrogen, as in *tri-iodobenzene*, $C_6H_3I_3$, *tri-iodomethane*, etc.

tri-ˈiodide: see TRI- 5 a and IODIDE.

triiodothyronine: see TRI- 5 c.

tri-jet (ˈtraɪdʒɛt). Also **trijet.** [f. TRI- + JET *sb.*[3]] An aircraft powered by three jet engines. Freq. *attrib.*, as ***tri-jet airbus, transport.***

1968 *Economist* 20 Apr. 24/3 Last month Eastern Air Lines and Trans World Airlines jumped in with orders to the Lockheed Aircraft Corporation for 94 of the new-look tri-jet transports. **1969** *New Scientist* 13 Mar. 554/2 The tri-jet air bus to carry 350 is on the way. **1970** *Time* 19 Jan. 44 Originally designed for shorter-range routes than the 747, the trijets are now being offered in stretched intercontinental versions. **1979** *Daily Tel.* 17 Apr. 8/8 Boeing..will be extremely busy introducing two new twin-jet airliners and possibly a tri-jet as well.

† **trike,** *v. Obs. rare*[−1]. [Derivation obscure. Some conjecture that it is the primitive of *trikel*, TRICKLE *v.*, and meant 'to flow down': cf. TRILL *v.*[2] 3; others that it may be for *strike*.] *intr.* To hang down, descend, fall in a flowing manner.

a **1310** in Wright *Lyric P.* (Percy Soc.) 35 Hire gurdel of bete gold is al, Umben hire middel smal, that triketh to the to.

trike. Colloq. abbrev. of TRICYCLE *sb.* and *v.* or (*rarely*) of TRICYCLIST. Hence **ˈtriker; ˈtriking** *vbl. sb.*

1883 *Sporting Life* 22 Apr. 6/5 Londoners call bicyclists 'bikes' and tricyclists 'trikes'. **1884** *Wheel World* Apr. 495/2 The makers of his new trike. **1885** *N. & Q.* 14 Nov. 386/1 Do you *bike* or *trike*? **1890** BARRÈRE & LELAND *Dict. Slang* II. 374/1 *Trike*, (common) a tricycle; *triking*, cycling. Do you bike or trike? do you ride a bicycle or a tricycle? **1901** *Pall Mall Gaz.* 15 May 1, I was further gratified with the intimation that the peccant triker had been discovered. **1912** A. S. M. HUTCHINSON *Happy Warrior* III. v. 148 I'm all mixed up in this awful trike, you know. **1939** X. HERBERT *Capricornia* xiii. 185 There is no fixed time for those who wish to come by horse or trike. Just roll up when you like. **1939–40** *Army & Navy Stores Catal.* 827/1 *Trike*..for ages 3 to 7 years. **1972** *Oxford Times* 4 Feb. 17 An Oxford doctor has condemned the three-wheeled invalid trikes as 'tin coffins'. **1977** *Times* 9 Aug. 5/7 Many disabled people are now turning from the 'to trike or not to trike' argument. **1984** *N.Z. Farmer* 23 Feb. 31/2 (*caption*) Honda farm bikes and trikes remain one of the strongest sellers in Motor Holdings' lineup.

b. A kind of ultralight aircraft.

1981 M. A. MARKOWSKI *Ultralight Aircraft* 45 The trike appears to be a viable approach to ultralight flight and allows thousands of hang gliders to be powered, as desired. **1982** *Sci. Amer.* July 63/1 A trike (from tricycle) is a pyramidal tubular frame that holds the engine, the pilot's seat and the landing gear.

Trike, var. TRIQUE *sb.* and *a.*

trikini (traɪˈkiːnɪ). Also **tri-kini, Tri-Kini.** [f. TRI-, after BIKINI b, with reference to BI-[2].] Any of various designs of ladies' swimsuit which consist of three main areas of fabric (as pants and a separate covering for each breast).

1967 *Scottish Daily Mail* 7 June 12 Some ingenious fellow has just come up with a Tri-Kini, best described as a handkerchief and two small saucers. The saucers, say the manufacturers, stick on with Velcro, the stuff which fastens at a touch. **1968** *Sunday Truth* (Brisbane) 8 Sept. 1/2 She is wearing the new trikini swimsuit which is to make its debut in Australia next summer. **1970** *Telegraph* (Brisbane) 20 Feb. 15/5 When is a bikini a trikini? When it's a suntanner of a swimsuit like this..deeply decolette [*sic*] and, to put it briefly, even briefer.

tril, obs. form of TRILL.

† **trilabe.** *Obs. rare*[−0]. [According to Mayne, 'f. Gr. τρεῖς three + λάβ-ειν to lay hold on'. Cf. ASTROLABE.] A surgical instrument with three expansible prongs: see quot.

1860 MAYNE *Expos. Lex.*, *Trilabe*, name of an instrument for extracting foreign bodies of sufficiently moderate size from the bladder through the urethra, having three branches capable of being expanded in the bladder, and then closed on the object to be withdrawn.

trilabiate to **trilaminate:** see TRI- 1.

† **trilapse, trelapse,** *a.* and *sb. Sc. Obs.* [f. L. *tri-*, TRI- + *laps-us* pa. pple. fallen, sb. a fall.]

A. *adj.* That has fallen for the third time into a sin or offence; also said of the offence.

1593 in *Maitl. Cl. Misc.* I. 56 James Pirrhie trilaps in adultery. **1597** *Ibid.* 128 Hellen Allan..confessis..that the samin fault is trelaps in hir persone. **1600** *Presbyt. Rec. Stirling* in Ferguson *Alex. Hume* (1899) 282 The penalties paid by adulterers and trelaps fornicaturs to be devoted to the reparatione of ye brig of Tullibody. **1651** *Humbie Kirk-sess. Rec.* in *Maitl. Cl. Misc.* I. 440 Declaring her to the session to be trilapse in fornication.

B. *sb.* A third lapse or fall (into a sin or offence).

1651 in *Maitl. Cl. Misc.* I. 441 Isobell Spence entred in sackcloth..to give satisfaction for her trilapse in [= into] fornication. **1725** *Presbyt. Rec.* in Cramond *Ann. Banff* (1893) II. 82 George Barclay had openly confessed his trelapse. **1776** in J. Mill *Diary* (1889) 133 This being a relapse to the woman and a trelapse to the man.

Hence † **triˈlapser (tre-)** *Sc. Obs. rare*[−1], one who lapses or falls a third time.

1649 *Rec. Dingwall Presb.* (S.H.S.) 148 Trelapsers in fornication be brought before the Presbyterie.

trilarcenous: see TRI- 2.

† **trilater,** *a. Obs. rare.* [ad. L. *trilater-us*: see next.] = next.

1570 BILLINGSLEY *Euclid* xvi. xxix. 453 To proue that an octohedron geuen, is tredecuple sesquialter to a trilater equilater pyramis inscribed in it.

trilateral (traɪˈlætərəl), *a.* and *sb.* [f. L. *trilater-us* three-sided + -AL[1]. Cf. F. *trilatéral.*]

A. *adj.* **1.** Contained by three sides; three-sided.

1660 BARROW *Euclid* I. Def. xx, Three sided or Trilateral figures are such as are contained under three right lines. **1788** T. TAYLOR *Proclus* I. 173 Euclid appears to me to have made a separate division into angles and sides, from considering this alone, that every triangle is not also trilateral. **1828** *Hutton's Course Math.* II. 136 The quadrilateral space *EAA'E'* is double the trilateral space *AA'F.* **1875** MERIVALE *Gen. Hist. Rome* xviii. (1877) 102 Two powers now remained to struggle for the dominion of the trilateral island [Sicily].

2. Pertaining to or concerning three countries, parties, etc., esp. with reference to the relations between Europe, the United States, and Japan; ***the Trilateral Commission*** (see quots. 1973, 1981).

1965 *Economist* 20 Feb. 758/1 Ethiopia. A trilateral agreement is being negotiated with the object of harnessing German and American help in forming an Ethiopian frontier defence force. **1973** *N.Y. Times* 2 Mar. 35/1 A group of distinguished private citizens in the United States, Japan and Europe are now organizing what they call 'the trilateral commission' to study the common problems of these three power centers. **1977** *Times* 28 Apr. 7/4 Mr Jimmy Carter..really believes in what has been called the trilateral system of America, Europe and Japan. **1981** *Washington Post* 18 Mar. A1/2 For the record, the Trilateral Commission is a New York-based policy group formed by Rockefeller in 1973 in a reaction to the nationalistic foreign economic policy of President Nixon, which disturbed some traditional U.S. allies. **1984** *Times* 5 Mar. 12/2 It was thanks to the complicated trilateral arrangement worked out in secret..that he was taken to Pakistan.

B. *sb.* A three-sided figure; a triangle.

1766 *Compl. Farmer* s.v. *Surveying*, Triangles are figures comprehended under three right lines, and..might be better called trilaterals. **1870** *Observer* 9 Oct., From the canal, round the trilateral of St. Denis, to the Seine about Argenteuil, the Prussian Guards..have their stations. **1885** LEUDESDORF *Cremona's Proj. Geom.* 31 It follows that the triangles (trilaterals) *bcd*, *b'c'd'* are also in perspective.

Hence **triˈlateralism; triˈlateralist;** also **trilateˈrality, triˈlateralness,** the quality of being trilateral; **triˈlaterally** *adv.*, in a trilateral form, triangularly.

1727 BAILEY vol. II, *Trilateralness*, the having three Sides. **1837–8** SIR W. HAMILTON *Logic* xi. (1866) I. 208 [A] triangle [is distinguished] from every other class of mathematical figures, by the single character of trilaterality. **1847** WEBSTER, *Trilaterally.* **1976** R. H. ULLMAN in *Foreign Affairs* Oct. 1 'Trilateralism'..is the latest attempt both to describe and to prescribe for the relationship between the United States and the other principal democratic, industrialized, market-economy states. **1977** *Studia Diplomatica* XXX. 231 Dr Kissinger can hardly be said to have been unaware of the 'Trilateralists'. **1977** *Foreign Policy* No. 29. 90 The original trilateralism, which links prominent citizens of the United States, Western Europe, and Japan in an international 'commission', arises from the shared ideological commitment of its members to liberal values and politics. The goals of Arab trilateralism, however, are not expressed in ideological terms. **1981** *Washington Post* 18 Mar. A1/2 Remember those dreaded, three-sided Trilateralists, the international conspirators headed by David Rockefeller who were going to take over the world? *Ibid.* A5/6 But old fears die hard, and the far right is ever-vigilant for signs of creeping Trilateralism within the citadel.

trilateration (traɪlætəˈreɪʃən). [f. TRI- + L. *later-*, *latus* side + -ATION.] A method of surveying analogous to triangulation in which each triangle is determined by the measurement of all three sides.

1948 *Bull. Géodésique* No. 10. 342 A network of triangles may be computed and adjusted from observed lengths of sides. The development of error in trilateration is different from that in triangulation..as the side error is not accumulative. **1952** G. BOMFORD *Geodesy* i. 34 It might be possible to use radar trilateration between ground points instead of ordinary geodetic triangulation. **1960** *Times* 4 Mar. 3/2 Experienced in first order triangulation, trilateration and astro-fixes. **1974** *Physics Bull.* Apr. 136/3 A geodetic network was established to an accuracy of 2 mm over the surface of the Laboratory II site using triangulation and trilateration.

trilby (ˈtrɪlbɪ). Also **Trilby.** Pl. **trilbies** or **trilbys.** [The title of a novel by George du Maurier published in 1894, and the name of its heroine.]

1. *colloq.* **a.** A jocular name for the foot (with reference to Trilby's feet, which were objects of admiration). ? *Obs.*

1895 *People* 7 July, An American paper has spent its energy of psychological investigation on the foot (I beg pardon, the trilby). **1907** H. E. DUDENEY *Canterbury Puzzles* 114 'Two feet—' he murmured. 'Somebody's Trilbys?' I inquired. **1932** U. SINCLAIR *Candid Reminiscences* I. v. 29 There was a book by the name of 'Trilby', which the ladies blushed to hear spoken of... I knew it had something to do with feet, because thereafter my father always called them 'trilbies'.

† **b.** A particular type of shoe. (Formerly a proprietary name in the U.S.) *Obs.*

1895 *Official Gaz.* (U.S. Patent Office) 16 Apr. 447/1 Boots, shoes and lasts. S. Weil & Co., New York... 'Trilby'. Essential feature—the word 'Trilby'. Used since October 1, 1894. **1895** *Montgomery Ward Catal.* Spring & Summer 509/3 The Trilby... The very latest in ladies' footwear. **1897** *Sears, Roebuck Catal.* 192/1 Our New Trilby... The accompanying cut is an exact reproduction of our new Trilby Shoe.

2. In full ***trilby hat***: a soft felt hat, esp. one of the Homburg type with a narrow brim and indented crown; any hat of a similar shape.

[**1895** *Bradford Daily Argus* 12 Nov. 1/8, I have been puzzling my head to account for the reason of so many soft hats being worn at present, and at last I have hit it. It is another phase of the 'Trilby' complaint. In one of the illustrations of the book Little Billee is 'discovered' wearing a hat of this description, so it has been seized upon by those worshippers at the shrine of Trilby, whom nature will not assist in the cultivation of a Svenjali [*sic*] beard or Taffy whiskers.] **1897** *Daily News* 6 Feb. 6/5 In the struggle Mr. Bennett lost his hat, a black 'Trilby'... Mr. Carr..was also wearing a black 'Trilby' hat. **1915** E. WALLACE *Man who bought London* iii. 33 He turned sharply to the young man in the trilby hat. **1927** W. DEEPING *Kitty* v. 63 The window-sill being a low one Mrs Sarah had a good view of Vernor Street, and the passing of the khaki caps, bowlers, 'Trilbys' and cloth caps. **1958** *Observer* 9 Feb. 11/5 Three men in trilbies and a woman with straggly hair. **1978** *Lancashire Life* Apr. 67/1 Fred was a dapper dresser, and I like to remember him in Summer, wearing a medium-grey lightweight suit, black patent shoes, a beautifully-arranged lilac-coloured pure silk cravat with a massive diamond stick-pin, and a natural straw Trilby. **1979** 'J. LE CARRÉ' *Smiley's People* (1980) xxi. 258 Toby..handed him a trilby hat.

Hence **ˈtrilbied, ˈtrilby-hatted** *adjs.*, wearing a trilby hat.

1966 *Punch* 12 Jan. 45/2 'Tell him about Indonesia, Dave,' cried a small, trilbied man. **1975** M. SIMPSON *Chrome Connection* ii. 25 The trilby-hatted husband..gave her a curious look.

trilemma (traɪˈlɛmə). [formed after DILEMMA: see TRI-.] A situation, or (in *Logic*) a syllogism, of the nature of a DILEMMA, but involving three alternatives instead of two.

1672 P. HENRY *Diaries & Lett.* 16 Feb. (1882) 250 Wee are put hereby to a Trilemma either to turn flat Independents, or to strike in with y[e] conformists, or to sit down in former silence. **1690** C. NESSE *O. & N. Test.* I. 375 Joseph.. prudently answers the..trilemma, the..three-horned argument. **1725** WATTS *Logic* III. ii. §6 This sort of argument may be..composed of three..members, and may be called a Trilemma. *a* **1860** SEARS (Worcester), We stand in a trilemma, and we must adopt one of three sets of conclusions. **1887** FOWLER *Deductive Logic* v. (ed. 9) 120 We may form a Trilemma, Tetralemma, &c., by increasing the number of antecedents or consequents or both.

Trilene (ˈtraɪliːn). *Pharm.* Also trilene. [f. TRI(CHLOROETHY)LENE.] A proprietary name for a medicinal grade of trichloroethylene, used as an analgesic and light anæsthetic.

1935 *Trade Marks Jrnl.* 13 Feb. 184/1 *Trilene*... Medicated preparations of trichlorethylene for human use. Imperial Chemical Industries Limited,.. Millbank, London. *Ibid.* 20 Feb. 214/1 *Trilene*... Trichlorethylene for veterinary and sanitary purposes. Imperial Chemical Industries Limited. **1941** *Brit. Med. Jrnl.* 21 June 925/1 We .. found that this firm was already manufacturing, under the trade name of 'trilene', a purified form of the substance specially prepared for medical purposes, though with no reference to inhalation or general anaesthesia. **1944** *Official Gaz.* (U.S. Patent Office) 18 Jan. 349/1 *Trilene* for anaesthetic for cleansing wounds and for the alleviation of pain. **1966** *New Statesman* 8 July 47/3 Where we had practised my wife was completely able to use the breathing for her own purposes, even under the sleepy drug. She never used her Trilene machine at all. **1971** H. PACY *Road Accidents* ii. 51 Trilene inhalers.. provide mild analgesia and are used by the casualties themselves. **1979** G. BOURNE *Pregnancy* (rev. ed.) xxiv. 365 The indications and the technique for Trilene analgesia are essentially similar to those described for nitrous oxide and oxygen analgesia.

triles, obs. f. TRELLIS.

tri-letter: see TRI- 1 b.

ˈtri-level, *a.* and *sb. N. Amer.* Also trilevel. [f. TRI- + LEVEL *sb.*] **A.** *adj.* Having or consisting of three levels; (of a house, etc.) having three storeys or floors on three levels. Cf. SPLIT-LEVEL *a.* **B.** *sb.* A tri-level house.

1960 V. PACKARD *Waste Makers* i. 8 Workingmen today.. want their tri-level house in the suburbs. **1965** P. WYLIE *They both were Naked* I. ii. 55 Coming down the staircase in Will's suburban home, a tri-level, if there's such a term. **1973** 'D. SHANNON' *No Holiday for Crime* iii. 34 Pershing Square with the tri-level parking lot under it. **1974** *Car & Locomotive Cycl.* (ed. 3) S1-25/1 *Tri-level car*, a flat car designed with integral superstructure of posts, bracings and decking to permit triple level loading of automobiles. **1976** *Casper* (Wyoming) *Star-Tribune* 29 June 16/5 (Advt.), Stretch out in over 2000 sq. ft. of tri-level located on 1.8 acres. **1979** *Arizona Daily Star* 5 Aug. (Advt. Section) 16/7 This tri-level showplace home is ideal for entertaining and family living. **1979** *United States 1980/81* (Penguin Travel Guides) 432 Today this tri-level arcade features chic boutiques and restaurants.

trilineal (traɪˈlɪniːəl), *a.* (*sb.*) *Geom.* [f. TRI- + post-cl.L. *līneālis* LINEAL.] = next. Also as *sb.* a trilineal figure.

1715 tr. *Gregory's Astron.* I. (1726) I. 45 The infinitely small trilineal Figures. **1807** HUTTON *Course Math.* II. 115 To each add the trilineal *IAE*. **1891** *Pall Mall G.* 20 Oct. 6/1 Dr. Barrett.. addressed the students,.. he said, 'Never mind about trilineal co-ordinates, go in for music.'

trilinear (traɪˈlɪniːə(r)), *a. Geom.* [f. TRI- + L. *līneāris* LINEAR, f. *līnea* line.] Of, contained by, or having some relation to, three lines (including curved as well as straight lines).

trilinear co-ordinates, a system of co-ordinates determining a point in a plane by its distances, measured in three fixed directions, from three fixed straight lines forming a triangle.

1715 tr. *Gregory's Astron.* III. (1726) I. 379 The trilinear Figure *ALS* is to the whole Ellipse, as the trilinear Figure *AGS* to the whole Circle. **1807** HUTTON *Course Math.* II. 115 The Sector or Trilinear Space contained by an Arc of the Curve and two Radii. **1896** *Yale Univ. Grad. Course Instr.* 70 A course in analytical geometry... It includes the use of determinants and trilinear coördinates.

trilineate (traɪˈlɪniːət), *a. Zool.* [f. TRI- + L. *līneāt-us* streaked, striped, f. *līnea* LINE: see -ATE[2] 2.] Marked with three lines or streaks. So **triˈlineated** *a.*

1802 SHAW *Gen. Zool.* III. 543 Trilineated Snake.. marked throughout the whole length by three black lines or narrow stripes.. Native of Africa. **1803** *Ibid.* IV. 472 Trilineated Sparus.. with the body marked on each side by three longitudinal spotted brown lines. **1891** *Cent. Dict.*, Trilineate.

trilingual (traɪˈlɪŋgwəl), *a.* [f. TRI- + L. *lingua* tongue, after *lingual*; cf. L. *trilinguis* in same sense.] Speaking or using, written or expressed in, or relating to three languages.

1834 *Encycl. Brit.* (ed. 7) VIII. 560/1 The trilingual, or rather trigrammatic stone of Rosetta. **1851** LAYARD *Pop. Acc. Discov. Nineveh* Introd. 13 What are called the Trilingual inscriptions of Persia. **1904** MORLEY in *19th Cent.* Oct. 578 Whatever we may think of.. the trilingual heresy [that worship could be offered only in three languages]. **1907** *Athenæum* 7 Dec. 719/1 The literature of England up to the end of the fourteenth century is trilingual, English, Latin, or Anglo-Norman.

trilingualism (traɪˈlɪŋgwəlɪz(ə)m). [f. TRILINGUAL *a.* + -ISM.] The ability to speak three languages; the use of three languages.

1934 H. V. MORTON *In Steps of Master* i. 5 And as you go into Jerusalem, glancing at the trilingualism everywhere, the words of St. John come into the mind. **1956** *Nature* 18 Feb. 343/2 If we take into consideration languages read as well as written, no language group can to-day avoid even trilingualism if it wishes to attain the highest standards of culture and scholarship. **1976** *Word 1971* XXVII. 388 The scope of this article constrains us from adding still a third dimension, where more than a language pair is involved, such as the Yaqui-English-Spanish trilingualism of Pascua, near Tucson, Arizona.

triˈlinguar, *a. rare.* [f. as TRILINGUAL *a.* + -AR.] **a.** Having, or uttered with, three tongues; three-tongued. **b.** = TRILINGUAL *a.*

1824 *New Monthly Mag.* XI. 424 We have no three-headed dog chained at the gate of Tartarus to startle the visitants by his tri-linguar latrations. **1824** [see TRIGRAMMATIC *a.*] **1830** MAUNDER *Dict.*, *Trilinguar*, consisting of three languages.

triliteral (traɪˈlɪtərəl), *a.* (*sb.*) [f. TRI- + L. *littera* letter + -AL[1].] Consisting of three letters.

1751 WESLEY *Wks.* (1872) XIV. 150 A [Hebrew] Root is usually triliteral, like [*pā'al*]. **1869** FARRAR *Fam. Speech* iii. (1873) 88 The root of the Semitic verb is always triliteral, or rather triconsonantic. **1884** H. D. TRAILL in *Macm. Mag.* Oct. 444/1 Ignoramus.. may annoy him even more than the triliteral Saxon.. 'ass'.

B. *sb.* A triliteral word or root.

1828 WEBSTER, *Triliteral, sb.*, a word consisting of three letters. **1839** PAULI *Analecta Hebraica* v. 41 Consonants were added to the original bi-literal words, and thus tri-literals arose. **1896** W. H. WARD in Hilprecht *Rec. Res. in Bible Lands* 180 The proper names of persons and cities resist the attempt to reduce them to Semitic triliterals or to Aryan roots.

Hence **triˈliteralism**, the use of triliteral roots, as in Semitic languages; **triliteˈrality** (cf. F. *trilittéralité*), **triˈliteralness**, triliteral character; **triˈliterally** *adv.*

1841 *Fraser's Mag.* XXIII. 484 May not this habit.. account for the Hebrew triliteralism? **1864** *Ann. Rep. Smithsonian Inst. 1863* 109 Their [*sc.* the Semitic languages'] most fundamental peculiarity is the triliterality of their roots, every Semitic verbal root containing just three consonants. **1874** SAYCE *Compar. Philol.* ii. 77 The Semitic languages.. entirely.. built upon the principle of triliteralism. **1875** WHITNEY *Life Lang.* xii. 248 The triliterality of the roots and their inflection by internal change. **1902** GRIFFITH in *Encycl. Brit.* XXVII. 728/1 The triliterality of Old Egyptian.

trilith (ˈtraɪlɪθ). Orig. (and still often) in Gr. form **trilithon** (ˈtraɪlɪθɒn). [ad. Gr. τρίλιθον, neut. of τρίλιθος adj., of three stones, f. τρι-, TRI- + λίθος stone; so mod.F. *trilithe.*] A prehistoric structure or monument consisting of three large stones, two upright and one resting upon them as a lintel.

α. **1740** W. STUKELEY *Stonehenge* iv. 22 This *adytum*.. is in truth compos'd of certain *compages* of stones, which I shall call *trilithons*, because made, each of two upright stones, with an impost at top. **1881** T. HARDY *What Shepherd Saw* in *Changed Man*, etc. (1913) 190 A Druidical trilithon, consisting of three oblong stones in the form of a doorway. **1904** WINDLE *Rem. Prehist. Age Brit.* 185 An ellipse of hewn sarsen trilithons, with mortise and tenon connections.

β. **1851** D. WILSON *Preh. Ann.* (1863) I. iii. 93 A trilith or complete cromlech, consisting only of three stones. **1852** WRIGHT *Celt, Rom. & Saxon* ii. 59 Stones.. arranged in what the French archæologists term triliths. **1867** PEARSON *Hist. Eng.* I. 78 Circles of monoliths or triliths, sometimes surrounding what seems an altar.

b. (in form **trilithon**) repr. Gr. τρίλιθον applied to the Jupiter temple at Bálbec, in the wall of which there are three gigantic stones lying end to end.

1847 LEITCH tr. *C. O. Müller's Anc. Art* §269. 262 Of the trilithon at Balbec there are to be seen stones as much as 60 feet in length. **1881** *Athenæum* 6 Aug. 174/2 She [Mrs. G. Sumner] attributes the trilithon temple of Baalbek.. to those mysterious Phœnician builders.

Hence **trilithic** (traɪˈlɪθɪk) *a.* (erron. **triliˈthonic**), pertaining to or of the nature of a trilith.

1834 *Gentl. Mag.* Feb. 175 Having what may almost be called the unique trilithonic construction. **1872** LATHAM *Eng. Dict.*, Trilithic.

†**trill**, *sb.*[1] *Obs. rare.* Also 6 tryle. Origin and meaning uncertain.

1558 *Cal. Anc. Rec. Dublin* (1889) 470 Wheare the bouchers of this cittie and ther servaunts dothe contynuallie cut trills out of every hyde,.. every person may laufully seise and take.. all and every suche tryle as shalbe founde. **1654** in W. M. Myddelton *Chirk Castle Acc.* (1908) 47 For makeinge trills and pullies for the weaver's loome.

trill (trɪl), *sb.*[2] Also 8 tril. [Goes with TRILL *v.*[3]; ad. It. *trillo*, beside *triglio*, 'a quaver or warble in singing' (Florio); so F. †*tril*, *trille.*]

1. *Mus.* **a.** A tremulous utterance of a note or notes, as a 'grace' or ornament: = TREMOLO or VIBRATO. **b.** A rapid alternation of two notes a degree apart; a shake.

1649 LOVELACE *Poems* 120 Far lesse be't Æmulation To passe me, or in trill or Tone Like the thin throat of Philomel. **1662** PLAYFORD *Skill Mus.* I. xi. (1674) 47 The Trill.. is upon one Note only. **1710** STEELE *Tatler* No. 222 ¶10, I.. have attributed many of his [a vocal musician's] Trills and Quavers to the Coldness of the Weather. **1785** BURNS *Cotter's Sat. Night* xiii, The sweetest far of Scotia's holy lays: Compar'd with these, Italian trills are tame. **1801** RANKEN *Hist. France* I. 488 The beats, the trills, the shakes, and accents of the Italians. **1886** *Appleton's Ann. Cycl.* XI. 87 This even and continuous roll [of the canary-notes] is as perfect as the trill of any instrument.

2. *transf.* A tremulous high-pitched sound or succession of notes, esp. in the singing of birds.

a **1704** T. BROWN *Praise Drunkenness* Wks. 1730 I. 37 The Drunkard's voice is hoarse and manly, not like the squeaking trils of an Eunuch. **1745** WARTON *Inscript. Hermitage* ii, Within my limits lone and still The blackbird pipes in artless trill. **1865** DICKENS *Mut. Fr.* III. xii, There was quite a fresh trill in his voice. **1884** MRS. C. PRAED *Zéro* iv, There was the trill and full chirrup of the chaffinch.

3. *Phonetics.* The pronunciation of a consonant, esp. *r*, with vibration of the tongue or other part of the vocal organs; a consonant so pronounced.

1848 A. J. ELLIS *Essentials Phonetics* 50 There may be three trills belonging to this group. *Ibid.* 51 Persons who are unable to execute the trill. **1867** A. M. BELL *Visible Speech* 55 The sign of 'trill'.. denotes a vibration of the *uvula*;.. of the point of the *tongue*;.. of the *lips*. **1877** SWEET *Handbk. Phonetics* §102 Trills are a special variety of unstopped consonants. **1889** A. J. ELLIS *Early Eng. Pronunc.* 643 Uvular trill.

trill, *sb.*[3] *dial.* [Variant of THRILL *sb.*[4], THILL[1].] The shaft of a cart or wagon. Also *attrib.*

1688 R. HOLME *Armoury* III. 339/2 The Trills, or Sides of the Cart, which the horse is to stand between. *Ibid.* 340/1 The Trill Horse, that next the Cart, and beareth the sides up with a Back band lying on the Trill Sadle. **1726** *Dict. Rust.* (ed. 3) s.v. *Cart*, The Trill-Hooks and Back-band, which holds the Sides of the Cart up to the Horse. **1766** *Compl. Farmer* s.v. *Spiky-roller*, Let the trills be placed just on the middle of each frame. [**1905** *Eng. Dial. Dict.*, *Thrill*, recorded from South Cheshire, but now 'less commonly used than formerly'. Also *Thrill-bars*, *Thrill-gears*; *Thrill-horse*, or *Thriller*, the shaft-horse.] [Randle Holme, with whom the Dictionary entries begin, was a native of Chester.]

†**trill**, *sb.*[4] *Obs.* [Cf. DRILL *sb.*[4], a furrow.] A hot-air channel in a green-house, etc.; a flue.

1707 MORTIMER *Husb.* (1721) II. 191 One part of it may have Trils made under the Floor to convey warmth from the Stoves made on the back side of the House, the better to preserve it from Cold or Dampness.

trill (trɪl), *v.*[1] Now *dial.* or *arch.* Forms: 4-6 tril(le, tryl(le, 6 tryll, 6- trill. [ME. *trille*: cf. Sw. and Norw. *trilla*, Da. *trilde*, *trille*, to roll, trundle, wheel; also EFris. *trullen*, *trüllen* to roll, turn round. See also TIRL *v.*[3]]

1. *trans.* To turn (a thing) round, to cause to revolve or rotate; = TIRL *v.*[3] 1. **a.** To twirl, twiddle, whirl, spin.

to trill the bones (slang): to throw the dice with a spinning motion; cf. 'whirl the bones', BONE *sb.* 5 a.

c **1386** CHAUCER *Sqr.'s T.* 308 But whan yow list to ryden any where Ye mooten trille [*v.r.* trylle] a pyn stant in his [the brazen horse's] ere. *Ibid.* 313 And whan ye come ther as yow list abyde, Bidde hym descende, and trille [*v.rr.* tryl, -le, tril] another pyn. **1530** PALSGR. 762/1, I trylle a whirlygyg rounde aboute, *je pirouette*... I tryll, *je jecte*. **1547** SALESBURY *Welsh Dict.*, *Troi whirligwgan*, tryll a whyrlygyg. *c* **1550** R. WEVER *Lusty Juventus* D iij, I wyll trill the bones while I haue one grote. **1570** LEVINS *Manip.* 123/43 To Tril, *circumuertere*. **1616** J. LANE *Cont. Sqr.'s T.* IV. 417 So taught her how to trill the pinn in th' eare, Which th' horse, at willes quicke call, heard anie wheare. **1873** WILLIAMS & JONES *Somerset. Gloss.*, *Trill*, to twirl. **1885** BURTON *Arab. Nts.* (1887) III. 141 Thereupon the Prince trilled the pin.

b. To roll, bowl, trundle (a ball, a hoop, etc.); to move (a thing) on wheels or castors. Also *fig.*

1408 CLIFTON tr. *Vegetius' De Re Milit.* IV. xvii. (MS. Digby 233, lf. 220 b/2) þese toures mot haue crafty whelus Imaad to trille hem liȝtliche to þe walles. *c* **1440** *Promp. Parv.* 502/2 Tryllyn, or trollyn, *volvo*, Cath. **1542** UDALL *Erasm. Apoph.* 42 b, Eris.. had trilled along the table a golden apple. *c* **1572** GASCOIGNE *Fruites Warre* lxvii, As fortune trilles the ball. **1642** HOWELL *For. Trav.* (Arb.) 29 As wise as he, who carried the coach-wheele upon his back, when he might have trilled it before him all along. **1650** —— *Giraffi's Rev. Naples* I. 91 The huge concourse of people.. which were so thick, that one might have trill'd a bal upon their heads. **1673-4** ALLESTREE *Let.* 7 Jan. in Fox Bourne *Locke* (1876) I. vi. 321, I had acknowledged the receipt of yours.. long since, had I not been trilled on in a constant expectation of being [etc.]. **1905** in *Eng. Dial. Dict.* s.v., (E. Kent) There now, let me see how nicely you can trill your hoop.

†**2.** *intr.* Of a wheel, ball, etc.: To revolve, spin, roll, trundle. *Obs.*

1531 ELYOT *Gov.* I. xxvii, If it [tennis-ball] trille fast on the grounde. **1681** RYCAUT tr. *Gracian's Critick* 142 Sometimes it [the ball] was tossed so high, that it was out of sight, anon so low.. it bounded and trilled on the ground.

Hence **ˈtrilling** *vbl. sb.*

c **1410** LOVE *Bonavent. Mirr.* xviii. (1908) 112 As we mowe see alday many men and wommen berynge bedes with trillynge on the fyngres and waggynge the lippes, bot the siȝt caste to vanytees.

trill, *v.*[2] *arch.* Forms: 4-6 trylle, 4-7 trille, (? 5 tryle), 6-7 tril, 6- trill. [Perh. a distinct sense-development of prec. But cf. the synonymous DRILL *v.*[2]; also Ger. *trillen* 'to flow whirling or rolling', cited by Grimm from a 17th c. writer, and taken by him as a form of *drillen* to turn.]

1. *intr.* Of tears, water, a stream: To roll, to flow in a slender stream, the particles of water being in constant revolution, with a more continuous motion than is expressed by *trickle*; to purl. (Sometimes (as in quot. 1613) including the notion of musical sound, as in TRILL *v.*[3])

13.. *St. Erkenwolde* 322 in Horstm. *Altengl. Leg.* (1881) 273 Teres trilled adoun & one þe toumbe lightene. *c* **1386** CHAUCER *Sompn. T.* 156 (Harl. MS.) With many a teere trilling [*v.rr.* triklyng, trynkelynge] on my cheeke. *a* **1541** WYATT *Poems, Compar. Love to Stream*, From these hie hilles as when a spring doth fall, It trilleth downe with still and suttle course. **1613** W. Browne *Brit. Past.* I. v, Two springs arise and delicately trill In gentle chidings through an humble dale. **1667** Dryden & Davenant *Tempest* II. iv, A cold sweat trills down o'er all my limbs. **1769** *De Foe's Tour Gt. Brit.* I. 230 Water, which trills through Marble Troughs, one below another. **1815** Scott *Guy M.* xxii, A little dell, through which trilled a small rivulet.

b. *intr.* To flow or run with thrilling effect. (Perh. meant for THRILL *v.*[1] 4 b.)

1740 Somerville *Hobbinol* I. 71 What Extasies of Joy Trill'd through thy Veins, when..they strok'd thy grizly Beard.

2. *trans.* To cause to flow in this way. † *trill off*, to drain off, drink up (*obs.*).

c **1485** *E.E. Misc.* (Warton Cl.) 65 One truth let ever thi tong tryle. **1589** Nashe *Almond for Parrat* 12 b, A boule of Beere..you tooke..from before him, and trilled it off without anie more bones. **1591** Sylvester *Du Bartas* I. v. 825 The other [Pelican]..Tears her own bowells, trilleth-out her blood To heal her young. **1649** G. Daniel *Trinarch.* To Rdr. 55 The Pumpe of Witt..trills a Coppie, that the Spunges may Lick vp what he hath Squeez'd. **1867** Aug. J. E. Wilson *Vashti* xxv, When I have trilled a fortune into that abhorred vacuum, my pocket, I shall go down to the Tigris, and catch the mate to Tobias' fish.

†**3.** *intr.* To fall or hang down in a flowing manner; to stream, trail. *Obs.*

a **1400** *Sir Beues* (E.) 1665 Hys heere tryllyd doun too hys ffoote. *c* **1440** *Brut* 462 A bawdrik of gold aboute his neck, trillyng doun behynde hym. **1609** Bp. W. Barlow *Answ. Nameless Cath.* 11 His Picture drawn with two ropes about his neck, and his bowels (like an other Iudas) trilling downe his body.

Hence '**trilling** *vbl. sb.* and *ppl. a.*

1567 Turberv. *Pyndara's Answ. to Tymetes* Epit., etc. 27 Not shed my trilling teares vpon thy moisted face? **1582** Stanyhurst *Æneis* II. (Arb.) 43 Tears with trilling shal bayne my phisnomye deepelye. **1637** B. Jonson *Sad Sheph.* II. ii, Twa trilland Brooks, each (from his Spring) doth meet. **1665** Hooke *Microgr.* xx. 129 The droppings or trillings of Lapidescent waters in Vaults under ground. **1713** Steele *Guard.* No. 50 ⁋2 The trilling of rivulets.

trill, *v.*[3] [Appears *c* 1667, ad. It. *trillare*, in Florio 1611 also *trigliare* (not in 1598), 'to quaver or warble in singing', cognate with *triglio*, *trillo*: see TRILL *sb.*[2] (It. *trillare* is usually referred to a German source: cf. TRILL *v.*[4])]

1. *intr.* To sing with vibratory effect; to sing a trill or shake, to 'shake'; of a voice, etc.: To sound with tremulous vibration.

1666–7 Pepys *Diary* 7 Feb., My wife..proud that she shall come to trill, and..I think she will. **1667** *Ibid.* 7 Sept., I did tell him of my intention to learn to trill. **1841** D'Israeli *Amen. Lit.* (1867) 402 This consonance trills in the simple carol of the African women. **1856** Capern *Poems* (ed. 2) 54 And music trilled o'er moor and mead. **1884** *St. James' Gaz.* 29 May 6/2 At least four nightingales..trilling in whole-hearted chorus.

2. *trans.* To utter or sing (a note, tune, etc.) with tremulous vibration of sound.

a **1701** Sedley *Poet. Pieces* Wks. 1722 II. 15 The Nightingale her mournful Story trills In yonder Hawthorn Shade. **1727–46** Thomson *Summer* 746 The sober suited songstress trills her lay. **1810** Scott *Lady of L.* IV. xxiv, So blithely he trilled the lowland lay. **1840** Dickens *Old C. Shop* xv, The lark trilled out her happy song. **1860** Gosse *Rom. Nat. Hist.* 28 Like that charming bird-voice, it was beautifully trilled or shaken. **1862** Miss Braddon *Lady Audley* ix, Sitting down to the piano to trill out a ballad.

b. To cause (an instrument or the voice) to vibrate with a tremulous sound.

1848 Dickens *Dombey* iii, The man who trilled the little bell of the Dutch clock as he went along. **1848** A. J. Ellis *Essentials Phonetics* 49 The tongue assumes precisely the same position as for *s*, but the tip is now trilled.

3. To pronounce (a consonant, esp. *r*) with a vibration of the tongue (or other vocal organ) and the corresponding auditory effect; = ROLL *v.*[2] 4 c.

1848 A. J. Ellis *Essentials Phonetics* 95 To show that the *r* is..trilled. **1873** J. A. H. Murray *Dial. S. Co. Scotl.* 120 R is in Scotch..in all positions trilled sharply with the point of the tongue. **1887** *Pronunc. Latin* (Camb. Philol. Soc.) 5 Trilled 'r' as in French (or Scotch): more strongly trilled than in English 'Opera', 'herring'.

Hence **trilled** (trɪld) *ppl. a.*, '**trilling** *vbl. sb.* and *ppl. a.*; whence '**trillingly** *adv.*, in a trilling manner, with trilling; also '**triller**, one who trills.

a **1700** Dryden (Todd), Am I call'd upon the grave debate, To judge of trilling notes and tripping feet? **1749** Fielding *Tom Jones* v. x, The sweet trilling of a murmuring stream. **1753** *Scots Mag.* XV. 40/2 Ye angels, catch the trilling sound. **1848** A. J. Ellis *Essentials Phonetics* 68 *Veer-ing, car-ing* [etc.] lose their trilled..*r*. **1854** Bushnan in *Circ. Sc.* (*c* 1865) I. 292/2 Its song is composed of several strains, each consisting of trilling and warbling notes variously modulated. **1873** T. L. K. Oliphant *Sources Stand. Eng.* 323 A triller of Italian trills must be known as a vocalist. **1887** Trilled [see sense 3]. **1887** *Eng. Illustr. Mag.* Sept. 779 As many finches, singing trillingly. **1888** Sweet *Eng. Sounds* 25 We have, lastly, the trilling of open consonants [especially English and German r]. **1894** *Outing* (U.S.) XXIV. 230/2, I had failed to subsist on the manna of the Covenanters or a high-trilled Te Deum.

†**trill**, *v.*[4] *Obs. rare.* [Etymology obscure Cf. MDu. *trillen*, *drillen* to move to and fro, vibrate, vacillate, Du. *trillen* to shiver, shake, EFris. *trillen* to shake or rock from side to side.] *trans.* To rock (a cradle).

c **1425** *Fest. of Ch.* viii. in *Holy Rood* (E.E.T.S.) App. 213 ȝit myȝt þe mylde may among Her cradel trille to and fro, And syng, Osye, thi song!

trill: see TIRL *v.*[3] (senses 1 b, 3).

†**tri'llado.** *Obs. rare.* [f. TRILL *sb.*[2] + -ADO.] A trilling or trill in music.

1721 D'Urfey *Operas*, etc., Pref., Equal with the buzzing and squeaking Trilladoes of the Italian.

trilles, obs. form of TRELLIS.

trillet ('trɪlɪt). [f. TRILL *sb.*[2] + -LET (? -ET[1]).] A little or tiny trill; also *fig.*

1867 G. Meredith *Vittoria* I. ii. 25 We require to be refreshed with quavers and crescendos and trillets. **1878** Lanier *To mocking-bird* 1 Trillets of humor,—shrewdest whistle-wit.

trillibub ('trɪlɪbʌb). *Obs.* exc. *dial.* Forms: 6 trylly-, trylybubbe, 7 trilla-, 6–9 trillibub; 6 trully-, trullibub(be, 7– trullibub. Cf. TROLLIBOBS, -BAGS. [Origin obscure.] Chiefly (now always) *pl.*: Entrails, the inwards of an animal.

Often in the alliterative collocation *tripes and trillibubs.*

1519 Horman *Vulg.* 155 b, Let vs haue trypis, chetterlyngis, and tryllybubbys ynough [*aulicoctia ad satietatem*]. **1542** Boorde *Dyetary* xvii. (1870) 276 All the inwardes of beestes and of fowles, as the..trypes, and trylybubbes. **1599** Massinger, etc. *Old Law* III. ii, I hope my guts will hold, and that's e'en all A gentleman can look for of such trillibubs. **1785** Grose *Dict. Vulg. T.*, *Tripes and trullibubs*, the entrails, also a jeering appellation for a fat man. **1823** Moor *Suffolk Words*, *Trullibubs*, a low coarse term among butchers for the entrails generally of animals. **1883** *Hampsh. Gloss.*, *Trullibubs*, the intestines.

b. Applied to a person or animal. (See also *Eng. Dial. Dict.* s.v. *trolly-bags.*)

1600 Dekker *Gentle Craft* iv, Run wife, bid your maids, your trullibubs, make ready my fine mens breakfasts. **1614** B. Jonson *Bart. Fair* I. iii, There cannot be an ancient Tripe or Trillibub i' the Towne, but thou art straight nosing it. **1785** [see above].

†**c.** In alliterative collocation *tricks and trillibubs.* In quot. 1632, *trilly bubkins* is a nonce diminutive. *Obs.*

1632 Brome *Novella* I. ii, Such Curles, such Purles, such Tricks and Trilly bubkins As Mayds would turne no Mayds almost to see 'hem! **1637** Shirley *Hyde Park* III. ii, I forgive thee, and forget thy tricks And trillabubs... Wenches must have their ways.

†**tri'llil**, *adv. Obs.* Also tri-, trylill, trill-lill. [A kind of onomatopœic prolongation of TRILL *v.*[2]] With the sound of flowing liquid. Hence † **trillil** *v.*, to drink with a trilling sound.

a **1592** Greene *Jas. IV*, Wks. (Rtldg.) 202 O Sir the wine runs trillill down his throat. **1599** Nashe *Lenten Stuffe* 40 Whereas in wodden Mazers, and Agathocles earthen stuffe, they trillild it off before. **1600** *Look About You* ix. C ij b, We'll drinke tryllil, Ifaith. **1609** Dekker *Ravens Alm.* B ij b, Amongst gentlemen that haue full pursses and those that crie trilill, let the world slide. **1635** Heywood *Philocoth.* 55 He that cryes trill-lill boyes, is a Rhetoritian.

trilling ('trɪlɪŋ), *sb.* [= Da., Sw. *trilling*, Norw. *trinnling*, Du. *drieling*, Ger. *drilling* triplet, f. TRI- + -LING.] One of a set of three. **a.** One of three children born at the same birth; a triplet. **b.** *Min.* A crystal composed of three individuals.

1846 Worcester, *Trilling*, one of three children born at the same birth. *For. Q. Rev.* **1864** in Webster (citing Wright). **1896** Chester *Dict. Min.*, *Tridymite*,..f. τρίδυμος, 'triplet', because often found in trillings.

trilling, *vbl. sb.* and *ppl. a.*: see TRILL *v.*[1–3].

trillion ('trɪljən). [= F. *trillion* (N. Chuquet, *c* 1484), It. *trillione*, from the stem of *million* with substitution of *tri-*: cf. *billion.*] The third power of a million; a million billions, i.e. millions of millions. Also, orig. in France and local U.S., a thousand 'billions', or 10^{12} (i.e. the traditional English billion: see BILLION): this sense is now standard in the U.S. and is increasingly common in British usage.

The terms *billion*, *trillion*, *quadrillion*, etc., up to *nonillion*, are explained by N. Chuquet, in his *Triparty de la Science des Nombres* (lf. 2 r) printed in *Bullettino di Bibliografia e di Storia delle Scienze Matematiche* XIII. 593 (Roma 1880); also in the *Arismetique* of Ét. de la Roche, 1520. Both of these early writers explain *billion*, *trillion*, etc. as successive powers of a million, the trillion being the third power of a million, 'a million of millions of millions', as formerly always used in England. According to Littré, it was only in the middle of the 17th c. that the 'erroneous' custom was established of dividing series of figures above a million into groups of three, and calling a thousand millions a billion, and a million millions a trillion, an entire perversion of the nomenclature of Chuquet and De la Roche.

1690 Locke *Hum. Und.* II. xvi. §6 [see BILLION]. **1696** Jeake *Arith.* 14 Others..call..the nineteenth place Trillion. **1706** W. Jones *Syn. Palmar. Matheseos* 8 Then the 3d. Point from Units stands under Trillions. **1802** in *Spirit Pub. Jrnls.* VI. 337 He wished also to purchase the words billions, trillions, and quadrillions, in order to make his constituents comprehend the immensity of their burdens, and the profundity of his arithmetic. **1806** Hutton *Course Math.* (1810) I. 5 Millions of millions, or bi-millions, contracted to billions, millions of millions of millions, or tri-millions, contracted to trillions. **1867** Denison *Astron. without Math.* 226 You will find the tons in..the earth [to be] 5842 with 18 cyphers after it or 5842 trillions of tons. **1919** *Evening Star* (Washington, D.C.) 12 Mar. 2/7 The consideration of reparations has introduced the word 'trillion' in recognizing money... In estimating the war losses of all the powers the first figures of one of the great powers aggregated a trillion francs and those of another power were slightly above a half trillion francs, namely, six hundred billion francs. **1971** *Daily Tel.* 30 Jan. 13 For the current calendar year the 'magic trillion' will be with us. The [American] budget assumed a 9 p.c. growth in GNP this year to $1,065,000 million. **1975** *New Yorker* 21 Apr. 48/1 About two trillion dollars' worth of insurance alone is currently in force. **1980** *Guardian Weekly* 30 Nov. 8/1 Plans to devote a trillion dollars to US military spending over the next five years. **1982** *Nature* 1 July 9/1 Compositions of many important trace species are in the parts per trillion (10^{-12}) by volume range.

Hence **trillionaire** (trɪljə'nɛə(r)) [after *millionaire*], one possessing property worth a trillion of pounds, dollars, or other standard coin.

1873 M. Collins *Miranda* I. 194 The trillionaire might turn patriot and pay the National Debt without feeling it. **1886** *Tinsley's Mag.* Oct. 323 A few trillionaires and struggling persons of that description.

trillionth ('trɪljənθ), *a.* and *sb.* [f. prec. + -TH[1].] **A.** *adj.* The ordinal adjective corresponding to 'trillion'. **B.** *sb.* One part out of a trillion.

1848 *Fraser's Mag.* XXXVII. 647 The millionth of a grain is a common dose; and a trillionth, octillionth, even a decillionth, very usual ones. **1851** Ruskin *Sheepfolds* 16 The seven-millionth or trillionth of its collective evidence.

‖**Trillium** ('trɪlɪəm). *Bot.* [mod.L. (Linnæus, 1753), in allusion to the triple leaves.] A genus (chiefly North American) of perennial endogenous herbs (N.O. *Trilliaceæ*, formerly referred to *Smilaceæ*) bearing a whorl of three thin short-stalked or stalkless leaves at the summit of a simple stem, with a solitary flower in the middle. In America also called *wake-robin.* Also, a plant of this genus.

1760 J. Lee *Introd. Bot.* (1788) 300 *Trillium*, Herb True-love of Canada. **1846** *Penny Cycl.*, *Suppl.*, Trillium. **1873** 'Susan Coolidge' *What Katy Did at Sch.* vii, Each walk..ended in some delightful discovery, trilliums, dog-tooth violets, apple-trees in blossom, or wild strawberries turning red. **1885** Gatty *Juliana H. Ewing* iii. 48 Trilliums are amongst the North American plants which have lately become fashionable. **1904** Farrer *Gard. Asia* 162 Tangles of bamboo, illuminated by the snowy stars of trillium.

‖**trillo** ('trɪləʊ). [It. (Florio, 1611), f. *trillare*, TRILL *v.*[3]] A shake or quaver· = TRILL *sb.*[2]

1651 Stanley *Poems* 201 Nightingales their trillo practise here. **1656** Blount *Glossogr.*, *Trillo*,..an excellent grace in singing; being an uniform trembling or shaking of the same Note. **1661** Pepys *Diary* 30 June, Myself humming to myself the trillo, and found by use that it do come upon me. **1721** D'Urfey *Two Queens Brentford* IV. i, The Relish and Story in't shall vie with all the Opera Trillo's in Europe. **1815** *Hist. J. Decastro* I. 232 A trillo from Old Comical threw her into convulsions.

b. *transf.* and *fig.*

1672 W. de Britaine *Interest Eng. in Dutch War* 25 My Genius never prompted me to the least Trillo of Grandeur. **1713** Addison *Guard.* No. 124 ⁋8 To dream On mossy pillows, by the trilloes Of a gentle purling stream.

trill-trill, *sb.* and *v.* Reduplication of TRILL *sb.*[2] and *v.*[3], representing a repeated or continued trill or trilling. So also **trill-rill** *int.*

1849 Cupples *Green Hand* xv, You heard a low, half-smothered, small sound, deeper down, as it were, fill up the break with its throbbing and trill-trilling, as if just *one* land-cricket or a grasshopper did it. **1859** Cornwallis *New World* I. 160 The trill trill of many a gaudy plumaged tenant of the woods. **1903** *Academy* 21 Feb. 186/2, I heard the thrush to-day..'Trill-rill!' he kept on trilling.

trilobal (traɪ'ləʊbəl, older 'traɪləʊbəl), *a.* [f. mod.L. *trilob-us* three-lobed + -AL[1].] = next; *spec.* applied to (man-made fibres having) a cross-section of this form.

1884 *Athenæum* 5 July 21/1 Trilobal are the windows, each lobe..counterchanged of three, like the Tresham shield. **1961** *Times Rev. Industry* Mar. 33/3 Bri-nylon 61..owes its softness of handle and subdued, silky lustre to the trilobal cross-section of the individual filaments. **1965** *Guardian* 31 Mar. 13/4 In America textured yarns of heavier denier tri-lobal..nylon have made a big hit in dress jersey. **1979** *Men's Wear* 24 May 34/1 Tri-lobal polyester and viscose do much the same.

trilobate ('traɪləʊbeɪt, traɪ'ləʊbət), *a. Nat. Hist.* [f. TRI- + mod.L. *lobātus*: see LOBATE.] Having or consisting of three lobes, three-lobed.

1785 Martyn *Rousseau's Bot.* xviii. 260 A trilobate capsule, of three valves and three cells. **1803** Shaw *Gen. Zool.* IV. 487 Trilobate Labrus [a fish] size of a Carp..native of the African seas. **1806** Galpine *Brit. Bot.* 61 Alchemilla... L[eaves] flat, trilobate, incised. **1877** Coues *Fur Anim.* ix. 274 The exterior pair [of incisors] are..obscurely trilobate.

So '**trilo,bated** *a.* = *trilobate*; **trilo'bation**, trilobate condition; **tri'lobe** *v.*, *trans.* to divide into three lobes; **trilobed** (-'ləʊbd) *a.* = *trilobate.*

1775 Ash, **Trilobated*, having three lobes. **1890** *Amer. Jrnl. Archæol.* VI. 594 Pointed windows..trilobated or with elaborate tracery. **1872** Nicholson *Palæont.* 161 In some cases..this *trilobation is only obscurely marked. **1826** Kirby & Sp. *Entomol.* xxx. III. 114 [The head] is *trilobed, each lateral lobe being divided into three smaller ones. **1872**

each lateral lobe being divided into three smaller ones. **1872** NICHOLSON *Palæont.* 160 Order Trilobita.—Crustaceans in which the body is usually more or less distinctly trilobed.

trilobe ('traɪləʊb), *a. rare.* [f. TRI- + LOBE.] Having three lobes, trilobate.

1931 *Antiquity* V. 272 One is reminded of the trilobe cranial amulet found in a La Tène context. **1950** A. L. ROWSE *Expansion Elizabethan England* i. 36 Pendennis and St. Mawes castles,..the latter a perfect..specimen of a Henrician fort of trilobe design, both planned by a German

trilobite ('traɪləʊbaɪt, 'trɪ-). *Palæont.* [ad. mod.L. *Trilobītes* (Walch, 1771), f. Gr. τρι-, TRI- + λοβ-ός lobe (of the ear, etc.) + -ITE[1].] A member of a large group of extinct arthropodous animals, characterized by a three-lobed body; allied to the extinct Eurypterids and the existing King-crabs (*Limulus*), and like them of doubtful affinity, having been usually classed as crustaceans, sometimes as arachnids; their remains are found abundantly in Palæozoic rocks, esp. the Silurian.

1832 J. GREEN *Monogr. Trilobites N. Amer.* 14 The fossil remains of the trilobite family. **1833** LYELL *Princ. Geol.* III. 195 A limestone, containing trilobites and other fossils of our mountain and transition limestones. **1842** H. MILLER *O.R. Sandst.* ix. (ed. 2) 209 The Trilobite has a wide geological range, extending from the upper Cambrian rocks to the upper Coal Measures. **1860** *All Year Round* No. 50. 563 A creature called a Trilobite, very much like an immense woodlouse. **1873** DAWSON *Earth & Man* iii. 44 The body was composed of numerous segments, each divided transversely into three lobes, whence they have received the name of Trilobites.

attrib. **1854** MURCHISON *Siluria* ix. 194 The trilobite-flags of Builth.

Hence **trilobitic** (-'ɪtɪk) *a.*, pertaining to, of the nature of, or containing trilobites.

1839 *Civil Eng. & Arch. Jrnl.* II. 148/2 Until we come to trilobitic schist. **1872** W. S. SYMONDS *Rec. Rocks* iii. 51 The absence of the trilobitic genus, Olenus, from the Menevian group. **1875** CROLL *Climate & T.* xviii. 294 Those strange trilobitic-looking fishes of that era.

† **'trilobous**, *a. Obs. rare.* [f. mod.L. *trilob-us* three-lobed + -OUS.] = TRILOBATE.

1753 CHAMBERS *Cycl. Supp.* s.v. *Leaf, Trilobous Leaf*, one divided into three lobes.

trilocular (traɪ'lɒkjʊlə(r)), *a. Nat. Hist.* [f. TRI- + L. *locul-us* small receptacle, dim. of *locus* place + -AR[1].] Having three cells or compartments, as the capsule of a plant, or the heart of a reptile. Also **tri'loculate** *a.* (*Cent. Dict.* 1891).

1753 CHAMBERS *Cycl. Supp.*, *Capsule*,..sometimes contains only one cell or cavity, sometimes more;..called *unilocular*;..*bilocular*, *trilocular*. **1785** MARTYN *Rousseau's Bot.* xvi. (1794) 185 Ipomæa has..a trilocular capsule. **1845** LINDLEY *Sch. Bot.* i. (1858) 16 [The pistil] is either *bilocular*, *trilocular*, *multilocular*, or otherwise. **1861** HULME tr. *Moquin-Tandon* II. II. 54 Amphibia... Their heart, trilocular or bilocular.

trilogical (traɪ-, trɪ'lɒdʒɪkəl), *a.*[1] [f. TRILOGY + -ICAL.] Of or pertaining to a trilogy. So **tri'logic** *a.*; **trilogist** ('trɪlədʒɪst), the author of a trilogy.

1866 FELTON *Anc. & Mod. Gr.* I. I. xi. 201 The trilogical form appears to have been an enlargement of the original tragic outline. **1889** HAIGH *Attic Theatre* 22 In it the trilogic form of composition is brought to the highest perfection. **1913** *Daily News* 8 Aug. 7/1 Mr. Onions is the first of the English trilogists to consummate his undertaking.

tri-logical (traɪ'lɒdʒɪkəl), *a.*[2] *rare.* [f. TRI- I + LOGICAL.] Relating to or dealing with three subjects of discourse.

1836-7 SIR W. HAMILTON *Metaph.* xli. (1870) II. 416 Kant..was the philosopher to whom we owe this tri-logical classification [of mental phenomena into knowledge, feelings, will].

trilogue ('traɪlɒg). [f. TRI- + Gr. λόγος word, discourse.] A group of three words or sayings (cf. next, 3), as the Welsh triads.

1834 MEDWIN *Angler in Wales* I. 283 These trilogues or triads..are easily retained in the memory.

trilogy ('trɪlədʒɪ). [ad. Gr. τριλογία (see def. 1), f. τρι-, TRI- + λόγος discourse: see -LOGY. Cf. F. *trilogie*.]

1. *Gr. Antiq.* A series of three tragedies (originally connected in subject), performed at Athens at the festival of Dionysus.

1836 THIRLWALL *Greece* III. xviii. 73 A trilogy, which comprised three distinct tragedies. **1842** BRANDE *Dict. Sc.* etc., s.v., All the plays of Æschylus, and the Henry VI of Shakspeare, are examples of a trilogy. **1850** GROTE *Greece* II. lxvii. (1862) VI. 25 To three serious dramas or a trilogy ..the tragic poet added a fourth or satyrical drama.

2. Any series or group of three related dramatic or other literary works.

1661 BLOUNT *Glossogr.* (ed. 2), *Trilogie*,..a speaking or writing in three parts. **1820** T. MITCHELL *Aristoph.* I. p. cxxvi, That immortal Trilogy of Plato, which has been embalmed by the tears of all ages. **1841** TRENCH *Parables* xxii. (1877) 376 These parables are thus a trilogy. **1875** JOWETT *Plato* (ed. 2) III. 679 The other great Platonic trilogy of the Sophist, Statesman, Philosopher. **1877** DOWDEN *Shaks. Prim.* vi. 90 The trilogy consisting of I and II Henry IV and Henry V.

3. *transf.* and *fig.* A group of three related utterances, sayings, subjects, etc.

1835 T. MITCHELL *Aristoph.*, *Acharn.* 249 *note*, What Theophrastus evidently intended for a trilogy of characters, ..each rising above the other in want of shame and an absence of decency. **1837** CARLYLE *Fr. Rev.* III. I. v, Thus they three, in wondrous trilogy, or triple soliloquy. **1879** FARRAR *St. Paul* I. 581 *note*, His fundamental trilogy of Christian virtues—faith, hope, love.

trilophodont to **triluminous**: see TRI- I.

trim (trɪm), *sb.* Also 6-7 **trym**, **trimme**, 7-8 **trimm**. [f. TRIM *v.*]

I. Nautical and Aeronautical senses.

1. The state of being trimmed or prepared for sailing; esp. the condition of being 'fully rigged and ready to sail' (Onions *Shaks. Gloss.*).

1590 SHAKS. *Com. Err.* IV. i. 90 The ship is in her trim, the merrie winde Blowes faire from land. *c* **1595** CAPT. WYATT *R. Dudley's Voy. W. Ind.* (Hakl. Soc.) 59 Our good shipp beinge putt in her best trym..Captaine Jobson caused the collers..to be advanced in the topps, poope and shrowdes of our shipp. **1628** DIGBY *Voy. Medit.* (Camden) 36, I found my shippe to be in perfect good trimme. **1874** BURNAND *My Time* xxix. 279 Their yacht..was kept in trim all the year round. **1878** BESANT & RICE *Celia's Arb.* xii, Don't let the boy think the vessel has got out of trim after all these years.

2. a. The most advantageous set of a ship in the water on her fore and aft line: also with qualification, as *good*, *better*, *best*, *bad trim*. **b.** Adjustment of the sails with reference to the direction of the wind and the ship's course. **c.** The condition of being properly balanced. **d.** The difference between the draught forward and the draught aft (cf. TRIM *v.* 13).

1614 GORGES *Lucan* III. 111 Of any ship to find the trimme, In wrought seas how she best might swimme. **1674** PETTY *Disc. Dupl. Proportion* 28 Different Velocities, arising from the different Trim of the same Ship,..the best Trim being that which makes least resistance. **1704** J. HARRIS *Lex. Techn.* I, *Trimm of a Ship*, is her best Posture, Proportion of Ballast, and hanging of her Masts, &c. for Sailing;..to find the best way of making any Ship to Sail swiftly, is called finding her Trim. **1748** *Anson's Voy.* Introd. 10 The discovery of her most eligible position in the water (usually stiled her Trim). **1764** REID *Inquiry* vi. §22 A ship requires a different trim for every variation of the direction and strength of the wind. **1769** FALCONER *Dict. Marine* (1789), *Out of Trim*, the state of a ship when she is not properly balanced for the purposes of navigation. **1793** SMEATON *Edystone L.* §170 They must..always be in sailing trim. **1839** *Civil Eng. & Arch. Jrnl.* II. 323/1 To preserve the trim of the ship, by keeping the centre of gravity in its proper position. *a* **1845** HOOD *Pain in Pleas.-Boat* 5 Bill, shift them bags of ballast aft—she's rather out of trim! **1867** SMYTH *Sailor's Word-bk.*, *Trim*, the set of a ship on the water, whether by the head or the stern, or on an even keel. It is by the disposition of the ballast, cargo, masts, and other weight which she carries, that a vessel is best adapted for navigation... *Trim of the hold*, the arrangement of the cargo, &c., by which a vessel carries sail well [etc.].

e. In vague non-technical use, The general appearance or look of a ship: cf. 4.

1757 GRAY *Bard* 73 In gallant trim the gilded Vessel goes. **1837** DISRAELI *Venetia* VI. ii, I cannot exactly make out its trim; it scarcely seems a merchant vessel.

f. The position of a submarine with respect to the angle between its longitudinal axis and the horizontal.

1917 *Chambers's Jrnl.* Aug. 557/2 When his boat was diving he had to be careful how he changed his position; otherwise the 'trim' was in danger of being upset. **1935** *Sun* (Baltimore) 14 Feb. 8/2 All ballast and emergency fuel dump tanks in the after part of the ship were dropped, and gas was valved from the forward gas cells in an effort to regain the trim. **1942** *Gen* 1 Aug. 3/1 Once out of the harbour the submarine dives for trim and, having caught the trim, she surfaces again. **1974** M. HEBDEN *Pride of Dolphins* II. ix. 186 Navigation..is what you will be chiefly responsible for. Navigation and trim. *Ibid.* III. ii. 224 Addams did a trim dive before he left.

3. The position of an aircraft with respect to the angle between its longitudinal axis and the horizontal; the condition of static balance of the aerodynamic forces on an aircraft in straight flight; a device or action used to maintain such balance. Freq. *attrib.*

1919 W. B. FARADAY *Gloss. Aeronaut. Terms* 17 *Trim*, the inclination to the horizontal of the longitudinal axis when the aerostat is floating freely at rest. **1935** C. G. BURGE *Compl. Bk. Aviation* 242/2 A trim of this kind may also be useful on a very powerful fighting aeroplane of small span. **1944** *Times* 3 Apr. 2/4 With the elevator trims gone, the Lancaster was tending to climb all the time. **1962** J. GLENN in *Into Orbit* 12 The enemy shell had knocked out part of my trim controls. **1968** M. WOODHOUSE *Rock Baby* xxvii. 250 Yancy corrected trim. We flew another mile. **1977** D. BEATY *Excellency* vi. 78 He studied the load and trim sheet. *Ibid.* 81 He took his right hand off the stick, grabbed the trim wheel to push it forward... He let go of the trim, brought his right hand back. *Ibid.* 82 With the aircraft so badly out of trim, the autopilot refused to cope. **1982** J. SAVARIN *Water Hole* 173 He found the trim to his liking, switched on the auto pilot and relaxed.

II. General senses.

4. a. Adornment, array; equipment, outfit; dress: usually in reference to style or appearance; hence sometimes nearly = guise, aspect.

1596 SHAKS. *1 Hen. IV*, IV. i. 113 They come like Sacrifices in their trimme. **1623** MASSINGER *Bondman* I. i, I'd court Bellona in her horrid trim As if she were a mistress. *a* **1646** VISCT. FALKLAND *Marr. Night* I. (1664) B ij b, A brave and Courtly Girle: has trim and dazle enough of white and red, to attract the eye. **1798** WORDSW. *Idiot Boy* xviii, She sees him in his travelling trim. **1818** SCOTT *Br. Lamm.* xxxii, Bucklaw, in bridegroom trim. **1838-9** FR. A. KEMBLE *Resid. in Georgia* (1868) 58 The Sunday trim of the poor people.

fig. **1637** HEYLIN *Antid. Lincoln.* Pref. A j b, One that conjectured of the house by the trimme or dresse, would thinke it very richly furnished. **1646** G. DANIEL *Poems* Wks. (Grosart) I. 38 The Earth doth now begin To flourish, in her Sweet and glorious Trimme. **1650** T. VAUGHAN *Anthroposophia* 65, I would not have Thee look here for the Paint, and Trim of Retorick. **1784** COWPER *Task* III. 357 Nature in her cultivated trim Dressed to his taste, inviting him abroad.

† **b.** *the trim*: the prevailing mode; the fashion. *Obs. rare.*

1603 DANIEL *Def. Ryme* F v, Being now the trym, and fashion of the times, to sute a man otherwise cannot but giue a touch of singularity. **1628** FORD *Lover's Mel.* I. iii, Not like a lady of the trim. **1638** —— *Fancies* IV. i, Is't possible? why, you are turned a mistress, A mistress of the trim.

† **c.** with *a* and *pl.* A piece of personal adornment, an ornament; a style of dress or array; also *fig. Obs.*

1579-80 NORTH *Plutarch* (1676) 228 For her Purple Gowns, or for other such pretty fine trims of Gold, as women use to wear. **1647** WARD *Simp. Cobler* (1843) 25 If I see a trimme, far trimmer than she that weares it. **1675** PENN *Eng. Pres. Interest* i, Civil Affairs..may be peaceably transacted under the different Liveries, or Trims of Religion.

d. The act of trimming or condition of being trimmed (cf. TRIM *v.* 9).

1608 ROWLANDS *Humors Looking Glasse* 4 Many antique faces passe, From Barbers chaire vnto his glasse, There to beholde their kinde of trim. *a* **1914** *Mod. colloq.* The barber will give you a trim. **1931** G. A. FOAN *Art & Craft of Hairdressing* iii. 134/1 It must be realized, however, that this is a shingle *trim*, that the work must be done more lightly, and that..less hair will be removed. **1955** H. D. STEINER *Crowning Glory* iii. 30 The main business of the hair dresser is to see that both the trim and set accord with the natural convolutions of the hair. **1977** D. BENNETT *Jigsaw Man* viii. 141 He left with two wigs and an appointment to come back for a trim. **1983** *Chicago Sun-Times* 15 Nov. 41/1 (*heading*) Too few trims in new budget.

e. = TRIMMING *vbl. sb.* 2a.

1665 SIR T. HERBERT *Trav.* (1677) 143 The gold..that was laid..upon the trim of Vests, was..in as perfect lustre as if it had been but newly done. **1948** H. PEPIN *Fund. Apparel Design* vi. 137/2 This asymmetrically balanced motif proved suitable for border trim on sleeve. **1964** [see BEADING *vbl. sb.* 2b]. **1982** W. BOYD *Ice-Cream War* I. i. 7 The women all wore white dresses with lacy trims and carried parasols.

f. The dressings of a house; 'the visible woodwork, as the base-boards, door and window-casings, etc.' (*Cent. Dict.*). *U.S.*

1884 *N. York Even. Post* 14 Apr. (Cent. D.), No wood having been used in construction except for floors, doors, and trim. **1885** HOWELLS *Silas Lapham* (1891) II. 54 The trim of the doors and windows was in light green and the panels in salmon.

g. A shop-window display. *U.S.*

1899 *Harman's Jrnl.* Feb. 7/1 The design for a [men's] furnishing trim..by Harry Harold of Milwaukee, Wis., a window trimmer, is a very clever arrangement. **1926** *Publishers' Weekly* 30 Jan. 328/1 A large red ribbon rosette, from which radiated white satin ribbons to a number of stands at each side of the trim. *Ibid.* 10 July 119/2 When Stone's trim was removed, Wheatly did his 'stuff'. **1945** J. BRADFORD *Retail Merchandiser's Handbk.* xi. 62 Try to liven up a window as much as possible by using new, bright, and flashy display trims.

h. Ornamental additions or finishings to a vehicle, piece of furniture, or other article; *spec.* the upholstery or interior lining of a motor car. Cf. TRIMMING *vbl. sb.* 2c. orig. *U.S.*

1922 *Automobile Trimmer & Painter* Aug. 50/1 The Franklin trim is designed to give a maximum degree of resiliency and durability in order to match these qualities in the rest of the car. **1936** C. W. SEAGER *Upholstered Furniture* vii. 54 Trim serves the double purpose of concealing the raw edges and seams and supplying a decorative note. **1950** POMEROY & WALKERLEY *Motor Year Bk.* 23 Throughout the range is an attractive style of trim incorporating contrasting piping round the edges of the seats. **1957** *Practical Wireless* XXXIII. 532/1 This model costs 98 guineas, and the bow-fronted cabinet is veneered in walnut with gilt trim. **1961** *B.S.I. News* Aug. 26/2 We have not had a single exhaust trim or exhaustor returned with a plating fault. **1962** *Which? Car Suppl.* Oct. 144/1 Leather upholstery and walnut trim. **1969** *Sears Catal.* Spring/Summer 6/2 Matching double handle handbag... Contrasting bar lightly touched with gleaming gold-color metal trim. **1971** 'D. HALLIDAY' *Dolly & Doctor Bird* vi. 85 The sofa..was one of a facing pair in oatmeal with hide trim. **1977** *Time* 4 July 6/3 But the new Soviet President let it be known that he was not pleased with the color of the trim on the wagon's seats.

i. *Cinemat.* A piece of film cut out during editing; *spec.* a very short piece cut out during the final stage of editing. orig. *U.S.*

1934 in WEBSTER. **1948** R. SPOTTISWOODE *Basic Film Techniques* iii. 31/2 If he has to unwind rolls of *trims* (or cut-out sections of shots), he will let them hang on the bins. **1959** W. S. SHARPS *Dict. Cinematogr.* 116/1 *Outs*, otherwise *Trims*, the material that is not included in the final edited version of a film. **1964** *Listener* 28 May 899/3 Theseus-Adonis and the Minotaur were separated by a film about Montreal made completely out of 'trims' from taped interviews and very rapid shots exemplifying the culture of cities. **1976** *Broadcast* 23 Aug. 6/2 The shop committee.. will consider releasing the trims once it has seen all the documentation. *Ibid.* 6/3 Thames..could also satisfy the union curiosity about the sheer quantity of trims—60 cans.

5. a. Condition, state, or order, esp. for work or action of any kind: usually qualified by an adj. (Now the chief general sense.)

1628 FELTHAM *Resolves* II. [I.] xlv. 132 If we looke vpon him, in another trimme of the minde: how smooth hee is. **1666** G. ALSOP *Maryland* Ded., I am so my self, and the world, as far as I can perceive, is not much out of the same trim. **1749** SMOLLETT *Gil Blas* XI. xiv, They had almost dined, and consequently were in a trim for disputing. **1782** COWPER *Gilpin* 162 The Calender, amazed to see His neighbour in such trim. **1803** WELLINGTON in Gurw. *Desp.* (1837) I. 476, I am in good marching trim. **1856** KANE *Arct. Expl.* II. i. 9, I can hardly keep my charts.. in any thing like decent trim. **1882** ROXBURGH in Jean L. Watson *R.S. Candlish* ii. 25 Matters were at length in trim for my settlement. **1891** *Field* 7 Mar. 344/2 With the excellent present trim of the water, and fish feeding, anglers should take advantage of the few days left.

b. Hence *in* (†*the*) *trim*, *into* (*to*) *trim*, in or into proper condition or order.

1827 SCOTT *Napoleon* lxv, Soldiers whose hearts were in the trim. **1828** —— *F.M. Perth* iii, One of your hermits that ..brings himself to trim by fasting and penance. **1879** RUSKIN *Hortus Inclusus* lvi. (1887) 68 [My] eyes, head, feet, and fingers, all fairly in trim. **1886** HUXLEY in *Life & Lett.* (1900) II. viii. 129, I will give him a dose of that remedy when once I get into trim. **1890** 'R. BOLDREWOOD' *Col. Reformer* (1891) 179 The barque was empty and the whaling gear in trim.

6. (orig. *fig.* from 2.) The nature, character, or manner of a person or thing; his or its 'way'.

1706 E. WARD *Wooden World Diss.* (1708) 31 Those that knew his Trim, us'd to load him well with Ale and Salmon. **1771** T. HULL *Sir W. Harrington* (1797) III. 53 Our brother ..never is ten minutes in the company of a woman without finding what he calls the trim of her. **1787** BECKFORD *Italy* (1834) II. 22 That I allow; but such, you know, is my trim and I cannot help it. **1818** SCOTT *Hrt. Midl.* xxxvii[i], His wife knows his trim, and I have not the least doubt that the matter is quite certain. **1824** R. STUART *Hist. Steam Engine* 206 The water which is heated under a great pressure.. is forced into [that] in the common boiler, and heats it to any degree suited to the nature or trim of the engine.

7. *U.S. slang.* A woman; sexual intercourse with a woman.

1955 *Amer. Speech* XXX. 302 *Chick, crazy freak, local talent, neat job, snatch, talent, trim, unfair sex, n.*, girl, usually pretty. Often used to refer to a woman of loose morals. [**1961** RIGNEY & SMITH *Real Bohemia* p. xvii, *Trim*, cunnilingus.] **1962** E. LACY *Freeloaders* vi. 125 The broad isn't worth it, no trim is. **1974** H. L. FOSTER *Ribbin', Jivin', & Playin' Dozens* v. 191 Female student: 'Somebody always askin for some trim and haven't even got anything.'

8. Special Comb.: **trim tab**, (*a*) *Aeronaut.* = *trimming tab* s.v. TRIMMING *vbl. sb.* 7 b; (*b*) *Naut.*, a hinged tab fitted to the trailing edge of a keel or rudder to facilitate steering.

1944 H. F. GREGORY *Anything a Horse can Do* 47 Elevator trim tab on an airplane—trimmed the craft so that when the hands were off the stick, the aircraft had no tendency to nose down or up. **1958** 'CASTLE' & 'HAILEY' *Flight into Danger* vii. 96 The speed slowly dropped. At 160 George adjusted the trim tabs. **1977** *Encycl. Aviation* 188/3 Most airplanes have hinged trim tabs whose incidence is controlled from the cockpit. **1978** *Detroit Free Press* 5 Mar. C21/5 (Advt.), 1977 Sea Ray 24' 233 Merc cruiser.. trim tabs—hydraulic.

trim, *a.* (*adv.*) Forms: 6– **trim**; also 6 *Sc.* **trume, trvme; trym, trymme, tryme;** 6–7 **trimme,** 7 **trimm, trimn.** [History obscure. OE. had an adj. *trum*, 'firm, stable, strong, sound, robust' (not known in the cognate langs.); whence also in prehistoric time the vb. **trum-jan*, OE. *trymman*, TRIM *v.* No example of *trum* is known after OE. times, but the negatives *untrum* infirm and *untrumnesse* infirmity survived to *c* 1200–1225. Afterwards, like TRIM *v.*, the adj. disappears till after 1500. The modern adj. *trim* does not answer in form, nor directly in sense, to *trum*; but in both it goes with the verb. It would appear therefore to be a deriv. of the verb (or, if both came down in ME., to have been conformed to the verb).]

In many early quotations it is difficult or impossible to infer the exact shade of meaning intended. Cf. TRIG *a.*[1]

1. In good condition or order; well prepared, furnished, or equipped; fit, competent, proper, suitable; hence, sound, good, excellent, fine, beautiful. (Often a vague term of approval.)

1503–13 [implied in TRIMLY *adv.* 1]. *c* **1530** H. RHODES *Bk. Nurture* 504 Better is it to beate a prowde man then for to rebuke him, For he thinkes in his owne conceyte he is wyse and very trim. **1567** DRANT *Horace, Art Poetry* A iv, For the sage ryghte seriouse wordes be trim. **1577** HOLINSHED *Chron.* II. 992/2, xl great carreuelles, and thirtene trymme Barques throughly furnished and appoynted with good mariners and men of warre. **1583** *Leg. Bp. St. Androis* 879 Ane burges man.. Having a trvme schop in the toun. *a* **1585** POLWART *Flyting w. Montgomerie* 551 (Harl. MS.) The blaired bucke and bystour.. Hes right trume [*v.r.* trim] teathe, somwhat sett in a thrawe. **1588** SHAKS. *Tit. A.* v. i. 96 'Twas trim sport for them that had the doing of it. **1590** SPENSER *F.Q.* III. i. 36 Fragrant violets, and Paunces trim. *Ibid.* 40 Sweet birdes.. Ay caroling of love and jollity, That wonder was to heare their trim consort. **1636** JAMES *Iter Lanc.* (Chetham Soc.) 6 Gilbert Stone, being for yᵉ time a trimme man of his penne. **1725** POPE *Odyss.* IV. 1032 The vessel rides,.. In all her tackle trim to quit the shore. **1817** BYRON *Beppo* xcvi, The ship was trim.

†**b.** (?) Firm. (But perh. sense 1.) *Obs.*

1549 COVERDALE, etc. *Erasm. Par. Jas.* i. 28 It taketh no rote in a briery place, ne in marice, nether in the sande.. but it requireth a pure, a trymme, and a substaunciall grounde. **1565** W. ALLEN in Fulke *Confut. Purg.* (1577) 449 Doe you not see here a trimme faith and a substantiall?

2. Neatly or smartly made, prepared, or arranged; elegantly or finely arrayed, dressed, or 'got up'; having a neat, spruce, or tidy appearance or effect. **a.** Of things: chiefly in sense 'neat, properly made and properly kept'; †formerly sometimes of dress, smart, pretty, beautiful.

c **1521** J. CLERK *to Wolsey* in Ellis *Orig. Lett.* Ser. III. I. 258, ij bokys.. coverd with clothe off gold.. the porteur, fascio[un] and tryme deckyng of the said bokis. **1542** UDALL *Erasm. Apoph.* 246 b, Fillyng vp as trymme as a trencher yᵉ space that stood voide. **1567** *Gude & Godlie B.* (S.T.S.) 37 Ȝe [= ȝe] set on schone vpone his feit, The quhilk are trim and wounder meit. **1574** tr. *Marlorat's Apocalips* 37 This place of Paradise was better furnished and trimmer than other places. **1675** HOBBES *Odyssey* 232, I him gave a purple double vest, A sword, and coat edged with fringes trim. **1717** BERKELEY *Tour Italy* Wks. 1871 IV. 537 Laurel hedges, but not so trim as ours. **1740** SOMERVILLE *Hobbinol* I. 150 See with what Pomp The gaudy Bands advance in trim Array. **1771** PENNANT *Tour Scotl. in 1769*, 31 The gardens are.. trim to the highest degree. **1789** MME. D'ARBLAY *Diary* 21 Aug., Captain Molloy's large boat.. was very trim and neat, and had all its rowers new dressed. **1840** DICKENS *Barn. Rudge* xxiii, Mr. Chester.. completely attired.. in the trimmest fashion of the day. **1849** MACAULAY *Hist. Eng.* ii. I. 201 The large and stately mansions, the trim villas. **1886** RUSKIN *Præterita* I. v. 168 The houses on each side with trim stone pathways up to them.

b. Of persons (rarely animals): Neat, 'trig', comely; neatly, smartly, or †finely dressed or adorned.

1548 UDALL, etc. *Erasm. Par. Matt.* vii. 50 The swyne is not the trymmer for the precioure stones. **1552** HULOET, Trymme, *bellulus, a, um*; loke in trycke... Trymme wenche gorgiously decked, *phalerata fœmina.* **1650** BULWER *Anthropomet.* 155 These paintings.. whereby the said women think themselves more trim and beautiful. **1681** W. ROBERTSON *Phraseol. Gen.* 1247/1 A very trim woman, *cultissima fœmina.* **1877** MAR. M. GRANT *Sun-maid* ii, He was rested from his long journey, trim, brushed, and polished. **1888** ANNA K. GREEN *Behind Closed Doors* iv, A trim and quiet girl came tripping to the door.

†**c.** 'Tight' (?), elegantly-shaped, well-made, handsome, good-looking. *Obs.*

1568 T. HOWELL *Newe Sonets* (1879) 146 So streight, so square, so trym was he, So fayre of forme, so wyse, so sage. **1578** LYTE *Dodoens* II. i. 148 Iupiter.. turned her into a trim heaffer. **1600** J. PORY tr. *Leo's Africa* VIII. 304 In the daytime he shall see none but trim and beautifull women. **1635** BROME *Sparagus Gard.* II. ii, I warrant you, is he a trim youth? **1649** G. DANIEL *Trinarch., Rich II* lxxviii, The Trimmest fellowes of this Regiment Envie'd the Gentry.

†**3.** In ironical use: cf. 'fine', 'nice', 'pretty', in similar use. *Obs.*

1569 J. SANFORD tr. *Agrippa's Van. Artes* 14 b, They.. haue spoken of nothinge but trimme trifles. **1573** G. HARVEY *Letter-Bk.* (Camden) 9 Here was stuf gud plenti to furnish up a trim tragedi. **1581** J. BELL *Haddon's Answ. Osor.* 66 Hath hee not made a trimme speake agaynst us? *a* **1586** SIDNEY *Arcadia* (1622) 370 A trim purchase you haue made of your owne shame. **1611** BEAUM. & FL. *Maid's Trag.* II. ii, And there's Another of 'em, a trim cheating souldier, I'le maul that Rascal. **1634** HEYWOOD & BROME *Witches Lanc.* III. Wks. 1874 IV. 217 O you are a trim mother are you not? **1680** OTWAY *Ca. Marius* IV. i, News quoth a? Trim News truly.

4. In parasynthetic combinations.

1873 B. HARTE *Fiddletown*, etc., *D. Varden* 87 Trim-bodiced, bright-eyed, roguish-lipped. **1840** DICKENS *Old C. Shop* xv, Then came the trim-hedged fields on either hand.

B. *adv.* †**1.** = TRIMLY 1. *Obs.*

c **1540** J. REDFORD *Mor. Play Wit and Sc.* (Shaks. Soc.) 37 His toong servth him now trym. **1549–62** STERNHOLD & H. *Ps.* xxxv. 26 Let not their hartes rejoyce and cry, There, there, this geare goeth trim. **1573** TUSSER *Husb.* (1878) 11 He plainly taught how good from naught may trim be tride. *c* **1613** MIDDLETON *No Wit like Woman's* v. i, Now the bells they go trim, they go trim.

2. = TRIMLY 2.

1529 *Supplic. to King* (E.E.T.S.) 49 Tryme decked horses, to ryde.. lyke a lorde. **1590** SPENSER *F.Q.* II. vi. 2 A litle Gondelay, bedecked trim With boughes and arbours woven cunningly. **1594, 1615** Trick and trim [see TRICK *adv.* 2]. **1742** COLLINS *Ode Manners* 17 Like a bride, so trim array'd.

3. *Comb.*, as *trim-cut*, *-dressed*, *-kept*, etc., adjs.

1813 SCOTT *Trierm.* II. v, Sick of flower and trim-dress'd tree, Long for rough glades, and forest free. **1861** THACKERAY *Four Georges* i. (1862) 23 The trim-cut forest vistas. **1873** MISS BROUGHTON *Nancy* III. 9 The little trim-swept drive. **1889** J. K. JEROME *Three Men in Boat* 77 The trim-kept villas on the other side.

trim (trɪm), *v.* Infl. **trimmed, -ing.** Forms: (1 **trymman, trymian, treman**), 6 **trymme, tryme,** (**treme**), **trym,** 6–7 **trimme,** 6– **trim,** (7 **trime**). [The existing senses of this verb begin early in the 16th c. Before 1550 the word had become exceedingly common in nearly all its chief senses. OE. had a verb *trymman* or *trymian*:—**trumjan* to make firm or strong, strengthen, confirm, set (a force) in array, settle, arrange, etc., f. OE. *trum* adj. firm, strong, sound, steadfast, stable, etc. So far as the *form* is concerned, *trymman*, *trymian* would naturally become *trym*, *trim* by 1500; the *sense* 'make fit, make ready, prepare, fit out' might also arise out of the OE. The difficulty is that not one certain example of the verb in any sense is known during the Middle English period, and that it comes upon the scene in the 16th c., like a new word, quickly laid hold of to supply many needs. But as no other source is known, it is generally held that *trim* is identical with the OE. *trymman*, and that the verb (perh. along with TRIM *a.*), must have been preserved in spoken use, or in some dialect, for four centuries, without appearing in the extant literature.

OE. had also the compounds *ȝetrymman* to confirm, strengthen, encourage, also intr. (for refl.) to grow strong, gain or recover strength, and *betrymian* to beset with a force, besiege, environ, with 3 examples as late as *c* 1225 (see BITRUM); *Genesis & Exodus*, *c* 1250, has also two instances of a vb. *trim-en* to 'be pregnant, conceive', or perhaps to 'give birth'; but none of these show any approach to the modern senses. The OE. senses and that in *Gen. & Ex.* are here prefixed as possibly bearing upon the later history.]

I. (Only OE.) †**1. a.** *trans.* To make firm or strong; to strengthen, confirm; to give as security; to arm or array (a force); to settle, arrange; to encourage, comfort, exhort.

a **800** *Cædmon's Gen.* 276 (Gr.) þæt he west and norð wyrcean ongunne, trymede ȝetimbro. *a* **800** *O.E. Chron.* an. 430 þæt he hiera ȝeleafan trymede. *c* **840** in Kemble *Cod. Dipl.* II. 5 Ic Berhtwulf.. ðas mine ȝesaldnisse trymme and fæstna in Cristes rode tacne. *c* **893** K. ÆLFRED *Oros.* IV. x. §2 þæs on merȝen Hannibal ȝefor to þære byriȝ, & beforan ðæm ȝeate his folc ȝetrymede, þe mon haett Collina... Ac hie hie butan þæm ȝeate anȝean Hannibal trymedon. *c* **897** —— *Gregory's Past. C.* xv. 88 Ne ȝe ðone weall ne trymedon ymb hiera hus on ðæm dæȝe þe him niððearf wæs. *c* **950** *Lindisf. Gosp.* John v. 31 ȝif ic cyðnisse ic trymmo [*perhibeo*] of mec. **971** *Blickl. Hom.* 91 Men ȝehyraþ myccle stefne on heofenum swylce þær man fyrde trymme & samniȝe. *a* **1000** *Ags. Ps.* (Th.) ciii. 15 Hlaf trymeð heortan mannes. **10..** *O.E. Chron.* an. 1052 Hi.. ȝerædon þæt man tremede gislas on æȝðer healfe.

†**b.** [(Early ME.) *intr.* To become pregnant, conceive; ? to bring forth. *Obs.* (Perhaps does not belong to this word.)

c **1250** *Gen. & Ex.* 1024 Bi ðan sal sarra selðe timen, Ðat ȝ[h]e sal of a sune trimen. *Ibid.* 1198 Ȝhe wurd wið child, on elde wac, And trimede and clepede it ysaac.]

II. (Mod.Eng.) †**2.** To put into proper condition for some purpose or use; to prepare, make ready; to dress; to get (land) into condition for cropping, to till; to cultivate (a tree). *Obs.*

1517 TORKINGTON *Pilgr.* (1884) 55 The bestys that we rode vpon, [were] ryght weke and ryght simple, and evyll trymed to Jorney with. **1523** LD. BERNERS *Froiss.* I. lix. 80 He raysed an engyn in yᵉ Castell, the which was not very great, but he trymmed it to a poynt [*orig.* lattrempa bien et apoint]. **1578** LYTE *Dodoens* VI. xxvii. 692 In Brabant.. the Corriers and Leather dressers.. do trimme and dresse Leather like Spanishe skinnes. **1593** SHAKS. *Rich. II*, III. iv. 56 He had not so trim'd And drest his Land, as we this Garden. **1645** in W. M. Williams *Ann. Founders' Co.* (1867) 98 Thomas Embry.. did trim and make up Brass Works for persons not free of the Company. **1725** DE FOE *Voy. round World* (1840) 71 Casks.. which their coopers assisted us to trim, season and fit up.

3. To fit out (a ship, etc.) for sea. *arch. spec.* †to caulk, clean, and dress a ship's bottom: see quot. 1711 (*obs.*).

c **1513** E. HOWARD in Ellis *Orig. Lett.* Ser. III. I. 147 Ther be redy.. a c. shippes of warre.. they be very well trymmed and will not faill to comme owte and fight with us. **1525–6** in Ellis *Orig. Lett.* Ser. III. I. 221 Our.. Sovereyn Lorde shall within fewe yerys loose his seyd Shypps.. except they be new kalkyd and trymmyd. **1542** *Lam. & Piteous Treat.* in *Harl. Misc.* (Malh.) I. 235 Seuen galleyes stronge and well trymmed. **1585** T. WASHINGTON tr. *Nicholay's Voy.* I. viii, The Arsenal,.. into which are hayled vppe and trymmed the gallies and other vessels. **1613** SHAKS. *Hen. VIII*, I. ii. 80 As rau'nous Fishes doe a Vessell follow That is new trim'd. **1711** W. SUTHERLAND *Shipbuild. Assist.* 165 To *trim* a Ship; to load and equip her, and put her into a condition for Sailing; also to calk, clean, and dress a Ship, and do any small matter in repairing her. **1850** BLACKIE *Æschylus* II. 258 Xerxes.. Trimmed vain fleets for thy undoing.

†**4.** To put (something broken, worn, or decayed) into good condition or working order; to repair, restore, put right. *Obs.*

c **1520** *Mem. Ripon* (Surtees) III. 204 Will'mo Caruer tremyng dorythes & lokes & alias. **1548** UDALL, etc. *Erasm. Par. Mark* i. 14 Who were also trymmyng and mendyng theyr nettes. **1569** SPARKE *Sir J. Hawkins' 2nd Voy.* (Hakl. Soc.) 11 He trimmed the maine mast of the *Iesus*, which in the storme aforesaid was sprong. *a* **1628** PRESTON *Breastpl. Love* (1631) 114 Your soules need to be trimmed every morning as well as the body. **1633** MUNDAY *Stow's Surv.* 905 The repairing and trimming of this Church.. was in the yeere of our Lord God 1600. *a* **1687** PETTY *Treat. Naval Philos.* I. ii, All the forementioned Incurvations are to be trimmed and repaired by reconciled lines.

5. *spec.* To put (a lamp, fire, etc.) into proper order for burning, by removing any deposit or ash, and adding fresh fuel; also, to cleanse or cut level (a wick); by extension, to renew the burned-out carbons or electrodes of (an arc lamp). Also *fig.*

1557 N. T. (Genev.) *Matt.* xxv. 7 Then all those virgins arose, & trymmed their lampes [So *Rhem.* (1582) & 1611; WYCLIF (1382) anourneden, (1388) araieden; TINDALE (1526), COVERDALE (1535), *Great* (1539), *Bishops'* (1568) prepared]. *a* **1701** MAUNDRELL *Journ. Jerus.* (1732) 71 The dayly employment of these Recluses is to trim the lamps. **1764** GOLDSM. *Trav.* 14 Where cheerful guests retire To pause from toil, and trim their evening fire. **1794** MRS. RADCLIFFE *Myst. Udolpho* xxvi, He stopped for a moment to trim the torch. **1819** WIFFEN *Aonian Hours* (1820) 134 Vesper has trimmed up his lamp for the night. **1902** SLOANE

Stand. Electr. Dict. App., *Trimming*, the renewal of the carbons in an arc lamp.

†**6.** To provide or furnish *with* what is necessary for the purpose in view; to equip, supply. *Obs.*

1523 WOLSEY in *St. Papers Hen. VIII*, VI. 188, 50,000 souldeours largely and plenteously furnished eskipped and trymmed. **1552** HULOET, Trymme a gardeyn wyth beddes. **1552–3** in Feuillerat *Revels Edw. VI* (1914) 93 Cupid shalbe a letell boy howe mvst be tremmed with a bow and arrows blinfelde. **1557** N. T. (Genev.) *Luke* xxii. 12 Then he shal shewe you a great hie chamber trimmed [1611 furnished]. **1630** J. LEVETT *Ord. Bees* (1634) 20 Do you not usually dresse and trim your hives with some hony, or other sweet liquor, before you put any swarm into them? **1667** PEPYS *Diary* 20 July, And..is married to him that is new come, and hath new trimmed the house.

7. To array, dress (const. *in* or *with* something); to make comely, adorn, dress *up* (also with *out*).

c **1516–21** DK. BUCKHM. *to Wolsey* in Ellis *Orig. Lett.* Ser. III. I. 216 He dowtid that I was not soo well trymmed as I wolde desir to be. **1525** LD. BERNERS *Froiss.* II. ccxlvii. [ccxliii.] 759 All the armorers in London were sette a worke to trymme men in their harnesse for the iustes. **1557** N. T. (Genev.) *Rev.* xxi. 2 That holy citie..prepared as a bryde trymmed for her housbande. **1604** T. WRIGHT *Passions* v. §1. 151 Salomon..exhorteth vs..not to looke vpon a woman trimmed and decked vp. **1697** DRYDEN *Virg. Georg.* III. 734 The Victim Ox..Trim'd with white Ribbons, and with Garlands drest. **1756** W. DODD *Fasting* (ed. 2) 10 To be deck'd and trimm'd out..in the pride of dress. **1903** N. MUNRO in *Blackw. Mag.* Jan. 81/1 She hastened to trim herself before the moon revealed her.

8. *spec.* To decorate (a hat, garment, etc.) with ribbons, laces, feathers, flowers, braids, embroideries, or the like, so as to give it a finished appearance; also, of a thing, to form the trimming of. Also *fig.*

1547 in Feuillerat *Revels Edward VI* (1914) 11, vj Black vellett Cappes..trymyd with damaske golde & Syluer. **1581** SIDNEY *Apol. Poetrie* (Arb.) 59 And who reades Plutarchs eyther historie or philosophy, shall finde, hee trymmeth both theyr garments, with gards of Poesie. **1793** MME. D'ARBLAY *Let.* May, Miss Kitty trimmed up her best cap, and tried [it] on. **1796** JANE AUSTEN *Pride & Prej.* xxix, When I have bought some prettier-coloured satin to trim it with fresh. **1859** *Habits Gd. Soc.* iv. (new ed.) 184 Her dress was white, trimmed down on either side with single roses. **1859** W. COLLINS *Q. of Hearts* iii, Trimmed with white braid.

9. a. To dress (the hair or beard); to clip (the hair), or to clip the hair of (a person); sometimes, to shave (a person); also, to dub (a cock).

1530 PALSGR. 762/2, I trymme, as a man dothe his heare or his busshe... Trymme my busshe, barber, for I intende to go amongest Ladyes to day. **1592** LYLY *Midas* III. ii, How sir will you be trimmed? wil you haue your beard like a spade, or a bodkin? **1607** *Nottingham Rec.* IV. 283 We present the barbr..for triming men in serves tyme vppon the Sabott Daye. **1611** BIBLE *2 Sam.* xix. 24 And Mephibosheth..had neither dressed his feete, nor trimmed his beard [COVERDALE (1535) combde, *Great* (1539) shauen, *Geneva* (1560), *Bishops'* (1568) dressed], nor washed his clothes. *a* **1625** in Strutt *Sports & Past.* (1801) III. vii. §20 A dunghill cock, neatly cut and trimmed for the battle. **1652** in *Verney Mem.* (1907) I. 485 The Razors and Sizars hee Trimmed withall. **1748** SMOLLETT *Rod. Rand.* lxiv, I sent for another barber and suffered myself to be trimmed. **1856** R. W. PROCTER *Barber's Shop* xxi. (1883) 203 The era of the flying barbers, when shops were few, and gentlefolk were trimmed at home.

b. *fig.* or in fig. context. To cheat (a person) out of money; to 'fleece'. *slang.*

1600 *Dr. Dodypoll* v. ii. in Bullen *O. Pl.* III. 158 The Marchant I perceive hath trimde you, Doctor, And comb'd you smoothlie. **1604** DEKKER *Newes from Graves-End* Ep. Ded. sig. C, Thou wouldst neuer haue gone to any Barbers in London..but haue bin trimd only there, for they are the true shauers, they haue the right Neapolitan polling. **1917** D. G. PHILLIPS *Susan Lenox* I. vi. 95 Guileful women, bent on trimming him for anything from a piece of plated jewelry to a saucer of ice cream. **1926** *Flynn's* 16 Jan. 639/1, I had simply trimmed a sucker for a few kale seeds. **1940** WODEHOUSE *Eggs, Beans & Crumpets* 155 Hearing her elders discuss..some burgeoning scheme for trimming the investors. **1955** *Publ. Amer. Dial. Soc.* XXIV. 94 Some of the big circuses carried their own *whiz mobs* to trim the crowds along the way. **1962** J. LUDWIG in R. Weaver *Canad. Short Stories* (1968) 2nd Ser. 254 Didn't she know he was going to get trimmed? But what did she care about money by that time?

c. *fig.* To reduce the size, amount, or number of; to eliminate (wasteful expenditure); to reduce the profits of. Also *absol.* orig. *U.S.*

1966 *Wall St. Jrnl.* 21 Nov. 2/2 General Motors Corp. will reduce previously scheduled overtime next month and trim its daily car production pace 3·7%. **1970** *Globe & Mail* (Toronto) 26 Sept. 33/2 If you really want to trim expenses, you can rent a camper. **1976** *National Observer* 13 Nov. 12/2 There is the argument over dollar levels of U.S. spending and what waste might be trimmed from the budget as well as what new items should be included. **1979** *Daily Tel.* 8 Nov. 21/1 Readicut trimmed. Readicut International reveals a 32·5 p.c. drop in interim pre-tax profits. **1981** *Times* 17 Apr. 1/4 British forces on the Continent are likely to be trimmed. **1982** *Times* 9 Jan. 17 (*heading*) American Telephone trims to compete.

10. *fig.* To beat, thrash, trounce; to defeat; also, to reprimand, reprove, upbraid, scold (cf. 'to give one a dressing').

App. at first an ironical use of sense 2, but afterwards often with allusion to 8, 9 or other sense: cf. the colloq. phr. *to trim one's jacket*, and the ironical use of DRESS *v.* 9, ARRAY *v.* 10. With quots. *a* 1518, 1638, cf. TRIM-TRAM *sb.*

a **1518** SKELTON *Magnyf.* 2234 Tushe! these maters..are but soppys in ale; Your trymynge and trampyng by me must be tangyd. *c* **1550** R. WEVER *Lusty Juventus* D j, Tell me.. who it was, And I wyl trim the knaue, by the blessed masse. **1638** FORD *Fancies* III. iii, *Sec.* My razor shall be my weapon, my razor. *Spa.* Why, has not come to the honour of a beard yet; he needs no shaving. *Sec.* I will trim him and tram him. **1748** SMOLLETT *Rod. Random* iii, None of your jaw, you swab,..else I shall trim your lac'd jacket for you. **1822** SCOTT *Nigel* xxxiii, Some that remember..how I trimmed them about the story of hearkening behind the arras. **1882** *Mrs. Raven's Tempt.* I. 232 Mrs. Raven stood trimming Worsfold and his wife about harbouring the woman. **1927** S. LEWIS *Elmer Gantry* iii. 40 No, gee, Judson, I guess you got me trimmed! **1950** WODEHOUSE *Nothing Serious* 152 Surely ..Rodney can trim a man with hay fever? **1977** *Chicago Tribune* 2 Oct. III. 16/9 Grand Valley of Michigan piled up 324 yards rushing and 90 yards passing to trim Northeastern Illinois 34–12.

11. a. To cut off the excrescences or irregularities of; to reduce to a regular shape by doing this. Also with the part removed as object. In quot. 1879 *absol.* Also with *up.* Also *fig.*

1594 CAREW *Huarte's Exam. Wits* ix. (1596) 120 A wodden chest knobby and nothing trimmed on the outside. **1664** EVELYN *Kal. Hort., Feb.* 60 Trim up your Palisade Hedges, and Espaliers. **1761** CHURCHILL *Apol.* Poems 1763 I. 72 See tortur'd Reason how they pare and trim And like Procrustes, stretch or lop the limb. **1879** BROWNING *Ivan Ivan.* 36 His axe now trimmed and toyed With branch and twig. **1885** *Law Times* LXXIX. 187/2 The farmer has..no inclination ..to trim the roadside hedges. **1891** *Labour Commission Gloss., Trimming castings*, the operation of trimming off with chisel and file the 'runners', i.e. rough edges of metal castings. **1893** J. A. HODGES *Elem. Photogr.* (1907) 105 The manner in which it [a print] has been trimmed and mounted.

b. *transf.* See quots.

1783 G. CARTWRIGHT *Jrnl.* 8 Oct. (1792) III. 29 As those birds [*sc.* eider-ducks] trim the shore along in the flight-times. **1895** *Funk's Standard Dict., To trim the shore*, to follow the shore-outline: said of fish. **1901** *Blackw. Mag.* Nov. 692/2 They [migrating birds] always 'trim' the shore —that is pass close over the headlands.

12. *Carpentry.* To bring (a piece of timber, etc.) to the required shape; *spec.* ***to trim in***, to fit or frame (one piece) to or into another; cf. TRIMMER 4, *trimming-joist* (TRIMMING *vbl. sb.* 7).

1679 MOXON *Mech. Exerc.* ix. 153 This Newel serves also for a Post to Trim the Stair-Case too. **1703** T. N. *City & C. Purchaser* 268 When Workmen fit a piece into other Work, they say they trim in a piece. **1833** LOUDON *Encycl. Archit.* §83 The whole properly trimmed (framed round, leaving a clear opening,) to the chimney shafts. **1842–76** GWILT *Encycl. Archit.* Gloss. s.v., A piece of workmanship fitted between others previously executed, which is then said to be *trimmed in* between them.

13. *Naut.* **a.** To distribute the load of (a ship or boat) so that she floats on an even keel; in quot. 1580, to steady, as with cargo or ballast.

to be trimmed (so much) ***by the head*** (or ***stern***), to be built or laden so as to draw (so much) more water at the bows than at the stern (or the reverse).

1580 H. SMITH in Hakluyt *Voy.* (1598) I. 448 With all hands she did lighten her sterne, and trimme her head. **1627** CAPT. SMITH *Seaman's Gram.* vi. 27 Trim the Boat is to keepe her straight. **1668** CULPEPPER & COLE *Barthol. Anat.* I. ix. 18 That so the Body may be equally as it were poised, and ballanced, or trimmed, as the Watermen speak of their boats. *c* **1720** PRIOR *Bibo & Charon* 5 Trim the boat, and sit quiet, stern Charon replied. **1800** *Local Act 39 & 40 Geo. III*, c. x §42 The Lighter trimmed so as to make the same swim at equal Marks at the Stem and Stern thereof. **1820** SCORESBY *Acc. Arctic Reg.* II. 475 For the purpose of trimming the ship more by the stern.

b. *intr.* (for *refl.* or *pass.*) of a ship or boat.

1861 HUGHES *Tom Brown at Oxf.* ii, While he had been sitting quiet and merely paddling,..the boat had trimmed well enough. **1889** WELCH *Naval Archit.* i. 7 When the excess draft is aft,..the vessel is said to trim by the stern.

c. *transf.* To adjust (the balance) so as to equalize it.

1817 JAS. MILL *Brit. India* II. v. i. 338 How easily the balance among those powers might have been trimmed. **1840** THIRLWALL *Greece* VII. liii. 23 The only way to secure the Macedonian ascendancy.., was to trim the balance of power. **1864** COBDEN *Speeches* (1878) 492, I wanted to trim the scales to prevent there being an undue preponderance in favour of the other side.

14. *Aeronaut.* **a.** To maintain or adjust the trim (sense 3) or inclination of (an aircraft or spacecraft, or part of one). Also *absol.*

1909 *Aero Manual* 40 Some..device is necessary to damp any oscillations that may take place in the line of flight..but hand operation of the steering devices must also be used to 'trim' the machine occasionally. **1921** *Discovery* Apr. 95/2 When trimmed up by the bow, the airship will be found to ride satisfactorily. **1924** *Flight* 13 Mar. 149/2 The pilot trims the tail by operating a hand pump..to increase or decrease its angle of incidence. **1942** *Tee Emm* (Air Ministry) II. 85 If he trims it to fly at a certain speed and power, it should stay at that speed despite bumps. **1958** 'CASTLE' & 'HAILEY' *Flight into Danger* vii. 103 Put full flap on, bring your airspeed back to 110 knots and trim to hold you steady. **1976** B. LECOMBER *Dead Weight* i. 12, I ease the throttles back a fraction and trim the nose a touch lower. **1978** *Nature* 5 Oct. 415/1 The spacecraft gyros were trimmed to the Ganymede celestial motion and Io was subsequently manoeuvered into the large slot.

b. *intr.* (for *refl.* or *pass.*) of an aircraft.

1921 *Techn. Rep. Advisory Comm. Aeronautics 1917–18* III. 1023 It should be noted that the ability to trim at high speeds is the one essential point of difference between a seaplane and a racing motor boat. **1923** *Flight* 31 May 295/2 In order..that the machine would trim correctly..the pilot was placed ahead of the wing, in which position he balances the rest of the machine.

15. *Naut.* **a.** To adjust (the sails or yards) with reference to the direction of the wind and the course of the ship, so as to obtain the greatest advantage. Const. *to.*

to trim by or ***on a wind***, to set the sails so as to sail as nearly as possible against the direction of the wind: see BY A. 9, B. 1 d. ***to trim full*** or ***sharp***: see FULL A. 11, SHARP *adv.* 2.

1624 CAPT. SMITH *Virginia* II. 24 Nor had we a Mariner nor any had skill to trim the sayles. **1627** —— *Seaman's Gram.* ix. 42 All your Sheats, Brases, and Tackes are trimmed by a winde. **1667** DRYDEN & DAVENANT *Tempest* I. i, Trim her right before the wind. **1669** STURMY *Mariner's Mag.* I. ii. 17 Thus have you all the Sails trimm'd sharp, full, and by a Wind. **1697** *Lond. Gaz.* No. 3315/1, I crouded Sail to Leeward to him, trimming my Sails on a Wind tho' I went before it. **1748** *Anson's Voy.* III. v. 342 That which was the stern of the proa, now becomes the head, and she is trimmed on the other tack. **1836** H. ROGERS *J. Howe* i. (1863) 8 The ..dexterous pilot..will trim his sails to every variation of wind. **1899** F. T. BULLEN *Log Sea-waif* 336 A little south-easterly breeze sprang up, to which we trimmed the yards.

b. *absol.* or *intr.* Also *fig.*

1697 DAMPIER *Voy.* (1729) I. 145 Next Morning we again trimm'd sharp, and made the best of our way to the *Lobos de la Mar.* **1706** E. WARD *Wooden World Diss.* (1708) 21 If the Wind and Tide of Affairs prove too violent, he then certainly trims about. **1833** R. MUDIE *Brit. Birds* (1841) I. 110 The kite feels the first action of the revolving air as if it were a breeze, trims to it, and is borne upward in a spiral. **1857** C. GRIBBLE in *Merc. Marine Mag.* (1858) V. 9 Trimmed on the starboard tack, and made all possible sail.

c. *transf.* and *fig.* To turn, adjust, adapt. Freq. in phr. ***to trim one's sails to the wind***, to adapt oneself to circumstances.

1779 COWPER *Pineapple & Bee* 12 Having wasted half the day, He trimmed his flight another way. **1821** SCOTT *Kenilw.* xxxiv, He could scarce have missed shipwreck, knowing..so little how to trim his sails to a court gale. **1847** EMERSON *Poems* (1857) 187 As the bird trims her to the gale, I trim myself to the storm of time. **1898** *Allbutt's Syst. Med.* V. 958 We must trim our treatment according to the phases and peculiarities of the individual. **1928** L. STRACHEY *Elizabeth & Essex* viii. 112 Burghley, trimming his sails to the changing wind, thought it advisable..to take the side of Essex in the matter of the Spanish ransoms. **1934** J. E. NEALE *Queen Elizabeth I* xiv. 229 She preferred to trim the country's sails to the winds when and how they blew, rather than set them at once for a storm that might not come. **1940** F. L. ALLEN *Since Yesterday* x. 275 *Fortune*..trimmed its sails so skillfully to the winds of conservatism that it not only became a mine of factual material for future historians but subtly broadened reactionary minds.

16. To stow or arrange (coal or cargo) in the hold of a ship, or carry it to the hatches when discharging; also to shift (coal) in a ship's hold, etc.; also, to arrange (coal) as it is loaded on a truck. Cf. *coal-trimmer* (COAL *sb.* 16).

1797 BAILEY & CULLEY *Agric. Northumberld.* 7 Trimming 2 s. 6 d. keelman's beer 1 s. 4 d. per chaldron. **1828** JOPLIN *Views Currency* 14 Corn can be warehoused at Hull, and trimmed and turned for about 2 s. per quarter per annum. **1838** *Civil Eng. & Arch. Jrnl.* I. 397/1 The coals cannot be trimmed in the ships so fast. **1884** *Manch. Guard.* 24 Jan. 5/1 The cargo was properly stowed and trimmed. **1886** J. BARROWMAN *Sc. Mining Terms* 68 To *Trim*, to arrange by hand the coals on a truck while being loaded.

17. a. *intr.* (also with *it*). To modify one's attitude in order to stand well with opposite parties; to move cautiously, or 'balance' between two alternative interests, positions, opinions, etc.; also, to accommodate oneself to the mood of the times.

1685 SOUTH *Serm.* (1697) I. 456 Gross, fulsome juggling with their Duty, and a kind of Trimming it between God and the Devil. **1687** DRYDEN *Hind & P.* III. 666 [Non-resistance] A passive term which..trims betwixt a rebell and a king. *a* **1700** B. E. *Dict. Cant. Crew*, *To Trim*, to hold fair with both sides. **1766** EARL MARCH in Jesse *Selwyn & Contemp.* (1843) II. 67 Lord Mansfield trimmed in his usual manner, and avoided declaring his opinion. **1888** BURGON *Lives 12 Gd. Men* II. ix. 217 Nothing knew he..of a disposition to trim with the times.

†**b.** *trans.* ***trim away***: To waste (time) in indecision. *Obs. rare.*

1687 DRYDEN *Hind & P.* III. 501 He who heard what every fool could say Would never fix his thoughts, but trim his time away.

c. *trans.* To modify according to expediency.

1885 *Daily Tel.* 6 Nov. (Cassell), Lord Hartington is not the sort of statesman to trim his opinions according to the expediency of conciliating or not conciliating.

trimachy ('trɪməkɪ, 'traɪ-). *rare.* [f. Gr. τρι-, TRI- + -μαχία, μάχη fight, battle, combat.] **a.** A series of three battles. **b.** 'A contest among three' (*Cent. Dict. Suppl.* 1909).

1887 F. M. CRAWFORD *Saracinesca* i, Count Bismarck had only just brought to a successful termination the first part of his trimachy; Sadowa and Sedan were yet unfought.

trimacular (traɪ'mækjʊlə(r)), *a. Nat. Hist.* [f. TRI- + L. *macula* spot + -AR[1].] Having or marked with three spots. So **tri'maculate** [mod.L. *trimaculāt-us*], **tri'maculated** *adjs.*

1769 PENNANT *Zool.* III. 206 The Trimaculated Wrasse. .. On each side of the lower part of the back fin were two large spots, and between the fin and the tail another. **1888** *Cassell's Encycl. Dict.*, *Trimacular.*

trimaran ('traɪməræn). [f. TRI- + CATA)MARAN *sb.*] A boat with a central hull and a float on each side.

1949 *Sun* (Baltimore) 27 Sept. 22/3 A trimaran showed running speed but little drive to windward. **1959**

Engineering 16 Jan. 86/2 The trimaran configuration, that is a main hull and two outriggers. **1966** T. PYNCHON *Crying of Lot 49* iii. 57 Metzger handed Oedipa aboard the about-to-be-hijacked vessel, a 17-foot aluminum trimaran. **1973** *Guardian* 18 May 18/1 [He] sailed out from England to New Zealand three years ago in a 22-foot trimaran, built and designed by himself.

trimastigate, -membral, etc.: see TRI- 1 a, c.

trimble, obs. form of TREMBLE.

†**'trimboat.** *Obs.* In 6 tryme-. [First element uncertain.] Some kind of fishing-boat used in the 16th c. on the Thames. So **trimnet** (**trimmenet**), and app. **trymle boat**: see quot.

1558 *Act 1 Eliz.* c. 17 §1 No person..withe any maner of..Trollnett Trimmenet Trymebote Stalbote Weblyster..or..any Heling Nett or Trymle Bote..shall take and kyll any yong Broode Spawne or Frye of Eeles Salmon Pyke or Pyckerell.

trimelic (traɪ'mɛlɪk), *a. Gr. Antiq.* [f. Gr. τριμελής (f. τρι-, TRI- + μέλος song, melody) + -IC.] Consisting of three melodies in different modes.

1850 MURE *Lit. Greece* III. 44 The celebrated trimelic or tripartite nome,..consisting of three parts or strophes, each in one of the three chief..modes..Dorian, Phrygian, and Lydian.

trime'llitic, *a. Chem.* [f. TRI- 5 + MELLITIC.] In ***trimellitic acid***, a colourless compound, $C_6H_3(COOH)_3$, unsymmetrical benzene-tricarboxylic acid, obtained by the oxidation of colophony by means of nitric acid. So named in 1870, by Baeyer, who prepared it from mellitic acid.

1872 WATTS *Dict. Chem.* VI. 813 Trimellitic Acid..is moderately soluble in water.., and crystallises..by slow evaporation in nodular groups of indistinct crystals.

†**trimenstre,** *a. Obs. rare.* [f. L. *trimenstris*, erron. form of *trimestris*: see TRIMESTER.] Ripening in three months.

c **1440** *Pallad. on Husb.* I. 260 Trymenstre seed in heruest forto sowe In londis cold is best.

So **tri'menstruous, tri'mensual** *adjs.* (*rare*$^{-0}$) [f. TRI- + MENSTRUOUS, etc.]: see quots.

1656 BLOUNT *Glossogr.*, *Trimenstruous*, of three moneths age. **1658** in PHILLIPS. **1891** *Cent. Dict.*, *Trimensual*, happening every three months.

trimeprazine (traɪ'mɛprəziːn). *Pharm.* [prob. f. TRIME(THYL + PR(OPYL + PHENOTHI)AZINE.] A henothiazine derivative that is used for its sedative and antihistaminic properties (usu. in the form of the tartrate); dimethyl (2-methyl-3-phenothiazin-10-ylpropyl)amine, $C_{18}H_{22}N_2S$.

1959 *Canad. Med. Assoc. Jrnl.* LXXX. 125/1 (*heading*) A new drug for control of itching—trimeprazine. **1977** *Proc. R. Soc. Med.* LXX. 627/1 Mild sedation, e.g. trimeprazine tartrate, is usually required for a few days until the child becomes used to the apparatus.

trimer ('traɪmə(r)). *Chem.* [f. TRI- + -MER.] A compound whose molecule is composed of three molecules of monomer.

[**1929** *Chem. Abstr.* XXIII. 3213 The supernatant liquid ..yielded 180, 20, 11, and 4g. of the di-, tri-, tetra- and pentamer, resp.] **1939** [see TETRAMER]. **1952** *Jrnl. Physical Chem.* LVI. 85 A reaction between 3 molecules of insulin of molecular weight 12,000..to give a 'trimer' of molecular weight 36,000..is postulated. **1969** W. R. R. PARK *Plastics Film Technol.* viii. 195 Even polystyrene films..can cause problems if they contain even relatively low percentages of residual monomers, dimers, or trimers. **1974** M. C. GERALD *Pharmacol.* xi. 198 This compound [*sc.* paraldehyde] is a trimer of acetaldehyde.., that is, three molecules linked in a ring.

Hence **tri'meric** *a.*; **,trimeri'zation**, the formation of a trimer from smaller molecules.

1938 *Jrnl. Chem. Soc.* 11 Polymerisation of βγ-dimethylbutadiene by sulphuric acid dissolved in acetic acid gives dimeric, trimeric and other low-molecular products. **1954** *Adv. Protein Chem.* IX. 419 A similar free energy change might be expected on dimerization and trimerization. **1972** A. A. R. SAYIGH et al. in Stille & Campbell *Condensation Monomers* v. 382 The value of these catalysts is limited because the same substances can act as catalysts for the trimerization of isocyanates. **1975** *Nature* 18 Dec. 576/2 The functional significance of the trimeric nature of the molecule is obscure.

trimerous ('trɪmərəs, 'traɪ-), *a.* [f. mod.L. *trimer-us* (ad. Gr. τριμερής, f. τρι-, TRI- + μέρος part) + -OUS.] Having, consisting of, or characterized by three parts: *spec.* **a.** *Bot.* Having the parts of the flower, or the leaves, in series or whorls of three. **b.** *Entom.* Consisting of three segments or joints, as the tarsi in certain insects (see *trimeran* below); of an insect, having such tarsi (= *trimeran*).

1826 KIRBY & SP. *Entomol.* III. xxxv. 685 Trimerous insects are those whose tarsi consist of only three joints. *Ibid.* IV. xlvii. 378 Tarsi mostly trimerous, rarely dimerous. **1845** LINDLEY *Sch. Bot.* viii. (1858) 129 *note*, *Trimerous* means that they [parts of a flower] are a power of 3. **1857** HENFREY *Bot.* 226 *Schizandraceæ*..calyx and corolla 3-merous. **1869** *Student* II. 12 Polymerous leaves may be dimerous, trimerous, etc. according to their number of meriphylls. **1875** BENNETT & DYER *Sachs' Bot.* 570 Among the dimerous and trimerous flowers of the orders Polycarpæ and Cruciferæ.

So **trimeran** ('trɪmərən) *Entom.*, *adj.* belonging to the division *Trimera* of beetles, or of hymenopterous insects, characterized by trimerous tarsi; *sb.* an insect of either of these divisions; **trimere** ('traɪmɪə(r)) *Zool.*, a division of the third order in the supporting reticular skeleton of extinct siliceous sponges; **trimerite** ('trɪməraɪt) *Min.*, a rare silicate of glucinum, manganese, and calcium, occurring in pinkish pseudo-hexagonal crystals, shown by their optical properties to be combinations of three triclinic individuals (*Cent. Dict.* 1891).

1842 BRANDE *Dict. Sci.*, etc., **Trimerans*, *Trimera*,..the name of a section of Coleopterous insects, including those which have each tarsus composed of three articulations. **1909** *Cent. Dict. Suppl.*, *Trimere. **1896** CHESTER *Dict. Names Min.* 274 **Trimerite*, Silicate of glucinum, manganese, and calcium, found in brilliant pinkish crystals.

trimesic (traɪ'mɛsɪk), *a. Chem.* [f. TRI- 5 + MES(ITYLENE + -IC.] In ***trimesic acid***, $C_6H_3(CO_2H)_3$, symmetrical benzene-tricarboxylic acid. (So named by Fittig, 1867, when he obtained it from mesitylenic acid, and found it to be tribasic.)

1889 ROSCOE & SCHORLEMMER *Chem.* V. 138 Trimesic acid..crystallizes in hard, transparent, thick prisms, which melt above 300°.

trimester (traɪ'mɛstə(r)). [ad. F. *trimestre* sb. (Cotgr., 1611), ad. L. *trimestris* adj., f. TRI- + *mensis* month.] A period or term of three months; *spec.* each of three such periods into which human gestation is divided.

1821 S. WESTON (*title*) A Trimester in France and Swisserland; or, a three months' journey..from Calais to Basle. **1895** *Current Hist.* (U.S.) V. 573 The cause of the insurgents seems to have made good progress in the third trimester of the revolt. **1907** *Westm. Gaz.* 6 Feb. 12/1 His two trimesters at Bonn University barely sufficed for him to attend a score of lectures. **1916** G. P. SHEARS *Obstetrics* ii. 27 Most writers divide pregnancy into three periods of three months each, three trimesters, as they are often called. **1938** A. L. MUDALIAR *Clin. Obstetrics* vi. 33 The signs and symptoms vary with the different periods of pregnancy, and we shall classify them into..the first, second and third trimesters of pregnancy. **1980** GATES & MECKEL *Newborn Beauty* (1981) iii. 79 During the first trimester you may feel nauseated, fatigued, and lose your appetite.

So †**trimestre** *a. Obs. rare*$^{-0}$ = next.

1623 COCKERAM, *Trimestre*, of three moneths.

trimestrial (traɪ'mɛstrɪəl), *a.* (*sb.*) [f. L. *trimestris* (see prec.) + -AL[1].] Consisting of or containing three months; occurring or appearing every three months. **b.** as *sb.* A quarterly publication.

1693 J. BEAUMONT *On Burnet's Th. Earth* II. 96 By others it's made Trimestrial, and by others to consist of Six Months. **1824** MEDWIN *Convers. Byron* I. 171 People who read nothing but these trimestrials. **1855** *Tait's Mag.* XXII. 630 The complaint of a trimestrial contemporary. **1865** MAFFEI *Brigand Life* I. 81 He levied a regular trimestrial tax upon all cattle-dealers.

Also (less correctly) **tri'mestral** *a.*

1824 BP. BLOMFIELD in *Mem.* (1863) I. iv. 101, I have been busier for the last three months than ever I was before for any trimestral portion of my life. **1829** GEN. P. THOMPSON *Exerc.* (1842) I. 52 The fiend is up again and doing, till Vishnu array himself in trimestral or monthly incarnation, to return him to his deep. [Referring to the *Quarterly Review*.] **1881** MRS. LYNN LINTON *My Love* xii, Their trimestrial visit..had to be paid.

trimetallic (traɪmɪ'tælɪk), *a.* [after BIMETALLIC: see TRI-.] Pertaining to or using three metals as currency. So **tri'metallism**, the use of a triple standard of currency.

1887 *Contemp. Rev.* Dec. 812 The metal coinage system of the world is not..'mono-metallic', nor 'bi-metallic', but 'trimetallic'. **1897** *Westm. Gaz.* 8 Oct. 2/3 Here is a correspondent in the *Times*..who asks, 'Why not Trimetallism?'

tri,meta'phosphate. *Chem.* [TRI- 5 a.] A triple polymer of a metaphosphate, sodium mono-metaphosphate being $NaPO_3$.

1894 MUIR & MORLEY *Watts' Dict. Chem.* IV. 107.

trimeter ('trɪmɪtə(r), 'traɪ-), *sb.* and *a. Pros.* Also 6 **trymeter**, 8 **trimetre**. [ad. L. *trimetrus* adj. and sb., a. Gr. τρίμετρος adj., f. τρι-, TRI- + μέτρον measure (see METRE *sb.*[1] 4).]

A. *sb.* A verse of three measures; i.e. in trochaics, iambics, or anapæstics, of three dipodies (= six feet); in other rhythms, of three feet; *esp.* the ***iambic trimeter***, the usual verse of the dialogue in ancient Greek plays.

1567 DRANT *Horace, Art Poetry* A viij, The foote of Syllabs shorte and long Iambus hath to name..and trymeter the verse (which of the same Consists) is cawld. *a* **1637** B. JONSON *Horace, Art Poetrie* 381 This foot yet, in the famous trimeters Of Accius and Ennius, rare appeares. **1789** T. TWINING *Aristotle's Treat. Poetry* (1812) II. 445 The hexameter is but one third longer than the Iambic trimeter; their respective times being 24, and 18. **1850** BROWNING *Christmas Eve* xviii, Or Turklike brandishing a scimetar O'er anapæsts in comic-trimeter. **1859** *Sat. Rev.* 20 Aug. 225/2 Mr. Whyte and..Mr. Thomas..have translated the *Inferno* into English trimeters.

B. *adj.* Of a verse: Consisting of three measures.

1706 PHILLIPS (ed. Kersey), *Trimetrum*,..a Trimeter Verse of three Measures, an Iambick of six Feet. **1886** C. A. BRIGGS *Messianic Proph.* v. 143 Psalm xviii..is of eight strophes, of fourteen trimeter lines each.

trimethoprim (traɪ'mɛθəʊprɪm). *Pharm.* [f. TRIMETH(YL + O(XY- + P(Y)RIM(IDINE, constituent parts of the systematic name (see quot. 1962).] An antibiotic, $C_{14}H_{18}N_4O_3$, that is usually given in conjunction with a sulphonamide, esp. in the treatment of malaria and of respiratory and urinary infections.

1962 *Jrnl. Medicinal & Pharmaceutical Chem.* V. 1107 Compound LXV, 2,4-diamino-5-(trimethoxybenzyl)-pyrimidine (B.W. 56-72, trimethoprim), has been selected for detailed study and clinical trial. **1968** *New Scientist* 17 Oct. 147/1 A tablet of Septrin actually contains two drugs, one old—a sulphonamide—and one 'new'—trimethoprim. **1974** R. M. KIRK et al. *Surgery* ii. 29/1 Trimethoprim acts synergistically with sulphonamides, since they interfere sequentially at two stages in bacterial synthesis of folic acid. **1977** *Lancet* 2 July 4/1 Much of the shigellosis could be successfully treated with ampicillin trihydrate and closely related antibiotics, or with cotrimoxazole (trimethoprim and sulphamethoxazole).

trimethyl (traɪ'mɛθɪl, -aɪl). *Chem.* [f. TRI- 5 + METHYL.] **a.** A formative denoting the presence of three methyl groups, CH_3, in a compound, as **trimethyl-arsine**, $As(CH_3)_3$, **trimethyl-phosphine**, $P(CH_3)_3$: see also *trimethylamine* below. **b.** *spec.* denoting the substitution of 3 methyl groups for 3 hydrogen atoms, in the substance designated by the rest of the name; e.g. **trimethylbenzene**, $C_6H_3(CH_3)_3$, in which 3 methyl groups have taken the place of 3 H atoms in benzene, C_6H_6; so **trimethyl-methane**, $CH(CH_3)_3$, from methane, CH_4, **trimethyl-carbinol**, $C(CH_3)_3.OH$, etc. Also used *attrib.* as **trimethyl phosphate**, $(CH_3)_3.PO_4$. Hence **trime'thylic** *a. attrib.* in same sense.

1866 ROSCOE *Elem. Chem.* xxxi. 281 Trimethylarsine is a colourless liquid. **1868** WATTS *Dict. Chem.* IV. 608 Trimethylphosphine is a transparent, colourless, mobile liquid, heavier than water, having a strong refracting power, and an indescribably nauseous odour. **1873** WATTS *Fownes' Chem.* (ed. 11) 767 Trimethyl-benzene is susceptible of three isomeric modifications.

Also **tri'methylamine**, the tertiary amine of methyl, $N(CH_3)_3$, in which all the 3 hydrogen atoms of ammonia, NH_3, are replaced by 3 methyl groups; a volatile liquid with a penetrating fishy odour; formerly also called ***trimethyl ammonia*** and ***trimethylia***.

tri'methylene, $CH_2\langle{}^{CH_2}_{CH_2}$ (with a single bond linking the two CH_2 groups), a colourless gas; ***trimethylene-diamine***, a poisonous ptomaine.

1857 MILLER *Elem. Chem.* III. 210 *Trimethylia*... This alkali..is found in considerable quantity in the roe of herrings. **1866** ODLING *Anim. Chem.* 87 Trimethylamine $(CH_3)_3N$, a frequent constituent of stale brine in which herrings and other fish have been pickled. **1872** GARROD & BAXTER *Mat. Med.* (1880) 408 The Hydrochlorate of Trimethylamine is a stable compound, in long needle-shaped crystals, very deliquescent, soluble in water and in alcohol.

trimetric (traɪ'mɛtrɪk), *a.* [f. TRI- + Gr. μέτρον measure (or, in sense 2, f. as TRIMETER) + -IC.]

1. *Cryst.* Applied to that system of forms having three unequal axes mutually at right angles: = ORTHORHOMBIC.

1837 DANA *Min.* 15 *Classis Trimetrica*, or the Trimetric System. **1873** WATTS *Fownes' Chem.* (ed. 11) 281 The bases of these monoclinic forms are identical in form with those of the trimetric system.

2. *Pros.* Consisting of three measures.

1889 *Amer. Jrnl. Philol.* July 224 The theory that the hexameter is a combination of two trimeters..is old and familiar;..a tetrameter (tetrapody) is assumed as the original verse, which became a trimeter (trimetric colon) as a result of..the combination.

tri'metrical, *a.* [f. as prec. + -AL[1].] **a.** *Pros.* = prec. 2. *rare*$^{-0}$. **b.** ***Trimetrical Classic***, a loose expression for the 'three-character classic', a Chinese elementary school-book written in lines of verse, each line consisting of three characters.

1828 WEBSTER, *Trimeter, Trimetrical*, consisting of three poetical measures. **1835** *Chinese Repository* July 105 The Trimetrical Classic. **1853** *North-China Herald* 21 May 168/1 (*heading*) Pamphlets published by the Insurgents. The Trimetrical Classic. [*Note*] Each line containing three words, and each verse four lines. **1900** A. H. SMITH in *Westm. Gaz.* 28 June 3/3 He was set the usual task in the Trimetrical Classic. **1908** *China's Millions* Mar. 40/1 For a nation to pass within the life-time of a generation from the Trimetrical Classic to the study of John Stuart Mill.

Trimetrogen (traɪ'mɛtrəʊgɒn). Also **trimetrogon.** [f. TRI- + *Metrogon* (see quot. 1944).] Used *attrib.* with reference to a technique in which aerial photographs are taken simultaneously by a camera pointing vertically downwards and two pointing obliquely in opposite directions.

1944 P. G. McCurdy et al. *Man. Photogrammetry* (Amer. Soc. Photogrammetry) xiii. 648 In the United States the tri-lens system of map compilation is now usually designated as the 'Trimetrogon' method. The word 'Metrogon' is the commercial name of the kind of lens generally used, but the method of compilation is not affected by the kind of lens. *Ibid.*, Either the K-17 or K-3B type cameras are used in the trimetrogon assembly. **1952** *Chambers's Jrnl.* Feb. 84/1 The planes..carried the marvellous trimetrogon aerial cameras, developed during the War, which make possible a thousandfold increase of speed and show the landscape in stereoscopic detail. **1969** G. C. Dickinson *Maps & Air Photographs* xv. 244 Something of the best of both worlds is obtained with photographs taken by multiple camera installations, the chief aim here being to reduce cost or time by increasing the area photographed during each run; well-known types are..the American Trimetrogon type where one vertical camera is flanked by two high oblique cameras giving continuous cover from horizon to horizon at each exposure.

trimillion, -millionaire: see TRI- 4 a.

trimle, obs. or dial. form of TREMBLE.

'trimly, *a. rare.* [f. TRIM *a.* + -LY¹.] Having a trim character.

1858 Mrs. Gore *Heckington* I. xiii. 274 Estates and mansions [so] left..are now..of rare occurrence in our trimly island.

trimly ('trɪmlɪ), *adv.* [f. TRIM *a.* + -LY².] In a trim manner.

†**1.** Effectively, thoroughly, soundly, properly; cleverly, featly, neatly, nicely; finely, well. *Obs.*

1503–13 Dunbar *Poems* liii. 200 Quhen I saw hir sa trimlye dance, Hir guid conwoy and countenance. **1556** Olde *Antichrist* 171 Being trymlye furnished in false wyles and lies. **1579–80** North *Plutarch* (1676) 489 Little showers ..which..make the Earth bring forth all things very trimly. **1600** Fairfax *Tasso* vi. xcvii, This formost hazard had she trimly past. **1623** Lisle *Ælfric on O. & N. Test.* Pref. 11 Harke ye..how trimly this sounds in English. **1679** C. Nesse *Antid. agst. Popery* 133 Scaliger truly and trimly told the Jesuits.

2. So as to be neat, elegant, or smart in appearance or effect; neatly; finely, smartly.

1523 [Coverdale] *Old God & New* (1534) P j, They shall haue trymly garnyshed & decked the aulters with many ymages. **1545** Elyot, *Candide uestitus*, trymmely apparayled... *Concinne*, properly, honestly, trymly. **1588** Parke tr. *Mendoza's Hist. China* 331 The women [with] their haire trimly kembed and dressed. **1645** Milton *Colast.* Wks. 1851 IV. 348 The stuff, though very cours and thredbare, garnisht and trimly fac't with the commendation of a Licencer. *c* **1728** Somerville *To A. Ramsay* 65 In all her richest head-geer trimly clad. **1879** Butcher & Lang *Odyssey* vii. 107 All manner of garden beds, planted trimly.

†**'trimmage.** *Obs. rare*⁻¹. [f. TRIM *v.* + -AGE.] = TRIMMING *vbl. sb.*

1693 *Lond. Gaz.* No. 2892/4 A Copper colour'd Coat with black Trimmage.

trimmed, *ppl. a.* [f. TRIM *v.* + -ED.]

1. That has been trimmed, in various senses of the verb. In sense 8 often as the second element in an instrumental combination, as ***blue-, ermine-, flower-, gold-, lace-trimmed***, etc.: see also these words.

c **1532** Du Wes *Introd. Fr.* in *Palsgr.* 922 A goodly lady meke, trymmed, *dame gaillarde, benigne, cointe.* **1649** in *Verney Mem.* (1907) I. 448 A paire of French trimed gloves. **1892** *Photogr. Ann.* II. 57 To mark the mount at each corner of the trimmed print.

b. ***trimmed joist***, a joist which is tenoned into a trimmer (sense 4); cf. *trimming-joist* s.v. TRIMMING *vbl. sb.* 7.

1876 *Encycl. Brit.* IV. Plate facing p. 482, Trimmed Joists. **1945** H. C. Bissill in N. W. Kay *Pract. Carpenter & Joiner* xvii. 361 (*caption*) Pictorial view of floor of a first-floor, with..bridging joists,..trimmer, trimming joist, and ..trimmed joist. **1966** A. T. Collins *Newnes Complete Pract. Woodworking* 96/1 A further use for the stopped housing is to join trimmed floor joists to a trimmer.

2. In Comb. with advbs. and preps. forming adjs., as ***trimmed-down, -up***.

1897 Kipling *Capt. Cour.* ix. 198 It's great to have a trimmed-up meal again. **1971** *Wall St. Jrnl.* 22 July w1/3 Last month the White House vetoed a public works measure, but an administration spokesman said there are signs the President might accept a trimmed-down plan.

trimmenet: see under TRIMBOAT.

trimmer ('trɪmə(r)). [f. TRIM *v.* + -ER¹.]

†**1.** app. A canopy. *Obs. rare.*

1518–19 *Rec. St. Mary at Hill* 303 As towchyng the tabernacles, trymmers, is that a wourkman shall se them & he to shew his best advice in it. *a* **1548** Hall *Chron., Hen. VIII* 73 Vnder yᵉ trimmer, anticke images of gold. **1559** *Dunmow Churchw. Acc.* lf. 42 b (MS.), For making ii yrons and iiii staples for the trymmer over the rood, iiᵈ.

2. One who trims; one who repairs, adjusts, makes neat or smart, etc.; *spec.* **a.** a tailor's, dressmaker's, or milliner's assistant; **b.** a finisher in coach-making; **c.** see quots. 1881, 1891. Often as second element, as in ***hat-trimmer***, etc.

1555 W. Watreman *Fardle Facions* ii. viii. 167 The yndians are..greate deckers and trimmers of them selues. **1580** Hollyband *Treas. Fr. Tong*, *Racoustreur*, a minder or trimmer of things. **1591** Percivall *Sp. Dict.*, *Afeytador*, a barber, a trimmer, a decker, *tonsor, fucator, ornator.* **1621** T. Williamson tr. *Goulart's Wise Vieillard* 115 That man a trimmer of a garden of pleasure. **1652** N. Culverwell *Treat.* i. xi. (1661) 88 He calls God..the Painter, and Trimmer of the Soul. **1850** Kingsley *Cheap Clothes* 17 If to the trimmer we return an answer that is considered 'saucy', we are fined 6*d.* or 1*s.* **1879** *Melbourne Argus* 24 Dec. 2/1 Trimmers [coachmaking] get from £2 10s. to £3 10s. per week. **1881** *Guide Worcester Porcelain Wks.* 8 The trimmer ..removes any superfluous glaze. **1891** *Labour Commission Gloss.*, *Trimmers*, skilled workmen engaged in shaping and pressing hosiery goods. **1902** Sloane *Stand. Electr. Dict.* App. s.v. *Trimming*, The work of a lamp trimmer frequently includes cleaning the feed rod of the upper carbon with a cloth so as to ensure smooth action of the clutch.

3. One who or that which cuts, clips, prunes, etc.; *spec.* †a barber (*obs.*); also, an implement or machine for trimming edges in industrial processes.

1583 Stubbes *Anat. Abus.* ii. (1882) 50 What say you of the barbers and trimmers of men? **1653** Urquhart *Rabelais* i. lv, At the going out of the halls..were the perfumers and trimmers, through whose hands the gallants past. **1751** Smollett *Per. Pic.* (1779) II. xl. 37 Peregrine mentioned this assassination to his own trimmer. **1810** *Sporting Mag.* XXXV. 263 The defendant's witnesses..described as croppers, dockers, nickers and trimmers [of horses]. **1876** Spurgeon *Commenting* 4 Calvin..was no trimmer and pruner of texts. **1883** R. Haldane *Workshop Receipts* Ser. ii. 99/2 Trimmers' paste requires to be smooth,..and possessed of great adhesive qualities. **1889** *Anthony's Photogr. Bull.* II. 364 With..the straight-edge to guide the knife or trimmer, cut first one side and then..the three others.

4. *Arch.* A short beam framed across an opening (as a stair-well or hearth) to carry the ends of those joists which cannot be extended across the opening; also, a brick-trimmer (BRICK *sb.*¹ 10). Also *attrib.*

1654 in E. B. Jupp *Carpenters' Co.* (1887) 316, 2 foote 9 inches from the backe of the Chimney to the Trimmer peece or binding Joyst. **1737** *Salmon's Country Build. Estimator* (ed. 2) 62 Remember to measure the Trimmers that support the Hearths taking the Length by the Girt of the Arching of them. **1833** Loudon *Encycl. Archit.* §234 Four-inch brick trimmer arches to be turned where required. **1897** F. C. Moore *How to build Home* iii. 32 'Trimmer'-beams enter the wall on each side of the chimney. *Ibid.* viii. 113 All hearths shall be constructed with trimmer-arches extending 20 inches from the chimney-breast to a 'skew back'. **1953** *Archit. Rev.* CXIV. 364/1 With the exception of the assembly hall and gymnasia, which are on solid load-bearing walls, the structure is carried on reinforced raft foundations with ground trimmer beams at the edges.

5. One who trims between opposing parties in politics, etc.; hence, one who inclines to each of two opposite sides as interest dictates.

Applied orig. in this sense to Lord Halifax and those associated with him (1680–90), but by him accepted in the sense 'one who keeps even the ship of state'; hence 'one who changes sides to balance parties' (J.).

1682 Dryden *Dk. Guise* Epil. 33, 38 We Trimmers are for holding all things even.—Yes—just like him that hung 'twixt Hell and Heaven... You Trimmers shou'd, to poize it, hang on t'other. **1682** *Character of a Trimmer* 2 A Trimmer, one neither Whigg nor Tory, is a Hater of Anti-christ, an Abominator of Enthusiasm. **1685** Evelyn *Mem.* 7 May, Those whom (by way of hateful distinction) they call'd Whiggs and Trimmers. **1704** *Faction Displ.* xiv, The Patriot's Soul disdains the Trimmer's Art. **1739** Wesley *Wks.* (1872) I. 183 Nor is it possible for all the trimmers between God and the world to elude the consequence. **1809** W. Irving *Knickerb.* v. i. (1849) 262 He who wavers in seeking to do what is right gets stigmatized as a trimmer. **1888** T. Hardy *Wessex T.* (1889) 201 One of the trimmers who went to church and chapel both.

6. One who or that which trims or trounces (see TRIM *v.* 10); a stiff competitor, fighter, etc.; a slasher; a stiff letter, article, bout, run, blow, throw of the ball, etc.; (chiefly *Austral.* and *N.Z.*) a good or impressive thing or person, a 'smasher'. *colloq.*

1776 Foote *Bankrupt* iii. Wks. 1799 II. 126 *Pep.* Don't you think the public would bear one skirmish more..? I have a trimmer here in my hand. *Plast.* To which I have as tart a retort. **1804** Nelson in Nicolas *Disp.* (1846) VI. 163, I shall write the Dey of Algiers a trimmer. **1816** Scott *Antiq.* xi, I will shew you his last epistle, and the scroll of my answer—egad, it is a trimmer! **1827** *Sporting Mag.* XXI. 141 Amongst the young hounds I noticed some trimmers. **1828** *Ibid.* XXII. 117 We found in Man Wood, and killed him [the fox] after a trimmer of fifty minutes. **1878** 'Ironbark' *Southerly Busters* 11, I thought thee a regular 'trimmer', I thought thee a generous man. **1882** *Daily Tel.* 17 May, Mr. H. was clean bowled by a trimmer from Barnes. **1943** N. Marsh *Colour Scheme* v. 92 'Running well, isn't she [*sc.* a car]?'.. 'She's a trimmer.' **1955** [see LAIR *v.*]. **1962** [see SHEILA]. **1970** *Private Eye* 13 Mar. 16 Jeez Valda Clissold, cripes she was a real little trimmer. **1970** *N.Z. Listener* 12 Oct. 13/5 Dave, you're a trimmer. You'll go places. Take a top seat.

7. One whose business is to stow the cargo or coal in loading a ship, or to shift it from one place to another in the hold; also, a mechanical contrivance for doing this; also, one who arranges the coal in loading trucks.

1836 Sir G. Head *Home Tour* 331 These men called trimmers, whose business it is to level the cargo as it comes tumbling below. **1890** *Sci. Amer.* 7 June 360/1 The coal handling plant..may be resolved into three parts: The elevators..; the trimmers, which take the coal from the elevators and deposit it upon the heaps; and finally the reloaders. **1891** *Labour Commission Gloss.*, *Trimmers*, men on board ship whose duty is to go into the coal bunkers of a vessel and to place the coals within reach of the fireman... When a ship is loading grain in bulk, the trimmers move the grain from the point under the hatchway to the ends of the ship.

†**8.** *pl.* Ropes and yards for trimming the sails of a ship: see TRIM *v.* 15. *Obs. rare*⁻¹.

1630 tr. *Camden's Hist. Eliz.* iv. 32 Their Masts and Trimmers ouerthrowne, their Cables cut.

9. *Angling.* **a.** (*a*) A float of cork, wood, etc., to which a line, with baited hook, is attached; used on lakes and ponds for taking pike; (*b*) a peg surmounted by a reel on which the line is wound, driven into the bank of a stream for the same purpose; a bank-runner.

1799–1815 [implied in *trimmer-angling, -fishing*: see b.]. **1840** Blaine *Encycl. Rur. Sport* §3638 The bank trimmer is much in use on the lakes of England, the lochs of Scotland, [etc.]. **1845** Lubbock *Fauna Norfolk* ii. 90 He launched his fleet of trimmers, pike finding a ready sale at his own door. **1854** L. Lloyd *Scandinav. Adv.* I. 189 Trimmers, or night-lines, were also much used in my vicinity. **1873** G. C. Davies *Mount. & Mere* iii. 18 The trimmers are baited with dead roach, and, luckily for the pike and the fair sportsman the eels get the largest share of the bait.

b. *attrib.* and *Comb.*, as ***trimmer-angling, -bait, -cork, -fishing, -hook, -line***.

1799 G. Smith *Laboratory* II. 264 An approved Method of Trolling, and Trimmer-fishing. **1815** T. F. Salter *Angler's Guide* (title-p.), Trolling, Bottom and Float-Fishing, Fly-Fishing, and Trimmer-Angling. **1840** Blaine *Encycl. Rur. Sport* §3638 A large hooked arrow armed with strong twine might be shot over the trimmer line... The cord [should be wound] on round the groove in the flat trimmer cork. *Ibid.* §3639 Let the trimmer-hook be sufficiently large. **1863** Atkinson *Stanton Grange* (1864) 194 The trimmer-bait had been taken by a nice half-pound trout. **1867** F. Francis *Angling* iv. (1880) 133 *note*, It is trimmer-fishing in disguise.

10. *Electronics.* A small adjustable capacitor usu. used for the fine adjustment of a larger capacitor to which it is connected. Also ***trimmer capacitor, condenser***.

1930 Moyer & Wostrel *Radio Construction & Repairing* (ed. 2) xviii. 331 'Trimmer' condensers which are out of adjustment..will impair the quality of sound reproduction. **1939**, etc. [see PADDER *sb.*² 3]. **1944** *Electronic Engin.* XVI. 362/2 This error can easily be compensated by the use of a two gang trimmer condenser across the two tuning condensers. **1965** *Wireless World* Sept. 422/2 The appropriate trimmer is first adjusted to give a low intermediate frequency. **1971** A. Margolis *Mod. Radio Repair Techniques* (1974) vi. 83 Usually, padder capacitors are found only in oscillator circuits. Trimmer capacitors are found in the RF circuits, mixer circuits and oscillator circuits.

11. *Aeronaut.* = *trimming tab* s.v. TRIMMING *vbl. sb.* 7 b.

1935 *Aircraft Engineering* Dec. 305/1 The effect of the trimmer on the drag of the whole tail must be kept in mind. **1947** A. C. Douglas *Gliding & Advanced Soaring* ii. 48 If the quick release is the one used for winching, usually below the thrust line, the machine may tend to ride high, necessitating a continual forward pressure on the stick. This may be tiring on long tows unless elevator trimmers are fitted. **1964** G. Lyall *Most Dangerous Game* ix. 62 Watching my hands wander round the cockpit, checking and setting... Trimmers to takeoff, throttle nut tensioned.

Hence **'trimmering** *vbl. sb.*, trimmer-fishing.

1870 *Observer* 9 Oct., Trimmering, trolling, live bait fishing, spinning, fly fishing.

attrib. **1888** Fenn *Dick o' Fens* x. *heading*, A trimmering expedition.

trimmill, obs. or dial. form of TREMBLE.

trimming ('trɪmɪŋ), *vbl. sb.* [f. TRIM *v.* + -ING¹.] The action of the verb TRIM.

1. a. Making trim, putting in order, equipment, preparation; repairing, putting right; *spec. Naut.* the fitting out, repairing, or cleaning the bottom of a ship: see TRIM *v.* 2–6.

1519–20 *Rec. St. Mary at Hill* 304 Paid for Trymmyng of the courten of our ladys tabernacle... Paid to a carpenter for Trymmyng of the peyse of the pyx. **1585** T. Washington tr. *Nicholay's Voy.* ii. vi. 36 The trimming and gathering of the mastick. *c* **1595** Capt. Wyatt *R. Dudley's Voy. W. Ind.* (Hakl. Soc.) 30 Such things which wee weare to have from the carvells for the speedie dispatchinge of our admeralls trimminge. *a* **1642** Sir W. Monson *Naval Tracts* ii. (1704) 254/2 Upon the return of the clean Squadron to Sea, whilst the other Squadron is in Trimming.

b. Adornment, decoration, dressing up; making neat or smart; also cutting, clipping, shearing (*lit.* and *fig.*); †*spec.* cutting of the hair (*obs.*).

a **1536** *Calisto & Mel.* A iij b, What trimyng what payntyng, to make fayrnes. **1554–5** in Feuillerat *Revels Q. Mary* (1914) 176 Counterfet pearle for the trymynge & garnishing of the womens hedpeces and fruntes of their visars. **1583** Stubbes *Anat. Abus.* ii. (1882) 50 They [the barbers] haue inuented such strange fashions and monstrous maners of cuttings, trimmings, shauings. **1638** *Archdeaconry Essex Min.* lf. 3 b (MS.) Edwardus Geary presentatus for tryming of men on the Saboath day in tyme of divine service. **1693** *Vestry Bks.* (Surtees) 258 For the Beadle's blew cote trimming and making, 19 s. 6 d. *a* **1700** B. E. *Dict. Cant. Crew*, *Trimming*, Cheating People of their Money. **1723** Mandeville *Fab. Bees* (1733) I. 320 To have them all whole and tight in the same Cloaths and Trimming must add to the comliness of the sight. **1886** C. Scott *Sheep-Farming* 171 Trimming is the modelling or clipping from time to time of the already rough shorn sheep.

c. *pl.* Pieces cut off in trimming something; parings, cuttings, scraps.

1805 R. W. DICKSON *Pract. Agric.* I. 116 Where there are coppices of young wood,..fences..may be formed at very small expence by the trimmings from them. **1846** SOYER *Cookery* 27 The trimmings of any description of game..may be used for making the above sauce. **1857** MILLER *Elem. Chem.* III. 667 The strongest glue..from the ears and refuse trimmings of thick hides in general. **1881** *Daily Tel.* 23 Feb., The scraps and trimmings of joints,..good meat, true meat, often cut from the primest parts of the animal. **1912** *Daily News* 21 Mar. 4 The bodger's fire of beech trimmings.

2. *concr.* Adornment, array; *esp.* **a.** Any ornamental addition to the bare fabric of a dress, etc. Also *fig.* Chiefly *pl.*

In quot. 1625 = the trappings of the sacrificial victim. Cf. quot. 1697 in TRIM *v.* 7.

1625 K. LONG tr. *Barclay's Argenis* IV. v. 255 Must this pompe, this attire, this beauty, be the trimmings to offer mee a Sacrifice to Sicilies infernall gods? *a* **1654** SELDEN *Table-T., Relig.* (Arb.) 102 Every Man has a Doublet: So every Man has his Religion: We differ about Trimming. **1684** *Contempl. St. Man* II. v. (1699) 178 What Fool is so sottish as to bestow precious Trimming upon a Penitential Garment? *a* **1713** ELLWOOD *Autobiog.* (1765) 24 Those unnecessary Trimmings of Lace, Ribbands, and useless Buttons. **1850** H. ROGERS *Ess.* II. iv. 205 Discourses.. garnished with a trimming of French terms and phrases. **1906** *Temple Bar Mag.* Jan. 33 Tunics..of darker grey with 'trimmings'.

b. *pl.* Accessories, usual accompaniments; e.g. to the bare fabric of a house, to a joint of meat, etc. Freq. in phr. ***all the trimmings.*** Also *fig.*

1612 T. BODLEY *Will* in Macray *Ann. Bodleian* (1880) 407 There shelues, deskes, seates, and other needeful trimings. **1828** MISS MITFORD *Village* Ser. III. 47 The leg of mutton and trimmings had been paid for over and over. **1837** DICKENS *Pickw.* xxxvii, A boiled leg of mutton with the usual trimmings. **1858** GEN. P. THOMPSON *Audi Alt.* II. lxx. 11 Style, which is only the trimmings of the dish. **1884** *St. James' Gaz.* 29 Apr. 4/2 Agricultural and mechanical implements, house trimmings, locks, latches, and hinges. **1927** D. PARKER in *New Yorker* 29 Oct. 93/1 He was praised, adored, analyzed, bestsold, argued about, and banned in Boston; all the trimmings were accorded him. **1946** M. DICKENS *Happy Prisoner* ix. 195 If he..had to start his illness all over again, with transfusions and penicillin and all the trimmings, it would be their fault. **1949** R. HARVEY *Curtain Time* 148 Turkey and all the trimmings. **1973** *Times* 25 Apr. 8/2 Those rich romantics or fantasists who still wish to enter matrimony with a gracious splash can hire for a day the ancestors, the family retainers, their own private stately home and all the trimmings, in the centre of London. **1981** 'W. HAGGARD' *Money Men* iii. 35 He had a passion for silverside, all the trimmings—carrots and onions and small sweet dumplings. **1984** *Times* 6 Apr. 21/2 Next week he unveils his..personal computer which is said to have all the trimmings but with a no-frills price.

c. The upholstery or interior lining of a motor vehicle. Cf. TRIM *sb.* 4 h.

1938 *Motor* 8 Nov. 2/1 (Advt.), 1937, colour scheme green, suitable leather trimming, comprehensively equipped. **1948** *Ibid.* 3 Nov. 385/1 The windscreen is slightly vee'd. Interior trimming is grey leather and the price is £3,775.

3. A beating, a drubbing; a sharp censure.

a **1518** [see TRIM *v.* 10]. **1675** V. ALSOP *Anti-Sozzo* Pref., They..would doubtless interpose, and bestow a deserved Trimming upon the Book, and make it doe Penance in its own sheets. **1763** LD. HALIFAX *Let.* 24 Sept., in *10th Rep. Hist. MSS. Comm.* App. I. 360 That superficial pert Gentleman has got a thorough trimming from the Duke. **1787** MRS. TRIMMER *Two Farmers* (1788) 21 It was a cruel trick and he deserves a good trimming for it. **1823** PYNE *Wine & Walnuts* (1824) I. xviii. 215 He expected another trimming on the usual topic, his vanity.

4. *Naut.* The adjustment of a ship's balance, load, sails, etc. as in TRIM *v.* 13, 15.

1627 CAPT. SMITH *Seaman's Gram.* viii. 34 The Master is to see the cunning of the ship, and trimming of the sailes. *Ibid.* xi. 54 The trimming of a ship doth much amend or impaire her sailing... To finde her trim, that is, how she will sail best.

5. The action of balancing or poising; the stowing or arrangement of cargo or coal in the hold of a ship in such a way as to keep her trim.

c **1796** T. TWINING *Trav. Amer.* (1894) 96 The wagon.. was so often depressed in the soft ground and old ruts on one side, that the passengers were obliged to press towards the other. Without this perpetual trimming we should certainly have been overturned. **1893** *Times* 10 July 13/6 The apparatus..has a working capacity of 100 tons per hour, and by it all trimming of the cargo is obviated. **1911** *Act 1 & 2 Geo. V*, c. 41 §1 Work done..in connection with the stowing or discharging of cargoes..or the trimming of coal on board that ship.

6. *fig.* Balancing between opinions or parties so as to remain in favour with both sides: see TRIM *v.* 17.

1696 C. LESLIE *Snake in Grass* (1697) 223 Having themselves serv'd all turns, that ever happen'd in their time,.. they had the Face to upbraid others for their Changing and Trimming. **1760** LAW *Spir. Prayer* II. 91 Management, prudence, or an artful trimming betwixt God and mammon, are here all in vain. **1827** SCOTT *Jrnl.* 22 Dec., An attempt to govern *par bascule*—by trimming betwixt the opposite parties. **1882** A. BAIN *Jas. Mill* iv. 194 The opposition was founded on Brougham's trimming to the Church.

7. a. *attrib.* and *Comb.*, as ***trimming-blade, -hook, -tool***; in sense 2 a, ***trimming-maker, -manufacturer, -merchant, -shop***. **b.** Special combs. (in some of which *trimming* may be the *ppl. a.*), as **trimming-basin**, a barber's basin; **trimming-board**, a board on which paper is trimmed; **trimming-can**: see quot.; **trimming flap** = *trimming tab* below; **trimming gear** *Aeronaut.*, apparatus for altering the angle of the tailplane of an aircraft; **trimming-joist**, a joist into which the end of a trimmer (sense 4) is fitted; **trimming-machine**: see quot.; **trimming-piece** = *trimming-joist*; **trimming plane** *Aeronaut.*, a control surface used to trim an aircraft; **trimming-room, -shear**: see quots.; **trimming spout**, a jointed spout delivering grain, sand, or the like from an elevator into a ship or truck, so as to distribute it over the available space (*Cent. Dict.*, *Suppl.* 1909); **trimming tab** *Aeronaut.*, an adjustable tab or aerofoil attached to a control surface, and used to trim the aircraft; *spec.* one which can be adjusted by the pilot in flight; **trimming-tank**, a water-tank in the bow or stern of a ship which is filled or emptied as the trim of the ship demands; **trimming wheel** *Aeronaut.*, a control wheel used to trim an aircraft by its action on the tailplane.

1683 *Lond. Gaz.* No. 1820/4 A Silver *Trimming-Bason and a Pot, two Silver Candle-sticks. **1868** *Rep. U.S. Commissioner Agric.* (1869) 255 Figure 8 represents the *trimming hook, and Figure 9 the *trimming blade. **1858** SIMMONDS *Dict. Trade*, **Trimming-can*, a small tin vessel with a spout, for pouring oil into a table-lamp. **1935** *Jrnl. R. Aeronaut. Soc.* XXXIX. 1038 The ailerons and elevators require *trimming flaps sufficient to enable the airplane to be flown 'hands off'. **1922** *Flight* XIV. 416/1 The tail plane, for which a very substantial worm *trimming gear is provided, has spars of straight taper, spindled out to an I section. **1933** *Aeroplane* 5 Apr. 606/1 There was some mechanical stiffness in the ailerons and no tail trimming gear had yet been rigged. **1667** PRIMATT *City & C. Build.* 81 Binding-Joysts with their *Trimming-Joysts. **1679** MOXON *Mech. Exerc.* viii. 137 These Joysts, Trimmers and Trimming Joysts, are all to be pinned into their respective Mortesses. **1877** KNIGHT *Dict. Mech.*, **Trimming-machine*, 1. a species of lathe for trimming the edges of stamped hollow-ware, such as sheet-metal pans... 2. (*Boot-making*), a machine for trimming the edge of uppers. **1819** *Lond. Post Off. Direct.* 84 Crooks' & Co. *Trimming-makers, 98 Wood-street. **1896** C. K. PAUL tr. *Huysman's En Route* II. vi. 262 The religious trimming-makers could trim these watered and plain silks with silver and gold. **1833** LOUDON *Encycl. Archit.* §234 The trimmer arch, *w*, is shown abutting against the *trimming piece. **1921** *Flight* XIII. 325/2 A *trimming plane is installed just ahead of the tail plane, which can be adjusted in flight from the pilot cabin by a wheel. **1881** *Guide Worcester Porcelain Wks.* 27 The ware.. is then taken..into the *trimming room, where any superfluous glaze is taken off. **1877** KNIGHT *Dict. Mech.*, **Trimming-shear*, a machine for trimming wool borders on ..mats. **1854** M. T. MORRALL *Hist. Needle Making* (ed. 2) 22 Which soon brought them [needles] into demand in the *trimming shops of London. **1935** *Aircraft Engineering* Dec. 297 The *trimming tab is quite revolutionary in its simplicity. **1942** W. SIMPSON *One of our Pilots is Safe* II. 42 To twist the trimming tab controls for rudder and elevator. **1950** *Engineering* 29 Sept. 269/3 All the control surfaces are provided with trimming tabs. **1903** *Q. Rev.* July 119 The *trimming-tanks..assist in keeping the boat on an even keel. **1941** D. MASTERS *So Few* 99 The *trimming wheel is a device which acts upon the tailplane in order to take the physical strain off the pilot. **1956** D. BARNHAM *One Man's Window* 153, I start turning the trimming wheel to ease me out of this dive.

'trimming, *ppl. a.* [f. as prec. + -ING².] That trims, in various senses of the verb; making trim, adorning, decorating; clipping, paring; *colloq.* or *slang*, 'stunning', 'rattling', excellent.

1559 MORWYNG *Evonym.* 187 We will referre amongste the trimmyng waters also, those waters wherwith whelkes and litle Pushes or Biles in the face, are made hoale. **1778** EARL CARLISLE in Jesse *Selwyn & Contemp.* (1844) III. 341 Such trimming gales as would make such a landsman as you stare. **1825** *Sporting Mag.* XV. 340, I did not minute this run, but..it must have been a trimming one. **1828** *Ibid.* XXI. 297 Lord Cleveland's hounds have..had a trimming day in their Bedale country. **1896** *Daily News* 31 Jan. 5/5 Expert dressmakers, forewomen, embroiderers, and trimming-women have been recruited for her wardrobe workroom.

b. Following a neutral or middle course between opposed principles or parties, esp. when this is done to stand in favour with both.

1683 *Trimmer Catechised* 1 You follow..the Old Trimming Jews..who sometimes worship God, and sometimes Baal. **1685** WOOD *Life* 23 Apr. (O.H.S.) III. 141 It was [a] luke-warm, trimming sermon. **1686** W. HOPKINS tr. *Ratramnus* Dissert. ii. (1688) 32 He now passeth at best but for a Trimming Catholick, with F. Cellot and his Friends. *c* **1780** SIR J. HARRIS in Bancroft *Hist. U.S.* (1876) VI. xlix. 359 An ambiguous and trimming answer was given. **1793** G. ROSE in *Ld. Auckland's Corr.* (1862) III. 165 The politics of his paper were very trimming.

Hence **'trimmingly** *adv.*

1718 *Free-thinker* No. 118 ¶3 He will neither philosophize Trimmingly..nor reason Intemperately. **1789** A. C. BOWER *Diaries & Corr.* (1903) 97 The next day I had the gout trimmingly [cf. quots. 1778–1828 above].

trimmle, obs. or dial. form of TREMBLE.

trimness ('trɪmnɪs). [f. TRIM *a.* + -NESS.] The quality or condition of being trim; neatness, smartness, spruceness, fineness.

1552 HULOET, Trymnes, *polities, ei.* **1565** COOPER *Thesaurus*, *Commendatur..verborum splendore et copia..* commended..for trimnes & plentie of woordes. **1576** FLEMING *Panopl. Epist.* 240 In turning them [his verses] in a foreigne tonge, much of their worthinesse and trimnesse is diminished. **1580** HOLLYBAND *Treas. Fr. Tong*, *Mignonneté*, trimmenesse, neatenesse, finenesse. **1727** BAILEY vol. II, *Trimness*, Neatness, Gayness, Spruceness in Dress. **1820** L. HUNT *Indicator* No. 61 (1822) II. 63 To shew the trimness of her ankles. **1886** J. R. REES *Diversions Bk.-worm* i. 8 The very wilderness..makes the trimness of other gardens appear paltry and forbidding.

trimnet: see under TRIMBOAT.

trimodal (traɪ'məʊdəl), *a.* [f. TRI- + MODE *sb.* + -AL.] Of a frequency curve or distribution: having three modes (MODE *sb.* 7 c). Of a phenomenon or property: described by such a distribution.

1927 *Jrnl. du Conseil* II. 354 Though the significance of the bimodal or trimodal selection in drift caught fish is open to argument, the fact of its existence is not. **1962** *Lancet* 5 May 968/1 The distribution of the values for 'relative incidence' is not a normal one but bimodal (or possibly even trimodal). **1978** *Nature* 3 Aug. 485/2 The results in Fig. 2 show a trimodal distribution when viability was determined after exposure to a standard dose of γ-radiation.

‖**'trimoda ne'cessitas.** *Old Eng. Hist.* Usually erron. **trinoda n.** [Late L., = *trimoda*, fem. of *trimodus* adj. 'of three kinds', (Isidore *Orig.* II. xvii, *De trimodo dicendi genere*), f. TRI- + *modus* mode, manner, *necessitas* necessity, exigency, need, obligation.

The phrase occurs only once, viz. in an OE. Charter attributed to K. Cædwalla of Wessex, 685–88, but actually in a MS. of about 975. Thence erroneously cited in 1614 by Selden as *trinoda necessitas*, whence in other 17th c. legal antiquaries and dictionaries, and thence in 19th c. historians and legal writers, and usually taken to mean *three-knotted* from L. *nōdus* knot. See article by W. H. Stevenson in *Eng. Hist. Rev.* Oct. 1914; also G. J. Turner in *Encycl. Brit.* (ed. 11) XXVII. 287/1.]

A collective appellation for the three great obligations upon land-holders in Anglo-Saxon times, of maintaining bridges and fortresses, and rendering military service, in OE. *brycgbót*, *burhbót*, and *fyrd*. (There was no collective OE. term for the three.)

c **975** *Charter of Cædualla* an. 680 in Kemble *Cod. Dipl.* I. 24 Ego cædualla rex..hanc donationis meæ cartulam scribere iussi, et absque trimoda necessitate totius christiani populi, id est arcis munitione, pontis emendatione, exercitii congestione, liberam perstrinxi. **1614** SELDEN *Titles of Honor* II. viii. 301 Those three; repairing of Bridges, Tax for Warre, and Castle gard, or repairing them: as of what no land should or could be discharged. They are called by a speciall name *Trinoda Necessitas* in a Patent by K. Cedwalla to Wilfrid first Bishop of Selesey. **1691** BLOUNT *Law Dict.* (ed. 2), *Trinoda necessitas*, i. Expeditio, Pontis, & Arcis reparatio. **1701** *Cowell's Interpr.*, *Trinoda Necessitas*, a threefold necessary Tax or Imposition, to which all Lands were subjected in Saxon Times. **1874** STUBBS *Const. Hist.* I. v. 95 The duty of 'burh-bot', which formed part of the *trinoda necessitas*, and was incumbent on every owner of land, threw the burden of repairing the fortifications on the land-owning townsmen of the particular *burh*. **1876** DIGBY *Real Prop.* i. 13 The *trinoda necessitas*, to which all lands were subject.

†**tri'modial,** *a.* *Obs. rare*$^{-0}$. [f. L. *trimodia* or *trimodium*, a measure of three modii or pecks, f. TRI- + *modius* peck + -AL¹.]

1656 BLOUNT *Glossogr.*, *Trimodial*, pertaining to a measure of three bushels.

trimontane (traɪ'mɒnteɪn), *a.* *nonce-wd.* [f. TRI- + L. *montānus*: see MONTANE, and cf. L. *Trimontium*, place-name.] Having, or having some relation to, three mountains or hills; in quots., belonging to Boston in Massachusetts. So **tri'mountain** *a.* in same sense; *sb.* (in *pl.*) a set or group of three hills.

1837 HAWTHORNE *Twice-told T.* (1851) II. i. 8 From this station,..Gage may have beheld his disastrous victory on Bunker Hill, (unless one of the tri-mountains intervened). **1840** —— *Biog. Sk., Mrs. Hutchinson* (1879) 169 The dusk has settled..upon..the Trimountain peninsula. **1885** E. C. STEDMAN in *Century Mag.* XXIX. 511 It has required some independence..for a trimontane [i.e. Bostonian] poet to be a progressive and speculative thinker.

tri'monthly, *a.* [TRI- 3.] **a.** Occurring every three months. **b.** Lasting or extending over three months.

1856 *Trans. Mich. Agric. Soc.* VII. 329 The Steamer Superior..made tri-monthly trips from Buffalo to Detroit. **1869** J. D. BURNS *Mem. & Rem.* vi. 104 Our trimonthly Communion. **1870** *Cornh. Mag.* July 66 The trimonthly homes of country squires. **1879** *Daily News* 1 Dec. 6/5 Annual as opposed to bi-monthly or tri-monthly budgets.

trimoric (traɪ'mɒrɪk), *a.* *Pros.* [f. TRI- + MORA¹ 3 + -IC.] Containing three *moræ*; having the length of three short syllables.

1901 P. GILES *Man. Compar. Philol.* §271 (ed. 2) 230 In the difference of accentuation between οἴκοι and οἶκοι we have probably traces of the difference between original dimoric and trimoric diphthongs. Final diphthongs when dimoric allow of the circumflex on a foregoing long syllable; when trimoric they do not.

trimorphic (traɪ'mɔːfɪk), *a.* [mod. f. Gr. τρίμορφ-ος (f. τρι-, TRI- + μορφή form) + -IC.] Having, or existing in, three forms: *spec.* **a.** *Bot.* Having flowers with pistils and stamens of three different relative lengths. **b.** *Zool.* Exhibiting three different forms (colorations, etc.) in different individuals of a species, or of a colony of polyps. **c.** *Cryst.* Of a substance: Occurring in crystals of three fundamentally different forms with the same chemical composition.

1866 DARWIN *Orig. Spec.* iv. (ed. 4) 111 The reciprocally dimorphic and trimorphic plants. **1870** NICHOLSON *Man. Zool.* 19 When two such distinct forms exist the species is said to be 'dimorphic', and when three are present it is called trimorphic. **1870** HOOKER *Stud. Flora* 147 Lythrum Salicaria.. Flowers trimorphic in respect of length of style and filaments in 3 sets of individuals. **1888** ROLLESTON & JACKSON *Anim. Life* 238 The worker bee is a dimorphic female; the soldiers and workers among the Termites are trimorphic with the fully-formed male and female.

So **'trimorph**, *Cryst.* a trimorphic substance, or each of its three different forms; **tri'morphism**, trimorphic condition, occurrence in three different forms (of a plant, animal, or crystalline substance); **tri'morphous** *a.* = *trimorphic.*

1860 WORCESTER, **Trimorphism*, the property of crystallizing in three different forms. *Dana.* **1862** DARWIN in *Life & Lett.* (1887) III. 301 If I can only prove..it [Lythrum] is a grand case of trimorphism, with three different pollens and three stigmas. **1866** —— *Orig. Spec.* ii. (ed. 4) 50 There are, however, other cases, namely of dimorphism and trimorphism,..which certain animals of either sex, and certain hermaphrodite plants, habitually present. Thus..the females of certain species of butterflies ..appear under two or even three conspicuously distinct forms. **1875** LUBBOCK *Wild Flowers* iii. 77 Of the foreign species of Oxalis some are dimorphous, some *trimorphous. **1878** GURNEY *Crystallogr.* 83 Titanium dioxide is trimorphous, for it not only crystallises as Anatase and Rutile, but also as Brookite. **1909** *Cent. Dict. Suppl.*, Trimorph.

'tri,motor. Also tri-motor. [f. TRI- + MOTOR *sb.*] An aeroplane fitted with three engines. Cf. TRI-JET.

1923 *Glasgow Herald* 1 Jan. 8 The aeroplane which it is proposed to use will be a tri-motor. **1931** *Technol. Rev.* Nov. 66/2 The Ford trimotors are *tin geese*, an amphibian is often a *duck.* **1936** *New Yorker* 14 Mar. 25/1 His favorite machines are a tri-motor Junker and a silver-and-black steel Immelmann. **1965** C. D. EBY *Siege of Alcázar* (1966) 13 The pueblo of Getafe..in 1936 boasts the busiest airport in Spain, but there are only a few silent trimotors on the airstrips. **1977** H. FAST *Immigrants* IV. 226 He lay awake most of the night, reliving his experience on the big trimotor plane. **1981** R. THOMAS *Mordida Man* xviii. 158 The old gentleman said he had flown in everything from Ford trimotors to 747s.

'tri-,motored, *a.* Also trimotored. [f. TRI- + MOTOR *sb.* + -ED[2].] Of an aeroplane: fitted with three engines.

1927 *Times* (Weekly ed.) 9 June 632/3 Tri-motored aeroplanes capable of landing on the water..were essential. **1929** *Sat. Even. Post* 7 Dec. 63/1 The giant tri-motored Ford planes of this line. **1968** MILLER & SAWERS *Technical Devel. Mod. Aviation* ii. 33 The totals..may suggest the general level of operating costs of the tri-motored aircraft in the United States in 1932–33. **1980** R. BUTLER *Blood-Red Sun at Noon* (1981) I. ii. 28 One of the big tri-motored Junkers.

trimountain: see TRIMONTANE.

Trimphone ('trɪmfəʊn). Also trimphone. [f. TRIM *a.* + PHONE *sb.*[2]] The proprietary name of a type of lightweight telephone with a high-pitched quavering (or 'warbling') ringing tone.

1965 *Times* 11 May 6/7 The new instrument is called a Trimphone and, in the words of the Post Office, it does not ring, it warbles. **1969** *Daily Tel.* 18 Apr. 23/2 The £1 charged is also removed from the cost of installing a Trimphone—the one that 'warbles'. **1973** *Trade Marks Jrnl.* 26 Sept. 1852/2 *Trimphone*..B 986,992. Telephones; telephone receivers; telephone transmitters; telephone dialling apparatus; and parts and fittings..for all the aforesaid..The Post Office. **1973** J. WAINWRIGHT *Pride of Pigs* 166 Quince hooked his fingers through the carrying handle of the Trimphone telephone handset. **1977** J. GARDNER *Werewolf Trace* i. 18 The trimphone whistled and Greg picked it up, nodding at the voice in his ear.

trimsie: see TRICKSY *a.* 1 (quot. 1577).

trim-tram ('trɪm'træm), *sb.* (*a.*) *Obs.* exc. *dial.* Also 9 *dial.* **trin tran.** [In I. app. f. TRIM *a.*, with varied reduplication; in II. and III., app. whimsical applications of I.; but perh. distinct words.]

I. (Cf. *flim-flam, jim-jam, whim-wham.*)

†**1.** app. A personal ornament of little value; a pretty toy or trifle; a gew-gaw. *Obs.*

1523 SKELTON *Garl. Laurel* 130 A trym tram for an horse myll it were a nyse thyng. *a* **1529** —— *El. Rummyng* 76 After the Sarasyns gyse, With a whym wham, Knyt with a trym tram, Vpon her brayne pan. **1548** PATTEN *Exped. Scotl.* Pref. c iv, From y[e] fondnes of his trimtrams and gugaws. **1560** BECON *Jewel of Joy* Wks. II. 19 b, A frenche hode wyth an edge of golde, besydes pearles and precious stons and suche other trime trames. **1667** F. VERNON *Oxonium* 24 [Undergraduates] making Trimtrams with Rushes and flowers.

†**2.** An absurd or silly device or practice; an absurdity; a piece of nonsense. *Obs.*

1533 MORE *Answ. Poysoned Bk.* Wks. 1114/2, I haue as you se so wel auoyded his ginnes and his grinnes & all his trimtrams. *c* **1550** R. WEVER *Lusty Juventus* in Hazl. *Dodsley* II. 66 Holy kneeling, holy censings, And a hundred trim-trams mo. **1568** W. FULWOOD *Enimie Idlenesse* I. B vij, Whether that sorcerers do vse to ryde vpon a Byzom, and practise such other like trim trams. **1582** STANYHURST *Æneis* II. (Arb.) 46 But loa, to what purpose do I chat such ianglerye trim trams? **1708** *Brit. Apollo* No. 16. 2/2, I have some Thoughts with an old Trim Tram To venture on the Marriage Whim Wham.

3. In riming jingles; sometimes referring to similarity or equal treatment of two of different position. Now *dial.* (Cf. *giff-gaff.*)

1583 MELBANCKE *Philotimus* D iij b, Trim tram, neither good for God nor man. *a* **1627** MIDDLETON & ROWLEY *Span. Gipsy* IV. iii, Trim, tram, hang master, hang man! **1681** T. FLATMAN *Heraclitus Ridens* No. 19 (1713) I. 131 Well, Trim tram, like Master like Man. **1760–62** SMOLLETT *Sir L. Greaves* xiii, They thought you as great a nincompoop as your squire—trim tram, like master, like man. **1877** T. GIBSON *Leg.*, etc. *Westmoreld.* 50 Trin tran, sike like master sike like man, A lazy life brings scant or scan.

†**4.** *attrib.* or as *adj.*

1615 SIR E. HOBY *Curry-combe* v. 223 Wee dare not say the Master and man might bee trim-tram and confederate. **1632** BROME *North. Lasse* I. v, What a Trim-tram trick is this? the Master and the man both brain-cras'd. **1762** BRIDGES *Burlesque Homer* (1772) 411 (Farmer) He's telling some long trim-tram story.

II. †**5.** A shrimp-net having a triangular wooden frame resting on the ground in front of the beam (*Funk's Stand. Dict.*). *attrib.* **trim-tram man**, one who uses this net in shrimping. *Obs.*

1590 *Cal. St. Papers, Dom.* 692 Regulations for hooks.. whitebait, shrimp leaps and trim trams. **1746** R. GRIFFITHS *Ess. Conserv. Thames* Index 277 Draggermen (or Trim-trammen).

III. 6. A lich-gate; also a gate which opens in a V-shaped enclosure, a kissing-gate. *dial.*

1842 *Church Builder* Apr. 45 *note*, In..parts of Devonshire and Cornwall Lichgates are called Trim-trams. **1893** *Wilts. Gloss.*, *Trim-tram*, a gate which swings in a V-shaped enclosure of post and rail, so as to prevent cattle from passing through.

‖**Trimurti** (tri'mu:rti). Also Tri-murti and with small initial. [Skr., f. *tri* three + *-mūrti* consisting or formed of.] **1.** In Hinduism, the gods Brahma, Vishnu, and Shiva, conceived as aspects of one ultimate reality. Also *transf.* Cf. TRIAD 2 b.

1836 J. F. DAVIS *Chinese* II. xiii. 107 Their own *Tri-murti*, or Triad of *Brahma, Vishnu*, and *Siva.* **1877** MONIER WILLIAMS *Hinduism* vii. 87 These three gods are the first and highest manifestations of the Eternal Essence, and.. constitute the well-known *Tri-mūrti*, or Triad of divine forms which characterises Hindūism. **1895** E. W. HOPKINS *Relig. of India* xvi. 447 The votaries of these subsects worshipped some, the rising sun, some the setting sun, while some again worshipped the noonday sun, and others, all three as a *tri-mūrti.* **1921** *Encycl. Relig. & Ethics* XII. 457/2 Serving as it does to reconcile rival monotheisms with one another and with the philosophic doctrine of the absolute, the theory of the Tri-mūrti presents no such close similarity to the Christian doctrine of the Trinity as to render derivation from Christian influences either necessary or probable. **1954** D. S. SARMA in K. W. Morgan *Relig. of Hindus* 34 The three most important functions of that Spirit, the creation, preservation, and destruction of the world, were associated with the great gods Brahmā, Vishnu, and Siva. Thus arose the doctrine of the Hindu Trinity, the Trimūrti. **1980** M. GILBERT *Death of Favourite Girl* ii. 23 Brahma, the creator, with Vishnu, the preserver and Siva, the destroyer..form the Trimurti—that is, the great Hindu Triad.

2. A statue with three faces representing Brahma, Vishnu, and Shiva.

1877 MONIER WILLIAMS *Hinduism* vii. 87 There is a well-known Tri-mūrti sculptured out of the rock in the caves of Elephanta, at Bombay. **1920** E. B. HAVELL *Handbk. Indian Art* III. i. 203 The Bodhisattva holds in his right hand Vishnu's blue lotus, and his tiara bears the three jewelled sun-discs like the Vishnu in the Trimūrti sculpture of Elephanta. **1953** B. ROWLAND *Art & Architecture of India* xvii. 188 The treatment of the subjects, ranging from the *Trimurti*..to a panel like the Betrothal of Siva and Pārvatī.. reveal the extraordinary ability and scope of the Dravidian sculptor. **1981** G. PRIESTLAND *Priestland's Progress* viii. 123 A statue with three faces, like the sublime Hindu *trimurti* in the cave temples of Elephanta.

trimuscular: see TRI- 1.

trin (trɪn). [perh. f. TRINE *sb.*, conformed to TWIN.] *pl.* Three children or young born at one birth: = TRINE *sb.* 3. Also *sing.* one of such; also *attrib.* or as *adj.* Cf. THRIN *sb.*

1831 *Blackw. Mag.* XXIX. 998 The teeming matron is near her time, and from her bulk you may back her for trins. **1844** STEPHENS *Bk. Farm* (1849) I. 597/2 In a small flock of 50 Leicester ewes, 48 of them had twins, and 2 trins. **1875** FURNIVALL in *Lovelich's Grail* I. 291 *note*, Trins are always born: two males and one female. **1887** —— in *J. Lane's Cont. Sqr.'s T.* p. viii. *note*, Spenser..made the fay-born trin brethren, Priamond, Dyamond, and Triamond, fight Camballo..to see which of them could win Canace.

b. *transf.* (*Min.*) A compound crystal of three individuals, a trilling.

1868 DANA *Min.* (ed. 5) 805 *Tridymite*,..in allusion to its compound forms of three individuals, or trins, from τρίδυμος.

Trinacrian (traɪ'neɪkrɪən), *a.* [f. L. *Trīnacria* Sicily, a. Gr. Τρινακρία, taken as f. τρι-, TRI- + ἄκρα point, cape; but orig. Θρινακίη, f. θρῖναξ trident.] Of Sicily, Sicilian; hence, three-pointed.

1640 HOWELL *Dodona's Gr.* (1645) 49 The Trinacrian Vespers, and Bartholomean Massacre, were nothing to this. **1667** MILTON *P.L.* II. 661 Vex'd Scylla bathing in the Sea that parts Calabria from the hoarce Trinacrian shore. **1871** RUSKIN *Fors Clav.* x. (1896) I. 201 Only the Trinacrian legs of [the Isle of] Man.

So **trinacrite** ('trɪnəkraɪt) *Min.*, a brown variety of PALAGONITE. (Now considered as a rock.)

1854 DANA *Min.* (ed. 4) II. 166 Trinacrite..is dull brown and cleavable or micaceous, and is mixed with.. Siderosilicite. **1868** WATTS *Dict. Chem.* V. 240 *Siderosilicite*, a mineral forming, together with trinacrite, a brown mass on the tufa..at Cape Passaro, the southernmost point of Sicily.

trinal ('traɪnəl), *a.* Also 6–7 trinall, 7 trienall. [ad. late L. *trīnāl-is* (Adamnan), f. L. *trīn-us*, pl. *trīnī* three each, threefold: see -AL[1].]

1. Composed or consisting of three parts; threefold; triple; trine.

1590 SPENSER *F.Q.* I. xii. 39 Singing before th' eternall Majesty, In their trinall triplicities on hye. **1622** P. HANNAY *Sonn.* xx, O Trinall-one, one God and Persons three. **1629** MILTON *Ode Nativity* 11 Wherwith he wont at Heav'ns high Councel-Table, To sit the midst of Trinal Unity. *a* **1843** SOUTHEY in *Fraser's Mag.* (1868) LXXVIII. 118 Tercets, or the trinal verse of Dante. **1871** FRASER *Life Berkeley* x. 396 The relations which contribute to form distance, and trinal extension. **1907** F. HARRISON *Philos. Common Sense* p. xxviii, The synthesis is necessarily dual, or often trinal, in idea.

†**2.** *Astrol.* = TRINE *a.* 2. *Obs. rare*$^{-1}$.

1561 EDEN *Arte Nauig.* II. vii. 33 Trinall aspecte, is when betwene the planettes shal be foure signes, which are .120. degrees.

3. *Gram.* Applied to a 'number' or inflected form expressing three. Also *absol.* as *sb.*

1853 *Proc. Philol. Soc.* (1854) IV. 60 A trinal as well as a singular, a dual, and a plural number. **1881** *Trans. Victoria Inst.* 26 The form of the plural in some languages shows that it was originally a trinal.

Hence **tri'nality**, the quality of being trinal.

1864 SHEDD *Hist. Chr. Doctr.* III. i. (1869) 243 Some of the theologies of pagan antiquity contain intimations of trinality in the Divine Being.

trinary ('traɪnərɪ), *a.* and *sb. rare.* [ad. late L. *trīnāri-us* of three kinds (Isidore *Orig.* III. vi): cf. L. *ternārius* TERNARY.]

A. *adj.* Consisting or composed of a set of three; threefold; triple; ternary.

1474 CAXTON *Chesse* IV. ii. (1883) 166 For the trynary nombre conteyneth iii parties whiche make a perfect nombre. **1882** G. ALLEN in *Nature* 17 Aug. 374 The inner palea exhibits rudiments of two sepals,..making up, with the outer palea, a single trinary whorl. **1884** MARY BOOLE in *Athenæum* 23 Aug. 238/1 Ascribing to the Eternal a dividedness projected from the trinary nature of the human faculties.

†**B.** *sb.* A set or group of three; a triad; a trio.

1596 FITZ-GEFFRAY *Sir F. Drake* (1881) 22 The gracefull Graces faire triplicitie, Of moderne Poets rarest trinarie. **1654** VILVAIN *Epit. Ess.* IV. lxxx. 83 In England a Trinary of Peers Renound for riches was in divers yeers.

trinch, trinchet: see TRENCH, TRINKET *sb.*[3]

trinck, trinckam, trinckle, etc.: see TRINK, TRINKUM, TRINKLE, etc.

Trin,coma'lee. Name of a harbour on the north-east coast of Sri Lanka: *attrib.* in **Trincomalee wood**: see quots.

1842 *Penny Cycl.* XXIV. 448/1 The Trincomalee-wood used at Madras for making the Massoola boats is the produce of Berrya Ammonilla. **1866** *Treas. Bot.* 138 The tree [*Berrya Ammonilla*] is a native of the Philippine Islands and Ceylon,..and is considered the best wood in the island for making oil casks... It is exported in large quantities under the name of Trincomalee wood.

trincum, trind: see TRINKUM, TREND *v.*

trindle ('trɪnd(ə)l), *sb.* Forms: 4–6 trindel, (5 -ylle, 6 -al, -ell, -ill(e; 4 tryndall, 5 -yl, -el, 5–6 -elle, -yll, -ylle, 6 -ell, -ull, tryndle, trynle, tryneyll, 7–9 *Sc.* trinle, 9 *Sc.* trinnel, trinnle), 6– trindle; also 8–9 *Sc.* trintle. [Early ME. *trindel*, a parallel form to TRENDLE, corresp. to MHG. *trindel*, from **trendilo-*; see also the various *trind-* forms under TREND *v.*, and cf. TRUNDLE *v.*]

1. A wheel; *esp.* a 'trundle' or lantern-wheel in a mill; also, the wheel of a wheelbarrow: = TRENDLE *sb.* 2, TRUNDLE *sb.* 1, 2. *Obs.* exc. *dial.*

c **1343** *Durham Acc. Rolls* (Surtees) 543 In j pari de Trindelis. [**1391** *Mem. Ripon* (Surtees) III. 106 In tryndallo pro j porta infra cymiterium, 3*d.*] **14..** *Nom.* in Wr.-Wülcker 696/13 *Hec troclia*, a trindylle. **1455–6** *Durham Acc. Rolls* (Surtees) 241 Pro j pare de le tryndylles empto pro molendino de Milburn. **1531** *Lett. & Papers Hen. VIII*, V. 180 For working of the tryndyll of the myll at Hampnes Castell. **1587** *Shuttleworths' Acc.* (Chetham Soc.) 41 For a pere of myllne trynles, ij[s] x[d]. **1594** *Ibid.* 89 For makinge of a whelebarrowe trindle iiij[d]. **1786** BURNS *The Inventory* 33 Ae auld wheelbarrow..I made a poker o' the spin'le, An' my auld mother brunt the trin'le. **1855** E. WAUGH *Sk. Lanc. Life* (1857) 65 He..order't th' wheelbarrow wi' spon-new trindle t' be fotcht.

†**b.** A spindle: cf. TRENDLE *sb.* 5. *Obs.*

1483 *Cath. Angl.* 393/2 A Tryndelle of A webster, *insubulus* (A. *infusillus*), *troclea.* *Ibid.* 412/2 A Weffer tryndylle, *insubulus, troclea.*

†**2.** A roll or coil (?) of wax taper, used for light in mediæval churches. (Its nature is disputed: see quots. 1796 and 1852.) *Obs.* exc. *Hist.*

(App. something different from TRENDLE *sb.* 3.)

1537 in *Reliquary* Jan. (1893) 40 Itm' ij new tryneylls of waxe lytylle wasted. **1547** Edw. VI. *Injunct.* §28 Also, that they shall take awaie, vtterly extincte, and destroye, all shrines,..candelstickes, tryndilles or rolles of waxe, pictures, paintynges [etc.]. **1559** Q. Eliz. *Injunct.* §23 Trindals, and Rolles of wax. [**1796** Pegge *Anonym.* (1809) 42 *Trindilles* or *trindals*..may mean cakes of wax, which being round are therefore called *trindles*, or *trundles*. **1852** Rock *Ch. of Fathers* III. ix. 237 In some..instances it is likely that these long strings of wax taper were..coiled up..into folds, so as to form what we are to understand by *trindles* or rolls of wax.]

† **3.** Something of rounded form, as a pellet of sheep's or goat's dung. *Obs.*

1607 Topsell *Four-f. Beasts* (1658) 203 The same Physitian prescribeth Goats trindles to be drunk in Wine against the Jaundise. **1660** Howell *Parly Beasts* 123 The very trindles drunck in wine are good against the Jaundise.

b. See quot. 1825. *dial.*

16.. in *Daily News* 27 Dec. (1911) 3/2 To make a Haggisse Puddinge. Take a Calfe Trindle, a quart of Creame, halfe a dozin Egges, a Manshett, a pound of Currans, with Cinamon, Ginger, Nuttmegge, Mace, and Cloves, and Suger, and a little Rose water. **1825** Jamieson, *Trinnel*, calf's guts.

4. *Bookbinding.* Each of several flat pieces of thin wood or metal, shaped something like toy horse-shoe magnets, by which (in pairs) the stitched, glued, and rounded back of a book is held flat while the front edge is ploughed.

On the withdrawal of the trindles, the back resumes its convex form and the front edge becomes concave.

1818 *Art Bk.-binding* 16 Put the trindles between the back of the book and paste-boards. **1885** C. G. W. Lock *Workshop Receipts* Ser. iv. 239/2 A piece of thin millboard or 'trindle' is put between the hind board and the book.

'trindle, *v. Obs.* or *dial.* Forms: see prec. [A parallel form to trendle. Form history not clear. The OE. *tryndyl-* seems to imply derivation from the grade *trund-*: see trend *v.*]

† **1.** *trans.* To make round, to round. (only OE.)

c **1000** Ælfric *Voc.* in Wr.-Wülcker 152/5 *Circumtectum*, tryndyled reaf.

2. *trans.* To cause (a wheel, etc.) to revolve; to cause (a ball, hoop, cask, etc.) to roll along a surface; to trundle.

1595 Barnfield *Cynthia* x, A golden Ball was trindled from aboue. **1637** Rutherford *Lett.* (1862) I. 272 He hath other things to do than to play with me and to trindle an apple with me. **1808–18** in Jamieson, *Trintle, trinle, v. a.*

3. *intr.* To revolve or turn round (as a wheel, spindle, etc.); to roll (as a ball, hoop, cylinder, etc.) along a surface.

c **1400** *Ywaine & Gaw.* 3259 Sir Ywain..strake his nek-bane right in sonder,..His hevid trindeld on the sand. **1530** Palsgr. 762/2, I tryndell, as a boule or a stone dothe, *je roulle.* **1815** Scott *Guy M.* xlviii, If we were ance out o' this trindling kist o' a thing. **1894** Black *Highl. Cousins* I. 35 Your ball strikes the face of the hill and..comes quietly trintle, trintle, trintling down the slope.

trindle-bed, -tail: see trundle-bed, -tail.

trine (traɪn), *a.* and *sb.* Also 4–7 tryne. [a. F. *trin, trine* (13th c. in Littré):—L. *trīn-us* threefold, f. *trēs, tria* three.]

A. *adj.* **1.** Threefold; triple.

trine compass, threefold space, i.e. heaven, earth, and sea.

c **1386** Chaucer *Sec. Nun's T.* 45 The eterneel loue and pees That of the tryne compas lord and gyde is. *c* **1450** *Cov. Myst.* ix. (1841) 88 Recomendyng me to that Godhyd that is tryne in trone. *a* **1550** Bellenden in *Bannatyne Poems* (Hunter. Cl.) 8/153 Thow Godheid trine, rignand in vnitie. **1656** Blount *Glossogr.*, *Trine, trinus*, of three years old, or pertaining to the number three. **1675** Baxter *Cath. Theol.* i. i. 40 By his Trine influx of Power, Wisdom, and Goodness. *a* **1711** Ken *Hymns Festiv.* Poet. Wks. 1721 I. 248 To teach the Faith of Godhead Trine. **1735** Berkeley *Reasons* §17 The trine dimensions of a cube generated by motion. **1868** Gladstone *Juv. Mundi* viii. (1870) 227 He [Zeus] is the governor of the air..; the eldest of the trine brotherhood.

b. ***trine immersion*** (also ***trin-immersion***), the immersion of a person three times in baptism, in the name of the three Persons of the Trinity. So ***trine affusion, aspersion.***

1637 Gillespie *Eng. Pop. Cerem.* ii. ix. 37 When the Arrians abused Trin-immersion in Baptisme. *Ibid.*, The Ceremony of Trin-immersion. **1657** J. Watts *Dipper Sprinkled* 54 She hath given over her old way of the Trine-immersion, and is upon the new path of Trine-aspersion. **1884** G. T. Stokes in *Contemp. Rev.* Apr. 600 If immersion cannot be used, trine affusion may suffice, accompanied by fasting.

2. *Astrol.* Denoting the 'aspect' of two heavenly bodies which are a third part of the zodiac, i.e. 120°, distant from each other. Also, Connected with or relating to a trine aspect. Also *fig.* Favourable, benign: cf. quots. 1581, 1614 in B. 2.

1477 Norton *Ord. Alch.* vi. in Ashm. *Theat. Chem. Brit.* (1652) 100 Cause them to looke with a Trine aspect. **1594** Blundevil *Exerc.* iv. xliv. (1636) 502 You shall find the Moone to be in a trine aspect with the Sunne. **1605** Drayton *Man in Moon* 459 How the Signes in their Triplicities, Be simpathizing in their Trine consents. **1609** C. Butler *Fem. Mon.* v. (1623) Lj, If hir Princely Grace Vouchsafe with Trine Aspect reply to make. **1790** Sibly *Occult Sc.* (1792) I. 143 A trine aspect, Δ.

B. *sb.* **1.** A group of three; a triad.

1552 Lyndesay *Monarche* 5681 Gregor, Ambrose, and Augustyne, With Confessoris, ane tryumphand tryne. **1591** Sylvester *Du Bartas* i. ii. 383 Rightly may we call those Trines (Fire, Aire and Water) but Heav'n's Concubines. *c* **1614** Sir W. Mure *Dido & Æneas* iii. 291 O furyes! O Vindictive tryne. *a* **1711** Ken *Hymns Evang.* Poet. Wks. 1721 I. 40 Believe, repent, and love, this easy Trine. **1874** A. J. Ellis in *Phil. Trans.* XXIII. 16 A *duodene*..consists of 12 tones, forming four *trines* of major Thirds arranged in three *quaternions* of Fifths.

b. *spec.* The Trinity; in first quot. = trinity 1 b.

a **1568** *Bannatyne Poems* (Hunter. Cl.) 79/7 Off a will, substance, and equalite,..To be laud in tryne and vnite. **1613** W. Browne *Brit. Past.* i. v, Thou by whose hand the sacred Trine did bring Us out of bonds. *a* **1711** Ken *Hymnarium* Poet. Wks. 1721 II. 68 O holy, holy, holy Trine, Me for thyself refine. **1827** Keble *Chr. Y.*, *Trin. Sunday*, Eternal One, Almighty Trine!

2. *Astrol.* A trine aspect. Phr. ***in trine.***

1581 N. Woodes *Conflict Consc.* ii. i. Biij, Now murthering Mars..With amiable tryne, apply to my beame. **1614** Tomkis *Albumazar* ii iii, Coniunctions, And fortunate aspects of Trine and Sextile. **1761** *Brit. Mag.* II. 465 The planets, with their conjunctions, oppositions, signs, circles, cycles, trines, and trigons. **1837** Whewell *Hist. Induct. Sc.* (1857) I. 176 When she was nearly in trine, and in sextile with the sun.

3. *pl.* Three children (or young) at a birth; triplets.

1628–9 *Faversham Par. Reg.* (MS.), Samuell..Elizabeth ..Marie..Trines of John Juyce [and] Susan. **1706** *All Saints, Canterb. Par. Reg.* (MS.), Jane and Mary 2 of ye trines of Wm Plummer [buried]. **1844** Stephens *Bk. Farm* II. 610 The two lambs which constituted the trines were.. taken away to relieve the ewes. **1867** J. Campbell *Balmerino* iv. v. 325 He..baptized in the parish three times trines.

† **trine,** *v.*[1] *Obs.* Also 4–5 tryne, 5 trien. [Aphetic f. ME. *atrīne-n, etrīne-n*, atrine:—OE. *æthrīnan* to touch, f. *æt-* at- + *hrīnan* to touch.] *trans.* To touch.

c **1200** *Trin. Coll. Hom.* 21 Whu shal þat wurðe, siððen wapman me ne trineð? **1340–70** *Alex. & Dind.* 132 Sent was a vois sone fro heuene, þat non trinde þe tres. **1393** Langl. *P. Pl.* C. xxi. 87 For alle hij were vnhardy þat houede þer oþer stode, To touche hym oþer to tryne [*v.rr.* trien, trine, trinen, turne] hym oþer to take hym doun and graue hym. *c* **1400** *St. Alexius* (Trinity) 429 Ac hy ne dorste hem tryne [*Laud* ouer him trine].

† **trine,** *v.*[2] *Obs.* Also 4–6 tryne, 5 treyne, trene; *pa. t.* 4 tron(e, 5 treyned, trynyd. [Of Scand. origin: cf. OSwed. *trina* (pret. *trān*) to go, step, march, Da. *trine*, older *trene* (pret. *trēn*).]

intr. To go, march, step. (Chiefly in allit. verse.)

13.. *E.E. Allit. P.* C. 101 Then he tron on þo tres & þay her tramme ruchen. ? *a* **1400** *Morte Arth.* 1757 With trompes thay trine, and trappede stedes. *Ibid.* 4189 Than the traytoure..Trynnys in with a trayne tresone to wirke. *a* **1400–50** *Alexander* 4888 He..Gas him vp be degreces to þe grete lawe, Trenes to þe topward þat touched to þe cloudis. **1560** Rolland *Crt. Venus* i. 189 [The twa] did tryne with diueris countenance.

b. *trans.* with cognate obj.

13.. *E.E. Allit. P.* A. 1112 To-warde þe þrone þay trone a tras. *Ibid.* B. 976 Trynande ay a hyȝe trot þat torne neuer dorsten. *a* **1400** *Pistill Susan* 225 But ȝit we trinet [*v.r.* trynyd] a trot, þat traytor to take. ? *a* **1400** *Morte Arth.* 4055 The trays of the traytoure he trynys fulle euenne.

c. apparently preserved in Rogues' Cant.

1622 Fletcher *Beggar's Bush* iii. iii, *Hig.*..Let the Quire Cuffin: And Herman Beck strine, and trine to the Ruffin. *Clause.* Now interpret this unto him. *Hig.*..Let the Constable, Iustice, and Divell go hang. **1815** Scott *Guy M.* xxviii, No wonder that you scour the cramp-ring, and trine to the cheat sae often. **1826** —— *Woodst.* xxxvi, We trine to the nubbing cheat to-morrow.

d. (Perh. arising from a shortening of the phrase *trine to the cheats* = go to the gallows, be hanged). To hang (*intr.* and *trans.*).

1567 Harman *Caveat* 37 Their end is..hanginge, whiche they call trininge in their language. *Ibid.* 85, I towre [see] the strummel [straw] trine [hang] vpon thy nabchet [cap]. *Ibid.* 86 Tryning on the chates..hange on the gallowes. **1608** Dekker *Lanthorne & Candle-light* Bij b, [From thence] to be Tryn'de on the Chates. **1610** Rowlands *Martin Mark-all* Eij, If you will make a word for the Gallous, you must put thereto this word *Treyning*, which signifies hanging; and so Treyning Cheate is as much to say, hanging things, or the Gallous. *a* **1700** B. E. *Dict. Cant. Crew*, *Trine*, to Hang; also Tyburn. *Ibid.* s.v. *Wap*, Let her trine for a Make,..let her hang for a Half-penny.

trine, *v.*[3] *rare.* [f. trine *a.* or *sb.*]

1. *trans.* To put or join in a trine aspect.

a **1700** Dryden *Pal. & Arcite* iii. 389 By fortune he [Saturn] was now to Venus trined, And with stern Mars in Capricorn was join'd. **1840** Browning *Sordello* iv. 603 'Tis done! and now deter Who may the Tuscan—once Jove trined for her—From Friedrich's path!

2. To make a trine or triad of.

1834 *Tait's Mag.* I. 658/1 The Isthmian *now* of each Eternity, Trining the has-been, being, and to-be.

† **'trinehood.** *Obs. rare*$^{-1}$. In 5 tryne-hode. [f. trine *a.* + -hood.] Threefold state; Trinity.

1471 Ripley *Comp. Alch.* Pref. i. in Ashm. *Theat. Chem. Brit.* (1652) 121 O Tryne hode in Deite.

† **'trinely,** *adv. Obs. rare*$^{-1}$. [f. trine *a.* + -ly[2].] Triply, in a threefold manner.

1606 Sylvester *Du Bartas* ii. iv. ii. *Magnif.* 1341 The greater World hath but one Sun to shine, The lesser but one Soule, both but one God, In Essence One, in Person Trinely-odde.

trinervate (traɪ'nɜːvət), *a. Nat. Hist.* [f. tri- + L. *nervus* nerve + -ate[2]; cf. mod.L. *trinervis.*] Having three nerves or veins. Also **tri'nerve, tri'nerved** *adjs.*, three-nerved.

1811 A. T. Thomson *Lond. Disp.* ii. (1818) 45 Thin, cordate..trinerved leaves. **1819** *Pantologia*, *Trinerve leaf*,.. having three nerves or unbranched vessels meeting in the base of the leaf. *Ibid.*, Trinervate. **1866** *Treas. Bot.*, *Trinerved, trinervis*, having three ribs, all proceeding from the base. **1891** *Cent. Dict.*, Trinervate..Trinerve.

trinfauld, var. thrinfald *Obs.*, threefold.

tring (trɪŋ). *Ornith. rare* [ad. mod.L. *tringa* (Linn.), generic name, formed app. after Gr. τρύγγας, name of some bird.] Any species of bird of the genus *Tringa* (which name is more frequent in use), commonly called Sandpipers. So **'tringine** *a.*, of or pertaining to the genus *Tringa*; **'tringoid** *a.*, resembling the genus *Tringa*.

[**1674** Ray *Words, Water Fowl* 90 Tringa major.] **1752** J. Hill *Hist. Anim.* 476 The red-legged Tringa. **1757** [see *coot-footed* s.v. coot *sb.*[1] 5]. **1757** *Phil. Trans.* L. 255 This bird is like in shape to most others of the tringa or snipe kind. **1796** Morse *Amer. Geog.* I. 212 Red coot footed Tring, *Tringa Rufa*. Spotted Tring, *Tringa maculata*. Little Trings of the sea shore. Sand Birds. **1816** J. Bigelow in *N. Eng. Jrnl. Med. & Surg.* V. 338 A species of plover or of tringa.

tringham: see trinkum.

tringle ('trɪŋg(ə)l). [a. F. *tringle* (16th c.), in Cotgr. *tringle, trangle*, 'a Curtaine-rod; and more generally, a peece of round yron, or wire, ..vsed for [various purposes]; also, a flat sticke, or lath-like peece of wood'. In OF. *tingle* beam (1328 in Godef.): cf. mod.Du. *tengel* flat lath.

Hatz.-Darm. derive the OF. from the Du. word; but as the latter is app. only mod.Du., and not mentioned even by Kilian (see Franck, Van Wijk), it may be from the Fr. word.]

a. *Arch.* (See quot. 1696.) **b.** A curtain-rod, or any long slender rod. Cf. trangle.

1696 Phillips (ed. 5), *Tringle*, a little square Member, which is directly upon every Triglyph, under the Platband of the Architrave; from whence hang down the Pendant Drops of the Dorick Order [**1706** (ed. Kersey), *adds*] A Curtain-Rod, a Lath that reaches from one Bed-post to another. **1704** in J. Harris *Lex. Techn.* I. **1881** W. E. Dickson *Organ-Build* xii. 151 A long rod or tringle of wood, connecting all these arms by pins passing through them and itself.

tringle, variant of trinkle *v.*[1], to trickle.

‖ **tringlette** (trɛ̃glɛt). [F. (1690 in Furetière), dim. of *tringle*: see above.] A pointed stick used to open the cames or grooved leaden bars which hold the panes in fretwork or diamond-paned windows (Knight *Dict. Mech.* 1877). (In Fr. also, the piece of glass in such a pane, Littré.)

tringum-trangum: see trinkum.

Trinidadian (trɪnɪ'dædɪən, -'deɪdɪən), *a.* and *sb.* [f. *Trinidad* + -ian; see Trinidado.]

A. *sb.* A native or inhabitant of Trinidad.

1910 L. O. Inniss (*title*) Trinidad and Trinidadians. **1948** *Trinidad Guardian* 24 June 1/2 (*heading*) Trinidadian faces fraud indictment. **1957** [see the adj. below]. **1966** *Listener* 23 June 923/3 White men in Trinidad had only taught the Trinidadians how to play cricket because there were not enough of their own sort to make a team. **1978** 'A. York' *Tallant for Disaster* ii. 25 A Trinidadian by birth, he was tall and thin.

B. *adj.* Of or pertaining to Trinidad or its inhabitants.

1934 A. Huxley *Beyond Mexique Bay* 20 This appeal for Trinidadian autarchy was warmly applauded. **1957** *Amer. Anthropologist* LIX. 817 Trinidad's social structure..shows these racial and national groups to be arranged in a hierarchy by Trinidadians... A consensus of Trinidadian opinion might arrange these groups as follows. **1971** *Advocate-News* (Barbados) 17 Sept. (Guyana Suppl.) p. iii/1 A Trinidadian sportsman has also been ordered to serve two six-month jail sentences. **1980** *Amer. Speech* LV. 31 Examples are Barbadian../basabasa/ 'fussy' and /kɔŋki/ 'boiled corn pudding', both also Trinidadian and Guyanese.

‖ **Trinidado** (trɪnɪ'dɑːdəʊ). *Obs.* or *arch.* [Sp. adj. from *Trinidad* (= Trinity) an island of the West Indies.] A kind of tobacco from Trinidad.

1599 Buttes *Dyets drie Dinner* Ep. Ded. Aaj b, Here is a Pipe of right Trinidado for him. **1600** Rowlands *Lett. Humours Blood* ii. 8 To drinke a pipe of Trinedado. **1889** Doyle *Micah Clarke* 180 A pipe of Trinidado is all I require.

Trinil ('triːnɪl). The name of a village in Java, used *attrib.* to designate the fossil remains found there by Eugène Dubois in 1891, esp. those of a hominid, *Homo erectus* or Java man. Cf. Java *a.*, pithecanthropus 2.

1896 *Jrnl. Anthropol. Inst.* XXV. 245 The Trinil skull in form and size very closely resembles the type of the anthropoid apes. **1898** E. Dubois in *Sci. Trans. R. Dublin Soc.* VI. 9 The human form of the Trinil femur is not sufficient to prove that it did not belong to the same individual as the skull-cap. *Ibid.* 12 The Trinil individual, if a human being, ought to have been a microcephalic idiot. .. The Trinil cranium..very much approaches the type of Anthropoid Apes. **1933** A. S. Romer *Man & Vertebrates* xi.

237 The teeth are essentially human in character but do not definitely settle the status of this Trinil man. **1960** C. WINICK *Dict. Anthropol.* 210/1 The Trinil man's teeth are large and his dental arch narrow. **1975** G. H. R. VON KOENIGSWALD in R. H. Tuttle *Paleoanthropology* 304 The famous hominid of the Trinil fauna is the classic *Pithecanthropus* or *Homo erectus*. *Ibid.* 305 It [*sc.* a skull] is not directly comparable to the Trinil skull cap.

† **trin-i'mmersion**: see TRINE *a.* 1 b.

Trinitarian (trɪnɪ'tɛərɪən), *a.* and *sb.* [f. 16th c. L. *trīnitāri-us* (f. *trīnitās* TRINITY) + -AN.

Trinitarius sb. occurs in Servetus, *2nd let. to Calvin a* 1553, also in Prince N. Radzivil *Let. to Calvin* 1564 (Calvin Wks. 1879 XX. 332). Cf. F. *trinitaire*, TRINITARY.]

A. *adj.* (In sense 3 with lower-case t.)

1. *Ch. Hist.* Belonging to the order of the Holy Trinity: see B. 1.

1628 L. OWEN *Unmask. Monks* 24 Of the Trinitarian Friars. In the time of..Pope Innocentius the third, the Friers who are called Trinitarians, began to shew themselues to the world. **1725** *Lond. Gaz.* No. 6355/1 Father Navajas, a Trinitarian Fryar. **1885** *Cath. Dict.* (ed. 3) s.v., At the dissolution there were eleven Trinitarian houses in England, five in Scotland, and one..in Ireland.

2. *Theol.* Relating to the Trinity; holding the doctrine of the Trinity (opp. to *Unitarian*).

In early use, *Trinitarian heretic*, one holding heretical views as to the Trinity: cf. B. 2 b.

1656 BLOUNT *Glossogr.*, *Trinitarian* hereticks, otherwise *New Arians* are those that deny the blessed Trinity, and all distinction of the Divine persons. **1775** ASH, *Trinitarian*, belonging to the Trinity, acknowledging the Trinity. **1838–9** HALLAM *Hist. Lit.* IV. IV. ii. §28. 37 We do not find much of importance written on the Trinitarian controversy. **1899** A. E. BURN *Introd. Creeds* ii. §6. 22 An unbroken traditional use of the Trinitarian [baptismal] formula.

3. Forming a trinity; consisting of or involving three in one; triple, threefold.

1812 *Reflector* II. 159 Our polygraphs, our trinitarian writing-desks. **1889** B. JONES in *Co-operative News* 22 June 644 The fund would not be there, if it were not for this trinitarian combination of effort [of labourer, capitalist, consumer]. **1910** *Daily News* 30 Dec. 4 France, Russia, and England do not constitute a trinitarian group or three-fold entity in foreign affairs.

4. Belonging to Trinity College (in Cambridge, Oxford, or Dublin). *nonce-use.*

a **1876** M. COLLINS *Pen Sketches* (1879) I. 50 Concerning Cam wrote our pleasant Trinitarian poet [Jas. Payn].

B. *sb.*

1. A member of the religious order of the Holy Trinity, founded in 1198 to redeem Christian captives from Muhammadans: = MATHURIN.

All the churches and houses of the order were dedicated to the Holy Trinity.

1628 [see A. 1]. **1656** BLOUNT *Glossogr.*, *Trinitarians*, a religious order. See *Mathurins*. *Ibid.*, *Mathurins*, Friers so called, being of the order of the Holy Trinity, whose principal institute is to redeem poor Christian Captives from the slavery of the Turk. **1688** R. HOLME *Armoury* III. 179/2 The Trinitarians, or Monks of the Order of the Trinity, begun Anno 1211. **1905** *Westm. Gaz.* 11 Sept. 3/1 Down Mark-lane and through Crutched Friars, where the famous Trinitarians of old had their monastery.

2. *Theol.* One who holds the doctrine of the Trinity of the Godhead; a believer in the Trinity.

1706 PHILLIPS (ed. Kersey) s.v., The Orthodox that believe the Trinity are also call'd Trinitarians by the Socinians. **1708** SWIFT *Abol. Chr.* Misc. 1731 I. 109 They make a Difference betwixt nominal and real Trinitarians. **1850** ROBERTSON *Serm.* Ser. III. iv. (1872) 45 There are.. Trinitarians who are practically Tri-theists, worshipping three Gods.

†**b.** In earlier use, 'applied particularly to certain sectaries whose opinion as to the Trinity was not orthodox' (Littré) = *Trinitarian heretic* in A. 2; including Antitrinitarians or Unitarians.

1565 HARDING *Confut. Apol.* 133 There are many other sectes..to witte, Osiandrines, Adiaphoristes, Antinomians, Newe Maniches,..Trinitarians. **1658** PHILLIPS, *Trinitarians*, a sort of Hereticks that deny the Mystery of the Trinity [**1706** (ed. Kersey) *adds*] and all distinction of the Divine Persons.

3. A member of Trinity College (Cambridge, Oxford, or Dublin). *nonce-use.*

1852 C. A. BRISTED 5 *Yrs. Eng. Univ.* (ed. 2) 48 The outcries of the Trinitarians waxed more and more boisterous. **1899** *Literature* 28 Jan. 89 Trinity College, Oxford... The story of each period is supplemented by a list of the most notable amongst contemporary Trinitarians.

Hence **Trini'tarianism**, the doctrine of Trinitarians; Trinitarian belief; **Trini'tarianize** *v. trans.* to make Trinitarian.

1775 ASH, *Trinitarianism*,..the doctrine of a Trinity of persons in the Godhead. *a* **1817** *Merivale's Reports* III. 357 A sect of Protestant Dissenters called Unitarians, professing themselves to be opposed to Trinitarianism. **1833** ARNOLD *Let.* 9 Mar., in Stanley *Life & Corr.* (1845) I. vi. 358 If we could get rid of the Athanasian Creed, and of some other instances of..the technical language of Trinitarianism, many Unitarians would have a stumbling-block removed. **1852** DE MORGAN in Graves *Life Sir W. R. Hamilton* (1889) III. 404 In your versification of the Te Deum you Trinitarianize it.

†**'Trinitary.** *Obs.* [ad. 16th c. L. *trīnitāri-us*: see TRINITARIAN. Cf. F. *trinitaire* (Calvin, 1560).] = TRINITARIAN B. 1, 2, 2 b.

1561 NORTON tr. *Calvin's Inst.* I. xiii. 39 The name of the Trinitie was so hatefull, yea so detestable to Seruetto, that he sayde, that all the Trinitaries, as he called them, were vtterly godlesse. **1581** ALLEN *Apol.* 20 These present Protestants, Anabaptists, Puritans, Trinitaries, and other wolues of what heare so euer,..daily decay and discouer their owne malice and folly. **1693** tr. *Emilianne's Hist. Monast. Ord.* 135 Of the Order of the Mathurines, or Trinitaries.

trinitrate (traɪ'naɪtrət). *Chem.* [f. TRI- 5 + NITRATE.] A compound formed from three molecules of nitric acid, HNO_3, by the replacement of the three hydrogen atoms by a trivalent element or radical; e.g. ***bismuth trinitrate***, $Bi'''(NO_3)_3$; ***glyceryl trinitrate***, $C_3H_5'''(NO_3)_3$, (= TRINITRIN).

1868 WATTS *Dict. Chem.* IV. 83 The [hydrated] trinitrates of aluminium and bismuth..evolve unaltered nitric acid. **1880** ROSCOE & SCHORLEMMER *Treat. Chem.* II. ii. 338 Bismuth Trinitrate..is obtained in large transparent triclinic prisms. **1912** THORPE *Dict. Appl. Chem.* (ed. 2) II. 773 The most important is glyceryl trinitrate, or nitroglycerin.

tri'nitride. *Chem.* [f. TRI- 5 + NITR(OGEN + -IDE.] A compound formed from hydrazoic acid or azoimide, HN_3, by replacement of the hydrogen by a metal; as ***sodium trinitride***, NaN_3.

1911 *Jrnl. Chem. Soc.* C. II. 693 Corrosion of some metals in Sodium Trinitride Solution.

tri'nitrin. *Chem.* [f. TRI- 5 + NITR(IC + -IN[1] (see ACETIN).] The compound ether or ester of glycerol or glycerin with nitric acid, $C_3H_5(O.NO_2)_3$, also called *glyceryl trinitrate* or more commonly and less correctly *nitroglycerin*; an oily liquid discovered in 1847, which when struck explodes violently; largely used in making dynamite and other explosives.

1866 ROSCOE *Elem. Chem.* xxxvi. 316 If the nitric acid employed..be concentrated, a new compound called Trinitrine or Trinitro-glycerine, is formed. **1898** *Allbutt's Syst. Med.* V. 996 Trinitrine should be prescribed if any sign of intolerance of the iodides be noticed.

trinitro- (traɪ'naɪtrəʊ), before a vowel **trinitr-**. *Chem.* [f. TRI- 5 + NITRO-.] **a.** A formative denoting that three nitro-groups, NO_2, have replaced three hydrogen atoms in the substance designated by the rest of the name, the nitrogen atoms being directly joined to carbon atoms; e.g. **trinitrophenol** or picric acid, $C_6H_2(NO_2)_3(OH)$, in which three H atoms of phenol have been replaced by three NO_2 groups, the N atoms directly joined to three C atoms. So **trinitrocresol**, $C_6H(CH_3)(OH)(NO_2)_3$, from cresol; **trinitronaphthalene**, $C_{10}H_5(NO_2)_3$ from naphthalene, $C_{10}H_8$, etc. Also *attrib.*, as ***trinitro carbolic acid***.

1851 *Q. Jrnl. Chem. Soc.* III. 75 A third compound is formed, in which 3 eq. of hydrogen are replaced by hyponitric acid: this is Trinitranisol. **1869** ROSCOE *Elem. Chem.* xxxix. 381 Tri-nitro-phenol [**1866**, xxxix. 336 tri-nitro carbolic acid] or picric acid, is a bright yellow crystalline body.

b. In earlier nomenclature, *trinitro-* included cases in which the nitrogen atoms of the NO_2 groups were attached by oxygen atoms to the carbon atoms of the substance designated by the rest of the name; such compounds are now called TRINITRATES; e.g. **tri,nitro'glycerin**, $C_3H_5(O.NO_2)_3$ (also TRINITRIN), now called *glyceryl trinitrate*. So **tri,nitro-'cellulose** or gun-cotton, a powerful explosive, considered to be $\{C_6H_7O_2(O.NO_2)_3\}_x$, derived from cellulose, $\{C_6H_{10}O_5\}_x$, by replacement of OH groups by $O.NO_2$ groups of nitric acid, $HO.NO_2$, the molecule being some unknown multiple of the formula. (See also quot. 1910.)

1864 MILLS in *Jrnl. Chem. Soc.* XVII. 158, I prepared trinitro-glycerin for this purpose. **1866** [see TRINITRIN]. **1875** H. C. WOOD *Therap.* (1879) 589 The true explosive gun-cotton, that which is alone adapted for gunnery, is tri-nitrocellulose. **1897** *Daily News* 9 Feb. 7/4 Mr. Maxim.. took the two most powerful smokeless explosives, nitro-glycerine and tri-nitro-cellulose. He mixed them by dissolving them in something which would dissolve both. **1910** WALKER & MOTT *Holleman's Org. Chem.* (ed. 3) 293 In the nitration of cellulose the final product is trinitro-oxy-cellulose..the formation of the trinitro-compound is accompanied by oxidation of the cellulose... $(C_{24}H_{40}O_{21})_x$.

trinitrotoluene (traɪ,naɪtrəʊ'tɒljuːiːn). [f. TRINITRO- + *toluene* s.v. TOLU-.] Any of three isomeric nitro derivatives, $CH_3C_6H_2(NO_2)_3$, of toluene, esp. the 2,4,6-isomer, used as a high explosive that is relatively insensitive to shock and can be conveniently melted. Abbrev. *T.N.T.* s.v. T 6 a. Also † **tri,nitro'toluol** [*toluol* s.v. TOLU-], in the same sense.

1908 *Chem. Abstr.* II. 459 The trinitrotoluene is preferable because it leaves no poisonous gases after explosion..and can be added to safety explosives. **1910** Trinitrotoluol [see TROTYL]. **1915** KIPLING *Fringes of Fleet* 21 We lay doggo in twelve-fathom water With tri-nitro-toluol hogging our run. **1916** *Yorkshire Post* 27 Mar. 5/1 Contact with tri-nitrotoluol may result in the occurrence of troublesome skin affections. **1917** *Causation & Prevention Tri-nitro-toluene* (*T.N.T.*) *Poisoning* (Nat. Health Insurance) 9 The material known commercially as T.N.T. is mainly composed of one of the three isomeric tri-nitro-toluenes. **1964** N. G. CLARK *Mod. Org. Chem.* xx. 402 All the existing substituents direct to one position in the nucleus, and the product is 2,4,6-trinitrotoluene, the well-known explosive TNT. **1973** 'A. HALL' *Tango Briefing* xviii. 227 It has the equivalent of one hundred tons of trinitrotoluene.

trinity ('trɪnɪtɪ). Forms: 3–6 **trinite, -yte,** (4 **trinte,** 4–6 **trynite, -yte,** 5 **trynete**), 4 **trini-, tryni-,** 5 **trynytee;** 4–5 **trenite,** (4 **-ete,** 4–6 **-yte,** 6 **-eti, -etee, -ytie);** 4–6 **trynitie,** 6 **triniti,** 6–7 **trinitie,** 6– **trinity.** Also β. 5 **ternyte,** 6 **ternitie.** [a. OF. *trinite* (in 11th c. *trinitiet, -itet*), also *trinetei, trenite, ternite* (= Pr., Sp. *trinidad*, Pg. *trindade*, It. *trinità*):—L. *trīnitāt-em* (nom. *trīnitās*) 'a triad, a trio', in Christian use from Tertullian (195–220), f. *trīnus*: see TRINE. Also in other langs. from L., e.g. Ir. *trionnoid*, Gael. *trionaid*, Welsh *trindod*; Ger. *trinität*.

L. *trīnitās* in Christian use rendered Gr. τριάς, used in this sense by Theophilus of Antioch, fl. 180, and by Clement of Alexandria, *c* 150–212. After Tertullian (*Adv. Prax.* xxv.) L. *trīnitās* is used by Cyprian, Hilary, Marius Victorinus, Priscillian, Jerome, Augustine, and others.]

1. The state of being threefold, threefoldness, threeness. **a.** in non-theological sense.

?*c* **1425** *Lucidarie* vi. (1909) 6 Nyne ordres of aungels.. Whi nyne of angels? For þe trynyte þat is in hem in þe nombre of nyne, þat is þries þre. **1850** ROBERTSON *Serm.* Ser. III. iv. (1872) 52 It is a trinity—a division in the mind of God.

b. *spec.* in theological use: applied to the existence of one God in three persons. (In early use esp. in phr. 'God in trinity', i.e. in threeness.)

a **1300** *Cursor M.* 2708 Toward him com childir thre, Liknes o god in trinité. *c* **1320** R. BRUNNE *Medit.* 1 Alle myȝty god yn trynyte, Now & euer wyþ vs be. *c* **1400** *Ywaine & Gaw.* 2205 Thorgh grace of god in trenyte, I sal the wreke of tham al thre. *c* **1450** *Merlin* i. 8 Belevest thow not in the fadir, sone, and holy goste, and that these thre persones be oon god in trynite? **1548–9** (Mar.) *Bk. Com. Prayer, Athanasian Creed*, So that..the vnitie in trinitie, and the trinitie in vnitie, is to be wurshipped. **1673** MILTON *True Relig.* Wks. 1851 V. 410 For terms of Trinity, Tri-unity, Co-essentiality, Tripersonality, and the like, they reject them as Scholastic Notions, not to be found in Scripture. **1719** WATERLAND *Vind. Christ's Div.* xxii. 336 As to Those who take Trinity and Tritheism for Synonymous Terms, They may go on to value Themselves upon it. **1907** SANDAY *Life Christ in Rec. Research* v. ix. 232 The doctrine of the Trinity is essentially a doctrine of Trinity *in* Unity. The basal truth is that God is one.

2. a. The three 'persons' or modes of being of the Godhead as conceived in orthodox Christian belief; the Father, Son, and Holy Spirit as constituting one God; the triune God. (Now always with capital T; often ***the Holy Trinity, the Blessed Trinity***.)

(There is possibly an instance of an early form *trineteð* = ONF. *trinitet*, in Layamon 29533; but both MSS. are defective, one reading merely *ðes nome*, and the other... *nete his name* (the rest being burnt).)

a **1225** *Ancr. R.* 26 Ʒette me ham, holi þrumnesse Trinite, iþe wurðschipe of þe. *a* **1300** *Cursor M.* 129 (Gött.) þat es, þe haly trinite, þat all has wroght wit his beute. **1390** GOWER *Conf.* III. 87 The hihe almyhti Trinite, Which is o god in unite. *c* **1450** LYDG. *Merita Missæ* 46 in *Lay Folks Mass Bk.* App. v. 149 Wershipe Ewyr the Ternyte. **1516** in *Acts Parlt. Scotl.* (1875) XII. 37/1 Ʒoure hienes..quhais grace..the trinite have in his blissit keping. **1587** GOLDING *De Mornay* xxxiv. (1592) 552 The Kingdome whose king is the Trinitie, whose Lawe is Charitie, and whose measure is eternitie. **1677** GALE *Crt. Gentiles* II. III. 48, I shal not denie but that these blind heathens..might have some..imperfect traditions concerning a Trinitie. **1827** HEBER *Hymn*, '*Holy, holy, holy*' i, God in three Persons, blessed Trinity! **1849** R. I. WILBERFORCE *Doctr. Holy Bapt.* (1850) 18 It was the Second, not the Third Person of the Ever-blessed Trinity who became the Incarnate Mediator.

b. A symbolical figure representing the three persons of the Godhead.

1496–7 *Rec. St. Mary at Hill* 33 Item, a gylt Table of the Trynete, for to sett on the high Aulter. **1503–4** *Ibid.* 252 Payd to the glasyng of þe gret vynddow vythe þe Trenyte in the southe yell [= aisle]. [*c* **1828** BERRY *Encycl. Her.* I. Gloss., *Trinity*, the heraldic device for the representation thereof is composed of roundles and lines.]

c. *ellipt.* The festival of the Holy Trinity; Trinity Sunday (see 6).

[**1215–30** *S. Osmundi Consuet.* xxi. 4 in *Reg. S. Osmund* (Rolls) I. 38 Festum Sanctæ Trinitatis.] *c* **1290** *St. Brendan* 229 in *S. Eng. Leg.* I. 225 þo com atte trinite þis gode man. **13..** *Guy Warw.* (A.) 705 It was at þe holy trinite, þerl dubbed sir Gij þe fre. **1624** LAUD *Diary* 6 June, Second Sunday after Trinity, I preached at Westminster. **1911** [see *Trinity Sunday*, sense 6]. **1981** BARTON & HALLIBURTON in *Believing in Church* iv. 90 From Trinity to Advent a series of *historiae* is appointed [to be read].

3. Any combination or set of three (persons, beings, things, principles, etc.) forming a unity, or closely connected; a trial, trio.

1542 *St. Papers Hen. VIII*, IX. 251 We might ones be joyned to gidre in a ternitie, as the Pope thEmpereur and the King of Portugal be. **1633** G. HERBERT *Temple, Starre* v, Then with our trinitie of light, Motion, and heat, let's take our flight. **1694** F. BRAGGE *Disc. Parables* iii. 84 The lust of the flesh, the lust of the eyes, and the pride of life;..that Trinity which the generality of men adore. *a* **1711** KEN *Hymns Festiv.* Poet. Wks. 1721 I. 268 Thus coalesce in sacred Lays, A Trinity, Love, Joy, and Praise. **1883** W. BINNS in *Chr. Globe* 13 Sept. 823/2 Siva, the destroying deity of the Indian trinity. **1906** PETRIE *Relig. Anc. Egypt*

xii. 79 The formal theology of the schools which grouped gods together in trinities or enneads.

4. In full, ***herb trinity*** (med.L. *herba Trinitatis*): an old name for **a.** the heart's-ease or pansy, *Viola tricolor*, from the three colours of the flower; **b.** *Anemone Hepatica*, from the three-lobed leaf.

1597 GERARDE *Herbal* I. ccxcix. 703 Harts ease is named.. of others *Herba Trinitatis* or Herbe Trinitie, by reason of the triple colour of the flowers. *Ibid.* II. ccclxxxvii. 1032 Noble Liuerwoort is called *Hepatica trifolia*,.. and Herbe Trinitie. *a* **1700** B. E. *Dict. Cant. Crew*, *Hearts-ease*,.. an Herb called by some the Trinity,.. or Pansies. **1864** *N. & Q.* 3rd Ser. V. 60/2 The well known name of Herb Trinity given to the *Anemone hepatica*.

5. Colloquial abbreviation for *Trinity College*.

1757 GRAY *Let.* 17 Apr., The Duke of Bedford is now here [Cambridge] to settle his son at Trinity. *c* **1765** —— *Satire* 11 The Master of Trinity To him bears affinity. **1874** K. H. DIGBY *Temple of Memory* iii. 39 To Cambridge he is gone.. with comrades three, Bound like himself for Trinity. **1933** D. L. SAYERS *Murder must Advertise* i. 12 'He was at Trinity. Your Trinity, I mean, not ours.' (Mr. Hankin was a Cambridge man.) **1982** M. YOUNG *Elmhirsts of Dartington* ii. 20 He became a 'Trinity man' expected to assume a definite character.. to distinguish him from King's men or Christ's men or John's men.

6. *attrib.* Dedicated to or connected with the worship of the Holy Trinity, as ***Trinity aisle***, ***altar***, ***guild***, ***light***; bearing a figure or symbol of the Trinity, as ***Trinity ring***, ***window***; occurring (blossoming, etc.) about the season of Trinity Sunday (see below), as ***Trinity fair***, ***honeysuckle***, ***tide***; belonging to or connected with the Trinity House (see below), as ***Trinity Brethren*** (sb. pl.), ***Corporation***, ***due***, ***high-water mark***, ***man***, ***pilot***, ***standard***, ***waterman***, ***yacht***; also † **trinity grass**, an old name for some species of trefoil; **trinity-herb** = herb trinity (see 4 a); **Trinity House**, shortened title of a guild or fraternity originally established at Deptford, incorporated in the reign of Henry VIII, formerly having the official regulation of British shipping, and now chiefly concerned with the licensing of pilots and the erection and maintenance of lighthouses, buoys, and other aids to navigation, on the coasts of England and Wales; **Trinity Monday** (*rare*), the day after Trinity Sunday; **Trinity Sunday**, the Sunday next after Whit-Sunday, observed as a festival in honour of the Trinity; **Trinity term**, the fourth of the terms or sessions of the High Court of Justice in England: see TERM *sb.* 5; since 1873 called officially ***Trinity Sittings***, and now beginning on the Tuesday following Trinity Sunday; also one of the university terms, which at Oxford is continuous with Easter term, the two being reckoned for most purposes as one.

1579 in Cranage *Churches Shropsh.* (1912) II. 945 Towards the reparations of the wyndoo in the *triniti ylle [= aisle]. **1536** in *Luton Trinity Guild* (1906) 214 Item payd to the paynter for makynge of a border for the *trenyte awter ..6*s.* **1860** COOTE *Admiralty Practice* 59 The Court will direct the attendance of the *Trinity Brethren to be written for. *Ibid.*, The Court is assisted by two elder Brethren of the *Trinity Corporation at the hearing of every suit for collisions. **1783** in *Late Meas. Ship-Owners in Coal-Trade* (1786) 63 *Trinity dues per Cocket. **1507** in *Charters &c. Edinb.* (1871) 191 Thair said *Trinite faires yeirlie to begin on the Monninday next eftir Trinitie Sonday. **1545** ELYOT, *Lagopus*, an herbe of the kynd of trefoyles called *trinitie grasse. **1657** C. BECK *Univ. Char.* L viij, Trinity grass or hare-foot. **1423** *Coventry Leet Bk.* 47 The brethren and systren of the *Trinyte guylde of Couentre. **1566** *Act 8 Eliz.* c. 13 §1 The.. Mayster Wardens and Assistauntes of the *Trinytie Howse.. shall.. set up suche.. Beakons, Markes and Signes for the Sea.. as to them shall seeme moost meete. *a* **1642** SIR W. MONSON *Naval Tracts* III. (1704) 339/1 A Master is to be chosen by the Trinity-House. **1842** QUEEN VICTORIA *Jrnl.* 29 Apr. (1980) 17 The Trinity-House steamer goes with us. **1979** *Bull. Yorks. Dial. Soc.* Summer 9 The station at the time was controlled by the Hull Trinity House. **1534** in *Luton Trinity Guild* (1906) 208 Item payd for xij li. wex for y^e *trenytie lyght.. 6*s.* **1698–9** *Act 11 Will. III*, c. 21 §2 Every Person.. who.. shall be employed in.. navigating any Lighter.. on the River Thames (*Trinity Man Fisherman Ballast Man.. excepted). **1771** *Order Bk. B. Junior Bursar Trinity Coll. Oxford* 39 (MS.) May 27 .. *Trinity Monday. Ordered that a general Court be held at Wroxton, Oct. 29. **1819** J. H. NEWMAN *Lett.* (1891) I. 37. **1867** FREEMAN in Stephens *Life* (1895) I. vi. 386 So we shall anyhow meet on Trinity Monday. *a* **1903** 'MERRIMAN' *Last Hope* i, The tottering headstones of certain master mariners and *Trinity-pilots. **1877** W. JONES *Finger-ring* 487 A rare and curious '*Trinity' ring, turned out of one piece of ivory. **1837** *Civil Eng. & Arch. Jrnl.* I. 33/1, 16 feet under the high-water of *Trinity standard. **1426–7** *Rec. St. Mary at Hill* 65 þe monday after *Trenite sonday. **1911** *Encycl. Brit.* (ed. 11) XXVII. 286 From Trinity Sunday onwards all Sundays until the close of the ecclesiastical year are reckoned as 'after Trinity'. **1540** *Act 32 Hen. VIII*, c. 21 §2 The full terme of the said *Trinitie Terme shall.. begynne.. the Fryeday next after Corpus Christi day. **1669** [see HILARY]. **1899** *Oxford Univ. Cal.*, May 20, Oxford Trinity or Act Term begins. May 30, Trinity Law Term begins. **1511** *Pilton Churchw. Acc.* (Som. Rec. Soc.) 61 Item for ij tapers agenst *trinyte tide.. xx^d. **1841** L. J. BERNAYS tr. *Couard's Serm. Ch. Hist.* xii. 154 During the coming Trinity tide. **1724** *Lond. Gaz.* No. 6249/9 Thomas Measant,.. *Trinity-Waterman. **1525–6** *Rec. St. Mary at Hill* 332 For mendyng of the *trynite wyndowe of the Sowthe side of the church. **1825** HONE *Every-day Bk.* I. 726 The *Trinity-yacht.. lay off St. George's.

Hence '**trinityhood** (*nonce-wd.*), the condition or character of being a trinity.

1886 *Trinitas Trinitatum* xxvii. 267 We have seen the Majesty of the Divine Trinityhood vindicated, in the triumph of the Second Adam over Satan.

triniunity, variant of TRINUNITY.

† **trink**, *sb.*^{1} *Obs.* Also (4 *pl.* **treinekys**), 4–6 **trynk**, **treinke**, 5 **trenke**, (**trimke**, **trymke**), 5–6 **trynke**, (6 **trungke**), 7 **trinck(e**, **trinke**. [Origin obscure. Known in AF. (or English in AF. context) from 14th c., and in use till 17th c.; but almost confined to legal enactments. It has been compared as to form with It. *trinca* a cable, Sp. *trinca* rope, cord, *trincas* lashings (Diez), but evidence of connexion with these is wanting.]

A kind of fixed fishing-net formerly used in the Thames and other rivers, concerning which ordinances were made from 14th c. onward.

1311 *Liber Horn City of London* lf. 221 b (MS.) Item ylia un autre manere de Reys qe um apele Treinekys la largesce de 1 pouz et di. **1344** *Letter Bk. F. London Recds.* lf. 80 b, Compertum est.. quod predicta retia vocata Treinkes non sunt largitatis in Mallio.. nisi dimidii pollicis ad plus. Ideo consideratum est quod comburantur. **1376** *Rolls of Parlt.* II. 331/2 Qe touz les Trynks par entre Loundres & la miere soient oustez. **1423** *Act 2 Hen. VI*, c. 12 §1 Salvez a chescun son droit & title en les Weres Kydelx & Trymkes avantditz. *Ibid.* c. 19 §1 Item ordeignez est & establiz qe la stacion des Reis & engines appellez Trynkes et de toutz autres maneres reis qe sont.. fichez & attachez.. soit toutoutrement defenduz... Purveux toutfoitz qe bien lise as possessours des ditz Trynkes.. peschier ovec eux.. les entraihantz et conveiantz par main come autres peschours [cf. TRINKER, quot. *c* 1485]. **1485** *Letter-Bk. L. Lond.* lf. 208 b, That the Nettes called Trenkes be of the largenes of ii Inches in the Masshe in the fore part and an Inche & half large.. in.. the later part. **1556** *Chron. Gr. Friars* (Camden) 10 This yere [1405] alle the kydelles and trungkes thorowgh-out the Temse from the towne of Stanes.. unto the watter of Medevey.. by the mayer & commonalte of London were dystrowyd and brent. **1630** *Lex Londinensis* (1680) 211 That no Trinckerman or other Fisherman shall buy any Trincke .. until he be allowed and thought fit by the Lord Major of London.. and seventeen Trinks allowed, and no more. [**1688** R. HOLME *Armoury* III. xxii. (Roxb.) 278/1 A Trink, was of old a Kind of Nett to fish withall.]

b. Short for *trink-boat*: see d.

1557 *Admir. Crt. Lib.* 27 (2) No. 131 Proprietarii duarum navicularum vocatarum ij Trynkes.

c. A fisherman who uses a trink; a trinkerman.

1630 *Lex Londinensis* (1680) 210 That no Trincke shall stand in any Byrth more than is allowed him to stand. *Ibid.* 212 That each Trincke shall every dark and foggy night hang forth out of his said Trinck-boat one Lanthorn. *Ibid.*, That every Trincke shall at all times and seasons take up.. his Anchor at the time of his leaving off from fishing.

d. *attrib.* and *Comb.*: **trink-boat**, a fishing-boat with a trink; **trink-cable**, a cable used with a trink; **trink-man** = TRINKERMAN; **trink-net** = *trink*.

1630 *Trinck-boat [see c above]. **1630** *Lex Londinensis* (1680) 212 That every *Trincke Cable be no more then twenty fathom long at the most. **1689** in Strype *Stow's Surv.* (1754) II. v. xxvii. 480/2 All *Trinke-Men shall yearly, at the Guildhall-Chappel, present themselves before the Lord-Mayor or Water-Bailiff. **1584** *Order Conserv. Thames* in Strype *Stow's Surv.* (1754) I. I. ix. 42/2 No Fishermen, Garthmen.. or Tynkermen, shall.. make any.. Stalker Nets, *Trynck Nets, Purse Nets, Casting Nets [etc.] except they be 2 Inches in the Mash.

† **trink**, *sb.*^{2} *Obs.* *rare*$^{-1}$. [? Nasalized form of TRICK *sb.* 8 a.] Style of adornment; fashion.

1575 LANEHAM *Let.* (1871) 36 Hiz beard smugly shauen; and yet hiz shyrt after the nu trink, with ruffs fayr starched, sleeked, and glistering like a payr of nu shooz.

trink, *sb.*^{3} *Sc.* and *dial.* Also 7 **trinck**. [perh. a. Norm. (Picard) *trenque*, *trencque*, northern form of OF. *trenche*, *tranche* TRENCH.] A trench, channel, watercourse (natural or artificial).

1592 *Aberdeen Regr.* (1848) II. 77 That na channell, stanes, sand, nor any uther thing be cassin in the trink of the watter, or within the fluid merk, out of schippis, craris, or bottis. **1603** *Ibid.* 239 That the haill trinck of the water salbe drawn doun the South syd of the Lochfeild croft.. and eist syd of the said loch in the auld trinck to be cassin deper and wyder, and that the water trinck on the south-vest syd of the said locht.. salbe stoppit and condamnit. **1812** J. HENDERSON *Agric. Surv. Caithn.* 200 The lower end in an oblong trink in the earth or floor. **1825** JAMIESON, *Trink*, *trenk*, app. synon. with Eng. *trench*. **1859–99** in *Eng. Dial. Dict.*

† '**trinker**. *Obs.* [f. TRINK *sb.*^{1} + -ER^1.] **a.** = TRINK *sb.*^{1} **b.** = TRINKERMAN. Also in comb. † **trinker-boat** = *trink-boat* (see TRINK *sb.*^{1} d).

c **1485** tr. *Act 2 Hen. VI*, c. 19 (MS. Harl. 4999, lf. 185 b), That the stacioun of nettis and engynes cald Trynkers and al other maner nettis whiche bien.. ficched and attached.. be al vtterly defended... Purveied alwey that it be lieful to the possessours of the saide Trynkers.. to fisshe with hem.. in drawyng and conveiyng bi hande as other fisshers don [cf. TRINK *sb.*^{1} quot. 1423]. **1615** E. S. *Britain's Buss* in Arb. *Garner* III. 650 Those pernicious Trinkermen, who with trinker-boats destroy the river of Thames, by killing the fry and small fish there.

So '**trinking**, the action of fishing with a trink.

1689 in Strype *Stow's Surv.* (1754) II. v. xxvii. 480/1 That no Person.. use or practice Trincking, Stow-boating, Trawling, or Catching of Fish, or Bait, on the Lord's-Day.. upon Forfeiture of 20*s.*

trinkerman ('trɪŋkəmən). Pl. **-men**. Also *erron.* 6–7 **tynker-**, 7–8 **tin(c)kerman**. See also TINKLERMAN. [f. TRINKER: cf. FISHERMAN.] A man who fishes with a trink (see TRINK *sb.*^{1}); the title of a class of fishermen on the Thames.

1538 *City of London Recds.* Jrnl. 14 lf. 111 (MS.) Fyrst yt ys agreed that the Trynkermen shal begynne to occupye theyre occupacion at Saynt James day. **1542** *Lett. & Pap. Hen. VIII*, XVII. 15 Considerations why the trynker men cannot save small brood and fry of fish. **1584** Tynkermen [see *trink-net*, TRINK *sb.*^{1} d]. **1615** [see TRINKER-*boat*]. **1720** STRYPE *Stow's Surv.* (1754) I. I. vii. 34/1 Whereas there are a certain Company of Fishermen, called Trinkermen (or Tynkermen) frequenting the River of Thames, eastward. **1868** in *Windsor Express* 22 Aug., The old fishermen—'trinkermen' as they are termed—in the tidal way are praying devoutly for a continuance of rain.

† '**trinkery**, *sb.* or *a.* *Obs.* *rare*$^{-1}$. [? f. TRINKET *sb.*^{1} Perh. error or misprint for *trinketry* or *trinkety*.] ? Adornment; in quot. *attrib.* or *adj.* Serving for adornment, ornamental.

1582 STANYHURST *Æneis* IV. (Arb.) 99 As yet in her pincking not pranckt with trinckerye trinckets.

trinket ('trɪŋkɪt), *sb.*^{1} Also 6 **tryn-**, **trinkett(e**, 7 **trinckett**. [Origin uncertain; has the form of a diminutive in -ET^1.

From the similarity of form, it has been suggested that this is the same word as TRENKET or *trynket*, a small knife, spec. a shoemaker's knife. But to such a transition of sense the general sense-history of the word from 1533 offers no confirmation. Another suggestion, supported by other words with *trink-* for *trick-*, is that this may be in some way related to TRICK *sb.* or *v.*; cf. esp. TRICK *sb.* 6 b; but here also evidence is wanting. Godefroy has a single instance of OF. *tryncle*, 1474, evidently denoting a piece of jewellery: cf. sense 2.]

† **1.** **a.** Any small article forming part of an outfit; usually *pl.* the tools, implements, or tackle of an occupation; paraphernalia, accoutrements, 'traps'.

a **1536** *Calisto & Mel.* A vj, I haue.. sene her trynkettes For payntyng thynges inumerable Squalmys & balmys. **1560** DAUS tr. *Sleidane's Comm.* 114 b, A conjuror.. had all his trynkettes and furniture concerning suche matters in a redinesse. **1573** TUSSER *Husb.* (1878) 36 Husbandlie furniture [in the stable].. A line to fetch litter, and halters for hed, With crotchis and pinnes, to hang trinkets ther-on, And stable fast chained, that nothing be gon. **1583** STUBBES *Anat. Abus.* II. (1882) 49 Cheese, fagots, pots, pannes, candles, and a thousand other trinkets besides. **1598** HAKLUYT *Voy.* I. 62 The poorer sort of common souldiers haue euery man his leather bag or sachell well sowen together, wherin he packs vp all his trinkets. **1606** S. GARDINER *Bk. Angling* 48 Sundrie and many are the trinkets that belong to fishing. **1693** DRYDEN *Juvenal's Sat.* VI. 212 Pack up with all your Trinkets, and away. **1787** W. TAYLOR *Poems* 67, I' se gie her.. A rock an' reel, pot, pan, an' wheel, An' mony mae usefu' trinkets.

† **b.** Applied to articles of food: A sweet, a dainty trifle. *Obs.*

1587 *Wills & Inv. N.C.* (Surtees) II. 158, xij lbs of synnamount comffettes 20/-. For banketinges disshes, as socatte and sewgar trinkettes, 10/-. **1822** SCOTT *Nigel* xxiii, Let Tim send the ale.. with a bit of diet-loaf, or some such trinket.

2. A small ornament or fancy article, usually an article of jewellery for personal adornment.

a **1533** LD. BERNERS *Gold. Bk. M. Aurel.* Let. v. (1535) Ff ij, But I wold wyt.. what goodly trinkettes ye hope to were in the straytnes of the Sepulchre. **1577** HARRISON *England* II. vii. (1877) I. 168 To receiue some other trinket newlie deuised by the fickle headed tailors. **1585** T. WASHINGTON tr. *Nicholay's Voy.* II. vii. 37 b, They were many chaines, tablets, and other trynkets of gold. **1674** tr. *Scheffer's Lapland* 89 The weight of the trinkets they [Lapp women] carry about them doth commonly weigh twenty pound. **1713** GAY *Fan* I. 115 Each trinket that adorns the modern dame, First to these little artists ow'd its frame. **1726** SWIFT *Gulliver* II. iv, Trinkets, of which the girl was very fond, as children at her age usually are. **1774** GOLDSM. *Nat. Hist.* (1776) VI. 396 The tortoise-shell of which such a variety of beautiful trinkets are made. **1849** MACAULAY *Hist. Eng.* iv. I. 473 Half as much as he proposed to expend in covering his wife with trinkets. **1863** KINGLAKE *Crimea* (1876) I. i. 14 Down to the giving of trinkets and ribbons, he was not forgetful.

† **3.** *fig.* Applied esp. to the decorations of worship, and to religious rites, ceremonies, beliefs, etc. which the speaker thinks vain or trivial. *Obs.*

1538 LONDON in *Lett. Suppress. Monasteries* (Camden) 224, I have pullyd down the image of your lady.. with all trynkettes abowt the same, as schrowdes, candels, images of wexe, crowches, and brochys. **1549** COVERDALE, etc. *Erasm. Par. Col.* i. 1 Iewishnes and supersticious Philosophie.. supersticiously also honouryng the Sunne, the Moone, and starres, with suche other smal trinkettes of this worlde. *a* **1591** H. SMITH *Serm.* (1625) 50 Then they invented purgatory, masses, prayers for the dead, and then all their Trinkets. **1655** FULLER *Ch. Hist* II. ii. §20 The Administration of that Sacrament was not loaded with those Superstitious Ceremonies.. of Crossing, Spittle, Oyl, Cream, Salt, and such like Trinkets.

4. *attrib.* and *Comb.*, as ***trinket-box***, ***-case***, ***-maker***.

1809 MALKIN *Gil Blas* IX. i. (Rtldg.) 309 A goldsmith's daughter! exclaimed I.. Can you think of tying me up to a trinket-maker? **1814** JANE AUSTEN *Mansfield Park* II. viii. 186 You would be.. welcome to any other in my trinket-box. **1825** T. HOOK *Sayings* Ser. II. *Sutherl.* I. 142 Repeating the question about Grace's trinket-box. **1841**

Mrs. Mozley *Lost Brooch* II. xv. 109 The trinket case was on the toilette table, and open. **1906** W. Churchill *Ld. R. Churchill* II. xvi. 250 The place-hunters and trinket-seekers who surrounded them.

† **ˈtrinket,** *sb.*^{2} *Obs.* Also 6 **trankett.** [Origin and history obscure.

App. a local word of Cheshire and Lancashire; possibly a particular use of prec.; but according to Ray 1691 from Welsh *trànked.* Owen Pugh (1832) has this word as '*tranced* an earthen vessel or cup, such a cup with a handle, as is in common use'; but no etymology of the word is known in Welsh, and it may have been borrowed from a neighbouring Eng. dialect.]

A small drinking vessel; a cup, mug; a porringer.

1541–2 *Will W. Davenport* (Bramhall, nr. Stockport) in *Lanc. & Chesh. Wills* (Chetham Soc. 1857) I. 80 In yᵉ kechen..xij pottengers, xij salsers, xv trankettis, iij potthookis. **1621** Gill *Logon. Angl.* (ed. 2) 37 *Trinkets*, instrumenta doliariorum quibus vinum ab uno vase exhauritur in aliud. **1691** Ray *N.C. Words* (E.D.S.), *Counterfeits and Trinkets*, porringers and saucers. *Chesh. Ibid., Trinket*, a porringer. *Chesh.* from Welsh *trànked.* **a 1700** B. E. *Dict. Cant. Crew, Trinkets*, Porringers. **c 1705** De Foe *True Relat. Appar. Mrs. Veal* Wks. 1840 V. 348 I'll warrant you, this mad fellow..has broke all your trinkets. But, says Mrs. Bargrave, I'll get something to drink [tea] in, for all that.

† **ˈtrinket,** *sb.*^{3} *Obs.* Also 6–7 **-ette, trinquet,** 7 **trinchet.** [Identical with (and prob. a.) F. *trinquet* (15–16th c. in Hatz.-Darm.) a foremast, also its sail; in Cotgr. 1611, 'properly the top or top-gallant on any mast'; in mod.F. dictionaries 'the foremast in a lateen-rigged vessel'. According to Hatz.-Darm., ad. It. *trinchetto* 'a small saile called a trinket' (Florio), 'the fore-sail' (Baretti); = Sp. *trinquete* 'the foremast, the fore saile' (Percival); Cat. *triquete*, Pg. *traquete* (Jal). Cf. also F. *trinquette* (15–16th c.), 'a triangular sail, a kind of lateen sail' (Littré), a fore-stay sail, a storm-jib; so Sp. *trinquetilla.* If the original application was to a sail, the meaning may have been a three-cornered sail, from L. *triquetrus*; but Jal takes the name as primarily designating a mast. See Diez, Littré, Jal.] A kind of sail; *esp.* the triangular sail before the mast, in a lateen-rigged vessel.

In Holland's Livy it represents L. *dolon*, which Isidore (xix. iii. 3) defines as 'minimum velum et ad proram defixum'.

1555 Eden *Decades* 195 They..sayle with twoo sayles as with the master sayle and the trinkette. **1596** Thomas *Lat. Dict.* (1606), *Dolo*, a small saile in a ship called a Trinket. **1600** Holland *Livy* xxxvi. xliv. 943 b, Hee set up the trinkets [L. *dolones*] or small sailes, meaning to make way into the deepe. **1648** Hexham *Dutch Dict., Focke, ofte Fockezeyl*, a small saile at the prow of a ship, called a Trinket. **1658** Earl Monm. tr. *Paruta's Wars Cyprus* 63 That they might keep company, they used only the Trinchet. *Ibid.* 134 The Turkish gallies sayled..with their Trinchet-sayl onely, very close together. **1697** Potter *Antiq. Greece* iii. xvi. (1715) 134 *Δόλων*, the Trinket, or small Sail in the Fore-deck.

b. See quots., and cf. Cotgr. cited in etymology above. (Perh. an error.)

1656 Blount *Glossogr., Trinquet*..is properly the top or top-gallant on any mast, the highest saile of a ship. So **1707** in *Glossographia Anglicana Nova.*

ˈtrinket, *sb.*^{4} *local.* [dim. of trink *sb.*^{3}: see -et^{1}.] A small or narrow channel or watercourse.

1880 *Antrim & Down Gloss., Trinket*, a small artificial water-course. **1888** H. C. Hart in *N. & Q.* 7th Ser. VI. 372/2 *Trinket*..is used about Dublin and also in the northern counties, with the sense of 'a little stream or watercourse by the roadside'. **1901** *Blackw. Mag.* Sept. 362/1 A smack drew through the fine mist in the Firth [of Forth], and sailing up the trinket, landed Provost Trail on the east pier-head.

† **ˈtrinket,** *v.*^{1} Chiefly *Sc. Obs.* Also 9 **trinquet.** [Origin unknown (unless connected with trinket *sb.*^{1} 3, or trick *sb.* or *v.*). Cf. also trinkle *v.*^{3}] *intr.* To have clandestine communications or underhand dealings *with*; to intrigue *with*; to act in an underhand way, prevaricate.

1647 [see *trinketing* vbl. sb. below]. **1651** *Mr. Love's Case* 37 Was there any such Article..by which he stood in Conscience bound to trinket with the declared and professed Enemies of the State? **1676** Fountainhall in M. P. Brown *Suppl. Dict. Decis.* (1826) III. 67 If the witness be found lying and trinketing in thir, it vilifies and derogates much from the weight and faith of his testimony. **a 1734** North *Exam.* i. ii. §63 (1740) 63 Had the Popish Lords.. not trinketed with the Enemies of that [the Crown] and themselves. **1819** Scott *Ivanhoe* xxxviii, Tampering and trinketing with hellish cures. **1821** —— *Kenilw.* xxxvi, A woman, who trinkets and traffics with my worst foes!

Hence † **ˈtrinketer^{1}**, one who has underhand dealings; a secret trafficker; an intriguer; † **ˈtrinketing** *vbl. sb.*, underhand dealing or trafficking.

1651 *Mr. Love's Case* 40 Mr. [Chr.] Love with the rest of his fellow *Trinketers, divided their thoughts and endeavors between doing of mischief..and the keeping themselves out of danger. **1821** Scott *Kenilw.* ix, If he becomes thus a trinketer with Satan. **1646** R. Baillie *Lett.* 1 Dec. (1841) II. 412 The King, all his lyfe, hes loved *trinketting naturally and is thought to be much in that action now with all parties. **1647** *Hamilton Papers* (Camden) 149 Some talk confidently of fresh trinketting with the King. **a 1716** South *Serm.* (1717) VI. 126 By their Tricks and Trinketting, between Party and Party. **1827** Scott *Surg. Dau.* i, To abhor all trafficking or trinketing with Papists.

ˈtrinket, *v.*^{2} *rare.* [f. trinket *sb.*^{1}] *trans.* To deck *out* with trinkets. Hence **ˈtrinketed** *ppl. a.* (*rare*).

1863 Sala *Capt. Dangerous* III. viii. 265 The Girls for sale are apparelled in a sumptuous manner, bathed, perfumed, and trinketed out. **1922** Joyce *Ulysses* 433 Her hands passing slowly over her trinketed stomacher.

trinketer^{1}: see trinket *v.*^{1}

† **ˈtrinketer^{2}**. *Obs.* [f. trinket *sb.*^{1} + -er^{1} 1.] One who attaches importance to trinkets: in quots. used contemptuously in reference to Romish religious observances, etc.: see trinket *sb.*^{1} 3.

1583 Melbancke *Philotimus* C iij, These two deludinge trinketters. **1659** Heylin *Certamen Epist.* 321 Neither of which (..necessity nor essentiallity) hath hitherto been ascribed to the Cross in Baptism, by any of the greatest Trinketers in the Church of Rome.

So † **ˈtrinketing** *a. nonce-wd.*, having to do with trinkets, toys, or trivial rites and ceremonies.

1679 Bp. Croft *Let. Popish Idol.* 23 Silly Women.. pleased with Toys, which makes the weaker Sex much incline to the trinketting Ceremonies of the Papists.

trinketry (ˈtrɪŋkɪtrɪ). [f. trinket *sb.*^{1} + -ry, after *jewelry.*] Trinkets collectively; articles of personal decoration or of ornament viewed as trinkets or toys. Also *fig.*

1810 Southey *Kehama* xiii. xiii, Ear-drop, nor chain, nor arm, nor ankle-ring, Nor trinketry on front, or neck, or breast. **1839–40** W. Irving *Wolfert's R.* (1855) 205 In those days there were no country stores in those parts, with their artificial finery and trinketry. **1892** *Critic* 23 Jan. 47/2 Plain, entirely accurate, not unmusical prose, unencumbered with the trickery and trinketry required by verse. **1911** F. N. Streatfeild *Remin.* xiii. 147 A General, with much trinketry on his manly bosom.

ˈtrinkety, *a. colloq. rare.* [f. trinket *sb.*^{1} + -y.] Of the nature of a trinket or thing of little importance; trivial, paltry.

1817 Scott *Let. to Miss J. Baillie* 26 Sept., in Lockhart *Life*, A series of little trinketty sort of business, and occupation, and idleness, have succeeded to each other.

‖ **Trinkhalle** (ˈtrɪŋkhalə). Also **trinkhalle.** [Ger., lit. 'drinking-hall'.] A place at a spa where medicinal water is dispensed for drinking; a pump-room. Also, an establishment at which (alcoholic) drink is served; a refreshment stall.

1873 G. H. Lewes *Diary* 16 Aug. in *Geo. Eliot Lett.* (1956) V. 427 Drinking seltserwasser at a Trinkhalle. **1971** D. MacKenzie *Sleep is for Rich* vi. 189 Chalice was waiting in the *trinkhalle* in an aura of stale tobacco smoke and beer.

† **trinkilo.** *Obs. rare.* App. perversion of trinket *sb.*^{1}, simulating a Sp. or It. form.

1631 Brathwait *Whimzies, Char. Pedler* 138 It is a pretty thing to observe how hee carries his trinkilo's about him.

trinking: see under trinker.

trinkle (ˈtrɪŋk(ə)l), *v.*^{1} *Sc.* and *dial.* Also 5–6 **trynkel,** 6 **-kle;** *β.* 6 **tringle, thringle.** [app. a nasalized modification of trickle *v.*^{1}]

1. *intr.* To trickle, to flow or fall drop by drop. Also *fig.* Hence **ˈtrinkling** *ppl. a.*

14.. *Chaucer's Sompn. T.* 156 (Camb. MS. Gg. 4. 27) With manye a tere trynkelynge [*v.rr.* trilling, triklyng] on myn cheke. **1513** Douglas *Æneis* ix. v. 58 With teris trynkeland our his chekis and face. **a 1600** Montgomerie *Sonn.* lv. 10 My trinkling teirs, the presents I propyne. **1687** Macfarlane *Geog. Collect.* (S.H.S.) III. 145 Burns..are seen trinkling down the green Hills. **1794** Burns *'O Mally's meek'* 14 Her yellow hair..Comes trinkling down her swan-white neck. **1828** *Craven Gloss., Trinkle*, to trickle. **1832** Motherwell *Jeanie Morrison* ix, Tears trinkled doun your cheek.

β. **1513** Douglas *Æneis* vi. xi. 14 The teris thringling [*ed.* 1553 trigling] furth our his chekis ran. **1535** Stewart *Cron. Scot.* (Rolls) II. 558 So mony teir come tringland fra his ene.

2. *trans.* To cause to trickle; to shed (tears).

a 1605 Montgomerie *Cherrie & Slae* (revision) iv, Quhairon Apollos paramouris Had trinklit mony a teir.

Hence **ˈtrinkle** *sb. Sc.* = trickle *sb.* 1.

1887 *Jamieson's Dict., Suppl., Trinkle*, a drop, series of drops, falling or fallen, as from a leaking vessel or a spout; a continuous dropping, or a slender thread of falling liquid;.. a trinkle of blood. **1905** in *Eng. Dial. Dict.*

ˈtrinkle, *v.*^{2} *dial.* [Altered f. tingle, tinkle.]

1. *intr.* To tingle, thrill.

1644 R. Baillie *Lett.* 2 Apr. (Bann. Cl.) II. 154 The maine chance is in the North, for which our hearts are trinckling.

2. To tinkle, make a tinkling sound.

1827 Coleridge in *Hone's Every-day Bk.* II. 115 The noises give an impulse to the icy trees, and the woods all round the lake *trinkle.* **1892** *Field* 28 May 805/2 The pilot.. watched her [a yacht] trinkling through the water.

† **ˈtrinkle,** *v.*^{3} *Obs.* Also 7 **-ckle,** 8 **-cle.** [app. orig. an alteration (erroneous or intentional) of trinket *v.*^{1}] *intr.* To treat secretly or in an underhand way, intrigue (*with*); = trinket *v.*^{1}

1672 Marvell *Reh. Transp.* i. 310 Others..have made it their business to trinkle with the Members of Parliament, for obstructing it. **1677** *Sec. Packet Advices to Men of Shaftesb.* 28 No Temporal Lordships must look to thrive by trinkling with them, unless they will truckle to 'em too. **1683** Temple *Mem.* Wks. 1731 I. 394 They were suspected to have trinkled at least with Holland about raising Seditions, and perhaps Insurrections in England. **1688** *Vox Cleri pro Rege* To Rdr., Let her [the Church] then take heed how she trinckles with the Crown, and be afraid of bringing down the Royal Thunder upon her own Head.

b. *trans.* ? To provoke, incite.

1685 Cotton tr. *Montaigne* III. 180 We have need to be trinckled and tickled by some such niping incitation as this. **1705** Hickeringill *Priest-cr.* ii. Wks. 1716 III. 91 Can you blame them therefore, by all Arts, to trinkle a Popishly-affected Prince..or some silly well-meaning Bigot, to draw his Weapon? *Ibid.* iii. 180 That such Wretches..would trincle the Tackers, and Priest-ridden Bigots, to endeavour to exclude all other English-Men from their Liberties.

ˈtrinklement. Now *dial.* Also 6 **trentill-, trintlment.** [Irregularly f. trinket *sb.*^{1} or OF. *tryncle* trinket, jewel (1474 in Godef.).] Adornment; in *pl.* 'trinkets, knick-knacks' (E.D.D., Lancash.).

1582–3 *Wills & Inv. N.C.* (Surtees) II. 61 Trentillment of houshold 10/- One siluer cupp 40/-. **1586** *Ibid.* 129 Wooden vessell, tubbes, and other trintlmentes of howsholde, 10/-. In the Seller. Tubbes, with other trintlmentes 10/-. **a 1675** Lightfoot *Rem.* (1700) 245 You see all the Trinklements of Popery, and the Pope and Friars hanging on. ? **1857** J. T. Staton *B. Shuttle* 8 (E.D.D.) Owd-fashunt, un valuable trinklaments.

trinklet (ˈtrɪŋklɪt). *rare.* Also 6 **trincklet.** [app. an alteration of trinket *sb.*^{1}, after diminutives in -let; cf. *giglet.*]

† **1.** ? A woman decked out with 'trinkets' or finery. *Obs. rare*$^{-1}$.

c 1550 *Pryde & Abuse Wom.* 52 in Hazl. *E.P.P.* IV. 234 Oure trotte, our trotte, our lustye trotte,..Is nowe become a trickynge one, And a wanton trincklet agayne.

2. = trinket *sb.*^{1} 2, 3.

1897 J. Kensit in *Westm. Gaz.* 15 Jan. 7/3 His lordship is now reintroducing the trinklets of Rome, by the wearing of a mitre upon his head. **1898** *Westm. Gaz.* 29 Nov. 5/2 A jewel robbery..the greater part of the jewels and trinklets.. being taken. **1909** *Nation* 6 Mar. 862 Ornaments of show, Trinklets and mirrors—these can go Outside.

trinkum (ˈtrɪŋkəm). Now *dial.* or *colloq.* Also 7 **trinckam, trinkom,** 8–9 **-cum,** 9 **-krum.** [app. a humorous alteration of *trinket*, with latinized ending.] A trinket.

1667 Cotton *Scarron.* iv. 125 Scarce had she thus dispos'd her trinckums, When up the Stairs, behold the Queen comes. **1699** J. Dunton *Life & Err.* (1818) II. xvii. 537 Good store of holy water..and of several other consecrated trinckams. **1774** *Poetry* in *Ann. Reg.* 224 Very fine ladies with very fine incomes, Which they finely lay out on fine toys and fine trincums. **1819** Scott *Let. to J. Richardson* 22 Aug., in *Lockhart*, He had a world of trinkums to get, for you know there goes as much to the man-millinery of a young officer of hussars as to that of an heiress on her bridal day. **1892** Sarah Hewett *Peas. Sp. Devon.* 136, I put a vew trinkrums about a 'undered yers old in a smal box.

Also reduplicated, **ˈtrinkum-ˈtrankum** (also **tringum-trangum, tringham trangham**) *slang* and *dial.*; also *attrib.*

a 1700 B. E. *Dict. Cant. Crew, Tringum-Trangum*, a Whim, or Maggot. **1702** Steele *Funeral* ii. ii, Come, come, this is not one of your Tringham Trangham witty things, that your poor poets write. **1718** Motteux *Quix.* i. iii. vi. (1749) 154 Toralva..comes after him bare-foot..with a pilgrim's staff in her hand, and a wallet at her back wherein ..she carry'd a piece of a looking-glass,..a broken pot with paint, and I don't know what other trinkums trankums to prink herself up. **1821** Galt *Ann. Parish* xii, Trinkum-trankum flowers and feathers. **1842** *Blackw. Mag.* LI. 23 Cheap gun shops, trinkum-trankum shops.

trinoctial: see tri- 1.

trinocular (traɪ-, trɪˈnɒkjʊlə(r)), *a.* [After binocular *a.* and *sb.*: see tri-.] Of a microscope or its body tube: having provision for a camera in addition to eyepieces for both eyes.

1960 *McGraw-Hill Encycl. Sci. & Technol.* VIII. 392/1 Trinocular bodies are binocular bodies with a third tube for a camera. **1970** R. P. Loveland *Photomicrography* I. iii. 121 The trinocular body tube can now be obtained from all of the microscope companies. **1972** *Sci. Amer.* Mar. 65/1 (Advt.), The ED-10 fits virtually any microscope. Whether monocular, binocular or trinocular.

trinodal (traɪˈnəʊdəl), *a.* [f. tri- + L. *nōd-us* knot, node + -al^{1}; cf. L. *trinōdis.*] **a.** Having three knots. *rare*$^{-0}$. **b.** *Bot.* Having three nodes (node *sb.* 2 b), as a stem. **c.** *Geom.* Having three nodes (node *sb.* 7), as a curve.

1656 Blount *Glossogr., Trinodal*.., that hath three knots, three-knotted. **1866** *Treas. Bot.* 1172 *Trinodal*, having three nodes only. **1873** Salmon *Higher Plane Curves* vi. (1879) 255 The other will be a trinodal quartic.

So **trinode** (ˈtraɪnəʊd), *Geom.* a combination of three nodes at one point of a curve; **triˈnodine** *a.* = *trinodal* a.

1866 J. B. Rose tr. *Ovid's Fasti* i. 612 Alcides grappled him; and broke With club trinodine,..The caitiff's head. **1891** *Cent. Dict.*, Trinode.

trinoda necessitas: see TRIMODA N.

trinomial (traɪˈnəʊmɪəl), *a.* and *sb.* [Formed with TRI- after BINOMIAL, q.v.]

A. *adj.* **1.** *Math.* Consisting of three terms, as an algebraical expression.

1704 J. HARRIS *Lex. Techn.* I, *Trinomial-Root*, in Mathematicks, is a Root consisting of three parts connected together by the Sign +; as *a* + *b* + *c*. See *Binomial.* **1743** EMERSON *Fluxions* 1. 83 The Fluents of the Trinomial or compound Binomial Fluxions. *c* **1865** *Circ. Sc.* I. 483/2 The ..multiplier will be trinomial.

2. *Nat. Hist.* Consisting of three terms, the first being that of the genus, the second that of the species, the third that of the subspecies or variety, instead of the two former only; involving or characterized by three terms, as a system of nomenclature. (Cf. BINOMIAL A. 2.)

1865 DARWIN *Lett.* (1903) I. 474, I have sometimes.. speculated on what nomenclature would come to, and concluded that it would be trinomial. **1884** *Nature* 10 July 257/1 More than ten years ago..Dr. Coues, in his 'Key to the North American Birds', first began to adopt the trinomial nomenclature which is now so generally accepted by American ornithologists.

3. Of the names of married women (esp. in the U.S.): consisting of three elements, the given, maiden, and husband's surname; also applied to those known by this style, whereby the maiden name is in some measure retained.

1966 *Listener* 2 June 806/3 A vast cast of trinominal cuckoos (Harriot Stanton Blatch, Carrie Chapman Catt, Elizabeth Gurley Flynn, Lucretia Coffin Mott, Rev. Anna Howard Shaw *et aliae*) flap across the stage, but hardly one is characterized by any human identifiable characteristic. **1981** *Economist* 28 Nov. 107/2 Mary Boykin Chesnut—and the reader cannot begin too soon to accustom himself to trinomial appellations.

B. *sb.* **1.** *Math.* An expression consisting of three terms connected by + or −.

1674 JEAKE *Arith.* (1696) 294 If three Quantities be conjoyned, and but three, they are sometime called Trinomials. **1706** W. JONES *Syn. Palmar. Matheseos* 171 To raise any Trinomial..to any given Power. *c* **1865** *Circ. Sc.* I. 473/1 The square of a binomial consists of three terms; that is, it is a trinomial.

2. *Nat. Hist.* The name of a subspecies or variety when composed of three terms (the names of the genus, species, and subspecies or variety).

1884 *Proc. Boston Soc. Nat. Hist.* 19 Mar. 166 According to recent lists all names are to be trinomials, either through duplication or addition.

Hence **triˈnomialism**, the trinomial system of nomenclature, or the use of trinomial names (see A. 2); **triˈnomialist**, one who uses or advocates this system; **trinomiˈality**, the quality or character of being trinomial; **triˈnomially** *adv.*, in a trinomial manner; by the use of trinomial names.

1884 *Academy* 5 July 13/3 Dr. Coues..showed how useful '*trinomialism' was in describing species which over the vast extent of North America varied to an extent hardly realised in the Old World. **1898** *Nature* 30 June 196/2 Mr. Blanford has not yet brought himself to accept the principle of trinomialism for birds. **1884** *Proc. Boston Soc. Nat. Hist.* 19 Mar. 168 Some *trinomialists disclaim responsibility for the repetition or duplication. **1891** *Cent. Dict.*, *Trinomiality. **1884** *Nature* 10 July 257/2 There has been.. a consensus of opinion..that they [the Yellow Wagtails] ought to be treated *trinomially.

trinominal (traɪˈnɒmɪnəl), *a. rare.* [f. TRI- + L. *nōminālis* NOMINAL.] Having three names; in *Nat. Hist.* = TRINOMIAL A. 2.

1674 BLOUNT *Glossogr.*, *Trinominal* (*trinominalis*), that hath three names. **1691** W. NICHOLLS *Answ. Naked Gospel* 90 No farther distant from Socinianism, than a Trinominal Diety is different from him that is personally one, without such nominal Distinction. **1882** OGILVIE (Annandale), *Trinominal, a.*, same as *Trinomial*.

†ˈ**trinomy**[1]. *Math. Obs. rare.* [formed with TRI- after BINOMY.] = TRINOMIAL B. 1.

1571 DIGGES *Pantom.* IV. xxi. Cc iij b, By reduction of the former Trinomye to a Binomye.

trinomy[2] (ˈtrɪnəmɪ). *rare.* [f. TRI- + Gr. -νομία, -NOMY.] A threefold law, rule, or arrangement.

1838 *Fraser's Mag.* XVIII. 556 Its greatest pivot consists in the fundamental trinomy of understanding, discerning, and contempering.

trinquet, var. TRINKET *sb.*[3] and *v.*[1] *Obs.*

trinsch, obs. Sc. form of TRENCH.

trintch, trinte, obs. ff. TRENCH, TRINITY.

trintle, Sc. and dial. variant of TRINDLE.

trintlment, obs. form of TRINKLEMENT.

trinucleate, -nucleotide: see TRI- 1 a.

triˈnundine. *Rom. Antiq. rare*[−1]. [ad. L. *trinundin-us*, f. TRI- + *nundina*: see NUNDINE.] A period including three successive nundines, i.e. seventeen days.

1891 FARRAR *Darkn. & Dawn* xix, Onesimus was doomed to the scourge, as well as to a trinundine of solitude on bread and water.

†**triˈnune, trin-une**, *a. Obs.* Also 7 trine une, triniune. [f. L. *trīn-us* (or its pl. *trīnī*) three each, TRINE + *ūnus* one.] Three in one: = TRIUNE. So †**triˈnuned** *ppl. a.*, combined as three in one; †**triˈnunion**, †**triˈnunionhood**, †**triˈnunity** (also triniunity), state of being triune, trinity in unity.

1620 T. GRANGER *Div. Logike* 73 That we are bound to worship the *trin-vne God with faith. **1681** J. SCOTT *Chr. Life* I. (1684) 10 The Mysterious Trin-un-Divinity. **1610** W. FOLKINGHAM *Art of Survey* I. iii. 5 Opall Paderas, with their *Trineuned luster. **1603** J. DAVIES *Microcosmos* 207 But that same onely-wise *Trin-vnion Workes Miracles, wherein all wonder lies. **1612** —— *Muse's Sacr.* (Grosart) 32/2 Who (were it possible) art more compleate in Goodnesse, then thine owne *Trin-vnionhood! **1650** F. CHEYNELL (*title*) The Divine *Trinunity of the Father, Son, and Holy Spirit. **1673** MILTON *True Relig.* 7 As for terms of Trinity, Triniunity, Coessentiality, Tripersonality, and the like, they reject them as Scholastic Notions, not to be found in Scripture. **1694** R. BURTHOGGE *Reason & Nat. Spirits* 279 He makes the same application of it to the Divine Trin-unity that Laurentius Valla doth.

trio (ˈtriːəʊ, ˈtraɪəʊ). [a. F. *trio* (*a* 1600 in Hatz.-Darm., according to whom) a. It. *trio*, f. *tre* three, 'formed in imitation of *duo*'.]

1. *Mus.* **a.** A composition for three voices or instruments; also, a company of three performers singing or playing such a composition.

1724 *Short Explic. For. Wds. in Mus. Bks.*, *Tria*, or *Trio*, Musick in Three Parts is so called, either for Voices or Instruments, or both together. **1727–41** CHAMBERS *Cycl.*, *Trio*, in music; a part of a concert wherein three persons sing; or more properly a musical composition consisting of three parts. **1775** MME. D'ARBLAY *Early Diary* (1889) II. 134 It seemed to be a sort of *trio* between an old woman, a young woman, and a young man. **1824** BYRON *Juan* XVI. xlv, Oh! the long evenings of duets and trios! **1885** 'MRS. ALEXANDER' *At Bay* iii, Mademoiselle Antoinette and Elsie, assisted by the singing-master, were performing a trio.

b. Name for a second or subordinate division of a minuet or other dance movement, or of a scherzo or march; commonly in a different key and style from the main division, which is repeated after it.

Supposed to be so called because originally written for three instruments or in three parts.

1840 *Encycl. Brit.* (ed. 7) XXI. 387/1 The term *trio* is also applied to a movement in ¾th time, which often follows the minuet in a piece of instrumental music. **1889** F. CORDER in Grove *Dict. Mus.* IV. 172/2 How the second minuet acquired the name of Trio is not quite clear. Bach only calls it so in the few instances in which it is written in three parts —as opposed to the minuet in two. *Ibid.* 173/1 By the time of Haydn the term Trio is firmly established, and even in his earliest works..there are two minuets, each with a trio.

2. A group or set of three: **a.** of persons.

[**1763** MRS. BROOKE *Lady J. Mandeville* (1820) 55 Foreseeing we should be a very awkward party to-day *à trio*, I sent..to ask three or four very agreeable girls..to come and ramble all day with us in the woods.] **1789** H. WALPOLE *Let. to Mrs. H. More* 22 Apr., The lady flowers and their lovers enter in pairs or trios. **1836** W. IRVING *Astoria* xliv. III. 38 The trio of Kentucky hunters, Robinson, Rezner, and Hoback. **1904** *Verney Mem.* II. 59 Chatting with this trio of charming cousins.

b. of things or animals; in quot. 1777 a stanza of three lines; in *Cricket*, three runs.

1777 tr. *Chesterfield's Lett.* I. xxxv. Misc. Wks. II. 110, I will tell you very frankly, I could as soon get off fifty thousand of his *trios* as fifty. **1856** KANE *Arct. Expl.* II. xiii. 132 [Walrus] surging in loving trios from crack to crack. **1873** EARLE *Philol. Eng. Tongue* (ed. 2) §109 The general adoption of this trio of vowel-sounds as the basis of phonology. **1882** *Daily Tel.* 24 June, At 237 Studd resumed in place of Ramsay, but was almost at once driven by Giffen for a trio.

c. *Cards.* At piquet, a combination of three aces, kings, queens, or knaves in one hand.

1891 in *Cent. Dict.*

3. *Comb.*, as **trio-sonata** [cf. It. *sonata a tre*], a sonata written in three parts, and often performed on four instruments.

1884 BELL & FULLER-MAITLAND tr. *Spitta's Johann Sebastian Bach* II. IV. iii. 106 The accompaniment..is arranged by one of the master's best pupils..who did the same thing in a trio-sonata of Bach's. **1934** (*title*) J.-M. Leclair: Trio-Sonata in B flat major for 2 violins, violoncello (ad lib.) & Piano. **1958** *Listener* 11 Dec. 1010/2 Purcell wrote two splendid sets of trio-sonatas. **1978** *Early Music* Oct. 561/1, I have chosen the trio sonata in C major for recorder, flute and basso continuo.

triobol (ˈtraɪəʊbɒl, traɪˈəʊbəl). Also in L. form triobolus. [ad. Gr. τριώβολον, f. τρι-, TRI- + ὀβολός OBOL.] An ancient Greek coin of the value of three obols, or half a drachma.

[**1693** tr. *Blancard's Phys. Dict.* (ed. 2), *Triobolon*, half a Dram.] **1837** WHEELWRIGHT tr. *Aristoph.* II. 190 She bates her tongue for my triobolus. **1842** *Smith's Dict. Grk. & Rom. Antiq.* s.v. *Drachma*, Specimens of the tetrobolus, triobolus, diobolus..are still found. **1887** B. V. HEAD *Hist. Numorum* 316 Tetradrachms, Drachms, and Triobols.

†**triˈobolar**, *a. Obs.* Also 6–7 triobular. [ad. med.L. *triōbulār-is* (Du Cange), f. L. *triōbol-us*: see prec. and -AR.] *lit.* Worth three obols; in use always *fig.*, of little or no worth, vile, paltry, mean, contemptible. (Cf. *twopenny-halfpenny*.)

1585 T. WASHINGTON tr. *Nicholay's Voy.* Ep. Ded., Common men, (I meane not triobular mates) men I say, of base descent and linage. **1593** ABP. BANCROFT *Daung. Posit.* II. iii. 48 Railing pamphlets; many of them but triobolar chartals. **1647** MAYNE *Serm. agst. False Proph.* 11 It may pass current amongst the Balladmongers for a triobolar Ballad.

Also †**triˈobolary** (also -ulary) *a.* in same sense.

1644 FEATLEY *Levites Scourge* 7 Libelled in all the triobulary pasquils printed the first and second weeke of October. **1653** GAUDEN *Hierasp.* 504 There are many such whining people, penurious protestants, triobolary Christians. **1700** T. BROWN *Amusem. Ser. & Com.* 48 Seeing their Qualities ridicul'd by every Triobolary Poet.

tri-octahedral, -ocular: see TRI- 2 b, 1.

trioctile (traɪˈɒktɪl, -taɪl). *Astrol.* [f. TRI- + L. *octo* eight, after *quartile*, *sextile*.] An aspect of two planets distant from each other three-eighths of the whole circle, i.e. 135 degrees; the sesquiquadrate.

1727–41 CHAMBERS *Cycl.* s.v. *Aspect*, To the five ancient aspects, the modern writers have added several more; as decile, containing the tenth part of a circle; tridecile,.. biquintile,..semisextile,..quincunx.., to the astrological physicians we owe octile, containing one eighth; and trioctile, containing three eighths. **1795** HUTTON *Math. Dict.*, *Trioctile*,..which some call the *sesquiquadrans*.

triod (ˈtraɪɒd). *Zool.* [ad. Gr. τρίοδος a place where three ways meet, f. τρι-, TRI- + ὁδός way.] Name for a simple triradiate sponge-spicule, consisting of three rays inclined at angles of 120°.

1887 SOLLAS in *Encycl. Brit.* XXII. 416/2 Fig. 12..*c*, triod (triaxon triactine).

triode (ˈtraɪəʊd), *a.* and *sb.* [f. TRI- + -ODE[2].]

†**A.** *adj. Telegr.* Permitting or involving the transmission of three signals simultaneously. *Obs.*

1886 [see HEXODE *a.*].

B. *sb. Electronics.* **a.** A thermionic valve having three electrodes (also ***triode valve***); also, an analogous semiconductor device with three terminals.

1919 W. H. ECCLES in *Electrician* 18 Apr. 475/2 It seems very natural to call a vacuous space containing three electrodes a 'tri-electrode', or, for short, a triode. **1919** *Nature* 30 Oct. 178/2 The internal action of a triode valve. **1923** *Mod. Wireless* June 304/2 The amplifier used consisted of a single Western Electric triode. **1943** C. L. BOLTZ *Basic Radio* x. 155 The thing which is most striking about the triode is the effect of grid voltage on the anode current. **1948** *Physical Rev.* LXXIV. 230/1 (*heading*) The transistor, a semi-conductor triode. **1962** D. F. SHAW *Introd. Electronics* xi. 220 One of the most important uses of the triode valve is for the amplification of a voltage. **1962** SIMPSON & RICHARDS *Physical Princ. Junction Transistors* viii. 191 The second type of avalanching triode..is obtained by connecting a base lead to either the n_1 or p_2 sections of the diode in Fig. 8.22. **1974** A. VAN DER ZIEL *Introd. Electronics* ix. 216 The vacuum triode is hardly ever used as a small-signal amplifier except at high temperatures, but it is still the only way to develop very large powers.

b. Comb.: **triode-hexode**, a valve containing a triode and a hexode in a single envelope, with separate anodes but a common cathode; similarly **triode-pentode**.

1937 A. T. WITTS *Thermionic Valves Mod. Radio Receivers* viii. 164 (*caption*) Circuit for the triode-hexode. **1952** E. ARMITAGE *Wireless Fundamentals* xviii. 325 Sometimes the beat oscillator valve and the mixer valve are both inside a single glass envelope as in the triode-hexode. **1936** MOYER & WOSTREL *Radio Receiving & Television Tubes* (ed. 3) iv. 156 (*caption*) Characteristic curves of triode section of triode-pentode tube.

triodontoid (traɪəʊˈdɒntɔɪd), *a.* (*sb.*) *Ichth.* [f. mod.L. *Triodon, -ont-* (f. Gr. τρι-, TRI- + ὀδούς tooth; so called from the divided upper jaw and undivided lower jaw, suggesting three teeth) + -OID.] Resembling or allied to the genus *Triodon* of plectognath fishes. **b.** *sb.* A fish of this genus or family.

1891 in *Cent. Dict.*

‖**Triœcia** (traɪˈiːʃɪə). *Bot.* [mod.L. (Linnæus), f. Gr. τρι-, TRI- + οἶκος house: cf. DIŒCIA, MONŒCIA.] The third order in the Linnæan class *Polygamia*, comprising plants having male, female, and hermaphrodite flowers on different individuals. Hence **triœcious** (-ˈiːʃ(ɪ)əs) *a.*, **triˈoicous** *a.*, belonging to this order, or having the flowers thus distributed (whence **triˈœciously** *adv.*); **triœcism** (-ˈiːsɪz(ə)m), triœcious character or condition.

1760 J. LEE *Introd. Bot.* II. xxvi. (1765) 138 **Trioecia*, comprehending such Plants as have the Polygamy on three distinct Plants. **1860** MAYNE *Expos. Lex.*, *Triœcius*, *Bot.* ..*triœcious. **1866** *Treas. Bot.*, *Triœcious, Trioicus*, having male flowers on one individual, female on another, and hermaphrodite on a third. **1891** *Cent. Dict.*, *Triœciously ..*Trioicous.

triole (ˈtraɪəʊl, ˈtriːəʊl). *Mus. rare.* [dim. of TRIO: cf. F. *triolet* TRIOLET.] = TRIPLET 2 c.

1880 S. LANIER *Sc. Eng. Verse* iii. (1909) 116 In the first bar a process exactly reversing that..described for the triole is used with singular effect. A triole..indicates that the three notes..are to be played in the time of two..[quavers]; but we may reverse this and indicate that two..[quavers] are to occupy the time of three..[quavers].

triolein (traɪ'əʊliːɪn). *Chem.* [f. TRI- 5 + OLEIN.] One of the glycerides of oleic acid, or oleates of glyceryl: see quots.

1855 *Q. Jrnl. Chem. Soc.* VII. 282 Berthelot.. prepared.. Triolein... It is identical with natural olein. **1868** WATTS *Dict. Chem.* IV. 195 Triolein is liquid at 100°. In contact with the air it gradually turns acid. **1873** —— *Fownes' Chem.* (ed. 11) 626 Oleic acid forms three glycerides, viz. monolein ..; diolein..; and triolein $(C_3H_5)(C_{18}H_{33}O_2)_3$, which are produced by heating oleic acid and glycerin together.

triolet ('traɪəlɪt, 'triː-). [a. F. *triolet* (1538 in Godef., used in senses 1 and 3), dim. of *trio*; but see Hatz.-Darm for a different origin.]

1. *Verse.* A stanza of eight lines, constructed on two rimes, in which the first line is repeated as the fourth and seventh, and the second as the eighth.

1651 P. CAREY (*title*) Trivial Poems, and Triolets. Written in obedience to Mrs. Tomkin's commands. **1836** F. MAHONY *Father Prout* (1860) 208 To his fostering care the poetry of France is indebted for.. the triolet. **1878** DOWDEN *Stud. Lit.* 394 This writer excels in sonnets, and that in triolets. **1880** F. HUEFFER in *Macm. Mag.* Nov. 51 Such a poem as the following triolet, by Mr. Robert Bridges, is perfect of its kind. 'When first we met we did not guess' [etc.].

†**2.** *Cards.* Term for one-third of the stakes at the game of Beast. *Obs.*

1680 COTTON *Compl. Gamester* xxiv. (ed. 2) 108 He that hath three of any sort, that is, three fours, three fives, three sixes, and so forth, takes up the Triolet.

‖**3.** *Mus.* = TRIPLET 2 c. *rare*⁻⁰. (Properly Fr.)

1888 in *Cassell's Encycl. Dict.*

triology (traɪ'ɒlədʒɪ). [f. TRI- + -OLOGY. (Not on Greek analogies.)]

1. = TRILOGY.

1837 *For. Q. Rev.* XIX. 447 Three tragedies thus formed together a Triology. **1898** *Westm. Gaz.* 14 Apr. 3/1 Mr. Meredith's 'Napoleon', the second instalment of his triology on France,.. appears in the current number of *Cosmopolis*. **1900** *Dundee Advertiser* 29 Nov. 2 Mr. Fenton treats the Epistles to the Romans, Corinthians, and Hebrews as a 'Triology' designed to show 'the Christian Faith in its Intellectual, Social, and Spiritual aspects'.

2. A doctrine or system of three or a triad.

1894 *Thinker* V. 346 The monotheistic idea of All-Father soon gave place to that of a triology.

trional ('traɪəʊnæl). *Pharm.* [f. TRI- 5 + ending of SULPH)ONAL, because it contains three ethyl groups.] Trade-name of the synthetic narcotic drug diethylsulphonemethylethylmethane, $CH_3(C_2H_5)C(SO_2C_2H_5)_2$, resembling sulphonal.

1889 *Jrnl. Chem. Soc.* LVI. 1233 Trional.. crystallises in lustrous tables, melts at 76°, and dissolves in 320 parts of cold water. **1896** *Allbutt's Syst. Med.* I. 225 By the substitution of Sulphonal of a molecule of ethyl (C_2H_5) for a molecule of methyl, trional is formed. **1913** THORPE *Dict. App. Chem.* (ed. 2) V. 530 Trional.. is employed in medicine for the same purpose as sulphonal and tetronal.

‖**Triones** (traɪ'əʊniːz), *sb. pl.* Also 7 in anglicized form trions. [L. *triōnēs* ploughing-oxen, also as here.] A name for the seven principal stars in *Ursa Major*, also called *Charles's Wain.*

1594 GREENE & LODGE *Looking Glass* G.'s Wks. (Rtldg.) 134/1 The fair Triones with their glimmering light Smil'd at the foot of clear Bootes' wain. **1615** CROOKE *Body of Man* 340 There are seauen wonders of the world,.. seauen greater and lesser Triones in heauen. **1654** VILVAIN *Epit. Ess.* VI. 51 The Heav'ns sevn Trions show. **1795** HUTTON *Math. Dict.*, *Triones*,.. Charles's Wain.

trionychoid (traɪ'ɒnɪkɔɪd), *a.* (*sb.*) *Zool.* [ad. mod.L. *Trionychoidea*, neut. pl., f. TRIONYX, generic name: see -OID.] Belonging to the suborder *Trionychoidea* of *Chelonia*, typified by the genus *Trionyx* of soft-shelled turtles. **b.** *sb.* A turtle of this suborder.

1886 GÜNTHER in *Encycl. Brit.* XX. 469/1 A distinct Trionycoid genus. **1889** NICHOLSON & LYDEKKER *Palæont.* II. liii. 1117 The marked resemblance of the palate and the general aspect of the Trionychoid skull to that of existing Pleurodira.

trionym ('traɪəʊnɪm). [f. Gr. τριώνυμ-ος having three names, f. τρι-, TRI- + ὄνομα name.] A name consisting of three terms; a trinomial name in botany or zoology; = TRINOMIAL B. 2. So **trionymal** (traɪ'ɒnɪməl) *a.* = TRINOMIAL A. 2, TRINOMINAL.

1656 BLOUNT *Glossogr.*, *Trionimal*.., that hath three names. [**1691** TOMLINSON in Ray *N.C. Words* s.v. *Brock*, The animal is trionymus, *badger, brock*, or *gray*.] **1884** COUES in *Auk* Oct. 321 *Trionym*, an onym consisting of three terms. **1884** J. A. ALLEN *ibid.* 352 Even a trinomial (or trionymal) system.. fails to meet the requirements of the case.

Trionyx ('traɪənɪks, traɪ'əʊnɪks). *Zool.* [mod.L. *triōnyx*, f. Gr. τρι-, TRI- + ὄνυξ nail; cf. Gr. τριώνυχ-ος having three nails.] Name of a genus of chelonian reptiles, so called because only three of the five toes have nails. There are several species, including *T. triunguis*, *sinensis*, *ferox*, the Nilotic, Chinese, and American Trionyx.

1835 KIRBY *Hab. & Inst. Anim.* II. xxii. 433 The Trionyx, also, a kind of tortoise, devours them [the young crocodiles] as soon as hatched. **1878** BELL *Gegenbaur's Comp. Anat.* 427 These are wanting in Trionyx. **1896** *List Anim. Zool. Soc.* 570 *Trionyx muticus*, Unarmed Trionyx; Hab. North America.

trioperculate to **triovulate**: see TRI- 1, 4 b.

trior, triour: see TRIER.

triose ('traɪəʊs). *Chem.* [f. TRI- 5 + -OSE².]

1. a. Group name of the sugars containing three atoms of carbon, $C_3H_6O_3$; the two possible cases are ***aldotriose***, $CH_2OH.CHOH.CHO$, and ***ketotriose***, $CH_2OH.CO.CH_2OH$. **b.** It has also been used as a group name and as a termination for the trisaccharides, i.e. those sugars which break up on hydrolysis into three simple sugars.

1894 MUIR & MORLEY *Watts' Dict. Chem.* IV. 531 [Sugars] are designated according to the number of carbon atoms they contain: thus, pentose containing C_5,.. Triose $C_3H_6O_3$, glycerose. **1894** M'GOWAN *Bernthsen's Org. Chem.* (ed. 2) 317 Sugars of the above [cane sugar] group are termed '*-bioses*', e.g. milk sugar is lacto-biose. Similarly raffinose is a '-triose', Mele-triose. **1895** *Athenæum* 26 Jan. 123/1 [A paper] 'Presence of a Triose in Starch Transformation Products' [was read].

2. Special Comb.: **triose phosphate**, any compound in which a hydrogen atom in the hydroxyl group of a triose is replaced by a phosphate group (PO_3^{2-}).

1934 *Chem. Abstr.* XXVIII. 3746 Triosephosphate was sepd. by fractional pptn. with EtOH and Me_2CO. **1982** R. A. HARRIS in T. M. Devlin *Textbk. Biochem.* vii. 336 Triose phosphate isomerase then catalyzes the reversible interconversion of dihydroxyacetone phosphate and glyceraldehyde 3-phosphate to complete the splitting stage of glycolysis.

trioxan (traɪ'ɒksæn). *Chem.* Also **-ane** (-eɪn). [f. TRI- + OX(A- + -ANE.] A cyclic trimer of formaldehyde, $(-CH_2 \cdot O-)_3$, obtained as colourless, pliant crystals that are combustible and very volatile at room temperature.

1915 P. E. SPIELMAN tr. *V. von Richter's Org. Chem.* I. 205 Hexachlorodimethyl Trioxan. **1919** *Decennial Index Chem. Abstr. 1907–16* 4643/2 *s*-Trioxane. **1964** [see *trioxymethylene* s.v. TRIOXY-]. **1978** P. S. & C. A. BAILEY *Org. Chem.* x. 268 It [*sc.* formaldehyde] is usually sold and transported as low-molecular-weight polymers, such as 1,3,5-trioxane, formalin, and paraformaldehyde.

trioxide (traɪ'ɒksaɪd). *Chem.* [f. TRI- 5 + OXIDE.] A compound of three atoms of oxygen with an element or radical; e.g. ***sulphur trioxide***, SO_3; ***nitrogen trioxide***, N_2O_3.

1868 FOWNES *Elem. Chem.* (ed. 10) 134 A series of oxides containing quantities of oxygen in the proportion of the numbers 1, 2, 3, united with a constant quantity of another element, are distinguished as *monoxide*, *dioxide*, and *trioxide* respectively. **1911** ROSCOE & SCHORLEMMER *Treat. Chem.* (ed. 4) I. 723 Boron Trioxide, B_2O_3,.. is obtained when boron burns in the air, or in oxygen.

trioxy- (traɪ'ɒksɪ). *Chem.* [f. TRI- 5 + OXY-².] A formative denoting the presence of three atoms of oxygen in a compound; most commonly used as a substitute for *trihydroxy-*, denoting that three hydroxyl groups, OH, have replaced three hydrogen atoms in the compound designated by the rest of the name; **trioxy'methylene** = TRIOXAN.

Thus pyrogallol, $C_6H_3(OH)_3$, is one of the three *trioxybenzenes*, being derived from benzene, C_6H_6, by the replacement of three hydrogen atoms by three OH groups.

1863 *Fownes' Chem.* (ed. 9) 494 Trioxethylenamine. **1880** MILLER *Elem. Chem.* III. 552 *Trioxynaphthalene*: $C_{10}H_5(OH)_3$, is formed in a similar manner. **1880** *Jrnl. Chem. Soc.* XXXVIII. 25 The distillate left a white amorphous residue.. which proved to be identical with trioxymethylene, $C_3H_6O_3$. **1900** SMITH *Richter's Org. Chem.* (ed. 3) II. 230 Trioxybenzoic acids, $(HO)_3C_6H_2CO_2H$. Three of the six possible isomerides are known. **1964** N. G. CLARK *Mod. Org. Chem.* x. 188 On distilling aqueous formaldehyde with a trace of sulphuric acid, trioxan ('trioxymethylene') is obtained.

trip (trɪp), *sb.*¹ Also 5 tryp, 5–7 trippe, 6 tryppe, 7–8 tripp. [f. TRIP *v.*]

(The order of the senses here is not chronological, but follows that of the verb.)

I. 1. a. The action or an act of tripping or moving lightly and quickly; a light lively movement of the feet; tripping gait or tread; the sound of this.

1600 in Bodenham *Eng. Helicon* O iij, More fine in trip, then foote of running Roe. **1694** DRYDEN *Love Triumph.* IV. i, Yonder comes Dalinda; I know her by her trip. **1747** R. FORBES *Lyon in Mourning* (1895) I. 117 Some.. used to take a dance in the cabin.. they could not prevail with her to take a trip. **1814** SCOTT *Wav.* xxxvii, He sometimes could distinctly hear the trip of a light female step. **1871** B. TAYLOR *Faust* (1875) I. xxii. 200 How each his legs in nimble trip, Lifts up and makes a clearance.

†**b.** *spec.* A kind of step in dancing. *Obs.*

1599 B. JONSON *Cynthia's Rev.* II. iv, Both the swimme and the trip are properly mine, euery body will affirme it, that has any iudgement in dancing.

†**c.** *fig.* app. A step *towards* accomplishing something. *Obs. rare.*

1682 BUNYAN *Holy War* 6 The King.. takes them in the very nick and first tripp that they made towards their design, convicts them of the treason [etc.].

2. *fig.* ***in the trip of a minute***, in the movement or passage of a minute, in a minute's space.

1728 VANBR. & CIB. *Prov. Husb.* IV. i. 59 They'll whip it up, in the Trip of a Minute. **1899** *Literature* 25 Nov. 515/1 Mr. Zangwill's [prologue] has caught the 'trip' of the old fashioned prologue.

3. A short voyage or journey; a 'run'. Apparently originally a sailor's term, but very soon extended to a journey on land. **a.** A short voyage or run of a ship, between two points, or to a point and back again; each of a series of short runs made by a ship or boat; hence also, a short voyage in a ship.

1691 T. H[ALE] *Acc. New Invent.* 12 [A vessel pronounced] not to be fit for her being adventured to Sea.. for more than a small tripp. *Ibid.* 15 Making a Tripp for England. **1743** BULKELEY & CUMMINS *Voy. S. Seas* 106 After three or four Trips return'd, and anchor'd where we came from. **1754** RICHARDSON *Grandison* IV. lvi, It will be what mariners call a *trip* to England. **1769** COOK *Voy. round World* II. i. (1773) 293 The little boat was obliged to make three trips before we could all get over to the rest of the party. **1773** *Life N. Frowde* 81 We were one Voyage to Dantzic and Hamburgh, another to Copenhagen and Stockholm,.. During all these Trips, my Polly and I wrote to each other. **1852** MRS. STOWE *Uncle Tom's C.* xxxi, The good steamer *Pirate*, which lay at the levee, ready for a trip up the Red River. **1867** SMYTH *Sailor's Word-bk.*, *Trip*, an outward bound passage or short voyage, particularly in the coasting trade. **1879** FROUDE *Caesar* xvi. 270 Two trips were required to transport the increased numbers.

b. A short journey or run on land; *esp.* each of a series of journeys or runs over a particular route.

(The meaning in quot. *c* 1440 is doubtful.)

[*c* **1440** *York Myst.* xviii. 133 An aungell.. bad me flee With hym and þe On-to Egipte. And sertis I dred me sore To make my smale trippe.] **1699** DAMPIER *Voy.* II. III. viii. 94, I pass'd the Isthmus twice, and was 23 days in the last Trip that I made over it. **1706** E. WARD *Wooden World Diss.* (1708) 53 If ever he make a Trip by Land, it's a Wonder. **1856** KANE *Arct. Expl.* II. xvi. 169 The food I could bring from the vessel by occasional trips with my dog-team. **1901** *Daily News* 3 Jan. 6/4 These two men work on eight-trip shifts, each trip consisting of an eastward and westward journey. **1906** *Ibid.* 22 Dec. 6 The 'bus-driver.. is paid by 'trip', and anxious to get his trips done.

c. A short journey (by sea or land) for pleasure or health, an excursion (more fully ***pleasure trip***); in later use often applied to such a journey whatever its length. Also applied to a passage by rail provided at a fare lower than the usual; a ***cheap trip***, an excursion; occas. short for 'party of trippers' or 'trip-train'.

This arose imperceptibly out of a or b, and it is not easy to fix its first use.

c **1749** LADY LUXBOROUGH *Lett. to Shenstone* (1775) 159 If you would take a trip to this little Retreat at this melancholy season. **1774** GOLDSM. *Nat. Hist.* (1776) I. 152 A passage over the Alps, or a journey across the Pyrenees, appear pretty trips or excursions, in the comparison. **1812** *Religionism* 25 Lectureship Will meet th' expences of a country trip. **1861** THORNBURY *Turner* (1862) I. 18 Later trips to Margate made him love Kent and the sea. **1880** *Sat. Rev.* 2 Oct. 423/2 On inquiring.. what it all means, he is told that 'a trip is in' from some large manufacturing town, and his peace is gone, for that day at least. **1884** *Times* (weekly ed.) 29 Aug. 14/1 [They] hurry off on flying trips to Kerry or Connemara.

†**d.** An account or description of a journey. *Obs.*

1712 SWIFT *Lett. Eng. Tongue* Wks. 1755 II. I. 189 Those monstrous productions, which under the name of trips, spies, amusements, and other conceited appellations, have over-run us for some years past.

e. Each run or voyage of a fishing vessel; also (*U.S.*) the catch or take of fish during a single run; the proceeds of a trip in fish.

1891 in *Cent. Dict.*

f. *Mining.* A train of cars run in and out of a mine as a single unit.

1909 in *Cent. Dict. Suppl.*

g. *colloq.* ***this*** (or ***that***) ***trip***: on this (or that) particular time; on the occasion specified.

1746 C. KNOWLES *Let.* 19 Sept. in J. S. McLennan *Louisbourg* (1918) x. 174 M. le Duc with all his force shan't have Louisbourg this Trip. **1902** S. E. WHITE *Blazed Trail* 188, I guess I'll let you off this trip. **1906** E. DYSON *Fact'ry 'Ands* ii. 18 Copped out that trip, didn't yeh?

h. *Racing.* The distance from start to finish of a race.

1959 *Times* 1 June 16/7 Dan Cupid is a stocky.. colt with .. little on public form to prove he can get the trip. **1969** *Australian* 24 May 34/5 Koranui: eighth to Deep Court over 14½f here last Sat. Looks tested at this trip from 24 yd. **1977** *Cork Examiner* 6 June 8/9 The highly fancied Pharly, who beat Crystal Palace three weeks ago in the Prix Lupin at Longchamp over a slightly shorter trip.

4. *Naut.* A single board or reach in tacking; a tack. Also *transf.* a run on land.

1700 T. BROWN *Amusem. Ser. & Com.* 34, I Tack'd about, and made a Trip over Moor-fields. **1708** *Constit. Watermen's Co.* lxi, If any Tilt-Boat-Master.. shall.. turn to Windward in any of the said Boats except one Trip in each particular Reach. **1722** CAPT. OGLE in *Lond. Gaz.* No. 6091/3 The wind took me a-head and I made two Trips. **1867** SMYTH *Sailor's Word-bk.*, *Trip*.. also denotes a single board in plying to windward.

5. *slang* (orig. *U.S.*). **a.** A hallucinatory experience induced by a drug, esp. LSD. Cf. *down trip* s.v. DOWN *a.* 1 e.

1959 N. MAILER *Advts. for Myself* III. 245, I took some mescaline... At the end of a long and private trip which no quick remark should try to describe, the book of *The Deer Park* floated into mind. **1960** J. GELBER *Connection* I. 23 All right, junkies. During our trip we will incorporate an allied art—the motion picture. **1966** *Daily Tel.* 10 Aug. 13/3 The tape-recorder picked up the horrifying moans and shrieks of one man who had made 33 pleasurable 'trips' with LSD and was encountering his first 'freakout,' or bad LSD experience. **1971** *Sci. Amer.* Sept. 240/3 One of the volunteers had a bad trip, entering a panicky and nearly psychotic state. **1975** I. MURDOCH *Word Child* 301 You were under the influence. He tried to talk to you... I said you were on a trip.

b. *transf.* and *fig.* An experience, esp. a stimulating one.

1966 *Time* 1 July 50 The Jefferson Airplane flies on weekends at a discothèque in Fillmore Auditorium, where projectors flash quivering, amoeba-like patterns on the walls to induce the dancers 'to take a 'trip'..without drugs'. **1968** L. W. ROBINSON *Assassin* (1969) xii. 128 Their passion was a long one.., as though they hated to come back, ever, from the rocking, tossing, sweet trip. **1970** *Time* 3 Aug. 32 Part of the message is in the drug argot that he [*sc.* Arthur Blessitt] raps out to his street audiences: 'You don't need no pills. Jes' drop a little Matthew, Mark, Luke, and John. Christ is the ultimate, eternal trip.' **1974** *Melody Maker* 13 July 3/7 The drums are bright shiny cab yellow by the way. It's a trip. **1978** G. VIDAL *Kalki* iv. 91 On the other hand, the shop itself was not only exotic, it was a trip, as the addicts say.

c. An activity, attitude, or state of mind, esp. one that is delusory or self-indulgent. Cf. *ego-trip* s.v. EGO 5.

1967 WENTWORTH & FLEXNER *Dict. Amer. Slang* Suppl. 708/2 *Trip*,..any activity, outing, period of time, or way of life. Some beat and student use since c 1965. **1969** [see BIT *sb.*[2] 4 i]. **1970** J. POPENOE *Inside Summerhill* 104 It [*sc.* a gang] was a great power trip for the 14-year-old boy who was the leader. **1972** V. FERDINAND in A. Chapman *New Black Voices* 470 It's an unbelievable trip to think that the absence of quality is the cause for the exclusion of Black writers when there is so much garbage being dumped on the heads of people by white publishers. **1974** K. MILLET *Flying* III. 282 Hoping is a trip, and it's hopeless anyway. **1977** *New Musical Express* 12 Feb. 8/2 Transcribed onto paper his words may sound like a speech by a musician with delusions of grandeur, but Piazzo ain't into that trip. **1979** R. L. SIMON *Peking Duck* xvi. 117, I shouldn't bother—politics was a sixties trip.

II. 6. a. 'A stroke or catch by which the wrestler supplants his antagonist' (J.); a sudden catching of a person's foot with one's own so as to cause him to lose his balance and stumble or fall.

1412–20 LYDG. *Chron. Troy* II. 1867 Sodeynly to make hym doun to falle, And with a trip, þrowe him on þe bake. **1530** PALSGR. 283/1 Tryppe in wrastlyng, *crochet, jambet. Ibid.* 762/2, I gyve one a tryppe, or caste my foote byfore hym to gyve hym a fall. **1697** DRYDEN *Virg. Georg.* II. 776 The Groom..stript for Wrestling, smears his Limbs with Oyl, And watches with a Trip his Foe to foil. **1760–72** H. BROOKE *Fool of Qual.* (1809) III. 20 [He] gave a slight trip to his..assailant, who instantly fell. **1825** SCOTT *Betrothed* xxxii, I knew the old De Lacy's back-trip as well as thou.

b. *fig.*

c **1430** *Hymns Virg.* (1867) 75 Til deep þee caste with a trippe of dissaite. **1601** SHAKS. *Twel. N.* v. i. 170 Or will not else thy craft so quickely grow, That thine owne trip shall be thine ouerthrow? **1660** WINSTANLEY *Eng. Worth.* Pref. 3 The trips that Writers cunningly give one another. **1884** SHARMAN *Hist. Swearing* iii. 39 Socrates..held at a just appreciation the trips and sallies of Athenian manhood.

c. In coursing: see quots.

1856 'STONEHENGE' *Brit. Sports* (ed. 2) I. III. viii. §2 A Trip or Jerk occurs when a dog in attempting to kill his hare, lays hold of her but loses her again; these score half-a-point. **1890** A. R. STARR in *Upland Shooting* 466 The trip is an unsuccessful effort to hold a rabbit, although the greyhound may touch him, or even tumble him.

7. a. A stumble or mis-step caused by striking one's foot against an object so as to lose one's equilibrium. †*to hang on the trip*, to hang on the point of falling or toppling over (*obs.*).

1681 COTTON *Wond. Peak* (ed. 4) 42 Jutting Stones that, by the Earth left bare, Hang on the trip, suspended in the air. **1687** A. LOVELL tr. *Thevenot's Trav.* III. 45 Elephants.. are the surest footed of all Beasts of Carriage,..it is very rare to see them make a trip. **1710** STEELE *Tatler* No. 231 ¶2 The poor Animal being now almost tired, made a second Trip. **1846** *J. Baxter's Libr. Pract. Agric.* (ed. 4) I. 419 If the [horse's] toe dig into the ground before the foot is firmly placed, a trifle will cause a trip and a fall. **1884** MARTINEAU in *Mem. Anna Swanwick* iii. (1903) 147 A bruise which I got through a trip-up and fall upon some rough rocks.

b. *fig.* Cf. TRIP *v.* 8 b, c.

1584 LYLY *Campaspe* I. ii, It is a signe by the trip of your tongue.. that you haue done that to day, which I haue not done these three dayes. (*Psyllus*) What is that? (*Manes*) Dined. **1649** G. DANIEL *Trinarch., Hen. IV* i, The Pulse of Nature neuer giues one trip.

c. *Mil.* A contrivance for tripping an enemy.

1862 *Catal. Internat. Exhib.* II. XI. 14/2 Trip for Checking Infantry and Cavalry..formed by laying the bands singly on the ground three or four feet apart, edge-wise and buttoned.

8. A mistake, blunder; a fault; a slip, lapse; a false step; a slip of the tongue. †*to take* or *have in a trip* (also †*to take trip*), to catch tripping, to detect in an error (*obs.*).

(In some cases *take in a trip* seems to have been misunderstood to mean 'take in a trap'.)

1548 UDALL, etc. *Erasm. Par. Mark* x. 63 Y^e other desired more to take him in a trip, then to be healed: to proue him, rather then to learne. **1551** ROBINSON tr. *More's Utop.* I. (1895) 91 [To] fynde some hole open to set a snare in, wherewith to take the contrarie parte in a trippe. **1579** FULKE *Refut. Rastel* 725 He is taken tardie in his owne trip. **1594** J. DICKENSON *Arisbas* (1878) 69 Thus fell Loue into a trip: Thus she galde him with a quip. **1604** N. D. *3rd Pt. Three Convers. Eng.* 214 Sutcliffe, being taken trip by E. O. ..beateth himselfe vp and downe pittifully. **1628** MILTON *Vacation Exerc.* 3 And mad'st imperfect words with childish tripps, Half unpronounc't, slide through my infant-lipps. **1773** J. BERRIDGE *Wks.* (1864) 130 A trip in one point would have spoiled all. **1841** BP. WILBERFORCE in *Croker Papers* (1884) 23 July, An occasional trip in the performance was what threw you out.

III. 9. a. *Mech.* A contrivance that trips (see TRIP *v.* 14); a projecting part of some mechanism which comes into momentary contact with another part so as to cause or check some movement. (Cf. TRIP-HAMMER.)

1906 *Westm. Gaz.* 6 Mar. 10/1 To protect trains in foggy weather, when the arms and lights of signals are obscured, the automatic train-stop has been installed... A little arm is raised to a vertical position and strikes a trip on the front motor-car of the passing train. By this operation current is cut off. **1907** *Daily Chron.* 8 Aug. 2/3 In dismounting the pedal is again held against the trip, and by it the rider swings himself comfortably out of the saddle to drop on his foot as the cycle is still moving along.

b. *Nuclear Sci.* (See quots.)

1962 *Gloss. Terms Nucl. Sci.* (*B.S.I.*) 122 *Trip*, a reduction in reactor power initiated by any of the safety circuits of the reactor. **1978** *Times* 1 Feb. 4/7 Reactors suffer occasional unscheduled shut-downs or 'trips' from a wide range of causes, such as fail-safe faults on protective equipment, operator errors and faults in conventional non-nuclear equipment.

IV. 10. *attrib.* and *Comb.* (in some cases perh. from the vb.-stem); in sense 3, as ***trip-card, -committee, -fund, -mileage, -taking***; in sense 9, describing an appliance for catching, releasing, or actuating some part, or a machine operated by such a device, as ***trip-coil, -cord, -cut-off, -die, -lever, -motion, -piece, -pin, -wagon, -wheel***; also **trip-bucket**, a bucket used for raising water from wells in Arabia, operated by a tripping device and pulled by animals; **trip-catch**, a catch which holds the trip or releasing device until it is tripped; †**trip-coat**, ? a turn-coat; **tripcock**, a device on a train which applies the brakes when engaged by a projection on the track, if the train is passing a signal set at danger; **trip-dial**, in a cyclometer, a dial on which the mileage of each trip is registered; **trip-engine**, a steam-engine having a *trip valve-gear* (*Cent. Dict. Suppl.* 1909); **trip-gear**, short for *trip valve-gear* (*Cent. Dict.* 1891); **trip-hook**, some instrument of torture (perh. an error; cf. GADGE *sb.*); **trip-line**, in *Lumbering*, a light line attached to the dog-hook, or to a cable, by which these are recovered or returned; **tripmeter**, an instrument which may be set to record the distance travelled by a vehicle during each trip; similarly ***trip (mileage) counter, trip (distance, mileage) recorder***; **trip money**: see quot.; **trip-rate**, the rate of payment by the trip: see *trip-system*; **trip-shaft**: see quot.; **trip-sill**: see quot.; **trip slip**, a strip of paper in which a car conductor registers the number of fares taken on each trip (*U.S.*); **trip switch** *Electr. Engin.* (see quot. 1924); **trip system**, a system of payment of men in charge of a train, omnibus, or the like by the trip or journey; †**trip-taker**, one who 'takes another in a trip', a fault-finder; **trip-train**, a mineral train which is intended to make a certain number of trips, out and home, in the day; also, an excursion train; **trip valve-gear**, a valve-gear in which the steam is cut off by the tripping of a lever which holds open the steam-valve. See also TRIP-HAMMER.

1926 T. E. LAWRENCE *Seven Pillars* (1935) xxxix. 229 He told me of the wheel over the well, with its machinery of leathern *trip-buckets, raised by oxen upon an inclined path of hard-trodden earth. **1959** W. THESIGER *Arabian Sands* x. 190 Villagers in the Hadhramaut use camels and oxen to raise the trip-buckets from which they water their cultivation. **1897** *Outing* (U.S.) XXX. 492/2 Road-rides are scheduled on cards distributed among the members. These *trip-cards are a commendable feature. **1880** TOLHAUSEN tr. *Uhland's Corliss-Engines* 193 The edge of a *trip-catch fastened on the eccentric strap, will approximately move on an elliptical path, and trip up against a steel catch-plate fastened on the extremity of the inlet valve-spindle. *a* **1619** FLETCHER *Mad Lover* I. i, Twenty of your *trip-coats turn their tippets. **1906** *Railway Mag.* Apr. 341/2 These automatic signals have a trigger, which, when the signal is at danger, should engage with a *trip cock on the vehicles of the train. **1968** O. S. NOCK *Railway Enthusiasts' Encycl.* VII. 274 Co-acting with each stop signal is a train stop, mounted beside the track... When the signal is at danger, the arm is raised. If a train overran a signal..a trip cock lever would strike the raised train stop arm. **1903** *Trans. Amer. Inst. Elect. Engin.* 657 (Cent. Supp.) *Trip-coil. **1959** *Motor Manual* (ed. 36) vii. 195 Another difference with the *trip counter is that it may be set to zero at any time. **1977** *Westworld* (Vancouver, B.C.) May–June 34/2 This gradual phasing-in of the changes means that by 1978 all instrumentation, speedometers, odometers and tripcounters will be entirely converted [to metric]. **1884** KNIGHT *Dict. Mech.* Supp., **Trip Cut Off*, an arrangement to disconnect one portion of the valve motion from the other, so as to allow the cut-off valve to close with great rapidity. **1907** *Daily Chron.* 27 Mar. 9/5 For all-round purposes a double cyclometer with '*trip' dial is preferable. **1955** *Motor* 7 Dec. 765/1 (*caption*) *Trip distance recorder re-setting (twist). **1884** *Pall Mall G.* 11 Sept. 4/1 At the mills and workshops ..weekly payments are received towards the *trip fund... The tickets are supplied..a fortnight beforehand, the trip committee being responsible for the issue and the payment of those actually used. **1846** BROWNING *Soul's Trag.* I. 333 The glowing *triphook, thumbscrew and the gadge. **1904** *Sci. Amer. Suppl.* 23 July 23880 On this stem is fixed a *trip lever, C, which holds B against A by the spring, D. **1905** *U.S. Dept. Agric., Logging terms*, **Trip-line*, a light rope attached to a dog hook, used to free the latter when employed in breaking a jam... *Syn.* throw line. *Ibid.*, *Haul back*, a light wire rope..used to return the cable. *Syn.*...trip line. **1966** T. WISDOM *High-Performance Driving* xi. 114 A driver..may..exchange his present speedo for a similar one with a *trip meter. **1972** O. SELA *Bearer Plot* xxi. 134 Elmer hunched over the bicycling machine... The tripmeter read 5.2 kilometres. **1909** *Westm. Gaz.* 17 June 4/2 The Jones Speedometer..registers up to sixty miles an hour, and is fitted with season and *trip mileage. **1959** *Motor Manual* (ed. 36) vii. 195 When a *trip mileage counter is also fitted this will be constructed on similar lines to the main counter. **1962** *Times* 8 May 16/5 The car is well equipped, and noteworthy points include..a *trip mileage recorder, brake servo warning light, twin screenwashers. **1970** *Motoring Which?* Apr. 55/1 All six cars had a speedometer, mileage recorder, trip mileage recorder, fuel gauge. **1891** *Labour Commission Gloss.* s.v. *Money*, **Trip money*, a term used on canals to mean a payment in addition to tonnage; a bonus given in addition to wages. **1907** *Daily Chron.* 27 Mar. 9/6 The 'Little *Trip Motion'. **1908** *Ibid.* 6 June 8/3 The trip motion.. consists of a catch which holds the cranks and pedals at a certain position. **1901** *Westm. Gaz.* 25 Nov. 8/3 Their grievance is that *trip rates paid them are inadequate, and do not admit of a fair wage. **1966** T. WISDOM *High-Performance Driving* xi. 114 Few speedometers these days are fitted with *trip recorders. **1977** *Daily Tel.* 14 Dec. 12/6 Instruments include a rev. counter, speedometer trip recorder, and large clock. **1864** WEBSTER, **Trip-shaft*, (Steam eng.), a supplementary rock-shaft, worked by hand, for starting an engine. **1905** *U.S. Dept. Agric., Logging terms*, **Tripsill*, a timber placed across the bottom of the sluiceway in a splash dam, against which rest the planks by which the dam is closed. **1876** *Scribner's Monthly* Apr. 910/2 The conductor, when he receives a fare, will immediately punch in the presence of the passenger, A Blue *trip slip for an 8 cent fare. *a* **1884** Trip-slip [see *bell-punch* s.v. BELL *sb.*[1] 12]. **1924** S. R. ROGET *Dict. Electr. Terms* 275/2 **Trip Switch*, a switch for closing the tripping circuit of a circuit breaker. **1977** *Times* 15 July 8/5 The British system includes a series of trip switches, making it a simple matter for the engineer watching the various loads at any time to isolate a power failure. **1894** *Labour Commission Gloss.* s.v., The *trip system on railways is the equivalent of the piece-work system in productive industries. **1556** ROBINSON tr. *More's Utopia* (Arb.) 35 *margin*, *Triptakers. **1897** *Daily News* 31 May 2/7 The second and fourth weeks in June being very largely given up to *trip-taking and rejoicing. **1894** *Labour Commission Gloss.* s.v. *Trip System*, The men working a *trip train are paid a full week's wages. **1907** *Daily News* 28 June 6 He had come by a trip train to Skegness. **1903** *Electr. Rev.* 8 Aug. 197 Engines with Corliss *trip-valve gear driven by separate eccentrics. **1874** RAYMOND *Statist. Mines & Mining* 405 From these the chargers can take the ore in quantities to suit. A *trip-wagon, holding one charge, is generally used. **1877** *Ibid.* 429 A fan B, to give the puffs of air; a *trip-wheel, lever, and spring to operate the fan.

trip, *sb.*[2] Also 4 **tryppe**, 5 **tripe**, 5–6 **trippe**, 6 *Sc.* **trype**, 7 **tripp**. [Etymology obscure: perh. related to *troop*.]

†**1.** A troop or company of men. *Obs. rare.*

(App. in contemptuous use.)

c **1330** R. BRUNNE *Chron.* (1810) 203 Me þouht kyng Philip inouh was disconfite, Whan he & alle his trip [orig. *tut sun hoste*] for nouht fled so tite. *a* **1578** LINDESAY (Pitscottie) *Chron. Scot.* (S.T.S.) II. 157 Think not it wilbe ane trype [*v.r.* troup] of men of weir of France that will..conqueis this realme.

2. a. A small flock (of goats, sheep, hares, etc.). *Obs.* exc. *local.*

1305 [implied in *tripherd*]. *a* **1400** *Sir Perc.* 186 Scho.. with hir tuke a tryppe of gayte, With mylke of thame for to bayte To hir lyves fode. *c* **1410** *Master of Game* (MS. Digby 182) v, þat men calle a trippe of tame swyne, and of wylde swyne it is called a soundre. *c* **1470** in *Hors, Shepe, & G.* etc. (Caxton 1479, Roxb. repr.) 31 A Trippe of gete. A Trippe of hares. *c* **1470** HENRYSON *Mor. Fab.* IV. xix. *Ibid.* v. (*Parl. Beasts*) xxxvi, Ane trip of lambis dansing on ane dyke. *Ibid.* VII. (*Lion & Mouse*) i, Ane trip of myis..Richt tait and trig, all dansand in ane gyis. **1513** DOUGLAS *Æneis* III. iv. 24 Trippis eik of gait, but ony keipar, In the rank gersis pasturing on raw. **1556** WITHALS *Dict.* (1568) 14 b/2 A flocke or trippe of goates. **1575** TURBERV. *Venerie* 235 Huntesmen vse to saye an Heard of harts and hindes, buckes and does: and a Trippe of Gotes and Geates. **1584** in *Five Crt. Rolls Gt. Cressingham, Norfolk* (ed. Chandler 1885) 80 A certeyn trippe of sheep. **1674** RAY *S. & E.C. Words.* 77 A Trip of sheep i.e. a few sheep, Norf. **1807** VANCOUVER *Agric. Devon* (1813) 101 They are generally owners of trips or small flocks of sheep, depastured upon Exmoor. *a* **1905** in *Eng. Dial. Dict.* (Norfolk), I ha' got a trip of sheep.

b. A small flock of wild-fowl.

1805 MACKINTOSH *Driffield Angler* 294 Trip of dotterel. **1826** COL. HAWKER *Diary* (1893) I. 291 A fine trip of wigeon. **1859** FOLKARD *Wild-Fowler* liii. 276 Trip after trip [of wild-fowl] passes over his head in rapid succession. **1893** *Daily News* 28 Feb. 5/4 Wild ducks..are seen hurrying across the lawn with large 'trips' of young ones.

3. *Comb.* †**tripherd**, a goatherd, or shepherd.

1305 *Compotus of Bolton Abbey* in Whitaker *Hist. Craven* (1805) 330 In pane pro triphyrdes sarculant' metent'. **1317** *Ibid.* 338 Pro Tripherds.

†**trip**, *sb.*[3] *Obs.* In 4–5 also **trippe, trype, trep.** [Derivation uncertain.]

a. ? A piece of rind of cheese. **b.** *E. Anglian dial.*: see quots. *a* 1825, 1849.

c **1386** CHAUCER *Sompn. T.* 39 Yif hym a busshel whete Malt or Reye A goddes kechyl or a trype [*v.rr.* trip, -pe, trep] of chese. **1823** MOOR *Suffolk Words* s.v., 'Is that a cream cheese?' 'No, it is only a trip.' *a* **1825** FORBY *Voc. E. Anglia, Trip, s.*, a small cheese, made in summer, to be eaten in its soft and curdy state, or it soon becomes dry, tough, and uneatable. **1849** RAYNBIRD *Agric. Suffolk* 301 *Trip*..differs from cream-cheeses as having no cream in, and being thicker.

†**trip**, *sb.*[4] *Obs. rare.* [Cf. THRIP (*a* 1700).] Threepence.

1600 T. HILL *Art Vulgar Arith.* III. x. 261 b, The same Vingtin is woorth our trip or English 3d.

Trip (trɪp), *sb.*[5] Colloq. abbrev. of TRIPOS 2 d.

1909 R. BROOKE *Let.* 18 May (1968) 170, I am a prisoner ..in a room where a hundred and eight damned fools are writing Greek verses for the classical Trip. **1925** W. DEEPING *Sorrell & Son* xxiv. 229, I want a first in the Science Trip. **1927** R. LEHMANN *Dusty Answer* III. i. 126 Trips. Labs. Lectures. Dons. Vacs. Chaperons. The voices gabbled on.

trip (trɪp), *v.* Also 4 **trep**, 4–6 **tryp(pe**, 4–7 **trippe**, 5 *Sc.* **treip**, 6 **trype**, 6–8 **tripe**, 8 **tripp**, 9 *dial.* **thrip.** [a. OF. *treper*, *triper*, *tripper* (12th c. in Godef.) to strike (the ground) with the foot in sign of joy or of impatience, to leap, dance, also to trample or strike with the feet; in Cotgr. 'to hop, skip, trip, or foot it up and downe; also to stampe, trample on, tread under foot'; = Pr. *trepar* to hop, spring (Diez); of Lower Frankish origin: cf. MDu. *trippen* (Kilian, Du. *trippelen*) to skip, trip, hop, LG. *trippen*, *trippeln*, Fris. *tripje*; in ablaut relation with Du. *trappen*, G. *trappen*, *trappeln*, in OE. *treppan* to tread, trample: cf. G. *treppe* step.]

I. To tread or step lightly or nimbly.

1. *intr.* To move lightly and nimbly on the feet; to skip, caper; to dance; †of a horse: to caper, prance (*obs. rare*⁻¹). *arch.*

c **1386** CHAUCER *Miller's T.* 142 In twenty manere koude he trippe [*v.r.* trip] and daunce After the scole of Oxenford[e] tho. —— *Sqr.'s T.* 304 This hors anoon bigan to trippe [*v.r.* tryppe] and daunce. *c* **1430** *Pilgr. Lyf Manhode* IV. ix. (1869) 180, j carolle, j trippe, j daunce. *c* **1560** A. SCOTT *Poems* (S.T.S.) v. 9 Now in May to madynis fawis With tymmer wechtis to trip in ringis. **1598** SHAKS. *Merry W.* v. v. 97 About him (Fairies) sing a scornfull rime, And as you trip, still pinch him to your time. **1610** —— *Temp.* IV. i. 46 Each one tripping on his Toe, Will be here with mop, and mowe. *c* **1633** MILTON *Arcades* 99 Nymphs and Shepherds dance no more..Trip no more in twilight ranks. **1796** R. P. KNIGHT in *New Ann. Reg., Poetry* 152 No fairies now, or dapper elves are seen, By Fancy's eye, light-tripping o'er the green. **1849** JAMES *Woodman* ii, He found the young sisters..tripping in the green wood with the fairies of nights.

b. *intr.* with *it*.

1579 LYLY *Euphues* (Arb.) 115 If [she have] no cunning to daunce, request her to trippe it, if no skill in musicke, profer hir the Lute. **1632** MILTON *L'Allegro* 33 Com, and trip it as ye go On the light fantastick toe. **1712** ARBUTHNOT *John Bull* IV. viii, The Family tripped it about, and capered like hail-stones bounding from a marble floor. **1833** HT. MARTINEAU *Brooke Farm* ix. 112 The young folks tripped it away on the grass.

†**c.** *transf.* Of the heart: To beat excitedly. *Obs.*

c **1430** *Pilgr. Lyf Manhode* II. cvi. (1869) 115 Myn herte hoppeth for ioye, and lepeth and trippeth.

†**d.** *trans.* To step or tread on. *Obs. rare.*

c **1380** *Sir Ferumb.* 241 Garyn his gode stede hym fette, þat was in spaygne iboȝt; þe erld lep vp wyþ oute lette, His styrop trepede he noȝt.

2. *trans.* **a.** To perform (a dance) with a light lively step. *rare.*

1627 DRAYTON *Nymphidia* xli, Eu'ry Mayde..The Horne-pype neatly tripping. **1660** F. BROOKE tr. *Le Blanc's Trav.* 406 They dance and trip Moresco Sarabrands to them again. **1812** LADY NAIRNE *Caller Herrin* in R. Ford *Harp Perthshire* (1893) 112 He can trip the spring fu' tightly.

b. To tread lightly and nimbly, dance upon.

1749 SHENSTONE *Irregular Ode* 72 The sportive graces trip the green. **1808** A. SHARPE in R. Ford *Harp Perthshire* (1893) 93 Ghosts of the slain trip Corunna's lone shore. **1887** P. M'NEILL *Blawearie* 43 Nannie had been a short time at the dance, and had tripped the floor with both the joiner and the blacksmith.

3. *intr.* To go, walk, skip, or run with a light and lively motion; to move with a quick light tread; also with *it*, and in phr. † *to trip and go*.

? *a* **1400** *Morte Arth.* 3713 Alle trompede they trippe one trappede stedys. *c* **1470** HENRYSON *Mor. Fab.* v. (*Parl. Beasts*) xi, The lark, the maueis..treipand fra tre to tre. **1576** FLEMING *Panopl. Epist.* 405 That you should in stormy weather, and durtie wayes,..come tripping to mee in your silcken sleppers. **1579** GOSSON *Sch. Abuse* (Arb.) 25 Trype and goe, for I dare not tarry. **1588** SHAKS. *L.L.L.* IV. ii. 144 Trip and goe, my sweete, deliuer this Paper into the hand of the King. **1712** TICKELL *Spect.* No 410 ⁋1, I dismissed my Coach at the Gate, and tripped it down to my Counsel's Chambers. **1870** ROCK *Text. Fabr.* I. 240 Hares tripping within a park. **1883** S. C. HALL *Retrospect* II. 173 She.. tripped before us up the stairs to the drawing-room.

b. *transf.* and *fig.*

1662 STILLINGFL. *Orig. Sacræ* III. i. §18 We see..with what facility the mind..trips over mountains, crosseth the ocean. *a* **1774** TUCKER *Lt. Nat.* (1834) II. 126 Vanity.. mingles among our vital juices, trips along the tongue, dances upon the eyes. **1854** ALFORD in *Life* (1873) 237 So many notes tripped backwards and forwards between us. **1884** W. C. SMITH *Kildrostan* 86 There's a nice breeze tripping on the Loch.

c. *Angling.* See quots.

1867 F. FRANCIS *Angling* i (1883) 8 The line [is] plumbed, so that the float shall carry the hook just off the bottom, now and then perhaps touching it, or 'tripping'. *Ibid.* ii. (1880) 66 The right depth..for the worm to trip or drag slowly over the bottom.

d. quasi-*trans.* = RUN *v.* 37 a.

1850 BLACKIE *Æschylus* II. 64 Far liefer would I lackey this bare rock Than trip the messages of Father Jove.

4. *trans.* To cause to trip or go nimbly; to send *forth* trippingly.

1598 E. GILPIN *Skial.* (1878) 20 Come trip the dice, haue at you box (Madame) Ile cast at all. **1616–61** HOLYDAY *Persius* (1673) 294 His dainty palate tripping forth his words. **1901** 'ZACK' *Dunstable Weir* 191 When her zot under the big fig tree, thripping her lace-bobbins in and out.

5. *intr.* **a.** To make a trip or short excursion. Also *to trip it*.

1664 ETHEREDGE *Comical Revenge* Prol., If you shou'd, we and our Comedies Must trip to Norwich, or for Ireland go. **1699** J. DUNTON *Life & Err.* (1818) II. 613 The gentleman who tripped lately to Ireland. **1767** H. WALPOLE *Let. to G. Montagu* 31 July, I shall trip to Paris in about a fortnight. **1878** M. C. JACKSON *Chaperon's Cares* I. xiii. 177 Persuaded Mr. Kirke to trip it to Brighton for the good of his health. **1892** BESANT in *Illustr. Lond. News* Summer No. 1 The trippers have not yet begun to trip.

b. *slang* (orig. *U.S.*). To experience hallucinations induced by a drug, esp. LSD. Also with *out*. Also *transf.* Cf. TRIP *sb.*[1] 5 a.

1966 [see PSYCHEDELIC *sb.* 2]. **1968** *Globe & Mail* (Toronto) 3 Feb. 25/1 'Trip with us,' coaxes Duke Edwards in a sandy voice... 'Trip with us—without the aid of LSD.' **1969** *Daily Tel.* 4 Sept. 23/2 He was asked if he took LSD, and answered: 'I have been tripping for three weeks.' **1971** [see MANDY, MANDY]. **1976** H. FERGUSON *Confessions of Long Distance Acid Head* 13 The bunch with whom I used to trip out and smoke pot with were form-mates of my brother. **1980** J. SCOTT *Gospel Lamb* iii. 45 Some of the people here were tripping already. Seemed a pity not to bust 'em.

II. To strike with the foot so as to cause stumbling (and derived senses).

(App. an English development of sense.)

6. *trans.* To cause to stumble or fall by suddenly arresting or catching the foot; 'to throw by striking the feet from the ground by a sudden motion; to strike the feet from under the body' (J.). Also with *up*, † *down*. Often with the heels, foot, etc., as object, esp. in the phrase ***to trip up one's heels***.

c **1425** *Cast. Persev.* 3426 in *Macro Plays* 179 He wende þat he schulde a levyd ay, tyl dethe trypte hym on his daunce. **1530** PALSGR. 762/2 Why dyd you tryppe him as he was ronnyng? **1592** GREENE *Art Conny Catch.* III. 32 The other following tript vp his heeles. **1592** SHAKS. *Ven. & Ad.* 722 The earth, in love with thee, thy footing trips. **1605** SHAKS. *Lear* I. iv. 95 *Ste.* Ile not be strucken, my Lord. *Kent.* Nor tript neither, you base Foot-ball plaier. *Ibid.* II. ii. 32, 126. **1627** DRAYTON *Nymphidia* lvii, A Stump doth trip him in his pace, Downe comes poore Hob vpon his face. *a* **1653** GOUGE *Comm. Hebr.* xi. 20 (1655) III. 84 The verb.. signifieth to supplant, or to trip down, which is oft done with the heel. **1711** ADDISON *Spect.* No. 42 ⁋1 The right adjusting of her Train, lest it should chance to trip up her Heels. **1786** MME. D'ARBLAY *Diary* 13 Aug., I have come on prodigiously..in the power and skill of walking backwards, without tripping up my own heels. **1828** SCOTT *F.M. Perth* iv, Henry Smith, parrying the blow.., tripping him at the same time, gave him a severe fall. **1884** BROWNING *Ferishtah, Shah Abbas* 144 What lay on floor to trip your foot?

b. *fig.* or in *fig.* context.

a **1548** HALL *Chron., Hen. VI* 122 b, The Frenchmen.. determined to trippe and deceiue them by their accustomed seruaunt, called master Treason. **1551** BP. GARDINER *Explic., Transubstantiation* 109 b, There was neuer man tryppyd himselfe more hansomely to take a fall, then this auctour doth. **1597** SHAKS. *2 Hen. IV*, v. ii. 87 To trip the course of Law, and blunt the Sword That guards the peace. **1653** HOLCROFT *Procopius* II. 29 The former fight, wherein not our cowardise, but some cross fortune tript us. *a* **1774** TUCKER *Lt. Nat.* (1834) II. 118 The free-thinker..loves to pick holes..to trip up an adversary at unawares. **1872** BLACKIE *Lays Highl.* 62 Hasty winter..Came, and tripped the summer's heels.

(*b*) *spec.* in *U.S. Sport*, to defeat.

1974 *State* (Columbia, S. Carolina) 15 Feb. 6-B/2 The Generals got goals from Mike Gaines and Eddie Hewbrank in the second overtime to trip Airport, 2–0. **1979** *Honolulu Advertiser* 8 Jan. C-2/4 In Rural AJA games, Wahiawa tripped Pearl Ridge 7–5.

†**c.** *intr. to trip at*: to attempt to trip or overthrow. *Obs. rare.*

1633 HEYWOOD *Eng. Trav.* v. Wks. 1874 IV. 87 Though their riots tript at my estate, They haue not quite ore-throwne it.

†**d.** *trans. to trip off*: to throw off. *Obs. rare.*

1674 N. FAIRFAX *Bulk & Selv.* 173 At the very time of my writing this, Half..should be fairly tript off.

e. In coursing: see quot., and cf. TRIP *sb.*[1] 6 c.

1859 STONEHENGE *Brit. Sports* (ed. 4) I. III. viii. §2 A tripping or jerking the hare to be reckoned one point... It has been said, when a hare is tripped or jerked that the dog ought to have held her.

7. To overthrow by catching in a fault or blunder; to detect in an inconsistency or inaccuracy.

1557 N. T. (Genev.) *John* xv. 20 *note*, To be diligent to espie fautes to trippe one in. **1586** J. HOOKER *Hist. Irel.* in *Holinshed* II. 105/1 Being tript by the councell in his tale, was committed to the Fleet. **1611** SHAKS. *Cymb.* v. v. 35 These her Women Can trip me, if I erre. *a* **1625** FLETCHER *Noble Gent.* III. i, He must..Be a better States-man than yourself that can Trip me in anything.

8. *intr.* To strike the foot against something, so as to hop, stagger, or fall; to stumble *over* an obstacle; to make a false step.

c **1440** *Promp. Parv.* 503/1 Tryppyn, or stoomelyn, *cespito.* **1530** PALSGR. 762/2 My horse stombled nat, he dyd but tryppe a lytell. **1579** G. HARVEY *Let. to Spenser* Wks. (Grosart) I. 23 A good horse that trippeth not once in a iourney. **1637** HEYWOOD *Dial.* Wks. 1874 VI. 291 Run not so fast, lest thou shouldst trip perhaps. *a* **1760** I. H. BROWNE *Design & Beauty* Poems (1768) 100 Tumblers trip but to conceal their art. **1833** MARRYAT *P. Simple* xvii, I tripped over my sword, and nearly fell on my nose. **1867** TROLLOPE *Chron. Barset* II. xlix. 61 He would have tripped at the upward step at the cathedral door had she not been with him.

fig. **1581** MULCASTER *Positions* xxxvii. (1887) 150 Neither will I touch the other two, vnles I fortune to trip vpon them by chaunce. *a* **1716** SOUTH *Serm.* (1744) XI. 167 They may sometimes out of infirmity trip into a perjury, a murder or an adultery.

b. Said of the tongue: To stumble in articulation; to falter in speaking.

1526 *Pilgr. Perf.* (W. de W. 1531) 163 b, To saye his seruyce with stoppynge & tryppynge of tonge. **1598** DRAYTON *Heroic. Ep.* ii. 9 With the earnest Haste, my Tongue oft trips. **1690** LOCKE *Hum. Und.* III. x. §33 Drinking..till his Tongue trips, and his Eyes look red, and his Feet fail him. **1706** PHILLIPS (ed. Kersey), To *Trip*, to stumble with the Feet, or falter with the Tongue.

c. *Horology.* Of an escape-wheel: To fail to release itself from the pallet; see also quot. 1850 s.v. TRIPPING *vbl. sb.* 2.

1850–79 [see TRIPPING *vbl. sb.* 2]. **1884** F. J. BRITTEN *Watch & Clockm.* 89 Gravity escapements were rather regarded with suspicion as having a tendency to trip.

9. *intr.* To fall into an error; to make a mistake or false step; to commit a fault, inconsistency, or inaccuracy.

1509 BARCLAY *Shyp of Folys* (1570) 39 Thy finger lay before thy lips, For a wise mans tonge without aduisement trips. **1584** B. R. tr. *Herodotus* I. 37 b, Least he were taken vp for triping and conuicted of a lye. **1726** SWIFT *Gulliver* IV. xi, After many endeavours to catch me tripping in some part of my story [etc.]. **1864** TENNYSON *Grandmother* vii, Jenny had tript in her time. **1871** TYNDALL *Fragm. Sc.* (1879) II. vii. 93 How I rejoiced when I found an author tripping.

III. †**10.** *Naut. intr.* To tack. *Obs. rare.*

1687 A. LOVELL tr. *Thevenot's Trav.* II. 188 Thus did we trip to and again in that Streight, the wind continually shifting and turning.

11. *Naut. trans.* To loose (an anchor) from its bed and raise it clear of the bottom by the cable or a buoy rope. Also *intr.* for *pass*.

1748 *Anson's Voy.* II. i. 112 We..set the sails, which fortunately tripped the anchor. **1797** S. JAMES *Narr. Voy. Arabia*, etc. 16 We tripped our small bower. **1825** H. B. GASCOIGNE *Nav. Fame* 50 A greater force each steady shoulder plys, The Anchor Trips, and from the mud does rise. **1840** R. H. DANA *Bef. Mast* xxv, Everything was sheeted home and hoisted up, the anchor tripped and cat-headed, and the ship under headway. **1882** NARES *Seamanship* (ed. 6) 199 Sail must be made before tripping the anchor. **1903** *Union Mag.* Oct. 447/1 The usual plan is to take in the chain till it is straight up and down and then to trip the anchor by paying the boat off.

12. *trans.* To tilt; *spec. Naut.* to give (a yard) the necessary cant in sending it down; also, to lift (an upper mast) in order that it may be lowered.

1840 R. H. DANA *Bef. Mast* xxiii, [The royal yards] were all tripped and lowered together. **1841** —— *Seaman's Man.*, *Tripping Line*, a line used for tripping a topgallant or royal yard in sending it down. **1886** *Encycl. Brit.* XXI. 821/1 (*Ship-building*) The chain then draws the bolt, and in falling trips the cradle from under the bottom.

13. *intr.* To tilt or tip up; of the floors of a ship, to be strained or twisted out of their horizontal position.

1869 SIR E. J. REED *Shipbuild.* ii. 23 The floors are comparatively free to trip, by the keelson riding along the keel. **1874** THEARLE *Naval Archit.* 72 The hogging strains peculiar to long, narrow ships tend to produce a tripping of the floors; or an alteration in the form of the space..enclosed by keel, keelson, and floors. **1888** ELWORTHY *W. Somerset Word-bk.*, *Trip*, v. i. to move on a pivot or fulcrum. A paving stone not evenly bedded when stepped upon is apt to log —this is to trip.

14. *trans.* To release (a catch, lever, or the like) by contact with a projection; to operate (a mechanism) in this way. Also more widely, to cause to operate or respond; *spec.* in *Electronics*, to cause (a bistable device) to change from one stable state to the other; *to trip out*, to render electrically disconnected, esp. as an automatic action. Cf. TRIP *sb.*[1] 9.

1897 *Daily News* 4 Nov. 6/4 An automatic parachute was to spread itself to make the descent and 'trip' the camera as it gracefully came to earth. **1936** *Sun* (Baltimore) 25 Jan. 5/8 It was eleven minutes after the electrical apparatus operating the gas generating equipment was tripped before physicians pronounced Foster dead. **1937** *Rev. Sci. Instruments* VIII. 414/2 It is necessary that at each incident pulse the circuit shall be tripped from one equilibrium state to the other. **1950** *Engineering* 20 Jan. 79/3 The gap was in the form of an expulsion tube..this arrangement helping to extinguish quickly the power-follow current so that the transformer was not tripped out. **1953** C. A. LINDBERGH *Spirit of St. Louis* II. vi. 307, I tripped by safety-belt buckle

..and rolled out over the high rim of the cockpit. **1961** *Ann. Reg. 1960* 396 This light in turn tripped more atoms until none were left in the excited state. **1967** *Electronics* 6 Mar. 126/2 When the critical temperature is reached, the resistance of the thermistor changes to allow the proper value of current to flow, and this trips a relay. **1972** P. CLEIFE *Slick & Dead* xxviii. 233 Tripping the quick-release of my harness, I leapt from my seat. **1977** *Daily Tel.* 25 Oct. 2/1 'The damn thing didn't even trip our noise meters,' he was quoted as having said after last week's three days of test landings and take-offs at Kennedy Airport. **1978** *Sci. Amer.* Mar. 146/3 When I tripped the switch *S1*, the ouputs from *Q* and *Q̄* of *IC 1A* changed states: the *Q* then produced a logical-1 signal. **1981** *New Scientist* 29 Oct. 295/2 Another tree..in East Sussex caused a similar fault, tripping out another 400 kV supergrid line feeding the south coast.

b. *intr.* Of a mechanism or the like: to undergo a sudden change of state; to operate or (also *trip out*) cease to operate.

1940 *Jrnl. Marine Res.* III. 73 When each water bottle trips there will be a sufficient jar..so that the recording stylus..will make a noticeable mark on the temperature depth trace. **1950** *Engineering* 20 Jan. 79/3 In the 14 years under review, sub-station transformers tripped out 140 times. **1977** *Times* 16 July 5/8 Three main power lines.. were hit by lightning... This caused four more lines to trip out as the safety devices to stop them overloading came into action. **1980** *Sci. Amer.* Mar. 36/1 The main feedwater pumps in the lower level of the turbine building tripped, interrupting the removal of heat from the primary system. **1981** *New Scientist* 29 Oct. 295/2 As other parts of the grid tripped out, power stations in the South and South-West struggled to meet what demand they could.

15. *Bot. trans.* To operate the pollination mechanism of (certain flowers) by disturbing the keel so that the anthers and style spring out of it.

1909 *Bull. Bureau Plant Industry, U.S. Dept. Agric.* No. 24. 9 Only a slight pressure on the keel is necessary to trip the flower. **1930** *Jrnl. Amer. Soc. Agronomy* XXII. 782 The flowers were left exposed and not tripped artificially. **1978** *Nature* 7 Sept. 54/1 Most inbred lines show poor seed set unless their flowers are visited by bees or artificially manipulated (tripped) and are therefore called auto-sterile.

tripack (ˈtraɪpæk). *Photogr.* Also **tri-pack**, †**-pak**. [f. TRI- + PACK *sb.*[1]] A set of three superimposed plates or films with different colour sensitivities and kept in contact, so that three separation negatives can be obtained at one exposure; also (*integral tripack*), a film having three such emulsions on the one base.

1911 *Brit. Jrnl. Photogr.* 3 Mar. (Suppl.) 19 (*heading*) The Ives Tripak system of colour photography. **1924** *Ibid.* Sept. (Suppl.) 36/1 It is fundamentally impossible to obtain satisfactory results by the tri-pack system. **1931** [see *separation negative* s.v. SEPARATION 17]. **1953** [see INTEGRAL *a.* 2]. **1957** R. W. G. HUNT *Reproduction of Colour* v. 47 (*caption*) Sensitization of the layers in Kodachrome, Ektachrome, Kodacolor and other similar integral tripacks. **1973** D. A. SPENCER *Focal Dict. Photogr. Technol.* 606 The coloured positive images may be produced..*in-situ* by using integral tripack material.

tripair, -paleolate: see TRI- 4 a, 1.

tripal, trypal (ˈtraɪpəl), *a.* and *sb.* [f. TRIPE *sb.*[1] + -AL[1].]

†**A.** *adj.* Of or pertaining to the tripes or entrails. *Obs. rare.*

1709 [W. KING] *Usef. Transact. Philos.* Mar.–Apr. 47 Microscopical Observations on the Membranes of the Intestines, and other Trypal Vessels.

B. *sb.* A tall, lanky, or slovenly person. *Sc.*

1809 SKINNER *Poems, Christmas Ba'ing* 4 But a lang trypall there was Snap, Cam' on him wi' a bend. **1871** W. ALEXANDER *Johnny Gibb* x. (*dial.*), Mair smeddum..nor the like o' that gawkie trypal.

tripalmitin (traɪˈpælmɪtɪn). *Chem.* [f. TRI- 5 + PALMITIN: cf. TRIACETIN.] A crystalline substance, also called *palmitin* or *glyceryl tripalmitate*, $C_3H_5(C_{16}H_{31}O_2)_3$, occurring in palm-oil and in many animal and vegetable fats and oils, and prepared synthetically by Berthelot.

1855 *Q. Jrnl. Chem. Soc.* VII. 283 Natural margarin and palmitin..as well as the artificial compounds identical with them, appear indeed to be trimargarin and tripalmitin. **1913** THORPE *Dict. App. Chem.* (ed. 2) IV. 78 By heating palmitic acid with glycerol, the mono-, di-, and tri- palmitins are prepared.

tripam, -pang, obs. forms of TREPANG.

†**trip-and-go, trip-go,** *sb. phr. Obs.* [See TRIP *v.* 3.] The action of tripping and going; one who trips and goes, or who uses this expression.

1532 MORE *Confut. Tindale* Wks. 685/2 [Water] receiueth shortly the steppes of euery man, yea and of euery woman to, but she gete her on a pace, with trip and go quikly and walke wonderous light. **1601** CHETTLE & MUNDAY *Death Earl Huntington* v. i. Kj, Should any of these no for-sooths, These pray awayes, these trip and goes, these tits, Deny mee. **1611** in *Coryat's Crudities* Panegyr. Verses h ij, So nimble Tom, the traueller Trip-goe.

tripapalty, -papillated: see TRI- 4 a, 1.

triparental: see TRI- 1 a.

tripart (ˈtraɪpɑːt), *a. rare.* [f. TRI- + PART *sb.*] = TRIPARTITE *a.*; threefold; in quot. 1592, taking place between three parties, three-sided.

1592 WYRLEY *Armorie* 137 Which tripart combate was so noblie fought As sick prince tooke pleasure it t'behould. **1630** GOODALL *Tryall Trav.* Ded., To the Thrice Noble And Illustrious Lady:..Elizabeth..These tripart tryalls of trauell are consecrated by Baptist Goodall. **1791** COWPER *Iliad* xv. 230 By distribution tripart we received Each his peculiar honours.

†**ˈtripart,** *v. Obs.* Also 6 **try-**. [f. TRI- + PART *v.*] *trans.* To divide into three parts.

Chiefly in pa. t. and pple. *triparted*, Sc. *-it*: cf. next.

1528 LYNDESAY *Dreme* 202 The Patrimonie and rent.. Quhilkis suld haue bene trypartit in to thre. **1567** *Gude & Godlie B.* (S.T.S.) 210 Quhy war ȝe sa vnnaturall, As..Tripartit and deuydit him? **1621** QUARLES *Esther* Div. Poems (1717) 134 He That's born, may challenge but one part of three Triparted thus.

So **triˈpartible** *a.* [f. TRI- + L. *partibilis* divisible], separable into three parts or pieces.

1860 WORCESTER cites GRAY.

triˈparted, *ppl. a.* [f. OF. *triparti* or L. *tripartitus*: see -ED.] = TRIPARTITE *a.*

1424 in *Calr. Pat. Rolls* VI. 29 The mair and the aldermen..be thise presents triparted..make and ordeyne thise constitutiouns and restreynts. *c* **1456** PECOCK *Bk. of Faith* (1909) 298 In the stories clepid Ecclesiastik Storie and Tripartid Stori. **1514** in *Eng. Gilds* (1870) 146 Vnto twoo parties of thes Indentourz triparted,..the seid Maister & brethern hath putt ye common seal. **1586** FERNE *Blaz. Gentrie* 175 As they [crosses] are to be seen biparted, or diuided into 2 parts, so also may they be borne in Armes, triparted ouer the whole feeld. **1688** R. HOLME *Armoury* III. 270/2 Some blazon this ..triparted, if it end in three points. **1866** *Treas. Bot.* 1172 *Triparted, Tripartite*, parted to the base in three divisions.

Hence **triˈpartedly** *adv.*

1569 *Reg. Privy Council Scot.* II. 5 That the articles of this treaty may be accorded tripartedlie.

tripartient (traɪˈpɑːʃɪənt), *a.* and *sb. rare.* [f. TRI- + L. *partient-em* dividing.] See quot.

1706 PHILLIPS (ed. Kersey), *Tripartient*, any Number that divides another into three equal Parts, without any Remainder. Hence **1721** in BAILEY; and in later Dicts.

triˌpartiˈsan, *a.* [f. TRI- + PARTISAN *a.*] Of, representing, or composed of members of, three (political or other) parties.

1959 *Economist* 14 Mar. 950/2 Candidates deliver brief speeches of equal length to an invited bi-partisan or tri-partisan audience. **1965** *Ibid.* 20 Feb. 731/1 The cross-currents of party strife over what should be a tripartisan policy. **1972** D. DAKIN *Unification of Greece* v. 76 Otho accepted a tripartisan cabinet of seven who had been recommended by Makriyannis.

tripartism (traɪˈpɑːtɪz(ə)m). [f. TRIPART(ITE *a.* + -ISM.] **1.** Division into three political parties or other groups. Also *transf.*

1954 B. & R. NORTH tr. *M. Duverger's Pol. Parties* II. i. 222 A tripartism analogous to that in England at the same period where the Socialist party was taking up a position alongside the two 'bourgeois' parties. **1964** *Listener* 1 Oct. 505/1 If different types of secondary school really were 'separate but equal', the attacks upon tripartism would lose much force.

2. A system under which representatives of three groups engage in consultation, negotiation, or joint action; *spec.* a system of economic planning by representatives of government, employers, and trade unions.

1961 *Guardian* 14 June 18/6 The Soviet insistence on tripartism and triunity. **1974** *Government & Opposition* IX. 405 The British flirtation with planning throughout the 1960s could be characterized as toothless tripartism. **1980** *Times* 17 May 14/3 Meetings with Ministers are not the 'tripartism' that the TUC wants.

tripartite (traɪˈpɑːtaɪt, ˈtrɪpɑːtaɪt), *a.* (*sb.*) Also 5 **trypartite, -tyte,** 5–6 **tripertite, -tyte.** [ad. L. *tripartīt-us*, f. *tri-* three + *partītus*, pa. pple. of *partīrī* to divide.]

1. Divided into or composed of three parts or kinds; threefold, triple.

c **1420** LYDG. *Assembly of Gods* 1031 Freewyll, Vertew & Vyce, as trypartyte [*rimes* lyght, wyght]. **1432–50** tr. *Higden* (Rolls) II. 161 Of the tripartite langage of Saxones,..the weste men of Englonde sownde and acorde more with the men of the este..then the men of the northe with men of the sowthe. *Ibid.* III. 275 Oon Socrates Cassiodorus commendethe in his story tripartite. **1592** WARNER *Alb. Eng.* VIII. xliii. (1612) 206 Of Brittish race and many, and of Saxon Princes some, Whose blood by Normaine mixture now is tripartite become. **1609** HOLLAND *Amm. Marcell.* 56 Hee divided the nights according to a tripartite or three-fold function, For sleepe, for affaires of State, and for his booke. **1647** CLEVELAND *Poems, Smectymnuus* 44 Like to an *Ignis fatuus*, whose flame Though sometimes tripartite, joynes in the same. **1745** J. MASON *Self Knowl.* I. ii. (1853) 14 Man is ..a tripartite Person; or a compound Creature made up of three distinct Parts, viz. the Body, which is the earthy or mortal Part of him, the Soul, which is the animal or sensitive Part; and the Spirit or Mind, which is the rational and immortal Part. **1848** GALLENGA *Italy* I. IV. iii. 468 Though still nominally tripartite, Italy, for all commercial and intellectual purposes, was one. **1861** O'CURRY *Lect. MS. Materials* 347 The Tripartite Life of St. Patrick. **1900** *Westm. Gaz.* 15 Feb. 10/1 The folding bicycle... This detachable machine is known as the 'Tripartite', because it is made to disconnect into three separate parts.

b. Involving, or of the nature of, division into three parts.

1576 FLEMING tr. *Caius' Dogs* (1880) 2, I wyll expresse and declare in due order, the grand and generall kinde of English Dogges,..making a tripartite diuision. **1596** HARINGTON (*title*) An Anatomie of the Metamorphosed Aiax. Wherein by a tripertite method is plainly, openly and demonstratiuely declared [etc.]. **1785** BURKE *Nabob of Arcot* Wks. 1842 I. 331 They prevailed on him to propose a tripartite division of that vast country. **1856** MERIVALE *Rom. Emp.* (1865) IV. xxxix. 370 The tripartite division of the earth's surface is a tradition of unknown antiquity. **1882–3** *Schaff's Encycl. Relig. Knowl.* I. 724 A tripartite division into philosophical, historical and practical theology.

2. Made in three corresponding parts or copies, as an INDENTURE (q.v.) drawn up between three persons or parties, each of whom preserves one of the copies.

1442 in *Proc. King's Counc. Irel.* (Rolls) 275 He was bounde by endenture tripartite to kepe the peas. *a* **1483** *Liber Niger* in *Househ. Ord.* (1790) 74 One indenture trypartite; the one to remayne with these Butlers purveyours.. the other parte, with the clerke of buttillary..the thirde parte to remayne in the countyng-house. **1592** WEST *1st Pt. Symbol.* §47 D, These deedes indented are not only bypartite..but also may be made tripartite, that is of three parts. **1643** BAKER *Chron., Hen. IV* 36 They [Earls of Northumberland and Worcester, and Henry Hotspur] agreed upon a Tripartite Indenture under their hands and seales, to divide the Kingdome into three parts. *a* **1743** SOMERVILLE *Sweet-Scented Miser* 62 By precedents a bond can write, Or an indenture tripartite.

3. Engaged in or concluded between three parties.

1497 in Ellis *Orig. Lett.* Ser. I. I. 50 The tripartite Warre ..determyned ayenst the said Turk, and how the Hungaries, Boyams, and the Polans..shall make werre by land [etc.]. **1577–87** HOLINSHED *Chron.* III. 862/1 The articles of the league tripartite, agreed betwixt the emperour, the king of England, and the French king. **1665** MANLEY *Grotius' Low C. Warres* 666 George Count Solmes, Ernestus of Nassau,..and Vere General of the English,.. Govern'd the Army by a Tripartite Command. **1775** L. SHAW *Hist. Moray* iii. (1882) 402 A parsonage..the patronage whereof was once tripartite between the King, Marshal, and Duffus. **1857** GEN. P. THOMPSON *Audi Alt.* I. xxiv. 88 The tripartite treaty which virtually exists among three of the leading powers of the world.

4. *Her.* **a.** Applied to the field when divided into three parts of different tinctures: = TIERCÉ. **b.** Applied to a cross or saltire when each of its members consists of three narrow bands with spaces between. Also TRIPARTED, †TRIPARTITED.

1796 STEDMAN *Surinam* II. xix. 79 The arms [of Surinam] are tripartite, which I apprehend to be some of those of the house of Somelsdyke, the West India company, and the town of Amsterdam.

5. Consisting of three parts or divisions, as a member or organ of an animal or plant.

a. *Zool.* and *Anat.*

1658 ROWLAND *Moufet's Theat. Ins.* 936 A black bill or beak, hardish, tripartite. **1668** CULPEPPER & COLE *Barthol. Anat.* IV. iv. 163 It is inserted into the three Intervals of the four upper Ribs, being tripartite. **1911** J. W. JENKINSON *Sea Urchin* 270 These larvae had a mouth and a typically tripartite gut.

b. *Bot.*: *spec.* of a leaf, etc., Divided into three segments nearly to the base. (Abbrev. *3-partite.*)

1753 CHAMBERS *Cycl. Supp.* s.v. *Leaf*, Tripartite Leaf. **1862** DARWIN *Fertil. Orchids* ii. 90 The stigmatic surface is differently shaped, being more plainly tripartite. **1870** HOOKER *Stud. Flora* 256 Solanum Dulcamara..leaves ovate or cordate, sometimes 3-partite.

6. *Math.* Involving three sets of variables.

1869 CAYLEY *Math. Papers* VI. 464 The quantic is unipartite, bipartite, tripartite, &c., according as the number of sets is one, two, three, &c.

B. *sb.* †**a.** A tripartite indenture (see 2). *Obs.*

b. A book, document, or treatise in three parts.

1480 *Coventry Leet Bk.* 445 The people..in Hasil-wode, ..throwen don thornes, ffirs, fern, brome; diggen turves, & such other; where be the tripartite they owe nothyng to haue there but comien of pasture to their bestes cominable. **1657** R. MOSSOM (*title*) The Preacher's Tripartite, in Three Books. **1788** GIBBON *Decl. & F.* xliv. (1836) 757 The tripartite [*tripertita*] of Aelius Paetus..was preserved as the oldest work of jurisprudence. **1861** O'CURRY *Lect. MS. Materials* 350 Father Colgan's deductions from the text of the Tripartite [cf. quot. 1861 in sense 1 above].

†**tripartite,** *v. Obs. rare.* [f. as prec.] *trans.* To divide into three parts, or among three persons.

c **1470** HARDING *Chron.* XV. i. (*MS. Ashm. 34*, lf. 13 b), Whanne he [Brutus] had the Ile alle Trypartytede [*v.r.* (*MS.*) tripertited; *ed.* 1543 tripertyed] He callede the Chyef logres aftir locryne. **1633** GERARD *Descr. Somerset* (1900) 103 Reginald Prouse whose son's daughters, married to the Earls of March Mortimer, to the Lord Zouche, and to the Earl of Pembrooke Hastings, tripartited these lands. **1641** J. JACKSON *True Evang. T.* III. 165 The Text at the first was tripartited, and two of those parts are already handled.

¶**b.** *erron.* To divide (in general).

1653 T. BROOKS *Precious Remedies* (1658) 275 *margin*, The Counsellor saith, A States-man should be thus tripartited, his will to God, his love to his Master, his heart to his Countrey, his secret to his friend, his time to businesse.

†**tripartited,** *ppl. a. Obs.* [f. as prec. + -ED[1].] Divided into or composed of three parts; made between three parties: = TRIPARTITE *a.*

1426 *Anc. Deed* A. 10383 (P.R.O.) in *Catalogue* IV. 547 This endenture tripartitit beres wittenes that [etc.]. **1486** *Bk. St. Albans, Heraldry* C vij b, Off a cros tripartitid florishid. *a* **1548** HALL *Chron., Hen. V* 68 b, A truce tripertited betwene the .ii. kynges and the duke and their countreys was determined. **1612** DRAYTON *Poly-olb.* xv. 257 In Britaine here we find, our Severne, and our Tweed, The tripartited ile doe generally divide. **1650** T. BAYLY *Herba Parietis* 3 So many tripartited walls, with benches for to sit upon.

tripartitely (see TRIPARTITE *a.*), *adv.* [f. TRIPARTITE *a.* + -LY^2.] In a tripartite manner; in or into three parts.

1656 W. D. tr. *Comenius' Gate Lat. Unl* §584 The Body [is divided] tripartitely into head, trunk, joynts or Limbs. 1752 J. HILL *Hist. Anim.* 561 The Dasypus, with the covering tripartitely divided. The African Armadillo.

tripartition (traɪpɑːˈtɪʃən). [f. L. *tripartītus*: see TRIPARTITE *a.* and -TION.] Division into three parts; partition among three; †*Arith.* division by three (*obs.*).

1652 SPARKE *Prim. Devot.* (1663) 293 St. Augustine giveth another and very proper tripartition. 1691 tr. *Emilianne's Frauds Rom. Monks* (ed. 3) 103 He divided the vast Revenues of his Abby into three parts... Almost all the Abbots of France, Germany and Italy..made a Tripartition of the Revenues of their Abbies. 1853 TH. ROSS *Humboldt's Trav.* III. xxxii. 309 The tripartition of the Cordilleras, and ..the spreading of their branches. 1908 J. MASSIE in *Daily Chron.* 14 May 4/4 It is the principle of this Bill—its tripartition of Irish University education—that I do not like.

†**triˈpartitory**, *a.* *Obs.* *rare*$^{-1}$. [f. as prec. + -ORY^2.] Composed of three ingredients: = TRIPARTITE *a.* 1.

1651 BIGGS *New Disp.* ¶246 The other three, in this tripartitory [*erron. printed* -atory] secretion shall even then be worse naughty packs then the solitary bloud.

†**triˈparty**, *v.* *Obs.* *rare.* = TRIPARTITE *v.*

1543 [see quot. *c* 1470 s.v. TRIPARTITE *v.*].

triparty *a.*, **tripaschal**: see TRI- 1 b, a.

tripe^1 (traɪp). Also 5 *Sc.* trip, 5–6 trippe, 6 tryppe, 5–8 trype. [a. OF. *tripe*, *trippe* entrails of an animal (13th c. in Hatz.-Darm.), mod.F. *tripe* (whence Sp., Pg. *tripa*): ulterior source uncertain.]

1. The first or second stomach of a ruminant, esp. of the ox, prepared as food; formerly including also the entrails of swine and fish.

plain tripe is the first stomach, paunch, or rumen, ***honeycomb tripe*** the second, or reticulum.

a. With *a* and *pl.* as an individual thing. Now *rare.* (Usually plural.)

a 1300 *Sat. People Kildare* xviii. in *E.E.P.* (1862) 155 Hail be ȝe hokesters dun bi þe lake wiþ..tripis and kine fete and schepen heuedes. 14.. *Nom.* in Wr.-Wülcker 741/30, 31 *Hoc strutum, Hec tripa*, a tripe. *c* 1483 CAXTON *Dialogues* 26/27 We shall breke our fast with trippes, Of the lyver, of the longhe. 1533 ELYOT *Cast. Helthe* (1541) 22 The inwarde of beastes, as trypes and chytterlynges. 1556 WITHALS *Dict.* (1568) 48b/2 *Omasum*, is one of the foure partes of the beastes mawe very fatte, calde a tripe. 1655 MOUFET & BENNET *Health's Impr.* (1746) 201 The Taste of Tripes did seem so delicate to the Romans, that they often killed Oxen for the Tripes sake. 1767 STERNE *Tr. Shandy* IX. xxi, 'I'm loaded with tripes', says the second. 1880 R. OWEN in *Sanctorale Catholicum* Mar. 133 Then the priest, bearing tripes hot from the spit, approached as if to give to Pionius.

b. *collect. sing.* as the name of this substance.

13.. *K. Alis.* 1574 (Bodl. MS.), Ribaudes festeþ also wiþ tripe. *c* 1430 *Two Cookery-bks.* 1. 18 Trype of Turbut or of Codelynge. Take þe Mawes of Turbut, Haddok, or Codelyng, & pyke hem clene [etc.]. 1682 DRYDEN *Abs. & Achit.* II. 473 To what would he on quail and pheasant swell That ev'n on tripe and carrion could rebel? 1771 GOLDSM. *Haunch of Venison* 82 At the bottom [of the table] was tripe, in a swinging tureen. 1840 DICKENS *Barn. Rudge* xxxi, A steaming supper of boiled tripe and onions.

c. ‖*tripe(s) à la mode de Caen*, a traditional French dish of tripe cooked with carrots, onions, and cow heels in cider or white wine. Also *tripe à la mode* (*du pays*).

1859 THACKERAY *Virginians* II. iii. 26 'And an orchard.. and a dish of tripe *à la mode du pays*!'.. Museau would.. return to the subject of Normandy, and cyder, and '*trippes* [sic] *à la mode de Caen*.' 1936 E. WAUGH *Waugh in Abyssinia* ii. 71 From time to time she would placard the town with news of some special delicacy—*Grand Souper. Tripes à la mode de Caen.* 1968 E. HYAMS *Mischief Makers* ii. 20 An improbable garden-restaurant where we sat eating *tripe à la mode.* 1970 SIMON & HOWE *Dict. Gastronomy* 376/2 The classical way of preparing tripe in France is *Tripe à la mode de Caen.*

2. a. The intestines, bowels, guts, as members of the body; hence, the paunch or belly including them. *arch.* or *low.* Commonly in *pl.*

c 1470 HENRYSON *Orpheus & Eurydice* 298 Ane grysly grype,..with his bill his baly thro[w] can bore, Baith maw, mydred, hart, lever, & tripe [*v.rr.* trype, trip], He ruggit owt. *a* 1529 SKELTON *Ph. Sparowe* 307 Of Inde the gredy grypes Myght tere out all thy trypes! *c* 1645 HOWELL *Lett.* (1650) II. lv. 71 The Turke when he hath his tripe full of pelaw, or of Muton and Rice, will go to natures cellar. 1774 J. COLLIER *Mus. Trav.* (1785) 82 Dead cats, rotten puppies, the tripe of a dead horse. 1806–7 J. BERESFORD *Miseries Hum. Life* (1826) xx. 250 Poor Margery's tripes Are the martyrs of gripes.

b. Applied opprobriously or contemptuously to a person; also *bag of tripe.*

1595 *Eng. Tripe-wife* (1881) 150 Saist thou me so, thou Tripe, thou hated scorne? 1614 B. JONSON *Bart. Fair* IV. v, *Alice.* Thou Sow of Smithfield, thou. *Ursula.* Thou tripe of Turnebull. 1614, 1785 Tripe or Trillibub [see TRILLIBUB]. 1822 COBBETT *Weekly Reg.* 349 Any great, bloated, squeaking, bag of tripe. 1825 JAMIESON s.v. *Trypal*, A tall, meagre person is denominated 'a long tripe o' a fallow'.

3. *transf.* and *fig.* (in various applications). Now applied esp. to artistic work, opinions, conversation, or the like: worthless stuff, rubbish.

1676 D'URFEY *Mad. Fickle* II. i. (1677) 11 You Dog,.. Udsbores, I'le beat thee into a Tripe. *a* 1704 T. BROWN *Contin. Quaker's Serm.* Wks. 1709 III. II. 4 Sowse us therefore, in the Powdering-Tub of thy Mercy, that we may be Tripes fit for the Heavenly Table. 1892 *Spectator* 24 Dec. 930/2 This book..very vulgar..it is a dish of literary and artistic 'tripe-and-onions'. 1895 CROCKETT in *Cornh. Mag.* Oct. 341 He swore that he could make a song..that would be worth a shopful of such 'tripe'. 1902 'T. LE BRETON' *Mod. Christian* viii. 80 She puts in six or seven pages of her own tripe. 1927 C. CONNOLLY *Let.* Aug. in *Romantic Friendship* (1975) 313 Ordinary talk is such ghastly tripe once voice and gesture are removed. 1935 I. MILLER *School Tie* xiv. 277 'I've tried hard, sir; really I have.' 'Tripe! You've tried to get out of work.' 1952 W. STEVENS *Let.* 24 Oct. (1967) 763 Non-objective art without an aesthetic basis seems to be an especially unpleasant kettle of tripe. 1963 [see CODSWALLOP]. 1973 W. H. CANAWAY *Harry doing Good* I. ii. 22 The group of girls who were watching some tripe on television.

4. *attrib.* and *Comb.*, as ***tripe-broth***, ***fritter***, ***sausage***, ***soup***; ***tripe-gut***; ***tripe-cart***, ***-house***, ***-shop***; ***tripe-dealer***, ***-dresser***, ***-monger***, ***-seller***, ***-selling***; ***tripe-like***, ***-visaged*** adjs.; **tripe-cheeks**, a person with coarse blowzy cheeks; **tripe-club**, a society which meets to eat tripe; **tripe-hound** *slang*, (*a*) an unpleasant or contemptible person; also *spec.* a newspaper reporter or an informant; (*b*) a contemptuous term for a dog; *spec.* in *Austral.* and *N.Z.*, a sheep-dog; **tripe-man**, one who prepares and sells tripe as a business; **tripe-stone** *Min.*, see quot. 1816; †**tripe-wife** *sb.*, a female tripe-dresser; hence †**tripe-wife** *v.*, *trans.* to make into, or like, a tripe-wife; **tripe-woman** = *tripe-wife sb.*

1747 tr. *Astruc's Fevers* 308 Physicians prescribe on this occasion anodyne lenient clysters of *tripe-broth. 1912 *Dollar Mag.* Dec. 182 Neither of us had seen a *tripe-cart before. 1599 PORTER *Angry Wom. Abingd.* H iij b, What needst thou to care, whipper-Ienny, *Tripe-cheekes. 1710 (*title*) The Swan *Tripe-Club: A Satyr on the High-Flyers. 1868 *Daily News* 19 June, The tripes of bullocks are purchased wholesale by the *tripe-dressers. 1906 *Breakfast Menu S.Y. 'Argonaut'* 9 July, *Tripe Fritters. 1659 TORRIANO, *Bottaccio*, the greatest *tripe-gut in an ox. 1923 J. MANCHON *Le Slang* 320 **Tripe-hound*,..un sale cabot, un clebs à poubelles. 1928 D. L. SAYERS *Unpleasantness at Bellona Club* xv. 176 If you'll call off your tripe-hounds, we'll let you have an interview and a set of photographs. 1933 L. G. D. ACLAND in *Press* (Christchurch, N.Z.) 23 Dec. 15/7 *Tripe-hound*, slang for sheep dog. This was common on South Canterbury stations in the 'nineties, and I always thought it a New Zealand word until I came across it in an English novel the other day, 'Early Closing', I think. In the novel the word was applied to a spaniel! 1935 J. BUCHAN *House of Four Winds* iv. 98 If your tripe-hounds had been worth their keep they would have seen me meet him. 1937 N. MARSH *Vintage Murder* viii. 87 You damned little tripe-hound. 1946 B. MARSHALL *George Brown's Schooldays* 123 Draw, you sorry tripehound, draw. 1966 'L. LANE' *ABZ of Scouse* 111 *Tripe-hound*, a mongrel dog. Also applied to a racing greyhound that persists in putting up a disappointing performance. 1897 *Allbutt's Syst. Med.* II. 941 Inflammation of the stomach and bowels accompanied by peculiar *tripe-like wrinklings of the mucous membrane. 1621 BP. MOUNTAGU *Diatribæ* 114 Cleon the Currier, and Agoracritus the *Tripe-man. 1851 MAYHEW *Lond. Labour* II. 7/2 These portions [of the bullock] form what is styled the tripe-man's portion. 1621 BP. MOUNTAGU *Diatribæ* 540 He..vseth κοιλίας belly, or, Inwards of a Beast, as speaking vnto him, whom hee maketh a *Tripe-monger. 1966 P. V. PRICE *France* II. 219 *Andouilles limousines.* *Tripe sausages, usually served grilled. 1981 'M. HEBDEN' *Pel is Puzzled* viii. 73 Andouillettes, the tripe sausage of the region. 1597 A. M. tr. *Guillemeau's Fr. Chirurg.* 54 b/2 A *Tripe-seller..had his membrane *Dura mater* cleft asunder. 1621 BP. MOUNTAGU *Diatribæ* 540 Hee..saith, *For not Tithing thy Tripes*, intending..that *Tripe-selling was his raising trade. 1829 MARRYAT *F. Mildmay* xx, My mother keeps a *tripe-shop. *a* 1735 ARBUTHNOT *Harmony in Uproar* Misc. Wks. 1751 II. 34 To invite you to eat a *Tripe-soup and Fricassey of Sheep's Trotters. 1816 CLEAVELAND *Min.* 122 Concreted sulphate of barytes... These stalactites..from some resemblance to the intestines, have received the name of *tripe stone. 1597 SHAKS. 2 *Hen. IV*, v. iv. 9 Thou damn'd *Tripe-visag'd Rascall. 1580 HOLLYBAND *Treas. Fr. Tong*, *Tripiére*, a *trype wife. 1595 *Eng. Tripe-wife* (1881) 146, I haue heard him that trickt the Tripe-wife sweare, till her husband abused him. *a* 1652 BROME *City Wit* IV. ii, Was not thy mother a notorious Tripe-wife? 1647 WARD *Simp. Cobler* 26 When I consider how women..haue *tripe-wifed themselves with their cladments. 1598 FLORIO, *Trippara*, a *tripe-woman.

Hence †**triped** (traɪpt) *a.* *Obs.* *rare*, made into or dressed as tripe.

1597 *Bk. Cookerie* B ij b, Triped mutton. Take a paunche of a Sheepe faire scowred [etc.].

†**tripe**^{2}. *Obs.* Forms: 5–6 trype, 6 tryp, trip, (7 trape), 7–8 tripe. [a. OF. *tripe* (1374 in Godef. *Compl.*; cf. also *triperie* 1275), 'étoffe de laine ou de fil travaillée comme le velours'; according to Littré, so called from its resemblance to the interior of the paunch of ruminants.] An imitation velvet of wool or thread; 'mock-velvet', velveteen, fustian. Also ***tripe of velvet*** (F. *tripe de velours*), and ***tripe velvet***; hence also †**triped (trypit, tript)** *a.* applied to velvet.

c 1430 *Brut* 459 Clothed in scarlet, with furred hodes, and round standynge cappes of Trype. 1542–3 *Acc. Ld. High Treas. Scot.* VIII. 176 Ane elne trype velvet, price xiiij *s.* 1565 in Hay Fleming *Reform. Scotl.* (1910) 609 Twa stuillis coverit with trypit wellwott. 1598 FLORIO, *Trippa*, a kinde of tripe veluet that they make womens saddles with, called fustian of Naples. 1612 *Inv.* in A. McKay *Hist. Kilmarnock* (1880) 308 Four cuschownis of tripe veluet. 1656 *Acts & Ordin. Parl.* c. 20 *Rates* (Scobell) 467 Fustians called.. Naples Fustians, Trape, or Velure plain. [cf. 1660 *Act 12 Chas. II*, c. 4 (*Schedule of Rates*) Naples fustians tript.] 1714 *Fr. Bk. of Rates* 80 Tripes of Velvet, per Piece of 10 Ells 03 10.

triped (ˈtraɪpɛd). [ad. L. *tripēs*, *-ped-is*, three-footed, three-legged, f. *tri-* TRI- + *pēs* foot.] A three-legged animal.

1916 *Daily Colonist* (Victoria, B.C.) 2 July 4/5 A three-legged chicken is the pride of a brood of a dozen hatched last week... The triped is quite lively and is putting lots of joy into the life of the Simpson barnyard. 1954 W. K. HANCOCK *Country & Calling* 14 Peter [*sc.* a horse] went permanently lame after a week or two of work; he was a triped, William said, and no use to a bush minister in his professional capacity. 1971 I. BROWN *Old & Young* xiv. 220 The small child is a quadruped... Then comes the erect and active biped. At last the codger limps along using a stick for an extra limb. As one who has reached the triped stage I am denied the pleasure of..exercise.

tripedal (ˈtrɪpɪdəl, ˈtraɪpɪdəl, traɪˈpiːdəl), *a.* *rare.* [ad. L. *tripedāl-is*, f. *tri-*, TRI- + *pēs*, *ped-* foot: see -AL^1.] †**a.** Having a length or extent of three feet. *Obs.* *rare*$^{-0}$. **b.** Having three feet, three-footed. So †**tripeˈdaneous** *a.* [f. L. *tripedāne-us* + -OUS] = sense a. *Obs.* *rare*$^{-0}$.

1623 COCKERAM, *Tripedall*, three foot long. 1656 BLOUNT *Glossogr.*, *Tripedanious*, *Tripedal*..that is three foot long. 1658 in PHILLIPS. 1856 *Chamb. Jrnl.* 29 Mar. 202/2 The "baked 'tato" man, with his brightly-polished..tripedal or quadrupedal apparatus. 1878 MISS J. J. YOUNG *Ceram. Art* (1879) 113 The Japanese dragon is a tripedal representative of the species.

‖**tripe de roche** (trip də rɔʃ). [F., 'rock tripe', from the appearance of the thallus.] A name originally given in Canada to various edible lichens of the genera *Gyrophora* and *Umbilicaria*, which afford a slightly nutritious but bitter and purgative food. Also called *rock tripe.*

1809 A. HENRY *Trav.* 221, I found a very high rock, and this covered with a lichen, which the Chipeways call *waac*, and the Canadians, *tripe de roche.* 1861 H. MACMILLAN *Footn. fr. Page Nat.* 99 A bitter and nauseous lichen, to which the name of *Tripe de Roche* (Gyrophora) has been given, as if in mockery.

tripela: see TRIPOLI (polishing powder).

tripelennamine (traɪpəˈlɛnəmiːn). *Pharm.* [f. TRI- + P(YRIDYL + E(THY)LEN(E + AMINE.] An antihistamine drug, $C_{16}H_{21}N_3$, given orally as the crystalline hydrochloride or citrate.

1947 *Jrnl. Amer. Med. Assoc.* 31 May 454/2 Granulocytopenia is believed not to have been described hitherto among the untoward side effects of tripelennamine hydrochloride, 'pyribenzamine' (N.N.R.) (N'-pyridyl-N'-benzyl-N-dimethylethylenediamine hydrochloride), therapy. 1962, 1974 [see PYRIBENZAMINE].

triˈpennate, *a.* *Bot.* *rare*$^{-0}$. [f. TRI- + PENNATE.] = TRIPINNATE.

1828 in WEBSTER. 1900 in B. D. JACKSON *Gloss. Bot. Terms.*

tripeptide (traɪˈpɛptaɪd). *Chem.* [Named by Fischer, 1902, f. TRI- 5 + PEPT(ONE + -IDE.] A compound containing the residues of three amino-acids united by the joining of NH in one residue to CO in another; e.g. alanyl-glycyl-glycine, $NH_2.CH(CH_3).CO-NH.CH_2.CO-NH.CH_2.CO.OH$, is a tripeptide formed from alanine, $NH_2.CH(CH_3).COOH$, and two glycine molecules, $NH_2.CH_2.CO.OH$.

1903 *Jrnl. Chem. Soc.* LXXXIV. I. 799 The ethyl ester is very easily formed when the tripeptide is acted on by alcoholic hydrochloric acid. 1908 PLIMMER *Chem. Const. Proteins* II. 23 Carbethoxyl-glycyl-glycyl-leucine ester.. was the first known representative of a tripeptide.

tri-personal (traɪˈpɜːsənəl), *a.* *Theol.* [f. TRI- + L. *persōna* PERSON + -AL^1.] Consisting of or existing in three persons: said of the Godhead (see PERSON *sb.* 7 a); also, relating to the three persons of the Godhead.

1641 MILTON *Reform.* II. Wks. 1851 III. 68 Thou..one Tri-personall Godhead, looke upon this thy poore and almost spent, and expiring Church. 1859 G. BUSH *Swedenborg's Doctr.* (1875) 25 Those who oppose the tripersonal scheme [of the Trinity] will be accused of rejecting a Trinity in any sense whatever. 1871 H. MACMILLAN *True Vine* iii. (1872) 88 In our creation as body, soul, and spirit, God exhibited the tri-personal aspect of His nature.

Hence **triˈpersonalism**, the doctrine or theory of three persons in the Godhead; **triˈpersonalist**, one who holds this doctrine; **tripersoˈnality**, the condition of being tripersonal, existence in three persons; **triˈpersonally** *adv.*, in a tripersonal manner, in three persons.

1886 N. F. RAVLIN *Progress. Th. Gt. Subj.* i. 14 Jesus..did not speak the truth, if the popular doctrine of *tripersonalism be true. 1846 WORCESTER cites CLISSOLD for

modern Jews, in opposition to the tripersonalists, consider the whole as attributes. **1673** MILTON *True Relig.* 7 *Tripersonality [see TRINUNITY]. **1836** CARLYON *Early Years* 290 The Tri-personality of the Deity is the very corner-stone of our religion. **1901** MOBERLY *Atonement & Personality* 154 The Three Persons are neither Three Gods, nor Three parts of God. Rather they are God Threefoldly, God *Tri-personally.

tripertite, obs. form of TRIPARTITE.

tripery (ˈtraɪpərɪ). [a. OF. *triperie* (13.. in Godef. *Compl.*), f. *tripe* TRIPE[1]: see -ERY.] **a.** A place where tripe is prepared or sold. †**b.** In contempt, Action pertaining to the tripes or entrails (*obs. rare*).

1611 COTGR., *Triperie*, a Triperie; a market, street, or shop wherein tripes are vsually sold. **1651** BIGGS *New Disp.* ¶150 To speake of that piece of Tripery, of washing the Guts with a Clyster. **1656** in BLOUNT *Glossogr.* [from Cotgr.]. **1854** *Q. Rev.* Sept. 282 Slaughter-houses, triperies, bone-boiling houses, gut-scraperies.

tripet, obs. form of TRIPPET.

tripetalous (traɪˈpɛtələs), *a. Bot.* [f. TRI- + L. *petalum* PETAL *sb.* + -OUS.] Having, or consisting of, three petals. Also † **triˈpetalose** *a. Obs.* So **triˈpetaloid**, **tripetaˈloideous** *adjs.* (of a six-parted perianth) having three of the segments petaloid.

[**1688** R. HOLME *Armoury* II. 118/1 *Tripetala*, or *Tetrapetala*, Flowers which consist of 3 or 4 leaves.] **1830** LINDLEY *Nat. Syst. Bot.* 283 The *tripetaloid flower and polyspermous fruit of Xyris. **1866** *Treas. Bot.* 1173 *Tripetaloid*, consisting of six parts, of which three resemble petals, and three are green and small. **1830** LINDLEY *Nat. Syst. Bot.* 254 These water-plants are readily distinguished from all other monocotyledons by their *tripetaloideous flowers. **1698** PETIVER in *Phil. Trans.* XX. 332 The Flowers [are] *tripetalose. **1704** J. HARRIS *Lex. Techn.* s.v. *Petala*, Plants are distinguished into Monopetalous, ..*Tripetalous, and Pentapetalous. *c* **1711** PETIVER *Gazophyl.* VIII. lxxi, A blew flowred tripetalous Plant, with Lilly Leaves. **1800** HURDIS *Fav. Village* 136 Fair tripetalous depending flowers.

tripey (ˈtraɪpɪ), *a. colloq.* Also **tripy**. [f. TRIPE[1] + -Y[1].] Inferior, trashy, rubbishy, worthless.

1955 E. BLISHEN *Roaring Boys* IV. 239 How you can tell them to paint in the same tripey way as me, I don't know. **1962** L. DAVIDSON *Rose of Tibet* x. 177 'Don't you like any of our books?.. What do you think of this one?' 'It looks a bit tripy to me.' **1968** R. JEFFRIES *Traitor's Crime* iv. 49 It's a case of the more tripey, the more relaxation. **1971** 'M. UNDERWOOD' *Trout in Milk* xiv. 145 The jury'll never convict on the tripey evidence the prosecution have brought.

tripgette, -go: see TREBUCHET, TRIP-AND-GO.

ˈtrip-ˌhammer. [f. TRIP *sb.*[1] or *v.* + HAMMER.] A massive machine-hammer operated by a tripping device, as a wheel with projecting teeth, a cam, or the like, by which it is raised and then allowed to drop; a tilt-hammer. Also *fig.*

1781 S. PETERS *Gen. Hist. Connecticut* 265 Anchor-making is done by water and tri-hammers. [**1809** (Oct. 14), A trip hammer was patented by the United States to John Smith, Otsego County, New York.] *a* **1817** T. DWIGHT *Trav. New-Eng.* (1821) II. 15 Here he built a shop; and set up the first trip-hammer in this part of the country. **1824** *Debates in Congress* 18 Feb. (1856) 1572 Our committee on manufactures, while it keeps in motion its wheels and triphammers, has kindly condescended to superintend our ploughs and sheep-folds. **1831** J. HOLLAND *Manuf. Metal* I. 128 A blast furnace, forge, trip-hammer, shop, and mills. **1848** LOWELL *Fable for Critics* 893 When the heart in his breast like a trip-hammer beats. **1854** EMERSON *Lett. & Soc. Aims, Eloquence* Wks. (Bohn) III. 190 What character, what infinite variety, belong to the voice! sometimes it is a flute, sometimes a trip-hammer.

attrib. *a* **1864** GESNER *Coal, Petrol.* etc. (1865) 321 To bore the well with an auger, instead of a trip-hammer motion. **1883** H. TUTTLE in *Harper's Mag.* Nov. 825/2 Chisels acting on the trip-hammer principle. **1896** KIPLING *Seven Seas, M'Andrew's Hymn* 45 Oh for a man to weld it then, in one trip-hammer strain.

triphane (ˈtraɪfeɪn). *Min.* [a. F. *triphane* (Haüy, 1801), f. Gr. τριφανής appearing threefold; so called from exhibiting three lustrous cleavages (Littré *Suppl.*).] A synonym of SPODUMENE.

1816 CLEAVELAND *Min.* 251 *note*, Spodumene. Jameson. Triphane, Hauy. **1819** *Gentl. Mag.* May 448/2 Triphane has been recently found by Dr. MacCulloch in the granite of Glen Elg. **1850** ANSTED *Elem. Geol., Min.*, etc. §415 Spodumene or Triphane, another felspathic mineral, with a yet larger proportion of silicate of lithia in the place of silicate of potash.

triphase, -phasic: see TRI- 1 b, a.

triphen-, tripheno-. *Chem.* [f. TRI- 5 + PHEN-, PHENO-.] A formative of names of compounds containing three radical groups formed from the benzene or phene group, C_6H_6, by loss of hydrogen atoms; e.g. ***triˈphenazine***,

$$C_6H_4\langle{N \atop N}\rangle C_6H_2\langle{N \atop N}\rangle C_6H_4.$$

1890 *Jrnl. Chem. Soc.* LVIII. 491 The dye..regarded by the author as triphenodioxazine. **1892** MUIR & MORLEY *Watts' Dict. Chem.* III. 830 Triphenazine Dihydride $C_{18}H_{12}N_4$.

triˈphenin. *Pharm.* [app. f. TRI- 5 (referring to the three carbon atoms in propionyl) + PHEN(ETIDIN + -IN[1].] Propionylphenetidin, $CH_3CH_2CO.NH.C_6H_4.OC_2H_5$, i.e. phenetidin, $NH_2.C_6H_4.OC_2H_5$, in which one of the hydrogen atoms of the amino-group, NH_2, is replaced by propionyl, CH_3CH_2CO; a synthetic drug with antipyretic and antineuralgic properties.

1896 *Merck's Ann. Rep.* 155 Triphenin..White crystalline flakes, freely dissolving in alcohol..melting point of 120–121° C. **1911** MAY *Chem. Synth. Drugs* 74 Para-propionyl-phenetidine (*Triphenin*) is similar to *phenacetin*.

triˈphenyl-. *Chem.* [f. TRI- 5 + PHENYL.] A prefix denoting that three phenyl groups, C_6H_5, are substituted for three hydrogen atoms in the substance designated by the rest of the name; e.g. ***triphenylacetic acid***, $C(C_6H_5)_3.CO_2H$, from acetic acid, $CH_3.CO_2H$. So **triphenylmethane**, $CH(C_6H_5)_3$, from methane, CH_4; **triphenylmethyl-**, $C(C_6H_5)$—, from methyl, CH_3. But this term may also indicate the presence of three phenyl groups and one methyl group, $(C_6H_5)_3(CH_3)$; **triphenylcarbinol**, $C(OH)(C_6H_5)_3$, from carbinol, CH_3OH; **triphenylamine**, formerly triphenylia, $N(C_6H_5)_3$, from ammonia, NH_3; **triphenylrosaniline**, $C(OH)\{C_6H_4.NH(C_6H_5)\}_2\{C_6H_3(CH_3).NH(C_6H_5)\}$, from rosaniline, $C(OH)\{C_6H_4.NH_2\}_2\{C_6H_3(CH_3).NH_2\}$; the hydrochloric acid derivative of this is a blue dye-stuff. So also **triˈphenylated** *a.*, containing three phenyl groups.

1858 FOWNES *Elem. Chem.* (ed. 7) 601 Triphenylamine. **1862** MILLER *Elem. Chem.* (ed. 2) III. 444 Triphenylia. **1871** *Jrnl. Chem. Soc.* XXIV. 143 An alcoholic solution of triphenylguanidine absorbs large quantities of cyanogen. **1880** FRISWELL in *Jrnl. Soc. Arts* 445 The hydrochloride of triphenylrosaniline. **1893** THORPE *Dict. App. Chem.* III. 874 Triphenylrosanilines. The triphenylated derivatives of ordinary rosaniline may be subdivided into two classes: crystalline and uncrystallisable blues. **1894** MUIR & MORLEY *Watts' Dict. Chem.* IV. 2 Tri-phenyl-benzene $C_{24}H_{18}$ i.e. $C_6H_3Ph_3$.

triphibian (traɪˈfɪbɪən). [Irreg. f. TRI- + AM)PHIBIAN *sb.*] One who or that which is capable of existing or operating in three different spheres, esp. on land, on water, and in the air. (An occasional word.)

1935 *Sun* (Baltimore) 26 Oct. 1/2 Constantinos Vlachos' invention, which he had intended should travel on the ground, in the air and on water, collapsed upon him in flames today as he was demonstrating it on the lawn of the Library of Congress. The device, which Vlachos, a resident of Washington, called a triphibian, has never been off the ground, his wife said. **1943** W. S. CHURCHILL in *Amer. Speech* (1944) XIX. 14/2 He [*sc.* Lord Mountbatten] is what I venture to call a complete triphibian. **1943** *Punch* 8 Sept. 197 (*caption*) Looking Eastward. Mr. Punch's portrait of a 'Triphibian'. **1977** H. OSMOND in A. Huxley *Moksha* viii. 39 Soon my dear friend [*sc.* A. Huxley], the wise and gentle triphibian, for that was his own definition of man, was no more.

triphibious (traɪˈfɪbɪəs), *a.* [Irreg. f. TRI- + AM)PHIBIOUS *a.*] Capable of living or operating on land, on water, and in the air; *spec.* of or pertaining to military operations involving land, sea, and air forces. Hence **triˈphibiously** *adv.* (*rare*).

1941 L. HORE-BELISHA in *Times* 4 Nov. 2/3 Whether or not amphibious—or rather triphibious—raids at unexpected points along the extensive coastline..would at this stage seriously distract the enemy was doubtful. **1950** A. DE SEVERSKY *Air Power* (1952) ii. 25 Either we shall continue to divide our national potential three ways to support an outlived triphibious method of war-making, or we shall concentrate it. **1964** D. MACARTHUR *Reminiscences* VI. 166 Ground, air, and sea operations were thoroughly co-ordinated. It was a new type of campaign—three-dimensional warfare—the triphibious concept. **1978** *Sci. Amer.* Dec. 29/2 In southeastern Asia, however, some 50 species of frogs have lengthened toes, arrayed in a still wider web, and swim the air—triphibiously. **1982** *Contemp. Rev.* Jan. 51 Their service is universal and triphibious.

triphilrie: see TRIFLERY.

triphony (ˈtrɪfənɪ). *Mus.* [ad. med.L. *triphōnia* (see below), f. Gr. τρι- three + φωνή voice.] In early mediæval music, Diaphony for three voices. (In quot. 1827 *gen.* A sound of three together.)

1827 CARLYLE *Germ. Rom.* II. 278 Then resounded a louder triphony of clear crystal bells. [**1889** ROCKSTRO in Grove *Dict. Mus.* App. s.v. *Diaphonia*, When a third Part was added, by doubling the Organum in the Octave above, the form of composition was called Triphonia.] **1899** *Spectator* 20 May 723 A service with the chants sung in unison, the organ accompanying with triaphony [*sic*].

triˌphosphoˈpyridine ˈnucleotide. *Biochem.* [f. TRI- + PHOSPHO- + PYRIDINE + NUCLEOTIDE.] = *nicotinamide-adenine dinucleotide* s.v. NICOTINAMIDE b.

1937 *Chem. Abstr.* XXXI. 718 (*heading*) Oxidation of Robison's ester with the aid of triphosphopyridine nucleotide. **1951** *Sci. News* XXII. 80 This reaction, which uses di- or tri-phosphopyridine nucleotide as a hydrogen carrier may thus be a key reaction in photosynthesis. **1962** [see DIPHOSPHOPYRIDINE NUCLEOTIDE].

triphthong (ˈtrɪfθɒŋ). Also 7 **triphthonge, tripthong**, 8 **triphthongue**. [f. TRI-, after DIPHTHONG; cf. F. *triphtongue* (1550 in Godef. *Compl.*).] A combination of three vowel sounds in one syllable; also loosely applied to a combination of three vowel characters, more correctly called TRIGRAPH. (Cf. DIPHTHONG.)

1599 MINSHEU *Span. Gram.* (1623) 9 A triphthong is a sounding of three vowels into one syllable with one breath together, and that after five sorts. *a* **1637** B. JONSON *Eng. Gram.* I. v, The Tripthong is of a complexion, rather to be fear'd than lov'd. **1668** WILKINS *Real Char.* 371 A common Assertion..That no one syllable can consist of three Vowels, and consequently that there can be no Tripthongs. **1706** PHILLIPS (ed. Kersey), Triphthongue. **1711** J. GREENWOOD *Eng. Gram.* 244 A Triphthong is, when three Vowels meet together in one Syllable; as *eau* in Beauty: but this we pronounce *Buty*. **1889** PITMAN *Man. Phonogr.* (new ed.) §41 The double vowels heard in the words *ice*, *owl*, *ay*, *boy*, and the triphthong *wī*, are represented by small angular marks.

Hence **triphthongal** (trɪfˈθɒŋgəl) *a.*, pertaining to or of the nature of a triphthong.

1748 *Phil. Trans.* XLV. 403, 7 vocal Notes or Vowels,.. struck, as one may say, in diphthongal or triphthongal Chords with each other.

triphyletic: see TRI- 1 a.

triphylite (ˈtrɪfɪlaɪt). *Min.* [f. Gr. τρι- three + φυλή tribe + -ITE[1], because it contains three bases.] A compound phosphate of iron, manganese, and lithium, occurring in greenish-grey or bluish crystals. Orig. called **triphyline** (ˈtrɪfɪlɪn) [ad. Ger. *triphylin* (Fuchs, 1834)].

1836 *R. D. & T. Thomson's Rec. Gen. Sci.* III. 476 Triphylline.., from its consisting of three phosphates. It is described by Fuchs as being crystalline, cleaving in four directions; one of the cleavages is vertical to the others. **1850** Triphylline [see TRIPLITE]. **1868** DANA *Min.* (ed. 5) 542 Triphylite and triplite, like other minerals containing protoxyd of manganese, undergo easy alteration by oxydation and hydration.

triphyllous (traɪˈfɪləs), *a. Bot.* [f. Gr. τρίφυλλ-ος (f. τρι-, TRI- + φύλλον leaf) + -OUS.] Having or consisting of three leaves; *spec.* of a calyx or corolla, trisepalous or tripetalous.

1760 J. LEE *Introd. Bot.* II. xxxii. (1765) 156 *Ranunculus*, with a triphyllous Calyx and polypetalous. **1762** EHRET in *Phil. Trans.* LIII. 82 At the base of this broad petal is situated an irregular unequal-divided triphyllous periantheum. **1866** *Treas. Bot.* 1173 *Triphyllous*, having the leaves in a whorl of three; also, having only three leaves.

ˈTriphysite. [f. TRI- + Gr. φύσις nature + -ITE[1] 1 a: see MONOPHYSITE.] See quot.

1874 J. H. BLUNT *Dict. Sects* (1886) 599/2 *Triphysites*, those divines who..A.D. 684, 688..declared a belief not only in Christ's distinct Divine and Human natures, but also in a third nature resulting from the union of the two.

†**tripilous**, *a. Obs. rare*[−1]. [f. L. *tri-* three + *pil-us* hair + -OUS.] Having three (anal) hairs.

1671 *Phil. Trans.* VI. 2255 Some of them [insects] had stings and were tripilous, and others not.

triping (ˈtraɪpɪŋ). *Sc.* [Perh. f. TRIPE[1] + -ING[1].] Coal as brought to the pit-head, not yet cleaned or graded.

1886 J. BARROWMAN *Mining Terms* 68 *Triping*, a kind of drossy coal. **1921** *Glasgow Herald* 21 Apr. 5 A 'triping' ton ..represents about 55 per cent. of round coal, 40 per cent. of dross, and 5 per cent. of dirt. **1923** *Ibid.* 22 Dec. 5 The miner produces what is known in the trade as 'triping'. **1924** *Ibid.* 6 Oct. 8 The coals are filled in the hutches at the coal face as 'triping'—large and small mixed.

tripinnate (traɪˈpɪneɪt), *a. Bot.* [f. TRI- + PINNATE.] Of a leaf: Triply pinnate; having leaflets pinnately arranged on tertiary petioles similarly arranged: see PINNATE *a.* 1 a, and cf. BIPINNATE. (Abbrev. *3-pinnate*.)

1760 J. LEE *Introd. Bot.* III. vi. (1765) 188 *Tripinnate*, or *Triplicato-Pinnate*, when a Petiole bears many Folioles, each of which are Bipinnate. **1870** HOOKER *Stud. Flora* 170 Daucus Carota; leaves 3-pinnate. **1880** GRAY *Struct. Bot.* iii. §4 (ed. 6) 104 Tripinnate or Thrice Pinnate leaves of a regular sort are rare.

So **triˈpinnated** *a.* in same sense; **triˈpinnately** *adv.*, in a tripinnate manner; **tripinnatifid** (-ˈætɪfɪd), **tripiˈnnatisect** *adjs.*, triply pinnatifid, or pinnatisect; tripinnately divided half-way, or quite, to the base.

1845 LINDLEY *Sch. Bot.* iv. (1858) 26*b*, *A*[*nemone*] *Pulsatilla* (Pasque Flower). Leaves tripinnatifid with linear acute segments. **1847** W. E. STEELE *Field Bot.* 95 *A*[*donis*] *autumnalis*..; leaves 3-pinnatifid. **1857** HENFREY *Elem. Bot.* §94 Where tripinnatisect leaves have filiform segments, the term dissected is usually employed. **1876** HARLEY *Royle's Mat. Med.* 583 Leaves tripinnated, with fine capillary segments like those of fennel. **1891** *Cent. Dict.*, Tripinnately.

ˈtripla. *Mus.* [a. L. *tripla*, fem. of *triplus*: see TRIPLE *a.*] Triple proportion between one note and another; triple time or rhythm. Also *attrib.*

1549 *Compl. Scot.* vi. 37 There vas mony smal birdis.. singand..in accordis of mesure of diapason prolations, tripla ande dyatesseron. **1597** MORLEY *Introd. Mus.* 29 Tripla .. is that which diminisheth the value of the notes to one third part: for three briefes are set for one. **1659** C. SIMPSON *Division-Violist* I. 8 Of Tripla's. Sometimes the Grounds themselves are Tripla-Time; consisting (usually) either of three Semibreves, or three Minims, or three Crochets to a Measure. **1728** R. NORTH *Mem. Music* (1846) 104 For songs he approved onely the soft vein, such as might be called a step tripla. **1944** W. APEL *Harvard Dict. Mus.* 608/2 Nominally, this proportion was *proportio tripla* (another name for such a *Nachtanz* was *Tripla*). **1980** *Early Music* Jan. 120/2 Whilst I applaud the attempt to maintain a definite relationship with the main pulse, the required effect might sometimes be a stately *sesquialtera* rather than a hectic *tripla*.

tripla: pl. of TRIPLUM.

†**'triplage**, *a. Obs. rare.* [app. f. TRIPLE + -AGE (irregularly used).] Triple, threefold.

1526 in Dillon *Customs of Pale* (1892) 85 Upon paine of m[l] markes to the kinge, and amendes to the partie grevid by triplage damage. *Ibid.*, By triplage freholdurs dammage.

†**triplar**, *a. Obs.* Also -are, -er. [ad. late L. *triplāris*, f. *triplus* TRIPLE.] = TRIPLE *a.*; cf. TRIPLA.

c **1470** HENRYSON *Orpheus & Eurydice* 227 (Bann. MS.) Thair leirit he tonis proportionat, As duplare, triplare [*v.r.* triplar, -er] and emetricus.

triplasian (traɪ'pleɪsɪən, -ʃən), *a. rare.* [f. Gr. τριπλάσι-ος three times as much or as many, threefold + -AN.] Threefold, triple. So **triplasic** (traɪ'plæzɪk) *a.* in same sense; **'triplasy** (see quot. 1900).

1678 CUDWORTH *Intell. Syst.* I. iv. 288 The Persian Magi to this very day, celebrate a Festival Solemnity in honour of the Triplasian (that is, the Three-fold or Triplicated) Mithras. *Ibid.* 290 The Persian Trinity (or Triplasian Deity). **1816** G. S. FABER *Orig. Pagan Idol.* II. 415 The triplasian Mithras. **1864** J. HADLEY *Ess.* v. (1873) 98 Beside these three ratios of arsis and thesis,.. Aristoxenus mentions two others: the triplasic, in which the two parts of the foot are as 3 to 1 [etc.]. **1900** B. D. JACKSON *Gloss. Bot. Terms*, *Triplasy*.., the division of an organ into three analogous structures (Fermond).

†**'triplate**, *ppl. a.* and *sb. Obs.* [ad. med.L. *triplāt-us*, pa. pple. of *triplāre* to triple (Johannes de Janua, *a* 1286).] **a.** *ppl. a.* Multiplied by three; triplicated, triple. **b.** *sb.* The product of a number multiplied by three. So †**'triplated** *ppl. a.*, triple, threefold; †**tri'plation**, multiplication by three, tripling.

c **1430** *Art of Nombryng* 17 Thow most trebille the digit, and that triplat is to be put vnder the .3.[rd.] next figure towarde the right honde. *Ibid.* 18 After-warde .. settyng away alle that is ouer the hede of the triplat nombre. *Ibid.*, Nother me shalle not cesse of the fyndynge of that digit, neither of his triplacioun, .. tille it come to the first figure. **1486** *Bk. St. Albans, Her.* E vij, Off tractis triplatit and quatriplatit othyrwyle... He berith golde a trace triplatit of Siluer. **1501** DOUGLAS *Pal. Hon.* I. xli, Fresche ladyis sang in voice virgineall .. Proportionis fine with sound celestiall, Duplat, triplat, diatesserial [etc.]. **1542** RECORDE *Gr. Artes* (1575) 167 Triplation is multiplying by 3. **1574** H. BAKER *Well-spring Sci.* (1617) 76 Example of Triplation. If you will triple $\frac{3}{5}$, you must diuide $\frac{3}{5}$ by $\frac{1}{3}$ [etc.].

triple ('trɪp(ə)l), *sb.* Forms: see next. [sb. use of TRIPLE *a.*; cf. OF. *triple* in sense 5 below (*c* 1450 in Godef. *Compl.*).]

1. a. A triple quantity, sum, or number; thrice as much or many; the product of a number multiplied by three.

c **1425** tr. *Arderne's Treat. Fistula* 30 Of alle þise herbes, .. take euen porcion, outtake of wodebynde, of whiche .. be taken þe triple or quadriple. **1557** RECORDE *Whetst.* N iij b, Multiplie that triple, by the same quotiente. And set it doune vnder the first triple. **1674** JEAKE *Arith.* (1696) 195 Triple the Root, and multiply this triple by the Root. **1789** T. TAYLOR *Proclus* II. 16 Not only the doubles, but also the triples, and all multiples of the same quantity. **1830** H. ANGELO *Remin.* I. 327 To add more than triple to his income.

b. A set or series of three; a triad.

1653 R. G. tr. *Bacon's Hist. Winds* 203 This triple of Principles hath been introduced by the Chymists. **1654** WHITLOCK *Zootomia* 464 The Sins, or Judgments of others may make this Triple of Petitions out of that unparallel'd Paterne. **1966** D. BENNETT *Stranger in his Grave* viii. 66, I wanted to .. lie naked in an air-conditioned room with a triple of aspirins inside me. **1981** *Northeast Woods & Waters* Jan. 11/2 We finally settled down and started to pick individual targets and stopped shooting at triples or whole flocks.

2. In technical and elliptical uses. †**a.** *Mus.* Triple measure or rhythm. *Obs.*

1597 MORLEY *Introd. Mus.* 9 Where it comprehendeth three semibriefes, as in a triple.

b. A triple star.

1890 C. A. YOUNG *Uranography* §32, 11 Monocerotis, a fine triple.

c. A magic lantern having three optical tubes combined in one.

1892 *Photogr. Ann.* II. 531 Optical lanterns. Single lanterns. Biunials and triples.

d. *Chem.* A group of three atoms or ions.

1952 *Jrnl. Chem. Physics* XX. 685/2 I_{123} is an integral involving a triple of atoms arranged as in the figure. **1977** *Sci. Amer.* July 95/2 (*caption*) A sodium cation (Na^+) might attract to its vicinity two independent solvated electrons, forming an 'ion triple'.

e. *Horseracing.* = TRIFECTA.

1972 *Britannica Bk. of Year* 733/3 *Triple, specif.*, a system of betting on races in which the bettor must pick the first, second, and third horses in this sequence in a specified race in order to win. **1976** *N.Y. Times* 21 Aug. 22 They had hit on a triple (picking the first three horses in the right order), and it was the young woman's turn to collect.

3. *Bell-ringing.* A peal rung on seven bells with the tenor, i.e. the eighth, behind; the bells interchanging each time in three sets of two.

1798 in *Gentl. Mag.* Apr. (1825) 298/2 A full and compleat peal of grandsire tripples, consisting of 5040 changes. **1872** ELLACOMBE *Ch. Bells Devon*, etc. iii. 238 A peal of 'London Union Triples'. **1902** *Westm. Gaz.* 23 Oct. 12/2 A boy of fourteen .. took part in ringing 1,260 changes, which constitutes a quarter-peal of Grandsire Triples.

†**4.** = TREBLE *sb.* 7 b. *Obs. rare*$^{-1}$.

a **1553** UDALL *Royster D.* (Arb.) 88 The Peale of belles rong by the parish Clerk, and Roister Doisters foure men. The first Bell a Triple.

†**5.** = TREBLE *sb.* 4. *Obs. rare*$^{-1}$.

1600 FAIRFAX *Tasso* XVIII. xxiv, The humaine voices sung a triple hie.

6. *Baseball.* A hit which enables the batter to reach third base.

1880 *Chicago Inter-Ocean* 21 June 8/4 In the fifth Farrell's two-baser, Ward's triple hit, Bradley's triple hit, and Walker's fumbled grounder gave the Champions two earned runs. **1887** *Chicago Tribune* 3 May 3/1 He made in succession a single, double, triple, and home run. **1926** [see HOME *a.* 4]. **1949** *Milwaukie* (Oregon) *Rev.* 4 Aug. 4/4 The hard working first sacker collected his first triple of the year. **1974** *Birmingham* (Alabama) *Post-Herald* 29 June A 14/2 With two out, Bill North singled and scored on Campaneris' triple.

7. = TREBLE *sb.* 2 j.

1981 W. H. HALLAHAN *Trade* v. 153 He poured himself another drink—a triple. **1981** G. MARKSTEIN *Ultimate Issue* 174 Welk poured them all triples. 'Salut,' he toasted.

triple ('trɪp(ə)l), *a.* (*adv.*) Forms: 6 tryple. (treeple), 7 tripill, 7–8 (9 *U.S.*) tripple, 6– triple. [a. F. *triple* (16th c. in Godef. *Compl.*), or ad. L. *triplus*, a. Gr. τριπλοῦς, = L. *triplex* threefold.]

A. *adj.* **1.** Consisting of three members, things, or sets combined; threefold; = TREBLE *a.* 1.

1551–2 in Feuillerat *Revels Edw. VI* (1914) 78 One sute of tryple aparrell of whighte satten. **1587** HARRISON *England* III. viii. in *Holinshed* I. 233/1 The triple tillage of an acre dooth cost 13 shillings foure pence before the saffron be set. **1589** PUTTENHAM *Eng. Poesie* II. i. (Arb.) 78 The Philosopher gathers a triple proportion, .. the Arithmeticall, the Geometricall, and the Musicall. *c* **1620** T. ROBINSON *M. Magd.* 1132 There stood ye Monarche of this tripple Isle. **1697** DRYDEN *Æneid* VI. 563 The triple porter of the Stygian sound, Grim Cerberus. **1776** WITHERING *Brit. Plants* (1796) II. 266 A triple thorn beneath the buds. **1847** GROTE *Greece* II. xxiii. III. 536 The trireme or war-ship with a triple bank of oars. **1874** H. H. COLE *Catal. Ind. Art S. Kens. Mus.* 127 Triple rows of chains.

2. Having three applications or relations; existing or occurring in three ways or characters; of three kinds; = TREBLE *a.* 1 b.

1567 GOLDING *Ovid's Met.* VII. (1603) 79 b, By triple Hecats holy Rites. **1587** *T. Norton's Calvin's Inst.* IV. xii. §15. 414 *margin*, [There is] a triple vse of fasting. **1651** HOBBES *Leviath.* II. xxxi. 187 From hence there ariseth a triple Word of God, .. to which Correspondeth a triple Hearing. **1675** BAXTER *Cath. Theol.* II. VIII. 173 The Sun .. whose triple Influx Motion, Light, and Heat, affecteth all things. **1860** MOTLEY *Netherl.* (1868) I. i. 10 Their choice was triple.

3. Three times as much or many; of three times the measure or amount; multiplied by three.

1550 CROWLEY *Last Trump.* 955 If any man do the desyre Him to defend in doinge wronge, Though he woulde geue the triple hire, Yet geue none eare unto his songe. **1557** RECORDE *Whetst.* E iij, For .9. is triple to .3: and .12. is triple to .4. **1614** RALEIGH *Hist. World* II. (1634) 478 Great conquests are won to repay the charges of Warre with triple interest. **1756** C. LUCAS *Ess. Waters* I. 169 The quantity should not be less than triple the weight of the solids consumed. **1793** SMEATON *Edystone L.* 195 The detached figure .. shews a part of the top of the wall .. to a triple scale. **1806** HUTTON *Course Math.* I. 344 Each pyramid is the third part of the prism, or the prism is triple of the pyramid.

†**4.** That is one of three; third. *Obs. rare.*

1601 SHAKS. *All's Well* II. i. 111 One [receipt] which .. He bad me store vp, as a triple eye, Safer then mine owne two. **1606** —— *Ant. & Cl.* I. i. 12 You shall see in him (The triple Pillar of the world) transform'd Into a Strumpets Foole.

5. Special collocations.

triple agent = *treble agent* s.v. TREBLE *a.* 3; ***triple alliance***, an alliance of three states or powers, esp. (usu. with catital initials) that of England, Sweden, and the Netherlands in 1668, of France, Great Britain, and the Netherlands in 1717, and of Germany, Austria-Hungary, and Italy in 1883; also *transf.*; also, an alliance of trade unions representing miners, railwaymen, and transport workers; ***triple bob major***, app. an error for *treble bob major*: see BOB *sb.*[5]; ***triple bond*** (*Chem.*) [BOND *sb.*[1] 13 e], a bond in which the two atoms 'share' three pairs of electrons rather than one pair; hence ***triple-bonded*** adj.; ***triple change*** (*Bell-ringing*), one in which three pairs of bells change places; ***triple concerto***, a concerto with three solo parts; ***triple counterpoint***, three-part counterpoint in which the parts may be interchanged without breaking the rules; ***triple cross***, the act of betraying one party in a transaction by pretending to betray the other, or of betraying a person who has betrayed another; so ***triple-crossing***; ***triple crown***, a threefold crown; *spec.* (*a*) the papal tiara; also, a heraldic bearing representing this = TIARA 2 b; (*b*) in horse-racing, the winning of the three races known as the 'Two Thousand Guineas', the 'Derby', and the 'St. Leger' (also *attrib.*); (*c*) also applied to several other instances of winning three victories in the Kentucky Derby, the Preakness Stakes, and the Belmont Stakes, and, in Rugby Union and hockey, the winning by England, Ireland, Scotland, or Wales of victory over each of the other three in the same season; ***triple entente*** (Fr.), an understanding as to political action between three powers; ***triple first***, at Cambridge University, a first class in three triposes; also, one who obtains this; ***triple fugue*** (*Mus.*), a fugue having three subjects; ***triple gown***: see quot.; †***triple grass***, the genus *Trifolium*; ***triple hat***, the papal tiara; †***triple Lady's traces***, a species of orchid with three tubers; ***triple jump***, an athletic long jump event, also known as the hop, step, and jump (cf. HOP *sb.*[2] 3 a); ***triple junction*** (*Geol.*), a region at which the boundaries of three lithospheric plates meet; (*Petrogr.*), a point where three grain boundaries meet at angles of approximately 120 degrees; ***triple line***, (*Geom.*), a line, plane, or point formed by the coincidence of three lines, planes, or points; ***triple mirror*** = *three-way mirror* s.v. THREE-WAY *a.* a; ***triple phosphate*** (*Chem.*), phosphate of ammonium and magnesium; ***triple pit*** (*Mining*), a shaft divided into three compartments lengthwise: see quot.; ***triple plane***: see *triple line*; ***triple play***, in baseball, play in which three men are put out; ***triple point***, (*a*) (*Geom.*), a point common to three branches of a curve, or at which the curve has three tangents: see *triple line*; (*b*) (*Physics*), the temperature and pressure at which the solid, liquid, and vapour phases of a pure substance can coexist in equilibrium; the point representing this state in a phase diagram (marked by the junction of three lines); more widely, an analogous state or point for any three phases of a substance; (*c*) (*Petrogr.*), an invariant point involving three phases, e.g. where kyanite, andalusite, and sillimanite are stable in the system Al_2SiO_5; †***triple progression*** (*Mus.*): see quot.; †***triple proportion***: = *triple ratio*; ***triple quartan*** (***ague***), a quartan ague in which the paroxysms occur in sets of three; ***triple ratio***, the ratio of three to one; ***triple rime*** (***rhyme***): see RHYME *sb.* 3 c (but in quot. 1872 = TERZA RIMA); ***triple rhythm*** (*Mus.*), a threefold rhythm consisting of one heavy and two light accents or beats; ***triple salt*** (*Chem.*), a salt containing three different bases; ***triple screw***, a screw having three consecutive threads of the same pitch (*Cent. Dict.* 1891); ***triple spacing***, the spacing of typewritten or other text so that two blank lines separate adjacent lines of text (see *triple-spaced*, sense C. 1 a below); ***triple star***, a treble star (see TREBLE *a.* 3); ***triple suspension*** (*Mus.*): see quot.; ***triple tail***, a fish, *Lobotes surinamensis*, in which the dorsal and anal fins are extended so as to resemble tails; ***triple tertian*** (***ague***): cf. *triple quartan*; ***triple time*** (*Mus.*), a rhythm of three beats in the bar (*transf.* in prosody); also ***compound triple time*** (see COMPOUND *a.* 2 f); ***triple tonguing***, the use of the tongue to achieve rapid articulation in groups of three notes on the flute and brass instruments; hence (as back-formation) ***triple-tongue*** vb. intr.; ***triple unite***: see UNITE; ***triple vaccine*** (*Med.*), (*a*) a vaccine containing three species of the *Salmonella* bacteria, used as a prophylactic against typhoid and paratyphoid; (*b*) a vaccine containing diphtheria and tetanus toxoids and the killed whooping cough organism, administered in early childhood as a prophylactic against conditions caused by these. Also TRIPLE TREE.

1968 J. WAINWRIGHT *Web of Silence* 94 Jackson figures he's created a double-agent. We don't agree. The way we see it, Schneller's maybe a *triple-agent. **1982** T. HEALD *Masterstroke* viii. 159 Something in Intelligence. Our Intelligence. Theirs too... A triple agent at least. **1668** TEMPLE *Lett.* xv. (1699) 56 Monsieur de Witt: Who, he said, hindred them from being received into the *Triple-Alliance. **1715** ADDISON *Drummer* v. i. (1722) 39 But here comes the Triple-Alliance [three Rogues]. **1799** *Monthly Rev.* XXX. 528 This design .. gave rise to the Triple alliance .. to support the treaty of Utrecht. **1868** G. DUFF *Pol. Surv.* 18 A triple commercial and political alliance between France, Belgium, and Holland. **1906** *Westm. Gaz.* 26 Oct. 2/3 The alleged renewal of the Triple Alliance between Germany, Austria-Hungary, and Italy. **1915** *Times* 9 Oct. 3/1 The conference of the Miners' Federation of Great Britain .. adopted unanimously the scheme of a triple alliance between railwaymen, transport workers, and miners. **1974** *Times* 8 Jan. (Europe Suppl.) p. ii/2 As Christmas approached, a state of affairs was fast developing reminiscent of that which occurred when the 'triple alliance' of miners, dockers and railwaymen sprang into being during the run-up to the General Strike of 1926. **1809** W. IRVING *Knickerb.* (1861) 42 The bells .. rang a *triple bobmajor on the joyful occasion. *a* **1845** BARHAM *Ingol. Leg.*, *Wedding-day* 94 The blithe 'College Youths' .. Accustomed, for years, to pull bell-ropes for wagers, Rang faster than ever; their 'triple-bob-majors'. **1889** G. M'GOWAN tr. *Bernthsen's Organic Chem.* i. 55 The constitutional formula for acetylene, C_2H_2, is assumed to be $CH \equiv CH$, according to which the carbon atoms are joined together by a *triple bond. **1971** *Nature* 10 Dec. 333/2 The CO molecule has a very stable triple bond which is difficult to dissociate. **1937** *Jrnl. Amer. Chem. Soc.* LIX. 2091/2 The carbon-oxygen bond [in BH_3CO] presumably involves resonance between double- and *triple-bonded structures. **1965** PHILLIPS & WILLIAMS *Inorg. Chem.* I. xiii. 484 In the most extreme cases there is some reason for saying that oxygen is triple-bonded. **1872** ELLACOMBE *Ch. Bells Devon* iii. 232 After 1677 .. Stedman .. appears to have introduced the method of double and *triple changes. **1879** GROVE *Dict. Mus.* I. 389/1 Sometimes concertos are written for more than one solo instrument, and are then known as double, *triple, etc., concertos as the case may be. **1932** *Daily Tel.* 8 Oct. 8/3 In March a triple concerto for flute, clarinet, bassoon and orchestra by J. R. Heath will be introduced. **1985** *Daily Tel.* 22 Jan. 9 The London Sinfonietta .. had played the Triple Concerto on the first night of the Tippett birthday celebration week. **1869** OUSELEY *Counterp.* xvii. 134 *Triple and quadruple counterpoints .. consist of three or four melodies so interwoven that any of them may become a correct bass to the others. **1876** STAINER & BARRETT *Dict. Mus. Terms*, *Triple counterpoint*, a counterpoint in three parts, so contrived that each part will serve for bass, middle, or upper part as required. **1971** J. AIKEN *Nightly Deadshade* vii. 76, I .. resolve to set a few subliminal tests for my fellow-conspirators .. in case they are working the *triple-cross. **1978** *Times* 25 Jan. 11/5 Anthony Price is a master of the double (or even triple) cross. **1922** S. LEWIS *Babbitt* xix. 236 'Kind of double-crossing.' 'It ain't. It's *triple-crossing. It's the public that gets double-crossed.' **1555** EDEN *Decades* 226 A *triple crowne much lyke the popes. **1593** SHAKS. *2 Hen. VI*, I. iii. 66. **1624** BEDELL *Lett.* iv. 78 In one scutchion with the crosse Keyes and triple crown in the crest. **1780**, **1894** [see TIARA *sb.* 2 b]. *a* **1854** H. REED *Lect. Eng. Hist.* viii.

(1855) 272 The triple crown of the papacy. **1897** *Daily News* 7 Sept. 5/1 What the sporting prophets love to call the 'triple crown',..the Two Thousand, the Derby, and the St. Leger. **1899** *Whitaker's Almanack 1900* 648/2 In their last match at Cardiff against Wales, Ireland won by a try to nothing, securing the triple crown with three straight victories as in 1894. **1901** *Daily Chron.* 20 July 9/1 The triple-crown winner stood a sound 6 to 4 on chance. **1946** M. C. SELF *Horseman's Encycl.* 413 Race horses which win the Kentucky Derby, the Preakness and the Belmont are said to win the Triple Crown. **1953** *Times* 10 Apr. 4/5 A victory for England [over Scotland at hockey] will mean that the meeting of Ireland and England in Dublin on April 18 will be a fight for the triple crown. **1974** *Sunday Tel.* 7 Apr. 36/7 Hockey history was made on the Cardiff University ground at Llanrumney where Wales won the Championship and took the Triple Crown for the first time since the quadrangular tourney began in 1903. **1976** *National Observer* (U.S.) 22 May 6/4 She may never win a Triple Crown race herself—no woman ever has—but she says she'll 'definitely ride again; it's in my blood'. **1978** *World of Tennis* (BP Yearbk.) 179 The Virginia Slims Championship is the first event in the Triple Crown (Wimbledon and Forest Hills are the others) which has replaced the Grand Slam at the pinnacle of achievement in women's tennis. **1979** M. BOYCE *I was There!* 47/2 Twelve..the number of times Wales have won the Triple Crown. **1979** *Harvard Gaz.* 23 Feb. 2 Zoo Captain Bill Renke is the only person to have won the tiddlywinks Triple Crown—the Singles, Pairs, and Team Championships. **1910** *Encycl. Brit.* IX. 949/1 (*heading*) The *Triple entente and the Triple Alliance. **1914** *Times* 5 Aug. 7/4 First came the Franco-Russian Alliance, and later on the Anglo-French, and the Anglo-Russian agreements, which paved the way for the diplomatic group known as the Triple Entente. **1876** STAINER & BARRETT *Dict. Mus. Terms* s.v. *Fugue*, Fugues have been divided..By number of subjects; as a double fugue, having two subjects; a *triple fugue, three subjects, &c. **1834** *Tait's Mag.* I. 720/2 The double or *triple gowns (the Judges with the double and triple salaries). **1562** BULLEYN *Bulwark, Bk. Simples* (1579) 32 *Trifolium*, called the three leaued grasse. [*margin*] *Triple grasse. **1840** CARLYLE *Heroes* iv. (1858) 285 You with your tiaras, *triple-hats,..stand on Devil's Lie, and are not so strong! **1964** M. WATMAN *Encycl. Athletics* 150/1 Basically, the rules for the *triple jump (formerly known as the hop, step and jump) are identical with those governing the long jump. **1972** *N.Y. Times* 4 June 4/7 The runner-up in the voting was John Craft, who set an American triple-jump record of 55-5. **1969** *Nature* 11 Oct. 125/2 Evolution of such *triple junctions can produce many of the changes which would otherwise appear to have been caused by a change in the direction or magnitude of the relative motion between plates. **1976** R. H. VERNON *Metamorphic Processes* v. 137 Three grains meet at a point ('triple junction'), the inter-facial angles closely approximating 120°. **1979** MALLORY & CARGO *Physical Geol.* xvii. 437 Examination of these triple junctions shows that the three branches of the junction may involve convergence, divergence, or translational (sideways) movement. **1982** ARAMAKI & UI in R. S. Thorpe *Andesites* iii. 260/1 Japan and the surrounding islands form three chains of island arcs which meet at a trench-trench-type triple junction located at *c.* 34° N and 142° E. **1611, 1785** *Triple Ladies traces [see LADY'S TRACES]. **1907** *Yesterday's Shopping* (1969) 110/2 *Triple folding mirrors..Size of glass, 9 by 9 in.—20/3. **1920** S. LEWIS *Main Street* xiv. 164 A real dressing-table with a triple mirror. **1967** 'K. O'HARA' *Unknown Man* iv. 29 She adjusted the triple mirror and took up the eye-liner. **1857** *G. Bird's Urin. Deposits* (ed. 5) 276 The *triple phosphate which is precipitated artificially from urine..is a neutral salt. **1899** CAGNEY tr. *Jaksch's Clin. Diagn.* vii. (ed. 4) 388 It [urine] deposits on standing a more or less abundant deposit of fat-laden and swollen leucocytes and triple-phosphate crystals. **1839** URE *Dict. Arts* 970 A shaft is to be divided into three compartments, one for the engine pumps, and two for raising coals,..which is denominated a *triple pit. **1869** *De Witt's Official Base Ball Guide* 42 Remarks concerning double and *triple plays will apply to the third baseman as much as to either of the other base-players. **1896** KNOWLES & MORTON *Baseball* 103 *Triple play*, a play in which the ball is handled quickly enough to retire three men. **1872** J. THOMSON in *Rep. Brit. Assoc. Adv. Sci. 1871* II. 32 We must suppose three curves (namely, the line between gas and liquid, the line between liquid and solid, and the line between gas and solid) to meet in one point... This point of pressure and temperature for any substance may then be called the *triple point for that substance. **1873** B. WILLIAMSON *Diff. Calc.* (ed. 2) xiv. §209 If the lowest terms in the equation of a curve be of the third degree, the origin is a triple point. **1879** [see *ice line* s.v. ICE *sb.* 8]. **1955** *Sci. Amer.* Mar. 52/3 In another change, the absolute temperature scale was redefined in terms of a single fixed reference point—the triple point of water. **1964** J. H. BROPHY et al. *Thermodynamics of Structure* ii. 20 If the specified temperature and pressure are the coordinates of point *D*, all three phases coexist in equilibrium with one another. Point *D* is called the *triple point*. **1966** [see *ice-point* s.v. ICE *sb.* 8]. **1978** *Nature* 14 Dec. 696/2 One possible reason..is that a solid-solid-liquid triple point could exist near 10^7 Pa..in the proposed phase diagram [of carbon]. **1979** K. G. COX et al. *Interpretation of Igneous Rocks* iii. 47 Figure 3.1 shows a one-component phase diagram for a substance such as H_2O. It consists of three fields in each of which a single phase exists. Each pair of fields meets in a curve along which two phases co-exist, and the three fields meet in a point U (so-called triple point) at which all three phases co-exist. **1983** D. S. BARKER *Igneous Rocks* iii. 28 The 'triple point' where liquid, vapor, and solid coexist in equilibrium has yet to be experimentally located for any silicate. **1801** BUSBY *Dict. Mus.*, **Triple Progression*, an expression in old music, implying a series of perfect fifths. **1557** RECORDE *Whetst.* Cj, Proportion..Doble, *Triple, Quadriple. *a***1696** SCARBURGH *Euclid* (1705) 180, 12 compared to 4 is Multiple Proportion, and named triple. **1625** HART *Anat. Ur.* II. v. 79, I went to a Canon who lay sicke of a *triple Quartane ague. **1727-38, 1866** *Triple rhyme [see RHYME *sb.* 3 c]. **1872** LOWELL *Dante* Prose Wks. 1890 IV. 158 In the form of the verse (triple rhyme) we may find an emblem of the Trinity. **1800** tr. *Lagrange's Chem.* I. 248 When the quantity of ammonia corresponds with that of the nitrate of magnesia necessary to form a *triple salt, the precipitation is then checked. **1868** WATTS *Dict. Chem.* V. 886 *Triple salts*, a name sometimes applied to salts containing three different bases, such as microcosmic salt. **1957** A. C. LLOYD et al. *Gregg Typewriting for Colleges* 2/1 In *triple spacing, typing appears on every third line with 2 blank lines between the typed ones. **1978** *Brit. Med. Jrnl.* 16 Dec. 1724/3 Typing should be on one side of the paper, with double or triple spacing between the lines. **1831** *Encycl. Brit.* (ed. 7) IV. 47/1 M. Struve has also taken notice of 52 *triple stars. **1876** STAINER & BARRETT *Dict. Mus. Terms* s.v. *Suspension*, Two suspended notes form a double suspension; three a *triple suspension, and so on. **1803** SHAW *Gen. Zool* IV. 80 The tail..appears as if composed of three distinct parts,..hence the name of Triurus, or *Triple-Tail, applied to this fish by Commerson. **1888** GOODE *Amer. Fishes* 148 The 'Flasher' or 'Triple-tail'..is spoken of by various authors as the 'Black Triple-tail'. **1822-34** *Good's Study Med.* (ed. 4) I. 607 The fifth species [of ague] consisting of double tertians, *triple tertians, unequal tertians, duplicate tertians. **1662** PLAYFORD *Skill Mus.* I. viii. (1674) 28 Pricks of Perfection are used for perfecting Notes, and are only used in the *Triple-Time. **1749** J. MASON *Numbers in Poet. Comp.* 74 If..we banish our slow Tunes, and sing only Triple-Time Tunes to pure Iambic Measure. **1880** G. M. HOPKINS *Let.* 5 Sept. (1935) 107 So far as I know triple time is in English verse a shy and late thing. **1889** F. TAYLOR in Grove *Dict. Mus.* IV. 174/1 When a bar of triple time consists of two notes only the accent is always on the longer note. **1951** W. MORUM *Gabriel* I. i. 7 He *triple-tongued up the scale to high C. **1967** *Crescendo* Feb. 23/3 The band stopped for several bars, and Charles *triple-tongued*—at breakneck tempo—and never faltered or slowed down once. **1879** GROVE *Dict. Mus.* I. 459/2 *Triple tongueing is also possible. **1951** W. MORUM *Gabriel* II. vi. 211 You could rattle out triple-tonguing stuff when you was a kid. **1961** C. W. MONK in A. Baines *Mus. Instruments* xi. 280 Rapid passages are managed by alternating 't' and 'k' in 'double-tonguing' and fast triplets by 'triple tonguing' 'ttk' (or 'tkt, ktk'). **1917** *Jrnl. Amer. Med. Assoc.* 22 Sept. 100/2 The reaction following the inoculation of the *triple vaccine was no different than when the typhoid vaccine was alone used. **1947** *Ann. Rev. Microbiol.* I. 327 A reinvestigation of the antigenicity of the strains routinely used for the preparation of typhoid and 'triple' vaccine..resulted in the introduction of strains rich in somatic antigen. **1970** PASSMORE & ROBSON *Compan. Med. Stud.* II. xxii. 22/2 The injection of the triple vaccine may be combined with three oral doses of poliomyelitis vaccine. **1982** *Times* 8 Sept. 1/4 Kate is to have her third triple vaccine against whooping cough, diphtheria and tetanus today.

B. *adv.* To three times the amount or extent; in a threefold manner; triply; thrice. See also C. 2.

1606-1897 [see C. 2]. **1641** in Cochran-Patrick *Rec. Coinage Scotl.* (1876) I. Introd. 31 Coining of the Stirling coper monie..could not have been done the ordinare way for triple more charges. **1643** R. BAILLIE *Lett. & Jrnls.* (1841) II. 71 Triple more already than ever was taught in Scotland. **1692** BENTLEY *Boyle Lect.* iii. 85 If we had double or triple as many.

C. Combinations.

1. The adjective in combination.

a. Parasynthetic combs., as ***triple-arched, -barbed, -barrelled, -bodied, -coloured, -crested, -crowned, -edged, -formed, -gemmed, -hatted, -hummocked, -lived, mirrored, -nerved, -piled, -rayed, -ribbed, -stranded, -throated, -tiered, -towered, -turreted***; **triple-awned**, in ***triple-awned grass***, = *three-awned* (THREE B. III. 2); **triple-spaced**, typed or formatted so that two blank lines separate adjacent lines of text; also as quasi-*adv.*; (see *triple spacing*, sense A 5 above). Also TRIPLE-HEADED.

1906 *Daily News* 4 Sept. 6 The construction of the *triple-aisled nave [of Strassburg Cathedral]. **1819** KEATS *Eve St. Agnes* xxiv, A casement high and *triple-arch'd there was. **1848** BUCKLEY *Iliad* 204 Wounding him on the shoulder with a *triple-barbed arrow. **1905** *Daily Chron.* 22 Sept. 1/7 He is now in a cell *triple-barred and double-locked. **1934** W. S. CHURCHILL *Marlborough* II. xxv. 561 Between their squadrons appeared the *triple-barrelled guns, which opened a remarkably rapid fire. **1977** *Navy News* Sept. 2/3 Up, up, and away goes H.M.S. Salisbury's Squid triple-barrelled mortar, the last firing mounting in the Royal Navy. **1840** BROWNING *Sordello* I. 201 The *triple-bearded Teuton come to life! **1583** MELBANCKE *Philotimus* D dj, The *triple-bodied Pluto. **1728** POPE *Dunc.* II. 248 At some sick miser's *triple-bolted gate. **1855** MILMAN *Lat. Chr.* XIV. x. (1864) IX. 358 The *triple-chorded harmony of faith, holiness, and charity. **1660** F. BROOKE tr. *Le Blanc's Trav.* 140 *Triple-coloured tortoises. **1667** MILTON *P.L.* XI. 897. **1717** FENTON *Odyss.* XI. Poems 126 To drag to light the *triple-crested Dog That guards Hell's massy Portal. **1679** BEDLOE *Popish Plot* Ep. A j b, Their *Tripple Crown'd Idol at Rome. **1776** DA COSTA *Conchology* 21 A *triple-edged spear or sword. **1606** SYLVESTER *Du Bartas* II. iv. II. *Magnificence* 921 A great Cornaline, Where some rare Artist..Hath deeply cut Time's *triple-formed Front. **1840** CARLYLE *Heroes* iv. (1858) 286 A black spectral Nightmare and *triple-hatted Chimera. **1876** G. M. HOPKINS *Poems* (1967) 64 The *triple-hummocked Giant's Stool. **1709-10** STEELE *Tatler* No. 118 ¶1 To deal with them as Evander did with his *triple-lived Adversary. **1939** R. CHANDLER *Big Sleep* vii. 45 There was perfume on the *triple-mirrored dressing table. **1970** R. RENDELL *Guilty Thing Surprised* iii. 38 Between the two mirrors stood a triple-mirrored dressing table. **1811** WILLDENOW *Bot.* (new ed.) §42 A leaf is said to be..*Triple-nerved.., when out of the side of the middle rib above the base there arises a nerve running towards the point. **1851** MRS. BROWNING *Casa Guidi Wind.* I. 830 On *triple-piled Throne-velvets sit at ease to bless the poor. **1847** LD. LINDSAY *Chr. Art* I. 124 Our Saviour is represented..distinguished by the *triple-rayed nimbus. **1847** W. E. STEELE *Field Bot.* 47 Root-leaves crowded..petals rounded, *triple-ribbed. **1946** R. CHANDLER *Let.* 6 Oct. (1981) 80 The silly little *triple-spaced half pages I type on. **1966** F. STEWART *Deadly Nightcap* iii. 40 There were margins of twenty degrees on either side of the typescript, and it was triple-spaced. **1978** M. H. CLARK *Stranger is Watching* xix. 81, I typed them triple-spaced. **1629** FORD *Lover's Mel.* IV. ii, The dog, whose *triple-throated noise Hath rous'd a lion from his uncouth den. **1807** J. BARLOW *Columbiad* VII. 267 Flames, *triple tier'd, and tides of smoke, arise, And fulminations rock the seas and skies. **1962** E. SNOW *Other Side of River* (1963) ii. 23 A balcony overlooking the Outer City gave a view of the distant, triple-tiered, blue-glazed round roofs of the Temple of Heaven. **1972** M. J. BOSSE *Incident at Naha* i. 11 He..went to his triple-tiered pipe rack. **1611** COTGR., *Fourchier à trois dents*, a *triple-toothed forke. *c***1828** BERRY *Encycl. Her.* I. Gloss. s.v. *Triple*, *Triple-towered, gate, double-leaved. *a***1550** in Baring-Gould & Twigge *West. Armory* (1898) 3 Barnestaple Towne: Arg: a *triple turreted tower gul: betweene 3 ogresses.

b. in combination with sbs., forming adjectives or attributive phrases, as ***triple-action, -compartment, -cylinder, -digit, -expansion*** (see EXPANSION 7), ***-hearth, -line, -lock, -rack, -shift, -threat, -wick***; **triple-screw**, having three screw-propellers.

1934 WEBSTER 725/2 A **triple-action die*, when in operation, has a movement, produced by springs or a triple-action press, of two punches, two matrices, or a punch and a matrix, within either the upper or lower half of the die. **1960** *Farmer & Stockbreeder* 29 Mar. (Suppl.) 11/1 From Steiner comes news of two brand new hair aids. The first is Pearl Foam, a triple-action shampoo which cleanses, adds lustre and protects the hair from the weather. **1974** M. TAYLOR tr. *Metz's Film Lang.* ix. 233 This triple-action construction gives the ending of the film..its true meaning. **1882** *Rep. to Ho. Repr. Prec. Met. U.S.* 293 The main working shaft, which is *tripple compartment. **1877** KNIGHT *Dict. Mech.*, **Triple-cylinder engine*, a steam-engine employing three cylinders. **1976** *N.Y. Times* 7 Mar. III. 15/6 The foot-dragging is caused by Argentina's *triple-digit inflation. **1979** *Time* 28 May 12 The cost of living for April had jumped a shocking 8·7%, more than 100% if projected over the entire year. The admission provoked howls of alarm that the country could be heading toward uncontrollable triple-digit inflation. **1882** *Engineering* 12 May 474/1, I may mention that within the last few weeks there has been a steamer completed to work at a pressure of 150 lb. per square inch with *triple expansion engines very similar to those fitted in the Aberdeen. **1886** *Pall Mall G.* 21 Sept. 13/2 These steamers..are provided with triple expansion engines. **1893** J. A. HODGES *Elem. Photogr.* (1907) 17 The '*triple-extension' type [of camera]. **1877** RAYMOND *Statist. Mines & Mining* 339 The Bennett Mill carries ten stamps, six *triple-hearth reverberatory roasting-furnaces [etc.]. **1889** RIDER HAGGARD *K. Solomon's Mines* 220 The Greys filed off in a *triple-line formation. **1895** *Daily News* 14 Mar. 5/5 The ticket will be dropped in a *triple-lock box. **1892** *Photogr. Ann.* II. 545 Large size (patent) *triple-rack telescopic front tubes. **1901** *Daily Mail* 30 Oct. 5/3 A series of six *triple-screw 14,865 ton battleships. **1939** W. H. BAUMER *Sports as taught & played at West Point* 40 Any backs who possess the three qualifications of being a good runner, passer and kicker to a marked degree are *triple-threat men. **1972** J. MOSEDALE *Football* v. 67 Football no longer requires the triple threat back—the player who can run and kick as well as punt. **1892** *Photogr. Ann.* II. Advt., *Triple Wick Lamps,..Four Wick Lamps.

2. The adverb in combination. **a.** with pa. pples. or adjs., as ***triple-compound, -compounded, -dyed, -endowed, -locked, -quick, -refined, -roomed, -turned, -twined***.

1897 *Daily News* 14 June 6/6 Two sets of *triple-compound engines, each self-contained. **1775** ADAIR *Amer. Ind.* 69 A double, or *triple-compounded [word]. **1606** SYLVESTER *Du Bartas* II. iv. II. *Magnificence* 729 Their long strong sarcels, richly *triple-di'd Gold-Azure-Crimsin. **1974** HAWKEY & BINGHAM *Wild Card* xiv. 123 The *triple-locked door to his apartment. **1951** L. MACNEICE tr. *Goethe's Faust* 226 How *triple-quick we spirits fly! **1824** MISS MITFORD *Village* Ser. I. (1863) 130 A *triple-refined taste. **1610** HEALEY *St. Aug. Citie of God* XV. xxvi. 566 The arke..had roomes aboue those vpper roomes, and so was called *triple-roomed, being three stories high. **1606** SHAKS. *Ant. & Cl.* IV. xii. 13 *Triple-turn'd Whore, 'tis thou Hast sold me to this Nouice. **1804** J. COLLINS *Scripscrap.* xi, Bath deems a *triple-twin'd Laurel thy Due.

b. with pres. pples., as ***triple-barking, -flashing***.

1733 SWIFT *On Poetry* 214 To Cerberus they give a sop, His *triple-barking mouth to stop. **1903** *Daily Chron.* 27 Feb. 7/7 A light vessel, say one showing a ten-mile range *triple-flashing red light.

c. with vbs., as ***triple-lock***.

1876 'MARK TWAIN' *Tom Sawyer* xxxii. 251, I had its big door sheathed with boiler iron..and triple-locked. **1976** B. BOVA *Multiple Man* xvi. 177 The first thing I did was..to make certain I was alone..after triple-locking the front door.

Hence (*nonce-wds.*) † '**triplefold** *adv.*, triply, threefold; † '**triplewise** *adv.*, in a triple manner.

1570 FOXE *A. & M.* (ed. 2) 36/1 To these is gyuen pardon from the Pope, double and triplefold more, then to any other good worke of charitie. **1594** MARLOWE & NASHE *Dido* V. i, Ganges..Whose wealthy streams may wait upon her [Troy's] towers, And triple-wise entrench her round about.

triple ('trɪp(ə)l), *v.* Forms: see TRIPLE *a.*; also 5 **threpil, -el, tryple.** [ad. med.L. *triplāre* (see TRIPLATE); cf. F. *tripler* (1484 in Godef. *Compl.*), Prov. *triplar*.]

1. a. *trans.* To make three times as great or as many as before; to multiply by three; to make threefold; to treble.

1375 (MS. 1487) BARBOUR *Bruce* XVIII. 30 And said, that he suld fecht that day, Thouch Tryplit or quadruplit [*Edin. MS.* (1489) tribill and quatribill] war thai. *a***1400-50** *Alexander* 1476 Þe bischop..Comandis to ilka creatour to crie þurȝe þe stretis, To thre dais on a thrawe be threpild [*v.r.* threpelytt] to-gedire. **1542** RECORDE *Gr. Artes* (1575) 115 To double the remayner of poundes, and triple the remayner of shillings. **1564** *Reg. Privy Council Scot.* I. 297 Thair abone impresonment to be tripled. **1620** in Foster *Eng. Factories Ind.* (1906) 208 Private traders..who confesse they triple their principall between that place and Bantam. **1655** *Clarke Papers* (Camden) III. 23 His Highnesse..tripled the guards, and scoured the citty and 4 miles round with horse. *a* **1774** GOLDSM. *Surv. Exp. Philos.* (1776) I. 128 The body goes on with the double impression, and receives also a new one which triples it. **1795** *Hist.* in *Ann. Reg.* 17/1 She was determined to double and even triple her army. **1820** LAMB *Elia* Ser. I. *Two Races of Men*, He will return them [books]..with usury; enriched with annotations, tripling their value. **1858** BUCKLE *Civiliz.* (1864) II. i. 119 The export of foreign commodities was tripled.

b. To fold in three thicknesses. *rare*$^{-0}$.

1573–80 BARET *Alv.* T 376 *Triple*, to..fold a thing three times.

c. *spec.* in *Mech.* To alter (a steam-engine) from single or double expansion to the triple-expansion type; also, to fit (a vessel, etc.) with triple-expansion engines.

1891 [see TRIPLING *vbl. sb.* 1 b].

2. To amount to three times as many as. *rare*$^{-1}$.

1589 in Hakluyt *Voy.* (1599) II. II. 145 Their losse I can assure you did triple ours, as well in quality as in quantity.

3. *intr.* To grow to three times the former number or amount.

1799 W. TAYLOR in *Monthly Rev.* XXVIII. 526 Our author hesitates whether wages have not tripled. **1805** SYD. SMITH in Lady Holland *Mem.* (1855) II. 15, I..was pleasing myself with the notion..that your income was tripling and quadrupling in value. **1839** *Times* 11 June, Within the last twenty years it [crime] has tripled.

4. *Baseball.* To hit a triple (see TRIPLE *sb.* 6).

1908 *Sporting News* 17 Sept. 4/5 The very next day he tripled with the bases full. **1972** *N.Y. Times* 4 June 3/1 Danny Thompson tripled, and consecutive singles by Rod Carew, Harmon Killebrew, Steve Braun and Bobby Darwin gave the Twins a 2–0 lead.

tripled ('trɪp(ə)ld), *ppl. a.* [f. prec. + -ED[1].] Made triple or threefold; multiplied by three.

1583 STUBBES *Anat. Abus.* II. (1882) 98 This tripled commandement,..Feede my sheepe, feede my sheepe, feede my sheepe. **1621** MIDDLETON *Sun in Aries* Wks. (Bullen) VII. 349 Behold yon Fountain with the tripled crown. **1698** DRYDEN *Ep. to Motteux* 35 Time, action, place, are so preserved by thee That even Corneille might with envy see The alliance of his tripled Unity. **1790** R. MERRY *Laurel of Liberty* (ed. 2) 30 They force its tripled walls.

'triple-decker *a.* [f. TRIPLE *a.*, after DOUBLE-DECKER.] **1.** Of sandwiches: consisting of three layers of bread and two layers of filling.

1946 *New Yorker* 16 Mar. 21/2 We are the land of the between-meals snack, of the triple-decker sandwich. **1973** *Cookery Year* (Reader's Digest Assoc.) 133/5 *Club sandwiches*, one of the best inventions of the American kitchen is this triple-decker sandwich.

2. Of bunk beds: arranged one above another in threes.

1979 *Arizona Daily Star* 5 Aug. A8/2 Rosenthal walked into a tin-roofed quonset hut jammed with triple-decker bunk beds. **1980** *Nat. Geographic* June 866 Those who need rest..retire..to homemade triple-decker triple beds.

‖**triplegia** (traɪ'pliːdʒɪə). *Path.* [mod.L., f. Gr. τρι- three + πληγή stroke; cf. HEMIPLEGIA.]

1899 *Allbutt's Syst. Med.* VI. 894 Hemiplegia..when added to the paraplegia of spinal origin, makes up a clinical picture of a triplegia. **1900–13** DORLAND *Med. Dict.*, *Triplegia*,.., hemiplegia with paralysis of one limb on the opposite side.

triple-headed, *a.* Having three heads; three-headed.

1581 A. HALL *Iliad* v. 87 Iuno..stricken so did stand By triple headed sheering shafte, ysent by Herculs hand. **1605** DRAYTON *Pastorals* iv. 30 Such monster-tamers..As haue tyde vp the triple-headed hound. *a* **1658** CLEVELAND *Wks.* (1677) 94 The Tripleheaded Turn-key of Heaven with the Tripleheaded Porter of Hell. **1775** ADAIR *Amer. Ind.* 29 Proserpine and Cerberus were triple-headed. **1847** LD. LINDSAY *Chr. Art* I. 84 The triple-headed, bat-winged, horned and hoofed monster of the later middle ages.

triple-'header. *U.S.* Also **tripleheader.** [f. TRIPLE *a.*, after DOUBLE-HEADER.] **1.** In baseball, etc., a sporting event at which three consecutive matches are staged. Also *transf.* and *fig.*

1961 in WEBSTER. **1970** *New Yorker* 3 Oct. 34/2 Anybody who can't straighten out a plain old two-league, six-division distribution of twenty-six teams, each of which plays games both inside and outside its own division..isn't in shape for a single Sunday TV triple-header. **1979** *Honolulu Advertiser* 8 Jan. C-2/3 Sheridan Midas Mufflers..annihilated Manoa 15–5 in the opener of a Honolulu AJA Senior Baseball tripleheader yesterday.

2. A situation, occurrence, etc., having three aspects or involving three participants.

1976 *New Yorker* 29 Mar. 16/1 In his first attempt at a tripleheader (writer-director-star) he gets bogged down in an overelaborate production. **1977** *Ibid.* 4 July 23/1 The Cooper-Hewitt Museum, which this year has been throwing new exhibitions at us almost faster than we can catch them, has most recently unveiled a triple-header. **1977** *Washington Post* 13 Jan. C 1/3 Sens. Donald Riegle (D-Mich.), Lowell Weicker (R-Conn.) and Herman Talmadge (D-Ga.) made it a triple-header with their divorce announcements—getting it done before the new congressional session began and, of course, a few months after election time.

tripleness ('trɪp(ə)lnɪs). *rare.* [f. TRIPLE *a.* + -NESS.] The quality or condition of being triple; triplicity.

c **1881** HORT in *Expositor* June (1907) 489 When there is tripleness and at the same time not mere co-ordination but progression.

tripler ('trɪplə(r)). *Electronics.* [f. TRIPLE *v.* + -ER[1].] Any device for producing an output whose frequency or whose voltage is three times that of the input.

1924 S. R. ROGET *Dict. Electr. Terms* 244/2 *Static frequency-changer*... Also called doublers and triplers in the cases of twice and three times the original frequency. **1947** L. B. YOUNG in C. G. Montgomery *Technique of Microwave Measurements* vi. 371 In this frequency range the push-pull tripler of Fig. 6.22 is used. **1973** G. J. KING *Newnes Colour Television Servicing Man.* I. i. 29/2 The final 24 kV potential is developed only when the tripler e.h.t. output is connected to the tube final anode.

triplet ('trɪplɪt). Also 8 **triplit.** [f. TRIPLE, after DOUBLET; cf. F. *triplet* (Littré).]

1. A set of three; three persons or things combined or united.

1733 SWIFT *Legion Club* 183 Such a triplet could you tell Where to find on this side hell? **1824** L. MURRAY *Eng. Gram.* (ed. 5) I. 444 A very frequent succession of words and phrases, in couplets, or triplets, is also a great blemish in composition. **1851** AIRY *Presid. Addr. Brit. Assoc.* 43 Observing stations should be selected..in triplets: the three stations of each triplet having relation to the north boundary, the centre, and the south boundary of the shadow. The Russian Government has..actually equipped six triplets.

2. In various specific uses. **a.** Three successive lines of verse, esp. when riming together and of the same length.

1656 EARL MONM. tr. *Boccalini's Advts. fr. Parnass.* II. xiv. (1674) 153 Berni, the Head of those Italian Poets, who have..written facetious things in Triplets. **1697** [see 3]. **1751** EARL ORRERY *Remarks Swift* (1752) 188 One of his strictest rules in poetry was to avoid triplets. **1800** MALONE *Life Dryden* 525 He sent a second messenger to the book-seller, with a very satirical triplet. **1862** BORROW *Wild Wales* lix. (1911) 311 He was a poet by nature, having a muse wonderfully glib at making triplets and quartets.

b. *pl.* Three children at a birth; *sing.* one of three at a birth.

1787 GARTHSHORE in *Phil Trans.* LXXVII. 351 [Of] triplets, or three born at once, we find comparatively..few instances in..any..country. **1860** TANNER *Signs Pregnancy* (1862) 110 The presence of three distinct [uterine] double sounds, not isochronous, warrants the diagnosis of triplets. **1905** *Daily News* 25 Jan. 9 His mother said she..had two other boys the same age..The troublesome triplet was remanded.

c. *Mus.* A group of three notes to be played in the time of two of the same time-value.

1801 in BUSBY *Dict. Mus.* **1848** RIMBAULT *Piano* 23 When three notes of one sort are joined together, and have the figure 3 placed over or under them, they are called a Triplet, ..and are to be performed in the time of two only of the same kind. **1862** ERNST PAUER *Programme* 8 Mar., With triplets continually increasing in rapidity.

transf. **1860** RUSKIN *Unto this Last* iv. §82 Triplets of birds and murmur and chirp of insects.

d. *Arch.* A window of three lights.

1849 FREEMAN *Archit.* II. I. vii. 180 The genuine triplet with the higher central light seems hardly to be found in Italy. **1868** *Daily News* 22 July, A window in the Abbey Church, consisting of a triplet of lancets at the west end of the nave.

e. A combination of three plano-convex lenses in a microscope, etc.; also, a microscope having three lenses.

1837 *Encycl. Brit.* (ed. 7) XV. 36 Sir David Brewster has made triplets in which two of the lenses are fluids and the third a solid. **1867** [see 3].

f. A counterfeit jewel: see quot., and cf. DOUBLET *sb.* 5.

1877 *Five Yrs.' Penal Servitude* iv. 274 A triplet is made as follows:—Two colourless topazes are prepared for the back and the front. Between these is neatly placed a piece of blue glass, and the three are stuck together with Venice turpentine.

g. A tandem bicycle for three riders.

1894 *Daily News* 3 Sept. 3/3 On a triplet, [they] started to create a record for their type of machine, and succeeded..in riding the fastest mile ever ridden at Herne-hill.

h. *Geom.* A system of three families of surfaces such that one of each family passes through each point of space.

1891 in *Cent. Dict.*

i. *Naut.* Three links between the cable and the anchor-ring.

1891 in *Cent. Dict.*

j. *Poker.* (See quot. 1864.)

1864 W. B. DICK *Amer. Hoyle* 164 *Triplets* are three cards of the same denomination, and rank higher than two pairs. For example;—three Deuces beat a pair of Aces and Kings. **1887** J. W. KELLER *Game of Draw Poker* 14 Full Hand—(Triplets accompanied by a pair)... A full hand beats a flush. **1950** [see SANDBAGGER 2].

k. (i) *Physics* and *Chem.* A multiplet (sense a) composed of three lines or energy levels. Freq. *attrib.*, esp. designating an atom with two unpaired electrons and $S = 1$.

1879 *Proc. R. Soc.* XXX. 29 The flame spectrum of magnesium was examined, a green triplet was observed. **1922** [see SINGLET 3 a]. **1934, 1937** [see INTERCOMBINATION]. **1950** G. HERZBERG *Spectra of Diatomic Molecules* (ed. 2) v. 216 Molecules with an even number of electrons have odd multiplicities (singlets, triplets,...) since S is integral. **1977** *Nature* 3 Nov. 15/1 The Earth has an atmosphere containing diatomic triplet oxygen..essential for life.

(ii) *Particle Physics.* A multiplet (sense b) of three sub-atomic particles.

1937 [SINGLET 3 b]. **1961** M. GELL-MANN in Gell-Mann & Ne'eman *Eightfold Way* (1964) 12 We have a triplet ρ of vector mesons coupled to the isotopic spin current and a singlet vector meson ω^0 coupled to the hypercharge current. **1968** [see OCTET, OCTETTE 3 c]. **1975** *Sci. Amer.* Oct. 40/1 The pion is a triplet with an average mass of ·137 GeV and three charge states: $+1$, 0 and -1.

3. *attrib.* and *Comb.*, as ***triplet condenser***, ***head***, ***rhyme***, etc.; **triplet code** *Genetics*, the accepted version of the genetic code in which amino-acids are specified by three successive nucleotides in a nucleic acid molecule; **triplet lily**, the American genus *Triteleia*, N.O. *Liliaceæ*, having the parts of the flower regularly arranged in threes.

1697 DRYDEN *Æneid* Ded. fj, I frequently make use of Triplet Rhymes. **1867** J. HOGG *Microsc.* I. i. 13 The first triplet achromatic object-glass. **1874** H. H. COLE *Catal. Ind. Art S. Kens. Mus.* App. 287 This bas-relief represents a god with several triplet heads and a great number of hands. **1884** MILLER *Plant-n.*, *Triteleia*, Triplet-Lily. **1892** *Photogr. Ann.* II. 548 Microscope and micropolariscope, fitted with Mr. Hughes's patent 5in. triplet condensers. **1900** *Daily News* 21 Apr. 6/3 New amateur triplet records were established..from two miles up to 28 miles. **1957** *Proc. Nat. Acad. Sci.* XLIII. 687 Such triplet codes..have an excess of information, since there are sixty-four different triplets for the twenty amino acids. **1976** P. COLLARD *Devel. Microbiol.* viii. 107 The correctness of the triplet code was soon verified by the elegant experiments of Nirenberg.

triple tree. *Cant.* Now *Hist.* or *arch.* [TREE *sb.* 4 b.] A gallows (in reference to its three parts).

a **1634** RANDOLPH *Hey for Honesty* IV. i, This is a Rascal deserves to ride up Holborn, and take a pilgrimage to the triple-tree, To dance in Hemp Derricks Caranto. **1707** J. STEVENS tr. *Quevedo's Com. Wks.* (1709) 181 Being come to the tripple Tree, he..set his Foot on the Ladder. **1862** SALA *Ship Chandler* i. 5 Busy as was the triple tree.., they could not hang all the rogues they convicted.

triplex ('traɪ-, 'trɪplɛks), *a.* (*sb.*) [a. L. *triplex*, *-plic-* threefold, f. *tri-* three + *plic-* to fold.]

1. a. Triple, threefold. Also *absol.* as *sb.*

1601 SHAKS. *Twel. N.* v. i. 41 The triplex..is a good tripping measure, or the belles of S. Bennet,..may put you in minde, one, two, three. [**1654** D. CAWDREY (*title*) Diatribe Triplex: or A threefold Exercitation Concerning 1. Superstition. 2. Will-worship. 3. Christmas Festivall.] **1655** HAMMOND (*title*) An account of Mr. Cawdry's Triplex Diatribe. **1656** S. HOLLAND *Zara* (1719) 71 So that now there is like to be a trouble in Triplex. **1911** W. TEMPLE *Nat. Personality* viii. 112 We are not so compelled to speak of three centres of consciousness in the Deity; rather we should speak of a triplex consciousness.

b. ***triplex board***, a type of cardboard consisting of three layers felted together by pressure without the use of adhesive.

1921 H. A. MADDOX *Dict. Stationery* 78 *Triplex board*, a cheap class of pasteboard or ticket board which derives its name from the fact that it comprises three layers. **1962** F. T. DAY *Introd. to Paper* iv. 46 In the case of Triplex boards one grade of pulp is used for the middle while the two outside sheets are made of a thinner substance to make up the finished board.

2. *Genetics.* Of a polyploid individual: having the dominant allele of any particular gene represented three times.

1921, etc. [see NULLIPLEX *a.*]. **1929** *Jrnl. Genetics* XXI. 138 If we assume 14/16 to be triplex for Y the unexpected ivory plant could then have arisen by (1) non-disjunction.., or (2) irregularity of disjunction in the equational division.

3. (Usu. with capital initial.) The proprietary name of a type of toughened or laminated glass, orig. *spec.* consisting of two layers of glass and a layer of celluloid between them.

1923 *Trade Marks Jrnl.* 28 Nov. 2495 Triplex. Use claimed from 2nd August 1912... Safety Glass in sheets. The Triplex Safety Glass Co. Ltd. **1927** M. ARLEN *Young Men in Love* II. 128 'I live in such a glass house, Peter!' 'Well, so does everyone else.' 'Oh, no, other people's are made of Triplex!' **1930** *Times Educ. Suppl.* 27 Dec. (Home & Classroom Suppl.) p. i/3 The car was fully equipped with three speeds,..Triplex glass screen, windscreen wiper,.. side curtains, and hood bag. **1935** L. MACNEICE *Poems* 40 Chromium dogs on the bonnet, faces behind the triplex screens. **1970** P. DICKINSON *Seals* i. 26 Even through that grimy and half-opaque triplex, the harbour had seemed awkwardly placed.

4. a. An apartment or other residence on three floors. Chiefly *U.S.*

1932 E. FERBER in *Hearst's Internat.* Mar. 18/1 Photographs in the magazines showed her glamorous apartment—triplex, with balcony overhanging the East River. **1978** *New York* 3 Apr. 91 (Advt.), 40' converted mansion, elevator, magnificent owner's triplex plus high income apartments. **1981** *Times* 3 Aug. 10/5 A 21-room 'triplex' (ie, on three floors) going for 'only' $9 million.

b. A building containing three self-contained residences or suites of rooms; also, one of the dwellings in such a building. Cf. DUPLEX *sb.* 1. Chiefly *N. Amer.*

1962 *Maclean's Mag.* (Toronto) 10 Mar. 37/1 They wanted to build three triplexes. 'Definitely not,' Reeve Fred Hall told Norman. **1971** A. BLAISDELL *Practice to Deceive* i. 2 She lived in one unit of a triplex. **1971** *Rand Daily Mail* (Home Owner) 27 Mar. 7/2 City dwellers are gravitating towards high density living (flat complexes..duplex and triplex..and so on). **1976** *Billings* (Montana) *Gaz.* 30 June

7-D/1 (Advt.), Accelerated depreciation is still available on this new brick tri-plex. This unit features a fantastic view. **1979** *Arizona Daily Star* 5 Aug. B 1/6 She observes construction workers working on a triplex where her display company's warehouses once stood.

Hence **tri'plexity** = TRIPLICITY.

1895 in *Funk's Stand. Dict.*

tripley, obs. form of TRIPLY *v.*

tripli- (trɪplɪ), short for *triplici-*, combining form of L. *triplex* TRIPLE, occurring in a few rare adjs. (chiefly *Bot.*), as **tripli'costate** = *tricostate* (TRI- 1 a); **'tripliform** = TRIFORM 1; **triplinerved** = TRINERVATE.

1866 *Treas. Bot.* 1173 *Triple-nerved, Triplinerved, Triplinervis*, the same as Triple-ribbed. **1869** INMAN *Symbolism* Introd. 12 One symbol was tripliform, the other single. **1879** WEBSTER Suppl., Triplicostate.

tripli'cand. *Sc. Law.* [ad. L. *triplicānd-*, gerund. stem of *triplicāre* to TRIPLICATE.] The tripling of the feu-duty for one year; a triple feu-duty so paid. Cf. DUPLICAND.

1898 *Mem. Jas. E. Fyfe* 39 The superior rubbed his hands over an annual duty of £30 an acre, with a triplicand every twenty-first year.

triplicate ('trɪplɪkət), *a.* and *sb.* [ad. L. *triplicāt-us*, pa. pple. of *triplicāre* (*rare*) to triple.]

A. *adj.* Threefold, triple; forming three exactly corresponding copies; consisting of or related to three corresponding parts.

1432–50 tr. *Higden* (Rolls) I. 239 A triplicate honor was ȝiffen to a kynge..hauenge victory, in his commenge to the cite of Rome. **1512** *Act. 4 Hen. VIII*, c. 19 §10 One parte of the seid Writyng triplicate to be indented shall remayne with the seid Commissioners. **1528** in Burnet *Hist. Ref.* (1679) I. Records II. iv. 25 Certain Expeditions Triplicat; the one unto the Prothonotar Gambora, the other unto Gregory de Cassali, and the third unto me. **1756** *Gentl. Mag.* Oct. 461/1 It was always customary to make double and triplicate bills of loading. **1862** BEVERIDGE *Hist. India* III. VIII. iii. 333 The conclusion of a triplicate treaty by the British government, the Maharajah, and Shah Shujah-ul-Moolk. **1902** W. M. ALEXANDER *Demonic Possession N.T.* iii. 61 There are..duplicate or triplicate narratives of these three cases.

b. ***triplicate proportion, ratio***: the proportion or ratio of cubes (third powers) in relation to that of the radical quantities.

1660 BARROW *Euclid* v. Def. x, When 4 magnitudes A, B, C, D are proportional, the first A shall have a triplicate ratio to the fourth D of what it had to the second B. **1674** PETTY *Disc. Dupl. Proportion* 44 Like pieces of Timber, that are in cubical or triplicate proportion of their Sides, are strong but according to duplicate proportion, or the Squares of their respective Sides. **1718** QUINCY *Compl. Disp.* 45 The Gravity of Bodies decreases in a Triplicate, but their Surface in a Duplicate Proportion of their Diameters. **1806** HUTTON *Course Math.* (1810) I. 314 The Ratio of the First [quantity] to the Third, will be duplicate or the Square of the Ratio of the First and Second; and the Ratio of the First and Fourth will be triplicate or the cube of that of the First and Second; and so on.

c. ***triplicate quartan*** (***ague***) = *triple quartan* (TRIPLE *a.* 5).

1822–34 *Good's Study Med.* (ed. 4) I. 613 Quartanus triplicatus. Triplicate quartan.

d. In combination, as ***triplicate-ternate*** (*Bot.*) = TRITERNATE.

1847 in WEBSTER. **1900** B. D. JACKSON *Gloss. Bot. Terms, Triplicate-ternate*, triternate (Crozier).

B. *sb.* **1.** One of three things exactly alike, *esp.* one of three copies of a document; *pl.* three things exactly alike.

1762–71 H. WALPOLE *Vertue's Anecd. Paint.* (1786) II. 23 *note*, There are three portraits of himself,..and three triplicates of his mistress. **1801** WELLINGTON in Gurw. *Desp.* (1837) I. 284, I have the honour to enclose the triplicate of a letter to the Governor of Bombay. **1835** BATMAN in Cornwallis *New World* (1859) I. 410, I busied myself in drawing up triplicates of the deeds of the land I had purchased. **1859** TENNENT *Ceylon* II. VII. v. 200 Not only a duplicate, but a triplicate of the desecrated relic were regarded with undiminished adoration both in Pegu and Ceylon.

b. ***in triplicate***: in three exactly corresponding copies or transcripts. Also *transf.*

1810 WELLINGTON in Gurw. *Desp.* (1838) VI. 170 Desire Captain Eliott to send his account of the expenditure in Triplicate. **1860** HOOK *Lives Abps.* II. vii. 412 The constitutions were written in triplicate. **1894** *Times* 7 Aug. 6/2 Many of the trains..were run in duplicate and triplicate.

†**2.** Triplicate ratio; third power, cube. *Obs. rare.*

1767 MURDOCH in *Phil. Trans.* LVIII. 28 The accelerative force of A..will be increased in the triplicate of that ratio.

triplicate ('trɪplɪkeɪt), *v.* [f. L. *triplicāt-*, ppl. stem of *triplicāre* (see prec.), f. *triplex*, triple.]

1. *trans.* To multiply by three; to increase threefold; to triple.

1623 COCKERAM, *Triplicate*, to triple, or doe a thing three times. **1652** BENLOWES *Theoph.* x. lxi, Could'st thou engross Cathaiahs Gems And more than triplicate Romes triple diadems. **1717** B. TAYLOR in *Phil. Trans.* XXX. 614 This Formula will also triplicate the number of true Figures in Z. **1871** *Daily News* 19 Jan., They have thus triplicated the defences of a tract they had judged to be exposed.

2. To make or provide in triplicate; to make the triplicate of; to repeat a second time.

1639 GENTILIS *Servita's Inquis.* (1676) 851 They might.. reply, and triplicate the same request with greater instance. **1653** R. SANDERS *Physiogn.* 249 Such a person usually reiterates and triplicates his words, to little purpose. **1879** G. MEREDITH *Egoist* xxxvi, We are in danger of duplicating [wedding-presents] and triplicating and quadruplicating.

Hence **'triplicating** *ppl. a.*

1906 *Hibbert Jrnl.* Apr. 598 Hegel's argument was a kind of trinity: i.e. it moved in a triplicating way,—thesis, antithesis and synthesis.

'triplicated, *ppl. a.* [f. prec. + -ED[1].] Made threefold; triple. ***triplicated proportion***, triplicate proportion.

1635 WINGATE *Λογαριθμοτεχνία* 69 Having three numbers given, to finde a fourth in a triplicated Proportion. **1678** [see TRIPLASIAN]. **1753** CHAMBERS *Cycl. Supp.* s.v. *Bridge*, The piers being only thirteen feet thick, yet serving to support an immense weight of a triplicated arcade. **1851** C. L. SMITH tr. *Tasso* XI. vii, The flaming quire Of Heaven in triplicated order dighted.

triplication (trɪplɪ'keɪʃən). [a. F. *triplication* (Godef.), or ad. L. *triplicātiōn-em*, n. of action from *triplicāre* to TRIPLICATE.]

1. The action or process of making threefold, or multiplying by three; also, the result of this.

1610 HEALEY *St. Aug. Citie of God* XIX. ii. (1620) 708 These twelve sects are produced by the triplication of these foure. **1674** JEAKE *Arith.* (1696) 24 Triplication..is to add the given number to the double of the same. **1798** W. PALGRAVE *Let.* in *Parr's Wks.* (1828) VIII. 103 The triplication of the assessed taxes. **1893** *Nation* (N.Y.) 23 Mar. 213/3 A duplication or triplication of teachers of theology entered into my ideal of the school.

2. a. *Civil* and *Canon Law.* The plaintiff's reply to the defendant's duplication, corresponding to the surrejoinder at common law. **b.** In *Common Law* sometimes applied (after Britton) to the rejoinder.

[**1292** BRITTON III. xiv. §6 Et si le pleyntif die, qe il fust seisi par acun feffement, a ceo soit respoundu par triplicacioun, cum desus est dit.] *a* **1577** SIR T. SMITH *Commw. Eng.* (1609) 67 Where the law is not doubtful, according to the matter conteyned in the declaration, answer, replication, rejoynder, or triplication, the Judge out of hand decideth it. **1651** G. W. tr. *Cowel's Inst.* 243 Our Lawyers call a Duplication, as well in the Chancery, as in other Courts a Rejoinder, and a Triplication a Sur-rejoinder. **1726** AYLIFFE *Parergon* 251 There are also Triplications, which the Plaintiff objects to the Defendant's Duplication. **1865** NICHOLS *Britton* II. 116 Nevertheless in some cases the plaintiff may have a valid replication..But the tenant may answer by way of triplication, that [etc.]. **1880** MUIRHEAD *Gaius* IV. §128 If this..for any reason be really inequitable to the pursuer, still another clause is necessary on the other side for his relief, which is called a triplication. **1895** POLLOCK & MAITLAND *Hist. Eng. Law* II. ix. §4. 613 The exception may be met by a replication, the replication by a triplication and so on *ad infinitum*.

transf. **1593** G. HARVEY *Pierces Super.* Wks. (Grosart) II. 112 For any my briefe Triplication, he will prouide a Quadruplication at large. **1621** [see DUPLICATION 3 b]. **1649** ROBERTS *Clavis Bibl.* 344 Eliphas his Triplication, or third Opposition against Job.

triplicative ('trɪplɪkeɪtɪv), *a.* [f. L. *triplicāt-*, ppl. stem of *triplicāre* to TRIPLICATE + -IVE.] Having the quality of tripling.

1839–52 BAILEY *Festus* (ed. 5) 509 The esoteric truths which nature veiled, Of the one triplicative essence.

triplicato- (trɪplɪ'keɪtəʊ), combining form repr. L. *triplicātus* TRIPLICATE, rarely used in a few botanical terms instead of the simple *tri-*, as **triplicato-pinnate** *a.* = TRIPINNATE, **triplicato-ternate** *a.* = TRITERNATE.

[**1753** CHAMBERS *Cycl. Supp.* s.v. *Leaf, Triplicato-ternatum*.] **1760** J. LEE *Introd. Bot.* III. vi. (1765) 188 *Triternate*, or *Triplicato-Ternate*; when a Petiole bears three Folioles that are each of them Biternate. **1866** *Treas. Bot.* 1173 *Triplicato-pinnate*, the same as Tripinnate.

triplicature ('trɪplɪkeɪtjʊə(r)). [f. L. *triplicāt-*, ppl. stem of *triplicāre* to TRIPLICATE, after DUPLICATURE: see -URE.] Triplication.

1891 in *Cent. Dict.*

Triplice ('triplitʃe). Also with lower case initial. [a. It. *triplice* triple; cf. TRIPLEX *a.* (*sb.*).] The Triple Alliance (see TRIPLE *a.* 5) of Germany, Austria-Hungary, and Italy, formed in 1882 against Russia and France. Also *transf.*

1896 *Daily News* 15 Dec. 5/3 The same demand has been made to the other members of the Triplice. **1897** *Ibid.* 6 Sept. 5/2 The Triplice desires peace at any cost. **1901** *Speaker* 20 Apr. 74/2 It would be misleading to call the *Triplice* a League of peace. **1908** *Daily Chron.* 30 July 3/6 A suggestion for a new alliance, a triplice of Britain, France, and Germany, in the interests of peace, was made by Mr. Prust, of Launceston. **1911** DJAVID BEY *Let.* 28 Oct. in R. S. Churchill *Winston S. Churchill* (1969) II. Compan. II. xvii. 1368 The attack of one of the triple alliance powers on our territory has turned the public opinion greatly against the triplice. **1947** *Hist. of The Times* III. x. 250 The conclusion that the Triplice..was weak as an Alliance, was forced to the forefront of Wallace's mind. **1979** E. INGRAM *Beginning of Great Game* ix. 263 The tsar forestalled Palmerston's attempt to erect a near-eastern triplice [of Britain, Austria and France].

Hence **'Triplicist**, a supporter of the Triplice; also *attrib.* or as *adj.*

1923 J. BUCHAN *Nations of To-day: Italy* 172 It was able to give a decidedly 'Triplicist' aspect to the enterprise. **1924** *Glasgow Herald* 15 Jan. 7 It is all to the credit of the Triplicists..and very little to that of the Allies.

†**tri'plicitate**, *v. Obs.* [f. late L. *triplicitāt-*, TRIPLICITY + -ATE[3].] *trans.* To triple.

1657 TOMLINSON *Renou's Disp.* 720 Efficacious in curing the Dropsie, if the quantity of Cypress be triplicitated.

triplicity (trɪ'plɪsɪtɪ). [ad. late L. *triplicitāt-em*, f. L. *triplex*, *-icem*: see TRIPLEX and -ITY. Cf. F. *triplicité* (14–15th c. in Hatz.-Darm.).]

1. The quality or condition of being triple; threefold character or existence; tripleness, three-foldness.

1555 EDEN *Decades* I One god whom we honour in triplicitie of person. **1624** HEYWOOD *Gunaik.* VI. 268 To this three-fold age, I compare the triplicitie of the Muses. **1690** BURNET *Th. Earth* III. 10 This triplicity of the heavens and the earth is the first, obvious, plain sence of the apostle's discourse. **1705** HEARNE *Collect.* 12 Dec. (O.H.S.) I. 126 The Triplicity of the Crownes. **1850** L. HUNT *Autobiog.* I. ii. 45 He was clergyman, physician, and lawyer, at once. How this singular triplicity came to take place, I cannot say.

2. A combination or group of three things, beings, or attributes; three things collectively; a triad, trio, triplet.

1585 S. R. (*title*) The Choise of Change: Containing the Triplicitie of Diuinitie, Philosophie, and Poetrie. **1590** SPENSER *F.Q.* I. xii. 39 Many an Angels voice Singing before th'eternall majesty, In their trinall triplicities on hye. **1607** TOPSELL *Four-f. Beasts* (1658) 451 The Panther..is joyned with the Lion and the Wolf, to make up the triplicity of ravening Beasts. **1660** WATERHOUSE *Arms & Arm.* 143 Solomon, Marcus Antoninus, and our late King James, a triplicity of unparalleld Majesties. **1899** F. M. CRAWFORD *Via Crucis* vi. 71 A most perfect triplicity of beauty, grace and elastic strength.

†**b.** A multiple by three; three times the amount. *Obs. rare*$^{-1}$.

1646 SIR T. BROWNE *Pseud. Ep.* IV. xii. 218 Affirming.. what receiveth motion in the seventh, to be perfected in the Triplicities; that is, the time of conformation..from motion unto the birth [is] treble.

3. *spec.* in *Astrol.* A combination of three of the twelve signs of the zodiac, each sign being distant 120° or the third part of a circle from the other two: = TRIGON 2 a.

Each of the four triplicities is named after one of the 'elements', of whose qualities it is supposed to partake; thus *airy t.* = Gemini, Libra, Aquarius; *earthy t.* = Taurus, Virgo, Capricornus; *fiery t.* = Aries, Leo, Sagittarius; *watery t.* = Cancer, Scorpio, Pisces.

1398 TREVISA *Barth. De P.R.* VIII. ix. (Bodl. MS.) lf. 80/1 þese howses beþ icleped þe howses of triplicite and somme of exaltacioun, for þilke signes þat accordeþ in one kinde makeþ triplicite and have .o. name. *c* **1532** DU WES *Introd. Fr.* in *Palsgr.* 1054 The sayd xii signes..ben devided by foure triplicites. **1584** R. SCOT *Discov. Witchcr.* XIII. vii. (1886) 243 In Aries, Leo, and Sagittarie is a certain triplicitie. **1650** R. GELL *Serm.* 8 Aug. 45 Talk not to them of fiery, aiery, watry, earthly triplicities. **1815** SCOTT *Guy M.* iii, I will calculate his nativity according to the rule of the 'Triplicities', as recommended by Pythagoras, Hippocrates, Diocles, and Avicenna. **1855** SMEDLEY, etc. *Occult Sciences* 307 The Four Triplicities is another distribution of the twelve signs into groups of three.

†**b.** *fig.* or *allusively. Obs.*

1573 G. HARVEY *Letter-bk.* (Camden) 140 So many influences and triplicityes of loove. **1647** *Husbandman's Plea agst. Tithes* 70 The fiery triplicitie..of Bishops, Priests, and Deacons. **1680** *Hon. Cavalier* 15 The Pope, the Fanatick, and the Turk, that Fiery Triplicity of the World.

triplicostate, -form, -nerved: see TRIPLI-.

tripling ('trɪplɪŋ), *vbl. sb.* [f. TRIPLE *v.* + -ING[1].]

1. The action of the verb TRIPLE.

1603 FLORIO *Montaigne* (1634) 94 It is a great..wonder for a man to double himselfe; and those that talke of tripling, know not, nor cannot reach unto the height of it. **1630** DELAMAIN *Grammelogia* **j, The doubling, tripling [etc.] of Circles. **1853** SIR W. R. HAMILTON *Lect. Quarternions* ii. 53 Two successive acts, of negatively doubling and negatively tripling, compound themselves into the single act of positively sextupling.

b. *spec.* See TRIPLE *v.* 1 c.

1891 *Times* 26 Oct. 4/3 There is a fair amount of tripling of engines in old vessels ordered.

2. *concr.* **a.** *pl.* Three children at a birth; triplets.

1858 LEWES *Sea-side Stud.* 246 This multiplication of individuals from one egg, this production of twins, or triplings, is a constant fact.

b. *Min.* A compound crystal made up of three independent individuals; a trilling, trin.

1895 STORY-MASKELYNE *Crystallogr.* §157 Such crystals are triple, quadruple, &c. hemitropes (or triplings, fourlings, &c.).

triplite ('trɪplaɪt). *Min.* [ad. Ger. *triplit* (Hausmann, 1813), f. Gr. τριπλοῦς threefold, in reference to its three cleavages: see -ITE[1].] A phosphate of iron and manganese (often containing fluorine), of a brown or blackish colour, with cleavage in three directions mutually at right angles.

1850 ANSTED *Elem. Geol., Min.* etc. §447 Hureaulite, Heterozite, and Triphylline, or Triplite, are phosphates of manganese and iron. **1868** DANA *Min.* (ed. 5) 543.

triplo- (trɪpləʊ), before a vowel **tripl-**, combining form repr. Gr. τριπλόος, τριπλοῦς threefold, triple; occurring in a few rare scientific terms. (Cf. TRIPLI-.) **triploblastic** (-ˈblæstɪk) *a.*, *Biol.* [Gr. βλαστός germ], having three germinal layers (epiblast, mesoblast, and hypoblast: cf. BLASTODERM) in the embryo; belonging to the division *Triploblastica*, a synonym of CŒLOMATA, including the majority of animals; cf. *diploblastic* s.v. DIPLO-. **triplo-caulescent** (-kɔːˈlɛsənt), **-caulous** (-ˈkɔːləs) *adjs.*, *Bot.* [L. *caulis* stem], having a tertiary system of axes or stem-branches. ‖**triˈplopia**, anglicized **ˈtriplopy**, *Path.* [Gr. ὤψ eye: cf. DIPLOPIA], an affection of the eyes in which objects are seen triple.

1888 *Cassell's Encycl. Dict.*, *Triploblastic. **1890** BILLINGS *Med. Dict.*, *Triploblastic*, having three germ-layers. **1900** B. D. JACKSON *Gloss. Bot. Terms*, **Triplo-caulescent*.. when a plant has a third (tertiary) system of axes. **Triplo-caulous*.. possessing ternary axes (Pax). **1860** MAYNE *Expos. Lex.*, **Triplopia*, a term for.. disordered vision in which objects are tripled. **1903** F. W. H. MYERS *Hum. Personality* I. 479 Cases, where ciliary spasm.. led to .. triplopia. **1863** ATKINSON tr. *Ganot's Physics* VII. vi. 463 A single eye may also be affected with *triplopy, but in this case the third image is exceedingly weak.

triploid (ˈtrɪplɔɪd), *sb.* and *a.* [ad. mod.L. *triploides*, f. Gr. τριπλό-ος: see prec. and -OID.]

A. *sb.* **1.** *Surg.* (See quot.) *rare* (? *Obs.*).

[**1706** PHILLIPS (ed. Kersey), *Triploides*.] **1750** *Mem. R. Acad. Surg. Paris* I. 162–3 The instruments hitherto used to raise the bones of the cranium depressed on the dura mater are.. the triploid... This instrument has three feet or branches like a tripod.

2. A triploid organism (see below).

1927 *Jrnl. Genetics* XVIII. 183 These five are all the configurations which have been seen among several hundred trivalents of triploids.. in *Datura* and *Canna*. **1957** R. A. BEATTY *Parthenogenesis & Polyploidy in Mammalian Devel.* iv. 59 Three of the young [rabbits] lived nearly a year, being the two 'triploids' and a presumed diploid male. **1973** [see OCTOPLOID *a.* (*sb.*)].

B. *adj. Genetics.* [Cf. -PLOID.] (Made up of somatic cells) containing three sets of chromosomes.

1911 *Ann. Bot.* XXV. 933 There is not, so far as I am aware, a single case of a species whose sporophyte has the triploid number of chromosomes. **1930** *Times Lit. Suppl.* 10 July 578/3 Triploid apples (e.g., Bramley's Seedling) fruit well. **1971** [see DIPLOID *a.*].

Hence **ˈtriploidy**, the state of being triploid.

1916 *Genetics* I. 237 It seems probable that we have in these plants examples of triploidy (21 chromosomes). **1961** *Lancet* 5 Aug. 318/1 A malformation syndrome associated with triploidy. **1976** *Cytogenetics & Cell Genetics* XVII. 144 Triploidy or diploid/triploid chimerism has been reported in man. **1982** *Annals Human Genetics* XLVI. 223 Human triploidy is a common condition.

triploidite (ˈtrɪplɔɪdaɪt). *Min.* [f. TRIPL(ITE + -OID + -ITE[1].] A hydrous phosphate of iron and manganese, allied to TRIPLITE.

1878 *Amer. Jrnl. Sc. & Arts* Ser. III. May 398 Triploidite .. occurs in crystalline aggregates whose structure is parallel-fibrous to columnar.

‖**triplum** (ˈtrɪplʊm). *Mus.* Pl. tripla. [med.L., neut. of *triplus* TRIPLE *a.*; cf. TREBLE *sb.* 4.] In thirteenth- and fourteenth-century polyphonic vocal music, the third voice part, next but one above the tenor.

1782, 1884 [see TREBLE *sb.* 4]. **1944** W. APEL *Harvard Dict. Mus.* 223/1 *Triplum, quadruplum* are other parts above the tenor, frequently of the same range as the duplum. **1954** *New Oxf. Hist. Music* II. xi. 354 The motet 'Salve virgo virginum/Est il donc ainsi/Aptatur' has 202 notes in the *triplum* (highest voice), 173 in the *motetus* (middle voice), and only 103 in the tenor. **1977** *Early Music* Apr. 185 A glance through the tripla and dupla of 13th-century motets is enough to show that rhythmic styles could be tolerated in music which made a nonsense of poetic scansion.

triˈplumbic, *a. Chem.* [f. TRI- 5 + L. *plumb-um* lead + -IC.] Containing three atoms of lead; e.g. ***triplumbic tetroxide***, Pb_3O_4.

1866–8 WATTS *Dict. Chem.* IV. 566 *Triplumbic phosphate*, $Pb^3P^2O^8$, is obtained as a white, earthy, amorphous precipitate. **1905** NEWTH *Inorg. Chem.* (ed. 11) 648 Triplumbic Tetroxide.. is obtained when lead carbonate, or monoxide, is subjected to prolonged heating in contact with air.

triply (trɪˈplaɪ), *sb. Sc. Law. Obs.* exc. *Hist.* [ad. OF. *triplique* (*treplicque*, 1392–3 in Godef. *Compl.*); cf. also REPLY, DUPLY, QUADRUPLY.]

A third reply; a pursuer's reply to a defender's rejoinder; a surrejoinder. Also *allusively*.

1531 in *10th Rep. Hist. MSS. Comm.* App. I. 71 Notwithstanding the rights, replies and triplies produced on the part of John Kynross, not proved. **1643** BAILLIE *Lett., to W. Spang* 7 Dec. (1841) II. 109 When, upon every proposition by itself, and on everie text of Scripture.. the replyes, and duplies, and triplies, are heard. **1678** SIR G. MACKENZIE *Crim. Laws Scot.* II. xxiii. §9 (1699) 253 After they have ended, His Majesties Advocat speaks, but there are no Duplys, or Triplys used. *a* **1693, 1760, 1820, 1881** [see DUPLY]. **1695, 1762** [see QUADRUPLY].

So **triˈply** *v.* [cf. OF. *tripliquer* (1310 in Godef.)], to make a triply or reply to a defender's rejoinder (*trans.* and *intr.*).

1504 in *Charters &c. of Stirling* (1884) 68 Till obiect, except, and aganesay, to repley, dupley, tripley, and quadrupley. **1662** *Justiciary Records* (S.H.S. 1905) 44 Triplied by Birnie. He oppones the answers. **1678** SIR G. MACKENZIE *Crim. Laws Scot.* I. xxiv. §4 (1699) 123 To which it was triplyed, that the Act of Parliament, discharging Usurary Wadsets doth not discharge Tacks. **1766** *State of Proc., Dk. Roxburgh v. Pringle* 7 Duplied for the Defender.. Triplied for the Pursuer, That as.. this Question must go to Proof [etc.].

triply (ˈtrɪplɪ), *adv.* [f. TRIPLE *a.* + -LY[2].] In a triple degree or manner; three times.

1660 R. COKE *Power & Subj.* 191 If he will purge himself he may do it triply. **1826** DISRAELI *Viv. Grey* II. ii, His large library table, once triply covered with official communications. **1885** MISS BRADDON *Wyllard's Weird* III. xxxi. 210 She had heard her husband proclaim himself triply an assassin.

Comb. **1785** MARTYN *Rousseau's Bot.* xxxii. (1794) 490 The common Fern.. has superdecompound, or triplypinnate fronds. **1819** *Pantologia, Triply-ternate*, triternate. **1865** MRS. L. L. CLARKE *Common Seaweeds* iii. 67 Fan-like, rose-coloured varieties, or triply-branched. **1899** RODWAY *Guiana Wilds* 27 A triply-armed clump of palms.

ˈtrip-madam. *Herb.* Also 7–8 **tripe-madam(e.** [a. F. *tripe-madame*, according to Hatz.-Darm. an alteration of the earlier *trique-madame*, TRICK-MADAM. Taken from De La Quintinye by Evelyn, and thence in later herbalists and horticulturists. The earliest Eng. form was PRICK-MADAM.] = TRICK-MADAM.

1693 EVELYN *De La Quint. Compl. Gard.* II. VI. 202 Tripe-Madam is one of our Sallet-Furnitures; it is used chiefly in the Spring when it is tender. **1707** MORTIMER *Husb.* (1721) II. 177 Trip Madam is propagated of Seeds, Cuttings, or Slips; 'tis used in Salads in Spring. **1879** PRIOR *Brit. Plants, Trip Madam*.. a plant used as a treacle or vermifuge, *Sedum reflexum*.

tripod (ˈtraɪpɒd), *sb.* and *a.* Also 7 **trypod**, 7–8 **tripode**. [ad. L. *tripūs*, *tripod-*, a. Gr. τρίπους, -ποδ- adj., three-footed, also as sb., f. τρι- three + πούς, ποδ- foot.]

A. *sb.* **1.** *Gr.* and *Rom. Antiq.* A three-legged vessel; a pot or cauldron resting on three legs; a similar ornamental vessel, often presented as a prize, or as a votive offering (see also 2).

[**1370** *Mem. Ripon* (Surtees) II. 130 Item unum tripod ferri.] *c* **1611** CHAPMAN *Iliad* XVIII. 308 He gaue command to his neare souldiers, To put a Tripod to the fire, to cleanse the festred gore From off the person. **1697** DRYDEN *Æneid* V. 146 Within the circle, arms and tripods lie, Ingots of gold and silver heap'd on high. **1791** COWPER *Iliad* VIII. 333 A tripod, or a chariot with its steeds. **1834** LYTTON *Pompeii* II. ix, In the centre.. was a small altar on which stood a tripod of bronze. **1853** HUMPHREYS *Coin-Coll. Man.* iv. (1876) 35 The principal type of the coinage of Crotona is the tripod.

2. *spec.* A vessel of this kind at the shrine of Apollo at Delphi, on which the priestess seated herself to deliver oracles. Hence *allusively*, the Delphic oracle; any oracle or oracular seat.

1603 HOLLAND *Plutarch's Mor.* 1356, I will not be affraid to affirme that this reason properly is the Tripode or three footed table as one would say, and Oracle of trueth. *c* **1645** HOWELL *Lett.* (1892) II. 637 Pythagoras, whom the Tripod [= oracle of Apollo] pronounc'd the wisest Man. **1790** BURKE *Fr. Rev.* 99 Dr. Price, in whom the fumes of his oracular tripod were not entirely evaporated. **1839** THIRLWALL *Greece* xliii. V. 271 He compelled the prophetess by threats to mount the tripod, and pronounce a declaration. **1874** SAYCE *Compar. Philol.* i. 4 He [the comparative philologist] is ready to take his seat on the tripod.

3. A seat, table, or other similar structure with three legs; *esp.* a three-legged stool.

1656 BLOUNT *Glossogr.*, *Tripode* (*tripodium*), a three footed stool, any thing that hath three feet. **1710** ADDISON *Whig Exam.* No. 1 ⁋3 Three legs is a joint-stool, called in the Sphinx's country a tripode. **1798** BLOOMFIELD *Farmer's Boy, Spring* 193 A friendly tripod forms their humble Seat. **1870** EMERSON *Soc. & Solit.* Wks. (Bohn) III. 2 Each must stand on his glass tripod, if he would keep his electricity. **1887** J. NICHOLSON *Beacons E. Yorksh.* 13 *note*, The brandrith is literally an iron tripod.

4. A three-legged support of any kind; *esp.* a frame or stand with three (diverging) legs, usually hinged at the top, for supporting a camera, compass, or other apparatus.

1825 J. NICHOLSON *Operat. Mechanic* 185 A sort of tripod, having a flat ring of brass for its upper, and another for its lower part. **1893** J. A. HODGES *Elem. Photogr.* (1907) 15 Cameras.. intended to be used whilst supported on a tripod, and designated 'stand-cameras'.

5. ***tripod of life, vital tripod*** (*fig.*): see quot.

1834 J. FORBES *Laennec's Dis. Chest* (ed. 4) 1 The heart, lungs, and brain constitute, according to the happy expression of Bordeu, the tripod of life. **1857** DUNGLISON *Med. Lex.*, *Tripod, Vital*. **1872** HUXLEY *Physiol.* i. 19.

6. *Anat.* and *Zool.* **a.** A bone or other structure with three processes; a tripodal bone, etc. **b.** A sponge-spicule with three equal rays (*Cent. Dict. Suppl.* 1909).

1888 ROLLESTON & JACKSON *Anim. Life* 883 *Plectellaria*, without shell,.. or with an incomplete one, either a basal tripod without ring,.. or a sagittal ring usually without tripod. **1891** *Cent. Dict.* s.v., The premaxillary bone of birds is a tripod.

7. *attrib.* and *Comb.*, as ***tripod-head***, ***-leg***, ***-top***; ***tripod-covering***, ***-mounted*** adjs.

1614 GORGES *Lucan* V. 173 Pythons Trypod-couering hide. **1872** C. KING *Mountain. Sierra Nev.* xii. 257 Playfully drumming the frail crest with our tripod legs. **1889** *Anthony's Photogr. Bull.* II. 160 A few duplicate screws for camera and tripod head.. will be of much use. **1893** *Photogr. Ann.* 40 There is no tripod-top screw to lose. **1900** *Westm. Gaz.* 25 May 4/2 A tripod-mounted gun.

B. *adj.*

1. Having or resting upon three feet or legs; three-footed, three-legged; of the form of a tripod.

tripod race (quot. 1870), a THREE-LEGGED race.

1715–20 POPE *Iliad* XXIII. 50 Th' attending heralds,.. With kindled flames the tripod-vase surround. **1779** FORREST *Voy. N. Guinea* 373, I found many Badjoo boats,.. all of them having the tripod mast. **1794** MRS. RADCLIFFE *Myst. Udolpho* xxvi, A tripod lamp that stood on the stairs. **1833** T. HOOK *Parson's Dau.* I. iv, A cedar bagatelle board.. on silver tripod stand. **1870** *Routledge's Ev. Boy's Ann.* July Suppl. 9/2 Tripod race. **1877** KNIGHT *Dict. Mech.*, *Tripod jack*, a screw-jack supported on three legs, connected to a common base-plate. **1939** *Oxoniensia* IV. 101 Thirty-seven base and body fragments of tripod pitcher.. buff ware, uniform in colour throughout, fairly well fired and hard. **1963** E. M. JOPE in Foster & Alcock *Culture & Environment* xiii. 342 Regional styles are still discernible among these glazed jugs, such as the tripod-pitchers of the twelfth century.

2. ? Uttered as from the tripod, oracular; or ? three feet long (*fig.*: cf. SESQUIPEDALIAN A. 1).

1798 EDGEWORTH *Pract. Educ.* (1811) II. 29 He may be taught with much care and cost to speak tripod sentences. **1834** MAR. EDGEWORTH *Helen* vii, Some pages of 'The Rambler'.. I liked not at all; its tripod sentences tired my ear.

tripodal (ˈtrɪpədəl), *a.* [f. L. *tripod-*, TRIPOD + -AL[1].] Of the form of, or pertaining to, a tripod; three-footed, three-legged (in quot. 1843, performed on three legs, i.e. with a staff to support one's steps: cf. Gr. τρίποδας ὁδούς, Æsch. *Agam.* 80); *Anat.* having three rays or processes, as a bone. So, in same sense, **tripodial** (trɪˈpəʊdɪəl), **triˈpodian**; **tripodic** (traɪˈpɒdɪk) (applied to a method of walking in some insects in which two legs on one side and one on the other move together), **triˈpodical** (in quot. 1643 *fig.* oracular, authoritative: cf. prec. A. 2).

1774 T. WEST *Antiq. Furness* (1805) 10 The *tripodal copper vessel. **1843** G. WILSON *Let.* in *Life* vii. (1860) 306 Yesterday I made a tripodal journey round the garden. **1872** COUES *N. Amer. Birds* 23 This is a three-pronged or tripodal bone. **1845** BIRCH in *Classical Museum* III. 418 Immediately before him is a *tripodial vessel or caldron. **1797** *Encycl. Brit.* (ed. 3) X. 252/2 The *tripodian lyre of Pythagoras. **1801** BUSBY *Dict. Mus.* (1811), *Tripodian*, a stringed instrument, said to have been invented by Pythagoras the Zacynthian, which, on account of the difficulty of its performance, continued in use but for a short time. It resembled in form the Delphic Tripod, whence it had its name. **1891** H. H. DIXON in *Nature* 8 Jan. 223/2, I have observed this '*tripodic' walk in earwigs, water scorpions, aphides, and some beetles. **1643** HOWELL *Twelve Treat.* (1661) 249 Judges.. whose judgement in points of Law shold be onely *tripodicall and sterling. **1656** BLOUNT *Glossogr.*, *Tripodical*, that hath three feet, three footed. **1850** *Ecclesiologist* X. 179 A sort of tripodical shallow vessel.

tripody (ˈtrɪpədɪ). *Pros.* [f. TRI-, after DIPODY.] A group or verse of three feet.

1883 JEBB *Oedipus Tyrannus* p. lxx, This verse forms a.. sentence of three dactyls, a dactylic tripody. **1891** *Harper's Mag.* Mar. 570/2 There are hundreds of [folk-songs] in Hungarian music consisting of dipodies, tetrapodies, tripodies, pentapodies, and hexapodies.

tri-pointed, -polar: see TRI- 1 c, a.

tripoli (ˈtrɪpəlɪ). Also with capital initial, and 7 -ie, 7–8 -y, (8 tripela). [= F. *tripoli* (16th c. in Godef. *Compl.*), f. *Tripoli*, a region in North Africa, or town of the same name in Syria, where found.] **1. a.** A fine earth used as a polishing-powder, consisting mainly of decomposed siliceous matter, esp. that formed of the shells of diatoms; called also *infusorial earth* or *rotten-stone*.

1601 HOLLAND *Pliny* XXXV. vi. II. 530 Tripolie or goldsmiths earth. **1665** HOOKE *Microgr.* Pref., With a little Tripoly, rub them till they come to be very smooth. **1777** G. FORSTER *Voy. round World* II. 355 A sort of tripoly, which is called rotten-stone by some miners. **1797** *Encycl. Brit.* (ed. 3) VII. 608/2 The common tripela, or Tripoli, used to polish glass and stones. **1830** LYELL *Princ. Geol.* I. 214 That admixture of clay and silica, called tripoli. **1869** tr. *Pouchet's Universe* (1871) 21 Some tripolis of a red colour are employed in house-painting.

b. *attrib.*

1677 PLOT *Oxfordsh.* 78 That very lasting brightness.. receiv'd from the Gold-smiths Tripoli-stone. **1825** J. NICHOLSON *Operat. Mechanic* 755 To polish Varnish.—This is effected with pumice-stone and Tripoli earth. **1839** G. ROBERTS *Dict. Geol.*, *Tripoli powder*.., used for polishing fossils, &c. It is itself the remains of fossil insects. **1868** DANA *Min.* (ed. 5) 199 Tripolite.. (*c*) *Tripoli slate* (Polishing slate..), a slaty or thin laminated variety, fragile.

2. A large, mild onion; also, the plant producing a bulb of this kind. Also *attrib.*

1822 J. C. LOUDON *Encycl. Gardening* III. i. 715 Tripoli, the largest onion grown; oval, light-red, tinged with green and brown, soft and mild. **1873** *Young Englishwoman* Sept. 446/2 The best varieties [of onion] for autumn sowing are the Tripoli, Giant Madeira, [etc.]. **1932** *Times Educ. Suppl.* 27 Feb. (Home & School Suppl.) p. iv/1 The following crops should be started as soon as possible:.. tripoli onions, shallots, [etc.]. **1951** *Dict. Gardening* (R. Hort. Soc.) III. 1425/2 Such onions as the Roccas, white Lisbon, and Tripoli.. are of no value for storing.

Hence 'tripolite *Min.*, an infusorial variety of opalsilica, constituting one of the kinds of tripoli; 'tripolith [Gr. λίθος stone], trade name for a kind of cement: see quot.

1868 DANA *Min.* (ed. 5) 199 Infusorial Earth, or Earthy Tripolite, a very fine-grained earth looking often like an earthly chalk, or a clay. **1882** *Athenæum* 30 Sept. 438/1 The new binding material 'tripolith',.. is composed of sulphate of lime (gypsum), coke powder, and precipitated oxide of iron.

tripoline, *a.* (and *sb.*) [In sense 1, f. *Tripoli*, the name of a city and port in North Africa (see also TRIPOLI): see -INE[2], [4]] **1.** Of or pertaining to tripoli or rotten stone.

1759 DA COSTA in *Phil. Trans.* LI. 193 The layers of fossil wood in this mountain, having been saturated with the Tripoline particles,.. thereby composed a stone.

2. (With capital initial.) Of or pertaining to Tripoli, now the capital of Libya. Also as *sb.*, a native or inhabitant of Tripoli. Cf. next.

1819 A. SALAMÉ *Narr. Exped. Algiers* 6 We found she was a Tripoline polacca, (I am sorry that she was not an Algerine). **1843** *Penny Cycl.* XXV. 256/1 The Tripoline cruisers seldom allowed a ship at sea to escape them if they thought they could make a prize of her with impunity. *Ibid.* In 1832, Yussuf, the last basha of the Caramanli family,.. having lost the affection of the Tripolines, after a reign of forty years,.. was obliged to abdicate. **1909** [see TRIPOLITAN *a.*].

Tripolitan (trɪ'pɒlɪtən), *a.* (and *sb.*) [ad. It. *tripolitano* (in sense a); in sense b, f. *Tripolitania* (see next).] **a.** = TRIPOLINE *a.* 2. **b.** = TRIPOLITANIAN *a.* Occas. as *sb.*

1783 MISS TULLY *Let.* 3 July in *Narrative Ten Years' Residence at Tripoli* (1817) 5 The Tripolitan dresses, almost covered with gold and silver,.. make a most superb appearance. *Ibid.* 3 Sept. 24 The Tripolitans carry the right hand from the breast to the forehead.. where they mean to be respectful. **1888** *Encycl. Brit.* XXIII. 575/2 The Tripolitan pirates soon became the terror and scourge of the Mediterranean. **1896** *Geogr. Jrnl.* VII. 150 The Tripolitan range of hills. **1909** G. W. FURLONG *Gateway to Sahara* i. 8 'Tripolitans' signifies the people of the territory, 'Tripoline' a dweller in the town of Tripoli. **1913** R. G. USHER *Pan-Germanism* xii. 184 From the ports on the Tripolitan coast.. a flank attack could be directed upon the English communications with Suez. **1928** V. G. CHILDE *Most Anc. East* ii. 25 In the very heart of the Sahara at In-Ezzan, just south of the Tripolitan borders.

Tripolitanian (trɪpɒlɪ'teɪnɪən), *sb.* and *a.* [f. *Tripolitania*: cf. -IAN.] **A.** *sb.* A native or inhabitant of Tripolitania, the region surrounding Tripoli in North Africa. **B.** *adj.* Of or pertaining to Tripolitania. Cf. prec., sense b.

1942 [see CYRENAICAN *a.*]. **1943** G. CASSERLY *Tripolitania* 5 When this book was begun no enemy stood on Tripolitanian soil. **1963** M. KHADDURI *Modern Libya* ii. 48 Native Tripolitanians were soon to enter the service and their number steadily increased. **1969** J. WRIGHT *Libya* v. 55 The Roman empire has been called 'a federation of municipalities' and the Tripolitanian townsmen derived more benefit from Roman rule than the countryman. **1978** A. MELVILLE-ROSS *Blindfold* x. 60 The Tripolitanians are very much afraid of the nomads. **1981** T. BARLING *Bikini Red North* i. 29 Do what you can with your Tripolitanian argot.

Tripolye (trɪ'pɒljə). Also **Tripolje**. The name of a village near Kiev in Russia, used *attrib.* to denote a neolithic culture typified by remains found there, which flourished in the western Ukraine and in eastern Romania during the late fourth and third millennia B.C.

1913 [see PLOSHCHADKA]. **1935** *Jrnl. R. Anthrop. Inst.* LXV. 113 In successful search for painted pottery of the Tripolye type. **1937** *Discovery* Jan. 27/1 The Tripolje culture, so called from the site in Southern Russia on which it was first found, has as its most characteristic feature painted pottery. **1957** G. CLARK *Archæol. & Society* (ed. 3) vi. 190 Significant differences have been noted between the composition of animal remains from sites of the Tripolje culture marked by painted and grooved pottery and from those of the neighbouring Ousatovo culture. **1970** BRAY & TRUMP *Dict. Archaeol.* 237/2 Tripolye culture came to an end with the expansion westwards of steppe cultures of kurgan or Single-Grave type.

tripos ('traɪpɒs). See also TRIPUS. [app. irreg. alteration of L. *tripūs* TRIPOD, after Greek words in -ος.]

†**1.** A three-legged vessel, seat, or frame: = TRIPOD A. 1, 3, 4. *Obs.*

1621 BURTON *Anat. Mel.* To Rdr. (1628) 41 Thales sent the golden Tripos.. to Bias, Bias to Solon, &c. **1697** W. DERHAM in *Phil. Trans.* XX. 4 For which purpose a Tripos may be best, whose Legs open and shut by Joynts at the Top. **1745** D. E. BAKER *ibid.* XLIII. 540 A most curious antique Tripos of Metal. **1827** G. HIGGINS *Celtic Druids* 27 They were made of thin laminæ of gold—something like the triposes of the ancient Peruvians.

†**b.** *spec.* = TRIPOD 2. *Obs.*

1589 GREENE *Menaphon* (Arb.) 22 Posting from Arcadia to the Tripos where Pithia sate. **1606** MARSTON *Parasit.* I. ii. B j, What, in the name of prophesie?.. Speake, thou three legd Tripos, is thy shippe of Fooles a flote yet? [perh. sense 2.] **1679** DRYDEN *Troil. & Cress.* Pref., The inspiration was still upon him, he was ever tearing it upon the tripos. **1756** J. KENNEDY *Curios. Wilton Ho.* (1786) 30 The two Griffins and the Tripos are the Symbols of Apollo. **1780** J. DUCHÉ *Disc.* (1790) I. xv. 285 Whatsoever the thrice-great Hermes delivered as oracles from his sacred tripos.

2. *Cambridge University.* Formerly: **a.** (With capital initial.) A bachelor of arts appointed to dispute, in a humorous or satirical style, with the candidates for degrees at 'Commencement' (corresponding to the TERRÆ FILIUS at Oxford): so called from the three-legged stool on which he sat. **b.** A set of humorous verses, originally composed by the 'Tripos', and (till 1894) published at Commencement after his office was abolished (in full, *tripos verses*: see e). **c.** The list of candidates qualified for the honour degree in mathematics, originally printed on the back of the paper containing these verses (in full, *tripos list*: see e).

1659–60 PEPYS *Diary* 26 Feb., Mr. Nicholas, of Queen's College [Cambr.], who I knew in my time to be Tripos with great applause. **1665** J. BUCK in Peacock *Stat. Cambr.* (1841) App. B. p. lxx, The Senior Proctor calleth up the Tripos, and exhorteth him to be witty, but modest withall. *Ibid.* p. lxxi, The Bedels also are to deliver the Tripos's Verses to the V.C., Noblemen, D[rs] etc. **1696** PHILLIPS (ed. 5), *Tripos*,.. the Name which is given at Cambridge, to him that is called the *Terræ Filius* at Oxford. **1797** *Cambr. Univ. Cal.* 157 A List of those who have received Honors, on commencing Bachelors of Arts; copied from the Triposes. **1841** PEACOCK *Stat. Cambr.* App. A. p. x. *note*, He was called the *bachelor of the stool*, or *tripos*, which gave the name to the day: he was generally selected for his skill and readiness in disputation, and was allowed.. considerable license of language. **1851** *Coll. Life t. Jas. I*, 89 Thos annual verses which still bear the name of tripos.

d. Hence, in current use: *orig.* The final honours examination for the B.A. degree in mathematics, consisting of two parts (formerly ***first*** and ***second tripos***, now the ***Mathematical Tripos***, Parts I. and II.); *later*, extended to the subsequently founded final honours examinations in other subjects (***Classical Tripos***, ***Theological Tripos***, etc.).

1842 *Cambr. Univ. Cal.* 27 First Tripos Day. On the Day after Ash-Wednesday, at one o'clock, the bell rings for the first Tripos... The second Tripos is on the Thursday after Midlent Sunday. **1865** *Reader* 4 Mar. 245/2 The Mathematical and Classical Triposes. **1875** in Willis & Clark *Cambridge* (1886) III. 234 The Oriental Triposes attract a fair number of Candidates. **1905** *Edin. Rev.* Oct. 440 Not only had three new Triposes been established.

e. *attrib.*, as ***tripos candidate***; **tripos day**, (*a*) either of the two days on which the 'Tripos' disputed; (*b*) a day on which a tripos (examination) is held; **tripos list**, the list of successful candidates in a tripos; **tripos paper**, †(*a*) a paper containing the tripos list (*obs.*); (*b*) any one of the papers of questions set in a tripos (examination); **tripos speech**, the humorous or satirical speech delivered by the 'Tripos'; **tripos verses** (see b above).

1904 *Expositor* Mar. 219 He develops into a *Tripos candidate. **1842** *Tripos day [see 2 d]. **1847** WEBSTER s.v. *Tripos-paper*, Tripos day, *tripos examination. **1901** *Q. Rev.* Apr. 598 His ordinary '*tripos' lectures kept strictly to business. **1841** PEACOCK *Stat. Cambr.* 71 *note*, The earliest *Tripos list which appears in the *Cambridge Calendar* is for the year 1753. **1818** MACAULAY in *Life & Lett. Z. Macaulay* xi. (1900) 343 Desirous to return loaded with medals or distinguished on the *tripos-paper. **1876** L. STEPHEN *Eng. Th. 18th C.* II. xii. vi. 360 He seems to have been suspended from his degree for a *tripos speech. **1828** GUNNING *Ceremonies Cambr.* 84 *note*, First Tripos. The Writers of the *Tripos Verses.

‖**tripot** (tripo). [Fr.] A gaming-house, a gambling-den.

1864 W. H. AINSWORTH *John Law* I. II. v. 290 The person before us.. is a suspected sharper, and a constant frequenter of tripots. **1883** 'OUIDA' *Wanda* I. vii. 264 A winner at a *tripot*, what a hero for you, mother mine. **1909** R. NEVILL *Light come, Light Go* viii. 236 The gaming-resorts of old Paris were filled with people whose reputations for probity were generally a good deal more than doubtful. In one of the best of these *tripots* a gentleman.. delayed the game by insisting on searching for a few pieces of gold which he had dropped on the floor. **1930** A. BENNETT *Imperial Palace* xlv. 319 The loss of sixty pounds odd.. in a Paris *tripot*.

tripot, erron. spelling of TRY-POT.

‖**tripotage** (tripɔtaʒ). [Fr.] **a.** Underhand dealings, intrigue. Also *fig.* **b.** *rare.* Pawing, handling, fingering.

In quot. 1853 perh. used mistakenly for *tripotée* large quantity.

1779 DR. WARNER *Let.* Mar. in J. H. Jesse *George Selwyn & his Contemporaries* (1844) IV. 38 An infinite deal of lying, on all sides, and *tripotage*. *Ibid.* 42 But it is all of a piece, such a cursed *tripotage*! **1853** C. BRONTË *Villette* III. xxxvi. 131 At last I got through my list. The patterns for the slippers, the bell-ropes, the cabas were selected—the slides and tassels for the purses chosen—the whole 'tripotage', in short, was off my mind. **1895** *Nineteenth Cent.* Oct. 548 The recent exposures of political *tripotage*. **1932** *Times Lit. Suppl.* 12 May 343/3 Beau Nash, though dabbling deeply in the *tripotage*, deprecated sensational ruins and suicides. **1958** J. LODWICK *Bid Soldiers Shoot* ii. 41 The freshly shaved Hirsch.. cornered the two women and subjected their not unwilling flesh to expert *tripotage*.

trippage ('trɪpɪdʒ). [f. TRIP *sb.*[1] + -AGE.] The act or process of making a series of short journeys over the same route; the number of such journeys made.

1941 *Sun* (Baltimore) 16 Oct. 7/2 Dairy officials pointed out that the new system would eliminate 'back trippage of drivers' and make for 'straight trippage'. Under the old system, most drivers made early morning deliveries and then, on collection days, repeated the routes to collect the money. The second trip will be eliminated under the daylight delivery system. **1972** *Daily Tel.* 5 Apr. 19/4 If milk distribution costs are to be stabilised, some means must be found to push up the trippage rate [of milk bottles]. **1979** *Ibid.* 6 Aug. 2/6 The average milk bottle makes 23 trips to and from the dairy and customer before it is lost or broken. .. Bottles are still used because their high trippage more than offsets other costs.

trippant ('trɪpənt), *a. Her.* [a. OF. *trippant*, pres. pple. of *tripper* to TRIP.] = TRIPPING *ppl. a.* 3.

1658 in Prestwich *Respublica* (1785) 192 A bucke trippant Gules, attired Or. *c* **1828** BERRY *Encycl. Her.* I. Gloss., *Trippant*, or *Tripping*, a term used to express a buck, antelope, hart, hind, &c. when represented with the right foot lifted up, and the other three feet, as it were, upon the ground, as if trotting. **1898** *Tit-Bits* 25 June 512/2 Crest, a stag trippant; arms, a chevron between three roundles.

trippe, obs. form of TRIPE[1].

tripped (trɪpt), *ppl. a.* [f. TRIP *v.* + -ED[1].]

1. *Bot.* Of a flower whose pollinating mechanism has been activated by tripping.

1914 *Bull. U.S. Dept. Agric.* No. 75. 5 In artificially tripped flowers.. 12 out of 34 tripped set seed. **1956** *Nature* 18 Feb. 334/2 The number of tripped florets was recorded and calyces marked each day. **1980** *Sabrao Jrnl.* XII. 104 The seed set of tripped flowers indicates the level of self-fertility.

2. Operated or caused to respond by contact with a projection or other object.

1921 *Conquest* Jan. 130/1 A roller which reacts the 'tripped' brushes or wipers. **1977** R. LUDLUM *Chancellor Manuscript* xxx. 320 Don't worry, there's a set of electronically tripped windows.. with.. bulletproof glass.

3. ***tripped-out***: under the influence of a hallucinogenic drug, esp. LSD. *slang.*

1973 *Listener* 15 Nov. 680/3 The tripped-out nudes in the penthouse flat. **1976** H. FERGUSON *Confessions of Long Distance Acid Head* 11 Everyone was gathered round talking about the arrangements they would make for their 'excursion' the following day. They cared so little for my tripped-out state that they turned out the light and left me in the darkened room.

tripper ('trɪpə(r)), *sb.* [f. TRIP *v.* + -ER[1].] One who or that which trips.

1. One who dances; one who moves with light, sprightly steps; in quot. *a* 1847 *transf.* applied to a shoe or slipper.

c **1380** WYCLIF *Wks.* (1880) 246 A daunsere, a trippere on tapitis. **1576** GASCOIGNE *Grief of Joye* iv. Wks. (Roxb.) II. 299 Dancyng delights are like a whyrlyng wheele.. Thes tryppers strive to throwe theire braynes awaye As wheeles voyde water. **1594** NASHE *Unfort. Trav.* Wks. (Grosart) V. 106 [The ostrich] outstrippeth the nimblest trippers of his feathered condition in footmanshippe. **1691** DRYDEN *King Arthur* IV. i, Ye Sylvan trippers of the green. *a* **1847** ELIZA COOK *When I wore red shoes* i, What were Cinderella's slippers To my pair of fairy trippers?

2. One who or that which causes to stumble. Also ***tripper-up***; *spec.* in *slang*: see quots. 1887, 1904.

1605 CAMDEN *Rem.* (1657) 76 A tripper, or supplanter. **1860** C. A. COLLINS *Eye-witness* vi. 81 He has either been tripped up, or has stumbled.. The tripper up.. will.. come in for certain remarks which are the reverse of complimentary. **1887** *Daily Chron.* 18 Nov. (Farmer), A witness at the East End inquest yesterday alluded to 'trippers up'... 'A man who trips you up and robs you'. **1904** SWEENEY *Scotland Yard* xii. 313 Women known as trippers up, who preyed on drunken seamen. **1905** W. E. GEIL *Yankee in Pigmy Land* iv. 44 Roots were encountered. They were regular trippers.

3. One who or that which stumbles (*lit.* and *fig.*).

1806 W. TAYLOR in *Ann. Rev.* IV. 560 A sipper is a tripper. **1856** *Titan Mag.* Nov. 415/1 Our [church] service is spoil'd by.. The trippers—the clippers—the impudent skippers. **1903** *Union Mag.* Nov. 513/1 Dr. Young's camel was a 'tripper' and it stumbled and threw the Doctor over its head.

4. a. One who goes on a trip, or short journey or voyage for pleasure; an excursionist. *colloq.*

cheap tripper, one who travels by a cheap trip.

1813 *Drakard's Paper* 3 Oct. in Ashton *Mod. Street Ballads* (1888) 80 Trippers to the seaside for a week. **1851** *Eliza Cook's Jrnl.* 19 July 177 The Tripper is the growth of railways and monster trains. **1872** HARTLEY *Yorkshire Ditties* Ser. II. 140 A lot of cheap trippers 'at's just com'd for a day. **1899** KITCHIN in *Ruskin in Oxford* etc. (1904) 154 The modern tripper leaves only desolation and dirty paper behind him.

b. *attrib.* and *Comb.*

1904 *Daily Chron.* 17 Sept. 3/1 These pictures were painted in tripper haunts. **1907** H. WYNDHAM *Flare of Footlights* xii, Pull us down to the island. The tripper element won't be so conspicuous there. **1909** *Westm. Gaz.* 7 Aug. 4/3 The tripper-thronged part of the island.

5. A street railroad conductor or other employee who is paid by the trip or journey. *U.S.*

1882 J. D. MCCABE *New York by Sunlight & Gaslight* 244 The 'trippers', as those men are called who only run three-quarters of a day, get $1·50. **1950** *Reading* (Pennsylvania) *Times* 28 Feb., They had refused to operate 'tripper' or extra, runs because five members of the union had been furloughed. The company said this situation resulted in the failure of nine 'tripper' runs to be made.

6. *Mech.* A contrivance for tripping; a trip.

1870 *Eng. Mech.* 14 Jan. 430/1 To each rod a tripper or pallet is affixed. **1893** *Jrnl. R. Agric. Soc.* Dec. 717 As soon as the sheaf has attained the required size it automatically raises a tripper. **1908** *Blackw. Mag.* Jan. 59/2 The tripper works the air-delay valve.

7. One who experiences hallucinations induced by a drug, esp. LSD. *slang* (orig. *U.S.*).

1966 T. Leary in *Playboy* Sept. 110/2 These episodes can be dealt with easily by an experienced guide who recognizes where the LSD tripper is caught. **1968** *New Scientist* 3 Oct. 38/3 LSD 'trippers'..need no sleep. **1972** *Village Voice* (N.Y.) 1 June 78/4 When I returned several days later, Wheeler's was in an uproar over the discovery of a dead tripper. **1979** B. Malamud *Dubin's Lives* i. 29 One of the swamis there, a secret acid tripper, got on my nerves.

tripper ('trɪpə(r)), *v. colloq. rare.* [f. the sb.] *intr.* To behave like a tripper (sense 4); to take trips or excursions.

1959 G. Jenkins *Twist of Sand* ii. 41 Trippering up and down the coast. **1974** 'S. Harvester' *Forgotten Road* iii. 37 They trippered around Istanbul for some days.

tripperish ('trɪpərɪʃ), *a. colloq.* [f. tripper *sb.* + -ish[1].] = trippery *a.* So '**tripperishness**.

1898 M. Sadler *Let.* 26 Sept. in M. Sadleir *Michael Ernest Sadler* (1949) x. 166 Stromness is prim little grey stone place of about 2,000 people—quite unspoiled... No obtrusive tripperishness. **1931** E. Waugh *Remote People* iv. 89 Do you think..it would be very vulgar and tripperish to make them scramble for them [*sc.* coins]? **1934** M. Allingham *Death of Ghost* xxi. 245 Nothin' tripperish about them. **1960** 'J. & E. Bonett' *No Grave for Lady* xi. 170 The atmosphere was rather tripperish. **1975** S. Lauder *Killing Time on Corvo* iii. 26 She was very sharp..and tripperish.

trippery ('trɪpərɪ), *a. colloq.* [f. tripper *sb.* + -y[1].] Of, pertaining to, or characterized by the presence of trippers (sense 4); touristy (somewhat *derog.*).

1924 C. Connolly *Let.* 22 Dec. in *Romantic Friendship* (1975) 41 Italy is so trippery in Spring. **1926** W. J. Locke *Old Bridge* ii. 18 'But let us see all we can to-night.'.. 'That wouldn't be fair to Florence. It's a bit trippery, isn't it?' **1928** *Daily Express* 11 Apr. 9/4 Venice,..the Queen of the Adriatic in its most trippery and least attractive garb. **1969** M. Pugh *Last Place Left* xix. 145 Wordsworth had complained of trippery overcrowding in this belt, more than a hundred years before. **1970** *Nature* 4 July 11/1 The trippery appurtenances and atmosphere which have been established in the neighbourhood [of the Niagara Falls]. **1971** *Country Life* 20 May 1234/3 All that is missing are the monkeys: even though Iguazu is very definitely far from trippery, they have taken themselves off.

trippet[1] ('trɪpɪt). Forms: 4–5 **tripet, trypet,** 5 **trepett,** 6 **tryppyt,** 7 **trippett,** 9 **-it,** 8– **trippet.** [In sense 1 a. OF. *tripot, -pout* (*a* 1350 in Godef.). But in 2–4 associated with or formed from trip *v., sb.*[1]]

†**1.** An evil scheme; a malicious trick or plot. *Obs.*

c **1330** R. Brunne *Chron. Wace* (Rolls) 2911 Ne schal nought Brenne bede me trypet [*Petyt MS.* treget]. *a* **1400** *Leg. Rood* viii. 41 Fouled is my fayre fruit, þat neuer dude tripet ne truit. *Ibid.* 480 Truyt and tripet to helle shal sterue.

†**2.** An act of tripping up, a trip. *Obs.*

1430–40 Lydg. *Bochas* vi. ii. (MS. Bodl. 263) 306 To his pride I [Fortune] gaff a gret tripet. *c* **1450** *Mankind* 113 in *Macro Plays* 5 Take yow here a trepett! *a* **1550** *Image Hypocr.* i. 456 in *Skelton's Wks.* (1843) II. 420/1 In your holy armes,..Devoutly to clipe it, To caste her with a tryppyt. **1714** Parkyns *Inn-play* (ed. 2) 42 The Hanging Trippet is when you put your Toe behind your Adversary's Heel, on the same side, with a design to hook his Leg up forwards, and throw him on his Back.

3. The piece of wood pointed at the ends used in tip-cat; the 'cat'; also the game itself. Also *attrib.*, as ***trippet-stick***. *north. dial.*

c **1440** *Promp. Parv.* 503/1 Trypet, *tripula, trita.* **1624** *N. Riding Rec.* (1885) III. ii. 199 Fr. Milnes ordered to be whipped for that he..did on Easter day last in the time of afternoon service play in the Churchyard at Aislaby at a game called Trippett. **1825** Brockett *N.C. Words, Trippit and Coit,* a game similar to spell and ore... Called *Trippit* and *Rack* in parts of *North.* The trippit is a small piece of wood obtusely pointed. **1828** *Craven Gloss., Trippet,* the 'cat' or piece of wood in the game of tip-cat... The player with his bat, called a trippet stick, strikes it smartly at the end, which causes it to rise in a rotatory motion, high enough to strike it before it falls. **1873** Harland & Wilkinson *Lanc. Leg.* 152 Trippet. This game is played in the fields..It is still practised by the colliers... The trippet is about two inches long, and is made of holly.

b. The trap used in trap-ball; the game of trap-ball.

1825 Brockett *N.C. Words.*

4. *Mech.* See quot. and cf. trip *sb.*[1] 9.

1877 Knight *Dict. Mech., Trippet* (Machinery), a projection intended to strike some object at regularly recurrent intervals.

trippet[2] ('trɪpɪt). Now *north. dial.* Also 6 **-ett, tripett,** 7–9 **tripet.** [Cf. OF. *trepied, tripié, tripier* (12th c. in Godef. *Compl.*), and trivet.]

A trivet.

1563 *Richmond Wills* (Surtees) 169 A gyrdle, a brandrett, a speitt, and a trippett. **1570** Levins *Manip.* 87/42 A Trippet, *tripus, odis, hic.* **1581** *Inv.* in *Trans. Cumb. & West. Arch. Soc.* X. 40 *Item.* Spitt and tripett. **1677** Gale *Crt. Gentiles* II. iii. 60 Which Machine was called from its three Pillars, Tripos, as it were of three feet, much of the same forme with the usual Tripet. **1820** Shelley *Hymn to Mercury* x. 7 Her household stuff and state, Perennial pot, trippet, and brazen pan. **1894** *Northumbld. Gloss., Tripet,* an iron grating placed on the top of (and across) the kitchen fire for pans to rest on; a trivet.

tripping ('trɪpɪŋ), *vbl. sb.* [f. trip *v.* + -ing[1].]

1. The action of the verb trip in transitive senses.

1591 Percivall *Sp. Dict., Traspie,* tripping, *supplantatio.* **1601** Breton (*title*) No Whippinge, nor Trippinge: but a kinde friendly Snippinge. **1760–72** H. Brooke *Fool of Qual.* (1809) I. 163 The mysteries of bruising, of wrestling, and of tripping. **1862** *Catal. Internat. Exhib.* II. xii. 26 Martin's patent anchor..easy tripping and fishing, great lightness. **1880** *Times* 12 Nov. 4/4 It was only lately that Rugby school abandoned the 'hacking' and 'tripping' which made football dreaded by anxious mothers.

b. *spec.* in *Bot.*: see sense 15 of the vb.

1909 *Bull. Bureau Plant Industry, U.S. Dept. Agric.* No. 24. 8 If fertile seed is to be produced in any quantity it is necessary that a certain explosive mechanism within the flower be released. The release of this mechanism, whether it be accomplished by insects or otherwise, is popularly called 'tripping'. **1930** *Jrnl. Amer. Soc. Agronomy* XXII. 782 When the flowers were left exposed and not tripped artificially the gain was 1:1·7 in favor of artificial tripping. **1978** *Nature* 7 Sept. 54/2 In artificial field bean pollination, manual tripping of open flowers is a recommended practice for increasing seed set in auto-sterile lines.

2. The action of the verb trip in transitive senses. Also ***tripping up***; in quot. 1857 *spec.* the curvature of a boat's keel.

1594 Nashe *Terrors Night* Wks. (Grosart) III. 273 Their daintie feete in their tender birdlike trippings, enameld (as it were) the dustie ground. **1603** Holland *Plutarch's Mor.* 1072 Answeres and oracles as touching..the tripping and stumbling of the foot. **1693** *Apol. Clergy Scot.* 14 [They] are very glad when they can discover the trippings of their Adversaries. **1733** S. Knight in *Bibl. Topogr. Brit.* (1790) III. 167 It is very easy to discover his trippings. **1828** Carlyle *Misc., Goethe's Helena* (1857) I. 145 Fine warblings and trippings on the light fantastic toe. **1840** Hood *Up Rhine* 36 Tripping up the Rhine, instead of taking my place at Woodlands. **1850** Denison *Clock & Watch-m.* 77 The hook at the end of the slope will not catch the tooth as it ought to do, and two or three teeth will slip past at once: this is called tripping. **1857** Colquhoun *Comp. Oarsman's Guide* 31 *Shear* is the rising of the gunwale of a boat towards head and stern; *gamber* is the same on the keel; otherwise called tripping up. **1879** *Cassell's Techn. Educ.* IV. 371/1 This error called 'tripping', is also produced if there is much space between the detent and the wheel. **1894** *Forum* (N.Y.) Oct. 158 Slips, hesitations, and tripping in speech, which, once made, could never be recalled.

b. *spec.* of drug-induced hallucinations: see 5 b of the vb.

1968 L. W. Robinson *Assassin* xii. 128 Their passion was a long one..as though they hated to come back..from the rocking, tossing, sweet trip... But no, the sweet tripping was not over. **1970** K. Platt *Pushbutton Butterfly* vi. 59 The girls weren't wearing brassieres... The skinnier ones just looked flat. Tripping didn't solve everything. **1980** *Times Lit. Suppl.* 24 Oct. 1203/4 When Christiane F. was thirteen years old, she began to frequent a youth club run by the Protestant Church in an overcrowded district of West Berlin. There she started smoking hashish, taking 'uppers and downers' and 'tripping' on LSD.

3. *attrib.* and *Comb.*, as ***tripping-block***; **tripping-line** (*Naut.*), a light line for tilting the yards (see trip *v.* 12); also, a line for manipulating a drogue; **tripping string**, a line set by burglars to trip possible pursuers.

1620 Shelton *Quix.* ii. iv. 26 What doe I know, whether ..the Deuill hath set any tripping-blocke before me, where I may stumble and fall? **1841** R. H. Dana *Seaman's Man., Tripping line,* a line used for tripping a topgallant or royal yard in sending it down. **1882** Nares *Seamanship* (ed. 6) 260 Drogues..are towed..mouth foremost by a stout rope, a small line termed a tripping-line, being fastened to the apex. **1891** *Daily News* 31 Dec. 4/7 The doors..having first been securely fastened..and tripping strings having been stretched across the pathways and lawn.

'**tripping,** *ppl. a.* [f. as prec. + -ing[2].] That trips, in various senses.

1. Moving quickly and lightly; light-footed; nimble. Also *fig.*

1567 Drant *Horace, Epist.* xiv. Ev, Thou hast no trippinge trull to mince it with the now That thou mighst foote it vnto her. **1568** *Satir. Poems Reform.* xlvi. 56 Thir tripand tyddis may tyne ws aw. **1684** Bunyan *Pilgr.* ii. Introd. Verses 185 When little Tripping Maidens follow God, And leave old doting Sinners to his Rod. **1708** Prior *Turtle & Sparrow* 37 The tripping Fauns and Fairies came. **1807** Scott *Let. to Southey* 1 Oct. in Lockhart *Life,* A tripping Alexandrine stanza. **1851** D. Jerrold *St. Giles* i. 2 A quick, tripping footstep sounds in the deserted street. **1880** Ld. Acton *Lett. to Gladstone* (1904) 6 You will find his conversation, easy and tripping as it is, very inferior to his writings.

2. Stumbling, erring, sinning.

1557 tr. *Bullinger's Decades* (1592) 296 The Lord beginneth..with the bridle to checke the mouth of his tripping Church. **1580** Hollyband *Treas. Fr. Tong, Chevaux qui brunchent,* stumbling or tripping Iades. **1646** Gataker *Mistake Removed* 31 The tripping toung sometimes tels truth. **1703** Rowe *Fair Penit.* Epil., The tripping Dame cou'd find no Favour. **1903** G. Matheson *Repr. Men Bible* Ser. ii. 287 Where the tripping are trodden down, where the weak are weeded out by the strong.

3. *Her.* Of a buck, stag, etc.: Walking, and looking toward the dexter side, with three paws on the ground and one fore-paw raised; the same as *passant* of other animals. ***tripping-counter*** = counter-trippant.

1562 Leigh *Armorie* 90 b, An Vnicorne trippyng, Sable. **1610** Guillim *Heraldry* iii. xiv. (1611) 131 He beareth Azure, three Buckes tripping. *c* **1828** Berry *Encycl. Her.* I. Gloss., *Tripping-counter,* or *counter-trippant,* is when two bucks, &c. are borne trippant contraryways, as if passing each other out of the field. **1864** Boutell *Her. Hist. & Pop.* x. 62 Stags,..when in easy motion, they are tripping. **1870** Rock *Text. Fabr.* i. 40 Two giraffes, with one leg raised—may be better described as tripping.

4. In names of mechanical appliances that trip or are tripped (cf. trip *v.* 14); as ***tripping-coil, -lever, -relay*** (*Cent. Dict., Suppl.* 1909); **tripping-valve**: see quot.

1877 Knight *Dict. Mech., Tripping-valve,* one moved recurrently by the contact of some other part of the machinery.

Hence '**trippingness**.

1827 *Examiner* 738/1 Too much of trippingness in the walk. **1890** Fanny Murfree *Felicia* xi, The basso could not forgive the soprano for the trippingness of her execution.

trippingly ('trɪpɪŋlɪ), *adv.* [f. prec. + -ly[2].] In a tripping manner.

1590 Shaks. *Mids. N.* v. i. 402 This Ditty after me, sing and dance it trippinglie. **1602** —— *Ham.* iii. ii. 2 Speake the Speech I pray you..trippingly on the Tongue. **1819** *Blackw. Mag.* IV. 719 Her songs came trippingly off the tongue. **1858** Capern *Ball. & Songs* 89 Down the hill, towards the mill, Turned the maiden trippingly.

trippist ('trɪpɪst). *colloq. rare.* [f. trip *sb.* + -ist.] = tripper *sb.* 4.

1792 *Gentl. Mag.* Dec. 1129/1 Allowing that this Tourist, or Trippist, has told the truth. **1886** *Modern Society* 16 Jan. 117 (Farmer) With returning appetite came the desire to the convivial ocean trippists to set sail again for the Mediterranean. **1895** *B'ham Inst. Mag.* Oct. 202 A testimonial illuminated on parchment by one of the lady trippists.

trippkeite ('trɪpkɪaɪt). *Min.* [ad. G. *trippkeit* (G. vom Rath 1880, in *Sitzungsber. d. Niederrheinische Ges. f. Natur- und Heilkunde* 209), f. the name of P. *Trippke* (1851–80), Polish or German mineralogist, its discoverer: see -ite[1].] An oxide of copper and arsenic, $CuAs_2O_4$, found as soft greenish blue tetragonal crystals.

1881 *Jrnl. Chem. Soc.* XL. 551 Minerals from the Veins of Copper-ore near Copiapo, in Chili.—*a.* Trippkeite. A cupric arsenite..occurring in small bluish-green crystals, in druses of a thick bed of red copper-ore mixed with malachite and copper pyrites. **1976** *Mineral. Abstr.* XXVII. 300/1 The crystal structure of synthetic trippkeite..was refined to R = 0·059.

tripple ('trɪp(ə)l), *sb. S. Africa.* [f. tripple *v.*[2]] A horse's gait, resembling the amble.

1880 Gillmore *On Duty* 296 A slow tripple—a pace similar to what is designated 'racking' in North America. **1887** Rider Haggard *Jess* (1899) 4 He put the tired nag into a sort of 'tripple' or ambling canter much affected by S. African horses. **1901** *Field* 9 Mar. 322/1 This 'tripple' is between a fast walk and slow trot.

'**tripple,** *v.*[1] *Obs.* exc. *dial.* [freq. of trip *v.* + -le 3.] *intr.* To trip, move lightly; to dance, skip.

c **1630** Risdon *Surv. Devon* §308 (1810) 315 Where, fearless of the hunt, the deer securely stood, And trippling freely, walk'd a burgess of the wood. **1851** W. Anderson *Rhymes* (1867) 42 (E.D.D.) He trippled, he danced, an' he sung.

'**tripple,** *v.*[2] *S. Africa.* [a. Du. *trippelen,* f. *trippen* to trip, skip.] *intr.* To go at a tripple.

1899 G. H. Russell *Under the Sjambok* iv. 49 They [Boers]..getting into their saddles, slowly trippled away (a kind of run, neither gallop, canter, or trot). **1903** *Longm. Mag.* Dec. 151 That easy hand canter usual in such Free State horses as do not tripple.

Hence '**trippling** *vbl. sb.* and *ppl. a.*; also '**trippler,** a horse that tripples.

1901 *Field* 9 Mar. 322/1 The Boer never rides his horse at the trot, but at a quick walk or canter, and a step peculiar to the country and called 'trippling', or, as we should style it, ambling. **1905** *Blackw. Mag.* Oct. 526/1 He could still hear the trippling patter of the other rider. **1909** R. Cullum *Compact* xi. 132 Can't I even persuade you to ride my 'tripler'?

trippy ('trɪpɪ), *a. colloq.* (chiefly *U.S.*). [f. trip *sb.*[1] + -y[1].] Of, pertaining to, or resembling a hallucinatory experience induced by a drug. Hence '**trippiness**.

1969 Fabian & Byrne *Groupie* (1970) xiv. 101 Joe asks if it's trippy, and I tell him that it is a bit. **1975** *Harper's Mag.* June 9 In my trippy daze, dope was the filter for the movie camera in my mind, the regulator of my psychic jets. **1976** *New Yorker* 19 Jan. 48 Robert Wise directed with tame, impersonal good taste; there's none of the blissful trippiness of being carried in the belly of a zeppelin, and none of the carnival vulgarity of the recent disaster thrillers. **1976** Logan & Woffinden *Illustr. New Musical Express Encycl. Rock* 96/1 In 1966 they [*sc.* The Grateful Dead] chose their name; in keeping with the band's image, it was a decision made under the influence of various drugs... The band thought it seemed vaguely appropriate, and certainly it had trippy connotations. **1978** *Maclean's Mag.* 13 Nov. 78 The trippy optimism of the '60s lent importance to such things as creativity and communication, which in the '70s have given way to matters of a homelier urgency. **1980** *New Age* (U.S.) Oct. 54 (Advt.), Trippy music for meditation, massage, free-form movement, tantric loving, and a relaxing environment.

triprosthomerous, -prostyle: see TRI- 1 a.

† **trip-skin.** *dial. Obs.* [Cf. TRIP *sb.*[3]] See quots.

a **1825** FORBY *Voc. E. Anglia* s.v. *Rock*, Wool.. is spun.. by being drawn out and formed into yarn by the finger and thumb, and pressed by the hand on the trip-skin. *Ibid.*, *Trip-skin*.. 1. A piece of leather, worn on the right hand side of the petticoat, by spinners with the rock, on which the spindle plays, and the yarn is pressed by the hand of the spinner. 2. The skinny part of roasted meat which before the whole can be dressed, becomes tough and dry, like a trip [cheese] overkept.

tripsome (ˈtrɪpsəm), *a.* [f. TRIP *sb.*[1] or *v.* + -SOME.] Characterized by tripping; nimble. Hence ˈ**tripsomely** *adv.*

1819 *Blackw. Mag.* V. 401 The shortened notes more tripsomely tipped over than in the modern airs. **1846** MRS. GORE *Eng. Char.* (1852) 52 He beholds the tripsome feet of Lady Clementina flit by him. **1847** —— *Castles in Air* xvi, An elf-like pigmy.. walking tripsomely by my side. **1890** *Sat. Rev.* 13 Dec. 688/2 Sprightly style and tripsome metre.

tript, variant of *triped* (see TRIPE[2]).

triptane (ˈtrɪpteɪn). [f. TRI- + *-p-* + BU)TANE.] A liquid branched paraffin used as a high-octane aviation fuel; 2,2,3-trimethylbutane, $CH_3C(CH_3)_2CH(CH_3)CH_3$.

1943 *Chem. & Engin. News* 25 Sept. 1561/1 Triptane is the most powerful hydrocarbon known for use in internal combustion engines. **1970** M. SMITH *Aviation Fuels* x. 65 Some of the best hydrocarbons, such as triptane, do not occur naturally in significant amounts.

tripterous (ˈtrɪptərəs), *a. Bot. rare*⁻⁰. [f. TRI- three + Gr. πτερόν wing, after DIPTEROUS.] Having three wings, or wing-like expansions.

1866 *Treas. Bot.*, *Tripterous*, three-winged. **1900** in B. D. JACKSON *Gloss. Bot. Terms*.

tripton (ˈtrɪptən). *Biol.* and *Oceanogr.* [ad. G. *tripton* (J. Wilhelmi 1917, in *Arch. für Hydrobiol.* XI. 115), f. Gr. τριπτόν, neut. of τριπτός that which is rubbed or pounded, f. τρίβειν to rub or pound.] The non-living part of the fine particulate matter suspended in water. Cf. SESTON.

1931 R. N. CHAPMAN *Animal Ecol.* xvi. 325 The dry organic matter has been selected as the measure because it eliminates a large amount of detritus ('Tripton' of Wilhelmi, 1917). **1957** G. E. HUTCHINSON *Treat. Limnol.* I. xvii. 897 The phytoplankton, or possibly bacteria associated with organic tripton, produce a good supply of thiamin. **1978** *Nature* 21 Sept. 194/1 As spring and summer pass, decaying organic matter (tripton) from the overlying water accumulates on or near the chemocline where its continued decomposition removed any dissolved oxygen from the overlying water mass.

triptote (ˈtrɪptəʊt), *sb.* and *a. Gram.* Also 7–8 triptot. [ad. L. *triptōta* (pl.) nouns that have only three case-endings, a. Gr. τρίπτωτα, pl. neuter of τρίπτωτο-ς with three case-endings, f. τρι-, TRI- + πτωτός falling (πτῶσις case). Cf. F. *triptote*.]

a. *sb.* A noun (or other word) used in three cases only. **b.** *adj.* Having only three cases.

1612 BRINSLEY *Pos. Parts* (1669) 102 *Q.* What words do you call Triptots? *A.* Such as have but three cases in the singular number. **1656** BLOUNT *Glossogr.*, *Triptote* (*triptoton*), a Noun having but three cases. **1658** in PHILLIPS. **1751** WESLEY *Wks.* (1872) XIV. 40 Triptots, which have three Cases; as, *opis*, *opem*, *ope*. **1886** *Encycl. Brit.* XXI. 651/1 The nominative of the so-called 'triptote' nouns has, as in classical Arabic, the termination *u*.

triptych (ˈtrɪptɪk). Also triptic. [f. TRI- after DIPTYCH; cf. Gr. τρίπτυχος consisting of three layers, and It. *triptica*, F. *triptyque* (Littré).]

1. a. *Antiq.* A set of three writing-tablets hinged or tied together. **b.** A card made to fold in three divisions. Also *attrib.*

1731 GALE in *Phil. Trans.* XXXVII. 161 The Diptychs and Triptychs that were covered with Wax, served only for common Occurrences. **1885** E. M. THOMPSON in *Encycl. Brit.* XVIII. 154/1 These triptychs then were *libelli* of three tablets of wood, cleft from one piece and fastened together, like the leaves of a book, by strings passed through two holes pierced near the edge. *Mod. Advt.*, Confirmation Triptych. A small-folding Triptych Certificate Card.

2. A picture or carving (or set of three such) in three compartments side by side, the lateral ones being usually subordinate, and hinged so as to fold over the central one; chiefly used as an altar-piece.

[**1848** MRS. JAMESON *Sacr. & Leg. Art* (1850) 227 In a tabernacle or triptica by Niccolo Frumenti, the central compartment represents the raising of Lazarus.] **1849** CURZON *Visits Monast.* 366 The most valuable reliquary of St. Laura is a kind of triptic. **1852** MRS. JAMESON *Leg. Madonna* Introd. (1857) 53 A Triptych is an altar-piece in three parts. **1896** *Church Times* 14 Aug. 154 There is no east window, but above the altar is an exquisite triptych.

3. *transf.* **a.** A set of three operas or pieces of music intended to be performed together.

1925 R. A. STREATFEILD *Opera* (ed. 5) xiii. 304 Puccini's last work is a so-called 'triptych', consisting of three one-act operas. **1928** *Grove's Dict. Mus.* (ed. 3) IV. 283/2 In this triptych the composer's technique is more elaborate than in 'Butterfly'. **1959** *Listener* 31 Dec. 1176/3 Any music that makes a strong visual suggestion like the Debussy orchestral triptychs. **1976** *New Yorker* 1 Mar. 90/1 This season, the triptych has been reassembled: a new 'Tabarro' and 'Suor Angelica' join the 1974 staging of 'Gianni Schicchi'. **1976** *Gramophone* Sept. 424/2 Ormandy's version (which offers 24 minutes' extra music in the form of *Feste romane*, the still more luridly coloured third leaf of the triptych) will do very nicely.

b. *Cinemat.* A sequence of film designed to be shown on a triple screen, using linked projectors.

1976 *Oxf. Compan. Film* 494/2 After the first presentation it [sc. *Napoléon*] was released in a truncated version from which the triptych sequences had been removed: Gance, disappointed by the poor reception, destroyed much of the original footage, including some of the triptych. **1980** *Times* 5 Dec. 11/5 The great triptych—Gance called it Polyvision—in no respect falls short... From the breath-catching moment when the screen is suddenly multiplied to reveal a great panorama of the Grand Army on the Alps, Gance's use of the triptych is light years in advance of anything three-projector Cinerama ever achieved. *Ibid.*, Sometimes the triptych image is a continuous panorama; sometimes it is split into different images. There are superimpositions and mirror images, the whole orchestrated with passion.

So in Fr. form ‖ **triptyque** (triptik), applied to a threefold card used as an international passport by associations of motorists.

1908 *Westm. Gaz.* 21 Jan. 4/2 The triptyque, or special card which opens the doors to half-a-dozen countries, and relieves its holder of much bewildering formula when touring abroad. **1909** *Daily Chron.* 9 July 8/3 The adoption of the triptyque, or international passport, for balloons and aeroplanes such as is now in use for motor-cars.

tripudiary (traɪˈpjuːdɪərɪ), *a. rare.* [f. L. *tripudi-um*: see TRIPUDIATE *v.* and -ARY[1].]

1. *Rom. Antiq.* Denoting a species of divination (called *tripudium*) from the behaviour of birds, esp. of the sacred chickens, when fed.

1646 SIR T. BROWNE *Pseud. Ep.* I. iv. 16 The conclusions of Southsayers in their Auguriall, and Tripudiary divinations, collecting presages from voice or food of birds. **1656** BLOUNT *Glossogr.*, *Tripudiary divination* was by bread rebounding on the ground, when it was cast unto birds, or chickens.

2. Of or pertaining to dancing. (*affected.*)

1819 H. BUSK *Vestriad* III. 396 Which from my data, dicta, and decrees, At once the art tripudiary frees.

So **triˈpudial** *a.* [cf. med.L. *tripudiālis* (1237 in Du Cange), OF. *tripudial* (13th c. in Godef.)] in sense 2 above.

1716 M. DAVIES *Athen. Brit.* II. 138 Theatrical Decorations of Musical, Comical, and Tripudial Interludes.

tripudiate (traɪˈpjuːdɪeɪt), *v.* Now *rare* and *affected.* [f. L. *tripudiāt-*, ppl. stem of *tripudiāre* (collat. form *tripodāre*), f. *tripudium* a beating the ground with the feet, a leaping or dancing, a religious dance (prob. f. *tri-* three + *pod-* (cf. Gr. ποδ-, foot). Cf. OF. *tripudier* (14th c. in Godef.).]

1. *intr.* To dance, skip, or leap for joy, or with excitement; to exult.

1623 COCKERAM, *Tripudiate*, to daunce. *a* **1641** BP. MONTAGU *Acts & Mon.* iii. (1642) 205 Such.. could not but jubilate, tripudiate, feele extraordinary motions and affections of joy. *a* **1670** HACKET *Cent. Serm.* (1675) 589 The Earth did rejoice and tripudiate when the Saviour came forth alive out of the belly of the Grave. **1891** *Sat. Rev.* 8 Aug. 158/1 He.. will.. tripudiate upon the platform because his party have made a long legislative score.

2. To trample, stamp, or jump (*on* or *upon*) in contempt or triumph.

1888 *Sat. Rev.* 5 May 524/1 On poor Colonel Slade.. he tripudiates with all the chivalry of the 'varray perfit gentil knight' of controversy that he is. **1891** *Ibid.* 7 Nov. 520/1 He tripudiates a little.. on the unfortunate Mediæval and Modern Languages Tripos. **1895** FARRAR *Gathering Clouds* I. 131 The people tore down the image, tripudiated on its shattered fragments.

So **triˈpudiant** *a.* [ad. L. *tripudiānt-em*, pres. pple. of *tripudiāre*: see above], dancing; *fig.* exultant, triumphant; **tripudiˈation** [ad. late L. *tripudiātiōn-em*, n. of action f. *tripudiāre*], the action of dancing or leaping, esp. in token of joy or excitement; exultation; **tripudist** (ˈtrɪpjʊdɪst), one given to 'tripudiating'.

a **1626** W. SCLATER *Exp. 4th ch. Rom.* (1650) Ep. Ded., A kinde of *tripudiant joy, and exultation of spirit. **1668** H. MORE *Div. Dial.* III. xxxvi. (1713) 283 How transported are my Spirits, how triumphant and tripudiant! **1870** *Sat. Rev.* 26 Feb. 275/1 Fast young peeresses and.. tripudiant matrons. **1623** COCKERAM II, Dancing, **Tripudiation*. **1629** H. BURTON *Truth's Triumph* 295 After a goodly flourish and triumphall tripudiation, as if the field were already won. **1709** J. JOHNSON *Clergym. Vade M.* II. 110 The word implies tripudiation, or immodest dancing. **1885** *Sat. Rev.* 12 Dec. 769/2 The rest of his speech was mere tripudiation. **1833** DOUCE *Dance of Death* i. 6 These riotous and irreverent *tripudists and caperers appear to have possessed themselves of the churchyards to exhibit their dancing fooleries.

‖ **tripudium** (trɪˈpjuːdɪəm). *Rom. Antiq.* [L.; see TRIPUDIATE *v.*] A ritual dance (see quots.). Also *transf.* and *fig.*

1909 in WEBSTER. **1922** W. R. HALLIDAY *Lect. Hist. Roman Relig.* iii. 46 A feature of this procession was the dancing of the armed priests... Their leaping dance, the *tripudium* or three step, was accompanied by the clashing of rods or spears against the shields. **1922** JOYCE *Ulysses* 50 The foot that beat the ground in tripudium. *Ibid.* 559 He runs to the piano and takes his ashplant, beating his foot in tripudium. **1923** L. PULLAN *Relig. since Reformation* viii. 239 The Tübingen school attempted.. at the same time 'to force Christian history into the Hegelian *tripudium* of thesis, antithesis, and synthesis'. **1938** B. SCHÖNBERG tr. *C. Sachs' World Hist. Dance* vii. 246 The weapon dances of the warriors and the priests of Mars who were grouped together under the name of *Salii*, which is equivalent to *saltantes* or dancers... The *Salii* stamped.. in repetends of three beats... From this tripedal character their dance takes the name of *tripudium*. As a choral dance.. it had a dance leader whose movements were answered by the two choruses of older and younger men as they walked around in a circle to the rhythmical beating of the shields. **1949** *Oxf. Classical Dict.* 789/1 At certain spots they [*sc.* the Salii] halted and performed elaborate ritual dances (*tripudium*, cf. Plut. *Num.* 13), beating their shields with their staves.

tripuhyite (trɪˈpuːɪaɪt). *Min.* [f. *Tripuhy*, name of a locality near Ouro Prêto, Minas Gerais, Brazil, where the first specimen was found: see -ITE[1].] An oxide of ferrous iron and antimony, $FeSb_2O_6$, found as aggregates of translucent, yellowish to dark brown, tetragonal crystals.

1897 HUSSAK & PRIOR in *Mineral. Mag.* XI. 302 From these schists, doubtless, is also derived the tripuhyite, although as yet this new mineral has only been found in fragments loose in the gravel. **1968** [see ORDOÑEZITE].

tripunctal to **tripupillate**: see TRI- 1.

‖ **tripus** (ˈtraɪpəs). [L. *tripūs*, a. Gr. τρίπους TRIPOD.] † **1.** *Obs. rare.* **a.** = TRIPOS 2 a. **b.** = TRIPOD A. 1.

1670 EACHARD *Cont. Clergy* 37 Wits.. who never.. were at all inspir'd from a Tripus's, Terræ-filius's, or Prævaricator's speech. **1697** BENTLEY *Phal.* (1699) 458 Gelon.. made a Golden Tripus of xvi Talents, and sent it to Delphi and Donary to Apollo.

2. *Zool.* A bone in the Weberian ossicles of cypriniform fishes, linking the ear and the swim-bladder.

1893 T. W. BRIDGE in *Phil. Trans. R. Soc.* B. CLXXXIV. 83 The horizontal process moves backwards or forwards with the lateral motion of the tripus. **1962**, **1970** [see INTERCALARIUM 2].

ˈ**trip-wire.** Also trip wire, tripwire. [f. TRIP *sb.*[1] or *v.* + WIRE *sb.*] **1. a.** A wire stretched near the ground in order to trip up enemies, trespassers, etc. Hence, a wire placed so that contact with it operates a weapon, flash-light, or other device.

1916 A. KNEBWORTH *Let.* 24 Feb. in Ld. Lytton *Antony* (1935) i. 21 He walks forward, he has found his landmark. He thinks he knows where the Huns are. He is coming to the Hun trip wire. He has cut the German trip wire. **1928** *Daily Mail* 3 Aug. 8/3 Trip-wires to ensnare the enemy. **1928** *Daily Tel.* 16 Oct. 18 A flash-light operated by means of a 'trip wire'. **1941** *Illustr. London News* 22 Feb. 233/1 (*caption*) The mine can be fired by various methods such as electric contact or time fuse—trip wire or impact. **1947** D. M. DAVIN *Gorse blooms Pale* 124 They had time.. to lace the stumps with barbed trip-wires. **1960** C. DAY LEWIS *Buried Day* v. 100 The window-cleaner's tricycle was built up to represent a German tank, which was laagering in a dell I had privily surrounded with trip-wires. **1974** *Times* 21 Jan. 12/5 There's a series of trip wires which set off rockets and flares if they are touched. **1978** 'F. PARRISH' *Sting of Honeybee* vi. 83 Dan wondered about dogs, electric fences, trip-wires, gin-traps.

b. *transf.* and *fig.*

1971 P. O'DONNELL *Impossible Virgin* vi. 117 He was operating on more than one level. He may have meant his offer, but he was laying trip-wires at the same time. **1976** LD. HOME *Way Wind Blows* xiv. 195 A Prime Minister.. is well-advised to search every question for the trip-wire which is usually well-concealed, but almost sure to be there, and to think up the riposte which will turn the tables on the Opposition. **1979** P. NIESEWAND *Member of Club* ix. 63 One other type of sensor.. sets up an invisible light beam... If someone walks across it, they interrupt the beam. It's a kind of optical tripwire.

2. *fig.* A comparatively weak military force employed as a first line of defence, whose involvement in hostilities will trigger the intervention of stronger forces. Freq. *attrib.* orig. *U.S.*

1957 *Observer* 1 Sept. 8/3 The German electorate are baffled as to whether Nato is meant to defend their soil, or provide the tripwire for a Soviet-American suicide pact. **1960** *Washington Post* 4 Apr. A 19 Stans suggested that a switch be made to the 'trip-wire' defense theory which would require but one American division. **1966** SCHWARZ & HADIK *Strategic Terminology* 115 Advocates of this modification ridicule the simple tripwire concept by saying that to all intents and purposes a single U.S. soldier could act as tripwire. **1969** *New Statesman* 11 Apr. 500/3 He [*sc.* King Hussein] is anxious to make a separate peace with the Israelis on the basis of a demilitarised West Bank, with an Israeli military tripwire on the Jordan. **1976** LD. HOME *Way Wind Blows* xii. 167 There was, however, a running argument among the professionals as to whether the line between the Warsaw Pact and the NATO forces should be thinly held (by a trip-wire) or more strongly manned. **1979** *Jrnl. R. Soc. Arts* CXXVII. 550/2 From the mid 1950s to the late '60s, the West relied on the so-called 'tripwire' strategy. Stated simply, this meant that any aggressive adventure on the part of the Soviet Union would be met by an overwhelming nuclear response. **1980** *Times* 24 May 15/2 What is profoundly discouraging is to find our work impeded by the old discredited trip-wires of the Cold War.

tripylæan, -ean (trɪpɪˈliːən), *a.* and *sb. Zool.* [f. mod.L. *Tripylæa*, neut. pl. (f. Gr. τρι-, TRI- + πύλη gate) + -AN.] **a.** *adj.* Belonging to the division *Tripylæa* of radiolarians, characterized by having three openings into the central capsule. **b.** *sb.* A radiolarian of this division.

1888 ROLLESTON & JACKSON *Anim. Life* 879 (*Radiolaria*) Some tripylean *Phaeodaria*, i.e. those with three apertures to the central capsule. **1902** *Cassell's Encycl. Dict., Supp.*, Tripylæan *a.* and *s.*

tripyramid to **triquaternion**: see TRI- 4 a–c, 2, 1 a.

Trique (ˈtriːkeɪ), *sb.* and *a.* Also Trike, Triqui. [Native name.] **A.** *sb.* **a.** An Indian people of Oaxaca, Mexico. **b.** The Mixtecan language spoken by this people. **B.** *adj.* Of or pertaining to this people or their language.

1891 D. G. BRINTON *Amer. Race* III. 148, I do not doubt that Orozcoy Berra was right in placing the Triquis in the same [Tequistlatecan] family. **1900** F. STARR in *Proc. Davenport Acad. Sci. 1899–1900* (1901) VIII. 142 Belmar gives in his *Essays* a brief sketch of the grammar, a list of phrases in Spanish and Triqui and a Spanish-Triqui vocabulary. *Ibid.*, The towns he mentions are none of them Triqui. *Ibid.*, San Andres Chicahuastla is the Triqui town where our work was done. **1911** *Bull. U.S. Bureau Amer. Ethnol.* No. 44. 52 Trike. This language, which belongs to the Zapotecan family, is spoken by a small tribe residing in the central part of the Mixtec area. *Ibid.* 53 Professor Starr .. says none of the towns mentioned by Orozco y Berra are Trike .. and that the real district of the Trike is situated in the high mountains of the districts of Tlaxiaco and Juxtlahuaca... They form a little island of Trike speech in the midst of the Mixtec area. **1952** J. R. SWANTON *Indian Tribes N. Amer.* 639 Trique, a tribe entered by Mason and Johnson as a substock of their Otomanguean stock. **1957** [see MAZATEC *sb.* and *a.*]. **1965** *Language* XLI. 67 The identifier tagmeme in Trique noun phrases. **1974** *Encycl. Brit. Micropædia* X. 130/1 *Trique*, Indians of Oaxaca, Mex., speaking a Mixtecan language... Some Trique men work outside the community as labourers... Trique religion includes both ancient Indian and Roman Catholic rites. **1977** T. A. SEBEOK *Native Languages Americas* II. 370 Trique. Mixtecan; 4,000 in Oaxaca (1952).

†**triquet**, *sb.* and *a.* *Obs. rare.* Also 6 tricquet. [f. L. *triquetrus*: see TRIQUETROUS.] **a.** *sb.* A triangle; in quot., a set of verses arranged in the form of a triangle. **b.** *adj.* Triangular.

1589 PUTTENHAM *Eng. Poesie* II. xi. (Arb.) 105–6. *Ibid.* 107–8 Of the Triangle or Triquet... A certaine great Sultan of Persia called Ribuska, entertaynes in loue the Lady Selamour, sent her this triquet reue[r]st pitiously bemoning his estate... To which Selamour to make the match egall,.. answered in a standing Triquet. **1656** BLOUNT *Glossogr.*, *Triquet* (*triquetrus*), having three corners, triangular.

‖**triquetra** (traɪˈkwɛtrə, -ˈkwiːtrə). [L., fem. of *triquetrus*: see Walde.] †**a.** A triangle. *Obs.* **b.** An ornament of triangular shape, formed of three interlaced arcs or lobes. Also *attrib.*

1586 FERNE *Blaz. Gentrie* 48 A coate-armor, wherin something would be borne resemblant somewhat to the signes of that art [heraldry], as Circles, Spheres, Triquetras, Pyramides, &c. **1706** PHILLIPS (ed. Kersey), *Triquetra*, a Triangle, or three-cornered Figure. **1845** PETRIE *Round Towers Irel.* II. iii. 323 That curious triangular figure, known among medallists by the name of triquetra .. formed by the ingenious interlacing of a single cord or line. **1887** J. R. ALLEN *Early Chr. Symbolism* 111 The foot [of the Irish Cross] is finished off .. with a triangular point and a triquetra knot.

triquetral (traɪˈkwɛtrəl, -ˈkwiːtrəl), *a.* [f. L. *triquetr-us* (see below) + -AL[1].] = TRIQUETROUS.

triquetral bone, (*a*) (in *pl*), small bones of irregular triangular form, sometimes found in the sutures of the skull; also called *Wormian bones*; (*b*) an approximately pyramidal bone of the wrist that articulates with the pisiform bone; = *cuneiform bone* (*a*) s.v. CUNEIFORM *a.* 1; also *ellipt.* as *triquetral*.

1646 PRYNNE *Laud* 124 Plate for the Chappell... A triquetrall Censor. **1804** SHAW *Gen. Zool.* V. 420 Triquetral Trunk-fish. **1861** HAGEN *Synopsis Neuroptera N. Amer.* 159 Abdomen triquetral. **1913** *Cunningham's Text-bk. Anat.* (ed. 4) 223 An exceptional case .. in which the centres for the capitate and triquetral bones were already present [at birth]. **1961** S. ZUCKERMAN *New Syst. Anat.* I. iv. 84 The triquetral bone forms a conspicuous prominence distal to the head of the ulna on the medial border of the dorsum of the hand. **1980** *Gray's Anat.* (ed. 36) 371/2 The palmar and dorsal surfaces of the carpal bones, apart from the triquetral and pisiform, are rough for the attachment of ligaments.

triˈquetric, *a. rare*[−0]. [f. TRIQUETR-A + -IC.] 'Pertaining to the triquetra' (*Cent. Dict.* 1891).

triquetrous (traɪˈkwɛtrəs), *a.* [f. L. *triquetrus* three-cornered, triangular + -OUS.] Three-sided triangular; in *Nat. Hist.* of triangular cross-section, three-edged, trihedral, triangularly prismatic or pyramidal.

1658 SIR T. BROWNE *Gard. Cyrus* ii. 40 The *lithostrota* or figured pavements of the ancients, which consisted not all of square stones, but were divided into triquetrous segments. **1752** J. HILL *Hist. Anim.* 27 The grey wood Spider, with a triquetrous body. **1826** KIRBY & SP. *Entomol.* III. xxxiii. 432 Almost universally they [the mandibles of insects] incline to a triquetrous or three-sided figure. **1870** HOOKER *Stud. Flora* 291 Lamium, Dead-nettle .. nutlets 3-quetrous. **1872** OLIVER *Elem. Bot.* App. 309 Fruits ovoid, acutely triquetrous.

Hence **triˈquetrously** *adv.*

1884 in STORMONTH *Dict.*

triquinate: see TRI- 2.

triradial (traɪˈreɪdɪəl), *a.* [f. TRI- + L. *radius* ray: see RADIAL and -AL[1].] = next. Hence **triˈradially** *adv.*

a **1886** FERGUSON *Ogham Inscript.* (1887) 123 They are triradial groups corresponding to the .. symbol of the Trinity. **1891** *Cent. Dict.*, Triradially.

triradiate (traɪˈreɪdɪət), *a.* (*sb.*) [f. as prec.: see RADIATE *a.* and -ATE[2] 2.] Having or consisting of three rays; radiating in three directions from a central point; three-rayed, trifurcate.

1846 PATTERSON *Zool.* 60 Three beautiful little semicircular horny saws, arranged in a triradiate manner, so that their edges meet in the centre. **1874** COOKE *Fungi* 36 The triradiate spores of Asterosporium. **1875** HUXLEY in *Encycl. Brit.* I. 754/2 Each pterygoid .. is a triradiate bone, with an anterior, an inner, and a posterior, or outer, ray.

B. *sb.* A triradiate sponge-spicule.

1887 SOLLAS in *Encycl. Brit.* XXII. 417/1 (*Sponges*) The shorter paired rays being termed basal, and the whole spicule a sagittal triradiate. **1911** A. DENDY in *Encycl. Brit.* XXV. 722/1 The triradiates and quadriradiates .. are not simple spicules, but spicule-systems formed of three or four rays each originating independently from its own scleroblast.

So **triˈradiated** (-eɪtɪd), *a.* = *triradiate*; **triˈradiately** *adv.*, in a triradiate manner (*Cent. Dict.* 1891); **triradiˈation**, radiation in three directions; also, a triradiate figure or structure.

1786 *Phil. Trans.* LXXVI. 160 The cavity .. is divided into .. chambers or compartments by solid transverse septa, which communicate with each other by a triradiated aperture. *c* **1900** *Buck's Handbk. Med. Sc.* II. 177 The callosal eminence.., the hippocamp, and the occipital eminence form an irregular triradiation.

triradius (traɪˈreɪdɪəs). Pl. -radii. [f. TRI- + RADIUS.] In dermatoglyphics, a point from which the dermal ridges radiate in three directions at angles of approx. 120 degrees.

1960 *New Scientist* 14 July 129 (*caption*) A finger-print on which a white line has been drawn joining the core of the pattern .. to the associated triradius. **1965** *Ibid.* 11 Feb. 345/2 There are discontinuities [in the fingerprint pattern], known technically as 'triradius points', where three ridges meet at a single junction. **1970** [see LOOP *sb.*[1] 4 h]. **1971** J. Z. YOUNG *Introd. Study Man* xxxix. 570 For genetic analysis counts are made from the triradius to the centre of the pattern. **1977** *Sci. Amer.* Dec. 141/1 The resulting patterns are known to the dermatologist respectively as loops, triradii and whorls.

trirectangular: see TRI- 1.

trireme (ˈtraɪriːm), *sb.* and *a.* Also 7 tryreme. [ad. L. *trirēmis*, f. *tri-* three + *rēmus* oar; cf. F. *trirème* (*c* 1352 in Godef. *Compl.*).]

A. *sb.* An ancient galley (originally Greek, afterwards also Roman) with three ranks of oars one above another, used chiefly as a ship of war.

1601 HOLLAND *Pliny* VII. lvi. I. 190 Aminocles the Corinthian built the first Trireme with three rowes of ores to a side. **1656** BLOUNT *Glossogr.*, *Trireme* (*trirēmis*), a Galley wherein every oare had three men to it, or a Galley that hath three oares on every side. **1662** J. BARGRAVE *Pope Alex. VII* (1867) 118 They having then no such ships as we have now, their byremes and tryremes being but pittiful boats. **1776** BURNEY *Hist. Mus.* I. 185 In the triremes, or vessels of three banks of oars, there was always a *tibicen*, or flute-player. **1868** *Smith's Dict. Gr. & Rom. Antiq.* (ed. 7) 262/1 Triremes .. were .. divided into two classes: the one consisting of real men-of-war, .. and the other of transports.

B. *adj.* Having three ranks of oars.

1697 POTTER *Antiq. Greece* III. xiv. (1715) 124 Trireme, quadrireme, and quinquereme Gallies, which exceeded one another by a Bank of Oars. **1839** THIRLWALL *Greece* VII. lvi. 165 A fleet was to be equipped of forty trireme galleys.

trirhombohedral, -rhomboidal: see TRI- 1 a, 2 b.

tris (trɪs), *sb. Chem.* Also Tris. [f. TRIS-.]

1. [f. *tris*hydroxymethylaminomethane.] The crystalline compound $(HOCH_2)_3CNH_2$, 2-amino-2-(hydroxymethyl)propane-1,3-diol, used as a buffering agent. Also ***tris buffer***.

1959 *Science* 20 Mar. 783/1 This compound is commonly known as 'trishydroxymethylaminomethane' or 'tris buffer'. **1964** *Biochim. & Biophysica Acta* XCII. 133 A uniform suspension of ghosts in 0·5 mM Tris. **1979** *Sci. Amer.* Mar. 102/2 The sodium current in a squid axon is abolished by applying a sizable dose of tetrodotoxin (and also replacing the sodium in the bathing medium with 'Tris' buffer).

2. [f. *tris*-2,3-dibromopropylphosphate.] The organophosphorus compound $(Br_2C_3H_5)_3PO_4$, which is used as a flame retardant.

1976 *St. Louis* (Missouri) *Globe-Democrat* 17 Sept. 6 B/1 A chemical nicknamed 'tris' that clothing manufacturers use as a flame retardant in children's pajamas causes mutations in the genes of bacteria. **1981** M. C. GERALD *Pharmacology* (ed. 2) xxx. 578 To date there is no evidence that Tris causes cancer in humans.

tris- (trɪs), *prefix*, repr. Gr. τρίς thrice (which occurs as prefix, τρισ-, in numerous Gr. compounds, chiefly adjs.): used in Eng. in a few technical words of various kinds, and in Chemistry.

1. See TRISAGION, TRISDIAPASON, TRISMEGIST, TRISOCTAHEDRON, TRISTETRAHEDRON.

2. *Chem.* †**a.** Used in the early part of the 19th century, after T. Thomson (*First Princ. Chem.* (1825) I. p. xx), prefixed to the modified name of the chlorous element or of the acid, denoting that three atoms or molecules, not of this element or acid, but of the other component, are present in the compound named; e.g. ***trisphosphuret of copper***, a compound of one atom of phosphorus and three atoms of copper; ***trisacetate of lead***, a compound of one molecule of acetic acid and three molecules of lead oxide. (Cf. TRI- 5 a, note.) *Obs.*

1836 [see TRISNITRATE]. **1848** R. D. THOMSON *School Chem.* 39 Greek numerals denote an increase in the base, as B_2O is a *Disoxide*, or *Dinoxide*, while BO is a *trisoxide*. The same nomenclature is applied to the acids.

b. Now used prefixed to the names of complex radicals or compounds, signifying that the whole complex is present thrice over, and not merely the single element or radical immediately following the prefix; e.g. ***tris-benzene-azophenol***, $C_6H_2(N{:}NC_6H_5)_3OH$, a compound containing three $N{:}NC_6H_5$ groups substituted in phenol, C_6H_5OH; ***tristhio-dimethyl-benzaldehyde***, $\{C_6H_3(CH_3)_2.CHS\}_3$, in which the whole group is present thrice.

1907 *Jrnl. Chem. Soc.* XCII. I. 800 Trisbenzeneazoresorcinol, $C_6H(OH)_2(N_2Ph)_3$.

trisaccharide (traɪˈsækəraɪd). *Chem.* [f. TRI- 5 + L. *saccharum* sugar + -IDE. (Not f. TRI- + SACCHARIDE.)] A carbohydrate which on hydrolysis reacts with $2H_2O$, yielding three molecules of monosaccharides (sugars having the general formula $C_nH_{2n}O_n$); e.g. *raffinose*, $C_{18}H_{32}O_{16}$, which yields dextrose, fructose, and galactose; *gentianose*, $C_{18}H_{32}O_{16}$, which yields fructose and two molecules of dextrose.

1910 ARMSTRONG *Simple Carbohydrates & Glucosides* 49 The best-known trisaccharide is raffinose, which is often found .. in the sugar beet.

trisacramentarian: see TRI- 4 b.

‖**trisagion** (trɪˈsægɪən, -ˈseɪgɪən). Also 4–9 in Lat. form trisagium; also 9 trishagion; also in masc. form trisagios. [a. Gr. (τὸ) τρισάγιον, the eucharistic hymn, neut. of τρισάγιος thrice holy, f. τρίς thrice + ἅγιος holy.] An ancient hymn, used especially in the Oriental Churches, beginning with a threefold invocation of God as holy. Also loosely applied to the 'angelic hymn' called TER-SANCTUS or SANCTUS, q.v.

1387 TREVISA *Higden* (Rolls) V. 11 He ordeyned þat trisagium, þat is, 'Sanctus, sanctus, sanctus,' schulde be songe at masse. **1635** PAGITT *Christianogr.* 99 The Trisagion being solemnly sung, the Copt Priest beginneth the Consecration. **1654–6** TRAPP *Comm. Isa.* vi. 1 The prophet Isaiah .. heareth the *trisagion* of the blessed angels. **1710** WHEATLEY *Bk. Com. Prayer* vi. §19 Of the Trisagium. *a* **1711** KEN *Christophil.* Poet. Wks. 1721 I. 483 O may I with Seraphick Heat Trisagions while I live repeat. **1885** *Notes on Angels* 56 In the Tris-Hagion or Ter Sanctus of the Communion Office. **1894** F. WATSON *Bk. Genesis true Hist.* v. 89 He [Isaiah] hears the Seraphim chanting the Trisagion.

trisazo (trɪˈsæzəʊ), *a. Chem.* [f. TRIS- + AZO-.] Containing three azo groups in the molecule.

1904 *Jrnl. Chem. Soc.* LXXXVI. I. 700 Black trisazo-dyes are obtained by diazotising acetyl-*p*-phenylenediamine, [etc.]. **1948** KIRK & OTHMER *Encycl. Chem. Technol.* II. 247 Naphthogene Blue 4R.., a trisazo dye. **1966** [see DISAZO-]. **1970** R. L. M. ALLEN *Colour Chem.* v. 62 Three of the various types of trisazo structure are of principal importance.

trisceptral, -sceptred, -schism: see TRI- 1 a, c, 4 c.

Triscuit (ˈtrɪskɪt). Also triscuit. [f. TRI-, irregularly after *biscuit*.] The proprietary name of a savoury cracker or biscuit.

1906 *Official Gaz.* (U.S. Patent Office) 27 Mar. 1324/2 Biscuit or crackers. The Natural Food Company .. The word 'Triscuit'. **1919** 'G. CUMBERLAND' *Set down in Malice* xiv. 174 They have .. studios .. where one has triscuits for breakfast. **1932** *Trade Marks Jrnl.* 23 Mar. 383/1 *Triscuit*.. Solid food products. The Shredded Wheat Company, Limited, Welwyn Garden City .. Manufacturers. **1937** G. FRANKAU *More of Us* viii. 93 Stern strong business-men Whom Shredded Wheat or Triscuit made that hearty They rarely failed to catch the ten-past-ten. **1980** *Times* 22 Dec. 12/7 Ketchup in a bottle, salt in a shaker, triscuits (a savory snack biscuit) in the box.

†**trisdiaˈpason.** *Mus. Obs.* [f. TRIS- + DIAPASON, after DISDIAPASON.] An interval of three octaves, a twenty-second; a note three octaves above or below a given note. (Cf. *tridiapason*, TRI- 4 a.)

1677 PLOT *Oxfordsh.* 293 And so will strike an under trisdiapason, or a 22[d]. **1706** PHILLIPS (ed. Kersey), *Tris-Diapason*, or *Triple-Diapason* .. a Chord, otherwise call'd a Triple Eighth.

trise, obs. form of TRICE *sb.*[2] and *v.*

trisect (ˈtraɪsɛkt), *a. Bot. rare.* [f. TRI- + L. *sect-us* cut, as in *palmatisect*, *pinnatisect*.] Of a leaf:

Divided into three lobes quite to the base, but not articulated so as to form separate leaflets.
1899 HEINIG *Gloss. Bot. Terms, Sect*, completely divided from margin to midrib into distinct parts, in comp. as *trisect*.

trisect (traɪˈsɛkt), *v.* [f. TRI- + L. *sect-*, ppl. stem of *secāre* to cut, after BISECT.] *trans.* To divide into three equal parts (esp. in *Geom.*); sometimes *gen.* to divide into three parts.
1695 ALINGHAM *Geom. Epit.* 44 Trisect any side..in the points *d* and *e*. *a* **1696** SCARBURGH *Euclid* (1705) 88 From hence 'tis manifest, how to trisect a Right angle. **1786** *Phil. Trans.* LXXVI. 16 Mr. Graham..perceived.. how very much more easy a given line was to bisect than to trisect or quinquesect. **1822** DE QUINCEY *Confess.* 146 Could not I have reduced it a drop a day, or by adding water, have bisected or trisected a drop? **1876** A. J. EVANS *Through Bosnia* ii. 48 We found the dwelling-houses trisected into a sleeping-room, a kitchen, and a store-room.
Hence **triˈsected** *ppl. a.* (in *Bot.* = TRISECT *a.*); **triˈsecting** *vbl. sb.*
1694 *Phil. Trans.* XVIII. 70 So the halving, trisecting, quartering, &c. is performed by extracting the Square Root, the Cubick, Biquadratick Roots, &c. of the Terms. **1809** CAVENDISH *ibid.* XCIX. 227 In trisecting, the greatest error we are liable to does not exceed that of bisection in a greater proportion than that of 4 to 3. **1828** WEBSTER, *Trisected*, divided into three equal parts. **1866** *Treas. Bot.* 1174 *Trisected*, cut deeply into three parts.

trisection (traɪˈsɛkʃən). [n. of action f. TRISECT *v.*, after L. *sectiōnem* SECTION: see -TION, and cf. F. *trisection* (1690 in Hatz.-Darm.).] The action of trisecting; division into three equal parts; rarely *gen.* division into three.
1664 POWER *Exp. Philos.* III. 187 The Trisection of an Angle. **1786** *Phil. Trans.* LXXVI. 16 The division of the arc of 90..required trisections and quinquesections. **1842** DE QUINCEY *Pagan Oracles* Wks. 1858 VIII. 193 Into this trisection I shall decompose the coarse unity of the question presented by Van Dale. **1885** LEUDESDORF *Cremona's Proj. Geom.* 295 The point *Q* is one of the points of trisection of the arc.

trisector (traɪˈsɛktə(r)). [f. TRISECT *v.* + -OR.] One who or that which trisects; *spec.* in quot. 1872, one who attempts the trisection of an angle.
1864 *Athenæum* 27 Aug. 276/3 The trisector of an angle. **1872** DE MORGAN *Budget of Paradoxes* 71 He is sometimes ranked with the trisectors.
So **triˈsectory** *a.*, having the property of trisecting: applied to certain curves used in the trisection of an angle (*Cent. Dict.* 1891); **triˈsectrix** [see -TRIX], a line that trisects; *spec.* a curve used in the trisection of an angle (*ibid.*, *Suppl.* 1909).

triseme (ˈtraɪsiːm), *a.* and *sb.* *Anc. Pros.* [ad. Gr. τρίσημος, f. τρι-, TRI- + σῆμα sign.] **a.** *adj.* = *trisemic* (see below). **b.** *sb.* A trisemic foot. So **trisemic** (traɪˈsiːmɪk) *a.*, containing, consisting of, or equivalent to three moræ or short syllables.
1885 GOODELL in *Trans. Amer. Philol. Assoc.* XVI. 88 This metre is logaœdic, trisemes and cyclic dactyls, as well as tribrachs and inverted trochees, being substituted freely for pure trochees. **1894** GILDERSLEEVE *Lat. Gram.* (ed. 3) 459 Syncopé and Protraction (triseme long).

trisensory to **tri-shaped**: see TRI- 1 a, c.

tri-service (traɪˈsɜːvɪs), *a.* Also tri-Service, Tri-Service. [f. TRI- + SERVICE *sb.*[1] 5 b.] Of, pertaining to, or representing the three armed forces, Army, Navy, and Air Force.
1959 *Times* 18 June (Queen in Canada Suppl.) p. vii/7 A unique experiment in military education, a tri-service college. **1977** *Globe & Mail* (Toronto) 1 Feb. 7/6 Much has been made of the damage supposedly done by unification. The opponents of it, both in the services, and in groups on the outside such as TRIO (Tri-Service Identities Organization), concentrated on this one issue. **1979** *Navy News* Feb. 1/5 The survey, which will be tri-Service, will cover all personnel, including Servicewomen. **1982** *Daily Tel.* 15 Dec. 24/4 The White Paper confirmed the maintenance of a sizeable tri-service garrison in the South Atlantic.

trisette, variant of TRESETTE.

trishaw (ˈtraɪʃɔː). Also trisha, tri-sha, tri-shaw. [f. TRI- + RICK)SHAW.] In the Far East, a light three-wheeled vehicle propelled by pedalling, freq. used as a taxi.
1946 *Sun* (Baltimore) 9 July 5/6 (*heading*) Trishaws may replace Singapore Rickshaws. *Ibid.*, The Rickshaw Association has asked permission for 2,000 additional trishaw licences to provide employment for former rickshawmen. **1955** [see PEDAL *v.* b]. **1961** *Guardian* 30 May 7/3 The Chinese trishaman..who failed to move out of his way. **1971** *Carry Singapore in your Pocket* (Singapore Tourist Promotion Board) (ed. 3) 71 *Trishaw*, a pedal bicycle with side-car attached. This typically Oriental mode of transport is fast dying out in Singapore but a short 'trishaw ride' is certainly worthwhile. **1972** *Daily Colonist* (Victoria, B.C.) 26 Mar. 49/3 The Chinese introduced a souped-up version of the jinricksha in the form of the tri-sha. These bicycle-powered two-seaters weave their way through George Town traffic, as common as taxis are to the streets of other cities. **1977** P. THEROUX *Consul's File* 79 The cycling noises approached... It was a trishaw, cruising for fares. **1979** R. CASSILIS *Arrow of God* IV. vi. 119 The tri-shaw man came over to help him.

†**trish-trash.** *Obs.* [A reduplicated form of TRASH *sb.*[1]; cf. MISH-MASH.] Trash, rubbish, worthless stuff.
1542-5 BRINKLOW *Lament.* 14 b, All the trishtrashe that Antichrist hath solde vs. **1583** GOLDING *Calvin on Deut.* cix. 669 That a man shall seeme a wolfe vnto vs, or that such trishtrash shall get the vpper hand of vs. **1602** *How to Choose Good Wife* II. i. C iv b, He that minds trish trash.

trishtubh, var. TRISTUBH.

trisilicate (traɪˈsɪlɪkət). *Chem.* and *Min.* [f. TRI- + SILICATE.] A compound of one or more basic oxides with silicon dioxide or silica, SiO_2: **a.** in early nomenclature denoting a compound of silicon dioxide with three equivalents of the base (see note s.v. TRI- 5 a); thus ***trisilicate of iron*** denoted a compound of three equivalents of iron oxide and one of silicon dioxide, then called silicic acid; **b.** now used for compounds derived from hypothetical *trisilicic* acids, formed of three molecules of silicon dioxide (SiO_2) with varying numbers of water molecules; e.g. $3SiO_2.2H_2O$; $3SiO_2.5H_2O$. **c.** In Mineralogy, denoting a silicate in which the oxygen in the silicon dioxide bears to the oxygen in the basic oxides the ratio 3:1. So **trisilicic** (traɪsɪˈlɪsɪk) *a.*: see b.
1850 DAUBENY *Atom. The.* (ed. 2) 112 Trisilicate of iron [denotes] 3 of base to 1 of silicic acid. **1868** WATTS *Dict. Chem.* V. 243 Silicates are sometimes distinguished by names which express directly the oxygen-ratio in the base and acid..1:3 Trisilicates. *Ibid.* 251 Bohemian glass-tubing consists of potassio-calcic trisilicate, $2(K^2O.3SiO^2)3(Ca''O.3SiO^2)$. **1902** MIERS *Mineralogy* 208 Albite, $Na_2O.Al_2O_3.6SiO_2$ or $NaAlSi_3O_8$... According to [its] oxygen ratio, therefore..Albite is a trisilicate. **1905** NEWTH *Inorg. Chem.* (ed. 11) 637 By the partial withdrawal of water from three molecules of silicic acid a number of hypothetical trisilicic acids may be derived... Felspar, or orthoclase, is a trisilicate, $Al_2K_2(Si_3O_8)_2$. **1911** ROSCOE & SCHORLEMMER *Treat. Chem.* (ed. 4) I. 920 Derivatives of trisilicic acid, $H_4Si_3O_8[3Si(OH)_4-4H_2O]$.

trisinuate, -ed: see TRI- 1 a.

triskaidekaphobia (ˌtrɪskaɪdɛkəˈfəʊbɪə). Also triske-, -decaphobia. [f. Gr. τρεῖσκαιδεκα thirteen + -PHOBIA.] Fear of the number thirteen.
1911 I. H. CORIAT *Abnormal Psychol.* II. vi. 287 Fear of the number thirteen (triskaidekaphobia). **1953** *N.Y. Times* 8 Nov. E2 A discussion in the U.N. last week on the number of members on a committee raised the question of triskaidekaphobia. **1967** *Daily Tel.* 14 Jan. 18/8 Thirteen people, pledged to eliminate triskaidecaphobia, fear of the number 13, today tried to reassure American sufferers by renting a 13ft plot of land in Brooklyn for 13 cents (10½d) a month. **1976** *Sunday Mail Color Mag.* (Brisbane) 1 Aug. 7/1 Mrs. Ratcliffe suffers from triskedekaphobia..the name psychologists have given for an inexplicable dread of a Friday falling on the 13th of the month. **1979** *Guardian* 13 July 11/6 I'm tempted to diagnose triskaidekaphobia or allergy to 13.

triskele (ˈtrɪskiːl). Also in quasi-Gr. form **triskelion** (trɪˈskɛlɪɒn), erron. ˈ**triskelos.** [f. Gr. τρι-, TRI- + σκέλος leg; cf. τρισκελής three-legged.] A symbolic figure consisting of three legs or lines radiating from a common centre.
1857 BIRCH *Anc. Pottery* (1858) I. 164 On some other Sicilian tiles the potter had placed the triskelos, or three legs, as an emblem of the country. **1880** B. HEAD *Guide Coins & Medals Brit. Mus.* 23 The Triskelion is supposed by some to be a symbol of the sun. **1885** *Athenæum* 27 June 826/2 Panels, on which were sculptured designs such as the 'sunsnake', the swastika, and the triskele. **1914** *Brit. Mus. Return* 110 The rare staters..bear respectively a triskeles of human legs..a wheel..and a crescent. **1973** T. PYNCHON *Gravity's Rainbow* (1975) I. 150 Pins, brooches, opalescent scorpions (her birth sign) inside gold mountings in triskelion. **1977** *Sci. Amer.* Dec. 168 (*caption*) Below, at the left, is another fragment of side-link mold with a decorative whorl and, at right, a triskelion decoration for a chariot linchpin.

trismegist (ˈtrɪsmɪgɪst), anglicized form of L. *trismegistus*, Gr. τρισμέγιστος 'thrice-greatest' (cf. F. *trismégiste*), title of the Egyptian Hermes (see HERMES 3): in quots. used allusively. So **trismeˈgistian, trismeˈgistic, -ical** *adjs.*, belonging or ascribed to, following, or having the character of Hermes Trismegistus.
1657 H. PINNELL *Philos. Ref.* A viij, He that listed himselfe a true Chymist, had faire hopes to become a great Trismegist. **1678** CUDWORTH *Intell. Syst.* I. iv. 307, Δεύτερον θεὸν, as the Hermaick or Trismegistick Writers call it, *The Second God. Ibid.* 323 Books, called Hermetical and Trismegistical. **1694** MOTTEUX *Rabelais* v. xlvi, Is this all that the Trismegistian Bottle's Word means? **1913** *19th Cent.* Jan. 178 The extant tractates and fragments of this Trismegistic literature.

‖**trismus** (ˈtrɪzməs). *Path.* [mod.L., ad. Gr. τρισμός = τριγμός a scream, also a grinding, rasping.] Tetanus or tonic spasm of the muscles of the neck and lower jaw, causing the jaw to close rigidly; lock-jaw. (Rarely extended to tetanus in general.)
1693 tr. *Blancard's Phys. Dict.* (ed. 2), *Trismus*, the grinding of the Teeth, or a Convulsion of a Muscle of the Temples, whereby the Teeth gnash whether one will or no. **1704** in J. HARRIS *Lex. Techn.* I. **1806** *Med. Jrnl.* XV. 44 This man had a slight cut in the palm of one of his hands.. which was healed several days prior to his seizure with trismus. **1897** *Trans. Amer. Pediatric Soc.* IX. 77 There is trismus of the hands and feet.

†**trisˈnitrate.** *Chem. Obs.* [f. TRIS- + NITRATE.] Old name for a nitrate supposed to contain three equivalents of basic oxide and one equivalent of nitric anhydride (then called nitric acid). Cf. TRIS- 2 a.
1836 *Pharm. R. Coll. Physic.* 217 Trisnitrate of Bismuth was formerly employed as a cosmetic under the name of magistery of Bismuth..represented to possess anti-spasmodic powers. **1850** DAUBENY *Atom. The.* iii. (ed. 2) 112 Trisnitrate of alumina [denotes] 1 of acid to 3 of the earth. **1876** HARLEY *Royle's Mat. Med.* 252 Trisnitrate of bismuth.

trisoctahedron (ˌtrɪsɒktəˈhiːdrən, -ˈhɛdrən). *Geom.* and *Cryst.* [f. TRIS- + OCTAHEDRON.] A solid figure having 24 faces, every three of which correspond to one face of an octahedron: either with triangular faces (= *triakisoctahedron*), or with trapezoidal faces (= *deltohedron*, *icositetrahedron*, or *trapezohedron*). Hence ˌ**trisoctaˈhedral** *a.*, pertaining to or having the form of a trisoctahedron.
1847 WEBSTER (citing DANA), Trisoctahedron. **1891** *Cent. Dict.*, Trisoctahedral.

trisome (ˈtraɪsəʊm). *Cytology.* [f. TRI- + -SOME[4].] A chromosome which is represented three times in a chromosomal complement; also, a trisomic individual.
1921 [see DISOME]. **1926** L. W. SHARP *Introd. Cytol.* (ed. 2) xvii. 388 Such $2n + 1$ forms are called 'simple trisomic' mutants; they have 11 disomes (normal pairs) and one trisome. **1944** [see MONOSOME 1]. **1979** *Nature* 27 Sept. 280/2 The failure to form trisomes indicates..that on intact RNA3 stable ribosome binding does not occur simultaneously at both the site near base 29 and the site near base 70.

trisomic (traɪˈsəʊmɪk), *a.* (*sb.*) *Cytology.* [f. as prec. + -IC.] Of or pertaining to a trisome. Also as *sb.*, a trisomic chromosome, cell, or individual.
1921 A. F. BLAKESLEE in *Amer. Naturalist* LV. 259 If the Globe and Poinsettia [*sc.* 'mutant' forms of *Datura stramonium*] could be combined to form a mutant with 3 chromosomes each in two of the 12 sets, such a mutant would be called a double trisomic mutant. **1924** *Genetics* IX. 194 Super-enlarged in general bears the same relation to enlarged as round-leaf globe to globe; i.e., the tetrasomic is an accentuated expression of the trisomic. **1939** *Jrnl. Genetics* XXXVIII. 382 Trisomics are of frequent occurrence and are known in almost every genus employed in genetic work. **1957** R. A. BEATTY *Parthenogenesis & Polyploidy in Mammalian Devel.* v. 79 Since the only abnormality would be the presence of one extra chromosome, the trisomic might have greater viability than the full triploid. *Ibid.* vi. 102 In triploid or trisomic *Drosophila*, the position of the centromere has been assessed in this way. **1974** *Nature* 1 Mar. 54/2 Aneuploid embryos found in this study included uniform monosomics and trisomics.
So ˈ**trisomy**, trisomic state; freq. with following numeral denoting the chromosome concerned, as ***trisomy-21*** (associated with Down's syndrome).
1930 *Bibliographia Genetica* VI. 15 Further observations ..disclosed a high degree of intraspecific variation resulting in polyploidy, trisomy, fragmentation of chromosomes [etc.]. **1961** G. ALLEN et al. in *Lancet* 8 Apr. 775/2 Several others [of the undersigned] believe that this is an appropriate time to introduce the term 'trisomy 21 anomaly' which would include cases of simple trisomy as well as translocations. **1963** [see DERMATOGLYPHICS]. **1965** [see DOWN'S SYNDROME]. **1970** PASSMORE & ROBSON *Compan. Med. Stud.* II. xxxi. 19/1 The relative frequency of trisomy 13–15 in abortuses indicates that it is less compatible with normal intra-uterine development than either trisomy 17–18 or mongolism. **1977** *Nature* 6 Jan. 65/2 Case 2.. showed an excess of α-globin synthesis smaller than expected for functional trisomy of the α-globin genetic region. **1979** *Ibid.* 4 Jan. 57/1 Although the patient had no features of the trisomy 21 syndrome, two first-degree cousins of his father had given birth to children with Down's syndrome.

trisonant: see TRI- 2.

trispast (ˈtrɪspæst). *rare.* [ad. L. *trispastos* (Vitruvius), a. Gr. τρίσπαστος adj., f. τρι-, TRI- + σπά-ειν to draw, pull.] An (ancient) apparatus with three pulleys for hoisting heavy weights.
1706 PHILLIPS (ed. Kersey), *Trispast* (Gr.), an Engine that consists of three Pulleys. **1819** in *Pantologia*; and in later Dicts.

tri-spear to **trisquare**: see TRI- 4 c, 1 a, 2.

trispective (traɪˈspɛktɪv). *Geom.* [f. after PERSPECTIVE: see TRI-.] A relation, analogous to *perspective* (PERSPECTIVE *sb.* 3 c) between three trigraphic ranges of points: see TRIGRAPHY.
1895 J. W. RUSSELL in *Proc. Lond. Math. Soc.* XXVI. 450 Three ranges situated as above may be said to be in trispective, *O* being the centre of trispective.

triss, trisselle, trissett: see TREST, TRESTLE, TRESETTE.

† **trist**, *sb.*[1] *Obs.* Also 3–5 triste, 4–5 **tryst(e**, (5 **thrist**). [App. etymologically related to TRAIST, TRUST; but the nature of the relation is not clear; see further under TRUST *sb.*] Confidence, faith; confident expectation, hope: = TRUST *sb.* 1, 2.

c **1200** *Trin. Coll. Hom.* 75 Trist to longe lif letteð þe mannes shrifte. **1303** R. BRUNNE *Handl. Synne* 7228 Of swych, here wombes are here Cryst; þat ys here loue, þat ys here tryst. *c* **1330** —— *Chron.* (1810) 103 My triste is laid on þe duke Roberd. *c* **1374** CHAUCER *Troylus* I. 98 (154) Thei hadde a relyk hight Palladion That was hire tryst [*v.rr.* trist, trost] a bouen euerichon. *c* **1380** WYCLIF *Sel. Wks.* III. 431 Siche signes drawen fro love of Crist þo þat setten so meche trist in hem. **1388** —— *Matt.* ix. 22 Jhesus turnede, and say hir, and seide, Douȝtir, haue thou trist [1382 trust]. *c* **1400** *Apol. Loll.* 30 He haþ no tryst of preching.. he haþ only þe name of prest. **1413** *Pilgr. Sowle* (Caxton) II. xliii. (1859) 49 Thylke also, that vppon the tryste of mercy haue leyn in theyr lustes to theyr lyues ende. *c* **1440** *York Myst.* xviii. 13 All my triste, lord, is in þe. **1483** *Cath. Angl.* 393/2 Triste, *fiducia ex bona consciencia est, confidencia temeritatis est, & cetera.*

† **trist**, *sb.*[2] *Obs.* Forms: 4 **tryste**, 4–5 **tryst, triste**, 5 **trest, treste, tryyst**. [a. OF. *triste* (12th c. in Godef.); cf. TRISTRE: in med.L. *trista, tristra*. Derivation obscure; perh. the same word as prec.] An appointed station in hunting.

c **1330** R. BRUNNE *Chron. Wace* (Rolls) 858 To venerye he gaf his tent; An herde of hertes sone þey met, At a triste [*v.r.* at triste] to schete, Brutus was set. **14..** *Voc.* in Wr.-Wülcker 613/22 *Statuncula*, a tryst. *c* **1440** *Promp. Parv.* 503/1 Tryyst, merke, *limes*, C.F. *meta*. **1470–85** MALORY *Arthur* XVIII. xxi. 764 They.. coude wel kylle a dere bothe at the stalke & at the trest. [**1607** COWELL *Interpr.*, *Tritis*, alias *Tristis*, is an immunitie from that attendance, in the forest, whereby euery man dwelling in the forest, is tyed to be readie, houlding of a Greyhound, when the Lord of the Forest is disposed to chace. **1799** *Sporting Mag.* XIII. 321 The diversion named the *Traist* or *Trista*. **1882** J. F. S. GORDON *Hist. Moray* III. v. 102 He.. sounded with his horn the death-note of many a deer in the trystas which he held with his nobles in the royal forests.]

b. *gen.* A station assigned; appointed place, rendezvous. Cf. TRYST *sb.* 4.

c **1330** R. BRUNNE *Chron.* (1810) 157 Acres þan is his [K. Richard's] triste, opon þe Sarazin feendes, To venge Jhesu Criste þiderward he wendes. *Ibid.* 179 þe Inglis at þer triste bifor þam bare alle doun, & R. als him liste þe way had redy roun.

trist, *sb.*[3]: see TRIST *a.*[2]

† **trist**, *a.*[1] *Obs.* Also 4 **tryst, tryste**, 5 **triste**. [Goes with TRIST *sb.*[1]]

1. Confident, sure: = TRUST *a.* 1.

1340–70 [implied in TRISTLY]. *c* **1400** *Ywaine & Gaw.* 3888 Of him ye myght be trist inogh.

2. Trusty, trustworthy, faithful: = TRUST *a.* 2.

c **1330** R. BRUNNE *Chron. Wace* (Rolls) 1108 Anacletus graunted wel, ȝyf Brutus wold be tryst as stel þat his lyf he wolde hym saue. *Ibid.* 3564 þe walles he reisede trist & trewe. *c* **1400** *Destr. Troy* 12634 To tryve out the truthe with his trist hond, On what buerne so was bold þe batell to take. **1540** *Registr. Aberdon.* (Maitl. Cl.) I. 416 Letter from þe King praying his trist consalour þe bischop and weilbelouit clarkis of Abirdene to consent.

trist, *a.*[2] (*sb.*[3]) (*obs.* or *arch.*); in ordinary use now only as Fr. ‖triste (trist). Also 5 **tryst, tryste**. [a. F. *triste* (10th c. in Godef. *Compl.*) = Prov. *trist, triste*, Sp., Pg. *triste*, It. *tristo*, ad. L. *tristis* sad, sorrowful, gloomy.]

1. Feeling or expressing sorrow; sad, sorrowful, melancholy.

c **1420** LYDG. *Thebes* 1956 Whan Tydeus hadde told his tale, Ethiocles, trist and wonder pale, his conceyt first in maner hath refreyned. **1474** CAXTON *Chesse* II. v. (1883) 71 Hyt apperteyneth not to a prynce that ony man shold departe sorowfull or tryste fro hym. **1513** DOUGLAS *Æneis* XI. vi. 2 Thyr messingeris, all trist and wobegon, Returnit haymwartis into thar maist neid. **1600** FAIRFAX *Tasso* XIII. xxix, A bitter sorrow by the hart him bit,.. sad, silent, trist, Alone he would all day in darknes sit. **1702** VANBRUGH *False Friend* I. i, I staid in Flanders, very trist for your loss. **1775** MISS BURNEY *Early Diary* (1889) II. 112 The Russian nobleman.. had a most *triste*, foreign countenance. **1820** W. IRVING *Life & Lett.* (1864) II. 18 The populace have a more triste and grave appearance. **1851** SIR F. PALGRAVE *Norm. & Eng.* II. 410 His hitherto cheerful countenance [was] *triste* and worn.

b. Characterized by or causing sorrow; sad, doleful, lamentable.

c **1450** *St. Cuthbert* (Surtees) 6741 Eftirward fell tyme triste. **1513** DOUGLAS *Æneis* X. v. 142 The comete stern sanguynolent, Wyth hys red cullour trist and violent. **1667** WATERHOUSE *Fire Lond.* 83 Not more trist to other parts of the World and to this nation in general, then to Me in particular. **1768** EARL CARLISLE in Jesse *Selwyn & Contemp.* (1843) II. 285 It is a *triste* reflection. **1888** 'P. CUSHING' *Blacksmith of Voe* II. xi. 267 What a trist fate, elenge, sombre, and pitiful!

2. Devoid of interest or liveliness; dull, depressing, dismal, dreary. (Only in form *triste*, as Fr.)

? **1756** H. WALPOLE *Lett.* Aug. (1846) III. 239 The great apartment is vast and triste, the whole leanly furnished. **1805** EMILY CLARK *Banks of Douro* II. 135 To live constantly at my house will be a situation too triste for you. **1835** *Court Mag.* VI. 188/2 A family going to Bath.. without introductions to the *élite* of the town, will pass a most *triste* and deplorable winter. **1894** MRS. H. WARD *Marcella* III. 158 Life was often triste and dull in the great house.

† **B.** *sb.*[3] Sadness, sorrow, affliction. *Obs. rare.*

a **1510** DOUGLAS *K. Hart* II. 380 That is ane sing [= sign] befoir ane hevie trist!

Hence **'tristeness**, dullness, dreariness. *rare.*

1866 MARK LEMON *Wait for the End* xxxiv. 442 The mirthfulness of the guests.. was in pleasing contrast to the tristeness of the morning gathering.

† **trist**, *v.* *Obs.* Forms: 3–5 **triste**, 4–6 **trist, tryst(e**, (6–7 *Sc.* **thrist**). *Pa. t.* 4 **tristide**, 5 **tristed**; usually contr. 3–5 **triste**, 5 **trist, tryst**. [Goes with TRIST *sb.*[1]: cf. TRAIST *v.*, TRUST *v.*]

1. *intr.* To have confidence; to confide, rely (*in, on, upon, to*): = TRUST *v.* 1.

a **1250** *Owl & Night.* 760 Ich kan wit & song manteine Ne triste ich to non oþer maine. *c* **1330** R. BRUNNE *Chron. Wace* (Rolls) 1697 He triste to mykel on his myght. *c* **1374** CHAUCER *Troylus* V. 1709 O Pandarus that in dremes for to triste Me blamed hast. *c* **1380** WYCLIF *Wks.* (1880) 347 Whoso faylip in feiþ he is fals to god, & tristiþ not to hijs treuthe. **1382** —— *Mark* vi. 50 He spak with hem, and seide to hem, Triste ȝe, I am; nyle ȝe drede. ? *a* **1400** *Arthur* 428 Arthour.. tryst on god, & was wel payd. *c* **1430** *Pilgr. Lyf Manhode* I. v. (1869) 3 Seint Peeter, in whom he wel triste, and certeyn wel mihte triste in him. *c* **1475** *Songs & Carols* (Percy Soc.) 11 Few be trew to tryst upon.

2. *trans.* To have confidence in, rely on: = TRUST *v.* 2.

a **1272** *Luue Ron* 56 in *O.E. Misc.* 94 Nis he neuer treowe ifunde. þat him tristeþ he is amed. **1390** GOWER *Conf.* II. 257 He tok to him suche as he triste In secre. **1430–40** LYDG. *Bochas* I. x. (MS. Bodl. 263) 48/2 As a brother sholde his brother triste. *a* **1500** *Childe of Bristow* 154 in Hazl. *E.P.P.* I. 116 Frendship, sone, is ylle to triste.

3. To expect confidently, hope: = TRUST *v.* 3. (Const. with clause, or *intr.* with *of*.)

c **1200** *Trin. Coll. Hom.* 217 Ich triste þat he nele neng bi mine wrihte. *a* **1400–50** *Alexander* 1344 Of þe takyng of tire tristed þai no lenger. **1433** *Rolls of Parlt.* IV. 425/1 He takith hym nowe so nygh, tristyng yat it shall lyke the Kyng.

4. To believe: = TRUST *v.* 4. (With simple obj. or clause.)

1340–70 *Alisaunder* 489 Sir, I tolde you trouth, trist yee no nooþer. *c* **1380** WYCLIF *Wks.* (1880) 33 þey.. dysceyuen.. lordis & ladies.. & maken hem to triste þat it is almes to distroye trewe men. ? *a* **1400** *Arthur* 545 þer ys no man wel nye, y tryste, þat can be waar of hadde wyste.

5. To give credit to (a person for goods); to supply (goods *to* a person) on credit: = TRUST *v.* 7. *Sc.*

1583 *Leg. Bp. St Androis* 1046 Ye wald doe weill gif ye wald thrist me... Ye salbe payit... Your tristene sall not be for nought. **1609** SKENE *Reg. Maj., Burrow Lawes* cxxx. 136 Browsters, Fleshers, and Baikers sall lenne (and thirst) to their neighbours aill, flesh, and bread, sa long as they buy fra them.

trist, obs. f. TREST, TRYST.

tristachyous: see TRI- 1 a.

Tristanesque (trɪstəˈnɛsk), *a.* [f. the name *Tristan*, the hero of Wagner's opera *Tristan und Isolde* (1865), + -ESQUE.] Resembling the music of *Tristan und Isolde*; *spec.* characterized by tonal ambiguity and chromaticism.

1942 *Scrutiny* XI. 5 Similarly the diatonic system decayed into the deliquescence of feeling and tonal instability which marks the Tristanesque music of the late nineteenth century. **1948** [see IMPRESSIONIST 2]. **1957** W. MELLERS *Man & his Music: Romanticism & 20th Cent.* I. ii. 46 (Consider the Tristanesque opening of the second piece). Liszt the romantic lover here recollects in tranquillity. **1962** *Times* 26 Jan. 16/5 The debt to Wagner was incurred a little later, in the thoroughly Tristanesque love duet towards the end of *A Village Romeo and Juliet*.

tri-state: see TRI- 1 b.

triste: see TRIST *a.*[2]

tristearin: see TRI- 5 a.

tristell, obs. f. TRESTLE.

† **tristen**, *v.* *Obs. rare.* [irreg. f. TRIST *v.* + -EN[5].] = TRIST *v.* Hence † **tristening** *vbl. sb.* (Cf. TRUSTEN.)

1382 WYCLIF *2 Cor.* i. 15 And in this tristnynge [1388 tristyng, *Vulg.* confidentia] I wolde firste come to ȝou. **1388** —— *Eph.* iii. 12 [see TRUSTEN].

tristene, Sc. f. *tristing* vbl. sb.: see TRIST *v.* 5.

tristesse. Also 4 **tristesce**, 5 **trystesse**, (**tristresse**), 6 **tristes**. Now only as F. (tristɛs). [ME. a. OF. *tristesce, -tece, -trece* (12th c. in Godef. *Compl.*), F. *tristesse*, = Prov. *tristicia, tristessa*, Sp., Pg. *tristeza*, It. *tristezza*:—L. *tristitia* sadness, f. *tristis* sad.] Sadness, grief, melancholy.

1390 GOWER *Conf.* II. 115 He withinne his thought conceiveth Tristesce, and so himself deceiveth. *c* **1425** LYDG. *Dance Macabre* x, Mine old ioyes been turned into tristesse. **1485** CAXTON *Paris & V.* 11 He ledde hys lyf in grete trystesse and sorowe. *c* **1489** —— *Blanchardyn* iv. 20 þe palays and the cyte were tourned from Ioye vnto tristresse. **1547** HOOPER *Declar. Christ* v. Eiij b, *Ezeb*.. signifithe ether affliction, rebellion, sorow, tristes, trauel, or peyne. **1797** SCOTT *Fam. Lett.* (1894) I. 6 If it will help to banish *Tristesse*, let me again assure you that every thought of my heart shall be directed to insure your happiness. **1856** EMERSON *Eng. Traits* xvi. 162 Nature.. too much by half for man in the picture, and so giving a certain *tristesse*.

tristetrahedron (ˌtrɪstɛtrəˈhiːdrɒn, -ˈhɛdrən). *Geom.* and *Cryst.* [f. TRIS- + TETRAHEDRON.] A solid figure having 12 faces, every three of which correspond to one face of the tetrahedron: either with triangular faces (= *triakistetrahedron*), or with trapezoidal faces. (Cf. TRISOCTAHEDRON.)

In recent Dicts.

† **'tristful**, *a.*[1] *Obs. rare*[−1]. In 5 **trystefull**. [f. TRIST *sb.*[1] + -FUL 1.] Trustworthy: = TRUSTFUL *a.* 1.

c **1440** *York Myst.* xxv. 514 Hayll! talker trystefull of trew tales!

tristful (ˈtrɪstfʊl), *a.*[2] *arch.* Also 5 **trystefull**. [f. TRIST *a.*[2] + -FUL 1.] Full of sadness; sad, sorrowful; dreary, dismal: cf. TRIST *a.*[2]

1491 CAXTON *Vitas Patr.* II. (W. de W. 1495) 180 b/1 Entryng in his hermytage he founde hym trystefull and sore to the deth. *c* **1500** *Melusine* 305 That message was the cause of the trystefull doleur of the departyng of his wyf. **1602** SHAKS. *Ham.* III. iv. 50 This solidity and compound masse, With tristfull visage as against the doome, Is thought-sicke at the act. **1748** RICHARDSON *Clarissa* (1811) VIII. lv. 251 How will thy tristful visage be illuminated by it! **1880** BROWNING *Dram. Idylls* Ser. II. *Pietro of Abano* xxi, Then did Peter's tristful visage lighten somewhat.

Hence **'tristfully** *adv.*; **'tristfulness**.

1847 in WEBSTER. **1880** W. WATSON *Prince's Quest* (1892) 31 The day, begun Tristfully, trailed an ever wearier wing. **1909** HARDY *Time's Laughingstocks* 152 In the bearing of each a passive tristfulness. **1914** C. MACKENZIE *Sinister Street* II. IV. ii. 877 For a whim of tristfulness, for the luxury of consummating the ineffable depression the house created in him.

tristich (ˈtrɪstɪk). *Pros.* [f. TRI-, after DISTICH; cf. Gr. τριστιχία a union of three verses, f. τρίστιχος three-rowed, f. τρι- three + στίχος row.] A group of three lines of verse; a stanza of three lines.

1813 T. BUSBY tr. *Lucretius* II. VI. *Comm.* p. ix, Much of the thought contained in the subjoined tristich of Ovid, is evidently derived from the original of this. **1864** PUSEY *Lect. Daniel* vi. 316, Ps. x.. has 3 tristichs (verses divided into 3). **1886** C. A. BRIGGS *Messianic Proph.* III. ii. 82 *note*, In the third part, a tristich, the three sons appear.

Hence **tristichic** (trɪˈstɪkɪk) *a.*, characterized by tristichs.

1882–3 *Schaff's Encycl. Relig. Knowl.* III. 1955 A closed train of thought which is unrolled after the distichic and tristichic ground-form of the rhythmical period.

tristichous (ˈtrɪstɪkəs), *a. Bot.* [f. Gr. τρίστιχ-ος (see prec.) + -OUS.] Arranged in, or characterized by, three rows or ranks.

1857 HENFREY *Elem. Bot.* §62 The tristichous or three-ranked arrangement, which is common among the Monocotyledons. **1887** *Jrnl. Educ.* Dec. 520 The quincuncial or tristichous arrangement could be.. indicated by fractions.

† **tri'stifical**, *a.* *Obs. rare*[−0]. [f. L. *tristific-us* adj., saddening (f. *tristis* sad + *-ficus*, -FIC) + -AL[1].]

1656 BLOUNT *Glossogr.*, *Tristifical*.., that makes sad or heavy.

tristigm to **tristigmatose**: see TRI- 4 a, 1 a.

tristil, -ill(e, obs. forms of TRESTLE.

† **'tristily**, *adv.*[1] *Obs.* Forms: see TRISTY *a.*[1] [f. TRISTY *a.*[1] + -LY[2].]

1. Trustfully, confidently, boldly; securely: = TRUSTILY 1.

c **1380** WYCLIF *Wks.* (1880) 42 Goo þei [friars] tristiliche for almes, and hem nediþ not to be a-schamyd. **1382** —— *Acts* ix. 27 Barnabas.. telde.. how in Damask he [Paul] dide tristily in the name of Jhesu. **1388** —— *Prov.* iii. 23 Thanne thou schalt go tristili in thi weie, and thi foot schal not snapere. *c* **1410** LOVE *Bonavent. Mirr.* (1907) 149 The euerelastynge lyf in heuene, that thei tristily hopen to haue by his gracious byheste.

2. Faithfully, truly: = TRUSTILY 2.

c **1330** R. BRUNNE *Chron. Wace* (Rolls) 4864 þer to han hated, & fomen ben, þat syþen han loued to-gedre wel, Tristiloker þan ony stel. **1380** *Lay Folks Catech.* 1181 þis is nedful to alle þat tristyly lyuys. *a* **1400** *Pistill of Susan* 340 (Cotton MS.) Telle me tristili [*other MSS.* treuwely, trewly, trwly], er þow þy lyfe tyne. *c* **1400** *Destr. Troy* 8739 A tabernacle triet & tristyly wroght.

3. Certainly, surely: = TRUSTILY 3.

? *a* **1366** CHAUCER *Rom. Rose* 1166 (Glasgow MS.) If she hadde an enemy, I trowe that she coude tristely [*v.r.* craftily] Make hym fulle soone hir frend to be. **1393** LANGL. *P. Pl.* C. IV. 498 He þat secheþ sapience fynde he shal þat foleweþ Tristilich a teneful tixt.

† **'tristily**, *adv.*[2] *Obs. rare.* In 5 **trystily**. [f. TRISTY *a.*[2] + -LY[2].] Sadly, sorrowfully.

c **1450** *St. Cuthbert* (Surtees) 4408 Elfride lay wakand all'ane, He thoght trystily and made his mane.

tristimulus (traɪˈstɪmjʊləs). [f. TRI- + STIMULUS.] Each of three reference colours (as red, green, and blue) which can be combined additively in specified proportions (*tristimulus* *values*) to produce any given colour. Usu. *attrib.*

1933 *Jrnl. Optical Soc. Amer.* XXIII. 359/2 The specification [for matching any given colour stimulus] consists of giving the amounts of each primary stimulus required for the match. This is known as the tristimulus system of color specification. **1937** G. S. MONK *Light* xvii. 336 The tristimulus values of the recommended standard source..for wave-length 4800 angstroms are given by the ordinates at that wave-length of the three curves. **1962** H. C. WESTON *Sight, Light & Work* (ed. 2) vii. 212 The vertical scale labelled Y refers to one of the tristimuli and the horizontal scale labelled X refers to another. **1976** C. REYNOLDS *Photoguide to Filters* 227 The CIE system is the tristimulus specification most widely used, and is ideally suited to defining the colour of filters.

† **'tristiness.** *Obs.* [f. TRISTY *a.*[1] + -NESS.] Trustiness, faithfulness.

1408 CLIFTON tr. *Vegetius De re milit.* (MS. Digby 233) lf. 185 b/1 Wheþer he haue good tristinesse in knyghthod.

† **tri'stitiate,** *v. Obs. rare*⁻¹. [f. L. *tristitia* sadness + -ATE[3].] *trans.* To affect with sadness, to sadden. So † **tri'stitious** *a. Obs. rare*⁻¹, full of sadness, sorrowful.

1628 FELTHAM *Resolves* II. [I.] xli. 122 Nor is there any whom Calamity doth so much tristitiate, as that hee neuer sees the flashes of some warming ioy. **1694** MOTTEUX *Rabelais* V. 248 Their plaisant Notes tristitious Thoughts confound.

† **'tristive,** *a. Obs. rare*⁻¹. [f. TRIST *a.*[2] + -IVE.] Sad, doleful, mournful.

1578 T. PROCTOR *Gorg. Gallery* P iv, Though death hath shapte his most untimely end Yet for his prayse my tristive tunes I send.

tristle, obs. form of TRESTLE.

† **'tristly,** *adv. Obs.* [f. TRIST *a.*[1] + -LY[2].] Confidently; securely; boldly: = TRUSTLY *adv.* 1.

1340-70 *Alex. & Dind.* 513 Þat þou mihte trystli trye þe treweste lawe. *a* **1400-50** *Alexander* 1632 He me thrett to be tra [= thra, thro], & for no thyng turne, Bot tyre me titely þarto & tristly to wend. **1408** CLIFTON tr. *Vegetius De re militari* (MS. Digby 233) lf. 183 b/2 No man dredeþ to fulfille in dede þat he tristly troweþ he hath wel lerned.

tristnynge: see TRISTEN.

† **tristour.** *Obs. rare*⁻¹. [a. OF. *tristur, -teur, -tor* (12th c. in Godef.), f. *triste* sad; = L. type **tristōr-em*: cf. F. *hauteur*.] Sadness, grief.

c **1380** *Sir Ferumb.* 2373 Þe Amiral hem tolde with tristour by him how it is y-went.

† **tristre.** *Obs.* Also 4 trystor, -ere, -er, 5 -yre, tristur. [a. OF. *tristre* (12th c. in Godef.), phonetic variant of *triste*, TRIST *sb.*[2] (In OF. *tristre* appears later than *triste*; but in ME. *tristre* is the earlier.)] = TRIST *sb.*[2]

a **1225** *Ancr. R.* 332 Tristre is þer me sit mid þe greahundes forte kepen þe hearde, oðer tillen þe nettes aȝean ham. **13..** *Gaw. & Gr. Knt.* 1146 A hundreth of hunteres, as I haf herde telle, of þe best; To trystors vewters ȝod. *c* **1410** *Master of Game* (MS. Digby 182) xv, þe baytyng of þe bull and huntyng of þe wilde boore,..with grehoundes at þe tristre. *c* **1460** *Towneley Myst.* xxx. 208, I stande at my tristur, when othere men shones. **1483** *Cath. Angl.* 393/2 Trystyre, *staciuncula* (A.).

† **tristsum,** *a. Sc. Obs. rare*⁻¹. [f. TRIST *a.*[2] + -SOME.] Sad, woeful, lamentable.

1567 *Satir. Poems Reform.* iv. 75 I wat it wald mak ony haill hairt sair For to reuolue my tristsum tragidie.

tristubh ('trɪʃtʊb). Also trishtubh. [Skr. *triṣṭubha*.] A Vedic metre of eleven syllables (see also quot. 1939).

1869, etc. [see JAGATI]. **1939** *Jrnl. Amer. Oriental Soc.* LIX. 159 Ordinarily, the Hindu metricians mechanically define any metrical pāda of eleven syllables as 'triṣṭubh', and any of twelve syllables as 'jagatī'. This cannot be accepted. .. What we shall call a triṣṭubh may have anywhere from ten to thirteen syllables, a jagatī from eleven to at least thirteen (possibly more). The distinction between the two is solely based on the cadence; a triṣṭubh always ends ◡—x..in western terms..in a catalectic diiambus. **1965** *Language* XLI. 11 Three instances are accounted for by the pāda.. two by the triṣṭubh cadence. **1971** *Ibid.* XLVII. 64 The last pada of the stanza in question is incontrovertibly triṣṭubh.

† **'tristy,** *a.*[1] *Obs.* Also 4 tristi, trysti, 4-5 trysty. [f. TRIST *a.*[1] + -Y[1].]

1. Trustful, confident: = TRUSTY *a.* 1.

c **1325** *Spec. Gy Warw.* 477 Put al þin hope in god almiht, And tristi hope to him þou haue. **1382** WYCLIF *Prol. Bible* iii. 4 This..shulde make men trysty in Goddis help.

2. Trustworthy, faithful: = TRUSTY *a.* 2.

13.. *E.E. Allit. P.* B. 763 If ten trysty in toune be tan in þi werkkez, Wylt þou mese þy mode & menddyng abyde? *c* **1375** *Cursor M.* 13365 (Fairf.) Þe bridegome dide þidder calle His maste tristi [*Cott.* specialiest] frendis alle. *c* **1450** *St. Cuthbert* (Surtees) 7806 Þai were tristy, and a bote bryng To lede þein his body. **1483** *Cath. Angl.* 393/2 Tristy, *ubi* trewe (*A.*).

b. Of things: Reliable; secure: = TRUSTY *a.* 2 b.

13.. *Cast. Love* (Halliw.) 690 On trysti [*v.r.* trusti] roche heo stondeth fast. **1340-70** *Alisaunder* 952 Till hee had take þe toune þat tristy was holde. *c* **1350** *Will. Palerne* 1147 Boþe partiȝes prestly a-paraylde hem..Of alle tristy a-tir þat to batayle longed.

† **'tristy,** *a.*[2] *Obs.* Also 5 trysty. [f. TRIST *a.*[2] + -Y[1].] Sad, sorrowful; in quot. 14.., dark or dull-coloured (= SAD *a.* 8).

? *c* **1400** LYDG. *Æsop's Fab.* III. 88 The sheepe condempned, tristy and pale of hewe. **14..** *Epiph.* in *Tundale's Vis.* (1843) 114 Ne forred with armyn nor with trysty gray. ? *a* **1600** in Ashm. *Theat. Chem.* (1652) 264 The King was tristy and heavy of cheere.

tristylous: see TRI- 1 a.

tri'substituted, *a. Chem.* [TRI- 5 c.] Containing three substituted atoms or radicals. So **trisubsti'tution.**

1904 *Jrnl. Phys. Chem.* Apr. 298 Trisubstituted acids are less associated than disubstituted acids, and these latter less than monosubstituted acids. *Mod.* Trichloracetic acid is a trisubstitution product.

‖ **trisul** (trɪ'suːl), **trisula** (trɪ'suːlə). [Skr. *triçūla*, f. *tri-* three + **çūla* spit, spear-head.] A three-pointed figure or ornament, used as an emblem of the Hindu god Siva, and also as a Buddhist symbol.

1871 ALABASTER *Wheel of Law* 249 On the great toe is the Trisul. **1876** J. FERGUSSON *Hist. Indian Arch.* I. iv. 97 The trisul or trident emblem which crowns the gateways may.. represent Buddha himself. **1905** *Protestant Observer* Aug. 117/3 The trisul appears on a large medal of the Great Exhibition, 1851, with two fishes (Pisces) under Victoria and Albert.

† **'trisulc, 'trisulk,** *a.* (*sb.*) *Obs.* [ad. L. *trisulcus* three-cleft, f. *tri-*, TRI- + *sulcus* furrow. Cf. F. *trisulce* (*trisulque*, 16th c. in Godef. *Compl.*).] Three-cleft, three-forked, trifurcate: esp. as an epithet of the lightning or thunderbolt, after L. *trisulcum fulmen* (Varro), *Jovis telum trisulcum* (Ovid), etc.

1609 HEYWOOD *Rape Lucrece* I. ii, That hand That flings the trisulke thunder. **1611** —— *Gold. Age* v. i, Jupiter.. Who thunder and the trisulke lightning beares. **1650** BULWER *Anthropomet.* xiv. 142 The Tongue of man is not double, or trisulke, or bisulke, as in some creatures. **1653** URQUHART *Rabelais* II. xxxii, Jupiter confound me with his trisulk lightning if I lie! **1656** BLOUNT *Glossogr.*, *Trisulk* (*trisulcus*), having three edges, or three furrows. **1658** in PHILLIPS.

B. *ellipt.* as *sb.* A thunderbolt.

1637 HEYWOOD *Dial.* iv. Wks. 1874 VI. 160 Hand once againe thy Trisulk, and retire To Oeta, and there kindle't with new fire. **1638** SIR T. HERBERT *Trav.* (ed. 2) 239 They ..never..looke upon him, least the fulgor of his aspect might peradventure prove no lesse formidable than the Trisulk of Iupiter. **1646** SIR T. BROWNE *Pseud. Ep.* II. vi. 100 If we consider the threefold effect of Jupiters Trisulk, to burn, discusse and terebrate.

trisulcate (traɪ'sʌlkət), *a.* [f. as prec. + -ATE[2].]

1. = prec. adj.

1719 D'URFEY *Pills* III. 322 Him, that hurls the Bolt trisulcate. **1866** J. B. ROSE tr. *Ovid's Met.* 61 By whose right hand are hurled The flames trisulcate.

2. *a. Bot.* Marked with three furrows or grooves, three-furrowed.

1891 in *Cent. Dict.* **1900** in B. D. JACKSON *Gloss. Bot. Terms.*

b. *Zool.* Divided into three digits, as a foot; tridactylous. (Cf. BISULCATE.)

1891 in *Cent. Dict.*

So **tri'sulcated** *a. rare* = 2 a above.

1703 PETIVER in *Phil. Trans.* XXIII. 1428 The Fruit which is about the bigness of a midling Nut, smooth, blackish and trisulcated.

trisulph-, trisulpho- (traɪsʌlf, traɪsʌlfəʊ). *Chem.* [f. TRI- 5 + SULPH(URIC.] A formative of the names of carbon compounds containing three SO_2 groups, or three $SO_2.OH$ groups, and derivatives of the latter. (TRISULPHONE, and TRISULPHONIC, with TRISULPHONATE, now also express these meanings.)

1867 GRIESS in *Jrnl. Chem. Soc.* XX. 101 Trisulphodiphenylenic Acid..its composition may also be expressed in two different ways, viz. $C_{12}H_6.S_3H_4O_{11}$, or $C_{12}H_6.S_3H_6O_{12}$. **1875** WATTS *Dict. Chem.* VII. 1111 $N^vH^2(SO^3K)^3$ Trisulphammonate of potassium... $ON^v(SO^3K)^3$ Trisulphoxyazate of potassium.

trisulphate (traɪ'sʌlfət). *Chem.* [f. TRI- 5 + SULPHATE.] A compound formed from three molecules of sulphuric acid, H_2SO_4, by replacement of the hydrogen by a metal or radical, and thus containing three SO_4 groups; e.g. ***aluminium trisulphate***, $Al_2(SO_4)_3$; ***glyceryl and hydrogen trisulphate***, $(C_3H_5)'''H_3(SO_4)_3$.

1880 ROSCOE & SCHORLEMMER *Treat. Chem.* II. ii. 312 Antimony Trisulphate, $Sb_2(SO_4)_3$,..crystallizes..in long glistening silky needles.

trisulphide (traɪ'sʌlfaɪd). *Chem.* [f. TRI- 5 + SULPHIDE.] A compound of an element or radical with three atoms of sulphur; e.g. ***boron trisulphide***, B_2S_3; ***arsenic trisulphide***, As_2S_3; ***potassium trisulphide***, K_2S_3.

1866 ROSCOE *Elem. Chem.* xxiv. 207 Metallic antimony occurs native, but its chief ore is the trisulphide. **1888** MUIR & MORLEY *Watts' Dict. Chem.* I. 516 Bismuth Trisulphide, Bi_2S_3, occurs native as bismuth glance. **1905** *Jrnl. Chem. Soc.* LXXXVIII. II. 245 Golden-yellow leaflets of arsenic trisulphide are formed.

trisulphone (traɪ'sʌlfəʊn). *Chem.* [f. TRI- 5 + SULPHONE.] A compound in which carbon radicals are linked to other carbon radicals by the intervention of three SO_2 groups, the sulphur atoms being directly joined to the carbon atoms; e.g. ***triethylsulphonemethylmethane***, $C(CH_3)(SO_2.C_2H_5)_3$; ***trisulphone acetone***, $(CH_3)_2C:\{SO_2-C(CH_3)_2\}_2:SO_2$. So **trisulphonic** (traɪsʌl'fɒnɪk) *a.*, in ***trisulphonic acid, amide, chloride***, etc., compounds of three $SO_2.OH$, $SO_2.NH_2$, $SO_2.Cl$, etc., groups with a trivalent element or radical, the sulphur being directly joined to the element or carbon of the radical; e.g. ***amine-trisulphonic acid***, $N(SO_2.OH)_3$; ***benzene-trisulphonic acid***, $C_6H_3(SO_2.OH)_3$; ***benzene-trisulphonic chloride***, $C_6H_3(SO_2Cl)_3$; **tri'sulphonate**, a salt of trisulphonic acid.

1874 SCHORLEMMER *Carbon Comp.* 199 A series of sulphonic acids..substitution products of marsh gas,..the third is methenyltrisulphonic acid, $CH(SO_3H)_3$. **1879** WATTS *Dict. Chem.* VIII. I. 259 Benzenetrisulphonic acid, $C^6H^3(SO^3H)^3 + 3H^2O$, crystallises in long flat deliquescent needles. **1886** *Jrnl. Chem. Soc.* L. 623 Benzenetrisulphonic chloride melts at 184°; the amide melts at 306°. **1892** *Ibid.* LXII. 614 Attempts to prepare a tetrasulphone by the action of sodium on haloid trisulphones and of phenylthiochloride on trisulphonates [gave] negative results.

trisyllabic (traɪ-, trɪsɪ'læbɪk), *a. erron.* triss-. [a. F. *trissyllabique* (16th c. in Godef. *Compl.*), f. L. *trisyllab-us*, a. Gr. τρισύλλαβος of three syllables, f. τρι- three + συλλαβή syllable: see -IC. For spelling cf. note s.v. DISYLLABIC.] Consisting of or involving three syllables. So **trisy'llabical** *a.* in same sense; **trisy'llabically** *adv.*, as or in three syllables; **tri'syllabism**, trisyllabic character; **tri'syllabize** *v.*, *trans.* to make trisyllabic.

a **1637** B. JONSON *Eng. Gram.* I. vii, All nouns *trisyllabic [are accented] in the first [syllable]. **1861** PALEY *Æschylus* (ed. 2) *Persians* 467 *note*, Trisyllabic form of the more Attic ᾄσσω. **1882** F. T. PALGRAVE in *Spenser's Wks.* (Grosart) IV. p. xxx, In some the..trissyllabic rhyme is used. **1656** BLOUNT *Glossogr.*, **Trisyllabical* (*trisyllabicus*), that hath three syllables. **1658** in PHILLIPS. **1801** CHENEVIX in *Phil. Trans.* XCI. 195 *note*, In trisyllabical nouns, the first or second syllable is usually accented. **1858** DE QUINCEY *Mrq. Wellesley* Wks. 1858 VIII. 20 *note*, The *Annesley* family..do not pronounce their name *trisyllabically..viz., Ann-es-ley, but as if *Anns* (in the possessive case) *-ley*. **1884** E. EINENKEL *St. Kath.* p. xxxii, The older forms..are not very remote from genuine *trisyllabism. **1866** *Pall Mall G.* 12 Apr. 9 The Marquis finds it convenient to *trisyllabize that plebeian appellation.

trisyllable (traɪ-, trɪ'sɪləb(ə)l), *sb.* (*a.*) *erron.* 7 tress-, 6- triss-. [f. TRI- + SYLLABLE: cf. Gr. τρισύλλαβος of three syllables, F. *trissyllabe* (16th c. in Godef. *Compl.*), Sp. *trisilabo*.] A word, or a metrical foot, of three syllables. In quot. 1718, trisyllabic or 'triple' rime (*nonce-use*).

1589 PUTTENHAM *Eng. Poesie* II. iii. (Arb.) 82 To euery bissillable they allowed two times, and to a trissillable three times, and to euery polisillable more, according to his quantitie. **1630** J. TAYLOR (Water P.) *Cast over Water* Wks. II. 158 When a tressillable a verse doth end, 'Tis harsh, 'tis paltry, and it doth offend. **1718** SWIFT *To Sheridan* 31 But now I find my Muse but ill able, To hold out longer in Trissyllable. *a* **1771** GRAY *Corr.* etc. (1843) 303 As to trissyllables, as their accent is very rarely on the last, they cannot properly be any rhymes at all. **1875** POSTE *Gaius* Pref. (ed. 2) 6 The word 'Gaius' is a trisyllable in the classical period. **1887** COOK *Sievers' O.E. Gram.* 133 [They] sometimes take *u* after the manner of the trisyllables.

B. as *adj.* = TRISYLLABIC. (In quot. 1817[1], having trisyllabic or 'triple' rimes.)

1766 BP. LOWTH *Larger Confut. Bp. Hare* 36 [Bentley] gives examples of trisyllable feet, namely, Bacchiac and Cretic feet, in English Verse. **1817** COLERIDGE *Biog. Lit.* 31 An innocent amusement from the riddles, conundrums, trisyllable lines, &c., &c., of Swift. *Ibid.* 178 Double and trisyllable rhymes, indeed, form a lower species of wit.

trit-: see TRITO-.

tritactic: see TRI- 2.

tritagonist (traɪ'tægənɪst). [ad. Gr. τριταγωνιστής an actor who plays the third part, f. τρίτος third + ἀγωνιστής combatant, actor.] The third actor in a Greek tragedy.

1890 *Athenæum* 28 June 841/3 Creon, although said to be the tritagonist, entered by the central door. **1907** A. E. HAIGH *Attic Theatre* 283 The tritagonist took what in modern times would be called the 'heavy' parts.

tritanopia (traɪtə'nəʊpɪə). *Ophthalm.* [mod.L., ad. G. *tritanopie* (J. von Kries 1911, in *Helmholtz's Handbuch der Physiol. Optik* (ed. 3) II. 341), f. *trit-*, var. TRITO- + AN- 10 + -OPIA.] A form of dichromatic colour-blindness marked by reduced sensitivity and discrimination in the blue and green parts of the spectrum. Hence **'tritanope**, one who has tritanopia; **trita'nopic** *a.*

1915 J. H. PARSONS *Introd. Study Colour Vision* II. i. 159, I shall adopt his [*sc.* v. Kries's] terms, viz., protanopes, blue and green parts of the spectrum. Hence **'tritanope**, one who has tritanopia; **trita'nopic** *a.*

1915 J. H. PARSONS *Introd. Study Colour Vision* II. i. 159, I shall adopt his [*sc.* v. Kries's] terms, viz., protanopes, deuteranopes, and tritanopes, corresponding respectively with v. Helmholtz' red-, green-, and blue-blind. *Ibid.* ii. 180 Cases of tritanopia or so-called blue-blindness are rare and mostly due to disease. *Ibid.* 304/1 (Index), Tritanopic vision. **1937** [see DEUTERANOPE]. **1955** *Jrnl. Optical Soc. Amer.* XLV. 614/1 The tritanopic luminosity function.. does not indicate any major shift in excitation peaks of the receptor substances. **1959** [see DICHROMAT, DICHROMATE *sb.*[2]]. **1965** *New Scientist* 14 Oct. 134/3 Tritanopic defects are described as autosomal dominant while tritanomaly is considered to be more or less recessive sex-linked. **1974** *Jrnl. Optical Soc. Amer.* LXIV. 1246/1 The tritanope's targets were formed of checks of pale violet and yellow-green and were compared to a blank field of violet. **1978** *Nature* 23 Nov. 390/1 When the eye has been adapted to a bright yellow light, a marked loss of sensitivity to short-wavelength stimuli may be recorded immediately after the extinction of the adapting field. This phenomenon.. was termed transient tritanopia by Mollon and Polden.

tritaph ('traɪtɑːf, -æ-). *Archæol.* [f. Gr. τρι-, TRI- + τάφος tomb: cf. *cenotaph.*] A group of three cists or chambers in a prehistoric tomb.

1904 WINDLE *Rem. Preh. Age Eng.* viii. 181 This circle.. consists of six symmetrically arranged sets of cysts, each a tritaph, i.e. two tangential and one radial.

† **'tritarchy.** *Obs. rare.* [f. Gr. τρίτ-ος third + -αρχία government.] Rule or government by three persons: irregularly used for TRIARCHY 2.

1647 M. HUDSON *Div. Right Govt.* II. iv. 96 Intestine and bloody dissentions.. created by the Tritarchie of Simon, Iohn, and Eleazer.

tritcherie, obs. form of TREACHERY.

‖ **trite** ('trɪtiː), *sb. Anc. Gr. Mus.* [a. Gr. τρίτη, fem. of τρίτος third (sc. χορδή string).] Name of the third string or note (counting from the highest) in each of the higher tetrachords.

1603 HOLLAND *Plutarch* Explan. Words, *Trite Diezeugmenon*, The third of disjuncts, a string or note in the scale of musicke C *sol fa ut. Trite Hyperbolæon*, A treble string; the third of Exceeding or treble; F *fa ut. Trite Synemmenon*, or *Syzeugmenon*, The third of the Conjuncts, a string or note in musicke, B *fa*, B *mi* in rule. **1776** BURNEY *Hist. Mus.* (1789) I. i. 16 *Trite*, the third string from the top of the two last tetrachords. **1801** in BUSBY *Dict. Mus.*

trite (traɪt), *a.* [ad. L. *trītus*, pa. pple. of *terĕre* to rub.]

1. Worn out by constant use or repetition; devoid of freshness or novelty; hackneyed, commonplace, stale.

a **1548** HALL *Chron., Hen. V* 40 b, Accordyng to the trite adage: He must liberally spende that will plentefully gayne. **1607** *Puritan* III. v. 162, I would not haue my Arte vulgar, trite, and common. **1654** WHITLOCK *Zootomia* 384 A Saying not triter than truer. **1762–71** H. WALPOLE *Vertue's Anecd. Paint.* (1786) V. 133 It is a trite observation, that gunpowder was discovered by a monk. **1818** SCOTT *Br. Lamm.* xviii, An art of building up a character for wisdom upon a very trite style of commonplace eloquence. **1837–9** HALLAM *Hist. Lit.* (1855) I. I. vii. §32. 407 The story told by Erasmus of Colet is also a little too trite for repetition. **1885** *Athenæum* 28 Mar. 401 The theme of Death can no more wear trite than the theme of Love.

2. Well worn; worn out by rubbing; frayed; of a road or path, well-trod, beaten, frequented.

1599 B. JONSON *Cynthia's Rev.* I. iii, If my behaviours had beene of a cheape or customary garbe; my accent, or phrases, vulgar; my garments trite. **1656** BLOUNT *Glossogr.*, *Trite*, worne, over-worne, old, threedbare, much used, common. **1682** SIR T. BROWNE *Chr. Mor.* I. §25 Unexpected Emergences, whereby we pass not our days in the trite road of affairs affording no Novity. **1855** *Fraser's Mag.* LI. 272 Specimens of the bronze coinage of the later empire;.. mostly trite and faceless. **1861** G. F. BERKELEY *Sportsm. W. Prairies* vii. 98 The woods were.. unbroken save by the straight trite line of hasty locomotion.

tritely ('traɪtlɪ), *adv.* [f. prec. + -LY[2].] In a trite or commonplace manner.

1691 WOOD *Ath. Oxon.* (L.), Other things are mentioned by Baleus and Pitseus very tritely, and with little satisfaction to the reader. **1870** *Pall Mall G.* 5 Dec. 10 Keeping order among the band—'order', as he tritely observed, 'being necessary everywhere'.

tritencephalon: see TRITO-.

triteness ('traɪtnɪs). [f. TRITE *a.* + -NESS.] The quality of being trite; commonplaceness.

1727 BAILEY vol. II, *Triteness*, wornness, the being much worn. **1755** JOHNSON, *Triteness*, staleness; commonness. **1780** *Mirror* No. 80 There is one class of writers to whom the charge of triteness does.. very little apply. **1791–1823** D'ISRAELI *Cur. Lit.* (1858) III. 63 *note*, Triteness and triviality are fatal to a proverb. **1910** *Scott. Hist. Rev.* Oct. 17 Telling his story with the triteness and circumspection of a lawyer.

triternate (traɪ'tɜːnət), *a. Bot.* [f. TRI- 2 + TERNATE *a.*] Thrice ternate: see quots. (Abbrev. *3-ternate.*) Hence **tri'ternately** *adv.*

1760 J. LEE *Introd. Bot.* III. vi. (1788) 202 Triternate, or Triplicato-Ternate; when a Petiole bears three Folioles that are each of them ternate. **1835** LINDLEY *Introd. Bot.* (1848) II. 360 *Triternate*, when the common petiole divides into three secondary petioles, which are each subdivided into three tertiary petioles, each of which bears three leaflets. **1856** A. GRAY *Man. Bot.* (1860) 20 A large triternately compound leaf. **1870** HOOKER *Stud. Flora* 168 Peucedanum officinale; leaves 3-ternately pinnate.

triterpane, -pene, -penoid: see TRI- 5 a.

tritheism ('traɪθiːɪz(ə)m). [f. TRI- + THEISM; cf. Gr. τριθεΐα (f. τρι-, TRI- + θεός God), F. *trithéisme* (1727 in Littré).] Belief in three Gods; *esp.* an interpretation of the doctrine of the Trinity according to which the three Persons are three distinct Gods. (Cf. next.)

1678 CUDWORTH *Intell. Syst.* I. iv. 604 This Trinity is no other than a kind of Tritheism, and that of gods independent and co-ordinate too. **1719** WATERLAND *Vind. Christ's Div.* Contents, This Assertion,.. that there is no Medium between Tritheism and Sabellianism. **1855** MACAULAY *Hist. Eng.* xvii. IV. 51 In his zeal against Socinians and Sabellians, he [Sherlock] used expressions which might be construed into Tritheism. **1910** SANDAY *Christologies* i. 12 The doctrine of the Trinity is not Tritheism.

tritheist ('traɪθiːɪst). [f. TRI- + THEIST; cf. F. *trithéiste* (Littré).] A believer in three Gods; *esp.* one who holds that the three Persons of the Trinity are three distinct Gods.

Chiefly in controversial use; applied *spec.* to a sect of Monophysites in the sixth century who denied the consubstantiality of the three Persons of the Trinity.

1608 WILLET *Hexapla Exod.* 323 They which hold not the distinction of three persons onely, but the diuision also of the substance, as the Tritheists. **1715** *Wodrow Corr.* (1843) II. 17 Roell is not thought Arian or Socinian in the great point of the Deity of Christ, but rather a Tritheist. **1850** ROBERTSON *Serm.* Ser. III. iv. (1872) 45 There are in almost every congregation.. Trinitarians who are practically Tritheists, worshipping three gods. **1903** H. L. GOUDGE *1 Cor.* Introd. 30 S. Paul certainly is no Tritheist; the Son and the Spirit never obscure the Father for a moment.

Hence **trithe'istic, trithe'istical** *adjs.*, of, pertaining to, or believing tritheism.

1698 SOUTH *Serm.* III. Ded. A iv b, Reprinting exploded Tritheistick Notions. **1708** H. DODWELL *Nat. Mort. Hum. Souls* 44 Our Adversaries will appear to be the Tritheistical Gobarus's, as to this Particular of the Heresies then condemned in the Tritheists. **1822** JEFFERSON *Writ.* (1830) IV. 354 Missionaries.. from the tritheistic school of Andover. **1827** ARNOLD in *Life & Corr.* (1844) I. ii. 50 The tritheistic notions of the Trinity.

tritheite ('traɪθiaɪt). Also 6–8 -it. [ad. Gr. τριθεΐτης, late L. *tritheīta* (Isidore), f. τρι- three + θεός god; cf. F. *trithéite.*] = TRITHEIST.

1585–7 T. ROGERS *39 Art.* v. (1633) 24 The Tritheites; which affirme the holy Ghost to be inferiour vnto the Father. **1597** HOOKER *Eccl. Pol.* v. xlii. §13 The blasphemies of Arrians, Samosatenians, Tritheits, Eutychians, and Macedonians. **1691** W. NICHOLLS *Answ. Naked Gospel* 98 Gregorius Paulus,.. was first a Tritheite, and afterwards an Unitarian. **1725** tr. *Dupin's Eccl. Hist. 17th C.* I. VI. v. 252 He [Servetus] crudely affirms, that they who distinguish three Persons in the Godhead, are Tritheites who admit of three Gods.

attrib. **1708** H. DODWELL *Nat. Mort. Hum. Souls* 42 The Author of the Tritheit Heresy, Johannes Philoponus. **1887** C. J. BALL in *Dict. Chr. Biog.* IV. 319/1 An approach to the Tritheite standpoint.

tritheocracy (traɪθiː'ɒkrəsɪ). *nonce-wd.* [f. TRI- + THEOCRACY.] Rule or government by three Gods; a group of three Divine beings exercising joint rule.

1850 BUSHNELL *God in Christ* 115 Father, Son and Holy Ghost are, in their view, socially united only and preside.. as a kind of celestial tritheocracy over the world.

trithing ('traɪðɪŋ), **thrithing** ('θraɪðɪŋ). Forms: 3 triting, 3–4, 8–9 trithing, 7 -e, 8 triding; 4 thrythyng, 7–8 thrithing: see also RIDING *sb.* [Late OE. **þriðing*, **þriding*, ad. ON. *þriðjung-r* 'thirding', third part. The form *thrithing* was still known to the 17th c. legal writers; but *trithing* is also found in early times, and in modern legal and historical works. The form **þriding* or **thriding* lost its initial after *east*, *west*, and *north*, as in 13th c. *Northredyng*, later *North Riding.*]

1. = RIDING *sb.* Now only *Hist.* Also in *comb.* **trithing-reeve** = *trithinger*: see below.

[*a* **1150** *Law Edw. Conf.* c. 31 Erant etiam alie potestates super wapentagiis, quas trehingas uocabant, scilicet super terciam partem prouincie. Et qui super ipsam dominabantur, uocabantur þrehinggrefes [*v.r.* trehingreues], ad quos deferebantur cause que non poterant diffiniri in wapentagiis.] *c* **1290** FLETA II. lxi. §23 Sciendum [est] quod aliæ potestates erant super wapentakia, quæ tritinga dicebantur, eo quod erat tertia pars provinciæ; qui vero super eos dominabantur, trithingreves vocabantur, quibus differebantur causæ quæ non wapentakiis poterint diffiniri in Schiram. **1295–6** Trithing [see RIDING *sb.* 1]. **1313–14** *Eyre of Kent* (1910) I. 32 De wapentagiis & Trithingis positis ad firmam. **1333** *York Memo. Bk.* (Surtees) I. 144 Artificiariorum in tribus trithingis infra comitatum Ebor. **1593** NORDEN *Spec. Brit., M'sex* I. 7 Yorkeshire.. is diuided into Rydings, which may be also called ðriþings, all which parts conteine in them certain hundreds in euerie of which was conteined ten teoþunges, of us called Tithings, conteining ten men, whereof it was also called tienmentale, a colledge or corporation of ten men. **1701** *Cowell's Interpr., Thrithing-Reve*, the third part of a County, or three or more Hundreds or Wapentachs, were called a *Triding* or *Trithing*; such sort of Portions are the Laths in Kent, the Rapes in Sussex, and the Ridings in Yorkshire. And those who govern'd these Trithings, were thereupon called *Trithing-Reves*, before whom were brought all Causes that could not be determined in the Wapentakes, or Hundreds. **1747** CARTE *Hist. Eng.* I. 309 Some mention another subdivision of counties into three portions called thence *trithings* (corruptly ridings). **1765** BLACKSTONE *Comm.* I. Introd. iv. 116 Where a county is divided into three of these intermediate jurisdictions, they are called trithings, which were antiently governed by a trithing-reeve. **1874** STUBBS *Const. Hist.* I. v. 100 *note*, In the trithing he sees the threefold division of the land allotted to the Norse odallers.

2. Division into three parts, tripartition. *rare*[−1].

1879 HAIGH in *Yorks. Arch. Jrnl.* V. 205 The distinct trithing of two of the divisions [in a dial] is evidence of knowledge of the complete Hindu system.

Hence † **'trithinger, 'thrithinger**, the governor of a trithing.

1314–15 *Rolls of Parlt.* I. 291/2 Viscountes, Thrythyngers, & autres Baillifs [de Counte de Nicole].

trithio- (traɪθaɪəʊ). *Chem.* [f. TRI- 5 + THIO-.] Prefix denoting that three atoms of sulphur have been substituted for three atoms of oxygen in the substance designated by the rest of the name; e.g. ***trithiocarbonic acid***, H_2CS_3, derived from carbonic acid, H_2CO_3; ***trithiocarbonate***, a salt of this acid. In many cases, however, *tri-* refers to the whole substance and not to the sulphur alone; e.g. ***trithio-acetaldehyde***, $(CH_3CHS)_3$, a compound of three molecules of thio-acetaldehyde, CH_3CHS.

1894 MUIR & MORLEY *Watts' Dict. Chem.* IV. 692 Tri-Thio-Citric Ether $C_3H_5O(CO.SEt)_3$.. Oil, smelling like mercaptan. **1899** SMITH *Richter's Org. Chem.* (ed. 3) I. 203 Trithio-formaldehyde $(CH_2S)_3$, melts at 216°. **1910** WALKER & MOTT *Holleman's Org. Chem.* (ed. 3) 348 Carbon disulphide.. With alkali-metal or alkaline-earth-metal sulphides it yields trithiocarbonates.

trithionic (traɪθaɪ'ɒnɪk), *a. Chem.* [f. TRI- 5 + Gr. θεῖον sulphur + -IC.] In ***trithionic acid***, $H_2S_3O_6$, an acid containing three atoms of sulphur in the molecule, discovered by Langlois in 1842 (*Ann. Chim. Phys.* IV. 77), known only in aqueous solution, which is inodorous, sour, and bitter, and in its salts, the **tri'thionates.**

1844 *Chem. Gaz.* II. 66 Berzelius.. separates the acids of sulphur into monothionic acids (sulphuric and sulphurous acids), dithionic acids.. trithionic acid (Langlois' sulphated hyposulphuric acid). **1848** *Ibid.* VI. 369 Trithionic Acid is obtained dissolved in water when the solution of the trithionate of potash is decomposed with the fluosilicate of potash. **1913** THORPE *Dict. Appl. Chem.* (ed. 2) V. 308 Trithionic acid.. on attempting to concentrate [the solution], even *in vacuo*, it decomposes into sulphur, sulphur dioxide, and sulphuric acid.

tritiated ('trɪtɪeɪtɪd, -ʃɪeɪtɪd), *a. Chem.* [f. TRITI(UM + -ATE[3] + -ED[2].] Containing tritium; having had an atom of ordinary hydrogen replaced by tritium. So **triti'ation**, the introduction of tritium into a compound or molecule in place of ordinary hydrogen.

[**1947** M. D. KAMEN *Radioactive Tracers in Biol.* vi. 127 A few drops of triterated water may be recovered.] **1956** *Nature* 25 Feb. 379/2 Analyses for tritium were carried out by combustion of the organic compound and conversion of the tritiated water to tritium. **1961** G. R. CHOPPIN *Exper. Nuclear Chem.* xi. 180 The Wilzbach method of tritiation involves the exposure of the unlabeled compound to a multicurie atmosphere of tritium gas for periods of time as long as two weeks. **1978** *Bull. Amer. Acad. Arts & Sci.* Feb. 11 He further developed novel methods for the accurate determination of tritiated compounds in tissues.

tritical ('trɪtɪkəl), *a.* [f. TRITE *a.*, with play on *critical.*] Of a trite or commonplace character.

1709 SWIFT (*title*) A Tritical Essay upon the faculties of the mind. **1762** [see TRITICALLY]. **1841** D'ISRAELI *Amen. Lit.* (1867) 285 To sermonise with a tedious homily or a tritical declamation. **1869** *Contemp. Rev.* X. 125 To have every book of the Bible dealt with.. with the same tendency to 'tritical' reflections.

Hence **triti'cality, 'tritically** *adv.*, **'tritical-ness**; so **'triticism** (after *criticism*; cf. also *witticism*).

1835 CARLYLE in *Corr. Carlyle & Emerson* 13 May (1883) I. 71 Our Ex-Chancellor has been promulgating *triticalities.. against the Aristocracy. **1762** STERNE *Tr. Shandy* VI. xi, 'Tis all tritical, and most *tritically put together. *c* **1714** POPE, etc. *Mem. M. Scriblerus* vii, A *Triticalness or Mediocrity in the Thought. **1824** SCOTT *Redgauntlet* Let. xii, Weary, flat, and stale *triticism.

triticale (trɪtɪ'keɪliː). Also Triticale. [f. mod.L. generic names *Tritic(um* wheat + *Se)cale* rye.] A hybrid cereal grass, of the genus × *Triticosecale*, produced by crossing various species or varieties of wheat and rye.

1952 *New Biol.* XIII. 44 A cross between wheat and rye.. is known as Triticale. **1968** *New Scientist* 24 Oct. 181/2 (*caption*) Triticale, a hybrid of wheat and rye developed at the University of Manitoba. **1974** A. J. HUXLEY *Plant & Planet* xxvii. 309 New races of the great seed plants.. have been created in the last few years, including a promising wheat/rye hybrid called triticale. **1979** *McGraw-Hill Yearbk. Sci. & Technol.* 414/1 Although triticale plants were first described in 1876, only in the mid-1960s did they begin to receive great interest from scientists and farmers. **1983** *New Scientist* 13 Jan. 98/1 From a slow start in the 1950s.. triticale is now growing on more than half a million hectares, in the USSR, Europe, the United States and South America.

†**tri'ticean**, *a. Obs. rare*$^{-0}$. [f. L. *trītice-us* wheaten (f. *trīticum* wheat) + -AN.] (See quot.)
1656 BLOUNT *Glossogr.*, *Triticean* (*triticeus*), wheaten, of wheat. 1658 in PHILLIPS.

triticeous (trɪ'tɪʃəs, -iːəs), *a.* [f. as prec. + -OUS.] Resembling a grain of wheat. ***triticeous cartilage*** or ***nodule*** (mod.L. *cartilago triticea*), *Anat.*, each of two small cartilaginous nodules one on each side of the larynx.
[1890 BILLINGS *Med. Dict.* s.v. *Cartilago*, *C[artilago] triticea*, a small cartilaginous nodule found in lateral thyrohyoid ligament on each side.] 1891 *Cent. Dict.* s.v., Triticeous nodule. *Ibid.*, *Triticeus*, the triticeous cartilage of the larynx.

triticin ('trɪtɪsɪn). *Chem.* [f. L. *trītic-um* wheat (in mod.Bot.L. a generic name, including couch-grass) + -IN[1].]
†**1.** Name given to the gluten of wheat by Hermbstaedt (*Erdmann's Jrnl. Techn. Chem.* (1831) XII. 11); also applied to a substance obtained from potato starch (see quot. 1838). *Obs.*
1838 T. THOMSON *Chem. Org. Bodies* 652 [In preparing amidin, or the soluble part of starch from potato starch] The triticin is retained by the cloth. 1860 MAYNE *Expos. L.*, *Triticin*, term by Hermbstædt for the gluten of wheat.
2. A carbohydrate, $C_{12}H_{22}O_{11}$ or $(C_6H_{10}O_5)_n$, obtained from the roots of couch-grass, *Triticum repens*, and so named by Müller (*Arch. Pharm.* (1873) II. 508); it is a tasteless hygroscopic powder, very soluble in water, and lævorotatory; when boiled with dilute acids it changes into lævulose.
1874 *Jrnl. Chem. Soc.* XXVII. 171 The quantity of triticin present in the dried roots of couch-grass varies from 3·5 to 7·8 per cent. 1888 *Ibid.* LIV. 246 From *Dracaena australis* the author has obtained a carbohydrate, 6 $C_6H_{10}O_5+H_2O$, which very closely resembles triticin. 1890 *Ibid.* LVIII. 227 Triticin..from the root of *Dracaena rubra*, melts at 140°... Triticin, from *Triticum repens*, melts at 160°.

triticoid ('trɪtɪkɔɪd), *a. Bot.* [f. as prec. + -OID.] Resembling the wheat-plant.
1858 *Jrnl. R. Agric. Soc.* XIX. I. 103 Henslow has also found a triticoid form of *Ægilops squarrosa*.

tritish ('traɪtɪʃ), *a.* Also **triteish**. [f. TRITE *a.* + -ISH[1].] Somewhat trite. So **tritism** ('traɪtɪz(ə)m), trite or commonplace character.
1779 T. TWINING in *Recreat. & Stud.* (1882) 60 The notes ..seem now and then to be tritish. 1785 *Rolliad* (1812) 137 A solid truth in the observation of Horace which its tritism does not destroy. 1980 *Times* 5 June 11/3 A good, if triteish, situation.

tritium ('trɪtɪəm). *Chem.* [mod.L., f. Gr. τρίτ-ος third + -IUM.] **1.** A radioactive heavy isotope of hydrogen, having two neutrons as well as a proton in the nucleus, which constitutes one part in 10^{18} of the naturally occurring element and is produced for use in fusion reactors and as an isotopic label. Symbols ^{3}H (H^3), T. Cf. DEUTERIUM, PROTIUM.
1933 UREY & MURPHY in *Jrnl. Chem. Physics* I. 513/2 If the H^3 isotope is discovered, we would recommend to the discoverer the consideration of the name tritium for it. 1959 *Sci. News* LI. 12, ^{3}He is obtained from the decay of tritium which in turn is the product of nuclear reactions involving neutrons from a reactor. 1962 [see SUPERHEAVY *a.* b]. 1972 *Sci. Amer.* Oct. 104/3 Large amounts of tritium (hydrogen 3)..are stockpiled for nuclear weapons and for research in fusion power. 1976 *Nature* 9 Sept. 103/1 Tritium ($t_{\frac{1}{2}}$ = 12·3 yr) is present on the Earth's surface mainly as HTO.
2. *attrib.* and *Comb.*
1934 *Sun* (Baltimore) 6 Oct. 20/6 Tritium water could be formed by the addition of two more atoms of hydrogen to the heavy water. 1953 J. BLISH in E. Crispin *Best SF* (1955) 345 The U.N.'s police would be glad to know that they could have access to a virtually inexhaustible stock of tritium bombs. 1966 *McGraw-Hill Encycl. Sci. & Technol.* XIV. 113/1 Tritium oxide, T_2O, has been prepared by oxidation of tritium gas with hot copper oxide. *Ibid.* 113/2 Tritium-labeled compounds may be prepared by ordinary synthetic chemical methods. 1979 *McGraw-Hill Yearbk. Sci. & Technol.* 153/2 Tritium-helium dating will eventually prove very useful in studying those physical processes which transport or redistribute substances in oceans.

trito- (trɪtəʊ, traɪtəʊ), before a vowel **trit-**, combining form repr. Gr. τρίτος third, occurring in several technical, mostly scientific, terms (usually corresponding to terms in PROTO-, and DEUTERO- or DEUTO-).
1. Generally.
trita'nomaly *Ophthalm.* [ANOMALY], a rare form of anomalous trichromatism marked by a reduced sensitivity to blue; hence **trita'nomalous** *a.*, having tritanomaly. ‖**tritencephalon** (-ɛn'sɛfəlɒn) [mod.L., f. Gr. ἐγκέφαλος brain], the third of the three primary cerebral vesicles of the embryo; also, the hindmost segment of the brain of an insect. **'tritocere** (-sɪə(r)) [Gr. κέρας horn], that tine of a deer's antler which is third in order of development (*Cent. Dict.* 1891). ‖**tritocerebrum** (-'sɛrɪbrəm), *erron.* -on [mod.L., f. L. *cerebrum* brain], = *tritencephalon*; hence **trito'cerebral** *a.*, pertaining to or constituting a tritocerebrum. **'tritocone**, the posterior external cusp of a premolar tooth. **'trito-I'saiah** [after DEUTERO-*Isaiah*], a later author to whom a third section of the book of Isaiah is attributed by some critics. **trito'mesal** *a.* [Gr. μέσος middle], applied to a series of cells in the wings of hymenopterous insects, now usually called the submedian second discoidal and first apical cells. **trito'toxin**: see quot. 1904 s.v. *prototoxin* (PROTO- 2 b). **trito'vertebra**, in Carus's nomenclature (1828), applied to the bones of the limbs reckoned as the third set of vertebræ; hence **trito'vertebral** *a.*, pertaining to or of the nature of a tritovertebra. **tri'tovum**, a third stage of an ovum, succeeding the deutovum. **tritozooid** (-'zəʊɔɪd), a tertiary zooid, produced from a deuterozooid.
1943 *Jrnl. Optical Soc. Amer.* XXXIII. 572/1 These [subjects] are diagnosed by most other tests as *tritanomalous or blue-yellow blind. *Ibid.* 574/2 These plates are invalid for the detection of tritanomaly. 1946 W. D. WRIGHT *Res. on Normal & Defective Colour Vision* xxiv. 297 The tritanomalous observer has poor hue discrimination in the blue-green wavelengths. 1956 *Jrnl. Optical Soc. Amer.* XLVI. 1075/1 *Tritanomaly, discovered by Engelking, seems to be very rare. 1965 Tritanomaly [see TRITANOPIA]. 1910 *Encycl. Brit.* XIII. 425/2 This anterior or 'brain' mass consists of three lobes (the prot-, deut-, and *tritencephalon of Viallanes). *Ibid.* 418/2 An 'intercalary' or *tritocerebral segment has been demonstrated..in various insect embryos. 1898 PACKARD *Text-bk. Entom.* 231 Viallanes first..divided the brain of adult insects into three regions or segments; i.e. the 'protocerebron', 'deutocerebron', and '*tritocerebron'. *Ibid.* 237 The œsophageal lobes (Tritocerebrum). 1896 *Proc. Zool. Soc.* 5 May 563 (*Premolars*) The antero-external cusp (protocone of Scott)..develops first, the antero-internal or deuterocone second, and the tetartocone third, the *tritocone being wanting. 1908 *Athenæum* 7 Nov. 565/2 A *Trito-Isaiah besides a Deutero-Isaiah. 1826 KIRBY & SP. *Entomol.* III. xxxv. 632 The medial areolets..form three distinct series; these may be called the protomesal, deuteromesal, and *tritomesal. *c* 1860 S. KNEELAND, JR. in *Amer. Cycl.* XIII. 424 (Cent. Dict.) [Carus] makes what he calls proto-, deuto-, and *trito-vertebræ. 1902 *Cassell's Encycl. Dict.*, *Supp.*, *Tritovertebral. 1877 HUXLEY *Anat. Inv. Anim.* vii. 385 In the Acarus of the Mouse, Claparède observed that the deutovum stage is followed by a *tritovum. 1861 J. R. GREENE *Man. Anim. Kingd.*, *Cœlent.* 74 The medusoids budded by *Sarsia* are, probably, *tritozoöids.
†**2.** In *Chemistry*, formerly used, after T. Thomson (*Syst. Chem.* (1804) I. 103), in naming the third oxide, sulphuret, iodide, etc. in a series in ascending order (cf. PROTO- 3 a, DEUTO- 1). *Obs.*
1806-1850 [see TRITOXIDE]. 1825 T. THOMSON *First Princ. Chem.* II. 481 Tritosulphuret of potassium.

‖**Tritoma** ('trɪtəmə, *incorrectly* traɪ'təʊmə). *Bot.* [mod.L. (J. B. Ker 1804, in *Curtis's Bot. Mag.* XX. 744), f. Gr. τρίτομος thrice-cut, f. τρι- three + -τομος cut; from the capsule splitting into three valves.] A genus of liliaceous plants (also called *Kniphofia*), natives of South Africa, with spikes of scarlet or yellow flowers; several species in cultivation are popularly called *flame-flower* or *red-hot poker*; KNIPHOFIA.
1804 *Curtis's Bot. Mag.* XX. 744 (*heading*) Glaucous-Leaved Tritoma. 1854 [see KNIPHOFIA]. 1871 J. C. PATTESON *Let.* 8 Mar. in C. M. Yonge *Life J.C. Patteson* (1874) II. xii. 514, I like both the red and the yellow tritoma. 1882 *Garden* 13 May 325/2 Tritomas..produce a grand effect in autumn. 1900 *Blackw. Mag.* Apr. 574/2 The tritomas, blazing up red-hot.

tritomite ('trɪtəmaɪt). *Min.* [ad. G. *tritomit* (P. H. Weibye 1850, in *Ann. d. Physik u. Chem.* LXXIX. 299), f. Gr. τρίτομος thrice-cut, in allusion to the shape of the cavities left by the crystals: see -ITE[1].] **a.** A borosilicate, fluoride, and hydroxide of cerium earths, calcium, and thorium found as brown trigonal crystals. **b.** *tritomite-Y*: an analogue of this in which yttrium largely replaces cerium.
1856 *Edin. New Philos. Jrnl.* III. 60 The tritomite here analysed was sent me by M. Wiborg of Brevig, labelled as thorite, which it also very closely resembled in appearance. 1962 *Amer. Mineralogist* XLVII. 9 Tritomite, a rare, metamict boro-silicate..is known only from the nepheline syenite pegmatites of Låven, Brevik, and Barkevik, in.. southern Norway. 1966 *Ibid.* LI. 156 The terms..spencite, [etc.]. should be dropped... Respectively, these minerals would be known as..tritomite-(Y), [etc.]... The Commission [on New Minerals and Mineral Names of the International Mineralogical Association] has approved this nomenclature.

Triton[1] ('traɪtɒn). Also 6–7 **tryton**. [a. L. *Trītōn*, Gr. Τρίτων, in sense 1.]
1. *Gr.* and *Rom. Myth.* Proper name of a sea-deity, son of Poseidon and Amphitrite, or of Neptune and Salacia, or otherwise of Nereus; also, one of a race of inferior sea-deities, or imaginary sea-monsters, of semi-human form.
1584 R. SCOT *Discov. Witchcr.* VII. xv. (1886) 122 They have so fraied us with bull beggers, spirits, witches,.. tritons, centaurs, dwarfes, giants, imps [etc.]. 1593 PEELE *Order of Garter* Wks. (Rtldg.) 585/2 A trump more shrill than Triton's is at sea. 1656 BLOUNT *Glossogr.*, *Triton*, a god of the sea, also a weathercock. 1661 J. CHILDREY *Brit. Baconica* 102 A Triton or Man-fish was taken on the shore of Portugal. *a* 1764 LLOYD *Chit-Chat* Poet. Wks. 1774 I. 193 Tritons which in the ocean dwell, And only rise to blow their shell. 1806 WORDSW. *Sonnet 'The world is too much with us'*, So might I..hear old Triton blow his wreathèd horn. 1887 BOWEN *Virg. Æneid* v. 824 Tritons swift on the deep with the hosts of Phorcus parade.
attrib. 1801 ELIZ. SCOT *Alonzo & Cora* 146 He prays the Triton-train To still the blustring winds, and smooth the main.
b. A figure of a Triton in painting, sculpture, etc.; in *Her.* represented as a bearded man with the hind quarters of a fish, and usually holding a trident and a shell-trumpet (cf. MERMAN).
1601 HOLLAND *Pliny* IX. v. I. 236 A certain sea goblin, called Triton, sounding a shell like a Trumpet or Cornet:.. in forme and shape like those that are commonly painted for Tritons. 1722 RICHARDSON *Statues, &c. Italy* 116 Upon the Decks of the Ships there are Tritons. 1849 CLOUGH *Amours de Voy.* III. ii, It looked at me there from the face of a Triton in marble.
c. *fig.* and *allusively*: esp. applied to a seaman, waterman, or person connected in some way with the sea; in quot. 1900 to a large ship. ***Triton of*** or ***among the minnows*** (and similar phrases): see MINNOW 1 b.
1589 NASHE *Anat. Absurd.* Epistle, My tongue is too to base a Tryton to eternise her praise. 1607 [see MINNOW 1 b]. 1638 SIR T. HERBERT *Trav.* (ed. 2) 12 Neptune sweld with rage in such impatience, that the Tritons (Marriners) grew agast. *a* 1704 T. BROWN *Walk round Lond.*, *Thames* Wks. 1709 III. III. 57 From their Lowzy Benches up started such a noizy multitude of old grizly Tritons. 1817 COLERIDGE *Lay Serm.* 387 The wretched ambition of figuring as the triton of the minnows. 1900 *Q. Rev.* Jan. 80 These vessels [Atlantic liners] are the Tritons of the Sea. 1908 *Nation* 26 Dec. 497/2 On his own side he is a Triton among the minnows.
2. *Zool.* **a.** A genus of marine gastropods with trumpet-shaped shells; an animal, or shell, of this genus or of the family *Tritonidæ*. Also called ***Triton's shell***.
1777 PENNANT *Zool.* IV. 61 Lepas. Acorn. Its animal the Triton. The shell multivalve. 1835 KIRBY *Hab. & Inst. Anim.* I. ix. 297 Others which live by prey, as the strombs, the helmet-shells, and the tritons. 1842 *Penny Cycl.* XXII. 53/2 *Triton variegatus*, the marine trumpet or Triton's shell. 1861 P. P. CARPENTER in *Rep. Smithsonian Instit.* 1860, 185 The *Personæ*, or Mask-shells, are Tritons with a broad thin inner lip and curiously twisted mouth.
b. An extensive genus (now divided) of newts; an animal of this genus or group.
1839 *Encycl. Brit.* (ed. 7) XIX. 160/2 Genus Triton, *Laur.* Aquatic salamanders... Commonly called newts... The crested triton... The spotted triton. 1861 HULME tr. *Moquin-Tandon* II. v. ii. 288 Triton, or Aquatic Salamander. 1909 *Contemp. Rev.* Apr. 446 The lost leg of a lizard, or the amputated leg of a triton, can be readily regenerated.
Hence (*nonce-wds.*) **'Tritoness**, a female Triton; **Tri'tonic** *a.*, of or pertaining to a Triton or Tritons; **'Tritonize** *v.*, *intr.* to play the Triton (see 1 c above); **'Tritonly** *adv.*, like or in the manner of a Triton.
1614 GORGES *Lucan* IX. 377 To her selfe the name she chose Of *Trytonesse. 1956 K. CLARK *Nude* vii. 271 A small tritoness,..recently emerged from the excavations in Ostia. 1836 *Foreign Q. Rev.* XVII. 161 To conjure up fairy scenes and *tritonic festivals. 1841 *Blackw. Mag.* XLIX. 486 There alone is that petty vanity of *tritonizing among the minnows properly rebuked. 1599 NASHE *Lenten Stuffe* Wks. (Grosart) V. 229 Mercuriall..hath..noysed the name of our Ilande and of Yarmouth so *Tritonly. 1888 G. MEREDITH *Hard Weather* 16 Is the land ship? we are rolled, we drive Tritonly.

triton[2] ('traɪtɒn). *Physics.* [f. TRIT(IUM + -ON[1].] A sub-atomic particle composed of one proton and two neutrons, the nucleus of the tritium atom.
1942 *Physical Rev.* LXII. 115/1 The nucleus Li^7 is pictured on the alpha-particle model as built up from an alpha-particle group and a triton (H^3) group. 1965 *Wireless World* Sept. 446/2 Semiconductor devices can be employed for counting other types of ionizing particles such as protons, deuterons, tritons, fission fragments, etc. 1976 *Nature* 29 Apr. 749/3 There have been rather few studies of the interactions of tritons with nuclei, mainly because tritons are highly radioactive, with a half-life of about 12 years.

tritonality (traɪtəʊ'nælɪtɪ). *Mus.* [f. TRI- + TONALITY.] The simultaneous use of three keys in a musical composition. Hence **tri'tonal** *a.*
1931 *Music & Lett.* Oct. 323 Atonalities, bitonalities, tritonalities and their peers are best heard and not seen. 1944 *Scrutiny* XII. 121 The Lydian [mode]..is harmonically treacherous owing to its imperfect tritonal fourth. 1963 *Listener* 17 Jan. 141/2 The third movement is at the opposite tritonal pole, F sharp.

tritone ('traɪtəʊn). *Mus.* [ad. med.L. *tritonus*, ad. Gr. τρίτονος, f. τρι-, TRI- + τόνος TONE.] An interval consisting of three whole tones; an augmented fourth. (Also formerly in Latin form.)
1609 DOULAND *Ornith. Microl.* 20 A Tritone doth exceed the Consonance of a Diatessaron. 1730 *Treat. Harmony* 7 The Leaps of the False Relations, viz. of a Tritonus, and of a Semidiapente are..forbidden. 1775 STEELE in *Phil. Trans.* LXV. 76 Tritones, or sharp fourths, above the upper

minims. **1789** BURNEY *Hist. Mus.* (ed. 2) III. vii. 344 The Tritonus..consisting of three tones, without the intervention of a semitone, is extremely difficult to sing. **1854** *Cherubini's Counterpoint* 11 It now remains to be demonstrated how and why the Tritone is a false relation in harmony.

tritonioid (traɪˈtəʊnɪɔɪd), *a. Zool.* [f. mod.L. *Tritonia*, generic name + -OID.] Resembling or allied to the genus *Tritonia*, belonging to the family *Tritoniidæ* of opisthobranchiate gastropods.

1891 in *Cent. Dict.*

tritonoid (ˈtraɪtənɔɪd), *a. Zool.* [f. mod.L. *Triton*, generic name + -OID.] Resembling or allied to the genus *Triton* (TRITON[1] 2 a); belonging to the family *Tritonidæ* of tænioglossate gastropods.

1891 in *Cent. Dict.*

tritonous (ˈtraɪtənəs), *a. rare*$^{-1}$. [f. TRI- + Gr. τόν-ος TONE + -OUS; cf. *monotonous*.] Consisting of three tones or notes.

1847 GOSSE *Birds Jamaica* 194 The Flycatcher..is pertinacious in its tritonous call.

tritor (ˈtraɪtə(r)). *Zool.* [a. L. *trītor* a rubber, grinder, f. *terĕre*, *trīt-* to rub, grind.] A specially hard and white ridge or prominence on the teeth of some fishes, as those of the genus *Chimæra*.

1889 NICHOLSON & LYDEKKER *Palæont.* xlviii. 950 One or more triturating ridges, or prominences, differing in appearance from the rest of the tooth, which may be conveniently termed tritors. **1897** PARKER & HASWELL *Zool.* II. 178 Each..tooth has its surface slightly raised into a rounded elevation.., known as a tritor.

† **ˈtritory.** *Obs. rare.* [ad. med.L. *trītōri-um*, f. L. *trīt-*, ppl. stem of *terĕre* to rub, thresh: see -ORY[1]. Cf. *Ælfric's Vocab.* (Wr.-Wülcker 107/2), '*Trītōrium*, þerscel', THRESHEL, a threshing-instrument, a flail, which separates the grain from the straw and chaff.] A vessel for separating liquids of different densities.

1660 tr. *Paracelsus' Archidoxis* I. x. 143 The Pure [Spirit] will Swim at top, Separate it by a Tritory, or Separating Glass. [**1693** tr. *Blancard's Phys. Dict.* (ed. 2), *Tritorium*, the same with *Infundibulum*. **1758** *Elaboratory laid Open* Introd. 30 *Tritoriums*, or separating funnels. **1860** MAYNE *Expos. Lex.*, *Tritorium*, term for a mortar; also a glass for separating oil from water in distillation; formerly used the same as *Infundibulum*, according to Ruland and Johnson, and Paracelsus.]

† **tritoxide** (traɪ-, trɪˈtɒksaɪd). *Chem. Obs.* [f. TRIT(O- + OXIDE.] The third of the series of oxides of a metal or radical, containing the next higher proportion of oxygen to the *deutoxide*. (Now expressed by *trioxide* or other term indicating the actual proportion: cf. PROTOXIDE, DEUTOXIDE.) Sometimes improperly used to denote a compound containing three proportions of oxygen (= TRIOXIDE).

1806 *G. Adams' Nat. & Exp. Philos.* I. App. 538 Minium, the tritoxide of lead. **1812** SIR H. DAVY *Chem. Philos.* 369 The dark brown oxide [of manganese]..must be a tritoxide or an oxide containing three proportions of oxygene. **1850** DAUBENY *Atom. The.* xi. (ed. 2) 371 In certain states of disease, a peculiar compound, called by Mulder the tritoxide of proteine, makes its appearance.

† **ˈtritrace.** *Obs. Cant.* [app. f. TRY *v.* + TRACE *v.*, with allusion to *trey-trace* (TREY *sb.* 3).] In ***troll hazard of tritrace***, name of an 'order of knaves': see TROLL *v.* 15 b.

† **ˈtrittle.** *Obs.* Also 6 **tryttle.** [Phonetic variant of TRATTLE *sb.*[2]] A pellet of sheep's or goat's dung: = TRATTLE *sb.*[2], TREDDLE.

1526 *Grete Herball* ccxxx. (1529) N iv b, Gottes tryttles or tordes. **1624** GEE *Foot out of Snare* 35 To gild-ouer and make acceptable any Pils, though being nothing else but sheeps trittles.

trittle-trattle, *int.* and *sb. Sc. rare.* In 6 **trittyll trattyll, -ill, -il.** [Reduplication of TRATTLE *sb.*[1], idle talk. Cf. TITTLE-TATTLE.]

A. *int.* An exclamation expressing contempt.

1529 LYNDESAY *Complaynt* 245 Now trittyll, trattyll, trolylow,..thow dois bot mow. **1535** —— *Satyre* 4366 *Dil.* Better bring hir to the Leitches heir. *Fol.* Trittill trattill! Scho may nocht steir.

B. *sb.* (in *pl.*) **a.** Foolish or idle talk; nonsense. **b.** Trifles, gewgaws, knick-knacks.

1563 WINȜET *Wks.* (S.T.S.) II. 82/15 That thow be nocht temerouslie sclanderit..be euery wane manis trittil trattilis. **1896** CROCKETT *Grey Man* ii. 13 At the fair..buying of trittle-trattles at the lucky-booths.

trit-trot. [Reduplication of TROT.] A word imitating the sound of trotting.

1818 M. EDGEWORTH *Let.* Sept. (1971) 89 The drollest trit-trot little walk she has. *c* **1840** *Maypole Song*, All round the maypole, trit-trit trot, Our fine maypole shall never be forgot. **1912** COUCH *Poison Island* xii. 75 There come wafted to our ears..the trit-trot of hoofs approaching.

trituberculate (traɪtjuːˈbɜːkjʊlət), *a. Comp. Anat.* [f. TRI- + L. *tūbercul-um* tubercle + -ATE[2].] Having three tubercles, as a tooth; relating to or characterized by such teeth. Also **trituˈbercular** *a.* So **trituˈberculism, trituˈberculy,** the condition of being tritubercular, or the presence of tritubercular teeth; **trituˈberculist,** one who holds that the molar teeth of mammals are modifications of tritubercular teeth.

1883 COPE in *Proc. Amer. Philos. Soc.* (1884) 324 The type of superior molar tooth..was triangular or *tritubercular. **1890** *Nature* 20 Mar. 466/2 The tritubercular molar consists of three cusps, cones, or tubercles, arranged in a triangle, and so disposed that those of the upper jaw alternate with those of the lower. **1835–6** *Todd's Cycl. Anat.* I. 563/1 Molars..with *tri-tuberculate transverse ridges. **1902** *Sat. Rev.* 6 Dec. 711/2 The..fossil Theromorpha with multituberculate teeth,..those with trituberculate teeth. **1890** *Nature* 20 Mar. 466/2 It appears probable..that '*trituberculism', as this type of tooth-structure may be conveniently termed, was developed from a simple cone-like tooth during the Mesozoic period. **1891** FLOWER & LYDEKKER *Mammals* ii. 32 We also find trituberculism differentiating into a secodont and a bunodont series. **1896** *Proc. Zool. Soc.* 5 May 590 There is no evidence to show that this type of upper molar arose in the way suggested by *trituberculists. **1888** H. F. OSBORN in *Amer. Nat.* 1068 The almost universal predominance of *trituberculy in the early geological periods. **1902** *Sat. Rev.* 6 Dec. 711/2 Mr. Beddard..gives..the rival theories of trituberculy and multituberculy.

triturable (ˈtrɪtjʊərəb(ə)l), *a. rare*$^{-1}$. [= F. *triturable* (16th c. in Godef. *Compl.*), f. *triturer* or late L. *trītūrāre* to TRITURATE: see -ABLE.] Capable of being triturated.

1646 SIR T. BROWNE *Pseud. Ep.* II. i. 53 Crystall..is..triturable, and reduceable into powder, by contrition.

tritural (ˈtrɪtjʊərəl), *a. rare*$^{-1}$. [f. L. *trītūra* TRITURE + -AL[1].] Adapted for trituration.

1901 *Proc. Zool. Soc.* 5 Mar. 172 The armoured Chelonian... The roof of the mouth between this tritural border is raised into a dome with the concavity downwards.

triturate (ˈtrɪtjʊəreɪt), *v.* [f. late L. *trītūrāt-*, ppl. stem of *trītūrāre* to thresh, f. L. *trītūra* TRITURE. Cf. F. *triturer* (16th c.).] *trans.* To reduce to fine particles or powder by rubbing, bruising, pounding, crushing, or grinding; to comminute, pulverize; also, to mix (solids, or a solid and a liquid) in this way. **a.** *Pharm.*, *Geol.*, etc.

[**1623** COCKERAM II, *To thresh corne*, triturate.] **1755** JOHNSON, *Triturable*..(from triturate). **1771** T. PERCIVAL *Ess.* (1777) I. 60 The mixture was well triturated in a marble mortar. **1796** KIRWAN *Elem. Min.* (ed. 2) II. 224 Sometimes brittle, sometimes tough according to the proportion of Mercury principally when triturated. **1826** HENRY *Elem. Chem.* II. 99 Triturate in a mortar, and put the mixture..into a phial. **1862** DANA *Man. Geol.* § 51. 49 Rock made from shells..triturated into a calcareous earth by the sea.

b. *Phys.* said of the action of the molar teeth, the gizzard, etc. upon the food.

1822 [see *triturating* below]. **1835–6** *Todd's Cycl. Anat.* I. 311/1 It [the food] is triturated..by the mandibles certainly [in Parrots]. **1851** CARPENTER *Man. Phys.* (ed. 2) 269 By the act of mastication..the food is triturated and mingled with the salivary secretion. **1881** DARWIN *Veg. Mould* 81 Worms swallow many little stones,..it is probable that they serve, like mill-stones, to triturate their food.

c. *fig.*

1848 LANDOR *Imag. Conv.* Ser. v. *Thiers & Lamartine*, At first we were tickled, at last we were triturated. **1881** *Scribner's Mag.* Aug. 542 The raw ingredients of our national admixture are supplied quite as rapidly as the whirl and stir of the popular system can triturate and commingle them.

Hence **ˈtriturated, ˈtriturating** *ppl. adjs.*

1777 COOK *Voy. Pacific* II. viii. (1784) I. 331 Where the shore is low, the soil is commonly sandy, or rather composed of *triturated coral. **1791** COWPER *Iliad* II. 508 The triturated barley grain First duly sprinkling. **1839** DARWIN *Voy. Nat.* xix. (1852) 439 Gorges..through which the whole vast amount of triturated matter must have been carried away. **1898** P. MANSON *Trop. Diseases* xxxv. 547 Three or four ten- to thirty-grain doses of well triturated thymol in cachets. **1822** J. PARKINSON *Outl. Oryctol.* 312 In this [fossil elephant's] tooth..there are only thirteen plates, nine..of which are seen on the *triturating surface. **1835–6** *Todd's Cycl. Anat.* I. 318/2 The triturating action of the gizzard. **1860** MAURY *Phys. Geog. Sea* (Low) § 41 The abrading, triturating power of water.

trituration (trɪtjʊəˈreɪʃən). [ad. late L. *trītūrātiōn-em*, n. of action from *trītūrāre* to TRITURATE; cf. F. *trituration* (14th c. in Godef. *Compl.*).] The action or process of triturating; reduction to fine particles or powder by friction; comminution, pulverization. **a.** *Pharm.*, *Geol.*, etc.

1646 SIR T. BROWNE *Pseud. Ep.* IV. vii. 197 A pumice-stone powdered is lighter then one entire,..for..abatement can hardly be avoyded in the Trituration. **1756** C. LUCAS *Ess. Waters* I. 46 Earths..are..reduced to the utmost tenuity by trituration or grinding. **1833** LYELL *Princ. Geol.* III. 2 Disputing..whether sand and pebbles were the result of aqueous trituration. **1872** YEATS *Techn. Hist. Comm.* 318 By the continual trituration of the runner, the ore is reduced and amalgamation effected.

b. *Phys.*: see TRITURATE *v.* b.

1731 BAILEY vol. II, *Trituration*, (in Physick) the action of the stomach on the food. **1740** CHEYNE *Regimen* 73 Blood Globules, by their Rotundity, Volubility, and Elasticity, resist Trituration, that is, Digestion. **1802** PALEY *Nat. Theol.* xvi. (1817) 140 Without the trituration of the gizzard; a chicken would have starved upon a heap of corn.

c. *transf.* A mass produced, or medicine prepared, by trituration.

1890 BILLINGS *Med. Dict.*, *Trituration*... 2. A preparation directed by the U.S. P[harmacopœia]... *T. of elaterin*, elaterin 10, saccharum lactis 90; triturate (U.S.P.). **1898** P. MANSON *Trop. Diseases* viii. 153 He injected bouillon containing a trituration of one of these flies into a guinea-pig.

d. *fig.*

1832 I. TAYLOR *Saturday Even.* 344 The royal Image and Superscription by the trituration and corrosion it undergoes in the common world becomes continually less and less distinct. **1856** MERIVALE *Rom. Emp.* (1865) IV. xl. 528 Wealthy nobles..whose means were in process of trituration under the pressure of the imperial imposts. **1909** *Edin. Rev.* July 214 This trituration of the people has produced a multitude of dialects.

triturator (ˈtrɪtjʊəreɪtə(r)). [a. late L. *trītūrātor*, agent-n. from *trītūrāre* to TRITURATE.] One who or that which triturates; an instrument or apparatus for triturating, esp. for grinding drugs.

1864 *Reader* 17 Dec. 770/2 Hammers or triturators. **1893** E. A. BUTLER *Household Insects* 137 The gizzard..appears to act more as a strainer than as a triturator.

ˈtriturature. *rare.* [f. late L. *trītūrāt-* (see TRITURATE) + -URE.] = TRITURATION.

1846 WORCESTER, *Triturature*, a wearing by rubbing or friction. *Smith.*

† **triture** (ˈtrɪtjʊə(r)), *sb. Obs.* [ad. L. *trītūra* a rubbing, a threshing, f. *trīt*, ppl. stem of *terĕre* to rub; cf. F. *triture* (1610 in Hatz.-Darm.).]

1. Friction or galling (of a yoke). *rare*$^{-1}$.

1607 J. CARPENTER *Plaine Mans Plough* 221 The oxe accustomed to the yoke or triture..dooth often..returne to the yoke againe.

2. Pounding or grinding; comminution; trituration.

1657 TOMLINSON *Renou's Disp.* 57 Humectation, Infection or Triture are wont to be reduced to Infusion. **1718** QUINCY *Compl. Disp.* 12 The continual Triture has the same Effects upon it, as repeated Sublimation. **1767** PERCIVAL in *Phil. Trans.* LVII. 226 The powder and the water were well incorporated by triture. **1790** WEDGWOOD *ibid.* LXXX. 308 To try whether this tedious process of solution could be expedited by triture or calcination, some of the mineral was rubbed in a mortar.

Hence † **ˈtriture** *v.*, *Obs.*, *trans.* to triturate.

1773 CLEGG in *Phil. Trans.* LXIV. 49 Four penny-weights of each of the astringents..were tritured in plain water.

† **trityl** (ˈtraɪtɪl). *Chem. Obs.* [ad. F. *trityle* (Chancel, 1853), so called as being the third of the series of alcohol radicals of the form C_nH_{2n+1}: see TRITO- and -YL, and cf. TETRYL, PENTYL, HEXYL, etc.] The radical C_3H_7, now called PROPYL. Hence † **ˈtritylene** = PROPYLENE, † **triˈtylic** *a.* = PROPYLIC, etc.

1854 *Q. Jrnl. Chem. Soc.* VI. 287 Propionic Alcohol..to which the author [Chancel] gives the name *Hydrate of Trityl.* **1856** FOWNES *Elem. Chem.* (ed. 6) 474 Trityl-alcohol, or hydrated oxide of trityl. We prefer the name propylic alcohol. **1857** MILLER *Elem. Chem.* III. 27 Tritylic or Propylic Alcohol $C_6H_8O_2$. *Ibid.* 28 Propylic (Tritylic) Ether ..C_6H_7O. *Ibid.* 190 *Tritylene, Propylene*... Reynolds obtained this gas mixed with marsh gas. **1868** WATTS *Dict. Chem.* V. 887 Trityl (better known as Propyl). *Ibid.* 888 One of the earliest..recognitions of the trityl-group is to be found in Chancel's note..(1853), which describes a trityl-alcohol. *Ibid.* 891 Tritylamine, or Propylamine... Bright, colourless, highly refracting, very mobile liquid. *Ibid.* 892 Tritylene, or Propylene, C_3H_6.

tritylodontoid (ˌtraɪtɪləʊˈdɒntɔɪd), *a.* and *sb. Palæont.* [f. mod.L. *Tritylodōn*, *-ont-* (f. Gr. τρι-, TRI- + τύλος knob + ὀδούς, ὀδοντ- tooth) + -OID.] **a.** *adj.* Resembling the genus *Tritylodon*, or belonging to the family *Tritylodontidæ*, of extinct monotreme mammals, found in the Triassic and Jurassic formations, and characterized by tritubercular molar teeth. **b.** *sb.* A member of this family.

In recent Dicts.

trium-ˈfeminate. *nonce-wd.* [f. L. *trium*, gen. pl. of *trēs* three + *fēmina* female, woman + -ATE[1], after TRIUMVIRATE.] A group of three women associated in government.

1873 M. COLLINS *Miranda* I. 75 These three formed a trium-feminate, and governed despotically that corner of the quarterdeck.

triumph (ˈtraɪəmf), *sb.* Forms: 4–7 **triumphe, tryumphe,** (5 **treyumphe, trihumphe, triumphee,** 6 **triump, tryhumphe, tryoumffe,** *Sc.* **trywmph, trieumph, treumph(e, trewmph),** 6–7 **tryumph,** 6– **triumph.** [ME. a. OF. *triumphe* (12th c.), F. *triomphe*, = Prov. *triomfe*, Sp. *triunfo*, Pg. *triumpho*, It. *trionfo*, ad. L. *triumph-us* (older form *triumpus*); cf. Gr. θρίαμβος hymn to Bacchus.]

1. *Rom. Hist.* The entrance of a victorious commander with his army and spoils in solemn procession into Rome, permission for which was granted by the senate in honour of an important achievement in war. Also *transf.*

[*c* **893** K. ÆLFRED *Oros.* II. iv. §2 Heora an consul.. forsoc þone triumphan [L. *triumphum*], þe him mon onȝean brohte.] *c* **1374** CHAUCER *Anel. & Arc.* 43 With his tryumphe and laurer corovned thus.. Let I this noble prince Theseus Towarde Athenes in his wey ryding. **1398** TREVISA *Barth. De P.R.* XVII. xlviii. (Tollem. MS.), The lauri tre is propirly halowed to triumphes, worshipe of victoures. *c* **1430** LYDG. *Min. Poems* (Percy Soc.) 25 Where is Julius, proudest in his empire, With his triumphes moost imperiall? **1593** SHAKS. *Rich. II*, III. iv. 99 What was I borne to this: that my sad looke, Should grace the Triumph of great Bullingbrooke? **1600** HOLLAND *Livy* III. lxiii. 131 This was the first time that ever any triumph was granted by the voices of the people, without the authoritie and assent of the Senatours. **1703** ROWE *Ulyss.* I. i, Where is the Triumph shall go forth to meet him? **1838–42** ARNOLD *Hist. Rome* III. xlvi. 321 Marcellus was anxious to obtain a triumph for his conquest of Syracuse.

†**b.** *transf.* in the 'philosopher's game'. *Obs.*

c **1600** *MS. Sloane 451* lf. 1 In it men fight and striue together by the art of comptynge.. whether may (the enimies kinge beinge taken) erect a triumphe in his aduersaries campe. *Ibid.* 1 b, You may make your triumphe, as well of your enimies men taken as of your owne vntaken. **1801** STRUTT *Sports & Past.* IV. ii. (1876) 415 It is.. certain that the great object of each player is to take the king from his opponent, because he who succeeds may make his triumph and erect his trophy.

2. *transf.* The action or fact of triumphing; victory, conquest, or the glory of this; also, a signal success or achievement. Also *fig.*

c **1400** *Sowdone Bab.* 913 Of the treyumphe he bare the flour In dispite of Mahounde. *c* **1412** HOCCLEVE *De Reg. Princ.* 3213 He.. hadde of folkes dethes suche pitee, That.. Al his tryumphe was to hym but peyne. **1548–9** (Mar.) *Bk. Com. Prayer, Visitation of Sick*, That thou mayest haue perfit victory and triumph against the deuil, sinne, and death. **1567** *Gude & Godlie B.* (S.T.S.) 59 For vs he sched his precious blude, With greit tryumph vpon the rude. **1632** LITHGOW *Trav.* III. 119 Like a naked table wherein nothing is painted: euen so is Thebes and her past tryumphs defac'd. **1735** POPE *Ep. Lady* 225 Wisdom's triumph is well-tim'd Retreat. *a* **1835** SIR D. SANFORD *Rise & Progr. Lit.* (1847) 40 Of that airy and extravagant spirit,.. the Attic comedy, in its first estate, was at once the triumph and the type. **1853** J. H. NEWMAN *Hist. Sk.* (1873) II. I. iv. 191 It was the triumph of civilization over brute force.

†**b.** *transf.* The subject of triumph. *Obs. rare.*

1671 MILTON *Samson* 426 Our Foes Found soon occasion thereby to make thee Thir Captive, and thir triumph.

†**3.** Pomp, as of the procession described in 1; splendour; glory; magnificence.

1494 FABYAN *Chron.* lxix. 47 After whiche victory.. the sayd Constantyne.. was receyued of the Senate with moost triumphe. **1560** ROLLAND *Seven Sages* 6 With all triumph hir funerall seruice Was dewlie done. **1671** MILTON *Samson* 1312 This day to Dagon is a solemn Feast, With Sacrifices, Triumph, Pomp, and Games. **1718** *Free-thinker* No. 68 ¶9 This Ceremony is not performed.. with the usual Pomp and Triumph.

†**4.** A public festivity or joyful celebration; a spectacle or pageant; *esp.* a tournament. *Obs.*

1502 ARNOLDE *Chron.* (1811) p. xli, At the same triumphe the Kinge made lvii Knightis. **1568** GRAFTON *Chron.* II. 682 When publique playes or open triumphes should be shewed, or set forth abrode in the stretes. **1593** SHAKS. *Rich. II*, v. ii. 52 What newes from Oxford? Hold those Iusts & Triumphs? **1630** *R. Johnson's Kingd. & Commw.* 290 Many Chambers full of Masking garments, and other abiliments for triumphs and pastimes both for Land and Water. **1660** F. BROOKE tr. *Le Blanc's Trav.* 276 The River Nile.. advances moderately, not doing any dammage: and when it comes they make a generall triumph. *a* **1721** PRIOR *Ode on Coronation* iv, His Peoples blessings greater than his own, And he that gives the Triumph triumphs least. **1825** HONE *Every-day Bk.* I. 1446 The printed descriptions of these processions [Lord Mayor's show] are usually entitled 'Triumphs'. [**1903** *Edin. Rev.* Apr. 459 Every event in life was made a pretext for fêtes, processions, and 'triumphs'.]

5. The exultation of victory or success; elation; joy; rapturous delight.

1582 N. LICHEFIELD tr. *Castanheda's Conq. E. Ind.* I. xxviii. 71 That the rest of the Fleete shoulde weye their Ankors, the which.. they did begin with great diligence and triumph that the Marriners made. **1604** R. CAWDREY *Table Alph.*, *Triumph*, great ioy outwardly shewed. **1667** MILTON *P.L.* VII. 180 Great triumph and rejoycing was in Heav'n When such was heard declar'd the Almightie's will. **1761** GRAY *Fatal Sisters* 54 Songs of joy and triumph sing! **1891** E. PEACOCK *N. Brendon* II. 57 There was triumph on his countenance.

b. *in triumph*, triumphant, rejoicing in victory or success; triumphantly. (Orig. *fig.* from 1.)

1593 SHAKS. *3 Hen. VI*, III. iii. 18 Let thy dauntlesse minde still ride in triumph, Ouer all mischance. **1667** MILTON *P.L.* x. 537 To see In Triumph issuing forth thir glorious Chief. **1697** DRYDEN *Virg. Georg.* III. 15, I, first of Romans shall in Triumph come From conquer'd Greece, and bring her Trophies home. **1810** SCOTT *Lady of L.* II. xix, Hail to the chief who in triumph advances!

c. *to ride triumph*, to ride at full tilt. ? *Obs.*

1761 STERNE *Tr. Shandy* IV. xvi, To have so many jarring elements breaking loose, and riding triumph in every corner of a gentleman's house.

†**6. a.** A trumpet blast of victory. **b.** *pl.* Shouts of triumph or exultation. *Obs.*

1566 STAPLETON *Ret. Untr. Jewel* Epistle, It is to blowe the Triumphe before the Victory. **1602** MARSTON *Ant. & Mel.* I. Wks. 1856 I. 10 Hark how Piero's triumphs beat the ayre. **1704** J. TRAPP *Abra-Mule* v. i, The loud Triumphs of the shouting Soldiers.

†**7.** A triumphal arch. Also *transf. Obs. rare.*

1644 EVELYN *Diary* 7 Nov., The people were now generally busye in erecting temporary triumphs and arches with statues and flattering inscriptions. **1656** EARL MONM. tr. *Boccalini's Advts. fr. Parnass.* I. lxxix. (1674) 107 Triumphs, Trophies, Statues, and such like things, which are so familiarly seen built in your Streets. **1658** *Hist. Christina Q. Swedland* 319 The triumphs or statues of Sugar with which they had adorned the table.

†**8.** *Cards.* **a.** = TRUMP *sb.*[2] 1. *Obs.*

terrestrial triumph = TAROC, TAROT.

1529 LATIMER *1st Serm. Card* in Foxe *A. & M.* (1563) 1300/2 The game that wee wyll playe at, shall bee called the triumphe... Lette therefore euery Christian manne and woman playe at these cardes, that they maye haue and obteyne the triumph; you must marke also that the triumphe muste apply to fetche home vnto hym all the other cardes, whatsoeuer sute they bee of. **1598** FLORIO, *Gérmini*,.. a kind of playing-cards which we call terrestriall triumphs. [**1606** SHAKS. *Ant. & Cl.* IV. xiv. 20 Shee.. has Packt Cards with Cæsars, and false plaid my Glory Vnto an Enemies triumph.]

†**b.** An obsolete card-game; = TRUMP *sb.*[2] 1 b.

1529 [see 8 a]. **1554** *Interlude Youth* C iv, At the cardes I can theche you to play, At the triump [*ed.* **1561** triumph], and one and thyrtye. **1594** CAREW *Huarte's Exam. Wits* viii. (1596) 112 Playing at Cent, and at Triumph. **1626** tr. *Boccalini's New-found Politicke* III. xiii. (*heading*), A Poetaster for playing at Cards, and deuising the Game called Triumph or Trump, is brought before Apollo.

9. *attrib.* and *Comb.*, as ***triumph-bough***, ***-day***, ***-hour***, ***-path***, ***-robe***, ***-salute***, ***-song***, ***-tear***, ***-tune***, ***-wise***; ***triumph-decking*** adj.; also †**triumph-church**, the Church triumphant; **triumph-gate**, the gate through which a triumphing general entered Rome; in quot. *transf.*

a **1637** B. JONSON *Sad Sheph.* I. ii, [Why should not] each of us cut down a *triumph-bough? *c* **1620** in Farr *S.P. Jas. I* (1847) 318 Shyne bright in the *Triumph Church, faire soule, That in the Militant has shyn'd so longe. **1593** SHAKS. *Rich. II*, v. ii. 66 For gay apparell gainst the *triumph day. **1827** POLLOK *Course T.* x. 109 Great triumph-day of God's Incarnate Son. **1646** SIR R. FANSHAW tr. *Guarino's Faithf. Sheph.* IV. iv. 165 Ye *triumph-decking Lawrell boughs, Empale my glorious and victorious brows. **1880** G. MEREDITH *Tragic Com.* (1881) 143 This handsome, undaunted, *triumph-flashing man. **1848** ELIZA COOK *Old Palace* i, Its *triumph-gates were flinging wide. **1892** R. F. TOWNDROW *Garden*, etc. 65 The elms are clad in *triumph-robes of gold. **1844** *Regul. & Ord. Army* 37 The forts and batteries from which *Triumph Salutes are usually fired. **1561** DAUS tr. *Bullinger on Apoc.* (1573) 154 b, The voyces of the glade and ioyfull sort, singing true and eternall *triumph-songes in heauen. *c* **1586** SIDNEY *Ps.* LXVI. i, All lands.. With *triumph tunes Gods honor sound. **1565** GOLDING *Ovid's Met.* IV. (1593) 95 In *triumph-wise accomplishing her hest.

triumph ('traɪəmf), *v.* Forms: see prec. sb. [a. OF. *triumpher* (13th c.), F. *triompher*, = Prov. *triomfar*, Sp. *triunfar*, Pg. *triumphar*, It. *trionfare*, ad. L. *triumphāre*, f. *triumphus* TRIUMPH.]

1. *intr.* To celebrate a Roman triumph.

1530 PALSGR. 762/2, I tryumphe for a conquest or a victorye gotten... It was a marvaylouse syght to se the Romanynes tryumphe, whan they had the vyctorie of their ennemyes. **1607** SHAKS. *Cor.* II. i. 194 Would'st thou haue laugh'd, had I come Coffin'd home, That weep'st to see me triumph? *a* **1656** USSHER *Ann.* vi. (1658) 675 Upon the Ides of December, Q. Pedius Triumphed for Spain. **1764** GIBBON *Misc. Wks.* (1814) IV. 375 He triumphed for his victories over the great Mithridates. **1846** KEIGHTLEY *Notes Virg., Bucol.* x. 26 The custom of the Roman generals, when triumphing and attired as Jupiter, to have their faces tinged with *minium*.

2. To be victorious; to prevail; to gain the mastery. Const. *over*, †*against*, †*on*, †*of*, †*in*.

1508 DUNBAR *Poems* vii. 2 Renownit, ryall, right reuerend and serene Lord, hie trywmphing in wirschip and valoure. *a* **1520** —— *Poems* xxxvii. 39 He deit triumphand, he raiss and wan the feild. **1548–9** (Mar.) *Bk. Com. Prayer, Private Baptism*, To triumph againste hym [the devil], the worlde, and the fleshe. **1590** SPENSER *F.Q.* II. x. 56 [Bunduca].. Triumphed oft against her enemis; And yet, though overcome.., Shee triumphed on death. **1593** SHAKS. *Lucr.* 77 Those two armies that would let him go Rather then triumph in so false a foe. **1610** HOLLAND *Camden's Brit.* (1637) 39 Nations twice triumphed of. **1667** MILTON *P.L.* XII. 452 He shall ascend With victory, triumphing through the aire Over his foes and thine. *c* **1708** LADY M. W. MONTAGU *Lett., to Miss A. Wortley* 27 Aug. (1887) I. 37 Destiny triumphs over all your efforts. **1838** THIRLWALL *Greece* II. xvi. 342 After praying them to remember his good will, if the cause of Greece triumphed, he rode away.

†**b.** *trans.* To cause to triumph. *Obs. rare.*

a **1571** JEWEL *On Thess.* (1611) 143 God.. hath triumphed the name of his Christ. **1582** N. T. (Rhem.) *2 Cor.* ii. 14 Thankes be to God, who alwaies triumpheth vs in Christ Iesus.

†**c.** To triumph over; to conquer. *Obs.*

1603 B. JONSON *Sejanus* I. i, We, that,.. were born Free, equal lords of the triumphed world, And knew no masters, but affections. **1626** MASSINGER *Rom. Actor* II. i, Two and thirty legions, that awe All nations of the triumphed world. **1667** MILTON *P.L.* x. 572 So oft they fell Into the same illusion, not as Man Whom they triumph'd once lapst.

†**3.** *intr.* To be in a state of pomp or magnificence. Cf. prec. 3. *Obs.*

1483 CAXTON *Gold. Leg.* 388 b/2 Thou shalt tryumphe as a quene in my royame. **1538** STARKEY *England* I. iv. 131 Yongur bretherne go a beggyng, where as the eldur hath tryumphyd and lyuyd in plesure. **1553** *Respublica* v. v. 1472 Making these newe Ladies of hir werie, We shoulde thrihumphe & reigne. **1568** [see TRIUMPHING *vbl. sb.*].

4. 'To rejoice for victory'; to be elated at another's defeat, discomfiture, or the like; 'to insult upon an advantage gained' (J.); hence, to rejoice, exult, be elated or glad; to glory.

1535 COVERDALE *Ps.* xii[i]. 2 How longe shal myne enemie triumphe ouer me? *Ibid.* xciii[i]. 3 How longe shal the vngodly tryumphe? **1565** JEWEL *Repl. Harding* (1611) 371 S. Paul triumphed of that thing that in the world was so deepely despised. **1572** tr. *Buchanan's Detection* O j, Quhen rage.. shall ragingly triumph vpon the goods and blude of poore subiectis. **1591** SHAKS. *1 Hen. VI*, I. vi. 8 France, triumph in thy glorious Prophetesse. **1594** —— *Rich. III*, III. iv. 91 Triumphing at mine enemies. **1617** MORYSON *Itin.* I. 74 They.. triumph of diuers Citizens borne heere. **1746** FRANCIS tr. *Hor., Sat.* II. iii. 48 Good sir, don't triumph in your own disease. **1825** SCOTT *Betrothed* viii, The laugh and the song.. which triumphed by anticipation over their surrender.

fig. **1593** SHAKS. *Lucr.* 12 To praise the cleare vnmatched red and white, Which triumpht in that skie of his delight. *Ibid.* 1388 In great commaunders, Grace, and Maiestie You might behold triumphing in their faces. **1593** —— *Rich. II*, III. ii. 77 The blood of twentie thousand men Did triumph in my face.

†**5.** *intr. Cards.* To trump. *Obs. rare.*

1563 [see TRIUMPHING *ppl. a.*]. **1626** B. JONSON *Fortunate Isles* Wks. 650/1 The four knaves entertain'd for the guards Of the kings and the queens that triumph in the cards.

Hence '**triumphed** *ppl. a.*

1603, **1626** [see sense 2 c].

triumphable ('traɪəmfəb(ə)l), *a. rare.* [f. prec. + -ABLE.] That may be triumphed in or over.

1768 *Woman of Honor* I. 157 No.. very triumphable success.

triumphal (traɪ'ʌmfəl), *a.* (*sb.*) [ad. L. *triumphālis*, f. *triumphus* TRIUMPH, or a. OF. *triumphal* (*trionfal*, 12th c. in Godef. *Compl.*), F. *triomphal*: see -AL[1].]

A. *adj.* **1.** Of, pertaining to, or of the nature of a triumph; celebrating or commemorating a triumph or victory.

triumphal arch (†*arc*), an arch (sometimes threefold) erected, first by the Roman emperors and also in modern times, in commemoration of a victory; also a temporary structure of this kind. ***triumphal chaplet***, ***garland***, ***wreath***, the laurel wreath worn by the victor at a Roman triumph. ***triumphal images***, the laurel-wreathed statues which a triumphing general might bequeath to his descendants. ***triumphal ornaments***, the insignia of triumphing generals, consuls, etc.; also, the privileges or distinctions bestowed on them.

1430–40 LYDG. *Bochas* IV. i. (MS. Bodl. 263) 211/2 The tryumphal [crowns] maked wer of gold Offred in tryumphes to worthi Emperours. **1463** ASHBY *Prisoner's Refl.* 209 Thou may be in heuyn menyall Seruaunt thorough thy tryumphall victory By mekenes and werkes merytory. **1495** *Trevisa's Barth. De P.R.* XVII. xlviii. (W. de W.) P ij/2 The lauri tree ..is properly halowed to triumphal worship of Conquerours. **1539** TONSTALL *Serm. Palm Sund.* (1823) 15 The crosse is now euery where amongest Christen men erected.. as an arche triumphal ageinst the deuyll. **1542** UDALL *Erasm. Apoph.* 254 b, The garlande triumphal [was made] of golde. **1550** SIR T. HOBY *Trav.* (1902) 36 A verie bewtifull triumphall arke of the Emperor Nerva. **1591** SAVILE *Tacitus, Agricola* (1622) 200 That all the honours of triumphall ornaments, image triumphall,.. should be awarded vnto him in Senat. **1601** HOLLAND *Pliny* XXII. iii. II. 115 The Chaplet Triumphall, which they ware who entred with triumph into Rome. **1681** *Lond. Gaz.* No. 1631/1 A Triumphal Arch was Erected near the first Gate. **1706** PHILLIPS (ed. Kersey), *Triumphal Crown*,.. a Crown at first made of Laurel, and afterwards of Gold, which the Cities usually sent to the Victorious General, to wear on the Day of his Triumphal Entry. **1776** GIBBON *Decl. & F.* xi. (1846) I. 323 The triumphal car of Aurelian.. was drawn.. either by four stags or by four elephants. **1835** T. MITCHELL *Acharn. Aristoph.* 1099 *note*, A triumphal ode in honour of Hercules. **1884** *Pall Mall G.* 28 Aug. 1/1 The Prime Minister has arrived at Midlothian after a triumphal progress.

†**2.** Victorious, triumphant. *Obs.*

1513 DOUGLAS *Æneis* VIII. iv. 47 Wyth proud spulȝe arryving triumphall. **1618** BOLTON *Florus* (1636) 31 He returned home to his Oxen, a tryumphall husbandman.

B. *sb.* †**1.** An ode of triumph or victory; a pæan. *Obs. rare.*

1589 PEELE *Eclogue* Wks. (Rtldg.) 561/2 Man, if triumphals here be in request, Then let them chant them that can chant them best. **1589** PUTTENHAM *Eng. Poesie* I. xxiii. (Arb.) 61 Our Triumphals written in honour of her Maiesties long peace.

†**2.** A token of triumph. *Obs. rare*[−1].

1671 MILTON *P.R.* IV. 578 The Fiend.. to his crew.. brought Joyless triumphals of his hop't success, Ruin, and desperation, and dismay.

†**3.** A triumphal car or chariot. *Obs. rare*[−1].

1633 SHIRLEY *Triumph Peace* Introd., The four triumphals, or magnificent chariots, in which were mounted the Grand Masquers.

†**4.** A triumphal celebration; a triumph. *Obs.*

1592 SYLVESTER *Tri. Faith* i, A sacred Virgin's stately Triumphals. **1675** G. R. tr. *Le Grand's Man without Passion* 37 As he makes her to assist at her Triumphals, he will have her the constant companion of her Labours.

Hence **tri'umphally** *adv.* Cf. TRIUMPHANTLY *adv.*

1897 F. THOMPSON *New Poems* 109 Thou dost thy dying so triumphally. **1984** *Miami Herald* 6 Apr. 2B/1 Mike Zeck returns triumphally as.. the local kid who actually did break into the business.

triumphalism (traɪ'ʌmfəlɪz(ə)m). [f. TRIUMPHAL *a.* + -ISM.] The sense of pride (often linked with ostentation) in the rightness and achievements of one's Church (used *pejoratively*). Also in extended sense.

1964 R. MCA. BROWN *Observer in Rome* 27, I am greatly impressed by the recognition of human failings in this prayer and by its exclusion of the 'triumphalism' that has often seemed to characterize the church. **1968** *N.Y. Times* 12 Jan. 25 Wayne H. Cowan, managing editor of the liberal Protestant journal, Christianity and Crisis, said the pastoral 'mutes the triumphalism of the past, but still places great emphasis on the mystery and infallibility of the church'. **1972** *Catholic Herald* 9 June 4 Nostalgia for the pre-Conciliar years of exclusivity and triumphalism. **1975** *New Yorker* 10 Mar. 83/1 This contrast is understandable, given what critics of the regime have labelled 'triumphalism'—something that goes way beyond mere ostentation on a colossal scale. **1977** P. JOHNSON *Enemies of Society* iv. 47 The loss of interest and confidence in the human mind and spirit is, to some extent, concealed by the gigantic triumphalism of late imperial architecture. **1981** G. PRIESTLAND *Priestland's Progress* i. 17 John V. Taylor, Bishop of Winchester,..is right when he seeks to turn us from shallow triumphalism or the reshuffling of old dogmas. **1983** *Times* 31 May 13/2 There would probably be an initial outbreak of Tory triumphalism, which would be distasteful and unnecessary.

Hence **tri'umphalist** *a.* and *sb.*, **triumpha'listic** *a.*

1967 H. CHADWICK *Early Church* 285 Towards such triumphalist assumptions a twentieth-century Christian is likely to be cool and reserved. **1967** *Times* 22 Apr. 12/5 The anxieties of the lingering triumphalists are increased. **1967** R. McA. BROWN *Ecumenical Revolution* vi. 115 It must be acknowledged that later Protestants themselves became as triumphalistic about their own confessions and traditions and denominations as they ever accused the Roman Catholic Church of being. **1970** *Daily Tel.* 2 Dec. 12/7 Elgar's unashamedly triumphalist setting of the National Anthem sounded a defiantly anachronistic note. **1973** *Listener* 19 Apr. 512/1 The busy, businesslike, triumphalist, materially successful France of today. **1980** *Focus* Summer 24/1 The triumphalist tends to interpret what God has done as his own achievement. **1982** *Sunday Tel.* 30 May 9/2 Churches have been stripped of baroque or Italianate furnishings, altars have been heaved forward, 'triumphalist' pictures and symbols stashed away. **1983** *Observer* 28 Nov. 8/3 The journalists..fed readers and viewers a diet of triumphalistic pap.

triumphancy (traɪ'ʌmfənsɪ). [f. TRIUMPHANT: see -ANCY.] The state or quality of being triumphant.

1592 WYRLEY *Armorie* 153 Which Hector like with great triumphancie Had conquerd kings through magnanimitie. **1652** SPARKE *Prim. Devot.* (1663) 287 His triumphancy,.. his translation from earth to heaven. **1701** BEVERLEY *Apoc. Quest.* 17 Constantines Victorious Triumphancy over Paganism. **1892** PATER *Wks.* (1901) VIII. 51 In all the triumphancy of his later days at Rome.

triumphand, Sc. form of TRIUMPHING *ppl. a.*

triumphant (traɪ'ʌmfənt), *a.* (*sb.*) [ad. L. *triumphānt-em*, pres. pple. of *triumphāre* to TRIUMPH, or a. F. †*triumphant*, *triomphant* (15th c.): see -ANT.]

1. Celebrating a triumph or victory; of, pertaining to, of the nature of, or befitting a triumph; triumphal. Now *rare*.

1531 ELYOT *Gov.* III. xxi, They wold haue set his image in triumphant apparaile within the capitole. *a* **1548** HALL *Chron., Hen. VIII* 48 b, An arche triumphante, whiche shalbe made at the place where the iustes shalbe. **1591** SHAKS. *1 Hen. VI*, I. i. 22 Like Captiues bound to a Triumphant Carre. **1651** H. L'ESTRANGE *Smectymnuomastix* 6 Let us..chant that triumphant Ode which..the Children of Israel sung upon the overthrow of the Egyptians in the red sea. **1719** DE FOE *Crusoe* (1840) I. xiv. 246 The triumphant feast..after a victory. **1876** FREEMAN *Hist. Sk.* 50 That long procession of triumphant virgins..bearing their gifts to their Lord on the knees of His Mother.

2. That has achieved victory or success; conquering; 'victorious; graced with conquest' (J.)

Church Triumphant: see CHURCH 4 b.

1494 FABYAN *Chron.* 442 Kyng Edwarde..gaue to the sayde Scottys batayll, and of them had tryumphaunte victorye. **1526** *Pilgr. Perf.* III. liv. (W. de W. 1531) 251 b, Let vs gyue praysynges to god for the chirche triumphant. **1575–85** ABP. SANDYS *Serm.* xiv. (Parker Soc.) 283 He is that triumphant prince, which hath most victoriously vanquished and thrown under foot our enemies. **1683** *Brit. Spec.* 134 Whilst in all other Provinces..Cruelty and Slaughter were Triumphant, the Christians here began to repair their demolished Churches. **1704** HEARNE *Duct. Hist.* (1714) I. 401 The Spartan State which became afterwards so Triumphant in Greece. **1819** BYRON *Mazeppa* I. i, The power and glory of the war..Had pass'd to the triumphant Czar. **1878** BROWNING *La Saisiaz* 267 There is no reconciling..Goodness with triumphant evil.

†**b.** *transf.* Of or gained by conquest. *Obs. rare*$^{-1}$.

c **1600** SHAKS. *Sonn.* cli, My soule doth tell my body that he may Triumph in loue, flesh..doth point out thee As his triumphant prize.

†**3.** Splendid; glorious; magnificent; noble; notable. *Obs.*

1494 in *Lett. Rich. III & Hen. VII* (Rolls) I. 394 A tryhumphant sight. **1568** GRAFTON *Chron.* II. 419 King Henrie maried Iane Duches of Briteyne..and with all triumphant pompe conueyed her through the Citie of London to Westminster. **1592** SHAKS. *Rom. & Jul.* v. iii. 83 Ile burie thee in a triumphant graue. **1606** —— *Ant. & Cl.* II. ii. 190 She's a most triumphant Lady, if report be square to her. **1696** PHILLIPS (ed. 5), *Triumphant*, Victorious, Magnificent, Pompous, Superb.

4. Rejoicing or exulting for or as for victory; triumphing; exultant.

1594 SHAKS. *Rich. III*, III. ii. 84 Thinke you, but that I know our state secure, I would be so triumphant as I am? **1604** R. CAWDREY *Table Alph.*, *Triumphant*, reioycing for the conquest. **1794** MRS. RADCLIFFE *Myst. Udolpho* xxxi, The cavaliero thought..he was to be called to no account, but was to go off triumphant. **1827** LYTTON *Pelham* lx, The papers..were filled with the most triumphant abuse and ridicule of the Whigs. **1907** *Verney Mem.* I. 206 The triumphant cries of an immense multitude.

†**B.** *sb.* [cf. obs. F. *triumphant* (Godef. *Compl.*).] One who triumphs; a victor, conqueror. *Obs.*

1562 J. SHUTE *Cambini's Turk. Wars* 18 b, The number of the triumphantes was in maner infinite, thei had no desyre but to robbe. **1629** J. M. tr. *Fonseca's Devout Contempl.* 242 Saint Chrysostome reports of the Roman Triumphantes, That some entred Rome in Chariots drawne with pyde Horses. **1696** AUBREY *Misc.* (1721) 185 It hath been observed, That after Triumphs, the Triumphants have been sick in Spirit. **1812** SOUTHEY *Omniana* I. 227 Triumphant generals in Rome wore Rouge... Our fair ever-blushing triumphants have secured to themselves the charm of picturesque cheeks.

triumphantly (traɪ'ʌmfəntlɪ), *adv.* [f. prec. + -LY².] In a triumphant manner; victoriously; exultantly; 'with insolent exultation' (J.); †magnificently.

a **1548** HALL *Chron., Hen. VIII* 194 He would be so triumphantly installed without makyng the kyng priuye. **1595** SHAKS. *John* II. i. 309 The dancing banners of the French, Who are at hand triumphantly displayed To enter Conquerors. **1675** TRAHERNE *Chr. Ethics* 438 A man, that sees and knows the glory of his high and heavenly estate, does all things triumphantly. **1791** BOSWELL *Johnson* 21 Mar. an. 1783, While he went on talking triumphantly, I was fixed in admiration. **1855** MACAULAY *Hist. Eng.* xv. III. 504 Walker's accusers..brought calumnious accusations which were triumphantly refuted.

†**triumphate**, *a.* *Obs. rare*$^{-1}$. [ad. L. *triumphātus*, pa. pple. of *triumphāre* to TRIUMPH.] Triumphed over, conquered.

1471 RIPLEY *Comp. Alch.* v. li. in Ashm. *Theatr. Chem. Brit.* (1652) 160 My doctryne therefore remember wyttyly, And passe forth toward the Syxth Gate, For thys the Fyfthe ys tryumphate.

triumphator ('traɪəmfeɪtə(r)). [a. L. *triumphātor* one who triumphs, a conqueror, agent-n. f. *triumphāre* to TRIUMPH. Cf. OF. *triomphateur* (14th c.).] A conqueror; *spec.* a Roman general who was granted a triumph; hence *transf.*

1611 SPEED *Hist. Gt. Brit.* IX. vi. §61 The most noble King of England, and Triumphator of Ireland. **1876** T. S. EGAN tr. *Heine's Atta Troll* etc. 80 Vict'ry is at last decided, And the day, the triumphator Treads..On the necks of all the mountains.

So †**tri'umphatrice**, *Obs. rare* [cf. F. *triomphatrice* (1769 in Littré)], a female who triumphs.

1430–40 LYDG. *Bochas* IV. Prol. vi. (MS. Bodl. 263) 207/2 Dilligence, cheef triumphatrice Of slogardie, necligence & slouthe.

triumpher ('traɪəmfə(r)). [f. TRIUMPH *v.* + -ER¹.] One who triumphs.

1. One who celebrated a Roman triumph.

1542 UDALL *Erasm. Apoph.* 305 Of whom [Cicero] Plinius ..saieth..[Thou] diddest as worthyly deserue to haue the garlande of a triumpher for thy toung, as euer had any other before for the swearde. **1661** MORGAN *Sph. Gentry* III. iv. 34 The Triumpher made his entrance in his Royall Chariot and was met by the Senators in their robes. **1737** L. CLARKE *Hist. Bible* (1740) I. IX. 609 On entering the capitol he did not, as other Triumphers used to do, put any of his captives to death.

2. A victor, conqueror.

1540 COVERDALE *Fruitf. Less.* v. (1593) Oo j, The glorious triumpher ascending vp to heauen with great victorie. **1603** H. CROSSE *Vertues Commw.* (1878) 17 An Antidote against pride, and a valiant tryumpher ouer flaming desires. **1760** C. JOHNSTON *Chrysal* (1822) III. 313 A vain ambition of triumphing over the triumpher. **1848** W. H. KELLY tr. *L. Blanc's Hist. Ten Y.* I. Introd. 17 In that uninterrupted succession of calamities..what are all these famous triumphers,..all these haughty distributers of empires?

triumpherate, **-ery**, obs. erron. ff. TRIUMVIRATE, TRIUMVIRY (by confusion with *triumph*).

triumphing ('traɪəmfɪŋ), *vbl. sb.* [f. TRIUMPH *v.* + -ING¹.] The action of the verb TRIUMPH.

1568 GRAFTON *Chron.* II. 255 There was great triumphyng and iustyng the space of .xv. dayes. **1623** in Foster *Eng. Factories Ind.* (1908) II. 240 In Goa ther hath bine great triumfinge and much rejoysinge att this newes. **1777** BRAND *Pop. Antiq.* App. 402 The antient Hoc-tide, an Old Saxon Word, importing the Time of Scorning or Triumphing. *c* **1850** NEALE *Hymns East. Ch.* (1866) 144 Thou..Hast made them [heaven and earth] one by..Thy triumphing.

'triumphing, *ppl. a.* [f. as prec. + -ING².] That triumphs, in various senses; triumphant.

1500–20 DUNBAR *Poems* lxxxvi. 19 Tryumphand tempill of the Trinite. *Ibid.* lxxxvii. 9 O hye trivmphing peradiss of joy. **1563** FOXE *A. & M.* 1297/2 For yᵉ chief (as their triumphing card) he [Latimer] limited the hart. **1618** G. STRODE *Anat. Mortalitie* 214 The blessed and triumphing Church in heauen. **1660** *Charac. Italy* 6 Her streets..did shine with triumphing Cæsars and Consuls in their trophæal Chariots. **1721** DE FOE *Mem. Cavalier* II. 293 With a triumphing Enemy at our Heels. **1868** LYNCH *Rivulet* CXL. i, With adoring homage..And spirit triumphing.

Hence **'triumphingly** *adv.*, triumphantly (now *rare* or *Obs.*).

1552 LYNDESAY *Monarche* 3937 He rose..On the thrid day, tryumphandlye. **1645** BP. HALL *Remedy Discontent* xvii. 97 The good soul..can triumphingly say, O Death, where is thy sting? **1680** C. NESSE *Church Hist.* 72 Free-grace..rides triumphingly over all the incapacities.

†**tri'umphous**, *a.* *Obs. rare.* [f. L. *triumph-us* TRIUMPH + -OUS.] = TRIUMPHANT. Hence †**tri'umphously** *adv.*

c **1468** in *Archæologia* (1846) XXXI. 337 The Duke adressid hym, horssid and armid, tryhumphoslye accompanyd wᵗ lordis unto the felde. **1501** DOUGLAS *Pal. of Hon.* Verses to Jas. IV, i, Triumphous laud with palme of victorie. **1546** *Primer Hen. VIII* 145 Jesus, a King most merveilous, Noble, excellent, & triumphous.

†**'triumphress.** *Obs. rare.* [f. TRIUMPHER + -ESS.] A female triumpher.

c **1780** MONSEY in Jeaffreson *Bk. Doctors* (1860) II. iv. 84 Kill the Triumphress, and avenge my wrong.

triumvir (traɪ'ʌmvə(r)). Also 7 -ver. Pl. -virs, or in L. form -viri (-vɪraɪ). [a. L. *triumvir*, usually in pl. *triumvirī* (also *trēsvirī*), back-formation from *trium virōrum*, gen. pl. of *trēs virī* three men.] *Rom. Hist.* One of three magistrates or public officers forming a committee charged with one of the departments of the administration; also, a member of the coalition of Pompey, Cæsar, and Crassus, B.C. 60 (first triumvirate), or of the administration of Cæsar, Antony, and Lepidus, B.C. 43 (second triumvirate).

1579–80 NORTH *Plutarch* (1595) 940 M. Anthony the Triumuir. **1600** HOLLAND *Livy* VI. xxi. 232 They created certaine *Quinqueviri* for the division of the Pomptine lands: and *Triumviri* for the planting of a colonie at Nepet. **1697** DRYDEN *Æneid* Notes 626 Virgil had..describ'd the Miseries which Rome had undergone betwixt the Triumvirs and the Common-wealth-Party. **1704** HEARNE *Duct. Hist.* (1714) I. 378 Three Men called *Triumviri* were yearly appointed to be Judges what Lands were Public and what Private. **1814** BYRON *Corsair* II. xv, Yet be the soft triumvir's fault forgiven. **1847** TENNYSON *Princ.* VII. 116 By axe and eagle sat, With all their foreheads drawn in Roman scowls..The fierce triumvirs.

b. *transf.* and *fig. pl.* Three persons (or things) associated in power or authority; cf. TRIUMVIRATE 2, 3; *spec.* in the French Revolution: see quot. 1895.

1619 PURCHAS *Microcosmus* v. 34 Those *Triumviri*, the Liver, Heart, and Braine. **1788** *Gentl. Mag.* Jan. 16/2 Those triumviri in the republick of letters, Lipsius, Casaubon, Scaliger. **1837** CARLYLE *Fr. Rev.* III. VI. vii, Saint-Just is standing motionless,..Couthon ejaculating, 'Triumvir?'.. Robespierre is struggling to speak. **1894** *Q. Rev.* July 98 Keble, Newman and Pusey have been called its Triumvirs. **1895** *Edin. Rev.* Oct. 388 The Triumvirs, as they were called,—that is, Robespierre, Couthon, and St. Just.

Hence **tri'umvirship**, triumvirate.

1597 BEARD *Theatre God's Judgem.* (1612) 411 In the beginning of his triumuirship. **1870** *Echo* 7 Nov., The narrow escape we have had from another Reign of Terror, under the triumvirship of..MM. Flourens, Pyat, and Blanqui.

†**tri'umviracy.** *Obs. rare.* [f. as TRIUMVIRATE: see -ACY.] = TRIUMVIRATE.

1678 R. L'ESTRANGE *Seneca's Mor.* (1776) 260 In the triumviracy he made use of his sword.

triumviral (traɪ'ʌmvɪrəl), *a.* [ad. L. *triumvirāl-is*, f. *triumvir*, TRIUMVIR.] Of or pertaining to a triumvir or a triumvirate.

1579 TWYNE *Phisicke agst. Fort.* I. xlii. 60 b, He was thought to haue condemned certayne in the Triumuiral proscription. *a* **1671** LD. FAIRFAX *Mem.* (1699) 82 The army had three Generals, Lesly, Manchester and Fairfax... This Triumviral Government. **1862** MERIVALE *Rom. Emp.* III. xxxi. 448 The triumviral commission which gave him the government of one third part of the empire.

triumvirate (traɪ'ʌmvɪrət). Also 6–7 -virat, 7 -verat, *erron.* triumpherate. [ad. L. *triumvirāt-us*, f. *triumvir*, TRIUMVIR: see -ATE¹.]

1. *Rom. Hist.* The position, office, or function of the triumviri, or of a triumvir; an association of three magistrates for joint administration: see TRIUMVIR.

1601 HOLLAND *Pliny* XXXV. xi. II. 546 A pretie jest.. reported.. as touching Lepidus: It happened during the time of his Triumvirat. **1606** SHAKS. *Ant. & Cl.* III. vi. 28 He frets That Lepidus of the Triumpherate, should be depos'd. **1718** ROWE tr. *Lucan* I. 182 The fierce Triumvirate combin'd in peace. **1841** W. SPALDING *Italy & It. Isl.* I. 89 Cæsar's..weaker rivals.., Antony and Lepidus, who had formed with him the Second Triumvirate.

2. By extension: Any association of three joint rulers or powers.

1584 *Leycesters Commw.* (1641) 86* What doe you thinke ..of this new Triumvirat so lately concluded about Arbella? *c* **1650** DENHAM *On Fletcher's Wks.* 30 When Jonson, Shakespear, and thyself,..swayed in the triumvirate of wit. **1741–2** H. WALPOLE *Lett. to Mann* (1834) I. 64 A triumvirate who hate one another more than any body they could proscribe. **1861** *Sat. Rev.* 23 Nov. 526 He wishes Germany to be ruled by a triumvirate of Ministers.

fig. **1643** SIR T. BROWNE *Relig. Med.* I. §19 There is in our Soul a kind of Triumvirate, or triple Government of three Competitors. **1649** MILTON *Eikon.* xxii. Wks. (1847) 323/2 That violent and lawless triumvirate within him, under the falsified names of his reason, honour, and conscience. **1898** C. MARTYN in *Voice* (N.Y.) 9 June 6/4 The third member in his triumvirate of powers was a robust conscience.

3. Less exactly, A group or set of three persons (*rarely* things) thought of together, but not necessarily associated in fact; a trio; *esp.* three persons of authority or distinction in any sphere.

1654 H. L'ESTRANGE *Chas. I* (1655) 145 June the 14. a Triumvirate of Libellers, Mr. Prin,..Dr. Bastwick,..and Mr. Burton..received a severe censure in the Star-chamber. **1748** RICHARDSON *Clarissa* Wks. 1883 VIII. 197 How I cursed the censoriousness of this plaguy triumvirate! A parson, a milliner, and a mantua-maker! **1873** LOWELL *Among my Bks.* Ser. II. 2 The great triumvirate of Italian poetry, good sense, and culture. **1898** W. GRAHAM *Lost Links* 117 The triumvirate of the young century [Byron, Shelley, Keats].

4. *attrib.* or as *adj.*

1586 T. B. *La Primaud. Fr. Acad.* I. 659 Brutus and Cassius..slew Cæsar: wherupon..the triumvirate war was opened against them. **1624** CAPT. SMITH *Virginia* V. 181 A petition..vnto the triumuerat Gouernors. **1849** *Morning Chron.* 3 Feb., A triumvirate leadership..Mr. Herries, Lord Granby, and Mr. Disraeli.

† **tri'umviry**. *Obs.* Also *erron.* triumphery. [? for L. *triumvirī*, pl. of TRIUMVIR.] = TRIUMVIRATE.

1588 SHAKS. *L.L.L.* IV. iii. 53 *Lon.* Am I the first yt haue been periur'd so? *Ber.* I could put thee in comfort, not by two that I know, Thou makest the triumphery. **1656** EARL MONM. tr. *Boccalini's Advts. fr. Parnass.* 222 The City pretor..accusing the Triumviry of having exceeded the bounds of their authority.

triunal (traɪ'juːnəl), *a. poet. rare.* [f. as next + -AL[1].] = next.

a **1711** KEN *Hymnarium* Poet. Wks. 1721 II. 64 In the same Hymn the mystic four Triunal God adore. **1855** BAILEY *Mystic* 13 The true, triunal God.

triune ('traɪjuːn, *occas.* traɪ'juːn), *a.* (*sb.*) [f. TRI- + L. *ūnus* one.] Three in one; constituting a trinity in unity. **a.** of the Godhead; also of heathen deities.

1635 QUARLES *Embl.* V. viii. 31 The Son and heir to heav'n's Tri-une Jehove. *a* **1711** KEN *Hymns Festiv.* Poet. Wks. 1721 I. 270 We firmly God Triune believe. **1832** I. TAYLOR *Saturday Even.* (1834) 471 The economy of human Salvation has..signalised the distinction of the Triune Nature. **1904** BUDGE *3rd & 4th Egypt. Rooms Brit. Mus.* 82 A figure of..a singing woman of Amen-Rā, adoring the triune form of the sun-god.

b. *gen.* (often with allusion to a.).

1705 PENN in *Pa. Hist. Soc. Mem.* X. 73 Humility, fear, and love are the triune qualities of a true Christian. **1867** GOLDW. SMITH *Three Eng. Statesmen* (1882) 8 The triune despotism of the Privy Council, the Star-Chamber, the Court of High Commission. **1874** L. MORRIS *Ode Fair Spring Morning* 55 Youth, dawn, springtide, triune miracle!

c. Being three at a birth; 'trin'. *rare*$^{-1}$.

1771 *Stanhope* (*Durham*) *Par. Register Baptisms* 21 Dec. (MS.), Thomas, William, and George, triune sons of Thomas Thistlewaite.

B. *sb.* A being that is three in one; a group of three things united; a trinity in unity.

1605 TIMME *Quersit.* II. ii. 108 It hath pleased the omnipotent Creator to..showe himself a Unitrine or Triune. *a* **1711** KEN *Sion* Poet. Wks. 1721 IV. 363 The great Triune in Counsel far above. **1866** R. S. CANDLISH *1st Ep. John* xlvi. 516 The 'three in one' unitedly, 'the Triune'. **1879** G. MEREDITH *Egoist* I. v. 67 She had money and health and beauty, the triune of perfect starriness.

triungulin (traɪ'ʌŋgjʊlɪn), *a.* and *sb. Entom.* [f. TRI- + L. *ungula* claw + -IN[2].] **a.** *adj.* Having three claws on each leg, as the larvæ of the *Meloidæ* or blister-beetles in their first stage. **b.** *sb.* A triungulin larva.

1891 *Cent. Dict.*, Triungulin, *n.* **1899** *Cambr. Nat. Hist.* VI. 270 The eggs of the blister-beetle..giving rise to little larvæ of the kind called triungulin, because each leg is terminated by three tarsal spines or claws. *Ibid.* 301 The young triungulins.

tri-'unial, *a.* (*sb.*) [f. TRI-, after BI-UNIAL.] Applied to a magic lantern having three optical tubes combined in one: also ellipt. as *sb.*

1891 *Daily News* 3 Dec. 5/5 A lecturer..who was provided..with what was described as 'a magnificent triunial'.

triunity (traɪ'juːnɪtɪ). Also **Triunity**. [f. TRIUNE + -ITY, or f. TRI- + UNITY.]

1. The state or attribute of being three in one. **a.** of the Godhead: cf. TRINITY 1 b.

1653 H. MORE *Conject. Cabbal.* (1713) 157 The Præexistence of the Soul, and the Triunity in the Godhead, which Pythagoras taught. **1673** [see TRINITY 1 b]. *a* **1711** KEN *Hymns Evang.* Poet. Wks. 1721 I. 271 We guess from Man's co-eval Three, At God's ador'd Triunity. **1825** COLERIDGE *Aids Refl.* (1848) I. 134 The Scriptural..idea of God will, in its development, be found to involve the idea of the Triunity.

b. *gen.*: cf. TRINITY 1 a.

1816 COLERIDGE *Lay Serm.* 340 There exists in the human being..no mean symbol of Tri-unity, in reason, religion, and the will. **1894** ILLINGWORTH *Personality* iii. (1895) 71 The family..its abstract triunity being..personally realised in father, mother, and child.

2. Three in one; a set or group of three constituting a unity. **a.** The Godhead conceived as three 'persons': = TRINITY 2.

1621 T. BEDFORD *Sin unto Death* 15 Nor is it possible to offend any one person of this Tri-vnitie, but the iniurie doth redound to them all. *a* **1834** COLERIDGE in *Lit. Rem.* (1839) IV. 210 Instead of one Tri-unity we might have a mille-unity... Sherlock..had not the clear idea of the Trinity.

b. *gen.* = TRINITY 3.

1646 *Unhappy Game Scotch & Eng.* 8 Then were it a Triunity, and not a Bi-unity.

So **tri,unifi'cation**, the action of making to be three in one; **tri'union** = *triunity*; **triuni'tarian**, a believer in the triunity of the Godhead: = TRINITARIAN B. 2.

1892 *Nation* (N.Y.) 20 Oct. 305/3 To secure..the *triunification of Germany. **1650** T. VAUGHAN *Anima Magica* To the Author, And fix the roving thoughts in one Inseperate *Triunion. **1819** G. S. FABER *Dispensations* (1823) I. 188 Jewish commentators..cannot be said to have any of (what the Socinians would call) the prejudices of the *Triunitarians. **1859** LD. ACTON *Lett.* (1909) 103 The triunion representing Germany in that triumvirate would also..be president of the new Germanic confederation.

trivage, dial. corruption of TRAVIS[2].

trival, obs. erron. form of TRIVIAL.

trivalent (traɪ'veɪlənt, 'traɪvələnt, 'trɪv-), *a.* and *sb.* [f. TRI- + L. *valēnt-em*, pr. pple. of *valēre* to be worth.] **A.** *adj.* **1.** *Chem.* Having the combining power of three atoms of hydrogen or other univalent element; combining with three atoms of a univalent element or radical.

1868 FOWNES *Elem. Chem.* (ed. 10) 251 Trivalent elements or Triads. **1876** TILDEN *Chem. Philos.* 143 The group PO_4 is trivalent, and so it holds together the two atoms of sodium and one atom of hydrogen in one molecule. **1880** CLEMINSHAW *Wurtz' Atom. The.* 260 The ammonia type [represented] the combination of a trivalent atom with three univalent atoms. **1888** MUIR & MORLEY *Watts' Dict. Chem.* I. 524 The atom of B [Boron] is trivalent in gaseous molecules.

2. *Cytology.* That is (part of) a trivalent.

1921 *Proc. Nat. Acad. Sci.* VII. 200 In the 8 remaining prophase or metaphase figures, not all the trivalent chromosomes could be distinguished from the bivalents or univalents into which they had divided, or from which they were composed. **1929** [see QUADRIVALENT *a.* 2]. **1976** *Genetical Res.* XXVIII. 55 We present data pertaining to..chromosome XVII trisomics of *S[accharomyces] cerevisiae* which demonstrate that trivalent meiotic association occurs with a high frequency.

3. *Immunol.* Of a vaccine: giving immunity to three forms of a disease.

1959 *New Scientist* 19 Feb. 395 (*caption*) Transfer of single strain vaccine pools to tanks to form final trivalent vaccine. **1961** *Guardian* 25 Oct. 3/5 A 'trivalent' form of vaccine will be used. This contains polio virus of all three types.

B. *sb. Cytology.* With pronunc. ('trɪvələnt). A multivalent consisting of three chromosomes.

1922 *Amer. Naturalist* LVI. 341 There are 12 sets of three united chromosomes each, and these trivalents can be arranged according to the size formula. **1936** *Hereditas* XXI. 305 In triploid hybrids..there was a high frequency of trivalents. **1975** [see QUADRIVALENT *sb.* 2].

Hence **trivalence** ('traɪvələns, 'trɪv-), the quality of being trivalent; also **tri'valency**.

1888 *Athenæum* 21 July 102/2 The trivalence of the metals of the aluminium group. **1888** *Jrnl. Chem. Soc.* LIV. 1071 The formula for benzene [was]..afterwards given up owing to the difficulty of explaining the trivalency of carbon which it involved. **1927** N. V. SIDGWICK *Electronic Theory of Valency* xv. 271 Trivalency [of carbon]..only arises under extreme compulsion, and is excessively unstable.

trivalve ('traɪvælv), *sb.* and *a. Nat. Hist.* [f. TRI- + VALVE, after *bivalve*.] **a.** *sb.* A shell having three valves. **b.** *adj.* Having three valves. Also **'trivalved**, † **tri'valvous**, **tri'valvular** *adjs.*

1776 DA COSTA *Conchology* 278 These Shells are *trivalves, and have two large valves, with a small valve placed between them, near to the hinge. **1891** *Cent. Dict.*, Trivalve, *a.* and *n.* **1856** W. CLARK *Van der Hoeven's Zool.* I. 190 Head *trivalved. **1681** GREW *Musæum* II. I. iv. 198 *Trivalvous, i.e. composed of three Sides or Plates joyned together by the length of the Shell. **1693** SIR T. P. BLOUNT *Nat. Hist.* 60 Bauhinus Pictures it [the Ginger plant]..with a trivalvous Cod. **1785** MARTYN *Rousseau's Bot.* xx. (1794) 278 Purslain has..a capsule of one cell..; in some species it opens horizontally, in others it is *trivalvular.

trivant, dial. var. TRUANT. Hence (*nonce-wds.*) **trivanting** *a.*, playing the truant; † **trivantly** *a.* or *adv.*, ? idle or idly.

1621 BURTON *Anat. Mel.* I. ii. III. xv. 181 These men..cannot distinguish betwixt a true Schollar, and..him that by reason of a voluble tongue, and some triuantly [*ed.* 1624 *adds* Polyanthean] helps, steales and gleanes a few notes from other mens haruests. **1624** *Ibid.* Democr. to Rdr. (ed. 2) 8 A trifler, a triuant, thou art an idle fellow. **1851-85** Trivant, trivent in *Eng. Dial. Dict.* from Chesh., Leic., Northants., and Oxf. [**1863** SALA *Capt. Dangerous* I. iv. 90 Those trifling and trivanting gentlewomen that pull diseases on to their pates with drums and routs, and late hours.]

trivariant (traɪ'vɛərɪənt), *a. Physical Chem.* [f. TRI- 5 + VARIANT *a.*] Applied to a system having three degrees of freedom or variable factors; e.g. one in which the temperature, pressure, and concentration of the components can be varied independently without destroying the nature of the system.

1902 TREVOR in *Jrnl. Phys. Chem.* VI. 136, I would therefore suggest..that when the variance is successively zero, one, two, three..the system be said to be in an Invariant, Univariant, Bivariant, Trivariant..state. [Cf. **1904** A. FINDLAY *Phase Rule and its Applications*.]

† **trive**, *v. Obs.*, nonce-abbreviation of CONTRIVE.

1573 TUSSER *Husb.* (1878) 137 Teach timelie to trauerse the thing that thou triue. *marg.* Triue for contriue.

trivector (traɪ'vɛktə(r)). *Geom.* [f. TRI- + VECTOR *sb.*] A set of three vectors, i.e. *radii vectores* (see RADIUS *sb.* 3 e) from the same point.

1869 CAYLEY *Math. Papers* VII. 400 We should have the focus and three points on the orbit; or (what is the same thing) three radius vectors from the focus, say a 'trivector'.

triverbal to **trivertebral**: see TRI- 1.

trivess, Sc. dial. form of TRAVIS[2].

trivet ('trɪvɪt). Forms: ? 1 trefet, 5 trevid, treued, trefet, -ett, 5-6 trevette, 5-9 trevet, 6 trevyt, treyvette, trivette, tryvette, 6-7 trevett, tryvet, trivett, 7 trifet, 7-9 trevit, (9 *dial.* trewit), 6- trivet. [*Trefet* occurs in a 12th c. copy of a 10th c. document (see below), otherwise it is not known till the 15th c.; it appears to be this word, and to represent L. *triped-em*, nom. *tripēs* three-footed, f. *tri-* three + *pēs*, *ped-*foot; cf. OF. *trepied*, *tripié*, *trespieds*, TRIPPET[2].

11.. *Rec. Gifts of Adeluuold* (*963-84*) in Birch *Cart. Sax.* III. 367, vi bidenfate & ii cuflas & þry troȝas & lead & trefet & ix winterstellas & i fedelsswin.]

1. A three-footed stand or support: = TRIPOD A. 3, 4. Now *rare* exc. as in b.

1526 *Pilgr. Perf.* (W. de W. 1531) 37 b, And by sayenge of theyr pater noster make a treuet go rounde about the hous. **1594** PLAT *Jewell-ho.* II. 23 A large Balneo, wherein you may place sixe or eight glasse bodies..each of them fastened to a leaden trivet, yt they may stand steady in the water. **1653** H. MORE *Antid. Ath.* II. ii. §14 (1712) 47 Who perceiving that his Iron Trevet..had three Feet and could stand expected also that it should walk. **1782** BECKFORD *Italy*, *&c.* (1834) I. v. 347 [They] shifted their trivets from cow to cow. **1888** DOUGHTY *Arabia Deserta* II. 146 Abdullah made a trivet of reeds, and balancing thereupon his long matchlock..he fired.

b. *spec.* A stand for a pot, kettle, or other vessel placed over a fire for cooking or heating something: orig. and properly standing on three feet; now often with one or two vertical projections by which it may be secured on the top bar of a grate.

1416 *Maldon, Essex, Court Rolls* Bundle 10 No. 3 Districtus est per 1 trevet, 1 patell. de eneo. *c* **1483** CAXTON *Dialogues* 8/5 The ladle of the pot about the fyre; Treuet for to sette it on. **1561** HOLLYBUSH *Hom. Apoth.* 36 Put the same into a newe pot, set it by the fyre vpon a treuet. **1683** MOXON *Mech. Exerc.*, *Printing* xi. ¶23 This Caldron is set upon a good strong Iron Trevet. **1755** HALES in *Phil. Trans.* XLIX. 342 In Devonshire, they set the pans of milk on trivets, making fires under them, to give the milk..a scalding. **1838** DICKENS *O. Twist* xii, He sat over the fire with a saveloy and a small loaf in his left hand..and a pewter pot on the trivet. **1875** M. COLLINS *Sweet & Twenty* I. xviii, A defiant kettle sang upon a trivet.

c. *Her.* A bearing representing the three-footed stand used in cooking, usually as viewed from above, the three feet being shown around the edge.

a **1550** in *Baring-Gould & Twigge's West. Armory* (1898) 3 Arg: a trivet sab. **1688** R. HOLME *Armoury* III. xiv. (Roxb.) 7/2 He beareth Argent, a three square Trevett, sable.

† **d.** *pl. dialectal* (**trewets, truets**): see quot.

1674 RAY *S. & E.C. Words* 77 *Trewets* or *Truets*, Pattens for Women, *Suff.*

e. Applied allusively to prehistoric stone structures. (See also quot. 1892 in 4.)

1596 SPENSER *State Irel.* Wks. (Globe) 643/1 These..greate stones..which some vaynlye term the old Gyaunts Trivetts.

† **2.** A three-footed vessel, as a pot, cauldron, etc.; chiefly *Antiq.* = TRIPOD A. 1. *Obs.*

1547-64 BAULDWIN *Mor. Philos.* (Palfr.) 10 Certaine fishers found a golden tresle or triuet. **1612** *North's Plutarch* 1231 Pausanias..offered a triuet of gold vnto the temple of Delphes. **1676** HOBBES *Iliad* IX. 118 Seven fire new Trevets.

† **b.** = TRIPOD A. 2. *Obs.*

1577-87 HOLINSHED *Chron.* III. 1238/1 Who suppose euerie blast of their mouth to come foorth of Trophonius den, and that they spake from the triuet. *a* **1641** BP. MOUNTAGU *Acts & Mon.* iii. (1642) 205 Shee [Cumana Sibylla] composed her selfe upon a golden Trifet, and..uttered what by Inspiration was suggested to her.

3. Phr. ***as right as a trivet***, thoroughly or perfectly right (in reference to a trivet's always standing firm on its three feet).

1835 HOOD *Dead Robbery* x, 'I'm right', thought Bunce, 'as any trivet'. **1837** DICKENS *Pickw.* I, 'I hope you are well, sir'. 'Right as a trivet, sir', replied Bob Sawyer. **1868** HELPS *Realmah* ii. (1876) 24 All goes as right as a trivet.

4. *attrib.* Three-footed; having three feet, legs, or supports: = TRIPOD B. 1.

1481-90 *Howard Househ. Bks.* (Roxb.) 45 To Tomas pewterer for..a trefet vesel iiij.d. **1700** DRYDEN *Ovid's Met.* VIII. *Baucis* 84 The Trivet-Table of a Foot was lame. **1892** H. OWEN in *Owen's Descr. Pembrokeshire* 254 *note*, [They call the stone *Gromlegh*..There are other stones..in the Countrey adioyneinge as *Legh y tribedd* neere Ricordstone..] 'The trivet (or tripod) stone',..so called because of its three supporters.

Hence **ˈtrivetwise** *adv.*, in the manner of a trivet.

1859 R. F. BURTON *Centr. Afr.* in *Jrnl. Geog. Soc.* XXIX. 418 The fireplaces are three stones or clods, placed trivetwise upon the ground.

trivet, variant of TREVAT.

trivia (ˈtrɪvɪə), *sb. pl.* [mod.L., pl. of L. *trivium* (see TRIVIUM), infl. in sense by TRIVIAL *a.* 6.] Trivialities, trifles, things of little consequence.

1902 L. P. SMITH (*title*) Trivia. **1920** *Glasgow Herald* 21 July 8 His [*sc.* Mr. Bennett's] method suggests the amount of human interest and knowledge that may lurk in the trivia of holiday experience. **1929** E. LINKLATER *Poet's Pub* xv. 175 He packed an attaché case with a few shirts,..some toilet trivia. **1947** AUDEN *Age of Anxiety* I. 20 Farouche they appear,..loitering through the..Nocturnal trivia. **1961** B. PYM *No Fond Return of Love* xix. 191 The rooms were furnished in a luxuriantly Victorian style, and filled with such nostalgic trivia as waxed fruit under glass, paper-weights, shell and seaweed pictures, and stuffed birds. **1978** *Sunday Times* 26 Feb. 33/7 Besides, trivia has its importance too. Or to put it another way, trivia have their importance too.

b. [In allusion to the quiz game *Trivia.*] Useless information or (knowledge of) matters of little importance. Freq. *attrib.*, as ***trivia game, question***, etc. Chiefly *U.S.*

1968 *Courier-Mail* (Brisbane) 27 June 2/4 A game called trivia, so called because it's trivial... The trivia game is sweeping the world. A kind of quiz or exchange of useless information. **1968** *Telegraph* (Brisbane) 8 July 22/2 Take one Trivia brain teaser with an Australian flavor—Who was the actor who played the part of Dad in the Dad and Dave film series? **1977** *Washington Post* 13 Mar. E6/1 If you are into trivia collecting, collect me. I'm a good bet to show up in some paperback quiz book one of these days. **1978** *Ibid.* 17 July C1/6 Today's trivia question. As..for instance, who is the heavyweight champion of the world? **1986** *Daily Tel.* 12 May 14/3 She [*sc.* Barbara Morgan]..was to be the answer to the space trivia question: 'Who was the back-up astronaut for Christa McAuliffe, the first teacher to fly in the space shuttle?'

trivial (ˈtrɪvɪəl), *a.* (*sb.*) [ad. L. *triviālis*, in sense 5 below, f. *trivium* (see TRIVIUM); cf. F. *trivial* (16th c. in Godef. *Compl.*).]

A. *adj.* **I. 1.** Belonging to the TRIVIUM of mediæval university studies.

1432-50 tr. *Higden* (Rolls) VI. 333 Sche..hade noble auditors and disciples, to whom sche redde the arte triviall [L. *trivium legeret*]. **1515** BARCLAY *Egloges* iv. (1570) Cvj/1 If they haue smelled the artes triuiall, They count them Poetes hye and heroicall. **1597-8** BP. HALL *Sat.* IV. i. 173 Hath..thrise rehearsed them in his triviall floare. **1807-8** SYD. SMITH *Plymley's Lett.* x. Wks. 1859 II. 178/2 The Protestants may likewise retain their trivial and grammar schools. **1904** KER *Dark Ages* 27 Plato does not allow the mediæval classification of Dialectic as a Trivial Art along with Grammar and Rhetoric.

†**2.** Threefold, triple. *Obs. rare*$^{-1}$.

Cf. late L. use of *triviālis* (Arnobius).

1432-50 tr. *Higden* (Rolls) I. 25 Giraldus of Wales, which describede Topographie of Irlonde, Itinerary of Wales, and the Lyfe of Kinge Henry the Secunde, under a triuialle distinccion [L. *sub triplici distinctione*].

†**3.** Placed where three roads meet. *Obs. rare*$^{-1}$.

1614 SELDEN *Titles Hon.* 129 Their other sacred Triuiall Statues.

4. *Zool.* Belonging to the TRIVIUM of an echinoderm.

1891 in *Cent. Dict.*

II. 5. Such as may be met with anywhere; common, commonplace, ordinary, everyday, familiar, trite. Now *rare* (passing into 6).

1589 NASHE *Pref. Greene's Menaphon* (Arb.) 9 A few of our triviall translators. **1610** HEALEY *St. Aug. Citie of God* VIII. v. 291 It is triuiall in the Schooles: 'Nothing is in the vnderstanding that was not first in the sense'. **1665** GLANVILL *Scepsis Sci.* i. 8 The most ordinary and trivial Phænomena in nature. **1704** F. FULLER *Med. Gymn.* (1711) 37 Explain the manner of this by a trivial Observation. **1827** KEBLE *Chr. Y.*, *Morning* xiv, The trivial round, the common task. **1895** MACEWEN *Life Dr. Cairns* 161 This..is now the trivial definition and ground principle.

6. a. Of small account, little esteemed, paltry, poor; trifling, inconsiderable, unimportant, slight.

1593 SHAKS. *2 Hen. VI*, III. i. 241 We haue but triuiall argument, More then mistrust, that shewes him worthy death. **1655** FULLER *Ch. Hist.* II. i. §5 To demurre to the Truth of his so frequent Miracles, being so Redundant in working them on Triviall Occasions. **1790** BURKE *Fr. Rev.* 94 They..are ready..to abandon for a very trivial interest what they find of very trivial value. **1869** FREEMAN *Norm. Conq.* III. xii. 251 The offence..could..be passed by as altogether trivial.

b. *Math.* Of no consequence or interest, e.g. because equal to zero; satisfying a given relation on a set with every member of the set; *spec.* applied to a subgroup of a given group that either contains only the identity element or is identical with the given group.

1915 R. D. CARMICHAEL *Diophantine Analysis* ii. 28 We have thus established the fact that Eq. (2) has at least one integral solution which is not trivial. **1941** BIRKHOFF & MACLANE *Surv. Mod. Algebra* vi. 135 The reflexive property is trivial (every group is isomorphic to itself by the identity transformation). **1949** S. KRAVETZ tr. *H. Zassenhaus' Theory of Groups* i. 10 $\mathfrak{G}$ and *e* are trivial subgroups of $\mathfrak{G}$. **1953** [see PROPER *a.* 5c(ii)]. **1957** L. FOX *Two-Point Boundary Probl.* vii. 192 If *y* vanishes at $x = 1$ then all the derivatives, if finite, are also zero, giving the trivial solution. **1971** G. GLAUBERMAN in Powell & Higman *Finite Simple Groups* i. 35 These subgroups..will therefore be non-trivial when *P* is not trivial. **1979** *Proc. London Math. Soc.* XXXVIII. 508 Strong spectrality is trivial since $A(K) = A$.

7. *Nat. Hist.* Applied to names of animals and plants: **a.** to a Latin name added to the generic name to distinguish the species: = SPECIFIC A. 5; **b.** to a name in common as distinct from scientific use: Popular, vernacular, vulgar.

a. 1759 B. STILLINGFL. *Misc. Tracts* (1762) Pref. 16 In the last edition of his *Systema naturæ* he [Linnæus] has mentioned above 1500 species of insects, has..given them classical, generical, and trivial or specifical names. **1815** KIRBY & SP. *Entomol.* (1843) I. 181 *Scolytus destructor*, whose trivial name well characterises the..severity of its ravages. **1902** C. D. SHERBORN *Index Animalium* p. vii, All trivial names are entered as if they were masculine, *e.g. nigra* will be found under *niger*.

b. 1815 BURROW *Elem. Conchol.* 193 The following List of English Trivial Names will be found useful to purchasers of shells, as dealers most frequently adopt them. *Ibid.* 194 Trivial Names. Linnæan Name. Lepas. English Name. Acorn Shell. **1901** *Spectator* 17 Aug. 216/1 The trivial name for the whole family of terns..is 'sea-swallow'.

8. *Chem.* Of the name of a chemical species: not systematic; often used in preference to the systematic name for reasons of convenience or tradition, as *neohexane* (systematic name *2,2,dimethylbutane*) or *formaldehyde* (systematic name *methanal*). Cf. SYSTEMATIC *a* 7.

1892 *Nature* 19 May 58/1 The extent to which familiar trivial names shall be retained in the official system [of chemical nomenclature] is therefore a matter of great importance. **1951** *Chem. & Engin. News* 23 July 3036/2 The alchemists used fanciful names; we would class them as 'trivial' names today. **1979** CLARK & MCKERVEY in Barton & Ollis *Comprehensive Org. Chem.* I. ii. 40 Several of these trivial names are still universally accepted... However, trivial names for alkanes containing multiple branching can become cumbersome.

III. 9. *Comb.*, as ***trivial-minded*** adj. (whence ***trivial-mindedness***).

1872 GEO. ELIOT in Cross *Life* (1885) III. 161 We should ..have patience with their trivial-mindedness. **1905** A. R. WALLACE *My Life* II. 383 Even in the most trivial-minded [I] was able to find some common ground of interest.

B. *sb.*

†**1.** = TRIVIUM 1 (in quot. *transf.*). *Obs. rare*$^{-1}$.

1432-50 tr. *Higden* (Rolls) I. 5 The triuialle [L. *trivium*] of the vertues theologicalle and quadriuialle of the cardinalle vertues.

2. *pl.* The three subjects of study constituting the TRIVIUM. Now only *Hist.*

1481, 1522 [see QUADRIVIAL A. 2, B. 2]. **1630** HALES *Gold. Rem.* (1673) 282 In the Trivials and Quadrivials, as old Clerks were wont to name them. **1691** WOOD *Ath. Oxon.* II. 181 Peter Heylyn..profiting in Trivials to a miracle, especially in Poetry. **1716, 1886** [see QUADRIVIAL B. 2].

3. A trivial matter; a triviality, trifle. Usually *pl.*

1715 M. DAVIES *Athen. Brit.* I. 288 'Tis scarce worth disputing..about such trivials. **1886** TUPPER *My Life as Author* 334 Take these twelve as samples of many more such trivials.

4. *Math.* 'A coefficient or other quantity not containing the quantities of the set considered' (*Cent. Dict.* 1891).

trivialism (ˈtrɪvɪəlɪz(ə)m). *rare.* [f. prec. + -ISM.] Trivial character, triviality; something of trivial character, a triviality.

1830 H. N. COLERIDGE *Grk. Poets* (1834) 6 It will be a matter of wonder..that such trivialisms..could ever pass for genuine poetry. **1882** OGILVIE cites CARLYLE.

trivialist (ˈtrɪvɪəlɪst). *rare.* [See -IST.]

1. A student of 'trivials': see TRIVIAL B. 2.

1716 M. DAVIES *Athen. Brit.* III. 3 Fitter for Veterans and Criticks in Closets and Libraries, than for Tyronists and Trivialists in Schools.

2. One who pursues or deals in trivialities.

1829 CARLYLE *Misc.* (1840) II. 173 Voltaire..was, therefore,..no Philosopher, but a highly accomplished Trivialist.

triviality (trɪvɪˈælɪtɪ). [f. L. type **triviālitāt-em*, f. *triviālis* TRIVIAL; cf. F. *trivialité* (Cotgr. 1611), It. *triuialità* (Florio 1598), Sp. *trivialidad*, Pg. *trivialidade*: see -ITY.]

1. The quality of being trivial; commonplace or trifling character.

1598 FLORIO, *Triuialità*, homelines, triuiality. **1817** COLERIDGE *Biog. Lit.* 106 My severest critics have not pretended to have found in my compositions triviality. **1862** BORROW *Wild Wales* lxxxix. III. 228 The loss of the house was a matter of triviality compared with that of the library. **1874** L. STEPHEN *Hours in Library* (1892) II. ii. 39 The genuine excellence which underlay the superficial triviality of Crabbe's verses.

2. With *a*, or (commonly) in *pl.*: Something trivial; a trivial matter, affair, characteristic, remark, etc.; a trifle.

1611 COTGR., *Trivialitez*, Triuialities; triuiall, sleight, common, homelie, ordinarie matters. *c* **1664** BARROW in Rigaud *Corr. Sci. Men* (1841) II. 37, I..find little but repetitions and trivialities. **1831** CARLYLE *Sart. Res.* I. xi. (1858) 45 A..Letter, full of compliments,..dining repartees, and other ephemeral trivialities. **1843** —— *Past & Pr.* III. vi, The Practical labour of England is not a chimerical Triviality. **1877** BLACK *Green Past.* v, Archery meetings and croquet parties and such trivialities.

trivialization (trɪvɪəlaɪˈzeɪʃən). [f. TRIVIALIZE *v.* + -ATION.] The act or process of trivializing.

a **1866** J. GROTE in *Jrnl. Philol.* (1874) V. 153 A still more important law..is that of *evaporation* or *trivialization*; by which I mean the gradual blunting of the force of a word. **1927** H. G. WELLS in *Sunday Express* 26 June 12 The greater danger of promiscuity and the trivialisation of the sexual life lies in a delayed marriage. **1949** KOESTLER *Insight & Outlook* xxviii. 380 By this process of trivialization and smug understatement, the universe itself becomes a silly thought. **1981** *Times* 21 May 4/7 The growing under-use of human abilities through trivialization of work and through unemployment is damaging to those who suffer from them.

trivialize (ˈtrɪvɪəlaɪz), *v.* [f. TRIVIAL + -IZE; cf. mod.F. *trivialiser* (Littré).] *trans.* To make trivial; to render commonplace or trifling.

1846 LANDOR *Imag. Conv.*, *Southey & Landor* Wks. II. 168/1 Milton has ennobled it [the sonnet] in our tongue, and has trivialised it in that [Italian]. **1895** W. PLATT *Women* 147 Trivialising marriage into the enjoyment of a mere instinct.

trivializer (ˈtrɪvɪəlaɪzə(r)). [f. TRIVIALIZE *v.* + -ER[1].] One who trivializes.

1960 F. RAPHAEL *Limits of Love* III. vi. 369 There was.. nothing the happy man thought about less than death, but nor was there anything the trivialiser was more eager to forget. **1980** *Times Lit. Suppl.* 12 Dec. 1405/3 Taylor has been a popularizer without being a trivializer.

trivializing (ˈtrɪvɪəlaɪzɪŋ), *ppl. a.* [f. as next + -ING[2].] That trivializes.

1961 *New Left Rev.* Mar./Apr. 13/2 Berger would..see all 'abstract' art as the product of a trivialising despair. **1966** *Economist* 28 May 970/3 He has serious doubts about the power of literary studies, as now practised, to act as a counterweight to the trivialising forces of our society. **1970** *Radio Times* 8 Oct. 66 It's true that television is endemically a trivialising medium, but it doesn't follow that it *has* to be it.

ˈtrivializing, *vbl. sb.* [f. TRIVIALIZE *v.* + -ING[1].] The action of TRIVIALIZE *v.*

1963 A. HERON *Towards Quaker View of Sex* v. 44 There is an almost overwhelming urge throughout society towards the trivializing of sexual actions. **1979** *Listener* 16 Aug. 220/3 Any such trivialising of the sacred back-fires. The gods will not be mocked.

trivially (ˈtrɪvɪəlɪ), *adv.* [f. TRIVIAL *a.* + -LY[2].] In a trivial manner.

1. Commonly, ordinarily, familiarly; in a commonplace or trite way. Now *rare* or *Obs.*

1625 BACON *Ess.*, *Greatn. Kingd.* (Arb.) 473 Neither is Money the Sinewes of Warre (as it is triuially said). **1647** TRAPP *Comm. Matt.* xi. 17 He is the best preacher, saith Luther, that delivereth himself vulgarly, plainly, trivially. *a* **1661** HOLYDAY *Juvenal* (1673) 211 He thinks it more unhappiness..to die with a divided carcase, then with a whole one:..the whole body being not usually so trivially exposed to scorn, as the head, when divided from the body. **1818** SOUTHEY in *Q. Rev.* XVIII. 9 Leah and Rachel were.. used almost as trivially for examples by poets as by theologians.

2. a. In a trifling, slight, or paltry way; in the way of trifling, frivolously.

1649 J. H. *Motion to Parl. Adv. Learn.* 26 Their youth so trivially spent. **1710** STEELE *Tatler* No. 207 ¶2 Minds which are not trivially disposed. **1858** O. W. HOLMES *Aut. Breakf.-t.* viii. (1883) 161 You speak trivially, but not unwisely.

b. Chiefly *Math.* In an inconsequential or uninteresting way.

1941 BIRKHOFF & MACLANE *Survey Mod. Algebra* vi. 148 The conclusion is trivially true. **1956** E. M. PATTERSON *Topology* ii. 35 Conditions (T.1) and (T.3) are satisfied trivially. **1977** *Language* LIII. 353 But it is trivially true that *all* features characteristic of creole speech will be removed if decreolization is carried far enough.

ˈtrivialness. Now *rare.* [f. as prec. + -NESS.] = TRIVIALITY 1.

a **1687** H. MORE *App. Def. Philos. Cabbala* xi. §1 As for the pretended Trivialness of the Fifth and Sixth Days work. **1732** STACKHOUSE *Hist. Bible* (1767) IV. VI. v. 212 The vast distance of the place and trivialness of the errand. **1855** MILMAN *Lat. Chr.* XIV. ii. (1864) IX. 77 In the puerility and trivialness of their wonders they even surpass the Western Hagiologies.

tri-ˈvided, *ppl. a. nonce-wd.* [f. TRI-, after *divided.*] Divided into three. So **tri-ˈvision** [after *division*], division into three.

1896 J. H. WYLIE *Hist. Eng. Hen. IV*, III. 388 Instead of di-vision they had tri-vision. **1900** —— in *Athenæum* 4 Aug. 146/2 Instead of three Popes and a tri-vided faith.

†**ˈtrivious,** *a. Obs. rare.* [f. L. *trivium* (see TRIVIUM) + -OUS.] = TRIVIAL *a.* 5, 6.

1583 MELBANCKE *Philotimus* Mjb, Intricate endles triuious toylings. **1677** GALE *Crt. Gentiles* II. IV. 219 Upon as sleight and trivious reasons.

trivirgate: see TRI- 1.

triviss, Sc. dial. variant of TRAVIS[2].

‖**trivium** (ˈtrɪvɪəm). [L. (f. *tri-*, TRI- + *via* way), a place where three ways meet; in med.L. in sense 1 below.]

1. In the Middle Ages, the lower division of the seven liberal arts, comprising grammar, rhetoric, and logic. (Cf. QUADRIVIUM.)

1804 RANKEN *Hist. France* III. iv. 308 They included all learning in the seven liberal arts; of which grammar, rhetoric, and dialectics, formed what they called Trivium. 1837 HALLAM *Hist. Lit.* I. I. i. §3. 3 The trivium and quadrivium, a course of seven sciences, introduced in the sixth century. 1886 S. S. LAURIE *Rise Universities* 64 The.. instruction given by Gerbert at Rheims about 1000 A.D. seems to have been simply a full and extended trivium.

2. *Zool.* The three anterior ambulacra of an echinoderm. (Cf. BIVIUM.)

1870 ROLLESTON *Anim. Life* 142 To divide the five rays [in *Asterias*] into a 'bivium', between which the madreporic tubercle lies, and a 'trivium', the two lateral arms of which lie on either side of the arm which is opposite to that tubercle. 1877 HUXLEY *Anat. Inv. Anim.* ix. 570 In the fossil genus, Dysaster, this separation of the ambulacra into trivium and bivium exists naturally.

trivoltine, trivoluminous: see TRI- 4 b, 1 a.

triwe, obs. form of TRUE.

tri-weekly (traɪˈwiːklɪ), *a.*, (*sb.*), and *adv.* [TRI- 3.]

A. *adj.* **a.** Occurring every three weeks, or lasting for three weeks. **b.** Usually, Occurring, appearing, or operating three times every week. Also *absol.* as *sb.*, a tri-weekly journal. orig. *U.S.*

1832 (May 17) W. T. BARRY in *Amer. State Papers* (1834) XV. 348 The line of stages connecting Philadelphia and Delaware with the Eastern shore of Maryland and Virginia, has been increased from a bi-weekly, to a tri-weekly line. 1843 *Penny Cycl.* XXVI. 14/2 Semi- or tri-weekly newspapers. 1851 C. CIST *Sk. Cincinnati in 1851* 74 These are all dailies, tri-weeklies, and weekly reissues of dailies. 1884 *U.S. Census* VIII. 111 Three months only the *Spy* ran as a tri-weekly, and but three months longer as a semi-weekly. 1895 R. H. SHERARD in *Bookman* Oct. 16/2 The tri-weekly supplement of *La Lanterne*. 1903 *Daily Chron.* 15 Jan., The tri-weekly expresses running across Siberia. 1978 D. DAICHES *Edinburgh* vi. 110 The *Caledonian Mercury* (a tri-weekly founded in 1720).

B. *adv.* **a.** Every three weeks. **b.** Three times a week.

1837 J. M. PECK *Gazetteer Illinois* (ed. 2) III. 180 The mail ..arrives here tri-weekly. 1884 G. P. KEESE in *Harper's Mag.* July 300/1 A line of..coaches has been established, leaving tri-weekly. 1901 *Daily News* 12 Jan. 5/3 In consequence of military restrictions..the advertisement sheet which has been appearing every week will be issued tri-weekly.

triwes, triws, obs. forms of TRUCE.

-trix, *suffix*, ending of Latin feminine agent-nouns (with stems in *-trīc-*, acc. *-trīcem*, whence Fr. *-trice*: see -TRICE), corresponding to masculines in *-tor*, as *adjūtrix* female helper, *bellātrix* female warrior, *imperātrix* female commander, empress, *inventrix* female discoverer, *vēnātrix* huntress, etc.; sometimes used adjectively, as *victrix* victorious, *ultrix* avenging. Several of these nouns were adopted in Eng., from ancient or mediæval Latin, in the 15th c. and later, as ADMINISTRATRIX, CONSOLATRIX, CREATRIX, EXECUTRIX, MEDIATRIX, PERSECUTRIX, TESTATRIX, etc.; and others formed on the analogy of them, as INHERITRIX, NARRATRIX, PERPETRATRIX, etc. In Geometry, words in *-trix* denote straight lines (*linea* being understood), as BISECTRIX, DIRECTRIX; more rarely curves or surfaces, as INDICATRIX, TRACTRIX. The suffix has occasionally been loosely used to form nonce-feminines to agent-nouns in *-ter*, as PAINTRIX instead of the regular *paintress*. The commoner suffix in Eng. is -TRESS: see also -TRICE.

trixie, trixsie, trixy, obs. ff. TRICKSY.

trizomal: see TRI- 1.

trizonal (ˈtraɪzəʊnəl), *a. temporary.* [f. TRI- + ZONAL *a.*] Of, pertaining to, or consisting of three zones; *spec.* with reference to the British, French, and American zones of occupation in West Germany at the end of the war of 1939–45. So **tri'zonia**, an area of three zones; *spec.* (with capital initial) West Germany as occupied by the Allies.

1947 *Sun* (Baltimore) 21 Nov. 2/8 Advance indications were that a stalemate at London would bring efforts to expand the present American-British occupation area in Western Germany into a 'trizonia' with France. 1947 *Richmond* (Va.) *Times-Dispatch* 28 Dec. II. 2-B/1 It [*sc.* the German Socialist party] views the proposed establishment of 'Trizonia' with many misgivings. 1948 *Times* 10 Jan. 4/4 Pending steps towards tri-zonal fusion, administrative reorganization must go on in the bizone to secure greater efficiency. 1948 *Sunday Times* 7 Mar. 1 Establishment of a trizonal régime in Western Germany. 1948 *News Chron.* 28 Aug. 1 He said the West German political situation, particularly the question of the formation of a trizonal area was discussed.

trizzie (ˈtrɪzɪ). *Austral. slang.* Also **trizzy.** [Orig. uncertain: perh. f. TREY *sb.* + -IE.] A threepenny piece.

1941 BAKER *Dict. Austral. Slang* 78 *Trizzie*, a 3d. piece. 1959 G. HAMILTON *Summer Glare* 31 My greatest pal now was John 'Trizzie' Peele... He always had a threepenny bit in his pocket which gave him his nickname. 1966 *Sunday Truth* (Brisbane) 23 Dec. 22/1 When you peppered the Christmas pud. with trey-bits this year we hope you remembered they will be scarcer next Yuletide and unless you hoard some there will be no trizzies at all for..the 1968 plum-duff... A trey-bit or a trizzy is Aussie slang for a three-penny-bit.

tro, troa, obs. ff. TROW *v.*

troad, obs. pa. pple. of TREAD *v.*; obs. f. TROD *sb.*

Troadic (trəʊˈædɪk), *a.* [(f. *Troad*, name of the region about Troy,) f. L. *Trōad-*, *Trōas*, a. Gr. Τρωάδ-, Τρωάς (contr. of Τρωϊάς) Trojan + -IC.] Of or pertaining to ancient Troy and its surrounding regions.

1932 *Antiquity* VI. 77 In the second half of the third millennium, the culture which we may call Troadic spread over a large part of Asia Minor. 1977 G. CLARK *World Prehistory* (ed. 3) IV. 157 That Troadic forms reaching Greece were transmitted by way of the Cyclades is confirmed by the occurrence on the mainland of..the ceramic fictiles of 'hour-glass' form.

troak, obs. f. TRUCK.

troan, var. TRON; dial. f. TRUANT.

troat (trəʊt), *v. Venery.* Also 7 **troyte, trout, throat;** 9 *erron.* **froat.** [Cf. OF. *trout* (Godef.), also *trut*, an interjection for urging on hunting dogs, asses, sheep. Cf. also ROUT *v.*[3] to bellow.] *intr.* To cry or bellow: said of a buck at rutting time; cf. BELL *v.*[4] 2, BELLOW *v.* 2, GROAN *v.* 2. Hence **'troating** *vbl. sb.* and *ppl. a.*

1611 COTGR. s.v. *Réer*, In tearmes of hunting we say, that ..the fallow troytes or croynes. *Ibid.*, *Rere*, to bellow as a Stag, to trout as a Buck. 1650 FULLER *Pisgah* III. ix. 338 Here ..the throating Bucks [are said] to lodge. *a* 1700 B. E. *Dict. Cant. Crew* s.v. *Buck*, A Buck Growneth or Troateth, makes a Noise at Rutting time. 1727 *Bradley's Fam. Dict.* s.v. *Buck-hunting*, He groans and troats, as a Hart belleth. 1847–78 HALLIWELL, *Troat*, to bellow, said of the buck. 1900 *Sporting Phraseology* in *Shooting Times* 15 Dec. 15/1 *Froating* or *troating*, call of buck.

b. Said of a swan.

1839 G. DARLEY *Nepenthe* I. (1897) 20 And [the swan] troats for joy, too proud for song.

troath, obs. f. TROTH.

trobel, -bil, -ble, -bul(l, -byll, obs. ff. TROUBLE.

†**trobellion,** obs. var. TOURBILLION, whirlwind.

c 1450 *Merlin* xx. 324 Merlin by crafte made soche a trobellion a-rise that ther lefte nother tente ne pavilon stondinge.

trobelows, -lys, obs. forms of TROUBLOUS.

Trobriand (ˈtrəʊbrɪənd). Used *attrib.*: Of, pertaining to, native to, or produced in the *Trobriand* Islands, a small group of coral islands in the Solomon Sea, now forming part of Papua New Guinea; **Trobriand Islander** = TROBRIANDER.

1922 B. MALINOWSKI *Argonauts W. Pacific* ix. 221 The big bay of Gatu, where once the crews of a whole fleet of Trobriand canoes were killed and eaten. 1935 —— *Coral Gardens & their Magic* II. VI. v. 232 The Trobriand phenomenon of a language of magic..fits into our theory of language. 1937 R. H. LOWIE *Hist. Ethnol. Theory* xiii. 231 The reader becomes saturated with the Trobriand atmosphere. 1951 E. E. EVANS-PRITCHARD *Social Anthropol.* iv. 74 Malinowski came to know the Trobriand Islanders well. 1956 R. REDFIELD *Peasant Society & Culture* 35 The many interrelations of custom, institution, and human need in Trobriand life. 1974 *Country Life* 11 Apr. 838/1 The bronze..can be appreciated..by anyone—atheist, Hottentot, Eskimo, Trobriand Islander.

Trobriander (ˈtrəʊbrɪændə(r)). [f. *Trobriand* (see prec.) + -ER[1].] A native or inhabitant of the Trobriand Islands.

1922 B. MALINOWSKI *Argonauts W. Pacific* ix. 220 The Trobrianders will sail deep, shaded bays. 1969 *Times* 22 Jan. 12/8 The difficulty of disentangling the Trobrianders' original beliefs from what they have been taught by Europeans.

trocar (ˈtrəʊkɑː(r)). Also 8 **trochart, (trois-quarts, -quart),** 8–9 **trocart, trochar.** [ad. F. *troquart, trois-quarts* (1694), *trocart* (1762), f. *trois* three + *carre* side, face of an instrument; so called from its triangular form.] A surgical instrument consisting of a perforator or stylet enclosed in a metal tube or cannula, used for withdrawing fluid from a cavity, as in dropsy, etc.

1706 PHILLIPS (ed. Kersey), *Trochar*, a Cane, or Pipe made of Silver, or Steel, with a sharp-pointed End, us'd in tapping those that are troubled with the Dropsy. 1739 HUXHAM in *Phil. Trans.* XLI. 644 A very small hollow Needle with Perforations, as in that used by some instead of the Trocar. 1744 WARRICK *ibid.* XLIII. 16 My Apparatus was a large Trois-quarts, made on purpose, and dipped in Oil; an Injector [etc.]. 1751 *Ibid.* XLVII. xl. 268 The common trocarts did not seem proper. 1758 J. S. *Le Dran's Observ. Surg.* (1771) 216 He perforated it with the *Troisquart*. 1861 HULME tr. *Moquin-Tandon* II. VI. iv. 304 The Ticks plunge their beaks into the skin in the same way as one may thrust in a trochar. 1876 GROSS *Dis. Bladder* 32 If abscesses point, they must be opened with the knife, or trocar.

attrib. 1863–76 CURLING *Dis. Rectum* 101 A sharp trocar-needle can be passed through the canula. 1905 ROLLESTON *Dis. Liver* 54 There was..fibrinous peritonitis around the site of the trocar punctures.

†**troch,** obs. Sc. form of THROUGH *prep.*

1573 TYRIE *Refut.* in *Cath. Tractates* (S.T.S.) 29 To expose thame self troch sic wane subterfugis.

troch, Sc. form of TROUGH; var. of TROCHE.

‖**trocha** (ˈtrɒtʃa). *Mil.* [Sp.] A strategic line of defences, as trenches, blockhouses, etc.; a military cordon.

1896 *Daily News* 9 Dec. 7/5 The Spanish force,..near Punta Brava [Cuba], on the western side of the trocha. 1898 *Ibid.* 13 Apr. 3/1 These trochas have at every corner and at frequent intervals along the sides what are called forts, but which are really small blockhouses. 1902 R. T. HILL in *Encycl. Brit.* XXVII. 306/1 A corps of 20,000 men was stationed on this *trocha* or military cordon.

trochaic (trəʊˈkeɪɪk), *a.* and *sb. Pros.* [a. F. *trochaïque* (*c* 1550 in Godef. *Compl.*), or ad. L. *trochaic-us*, ad. Gr. τροχαϊκός, f. τροχαῖος: see TROCHEE.]

A. *adj.* **1.** Of a verse, rhythm, etc.: Consisting of, characterized by, or based on trochees.

1589 PUTTENHAM *Eng. Poesie* II. xiii. (Arb.) 136 Verses where the sharpe accent falles vpon the first and third, and so make the verse wholly Trochaicke. 1776 BURNEY *Hist. Mus.* (1789) I. vi. 73 The dialogue admitted, occasionally, Trochaic verses. 1835 T. MITCHELL *Acharn. Aristoph.* 190 *note*, In the structure of the comic trochaic tetrameter catalectic, the nice points of tragic verse are freely neglected.

2. Of a foot, etc.: Of the nature of a trochee; consisting of a long (or an accented) followed by a short (or an unaccented) syllable.

trochaic spondee, a spondee having the accent or *ictus* upon the first syllable.

1756–82 J. WARTON *Ess. Pope* II. 213 An intermixture of those different feet (iambic and trochaic particularly) into which our language naturally falls. 1827 TATE *Grk. Metres* in *Theatre of Greeks* (ed. 2) 426 In the two following lines will be found specimens of..the Trochaic Spondee in all its places. 1888 H. W. CHANDLER *Elem. Grk. Accentuation* I. i. (ed. 2) 2 A word with a trochaic ending and accented penultimate must be properispome.

B. *sb.* A trochaic verse or foot.

1693 DRYDEN *Juvenal* Ded. (1697) 44 One Poem consisted only of Hexameters; and another was entirely of Iambiques; a third of Trochaiques. 1756–82 J. WARTON *Ess. Pope* (ed. 4) I. ii. 55 He conjures the powers below in beautiful trochaics. 1827 TATE *Grk. Metres* in *Theatre of Greeks* (ed. 2) 427 This nicety of structure in the long Trochaic of Tragedy.

Also **tro'chaical** *a. rare* (*lit.* and *fig.*); hence **trochai'cality**, trochaic character.

1755 JOHNSON, *Trochaical*, consisting of trochees. 1910 *Sat. Rev.* 18 June 791/1 A trochee of quite excessive trochaicality. 1930 R. CAMPBELL *Poems* 10 Jack Squire through his own teardrops sploshes In his great flat trochaical goloshes.

trochal (ˈtrɒkəl, ˈtrəʊkəl), *a.* [f. Gr. τροχ-ός wheel + -AL[1].]

1. *Zool.* Resembling a wheel; rotiform: as the ***trochal apparatus, disk,*** or ***organ*** of the Rotifera, an organ of locomotion consisting of two rings of cilia surrounding the mouth. **b.** Having a trochal apparatus, as a rotifer: = TROCHATE (*Cent. Dict.*).

1841–71 T. R. JONES *Anim. Kingd.* (ed. 4) 482 The space between the two layers of the trochal disk. 1888 ROLLESTON & JACKSON *Anim. Life* 632 Class Rotifera. Unisegmental Vermes with a retractile trochal apparatus at the anterior end of the body. 1899 *Syd. Soc. Lex.*, *Trochal organ*, the characteristic oral organ of the Rotifera.

2. Revolving like a wheel or top. *rare*⁻⁰.

1891 in *Cent. Dict.*

trochalopod (ˈtrɒkələʊpɒd, trəʊˈkæləpɒd), *sb.* (*a.*) *Entom.* [f. mod.L. *Trochalopod-a*, neut. pl., f. Gr. τροχαλός adj. running, rolling + πούς, ποδ- foot.] A member of the *Trochalopoda*, a group of heteropterous insects in which the posterior coxæ have a rotary motion. **b.** *adj.* Belonging to the *Trochalopoda*. Also **trochalopodous** (trɒkəˈlɒpədəs) *a.*

1870 *Ann. & Mag. Nat. Hist.* Sept. 233 The coxæ of trochalopodous Heteroptera are round. 1909 *Cent. Dict. Suppl.*, Trochalopod.

trochanter (trəʊˈkæntə(r)). *Anat.* and *Zool.* [a. F. *trochanter* (Paré, 16th c.), a. Gr. τροχαντήρ (in sense 1), f. τρέχειν to run.]

1. A protuberance or process in the upper part of the thigh-bone, serving for the attachment of certain muscles; usually, as in man, two in number, the ***great trochanter*** (*t. major*) for the external rotator muscles, and the ***lesser trochanter*** (*t. minor*) for the ilio-psoas muscle.

1615 CROOKE *Body of Man* 997 The great Trochanter.. the lesser Trochanter. These two processes are ioyned together by a line which buncheth out behind. 1741 MONRO *Anat. Bones* (ed. 3) 279 The Muscles inserted into these two Processes being the principal Instruments of the rotatory Motion of the Thigh, have occasioned the Name of Trochanters to the Processes. 1881 MIVART *Cat* 282

Between the great trochanter and the tuberosity of the ischium.

2. *Entom.* The second joint of an insect's leg, next to the coxa (COXA 2); sometimes consisting of two joints (cf. TROCHANTIN b).

1816 KIRBY & SP. *Entomol.* xxii. (1818) II. 286 These legs .. vary in larvæ of the different orders; but they seem in most to have joints answering to the hip (*coxa*); trochanter; thigh (*femur*); shank (*tibia*); foot (*tarsus*), of perfect insects. **1861** HULME tr. *Moquin-Tandon* II. VI. i. 310 Each limb [of the Sarcoptus Scabiei] consists of a hip, trochanter, small trochanter, thigh, leg, and tarsus.

Hence **trochanteral** (-'kæntərəl), **trochanterian** (-'tɪərɪən) (*rare*$^{-0}$) [F. *trochantérien*], **trochanteric** (-'tɛrɪk) *adjs.*, pertaining to a trochanter; *trochanteric fossa* = digital fossa (see DIGITAL A. 2).

1842 E. WILSON *Anat. Vade M.* (1851) 254 The trochanteric fossa of the femur. **1857** DUNGLISON *Med. Lex.*, *Trochanterian.* **1890** HUMPHRY *Old Age* 16 Liability to fracture .. especially remarkable in the trochanteric part and neck of the thigh-bone. **1961** WEBSTER, Trochanteral. **1967** J. H. SUDD *Introd. Behaviour Ants* ii. 15 The coxal and trochanteral joints.

trochantin (trəʊ'kæntɪn). *Anat.* and *Zool.* [a. F. *trochantin*, f. *trochanter* (see above).] **a.** The lesser trochanter: see TROCHANTER 1. *rare*$^{-0}$. **b.** *Entom.* The proximal joint of the trochanter (TROCHANTER 2) when two-jointed. Hence **trochan'tinian** *a.* [F. *trochantinien*], pertaining to the trochantin.

[**1857** DUNGLISON *Med. Lex.* s.v. *Trochanter*, Chaussier, by the word *trochanter*, means the larger process; the smaller he calls *trochantin.*] *Ibid.*, *Trochantinian.* **1898** PACKARD *Text-bk. Entomol.* 95 The coxa usually has a posterior subdivision or projection, the trochantine; sometimes, as in Mantispa, the trochantine is obsolete.

trochar, -art, variants of TROCAR.

trochate ('trəʊkeɪt), *a. Zool. rare.* [f. as TROCHAL + -ATE^{2}.] **a.** Furnished with a trochal apparatus, as a rotifer. **b.** = TROCHAL 1.

1891 in *Cent. Dict.*

†**troche**, *sb.*^{1} *Venery. Obs.* Also 7 troch, in Dicts. *erron.* torch. [a. OF. *troche* (13th c. in Godef.) cluster, mass, also in sense 2 below; in Twety *Art de Venerie* (*a* 1327) in sense 1, with which cf. OF. *trocheure* (14th c. in Godef. *Compl.*), F. *trochure.* Cf. also TROCHED, TROCHING.]

1. A cluster of three or more tines at the summit of a deer's horn; distinguished from a *fourche* (*i.e.* fork) of two tines.

c **1410** *Master of Game* (MS. Digby 182) xxxiii, And þenne þe lorde shulde take vppe þe hertes heede by þe reght syde bitwene þe sureale and þe fourche or troche. **1586** FERNE *Blaz. Gentrie* 194 As a perfect wood-man .. to name the Sommeites, troches, or tynes, of the hornes. **1623** COCKERAM I. s.v. *Pollard*, Torch. **1651** DAVENANT *Gondibert* II. xxxiv, His [a stag's] spacious Beame .. From Antlar to his Troch had all allow'd.

2. An ornamental button consisting of or set with three or more jewels in a bunch.

1434 in Rymer *Fœdera* (1710) X. 593/2 Withynne which Tablet ar xl Troches, iche Troche conteynyng iv Peerles. **1576** in Nichols *Progr. Q. Eliz.* (1823) II. 2 A border containing vii buttons or troches of gold, in every of them iii smale rubyes, and viii buttons or troches of golde, in every of them iv mene perle. **1625** in Rymer *Fœdera* (1726) XVIII. 238/1 A Cupp of Goulde with a Cover .. garnished with .. one and twentie Troches of Pearles, three Pearles in every Troche.

Hence †**troche** *v. Obs.*, *intr.* to develop a troche or troches.

1413–22 *Venery de Twety* in *Rel. Ant.* I. 151 Now wyl we speke of the hert, .. Whan an hert hath .. forched on the one syde, and troched on that other syde, than is he an hert of .x. and of the more. And whan .. that he hath troched on boothe parties of the hed, he is of xij. and of that lasse. *c* **1450** in *Twici's Art of Hunting* etc. (1908) 108 When he trochithe on that one side of v & on the other side of vj he is of xvj de greynders.

troche (trəʊʃ, trəʊtʃ, trəʊk), *sb.*^{2} *Pharm.* Forms: *pl.* 6 troschies, (trocis), 7 trosches, trotches, 7–8 trochies, 7– troches; *sing.* 7 trosche, 7– troch, troche. [An altered form of TROCHISK, originating in the plural *troschies*, *trochies*, taken as *trosches*, *troches*, implying a sing. *troschie*, *trochie*, in vulgar and commercial use often pronounced and sometimes written *trochee* ('trəʊkiː), like TROCHEE. The spellings *trosch*, *troche* simulate French, and the pronunciation ('trəʊkiː) is conformed to that of L. *trochiscus.*]

A flat round tablet or lozenge, made of some medicinal substance powdered, worked into a paste with mucilage or the like, and dried; = TROCHISK.

α. **1597** GERARDE *Herbal* II. ccxcvi. 696 Troschies, or little flat cakes. **1714** *Phil. Trans.* XXIX. 68 The Trochies made of the Gall .. a Cordial Sudorifick.

β. **1601** HOLLAND *Pliny* XX. xviii. II. 68 There bee certaine ordinarie trosches made of Poppie seed beaten into pouder, which with milke are .. vsed by way of a liniment to bring sicke patients to sleepe. **1639** T. DE GRAY *Compl. Horsem.* 234 Make of it little cakes or trotches, as broad as a groat. **1656** RIDGLEY *Pract. Physick* 260 Troches of Capers, of Harts-tongue. **1681** GREW *Musæum* III. I. v. 297 A little round, flat, and blackish Stone, resembling a Medicinal Troch. **1769** PENNANT *Zool.* III. 22 The medicine was .. given in form of a powder or troche. **1811** A. T. THOMSON *Lond. Disp.* (1818) 709 *Trochisci.* Troches .. are little cakes or tablets composed of powders combined with sugar and mucilage. [**1857** DUNGLISON *Med. Lex.*, *Trochiscus* .., a troch or round table ..; a solid medicine, prepared of powders, incorporated by means of mucilage, crumb of bread, juices of plants, &c.] **1875** H. C. WOOD *Therap.* (1879) 19 Troches, or lozenges, are gummy pellets or disks, so made as to dissolve slowly in the mouth.

trocheameter (trɒkiː'æmɪtə(r)). [app. erron. f. Gr. τροχός wheel (cf. τροχιά wheel-track) + -METER.] = TRECHOMETER.

1857 LIVINGSTONE *Trav.* iii. 59 Our trocheame[te]r showed that we had made but twenty-five miles. *Note.* This is an instrument which, when fastened on the waggon-wheel, records the number of revolutions made. **1903** J. G. C. ANDERSON *Journ. Pontus* vii. 47 An accident happened to my trocheameter, so that I am unable to give the exact length of this section of the road.

†'**troched**, *a. Venery. Obs.* [ad. OF. *troche* (14th c. in Godef.), as if f. TROCHE *sb.*^{1} + -ED^{2}.] Having a 'troche', as a deer's horn; also said of the deer.

c **1410** *Master of Game* (MS. Digby 182) xxiv, If he be troched of iii. he is an herte of xii. **1413–22** *Venery de Twety* in *Rel. Ant.* I. 151 Whan he is troched on boothe sydes of .vi. than is he of .xxiij. atte fulle. **1611** COTGR. s.v. *Troché*, *Teste de cerf trochée*, Troched, or whose top is diuided into three or foure small branches.

b. Also (by analogy) said of a tower furnished with pinnacles or battlements. *rare.*

13.. *E.E. Allit. P.* B. 1383 With koynt carneles aboue, coruen ful clene, Troched toures bitwene twenty spere lenþe. **13..** *Gaw. & Gr. Knt.* 795 A better barbican þat burne blusched vpon neuer; And innermore he be-helde þat halle ful hyȝe, Towre telded bytwene trochet ful þik.

trochee ('trəʊkiː). *Pros.* Also in Gr.-Lat. form 6 trocheus, 6–7 (9) trochæus. [ad. L. *trochæus*, ad. Gr. τροχαῖος, prop. adj. (*sc.* πούς foot) running, tripping, f. τρόχος a running, course, f. τρέχειν to run; cf. F. *trochée* (1572 in Hatz.-Darm.).] A metrical foot consisting of a long followed by a short syllable; in accentual verse, of an accented followed by an unaccented syllable. Also called CHOREE.

1589 PUTTENHAM *Eng. Poesie* II. xiii. (Arb.) 133 For your Trocheus of a long and short ye haue these words *mānĕr*, *brōkĕn*, *tākĕn*, *bōdiĕ*, *mēmbĕr*, and a great many moe. **1603** HOLLAND *Plutarch's Mor.* 1259 A Trochæus was put in stead of a Pæon. **1603** DANIEL *Def. Rhyme* G j b, If we shold say the state of China, which neuer hard of Anapestiques, Trochies, & tribracques, were grosse, barbarous, and vnciuile. *a* **1771** GRAY *Corr.* etc. (1843) 240 The measure .. is Dimeter-Iambic, but admits of a Trochee, Spondee, Amphibrachys, Anapæst, &c. in almost every place. **1803** COLERIDGE *Met. Feet* i, Trochee trips from long to short.

†**b.** = TRIBRACH. *Obs. rare*$^{-1}$.

1586 W. WEBBE *Eng. Poetrie* (Arb.) 69 A foote of 3 sillables .. is either simple or myxt. The simple is eyther *Molossus*, that is of three long, .. or *Trochæus*, that is of 3 short.

trochee, trochies: see TROCHE *sb.*^{2}

'**troche(e)ize**, *v.* [f. TROCHEE + -IZE.] *trans.* To turn into a trochee, to make trochaic.

a **1834** COLERIDGE *Notes & Lect.* (1849) I. 319 A dibrach .. trocheized .. by the *arsis* or first accent damping, though not extinguishing, the second. **1907** OMOND *Eng. Metrists* ii. 83 An Italian priest said to him, 'You dactylize and trocheeize every thing.

trochid ('trɒkɪd). *Zool.* [f. mod.L. *Trochidæ*, f. *Trochus*, generic name: see TROCHUS and -ID^{3}.] A mollusc of the family *Trochidæ*; a top-shell.

1861 P. P. CARPENTER in *Rep. Smithsonian Instit.* 1860, 215 The shells are not pearly as in the Trochids. *Ibid.* 216 A conical Trochid.

trochiferous (trəʊ'kɪfərəs), *a. Zool. rare*$^{-0}$. [f. Gr. τροχός wheel (see TROCHUS) + -[I]FEROUS.] Bearing a wheel-like or trochal organ, as a rotifer; rotiferous.

1899 in *Syd. Soc. Lex.* **1909** in *Cent. Dict. Suppl.*

trochiform ('trɒkɪfɔːm), *a. Zool.* [f. TROCHUS + -[I]FORM.] Having the form of a trochus or top-shell; top-shaped; = TROCHOID *a.* 2.

1822 J. PARKINSON *Outl. Oryctol.* 250 The single trochiform shell, *Trochus Anglicanus* of Lister. **1875** C. C. BLAKE *Zool.* 257 The shell is ear-shaped, spiral, or trochiform.

†'**trochil**. *Obs.* Also 7 -yle. [ad. L. *trochilus.*] = TROCHILUS^{1} 1.

1604 DRAYTON *Owle* 411 For the base Trochyle thinketh it no payne, To scowre vile Carion for a savoury gayne. **1638** SIR T. HERBERT *Trav.* (ed. 2) 323 He [the crocodile] opens his chaps to let the little Trochil pick his teeth, which give it feeding.

trochile, anglicized form of TROCHILUS^{2}.

trochilic (trəʊ'kɪlɪk), *a.* and *sb. rare.* ? *Obs.* [f. Gr. τροχίλος, taken in sense of τροχός wheel + -IC.] **a.** *adj.* Of or pertaining to rotary motion; relating to wheels. **b.** *sb.* The science or art of rotary motion. Also **trochilics**.

1570 DEE *Math. Pref.* c iv b, Bycause the frute hereof .. is in Wheles, it hath the name of *Trochilike*: as a man would say, Whele Art. **1605** CAMDEN *Rem.* 138 By Arte Trochilick. **1641** WILKINS *Math. Magick* II. xiv. (1648) 265 Some principles in Trochilicks, or the art of wheel-instruments. **1646** SIR T. BROWNE *Pseud. Ep.* v. xviii. 260 Horologies composed by Trochilick or the artifice of wheeles. **1648** PETTY *Advice to Hartlib* 6 Making Watches and other Trochilick motions. **1696** in PHILLIPS (ed. 5).

trochilidine (trəʊ'kɪlɪdaɪn), *a. Ornith.* [f. mod.L. *Trochilidæ* (f. *Trochilus*: see next) + -INE^{1}.] Belonging to or characteristic of the family *Trochilidæ* or humming-birds. So **tro'chilidist**, one who studies the *Trochilidæ*.

1861 GOULD *Trochilidæ* III. Pl. 142 The name of Floresi will also always be held in high regard among Trochilidists for the fine collections of Humming-Birds obtained by him. **1881** NEWTON in *Encycl. Brit.* XII. 358/1 *note*, 'Trochilidists' in giving their measurements do not take these extraordinary developments into account. **1885** *Proc. Zool. Soc.* 1 Dec. 887 The characters presented in the Trochilidine skeleton.

‖**trochilus**^{1} ('trɒkɪləs). *Ornith.* Also *erron.* 7–9 troculus, 8 trochulus. [L. *trochilus*, a. Gr. τροχίλος, f. τρέχειν to run.]

1. A small Egyptian bird (not certainly identified) said by the ancients to pick the teeth of the crocodile. Also *allusively* (in quot. 1856 *attrib.*).

1579 LYLY *Euphues* (Arb.) 44 The birde Trochilus lyueth by the mouth of the Crocodile and is not spoyled. **1596** LODGE *Marg. Amer.* (Hunter Cl.) 48 Why the swanne hateth the sparrow, the eagle the *Trochilus*, the asse the bee [etc.]. **1615** G. SANDYS *Trav.* II. 100 A little bird called *Troculus*, doth feede her selfe by the picking of his teeth. *a* **1658** CLEVELAND *Char. Country-Comm.-Man* Wks. (1687) 74 So the poor Souldiers live like Trochilus, by picking the Teeth of this sacred Crocodile. **1856** R. A. VAUGHAN *Mystics* (1860) II. IX. iii. 134 This troculus service—the picking the teeth of the gorged ecclesiastical crocodile. **1910** THOMPSON tr. *Aristotle's Hist. Anim.* 612 When the crocodile yawns, the trochilus flies into his mouth and cleans his teeth.

2. An alleged name for some species of wren, or other small European bird.

[**1678** RAY *Willughby's Ornithol.* II. xi. 227 The golden-crown'd Wren: Regulus cristatus... The Trochilus of Pliny and Aristotle.] **1706** PHILLIPS (ed. Kersey), *Trochilus*, the fin-footed Runner; a Bird so call'd because it always runs; a Wren.

3. A Linnæan genus of American birds, originally including all the then known humming-birds; now greatly restricted.

In first quot. app. used for some other small bird.

1672 JOSSELYN *New Eng. Rarities* 7 The Troculus, a small bird, black and white, no bigger than a Swallow. **1752** J. HILL *Hist. Anim.* 502 The gold and purple Trochilus. The yellow Humming-bird. **1796** STEDMAN *Surinam* II. xxv. 219 The trochulus, or humming-birds, were so thick among the tamarind-trees, that they resembled a swarm of bees.

‖'**trochilus**^{2}. *Arch.* Also 7–8 anglicized as trochile ('trəʊkaɪl). [L., app. the same word as prec.: cf. Gr. τροχιλία the sheaf of a pulley.] A concave moulding; = SCOTIA, CASEMENT 1: esp. in classical architecture.

1563 SHUTE *Archit.* D iij, The nethermost Trochilus or Scotia. **1664** EVELYN tr. *Freart's Archit.* 125 Trochile is that cavity appearing next to the Torus. **1789** P. SMYTH tr. *Aldrich's Archit.* (1818) 117 At Tivoli, the ends of the channels and the cavity of the trochile or casement are not round but square. **1842–76** GWILT *Archit.* Gloss., *Trochilus*, .. an annular moulding whose section is concave like the edge of a pulley .. more commonly called a *scotia.* **1845** PARKER *Gloss. Archit.* 330 *Scotia*, or *Trochilus*, a hollow moulding constantly used in the bases of columns, &c., in classical architecture.

trochin ('trəʊkɪn). *Anat. rare*$^{-0}$. [a. F. *trochin* (Chaussier), app. arbitrarily f. TROCHANTER; cf. TROCHANTIN.] (See quot.) Hence **tro'chinian** *a.* [F. *trochinien*].

1857 DUNGLISON *Med. Lex.*, *Trochin*... Chaussier has given this name to the smaller of the tuberosities at the upper extremity of the os humeri; because it gives attachment to one of the rotator muscles of the arm,—the subscapularis. *Trochinian*, that which belongs or relates to the trochin.

†'**troching**. *Venery. Obs.* [f. TROCHE^{1} + -ING^{1}.] A 'troche', or troches collectively; a branching into a troche.

c **1410** *Master of Game* (MS. Digby 182) ii, If þer be thre or .iiii. or mo, it is ycleped trochynge. *Ibid.* xxiv, þe trochynge .. hye and gret. **1660** HOWELL *Parly of Beasts* iv. 62 Such branch'd horns, such spilters [*sic*] and trochings on their heads, as that goodly Stagg bears. **1678** PHILLIPS (ed. 4), *Trochings*, .. the small little branches on the top of the Deers-head, divided into three or four.

†**tro'chiscate**, *v. Obs.* [f. L. *trochisc-us* (see next) + -ATE^{3}.] *trans.* To make into 'trochisks'.

1657 TOMLINSON *Renou's Disp.* 580 [Pills] of .. choyce Rhabarb, Agarick trochiscated. **1662** H. STUBBE *Ind. Nectar* vi. 112 Half a dram of Rhubarb trochiscated.

‖**tro'chiscus.** *Pl.* -isci. [L.] = next.

†**trochisk** ('trəʊkɪsk). *Obs.* Forms: 5 trocis, 6 -cysce, -cyske, -cisque, 6–7 -ciske, -chiske, -chisce, -chisque, -chis, 7 -cisk, -chisc(k, -chisch,

-chisq, 7–8 trochisk, (*erron.* 5 -ciste, 6 -chist, 7–8 -chiste); also, in L. form **trochiscus.** [a. F. *trochisque* (*trocisque*, *trocisse*, 1425 in Godef. *Compl.*) = It. *trochisco*, Ger. *trochisk*; ad. L. *trochiscus*, a. Gr. τροχίσκος small wheel, small globe, pill, lozenge, dim. of τροχός wheel.]

A medicated tablet or disk; a (round or ovate) pastille or lozenge; = TROCHE *sb.*[2]

c **1400** *Lanfranc's Cirurg.* 211 þou schalt purge him with trocis de turbit, or wiþ anoþer medicyn þat purgiþ fleume. *c* **1425** tr. *Arderne's Treat. Fistula* (E.E.T.S.) 91 When..it is cold..enforme þerof trocistes. **1525** tr. *Jerome of Brunswick's Surg.* F j b/2 Therof make a trocysce. **1541** R. COPLAND *Guydon's Formul.* U ij b, Trociskes..be put to powdre, and with swete wyne incorporate, and be made to trociskes. **1545** RAYNOLD *Byrth Mankynde* R ij, Temper the hole masse into litell roundels or trociskes. **1576** BAKER *Jewell of Health* 109 Let Trochistes or lytle flat balles be made therof. **1612** WOODALL *Surg. Mate* Wks. (1653) 64 Trochisks of Minium..mundifie sordid ulcers. **1625** GILL *Sacr. Philos.* i. 17 Poysons..rightly used..may be helpefull ..: as it appeares in the trocisks of the vipers flesh. **1658** ROWLAND *Moufet's Theat. Ins.* 1056 The Dose is one Trochis, with one ounce of wine. **1665** G. HARVEY *Advice agst. Plague* 21 Perfume your sheets..by burning the said Trochisces in a warming pan. **1748** tr. *Vegetius' Distemp. Horses* 136 Give him..one Trochisk a Day dissolved in Water.

trochite ('trɒkaɪt, 'trəʊkaɪt). *Palæont.* Now *rare* or *Obs.* [ad. mod.L. *trochītēs*, f. Gr. τροχός wheel: see -ITE[1].] A name for the detached wheel-like joints of encrinites: = ENTROCHITE, ENTROCHUS.

1676 BEAUMONT in *Phil. Trans.* XI. 726 One Trochite.. has round inlets or sockets. **1815** W. PHILLIPS *Outl. Min. & Geol.* (1818) 141 Transition Limestone..contains petrifactions of marine animals, as corallites, encrinites, pentacrinites, entrochites, and trochites. **1853** TH. ROSS *Humboldt's Trav.* III. xxxii. 391 A heap of turbinites and trochites.

Hence **trochitic** (trəʊ'kɪtɪk) *a.* (*rare*⁻⁰), of the nature of or pertaining to a trochite or trochites.

1891 in *Cent. Dict.*

trochiter ('trɒkɪtə(r)). *Anat. rare*⁻⁰. [a. F. *trochiter* (Chaussier), altered from TROCHANTER.] (See quot.) Hence **trochi'terian** *a.* [F. *trochitérien*].

1857 DUNGLISON *Med. Lex.*, *Trochiter*.., the larger of the two tuberosities at the upper extremity of the os humeri; so called because it affords insertion to rotator muscles—Chaussier. *Trochiterian*, in the language of Chaussier, means any thing belonging or relating to the trochiter.

‖**trochlea** ('trɒkliːə). *Anat.* [L. *trochlea*: cf. Gr. τροχιλία, -χιλέα, -χαλία sheaf of a pulley.] A pulley-like structure or arrangement of parts, with a smooth surface upon which some other part, as a bone or tendon, slides;

spec. (*a*) the surface of the inner condyle of the humerus at the elbow-joint, with which the ulna articulates; (*b*) the cartilaginous loop through which the superior oblique muscle of the eye passes; (*c*) the orifice of the metathorax in hymenopterous insects, through which the tendon of the abdomen passes.

1693 tr. *Blancard's Phys. Dict.* (ed. 2), *Trochlea*, the same that *Bathmis*. **1826** KIRBY & SPENCE *Entomol.* xxxvi. III. 701 Here the upper orifice in the trunk is the pulley (*trochlea*), the tendon is the rope (*funiculus*), and the abdomen is the weight to be lifted. **1854** OWEN *Skel. & Teeth* (1855) 64 The distal end of the tibia forms a transverse pulley or trochlea. **1857** DUNGLISON *Med. Lex.*, *Trochlea*, a pulley;..for example, the articular surface at the lower extremity of the os humeri; so called from its forming a kind of pulley on which the ulna moves... Also, the cartilaginous pulley over which the tendon of the trochlearis muscle passes, at the upper and inner part of the orbit.

trochlear ('trɒkliːə(r)), *a.* [ad. mod.L. *trochleār-is*, f. *trochlea*: see prec. and -AR.]

1. *Anat.* Belonging to or connected with a trochlea, as a muscle, nerve, etc.; forming a trochlea, pulley-like, as a surface of a bone, etc.

trochlear fossa, t. spine, parts of the frontal bone connected with the trochlea of the eye. ***t. muscle***, the superior oblique muscle of the eye. ***t. nerve***, each of the fourth pair of cranial nerves, the motor nerves for the trochlear muscles. ***t. nucleus***, a nucleus in the brain from which the trochlear nerve arises.

1681 tr. *Willis' Rem. Med. Wks.* Vocab., *Trochlear muscle*, a muscle made almost like a windlas or pully. **1808** BARCLAY *Muscular Motions* 304 In many cases..the particular direction in which several muscles act..is regulated by trochlear ligaments or pulleys. **1870** N. F. HELE *Aldeburgh* iv. 29 A trochlear end of a humerus. **1875** SIR W. TURNER in *Encycl. Brit.* I. 840/2 The patella moves up and down the trochlear surface of the femur.

2. *Bot.* Pulley-shaped; circular and contracted in the middle like the wheel of a pulley, as the embryo of *Commelynaceæ*.

1830 LINDLEY *Nat. Syst. Bot.* 255 It [Spiderwort] has scarcely any affinity with Palms, except in its trochlear embryo.

So **trochleariform** (-'ærɪfɔːm) *a.*, *Bot.* [f. mod.L. *trochleāri-s* + -FORM; irreg. for **trochleiform*, f. TROCHLEA + -FORM] = sense 2 above; ‖**trochlearis** (-'ɛərɪs), *Anat.* [mod.L. (see above), sc. *musculus* or *nervus*], the trochlear muscle, also the trochlear nerve; '**trochleary** *a.*, *Anat.* (*rare*) = sense 1 above; '**trochleate** *a.*, *Bot.* = sense 2 above (*Cassell's Encycl. Dict.* 1888).

1895 *Funk's Stand. Dict.*, *Trochleariform. **1693** tr. *Blancard's Phys. Dict.* (ed. 2), **Trochlearis*, the upper, or greater oblique Muscle of the Eye. **1842** *Penny Cycl.* XXII. 78/2 The pulley of the trochlearis muscle of the eye. **1890** BILLINGS *Med. Dict.*, *Trochlearis*...2. Trochlear nerve. **1828** WEBSTER, **Trochleary*, pertaining to the trochlea; as, the trochleary muscle,..the trochleary nerve... *Parr.*

trocho- (trɒkəʊ), before a vowel **troch-** (trɒk), combining form repr. Gr. τροχός wheel, disk; occurring in several scientific words. **trocheidoscope** (-'kaɪdəskəʊp) [after KALEIDOSCOPE *sb.*], a rotating disc with coloured sectors, for showing combinations of colours (*Cassell's Encycl. Dict.* 1888). **trochelminth** ('trɒkɛlmɪnθ) [Gr. ἕλμινς, ἑλμινθ- worm], a rotifer. '**trochoblast** [Gr. βλαστός germ], one of the embryonic cells giving rise to the prototroch in the trochophore larva of marine annelids. ˌ**trochoce'phalic** (-sɪ'fælɪk) *a.* [Gr. κεφαλή head], having a round form of skull due to permature union of the parietal and frontal bones; so **trochocephaly** (-'sɛfəlɪ), the condition of being trochocephalic. **trochoceracone** (-'sɛrəkəʊn) [Gr. κέρας horn, κῶνος cone], a nautiloid shell with loose flattened coils, as those of the fossil genus *Trochoceras*; so **trochoceran** (trəʊ'kɒsərən) *a.*, having the form or character of such a shell (*Cent. Dict. Suppl.*). ˌ**trochocœlomate** (-sɪ'ləʊmət) *a.*, belonging to the *Trochocœlomata*, a proposed division of *Metazoa*, containing animals having radiated cœlomes (= *radiata*). **tro'chometer** [-METER] = TRECHOMETER (Worcester 1846). '**trochophore** (-fɔə(r)) [Gr. -φόρος bearing], '**trochosphere** (-sfɪə(r)), a larval form constituting a stage in the development of most molluscs and of certain worms, esp. marine annelids, characterized by a spheroidal body with a ring of cilia; also *attrib.*; hence **trochospheric** (-'sfɛrɪk), -'**spherical** *adjs.*, pertaining to or having the form of a trochosphere. **trochozoon** (-'zəʊɒn) [Gr. ζῷον animal], one of the *Trochozoa*, a collective name for those molluscs, annelids, etc. which pass through a trochosphere larval stage, or for such larvæ; also for a hypothetical ancestral group of animals from which these are assumed to be derived.

1904 *Amer. Nat.* July–Aug. 500 Cells..identical in origin with the 'primary *trochoblasts' of the annelids. **1878** BARTLEY tr. *Topinard's Anthrop.* v. 176 *Trochocephalic, very round skull. *Ibid.* Index 547/1 *Trochocephaly. **1884** HYATT in *Proc. Boston Soc. Nat. Hist.* 5 Mar. 113 We can readily transform a protocoelomate into a *trochocoelomate by destroying the horizontal parts of the partitions between the ampullae. **1892** J. A. THOMSON *Outlines Zool.* xi. 182 By far the most important larval form among Annelids is that known as the Trochosphere or *Trochophore. **1909** J. W. JENKINSON *Experim. Embryol.* 213 Eight instead of the usual four macromeres were found in the Trochophore larva. **1883** E. R. LANKESTER in *Encycl. Brit.* XVI. 648/1 [In the Limpet the] Diblastula..acquires a ciliated band, and becomes a nearly spherical *Trochosphere. **1888** ROLLESTON & JACKSON *Anim. Life* 454 The Mollusca with the exception of *Cephalopoda* pass through a typical larval development, in two stages—a Trochosphere and a Veliger stage. **1899** *Syd. Soc. Lex.*, *Trochospheric. **1891** *Cent. Dict.*, *Trochospherical. **1890** *Nature* 22 May 94/1 The author's conclusions are, that the *Balanoglossus*..has originated from a *trochozoon which acquired some features in common with worms.

trochoid ('trɒkɔɪd, 'trəʊkɔɪd), *sb.* and *a.* [ad. Gr. τροχοειδής round like a wheel, f. τροχός wheel + εἶδος form: see -OID; cf. F. *trochoïde* (1658 in Hatz.-Darm.).] **A.** *sb.*

1. *Geom.* A curve traced by a point on or connected with a rolling circle; *orig.* = CYCLOID 1: now usually restricted to the *curtate* and *prolate cycloids*, traced respectively by points within and without the circle; also extended to curves similarly generated by a circle rolling upon another circle, either inside it (HYPOTROCHOID) or outside it (EPITROCHOID).

1704 J. HARRIS *Lex. Techn.* I. s.v., A Curve Line..called a Cycloid or Trochoid. **1711** W. SUTHERLAND *Shipbuild. Assist.* 59 The Cycloids or Trochoids. **1867** DENISON *Astron. without Math.* 86 *note*, That curve is called a trochoid, but when the tracing point is on the circumference it becomes a cycloid. **1881** C. W. BOURNE in *Eng. Mech.* No. 874. 377/1 The bar AB is jointed to a bar BC, so that while AB revolves round A as centre, BC can also revolve round B as centre, then a curve will be described by the point C... Every such curve is comprised under the name 'trochoid'.

2. *Zool.* A gastropod of the family *Trochidæ*; a top-shell.

1839 *Penny Cycl.* XIV. 317/2 Mollusca... Class III. Gastropoda... Order 6. Pectinibranchiata. Family of Trochöids.

3. *Anat.* A trochoid articulation, a pivot-joint.

1860 in WORCESTER; hence in later Dicts. [Cf. quot. 1857 in B. 3.]

B. *adj.*

1. *Geom.* = TROCHOIDAL 1. *rare*⁻⁰.

1882 OGILVIE (Annandale), *Trochoid*, *a.* 1. Trochoidal.

2. *Conch.* Top-shaped, conical with flat base, as the shells of the genus *Trochus* or family *Trochidæ*; *Zool.* belonging to the family *Trochidæ*.

1859 J. R. GREENE *Man. Anim. Kingd.*, *Protozoa* 16 If.. the spiral passes obliquely round an axis, the shell assumes a more or less pyramidal form, and is termed 'trochoid'. **1861** P. P. CARPENTER in *Rep. Smithsonian Instit.* 1860, 213 The..African group *Collonia* have small Trochoid shells.

3. *Anat.* Applied to a pivot-joint, in which one bone turns upon another with a rotary motion.

1857 DUNGLISON *Med. Lex.*, *Trochoid*.., an articulation, in which one bone turns upon another, like a wheel upon its axle. **1860** MAYNE *Expos. Lex.*, *Trochoides*,..resembling a wheel: trochoid. *Anat.* Applied to a movable connexion of bones in which one bone rotates upon another, as the first cervical vertebra upon the odontoid process of the second.

trochoidal (trəʊ'kɔɪdəl), *a.* [f. prec. + -AL[1].]

1. *Geom.* Having the form or nature of a trochoid; pertaining or relating to trochoids: see prec. A. 1.

1799 YOUNG in *Phil. Trans.* XC. 137 A similar chord bent into a trochoidal curve. **1861** W. FROUDE *Rolling of Ships* (1862) 23 The wave would be more accurately represented by some member of the cycloidal or trochoidal family than by the curve of sines.

2. *Conch.* = TROCHOID B. 2. *rare*⁻⁰.

1891 in *Cent. Dict.*

3. *Anat.* = TROCHOID B. 3. *rare*.

1882 OGILVIE (Annandale) s.v. *Trochoid*, A trochoidal articulation.

Hence **tro'choidally** *adv.*, in a trochoidal manner or course.

1855 DE MORGAN in Graves *Life Sir W. R. Hamilton* (1889) III. 519 A book..showing that the earth moves trochoidally if the sun has motion.

trochotron ('trɒkəʊtrɒn). *Electronics.* [f. TROCHO(IDAL *a.* + -TRON.] A type of magnetron in which there are a number of anodes at different angular positions around the central cathode, with the electron beam able to be switched from one anode to another.

1947 ALFVÉN & ROMANUS in *Nature* 1 Nov. 614/1 Research on valves with cycloidal or trochoidal electronic motion has been carried out... The development of the valves, which are called 'trochotrons', has been carried out by G. Hambraeus and..T. Wallmark. **1962** *Jrnl. Brit. Inst. Electr. Engineers* XXIII. 99/1 The Trochotron is a hot-cathode multi-electrode tube containing a number of open box electrodes and operating in a constant magnetic field. **1980** *Jrnl. Nuclear Materials* XCIII–XCIV. A. 352/2 The property of stigmatic focusing used in the trochotron mass spectrometer..is conserved in this device.

‖**trochus** ('trəʊkəs, 'trɒkəs). Pl. **trochi** (-kaɪ), also **trochuses.** [L., a. Gr. τροχός, f. τρέχειν to run.]

1. *Gr.* and *Rom. Antiq.* A wheel or hoop, used in athletic exercises or as a plaything.

1706 PHILLIPS (ed. Kersey), *Trochus*, a Wheel, a Top for Children to play with. **1734** tr. *Rollin's Anc. Hist.* (1768) I. Pref. 88 The exercises of leaping, throwing the dart, and that of the trochus or wheel. **1847** LEITCH tr. *C. O. Müller's Anc. Art* §351. (1850) 427 Ganymede with trochus.

†**2.** = TROCHE[2]. *Obs. rare*⁻¹.

1748 tr. *Vegetius' Distemp. Horses* 85 Three Trochus's or Cakes of Sinoper.

3. *Zool.* **a.** A genus of gastropod molluscs, having a top-shaped or conical shell; the type of the family *Trochidæ* or top-shells.

1753 CHAMBERS *Cycl. Supp.*, *Trochus*,..a genus of shells. **1774** GOLDSM. *Nat. Hist.* (1776) VII. 33 The trunk of the Trochus is fleshy, muscular, supple, and hollow. **1851** WOODWARD *Mollusca* (1856) 12 The trochi and purpuræ are found at low-water, amongst the sea-weed. **1859** H. KINGSLEY *G. Hamlyn* xxxiv. (1894) 325 They fell to gathering shells... Trochuses, as big as one's fist.

attrib. and *Comb.* **1774** GOLDSM. *Nat. Hist.* IV. 22 Snails of the trochus kind. **1889** *Science-Gossip* XXV. 168 Trochus-shaped rotulites.

b. The internal ring of cilia in the trochal organ of a rotifer.

1888 ROLLESTON & JACKSON *Anim. Life* 632 The trochal apparatus..appears to consist typically of an internal præoral ring of long cilia, the trochus, and an external ring of finer cilia, the cingulum.

trock, trocker, Sc. ff. TRUCK, TRUCKER.

‖**trockenbeerenauslese** ('trɔkənbeːrən ˌausleːzə). Pl. -lesen. [Ger., f. *trocken* dry + *beeren* pl. of *beere* BERRY *sb.* grape + *auslese* selection, choice (wine).] (A) sweet German white wine of superior quality, made from individually selected grapes affected by noble rot.

1963 *Times* 8 Feb. 12/5 Beerenauslesen and Trockenbeerenauslesen. These latter terms mean, respectively, wines made from selected over-ripe single grapes and those made from over-ripe single grapes which are in effect sun-dried raisins, in a state of *pourriture noble*. **1964** *Harper's Bazaar* Nov. 146/3, I do not think a white wine, except a Trockenbeerenauslese..should be expected to last so long. **1972** W. GARNER *Ditto, Brother Rat!* i. 5, I drank so many good wines my tastebuds stopped performing for anything less than a *Trockenbeerenauslese*.

trocle, obs. form of TRUCKLE.

troco ('trəʊkəʊ). [app. altered from It. *trucco* 'a billiard-boord, also the play at billiards' (Florio,

1611); or Sp. *truco* the game of TRUCKS, q.v.] See quot.

[**1598** FLORIO, *Trucco*, a kinde of play with balles vpon a table called billiards; but properly a kinde of game vsed in England with casting little bowles at a boord with thirteene holes in it.] **1882** OGILVIE (Annandale), *Troco*, an old English game revived, formerly known as 'lawn-billiards'.. played on a lawn with wooden balls and a cue ending in a spoon-shaped iron projection. [But app. never so called in English. See TRUCKS.]

troctolite ('trɒktəʊlaɪt). *Min.* Also trok-. [ad. Ger. *troktolit* (Von Lasaulx, 1875), f. Gr. τρώκτης a kind of sea-fish (taken as = trout) + λίθος stone: see -LITE.] (See quot. 1892.)

1883 *Science* I. 342/2 The term 'troktolite' is the equivalent of the more common 'forellenstein'. **1892** *Chambers' Encycl.* X. 301 *Troctolite* (trout-stone), a variety of Gabbro, composed almost entirely of white felspar.. and dark olivine.

troculus, erron. form of TROCHILUS[1].

trod (trɒd), *sb.* Now *dial.* Forms: 1- trod; 6 troad, trood, trodd, -e, 6-7 trode. [OE. *trod* neut. (also *trodu* fem., acc. *trode*) = ON. *troð* treading, trampling, OHG. *trota* winepress (cf. mod. Norw. dial. *trod* fem. foot-board, step), f. ON. *troða*, Goth. *trudan* to tread, ablaut variants of WGer. *tredan* to tread.]

†**1.** Tread, footprint, track, trace. *Obs.*

Beowulf (Z.) 843 Secga æneȝum þara þe tir-leases trode sceawode, hu he..on weȝ þanon..feorh-lastas bær. **946-961** *Laws of Edgar* I. c. 5 Gyf him hundred bedrife trod on oðer hundred. *a* **1225** *Ancr. R.* 380 (MS. Titus) Þe dunes underuoð þe trodes [*v.r.* treden] of him suluen. *c* **1420** *Chron. Vilod.* 513 Þey nyste neuer where he was a-go, Ne of his trodus no sygne þer nasse. **1551** SIR R. BOWES in *Eng. Border Hen. VIII* (1847) II. 18 They may lawfullye followe there [stolen] goodes either wth a sleuthe hounde the trodd thereof, or ellse by suche other meanes as they best can devise. **1563** in Bp. W. Nicholson *Leg. Marchiarum* (1705) 127 Providing the Parties grieved to follow their lawful Trode with Hound and Horn, with Hue and Cry and all other accustomed manner of fresh Pursuit.

b. *hot-trod*: see HOT *a.* 12.

2. A trodden way; a footpath, path, way. *dial.*

1570 LEVINS *Manip.* 155/32 A Trod, path, *callis, is, hæc.* *a* **1575** PILKINGTON *Expos. Neh.* iv. 13 (1585) 60 God and the world cannot be friends: and that maketh so few Courtiers to tread this trodde. **1578** *Paradise Dainty Devises* A iij, And takes us from the trod, which guides to en[d]lesse gayne And sets us in the way that leades to lasting payne. **1596** SPENSER *F.Q.* VI. x. 5 He chaunst to come, far from all peoples troad. **1642** H. MORE *Song of Soul* IV. xxvii, Thus in the middle trod I safely went, and fairly well have row'd. **1678** PHILLIPS (ed. 4), *Trode*, (old word) signifying a path. **1825** BROCKETT *N.C. Words, Trod*, a foot path through a field. **1897** *Speaker* 4 Sept. 260/2 The lane and 'trod' must have saved me the mile or more.

3. The tread of a wheel (TREAD *sb.* 10 b). *dial.*

1797 CURR *Coal Viewer* 20 The rim [of the corf wheel] is 1½ inches broad on the trod or face. **1825** J. NICHOLSON *Operat. Mechanic* 645 Making the wheels and spokes of cast iron, with hoops, tyres, or trods, of malleable iron.

4. *Comb.*, as †**trod-gate**, †**trod-way**, trodden way or track.

a **1400-50** *Alexander* 2988 Alexander..Ay trottis him to þe trod-gate [*Dublin MS.* troyde-gate] as him þe torche wyssis. **1661** J. CHILDREY *Brit. Baconica* 164 The Coals grow so near the surface..that the Cart wheels turn them up in the trod-ways.

trod (trɒd), *ppl. a.* [Shortened from TRODDEN.] = TRODDEN: chiefly as second element; also with adv., as *trod-down*.

1632 MILTON *L'Allegro* 131 Then to the well-trod stage anon. **1638** W. LISLE *Heliodorus* x. 177 To see their trod-downe fellowes hurt. **1897** H. N. HOWARD *Footsteps Proserpine* 48 Mingled with elf-trod moss.

trod, *v. Obs.* or *dial.* [f. TROD *sb.*] **a.** *trans.* To follow the footprints or track of; to track, trace. **b.** *intr.* (*U.S.*) To pursue a path.

a **1225** *Ancr. R.* 232 Betere is þe þet troddeð wel & ofsecheð wel ut his owune feblesce þen he þet meteð hu heih is þe heouene. **1619** SIR J. SEMPIL *Sacrilege Handled* App. 49 To trode Tithes then vp as neare as may be, euen to Adam, from the Law. **1825** JAMIESON s.v., To 'trod a thief'. **1909** *N. York Observer* 2 Sept. 316/1 Trodding to Self-Support. The Home Mission Committee of Buffalo Presbytery has set itself earnestly to the task of bringing its dependent churches to self-support.

trod (trɒd), pa. t. and pple. of TREAD *v.*; obs. pa. pple. of TROW *v.*

trodden ('trɒd(ə)n), *ppl. a.* [Late ME. *troden*, taking the place of OE. and ME. *treden*, pa. pple. of TREAD; imitating such pa. pples. as *holpen, stolen*, from *help, steal*.] That has been walked, stepped, or trampled upon (also *fig.*): see senses of TREAD *v.* Also in comb, as DOWN-TRODDEN.

1545 ELYOT, *Pressatus*, oppressed, charged, troden downe. **1590** SPENSER *F.Q.* I. iii. 10 The troden gras, In which the tract of peoples footing was. **1700** DRYDEN *Ovid's Met., Acis, Polyphemus*, etc. 94 More revengeful than a trodden snake. **1760-72** H. BROOKE *Fool of Qual.* (1890) I. p. x, I was as a trodden worm, and turned. *a* **1849** J. C. MANGAN *Poems* (1859) 421 There's hope, too, for his trodden thralls.

b. Of a path, etc.: Formed or marked by treading; beaten.

1576 FLEMING *Panopl. Epist.* 226 *margin*, Pouertie the troden path to vertuous conuersation. **1615** W. LAWSON *Country Housew. Gard.* (1626) 19 To walke in the plaine trodden path. **1870** MORRIS *Earthly Par.* III. IV. 34 Now by trodden way and wild Goes Heimir long.

trode, arch. pa. t. and pple. of TREAD *v.*

†**trod-net.** *Obs.* Also 6 trodenette. [Origin uncertain.] Some kind of fishing-net.

1523 FITZHERB. *Surv.* 10 b, In some rinnyng waters, the lordes tenauntes haue lybertie by custome to fysshe with shouenettes, trodenettes, small pytches, and suche other. **1562-77** LEIGH *Surv.* (1596) F iv, Fishing, with..casting nets..trod-nets, and such like.

troe, obs. form of TROW.

troepie: see TROOPIE.

trofe, troffe, obs. forms of TROUGH, TURF.

trofel, -fil, -fle, obs. forms of TRIFLE.

trog (trɒg). *slang.* [Abbrev. of TROGLODYTE.]

1. A speleologist. *rare.*

1955 *People* (Austral.) 7 Sept. 23/3 These are the trogs, as they cosily call themselves,..members of the Sydney Speleological Society, the Sydney University Speleological Society, [etc.].

2. One of a despised social group; a lout, a boor, a hooligan, an obnoxious person.

1956 L. MCINTOSH *Oxford Folly* 15 This charm school would have been rather a brilliant thing to do... After all, these trogs lead such dreary lives. **1957** J. I. M. STEWART *Use of Riches* I. ii. 23 You've been listening to some disgusting trog being beastly about Rupert, and now you're parroting him. **1960** D. POTTER *Glittering Coffin* vi. 89 Trinity..infrequently admits a 'trog' (in other words a grammar school boy). **1961** M. DICKENS *Heart of London* III. 277 Nobody mixes, I mean really *mixes* with the trogs. **1962** J. FLEMING *When I grow Rich* xv. 173 One of the trogs appointed himself foreman. **1967** *Guardian* 30 May 2/4, I am thoroughly disgusted. Yesterday I saw two long-haired trogs, one with a ribbon in his hair, wearing the red frock-coats of the Chelsea Pensioners. **1981** M. DUFFY *Gor Saga* 87 He'd given her the morning after pill and the little trog had just kept it... She would stick him with a paternity order. **1983** *Granta* VII. 17 The scowling vandals, bus-stop boogies, and soccer trogs malevolently lining the streets.

3. (See quot. 1958.) *N.Z.*

1958 *Tararua* XII. 28 For shelter, hillmen may seek a *trog*, a large overhanging boulder or bluff giving shelter like a cave. **1971** *N.Z. Listener* 19 Apr. 56/5 They found a possie in a bit of a trog and boiled-up.

4. A teenager who camps out or lives in caves. *temporary.*

1965 *Sun* 8 June 7/7 For Mods and Rockers you can now read Trogs and Thunderbirds... A teenager I know explained it to me yesterday: 'Mods do a lot of sleeping out, camping.' **1966** *Daily Tel.* 14 Apr. 23/3 The young people, who called themselves 'trogs' after the word troglodyte, cave dweller, could be found in the caves at weekends with about 50 permanent 'residents'.

trögerite ('trɜːgəraɪt). *Min.* [Named (1871) after R. Tröger of Neustädtel, Saxony: see -ITE[1].] A hydrous arseniate of uranium, occurring in thin lemon-yellow tabular crystals.

1872 DANA *Min.* App. i. 16.

troget, -eter, -ettar, var. TREGET, TREGETOUR.

trogh(e, troght, obs. ff. TROUGH, TROTH.

troglo- ('trɒgləʊ), combining form of Gr. τρώγλη hole, used in the names of various groups of organisms found in caves, as **troglo'bion(t)**, **'troglobite** [a. G. *troglobie* (J. B. Schiner in A. Schmidl *Grötten und Höhlen von Adelsberg* (1854) 240), f. Gr. βιῶν living], an animal living entirely in the dark parts of caves; hence **troglo'bitic, -bi'otic** *adjs.*; **'troglophil(e)** [a. Ger. (J. B. Schiner *loc. cit.*: see -PHIL, -PHILE], a cave-dwelling animal that does not live entirely in the dark; **'trogloxene** [a. Fr. *trogloxène* (E. G. Racovitza 1907, in *Arch. Zool. Expér. & Gén.* 4th Ser. VI. 437), f. Gr. ξένος guest], an animal that spends occasional short periods in dark caves.

1924 *Glasgow Herald* 13 Dec. 4 Permanent cave-dwellers (the troglobions), like the Dalmatian Proteus newt. **1927** *Ibid.* 2 July 4 The three groups have received various names, such as troglobionts, troglophils, and trogloxenes. **1982** MOYLE & CECH *Fishes* xxxi. 444 Most cave waters containing troglobiotic fishes have at least intermittent connections to the outside. **1953** HAZELTON & GLENNIE in C. H. D. Cullingford *Brit. Caving* ix. 268 The family Dendrocoelidae includes a large number of troglobites. *Ibid.* 270 The genus *Candona*..includes many troglobite species. **1971** WEBSTER Add., Troglobitic. **1924** *Glasgow Herald* 13 Dec. 4 We include many of the bats as troglophils. **1947** *Sci. News* V. 52 The troglophili actively seek out and prefer the underground dark. **1953** HAZELTON & GLENNIE in C. H. D. Cullingford *Brit. Caving* ix. 268 Only those species which find the cave temperature suitable can become troglophiles. **1965** B. E. FREEMAN tr. *Vandel's Biospeleology* vii. 66 Its grey colour and the presence of eyes indicate that this planarian is a troglophile. **1927** Trogloxene [see *troglobiont* above]. **1965** B. E. FREEMAN tr. *Vandel's Biospeleology* ix. 142 Until quite recently all crabs which had been found in caves were trogloxenes or at most troglophiles.

troglodyte ('trɒg-, 'trəʊgləʊdaɪt), *sb.* (*a.*) Also 6-8 -ite. [ad. L. *trōglodyta*, ad. Gr. τρωγλοδύτης, f. τρώγλη hole + δύειν to get or go into.]

1. One of various races or tribes of men (chiefly ancient or prehistoric) inhabiting caves or dens (natural or artificial); a cave-dweller, cave-man.

1555 W. WATREMAN *Fardle of Facions* I. vi. 93 The Troglodites myne them selues caues in the grounde, wherin to dwell. **1614** RALEIGH *Hist. World* I. (1634) 52 Which Regions..(I mean that of Niger, and that of Prester John and the Troglodytes). **1642** HOWELL *For. Trav.* (Arb.) 51 They were Troglodites, and had no dwelling but in the hollowes of the rocks. **1842** W. C. TAYLOR *Anc. Hist.* xii. §4 (ed. 3) 336 Some.. Cappadocians were and continue to be Troglodytes, or dwellers in caves. **1851** D. WILSON *Preh. Ann.* (1863) I. ix. 251 The Troglodytes of post-pliocene ages.

2. Applied to various species of animals. †**a.** Some kind of deer or other horned quadruped. *Obs.* **b.** A bird of the genus *Troglodytes*; a wren. *rare*$^{-0}$. **c.** An anthropoid ape of the genus *Troglodytes*, as a gorilla or chimpanzee.

1661 LOVELL *Hist. Anim. & Min.* Introd., The hornes, in the stagge are ramous,..the Phrygian have moveable hornes, the Troglodyte direct to the earth. [**1706** PHILLIPS, *Troglodytes* or *Passer Troglodytes*, a little Bird call'd a Wren.] **1774** GOLDSM. *Nat. Hist.* (1862) I. VII. i. 491 The Troglodyte of Bontius, the Drill of Purchas, and the Pigmy of Tyson, have all received this general name—oran-outang.

d. Applied allusively to an animal or plant.

1817 KIRBY & SP. *Entomol.* (1818) II. xxi. 265 The caterpillar of another moth (*Noctua subterranea*, F.).. remains, a true Troglodyte,..in its cell under ground. **1845** LONGF. *To a Child* 99 The cavernous..homes Of wandering ..tribes of ants..These hapless Troglodytes. **1856** GRINDON *Life* iii. (1875) 29 That sullen troglodyte, the *Lathræa*, of the woods.

3. *fig.* A person who lives in seclusion; one unacquainted with the affairs of the world; a 'hermit'. Also, a dweller in a hovel or slum; a person of a degraded type like the prehistoric or savage cave-dwellers.

1854 H. ROGERS *Ess.* II. i. 11 Some would make him.. such a very Troglodyte in metaphysics that he was not properly acquainted even with such writers as Descartes or Hobbes. **1879** G. MACDONALD in *Graphic* Christmas No. 5 The girl who had been from her very birth a troglodyte, stood in the glory of a southern night. **1905** *Sat. Westm. Rev.* 25 Feb. 3 A belief worthy only of troglodytes inaccessible to Imperial..thought.

4. *attrib.* or *adj.* That is a troglodyte, cave-dwelling; of or belonging to a troglodyte or troglodytes.

1704 SWIFT *T. Tub* x. (1709) 119 Hear the words of the famous Troglodyte Philosopher. **1785** LATHAM *Gen. Synopsis* V. 229 Troglodyte Rail... These inhabit New Zealand. **1827** BUCKINGHAM *Trav. Mesopot.* I. 58 Large caves, and smaller grottoes;..any other Troglodyte habitations. **1873** H. SPENCER *Stud. Sociol.* vi. 119 Aboriginal man, of troglodyte or kindred habits.

Hence (or from the L. or Gr.) **'troglo,dytal** *a.*, pertaining to or characteristic of a troglodyte; †**'troglodytan** = *troglodyte* (sense 1); **'troglodytish** *a.*, resembling or characteristic of a troglodyte; **'troglody,tism**, the condition of a troglodyte, the habit of dwelling in caves.

1845 S. JUDD *Margaret* II. i. (1871) 160 Coming up from their dark *troglodytal abodes. **1607** TOPSELL *Four-f. Beasts* (1658) 225 People of Arabia called *Erembi*, which some call *Ichthyophagans*, and **Troglodytans*. **1866** *Sat. Rev.* 3 Mar. 256/2 The most perfect type of *troglodytish women does not care even for theology or religion. **1867** *Chambers' Encycl.* IX. 557/1 Perhaps we shall not be far wrong if we regard *Troglodytism as the primitive state of all.. mankind.

troglodytic (trɒg-, trəʊgləʊ'dɪtɪk), *a.* Also 6 -it-. [ad. L. *trōglodytic-us*, a. Gr. τρωγλοδυτικός, f. τρώγλη: see prec. and -IC.]

1. Inhabited or frequented by troglodytes; pertaining to or characteristic of a troglodyte.

1585 T. WASHINGTON tr. *Nicholay's Voy.* IV. xi. 122 b, The part of this Arabia bordering vpon Ethyopia by the auncients called Trogloditick. **1665** SIR T. HERBERT *Trav.* (1677) 36 Upon the Æthiopick or Trogloditick shoar. **1841** W. SPALDING *Italy & It. Isl.* I. 313 In the deep rocky valley of Ispica, are cliffs cut out into numerous habitations... This curious Troglodytic city, still occupied by a few peasants. **1874** WITHROW *Catacombs of Rome* (1877) 152 So habituated did he become to this troglodytic existence.

2. Having the habits of a troglodyte; cave-dwelling.

1676 EVELYN in *Aubrey's Nat. Hist. Surrey* (1719) I. Pref. 8 In the sandy Banks about Albury, do breed the Troglodytic Martines, who make their Boroughs in the Earth. **1833-4** J. PHILLIPS *Geol.* in *Encycl. Metrop.* (1845) VI. 698/2 Many parts of the Mediterranean shores were anciently possessed by Troglodytic nations. **1894** WINDLE *Tyson's Philol. Ess. Pygmies Introd.* I. 21 These tribes..are said to be pigmy in stature, troglodytic, and still in the Stone Age.

3. Resembling a troglodyte; of a degraded type like the cave-dwellers; also *fig.* not interested in or conversant with affairs.

1871 J. A. SYMONDS in *Life* (1895) II. 77 Uttering..these little bat squeaks of a Troglodytic creature. **1886** STEVENSON *Dr. Jekyll* ii. (ed. 2) 25 God bless me, the man seems hardly human! Something troglodytic..? **1910** *Blackw. Mag.* Feb. 169/2 A respectable troglodytic peer.

So **troglo'dytical** *a.*

1841 T. A. TROLLOPE *Western France* I. ix. 164 The whole [calcareous bank]..is hollowed out into a vast number of.. troglodytical habitations.

troglodytid (trəʊˈglɒdɪtɪd). *Ornith.* [f. mod.L. *Troglodytidæ*, f. *Troglodytes*, generic name: see TROGLODYTE and -ID[3].] A bird of the family *Troglodytidæ*, including wrens, mocking-birds, etc. So **troglodytine** (trəʊˈglɒdɪtaɪn) *a.*, belonging to the subfamily *Troglodytinæ*; **troglodytoid** (trəʊˈglɒdɪtɔɪd) *a.*, akin to the *Troglodytidæ*.

1890 *Field* 12 Apr. 517/3 Other families may be ultimately added to this Troglodytine group. **1895** *Funk's Stand. Dict.*, Troglodytid..Troglodytoid.

trogon (ˈtrəʊgɒn). *Ornith.* [mod.L., Gr. τρώγων, pr. pple. of τρώγειν to gnaw.] A bird of the genus *Trogon* or family *Trogonidæ*, widely distributed in tropical and subtropical regions, esp. in the New World, and characterized by soft plumage of varied and usually brilliant colouring.

1792 SHAW *Mus. Lever.* 177 The Leverian Trogon... Violaceous Trogon with a gloss of green-gold; wings black; abdomen white. **1838** J. GOULD *(title)* A Monograph of the Trogonidæ, or Family of Trogons. **1879** E. P. WRIGHT *Anim. Life* 277 The Golden Trogon (*Trogon resplendens*) has the greater portion of its plumage apparently composed of burnished gold. **1907** *Spectator* 23 Mar. 452/1 In the Miocene period..among the birds of French forests were trogons and parrots. **1910** *Q. Rev.* July 137 The beautiful Central American Quezal, or King of the Trogons, ranges.. from greenish bronze, through golden green, green, indigo, to purple and then into grey-black.

Hence **trogonid** (trəʊˈgəʊnɪd), a bird of the family *Trogonidæ*; **trogonine** (ˈtrəʊgənaɪn), **trogonoid** (ˈtrəʊgənɔɪd) *adjs.*, belonging to or having the characters of the *Trogonidæ*.

1890 H. SEEBOHM in *Ibis* Jan. 31 In the Picine arrangement, whether typical or Trogonine, the front plantar does not lead to the second toe. **1891** *Cent. Dict.*, Trogonoid. **1895** *Funk's Stand. Dict.*, Trogonid.

trogositid (trəʊgəʊˈsaɪtɪd), *sb.* and *a. Entom.* [ad. mod.L. *Trōgosītidæ*, f. *Trōgosīta*, name of the typical genus, f. Gr. τρώγειν to gnaw + σῖτος grain.] **a.** *sb.* A clavicorn beetle of the family *Trogositidæ*. **b.** *adj.* Belonging to the *Trogositidæ*. So **trogositoid** (trəʊgəʊˈsaɪtɔɪd) *a.*, allied to the *Trogositidæ*.

1895 in *Funk's Stand. Dict.*

Troian(e, -en: see TROJAN.

Troic (ˈtrəʊɪk), *a.* [ad. Gr. Τρωικός, f. Τρώς, name of the mythical founder of Troy.] Pertaining or relating to ancient Troy; Trojan.

1831 KEIGHTLEY *Mythol. Anc. Greece* (1854) 440 Contains much Troic matter. **1878** GLADSTONE *Homer* ii. 32 The Troic expedition.

troich, obs. Sc. f. TROUGH.

Troie, obs. f. TROY.

‖**troika** (ˈtrɔɪkə). [Russ. *troĭka*.] **1.** A Russian vehicle drawn by three horses abreast.

1842 tr. *Kohl's Russia* xxv. 202 One of his [Orlowsky's] best, and best-known pictures is his 'Courier'. A Russian troika is carried on at full speed by three wild horses. **1904** *Daily Record & Mail* 22 Apr. 4, I crossed the Baikal in a troika, a basket sleigh on wooden runners, drawn by three horses abreast.

2. A group or set of three persons (*rarely* things) or categories of people associated in power; a three-person commission or administrative council. Also *attrib.*

1945 [see *N.K.V.D.* s.v. N II. 1]. **1954** C. P. SNOW *New Men* xl. 286 Faith, hope, and hate: that was the troika which rushed him on. **1957** *Times Lit. Suppl.* 15 Nov. 682/1 The so-called *troika*, or commission of three, which authorized summary executions. **1961** *Guardian* 6 June 1/2 Experience of the United Nations action in the Congo..had convinced the Soviet Government of the need for the troika principle to be applied to all international action. **1961** *New Statesman* 9 June 901/2 Krushchev's central doctrine of the 'Troika', the principle of triple-harness—Communist, western and uncommitted—in the administrative, as well as in the policy-making, organs of the UN. **1969** A. ARENT *Laying on of Hands* (1971) ix. 91 The landed gentry. Part of the troika who, with the army and the Church, run Spain. **1971** *Nature* 26 Feb. 585/1 Every chemistry department, after all, is now at least a troika of inorganic, physical and organic chemistry. **1974** T. P. WHITNEY tr. *Solzhenitsyn's Gulag Archipelago* I. I. vii. 281 Real scope entered the picture with the twenties, when *permanently* operating *Troikas*—panels of three, operating behind closed doors—were created to bypass the courts permanently. **1976** *Church Times* 23 Jan. 9/1 The editorship is now a troika consisting of David Jenkins, John Drury and James Mark. **1976** M. J. LASKY *Utopia & Revolution* (1977) ii. 92 Ideas, images, and ideology never quite manage to be harnessed into a controllable troika.

†**troil**, *v. Obs. rare.* [a. OF. *troillier*, *truillier*, *treuiller* (*c* 1250 in Godef.), ad. MHG. *trüllen*.] *trans.* To dupe, beguile, deceive.

1393 LANGL. *P. Pl.* C. XXI. 321 Thus with treison and with trecherie þow troiledest hem boþe.

troilism (ˈtrɔɪlɪz(ə)m). [Perh. f. F. *trois* three: see -ISM.] Sexual activity in which three persons take part simultaneously. Also *transf.* Hence **ˈtroilist** *a.*

[**1941** *Dorland's Med. Dict.* (ed. 19) 1544/2 *Troilism*,..a psychotic sexual manifestation in which the patient desires the sexual partner of the person for whom he has homosexual yearnings.] **1951** *Ibid.* (ed. 22) 1622/2 *Troilism*, ..paraphilia practised by three persons, by two women and a man, or by two men and a woman. **1973** *Sunday Times* 14 Oct. 18/4 Wife-swapping and troilism are mostly in the writers' imaginations, not part of their life. **1976** *Times Lit. Suppl.* 20 Feb. 191/1 The troilist encounter in the film *Performance* is breathlessly mentioned as taking place in 'a great big bed'. **1983** V. GLENDINNING *Vita* 197 Emotional troilism always attracted her.

troilite (ˈtrəʊɪlaɪt). *Min.* [f. the name of Dominico Troili, who described a meteorite containing this mineral which fell in 1766 (Dana): see -ITE[1].] A sulphide of iron found in meteorites.

1868 DANA *Min.* (ed. 5) 57. **1903** *Daily Chron.* 12 Sept. 3/1 Troilite..is one of the dozen or so minerals found in meteorites that are not found on our earth.

troillebastone, variant of TRAILBASTON.

trois, troiss: see TROY (weight), TRUSS.

trois point (trwɑ pɔɪnt). [F. *trois* three + POINT *sb.*[1] B. 3 g.] The third point from the outer end in either table of a backgammon-board.

1745 HOYLE *Backgammon* viii. §7. 50, 5 Men upon his Adversary's Ace Point, and 3 Men upon his Adversary's Trois Point. **1870** HARDY & WARE *Mod. Hoyle, Backgammon* 143 You must then endeavor to secure your adversary's cinque, quatre, or trois point.

trois-quart(s: see TROCAR.

‖**trois-temps** (trwɑtɑ̃). [Short for F. *valse à trois temps* waltz in triple time.] The ordinary form of waltz, as distinguished from the more rapid DEUX-TEMPS. Also ***trois-temps waltz***.

1859 *Habits of Gd. Society* v. (new ed.) 209, I was at a public ball at Caen..and was amused to find the *trois-temps* danced with a peculiar shuffle, by way of compromise between conscience and pleasure. *Ibid.*, They..danced a polka, a gallop and a *trois-temps* waltz.

troite, obs. form of TROUT.

Trojan (ˈtrəʊdʒən), *a.* and *sb.* Also 4 Troien, 4-5 Troiane, 4-6 Troyan, 4-7 Troian, 5 Troienne, 6 Troyane, -en(e. [Formerly *Troyan*, *Troian* (ˈtrɔɪən); ad. L. *Trōiānus*, f. *Trōja* Troy.

The spelling *Troian* app. stood originally for *Troyan*; later it prob. represents *Trojan*.]

A. *adj.* **1. a.** Of or pertaining to ancient Troy or its inhabitants.

c **1374** CHAUCER *Troylus* II. 825 Antigone..Gan on a troyan lay to syngin clere. **1412-20** LYDG. *Chron. Troy* II. 8591 For Achilles þou3t it dide hym good With his swerde Troyan blood to schede. **1490** CAXTON *Eneydos* xxv. 91 The troienne folke is alle..descended of the forsworne laomedon. **1581** A. HALL *Iliad* v. 92 Through all the camp Troyene So honord..as he King Priams sonne had bene. **1649** OGILBY tr. *Virgil's Georgicks* I. (1684) 72 Long since enough we with our Blood did pay What might the Trojan Perjury defray. *a* **1721** PRIOR *Pallas & Venus* 1 The Trojan Swain had judg'd the great Dispute. **1835** THIRLWALL *Greece* I. 149 We..pass..out of the mythical circle..into that of the Trojan war.

b. *Trojan horse*: according to epic tradition, the hollow wooden horse in which Greeks were concealed to enter Troy; *fig.* a person, device, etc., insinuated to bring about an enemy's downfall; a person or thing that undermines from within; also *attrib.*

1574 R. BRISTOW *Motives* (1599) 7 b, The Troian horse. **1837** S. S. PRENTISS in G. L. Prentiss *Memoir of S.S. Prentiss* (1858) I. viii. 188 He cannot so easily introduce his Trojan horse within these walls [seating of contested members in Mississipi House]. I, for one, will hurl a spear against its hollow sides. **1940** *Sun* (Baltimore) 13 May 1/4 Alarmed by the success of Germany's 'Trojan horse' and parachute-troop tactics. **1963** *Listener* 17 Jan. 112/2 The strengthening of the 'special links' between London and Washington made Britain's possible entry into the Common Market 'more than ever likely to be that of a Trojan horse'. **1974** *Datamation* Jan. 57/1 A 'Trojan Horse' technique was used to compromise the security of a campus time-sharing computer system... A computer operator used it..erasing all trace of the illicit Trojan Horse code. **1979** A. BOYLE *Climate of Treason* iii. 96 This ambitious Trojan Horse strategy called for the recruitment and indoctrination of compliant intellectuals. **1981** *Courier-Mail* (Brisbane) 27 July 5/4 The 'Trojan horse' technique involves smuggling into a computer system an illegal set of instructions.

2. *Astr.* The epithet of two groups of asteroids which are at the same distance as Jupiter from the sun and approximately 60 degrees ahead of it and 60 degrees behind it in their orbit, so that with the sun and Jupiter they occupy positions of stability at the corners of two equilateral triangles. [So called because the first ones to be discovered were named after heroes of the Trojan War.]

1913 *Jrnl. Brit. Astron. Assoc.* XXIII. 214 Masculine names are reserved for [minor] planets of peculiar interest, viz., those that pass very near the Earth..or have the same period as Jupiter (the Trojan group). **1918** *Mem. R. Astron. Soc.* LXII. 79 The four asteroids—Achilles, Patroclus, Hector, and Nestor—are the Trojan planets. **1979** *Daily Tel.* 17 Apr. 8/6 *(caption)* Troy is one of the two groups of so-called Trojan satellites which always form equilateral triangles between themselves, the sun and Jupiter.

B. *sb.* **1.** An inhabitant or native of Troy. (In quot. 1910 used allusively.)

[*c* **893** K. ÆLFRED *Oros.* I. viii. §4 Ymb ealra þara Troiana ȝewin to aseceȝenne.] *c* **1330** R. BRUNNE *Chron. Wace* (Rolls) 158 Of manyon he reknes & sayes, both of Troiens & of Gregeis. *c* **1385** CHAUCER *L.G.W.* 933 *Dido*, The hors.. Thour which that many troyan [*v.r.* many a troian] muste sterue. **1503** HAWES *Examp. Virt.* vii, To the Troyans story lette hym resort. **1579** E. K. *Gloss. Spenser's Sheph. Cal.* July 147 Paris, who thereupon with a sorte of lustye Troyanes, stole her [Helena]. *c* **1620** T. ROBINSON *Mary Magd.* 122 Thousand Hellens faire,..And as many Troians braue. **1835** THIRLWALL *Greece* I. 33 The Pelasgians..in the Trojan war..side with the Trojans against the Greeks. **1910** M. G. KYLE *Fundamentals* 31 The Hittites have in one respect been the Trojans of Bible History.

2. *colloq.* **a.** A merry or roystering fellow; a boon companion; a person of dissolute life; also (in later use only) as a vague term of commendation or familiarity: a good fellow (often with the alliterative epithet *true* or *trusty*). Cf. GREEK *sb.* 5.

[**1588** SHAKS. *L.L.L.* v. ii. 681 Fellow Hector..Vnlesse you play the honest Troyan, the poore Wench is cast away.] **1600** KEMP *Nine Daies Wond.* C ij, He was a kinde good fellow, a true Troyan. **1663** BUTLER *Hud.* I. i. 620 There they say right, and like true Trojans. **1762** BP. FORBES *Jrnl.* (1886) 208, I was most hospitably entertained by that honest old Trojan Mr. Sutherland. **1827** SCOTT *Surg. Dau.* v, None are so scrupulous as I am about making promises. I am as trusty as a Trojan for that. **1888** F. COWPER *Captain of Wight* (1889) 84 Eustace, my Trojan, don't you call me a goose again.

b. A brave or plucky fellow; a person of great energy or endurance: usu. in phr. ***like a Trojan***.

[**1387** TREVISA *Higden* (Rolls) II. 225 3if we wil mene þat þey [the people of Ilium] beeþ stronge we clepeþ hem Troians.] **1846** NEWMAN in Ward *Life* (1912) I. iii. 114 Working like a Trojan. **1882** JAMIESON, *Trojan*, a name applied to a person of uncommon size, strength, daring, or endurance. **1897** G. ALLEN *Type-writer Girl* xvii. 179, I worked hard at that gown... Dear little Elsie helped me with it like a Trojan.

3. *Entom.* A name given by Linnæus to certain species of butterflies, chiefly tropical, distinguished by crimson spots on the wings from allied species called *Greeks*.

1832 T. BROWN *Bk. Butterflies & M.* (1834) I. 142 The Imperial Trojan. *Papilio Priamus.* **1863** BATES *Nat. Amazon* iii. (1864) 62 Those species of Papilio..so conspicuous in their velvety black, green, and rose-coloured hues, which Linnæus..called 'Trojans'.

4. *Astr.* A Trojan asteroid.

1918 *Mem. R. Astron. Soc.* LXII. 80 The inclinations of the orbits of the Trojans and Jupiter vary through a quite considerable range. **1954** C. PAYNE-GAPOSCHKIN *Introd. Astron.* (1956) ix. 234 The theory of the 'Trojans' is a beautiful special application of the dynamical 'Problem of Three Bodies'. **1979** *Icarus* XL. 341/1 There seem to be three times more Trojans at the leading Trojan point.

5. *U.S.* The proprietary name of a make of contraceptive sheath.

First registered as a proprietary term in the U.S. on 26 Apr. 1927.

1951 *Official Gaz.* (U.S. Patent Office) 17 Apr. 757/1 Trojan... For Prophylactic Membranous Articles for the Prevention of Contagious Diseases. **1962** A. LURIE *Love & Friendship* xiv. 264 'Why "Trojans"?' she asked, picking up a small box... 'They lost the war, after all.' **1973** M. AMIS *Rachel Papers* 202 After some neck-ricking soixante-neuf and a short period inside her unsheathed, I clawed at the little pink holder and took its final trojan.

Hence **ˈTrojanry** (*nonce-wd.*), body or company of Trojans. See also TROYANISH, TROYISH.

1667 COTTON *Scarron.* IV. 135 Dido..Ran..to spie, What was become o' th' Trojanry.

†**troke, truke,** *v. Obs.* (exc. *dial.*) Forms: 1 trucian, 2-3 truke, 3 trukie, 3-4 troke, 5 truche, (8 *dial.* truck). [OE. *trucian*, ulterior origin unascertained.]

1. *intr.* To fail; to be wanting or lacking.

c **1000** ÆLFRIC *Hom.* (Th.) II. 42 Ne trucað heora nan ana ðurh unmihte. *c* **1205** LAY. 16416 Þa iseh Hængest þæt his help trukede [*c* **1275** trokede]. *a* **1225** *Ancr. R.* 68 Bute 3if þe ilke þridde, oðer stu[n]de trukie. *c* **1250** *Gen. & Ex.* 105 Til domes-dai ne sal it troken. *a* **1800** PEGGE *Suppl. Grose* s.v., A cow is said to truck when her milk fails. North.

b. with dative of person.

c **1122** *O.E. Chron.* an. 1090, He underȝeat þæt his ȝeswerene men him trucedon. *a* **1225** *Ancr. R.* 230 3if bileaue him trukede. *a* **1240** *Lofsong* in *Cott. Hom.* 213 Bihold, heie louerd, hu monnes help trukeð me.

c. To fail or be unable *to do* something. *rare*[−1].

a **1400-50** *Alexander* 1988 Loo here a gloue full of graynes ..And þou truches [*Dubl. MS.* And yf þou thynkes] þaim to tell [L. *quod si facere non valebis*], þen [etc.].

2. *trans.* To deceive, beguile.

c **1175** *Lamb. Hom.* 35 Heo us truket þenne we lest weneð. *a* **1225** *Juliana* 7 Ah ha truste upon him þat ne truked na mon. **13..** *Sir Beues* (A.) 3268 Ful wel him þou3te..þat him trokede a gret gile, For he was in þe castel be-loke.

Hence †**troking (truking)** *vbl. sb.*, failure, lack; deceit; also †**troke (truke)** *sb.* (*rare*[−1]), failure, want, lack.

c **1175** *Lamb. Hom.* 79 Ierusalem bitacneð griþes sihþe, and ierico trukinge of lihte. *a* **1225** *Ancr. R.* 12 Þis nis bute a trukunge & a fals gile. *c* **1250** *Gen. & Ex.* 3508 Help ðe nedful ðat he ne be dead, for truke of ðin helpe.

troke, troker, Sc. ff. TRUCK, TRUCKER[1].

trokel, -ell, -ill, obs. forms of TRUCKLE.

† **'troker, 'truker.** *Sc. Obs.* Forms: 5–6 **truker,** 6 **trukour, treukour, truikour, -er, trouker, trucour,** 7 **trewker.** [f. TROKE *v.* + -ER[1].] A deceiver, cheat; a rascal, rogue.

c **1470** HENRYSON *Mor. Fab.* IX. (*Wolf & Fox*) xxii, Staf or sting yone truker for to strike. **1530** LYNDESAY *Test. Papyngo* 1001 Agane our wyll, those treukouris bene intrusit. **1535** STEWART *Cron. Scot.* (Rolls) II. 511 With diligence and bissie cuir tha woik, And mony trucour in the tyme tha tuik. **1560** ROLLAND *Seven Sages* 78 The treuth now ȝe haue spyit Of that Truikour. *a* **1578** LINDESAY (Pitscottie) *Chron. Scot.* (S.T.S.) I. 221 Thir fallis trukeris quhilk cause ȝour grace to beleif ewill on my handis. *a* **1585** POLWART *Flyting w. Montgomerie* 225 Thy doytit dytings soone denie, Trouker, or I thy trumperie trie.

b. *attrib.* or as *adj.*

1596 DALRYMPLE tr. *Leslie's Hist. Scot.* VIII. (S.T.S.) II. 58 Mony at this tyme mony trukour tragidies in the cuntrie stiret vp. **1650** *Dalgety Sess. Rec.* in W. Ross *Past. Wk. in Covenant. Times* ix. (1877) 172 William Skinstone..did sclandour him in calling him a trewker lowne.

troktolite, variant of TROCTOLITE.

troland ('trəʊlənd). [The name of L. T. *Troland* (1889–1932), U.S. psychologist and physicist.] A unit of retinal illumination, being the illumination produced by a surface with a luminance of one candela per square metre when the pupil has an area of one square millimetre; orig. called a *photon* (PHOTON[1] 1).

1944 *Jrnl. Optical Soc. Amer.* XXXIV. 254/2 [Report by the Committee on Colorimetry.] A special unit of retinal illuminance, the photon, was introduced by Troland in 1917 and has been employed to some extent, but its use is circumscribed by the danger of confusion with the elementary quantum of radiant energy which is generally called the photon. The renaming of the unit of retinal illumination as the troland, in honor of Dr. L. T. Troland, its originator and chairman of the Committee..in 1921–22, is recommended. **1976** *Nature* 19 Feb. 570/1 We have.. measured sensitivity to short wavelengths after adaptation to retinal illuminances that varied over the range 1·1–6·0 log trolands.

troll (trəʊl), *sb.*[1] Also 6 **trowell,** 7 **trole, troul, trowle,** 7–9 **trowl.** [app. f. TROLL *v.*; but in some uses the derivation is uncertain.]

1. The act of trolling; a going or moving round; routine or repetition.

1705 ROWE *Biter* I. i, Make up the Troll of the Sentence, as merrily conceited Persons are us'd to do. **1790** BURKE *Fr. Rev.* 274 The troll of their categorical table might have informed them that there was something else..besides substance and quantity.

2. A song the parts of which are sung in succession; a round, a catch.

1820 W. IRVING *Sketch Bk., Little Britain* (1865) 306 The famous old drinking trowl from Gammer Gurton's Needle. **1856** KANE *Arct. Expl.* I. xix. 233 It is sad..to miss..the joyous troll of his ballads.

†**3.** A little wheel; *spec.* an angler's reel or winch on a fishing-rod. *Obs.*

[Cf. OF. *trueil* (Godef. *Compl.*), F. *treuil* windlass, winch.]

1570 LEVINS *Manip.* 57/15 A Trowell, *rotula.* **1662** VENABLES *Experienced Angler* iv. 47 With your troul wind up your line till you think you have it almost streight. **1670–1** *Act 22 & 23 Chas. II,* c. 25 §6 If any person..shall..use any ..Nett..Angle, Haire Noose, Troll or Speare.

4. *Angling.* **a.** The method of trolling in fishing for pike, etc.: see TROLL *v.* 13.

1681 CHETHAM *Angler's Vade-m.* xli. §7 (1689) 312 It's not so good for the Trowl as snap. **1688** R. HOLME *Armoury* II. 324/2 *Trowl,* a fishing for a Pike: and this is by walking, and the line to run on a winch, that it may be winded up, or let out at pleasure. **1794** *Sporting Mag.* III. 247 Both at trowl and snap, cut away one of the fins. **1847** T. BROWN *Mod. Farriery* 902 At both troll and snap some persons have two or more swivels to their line.

b. A lure used in trolling, as a *trolling-spoon* (see TROLLING *vbl. sb.* 4).

1869 *Cornh. Mag.* Apr. 419 The many artificial trolls which have been..invented for salmon and trout-angling.

5. A kind of low cart: = TROLLEY *sb.* 1. *local.*

1663 [implied in *trollful*: see below]. **1810** *Hull Improv. Act* 56 Any cart waggon sledge troll dray. **1870** *Murray's Handbk. E. Counties* 224/2 They [the 'rows' of Yarmouth] are traversed by..a sort of horse-wheelbarrow, called 'trolls' or 'trolly-carts'. **1882** BUCKLAND *Notes & Jottings* 192 When the trawlers [at Yarmouth] come in laden with fish they transfer them to very large boats..and thence into trolls, which are backed into the water.

6. *attrib.* and *Comb.*: **troll-line** = *trawl-line* (see TRAWL *sb.* 4); **troll-plate** (see quot.).

1888 EARLL in Goode *Amer. Fishes* 195 The smack fishermen of Charleston catch a few on *troll-lines during.. spring and early summer. **1877** KNIGHT *Dict. Mech.,* **Troll-plate* (*Machinery*), a rotating disk employed to effect the simultaneous convergence or divergence of a number of objects; such as screw-dies in a stock, or the jaws of a universal chuck.

Hence **'trollful,** as much as fills a troll (sense 5).

1663 P. HENRY *Diaries & Lett.* (1882) 143 August 1. Hay carry'd in out of ye great meadow, three trolefuls.

troll (trəʊl), *sb.*[2] Also **trold, trolle.** See also TROW *sb.*[4] [a. ONorse and Swed. *troll,* Da. *trold* (whence Da. *trylla, trylde,* Sw. *trolla* to charm, bewitch, ON. *trolldómr* witchcraft).

(Adopted in English from Scandinavian in the middle of the 19th c.; but in Shetland and Orkney, where the form is now TROW (in 1616 *troll*), it has survived from the Norse dialect formerly spoken there.)]

a. In Scandinavian mythology, One of a race of supernatural beings formerly conceived as giants, now, in Denmark and Sweden, as dwarfs or imps, supposed to inhabit caves or subterranean dwellings: see quotations, and cf. TROW *sb.*[4]

1616 *Dittay Sheriff Court Shetland* 2 Oct. (Jam. s.v. *Trow*), The said Catherine for airt and pairt of witchcraft and sorcerie, in hunting and seeing the Trollis ryse out of the kyrk yeard of Hildiswick.

1851 BORROW *Lavengro* xxx. (1911) 188 A laidly Trold has dragged it there. **1856** EMERSON *Eng. Traits, Ability* Wks. (Bohn) II. 34 The Scandinavian fancied himself surrounded by Trolls—a kind of goblin men, with vast power of work and skilful production. **1865** BARING-GOULD *Werewolves* iv. 40 In the Hrolfs Saga Kraka, we meet with a troll in a boar's shape, to whom divine honours are paid. **1865** WHITTIER *Tent on Beach, Kallundborg Church* 14 But the sly Dwarf said, 'No work is wrought By Trolls of the Hills, O man, for naught.' **1867** BRANDE & COX *Dict. Sc.,* etc. s.v., These Trolls are superior to man in strength and stature, but far beneath him in mind. **1869** TOZER *Highl. Turkey* II. 273 A boy's escape from a Troll or an enchanted horse.

b. *attrib.* and *Comb.* That is a troll, as ***troll-maiden, -wife, -woman***; belonging to or inhabited by trolls, as ***troll-garden, -land, -marsh***; also ***troll-like*** adj.; **troll-bull,** a supernatural being in the form of a bull; **troll-drum,** a drum used in Lappish magical rites; **trollman,** a magician or wizard.

1902 *Folk-Lore* June 185 On 'Old Holy Kings' Night' black *troll-bulls come up from the sea and visit the byres. **1894** *Jrnl. Hellenic Stud.* XIV. 270 In Lapland..designs of this character ornamented the *troll-drums of the magicians till within a recent period. **1864** KINGSLEY *Rom. & Teut.* i. (1875) 1 Fancy to yourself a great *Troll-garden. **1886** J. CORBETT *Fall of Asgard* I. 65 This is no *Troll-land, but a fair place that Thor has kept for you. **1954** J. R. R. TOLKIEN *Two Towers* iv. 66 A large Man-like, almost *Troll-like, figure. **1978** *Trans. Yorks. Dial. Soc.* LXXVIII. 18 Joseph is a troll-like figure, the foil to Heathcliff's gigantic, elemental being. **1886** J. CORBETT *Fall of Asgard* 36 They had wanted to drive her away for a *troll-maiden. **1865** BARING-GOULD *Werewolves* viii. 108 Property..imparted to them by the *Trollmen. **1886** J. CORBETT *Fall of Asgard* I. 59 Over the lake..and over the *Troll marsh to the valley. **1851** THORPE *Northern Mythol.* I. 113 Hedin met in the forest a *Troll-wife riding on a wolf, with a rein formed of serpents. **1862** H. MARRYAT *Year in Sweden* II. 390 Herve Ulf, on his way to matin-song, was accosted by a *Trolle woman.

troll (trəʊl), *v.* Forms: 4–5 **trolle,** 6 **trol,** 6–7 **trole,** 6– **troll;** 5–9 **trowl,** 6–7 **trowle, troule,** 6–8 **troul;** 5–9 **trull,** (5 **trulle);** 8–9 *Sc.* **trow.** [A word or series of words of uncertain origin, and of which all the senses do not go closely together. It is generally derived from OF. *troller,* a hunting term, 'to quest, to go in quest of game, without purpose', of which Godefroy has one instance. This survives in mod.French (see Littré). Godefroy has also one example of *traller,* in Littré *trôler* 'to lead or walk in all directions indiscriminately, to run here and there, to run about, ramble'. These may well be the same word, and *trôler* is by many referred to Ger. *trollen* 'to roll', though the senses are not the same. Both senses are found in English, but the word has also other senses not found in German or French.]

I. 1. *intr.* To move or walk about or to and fro; to ramble, saunter, stroll, 'roll'; *spec.* (*slang*) of a homosexual: to walk the streets, or 'cruise', in search of a sexual encounter; cf. sense 13.

1377 LANGL. *P. Pl.* B. XVIII. 296 And þus hath he trolled [*v.r.* tollid] forth þis two & thretty wynter. [**1561**: see 15 b.] **1691** tr. *Emilianne's Frauds Rom. Monks* (ed. 3) 107 Another sort of Pilgrims..who spend their time in trouling from one place of Devotion to another. **1942** E. LANGLEY *Pea Pickers* I. iii. 41 Past rows of hawthorn hedges in leaf, but lacking flowers, we trolled. **1967** A. WILSON *No Laughing Matter* III. 201 At first..I just got myself picked up... But later I started trolling. **1967** *Listener* 21 Dec. 814/3 They all come trolling on in form-hugging black and do evocative things with chairs and ladders and planks of wood. **1981** R. BARNARD *Sheer Torture* xi. 120, I trolled off quite happily and entered the house.

2. *trans.* To move (a ball, bowl, round body) by or as by rolling; to roll, bowl, trundle; to turn over and over, or round and round; to roll (the eyes); to throw (dice); *spec.* to trundle (a bowl) at the game of bowls (also *absol.*); also, to knock *down* by bowling.

c **1425** *St. Eliz. of Spalbeck* in *Anglia* VIII. 117/12 Sche myghte not holde hir heed vpon a pillow..but..trollid it hyderwarde and þyderwarde. *c* **1450** *Two Cookery-bks.* 95 Put all in a treen boll, and trull [*v.r.* twille] hit to-gidre with thi honde. **1572** [see TROLL-MADAM]. **1599** PORTER *Angry Wom. Abingd.* (Percy Soc.) 8 Let them trowle the bowles vppon the greene; Ile trowle the bowles in the buttery. **1628** LE GRYS *Barclay's Argenis* 77 Shee trowled her angry eyes on euery side. **1647** FANSHAW *Civ. Wars Rome* Poems 301 The forbidden Dice to trowle. **1665** T. A. *Excell. Roy. Hand* 9 Taking a few Pease out of his Pocket,..he troll'd them along the Floor. **1699** J. DUNTON *Life & Err.* (1818) II. 594 The Duke was then flinging the first bowl. Next trowled the Bishop. **1821** GALT *Ann. Parish* xlv, The sinner..who loves to troll his iniquity like a sweet morsel under his tongue. **1822** SCOTT *Nigel* xxi, As I was wont to trowl down the ninepins in the skittle-ground. **1841** THACKERAY *Drum* I. iii, My Grandsire was trolling the [drum-]sticks.

3. *intr.* To roll; also, to turn round and round; to spin, whirl.

1581 MULCASTER *Positions* xix. (1887) 80 Children when they had their whirling gigges vnder the deuotion of their scourges, caused them to troule about the broad streates. **1626** BRETON *Fantasticks, Easter Day* (1857) 330 The Lovers eyes doe troule like Tennis balls. **1664** POWER *Exp. Philos* I. 18 Mites..trolling to and fro with this mealy dust ..sticking to them. **1730** SWIFT *Death & Daphne* 88 How pleasant on the Banks of Styx, To troll it in a Coach and Six! **1818** SCOTT *Hrt. Midl.* l, This is Lady—Lady—these tamn'd Southern names rin out o' my head like a stane trowling down hill. **1855** SINGLETON *Virgil* I. 80 Waggons.. That lazy troll.

II. 4. a. *intr.* To move nimbly, as the tongue in speaking; to wag. Also said of a person. *Obs.* or *arch.*

a **1616** BEAUMONT *Ex-ale-tation of Ale* xxxiv, Fill him but a boule, it will make his tongue troule. **1638** FORD *Fancies* III. iii, His tongue trouls like a mill-clack. **1828** *Blackw. Mag.* XXIV. 166 See how she trolls with the tongue.

b. *trans.* To move (the tongue) volubly. ? *Obs.*

1667 MILTON *P.L.* XI. 620 To sing, to dance, To dress, and troule the Tongue, and roule the Eye. **1747** [? UPTON] *New Canto Spencer's F.Q.* xviii. 12 How they troul the Tongue and roll the Eye.

†**5.** *fig. trans.* To turn over in one's mind; to revolve, ponder, contemplate. *Obs. rare*[−1].

1685 F. SPENCE tr. *Varillas' Ho. Medicis* 107 His Holiness .. had trolled in his understanding so black a crime.

III. †**6.** *trans.* To cause to pass from one to another, hand round among the company present; esp. in phrase *to troll the bowl.* Hence ***troll-the-bowl*** as sb., a tippler, carouser. *Obs.*

1575 *Song* in *Gammer Gurton* II. Bj b, Then dooth she trowle, to mee the bowle. **1599** PORTER *Angry Wom. Abingd.* Bij b, Where be..these trowle the bowles, these greene men? **1600** DEKKER *Gentle Craft* (1862) 4 Trowl the bowl, the jolly nut-brown bowl. **1819** SCOTT *Ivanhoe* II. vi. 88 Come, trowl the brown bowl to me.

†**7.** *intr.* Of the vessel or its contents: To move or pass round the company; to circulate, be passed round. *Obs.*

1620 MIDDLETON *Chaste Maid* III. ii. 77 Now the cups troll about To wet the gossips' whistles. **1651** *Miller of Mansf.* 9 Nappie Ale..in a browne Bole Which did about the Board merrily trowle. **1808** SCOTT *Marm.* VI. Introd. 65 The wassel round, in good brown bowls, Garnish'd with ribbons, blithely trowls.

†**8.** *intr.* To come *in* abundantly like a flowing stream; to 'roll' in. *Obs.*

1576 GASCOIGNE *Steele Gl.* (Arb.) 68 He that can winke at any foule abuse As long as gaines come trouling in therwith. *a* **1627** MIDDLETON & ROWLEY *Spanish Gypsy* I. (1653) C ij, This little Ape gets money by the sack full, It troules upon her. **1630** J. TAYLOR (Water P.) *Jack-a-Lent* Wks. I. 117/1 The pide-coat Mackrell, Pilchard, Sprat, and Soale, To serve great Jacke-a-Lent amaine doe trole. **1689** HICKERINGILL *Ceremony-Monger* Concl. iii. Wks. 1716 II. 482 The Council of Sardica..saw this Develish Mischief coming trowling into the Church.

†**9.** *trans.* To cause to roll or flow (*in*). *Obs.*

1573 TUSSER *Husb.* lix. (1878) 137 That trustily thriftines trowleth to thee. **1599** NASHE *Lenten Stuffe* (1871) 40 To trowl in cash throughout all nations.

IV. 10. a. *trans.* To sing (something) in the manner of a round or catch; to sing in a full, rolling voice; to chant merrily or jovially. Const. *forth, out.* Cf. ROLL *v.*[2] 4 b and TROLLY-LOLLY *int.*

Perh. originally *fig.* from 6 = to sing in succession, as a round or catch (each line being as it were passed on to the next singer).

1575, 1586 [see TROLLING *vbl. sb.* 2]. **1610** SHAKS. *Temp.* III. ii. 126 Will you troule the Catch You taught me but whileare? **1672** SHADWELL *Miser* I, If thou wert just now trolling out Hopkins and Sternhold. **1813** SCOTT *Rokeby* III. xxviii, But, hark! our merry-men so gay Troll forth another roundelay. **1863** GEO. ELIOT *Romola* ix, He could touch the lute and troll a gay song. **1881** R. L. STEVENSON *Virginibus Puerisque* 283 But let him feign never so carefully, there is not a man but has his pulses shaken when Pan trolls out a stave of ecstasy and sets the world a-singing. **1933** H. ALLEN *Anthony Adverse* III. IX. lxiv. 1190 At Anthony's suggestion they left off the doleful ballads which at first engrossed them and took to trolling more cheerful lays. **1951** N. M. GUNN *Well at World's End* xiv. 99 He felt like a voyageur..trolled a note or two and lifted his tweed hat as if it were a sombrero. **1977** *Rolling Stone* 16 June 69/2 When the Diamonds trolled 'Them Never Love Poor Marcus', I was moved.

b. *intr.* To sing in this way; to carol, warble.

1879 STEVENSON *Trav. Cevennes* 132 He trolled with ample lungs. **1881** —— *Virg. Puerisque* 281 Pan, the god of Nature,..trolling on his pipe until he charmed the hearts of upland ploughmen.

11. *intr.* Of bells: To give forth a recurring cadence of full, mellow tones; of a song: to sound or be uttered in a full, rolling, or jovial voice; *transf.* of a tune: to be present in or recur constantly to the mind, to 'run in one's head'.

1607 [see TROLLING *ppl. a.*]. **1678** DRYDEN *Kind Keeper* III. i, I have had..a Tune trouling in my Head. **1682** H. ALDRICH *Upon Christ Church Bells Oxf.,* O the bonny Christ Church Bells..they..trowle so merrily, merrily. **1813** [see TROLLING *ppl. a.*] **1890** BARRIE *My Lady Nicotine* xxx. 239

He strolled away, an air from 'The Grand Duchess' lightly trolling from his lips.

12. *trans.* To utter nimbly or rapidly; to recite in a full rolling voice. Also *intr.* of speech.

1625 B. JONSON *Staple of N.* IV. iv, If he runne To his Iudiciall Astrologie, And trowle the Trine, the Quartile and the Sextile. **1709** MRS. MANLEY *Secret Mem.* I. 185 The old Ones Discourse trouls all upon Virtue. **1850** L. HUNT *Autobiog.* III. xix. 50 They speak well out, trolling the words clearly over the tongue. **1874** BLACKIE *Horæ Hellen.* 292 Greek trimeters may be trolled off from the British tongue, as glibly as any hexameters. **1948** J. BERRYMAN *Dispossessed* 77 Now Tell me. Troll me the sources of that Song—Assigned last week—by Blake. **1971** K. MILLETT *Sexual Politics* (1972) II. iii. 137 The old scholar chuckles while trolling the more rakish passages of Catullus.

V. 13. *Angling. intr.* To angle with a running line (? *orig.* with the line running on a 'troll' or winch); also (*trans.*) to fish (water) in this way; *spec.* **a.** to fish for pike by working a dead bait (usually on a gorge hook) by a sink-and-draw motion; **b.** (*trans.* and *intr.*), to angle with a spinning bait: = SPIN *v.* 12 a, b; **c.** in *U.S.* and *Sc.* use (perh. through association with *trail* or *trawl*), to trail a baited line behind a boat. Also *fig.*

In quot. 1606 perh. confused with TRAWL.

1606 S. GARDINER *Bk. Angling* 28 Consider how God by his Preachers trowleth for thee. **1651–7** [see TROLLING *vbl. sb.* 3]. **1675** CROWNE *Country Wit* v, Here have I been angling and trowling for my Father-in-law, and have had him at my hook all day. **1682** NOBBES *Compl. Troller* (1822) 226 In some places, they troll without a rod, or playing the bait, as I have seen them throw a line out of a boat, and so let it draw after them as they row. **1711** GAY *Rural Sports* I. 264 Nor drain I ponds the golden carp to take, Nor trowle for pikes, dispeoplers of the lake. **1764** GOLDSM. *Trav.* 187 The peasant..With patient angle trolls the finny deep. **1814–24** COL. HAWKER *Instr. Yng. Sportsm.* 173 Trolling, or spinning a minnow, is the other most general mode of trout fishing. **1831** *Encycl. Brit.* (ed. 7) III. 144/2 *Trolling*, in the more limited sense of the word, signifies catching fish with the gorge-hook, which is composed of two, or what is called a double eel-hook. **1864** WEBSTER, *Troll*,..to angle..with a hook drawn along the surface of the water. **1881** *Harper's Mag.* Nov. 831, I troll a cast of flies. **1891** LANG *Angling Sk.* 5 Trolling a minnow from a boat in Loch Leven—probably the lowest possible form of angling. **1966** E. LINDALL *Time too Soon* iv. 51 Kamindo had rebuffed him when he had trolled for information. **1984** *Monitor* (McAllen, Texas) 1 May 6A/3 It will troll the Earth's upper atmosphere for magnetospheric, atmospheric and gravitational data.

†14. *fig. trans.* To draw on as with a moving bait; to entice, allure. *Obs.*

1565 GOLDING *Ovid's Met.* II. (1593) 33 They troll me downe to lower waies. **1638** FORD *Lady's Trial* v. I foster a decoy here, And she trowls on her ragged customer. **1684** J. GOODMAN *Winter-even. Confer.* I. (1705) 21 The hopes he is fed withal trowls him on.

VI. †15. *Phrases.* **a.** *Hawking.* (?)

a **1529** SKELTON *Ware the Hauke* 116 With troll, cytrace [? trytrace], and trouy, They ranged, hankin bouy. **1575** R. B. *Appius & Virginia* Bj, With hey tricke, how trowle, trey trip, and trey trace Trowle hazard in a vengeance.

†b. ***troll and troll by, troll hazard, troll with,*** as sbs., names for various 'orders of knaves': see quot. and cf. sense 1. *Obs. Cant.*

1561 AWDELAY *Frat. Vacab.* (E.E.T.S.) 12 Troll and Trol by, is he that setteth naught by no man nor no man by him. Troll with is he that no man shall know the seruaunt from y[e] Maister... Troll hazard of trace is he that goeth behynde his Maister as far as he may see hym... Troll hazard of tritrace, is he that goeth gaping after his Master.

troll, obs. form of TROWEL.

trolldom ('trəʊldəm). [= Sw. *trolldom* :—ONorse *trolldómr*: see TROLL *sb.*[2] and -DOM.] The practice of trolls, witchcraft.

1891 ATKINSON *Moorland Par.* 76 *note*, The entire category of 'trolldom' or witchcraft.

trolleite ('trɒliːaɪt). *Min.* [ad. Sw. *trolleit* (Blomstrand, 1867), named after the Swedish chemist Trolle-Wachtmeister: see -ITE[1].] A hydrous aluminium phosphate, occurring in pale green compact masses.

1868 DANA *Min.* (ed. 5) 577.

troller ('trəʊlə(r)). Forms: see TROLL *v.* [f. TROLL *v.* + -ER[1].]

1. One who trolls catches, songs, etc.: see TROLL *v.* 10.

a **1734** NORTH *Lives* (1826) II. 205 He was a great troller of songs. **1824** MISS MITFORD *Village* Ser. I. (1863) 113 A troller of profane catches.

2. *Angling.* One who trolls for pike, etc.: see TROLL *v.* 13.

1651–7 T. BARKER *Art of Angling* (1659) 30 The best Trouler for a Pike within this Realm of England. **1682** NOBBES (*title*) The Compleat Troller, or the Art of Trolling. **1820** T. F. SALTER (*title*) The troller's guide; a practical treatise on the art of trolling or fishing for jack and pike. **1894** *Field* 1 Dec. 838/2 The trollers killed ten.

b. A trolling-rod.

1688 [see *trolling-rod* s.v. TROLLING *vbl. sb.* 4].

trolley, trolly ('trɒlɪ), *sb.* Also **trawley**. [? f. TROLL *v.*; cf. *lorry, rolley, rulley*.]

1. Locally applied to a low cart of various kinds, e.g. a costermonger's cart; at Yarmouth, a narrow cart or sledge adapted for the 'rows' or narrow alleys (ROW *sb.*[1] 4 c). Cf. TROLL *sb.*[1] 5 and *trolley-cart* in 4 below.

1823 MOOR *Suffolk Words* s.v., Sich roads! We got rarely jounced i' the trolly. **1870** *Pall Mall G.* 25 Aug. 4 The prisoner was leading his horse in a trolly along Fairfield-road, Bow.

2. a. A low truck without sides or ends, esp. one with flanged wheels for running on a railway, or a track of rails in a factory, etc. Cf. BOGIE 1.

1858 SIMMONDS *Dict. Trade*, *Trolley*, a kind of railway vehicle. **1861** SMILES *Engineers* II. 201 The goods in the London Docks are hauled in trollies, waggons or hand-barrows from ship to ship. **1862** MRS. H. WOOD *Mrs. Hallib.* xix, I'll send in a trolley of coal. **1881** RAYMOND *Mining Gloss.* s.v., The two-wheeled trolly is used in a rolling-mill to wheel the puddle-balls to the squeezer. **1881** H. W. NICHOLSON *From Sword to Share* xxv. 182 The train..was made up of some dozen sideless trucks, or trawleys. **1885** *Law Times* 16 May 47/1 A porter..put all the luggage on a trolley..and wheeled the trolley on to the platform.

b. In fig. phr. ***off one's trolley***, crazy. Cf. ROCKER[1] 2 c. *slang.*

1896 ADE *Artie* x. 92 Any one that's got his head full o' the girl proposition's liable to go off his trolley at the first curve. **1903** A. H. LEWIS *Boss* xix. 264 She's off her trolley. She toins sick; an' in a week she croaks. **1949** N. R. NASH *Young & Fair* II. ii. 66 If you suspect Patty, you're off your trolley! **1976** *National Observer* (U.S.) 4 Sept. 13/3 Anybody who buys a luxury liner for use as a floating hotel is off his trolley. **1983** *Times* 5 Feb. 3/1 The London college gym mistress who is suing her former lover for libel in the High Court, heard a lawyer say yesterday that she had 'gone off her trolley' about the affair.

c. A small table or stand on wheels or castors for use in serving food, transporting light objects, luggage, etc. Freq. as the second element in Combs. ***supermarket trolley***: see SUPERMARKET 2 b; also *ellipt.*

1937, etc. [see *tea-trolley* s.v. TEA *sb.* 9 c]. **1944** D. WELCH *In Youth is Pleasure* ii. 39 Some [waiters] carried trays poised high in the air; others trundled chromium trolleys with glass shelves, on which brilliant little cakes were piled. *a* **1948** —— *Voice through Cloud* (1950) iv. 39 When the porters..started to wheel him out of the ward, he sat up on the trolley, so that the red blankets fell off him. **1949** S. SMITH *Holiday* xiii. 173 The semolina pudding came in on the trolly. **1963** [see *hostess trolley* s.v. HOSTESS 4]. **1973** J. WILSON *Truth or Dare* ii. 24, I couldn't help noticing what she'd got in her trolly: sausages, luncheon meat *and* a tub of marge. **1977** *Lancs. Life* Nov. 107/1 (*caption*) A good trolley is an invaluable aid to efficient hostessmanship. **1982** *Amer. Speech* LVII. 154 *Trolley*, surgical dressing cart (British).

3. a. A grooved metallic pulley which travels along, and receives current from, an overhead electric wire, the current being then conveyed by a *trolley-pole* or other conductor to a motor, usually that of a car on a street railroad; also called *trolley-wheel* (see 4). Also applied to any pulley running along an overhead track, as in a *trolley-scale* (see 4).

1891 in *Cent. Dict.* **1902** SLOANE *Stand. Electr. Dict.* s.v., Trolleys are principally used on electric railroads. **1909** *Cent. Dict. Suppl.* s.v. *Abattoir scales*, The meat, suspended from hooks attached to a trolley traveling on a telpherage system or overhead track, is run upon a short section of track which forms the weighing-platform of the scales... Another form of scale employs a trolley for weighing materials in transit, with a scale-beam attached directly to the trolley and traveling with it. Called a *trolley-scale*.

b. Short for *trolley-car*: see 4. *U.S.*

1891 *Month* LXXIII. 24, I jumped off the trolley. **1908** *Daily Chron.* 20 Jan. 4/4 To go anywhere in Boston you must take a tram..(they call it a trolley).

4. *attrib.* and *Comb.*, as ***trolley-journey, -load, system***; **trolley-bar** = *trolley-pole*; **trolley-bus** (**† trolli-bus**), a trackless passenger vehicle that gets its power from an overhead cable by means of a pole and trolley (see 3); also *attrib.*; **trolley-car** (*U.S.*), an electric car driven by means of a trolley (see 3); **trolley-cart** (*local*), a Yarmouth trolley (see 1); **trolley coal**, coal conveyed on trolleys or street trucks for sale; **trolley-ear, trolley-hanger**, a contrivance for supporting and insulating a trolley-wire; **trolley-frog** (see quot.); **trolley-harp, trolley-head**, the holder at the end of a trolley-pole which supports the trolley-wheel; **trolley-hook**, a hook used for replacing a trolley-wheel when it slips off the wire (*Funk's Stand. Dict.* 1895); **trolley-line**, a line of electric cars run by means of trolleys (*ibid.*); **trolleyman**, a man employed to drive a trolley or a trolley-car; **trolley-pole**, a hinged pole on an electric car, supporting the trolley (see 3), and conveying the current from the overhead wire; **trolley-rail**, a rail conveying current to the motors on an electric railway; **trolley-road**, an electric tram-line worked on the trolley system (*U.S.*); **trolley-scale**, a scale for weighing meat or other commodities, in which the scale-beam is attached to a trolley travelling on an overhead track, as in a market or warehouse; **trolley shop**, a trolley (see 2 c) from which goods are sold, esp. in a hospital; **trolley-wheel** = sense 3; **trolley-wire**, an overhead electric wire supplying current to the trolleys of electric cars.

1891 *Pall Mall G.* 30 Oct. 6/2 On the top of the car is a '*trolley bar'. **1921** *Daily Colonist* (Victoria, B.C.) 13 Oct. 11/7 The *trolley-buses..are of the single-deck type, with seats for twenty-four passengers. **1927** *Daily Express* 20 July 9/6 The 'trolli-bus' traffic receipts last week..were £400 more than the receipts for the corresponding week last year. **1939** J. B. PRIESTLEY *Let People Sing* i. 13 He climbed into a trolley-bus, which after a mile or so stopped at a large gateway. **1961** C. WILLOCK *Death in Covert* xii. 224 A clang and ring that reminded him incongruously of vibrating trolley-bus wires. **1978** *Country Life* 13 Apr. 956/2 The nearly extinct tram and trolley bus will be revived. **1895** *Pop. Sci. Monthly* Apr. 758 The lazy barges will perhaps rival in bustle the *trolley car on land. **1865** *Daily Tel.* 25 Aug., Yarmouth ingenuity..hit upon the notion of the '*trolly cart'..a sledge, about 12 ft. long, but not much more than a yard in breadth, mounted upon wheels less than 3 ft. high. **1890** *Daily News* 18 Mar. 4/6 They further increased the price of house coal by 2s. a ton, and *trolly coal by 1s. 6d. per ton. **1898** HOUSTON *Dict. Electr.*, **Trolley Ear*, a metal piece supported by an insulator to which the trolley wire is fastened. **Trolley Frog*, the device to which the trolley wire is attached, employed for causing a car to deviate from one line to another. *Ibid.* s.v. *Hanger*, A *trolley hanger on a straight trolley line. **1904** *Electr. World & Engin.* 18 June 1167 *Trolley-harp. **1896** A. MORRISON *Child of the Jago* 190 To start..on a *trolley journey. **1898** *Daily News* 22 Oct. 3/5 A *trolley-load of foreign silks, velvets, and fancy woollen goods. **1897** *Ibid.* 23 Feb. 7/4 The number on strike at Sunderland is 111, including 51 *trolleymen. **1900** *Ibid.* 11 June 3/2 The strike of street trolley (electric tramcar) men [at St. Louis]. **1895** *Funk's Stand. Dict.*, *Trolley-pole. **1897** *Daily News* 19 July 8/4 The electricity is transmitted to the motors on the car by means of trolley poles, or 'fishing rods', which..glide along the wire as the car runs. **1897** *Trans. Amer. Inst. Electr. Engin.* 355 *Trolley-rail. **1895** *Information* 6 July 3/2 This electric railroad is practically a very heavy and substantially built *trolley road. The trolley wire..is hung from very heavy poles. **1909** *Trolley-scale [see 3]. **1958** *Times* 7 July (Suppl.) p. xix/1 Volunteer nurses ..still give invaluable aid in hospital wards; volunteers take round *trolley-shops. **1974** *Country Life* 4 Apr. 797/1 We [*sc.* the Red Cross] organize out-patients' canteens. Trolley shops. Libraries. **1892** *Daily News* 4 Oct. 5/1 An intramural elevated railway is being constructed... Its cars will be moved by electric traction on the '*trolley' system. **1891** *Pall Mall G.* 30 Oct. 6/2 A small grooved '*trolley wheel'.. runs against the under side of the overhead wire. **1895** *Trolley wire [see *trolley road*].

Hence **'trolley** *v.*, *trans.* to convey by trolley; *intr.* to travel by trolley; **'trolleyful**, as much or many as a trolley will hold; **'trolleyize** *v. trans.* to adapt to the trolley system, as a tramline (*U.S.*).

1882 W. E. BAXTER *Winter in India* viii. 84 Mr. Prestage ..had arranged that we should be '*trollied' down the mountains instead of going in the train. **1900** *Daily News* 21 Mar. 5/4 These two officers trollied along the line..till they got close to Springfontein Station. **1936** 'M. INNES' *Death at President's Lodging* xiii. 234 Ah, well, my picture of Háveland trolleying his own bones plus corpse up the garden path was no doubt, as you suggested, a bit steep. **1978** P. MCCUTCHAN *Blackmail North* vi. 69 Stocks being trolleyed in from freighter aircraft. **1889** KIPLING *From Sea to Sea* (1899) II. xxvii. 34 The cans..were..slidden along by the *trolleyful. **1900** *Daily News* 21 May 4/1 A procession of three hundred young men dragging a trolleyful of ladies. **1895** *Pop. Sci. Monthly* Apr. 751 Every species of tramway ..becomes *trolleyized.

troll flower. Also 6 trol flower. [tr. Ger. *trollblume* (whence app. mod.L. generic name *Trollius*, C. Gesner *c* 1555, and F. *trolle*); app. f. stem of *troll-en* to roll, in reference to the globular shape of the flower. (Dr. Prior's statement in quot. 1879 appears to be erroneous.)] A book-name for the Globe-flower (*Trollius europæus*).

1578 LYTE *Dodoens* III. lxxii. 418 Byside these kindes of Ranunculus is yet another strange kinde.., the whiche is called Troll flowers. *Ibid.* 419 The Trol flowers grow upon the mountaynes of Switserlande. **1879** PRIOR *Pop. Names Brit. Plants* (ed. 3), *Troll-flower*, the globe-flower, from Sw. *troll*..a malignant supernatural being, a name..given to this plant on account of its acrid poisonous qualities.

'trollibags, -bobs. *dial.* Also trolle-, trolly-, -bags, -bods. [Variant of TRILLIBUB.] Entrails, intestines: generally with *tripes*.

1824 MACTAGGART *Gallovid. Encycl.* s.v. *Raens*, And when he fins a sheep fa'en aval, Her trolly-bags he can unravel. *a* **1825** FORBY *Voc. E. Anglia*, *Trollibags s.*, the intestines. **1828** *Craven Gloss.*, *Trollibobs*..is generally preceded by tripes; as 'tripes and trollibobs', intestines. **1876** *Whitby Gloss.*, *Trollebods*, a roll or complication of entrails. **1876** *Mid-Yorks. Gloss.*, *Trollybods*..entrails.

trolling ('trəʊlɪŋ), *vbl. sb.* Also 5–9 trowling, 6–8 trouling. [f. TROLL *v.* + -ING[1].] The action of the verb TROLL in its various senses.

I. 1. a. Rolling, revolution.

c **1440** *Promp. Parv.* 503/1 Trollynge, or rollynge, *volucio.* **1613** DAY *Dyall* v. (1614) 98 Concerning the Heavens they perceived such aequabilitie of motion, such turning and trolling of them.

†b. 'Rolling' or 'streaming' in; abundant influx. *Obs.*

1614 T. ADAMS in Spurgeon *Treas. Dav.* Ps. xiv. 1 Extortion batters in the usurer's affections by the trolling in of his moneys.

II. 2. Singing in the manner of a round, or in a jovial style; in quots. applied contemptuously to antiphonal singing.

1575 *Brieff Disc. Troubles Franckford* (1846) 206 The trollinge and descantinge of the Psalmes. **1586** in Neal *Hist.*

Purit. (1732) I. 480 The service of God is grievously abused by..ringing and trowling of psalms from one side of the Choir to another.

III. 3. *Angling.* The action or practice of fishing by the methods described s.v. TROLL *v.* 13.

But in *trolling-line* (quot. 1888 in 4), app. confused with *trawling*; cf. TRAWLING, TRAWL-NET, TROLLNET.

1651–7 T. BARKER *Art of Angling* (1820) 22 The manner of his trouling was with a hasell rod. **1682** [see TROLLER 2]. **1725** T. TAYLOR in *Portland Papers* VI. (Hist. MSS. Comm.) 88 The late Duke..took great delight in that kind of fishing for them [pike] which is termed 'trowling'. **1787** BEST *Angling* (ed. 2) 43 The walking bait is that which the fisher attends to himself, and is called trowling. **1860** G. H. K. *Vac. Tour.* 167 If you..will go and spin a butterfish for lythe,..you will there first discover what sport trolling can be. **1888** GOODE *Amer. Fishes* 62 In trolling from a boat at least 300 feet of line should be used. **1910** H. T. SHERINGHAM in *Encycl. Brit.* II. 28/2 The use of the drop-minnow, which is trolling on a lesser scale.

4. *attrib.* and *Comb.* (In sense 3), as ***trolling-bait, -fly, -hook, -line, -rod, -spoon, -tackle***; **trolling motor** *U.S.*, a motor suitable for a boat used in trolling (see TROLL *v.* 13 c); **trolling pole** *N. Amer.*, a horizontal pole rigged on each side of a fishing boat in order to keep the lines clear of the propeller.

1891 *Cent. Dict.*, **Trolling-bait.* **1898** *Blackw. Mag.* Nov. 630/1 Many reaches of the Tay are fished by *trolling-fly. **1891** *Cent. Dict.*, *Trolling-hook. **1701** *Cowell's Interpr.* s.v. *Trawlerman*, To trowle or trawle with a *Trowling-line for Pikes. **1888** GOODE *Amer. Fishes* 187 They live at sea and are caught by the use of trolling-lines. **1964** M. WEEKS *Compl. Boating Encycl.* 530/1 **Trolling motor*, a low-powered, slow-speed motor used for trolling. **1980** *Outdoor Life* (U.S.) (Northeast ed.) Oct. 26/1 The latest high-thrust, 12-volt electric trolling motor, Thruster Plus from Mercury Marine, is the most efficient that I've tested to date. **1960** M. SHARCOTT *Place of Many Winds* v. 97 Fishermen cut their *trolling poles from the forest... The poles must be between thirty and fifty feet long. **1688** R. HOLME *Armoury* III. 103/1 A *Trowling Rod, or a Trowler, hath a ring at the end of the Rod for the Line to run through, when it runs off a Reele. **1844** J. T. HEWLETT *Parsons & W.* xi, I..bought a short, strong trolling-rod. **1883** *Century Mag.* XXVI. 382 The Florida bass are taken with the hand-line and *trolling-spoon. **1910** H. T. SHERRINGHAM in *Encycl. Brit.* II. 28/2 (*Angling*), The traditional form of *trolling-tackle was such that the bait had to be swallowed by the pike before the hook would take hold.

'trolling, *ppl. a.* [f. TROLL *v.* + -ING².] That trolls, in various senses of the vb.; rolling.

1581 A. HALL *Iliad* IV. 73 A wood ful fit to forge the trolling wheeles Of chariots. **1607** *Lingua* v. ix. Ljb, The pleasing changes that a well tun'd Corde Of trowling bells will make. **1659** WOOD *Life* (O.H.S.) I. 287 His voice was a bass,..very strong and exceeding troulling, but he wanted skill. **1813** T. BUSBY *Lucretius* II. v. 1792 Relieved by many a trolling song.

trollius ('trɒlɪəs). Also Trollius. [mod.L. (J. C. Buxbaum *Plantarum Minus Cognitarum Centuria I* (1728) 15): see TROLL FLOWER.] A perennial herb of the genus of this name, belonging to the family Ranunculaceæ, native to Europe, Asia, and North America, and bearing yellow or orange globe-shaped flowers. Also *attrib.* Cf. *globe-flower* s.v. GLOBE *sb.* 10 b.

1899 in E. T. Cook *Century Bk. Gardening* 142/1 It must be a sorry garden that fails to satisfy the Trollius. **1952** BATES & LOWTHER *Breeding Birds Kashmir* 191 We found one [*sc.* a wagtail's nest] in a tuft of *trollius* leaves. **1962** R. PAGE *Education of Gardener* viii. 236 We planted its [*sc.* a stream's] banks..with..clumps of different varieties of yellow trollius. **1978** R. GORER *Growing Plants from Seed* vi. 76 Plants with hard, shiny seeds, such as..trollius, tiarella, and saxifraga all do best if sown outside in autumn.

† **'troll-madam.** *Obs.* Forms: 6 **troule in madame, trol in madam, trowe maddam, trolemadame,** 7 **trol-madame, troll-my-dame, troll-medam, trou-madam,** 8 **troll-madame,** 8–9 **trou-madame.** [app. an alteration of F. *trou-madame* (f. *trou* hole) by association with TROLL *v.*] A game played by ladies, resembling bagatelle: see quot. 1572. = HOLE *sb.* 10 a.

1572 J. JONES *Bathes Buckstone* 12 The Ladyes, Gentle Women, Wyues and Maydes maye..haue in the ende of a Benche eleuen holes made, intoo the which to trowle pummetes or Bowles of leade..or also of Copper, Tynne, Woode..the pastyme Troule in Madame is termed. *margin*, Trol in Madam. **1573** in Gage *Hengrave* (1822) 199 A frame of wood upon wᶜʰ they play wᵗʰ pellets, called trowe maddam. **1606** HOLLAND *Sueton.* Annot. 18 The game of young Gentlewomen called of some Trol-Madame. **1611** SHAKS. *Wint. T.* IV. iii. 92 A fellow (sir) that I haue knowne to goe about with Troll-my-dames. **1666** *Third Advice to a Painter* 19 He plays with Danger, and his Bullets trouls, As 'twere at Trou-Madam through all the holes. **1689** *Lond. Gaz.* No. 2503/4 If any Persons have occasion for Tables, and Table-men,..and Troll-Madams, they may be furnished. **1774** H. WALPOLE *Let. to C'tess Upper Ossory* 30 July, I would not for the world have a table of trou-madame without a king and a queen. **1819** *Blackw. Mag.* IV. 564 A harmless quiet kind of sport, like shuttlecock, or trou-madame, or nine-pins.

† **'trollnet.** *Obs. rare*⁻¹. A kind of net declared illegal in the Act cited.

It is doubtful whether it is connected with TRAWL, TRAWLER, TRAWL-NET, or TRAIL *v.*, since it seems to relate to fishing for river fish which are not caught with drag-nets or by trawling; but cf. *trawler-man* (TRAWLER 3).

1558 *Act 1 Eliz.* c. 17 §1 No Person..withe any..Crele, Rawe, Fagnett, Trollnett..shall take..Spawne or Frye of Eeles, Salmon, Pyke or Pyckerell.

† **tro'lloll,** *v. Obs. rare*⁻¹. [Reduplicated form of TROLL *v.*] *intr.* (with *it*). To sing in a rollicking style, to troll.

a **1734** NORTH *Examen* I. ii. §130 (1740) 101 They got drunk and trolloll'd it bravely.

trollop ('trɒləp), *sb.* Also 7 **trolops,** *dial.* 7–9 **trallop,** 9 **trollops, trallops.** [? Connected with TROLL *v.*; for the termination cf. *gallop, wallop.*]

1. An untidy or slovenly woman; a slattern, slut; also, sometimes a morally loose woman, a trull.

In quot. 1615 *transf.* of hounds.

1615 WITHER *Sheph. Hunt.* Ecl. ii, Such wide-mouth'd Trollops that 'twould doe you good To heare their loud-loud Echoes teare the Wood. **1621** BRATHWAIT *Nat. Embassie*, etc. (1877) 196 The Parsons wife, a lusty Trolops. *a* **1626** MIDDLETON *Mayor of Queenborough* IV. i. 4 To greet thy grace, thy queen, and her fair trollops. **1682** in *East Anglian* Sept. (1904) 327 Many rayleing opprobrious Speeches and Invectives against the said Elizabeth, calling her Tripe and Trallop. **1742** FIELDING *Jos. Andrews* I. viii, That impudent trollop, who is with child by you. **1846** D. JERROLD *Mrs. Caudle's Curtain Lect.* xxxii, But for that trollop..her quarter's up on Tuesday, and go she shall. **1887** JESSOPP *Arcady* vii. 210 The husband of a dirty trollop who can neither cook nor sew.

2. Anything draggling, or hanging loosely and untidily. *Sc.*

1872 WEDGWOOD *Dict. Eng. Etym.* (ed. 2), *Trollop*, a large piece of rag, especially wet rag. **1882** JAMIESON, *Trollop*, a large, unseemly, straggling mass of anything.

Hence **'trollop** *v., intr.* (*a*) (*Sc.*) to hang loosely and untidily, to draggle; (*b*) (*colloq.*), to act or dress like a trollop, to be slovenly; *spec.* to walk in a slovenly way, to slouch; † **trollo'pee**, name for a loose dress worn by women in the 18th century; **'trolloping, 'trollopish, 'trollopy** *adjs.*, like or characteristic of a trollop, ungainly, slovenly.

1854 M. DODS *Early Lett.* (1910) 63, I felt deeply moved for her, thinking she would *trollop away home. **1870** 'OUIDA' *Puck* I. vii. 113 There's allus a lot of..bad wimmin a trolloping about. **1872** WEDGWOOD *Dict. Eng. Etym.* (ed. 2) s.v., Banff, *trollop*, to hang in a wet state; 'The bairn cam in wee 'ts frockie a' trollopin' aboot its leggies'. **1882** JAMIESON, To *Troll, Trollop*,..to walk, work, or dress in a slovenly manner. **1925** *Chambers's Jrnl.* 23 May 397/2 We'll go very slow and he can trollop behind. **1756** *Connoisseur* No. 134 ¶7 A burgess's daughter..who appeared in a *Trollopee or Slammerkin, with treble ruffles to the cuffs. **1762** *Songs Costume* (Percy Soc.) 240 With your flounces and furbelows, sacks, trollopees. **1733** DUCHESS OF QUEENSBERRY *Let. to Swift* 10 Nov., I did not cut and curl my hair like a sheep's head, or wear one of their *trolloping sacks. **1773** GOLDSM. *Stoops to Conq.* I. ii, The daughter, a tall trapesing, trolloping, talkative May-pole. **1876** MISS BROUGHTON *Joan* iv, With such a trolloping length of uncurled curls down their backs. **1864** WEBSTER, *Trollopish. **1748** RICHARDSON *Clarissa* (1811) VIII. xli. 157 Their gowns, made to cover straddling hoops, hanging *trollopy, and tangling about their heels. **1864** MISS YONGE *Trial* II. 133 In the front.. stood a trollopy-looking girl.

Trollopian (trɒ'ləʊpɪən), *a.* and *sb.* Also **-ean.** [f. the name *Trollope* (see below) + -IAN.]

A. *adj.* **1.** Of, pertaining to, or characteristic of the English novelist Frances Trollope (1780–1863) (mother of Anthony) or her writings.

1847 W. HOWITT in *Howitt's Jrnl.* 9 Jan. 18/1 Mrs. Trollope was introduced to the court circles—everything was shown to her, and the urbane minister was so particularly polite, that, instead of a Trollopean laughter, there was nothing but laudation.

2. Of, pertaining to, or characteristic of the English novelist Anthony Trollope (1815–82) or his writings.

1903 G. GISSING *Private Papers Henry Ryecroft* 213 Any Trollopean work that lay upon the counter. **1907** HARDY *Let.* 29 Sept. in *One Rare Fair Woman* (1972) 134 *Our Fatal Shadows*..shows I think a great advance upon your previous novels... It is quite Trollopian. **1939** C. S. LEWIS *Let.* 24 Nov. (1966) 171 The Curé and the whole cathedral surroundings in Tours are almost Trollopian. **1957** *Times Lit. Suppl.* 25 Oct. 637/4 A Trollopean setting and situation, a cathedral town and a Dean's daughter about to be married. **1980** *Daily Tel.* 12 July 9/2 The 'Strangers and Brothers' sequence..was a conscious effort to write a social history in novel form on a Trollopian scale. **1983** M. DUGGAN *Runcie* xii. 173 The paper's Trollopian report next day—' "Good Heavens!" cried the chaplain.'

B. *sb.* A student or admirer of Anthony Trollope or his writings.

1910 A. D. GODLEY *Reliquiae* (1926) II. 316 In Trollope one remembers the characters, but I never met more than one Trollopian who knew the plots apart. **1946** *N. & Q.* 23 Feb. 67/1 We receive..from the University of California Press the first number of '*The Trollopian*: A Semi-annual Journal Devoted to Studies in Anthony Trollope and His Contemporaries in Victorian Fiction'. **1969** J. GROSS *Rise & Fall Man of Lett.* ix. 245 Michael Sadleir..well known as biographer, bibliographer, Trollopean, and author of *Fanny by Gaslight*.

trolly ('trɒlɪ), *sb.*¹ Also 7–8 **trolly-lolly.** [Cf. Flemish *tralje, traalje*, trellis, lattice, mesh, network (De Bo). *Kant* (q. 1882) is Flem. for 'edge, border, lace, point'.] **1.** Name of a kind of lace: see quots. Also *attrib.*

a **1700** B. E. *Dict. Cant. Crew, Trolly-lolly*, coarse Lace once much in fashion, now worn only by the meaner sort. **1756** MRS. DEWES in *Mrs. Delany's Life & Corr.* (1861) III. 434 She is..dressed much better than I ever saw her. I fancy her friend Mrs. Egerton has vamped her up with a trolly hood. **1882** CAULFEILD & SAWARD *Dict. Needlework* 501 *Trolly Laces*..are Pillow Laces, made in Normandy, in Flanders, and in Buckinghamshire, and Devonshire,..their ground..is an imitation of the Antwerp Trolly Net or Point de Paris Ground, and is made with twists, while the pattern is outlined with a thick thread like that used in the old Flemish Laces, and known as Trolle Kant. **1891** *Cent. Dict.* s.v. *Trolley*, Honiton lace made with a trolley ground. **1895** *Funk's Stand. Dict.* s.v. *Trolley, T[rolley]-thread*, one of the threads outlining the pattern of trolley-lace.

2. [Perh. a different word: cf. *trolleywags* trousers (Barrère & Leland *Dict. Slang*)]. *pl.* Ladies' drawers or knickers. *dial.* and (*schoolgirls'*) *slang*.

1891 J. BARON *Blegburn Dickshonary* (rev. ed.) 68 *Trollys* (female underclothing). That's as near as th' payson'll come to th' meeanin' o' this word; aw co'em wimmen's treawsis, an' he co's 'em drawers, which is *wheere* they're kept. **1934** B. PYM *Diary* 8 Jan. in Holt & Pym *Very Private Eye* (1984) I. 33, I bought a peach coloured vest and trollies to match. **1971** M. WOBER *Eng. Girls' Boarding Schools* vi. 148 Items of clothing earned names, thus 'trolleys' for underwear, 'B squared' for brassieres.

trolly ('trɒlɪ), *sb.*² *dial.* [Alteration of TROLLOP *sb.*: cf. also TRULL.] = TROLLOP *sb.* 1. Also *comb.* in **trolly-mog, trollimog** [cf. MOGGY 2] in the same sense.

1851 T. STERNBERG *Dial. & Folk-Lore Northants.* 117 *Trolly-mog*, a dirty, slovenly female. **1854** A. E. BAKER *Gloss. Northants. Words & Phrases* II. 357 Oh! what a *trolly* she is! **1876** J. HARTLEY *Yorksher Puddin* 164 He's pickt up some idle trolly. **1901** F. E. TAYLOR *Folk-Speech S. Lancs.* s.v. *Troll, Trolly*, a loose woman; a trull. **1925** W. DE LA MARE *Broomsticks* 130 That old trollimog what lives in Hogges Bottom. **1974** P. WRIGHT *Lang. Brit. Industry* xvii. 163 Untidy housewives abound, judging by all the so-called *slatterns, trolly-mogs, slovens* and *tosspots*.

trolly, variant of TROLLEY.

trolly-lolly ('trɒlɪ'lɒlɪ), *int.* [Cf. TROLLOLL.] A refrain of a song, expressing careless gaiety or jollity. Also in nonce (threatening) use as *vb. trans.* (quot. 1723). So † **trolylow** (also as an expression of contempt), **trolo'lay** *Sc.* (in conjunction with HOGMANAY). Also † **trolly trolly** (? *int.* or *a.*), expressing contempt.

1362 LANGL. *P. Pl.* A. VII. 109 Þenne seten summe and songen atte ale, And holpen him to herien wiþ 'Hey! trolly-lolly!' [**1377** B. VI. 118 'how! trolli-lolli!' **1393** C. IX. 123 'hoy! troly! lolly!']. **1529** LYNDESAY *Complaynt* 245 Now trittyll, trattyll, trolylow,..thow dois bot mow. *c* **1530** *Hickscorner* 690, I was not gladde, perde! but now: Hey, trolly, lolly! Let us se who can descaunt on this same. **1567** *Triall Treas.* (1850) 5 Hey howe, troly lowe; hey dery, dery. *a* **1693** *Urquhart's Rabelais* III. xxxvi. 298 Wishy, washy; Trolly, trolly. **1723** *Case of Edward Collins* 11 She said to her I'll trolly-lolly you. **1792** *Caledonian Mercury* 2 Jan. (Jam. s.v. *Hogmanay*), The cry of *Hogmanay Trololay*, is of usage immemorial in this country.

trolops: see TROLLOP.

‖ **tromba marina** ('trɒmba ma'rina). [It., = marine trumpet.] = ***trumpet marine, marine trumpet*** s.v. TRUMPET *sb.* 2 b.

The identification in quot. 1776 is erron.

1776 [see SEA-TRUMPET 2]. **1838** [see TRUMPET *sb.* 2 b]. **1948** G. B. SHAW *How to become Mus. Critic* (1960) 325, I should rather like to hear the *tromba marina*. **1976** D. MUNROW *Instruments Middle Ages & Renaissance* 30/2 A French sculpture of the twelfth century gives us our first glimpse of the tromba marina: the three-sided body is about four feet long and tapers towards the pegbox... By the fifteenth century it had acquired two strings of unequal length.

‖ **trombash** ('trɒmbæʃ). Also **trum-.** [Native name in the Sudan.] A kind of boomerang used by the Sudanese. Also *fig.*

1867 BAKER *Nile Tribut.* xx. (1872) 346 A curious weapon, the *trombash*, used by these people. **1876** C. C. LONG *Central Africa* xvii. 237 Central Africa is a deadly pestiferous country, in spite of the 'trumbash' to the contrary by travellers. **1884** A. GREGORY in *Fortn. Rev.* Mar. 382 They use many weapons, lances and sickle-bladed knives and trumbashes, a kind of boomerang with mischievous-looking iron prongs and points.

† **'trombe**¹. *Obs. rare.* Also **trompe, trumbe.** [ad. It. *tromba* a hand-grenade, *tromba di fuoco* 'a kind of casting wild-fier' (Florio, 1598); cf. obs. F. *trombe* a hollow humming-top.

With *trompe* cf. TRUMP *sb.*¹ hollow tube, trumpet, etc.]

a. A hollow tube filled with explosives; a hand-grenade. **b.** A mortar for firing rockets.

1560 WHITEHORNE *Ord. Souldiours* xxix. 39 b, Trombes or trunkes of fyre. *Ibid.*, Putte in the trumbe a handfull of serpentine poulder vnmixte. **1588** LUCAR tr. *Tartaglia's Colloq. Arte Shooting* App. 85 How you may make a Trunke or Trombe which will shoote fireworkes. **1591** *Garrard's Art Warre* 317 For preparations against the assault you must not be destitute of all sorts of artefficial fire, as Trompes, Granades, Bullets.

Trombe² (trɒmb, ‖ trɔ̃b). *Archit.* The name of Felix *Trombe*, 20th-c. Frenchman, used *attrib.* and in conjunction with that of his collaborator

J. *Michel* to designate a masonry wall of a kind designed by him, having glass sheeting fixed a small distance in front of it so as to absorb solar radiation, and usu. ventilated internally to release the heat into the building.

1978 *Washington Post* 4 Nov. E33/2 One of its simple forms is the Trombe wall. This consists of a masonry wall just inside a large south-facing glass wall or window. **1980** *Family Handyman* Sept. 83/1 Since these shutters can be motor-controlled from a remote position, you can install them in front of a trombe wall or other passive solar heat collector. **1980** J. J. Greenland in H. J. Cowan *Solar Energy Applications in Design of Buildings* v. 130 A recent development which makes use of solar energy and thermal inertia without excessive loss of heat through glass is the Trombe-Michel solar wall. **1984** *Christian Sci. Monitor* 14 Feb. 21/3 A 'Trombe wall' solar-heating system..helps warm the big structure's lab.

trombe, variant of trompe², blast apparatus.

trombiculid (trɒmˈbɪkjʊlɪd), *a.* (and *sb.*) [a. mod.L. family name *Trombiculidæ*, f. generic name *Trombicula* (A. Berlese *Acari Nuovi* (1905) IV. 155), f. *Trombi-dium* (see trombidiid *a.* and *sb.*) + -culus: see -id³.] Of or pertaining to a mite of the family Trombiculidæ, which includes several species having parasitic larvæ which cause or transmit disease in man and other mammals. Also as *sb.*, a mite of this kind.

1950 R. Matheson *Med. Entomol.* (ed. 2) iv. 133 Trombiculid mites and disease: The attacks of various species of mites..usually result, in man, in a marked dermatitis accompanied by intense itching. **1957** *New Scientist* 14 Nov. 33/1 A trombiculid does not feed on a mammal more than *once* in its lifetime. **1962** Gordon & Lavoipierre *Entomol. for Students of Med.* xlv. 267 The association of trombiculid mites with scrub typhus has been suspected well over a century ago by the Japanese physician Ohtomo. **1978** *Jrnl. R. Soc. Med.* LXXI. 507 The causative organism..is transmitted by the larvae (or chiggers) of several species of trombiculid mites.

trombidiid (trɒmˈbɪdɪɪd), *a.* and *sb. Zool.* [ad. mod.L. *Trombidiidæ*, f. *Trombidium*, the typical genus: see -id³.] **a.** *adj.* Of or pertaining to the *Trombidiidæ*, a family of mites. **b.** *sb.* A mite of this family.

1891 in *Cent. Dict.*

trombolite, variant of thrombolite.

trombone (ˈtrɒmbəʊn, trɒmˈbəʊn), *sb.* [ad. It. *trombone* 'a bace or great sackbut, a great trump' (Florio, 1598), also, a blunderbuss, augmentative of *tromba* trumpet. Cf. F. *trombon* (16th c. in Godef.).]

1. *Mus.* **a.** A large loud-toned brass instrument of the trumpet kind, consisting of a long tube bent twice upon itself, and ending in a bell mouth; the U-shaped bend nearer the mouth-piece is of double telescoping tubes, sliding upon one another, so that the length of the sounding tube may be adjusted to produce the desired note.

It is also made with valves and pistons instead of the slide (*valve-trombone*).

1724 *Short Explic. For. Wds. Mus. Bks.*, *Trombone*, a very Large or Bass Trumpet, though more properly a Sackbut. **1813** *Examiner* 10 May 303/2 Every violin, bassoon, and trombone. **1856** Mrs. C. Clarke tr. *Berlioz' Instrument.* 151 There are four kinds of trombones, each of which bears the name of the human voice to which it bears the nearest resemblance in quality of tone and compass. **1881** Broadhouse *Mus. Acoustics* 234 The Trumpet..and the Trombone its natural bass. **1889** W. H. Stone in Grove *Dict. Mus.* IV. 176 In a.d. 1520 there was a well-known Posaunenmacher named Hans Menschel, who made slide Trombones as good as, or perhaps better, than those of the present time. **1892** Symonds *Life Michel Angelo* (1899) II. xi. 65 A sense-deafening solo on a trombone.

attrib. **1886** *Academy* 16 Oct. 267/1 Why..are Handel's trombone parts persistently ignored? **1893** B. Abbotsford *But* vii. 40 The 'it' [man] with the trombone voice. **1906** Kropotkin *Mem. Revolutionist* (1908) I. viii. 47 Behind each one of us a violinist or a trombone player stands. **1908** *Westm. Gaz.* 23 July 4/2 It does not concern them whether the [motor-engine] cylinders are as big as beer-barrels, or the stroke as elongated as a trombone-slide.

b. One who plays this instrument.

1848 Dickens *Dombey* xxxi, An artful trombone lurks and dodges round the corner.

c. A reed-stop in the organ of similar tone.

1837 *Stranger's Guide York* (ed. 6) 78 Trombone..Wood open diapason.

‖**2.** (tromˈbone), pl. **tromboni** (-ni). = blunderbuss 1.

1754 Richardson *Grandison* (ed. 7) III. 258, I beat down his Trombone, a kind of Blunderbuss, just as he presented it at me. **1794** Mrs. Radcliffe *Myst. Udolpho* xxxi, When we came up, we fired our tromboni, but missed. **1797** —— *Italian* xxi, He fired his trombone in the air, when every rock reverberated the sound. **1843** Borrow *Bible in Spain* xxxiii, He then discharged his trombone just over my head.

3. A green or yellow pear-shaped pumpkin belonging to the Australian variety of this name.

1946 *Jrnl. Agric.* (S. Austral.) Jan. 275 The trombone is not such a good cropper unless it can be watered in hot weather. **1969** *Ibid.* Jan. 208 By far the most popular pumpkin variety in South Australia is the Trombone. It is typically pear-shaped with a curved neck. **1978** *Guardian* 10 Nov. 21/8 According to one reader, a trombone is a non-spherical pumpkin much used in chutneys and pickles. Another, equally well versed in Australian horticulture, tells me that it is a long-necked marrow with a bulbous end (hence the name) which is cooked and treated exactly like vegetable marrow.

Hence **trombonist,** = 1 b; **trombony** *a. colloq.*, pertaining to or characterized by the trombone.

1891 *Cent. Dict.*, *Trombonist. **1897** *Weekly Sun* 19 Sept. 3/4 A trombonist in our tontine band. **1908** *Times* 8 July 7/2 Herr Steidl..showed us how a trombonist and a clarinetist ought to be educated. **1899** A. Layard *Musical Bogeys* 44 The *Trombony Bogey is terribly thin. **1913** *Daily News* 6 Sept. 6 The Prelude to Act III of 'Lohengrin'..is a tromboney piece of music.

trombone, *v.* [f. prec. sb.]

1. *trans.* To move to and fro as in playing the trombone (*humorous*). *rare*

1879 Harlan *Eyesight* vi. 70 The age..when we commence to 'trombone our newspaper' in search of the receding near point of distinct vision. **1893** W. H. Hudson *Idle Days Patagonia* xi, The redskin..is never observed to trombone his newspaper.

2. *intr.* To play the trombone; also *transf.* to make a sound like a trombone. So **tromˈboning** *vbl. sb.*

1864 J. A. Grant *Walk across Africa* ix. 196 When standing here, the hoarse tromboning of the hippopotamus, wishing to come out to graze, echoed from out these rushes. **1866** J. Macgregor *Thousand Miles in Rob Roy Canoe* (ed. 2) iii. 48 Crowds of gaping peasants..jostled against bands drumming and tromboning.., and marching in a somewhat ricketty manner over the undoubtedly rough pavement. **1888** H. Drummond *Tropical Africa* i. 18 The hippopotami ..tromboning at us within pistol-shot kept us awake. **1958** R. Harris in P. Gammond *Decca Bk. Jazz* iii. 44 There was one man..who created a legend of tail-gate tromboning—the one and only Kid Ory. **1960** *New Oxf. Hist. Music* III. xii. 426 'Die pusauner pusaunoten über einnander mit dreyen stymmen, als man sunst gewonlichen singet' ('the trombonists tromboned together in three parts as one is otherwise accustomed to sing'). **1967** *Listener* 26 Jan. 144/3 A contentious fugal start and imperious tromboning herald the story-telling with a piquant sense of expectation.

trome, variant of trume.

tromino (ˈtrɒmɪnəʊ). [f. tr(i- + d)omino by deliberately false analogy (see quot. 1961).] Any planar shape formed by joining three identical squares by their edges.

1954 S. W. Golomb in *Amer. Math. Monthly* LXI. 676 It is impossible to cover the checker board with 21 *straight* trominoes, and a monomino in the upper left-hand corner of the board. **1961** [see pentomino]. **1979** *Sci. Amer.* Apr. 19/1 The games played with the two 3-cell animals (the trominoes) are slightly more difficult to analyze.

trommel (ˈtrɒm(ə)l). *Mining. U.S.* [a. G. *trommel* drum.] A rotating cylindrical sieve or buddle used for washing and sizing ores.

1877 in Knight *Dict. Mech.* **1886** tr. *Callon's Lect. Mining* xxiii. III. 27 A trommel is a barrel in the form of a cylinder or of a truncated cone, horizontal or slightly inclined.

tromometer (trəʊˈmɒmɪtə(r)). [f. Gr. τρόμος trembling + -meter.] An instrument for measuring or detecting faint earth-tremors. Hence **tromometric** (trɒməʊˈmɛtrɪk), **tromoˈmetrical** *adjs.*, of or pertaining to the tromometer or its use; **tromometry** (trəʊˈmɒmɪtrɪ), the measuring of earth-tremors, the scientific use of the tromometer.

1878 *Nature* 12 Sept. 533/1 The instruments, particularly the tromometer, were continually agitated. **1883** J. Milne in *Trans. Seismol. Soc. Japan* VII. i. 13 As to the cause of tromometric movements we have a field for speculation. **1887** G. H. Darwin in *Fortn. Rev.* Feb. 271 The 'normal tromometer' of Bertelli..is a simple pendulum,..with an arrangement for observing the dance of the pendulum-bob with a microscope. **1895** *Funk's Stand. Dict.*, Tromometry. **1898** *Nature* 1 Dec. 104/2 The subject to which he [Rossi] devoted the greatest attention was perhaps tromometry, in connection with which he devised many instruments. **1901** *Daily Record & Mail* 22 July 7 'Tromometric' observations (states 'Science Siftings') have been made at the observatory near the summit of Mount Etna.

tromp (trɒmp), *v.* Var. (orig. and chiefly *U.S.*) of tramp *v.*¹ Hence **ˈtromping** *vbl. sb.*

1892 *Dial. Notes* I. 234 Tromp = tramp. **1895** S. Crane *Red Badge of Courage* x. 105 Yeh wanta go trompin' off. **1902** *Dial. Notes* II. 248 He *tromped* my toe. **1929** W. Faulkner *Sanctuary* (1981) viii. 95 You'll tromp on a loose boa'd and find yoself downstairs befo you know hit. **1940** J. Stuart *Trees of Heaven* 251 Somebody has..tromped the vines into the ground. **1952** E. Ferber *Giant* xx. 334 You want to look out, Bick, she don't get tromped the way they're milling around today. **1953** R. Mais *Hills were Joyful Together* i. xi. 109 White-robed figures..sang hymns and clapped their hands, and some shook tambourines, and they tromped, jumping and grunting rhythmically. *Ibid.*, And while the singing and tromping was going on on the river bank, the initiates for baptism came down one by one from a high rock. **1962** J. Steinbeck *Trav. with Charlie* i. 12 About that time hurricane Donna was reported tromping her way out of the Caribbean. **1968** J. Crist *Private Eye, Cowboy & Very Naked Girl* 193 Beatniks tromping grapes in the buff. **1974** J. Irving *158-Pound Marriage* v. 117 Edith heard Frau Reiner and the Chetniks whispering and tromping about in the living room. **1975** *New Musical Express* 24 May 20/1 Heat and noise and darkness and a steady, muffled tromping that you can feel through your feet. **1976** M. Machlin *Pipeline* xlvii. 491 He wouldn't care who he tromped on to get there, either. **1979** *United States 1980/81* (Penguin Travel Guides) 501 Tromping through the ice plants is a botanical education in itself.

tromp, obs. form of trump; var. trompe.

†**ˈtrompant,** *a. Obs. rare*⁻¹. [a. F. *trompant*, pres. pple. of *tromper*: see trump *v.*²] Cheating, deceiving, dishonest.

1605 *Lond. Prodigal* iv. ii, Him..Who makes a trompant life his daily sport.

trompat, -er(e, obs. forms of trumpet, -er.

†**trompe**¹. *Obs. rare*⁻¹. [a. OF. *trompe* (Godef.), f. *tromper* to deceive: cf. trump *v.*²] Deceit, deception.

1547 *Bk. Marchauntes* a vij, Beholde here the trompe the paynted glosse of theyr malycyousnes.

‖**trompe**² (trɔ̃p). Also **trombe, tromp.** [F. *trompe, trombe.*] An apparatus for producing a blast, in which water falling in a pipe carries air into a receiver, where it is compressed, and thence led to the blast-pipe; a water blowing-engine. Also *attrib.*

1828 Webster, *Tromp*, a blowing machine formed of a hollow tree, used in furnaces. **1839** Ure *Dict. Arts* 824 The trompe, or water-blowing engine. *Ibid.* 825 The ordinary height of the trompe apparatus is about 26 or 27 feet to the upper level of the water cistern. **1881** Raymond *Mining Gloss.*, *Trombe* or *Trompe*, (Fr.), an apparatus for producing an air-blast by means of a falling stream of water, which mechanically carries air down with it, to be subsequently separated and compressed in a reservoir or drum below. **1894** Bowker in *Harper's Mag.* Jan. 418 About the middle of the seventeenth century the tromp was introduced.

trompe, obs. f. trump; var. trombe¹ *Obs.*

‖**trompe l'œil** (trɔ̃p lœj). Also **trompe-l'œil,** *erron.* d'œil. [Fr., lit. 'deceives the eye'.] Deception of the eye, an illusion, *spec.* in *Art* with regard to the material reality of the object(s) represented, a (usu. still-life) painting, plaster ornament, etc., intended to give an illusion of reality. Also *fig.* and *attrib.* passing into *adj.*

1889 C. H. Stranahan *Hist. French Painting* vii. 457 The public of connoisseurs who care not for any tricks of 'trompe l'œil', but for art. **1926** A. Huxley *Ess. New & Old* 171 Their taste ran to *trompe l'œil* pictures of fighting giants. **1927** E. Bowen *Hotel* x. 118 The hill..by some *trompe-l'œil* of twilight seemed to topple. **1928** *Observer* 19 Feb. 5/1 The nearest approach to realistic treatment is Mr. Cedric Morris's picture of a luxurious flowery meadow in North Africa, but this realism is not carried to the point of a *trompe l'œil.* Paint is made to tell as paint, and not as a substitute for the thing represented. *a* **1934** R. Fry *Last Lect.* (1939) 207 The carefully exposed reflection of the fallen soldier in the retina of his shield, which is very much in agreement with the puerile stories of *trompe-d'œil*—like that of the 'Grapes of Zeuxis'—which were the stock in trade of art critics like Pliny. **1936** A. Huxley *Eyeless in Gaza* xviii. 231 And the Museum of Sexology: such photographs and wax models—almost too *trompe-l'œil.* **1957** *Listener* 24 Oct. 658/3 Details may be solid, trompe l'œil, or flat. **1961** E. Taylor *In Summer Season* i. 11 Facing her, as she turned the stairs, was a *trompe-l'œil* panel, designed to lengthen the passage into an endless arcade. **1964** S. Sontag in *Evergreen Rev.* Dec. 76 Plato's view that all art is an elaborate *trompe l'œil*, and therefore a lie. **1968** *Ideal Home* Nov. 31 The dining-room has *trompe l'œil* marbling. **1970** *New Scientist* 11 June 530/1 *Trompe d'œil* effects such as false perspectives painted on walls are common. **1974** G. Butler *Coffin for Canary* xii. 147 Olivia had told her own story and had told it badly... She had led those who listened to her up to a blank wall and confronted them with a *trompe l'œil.* **1978** R. Barnard *Unruly Son* xv. 155 Shelves and books had been painted on the wall, making a perfect *trompe l'œil.*

tromper, tromperie, -ery, trompet, -ette, obs. ff. trumper, trumpery, trumpet.

‖**trompille** (‖trɔ̃pij, trɒmˈpiːl). *rare*⁻⁰. [F., f. *trompe*, trompe²; cf. F. *trompillon.*] Each of the holes or tubes by which air is admitted to the water-pipe of a trompe.

1828 Webster, *Trompil*, an aperture in a tromp. **1891** *Cent. Dict.*, Trompille.

trompour, -e, obs. ff. or var. trumper.

tron (trɒn), **trone** (tron), *sb. Sc.* and *north. dial.* Also 6 **tronne, throne, troyne,** 7, 9 **troan.** [ME. a. OF. *trone* (Godef.):—L. *trulina*, a. Gr. τρυτάνη balance, pair of scales.]

1. (Chiefly *Sc.*) A weighing machine; a pair of scales or other machine for weighing merchandise; a public weighing apparatus in a city or (burgh) town; also called 'the king's trone'. Now *Hist.*

[*c* **1290** *Fleta* ii. xii. §15 Quod fideliter colligant..ulnas, tronas, stateras, et pondera cujuslibet generis, tam pro pane quam pro aliis rebus venalibus provisa et habita. **1365** *Stat. David II*, c. 39 in *Acts Parlt. Scot.* (1844) I. 139/1 Extitit ordinatum, quod sit trona ad lanas ponderandas in burgis Regiis, per singulos portus Regni.] **1477** in *Charters &c. Edinb.* (1871) 141 Sic like gudis that suld be weyit to be vsit at the Ouer Bow, and a trone set thare. *a* **1500** in *Arnolde's Chron.* (1811) 101 The marchaunt may make his wolle to be weyen at the kyngis trone yf he will. **1609** Skene *Reg. Maj.*, *Stat. David II* 44 (see 1365 above) The Chalmerlane sall cause..mak ane Trone for weying of woll in all the Kings burghis. **1742** in J. Paterson *Hist. Regality Musselburgh* (1857) 82 Repair the cross and the trone in the town of Musselburgh. **1824** G. CHALMERS *Caledonia* III. VI. viii. 654 The trone for weighing goods being established at the bottom of the tower, the Church obtained the name of the Trone Church. *a* **1850** J. GRAY *Arithm.* (ed. 100) 12 The Tron Pound kept at Edinburgh is equal to 9622·67 Troy Grains; it varies, however, in different places and for different purposes. **1886** MASSON *Edinb. Sk.* 29 Markets.. each having its own 'tron' or weighing apparatus.

b. The post of this was used as a pillory, or place of public exposure and punishment of offenders.

1449 *Sc. Acts Jas. II*, c. 9 (1814) II. 36/1 And fra þai [beggars] haf no^t^ to lefe aponne þat þar eris be nalyt to þe trone or to ane vthir tre and cuttit of and bannyst þe cuntre. **1515** *Burgh Rec. Edinb.* (1869) I. 156 He was adiugeit to be had to the trone and thair strikkin throw the hand and banist this towne. **1650** *Acts Sederunt* 6 Feb. (1790) 69 They ordain the said John Rob to be sett upon the Trone with a paper upon his head, bearing thir words; (This John Rob is sett heir for being an false informer of witnesses), and ordaines his lugg to be nailed to the Trone be the spaice of ane hour. **1731** *Gentl. Mag.* Mar. 123/2 He shall have his Lugs tacked to the muckle Trone with a Nail of twal a Penny.

c. Contextually, The place where the tron was set up; a market-place, market; in quot. 1821 *fig.*

1500–20 DUNBAR *Poems* lxxxii. 24 At your hie Croce, quhair gold and silk Sould be, thair is bot crudis and milk; And at ȝour Trone bot cokill and wilk. *a* **1572** KNOX *Hist. Ref.* Wks. 1846 I. 121 The Englismen seing no resistance, hurlled.. cannounes up the calsay to the Butter-throne. **1725** RAMSAY *Gentle Sheph.* I. ii, I'll.. win the vogue at market, tron, or fair, For halesome, clean, cheap, and sufficient ware. **1821** GALT *Ann. Parish* xxxvii, Irville.. is an abundant trone for widows and other single women. **1891** H. HALIBURTON *Ochil Idylls* 65 At the very trons in touns It [snow]'s knee-deep lyin.

d. Short for *tron weight*: see 3.

1801 RANKEN *Hist. France* I. I. v. 429, 1200 bundles of hay, of 4 pounds weight each.. is.. 327 stone Trone on the Scotch acre.

2. (*pl.*) *north. dial.* A weighing-machine; a pair of scales, a steelyard or spring balance.

1825 BROCKETT *N.C. Words*, *Trones*, a steel yard. **1863** MRS. TOOGOOD *Yorksh. Dial.* (MS.), Go and borrow the trones to weigh the hay.

3. *attrib.* **tronman (trone-man)**: see quot. 1808–25; **tron(e-pound**, the pound of *tron weight*, varying locally from 21 to 28 ounces avoirdupois; so **tron(e-stone** (see quots.); **tron(e weight**, the standard of weight used at the tron.

1808–25 JAMIESON, **Trone-men*, the name given to those who carry off the soot sweeped from chimneys, because they had their station at the *Trone*, Edinburgh. **1896** SMEATON *Ramsay* vii. 182 Tronmen with their bags of soot. **1683** *Repr. Advantages Manuf. Woollen-cloath* 4 Wooll (not worth 8 sh. Scots the *Trone-pound). **1565** *Reg. Privy Council Scot.* I. 375 Fourtie thowsand *troyne stane wecht. **1795** HUTTON *Math. Dict.*, *Trone-Stone*, in Scotland, according to Sir John Skene, contains 19½ pounds. **1882** OGILVIE (Annandale) s.v. *Trone*, The later tron stone.. contained 16 tron pounds, the tron pound being equivalent to 1·3747 lbs. avoirdupois. **1593** *Reg. Mag. Sig. Scot.* 815/1 Cum potestate crucem foralem cum lie trone et *trone-wechtis habendi. **1618** *Sc. Acts Jas. VI* (1816) IV. 587/2 That Weght called of old the Trone weght to be allvtterlie abolisched. **1799** J. ROBERTSON *Agric. Perth* 346 Cheese.. sold by tron weight, having twenty-one ounces to the lb. **1812** SIR J. SINCLAIR *Syst. Husb. Scot.* I. 58, 150 to 200 stone of hay, trone weight, is carried by each two-horse cart, to.. Perth and Dundee.

Hence **tron (trone)** *v.*, *trans.* to weigh at the tron.

1609 SKENE *Reg. Maj.* I. 152 Tronars sould be challenged, that they keip not their office in troning.. of wooll, bot they trone the samine to some men, and not to others. **1861** RILEY *Liber Albus* 124 That no foreign merchant or other shall sell or buy any wares that ought to be weighed or troned, except by our own beam or tron.

tron, obs. f. THRONE; pa. t. of TRINE *v.*² *Obs.*

-tron (trɒn), *suffix. Physics.* The ending of ELECTRON² (but cf. Gr. -τρον instrumental suffix), used: **a.** in the names of some kinds of thermionic valves and other electron tubes, as *kenotron* (1915), *pliotron* (1915), *ignitron* (1933); **b.** in the names of a few sub-atomic particles, as *positron* (1933), *negatron* (1934), *mesotron* (1938): cf. -ON¹; **c.** in the names of devices and machines, *spec.* particle accelerators, as *cyclotron* (1935), *betatron* (1941), *phantastron* (1943), *levitron* (1960).

1939 *Nature* 8 Apr. 602/1 *-tron* should be restricted to signify either an instrument or a particle, but not both... *-on* taken by itself.. seems the most natural ending for a particle. **1949** *Ibid.* 13 Aug. 263/2 The Amsterdam conference [of the International Union of Physics] attempted to dispose of the curious modern theory that the ancient Greek termination for a fundamental particle was '-tron'. It blessed the word 'meson' as against its rivals.

trona ('trəʊnə). *Min.* [a. Swed. *trona* (1773), app. from Arabic *ṭrōn*, apocopate form of *naṭrūn*, NATRON, ad. Gr. νίτρον soda (Dozy).] Native hydrous sodium carbonate, found in various places in N. Africa and America.

1799 KIRWAN *Geol. Ess.* 497 The trona was not deprived of its water of crystallization. **1850** ANSTED *Elem. Geol., Min.* etc. §371 Trona, Urao, Hydrous sesqui-carbonate of soda. **1866** LAWRENCE tr. *Cotta's Rocks Class.* (1878) 51 Trona.. forms a crust on the ground on mountain slopes.. in Peru.

tronage ('trəʊnɪdʒ). [a. AF. *tronage*, f. OF. *trone* TRON: see -AGE.] The weighing of merchandise at the tron; a charge or toll upon goods so weighed; the right of levying such charge.

[**1200** *Rot. Chart.* (1837) 35/2 Teneant predictam feriam .. cum stallagio et theloneo, pesagio et tronagio, et cum omnibus aliis libertatibus. **1290** *Rolls of Parlt.* I. 47/2 Mercatores.. conqueruntur quod per deceptionem tronagii, & suptilitatem manuum ponderantium, decipiuntur de Catallis suis. **1347–8** *Ibid.* II. 213/1 Les ditz Citeinz ount este quitz de tronage, pesage des leins, & de merces.]

a **1325** *MS. Rawl. B.* 520 lf. 20 b, þe lord king grauntez þat .. of.. tollage, tronage, passage, pontage.. lith fram nou forth ward assise of nouele disseisine. *a* **1500** in *Arnolde's Chron.* (1811) 100 To tronage perteinen thoos thingis that shalbe weyen by the trone of ye kyngis. **1603** STOW *Surv.* 564 It [London] auayleth the prince in Tronage [*ed.* 1598 Tonnage], Poundage and other her customes, much more then all the rest of the realme. **1607** COWELL *Interpr.*, *Tronage*.. is a kind of tolle.. taken (as it seemeth) for weying. **1766** ENTICK *London* (1776) I. 334 The tronage, that is to say, the weighing of lead. **1860** *All Year Round* No. 76. 614 Here, was formerly kept the royal steelyard, or beam, for the tronage of imports.

Hence **'tronager** = TRONER.

1885 H. HALL *Hist. Custom-Revenue Eng.* II. vi. 123 The sacks.. and the bales.. were successively weighed at the 'beam' by a special officer, the 'tronager' or 'tronour'.

tronc (trɒŋk, ‖trɔ̃). [a. Fr., = collecting box.] In hotels and restaurants, a common fund into which tips and service charges are paid for distribution to the staff. Also *attrib.*

1928 *Observer* 15 Jan. 6/1 The staff are paid on the tronc, or pooling system, whereby all tips are divided. **1960** *Times* 15 Jan. 9/3 The value of a point was set each week according to the amount in the *tronc*. **1964** *Observer* (Colour Suppl.) 13 Dec. 33/1 In all *troncs* (pooled tips, which the *tronc* head waiter distributes according to the number of points each waiter has) they declare an average figure to the Income Tax. **1976** *Rhyl Jrnl. & Advertiser* 9 Dec. 20 (Advt.), Chef —Royal Lido, Prestatyn. Applications are invited for this permanent post at a salary in accordance with Miscellaneous grade 6.. plus an annual supplement of £312 and a percentage of tronc. **1981** *Times* 11 June 14/6 The money was massaged by managements and distributed on their behalf to staff.. or paid into an independent tronc fund.

troncheon, -ion, -on, -oun, troncke, trondle, obs. ff. TRUNCHEON, TRUNK, TRUNDLE.

trondhjemite ('trɒndheɪmaɪt). *Petrogr.* [ad. G. *trondhjemit* (V. M. Goldschmidt 1916, in *Skrifter udgivna af Vidensk. i Christiania* (Matem.-Naturv. Klasse) No. 2. 77), f. *Trondhjem* (now *Trondheim*), name of a city in western Norway: see -ITE¹.] Any leucocratic tonalite, esp. one in which the plagioclase is oligoclase.

1922 *Jrnl. Geol.* XXX. 406 The acid phase is represented by 'trondhjemite' (new name) which Kjerulf calls an oligoclase-granite, and which might as well be characterized as a granodiorite. **1978** *Nature* 12 Oct. 538/2 The metabasaltic sequences may be of considerable thickness and in many areas are associated with intrusive cumulate gabbros, trondhjemites and minor developments of serpentinised peridotites. **1979** F. BARKER *Trondhjemites, Dacites, & Related Rocks* i. 1 The author suggests that the IUGS definition of trondhjemite as leucotonalite be followed, except that andesine-bearing leucotonalite be termed calcic trondhjemite, and that albite-bearing leucotonalite, as well as the oligoclase variety, be termed trondhjemite.

trone: see TRON.

trone, obs. f. THRONE; pa. t. of TRINE *v.*² *Obs.*

'troner. *Sc.* and *north. dial. Obs.* exc. *Hist.* Forms: 5 tronner, 5–7 tronar, 7 -our, 8 -or. [ad. med.L. *tronārius*, f. *trona* TRON.] An official who had charge of the weighing of merchandise at the tron.

[**1365** *Stat. David II*, c. 39 in *Acts Parlt. Scot.* (1844) I. 139/1 Et sit in quolibet loco tronarius.] *c* **1450** *Iter Camerar.* c. 15 in *Acts Parlt. Scot.* (1844) I. App. iv. 698/2 Of Tronaris. At þai keip nocht þar office in assayande woll bot sum þai assay and oþer sum þai spar for mede in scath to þe king. **1507** *Reg. Privy Seal Scotl.* I. 219 Tronaris and uther officiaris. **1609** [see COCKET *sb.*¹ 1 b, TRON *v.*]. **1789** BRAND *Hist. Newcastle* II. 150 *note*, The office of tronor and poisor of Newcastle upon Tyne. **1885** [see TRONAGER].

†**'trongle**, *v. Obs. rare*⁻¹. [Echoic.] In vbl. sb. **'trongling**, a ringing or tingling in the ears.

1398 TREVISA *Barth. De P.R.* XI. ii. (Tollem. MS.) In eeren wynde makeþ also whistelynge and tronglynge [*Bodl. MS.* trongelinge] and ryngynge [*orig.* sibilum et tinnitum].

tronion, obs. form of TRUNNION.

‖**tronk** (trɒŋk). [Cape Dutch, ad. Pg. *tronco* trunk, stock (of a tree), the stocks, by extension 'prison'. (Unknown in Du. of Holland.)] A prison.

1693 *Gov. Rec. Fort St. George, Madras*, The justices.. committed him to the Custody of the Talliars in the Trunke, but on the 21 September last, he made his escape by breaking through the Prison wall. **1863** LADY DUFF GORDON *Lett. fr. Egypt*, etc. (1875) 259 He.. informed me he had just been in the Tronk. **1897** *Daily News* 31 Mar. 6/4 Discomfort inflicted by the Boers on their prisoners in the tronk at Pretoria. **1905** *Blackw. Mag.* Sept. 389/1 You shall be caught. You shall go to tronk.

tronk, tronke, obs. forms of TRUNK.

tronsoun, obs. form of TRUNCHEON.

troo, obs. or Sc. form of TROW *v.*

troocheman, obs. f. TRUCHMAN, interpreter.

trood, obs. f. TROD (*sb.*, and pa. t. of TREAD *v.*).

trookyll, obs. form of TRUCKLE.

troolie ('tru:lɪ). Also 8 troelie, 9 troely, (in Dicts.) trooly. [Corruption of Tupi *tururi*.] A name for the immense entire leaf of the bussu-palm (*Manicaria saccifera*), often thirty feet in length and four or five in breadth, used in the lower Amazon region for thatching. Also, the tree itself. Also *attrib.*, as ***troolie leaf, palm, tree***; **troolie hut**, a hut thatched with troolies.

1769 E. BANCROFT *Guiana* 13 Troelies are a leaf near thirty feet in length, serving for the thatch of houses. *Ibid.* 103 Troolies are, perhaps, the largest leaves.. hitherto discovered. **1825** WATERTON *Wand. S. Amer.* I. (1903) 12 The troely, one leaf of which will defend thee from both sun and rain [*Note* (1903) The Troolie palm]. *Ibid.* (1882) 30 The low and swampy parts near creeks where the troely tree grows. **1847** M. J. HIGGINS *Ess.* (1875) 227 An Indian.. barn, open at the sides, and thatched thickly with troolie leaves at the top. **1899** RODWAY *Guiana Wilds* 20 Lying on the bed in the troolie hut.

trooly, troone, obs. ff. TRULY, THRONE.

troop (tru:p), *sb.* Forms: 6 trowp, (troppe), 6–7 troup, trowpe, troope, 6–8 troupe, (7 trope), 6– troop. [a. OF. *trope* (13th c.), F. *troupe* (16th c.), = Prov. *trop*, Sp., Pg. *tropa*, It. *truppa*, prob.:—late L. *troppus* 'flock', of which the ulterior origin is uncertain.]

1. a. A body of soldiers.

1545 LISLE in *St. Papers Hen. VIII*, I. 829 Your enymyes .. assemblyd more and more in gret troupes. **1598** BARRET *Theor. Warres* III. i. 42 Your Musketiers being deuided into sundrie troupes, of 30, 40 or 50 in a troupe. **1610** HOLLAND *Camden's Brit.* (1637) 527 Amid the thickest troupes of his enemies in the battaile of Agincourt. **1794** MRS. RADCLIFFE *Myst. Udolpho* xv, The travellers frequently distinguished troops of soldiers moving at a distance. **1838** LYTTON *Leila* II. ii, In this troop.. rode many of the best blood of Spain. **1852** THACKERAY *Esmond* III. vii, Esmond perfectly well remembered seeing the old lady sitting up in the bed.. that morning when the troop of guard came to fetch her.

b. A number of persons (or things) collected together; a party, company, band.

1584 R. SCOT *Discov. Witchcr.* X. ix. (1886) 150, I marvell againe, that no bodie else heareth nor seeth this troope of minstrels. **1601** ? MARSTON *Pasquil & Kath.* II. 95 The glooming morne.. hath.. forc'd the sacred troupes of sparkling stars into their priuate Tents. **1615** G. SANDYS *Trav.* 42 Liuing in wandring troupes according to the Scythian Nomades. **1711** ADDISON *Spect.* No. 130 ¶1 We saw at a little Distance.. a Troop of Gipsies. **1833** HT. MARTINEAU *Manch. Strike* i. 1 The children dispersed in troops.

c. Of animals: A herd, flock, swarm; *esp.* a group of apes or monkeys.

1587 MASCALL *Govt. Cattle* (1596) 237 Fold for sheepe... Make your pennes.. in some drie ground, and make also partitions thereinto to receiue small troups of forty or moe. **1604** E. G[RIMSTONE] *D'Acosta's Hist. Indies* IV. xxxiii. 299 In Peru there is such store of pastures and feelings, as.. every man feedes his troupes where he pleaseth. **1719** DE FOE *Crusoe* (1840) I. xx. 358 We perceived two or three troops of wolves. **1812** CARY *Dante, Parad.* XXXI. 6 A troop of bees. **1847** TENNYSON *Princ.* IV. 150 As flies A troop of snowy doves athwart the dusk. **1929** R. M. & A. W. YERKES *Great Apes* vii. 71/1 Some observers assert that troops [of gibbons].. will abandon a wounded comrade. **1951** R. CAMPBELL *Light on Dark Horse* v. 84, I blundered into the middle of a huge troop of baboons. **1965** *Listener* 10 June 863/1 Another of the characteristic features of the primates is the size of the group or 'troop' as it is called.

d. Used to indicate a great number; a 'lot'; esp. in *pl.* 'flocks', 'swarms'.

1590 SHAKS. *Com. Err.* V. i. 81 A huge infectious troope Of pale distemperatures, and foes to life. **1596** DALRYMPLE tr. *Leslie's Hist. Scot.* IX. (S.T.S.) II. 193 Our folkis, in hope to obteine the hous, in troupis rinis to, bot agane ar dung doune. **1605** SHAKS. *Macb.* V. iii. 25 That which should accompany Old-Age, As Honor, Loue, Obedience, Troopes of Friends. **1658** *Whole Duty Man* xvii. §18 We find this sin of self-love set by the Apostle in the head of a whole troop of sins. **1794** LD. AUCKLAND *Corr.* (1862) III. 198 Lady Auckland and the troop are all in perfect health. **1881** BESANT & RICE *Chapl. of Fleet* II. i. (1883) 120 There is no time, for a woman, like the time when she.. is courted by a troop of lovers.

†**e.** A company of performers: = TROUPE.

1779 SHERIDAN *Critic* I. i, Your first inquiry would be, whether they had brought a theatrical troop with them. **1835** T. MITCHELL *Acharn. Aristoph.* 1043 *note*, This prize-feast is.. a frequent source of encouragement to his orchestral troop.

2. *pl.* **a.** Armed forces collectively. Also *fig.*

1598 BARRET *Theor. Warres* 136 Fraunce and Flanders, too full of his pencionary troupes. **1605** SHAKS. *Lear* IV. v. 16 Our troopes set forth to morrow. **1671** LADY M. BERTIE in *12th Rep. Hist. MSS. Comm.* App. v. 22 My brother Peregrine and all the troopes are to show in Hide Parke before the Prince of Orange. **1732** LEDIARD *Sethos* II. VIII. 143 Certain sums of money to raise troops. **1835** T. MITCHELL *Acharn. Aristoph.* Introd. p. xvii, It was a war of native and self-paid troops against troops foreign and purchased. **1854** COBDEN *Speeches* (1878) 319 The courage displayed by our troops.

b. The members of a mob or gang collectively. *U.S. slang.*

1932 *Daily Progress* (Charlottesville, Va.) 7 Apr. 4/4 *Troops*, mob or gang. 1963 *Listener* 4 Apr. 585/2 On the trip back he was met by 'the troops'. With quick dispatch they placed four bullets in the back of his head, disposed of the weapon in a nearby alley, and were gone.

3. a. *Mil. spec.* A subdivision of a cavalry regiment commanded by a captain, corresponding to a *company* of foot and a *battery* of artillery.

1590 SIR J. SMYTH *Disc. Weapons* Ded. 5 b, Souldiors.. disordering themselues vpon euery light occasion both in battallion, squadron and troupe. 1641 EVELYN *Diary* 12 Sept., Here were now 16 companies and 9 tropes of horse. 1703 MARLBOROUGH *Lett. & Disp.* (1845) I. 117 Lord Raby's regiment of dragoons..is of eight troops. 1832 *Regul. Instr. Cavalry* III. 45 *Troop*—The half of a Squadron. Troops are called Right and Left in each Squadron.

b. The command of a troop.

1813 WELLINGTON in Gurw. *Desp.* (1838) XI. 187 Just at this moment there is a troop vacant for purchase in the regiment of Life Guards. 1842 THACKERAY *Fitz-B. Pap.* Pref. (1887) 14 His papa would have purchased him a troop —nay, a lieutenant-colonelcy—some day, but for his fatal excesses.

c. A company of Scouts comprising not less than three patrols of six Scouts each.

1908, etc. [see PATROL *sb.* 3 b]. 1959 E. H. CLEMENTS *High Tension* x. 167, I ran a Scout Troop in that town and he was one of my troop. 1980 W. MAXWELL *So Long, see You Tomorrow* iii. 28 Were we in the same Boy Scout troop?

4. *Mil.* A signal on the drum for troops to assemble in readiness for marching; the assembly. (Cf. quot. 1667 in TROOP *v.* 1.)

1688 R. HOLME *Armoury* III. xix. (Roxb.) 153/2 The drumer is to beat all maner of beats, as a Call, a Troope, a March, a Preparative. 1706 PHILLIPS (ed. Kersey) s.v., The Troop, which is the second beat of the Drum,..for the Men to repair to their Colours. 1803 *Instruct. Infantry* (ed. 3) 13 The Music plays the Troop. 1845 S. JUDD *Margaret* I. xiii, Tony's beat of the troop was the signal for the soldiers to assemble.

5. *attrib.* and *Comb.*: in sense 2, as ***troop-boat, column, -ship, -steamer, -traffic, -train, -transport***; in sense 3, as ***troop-gelding, -leader*** (cf. LEADER[1] 6), ***-leading, -orderly, sergeant (-major), -stable***; also ***troop-lined, -thronged*** adjs.; **troop-bird** (*U.S.*), a troopial (Worcester 1860, citing Gray); **troop-boot** (*U.S.*), a cavalry boot; **troop-carrier**, a large aircraft or armoured vehicle for transporting troops; hence **troop-carrying** *a.*; **troop-fowl** (*local U.S.*), a scaup-duck; **troop-horse**, (*a*) a cavalry horse; †(*b*) *collectively*, horsemen for a troop.

1816 in *Century Mag.* LIX. 623/1 He had taken ten gun-boats from the Neapolitans, and several *troop-boats. 1885 E. CUSTER *Boots & Saddles* x. 107 The general..wore *troop-boots reaching to his knees. 1923 *Daily Mail* 23 June 5 Among landplanes there are huge new *troop-carriers capable of carrying 25 fully equipped soldiers. 1958 *Ibid.* 18 July 1/1 Israel's permission to ferry troop-carriers through her air-space was not..fully cleared. 1964 L. DEIGHTON *Funeral in Berlin* vi. 38 A Volkspolizei troop carrier was parked at the roadside. 1976 A. WHITE *Long Silence* ix. 84 We could hear..the engines of motor-cycles, lorries and troop-carriers. 1937 L. HART *Europe in Arms* iii. 32 A force of 1200 men together with 150 machine-guns and 18 light field-guns was carried 100 miles in *troop-carrying aircraft. 1977 M. GILBERT *Winston S. Churchill* IV. Compan. I. 654 The first use of troop-carrying aeroplanes during a military campaign took place on 21 February 1923. 1702 *Lond. Gaz.* No. 3790/8 A bright-bay *Troop-Gelding 15 hands and half high. 1640 *Bk. War Comm. Covenanters* 1 The Committie ordaines, that, the *troupe horss to be leviat furth of the Stewartrie for the service of the publict. 1856 LEVER *Martins of Cro' M.* xxxvi, The sound of troop-horses passaging to and fro..now interrupted the colloquy. 1832 *Regul. Instr. Cavalry* II. 29 The *Troop Leaders are to be on the pivot flank. 1889 *Pall Mall G.* 3 July 4/3 The procession followed the *troop-lined route. 1896 *Westm. Gaz.* 10 Mar. 5/3 He was *troop orderly that day. 1688 R. HOLME *Armoury* III. xviii. (Roxb.) 134/1 The *Troup, or Holster pistall, this is longer then the fore said [girdle pistol] by as much againe. 1838 JAS. GRANT *Sk. Lond.* 92 The Troopers ..being allowed..to call for as much tobacco, technically termed '*Troop-sand', as they could consume at the sitting. 1853 STOCQUELER *Milit. Encycl.* s.v. *Serjeant-Major*, A *Troop Serjeant-major receives 3s. [per day]. 1889 W. S. GILBERT *Foggerty's Fairy* etc. (1892) 108 He was now troop-sergeant, and one of the smartest men in the squadron. 1862 THACKERAY *Philip* xvi, I certainly did suffer most cruelly on board that horrible *troop-ship. 1855 WHYTE MELVILLE *Gen. Bounce* xx, Their task consisted of lounging about a *troop-stable, attired in undress uniform, to watch the men cleaning and 'doing up' their respective horses. 1862 *Catal. Internat. Exhib.* II. XII. 13 Model of Government *troop steamer for the Lower Indus. 1893 GOSSE *Questions at Issue* 270 The breaking-out of cholera in a *troop-train.

troop (truːp), *v.* [f. prec. sb.]

1. *intr.* To gather in a company; to come together; to flock, assemble.

1565 COOPER *Thesaurus*, *Agglomero*,..to prease or gather thicke to gether, as souldiours doe: to trowpe. 1588 SHAKS. *Tit. A.* II. i. 113 There will the louely Roman Ladies troope. 1604 E. G[RIMSTONE] *D'Acosta's Hist. Indies* IV. xxxiii. 300 These wilde kine have so multiplied..that they troupe together in the fields and woods by thousands. 1667 MILTON *P.L.* VII. 297 As Armies at the call Of Trumpet.. Troop to thir Standard. 1795 BURKE *Let. to W. Elliot* Wks. 1842 II. 244 Multitudes, hardly thought to be in existence, would appear, and troop about him. 1799–1805 WORDSW. *Prelude* v. 260 She left us destitute, and, as we might, Trooping together.

†2. a. *trans.* To gather or assemble (individuals) into a troop or company. Also *refl.* To associate or consort *with* a number of others, to go in company. *Obs.*

c 1590 GREENE *Fr. Bacon* vii. 3 The king..trooped with all the western kings That lie alongst the Dantzic seas by east. *Ibid.* xii. 16, I came not, troop'd with all this warlike train. 1590 —— *Orl. Fur.* Wks. (Rtldg.) 91/2, I vow..To troop myself with such a crew of men As [etc.]. 1620 [G. BRYDGES] *Horæ Subs.* 410 Amongst some of them hee should troope himselfe.

b. *intr.* To associate *with*.

1592 SHAKS. *Rom. & Jul.* I. v. 50 So shewes a Snowy Doue trooping with Crowes, As yonder Lady ore her fellowes showes. 1605 —— *Lear* I. i. 134 All the large effects That troope with Maiesty. 1864 LOWELL *Fireside Trav.* 195 The descendants of Sabine pigeons..trooping with noisy rooks and daws. 1880 KINGLAKE *Crimea* VI. ix. 299 He would troop with the accusing throng.

3. *intr.* To walk, go, pass; *colloq.* (with *off*, *away*, etc.) to go away, 'be off', 'pack'. Cf. MARCH *v.*[2] 2.

1590 SHAKS. *Mids. N.* III. ii. 382 And yonder shines Auroras harbinger; At whose approach Ghosts wandring here and there, Troope home to Church-yards. 1700 T. BROWN *Amusem. Ser. & Com.* 32, I thought 'twas Time to troop off to an Eating-House. 1708 MRS. CENTLIVRE *Busie Body* IV. ii, Get out of my house,—go troop. 1782 ELIZ. BLOWER *Geo. Bateman* I. 147 Pack up your cloaths, Miss Pert, for..you shall troop from hence to-morrow. 1860 G. MEREDITH *Evan Harrington* xlv, The place is ours till we troop.

4. *intr.* To march in rank; to walk or pass in order. Also *fig.* Now somewhat *colloq.*

1592 WYRLEY *Armorie* 148 Now close to troupe, then goodly to deraine. 1598 BARRET *Theor. Warres* III. ii. 70 Sundry small troupes, trouping round about the battell. 1635 BARRIFFE *Mil. Discip.* lxxiii. (1643) 199 Those files which formerly gave fire in the meane time trooping backe. 1682 H. ALDRICH *Upon Christ Church Bells Oxf.*, Y[e] verger troops before y[e] Deane. 1698 FRYER *Acc. E. India & P.* 130 My Indians..trouped by three or four wretched Towns. 1820 W. IRVING *Sketch Bk.* I. 63 (*R. van Winkle*) He was generally seen trooping like a colt, at his mother's heels. 1883 S. C. HALL *Retrospect* II. 40 The days..trooped forward as peacefully as..the soft white clouds. 1893 *Nation* (N.Y.) 22 June 453/2 As the spring months troop by, they bring a succession of fruits.

b. *trans.* To cause to march in a troop.

1872 T. COOPER *Life* 238 At six we were trooped off.

5. *intr.* To come or go in great numbers; to pass in flocks or troops; to flock (*in*, *out*, etc.).

1610 BOLTON *Elem. Armories* 51 The rest of proofes which troup-vp close to their quarter,..who can but embrace? 1629 MILTON *Christ's Nativity*, *Hymn* xxvi, The flocking shadows pale Troop to th' infernall jail. 1784 COWPER *Task* v. 61 Now from the roost..Come trooping at the house-wife's well-known call The feather'd tribes domestic. 1862 MRS. H. WOOD *Mrs. Hallib.* I. xiv, All the children trooped in at once. 1910 A. M. FAIRBAIRN *Stud. Relig. & Theol.* II. VIII. iii. 519 The address delivered, the Jews trooped out of the synagogue.

6. *trans.* (*Mil.*) *to troop the colour* (or *colours*): to perform that portion of the ceremonial known as Mounting of the Guard in which the colour is received. Also *absol.*

The first Standing Order on the subject (but not containing the word) is dated May 1755; but the appellation may date back to Marlborough's time, as it is known that there were Campaign orders on the subject of Mounting of the Guard which do not appear to have been preserved. See 'General Regulations, Orders, and Warrants, 1717–1766', MS. in the Ministry of Defence Library, in which the ceremonial is fully described.

1803 *Instruct. Infantry* (ed. 3) 11 To Troop or send for the Colours. 1816 *Chron.* in *Ann. Reg.* 8/1 After the trooping of the colours had taken place the detachment..received the Eagles. 1861 G. F. BERKELEY *Sportsm. W. Prairies* xiv. 233 In mounting guard they 'troop' as much as we do. 1893 *Times* 5 June 6/1 The ceremony called trooping the colour which dates back to the times of Marlborough. 1894 *Ibid.* 1 June 10/1 First the colour was trooped, and then followed a march past in column.

7. To transport (troops).

1882, 1894 [see TROOPING *vbl. sb.* b.].

trooper (ˈtruːpə(r)). [f. TROOP *sb.* + -ER[1].]

1. a. A soldier in a troop of cavalry; a horse soldier.

The term was used in connexion with the Covenanting Army which invaded England in 1640. It was used in the English Army in 1660. In the first establishment of Horse Regiments after the Restoration, the strength of a troop of horse was 1 Captain, 1 Lieutenant, and 60 Troopers.

1640 *Bk. War Comm. Covenanters* 1 That ilk trouper have for the twa pairt of the 40 dayes lone appoyntit be the Committie of Estaites xviij libs. 1694 LUTTRELL *Brief Rel.* (1857) III. 296 [They] were all mounted on gray and white horses, and new clothed, and are more like troopers than dragoons. 1703 MARLBOROUGH *Lett. & Disp.* (1845) I. 164 The troopers might embark with the two regiments of foot. 1844 H. H. WILSON *Brit. India* I. 199 The escort..consisted of but two companies of native infantry and sixteen troopers. 1877 *Field Exerc. Infantry* 331 Two or more troopers should be with each support, to carry intelligence.

b. In various colloq. and slang phrases, esp. ***to swear like a trooper.***

1739–40 RICHARDSON *Pamela* (1740) I. 239 She curses and storms at me like a Trooper. 1785 GROSE *Dict. Vulg. T.* s.v., You will die the death of a trooper's horse, that is with your shoes on, a jocular method of telling any one he will be hanged. 1810 *Sporting Mag.* XXXVI. 122 The fellow.. swore like a trooper. 1812 LADY GRANVILLE *Lett.* 12 Sept. (1894) I. 41 William Lamb laughs and eats like a trooper. 1842 S. LOVER *Handy Andy* xli, Jack was heard below, swearing like a trooper. 1854 BADHAM *Halieut.* 443 A friend of his, 'eques fortissimus', i.e. one who lied like a trooper. 1884 SYMONDS *Shaks. Predecess.* iv. 160 Juventus..swears like a trooper.

c. A brave or stalwart person. *colloq.*

1951 R. CAMPBELL *Light on Dark Horse* 230 Nina Hamnett (she was a fine trooper).

2. A horse ridden by a trooper; a troop-horse; a cavalry horse.

1640 SIR J. LESSLEY in *Antiq. Rep.* (1809) IV. 436 The tag'd tail'd trooper that stands in the staw. 1791 'G. GAMBADO' *Ann. Horsem.* iv. (1809) 84 Instead of his capering like a Trooper, he hangs down his head and tail. 1855 WHYTE MELVILLE *Gen. Bounce* xx, How he gave it you ..about riding that old trooper instead of your own charger! 1901 *Field* 9 Feb. 163/3 These expenses take too much off the price paid for a trooper.

3. a. In Australia: A mounted policeman.

1830 *Hist. Rec. Austral.* (1922) 1st Ser. XV. 770 The Mounted Police, which at present consists of about 68 Troopers. 1858 MCCOMBIE *Hist. Victoria* viii. 100 A violent effort [was] made by the troopers on duty to disperse an assemblage which occupied the space of ground in front of the hustings. 1864 J. ROGERS *New Rush* II. 51 A trooper spies him snoring in the street.

b. More fully ***state trooper.*** *U.S.* A mobile state policeman.

1911 *Ann. Rep. 1910* (Pennsylvania Dept. State Police) 16 On arrival of the detail, the mob of foreigners proceeded to stone and shoot at Troopers... Three of the Troopers.. fired at their assailants, wounding two Italians. 1941 [see STATE *sb.* 38 e]. 1977 *New Yorker* 3 Oct. 43/1, I slowed the car and pulled over..and a state trooper pulled up behind us... The trooper said, Do you need any help.

c. A paratrooper. orig. *U.S.*

1942 *Yank* 14 Oct. 2 English neighbors tasted this clannishness soon after the troopers settled in their midst. 1974 C. RYAN *Bridge Too Far* III. iii. 156 Of the sixteen paratroopers, pilot and co-pilot, only Johnson and two other troopers got out.

4. A troop-ship.

1872 'ALIPH CHEEM (Yeldham) *Lays of Ind* (1876) 204 The gallant trooper 'Crocodile' is getting under weigh. 1880 *World* 13 Oct., Of those in the Euphrates, one of the Imperial troopers, four were down simultaneously with sunstroke. 1896 NEWNHAM-DAVIS *Three Men & a God* 79 The last hired trooper of the season was going home in the early spring, taking in her a draft of the regiment. 1942 *R.A.F. Jrnl.* 16 May 11, I saw the empty trooper, scrubbed and waiting. 1981 J. BARNETT *Firing Squad* II. 114 First objective, a decent cabin on the trooper.

†5. *Cant.* A half-crown. *Obs.*

a 1700 B. E. *Dict. Cant. Crew*, *Trooper*, a half Crown.

Hence **trooperˈess** (*rare*), a female trooper.

1924 GALSWORTHY *White Monkey* II. iv. 152 When she was..lying to them like a trooperess. 1927 *Daily Express* 2 Sept. 3 The stories related of the coarse, swearing 'trooperess' are astounding.

troopial, troupial (ˈtruːpɪəl). *Ornith.* [ad. F. *troupiale* (Brisson 1760), f. *troupe* troop, from its living in flocks.] A name given to various species of birds of the American family *Icteridæ*; *esp.* the icteric oriole. Also *attrib.*

[1825 WATERTON *Wand. S. Amer.* (1882) 26 You hear the pretty songster called Troupiale pour forth a variety of sweet and plaintive notes.] 1825 BONAPARTE *Amer. Ornith.* I. 27 Yellow-headed Troopial. *Ibid.* 28 Red-winged Troopial. *Ibid.* 31 All the species of Troopial are peculiar to America. 1863 BATES *Nat. Amazon* vii. (1864) 168 Flocks of a handsome bird belonging to the Icteridæ or troupial family. 1892 W. H. HUDSON *Nat. La Plata* 283 A scarlet-breasted troupial of La Plata. 1895 NEWTON *Dict. Birds*, Troopial.

troopie (ˈtruːpɪ). *colloq.* Also (*S. Afr.*) troepie. [f. TROOP *sb.* + -IE.] In South Africa and Rhodesia (Zimbabwe): a private soldier, esp. a national serviceman without rank.

1972 *Eng. Use in S. Afr.* May, Some of the troopies with particularly dirty habits..receive the title *vuilgat*. 1976 [see *request programme* s.v. REQUEST *sb.*[1] 11]. 1980 *Observer* 3 Aug. 10/1 The FN rifle carried by troopies in the bush.

trooping (ˈtruːpɪŋ), *vbl. sb.* [f. TROOP *v.* + -ING[1].] The action of the verb TROOP.

1809 *Howell's St. Trials* I. 142/2 Not for any assemblings or troopings by them formerly made within the kingdom of England, but [etc.]. 1816 [see TROOP *v.* 6]. 1885 *Manch. Exam.* 8 June 4/7 The chief event..was the trooping of the colours on the Horse Guards Parade. 1888 STEVENSON *Black Arrow* 167 The great trooping of black clouds, and the cold squalls that followed one another. 1893 L. KILLEEN *Soldiers at Sea* 32 When the trooping is over for the year, the troopships lie idle in Portsmouth Harbour. 1907 *Westm. Gaz.* 2 Dec. 12/1 The completion of a dream of 'trooping', by means of which the South-Western moves our sailors and soldiers to and from the coast in any part of England without detraining for other lines.

b. *attrib.*

1647 *Caldwell Pap.* (Maitl. Cl.) I. 110 Quhat they depursed..for trouping horses furnishit be them, quartering of troupers, and monethlie mantinance. 1696 *Lond. Gaz.* No. 3147/4 A Trooping Saddle trimmed with blue. 1882 *Pall Mall G.* 24 June 8/1 The preparation of the *Serapis* and *Crocodile* for the Indian trooping season can be suspended if found necessary, and they can be employed as supplementary transports. 1894 *Scott. Leader* 17 May 5 The Admiralty has chartered two P. & O. steamers..to begin the trooping service in September.

ˈtrooping, *ppl. a.* [-ING[2].] That troops.

1582 STANYHURST *Æneis* III. (Arb.) 83 Heere..fields of Salent with trouping clustered armye Lyctius Idomeneus dooth keepe. 1728–46 THOMSON *Spring* 135 The little trooping birds. 1823 CHALMERS *Serm.* I. 24 His people.. come in trooping multitudes around him. 1843 J.

MARTINEAU *Chr. Life* (1867) 464 Whose trooping images the dawning light does not disperse.

†**'troopmeal,** *adv. Obs. rare.* [f. TROOP *sb.* + -MEAL.] By troops, in a troop or troops.

1600 HOLLAND *Livy* v. xxx. 200 The Nobles old and young, came troup-meale..into the hall. *c* **1611** CHAPMAN *Iliad* XVII. 634 So troope-meale Troy pursu'd a while.

'troopwise, *adv. rare.* [f. TROOP *sb.* + -WISE.] By or in troops.

1820 W. TOOKE tr. *Lucian* I. 560 *note*, Wolves are frequently seen going troopwise.

troose, var. TROUSE, trews, trousers.

troostite ('tru:staɪt). [Named after Prof. G. Troost of Nashville, Tennessee: see -ITE[1].]

1. *Min.* A variety of WILLEMITE, with admixture of iron and manganese, occurring in reddish hexagonal crystals.

1835 C. U. SHEPARD *Treat. Min.* II. 247 Troostite..is found at Sterling (N.J.) associated with Franklinite. **1850** ANSTED *Elem. Geol., Min.* etc. §448 Troostite, or Troolite, is a variety [of Bi-silicate of Manganese] containing iron. **1868** DANA *Min.* (ed. 5) 262 Willemite..Silicate of Zinc... The crystals of..New Jersey are often quite large, and pass under the name of *troostite*.

2. *Metallurgy.* A transitional constituent of steel: cf. MARTENSITE, PEARLITE 2, SORBITE[2].

1902 *Encycl. Brit.* XXIX. 572/2 Austenite, troostite, sorbite, and other constituents [of iron] have also been described.

Hence **troostitic** (-'ɪtɪk) *a.*, pertaining to or consisting of troostite (*Cent. Dict. Suppl.* 1909).

trooze, variant of TROUSE, trews, trousers.

†**tro'pæan,** *a. Obs. rare*[−1]. [f. L. *tropæ-us* adj. (Pliny) + -AN: cf. Gr. τροπαία '(sc. πνοή) an alternating wind, one which blows back from sea to land' (L. & Sc.), f. τρόπος turning.] Blowing from sea to land; ***tropæan winds***, sea-breezes.

1686 PLOT *Staffordsh.* 44 The frequent rains brought by the Tropæan winds from the Irish Seas.

tropæolaceous (trəʊpi:əʊ'leɪʃəs), *a. Bot.* [f. mod.L. *Tropæolāce-æ* (f. TROPÆOLUM) + -OUS: see -ACEOUS.] Belonging to the Natural Order *Tropæolaceæ*, typified by the genus *Tropæolum*; regarded by some as a division of *Geraniaceæ*.

1909 in *Cent. Dict. Suppl.*

tropæolin (trəʊ'pi:əlɪn). Also **-ine.** [f. next + -IN[1], -INE[5]; from the resemblance of the colour to that of the flowers of some species of *Tropæolum*.] Any one of several orange dyes, of complex composition, belonging to the class of sulphonic acids.

1880 FRISWELL in *Jrnl. Soc. Arts* 446 This body has been used as a dye, under the name of Tropæoline O. **1881** WATTS *Dict. Chem.* VIII. 1857 Diazinsulphonic Acids.. Sulphoxybenzenephenols... Some of them are dye-stuffs, known in commerce as tropæoline, chrysoïdine, roccelline, &c. **1897** *Allbutt's Syst. Med.* II. 522 Watery solution of tropæolin.

‖**Tropæolum** (trəʊ'pi:ələm). *Bot.* Pl. **-a** (and in Eng. form **-ums**). [mod.L. (Linnæus, 1737), f. Gr. τρόπαιον trophy; so called from the resemblance of the leaf to a shield and the flower to a helmet.] A South American genus of herbs (N.O. *Tropæolaceæ* or *Geraniaceæ*), mostly of trailing or climbing habit, with irregular spurred flowers, usually deep orange or yellow; several species are cultivated as ornamental plants, and are commonly called Indian Cress, and (erroneously) Nasturtium.

1785 MARTYN *Rousseau's Bot.* xxxi. (1794) 481 The nectary is found on the calyx in *Tropæolum*. **1815** J. SCOTT *Vis. Paris* (ed. 2) App. 287 The hedges are interlaced with twining *Tropæola, Passion flowers*, and *Convolvuli*. **1866** *Treas. Bot.* 1178/1 The Tropæolums are remarkable for possessing an acrid taste, similar to that which exists among the *Cruciferæ*. **1901** *J. Black's Carp. & Build., Home Handicr.* 45 Passion flowers, convolvuluses, and tropæolums running up and around the window.

‖**tropæum** (trəʊ'pi:əm). Also 6 **tropheum,** 7–9 **trophæum,** 9 **tropæon.** [L. *tropæum, trophæum*, ad. Gr. τρόπαιον trophy.] = TROPHY. (Now only *Antiq.*, in *lit.* sense.)

1549 *Compl. Scot.* xvii. 149 This last tryumphe of laure tre vas callit *tropheum*, quhilk singnifeis ane ioyful victoree. **1570–6** LAMBARDE *Peramb. Kent* (1826) 307 They..enacted in their Chapter house, that..Saint Cuthbertes feast (as a Tropheum of their victorie) shoulde be holden double, both in their Church and Kitchen. **1847** LEITCH tr. *C. O. Müller's Anc. Art* §200 (1850) 189 Below, a tropæon is erected by Roman legionaries and auxiliaries. **1901** *Athenæum* 5 Jan. 24/2 [The] massive foundations..are too deep and strong for anything but a very large tower of trophæum.

tropal ('trəʊpəl), *a. Geom.* [f. L. *trop-us* TROPE *sb.* + -AL[1].] Pertaining to or constituting a trope: see TROPE *sb.* 8.

1875 CAYLEY *Math. Papers* IX. 519 The quartic surface has also four tropes (planes which touch the surface along a conic)... The conic of contact or tropal conic in each plan being the intersection of the plane with the before-mentioned quadric surface. *Ibid.* 520 Ordinary tropal planes each touching the surface in a proper conic.

tropane ('trəʊpeɪn). *Chem.* Also †**tropan.** [ad. G. *tropan*, f. *tropeïn* TROPEINE: see -ANE 2 b.] A saturated bicyclic tertiary amine which is a basic liquid obtained from various plants and the parent of a series of compounds which includes atropine, cocaine, and related alkaloids; 8-methyl-8-azabicyclo-[3.2.1]octane, $C_8H_{15}N$.

1919 *Chem. Abstr.* XIII. 592 The residual sirup solidifies in a few days to needles, somewhat deliquescent in air of the HCl salt of tropan. **1923** *Ibid.* XVII. 1643 (*heading*) The spectrochemistry of derivatives of tropane. **1951** A. GROLLMAN *Pharmacol. & Therapeutics* i. 34 The alkaloids of the atropine group of drugs may be considered as derived from a combination of a piperidine and pyrrolidine ring designated as tropane. **1981** *Phytochemistry* XX. 497/1 Tropane alkaloids are known to occur in *Anthocercis littorea* [etc.].

‖**troparion** (trəʊ'pærɪɒn, -'ɛərɪɒn). Pl. **-ia.** [a. Gr. τροπάριον, dim. of τρόπος TROPE *sb.* (sense 5).] In the Greek Church: A short hymn, or a stanza of a hymn; also, = TROPER.

1850 NEALE *Hist. Eastern Ch.* I. 832 *note* b, A Canon, in the usual services, consists of nine odes; each ode is divided into an uncertain number of troparia, generally three, four, or five. *Troparion* is the generic term for all the short hymns of which the services of the Greek Church almost entirely consist. **1876** STAINER & BARRETT *Dict. Mus. Terms* (1898), *Troparion*, an office-book of the Greek Church containing the sequences or chants sung after the lessons.

tropary, tropery ('trəʊpərɪ). *Eccl.* [ad. med.L. *troparium, troperium*, f. L. *tropus* TROPE *sb.* (sense 5).] = TROPER.

14.. *Nom.* in Wr.-Wülcker 719/34 *Hic troporius*, a tropery. **1725** J. LEWIS *Life Pecocke* (1744) 158 It was usual to swear on the tropery or t[r]oper, a book of sequences. **1882** *Church Q. Rev.* 276 A very considerable number of the Service Books in use..in Anglo-Saxon times survive... They consist of Sacramentaries or Missals, Troparies, Passionals [etc.].

trope (trəʊp), *sb.* Also 6 **troope,** 7 **trop.** [ad. L. *tropus* a figure of speech, ad. Gr. τρόπος a turn, f. τρέπειν to turn; cf. F. *trope* (1554 in Godef. *Compl.*). Sometimes app. repr. Gr. τροπή (cf. 3).]

1. *Rhet.* A figure of speech which consists in the use of a word or phrase in a sense other than that which is proper to it; also, in casual use, a figure of speech; figurative language.

1533 TINDALE *Supper of Lord* C v, If ye be so sworne to the litteral sense in this matter, that ye will not in these wordes of Christe, Thys is my bodye, &c., admitte in so playne a speache anye troope. **1573** TUSSER *Husb.* xxviii. (1878) 68 Christmas is onely a figure or trope. *a* **1638** MEDE *Wks.* (1672) 349 That usual Trope of Scripture, by a part, or that which is more notable or obvious in any kind or rank of things, to imply the rest. **1693** DRYDEN *Juvenal* (1697) p. liii, Where the Trope is far fetch'd, and hard, 'tis fit for nothing but to puzzle the Understanding. **1779** SHERIDAN *Critic* I. i, Your occasional tropes and flowers suit the general coarseness of your stile, as tambour sprigs would a ground of linsey-wolsey. **1783** BLAIR *Lect. Rhetoric* xiv. I. 275 Tropes ..consist in a word's being employed to signify something that is different from its original and primitive meaning; so that if you alter the word, you destroy the Figure. **1837** MACAULAY *Ess., Bacon* (1887) 428 Irony is one of the four primary tropes. **1876** GLADSTONE *Homeric Synchr.* 262 To treat as a poetical trope this idea of kings as god-born or god-reared. **1888** BRYCE *Amer. C.* III. cxi. 597 [American] rhetoric is Rhodian rather than Attic, overloaded with tropes and figures.

attrib. **1799** HAN. MORE *Fem. Educ.* (ed. 4) I. x. 221 By this negligence in the just application of words, we shall be.. much misled by these trope and figure ladies.

†**2.** In Gregorian Music, A short distinctive cadence at the close of a melody. *Obs.*

1603 HOLLAND *Plutarch's Mor.* 1358 To let passe therefore the five positures of the Tetrachords, as also the first five tones, tropes, changes, notes or harmonies. **1605** BACON *Adv. Learn.* II. v. §3 Is not the trope of music, to avoid or slide from the close or cadence, common with the trope of rhetoric of deceiving expectation? **1626** —— *Sylva* §113.

†**3.** [= Gr. τροπή.] The 'turning' of the sun at the tropic; also = TROPIC A. 2. *Obs. rare.*

1677 GALE *Crt. Gentiles* II. IV. 258 The Sun has..its annual Tropes and Vicissitudes, what they call Solstices, whereby it is nearer to or remoter from us. **1735** H. BROOKE *Univ. Beauty* IV. 169 Now 'thwart the trope, or zone antartic steer.

†**4.** *Logic.* = MOOD *sb.*[2] 1. *Obs. rare.*

1656 STANLEY *Hist. Philos.* VIII. (1701) 315/1 Of Moods or Tropes there are two kinds, one of Indemonstrables,..the other of Demonstrables.

5. In the Western Church, A phrase, sentence, or verse introduced as an embellishment into some part of the text of the mass or of the breviary office that is sung by the choir.

(Tropes were discontinued at the revision of the missal under Pope Pius V in the 16th cent.)

1846 MASKELL *Mon. Rit.* I. p. xxxvii, The Tropes..were ..sung either before or after the Introit and Hymns in the service of the Mass. **1853** ROCK *Ch. of Fathers* IV. xi. 21 A ..practice..had..grown up..in the north and western quarters of Christendom..of weaving certain pious sentences, called by the Romans 'festive praises', by the Franks 'tropes', between the words of the psalm in the introit at mass. **1894** W. H. FRERE *Winchester Troper* p. ix, 'Trope'..is the regular word to describe additions to the Introit, Offertory and Communion, and is also more rarely found in connection with the Ite missa est or Benedicamus at the close of Mass.

6. In the Moravian Church, One of the three divisions forming the 'Unity of the Brethren'.

[**1780** B. LA TROBE tr. *Cranz's Hist. Brethren* 355 In.. 1749..the administration of the Reformed tropus in the Unity of the Brethren was tendered to, and accepted by, the Bishop of Sodor and Man, Thomas Wilson.] **1809** BOGUE & BENNET *Hist. Dissenters* (1833) II. i. 64 The three different classes of persons who compose the Unity, bear among the brethren the name of tropes or tropuses.

7. In Greek Philosophy: see quots.

1866 FERRIER *Grk. Philos.* I. xv. 467 Of these tropes or Sceptical arguments Sextus enumerates ten. **1910** R. D. HICKS *Stoic & Epicurean* 376 Ænesidemus undertook to arrange the whole material at the disposal of the Sceptic in his contention against the dogmatic position under ten heads or tropes. The word trope properly denotes procedure; the ten tropes were intended to contain the means of refuting dogmatism in all possible forms, and to provide directions for stating every line of available argument which could lead to negative conclusions and paralyse assent.

8. *Geom.* The reciprocal of a node on a curve or surface; in different cases, a multiple tangent or tangent plane, or a plane or developable surface touching the given surface in a particular way.

1869 CAYLEY *Math. Papers* VI. 330 Using 'trope' as the reciprocal term to node. **1875** [see TROPAL].

trope (trəʊp), *v.* [f. TROPE *sb.* 5.] *trans.* To introduce (a trope) as an embellishment; to embellish with a trope or tropes; to add as a trope to. Hence **troped** *ppl. a.*

1894 W. H. FRERE *Winchester Troper* p. xv, The Winchester Tropers..originally contained only a long jubilum on *per*manebit, but later in MS. CC the words were added and the trope troped. **1922** MADAN & CRASTER *Summary Catal. Western Manuscripts Bodleian Library* II. I. 149 These flyleaves I understand from Mr. Bannister to come from a non-monastic breviary, and, as he does not find a troped office for St. K. in English breviaries, I should have supposed them French. **1959** *Listener* 24 Dec. 1134/3 The final word 'portum', set to a long melisma, is troped 'portum in ultimo, da nobis iudicio'. **1977** *Gramophone* Sept. 469/3 The choir missed a golden opportunity by not singing *O come, O come, Emmanuel* in its original fifteenth-century French Franciscan version, as a two-part troped litany.

tropee, obs. form of TROPHY.

tropeic (trəʊ'pi:ɪk), *a. Ichth.* [f. Gr. τρόπις keel + -IC.] Applied to the ventral fold in certain sharks.

1895 in *Funk's Stand. Dict.*

tropeine ('trəʊpi:aɪn). *Chem.* [Arbitrarily altered from TROPINE.] Generic name for the esters or compund ethers of tropine.

1883 *Science* I. 401/2 A series of derivatives, called by the author tropeines, results from the action of various organic acids with hydrochloric acid upon tropine. **1895** in *Funk's Stand. Dict.*

†**tropel.** *Obs. rare.* Also (*pl.*) 5 **troplys,** 7 **trowples.** [a. OF. *tropele* (*a* 1200 in Godef.), dim. f. OF. *trope* TROOP: see -EL[2].] A small troop or company.

1375 BARBOUR *Bruce* XIII. 275 Thai scalit in tropellis [*v.rr.* troplys, trowples] ser. *c* **1400** *Laud Troy Bk.* 5577 Paris come thenne with his tropel, With alle his knyghtes hardi and fel.

troper ('trəʊpə(r)). *Eccl.* (now only *Hist.*). Also 5 **tropere, tropoure, tropure,** 8 **tropar.** [OE. *tropere*, ad. med.L. *troperium* (see TROPARY); cf. OF. *tropier, troper* (12th c. in Godef.).] A book containing tropes (TROPE *sb.* 5); also, a book containing sequences; a sequencer.

a **1073** *Charter Bp. Leofric* in Thorpe *Charters* 430, II. fulle sangbec..& I. tropere & II. salteras. *a* **1400–50** *Alexander* 1568 With tablis & t[r]opoures. *c* **1400** *Laud Troy Bk.* 9369 The Bible ne no Missale,..The Grael ne the Tropere. *c* **1475** *Pict. Voc.* in Wr.-Wülcker 755/3 *Hoc troparium*, tropere. *a* **1746** LEWIS in Gutch *Coll. Cur.* II. 169 A Tropery, or book of Sequences. It was called in English a T[r]oper. **1894** W. H. FRERE *Winchester Troper* p. vi, The Tropers practically represent the sum total of musical advance between the ninth and the twelfth century.

tropery: see TROPARY.

troph-, var TROPHO- before a vowel.

†**tro'phæal,** *a. Obs* [f. L. *trophæ-um* TROPHY + -AL[1].] Pertaining to or adorned with trophies.

1646 J. GREGORY *Notes & Obs.* (1650) 163 He stiled himself thus Augustus Cæsar Octavianus Trophaeall. **1660** *Charac. Italy* 6 Her streets of old did shine with trumphing Cæsars and Consuls in their trophæal Chariots.

trophæum: see TROPÆUM.

trophal ('trəʊfəl), *a. Zool.* [f. TROPH-I + -AL[1].] Pertaining to or forming the trophi.

1902 D. SHARP in *Encycl. Brit.* XXIX. 500/1 The appendages of the posterior three, or trophal, segments become the parts of the mouth.

trophallaxis (trɒfə'læksɪs). *Ent.* [f. TROPH- + Gr. ἄλλαξις exchange.] The mutual exchange of food material by adult insects and larvæ. Hence **tropha'llactic** *a.*

1918 W. M. WHEELER in *Proc. Amer. Philos. Soc.* LVII. 322 In *Belonogaster* the feeding of adults and larvæ is reciprocal... As the relationship is clearly coöperative or mutualistic, I suggest the term *trophallaxis.* **1919** W. OSLER *Old Humanities* ii. 13 The nursing function..is really trophallactic... The larva is provided with..an ambrosia greedily lapped up by the nurse. **1931** W. C. ALLEE *Animal Aggregations* xix. 388 'Trophallaxis' is the bond that unites parent and offspring in the social insects. **1940** *Jrnl. Compar. Psychol.* XXIX. 456 This process..may be represented as the outcome of a simple conditioned response based upon trophallactic relations in the bivouac. **1978** R. J. ELZINGA *Fund. Entomol.* vii. 186 Trophallaxis plays a greater role in ants than it does in the social wasps.

trophe, -ee, obs. forms of TROPHY.

trophesy (ˈtrɒfɪsɪ). *Path.* [irreg. f. Gr. τροφή nourishment, with ending app. after *dropsy, palsy.*] 'Defective nutrition due to disorder of the trophic nerves' (Dorland *Med. Dict.* 1900–13). Hence **trophesial** (trəʊˈfiːʃ(ɪ)əl, -zɪəl) *a.*, pertaining to trophesy; in quot. 1899, pertaining to nutrition: = TROPHIC.

1883 E. C. MANN *Psychol. Med.* 349 (Cent. Dict.) Excessive thought, with mental anxiety,..is much more exhausting, and therefore more commonly followed by trophesies. **1891** *Cent. Dict.*, Trophesial. **1899** *Allbutt's Syst. Med.* VIII. 408 A morbid cerebral condition impairing psychical and trophesial function. *Ibid.* 409 The trophesial function of the cortex.

‖**trophi** (ˈtrəʊfaɪ), *sb. pl. Zool.* [mod.L., pl. of *trophus*, a. Gr. τροφός feeder, f. τρέφειν to nourish.] A collective name for the mouth-parts in insects, as organs for seizing and preparing the food. Also applied to the parts of the pharynx in rotifers, having a similar function.

1826 KIRBY & SP. *Entomol.* xxxiii. III. 355 *Trophi*, the different instruments or organs contained in the mouth, or closing it, and employed in manducation or deglutition. They include the *Labrum, Labium, Mandibulæ, Maxillæ, Lingua*, and *Pharynx.* **1833** LYELL *Princ. Geol.* III. 277 The antennæ, tarsi and trophi are generally very obscure or distorted. **1888** ROLLESTON & JACKSON *Anim. Life* 633 Class Rotifera... The mouth leads into an oesophagus, followed ..usually directly by a muscular pharynx or mastax containing the chitinous jaw-apparatus or 'trophi'... The shape of the 'trophi' is variable.

trophic (ˈtrɒfɪk), *a.* (*sb.*) [ad. Gr. τροφικός, f. τροφή nourishment: see -IC. Cf. F. *trophique.*]

A. *adj.* **1.** *Biol.* **a.** Of or pertaining to nutrition; *spec.* of certain nerves and nerve-centres, Concerned with or regulating the nutrition of the tissues.

1873 A. FLINT *Physiol. Man, Nervous Syst.* ii. 80 Centres attached to the sensory system of nerves, which have, as far as we know, a purely trophic influence over the nerves. **1875** H. C. WOOD *Therap.* (1879) 559 Nerves which preside over nutrition,—the so-called trophic nerves. **1894** *Lancet* 3 Nov. 1030 The large amount of wasting of the muscles..might suggest the possibility of a trophic lesion. **1899** *Allbutt's Syst. Med.* VII. 124 Another affection of the lower limbs, possibly trophic,..is rupture of the tendo Achillis.

b. *Ecol.* Of or pertaining to the feeding habits of, and the food relationship between, different types of organisms in the food-cycle; so ***trophic level***, any of a hierarchy of levels of an ecosystem, each consisting of organisms sharing the same function in the food-web, and the same relationship to the primary producers.

1942 *Ecology* XXIII. 407/2 Food-cycles rarely have more than five trophic levels. **1957** *Ecol. Monogr.* XXVII. 55 (*heading*) Trophic structure and productivity of Silver Springs, Florida. **1974** R. H. BRITTON in R. Goodier *Natural Environment of Shetland* 123 The nutrient poor categories (dystrophic and oligotrophic) are by far the most numerous and..eutrophic and brackish lochs are rather rare... The lochs within each trophic category can be further subdivided according to their superficial area. **1976** *Nature* 22 July 284/1 The trophic base of the arthropod fauna is wind-blown detritus. **1980** *Jrnl. R. Soc. Arts* Feb. 140/2 While they are trophic levels—top carnivore, herbivore, plants, microorganisms—none is dominant.

2. Of a hormone: stimulating the production of another hormone from a specific gland; = TROPIC *a.* 4b.

1945 I. S. KLEINER *Human Biochem.* xxiii. 503 Another hormone of this gland which produces its effect by influencing a different structure, i.e., a 'trophic' hormone, is the adrenotrophic factor. **1965** LEE & KNOWLES *Animal Hormones* ii. 19 The site of production of the trophic hormone controlling the adrenal cortex is still in doubt. **1975** *Nature* 27 Nov. 340/2 The existence of a human cell line showing severalfold stimulation by androgens in a defined system, free from the effects of other trophic hormones, should provide a useful reagent for the further study of the mechanism of androgen action.

B. *sb. Biol.* Something that promotes nutrition.

1893 E. S. D'ODIARDI *Med. Electricity* 54 The second class is composed of trophics, or nutrients, *i.e.*, promoters of nutrition.

So **'trophical** *a.* (*rare*) = *trophic* adj.; hence **'trophically** *adv.*, in relation to nutrition.

1857 DUNGLISON *Med. Lex., Trophical Nerves*, the organic nerves, or nerves of the sympathetic system. **1900** *Lancet* 23 June 1779/2 This..implies continuity of the protoplasm of one neurone with another, but trophically and genetically the two are independent.

-trophic (ˈtrəʊfɪk, ˈtrɒfɪk), *suffix.* [See TROPHIC *a.*] **1.** Forming adjs.: (*a*) with the senses 'characterized by nutrition (of a certain kind)', 'finding nourishment in', as in *autotrophic* adj. s.v. AUTO-[1], HETEROTROPHIC, LECITHOTROPHIC *adjs.*, *psychrotrophic* adj. s.v. PSYCHRO-; also 'controlled by', as in NEUROTROPHIC *a.*; (*b*) with the sense 'maintaining or supporting (a gland, tissue, etc.)' and hence 'regulating', esp. in the epithets of hormones, as GONADOTROPHIC, SEBOTROPHIC *adjs.* Cf. -TROPIC.

1943 *Endocrinology* XXXIII. 407 The use of -tropic as in *gonadotropic*..reverses and confuses a clear, practical pre-established usage in the broad field of biology... -Trophic, even if not perfectly apt, is close enough in meaning and is free from confusion. **1950** *Lancet* 2 Dec. 708/2 It is becoming current practice to speak of the action of a hormone in controlling an endocrine gland as trophic (e.g., thyrotrophic hormone..)... This is surely a misuse of words, from a confusion between trophic action..which is concerned with nutrition,..and tropism..., which connotes control... Is it too late to revert to thyrotropic..and the like? **1971** *Ibid.* 25 Sept. 701/2 For good or ill, -trophic is all but universal [in the names of hormones], though I saw corticotropic recently in a new edition of a student's biochemistry book from the States.

trophied (ˈtrəʊfɪd), *a.* Also 8 trophy'd. [f. TROPHY *sb.* or *v.* + -ED.]

1. Adorned with a trophy or trophies. Also *fig.*

1622 DRAYTON *Poly-olb.* xxx. 159 From whose stone-trophied head, it [the echo] on to Wendrosse went. **1718** ROWE tr. *Lucan* VIII. 1122 The Name that wont the trophy'd Arch to grace. **1798** S. ROGERS *Epist. Friend* 200 Thro' trophied tombs of heroes and of kings. **1844** H. G. ROBINSON *Odes Horace* I. xii, The peaceful reign Of Numa, or the proudly trophied state Of Tarquin. **1905** CAPT. GLASFURD *Rifle Ind. Jungle* 387 That mighty head shall be accorded the post of honour on already well-trophied walls.

2. Formed into or constituting a trophy.

1805 SOUTHEY *Madoc* II. 197 He sits upon a throne of trophied skulls. *a* **1843** —— *Comm.-pl. Bk.* IV. 55/1 The trophied armour damp gleaming to the central fire. **1887** *Daily News* 16 May 5/7 The Exchange was..tastefully decorated, each window..having its trophied flags and shield.

trophilegic (trɒfɪˈlɛdʒɪk), *a. Biol.* [irreg. f. Gr. τροφή nourishment + L. *legĕre* to gather, to collect + -IC. (Perhaps suggested by L. *frūgilĕgus* fruit-gathering.)] Collecting nutriment.

1898 *Nature* 3 Nov. 15/1 The trophilegic action of the fronds [of ferns], in connection with which certain arrangements have been observed, destined to facilitate the passage of water to the roots.

trophism (ˈtrɒfɪz(ə)m). *Phys.* [f. Gr. τροφή nourishment + -ISM.] The process of nutrition of the tissues; 'direct trophic influence' (Dorland *Med. Dict.* 1900–13).

1878 A. HAMILTON *Nerv. Dis.* 444 Various depraved conditions of sensibility, motility, and trophism may follow.

tropho- (ˈtrɒfəʊ, ˈtrəʊfəʊ), also, before a vowel, **troph-**, combining form repr. Gr. τροφή nourishment, f. τρέφειν to nourish: entering into various technical terms, chiefly of biology and allied sciences. **tro'phectoderm** *Embryol.* = *trophoblast*; hence **trophecto'dermal** *a.*; **tropho'biont** *Ent.* [f. Gr. βιουντ-, βιῶν living], an insect which produces a secretion used as food by another; **'trophoblast** [-BLAST], a layer of cells external to the embryo, having the function of supplying it with nourishment; also applied by some to the morbid growth in cancer, as held to be an abnormal development of the same tissue; hence **tropho'blastic** *a.*, relating to or consisting of trophoblast; **tropho'calyx** [CALYX], a cup-shaped body from which the placenta is developed in certain mammals, as bats and moles; †**tropho'chromatin** *Cytology* [f. CHROMATIN: cf. G. *trophochromatisch* (W. Lubosch 1902, in *Ergebnisse Anat. und Entwicklungsgeschichte* XI. 783)], chromatin which was thought to be concerned only with the regulation of the metabolism and growth of the cell, and not with its reproduction (*obs.*); **'trophocyte** (-saɪt) [-CYTE], each of a set of cells forming one of the constituents of the fatty tissue in adult insects; **'trophodisc, -disk**, a disk-shaped body from which the placenta is developed in certain mammals, as rabbits; ‖**tropholecithus** (-ˈlɛsɪθəs) [mod.L., f. Gr. λέκιθος yolk], the nutritive yolk of an ovum; hence **tropho'lecithal** *a.*; **tro'phology** [-LOGY], that department of physiology which deals with nutrition; **tropho'lytic** *a.* [-LYTIC], (of part of a lake) characterized by the decomposition of organic matter; opp. TROPHOGENIC *a.* 2; ‖**tropho'nema** (pl. -'nemata) [mod.L., f. Gr. νῆμα thread], each of the glandular villi of the uterus in certain viviparous fishes, which supply nutriment to the embryos; ‖,**trophoneu'rosis** (-ˈrəʊsɪs), pl. **-oses** (-ˈrəʊsiːz) [NEUROSIS], any one of a class of functional disorders due to derangement of the trophic action of the nerves; hence **trophoneurotic** (-ˈrɒtɪk) *a.*, pertaining to or of the nature of trophoneurosis; **tropho-'nucleus** *Zool.*, a large nucleus present in some flagellated protozoa, esp. trypanosomes, which regulates the metabolism and growth of the cell; **tro'phopathy** [Gr. -παθεια suffering], any derangement of nutrition, esp. of a tissue; **'trophophore** (-fɔə(r)) [ad. Gr. τροφοφόρος bringing nourishment], any one of the wandering amœboid nutritive cells in a sponge which give rise to gemmules or embryos; **trophophoric** (-ˈfɒrɪk) *a.* [f. as prec. + -IC], having the function of supplying provisions; **trophophorous** (-ˈfɒfərəs) *a.* [f. as prec. + -OUS], pertaining to or of the nature of a trophophore; **'trophoplasm** (-plæz(ə)m), Nägeli's term for that portion of the protoplasm of a germ or cell which is supposed to furnish nutriment to the *idioplasm*; hence **tropho'plasmic** *a.*, pertaining to or of the nature of trophoplasm; **'trophoplast**, Meyer's term for a specialized granule of protoplasm in a vegetable cell: = PLASTID 2; ,**tropho'pollen** [cf. *trophosperm* below], a proposed name for the partition of the loculus of an anther; **'trophosome** (-səʊm) [Gr. σῶμα body], the aggregate of nutritive zooids of a hydrozoan (distinguished from *gonosome*); hence **tropho'somal** *a.*; **'trophosperm** [ad. F. *trophosperme* (Richard, *a* 1819), f. Gr. σπέρμα seed], a proposed name for the placenta of a seed-vessel; **'trophosphere**, a spherical body (consisting of the *trophoblast* and the *trophospongia*) from which the placenta is developed in certain mammals, as hedgehogs; ‖**trophospongia** (-ˈspɒndʒɪə) [mod.L. (Hubrecht), f. Gr. σπογγιά sponge], a compact layer of cells between the trophoblast and the decidual tissue; hence **tropho'spongial, -ian** *adjs.*; ‖**tropho'taxis** [mod.L.: cf. TAXIS 6], = *trophotropism*; **tropho'thylax** *Ent.* [f. Gr. θύλακ-ος pouch] (see quot. 1971); **tropho'tropic** *a.*, pertaining to or exhibiting trophotropism; **tro'photropism** [Gr. -τροπος turning: after *heliotropism*, etc.], reaction of an organism or cell to the stimulus of a source or supply of food by movement towards or away from it (*positive* or *negative t.*); **trophozoite** (-ˈzəʊaɪt) [Gr. ζῷον animal: cf. -ITE[1] 3], a sporozoon (endoparasitic protozoon) in its growing stage, when it is absorbing nutriment from its host; **trophozooid** (-ˈzəʊɔɪd), a nutritive zooid of any colonial organism, as a hydrozoan.

1932 M. T. HARMAN *Textbk. Embryol.* vii. 134 Supposedly the *troph-ectoderm produces an enzyme which digests the maternal tissue until the embryo is entirely imbedded. **1980** *Nature* 10 Apr. 550/2 It was recently found that the inner cell mass of the early blastocyst is also totipotent and can form trophectoderm when isolated by immunosurgery. **1978** *Ibid.* 7 Sept. 10/3 The strange distribution of this determinant does not fit in with any preconceived notions of *trophectodermal formation or differentiation. **1913** E. WASMANN in *Ann. Rep. Smithsonian Inst. 1912* 464 We distinguish..*trophobionts or food-producing animals of the ant. **1978** R. J. ELZINGA *Fund. Entomol.* vii. 173 These trophobionts are protected by their hosts and are analogous to domestic cows, for they yield food sugar solutions..upon request. **1889** HUBRECHT in *Q. Jrnl. Microsc. Sci.* Dec. 299 This striking difference between somatic mesoblast and *trophoblast becomes still more accentuated in the next developmental phases. *Ibid.* 385 If we agree..to designate the outer layer alone as trophoblast, the outer layer plus a thin layer of somatic mesoblast without blood-vessels as diplotrophoblast [etc.]. **1907** *Contemp. Rev.* Sept. 411 A cancer is 'irresponsible trophoblast'. **1889** HUBRECHT (as above) 301 Mesoblastic warts, ridges, and outgrowths being soon surrounded on three sides by the *trophoblastic proliferation. **1907** *Contemp. Rev.* Sept. 410 The trophoblastic theory of cancer. **1889** HUBRECHT (as above) 359 The *trophocalyx (as this specialized region may conveniently be called, both in the bat and the mole, per analogiam with the trophosphere of the hedgehog and the trophodisc of the rabbit). **1909** *Q. Jrnl. Microsc. Sci.* LIII. 282 Mesnil ('05) uses a terminology which also has a physiological foundation..; trophochromidia, for chromidial structures of a vegetative function; idiochromidia, for chromidia which enter into the formation of gametes. [*Note*] Cf. Lubosch's ('02) terms, '*trophochromatin' and 'idiochromatin'. **1947** *Ann. Rev. Microbiol.* I. 2 In amœboid forms special interest attaches to the structure and division of the nucleus. A distinction may be made between the 'trophochromatin' which stains intensely with iron haematoxylin, but takes no part in the formation of the chromosomes, and the 'idiochromatin' out of which the chromosomes are formed. **1904** *Jrnl. Roy. Microsc. Soc.* Oct. 527 Imaginal Adipose Tissue in Muscidæ.—Ch. Pérez has made a study of this tissue, which consists of two kinds of elements—*trophocytes and œnocytes. **1889** HUBRECHT (as above) 323 Corresponding regions of the rabbit might be indicated by the name of *trophodisc, that of the bat and mole of trophocalyx. **1891** *Cent. Dict.*, *Tropholecithal. **1879** tr. *Haeckel's Evol. Man* I. viii. 216 The nutritive yolk (*vitellus nutritivus*, or **tropholecithus*)..is a mere appendage of the true egg-cell, and contains hoarded food-substance,..so that it forms a sort of storehouse for the embryo in the course of its evolution. **1890** BILLINGS *Med. Dict.*, **Trophology*, science of nutrition. **1957** *Tropholytic [see TROPHOGENIC *a.* 2]. **1975** G. A. COLE *Textbk. Limnol.* ii. 10/1 Below the trophogenic layer is a darker tropholytic region..where respiration and decomposition predominate. **1891** *Proc. Roy. Soc.* 19 Mar. 363 We propose to term the villiform structures of the uterine mucous membrane in Selachians, which essentially secrete nutriment, **trophonemata*. *Ibid.* 365 Transverse sections of a trophonema shew [etc.]. **1857** DUNGLISON *Med. Lex.*, **Trophoneuroses*, morbid conditions of the process of nutrition, owing to modified nervous influence. **1876** tr. *Wagner's Gen. Pathol.* 292 Many forms of disease rarely occurring, but..highly characteristic and very evident to the senses, tropho-neuroses. **1896** *Allbutt's Syst. Med.* I. 179 Facial hemi-atrophy and scleroderma from their distribution would suggest a trophoneurosis. **1891** *Cent. Dict.*, *Trophoneurotic. **1897** *Allbutt's Syst. Med.* II. 47 The so-called 'varieties' or 'forms' of leprosy..(2) the *smooth* (also called 'anæsthetic', 'non-tuberculated', 'tropho-neurotic', etc.). **1906** H. M. WOODCOCK in *Q. Jrnl. Microsc. Sci.* L. 182 This is revealed..in the sharp resolution of the nuclear material into trophic and kinetic constituents, which are practically separate and independent, at any rate, during the trypanosome phase... The fertilisation spindle or definitive nucleus is to be regarded as representing the trophic portion, and it will be convenient, therefore, to distinguish it as the *trophonucleus. **1964** M. HYNES *Med. Bacteriol.* (ed. 8) xxviii. 436 Stained preparations [of *Trypanosoma gambiense*] show two nuclear structures; the one, larger and centrally placed, is known as the macronucleus or trophonucleus and the other, smaller, placed at the posterior end, is known as the micronucleus or kinetoplast. **1890** *Lancet* 8 Mar. 535 The belief of the writers that *trophopathy..has more to do with the cause of the so-called incurable diseases than the profession gives credit to. **1890** BILLINGS *Med. Dict.*, *Trophopathies*, disorders of nutrition. **1891** *Cent. Dict.*, *Trophophore, *Trophophorous. **1892** LD. LYTTON *King Poppy* i. 67 *note*, Official ranks, civil, military, and *trophophoric. **1893** tr. *Weismann's Germ-Plasm* I. i. 38, I shall..call the vital substance of the cell the 'formative plasm' or morphoplasm (Nägeli's '*trophoplasm'), in contrast to the idioplasm. [**1899** *Allbutt's Syst. Med.* VI. 718 [The axis cylinder] is a prolongation of the achromatic amorphous substance, called also trophoplasma.] **1903** *Bot. Gaz.* May 340 Everything seems to point to the ooplasm as *trophoplasmic in character. **1885** GOODALE *Physiol. Bot.* (1892) 287 General Term..*Trophoplast. Special Terms.. anaplast, autoplast, chromoplast. **1889** *Science* 22 Nov. 355/1 The nucleus and other granules (the trophoplasts) within the cell... Each protoplast possesses the organs necessary for continuous transmission; the nucleus for new nuclei, the trophoplasts for new granules of all kinds. **1832** LINDLEY *Introd. Bot.* I. ii. 126 That part of the anther.. which is called..the *trophopollen by Turpin. **1870** NICHOLSON *Man. Zool.* 26 The individual Campanularia consists of a series of nutritive zooids, collectively called the '*trophosome'. **1888** ROLLESTON & JACKSON *Anim. Life* 245 The Sea-fir..forms a fixed colony or *hydrosoma*... The hydrosome consists of a number of *hydranths* or nutritive zooids collectively forming the *trophosome* and connected to one another by a branching *cœnosarc*. **1819** LINDLEY tr. *Richard's Observ. Fruits & Seeds* 6, I substitute the name of **Trophosperm* for that of *Placenta*, which botanists have given to the internal part of the pericarp, on which the seeds are immediately attached. **1889** HUBRECHT (as above) 322 These two together [the trophoblast and the trophospongia], forming in Erinaceus a sphere which is shut off from the uterus lumen by the fusion of the lips of the decidua reflexa, should be indicated by the name of *trophosphere. *Ibid.*, It is to this cell-mass of which we have just traced the maternal origin, that I propose to give the name of *trophospongia. *Ibid.* 326 The topography of the *trophospongian region. **1897** C. B. DAVENPORT *Exper. Morphol.* i. §3. 39 Chemotaxis is, therefore, in some cases, a response to the stimulus afforded by substances which can be employed by the organism as food; under which circumstances it can be called '*Trophotaxis'. **1920** WHEELER & BAILEY in *Trans. Philos. Soc.* XXII. 258 The sternal portion of the first abdominal segment is transversely elliptical..and furnished with a food-pouch, the *trophothylax. **1971** E. O. WILSON *Insect Societies* iv. 55/1 The nurse worker first pushes the fragment deep within the trophothylax, the special food pouch located on the lower surface of the thorax just behind the head (and found only in pseudomyrmecine [ant] larvae). **1891** *Cent. Dict.*, *Trophotropic. **1887** GARNSEY & BALFOUR tr. *De Bary's Fungi*, etc. ix. 449 *Trophotropism.—Vegetating plasmodia spread out on surfaces which yield little or no nutriment move towards bodies which contain nutrient substances as soon as they are offered to them. **1906** *Lancet* 27 Oct. 1161/2 The problem of digestion is intimately related to ..'trophotropism', both positive and negative. **1900–13** DORLAND *Med. Dict.* (ed. 7), *Trophozoïte. **1909** *Cent. Dict. Suppl.*, Trophozoite. **1888** W. A. HERDMAN in *Encycl. Brit.* XXIII. 615/2 Nutritive forms (*trophozooids) which remain permanently attached to the nurse, and serve to provide it with food.

trophogenic (trɒfəʊ-, trəʊfəʊˈdʒɛnɪk), *a.* [f. TROPHO- + GENIC.] **1.** *Ent.* Arising from an insect's feeding habits or diet.

1928 W. M. WHEELER *Social Insects* viii. 193 The castes may be blastogenic..in some groups of social insects, and trophogenic..in others. **1980** *Insectes Sociaux* XXVII. 80 The autogenic determination which separates queen and worker castes is succeeded by the larval trophogenic determination which is also at the origin of the soldiers.

2. Of part of a lake: characterized by the photosynthetic production of oxygen and organic matter. Opp. *tropholytic* adj. s.v. TROPHO-. [tr. G. *trophogen* (E. Naumann *Limnologische Terminol.* (1931) 696).]

1957 G. E. HUTCHINSON *Treat. Limnol.* I. ix. 583 Oxygen, produced by photosynthesis in the trophogenic layers of the lake, and methane, produced by anaerobic decomposition in the tropholytic layers. **1979** *Ecol. Modelling* VI. 1 (*heading*) The modelling of ^{32}P kinetics within the trophogenic zone of a small lake.

So **troˈphogeny**, the determination of an insect's development by its feeding habits.

1923 W. M. WHEELER *Social Life among Insects* vi. 253 It was formerly supposed that all termite eggs were alike and therefore produced young larvae which..took on the various caste characters as a result of differences in feeding (trophogeny). **1938** *Times Lit. Suppl.* 5 Mar. 159/1 Are the castes of ants determined by the diet of the larvae, that is, trophogeny, or in the egg, that is blastogeny?

Trophonian (trəʊˈfəʊnɪən), *a.* [f. L. *Trophōnius*, Gr. Τροφώνιος, proper name (see below) + -AN.] Pertaining to Trophonius, the mythical builder of the original temple of Apollo at Delphi, who after his death was worshipped as a god, and had an oracle in a cave in Bœotia, which was said to affect those who entered with such awe that they never smiled again: hence *allusively*.

1792 in Morse *Amer. Geog.* (1794) I. 398 Two young ladies..who had heroism enough to make the trophonian [*mispr.* trophimium] tour with us. **1796** BURKE *Regic. Peace* i. Wks. VIII. 109 There is great danger that they who enter smiling into this Trophonian cave, will come out of it sad and serious conspirators. **1896** GOSSE in *Contemp. Rev.* Jan. 87 His face had the solemn Trophonian pallor, the look of the man who has seen death in the cave.

trophy (ˈtrəʊfɪ), *sb.* Forms: 6–7 **trophe, -ee, -ey, -æ,** (6 **-æe**), 7 **-ea, -ie, -ye,** (**tropee, -æe**), 7– **trophy.** See also TROPÆUM. [a. F. *trophée* (15th c. in Hatz.-Darm.), ad. post-cl.L. *trophæum*, cl.L. *tropæum*, ad. Gr. τρόπαιον, neut. of τροπαῖος, f. τροπή turning, putting to flight, defeat.]

1. *Gr.* and *Rom. Antiq.* A structure erected (originally on the field of battle, later in any public place) as a memorial of a victory in war, consisting of arms or other spoils taken from the enemy, hung upon a tree, pillar, etc. and dedicated to some divinity. Hence applied to similar monuments or memorials in later times.

1550 T. NICHOLS *Thucydides* I. 36 The Athenians dyd make and set vp their Trophe or signe of victorye, pretending to haue had the better. **1638** JUNIUS *Paint. Ancients* 145 Religion..hindering the Rhodians to deface this monument, because dedicated tropæes might not be removed. **1697** DRYDEN *Æneid* VII. 254 Around the posts hung helmets, darts, and spears, And captive chariots, axes, shields, and bars, And broken beaks of ships, the trophies of their wars. **1700** PRIOR *Carmen Seculare* 369 Let every Sacred Pillar bear Trophies of Arms, and Monuments of War. **1776** GIBBON *Decl. & F.* ii. (1788) I. 45 Alexander erected the Macedonian trophies on the banks of the Hyphasis. *a* **1854** H. REED *Lect. Eng. Hist.* iv. (1855) 146 The banners of the ships of Spain hung out as trophies from the battlements of the Cathedral of St. Paul. **1881** JOWETT *Thucyd.* I. 159 The Athenians..raised a trophy on the place from which they had just sailed out to their victory.

b. *transf.* A painted or carved figure of such a memorial; by extension, an ornamental or symbolic group of any objects, or a representation of such a group in decorative art.

1634 SIR T. HERBERT *Trav.* 64 The Trophies of his Ormus Victory..painted in Gold..wherein are set downe ..the assaults and massacres of the Ormusians. **1688** *Lond. Gaz.* No. 2363/4 A Steel Sword, the Hilt cut with Trophies, the Trophies black, the Ground inlaid with Gold. **1716** LADY M. W. MONTAGU *Let. to C'tess Mar* 14 Sept., Near the Empress was a gilded trophy wreathed with flowers. **1753** CHAMBERS *Cycl. Supp.*, *Trophy*, in architecture, an ornament which represents the trunk of a tree, charged.. with arms or military weapons. **1848** THACKERAY *Bk. Snobs* xxvi, His gorget, sash, and sabre of the Horse Marines, with his boot-hooks underneath in a trophy.

2. a. *transf.* Anything taken in war, or in hunting, etc.; a spoil, prize: esp. if kept or displayed as a memorial. Also *fig.*

1513 DOUGLAS *Æneis* XI. iv. 75 For all the Tuscane menȝe ..Greyt trophe and rich spulȝe hyddir bringis. **1599** B. JONSON *Cynthia's Rev.* I. ii, That trophæe of selfe-loue, and spoile of nature. **1612** DRAYTON *Poly-olb.* iv. 317 For a Trophy brought the Giants coat away, Made of the beards of Kings. **1681** FLAVEL *Right. Man's Ref.* x. 244 They are.. not left as a prey and trophy to their enemy. **1788** GIBBON *Decl. & F.* lxiii. (1846) III. 580 A defeat and a wound were the only trophies of his expedition. **1810** SCOTT *Lady of L.* I. xxvii, All around, the walls to grace, Hung trophies of the fight or chase. **1860** MAURY *Phys. Geog. Sea* (Low) xiv. §586 It was upon this plateau that Brooke's sounding apparatus brought up its first trophies from the bottom of the sea. **1895** J. G. MILLAIS *Breath fr. Veldt* (1899) 322 Sable antelope, the heads of which are, to my thinking, the finest trophies that Africa produces.

b. *fig.* Anything serving as a token or evidence of victory, valour, power, skill, etc.; a monument, memorial.

1569 SPENSER *Vis. Bellay* xi, She raisde a Trophee ouer all the worlde. **1644** MILTON *Areop.* (Arb.) 31 Whereof this whole Discourse..will be a certaine testimony, if not a Trophey. **1661** SECRETARY NICHOLAS *Let.* 18 Nov. in *Remembrancia* (London, Town Clerk's Office), The officers of the Trained Bands of the City had been put to great expense and charges in providing themselves with trophies and other necessaries. **1675** TRAHERNE *Chr. Ethics* 397 Hands, hearts, and souls, our victories, And spoils, and trophies, our own joyes! **1750** GRAY *Elegy* 38 If Mem'ry o'er their Tomb no Trophies raise. **1847** EMERSON *Poems, Ode to Beauty* 89 The leafy dell, the city mart, Equal trophies of thine art. **1871** MACDUFF *Mem. Patmos* xxi. 292 The triumphs and trophies of intellect.

3. *attrib.* and *Comb.*, as *trophy-badge*, *-bearer*, *decoration* (see 1 b), *flag*, *-hunter*, *-hunting*, *-work*; **trophy-cress** = *trophywort*; **trophy-lock**, 'a lock of hair cut from the head of a slain enemy, used to adorn a weapon or shield' (*Cent. Dict.* 1891); **trophy-money, trophy-tax**, a tax formerly levied in each county for incidental expenses connected with the militia, etc.; now only in the City of London as an annual payment met out of Rates Funds, and distributed to the various City Territorial and Volunteer Reserve units: see quot. 1727–41, and cf. quot. 1661 in 2 b; **trophy-wort**, a book-name for the genus TROPÆOLUM.

1891 WESTERMARCK *Hist. Human Marr.* (1894) 172 Many ornaments are really nothing but *trophy-badges. **1614** T. WHITE *Martyrd. St. George* C iij b, Thou..the..name dost gaine Of *Trophee-bearer. **1888** *Cassell's Encycl. Dict.*, **Trophy-cress*, the genus Tropæolum. **1891** *Cent. Dict.* s.v. *Decoration*, **Trophy decoration*, decoration by means of groups of arms, musical instruments, scrolls, tools of painting and sculpture, and the like, or what may by extension be called trophies, especially in Italian decorative art. **1663** BUTLER *Hud.* I. II. 1121 The Squire in State..bore The *Trophee-Fiddle and the Case. **1898** G. MEREDITH *Odes Fr. Hist.* 78 To clasp his *trophy flag, and call him Saint. **1909** *Westm. Gaz.* 16 Apr. 3/3 He interweaves.. many little incidents that would escape the notice of the mere *trophy-hunter. **1899** W. H. FURNESS *Folk Lore Borneo* 15 That savage love of *trophy-hunting which seems inborn in mankind. **1664** in J. Croft *Excerpta Ant.* (1797) 21 Item, paid for *Trophye Money, 3*l.* 8*s.* 8*d.* **1727–41** CHAMBERS *Cycl.*, *Trophy money*, a duty paid annually.. towards providing harness, drums, colours, etc., for the militia. **1766** ENTICK *London* IV. 29 In 1682 a suit was commenced with the college..for trophy-money. **1897** *Outing* (U.S.) XXX. 227/1 The occasional sailor has no chance in the *trophy races. **1901** *Daily Chron.* 24 July 5/2 The '*Trophy Tax', or, to give it its full designation, the Trophy Tax Militia Rate..is peculiar to the City of London, and is a relic of the old train-band system. **1708** *New View Lond.* II. 491/2 A neat white marble monument, enricht with *Trophy work, an Urn, Cherub and Palm branches. **1866** *Treas. Bot.*, *Trophywort, *Tropæolum.*

Hence **ˈtrophyless** *a.*, without a trophy.

1897 *19th Cent.* May 703 The disappointment at returning trophyless.

ˈtrophy, *v.* [f. prec. sb.] *trans.* (chiefly *pass.*) †**a.** To transform into a trophy. *Obs. rare*$^{-1}$. **b.** To bestow a trophy upon, celebrate with a trophy. **c.** To adorn with a trophy or trophies; also *fig.* (See also TROPHIED.)

1599 B. JONSON *Cynthia's Rev.* V. xi, And so, swolne Niobe..was trophæed into stone. **1631** HEYWOOD *2nd Pt. Fair Maid of W.* I. i, If it prove as I have fashion'd it, I shall be trophide ever. **1632** —— *1st Pt. Iron Age* IV. Wks. 1874 III. 328 You beare your selfe more equall then you ought, With one so trophy'd. **1806** MOORE *Epist.* ix. 159 Heroes, trophied high In ancient fame. **1816** BYRON *Ch. Har.* III. xvii, Is the spot mark'd with no colossal bust? Nor column trophied for triumphal show? **1825** CAMPBELL *Poems, Stanzas Spanish Patriots* i, Looking on your graves, though trophied not, As holier hallow'd ground than priests could make the spot! **1847** R. W. HAMILTON *Disq. Sabbath* ii. (1848) 55 The Sabbath of the old covenant..descends to us trophied with holy illustrations.

tropic (ˈtrɒpɪk), *sb.* and *a.*[1] Forms: 4 **tropik**, 6 **-ycque(-we), -yk(e,** 6–7 **-ike, -ique, -icke,** 6–8 **-ick,** 7– **tropic.** [ad. L. *tropicus*, a. Gr. τροπικός pertaining to the 'turning' of the sun at the solstice, tropical (hence as sb. (sc. κύκλος circle) the tropic); also, of the nature of a trope, figurative, f. τροπή turning. Cf. F. *tropique* (16th c.).] **A.** *sb.*

I. 1. *Astr.* †**a.** Each of the two solstitial points, the most northerly and southerly points of the ecliptic, at which the sun reaches his greatest distance north or south of the equator, and 'turns' or begins to move towards it again; also (*loosely*), each of the two signs (Cancer and Capricorn) at the beginning of which these points occur. *Obs.*

In quot. 1662 erroneously extended to include the equinoctial points.

c **1391** CHAUCER *Astrol.* I. §17 This signe of cancre is cleped the tropik of Somer, of *tropos*, þat is to seyn Agaynward, for thanne by-gynneth the sonne to passe fro vs-ward. **1579** E. K. *Gloss. Spenser's Sheph. Cal.* Nov. 15 The sonne draweth low..toward his Tropick or returne. **1615** G. SANDYS *Trav.* 98 The Sunne performing his course in the winter Tropick. **1662** STANLEY *Hist. Chaldaic Philos.* (1701) 17/2 In Aries is the Spring Tropick, in Capricorn the Winter, in Cancer the Summer, in Libra the Autumnal.

b. Each of two circles of the celestial sphere (*tropic of* CANCER and *tropic of* CAPRICORN), parallel to the equinoctial or celestial equator, and distant about 23° 28′ north and south of it, touching the ecliptic at the solstitial points.

1503 *Kalender of Sheph.* I ij, The other two [circles] ar namyt tropycqwes, the oon of sommer the other of wynter. **1555** EDEN *Decades* 183 The soonne..remaynynge continually betwene the two tropykes of Cancer and Capricorne. **1561** —— tr. *Cortez' Arte Nauig.* I. xv. 16 The Estiuall or sommer Tropyke. **1607** TOPSELL *Four-f. Beasts* (1658) 112 Other by the Dogs, do understand the two Tropicks, which are (as it were) the two porters of the Sun for the South and North. **1625** N. CARPENTER *Geog. Del.* I. vi. (1635) 144 The Tropicks are Parallels bounding the Suns greatest declination. **1658** WALLER *On Cromwell's Death* 21 Under the Tropick is our Language spoke. **1837** WHEWELL *Hist. Induct. Sc.* (1857) I. 114 Where the sun's path touches the tropics. **1868** LOCKYER *Elem. Astron.* iii. (1879) 65 At 23½° on either side of the equator are the Tropics.

c. *fig.* Turning-point; limit, boundary. (In quot. 1635 otherwise used: cf. 2 c.)

1635 QUARLES *Embl.* III. vii. (1718) 155 Our equinoctial hearts can never lie Secure, beneath the tropicks of that eye. *a* **1639** WOTTON *Charac. Kings Eng.* in *Reliq.* (1651) 166 States have their Conversions and Periods as well as Naturall Bodies, and we were come to our Tropique. **1670** EACHARD *Cont. Clergy* 54 It was a zodiacal mercy!..for Christ keeps within the tropicks; He goes not out of the pale of the church. **1844** N. PATERSON *Manse Garden* 63 Let rest and fatigue be your tropics and you will travel with unabated vigour over the undulating line of your ecliptic.

2. a. *Geog.* Each of two parallels of latitude on the earth's surface (corresponding to the celestial circles, 1 b, and called likewise *tropic of Cancer* and *tropic of Capricorn*), distant about 23° 28′ north and south of the equator, being the boundaries of the torrid zone.

1527 R. THORNE in Hakluyt *Voy.* (1589) 252 From the Tropickes to both the Poles. **1604** E. G[RIMSTONE] *D'Acosta's Hist. Indies* II. iv. 87 In Regions which lie without the Tropicks. *c* **1645** HOWELL *Lett.* (1688) III. 409 Our late Navigators..who use to cross the Equator and Tropiques so often. **1711** ADDISON *Spect.* No. 170 ¶13 It is a Misfortune for a Woman to be born between the Tropicks. *a* **1780** WATSON *Philip III* (1839) 175 Countries..on this side of the northern tropic. **1878** HUXLEY *Physiogr.* xx. 356 The boundaries of these zones are called tropics.

b. *pl.* With *def. art.*: The region between (and about) these parallels; the torrid zone and parts immediately adjacent.

1837 W. IRVING *Capt. Bonneville* III. 145 The Mississippi; whose rapid current traverses a succession of latitudes..in a few days..almost from the frozen regions to the tropics. **1854** EMERSON *Lett. & Soc. Aims, Resources* Wks. (Bohn) III. 203 The tropics are one vast garden. **1880** HAUGHTON *Phys. Geog.* iii. 130 The warm waters of the tropics are carried, bodily, into the temperate zone.

Comb. **1887** *Daily News* 7 Nov. 3/1 That pulmonary disease..generally..fatal to the tropic-born anthropoids.

c. *fig.* in allusion to the excessive heat or luxuriant growth of the tropics.

1641 J. JACKSON *True Evang. T.* I. 38 The sixt Persecution ..did so scorch within the Tropicks of the Church, that many thousands suffered. **1893** *N.Y. New-Church Messenger* 19 Apr. 244 Mastodon-affections..swarming through the tropics of his soul.

II. †**3.** *pl.* [tr. L. *tropicī* (Athanasius, etc.).] Name for a sect who interpreted Scripture, or certain passages of Scripture, metaphorically. (Cf. TROPIST.) *Obs.*

1585-7 T. ROGERS *39 Art.* v. (1633) 23 Some affirme the holy Ghost to be but a meere creature, as did Arius,..the Tropickes, [etc.].

†**4.** Tropical or metaphorical uses of words; tropes. *Obs.*

1697 tr. *Burgersdicius his Logic* I. xxvi. 104 The Change of the Word, from its proper Signification, as in the Tropicks.

B. *adj.*

I. 1. *Astr.* **a.** Connected with the sun's 'turning back' towards the equator at the solstices; pertaining to the tropics, or to either tropic (in sense A. 1 a or b): = TROPICAL 1. ***tropic circle*** or ***line*** = A. 1 b; ***tropic point*** = A. 1 a. Now *rare* or *Obs.*

1551 RECORDE *Cast. Knowl.* (1556) 24 These other two cyrcles..are called the twoo Tropike cyrcles after the greeke deriuation. **1616** *Marlowe's Faust.* vi. Wks. (Rtldg.) 117/2 He views the clouds, the planets, and the stars, The tropic Zones. **1667** MILTON *P.L.* x. 675 Som say the Sun Was bid turn Reines from th' Equinoctial Rode..Up to the Tropic Crab. **1667** DRYDEN *Sir Martin Mar-all* v. i, I have seen your hurricanos and your calentures, and your ecliptics and your tropic lines. **1701** *Stanley's Hist. Philos.* Biog. bj, Stanley..thinks his Gnomon did only note the Tropick and Equinoctial Points.

†**b.** *fig.* or *allusively*. Of or pertaining to turning (in quot., in allusion to *Jas.* i. 17). *Obs.*

1677 GALE *Crt. Gentiles* II. IV. 258 It casts various shadows and causeth varietie of Seasons,..such is the ἀποσκίασμα or tropic shadow of the sun. But now the immutable God admits no such tropic shadows or variations.

2. *Geog.* **a.** Belonging to the tropics (in sense A. 2 or 2 b): = TROPICAL 2.

1799 WORDSW. *Ruth* vii, No dolphin ever was so gay Upon the tropic sea. **1806** MAURICE *Fall of Mogul* II. iv. 53 Relentless as the tropic whirlwind's rage. **1855** KINGSLEY *Westw. Ho!* xxv, The rapid tropic vegetation has reclaimed its old domains. **1875** BENNETT & DYER *Sachs' Bot.* 832 The vital conditions of all plants growing at a great elevation and in Arctic countries must be different from those growing in the lowlands of the Tropic and Temperate zones.

b. *fig.* = TROPICAL 2 c.

[**1802** WORDSW. *Sonn.*, '*We had a female Passenger*' 10 Yet still her [a negro's] eyes retained their tropic fire.] **1887** *Daily News* 29 June 5/2 Spring completely lost its way..and it was winter,..till this tropic time came upon us unawares.

3. a. tropic bird, any bird of the family *Phaethontidæ*, comprising sea-birds resembling terns, widely found in tropical regions, and characterized by webbed feet, rapid flight, and varied coloration.

1681 GREW *Musæum* I. IV. iii. 74 The Tropick Bird. So called because said never to be seen but between the Tropicks. **1756** P. BROWNE *Jamaica* 482 The Tropic Bird.. breeds on the most desolate rocks and lonely places and is seldom seen near any inhabited shores. **1825** WATERTON *Wand. S. Amer.* II. (1903) 64 Sometimes..the tropic bird comes near enough to let you have a fair view of the long feathers in his tail. **1896** NEWTON *Dict. Birds* 990 The Yellow-billed Tropic-bird, *P[haethon] flavirostris. Ibid.* 991 The Red-tailed Tropic-bird, *P. rubricauda* or *phœnicurus*.

b. tropic crow: see quot.

1781 LATHAM *Synopsis Birds* I. I. 384 Tropic [1809 SHAW, Tropical] Crow. Length twelve inches and a half..From O-wy-hee..in the South Seas.

c. tropic grape, the gulf-weed: = SEAGRAPE 6.

1850 MISS PRATT *Comm. Things Sea-side* ii. 111 The Seagrape is an olive-green weed, with long slender leaves, and berries about as large as a pea, from which it derived its name of Tropic Grape. **1852** TH. ROSS *Humboldt's Trav.* I. iii. 129 To the north of the Cape Verd Islands we met with great masses of floating seaweeds. They were the tropic grape (*Fucus natans*), which grows..only from the equator to the fortieth degree of north and south latitude.

II. 4. Also with pronunc. (ˈtrəʊpɪk). **a.** *Biol.* [Properly the second element of GEOTROPIC, HELIOTROPIC, etc. used as an inclusive or generic term (cf. -TROPIC, TROPISM).] Pertaining to, consisting in, or exhibiting tropism.

1903 T. H. MORGAN *Evol. & Adapt.* xi. 399 Another instinct, that appears to be due to a tropic response, is the definite time of day at which some marine animals deposit their eggs.

b. Of a hormone: = TROPHIC *a.* 3.

1955 R. M. DE COURSEY *Human Organism* xviii. 433 The hypophysis or pituitary gland has been called the master gland of all the endocrines because through its tropic hormones it exerts a regulatory effect over the activity of other endocrine glands. **1965** LEE & KNOWLES *Animal Hormones* ii. 19 The hormones secreted by the adenohypophysis may be divided into those which control the secretion of other endocrine glands and are named trophic (or tropic) hormones; the remainder act without the mediation of another endocrine gland. **1982** *Jrnl. Clinical Endocrinol. & Metabolism* LIV. 367/1 Rates of [^{14}C]acetate incorporation into steroids are increased by tropic hormones.

ˈtropic, *a.*[2] *Chem.* [Arbitrarily formed from ATROPIC: cf. TROPINE.] In ***tropic acid***, an acid forming a constituent of atropine.

1881 WATTS *Dict. Chem.* VIII. 2062 *Tropic acid*, $C^9H^{10}O^3$ = $CH^2(OH).CH(C^6H^5).CO^2H$. This acid, one of the proximate constituents of atropine, has lately been prepared synthetically from atropic acid. **1882** *Nature* 2 Feb. 315/1 By decomposing atropine he obtained tropic acid and tropine, and by recombining these products he again formed atropine.

-tropic (ˈtrɒpɪk, ˈtrəʊpɪk), *suffix.* [f. Gr. τροπή turning (sb.) + -IC.] Forming adjs. with the senses: (*a*) 'turning or attracted towards', as in GEOTROPIC, HELIOTROPIC, SYMPATHICOTROPIC *adjs.*; (*b*) 'affecting', as in NEUROTROPIC, PSYCHOTROPIC *adjs.* (in epithets of hormones used interchangeably with -TROPHIC, q.v.).

tropical (ˈtrɒpɪkəl), *a.* and *sb. pl.* [f. as TROPIC *a.*[1] + -AL[1]. Cf. mod.F. *tropical.*]

A. *adj.* **1.** *Astr.* Pertaining or relating to the tropics, or either tropic (in sense A. 1 a or b). Chiefly in ***tropical year***, the interval between two successive passages of the sun through the same 'tropic' or solstitial point (or, equivalently, through the same equinoctial point); the natural year of the seasons, as reckoned from one (winter or summer) solstice or (vernal or autumnal) equinox to the next. So ***tropical month***, the time taken by the moon in passing from either tropic (or either equinoctial point) to the same again.

1527 R. THORNE in Hakluyt *Voy.* (1589) 252 The quantitie of the earth vnder the Equinoctiall to both the Tropicall lines. **1594** BLUNDEVIL *Exerc.* III. I. xxxviii. (1636) 353 The Astronomicall yeere is either Tropicall or Syderall. **1662** STANLEY *Hist. Chaldaic Philos.* (1701) 17/2 Tropical [signs] are those to which when the Sun cometh he turneth back. **1715** tr. *Gregory's Astron.* (1726) I. 408 The Tropical Year is that space of time wherein the same Seasons of the Year return again. **1812** WOODHOUSE *Astron.* xxxi. 305 The tropical revolution of the Moon, or the revolution with respect to the equinoxes. **1834** *Nat. Philos.* III. *Astron.* i. 41/1 (Usef. Knowl. Soc.) The year from equinox to equinox is called the equinoctial year, or sometimes the tropical year. **1868** LOCKYER *Elem. Astron.* v. (1879) 203 The tropical month is the revolution of the moon with respect to the moveable equinox.

2. a. *Geog.* Pertaining to, occurring in, or inhabiting the tropics; belonging to the torrid zone.

1698 FROGER *Voy.* 3 At three o'clock in the morning we passed the tropick of Cancer;..and in the afternoon performed the ceremonies of Tropical baptism or duckings, which are commonly us'd by mariners in those places. **1699** DAMPIER *Voy.* II. I. ii. 33 Many reasons..beside the accidental ones from the make of the particular Countries, Tropical Winds, or the like. *a* **1700** SALMON (J.), The pine-apple is one of the tropical fruits. **1788** GIBBON *Decl. & F.* l. (1846) V. 2 The face of the desert..is scorched by the direct and intense rays of a tropical sun. **1851** CARPENTER *Man. Phys.* (ed. 2) 67 The highest temperature which the soil usually possesses in tropical climates, is about 126°. **1862** DANA *Man. Geol.* 615 Coral formations are most abundant in the tropical Pacific. **1880** HAUGHTON *Phys. Geog.* vi. 272 The second and third of the sub-orders are confined to the tropical forests of South America.

b. *Path.* Applied to diseases to which one is liable in tropical regions.

1828 WEBSTER, *Tropical.* 2. Incident to the tropics; as, tropical diseases. **1843** R. J. GRAVES *Syst. Clin. Med.* xi. 118 [Salivation] has been also very extensively recommended by army and navy surgeons, in the treatment of tropical fevers. **1893** A. DAVIDSON *Hygiene & Dis. Warm Climates* xvii. 613 Tropical Liver. **1905** *Daily Chron.* 9 Oct. 5/3 The notorious disease known in Germany as 'tropencholer', or tropical frenzy. **1934** *Discovery* July 207/1 The practical certainty of infection from tropical anaemia or 'hookworm'. **1944** *Living off Land* v. 101 The most insignificant scratch or wound should be tended carefully—it might cause immediate infection and numerous large tropical sores. **1969** EDINGTON & GILLES *Path. in Tropics* x. 435 Tropical splenomegaly syndrome may in some patients end up in lymphosarcoma. **1974** Tropical bubo [see LYMPHOGRANULOMA]. **1980** F. A. NWAKO *Textbk. Paediatric Surg. in Tropics* lxv. 368/1 The acute tropical ulcer may be complicated by tetanus and gas-gangrene.

c. *fig.* Like the climate or growth of the tropics; very hot, ardent, or luxuriant.

1834 *Tait's Mag.* I. 383/1 Home he came, after an absence of fifty years, in a hissing hot fit of tropical rage. **1850** S. DOBELL *Roman* vi. Poet. Wks. (1875) 85 My fierce and tropical fancy, Hot with swift pulses. **1880** 'OUIDA' *Moths* I. 174 We Russians have a passion for tropical houses. *Mod.* The heat was perfectly tropical.

d. Of clothing, fabric, etc.: suitable for wearing or using in hot climates; lightweight and porous; also more fully ***tropical weight***. Of a (weight of) fabric freq. in *attrib.* use.

1792 W. BLIGH *Voy. to South Sea* ii. 26, I gave orders for their light tropical clothing to be put by, and made them dress in a manner more suited to a cold climate. **1920** W. J. LOCKE *House of Baltazar* x. 121 The tropical drill material which had clothed the troops in Hong Kong. **1924** R. MACAULAY *Orphan Island* ii. 31 [We] can be ready in a fortnight. It will take us about that to get our tropical outfit. **1925** in C. Allen *Tales from Dark Continent* (1979) iii. 43 Tropical weight dress coat. **1931** E. WAUGH *Remote People* 150 They dried themselves, combed their hair, put on smart tropical suits, and called for dinner. **1938** —— *Scoop* I. iii. 57 William had acquired..six suits of tropical linen. **1942** R. CHANDLER *High Window* iii. 24 A tropical worsted suit. **1945** E. WAUGH *Brideshead Revisited* II. i. 200, I discarded the experiences of those two years with my tropical kit. **1966** P. O'DONNELL *Sabre-Tooth* i. 8 He wore the tropical uniform of the United States Army. **1971** 'J. MAYO' *Asking for It* v. 18, I unpacked a cream shirt, my tropical-weight brown suit and put them on. **1972** 'W. HAGGARD' *Protectors* viii. 93 He wore a tropical suit and a spotted bow tie. **1978** L. BLOCK *Burglar in Closet* i. 4 My suit was a tropical worsted. **1981** G. MACBETH *Kind of Treason* xviii. 178 Mountbatten..was.. in immaculate tropical kit.

3. *Zool.* (transf. from 1 or 2.) Used to describe the position of certain spines in the skeleton of some radiolarians: see quot.

1888 ROLLESTON & JACKSON *Anim. Life* 874 *note*, Imagine a globe with an axis of rotation, and five circles inscribed on it, an equatorial, two tropical and two polar. The twenty spines lie four in each of these circles, the equatorial and polar spines in the same meridian lines,..the tropical in meridian lines exactly intermediate.

4. Pertaining to, involving, or of the nature of a trope or tropes; metaphorical, figurative.

1567 MAPLET *Gr. Forest* 97 To sende ouer Owles to Athens. In Tropicall sense, ment of such as bestow largely vpon them that haue no neede. **1620** T. GRANGER *Div. Logike* 19 Whether the words bee plaine, and proper, or tropicall, and figuratiue. **1646** SIR T. BROWNE *Pseud. Ep.* III. iii. 111 A strict and literall acception of a loose and tropicall expression. **1725** WATTS *Logic* I. iv. §7 They are used in a figurative or tropical Sense, when they are made to signify some things, which only bear either a Reference or a Resemblance to the primary Ideas of them. **1819** G. S. FABER *Dispensations* (1823) II. II. v. 190 The great sheet let down from heaven was as perfect a tropical hieroglyphic as any invented by the ingenuity of Moses. **1862** H. SPENCER *First Princ.* xv. (1875) 349 These [writings] had been partially differentiated into the kuriological or imitative, and the tropical or symbolic.

5. *Math.* ? Relating to the number of values of a function corresponding to one value of the variable.

1887 CAYLEY *Math. Papers* XII. 433 We wish to know whether *u* is a monotropic function of *z*. It will not be so if we have a tropical point,..such that [etc.].

B. *sb. pl.* Tropical clothes (see sense A. 2 d above).

1934 G. B. SHAW *Too True to be Good* III. 85 Aubrey, in white tropicals, comes strolling along the beach. **1980** J. HONE *Flowers of Forest* III. i. 221 Dressed in immaculate linen tropicals and some kind of old boy's tie.

tropicalian (trɒpɪˈkeɪlɪən), *a.* *Zoogeog.* [f. mod.L. *Tropicalia* (f. Gr. τροπικός tropic + ἅλς sea) + -AN.] Belonging to the marine region called *Tropicalia*, comprising the seas between the isocrymes of 68° F. on each side of the equator.

1888 *Proc. Biol. Soc. Washington* II. 34 (Cass. Supp.) Generic and specific modifications of the Arctalian and Tropicalian realms.

tropicalize (ˈtrɒpɪkəlaɪz), *v.* Chiefly in *pass.* or as *pa. pple.* ˈtropicalized. [f. TROPICAL + -IZE.]

1. *trans.* To make tropical; to give a tropical character to.

1885 LADY BRASSEY *The Trades* 125 Vegetation not unlike a patch of British fern suddenly transferred to a temperature of about fifty degrees above what it is accustomed to,—and thus, as it were 'tropicalised'. **1888** *Harper's Mag.* Sept. 616 The architecture is a tropicalized Swiss style.

2. To make suitable for use under tropical conditions.

1941 W. S. CHURCHILL *Second World War* (1950) III. 760 The German tanks recently captured by the Tobruk garrison... Are they tropicalised, desert-worthy, and fitted for use in the very hot weather? **1947** *Short Wave Mag.* V. 234/1 All components are tropicalised. **1972** *Daily Tel.*

(Colour Suppl.) 20 Oct. 50 All the woodwork in a Rolls..is 'tropicalised' by three coats of lacquer making it impervious to changes in temperature and humidity. **1978** *Gramophone* Jan. 1335/3 The massive mains transformer is fully tropicalized and the primary winding is adjustable for input voltages of 110–120 and 220–240V AC. **1981** *Hi-Fi Answers* Jan. 7/2 The manufacturer of the British amplifier made a 'Point' of claiming that his equipment had been tropicalised.

Hence ˌ**tropicaliˈzation**.

1944 *Sun* (Baltimore) 24 Sept. 5/4 For a year past our modern battleships have been undergoing a further measure of modernization and tropicalization to meet the rapid wartime changes in technical apparatus. **1980** *Nature* 7 Feb. p. xii/1 Virtually any required type of impregnation, tropicalisation, potting or moulding (in epoxy, polyester or polyurethane) can be supplied.

tropically (ˈtrɒpɪkəlɪ), *adv.* [f. as prec. + -LY².] In a tropical manner.

1. In the way of a trope; metaphorically, figuratively.

1564 J. RASTELL *Confut. Jewell's Serm.* 140 The body of Christ is, onlye figuratiuelye,..tropicallie, imaginatiuelie, in the Sacrament. **1602** SHAKS. *Ham.* III. ii. 247 *King.* What do you call the Play? *Ham.* The Mouse-trap: Marry how? Tropically. **1646** SIR T. BROWNE *Pseud. Ep.* III. iii. 111 Spanish Mares, whose swiftnesse [is] tropically expressed from their generation by the wind. *a* **1703** BURKITT *On N.T.* Gal. v. 24 The work of mortification (called here tropically, a crucifixion). **1809** W. IRVING *Knickerb.* v. ix. (1849) 302 It is tropically observed by honest old Socrates, that heaven infuses into some men..a portion of intellectual gold. **1879** R. T. SMITH *St. Basil* 91 There are multitudes of expressions applied in Scripture to God, which we agree are to be tropically taken.

2. In a way characteristic of the tropics; with tropical heat, luxuriance, or violence.

1852 HAWTHORNE *Blithedale Rom.* xvii. (1885) 173 The sunshine lay tropically there. **1886** *Pall Mall G.* 10 June 9/1 The rain..continues, although not quite so tropically. **1896** *Academy* 11 July 27/1 Hume's tropically coloured account of what..he called 'the Irish rebellion'.

tropicana (trɒpɪˈkɑːnə), *sb. pl.* [f. TROPIC *sb.* and *a.*¹ + ANA *suff.*] Things associated with or characteristic of tropical regions; objects from the tropics.

1960 *Spectator* 1 July 12/2 Cockfighting is part of the exotic tropicana Haiti offers to American tourists. **1969** 'G. BLACK' *Cold Jungle* xii. 165 An astonishing display of tropicana, palms, bamboo, a couple of flame trees. **1976** *Listener* 29 Jan. 121/3 'That slice of the mind which is pure tropicana'—a mixture of Kipling and Maugham.

tropicopolitan (ˌtrɒpɪkəʊˈpɒlɪtən), *a. Nat. Hist.* [f. TROPIC, after COSMOPOLITAN.] Belonging to or inhabiting the whole of the tropics, or tropical regions generally.

1878 P. L. SCLATER in *19th Cent.* Dec. 1050 'Tropicopolitan' forms, by which I mean tropical forms that are found in the tropics of both hemispheres. **1879** A. R. WALLACE *ibid.* Feb. 254 The tropical land..which afforded the passage of the tropicopolitan forms from one continent to the other. **1895** C. DIXON in *Fortn. Rev.* Apr. 652 We have many tropicopolitan families that are confined absolutely to the great equatorial zone round the entire earth.

tropidial (trəʊˈpɪdɪəl), *a. Zool.* [f. Gr. τρόπις, τροπιδ- keel + -IAL.] Pertaining to the *tropis* or keel of a C-shaped sponge-spicule.

1887 SOLLAS in *Encycl. Brit.* XXII. 418/1 (*Sponges*) The pterocymba is subject to considerable modifications;..the pteres may be lamellar or ungual; additional lamellæ (tropidial pteres) may be produced by a lateral outgrowth of the keel.

tropidine (ˈtrɒpɪdaɪn). *Chem.* [Arbitrary formation from TROPINE.] A colourless oily alkaloid obtained from tropine by the action of acids. So **troˈpilidine**, a liquid hydrocarbon, C_7H_8, obtained by the dry distillation of tropine with quicklime (Webster, 1911).

1883 *Science* 11 May 401/2 When distilled with soda-lime, tropine is decomposed, giving methylamine and tropilidine (C_7H_8); and, when treated with fuming hydrochloric acid, a volatile base, tropidine ($C_8H_{13}N$), is formed. **1890** BILLINGS *Med. Dict.*, *Tropidine*, $C_8H_{13}N$, a liquid basic substance obtained from tropine by heating with strong hydrochloric acid in a sealed tube.

tropidosternal (ˌtrɒpɪdəʊˈstɜːnəl), *a. Ornith.* [f. mod.L. *Tropidosterni* pl. (f. Gr. τρόπις, -ιδ- keel + στέρνον, L. *sternum* breast-bone) + -AL¹.] Belonging to the division *Tropidosterni* (= *Carinatæ*) of birds; having a keeled breast-bone.

In recent Dicts.

tropilidine: see TROPIDINE.

tropine (ˈtrəʊpaɪn). *Chem.* [Arbitrarily formed from ATROPINE.] An alkaloid forming a constituent of atropine.

1881 WATTS *Dict. Chem.* VIII. 2062 *Tropine*, $C^8H^{15}NO$. This base, which Kraut obtained, together with atropic acid, by the action of baryta-water on atropine, may also be extracted..from the residues of the preparation of atropine.

troping (ˈtrəʊpɪŋ). [f. TROPE *sb.* + -ING¹.]

a. Figurative or metaphorical speech or conversation. **b.** The composition or use of tropes (sense 5).

1678 DRYDEN *Kind Keeper* v. i, Will you leave your Troping, and let me pass? **1907** J. M. MANLY in *Mod. Philol.* IV. 593 It was an age of troping. Tropes—that is, insertions in the authorized liturgy—were composed by the hundreds, and of all conceivable varieties.

‖**tropis** (ˈtrəʊpɪs). *Zool.* Pl. **tropides** (ˈtrɒpɪdiːz). [mod.L., a. Gr. τρόπις keel.] The 'keel' or middle part of a *cymba* or C-shaped sponge-spicule, between the *proræ* or 'prows'.

1887 SOLLAS in *Encycl. Brit.* XXII. 471/2 (*Sponges*) A truly C-shaped spicule... The back of the 'C' is the keel or *tropis*; the points are the prows or *proræ*.

tropism (ˈtrɒpɪz(ə)m, ˈtrəʊpɪz(ə)m). *Biol.* [The second element of HELIOTROPISM, GEOTROPISM, etc., used as an inclusive or generic term.] The turning of an organism, or a part of one, in a particular direction (either in the way of growth, bending, or locomotion) in response to some special external stimulus, as that of light (*phototropism, heliotropism*), heat (*thermotropism*), gravity (*geotropism*), etc.

1899 C. B. DAVENPORT *Morphology* II. 480 All cases of true tropism are cases of response to stimuli: such are chemotropism, hydrotropism, thigmotropism, traumatropism, rheotropism, geotropism, electrotropism, phototropism and thermotropism. **1909** J. W. JENKINSON *Experim. Embryol.* 273 The outgrowth and anastomoses of nerves, glands, ducts, the concrescence of layers may be tropisms of various sorts.

tropist (ˈtrəʊpɪst). *rare*⁻⁰. [f. as TROPE *sb.* + -IST; cf. F. *tropiste* (Calvin, 1560).] **a.** A member of a sect who interpreted Scripture or some passage of Scripture in the way of trope or metaphor: see TROPIC *sb.* 3. **b.** One who deals in tropes or metaphors.

1727–41 CHAMBERS *Cycl.*, *Tropists*, or *Tropici*, the name of a sect... The reason of the name tropist was that they explained the scripture altogether by tropes and figures of speech... The Romanists also give the appellation tropists to those of the reformed religion, in regard of their construing the words of the eucharist figuratively. **1775** ASH, *Tropist*, one who deals in tropes, one who explains the scriptures by tropes and figures.

tropistic (trəʊˈpɪstɪk), *a. Biol.* [f. TROPISM: see -ISTIC.] Pertaining to or constituting tropism. Hence **troˈpistically** *adv.* [see -ICALLY], in the way of tropism.

1910 F. KEEBLE *Plant-Anim.* ii. 41 We may use the term tropistic to describe the reactions of both fixed and free organisms to directive stimuli. *Ibid.* 52 Responding tropistically to unilateral light.

trople, variant of TROPEL *Obs.*

tropo (ˈtrəʊpəʊ), colloq. abbrev. of TROPOSCATTER.

1966 [see BILL-BOARD, BILLBOARD 2]. **1976** *Offshore Engineer* July 5/1 There is little hope of a similar development in the UK sector, since the Post Office has provided the tropo facility and would be reluctant to offer an alternative.

tropo-, combining form repr. Gr. τρόπος turning, etc. (see TROPE *sb.*), occurring in a few modern technical terms. **tropoˈcollagen** (trəʊ-) *Biochem.* [so called from its being able to turn into collagen], the molecular constituent of collagen fibrils, formed of three supercoiled polypeptide chains; **tropometer** (trəʊˈpɒmɪtə(r)) [-METER], an instrument for measuring the angle of turning or torsion of some part of the body, as the eye-ball or a long bone; **tropophil** (ˈtrɒpəʊfɪl), **tropophilous** (trəʊˈpɒfɪləs) *adjs.* [Gr. -φιλος loving], applied to a plant adapted to a climate which is alternately moist and dry (or cold, the physiological effect of cold being similar to that of dryness); so **tropophyte** (ˈtrɒpəʊfaɪt) [Gr. φυτόν plant], a tropophilous plant; whence **tropophytic** (-ˈfɪtɪk) *a.*; **tropo-stereoscope** (trɒpəʊˈsterɪəʊˌskəʊp), a stereoscope with an arrangement for rotating the figures so as to bring them into some required position, in experiments on vision; **tropoˈtaxis** (trəʊ-) *Biol.* [mod.L., coined in Ger. (A. Kühn *Die Orientierung der Tiere im Raum* (1919) 60)], a taxis in which an animal's movement is in response to the difference in stimulation of two symmetrically placed receptors; hence **tropoˈtactic** *a.*, **-ˈtactically** *adv.*

1954 J. GROSS et al. in *Proc. Nat. Acad. Sci.* XL. 679 We adopted the term '*tropocollagen' to denote the thin, long particles. *Ibid.*, In the present paper is summarized the evidence..that the various morphologically distinguishable forms of collagen are mutually interconvertible and that the unit of collagen structure involved in these changes of aggregation is the tropocollagen particle. **1971** *Nature* 16 Apr. 437/1 It is usually accepted that collagen is composed of tropocollagen molecules 2900 Å long, 15 Å wide. **1982** J. F. VAN PILSUM in T. M. Devlin *Textbk. Biochem.* xxi. 1050 The above classifications of collagens are based on the amino acid sequence and composition of the peptide chains in the tropocollagen molecule. **1881** *Athenæum* 11 June 787/1 The *tropometer, an instrument for measuring the angle of torsion of the humerus. **1902** I. B. BALFOUR in *Encycl. Brit.* XXV. 439/2 Parasitism..occurs in..*tropophil woods of temperate regions, and alpine slopes. **1900** B. D. JACKSON *Gloss. Bot. Terms*, **Tropophilous*,..loving change of condition, as Tropophytes. **1903** tr. *Schimper's Plant-Geog.* I. i. 21 The vegetation of districts with climates alternately damp and dry or cold, is alternately of a hygrophilous and of a xerophilous character; it is therefore tropophilous. **1900** B. D. JACKSON *Gloss. Bot. Terms*, **Tropophyte*. **1903** tr. *Schimper's Plant-Geog.* I. i. 3 It appears..necessary to place in a third category all plants whose conditions of life are, according to the season of the year, alternately those of hygrophytes or of xerophytes. All such plants, including..the great majority of the plants composing the Central European flora, should be termed tropophytes. *Ibid.*, There are hygrophytic, xerophytic, and *tropophytic climates. **1901** TITCHENER *Exper. Psychol.* I. II. 272 Ludwig's *tropostereoscope..is..a refined form of the tube stereoscope. **1940** FRAENKEL & GUNN *Orientation of Animals* vii. 89 Arthropods..are, above all, the animals which have eyes suitable for *tropo-tactic behaviour. **1979** *Experientia* XXXV. 1457/1 Widely separated nares..would appear to be an adaptation for tropotactic olfactory perception. **1940** FRAENKEL & GUNN *Orientation of Animals* vii. 78 The paired receptors of an animal which behaves *tropotactically have been compared with the paired reins of a horse. **1934** *Tropotaxis [see TELOTAXIS]. **1979** *Experientia* XXXV. 1457/2 Tubenosed fruit bats locate ripe fruit from among unripe fruit by olfaction, and since detection..has to be made while on the wing, it seems likely that tropotaxis is beneficial.

†ˌ**tropoloˈgetically**, *adv. Obs. rare*⁻¹. [Extended form of TROPOLOGICALLY, after *apologetically*.] = TROPOLOGICALLY 1.

1652 URQUHART *Jewel* Wks. (1834) 292, I could have enlarged this discourse..tropologetically, by metonymical, ironical, metaphorical and synecdochical instruments of elocution.

tropologic (trɒpəˈlɒdʒɪk), *a.* [ad. late L. *tropologicus* (Jerome, *a* 400), = late Gr. τροπολογικός (*c* 1160), f. τρόπος trope: see -LOGIC. Cf. F. *tropologique* (Godef. *Compl.*).] = next (in either sense).

c **1380** WYCLIF *Sel. Wks.* II. 277 Þe þridde witt is tropologik, þat bitokeneþ witt of vertues. **1388** — *Gen. Prol. Bks. Proph.* 226 Moral ether tropologik [vndurstondyng of scripture] techith what we owen to do to fle vices, and kepe vertues. **1677** GALE *Crt. Gentiles* II. III. 153 These mystic Divines glorie in their Tropologic, Anagogic and Allegoric explication of Scripture: Neither is there any so plain, literal, or historic, but they have some tropologic or mystic sense for it. **1884** *Expositor* Jan. 45 The three traditional divisions of the mystic sense into allegoric, tropologic or moral, and anagogic or spiritual.

tropological (trɒpəʊˈlɒdʒɪkəl), *a.* [f. as prec. + -AL¹.] Belonging to or involving tropology.

1. Metaphorical, figurative: = TROPICAL 4.

1555 EDEN *Decades* 44 *margin*, Here nedeth sum tropologicall interpretour. **1621** BURTON *Anat. Mel.* III. iv. I. iii. (1628) 607 Tropological, allegorical expositions, to salve all appearances. **1862** NEALE *Hymns East. Ch.* 24 The ingenuity of some tropological applications.

2. Applied to a secondary sense or interpretation of Scripture, relating or applied to conduct or morals.

1528 TINDALE *Obed. Chr. Man* 129 They devide yᵉ scripture in to iiij senses, yᵉ literall, tropologicall, allegoricall, anagogicall. **1607** R. C[AREW] tr. *Estienne's World of Wonders* 255 To reduce all they haue to say, to certaine Allegoricall, Anagogicall, and Tropologicall senses. **1734** WATERLAND *Doctr. Trinity* vii. §6. 438 Such a kind of Exercise I take many of those Allegorical Comments (Those especially of the Tropological kind) to have been. **1882–3** *Schaff's Encycl. Relig. Knowl.* I. 784 The moral, or tropological [sense of Scripture] teaches what to do.

tropoˈlogically, *adv.* [f. prec. + -LY².] In a tropological manner (in either sense of the adj.).

1549 CHALONER *Erasm. Praise Folly* N iv b, Moralisyng the same bothe Allegorically, Tropologically, and Anegogically. **1678** CUDWORTH *Intell. Syst.* I. iv. §32. 512 This was the General opinion concerning the Greekish Fables, that some of them were Physically, and some Tropologically Allegorical. **1730** WATERLAND *Script. Vind.* Pref. 18 The Law about the Sabbath..may be supposed..tropologically to denote the Rest of the Soul and its Cessation from Sin. **1888** SCHAFF *Hist. Chr. Ch.* VI. I. xxxii. 139 Jerusalem means..allegorically the good, tropologically virtue, anagogically reward.

tropologize (trəʊˈpɒlədʒaɪz), *v. rare*⁻¹. [f. as TROPOLOGY + -IZE.] *trans.* To convert by a trope or metaphor; to use in a tropological sense.

1678 CUDWORTH *Intell. Syst.* I. iv. §33. 520 If Athena or Minerva be tropologized into Prudence, then let the Pagans show what substantial essence it hath, or that it really subsists according to their tropology.

tropology (trəʊˈpɒlədʒɪ). [ad. late L. *tropologia* (Jerome, *a* 400), a. late Gr. τροπολογία (Justin Martyr, *a* 160), f. τρόπος trope: see -LOGY. Cf. F. *tropologie* (*a* 1300 in Godef. *Compl.*).]

1. 'A speaking by tropes' (Blount, 1656); the use of metaphor in speech or writing; figurative discourse.

1519 HORMAN *Vulg.* 98 b, The figuris of construction and locucion: and specially allygoris: and tropologies: & anagogies. **1613** PURCHAS *Pilgrimage* (1614) 88 Those, that by Allegories and Tropologies peruert and obscure the Historie of their Gods. **1678** [see TROPOLOGIZE]. **1873** F. HALL *Mod. Eng.* vi. 170 But, whether due to tropology, or to whatever other cause, multivocals, as conducing to brevity and expressiveness, are unwisely condemned, or deprecated, except where they entail ambiguity.

2. A moral discourse; a secondary sense or interpretation of Scripture relating to morals (cf. TROPOLOGICAL 2).

1583 FULKE *Defence* 47, I can not, following both the storie, and the tropologie or doctrine of maners, comprehend both briefly. **1706** PHILLIPS (ed. Kersey), *Tropology*,.. a Moral Discourse tending to the Reformation of Manners. **1896** LINA ECKENSTEIN *Woman under Monast.* 113 The four-square pattern of ecclesiastical usage, namely according to the letter, allegory, tropology and anagogy.

3. A treatise on tropes or figures of speech.

a **1667** JER. TAYLOR *Serm.* Wks. 1831 IV. 160 Vocabularies, tropologies, and expositions of words and phrases. **1768** J. BROWN (*title*), Sacred Tropology.

tropolone ('trɒpələʊn). *Chem.* [f. TROP(ILIDINE + -OL + -ONE.] A water-soluble, colourless crystalline compound, $C_7H_6O_2$, which is an enolic ketone whose molecule is formed by a ring of seven carbon atoms and which is the parent of a series of compounds derived from various plants (as colchicine and the thujaplicins); also, any derivative of this.

1945 M. J. S. DEWAR in *Nature* 13 Jan. 51/1 If stipitatic acid actually has the resonating structure (I) or (II), it represents a new type of aromatic system; the parent *cyclo*heptatrienolone might be termed 'tropolone'. **1964** *New Scientist* 4 June 613/1 One group of compounds extracted [from timber], the tropolones, was found to be comparable in fungicidal effect to the synthetic fungicides. **1981** *Tetrahedron* XXXVII. Suppl. No. 9. 426/1 The 1,3,2-benzodioxaarsole ether of tropolone.. illustrates the possibility of modelling extremely rapid rearrangements.

tropometer: see TROPO-.

tropomyosin (trɒpəʊ-, trəʊpəʊ'maɪəsɪn). *Biochem.* [f. TROPO- + MYOSIN.] Any of a group of crystallizable proteins related to myosin; *esp.* one found together with troponin in the thin filaments of myofibrils which is instrumental in the mechanism of muscle contraction.

1946 K. BAILEY in *Nature* 23 Mar. 369/1 The exact relation of tropomyosin to myosin itself is equally obscure, but the analytical and structural similarities indicate that it is a species of myosin differing mainly in the length of the polypeptide chain. In proposing the present name, we have deemed it desirable to retain the word 'myosin' and to add a prefix which suggests this specific relationship. **1973** *Nature* 5 Oct. 235/3 The finding of non-muscle tropomyosins, of course, raises more questions than it answers. **1979** *Sci. Amer.* May 94 (*caption*) In muscle cells tropomyosin regulates the ability of actin filaments to form cross bridges with adjacent myosin filaments. **1982** J. F. VAN PILSUM in T. M. Devlin *Textbk. Biochem.* xxi. 1006 Tropomyosin is a rod-shaped molecule found associated with the actin filaments.

tropone ('trəʊpəʊn). *Chem.* [TROP(ILIDINE + -ONE.] A viscous hygroscopic oil, C_7H_6O, which is a cyclic ketone of aromatic character and of which tropolone is the hydroxylated derivative.

1951 *Jrnl. Amer. Chem. Soc.* LXXIII. 876/1 We wish to report the synthesis of 2,4,6-cycloheptatrien-1-one (tropone).. and evidence bearing on its aromatic character. **1981** *Jrnl. Org. Chem.* XLVI. 3575/1 The cycloadducts from 8-azaheptafulvenes and sulfenes, as well as those from tropone and arylsulfenes, readily undergo metalation.

troponin ('trəʊpənɪn, 'trɒ-). *Biochem.* [f. TROPO(MYOSIN + *-n-* + -IN[1].] A globular protein complex consisting of three subunits (*troponin C, I,* and *T*) which is related to and occurs with tropomyosin in the thin filaments of muscle tissue and is important in the mechanism of muscle contraction.

1966 EBASHI & KODAMA in *Jrnl. Biochem.* (Tokyo) LIX. 425/1 Tropomyosin-like protein, or 'native' tropomyosin.. has been shown to consist of two different proteins, *viz.*, tropomyosin of Bailey type and a globular protein promoting the aggregation of tropomyosin, named troponin. **1982** *Sci. Amer.* June 52/3 Troponin *c* is probably found only in cardiac and skeletal muscle; the troponinlike protein in other tissues is calmodulin.

tropopause ('trɒpə-, 'trəʊpəʊpɔːz). *Meteorol.* [f. TROPO(SPHERE + PAUSE *sb.*] The upper limit of the troposphere, separating it from the stratosphere, at which the lapse rate falls to zero.

1919 *Geophysical Mem.* (Meteorol. Office) No. 13. 59 The terms 'tropopause' and 'lapse-limit' have been suggested to denote the plane of cessation of the vertical temperature gradient. **1922** *Encycl. Brit.* XXXI. 930 In a cyclone the tropopause is low, in an anticyclone high. **1947, 1971** [see JET STREAM a]. **1982** *New Scientist* 17 June 788/1 Venus's tropopause.. is much higher than that of the Earth,.. some 70 kilometres above the Venusian surface.

tropophil to **tropophytic**: see TROPO-.

troposcatter ('trɒpəʊ-, 'trəʊpəʊskætə(r)). [f. TROPO(SPHERIC *a.* + SCATTER *sb.*] The scattering of radio waves by clouds and local variations in the troposphere so as to extend the range of radio communication.

1959 *Britannica Bk. of Year* 547/1 Tropo-scatter. **1962** *Aeroplane* 7 June 19/2 For VHF ground-air improvements the team suggested the investigation of mountain-top sites and tropo-scatter methods to provide better coverage. **1967** *Technology Week* 23 Jan. 45/1 (Advt.), The Pacific Scatter System.. uses ionoscatter, troposcatter, microwave, and vhf. **1976** *Times* 26 May 16/8 High levels of production of oil from the North Sea are dependent on advances in the use of troposcatter.

troposphere ('trɒpə-, 'trəʊpəʊsfɪə(r)). *Meteorol.* [f. TROPO- + SPHERE *sb.*] The lowest region of the atmosphere, extending to a height of 8 to 18 km. and marked by convection and a general decrease of temperature with height.

1914 *Q. Jrnl. R. Meteorol. Soc.* XL. 108 M. Teisserenc de Bort discovered that the atmosphere is divided into two parts, the troposphere, which extends from the surface to about 7 miles, and the stratosphere, which lies above. **1922** *Nature* 2 Feb. 141/1 In the lower layer, called the troposphere, the atmospheric gases are kept well mixed up by winds and convection. **1951** [see *exosphere* s.v. EXO-]. **1982** *New Scientist* 21 Jan. 151/1 Dust in the troposphere, the lowest layer of the atmosphere, is soon washed out by rain.

Hence **tropo'spheric** *a.*, of, pertaining to, or involving the troposphere; ***tropospheric scatter*** = TROPOSCATTER.

1939 *Proc. IRE* XXVII. 634 It is believed that most of the tropospheric reflections occur at air-mass boundaries or other similar discontinuities. **1955** *Ibid.* XLIII. 1336 (*heading*) Some tropospheric scatter propagation measurements near the radio horizon. **1966** *Electronics* 17 Oct. 137 The system.. is a wideband tropospheric scatter and microwave network consisting of 100 sites. It hops across the Mediterranean from the center of Spain to eastern Turkey, covering 6,000 miles and five nations. **1973** *Guardian* 18 May 18/5 With tropospheric fallout there is a steep rise in the level of iodine 131 in milk.

tropostereoscope to **tropotaxis**: see TROPO-.

troppo ('trɒpəʊ), *a. Austral. slang.* [f. TROPIC *sb.* and *a.*[1] + -O[2].] Mentally ill through spending too much time (orig. on war service) in the tropics; (hence simply) crazy, mad. Esp. in phr. ***to go troppo***.

1943 G. JOHNSTON *New Guinea Diary* 222 'A man must be going troppo,' he remarks quietly. **1958** R. STOW *To Islands* i. 19 'Terry thinks he's going troppo.' 'Troppo?' 'It's not in the Nurse's Encyclopaedia. Means going queer from being too long in the tropics.' **1968** S. L. ELLIOTT in E. Hanger *Three Austral. Plays* I. i. 33 Only fourteen months here and he's troppo... Know what he does this morning?.. Gets out of bed at reveille and goes off to shave with his spoon and fork. **1975** *Sun-Herald* (Sydney) 30 Nov. 131 Aunty Jack.. could bring a badly-needed fresh burst of local comedy (in a troppo way) to our screens.

tropylium (trə'pɪlɪəm). *Chem.* [f. TROP(OLONE + -YL + -IUM.] The cation $C_7H_7{}^+$ consisting of a ring of seven =CH− groups. Usu. *attrib.*

1954 *Jrnl. Amer. Chem. Soc.* LXXVI. 3204/2 The value.. indicates that the tropylium ion is about as strongly acidic as acetic acid when water is the reference base. **1982** T. W. G. SOLOMONS *Fund. Org. Chem.* xi. 375 Tropylium bromide, C_7H_7Br, is insoluble in nonpolar solvents but dissolves readily in water.

†**troque** (trəʊk). *Obs. rare.* [ad. L. *trochus*, a. Gr. τροχός: see TROCHE[2], TROCHUS.] A hoop: = TROCHUS 1.

1743 FRANCIS tr. *Hor., Odes* III. xxiv. 58 More skill'd in.. The whirling troque, or law-forbidden dice. **1746** —— *Art Poetry* 515 The bounding Ball, round Quoit, or whirling Troque.

tros, tross, trosse: see TRUSS.

trossers: see TROUSERS.

trost, trosty, obs. ff. TRUST, TRUSTY.

trostell, -yle, obs. ff. TRESTLE.

trot (trɒt), *sb.*[1] Also 3–7 trott, 5–6 trotte, 5–7 trote. [a. F. *trot* (12th c. in Godef. *Compl.*), verbal sb. of *trotter* to TROT.]

I. 1. a. A gait of a quadruped, originally of a horse, between walking and running, in which the legs move in diagonal pairs almost together, so that in a slow trot there is always one foot at least on the ground, but in a fast trot one pair leaves the ground before the other reaches it, all four feet being thus momentarily off the ground at once; hence applied to a similar gait of a man (or other biped), between a walk and a run.

a **1300** *Cursor M.* 15872 (Cott.) His [Christ's] hend þai band and ledd him forth, A-trott and noght þe pas [2 *MSS.* a-pas, a pas]. **13..** *E.E. Allit. P.* B. 976 Trynande ay a hyȝe trot þat torne neuer dorsten. *c* **1386** CHAUCER *Can. Yeom. Prol. & T.* 22 His hat heeng at his bak doun by a laas For he hadde riden moore than trot [*v.rr.* trote, trotte] or paas. *c* **1425** *Cast. Persev.* 3100 in *Marco Plays* 169 Now dagge we hens a dogge trot. *a* **1547** SURREY *Æneid* IV. 957 Redouble gan her nurse Her steppes, forth on an aged womans trot. **1590** BARWICK *Disc. Weapons* 9 b, They retired a soft trote: their enemies.. made after them with more speed. **1638** SIR T. HERBERT *Trav.* (ed. 2) 35 Our Chariot drawn by 2 Buffolls who by practise are nimble in their trot. **1737** BRACKEN *Farriery Impr.* (1757) II. Index s.v., A good Trot may be judged of by the Ear. **1755** JOHNSON, *Trot*, The jolting high pace of a horse. **1780** *Mirror* No. 92 A smart young man.. passed by in his carriage at a brisk trot. **1818** SCOTT *Rob Roy* v, His [a fox's] drooping brush, his soiled appearance, and jaded trot, proclaimed his fate impending. **1835** ALISON *Hist. Europe* (1849–50) V. xxviii. §3. 124 The pontoons arrived at a quick trot, from Dietikon. **1845** FORD *Handbk. Spain* I. 52 Their pace is the peculiar '*paso Castellano*', which is something more than a walk and less than a trot.

†**b.** An action of trotting; a journey or expedition on horseback. *Obs.*

a **1670** SPALDING *Troub. Chas. I* (1850) I. 186 The barronis.. rydis fra Turreff to New Abirdein,.. Thay plunder the laird of Kermok... The covenanteris, heiring of this trot of Turref.. began to hyde thair goodis. **1676** COTTON *Angler* II. ii. 22 I'le make as bold with your meat; for the Trot has got me a good stomach.

c. The sound of a horse, etc., trotting.

1858 CAPERN *Ball. & Songs* (1859) 138 The lime-team's trot, And milkmaid's carol.. Are the chief sounds. **1882** 'OUIDA' *In Maremma* I. 6 The trot of the chargers and the clash of the steel had passed into silence.

d. *transf.* and *fig.* Freq. in phr. ***on the trot***, (*a*) continually moving without intervals for rest; on the go; (*b*) in uninterrupted sequence, in succession; (*c*) on the run, escaping from confinement, etc.

a **1625** FLETCHER & MASS. *Custom of Country* IV. iv, Nor am I able to endure it longer,.. I am at my trot already. **1646** JENKYN *Remora* 28 Shall we go a dull Asses trot heavenward? **1697** DRYDEN *Virg.* Ded. (1721) I. 20 The Virtuoso's Saddle, which will be sure to amble, when the World is upon the hardest Trott. **1822** W. IRVING *Braceb. Hall* (1823) I. xiv. 103 One of those who eat and growl, and keep the waiter on the trot. **1892** G. MEREDITH *Poet. Wks.* (1912) 454 Away on the trot of thy servitude start. **1952** M. TRIPP *Faith is Windsock* vii. 106 Two kites on the trot with crook engines. **1956** *People* 13 May 13/5, I want to be between those posts again when Manchester City reach Wembley next year for the third time on the trot! **1958** M. PUGH *Wilderness of Monkeys* 176, I eloped with one of the boys and we went on the trot from the approved school. Then it came time for his National Service and he went on the trot from the Army. **1973** *Times* 12 Apr. 12/6 Bookmakers lost money for five weeks on the trot. **1982** G. LYALL *Conduct Major Maxim* ii. 16 'He's on the trot,' Maxim guessed. 'Oh *Christ*, Jim, you can get a district court for that, aiding a deserter.'

e. *the trots* († ***trot***), diarrhœa; also *fig. colloq.* Cf. RUN *sb.*[1] 14 f.

1808 E. WEETON *Let.* 10 June in *Jrnl. of Governess* (1969) I. 94, I should perhaps be running over to Mr. Ridyard's so *very* often, that ten to one my brother would be.. asking what was the matter with me that I was so *often hastily taken*; saying he was sure I was ill of the trot. **1904** in P. Fleming *Bayonets to Lhasa* (1961) xv. 205 He suffers continually from the trots (diarrhoea) which have completely shattered his nerves. **1936** J. G. COZZENS *Men & Brethren* II. 181, I often used to have to hot-foot it over to chapel—a kind of spiritual trots—and pray fervently. **1977** C. MCCULLOUGH *Thorn Birds* xi. 249 'Go easy on the water at first,' he advised. 'Beer won't give you the trots.'

2. A trotting-race. In *pl.* (*colloq.*, orig. *Austral.* and *N.Z.*), a series of trotting-races held at a fixed time on a regular course.

1856 *Porter's Spirit of Times* 25 Oct. 128/2 Nothing would have given the lovers of the trotting turf more pleasure than to witness a trot of three miles. **1891** *Auckland Star* 1 Oct. 8/6 Spring Meeting... Handicap Maiden Trot, of 40 sovs; second horse to receive 5 sovs from stakes... Selling Trot. .. Pony Trot Handicap. **1893** *Scott. Leader* 12 June 1 Grand Handicap Trot—First, £10; Second, £3; Third, £2. **1899** *Bulletin* (Sydney) 21 Jan. 24/2 At the recent big M.L. trots horses well-known this side carried off their full share of prize-money. **1905** A. C. RICE *Sandy* 215 Nelson wants the fellow to drive for him at the fall trots. **1934** T. WOOD *Cobbers* ii. 19 We're proud of the Trots in Perth. It's the best course in the world. **1959** *N.Z. Listener* 16 Jan. 14/4 An oddball like myself, wholly uninterested in racing, even night trots. **1968** *Globe & Mail* (Toronto) 17 Feb. 43 Sixth race—Trot, mile. Purse $3,000. **1976** *National Observer* (U.S.) 2 Oct. 7/1 He won the Empire Trot at Syracuse two weeks ago. **1977** *New Yorker* 19 Sept. 131/1 No doubt remembering the crush of more than forty thousand when the trots opened at Meadowlands a year ago, many people stayed away.

3. † ***Irish trot*** (*obs.*), ***Turkey trot***, names of dances. Also † ***shake a trot*** (*Sc. obs.*).

1549 *Compl. Scot.* vi. 66 In the fyrst, thai dancit al cristyn mennis dance, the northt of scotland, huntis vp,.. schaik a trot. **1652** *News fr. Lowe-Countr.* 7 The Scottish Jigg, the Irish Trot.

4. A toddling child; also, a small or young animal. *colloq.* Hence **'trottie**, a little toddling child.

1854 THACKERAY *Newcomes* x, Ethel romped with the little children—the rosy little trots—and took them on her knees, and told them a thousand stories. **1895** SKELTON *Table-Talk* iv. 72 Black, hairy little trots.. with their big bills and their big feet. **1905** *Contemp. Rev.* July 62 A practising school is maintained, partly of grave little trots from outside and partly of little boarders. **1924** 'L. MALET' *Dogs of Want* vii. §6 Darling girls, from the time when they were the tiniest trotties till now.

5. *U.S.* A literal translation of a text used by students; a 'crib'. Cf. HORSE *sb.* 13, PONY *sb.* 3. (*College slang.*)

1891 in *Cent. Dict.* **1924** P. MARKS *Plastic Age* 299 I'm talking about the copying of math problems and the using of trots. **1975** B. MEGGS *Matter of Paradise* (1976) VII. v. 173 Somebody suggested.. that he get a trot. An absolutely forbidden interlinear translation. The Latin on one line; the English right below it. **1984** *Times Lit. Suppl.* 27 Apr. 44/2 The translations are rarely better than lame trots.

6. *Austral. colloq.* A sequence, a succession, esp. in a game of chance; a run of luck of a specified kind. See 1 d above.

1911 L. STONE *Jonah* 216 A trot or succession of seven tails followed, and the kip changed hands rapidly. **1919** W. H. DOWNING *Digger Dialects* 51 *Trot*, an experience (e.g. 'a rough trot'; 'a bad time'). **1937** J. A. LEE *Civilian into Soldier* 99 Sometimes a man would succeed daringly, doubling up and breaking the ring with a long run of heads, 'throwing a trot'. **1949** L. GLASSOP *Lucky Palmer* 177 He was 'Lucky' Palmer, having a bad trot at the moment, admittedly, but still 'Lucky' Palmer. **1966** P. MATHERS *Trot* 90 He.. had had a tough trot, humped the bluey, been through it all. **1974** D. R. STUART *Prince of my Country* v. 33 He's had a damn good trot, old Marney.

II. 7. a. *Fishing.* (Perhaps a different word: cf. TRAT.) A long-line lightly anchored or buoyed, with baited hooks hung by short lines or snoods a few feet apart; a trawl-line; also called a *trot-line*; also, each of the short lines attached to this.

1858 [see *trot-line* in 8]. **1883** *Fisheries Exhib. Catal.* 10 Floating Trots and Spillers. **1884** *St. James's Gaz.* 18 Jan. 6/2 A 'trot' is a line some twenty yards long. **1886** R. C. LESLIE *Sea-painter's Log* x. 199 Much longer lines than the trots just described are used for flounders.

b. *Naut.* (See quot. 1976.)

1923 *Man. Seamanship* (Admiralty) II. 107 When several targets are secured in line to a trot, only the ends of the trot need be marked by lights. **1950** G. HACKFORTH-JONES *Worst Enemy* iii. 202 The old ship parted her moorings and drifted down on to a destroyer trot. I had to let go two Admiralty-pattern anchors that were last used in the Crimean War. **1976** *Oxf. Compan. Ships & Sea* 893/1 *Trot*, a multiple mooring for small boats or yachts. The base mooring is laid in a straight line and from it individual moorings rise at intervals spaced to allow the boats room to swing with the tide.

III. 8. *attrib.* and *Comb.* **trot-boat** (see quot. 1955); **trot-line** = sense 7; **trot-rope**, a rope securely pegged down at each end, on which runs a sliding ring to which a horse is tethered, enabling him to graze a strip the length of the rope (*Cent. Dict. Suppl.* 1909).

1945 'N. SHUTE' *Most Secret* vi. 124, I can get the *trot boat down each evening. **1955** *N. & Q.* Sept. 402/2 A 'trot-boat' is a boat of any size which makes routine visits to discharge or embark passengers, stores, etc., at ships secured to the buoys. **1826** 'NONIUS NONDESCRIPT' *The*—— 18 Feb. 10 As full of noozes and strings as a fisherman's *trot line. **1858** in A. E. Lee *Hist. Columbus, Ohio* (1892) I. 146 Father went down to the river to examine a trotline.

trot (trɒt), *sb.*[2] Forms: α. 4 **trate**, 4–6 **trat, tratte**; β. 6 **trott, trotte, trote**, (8 **trout**), 6– **trot**. [AF. *trote* occurs twice in Gower's French *Mirour de l'Omme*, ll. 8713 and 17900 ('la viele trote q'est jolie'), but the ME. instances have all *trat(e, tratte*, and the word has not been found in Continental French either as *trote* or *tratte*, so that the derivation is uncertain. It can hardly be connected with TROT *sb.*[1], or with OF. *baudetrot*, BAWDSTROT.] An old woman; usually disparaging: an old beldame, a hag.

α. *c* **1350** *Will. Palerne* 4769 þat þo tvo trattes þat William wold haue traysted. *c* **1380** *Sir Ferumb.* 1370 þan ful doun þat olde trate in-to þe salte see. *c* **1460** *Towneley Myst.* xvi. 394 Gett out of thise wonys! ye trattys, all at onys. **1513** DOUGLAS *Æneis* IV. xi. 114 Thus said Dido; and the tother, with that, Hichit on furth with slaw pase lyke ane trat. **1570** LEVINS *Manip.* 37/14 A tratte, *anus*.

β. **1530** PALSGR. 642/1 Se yonder olde trot howe she mumbleth, *auisez ceste vielle* [etc.]. **1596** SHAKS. *Tam. Shr.* I. ii. 79 Marrie him to a Puppet or an Aglet babie, or an old trot with ne're a tooth in her head. **1598** DRAYTON *Heroic. Ep.* xiii. 105 And call me, Beldam, Gib, Witch, Night-mare, Trot, With all despight that may a Woman spot. **1654** WHITLOCK *Zootomia* 78 An old Trot (that boasted of her Giftishnesse in Waterology). **1719** D'URFEY *Pills* V. 74 You are.. A fulsome Trot and good for nought. *a* **1845** HOOD *Forget-me-nots* ii, Some strange, neglectful, gossiping old Trot. **1906** E. V. LUCAS *Listener's Lure* (1910) 282 Miss Graham got an old trot after a good deal of messing about.

Trot (trɒt), *sb.*[3] and *a.* Colloq. abbrev. of TROTSKYIST *sb.* and *a.*, TROTSKYITE *a.* and *sb.*

1962 D. LESSING *Golden Notebk.* IV. 451, I was a hundred per cent party member, and there was Harry, a dirty Trot, so there were high words and we parted for ever. **1970** G. GREER *Female Eunuch* 22 The most telling criticisms will come from my sisters of the left, the Maoists, the Trots. **1976** *Times* 29 Dec. 8/8 A true Trot ought to believe in worldwide revolution. **1983** 'J. LE CARRÉ' *Little Drummer Girl* iv. 80 Some kind of loony Trot splinter group.

trot (trɒt), *v.* Forms: see TROT *sb.*[1]; also 5 **tret**. [ME. a. OF. *troter* (12th c. in Hatz.-Darm.), F. *trotter* (Prov., Sp., Pg. *trotar*, It. *trottare*) to TROT. A med.L. deriv. *trottare* appears *c* 1150 in Thesaurus of Thomas.]

I. 1. *intr.* Of a horse, and occasionally other quadrupeds: To go at the gait called the trot (see TROT *sb.*[1] 1). Also said of a man.

to trot all (see ALL C. 4), *altogether* (ALTOGETHER B. 2), *high* (HIGH *adv.* 1 b), *large* (LARGE B. 6), *rough* (ROUGH *adv.* 1), *short* (SHORT C. 4); *to trot out*, to trot with extended action (opposed to *trot short*).

1362 LANGL. *P. Pl.* A. II. 135 Fauuel fette forþ Foles of þe beste, And sette.. fals on a sysoures backe þat softly trotted. *c* **1386** CHAUCER *Merch. T.* 294 No man fynden shal Noon in this world, that trotteth [*v.r.* (*Petw. MS.*) treteþ] hool in al Ne man ne beest. *c* **1410** *Master of Game* (MS. Digby 182) iv, Somtyme þei [roe-deer] trotteth and goth a paas. **14..** *Beryn* 939 As hors þat evir trottid.. It were hard to make hym aftir to ambill well. *c* **1450** *Merlin* 279 A Curroure trottynge on foote. **1553** T. WILSON *Rhet.* 61 Trotte sire and trotte damme, how should the fole amble? *c* **1566** *Merie Tales of Skelton* in S.'s *Wks.* (1843) I. p. lx, Hee was a litell olde fellowe, and woulde lye as fast as a horse woulde trotte. **1633** MARMION *Antiquary* I, You'll hardly find.. beast that trots sound of all four: There will be some defect. **1674** *Lond. Gaz.* No. 882/4 A light gray Mare about fourteen hands high, five years old, trots altogether. **1675** *Ibid.* No. 959/4 A Brown Bay Nag,.. Trots all. **1676** *Ibid.* No. 1107/4 Gray Mare,.. trots rough. **1677** *Ibid.* No. 1222/4 A Sorrel Chesnut Gelding.., paces little, but trotteth high. **1706** Trot out [see SHORT C. 4]. **1856** MISS MULOCK *J. Halifax* ii, He took me on his back.. and fairly trotted with me down the garden-walk. **1859** GEO. ELIOT *A. Bede* I. i, Gyp with his basket, trotting at his master's heels. **1883** H. CRAIG in *Harper's Mag.* Aug. 346/1 She trotted a mile in the unparalleled time of 2.10¼. **1897** *Daily Chron.* 23 Aug. 8/2, I trotted down the wicket very slowly.

b. *transf.* Of a rider, etc., or of a vehicle.

c **1386** CHAUCER *Wife's Prol.* 838 Amble, or trotte [*v.r.* trote], or pees, or go sit doun, Thou lettest oure disport. *a* **1450** *Le Morte Arth.* 3339 Arthur with knyghtis fully xiiij .. With helme, sheld, And hauberke shene; Ryght so they trotted vppon þe grownde. **1599** SHAKS. *Hen. V*, III. vii. 86, I will trot to morrow a mile. *c* **1682** CLAVERHOUSE in *15th Rep. Hist. MSS. Comm.* App. VIII. 270 The smith at Menegaff,.. after whom the forces has troted so often. **1688** R. HOLME *Armoury* III. xix. (Roxb.) 186/2 Words of command about wheelings of Horsmen... Trot large, and wheele to the left. **1807** CRABBE *Par. Reg.* I. 487 Who trots to market on a steed so fine. **1833** *Regul. Instr. Cavalry* I. 66 '*Trot Out*'—Increase gradually to the trot of manœuvre, 8½ miles per hour. When steady, '*Trot Short*'—Collect the horses to the school pace again. **1833** T. HOOK *Parson's Dau.* I. iii, At Windsor.. a royal coach may be often seen trotting about the town. **1913** *Times* 14 May 6/2 The Brigade was an imposing picture as it trotted past the King.

c. *transf.* and *fig.*

c **1430** *Pilgr. Lyf Manhode* III. xl. (1869) 157 Alwey j muste make the chyn trotte, and the throte gaape. **1600** SHAKS. *A.Y.L.* III. ii. 331 Time.. trots hard with a yong maid, between the contract of her marriage, and the day it is solemnizd. **1612** DEKKER *If it be not good* Wks. 1873 III. 275 Vncle write that. *Oct.* Fast as my pen can trot. **1671** R. MACWARD *True Nonconf.* 273 Your loftie Pindarick.. doth trote more rudely, and lamely, then our hobling meeter. *a* **1758** RAMSAY *Generous Gentl.* iii, She lean'd upon a flow'ry brae, By which a burnie trotted. **1852** THACKERAY *Esmond* II. xi, We college poets trot.. on very easy nags. **1893** SALTUS *Madam Sapphira* 31 A woman is never led astray. She trots, or gallops or bolts astray, but never is she led.

†**d.** In the alliterative phrases *trot and tremble, tremble and trot*. *Obs. rare.*

c **1425** *Cast. Persev.* 459 in *Macro Plays* 91 Now I sytte in my semly sale; I trotte & tremle in my trew trone. *c* **1485** *Digby Myst.* (1882) III. 555 A! how I tremyl and trott for ȝese tydynges!

2. *intr.* To go or move quickly; to go briskly or busily; to bustle; to run. Also *refl.*, and with *it*. Now *colloq.*, implying short, quick motion in a limited area. Freq. with specifying adv. or advb. phr.; *absol.* also (contextually) to depart, to leave. Cf. TODDLE *v.* 2 b.

Also *trans.* in *to trot one's terms*, at Durham University, to keep one's terms as a day-student: cf. TROTTER 2. (N.E.D.)

c **1416** HOCCLEVE *Balade to Henry V* 8 The scantnesse [of gold] Wole arte vs three to trotte vn-to Newgate. *c* **1440** *York Myst.* xxviii. 204 Do trottes on for that traytoure apas. **1530** PALSGR. 763/1, I have doone naught sythe syxe of the clocke in the mornyng but trotte aboute from place to place. *a* **1553** C. BANSLEY *Treat.* xii. (Percy Soc.) 5 Sponge up your vysage, olde bounsynge trotte, and tricke it wyth the beste, Tyll you tricke and trotte youre selfe to the devyls trounsynge neste. **1581** T. HOWELL *Deuises* E ij b, Wante makes the olde wyfe trot. *c* **1645** HOWELL *Lett.* (1753) 126 Som.. find the Table ready laid; but som Must for their commons trot. *a* **1704** T. BROWN *Alsop's State of Conform.* Wks. 1711 IV. 116 If you'd have me trot it to the East-Indies,.. 'tis no sooner said, than done. **1774** C. KEITH *Farmer's Ha!* ix, Now lasses round the ingle trot, To make the brose. **1825** T. HOOK *Sayings* Ser. II. *Man of Many Fr.* (Colburn) 125, I will trot myself off for the moment, and be back immediately. **1847** C. BRONTË *Jane Eyre* II. viii. 203 In case I married Miss Ingram, both you and little Adèle had better trot forthwith. **1862** in N. Longmate *Hungry Mills* (1978) viii. 108, I.. trot down to a butcher in a better neighbourhood. **1863** MRS. C. CLARKE *Shaks. Char.* xvi. 402 She.. will keep her husband trotting. **1883** *Durham Univ. Jrnl.* 17 Dec. 141 'To trot one's terms' was, we believe originally, a Dublin phrase. **1899** O. WILDE *Importance of being Earnest* II. 74 *Chasuble*... At what hour would you wish the ceremony performed? *Jack*. Oh, I might trot round about five if that would suit you. **1954** J. R. R. TOLKIEN *Fellowship of Ring* I. ix. 166 No time for talking. I must be trotting. **1960** *Cambr. Rev.* 7 May 506/2 It is not true to suppose that the setting-up of machinery for psychiatric consultation merely encourages the 'neurotic' to trot along to the psychiatrist at the least excuse. **1984** *Your Computer* May 25/2 You can.. trot up to the Registry with that reference number and get a copy of his death certificate very quickly.

†**3.** *trans.* **a.** To trot upon (something) (*rare*). **b.** To make, describe, or execute by trotting; to go through at a trot. **c.** To follow, traverse (a path) as if by trotting (*rare*). *Obs.*

1599 SHAKS. *Hen. V*, III. vii. 16 My horse.. bounds from the Earth.. he trots the ayre. **1602** MARSTON *Antonio's Rev.* III. i. Wks. 1856 I. 104 The black jades of swart night trot foggy rings Bout heavens browe. **1612** *Two Noble K.* v. iv. 68 On this horse is Arcite Trotting the stones of Athens. **1633** FORD '*Tis Pity* I. ii, I have seen an ass and a mule trot the Spanish pavin with a better grace. **1638** SIR T. HERBERT *Trav.* 58 He.. was.. compell'd to trot the knotty path of inevitable destinie.

4. *trans.* To cause to trot; to lead or ride at the trot. Also *fig.*

1592 WARNER *Alb. Eng.* VIII. xxxviii. (1612) 189 Whether that he trots, or turnes, or bounds his barded Steede. *a* **1628** G. CARLETON *Life B. Gilpin* (1636) 66 He commanded William Airy.. to trott the horses up and downe. **1684** R. H. *School Recreat.* 21 Trot him about in your hand a good while; Then offer to mount. **1884** *Daily Chron.* 25 Oct. (Cassell's) The whips trotted the pack to Gravel-hill. **1886** *Sat. Rev.* 6 Mar. 315/1 The public.. is being trotted up and down in front of Home Rule in the belief that, like a nervous horse, it can be familiarized with the alarming object.

b. *to trot out*: To lead out and show off the paces of (a horse); hence *fig.* to bring forward (a person, an opinion, etc.) for or as for inspection or approval; to exhibit, show off. *colloq.*

1838 LYTTON *Alice* VII. iii, His guest, to be shown off.. and trotted out before all the rest of the company. **1841** SIR G. STEPHEN *Adv. Search Horse* (ed. 6) p. xxiv, A little cross-bred, vicious beast.. was 'trotted out' before a circle of ladies and gentlemen, to be admired. *Ibid.* ii. 46 He is trotted out, admired, and purchased. **1848** THACKERAY *Bk. Snobs* xxv, She began to trot out scraps of French. **1884** *Manch. Exam.* 20 Aug. 5/1 The fine old historical commonplaces were trotted out.

c. To draw out (a person) in conversation so that he appears ridiculous; to make game of, make a butt of. Chiefly with *out*.

1818 *Blackw. Mag.* III. 527 Menippus, accordingly, would fain trot Dr. Chalmers. **1848** THACKERAY *Van. Fair* xxxiv, You want to trot me out, but it's no go. **1888** BURGON *Lives 12 Gd. Men* II. x. 298 [He] trotted out his neighbour to his heart's content.

d. To conduct or escort (a person) *to* or *round* a place. *to trot out* (a woman), to walk out with, as a lover; also (*N.Z.*) simply *trot*. *slang.*

1888 'J. S. WINTER' *Bootle's Childr.* xiv, I've trotted 'em out, all sorts of girls—but I never could.. tie myself to any one of 'em. **1898** 'MERRIMAN' *Roden's Corner* vi. 60 Perhaps you'll trot us round the works. **1902** *Daily Chron.* 23 Aug. 6/7 He gave religious instruction.. in his school, and on saints' days 'trotted' the children to church. **1946** F. SARGESON *That Summer* 33 I've got a job in a grocer's shop and I'm trotting a sheila. **1964** B. CRUMP in *Weekly News* (Auckland) 21 Oct. 46/6, I didn't know she was going steady with you... If I'd known you were trotting her [etc.].

e. To jog (a child) on one's knee; to 'give a ride' to.

1853 HAWTHORNE *Tanglewood Tales* (Chandos) 193 He had trotted him on his knee when a baby. **1887** AUG. J. E. WILSON *At Mercy of Tiberius* 79, I trotted her on my knee.

f. To bid against at an auction in order to force up the price; to make or accept a spurious bid for (an item at auction) in order to force up the price. Also with *up*. *slang.*

1864 HOTTEN *Slang Dict.* 262 *Trot*, to 'run up', to oppose, to bid against at an auction. *Ibid.*, 'We *trotted* him up nicely, didn't we?' *i.e.*, we made him (the private buyer) pay dearly for what he bought. **1955** W. MANKOWITZ *Make me an Offer* viii. 64 'But it's no good to you?'.. 'Only if it goes reasonable —not if the reserve is high. And not.. if it's trotted.' 'We don't do that sort of thing in the country, you know.'

g. *to be able to trot a mouse on it* and varr.: said of particularly strong or thick liquid food or drink. *dial.*

1936 'N. BLAKE' *Thou Shell of Death* xiii. 229 A cup of tea, sir, after your journey... It's nice strong tea, so it is. Ye could trot a mouse on it. **1970** H. MCLEAVE *Question of Negligence* i. 3 That's the way they make it [*sc.* tea] in Scotland... Sweet as a sheep's eye and strong enough to trot a mouse on. **1975** *Times* 17 May 10/8 A bowl of parsnip soup —'so thick you could trot a mouse on it', as the country saying goes.

II. 5. *intr.* To fish with a trot-line. (Perhaps a different word: cf. TROT *sb.*[1] 7.) *dial.*

1864 *Daily Tel.* 18 May, They are trawlers, trotters, dredgers, and shrimpers, and their fathers have trawled, trotted, dredged, and shrimped ever since Earl Godwin. **1884** *St. James's Gaz.* 18 Jan. 6/2 The eel-spearer.. digging himself a good supply of bait, goes 'trotting' for flounders.

trot-cosy, -cosey, -cozy. *Sc.* [app. f. TROT *v.* + COSY *a.*] A kind of cloak with a hood, worn when travelling in cold weather.

1814 SCOTT *Wav.* xxix, At length the tall ungainly figure and ungracious visage of Ebenezer presented themselves. The upper part of his form.. was shrouded in a large greatcoat, belted over his under habiliments, and crested with a huge cowl of the same stuff, which, when drawn over the head and hat, completely overshadowed both, and being buttoned beneath the chin, was called a trot-cozy. **1818** —— *Rob Roy* xxvi, He roared to Mattie to 'air his trot-cosey, to have his jackboots greased.. and to see that his beast be corned, and a' his riding gear in order.' **1867** A. DAWSON *Rambling Recoll.* (1868) 31 Mr. More..—trotcosey enveloping his head.

†**trotevale, -uale.** *Obs. rare.* Also **trotouale, trotyuale.** [Derivation unascertained. The word occurs 4 times in R. Brunne *Handlyng Synne*, and once in Map's *Body & Soul*; no OF. equivalents. In *Piers Plowman* B. XVIII. 142, C. XXI. 146, *waltrot, walterot* appears to have the same elements in reversed order: see Skeat's *Notes*, p. 407, where the word is discussed, and conjectures put forth, but with little success.] Idle tale-telling, vain talk.

a **1300** *Body & Soul* in *Map's Poems* (Camden) 337 Al ye maden troteuale [*printed* trotenale], that I haved seid biforn. **1303** R. BRUNNE *Handl. Synne* 48 Yn gamys, & festys, & at þe ale, Loue men to lestene troteuale [*v.rr.* trotouale, to telle trotyuale]. *Ibid.* 8080 þenkeþ on þys tale, And takeþ hyt for no troteuale! *Ibid.* 5970. *Ibid.* 9244.

troth (trəʊθ, trɒθ, trɔːθ), *sb. arch.* Forms: α. 2–5 **trowþe**, 3 (*Orm.*) **trowwþe**, 3–5 **trouþe**, 4–5 **trowþ, trowthe**, 4–6 **trouthe**, 4–6 (*Sc.* 4–) **trowth, trouth**, 5 **trouþ**, (**trowith, -yth**, 5–6 **trougth**, 6 **trowgthe, trough**). (Also 4 **troutht, trout, troght**, 4–6 **trought(e**, 6 **trowht, trouht**; 4 **throwth, throut**, 5 **throuth, throughte.**) β. 5 **trothe**, 6–7 **troath**, 6– **troth**. γ. 4 **trawþe, trauþ(e**, 5 **trauthe, trawethe**, 5–6 **trawth(e**. [Early ME. *trowþe, trouþe*, for OE. *tréowþ*, TRUTH, app. due to the shifting of *éo* to *eó*, with subsequent loss of the unaccented *e*. Cf. TROW *v.*, and the development of ME. and mod. *four* from OE. *féower*, and of ME. *fourti*, and *forty* from OE. *féowertiȝ*. *Trowth, troth* were thus originally phonetic variants of OE. *tréowþ*, TRUTH, which hardly survived the 16th c. except as midland and northern dialect forms, and in special archaic locutions as 'to plight one's troth', 'wedded troth', 'by' or 'upon my troth', and in some combinations, as *trothless*, *troth-plighted*. Cf. also BETROTH. *Trawthe*, *trauth* are specially northern forms in which *aw*, *au* take the place of *ow*, *ou*. They are cited in the English Dialect Dictionary from Yorkshire.]

I. 1. Faithfulness, good faith, loyalty; honesty: = TRUTH *sb.* 1, 4. ? *Obs.*

α. *c* **1175** *Pater Noster* 42 in *Lamb. Hom.* 57 Mid al þis haue þu charite and soðfeste leaue and trowðe lef. *a* **1275** *Prov. Ælfred* 506 in *O.E. Misc.* 132 On him þu maist þe tresten, ȝif is trowþe deȝh. *c* **1325** *Spec. Gy Warw.* 1033 To serue hym [Christ] and hys moder dere In trowþe, loue, and in charite. **1340–70** *Alex. & Dind.* 910 For-þy vs kenneþ our kinde to a-corde in trowþe. **1448** HEN. VI *Will* in Willis & Clark *Cambridge* (1886) I. 379 His high trought and feruent zele. **1474** CAXTON *Chesse* II. iv. (1883) 48 He knewe well the trouth of his felawe. *a* **1548** HALL *Chron.*, *Hen. VI* 164 Many thynges..declared the duke of Yorkes trought and innocencye in this case.

β. **1568** GRAFTON *Chron.* II. 766 The Lord Hastings, whose troth towarde the king no man doubted. **1620** J. WILKINSON *Courts Leet* 139, I shall sweare that I will bee true liege man and true faith and troth beare to our soveraigne lord the king. **1664** BUTLER *Hud.* II. ii. 227 These thinking they're obliged to Troth In Swearing, will not take an Oath. **1866** NEALE *Sequences & Hymns* 130 Wedded troth remains as firm, and wedded love as pure. **1905** C. WHITLEY in *Disraeli's Bentinck* Introd. 15 His..followers lacked either troth or cordiality.

b. *by* (rarely *upon*) *my troth*, as a form of asseveration. See also TRUTH 1 b.

α. *c* **1374** CHAUCER *Troylus* V. 1001 If þat I sholde of any Grek han rouþe, It shulde be youre seluen, by my trouþe. **14..** *Beryn* 116 Kit, how likith the? Be my trowith, wondir wele. *c* **1518** SKELTON *Magnyf.* 1669 Ye, by my trouthe, I shall waraunt you. **1564** in *Child-Marriages* 64 Bie my faith and trouth, I will marry the.

β. **1555** in Foxe *A. & M.* (1576) 1604/2 No, by my troth my Lord, we can do no good. **1599** SHAKS. *Much Ado* II. iii. 103 By my troth my Lord, I cannot tell what to thinke of it. **1704** SWIFT *Batt. Bks.* Misc. (1711) 236 By my Troth, said the Bee, the Comparison will amount to a very good Jest. **1820** COMBE *Consol.* II. (Chandos) 158 Nay, if you swear, Sir, by my troth, The Echo will repeat the oath. *a* **1839** PRAED *Everyday Char.*, *Quince* 45 Old Quince averred, upon his troth, They were the ugliest beasts in Devon.

γ. **13..** *E.E. Allit. P.* B. 63 On hade boȝt hym a borȝ he sayde by his trawþe. *c* **1400** *Destr. Troy* 1749 And now is tyme, by my trauthe, to take it on hond.

2. One's faith as pledged or plighted in a solemn agreement or undertaking; one's plighted word; the act of pledging one's faith, a promise, covenant. Chiefly in phr. *to plight one's troth*, to pledge one's faith; to make a solemn promise or engagement; *spec.* to engage oneself to marry. = TRUTH 2.

α. *a* **1225** *Ancr. R.* 54 þerefter of þen ilke weren trouðen tobrokene. *Ibid.* 310 *Pepigimus cum morte fedus*..we habbeð trouðe ipluht deaðe. **1303** R. BRUNNE *Handl. Synne* 8360–1 Trouþe þat men alle day breke,..fals trouþes, and fykyl,.. are ȝyue mechyl. *c* **1386** CHAUCER *Frankl. T.* 746 Ye shul youre trouthe holden. *c* **1430–40** *Anturs of Arth.* 465 (Thornton MS.) Here my trouthe I ȝow plyghte, I salle feghte withe ȝone knyghte. *a* **1440** *Sir Eglam.* 246 'ȝys', seyde the erle, 'here myn honde!' Hys trowthe to hym he strake. **1543–4** *Act 35 Hen. VIII*, c. 12 The..Frenche King nothing regarding his honor, othe, trouthe, promyse, and fidelitie. **1552** HULOET, Plyght fayeth and trougth in matrimonye, *sponso.* **1564** in *Child-Marriages* 201 Therapon they plightid their trouthes together, and kissed together, and after dronk, and made mery.

β. *c* **1420** *Anturs of Arth.* xxxvi. (Ireland MS.), I wille countur with the knyȝte,..Ther-to my trothe y the plyȝte. **1515** *Acc. Ld. High Treas. Scot.* V. 36 Item, to David Cameroun for to pas to the day of troth, and erandis to the Lord Dakkir, to his expensis, xlij s. **1578** T. N. tr. *Conq. W. India* 7 She demaunded him as hir husband by faith and troth of hand. **1600** HOLLAND *Livy* XXI. vii. 397 They observed their troth and loyaltie with their allies. **1724** RAMSAY *Tea-t. Misc.* (1733) II. 149 Give me back my maiden-vow And give me back my troth. **1848** LYTTON *Harold* VI. i, Gryffyth will never keep troth with the English. **1872** YEATS *Techn. Hist. Comm.* 188 Betrothal rings, set with pearls and gems, were worn by maidens who had plighted their troth.

γ. *c* **1375** *Cursor M.* 3240 (Fairf.) Of þi trauþ I make þe free. *c* **1400** *Destr. Troy* 1749 And now [is] tyme, by my trauthe, to take it on hond. *Ibid.* 10110 Vntrew of his trawth trust neuer after. *c* **1420** *Avow. Arth.* xxx, Ther-to grawuntus the knyȝte, And truly his trauthe pliȝte.

†**3. a.** Faith, trust, confidence. (Cf. TRUTH 3 a.)

α. *c* **1200** ORMIN 4015 He wass Drihhtin swiþe lef þurrh trowwþess rihhtwisnesse. *Ibid.* 18857 Hæþenn trowwþe on hæþenn Godd. *a* **1300** *Cursor M.* 2387 (Cott.) Abram þat o trouth was tru. **13..** *Ibid.* 18678 (Gött.) þair mistrovth..Es strinthing of vr troght to-day. *a* **1400** *Religious Pieces fr. Thornton MS.* (1867) 10 þe firste vertu es trouthe wharethurghe we trow anely in Godd... Trouthe es begynnynge of all gude dedis. *c* **1425** WYNTOUN *Cron.* VI. xviii. 2205 Makbeth aye In fantown fretis had gret fay, And trowth had in swylk fantasy.

γ. *c* **1375** *Cursor M.* 2525 (Fairf.) Abraham þat was in trauþe strange.

†**b.** Belief; *spec.* a form of religious belief, a creed. (Cf. TRUTH 3 b.) *Obs.*

c **1200** ORMIN 1347 ȝiff þatt tu willt..Wiþþ fulle trowwþe lefenn Al þæt tatt wass bitacnedd tær. *Ibid.* 6953 Forrþi þatt teȝȝ þatt time ȝet unnderrstodenn littleswhatt Off all þe rihhte trowwþe. *a* **1340** HAMPOLE *Psalter* i. 6 Fals cristen men, þat has þe trouth of ihū crist withouten luf & goed werkes. **1340** —— *Pr. Consc.* 4228 þai lyved in fals trowthe. *c* **1375** *Lay Folks Mass Bk.* (MS. B.) 414 þis is þo trouthe of holy kirk. *c* **1400** MAUNDEV. (Roxb.) xxxiv. 154 If all þai be of diuerse lawes and diuerse trowyngs, þai hafe sum gude poyntes of oure trowth. **1481** CAXTON *Myrr.* III. xii. 159 In this only veryte, he [Plato] preuyd the right trouthe, ffor he preued his power, his wisedom, and his goodnes..that is the fader, the sone, and the holy goste.

II. †**4.** Truth, in various senses: see TRUTH 5–14.

α. *c* **1300** *Cursor M.* 22789 (Edin.) Of þis trowþe hard es trowþe to find. **13..** *Ibid.* 18710 (Cott.) He badd..his disciplis..Oueral þis werld his trouth to teche. *c* **1386** CHAUCER *Man of Law's T.* 532 He wolde enquere Depper in this, a trouthe for to lere. **1387** TREVISA *Higden* (Rolls) III. 221 God..is cause of al þing..and liȝt of sooþnesse, and of trowþe [*v.rr.* trouthe, truthe], and welle of grace. **1390** GOWER *Conf.* III. 151 Hou so that the cause wende, The trouthe is schameles ate ende. *c* **1400** *Apol. Loll.* 13 In two maner of þing, is [a man] seid iust; first sympli, or after trowþ... In þe secound maner..onli in name. **14..** in *Babees Bk.* (1868) 332 Deame þee best in euery doute Tyl þe trouthe be tryed oute. **1422** tr. *Secreta Secret.*, *Priv. Priv.* 211 He sholde bene sothefaste in worde and dedd, and lowe throuth abowe al thynge, and hate lesynge. **1436** *Pol. Poems* (Rolls) II. 204 Go furthe, libelle,..And pray my lordes the to take in grace.., if that not variaunce Thow haste fro troughte. **1470–85** MALORY *Arthur* I. iii. 38 Telle me the trouthe... Syre saide she I shalle telle you the trouthe... That is trouthe..as ye say. *a* **1533** LD. BERNERS *Huon* cxxxix. 521, I shall neuer haue ioye..tyll I maye knowe the trought. **1545** *Plumpton Corr.* (Camden) 250 Send forth your excuse..with a letter of the trough of your sicknes. **1593** Q. ELIZ. *Boethius* V. pr. i. 103 Aristotle..hath defynd it [chance] in a neere reason to breefenes & trouth.

β. **1538** STARKEY *England* I. ii. 30 Thys ys of trothe. **1553** T. WILSON *Rhet.* (1580) 173 When perfite judgement is wantyng, the trothe can not be knowne. **1600** HOLLAND *Livy* XXIV. XXX. 529 They reported other newes besides, as well lies as troths. **1663** COWLEY *Country Mouse* 56 Plainly, the troth to tell, the Sun was set.

γ. **13..** *E.E. Allit. P.* A. 494 For al is trawþe þat he con dresse, And he may do no þynk bot ryȝt. *Ibid.* B. 1490 Hit [the sacred candlestick] watz..wont..in temple of þe trauþe trwly to stonde. *c* **1420** *Sir Amadace* (Camden) xxix, Butte the trauthe fulle litulle thay wote. **1432–50** tr. *Higden* (Rolls) III. 221 The philosophres knowenge the trawthe of God profite moche to the cognicion of trawthe. **1504** *Plumpton Corr.* (Camden) p. lxiv, All that ys afore rehersed..we wyll ..yf nede be, depely depose afore the kynge and hys counsell, that yt is matter of trawth.

b. *in troth* (*arch.*), †*of* (*a*) *troth* (*obs.*): truly, verily, indeed: = *in truth, of* (*a*) *truth* (TRUTH 14).

α. *a* **1380** *Pistill of Susan* 187 Heo was in trouþe, as we trowe, tristi and trewe. *c* **1475** *Partenay* 1568 Many merueles of trought cam ther ryght. **1508** FISHER *Penit. Ps.* xxxviii. Wks. (1876) 60 This of a trouth is a grete mysery wherof..Dauyd maketh his complaynte. **1546** J. HEYWOOD *Prov. & Epigr.* (1867) 50 But of trough I thought, better to haue then wishe. **1789** BURNS *To Dr. Blacklock* ii, I lippen'd to the chiel in trouth.

β. *a* **1566** R. EDWARDES *Damon & Pithias* (1571) Bj, Tell me of troth, Is not that great Wisdom as the world goth? **1607** SHAKS. *Cor.* I. iii. 118 In troth I thinke she would. **1660** R. COKE *Power & Subj.* 205 Divers sums of money (which in troath were the oblations and offerings). **1727** GAY *Begg. Op.* I. viii, A mighty likely speech in troth. **1756** FOOTE *Eng. fr. Paris* I. Wks. 1799 I. 98 In gude troth, not a mighty booty.

γ. **1432–50** tr. *Higden* (Rolls) II. 365 The faders of whom were not knowen in trawthe.

c. Also *ellipt.* or as *int.* = TRUTH 14 c. *arch.*

α. **1719** RAMSAY *To Arbuckle* 48 And trouth I think they're in the right on't. **1728** —— *A Character* iv, And trowth the picture I have drawn Is very like. **1786** BURNS *Brigs of Ayr* 129 Fine Architecture, trowth, I needs must say't o't.

β. **1603** SHAKS. *Meas. for M.* II. ii. 60 Troth sir, shee hath eaten vp all her beefe, and she is her selfe in the tub. *a* **1627** MIDDLETON, etc. *Widow* II. i, Troth, and I would have my will then, if I were as you. **1741** RICHARDSON *Pamela* (1824) I. xxiii. 34 Troth, sir, said he,..I never knew her peer. **1843** LYTTON *Last Bar.* I. i, 'Troth', answered Master Heyford [etc.].

III. 5. *attrib.* and *Comb.*, as *troth-breaker*, *-breaking*, *-keeping*, *-kiss*, *-ring*; *troth-contracted*, *-like*, *-telling* adjs.

1648 HERRICK *Hesper.*, *To His Mistresse* ii, Promise, and keep your vowes, Or vow ye never; Loves doctrine disallowes *Troth-breakers ever. **13..** *Cursor M.* 26234 (Cott.) Fals wijtnes and *trouth breking. **1464** *Paston Lett.* II. 159 Master Constantyn sewyd hym for feyth and trowth brekyng. **1633** FORD *Broken H.* II. iii, Intercourse of *troth-contracted loves. **1605** VERSTEGAN *Dec. Intell.* viii. (1628) 253 A mouth of *troth-keeping or loyaltie. **1844** MRS. BROWNING *Lay Brown Rosary* II. 64, I was betrothed that day; I wore a *troth-kiss on my lips, I could not give away. **1544** BETHAM *Precepts War* II. xl. K viij, Such other thynges are to be feyned, whyche appere *trouthlyke. **1856** MRS. BROWNING *Aur. Leigh* IX. 100, I had sooner cut My hand off (though 't were..promised a duke's *troth-ring). **1673** WYCHERLEY *Gentl. Dancing-Master* IV. i, The *troth-telling Trojan gentlewoman of old was ne'er believed till the town was taken.

troth, *v. Obs.* or *arch.* [f. TROTH *sb.* or aphetic f. BETROTH *v.*] *trans.* To plight one's troth to; to engage in a contract, esp. of marriage: = BETROTH 1, 2, 4 a. Hence **'trothed** *ppl. a.*, **'trothing** *vbl. sb.* and *ppl. a.* (See also TRUTH *v.* 2.)

1422 tr. *Secreta Secret.*, *Priv. Priv.* 190 A gentill-man of the contrey had hyr trouthid. **1565** COOPER *Thesaurus*, *Coemptio*,..a solemnitie of the ciuill lawe where the woman and man commyng together at a trothyng, as it were, bye one the other. **1567** DRANT *Horace*, *Epistles* II. ii. H iv, Too Orators..th' one was to the other, In mutuall prayse for both their gaynes a faste ytrothed brother. **1599** SHAKS. *Much Ado* III. i. 38 So saies the Prince, and my new trothed Lord. **1605** *Tryall Chev.* II. i. in Bullen *O. Pl.* III. 288, I scorne..to give answere to such a trothing question. **1893** F. THOMPSON *Love in Dian's Lap* I. Poems 4, I reach back through the days A trothed hand to the dead.

'trothful, *a. arch. rare.* [f. TROTH *sb.* + -FUL.] Full of 'troth' or loyalty, faithful, trusty; trustworthy, truthful.

a **1380** *Minor Poems fr. Vernon MS.* xxviii. 9 Heil trewe, trouþeful and tretable. **1861** LYTTON & FANE *Tannhäuser* 13 Trothful men..Aver he was the fairest-favour'd knight.

trothless ('trəʊθlɪs), *a.* [f. as prec. + -LESS.]

1. Destitute of 'troth' or loyalty; faithless, perfidious, disloyal. *arch.*

α. *c* **1200** ORMIN 188 He shall turrnenn þurrh hiss spell þe trowwþelæse leode. **1513** DOUGLAS *Æneis* IV. vii. 8 Thow throuthles wycht.

β. **1567** DRANT *Horace*, *Art Poetry* A iv, Let Ino still be sad, Ixie trothlesse, lo wandring. **1594** LODGE *Wounds Civil War* III. i. D iij b, The trustfull man that builds on trothles vowes. **1647** TRAPP *Comm. Matt.* viii. 32 [Drunkenness] making the understanding ignorant, the strong staggering, the trusty trothless. **1887** SWINBURNE *Locrine* I. i. 68 No coward indeed, but faithless, trothless.

†**2.** Destitute of truth; false, mendacious; incredible, untrustworthy. *Obs.*

α. **1390** GOWER *Conf.* III. 151 Bot what thing that is troutheles, It mai noght wel be schameles.

β. **1592** GREENE *Groat's W. Wit* (1874) 13 Trothlesse toungs of men. **1601** DEACON & WALKER *Answ. Darel* 60 To trauerse the trueth of their trothlesse tales. *Ibid.* 75 Will you leaue the law, and the testimonies, and trot after a blind and a trothlesse lad for the reuelation of these hidden truthes?

†**'trothly**, *adv. Obs. rare*[-1]. In 5 **trouþly**. [f. as prec. + -LY[2].] Faithfully, loyally.

c **1425** *Cursor M.* 19950 (Trin.) Noon wol he awey cast þat trouþly [*v.r.* traistili] wol him loue & last.

troth-plight ('trəʊθplaɪt), *sb. arch.* Forms: see TROTH, TRUTH, PLIGHT *sb.*[1], *v.*[1] [f. TROTH *sb.* + PLIGHT *sb.*[1]] The act of plighting troth, or troth plighted; a solemn promise or engagement, esp. of marriage; betrothal.

[**13..** *Cursor M.* 28485 (Cott.) Broken..my trouth plight.] **1513** DOUGLAS *Æneis* X. xii. 82 A Greik,..That fugityve..Had left hys spowsal trewth plycht oncompleit. **1570** FOXE *A. & M.* (ed. 2) 265/2 That all debtes, that were owyng through trouth plyght, should not be pledid in spirituall but in temporall court. **1611** SHAKS. *Wint. T.* I. ii. 278 A Name As ranke as any Flax-Wench, that puts to Before her troth-plight. **1818** SCOTT *Br. Lamm.* xix. [xx], The lovers going through an emblematic ceremony of their troth-plight... They broke betwixt them the thin broad-piece of gold. **1881** SWINBURNE *Mary Stuart* I. i. 52 To set again the seal on our past oaths And bind their trothplight faster than it is With one more witness.

attrib. **1550** *Reg. Gild Corp. Chr. York* (1872) 228 *note*, A trouth-plighte ryngе. *a* **1652** BROME *Queenes Exch.* II. i, A very trothplight qualm.

'troth-plight, *pa. pple.* and *ppl. a. arch.* [f. as prec. + *plight*, pa. pple. of PLIGHT *v.*[1]] Engaged by a 'troth' or covenant, esp. of marriage; betrothed, affianced.

c **1330** R. BRUNNE *Chron.* (1810) 153 Whan þei were trouth plight, & purueied þe sposage. **1393** LANGL. *P. Pl.* C. VII. 208 Ich serued symme at þe style, And was his prentys yplyght [*v.r.* truþeplith]. **1491** CAXTON *Vitas Patr.* (W. de W. 1495) I. xlviii. 93 b/2 The doughter of a noble Romayne; whyche some tyme was fyaunced and trouthplyght in maryage to a noble man of Rome. **1513** DOUGLAS *Æneis* X. xii. 87 The purpour brycht, Quhilk of his trewth plycht lufe he bair in sing. **1599** SHAKS. *Hen. V*, II. i. 21 He is marryed to Nell Quickly, and certainly she did you wrong, for you were troth-plight to her. **1633** HEYWOOD *Eng. Trav.* III. Wks. 1874 IV. 57 Shee a Prostitute? Nay, and to him my troath plight, and my Friend. **1887** SWINBURNE *Locrine* I. ii. 33, I that was trothplight servant to thy sire. **1896** MORRIS *Poems by the Way* (1898) 119 There are troth-plight maids unwed.

troth-'plight, *v. arch.* [f. as prec. + PLIGHT *v.*[1]] *trans.* To plight one's troth to; to engage, or engage oneself to, in order to pledge marriage; to betroth, affiance: = TROTH *v.* †In quot. 1470–85, to plight one's troth, engage (*to do* something).

[**1303** R. BRUNNE *Handl. Synne* 8363 ȝyf þou a womman trouþe plyght.] *c* **1440** *Promp. Parv.* 504/1 Trutheplytyn (*K.*, *S.* truplytyn, *P.* trouthplityn), *affido*, C. F. **1470–85** MALORY *Arthur* VII. xxii. 247 And thenne they trouth-plyte eche other to loue, and neuer to faylle whyles their lyfe lasteth. **1494** FABYAN *Chron.* VII. 676 Fraunceys,..whose doughter..Maximylian had before trouth plyted for his lawfull wyfe. **1601** MUNDAY *Downfall Robt. Earl of Huntington* I. ii. A iv b, Marian, daughter to Lord Lacy, Is troth-plighted to wastfull Huntington. **1825** SCOTT *Betrothed* xxix, Not married, perhaps, but engaged—troth-plighted. **1878** SUSAN PHILLIPS *On Seaboard* 75 Hand in hand, Troth-plighted, we two heard the midnight chime.

So †**'troth-,plighting**, the action of plighting troth, engagement, betrothal: = TROTH-PLIGHT *sb.*

c **1440** *Jacob's Well* 52 þowȝ non othe be made, ne trewthe plyȝtyng, ne no fleschly knowyng, ne no wytnes be þere. *c* **1477** CAXTON *Jason* 127 The fyansailles and trouthplighting of Iason and Creusa. **1530** PALSGR. 283/1 Trouth plyghtyng, *fianceailles*.

'trotlet. *nonce-wd.* [f. TROT *sb.*[1] + -LET.] A diminutive trot.

1879 STEVENSON *Trav. Cevennes* 38 A prick, and she broke forth into a gallant little trotlet that devoured the miles.

Trotskyism ('trɒtskɪɪz(ə)m). Also †**Trotskysm**, †**Trotzkyism.** [f. Leon *Trotsky*, the assumed name of Lev Davidovich Bronstein (1879–1940), Russian revolutionary and politician + -ISM.] The political or economic principles of Trotsky; a form of Marxism urging world-wide revolution, as advocated by Trotsky.

1925 tr. Trotsky in *Times* 30 Jan. 11/4, I cannot..accept the accusation of trying to pursue my own line of policy (Trotskyism). **1925** —— in M. Eastman *Since Lenin Died* 155, I can nowise accept, however, the accusation that I have pursued a special line (Trotskysm) and tried to revise Leninism. **1930** W. H. CHAMBERLIN *Soviet Russia* iv. 76 There would seem to be little political future in Russia for Trotzkyism. **1942** E. WAUGH *Put out More Flags* 48 She believed in a People's Total War; an uncompromising girl whom none of them liked; a suspect of Trotskyism. **1963** [see CAPITULATIONISM]. **1977** *Belfast Tel.* 24 Jan. 9/8 Trotskyism is installed as official doctrine and the pro-Soviet sympathies of some of our trade union leaders go unrebuked.

Trotskyist ('trɒtskɪɪst), *sb.* and *a.* Also Trotskist, †Trotzkyist. [f. *Trotsky* (see prec.) + -IST.] **A.** *sb.* A follower or supporter of Trotsky or Trotskyism. **B.** *adj.* Of, pertaining to, or characteristic of Trotsky or Trotskyism.

1927 *Daily Tel.* 22 Nov. 9/2 The adoption of the word 'Russia' by the Trotskyists. *Ibid.* 6 Dec. 11 The struggle between the Trotskists and the Stalinites. **1930** W. H. CHAMBERLIN *Soviet Russia* iv. 74 The Party Congress..laid down the rule that adherence to the views of the Trotzkyist opposition was inconsistent with membership in the Communist Party. **1937** KOESTLER *Spanish Testament* ix. 178 The P.O.U.M.—the Trotskyist Party—was even more unrestrained in its agitation. **1949** [see DIVERSIONIST]. **1959** *Daily Tel.* 15 Apr. 17/5 The recently formed Trotskyist organisation known as the Socialist Labour League. **1973** 'I. DRUMMOND' *Jaws of Watchdog* x. 136 Trotskyists, anarchists and the lunatic fringe of the Underground. **1980** *Washington Post* 6 July C1/2 On the left there are well over 40 different organizations—Leninist, Stalinist, Trotskyist.

Trotskyite ('trɒtskɪaɪt), *a.* and *sb.* Also Trotskiite. [f. *Trotsky* (see TROTSKYISM) + -ITE[1].] = TROTSKYIST *sb.* and *a.*

1919 *Mr. Punch's Hist. Great War* 210 Which am I..Pro-German or Pro-Trotskyite? **1920** [see LENINITE *a.* and *sb.*]. **1953** *Encounter* Nov. 30/2 Young X. starts as a Communist, is soon disillusioned, founds a Trotskyite opposition group of ten people [etc.]. **1957** V. NABOKOV *Pnin* vii. 184 Russian emigration was made to mean by astute communist propaganda a vague and perfectly fictitious mass of so-called Trotskiites (whatever these are), ruined reactionaries, [etc.]. **1977** M. WALKER *National Front* viii. 210 The Trotskyite parties..are too small and too dependent upon the intelligentsia to present any credible revolutionary threat. **1978** *Jrnl. R. Soc. Arts* CXXVI. 671/1 Their activities were compared to those of the Trotskyites in 1923.

trottee (trɒ'tiː). *nonce-wd.* [f. TROT *v.* + -EE.] One who is trotted out (see TROT *v.* 4c).

1818 *Blackw. Mag.* III. 527 There is something about the Doctor that all at once converts the trotter into the trottee. **1819** LOCKHART *Peter's Lett.* lxxi. III. 246, I had the good sense..to perceive the danger of the practice,..and..hope never to fill the roll either of Trotter or Trottee.

trotter ('trɒtə(r)). [f. TROT *v.* + -ER[1]; cf. med.L. *trotārius* (Du Cange), OF. *trotier* (Godef.).]

1. A horse (or other quadruped) which trots; *spec.* a horse especially bred and trained to the trot.

1381–2 [see 6]. **1391–2** *Earl Derby's Exped.* (Camden) 143 Pro duobus equis trotters cum duabus sellis per ipsum emptis. **1452** *Test. Ebor.* (Surtees) III. 137, j equi basii, trotter, xs. **1592** GREENE *Maiden's Dream* Wks. (Rtldg.) 279/1 His stable full of coursers.., Trotters whose manag'd looks would some affright. **1679** *Lond. Gaz.* No. 1412/4 A black brown Gelding about 15 hands,..a Trotter only. **1776** *Pennsylv. Even. Post* 26 Mar. 154/2 A Dark Brown Coloured Horse..a natural trotter. **1812** *Sporting Mag.* XXXIX. 31 A trotter constantly habituated to that pace. **1858** O. W. HOLMES *Aut. Breakf.-t.* ii, Compare the racer with the trotter. **1890** W. P. LETT in *Big Game N. Amer.* 88 The Caribou is the champion trotter of America. **1898** DOYLE *Trag. Korosko* v. 110 Most of them [camels] were beautiful creatures, true Arabian trotters.

b. A trotting-cart, a sulky.

1902 *Times* 4 Apr. 9/6 He would come up in the morning in his 'trotter'.

2. One who moves or goes about briskly and constantly; see TROT *v.* 2.

spec. (*Univ. slang*) a tailor's assistant who goes round for orders; also, a tailor's, dressmaker's, or milliner's girl messenger; at *Dublin University*, one who goes to Dublin for a degree, without residence (cf. *term-trotter*, at Oxford: see TERM *sb.* 17); at *Durham University*, a day-student (cf. TROT *v.* 2). (N.E.D.)

1562 J. HEYWOOD *Prov. & Epigr.* (1867) 140 Neede makth tholde wyfe trot: is she a trotter now? **1580** HOLLYBAND *Treas. Fr. Tong, Gaste-pavé*, a trotter vpon the pauements, a walker by the streets. **1605** *Tryall Chev.* II. i. in Bullen *O. Pl.* III. 288 And this trotter is my ryval and loves Thomasin. **1765** FOOTE *Commissary* I. Wks. 1799 II. 17 That eternal trotter after all the little draggle-tail'd girls of town. **1860** *Slang Dict.*, *Trotter*, a tailor's man who goes round for orders. *University*. **1883** *Durham Univ. Jrnl.* 17 Dec. 141 We suspect that the ingenious inventor of the name 'trotter' was well aware that the name had a ridiculous sound. **1897** *Daily News* 23 Feb. 3/1 She was a Trotter..she trotted to and fro between the East and the West, with patterns to match—silks, stuffs, and so on.

3. Usually *pl.* The feet of a quadruped, esp. those of sheep and pigs as used for food; also *humorously*, the feet of a human being.

(Quot. *c* 1358 doubtfully belongs here.)

[*c* **1358** in *Eng. Hist. Rev.* Oct. (1909) 742 Item in duro pisce frisc. vd o. Item in trotters viijd.] **1522** SKELTON *Why not to Court* 908 The chefe of your fayre Myght stand nowe by potters, And suche as sell trotters. *c* **1550** LACY *Wyl Buck's Test.* (Halliw.) 58 For to make the Trotters of the Bucke. Take the foure fete, and skalde them [etc.]..and that ben the trotters. **1602** CAREW *Cornwall* I. 24 Not the dammes Foale, but the dames Trotters, be trusted vnto. **1630** *R. Johnson's Kingd. & Commw.* 174 He steales the sheepe; and gives the Trotters for Gods sake. *a* **1650** *Anc. Poems*, etc. (Percy Soc.) 164 Two calves' feet, and a bull's trotter. **1755** *Gentl. Mag.* XXV. Pref., Finding out that some bald pated drone of a monk laid up his useless trotters in the corner of his Abbey, about 500 years ago. **1775** ADAIR *Amer. Ind.* 309 They will fasten the paws and trotters of panthers, bears, and buffalos, to their feet and hands. **1851** MAYHEW *Lond. Labour* I. 158/2 For supper there is a sandwich, a meat pudding, or a 'trotter'. **1872** MARY JEWRY *Every-day Cookery* 72/2 Perfectly cleanse and blanch the trotters.

4. See quot.

1864 *Daily Tel.* 18 May, 'The..trotters'—fishermen who ..trot for whelks to sell as bait to the North Sea cod-smacks.

5. One who trots another out in conversation: see TROT *v.* 4c.

1818–19 [see TROTTEE].

6. *attrib.* and *Comb.*, as ***trotter-bone***, ***-girl*** (see sense 2), †***-saddle***, ***-stall***; **trotter-boiler**, one whose business is to treat the hoofs of animals by boiling; **trotter-cases**, *sb. pl.* boots or shoes (*slang*); **trotter-pie**: see quot.; **trotter skirt** (see also TROTTEUR), a short, neat walking skirt.

1883 R. HALDANE *Workshop Receipts* Ser. II. 301/1 Some [glue-making materials] that come from the *trotter-boilers ..have been limed already. **1799** G. SMITH *Laboratory* II. 407 Take *trotter-bones; calcine and beat them to a fine powder, wherewith rub the spots on both sides. **1869** *Daily News* 23 Aug., The original floor..was laid with 'trotter bones',..closely packed and driven into the ground to the depth of from three to four inches. **1821** HOOD *Sent. Journ.* Wks. 1862 I. 34 A young gentleman in very tight *trotter-cases,..his feet gave evident signs of suffering. **1838** DICKENS *O. Twist* xviii, 'Japanning his trotter-cases'.. rendered into plain English signifieth, cleaning his boots. **1903** *Westm. Gaz.* 10 Aug. 10/1 The streets of Soho are unusually quiet; the *trotter girl, with her bundle of coats or trousers, is almost a curiosity. *a* **1693** *Urquhart's Rabelais* III. xviii. 151 We were..eating a Bushel of *Trotter-pies [*orig.* goudiveaulx (see Cotgr.)]. **1381–2** *Durham Acc. Rolls* (Surtees) 592 Pro reparacione j *trottersadill. **1909** *Westm. Gaz.* 15 Feb. 5/3 A..gown..for roller skating or merely for walking [with] a *trotter skirt. **1595** *Enq. Tripe-wife* (1881) 148 Since I trotted from my *trotter stall, And figd about from neates feete neatly drest: I finde no pleasure nor content at all.

Hence **'trotteress** (*nonce-wd.*), a female trotter (in ***globe-trotteress***: cf. *globe-trotter* s.v. GLOBE *sb.* 10b).

1892 MARIANNE NORTH *Recoll. Happy Life* (ed. 2) II. 213 Lady A. joined our three pairs of hands and blessed us—'Three globe trotteresses all at once!'

‖**trotteur** (trɔtœr), fem. **trotteuse** (trɔ'tœz). [Fr.] = TROTTER: see *trotter skirt* (prec. 6).

1904 *Daily Chron.* 6 Feb. 9/1 The short trotteuse costume is quite out of place at a wedding. *Ibid.* 20 Feb. 8/5 The trotteuse skirt..is being more and more worn. **1909** *Westm. Gaz.* 29 May 15/2 Seaside dresses..are short, and the pleated trotteur skirt can scarcely be improved upon. **1910** *Ibid.* 15 Apr. 5/3 The black and white check 'trotteur'.

trottie, var. TROTTY *a.*

trottie: see TROT *sb.*[1] 4.

trotting ('trɒtɪŋ), *vbl. sb.* [f. TROT *v.* + -ING[1].]

a. The action of the verb TROT in various senses; *spec.* in *U.S.*, a trotting-race.

14.. *Beryn* 2402 Yeur rennyng & yeur trotting, in-to an esy pase I shall turn. **1470–85** MALORY *Arthur* III. xiii. 116 A lytel afore mydnyȝt they herd the trottynge of an hors. **1581** MULCASTER *Positions* xxiv. (1887) 98 Trotting.. shaketh the bodie to violently. **1646** SIR T. BROWNE *Pseud. Ep.* IV. vi. 193 Animalls..move *per latera*,..or *per diametrum*,..lifting the foot before, and the crosse foot behinde, which is succussation or trotting. **1787** 'G. GAMBADO' *Acad. Horsem.* Title-p., Instructions for Walking, Trotting, Cantering, Galloping. **1873** H. E. P. SPOFFORD *Pilot's Wife* in *Casquet Lit.* IV. 13/2 She and the nurse made such a racket.., with their shshshing and trotting and patting and stirring and sipping. **1882** *Standard* 26 Sept. 2/2 At Lynn and other parts of the Wash they [whelks] are caught by a mode of fishing designated 'trotting'. Green crabs are threaded together and let down into the water, and the whelk,..while sucking the meat out of the crabs, is easily drawn to the surface. **1883** F. M. CRAWFORD *Dr. Claudius* v, 'Do you have much racing in America?'..'Yes. Trotting. Ag'd nags in sulkies. See how fast they can go a mile.' **1969** *Daily Tel.* 5 May 19/2 The most common is 'trotting'—taking non-existent bids to force up the price.

b. *attrib.* as ***trotting-match***, ***-race***, ***-sulky***, ***-term*** (see TROT *v.* 2), ***-track***, ***-turf***.

1822 *Sunday Times* 20 Oct. 3/2 The roan trotting match for 500 sovereigns. **1840** BLAINE *Encycl. Rur. Sports* §1046 Formerly it was a maxim in trotting races, that weight did not form a considerable object. *Ibid.* §1049 The distances of this trotting match were [etc.]. **1863** 'OUIDA' *Held in Bondage* (1870) 41 The certainty that Vane Steven's roan filly would lose the trotting-match. **1883** *Durham Univ. Jrnl.* 17 Dec. 141 I'm going to keep a trotting term. **1888** LIGHTHALL *Yng. Seigneur* 74 The horse-trader's trotting-sulky was standing at the door. **1893** *Outing* (U.S.) May 98/1 The perfect trotting track of the present time is built [etc.]. *Ibid.* 99/1 This early heroine of the trotting turf.

'trotting, *ppl. a.* [f. as prec. + -ING[2].] That trots, in various senses.

trotting butcher, a butcher who goes his rounds on horseback. ***trotting seconds hand***, in a watch, a hand which registers the seconds on the minute-divisions of the dial, pausing on each.

c **1425** *Eng. Conq. Irel.* 88 Vnnethe he [Henry III] wold ryde any amblynge hors, bot myche trottynge hors, for to trauaylle hys body the more. **1480** in *Cely Papers* (1900) 55, I whowlde awise yow brynge hower aull yowr trottyng hors. **1523** FITZHERB. *Husb.* §77 The .ix. propertyes of a foxe,.. the .vii. to be shorte-trottynge. **1579** J. JONES *Preserv. Bodie & Soule* I. xv. 28 Blinde bittels, flattering fellowes, trotting trulles, and wilful murtherers. **1660** BLOUNT *Boscobel* 23 The valiant Earl of Cleveland (who being above 60 years of age had marched 21 dayes together upon a trotting horse). **1725** RAMSAY *Gentle Sheph.* I. ii. Prol., A trotting burnie wimpling through the ground. **1842** MRS. F. TROLLOPE *Visit to Italy* I. i. 2 Inferences..deduced by trotting travellers from the aspect of the scenes through which they passed. **1851** MAYHEW *Lond. Labour* I. 175/2 The trotting butcher is..not likely to be succeeded by any in the same line, or..'ride' of business. **1888** BRYCE *Amer. Commw.* III. 528 *note*, The trotting horse is driven, not ridden. **1900** *Jeweller's Catal.*, The Nurse's Watch, with long trotting seconds hand for taking the beats of the pulse.

trottle: see TRATTLE *sb.*[2]

‖**trottoir** (trɔtwar). [F. (16th c.), f. *trotter* to TROT + *-oir*, L. *-ōrium*.] A paved footway on each side of a street; a pavement. Also *attrib.*

1792 A. YOUNG *Trav. France* I. 150 The streets..are wide, and very well paved, with the addition, uncommon in France, of *trotoirs*. **1804** *Edinb. Rev.* Jan. 337 A neat *trottoir* of flat stones runs before the doors. **1828** H. BEST *Italy as it is* 88 Milan is well paved, though there are no *trottoirs*, or foot passengers' pavements. **1832** MRS. F. TROLLOPE *Dom. Mann. Amer.* xxx. (1839) 293 The *trottoir* paving, in most of the streets, is extremely good, being of large flag stones, very superior to the bricks of Philadelphia. **1864** G. MUSGRAVE *Ten Days Fr. Parsonage* I. i. 22 Water-carts..irrigating.. the splashed..pedestrians on the trottoir.

Hence **trottoired** *a.*, furnished with a trottoir.

1858 MAYHEW *Upper Rhine* iv. (1860) 185 The streets.. are mostly broad and trottoired.

trotty ('trɒtɪ), *a. colloq.* Also **trottie**. [f. TROT *sb.*[1] + -Y[1].] **a.** Of daintily small proportions. **b.** Of a person: agreeable, amenable.

1891 'L. MALET' *Wages of Sin* II. v. i. 165 Some of the little silk shifties and night-i-gowns were simply too trottie for words. *a* **1913** F. ROLFE *Desire & Pursuit of Whole* (1934) xi. 109 'I can't tell you how trotty we think it of you!' ..bibbled the woman. **1928** GALSWORTHY *Swan Song* I. i. 4 Trotty little ladies with dresses tight blown about trotty little figures.

trotyl ('trəʊtɪl). [f. TRINI)TROT(OLUENE + -YL.] = TRINITROTOLUENE.

1910 *United Service Mag.* Feb. 554 A new explosive for shells, mines and torpedoes is being manufactured... It is known commercially as 'Trotyl', its full name being Trinitrotoluol. **1922** *Encycl. Brit.* XXXI. 50 Trinitrotoluene (TNT) which is known officially as Trotyl is..very similar in its action to picric acid and had been discovered by Wilbrand in 1863. **1981** *Chem. Abstr.* 7 Sept. 121/2 (*heading*) Initial phase of the initiation of the detonation process in pressed trotyl.

trou, trouage, trouant: see TROW, TREWAGE, TRUANT.

troubadour ('truːbədʊə(r), -dɔə(r)). [a. F. *troubadour* (16th c. in Godef. *Compl.*), ad. Prov. *trobador* (= Cat. *trobador*, Sp., Pg. *trovador*, It. *trovatore*), agent-n. f. Prov. *trobar*, Sp., Pg. *trovar*, It. *trovare*, F. *trouver* to find, invent, compose in verse; cf. TROUVÈRE.

The origin of the verb itself is questioned. As it exists in most of the Romanic langs., it is generally held to be late popular L. Diez explained it as formed by metathesis from L. *turbāre* to disturb, through the sense 'turn up'. Cf. for the form F. *troubler*, OF. *trubler*, from late L. **turbulāre*: see *Etymol. Wörterbuch* ed. 4, s.v.; cf. also the Neapol. *controvare* from L. *conturbāre*. Another conjecture in Du Cange would take the Romanic forms from med.L. *tropus*, TROPE *sb.* 5, a verse or versicle, whence **tropāre*. Both of these, and other conjectures, present difficulties.]

One of a class of lyric poets, living in southern France, eastern Spain, and northern Italy, from the 11th to the 13th centuries, who sang in Provençal (*langue d'oc*), chiefly of chivalry and gallantry, sometimes including wandering minstrels and jongleurs.

1727–41 CHAMBERS *Cycl.* s.v., The poesy of the troubadours consisted in sonnets, pastorals, songs [etc.]. **1767** PERCY *Rel. Anc. Eng. Poetry* (ed. 2) I. p. xxvii, The Troubadours of Provence..are supposed to have led the way to the poets of Italy, France, and Spain. **1801** STRUTT *Sports & Past.* III. iii. 162 The troubadours brought with them into the north a new species of language called the Roman Language... It evidently originated from the Latin, and was the parent of the French tongue. **1833** LONGF. *Outre-Mer* Prose Wks. 1886 I. 94 The lyre of the Troubadour seems to have responded to the impulse of momentary feelings only,—to the touch of local and transitory circumstances. **1884** TENNYSON *Becket* Prol., I am a Troubadour, you know, and won the violet at Toulouse.

b. *transf.* One who composes or sings verses or ballads; also, a composer or writer in support of some cause or interest.

1826 J. M. SHERER *Refl. Ramble Germany* Introd. 24 At the inn here I found a young German troubadour. He sung ballads for me, accompanying himself on the guitar. **1840**

DICKENS *Old C. Shop* li, He's quite a Troubadour, you know. **1861** GOLDW. SMITH *Inaug. Lect.* 32 Novels and poems by the troubadours of the landed interest. **1869** B. TAYLOR *Byeways of Europe* I. 227 The Majorcans still have their troubadours, who are hired by languishing lovers to improvise strains.

c. *attrib.*

1883 *Chambers's Encycl.* IX. 560/2 The extent of territory on which the troubadour poetry was cultivated—viz... France south of the Loire; Catalonia, Valencia, and Aragon in Spain; and part of Upper Italy. **1887** MISS R. H. BUSK *Folk-Songs Italy* 122 The influence of the troubadour songs of Provence is scarcely felt beyond the region of Piedmont in the songs of the people. **1898** LADY MARY LOYD tr. *Uzanne's Fashion in Paris* iii. 55 Towards the close of the [First] Empire, when troubadour fashions came in. **1902** CHAYTOR *Troubadours Dante* Introd. 19 The great feature of the troubadour love-poetry is the glorification of the married woman.

Hence **'troubadourish** *a.*, pertaining to, or having the character or style of a troubadour, or of the poetry of the troubadours (whence **'troubadourishly** *adv.*); **'troubadourism**, the character, principles, or style of the troubadours; **'troubadourist**, one who writes in the style or studies the productions of the troubadours (in quot. *attrib.*).

1849 *Fraser's Mag.* XL. 448 'Effeminate and *troubadourish', I thought. **1864** PEARSON in *Spectator* 245/2 Blondel..maintained the honours of his troubadourish name by a patriotic Latin poem 'Complanctus Bonorum Gallicorum'. **1905** *Daily Chron.* 17 May 3/3 The troubadourish, unworldly, exquisite passionateness of it all. **1880** G. MEREDITH *Tragic Com.* xiii. (1892) 184 The pleading was not done *troubadourishly, in soft flute-notes. **1898** LADY MARY LOYD tr. *Uzanne's Fashion in Paris* Introd. 7 The stiff lines and starched manners of a sham *Troubadourism. **1901** *Daily Chron.* 18 Dec. 3/6 Tiptoft, whose..career..is entirely lacking in *troubadourist qualities, good or bad.

† **'troublable**, *a. Obs. rare*$^{-1}$. [f. TROUBLE *v.* + -ABLE.] Troublesome, grievous.

c **1374** CHAUCER *Boeth.* IV. met. ii. 92 (Camb. MS.) Trowblable [*Add. MS.* troublable] Ire þat arayseth in hym the floodes of trwblynges tormentith..hyr thowht.

† **'troublance.** *Obs.* Also 5 **turbulaunce, turblaunce**, 6 **trublance**, 7 **trubellance.** [a. OF. *trublance, troblance* (13th c. in Godef.), f. *trubler, trobler* to TROUBLE. With the earlier examples cf. the *β*-forms of TROUBLE; *turbulaunce* is conformed to L. *turbulentia*.] The action of troubling or state of being troubled; disturbance; trouble, sorrow, pain. (In later use only *Sc.*)

c **1400** LOVE *Bonavent. Mirr.* (1907) 287 With grete ioye.. of the blessed presence of her lorde; but..with grete drede and turbulaunce of his aweie passynge. *c* **1425** *Orolog. Sapient.* iv. in *Anglia* X. 353/44 The periles of turblaunce of þis noyous worlde. **15..** *Aberdeen Regr.* (Jam.), Conwickit for the trublance of him in wordis, calland him koffcaryll one the oppin gait. **1627** *Dumbarton Burgh Rec.* in J. Irving *Hist. Dumbartonshire* (1860) 475 The sd R^t M'Cawlay..to pay unlaw, and find caution for trubellance in tyme coming. **1819** W. TENNANT *Papistry Storm'd* iv. (1827) 127 The tipsy sutors..wi' their iron grapples, grippit His flesh, and unto troublance nippit, Garrin' him scream.

trouble ('trʌb(ə)l), *sb.* Forms: 3-7 **truble**, (3 **trubuil**), 4-6 **troble, -el(l, -il(l, -yll, -ul, trowble**, (5 **thruble, trobbyll**), 5-6 **trubel, trubble, troubel(l, trowbel, (-ill, -yll, -ul(l)**, 4- **trouble.** *β*. 4-6 **turble, -el, -ill**, 5 **torble, -el, tourbel.** [ME. a. OF. *truble, turble* (12th c.), *torble, tourble, troble* (13th c.), F. *trouble* (15th c.), f. *tourbler, troubler* to TROUBLE.]

1. a. Disturbance of mind or feelings; worry, vexation; affliction; grief; perplexity; distress.

Now often also in lighter use, expressing any degree, however slight, of embarrassment or 'bother', or a condition of suffering some inconvenience or discomfort.

c **1230** *Hali Meid.* 29 Godes spuses þat ise swote eise wiðute swuch trubuil. *c* **1430** LYDG. *Min. Poems* (Percy Soc.) 14 Out of the lond he put awey alle trobelle, And made of newe oure joies to be dobelle. **1509** FISHER *Fun. Serm. C'tess Richmond* Wks. (1876) 299 The greuaunce trouble and vexacyon of the good persone hath gretter cause of pyte ..than of the euyll persone. **1535** COVERDALE *Ps.* lxxxv[i]. 7 In the tyme of my trouble I call vpon the. **1611** BIBLE *Job* v. 7 Man is borne vnto trouble [*earlier vv.* labour, travail], as the sparkes flie vpward. **1667** MILTON *P.L.* v. 96 The trouble of thy thoughts..in sleep. **1719** DE FOE *Crusoe* II. vi, In trouble to be troubled Is to have your trouble doubled. **1818** SCOTT *Hrt. Midl.* xxiii, Her head was so carried with pain of body and trouble of mind. **1910** *Stage Year Bk.* 23 There are two services [of electricity] installed, to prevent trouble in case of a breakdown on the mains. *Mod.* The family were in great trouble on account of the death of the eldest son.

b. With *a* and *pl.* An instance of this; a misfortune, calamity; a distressing or vexatious circumstance, occurrence, or experience.

1515 BARCLAY *Egloges* iv. (1570) C v/2 Graunt me a liuing sufficient.. And voyde of troubles. **1560** DAUS tr. *Sleidane's Comm.* 208 The Ambassadors were in a pecke of troubles. *a* **1591** H. SMITH *Serm.* (1637) 244 Troubles come in an hundred wayes. **1602** SHAKS. *Ham.* III. i. 59 To take Armes against a Sea of troubles. **1612** BRINSLEY *Lud. Lit.* iii. (1627) 20 The trouble is this: that when as my children doe first enter into Latine, many of them will forget to reade English. **1861** PALEY *Æschylus* (ed. 2) *Choeph.* 683 *note*, At the very time when his troubles seemed at an end. **1863** READE *Hard Cash* I. 5 She was determined to share his every trouble.

c. *transf.* A thing or person that gives trouble; an occasion or cause of affliction or distress.

1591 SAVILE *Tacitus, Hist.* IV. lxxvi. 228 The Germans.. were..a kinde of vnprofitable troubles of a campe. **1610** SHAKS. *Temp.* I. ii. 152 Alack, what trouble Was I then to you? **1611** BIBLE *Isa.* i. 14 Your appointed Feasts..are a trouble vnto me, I am weary to beare them. **1709** POPE *Ess. Crit.* 502 Then most our trouble still when most admir'd. **1859** TENNYSON *Geraint & Enid* 1619 The useful trouble of the rain.

† **d.** Harm, injury, offence. *Obs.*

1463 ASHBY *Prisoner's Refl.* 255 Seyntes..That suffred trowbyll with out resystence. **1568** GRAFTON *Chron.* II. 281 The Flemynges did the French men great trouble.

e. ***my troubles***, a dismissive exlamation: 'don't worry about me': 'I don't care'. *Austral. colloq.*

1895 C. CROWE *Austral. Slang Dict.* 89 *My troubles*, what do I care. **1905** N. SPIELVOGEL *Gumsucker on Tramp* 90 Off again; round Leuwin Cape; rough seas; My Troubles! I'm coming home. **1947** G. CASEY *Wits are Out* 44 'You better lay off Kitty while the old man's about, or there'll be one more out-of-work motor salesman kicking round the city,' Syd suggested. 'My troubles!' Jerry jeered.

f. Usu. with qualifying noun: faulty working of apparatus or machinery, esp. on a motor vehicle; a problem caused by this (*engine trouble*, etc.). Also applied *transf.* to personal relations, as *wife trouble*.

1902 *Trans. Inst. Naval Archit.* XLIV. 213 Although it seems to fit the water tube troubles, it does not answer so well with the furnace troubles. **1909** *Westm. Gaz.* 26 Oct. 2/1 The only other serious difficulty [with the Wright biplane] seems to be what is known, generically, as 'engine trouble'... The forms that this 'engine trouble' takes are various, as every motorist knows. **1981** P. AUDEMARS *Gone to her Death* iii. 61 The local garagist..has wife trouble, because she has the money he needs.

g. ***trouble and strife***, rhyming slang for: (*a*) 'life' (*rare*); (*b*) 'wife'.

1908 'DOSS CHIDERDOSS' in *Sporting Times* 11 July 1/3, I shouted, 'Your "bees", or your "trouble and strife"!' Like the hero in 'Highwayman Harry'. **1929** J. B. PRIESTLEY *Good Companions* III. ii. 611 The old trouble-and-strife, eh? **1949** A. WILSON *Wrong Set* 62 'Thanks for looking after my old trouble and said strife' said Bruce. **1959** J. OSBORNE *Paul Slickey* II. x. 86 My posh trouble-and-strife, I'll be hers. **1977** G. FISHER *Villain of Piece* i. 7 It's the old trouble and strife—wife. I want to see her all right.

h. ***trouble at*** (***the*** or ***t'***) ***mill***: an industrial dispute, as at a Midlands or North Country textile mill; also *transf.* and *fig.*, alluding to any disagreement or problem at work, home, etc.

1967 'J. WINTON' *H.M.S.Leviathan* xx. 333 He replaced the receiver, and assumed a passable Yorkshire accent. 'Ah'm sorry, lass, but there's trouble down at t'mill... It looks as if we've got to go to sea in a hurry.' **1977** *New Scientist* 14 Apr. 84/1 This latter-day trouble at t'mill seems to stem from a dispute about what we mean by such expressions as 'use water' or 'abstract water' [at a water-mill]. **1982** *Times* 26 Aug. 16/7 Stanley has trouble at mill. A G Stanley Holdings..has dropped into losses at the interim stage..mainly because of continued problems at its Holmes Chapel wallpaper mill. **1984** *Times* 15 Sept. 8/1 There's trouble at t'mill in the board room of Grimsby Town Football Club.

2. a. Public disturbance, disorder, or confusion; with *a* and *pl.* an instance of this, a disturbance, an agitation.

[**1378** *Rolls of Parlt.* III. 43/1 Le Roialme en diverses parties est mys en grant troboill.] *c* **1400** *Apol. Loll.* 87 Mansleyng, þeft,..corrupcoun,..troubyl[l], periury. *c* **1435** *Chron. London* (Kingsford 1905) 85 To eschew Rebellion, dysobeyssaunce and Trouble. *c* **1460** FORTESCUE *Abs. & Lim. Mon.* xvii. (1885) 153 Wheroff hath comyn..mony gret trowbels and debates. **1550** LATIMER *Last Serm. bef. Edw. VI*, 105 It maketh troble and rebellion in the realme. **1651** HOBBES *Leviath.* II. xxx. 184 It is a hard matter to know who expecteth benefit from publique troubles. **1760-72** H. BROOKE *Fool of Qual.* i, [Then] the troubles happened: and Cromwell assumed the regency. **1855** MACAULAY *Hist. Eng.* xvii. IV. 105 They were to be allowed to exercise any profession which they had exercised before the troubles.

β. *c* **1440** *Promp. Parv.* 497/1 Torble, or torblynge.., *turbacio.* **1463** *Plumpton Corr.* (Camden) p. lxix, When any turble or enterprise was like to fall hurt or scaythe to the Kings people.

b. ***the troubles, the Troubles.*** Any of various rebellions, civil wars, and unrest in Ireland, *spec.* in 1919-23 and (in Northern Ireland) since the early 1970s.

1880 W. H. PATTERSON *Gloss. Words Antrim & Down* 109 *Troubles, the*, the Irish rebellion of 1641. **1922** JOYCE *Ulysses* 237 Times of the troubles... Somewhere here Lord Edward Fitzgerald escaped from major Sirr. *Ibid.* 613 He vividly recollected when the occurrence alluded to took place..in the days of the land troubles..early in the eighties. **1923** *Times Lit. Suppl.* 11 Oct. 661/3 A weak Government.., a new wave of nationalist exaltation, an untrained army of youths brought up on war rations..—these factors were sufficient to account for the troubles of 1919-21. **1942** E. WAUGH *Put out More Flags* iii. 235 The ruins of a police barracks, built to command the road through the valley, burnt in the troubles,..were one green with the grass. **1949** C. GRAVES *Ireland Revisited* vi. 57 'This was where Michael Dwyer was in keeping during the 'Troubles,' Mackey vouchsafed. ('In keeping' means being on the run.) **1959** *Listener* 2 July 32/1 The complicated political and personal passions inspired by 'the troubles'. **1968** M. COLLIS *Somerville & Ross* xxv. 258 As the Troubles were over more than ten years before [1936], how came it that Admiral Boyle, living in quiet retirement and much liked by high and low, was singled out? **1981** M. KENYON *Zigzag* i. 6 Before the new Troubles..he had fallen in love with romantic Ireland.

3. Pains or exertion, esp. in accomplishing or attempting something; care, toil, labour. Phr. ***to put to (the) trouble, to take (the) trouble.***

1577 B. GOOGE tr. *Heresbach's Husb.* 35 b, Lupines..This pulse requireth least trouble. **1662** J. DAVIES tr. *Olearius' Voy. Ambass.* 248 That trouble we had been at, put us all in a sweat. **1729** LAW *Serious C.* iii. (1732) 31 If it costs me no pains or trouble. **1830** R. J. RAYMOND *Oh! Men what Silly Things You Are* (song) 3 She marks you down, fly where you will..Can wing you, feather you or kill, Just as she takes the trouble. **1840** MISS MITFORD in L'Estrange *Life* (1870) III. vii. 108 To be quit of the trouble and expense of the garden. **1856** *Titan Mag.* Dec. 525/1 He..did not care to put himself to the least trouble. **1866** DK. ARGYLL *Reign Law* vii. (1871) 366 Wherever we take the trouble to trace any.. phenomenon through the sequences of cause and effect. **1912** *Oxford Mag.* 14 Nov. 78/1 To save themselves the trouble of thinking.

4. a. A disease, disorder, ailment; a morbid affection.

1726 *Wodrow Corr.* (1843) III. 267 Riding..agrees much with my trouble which I am not altogether free of. **1897** *Allbutt's Syst. Med.* III. 882 Perityphlitis due to trouble in the cæcum. **1899** *Ibid.* VIII. 16 Writer's cramp and like troubles.

b. A woman's travail. (Also of an animal.) *dial.* or *euphem.*

a **1825** FORBY *Voc. E. Anglia* s.v., She is now in her trouble. **1877** H. SMART *Bound to Win* i, Calvert came..and told me Veturia [the mare] was getting very close upon her trouble. **1889** M. GRAY *Annesley* III. i. 95 He rode over the bleak downs to help Daniel Pink's wife in her trouble. **1896** A. LILBURN *Borderer* xxix. 219 Come now, my canny woman, you must try and drink this, or you'll never win through your trouble. **1901** M. E. FRANCIS *Pastorals Dorset* 162 When I'm over my trouble I'll come to see you.

5. In various other special applications, euphemistic, colloquial, dialectal, or vulgar.

a. Unpleasant relations with the authorities, esp. such as involve arrest, summons before a magistrate, imprisonment, or punishment; e.g. ***to bring oneself into trouble, to get into trouble; to be in trouble***, to be in gaol (*slang*). Also ***to ask for trouble***: see ASK *v.* 16 b. Similarly, ***to look for*** (or ***seek***) ***trouble.***

1560 DAUS tr. *Sleidane's Comm.* 115 Lest they should both offend the Mayor, and bring themselues in trouble. *a* **1562** CAVENDISH *Wolsey* (1893) 266 This gentilman..who hathe byn late in troble in the Tower of London. **1837** J. D. LANG *New S. Wales* II. 34 His wife very soon got into trouble, as it is technically termed in the colony; i.e. into the commission of some crime or misdemeanour, which issues in..flagellation, or imprisonment, or transportation, or death by the law. **1899** MARY JOHNSTON *Old Dominion* vii, My friend has been in trouble..He will not make the worse conspirator for that. **1901** MERWIN & WEBSTER *Calumet 'K'* 134 We've got to build the belt gallery—and we'll have no end of a time doing it if the C. & S.C. is still looking for trouble. **1905** *N.Y. Even. Post* 29 Aug. 2 In the possible chance of rounding up all who might be seeking trouble, the police temporarily sequestered and searched 140 Chinamen. **1912** 'AURORA' *Jock Scott, Midshipman* xiv. 165 But if you are artful you don't often get 'bowled out', unless one of the 'crushers' has a 'down' on you, and is 'looking for trouble'. *a* **1915** *Mod.* Take care what you say, or you'll get into trouble. **1922** E. O'NEILL *Anna Christie* (1923) I. 25, I ain't looking for trouble. **1947** W. MOTLEY *Knock on Any Door* 152 Swollen out in their own importance they walked along West Madison looking for trouble.

b. Said of the condition of an unmarried woman with child.

1891 T. HARDY *Tess* xxxi, On no account do you say a word of your Bygone Trouble to him... Many a woman —some of the Highest in the Land—have had a Trouble in their time. **1891** *Daily News* 26 Jan. 7/2 She said she consented to come to London to be married to the prisoner as she believed she was in trouble.

c. *U.S. colloq.* or *slang.* Public festivity; interruption or disturbance of ordinary work.

1884 C. T. BUCKLAND *Sk. Social Life India* iii. 66 A day of rest comes in between each day of pleasure, or 'trouble' as the Yankees more rightly call it. **1897** FLANDRAU *Harvard Episodes* 313 That particular quarter..was not..the most decorous on Class Day. There is always more or less, what is technically known as 'trouble'..on Class Day afternoon.

6. *Mining.* A dislocation in a stratum; a fault (usually small).

1672 SINCLAIR *Misc. Obs. Hydrostaticks* (1683) 267 That alteration..was not occasioned by any Gae, or trouble. *Ibid.* 276 Gae's, and Dykes..being the occasion of so much Trouble, in the working of Coal,..the Coal-hewers call them ordinarily by that name Trouble. **1789** BRAND *Hist. Newcastle* II. 680 *note*, Troubles [are] dikes of the smallest degree;..strata are generally altered by a trouble, from their regular site to a different position. **1859** R. HUNT *Guide Mus. Pract. Geol.* (ed. 2) 228 The effects of these movements will be visible in faults, troubles, dykes, throws, or heaves (as in different localities they are named).

7. *attrib.* and *Comb.*, as ***trouble-bearer, -cup, -maker, -shirker; trouble-free, -giving, -haunted, -proof, -saving, -tost, -void*** adjs.; ***trouble-making*** ppl. adj. and vbl. sb. (See also TROUBLE *v.* 6.) **trouble-hunter**: *spec.* = TROUBLE-SHOOTER 1; also **trouble hunting** *vbl. sb.*; **trouble lamp, light** *N. Amer.*, a portable lamp (esp. one carried on a motor vehicle), by the light of which roadside repairs, etc., can be done; **trouble man** *U.S.* = TROUBLE-SHOOTER 1; **trouble spot**, a place where difficulties frequently occur; a scene of (impending) conflict.

1909 *Daily Chron.* 14 Apr. 7/5 A laugh is the best trouble bearer. **1850** STRUTHERS *Poet. Wks.* II. 244 Quaff'd it must be, life's trouble-cup. **1648** HERRICK *Hesper.*, *Content, not Cates* 7 A little pipkin.. Set on my table, trouble-free. **1893** *Westm. Gaz.* 3 Feb. 1/3 A most trouble-giving class. **1807** WORDSW. *White Doe* VII. 151 All now was trouble-haunted ground. **1910** Trouble-hunter [see HELL-BENT *a.* and *adv.*]. **1924** *New Eng. Telephone Topics* XVIII. 288 Repairmen, the 'trouble hunters', are at work constantly. **1882** T. D. LOCKWOOD *Pract. Information for Telephonists* 135 Every movement made for an accurate preliminary test frequently saves an hour of happy-go-lucky trouble hunting. **1916** *Daily Colonist* (Victoria, B.C.) 9 July 12/4 If a car is not equipped with an extension trouble lamp, it is well to provide among the accessories a pocket flash lamp. **1927** W. FAULKNER *Sartoris* III. 196 He was doing something to the engine of it [*sc.* a car] while the house-yard-stable-boy held a patent trouble-lamp. **1952** *Sun* (Baltimore) (B ed.) 5 Jan. 7/4 Their headlights went out... A door slammed shut and cut the wire on the trouble light. **1979** *Arizona Daily Star* 1 Apr. H3/1 He just happened to have a siphon hose; also a trouble light with a cord that seemed long enough to reach back to his home in Mexico City. **1923** *Time* 28 May 1/2 (*heading*) Chief trouble maker. **1931** KIPLING *Limits & Renewals* (1932) 191, I took stock o' them, to spot the funny-men an' trouble-makers. **1955** 'A. GILBERT' *Is She Dead Too?* ii. 40 A snooper, or trouble-maker, that was Margaret Reeve. **1981** W. EBERSOHN *Divide Night* xiii. 175 A more disciplined age where trouble-makers who went against the government would be dealt with firmly. **1920** S. LEWIS *Main St.* xvi. 202, I certainly hope you don't class yourself with a lot of trouble-making labor-leaders! *a* **1974** R. CROSSMAN *Diaries* (1975) I. 77 Manny wouldn't allow it, for fear—as he put it—that the questions raised would be used for trouble-making. **1889** *Cassell's Family Mag.* June 410/1 A special band of what the Americans call 'Trouble-men', who are prepared to attend at once to sudden calls for assistance. **1953** *Herald* (Belle Glade, Florida) 13 Feb. 1/1 According to Florida Power & Light district manager C. A. Chase, FPL's 'Troubleman' J. J. McCarley located the difficulty, and repair crews worked until 2 am Wednesday repairing broken circuits and restoring service. **1878** A. PAUL *Random Writ.* 202 We think ourselves giants and trouble-proof until it [illness] overtakes us. **1908** A. S. M. HUTCHINSON *Once aboard Lugger* v. vii. 268 These light-hearts, these trouble-shirkers. **1956** M. E. W. GOSS in R. K. Merton *Student-Physician* IV. 258 The regular duties.. included the unwritten obligation to assist in.. assessing the 'trouble-spots' and suggesting possible solutions. **1963** *Listener* 7 Feb. 260/2 Sir David Eccles wants £200,000,000 a year pumped into the trouble-spots [*sc.* areas of heavy unemployment]. **1981** T. BARLING *Bikini Red North* ii. 41 It should be quiet enough, being so far from Montmartre and the other trouble spots. **1608** SYLVESTER *Du Bartas* II. iv. III. *Schism* 506 Art not thou hee that sow'st the Isaacian Plain With Trouble-Tares? **1850** TENNYSON *In Mem.* lxv, I lull a fancy trouble-tost. **1559** *Mirr. Mag.*, *Mortimers* xiv, Seldome ioye continueth trouble voyde.

Hence †'**troubleful** *a.*, full of trouble, troublesome (*obs.*); '**troubleless** *a.*, free from trouble.

1588 J. HARVEY *Disc. Probl.* 71 To what end.. haue they breathed out so loude, boisterous, and troublefull blasts? **1838** MARY HOWITT *Birds & Flowers*, *Birds* ii, In a troubleless delight!

†'**trouble**, *a.* *Obs.* Forms: 4–5 trouble, -el, -ele, trowble, (4 turble), 5 trobil, trobille, trowbul, *Sc.* trubill. [a. F. *trouble* (in 12th c. *truble*, *turble*, 13th c. *tourble*, *troble*, *trouble*), according to Hatz.-Darm.:—late pop.L. **turbulum*, for cl.L. *turbidum*, whence *troubler* to TROUBLE. A genuine adjectival form, but perh. sometimes standing in Eng. for *troublé*, TROUBLY.]

1. Of water, wine, etc., Troubled, turbid, muddy, thick; of air, etc., Misty, murky, cloudy, not clear; in quot. *c* 1400[1], dim, dusky.

a **1327** *On Dreams* in *Rel. Ant.* I. 263 Water thikke ant trouble. *c* **1400** *Rom. Rose* 7116 As moche as.. The sunne sourmounteth the mone, That troubler is, and chaungeth sone. *c* **1400** MAUNDEV. (1839) viii. 108 Þere is a welle that iiij. sithes in the ȝeer chaungeth his colour: somtyme grene, somtyme reed, somtyme cleer, & somtyme trouble [*Roxb.* trublee]. *Ibid.* xiv. 157 The gode dyamandes.. ben of trouble colour. *c* **1450** *Merlin* 236 Thei loked towarde Lanneriur, and saugh the eyr trouble, and thikke of duste. **1482** WARKW. *Chron.* (Camden) 24 Whenne it betokenethe battayle it rennys foule and trouble watere [cf. quot. 1605 s.v. TROUBLY 1].

2. Disturbed, distressed, confused; marked by disturbance or confusion; troublous, restless, unquiet.

c **1374** CHAUCER *Boeth.* IV. pr. iv. 107 (Camb. MS.) Alle thingys semen to be confus and trouble [*Add. MS.* trouble] to vs men. *c* **1386** —— *Clerk's T.* 409 With stierne face and with ful trouble cheere. *c* **1430** *Pilgr. Lyf Manhode* IV. xvii. (1869) 184 Þe anguishe þat so harde presseth troubel herte.

3. Turbulent, tempestuous, stormy, violent.

c **1374** CHAUCER *Boeth.* I. Met. vii. 19 (Camb. MS.) The trowble [*Add. MS.* trouble] wynde þat hyht Auster. *c* **1470** HENRY *Wallace* VII. 182 Trubbill weddyr makis schippis to droune. **1509** *Payne Evyll Marr.* 95 Like perilous Caribeis of the trouble see.

Hence '**troubleness**, troubledness, turbidity.

c **1380** WYCLIF *Serm.* Sel. Wks. II. 333 Þe wynd of Goddis lawe shulde be cleer, ffor turblenes in þis wynde mut nedis turble mennis lif. **14..** *Beryn* 1417 Of hertis trobilnes I had nevir knowlech, but of al gladnes. **1482** *Monk of Evesham* (Arb.) 73 They sofryd greuys and varyante trowbulnes of the eyre.

trouble ('trʌb(ə)l), *v.* Forms: see TROUBLE *sb.* [ME. a. OF. *trubler*, *trobler*, *torbler*, *tourbler*, *turbler* (11–14th c.), F. *troubler*:—late L. **turbulāre*, f. **turbulus* = cl.L. *turbidus* TURBID.]

I. 1. *trans.* To disturb, agitate, ruffle (water, air, etc.); *esp.* to stir up (water) so as to make it thick or muddy; to make (wine) thick by stirring up the lees; to make turbid, dim, or cloudy. Now *rare* or *arch.*

1340 HAMPOLE *Pr. Consc.* 4319 He sal trobel þe se when he wille, And pees it and make it be stille. **1382** WYCLIF *Ezek.* xxxii. 2 Thou.. trublist to gidre watris with thi feet. **1422** tr. *Secreta Secret.*, *Priv. Priv.* 230 Tho that haue eyen discolourid and trowbelid. **1534** TINDALE *John* v. 4 For an angell went doune.. and troubled the water. *a* **1550** in *Dunbar's Poems* (S.T.S.) 315 He trublit all the air. **1579** GOSSON *Sch. Abuse* (Arb.) 56 The fishe Sepia can trouble the water. **1596** SHAKS. *Tam. Shr.* v. ii. 141 Like a fountaine troubled, Muddie, ill seeming, thicke. **1660** DRYDEN *Astr. Red.* 272 As those lees, that trouble it, refine The agitated soul of generous wine. **1859** GULLICK & TIMBS *Paint.* 231 In the application of paint,.. to avoid unnecessarily mixing, or, as it is called, 'troubling', 'saddening', or 'tormenting' the tints. **1878** HUXLEY *Physiogr.* 170 Its [the sea's] surface is ordinarily more or less troubled with waves.

†**b.** *intr.* for *pass.* Of water, to grow turbid; of the sun or sky, to grow dark, cloudy, or stormy; of a storm, to rage. Also *fig.* *Obs.*

1390 GOWER *Conf.* VIII. 3009* But hou so that it trowble in their [= the air], The Sonne is evere briht and feir. *c* **1400** MAUNDEV. (1839) v. 52 Put a drope of bawme in clere water.. & stere it wel;.. And ȝif þat the bawme be fyn.. the water schall neuere trouble. *c* **1400** *Destr. Troy* 7619 A thondir with thicke Rayn thrublit in þe skewes. **1568** GRAFTON *Chron.* II. 885 The British affayres.. began now again to flow out and to trouble.

2. *trans.* To disturb, derange; to interfere with, interrupt; to hinder, mar. *Obs.* or *arch.*

c **1330** R. BRUNNE *Chron. Wace* (Rolls) 4764 (Petyt MS.) Þe feste was turbled & mirth aweye. *c* **1470** HENRY *Wallace* VIII. 1462 Your fredom we sall trowbill na ma. **1558** KNOX *First Blast* (Arb.) 13 By her babling she troubled the hole assemblie. **1607** SHAKS. *Cor.* v. vi. 129 Trouble not the peace. **1642** JER. TAYLOR *Episc.* (1647) 195 Lucius.. troubled the affayre by his interposing. **1713** ADDISON *Guardian* No. 99 ¶4 Such who.. might.. trouble and pervert the course of justice. **1832** TENNYSON *Lotos-Eaters* 119 And we should come like ghosts to trouble joy.

II. 3. To put into a state of (mental) agitation or disquiet; to disturb, distress, grieve, perplex.

a **1225** *Ancr. R.* 268 Þu nouhst nout sturien ne trublen þine heorte. **1340** *Ayenb.* 104 Wyþ-oute him to trobli, wyþ-oute him to chongi, wyþ-oute him remue ine none manere. **1382** WYCLIF *John* xii. 27 Now my soule is troublid. *c* **1440** *Generydes* 54 Sore trobelyd in his mynde. **1526** TINDALE *John* xiv. 1 Lett nott youre hertes be trubled. **1538** STARKEY *England* I. i. 20 Let thys dyuersyte of sectys.. no thyng trowbul vs at al. **1657** *North's Plutarch, Add. Lives* (1676) 8 Orators who do break their brains to utter good things, and never trouble their heads in the least to do them. **1715** DE FOE *Fam. Instruct.* I. iii. (1841) I. 57 Husband, I believe something troubles thee. **1866** G. MACDONALD *Ann. Q. Neighb.* xxiii. (1878) 417, I was troubled in my own mind. **1875** JOWETT *Plato* (ed. 2) IV. 133 No such perplexity could ever trouble a modern metaphysician.

β. *c* **1380** WYCLIF *Sel. Wks.* II. 328 And þerfore Petre biddiþ Cristen men, Be not turblid bi þer manas. *c* **1450** *St. Cuthbert* (Surtees) 2850 Turbyld in spirit he chaunged his mode.

†**b.** *intr.* for *pass.* To be disturbed or agitated; to be in or get into an unsettled state. *Obs.* *rare*[−1].

1618 BOLTON *Florus* IV. iii. (1636) 295 In the change of the government of the Romans,.. the world troubled throughout, and the whole body of the Empire was turmoiled with all sorts of perils.

4. *trans.* To do harm or hurt to; to injure; to molest, oppress.

1375 BARBOUR *Bruce* I. 479 And swa trowblyt the folk saw he, That he tharoff had gret pitte. *c* **1475** *Rauf Coilȝear* 136 For sa troublit with stormis was I neuer stad. **1526** TINDALE *Matt.* xxvi. 10 Why trouble ye the woman? **1567** *Gude & Godlie B.* (S.T.S.) 107 The fleand dartis,.. To trubill the, sall haif na mycht. **1667** MILTON *P.L.* XII. 209 God looking forth will trouble all his Host And craze thir Chariot wheels. **1711** in *Nairne Peerage Evid.* (1874) 143 From all citing conveening judging fyning or otherways molesting and troubling the saids heritors tennents possessors and occupiers. **1855** SINGLETON *Virgil* I. 246 Swans.. Whom, swooping from the region of the skies, Jove's bird was troubling. **1912** *Times* 19 Oct. 5/4 No individual.. shall be proceeded against or troubled in his person or property.

absol. *c* **1570** R. ROBINSON *Gold. Mirr.* (Chetham Soc.) Introd. 7 Stormes that troubleth sore. **1611** BIBLE *Job* iii. 17 There the wicked cease from troubling.

b. Of disease or ailment: To cause bodily derangement, pain, or inconvenience to; to afflict; sometimes in weakened sense, to affect. (Often in *pass.* with *with*; also *fig.*)

c **1400** tr. *Secreta Secret.*, *Gov. Lordsh.* 72 Þy stomak shal fille hym with euyl humours.., and þat shall trobbyl þy brayn with euyll fumosyte. *Ibid.* 80 Wyn þat ys takyn abundanly.. lettys þe vnderstondynge,.. troblys þe brayn. **1508** DUNBAR *Poems* iv. 2, I.. Am trublit now with gret seiknes. *a* **1548** HALL *Chron.*, *Hen. IV*, 32 b, His pange so sore troubled him that he lay as though al his vitall sprites had bene from him departed. **1595** SHAKS. *John* v. iii. 3 This Feauer that hath troubled me so long, Lyes heauie on me. **1604** —— *Oth.* III. iii. 414 Being troubled with a raging tooth, I could not sleepe. **1684** BUNYAN *Pilgr.* II. 84 He said, That Mercy was a pretty Lass; but troubled with ill Conditions. **1751** JOHNSON *Rambler* No. 153 ¶19 All whom I intreat to sing are troubled with colds. **1899** *Allbutt's Syst. Med.* VIII. 842 For many years he has had an ulcer.. which troubles him.

5. To distress *with* something disagreeable and unwelcome; to vex, annoy; to tease, plague, worry, pester, bother. †Also *intr.* with *with* (obs.).

1515 *Plumpton Corr.* (Camden) 213 If they may find any hole or colur therin, they will troble with me for the same. **1538** AUDLEY in *Lett. Suppress. Monasteries* (Camden) 247 Thus I trobill you with my sutes. **1560** DAUS tr. *Sleidane's Comm.* 23 b, [He] besecheth him and his adherentes to trouble the church no more. **1590** SHAKS. *Com. Err.* III. i. 62 Your towne is troubled with unruly boies. **1611** —— *Wint. T.* II. i. 1 Take the Boy to you: he so troubles me, 'Tis past enduring. **1794** NELSON in Nicolas *Disp.* (1845) I. 440, I made.. thirteen scaling ladders,.. for I think the Troops will be troubled in getting up the wall, 'because the earth is too loose. **1885** 'MRS. ALEXANDER' *Valerie's Fate* ii, 'He would trouble me no more.' 'Does he really trouble you, Valerie?' 'Yes, really. I am frightened and nervous when I go out.'

b. In lighter sense: To put to inconvenience, incommode; often used hyperbolically by way of courtesy: 'to give occasion of labour to: a word of civility or slight regard' (J.). Usu. const. *with*: also with *inf.* (esp. in a formula of polite or quasi-polite request), to give (one) the trouble *to do* something (cf. c, d).

1516 Q. MARGARET in Mrs. Wood *Lett. Illustr. Ladies* (1846) I. 221, I pray you send me word, for I will trouble you no more with my sending. **1612** BRINSLEY *Lud. Lit.* iii. (1627) 12 It seemeth to mee.. unreasonable.. that the Grammar Schooles should bee troubled with teaching A.B.C. **1669** STURMY *Mariner's Mag.* I. 14 He will not be troubled with small Fractions.. which breedeth no great error. **1708** ARBUTHNOT in *Lett. Eminent Persons* (1813) I. 180, I shall trouble you to give my services to my friends at Oxford. **1711** STEELE *Spect.* No. 142 ¶1, I will not trouble you with more Letters at this time. **1875** JOWETT *Plato* (ed. 2) I. 294 Let me trouble you with one more question. *Mod.* May I trouble you to pass the mustard? I'll trouble you to wipe your feet the next time you come into the house.

c. With *for*: To pester with requests, ask importunately, importune; hence (usually) in lighter use, in a formula of polite request: to give (one) the trouble of passing or handing something.

1516 Q. MARGARET in Mrs. Wood *Lett. Illustr. Ladies* (1846) I. 221, I shall trouble you no more for no money. **1755** JOHNSON, *To Trouble*... 9. (In low language.) To sue for a debt. **1844** DICKENS *Mart. Chuz.* vi, The new pupil who 'troubled' Mr. Pecksniff for the loaf. **1894** H. NISBET *Bush Girl's Rom.* 30 I'll trouble you, Shafton, for another of those good cigars.

d. *refl.* To take the trouble, take pains, exert oneself (*to do* something).

1500–20 DUNBAR *Poems* xx. 6 Trubill nevir thy self,.. Vthiris to rewill, that will not rewlit be. **1621** T. WILLIAMSON tr. *Goulart's Wise Vieillard* 49 Pilots.., without much troubling themselues, or stirring from their places, sit quietly at the sterne, and holding the Rudder,.. doe cond and carry their Ships.. to their vnlading port. **1845** R. MONCKTON MILNES in *Life* (1891) I. viii. 357 He had never troubled himself.. to understand the question. **1855** MACAULAY *Hist. Eng.* xv. III. 581 The officer never troubles himself to ascertain whether the arms are in good order.

e. *intr.* for *refl.* = prec. sense. *mod. colloq.*

1880 MCCARTHY *Own Times* III. xl. 206 He would have allowed reform to go its way for him, and never troubled. **1884** W. C. SMITH *Kildrostan* 50 Do not trouble to bring back the boat.

III. 6. The verb-stem in comb., prefixed to sbs., forming sbs. with sense 'one who or that which troubles, disturbs, or mars the peace or enjoyment of'; as †*trouble-belly* (gutwort, *Globularia Alypum*), *trouble-cup*, *trouble-feast* (also attrib.), *trouble-house*, *trouble-mirth*, *trouble-rest*, *trouble-state*, *trouble-tomb*, *trouble-town*, *trouble-world*. (Mostly *rare* or *Obs.*)

1668 WILKINS *Real Char.* 112 Guttwort, *Trouble-belly. *a* **1610** HEALEY *Theophrastus* (1636) 70 Then he railes on the Fidler as a *trouble-cup. **1603** FLORIO *Montaigne* III. ix. (1632) 562 This *trouble-feast reason. **1630** LENNARD tr. *Charron's Wisd.* (1658) 52 A little trouble-feast, a tedious and importunate parasite. **1691** tr. *Emilianne's Frauds Rom. Monks* (ed. 3) 226 The old Fryer was a *Turba Festa*, a meer Trouble-Feast to talk so at random. **1608** DOD & CLEAVER *Expos. Prov.* xi–xii. 100 This unthrifty *trouble-house. **1643**, **1690** [see *trouble-town*]. **1874** T. HARDY *Far fr. Madding Crowd* xxxv, 'Tis well to say 'Friend' outwardly, though you say 'Troublehouse' within. **1598** SYLVESTER *Du Bartas* II. i. III. *Furies* 328 Th' other Furie.. Foule, *trouble-rest. **1604** DANIEL *Civ. Wars* IV. xxiv, Those faire bayts these *Trouble-States still vse. **1822** LAMB *Elia* Ser. II. *Detached Th. Bks.*, They covered [Shakespeare's effigy] over with a coat of white paint... I think I see them.. these sapient *trouble-tombs. **1619** J. DYKE *Counterpoison* 23 What breedeth these *trouble-townes but couetousnesse? **1643** TRAPP *Comm. Gen.* xxxiv. 30 Many such trouble-houses and trouble-towns there are abroad. **1690** C. NESSE *O. & N. Test.* I. 319 Branding his sons with the black name of trouble-houses, and trouble-towns. **1663** *Flagellum or O. Cromwell* Pref., *Trouble-worlds. **1691** WOOD *Ath. Oxon.* II. 101 John Lilbourne [was] naturally a great trouble-world.

troubled ('trʌb(ə)ld), *ppl. a.* [f. prec. + -ED[1].]

1. Physically agitated; of the sea, sky, etc., stormy; of water, wine, etc., stirred up so as to diffuse the sediment, made thick or muddy, turbid.

troubled waters (*fig.*), a state of agitation or disquiet.

1388 WYCLIF *Josh.* xiii. 2 The troblid flood that moistith Egipt. **1581** J. WALKER in *Confer.* IV. (1584) F fiij, It is troubled water when we mingle our workes and righteousnes with Gods. **1611** BIBLE *Isa.* lvii. 20 The wicked are like the troubled sea, when it cannot rest, whose waters cast vp myre and dirt. **1632** LITHGOW *Trav.* I. 12 The Riuer Tyber [is] of a troubled and muddy colour. **1796** KIRWAN *Elem. Min.* (ed. 2) I. 334 Jargon... Heated to redness, and quenched in water, it becomes rifty, and troubled. **1855** MACAULAY *Hist. Eng.* xx. IV. 535 The sky was dark and troubled. **1864** G. MUSGRAVE *Ten Days Fr. Parsonage* II. iii. 98 An inadvertent inquiry would have brought us into troubled waters.

2. Disturbed; disquieted; disordered; agitated; afflicted. Also *absol.*

a **1325** *Prose Psalter* l. 18 [li. 17] Trubled gost is sacrifice to God. *c* **1450** CAPGRAVE *Life St. Aug.* xv. 21 Augustine with a troubled mynde be-gan to loke up-on his felaw Alipius, and..cried: What suffir we? **1535** COVERDALE *2 Esdras* xv. 8 The innocent bloude of the troubled crieth vnto me. **1611** BEAUM. & FL. *Philaster* III. i, Medicine for a troubled mind. **1651** HOBBES *Leviath.* II. xxiii. 126 Some private partie of a troubled State. **1728** ELIZA HEYWOOD tr. *Mme de Gomez's Belle A.* (1734) II. 31 Philosophy could give his troubled Thoughts but little ease. **1849** MACAULAY *Hist. Eng.* vi. II. 127 The historian of this troubled reign. **1885** 'MRS. ALEXANDER' *At Bay* vii, I wandered about the old scenes like a troubled ghost. **1894** HALL CAINE *Manxman* III. xxi, She slept a troubled sleep.

troubledly ('trʌb(ə)ldlɪ), *adv. rare.* [f. prec. + -LY[2].] In a troubled or agitated manner; in quot. 1624, in a disorderly way, confusedly (*obs.*).

1599 NASHE *Lenten Stuffe* 23 So troubledly bemudded with griefe and care. **1624** BP. HALL *Art Divine Medit.* xvi, Our Meditation must proceed in due order; not troubledly, not preposterously. **1630** LENNARD tr. *Charron's Wisd.* Pref. A ij a, He that carieth himselfe troubledly, disquietly, malcontent, fearing death, is not wise. **1891** H. C. HALLIDAY *Someone must suffer* II. ii. 51 He answered troubledly.

troubledness ('trʌb(ə)ldnɪs). *rare.* [f. as prec. + -NESS.] The quality or condition of being troubled, disturbed, or disquieted; also, turbidity.

c **1530** *Judic. Urines* II. xii. 40 b, That same thycknes & trublydnes. **1631** *Celestina* xx. 191 With so great importunity, and troubledness of minde. *a* **1681** WHARTON *Causes Earthquakes* Wks. (1683) 323 Putrefaction and Troubledness of the Waters of Pits and Wells.

† **'troublement.** *Obs. rare.* [a. F. *troublement*, f. *troubler* to TROUBLE: see -MENT.] The act of troubling or condition of being troubled.

1484 CAXTON *Chivalry* 84 Ire is in courage troublement and remembraunce of wycked wil. *c* **1557** ABP. PARKER *Ps.* xviii. L iv, They did preuent with troublement, the day of my great stresse.

troubler ('trʌblə(r)). Forms: see TROUBLE *sb.*: also 4 -ere, 5–6 -ar(e. [ME. a. OF. *trobleor*, F. *troubleur* (13th c.), *tourbleur* (15th c.), f. *trobler*, etc.: see TROUBLE *v.*] One who or that which troubles (in any sense); a disturber; an oppressor.

1382 WYCLIF *Isa.* xix. 20 They shul crien to the Lord fro the face of the trublere. *c* **1440** *Promp. Parv.* 497/1 Torbelare, or he þat makythe debate, *turbator*. **1547–64** BAULDWIN *Mor. Philos.* (Palfr.) 140 Conscience..is..an inward troubler or tormentor. **1594** SHAKS. *Rich. III*, I. iii. 221 The troubler of the poore Worlds peace. **1624** MIDDLETON *Game at Chess* I. i, Yon troubler of all Christian waters. **1710** HUME *Sacred Success.* (1716) 108 That troubler of the Church. **1869** TROLLOPE *He knew*, etc. xxv. 195 That pernicious troubler of the peace of families.

'trouble-shooter. orig. *U.S.* [f. TROUBLE *sb.* + SHOOTER.] **1.** A person who traces and corrects faults in machinery and equipment (orig. *spec.* on a telegraph or telephone line). Cf. *trouble-hunter, man* s.v. TROUBLE *sb.* 7.

1905 *Strand Mag.* Mar. 268/1 A good looking young 'trouble-shooter'—as a mender of telephone lines is called —had..asked her to marry him. **1913** *Red Cross Mag.* Jan. 34/1 Among them are..the 'trouble shooters', highly trained men who are responsible for the repairing of any breaks in the plant or equipment. **1931** B. STARKE *Touch & Go* xv. 248 A trouble-shooter for the telephone lines. **1945** H. D. SMYTH *Gen. Acct. Devel. Atomic Energy Mil. Purposes* xi. 121 Particularly in the early stages of operation the Berkeley men stationed at Clinton were invaluable as 'trouble-shooters' and in instructing operators. **1951** *Engineering* 2 Feb. 133/2 Manufacture..by fully-automatic machine shops..with only a few skilled men as 'trouble-shooters'. **1959** H. HOBSON *Mission House Murder* xxi. 140 A post office electronics expert and trouble-shooter.

2. One who specializes in removing or solving difficulties; esp. a mediator in diplomatic or industrial affairs.

1927 *Sat. Even. Post* 15 Jan. 153/3 With the 'Trouble-Shooters' of the North Atlantic Icebergs... Locating and destroying them is the perilous and never-ending duty of the United States Coast Guard cutters. **1933** R. C. MAYER *How to do Publicity* xi. 134 The 'trouble-shooters' in publicity deal mostly with such emergencies. **1940** R. S. LAMBERT *Ariel & all his Quality* iii. 77 The light had gone out of the Talks... His successors were chosen to be what Americans call 'trouble shooters'. **1953** W. R. BURNETT *Vanity Row* iii. 21 He needed an expert trouble-shooter, untainted by police politics. **1962** R. BUCKMINSTER FULLER *Epic Poem on Industrialization* 24 Self-helpless old fashioned business War forced to call in..Professional Trouble-shooters. **1971** H. WILSON *Labour Govt.* ix. 136 The appointment of an industrial relations 'trouble-shooter' for the industry.

Also **'trouble-shooting** *vbl. sb.* and *ppl. a.*; hence (back-formation) **trouble-shoot** *v. trans.* and *intr.*, to solve (a problem), to repair; to mediate.

1918 V. W. PAGÉ *Aviation Engines* 9 Special attention has been paid to instructions on tool equipment, use of tools, trouble 'shooting' and engine repairs. **1938** E. B. WHITE *Let.* 18 Nov. (1976) 186 This place teems with trouble of one sort and another. I am up every morning at twenty past six, trouble shooting. **1941** *Daily Progress* (Charlottesville, Virginia) 19 Aug. 1 (*heading*) Judge Rosenman..is now in capital, trouble-shooting the bottle-neck. **1957** V. PACKARD *Hidden Persuaders* xviii. 208 One firm that provides psychological bug-hunting services to industry cited the service it performed in trouble-shooting an employee problem in Ohio. **1964** S. BRITTAN *Treasury under Tories* ii. 53 The Cabinet's *Economic Policy Committee*.., over which the Chancellor presides, is mainly a trouble-shooting body. **1969** *Daily Colonist* (Victoria, B.C.) 8 June 2/7 (Advt.), Analyst—reporting to the President—required for troubleshooting all facets of the Victoria winery operation. **1977** P. DICKINSON *Walking Dead* IV. ii. 255 His official status in the Company was a string of vague general nouns, but his job was trouble-shooting. **1978** R. LEWIS *Inevitable Fatality* i. 19 I'm a business consultant... My forte is to troubleshoot, to get in and out again.

troublesome ('trʌb(ə)lsəm), *a.* Forms: see TROUBLE *sb.* [f. TROUBLE *sb.* + -SOME[1].] Full of, characterized by, or causing trouble.

† **1.** Full of disturbance or tumult; disturbed, disorderly, unsettled, troublous. *Obs.*

a **1548** HALL *Chron., Hen. IV*, 19 His painfull and busi wanderyng, his troblesome and vncertaine abidyng. **1553** in Hakluyt *Voy.* (1599) II. 111 There arose in the ship such a troublesome disturbance, that all the ship was in an vprore with weapons. **1560** DAUS tr. *Sleidane's Comm.* 98 The state of Christendom was troublesome. **1687** ALDWORTH in *Magd. Coll. & Jas. II* (O.H.S.) 63 In troublesome times.

† **b.** Causing or inclined to cause disturbance; turbulent. *Obs.*

1552 HULOET, Troublesome, or full of troublynge, or who troubleth muche, *vexabundus*. **1591** SAVILE *Tacitus, Hist.* I. lxvii. 37 His froward and troublesome disposition. **1687** H. HOLDEN in *Magd. Coll. & Jas. II* (O.H.S.) 124 The Crowd ..was very troublesome.

† **c.** Characterized by physical disturbance or agitation; stormy. *Obs.*

1560 DAUS tr. *Sleidane's Comm.* Pref. 2 b, In so many troublesome stormes, and tempestes full of pearil. **1610** HOLLAND *Camden's Brit.* (1637) 697 It is a troublesome River and dangerous even in Summer time. **1623** LISLE *Ælfric on O. & N. Test.* Pref., A troublesome and tempestuous sea.

2. Full of trouble, affliction, or distress; troubled, sorrowful. *arch.*

1552 *Bk. Com. Prayer, Public Baptism Infants*, That they ..maye so passe the waues of thys troublesome world, that [etc.]. **1575–85** ABP. SANDYS *Serm.* (Parker Soc.) 321 Heretics, by whom it [marriage] hath been not only misliked as troublesome, but utterly condemned as unclean. **1614** RALEIGH *Hist. World* IV. vi. §4. 281 So many Darts..as tooke away his..hopes, together with his troublesome life. **1734** ARBUTHNOT *Let. to Swift* 4 Oct., I am going out of this troublesome world. **1853** LYNCH *Self-Improv.* ii. 43 Christianity is..plainly designed for a troublesome world.

† **b.** Troubled in mind, having trouble. *rare*[−1].

1596 DALRYMPLE tr. *Leslie's Hist. Scot.* v. (S.T.S.) I. 289 For the cleir cloudis to the dulfull was pleisant, and to the trublesum happie.

3. Giving trouble; causing annoyance; vexatious, distressing, worrying, bothering.

1573 G. HARVEY *Letter-bk.* (Camden) 4, I hope you wil haue me excusid thouh I be trubblesum to your waihtier affaiers. **1598** SHAKS. *Merry W.* I. i. 325 Ile rather be vnmannerly, then troublesome. **1604** E. G[RIMSTONE] *D'Acosta's Hist. Indies* II. xiii. 112 Why are not the nightes in summer at Peru, as hotte and troublesome as in Spaine? **1662** J. DAVIES tr. *Olearius' Voy. Ambass.* 97 This small mony..is troublesome in the telling and handling. **1747** WESLEY *Prim. Physic* (1762) 84 If the Cough be very troublesome. **1839** THIRLWALL *Greece* xlv. VI. 33 If the barbarians were troublesome neighbours.

4. Involving labour or effort; toilsome, laborious, difficult; tiresome, wearisome, oppressive. Now *rare.*

1576 FLEMING *Panopl. Epist.* 243 An office of exceeding great authoritie, and maruellous troublesome. **1600** J. PORY tr. *Leo's Africa* v. 236 Their streetes either descend or ascend, which is verie troublesome to them that haue any busines in the towne. **1632** LITHGOW *Trav.* VI. 253 Leauing our troublesome way. **1780** *Mirror* No. 97 ¶ 30 When I first got the multiplication-table by heart..it was a plaguy troublesome job. **1836–41** BRANDE *Chem.* (ed. 5) 485 Phosphorus may be purified by careful distillation, but the process is troublesome and dangerous.

† **b.** Painstaking, laborious. *Obs. rare.*

1818 MOORE *Mem.* (1853) II. 245 A most learned and troublesome practician.

troublesomely ('trʌb(ə)lsəmlɪ), *adv.* [f. prec. + -LY[2].] In a troublesome manner.

† **1.** In a disturbed or disorderly manner; confusedly. *Obs.*

1561 T. NORTON *Calvin's Inst.* IV. 25 They were wonte.. to be present at the election..that nothyng should be troublesomely done. *a* **1699** R. GILPIN in Spurgeon *Treas. Dav.* Ps. cxix. 32 When the mind is so distracted..it acts troublesomely.

2. So as to cause trouble; annoyingly, distressingly, vexatiously; oppressively; tiresomely.

1591 PERCIVALL *Sp. Dict.*, *Molestamente*, troublesomely. **1641** MILTON *Reform.* I. Wks. 1851 III. 4 [Peter] falling troublesomely upon the..alwise, and unexaminable intention of Christ. **1663** BOYLE *Usef. Exp. Nat. Philos.* II. v. xviii. 273 Wonderful cures..by the long use of this Decoction, notwithstanding its..troublesomely heating Quality. **1689** SHADWELL *Bury F.* I, More troublesomly ill-bred with his formality, than a high-shoo'd peasant with his roughness. **1870** W. CHAMBERS *Winter Mentone* iv. 54 Troublesomely cold and wet weather.

† **b.** In a condition of trouble or distress. *Obs.*

1625 K. LONG tr. *Barclay's Argenis* I. x x. 56 The night being troublesomely spent betweene hope and feare.

troublesomeness ('trʌb(ə)lsəmnɪs). [f. as prec. + -NESS.] The quality or condition of being troublesome.

† **1.** Disturbed or unsettled state; confusion, disorderliness. *Obs.*

1561 T. NORTON *Calvin's Inst.* I. xv. (1634) 79 As though Reason also did not dissent from it selfe... But..that troublesomenesse proceedeth of the corruption of nature. **1655** FULLER *Ch. Hist.* III. iv. §27 The troublesomness of the times. **1715** in Black *Hist. Brechin* (1867) 126 Taking into.. consideration the troublesomeness of the times.

† **b.** Disposition to cause disturbance; turbulence. *Obs.*

1591 TURNBULL *Exp. Jas.* 167 b, Prosperous estate.. which by brauling, contention and troublesomnes is hindered. **1657** in *Eng. Hist. Rev.* Oct. (1910) 727 Filled with passion and troublesomness of spirit.

† **c.** Physically disturbed or agitated state. *Obs.*

1648 HEXHAM II. s.v. *Zee*, The troublesomenesse, or the swelling of the Sea. **1652–62** HEYLIN *Cosmogr.* IV. (1682) 149 Exposed..to the troublesomeness of sudden tempests. **1658** ROWLAND *Moufet's Theat. Ins.* 953 By the troublesomenesse of the air they are dispersed hither and thither.

† **2.** Trouble, affliction, distress. *Obs.*

1561 T. NORTON *Calvin's Inst.* II. x. (1634) 202 He suffered much troublesomenesse by his childrens wives. **1604** T. WRIGHT *Passions* II. Pref. 47 Troublesomenesse or disquietnesse of the soule. *a* **1639** W. WHATELEY *Prototypes* II. xxvi. (1640) 44 To inflict disquietment and troublesomenesse upon men in their labour.

3. The quality of giving trouble; vexatiousness, annoying character; toilsomeness; oppressiveness.

1548 UDALL, etc. *Erasm. Par. Matt.* xii. 74 Offended with this importunitie and troublesumnes. **1608** D. T[UVIL] *Ess. Pol. & Mor.* 79 The troublesomnesse of labor. **1630** J. TAYLOR (Water P.) *Heaven's Blessing* Wks. III. 116/1 For the auoyding of the troublesomenesse of Boats and Wherries. **1764** HARMER *Observ.* I. i. 6 Even grammarians derive.. summer from a root which points out the troublesomeness of its heats. **1787** W. MARSHALL *Norfolk* I. 375 Many farmers..dislike the noise and troublesomeness of these animals. **1881** MISS BRADDON *Asph.* i. 5 With the air of a sinner who gloried in her troublesomeness.

troubling ('trʌblɪŋ), *vbl. sb.* [f. TROUBLE *v.* + -ING[1].] The action of the verb TROUBLE, or an instance of this (in various senses).

c **1340** HAMPOLE *Prose Tr.* 17 A fantasie caused of trubblyng of þe brayne. *c* **1374** [see TROUBLABLE]. *c* **1400** LOVE *Bonavent. Mirr.* (1907) 92 With moche noyse and turblynge prayer wil not wele and deuoutly be seide. *c* **1400** MAUNDEV. (Roxb.) vii. 23 Þer es na trubling of þe aer thurgh raynes. *c* **1440** *Jacob's Well* 97 Þe feend..louyth dyscord & trubelyng of pes. **1530** PALSGR. 283/1 Troublyng of ones mynde, *distraction*. **1611** BIBLE *John* v. 4 Whosoeuer then first after the troubling of the water stepped in, was made whole. **1617** MORYSON *Itin.* I. 208, I thinke they would not haue denied vs wine,..yet to auoide troubling of them, my selfe and my brother carried some flaggons of rich wine. **1842** PARNELL *Chem. Anal.* (1845) 44 A faint troubling in strong solutions. **1878** F. FERGUSON *Life Christ* xviii. 174 The medicinal properties..would be intensified at the time of the periodical natural troublings.

'troubling, *ppl. a.* [f. as prec. + -ING[2].] That troubles; causing trouble.

a **1325** *Prose Psalter* li[i]. 4 Þou louedest alle trubland wordes. **1552** HULOET, Troublynge, *angens*. *a* **1684** LEIGHTON *Comm. 1 Peter* v. 7 Wks. (1868) 291 The troubling cares of men. **1851** LYNCH *Sabbath Medit.* in *Lett. to Scattered* (1872) 157 A third troubling thought. **1871** HOWELLS *Wedd. Journ.* (1892) 66 They disposed of their troubling bags and packages.

† **'troublish,** *a. Obs. rare.* [f. TROUBLE *a.* + -ISH[1].] Somewhat 'troubled' or turbid.

c **1530** *Judic. Urines* II. iii. 18 Whye it is thyckysshe and trublysshe, is bycause that the humours..are all distempred.

troublous ('trʌbləs), *a.* Now only *literary* or *arch.* Forms: see TROUBLE *sb.*; also 5 -ose, -ows, (-es, -ys, 5–6 -is), 6 -us. [a. OF. *troubleus, -eux*, *torbleus* (12th c. in Godef.), f. *trouble* TROUBLE: see -OUS.]

† **1.** Of water or other liquid: Troubled, turbid, thick, muddy. *Obs.*

1495 *Trevisa's Barth. De P.R.* XVIII. xxxix. (W. de W.) cc vj/2 The horse..hath lykynge..to drynke trowblous [*MS.* troubly] and thycke water. **1527** ANDREW *Brunswyke's Distyll. Waters* B ij, Other lyquor..which ye wyl puryfye from all trowblous and vnclere substaunces. **1544** PHAER *Pestilence* (1553) L viij, Thick wyne and troubleous.

2. Characterized by trouble, agitation, or disturbance; disordered, disturbed, unsettled, confused.

c **1449** PECOCK *Repr.* III. vii. (Rolls) 318 Like troubelose tyme was in Ierusalem. **1555** BALE in Strype *Eccl. Mem.* (1721) III. App. xxxix. 107 The state of our Church..is troublous at this present. **1675** TRAHERNE *Chr. Ethics* 363 That troublous times are the seasons of honour, and that a warlike-field is the seed-plot of great and heroical actions. **1840** CARLYLE *Heroes* iv. (1858) 274 There are long troublous periods, before matters come to a settlement.

1878 BROWNING *La Saisiaz* 599 The millions..live their calm or troublous day.

b. Of persons or their attributes: Causing disturbance; turbulent, disorderly; restless, unquiet.

1450–1530 [implied in TROUBLOUSNESS]. *c* **1485** *Digby Myst.* (1882) III. 1611 Thow froward Kyng, trobelows and wood. **1550** LATIMER *Last Serm. bef. Edw. VI*, (1562) 115 They..accused hym..that he was a sedicious fellow, and a troublous preacher. **1855** MOTLEY *Dutch Rep.* I. II. vi. 501 Troublous and adventurous spirits, men of broken fortunes ..and boundless desires.

c. Of the sea, wind, etc.: Tempestuous, stormy, violent.

1482 *Cely Papers* (Camden) 123 Here was noon passage.. the wynd was so contrary and the see soo trublys. *a* **1548** HALL *Chron., Hen. VIII*, 48 The wynde was troblous and the wether foule. **1610** HOLLAND *Camden's Brit.* (1637) 305 The sea is..rough, and troublous. **1742** COLLINS *Ode Evening* 46 Winter yelling thro' the troublous air. **1855** SINGLETON *Virgil* I. 364 He hunts the storms, and swims through troublous clouds.

3. Causing trouble or grief; painful, grievous; vexatious, troublesome.

1463 ASHBY *Prisoner's Refl.* 250 With hys trowbelous hurt. **1465** MARG. PASTON in *P. Lett.* II. 211 I..trost..that ye shall overcome your enemys and your trobelows maters. **1535** COVERDALE *Ezek.* xiv. 21, I sende my foure troublous plages vpon Ierusalem: the swearde, honger, perlous beestes and pestilence. **1651** BIGGS *New Disp.* ¶273 A difficulty of breathing, troublous to life. **1747** UPTON *New Canto Spenser's F.Q.* xxii, Bowers, that exclude the troublous Light. **1880** MCCARTHY *Own Times* IV. li. 79 Mr. Walpole took on himself the management of the Home Office, little knowing what a troublous business he had brought upon his shoulders.

†**b.** Expressing or indicating trouble or grief; sad, sorrowful. *Obs. rare.*

1535 COVERDALE *2 Kings* viii. 11 The man of God loked earnestly, & made a troublous countenaunce, & wepte. **1590** MARLOWE *2nd Pt. Tamburl.* IV. i, As when an herd of lusty Cimbrian bulls..Fill all the air with troublous bellowing.

Hence **'troublously** *adv.*; **'troublousness.**

1538 ELYOT, *Fluctuation*, *troublously, doubtfully. **1548** UDALL *Erasm. Par. Luke* xii. 106 To bee troubleously vexed with the care of suche thynges is a poynte..of mystrustfulnesse towardes god. **1573–80** BARET *Alv.* S 635 The sea riseth vp troublouslie with great sourges, *vnda exæstuat vorticibus*, Virg. **1897** F. THOMPSON *New Poems* 6 Their orbs are troublously Over-gloomed. **1450–1530** *Myrr. our Ladye* 45 When goddes seruantes ar besy..in hys seruyce: they with theyre vanyte & *troubelousnes pulle downe theyre myndes. **1577** *St. Aug. Manual* (Longman) 37 Let the troubleousnesse of the flesh cease. **1846** H. W. TORRENS *Rem. Milit. Hist.* 179 His worst troublousness had something quiescent in it.

†**troubly**, *a. Obs.* Forms: 4 trubli, -byly, 4–5 troubli, trobli, -bly, trublee, 4–6 trowbly, trubly, 4–7 troubly, 5 trow-, trobely. [f. TROUBLE *sb.* + -Y[1] or -LY[1]: cf. *cloudy*, *muddy*.]

1. = TROUBLE *a.* 1.

c **1380** WYCLIF *Serm.* Sel. Wks. I. 14 þese fisheris of God shulden waishe þere nettis in þis ryuer, for Cristis prechours shulden..not medle wiþ mannis lawe, þat is trobly water. *c* **1400** Trublee [see TROUBLE *a.* 1]. **1422** tr. *Secreta Secret., Priv. Priv.* 229 Tho that bene Pale and trowbely y-colurid. **1450–80** tr. *Secreta Secret.* xlv. 28 The eyre wexith trobely. *c* **1530** *Judic. Urines* II. i. 11 b, *Rubeus & subrubeus color* with a thycke and a trowbly bodye, sheweth grete dysturblynge of the humours. *Ibid.* vii. 28 Trubly. **1605** STOW *Annals* 707 When it betokeneth battaile, [it] runneth foule, and troubly water; and when it betokeneth dearth or pestilence, it runneth cleare [cf. TROUBLE *a.* 1, q. 1482].

2. = TROUBLE *a.* 2.

c **1340** HAMPOLE *Prose Tr.* 31 þe trubylyere þat þou hase bene owtwarde with actyfe werkes, the mare brynnande desyre þou sall hafe to Godd. *c* **1412** HOCCLEVE *De Reg. Princ.* 2 The restles bisynesse Which that this troubly world hath ay on honde. **1421** —— *Compl.* 302 This troubly lyfe hathe all to longe enduryd. **14..** in *Hist. Coll. Citizen Lond.* (Camden) 188 He..passyde owte of thys wrecchyde and false trobely worlde.

3. = TROUBLE *a.* 3.

1398 TREVISA *Barth. De P.R.* XIII. xxii. (Bodl. MS.), Whanne þe see is aboue troublye and to hiȝe bi windes and stormes. ? *c* **1400** LYDG. *Æsop's Fab.* ii. 44 þou..Sekest occasion by trobly violence Ayenst me. **1430–40** —— *Bochas* IX. xxiii. (MS. Bodl. 263) lf. 427/2 Who may the furies of fortune appese Hir troubli wawes to make hem calm and pleyne? **1513** DOUGLAS *Æneis* IV. v. 133 He chasis the windis away, And trubly cluddis dividis in a thraw.

Hence †**'troubliness**, troubled or disturbed condition; turbidity.

c **1530** *Judic. Urines* II. iii. 18 Vryne..with a trublynes.. sheweth a wombe fluxe.

trouchman, obs. form of TRUCHMAN.

troucht, obs. Sc. form of TROUGH.

troucit, obs. Sc. f. *trussed*, pa. pple. of TRUSS *v.*

‖**trou-de-loup** (trudəlu). *Mil.* [F., lit. 'wolf-hole, wolf-pit'.] In field fortification, a conical pit with a pointed stake fixed vertically in the centre, rows of which are dug before a work to hinder an enemy's approach. Usually *pl.* **trous-de-loup** (trudəlu).

1789 REES *Chambers' Cycl.*, *Trous-de-loup*...are round holes, about six feet deep, and pointed at the bottom, with a stake placed in the middle. They are frequently dug round a redoubt. **1828** J. M. SPEARMAN *Brit. Gunner* (ed. 2) 400 Trous-de-loup... Diameter of the base, 4 feet 6 inches. Depth, 6 feet. Picket, 6 feet long. **1862** *Catal. Internat. Exhib.* II. XI. 14 This kind of obstacle would, on service, be found to occasion much more confusion than crows-feet, trous-de-loup, &c.

troue, trouel, obs. forms of TROW, TROWEL.

trough (trɒf, -ɔːf), *sb.* Forms: 1–2 troȝ, (troh), 4 trowȝ, trouȝ, 4–6 trowe, 4–7 (8–9 *dial.*) trow, 5–6 trogh, troghe, *Sc.* trouch (also 9 *Sc. dial.*), 5–7 troughe, trowgh, trowghe, (5 troȝ, troue, trowh, trowegh, 6 trouthe, troh, trogh, troght, *Sc.* troch (also 9 *Sc. dial.*), trowch, -t, truch, troich, troucht, troycht, troyt, 7 traught), 5– trough; *β.* 6 troffe, troofe, 7 trof, trofe, trouff; *γ.* 5 throwhe, 6 throuh, *Sc.* throch, -t, 7 through. [Com. Teutonic: OE. *troȝ*, OFris. *trog*, OS. *trog* (MLG., LG., EFris. *trog*, MDu. *troch(-gh)*, Du. *trog*), OHG., MHG. *troc* (*trog*), Ger. *trog*, ON. *trog* (Sw. *tråg*, Da. *trug*, Norw. dial. *trog*, *trugh* (*traug*, *trau*):—OTeut. **truȝoz*, Indo-Eur. **druko-*, deriv. of *dru*, TREE, wood, timber; primary meaning 'wooden vessel'.]

1. a. A narrow open box-like vessel, of V-shaped or curved section, made of wood, stone, metal, or earthenware, and often a fixture, to contain liquid; *esp.* a drinking-vessel for domestic animals; also, a tank or vat used for washing, kneading, brewing, tanning, fulling, and various other purposes. (Often with prefix, as *drinking-*, *hog-*, *horse-*, *kneading-*, *pig-*, *water-trough*, etc.: see the first element.)

a. c **725** *Corpus Gloss.* (O.E.T.) 425 *Canthera*, troȝ. *a* **800** *Erfurt Gloss.* 1140 *Albeus* (*v*), *genus vasis*, troȝ. *c* **950** *Lindisf. Gosp.* John xiii. 5 Soðða sende þat uæter in troȝ and ongann geðoa foet ðara ðegna. *c* **1000** *Sax. Leechd.* II. 68 Do on troh hate stanas. *Ibid.* 326 ȝecnua ealle wel, leȝe on hatne stan on troȝe, ȝeot hwon wæteres on. **11..** *Rec. Gifts of Adeluuold* (963–84) in Birch *Cart. Sax.* III. 367, vi bidenfate & ii cuflas & þry troȝas & lead & trefet. *c* **1325** *Gloss. W. de Bibbesw.* in Wright *Voc.* 155 *De un rastuer*, a douwribbe, *le auge*, a trow. **1382** WYCLIF *Gen.* xxiv. 20 She, heldynge out the water pot into the water trowis,..ȝaue to alle the camelis. *c* **1386** CHAUCER *Reeve's T.* 123 Thanne wil I be bynethe..And se how þat the Mele falles doun In to the trough [*v.rr.* trogh, trow, troughe]. *c* **1410** *Master of Game* (MS. Digby 182) xxxiii, þe trowegh fillede with clene water. *c* **1460** *Registr. Aberdon.* (Maitl. Cl.) II. 85 In brasina vnum plumbum cum cuppa que dicitur Masfate vel caldarium. et algeam que dicitur le trovch. **1485** *Naval Acc. Hen. VII* (1896) 51 Moldyng trowghes [for leaden shot]. *a* **1500** *Kyng & Hermit* 486 in Hazl. *E.P.P.* I. 32 Till two trowys he gan him lede; Off venyson there was many brede. **1502** ARNOLDE *Chron.* (1811) 188 Take iij. C. weight orchell drye grounde and doo it in a trouthe. **1535** *Aberdeen Regr.* XV. (Jam.), Ane troycht & tua aiking buyrdis. **1536** *Abstr. Protocols Town Clerks Glasgow* (1897) IV. 87 Ane lyme trowcht. **1546** *Inv. Ch. Goods* (Surtees No. 97) 132 One stone troght. ? *a* **1550** *Freiris of Berwyk* 210 in *Dunbar's Poems* (S.T.S.) 292 Hyd ȝou..Into ȝone troich... It held a boll of meill quhen that we buke. **1583** in Wadley *Bristol Wills* (1886) 234 My howse wch I [a tanner] nowe dwell in wth vates and trowes. **1632** in E. B. Jupp *Carpenters' Co.* (1848) 301 All manner of traughts for Bakers. **1710–11** SWIFT *Jrnl. to Stella* 25 Mar., We have let Guiscard be buried at last, after shewing him pickled in a trough this fortnight for two pence apiece. **1789** MRS. PIOZZI *Journ. France* I. 245 The old original trough at the corner of the road. **1815** J. SMITH *Panorama Sci. & Art* II. 534 In troughs of water mixed with fuller's earth. **1859** G. MEREDITH *Juggling Jerry* x, You shan't beg from the troughs and tubs.

β. **1545** JOYE *Exp. Dan.* iv. 56 The vnthrifty sone..at last was compelled to come to the hoggis troffe for hunger. **1574** N. DANIEL in Grosart *Spenser's Wks.* I. 422 A pulpitt, many swynes troofe better. **1620** *Inv.* in *Essex Rev.* (1907) XVI. 206 A payer of Quarnes, a kneadinge trof, and shellves 2*s.* **1626** *Ibid.* (1906) XV. 67 One knedinge trofe. **1688** R. HOLME *Armoury* III. xx. (Roxb.) 246/2 A Tallow Trough, and of some termed a Trouff, it is to let the Tallow in working drop or run into it.

γ. c **1440** *Promp. Parv.* 503/2 Throwhe, vessel (*K.*, *S.* trow, *P.* trough), *alveus*. *a* **1539** *Cartular. Abb. de Rievalle* (Surtees) 340 The Bruehouse vi kelynge throuhs of lede, ii coper vesselles. **1560** *Aberdeen Regr.* (1844) 329 Lawaris and throchtis of brass. *a* **1660** *Contemp. Hist. Irel.* (Ir. Archæol. Soc.) I. 254 Some..burned the through, broke the kievve, demolished the house.

b. A small vessel of similar shape used in chemistry, photography, microscopy, etc.

1819 *Pantologia* s.v., In [operations with] gasses absorbable by water the trough must be filled..with mercury. **1826** Pneumatic trough [see PNEUMATIC 2]. **1827** FARADAY *Chem. Manip.* i. 20 The mercurial trough. **1831** BREWSTER *Nat. Magic* iv. (1833) 79 A trough having two of its sides parallel, and made of plate glass. **1853** W. GREGORY *Inorg. Chem.* (ed. 3) 68 Closing the tube with the finger, and inverting it, with the open end under water in a basin or trough.

c. *fig.* In contempt, A person who is a mere receptacle for liquor; a toper.

1613 FLETCHER, etc. *Captain* IV. iii, This drunken trowgh has killed him. **1899** LUMSDEN *Edinb. Poems & Songs* 131 A thae trochs are drucken slochs.

d. *fig.* A place where food is provided, *spec.* a dining-table; hence, a meal. *colloq.*

1901 'H. MCHUGH' *John Henry* 95 We left the mob just as all hands were paddling off to the ice-cream trough. **1915** F. M. HUEFFER *Good Soldier* I. iii. 38 Why shouldn't we all eat out of the same trough—that's a nasty New York saying. **1930** WODEHOUSE *Very Good, Jeeves!* iv. 96 The Bellinger.. had sung us a few songs before digging in at the trough. **1965** *New Statesman* 14 May 777/1 Things are a bit different at the old trough these days. **1981** 'M. INNES' *Lord Mullion's Secret* viii. 68 If he didn't stir his stumps he would be late for the trough.

e. In various *fig.* phrases applied to a ready source of income, esp. one shared by unscrupulous persons. *colloq.*

1906 J. LONDON *Let.* 20 Oct. (1966) 212 All I can tell you is, that you've got your feet in the trough. **1971** P. TAMONY *Americanisms* (typescript) No. 28. 2 Local pimps and fast-buck boys who had hustled to the troughs for fat-staff salaries. **1974** L. DEIGHTON *Spy Story* iv. 47 I'm going to find out what it's costing. We can't go on eating our heads off at the public trough. **1981** J. D. MACDONALD *Free Fall in Crimson* xvi. 186 The money would come..to Josie, and you would be able to stay in the trough.

2. In spec. uses: **a.** An oblong vessel containing the water in which a grindstone runs; also *transf.* the stone itself, or the place where it stands; a workman's compartment in a grindery.

1725 T. THOMAS in *Portland Papers* VI. (Hist. MSS. Comm.) 144 Most of their wheels and troughs (as they call those places where these grindstones are). **1743** in H. S. Wyndham *Ann. Cov. Gard. Theatre* (1906) II. 312 A grindstone handle and trough. **1839** S. ROBERTS *Tom & Charles* in *Yorkshire Tales* 130 The building itself is generally the property of one person, but he lets off, to different grinders, what are denominated the Troughs, or the parts in which each grinding-stone is fixed. **1884** W. H. RIDEING in *Harper's Mag.* June 79/1 The lower part of the stones touches a long vessel containing water, and by a technical peculiarity each stone is called a 'trough'. **1892** *Labour Commission Gloss.* s.v., It is customary to speak of the trough not only as the actual vessel..but as..the portion of the room containing the trough. In this sense..local.

b. An oblong box with divisions serving as the cells of a voltaic battery; also short for *trough-battery*.

1806 *Med. Jrnl.* XV. 150 Having constructed a very powerful Galvanic trough, I have tried its effects..with very satisfactory results. *Ibid.* 153 My trough contains about 1280 square inches of metallic surface; at first I did not use above four or five pair of plates. **1815** J. SMITH *Panorama Sci. & Art* II. 277 This apparatus..combines the principle of the battery with glasses and that of the common trough. **1866** R. M. FERGUSON *Electr.* §79 The inner surface of the trough is coated with an insulating substance.

c. *Mining.* (*a*) An oblong tank in which ores are washed; a rocker or buddle; (*b*) A passage cut through a wall or pillar of coal: = THIRLING *vbl. sb.*[1] 2 (*Cent. Dict. Suppl.* 1909).

1877 KNIGHT *Dict. Mech.*, *Trough*.., a frame, vat, buddle, or rocker in which ores or slimes are washed and sorted.

d. See quot.

1877 KNIGHT *Dict. Mech.*, *Trough*,..the tray or vat containing the metallic solution used in electro-plating.

e. *Typog.* A metal-lined box in which stones, inking-rollers, and forms are washed.

1891 in *Cent. Dict.* **1892** *Labour Commission Gloss.* s.v., A trough in the printing industry is a box, lined with lead, with pieces of wood laid across for stones to rest on; the water runs off from the stone into the trough.

3. †A small primitive boat; sometimes app. a canoe hollowed out of a solid block of wood (*obs.*); also locally applied to various kinds of boats or barges: see TROW *sb.*[2]

c **893** K. ÆLFRED *Oros.* II. v. §6 He eft wæs biddende anes lytles troȝes æt anum earman men. **1531–2** *Act 23 Hen. VIII*, c. 12 §1 Their troughes barges botes and other vessells passing..on the said River of Severne. **1555** R. TOMSON in Hakluyt *Voy.* (1600) III. 454 A great caue or ditch of water ..where come euery morning at the break of the day twentie or thirtie Canoas, or troughes of the Indians. **1570** LEVINS *Manip.* 217/24 A Trough, bote, *linter*. **1574** R. EDEN tr. *Taisner's De Natura Magnetis* Ded., If none had proceeded further then the inuentions of our predecessors, we..had yet haue sayled in troughes or in boates. **1633** T. STAFFORD *Pac. Hib.* III. xvii. (1810) 658 No boats nor troughs to passe them over into Connaght. **1869** *Pall Mall G.* 21 Sept. 6 In Weymouth Bay..Four fishermen went out in a boat known as a 'trough', a little flat-bottomed craft, to fish for herrings.

4. a. A stone tomb or coffin. Cf. THROUGH *sb.*[1] 2. Now *dial.*

1494 FABYAN *Chron.* VI. ccxiii. 230 In case that ye may kepe my body from tourment,..laye it in a troughe of stone, and hyll it with lede close and iuste [cf. quot. *c* 1400 s.v. THROUGH *sb.*[1] 2 *β*]. **1610** HOLLAND *Camden's Brit.* (1637) 486 A little trough or coffin, very cunningly and finely wrought of Marble. *a* **1682** SIR T. BROWNE *Tracts* ix. 155 In one of the Mounts..there were found three Troughs containing broken Bones. **1876** *Mid-Yorks. Gloss.*, *Trough*.., a coffin, of old shape; a stone cistern.

†**b.** App. confused with THROUGH *sb.*[1] 3, a flat grave-stone. *Obs.*

1501 *Bury Wills* (Camden) 83 Also I wyll that the tabernacle of Seynt Jamys..and the troues of the auter ther by, be well and suffyciently peyntyd. **1588** *Knaresborough Wills* (Surtees) I. 163 My bodye to be buryed in Fuiston churche yeard under my grandfather trough.

5. A channel, pipe, or trunk for conveying water; a conduit; a gutter fixed under the eaves of a building; *Sc.* (*pl.*) the channel conducting the water to a mill-wheel. Now *dial.* (usually *trow*).

1398 TREVISA *Barth. De P.R.* XVII. cxxi. (Tollem. MS.), Trowes and condites made of pine tre, and leyde deep under erþe dureþ many ȝeres. **1554** *Burgh Rec. Edinb.* (1871) II. 309 The beitting and mending of the fyve Commoun Mylnis, making of thair haill watter wallis, scheitts and trouchtis. **1555** W. WATREMAN *Fardle Facions* Pref. 10 By conduicte of pipes and troughes, and such other conueyance. **1678** PHILLIPS (ed. 4), *Trough*,..a hollow thing made of Boards, and lying open for the Conveyance of Water. **1792** A. YOUNG *Trav. France* 137 All the houses at Nancy have tin eave troughs and pipes. **1808–18** JAMIESON, *Trow*, the wooden spout in which water is carried to a mill-wheel. **1825** *Ibid.*, *Trows* s. pl., properly..the troughs which conduct the water to the mill-wheel. **1881** RAYMOND *Mining*

Gloss., *Trow*, a wooden channel for air or water. **1901** LAWSON *Remin. Dollar Acad.* 112 He washed himself.. in the small lade or 'trows' which conveyed the water from the burn at the bleaching-green.

6. a. A hollow or valley resembling a trough; the bed or channel of a stream, or the depressed tract through which it flows; *spec.* in *Geol.* a basin-shaped depression, a syncline (longer than broad).

1513 DOUGLAS *Æneis* IX. i. 76 Lyke as sum tyme Ganges, the flude Indane,.. In hys deip trowch now flowis esely. **1719** HAMILTON *Ep. to Ramsay* 24 July xvii, Mony a lang and weary wimple, Like trough of Clyde. **1796** W. MARSHALL *W. England* II. 175 Mountain heights.. partially severed by deep rich Vallies or 'Troughs'—as they are called. **1819** LOCKHART *Peter's Lett.* lxxiv. III. 299 The whole valley, or strath, or trough of the Clyde. **1854** MURCHISON *Siluria* viii. 155 These schists and limestones are overlain in the contiguous troughs by other rocks. **1862** W. CORY *Lett. & Jrnls.* (1897) 78 The long troughs of woodland where the deer and the streamlets wander. **1883** *Good Words* July 438/2 It is therefore a question how far the ocean troughs may have the antiquity assigned to them.

b. In full ***trough of the sea***, the hollow on the surface between two waves. Also *fig.*, esp. as ***in a*** (or ***the***) ***trough***.

a **1625** *Nomenclator Navalis* (Harl. MS. 2301), *Ye Trowgh of the Sea*.. when wee lay a Shipp vnder the Sea, (.. her broadeside to the Sea) wee saie shee lies in ye Trowgh of the Sea. **1699** DAMPIER *Voy.* II. III. 64 The ship by the mistake of him that con'd, broched to, and lay in the trough of the Sea. **1762–9** FALCONER *Shipwr.* II. 890 Still in the yawning trough the vessel reels, Ingulf'd beneath two fluctuating hills. **1856** MRS. STOWE *Dred* xvii, Tom.. never is himself; always up on a wave, or down in the trough. **1886** FROUDE *Oceana* ii. 21 The engines stopped, the ship lay rolling in the trough of the sea broadside on to the waves. **1942** C. S. LEWIS *Let.* 20 Jan. (1966) 199 Sorry you're in a trough. I'm just emerging.. from a long one myself. **1958** *Sunday Times* 9 Nov. 15/3 E. Nesbit.. has therefore been 'in the trough'—widely read, ardently admired, but neglected as a subject for critical appraisals. **1977** *Listener* 28 July 123/3 At the moment his [*sc.* E. M. Forster's] reputation is in the trough; it is said that he is a slight talent, overpraised for extraneous reasons.

c. *Meteorol.* A line or elongated region of lower barometric pressure between two regions of higher.

1882 W. MARRIOTT in *Standard* 26 Dec. 7/4 At right angles to the path of a cyclone there is always a line running through the centre, called the trough, where the barometer reading is the lowest. **1887** R. ABERCROMBY *Weather* ii. (1888) 30 If we look at the barometer-trace at any one place, the 'ups' and 'downs' suggest the analogy of waves, so that the lowest part of a trace may be called a 'trough'. **1904** *Westm. Gaz.* 10 May 6/2 A long trough of low barometric pressure now lies over the southern parts of our islands.

d. *Econ.* The lowest level of economic activity or prosperity reached during a recession.

1916 G. B. SHAW *Androcles & Lion* Pref. p. lxvi, Basing.. our whole industrial system on successive competitive waves of overwork with their ensuing troughs of unemployment. **1930** *Economist* 29 Mar. 691/1 We are, in fact, in the trough of a depression. **1960** *Ibid.* 8 Oct. 161/2 Even if the recession does not reach its trough until well into the spring. **1981** *Daily Tel.* 9 July 1/6 There is now firmer evidence that the trough in the recession has been reached, said the Treasury yesterday.

e. Hence, the lowest point in a period of any varying quantity; the time when this occurs. Also, the representation of this state on a graph; a point in a wave-form at which the varying quantity is a minimum. Cf. CREST *sb.*[1] 7 e, PEAK *sb.*[2] 5 e.

1938 *British Birds* XXXII. 214 This is followed by a more or less distinct trough, after which numbers rapidly increase to a higher autumn peak by mid September. **1958** *Listener* 16 Oct. 605/1 Absence of distortion and the avoidance of marked peaks and troughs in the amplitude-frequency characteristic. **1971** *Physics Bull.* Aug. 462/2 Such currents tend to pile electrons in the potential troughs of the wave and denude the crests. **1976** *Daily Tel.* 22 Mar. 7/1 Chromatography splits the sample into its volatile chemical constituents, and draws an alpine graph with heady peaks and troughs to represent the chemicals coming through.

7. *attrib.* and *Comb.*, as ***trough form, frame, -meat, plate*** (sense 2 b), ***-sailing*** (see sense 3), ***-stone***; ***trough-like, -shaped*** adjs.; also **trough battery**, a voltaic battery consisting of a number of cells in a trough (sense 2 b); **trough-closet**: see quot.; **trough core**, *Geol.*: see quot.; **trough-current**, the current produced by a moving vessel; **trough fault**, *Geol.*: see quot.; **trough flooring**, steel troughing riveted together to form the floor of a bridge; **trough garden**, a miniature garden comprising a group of small plants, often alpine ones, grown in a trough-like container of real or imitation stone; cf. *sink garden* s.v. SINK *sb.*[1] 14; **trough girder**, an iron girder shaped like a trough; **trough gutter**, a box-like channel for drainage; a rain-water pipe of this form; **trough-joint, trough limb**, *Geol.*: see quots.; **trough mercury**, the mercury used in a pneumatic trough; **trough roof**, *U.S.*: see quot.; **trough shell**, a mollusc of the family *Mactridæ*.

1841 *Encycl. Brit.* (ed. 7) XXI. 665/2 A valuable modification of the '*couronne des tasses*', called the *trough battery. **1878** G. PRESCOTT *Sp. Telephone* 260 A trough battery of six cells. **1870** CORFIELD *Treatm. Sewage* 121 What are called *trough-closets have been erected in Liverpool... A long trough is placed below and behind the seats of a series of closets. **1911** *Encycl. Brit.* X. 598 The innermost strata in a fold constitute the 'core', arch-core, or *trough core. **1843** *Mech. Mag.* XXXVIII. 70/1 The *trough-current can only act against the front of the screw and the bevelled or slanting sides of the recess. **1883** GRESLEY *Gloss. Coal Mining*, **Trough fault*, a wedge-shaped fault, or, more correctly, a mass of rock, coal, &c., let down in between two faults. **1911** *Encycl. Brit.* IV. 538 The *trough flooring, 3/8 in. thick and 6 in. deep, is rivetted to the longitudinals. **1876** PREECE & SIVEWRIGHT *Telegraphy* 244 In the *trough form of battery this [short circuit] is caused by leakage. **1827** FARADAY *Chem. Manip.* xv. (1842) 318 A flap fixed to this end of the *trough frame, which.. may be used when there is occasion. [**1923** *Times* 31 May 10/7 Mr. Clarence Elliot's attempt at providing miniature alpine gardens in old stone troughs.. would undoubtedly provide much interest where space was too limited for real gardening.] **1935** C. ELLIOTT *Rock Garden Plants* 288 An invaluable small thing for spilling about and filling up odd sunny corners, and perfect on the *trough rock garden. **1950** W. E. SHEWELL-COOPER *Home, Window & Roof Gardening* viii. 70 The Trough Garden.. can be a great joy to the rock garden lover. **1979** M. SOAMES *Clementine Churchill* xxviii. 471 Here Clementine made a 'trough' garden. **1883** *Specif. Alnwick & Cornhill Railw.* 48 The superstructure is to consist of two wrought-iron *trough girders carrying the rails. **1856** BREES *Gloss. Terms*, **Trough gutter*, a sort of sunk or enclosed gutter, about 8 or 10 inches wide, and adopted with advantage in exposed situations. The wooden trunks employed as gutters for sheds and common buildings.. are also known by this name. **1865** PAGE *Handbk. Geol. Terms* (ed. 2), **Trough-joint*, the fissure or joint which frequently accompanies the abrupt bending of strata passing through the middle of the curvature. **1839** DE LA BECHE *Rep. Geol. Cornwall*, etc. iii. 43 These rocks rested in a *trough-like cavity extending east and west. **1869** TOZER *Highl. Turkey* II. 109 A trough-like depression between two ridges. **1911** *Encycl. Brit.* X. 598 In a fold of this kind we have an 'arch limb', a middle limb, and a floor or '*trough limb'. **1844** H. STEPHENS *Bk. Farm* II. 71 The whole have hay or *trough-meat.. on wet or stormy nights. **1827** FARADAY *Chem. Manip.* xx. (1842) 554 These chemical cleansings of the *trough mercury are intended to destroy the disposition which exists in impure mercury to form films upon its surface. *Ibid.* xvii. (1842) 457 The wires are soldered to plates equal in size to those of the troughs,.. though they may not touch the *trough plates. **1905** *U.S. Dept. Agric., Bureau Forestry* Bulletin lxi, **Trough roof*, a roof on a logging camp or barn, made of small logs split lengthwise, hollowed into troughs and laid from ridge pole to eaves. **1855** J. D. MACLAREN in *Mem.* vii. (1861) 134, I could almost resume the bathing and the *trough-sailing. **1871** NESBITT *Catal. Slade Coll. Glass* 77 A *trough-shaped spout. **1867** LOVELL *Edible Mollusks* 152 *Mactra solida*, Linnæus. *Trough shell. **1470–1** *Durham Acc. Rolls* (Surtees) 643 Pro nova factura unius le *Troughstane pro aqueductu in gardino. **1587** *Wills & Inv. N.C.* (Surtees) II. 157 In the brewhowsse. One brew lead.. j maskefatte and a trogh-stone. **1854** MURCHISON *Siluria* xiii. 329 Yellow sandstones.. extensively used as.. trough-stones.

Hence **'troughful**, as much as a trough will hold; **'troughster**, one who feeds at a trough, a pig; **'troughwise** *adv.*, as or like a trough; **troughy** ('trɒfɪ, -ɔː-) *a.*, characterized by troughs.

1877 *Honourable Miss Ferrard* I. v. 128 A *troughful of buttermilk. **1891** *Daily News* 30 Oct. 5/6 Wheaten flour, which I distributed among them by troughfulls. **1892** G. MEREDITH *Ode to Comic Spirit* 19 The poor smoke Struck from a puff-ball, or the *troughster's grunt. **1551** ROBINSON tr. *More's Utop.* I. (1895) 31 The shyppes that they founde fyrste were made playne, flatte, and broade in the botome, *troughewyse. **1877** BEER *Prophet of Nineveh* I. iv. 58 She plunges heavy in the *troughy seas.

trough (trɒf, -ɔː-), *v.* [f. prec. sb.]

1. *trans.* †**a.** To furnish with a trough or troughs for irrigation or drainage. *dial. Obs.* **b.** *Geol.* To form into a trough or into the shape of a trough. **c.** To treat in some way in a trough; to stain, gauge, or mould in a trough.

1668 *Demise of Coal Mine* (Arncliffe Hall MSS.), To carry a sough or watergate through the demised ground.. and to leave the same trowed and scoured. **1839** MURCHISON *Silur. Syst.* I. xxix. 388 This spur reposes conformably on the Old Red Sandstone.. being troughed between the latter and the ridge of Old Red Sandstone to the South of it. **1872** W. S. SYMONDS *Rec. Rocks* viii. 277 The Pilton rocks are rolled and troughed to a great extent about Ashford. **1881** GREENER *Gun* 254 The same method of troughing is required to brown them a dark brown. **1887** *Daily News* 20 May 3/2 Sword-bayonets.. in store were re-tested,.. being sprung round a curved block 2½ inches high,.. troughed and gauged. **1905** *Daily Chron.* 25 July 4/4 Cottages which have unusual features..—concrete troughed between upright timbers.

2. *intr.* To feed at or as at a trough; to feed swinishly.

1748 RICHARDSON *Clarissa* (1811) VIII. 168 What miry wallowers the generality of men of our class are in themselves, and constantly trough and sty with.

†**3.** *Mining.* Of a vein: To dip. *Obs. rare.*

1747 HOOSON *Miner's Dict.* R ij, When Veins or Pipes take a chop up higher than ordinary into their proper Lids, whethersoever the Lids be Stone, Mixt-beds, &c., this is opposite to Troughing or Choping down.

Hence **troughed** (trɒft, -ɔː-) *ppl. a.*, **troughing** ('trɒfɪŋ, -ɔː-) *vbl. sb.* and *ppl. a.*

1897 *Daily News* 31 Dec. 2/1 A rather lumbering looking 'troughing' machine automatically scours the edges with emery until the embryo sword-bayonet will just fit in flat into a gauge or 'trough'. **1898** G. MEREDITH *Odes Fr. Hist.*, *Napoleon* vi, Heap over heap [of horses and men] Right through the troughed black lines turned to bunches or shreds, or a fog.

trough, obs. form of TROTH.

troughing ('trɒfɪŋ, -ɔː-), *sb.* [f. TROUGH *sb.* + -ING[1] 1 g.] Troughs collectively; provision of troughs; a set or system of troughs.

1825 J. NICHOLSON *Operat. Mechanic* 85 The openings in the bottom of the troughing should be of iron. **1904** *Daily Chron.* 31 Dec. 6/7 On the walls of the tunnels 153 miles of troughing have been fixed to carry the cables.

trought(e, obs. form of TROTH, TROUT.

trougth, obs. form of TROTH.

trouker, troukle, obs. ff. TRUCKER, TRUCKLE.

troul, obs. form of TRAWL, TROLL, TRULL.

trou-madam: see TROLL-MADAM.

troump, -ar, -ate, -erie, -etter, obs. ff. TRUMP, TRUMPER, TRUMPET, TRUMPERY, TRUMPETER.

trounce (traʊns), *v.*[1] Also 6–7 **trounse**, 7 **trownse, -ce**. [Of obscure origin; usually compared with OF. *troncer*, *troncher*, Cotgr. *troncir*, *tronchir* to cut, cut off a piece from, retrench, f. *tronce*, *tronche* stump or stock of wood (14th c. in Godef.): cf. *tronc* TRUNK, and *tronçon* TRUNCHEON. But the OF. and Eng. vbs. do not agree in sense. See also *Eng. Dial. Dict.*]

†**1. a.** *trans.* To trouble, afflict, distress; to discomfit, harass. *Obs.*

1551 BIBLE *Judg.* iv. 15 But the Lorde trounsed [1611 discomfited] Sisara and all his charettes, and all hys hoste with the edge of ye swerde, before Barak. **1553** *Respublica* III. iii. 652 Lorde Ihese Christe whan he was I-pounst & I-pilate, Was ner zo I-trounst as we [ignoram people] have been of yeares Late. **1570** FOXE *A. & M.* (ed. 2) 408/2 If any do speake against them, he is miserablye tossed & trounsed for his labour. **1646** TRAPP *Comm. John* ii. 16 The churchwarden of Ipswich was much trounced and troubled in the High-commission. **1655** GURNALL *Chr. in Arm.* I. 111 Joseph's mistresse first tries to draw him to gratifie her lust; that string breaking, she hath another to trounce him and charge him.

b. *intr. Obs. rare*[−1].

1589 *Rare Triumphs Love & Fortune* IV. (Roxb.) 119 Oh, terrible tormentes that trounce in my toe!

2. To beat, thrash, belabour, cudgel; to beat by way of punishment, to flog.

1568 *Hist. Jacob & Esau* II. ii. C ij, There was neuer none trounced as I shal trounce that elf. **1621** MOLLE *Camerar. Liv. Libr.* II. iv. 85 He tug'd and trownst his aduersarie. **1748** SMOLLETT *Rod. Rand.* xxii. (1804) 149 Flattered with the hopes of seeing a bailiff trounced. **1820** *Gentl. Mag.* XC. I. 412 The common provincial phrase of 'I'll trounce you', meaning to beat or bruise with a stick or fists. **1887** BESANT *The World went*, etc. xxi. 169 One after another, they were tied up.. and soundly trounced.

3. a. To inflict chastisement upon; to punish; also, to get the better of, defeat.

1657 HOWELL *Londinop.* 40 How Rich. the first trounced her for murthuring the Jews. *a* **1704** T. BROWN *Comm.-Place-Bk.* Wks. 1709 III. II. 136 The Gods Neptune and Apollo trounc'd Laomedon for cheating 'em of their Hire. **1833** MARRYAT *P. Simple* lxiv, We will set to and trounce that scoundrel of an uncle. **1859** J. R. GREEN *Lett.* I. (1901) 28 You honour a man.. by condescending to an encounter, even though you trounce him. **1878** BROWNING *Poets Croisic* xlv, Who chides.. the unchilded monarch shall be trounced For irreligion.

b. To punish by legal action or process; to indict, to sue at law. Now *dial.*

1638 FORD *Fancies* IV. i, The court shall trounce thee. **1678** BUTLER *Hud.* III. iii. 683, I would so trounce her, and her Purse, I'd make her kneel for better or worse. **1681** DRYDEN *Spanish Fryar* IV. i, I'll trounce you for offering to corrupt my Honesty. *a* **1700** B. E. *Dict. Cant. Crew*, *Trounc'd*... Cast in Law. **1730–6** BAILEY (folio), *Trounce*, to sue at law. **1755** JOHNSON, *Trounce*, to punish by an indictment or information. **1818** MOORE *Fudge Fam. Paris* vi. 206 Who shall describe.. Thy candour, when it falls to thee To help in trouncing for a libel? **1830** DE QUINCEY *Bentley* Wks. 1857 VII. 98 He 'trounced' Colbatch, who was sentenced to pay 3*s.* 6*d.*, together with 2*s.* 6*d.* arrears, and £20 costs. **1888** ELWORTHY *W. Somerset Word-bk.*, *Trounce*, to summon before a magistrate; to sue at law.

c. To defeat heavily at a sport. *colloq.*

1942 BERREY & VAN DEN BARK *Amer. Thes. Slang* §649/5 *Defeat decisively*,.. trample (on), trounce, walk on [etc.]. **1951** *Sport* 27 Jan.–2 Feb. 3/1 He was omitted from the side trounced 4–0 at Reading. **1972** J. MOSEDALE *Football* v. 64 Green Bay teams had trounced AFL entries the previous two years.

4. To assail or attack with rebuke or abuse; to censure; to scold severely.

1607 R. C[AREW] tr. *Estienne's World of Wonders* 2 These learned Latin authors haue been trounced by these dangerously conceited and proud presumptuous censurers. **1673** MARVELL *Reh. Transp.* II. Wks. 1776 II. 261 Had not Mr. Killigrew foreseen that they must.. fall to dirt of themselves, he would ere this.. have trounced the author. **1865** *Star* 6 Jan., He deals chiefly with the best-named folly and trounces it most severely. **1894** BESANT *Equal Woman* 127 He very finely trounced the Public for daring to like these favourites.

Hence **trounced** (traʊnst) *ppl. adj.*

1898 *Blackw. Mag.* Oct. 469/1 The howling of trounced sailors.

trounce, *v.*[2], a dialectal or quasi-dialectal variant of *traunce*, TRANCE *v.*[2]; also *trans.* in causal sense. Hence **trouncing** *ppl. a.*

1566 DRANT *Horace, Sat.* vi. D vj, In cytie, I must set vppon my golde bespangled mule, In deeper way, a trounsinge steede, whome vneth ought can rule. **1824** SCOTT *Redgauntlet* ch. xi, They behoved to trounce us away to be tried at Carlisle. **1824** MACTAGGART *Gallovid. Encycl.* 166 The Prince of Darkness trounces through the world in the form of a black dog. **1887** *Charity Organis. Rev.* Nov. 416 The young woman refused to pay, and trounced off to a.. hospital.

trouncer ('traʊnsə(r)). [f. TROUNCE *v.*[1] + -ER[1].] One who trounces; *spec.* an odd man (see ODD A. 9 d); an assistant to a carman, drayman, or lorry-driver; †on a man-of-war: see quot. 1867 (*obs.*).

c **1630** DR. TRIPLET in Aubrey *Brief Lives* (1898) I. 264 When this well truss't trounser Into the school doth enter. **1867** SMYTH *Sailor's Word-bk.*, *Trouncer*, an old word for a waister. [*Ibid.*, *Waisters*.. had little else of duty but hoisting and swabbing the decks.] **1896** BOOTH in *Westm. Gaz.* 26 Mar. 2/1 Brewhouse men, cellar men, yardmen, coopers, filings-makers, draymen, and trouncers. **1898** A. LANG in *Longm. Mag.* Nov. 92 My friend and constant 'trouncer'.. has been pitching into me. **1913** M. S. REEVES *Round about Pound a Week* i. 2 Some of the more enviable and settled inhabitants of this part of the world [*sc.* Kennington].. generally are somebody's labourer, mate, or handyman. Painters' labourers.. trouncers for carmen, are common amongst them. **1923** *Weekly Dispatch* 30 Sept. 3 It was stated that a 'trouncer' was a coal carman's assistant. **1953** *Word for Word* (Whitbread & Co.) 35/2 *Trouncer*, the drayman's mate; so-called because, before the improvement of roads under Telford and MacAdam, he had to 'trounce', i.e., push and manhandle the dray over the innumerable potholes and hazards.

trounchen, obs. form of TRUNCHEON.

trounchman, obs. corrupt f. TRUCHMAN.

trouncing ('traʊnsɪŋ), *vbl. sb.* [f. TROUNCE *v.*[1] + -ING[1].] The action of TROUNCE *v.*[1]; a beating, thrashing; also *fig.* Also *attrib.*

a **1553** C. BANSLEY *Treat.* xii. (Percy Soc.) 5 Tyll you tricke and trotte youre selfe, to the devyls trounsynge neste. *c* **1580** JEFFERIE *Bugbears* Epil. in *Archiv Stud. Neu. Spr.* (1897), With rowsynges, with bownsynges, with trownsynges. **1803** R. ANDERSON *Cumberld. Ball.* 64 In a passion I flew, And gave her a trouncin. **1867** *Routledge's Ev. Boy's Ann.* Aug. 3 Cheltenham gave Marylebone a fine trouncing.

troune, trounson, troup, -e, obs. ff. THRONE, TRUNCHEON, TROOP.

‖**troupe** (truːp). [F. (16th c.), = OF. *trope* (13th c.): see TROOP *sb.*] A company, band, troop; *esp.* a company of players, dancers, or the like.

1825 *N.Y. Evening Post* 6 Dec. 2 The whole troupe were equally excellent. **1847** W. IRVING in *Life & Lett.* (1864) IV. 32, I have attended the opera.. the troupe [is] very fair. **1906** E. V. LUCAS *Listener's Lure* (1910) 181 A troupe of jumping dogs.

trouper ('truːpə(r)). Also trooper. [f. TROUPE + -ER[1].] **1.** An actor or performer belonging to a troupe.

1890 B. HALL *Turnover Club* 160 As the 'troupers' come into the station where I sat, they were a sorry-looking lot. **1912** L. J. VANCE *Destroying Angel* (1913) vi. 77 I'm as superstitious as any trooper in the profession. **1946** *Boston Transcript* Sept. 6/2 A little knot of interested troupers were looking on as Joe and I met. **1973** 'D. RUTHERFORD' *Kick Start* i. 8 A good trouper can still shimmy in her fifties.

2. *transf.* A reliable, uncomplaining person; a staunch supporter or colleague. Freq. with qualifying adj., as *good trouper*. *colloq.*

1959 P. BULL *I know Face* xi. 194 The phrase 'she's a trouper' now has an old-fashioned and faintly derogatory air and is usually bandied about when someone continues to play with a high temperature or a shattering bereavement. **1961** *Times* 6 July 5/5 Chapman is a good trouper, and.. he has a fine record of consistency in match and stroke play. **1976** D. FRANCIS *In Frame* iv. 70, I don't think you're selfish at all. In fact, Maisie, I think you're a proper trouper.

troupial, var. TROOPIAL.

trous, obs. f. TRUSS.

trous-de-loup, pl. of TROU-DE-LOUP.

trouse (traʊs), *sb.*[1] Now *dial.* Forms: 1 trus, 3–4 trous, 6–7 trousse, trowse, 5– trouse. [OE. *trus*, perh. a. OIcel. *tros* rubbish, fallen leaves and twigs, ON. and Norw. *tros*, Sw. *trås*, perh. in ablaut relation with *tras* twig, sprout: see TRASH *sb.*[1]; but the ON. word is applied only to twigs, etc. used for burning.] Brushwood, cuttings from hedges or copses; = TRASH *sb.*[1] 1.

978 *Charter Bp. Oswald* in Kemble *Cod. Dipl.* III. 169 Ðæt mylenstall and vi. æcras ðærto, and vi. foðra truses ælce geare on Bloccanlea. **1293** *Anc. Deed* A. 9277 (P.R.O.), Dederunt.. dicto Hamundo.., trous de alnetis et spinis ad claudendum schidstauid yord. *a* **1310** in Wright *Lyric P.* xxxix. 110 For hope of ys thornes to dutten is doren, He mot myd is twy-byl other trous make. **1458** *Anc. Deed* A. 7587 (P.R.O.), To take als moche wode & trouse vpone þe seid londe growyng as is sufficiaunt for closure of alle þe seid londes. **1523** FITZHERB. *Husb.* §126 Lay thy small trouse or thornes, that thou hedgeste withal, ouer thy quicke-settes. **1573** *Nottingham Rec.* IV. 149 Fellyng of trouse.. in the nere Coppy. **1600** HOLLAND *Livy* VI. x. 223 They provided themselves out of the fields of a number of faggots, of brushwood, and such like trousse, and so.. filled up the ditches close to the wals. **1610** *Nottingham Rec.* IV. 301 To fetch any trowse or tinsell out of the same woodes. **1691** *Blount's Law Dict.* (ed. 2), *Tinet*,.. Trouse, Brushwood and Thorns to make and repair Hedges. **1881** MISS JACKSON *Shropsh. Word-bk.* s.v., 'That rough trouse ool be rar' stuff fur breastin' the 'edge to keep the ship [*i.e.* sheep] out.'

Hence †**trouse** *v. Obs.*, to cut brushwood (cf. TRASH *v.*[3]); †'**trousing** *vbl. sb.* (in quot. *attrib.*).

1512 *Nottingham Rec.* IV. 454 A trowsyng ax. **1787** GROSE *Provinc. Gloss.* s.v., Trousing a hedge or faggot; trimming off the superfluous branches. *Warw.*

trouse (truːz, traʊz), *sb.*[2] Now *Hist.* and *arch.* [App. taken in 16th c. from Irish (and Sc. Gaelic) *triubhas*, recorded *c* 1500 (see quot.), orig. pronounced *trīwăs* or *trīwăs*, in mod.Irish pronunc. *trūs* (see TREWS). (The quot. of 1306, from its early date and late form, is doubtful, and may not belong to this word.) The 16th and 17th c. quots. here and under TREWS refer to it as worn by the Celts. It has been held to be derived from OF. *trousse* TRUSS, etc. q.v., but a careful examination of OF. literature by M. Antoine Thomas shows no trace of *trousse* in the sense assumed, which appears, later than in English, in Miège's *Dict.* 1679. The thing is said by Littré to have been worn (? in 17th c.) by young pages and by certain novices, and to survive in certain expressions, as *il avait quitté les trousses*, and *être aux trousses de l'ennemi*.

As to the ulterior history, Prof. Bergin of Dublin thinks well of the suggestion in Holder *Alt-celt. Sprachsch.* II. 1974, that the Celtic *triubhas* represents OF. *trebus* 'sorte de chaussure ou de chausse' (13th c., Godef.), from late L. *tubrācōs* 'tubrucos vocatos quod tibias braccasque tegant' (Isidore *Orig.* XIX. xxii. 30). 'Tubraci quod a braccis ad tibias usque perveniant', which appears later as *tribraci*.

Miège *F. Dict.* (1679) has '*Trousses, sorte de chausses*, trunk-breeches'.]

1. Originally, A close-fitting article of attire for the buttocks and thighs (divided below so as to form a separate covering for each thigh), to the lower extremities of which stockings (when worn) were attached; *spec.* = TREWS. In later use drawers, or knee-breeches.

α. sing. **6 trowes, trwse, 7 trous, trouze, 7–8 trowze, 8 trowse, 6– trouse.**

[**1306** *Pleas of Crown* (*Irel.*) *34–5 Edw. I*, m. 10 d, Vnum crannoc.. vnus arcus cum sagittis.. vna spartha (unum par) [so app.; MS. faint] s[o]tularium cum trues.. precii vnius denarii et oboli. *c* **1500** in W. Stokes *Irish Glosses, Tract on L. Declen.* (1860) 12 Hee brace gl. *tribus*.]

1578 in Sharp *Cov. Myst.* 37 Pd. for a trwse for Judas ijs. viijd. **1581** Trowes [see TREWS]. **1630** *Conceits, Clinches*, etc. (1860) 8 A jellous wife was like an Irish trouze, alwayes close to a mans tayle. **1633** *Spenser's State Irel.* 48 The leather quilted Iacke.. for any occasion of suddaine service,.. to cover his trouse [*Add. MS.* thinn breeche] on horsebacke. **1676** WISEMAN *Chirurg. Treat.* I. xviii. 85 The Trowze being made, I saw it laced on... The lower part of the Trowze was tacked to a Cotton Stocking he put on that Leg. *c* **1730** BURT *Lett. N. Scotl.* xxii. (1818) II. 84 Few besides gentlemen wear the trowze, that is, the breeches and stockings all of one piece. **1746** Trowse [see TREWS]. **1775** F. GREGOR tr. *Fortescue De Laudibus* xxxv. 125 Nor do they [French common people] wear any Trowse, but from the Knees upwards; their Legs being exposed and naked. **1813** JAS. GRANT *Orig. Gael* (1814) 213 Strabo describes the clothing of the Gauls as consisting of.. a sort of breeches, which covered the inferior members of the body, similar to the *triumhas* or trouse of the Gael. **1852** *Meanderings of Mem.* I. 86 The belted blouse Of velvet black, and closely-fitting trouse.

β. pl. **6–7 trouzes, 7 troussses, trooses, troosses, troozes, truzes, trusses, 7–8 trowzes, 7–9 trowses, 8 truses, 6– trouses.**

1581 DERRICK *Image Irel.* II. E iij b, His skirtes be verie shorte, with pleates set thicke about, And Irishe trouzes more to put, their straunge protractours out. **1586** D. ROWLAND *Lazarillo* II. (1672) T iv, A Gentleman-Usher with handsom Trouses, a neat Doublet, a good Cloak, and a comely bonnet. **1601** HOLLAND *Pliny* VII. xliii. I. 177 In his youth he was a poore souldier, and served as a footman in his single trousses and grieves. **1612** R. DABORNE *Chr. turned Turke* 1409 S'hart, a French slop, these are none of the Iewes trouses. **1622** *Relat. Eng. Plantation* in Arber *Story Pilgrim Fathers* (1897) 453 They had most of them long hosen up to their groins, close made; and above their groins to their waist, another leather. They were altogether like the Irish trouses. **1625** B. JONSON *Staple of N.* I. i, Hee walks in his Gowne, wastcoate, and trouses, Expecting his Taylor. **1634** SIR T. HERBERT *Trav.* 146 Their [Persians'] breeches are like Irish troozes, hose and stockings sowed together. **1673** *Lond. Gaz.* No. 807/4 A Cook,.. in a sad coloured Stuff Coat and Trowses. **1741** in *Scott. Hist. Rev.* Apr. (1905) 303 The prisoner was going to the field in truses, Contrary to orders. **1747** CARTE *Hist. Eng.* I. 20 The inhabitants of those provinces, who wore Braccæ, trowses striped and of various colours serving for both hose and breeches. **1834** PLANCHÉ *Brit. Costume* 234 The close hose, fitting exactly to the limbs, in fact, the Norman chausses, were.. revived [Henry VIII] under the.. name of trouses.

†**2.** (*pl.*) = TROUSERS 2. *Obs.*

1679 V. ALSOP *Melius Inquir.* I. i. 60 The Papists.. maliciously reproach the Scripture.. when they call it.. a Leaden Dagger, a pair of Seamans Trowzes, a movable Dyal. **1705** ELSTOB in *Hearne's Collect.* 30 Nov. (O.H.S.) I. 107 His trowzes wch with loops emboss'd he tyes. **1820** *Acc. Coronation Geo. IV*, The King's Trowses.

3. *Comb.*, as **trouse-like** *a.* or *adv.*

1650 BULWER *Anthropomet.* Pref., Their colour'd thighs Trous-like being died black.

Hence †**troused** *a. Obs. rare*[−1], wearing the trouse (cf. *kilted*, *plaided*).

1612 DRAYTON *Poly-olb.* xviii. 638 The trowzed Irish led by their uniust Tyrone.

trouser to **trouser-wearer**: see TROUSERS.

trousering ('traʊzərɪŋ). [f. TROUSER(S + -ING[1] 1 g.] Cloth suitable for making trousers; a species of this. Chiefly *pl.*

1883 *Daily News* 24 Sept. 2/6 Worsted coatings and trouserings, fancy twills, diagonals, and other fabrics suitable for the leading markets. **1899** O. SEAMAN *In Cap & Bells* (1900) 46 We sit in sable Trouserings and Boots.

trousers ('traʊzəz), *sb. pl.* Forms: 7–8 trossers, trowzers, 7– trowsers, trousers, 8 trouzers. See also STROSSER. [An extended form of TROUSE *sb.*[2], cf. other words indicating a pair, as *tweezers*; perh. directly after DRAWERS.]

†**1.** = TROUSE *sb.*[2] 1, TREWS. *Obs.*

[**1599**: see STROSSER.] **1613** FLETCHER *Coxcomb* II. iii, I'le haue you flead and trossers made of thy skin to tumble in. **1633** T. STAFFORD *Pac. Hib.* I. xviii. (1821) 191 Cloathed in a simple mantle, and torne trowsers. **1676** WISEMAN *Chirurg. Treat.* I. xviii. 85 By laced Stockings and Trowzers the Swellings in his Legs and Thighs went off. **1752** C. STEWART in *Scots Mag.* (1753) 293/1 Stewart had on blue and white trowsers. **1776** GIBBON *Decl. & F.* xi. I. 315 The emperor Tetricus.. as well as his son, whom he had created Augustus, was dressed in Gallic trowsers, a saffron tunic, and a robe of purple. **1778** LD. CARLISLE *Let.* 21 June in *15th Rep. Hist. MSS. Comm.* App. VI. 345 The gnats in this part of the river [Delaware] are as large as sparrows; I have armed myself against them by wearing trousers, which is the constant dress of this country. **1789** M. MADAN *Persius* (1795) 80 *note*, The bracca was a peculiar dress of the Medes, which like trowzers, reached from the loins to the ankles. **1834** PLANCHÉ *Brit. Costume* 8 They wore close trousers, which they called *bracæ*; these trousers, an article of apparel by which all barbaric nations seem to have been distinguished from the Romans, being made of their chequered cloth, called *breach* and *brycan*, and by the Irish, *breacan*.

2. a. Orig., a loose-fitting garment of cloth worn by men, covering the loins and legs to the ankles; sometimes said to have been worn over close-fitting breeches or pantaloons; now applied generally to any two-legged outer garment worn by both sexes, and extending from the waist usu. to the ankles. (Also *a pair of trousers*.) Cf. TROUSE *sb.*[2] 2, PANTALOON 3 c.

In early use esp. worn by sailors, later by soldiers, and gradually becoming common from about 1820. Subsequently distinguished from *breeches* chiefly by covering the whole leg, and by not being shaped so as to fit tightly: cf. BREECH.

1681 *Lond. Gaz.* No. 1661/4 John Clarke, a stout Man,.. in.. a pair of Buck skin Leather Breeches.. (sometimes wearing Trousers over his Breeches) rid away on a Grey Gelding. **1718** OZELL tr. *Tournefort's Voy. Levant* I. Life 9 All he could afford himself was a Thrum-cap, Linen Trowzers, and a Pair of Wooden Shoes. **1731** *Gentl. Mag.* Nov. 474/2 Instead of Breeches, he proposes that the Ladies should wear Trowsers, which will be particularly convenient for those who have not handsome Legs. **1742** J. PARRY *True Anti-Pamela* 216 *note*, Trowzers are commonly worn by those that ride Post down into the North, and are very warm; at the same Time, they keep the Coat, Breeches, &c., very clean, by being wore over them. **1748** *Anson's Voy.* I. iii. 29 Orellana and his companions.. having prepared their weapons, and thrown off their trouzers and the more cumbrous part of their dress, came all together on the quarter-deck. **1768** WALES in *Phil. Trans.* LX. 108 Breeches made of seal, or deer skin, much in the form of our seamens short trousers. **1772** COOK *Voy. S. Pole* I. ii. (1777) I. 20, I .. gave to each man the fearnought jacket and trowsers allowed them by the Admiralty. **1786** *Gentl. Mag.* Sept. 814/1 Twenty-five boys belonging to the Marine Society, in new jackets and trousers. **1814** WELLINGTON in Gurw. *Desp.* (1838) XI. 504, I beg leave to recommend that 20,000 shirts, 20,000 pairs of socks or stockings and 6,000 pairs of trousers should be sent out to Tarragona. **1869** E. A. PARKES *Pract. Hygiene* (ed. 3) 415 Shortly before or during the Peninsular war trousers were introduced.

b. The loose bag-like drawers or pantaloons worn by both sexes in Muslim countries.

1775 R. CHANDLER *Trav. Asia M.* xix. 66 Their ladies wear.. large trowsers or breeches, which reach to the ancle. **1810** E. D. CLARKE *Trav. Russia* (1839) 62/1 The dress of a Cossack girl is elegant; a silk tunic, with trousers fastened by a girdle of solid silver [etc.]. **1815** ELPHINSTONE *Acc. Caubul* (1842) II. 57 The Murwuts.. are tall, fair men, and wear a pair of loose trowsers, something thrown over their shoulders, and a handkerchief tied round their heads. **1882** FLOYER *Unexpl. Baluchistan* 256 He had the ordinary white calico trowsers. **1913** D. BRAY *Life-Hist. Brahui* ii. 31 A girl should be put into trousers as soon as she is two, or at the most four.

c. White frilled or trimmed drawers reaching to the ankles (or nearly so), worn by women and girls, and young boys, about the second quarter of the 19th c.; pantalettes.

1820 M. WILMOT *Let.* 3 May (1935) 57 Catharine.. has not one frock, or pair of trousers fit to wear, now that summer is coming. **1821** SHELLEY 15 Aug. in Ingpen *Life* (1909) II. xix. 900 She was prettily dressed in white muslin, and an apron of black silk, with trousers. **1838** DICKENS *Nich. Nick.* xiv, Her little girls.. wore little white trousers with frills round the ancles. **1844** *Ladies' Hand-bk. Haberdashery* 56 Ladies' Wearing Apparel... Trowsers with Worked Bottoms. **1859** GEO. ELIOT *A. Bede* xii, His hearty affection for the Rector dated from the age of frocks and trousers. **1873** J. ASHBY-STERRY *Shuttlecock Papers* 95 Girls.. in short frocks, frilled trousers, and broad blue sashes.

d. Applied to the hair on the hind legs of certain dogs, esp. those of long-coated breeds.

1948 C. L. B. HUBBARD *Dogs in Britain* 464 Trousers.—The hair on the hindquarters of any dog. **1949** L. E. NAYLOR *Poodles* v. 44 They [*sc.* poodles] enjoy having any kind of smart clip, because they dislike their trousers being muddy. **1962** R. H. SMYTHE *Anat. Dog Breeding* vii. 133 The loose trousers wrinkled round the knees and pasterns of the Dachshund.

3. In various colloq. phrases. **a.** ***anything in trousers***, etc.: any man, whether eligible, suitable, or not.

1887 *Lantern* 14 May 3/1 They go crazy over everything that wears trousers. **1979** A. PRICE *Tomorrow's Ghost* i. 9 Anything in trousers was as much Target for Tonight to Marilyn Francis as Marilyn Francis was for anything in trousers.

b. ***not in these trousers***: certainly not.

1920 P. GIBBS *Realities of War* IV. vii. 189 'Come up and have a look, Jack,' he said to one of the blue-jackets. 'Not in these trousers, old mate!' said that young man. **1929** R. C. SHERRIFF *Journey's End* III. ii. 71 She said, 'Not in these trousers'—in French. **1939** J. CARY *Mister Johnson* 247 You think perhaps we leave the money in the till and you tief 'em. Not in these trousers, Mister Poldedoodle.

c. ***to wear the trousers***: to be the dominant member of a household. Also *transf.* Cf. BREECH *sb.* 2, PANTS *sb. pl.* 1 e.

1931 R. CAMPBELL *Georgiad* i. 11 It is you must 'wear the trousers' now. **1959** J. L. AUSTIN *Sense & Sensibilia* (1962) ii. 15 It is essential to realize that here the notion of perceiving *in*directly wears the trousers. **1963** A. HERON *Towards Quaker View of Sex* iii. 33 A married couple where the woman 'wears the trousers'.

d. ***(to catch) with one's trousers down***: in a state of embarrassing unpreparedness. Cf. PANTS *sb. pl.* 1 c. *slang.*

1966 *Guardian* 31 Mar. 14/8 Catch them with their trousers down. **1967** 'F. CLIFFORD' *All Men are Lonely Now* II. vii. 234 By that time the shooting will seem to be as haphazard as can possibly be, as if we'd almost been caught with our trousers down. **1980** J. GARDNER *Garden of Weapons* II. vii. 186 A job... Took us by surprise: with the trousers down.

4. a. In sing. form **trouser**, in various senses. (See also attrib. and combinations in 5.)

[**1609**: see STROSSER.] **1702** ADDISON *Dial. Medals* i. Wks. 1766 III. 17 Of the old British Trowser. **1823** SCOTT *Quentin D.* Introd., All the rest was mustache, pelisse, and calico trowser. **1885** STEVENSON *Dynamiter* i. 2, I have scarcely a decent trouser in my wardrobe.

b. A single leg of a pair of trousers (in quots. *transf.*).

1893 MARY CHOLMONDELEY *Diana Tempest* v, A little palm near had its one slender leg draped in an *impromptu* Turkish trouser, made out of an amber handkerchief. **1899** —— *Red Pottage* ix, One melancholy Scotch fir embarrassed by its trouser of ivy.

5. *attrib.* and *Comb.* (more usually in sing. form *trouser*), as ***trouser-brace*** (BRACE *sb.*[2] 9 b), ***-button***, ***-finisher***, ***-fly***, ***-hem***, ***-knee***, ***-leg***, ***-lining***, ***-making***, ***-pocket***, ***-seat***, ***-wearer***; ***trouser-wearing*** adj.; also **trouser-band**, the waistband of a pair of trousers; **trouser-bottoms** *pl.*, the lower parts of the legs of a pair of trousers; †**trouser breeches**, = sense 1; **trouser-clips** *pl.*, clips (of various kinds) used by cyclists to confine the trousers round the ankles; **trouser-cuff**, the turn-up on a trouser-leg; **trouser-press**, a contrivance for pressing the legs of trousers so as to produce a crease; **trouser-presser**, a workman engaged in ironing trousers; also = *trouser-press*; **trouser-stockings**, ? waterproof overalls or leggings used by fishermen; **trouser-strap**, a strap passing beneath the instep and attached at each end to the bottom of the trouser-leg; **trouser-stretcher**, a device for stretching trousers so as to take out any 'bagginess'; **trouser suit**, a woman's suit consisting of matching jacket and trousers; hence **trouser-suited** *a.*; **trouser zip**, a zip used as a fastening, usu. at the front of a pair of trousers.

1892 ZANGWILL *Childr. Ghetto* I. 221 His blue bandana.. tied round his *trouser-band. **1896** A. MORRISON *Child of the Jago* 126 He gave a hitch to his trousers-band. **1920** D. H. LAWRENCE *Women in Love* xxiv. 388 He..pulled on his boots. They were sodden, as were his socks and *trouser-bottoms. **1973** A. ROSS *Dunfermline Affair* 116 My trouser bottoms were wet. **1875** BEDFORD *Sailor's Pocket Bk.* viii. (ed. 2) 286 The shoulder-strings..cross behind like *trouser-braces. **1762–71** H. WALPOLE *Vertue's Anecd. Paint.* (1786) II. 1 James..hated novelties. He..hunted in the most cumbrous and inconvenient of all dresses, a ruff and *trowser breeches. **1898** *Daily News* 22 Nov. 7/3 Stanley once characterised the Heligoland Treaty as follows: 'England received in exchange for a *trouser-button a new suit of clothes'. **1895** *Army & Navy Co-op. Soc. Price List* 1379/2 Lucas's *Trouser Clips. Per pair 0/3. **1908** H. G. WELLS *War in Air* ii. 33 A small, dissolute-looking shop in the High Street, adorned with..a display of bells, trouser-clips, oil cans..and other accessories. **1970** K. GILES *Death in Church* i. 11 Horace Drood adjusted his trouser clips and resentfully pedalled off. **1931**, etc. *Trouser-cuff [see CUFF *sb.*[1] 2 d]. **1942** C. BARRETT *On Wallaby* v. 90, I had fifteen-inch trouser cuffs, while my coat sleeves were about half-mast high. **1982** H. ENGEL *Murder on Location* (1983) xxiii. 207, I squeezed water from my shoes and trouser cuffs. **1887** W. WESTALL *Her Two Millions* li, She was a *trousers finisher. **1922** JOYCE *Ulysses* The slits of his buttoned *trouserfly. **1896** MRS. CAFFYN *Quaker Grandmother* 251 John..flicked an atom of fluff off his *trouser-knee. **1849** CUPPLES *Green Hand* xiii. (1856) 130 One of his long *trowser-legs. **1901** G. DOUGLAS *House w. Green Shutters* 239 They stopped—their trouser-legs flapping behind them. **1909** ELIZ. L. BANKS *Myst. Fr. Farrington* 37 A strip of his *trousers-lining. **1906** *Daily News* 8 Mar. 6 Her work of *trousers-making yields her a good deal less than a penny an hour. **1852** J. S. COYNE *Box & Cox married & Settled* 9, I demand your card, sir?.. You'll find it in my left-hand *trowsers' pocket. **1856** GEO. ELIOT *Ess.* (1884) 106 His hands stuck in his trouser-pockets. **1898** W. W. JACOBS *Sea Urchins, Money-changers* (1906) 223 The fare..rose slowly and felt in his trousers-pocket. **1905** H. A. VACHELL *The Hill* iii. 49 He possessed a *trouser-press. **1887** *Pall Mall G.* 4 Nov. 8/1 They had heard Allman, the *trousers-presser, say, 'Now, gentlemen, I'm going to talk sedition'. **1906** *Daily Chron.* 25 Apr. 8/2 The crease..savours of the automatic trousers-pressers,.. rather than of the hot iron of the tailor. **1923** D. H. LAWRENCE *Ladybird* 243 He would have slid the whole way down on his *trouser-seat. **1960** WODEHOUSE *Jeeves in Offing* viii. 90 Gives a woman a start, naturally, to come into her son's bedroom and observe an alien trouser-seat sticking out from under the dressing table. **1883** *Fisheries Exhib. Catal.* 45 The *Trouser-Stockings..and Cork Jackets are indispensable adjuncts. **1841** *Civil Eng. & Arch. Jrnl.* IV. 176/2 Improved apparatus to be attached to trowsers, commonly called *trowser-straps. **1860** E. FALKENER *Dædalus, Mod. Art* ii. 202 German hobnailed boots and leather trouser-straps. **1939** *Vogue* Dec. (Advt., verso front cover), Digby Morton, famous tailleur, created this *trouser suit in a bright tartan 'Viyella'. **1975** D. LODGE *Changing Places* v. 174 She was waiting for him..in a cream-coloured trouser-suit. **1973** 'D. HALLIDAY' *Dolly & Starry Bird* iv. 47 The girls were thin, *trouser-suited and purposeful, with Pat Nixon hairdos. **1897** MARY KINGSLEY *W. Africa* 590 Xenia, who is the one and only *trouser wearer in our band, spends fifty per cent. of the night on one leg struggling to get the other in or out of these garments. *c* **1820** HUGH BOURNE *Let.* in *N. & Q.* 9th ser. IX. 489/2 That *trousers-wearing, beer-drinking Clowes will never get to heaven. **1966** *Olney Amsden & Sons Ltd. Price List* 44 Lightning *Trouser Zipps. **1976** P. DICKINSON *King & Joker* vi. 70 'Shall I show you something, little girl?' he whispered. His hand was at his trouser-zip.

Hence **'trouser** *v. slang, trans.* to put (money, etc.) into the trouser-pocket, to pocket; **'trouserdom**, the realm of trousers; the wearing of trousers; **'trousered** (-əd) *a.*, wearing or dressed in trousers; also *fig.*; **'trouserettes**, (*a*) girls' 'knickerbockers'; (*b*) short trousers; **trou'serian** *a. nonce-wd.*, of or pertaining to trousers; **'trouserless** *a.*, without trousers; wearing or having no trousers.

c **1890** G. H. KINGSLEY *Sport & Trav.* vi. (1900) 183 The sheriff *trousered the dollars! **1892** *Labour Commission Gloss.* s.v., To trouser is to put money into one's pocket, that is, to earn; a slang expression used by cabmen. **1882** *Pall Mall G.* 27 Oct. 2 The regeneration of feminine attire will never be compassed by the way of *trouserdom. **1789** M. MADAN *Persius* (1795) 81 The *trowzer'd Medes. **1825** COBBETT *Rur. Rides* (1885) I. 319 The tarred, and trowsered, and blue-and-buff crew whose very vicinage I.. detest. **1878** STEVENSON *Inland Voy.* 49 My pipe..was.. pretty well 'trousered', as they call it [cf. Fr. *culotter un pipe*]. **1895** L. DOUGALL *Question of Faith* 277 The roadside elms, trowsered to the ground with brush of branches. **1874** J. ASHBY-STERRY *Tiny Trav.* 284 Troublesome Twelve in.. the frilliest of frilled *Trouserettes. **1896** *Godey's Mag.* Apr. 387/2 Bloomers, very short tunics, or trouserettes. **1924** W. DE LA MARE *Ding Dong Bell* 30 A little boy in velveteen trouserettes. **1961** *New Statesman* 28 Apr. 658/2 The huge arthritic waiters stared..at Mart's rather strange check pantaloons. A party of secure business people were eating lobsters, and one of them..giggled at these semi-tropical trouserettes. ? *c* **1820** L. HUNT *Secret Existing Fashions* Ess. (1887) 276 Round comes the kindly *trouserian veil,..the legs retreat..into retirement. **1848** A. H. CLOUGH *Bothie of Toper-na-Fuosich* v. 33 A heavy pea-coat his *trouserless trunk enwrapping. **1857** in Ld. Dufferin *Lett. High Lat.* vii. 124 Before I knew where I was, I found myself sitting on a chair, in my shirt, *trowserless.

trousies ('traʊzɪz), *sb. pl.* Also **trowsies**. Dial. or colloq. var. of TROUSERS *sb. pl.* 2 a.

1886 H. BAUMANN *Londinismen* 219/2 *Trousies*,..trousers. **1913** H. KEPHART *Our Southern Highlanders* xiii. 285 The ancient syllabic plural is preserved in beasties (horses), nesties, posties, trousies (these are not diminutives). **1924** H. DE SELINCOURT *Cricket Match* viii. 200 Mind now, or you'll spill the beer over your trousies. **1958** A. HUNTER *Gently through Mill* v. 52 It spoils the set of my nice new trousies! **1974** J. AIKEN *Midnight is Place* v. 146 You'll want clothes..canvas trowsies and some old slops of shoes.

trouss, obs. f. TRUSS.

troussage, var. TRUSSAGE *Obs.*

trousse, obs. f. TRUCE, TRUSS.

‖**trousseau**[1] (truso, 'truːsəʊ). Also 3 **trusseau**. [F. (13th c.), dim. f. *trousse* TRUSS *sb.*; cf. TRUSSELL.]

1. †**a.** A bundle; cf. TRUSSELL 1. *Obs.* **b.** A bunch of keys. *rare.* (perhaps only as Fr.)

a **1225** *Ancr. R.* 168 Noble men & gentile ne bereð nout packes, ne ne uareð nout itrussed mid trusseaus [*v.r.* trusses], ne mid purses... Trusseaus, & purses, baggen, & packes beoð alle eorðliche weolen, & worldliche renten. **1847** DE QUINCEY *Sp. Mil. Nun* § 5 There lay the total keys, in one massive *trousseau*, of that monastic fortress, impregnable even to armies from without.

2. A bride's outfit of clothes, house-linen, etc. Also *attrib.*

[**1817** LADY MORGAN *France* I. (1818) I. 27 An *armoire*.. held the bridal wardrobe, or rustic *trousseau*.] **1833** T. HOOK *Widow & Marquess* iv, The trousseau is ready, and the day fixed. **1855** MRS. GASKELL *North & S.* i, I have spared no expense in her trousseau. **1880** 'OUIDA' *Moths* III. 293 Claire has got the coffer for her doll's trousseau. **1896** *Westm. Gaz.* 28 Mar. 3/2, I have just seen some of the trousseau gowns of a much-talked-of April bride-elect.

Trousseau[2] (truso). *Med.* [The name of A. *Trousseau* (1801–67), French physician, who described the sign in 1862 (*Clin. Med. de l'Hôtel-Dieu de Paris* II. xliv. 113).]

Trousseau's sign: spasm of a muscle evoked by pressure on the nerve supplying it, as seen in cases of tetany.

1887 VICKERY & KNAPP tr. *A Strümpell's Text-bk. Med.* 748 Another very characteristic symptom [of tetany] was discovered by Trousseau—'Trousseau's sign'. It is..this: a fresh paroxysm can at any time be artificially excited by pressure upon the larger arteries and nerves of the arm. **1981** *Brit. Med. Jrnl.* 14 Nov. 1315/2 Trousseau's sign, while dramatic for the doctor, is very painful for the patient.

troust, abbrev. f. **trouest*, *trowest*: see TROW *v.*

trout (traʊt), *sb.*[1] Forms: 1–2 **truht**, 3 **troit**, 4 **trouȝt(e**, **trouhte**, **troȝte**, 4–5 **trote**, 4–6 **trute**, **trowte**, 4–7 **troute**, 5 **trowȝt(e**, **trowyt**, **troughte**, **trouth(e**, **troyte**, **(tryotht)**, 6–7 **trowt**, **trought**, (7 **trowet**, **troot**), 6– **trout**. [OE. *truht*, ad. late L. *tructus*, *tructa*, *truta*, *trutta*, etc. = Gr. τρώκτης gnawer, also the name of a sea-fish, f. τρώγειν to gnaw; the forms *troit*, *troute*, etc. correspond to OF. *troite*, *troute*, etc., F. *truite* (13th c.).]

1. a. A well-known freshwater fish of the genus *Salmo*, esp. *S. fario*, the common trout, inhabiting most rivers and lakes of the temperate or colder parts of the northern hemisphere; it is distinguished by numerous spots of red and black on its sides and head, and is greatly valued as a sporting fish and on account of its edible quality. See also 3.

†***whole*** or ***sound as a trout***: cf. *sound as a roach* (ROACH *sb.*[1] 1 b). *Obs.*

c **1050** *Suppl. Ælfric's Voc.* in Wr.-Wülcker 180/37 *Tructa*, truht. *a* **1100** *Ags. Voc.* ibid. 319/15 *Tructa*, truht. **1290** in *Archæologia* XV. 354 Pro uno paner. gurnardi..pro iiij troites. *a* **1300** *Cursor M.* 11884 (Cott.) Bi þat þou þar-of cum vte þou sal be hale sum ani trute [*v.r.* troute]. **1375** BARBOUR *Bruce* II. 577 Gynnys, to tak geddis & salmonys, Trowtis, elys and als menovnys. **1387** TREVISA *Higden* (Rolls) I. 423 Perche and trouȝtis. *c* **1420** *Liber Cocorum* (1862) 50 Trowȝtes..Wele soþun and hakked. *a* **1450** *Fysshynge wyth an angle* (1883) 22 For þe Trowte. The trowyt ys a deyntet fyche and a fre bytyng. *c* **1518** SKELTON *Magnyf.* 1624, I am forthwith as hole as a troute. **1525** LD. BERNERS *Froiss.* II. cxiii. 325 Pastyes of samonde, troutes, and elys, wraped in towels. **1589** [? LYLY] *Pappe w. Hatchet* 3, I..will giue them line enough like a trowte. *a* **1616** BEAUM. & FL. *Scornf. Lady* III. ii, Leave off your tickling of young heirs like Trouts. **1635** SWAN *Spec. M.* (1670) 347 When we speak of one who is sound indeed, we say that he is sound as a Trout. *a* **1677** HALE *Prim. Orig. Man.* II. vii. 200 River-Fish, as Trouts..will alter their figure, some for the better and some for the worse, being put into Ponds. **1727–46** THOMSON *Summer* 253 They sportive wheel, or sailing down the stream Are snatched immediate by the quick-eyed trout. **1735** SOMERVILLE *Chase* IV. 371 The crimson-spotted Trout, the River's Pride, And Beauty of the Stream. **1790** SCOTT *Let. to W. Clerk* 3 Sept. in *Lockhart*, Two miles from an excellent water for trouts. **1839** DOUGLAS in *Proc. Berw. Nat. Club* I. 185 The trouts were scarcely covered in the small pools. **1860** GOSSE *Rom. Nat. Hist.* 6 The streams..where the trout displays his speckled side as he leaps from pool to pool. **1885** *Good Words* 255/2 He may guddle trouts in a stream.

b. *collective sing.* (in sporting use taking the place of the pl.).

1602 CAREW *Cornwall* II. 105 b, The pond will moreouer keepe Shote, Seale, Trought, and Sammon, in seasonable plight, but not in their wonted reddish graine. **1609** in *Craven Gloss.* (1828), 33 pearch and troot from Mawater for my Ld. Judge. **1789** MRS. PIOZZI *Journ. France* I. 41 The trout..there have been over praised. **1849** JAMES *Woodman* ii, She was exceedingly fond of trout. **1875** W. MCILWRAITH *Guide Wigtownshire* 24 Pike and trout are to be had in the lochs.

2. Used as a name of various fish (chiefly *Salmonidæ*) resembling the trout in appearance or habits. Now *local.*

1604 E. G[RIMSTONE] *D'Acosta's Hist. Indies* III. xv. 164, I have not seene any *Besugues* there, nor trowts. **1854** BADHAM *Halieut.* 313 Of salars caught in the Ribble, those of the first year are called smolts; those of the second year, sprods; those of the third, trouts. **1884** MATHER in *Century Mag.* Apr. 908/1 The name of 'trout' is also applied..to a salt-water fish called 'squeteague'. **1891** G. H. KINGSLEY *Sport & Trav.* (1900) 456 Char, known to the natives [of Colorado] by the name of trout. **1897** *Outing* (U.S.) XXX. 217/2 In the South, he [the black bass] is commonly called 'trout'.

3. With defining prefix, as the name of various species of the genus *Salmo* (or of the allied genus *Salvelinus*), and occasionally of other genera.

bastard trout (*U.S.*), a squeteague or weak-fish, *Cynoscion nothus*; **brook trout**, *Salmo fario*; in *U.S.*, *S. fontinalis*, or *S. irideus*, the rainbow trout; **brown trout**, *S. fario*; **Dolly Varden trout** (*U.S.*), *Salvelinus Malma*; **grey trout**, *Salmo trutta*; in *U.S.* the squeteague; **lake trout**, *S. ferox* (the great lake trout); in *U.S.*, (*a*) *S. confinis* (the North American lake trout), inhabiting the deepest waters of the great lakes; (*b*) = next; **Mackinaw** or **Namaycush trout**, *S. Namaycush*, of Lake Huron and Lake Superior; **rainbow trout**, *S. irideus*, a Californian species, now introduced in British trout-streams; **red-bellied trout**, the char, *S. salvelinus*; also *S.* or *Fario erythrogaster*, of the lakes of New York State and Pennsylvania; **red-spotted trout**, *S. fontinalis* or *S. salvelinus*; **rock trout**, *Chirus constellatus*

(ROCK *sb.*[1] 9 d); † **skegger trout** = SKEGGER; **speckled trout**, *S. fontinalis*; **white trout**, (*a*) a variety of *S. fario*; (*b*) the weak-fish (*Cynoscion nothus*); **yellow trout**, a name used in Scotland for the brown trout. See also BULL-TROUT, SALMON-TROUT, SEA-TROUT.

1661 LOVELL *Hist. Anim. & Min.* 228 Both the Salmon and gray trouts are very pleasant, and good for sound persons, but in agues they are not comparable to the Perch. **1668** CHARLETON *Onomast.* 163 *Trutta Lacustris*, the Lake-Trout. **1794** *Statist. Acct. Scotland* XIII. xxiii. 345 Fish are not plenty in this river; a few salmon, sea trout, yellow trout, and flounders, are caught in it. **1830** *Cabinet Nat. Hist.* I. 147 In the outlet..from the lake, none of the lake trout were ever found. **1836** YARRELL *Brit. Fishes* II. 31 The Grey Trout. *Ibid.* 60 The Great Lake Trout of Loch Awe..was shortly noticed by Pennant..as a native of Ullswater Lake in Cumberland, and of Lough Neagh in Ireland. *Ibid.* 74 This species has been called a Red-bellied Trout. **1839** T. T. STODDART *Songs & Poems* 51 Is the yellow trout at feed? **1861** *Act 24 & 25 Vict.* c. 109 §4 All migratory fish of the genus salmon,..that is to say, harvest cock, sea trout, white trout, sewin, buntling [etc.]. **1868** *Rep. U.S. Commissioner Agric.* (1869) 322 It is..rank folly to allow so great a delicacy as the speckled brook trout (*Salmo fontinalis*) to become extinct. *Ibid.* 330 The commission has..bred salmon, trout, lake trout (*Salmo toma*), and land-locked salmon (*S. Gloveri*). **1881** *Cassell's Nat. Hist.* V. 115 The Grey Trout (*Salmo Cambricus*). **1883** *Fisheries Exhib. Catal.* 204 Brook Trout, Lake Trout,..Rainbow Trout, Rangeley Trout. **1884** GOODE, etc. *Nat. Hist. Aquatic Anim.* 468 According to the latest system..the second group [of the old genus *Salmo*] includes the Chars, or Red-spotted Trout, and the gray-spotted species known as Salmon Trout, or Lake Trout. These are assigned to the genus *Salvelinus*. *Ibid.* 504 The Dolly Varden Trout—*Salvelinus Malma*,..known in the mountains as 'Lake Trout', 'Bull Trout', 'Speckled Trout', and 'Red-Spotted Trout'. **1884** *St. James's Gaz.* 23 Feb. 5/2 Like mice in a house, the little brook-trout are often almost under your feet. **1884** *Sat. Rev.* 12 July 61/1 Mr. Thomson caught one sixteen-pounder, which seized a yellow trout he was playing. **1888** GOODE *Amer. Fishes* 120 The Silver Squeteague, *Cynoscion nothum*, called at Charleston the 'Bastard Trout'. The 'White Trout'..is caught with hook and line.

4. *slang.* †**a.** Originally in the alliterative phrase ***true*** or ***trusty trout***, a confidential friend or servant; so ***humble trout***. *Obs.*

c **1661** *Roxb. Ball.* (1883) IV. 518, I was a trusty trout In all that I went about. **1682** *New News fr. Bedlam* 30 They are all very honest Fellows, true Trouts. **1688** SHADWELL *Sqr. Alsatia* I. i, Your humble Trout, good noble squire.

b. ***old trout***: a derogatory term for an old woman. Cf. TROT *sb.*[2]

1897 'S. GRAND' *Beth Book* (1898) xxxix. 364 They said..they were blessed if they'd go near the old trout again. **1914** D. BEATTY *Let.* 16 Feb. in W. S. Chalmers *Life & Lett. David, Earl Beatty* (1951) vi. 127 There were some funny old trouts and some spritely young ones, but no raving beauties. **1932** S. GIBBONS *Cold Comfort Farm* xvi. 224 'Serve her right, the old trout,' muttered Flora. **1956** 'A. GILBERT' *And Death came Too* ii. 33 She and her husband always went south to stay with her mother-in-law, an old trout called Lady Dingle. **1972** V. CANNING *Rainbird Pattern* iii. 50 She wasn't such a bad old trout. For all her money and position, life hadn't been all good to her.

5. a. *attrib.* and *Comb.*, as ***trout-angler***, ***-angling***, ***-brook***, ***farm***, ***-hole***, ***-hook***, ***-line***, ***-net***, ***ova***, ***-pond***, ***-preserve***, ***-rod***, ***-spawn***, ***-spear***, ***-stream***, ***-worm***; objective and obj. gen., as ***trout-breeder***, ***-catcher***, ***-fisher***, ***-fishing***, ***-pirate***, ***-rearing***, ***-tickler***; also ***trout-coloured***, ***-famous***, ***-haunted*** adjs.; ***trout-like*** adj.

1538 ELYOT, *Fuscina*..a troute speare, an yele speare. **1555** [see EEL-SPEAR]. **1591** SYLVESTER *Du Bartas* I. vi. 653 Kennet, whose Trout-famous Drift..by Hungerford doth hasten. **1653** R. SANDERS *Physiogn.* 35 A greenish eye, a trout-nose, a great mouth. **1653** WALTON *Angler* v. 126, I shall tel you a little more of Trout fishing before I speak of the Salmon. *Ibid.* 128 In Hamp-shire..they use to catch Trouts in the night by the light of a Torch or straw, which when they have discovered, they strike with a Trout spear. **1668** WILKINS *Real Char.* 140 [These] may be stiled the Trout-kind. **1727** BAILEY vol. II, *Trout-coloured* (spoken of Horses) is White speckled with Spots of Black, Bay, or Sorrel, particularly about the Head and Neck. **1751** FIELDING *Amelia* I. III. xii. 271 It is placed among Meadows washed by a clear Trout Stream. **1770** S. FOOTE *Lame Lover* I. 15 Oh! clear as a trout-stream. **1799** A. YOUNG *Agric. Lincoln.* 4 A narrow vale, through which runs a trout stream. **1807** W. IRVING *Salmag.* xi. 2 July (1855) 115 Trout-fishing was my uncle's favourite sport. **1839** T. C. HOFLAND *Brit. Angler's Man.* ii. (1841) 11 He [the peacock red worm] is a good trout-worm. **1839** *Spirit of Times* 15 June 170/3 Surely a trout rod of fourteen ounces is not likely to fatigue (by the difference of weight in ash and willow) in the last hours of fishing. **1840** *Ibid.* 5 Sept. 319/1 Get a couple of dozen of trout hooks of assorted sizes. *Ibid.* 319/2 They know every trout hole or deer stand within twenty miles. **1842** W. P. HAWES *Sporting Scenes* I. 189 A scow, chiefest for a trout-pond. **1845** J. COULTER *Adv. Pacific* vii. 78 They can be caught with small trout hooks, carefully baited. **1849** THOREAU *Week Concord Riv.* 323 Trout-fishers from distant cities had arrived before us. **1868** *Rep. U.S. Commissioner Agric.* (1869) 327, I hatched about five hundred thousand trout last season, and sold about five hundred thousand impregnated trout spawn. *Ibid.* 328 A fountain capable of filling constantly a two-inch pipe will sustain a trout preserve which may prove a source of pleasure and profit. *Ibid.* 337 Experimental and initiatory practice in trout-rearing is becoming common upon Long Island. **1883** W. E. NORRIS *No New Thing* I. i. 9 His gun, and a trout-rod, and some other things. **1884** JEFFERIES *Life of Fields* 199 The swan is a well-known trout-pirate. **1887** HISSEY *Holiday on Road* 7 By the side of a trout-haunted stream. **1887** in W. Whitman *Daybks. & Notebks.* (1978) II. 509 A trout pond formed the boundary. **1894** *Field* 9 June 833/3 Fine trout given our society by Mr. A., the trout breeder. **1897** *Outing* (U.S.) XXX. 324/2 In this place one can..trace..the trout-brook to its source. **1904** GALLICHAN *Fishing Spain* 185 The Portuguese peasant lads are expert trout-ticklers. **1904** *Pilot* Apr. 330/1 It is clear..that the really desirable *requies senectæ* will be afforded by a trout farm. **1906** *Westm. Gaz.* 28 Apr. 14/3 The appearance of the may-fly..is eagerly looked forward to every year by the trout-angler. **1910** H. T. SHERINGHAM in *Encycl. Brit.* II. 28/2 (*Angling*) Grayling injure a trout stream by devouring trout-ova and trout-food. **1936** *Discovery* Feb. 43/1 It is common knowledge to most trout-fishers that the May Fly has steadily decreased over many parts of the country in recent years.

b. Special Combs.: **trout-fly**, (*a*) the may-fly; (*b*) an artificial fly for trout-fishing; **trout-lily** *U.S.*, the yellow dog's-tooth violet, *Erythronium americanum*; cf. ERYTHRONIUM; **trout-line**, (*a*) a line used in trout fishing; (*b*) *U.S.* = *trot-line* (TROT *sb.*[1] 8); **trout-louse**, a fish-louse parasitic on the trout, also called *sug*; **trout-perch**, the black bass (*local, U.S.*); also a trout-like fish (*Percopsis guttatus*) of the rivers and Great Lakes of U.S., having the mouth and scales like those of a perch; **trout-spoon**, a small spoon-bait for trout-fishing (*Cent. Dict.* 1891); **trout-stone**, *Min.* (G. *forellenstein*) = TROCTOLITE.

1744–50 W. ELLIS *Mod. Husbandm.* III. II. xiii. 84 The Caddis or *Trout Fly,..certainly the best natural Baits of all others for taking Trouts. **1787** BEST *Angling* (ed. 2) 109 They [salmon] will rise at anything gaudy, and where they are plenty, at Trout flies. **1888** GOODE *Amer. Fishes* 466 The young fish rise freely to trout-flies in rapid water. **1910** H. T. SHERINGHAM in *Encycl. Brit.* II. 28/2 Grayling will take most small trout-flies. **1909** *Cent. Dict.* Suppl. 729/2 **Trout-lily*, the yellow dog-tooth violet. **1943** R. PEATTIE *Great Smokies* 275 The spring beauties and trout lilies..herald the blooming season. **1975** M. C. DAVIS *Near Woods* ix. 148 Almost all the trout-lilies emerging had but single leaves. **1789** J. WOODFORDE *Diary* 15 July (1927) III. 121 Busy..in making up some new *Trout lines and for Eels. **1839** *Spirit of Times* 13 July 217/1 We have..bought an assortment of trout-lines and flies. **1912** *Dialect Notes* III. 592 *Trout-line, n.*, a trot-line. *Trout-line* has grown from the belief that there was something incorrect about *trot-line*. The line, of course, is not used in catching trout. **1934** *Sun* (Baltimore) 9 July 11/3 Crabs are reported to be so scarce that trout-line crabbers are able to catch only two barrels daily. **1653** WALTON *Angler* iii. 90 In winter..many of them have sticking on them Sugs, or *Trout lice, which is a kind of worm. **1883** *Century Mag.* July 376/2 A description of a Carolina bass was sent to Lacépède under the local name of trout, or *trout-perch, who accordingly named it salmoides, meaning trout-like. **1892** *Trout-stone [see TROCTOLITE].

Hence **'trouted** *a.* [cf. F. *porcelaine truitée*], see quot.; **'troutful** *a.*, full of or abounding in trout; **'troutless** *a.*, without trout, devoid of trout (whence **'troutlessness**); **'trouty**, a troutlet.

1783 JUSTAMOND tr. *Raynal's Hist. Indies* III. 153 The *trouted china, which no doubt is called so from the resemblance it bears to the scales of a trout. *a* **1661** FULLER *Worthies, Hants.* (1662) II. 1 Clear and fresh rivulets of *troutful water. **1891** ATKINSON *Moorland Par.* 197 Our troutful little stream of the Esk. **1865** KINGSLEY in *Life & Lett.* (1879) II. 180, I catch a trout now and then..so I am not left *troutless. **1904** GALLICHAN *Fishing Spain* 15 He maintains that the Bidasoa will be troutless in two years. **1879** *Daily News* 25 Nov. 5/2 Dynamite, disease, pollution of rivers, have destroyed their thousands since Thomas Stoddart wrote a sad song on the *troutlessness of Yarrow. **1848** *Fraser's Mag.* XXXVIII. 73 My wilfulness that bright day..was rewarded with a few *trouties.

† **trout**, *sb.*[2] *dial. Obs.* Also 5 **trowtt**. [Of uncertain origin.] *pl.* (See quot. 1691.) So † **trout** *v. Obs.*, to curdle, coagulate.

1483 *Cath. Angl.* 395/1 To Trowtt, *coagulare*. Trowttis, *coagulum*. **1683** G. MERITON *Yorks. Dialogue* 402 (E.D.S.) Ile give um some Trouts, reach me hither th' Bowl. **1691** RAY *N.C. Words* 77 *Trouts*, Curds taken off the Whey when it is boiled: a Rustick word. In some places they call them Trotters.

trout, obs. form of TROAT *v.*, TROTH.

trouter ('traʊtə(r)). [f. TROUT *sb.*[1] + -ER[1].] One who fishes for trout; a trout-fisher.

1830 HOWITT *Seasons* (1837) 122 Cloudy weather, a little windy, especially from the South, is in high favour with the trouter. **1854** *Fraser's Mag.* L. 397 However well a trouter may get on by keeping to the banks of his river, the salmon fisher can rarely be successful by fishing from dry land. **1887** *Macm. Mag.* June 107/1 Your dry-fly man is inclined to look upon the great mass of trouters..with something akin to complacent and patronizing compassion.

trouthe, obs. form of TROTH, TROUGH.

'troutiness. [f. TROUTY *a.* + -NESS.] The condition or quality of being 'trouty'; speckledness, spottiness.

1895 R. GRAHAM *Notes Menteith* v. 72 A..much patched coat of various shades of troutiness and stages of decay.

trouting ('traʊtɪŋ). [f. TROUT *sb.*[1] + -ING[1].] Fishing for trout, trout-fishing.

a **1768** ERSKINE *Inst. Law Scot.* II. ix. §13 Depriving him of the pleasure of trouting. **1827** SCOTT *Surg. Dau.* v, The game was plenty, and the trouting in the brook such as had been represented by advertisement.

b. *attrib.*

1806 *Gazetteer Scotl.* (ed. 2) 558 Venny or Finny; a small rivulet of Angus-shire,..is a fine trouting-stream. **1833** J. RENNIE *Alph. Angling* 64 A trouting-rod is usually made from twelve to fifteen feet. **1883** *Fisheries Exhib. Catal.* (ed. 4) 176 Salmon Lines, Deep Sea Lines, Trouting Lines. **1896** *Westm. Gaz.* 16 Sept. 3/3 The one good trouting loch in Scotland is Loch Leven.

c. as *pres. pple.* (chiefly after *go*).

a **1845** HOOD *To I. Walton* 65 Sham flies to go trolling and trouting. **1866** ALGER *Solit. Nat. & Man* III. 181 The loneliness of Izaak Walton trouting in a secluded glen. **1899** *Q. Rev.* Jan. 88 At Villeneuve he goes trouting in the dark with the servant of the inn.

troutlet ('traʊtlɪt). [f. as prec. + -LET.] A little or tiny trout. Also *attrib.*

1829 HOOD *Eugene Aram* i, There were some that ran and some that leapt, Like troutlets in a pool. **1879** SENIOR *Trav. & Trout Antipodes* (1880) 121 By the 15th of June three thousand young salmon and fifty troutlet immigrants were swimming about, strong, contented, and merry. **1881** G. ALLEN *Vignettes fr. Nat., Mountain Tarn* 175 If ever a young Llyn Gwernant troutlet..leaps the cascades.

troutling ('traʊtlɪŋ). [f. as prec. + -LING[1].] = prec.

a **1739** JARVIS *Quix.* I. I. ii, If there be many troutlings,..they will supply the place of one trout. **1856** 'STONEHENGE' *Brit. Sports* I. v. iii. §13 In using the Spinning-Tackle with the parr-tail or troutling as a bait, it is spun exactly as for trout. **1889** H. C. PENNELL *Fishing* 100 The catching and eating of half a dozen troutlings.

Trouton ('traʊtən). *Physics.* [The name of F. T. *Trouton* (1863–1922), Irish physicist, who published the observation in 1884 (*Phil. Mag.* XVIII. 54).] ***Trouton's law*** or ***rule***: the observation that for many substances the latent heat of vaporization of one mole, divided by the absolute temperature of the boiling point, is a constant (***Trouton('s) constant***) equal to approximately 88 joules per kelvin.

1899 J. WALKER *Introd. Physical Chem.* xii. 124 If the substance is in the state of vapour, the heat of vaporisation must be added to the thermochemical data for the liquid. This correction is often considerable, amounting approximately to one-fourth of the value of the boiling point of the substance on the absolute scale (Trouton's rule). **1901** *Jrnl. Chem. Soc.* LXXX. II. 372 The author states that if the heat of fusion is added to the heat of vaporisation for the determination of Trouton's constant, the quotient then obtained agrees with that found for dissociation. **1922** GLAZEBROOK *Dict. Appl. Physics* I. 561/2 It was shown by Despretz in 1823 that some relationship of the form given above by Trouton held, and later Pictet (1876), Ramsay (1877), rediscovered it independently, but it is now generally referred to as Trouton's law. **1966** [see POLAR *a.* 3 b]. **1982** A. M. LESK *Introd. Physical Chem.* iv. 71 Enthalpies of vaporization of unassociated substances follow Trouton's rule.

trouty, *sb.*: see after TROUT *sb.*[1]

trouty ('traʊtɪ), *a.* [f. TROUT *sb.*[1] + -Y.] Full of, abounding in, or containing trout.

1676 COTTON *Walton's Angler* II. ii. 17 Little inconsiderable Rivers, as Awber, Eroways, and the like, scarce worth naming, but Trouty too. **1831** *Blackw. Mag.* XXX. 965 Heavens! among the gravel what a trouty congregation! **1883** STEVENSON *Across the Plains* i. (1892) 74 Every trouty pool along that mountain river.

b. Speckled like a trout.

1895 [implied in TROUTINESS].

‖**trouvaille** (truvɑj). [Fr., f. *trouver* to find.] A lucky find; a windfall.

[**1753** LADY LUXBOROUGH *Lett. to Shenstone* 12 Dec., I..should else have stolen a word from the French and have said *une trouvaille*.] **1842** THACKERAY *Profess. Fitz-Boodle* i, The *plebs* have robbed us of that trade among others, nor, I confess, do I much grudge them their *trouvaille*. **1848** —— *Van. Fair* xi, My dear, you are a perfect *trouvaille*. **1881** *Blackw. Mag.* Apr. 523 The trouvaille proved to be the first edition of Shakspere.

‖**trouvère** (truvɛr), **trouveur** (truvœr). [OF. *trovere*, *-eur*, *truveur* (12th c. in Godef.), F. *trouvère*, *trouveur* (= Prov. *trobaire*), f. *trouver*: cf. TROUBADOUR.] One of a school of poets who flourished in Northern France from the 11th to the 14th c., whose works are chiefly epic in character. They produced the *chansons de geste*, *fabliaux*, etc. Cf. TROUBADOUR.

1795 SOUTHEY *Joan of Arc* IV. 175 Meantime the Trouveur struck the harp; he sung Of Lancelot Du Lake. **1833** LONGF. *Outre-Mer* Prose Wks. 1886 I. 94 The great mass of the poetry of the Trouvères is of a narrative or epic character. **1887** LOWELL *Old Eng. Dram.* (1892) 7 One French Miracle Play of the thirteenth century, by the trouvère Rutebeuf. **1889** DOYLE *Micah Clarke* 208 A king of bards and trouveurs.

trouwe, **trouzed**, obs. ff. TROW *v.*, TROUSED.

trove (trəʊv). Short for TREASURE-TROVE (q.v.), in sense 'a valuable find'. Hence, a source of treasure, a reserve or repository of valuable things.

1888 KIPLING *Plain Tales* xiii. 94 The value of her trove struck her, and she cast about for the best method of using it. **1901** —— *Kim* i. 11 Delighted as a child at each new trove. **1909** G. W. YOUNG *Wind & Hill* Ded., A kingdom..More rich than childhood's fairy trove. **1976** *Publishers Weekly* 13 Sept. 97/1 Reaching back to the fifth century and up to today, the authors find a trove of artists whose work merits acknowledgment. **1982** *Sci. Amer.* Aug. 30A/1 Kingdon has himself visited 105 of those areas. He returns with his trove of image and understanding.

trove, obs. Sc. and north. form of TURF.

trover (ˈtrəʊvə(r)). *Law.* [subst. use of OF. *trover* (11th c.), F. *trouver* pres. inf., to find.] The act of finding and assuming possession of any personal property; hence (in full, ***action of trover***), an action at law to recover the value of personal property illegally converted by another to his own use.

Originally the action was brought for damages against one who had found and refused to give up the goods of the plaintiff on demand; this refusal constituted 'conversion' (CONVERSION 7); hence the action was called ***trover and conversion***. Later, the finding became a legal fiction, and it was only necessary to prove the ownership and detention of the goods.

1594 WEST *2nd Pt. Symbol., Chancerie* §148 They came to the handes and possession of your poore suppliant.. by way of trover. **1615, 1712, 1765** [see CONVERSION 7]. **1678** BUTLER *Hud.* III. iii. 648 Whether I should.. bring my Action of Conversion And Trover for my Goods? **1749** FIELDING *Tom Jones* XII. iv, Some perhaps would have given nothing [for the pocket-book] and left the Fellow to his Action of Trover. **1848** ARNOULD *Mar. Insur.* I. iv. (1866) 195 The policy, when effected, becomes in law the property of the assured, who may maintain trover for it. **1876** LOWELL *Among my Bks.* Ser. II. 323 In this sense the author of a dictionary might bring an action of trover against every other author who used his words.

†**ˈtrovy**, *int. Obs.* [? a. OF. *trové*, pa. pple. of *trover*, F. *trouver* to find.] ? A call in hawking.

a **1529** SKELTON *Ware the Hauke* 116 With troll, cytrace, and trouy, They ranged, hankin bouy.

†**trow** (trəʊ), *sb.*[1] *Obs. rare.* [f. TROW *v.* (cf. Norse, Sw., Dan. *tro*).]

1. Belief; faith, trust.

c **1300** *Cursor M.* 22722 (Edin.) þai þat war in dred and dout, þar-of wit trow [*v.rr.* trouth, trouþe] he broht þaim out. [**1883** G. STEPHENS *Bugge's Stud. N. Mythol.* 149 Teaching of the new trow by help of the old.]

2. Fancy, supposition.

14.. *Beryn* 38 For they that loven so passyngly, such trowes þey have echone. *a* **1536** *Calisto & Melib.* A iv, Her lyttyll handis in meane maner this is no trow.

3. Faith as pledged, covenant: = TROTH *sb.* 2.

1515 *Acc. Ld. High Treas. Scot.* V. 40 For keeping the day of trow. **1634** *Malory's Arthur* IX. viii. (1816) I. 375 Then sir Plenorius yielded him and his tower, and all his prisoners at his will; and then sir Launcelot received him, and took his trow [1470–85 trouthe].

trow (trəʊ, locally trou, traʊ), *sb.*[2] *local.* [Dial. variant of TROUGH.] A name for various kinds of boats or barges: *spec.* **a.** Formerly, on the Severn, a large flat-bottomed sailing barge; **b.** in the south of Scotland and north of England, a double canoe or boat used in spearing salmon by torch-light (also *pl.* const. as *sing.*): see quot. 1825 (? *obs.*); **c.** on the south coast of England, a small flat-bottomed boat used in herring-fishing. **d.** *attrib.*, as ***trow-fisher***, ***-lock***; also TROWMAN.

c **1330** R. BRUNNE *Chron. Wace* (Rolls) 10218 Arthur.. gadered botes, chalans, & trowes. **1479** *Office Mayor of Bristol* in *Eng. Gilds* (1870) 424 Such as bryngeth whete to towne, as wele in trowys, as otherwyse, by lande and by watir. **1778** WESLEY *Wks.* (1872) XI. 144 Are there fewer trows or barges employed on rivers and canals? **1825** JAMIESON, *Trows*,.. used in Roxb. and other southern shires, to denote two pieces of wood, each formed like the half or section of an ellipsis, fenced with upright boards, so as to prevent the entrance of water. These two are conjoined... An interstice is left between the two sections, so that the water is seen distinctly through it. This sort of vessel.. is used.. in night-fishing on rivers for salmon. **1835** 'STEPHEN OLIVER' *Rambles Northumb.* 154 'The trows'.. used in spearing salmon in parts of the river where they cannot be taken with a net. The trows consist of.. two narrow boats,.. connected at the top by a piece of flat board. *Ibid.* 155 Some of the old trow-fishers here are of opinion [etc.]. **1838** SIMMS *Public Wks. Gt. Brit.* ii. 14 The trow-lock [in the Gloucester and Berkeley canal] is eighty-one feet six inches long. **1875** *Bristol Times* 17 June (E.D.D.), The Fanny was a ketch-rigged (two-masted) trow, of 120 tons.., and was used for trading purposes. **1888** ELWORTHY *W. Somerset Word-bk.* s.v., On the south coast about Sidmouth a small fishing-boat is a trow. **1899** *Daily News* 13 Feb. 7/3 The trow 'Flower of the Severn',.. moored in the river, was carried away by the tide and wrecked.

†**trow**, *sb.*[3] *Obs. rare.* Also trew. [a. OF. *trëud*, *trëu*, *trou*, etc. (Roland, 11th c.):—L. *tribūt-um* TRIBUTE.] = TREWAGE, toll.

c **1380** *Sir Ferumb.* 1732 ȝe mote furst.. þe truwage make fyn þat to þis brigge longeþ.. do tell me wat is þe trow. *Ibid.* 4471 Tel me, sire,.. Of þys passage what ys þe trow? *Ibid.* 4477 My trew þay sayde þay wolde pay.

trow (trou), *sb.*[4] *Orkney* and *Shetl.* [= Swed. *troll*: see TROLL *sb.*[2]] = TROLL *sb.*[2]

1640 *Orkney Witch Trial* in *Abbotsford Cl. Misc.* I. 167 ȝe ansuered hir againe, that it was but the Trow that haid gripped her. **1643** *ibid.* 173 Knoweing that the said Thomas was lying seik in his hous, ȝe said that it was the sea trow or spirit that was lying vpoun him. **1701** BRAND *Descr. Orkney* etc. (1703) 115 They tell us that several such Creatures do appear to Fishers at Sea, particularly such as they call *Sea-Trowes.* **1822** SCOTT *Pirate* v, Other [magicians] dealt with spirits of a different and less odious class—the ancient dwarfs, called, in Zetland, Trows, or Drows, the modern fairies, and so forth. **1868** D. GORRIE *Summ. & Wint. Orkneys* v. 168 The trows, or drows,.. resembled the *daoine shith* of the Highlanders, in the malevolent feelings which they.. entertained towards mankind. **1883** R. M. FERGUSSON *Rambling Sk. Far North* xvii. 121 It was an unlucky moment when a fisherman cast his eyes on a sea-trow; panic and fear seized him.

trow (trəʊ), *v. arch.* Forms: α. 1 trúwian, 4 truu, 4–5 tru, 4–6 (8–9 *Sc.*) true. β. 1 tréowan, tréowian, 3 treowe, 3–6 (9 *Sc.*) trew, 4 ? *Sc.* treu. γ. 3–5 trowen, (3 (*Orm.*) trowwenn, 4 trouwe), 3–6 (8 *Sc.*) trou, 4–7 trowe, (4 *Sc.* throw, throu), 5 troue, 5–7 tro, (8 tro'), 5, 9 *Sc.* troo, 6–7 troe, troa, 4– trow. δ. (*north. dial.*) 4 trau, (tray), 4–5 traue, trawe, traw, (5 traywe). Pa. t. and pple. trowed (trəʊd); also *pa. t.* 3–5 -ede, 4–6 *Sc.* -it, etc.; 4 troud, 4–6 trowd, 6 troude; *pa. pple.* 4 troud, troude, trod, trawet, 5 trawt; (4 (?) trowen). [OE. had more than one type: (1) OE. *trúwian*, f. *trúwa* sb. 'faith, belief' = OS. *trûon* (MLG. *truwe*), OHG. *trû(u)ên* (MHG. *trûen*, *truuen*, Ger. *trauen*), ON. *trúa* (Sw. and Norw. *tro*), Goth. *trauan*, OTeut. **trûwian*, from base *trû-*, orig. 'strong, firm, sure'; (2) OE. *tréowan*, *tréowian*, from *tréowe* 'faith, belief', with the ablaut grade **tréu(w)*; cf. OS. *tre(u)wa*, OWFris. *trouwa* (MLG., MDu., Du. *trouwen* to believe, trust, espouse). Of the two OE. forms, *trúwian* was the earlier and more usual; but its place was mainly taken in ME. by *trowen*, with its variants *traue*, *traw*, from *tréow(i)an*. In some of the ME. forms, *trúwian* and *tréow(i)an* appear to run together.]

†**1.** *trans.* (orig. *intr.* with *dat.*; cf. 2). To trust, have confidence in, believe (a person or thing).

α. *c* **897** K. ÆLFRED *Gregory's Past. C.* ix. 58 Swiðe eaðe mæȝ on smyltre sæ unȝelæred scipstiora ȝenoh ryhte stieran, ac se ȝelæreda him ne truwað on ðære hreon sæ & on ðæm miclan stormum. **13..** *Cursor M.* 4366 (Cott.) And for he es traist o mi leute Of all his god he trues me. **1728** RAMSAY *Fables* xii. 12 His colour's green, If ane may true his ain twa een.

β. *Beowulf* (Z.) 1166 ȝehwylc hiora his ferhþe treowde, þæt he hæfde mod micel. *c* **888** K. ÆLFRED *Boeth.* xxxvii. §2 Yrnað ealle endemes ða ðe hiora ærninge trewað. *a* **1000** *Cædmon's Gen.* 2318 Ic eow treowiȝe ȝif ȝe þæt tacen ȝegað. *c* **1175** *12th c. Hom.* 136 3yf he þa bote deþ..& on Gode trywiȝe. **1375** BARBOUR *Bruce* II. 326 He that will trew His fa, It sall him sum tyme rew.

γ. *c* **1250** *Gen. & Ex.* 1092 Loth hem warnede,.. Oc he ne troweden him. *c* **1275** LAY. 3413 Wan hii þe troueþ alre best. **13..** *Cursor M.* 5212 (Gött.) þis es þe soth, trou [*Cott.* tru] ȝe me. *c* **1400** MAUNDEV. (1839) xx. 221 And all be it that sum men wil not trow me, but holden it for fable. **1500–20** DUNBAR *Poems* xxxii. 40 The silly thing trowd him, allace! The lame gaif creddence to the tod. *c* **1600** MONTGOMERIE *Cherrie & Slae* 842 Suld not I trow my ain twa een? *a* **1829** *Parcy Reed* xviii. in Child *Ballads* VII. (1890) 26/2 The three false Halls of Girsonsfield, They'll never be trusted or trowed again.

δ. **13..** *Cursor M.* 5151 (Cott.) If þat þou noght traues me,.. come þi-self and se. *c* **1460** *Towneley Myst.* iii. 45 To those that wille hym trawe.

†**b.** *refl.* To trust oneself *to* a person. *Obs. rare.*

α. *c* **950** *Lindisf. Gosp.* John ii. 24 Se hælend ne lefde *vel* ne truȝude hine seolfne him *vel* ðæm, foreðon he uiste alle.

γ. **1388** WYCLIF *ibid.*, But Jhesus trowide not hym silf to hem, for he knewe alle men.

†**2.** *intr.* with prep. To believe *in* or *on*; to have confidence *in*; to trust *to*. *Obs.* or *rare arch.*

α. *c* **1000** ÆLFRIC *Saints' Lives* xxv. 446 Ða burhware.. truwodon to þam wealle. *c* **1300** *Cursor M.* 19883 (Edin.) Truis tu in god?

β. *c* **1000** *Ags. Ps.* (Th.) cxvii[i]. 8 God ys on Dryhten ȝeorne to þenceanne, þonne on mannan wese mod to treowianne.

γ. *c* **1205** LAY. 2351 He nom his enne hired mon þe he wel trowede on. *c* **1330** R. BRUNNE *Chron. Wace* (Rolls) 2855 Trowe til vs & oure consayl! **1340–70** *Alex. & Dind.* 829 3if alle þe lorus.. Ben trewe to be trowen on & trysty to leue. **1375** BARBOUR *Bruce* I. 490 Gyff that ȝe will trow to me. *c* **1385** CHAUCER *L.G.W.* 1707 (*Lucrece*) It is no nede To trowyn on the word but on the dede. *c* **1400** tr. *Secreta Secret., Gov. Lordsh.* vi. 52 A trew discret man.. to whom he may trowe to ordeyne þe besynesse of his godys. *c* **1449** PECOCK *Repr.* I. xviii. (Rolls) 102 Thei wolen not trowe to his teching. *c* **1460** *Towneley Myst.* xx. 434 Bot trow in god, that you has wroght. *c* **1470** HENRY *Wallace* II. 235 In Inglismen, allace, quhi suld we trow? **1522** *World & Child* C vij, The xij. artycles of the fayth That mankynde must on trowe. **1552** ABP. HAMILTON *Catech.* (1884) 14 We suld trow in the sonne of God. **1870** MORRIS *Earthly Par.* III. IV. 369 Vague tales, wherein I was well fain to trow.

δ. **13..** *Cursor M.* 13671 (Cott.) Traus [*Fairf.* trawes] þou in godd sun or nai?

†**b.** *trans.* To believe in (a doctrine, etc.). *Obs.*

1340–70 *Alex. & Dind.* 841 Hit semeþ.. þat ȝe no giuen of no gome no none godus trowe. *c* **1380** WYCLIF *Wks.* (1880) 422 Oon article of bileue.. is to trowe hooly chirche. *c* **1400** MAUNDEV. (Roxb.) xv. 66 þe Sarzenes trowes þe incarnacioun. **1513** DOUGLAS *Æneis* VI. Prol. 81 We trow a God, regnand in personis thre.

3. *trans.* To believe (a statement, etc.); to give credence to, accept as true or trustworthy.

α. *a* **1300** *Cursor M.* 14708 (Cott.) Qua wil noght tru [*Gött.* trou, *Fairf.* traw, *Trin.* trowe] þat i tell.

β. *c* **1250** *Gen. & Ex.* 2037 Pvtifar trewið hise wiwes tale.

γ. *c* **1200** ORMIN Ded. 134, I wollde bliþeliȝ þatt all Ennglisshe lede.. shollde itt trowwenn. **1413** *Pilgr. Sowle* (Caxton) I. iii. (1859) 4 Such thynges wold I nought haue trowyd, yf I had nought seen it my self. **1450–80** tr. *Secreta Secret.* xvi. 14 Trowe not lightly alle that that men wille telle the. **1536** BELLENDEN *Cron. Scot.* (1821) II. 272 We may nocht trow ane wourd he sayis. **1605** SHAKS. *Lear* I. iv. 135 Speake lesse then thou knowest,.. Learne more then thou trowest. **1816** SCOTT *Antiq.* xxi, I hae garr'd him trow mony a queer tale. *a* **1818** MACNEILL *Poems* (1844) 102 She trou'd ilka word that the fause loon did say. **1876** MORRIS *Sigurd* II. 79 Men trowed his every word.

δ. **13..** *E.E. Allit. P.* B. 662 Saré laȝez, Not trawande þe tale.

†**b.** with *obj.* and *compl.* To believe or suppose (a thing or person) to be (so and so); also with *compl. inf.* (*to be..*, or *to do* something). *Obs.*

γ. *a* **1275** *Prov. Ælfred* 164 in *O.E. Misc.* 113 For wanne he is lif alre beste trowen, þenne sal he letin lif his oȝene. *c* **1400** tr. *Secreta Secret., Gov. Lordsh.* xxix. 63 Yf þe nedys of a woman, drawe to þe to here þat þow trowys trewe, and þat þou demys good. *c* **1460** *Play Sacram.* 559, I trowe best we mak a crye. **1581** A. HALL *Iliad* IV. 69 Thou Agamemnon trowes Vs dastards and faint hearted folke. **1596** DALRYMPLE tr. *Leslie's Hist. Scot.* VIII. (S.T.S.) II. 59 The chanceller trowit al to be trew.

δ. **13..** *E.E. Allit. P.* A. 282, I trawed my perle don out of dawez. **1432–50** tr. *Higden* (Rolls) II. 121 Of whom somme men trawe that cite to have taken name.

†**c.** Phr. ***to trow*** (in passive sense): to be believed or thought (so and so). Also ***at trow*** (AT *prep.* 39), in quot. *a* 1340, worthy of belief, credible.

13.. *Cursor M.* 27126 (Cott.) And es he for a fule to trou [*Fairf.* traw]. *a* **1340** HAMPOLE *Psalter* xcii. 7 *Testimonia sua credibilia facta sunt nimis...* þi biddyngis ere mykil made at trow. **1596** SPENSER *F.Q.* V. ii. 34 How much it doth overflowe, Or faile thereof, so much is more then iust to trowe.

4. with *obj. cl.* To believe, think, be of opinion, suppose, imagine; sometimes, to believe confidently, feel sure, be assured. †***trow you what..*** (?) 'what do you think..?'

α. *c* **1000** *Ælfric's Past. Ep.* iii. in Thorpe *Ags. Laws* II. 364 Ic truwiȝe þeah þæt sum wurðe abirrd þurh God. *a* **1818** MACNEILL *Poems* (1844) 96, I pree'd it aft as ye may true!

γ. *c* **1200** ORMIN 6946 þeȝȝ munndenn trowwenn þatt te child Josæpess sune wære. **1362** LANGL. *P. Pl.* A. I. 133 þis I trouwe beo treuþe! *a* **1400** *Prymer* (1891) 83 Trowest þou auȝt that a deed man schal lyue aȝen? **14..** *Cov. Corp. Christi Pl.* I. 883, I tro there wolbe a carefull syght. *c* **1470** HENRY *Wallace* II. 391, I trow thow be sum spy. **1526** TINDALE *Luke* xvii. 9 Doeth he thanke that servaunt be cause he did that which was commaunded vnto hym? I trowe not. **1533** BELLENDEN *Livy* III. v. (S.T.S.) 256 þe hevynnis apperit birnand; The erde trymblit..; men trowis ane kow spak. **1588** SHAKS. *L.L.L.* v. ii. 279 Trow you what he call'd me? **1590** SPENSER *F.Q.* II. v. 13 And henceforth by this daies ensample trow, That hasty wroth, and heedlesse hazardry, Doe breede repentaunce late, and lasting infamy. **1613** SHAKS. *Hen. VIII*, I. i. 184 As I troa Which I doe well; for I am sure [etc.]. **1637–50** ROW *Hist. Kirk* (Wodrow Soc.) 451, I used.. to.. cast up the whyte of my eyes, so that any bodie wold have trowed that I was blind. **1786** BURNS *A Dream* ii, The poets.. Wad gar you trow ye ne'er do wrang. **1818** SCOTT *Rob Roy* iv, I trow he's a dealer in cattle. **1872** THIRLWALL *Rem.* (1878) III. 254 Can anything be more clearly proved..? I trow not.

δ. *c* **1400** *Destr. Troy* 3351 Ne trawes not, tru lady, þat I take wolde Thy ladyship to losse.

b. Parenthetically or at the end of a sentence (often merely expletive), as ***I trow*** (in assertions) = 'I suppose', 'I ween'; †also rarely in questions (where the sense is not clear).

α. **13..** *Cursor M.* 371 (Cott.) þarfor scaples was it [I] tru [*Fairf.* traw].

γ. [**1423** JAS. I *Kingis Q.* xi, Bot now, how trowe ȝe? suich a fantasye Fell me to mynd.] *c* **1491** *Chast. Goddes Chyld.* 35 Thyse wordes I trowe shall suffyse. **1549** LATIMER *Ploughers* (Arb.) 20 Who trowe you is a faythefull seruante? **1577** NORTHBROOKE *Dicing* (1843) 71 No man is so foolishe, I trowe, so to doe. **1598** SHAKS. *Merry W.* I. iv. 140 Who's there, I troa? **1676** MARVELL *Gen. Councils* Wks. (Grosart) IV. 138 Did not this Historian, trow you, deserve [etc.]? **1678** BUNYAN *Pilgr.* I. 174 But I tro, you will put some difference between Little-faith and the Kings Champion. **1748** RICHARDSON *Clarissa* (1811) IV. xxxv. 224 What is become of Lord M. I trow, that he writes not to me? **1798** COLERIDGE *Anc. Mar.* VII. iii, Why, this is strange, I trow! **1852** H. ROGERS *Ecl. Faith* (1853) 438 A sceptic is not to be startled by paradoxes, I trow.

†**c.** Also simply *trow* (ellipt. for *I trow* or *trow you*). *Obs.*

1553 *Respublica* IV. ii. 998 Was not he drownde, trowe, last yeare? **1601** B. JONSON *Ev. Man in Hum.* (Qo.) IV. i. I iv, Where are these villaines troe? **1620** SHELTON *Quix.* II. x. 57 And haue you euer seene her, trow? **1636** HEYWOOD *Challenge* I. Wks. 1874 V. 14 How came you by them tro? honestly? **1741** RICHARDSON *Pamela* I. 57 What could you have done to him, tro'?

†**5.** *intr.* or *absol.* To believe; to hold a belief; to have or exercise faith. *Obs.*

α. *c* **1300** *Cursor M.* 19530 (Edin.) Simon [Magus] lete als þoȝ he truwid, And baptizid him.

γ. *c* **1200** ORMIN 2820 & tu full ædiȝ wurrþenn arrt, Forr þatt tu mihhtesst trowwenn. *c* **1330** R. BRUNNE *Chron. Wace* (Rolls) 7358 He asked þenne how þey trowd, & what þer Godes name hight. *c* **1440** *York Myst.* xxi. 162 What man þat trowis and baptised be. **1573** TYRIE *Refut.* in *Cath. Tractates* (S.T.S.) 12 Befoir a thousand yeiris.. wes thair peple of God that trowit as thay did.

†**6.** *trans.* To expect, hope. Usually with *inf.*; less commonly with *obj. cl.*; rarely with *simple obj.*

γ. **1340–70** *Alisaunder* 919 þei trowed no tresoun untruly too haue. *c* **1470** HENRY *Wallace* IX. 1266 Fra Fyff was tynt, the war thai trowyt to speid. **1470–85** MALORY *Arthur* X. xii. 432 Shewe me the Knyght, & I trowe I shalle bere hym doune. **1575** *Durham Depos.* (Surtees) 301 She.. was sore sike.., so that none of hir frendes trowed hir life. *c* **1600** MONTGOMERIE *Sonn.* xxviii. 11 Vhair sho [an ass] troude hir maister suld hir treit, They battound hir.

†**7.** To prove to be true; to vouch for; to verify; to ascertain. *Obs. rare.*

β. *a*901 *Laws of Alfred* c. 33 ȝif he hine treowan [*v.r.* treowian] wille.

γ. *c*1330 R. BRUNNE *Chron.* (1810) 258 Þe letter forth þei nam, to trowe þer sayng. *Ibid.* 339 Blissed be þou God,.. þi word is wele trod, I say it, bi William. 1603 *Philotus* iii, First try the treuth, then may ȝe trow, Gif I mynd to desaue.

trow: see THROW *v.*[1], TREE, TROLL, TROUGH.

†**'trowable**, *a. Obs.* [f. TROW *v.* + -ABLE.] That can be 'trowed' or believed; credible.

*a*1340 HAMPOLE *Psalter* xcii. 7 Þi witnessyngis ere made trowabile ful mykil. *c*1440 *Alphabet of Tales* 154 It is not trowable at he þat I hafe luffid so lang, att I sulde not be luffid of hym agayn. 1533 BELLENDEN *Livy* IV. viii. (S.T.S.) 75 It is als nocht trowabil þat sic exempil suld be Introducit be ane patriciane.

trowage, variant of TREWAGE *Obs.*

trowan, -ande, -ane, -ant, obs. ff. TRUANT.

trowandise, -yse, etc., var. TRUANDISE *Obs.*

trowch, obs. Sc. form of TROUGH.

trowe, var. THROW *sb.*[1] *Obs.*; obs. f. TROW, TRUE.

trowean, obs. form of TRUANT.

†**trowed**, *ppl. a. Obs.* [f. TROW *v.* + -ED[1].] Believed to be such; supposed, reputed.

*c*1410 LOVE *Bonavent. Mirr.* xv. (1908) 100 Joseph.. his trowed fader.

trowel ('traʊəl), *sb.* Forms: 4-5 **trowelle**, 4-7 **truel**, 5 **trowylle**, 7 **trewel**, 5-8 **trowell**, 6 **truell**, 6-7 **trewell**, 8 **trouel**, 5- **trowel**; also 4 **trulle**, 5 **troll(e**, 7 **trull**, **trule**. [ME. *truel*, a. OF. *truele* (13th c.), F. *truelle* (14th c.), ad. vulgar or late L. *truella* (1163 in Du Cange), for cl.L. *trulla*, dim. of *trua* stirring-spoon, skimmer, ladle, whence the monosyllabic form.]

1. a. A tool consisting of a flat (or, less commonly, rounded) plate of metal or wood, of various shapes, attached to a short handle; used by masons, bricklayers, plasterers, and others for spreading, moulding, or smoothing mortar, cement, and the like.

to lay it on with a trowel, to express a thing coarsely or bluntly; now *spec.* to flatter excessively or grossly.

1344 *Pipe Roll 18 Edw. III*, m. 45 (P.R.O.) In.. iiij. hamers, iiij. Trowellis, vj hirdellis pro lymeputtes.. xxx. ladlis pro cemento fundendo. 1382 WYCLIF *Amos* vii. 7 Loo! the Lord stondynge on a wall teerid, or morterd, and in the hond of hym a truel [*v.r.* trulle] of masoun. 1398 TREVISA *Barth. De P.R.* II. iv. (Harl. MS. 614) lf. 8 b/1 Aungels.. ben seen to haue trollis & hangynge plometis and mesuris & towles & werke men. *c*1440 *Pallad. on Husb.* I. 415 The parget of thy wough be strong & bryght; The trewel first ful ofte hit most distreyne. 1533 ELYOT *Cast. Helthe* Pref. (1539) 1, I toke my penne in the stede of a truell. *c*1570 *Pride and Lowl.* (1841) 32 A Brick-layer,.. A trewell at his gyrdle weared he. 1600 SHAKS. *A. Y. L.* I. ii. 112 Well said, that was laid on with a trowell. 1693 EVELYN *De la Quint. Compl. Gard.* II. 110 The said Gum must be kept hot,.. to be apply'd with a kind of Wooden Trule. 1719 *Free-thinker* No. 118 ¶8 Mr. Thornhill [cannot] paint the Cupolo of Paul's with a Trowel. 1836 THIRLWALL *Greece* III. xxii. 237 They supplied the place both of hods and trowels with their hands. 1887 RUSKIN *Præterita* II. x. 362 The instrument I finally decided to be the most difficult of management was the trowel.

b. A culinary ladle or slice of this shape. Cf. *trowel-slicer* in 2.

1773 *Lond. Chron.* 7 Sept. 248/3 Fish and pudding trowells. 1855 H. CLARKE *Dict.*, Fish-trowel.

c. A tool of this kind used in gardening, having a hollow, scoop-like, semi-cylindrical blade.

1796 C. MARSHALL *Garden.* iv. (1813) 52 Plants.. are best put in by a small spade or trowel. 1846 J. BAXTER *Libr. Pract. Agric.* (ed. 4) II. 119 The compound is firmly pressed into the moulds with a gardener's trowel. 1855 DELAMER *Kitch. Gard.* (1861) 16 The English trowel is excellent for many purposes; but besides it, it will be found convenient to have one or two long, narrow ones.

d. An elastic flat steel instrument used in spreading the paint in the manufacture of oilcloth.

1845 G. DODD *Brit. Manuf.* 4th Ser. v. 128 The workman holds in his right hand a kind of trowel, consisting of a long narrow blade, about a foot in length, decreasing in width towards one end, and having at the other a handle which bends back over the blade. With this trowel.. the workman draws the paint over the canvas, smoothing it repeatedly. 1881 [implied in TROWELLER].

e. See quot.

1892 GREENER *Breech Loader* 180 A properly-made trowel will load millions of cartridges before the holes become so worn that it has to be discarded. The author uses this counting trowel in loading all his cartridges.

2. *attrib.* and *Comb.*, as ***trowel-handling***, ***-planting***, ***-slicer*** (cf. 1 b); ***trowel-shaped*** adj.; **trowel-bayonet**, a bayonet resembling a mason's trowel, which may be used as a light entrenchment tool, or when detached from the rifle, as a hatchet (Knight *Dict. Mech.* 1877); **trowel-beak**, a bird, a Sumatran broadbill, *Corydon sumatranus* (*Cent. Dict.* 1891); **trowel-gauge**, an instrument for setting the nippers on a cotton-combing machine; **trowel-man**, one who uses a trowel; *spec.* a mason, bricklayer, or the like; also *fig.*

1902 THORNLEY *Cotton Combing Mach.* 151 In setting the nippers great assistance is rendered by the use of a *trowel gauge. 1887 RUSKIN *Præterita* II. x. 362 *note*, A piece of *trowel-handling as subtle as spreading the mortar under a brick. 1632 B. JONSON *Magn. Lady* II. vii, A hard-handed, and stiff ignorance, worthy a *Trewel, or a Hammer-man. 1737 *Salmon's Country Builder's Estimator* (ed. 2) 69 A Trowel-man and Labourer.. can perform one Rod of rough Work in five Days. 1756 *Monitor* No. 73 II. 203 It has been the general defect of English politicians to proceed without a plan; ignorant trowel-men in the service of the state. 1815 J. SMITH *Panorama Sci. & Art* II. 657, 7. Furrow planting. .. 8. Dibbling... 9. *Trowel planting. 1776 WITHERING *Brit. Plants* (1796) III. 573 [*Cochlearia danica*] All the leaves *trowel-shaped. 1897 MARY KINGSLEY *W. Africa* 454 Broad, trowel-shaped, almost triangular daggers. 1862 *Catal. Internat. Exhib., Brit.* II. No. 6504 A very large bread knife, and *trowel slicer.

Hence **'trowelful**, as much as can be taken up on a trowel (also *fig.*).

1580 HOLLYBAND *Treas. Fr. Tong.* s.v. *Truellée*, A trowell full of plaster or morter. 1801 LD. MINTO *Let.* in *Edin. Rev.* Apr. (1896) 405 Cramming Nelson with trowelfuls of flattery. 1843 LD. COCKBURN *Circuit Journeys* (1883) 184 Not one trowelful of lime.

trowel ('traʊəl), *v.* [f. prec. sb.]

1. *trans.* To spread, smooth, or dress (a surface) with or as with a trowel; to form or mould with a trowel; in quot. *c* 1670, to coat thickly *with*.

*c*1670 LD. ORRERY in *Daily Chron.* 12 June (1903) 3/3 The Women are never old, for the Wrinkles are well filled up by Paint,.. the Women trowel themselves with red. 1703 MOXON *Mech. Exerc.* 249 They finish the Plastering.. either by Trowelling and brishing it over with fair Water, or else by laying a thin Coat of fine stuff.. and.. Trowelling and brishing it. 1774 GOLDSM. *Nat. Hist.* VIII. IV. iii. 99 They [wasps] stick their load of paste on that part where they make their walls and partitions; they tread it close with their feet, and trowel it with their trunks. 1842 *Civil Eng. & Arch. Jrnl.* V. 337/2 After being properly trowelled, it is jointed to imitate stone.

2. To put, place, or move (something) with or as with a trowel; to lay on with a trowel, i.e. thickly or clumsily; often *fig.* of flattery or laudation.

1772 NUGENT tr. *Hist. Friar Gerund* I. 502 The good gentleman trowels on himself the plaister of praise without reserve. 1792 COLERIDGE *Lett., to G. Coleridge* 24 If ever hog's lard is pleasing it is when our superiors trowel it on. 1841 THACKERAY *Men & Pictures* 111 The skies are trowelled on; the light-vapouring distances are as thick as plum-pudding. 1898 HOLLINGSHEAD *Gaiety Chron.* i. 45 Mortar and cement were trowelled into their proper places.

Hence **'trowelled** *ppl. a.*; ***trowelled stucco***, stucco of the best description intended to be painted; **'trowelling** *vbl. sb.*; also **'troweller**, one who uses a trowel.

1823 P. NICHOLSON *Pract. Build.* 375 *Trowelled-stucco is a very neat kind of work, much used in dining-rooms, vestibules, stair-cases, &c. 1913 *Daily News* 31 Mar. 6 The roof.. has a fall of 5 in. in 13 ft. and was simply left with a trowelled finish. 1611 COTGR., *Truelleur*, a *Troweller; a Plaisterer, or any one that workes with a Trowell. 1881 *Instr. Census Clerks* (1885) 80 Floor Cloth, Oil Cloth Manufacture... Oil Skin Maker, Dealer. Silk Oiler. Trowler. 1630 *R. Johnson's Kingd. & Commw.* 598 Their Painting is meere steyning or *trowelling in respect of ours.

trowell, obs. form of TROLL *sb.*[1]

trowe maddam, var. TROLL-MADAM *Obs.*

trowent, -tyze: see TRUANT, TRUANDISE.

†**'trower.** *Obs. rare*[−1]. In 4 truer(e, trawere. [f. TROW *v.* + -ER[1].] A believer.

*c*1300 *Cursor M.* 21092 (Edin.) Thomas.. þat he ne moȝte noȝte tru wiþ here, Wiþ eie he was made lele truer [*v.rr.* truere, trawere].

trowes, obs. pl. of TREE; obs. f. TRUCE.

trowet, trowht, obs. forms of TROUT, TROTH.

trowie ('traʊɪ), *a. Orkney* and *Shetl.* [f. TROW *sb.*[4] + -IE, -Y.] Of or pertaining to the 'trows' or trolls; elfin; also, influenced by a 'trow'. So **'trowist** (*nonce-wd.*), a person credited with acquaintance with 'trows' and power to avert their influence.

1793 *Statist. Acc. Scotl.* VII. 396 Sponges are found upon the shore in great plenty, shaped like a man's hand, and called by the people Trowie Gloves. 1825 JAMIESON, *Trowie* adj., sickly, *Orkn.*... Shall we view this as signifying 'under the malign influence of the Trow, or daemon'? 1840 *New Statist. Acc. Scot.* (1845) XV. 142 (*Shetland*) When a cow or sheep happens to turn sick or die, it is firmly believed.. that the real animal has been taken away and something of a trowie breed substituted in its place. 1895 J. J. HALDANE BURGESS *Shetland Folklore* 99 He at once sent for an old woman who was celebrated as a 'trowist'. *Ibid.* 101 He.. found lying on the ground and half-hidden among the heather, a beautifully-wrought 'trowie' dart or arrow.

trowing ('trəʊɪŋ), *vbl. sb. Obs.* or *arch.* [f. TROW *v.* + -ING[1].] The action of the verb TROW; belief; faith, creed; opinion, notion, idea. † ***to trowing***, to be believed, worthy of belief (cf. *to trow*, TROW *v.* 3 c).

*a*1300 *Cursor M.* 25088 (Cott.) To haf wit santes communing; þis es a pointe of vr truing [*Gött.* truyng, *Fairf.* trowing]. 1303 R. BRUNNE *Handl. Synne* 498 For whan þou trowyst yn a fals þyng þe deuyl hyt shewyþ for þat trowyng. 1387 TREVISA *Higden* (Rolls) III. 401 Nectanabus seide þis sawe, and was a wicche, and þerfore it is nevere þe bettre to trowynge. *Ibid.* V. 89 So seiþ martilogie, þat is more to trowynge [L. *credendum*] þan cronicles of auctours þat beeþ nouȝt i-knowe. *Ibid.* VI. 195 It is nouȝt to trowynge [L. *opinandum*] þat þis Iohn is Iohn the Ermyte. *c*1400 MAUNDEV. (Roxb.) xxxiv. 154 Þ ai be of diuerse lawes and diuerse trowyngs. *c*1449 PECOCK *Repr.* I. i. (Rolls) 5 Thre trowingis or opinions ben causis.. of manie.. errouris. 1491 CAXTON *Vitas Patr.* I. c. (W. de W. 1495) 131 b/2 By the thynges passed he had some trowynge of those that were to come. *c*1570 in Redforde *Play Wit & Sc.* (Shaks. Soc.) 57 Ever in trowing and never in knowinge.

So †**'trowing** *ppl. a. Obs.*, believing; in first quot. as *sb.* one who believes.

*a*1300 *Cursor M.* 18719 (Cott.) Þe truand [*Fairf.* trawande] and þe baptist bath þai sal be saue. *c*1400 *Apol. Loll.* 61 Crist is end of þe lawe to riȝtfulnes to ilk man trowing. 1483 *Cath. Angl.* 394/2 Trowinge, *credulus.*

trowith, obs. f. TROTH.

trowkle, obs. f. TRUCKLE.

trowl, obs. f. TRAWL, TROLL, TRULL.

trowlesworthite ('trəʊlzwəθaɪt). *Min.* [f. the name of Trowlesworthy Tor, Devonshire, where found: see -ITE[1].] An altered granite in which fluorite, orthoclase, and tourmaline have taken the place of the original quartz, feldspar, and mica.

1884 BONNEY in *Q. Jrnl. Geol. Soc.* XL. 7 A rock-specimen exhibited by Mr. R. N. Worth,.. and by him named Trowlesworthite. It consisted chiefly of reddish orthoclase, purple fluor, and black schorl, in intimate association with quartz, and was found.. as a loose block on Trowlesworthy Tor.

'trowling. *Orkney* and *Shetl.* [f. TROW *sb.*[4] + -LING[1].] A young or infant 'trow' or troll.

1840 *New Statist. Acc. Scot.* (1845) XV. 142 (*Shetland*) Females newly confined must.. be watched.. lest they be carried off to perform the office of wet-nurse to some trowling of gentle blood.

trowly, obs. Sc. form of TRULY.

trowman ('trəʊmən). *local.* [f. TROW *sb.*[2] + MAN *sb.*[1]] The master or captain of a trow: see TROW *sb.*[2] a.

1429 *Rolls of Parlt.* IV. 345/2 The owners.. and the saide trowmen. 1505 *Sel. Cas. Crt. Star Chamber* (Selden Soc.) I. 220 During which xl yeris I occupyed vppon the seide Ryuer as a Trowman. 1641 J. TAYLOR (Water P.) *Last Voy.* B vij, Usually much abused by Trow-men. 1752 *Deed* in Miss Jackson *Shropsh. Word-bk.* s.v., This Indenture made.. Between John Rogers of the Town of Shrewsbury.. Trowman and [etc.].

trown, trownsciown, trowple, trowse, trowth: see THRONE, TRUNCHEON, TROPEL, TROUSE, TRUSS, TROTH.

troxidone ('trɒksɪdəʊn). *Pharm.* [f. TR(I- + OX- + -ID(INE + -ONE, elements of the systematic name (see quot. 1952).] An anticonvulsant drug, $C_6H_9NO_3$, used chiefly in treating petit mal epilepsy. Cf. TRIDIONE.

1952 *Brit. Pharmaceutical Codex 1949* Suppl. 78 Troxidone... *Synonym*: Trimethadone. Troxidone is 3:5:5-trimethyloxazolidine-2:4-dione. 1970 PASSMORE & ROBSON *Compan. Med. Stud.* II. v. 60/1 In patients undergoing electroconvulsion treatment the seizure patterns are not modified by troxidone as they are by phenobarbitone and phenytoin.

Troy[1] (trɔɪ). The name of an ancient city in Asia Minor, besieged and taken by the Greeks; in comb. ***Troy-bane***, ***-jousting***; **Troy-fair**, **Troy-town** (also simply †**Troy**), *fig.* a scene of disorder or confusion (now *dial.*).

*a*1520 *Vox Populi* 522 in Hazl. *E.P.P.* III. 286 And Pauper he above satte In the seate of Habrahams lappe, And was taken from thys Troye, To lyve allwaye with God in ioye. 1606 HOLLAND *Sueton.* 130 He represented besides, many Cirq-games,.. interposing.. the Troie-justing and Turnament. 1652 BENLOWES *Theoph.* I. xii, Does Troy-bane Hellen.. with Angels share? 1678 OTWAY *Friendship in F.* v. i, And for the Cittern, if ever Troy Town were a Tune, he master'd it upon that Instrument. 1870 *N. & Q.* 4th Ser. VI. 300/1 Troy Fair. I heard this phrase lately employed.. to describe a time of household confusion. *Ibid.* 401 In this part of Devonshire a room with its furniture disarranged is said to be 'like Troy Town'. 1880 *W. Cornwall Gloss.*, *Troy town*, a maze; a labyrinth of streets. 'I lost my way; 'twas a regular Troy town'.

troy[2] (trɔɪ). Forms: 4-6 **troye**, 5 **troie**, 5- **troy**; also *Sc.* 5-7 **trois**, 6 **troiss**, **troyis**, (**troce**). [The received opinion is that it took its name from a weight used at the fair of Troyes in France, which is favoured by the Scottish forms, *trois*, *troiss*, *troyis*.] ***troy weight*** (†***weight of Troy***), also ellipt. *troy*: The standard system of weights used for the precious metals and precious stones; formerly also for bread. Also attrib., ***troy ounce***, ***pound***, etc. (also ***ounce troy***, ***pound troy***, etc.). Cf. TOWER POUND.

The pound troy contains 5760 grains, and is divided into 12 ounces. Cf. AVOIRDUPOIS.

1390–1 *Earl Derby's Exped.* (Camden) 100 Pro j chargeour, iij diocis, et j sawcere, ponderis xx marc. de troye. **1423** *Rolls of Parlt.* IV. 256/2 Silver is bought atte pris of xxxii s. the pound of troie. **1458** Agnes Paston in *P. Lett.* I. 422 To do make me vj. sponys, of viij. ounce of troy wyght. **1488–91** *Acc. Ld. High Treas. Scot.* I. 168 The cunȝeing of fifty tua Trois pundis and ane halue vnce of brokin siluer. **1542** Recorde *Gr. Artes* (1575) 202 Of Ounces after Troye rate.. 12 doe make 1 pounde. **1565** *Reg. Privy Council Scot.* I. 413 That thair be cunyeit ane penny of silver..of wecht ane unce, troce wecht. **1573** *Aberdeen Regr.* (1848) II. 10 A troiss pund of brass, pryce v s. **1582** *Reg. Privy Council Scot.* III. 481 Quhilk [penny] suld wey ane quarter unce troyis wecht. **1641** in R. W. Cochran-Patrick *Rec. Coinage Scotl.* (1876) I. Introd. 32 The once trois of bullione. **1688** R. Holme *Armoury* III. 259/2 [By] Troy Weight..are Weighed..Bread, and all manner of Corn and Grain. **1825** J. Nicholson *Operat. Mechanic* 759 Take an exact troy ounce of the ore. **1868** Rogers *Pol. Econ.* iii. (1876) 29 In the rough, it may be said that the cost of producing a pound Troy of gold is fifteen-and-a-half times as great as that of producing a pound Troy of silver.

b. *fig.* in allusion to the pound troy being less than the pound avoirdupois.

1599 Massinger, etc. *Old Law* IV. i, There was Cressid was Troy weight, and Nell was avoirdupois. **1647** Ward *Simp. Cobler* (1843) 38 Heads.., who will weigh Rules by Troyweight, and not by the old Haber-du-pois. **18..** J. Parker in W. Adamson *Life* i. (1902) 4 No namby-pamby speaker, weighing words in troy scales and mincing syllables as if afraid of them. **1906** *Daily Chron.* 21 Dec. 9/2 Years and years of troy-weight legislation have left unrectified the avoirdupois anomaly.

†**Troyan(e, -en(e**: see Trojan.

'**Troyanish**, *a.* and *sb.* Also troi-. = Trojan (q.v.). So '**Troyish** *a. Obs.*

*c*893 K. Ælfred *Oros.* I. x. §4 Pentesilia, sio on þæm *Troianiscan ȝefeohte mære ȝewearð. *c*1205 Lay. 416 þat Troynisce folc. *Ibid.* 809 Iherden hit Troynisce [*c*1275 Troynisse]. *c*1384 Chaucer *Ho. Fame* I. 201 Iuno.. That hast y-hated al thy lyfe Alle the Troianysshe [*v.r.* Troyanyssh] bloode. **1412–20** Lydg. *Chron. Troy* III. 219 On Troyanysche grounde. *a*900 tr. *Bæda's Eccl. Hist.* IV. xvi. (1890) 307 ȝelice þy *troiscan wæle. *c*1205 Lay. 410 Ah he hefde muchele strengþe of meren his cunne, of þan Troyscen monnen.

troycht, obs. Sc. f. trough.

troylebaston, var. trailbaston.

troyne, obs. f. throne, tron, trone.

troyte, obs. f. troat, trout *sb.*[1]; obs. Sc. f. trough.

tru, obs. form of trow *v.*, truce, true.

truage, variant of trewage *Obs.*

truan, obs. form of truant.

truancy ('tru:ənsɪ). Also truantcy. [f. truant + -cy.] The action, or an act, of playing truant; truant conduct or practice.

1784 Mme. D'Arblay *Diary* 24 Apr., I had many flattering reproaches for my late truancy from these parties. **1858** Carlyle *Fredk. Gt.* VII. iii. (1872) II. 270 Suggesting to him idle truantcies or worse. **1905** W. B. Boulton *Life Gainsborough* 12 The boy..brought back..a collection of sketches as the result of the day's truancy.

†**truandal.** *Obs. rare.* [OF. *truandaille*, f. *truand*, assemblage of beggars.] *pl.* Beggars; camp-followers.

1523 Ld. Berners *Froiss.* I. xvii. 7b/2 They are all a horsbacke, without it be the truandals [orig. *la truandail*] and laggers of ye oost, who folow after a foote.

†**truandise.** *Obs.* Forms: 3 truw-, 4 treu-, trowandise, -is, truandis, 4–5 -ise, 5 trewaundise, trowandyse, -aundyse, -antyse, -entyze, truaundise, trwandyse, -aundise, 5–6 trewandise, -yse, 6 truantisse. [a. OF. *truandise* (13th c. in Godef.), f. *truand* truant (q.v.) + *-ise*, suffix:—L. *-itia*: see -ise[2].]

1. Fraudulent begging; vagabondage; roguery, knavery.

*a*1225 *Ancr. R.* 330 Mid iseli truwandise heo hut [= hides] euer hire god, & scheaweð forð hire pouerte. *c*1400 *Rom. Rose* 3954 Which han assailed hym to shende, And with her trowandyse to blynde. *c*1430 *Pilgr. Lyf Manhode* III. xxiii. (1869) 148 Whan I make hem thus to bere the dish of trewaundise. **1547** *Bk. Marchauntes* c vij b, Thus can these fyne marchants by wyls [= wiles] and trewandise fructifie at the expence of other.

2. Idle or loitering ways or habits; idleness.

*a*1300 *Cursor M.* 253 þoo..þat won..es to wast þair liif in trofel and truandis [*Gött.* trowandis, *Trin.* trewandise]. *c*1400 *Rom. Rose* 6664 Seynt poule..bade thappostles forto wirche And wynnen her lyflode in that wise And hem defended truaundise. *c*1440 *Jacob's Well* 104 Whanne þou ..in tyme of lernyng, ȝeuyst þe to trowaundyse.

truant ('tru:ənt), *sb.* (*a.*) Forms: α. 3– truant, 4 -ont, (*pl.* -ons), truan, 4–5 truaunt, 5 truwaunt(e, (trwaunt), truaund, 6 -ande, (-ent), 6–7 truand. β. 4–6 trewaunt, 5 -aund(e, 5–6 -ante, 6 -ande, (trewnt), 6–7 trewant, -and, 7 treuant. γ. 4–5 trowaunt, 5 -ande, (-awnt, -ent, -ean, trovwont, trownt), 5–6 trowan(e, 6 -ant, trouant. δ. *dial.* 8–9 troant, 9 troan, trawn, trown. See also trivant. [ME. a. OF. *truant*, F. *truand* adj. (12th c. in Godef.), (now only) as sb. = Prov. *truan*, Sp. *truhan*, Pg. *truão*; prob. from a Celtic source (Thurneysen): cf. Welsh *truan* wretched, a wretch, Gael. *truaghan* wretched, *trudanach* vagabond.]

A. *sb.* †**1.** One who begs without justification; a sturdy beggar; a vagabond; an idle rogue or knave. (Often a mere term of abuse.) *Obs.*

*c*1290 *S. Eng. Leg.* I. 60/240 Manie heolden him [St. Francis] a truant. **1340** *Ayenb.* 174 þe truont..þet sseweþ hare pouerte and hare ziknesse..uor to habbe þe elmesse. *c*1425 tr. *Arderne's Treat. Fistula* 100 Ribaldez and trowans ..þat felawshypeþ þam by þe waiez to pilgrimez, þat þai may robbe þam of þair siluer. *c*1489 Caxton *Sonnes of Aymon* xxii. 490 Now shall I be a goode trewaunt, for I can well aske brede whan me nedeth. **1526** *Pilgr. Perf.* (W. de W. 1531) 224 b, Obey your..rulers, although they be trewantes, that is to saye..though they..be not so good and vertuous as they sholde be. **1599** Shaks. *Much Ado* III. ii. 18 Hang him truant, there's no true drop of bloud in him to be truly toucht with loue. **1656** Blount *Glossogr.*, *Truand* (Fr.), a common beggar, a lazie rascal, a vagabond; a knave, a scowndrel. [**1895** J. C. Beckwith tr. *Hugo's Notre Dame* II. vi. I. 147 Such law as you mete to the Truands (vagabonds and outlaws), the Truands mete to you.]

2. a. A lazy, idle person; *esp.* a child who absents himself from school without leave; hence *fig.*, one who wanders from an appointed place or neglects his duty or business.

*c*1449 Pecock *Repr.* II. xii. (Rolls) 219 Truauntis in the scole of God. *a*1548 Hall *Chron.*, *Hen. V* 61 b, I am not so loiteryng a truand as to forgette so good a lesson. **1591** Shaks. *1 Hen. VI*, II. iv. 7. **1596** —— *1 Hen. IV*, V. i. 94, I haue a Truant beene to Chiualry. **1697** Dryden *Virg. Georg.* IV. 160 When the Swarms..loath their empty Hives, and idly stray,..take A timely Care to bring the Truants back. **1770** Goldsm. *Des. Vill.* 198 The village master..A man severe he was,..I knew him well, and every truant knew. **1856** Kane *Arct. Expl.* I. xxix. 398 One of our dogs, a truant from Morton's team.

b. Phr. *to play truant*; also formerly †*to play the truant*, *-s* (obs.). Const. *from*, *to*.

1560 *Nice Wanton* A ij, Be ye not ashamed the treauandes to play? **1598** Shaks. *Merry W.* V. i. 27 Since I pluckt Geese, plaide Trewant, and whipt Top, I knew not what 'twas to be beaten, till lately. **1642** Rogers *Naaman* 93 That so they may shun this sharpe Schoolemaster by playing the trewants. **1834** Medwin *Angler in Wales* I. viii. 129, I was scarcely breeched when I used to play the truant. **1887** Bowen *Virg. Æneid* V. 845 Rest those brows, let wearied eyes play truant to toil.

B. *adj.* **1. a.** That is a truant, or plays truant; idle, lazy, loitering, *esp.* of a child, staying from school without leave; hence, wandering, straying.

*a*1550 *Hye Way to Spyttel Ho.* 43 in Hazl. *E.P.P.* IV. 24 These trewant beggers begging fro place to place. **1561** Awdelay *Frat. Vacab.* (1869) 13 A Trewand knaue that faineth himselfe sicke when he should woorke. **1615** A. Stafford *Heav. Dogge* 59 To behold an austere.. Philosopher..quake at the name of death, even as a treuant boy does at the name of his Tutor. **1784** Cowper *Task* I. 114 E'er since, a truant boy, I passed my bounds. **1791** E. Darwin *Bot. Gard.* I. 54 Down the steep slopes He led.. The willing pathway, and the truant rill. **1793** (ed. 1) Wordsw. *Descr. Sketches* 49 Through her truant pathway's native charms. **1824** W. Irving *T. Trav.* I. II. vii. 259 This freak of fancy made me more truant from my studies than ever. **1869** Tozer *Highl. Turkey* I. 318 We recovered the truant saddle.

b. Characterized or marked by truancy or idleness; befitting a truant or idler.

1602 Shaks. *Ham.* I. ii. 169 But what in faith make you from Wittemberge? *Hor.* A truant disposition, good my Lord. **1649** Milton *Eikon.* xvi. 152 Wee are not..to distrust God in the removal of that Truant help to our Devotion, which by him was never appointed. **1803** Scott *Let. to G. Ellis* 25 May in *Lockhart*, My truant days spent in London having thrown me a little behind.

†**2.** Trivial, trite; idle, vain. *Obs. rare.*

*a*1572 Knox *Hist. Ref.* III. Wks. 1848 II. 141 We should nott wonder albeit that the auld trowane verse be trew, *Patrem sequitur sua proles.* **1682** Oldham *8th Sat. Boileau Imit.* 49 So fam'd for many a truant jest On wiving.

C. *Comb.*, as *truant-like* adj.; **truant-inspector**, a school attendance officer; **truant officer** *U.S.* = *truant-inspector*; **truant-school**, an industrial school to which truant or other children may be sent by order of a magistrate.

1583 Melbancke *Philotimus* M j, A trewantlike barrister. **1628** Ford *Lover's Mel.* I. i, If my experience hath not, truant-like, Mispent the time..For bettering my mind. **1872** C. L. Brace *Dangerous Classes N.Y.* 348 The Massachusetts system of 'Truant-schools'—that is, Schools to which truant officers could send children habitually truant—does not seem so applicable to New York. **1882** *Standard* 31 Aug. 2/4 Truant Schools have..been doing good work in checking truancy. **1891** E. Kinglake *Australian at H.* 22 Attendance officers, called truant inspectors, go and examine the books of the state schools periodically, and then visit the parents of those children who have not fulfilled the required conditions. **1911** G. F. Ward in S. M. Kingsbury *Labor Laws* 181 The truant officer finds that no certificate has been issued from the central office. **1972** T. Kochman *Rappin' & stylin' Out* 249 What do you do when you ditch school and..a truant officer walks up.

Hence '**truantness** (**truanness**), truancy.

1483 *Cath. Angl.* 394/2 Trowannes, *trutannitas.* **1658** J. Jones tr. *Ovid's Ibis* 52 Boys will excuse the fault of Treuantness by the sin of lying.

'**truant**, *v.* Forms: see the sb. [ME. f. prec.: cf. obs. F. *truander* (12th c. in Godef. *Compl.*), f. *truand* truant.]

†**1.** *intr.* To play the vagabond or rogue. *Obs.*

*c*1400 *Rom. Rose* 6721 Somme maner crafte..Thurgh which without truaundyng He may..haue his lyuyng. *c*1430 *Pilgr. Lyf Manhode* III. xxiii. (1869) 148 Wel thei kunne glooven maungepayn whan thei wolen trewande therwith. *c*1440 *Promp. Parv.* 503/2 Trovwonton (*S.* trownton, *P.* trowantyn), *trutannizo*, Cath.

2. *intr.* To idle, play truant (esp. from school); to wander, stray. Also with *it*.

1580 Lyly *Euphues* (Arb.) 279 What made the Gods so often to trewant from Heauen? **1637** Heywood *Dial.* Wks. 1874 VI. 285, I must..truly study man, (A booke in which I yet have truanted). **1642** Fuller *Holy & Prof. St.* I. ix. 24 He will not truant it now in the afternoon. **1748** Richardson *Clarissa* (1811) V. i. 6 Her good angel is gone a journey: is truanting at least. **1879** M. Pattison *Milton* xii. 143 He returned with concentrated ardour to woo the muse, from whom he had so long truanted.

†**3.** *trans.* To waste or idle away (time); to spend in truanting. *Obs.*

1597 *1st Pt. Return fr. Parnass.* III. i. 1115 In trewantinge there time, wastinge whole years. **1638** Ford *Fancies* III. iii, I dare not be the author Of truanting the time. **1708** Ozell tr. *Boileau's Lutrin* III. 120 A heedless Troop of wanton Boys ..In idle Pastime truanting the Day.

b. To play truant from. *dial.*

1899 Crockett *Kit Kennedy* xii. 95 Kit Kennedy,..Ye troaned the schule yesterday.

Hence '**truanting** *ppl. a.*

1634 Rainbow *Labour* (1635) 25, 't has given the truanting world a desired play-day.

'**truanting**, *vbl. sb.* [f. truant *v.* + -ing[1].] The action of the verb truant; an instance of this.

*c*1400 [see truant *v.* 1]. **1532** More *Confut. Tindale* Wks. 574/2 With three strypes for hys tarying and trewaunting by the way. **1630** Lennard tr. *Charron's Wisd.* III. xiv. §12 (1670) 443 To save themselves from the rigour of the punishment, they have recourse to..false excuses,..flights, truantings. **1884** Hunter & Whyte *My Ducats* xx. (1885) 286 The sense of truanting gave a..spice of excitement to his reflections.

truantism ('tru:əntɪz(ə)m). [f. truant *sb.* + -ism.] The practice of a truant; truancy.

1812 J. J. Henry *Camp. agst. Quebec* 13 His own education, though made by his truantisms..an incorrect one. **1875** G. Dawson *Shaks. Lect.* (1888) 117 He.. neglected his studies with that persistent truantism some great men have been guilty of.

truantly ('tru:əntlɪ), *a.* and *adv.* Now *rare.* [f. as prec. + -ly[1], -ly[2].]

A. *adj.* Having the qualities of a truant; characteristic of or befitting a truant.

1579 Twyne *Phisicke agst. Fort.* I. cv. 131 b, You, like wilful and truently children, can neuer learne wisedome without whipping. **1651** Jer. Taylor *Serm. for Year* I. Ep. Ded. 5 The Spirit of a man is truantly, and trifling. **1690** C. Nesse *O. & N. Test.* I. 125 For his truantly tricks [he] is turned down into the lowest form.

B. *adv.* After the manner of a truant.

1822 Scott *Nigel* xxviii, Idle and truantly disposed.

truantness: see after truant *a.*

truantry ('tru:əntrɪ). Forms: 5 trewaundrie, trwandrye, truantrye, 6 trewantrie, 7– truantry. [a. F. *truanderie* (13th c. in Godef. *Compl.*), f. *truand* truant: see -ry.]

†**1.** Fraudulent begging; knavery, roguery. *Obs.*

1426 Lydg. *De Guil. Pilgr.* 17828 Thys dyssh that I holde in myn hond, (In ffrenche callyd 'Coquynerye' And in ynglyssh 'Trwandrye'). *c*1430 *Pilgr. Lyf Manhode* III. xxii. (1869) 147 This hand heere is cleped coquinerie; Trewaundrie bi name j cleyme it.

2. Idleness, truancy; the practice, or an act, of playing truant.

1481 Caxton *Reynard* iv. (Arb.) 8 Yf the scolers were not beten..and reprised of their truantrye, they shold neuer lerne. **1581** Mulcaster *Positions* xl. (1887) 225 In the maisters house..children may..be lesse subiect to loytering and trewantrie. **1685** Cotton tr. *Montaigne* I. 301 An understanding Tutor, who..knew discreetly to connive at this and other truantries. **1811** L. M. Hawkins *C'tess & Gertr.* I. 166 Her frequent..truantries from the place where she ought to have been. **1887** Stevenson *Mem. & Portraits* ii. 27 Infinite yawnings during lecture and unquenchable gusto in the delights of truantry.

'**truantship.** *rare.* [f. truant *sb.* + -ship.]

a. Truancy. **b.** with possessive, as a mock title.

*a*1568 Ascham *Scholem.* I. (Arb.) 27 If the childe haue done his diligence, and vsed no trewandship. **1592** Nashe *Four Lett. Confut.* Wks. (Grosart) II. 264, I would teach thy old Trewantship the true vse of words.

†**trub.** *Obs.* or *dial.* Also 8–9 trubbe. [app. short for *truffle*, OF. *truffe* (Sp., Pg. *trufa*), or for L. *tūber*.]

1. A truffle.

1668 Wilkins *Real Char.* II. iv. §3. 70 Imperfect Herbs.. Without a Stem,..growing..in the ground, being esculent, ..Trubs, Trufle. **1673** Ray *Journ. Low C.* (1738) I. 346 A kind of subterraneous musheroom, which our herbarists English Trubs, or after the French name Trufles. **1693** Robinson in *Phil. Trans.* XVII. 825 Ludovicus Romanus.. affirms, That Thirty Camels Load of these Truffles or Trubs..have been..sold at Damascus in two or three days. **1727–41** Chambers *Cycl.* s.v. *Truffles*, Bradley calls them underground edible mushrooms, or Spanish trubbes. **1860** Mayne *Expos. Lex.*, *Trubs*,..common name for the *Lycoperdon tuber.* **1866** *Treas. Bot.*, *Trubs*, or *Trubbes*, truffles.

2. 'A little squat woman' (Phillips 1706); also, 'a slut, sloven; a wanton; an opprobrious term' (*Eng. Dial. Dict.*). Also **'trubkin, 'trub-tail.**

1625 PURCHAS *Pilgrims* IX. xvi. §3. 1622 The Dogges.. satiate with the Womans flesh.., who was a short fat trubkin. **1706** PHILLIPS (ed. Kersey), *Trub* or *Trub-tail*, a little squat Woman. **1746** *Exmoor Scolding* 104 (E.D.S.) Andra wou'd ha' had a Trub in tha.

Trubenized ('truːbənaɪzd). [f. *Tru-*, of unknown origin + *-ben-*, said to be f. the name of *Benjamin* Liebowitz, inventor of the process + -IZE + -ED[1].] A proprietary name for clothing, esp. shirt collars, made durably stiff by a special process in manufacture.

No longer a proprietary name in the U.S.

1933 *Official Gaz.* (U.S. Patent Office) 26 Dec. 879/2 S. Liebovitz & Sons, Inc., New York... *Trubenized* for dress and negligee shirts and collars. **1939** *Trade Marks Jrnl.* 26 July 1051 *Trubenised*... All goods included in Class 25. Trubenising Limited,..High Holborn, London. **1955** *Radio Times* 22 Apr. 27/3 Shirt..25/6d. with soft collar (or 26/6d. with 'Trubenised' collar). **1969** A. J. HALL *Stand. Handbk. Textiles* (ed. 7) i. 45 Actually this solubility is not a serious disadvantage..for it enables acetate fibres to be employed in the 'Trubenised' process.

Trubetzkoyan (truːbɛtˈskɔɪən), *a.* Also Trubetskoyan. [f. the name of Nikolai Sergeevich *Trubetzkoy* (1890–1938), Russian linguist + -AN.] Of or pertaining to Trubetzkoy or his theory and methodology.

1940 *Language* XVI. 248 The first part is very largely Trubetzkoyan. **1951** *Ibid.* XXVII. 333 Martinet presents an outline of fairly orthodox Trubetskoyan phonology. **1964** R. H. ROBINS *Gen. Linguistics* iv. 177 Without the use of further Trubetzkoyan concepts like neutralization. **1977** *Language* LIII. 427 The Trubetzkoyan era, however, was to be closed in a most dignified manner by his virtually finishing the manuscript of his famous encyclopaedic *Grundzüge der Phonologie*.

trublance, truble, etc., obs. ff. TROUBLANCE, TROUBLE, etc.

†**truble.** *Obs. rare.* [a. F. *truble* kind of net (13th c. in Littré).] A small net for catching fish in ponds and stews.

1600 SURFLET *Countrie Farme* IV. xiii. 646 Taking..little fish with the shouenet, small net, called a truble and line. *Ibid.* xvi. 650 The gudgeon is taken with a hooke or the little net called a truble.

truce (truːs), *sb.* Forms: α. *sing.* 4 truwe, 4–5 trewe, 5 tru, 5–6 trew, 5–7 true. β. *pl.* 3 triwes, triws, 4 treus, treuwes, *Sc.* trowis, 4–6 trewes, trues, 5 trewys, triew(i)s, trieux, tryew(e)s, trowes, truwes, -ys, trwes, trwys, trux, 5–6 trews, treux, 5 (5–7 *Sc.*) trewis, 6 treuis, -ys; treuges. γ. 5 trewysse, truyse, 5–6 trewse, truxe, 5–7 truse, 6 trewice, -yce, treuce, trewce, trwce, trusse, 7 trousse, 5– truce. [ME. *trewe* and *triewe*, mostly in pl. form *trewes* and *triewes*:—OE. *tréow* sb. masc. (fem. pl. *tréwa*), 'truth or fidelity to a promise, good faith, assurance of faith or truth, promise, engagement, covenant, league', = OEFris. *tríuwe*, OWFris. and MDu. *trouwe* (Du. *trouw*), OS. *treuwa*, *tríuwa*, OHG. *tríuwa* (MHG. *triuwe*, Ger. *treue*):—WGer. **trewwa*, Goth. *triggwa* 'covenant' (whence late L. and Romanic *tregua*, *treuga*, F. *trêve*); also, in ablaut form, OE. *trúwa* sb. masc. and pl. *-an*; = ON. *trúa*, *trú*, Norw. *trū*, Sw. *trōa*: see TRUE *a.* Already in OE. the pl. *tréwa* was often used in the sense of the sing.; this became still more frequent with the ME. pl. *trewes*, *triues*, *triwes*, *trues*, and finally this, as *trews*, *trewse*, *truse*, *truce*, became the received sing. (app. in reference to the pledges or engagements given by both parties), with a new pl. *truses*, *truces*, when required. Cf. *cherries*, *pease*. See also *trève* from French, and the rare *treuges* after MLat. *treugas*.]

1. a. A suspension of hostilities for a specified period between armies at war (formerly also between combatants in a private feud or quarrel); a temporary peace or cessation from arms; an armistice; also, an agreement or treaty effecting this.

to †*take*, †*cry*, *call* (*a*) *truce*, to make, call for a truce. *flag of truce*: see FLAG *sb.*[1] 1 b.

α. *c* **1330** R. BRUNNE *Chron.* (1810) 193 If þou pes wille ȝerne,..& trewe for seuen ȝere, I consent þertille. *Ibid.* 275 For þre days trewe þe Inglis him hete. *c* **1374** CHAUCER *Troylus* IV. 1284–6 (1312–4) It is now a truwe..And er þat truwe is don I shal ben here. *c* **1400** *Destr. Troy* 7874 Then takyn was the true. *Ibid.* 8372 For a trew to be takon of a tyme short. **1494** FABYAN *Chron.* VI. clxxxi. 179 To requyre a trewe or trewse for .iii. monethes. **1575** CHURCHYARD *Chippes* (1817) 91 But ere the heate, of this great skirmishe grew, The Dowager, with trumpet tooke a trew.

β. *a* **1225** *Ancr. R.* 286 He..brekeð þe triws, & awrekeð him of þe, oðer of him seoluen. **1297** R. GLOUC. (Rolls) 10005 He..triwes nom of saladin. *c* **1330** R. BRUNNE *Chron. Wace* (Rolls) 7843 þorow trist of trues..þey sette a day of Parlement. *c* **1375** *Cursor M.* 26768 (Fairf.) As trewes þat is tane. **1387** TREVISA *Higden* (Rolls) II. 413 Whan Hector was i-buried, were trewes i-take for a ȝere. —— VIII. 337 Trewes [*v.r.* truwes] were i-take bytwene þe kynges. **1442** *Rolls of Parlt.* V. 44/2 Ayenst þe fourme of trieux..betwixt ..England and Scotland had and concludyd. **1483** in Rymer *Foedera* (1711) XII. 174/1 By thies Presentis is made.. assured Treux and Abstinence of Werre for oon hool Yere. **1483** CAXTON *Gold. Leg.* 306 b/1 The Crysten men tooke triews for thre dayes. **1496** *Act 12 Hen. VII*, c. 13 §15 After the seid perfite peas be had and concluded, or such abstynence of Warre, Trux and Peax for a tyme be had and made. **1524** *Carew MSS.* (1867) I. 25 The patched and inhonorable treuges, which by inforcement of pure necessity be tolerated. **1596** DALRYMPLE tr. *Leslie's Hist. Scot.* I. (S.T.S.) I. 75 Trues ar bund, mariages ar maid with sum of the Inhabitouris.

γ. **14..** in *Wars Eng. in France* (1864) II. 526 The tyme that the last truxe was take betwene Herre the VI...and his aduersarie of Fraunce. *c* **1440** *Generydes* 5882 To graunt them truse for ij monethis day. *c* **1440** *Promp. Parv.* 503/2 Truwys, or truce of pees. **1483** *Cath. Angl.* 393/1 Trewysse, *inducie*. **1494** Trewse [see a]. **1538** CROMWELL in Merriman *Life & Lett.* (1902) II. 124 To offer therfor a longer treux. **1552** HULOET, Trewice, *fœdus*,..*induciæ*. **1560** DAUS tr. *Sleidane's Comm.* 41 Yᵗ eyther a suer peace, or els a long treuce may be taken. **1613** PURCHAS *Pilgrimage* (1614) 634 They obserue three dayes in a week truce, when euery man may travell or barter safely. **1621** in Foster *Eng. Factories Ind.* (1906) 306 Truse taken betwene the Mogull and them. *a* **1780** WATSON *Philip III* (1839) 145 To put a period to the miseries attendant upon war, by a peace or truce. **1875** STUBBS *Const. Hist.* II. xiv. 148 A truce which in the following November became a permanent peace.

b. Loosely or vaguely: Cessation or absence of hostilities (without limitation of time); peace.

1377 LANGL. *P. Pl.* B. XVIII. 416 Trewes, quod treuth.. Clippe we in couenaunt, & vch of vs cusse other. **1456** SIR G. HAYE *Law Arms* (S.T.S.) 164 Nocht brekand gude faith, and, namely, fra trewis be gevin our, and diffiaunce maid. **1535** COVERDALE *1 Macc.* vi. 49 The kynge toke truce with them that were in Bethsura. **1578** T. NORTON *Calvin's Inst.* Table RRRR vj/1, I will put my couenaunt betwene me and thee: and betwene thy seede after thee..by an euerlasting truce. **1598** SYLVESTER *Du Bartas* II. ii. I. *Ark* 377 Behold the peacefull Dove Brings in her beak the Peace-branch, boading weal And truce with God.

†**c.** A document recording the terms of a truce. *Sc. Obs. rare.*

1502 *Acc. Ld. High Treas. Scot.* II. 350 To illumyn the trewis and the conjunct infeftment.

†**d.** *Sc. Law.* A suspension of judicial proceedings; a stay. *Obs.*

1609 SKENE *Reg. Maj.* II. 112 And therfore this time is called *induciæ deliberatoriæ*, because..the pley ceases, and stayes: and trewis are taken betwixt the parties.

†**e.** *day of truce*, a court held by the Wardens of the Marches (of England and Scotland), or the day appointed for this, on which a truce was observed. Also called *truce-day* (see 4).

1486–7 *Plumpton Corr.* (Camden) 56 Ye prepared yourselfe to have ridden with me to this day of trewe. **1564** *Reg. Privy Council Scot.* I. 282 Accustumat to serve and await upoun the wardane at all dayis of trew. **1863** S. S. JONES *Northumberland* 162 The days of Trews, or Warden Courts, had to be held frequently.

f. *truce of God*, a suspension of hostilities between armies, or of private feuds, ordered by the Church during certain days and seasons in mediæval times. Hence *allusively*.

[*a* **867** in Mansi *Concilia* XV. 448 Pax vero illa quam treguam Dei dicimus, fideliter observetur.] **1727–41** CHAMBERS *Cycl.*, *Truce of God*, *Treuga Dei*, is a phrase famous in the histories of the xiᵗʰ century, when the disorders and licences of private wars..obliged the bishops of France to forbid such violences within certain times, under canonical pains. **1828** SCOTT *F.M. Perth* xxxiv, The Church of Rome..had decided that during the holy season of Easter..the sword of war should be sheathed, and angry monarchs should respect the season termed the Truce of God. **1870** LOWELL *Study Wind.* I. 20 It was Sunday, and I gave him the benefit of its gracious truce of God.

g. A temporary pause or respite during a game. Hence, used to demand such a truce (cf. sense 2 b).

1870 [see FAIN *v.*[2]]. **1959** I. & P. OPIE *Lore & Lang. Schoolch.* viii. 142 Children were sensitive to the difference between making a truce and surrendering.

2. a. Figurative and allusive uses (from 1).

1560 DAUS tr. *Sleidane's Comm.* 140 b, He would now take occasion to breake that treuce of Religion. **1590** SHAKS. *Com. Err.* II. ii. 147 Keepe then faire league and truce with thy true bed. **1606** —— *Tr. & Cr.* II. ii. 75 The Seas and Windes (old Wranglers) tooke a Truce. **1647** N. BACON *Disc. Govt. Eng.* I. lxiv. (1739) 137 The King foresaw the storm, and thought it safest first to cry truce with the people. *a* **1711** KEN *Hymns Evang.* Poet. Wks. 1721 I. 52 But jealous Fears no Truce with Tyrants make. **1849** MACAULAY *Hist. Eng.* ii. I. 159 Between the bigoted followers of Laud and the bigoted followers of Calvin there could be neither peace nor truce.

†**b.** *king's truce*: a cry for the discontinuance of a game. *Obs.*

1608 DAY *Hum. out of Br.* IV. iii, *Hort.* What haue I catchd you? *Pa.* Kisse her and let her goe. *Host.* Kings truce till I breath a little.

3. a. Hence, Respite or intermission (more loosely, freedom or liberty) from something irksome, painful, or oppressive.

1567 DRANT *Horace, Epistles* To Rdr., To take truce with myne other studyes,..and to become a sillye translator rythmical. **1598** J. DICKENSON *Greene in Conc.* (1878) 160 Till death gaue truce to hir distresses. **1667** MILTON *P.L.* II. 526 Where he may..find Truce to his restless thoughts. **1713** SWIFT *Imit. Hor.* I. vii. 130 Truce, good my lord, I beg a truce,..Your raillery is misapply'd. **1859–69** HEAVYSEGE *Saul* (ed. 3) 337 Let us dry these unavailing tears, And, with such truce to sorrow as we may, Wend each..his..several road.

b. In interjectional phrase (*a*) *truce with*, now usually (*a*) *truce to*, enough of, have done with.

1700 CONGREVE *Way of World* II. v, Truce with your Similitudes: For I am as sick of 'em ——. **1757** MRS. GRIFFITH *Lett. Henry and Frances* (1767) II. 150 But a truce with the subject, for I am determined to never mention it more. **1786** tr. *Beckford's Vathek* (1868) 90, I am going on affairs of emergency, a truce therefore to parade! **1835** LYTTON *Rienzi* II. i, A truce to this light conversation. **1846** BROWNING *Soul's Trag.* I. 142 Truce with toying for this once! **1878** —— *La Saisiaz* 249 Truce to such old sad contention.

4. *attrib.* and *Comb.* **a.** attrib., as *truce-day* (†*true-day* = day of truce), *-flag*, *-note*, *-place* (*true-place*). **b.** objective, as *truce-bearer*, *-breaker*, *-maker*, *-taker*; *truce-breaking*, *-hating*, *-making*, *-taking* sbs. and adjs.

1853 HICKIE tr. *Aristoph.* (1887) I. 11 This *truce-bearer would not so easily have escaped. **1534** TINDALE *2 Tim.* iii. 3 Vnkinde, *truce-breakers, stubborn. **1625** K. LONG tr. *Barclay's Argenis* I. xx. 61 The Herald..rehearses a long prayer, contayning many curses against Truce-breakers. **1949** KOESTLER *Promise & Fulfilment* II. v. 265 The Egyptians having officially been branded as truce-breakers. **1592** TIMME *Ten Eng. Lepers* vii. I j, A wilful *trucebreaking and perjurie. **1719** *Free-thinker* No. 110 ¶1 An unjust, Truce-breaking Prince. **1587** FLEMING *Contn. Holinshed* III. 1413/2 Slaine..by a Scot..as they met vpon a *true daie. **1610** HOLLAND *Camden's Brit.* I. 403 In a tumult upon a True-day in the midle marches. **1876** T. HARDY *Ethelberta* (1890) 376 A little tufted white feather..like a *truce-flag between the blood of noble and vassal. **1591** SYLVESTER *Du Bartas* I. ii. 251 *Truce-hating Twins. **1552** HULOET, *Trewice maker, *symmachus*. **1523** LD. BERNERS *Froiss.* I. clxii. 197 Without any peace or *trewse makynge. **1810** SCOTT *Lady of L.* VI. xxi, Clarion and trumpet..Rung forth a *truce-note. **1674** BLOUNT *Glossogr.*, **True-place*, i.e. a place of Parley and Conference in Northumberland, antiently so called. **1483** *Cath. Angl.* 393/1 *Trews taker. **1533** *Acc. Ld. High Treas. Scot.* VI. 138 For keping of gude reule during the *trewis taking. **1581** MARBECK *Bk. of Notes* 471 This tranquilitie of the sea..as a trewes taking in the Winter, called the Halcions daies.

truce (truːs), *v.* Now *rare.* Also 6 truse. [f. prec. sb.]

1. *intr.* To make a truce.

1569 STOCKER tr. *Diod. Sic.* III. v. 109 Who after that victorie, trused with the Aretians. **1731** FIELDING *Mod. Husb.* II. xi, If you please, my lord, to truce with your proposals. **1893** E. L. WAKEMAN in *Columbus* (*Ohio*) *Dispatch* 25 May, The factions had attacked each other, retreated, parleyed, blarneyed, scorned, truced.

2. *trans.* To bring to an end by or as by means of a truce; to put an end to.

1618 MIDDLETON *Peacemaker* Wks. (Bullen) VIII. 326 Spain..betwixt whom and England the ocean ran with blood.., nor ever truced her crimson effusion. **1706** T. BAKER *Tunbr. Walks* II. i, We may truce the debate.

truceless ('truːslɪs), *a.* [f. TRUCE *sb.* + -LESS.] That is without truce; unceasing in hostility; also *fig.*

1631 FULLER *David's Sin* v, With truceless war each other doth oppose. **1747** B. SOWDEN *Death Gardiner* in Doddridge *Life Col. Gardiner* App. ii. 198 Dissolv'd in truceless grief she lay. **1852** LD. COCKBURN *Jeffrey* I. 202 His whole session was one keen and truceless conflict. **1886** E. KING in *Flaubert's Salammbô* p. xv, The truceless war between the Carthaginians and those barbarian mercenaries.

truceman, obs. variant of TRUCHMAN.

truch, obs. Sc. form of TROUGH; obs. f. TRUSH.

truche, variant of TROKE *v. Obs.*, to fail.

truchman ('trʌtʃmən). Forms: 5 tourcheman, (6 trooche-, truce-, trowch-, trounch-, trush-, treush-man, *Sc.* trwcheman, trunsche-), 6–7 truche-, trouch(e)-, (trunch-), treuch-, 7 trudgeman, 6– truchman. [ad. med.L. *turchemannus*, F. *trucheman* (Cotgr. 1611), *truchement* = It. *turcimanno*, Sp. *trujaman*, ad. Arab. *turjamān* (also *tarjumān*, *tarjamān*), interpreter, the same word which through Gr. and med.L. appears as DRAGOMAN. The Arabic letter *jim* which is now generally *j* was orig. *g*, like Heb. *gimel*, the early form of the word being *targumān*, f. *targama* to translate: cf. TARGUM.] An interpreter.

1485 CAXTON *Paris & V.* (1868) 77 Thenne sayd parys vnderstondeth he mouryshe and they sayd nay but..yf he wold speke to hym they should find tourchemen ynough. **1525** LD. BERNERS *Froiss.* II. clxxi. [clxvii.] 503 They..toke a truchman that coulde speke Italyan, and commanded hym to go to the crysten host. **1575** GASCOIGNE *Flowers, Maske Visct. Mountacute* Wks. 1907 I. 85 He may your Trounchman bee, Your herald and ambassador. **1577** STANYHURST *Descr. Irel.* in Holinshed (1808) VI. 4 If a traveller of the Irish had..spoken Irish, they would command him..to..speake English, or els bring his truchman with him. **1578** in Feuillerat *Revels Q. Eliz.* (1908) 287 Torche bearers with the troocheman. **1613** PURCHAS *Pilgrimage* v. xvii. (1614) 543 Suborning his Trudge-man..to poyson or murder him by the way. **1679** BLOUNT *Anc. Tenures* 17 Beneath Whittington in Shropshire, one Wrenoc..held Lands by the service of being Latimer, that is, Trucheman or Interpreter, between the English and the Welshmen. **1888** DOUGHTY *Arabia Deserta* I. 175 Their truch-man in entering Moses' valley had paid out presents to the Howeytât sheykhs.

b. *fig.*

1585 JAS. I *Vranie* 124 Poets..Dame Naturs trunchmen, heauens interpretes trewe. **1637** SUCKLING *Aglaura* II. i, Our soules..will not need that duller truch-man Flesh. *a* **1649**

DRUMM. OF HAWTH. *Cypress Grove* Wks. (1711) 126 Formed..to be the interpreter and trunchman of His creation. *a* **1680** BUTLER *Rem.* (1759) II. 405 He is a Truch-Man, that interprets between learned Writers and gentle Readers.

Hence †'**truchmanry** *Obs.*, the office or function of an interpreter; so † **truch sprite** *nonce-wd.*, a spirit acting as interpreter or messenger; †'**truchwoman** *Obs.* [cf. *Mussulwoman*], a female interpreter.

1573 in Feuillerat *Revels Q. Eliz.* (1908) 217 For the Tronchwoman's Heade and for vii Hatbandes for the men Maskers. **1582** STANYHURST *Æneis* IV. (Arb.) 107 Latelye toe mee posted from Ioue thee truch sprit, or herrald Of Gods. **1663** SIR G. MACKENZIE *Religio Stoici* 97 To teach that sensual croud, by the trunchmanrie of sense.

trucial ('truːʃ(ɪ)əl), *a.* [f. TRUCE *sb.* + -IAL.] Of, pertaining to, or bound by a truce; used only with reference to the maritime truce made in 1835 between the British Government and certain Arab sheikhs of the Oman Peninsula.

The truce was renewed several times. In 1853 it was succeeded by a Treaty of Perpetual Peace, but the territories to which it had applied continued to be known as the ***Trucial States*** until 1971, when they became the United Arab Emirates.

1876 *Aitchison's Coll. Treaties* (ed. 2) VII. 44 The possessions of the so-called trucial Chiefs of the maritime tribes of the Persian Gulf. **1891** G. N. CURZON *Persia* II. 452 Adjoining the Trucial states upon the West is the rugged promontory of El Katr. **1911** L. FRASER *India under Curzon* 82 We..bound them by a truce..so that to this day they are known as the Trucial Chiefs of Oman. **1927** P. COX in *Lett. Gertrude Bell* II. 506 We had treaties of old standing..with the Sheikhs of the Pirate (now the Trucial) Coast of Oman. **1930** A. RIHANI *Around Coasts of Arabia* 354 In Trucial Oman also the five independent Sheikhs agree not to enter into correspondence or agreement with any power other than the British Government. **1957** *Times* 24 Aug. 5/4 The Government are prepared to prop up even the ailing and backward sheikhs of the Trucial coast. **1971** *Daily Colonist* (Victoria, B.C.) 15 Aug. 1/4 The announcement of independence had been expected for some time—ever since six of the seven trucial coast emirates agreed to federate without Bahrain when the British military forces depart at the end of this year.

trucidation (truːsɪ'deɪʃən). *rare.* [ad. L. *trucīdātiōn-em*, n. of action f. *trucīdāre* to cut to pieces, kill cruelly, slaughter.] A cruel killing or murdering; in use *humorous*: slaughter.

1623 COCKERAM, *Trucidation*, a cruell murder. [Whence in subsequent dicts.] **1883** STEVENSON *Lett.* (1901) I. 267, I loathe the snails: but from loathing to actual butchery, trucidation of multitudes, there is still a step that I hesitate to take.

truck (trʌk), *sb.*[1] Also 6–7 trucke, 8–9 *Sc.* troke, trock. [a. F. *troque*, †*troq*, *troc* (16th c.), AF. *truke* (1364), f. *troquer*: see TRUCK *v.*[1]]

1. a. The action or practice of trucking; trading by exchange of commodities; barter. Often ***in truck (for, †of), by truck for.***

[**1364** *Vintner's Co. Charter* in *Pat. Roll 38 Edw. III*, m. 44 (P.R.O.) Si mettent pris sur les vins par Truke ou par eschaunges.] **1553** in Hakluyt *Voy.* (1598) I. 228 No commutation or trucke to be made by any of the petie marchants, without the assent abouesaid. **1567** HAWKINS *Let. to Eliz.* 16 Sept. (St. Pap. Dom. XLIV. 7, P.R.O.) To ..sell them [negroes] in the West Indyes in trvcke of golde peirels and Esmeraldes. **1625** PURCHAS *Pilgrims* x. i. 1674 The Moores gave them in trucke for them againe black Moores. **1667** in Magens *Insurances* (1755) II. 437 If..any ..shall buy, or get to themselves by Truck, or any other way, such Ship or Goods. **1747** *Gentl. Mag.* Apr. 173/2 Their trade is managed by truck, or bartering one commodity for another. **1861** *Sat. Rev.* 14 Dec. 609 The mind has organs and functions..ranging beyond the things of avoirdupois and truck.

b. *transf.* and *fig.*

1741 tr. *D'Argens' Chinese Lett.* xxxix. 300 There's a Place at Moscow for the Truck and Barter of Images, and the Money given is in Proportion to the Size of the Figure. **1784** COWPER *Task* II. 741 Precedence went in truck, And he was competent whose purse was so. **1796** MRS. M. ROBINSON *Angelina* II. 128 My girl has money, my Lord has a title; —'tis a sort of truck, Sir Clifford.

c. with *a* and *pl.* (*a*) A traffic, trade. (*b*) An act of trading; a bargain or deal.

1638 *Diary Citizen Exeter* (ed. Brushfield, 1901) 16 For 30 yards Canvas..for wch I set nothing bec[ause] taken in a truck. **1642** TASMAN *Jrnl.* in *Acc. Sev. Late Voy.* I. (1694) 134 They indeavoured to begin a Truck or Merchandize with the yacht. **1678** R. L'ESTRANGE *Seneca's Mor.* (1702) 47 This for That, is rather a Truck than a Benefit. **1749** CHESTERF. *Lett.* 14 Nov., Utility..established a truck of the little *agré mens* and pleasures of life. **1851** MAYHEW *Lond. Labour* I. 417/1 There's Paddy in the truck too; he makes a good thing.

2. The payment of wages otherwise than in money; the system or practice of such payment, the *truck system* (see 5); in quots. 1879, 1911, goods supplied in lieu of wages.

1743 *Ir. Act 17 Geo. II*, c. 8 §6 In case any person or persons..shall pay any such artificer, workman, servant or labourer..their wages, or other price agreed on, or any part thereof, either in goods or by way of truck, or in any other manner than in ready money. **1766** *Museum Rust.* VI. 420 The workmen alledged, that the clothiers..had..obliged them to take goods in truck, at exorbitant prices. **1879** *Cassell's Techn. Educ.* IV. 12/2 Wages are largely paid in truck, in defiance of the law. **1886** *Act 49 & 50 Vict.* c. 40 §1 The provisions of the Acts relating to truck. **1911** *Daily News* 13 Oct. 3 She pays 2s. 9d. as well as a small amount of 'truck', worth a few pence, for getting the whole of her washing done by a washerwoman.

3. a. 'Traffic', intercourse, communication, dealings. Now usu. in negative contexts: ***to have no truck with*** (a person or thing), etc.

a **1625** FLETCHER *Chances* II. i, Hark ye Frederick, What truck betwixt my infant——? **1790** MORISON *Poems* 106 Nor does our blinded master see The trocks between the Clerk and she. **1809** J. SKINNER *Ep. to Capt. R. B.* xv, Ye and I have had a trock This forty year. **1866** *N. & Q.* 3rd Ser. IX. 400/1 [In Suffolk] A man who has left off courting a girl, says that he has 'no more truck along o'har'. **1894** *Blackw. Mag.* June 748 You would think he is a Christian to see the troke there is between that beast and my man. **1899** R. WHITEING *No. 5 John Street* xxvi. 259 Fust time in 'er life..she's ever 'ad any truck with any of them sort. **1929** H. S. WALPOLE *Hans Frost* III. iii. 333, I don't want to have any truck with the world at all. **1938** M. K. RAWLINGS *Yearling* xi. 112 Mebbe your Ma's right. Mebbe you hadn't ought to have no truck with the Forresters. **1948** *Mind* LVII. 17 Others will have no truck with images, and declare that when we remember we are directly apprehending the past occurrence. **1952** J. L. WATEN *Alien Son* 97 She would have no truck with so-called midwives who practised spells and incantations. **1960** 'J. & E. BONETT' *No Grave for Lady* i. 13 Wasn't there a story going about..that Lotte Liselotte was having truck with him? **1975** S. HEANEY *North* II. 58 We tremble near the flames but want no truck With the actual firing.

b. *pl.* Small matters of business or work; odd jobs, errands, chores. *Sc. dial.*

1808–18 JAMIESON s.v. *Troke, Troques*, or *trockies*, pl. Small pieces of business that require a good deal of stirring. **1894** 'IAN MACLAREN' *Bonnie Brier Bush, Lachlan Campbell* iii, A'll come for ye as sune as a' get..ma little trokes feenished.

4. † **a.** Commodities for barter. *Obs.*

1555 EDEN *Decades* 281 The Tartars..bringe none other wares then truckes or droues of swyfte runnynge horses and clokes made of whyte feltes. **1621** in Foster *Eng. Factories Ind.* (1906) 233 The[y] would not geve 2s. a pece neither in money nor truck. **1688** CLAYTON in *Phil. Trans.* XVII. 792 They must carry all sort of Truck that trade thither, having one Commodity to pass off another. **1770** SIR J. BANKS *Jrnl.* (1896) 332 The boat with some truck was sent ashore..in hopes of purchasing some trifling refreshment for the sick.

b. Small articles of a miscellaneous character; sundries; stuff; chiefly in depreciative use: odds and ends; things of little value; trash, rubbish. (Rarely *pl.*) Also *fig.*

1785 SHIRREFS *Poems* (1790) 250 Scales, compasses, and ither trocks. **1792** in *Hist. Broughton Place U.P. Ch.* (1872) 20 Your Priests wear bands an' pouther'd hair, An' sick vain troke. **1834** J. HALL *Kentucky* I. 221 Several bouncing girls ..were clearing away the truck of the evening meal. **1840** R. H. DANA *Bef. Mast* xxx, Spent all his time in the bush and along the beach, picking up flowers and shells, and such truck. **1871** W. ALEXANDER *Johnny Gibb* i, Is their trock a' in noo, I won'er? **1890** L. C. D'OYLE *Notches* 67 What cooking utensils and other 'truck' we thought we needed. **1897** KIPLING *Captains Courageous* i, I can't smoke the truck the steward sells.

c. *U.S.* Market-garden produce; hence as a general term for culinary vegetables.

1784 *Maryland Jrnl.* 14 Dec., Advt. (Thornton), A large Room..for his Customers to lodge in, and deposit their Market-truck. **1822** J. FLINT *Lett. Amer.* 264 Truck.. Culinary vegetables. **1870** S. LANIER *Nine fr. Eight* 2, I was drivin' my two-mule waggin, With a lot of truck for sale. **1885** *Blackw. Mag.* Sept. 330/1 He is laying out the back land in truck or early vegetables. **1902** *Ibid.* Apr. 498/1 'Truck' means briefly such things as can be grown for the Northern markets—cucumbers, cabbages, sweet potatoes, strawberries, tomatoes, &c.

5. *attrib.* and *Comb.*; in sense 2, as ***truck act, law, principle, system***; in sense 4 c, ***truck-farm, -farmer, -farming, -garden, -gardener, -gardening, -patch, -produce***; also **truck crop** *U.S.* = sense 4 c; **truck-economy**: see quot.; **truck-house**, in North America, a store-house for trading with Indians; also, any storage building (*Funk's Stand. Dict.* 1895); **truck-knight, -man**: see quots.; **truck-master**, (*a*) one who is in charge of a truck-house; (*b*) an employer who uses the truck system; **truck-shop**, a shop at which vouchers given instead of wages may be exchanged for goods, a tommy-shop; **truck-store** = prec.; also, a greengrocery shop (*local U.S.*).

1895 *U.S. Dept. Agric. Yearbk. 1894* 133 Soils having over 10 or 12 per cent of clay are too heavy and too retentive of moisture for the early *truck crops. **1937** *Sun* (Baltimore) 17 Feb. 7/8 Payments for truck-crop growers have been increased. **1972** R. G. KAZMANN *Mod. Hydrol.* (ed. 2) iv. 109 Higher-valued crops such as truck crops are valuable enough to justify far more than this expenditure. **1889** R. T. ELY *Introd. Pol. Econ.* I. vii. 50 *Truck-economy is the term used to denote the period which precedes the use of money. **1866** *N. & Q.* 3rd Ser. IX. 323/1 A truck garden, a *truck farm, is a market-garden or farm. **1969** *Observer* (Colour Suppl.) 19 Jan. 8/3 It was a truck farm, which you call a market-garden, don't you, or a nursery? **1976** *New Yorker* 17 May 34/1 Sold their..duplex and moved to a coöperative truck farm. **1877** A. DOUAI *Better Times* (1884) 7 The *truck-farmers from Virginia down to Florida. **1979** *Amer. Poetry Rev.* Mar./Apr. 24/1 A few children of Japanese truck farmers and some of us from Youngstown and White Center helped preserve what I snobbishly prefer to think of as peasant vitality. **1885** *Blackw. Mag.* Sept. 331/1 The river-bluffs are admirably suited for *truck-farming. **1891** *N.Y. Weekly Witness* 22 Apr. 2/2 A distinction is made between truck-farming and what is known as market-gardening... Truck-farming is defined as the production of green vegetables on tracts remote from market. **1973** *Publ. Amer. Dial. Soc.* LX. 10 Raised and lives in Williston, an unincorporated community..mainly devoted to fishing, tugboating, and truck farming. **1866** *Truck garden [see *truck farm*]. **1868** LOSSING *Hudson* 394 Numerous 'truck' gardens, from which the city draws vegetable supplies. **1889** L. H. BAILEY (*title*) The Horticulturist's Rule-Book. A Compendium of Useful Information for Fruit-Growers, *Truck-Gardeners, Florists, and Others. **1890** *Boston* (Mass.) *Jrnl.* 12 Apr. 2/4 During their two years' residence they have done all of their own work and *truck-gardening. **1731** *Massachusetts Stat.* 9 Nov., The Indians..have their dependance on this government for supplies..several *truck-houses having been erected..for that purpose. **1753** DOUGLASS *Brit. Settlem. N. Amer.* 228 Some place of Strength, Security, or Retreat for our Indian traders under the name of a Trading or Truck-House. **1625** F. MARKHAM *Bk. Hon.* II. viii. §2 Dunghill or *Truck-Knights, whose Honors haue no other assent or scale to rise by, but onely their wealth and purchase trucking and bargaining with gold or other merchandise. **1914** *Daily News* 24 Mar. 6 For practical purposes the present *Truck Laws are a dead letter. **1864** WEBSTER, **Truckman*, 1. One who does business in the way of barter and exchange. **1694** *Massachusetts Stat.* 13 June, That all trade with the said Eastern Indians be managed and carried on at the charge of and with the public stock..by suitable *truck masters. **1767** T. HUTCHINSON *Hist. Mass.* II. iii. 318 The charge of trading houses, truckmasters, garrisons, and a vessel employed in transporting goods. **1906** *Daily Chron.* 22 June 5/2 The wool was given out, and the payment in tea or groceries for the manufactured article was made from the shop of a truck master. **1829** T. FLINT *G. Mason* iii. 33 A garden, or, as the people call it, a *truck patch, was also prepared. **1837** SYD. SMITH *2nd Let. Archd. Singleton* Wks. 1859 II. 285/1 Recommending the *truck principle to the Bishops, and offering to pay them in hassocks, cassocks, aprons, shovel-hats [etc.]. **1890** L. C. D'OYLE *Notches* 145 The proximity of the camp would ensure them a ready market for all '*truck' produce. **1845** DISRAELI *Sybil* III. i, The Butty generally keeps a Tommy or *Truck shop and pays the wages of his labourers in goods. **1886** *Appleton's Ann. Cycl.* 84/1 In Liége..employers compelled the labourers to purchase supplies from their *Truck stores, at prices from 50 to 90 per cent. above..retail rates. **1830** COBBETT *Rur. Rides* (1885) II. 352 In the iron country..the *truck or tommy system generally prevails. **1869** *Adam Smith's W.N.* I. x. II. I. 150 *note*, The truck system..is now uniformly illegal. **1740** DOUGLASS *Disc. Curr. Brit. Plant. Amer.* 4 All Commerce naturally is a *Truck Trade exchanging Commodities which we can spare (or their Value) for Goods we are in want of. **1794** *Gaz. U.S.A.* (Philad.) 6 Jan. (Thornton), It is a truck trade that is proposed.

truck (trʌk), *sb.*[2] Also 7 trucke. [app. deriv. of L. *trochus* = Gr. τροχός: see TROCHUS, or short for TRUCKLE, a. AF. *trokle*:—L. *trochlea.*]

1. A small solid wooden wheel or roller; *spec. Naut.* one of those on which the carriages of ships' guns were formerly mounted.

1611 FLORIO, *Rigolo*, a little wheele vsed vnder sleds. Gunners call it a trucke. **1627** CAPT. SMITH *Seaman's Gram.* xiv. 65 If for Sea she [gun carriage] haue Trucks, which are round intier peeces of wood like wheeles. **1727** A. HAMILTON *New Acc. E. Ind.* I. xxii. 269 Those Priests had erected a Scaffold on two Axle-trees, that had Trucks fitted for them like the Carriage of Ship Guns. **1860** *All Year Round* No. 67. 404 At another of the guns, a shot came in and took off the truck (or, as a shore-going person would say, 'the wheel'). **1883** [implied in *truck gun*, 4].

2. *Naut.* **a.** A circular or square cap of wood fixed on the head of a mast or flag-staff, usually with small holes or sheaves for halliards.

1626 CAPT. SMITH *Accid. Yng. Seamen* 13 The maine top gallant sayle yeard, the trucke or flagge staffe. **1627** —— *Seaman's Gram.* iv. 18 The Trucke is a square peece of wood at the top wherein you put the Flag-staffe. **1697** DAMPIER *Voy.* (1729) I. 414 At our Main-top-mast head, on the very top of the truck of the Spindle. **1774** *Westm. Mag.* II. 429 What surprise he declar'd at the Boy on the truck! **1840** R. H. DANA *Bef. Mast* viii. 18 We painted her, both inside and out, from the truck to the water's edge. **1899** F. T. BULLEN *Log Sea-waif* 192 The second mate..ordered me to go up and reeve the signal halliards in the mizzen truck.

b. One of the small wooden blocks through which the rope of a parrel is threaded to prevent its being frayed against the mast. **c.** See quot. *c* 1635. **d.** A similar block lashed to the shrouds to form a guide or fair-leader for running rigging.

a **1625** *Nomenclator Navalis* (Harl. MS. 2301) s.v., Those little round thinges of Wood which belong to the *Parrells*, are called *Trucks*. **1627** CAPT. SMITH *Seaman's Gram.* v. 20 Parrels are little round Balls called Trucks, and little peeces of wood called ribs, and ropes. *c* **1635** CAPT. N. BOTELER *Dial. Sea Services* iv. (1685) 236 When the Main-capstan is not able to purchase in the Cable..they use to take a Hawser, and open a Strond thereof, and so put in Nippers, (which are small Ropes with a small Truck at one end) and with them they bind fast this Hawser to the Cable. **1688** R. HOLME *Armoury* III. xv. (Roxb.) 42/1 The Trucks are the little round things of wood made with holes through, to turne vpon a rope as aforesaid. **1711** W. SUTHERLAND *Shipbuild. Assist.* 135 Trucks for Shrouds—42.

3. A wheeled vehicle for carrying heavy weights; variously applied. **a.** A strong flat open trolley for carrying blocks of stone or the like; a lorry. **b.** A light two-wheeled hand-propelled vehicle; a hand-cart. **c.** An open railway wagon. **d.** A bogie truck; = LOGIE 2. **e.** A low barrow of various types, with one to four wheels; as that used on railway platforms for moving luggage, etc. **f.** A small barrow, with two stout low wheels and a projecting plate or lip in front, used for moving sacks or other heavy packages.

1774 *Hull Dock Act* 46 Any truck or cart, sledge waggon, dray. **1815** *Chron.* in *Ann. Reg.* 47/2 A baker's boy was wheeling his truck of bread along the road. **1838** N. WOOD *Railroads* 209 Truck for the conveyance of general merchandise. **1843** *Proc. Inst. Civil Eng.* 99 A 'bogie' engine, having a four-wheeled truck to support one end of the boiler. **1844** DICKENS *Mart. Chuz.* ix, There were more trucks near Todgers's than you would suppose a whole city could ever need. **1866** R. M. BALLANTYNE *Shift. Winds* xxiv. (1881) 274 Porters are hurrying to and fro with luggage on trucks. **1888** F. HUME *Mme. Midas* I. v, Another truck was waiting to take it to the main shaft, from whence it went up to the puddlers.

g. A motor vehicle for carrying goods, troops, etc., by road. Cf. LORRY *sb.* 1 b. orig. *U.S.*

1916, etc. [see *motor-truck* s.v. MOTOR *sb.* 5 a]. **1930** [see LORRY *sb.* 1 b]. **1932** G. GREENE *Stamboul Train* I. i. 3 The passengers cross the quay..round..abandoned trucks. **1950** *Times* 27 Apr. 6/7 Many soldiers in the last war will remember that 'gas' might or might not be petrol and a 'truck' might or might not be a lorry. So it is to-day with 'gearbox', 'transmission', and many others. **1961** L. VAN DER POST *Heart of Hunter* vii. 112 One of the foremost ranchers near Gemsbok Pan was in the Union and coming back by truck across the desert. **1976** *Economist* 16 Oct. 92/1 Of European sales nearly 200,000 were glorified cars, about 400,000 medium-sized vans (up to 3.5 tonnes) and some 240,000 trucks (over 3.5 tonnes). **1984** *Times* 8 Feb. (Energy Suppl.) p. iv./2 This step by the manufacturers to put electric vans and trucks into serious production..has vindicated the enthusiasm of the..Electric Vehicles Association. **1984** *N.Z. Truth* 23 May 33/3 The new ERF M16, ERF's bid for sales in the mid-size truck market, is on its way to becoming a big seller in Europe.

h. An axle unit of a skateboard to which the wheels are attached.

1976 A. CASSORLA *Skateboarder's Bible* 12 The average board came with trucks featuring one cushion rather than two. **1977** *Montgomery Ward Catal.* Spring–Summer 509/1 Heavy duty double-action die-cast trucks. **1978** *Globe & Mail* (Toronto) 15 Aug. 5/2 The wheels are lined with fibrous or plastic material to reduce noise, and steerable axles called trucks are supposed to eliminate squealing on curves and costly wear on rails.

4. *U.S.* A popular dance (see quots.). Cf. TRUCK *v.*[2] 5, TRUCKING *vbl. sb.*[2] 2.

1935 *Sun* (Baltimore) 15 Nov. 14/6 The truck, or truckin', that jerky yet rhythmic dance which combines a bend of the body, a tightening of the hand muscles and a slight strut with the legs, hit the theaters, sidewalks, gin taverns and dance floors of Harlem last summer. **1937** *N.Y. Amsterdam News* 4 Sept. 12/2 Add a bit of the Shag, the new dance sensation that has pushed the 'Truck' out of the limelight, throw in a bit of the Suzi-Q for a spice and then top it all off with the 'Truck'.

5. *attrib.* and *Comb.*, as ***truck-barrow***, ***-boy***, ***construction***, ***-driver***, ***-horse***, ***-load***, ***-man***, ***-porter***, ***-proprietor***, ***-wagon***, ***-wheel***; ***truck-like*** adj.; **truck-bolster**, the cross-beam of a bogie truck on which the weight of the carriage rests (*Cent. Dict.* 1891); **truck-end** *slang rare*⁻¹, the buttocks; **truck frame** *U.S.*, the frame of a bogie; **truck-gun**, a gun mounted on trucks (see sense 1); **truck-jack**: see quot.; **truck-light**, in the U.S. Navy, a mast-head signalling light; **trucklot** *N. Amer.*, a quantity of goods sufficient to fill a truck and sold at a lower rate than a smaller quantity; **truck mixer** (see quot. 1954); **truck stop** chiefly *U.S.*, an establishment which provides refreshments for truck-drivers and fuel and servicing for their trucks; **truck-windlass**, a windlass mounted on a truck (*Funk's Stand. Dict.* 1895).

1849 CRAIG, **Truck-barrow*, in Ropemaking, a sort of barrow with three wheels, used to take hauls of yarn from the yarn-house. **1900** *Engineering Mag.* XIX. 705 Castings keep coming in until there is a perfect wilderness of them piled about, through which the *truck-boy winds his tortuous way. **1901** *Daily News* 16 Jan. 6/5 Colossal expenditure on track improvements, *truck construction, and increased power of locomotives. **1907** *Ibid.* 17 Apr. 4 All sorts and conditions of people,..business men, *truck drivers, workgirls, policemen, Army men, everybody. **1931** E. WILSON *Axel's Castle* viii. 278 At Marseilles, he manages to live by unloading cargo and helping truck-drivers. **1973** 'R. MACLEOD' *Burial in Portugal* iii. 71 A truck driver leaned out of his cab and shouted a greeting. **1913** D. H. LAWRENCE *Sons & Lovers* iii. 53 But six shillin' wearin' his *truck-end out on a stool's better than ten shillin' i' th' pit. **1850** *Rep. Comm. Patents 1849* (U.S.) I. 164, I claim the shapes and combinations of the *truck frame pieces. **1942** W. FAULKNER *Go down, Moses* 145 He nudged the log to the edge of the truckframe. **1883** *Daily News* 31 Aug. 6/6 One of the old class of corvettes with *truck guns. **1839** *Spirit of Times* 27 July 246/1 Indeed many of their *truck horses are equal to those used on the road. **1894** S. FISKE *Holiday Stories* (1900) 21 What does it cost to keep a truck-horse? **1877** KNIGHT *Dict. Mech.*, **Truck-jack*, a lifting-jack suspended from a truck-axle to lift logs or other objects so that they may be loaded on to a sled or other low-bodied vehicle. **18..** *Army & Navy Reg.* (U.S.A.) XXIV. 277 (Cent. Supp.) *Truck-light. **1895** *Daily News* 8 Apr. 6/4 The third-class passenger for a long time had to be content with a *truck-like carriage, with low sides, and seldom roofed. **1862** *Sat. Rev.* 18 Feb. 157 The great London firms have sent off many railway *truck-loads of their publications. **1943** *Sun* (Baltimore) 15 July 12/3 The regulation covers sales of berries at country shipping points, effective July 13, and carlot and *trucklot sales at any receiving point. **1970** *Toronto Daily Star* 24 Sept. 16/3 (Advt.), Attention! all Trucklot Buyers!!.. Prices in this section apply on normal mixed truckloads. **1787** M. CUTLER in *Life*, etc. (1888) I. 306 By them..licensing retailers, taverns, carters, *truckmen,..are regulated. **1854** EMERSON *Lett. & Soc. Aims*, *Eloquence* Wks. (Bohn) III. 192 Ought not the scholar to be able to convey his meaning in terms as ..strong as the porter or truckman uses to convey his? **1901** *Scotsman* 11 Apr. 8/1 The truckman..delivered the gold from the Assay office to the steamship. **1954** *Gloss. Highway Engin. Terms (B.S.I.)* 49 **Truck mixer*, a concrete mixer mounted on a self-propelled chassis, capable of mixing materials during transit from a batching plant to the point of placing. **1976** *Milton Keynes Express* 9 July 16/1 (Advt.), Experienced class II H.G.V. driver required to operate a truck mixer in the Milton Keynes area. **1961** *Amer. Speech* XXXVI. 271 Somewhere on your *run* you will spend some time at a **truck stop*..while the *hasher* serves your *diesel* or *Joe* or *Java*. **1973** P. BERTON *Drifting Home* vi. 91 Now it is a hodge-podge: tavern, gas station, motel, snack bar, grocery store. Carmacks has become a truck stop. **1897** *Outing* (U.S.) XXX. 351/2 At Baddeck our camping outfit was packed upon a *truck-wagon. **1825** J. NICHOLSON *Operat. Mechanic* 423 The motion given to the *truck-wheels of the spinning-machine. **1909** *Daily Chron.* 25 Sept. 7/6 Lad wanted for *truck work.

Hence **'truckful**, as much as fills or loads a truck.

1836 DICKENS *Pickw.* xxi. 213 He had moved in all his furniture—it wasn't quite a truck-full. **1893** *Columbus (Ohio) Dispatch* 12 Oct., Cigars are pouring in by the truckful and the cigarettes are innumerable. **1900** *Daily News* 1 Aug. 6/6 The truckful of sick and wounded left at Bloemfontein Station.

truck (trʌk), *v.*[1] Forms: 3 trukie, 5 trukke, 6–7 trucke, (7 trucque, 8 *Sc.* troak), 8–9 *Sc.* troke, trock, 9 *Sc.* troque, 6– truck. [ME. *trukie*, a. F. *troquer* to truck, shop, barter, exchange (Cotgr.), Norman-Picard form of OF. **trocher*, in med.L. *trocāre* (1257 in Cartulary, Hatz.-Darm.), Fr. has also verbal sb. *troc*, †*troq* barter, Pg. *troca* = Sp., Pg. *trocar*, It. *truccare* (Florio, 1598): of unknown origin: see suggestions in Diez.

In 13th c., and in *Promp. Parv.*, but rare before 1580.]

1. *trans.* To give in exchange *for* something else; to exchange (one thing) *for* another; also, to exchange (a thing) *with* a person (also *absol.*).

a **1225** *Ancr. R.* 408 Vndeore he makeð God, & to unwurð mid alle, þet for eni worldliche luue his luue trukie. *c* **1230** *Hali Meid.* 5 And trukie for a mon of lam þe heuenliche lauerd. **1598** SYLVESTER *Du Bartas* II. ii. II. *Babylon* 485 Trade..with hardy luck Doth words for words barter, exchange and truck. **1614** B. JONSON *Bart. Fair* II. vi, S'blood, how braue is he? in a garded coate? you were best trucke with him. *c* **1645** HOWELL *Lett.* (1650) II. 105 To truck the Latine for any other vulgar Language, is but an ill barter. **1698** FARQUHAR *Love & Bottle* I. i, What, slighted! despised! my honourable love trucked for a whore! **1706** E. WARD *Wooden World Diss.* (1708) 23 Let him truck Jackets with any of his Barge-men. **1819** KEATS *K. Stephen* I. iii. 11, I would not truck this brilliant day To rule in Pylos with a Nestor's beard. **1827** BARRINGTON *Pers. Sk.* II. 305 Revolutions have been effected..dynasties annihilated, and kings trucked, with as little confusion as the exchanging a gig horse.

2. To exchange (commodities) for profit; to barter. Const. *for* a thing, *with* a person.

c **1440** *Promp. Parv* 503/2 Trukkon, roryn, or chaungyn, *cambio, campso*. **1588** PARKE tr. *Mendoza's Hist. China* 329 They..brought with them many curious thinges..to truck for other thinges. **1650** FULLER *Pisgah* II. ii. 80 They kept swine to truck and barter with other nations. *c* **1660** D. NORTH in R. North *Lives* (1826) II. 306 The seamen trucked some tobacco with them for their capeaks, or furred caps. **1774** *Phil. Trans.* LXIV. 380 For blanketing, fire-arms.. and ammunition, they truck the greatest part of their furs. **1817–18** COBBETT *Resid. U.S.* (1822) 40 My own stock being gone, I have trucked turnips for apples. **1884** *St. James' Gaz.* 19 Dec. 4/1 When the smacksmen have no money he [the skipper] will tempt them to 'truck' the stores of their vessel.

fig. *c* **1645** HOWELL *Lett.* (1650) III. 3 Since we are both agred to truck Intelligence [etc.]. *a* **1774** FERGUSSON *Butterfly in Street* 41 How cou'd you troke the mavis' note For 'penny pies all piping hot'? **1896** J. LUMSDEN *Poems* 171 A' the news the country offered Crinch for crinch they trockit thrang.

†**b.** To acquire by barter. *Obs. rare.*

1553 S. CABOT *Ordinances* in Hakluyt *Voy.* (1589) 261 All wares and commodities trucked, bought or giuen to the companie. **1600** HAKLUYT *Voy.* III. 326 Fiue or sixe pounds weight of siluer which he had trucked and traffiqued with Indians. **1631** J. ROUS *Diary* (Camden) 67 Fish, either bought or trucked at Norwich.

c. To dispose of *to* a person by barter. ? *Obs.*

1686 *Col. Rec. Pennsylv.* I. 187 Nicho. Skull hath sould and trucked to and with yᵉ Indians severall quantities of Liquors. **1755** T. PRINCE *Ann. New Eng.* II. ii. (1826) 317 That no person give, sell, truck or send any Indian corn to any English out of this jurisdiction. **1819** WIFFEN *Aonian Hours* (1820) 47 No selfish ministers,..for place, Truck to a crown their dignity of mind.

†**d.** To deal or traffic in (a commodity). *rare.*

1715 BENTLEY *Serm.* x. 358 The very Sins of the Living, the Wages of Damnation, were negotiated and truck'd by the wicked Politic of Popery.

†**e.** To carry *about* for sale; to hawk, peddle.

1681 R. KNOX *Hist. Ceylon* IV. ix. 157 We shewed him.. the Cotton Yarn which we had trucked about the Country.

3. To barter away (what should be sacred or precious) *for* something unworthy; = BARTER *v.* 2 b.

1649 G. DANIEL *Trinarch.*, *Hen. V*, cccxxviii, The Painted Apple, for his part In Paradice; France truck't, for a faire face. **1706** DE FOE *Jure Div.* v. 9 Liberty's too often truck'd for Gold. **1726** W. REEVES *Serm.* (1729) 160 He will not.. truck his religion for preferment. **1781** COWPER *Expost.* 374 Having trucked thy soul, brought home the fee. **1829** J. STERLING *Ess.*, etc. (1848) I. 124 Many of..the Spaniards.. were willing to truck the independence of their country for the political benefits promised by the invaders.

b. *to truck away*: to dispose of by barter.

1631 SANDERSON *Serm.*, *Ad Aulam* i. (1660) II. 6 For the obtaining whereof they truck away their precious souls. **1657** R. LIGON *Barbadoes* (1673) 119 His men..(for some Commodities useful to themselves) had truckt away the greatest part of his Bisket. **1796** BURKE *Regic. Peace* iv. Wks. IX. 110 Some of our Kings have..trucked away, for foreign gold, the interests and glory of their crown.

4. *intr.* To trade by exchange of commodities; to barter. Const. *for* a thing *with* a person.

1594 [see TRUCKING *vbl. sb.*[1]]. **1599** HAKLUYT *Voy.* II. 227 Neither would they take money for their fruite but would trucke for olde shirtes or pieces of olde linnen breeches. **1623** LISLE *Ælfric on O. & N. Test.* To Rdr. 3 Wee liue here as on the great Bursse and Exchange of the World, trucquing and trading as it were by the Merchant Waters thereof. **1697** DAMPIER *Voy.* (1720) I. 41 Spaniards who lived there to truck with the Indians for gold. **1797** S. JAMES *Narr. Voy.* 162 He would either sell them to him, or truck with him for any thing. **1854** R. G. LATHAM *Native Races Russian Emp.* 181 Chinese..tobacco, for which they truck with the Russians.

5. *intr. fig.* or in fig. context: To bargain or deal *for* a commodity, *with* a person; to negotiate; also to have dealings *in*, to trade; esp. of dealings of an underhand or improper character: to traffic.

1615 JACKSON *Creed* IV. III. vii. §6 A city which is above, whose commodities cannot be purchased with gold or silver ..much less may we truck for them with our unclean worldly delights. **1640** in Rushw. *Hist. Coll.* III. (1692) I. 122 He hath most unworthily trucked and chaffered in the meanest of them. *a* **1656** USSHER *Ann.* vi. (1658) 500 [She] trucked with the army..and brought it over to her husband as her dowry. **1664** in Howell *State Trials* (1816) VI. 607 Here is Wild commits a robbery, you come and truck with Wild, and agree with him that Mr. Tryon shall let him go. *a* **1774** FERGUSSON *Election* Poems (1845) 43 Ye louns! that troke in doctors' stuff. **1824** SCOTT *St. Ronan's* xxxi, She must go on troking wi' the old carrier, as if there was no post-house in the neighbourhood. **1904** *Daily News* 7 Dec. 11 Private communities have no business to 'truck with' the State.

b. In weakened sense: To have dealings or intercourse *with*, to have to do *with*, be on familiar terms; †*spec.* of sexual intercourse. Now *dial.*

1622 F. MARKHAM *Bk. War* II. iv. 54 If he haue..the vnderstanding of other Languages he is an inestimable Iuell, for so he shall be able to trucke with strangers for the benefit of his Company. **1624** MASSINGER *Parl. Love* II. i, Truck with old ladies That nature hath given o'er. *a* **1658** CLEVELAND *Mixt Assembly* 86 If they two truck together, 'twill not be A Child-birth, but a Goal-delivery. *a* **1704** T. BROWN *Sat. Quack* 95 Wrinkled witches, when they truck with hell. **1719** HAMILTON *Ep. to Ramsay* 24 July v, To troke with thee I'd best forbear 't. **1787** W. TAYLOR *Poems* 132 Me ..wuss me hae never Enbowr see, Nor wi' sic Lady trockit. **1815** SCOTT *Guy M.* xi, He held ower muckle troking and communing wi' that Meg Merrilies, wha was the maist notorious witch in a' Galloway. **1893–4** *Northumbld. Gloss.*, *Troke*, to truck, to negotiate with, to be on familiar terms.

6. *intr.* To walk about on petty business; to potter. *Sc.*

1864 GILFILLAN *Jrnl.* in Watson *Life* (1892) 384, I troked about Edinburgh for a day or two. **1871** W. ALEXANDER *Johnny Gibb* xxxix, Tak' a girse parkie or twa, an' trock aboot amo' nowte beasts. **1892** STEVENSON & L. OSBOURNE *Wrecker* vi, Going troking across a continent on a wild goose chase. **1894** Traikings and trokings [see *traiking* s.v. TRAIK *v.*].

7. *trans.* To pay (an employee) otherwise than in money; to pay or deal with on the truck system (with the implication of profiting by the transaction). Also *intr.*

1871 A. S. HARVEY in *Gd. Words* 610 A large proportion of the trade is in the hands of middlemen, called 'foggers', —those who truck being known as 'pettifoggers',—each of whom employs a certain number of nailmakers. *Ibid.* 614 He ..works on,..trucked by the same merchant from boyhood to manhood, from manhood to old age. *Ibid.* 615 The very paupers used to be 'trucked', the inspectors..gave the paupers their relief in kind. **1879** ESCOTT *England* I. 265, 25,000 hands are employed, and, speaking roughly, about 14,000 are trucked.

¶**8.** *intr.* = TRUCKLE *v.* 2 a. *Obs. rare.*

1665 *Surv. Aff. Netherl.* 174 Their Towns..ready to submit to any new Masters, rather than Truck under Amsterdam. **1674** STAVELEY *Rom. Horseleach* Ep. Ded., Amsterdam supplanted Antwerp,—Flanders trucked under Holland.

Hence **'trucking** *ppl. a.*, that trucks or barters.

1776 ADAM SMITH *W.N.* I. ii. (1869) I. 16 This same trucking disposition..originally gives occasion to the division of labour. **1871** A. S. HARVEY in *Gd. Words* 611 In the hosiery trade the trucking middlemen undersell the cash-paying masters.

truck, *v.*[2] [f. TRUCK *sb.*[2]]

1. *trans.* To put on or into a truck; to convey by means of a truck or trucks. Now usu. with reference to TRUCK *sb.*[2] 3 g.

1809 [see *trucking* below]. **1864** *Pall Mall G.* 4 Sept. 10/2 At stations where cattle are trucked, special accommodation for trucking them quietly and carefully,..ought to be provided. **1865** *Ibid.* 29 Sept. 7/2 A farmer in Perthshire, having lost one or two animals from the plague, immediately trucked off the rest to London for the Monday morning's market. **1884** *West Morn. News* 6 Aug. 1/2 Lots can be trucked..to any part of the West of England. **1935** *Motion Picture* Nov. 80/3 The heavy electrical equipment was trucked in. **1943** *Sun* (Baltimore) 28 Apr. 8/3 The fighters are trucked in crated from cargo ships. **1954** [see FAT *sb.*[2] 1 b]. **1969** A. LURIE *Real People* 108 He has trucked all his equipment..up here at considerable expense. **1982** L. KALLEN *C. B. Greenfield* iv. 47 The produce, trucked in daily from their own upstate farm, was fresh.

2. *intr.* To drive or take charge of a truck, to act as a truck-driver. *U.S. colloq.*

1907 *Black Cat* June 3, I been truckin' fer you, or rather fer your father and uncle, eighteen years, and that's the first time any one's ever accused me of droppin' anything. **1976** M. MACHLIN *Pipeline* xi. 135 If he stayed with the private contractors who were trucking for Denali, it was improbable he would be recognized.

3. a. *U.S. slang.* Of a vehicle: to proceed. Hence of a person: to go (by truck or otherwise); to move or stroll.

1925 C. R. COOPER *Lions 'n' Tigers* v. 109 One by one the big wagons were trucking toward the first smoking torch at a corner of the grounds. **1938** *Better English* Nov. 51 *Truck, truck on down,* to go somewhere. **1941** STEINBECK & RICKETTS *Sea of Cortez* xxiv. 237 We said good-by to Tiburoń and trucked on down toward Guaymas. **1970** T. WOLFE *Radical Chic & Mau-Mauing Flak Catchers* 131 They would truck around in the pimp style, too. **1979** *United States 1980/81* (Penguin Travel Guides) 148 You'll still find plenty of people trucking through the streets in flannel shirts, blue jeans, cowboy hats, and boots.

b. Slang phr. *to keep on trucking*, to persevere: a phrase of encouragement.

1972 *Sat. Rev.* (U.S.) 28 Oct. 12 One poster.. shows the famous R. Crumb cartoon characters and bears the caption: 'Let's Keep on Truckin'.' **1976** *Southern Even. Echo* (Southampton) 6 Nov. (Advt. Suppl.) 5/4 'To keep in business he's just got to keep on truckin'.' For Karl, and his kind, that can mean upwards of 200,000 miles a year. **1977** *New Yorker* 27 June 79/1 Feels like I frosted the ends of my toes a bit, but they're far from my heart, so I'll keep on truckin.

4. *Cinematogr.* = TRACK *v.*[1] 3 e.

1929 [see DOLLY *sb.*[1] 4 h]. **1942** *Amer. Cinematographer* June 283/2 The camera would start at a long shot, and truck rapidly down toward the background. **1948** A. HUXLEY *Ape & Essence* (1949) 151 Dr. Poole and Loola enter the shot, and the Camera trucks with them as they come striding down the slope. **1961** G. MILLERSON *Technique Television Production* iii. 25 (*caption*) Two methods of trucking sideways are shown.

5. To dance the truck. *U.S. slang.*

1937 *Amer. Speech* XII. 183/1 Only negroes can really truck. **1966** M. & J. STEARNS in A. Dundes *Mother Wit* (1973) 614/2 Sweetie May trucks provocatively onstage. **1972** W. M. ESTES *Streetful of People* vii. 238 Toward the end of the number, the girls turned rosy red and started truckin'.

Hence **trucked** *ppl. a.*; *trucked-in* adj., brought by truck.

1940 *Sun* (Baltimore) 16 Apr. 15/5 Offerings during forenoon rounds in the sheep pens consisted of a few lots of trucked-in native spring lambs. **1966** T. PYNCHON *Crying of Lot 49* iii. 56 The trucked-in white sand. **1977** *Time* 7 Mar. 54/3 Lack of green grazing land and hay is also forcing cattlemen either to sell off their thin animals at low prices or fatten them on expensive trucked-in feed.

†**truck**, *v.*[3] *Obs. rare*[−1]. [Cf. It. *truccare* 'to trudge, to skud, or pack away' (Florio, 1598).] *intr.* To trudge, tramp.

1631 BRATHWAIT *Whimzies, Wine-soaker* 102 If he.. fall into a gravell-pit hee taxeth the citie for her governement, for leaving her cellar doores so wide open at that time a night. Yet on hee trucks, if he can mount the pit.

truck, var. TRUG[2] *Obs.*; dial. var. TROKE *v.*

†**truckage**[1]. *Obs. rare.* In 7 truccage. [f. TRUCK *v.*[1] + -AGE.] The action of trucking; exchange, barter.

1641 MILTON *Reform.* II. 15 If such Divine ministeries as these must.. not passe to and fro.. without the truccage of perishing Coine.

truckage[2] ('trʌkɪdʒ). [f. TRUCK *sb.*[2] or *v.*[2] + -AGE.] Conveyance by truck or trucks, or the cost of this; also, supply of trucks collectively (cf. TONNAGE *sb.* 5).

1830 W. S. MOORSOM *Lett. from Nova Scotia* iii. 80 Away scamper a dozen proud nags waiting for truckage. **1846** WORCESTER, *Truckage*,.. expense of conveying by trucks. **1883** JONCAS *Fisheries Canada* 28 (Fish. Exhib. Publ.) The erection and repairs of buildings, tin and iron work, boat-building, fuel-cutting, truckage, and other expenditure. **1901** *Daily Chron.* 11 Nov. 5/6 Unless a further amount of truckage can be allotted immediately, the inhabitants will have to go extremely short.

trucker[1] ('trʌkə(r)). [f. TRUCK *v.*[1] and *sb.*[1] + -ER[1]. Cf. F. *troqueur* (17th c.).]

1. One who trucks or barters; a barterer, bargainer; *Sc.* an itinerant dealer, a pedlar; †also, as a term of reproach: a haggler, huckster, trafficker (*obs.*).

1598 FLORIO, *Barattiere*,.. a trucker, a marter, an exchanger. **1622** MABBE tr. *Aleman's Guzman d'Alf.* II. 239 This silly foole was a kinde of trucker of commodities. **1632** MASSINGER *City Madam* III. i, I know them—swaggering, suburbian roarers, Sixpenny truckers. **1660** J. LLOYD *Prim. Episc.* 31 The sacrilegious truckers, which would have the reverend Clergy live upon their leavings and scraps. *c* **1790** in Ramsay *Scot. in 18th C.* (1888) II. xi. 323 *note*, Every year there came a set of *troquers* or *trockhers* (barterers, Fr. *troquer*) from Ireland with horse-loads of linen, which they bartered for the miner's old clothes. **1802** JOANNA BAILLIE *Ethwald* II. I. iii, Come on, base trokers of your country's blood. **1816** SCOTT *Antiq.* iii, Brokers and trokers, those miscellaneous dealers in things rare and curious.

2. *U.S.* One who grows 'truck' or garden produce for market; a truck-gardener or truck-farmer.

1868 *Norfolk* (Virginia) *Jrnl.*, The truckers in this neighborhood. **1882** *Philad. Even. Star* 2 May, Norfolk truckers are picking their strawberries. **1890** *Boston* (Mass.) *Jrnl.* 10 Apr. 2/4 Southern vegetables are looking very well and the truckers are hopeful.

3. *attrib.*, as *trucker-fashion*; also †**trucker-cloth**, ? cloth for trucking; cf. *trucking-cloth.*

1536 *Somerset Medieval Wills* (Som. Rec. Soc.) 34 To my brother Edward a Trucker cloth. **1543** *Ibid.* 75 To John Burges my prentice, a trucker cloth. **1881** A. WATT in *Mod. Scott. Poets* III. 137 In true troker fashion, she ca'd at ilk dwellin'.

'**trucker**[2]. [f. TRUCK *sb.*[2] + -ER[1].]

1. A labourer who uses a truck.

1853 DICKENS *Down with Tide* in *Househ. Words* 5 Feb. 484/2 The Truckers.. whose business it was to land more considerable parcels of goods than the Lumpers could manage. **1878** F. S. WILLIAMS *Midl. Railw.* 640 No sooner is the train marshalled in its dock.. than the 'truckers' bring forward the goods to be loaded. **1895** *Westm. Gaz.* 30 May 5/3 Two wagonettes, in each of which thirty dock labourers had been driven from the East End at the expense of a lucky 'trucker'.

2. A (long-distance) lorry-driver. orig. and chiefly *U.S.*

1961 *Amer. Speech* XXXVI. 273 A fast-driving trucker. **1963** *Times* 2 Feb. 9/6 'Truckers, the real night drivers, are a race apart and 99 per cent honest,' said Taffy. **1966** B. H. DEAL *Fancy's Knell* (1967) vi. 84 There was the barbecue and good coffee. Truckers often stopped here. **1971** *Maclean's Mag.* Sept. 72/3 Most truckers.. name their rigs after their girl friends. **1978** S. BRILL *Teamsters* i. 14 The special nature of their work gives these truckers and warehousemen a stranglehold on the nation's economic life. **1984** *Gainesville* (Florida) *Sun* 30 Mar. 11A/1 The chase started when truckers on I-75 radioed troopers about a late-model Chevrolet station wagon that was weaving on the highway. **1984** *More* (Auckland) May 81/3 And then there are some hardcore longterm truckers who have seen several seasons come and go.

truckie ('trʌkɪ). *Austral.* and *N.Z. colloq.* [f. TRUCK *sb.*[2] + -IE.] = TRUCKER[2] 2.

1958 *Coast to Coast 1957–8* 201 The truckie looked upwards. 'Whaddya want, mate?' **1968** *Sunday Mail* (Brisbane) 9 June 5/3 Since April last year, more than 50 truckies had appeared in the courts in Queensland on 'pep' pill charges. **1970** P. CARLON *Souvenir* vi. 56 In the truckies' café.. the waitress remembered them. **1970** *N.Z. Listener* 21 Dec. 8/4 Another time you'll thumb a truck—truckies will generally stop for you. **1976** *Telegraph* (Brisbane) 24 June 20/2 Detectives have begun a blitz on interstate truckies in a bid to catch color television thieves. **1978** O. WHITE *Silent Reach* viii. 83 We are evacuating this camp... Regular truckies stand to their vehicles.

trucking ('trʌkɪŋ), *vbl. sb.*[1] [f. TRUCK *v.*[1] + -ING[1].] The action of TRUCK *v.*[1]; exchanging, bartering, trafficking, bargaining; dealings, intercourse; also *spec.* the giving or receiving payment of wages in kind.

1594 CAREW *Huarte's Exam. Wits* xiii. (1616) 216 Manie .. by trafficking and trucking, within few dayes haue lost their principall. **1624** MASSINGER *Renegado* II. vi, Pray you, help me to some trucking With your last she-customer. **1661** *Colet's Serm. Conf. & Ref.* II. 27 Unloose your selves from the worldly bondage, from trucking with the world. **1705** VANBRUGH *Confed.* II. i, You like your neighbour's [wife] better... What a pity it is the law don't allow trucking. **1755** RAMSAY *To Jas. Clerk* 11 To fend by troaking, buying, selling. **1818** SCOTT *Rob Roy* xxvi, He was here about some Jacobitical papistical troking in seventeen hundred and seven. **1830** COBBETT *Rur. Rides* (1885) II. 354 The workman.. if he will have liquor,.. must get it by trucking with the goods that he has got at the tommy shop. *a* **1867** SIR A. ALISON *Autobiog.* (1883) I. ii. 30 Our.. interchange of little purchases or troking as we called it.

b. *U.S.* The cultivation of 'truck' or vegetables.

1897 *Philad. Jrnl. Fine Arts* June, About one half [of the grounds] is used for trucking and pasture purposes.

c. *attrib.* in sense 'used for truck or barter', as †*trucking-cloth, -house, -stuff.*

1675 in Hubbard *Narrative* I. (1865) 78 He or they.. shall receive for their Pains, forty *Trucking-cloth Coats. **1632** *Rec. Crt. Assistants Mass. Bay* (1904) II. 23 There shalbe a *trucking howse.. in euery plantacion whither the Indians may resorte to trade. **1648** B. PLANTAGENET *Descr. New Albion* 23 To reduce all their trading to five Ports or Pallisadoed trucking houses. **1755** T. PRINCE *Ann. New Eng.* II. ii. (1826) 395 There shall be a trucking house in every plantation. **1624** *Good News fr. New Eng.* in Arber *Pilgrim Fathers* (1897) 533 We were worn out of all manner of *trucking stuff, not having [therefore] any means left to help ourselves by trade.

trucking ('trʌkɪŋ), *vbl. sb.*[2] [TRUCK *v.*[2] + -ING[1].]

1. The action of conveying by truck. Now chiefly *U.S.*, the conveyance of goods by means of a lorry or other motor vehicle; lorry-driving.

1809 R. LANGFORD *Introd. Trade* 73 Wharfage and Shipping Marking £1 16*s.* 7*d.*, Trucking.. £1 10*s.* **1891** *Echo* 10 Mar. 3/2 On the quays.. the snow is a foot deep, and trucking from the sheds to the ship has been delayed. **1909** *Dundee Advertiser* 24 Nov. 7 Miners.. have struck work owing to a difference with the management regarding the trucking of coal. **1947** [implied at PARLAY *v.* 2]. **1955** *Amer. Speech* XXX. 91 In trucking, *twin screws* mean that there are two sets of rear wheels that are powered. **1961** *Ibid.* XXXVI. 271 Both the [lumbering] industry and the comparative isolation encourage trucking. **1968** *Globe & Mail* (Toronto) 3 Feb. B5/1 Parts one and two of the act, introduced last year, have been implemented and deal mainly with railways. Part three, dealing with trucking, has not yet become law. **1978** *New York* 3 Apr. 88/1 (Advt.), Quick (but careful) Trucking—Immediate Service.

b. *attrib.*

1947 Trucking firm [see PARLAY *v.* 2]. **1955** *Amer. Speech* XXX. 91 Some of the words and terms of the trucking industry have been carried over from earlier days of teamsters and steamboat men. **1962** 'E. MCBAIN' *Heckler* iv. 35, I.. work for the trucking company. **1969** G. LYALL *Venus with Pistol* ix. 50 I'm in the trucking business. **1978** S. BRILL *Teamsters* i. 14 He had negotiated a national trucking contract.

2. The action of dancing the truck. *slang.*

1935 [see TRUCK *sb.*[2] 4]. **1938**, etc. [see SUSIE-Q]. **1944** C. CALLOWAY *Hepsters Dict.* in *Of Minnie the Moocher* (1976) 260 *Trucking*, a dance introduced at the Cotton Club in 1933. **1959** 'F. NEWTON' *Jazz Scene* iv. 60 The Black Bottom, Charleston, Lindy Hop, Big Apple, Truckin' and the rest.. have been mainly temporary crazes. **1971** E. BULLINS in W. King *Black Short Story Anthol.* (1972) 70 The dancers upon the concrete were blocks away, souls in time to the trotting and trucking of the savage song of the threshing floor.

3. *Cinematogr.* (In sense 3 of the vb.) **trucking shot** = *tracking shot* s.v. TRACKING *vbl. sb.* 5.

1948 A. HUXLEY *Ape & Essence* (1949) 46 We.. enjoy a trucking shot of mortuary gazebos. **1959** W. S. SHARPS *Dict. Cinematogr.* 91/2 *Dollying*, otherwise *Tracking, Travelling* or *Trucking*, the moving of a camera on a *dolly* or *camera truck* during *shooting*.

truckle ('trʌk(ə)l), *sb.* Forms: 5 trokel, -ill, trookyll, trokle, *pl.* trokleys, 5–6 trokell, trocle, 6 troukle, -cle, trowkle, truckill, 7 truckel, trukle, trickle (also 9 *dial.*), 6– truckle. [= AF. *trocle, trokle*, ad. L. *trochlea* = Gr. τροχιλία, τροχιλέα, etc., sheaf of a pulley: see TROCHLEA.]

1. A small wheel with a groove in its circumference round which a cord passes; a pulley, a sheave.

1417 in *For. Acc. 8 Hen. V*, D/2, j apparaille ix pullifs vj Trokles. *Ibid.* G/1 Eiusdem Nauis j apparatu ix Pullifs vj Trocles j securi. **14..** *MS. Digby 233* lf. 221/2 þanne drawe þei & wyndeþ vp þe lasse toure with ropes & trokelus. **1545** ELYOT, *Artemon*, a troukle wherby ropes dooe runne. It maye also be taken for any instrument that hath troucles. **1592** R. D. *Hypnerotomachia* 8 With what Cranes, winding beames, Trocles, round pullies, Capres. *a* **1693** *Urquhart's Rabelais* III. xvi. 132 A Truckle for a Pully. **1761** STERNE *Tr. Shandy* III. xx, A truckle for a pully. **1904** ANSTRUTHER THOMSON *Remin.* II. v. 135 They hoisted him and then let the truckle go with a run.

2. A small roller or wheel placed under or attached to a heavy object to facilitate moving it; a castor on a piece of furniture. Now *dial.*

1459 [see TRUCKLE-BED]. **1519** HORMAN *Vulg.* 244 b, This house may be remoued with trocles, & slyddis. **1617** HIERON *Wks.* (1619–20) II. 351 Thou which canst not goe alone, maist be allowed to goe by truckles, or as thou art led by anothers hand. **1655** tr. *Com. Hist. Francion* IX. 14 He showed them a great round chair very ancient, which had truckles under it to move withall. **1706** PHILLIPS (ed. Kersey), *Truckle*, a little running Wheel. **1837** *Penny Mag.* VI. 338 [A wooden horse] placed on a stand made moveable by truckles. **1888** ELWORTHY *W. Somerset Word-bk.*, *Truckle*, .. 2. a caster. 'The very chairs 'ad a-got truckles to 'em'.

3. Short for TRUCKLE-BED.

1637 HEYWOOD *Royall King* III. vii, A close roome, with a standing bed in 't, and a truckle too. **1664** BUTLER *Hud.* II. ii. 40 With knocking loud and bauling, He rous'd the Squire, in Truckle lolling. **1707** PRIOR *Sat. Poets* 76 No Friend.. but trusting Landlady, Who stows you on hard Truckle, Garret high. **1826** SCOTT *Woodst.* xxi, His.. attendant.. deposited himself on his truckle. **1851** W. ANDERSON *Rhymes* (1867) 143 (E.D.D.) A wee truckle filled wi' fusionless strae.

4. A low-wheeled car; a truck. Chiefly in Irish use.

1689 *Irish Procl.* 14 Sept., [Not] to.. meddle with any of their horses, carts, truckels, or other their tacklings. **1751** R. PALTOCK *P. Wilkins* (1884) I. 118, I no sooner unloaded but down went I again with my cart, or truckle rather, to the lake, and brought from thence on it my other chest. **1807** P. GASS *Jrnl.* 240 Our waggons and truckles to transport the baggage and canoes. **1880** *Antrim & Down Gloss.*, *Truckle*, a small car, in common use before the introduction of the present farm-carts.

5. A small barrel-shaped cheese. *dial.*

a **1813** [see *truckle-cheese* in 6]. **1850** *Jrnl. R. Agric. Soc.* XI. II. 705 Besides these cheeses, some small ones are made, called 'truckles'. **1891** *Catal. Oxf. Agric. Show* 45 The best lot of Cheese not less than ½ cwt. (Truckles excepted). **1901** *Scotsman* 9 Oct. 10/2 For cheddar truckles.

6. *attrib.* and *Comb.*, as *truckle-car, -cheese* (= 5), *-wheel.* See also TRUCKLE-BED.

1748 MRS. DELANY *Life & Corr.* (1861) II. 491 *Truckle-car (what they [Irish] make use of for carrying goods) drawn by one horse and the wheels not three foot high. *a* **1813** in Ellis *Brand's Pop. Antiq.* I. 55 A piece of *Truckle Cheese. **1891** *Catal. Oxf. Agric. Show* 45 The best lot of 3 Loaf or other Truckle Cheese (not Stilton). **1533** *Lett. & Pap. Hen. VIII*, VI. 503, 4 carpenters.. making of *truckill whelis. **1706** *Phil. Trans.* XXV. 2253 Near the one End.. let a little Truckle-wheel.. be fastened to the Rular by a Pin.

'**truckle**, *v.* Also 8 *Sc.* trockle. [f. *truckle* in TRUCKLE-BED.]

†**1.** *intr.* To sleep in a truckle-bed. Const. *under* (*beneath*) the person occupying the high bed, or the high bed itself. Also *fig. Obs.*

1613 BEAUM. & FL. *Coxcomb* I. vi, I'll truckle here, boy; give me another pillow. **1655** R. BOREMAN *Mirr. Mercy & Judgm.* 21 Who had the custody of him at the house of master Foster, Keeper of the Prison, and truckled under him every night. **1657** HOWELL *Londinop.* 399 [St. Paul's] having a large Church.. truckling, as one may say, under her Chancel. **1658** E. PHILLIPS *Gard. Tulips* 51 The Knight keeps to his Lady in the high bed, and never truckles. **1674**

N. FAIRFAX *Bulk & Selv.* 21 Such a kind of somewhatkin, as truckles beneath the very tinyness of an half nothing.

2. *fig.* †**a.** To take a subordinate or inferior position; to be subservient, to submit, to give precedence. Const. *under*, *to*. *Obs.*

1667 PEPYS *Diary* 2 Sept., He will never..truckle under any body or any faction, but do just as his own reason and judgment directs. **1671** MARVELL *Corr.* Wks. (Grosart) II. 395 We truckle to France in all things, to the prejudice of our honour. **1681** EVELYN *Let. to Pepys* 5 Dec., in *Mem.* (1819) II. 216 Unlesse it be, that we designe to truckle under France. *a* **1704** T. BROWN *Praise Poverty* Wks. 1730 I. 92 Publick good is made to truckle to private gain. **1738** tr. *Guazzo's Art Conversation* 66 Where Sense imperious bears the Sway, Reason must truckle and obey.

b. To submit from an unworthy motive; to yield meanly or obsequiously; to act with servility. Const. *down*, *to* a person, *for* an object.

1680 C. NESSE *Church-Hist.* 285 His sordid spirit truckles and crouches. *a* **1715** EARL HALIFAX *Man of Hon.* Poems (1779) 226 Those that meanly truckle to your power. **1789** PARR *Tracts Warburton*, etc. 184, He was..too proud to truckle to a Superior. **1809** —— *Char. Fox* Wks. 1828 IV. 111 Ambition..which..truckles for office by the barter of principle. **1842** THACKERAY *Miss Tickletoby* ix, These nobles..were the first to truckle down to him when he came to assert..his right. **1858** FROUDE *Hist. Eng.* III. xiv. 223 The short years which might have been his, had he..denied his faith and truckled to the time. **1885** R. L. & F. STEVENSON *Dynamiter* i, Doubtful people of all sorts and conditions begging and truckling for your notice.

c. To submit or give way timidly; in quot. 1840, to quail, cower, be daunted.

1837 CAMPBELL *Hybrias* i, With these I make..all around me truckle. **1840** DICKENS *Barn. Rudge* xxiii, Hugh truckled before the hidden meaning of these words. *a* **1845** HOOD *Jack Hall* xii, To my commands The strongest truckles.

†**3.** *trans.* To cause to truckle. *Obs. rare*$^{-1}$.

1687 *Good Advice* 9 They..compell men to truckle their tender Consciences to the Grandure and Dominion of their Doctors.

†**4.** *intr.* and *trans.* To move on truckles or castors; = TRUNDLE *v.* 3 a, b. *Obs.*

1656 [see TRUCKLING *ppl. a.*]. **1796** MME. D'ARBLAY *Camilla* III. xiii, Tables with two legs, and chairs without bottoms, were truckled from the middle to one end of the room.

¶**5.** *intr.* To traffic, deal. = TRUCK *v.*^{1} 5, 5 b. Const. *with*. *rare.*

1806 FELLOWES tr. *Milton's 2nd Defence* (1848) 293 Those money-changers..do not merely truckle with doves, but with the Dove itself, with the Spirit of the Most High. **1909** *Q. Rev.* July 284 He declined to truckle with any practices tending, as he thought, towards Rome.

truckle, obs. form of TRICKLE *v.*

'truckle-bed. [TRUCKLE *sb.* 2.] A low bed running on truckles or castors, usually pushed beneath a high or 'standing' bed when not in use; a trundle-bed. So **truckle bedstead**.

1459 *Stat. Magd. Coll. Oxf.* xlv, Sint duo lecti principales, et duo lecti rotales, Trookyll beddys vulgariter nuncupati. **1531** in *Rec. St. Mary at Hill* 45 Item, an olde lytell coueryng for a lytell Trokell bed. **1597** BP. HALL *Sat.* II. vi. 5 First that He lie vpon the Truckle-bed, Whiles his yong maister lieth ore his hed. **1598** SHAKS. *Merry W.* IV. v. 6 There's his Chamber, his House, his Castle, his standing-bed and truckle-bed. **1662** PEPYS *Diary* 1 May, To bed all alone, and my Will in the truckle bed. **1755** SMOLLETT *Quix.* (1803) IV. 273 Sancho slept that night in a truckle-bed, in the apartment of Don Quixote. **1807** SIR R. C. HOARE *Tour Irel.* 302 Numbers [of peasants]..have not a bedstead, nor even what is called a truckle bed frame. **1831** CARLYLE *Sart. Res.* I. iii, Wretchedness cowers into truckle-beds, or shivers hunger-stricken into its lair of straw. **1895** RIDER HAGGARD *Heart of World* vii, A few chairs, a rough washing-stand, and two truckle bedsteads of American make.

truckler ('trʌklə(r)). [f. TRUCKLE *v.* + -ER^1.] One who truckles (in sense 2 b of the verb).

1827 SCOTT *Napoleon* Introd. Wks. 1870 IX. 31 These trucklers to fortune. **1848** KINGSLEY *Saint's Trag.* III. iii, The wonder Of timid trucklers. **1872** GEO. ELIOT *Middlem.* xliv, I should be a base truckler if I allowed any consideration of personal comfort to hinder me.

truckling ('trʌklɪŋ), *vbl. sb.* [f. TRUCKLE *v.* + -ING^1.] The action of the verb TRUCKLE; mean submission.

c **1665** MRS. HUTCHINSON *Mem. Col. Hutchinson* (1846) 475, I am free from any truckling with them. **1820** L. HUNT *Indicator* No. 55 (1822) II. 22 He had a grudge against Milton for what he called his trucklings about Pandæmonium. **1848** THACKERAY *Bk. Snobs* iii, The habit of truckling and cringing. **1888** BURGON *Lives 12 Gd. Men.* I. ii. 140 The base truckling of an ungodly age, ever ready to surrender what is unpopular.

'truckling, *ppl. a.* [f. as prec. + -ING^2.] That truckles; †that is subordinate or inferior (*obs.*); meanly submissive, servile.

1656 [see *standing-stool*, STANDING *vbl. sb.* 11]. **1665** TEMPLE *Let. to Ld. Arlington* Wks. 1731 II. 6 Their last Resourse, which is the Protection of France,..or else a perfect truckling Peace with England. **1701** SWIFT *Contests Nobles & Com. Athens & Rome* ii, A small truckling state, of no name or reputation. **1728** RAMSAY *Epist. to Burchet* v, The like of you..Should gar the trockling rogues look blue. **1796** BURKE *Regic. Peace* i. Wks. VIII. 87 In small truckling states a timely compromise with power has often been the means..of drawling out their puny existence. **1823** SCOTT *Peveril* xvii, Unworthy or truckling compliance with tenets which my heart disowns. **1868** FARRAR *Silence & V.* iii. (1875) 64 Our beloved English Church..may, even yet, be unable to escape..the Nemesis..due to the sluggish impotence and truckling worldliness of her 18th Century.

Hence **'trucklingly** *adv.*, in a truckling manner.

1831 *Fraser's Mag.* III. 605 He would joyfully, thankfully, trucklingly accept it. **1857** *Tait's Mag.* XXIV. 30, I could conceive women..unhappy; but not meanly, timidly, trucklingly miserable.

trucks (trʌks). *Obs.* exc. *Hist.* Also (? *erron.*) 7–8 **truck.** [ad. It. *trucco* (see below), Sp. *troco*.] An early form of billiards, in which an upright mark called the king was placed near one end of the table. Cf. TROLL-MADAM and TRUNK *sb.* 16.

[Cf. **1598** FLORIO, *Truccare*,..to play at billiards. *Trucco*, a kinde of play with balles vpon a table called billiards, but properly a kinde of game vsed in England with casting little bowles at a boord with thirteene holes in it.]

1671 SKINNER *Etymol.*, *Truck*, Biliers or Biliards. **1674** COTTON (*title*) The Compleat Gamester: or, Instructions how to play at Billiards, Trucks, Bowls, and Chess. **1688** R. HOLME *Armoury* III. 263/1 *Truck*, is an Italian Game, and is not very unlike Billiards, the Table..hath 3 holes at each end, besides the corner holes. **1736** AINSWORTH *Lat. Dict.*, Truck (the play), *ludus tudicularis*. **1801** STRUTT *Sports & Past.* IV. i. §16 The Italian method of playing, known in England by the name of Trucks,..had its king at one end of the table.

truckster ('trʌkstə(r)). *rare.* [f. TRUCK *v.*^{1} + -STER.] A base trafficker; cf. TRUCK *v.*^{1} 3.

1843 *Knickerbocker* XXII. 38 All relics of a former age.. exposed for sale in the windows of the trucksters. **1868** TUCKERMAN *Collector* 83 Many a poet..has degenerated into a hack, a truckster, and a mercenary penman. **1916** H. J. LASKI in *Holmes-Laski Lett.* (1953) I. 40 It gets very nauseating to have the measure of progress taken as a commercial truckster might measure it. **1931** A. UTTLEY *Country Child* v. 69 He had a pack on his back containing.. all the odds and ends of the truckster.

truculence ('tru:k-, 'trʌkjʊləns). [ad. L. *truculentia* savageness, ferocity, f. *truculentus* TRUCULENT: see -ENCE.] The condition or quality of being truculent; fierceness, savageness.

1727 BAILEY vol. II, *Truculence*, *Truculentness*, cruelty, savageness, sternness. **1877** D. M. WALLACE *Russia* vi. 83 The entire absence of obsequiousness or truculence in his manner. **1890** GLADSTONE *Sp. Ho. Comm.* 28 Nov., He sometimes accompanies the temperance of language with a truculence of action.

truculency ('tru:k-, 'trʌkjʊlənsɪ). [f. as prec.: see -ENCY.] = prec.

1569 J. SANFORD tr. *Agrippa's Van. Artes* 111 The truculencie of the Beare. **1630** BRATHWAIT *Eng. Gentlem.* (1641) 88 It was Saint Augustine's prayer unto God that he would root out of him all..truculencie. **1855** MILMAN *Lat. Chr.* XIV. iv. (1864) IX. 188 They have more of Juvenal..of his pitilessness, of his bitterness, it may be said of his truculency, than of Catullus. **1864** CARLYLE *Fredk. Gt.* XVII. v. IV. 556 Friedrich's First Campaign..will by no means check the Austrian truculencies.

truculent ('tru:k-, 'trʌkjʊlənt), *a.* [ad. L. *truculentus*, f. *trux* (*truc-em*) fierce, savage; cf. obs. F. *truculent* (Cotgr. 1611).]

1. Characterized by or exhibiting ferocity or cruelty; fierce, cruel, savage, barbarous.

c **1540** tr. *Pol. Verg. Eng. Hist.* (Camden) I. 105 Havinge attained libertie, [Britain] entered into moste truculent warrs. **1607** TOPSELL *Four-f. Beasts* (1658) 10 His aspect and countenance was fierce, truculent, and fearful. *Ibid.* 254 Many Horses by their seed and stones are made very fierce, truculent, and unruly. **1670** BAXTER *Cure Ch.-Div.* 4 It is the character of a truculent people..that they regard not the person of the old. **1722** WOLLASTON *Relig. Nat.* vi. 141 Convulsed and agonizing under the knife of some truculent villain. **1889** JESSOPP *Coming of Friars* i. 4 The truculent ruffianism that pretended to be animated by the crusading spirit.

b. Of speech or writing: Violent; rude; scathing; savage; harsh.

1850 MARSDEN *Early Purit.* (1853) 204 Pamphlets.. scarcely less truculent or less contemptuous of the Christian virtues. **1868** MILMAN *St. Paul's* xvii. 416 The broader and more truculent satire of Ulrich Hutten. **1872** MORLEY *Voltaire* iii. (ed. 2) 120 Voltaire is never either gross or truculent.

†**c.** *transf.* Of a disease: Destructive; deadly. *Obs. rare.*

1665 G. HARVEY *Advice agst. Plague* x, More or less truculent Plagues.

¶**2.** (In catachrestic use, associated with TRUCK *sb.*^{1}, *v.*^{1}, TRUCKLE *v.*) Mean, base, mercenary.

1825 BENTHAM *Ration. Rew.* 62 A truculent exchange not only of truth, but of sincerity, for money. **1884** J. T. DAVIDSON *Talks Yng. Men* viii, The mean dastard [Ahab] sent back the truculent reply: 'My lord, O king, according to thy saying, I am thine, and all that I have'.

3. Comb., as ***truculent-looking***.

1828 SCOTT *F.M. Perth* xvii, This ungainly and truculent-looking savage. **1866** HOWELLS *Venet. Life* viii, That truculent-looking craft.

So †**trucu'lental** *a. Obs. rare*$^{-1}$.

1593 G. HARVEY *Pierce's Super.* ***j, A glorious, and brauing Knight, That would be deem'd a truculental wight.

'truculently (see the adj.), *adv.* [f. TRUCULENT + -LY^2.] In a truculent manner; savagely.

1654 VILVAIN *Epit. Ess.* I. 86 Most truculently butchered. **1837** CARLYLE *Misc. Ess., Diam. Neckl.* xiv. (1872) V. 186 How fares it with his Eminence..at times truculently stamping? **1868** M. E. G. DUFF *Pol. Surv.* 179 Often beaten ..from the firm land, he always returned again, truculently fought again.

So **'truculentness** (*rare*$^{-0}$) = TRUCULENCE.

1727 [see TRUCULENCE].

†**'truddle**, obs. form of TREADLE.

1667 in Pettus *Fodinæ Reg.* (1670) 37 One large new Wheel, that carrieth three Pair of bellows, with Swords, Beams, Truddles.

Trudeaumania (tru:dəʊ'meɪnɪə). [f. the name of Pierre Elliott *Trudeau* (b. 1919), former Prime Minister of Canada + -MANIA.] Enthusiastic or exaggerated admiration for Trudeau.

1968 *Listener* 4 July 5/1 With the phenomenal climb to power of Mr Trudeau a tremendous cult has developed among younger Canadians. It's known as Trudeaumania or Trudolatry. **1971** *Maclean's Mag.* Oct. 28/1 Far more accomplished than Pierre Trudeau, who merely observed the phenomena named Trudeaumania and was shrewd enough to take advantage of it. **1976** *Time* 22 Mar. 32/1 Trudeaumania has long since faded away in Canada.

trudge (trʌdʒ), *v.*^{1} Also 6 tredge, 6–7 (8–9 *dial.*) tridge, 7 trug. [Of obscure origin. Skeat suggests F. *trucher* to beg from laziness (in Oudin, 16th c.), but this does not agree in sense.]

1. *intr.* To walk laboriously, wearily, or without spirit, but steadily and persistently; 'to jog on; to march heavily on' (J.). Sometimes merely an undignified equivalent of 'walk', 'go on foot'.

1547 *Bk. Marchauntes* e j b, If the belles rynge in any place ..for an obit, than oure gentyl gallants trudge apace. *c* **1550** in Strype *Mem. Cranmer* (1694) App. xlix. 138 Some of their carcases standith on the gates, And their heads..on London bridge, Therefore, ye Traytors, beware your pates, For yf ye be founde, the same way must ye tridge. **1573** TUSSER *Husb.* (1878) 21 Good husband he trudgeth, to bring in the gaines, Good huswife she drudgeth, refusing no paines. **1622** MABBE tr. *Aleman's Guzman d'Alf.* I. 219, I..trugg'd along with my sore legge. **1685** EVELYN *Mrs. Godolphin* (1888) 122 Wherever a certaine Lady goes,—I must trudge. **1709–10** STEELE *Tatler* No. 137 ⁋3, I was the other Day trudging along Fleet street on Foot. **1795** WOLCOTT (P. Pindar) *Royal Visit Exeter* II. xi, Now tridg'd to aldermen and may'r, 'Squire Rolle. **1856** R. A. VAUGHAN *Mystics* (1860) II. xi. i. 216 From house to house he trudges in the snow, visiting poor widows. **1880** L. OLIPHANT *Gilead* i. 18 We were perpetually meeting them trudging behind their loaded mules.

b. Also with *it*.

1649 G. DANIEL *Trinarch., Hen. V*, clxxxv, The Ragged Squad..will trudge it out And Combat all the world, if Harrie lead. **1787** *Minor* IV. i. 203 So my mentor and I trudged it on foot to Oxford. **1806** SURR *Winter in Lond.* I. 194 Give me your arm, we'll trudge it.

c. *spec.* To go away, be off, depart.

1547–64 BAULDWIN *Mor. Philos.* (Palfr.) 77 The cowardly ..souldier..betaketh him to his feete, & trudgeth away. **1562** *Jack Juggler* (1873) 50 Be tredging, or in faith you bere me a souse. **1573** *New Custom* I. ii, Hence out of my sight, away, packing, trudge. **1623–34** FLETCHER & MASS. *Lover's Progr.* I. ii, 'Tis time for me to trudge. **1824** SCOTT *Let. to Ld. Montagu* 14 Apr., in *Lockhart*, A dog of a banker has bought his house.., and I fear he must trudge.

d. *fig.*

1573 TUSSER *Husb.* (1878) 177 If pennie for all thing be suffred to trudge, Trust long, not to pennie, to haue him thy drudge. **1575** R. B. *Appius & Virg.* B iij b, By beuty of Virginia, my wisdome all is trudged. **1683** KENNETT tr. *Erasm. on Folly* 54 Trudging after learning. **1763** JEFFERSON *Corr.* Wks. 1859 I. 185 All things here appear to me to trudge on in one and the same round. **1856** J. RICHARDSON *Recoll.* I. iv. 86 [The other masters at Eton] trudged leisurely on in the beaten track of school literature.

2. *trans.* **a.** To perform (a journey) or travel over (a distance) by trudging; to tramp; to trudge along or over.

1635 PAGITT *Christianogr.* 190 They..are constrained to trudge no small journeyes, to begge their wages. **1884** BROWNING *Ferishtah, Two Camels* 37, I shall trudge The distance. **1886** HALL CAINE *Son of Hagar* III. iii, Drayton.. trudged the floor uneasily.

b. To trudge with (a burden); to drag *about*.

1883 W. H. BISHOP in *Harper's Mag.* Mar. 504/2 A few old men trudge about their bake-ovens and water jars and strings of dried squash.

3. The vb.-stem used *advb.*: cf. TRAMP *v.*^{1} 7.

1904 MAX PEMBERTON *Red Morn* xx, Trudge, trudge, trudge upon the muddy path she went.

Hence **'trudging** *vbl. sb.* and *ppl. a.*; also **'trudger**^{1}, one who trudges.

a **1849** H. COLERIDGE *Poems* (1850) II. 379 Dear..To weary *trudger by the long black lake. **1896** *Blackw. Mag.* Feb. 224 The steadiest trudger along life's road. **1570** *Marr. Wit & Science* v. iii, Such *trudging and such toyle..was neuer seene. **1653** MILTON *Hirelings* Wks. 1851 V. 369 To save them the trudging of many miles thither. **1728** MORGAN *Algiers* I. Pref. 15 My Trudgings have been so misguided, by an Ignis Fatuus. **1828** P. CUNNINGHAM *N.S. Wales* (ed. 3) II. 197 After three hard weeks of toilsome trudging over rugged hills. **1584** R. SCOT *Discov. Witchcr.* XIV. viii. (1886) 310 He set forward on his journey a good trudging pase. **1716** GAY *Trivia* I. 118 The griping Broker ..laughs at Honesty, and trudging Wits. **1848** DICKENS *Dombey* xviii, His trudging wife..loiters to see the company come out.

trudge, *v.*^{2}: see TRUDGEN.

trudge (trʌdʒ), *sb.* [f. TRUDGE *v.*^{1}]

1. A person who trudges; a trudger.

1748 SMOLLETT *Rod. Rand.* xxx, Nor would he be a tennis-ball, nor a shuttle-cock, nor a trudge, nor a scullion.

1775 JEKYLL *Corr.* (1894) 22 Miss would have felt the absence of her fellow-trudge in clambering stiles and scrambling through hedges.

2. An act of trudging; a laborious or wearisome walk; a 'tramp'.

1835 J. BROWN *Lett.* (1907) 32 You say nothing of your body and how it fared in your darkness trudge. **1871** L. STEPHEN *Playgr. Eur.* iv. III. 257 We reached the mule track, and a steady trudge along it led us back.

†**3.** (Meaning uncertain: ? error for *thrutch.*)

1579 LYLY *Euphues* (Arb.) 137 One thing said twice (as we say commonly) deserveth a trudge.

†**trudge,** *a. Obs. rare*⁻¹. [f. as prec.] ? That trudges (as in service or attendance upon one).

1602 F. HERING *Anat.* 14 Those old Suresbies and Trudge blew-coats, Antimony and Mercury Precipitate.

trudge-man, obs. variant of TRUCHMAN.

trudgen ('trʌdʒən). Also *erron.* trudgeon. [f. proper name *Trudgen*: see below.] In full ***trudgen stroke***: applied to a kind of hand-over-hand or double over-arm breast-stroke in swimming: so ***trudgen swimmer***. Hence **trudge** *v.*³, *intr.* to swim with this stroke; whence **'trudger²**.

1893 *Westm. Gaz.* 3 Oct. 5/2 Thompson adopted the old-fashioned 'trudgeon' stroke in his spurt. **1902** J. A. JARVIS *Swimming* vi. 35 The best trudgen swimmers use a similar, though shorter leg kick, to that made when swimming over arm. *Ibid.*, I am firmly convinced that the present records at all distances will be wiped out, and fresh ones put in their place by 'trudgers'. **1904** RALPH THOMAS *Swimming* 40 Hand-over-hand or Indian stroke. In this each hand (or arm) is alternately raised above the surface of the water, thrust forward and brought sharply back under water to the loins. There are many varieties, one of which is called the trudgen. *Ibid.* 418 *note*, John Trudgen..in 1863..went to Buenos Ayres... While there he learnt 'to trudge' from the natives. **1905** *N. & Q.* 10th Ser. IV. 205/1 The trudgeon-stroke..appears to date from 1868, when it was popularized by a Mr. Trudgen.

trudgeon ('trʌdʒən). *rare*⁻¹. [App. nonce-wd. f. TRUDGE *v.*¹] ? One who trudges; a toddling child.

1814 W. IRVING in *Life & Lett.* (1864) I. 308 To take holiday and go to the country with his wife and little trudgeons.

trudger¹, ²: see after TRUDGE *v.*¹, TRUDGEN.

true (tru:), *a.* (*sb.*, *adv.*). Forms: *α.* 1 (ʒe)tríewe), 1–3 tréowe, 1–4 trýwe, 3 treouwe, 3–4 triwe, 3–7 trewe, trew, 4–7 treu, 5 treewe, triew(e. *β.* 3 (*Orm.*) trowwe, 5 trowe, 5–6 trow; 5 traw. *γ.* 3–5 truwe, 4–5 trwe, 4–7 tru, 6 trw, 5– true. [OE. (strict WS. (*ʒe*)*tríewe*, commonly *tréowe* (ME. also *truwe*) = OS. (*gi*)*trûui*, OEFris. *triuwe*, OWFris. *trouwe*, (MDu. (*ghe*)*trûwe*, (*ghe*)*trouwe*, Du. *getrouw*), OHG. (*ga*)*triuwu*, (Ger. *treu*), ON. *tryggr*, Goth. *triggws*; repr. WGer. **trewwj-*, lit. 'having or characterized by good faith', deriv. of the sb. which is represented by OE. *tréow*, *trúw*, OHG. *triuwa*, Goth. *triggwa* faith, covenant: see TRUCE.]

A. *adj.* **1. a.** Of persons: Steadfast in adherence to a commander or friend, to a principle or cause, to one's promises, faith, etc.; firm in allegiance; faithful, loyal, constant, trusty. Somewhat *arch.*

a **1000** *St. Guthlac* 1269 (Gr.) Se wuldormaʒo..spræc..to his treowum ʒesiðe. *c* **1205** LAY. 8851 Mildeliche spæc þus þe treowe cniht Androgeus. *c* **1250** *Hymn Virg.* 2 in *Trin. Coll. Hom.* App. 257 þu ert leuedi swuþe treowe..þi loue is euer iliche neowe. **1303** R. BRUNNE *Handl. Synne* 2320 May y þan trust to þy sawe þat þou be now my trew felawe? **1388** WYCLIF *Luke* xvi. 10 He that is trewe in the leeste thing, is trewe also in the more. **1450–80** tr. *Secreta Secret.* 19 Kepe wel thi feith and thi word euermore..gret worshipe vnto hem þat so trewe are founden in here feith. **1476** *Surtees Misc.* (1888) 35 To all trewe Christen men. *a* **1533** LD. BERNERS *Huon* xcv. 307 Ye haue done as a trew subjet ought to do to his lorde. **1646** *Hamilton Papers* (Camden) 119 Your Grace's humblest truest seruant, R. Moray. **1821** SHELLEY *Bridal Song* i, Never smiled the inconstant moon On a pair so true. **1847** TENNYSON *Princess* iv. 80 Bright and fierce and fickle is the South, And dark and true and tender is the North.

b. *transf.* of personal attributes or actions. Somewhat *arch.*; often passing into sense 2 or 5.

a **800** [see TRUE-LOVE 1]. *c* **1200** ORMIN Introd. 69 Trigg & trowwe griþþ & friþþ. *c* **1275** *Passion our Lord* 45 in *O.E. Misc.* 38 Alle men he tauhte to holde treowe luue Erest to god almyhti. **13..** *Cursor M.* 4422 (Gött.) Ille es þe quit þi treu seruis. **1454** *Cal. Anc. Rec. Dublin* (1889) 281 That they shall do trewe execucion. *c* **1560** A. SCOTT *Poems* (S.T.S.) ix. 14 Ane trewar hairt may no man haif. **1667** MILTON *P.L.* III. 104 What proof could they have givn..Of true allegiance? **1832** TENNYSON *Miller's Dau.* 216 Round my true heart thine arms entwine.

c. Const. *to* (in early use with simple dative).

Beowulf (Z.) 1165 Æʒ-hwylc oðrum trywe. *c* **1200** ORMIN 6177 þin laferrd birrþ þe buhsumm beon & hold & trigg & trowwe. *c* **1350** *Will. Palerne* 596 And be tristy and trew to ȝow for euer-more. *c* **1400** *Trevisa's Higden* (Rolls) V. 447 (MS. *γ*) þanne doo as þou hast byhote, and be truwe [*v.r.* trewe] to hym þat so haþ þe i-holpe. *a* **1450** *Knt. de la Tour* (1906) 97, Y haue founde you..not true vnto me. **1583** MELBANCKE *Philotimus* E ej, I will bee as true to thee as the begger to his dishe. **1602** SHAKS. *Ham.* I. iii. 78 This aboue all; to thine owne selfe be true:..Thou canst not then be false to any man. **1678** WANLEY *Wond. Lit. World* v. ii. §82. 472/2 A Prince more just and true to his word. *a* **1721** PRIOR *Song 'Still, Dorinda'* iv, To my vows I have been true. **1849** MACAULAY *Hist. Eng.* ii. I. 258 Hyde had been true to his Tory opinions. **1855** *Ibid.* xi. III. 1 True..to the cause of civil freedom.

d. *fig.* of things: Reliable; constant; †sure, secure (*obs.*).

c **1205** [see TRULY 1 b]. *c* **1330** R. BRUNNE *Chron.* (1810) 73 þe pes to ȝeme & gyue with lawes trewe als stele. *c* **1425** *Cursor M.* 59 (Trin.) For whenne þou wenest hit trewest [*v.r.* truyst] to be, þou shalt from hit or hit from þe. *a* **1733** BARTON BOOTH *Song, 'Sweet are the charms of her I love'* ii, True as the Needle to the Pole, Or as the Dial to the Sun. **1791** COWPER *Iliad* vi. 60 Steel Of truest temper. **1872** DORA GREENWELL *Liber Hum.* (1875) 209 To the rock the root adheres, In every fibre true.

2. In more general sense: Honest, honourable, upright, virtuous, trustworthy (*arch.*); free from deceit, sincere, truthful (cf. 3 d); of actions, feelings, etc., sincere, unfeigned (now passing into or merged in 5). See also TRUEMAN.

a **1012** *Laws of Ethelred* III. c. 9 Buton he habbe tweʒra trywra manna ʒewitnesse. *c* **1200** *Vices & Virt.* 45 Be trewe mann and halt tin god. *a* **1225** *Ancr. R.* 2 þeos riwle is cherité of schir heorte and cleane inwit, and trewe bileaue. **1297** R. GLOUC. (Rolls) 859 Men triwest [*v.r.* trewest] we [*v.r.* me] seþ And best me mai to hom truste þat of lest wordes beþ. *c* **1380** WYCLIF *Eng. Wks.* (1880) 321 As lif of a trew plow man..is betere preyere to god þen preyere of any ordre þat god loueþ lesse. *c* **1385** CHAUCER *L.G.W.* 464 (*Balade*) A trewe man..Hath nat to parte with a theuys dede. **1446** LYDG. *Two Night. Poems* ii. 69 Triewe meanyng rooted so withynne, Fer from the conceyte of any maner synne. *c* **1460** FORTESCUE *Abs. & Lim. Mon.* xiii. (1885) 141, iij. or iiij. theves..haue sett apon vj. or vij. trewe men, and robbed hem all. **1484** CAXTON *Fables of Alfonce* ii, He is..reputed..for a good man and trewe. **1599** SHAKS. *Much Ado* I. i. 27 There are no faces truer, then those that are so wash'd, how much better is it to weepe at ioy, then to ioy at weeping? **1611** BIBLE *Gen.* xlii. 11 We are true men: thy seruants are no spies. *c* **1614** SIR W. MURE *Dido & Æneas* I. 715 Her waxen heart, touch't with a trew remorse. **1710** ADDISON *Tatler* No. 250 ¶8 Good Men and true for a Petty Jury. **1847** HELPS *Friends in C.* I. 8 A true man does not think what his hearers are feeling, but what he is saying. **1865** DICKENS *Mut. Fr.* III. v, Your own father has not a truer interest in you.

3. a. Of a statement or belief: Consistent with fact; agreeing with the reality; representing the thing as it is.

c **1205** LAY. 4443 Belin ihærde sugge þurh summe sæȝ treowe Of his broðer wifðinge. **1382** WYCLIF *John* xxi. 24 We witen, for [**1388** that] his witnessing is trewe. **1393** LANGL. *P. Pl.* C. I. 100 Al þe world wot wel hit myȝte nat be trywe. *c* **1489** CAXTON *Sonnes of Aymon* xvii. 396 'Syr, wyte that charlemagne is come wyth his oost'... 'Is it true?' said mawgis. *a* **1529** SKELTON *Dk. Albany* 4 These tidinges newe Whiche be as trewe As the gospell. *a* **1584** MONTGOMERIE *Cherrie & Slae* 1018, I..Thocht all thair tales was trew. **1608** WILLET *Hexapla Exod.* 839 The truer opinion. **1710** BINGHAM *Chr. Antiq.* xx. vii. §10 The fact was too true, and the charge too well-grounded, to be denied of them all in general. **1759** JOHNSON *Rasselas* xlvii, The same proposition cannot be at once true and false. **1858** LARDNER *Handbk. Nat. Phil.*, etc. 16 This will be true, however shallow the vessel..and however narrow the tube.

b. Often in phr. ***it is true*** (also inverted, ***true it is***), introducing a statement; also ellipt. or interjectionally, *true*, introducing or in reply to a statement; usually in concessive sense: = truly, verily, certainly, doubtless.

1594 T. B. *La Primaud. Fr. Acad.* II. 13 True it is, that we haue now taken in hand a very long piece of worke. **1604** SHAKS. *Oth.* I. iii. 79 That I haue tane away this old mans Daughter, It is most true: true I haue married her. **1611** BIBLE *Dan.* iii. 24 They answered and said vnto the king: True, O king. **1724** DE FOE *Mem. Cavalier* (1840) 173 It is true, we were all but young in the War. **1784** COWPER *Task* III. 210 True; I am no proficient, I confess, In arts like yours. **1859** RUSKIN *Two Paths* i. §1 It is true that the art which carves and colours the front of a Swiss cottage is not of any very exalted kind; yet [etc.].

c. ***come true***: to be verified or realized in actual experience; to be fulfilled. ***hold true***: see HOLD *v.* 23 c.

1819 SHELLEY *Questions* 7 To patch up fragments of a dream, Part of which comes true. **1875** MORRIS *Æneid* VIII. 580 While yet my fear is unfulfilled, and hope may yet come true. **1879** M. J. GUEST *Lect. Hist. Eng.* xxi. 206 His prophecy had come true.

d. *transf.* Speaking truly, telling the truth; trustworthy in statement; veracious, truthful. (Not always distinguishable from 2.) Also *fig.*

a **1300** *Cursor M.* 6599 (Cott.) All er yee tru, þis es your saghes, Es nan of yow þat þis calf knaues. *c* **1440** *Promp. Parv.* 503/2 Truwe mann, or woman, *verax*. *c* **1460** *Towneley Myst.* vii. 77 That thay be traw of thare tong, And bere no fals witnes. **1526** TINDALE *Matt.* xxii. 16 Master, we knowe that thou arte true, and that thou teachest the waye of god trueli. **1611** BIBLE *Prov.* xiv. 25 A true witnesse deliuereth soules: but a deceitfull witnesse speaketh lyes. **1634** MILTON *Comus* 170 This way the noise was, if mine ear be true. **1697** DRYDEN *Virg. Past.* II. 33 If the Glass be true, With Daphnis I may vie. **1850** TENNYSON *In Mem.* lxxxv. 5 O true in word, and tried in deed.

e. Phr. ***true for you*** [after Ir. *is fíor duit*]: an expression of assent to something said by another. (Stressed on *for.*) *Anglo-Ir.*

1835 R. M. BIRD *Hawks of Hawk-Hollow* I. xix. 247 'You are Tapes, the pedler.'.. 'True for you, captain Gilbert!' cried the other, with a stare. **1901** J. BARLOW *From Land of Shamrock* 63 They would not, thrue for you. **1980** J. O'FAOLAIN *No Country for Young Men* xv. 329 You're right there... True for you.

f. Purporting to be true. Freq. in collocations used *attrib.* to designate popular magazines which contain (remarkable) stories which purport to be true, as ***true confessions, story***; also ***true-life story***, etc.

1926 A. HUXLEY *Jesting Pilate* IV. 260 He walked up and down the train..peddling..True Story Magazines. **1937** [see *pulp magazine* s.v. PULP *sb.* 5 c]. **1957** C. MACINNES *City of Spades* II. x. 170 Barbara was..reading a 'true story' magazine. **1958** *Times Lit. Suppl.* 7 Feb. 72/3 She writes well, and—somewhat unusually for a social worker—quotes poetry. She seasons her facts with many 'true-life' stories. **1965** M. SPARK *Mandelbaum Gate* vii. 303 Love, love-affairs, men and women and true-life stories formed the daily entertainment and talk of their week's travelling. **1967** 'T. WELLS' *What should you know of Dying?* ii. 30 [She] was reading a true confessions magazine. I didn't think they even printed them any more.

g. Colloq. phr. *so* (..) ***it isn't true*** and varr.: to an almost incredible extent.

1963 *Daily Herald* 25 Apr. 7/6 The Princess was so calm it wasn't true. She was so relaxed. **1964** 'A. GARVE' *Ashes of Loda* i. 14 He's..so incompetent about ordinary day-to-day living it's just not true. **1970** R. RENDELL *Guilty Thing Surprised* ix. 103 You may be only thirty-six but you're so dead old-fashioned it isn't true. **1982** BARR & YORK *Official Sloane Ranger Handbk.* 8/1 Sloane Britain is so heavily weighted towards the South and the West it's not true.

4. a. Agreeing with a standard, pattern, or rule; exact, accurate, precise; correct, right.

c **1550** CHEKE *Matt.* x. 5 (1843) 46 An Apostol, if ye wold have yᵉ trutorn of yᵉ naam is as much to sai as a frosent. **1570** DEE *Math. Pref.* a iv b, Of the Variacion of the Compas, from true North. **1583** STUBBES *Anat. Abus.* II. (1882) 77 Such as can scarcely read true English. **1651** HOBBES *Leviath.* III. xxxv. 217 The truest Translation is the first. **1674** RAY *Collect. Words, Smelting Silver* 114 Where the furnace is come to a true temper of heat. *a* **1721** PRIOR *Protogenes & Apelles* 54 Apelles drew A Circle regularly true. **1782** COWPER *Gilpin* 72 He..hung a bottle on each side To make his balance true. **1822** IMISON *Sc. & Art* I. 98 Clocks and watches..so regulated as to measure true equal time. **1850** TENNYSON *In Mem.* xcvi. 8 One indeed I knew ..Who touch'd a jarring lyre at first, But ever strove to make it true.

b. In more general sense: Of the right kind, such as it should be, proper. (Cf. 5.)

1340–70 *Alex. & Dind.* 513 þat þou miht trystli trye þe treweste lawe... þat þou miht..þe beste lawe kenne. **1435** *Coventry Leet Bk.* 182 Yif the cardwiredrawer were.. disseyued withe ontrewe wire..then wold he sey vnto the smythier..'Sir, amende your honde, or, in feithe, I wille no more bye of you'. And then the smythier, lest he lost his Custemers, wolde make true goode. *c* **1600** SHAKS. *Sonn.* lxii, Me thinkes no face so gratious is.., No shape so true. **1677** YARRANTON *Eng. Improv.* 51 The Land in this Mannor is sound, rich, dry, and good, and that is the true Land to bear Flax. *a* **1770** JORTIN *Serm.* (1771) II. i. 12 To place things in their true order. **1911** H. WACE *Proph. Jew. & Chr.* v. 92 Facts thus placed in their true bearings.

c. That is rightly or lawfully such; rightful, legitimate.

c **1400** *Destr. Troy* 5411 How Thelaphus tide to be treu kyng. **1593** SHAKS. *3 Hen. VI*, I. ii. 23 An Oath is of no moment, being not tooke Before a true and lawfull Magistrate. **1681** DRYDEN *Abs. & Achit.* 921 The true successor from the court removed. **1790** BURKE *Fr. Rev.* 322 By the laws of nature the occupant and subduer of the soil is the true proprietor.

d. Accurately placed, fitted, or shaped; exact in position or form, as an instrument, a part of mechanism, or the like.

1474 *Coventry Leet Bk.* 400 That his weyghtes be sised & sealed and true beme. **1551** RECORDE *Pathw. Knowl.* I. xxiv, More easyly..may you..make any suche line with a true ruler. **1664** BUTLER *Hud.* II. iii. 1019 I'll make them serve for perpendiculars As true as e'er were us'd by bricklayers. **1726** LEONI tr. *Alberti's Archit.* I. 38/2 We must use a Square Rule..of a very large Size, that our strait Lines may be the truer. **1875** *Carpentry & Join.* 43 A strip required to be cut and planed up perfectly true and even on its sides and ends. **1897** PEMBERTON *Compl. Cyclist* 87 A wheel which will remain perfectly true.

e. ***true to***: consistent with, exactly agreeing with, 'faithful to' (cf. 1 c). Also ***true to type***.

a **1735** ARBUTHNOT (J.), A translation nicely true to the original. **1835** *Athenæum* 16 May 372/1 Another character—true to life—is Mrs. Hollis, the fruiterer. **1840** DICKENS *Old C. Shop* i, Be true to your time in the morning. **1872** J. M. LANGFORD *Let.* 11 Mar. in *Geo. Eliot Lett.* (1956) V. 254 One feels them all to be true to life. **1883** MORFILL *Slavonic Lit.* i. 15 The dialects of a language are truer to its spirit than its literary form. **1885** *Athenæum* 23 May 661/2 The incident is very true to life and graphically described. **1929** *Oxford Poetry* 10 Say he died true to type: and then erect A cenotaph; he liked to be select. **1960** *Farmer & Stockbreeder* 1 Mar. 80/2 This was indeed a true-to-type Devon: a good, compact animal with nice fleshing and conformation. **1980** K. FOLLETT *Key to Rebecca* xvii. 193 His preference for 'true-to-life' murders, as opposed to implausible country-house killings.

f. Conformable to reality, natural: = *true to nature*.

1870 HUXLEY *Lay Serm.* i. 1 That truest of fictions, 'The History of the Plague Year'. **1894** S. G. GREEN in *Sunday at H.* June 527, I do not object to fiction provided it be true.

g. Remaining constant to type; not subject to variation. (Cf. C. 3 b.)

1839 DARWIN *Voy. Nat.* viii. (1873) 146 This breed is very true. **1859** —— *Orig. Spec.* iv. (1860) 84 Can we wonder, then, that Nature's productions should be far 'truer' in character than man's productions?

h. Of the wind: Steady, constant, uniform in direction and force.

1894 *Dundee Advertiser* 11 July 6/1 The Britannia was now 400 yards ahead... The wind was continuing true.

i. Of bearings: measured relative to true North.

1834 [see AZIMUTH 2 a]. **1912** [see PROJECTION *sb.* 7 b]. **1969** G. C. DICKINSON *Maps & Air Photographs* viii. 125 Bearings measured relative to true north are called true bearings.

j. Of the ground or other surface prepared for ball games: free from unevenness, level and smooth.

1851 in W. G. Grace *W. G.'s Little Bk.* (1909) i. 5 A man is but half a player who is only prepared for true grounds. **1895** H. G. HUTCHINSON *Golf* (ed. 5) xii. 309 The putting-greens are very good and true. **1934** W. J. LEWIS *Lang. Cricket* 297 It [*sc.* the wicket] is said, with regard to its condition, to be *hard* when firm..*plumb* or *true* when it is perfectly level and the ball behaves normally. **1965** L. R. BENAUD *Young Cricketer* 86/1 Pitches of today seem to have changed from those of Bulli soil days..when..one played on a true, black, shiny strip as hard as concrete.

5. a. Real, genuine; rightly answering to the description; properly so called; not counterfeit, spurious, or imaginary; also, conforming or approaching to the ideal character of such.

1398 TREVISA *Barth. De P.R.* XVI. xlvii. (Bodl. MS.) lf. 176/2 Stones..þat bene fals..seme moste liche..to ham þat bene trew. [*c* **1440** *Promp. Parv.* 503/2 Trvwe, in belevynge, *catholicus*.] *c* **1470** HENRY *Wallace* I. 22 His forbearis..Of hale lynage, and trew lyne of Scotland. **1526** TINDALE *1 John* ii. 8 The darknes is past, and the true lyght nowe shyneth. **1535** COVERDALE *1 John* v. 20 This is the true God, and euerlastinge life. **1562** A. SCOTT *Poems* (S.T.S.) i. 21 Caus his trew Kirk be had in reuerence. **1589** PUTTENHAM *Eng. Poesie* I. xii. (Arb.) 43 Vntrue praise neuer giueth any true reputation. **1680** OTWAY *Orphan* I. i, The World has not A truer Soldier, or a better Subject. **1697** DRYDEN *Virg. Georg.* IV. 598 He turns agen To his true Shape. **1781** COWPER *Truth* 176 True Piety is cheerful as the day. **1828** SCOTT *F.M. Perth* ii, The best armourer that ever made sword, and the truest soldier that ever drew one. **1849** MACAULAY *Hist. Eng.* vi. II. 16 It was thought that the flocks..would soon return to the true fold. **1854** MOSELEY *Astron.* xx. (1874) 93 About the equinox the time of true noon precedes the time of mean noon. **1891** FARRAR *Darkn. & Dawn* liii, You may yet find the true criminals.

b. In scientific use: Conformable to the type, or to the accepted idea or character of the genus, class, or kind; properly or strictly so called.

1578 LYTE *Dodoens* III. lxviii. 408 True Maydenheare, Ladies heare, Venus heare. **1704** F. FULLER *Med. Gymn.* (1711) 201 The true skin, and all its innumerable Glands. **1741** MONRO *Anat. Bones* (ed. 3) 222 The Ribs are commonly divided into True and False. The True Costæ are the seven superior of each Side. **1809** *Med. Jrnl.* XXI. 274 In all cases of true hydrophobia. **1841** *Penny Cycl.* XXI. 415/1 The *Lanianæ*, or true Shrikes. **1855** PHILLIPS *Man. Geol.* 513 Masses of true granite. **1899** *Allbutt's Syst. Med.* VIII. 825 True nerve tumours are exceedingly rare.

c. *true bill* (in *Law*), a bill of indictment found by a Grand Jury to be supported by sufficient evidence to justify the hearing of a case: see BILL *sb.*[3] 4. Hence *allusively*, a true statement or charge (*true* being loosely taken in sense 3).

1591 LAMBARDE *Eiren.* IV. v. 484 An Enditement in their [Jurors'] finding of a Bill of accusation to be true. **1659** *Termes de la Ley* 135 b, *Indictment*..is a Bill..exhibited by way of accusation..and preferred unto Jurors, and by their verdict found presented to be true before a Judge. **1769** BLACKSTONE *Comm.* IV. xxiii. 305 If they [the grand jury] are satisfied of the truth of the accusation, they then endorse upon it, 'a true bill'; antiently, '*billa vera*'. The indictment is then said to be found. **1809** MALKIN *Gil Blas* IX. vi. (Rtldg.) 321 Him they taxed with the plotted massacre, and the bill was a true one. **1852** SMEDLEY *L. Arundel* lii, A true bill, by all that's unlucky!

d. *true left* (or *right*): the side which is on the left (or right) as one looks down from a hill or mountain, or downstream.

1910 J. BUCHAN *Prester John* x. 177 We followed a narrow shelf on its left side (or 'true right', as mountaineers would call it). **1929** —— *Courts of Morning* III. iv. 344 Six men were perched high up among the rocks on the right side (what mountaineers would call the 'true left') of the couloir. **1971** *N.Z. Listener* 19 Apr. 55/2 An acquaintance asked..what the reporter had meant by the 'true left' bank of the river. I explained that it was the one on the lefthand side as you looked downstream.

B. *sb.* (absol. use of the adj.)

†**1. a.** A faithful, loyal, or trusty person; a 'true man'. *Obs.*

13.. *Gaw. & Gr. Knt.* 2354 Trwe mon [= must] trwe restore. *c* **1400** *Destr. Troy* 11976 A! traytor vntrew, how toke þou on honde þat trew to be-tray? *c* **1470** *Golagros & Gaw.* 356 Thus with trety ye cast yon trew vndre tyld.

b. *spec.* Nickname for a member of the Protestant or Whig party in the 17th c.: cf. *true blue* (see BLUE *sb.* 8). *Obs.*

a **1734** NORTH *Exam.* II. v. §68. (1740) 357 Most of the eminent Fanatics in England, with all their Trues and True-blues.

2. *the true*: That which is true; truth, reality.

1812 CRABBE *Tales* xi. 388 If sleep one moment closed the dismal view, Fancy her terrors built upon the true. **1874** GEO. ELIOT *Coll. Breakf. P.* 13 Yearning for that True Which has no qualities.

3. Accurate position or adjustment (in phr. *out of true* or *the true*): cf. sense 4 d above, and TRUTH *sb.* 6. Hence *out-of-true* sb., the extent to which a part is out of exact alignment. Cf. TRUTH *sb.* 6.

1876 J. ROSE *Compl. Pract. Machinist* vi. 86 If the face plate of the lathe is a trifle out of true, the eccentric will only be out to an equal amount. **1890** W. J. GORDON *Foundry* 51 The bottom member would be out of the true as it expanded unequally. **1895** J. T. USHER *Mod. Machinist* xxi. 199 The eccentric is..held on the arbor while it is being turned in precisely the same way as it is held on the crank-shaft or axle of the engine, thereby avoiding the tendency to spring it out of true after it is turned, which often happens when it is held for turning by other means. **1970** K. BALL *Fiat 600, 600D Autobook* vi. 59/1 The out-of-true at bearing seats must not exceed ·0008 inch.

C. *adv.*

1. Faithfully; †honestly; †confidently: = TRULY 1, 2.

1303 R. BRUNNE *Handl. Synne* 1912 Þere ys no solas vndyr heuene..þat shuld a man so moche glew As a gode womman þat loueþ trew. **13..** [see B. 1]. *a* **1425** *Cursor M.* 4913 (Trin.) Þing þat we truly bouȝt And so is oure trewe geten þing. *c* **1470** HENRY *Wallace* I. 86 Ressawide he was and trastyt werray trew. *c* **1555**, **1633** [see *true-dealing, true-meaning*, in D. 2].

2. In accordance with fact; truthfully; rightly: = TRULY 3.

a **1300** *Cursor M.* 18420 (Cott.), I hight þe tru þat þou þis ilk dai sal be..in paradis wit me. *c* **1450** *Merlin* i. 7 The gode woman that spake with me seyde full trewe. **1526** TINDALE *John* xix. 35 He knoweth that he sayth true. **1638** BAKER tr. *Balzac's Lett.* (vol. II.) 142 Tell mee true, Did you not [etc.]? **1711** ADDISON *Spect.* No. 58 ¶13 If he tells me true. **1883** *Athenæum* 17 Feb. 217/1 If report speak true.

3. a. Exactly, accurately, correctly: = TRULY 4.

1530 PALSGR. 698/2 *Sauf vostre grace*, or *saulue vostre grace*, for I fynde bothe, but *saulue* is trewer written. **1660** BLOOME *Archit.* A c, Sima being made true Square. **1687** A. LOVELL tr. *Thevenot's Trav.* I. 35 They shoot at a mark very true with a Bow and Arrow. **1765** WESLEY *Wks.* (1872) XIV. 335, I want the people called Methodists to sing true the tunes..in common use. **1835** SIR J. ROSS *Narr. 2nd Voy.* viii. 119 The wind had continued true north. **1850** LYNCH *Theo. Trin.* xii. 232 Thy love in ours is imaged true As skies in water clear.

b. In agreement with the ancestral type; without variation: in phr. *to breed true*. (Cf. A. 4 g.)

1859 DARWIN *Orig. Spec.* i. (1860) 19 Every race that breeds true. **1868** —— *Anim. & Pl.* I. vii. 242 The Spanish breed has long been known to breed true. **1912** *Chambers's Jrnl.* Dec. 810/2 Each variety breeds 'true' in breeders' parlance. **1967** *Listener* 3 Aug. 142/1 But there are two regularities which are equally impressive: organisms breed true, and their structures are orderly.

4. Really, genuinely; authentically. (Cf. TRULY 5.)

a **1586**, **1847** [see *true-felt, true-heroic*, in D. 2]. **1895** *Daily News* 17 Dec. 5/1 Miss Rushton does not say what paper or letter is true signed.

D. Combinations.

1. The adj. in comb.: **a.** parasynthetic, as *true-blooded*, *-breasted*, *-eyed*, *-paced*, *-souled*, *-spirited*, *-stamped* (having the true stamp, genuine), *-toned*, *-tongued* adjs.: see also TRUE-HEARTED; **b.** with other adjs., as *true-like*, *-seeming*; **c.** with sbs.: **true-metal** *a.*, like that of genuine metal; †**true-stitch**, a kind of embroidery exactly alike on both sides (*obs.*); **true-tongue**, one having a true tongue, a truthful person, truth-teller; †**true-wit** (**tru-witt**), a genuinely witty person, a real 'wit' (*obs.*).

1818 COBBETT *Pol. Reg.* XXXIII. 598 They are more *true-blooded. **1605** *1st Pt. Ieronimo* I. iii, O my *true brested father. **1883** MRS. PLUNKETT in *Harper's Mag.* Jan. 240/2 Some *true-eyed artist. **1588** FRAUNCE *Lawiers Log.* I. ii. 5 Plato..ascribeth truth to God and Gods children, leaving nothing but *truelike to mortall men. **1611** SHAKS. *Cymb.* I. vi. 166 He is one The *truest manner'd. **1868** J. H. BLUNT *Ref. Ch. Eng.* I. 449 This is the *true-metal ring of the Book of Common Prayer. **1648** HERRICK *Hesper.*, *Farewell to Sack* 35 Before they sing Their *true-pac'd numbers. **1590** SPENSER *F.Q.* I. i. 38 The falsest twoo, And fittest for to forge *true-seeming lyes. **1824** MISS MITFORD *Village* Ser. I. (1863) 222 The equally apocryphal but still truer-seeming History of the Plague. **1854** GRACE GREENWOOD *Haps & Mishaps* 37 A *true-souled old man. **1684** OTWAY *Atheist* I. i, A dozen..jolly, *true-spirited..Friends. **1678** DRYDEN *All for Love* I. i, The..rugged Virtue Of an old *true-stampt Roman. **1598** B. JONSON *Case is Altered* II. iii, What, *true-stitch, sister! both your sides alike! **1664** HAWKINS *Youths Behav.* II. 7 True-Stitch, Sattin stitch, Queen-stitch [etc.]. **1907** *Daily Chron.* 21 Nov. 5/3 Her..E flat rang out clear and perfect like a *true-toned bell. **1377** LANGL. *P. Pl.* B. III. 320 Thanne worth *trewe-tonge a tidy man þat tened me neuere. *c* **1369** CHAUCER *Dethe Blaunche* 927 Of eloquence was neuer founde So swete a sownynge facounde, Ne *trewer tonged. **1651** CHARLETON *Ephes. & Cimm. Matrons* II. (1668) 60 Transformed from an Ideot, a Bartholmew-Cokes, a Clown, to a Bon Esprit, a Virtuoso, a *Truwitt.

d. Appositively: **true-false** *a. Educ.* and *Psychol.*, denoting a type of test question constructed so that only the words 'true' or 'false' (or another pair of opposites) are acceptable responses; characterizing a test that uses this technique.

1923 P. B. BALLARD *New Examiner* vii. 80 The new examination comprised three tests, the first of which was of the True-False type. **1957** D. L. BOLINGER in *Publ. Amer. Dial. Soc.* XXVIII. 24 Yes-no Qs are essentially true-false Qs. **1965** N. E. GRONLUND *Measurement & Eval. in Teaching* viii. 127 Some of the variations..deviate considerably from the simple true-false pattern. **1974** in H. G. Macintosh *Techniques & Probl. Assessment* iii. 25 Other word pairs relating to the statement such as 'greater than-less than'..'faster-slower' and so on. It is the possibilities offered by these other pairs which make the true/false form a particularly useful one.

2. The adv. in comb.: **a.** with ppl. adjs., as *true-begotten*, *-dealing*, *-derived*, *-devoted*, *-disposing*, *-divining*, *-felt*, *-made*, *-meaning*, *-meant*, *-ringing*, *-run*, *-speaking*, *-spelling*, *-strung*; see also TRUE-BORN, -BRED; **b.** with other adjs., as *true-heroic*, *-noble*, *-sweet*, *-sublime*.

1596 SHAKS. *Merch. V.* II. ii. 36 O heauens, this is my *true begotten Father. **1708** MRS. CENTLIVRE *Busie Body* I. i, He ..scarce believes there's a true-begotten child in the city. *c* **1555** HARPSFIELD *Divorce Hen. VIII* (Camden) 94 Like an honest *true-dealing man. **1594** SHAKS. *Rich. III*, III. vii. 200 To draw forth your Noble Ancestrie..Vnto a Lineall *true deriued course. **1591** —— *Two Gent.* II. vii. 9 A *true-deuoted Pilgrime is not weary To measure Kingdomes with his feeble steps. **1594** —— *Rich. III*, IV, iv. 55 O vpright, iust, and *true-disposing God. **1588** —— *Tit. A.* II. iii. 214 To proue thou hast a *true diuining heart. *a* **1586** SIDNEY *Arcadia* I. (1622) 40 Such tokens of *true-felt sorrow. **1847** TENNYSON *Princess* Concl., Why Not make her *true-heroic —true-sublime? **1598** DRAYTON *Heroic. Ep.*, *O. Tudor to Q. Cath.* 44 By Frances conquest, and by Englands oth, You are the *true made dowager of both. **1633** T. ADAMS *Exp. 2 Peter* ii. 18 A thief lighting into *true-meaning company. **1603** SHAKS. *Meas. for M.* I. iv. 55 Of an infinite distance From his *true meant designe. **1601** CHESTER *Love's Mart.*, *Poet Ess.* Title-p., The *true-noble Knight. **1907** *Daily Chron.* 23 Feb. 3/2 These *true-ringing, rough-hewn epistles. **1893** *Bailey's Mag.* Oct. 273/1 Was the race a *true-run one? **1570–6** LAMBARDE *Peramb. Kent* (1826) 290 The opinion of any one *true speaking man. **1604** MIDDLETON *Father Hubburd's T.* Wks. (Bullen) VIII. 53 A *true-spelling printer. **1598** SYLVESTER *Du Bartas* II. i. III. *Furies* 55 This mighty World did seem an Instrument *True-strung, well-tun'd. **1593–4** —— *Profit Imprisonm.* 766 That this world's fained sweet..Should be preferr'd before these seeming-sowrs, that make us Taste many *true-sweet sweets. *c* **1600** SHAKS *Sonn.* lxxxii, Thy *true telling friend. **1821** CLARE *Vill. Minstr.* (1823) I. 26 *True-thought legends.

true, *v.* [f. TRUE *a.*]

†**1.** *trans.* To prove true, verify. *Obs. rare*$^{-1}$.

1647 WARD *Simp. Cobler* (1843) 81 Easilier told than tryed or trued.

2. To make true, as a piece of mechanism or the like; to place, adjust, or shape accurately; to give the precise required form or position to; to make accurately or perfectly straight, level, round, smooth, sharp, etc. as required. Often with *up*.

1841 *Civil Eng. & Arch. Jrnl.* IV. 234/1 An apparatus for 'truing up' the wheels of carriages and engines on railways. **1875** KNIGHT *Dict. Mech.*, *Marble-finishing Machine*, one for truing and molding the edges of marble slabs for mantels, tables, etc. **1881** GREENER *Gun* 267 The common barrels are done at half the cost of the best..by grinding them without turning and trueing them in the lathe. **1888** HASLUCK *Model Engin. Handybk.* (1900) 84 The next thing is to true up the valve-face on the cylinder.

Hence ˈ**truing** *vbl. sb.* (also *attrib.*).

1851–4 TOMLINSON *Cycl. Arts* (1867) II. 40/1 The trueing of the lenses..being completed, the polishing is next proceeded with. **1877** KNIGHT *Dict. Mech.*, *Truing-tool*, a device for truing the face of a grindstone, or any other surface. **1897** PEMBERTON *Compl. Cyclist* iii. 82 [The 'jointless' rim] takes even less trueing than a good wood rim.

† **true**, variant of TREWE *Obs.*, tribute.

c **1330** R. BRUNNE *Chron. Wace* (Rolls) 5605 Þe true to Rome gyue he [Arviragus] nolde, For he dedeyned of hem to holde.

true, obs. form of TROW *v.*, TRUCE.

true blue: see BLUE *a.* 1 e, 6 b, *sb.* 8.

ˈ**true-born**, *a.* Born of a true or pure stock; legitimately born; having the sterling qualities associated with such descent.

1591 SHAKS. *1 Hen. VI*, II. iv. 27 Let him that is a true-borne Gentleman..From off this Bryer pluck a white Rose with me. **1593** —— *Rich. II*, I. iii. 309 Though banish'd, yet a true-borne Englishman. **1645** FULLER *Gd. Th. in Bad T.* (1841) 54 He will acknowledge us to be no bastards, but his trueborn children. **1701** DE FOE (*title*) The True-Born Englishman. **1812** BYRON *Ch. Har.* II. lxxxiii, If Greece one true-born patriot still can boast.

ˈ**true-bred**, *a.* **a.** Bred of a true or pure stock; of the true breed; thoroughbred. **b.** Having or manifesting true breeding or education.

1596 SHAKS. *1 Hen. IV*, I. ii. 206, I know them to bee as true bred Cowards as euer turn'd backe. **1690** DRYDEN *Don Sebast.* I. i, He is a substantial true-bred beast. **1809** JEFFERSON *Writ.* (1830) IV. 126 True-bred shepherd's dogs. **1886** C. SCOTT *Sheep-Farming* 183 In a true-bred sheep the staple of the wool is of an equal length and texture on all parts of the body. **1911** W. P. KER *Eng. Lit.*, *Mediaeval* viii. 210 He writes of it in true-bred language.

†ˈ**truefast**, *a. Obs.* [OE. *tréowfæst*, f. *tréowe*, TRUE + *fæst*, FAST *a.*] Faithful. Hence †**truefastness** *Obs.*, faithfulness.

c **950** *Lindisf. Gosp.* Matt. xxv. 21 Wel ðe la god ðegn and trewufæst. *a* **1000** *Ags. Ps.* (Th.) cx. 5 [cxi. 7] Wærun his bebodu ealle treowfæste. *c* **1175** *Lamb. Hom.* 89 Þa weren þer igedered wiðinne þere buruh of ierusalem trowfeste men of elchere þeode. *Ibid.* 99 Þe halie gast..onlihte ure mod.. mid gode dedan and trewfestnesse. **1532** *Thynne's Chaucer*, *Lydgate's Ball. our Lady* 78 O trustie turtle truefastest [*MSS.* trewest] of all true.

† **ˈtrueful**, *a. Obs. rare.* In 4 treuful, 4–5 truful. [f. TRUE + -FUL.] Full of truth or loyalty, faithful. Hence † **ˈtruefully** *adv. Obs.*, faithfully.

13.. *Cursor M.* 20628 (Cott.) All..þat þe seruis treufulli [*v.r.* trufully]. **1435** MISYN *Fire of Love* II. iii. 74 Truful lufe in mynde is risyn.

† **ˈtruehead.** *Obs. rare.* In 3 **trewehede, (trywede)**, 4 **trewhede**, 5 **trowhede**. [f. OE. *tréowe*, TRUE + *-hede*, -HEAD.] Faithfulness, fidelity.

1297 R. GLOUC. (Rolls) 7370 He wolde þat alle men iseye is trewehede [*v.r.* trywede]. *c* **1375** *Cursor M.* 97 (Fairf.) Of hir godenes and hir trew hede.

true-hearted (ˈtruːˈhɑːtɪd), *a.* Having a true heart; faithful, loyal; honest, sincere.

1471 MARG. PASTON in *P. Lett.* III. 30 Remembyr ho[w] keynd and true hartyd he hath ben to us to hys powre. **1535** COVERDALE *Ps.* xcvii. 11 A ioyfull gladnesse for soch as be true herted. **1608** CHAPMAN *Byron's Consp.* II. i, To be reputed a true harted subiect. **1760–72** H. BROOKE *Fool of Qual.* (1809) III. 21 His downright and true-hearted kindness to me. **1855** MACAULAY *Hist. Eng.* xviii. IV. 196 The son of one of the bravest and most truehearted of Scottish patriots.

Hence ˌ**true-ˈheartedness**.

1608 HIERON *Wks.* I. 694 Encrease..loyalty and true-heartednesse in his subiects. **1858** LADY MORGAN *Autobiog.* (1859) 222 *note*, The same nobleness of soul,..the same single-mindedness, the same true-heartedness, were always present [in Ary-Scheffer].

trueish (ˈtruːɪʃ), *a. colloq.* Also **true-ish**. [f. TRUE *a.* + -ISH[1].] Partly true, almost true.

1980 I. MURDOCH *Nuns & Soldiers* v. 326 'So you think it's true?' 'I think it may be trueish. There's something.' **1981** T. HEALD *Murder at Moose Jaw* iv. 44 'True,' said Bognor. 'Or at least true-ish.'

truel, obs. form of TROWEL.

true-love (ˈtruːlʌv). Forms: 1 **tréowlufu**, 4–5 **trulofe**, 4–6 **trewelove**, **trewlove**, 5 **treulofe**, **trewluf**, **-lufe**, *pl.* **-luffes**, **treue loue**, 6 **tru-**, **treulove**, 6–8 **truelove**, 6– **true love**, 7– **truelove**. [f. OE. *tréowe*, TRUE + *lufu*, LOVE.]

1. Faithful love. Usually as two words (see TRUE *a.* 1 b), exc. *attrib.* (see 5).

a **800** CYNEWULF *Christ* 538 Wæs seo treow lufu, hat æt heortan. **1813** SCOTT *Trierm.* II. xvii, To plead their right, and true-love plight.

2. A faithful lover; one whose love is pledged; a sweetheart, beloved.

c **1385** CHAUCER *L.G.W.* 2542 (*Phillis*) This is he..That was his trewe loue In thought & dede. *c* **1460** *Quia amore langueo* 17 in *Pol. Rel. & L. Poems* (1866) 151, I am treulove that fals was neuer, My sistur, mannys soule, I loued hyr thus. *a* **1586** SIDNEY *Arcadia* Poems (Grosart) II. 128 My true-love hath my heart, and I haue his. ? **16..** *Friar of Orders Gray*, I pray thee, tell to me If ever at yon holy shrine My true love thou didst see. ? **17..** *Song*, '*Wala*; *wala, up the bank*' (Jam.), I leant my back unto an aik, I thought it was a trusty tree; But first it bow'd, and syne it brak, And sae did my true-love to me. **1871** PALGRAVE *Lyr. Poems* 73 My one true-love, My only.

†**3.** An ornament or figure symbolic of true love; a TRUE-LOVE KNOT. *Obs.*

13.. *Gaw. & Gr. Knt.* 612 Tortors & trulofez entayled so þyk. *c* **1420** *Anturs of Arth.* 354 (Thornton MS.) His mantylle..Trofelyte and trauerste wythe trewloues in trete. **1509** *Will* (MS. Prerog. Crt. Canterb.), Another standing Cupe gilt and enameled wt blew Trulovys in the botom. *a* **1550** *Image Hypocr.* I. 404 in *Skelton's Wks.* (1843) II. 419/1 Gay gloves..Wroughte with true loves. **1575** LANEHAM *Let.* (1871) 38 His napkin, edged with a blu lace, & marked with a trulooue, a hart, and A.D. for Damian.

4. A name for the Herb Paris (*Paris quadrifolia*), the whorl of four leaves with the single flower or berry in the midst suggesting the figure of a true-love knot. Also † ***herb true-love***, ***true-love flower***; † **true-love grass**, four-leaved clover. Also, †the North American genus *Trillium* (*obs.*).

13.. *Test. Christi* 126 (Vernon MS.) in Herrig's *Archiv* LXXIX. 428 A foure-leued gras..Whon þeose four leues togeder ben set A trewe-loue men clepen hit. *c* **1386** CHAUCER *Miller's T.* 3692 Vnder his tonge a trewe loue he beer For ther-by wende he to ben gracious. *c* **1400** *Emare* 125 Portrayed þey wer wyth trewe-loue-flour. **1448** *Paston Lett.* IV. 17 Floweris of sylver on the bukkelis made of iiij. lyke a trewlove. **1578** LYTE *Dodoens* I. v. 10 The seede [of Hound's-tongue] is flat and rough, three or foure together like to a trueloue, or foure leaued grasse. **1597** GERARDE *Herbal* II. lxxxv. §6. 329 One Berrie is also called herbe Trueloue, and herbe Paris. *a* **1674** ? HERRICK *Fairie Kings Diet* 4 The outside of his doublet was Made of the foure-leaued trueloue grass. **1760** LEE *Introd. Bot.* Tab. i, *Trillium*, Herb Truelove of Canada. **1838** MARY HOWITT *Birds & Fl., Summer Woods* iv, There grows the four-leaved plant, 'true love', In some dusk woodland spot.

5. *attrib.* (usually in sense 1; in quot. *c* 1430, in sense 3). See also sense 4, and next.

c **1430** *Syr Gener.* (Roxb.) 173 Of trewloue werk wroght ful wele. **1593** SHAKS. *Rich. II*, v. i. 10 And wash him fresh againe with true-loue Teares. **1602** —— *Ham.* IV. v. 39 Which bewept to the graue did go, With true-loue showres. **1818** SCOTT *Hrt. Midl.* xxxv, 'A sincere weel-wisher of mine, sir'... 'O, I understand,'..—'a true-love affair'.

true-love knot, true lover's knot. Also †**true-love's knot** (*obs.*). A kind of knot, of a complicated and ornamental form (usually either a double-looped bow, or a knot formed of two loops intertwined), used as a symbol of true love; a figure of this. Also *fig.* or *allusively*.

α. **1495** *Will J. Rogers* (Somerset Ho.), Treue loue knottes. **1591** SHAKS. *Two Gent.* II. vii. 46 Ile knit it vp in silken strings, With twentie od-conceited true-loue knots. **1643** WITHER *Campo Musæ* 74 A Peace, that by a true-love-knot, shall knit Three Nations..into One. **1877** W. JONES *Finger-ring* 414 True-love knots were common [on rings].

β. **1530** PALSGR. 283/1 Treweloves knotte, *neu damours*. **1583** STUBBES *Anat. Abus.* I. (1877) 74 Sleeues..tyed with true-loues knottes (for so they call them). **1662** HIBBERT *Body Div.* II. 145 The Lords brother, tyed unto him with a true-loves-knot. **1664** BUTLER *Hud.* II. i. 566 I'll carve your name on Barks of Trees, With True-loves knots, and Flourishes.

γ. **1615** BRATHWAIT (*title*) Loves Labyrinth: or The true-Louers knot. **1679** LOGAN *Treat. Hon.* II. 177 Or, on a Cheveron, Gules, a true Lovers Knot of the first. **1865** DICKENS *Mut. Fr.* I. x, Splendid cake, covered with Cupids, silver, and true-lover's knots. **1906** *Lady* 12 July 82/1 Pretty but simple hair ornaments are true-lovers' knots of sequined gauze, very stiffly wired.

truely, obs. form of TRULY.

† **ˈtrueman.** *Obs.* Forms: see TRUE *a.* [The phr. *true man* written as one word; cf. *oldman*, OLD MAN I.] A faithful or trusty man; an honest man (as distinguished from a thief or other criminal).

1297 R. GLOUC. (Rolls) 7274 Ac þe gode trywemen of þe lond wolde abbe ymad king..edgar aþeling. **1303** R. BRUNNE *Handl. Synne* 1337 Þys fals men..þat, for hate, a trewman wyl endyte, And a þefe for syluer quyte. *c* **1400** *Destr. Troy* 11157 Wacchemen for to wale, wacches to kepe, Of trewmen in towres, for treason of other. **1583** MELBANCKE *Philotimus* Y ij, Thou art like a Thiefe, that thinkes euerye Tree a trueman. **1647** A. ROSS *Myst. Poet.* xiii. (1675) 326 Thieves..use to stand nearer the Altar of Occasion, than True-men many times do.

trueness (ˈtruːnɪs). Forms: see TRUE *a.* [OE. *tré(o)wnes*, f. *tréowe*, TRUE + -NESS.]

I. †**1.** Trust, confidence; object of trust. Only *OE.*

c **888** K. ÆLFRED *Boeth.* xlii. (1899) 149 Drihten ælmihtiᵹa God,..þu eart min sceoppend, & min alesend,..min trewnes, & min tohopa.

†**2.** = TRUCE *sb.* I. *Obs. rare.*

a **1400** *Siege of Troy* 1058 in *Archiv neu. Spr.* LXXII. 34 Þeo folk of Grece on heore side Beden Treowenes [*v.r.* truce] for to abyde.

II. The quality of being true; truth (in various senses).

3. Faithfulness, loyalty: = TRUTH I.

c **1290** *Beket* 487 in *S. Eng. Leg.* I. 120 Wel þov wost þat ech of us..Trewenesse we þe sworen ase riȝt was. **1297** R. GLOUC. (Rolls) 738 Ac god þouȝte ȝut on hire vor hire triwenesse [*v.rr.* trewnesse, treweness, trunesse]. **1583** GOLDING *Calvin on Deut.* viii. 46 God shall..continue faithfull and his trewnesse shall be knowen. **1612** BACON *Ess., Faction* (Arb.) 83 The euen carriage betweene two factions, proceedeth not alwaies of moderation, but of a truenesse to a mans selfe, with end to make vse of both. **1909** P. C. SIMPSON *Life Rainy* v. 111 A shrewd, hardheaded race ..with..not only trueness but deep tenderness of heart.

4. Conformity with fact or reality; verity: = TRUTH 5.

1587 GOLDING *De Mornay* xxxiv. (1592) 550, I hope I haue now shewed the truenesse and substantialnesse of the Christian Religion, and the vanitie & wickednesse of al other Religions. **1861** H. BONAR *God's Way of Peace* viii. (1868) 91 The trueness of the Father's testimony.

5. Conformity to a standard; accuracy, exactitude: = TRUTH 6.

1594 BLUNDEVIL *Exerc.* v. (1636) 592 There were no way ..to be compared vnto it, neither for the truenesse, easinesse, nor readinesse of working thereby. **1805** LUCCOCK *Nat. Wool* 176 A far more valuable quality..which the wool-grower should observe..called the trueness of the hair.

6. Genuineness; reality, actuality: = TRUTH 7.

1613 PURCHAS *Pilgrimage* IX. xv. (1614) 912 They make this..one of the Markes of the truenesse and Catholicisme of their Church. **1622** MABBE tr. *Aleman's Guzman d'Alf.* II. (1623) 198 That seeing the truenesse of the stampe, she might be the sooner molded to entertaine the motion. **1833** CHALMERS *Const. Man* (1835) I. II. i. 151 The objective trueness of the things which are perceived.

truepenny (ˈtruːpɛnɪ). *arch.* A trusty person, an honest fellow (compared to a coin of genuine metal); as *adj.* true, genuine. *colloq.*

1589 *Hay any Work* A ij b, You haue shewed reuerende Martin to be truepenie in deede. **1595** *Enq. Tripe-wife* (1881) 152 Mother Messingham, the old true peny for trimming of a Tripe. **1602** SHAKS. *Ham.* I. v. 150 Art thou there truepenny? *a* **1825** FORBY *Voc. E. Anglia*, *True-penny*, s. Generally, 'Old True-penny',..hearty old fellow; staunch and trusty; true to his purpose or pledge.

attrib. **1906** *Westm. Gaz.* 26 May 4/2, I send you away to Spain With a catch in your ears from London, a truepenny pavement strain.

truer (ˈtruːə(r)). [f. TRUE *v.* + -ER[1].] An instrument for truing a piece of mechanism or the like.

1877 KNIGHT *Dict. Mech.* s.v. *Truing-tool*, A grindstone-truer, for keeping the face in good shape.

truer, compar. of TRUE *a.*; var. TROWER *Obs.*

trues, obs. form of TRUCE.

† **ˈtrueship.** *Obs.* Forms: see TRUE *a.* and -SHIP. [f. TRUE + -SHIP.] Faithfulness, fidelity.

c **1175** *Lamb. Hom.* 107 ȝif þe alde bið butan treuscipe. *a* **1225** *Ancr. R.* 8 Edmodnesse, & þolemodnesse, treoweschipe, & holding of ðe tene olde hesten. *a* **1250** *Owl & Night.* 1344, & mayde may luue cheose þat hire trevschipe ne forleose.

† **true-table**, app. an error for *trey-table*: see TREY *sb.* 3.

1646 EVELYN *Diary* (1827) I. 384 There is also..a tavern, and a true-table.

trueth, trufel, obs. forms of TRUTH, TRIFLE.

† **truff**, *sb.*[1] *Obs.* Forms: 4, 8 *Sc.* truf, 5–7 truffe, (6 *Sc. pl.* trufis), 7–8 truff. [a. F. *truffe* a truffle (1370 in Godef. *Compl.*), in OF. also figuratively *trufe* a cozening, cheating, etc. (1265 in Godef.) in which sense it is first recorded in English: see TRUFFLE.]

1. An idle tale or jest. Cf. TRIFLE *sb.* I.

1483 CAXTON *Gold. Leg.* 272b/1 In the same errour Austyn fylle..and was broughte to byleue the truffes and Iapes. **1494** FABYAN *Chron.* VII. 440 The Scottis in despyte of yᵉ Englysh men,..and also to theyr more derysyon made dyuerse truffys, roundys, & songys. **1513** DOUGLAS *Æneis* VIII. Prol. 170 Than wol I tene at I tuk to sic trufis [*ed.* 1553 truffuris] tent. **1611** SPEED *Hist. Gt. Brit.* IX. xii. §29 Playing vpon the English Truffes and Rounds.

2. A truffle. *rare.*

1633 HART *Diet Diseased* I. xiii. 47 Those roots, commonly called Puffes, or Truffes. **1669** *Phil. Trans.* IV. 1013 Other odd things in Nature, as Truffs, Mushroms. **1672** EVELYN *Fr. Gard.* 260 Concerning Morilles and Truffs.

truff, *sb.*[2] Local name for the bull-trout, *Salmo eriox*. Also ***sea-truff***.

1818 *Sporting Mag.* II. 158 What some call 'truffs', others sea-trout. **1865** COUCH *Brit. Fishes* IV. 211 Sea Trout. Grey Trout. Bull Trout. Sea Truff. Pugtrout. **1880** in Elworthy *W. Somerset Word-bk.* (1888) s.v., They've a-catcht a little truff, not five.

† **truff**, *v. Obs.* Forms: see TRUFF *sb.*[1] [ad. OF. *truffer*, *trufer* to mock, deride, gibe at (13th c.); cf. med.L. *trufare*, *truphare* to mock, It. *truffare* to cozen, cheat (Florio); see TRUPHANE.]

1. *trans.* To deceive, befool. Hence **ˈtruffing** *vbl. sb.*

c **1375** *Sc. Leg. Saints* i. 242 Sa cuth he deile with trufinge. **1657** C. BECK *Univ. Char.* L viij b, To truffe, *v.* gird.

2. *intr.* To trifle *with*.

1485 CAXTON *Chas. Gt.* II. II. x. 119 Ye haue seen how he truffed wyth me.

3. *trans.* *Sc.* To obtain by deceit; to steal, pilfer.

1720 A. PENNECUIK *Helicon* (ed. 2) 66 I've truf'd you a Ladies Shirt from the Hedge. **1721** RAMSAY *Lucky Spence* vi, Be sure to truff his pocket-book.

Hence † **ˈtruffer** [cf. OF. *trufeor*, *truffour* (*c* 1170 in Godef.)], one who 'truffs'; so † **ˈtruffery** [a. OF. *truf(f)erie* (*c* 1230 in Godef.)], a mockery, trifle, thing of no importance.

c **1450** *Mirour Saluacioun* 2225 The first two causes pilat helde bot a truferye. **1553** Truffuris [see TRUFF *sb.*[1] I, quot. 1513]. **1728** RAMSAY *Fables* xvii. 8 The hand of this young foolish truffer.

truff, Sc. form of TURF.

truffille, obs. form of TRIFLE.

truffle (ˈtrʌf(ə)l, ˈtruːf(ə)l). Also 7–8 **trufle**, **treuffle**, 8 **troufle**. [app. a derivative of Fr. *trufe*, *truffe* (1370 in Hatz.-Darm.), Comask. *treufol*, Genev. *trufola*, in same sense; of unsettled etymology. According to Diez and Hatz.-Darm., prob. repr. L. *tūber-*, supposed to have been altered at an early date to **tūfer-*, whence **tūfre*, *trūfe*, *tuffe*. The change of gender has been accounted for by supposing the neuter pl. *tūbera* to have been treated as a fem. sing. (cf. BIBLE, ARMS); according to Graff *tūbera* appears as a fem. sing. in some Ger. glossaries of the 9th c. A form without *r* is found in Swiss Romand and Languedoc *tufelle*, *tufeda*. Cf. also the Eng. contraction TRUB.

But this derivation is by no means certain; a longer form appears in It. *tartuffo*, Milanese *tartuffel*, Ven. *tartuf*, *tartufola*, Piemont *tartifla*, Rheto-Rumansch *tartufe*, Languedoc *tartifle*, Berry *tartrufle*. These mean 'potato', and have been explained by Miège as = *terræ tuber*; whence Ger. *kartoffel*, dial. *tartoffel*, Icel. *tartuflur* pl. potatoes. See the word in Diez, Scheler, and Littré.]

1. a. Any one of various underground fungi of the family *Tuberaceæ*; *spec.* an edible fungus of the genus *Tuber*, a native of Central and Southern Europe, esteemed as a delicacy; esp. *T. æstivum* or *cibarium*, the Common (English) Truffle, and *T. melanosporum*, the French Truffle, which have a black, warty exterior, and vary in size between that of a walnut and that of a large potato, which they more or less resemble in shape.

1591 SPARRY tr. *Cattan's Geomancie* B ij, The Topas and the Truffle haue power of Chastity, and to subdue the flesh. **1644** EVELYN *Diary* 30 Sept., Here we supped.., having amongst other dainties, a dish of trufles, an earth nut found by an hogg train'd to it. **1691** Ray *Creation* II. (1692) 99 By tying a Cord to the hind-leg of a Pig, and driving him before them..observing where he stops and begins to root,..they are sure to find a Trufle. **1726** Arbuthnot *It cannot rain*, etc. 10 A Dog is an Ass to him [Peter the Wild Boy] for finding Troufles. **1742** Pope *Dunc.* IV. 558 Thy Truffles, Perigord! thy Hams, Bayonne! **1847** Thackeray *Mrs. Perkins's Ball* ¶17 Such a quantity of goose-liver and truffles. **1866** *Treas. Bot.* s.v., Applied generally, the name Truffle (or Trubs) comprises all the Fungi which belong to the natural orders *Hypogæi* and *Tuberacei*.

fig. **1897** *Literature* 20 Nov. 155/1 A thin, ancient-looking octavo,..rooted up with other literary truffles.

b. *attrib.* and *Comb.*, as ***truffle-bed***, ***-grower***, ***-hunter***, ***-hunting***, etc.; ***truffle-like***, ***-stuffed*** adjs.; **truffle-beetle**, a beetle whose subterranean larvæ feed on the truffle; **truffle-dog**, **-pig**, a dog or pig trained to discover truffles; also *fig.*; **truffle hound** = *truffle dog*; **truffle-worm**, the larva of an insect infesting the truffle: see quots.

1726 Bradley *Gardening* App. 38 No Herb or plant is ever seen to grow upon a Truffiery or *Truffle bed. **1885** F. Whymper in *Girl's Own Paper* Jan. 169/1 A trained hog, when it has discovered a truffle bed, is immovable. **1899** Sharp in *Cambr. Nat. Hist.* VI. v. 222 The larvae of the group Anisotomides are believed to be chiefly subterranean in habits; that of *A. cinnamomea* feeds on the truffle, and the beetle is known as the *truffle-beetle. **1855** S. Whiting *Heliondé* ii. 47 'If they should see you digging into the surface of the Sun' (he might have added 'like a *truffle dog') 'they will certainly think you are demented.' **1874** Lisle Carr *Jud. Gwynne* I. iv. 114 As a truffle-dog noses out the dainty objects of his search. **1899** Hale *Lowell & Friends* xiv. 254 The reader is not necessarily an authority in language. He is a scout or truffle-dog who brings the result of his exploration to the authorities. **1898** *Gard. Mag.* 3 Sept. 572/2 The Agricultural Society of the Department of the Lot awards prizes at its shows to *truffle growers. **1975** J. Grigson *Mushroom Feast* 134 There is the whole business of truffle pigs and *truffle hounds. *a* **1793** G. White *Observ. Veg.* in *Selborne*, etc. (1837) 487 A *truffle-hunter called on us, having in his pocket several large truffles found in this neighbourhood. **1885** F. Whymper in *Girl's Own Paper* Jan. 169/1 In Upper Provence a hog trained to *truffle-hunting is worth the equivalent of eight pounds sterling. **1898** P. Manson *Trop. Diseases* xxxvii. 573 Moulded into *truffle-like masses. **1915** *N.E.D.*, *Truffle-pig. **1975** [see *truffle-hound*]. **1841** Thackeray *Mem. Gormandising* Wks. 1900 XIII. 589 Fat *truffle-stuffed partridges. **1753** Chambers *Cycl. Supp.*, **Truffle-worms*,..a species of fly-worm which is found in Truffles. **1888** *Cassell's Encycl. Dict.* s.v., A species of Leiodes deposits its ova in it, which in the pupa state feed upon the substance of the truffle; in this state they are called truffle-worms.

2. A type of confectionery made of a mixture of chocolate and cream, freq. flavoured with rum, shaped into a ball and covered with powdered chocolate.

1926–7 *Army & Navy Stores Catal.* 54/2 Chocolates.. Truffles—lb. 4/3. *c* **1938** *Fortnum & Mason Price List* 8/1 Truffles, with fresh cream (perishable)..Truffles, Rum Flavoured. **1944** D. Welch *In Youth is Pleasure* iv. 61 He imagined the aromatic acrid dust..sticking to [the heart] and coating it..as bright-coloured bitter cocoa powder clings to the rich dark truffle. **1951** *Good Housek. Home Encycl.* 407/1 (*heading*) Chocolate truffles. *Ibid.* 675/1 Turkish delight and marshmallows, chocolates and truffles. **1974** J. Stubbs *Painted Face* xiii. 168 [His] only acquaintance with truffles had been the chocolate variety.

Hence **truffled** (ˈtrʌf(ə)ld) *a.*, cooked, garnished, or stuffed with truffles; † **ˈtrufflery**, a truffle-bed; **truffˈlesque** *a.* (*nonce-wd.*), resembling that of truffles; **ˈtruffling** *vbl. sb.*, gathering truffles.

1837 M. Donovan *Dom. Econ.* II. 131 The liver and thighs of geese,..made into pies, and properly truffled,.. are reckoned a most delicate article. **1902** Elinor Glyn *Refl. Ambrosine* II. viii, Truffled partridge in aspic. **1726** *Trufflery [see *truffle-bed* above]. **1841** Thackeray *Mem. Gormandising* Wks. 1900 XIII. 583 A *trufflesque odour was left in the room. *Ibid.* 588 Some faint trufflesque savour. **1859** *Times* 14 Feb. 5/5 Many of these..people [poor labourers in Wiltshire] live by truffling and poaching, in the absence of farmer's employment.

truffle, trufle, truful, obs. forms of trifle.

trug[1] (trʌg). *local.* Also 6–8 **trugg.** [? Dialectal variant of trough.]

1. An old local measure for wheat, equal to two-thirds of a bushel. Also *attrib.*, **trug-corn**, **trug-wheat**: see quots.

[*c* **1350** in Blount *Law Dict.* (1670) s.v., Tres Trugge frumenti vel avenae faciunt 2 Bushels infra Prebendam de Hunderton in Ecclesia Heref.] **1670** Blount *Law Dict.* s.v., At Lempster at this day the Vicar has Trug Corn allow'd him for Officiating at some Chappels of ease. **1676** Coles *Dict.*, *Trug*, three trugs make two bushels. **1866** *N. & Q.* 3rd Ser. X. 415/2 There is in the parish of Leominster, a payment of the nature of tithe, which is known as trug-wheat.

2. A shallow wooden tray or pan to hold milk; also a tray or hod for mortar; also (*northern dial.*), a wooden coal-box.

1580, 1630 [implied in trugger]. **1600** in W. F. Shaw *Mem. Eastry* (1870) 226 Item in the mylke house..two dowsin of bowles and Truggs. **1630** *Will W. Buncker* (C. C. Canterb. MS.), Two milke trugges [and] two milk boules. **1674** Ray *S. & E.C. Words* 77 *A Trug*, a tray for milk or the like, *Suss. Dial.* **1706** Phillips (ed. Kersey), *Trugg*, (Country-Word) a Milk-Tray or such like Vessel, a Hod to carry Mortar in. **1847–78** Halliwell, *Ash-trug*, a coal-scuttle. *North.* **1878–81** *Cumberld. Gloss.*, *Trug*, a wooden coal-box.

3. A shallow oblong basket made of wooden strips with a handle from side to side, chiefly used for carrying fruit, vegetables, and the like; also ***trug-basket***.

1862 M. A. Lower in *Athenæum* 30 Aug. 281 A trug-basket,..a vessel..almost peculiar to the county of Sussex. Some such trugs were sent to the Great Exhibition of 1851. **1882** *Ibid.* 26 Aug. 271/2 A Sussex trug..is a flat basket, not of wicker, but of flakes of sallow, braced with ash and furnished with a handle of the latter wood. **1909** *Spectator* 10 July 49/1 She descends with a huge wooden trug half filled with maize.

trug[2]. *Obs.* exc. *dial.* Also 6–7 **trugge**, 7 **truck.** [? ad. It. *trucca* 'a fustian or rogish word for a trull, a whore, or a wench' (Florio); perh. cognate with truck *sb.*[1]] A prostitute; a trull.

1592 Greene *Upst. Courtier* G j, You Tom tapster..haue your trugges to draw men on to villanie. **1620** tr. *Boccaccio's Decam.* VI. x. 18 b, One of the Hostesses Female attendants, a gross fat Trugge. **1631** Brathwait *Whimzies* 139 Would you have a true survey of his family..? you shall finde them subsist of three heads: himselfe, his truck, and her misset. *a* **1700** B. E. *Dict. Cant. Crew*, *Trug*, a dirty Puzzel, an ord'nary sorry Woman. **1883** *Hampsh. Gloss.*, *Trug*, a trull, low female companion.

† **b.** A catamite. *Obs. rare.*

c **1608** Healey *Disc. new World* III. vii. §2. 194 Euery other house keepes sale Trugges or Ganymedes. *a* **1630** J. Taylor (Water P.) *Bawd* Wks. II. 93/2 A cursed Catalogue of those veneriall caterpillars..with the number of trugs which each of them kept.

Hence † **ˈtrugging-house**, † **ˈtrugging-place**, a brothel.

1591 Greene *Dict. Coosnage* Wks. (Grosart) X. 37 The whoore house, a Trugging place. **1592** —— *Blacke Bkes. Messenger* Wks. (ed. Huth) XI. 12 This olde Letcher..had a trugging house in Petticote Lane to a Trugging house there.

trug, obs. form of trudge.

† **ˈtrugger.** *Obs.* [f. trug[1] (sense 2) + -er[1].] A maker of trugs.

1580 *Reg. St. Alphage, Canterb.* (MS.), Sonne of John Harman, trugger. **1630** *Canterb. Marriage Licences* (MS.), Giles Reinold's of Great Chart, trugger.

† **trugˈmallion.** *Obs.* Also trugmullion. [f. trug[2]; cf. *tatterdemalion*, *rampallion*, etc.] = trug[2].

1715 tr. *C'tess D'Aunoy's Wks.* 414, I, cry'd the Charming King, I Marry such a Trugmullion as this! **1719** D'Urfey *Pills* V. 308 Tarpaulins, Trugmallions, Lords, Ladys.

truiff, obs. Sc. form of turf.

truikour, obs. Sc. form of trucker.

truing: see true *v.*

truis, variant of trews.

ˈtruish, *a. rare.* [f. true *a.* + -ish[1].] Somewhat true.

1659 Gauden *Tears Ch.* II. xvi. 198 Something that seems truish and newish. **1869** Mrs. Oliphant *Hist. Sk. Reign Geo. II* (1879) I. 140 It was truish sentiment in its way.

truism (ˈtruːɪz(ə)m). Also 8 **trueism.** [f. true *a.* + -ism.] A self-evident truth, esp. one of slight importance; a statement so obviously true as not to require discussion.

1708 Swift *Remarks Bk.* vii. Wks. 1841 II. 190/2 The title of this chapter [is] a truism. **1757** Mrs. Griffith *Lett. Henry & Frances* (1767) I. 135, I have..often illustrated the latter part of this trueism. **1817** Malthus *Popul.* III. App. 338 Truisms..of the same kind as the assertion that man cannot live without food. **1880** L. Stephen *Pope* ii. 25 Maxims, some of which strike us as palpable truisms.

b. (without article) Truistic statement.

1812 Shelley *Let. to Eliz. Hitchener* 20 Jan., You..tell me truism when you egotize at all. **1861** Max Müller *Chips* (1880) I. xiii. 312 The fear of truism in our modern writers.

Hence **truisˈmatic** *a.* (*rare*$^{-0}$) = next.

1860 Worcester cites *Edinb. Rev.*

truistic (truːˈɪstɪk), *a.* [f. truism: see -istic.] Having the character of a truism; trivially self-evident. (In quot. 1885, Dealing in or uttering truisms.)

1844 F. D. Maurice in W. Ward *W. G. Ward & Oxford Movem.* (1889) 321 Merely truistic statements. **1885** *Pall Mall G.* 30 May 2/1 It is the fashion nowadays to be truistic. **1902** *Athenæum* 11 Jan. 52/3 To a trained psychologist this statement looks truistic and commonplace.

So **truˈistical** *a.*, in same sense.

1858 *Brit. Q. Rev.* LVI. 444 While some are true, not to say truistical, others are as utterly false. **1906** *Hibbert Jrnl.* July 788 Quite obvious..in fact, almost suspiciously truistical.

† **truit, truyt.** *Obs. rare.* [?] ? Wrong, injury.

a **1400** *Leg. Rood* viii. 41 Fouled is my fayre fruit, þat neuer dude tripet ne truit. *Ibid.* 480 Rihtful schul ryse to riche restyng, Truyt and tripet to helle shal sterue.

‖ **truite au bleu** (trɥit o blø). *Cookery.* [Fr., lit. 'trout in the blue'.] Trout cooked with vinegar, which turns it blue.

[**1861** Mrs. Beeton *Bk. Househ. Managem.* 44 *Au-bleu*, fish dressed in such a manner as to have a *bluish* appearance.] **1935** M. Morphy *Recipes of All Nations* 37 *Truite au bleu*... One of the most popular ways of cooking them is 'au bleu'—the boiling vinegar in which they are plunged turning them a vivid blue. **1966** B. Glemser *Dear Hungarian Friend* iv. 76 He offered her blue trout, *truite au bleu Duna*. **1978** *Chicago* June 236/2 The Chicago branch of the Paris house offers wonderful dishes like truite au bleu (trout are killed immediately before poaching and sauced with hollandaise at the table).

‖ **truite bleue** (trɥit blø). Also *erron.* **truite bleu.** [Fr., lit. 'blue trout'.] = prec.

1907 E. Glyn *Three Weeks* i. 18 She ate a delicate *truite bleu*. **1948** Wodehouse *Uncle Dynamite* iv. 56 It was a relief when the waiter, arriving with *truite bleue*. broke a tension which had begun to be uncomfortable. **1980** 'M. Harris' *Treasure of Sainte Foy* ix. 123 The prix-fixe is Truite Bleue, then Cassoulet..salad, fruit, and cheese.

truke, var. troke.

trule, obs. f. trowel.

† **trule.** *Sc. Obs.* [Cf. troll *v.* to roll, trundle.] A game app. played with balls or bowls.

c **1508** Dunbar *Poems* xiv. 22 Sa mony lordis, so mony naturall fulis, That better accordis to play thame at the tralis, Nor seis the dulis that commonis dois sustene.

trull (trʌl). Also 6 trowle, 6–7 trulle, trul, 7 troul. [= Ger. *trulle*, Swiss *trolle*, Swabian *trull*.]

1. A low prostitute or concubine; a drab, strumpet, trollop.

1519 *Interl. Four Elements* (Percy Soc.) 46, I shall apoynt you a trull of trust, Not a feyrer in this towne! **1591** Greene *Disc. Coosnage* (1592) 15 These common truls..walke abroad..as stales to draw men into hell. **1632** Chapman & Shirley *Ball* II. i, Have you as much left..as will Keep you and this old troul a fortnight longer? **1737** Swift *Proposal Badges to Beggars* Wks. 1761 III. 337 He and his trull, and his litter of brats. **1871** Morley *Crit. Misc.* 255 Coarse orgies with the trulls of Wapping.

attrib. **1898** G. Egerton *Fantasias* 144 Singing a song of the trull forces of nature.

† **2.** A girl, lass, wench. *Obs.*

1560 Ingelend *Disob. Child* (Percy Soc.) 26 This mynion here, this myncing trull. **1573** Tusser *Husb.* (1878) 85 Sow pease (good trull) the Moone past full. *a* **1600** J. Wootton *Jigge* in *Eng. Helicon* G vj, Heard to each Swaine, seen to each Trull.

trull, trulle, obs. ff. troll *v.*, trowel.

trullibub, variant of trillibub.

† **trulliˈzation.** *Obs. rare*$^{-0}$. Also **-iss-.** [ad. L. *trullissātiōn-em* (n. of action f. *trullissāre* to plaster, f. *trulla* trowel), F. †*trullization*, *trullisation* (1691 in Hatz.-Darm.).] (See quots.)

1656 Blount *Glossogr.*, *Trullissation* (*trullisatio*), a pargetting or plaistering with mortar or loam. **1727–41** Chambers *Cycl.*, *Trullization*, in the ancient architecture, the art of laying on strata or layers of mortar, gypsum, or the like, with the trowel.

‖ **trullo** (ˈtrullo). Pl. **trulli.** [It.] In Apulia, a small round house built of stone, with a conical roof.

1909 in Webster. **1925** L. V. Bertarelli *Southern Italy* iii. 380 *Alberobello* is a curious village of 'trulli'... These are round huts of stone without mortar, with conical roofs. **1932** *Antiquity* VI. 408 Away in the distance another trullo is visible... No stables or barns are these. We have arrived in 'trulli land'. These trulli are human habitations. **1958** P. Kemp *No Colours or Crest* xii. 252 We lived in a *trullo*, one of the beehive-shaped dwellings that are typical of the Apulian hill country. **1968** S. Jay *Sleepers can Kill* xiii. 134 Those round Trulli houses they have in Southern Italy. **1981** *Italy* (Michelin Tourist Guide) 243 The *Trulli.*—In these..can be seen traces of prehistoric Saracen and Christian civilisations, similar to the *nuraghi* of Sardinia.

† **ˈtrully.** *Obs. rare.* [f. trull + -y.] A trull.

1711 E. Ward *Quix.* I. 32 Poor Tinker-like, without a Trully, Must beat the dusty Road but dully.

truly (ˈtruːlɪ), *adv.* (*sb.*) Forms: 1 tréowlíce, 3 treo-, treou-, trouliche, 3–6 treu-, trew-, etc., -lich(e, -ly, etc. (see true *a.* and -ly[2]), 5 treoly, 5–6 trulye, 5–8 truely, 6–7 trulie, (7 trooly), 4– truly. [OE. *tréowlíce*, ME. *treulich*, etc., f. *tréow*, *treu*, true: see -ly[2].] In a true manner (in various senses of the adj.).

1. a. Faithfully, loyally, constantly, with steadfast allegiance. *arch.*

a **1000** *Ags. Ps.* (Th.) xi. 6 [xii. 5] Ic do swyðe treowlice ymb hy. *c* **1205** Lay. 20000 Alle heo sworen þene að, Trouliche [*c* **1275** Treuliche] þat heo wolden Mid Arðure halden. **1297** R. Glouc. (Rolls) 2070 Conan..bihet him to serui triweliche. *a* **1300** *Cursor M.* 81 (Cott.) Qua truly [*v.rr.* treuli, trewely] loues þis lemman, þis es þe loue bes neuer gan. **13..** *Ibid.* 1062 (Gött.) Rightwis [Abel] was, and goddes freind, And treuli gaf he him his tend. *c* **1380** Wyclif *Sel. Wks.* III. 152 Hit were better þat lewid men diden to lordes þis offis..for better and lighter and treulier schulde hit be done. *c* **1400** *Brut* ccxli. 350 Alle þe conauntes ..schulde be trewly kept. **1563** Win3et *Four Scoir Thre Quest.* Wks. (S.T.S.) I. 121 The haill Kirk of God, professing trewlie Christ Iesus. **1611** Shaks. *Cymb.* III. v. 110. **1852** M. Arnold *Second Best* 24 An impulse..To the words, 'Hope, Light, Persistence', Strongly sets and truly burns.

† **b.** With steadfast faith or assurance; confidently. In quot. *c* 1275, ? so as to be safe or trustworthy; securely (cf. true *a.* 1 d). *Obs.*

c **1275** Lay. 11898 And wel he makede his castles Treuliche [*c* **1205** Treowe] and faste. *c* **1325** *Spec. Gy Warw.* 208 þu shalt..bileue also And treuliche in þin herte do, þat god had neuere biginning Ne neuere shal haue ending. *c* **1375** *Sc. Leg. Saints* i. (*Petrus*) 485 Gyf he liffis, he ma spek, and ga,..And gyf he na may, trewis trewly þat ȝe se is all fantassy. *a* **1548** HALL *Chron., Edw. IV* 202 b, Trustynge truely that all thynges were at a good poynt.

†**2.** Honestly, honourably, uprightly. *Obs.*

1362 LANGL. *P. Pl.* A. I. 155, 156 Bote ȝe liuen trewely and eke loue þe pore, And such good as God sent Treweliche parten. **1453** *Dunfermline Regr.* (Bann. Cl.) 340 To gife and to pay lelly and treuly but fraude or gille a hundreth pundis. **1530** PALSGR. 358, I holde with them that deale trewly. **1558** in Foxe *A. & M.* (1570) 2249/2, I am a poore woman and do liue by my hands, gettyng a peny truly.

3. In accordance with the fact; truthfully; correctly (in reference to a statement).

1303 R. BRUNNE *Handl. Synne* 2712 Trewely to swere hys oþe. *c* **1400** *Ywaine & Gaw.* 329 By that well hinges a bacyne ..With a cheyne, trewly to tell. *a* **1548** HALL *Chron., Hen. VIII* 228 b, The people thus instructed (or as I may trulier speake) deceiued. **1599** SHAKS. *Much Ado* I. i. 180 Tell me truely how thou lik'st her. *Ibid.* IV. i. 76 Bid her answer truly. **1607** —— *Cor.* v. iv. 27. *a* **1718** PENN *Truth Rescued* II. Wks. 1726 I. 494 [Words] truliest apply'd to Himself. **1766** GOLDSM. *Vic. W.* xvii, An elegy that may truly be called tragical. **1875** JOWETT *Plato* (ed. 2) I. 88 Unable to decide which of you speaks truly.

4. a. In accordance with a rule or standard; exactly, accurately, precisely, correctly.

1375 in Horstm. *Altengl. Leg.* (1878) 138/2 Fro Moyses to Dauid kyng Fyue hondred & two [years],..To kounten riȝt trewely. **1486** *Bk. St. Albans, Her.* e v, Trulier they shal be blasit on this wyse. **1535** JOYE *Apol. Tindale* (Arb.) 20 Correcking a false Copie..that thei mought be the trwelyer printed agen. **1696** WHISTON *Th. Earth* II. (1722) 131 The little Planets about Jupiter move in Orbits truly Circular. **1787** BEST *Angling* (ed. 2) 10 A long rod is..of more use.. provided it is truly made. **1875** KNIGHT *Dict. Mech.* 593/2 To make the spindle run truly.

b. Rightly, justly, duly; as it ought to be, properly; often in phrase ***well and truly***; now also for colloq. emphasis: decisively, 'good and proper' (GOOD *adv.* d).

1417 *York Memo. Bk.* (Surtees) I. 182 Sufficiant recorde that he es wele and lely and treuly partyd fra thiens whare he come fra. **1458** J. JERNYNGAN *Let.* 1 June in N. Davis *Paston Lett.* (1976) II. 341 There was not so gret a batayle vpon þe se þis xl wyntyr; and for sothe we were wele and trewly bette. **1477** in *N. & Q.* (1975) July 290/2 The forme of this present lettre whiche ben wel and truly correct. **1521** B. ANSLAY tr. *C. de Pisani's Bk. Cyte of Ladyes* I. xiii, He shall reward them that well and truely maynteyneth hym. **1531** TINDALE *Exp. 1 John* ii. (1537) 29 Wyl ye therfore worship saintes truely? **1596** DALRYMPLE tr. *Leslie's Hist. Scot.* VII. (S.T.S.) II. 47 Quhen he saw [them]..as tha war worthie, treulie tormented. *a* **1647** HABINGTON *Surv. Worc.* in *Worcs. Hist. Soc. Proc.* III. 535 After whose death it [some land] returned truely to the monastery. **1760** STERNE *Tristram Shandy* I. xv. 82 The said intended marriage..to be well and truly solemnized and consummated. **1849** RUSKIN *Sev. Lamps* Introd. 4 Every action..is capable of a peculiar dignity..which we sometimes express by saying that it is truly done (as a line or tone is true). **1895** *Funk's Standard Dict.* s.v. *well* adv., *Well and truly* (Law), conformably to duty; heedfully; used in oaths and affirmations. **1935** *Discovery* Oct. 314/1 The great principle is laid well and truly down—not to attempt to hurry. **1948** G. V. GALWEY *Lift & Drop* iv. 72, I am—well and truly married. **1971** D. POTTER *Brit. Eliz. Stamps* iii. 41 As soon as the cup was well and truly won by England. **1973** *Guardian* 16 Feb. 13/8 British Brussels is well and truly split on the issue of the TUC's participation in Europe.

c. Rightfully, legitimately. *Obs.* or merged in 5.

1605 SHAKS. *Macb.* v. ii. 26 To giue Obedience, where 'tis truly ow'd. **1611** —— *Wint. T.* III. ii. 135 His innocent Babe truly begotten.

d. In accordance with nature, naturally.

1600 SHAKS. *A.Y.L.* III. iv. 55 If you will see a pageant truely plaid. **1884** CHURCH *Bacon* ix. 219 A sketch so truly and forcibly drawn.

e. Without cross-breeding; purely; also, without variation from the ancestral type.

1854 *Poultry Chron.* II. 63 Very fine truly-bred birds. **1859** DARWIN *Orig. Spec.* i. (1866) 17 The greyhound, bloodhound, [etc.] propagate their kind truly.

5. a. Genuinely, really, actually, in fact, in reality; sincerely, unfeignedly.

c **1380** WYCLIF *Wks.* (1880) 5 Men þat trewly dispisen synne. **1591** SHAKS. *Two Gent.* v. iv. 76, I doe as truely suffer, As ere I did commit. **1682** NORRIS *Hierocles* 35 So may we learn to know what we ourselves truly are. **1711** STEELE *Spect.* No. 79 ¶9 A Mind truly virtuous. **1857** MILLER *Elem. Chem.* (1862) III. 236 The view that they were truly alcohol radicles. **1874** MOTLEY *Barneveld* II. xviii. 276 Nothing could be more truly respectable. **1908** MISS FOWLER *Betw. Trent & Ancholme* 231 She truly believed..that he [her donkey] liked the thistles best.

b. Used to emphasize a statement (sometimes as a mere expletive): Indeed, forsooth, verily.

c **1205** LAY. 20720 Arður [etc.] þene wude al bileien.. Treo uppen oðer Treoliche faste. *c* **1300** *Cursor M.* 23952 (Edin.) Of hir trewlik es al mi tale. *a* **1400–50** *Alexander* 2094 'Bot treuly, ser', quod þe duke, 'gret tresore me thinke At Alexander þe athill'. *c* **1470** HENRY *Wallace* III. 268 Ane awfull chyftane trewly he is ane. **1598** SHAKS. *Merry W.* I. i. 322 Truely I will not goe first: truely-la: I will not doe you that wrong. **1641** BROME *Jov. Crew* III. Wks. 1873 III. 399 Never in our lives trooly. **1781** COWPER *Truth* 521 Charge not a God with such outrageous wrong. Truly, not I. **1821** SCOTT *Kenilw.* xli, 'Is he dead?' 'Ay, truly is he'. **1869** RUSKIN *Q. of Air* iii. §146 A wide freedom, truly!

†**c.** Hence as quasi-*sb.* in phr. ***by*** (***upon***) ***my truly***, ***in*** (***good***) ***truly***, used as a kind of oath or asseveration. (In quot. 1594, ? a person who uses 'truly' as an asseveration.) *colloq. Obs.*

1580 G. HARVEY *Two Lett.* Wks. (Grosart) I. 42 By my truly, I was neuer so scared in my lyfe. **1594** NASHE *Unfort. Trav.* Wks. (Grosart) V. 86 Hee..was one of those trecherous brother Trulies. **1604** WEBSTER *Westw. Hoe* II. i, Have you a new pen for me, master? for, by my truly, my old one is stark naught. **1672** WYCHERLEY *Love in Wood* I. i, Patience,..'tis a necessary virtue for a widow without a jointure, in truly. **1697** VANBRUGH *Relapse* v. v, Why, in good truly, as a body may say, he is but a slam. **1795** *Jemima* I. 110 Part, repeated Rosina, yes, by my truly must we.

d. In phr. ***yours truly***, the most formal of the phrases used in subscribing a letter; hence humorously = 'myself'.

[**1638** BAKER tr. *Balzac's Lett.* (vol. II.) 15 And with this I solemnly assure you that I truely am Sir Y^rs &c.] **1788** BURNS *Let. to R. Brown* 24 Feb., Believe me to be, My dear Sir, yours most truly, R. B. **1817** SCOTT *Let. to Miss J. Baillie* 26 Sept., in *Lockhart*, Yours truly, W. S. **1849** THACKERAY *Pendennis* iii, Give the young one a glass,..and score it up to yours truly. **1850** DE MORGAN *Let. to Sir J. Herschel* 26 Mar. in *Mem.* vii. (1882) 209 Yours very truly, A. De Morgan.

Truman ('tru:mən). The name of Harry S. *Truman* (1884–1972), U.S. President 1945–53, used *attrib.* in **Truman Doctrine**, the principle first enunciated by Truman in March 1947 that the United States should 'support free peoples who are resisting attempted subjugation'.

1947 *Sun* (Baltimore) 2 Apr. 18/1 At some time, at some point, the Soviet may not take kindly to our extension of the 'Truman Doctrine' to areas bordering upon her claimed sphere of influence. **1948** *Labour Monthly* Aug. 237 The Truman Doctrine aims at making Europe safe against socialism. **1958** *Polit. Sci. Quarterly* LXXIII. 321 The broad terms of the Truman doctrine merely claimed a broad right to intervene, even though there was no intention to exercise this right in full. **1964** MRS. L. B. JOHNSON *White House Diary* 10 Mar. (1970) 82 President Truman..said, 'It [*sc.* the Truman Doctrine] was all the Marshall Plan... It's just that the Greeks like the Jews and the Irish can holler louder than anybody else, if you have heard more about the Truman Doctrine than you have the others.' **1977** *Time* 6 June 14/1 By early 1947 Soviet adventurism had inspired the Truman Doctrine, with its pledge of military help to any free people threatened by Communist aggression.

trumbash, var. TROMBASH.

trumbe, var. TROMBE[1] *Obs.*; obs. Sc. f. TRUMP.

trumbill, trumle, obs. forms of TREMBLE.

†**trume, trome**, *sb. Obs.* Forms: 1 truma; 3–4 trume, trome, (4 trun; cf. SHELTRON[1]). [OE. *truma*, app. a derivative of the adj. *trum* firm, strong, able to resist (neither *truma* nor *trum* appears outside English.)

Notwithstanding a suspicious likeness in form and sense to L. *turma* 'troop, squadron, crowd, throng', the OE. derivatives of *truma* (e.g. *ȝetruma, antruma, trymman*, to TRIM, etc.) show it to be a native word.]

A body of persons, esp. of troops, etc. in battle array; a troop; a company, band; a crowd, multitude. Cf. THRUM *sb.*[1]

c **893** K. ÆLFRED *Oros.* v. xii. § 5 He hæfde eahta & eahtatiȝ coortana, þæt we nu truman hatað. **1205** LAY. 26968 Romleoden ræsden to..Breken Bruttene trume. *c* **1230** *Hali Meid.* 21 þat eadi trume of schimerinde meidenes. *c* **1300** *Havelok* 8 Hauelok was a ful god gome, He was ful god in euerie trome. *c* **1380** *Sir Ferumb.* 2372 þe Ameral þyderward haþ him nome, To þe feldeward þan ful riȝt; & wan he sawe þat huge trome, His herte anon gan lyȝte. *Ibid.* 5432 Wanne hire hostes were to-gadre y-come, þanne was ther an huge trome, iij hundred þousent & mo.

†**trume, trome**, *v. Obs. rare*[−1]. [f. prec.] ? *intr.* To assemble in a troop.

? *a* **1400** *Morte Arth.* 3592 Nowe bownes the bolde kynge ..Gers trome and trusse, and trynes forth aftyre.

trumeau (trymo). Pl. **trumeaux**. [Fr., lit. 'calf of the leg'.] **1.** Also ***trumeau mirror***. A pier-glass.

1883 J. W. MOLLETT *Illustr. Dict. Art & Archæol.* 327/1 *Trumeau*, a pier looking-glass. **1941** *Amer. Speech* XVI. 27 'Über dem Kamin..ist ein Trumeau-Speigel.'.. Cf. 'Trumeau' in Cent. Dict., also in Webster's; not in NED. Nowhere do I find any reference to 'Trumeau Mirror'. **1969** *Canad. Antiques Collector* May 11/1 The trumeau at the left is one of a pair flanking the dining room entrance. **1974** S. SHELDON *Other Side of Midnight* xiv. 278 From mantel top to ceiling rose a heavily carved trumeau mirror.

2. *Archit.* A stone pillar supporting the middle of the tympanum of a doorway, esp. in a church.

1890 C. H. MOORE *Gothic Archit.* vii. 262 After the eleventh century the principal portals of great monastic and cathedral churches were commonly divided into two openings by *trumeaux*, or pillars of stone, affording place for sculpture, which consisted usually of a statue with more or less subordinate carving. **1936** A. W. CLAPHAM *Romanesque Archit.* iv. 100 The 'trumeau' at Moissac, also with its superimposed pairs of lions, stands parent to the extraordinary creation at Souillac. **1968** M. JAY tr. *Bazin's Hist. World Sculpture* (1970) vii. 266 (*caption*) *Trumeau* of the old portal, church of Souillac. **1977** *New York Rev. Bks.* 12 May 8/4 The only other Romanesque church with two portals, which originally included trumeaux, is St. Lazare at Autun.

[**trummelett**, misreading for TRAMMELET.]

trump (trʌmp), *sb.*[1] Also 3–6 trompe, 6 (8–9 *arch.*) tromp, 4–5 troumpe, 4–7 trumpe, (5 trommpe, trumppe); β. 6 *Sc.* trum, trumme, trumb(e. [ME. a. F. *trompe* (12–13th c. in Hatz.-Darm.) = Prov. *tromba, trompa*, It. *tromba*; ulterior derivation uncertain.]

1. = TRUMPET *sb.* 1. *arch.* and *poet.*

1297 R. GLOUC. (Rolls) 8166 Of trompes & of tabors þe sarazins made þere So gret noyse. *a* **1300** *Cursor M.* 15011 (Cott.) Wit harp and pipe, and horn and trump. **1303** R. BRUNNE *Handl. Synne* 4770 As Dauyd seyþ yn þe sautere,.. Wurschepe God, yn troumpes, and sautre. *c* **1375** *Sc. Leg. Saints* xiv. (*Lucas*) 78 þat þe angel his trumpe sal blav, And ger þame ryse þat lyis law. **1382** WYCLIF *1 Cor.* xv. 52 In the laste trumpe; forsoth the trumpe schal synge. —— *1 Thess.* iv. 15 In the voys of archaungel, and in the trumpe of God. *c* **1440** *Alphabet of Tales* 306 He sett þis trompe to his mouthe & began to blaw. **1526** *Pilgr. Perf.* (W. de W. 1531) 214 b, The day of the sounde of the claryon & trumpe of god. **1622** DRAYTON *Poly-olb.* xix. 141 With their crooked trumps his Tritons Neptune sent. **1748** THOMSON *Cast. Indol.* I. xxviii, Withouten tromp was proclamation made. **1805** SCOTT *Last Minstr.* VI. xxxi, When louder yet, and yet more dread, Swells the high trump that wakes the dead! **1835** LYTTON *Rienzi* v. iii, Like a king in his pomp, To the blast of the tromp, And the roar of the mighty drum.

β. **15..** *Aberdeen Regr.* (Jam.), To play vpoune the trum nychtly, to convene the waich at ewin. **1549** *Acc. Ld. High Treas. Scot.* IX. 281 Foure Duchemen quha with thair trumbis playit before Ladye Barbara. *Ibid.* 283 For ane trumme..to convene hors and pyonaris.

b. = JEWS' HARP, JEWS' TRUMP. Now *Sc.* and *north. Ireland.* ***tongue of the trump***: see TONGUE *sb.* 14 c.

1549 *Compl. Scot.* vi. 65 The thrid [shepherd] playit on ane trump. **1670** NARBOROUGH *Jrnl.* in *Acc. Sev. Late Voy.* I. (1694) 63, I gave them a Hatchet and Knives, and Beads, and Toys, Trumps etc. **1774** [see JEWS' HARP]. **1830** SCOTT *Demonol.* 314 She played on a Jews harp called in Scotland a trump.

c. ***trump marine*** = trumpet marine: see TRUMPET *sb.* 2 b.

1667 PEPYS *Diary* 24 Oct., We in to see..one Monsieur Prin play on the trump-marine, which he do beyond belief. **1863** THORNBURY *True as Steel* II. 164 Some blew hideous discord from the square-mouthed trump marine (a sort of bassoon). [An error.]

d. *transf.* in reference to a sound like that of a trumpet.

1809 W. IRVING *Knickerb.* IV. ii. (1861) 117 Wilhelmus Kieft..availed himself of that musical organ or trump which nature has implanted in the midst of a man's face. **1895** J. G. MILLAIS *Breath fr. Veldt* (1899) 26 At sunset their [cranes'] hoarse trumps may be heard as they wing their flight to some solitary spot.

e. *slang* or *vulgar*. The act of breaking wind audibly.

1903 in FARMER & HENLEY *Slang*.

†**2.** *transf.* One who plays a trump, a trumpeter.

13.. *Sir Beues* (A.) 3793 þe trompes gonne here bemes blowe. **1473–4** *Acc. Ld. High Treas. Scot.* I. 14 Gevin to James sadillare for a sadill to the Kingis trompis.

†**3.** *transf.* A hollow tube or pipe; *spec.* (*a*) the convoluted windpipe of the crane; (*b*) the trunk of an elephant; the proboscis of an insect. *Obs. rare.*

c **1440** *Pallad. on Husb.* IX. 179 To ha made Trumpis of cley bi potters. *c* **1460** J. RUSSELL *Bk. Nurture* 431 The Crane..of hyre trompe in þe brest loke þat ye beware [in carving]. **1648** HEXHAM II, *Rotel ofte russel*, the Trumpe or Snout of an Elephant. **1750** *Phil. Trans.* XLVI. 545 So that it [the Bee] does not suck, but laps or licks with its rough Fang or Tromp, like a Dog.

4. *fig.* One who or that which proclaims, celebrates, or summons loudly like a trumpet; esp. in ***trump of fame*** and the like (cf. quot. *c* 1384 in TRUMP *v.*[1] 2). *arch.* and *poet.*

1531 ELYOT *Gov.* III. xix, Howe moche worthyar had he [Cato] bene to haue hadde Homere, the trumpe of his fame immortall, than Achilles. **1548** UDALL, etc. *Erasm. Par. Matt.* iv. 33 The trumpe of the voyce of the gospell. **1575** R. B. *Appius & Virg.* Prol., Who doth desire the trump of fame, to sound vnto the Skies. **1630** QUARLES *Funeral Elegies* xiii, When the latest breath of fame Shall want her Trumpe, to glorifie a name. **1741–2** GRAY *Agrippina* 122 Say we sound The trump of liberty. **1827** KEBLE *Chr. Y.*, *1st Sun. Adv.* i, Awake—again the Gospel-trump is blown.

5. *Comb.*, as ***trump-like*** adj., ***trump-maker***.

1609 *Reg. Mag. Sig. Scot.* 57/2 Confectoris instrumentorum lusorialium lie trumpmaker. *c* **1611** CHAPMAN *Iliad* II. 419 A breast of brasse, a voyce Infract and trumplike.

trump (trʌmp), *sb.*[2] Also 6 troumpe, 6–7 tromp(e, trumpe. [Corruption of TRIUMPH *sb.*, in senses 8, 8 b.]

1. a. A playing-card of that suit which for the time being ranks above the other three, so that any one such card can 'take' any card of another suit; *spec.* the card, usually that last turned up by the dealer, determining this suit; also, *pl.* (formerly also in *sing.*), the suit thus determined.

1529 LATIMER *1st Serm. on Card* in Foxe *A. & M.* (1563) 1302/2 Heartes is trumpe. —— *2nd Serm.* ibid. 1306/1 Cast thy tromp vnto them both, and gather them all three together. **1575** *Gamm. Gurton* II. ii. B iv, There is 5 trumps beside the Queene. **1607** HEYWOOD *Wom. Kild w. Kindn.* Wks. 1874 II. 123 *Anne.* What's trumpes? *Wend.* Harts. **1656** EARL MONM. tr. *Boccalini's Advts. fr. Parnass.* I. ii. (1674) 4 Every the least Trump did take all the best Coat-Cards. **1779** WARNER in Jesse *Selwyn & Contemp.* (1844) IV. 254, I won the first trick and led a trump. **1849** HANNAY (*title*) Hearts are Trumps. **1885** PROCTOR *Whist* vii. 88 With good plain cards and five trumps you need never hesitate to lead trumps.

†**b.** An obsolete card-game, known also as ruff.

1529 LATIMER *1st Serm. on Card* in Foxe *A. & M.* (1563) 1303/1 There be many one that breaketh this carde,.. and playeth there with oftentimes at the blinde trompe, wherby they be no winners but great losers. **1575** *Gamm. Gurton* II. ii. B iv, We be fast set at trumpe, man, hard by the fyre. **1598** FLORIO, *Trionfo*,.. also a trump at cards, or the play called trump or ruff. **1688** R. HOLME *Armoury* III. xvi. (Roxb.) 72/1 Ruffe and Honors, and Whisk, which are generally amongst the Vulgar Termed Trump. **1798** *Sporting Mag.* XII. 299 Laws of the game of Trumps. [**1807** DOUCE *Illustr. Shaks.* II. 96 The old card game of trump.. bore a very strong resemblance to our modern whist.]

c. An act of trumping; the taking of a trick with a trump card.

1853 LYTTON *My Novel* I. xii, Parson.. mixes all the cards together again, and.. groans,.. 'The cruelest trump!'

2. a. *fig.* and in *fig.* context. ***to turn up trumps***, to turn out well or successfully (*mod. colloq.*).

1595 *Locrine* IV. ii, She.. snatcht vp a fagot stick.. and came furiously marching towards me,.. thundering out.. Thou drunken knaue, where hast thou bin so long?.. and so shee began to play knaues trumps. **1621** BURTON *Anat. Mel.* III. iii. I. ii. (1651) 602 They turned up trumpe, before the Cards were shuffled. **1641** HOLLIS in Rushw. *Hist. Coll.* III. (1692) I. 346 To be honest when every body else is honest, when Honesty is in fashion, and is Trump, as I may say, is nothing so meritorious. *a* **1734** NORTH *Exam.* III. vi. §63 (1740) 470 The same Card was going to be Trump in the factious Game against King Charles II. **1785** GROSE *Dict. Vulg. T.* s.v. *Trump*, Something may turn up trumps, something lucky may happen. **1819** M. WILMOT *Let.* 3 Sept. (1935) 17 A little converted Jew.. who received us into his house at a moderate rate and has turned up such *trumps* that I must introduce him to you. **1862** W. W. COLLINS *No Name* IV. viii, Instances.. of short courtships and speedy marriages, which have turned up trumps—I beg your pardon—which have turned out well, after all. **1890** J. HATTON *Order of Czar* II. II. xiii. 159 Nitrates have turned up trumps.

†**b.** *fig.* An obstruction, a hindrance: in phr. (***to cast***) ***a trump in*** (one's) ***way***. *Obs.*

1529 LATIMER *1st Serm. on Card* in Foxe *A. & M.* (1563) 1302/2 We wil fyrst cast a trumpe in theyr way, and play with them at cardes who shall haue the better. *a* **1548** HALL *Chron., Edw. V* 2 Euery one of these castes had been a troumpe in the duke of Gloucesters waye. **1577–87** HOLINSHED *Chron.* III. 855/2 He thought good first to send him some whither out of the waie, least he might cast a trumpe in his waie.

c. ***to put*** (one) ***to*** (†***upon***) ***his trump*** or ***trumps***: To oblige a card-player to play out his trumps; *fig.* 'to put to the last expedient' (J.).

1559 *Mirr. Mag., Jack Cade* xx, Ere he took me, I put him to his trumpes. **1584** LYLY *Campaspe* III. iv, Doeth not your beauty put the painter to his trump? **1681** DRYDEN *Span. Friar* IV. i, We are now put upon our last trump. **1697** DAMPIER *Voy.* (1729) I. 526 The Wind.. oft put us to our trumps to manage the Ship. **1751** R. PALTOCK *P. Wilkins* xiv. (1883) 46/2 The strangeness of her dress put me to my trumps, to conceive either what it was, or how it was put on. **1824** W. IRVING *T. Trav.* I. I. ii. 9 Whether such an unexpected accession of company.. would not put the housekeeper to her trumps to accommodate them. **1907** W. JAMES *Pragmatism* iv. 142 A bit of danger or hardship puts us agreeably to our trumps.

3. a. *colloq.* as a term of hearty commendation: A person of surpassing excellence; a first-rate fellow; a 'brick'.

[**1762** T. BRYDGES *Burlesque Homer* I. (1797) 37 But I, in spite of all his frumps, Shall make him know I'm king of trumps.] **1819** *Sporting Mag.* IV. 236 The Irish trump again got the throw. **1829** *Chron.* in *Ann. Reg.* 65/1 Girls of dissolute character.. called out.. 'Good bye, Tom! God bless you, my trump!' **1837** DICKENS *Pickw.* xli, You're a trump. **1867** TROLLOPE *Chron. Barset* I. xv. 127 Nobody knows better than you what a trump I got in my wife. **1894** DU MAURIER *Trilby* II. 257 Taffy, what a regular downright old trump you are!

b. *Austral.* and *N.Z. slang.* A person in authority.

1937 PARTRIDGE *Dict. Slang* 912/2 *Trump of the dump, the*, anyone in authority: New Zealanders': in G[reat] W[ar]. **1941** BAKER *Dict. Austral. Slang* 78 *Trump*, a commanding officer. Diggers' slang. **1950** *Landfall* (N.Z.) IV. 126 The hoops are on the last cask by 11.45, and the trump calls out all hands to load the railway wagon. *Ibid.* 127, The trump comes in and calls us gentlemen and wishes us the very best. **1974** D. STUART *Prince of my Country* xiv. 142 There's a blackfeller or two knows which is which, shafters, and pin, and body, and leaders, the trump says.

4. *attrib.* and *Comb.*, as ***trump card*** (also *fig.*), ***lead***, ***suit***; ***trump-like*** adj.; **trump signal**, at Bridge and Whist, a call for trumps: see CALL *v.* 22 d (*Funk's Stand. Dict.*, 1895).

1822 BYRON *Juan* VIII. xxv, 'The best Intentions'.. form all mankind's *trump-card. **1876** A. CAMPBELL-WALKER *Correct Card* (1880) 65 After the dealer has taken the trump card into his hand. **1884** *Times* (weekly ed.) 10 Oct. 9/3 The trump card which the Radicals played was the general remission of taxes. **1870** HARDY & WARE *Mod. Hoyle* 25 *Trump leads, without strength in trumps can only be justified [etc.]. **1836–9** DICKENS *Sk. Boz, Making a Night of it*, A certain *trump-like punctuality in turning up just in the very nick of time. **1901** C. J. MELROSE *Bridge Whist* 41 His partner must.. be on the alert to lead trumps through the opponent's strength, and to look out for a *trump signal from his partner. **1964** FREY & TRUSCOTT *Official Encycl. Bridge* 634/1 Some players use the trump signal whenever they hold three trumps. **1861** *Macm. Mag.* Dec. 130 No trump is turned up, the *trump suit being determined in another way. **1862** 'CAVENDISH' *Whist* (1879) 10 Any one may inquire what the trump suit is, at any time.

Hence ˈ**trumpless** *a.* (*nonce-wd.*), having or containing no trumps.

1899 A. MAINWARING *Cut Cavendish* 51 'Chicane', i.e. a trumpless hand, counts twice the value of the trump suit.

†**trump**, *sb.*[3] *Sc. Obs. rare.* [(?) Back-formation from TRUMPERY.] A thing of small value, a trifle; *pl.* goods of small value, trumpery.

1513 DOUGLAS *Æneis* V. xii. 47 From distructioun deliuer.. Thir sobir trumpis, and mene grayth of Troianis. *Ibid.* VIII. Prol. 107 Ten tendis ar a trump, bot gif he tak ma, Ane kinrik of paroch kyrkis cuppillit with commendis.

trump (trʌmp), *v.*[1] Forms: see TRUMP *sb.*[1]; also 4 *Sc.* **trwmp**. [ME. a. OF. *tromper* (12th c. in Godef.), f. *trompe*, TRUMP *sb.*[1]]

1. *intr.* To blow or sound a trumpet: = TRUMPET *v.* 1. Also with *up*. ? *Obs.* or *arch.*

13.. *Coer de L.* 3892 They trumpyd, and her baners displaye. **13..** *Cursor M.* 21307 (Cott.) An.. ringes.., dinnes þe toþer, trumpes þe thrid. **1375** BARBOUR *Bruce* VIII. 293 He left his amonystyng, And gert trumpe to þe assemble. *Ibid.* XII. 491 He gert trwmp vp to the assemble. **1377** LANGL. *P. Pl.* B. XIII. 230, I can noither tabre ne trompe, ne telle none gestes. *c* **1470** HARDING *Chron.* CCXXX. (MS. Lansd. 204 lf. 219 b), The kynge.. trumped vp and home he rode in hy. **1513** DOUGLAS *Æneis* XI. viii. 17 Tharfor trump vp, blaw furth thyne eloquens. **1535** COVERDALE *2 Chron.* xiii. 15 The prestes tromped with the trompettes.

b. To give forth a trumpet-like sound; *spec.* to break wind audibly (*slang* or *vulgar*).

c **1425** WYNTOUN *Cron.* VI. ii. 176 In publik placis ay fra þat day Scho wes behynde þan trumpande ay; Sa wes scho schamyt in ilk steid. **1552** HULOET, Trump or let a crackke, or fart, *crepo*. **1598** FLORIO, *Trombeggiare*,.. to snort, to trump or bray as an asse. **1719** D'URFEY *Pills* I. 35 She who doth Trump, Through defect in her rump. **1798** R. CUMBERLAND *Aristoph. Clouds* ii, I too.. under sufferance trump against your thunder:.. my frights.. Have pinch'd and cholick'd my poor bowels so. *a* **1845** [see *trumping* below].

2. *trans.* To proclaim, celebrate, or extol by, or as by, the sound of a trumpet: = TRUMPET *v.* 2 b. Now *rare* or *Obs.*

c **1384** CHAUCER *H. Fame* III. 539 Take forth thy trumpe,.. That is cleped sklaundre.. For thou shalt trumpe alle the contrarie Of that they han don wel or fayre. **1422** tr. *Secreta Secret., Priv. Priv.* 163 The trues [= truce] weryn trumped vp for that day. **1548** UDALL *Erasm. Par. Luke* iv. 52 That the fathers glorye may be.. troumped abrode by the sonne. **1686** F. SPENCE tr. *Varillas' Ho. Medicis* 231 This infirmity.. trumpt him up the aversion of such people as knew not otherwise his merit. **1847** L. HUNT *Men, Women, & B.* II. i. 4 See also how Pope, and Swift, and others, trumped up Lord Bolingbroke for a philosopher!

¶ **3.** *intr.* To march or go (as at the sound of a trumpet). Cf. quots. 1375, *c* 1470 in sense 1. *Obs.*

1513 DOUGLAS *Æneis* XI. ix. 4 Eneas all his ost and haill army Hes rasyt, trumping to the town in hy. *Ibid.* xiii. 99 Bot this Orsilochus fled hyr in the feyld, And gan to trump with mony a turnyng went.

Hence ˈ**trumping** *vbl. sb.* and *ppl. a.*

13.. *K. Alis.* 924 (Bodl. MS.), Þer was trumpyng & tabouryng. **1398** TREVISA *Barth. De P.R.* IX. xxvii. (Bodl. MS.) lf. 97 b, By trumpinge þe peple was icleped to þis feste þat hatte neomenia. **1631** P. FLETCHER *Sicelides* III. iv. F ij b, Thou bluebeard Neptune, and thou trumphing [*sic*] Triton. *a* **1845** HOOD *Schoolboy Joys & Griefs*, Six small Boys; Who ever and anon declare their joys, With trumping horns, and juvenile huzzas.

†**trump**, *v.*[2] *Obs.* Also 4 *Sc.* **trwmp**, 6 **trumpe**, 6–7 **tromp(e**. [a. F. *tromper* (14th c.), of uncertain origin; perh. the same word as prec.: see Littré.] *trans.* To deceive, cheat.

In quot. 1629, perh. identified with TRUMP *v.*[3]

1375 BARBOUR *Bruce* XIX. 712 Than sall we all be at our will, And thai sall let thame trwmpit [*v.r.* trumpyt] Ill. **1513** DOUGLAS *Æneis* I. vi. 82 That fals man,.. With wanhope trumpit the lele luwair. **1584** J. CARMICHAEL *Lett.* in *Wodrow Soc. Misc.* (1844) 415 To haif bein trompit with fair words. **1598** DALLINGTON *Meth. Trav.* E iij, They very wrongfully tromped the heires of Edward the third, of their enioying this Crowne of France. **1629** B. JONSON *New Inn* I. i, When she [Fortune] is pleas'd to trick or tromp mankind.

trump, *v.*[3] [f. TRUMP *sb.*[2]

Appears first in figurative senses (2–3); in some early quots. it may have been confused with TRUMP *v.*[2]; but the sense-development is not quite clear.]

I. 1. *Cards.* **a.** *trans.* To put a trump upon; to take with a trump.

1598 FLORIO, *Trionfare*,.. to trump at cards. **1680** COTTON *Gamester* xi. 87 A Card that is trumped by the follower, if the next player hath none of the former suit he must trump it again. **1778** C. JONES *Hoyle's Games Impr.* 58 If your Partner forces you to trump a Card early in the Deal. **1837** DICKENS *Pickw.* vi, Miller ought to have trumped the diamond. **1862** 'CAVENDISH' *Whist* (1879) 70 You may sometimes discontinue a suit if you suspect it will be trumped.

b. *absol.* or *intr.* To play a trump; to take a trick with a trump. ***trump out***, to play out one's trumps.

1680 COTTON *Gamester* x. 82 You ought to have a special eye to what Cards are play'd out, that you may know.. how to trump securely. **1746** HOYLE *Whist* (ed. 6) 15 Do not trump out. *Ibid.* 79 If your Partner calls.., you are to trump to him. **1862** 'CAVENDISH' *Whist* (1879) 108 It is an advantage to trump when you are weak.

2. *fig.* or in fig. context: in quot. 1586, ? to 'put to one's trumps', to nonplus; now usually, to beat, to 'cap'.

1586 FERNE *Blaz. Gentrie* 190 If you be not trumped, in the blazonne of this coate, I care not to what I put you. *a* **1612** HARINGTON *Epigr.* IV. xii, An odious play, and yet in Court oft seen, A sawcy Knave, to trump both King and Queene. **1681** DRYDEN *Princess of Cleves* Prol. 35 But since they're at renouncing, 'tis our parts, To trump their diamonds, as they trump our hearts. **1860** THACKERAY *Lovel* iii, I trumped her old-world stories.. with the latest.. intelligence. **1880** S. WALPOLE *Hist. Eng.* III. 296 The Liberals set themselves to trump his [Peel's] best cards.

II. †**3.** ***trump in*** (one's) ***way*** (cf. TRUMP *sb.*[2] 2 b): **a.** *trans.* To cast in one's way as a hindrance or obstruction; in quot. 1553, to allege against one (cf. 5 b). *Obs.*

1553 BALE *Gardiner's De vera Obed.* H j b, And that, that is fondly layed to the husbandes charge after he is divorced, because he perfourmed not his promyse, that he ought not to haue made: shall that.. be.. earnestly tromped in my waye? **1583** GOLDING *Calvin on Deut.* vi. 34 To ouercome all that euer the deuill trumpeth in our way. **1607** *Schol. Disc. agst. Antichr.* I. iv. 178 Sathan is suffered to trompe hinderances in their way.

b. *intr.* To get in one's way; to obstruct or impede one. *Obs.*

1570 FOXE *A. & M.* (ed. 2) 1146/2 But here now commeth Syr Thomas More trumpyng in our way. **1650** WELDON *Crt. Jas. I* 53 For all their setting their Cards.. to their owne advantages.., there was one Knave in the Packe would cousen their designes, and Trump in their way.

†**4.** To impose or thrust (something) *upon* a person. *Obs.*

1694 LESLIE *Short Meth. w. Deists* (1699) 3 Authors have been Trump'd upon us, Interpolated and Corrupted. *a* **1704** T. BROWN *Dial. Dead, Reas. Oaths* Wks. 1711 IV. 96 There are abundance of ill-affected Men.. that have trumped that unlucky Card upon the Dr. *a* **1716** SOUTH *Serm.* (1727) VI. 104 A sort of odd ill-natur'd Men, whom neither Hopes nor Fears.. can prevail upon to have any.. forlorn.. Kinswomen of any Lord or Grandee.. trump'd upon them.

b. *intr.* ? To impose *upon*. *Obs. rare.*

a **1716** SOUTH *Serm.* (1727) IV. 384 Fit for nothing but to be trumped and trampled upon, to be led by the Nose.

5. ***trump up*** (trans.). †**a.** ? To put (one) off *with*. *Obs. rare*$^{-1}$.

1634 MASSINGER *Very Woman* II. iii, Hang honesty! Trump me not up with 'honesty'!

†**b.** To bring up, bring forward, allege. *Obs.*

1697 T. SMITH in *Lett. Lit. Men* (Camden) 252 When the Benedictine Monks were so busy to trump up old charters of exemption and priveleges. *a* **1704** T. BROWN *Laconics* Wks. 1711 IV. 14 The Cavaliers.. us'd to trump up the 12th of the Romans upon the Parliament; the Parliament trump'd it upon the Army. **1710** PALMER *Proverbs* 333 Necessity is trump'd up for a plea. **1712** ADDISON *Spect.* No. 507 ¶2 To husband a lie, and trump it up in some extraordinary emergency. **1772** *Town & Country Mag.* 128 B[olland] trumped up an imaginary debt against him.

c. To get up or devise in an unscrupulous way; to forge, fabricate, invent.

1695 W. W. *Colbatch's New Lt. Chirurg. Put out* 64 His Pouder being.. disgraced, he was obliged to trump up another Medicine to supply its Defect. **1726** C. D'ANVERS *Craftsman* No. 3 (1727) 22 They.. forewarn us to beware of impostures trumpt up in imitation of their approved remedies. *a* **1774** TUCKER *Lt. Nat.* (1834) II. 328 Their very existence is mere hypothesis, trumped up to serve a turn. **1794** GODWIN *Cal. Williams* 277 If.. those servants could trump up such accusations. **1809** MALKIN *Gil Blas* IV. vii. ¶16 You have trumped up a cock-and-bull story. **1885** HOWELLS *Silas Lapham* viii, She had not.. courage to confess.. why she had come, but trumped up an excuse.

Hence **trumped** (trʌmpt) *ppl. a.* (only in *trumped-up*, in sense 5 c).

1728 FIELDING *Love in Several Masques* V. xii. 76, I know my Title to be secure, it must be some trumped-up Cheat. **1777** *Sixteenth Ode of Third Bk. Horace Imit.* 21 A Pamphlet fill'd with trump'd-up stories. **1800** COLERIDGE *Wallenst.* II. iii, A trumped up Spanish story. **1878** BOSW. SMITH *Carthage* 302 Three hundred.. youths were thrown into prison.. on a trumped-up charge.

†**trumpa** (ˈtrʌmpə). *Obs.* [ad. F. *trumpeau*, *trumpo*.] = SPERM WHALE.

1625 PURCHAS *Pilgrimes* III. 471 The third sort of Whale is called Trumpa, being as long as the first, but thicker forwards. **1851** H. MELVILLE *Moby Dick* I. xxxi. 215 This [sperm] whale, among the English of old vaguely known as the Trumpa whale.

trumper[1] (ˈtrʌmpə(r)). Forms: 4 **trompor**, **-er**, **trumpour**, 4–5 **trompour(e**, 5 **trumpowre**, 5– **trumper**. [a. OF. *trompeor*, *-peur*, *-pour*, *trumpeur*, etc. (13th c.), f. *tromper*, TRUMP *v.*[1]]

†**1.** A trumpeter. *Obs.*

13.. *K. Alis.* 3426 For the noise of the taboures, And the trumpours [*Bodl. MS.* trumpes] and jangelours. *c* **1330** *King of Tars* 499 Trompors gunne heore bemes blowe. *a* **1440** *Sir Degrev.* 661 Trompers tromped to the mete. **14..** *Nom.* in Wr.-Wülcker 693/7 *Hec tubicina*, a trumper. *Ibid.* 696/30 *Hic tubicen*, a trumper. **1483** *Cath. Angl.* 395/2 A Trumper, *buccinator*.

2. *slang* or *vulgar*. (Cf. TRUMP *sb.*[1] 1 e, *v.*[1] 1 b.)

1836–48 B. D. WALSH *Aristoph., Clouds* 313.

†ˈ**trumper**[2]. *Obs.* Forms: 5 **trompour**, **-er**, **-eur**, 6 **trumpour**, **-ir**, **troumpar**, 6– **trumper**. [a. F. *trompeur* (13–14th c. in Godef. *Compl.*), f. *tromper*, TRUMP *v.*[2]] A deceiver, impostor, cheat. (In quot. 1456 app. a trifler: cf. TRUMPERY.)

a **1450** *Knt. de la Tour* (1906) 33 He nis not so trewe a knight as we wende, for he is but a tromper and a iaper. **1456** SIR G. HAYE *Law Arms* (S.T.S.) 287 For syk maner of tromperyis, a prince sulde nocht juge na thole bataill to be. Bot he suld.. punys sik trompouris, that.. gage bataill for sik fule causis. **1560** ROLLAND *Seven Sag.* 37 Fy Trumpour that did sic ane deid. **1571** in Calderwood *Hist. Kirk* (Wodrow Soc.) III. 104 The most vile carion,.. the greatest trumper in all Europ. **1603** *Philotus* l, How durst thow trumper be sa bald To tant or tell, that he was ald?

trumpery ('trʌmpəri), *sb.* (*a.*) Forms: 5–6 **tropery(e**, (6 **tromperey, troumperie, trumprie**), 6–7 **tromp-, trumperie**, 6– **trumpery**. [a. F. *tromperie* (14th c. in Godef. *Compl.*), f. *tromper* TRUMP *v.*[2]: see -ERY 1.]

† **1.** Deceit, fraud, imposture, trickery. *Obs.*

1456 SIR G. HAYE *Law Arms* (S.T.S.) 226 Sa that thare be na trompery. *a* **1578** LINDESAY (Pitscottie) *Chron. Scot.* (S.T.S.) I. 141 They concordit alltogither in trumperie and fallsit. **1677** GALE *Crt. Gentiles* II. III. 78 Their Ethics were but false or..imperfect ideas of Vertues..their politics were but carnal and so false reasons of State..and therefore stiled in the Scripture tromperie, deceit, and lies. **1847** DISRAELI *Tancred* II. iv, Irish Papists denouncing the whole movement as fraud and trumpery.

pl. **1481** CAXTON *Godeffroy* clxiii. 241 His fayr wordes full of tromperyes and deceytes. **1598** DALLINGTON *Meth. Trav.* H j b, He left none of his trumperies and double dealings vnreuealed. **1646** SIR T. BROWNE *Pseud. Ep.* VII. xii. 362 He runnes into corners, exercising minor trumperies, and acting his deceits in Witches, Magicians, Diviners. **1687** R. L'ESTRANGE *Brief Hist. Times* I. 140 How was the Justice of the Nation, Abus'd, and Impos'd upon by the Trumperies of Confederacy.

2. 'Something of less value than it seems'; hence, 'something of no value; trifles' (J.); worthless stuff, trash, rubbish. (Usually *collective sing.*; also, now rarely, *pl.*)

a. Applied to material objects (see also c, d, e).

1531 *Test. Ebor.* (Surtees) V. 324 A tub, a hogeshed w[t] other trumperie, viij d. **1611** SHAKS. *Wint. T.* IV. iv. 608, I haue sold all my Tromperie: not a counterfeit Stone, not a Ribbon, Glasse, Pomander, Browch..to keepe my Pack from fasting. **1789** MRS. PIOZZI *Journ. France*, etc. II. 353 A heap of trumpery fit to furnish out the shop of a Westminster pawnbroker. **1807** W. IRVING *Salmag.* vi. (1824) 90 An abundance of trumpery and rubbish, with which the house is encumbered,..every room, and closet, and corner, is crammed with three-legged chairs, clocks without hands, swords without scabbards [etc.].

pl. *a* **1618** RALEIGH *Invent. Shipping* 41 Silver, Cut works, Cambricks, and a world of other trumperyes. **1848** THACKERAY *Van. Fair* xliv, Drawers and cupboards crammed with the dirty relics and congregated trumperies of a couple of generations of Lady Crawleys.

b. Applied to abstract things, as beliefs, practices, discourse, writing, etc.: Nonsense, 'rubbish'.

1456 SIR G. HAYE *Law Arms* (S.T.S.) 287 For gif fulis.. be sa daft that thai wage bataill for lytill, evyn as to say..that he dauncis or syngis better na he dois, or for syk maner of tromperyis. **1578** LYTE *Dodoens* III. lx. 401 The blacke spottes growing on the backside of the leaues [of 'male fern': cf. FERN-SEED]..some do gather thinking to worke wonders, but to say the trueth, it is nothing els but trumperie and superstition. **1693** DRYDEN *Juvenal* vi. 191 With all their Trumpery of Charms. **1726** DE FOE *Hist. Devil* I. ii. (1840) 23 All the metaphysical trumpery of the schools. **1846** D. JERROLD *Mrs. Caudle's Curt. Lect.* viii, I'd put an end to free-masonry and all such trumpery.

c. Applied contemptuously to religious practices, ceremonies, ornaments, etc. regarded as idle or superstitious. (Cf. TRINKET *sb.*[1] 3.) Now *rare* or merged in general sense.

1542–5 BRINKLOW *Lament.* 15 b, Pardons, and other of their tromperye, hath bene bought and solde. **1566** in Peacock *Eng. Ch. Furniture* (1866) 95 Banner clothes, crosse clothes, with the rest of the trash as vestments albes and such lik tromperie—wear defacid..by the said churchwardens. **1667** MILTON *P.L.* III. 475 Embryos, and Idiots, Eremits and Friers White, Black and Grey, with all thir trumperie. **1756** C. LUCAS *Ess. Waters* III. 12 This City is famed for.. reliques of saints, and such like holy trumpery. **1824** SOUTHEY *Bk. of Ch.* (1841) 267 St. Francis, St. Dominic, and their fellows, must dislodge with all their trumpery.

pl. **1548** *Luther's Art. Faith* Pref. A v, Our juglynge tromperies. **1625** PURCHAS *Pilgrims* IX. vii. §1. 1487 Wearied with the trumperies of the Religion of Mahumet. **1704** J. PITTS *Acc. Mohammetans* vi. (1738) 55 They blame the Papists for having so many Trumperies in their Churches.

d. Showy but unsubstantial apparel; worthless finery.

1610 SHAKS. *Temp.* IV. i. 186 The trumpery in my house, goe bring it hither For stale to catch these theeues. **1801** MAR. EDGEWORTH *Out of Debt* iii, 'You have brought me to the gallows, and all for this trumpery', cried he, snatching her gaudy hat from her head. **1851** C. BRONTE in Mrs. Gaskell *Life* (1857) 364 It would be no shame for a person of my means to wear a cheaper thing;..if you..call it 'trumpery' so much the worse.

e. *Gardening.* Weeds or refuse, such as hinder the growth of valuable plants. *Obs.* exc. *dial.*

1669 WORLIDGE *Syst. Agric.* (1681) 214 Broom, Furze, Heath, and other suchlike trumpery, that delight only in barren Lands. **1707** MORTIMER *Husb.* (1721) II. 387 Finish your last Weeding, and cleanse your Garden of Trumpery. **1758** R. BROWN *Compl. Farmer* II. (1760) 30 It occasions its running to May-weed, and other trumpery. **1888** in ELWORTHY *W. Somerset Word-bk.*

f. Applied to a person, esp. a woman: cf. TRASH *sb.*[1] 4. ? *Obs.* exc. *dial.*

1738 SWIFT *Pol. Conversat.* iii. 195 For Want of Company, welcome Trumpery. **1766** GOLDSM. *Vic. W.* xxi, Out, I say;..tramp, thou infamous strumpet.. What! you trumpery, to come and take up an honest house without cross or coin to bless yourself with! **1852** MRS. STOWE *Uncle Tom's C.* xviii, Get out wid ye, ye trumpery—I won't have ye round!

B. *attrib.* or *adj.* Of little or no value; trifling, paltry, insignificant; worthless, rubbishy, trashy.

1576 FLEMING *Caius' Dogs* (1880) 16 A Hare..was seene ..playing with his former feete vppon a tabbaret... This is no trumpery tale, nor trifling toye. **1748** H. WALPOLE *Lett.* (1845) II. 229 Mr. Ashurst..has built a trumpery new house. **1781** —— *Let. to W. Mason* 14 Apr., Dr. Johnson's 'Life of Pope'..is a most trumpery performance. **1810** SCOTT *Let. to Miss J. Baillie* 23 Nov., in *Lockhart*, I hope you will set some value upon this little trumpery brooch, because it is..a Scotch harp, and set with Iona stones. **1865** M. ARNOLD *Ess. Crit.* viii. (1875) 323 The accents of a trumpery rhetorician. **1869** TROLLOPE *He knew*, etc. xvi, It seems a trumpery quarrel,—as to who should beg each other's pardon first.

Hence **'trumperiness**.

1868 A. K. H. BOYD *Less. Mid. Age* 271 How these things impress the lover of Gothic who dwells in a country of churches of inexpressible trumperiness and shabbiness!

trumpet ('trʌmpɪt), *sb.* Also 4–6 **trompette, -et, trumpette**, 5 **trompett, troumpette**, 6–7 **trumpett**; *Sc.* 5 **trompat, troumpat(e, trumpate**, 5–6 **trumpat**, 6 **-ait**. [a. F. *trompette* (14th c.), dim. f. *trompe*, TRUMP *sb.*[1]]

1. a. A musical wind-instrument (or one of a class of such) of bright, powerful, and penetrating tone, used from ancient times, especially for military or other signals, and in modern times also in the orchestra; it consists of a cylindrical or conical tube, usually of metal (anciently also of horn or wood), straight or curved (or bent upon itself), with a cup-shaped mouthpiece and a flaring bell.

The natural tones of the instrument are the series of harmonics produced by varying force of breath; in modern forms of it additional tones are obtained by means of slides, crooks, valves, or keys.

13.. *Coer de L.* 303 Trumpettes began for to blowe, Knyghtes justed in a rowe. **1390** GOWER *Conf.* III. 217 Ech of hem ek a trompette Bar in his other hond. *c* **1470** HENRY *Wallace* VIII. 1021 Thai within..defyit Wallace, And trumpattis blew with mony werlik soun. **1533** GAU *Richt Vay* (S.T.S.) 71 Our lord sal thane command ane archangel to blaw the trumpait of God. **1535** COVERDALE *Ezek.* xxxiii. 4 Yff a man now heare the noyse off the trompet & will not be warned. **1606** SHAKS. *Tr. & Cr.* I. iii. 213. **1638** SIR T. HERBERT *Trav.* (ed. 2) 135 In another [mosque] sleeps Sandant-Emyr-amahow..; with many moe, who are like to sleep till the Trumpet raise them. **1788** GIBBON *Decl. & F.* xli. (1869) II. 506 The general's trumpet gave the signal of departure. **1844** THIRLWALL *Greece* VIII. lxiv. 317 Before the games began, after silence had been bidden by the sound of the trumpet, proclamation was made by a herald. **1889** W. H. STONE in Grove *Dict. Mus.* IV. 181 The simple or Field Trumpet is merely a tube twice bent on itself, ending in a bell... The modern orchestral or slide Trumpet..is twice turned or curved, thus forming three lengths. *Ibid.* 182 It [the tempering of the notes] is quite impossible on the Valve Trumpet.

† **b.** Distinguished from *trump*, as being smaller.

c **1407** LYDG. *Reson & Sens.* 5589 And for folkys that lyst daunce Ther wer trumpes and trumpetes. *c* **1440** *Promp. Parv.* 504/1 Trumpet, or a lytylle trumpe, that clepythe to mete, or men togedur, *sistrum*.

c. *feast of trumpets*, a Jewish festival observed at the beginning of the month Tisri, blowing of trumpets being a prominent part of the solemnities.

1560 BIBLE (Genev.) *Num.* xxix. (*heading*) 1 The feast of trumpets. **1611** *Ibid.*, The offering at the feast of Trumpets. **1903** W. BRIGHT *Age of Fathers* II. xxxiii. 192 Chrysostom was..indignant at the numbers that flocked to the festivals of 'Trumpets' or 'Tabernacles'.

2. Something of the nature of or resembling a trumpet. **a.** A reed-stop on the organ, of powerful tone resembling that of a trumpet.

1659 LEAK *Waterwks.* 31 To make Organs, or Trumpets of Organs, to Sound. **1660** *Specif. Organ* in Grove *Dict. Mus.* II. 591 Great Organ. 10 stops... 10. Trumpet... Eccho Organ. 4 stops... 19. Trumpet. **1688** in E. J. Hopkins *Organ* (1870) 453 Trumpett, of mettle. **1776** HAWKINS *Hist. Mus.* IV. I. x. 149 Of the stops of an organ, the most usual are the..Trumpet [etc.]. **1876** HILES *Catech. Organ* x. (1878) 70 *Trumpet, Tromba*, a striking reed stop of clear, penetrating tone.

b. *trumpet marine, marine trumpet* [tr. Ital. *tromba marina*, F. *trompette marine*], a large obsolete musical instrument of the viol kind, played with a bow, and having a single thick string passing over a bridge fastened at one end only, the other vibrating against the body, and producing a tone like that of a trumpet.

1675 *Lond. Gaz.* No. 961/4 A Rare Concert of four Trumpets Marine, never heard of before in England. **1748** tr. *Molière's Le Bourg. Gent.* II. i, The Trumpet-Marine is an Instrument that pleases me, and is very harmonious. **1838** G. F. GRAHAM *Mus. Comp.* App. 78 In Europe, in the last century, the only remnant of the most ancient monochord was the tromba-marina (trumpet-marine).

c. A conical tube with a wide mouth, used for increasing the force and carrying power of the voice: = SPEAKING-TRUMPET. **d.** A similar apparatus for conveying sound to the ear of a partially deaf person: = EAR-TRUMPET, HEARING-TRUMPET.

1696 PHILLIPS (ed. 5), *A Speaking Trumpet*, a Trumpet about Eight Foot, and sometimes Six Foot long, straight and very wide at the end... It carries the Voice so as to be distinctly heard above a Mile. **1774** GOLDSM. *Retal.* 146 When they judged without skill, he was still hard of hearing; When they talked of their Raphaels, Corregios, and stuff, He shifted his trumpet, and only took snuff. **1849** CUPPLES *Green Hand* xiv, 'Stand by to let go the larboard anchor!' I sang out through the trumpet. **1883** S. C. HALL *Retrospect* II. 46 So deaf that a trumpet was constantly at her ear.

e. = HORN *sb.* 15 a. Now *Hist.*

1899 *Strand Mag.* Dec. (Advt.), p. xxxv/1 The Gramophone. Berliner's Patent... Length of Trumpet 16 inches. **1904** *Science Siftings* 26 Mar. 353/1 These are again transferred into sound..and transmitted to the audience through a huge trumpet. **1922** S. A. MAYCOCK *Handbk. Gramophone* iii. 18 The hornless models certainly look neater than the instruments which are fitted with trumpets. **1947** F. W. GAISBERG *Music on Record* vi. 81 For the first time they heard sibilants emerge from the trumpet, loud and hissing!

3. *fig.* A means or agent (real or imaginary) which proclaims, celebrates, or gives warning of something. ***to blow one's own trumpet***, to sound one's own praises, boast, brag.

1447 BOKENHAM *Seyntys* (Roxb.) 35 Whan it was knowe.. And be the trumpet of fame aboute blowe. **1513** DOUGLAS *Æneis* I. Prol. 346 Venerable Chaucer, principall poet but peir, Hevinlie trumpat, horleige and reguleir. **1560** DAUS tr. *Sleidane's Comm.* 264 The decree of Wormes was the trompet of this warre. **1576** FLEMING *Panopl. Epist.* 59, I will..sound the trumpet of mine owne merites. **1644** MILTON *Areop.* (Arb.) 68 Why..was this Nation chos'n.. that out of her..should be..sounded forth the first tidings and trumpet of Reformation to all Europ? **1783** WOLCOTT (P. Pindar) *Odes to R.A.'s* vi, Sound their own praise from their own penny trumpet. **1803–6** WORDSW. *Ode Intim. Immort.* 25 The cataracts blow their trumpets from the steep. **1854** MAYNE REID *Young Voyageurs* v. 71 They may live to 'blow their own trumpet' a long while yet. **1887** W. S. GILBERT *Ruddigore* I. 12 You must stir it and stump it, And blow your own trumpet. **1902** ELIZ. L. BANKS *Newspaper Girl* 22 It was with a great flourish of newspaper trumpets that I started off. **1952** A. BUCKERIDGE *Jennings & Darbishire* ii. 27, I vote we're not allowed to vote for ourselves because my father says it's swanking to blow your own trumpet. **1983** P. ROBERTS *Tender Prey* xiv. 165, I was not averse to blowing my own trumpet. Modesty is a fool's game.

4. a. *transf.* One who blows or plays on a trumpet; a trumpeter.

1390–1 *Earl Derby's Exp.* (Camden) 114 Dati a le Trumpet de dono domini ibidem, xxiiij s. viij d. *a* **1450** *Le Morte Arth.* 2723 The trompettis vppon the wallis went. **1560** DAUS tr. *Sleidane's Comm.* 225 b, The Duke of Brunswicke sendeth a trompet to Duke Moris, and desyreth a communication. **1617** MORYSON *Itin.* I. 106 Our guard of horse left vs, and their trumpet asked of euery man a gift in curtesie. **1752** J. LOUTHIAN *Form of Process* (ed. 2) 233 The Judges..set out..for their respective Districts, attended with a Macer of Court and two Trumpets. **1855** MOTLEY *Dutch Rep.* I. ii. (1864) I. 178 Nevers sent a trumpet, after the battle, to the Duke of Savoy, for the purpose of negotiating concerning the prisoners.

b. *fig.* = TRUMPETER 2. Cf. 3 above.

1549 CHALONER *Erasm. Praise Folly* A ij, What..maie be ..better fittyng, than dame Foly to praise hir selfe, and be hir owne trumpet? **1577** *F. de L'isle's Leg.* G viij, Munkes and such other trumpets of sedition. **1595** SHAKS. *John* I. i. 27 So hence: be thou the trumpet of our wrath. **1709** STEELE *Tatler* No. 52 ¶ 4 He must in some Measure be the Trumpet of his Fame.

5. A sound like that of a trumpet; the loud cry of certain animals, esp. the elephant; the shrill hum of the gnat or mosquito.

1850 R. G. CUMMING *Hunter's Life S. Afr.* (1902) 86/2 He [the elephant] charged with a terrific trumpet. **1852** MUNDY *Our Antipodes* (1857) 195 The shrill scream of the heron, and the rough trumpet of the pelican. **1896** J. H. SKRINE in *Speaker* 25 July 98/2 The steed..neighed his trumpet. **1911** *Blackw. Mag.* Nov. 707/1 Suddenly there comes the well-known trumpet of the crane.

6. Something shaped like a trumpet.

* *natural.* **a.** = *trumpet-shell* (see 7); also called SEA-TRUMPET (1).

1668 CHARLETON *Onomast* 180 *Bucciuum*..the Trumpet. **1713** PETIVER *Aquat. Anim. Amboinæ* Tab. vii, *Buccinum Amboin. rarum, nubulis castaneis*: *Nobis*, Brown Amboina Trumpet. **1895** *Edin. Rev.* Oct. 355 Cuttles and squids.. crown-melons and fighting trumpets.

b. Applied to a plant having trumpet-shaped flowers; in quot. 1705 app. = *trumpet-daffodil* (see 7). Also *pl.* a name for a species of pitcher-plant, *Sarracenia flava* (cf. *trumpet-leaf* in 7). Also *gen.* a trumpet-shaped blossom or part of a blossom (as the tubular *corona* of a daffodil).

1705 tr. *Cowley's Plants* Wks. 1711 III. 344 Then a gay Flow'r for Shape the Trumpet nam'd. **1883** MRS. G. L. BANKS *Forbidden to Marry* v, The white and rosy trumpets of the bindweed. **1884** MILLER *Plant-n.*, Trumpets, *Sarracenia flava*. **1904** *Daily Chron.* 8 Mar. 8/5 The White Queen [narcissus], a novelty with white perianth and trumpet of pale chrome.

** *artificial.* **c.** A funnel-shaped conductor in a spinning-machine, etc.; also called *trumpet-mouth* (see 7). **d.** The flaring mouth of an automatic coupling on a railway car. **e.** (See quot. 1877[2].)

1877 KNIGHT *Dict. Mech.*, *Trumpet*... 4. (*Spinning.*) *a.* The funnel which leads a sliver to the cylinders of a drawing-machine, or which collects a number of combined rovings, and leads them to condensing cylinders. *b.* A funnel-shaped conductor used in many forms of thread-machines [etc.]... 5. (*Railway.*) The flaring mouth of a railway-car draw-head which directs the entering coupling-link. **1877** G. F. MACLEAR *St. Mark* xii. (1879) 139 This treasury, according to the Rabbis, consisted of thirteen brazen chests, called 'trumpets', because the mouths..were wide at the top and narrow below.

f. *Metallurgy.* A vertical tube with a bell mouth and a refractory lining, through which metal is poured into runners in uphill casting.

1923 HARBORD & HALL *Metallurgy of Steel* (ed. 7) I. i. 37 At one time it was generally considered that sounder ingots could be obtained by bottom casting, but opinions are now much divided as with bottom pouring there is..some danger of the refractory lining of the trumpet..being carried into the steel. **1929** W. LISTER *Pract. Steelmaking* xxxviii. 370 In this trumpet no wet clay or ramming is used and no weights or clamps are required. **1973** *Times* 12 Feb. (Anchor Project Suppl.) p. ii/6 Mould preparation will be done in a separate bay which is well designed for mould cooling and equipped for..preparation of trumpets and runners for up-run teeming.

7. *attrib.* and *Comb.* **a.** Simple attrib., as ***trumpet-blare***, ***-blast***, ***-bray***, ***-clang***, ***-clangor***, ***-flourish***, ***music***, ***-note***, ***-peal***, ***signal***, ***-sound***, ***stop*** (= sense 2a), ***tone***, ***-voice***, ***-word***. **b.** Objective, as ***trumpet-blowing*** adj. and sb.; instrumental, as ***trumpet-hung*** adj. (cf. 6b); parasynthetic and similative, as ***trumpet-flowered***, ***-loud***, ***-toned***, ***-twisted***, ***-voiced*** adjs.; also ***trumpet-like*** adj. **c.** Special Combs.: **trumpet animalcule**, an infusorian of the genus *Stentor* or family *Stentoridæ*, so called from its shape; **trumpet-ash** = *trumpet-creeper* (Cent. Dict. 1891); **trumpet-banner**, a small banner attached to a trumpet, formerly used by heralds; **trumpet-bird** = TRUMPETER 5b; **trumpet-call**, a call or summons sounded on a trumpet; also *fig.*; **trumpet-cheek**, a cheek inflated or distended as in blowing a trumpet; **trumpet-conch** = *trumpet-shell* (Cent. Dict. 1891); **trumpet creeper**, a climbing shrub of the genus *Tecoma* (N.O. *Bignoniaceæ*), *esp.* the common trumpet-flower, *T. radicans* (formerly *Bignonia radicans*), of the Southern U.S., with scarlet trumpet-shaped flowers; **trumpet daffodil**, a variety of daffodil with conspicuous 'trumpet' or tubular *corona* (cf. 6b); **trumpet-fish**, name for various fishes with long tubular snout, *esp.* the bellows-fish or sea-snipe (*Centriscus scolopax*) and the tobacco-pipe fish (*Fistularia*); **trumpet-flower**, name for various plants with large or showy trumpet-shaped flowers, esp. of the genera *Tecoma* (see *trumpet-creeper* above) and *Bignonia*, also species of *Catalpa*, *Brunfelsia*, *Datura*, *Solandra*, etc.; **trumpet-fly** (see quot.); **trumpet-gall**, a small trumpet-shaped gall found on grape-vines in U.S. (*Cent. Dict.*); **trumpet-gourd**, a trumpet-shaped variety of the common gourd (*Lagenaria vulgaris*); **trumpet-grass** = *trumpet-weed*; **trumpet-guide** = sense 6c (*Cent. Dict. Suppl.* 1909); **trumpet honeysuckle** (see HONEYSUCKLE 2); **trumpet hypha** (pl. **hyphæ**), *Bot.* (see quot.); **trumpet-jasmine** = *trumpet-creeper* (Cent. Dict.); **trumpet-keck** (see KECK *sb.*); **trumpet lamp**, 'miner's term for a *Mueseler* or Belgian safety-lamp' (Gresley *Gloss. Coal Mining* 1883); **trumpet-leaf**, name for species of pitcher-plant (*Sarracenia*) with leaves resembling trumpets rather than pitchers; **trumpet-lily**, the white arum-lily (see ARUM b); also some species of *Lilium*; **trumpet-lug** *Archæol.*, a type of tubular handle with expanded ends, found on British neolithic pottery; **trumpet-major**, the chief trumpeter of a band or regiment; **trumpet medium**, a spiritualistic medium in whose seances a trumpet megaphone is used; **trumpet milkweed** = *trumpet-weed* (*c*); **trumpet-mouth**, the 'mouth' or expanded end of a trumpet, or something resembling this (in quot. 1835 = sense 6c); **trumpet-mouthed** *a.*, (*a*) = *trumpet-tongued*, *-voiced*; (*b*) having a wide opening like the mouth of a trumpet; **trumpet narcissus** (cf. *trumpet daffodil* above); **trumpet pattern**, in medieval art: a shape resembling that of a horn; **trumpet-pipe**, (*a*) name for a particular pattern of musket; (*b*) a pipe of the trumpet-stop on an organ; **trumpet reed**, a West Indian species of reed, *Arundo occidentalis*; **trumpet seance**, a spiritualistic seance in which a trumpet megaphone is used; **trumpet-seaweed** = *trumpet-weed* (*a*); **trumpet-shaped** *a.*, of the shape of a trumpet; in *Nat. Hist.* tubular with one end dilated; **trumpet-shell**, a shell of the genus *Triton* or family *Tritonidæ* (see TRITON 2a), or any other shell which can be blown like a trumpet; **trumpet-snail** = RAM'S HORN 6; **trumpet spiral** (see quot. 1959); cf. *trumpet pattern* above; **trumpet style** *Jazz*, a style of piano-playing imitative of a trumpet; **trumpet-tongued** (-tʌŋd) *a.*, 'having a tongue vociferous as a trumpet' (J.), loud-voiced; so **trumpet-tongue** *v.*, *trans.* to proclaim loudly; **trumpet-tree**, a West Indian and South American tree (*Cecropia peltata*, N.O. *Artocarpaceæ*), with hollow stem and branches which are used for wind-instruments; **trumpet-vine** = *trumpet-creeper*; **trumpet-weed**, (*a*) a large S. African seaweed, *Ecklonia buccinalis* = SEA-TRUMPET 3; (*b*) a N. American species of hemp-agrimony, *Eupatorium purpureum*, with hollow stems which children blow through like trumpets; (*c*) a N. American species of lettuce, *Lactuca canadensis*; **trumpet-wood** = *trumpet-tree*.

1891 *Cent. Dict.*, *Trumpet-animalcule. **1895** L. WRIGHT *Pop. Handbk. Microscope* viii. 154 The largest animals of this type are the *Stentors* or Trumpet-Animalcules. **1503** *Acc. Gt. Wardrobe* in *Calr. Doc. rel. Scotl.* IV. 441 Item, vij *trumpetbaners pro v trumpetters et ij shakbotters. **1586** FERNE *Blaz. Gentrie* 161 The..French king, for want of a Hereald..was constrained to subbornate a vadelict, or common seruing man, with a trumpet banner..in steede of a better cote-armour of Fraunce. **1896** NEWTON *Dict. Birds* 992 Messrs. Sclater and Salvin in their *Nomenclator*..admit 6 species of *Trumpet-birds. **1865** KINGSLEY *Herew.* xv, The streets..rang with clank, and tramp, and *trumpet-blare. **1837** CARLYLE *Fr. Rev.* I. IV. ii, As it [the edict] sounds out..accompanied with *trumpet-blast. **1879** FARRAR *St. Paul* I. 582 Their faith had been as a trumpet-blast through all the Mediterranean coasts. **1856** *Mem. F. Perthes* II. xxiv. 362 The *trumpet-blowing angels. **1859** TENNYSON *Vivien* 416 Such a song, such fire for fame, Such trumpet-blowing in it. **1815** SCOTT *Waterloo* vii, Cannon-roar and *trumpet-bray. **1808** —— *Marm.* I. xii, Loudly flourish'd the *trumpet-call. **1909** *Blackw. Mag.* Mar. 402/1 His name was still a trumpet-call. **1693** DRYDEN *Juvenal* iii. 64 The Minstrels of a Country Show..By *Trumpet-Cheeks and Bloated Faces known. **1808** SCOTT *Marm.* v. xxv, And voice of Scotland's law was sent In glorious *trumpet clang. **1597** SHAKS. *2 Hen. IV*, v. v. 42 There roar'd the Sea: and *Trumpet Clangour sounds. **1818** W. P. C. BARTON *Compendium Floræ Philadelphicæ* II. 43 *Trumpet Creeper... Flowers red and orange. **1857** A. GRAY *First Less. Bot.* (1866) 34 By these rootlets..the Trumpet Creeper, the Ivy [etc.] fasten themselves firmly to walls. **1895** *Outing* (U.S.) XXVII. 220/1 Trumpet creepers, yellow as gold, and starry blue passion flowers. **1895** *Daily News* 25 Apr. 5/2 The great white and yellow *trumpet daffodils. **1668** WILKINS *Real Char.* 137 *Trumpet-fish. **1683–4** ROBINSON in *Phil. Trans.* XXIX. 479 The *Scolopax* or *Trombetta*, call'd by our Seamen the Bellows or Trumpet-Fish. **1871** KINGSLEY *At Last* vi, The good people of Trinidad believe that the fish which makes this noise is the trumpet-fish, or Fistularia. **1811** SCOTT *Vis. Don Roderick* lvi, Thrills the loud fife, the *trumpet-flourish pours. **1844** *Regul. & Ord. Army* 29 Trumpets sounding twice the Trumpet-flourish. **1731** MORTIMER in *Phil. Trans.* XXXVII. 175 *Bignonia Fraxini foliis, coccineo flore minore.* The *Trumpet-Flower. **1812** *New Bot. Gard.* I. 93 The Trumpet Flower, or Scarlet Jasmine. **1847** LONGF. *Ev.* II. ii. 80 The trumpet-flower and the grape-vine Hung their ladder of ropes aloft. **1857** HENFREY *Elem. Bot.* 353 The *Trumpet-flowered climbers form striking features of American forests. **1752** J. HILL *Hist. Anim.* 31 The blackish Œstrus, with a yellow breast... We call it the grey fly from it's colour, or the *trumpet fly from the noise it makes in the heats of summer. **1879** *Trumpet-gall [see *nail-gall* s.v. NAIL *sb.* 14a]. **1908** V. L. KELLOGG *Amer. Insects* 470 Trumpet-galls on leaves of California white oak. **1884** *De Candolle's Orig. Cultiv. Pl.* 245 The pilgrim's gourd,..the long-necked gourd, the *trumpet gourd, and the calabash. **1850** MISS PRATT *Comm. Things of Sea-side* II. 119 Thunberg..calls it [*sc.* the Sea-trumpet] the *Trumpet-grass. **1731** P. MILLER *Gardeners Dict.* s.v. *Periclymenum*, *Trumpet Honeysuckle... We have but one species of this Plant at present,..Virginian Scarlet Honeysuckle. **1753** *Trumpet honey-suckle [see HONEYSUCKLE 2]. **1882** *Garden* 3 June 383/1 The North American Trumpet Honeysuckle ..one seldom sees outside a greenhouse. **1870** MRS. WHITNEY *We Girls* xi, Its..splendid vista of *trumpet-hung bignonia vines. **1900** B. D. JACKSON *Gloss. Bot. Terms*, **Trumpet-hyphae*, tubes in Laminarieae having swollen portions with transverse septa (F. Oliver). **1861** A. WOOD *Class-Bk. Bot.* (ed. 10) 222 *S. Gronovii.* *Trumpet-leaf..in swampy pine woods. **1884** MILLER *Plant-n.*, *Trumpet-leaf*, the genus *Sarracenia*. **1814** ANNE PLUMPTRE tr. *Langsdorff's Voy. & Trav.* II. 104 *Anas Glacialis*... The harmonious *trumpet-like noise of this bird distinguishes it from every other species of duck. **1825** *Green Ho. Comp.* I. 57 Tube-shaped or long trumpet-like flowers. **1862** SHIRLEY *Nugæ Crit.* i. 89 The shrill trumpet-like call of the wild swan. **1878** F. FERGUSON *Life Christ* 465 The thirteen trumpet-like boxes in which the gifts of the people were received. **1857** HENFREY *Elem. Bot.* 397 *Richardia africana* is the white-spathed '*Trumpet-lily' of our conservatories. **1884** MILLER *Plant-n.*, *Lilium eximium*, Transparent Trumpet Lily... [*L.*] *longiflorum*, Common Trumpet Lily. *Ibid.*, *Richardia* (*Calla*) *æthiopica*, Lily-of-the-Nile, Trumpet Lily, White Arum-Lily. **1857** G. W. THORNBURY *Songs Cavaliers & Roundh.* 56 Blow the organ *trumpet-loud. [**1932** S. PIGGOTT in *Archaeol. Jrnl.* LXXXVIII. 76 The horizontally perforated lug..exhibits a 'trumpet-ended' variety at Windmill Hill and Hembury.] **1937** —— in *Antiquity* XI. 450 More important was the occurrence of a type of lug or tubular perforated handle with expanded ends, which the writer distinguished as a '*trumpet-lug' in 1932... At Hembury it was present as a recurrent feature. **1972** L. ALCOCK *By South Cadbury* v. 109 These suspension tubes —trumpet lugs to give them their technical name—are seen again on pottery from sites like Windmill Hill in Wiltshire. **1855** HYDE CLARKE, **Trumpet-major*, head trumpeter. **1902** *Westm. Gaz.* 26 May 8/2 There died at Shrewsbury yesterday Trumpet-Major Thomas Monks, who sounded the 'Charge' for the Heavy Brigade at Balaclava. **1912** *Nash's Mag.* July 553/2 Last year the wonderful *trumpet medium, Mrs. Wreidt, spent some time at 'Julia's Bureau'. **1968** B. STEIGER *Voices from Beyond* iii. 58 Trumpet mediums always seem to be popular at Spiritualist camps. **1835** URE *Philos. Manuf.* 153 A copper funnel, or *trumpet mouth, for conducting the sliver delivered by the second rollers. **1839** *Civil Eng. & Arch. Jrnl.* II. 231/2 The smoke pipe..having a wide, or trumpet mouth. **1899** R. MUNRO *Prehist. Scotl.* vi. 203 Its present mode of attachment to the trumpet-mouth is evidently modern. **1767** A. YOUNG *Farmer's Lett.* ii. 43 These are facts which speak *trumpet mouthed in favour of this..measure. **1895** *Daily News* 31 May 5/2 What Mr. Burns described as a trumpet-mouthed approach to the Houses of Parliament and Westminster Abbey. **1818** SCOTT *Br. Lamm.* xxiii[i], What had his memory to do with the degeneracy of the *trumpet music? **1904** *Daily Chron.* 8 Mar. 8/5 Weardale Perfection, an exquisite *trumpet narcissus. **1813** SCOTT *Trierm.* III. x, A wild and lonely *trumpet note. **1887** J. HUTCHISON *Lect. Philippians* i. 7 It is not a trumpet-note of defiance like the Epistle to the Galatians. **1937** *Burlington Mag.* Feb. 99/1 We find that admirable curling *trumpet-patterns..in the brilliant manuscripts of the early Church in Ireland and Northumbria. **1954** M. RICKERT *Painting in Brit.: Middle Ages* 232 *Trumpet pattern*, two whorls..joined across the open side by a curved line. **1965** L. N. VALENTINE *Ornament in Medieval Manuscripts* 51 '*French horn*', a trumpet pattern combined with a helix shape. **1804** J. GRAHAME *Sabbath*, etc. (1808) 56 The battle's *trumpet-peal. **1844** *Regul. & Ord. Army* 99 For long-fore or *trumpet-pipe. **1855** E. J. HOPKINS *Organ* xxii. 123 The tubes of the Trumpet-pipes are usually..of tin or metal,..occasionally..of zinc or wood. **1866** *Treas. Bot.* 963 *Trumpet [Reed], *Arundo occidentalis*. **1912** *Nash's Mag.* July 544/1 The sitting took place at 'Julia's Bureau'. It was a *Trumpet Séance, and Mrs. Wreidt..was the medium. **1931** *Daily Express* 15 Oct. 7/3, I am aware you are giving trumpet seances. **1968** B. STEIGER *Voices from Beyond* iii. 58 At trumpet seances—almost invariably conducted in the dark—the horn rises, ostensibly lifted by spirit hands. **1884** MILLER *Plant-n.*, *Ecklonia buccinalis*, Cape *Trumpet-Sea-weed, Horn-plant. **1767** ELLIS in *Phil. Trans.* LVII. 420 The figure of one of the *trumpet-shaped suckers highly magnified. **1861** BENTLEY *Man. Bot.* 446 Perennial boggy plants, with pitcher or trumpet-shaped leaves. **1887** RIDER HAGGARD *Jess* i, Long trumpet-shaped flowers. **1753** CHAMBERS *Cycl. Supp.*, *Trumpet-Shell, *Buccinum*. **1890** H. DRUMMOND in *Life* xv. (1899) 386 The great trumpet-shell, now rare [in Tongoa, New Hebrides]. **1864** ENGEL *Mus. Anc. Nat.* 98 *Trumpet signals are better fitted for transmitting orders to a great distance, than verbal messages through a speaking-trumpet. **1901** E. STEP *Shell Life* 320 The Ram's Horn or *Trumpet-snail, so frequently introduced in fresh-water aquaria. **1965** tr. *H. Janus' Young Specialist looks at Land & Freshwater Molluscs* IV. 70 Family Planorbidae (Ram's-horn or Trumpet Snails). **1718** ROWE tr. *Lucan* 224 At once the warriors shouts and *Trumpet-sounds surprise. **1823** SCOTT *Quentin D.* xxi, Summoned together, by war-cry and trumpet-sound, to assist in repelling a desperate sally. **1936** A. W. CLAPHAM *Romanesque Archit.* i. 9 Certain Celtic motives such as the *trumpet-spiral. **1959** E. A. FISHER *Anglo-Saxon Archit. & Sculpt.* 73 Both single and double spirals were common in Celto-British art... Sometimes the connecting C-line would be double and wider apart in the middle resembling two trumpets joined at their wide ends —hence the term *trumpet spiral*. **1795** MASON *Ch. Mus.* i. 64 Instead of using either the *Trumpet stop or the full organ, he will modulate on..the more delicate and softer series of Pipes. **1876** HILES *Catech. Organ* x. (1878) 71 *Trompette Harmonique*, a Trumpet stop..made to overblow, by a strong and copious wind; they sound the octave, or the super octave above the usual note. **1946** R. BLESH *Shining Trumpets* xiii. 320 Hines's *trumpet style..was based on Louis Armstrong's trumpet phrasing. **1959** 'F. NEWTON' *Jazz Scene* vii. 130 Players attempted the feat of adapting the piano to the vocalising style of the other instruments (the so-called 'trumpet style'). **1977** *New Yorker* 6 June 120/1 The so-called trumpet style of jazz piano playing, which Earl Hines originated in the late twenties, consists of hornlike single-note melodic lines in the right hand and on-and-off-the-beat chords, single notes, and countermelodic lines in the left hand. **1841** T. H. WHITE *Fragm. Italy & Rhineland* 9 Well may they dread to waken its [the Bible's] *trumpet tones! **1854** J. S. C. ABBOTT *Napoleon* (1855) I. i. 25 Those *trumpet-toned proclamations which..electrified Europe. **1880** BURTON *Reign Q. Anne* I. i. 27 Friends can confide their thoughts..to each other without their being *trumpet-tongued by..unscrupulous parasites. **1605** SHAKS. *Macb.* I. vii. 19 His Vertues Will pleade like Angels, *Trumpet-tongu'd against The deepe damnation of his taking off. **1775** J. ADAMS in *Fam. Lett.* (1876) 52 It will plead..with more irresistible persuasion than angels trumpet-tongued. **1860** PUSEY *Min. Proph.* 453 That Day of the Lord..shall, trumpet-tongued, proclaim the holiness and justice of Almighty God. **1756** P. BROWNE *Jamaica* 111 The *Trumpet-Tree... The trunk and branches are hollow,..stopped from space to space with membranous septæ... The smaller branches..serve for wind instruments. **1871** KINGSLEY *At Last* v, A tall stick, thirty feet high, with a flat top of gigantic curly horse-chestnut leaves, which is a Trumpet-tree. **1895** W. B. YEATS *Poems* 12 Many a *trumpet-twisted shell. **1717** *Petiveriana* III. 255 Scarlet *Trumpet-Vine. Makes a fine Arbour. **1883** *Peterson Ladies' Nat. Mag.* June 460/2 The great porch in front..[was] destitute of railing or ornament, but the creeping trumpet vine. **1978** *Detroit Free Press* 16 Apr. (Gardening Guide) 14/2 Trumpet vine is another woody vine that bears striking flowers. **1818** BYRON *Ch. Har.* IV. xcviii, Yet Freedom! yet..Thy *trumpet-voice, though.. dying, The loudest still the tempest leaves behind. **1902** *Athenæum* 4 Jan. 6/2 Howel Harris, the *trumpet-voiced revivalist. **1830** *Huntingdon* (Pa.) *Courier* 15 Sept. 4/5 American Remedies Wanted..Gravel Wort or *Trumpet Weed. **1856** GRAY *Man. Bot.* (1860) 186 *Eupatorium purpureum* (..Trumpet-Weed). **1866** *Treas. Bot.* 1179 *Trumpet-weed*, the name of a seaweed, *Ecklonia buccinalis*,.. very common..at the Cape of Good Hope... The stem of this seaweed, says Dr. Harvey, which is hollow in the upper portion, is when dried..used..as a siphon, and by the native herdsmen is formed into a trumpet for collecting the cattle in the evening... The name is also applied in America to *Eupatorium purpureum*. **1888** EGGLESTON *Graysons* xx, Shaded by the broad-leaved horse and trumpet weeds in the fence-row. **1836** LOUDON *Encycl. Plants* 826 *Cecropia.* From κεκραγω, to cry out, a sort of translation of the English word *trumpet-wood. This tree has the trunk and branches hollow everywhere... The leaves are large, peltate. **1827** G. DARLEY *Sylvia* 117 The wild reed breathes no *trumpet-word.

Hence **'trumpetless** *a.*, without a trumpet, without trumpeting; **'trumpetry**, trumpets collectively; trumpeting; **'trumpety** *a.* (*colloq.*), having the tone or style of a trumpet, blaring.

a **1711** KEN *Edmund* Poet. Wks. 1721 II. 321 It was impossible the Beast to rein, While *trumpetless the Pagans did remain. **1860** THACKERAY *Round. Papers* v, Cornhill.. has witnessed every ninth of November..a prodigious annual pageant, chariot, progress, and flourish of *trumpetry. **1884** *Sat. Rev.* 14 June 778/1 The blare of modern trumpetry. **1822** *Examiner* 810/2 The music..was altogether too clanging and *trumpetty—the word is a good word. **1896** *Pall Mall G.* 8 Jan. 1/3 A good stirring military song with an inspiriting trumpety air.

'trumpet, *v.* [f. TRUMPET *sb.*; cf. F. *trompeter* (14th c. in Godef. *Compl.*).]

1. *intr.* To blow or sound a trumpet.

1530 PALSGR. 763/1, I trompet, I blowe or sownde in a trumpet, *je sonne vne trompette.* **1535** COVERDALE *2 Chron.* v. 13 As yf one dyd trompet and synge. **1672** VILLIERS (Dk. Buckhm.) *Rehearsal* IV. i. (Arb.) 91 It [the Play] shall Drum, Trumpet, Shout and Battel, I gad, with any the most warlike Tragœdy we have. **1862** DICKENS *Somebody's Luggage* ii, Practising soldiers trumpeted and bugled. **1913** SIR H. JOHNSTON *Pioneers Australia* iv. 135 The seamen.. trumpeted back..in reply.

b. To emit a sound like that of a trumpet; used esp. in reference to the cry of an elephant when enraged or excited; also, to the musical piping of a mosquito or gnat when about to bite.

1828 CAPT. MUNDY *Pen & Pencil Sk.* (1832) I. ii. 112 My elephant suddenly raised his trunk and trumpeted several times. **1860** GOSSE *Rom. Nat. Hist.* 258 He..drives off the alarmed animal trumpeting shrilly with rage and pain. **1872** DARWIN *Emotions* vi. 168 The keeper ordered the old and the young elephant to trumpet. **1900** *Pilot* 22 Sept. 357/2 Anopheles, a mosquito that does not trumpet.

2. *trans.* **a.** To sound on a trumpet; to utter with a sound like that of a trumpet.

1729 YOUNG *Merchant* II. ix, She trumpets shrill her dread command. **1854** *Poultry Chron.* II. 84 An old..black cock, who could never utter the least sound without trumpeting a prolonged *finale.* **1875** BUCKLAND *Log-bk.* 355 He seems to have trumpeted the order. **1886** F. HARRISON *Choice Bks.* ii. 29 A passage of Homer, rolling along in the hexameter or trumpeted out by Pope.

b. *fig.* To announce or publish as by sound of trumpet; to proclaim, celebrate, or extol loudly; to noise abroad. Also with *forth.*

1604 SHAKS. *Oth.* I. iii. 251 That I loue the Moore,..My ..storme of Fortunes, May trumpet to the world. **1608** —— *Per.* I. i. 145 He must not liue to trumpet foorth my infamie. **1702** C. MATHER *Magn. Chr.* IV. I. (1852) 14 Commenius, the fame of whose worth hath been trumpetted as far as more than three languages could carry it. **1756** H. WALPOLE *Lett. to Mann* 23 Feb., They trumpeted the story all over the town. **1841** THACKERAY *Gt. Hoggarty Diam.* ix, This I state not to trumpet my own praises. **1856** DOVE *Logic Chr. Faith* III. iii. 148 Atheism may trumpet forth her astounding discovery.

c. To summon or denounce formally (cf. F. *trompeter*, and HORN *v.* 5), or to drive away, by sound of trumpet.

1680 SIR R. SOUTHWELL in *Cal. Ormonde MSS.* IV. 579 The Duchess of Soissons is trumpetted, which is the manner of citation used in like cases... And if she appear not at the third trumpetting, her crimes and sentences will be pronounced. **1795** BURKE *Regic. Peace* iv. Wks. IX. 52 They drummed and trumpeted the wretches out of their Hall.

trumpeted ('trʌmpɪtɪd), *ppl. a.* and *a.* [f. TRUMPET *v.* and *sb.* + -ED.]

I. 1. Sounded on a trumpet; *fig.* celebrated as with a trumpet, greatly extolled or boasted of.

1611 COTGR., *Trompetté*, trumpetted, or noised abroad; published, or proclaymed with sound of Trumpets. **1775** MME. D'ARBLAY *Early Diary, Let. to Crisp* 19 Nov., Giving ..his opinion in disfavour of so trumpeted a character. **1804** LARWOOD *No Gun Boats* 34 A complete Destruction of this trumpeted Flotilla. **1908** *Athenæum* 29 Aug. 236/1 Some of the most trumpeted names are..authors of no.. consequence.

II. [f. the sb.] **2.** Furnished with a trumpet (or something likened to one).

1841 L. HUNT *Seer* (1864) 4 The gnat,..airy, trumpeted, and plumed.

3. Formed like a trumpet; made with one end expanded; funnel-shaped.

1889 *Philos. Mag.* Aug. 95 Their [the wires'] ends were passed into two small trumpeted holes in a stout brass plate.

trumpeter ('trʌmpɪtə(r)). Forms: 5–6 *Sc.* **trumpatour(e, 6 trompetor, -etter, -atere, troumpetor, trumpetor, -ettor, -etour, -ettour, -ytar, -yter, -itour, 6–7 -etter, 6– trumpeter.** [f. TRUMPET *sb.* or *v.* + -ER[1], or a. F. *trompeteur* (Palsgr. 1530), f. *trompeter* to TRUMPET.]

1. One who sounds or plays upon a trumpet; *spec.* a soldier in a cavalry regiment who gives signals with a trumpet; also, one who has a similar function in a war-ship (? *obs.*); in quot. 1673, a herald.

1497 *Acc. Ld. High Treas. Scot.* (1877) I. 326 For their Pasche reward..to Thome Pringil and his brodir trumpatouris, xxviij s. **1533** *Ibid.* (1905) VI. 95 To Juliane and the laif of the trumpatouris in Dunbar. **1555** EDEN *Decades* 117 The gouernour commaunded the trumpitour to blowe a retraite. **1581** MULCASTER *Positions* xv. (1887) 70 Trumpetters, and those that play vpon winde instruments. **1627** CAPT. SMITH *Seaman's Gram.* viii. 35 The Trumpeter is..to attend the Captaines command, and to sound either at his going a shore, or comming aboord, at the entertainment of strangers, also when you hale a ship, when you charge, boord, or enter. **1673** TEMPLE *Let. to Dk. Florence* Wks. 1731 II. 291 A Trumpeter arrived from Holland, bringing full and entire Powers to the Ambassador of Spain, to treat here of a Peace. **1855** MACAULAY *Hist. Eng.* xvi. III. 680 A trumpeter was sent to summon the place. *Ibid.* xxi. IV. 654 Keyes..had formerly been trumpeter of the corps.

2. *fig.* One who gives the signal for, proclaims, or extols something as by sound of trumpet.

1581 J. HAMILTON in *Cath. Tract.* (S.T.S.) 84 Thir seditius trumpeters brocht hir maiestie in disdane of the peple. **1599** *Broughton's Let.* A ij, A clamorous trumpetor of his owne praises. **1793** BURKE *Policy of Allies* Wks. VII. 198 Subordinate instruments and trumpeters of sedition. **1796** GROSE *Dict. Vulgar T.* s.v., His trumpeter is dead, he is therefore forced to sound his own trumpet. **1869** FREEMAN *Norm. Conq.* (1875) III. xi. 33 Osbert, Prior of Westminster, the special trumpeter of Eadward's renown.

3. *trumpeter's muscle*, †also simply *trumpeter* (obs.) = BUCCINATOR.

1615 CROOKE *Body of Man* 754 Muscles..common to the Cheekes and the Lippes are foure, two on either side called *Quadratus* and *Buccinator*, the square muscle and the Trumpeter. **1758** J. S. *Le Dran's Observ. Surg.* Dict. (1771) B b ij b, *Buccinator*, the..Muscle of the Cheek, called the Trumpeter's Muscle. **1875** SIR. W. TURNER in *Encycl. Brit.* I. 837/2 The buccinator..compresses the cheeks, and drives the air out of the cavity of the mouth as in playing a wind instrument; hence the name, 'trumpeter's muscle'.

4. Applied to **a.** a braying ass (*humorous*); **b.** a broken-winded horse: cf. ROARER[1] 2.

1638 SIR T. HERBERT *Trav.* (ed. 2) 133 We jogged leasurely on upon our Portugall Trumpetters,..sometimes braying out. **1785** GROSE *Dict. Vulgar T.* s.v., The King of Spain's trumpeter, a braying ass. **1844** STEPHENS *Bk. Farm* II. 227 There are many degrees of broken wind, which receive appellations according to the noise emitted by the horse; and on this account he is called a..trumpeter.

5. Name given to various birds, from their loud note suggesting the sound of a trumpet.

a. A variety of domestic pigeon. **b.** Any species of the South American genus *Psophia* or family *Psophiidæ*, allied to the Cranes. † **c.** 'An obsolete name in Tasmania for the black Crow-Shrike, *Strepera fuliginosa*' (Morris *Austral Eng.*). **d.** = *trumpeter-swan*: see 7. **e.** (See quot. 1897.)

a. 1725 *Bradley's Fam. Dict.* s.v. *Pigeon*, Many sorts of pigeons, such as..Owls, Spots, Trumpeters. **1859** DARWIN *Orig. Spec.* i. (1860) 21 The trumpeter and laugher, as their names express, utter a very different coo from the other breeds.

b. 1747 tr. *De la Condamine's Trav. S. Amer.* 87 The bird called Trompetero by the Spaniards..is the same with the Agami..the noise it occasionally makes..has earned it the title of trumpeter. **1843** *Penny Cycl.* XXV. 317/2 *Trumpeter* .., the vulgar name for *Psophia crepitans.* **1879** E. P. WRIGHT *Anim. Life* 326 The Trumpeters, or *Psophiidæ*, are ..found only in the Great Amazon Valley.

c. 1827 HELLYER in Bischoff *Van Diemen's L.* (1832) 177 We..occasionally heard the trumpeter or black magpie.

d. 1891 *Cent. Dict.*, *Trumpeter*... 5. The trumpeter-swan. **1899** *Daily News* 4 May 8/2 The cry of the Trumpeter..is ..far-reaching and sonorous, and like the note of a horn.

e. 1897 *Month* Apr. 417 The Canada goose, sometimes called, from its note, the 'trumpeter'.

6. a. = *trumpet-fish* (see TRUMPET *sb.* 7). ? *Obs.* **b.** Any species of the genus *Latris*, comprising large food-fishes of Australia, Tasmania, and New Zealand: so called from the sound they utter when taken out of water.

1756 P. BROWNE *Jamaica* 441 The Trumpeter or Trumpet Fish..is frequent in the harbours of Jamaica. **1834** *Van Diemen's Land Ann.* 30 The most admired fish of the Island may be considered the Trumpeter. **1883** E. P. RAMSAY *Food Fishes N.S. Wales* 13 (Fish. Exhib. Publ.) Among the best are the trumpeters (*Latris*), of which there are several species... The Hobart trumpeter (*L. hecateia*).. in a smoked and dried state forms an article of export from Tasmania to the other colonies. **1883** *Roy. Comm. Fisheries Tasmania* 35 (Morris) The bastard trumpeter (*Latris Forsteri*)..Scarcely inferior to the real trumpeter.

7. *attrib.*, esp. in names of certain birds and fishes (cf. 5, 6): **trumpeter hornbill**, an African bird of the genus *Bycanistes*; **trumpeter perch**, a small Australian food-fish, *Therapon cuvieri*; **trumpeter swan**, a large N. American species of swan, *Cygnus* (*Olor*) *buccinator*; **trumpeter whiting**, an Australian fish, *Sillago bassensis*.

1899 F. V. KIRBY *Sport E.C. Africa* viii. 95 In the vicinity of this Kraal the great *trumpeter hornbill abounds, his hideous cries resounding through the dense forest. *Ibid.* xiii. 142, I..missed two shots..at a couple of lesser trumpeter hornbills (*Bycanistes buccinator*). **1669** DRYDEN *Tyrannic Love* IV. i, A *trumpeter-hornet to battle sounds loud. **1883** E. P. RAMSAY *Food Fishes N.S. Wales* 13 (Fish. Exhib. Publ.) The *trumpeter perch (*Therapon cuvieri*), was formerly very numerous in Port Jackson... It is a small, delicious fish, and prettily striped. **1842** *Penny Cycl.* XXIII. 375/1 The *trumpeter swan, *Cygnus Buccinator.* **1874** J. W. LONG *Amer. Wild-fowl* xxii. 227 The *cygnus buccinator*, or trumpeter swan, the largest of its kind, and most common to the valley of the Mississippi. **1882** TENISON-WOODS *Fish N.S. Wales* 65 The *trumpeter whiting (*Sillago bassensis*).. the most common species in Brisbane.

trumpeting ('trʌmpɪtɪŋ), *vbl. sb.* [f. TRUMPET *v.* + -ING[1].]

1. The action of the verb TRUMPET.

a. Blowing of a trumpet or trumpets; utterance of a sound like that of a trumpet.

1535 COVERDALE *1 Esdr.* v. 66 Then came the enemies.. to knowe what that trompettynge and noyse of shawmes might be. **1848** B. WEBB *Continental Ecclesiol.* 277 There was a great deal too much trumpeting and kettle-drumming in the orchestra. **1850** R. G. CUMMING *Hunter's Life S. Afr.* (1902) 90/1 Crash came a second charge of elephants.. accompanied by a trumpeting which caused our ears to tingle. **1861** J. LAMONT *Seahorses* v. 74 The sonorous bellowing and trumpeting of a vast number of walruses. **1881** MISS YONGE *Lads & Lasses Langley* iii, The door..had ..a trick of squeaking and trumpeting.

b. The action of proclaiming as by sound of trumpet.

1878 BAYNE *Purit. Rev.* xi. 487 The Lords Spiritual..for all their trumpeting of the duty of passive obedience, reminded Charles of the limitations of his prerogative when he tried to show mercy to the Presbyterians. **1885** *Pall Mall G.* 7 May 3/2 There was a great deal of party trumpeting on both sides.

2. *Mining.* A channel or passage-way made in a shaft by a partition of brickwork, boarding, etc., for ventilation or other purpose.

1839 URE *Dict. Arts* 985 There is a simple mode of conducting air from the pit bottom to the forehead of the mine, by cutting a ragglin, or trumpeting, as it is termed, in the side of the gallery.

So **'trumpeting** *ppl. a.* (in various senses: see the vb.).

1849 CUPPLES *Green Hand* xvi, Lifting his trunk..with a sharp trumpeting scream. **1852** THACKERAY *Esmond* II. iii, The Princess Anne..was proclaimed by trumpeting heralds ..from Westminster to Ludgate Hill. **1859** TENNYSON *Elaine* 138 The tiny-trumpeting gnat can break our dream. **1880** G. MEREDITH *Tragic Com.* (1881) 12 His publication of a trumpeting book fell appallingly flat.

trumpetless to **trumpetry**: see after TRUMPET *sb.*

† **trumpe'ttier.** *Obs.* [f. TRUMPET + -IER, -EER[1].] = TRUMPETER.

1609 HOLLAND *Amm. Marcell.* 6 Having..heard the trumpettiers and cornettiers sound.

trumph (trʌmf). Sc. and north. var. of TRUMP *sb.*[2] Phrases: † *to play trumph about* (obs.): to vie in achievements *with*; *what's trumph?* what is happening? what is the news?

1777 R. FORBES *Ulysses' Answer* 29 Achilles played na' trumph about Wi' him, he says; but judge ye. **1819** J. BURNESS *Plays, Poems* 286 Again Will deals the cartes about Says he, Lads, hearts is trumph. **1895** J. NICHOLSON *Kilwuddie* (ed. 3) 173 A lass that has that wi' the lads should be trumph. **1908** E. M. SNEYD-KYNNERSLEY *H.M.I.* iii. 30 Corners denoted the 'Jack of trumph'. **1955** W. P. MILNE *Eppie Elrick* xxx. 272 Fat's lickly tae be trumph noo? **1969** J. T. R. RITCHIE *Golden City* 76 Ye turn the tope card over to see what's to be trumph.

truncage ('trʌŋkɪdʒ). *Hist.* [ad. med.L. *truncāgium*, f. L. *truncus* TRUNK: see -AGE.] The furnishing of a trunk of a tree for the king's hearth, as a condition of the tenure of certain lands, e.g. at Bamburgh.

[**1212** *Exch. K.R., Knights' Fees* 2/2 m. 5 (P.R.O.) Thomas de Bedinhale..cariabit truncas ad castellum de Banburg. **1235** *Ibid.* 2/20 m. 4 Thomas de Bedenhal..facit truncagium castello de Bamburg' annuatim.] **1893** BATESON *Hist. Northumb.* I. 36 (*Bamburgh*) The truncage due to the castle from the several townships had by that time been commuted for the annual sum of £4. 19*s.* 4½*d.*

truncal ('trʌŋkəl), *a.* Also **trunkal**. [f. L. *truncus* TRUNK + -AL[1].] Pertaining to, or of the nature of, a trunk; situated in or affecting the trunk.

1847 WEBSTER, *Truncal*, pertaining to the trunk or body. **1860** A. PHELPS *Still Hour* xi. 67 A Christian's life, so conducted, must languish, as a tree does whose fibrous roots are stripped off, leaving only its truncal roots..for its nourishment. **1875** H. C. WOOD *Therap.* (1879) 651 Internal trunkal inflammations, such as pneumonia and pleurisy.

truncate ('trʌŋkeɪt), *a.* [ad. L. *truncāt-us*, pa. pple. of *truncāre*: see TRUNCATE *v.*]

† **1.** Cut short, mutilated. *Obs.* (exc. as in 2).

1579–83 [implied in TRUNCATELY].

2. In scientific and technical use: = TRUNCATED 2.

1716 E. HALLEY in *Phil. Trans.* XXIX. 408 Like truncate Cones or Cylinders. **1785** MARTYN *Rousseau's Bot.* xxi. 305 The Tulip Tree..is remarkable for the shape of its leaves, having the middle lobe of the three truncate, or cut transversely at the end. **1826** KIRBY & SP. *Entomol.* IV. xlvi. 333 Elytra..Truncate... When they are shorter than the abdomen and transverse at the end. **1839** DARWIN *Voy. Nat.* i. (1879) 2 Successive steps of tableland, interspersed with some truncate conical hills [i.e. kopjes]. **1872** COUES *N. Amer. Birds* 38 A rectrix broad to the very tip, and there cut squarely off, is truncate.

b. In combination with another adj. of form, as *truncate-turbinate*; = TRUNCATO-.

1887 W. PHILLIPS *Brit. Discomycetes* 354 Cups subtipitate, truncate-turbinate.

truncate ('trʌŋkeɪt, trʌŋ'keɪt), *v.* [f. L. *truncāt-*, ppl. stem of *truncāre*, f. *truncus* TRUNK.] **a.** *trans.* To shorten or diminish by cutting off a part; to cut short; to maim, mutilate. Also *fig.*

1486, 1572 [implied in TRUNCATED 1]. **1727** BAILEY vol. II, *Truncate*, to cut shorter, to maim. **1755** JOHNSON *Dict.* Pref. ¶70 The examples are too often injudiciously truncated. **1852** W. R. WILLIAMS *Relig. Progr.* iii. (1854) 53 It wrongs man by truncating his nature of conscience and immortality. **1911** *Athenæum* 16 Sept. 318/2 He..never wrote short stories, only truncated long ones.

b. In scientific and technical use: *spec.* in *Cryst.* to 'cut off' or replace (an edge or solid angle) by a plane face, esp. so as to make equal angles with the adjacent faces. Chiefly in *pa. pple.*: see TRUNCATED 2.

1758 REID tr. *Macquer's Chem.* I. 97 Pyramids..some of which..are obtuse as if truncated. **1830** LYELL *Princ. Geol.* I. 393 If this gulf were..choked up,..so that new explosions ..should truncate the cone once more. **1883** *Encycl. Brit.* XVI. 348/1 The faces of one hexagonal prism would truncate the lateral edges of the rhombohedron, while the faces of the other..would truncate its lateral solid angles.

c. *Math.* To cut short or approximate (a series, etc.) by ignoring all the terms beyond a chosen term. Also *absol.*

1955 M. LOÈVE *Probability Theory* xvi. 233 We truncate X [*sc.* a random variable] at $c > 0$..when we replace X by X^c $= X$ or 0 according as $|X| < c$ or $|X| \geq c$. **1966** J. H. CADWELL *Topics Recr. Math.* xiv. 157 Because of the steadily decreasing terms, when the series is truncated the error incurred is of smaller magnitude than the first term omitted. **1968** P. A. P. MORAN *Introd. Probability Theory* ii. 78 It is also sometimes useful to exclude more than one of the possible values of i, and in this case it is more often necessary to truncate at the other end. **1981** *Nature* 5 Nov. 14/3 The series in equation (1) should extend to $m = n = \infty$, but in practice the series is truncated at a maximum value..of m and n, usually in the range 8 to 15.

Hence **truncating** *ppl. a.*, that truncates; *spec.* said of a plane that replaces an edge or solid angle.

1805–17 R. JAMESON *Char. Min.* (ed. 3) 118 These new planes are named Truncating Planes, and the edges which they form with the other planes Truncating Edges. **1882** RUSKIN *Bible of Amiens* iii. 95 These two truncating and guarding rivers.

truncated (ˈtrʌŋkeɪtɪd, -ˈkeɪt-), *ppl. a.* [f. L. *truncāt-us*, pa. pple. of *truncāre* (see prec.) + -ED[1] 2, or f. prec. + -ED[1].] Cut short (actually or apparently); having a part cut off, or of such a form as if a part were cut off.

1. *Her.* Of a cross or tree: Having the arms or boughs cut off, so as not to extend to the boundaries of the shield; couped. ? *Obs.*

1486 *Bk. St. Albans, Her.* C vj b, A cros truncatid, And hit is calde trunkatid for his made of ij treys the boys [= boughs] cut a Way. **1572** BOSSEWELL *Armorie* II. 95 b, These trees are truncated, that is to saie, ye boughes cut of from the body, and laide in the forme of a Saltier. The endes whereof may not touch the Angles of the shield.

2. In modern scientific and technical use. (Const. as *adj.* preceding the noun, or as *pa. pple.* following the noun.) **a.** *Geom.*, etc. Of a figure: Having one end cut off by a transverse line or plane; *esp.* of a cone or pyramid: Having the vertex cut off by a plane section, esp. one parallel to the base: thus ***truncated cone*** or ***pyramid*** = FRUSTUM of a cone or pyramid.

1704 J. HARRIS *Lex. Techn.* I, *Truncated Pyramid* or *Cone*, is one whose top is cut off by a Plane parallel to its Base; and therefore the Figure of the truncated top must always be similar to the Base. **1827** FARADAY *Chem. Manip.* ii. (1842) 26 Weights..constructed in sets, each weight..having the form of a truncated cone. **1831** R. KNOX *Cloquet's Anat.* 581 The Cartilages of the apertures of the Nose..represent an ellipse truncated posteriorly. **1840** LARDNER *Geom.* 68 A trapezium is a truncated triangle. *Ibid.* 166 A figure formed by the section of a prism by a plane not parallel to its base is called a truncated prism. **1868** LOCKYER *Guillemin's Heavens* (ed. 3) 73 The southern horn of the crescent was truncated.

b. *Cryst.* and *Solid Geom.* Of an edge or solid angle: Cut off or replaced by a plane face, esp. one equally inclined to the adjacent faces; also said of a solid figure having its edges or angles thus cut off.

1796 KIRWAN *Elem. Min.* (ed. 2) I. 128 [Fluor] the angles or edges rarely truncated or bevilled. **1823** H. J. BROOKE *Introd. Crystallogr.* 24 When an edge, or solid angle, is replaced by one plane, it is said to be *truncated*. When an edge is replaced by two planes, which respectively incline on the adjacent primary planes at equal angles, it is *bevilled*. **1863** GEO. ELIOT *Romola* xxvi, The wide doorway, standing at the truncated angle of a great block..of houses. **1875** BENNETT & DYER *Sachs' Bot.* 51 The separate crystalloids are thin plates, single regular rhombs, often with truncated angles. **1891** *Cent. Dict.* s.v. *Truncate* v., Truncated cube, cuboctahedron, dodecahedron [etc.].

c. *Nat. Hist.* Appearing as if the tip or end were cut off transversely; terminating in a flat or broad edge or surface instead of a point.

1752 J. HILL *Hist. Anim.* 3 The Enchelis, with the head small, and the tail truncated. **1753** CHAMBERS *Cycl. Supp.* s.v. *Leaf*, *Truncated Leaf*, that whose summit or point seems to have been cut off, or is terminated by a strait line in a transverse direction. **1816** STEPHENS in Shaw *Gen. Zool.* IX. II. 236 Quills dusky black; the points..truncated. **1835** J. DUNCAN *Beetles* (Nat. Libr.) 184 The elytra are short and truncated at the extremity. **1899** *Allbutt's Syst. Med.* VIII. 774 These truncated hairs are of..importance for diagnosis.

d. So in *Architecture*, *Geology*, etc.

1723 CHAMBERS tr. *Le Clerc's Treat. Archit.* I. 114 Pediments..supported by an Entablature truncated in the middle. **1727–41** CHAMBERS *Cycl.* s.v. *Roof*, Sometimes it is truncated; that is, instead of terminating in a ridge or angle, it is cut square off at a certain heighth. **1829** SCOTT *Anne of G.* xi, A truncated column of marble, having its base sculptured with hieroglyphical imagery. **1830** LYELL *Princ. Geol.* (1872) I. II. xxiii. 588 The summit of the loftiest peak is truncated. **1869** BOUTELL *Arms & Arm.* ii. (1874) 11 In some [Assyrian] examples, the raised upper crest-like part of the helm is seen to have been bent backwards and truncated.

e. *Statistics.* Of a frequency distribution or sample: obtained by disregarding values of the variate greater than or less than some chosen value. Of a variate: treated in this way.

1931 R. A. FISHER *Truncated Normal Distribution in Math. Tables* (Brit. Assoc. Adv. Sci.) I. p. xxxiii, The frequency of the truncated distribution in the range dx. **1952** A. HALD *Statistical Theory with Engin. Applications* vi. 146 The cumulative distribution functions of three truncated distributions..with degrees of truncation of 10, 30 and 50% respectively. **1971** C. R. HEATHCOTE *Probability* v. 240 Truncated variables are often easier to handle than the original ones, and..under wide conditions, the two sequences have the same asymptotic behaviour.

f. Of soil: having lost the upper horizon(s) as a result of rapid erosion.

1938 A. B. YOLLAND tr. *A. de Sigmond's Princ. Soil Sci.* xiv. 206 These truncated forest soils possess a peculiar dynamics of their own. **1941** H. JENNY *Factors of Soil Formation* v. 100 Owing to differences in color of the *A* and *B* horizons, truncated profiles are often readily discernible on freshly plowed slopes. **1976** L. F. CURTIS et al. *Soils Brit. Isles* 315 Truncated podzols. Here the surface soil has the characters of a B horizon.

3. Maimed, mutilated; also *fig.*

1731 BAILEY, *Truncated*, cut shorter, maimed, mangled. **1791–1823** D'ISRAELI *Cur. Lit.* (1858) III. 181 All the Italian editions continued to be reprinted in the same truncated condition. **1845** R. W. HAMILTON *Pop. Educ.* v. (ed. 2) 97 The truncated frame of man is without power of locomotion or external action. **1890** J. STALKER *Imago Christi* v. (1891) 104 It is a truncated and most imperfect friendship when this region is closed.

truncately (ˈtrʌŋkeɪtlɪ), *adv.* [f. TRUNCATE *a.* + -LY[2].] In a truncate manner or form; in quots., in a mutilated form, with omission of something essential.

1579 FULKE *Heskins' Parl.* 62 Augustines wordes, not truncately and by peece meale rehearsed nor altered. **1583** —— *Defence* Answ. to Pref. 62 The doctors you quote without iudgment fraudulently, falsly, truncately, and otherwise abusiuely.

truncation (trʌŋˈkeɪʃən). [ad. late L. *truncātiōn-em*, n. of action f. L. *truncāre* to TRUNCATE; cf. OF. *troncacion* (1495) in Godef.).]

1. The action of truncating; cutting short; maiming, mutilation. Also *fig.*

1579 FULKE *Heskins' Parl.* 262 The alteration, falsification, and truncation of Tertullians wordes. **1611** COTGR., *Troncation*, a truncation, trunking, mutilation, cutting off. **1637** PRYNNE *Huntley's Breviate* 48 Decreeing judgment of death, or truncation of members. *a* **1682** SIR T. BROWNE *Tracts* xiii. (1684) 204 Singular inhumanities in Tortures..The living truncation of the Turks. **1779–81** JOHNSON *L.P.*, *Cowley* Wks. II. 69 In the Davideis are some ..verses left imperfect..in imitation of Virgil, whom he supposes not to have intended to complete them: that this opinion is erroneous, may be probably concluded, because this truncation is imitated by no subsequent Roman Poet [etc.]. **1903** F. W. H. MYERS *Hum. Personality* II. 301 If it [death] be..a sheer truncation of moral progress.

2. a. In scientific and technical use: The process of truncating, or condition of being truncated; diminution by or as by cutting off an end or point, so that the object terminates in a straight edge or plane surface instead; *spec.* in *Cryst.* replacement of an edge or solid angle by a plane face, esp. one equally inclined to the adjacent faces.

1796 KIRWAN *Elem. Min.* (ed. 2) II. 203 White Lead Ore ..Occurs..crystalized in..prisms, or pyramids, with or without truncations. **1803** H. J. BROOKE *Introd. Crystallogr.* 86 The rhomboid being converted into a six-sided prism by the truncation of all its solid angles, or of its terminal solid angles and its lateral edges. **1853** KANE *Grinnell Exp.* xlv. (1856) 416 The truncation of the muzzle..set their faces in almost perfect and human-like oval. **1861** W. POLE in *Macm. Mag.* III. 184/2 The corresponding facet..formed by the truncation of the lower..pyramid, is..called the collet. **1874** LYELL *Elem. Geol.* xxviii. 495 Similar.. catastrophes have caused..the truncation..of some large cones in Java.

b. *transf.* The place or part where something is truncated.

1805–17 R. JAMESON *Char. Min.* (ed. 3) 117 When we observe on a fundamental figure, in place of an edge or angle, a small plane, such a plane is denominated a Truncation. **1853** PHILLIPS *Rivers Yorksh.* iv. 135 The 'High Peak'..is at the truncation of an interior range of hills. **1897** HAZLITT *Suppl. Coinage European Cont.* 29 This Portuguese piece has under the truncation of the bust the name of W. Wyon as the engraver.

c. *Statistics.* The cutting off of a frequency distribution at a certain value of the variate.

1937 YULE & KENDALL *Introd. Theory of Statistics* (ed. 11) vi. 103 We can picture it as a slightly skew distribution which has been cut off on the left owing to the inadmissibility of negative values of the variate. Discontinuous variates not infrequently give rise to this effect of truncation. **1952** [see TRUNCATED *ppl. a.* 2 e].

d. The loss or removal of the upper horizon(s) of a soil by erosion.

1941 H. JENNY *Factors of Soil Formation* v. 100 An example of widespread truncation is provided by the Cecil series of the Piedmont Plateau. **1972** J. G. CRUICKSHANK *Soil Geogr.* iv. 133 Loss of surface horizons by erosion (truncation) is more common in Oxisols [than in Spodosols].

e. *Math.* The cutting short of a numerical computation or expression before its natural end (if any). Usu. *attrib.* in ***truncation error.***

1952 D. R. HARTREE *Numerical Analysis* x. 223 The solution of the set of equations..is not, of course, the solution of the partial differential equation on account of the truncation error of the approximation. **1968** FOX & MAYER *Computing Methods for Scientists & Engineers* x. 205 For the fourth-order Runge-Kutta method the truncation error is the factor h^5 multiplying a rather complicated expression involving derivatives of $f(x, y)$. **1973** [see ROUNDING *vbl. sb.*[1] 1 c].

truncato- (trʌŋˈkeɪtəʊ), combining form of L. *truncātus* TRUNCATE, used with other adjs. of form in sense 'truncately'.

1852 DANA *Crust.* II. 698 Abdomen..broad truncato-rotund at apex. **1891** *Cent. Dict.*, *Truncatosinuate*, in *entom.*, truncate, with a sinus or slight inward curve on the edge of the truncation.

truncator (ˈtrʌŋkeɪtə(r)). *rare.* [a. L. *truncātor*, agent-n. f. *truncāre* to TRUNCATE: see -OR.] One who truncates; a mutilator.

1579 FULKE *Heskins' Parl.* 184 Heskins, the impudent falsifier, truncator,..peruerter,..of Augustine.

truncature (ˈtrʌŋkətjʊə(r)). Now *rare.* [f. TRUNCATE *v.* + -URE.] = TRUNCATION 2.

1828 STARK *Elem. Nat. Hist.* II. 56 Shell oval, oblong, or turreted;..columella smooth, straight, without truncature or widening at the base. **1854** KELLY & TOMLINSON tr. *Arago's Astron.* 75 One horn of its [Mercury's] crescent is truncated; and it is this truncature that has enabled us to determine the period of its rotation. **1866** *Contemp. Rev.* July 452 Crystals are characterized by the truncatures of their angles, and the bevelment of their edges.

†**trunch,** *sb. Obs. rare.* [ad. F. *tronche* fem.:—pop.L. **trunca* for *truncus* stump of a tree, TRUNK (14th c. in Godef.).]

1. = TRUNCHEON *sb.* 3.

1590 L. LLOYD *Diall Daies* Oct. 14 Tipstaves..with silver trunches and staves to go before.., and to keep the people in order.

2. A post, stake.

1622 W. BRADFORD *Relat. New Eng.* 12 Little trunches knockt into the ground, and small stickes laid over, on which they hung their Pots.

trunch (trʌnʃ), *a.* Now *dial.* [app. shortened f. TRUNCHEON *a.*; cf. L. *truncus* maimed, mutilated.] Short and thick. Also in comb. ***trunch-made.*** Cf. TRUNCHEON *a.*

1683 *Lond. Gaz.* No. 1842/8 Lost.., a Black Gelding,..a thick trunch Horse. *a* **1825** FORBY *Voc. E. Anglia*, *Trunch, trunch-made*,..short and thick, compact and squab in figure.

Also **trunched** (trʌnʃt), **'trunchy** *adjs.* in same sense (*U.S.*). *rare.* ? *Obs.*

1787 M. CUTLER in *Life*, etc. (1888) I. 267, I saw a short, *trunched old man, in a plain Quaker dress. **1778** *Maryland Jrnl.* 21 July Advt. (Thornton), A thick, *trunchy fellow. **1789** *Ibid.* 21 Apr., A trunchy well-set bright-bay horse.

truncheon (ˈtrʌnʃən), *sb.* Forms: 4 **tronsoun, trounsoun, trunsoun, -ioune,** *Sc.* **trwnsown,** 5 **trounson;** 4–5 **tronchoun, -eoun, -en,** 4–7 **tronchon,** 5–7 **troncheon,** 6–7 **tronchion,** (5 **trounchen, tronchown, -yn, trenchoune,** 6 **tronchone, trenshon,** 7 **trouncheon);** *Sc.* 4–5 **trunschoun,** 5 **trunscyoune,** 6 **townsciown, trunscheon, -e;** 6–8 **trunchion,** 6– **truncheon,** (5–6 **trunchoun, -on, -en, -in, -yn, -yne).** [ME. a. OF. *trunçun, tronchon,* F. *tronçon* a piece cut or broken off, a stump (11th c. in Godef.), f. late L. type **trunciōn-em*, f. L. *truncus* TRUNK.]

1. A piece broken or cut off, a fragment. Also *fig. Obs.* or *arch.*

13.. *Seuyn Sag.* (W.) 819 Of the adder he fond mani tronsoun. *a* **1450** *Le Morte Arth.* 3071 One hytte hym vpon the olde wounde With a tronchon of an ore. **1570** LEVINS *Manip.* 164/29 A Trenshon, *fragmentum.* **1587** MASCALL *Govt. Cattle, Oxen* (1627) 18 Small trunchions of coleworts sod in sallet oyle and..brine. **1611** COTGR., *Tronçonneur*,.. a cutter of things into truncheons or lumpes. **1882** STEVENSON *New Arab. Nts.* II. i. 7 A huge truncheon of wreck half buried in the sands. **1892** —— *Across the Plains* 240 [They] set before him truncheons of tales upon their lighted theatre.

b. *spec.* A fragment of a spear or lance; a piece broken off from a spear. *Obs.* or *arch.*

13.. *Sir Beues* (A.) 827 On a tronsoun [*v.rr.* tronchen, tronchyn, tronchon, trunchyn] of is spere þat heued a stikede for to bere. **13..** *K. Alis.* 2149 (Bodl. MS.) þe spere tobrast on two trunsoun. *Ibid.* 3740 A gentyl kniȝth..Had on hym many wounde And a trunchoun in his flaunche. *c* **1400** MAUNDEV. (1839) xxii. 238 þei breken here speres so rudely þat the tronchouns fleu in sprotes and peces all aboute the halle. **1470–85** MALORY *Arthur* I. xxii. 69 He smote Gryflet..and brake the spere that the troncheon stack in his body. **1596** SPENSER *F.Q.* IV. iii. 12 Therewith asunder in the midst it brast, And in his hand nought but the troncheon left. **1697** DRYDEN *Æneid* XI. 16 His brazen buckler on the left was seen: Truncheons of shiver'd lances hung between. **1825** SCOTT *Talism.* xxviii, Sir Kenneth's lance..had wounded him deep in the bosom,..leaving the truncheon of the lance fixed in his wound.

c. The shaft of a spear. *Obs.* or *arch.*

13.. *K. Alis.* 2154 Alisaundre..him mette with speris egge; Through brunny and scheld, to the akedoun, He tobarst atwo his tronchon. **13..** *Guy Warw.* (A.) 3093 þurch þe bodi he bar a trounsoun. **1600** HOLLAND *Livy* XXXV. v. 891 Their captaines..laying about with their truncheons [L. *hastile*] upon the backs of them that so trembled for feare,.. forced them againe into their ranks. **1805** SCOTT *Last Minstr.* I. xix, A fancied moss-trooper, the boy The truncheon of a spear bestrode.

2. A short thick staff; a club, a cudgel. *Obs.* or *arch.* exc. as in 3.

13.. *Sir Beues* (A.) 1428 At þe prisoun dore Beues fond A tronsoun, þat he tok in is hond. **14..** *Stockh. Med. MS.* II. 709 in *Anglia* XVIII. 324 He beryth his seede, Lik a trwnsown or a pestell. *c* **1500** *Lancelot* 2890 O gret trownsciown In til his hond. **1593** SHAKS. *2 Hen. VI*, IV. x. 52 Thy legge a sticke compared with this Truncheon. *c* **1618** MORYSON *Itin.* IV. (1903) 449 A Castle of wood.. which the Senatours Armed with tronchions did assault and take. **1682** N. O. tr. *Boileau's Lutrin* III. 113 A Truncheon strong Confirms his staggering steps. **1725** POPE *Odyss.* XI. 707 Stern beasts in trains that by his truncheon fell. **1756** MRS. DELANY in *Life & Corr.* (1861) III. 451 You walk with your stick as with a truncheon, whilst we poor invalids make use of ours as a walking-staff.

3. A staff carried as a symbol of office, command, or authority; a marshal's baton; most freq. in modern usage, a short staff or club with which a police constable is armed.

1573 in Feuillerat *Revels Q. Eliz.* (1908) 203 A Trunchin for the dictator. **1603** SHAKS. *Meas. for M.* II. ii. 61 Not the Kings Crowne; nor the deputed sword, The Marshalls Truncheon, nor the Iudges Robe Become them with one halfe so good a grace As mercie does. **1728** MORGAN *Algiers* I. iii. 43 An express Embassy, attended with an Ivory Truncheon and a Triumphal Robe. **1843** LYTTON *Last Bar.* VII. iii, You are come.. to take the command of the troops.., and into your hands, I resign this truncheon. **1855** MACAULAY *Hist. Eng.* xiv. III. 412 For his religion [Schomberg] had resigned a splendid income, had laid down the truncheon of a Marshal of France. **1880** MCCARTHY *Own Times* IV. li. 82 Stones were thrown on the one side and truncheons used on the other.

†**b.** *fig.* Cf. TRUNK *sb.* 1 b, quot. 1586. *Obs.*

1601 ? MARSTON *Pasquil & Kath.* IV. 115 For such a one to yoke her free sweet youth Vnto a Lowne,.. A gilden Trunchion, fie! 'tis slauish vile.

4. †**a.** The stem or stock of a tree. *Obs. rare.*

c **1449** PECOCK *Repr.* I. vi. (Rolls) 28 Tho bowis grewen out of stockis or tronchons, and the tronchons or schaftis grewen out of the roote.

b. A length cut from a plant, esp. one used for grafting or planting; a stout cutting. Now *rare.*

1572 MASCALL *Plant. & Graff.* (1592) 17 An other way to set Mulberies.., cut.. great Mulberie bowes or stockes, asunder in yᵉ bodie (with a saw) in troncheons a foot long or more,.. make a.. furrow in good earth well and deepe, so that ye may couer.. your troncheons. **1664** EVELYN *Sylva* I. xviii. (1729) 86 [Alders] are propagated of Trunchions.. the Trunchions being set as big as the Small of one's Leg. **1725** *Bradley's Fam. Dict.* s.v. *Lime tree*, The Truncheons make far better Coal for Gun-Powder, than that of Alder it self. *Ibid.* s.v. *Sallow*, When you Graft Sallow, take a Truncheon as big as your Wrist, of two Foot and an half long. **1855** SINGLETON *Virgil* I. 127 Neither wild truncheons on the olive graft.

†**5.** An intestinal worm, short and thick in form, parasitic in horses. *Obs.*

c **1440** *Promp. Parv.* 504/1 Trunchon, wyrme, *lumbricus.* **1530** PALSGR. 283/2 Trunchon a worme. **1565** BLUNDEVIL *Horsemanship* IV. xcvi. (1580) 43 In a Horses guts do breede three kinds of wormes:.. The third be short and thicke, like the end of a mans little finger, and therefore be called Troncheons. *c* **1720** W. GIBSON *Farrier's Guide* II. xxxix. (1738) 142 Several Kinds of Vermin bred in the bodies of Horses, which go under the Denomination of Bots, Worms and Trunchions. **1748** tr. *Vegetius' Distempers Horses* 84 Another Drench for Worms, Botts and Truncheons.

†**6.** 'The solid part of a horse's tail, towards the croup' (Littré s.v. *Tronçon*). *Obs. rare*$^{-1}$.

1639 T. DE GRAY *Compl. Horsem.* 24 The hams dry, and streight, the trunchion small, long, well set on, and well couched.

¶**7.** Erroneously used for TRUNCHEOUR, TRENCHER[1] 2 or 3. *Obs.*

1548 *Acc. Ld. High Treas. Scot.* IX. 167 For serving of his gracis tabill upoun tuelf sylver truncheones. **1739** 'R. BULL' tr. *Dedekindus' Grobianus* 131 Trojans their Tables ate, eat thou thy Truncheon.

8. *attrib.* and *Comb.*, as ***truncheon-bearer***, ***-fashion***, ***officer***, ***-sceptre***; **truncheon-snake** (see quot.); **truncheon-wise** *adv.*, in the manner or form of a truncheon.

1896 *Westm. Gaz.* 18 Feb. 5/2 Yesterday was a busy.. day for *truncheon-bearers all over London. **1912** S. R. DRIVER in *Expositor* Jan. 35 Out of Machir came down truncheon-bearers. **1750** R. POCOCKE *Trav.* (1888) 71 A sceptre.. in the *truncheon fashion, having a round head guarded with points. **1708** *Mem. Right Villanous John Hall* 11 Out jump Four *Trunchion Officers. **1814** *Sporting Mag.* XLIV. 147 Brandishing his *truncheon-sceptre. **1736** MORTIMER in *Phil. Trans.* XXXIX. 254 *Vipera fusca*: The brown Viper in Virginia: In Carolina it is called the *Truncheon-Snake. **1572** MASCALL *Plant. & Graff.* (1592) 43 Certaine.. trees.. which in cutting the great branches therof *truncheon wise, doe renew againe.

Hence **'truncheoner, 'truncheonist** (*nonce-wds.*), one who bears a truncheon.

1613 SHAKS. *Hen. VIII*, v. iv. 54, I.. hit that Woman, who cryed out Clubbes, when I might see from farre, some forty Truncheoners [*Wks.* (ed. Johnson, 1765) truncheoneers] draw to her succour. **1854** *Tait's Mag.* XXI. 372 Circumscribed.. by 184 B and his co-truncheonists.

†**truncheon**, *a. Obs. rare*$^{-1}$. [? attrib. use of TRUNCHEON *sb.*] = TRUNCH *a.*

1611 COTGR., *Retroussé*, thicke and short, druggellie, trunchion.

'truncheon, *v.* Forms: see TRUNCHEON *sb.* [a. F. *tronçonner* (12th c. in Godef.), f. *tronçon*, TRUNCHEON *sb.*]

†**1.** *trans.* To reduce to 'truncheons' or fragments; to break in pieces; to shatter. Also *fig.*

c **1477** CAXTON *Jason* 16 Thus began the bataylle.. with speris that sone were tronchoned. *Ibid.* 35 b, She fill doune ..alle thurghe smyten and tronchoned with amerouse sorowe. *c* **1500** *Melusine* xxxvi. 286 The Saudan valyauntly smote geffray, & tronchoned hys spere vpon his shild.

†**b.** *spec.* To carve (an eel): the proper term for this. Cf. TRANCH *v. Obs.*

1486 *Bk. St. Albans* F vij b, An Ele trounsoned. **1787** BEST *Angling* (ed. 2) 169 *Trounchen an eel*, cut him up. **1853** BADHAM *Halieut.* 343 He gobbets trout, truncheons eel, fins chub, tusks barbel [etc.].

2. To beat with a truncheon, to baton.

1597 SHAKS. *2 Hen. IV*, II. iv. 154 If captaines were of my minde, they would trunchion you out, for taking their names vpon you. **1839** *Morn. Herald* 20 July, They are occasionally truncheoned by the police.

Hence **'truncheoning** *vbl. sb.*

c **1477** CAXTON *Jason* 15 b, Whan hit cam to the tronchoning of their speris.

truncheoned ('trʌnʃənd), *a.* [f. TRUNCHEON *sb.* + -ED[2].] Furnished or armed with a truncheon.

1761 GOLDSM. *Cit. W.* cix, The brickdust man took up as much room as the truncheoned hero. **1821** *Blackw. Mag.* X. 698 Truncheoned and uniformed as becomes a man of his military habits. **1839** *Morn. Herald* 11 July, The truncheoned police of the metropolis. **1883** HALL CAINE *Cobwebs Crit.* vii. 202 A city-marshal broke his leg.. while walking truncheoned from the Mansion House.

[**truncheoneer**, a suggested reading for *truncheoner* (see after TRUNCHEON *sb.*).]

†**truncheour**, obs. form of TRENCHER[1].

1511–12 *Acc. Ld. High Treas. Scot.* IV. 321 To Johne Aitkyne, goldsmith,.. to mak foure gret truncheouris.. threttein small truncheouris and five saltfattis.

†**'trunchfiddle**. *Obs. rare*$^{-1}$. [? f. TRUNCH *a.* + FIDDLE *sb.*, or ? for **trunkfiddle*: cf. next and *trunk-wame* (TRUNK *sb.* 18).] (?)

1589 *Hay any Work* 6 He might freely.. florish with his 2. hand sword. O tis a sweete trunchfiddle.

†**'trunch-hole**. *Obs. rare*$^{-1}$. ? = *trunk-hole*: see TRUNK *sb.* 18, and cf. sense 10 e.

1683 R. D. *State of Turkey* 153 The.. crew.. clapt an iron spike into the trunch-hole of the prow.

trunchman, obs. corrupt f. TRUCHMAN.

trunchy: see after TRUNCH *a.*

‖**truncus** ('trʌŋkəs). [L.: see TRUNK.]

a. *Anat.* The trunk or main stem of a vessel or nerve. **b.** *Zool.* The trunk or body of an animal, without the head, limbs, and tail; in *Entom.* the thorax. **c.** *Bot.* The trunk or stem of a tree.

1693 tr. *Blancard's Phys. Dict.* (ed. 2), *Truncus*, in general ..that part of the great Artery and *Vena Cava*, which descends from the Heart.. more especially.. those Branches which are sent from the great Trunk to the *Viscera.* **1706** PHILLIPS (ed. Kersey), *Truncus*, (Lat.) the Stem or Stock of a Tree without the Boughs; a Body without a Head. **1875** HUXLEY & MARTIN *Elem. Biol.* (1883) 177 As the truncus becomes more and more distended, the longitudinal valve.. tends more and more completely to shut off the openings of the pulmonary arteries.

trundle ('trʌnd(ə)l), *sb.* Also 6–7 trundel(l), 7 trondle, 8–9 *Sc.* truntle, 9 *dial.* trunnel, -nle. [A parallel form to TRENDLE, TRINDLE *sb.*]

I. Something that trundles or is trundled.

1. A small wheel, roller, or revolving disk; *esp.* a small but massive wheel adapted for supporting a heavy weight, as the wheel of a castor.

1564, 1602 [see TRUNDLE-BED β]. **1668** WILKINS *Real Char.* 257 Wheel, Truckle, Trundle. **1669** STURMY *Mariner's Mag.* II. vi. 68 Points, Halfs, and Quarters, which is on the two Trundles. **1833** J. HOLLAND *Manuf. Metal* II. 16 They are submitted to the buff, which is a trundle of wood covered with thick soft leather, and made to revolve rapidly.

b. *Organ-building.* In the draw-stop action, A roller with two arms by the rotation of which a slider is drawn or replaced.

1876–98 STAINER & BARRETT *Dict. Mus. Terms* 342 When the stop is pulled out, the arms *aa* draw the trace *b* from right to left, the end of the trundle *c* being attached to the trace is moved in a similar direction, whilst the other end of the trundle *d* moves in an opposite direction, and draws out the slider. **1881** W. E. DICKSON *Organ-Build.* x. 130 The connection of these horizontal draw-bars with the vertical levers will be effected by squares or bell-cranks of a form known as 'trundles'.

2. A device consisting of two discs turning on an axle, and connected by a series of parallel staves cylindrically arranged, which engage with the teeth of a cog-wheel; a lantern-wheel. In early use, each of such discs (= *trundle-head* (*a*): see 7). Also, each of the staves of this device.

1611 COTGR., *Lanterne à pagnons*, a paire of trundles, or trundle heads; that which is turned about by the cog wheele of a Mill. **1660** R. D'ACRES *Art Water-drawing* 13 Great wooden wheels with Coggs in them, working Trundles with round staves in them. **1764** J. FERGUSON *Lect.* iii. 35 A winch six inches long, fixt on the axis of a trundle of 8 staves or rounds. **1801** BOURNON in *Phil. Trans.* XCI. 186 They form a kind of indented cylinders, which have some resemblance to the trundle of a mill. **1829** *Nat. Philos.* I. *Mechanics* II. vii. 30 (Usef. Knowl. Soc.) The cylindrical teeth or bars of the lantern are called trundles or spindles. **1861** SMILES *Engineers* II. 125 He employed cast iron pinions, instead of the wooden trundles formerly used.

3. A low truck or carriage on small wheels. ? *Obs.*

1664 EVELYN *Sylva* (1679) 22 [In replanting a tree] You may weigh up, and place the whole weighty Clod upon a Trundle to be convey'd, and Replanted where you please. **1766** *Compl. Farmer*, *Trundle*, a sort of carriage with low wheels, for carrying heavy and cumbersome loads.

4. An embroiderer's quill of gold thread; in *Her.*, a charge representing this.

c **1828** BERRY *Encycl. Her.* I. Gloss., *Trundles*, quills of gold thread used by embroiderers, and borne by them in the Arms of their Company. **1894** *Parker's Gloss. Her.* 225 Embroiderers' Broaches, Trundles, and Quill... The Trundle represents a quill of gold thread, two of which are represented in the arms of the London company.

II. An act of trundling (*lit.* or *fig.*).

5. An act of trundling or rolling; an impulse that causes something to roll.

1893 Q. COUCH *Delect. Duchy* 95 They.. gave the stone a trundle.

6. *fig.* A going along or away; a course; departure: in phr. ***to run*** or ***take one's trundle***, to take one's course. *dial.*

1675 V. ALSOP *Anti-Sozzo* 388, I resolved he should run his Trundle. **1821** CLARE *Vill. Minstr.* I. 41 So take your trundle now, and good luck may ye see! *Ibid.* II. 97 Ye're each at once as free To take your trundle as ye us'd to be.

III. 7. *attrib.* and *Comb.* (in some cases perh. directly from the vb.): **trundle-head**, (*a*) each of the discs of a trundle (sense 2); (*b*) = sense 2; (*c*) *Naut.* (see quot. 1867); **trundle-shot**, a shot consisting of a bar of iron with sharpened ends and a ball of lead attached near each end so as to cause it to turn in its flight; **trundle-wheel** = sense 2. See also TRUNDLE-BED, -TAIL; also *trunnel-head*, *-hole* s.v. TRUNNEL.

1611 *Trundle heads [see 2]. **1766** *Compl. Farmer* s.v. *Madder*, The trundle-head, thirteen inches semi-diameter, furnished with eighteen rounds, each a foot long, and two inches diameter: the ends of this trundle-head are two inches and a half thick. **1867** SMYTH *Sailor's Word-bk.*, *Trundle-head*, the lower drum-head of a capstern, when it is double, and worked on one shaft both on an upper and lower deck. **1627** CAPT. SMITH *Seaman's Gram.* xiv. 67 *Trundle shot is.. a bolt of iron sixteene or eighteene inches in length; at both ends sharpe pointed, and about a handfull from each end a round broad bowle of lead. **1807** JOYCE *Sci. Dial.* xvii. (1846) 47 A small *trundle wheel made to work in the cogs. **1839** *Civil Eng. & Arch. Jrnl.* II. 357/2 A part of an ancient trundle wheel was found a few days ago in Chalmerston Moss.

'trundle, *v.* Forms: see prec. [A parallel form to TRENDLE, TRINDLE *v.*; cf. OF. *trondeler* to fall rolling (Godef.), 'to trundle as a ball' (Cotgr. 1611).]

I. 1. a. *trans.* To cause to roll along upon a surface, as a ball, hoop, or other globular or circular object; to roll, bowl. Also *fig.*

1598 FLORIO, *Carrucolare*, to trundle or rowle. **1601** HOLLAND *Pliny* VIII. vii. I. 196 One Elephant did wonders: ..hee caught from them their targuets and bucklers perforce, flung them aloft into the aire, which as they fell, turned round, as if they had beene trundeled by art. **1630** J. TAYLOR (Water P.) *Pennilesse Pilgr.* Wks. I. 122/2 There did we trundle down health after health. **1698** VANBRUGH *Æsop* III. i, I could tell my mother's pedigree before I could speak plain; which, to show you.. the strength of my memory, I'll trundle you down in an instant. **1760–72** H. BROOKE *Fool of Qual.* (1809) III. 92 Various exercises.., such as wrestling .., and tossing or trundling leaden balls. **1798** COLERIDGE *Fears in Solit.* 114 Terms which we trundle smoothly o'er our tongues. **1824** MISS MITFORD *Village* Ser. I. (1863) 109 George Hearn, the little post-boy, trundling his hoop at full speed. **1832** COBBETT *Rur. Rides* (1885) II. 380 Sitting round a dirty board, with potatoes trundled out upon it, as the Irish do. **1901** R. ANDERSON *Hist. Kilsyth* vi. 50 [He] trundled an orange across the floor.

b. *intr.* To move along on a surface by revolving; to roll. Also *fig.*

1629 B. JONSON *New Inn* II. i, To be cropp'd.. Close to his head to trundle on his pillow. *a* **1661** FULLER *Worthies*, *Cornw.* (1662) I. 201 His Round-Table,.. the tale whereof hath Trundled so smoothly along for many ages. **1711** ADDISON *Spect.* No. 253 ¶10 A Description in Homer's Odyssey, where Sisyphus is represented lifting his Stone up the Hill.. it is heaved up by several Spondees.. and at last trundles down in a continual Line of Dactyls. **1840** DICKENS *Barn. Rudge* v, Occasionally a hat or wig.. came spinning and trundling past him.

c. *Cricket.* (*trans.* or *absol.*). To bowl. *colloq.* The ball was originally trundled along the ground.

1849 *Punch* 14 July 12/1 In those Days.. they did moderately trundle the Ball under-hand; but now they fling it over-handed from the Elbow. **1861** *Baily's Mag.* July 140 Such bowling as was trundled by Mr. Lyttelton and Mr. Salter in this innings is rarely witnessed in a University match. **1870** *Ibid.* Dec. 213 Six out of the eleven have trundled the ball. **1882** [see TRUNDLER b, *trundling* below]. **1898** G. GIFFEN *With Bat & Ball* iii. 47 The bowlers, too, trundled with that specially placed on-field in their mind's eye. **1959** *Punch* 3 June 747/2 Four of the team bowl leg-spinners.., and Gupte is reported to be the best of his type now trundling.

2. a. *trans.* To cause to rotate; to twirl, spin, whirl (something held in the hand); *spec.* to twirl (a mop) so as to free it from water. Cf. ROLL *v.*[2] 5.

a **1756** [see *trundled* below]. **1787** COLMAN *Prose on Sev. Occas.* III. 277 While Footmen, women grown.. Shall darn old hose, sweep rooms, and trundle mops. **1864** SIR F. PALGRAVE *Norm. & Eng.* IV. 60 Instead of trundling the theodolite they yoked the oxen. **1883** H. J. POWELL

Glassmaking 65 The English workman attains the same result by trundling the glass during reheating.

b. *intr.* for *pass.*

1782 [see *trundling* below].

3. a. *intr.* To move or run on a wheel or wheels. (Cf. ROLL *v.*^{2} 12 c.)

1688 R. HOLME *Armoury* III. xiv. (Roxb.) 16/2 Such are termed Truckle beds, because they trundle under other beds. **1768** TUCKER *Lt. Nat.* (1834) I. 59 To see the wheelbarrow trundle. **1824** *Blackw. Mag.* IV. 95 The night coaches and mails were now trundling in. **1882** J. HAWTHORNE *Fort. Fool* I. xiv, Numbers of fine carriages.. trundle up.

b. *trans.* To draw or push along on a wheel or wheels, as a wheelbarrow, vehicle, etc.

1825 SCOTT *Let.* 7 June, A light barouche..which two horses will trundle along like a bowl. **1862** SALA *Seven Sons* II. iii. 80 [He] was trundling a wheelbarrow full of sand. **1886** H. F. LESTER *Under two Fig Trees* 128 If nurse..was requested..to trundle the perambulator.

4. a. *trans.* To convey in a wheeled vehicle, to wheel.

1773 GOLDSM. *Stoops to Conq.* II. *ad fin.*, I'll clap a pair of horses to your chaise that shall trundle you off in a twinkling. **1842** J. WILSON *Chr. North* (1857) I. 142 The children are all trundled away out of the cottage. **1847–8** H. MILLER *First Impr.* ix. 156 As many bricks as an Irish labourer would trundle in a wheel-barrow. **1869** DICKENS *Lett.* (1880) II. 413 The Bath chairs trundling the dowagers about the streets.

b. *intr.* To go in a wheeled vehicle (in quot. 1909, on a bicycle or tricycle).

1840 DICKENS *Barn. Rudge* xxii, Mr. Tappertit trundled off with the chaise. **1909** *Spectator* 31 July 164/2 On my trusty 'Rover' I trundle down the brae.

5. a. *fig.* (*intr.*) To go, walk, or run easily or rapidly; to go away, 'be off'; also, to walk unsteadily or with a rolling gait.

1680 V. ALSOP *Mischief Impos.* iv. 27 Some may come [to their own Parish-church] out of custom, because they have used to trundle thither down the hill. **1700** CONGREVE *Way of World* I. ii, *Bet.* They are gone, sir, in great anger. *Peb.* Enough, let 'em trundle. *a* **1754** FIELDING *Fathers* IV. i, The next morning down trundled her and I to Dirty Park. **1820** LADY GRANVILLE *Lett.* 22 Aug., She..trundled out of the House. **1872** C. KING *Mountain. Sierra Nev.* x. 220 Sarah Jane rolled, I might almost say, trundled in.

b. *trans.* To carry or send off, turn out, dismiss.

1794 WOLCOTT (P. Pindar) *Dinah* 99 Wks. 1816 III. 315 Off were the couple trundled—man and maid. **1818** SCOTT *Br. Lamm.* xxi, The women..always contrived to trundle me out of favour before the honeymoon was over.

II. [back-formation from *trundle-bed*.]

†**6.** *intr.* To occupy a trundle-bed; = TRUCKLE *v.* 1. *Obs. rare*$^{-1}$.

c **1626** *Dick of Devon.* IV. i. in Bullen *O. Pl.* II. 61 You and your brother Manuell lay in the high Bed, and I trondling underneath.

Hence **trundled** ('trʌnd(ə)ld) *ppl. a.*, **'trundling** *vbl. sb.* and *ppl. a.*

a **1637** B. JONSON *Horace, Art Poetrie* 568 Who's unskilful at the coit, or ball, Or trundling wheele. **1674** N. FAIRFAX *Bulk & Selv.* 68 As a Coach may be so tickly set..as to give it self a trundling. *a* **1756** MRS. HAYWOOD *New Present* (1771) 256 The house-maid then, with a trundled mop, dries the floor very neatly. **1782** COWPER *Gilpin* 139 Just like unto a trundling mop. **1803** R. COUPER *Tourifications* xvi. II. 121 The extremity of this avenue was crossed by a fine little clear trundling rivulet. **1861** W. J. PROWSE in *Bell's Life* 10 Nov. 6/3 But however good their trundling—pitch or pace, or break, or spin—Still the monarch of all bowlers, to my mind, was Alfred Mynn! **1862** *Baily's Mag.* Apr. 260 The Eleven then commenced batting to the trundling of Moore and Conway. **1882** *Daily Tel.* 19 May, Making a slashing drive to the off for 4 from the same trundling. **1908** *Chron. Lond. Mission. Soc.* Mar. 47/2 Trundling carts threw up clouds of choking dust.

trundle, obs. form of TREENAIL.

'trundle-bed. Forms: α. 6 trendyll-, trindle-, tryndle-, trindell-; β. 6 trundell-, 6– trundle-; cf. TRENDLE, TRINDLE, TRUNDLE. [TRUNDLE *sb.* 1.] = TRUCKLE-BED.

α. **1542** *MS. Acc. St. John's Hosp., Canterb.*, For makyng a trendyll bed iiij^{d}. **1560** DAUS tr. *Sleidane's Comm.* 232 He slept quietly in the trindle bed. **1599** *Nottingham Rec.* IV. 250, j. trindle bedd; one mattrice.

β. **1564** *Knaresborough Wills* (Surtees) I. 96, j trundell bedd. **1602** *2nd Pt. Return fr. Parnass.* II. vi. 979 When I was in Cambridge, and lay in a Trundlebed vnder my Tutor. **1667** PEPYS *Diary* 9 Oct., My wife and I in the high bed in our chamber, and Willet in the trundle-bed. **1727** DUDLEY in *Phil. Trans.* XXXIX. 68, I thought at first my Servants.. were haling along a Trundle-bed. **1852** MRS. STOWE *Uncle Tom's C.* iv, Aunt Chloe..had been busy in pulling out a rude box of a trundle-bed.

So †**'trundle 'bedstead** *Obs.*

1590 in *Archæologia* XL. 326 Itm. a trundell bedsted and a boulster. **1686** in *Essex Rev.* (1906) XV. 173 One trundle beadsted.

trundler ('trʌndlə(r)). [f. TRUNDLE *v.* + -ER^{1}.]

a. One who or that which trundles.

1648–60 HEXHAM *Dutch Dict.*, *Een Roller*, a Roler, or a Trundler. **1879** SALA *Paris herself again* (1880) I. xviii. 326 A friendly trundler of a Bath-chair..came to my assistance.

b. *Cricket.* A bowler. (See TRUNDLE *v.* 1 c.) *colloq.*

1871 [see SNICK *v.*^{2} 2 b]. **1882** *Daily Tel.* 27 May, Each trundler sent up five overs for one single run. **1895** *Westm. Gaz.* 1 Mar. 5/2 The two greatest Australian batsmen were seen playing the balls of England's two most famous trundlers.

trundle-tail. *Obs.* or *arch.* Forms: 5 tryndel-, 6–8 trundle-, 6–9 trindle-, 7 trondle-, trendle-.

1. A dog with a curly tail; a low-bred dog, a cur. Also *attrib.*

1486 *Bk. St. Albans* F iv b, Myddyng dogges. Tryndeltayles, and Prikherid curris. **1599** NASHE *Lenten Stuffe* 29 A trundle-taile tike or shaugh or two. **1602** *2nd Pt. Return fr. Parnass.* II. v. 872 All kinde of dogges..trindle tailes, prickeard curres, small Ladies puppies. **1605** SHAKS. *Lear* III. vi. 73 Hound or Spaniell,..Or Bobtaile tight, or Trondle taile. *a* **1639** WEBSTER *Appius & Virg.* III. iv, Amongst curs a trendle tale. **1820** SCOTT *Monast.* xxiv, The very brutes are degenerated..our hounds are turnspits and trindle-tails.

b. Applied contemptuously to a person.

1614 B. JONSON *Bart. Fair* II. v, Doe you sneere, you dogs-head, you Trendle tayle! **1632** ROWLEY *Woman Never Vexed* II. i. 18 How now my fine Trundletayles; My wodden Cosmographers. **1706** PHILLIPS (ed. Kersey), *Trundle-tail*, a Wench that runs fisking up and down with a draggled Tail.

2. (as two words) A curly tail (of a dog).

a **1625** FLETCHER *Love's Cure* III. iii, Like a poor cur, clapping his trindle tail Betwixt his legs. **1651** OGILBY *Æsop* (1665) 205 Rough with a trundle Tail, a Prick-ear'd Cur.

trunel, obs. form of TREENAIL.

trunes(se, trunisse, obs. ff. TRUENESS.

trunion, variant of TRUNNION.

trunk (trʌŋk), *sb.* Forms: 5–7 tronk, tronke, troncke, (7 tronck), 5–7 trunke, 6 trounk, trounke, (tronque, troonke, trouncke), 6–7 truncke, 6–8 trunck, 6– trunk. [a. F. *tronc* (12th c.), ad. L. *truncum*, acc. of *truncus* main stem or stock of a tree, the human body, a piece cut or broken off, etc. In branch III app. associated with TRUMP *sb.*^{1}, F. *trompe*. With IV cf. TRUNK-HOSE.]

I. The main part of something as distinguished from its appendages.

1. a. The main stem of a tree, as distinct from the roots and branches; the bole or stock.

1490 CAXTON *Eneydos* iv. 17 Eneas..hewe the troncke of a tree oute of the whiche yssued bloode. **1605** CAMDEN *Rem.* 161 A golden truncke of a tree. **1615** W. LAWSON *Country Housew. Gard.* (1626) 14 Cut away all his twigs..burying his trunck in the crust of the earth. **1697** DRYDEN *Virg. Georg.* III. 580 With Trunks of Elms and Oaks the Hearth they load. **1787** WINTER *Syst. Husb.* 103 The roots of trees grow in proportion to their trunks and branches. **1872** YEATS *Techn. Hist. Comm.* 21 These were formed from a single trunk of oak.

b. *fig.* or in fig. context.

1586 A. DAY *Eng. Secretary* I. (1625) 140 In stead of a louing and contented husband, to giue her a withered old Truncke. *Ibid.* II. 97 For his stature, a dwarffe; for his person, a trunke; for his qualities, a dog. **1603** SHAKS. *Meas. for M.* III. i. 72 You consenting too't, Would barke your honor from that trunke you beare, And leaue you naked. **1663** BP. PATRICK *Parab. Pilgr.* xv. (1687) 117 His endowments were divine;..yet blocks and trunks are wont now to lift up themselves higher in their own conceit than he could be tempted to do. **1839** H. ROGERS *Ess.* II. iii. 140 While the trunk of the language remains the same, the twigs and frailer branches are torn away by the storm. **1876** C. M. DAVIES *Unorth. Lond.* 81 Different offshoots which had from time to time separated themselves from the main trunk of Presbyterianism.

c. *transf.* The shaft of a column; also, the dado or die of a pedestal.

1563 SHUTE *Archit.* C ij b, Scapus,..being the troncke or body of the pillor. **1664** EVELYN tr. *Freart's Archit.* 124 [The Pedestal] is likewise called Truncus the Trunk..also Abacus, Dado, Zocco, etc. **1727–41** in CHAMBERS *Cycl.* **1842–76** in GWILT *Encycl. Archit.* Gloss.

d. (See quot. 1950.) Cf. *trunk dial*, sense 18.

1899 F. J. BRITTEN *Old Clocks and Watches* 316, I am able to give an engraving of a very early specimen of a long-case clock... This case is of oak and panelled. The head is fixed on the trunk, and will not take off. **1950** D. DE CARLE *Watchmakers' & Clockmakers' Encyclopædic Dict.* 188/1 *Trunk*, refers to the body or main part of the case of a long-case clock. The case is formed of three parts, the trunk, the Hood..and the Plinth. **1978** *Times* 17 June 9/5 A dial clock is basically a clock with a round dial which hangs on the wall, or a round dial with a trunk underneath, which is called a trunk dial or drop dial.

2. a. The human body, or that of an animal, without the head, or esp. without the head and limbs, or considered apart from these; in *Entom.* the thorax. Also *transf.* and *fig.*

1494 FABYAN *Chron.* VI. clxiii. 156 There was heddys, armys, leggys, and trunkys of dede mennys bodyes, lyinge as thycke as flowres growe in tyme of May. *Ibid.* VII. 495 His hed stryken of, & the trunke of his body hanged by chaynes vpon ye common gybet of Parys. **1541** R. COPLAND *Galyen's Terap.* 2 G ij, In diuiding ye tronke which is betwene the necke & the legges, is two great capacytees. **1593** SHAKS. *2 Hen. VI*, IV. x. 90 There [will I] cut off thy most vngracious head;..Leauing thy trunke for Crowes to feed vpon. **1610** HOLLAND *Camden's Brit.* (1637) 336 His head smitten off, and the truncke of his body throwen into the fire. **1711** ADDISON *Spect.* No. 229 ¶1 The Trunk of a Statue which has lost the Arms, Legs, and Head. **1715** ROWE *Lady Jane Gray* v. *ad fin.*, Blasted be the hand That struck my Guilford! Oh, his bleeding trunk Shall live in these distracted eyes for ever! **1804** ABERNETHY *Surg. Obs.* 26 The front, or back part of the trunk of the body. **1826** KIRBY & SP. *Entomol.* xxviii. III. 48 The second portion of the body is the Trunk, which is interposed between the head and the abdomen. **1837** EMERSON *Address, Amer. Schol.* Wks. (Bohn) II. 175 The state of society is one in which the members have suffered amputation from the trunk. **1870** ROLLESTON *Anim. Life* 7 In the trunk [of the Rat] we observe that the spines of the dorsal vertebræ..point backwards. **1913** *Times* 9 Aug. 4/1 A tendency to hairlessness on the trunk and limbs.

†**b.** *Her.* The head of a beast cut off immediately behind the horns or ears, i.e. caboched; cf. TRUNKED *ppl. a.*^{1} 2. *Obs. rare*$^{-1}$.

1486 *Bk. St. Albans, Her.* b v, Tronkys be calde in armys any bestys hede or neck Ykytt chagikli [= jaggedly] a sonder.

†**3.** A dead body, a corpse; also, the body considered apart from the soul or life. *Obs.*

1588 SHAKS. *Tit. A.* v. iii. 152 Vnckle draw you neere, To shed obsequious teares vpon this Trunke. **1605** —— *Lear* I. i. 180 If on the tenth day following, Thy banisht trunke be found in our Dominions. **1611** B. JONSON *Catiline* v. vi, His troops Couer'd that earth, they had fought on, with their trunkes. **1709** STEELE *Tatler* No. 83 ¶3 This poor meagre Trunk of mine is a very ill Habitation for Love.

4. a. *Anat.* The main body or line of a blood-vessel, nerve, or similar structure, as distinct from its branches; also *transf.* the main line of a river, railway, telegraph or telephone, road or canal system; see *trunk-drainage*, *-glacier*, *-line*, etc. in 18. Also *fig.*

1615 CROOKE *Body of Man* 906 The lesser Trunke creepeth along the inside of the Legge..and in his progresse sprinkleth diuers surcles into the skine. **1707** FLOYER *Physic. Pulse-Watch* 352 The Arteries join'd on each side in the same Original Trunk. **1817** J. BRADBURY *Trav. Amer.* 246 Small rivers that fall immediately into the great trunk of the Mississippi. **1841–71** T. R. JONES *Anim. Kingd.* (ed. 4) 156 The ovigerous canals..uniting on each side of the body into two principal trunks. **1843** R. J. GRAVES *Syst. Clin. Med.* xxx. 396 Not only the nervous filaments..may be affected, but also the main trunk of the nerve. **1876** GEO. ELIOT *Dan. Der.* xxviii, Like the main trunk of an exorbitant egoism.

b. *pl.* In Stock Exchange language, short for Grand Trunk Railway of Canada, or its stock.

1892 *Pall Mall G.* 9 Feb. 5/3 Trunks have risen, partly in sympathy with American, and also on a much better traffic than was expected. **1898** *Westm. Gaz.* 1 Dec. 8/1 A bull account in Trunks is always followed by a bad revenue statement.

c. *Teleph.* (*a*) A telephone line connecting two exchanges a long way apart or in different telephone areas; also (*U.S.*), a line connecting exchanges within the same area (cf. *toll call* s.v. TOLL *sb.*^{1} 3); (*b*) a line connecting selectors or the like of different rank within an exchange.

1889 PREECE & MAIER *Telephone* 249 This switchboard is required to distribute the trunks between the different offices [*sc.* exchanges], and also to enable the testing of all the trunk and subscribers' lines to be carried on from one central point. **1908** *Jrnl. Inst. Electr. Engineers* XLI. 120 In America the *local* term remains the same, the *junction* is called 'trunk', and our *trunk* is called a 'toll' or 'long-distance' line. **1921** W. AITKEN *Autom. Telephone Syst.* I. 4 The designation of the lines interconnecting apparatus at different switching stages..is somewhat confusing. The American generally speaks of these as trunks, which practically is equivalent to our junctions... For example, the circuits between first and second preselectors,..second and third selectors, and third selectors and connectors, are all trunks or junctions... Very commonly the lines between exchanges in this country [*sc.* Britain], and for the use of which an extra charge is made.., are known as trunks. For these the American terms toll line or long-distance line is used. **1925** WRIGHT & PUCHSTEIN *Telephone Communication* ii. 33 It is necessary in central-energy systems to serve districts of more than ten thousand lines by means of a number of central offices connected by trunk circuits or trunks. **1966** *McGraw-Hill Encycl. Sci. & Technol.* XIII. 433/1 When the extension user dials the first digit, the wipers of the first selector step upward to the level corresponding to the digit dialed, and automatically step around in a horizontal arc..until they find an idle trunk. **1978** *Sci. Amer.* June 90/2 A modern telephone exchange is connected not only to its own subscribers but also, through special lines called trunks, to other exchanges serving other subscribers. **1978** P. H. SMALE *Telecommunication Syst. I* vii. 60 There are various grades of exchange in order of importance... There are also various grades of interconnecting line, for example subscribers lines, junctions and trunks, and again the number gets fewer as length, importance and cost increase.

(*c*) *pl.* The operators who deal with trunk calls. *colloq.*

[**1889** PREECE & MAIER *Telephone* xx. 353 As the trunk operators had too much to do..a special plan was arranged by which a subscriber requiring a connection to another town mentions the word 'trunk' to the ordinary operator.] **1947** N. CARDUS *Autobiogr.* III. 233 He rang me up at my Manchester house; he was speaking from Harrogate. When 'trunks' gave me notice of his call I expected something urgent. **1977** C. MCCULLOUGH *Thorn Birds* ix. 203 Give me trunks, please, switch... I want to put an urgent call through.

†**5.** The scale of a map or plan; see SCALE *sb.*^{3} 9. *Obs. rare.*

1561 EDEN *Arte Nauig.* III. ii. 58 This the Maryners call the truncke or scale of leaques. **1574** BOURNE *Regiment for Sea* xviii. (1577) 47 b, As you may see in measuring it by the trunke of your carde there. **1594** BLUNDEVIL *Exerc.* VII. xxviii. (1636) 692 To know the distance of places,..there is wont to be set downe in the Mariners Card, a scale, otherwise called by the Mariners a Trunk.

II. A chest, box, case, etc. (supposed to have been orig. made out of a tree-trunk).

†**6.** A chest, coffer, box. *Obs.* in *gen.* sense.

1462 *Mann. & Househ. Exp.* (Roxb.) 150 Item, payd ffor a new tronke ffor my lord whych was delyvared to Willyam off Wardrope x. s. **1494** FABYAN *Chron.* cxxxi. 113 He ordeyned a cheste, or trunke of clene syluer, to thentent yt all suche iuellys and ryche gyftes..shuld therein be kepte. **1591** GREENE *Art Conny Catch.* III. (1592) 34 At the beds feete stood a hansome truncke, wherein was very good linnen. *a* **1648** LD. HERBERT *Autobiog.* (1824) 190 Having the copies of all my dispatches in a great trunk in my House in London. **1687** A. LOVELL tr. *Thevenot's Trav.* I. 62 So curious and elaborate a Work might deserve a better Fate, than to lye moulding in the bottom of a Trunk. **1702** ADDISON *Dial. Medals* ii. (1726) 51 The little trunk she holds in her left hand is the *acerra*.., in which the frankincense was preserv'd. **1726** SHELVOCKE *Voy. round World* Pref. 17 No chests, boxes, or trunks, which shall be found in the ship when taken, shall be open'd.

7. a. A box, usually lined with paper or linen, and with a rounded top, for carrying clothes and other personal necessaries when travelling; originally covered with leather, now often of canvas, painted metal, etc. Cf. PORTMANTEAU I.

1609 *Shuttleworths' Acc.* (Chetham Soc.) 181 To the porter, for the carridge of the gentlewomens truncke..xv^d. **1662–3** PEPYS *Diary* 8 Jan., We were forced to send for a smith, to break open her trunk. **1709** STEELE & ADDISON *Tatler* No. 93 ¶3 He had got his Trunk and his Books all packed up to be transported into Foreign Parts. **1773** GOLDSM. *Stoops to Conq.* II. i, I like to see their horses and trunks taken care of. **1841** THACKERAY *Gt. Hoggarty Diam.* viii, Away I went..with a couple of bran new suits from Von Stiltz's in my trunk. **1859** W. COLLINS *Q. of Hearts* iii, Ring the bell, and have your trunks packed.

b. *N. Amer.* The luggage compartment of a motor vehicle; = BOOT *sb.*^{3} 4 c.

[**1929** *Hearst's Internat. Mag.* Nov. 210 (Advt.), Six wire wheels and trunk rack standard equipment. **1930** *Automobile Topics* 6 Dec. 359/3 Rear-end trunks were larger and more prevalent. In one line of cars they were designed into the rear of the body itself.] **1931** *Amer. Home* Apr. 197 The luggage belongs in the trunk on the rear of the car. **1937** *Sat. Even. Post* 2 Oct. 28/3 The enlarged trunks will hold enough luggage to carry you around the world. **1951** J. W. VALE *Mod. Auto Body & Fender Repair* xiii. 162 The deck compartment, sometimes referred to as the rear trunk compartment or the turtle back..may be repaired in the same way. **1960** *Times* 14 Sept. 12/6 When we hired a car in California we found that a car..bristles with surprises. You ..find the spare wheel in the trunk. **1964** MRS. L. B. JOHNSON *White House Diary* 24 Apr. (1970) 119 Lyndon had transferred to an open convertible. Along the way he made three unscheduled stops, standing on the trunk of his car. **1968** *Globe & Mail* (Toronto) 17 Feb. 49/9 (Advt.), Extra lighting inside, in hood, in trunk. **1975** N. LUARD *Robespierre Serial* v. 34 The Belgian unlocked the trunk, stood by the porter while he lifted out two suitcases.

8. a. A perforated floating box in which live fish are kept.

c **1440** *Promp. Parv.* 504/1 Trunke, for kepynge of fysche, *gurgustium*. **1450–1** *Abingdon Rolls* (Camden) 130 In factura j tronke pro piscibus custodiendis. **1540** in *Sel. Pleas Crt. Admiralty* (1894) I. 99 He toke the tronke in his hands and hallyd it up to the land and there put forth alle the fysh that was in the tronke into a basket. **1674** tr. *Scheffer's Lapland* 70 Fishes also, of which they have so great draughts, that they are forced to keep them in trunks and ponds. **1766** BLACKSTONE *Comm.* II. xxv. 393 If the pheasants escape from the mew, or the fishes from the trunk,..they become *ferae naturae* again. **1898** J. K. FOWLER *Rec. Old Times* 108 In the midst was a large shallow pond,..in which was kept an eel trunk, consisting of a strong iron-bound box about four feet long and two feet wide and deep, perforated with holes, and a lid fastened with lock and key... In this trunk or box were kept live eels, the trunk having a strong iron chain attached to it..; this enabled the trunk to be hauled up a sloping bank.

b. An open box or case (containing from 80 to 90 lb.) in which fresh fish are sold wholesale.

1883 S. PLIMSOLL in *19th Cent.* July 147 The box, which is called by many names, as 'van', 'machine', 'tank', 'trunk', &c. **1883** *Daily News* 27 July 7/1 Soles and such fish are sold in open boxes, without any covering whatever, called trunks. **1909** *Times* 12 Aug. 11/6 Two trunks of plaice made the remarkably high price of £3 10s. per trunk.

c. A net or trap for lobster-catching. *dial.*

1835 'S. OLIVER' *Rambles Northumbld.* v. 210 For catching lobsters the fishermen of Holy Island mostly use small hoop-nets, called by them trunks. **1867** SMYTH *Sailor's Word-bk.*, *Trunk*,..an iron hoop with a bag, used to catch crabs and lobsters.

9. *Mining.* A long shallow trough in which lead or tin ore is dressed.

1653 MANLOVE *Lead Mines* 273 (E.D.S.) The miner's Tearms..Fleaks, Knockings, Coestid, Trunks and Sparks of oar. **1839** DE LA BECHE *Rep. Geol. Cornw.* etc. xv. 579 The trunk was a pit ten feet long, three wide, and nine inches deep. **1839** URE *Dict. Arts* 1244 The rough is washed in buddles..the slimes in trunks. **1851** TAPPING *Manlove's Lead Mines* Gloss. s.v., The trunks are agitated with water, and thereby the metals separated from the base minerals.

10. a. A box-like passage for light, air, water, or solid objects, usually made of boards; a shaft, conduit; a chute. Now chiefly *techn.*

1610 NORTH *Plutarch* 1117 He was newly come from Trophonius truncke or hole. **1632** in E. B. Jupp *Carpenters' Co.* (1887) 301 Truncks for bringing in of light into mens howses..trunckes for Jackeweights or conveyance of water. **1642** C. VERNON *Consid. Exch.* 42 Which Bill they..put.. downe through a Trunke made for that purpose, into the Chamberlaines Court. **1747** HOOSON *Miner's Dict.* H j, As to ..having the Trunks in the Roof of the Drift, that never does well. **1759** SMEATON in *Phil. Trans.* LI. 126 A trunk, for bringing the water upon the wheel, was fixed. **1861** R. WILLIS in Willis & Clark *Cambridge* (1886) III. 173 An opening or horizontal trunk through the rising seats, by which the solar ray may be directed upon the Lecture-table. **1886** *Act. 49 & 50 Vict.* c. 38 §6 Any bridge, waggon-way, or trunk for conveying minerals or other product from any mine or quarry. **1888** ELWORTHY *W. Somerset Word-bk.*, *Trunk*..a wooden tube much used in corn mills to convey grain or flour to or from the mills. Any wooden tube.

b. *spec.* A chute through which coal is emptied from the wagons into lighters, etc. *dial.*

1725 T. THOMAS in *Portland Papers* VI. (Hist. MSS. Comm.) 104 Those [steathes] that are covered with timber work are called trunks. **1893–4** *Northumbld. Gloss.*, *Trunk-staith*, a coal-spout at a shipping place. In former times a coal-staith was called a 'dyke', or trunk if a shoot or spout was used.

c. *Organ-building.* Short for *wind-trunk*.

1852 SEIDEL *Organ* 44 The principal canal..into which the wind passes from the bellows, is called the trunk.

d. In a steam-engine, A tubular piston-rod large enough to allow of the lateral movement of the connecting-rod when jointed directly to the piston.

1859 RANKINE *Steam Engine* (1861) 481 In large engines there are sometimes more than one piston rod and stuffing-box, and sometimes a tubular piston rod called a trunk.

e. *Naut.* A water-tight shaft passing through the decks of a vessel, for loading, coaling, etc.

1862 *Catal. Internat. Exhib.* II. XII. 2/1 The lower deck.. is made of iron, water-tight, and fitted with water-tight trunks, to communicate with the upper deck, so that access can be had at all times distinct from the other decks. **1877** W. H. WHITE *Man. Naval Archit.* i. 29 Where openings have to be made in a watertight deck or platform, either watertight covers must be fitted to the openings or water-tight trunks, carried to a sufficient height above the load-line, must be built around them.

f. See quot.

1877 KNIGHT *Dict. Mech.*, *Trunk* 5 (Hatting), the conduit, tube, or guiding-box which guides the air-currents and directs the fur fibers from the picker to the cone, in hat-body forming machines.

g. *Salt-making.* A box-like cover placed over an evaporating-pan.

1885 C. G. W. LOCK *Workshop Receipts* Ser. IV. 155 In.. Cheshire..the evaporating-pans are at times employed quite open and exposed to the sky, but nowadays they are mostly surrounded with sheds,..furnished with ventilating openings in the roof... On the Continent, all except the fine and butter-salt pans are generally covered in with wooden trunks, flat on top with sides converging upwards, thus forming an elongated truncated cone about 5 ft. high over the pan.

h. The water-tight case in which the centreboard of a sailing-boat works.

1894 *Westm. Gaz.* 20 Aug. 7/2 The centre board had not been lost, but had been jammed in the trunk and was held fast. **1897** *Outing* (U.S.) XXX. 228/2 The centerboard trunk is made long so that the board may be dropped at any desired point forward or aft.

i. *U.S.* A floodgate or sluice controlling the flow of water into and out of rice-fields.

1856 in *Documentary Hist. Amer. Industr. Society* (1910) I. 120 Trunk-minders undertake the whole care of the trunks. **1903** 'P. PENNINGTON' *Woman Rice Planter* (1913) i. 8 Each field has a very small flood-gate (called a trunk), which opens and closes to let the water in and out. **1939** *Sat. Even. Post* 10 June 37/2, I opened all my rice-field trunks, so that the flowed field inside would equalize the pressure from the flood outside, thus saving my banks.

III. A pipe or tube.

†**11.** A cylindrical case to contain or discharge explosives or combustibles; the barrel of a mortar, the case of a rocket, etc. *Obs.*

1548 *Privy Council Acts* (1890) II. 177, ij dosan of tronques for wild fyer. **1581** STYWARD *Mart. Discipl.* I. 12 To haue such gouernours as are..skilfull..in the making of trunkes, bawles, arrowes, and all other sortes of wilde fire. **1634** I. B. *Myst. Nat. & Art* 57 Fire-works..as Crackers, Trunks, etc. *a* **1660** *Contemp. Hist. Irel.* (Ir. Archæol. Soc.) I. 61 None could passe the same without eminent danger of fallinge under the fumie reache of that murtheringe troncke. *Ibid.* 102 Within the truncke some wilde fire in maner and forme of a bombe and granados. **1799** G. SMITH *Laboratory* I. 7 The cases, or trunks, of rockets.

†**12.** A pipe used as a speaking-tube or ear-trumpet. *Obs.*

1546 BALE *Eng. Votaries* I. (1550) 70 The roode spake these wordes, or else a knaue monke behynde hym in a truncke through the wall. **1589** PUTTENHAM *Eng. Poesie* III. xxv. (Arb.) 311 Not to heare but by a trunke put to his eare. **1631** SHIRLEY *Traitor* III. i, Ha! are there no trunks to convey secret voices? **1680** C. NESSE *Church-Hist.* 75 Which ..did but pass through him as a trunk through which a man speaks. **1704** SWIFT *Battle of Bks.* Misc. (1711) 245 They whisper to each other thro a large hollow Trunk.

†**13.** A hollow tube from which a dart or pellet is shot by blowing; a blow-gun, a pea-shooter.

1553 EDEN *Treat. Newe Ind.* (Arb.) 20 They..blowe them [arrows] oute of a trunke as we doe pellets of claye. *a* **1652** BROME *New Acad.* IV. i, All my..tops, gigs, balls, cat and catsticks, pot guns, key guns, trunks, tillers, and all. **1755** B. MARTIN *Misc. Corr.* Oct. 170 Two youths..in the gallery of Covent-garden Play-house..shooting Peas thro' a Tin Trunk in the Faces of the Audience. **1801** STRUTT *Sports & Past.* IV. iv. §1 A substitute for the gun,..a long hollow tube called a trunk.

†**14.** More fully *perspective trunk*: A telescope; cf. *trunk-glass*, *-spectacle* in 18.

1610 I. HEYDON in *Camden's Lett.* (1691) 130 With one of our ordinary Trunks I have told eleven stars in the Pleiades. **1620** B. JONSON *New World in Moon* Wks. (Rtldg.) 615/1 From the Moon!.. Oh, by a trunk! I know it, a thing no bigger than a flute-case: a neighbour of mine, a spectacle-maker, has drawn the moon through it at the bore of a whistle. **1620** WOTTON *Let. to Bacon* in *Reliq.* (1651) 414 A long perspective-trunke with the convexe glasse fitted to the said hole [in a camera obscura], and the concave taken out at the other end.

15. a. The elongated proboscis of the elephant; also *transf.* the prolonged flexible snout of the tapir, etc.

c **1565** R. BAKER in Hakluyt *Voy.* (1589) 150 The Elephant ..With water fils his troonke right hie, and blowes it on the rest. **1613** PURCHAS *Pilgrimage* (1614) 816 There was another strange creature in Nicaragua..like a blacke Hogge, with..a short truncke or snowt like an Elephant. **1687** A. LOVELL tr. *Thevenot's Trav.* III. 45 An Elephant..his Governour can make him do what he pleases with his Trunck. **1774** GOLDSM. *Nat. Hist.* (1776) IV. 273 Two tame elephants..that caress the indignant animal with their trunks. *c* **1850** *Arab. Nts.* (Rtldg.) 685 The trunks, ears, and other parts of these elephants, were painted red and other colours.

b. *slang.* The human nose.

a **1700** B. E. *Dict. Cant. Crew*, *Trunk*, a Nose. **1785** GROSE *Dict. Vulg. T.*, *Trunk*, a nose [in various phrases]. **1901** LAWSON *Remin. Dollar Acad.* 87 The deep bass rumbling sound, which was emitted from his trunk.

†**c.** The long pointed bill of the heron. *Obs. rare*$^{-1}$.

1575 TURBERV. *Falconrie* 160 A live hearon uppon the upper part of whose bill or truncke you must convey the joynt of a reed or cane.

d. The proboscis of some molluscs; also the proboscis of various insects. Now *rare* or *Obs.*

1661 LOVELL *Hist. Anim. & Min.* Introd., The Mollusca, ..some have acetabula, and two long trunks, which they use as anchors in storms. **1664** POWER *Exp. Philos.* I. 2 At his [the flea's] snout is fixed a Proboscis, or hollow trunk or probe. **1692** BENTLEY *Boyle Lect.* 125 Insects, which wound the tender buds with a long hollow trunk, and deposit an egg in the hole. **1805** PRISC. WAKEFIELD *Dom. Recreat.* i. (1806) 5 There is as great a variety in the trunks of insects as in their antennae.

†**16.** *pl.* Also ***small trunks***: an old game: = TROLL-MADAM; cf. TRUCKS. *Obs.*

1607 *Christmas Prince* II. (1816) 45 Why say you not that Munday will bee drunke, Keepes all vnruly wakes, and playes at trunkes? **1611** COTGR., *Trou Madame*, the Game called Trunkes, or the Hole. **1621** BURTON *Anat. Mel.* II. ii. IV, The ordinary recreations which we haue in Winter..are Cardes, Tables,..the Philosophers game, small trunckes [etc.]. **1654** GAYTON *Pleas. Notes* IV. iv. 196 Billiards, Kettle-pins, Noddy-boards, Tables, Truncks, Shovell-boards, Fox and Geese, or the like. **1706** PHILLIPS (ed. Kersey), *Trunks*, a kind of Play otherwise call'd Troll-Madame and Pigeon-holes. **1854** MISS BAKER *Northampt. Gloss.*, *Nine-holes*, or *Trunks*, a game played with a long piece of wood or bridge with nine arches cut in it... Each player has two flattened balls, which he aims to bowl edge-ways under the arches; he scores the number marked over the arch he bowls through.

IV. 17. *pl.* †**a.** = TRUNK-HOSE. *Obs.*

1583 *Rates of Custome Ho.* F j, Truncks the dosen xii. s. **1610** B. JONSON *Alch.* III. iii, Sixe great slopps, Bigger then three Dutch hoighs, besides round trunkes. **1652** in *Verney Mem.* (1907) I. 490 There are Pages in trunks that ride behind the coches..cloath trunks billited or garded with velvet. **1672** *Lond. Gaz.* No. 656/4 His Trunks and Stockings are of grey Worsted.

b. Short breeches of silk or other thin material; in theatrical use, often worn over tights; in quot. 1896 applied to ordinary breeches or knickerbockers.

1825 HONE *Every-day Bk.* I. 1463 Theatrical 'trunks', or short breeches. **1837** DICKENS *Pickw.* xv, The appearance of Mr. Snodgrass in blue satin trunks and cloak, white silk tights and shoes, and Grecian helmet. **1874** R. BUCHANAN *Kitty Kemble* 86 A slim fairy prince in trunks and tights. **1896** CROCKETT *Grey Man* xvi, David had donned the trunks and laid by the bairn's kilts. **1906** N. MUNRO in *Blackw. Mag.* Dec. 802/1 A right smart Alick in short trunks.

c. orig. *U.S.* Short tight-fitting drawers worn by swimmers and athletes. ***swimming trunks***: see SWIMMING *vbl. sb.* 6.

1883 *Pall Mall G.* 26 July 7/1 Captain Webb attempted his perilous feat of swimming the Niagara Rapids... He wore a pair of silk trunks. **1889** GUNTER *That Frenchman* xi, Black-velvet trunks cover his [the wrestler's] hips and thighs. **1891** *Daily News* 30 May 5/5 The men are together in front of Harvard boathouse in caps, 'sweaters', trunks, and canvas shoes. **1894** RALPH in *Harper's Mag.* Aug. 341 Nude bathing will not be permitted... The use of tights or 'trunks' will not be allowed. **1941** BAKER *Dict. Austral. Slang* 78 *Trunks*, swimming shorts. **1956** P. SCOTT *Male Child* I. vi. 86 Except for a pair of swimming trunks he was naked. **1964** L. DEIGHTON *Funeral in Berlin* xviii. 107 A blond man in very small knitted swimming-trunks. **1982** S. B. FLEXNER *Listening to Amer.* 61 Men's *trunks* had been in use by professional swimmers and athletes since the 1880s.

d. Knickers; underpants with short legs.

[**1926–7** *Army & Navy Stores Catal.* 705/1 Gent's underwear..Trunk drawers— 18/6.] **1936** [see *ankle-sock* s.v. ANKLE *sb.* 3]. **1970** *Kay & Co.* (Worcester) *Catal.* *1970–71* Autumn–Winter 452 *Meridian trunks.* New style with shorter leg and continental front.

V. 18. *attrib.* and *Comb.*, as, in senses 1 and 2, ***trunk-armour***, ***-bark***, ***-bone***, ***-diameter***, ***-muscle***, ***-rib***, ***-root***, ***-scar***; in senses 4 and 4 b, ***trunk-dealer***, ***-drainage***, ***exchange***, ***-glacier***, ***-jack*** (JACK *sb.*^{1} 15 d), ***-market*** (MARKET *sb.* 1 d), ***-road***, ***route***, ***-sewer***, ***-sheath***, ***stream***, ***-telegraph***, ***-telephone***, ***-traffic***, ***-train***, ***-wire***; in sense 4 c, ***trunk circuit***; in senses 6 and 7, ***trunk-boot*** (BOOT *sb.*^{3} 4 c), ***-buddle*** (see quot.), ***-castor***, ***-check***, ***-lid***, ***-liner***, ***-lock***, ***-mail*** (MAIL *sb.*^{2}), ***room***, ***-seller***, ***-shop***, ***strap***; in sense 10 (c and d), ***trunk-hole***, ***-piston***, ***-plunger***; in sense 15, ***trunk-bearer***; ***trunk-nosed*** adj.; also **trunk-alarm**, an alarum which sounds when the trunk-lid is lifted (Knight *Dict. Mech.* 1877); **trunk-back** = *trunk-turtle* (*U.S.*); **trunk-band**, *Organ-building*, a shallow box in the horizontal bellows to which the wind-trunk is attached; also called *trunk-lining*; †**trunk-board**, a platform for a trunk or trunks at the back of a carriage; **trunk-**

brace, a support or stay for a trunk-lid, to prevent it from falling again when raised (Knight); **trunk-cabin**, a ship's cabin partly above and partly below the upper deck; cf. sense 10 e and *trunk-deck* (*Cent. Dict.* 1891); **trunk-call**, a call from one telephone exchange to another; **trunk-case**, that part of a chrysalis case which covers the thorax; **trunk-deck**, the top of a hatchway trunk projecting above the deck, or a row of these joined so as to form a kind of raised deck (*Cent. Dict. Suppl.* 1909); **trunk dial**, a clock having a long case to accommodate the pendulum; **trunk dialling** (see quot. 1971); **trunk-engine**, an engine having a tubular piston-rod; see sense 10 d; †**trunk-glass** = sense 14; **trunk-leg, -limb**, in Crustaceans, a leg attached to the thorax; **trunk-light**, a skylight placed over a trunk or shaft (*Cassell's Encycl. Dict.* 1888); **trunk-lining**, (*a*) = *trunk-band*; (*b*) material for lining trunks: cf. TRUNK-MAKER; **trunk-machine**, a tube or shaft for the conveyance of cotton from one machine to another during the preparatory processes (*Cent. Dict. Suppl.* 1909); **trunk main**, a large pipe for the conveyance of water, etc. under pressure, as distinguished from the reticulation of smaller mains fed therefrom; † **trunk-manna**: see quot.; **trunk murder**, a murder after which the body is hidden in a trunk; also **trunk murderer**; **trunk-nail**, a short nail with broad convex brass head used for ornamenting trunks and coffins (Knight); **trunk-nose**, the sea-elephant or elephant-seal (*Funk's Stand. Dict.* 1895); **trunk-road**, a main road; *spec.* in ***Grand*** (also ***Great***) ***Trunk Road***, the great highway between Calcutta and Amritsar constructed during the British Raj; **trunk-rod**, a fishing-rod composed of short joints for convenience in packing (*U.S.*); †**trunk-saddle**, ? a packsaddle adapted for carrying a trunk or chest; † **trunk sleeve**, a full, puffed sleeve; cf. sense 17 a; so **trunk slops** (SLOP *sb.*[1] 4); †**trunk-spectacle** = sense 14; **trunk-staithe**, a wharf at which coal is loaded into vessels by a trunk or shoot; **trunk-stay** = *trunk-brace* (Knight); **trunk-turtle**, the Leathery Turtle or Leather-back, *Dermatochelys* (*Sphargis*) *coriacea*, of warm seas, having a flexible leathery carapace with osseous deposits and several longitudinal ridges; **trunk-valve**, in a steam-engine, a D slide-valve long enough to cover direct steamports when placed near the end of the cylinder (*Cent. Dict. Suppl.* 1909); †**trunk-wame**, a fiddle (*dial.*); **trunk-way**: see quot.; **trunk-weed**, ? a species of sea-weed; **trunk-work**, secret or clandestine action, as by means of a trunk. See also TRUNK-FISH, TRUNK LINE, -MAKER.

1854 OWEN *Skel. & Teeth* in *Orr's Circ. Sc.* I. *Org. Nat.* 165 In these colossal armadillos..the *trunk-armour was in one immovable piece, covering the back and sides, and was not divided by bands. **1883** S. GARMAN *Rept. & Batrach. N. Amer.* Introd. 6 Sea Turtles are numerous off the coasts of Florida. '*Trunk-backs' or 'Leather-backs', *Sphargis*, are the largest. **1876** STAINER & BARRETT *Dict. Mus. Terms*, *Organ Construction*, On it [the middle board] rests a strong ridge called the *trunk-band or lining, to which the wind trunks can be at any point joined. **1881** W. E. DICKSON *Organ-Build.* vi. 73 A shallow box, say 4 inches deep, upon the middle board, of the same size as the top board. This is called a trunk-band, and is introduced to allow of fixing the wind-trunks. **1880** C. R. MARKHAM *Peruv. Bark* 37 It [*Cinchona Condaminea*] once yielded great quantities of thick *trunk bark, but..is now almost exterminated. *Ibid.* 81 From the trunk-bark of a plant of this species [*Cinchona Calisaya*]..he obtained..5 per cent. of alkaloids. **1861** P. P. CARPENTER in *Rep. Smithsonian Inst.* 1860, 174 The shell of the *Trunk-bearers may almost always be known by a notch or canal at the base. **1819** B. H. LATROBE *Jrnl.* (1905) 224 A girl of thirteen or fourteen years old sat up on the *trunk board behind. **1904** *Westm. Gaz.* 23 Sept. 7/3 A second skull ..but no trace of *trunk bones can be found. **1794** W. FELTON *Carriages* (1801) II. 54 The carriage..; an iron coach-box on a square *trunk-boot, raised on neat, carved blocks. **1839** URE *Dict. Arts* 751 The *trunk buddle is.. composed of two parts; of a cistern or box into which a stream of water flows, and of a large tank with a smooth level bottom. **1878** F. O. DAVENPORT *On Man-of-War* 197 The captain had a small *trunk cabin, a little higher and abaft ours. **1910** *Times* 19 Aug. 4/6 The telephone is still open, but ..a message into the country usually involves a *trunk call. **1826** KIRBY & SP. *Entomol.* III. xxxi. 250 The *Trunk-case, divided into the thorax, or upper surface, extending from the head to the dorsal segments of the abdomen. **1877** KNIGHT *Dict. Mech.*, *Trunk-caster. **1906** M. NICHOLSON *House of 1000 Candles* iii, I gave him my *trunk-checks. **1896** *Trunk circuit [see TRUNKING *vbl. sb.*[2] 2]. **1921** *Jrnl. Inst. Electr. Engineers* LIX. 390/2 (*caption*) Trunk circuits radiating from London to provincial towns. **1909** *Westm. Gaz.* 3 Mar. 9/1 *Trunk dealers received another disappointment in the traffic, which showed a decrease. **1896** *Nautical Mag.* LXV. 1076 Oscar II..a *trunk deck vessel of the type invented by Mr. W. Hök. **1884** F. J. BRITTEN *Watch & Clockm.* 274 Generally *trunk dials have half seconds pendulums. **1952**, etc. *Trunk dialling [see *subscriber trunk dialling* s.v. SUBSCRIBER 3]. **1959** *Ann. Reg. 1958* 505 Trunk dialling from Bristol began in December. **1971** *Gloss. Electrotechnical, Power Terms* (*B.S.I.*) III. ii. 20 *Trunk dialling*, control of an exchange's automatic switching equipment from an exchange in another multi-exchange area over trunk or toll circuits. **1976** *Times* 20 Dec. (Istanbul Suppl.) p. iv/3 Although international trunk-dialling is promised..it can take anything up to 15 minutes to get a dialling tone..in Istanbul. **1909** *Chamb. Jrnl.* Sept. 561/2 The Rajah-tree..with a *trunk-diameter of six or eight feet. **1864** C. S. READ in W. White *Norfolk* 67 Some better system of *trunk drainage should be at once adopted. **1864** WEBSTER, *Trunk-engine. **1867** SMYTH *Sailor's Word-bk.*, *Trunk-engine*, a direct-acting steam-engine, in which the end of the connecting-rod is attached to the bottom of a hollow trunk, passing steam-tight through the cylinder cover. **1908** *Daily Chron.* 9 Dec. 1/4 Telephonists employed in *trunk exchanges. **1860** TYNDALL *Glac.* I. xiv. 99 The medial moraine of the *trunk glacier. **1875** *Wond. Phys. World* I. ii. 55 To coalesce in one great trunk-glacier. **1613** M. RIDLEY *Magn. Bodies* 28 A thing worthy of better observation from the *Truncke-glasse. **1881** W. E. DICKSON *Organ-Build.* v. 60 In one of these cheeks a *trunk-hole may have to be cut for the entrance of the wind. **1902** *Encycl. Brit.* XXX. 479/2 Of the corresponding pairs of appendages ..three..may be all maxillipeds or may help to swell the number of *trunk-legs. **1905** *Daily Chron.* 4 Oct. 9/7 *Trunk Liner wanted; must be used to glue work. **1876** *Trunk-lining [see *trunk-band*]. **1907** *Times* 29 Mar. 6/2 Second-hand booksellers..know more about books, have a sounder judgment as to what is literature and what is trunk-lining. **1677** MOXON *Mech. Exerc.* ii. 21 Chest Locks, *Trunk Locks, Pad-locks, &c. **1771** SMOLLETT *Humph. Cl.* 17 Apr., Tell Gwyllim that she forgot to pack up my flannels and wide shoes in the *trunk mail. **1820** SCOTT *Monast.* xv, I hope, a'gad, they have not forgotten my trunk-mails of apparel. **1663** BOYLE *Usef. Exp. Nat. Philos.* II. iv. 101 The Calabrians..by Incisions obtain from the common Ash Tree..a sweet Juice, so like to the Manna..that the Natives call it in their Language, *Manna del corpo*, or *Trunk-manna. **1902** *Westm. Gaz.* 3 Apr. 9/1 A *Trunk market wit. **1907** *Ibid.* 25 Mar. 9/3 Just come into the Trunk market for a second. **1884** *Birmingham Daily Post* 23 Feb. 2/4 Trunk-moulding machine, 32 in. long, with dies complete. **1905** *Daily Mail* 15 Apr. 5/4 (*heading*) The *trunk murder. How the bodies were found. **1936** G. GREENE *Journey without Maps* I. i. 11 Another clue in a trunk murder case. **1976** S. HYNES *Auden Generation* v. 136 The crimes..are actual-sounding crimes: a trunk murder at Paddington station, a girl killed on Streatham Common. **1925** P. SELVER tr. *K. Capek's Lett. from Eng.* 54 At Madame Tussaud's..in the catalogue I found..Arthur Devereux, hanged 1905, known as the '*trunk murderer', because he hid the corpses of his victims in trunks. **1962** G. BUTLER *Coffin in Oxford* xiv. 176 Discovered your trunk murderer yet? **1872** HUMPHRY *Myology* 32 Where the fibres diverge from the *trunk-muscle. **1899** *Allbutt's Syst. Med.* VIII. 59 Rarely the spasm [of tetany] begins in the trunk muscles. **1887** KIPLING *From Sea to Sea* (1899) I. 114 The Englishman..took off his hat to the tun-bellied, *trunk-nosed God of Good-Luck. **1900** —— in *Daily News* 9 Mar. 6/2 The temple wherein the 'tun-bellied', 'trunk-nosed' god Ganesha (the divine Elephant) receives his worshippers. **1888** HASLUCK *Model Engin. Handybk.* (1900) 108 The feed-pump..is on the *trunk principle. **1885** NICHOLSON *Man. Zool.* (ed. 4) 495 The anterior *trunk-ribs [of the *Dinosauria*] were double-headed. **1848** J. BOURNE *Let.* 24 Apr. in *Railways in India* (ed. 2) 19 The grand *trunk road, connecting Calcutta with the north west provinces..is already a railway all but the rails. **1851** *Ret. Public Works India* 146 in *Parl. Papers* XLI. 513 Documents..report the progress of the works on the Great Trunk Road. **1861** HUGHES *Tom Brown at Oxf.* xlvi, Englebourn was situated on no trunk road. **1869** E. A. PARKES *Pract. Hygiene* (ed. 3) 398 In India, on some of the trunk roads there are regular halting grounds. **1888** KIPLING *Departmental Ditties* (1890) 19 All those hairy gentlemen..Swaggered down the Grand Trunk Road into Bow Bazar. **1890** R. S. FERGUSON *Hist. Cumberld.* x. 149 The trunk-road itself passes Waverton. **1931** J. W. GREGORY *Story of Road* xviii. 274 In 1839 it was decided to construct a metalled road, the Grand Trunk Road, from Calcutta to Delhi... By 1849 about £300,000 had been spent on it. **1937** *Archit. Rev.* LXXXI. 155 The Trunk Roads Act comes into operation on April 1st. **1974** *Listener* 2 May 574/3 Bentinck's Governor-Generalship..was not a complete failure, as the Great Trunk Road shows. **1893** *Outing* (U.S.) XXII. 121/2 *Trunk rods made to pack in small space often have six or seven [joints]. **1698** J. VERNEY *Let.* 16 June in M. M. Verney *Verney Lett.* (1930) I. iii. 31 The little long room that is under the *Trunk room of the Purple Chamber. *a* **1752** LD. VERNEY *Will* in *Ibid.* II. xxxiii. 246, I give to her..all the money & Jewels in the cabinet in the Trynk Room. **1860** J. G. HOLLAND *Miss Gilbert's Career* (1866) 293 Cheek was..led to the trunk-room of the lodging-hall. **1952** E. WILSON *Lilly's Story* i, in *Equations of Love* 133 A trunk-room full of the trunks which accompany a large English family in migration. **1970** *Times* 2 June (Container Suppl.) p. i/5 Container ships,..capable of carrying as much general cargo in a year on a trunk-route shuttle service as an entire fleet of traditional break-bulk cargo liners. **1671** GREW *Anat. Plants* iii. App. §1 *Trunk-Roots are of two kinds:..those that vegetate by a direct descent... The other sort..shoot forth at right Angles with the Trunk. **1569** in *Richmond Wills* (Surtees) 219 In his owen stable..iiij hackney sadles..one *troncke sadle. **1857** GOSSE *Omphalos* xii. 364 The Palm and the Tree-fern show, in their *trunk-scars, evidences of organs which have completely died away and disappeared. **1855** TROLLOPE *Warden* xvi. 264 He remembered the shop distinctly; it was next door to a *trunk-seller's. **1899** *Daily News* 6 Dec. 6/6 We cannot possibly deal with local floodings..unless you give us the necessary additional *trunk sewers. **1893** A. S. ECCLES *Sciatica* 15 The nerves of the *trunk-sheath have been stimulated by the cold impression. **1596** SHAKS. *Tam. Shr.* IV. iii. 142 A loose bodied gowne..With a small compast cape..a *trunke sleeue. **1603** FLORIO *Montaigne* II. xii. (1632) 301 They make trunk-sleeves of wyre and whale-bone bodies. **1606** MARSTON *Parasit.* IV. Fiij b, A simple, country Ladie, wore gold buttons, trunck sleeues, and flaggon bracelets. **1592** NASHE *P. Penilesse* (ed. 2) 6 b, A pair of *trunke slops, sagging down like a Shoomakers wallet. **1613** M. RIDLEY *Magn. Bodies* 1 The foure attenders vpon Iupiter, lately discouered by the *trunke spectacle. **1625** N. CARPENTER *Geog. Del.* I. iv. (1635) 79 Many [stars] haue lately beene discouered, by reason of the Trunk-spectacle lately found out. **1789** BRAND *Hist. Newcastle* II. 256 *note*, When the waggons are emptied into a keel or vessel by a spout, it is called a *trunk staith. **1887** KIPLING *From Sea to Sea* (1899) I. 40 Jey Singh..would have hanged those Globe-trotters in their *trunk-straps. **1970** *Country Life* 31 Dec. 1296/2 The hood, when up, was secured to the front mudguards by two stout trunk straps. **1860** TYNDALL *Glac.* I. xxi. 149 All the glaciers..are suddenly turned aside where they meet the great *trunk stream. *Ibid.* II. x. 287 The width of the trunk stream is a little better than one-third of that of its tributaries. **1903** *Daily Chron.* 7 Oct. 7/1 An underground *trunk telegraph line to Scotland. **1909** *Westm. Gaz.* 17 Apr. 9/4 Sunday duty by females in the *trunk telephone department should be abolished. **1899** *Ibid.* 32 Aug. 4/3 It is no light task to make up a *trunk train in such satisfactory proportions. **1697** DAMPIER *Voy. round World* (1699) 103 There are 4 sorts of Sea-turtle, viz. the *Trunk-turtle, the Loggerhead, the Hawks-bill and the Green-turtle. **1735** MORTIMER in *Phil. Trans.* XXXIX. 117 *Testudo Arcuata*: The Trunk-Turtle. **1827** ROBERTS *Voy. Centr. Amer.* 94 A trunk-turtle, a species of immense size and exceedingly fat. **16..** *Poems, Ballads*, etc. (Percy Soc.) 196, I pray who's this we've met with here, That tickles his *trunk weam?.. If he'll play,..We'll dance you Jumping Joan. *a* **1825** FORBY *Voc. E. Anglia*, **Trunk-way*, a water course through an arch of masonry, turned over a ditch before a gate. The name arose no doubt, from the trunks of trees used for the same purpose in ancient and simpler times. **1730** CAPT. W. WRIGLESWORTH *MS. Log-bk. of the 'Lyell'* 5 May, At 6 this morning Saw a bunch of *Trunk Weeds. **1885** *List of Subscribers, Classified* (United Telephone Co.) (ed. 6) 8 The very great cost of running and maintaining the *Trunk wires between the different Exchanges. **1897** *Daily News* 20 Jan. 10/4 The Postmaster-General..states that..efficient working of the trunk wires is engaging his earnest attention. **1611** SHAKS. *Wint. T.* III. iii. 75 This has beene some staire-worke, some *Trunke-worke, some behinde-doore worke. **1920** 'K. MANSFIELD' *Let.* 25 Sept. (1928) 46, I heard again from Methuen to-day. They now say they'd like 2 books for next spring. I think there must have been some trunk work, some back stair work in this on your part.

Hence **'trunkie** *Sc.*, a little trunk (sense 7).

1728 RAMSAY *Bob of Dunblane* i, Gang to the ground of ye'r trunkies, Busk ye braw.

† **trunk**, *v.*[1] *Obs.* [ad. L. *truncāre*: see TRUNCATE *v.*] *trans.* To cut a part off from; to cut short, truncate; to lop, clip, prune.

c **1440** *Pallad. on Husb.* IV. 86 Ek summe her aged vynes welle repare, And trunke hem of al hie abouen grounde. *a* **1550**–*c* **1828** [see TRUNKED *ppl. a.*[1] 2]. **1586** FERNE *Blaz. Gentrie* II. 38 His coate-armor rased, his Sheeld reuersed, his Speare truncked, his spurres hewed from his heeles. **1611** [see TRUNKING *vbl. sb.*[1]]. **1688** R. HOLME *Armoury* III. xxii. (Roxb.) 274/1 Termes used by Tobacconists... Trunk it, is to make it in Order for the boxes.

trunk (trʌŋk), *v.*[2] [f. TRUNK *sb.*]

1. *trans.* To shut up as in a trunk; to imprison. *rare.*

1608 MIDDLETON *Fam. Love* II. iv, I thought thou had'st been cabin'd in thy ship, Not trunk'd within my cruel guardian's house.

2. *Mining.* To dress (lead or tin ore) by agitating it in water; cf. TRUNK *sb.* 9.

1758 BORLASE *Nat. Hist. Cornw.* 204 What runs off to the hindermost part of the pit..and..is slimy..must be trunked, buddled, and tozed, as the slimy tin. **1778** PRYCE *Min. Cornub.* 238 In order to clear the earthy sordes from the slime or loobs, it may be trunked. **1839** DE LA BECHE *Rep. Geol. Cornw.*, etc. xv. 579 In 1778 we find that the slime and tails, after having been allowed to dry, were trunked and framed. **1881** [see TRUNKING *vbl. sb.*[2]].

3. To cover or enclose as with a casing; see quots.

1838 *Civil Eng. & Arch. Jrnl.* I. 383/2 The road-way is then to be floored or trunked over with five courses of dry heathy sods. **1883** [see TRUNKING *vbl. sb.*[2] b].

4. Of an elephant: To pick *up*, pull, or pluck with the trunk. *nonce-use.*

1901 *N. & Q.* 9th Ser. VII. 165/1 The elephants went past a garden with cabbages in it, and did not they trunk them up!

trunkal, variant of TRUNCAL.

'trunk-,breeches, *sb. pl.* Now only *Hist.* = TRUNK-HOSE.

1662 BAGSHAW in *Acc. Baxter's Suspension* 43 The Trunk-Breeches, and Wooden Daggers of our Ancestors. **1691** T. H[ALE] *Acc. New Invent.* p. xlvi, To make the..writing of Politicks..grow as much out of Fashion as the garb of Trunk-breeches. **1735** BYROM *Jrnl. & Lit. Rem.* (1855) I. II. 621 John..brought my trunk-breeches, which had been forgotten. **1755** SMOLLETT *Quix.* (1803) IV. 108, I have, ever since I was born, longed to see father in laced trunk-breeches. **1809** W. IRVING *Knickerb.* VI. v. (1849) 341 These were short fat men, wearing exceeding large trunk-breeches. **1850** *N. & Q.* 1st Ser. I. 489/1.

trunked (trʌŋkt), *ppl. a.*[1] [f. TRUNK *v.*[1] + -ED[1].]

†**1.** Cut short, truncated; lopped; mutilated. *Obs.* exc. as in 2.

1551–2 in Feuillerat *Revels Edw. VI* (1914) 79 A payre of sleves trunked. **1559** W. CUNNINGHAM *Cosmogr. Glasse* 36 They be named Colures, or trunckid circles. **1586** J. HOOKER *Hist. Irel.* in *Holinshed* II. 24/1 By reason they had beene so long couered,..buried vnder the sands, they stood as trunked and polled trees. **1590** SPENSER *F.Q.* II. v. 4 The sharpe steele..from the head the body sundred quight... The truncked beast fast bleeding did him fowly dight. **1594** ? GREENE *Selimus* Wks. (Grosart) XIV. 249 My blood, Streaming in riuers from my tronked armes.

2. *Her.* (*a*) Having the extremities cut off smoothly: = COUPED. (*b*) Of the head of a beast: Cut off close behind the horns; = CABOCHED.

a **1550** in Baring-Gould & Twigge *W. Armory* (1898) 4 A fesse trunked betweene 3 escalops sab. **1610** BOLTON *Elem.*

Armories 111 Of that maim'd, or truncked kinde, are this, and the like. **1610** GUILLIM *Heraldry* III. iv. 95 Argent; two Billets Raguled, and Truncked, placed Saltireways. *Ibid.* xiv. 128 These horned beasts.. haue also their heads borne Trunked [*ed.* 1638 *adds* Which of some Armorists is blazoned Cabossed]. **1766–84** PORNY *Heraldry* (ed. 4) Gloss., *Trunked*.., is applied to Trees, &c. that are couped or cut off smooth. *c* **1828** BERRY *Encycl. Her.* I. Gloss. s.v. *Trunk*, When the tree is borne couped of all its branches, and separated from its roots, it is then termed trunked. *Ibid.*, *Trunked*,.. is likewise used in the same sense as *cabossed*, or *caboshed*, that is, showing only the head or face of a beast.

trunked (trʌŋkt, *poet.* ˈtrʌŋkɪd), *a.* and *ppl. a.*^{2} [In branch I, f. TRUNK *sb.* + -ED^2; in branch II, f. TRUNK *v.*^{2} (sense 2) + -ED^1.]

I. 1. Having a trunk, as a tree; usually in compounds, as ***straight-trunked***, etc., for which see the first element.

1640 HOWELL *Dodona's Gr.* 48 Strong and well trunked Trees of all sorts. **1852** *Meanderings of Mem.* I. 132 The trunkĕd forest's deep Where graces dance. **1905** HOLMAN-HUNT *Pre-Raphaelitism* II. 74 The trees were mightily trunked and limbed.

b. *Her.* Having the trunk of a tincture different from the rest of the tree.

1678 PHILLIPS (ed. 4), *Trunked*, in Heraldry Trees growing on a Stock, are said to be Trunked. *c* **1828** BERRY *Encycl. Her.* I. Gloss., *Trunked* is.. said of a tree, the main stem of which is borne of a different tincture from the branches.

2. Having a trunk or proboscis; proboscidiferous.

a **1794** SIR W. JONES *Tales* (1807) 182 In vain their high-priz'd tusks they gnash'd; Their trunked heads my Geda mash'd. **1899** BEAZLEY & PRESTAGE *Disc. Guinea* (Hakl. Soc.) II. 337 The Proboscidians, or trunked Pachyderms. **1913** A. G. THACKER tr. *Buttel-Reepen's Man & Forerunners* ii. 15 Great trunked mammals, precursors of our modern elephants.

3. Wearing trunks (TRUNK *sb.* 17 a). *rare.*

1904 M. HEWLETT *Queen's Quair* I. vi, The Queen and her maids braved it as saucy young men, trunked, puffed, pointed, trussed and doubleted.

II. 4. *Mining.* Washed in a trunk (see TRUNK *sb.* 9, *v.*^{2} 2).

1828 HENWOOD in *Trans. R. Geol. Soc. Cornwall* (1832) IV. 158 The operator.. spreads on the jagging board from two to three quarts of the trunked slime.

trunker (ˈtrʌŋkə(r)). [f. TRUNK *sb.* or *v.*^{2} + -ER^1.]

1. (See quot. 1921). Cf. TRUNK *v.*^{2} 2.

1881 *Instructions to Census Clerks* (1885) 84 Copper miner... Trunker. **1921** *Dict. Occup. Terms* (1927) §056 *Trunker*, separates slimes from ore by running mixture into and out of a long box, launder or trunk.

2. a. A long-distance lorry-driver; *spec.* one who drives at night, and is not responsible for loading or unloading his vehicle.

1954 in P. G. Hollowell *Lorry Driver* (1968) vii. 192 *Trunker*, night driver. **1958** *Times* 12 Apr. 7/6 The long-distance night lorry driver, or trunker. **1959** *Manch. Guardian* 20 July 2/3 We night trunkers.. pull out of the depot at seven or eight in the evening. **1968** P. G. HOLLOWELL *Lorry Driver* vii. 176 Although the trunker is a long distance driver and a night worker he is for the most part able to organize his leisure life as he has regular runs. He is not as able to do this as is the shunter who has the greatest rate of participation in associational groupings.

b. A lorry used for long journeys along trunk roads.

1965 M. RUSSELL *No Through Road* 20, I could see the.. cars on the A.1 highway and hear the scream of the all-night trunkers. **1969** *Jane's Freight Containers 1968–69* 10 (Advt.), By freight-liner any number of Abel Air containers are carried by rail to terminals where they are readily transferred to trunker or local delivery units. **1979** *Navy News* Sept. 34/1 (Advt.), Driving artics., trunkers or vans or sorting and loading back at base.

ˈtrunk-fish. Any fish of the genus *Ostracion* or family *Ostraciontidæ*, inhabiting tropical seas, and having the body of angular cross-section and covered with bony hexagonal plates; a coffer-fish.

1804 SHAW *Gen. Zool.* V. 420 Triquetral Trunk-fish. **1835** *Encycl. Brit.* (ed. 7) XII. 229/2 The horned trunk-fish, *Ostracion cornutus*, a native, like most of the genus, of the Indian and American seas. **1851** GOSSE *Nat. Hist., Fishes* 288 The Trunk-fishes.. have the body angular, four or three-sided, covered with angular plates of solid bone soldered together, and forming a sort of inflexible box, with openings for the mouth, the fins, the tail, and the gill-aperture. **1876** GOODE *Fishes Bermudas* 23 The locomotion of the trunk-fishes is very peculiar.

trunkful (ˈtrʌŋkfʊl). [f. TRUNK *sb.* + -FUL.] As much or as many as a trunk will hold.

1707 HEARNE *Collect.* 25 Oct. (O.H.S.) II. 65 A whole trunkful of papers. **1883** *Century Mag.* XXVI. 370 A trunkful of dresses fresh from Worth's. **1897** MARY KINGSLEY *W. Africa* xii. 259 Some [elephants] drew up trunkfuls of water and syringed themselves and each other.

ˈtrunk-hose. Now only *Hist.* [f. TRUNK (*sb.* or *v.*^{1}) + HOSE.

The sense of 'trunk' here, as in the later *trunk-breeches*, and the earlier TRUNK *sb.* 17, appears to be uncertain. Various suggestions have been made, e.g. that trunk refers to the trunk of the body, or that it is TRUNK *sb.* 13, 'a hollow tube or pipe'; or that it is = *truncate* or *truncated*, as being, as it were, cut short. Early explanations have not been found: the term may have been of vulgar origin.]

Full bag-like breeches covering the hips and upper thighs, and sometimes stuffed with wool or the like, worn in the 16th and early 17th c.

1637 HEYWOOD *Royall King* Epil. 9 Those Trunke-hose, which now the age doth scorn, Were all in fashion, and with frequence worne. **1694** LD. MOLESWORTH *Acc. Denmark* 162 In the habit of the North-Holland Boors, with great Trunk-hose, short Doublets. **1735** BYROM *Jrnl. & Lit. Rem.* (1855) I. II. 616 Put on my boots and coat and trunk-hose. **1907** *Verney Mem.* I. 53 His.. trunk hose slashed and lined with dull red.

b. *attrib.*, in sense 'wearing trunk-hose'; hence, old-fashioned, out-of-date.

a **1643** W. CARTWRIGHT *Ordinary* II. i. (1651) 24 The trunck-hose Justices will try all means To bind you to the Peace. **1647** J. BERKENHEAD *Pref. Verses in Beaumont & Fletcher's Wks.* e j b, You Two thought fit To weare just Robes, and leave off Trunk-hose-Wit.

Hence †**ˈtrunk-hosed** *a.*, wearing trunk-hose.

1621 FLETCHER *Wild Goose Chase* v. v, I would the trunk-hos'd woman would go with me. **1631** BRATHWAIT *Whimzies, Metall-man*, 61 A Metall-man.. that walking trunk-hos'd goblin.

†**ˈtrunking**, *vbl. sb.*^{1} *Obs.* [f. TRUNK *v.*^{1} + -ING^1.] The action of TRUNK *v.*^{1}; truncation.

1611 COTGR., *Troncation*, a truncation, trunking, mutilation, cutting off.

ˈtrunking, *vbl. sb.*^{2} [f. TRUNK *v.*^{2} + -ING^1.]

1. The action of TRUNK *v.*^{2}: **a.** in sense 2; also *attrib.*

1838 *Civil Eng. & Arch. Jrnl.* I. 409/2 The engine was working.. a trunking machine. **1839** DE LA BECHE *Rep. Geol. Cornw.*, etc. xv. 579 The trunking by machinery.. was introduced at St. Ives, according to Mr. Henwood, about the year 1825. **1839** URE *Dict. Arts* 1245 The portion B is to be washed again in the trunking-box. **1881** RAYMOND *Mining Gloss.*, *Trunking* (Cornw.), separating slimes by means of a trunk. **1884** C. G. W. LOCK *Workshop Receipts* Ser. III. 53/1 A revolving 'trunking' apparatus.

b. in sense 3. Also *concr.*, *spec.* a system of ducts or trunks (sense 10), esp. for cables or purposes of ventilation.

1838 *Civil Eng. & Arch. Jrnl.* I. 383/2 Perfect drainage and good trunking,.. if these are not attained, roads constructed on bog will lose their shape, become ruinous, and soon go to decay. *Ibid.*, Upon this trunking is to be laid a soling. **1883** *Science* II. 99/1 A 'trunking' or wooden covering is then placed over them to protect them from snow and the feet of any one walking about the yard. **1923** *Man. Seamanship* (Admiralty) II. 284 The quantity of air supplied by a fan depends greatly on.. the size and tortuosity of the trunking. **1950** *Engineering* 3 Feb. 123/1 Forced draught fans.. arranged to draw air.. and discharge it to the boilers through suitable trunking. **1963** *Times* 11 May 8/1, 60 electricians were dismissed for refusing to work on the trunking of electric cables on the frigate Mohawk. **1977** *Timber Trades Jrnl.* 17 Dec. 36/2 To blow the by-products from the hopper into a storage silo via trunking is.. becoming a more common practice.

c. The driving of lorries on long journeys along trunk roads.

1968 P. G. HOLLOWELL *Lorry Driver* iii. 64 Trunking, being a night driving job, is heavy on the eyes, and also requires quick response to meet crises particularly on runs where the schedules are tight. **1974** P. WRIGHT *Lang. Brit. Industry* ii. 31 *Trunking* used to mean only night driving, but now, because of improved roads and speeds enabling travel to and from a far unloading point in one day, it includes *day-trunking*.

2. *Teleph.* [f. TRUNK *sb.*] The use or arrangement of trunks (sense 4 c). Freq. *attrib.*

1896 *Jrnl. Inst. Electr. Engineers* XXV. 639 Facilities for through trunking—*i.e.*, connecting two or more trunk circuits at intermediate offices to provide communication between towns not directly connected. **1933** *Discovery* Apr. 132/2 When all the direct junctions to an exchange are engaged, subsequent calls to that exchange are passed (or 'routed') through a central exchange. This feature of the system is termed 'alternative trunking'. **1947** *Electronic Engin.* XIX. 66 Automatic telephony is dealt with almost entirely by means of trunking diagrams and trunking calculations. **1979** DANIELSON & WALKER *Telecommunications Systems for Technicians I* ix. 79 A trunking diagram showing the connection of a subscriber to a desired number in a four-digit (up to 9999) exchange.

trunkless (ˈtrʌŋklɪs), *a.* [f. TRUNK *sb.* + -LESS.] Having no trunk; *esp.* without a body, or severed from the body, as a head.

1631 WEEVER *Anc. Fun. Mon.* 279 Their trunklesse faces. **1682** J. BANKS *Anna Bullen* v. i. 78 The Trunkless Head with darting Eyes beheld her. **1820** *Examiner* No. 630. 290/1 The exhibition of their trunkless heads. **1897** *Daily News* 18 Feb. 2/2 The woolly elephant is trunkless. **1897** *Naturalist* 243 A generation.. that lops its oaks into trunkless brush-wood.

trunk line. 1. A main railway line. Also *fig.*

1843 R. WILSON *Let.* 13 Jan. in W. F. Cooke *Electric Telegraph* (1857) I. 219 Mr. Cooke's first object.. would be to get the Telegraph laid down on the Croydon or some other trunk line. **1851** DICKENS *Our School* in *Househ. Words* 11 Oct. 81/1 The Railway had cut it up... A great trunk-line had swallowed the playground. **1858** SIMMONDS *Dict. Trade*, *Trunk-line*, the main line of a railway, separate from the branch lines or feeders. **1861** *Sat. Rev.* 7 Sept. 236 The trunk lines already in existence are substantially all that the country requires. **1888** B. F. C. COSTELLOE *Ch. Cath.* 19 Great trunk lines of liturgical tradition.

2. *Teleph.* = TRUNK *sb.* 4 c (*a*).

1883 *Pall Mall Gaz.* 6 Dec. 12/2 The cost of laying a trunk line overhead averages about £25 a mile. **1893** PREECE & STUBBS *Man. Telephony* xxi. 336 The main trunk lines—those connecting [London] with the various provincial exchanges—are invariably metallic. **1926** T. E. LAWRENCE *Seven Pillars* cxi. 590 Young and I cut the telegraph, here an important network of trunk and local lines. **1964** M. MCLUHAN *Understanding Media* xxx. 306 Radio's use of the telephone in a glorified form of the old trunk-line wire-tapping. **1980** *Wall St. Jrnl.* 26 Nov. 10/2 The Federal Communications Commission voted to authorize American Telephone & Telegraph Co. to install an optical-fiber telephone trunk line between Washington and N.Y.

3. A large or main pipeline for oil or gas, esp. one from a production field to a refinery or terminal.

1896 REDWOOD & HOLLOWAY *Petroleum* II. VII. 475 As soon as the well is found to yield, the tank is connected by a 2-inch pipe with the trunk line. **1925** A. B. THOMPSON *Oil-Field Exploration & Devel.* II. xix. 1092 Long-distance trunk lines entail nearly as much work in surveys and construction as a railway. **1975** *Offshore* Sept. 195/2 The compressor will push the gas shoreward through a 67 mile, 42 inch diameter trunkline to a platform in West Cameron block 167 offshore Louisiana.

ˈtrunk-ˌmaker. One whose business is the making of trunks (TRUNK *sb.* 7); often with allusion to the use of the sheets of unsaleable books for trunk-linings.

a **1704** T. BROWN *Laconics* Wks. 1711 IV. 2 *The True-born Englishman* had dy'd silently among the Grocers and Trunk-makers, if the Libeller had not help'd off the Poet. *a* **1734** NORTH *Exam.* III. vii. §38 (1740) 530 The Trunk-maker, who pretended to be the right Heir Male of the noble Family of the Piercies. **1764** G. WILLIAMS in Jesse *Selwyn & Contemp.* (1843) I. 321, I hear he has been a pamphleteer, though as yet only to the benefit of the trunk-maker and pastrycook. **1845** J. COULTER *Adv. Pacific* xiv. 211 The hitting of the stick is so very rapid, that it resembles nothing that I know of more accurately than a trunk-maker driving in his nails. **1890** *Globe* 1 July 7/2 'All round St. Paul's, not forgetting the trunkmaker's daughter'. By the trunkmaker was understood, in the latter part of the last and the former part of the present century, the depository for unsaleable books.

ˈtrunnel, dial. form of TRUNDLE *sb.* Also in comb. **trunnel-head** *U.S.*, a circular plate or disc at the head of a coke-oven or in a furnace; **trunnel-hole**, the aperture or throat of a puddling furnace in which this disc works.

1819 E. EVANS *Pedestrious Tour* 270 The cogs, wallower, the trunnel-head and the stones [of a grist-mill]. **1839** *Knickerbocker* XIII. 345 Mill-wheels, and trunnel-heads. **1868** JOYNSON *Metals* 16 The opening at the top of the furnace, called the throat or trunnel-hole. **18..** *Amer. Manuf.* LXII. 626 (Cent. Suppl.) The trunnel-head, or ring, is a much more important part of a coke oven than most people imagine.

trunnel, -ell, variants of TREENAIL.

trunnion (ˈtrʌnjən). Chiefly in *pl.* Also 7–9 trunion, 8 tronion. [ad. F. *trognon* core of fruit, stump, trunk of a tree (14th c. in Godef. *Compl.*); of uncertain origin.]

1. Each of a pair of opposite gudgeons on the sides of a cannon, upon which it is pivoted upon its carriage. (Disused in large modern guns.)

a **1625** *Nomenclator Navalis* (Harl. MS. 2301), *Trunnions* are those knobbs which come from the side of the Ordnance and doe beare them vpp vpon the Cheekes of the Carriages. **1690** J. MACKENZIE *Siege London-Derry* 17/1 The rest attending the Lord Kingston till they had broke the Trunnions, and nailed the heavier Guns. **1781** JUSTAMOND *Priv. Life Lewis XV*, III. 389 They broke off the trunnions of the canon. **1794** NELSON in Nicolas *Disp.* (1845) I. 430 The Agamemnon's two twenty-four pounders are both ruined: one split up to the rings; the other with the trunnion knocked so much off, that it is useless for shot. **1890** W. J. GORDON *Foundry* 26 One of the strangest of the very latest developments of modern gunnery is the abolition of the trunnions.

b. Each of any similar pair of opposite pins or pivots on which anything is supported; *spec.* in the oscillating steam-engine, a hollow gudgeon on each side of the cylinder, upon which it is pivoted, and through which the steam passes into and out of the cylinder; also, a single projecting pivot.

1727 *Bradley's Fam. Dict.* s.v. *Chimney*, They fit two Trunnions or Knobs to the Middle of this Swipe. **1831** J. HOLLAND *Manuf. Metal* I. 88 The centre of the pivots or trunnions on which it [the large metal helve] works. **1833** *Ibid.* II. 215 The bar-handle acting.. upon a fulcrum or mouth-piece of solid iron, the top of which works against a trunnion under the middle of the press head. **1867** J. HOGG *Microsc.* I. ii. 82 The tripod-stand gives a firm support to the trunnions. **1873** W. S. MAYO *Never Again* xxii, This vessel I shall hang on trunnions, and keep in constant revolution while the glass is in a liquid state. **1895** *Model Steam Engine* 21 In a real engine, the centres on which the cylinders oscillate are called trunnions.

†**c.** *transf.* A pin or peg of wood; a treenail. *Obs. rare.*

1627 CAPT. SMITH *Seaman's Gram.* ii. 4 Those plankes are made fast with good Treenailes and Trunnions of well seasoned timber.

2. *attrib.* and *Comb.*, as ***trunnion-hole***, ***-joint***, ***-lathe***, ***-piece***, ***-pin***; **trunnion-band**, the band on which the trunnions are fixed; **trunnion-box**, a metal case fixed over the trunnion to prevent the gun leaving the carriage; **trunnion-carriage**, the top carriage of a mortar (Webster, 1911); **trunnion-chain**, a chain for slinging a cannon by the trunnions (ibid.); **trunnion-cradle**, branching arms in certain gun-carriages, in the extremities of which the trunnions play (ibid.); **trunnion-ledge, -level**, a small ledge on the trunnion of a heavy gun, parallel with the axis, as a guide to the elevation or depression of the piece (*Cent. Dict. Suppl.* 1909); **trunnion-plate**, an iron plate on the cheek of a wooden gun-carriage, on which the trunnion plays; also, a strengthening shoulder reinforcing the trunnion (*Cent. Dict.* 1891); **trunnion-ring**, the raised band or moulding encircling a cannon a little in front of the trunnions; **trunnion-rule**, an instrument for determining the distance from the trunnions to the base-ring (*Cent. Dict. Suppl.*); **trunnion-sight**, a front sight placed on the trunnion-band; **trunnion-square**, an instrument for determining whether the trunnions are perpendicular to the axis of the gun; **trunnion-valve**, a steam-valve situated in or attached to the trunnion of an oscillating cylinder.

1812 WELLINGTON in Gurw. *Desp.* (1838) IX. 131 It is recommended by the officers of the artillery that they should be fitted with strong iron *trunnion boxes, to secure the guns. **1795** BURKE *Let. to Ld. Auckland* Wks. IX. p. xxii, Those planks of tough and hardy oak, that used for years to brave the buffets of the Bay of Biscay, are now turned, with their warped grain and empty *trunnion-holes, into very wretched pales. **1859** F. A. GRIFFITHS *Artill. Man.* Plate (1862) 112 Trunnion hole. **1876** ROUTLEDGE *Discov.* 14 The *trunnion joints are easily packed, so that no leakage takes place. **1877** KNIGHT *Dict. Mech.*, **Trunnion-lathe*, a machine-tool for turning off the trunnions of ordnance or oscillating steam-cylinders. **1859** F. A. GRIFFITHS *Artill. Man.* (1862) 190 The *trunnion piece is made from a solid forging, and after being bored and turned, is shrunk in its place on the gun. **1888** HASLUCK *Model Engin. Handybk.* (1900) 27 The upper hole..takes the trunnion or pin on which the cylinder oscillates. Fig. 13 shows this *trunnion pin. **1644** NYE *Gunnery* (1670) 42 The Base-ring, the *Trunnion-ring, or Rings. **1868** *Rep. to Govt. U.S. Munitions War* 81 The Whitworth gun..is manufactured of one material (except the trunnion-ring).

Hence **ˈtrunnioned** *a.*, provided with trunnions (Webster, 1864); **ˈtrunnionless** *a.*, having no trunnions.

1890 W. J. GORDON *Foundry* 26 A trunnionless gun has a curious crippled look about it.

†**trunnion**, (?) perversion of TRIN-UNION or TRI-UNION, used as an asseveration or oath.

1577 *Misogonus* IV. ii, Gods trunnion, Alison, go thy wayes and fatch me hether my gose spitt.

trunsch(e)our, -owr, obs. Sc. ff. TRENCHER.

truntle, truont: see TRUNDLE, TRUANT.

†**truphane**. *Sc. Obs.* [app. ad. OF. *truf(f)ant* deceiver, f. *truf(f)er, trupher* to mock: see TRUFF *v.*, *truf(f)e*, TRUFF *sb.*[1] Or it might directly represent a med.L. **truf(f)ānus*, f. med.L. *truf(f)a, trupha* fraud, cheatery (Du Cange): cf. *pagānus*.] A deceiver, an impostor.

?*a***1500** *Colkelbie Sow* 145 (Bann. MS.) A tyrant, a tormentour, A truphane, and a tratlour.

†**trupt**, *int. Obs.* An exclamation expressing contempt. Cf. TPROT.

*c***1380** *Sir Ferumb.* 1872 ȝea, trupt..y set noȝt by þy sawes.

trus, obs. form of TRUSS.

†**trusatile** (ˈtruːsətɪl, -taɪl), *a. Obs. rare.* [ad. L. *trūsātil-is*, f. *trūsāt-*, ppl. stem of *trūsāre* to push strongly, freq. of *trūd-ēre*: see -ATILE, and cf. *versatile*.] That may be pushed; worked or driven by pushing.

1715 tr. *Pancirollus' Rerum Mem.* II. xxii. 399 Mills, or Versatile, or Trusatile Engines..which were turn'd about either by Men or Beasts.

truscottite (ˈtrʌskətaɪt). *Min.* [ad. Du. *truscottiet* (P. Hövig 1914, in *Jaarboek van het Mijnwezen in Nederlandsch Oost-Indië* XLI. 202), f. the name of S. J. *Truscott* (1870–1950), English mining engineer: see -ITE[1].] A hydrated basic silicate of calcium and manganese occurring as crystals of the hexagonal system that are typically pearly white.

1925 *Mineral. Mag.* XX. 466 Truscottite... Pearly white scales from the Lebong Donok gold-silver mine, Benkulen, Sumatra. **1979** *Ibid.* XLIII. 333/1 Truscottite and reyerite are of interest not only as natural minerals, but also because of their potential formation in cements hydrated at elevated temperatures and pressures, as in the casings of deep geothermal wells.

truse, trush, obs. forms of TRUCE, TRUSS.

trush (trʌʃ). *local.* Also 7 **thruch**, 8 **truch, thurse, truss, trouss.** [A local form of *turse*, TRUSS *sb.*] A round cushion made of matted flags, for kneeling on in church.

1621 in *Archæol. Cant.* (1902) XXV. 18 She abused Sibil Martin in taking of her trush from her that she sat upon. **1695** KENNETT *Paroch. Antiq.* Gloss., *Basse*,..the round matted cushion of flags used for kneeling [upon] in churches.., in Kent a trush. **1699** *Churchw. Acc. Holy Cross, Canterb.*, Paid for a Thruch for yᵉ Minister, 00. 01. 06. **1709** *Ibid.*, Pd. for twelve Thurses, 00. 09. 00. **1734** *Ibid.*, Paide Tho. Strouts Bill for truches, 0. 12. 0. **1719–21** *Overseers' Acc. Holy Cross, Canterb.*, Pd Goody Arnell for 4 Trusses for har to Chilldren..00.03.09. **1887** *Kent Gloss.* s.v., In the old Churchwardens' Accounts for the parish of Eastry the entry frequently occurs 'To mending the trushes'; and the word is still occasionally used.

†**trush-trash.** *Obs. rare*⁻¹. [A reduplication of TRASH *sb.*[1]; cf. RIFF-RAFF.] = TRISH-TRASH.

1582 STANYHURST *Æneis* IV. (Arb.) 118, I purpose..toe put in fyre brands this Troian pedlerye trush trash.

trusion (ˈtruːʒən). Now *rare* or *Obs.* [ad. med.L. *trūsiōn-em*, n. of action f. *trūdĕre* to push, thrust. In sense 1 app. short for *intrusion*.]

1. *Law.* Illegal entry; = INTRUSION 2.

*a***1604** HANMER *Chron. Irel.* (1809) 349 It was agreed, that his wife should not be endowed, because that her husband had not entred by the King, but rather by trusion.

2. The action of pushing or thrusting.

1656 tr. *Hobbes' Elem. Philos.* (1839) 214 Pulsion;..when the motions of the movent and moved body begin both together..may be called trusion or thrusting and vection. **1678** CUDWORTH *Intell. Syst.* I. v. §5. 888 As Engines and Machines move, by Trusion or Pulsion. **1729** DESAGULIERS in *Phil. Trans.* XXXVI. 132 If..the Point of Trusion be taken at C.

trusle, obs. form of TRESTLE.

truss (trʌs), *sb.* Forms: 3–8 **trusse**, (4–6 **trosse**, **trus**, 5 **truse**, *Sc.* **troiss**), 9 (in sense 5) **tross**, 7– **truss.** *β. Sc.* 5 **turss**, 5–7 **turs**, 7 **turse, tirrs.** [a. F. *trousse*, OF. also *torse, trusse, tourse* (12–15th c. in Godef.), Prov. *trossa*, Sp. *troxa*, Pg. *trouxa*; according to Scheler and Hatz.-Darm. vbl. sb. from *trousser* to TRUSS.]

1. a. A collection of things bound together, or packed in a receptacle; a bundle, pack; †in quot. 1577–87 *collect.* baggage. Now chiefly *technical.*

12.. *Ancr. R.* 168 (MS. C.) Noble men & gentile..ne uareð nout itrussed mid trusses [*Cott. Nero* trusseaus], ne mid purses. **1390** GOWER *Conf.* III. 194 The paien rod upon an asse, And of his catell more and lasse With him a riche trusse he ladde. *c***1400** *Rom. Rose* 4004 Undir his heed no pilowe was, But in the stede a trusse of gras. **1472** *Rental Bk. Cupar-Angus* (1879) I. 162 A turs of fresche ate fodder. **1562** BULLEYN *Bulwark, Dial. Soarnes & Chir.* 46 Knede it with a little Beane meale, and roule theim vp into a trosse. **1577–87** HOLINSHED *Chron.* (1807) II. 342 They spoiled the carriage and trusse of the said barons. **1622** MALYNES *Anc. Law-Merch.* 199 Commodities..packt vp in Bundels, Trusses, Cases, Coffers or Packes. **1712** TICKELL *Spect.* No. 410 ⁋2 She..devoured a Trusse of Sallet.

fig. **1531** ELYOT *Gov.* I. xiv, Lerned men..whiche..haue ..perused the great fardelles and trusses of the moste barbarouse autours, stuffed with innumerable gloses. **1878** VILLARI *Machiavelli* (1898) I. 3 The Commune was merely a truss of minor associations, badly bound together.

b. *spec.* A bundle of hay or straw; in technical use, of a definite weight, varying at different times and places: see below.

The *truss of hay* is usually a compact mass of hay, approximately cubical, cut from the stack, and tied; now generally, in England, of old hay, 56 lbs.; of new hay, 60 lbs.; *a truss of straw*, 36 lbs.

1483 in *Acta Audit.* (1839) 123*/2 Thre hundreth turss of hay. **1561** in *Reg. Mag. Sig. Scot.* 1587 401/1, 20 laid of cane peitis, ane turs of stray. **1608–9** *Shuttleworths' Acc.* (Chetham Soc.) 180 Towe trusses of haye, ijˢ. **1609** *Ibid.*, A trusse of strawe, vᵈ. **1688** R. HOLME *Armoury* III. 73/1 A Truss of Hay, as much as can be tied together in an Hay Rope, for a Man to carry on his shoulder. **1727–41** CHAMBERS *Cycl.* sv., A truss of hay is to contain fifty-six pounds,..thirty-six trusses make a load. In June and August the truss is to weigh sixty pounds. **1846** *J. Baxter's Libr. Pract. Agric.* (ed. 4) II. 63 Result.—On the acre sown with nitrate, 7 sacks 1 bushel of wheat, 50 trusses of straw. On the acre without manure, 6 sacks, 40 trusses of straw. **1862** MISS BRADDON *Lady Audley* x, A waggon laden with trusses of hay. **1866** ROGERS *Agric. & Prices* I. ii. 16 The hay was, as at present, cut into trusses.

†**c.** Applied to a person, in contempt or ridicule. *Obs. rare.*

1585 LUPTON *Thous. Notable Th.* (1675) 270 A Truss, a Rawbon, a Skeleton, a Doudy slut,..blinded by besotting lust, he admires all.

2. *Naut.* A tackle by which the centre of the yard was hauled back and secured to the mast; in mod. use extended to an iron fitting, consisting of a ring encircling the mast, with a goose-neck by which the yard is secured. Cf. *truss-parrel, -rope, -tackle* in 8. (The earliest use.)

1296 *Acc. Exch. K.R.* 5/20 m. 5 In vna Corda, et vnum par de Trusses Inuentis in domo Iohannis de Pytingtone. **1336–7** *Acc. Exch. K.R.* 19/31 m. 4 (P.R.O.) In diuersis cordis de Russhewale cum schiuis et Trussis pro vno rakke inde faciendo. *Ibid.* m. 5 In iiijᵒʳ poleyns emptis ad eandem [galeam] pro trusses..xvj. d. **1420** in *For. Acc. 3 Hen. VI*, F/2 *dorso*, j. hauser pro Prialle ropes j. hauser pro trusses. **1582** N. LICHEFIELD tr. *Castanheda's Conq. E. Ind.* 71 Other some vering the trusses. *a***1625** *Nomenclator Navalis* (Harl. MS. 2301), *Trusses* are Roapes which are made faste to the Parrell of the yardes and are vsed to two vses, one to bind fast the yarde to the Mast when shee rowles either a hull or at an Anchor; the other is to hale downe the Yards in a Storme, or Gust. **1704** J. HARRIS *Lex. Techn.* I, *Trusses*.. belong to the Main-yard, Fore-yard and Missen. **1840** R. H. DANA *Bef. Mast* xxvi, Running trusses on the yards. **1841** —— *Seaman's Man.* iv. 22 Lower yards are rigged now with iron trusses and quarter-blocks. **1867** SMYTH *Sailor's Word-bk.* s.v., The trusses or parrels of the lower yards serve to bind them to their masts, and are bowsed taut when the yards are trimmed, in order to arrest motion and friction. But the introduction of an iron goose-neck, centering and securing the yard well free of the mast, very much supersedes the use of trusses.

†**3. a.** A close-fitting body-garment or jacket formerly worn by men and women; cf. *trussing-bolster, trussing-coat*, s.v. TRUSSING *vbl. sb.* 3. *Obs.*

1563 FOXE *A. & M.* 1377/2 Mayster Ridley..sayd to his brother: it wer best for me to go in my trusse styll. No (quod his brother), it wyll put you to more payne: and the trusse wil dooe a poore manne good. **1585** HIGINS *Junius' Nomenclator* 164/2 *Strophium*, a womans breast trusse or stomacher. **1591** HARINGTON *Orl. Fur.* XXVI. lviii, She still did weare A slender trusse beneath her womans weed. **1612** DRAYTON *Poly-olb.* xii. 269 Puts off his Palmer's weede vnto his trusse, which bore The staines of ancient Armes.

b. *pl.* Close-fitting breeches or drawers, covering the buttocks and tops of the thighs: = TROUSE[2].

1592 NASHE *P. Penilesse* Wks. (Grosart) II. 31 We..of the vesture of saluation make some of vs Babies and Apes coates, others straight trusses and Diuells breeches. **1598** FLORIO, *Cotigie*, leather hosen, or trusses such as our elders were woont to weare. **1631** SHIRLEY *Schoole Complement* I. i. C iij, *Gasp.* Canst be close? *Gor.* As..a paire of Trusses to an Irish mans buttockes.

4. A surgical appliance serving for support in cases of rupture, etc., now usually consisting of a pad with a belt or spring to produce equable pressure on the part.

1543 TRAHERON *Vigo's Chirurg.* (1586) 118 Let the spunge be bounde upon a trusse, made by a good artificer. **1552** HULOET, Trusse for a wrestler, or diseased body, *strigil.* **1580** HOLLYBAND *Treas. Fr. Tong*, *Vne Trousseure*,..a trusse as such as be broken do vse. **1601** HOLLAND *Pliny* XXVII. vii. II. 277 If wormewood be worne in a trusse to the bottome of the belly, it allayeth the swelling in the share. **1696** *Lond. Gaz.* No. 3227/4 He..wears a Truss, being bursten. **1876** GROSS *Dis. Bladder* 99 Compression of the perineum with a spring truss.

5. *Gardening.* A compact cluster or head of flowers growing upon one stalk.

1688 R. HOLME *Armoury* II. 70/2 These Auricula's..bear a great Truss of many flowers. **1859** DARWIN *Orig. Spec.* v. (1860) 145, I have recently observed, in some garden pelargoniums, that the central flower of the truss often loses the patches of darker colour in the two upper petals. **1885** H. O. FORBES *Nat. Wand. E. Archip.* 108 A shrubby species of Cassia bearing large trosses of bright golden flowers.

6. a. *Building*, etc. A framework of timber or iron, or both, so constructed as to form a firm support for a superincumbent weight, as that of a roof or bridge.

1654 in E. B. Jupp *Carpenters' Co.* (1887) 316 When any Chimney..shalbe sett vpon a trusse of timber That it be sett two foote 6 inches from the vpside of the trusse to the vpside of the floore. **1751** LABELYE *Westm. Br.* 87 The Wooden Trusses, or rather Arches under its Roof. **1840** *Civil Eng. & Arch. Jrnl.* III. 125/1 These bridges are built on piers far apart and formed of a truss..of continuous trellis work.

b. *Arch.* A projection from the face of a wall, often serving to support a cornice, etc.; a kind of large corbel or modillion.

1519 HORMAN *Vulg.* 241 Make me a trusse (*podium, suggestum, vel pulpitum*) standynge out vpon gargellys that I may se about. **1812** RICKMAN *Archit.* (1862) 11 A truss is a modillion enlarged, and placed flat against a wall, often used to support the cornice of doors and windows. *Ibid.*, A Console is an ornament like a truss carved on a key-stone.

c. *Ship-building.* (*a*) See quot. 1823. (*b*) See quot. *c* 1860; also called *truss-piece* (see 8).

1823 CRABB *Technol. Dict.*, *Truss* is also the name of short pieces of carved work fitted under the taffrail, in the same manner as the terms. *c***1860** H. STUART *Seaman's Catech.* 70 The trusses are diagonal shores crossing each other, and resting against the abutments. **1874** THEARLE *Naval Archit.* 34 Besides these plate riders, a complementary set of diagonal wood internal frames, termed trusses, are fitted between the thick strakes or clamps under the orlop deck beams and the binding strake over the floor heads.

†**7.** Name of some game. Cf. TRUSS-A-FAIL. *Obs. rare*⁻¹.

1627 W. HAWKINS *Apollo Shroving* v. iv, The waues.. play at trusse and at leapfrogge on one anothers backe.

8. *attrib.* and *Comb.* Of, pertaining to or constituting a truss, in sense 2, as ***truss-line, -pendant, -pulley, -rope, -tackle*** (see quots.); in sense 6, as ***truss centre, frame, framing, girder, post, rib***; furnished with or supported by a truss or trusses, as ***truss-bridge, -roof***; also ***truss-maker***; ***truss-bound, -galled*** adjs.; **truss-band** *Naut.*, one of two iron bands by which an iron truss (sense 2) is fastened to the yard; **truss-beam**, a beam forming part of a truss; also a beam, or iron frame used as a beam, strengthened with a tie-rod or struts, so as to form a truss; †**truss-bed**, ? = *trussing bed* (see TRUSSING *vbl. sb.* 3); **truss-block**, a block between a beam and a tie-rod in a truss, serving to keep them apart (*Cent. Dict.* 1891); **truss-bolt**, a bolt or iron rod forming part of a truss (see quot.); **truss-hoop**, (*a*) *Naut.* (see quot. 1867); (*b*) *Coopering* = *trussing-hoop* (see TRUSSING *vbl. sb.* 3); **truss-parrel** *Naut.*, a parrel encircling a mast, forming part of or connected with a truss (sense 2); **truss-partition** (see quots.); **truss-piece** (see quot.); **truss-plank**, 'in a railway passenger-car, a wide piece of timber fastened on the inside of the car to the posts of the frame directly above the sills' (*Cent. Dict.*); **truss-rod**, a tie-rod forming part of a truss; **truss-work**, work consisting of trusses.

1909 *Cent. Dict. Suppl.* (lettering of figure s.v. *Truss*), *a*, truss; *b*, *b*, *truss-bands; *c*, truss-parrel. **1877** KNIGHT *Dict. Mech.*, **Truss-beam*, an iron frame serving as a beam, girder, or summer; a wooden beam or frame with a tie-rod to strengthen it against deflection. **1541** *Test. Ebor.* (Surtees) VI. 142 Towe *trusbeddes of the best. **1883** *Man. Seamanship for Boys' Training Ships R. Navy* (Admiralty) (1886) 26 Trestletrees are two pieces of hard wood, standing fore and aft... On their after ends an eye-bolt is driven from the lower side, for attaching the *truss blocks to. **1825** J. NICHOLSON *Operat. Mechanic* 563 Either with one king-bolt in the middle, or with a *truss-bolt at one-third of the length from each end. **1778** [W. MARSHALL] *Minutes Agric.* 16 Jan. an. 1776, To hinder the rats from harbouring in *truss-bound straw, and gnawing the bands. **1840** *Civil Eng. & Arch. Jrnl.* III. 125/2 Wood for small *truss bridges. **1735** J. PRICE *Stone Br. Thames* 7 A fram'd *Truss Center. **1874** THEARLE *Naval Archit.* 34 These *truss frames are the same thickness as the binding strakes, and are placed at an angle of 45 degrees in an opposite direction to the plate riders. **1825** J. NICHOLSON *Operat. Mechanic* 91 A large timber,.. which is supported at its ends in the side walls, and has a *truss-framing applied to the back of it, like the framing of a roof. **1679** *Lond. Gaz.* No. 1410/4 A Cart Gelding *truss-gall'd on the sides. **1825** J. NICHOLSON *Operat. Mechanic* 569 When the flooring is to be very stiff and firm, it is necessary to introduce *truss girders. **1867** SMYTH *Sailor's Word-bk.*, **Truss-hoops*, [or] clasp-hoops for masts or spars .. are open iron hoops, so made that their ends, being let into each other, may be well fastened by means of iron wedges or forelock keys. **1877** KNIGHT *Dict. Mech.*, *Truss-hoop*, one placed around a barrel to strain the staves into position. **1407** *Acc. Exch. K.R.* 44/11(1) m. 5 *dorso*, ij Bowelynes, ij Stetynges debiles, ij *Truslynes debiles. **1776** *Court & City Reg.* 167/1 *Truss-maker, Alexander Reid. **1824** WATT *Bibl. Brit.*, *Sheldrake, Timothy*.. Truss-maker to the East India Company, and the Westminster Hospital. **1411** *Acc. Exch. K.R.* 44/17 m. 2 (P.R.O.) Vn Bowespret, vn Rakke, vn *trusp[ar]aille.. vn Canone de Ferre. **1485** *Naval Acc. Hen. VII* (1896) 39 Maine perells..j, Truss perells..j. **1823** P. NICHOLSON *Pract. Build.* 595 **Truss-partition*, one with a truss, generally consisting of a quadrangular frame, two braces, and two queen-posts, with a straining piece between the queen-posts, opposite the top of the braces. **1856** S. C. BREES *Gloss. Terms*, *Truss-partition*, a partition in which trussing is employed as well as the regular quartering. **1867** SMYTH *Sailor's Word-bk.*, **Truss-pendant*, that part of a rope-truss into which the truss-tackle blocks are seized. **Truss-pieces*, the fillings in between the frame compartments of the riders, in diagonal trussing. **1823** P. NICHOLSON *Pract. Build.* 231 **Truss-post*, any of the posts of a trussed roof. **1357** in *Pipe Roll 32 Edw. III*, m. 34/2, j. wynding-rope, j. ȝerderope, ij. *trusspoliues. **1417** in *For. Acc. 8 Hen. V*, G/1, j. slynge, iiij Trusse Polleys, j henge pulley. **1735** J. PRICE *Stone Br. Thames* 7, 7 Pair of these *Truss Ribs. **1873** J. RICHARDS *Wood-Working Factories* 8 The *truss rods are generally in the way of the belts,..in nearly all cases it is both better and cheaper to provide strength in the girders without trussing them. **1842–76** GWILT *Encycl. Archit.* Gloss., **Truss Roof*, a roof formed of a tiebeam, principal rafters, king post or queen post, and other necessary timbers to carry the purlins and common rafters, etc. **1336** *Exch. Acc.* 19/31 m. 4 (P.R.O.) Et in xx. petris cordi de canabo..pro duobus *Trusseropes inde faciendis. **1417** in *For. Acc. 8 Hen. V*, G/1 De..ij. Prialle ropes debilibus j. Trusse rope. **1569** in *Richmond Wills* (Surtees) 226 Two pare of trusse roips. **1867** SMYTH *Sailor's Word-bk.*, **Truss-tackle*, a gun-tackle purchase applied to the ends of the truss-pendants, to bowse them taut home to the mast. **1884** *Harper's Mag.* Nov. 826/2 A triple-arch roof supported by iron *truss-work.

†**truss**, *a.* *Obs.* [attrib. use of prec. sb. in similative sense; cf. TRUSSED 1 b.] Of a thick rounded form, like a bundle or parcel; neatly and compactly framed; tight, compact; in quot. *a* 1722, shrunken, shrivelled.

1674 *Lond. Gaz.* No. 909/4 A truss well underlaid Horse. **1699** DAMPIER *Voy.* II. II. 62 The Tigre-Cat is about the bigness of a Bull-Dog, with short Legs, and a truss Body. **1709** *Lond. Gaz.* No. 4608/4 A truss well set Lad, about 16 years of Age. *a* **1722** LISLE *Husb.* (1752) 265, I..observed the cod [of the ox] to be truss. **1825** COBBETT *Rur. Rides* (1830) I. 85 A pretty, little, oldish, smart, truss, nice cockney-looking gentleman.

truss (trʌs), *v.* Forms: 3–7 trusse, (3–6 trosse, 4–5 tros(e), 4–5 trus, (truse, 5 trush, trusshe), 6 trousse, trowse, 6– truss. *β. Sc.* 4–6 turss, 5 twrss, 6 turs, turse. Pa. t. and pple. trussed (trʌst); also 5–7 trust, 6 truste; *β. Sc.* 4–6 tursit, 5 -id, -ed, 6 turst. [ad. F. *trousser*, in OF. also *trusser* (*Chanson Roland*, 11th c.), *trosser*, *torser*, *tourser* 'to trusse, tucke, packe up, to bind or gird up or in' (Cotgr.) = Pr. *trossar* (and med.L. *trossare*), OSp. *trossar*, Sp. *troxar*, Pg. *trouxar* (Diez), of disputed etymology; referred by Diez to the late L. ppl. stem *tort-* or *tors-* of L. *torquēre* to twist. But the sense in the mod. langs. presents difficulties, and other derivations have been conjectured; see Diez, Littré, Scheler, Hatz.-Darm.]

1. *trans.* To tie in a bundle, or stow away closely in a receptacle; to bundle, pack. Also with *up*. (With the stuff, or the bundle or receptacle, as obj.) Now *rare* or *Obs.*

c **1300** *Havelok* 2017 He wolden..trusse al þat he mihten fynde..in arke or in kiste. **13..** *Gaw. & Gr. Knt.* 1129 þay ..Tyffen her takles, trussen her males. **1375** BARBOUR *Bruce* XVII. 859 He gert turss his geir. *c* **1386** CHAUCER *Prol.* 681 But hood..wered he noon, For it was trussed vp in his walet. *a* **1450** *Songs & Carols* (Warton Cl.) 43 Fowre and xx good arwys trusyd in a thrumme. *a* **1450** *Brut* 435 The Frensshe men..trussid hir packe and went her wey. *a* **1533** LD. BERNERS *Huon* li. 173 They shall gyue me bothe gownes and mantelles, so that thou shalt haue myche a do to truss them in my male. **1557** N. T. (Genev.) *Acts* xxi. 15 We trussed vp our fardeles [1611 tooke vp our cariages] and went vp to Ierusalem. **1623** BINGHAM *Xenophon* 69 They trussed vp their baggage, and..marched forth. **1725** DE FOE *Voy. round World* (1840) 119 A bundle of plants, such as he had trussed up together. **1861** *Our Eng. Home* 105 Officers ..whose duty it was to..truss the beds in sacks or hides.

b. *fig.* (See also TRUSSED 1 b.)

c **1394** *P. Pl. Crede* 618 Of þat blissinge..þei may trussen her part in a terre powȝe! *c* **1425** *Cast. Persev.* 1637 in *Macro Plays* 125 þat curteys qwene..in here was trussyd þe trinite. **1500–20** DUNBAR *Poems* xiii. 38 Sum in his toung his kyndnes tursis. **1579** E. K. in *Spenser's Sheph. Cal.* Ded., What in most English wryters vseth to be loose,..in this Authour is well grounded, finely framed, and strongly trussed vp together. **1664** OWEN *Vind. Animad. Fiat Lux* i, Trussing up such a fardel of trifles and quibbles.

†**c.** To charge or burden with a bundle or pack, or a number of such; to load (a pack-horse, etc.); to lade (a ship). *Obs.*

a **1225** *Ancr. R.* 166 Noble men & gentile ne bereð nout packes, ne ne uareð nout itrussed mid trusseaus. **13..** *K. Alis.* 850 (Bodl. MS.) þe..kniȝttes..trusseden her somers And lepen vpon her destrers. *c* **1400** *Destr. Troy* 12313 Tho shippes to shilde o þe shyre whaghes,..And tyrn hom to takle, & trusse for the sea. *a* **1533** LD. BERNERS *Huon* cxxx. 478 They..trussyd & newe wyttelyd theyr shyppes. **1570** LEVINS *Manip.* 193/28 To Trusse, *sarcinare*.

d. *Naut.* To furl (a sail). Also *absol.* (? *Obs.*)

a **1400** *Morte Arth.* 3655 The maryners..Of theire termys they talke, how thay ware tydd, Towyne trvsselle one trete, trvssene vpe sailes. *c* **1400** [see TRUSSING *vbl. sb.* 1]. *c* **1515** *Cocke Lorell's B.* (Percy Soc.) 12 Some wounde at yͤ capstayne,..some dyde trusse and thrynge. **1594** GREENE & LODGE *Looking Gl.* G.'s Wks. (Rtldg.) 134 Our topsails up, we truss our spritsails in. **1867** SMYTH *Sailor's Word-bk.*, *Brails*, ropes..fastened to the outermost leech of the sail, in different places, to truss it close up as occasion requires. *Ibid.*, *Truss up, to*, to brail up a sail suddenly; to toss up a bunt.

†**e.** *trans.* and *intr.* To become shrunken and compact; cf. TRUSS *a.*, TRUSSED 1 b. *Obs. rare.*

1552 HULOET, Trusse vp as a cow or like best doth of milke, *subducere lac. Ibid.*, Trused vp as a bitch, or cow is of milke, *subductus*. Trussed vp, to be, of milche, *subducor*. **1693** [see TRUSSED *ppl. a.* 1 b].

†**2.** To pack up and carry away; to convey or take with one in a pack; to carry off. (In later use only *Sc.*) *Obs.*

a **1300** *Cursor M.* 4911 Ne haue we wit us trussed noght, Bot thing þat we ha lele boght. *c* **1400** MAUNDEV. (Roxb.) viii. 30 þam behoues also trusse þaire vitailles with þam thurgh þe forsaid desertes. **1422** tr. *Secreta Secret., Priv. Priv.* 162 Hare golde, Syluyr, armure, and Iowell with ham thay tursid. **1535** STEWART *Cron. Scot.* (Rolls) II. 342 Tha left na gude that tha mycht turs awa. **1567** *Gude & Godlie B.* (S.T.S.) 195 Preistis, keip no gold..Nor ȝit twa coittis with ȝow turs.

†**3.** *intr.* or *absol.* To pack up one's clothes, etc. in readiness for a journey: = PACK *v.*[1] 2 c. Also *fig.* *Obs.*

1297 R. GLOUC. (Rolls) 9978 Vaste he [King Philip] let trossi, to france uor to drawe. *c* **1375** *Cursor M.* 21115 (Fairf.) þai bad him trusse & make him boun. **1470–85** MALORY *Arthur* XX. xviii. 829 They trussed and payd alle that wold aske hem, and holy an honderd kynghtes departed with sir launcelot. **1696–7** EVELYN *Let. to Bohun* 18 Jan., And so you have the history of a very old man... I..am now every day trussing up to be gon.

†**4.** *intr.* To take oneself off, be off, go away, depart: = PACK *v.*[1] 10 b; sometimes simply to go.

1362 LANGL. *P. Pl.* A. II. 194 Lyȝere..nas nouȝwher welcome..Bote ouur al i-hunted and hote to trusse. *c* **1440** *York Myst.* xxiii. 151 A! lord, late vs no forther trus. *c* **1518** SKELTON *Magnyf.* 1774 As for all other, let them trusse and packe. **1592** BABINGTON *Notes on Gen.* xii. § 10 She trusseth vp and away with him whither God should appoint. **1721** RAMSAY *Richy & Sandy* 73 Let us truse and hame o'er bend.

†**b.** *refl.* in same sense: = PACK *v.* 10 a. *Obs.*

a **1400–50** *Alexander* 1143 And þen he trussys hym to tyre & þar hys tentes settes. *c* **1400** *Sowdone Bab.* 1707 Trusse the forth eke. *c* **1440** *Partonope* 3692 Therto eche man trusse hym home.

†**c.** *trans.* To 'send packing', drive off, put to flight. *Obs. rare.*

c **1475** *Partenay* 2154 The Brehaignons went out thaim Faste trussing [F. *destruisant*]. **1596** DALRYMPLE tr. *Leslie's Hist. Scot.* IX. (S.T.S.) II. 183 Al scotis..suld be turssed away to Scotland.

5. *trans.* To make fast to something with or as with a cord, band, or the like; to bind, tie, fasten; †also, to put on, gird on (clothing, etc.): cf. 6. Now *rare.*

a **1225** *Ancr. R.* 322 Ich chulle..trussen al þi schendfulnesse o þine owune necke. **13..** *K. Alis.* 5477 Bodl. MS.) þe kyng..dooþ on a Borel of a squyer,..And trusseþ a male hym bihynde. *c* **1400** *Destr. Troy* 5293 Teutra the true kyng was trust on a litter. **1575** R. B. *Appius & Virg.* E ij b, Goe trusse him to a tree. **1646** H. LAWRENCE *Comm. Angells* 113 They would..let him trusse on their armour. **1698** FRYER *Acc. E. India & P.* 20 Only a Clout..trust with a String about their Waists. **1813** SCOTT *Rokeby* v. xxxvi, Round his left arm his mantle truss'd, Received and foiled three lances' thrust.

b. *spec.* To tie the 'points' or laces with which the hose were fastened to the doublet. (With the hose, the points, or the person as obj.) Cf. 6. *Obs.* exc. *Hist.*

c **1460** J. RUSSELL *Bk. Nurture* 898 Strike his hosyn vppewarde his legge..þen trusse ye them vp strayte. *c* **1530** H. RHODES *Bk. Nurture* in *Babees Bk.* (1868) 70 Help to araye him, trusse his poyntes, stryke vp his Hosen. **1598** B. JONSON *Ev. Man in Hum.* I. iii, *Steph.* Helpe to trusse me... He dos so vexe me—. *Bray.* You'll be worse vex'd, when you are truss'd... Best keepe vn-brac'd. **1632** MASSINGER *Maid of Hon.* I. i, In the time of trussing a point, he can undo Or make a man. **1822** SCOTT *Nigel* xvii, Let me have the honour of trussing you. Now, observe, I have left several of the points untied of set purpose. **1856** DORAN *Knights & Days* ix. 139 Guy trussed his points, pulled up his hose.

6. To confine or enclose (the body, or some part of it) by something fastened closely round; to bind or tie up; to gird; to fasten up (the hair) with ribbon, pins, combs, etc.; to adjust and draw close the garments of (a person); hence contemptuously in reference to dress. Also with *up*. (Cf. 5 b.) ? *Obs.*

1340 [see TRUSSING *vbl. sb.* 1]. *c* **1440** *Promp. Parv.* 504/2 Trussyn, and byndyn, as menn done soore lymys, *fascio*. **1560** BIBLE (Genev.) *Jer.* i. 17 Trusse vp thy loynes. **1610** G. FLETCHER *Christ's Vict.* I. lxv, Now she would sighing sit, ..in sack cloth trust. **1712** BUDGELL *Spect.* No. 277 ¶7 How ridiculously..we have all been trussed up.., and how infinitely the French Dress excels ours. **1736** AINSWORTH *Lat. Dict.* (1783) I, To truss up the hair of one's head, *caesariem, vel comam, in nodum colligere*. **1833** J. HOLLAND *Manuf. Metal* II. 32 The combs used by the lower class of females for trussing their hair.

†**b.** To insert closely, to tuck. *Obs.*

1523 LD. BERNERS *Froiss.* I. xvii. 18 Bitwene the saddyll and the pannell, they trusse a brode plate of metall. *a* **1550** in *Archæologia* IV. 313 To trusse the endes of the said sheete under every end of the bolster. **1638** GUILLIM *Heraldry* III. xx. (ed. 3) 231 Fowles having long shankes doe (in their flight) stretch forth their legges..; but such as are short legged doe trusse their feet to the middest of their bodies. **1651** tr. *De-las-Coveras' Don Fenise* 114 This woman.. trussing up her garment turned her legs into wings and fled.

7. To fasten up on a gallows or cross, to hang as a criminal; to 'string up'. (Chiefly with *up*.) *arch.*

1536 *Remedy Sedition* B iij b, He was forthwith truste vppe. **1600** HOLLAND *Livy* XXVIII. xxxvii. 696 He commanded them to be roundly trussed up and crucified [*cruci affigi*]. **1618** BOLTON *Florus* III. xix. (1636) 234 He bound the remaynes of those strong theeves in chaines..and trussed them on gallowses. *a* **1721** PRIOR *Vicar of Bray & Sir T. Moor* 426 To be trussed up..as a Traytor. **1818** SCOTT *Hrt. Midl.* xxiii, If they must truss me, I will repent of nothing so much..as of the injury I have done my Lily. **1882** STEVENSON *Fam. Stud. Men & Bks.*, *Villon* (1905) 162 How or when he died, whether decently in bed or trussed up to a gallows, remains a riddle.

†**b.** *intr.* for *pass.* To be hanged: cf. *to hang.*

1592 *Arden of Feversham* III. vi, If thou beest tainted.. And come in question, surely, thou wilt trusse. **1601** F. GODWIN *Bps. of Eng.* 275 The halter was..about the yoong mans necke and he euen ready to trusse.

8. To fasten the wings or legs of (a fowl or other animal) to the body with skewers or otherwise, in preparation for cooking.

[*c* **1450** *Two Cookery-bks.* 81 Take a kydde..fle him, and larde him, and trusse his legges in þe sides, and roste him.] **1704** SWIFT *Batt. Bks.* Misc. (1711) 266 As when a skilful Cook has truss'd a Brace of Woodcocks. **1796** MRS. GLASSE *Cookery* v. 90 Take a fat pig,..slit and truss him up like a lamb. **1846** *J. Baxter's Libr. Pract. Agric.* II. 221 The Higgler's method of Killing, Picking, and Trussing Fowls.

b. *transf.*

1899 *Allbutt's Syst. Med.* VIII. 9 The patient must.. make the shoulder blades meet by trussing back the elbows.

9. Of a bird of prey: To seize or clutch (the prey) in its talons; *spec.* to seize (the quarry) in the air and carry it off. *arch.* (and *Her.*) Also *fig.*

1567 GOLDING *Ovid's Met.* VI. (1593) 144 As when the scarefull erne With hooked talents trussing up a hare among the ferne, Hath laid her in his nest. **1575** TURBERV. *Falconrie* 50 If shee strike hir or stoupe hir or trusse hir then suffer hir to kill it. **1590** SPENSER *F.Q.* I. xi. 19 As hagard hauke..His wearie pounces all in vaine doth spend To trusse the pray too heavy for his flight. **1649** G. DANIEL *Trinarch., Hen. IV* ccxxxiv, A young Eagle..rather Chus'd..at Armed Cranes to flye; Or trusse a farr-seen Swan. **1667** DRYDEN *Maiden Queen* III. i, So—at last he has truss'd his Quarry. **1742** SOMERVILLE *Field Sports* 210 The vigorous hawk..Truss'd in mid-air bears down her captive prey. **1864** BOUTELL *Her. Hist. & Pop.* xvi. §2 (ed. 3) 274 A cormorant trussing a fish all ppr. **1867** J. B. ROSE tr. *Virgil's Æneid* 266 So stoops the bird of Jove..To truss the snowy swan or dusky hare. **1883** HARTING *Perf. Bk. Kepinge Sparhawkes* Gloss. 49 *Truss*, to clutch the quarry in the air instead of striking it to the ground. **1910** RADCLIFFE in *Encycl. Brit.* X. 143/1 A hawk is said to 'truss' a bird when she catches it in the air, and comes to the ground with it in her talons.

transf. **1470–85** MALORY *Arthur* XIV. vi. 649 The lyon took his lytel whelp and trussed hym, and bare hym there he came fro. **1855** BROWNING *Fra Lippo* 88 The wind doubled me up, and down I went. Old Aunt Lapaccia trussed me with one hand.

10. To tighten up (a bell) on its stock after it has worked loose. ? *Obs.*

1468–1540 [see TRUSSING *vbl. sb.* 1]. **1545** *Churchw. Acc. St. Dunstan's, Canterb.*, For yerone [iron] worke to trowse the bellys xij d. **1622–3** in Swayne *Sarum Churchw. Acc.* (1896) 175 For newe Trussinge the 2 3 4 and 5 bells, 5 s.

11. To compress the staves of (a cask) into the required shape and position by means of a *trussing-hoop* (see TRUSSING *vbl. sb.* 3).

1535 COVERDALE *Jer.* xlviii. 12, I shall sende hir trussers to trusse her vp, to prepare and season hir vessels. **1688** R. HOLME *Armoury* III. 108/1 Trussing a Barrel, is putting it together from Boards or Staves within a Hoop. **1883** *Fisheries Exhib. Catal.* 83 Apparatus for heating casks before being trussed.

12. *Building*, etc. **a.** ***truss over***: see quot. ? *Obs.*

1703 T. N. *City & C. Purchaser* 109 Instead of Arching, they truss-over, or over-span, as they phrase it, i.e. they lay the end of one Brick about half way over the end of another, and so, till both sides meet within half a Bricks length, and then a bonding Brick at the top finishes the Arch. *Ibid.* 198 A kind of Bench,.. upon which they lay the largest Stones, and so truss them over,.. after the manner of Clamps for Bricks.

b. To support or strengthen with a TRUSS (*sb.* 6).

1823 [see TRUSSING *vbl. sb.* 1]. **1847** SMEATON *Builder's Man.* 77 It is not necessary to truss all the rafters in a roof. **1889** *Daily News* 15 July 6/3 This new safety ladder, securely trussed on springs and wheels.

†**truss-a-fail.** *Obs. rare*$^{-1}$. App. the name of some game. Cf. TRUSS *sb.* 7.

a **1658** CLEVELAND *Model New Relig.* 9 Or do the Iuncto leap at truss-a-fail?

†**'trussage.** *Obs.* Also 6 troussage, (trosache). [a. OF. *troussage* (14th c. in Godef.), f. F. *trousser* to TRUSS: see -AGE.] Articles 'trussed' or packed up, collectively; baggage; *spec.* booty carried off. Also *attrib.*

c **1500** *Melusine* xxi. 132 Who that myght flee, fledd toward theire folke that lede theyre proye, oxen, kyn & shep, swynes & othre troussage [orig. *troussages*]. **1527** *Acc. R. Gibson* in *Lett. & Pap. Hen. VIII* §45 lf. 23 (P.R.O.), For trosache kasis. *a* **1548** HALL *Chron., Hen. VIII* 119b, The Frenchmen were readye to depart with trussages and cariages.

trusse, obs. form of TRUCE, TRUSS.

trussed (trʌst), *ppl. a.* [f. TRUSS *v.* + -ED[1].]

1. Packed, tied up, etc. (see the vb.); in quot. 1904, with 'points' trussed (TRUSS *v.* 5b). †***trussed bed, bedstead***: cf. *trussing bed*, etc. (TRUSSING *vbl. sb.* 3).

c **1440** *Promp. Parv.* 504/1 Trussyd, of fardel, ..*fardellatus, sarcinatus*. Trussyd vp, and bowndyn, ..*fasciatus*. **1530** *Test. Ebor.* (Surtees) V. 297 A trust bed with a fedder bed. ? **1537** *Rutland MSS.* (1905) IV. 279 A truste bedsted for my Lord to cary to the Court, vij *s*. **1552** HULOET, Trussed, *suffarcinatus*... Trussed, beaten, layed, or stopped hard together, *stipatus*. **1578** LYTE *Dodoens* v. lxxx. 650 Clusters of many berries.. thicke set and trussed togither. **1890** DOYLE *White Company* iii, His robe was much too long and loose.. so that even with trussed-up skirts he could make little progress. **1904** M. HEWLETT *Queen's Quair* I. vi, The Queen and her maids braved it as saucy young men, trunked, puffed, pointed, trussed and doubleted.

b. *fig.* Knit together, compactly framed or formed. (Usually const. as *pa. pple.*, often with *well* or other adv.) ? *Obs.*

1548 ELYOT, *Compactilis*, that is well compacted and trussed togither, shorte and rounde. **1676** *Lond. Gaz.* No. 1080/4 A bay Nag,.. short necked, well trussed. **1693** *Ibid.* No. 2916/4 She has lately had Puppies, and is not yet fully Truss'd.

c. *Cookery.* Of a fowl, etc.: see TRUSS *v.* 8. Also in *Her.*: see quot. *c* 1828.

1828 SCOTT *F.M. Perth* viii, 'It's all here', said the little man, expanding his breast like a trussed fowl. *c* **1828** BERRY *Encycl. Her.* I. Gloss., *Trussed*, Close, or Complicated, are terms unnecessarily introduced into blazon when birds are borne with their wings closed to the body; which is ever implied when the contrary is not expressed. **1900** MRS. GLYN *Visits Eliz.* (1906) 59 He does look like a trussed pigeon.

2. *Building*, etc. Furnished, supported, or strengthened with a truss or trusses.

1840 H. SPENCER *Autobiog.* (1904) I. xi. 164 Experiments on trussed beams. **1853** SIR H. DOUGLAS *Milit. Bridges* vii. (ed. 3) 307 On trussed and suspension bridges. **1873** MEDLEY *Autumn Tour U.S. & Canada* ix. 146 Trussed girders are preferred [in bridge-building].

trussel, -ell, obs. forms of TRESTLE.

†**trussell.** *Obs.* Also 5 trusselle, 5–9 trussel; *Sc.* 6 tursall, 6–7 tursell. [a. OF. *troussel*, earlier *torsel, toursel*, mod.F. *trousseau*, dim. of *trousse*, vbl. sb. of *trousser*: see TRUSS.]

1. A bundle, package; in quot. *a* 1400, a furled sail. Cf. TROUSSEAU[1].

? *a* **1400** [see TRUSS *v.* 1 d]. **1426** LYDG. *De Guil. Pilgr.* 2755 And at the gate for to se Trussellys, ffardellys, in that place. Or any marchaunt in hey passe, He mvste vntrusse hem & vnbynde. *c* **1460** *Towneley Myst.* ii. 170 Lay downe thi trussell apon this hill.

2. The puncheon for making the impress on the upper side of the coin; cf. PILE *sb.*[4] 1.

[**1300**: see PILE *sb.*[4] 1.] **1473** *Chancery Enrolments, Durham* 3/49 m. 6 (P.R.O.) We.. haue.. licencid oure welbelouyd William Omorighe.. to make graue and prynte ij dosene Trussellys and j dosene Standerdys for penys and iiij Standerdys and viij Trussellys for half penys. **1484** *Chancery Warr.* Ser. 1. File 1531. No. 5767 (P.R.O.) Receptis.. tribus standardis et novem trussellis ruptis.. tria standarda et novem trussellos de novo fieri.. faciatis. **1562–3–1605** [see PILE *sb.*[4] 1, PUNCHEON[1] 3]. **1611** COTGR., *Trousseau*, a Trussell; the vpper yron, or mould, thats vsed in the stamping of coyne. **1817** RUDING *Ann. Coinage* I. 67, III. 24. **1876** COCHRAN-PATRICK *Rec. Coinage Scotl.* I. Introd. 49 The 'flan' being placed on the 'pile', the 'trussell' was applied to the upper side of it by means of a twisted wand, or by the hand, and the moneyer then struck the end of the puncheon with the hammer until the impression was produced on the 'flan'.

trusser ('trʌsə(r)). [f. TRUSS *v.* + -ER[1].]

†**1.** A receptacle or appliance in or with which something is 'trussed'; a bundle, package; a bandage. *Obs.*

1519 HORMAN *Vulg.* 30 The bounche or botche.. can vnneth be bounde vp with a trussar. *a* **1548** HALL *Chron., Hen. VIII* 17 Byndyng of males and fardelles, trussyng of coffers and trussers.

2. One who or that which trusses, in various senses: see the verb. *spec.* **a.** One who trusses a cask.

1535 [see TRUSS *v.* 11].

b. A person employed in trussing poultry, etc.

1857 A. MATHEWS *Tea-Table Talk* II. 96 It [*sc.* a chicken] had apparently made a vigorous struggle for continued existence, which struggle had evidently distorted its form out of the power of the trusser to regulate. **1903** *Daily Chron.* 16 Sept. 8/6 Poultry.—Wanted a trusser for best-class work. **1906** *Daily News* 14 Dec. 7 The removal of this favourite bone by the trusser.

c. A person employed in, or a machine for, trussing hay or straw.

1889 *Engineer* LXVII. 292 Hay and straw trussers. **1890** *Univ. Exhib. Guide* June 29/2 The Straw Trusser.. was shown at work attached to the Steam Thrashing Machine. **1892** T. B. F. EMINSON *Epidemic Pneumonia at Scotter* 49 The trussers.. were engaged trussing the hay for sale.

3. A plant that produces trusses of blossom: usually with qualifying adj. expressing the quality of the trusses.

1843 *Florist's Jrnl.* (1846) IV. 153 The flowers are extra-sized, and it is a very fine trusser. **1882** *Garden* 11 Mar. 160/3 This.. red ground Polyanthus.. is a noble trusser.

†**'trussery.** *Obs. rare*$^{-1}$. [f. TRUSS *sb.* + -ERY.] Things 'trussed' or packed, baggage.

a **1548** HALL *Chron., Hen. VIII* 65 A great numbre of rascal & pedlers, & Iuellers.. brought ouer.. diuerse merchandise vncustomed, all vnder the colour of the trussery of the Ambassadours.

trussing ('trʌsɪŋ), *vbl. sb.* [f. TRUSS *v.* + -ING[1].]

1. The action of the verb TRUSS, in various senses.

1340 *Ayenb.* 176 Ynoȝ þer is of ydelnesse aboute hire heaued, to kembe, to wesse, ine trossinge. *c* **1400** *Destr. Troy* 4653 All turnyt þaire tacle with trussyng of sailes. **1468–9** in Swayne *Sarum Churchw. Acc.* (1896) 11 Pro le trussyng magne campane ad thascum x d. **1540** *Churchw. Acc. St. Giles, Reading* 59 For trussing of the greate bell. **1615** LATHAM *Falconry* (1633) Explan. Words, *Trussing* is when a Hawke raiseth a fowle aloft, and so descendeth downe with it to the ground. **1670** EACHARD *Cont. Clergy* 75 Let your loins be girded... There must be a holy girding and trussing up for heaven. **1694** R. L'ESTRANGE *Fables* clxxvii. (1714) 190 The Trussing up of Thieves is the Security of Honest Men. **1823** P. NICHOLSON *Pract. Builder* 124 To frame timbers, so that their external surfaces shall keep this position, is the business of trussing. **1852** MRS. STOWE *Uncle Tom's C.* iv, Not a chicken, or turkey, or duck.. but looked grave when they saw her approaching,.. she was always meditating on trussing, stuffing, and roasting.

2. *concr.* The timber or other material forming a truss (TRUSS *sb.* 6); a work or structure consisting of trusses.

1840 *Civil Eng. & Arch. Jrnl.* III. 43/1 A plan of the trussed foot-bridge.. exhibiting the trussing and cast iron frames. **1890** W. J. GORDON *Foundry* 48 A platform of temporary girders.. strengthened by supplementary trussing.

3. *attrib.* Adapted or used for 'trussing', packing, or tying up (*obs.* exc. *Hist.*), as ***trussing chest, coffer, gear, mail, -needle, point, -thread***; adapted for being 'trussed' or packed up for travelling (*obs.* exc. *Hist.*), as ***trussing bed, bedstead, chalice***; used for trussing (in various senses of the verb), as (sense 1 d) ***trussing-rope***, (sense 10) ***-key, -nail***, (sense 11) ***-hoop, -machine***, (sense 12 b) ***-bar, -bolt, -piece, -rod***; also †**trussing-bolster**: see quot., and cf. TRUSS *sb.* 3 a; †**trussing-coat**, a padded jacket worn under armour.

1843 *Penny Cycl.* XXV. 318/2 So long as it [the beam] retains this curvature the weight laid upon it must eventually press upon the *trussing-bars. **1398** *Will John of Gaunt* in Armitage Smith *Life* (1904) 426 Lits faitz pur mon corps, appelles en Engleterre *trussyng beddes. **1482** MARG. PASTON in *P. Lett.* III. 286 A litel white bedde.. for a trussyng bedde. **1572** in Whitaker *Hist. Craven* (1812) 327 One trussing bedd for the field. **1861** *Our. Eng. Home* 105 Portable beds were often called 'trussing' beds. **1534** *Inv. Wardr. Kath. Arragon* in *Camden Misc.* (1855) 34 A lytille *trussinge bedsteede.. withe two lether cases to trusse it in. **1910** E. R. SUFFLING *Eng. Ch. Brasses* 110 *Trussing-Bolster, a padded belt for equalising and taking the weight of the heavy cuirass. **1843** *Penny Cycl.* XXV. 319/2 Through these eyes were passed vertical bars or *trussing-bolts. **1440** in Peacock *Eng. Ch. Furniture* (1866) 182 My *trushing challis and my highest guilt chalis. **1540** *Act 32 Hen. VIII* c. 14 Item for a *trussyng cheste ii. s. *a* **1562** CAVENDISH *Wolsey* (1893) 257 Syttyng uppon a trussyng chest. **1884** *Leisure Hour* Apr. 233/1 Large trunks, used for general packing.. were called trussing-chests. **1493** *Will of W. Oseney* (Somerset Ho.), A *trussing coat. **1387** TREVISA *Higden* (Rolls) VII. 385 His malys.. his bouges and his *trussynge cofres. **1485** in *Ripon Ch. Acts* (Surtees) 368, ij trussyng coffers 3s... unum magnum trussyng mayle precii 2s. **1466** *Mann. & Househ. Exp.* (Roxb.) 367, I payd fore viij. heles [= ells] of kanas for *trosenge gere, xx.d. **1688** R. HOLME *Armoury* III. 108/1 *Trussing Hoop, is a large strong Hoop.. first put about the Barrel staves to draw them to their compass. **1621–2** in Swayne *Sarum Churchw. Acc.* (1896) 172, ix *trussinge keyes. **1877** KNIGHT *Dict. Mech.*, *Trussing-machine, one for drawing the truss-hoops upon casks. **1883** *Fisheries Exhib. Catal.* 83 Trussing machine and accumulator. **1485** *Trussyng mayle [see *trussing coffer* above]. **1621–2** in Swayne *Sarum Churchw. Acc.* (1896) 172 One Hundred of *Trussinge nayles 10d. **1846** SOYER *Cookery* 149 To try when done run a *trussing needle into them. **1823** P. NICHOLSON *Pract. Builder* 595 **Trussing-pieces*, such timbers in a roof as are in a state of compression. **1548** ELYOT, *Strigmentum*.. it maie be vsed for a *trussyng pointe. **1843** *Penny Cycl.* XXV. 319/1 A formula for calculating the size of the iron *trussing-rods. **1420** in *For. Acc. 3 Hen. VI*, G/2 *dorso*, j haunser pro *trussynge rope. **1369–72** *Exch. Acc. K.R.* Bundle 178 No. 16 m. 4 (P.R.O.), lxiiij lb. fili pro cordis balistarum, lij lb. *trussyngthred, lj lb. di. trenchefyll.

†**'trussure.** *Obs.* [a. OF. *trusseure* (Cotgr. *troussure, -eure*), med.L. **trossātūra*, f. *trossare* to TRUSS: see -URE.] ? = TRUSS *sb.* 2.

1295 *Acc. Exch. K.R.* 5/8 m. 13 (P.R.O.) In j ancora et .j. Cable emptis de Hugone Kelinge. Et xxij. s. in Trussurs, Girdelinges [etc.] emptis de eodem.

trust (trʌst), *sb.* Forms: α. 3–6 truste, 3– trust; β. 4–7 trost, 5 troste. See also TRAIST *sb.*, TREST *sb.*[1], TRIST *sb.*[1] [Early ME. *trost(e, truste*, ad. ON. *traust* sb. neut.: see TRUST *a.*]

1. a. Confidence in or reliance on some quality or attribute of a person or thing, or the truth of a statement. Const. *in* (†*of, on, upon, to, unto*).

α. *a* **1225** *Ancr. R.* 274 Me haueð truste to Godes helpe þet euer is neih bute ȝif bileaue trukie. *a* **1240** *Ureisun* in *Cott. Hom.* 187 As mi trust is þer to hit beo mi lechunge. **13..** *Guy Warw.* (A.) 7242 He a lappe rent out anon Of his brini, þat alle his trust was on. **1484** CAXTON *Fables of Auian* i, He is wel a fole that setteth his hope and truste in a woman. **1505** in *Mem. Hen. VII* (Rolls) 275 Don Fernando of Aragon hathe no confidens nor truste unto the Kynge of Romaynes. **1605** STOW *Ann.* 671 A staffe of reede, of the which there is no trust. **1611** SHAKS. *Wint. T.* IV. iv. 607 Ha, ha, what a Foole Honestie is! and Trust (his sworne brother) a very simple Gentleman. **1729** BUTLER *Serm.* Wks. 1874 II. 189 To see and know and feel that our trust was not vain. **1823** SCOTT *Quentin D.* xiii, The honour and trust which were about to be reposed in him. **1860** TYNDALL *Glac.* I. xix. 134 We had.. to get round overhanging ledges, where our main trust was in our feet.

β. **1382** WYCLIF *Prov.* iii. 5 Haue trost in the Lord, of al thin herte. —— *Isa.* xxxi. 1 Hauende trost [1388 trist] vpon foure horsid carres. *c* **1440** *Promp. Parv.* 503/1 Troste, *confidencia, fiducia*. **1648** *Hamilton Papers* (Camden) 228 The trost reposid in me bi your Lordshipe.

b. ***take on*** or ***upon trust*** (†***receive, take up in trust, take up upon trust***), to accept or give credit to without investigation or evidence.

1641 *Nicholas Papers* (Camden) 4 Being constrayned to take upp all my intelligence concerning Parliament affaires upon trust.. from others. *c* **1645** HOWELL *Lett.* (1650) I. 67 Ey-witnesses of those things which other receive but in trust. *Ibid.* II. *The Vote* I ij b, Scribling Pamphletors.. thrust Lame things upon the world, t'ane up in trust. **1662** STILLINGFL. *Orig. Sacræ* I. iv. §5 The story was taken upon trust by Herodotus, Pliny, and many others. **1797** GODWIN *Enquirer* I. vi. 36 Active spirits.. take.. little upon trust. **1824** *Examiner* 353/1 That numerous body who take things on trust. **1869** J. MARTINEAU *Ess.* II. 98 Take what is set before him on trust.

c. *transf.* with possessive: That in which one's confidence is put; an object of trust.

1526 *Pilgr. Perf.* (W. de W. 1531) 8 b, Let hym be all your trust. **1560** BIBLE (Genev.) *Ps.* xl. 4 Blessed is the man, that maketh the Lord his trust. **1866** BRYANT *Death Abraham Lincoln* i, The sword of power, a nation's trust.

2. Confident expectation of something; hope.

[*c* **1200**: see TRIST *sb.*[1]] *c* **1400** *Destr. Troy* 8689 þai had no hope of þere heale.. all hor trust þan was tynt. **1523** LD. BERNERS *Froiss.* I. xviii. 22 They were all the weeke, without heryng of any worde of the scottis, vpon trust they shulde repasse agayn.. the same way. *a* **1548** HALL *Chron., Hen. IV* 28 This prince was sent thither, in trust of sauegard, in hope of refuge, and in request of aide and comfort against his euill willers. **1667** MILTON *P.L.* II. 46 His trust was with th' Eternal to be deem'd Equal in strength. **1864** J. MARTINEAU *Ess., Addr.*, etc. (1891) IV. 563 The trusts of eighteen centuries and the sighs and hopes of more.

3. Confidence in the ability and intention of a buyer to pay at a future time for goods supplied without present payment: = CREDIT *sb.* 9 a. Chiefly in phrases ***on, upon,*** †***of trust***.

1573 TUSSER *Husb.* (1878) 134 At first hand he buieth that paieth all doune.. At third hand he buieth that buieth of trust. **1649** BP. HALL *Cases Consc.* (1650) 26 Those who are able to pay downe ready money.. know to expect a better pennyworth, then those that runne upon trust. **1681** in *New Mills Cloth Manuf.* (S.H.S.) Introd. 85 Cloath will be.. delivered out to the merchants and after 12 months trust they will be paying [etc.]. **1758** JOHNSON *Idler* No. 26 ¶8 My master lived on trust at an ale-house. **1829** COBBETT *Adv. Yng. Man* ii. 63 The man therefore who purchases on trust not only pays for the trust, but he also pays his due share of what the tradesman loses by trust.

fig. **1821** BYRON *Sardan.* II. i. 596, I am content To be beloved on trust for what I feel. **1865** RUSKIN *Sesame* i. §1, I had even intended to ask your attention for a little while on trust.. until [etc.].

4. The quality of being trustworthy; fidelity, reliability; loyalty, trustiness. Now *rare*.

1470–85 MALORY *Arthur* XXI. v. 850 Comfort thyself.. and doo as wel as thou mayst, for in me is no truste for to truste in. *c* **1489** CAXTON *Sonnes of Aymon* vii. 166 There ys noo truste in hym And therfore I wyll kepe me from hym. **1590** MARLOWE *Edw. II*, III. ii, Our friend Levune, faithful and full of trust. **1592** SHAKS. *Rom. & Jul.* III. ii. 85 There's no trust, no faith, no honestie in men. **1620** MAY *Heir* III. (1622) D iv, Well I beleeue thee wench, and will reward Thy trust in this. **1695** PRIOR *Ode Queen's Death* iv, Fair Albion shall, with faithful Trust, Her holy Queen's sad Reliques guard. **1821** BYRON *Mar. Fal.* II. i, You have done well.—I thank you for that trust.

5. a. The condition of having confidence reposed in one, or of being entrusted *with* something; esp. in the phrases ***in trust, to*** one's ***trust, under trust.***

a **1548** HALL *Chron., Edw. V* 11, I dare putte no persone earthely in truste with his kepyng, but my selfe onely. **1577** HANMER *Anc. Eccl. Hist., Socrates* I. xxvi, He putteth the priest..in trust with his testament. **1609** SKENE *Reg. Maj.* II. 131 Murther..of our Soveraine Lords lieges, quhere the persone slaine is vnder the trust, credit, assurance, and power of the slayer, is treason and lese majestie. [*Margin*] Slauchter vnder trust. **1611** BIBLE *1 Thess.* ii. 4 As we were allowed of God to bee put in trust with the Gospel. —— *1 Tim.* vi. 20 O Timothie, keepe that which is committed to thy trust. **1675** tr. *Camden's Hist. Eliz.* II. (1688) 174 Such Letters I should never have committed to Barker's Trust. **1817** W. SELWYN *Law Nisi Prius* (ed. 4) II. 821 A devisee or executor in trust, who has acted, may be examined as a witness in support of the will. **1818** SCOTT *Br. Lamm.* xvii, The celebrated case of Sir Coolie Condiddle of Condiddle, who was tried for theft under trust.

b. The obligation or responsibility imposed on one in whom confidence is placed or authority is vested, or who has given an undertaking of fidelity.

1535 COVERDALE *Micah* vii. 20 Thou shalt kepe thy trust with Iacob, and thy mercy for Abraham, like as thou hast sworne vnto oure fathers longe agoo. *a* **1548** HALL *Chron., Rich. III* 27 The man..beynge hindered and kepte vnder by sir Richarde Ratcliffe and sir Willyam Catesbye, which..kept him by secrete driftes out of al secrete trust. *a* **1661** FULLER *Worthies* (1840) I. 402 His youth spent in some military employments of good trust. **1770** *Junius Lett.* xxxvii. (1820) 182 Until parliament itself betrays its trust, by contributing to establish new principles of government. **1784** J. BROWN *Hist. Brit. Ch.* (1820) II. vi. 289 Bringing them into places of power and trust. **1849** MACAULAY *Hist. Eng.* vii. II. 236 Grave apprehensions that, if Roman Catholics were made capable of public trust, great evils would ensue. **1907** *Verney Mem.* I. 72 A breach of trust.

c. The condition of that which is entrusted to some one. Only in phrase ***in*** (†***on***) ***trust.***

1425 W. PASTON in *P. Lett.* I. 20 The whiche procuracie and appelle I shal sende to yowr persone,..with moneye onward, on trust. **1596** SPENSER *F.Q.* v. iv. 2 To knights of great emprise The charge of Justice given was in trust, That they might execute her iudgements wise. **1608** SHAKS. *Per.* I. iii. 13 His sealed Commission, left in trust with mee. **1664** BUTLER *Hud.* II. I. 507 To make over In trust your fortune to your Lover. **1827** JARMAN *J. J. Powell's Devises* (ed. 3) II. 17 A gift to a college, in trust for another charitable object. **1858** O. W. HOLMES *Aut. Breakf.-t.* ii. (1891) 49 Put not your trust in money, but put your money in trust.

d. (with *pl.*) A duty or office, also a thing or person, entrusted to one.

1643 CHAS. I *Treaty at Oxford* Wks. 1662 II. 282 Those Trusts which the Law of the Land hath settled in the Crown alone. **1684** *Scanderbeg Rediv.* iii. 32 It was not fit two such great Trusts, as Marshal and General should both be managed by one Person. **1750** JOHNSON *Rambler* No. 71 ¶ 14 The few moments remaining are to be considered as the last trust of heaven. **1822–34** *Good's Study Med.* (ed. 4) II. 463 The digestive powers, or some of them, do not perform their trust as they should do. **1844** G. N. BRIGGS in *Massachusetts Acts* 363 Public offices are public trusts, created for the benefit of the whole people, and not for the benefit of those who may fill them. **1898** SOPHIA M. PALMER in Ld. Selborne *Mem.* I. p. v. (*Notice*) These Memorials are a Trust.

e. ***on trust***: (of a dog) obeying the command to trust (see TRUST *v.* 1 b). Also ***to play 'Trust'***.

1932 C. MORGAN *Fountain* i. 4 In Lewis's compartment were two former sergeants of marine, Lapham and Shordey, upright in opposite corners like dogs on trust. **1939** C. DAY LEWIS *Child of Misfortune* 196 Eve was trying to teach her puppy to play 'Trust' with a piece of biscuit. **1970** [see PAID *ppl. a.* 4 a].

6. *Law.* The confidence reposed in a person in whom the legal ownership of property is vested to hold or use for the benefit of another; hence, an estate committed to the charge of trustees; also *transf.* a trustee; a body of persons appointed as trustees; in quot. 1712, the position or relation of a trustee.

1442 *Rolls of Parlt.* V. 57/1 The seid Feffees haue no title ner interest therynne, but only upon trust, and to his use, to execute his will. **1455** *Ibid.* 295/1 Londes or Tenementes of which we were enfeoffed by them of trust, in which we had never title..but onely by the feoffement made by us in trust. **1544** tr. *Littleton's Tenures* (1574) 96 b, If a manne enfeoffe another in hys lande vppon truste. **1628** COKE *On Litt.* 272 b, An Vse is a Trust or Confidence reposed in some other. **1712** STEELE *Spect.* No. 402 ¶ 3, I am in a Trust relating to this Lady's Fortune. **1797** MRS. A. M. BENNETT *Beggar Girl* (1813) I. 96 Both Mr. Frazer and doctor Cameron were trusts to a will made a few years back. **1828** HOOD *Kilmansegg, Marriage*, It tipp'd the post-boy and paid the trust. **1873** *Iron* 3 May 493/1 The trustees of the Submarine Cables Trust.

7. *Commerce.* **a.** See quot.

1882–93 BITHELL *Counting-ho. Dict.* s.v., The 'Trusts' instituted in the City.., such as the 'Foreign and Colonial Securities Trust' [etc.]; in all these instances, a certain capital is subscribed..which is placed in the hands of trustees to be invested.

b. A body of producers or traders in some class of business, organized to reduce or defeat competition, lessen expenses, and control production and distribution for their common advantage; *spec.* such a combination of commercial or industrial companies, with a central governing body of trustees which holds a majority or the whole of the stock of each of the combining firms, thus having a controlling vote in the conduct and operation of each. Cf. *trust-certificate* in 8 b.

1877 J. WANAMAKER in J. H. Appel *Business Biogr. John Wanamaker* (1930) x. 137 Why should not individual ownership be permitted to grow peaceably and equally with industries that are bunched into trusts? **1887** *Pall Mall G.* 2 Nov. 6/1 A high customs tariff offers a special temptation to indulge in corners, pools, and trusts. *Ibid.* 16 Nov. 12/1 A distillers' 'trust' has been formed..in order to regulate the production and price of spirits, and another large section of the trade have combined to curtail the production. **1888** BRYCE *Amer. Commw.* III. 415 Those anomalous giants called Trusts,—groups of individuals and corporations concerned in one branch of trade or manufacture, which are placed under the irresponsible management of a small knot of persons, who, through their command of all the main producing or distributing agencies, intend and expect to dominate the market. *a* **1890** in G. B. Shaw *Fabian Ess. Socialism* 94 A trust is defined..as a combination to destroy competition and to restrain trade. **1894** W. T STEAD *If Christ came to Chicago* 191 The Gas Trust is as arbitrary as any Persian satrap in its dealings with the citizens.

8. a. *attrib.* and *Comb.*, as ***trust-betrayer, -breaker***; ***trust-breaking, -winning*** adjs.; also in sense 6, ***trust-beneficiary, -estate, -fund, -gift, -money, -right***; in sense 7 b, ***trust-maker, -regulation, -share***; ***trust-bolstering, -controlled, -ridden*** adjs.

1675 COTTON *Scoffer Scoft* 28 And like a treacherous Trust-breaker, Lewdly embezzel'd your Exchequer. **1766** BLACKSTONE *Comm.* II. xx. 337 They now consider a trust-estate..as equivalent to the legal ownership. **1776** ADAM SMITH *W.N.* II. iii. (1869) I. 341 The..allotment..of this fund..is not always guarded by any..trust-right or deed of mortmain. **1780** J. FIFE *Let.* 29 Feb. in A. & H. Tayler *Lord Fife & his Factor* (1925) v. 121 After his death, you know how I was involved in a trust-fund. **1802–12** BENTHAM *Ration. Judic. Evid.* (1827) II. 114 The hypocritical and trust-breaking humanity of judges. **1827** JARMAN *J. J. Powell's Devises* (ed. 3) II. 99 He gave several pecuniary legacies out of his said trust monies and personal estate. **1855** DICKENS *Dorrit* II. x, Plunderers, forgers, and trust-betrayers of many sorts. **1862** *Harper's Mag.* Aug. 337/1 Mr. Pennington has a considerable practice as a lawyer and a handsome private estate. He has, as a consequence, many trust funds. **1872** TALMAGE *Serm.* 291 The heroes of this country are fast getting to be those who have most skill in swallowing 'trust-funds'. **1880** MUIRHEAD *Gaius* Digest 495 A request to heir, legatee, or even a trust-beneficiary, to give effect to the truster's wishes. *Ibid.* II. §271 A legacy cannot be charged upon a legatee, but a trust-gift may. **1881** M. A. LEWIS *Two Pretty G.* II. 201 All the more trust-winning, solid qualities. **1892** *Daily News* 21 Dec. 7/3 Trust shares received a smart shock. Banks are reported unwilling lenders on some trust securities. **1896** S. PLIMSOLL in *Westm. Gaz.* 3 June (1898) 7/1, I would rather than see our English shopkeepers and manufacturers dragged..to a similar position, see those trust-makers one and all hanging from lamp-posts. **1901** SIR C. FURNESS *Ibid.* 22 Feb. 6/2 An object-lesson..as to the trust-bolstering effect of the tariff. **1901** *Spectator* 20 July 77/2 The Trustmakers are seeking monopoly. **1902** *Daily Chron.* 26 Apr. 5/1 Weep as you think of these Trust-ridden isles! **1902** *Westm. Gaz.* 28 Aug. 1/3 The striking fact is that President Roosevelt should have thrown himself into the Anti-Trust or Trust-regulation movement. *Ibid.* 5 Nov. 5/1 The whole of the share capital will stand in the names of five voting trustees... These voting trustees will issue voting trust share certificates which will be negotiable and will entitle the holders of them to all dividends declared upon the shares, but all voting powers upon the shares are reserved to the voting trustees. **1908** *Ibid.* 5 Nov. 2/1 All 'articles entering into competition with Trust-controlled products'.

b. Special combs.: **trust-buster** *colloq.* (orig. *U.S.*), one who works for the dissolution of trusts (sense 7 b); *spec.* a government official responsible for the enforcement of legislation against trusts; hence **trust-busting** *vbl. sb.* and *ppl. a.*; **trust-certificate** (in full ***trust-share certificate***), a negotiable certificate issued by the controlling board of a trust (sense 7 b), which entitles the holder to all dividends declared upon the surrendered shares which it represents, but gives him no voting power; **trust company**, a company formed (originally in *U.S.*) for the purpose of exercising the functions of a trustee, with which other financial activities were later combined; **trust corporation** *Law*, a corporation empowered to act as a trustee; **trust deed**, a deed of conveyance by which a trust (sense 6) is created, and its conditions set out; **Trust House**, a hotel owned by a company called Trust Houses, which was founded in 1903 to restore the traditional high standards of the best of the old coaching inns, and merged with Forte Holdings Ltd. in 1970 to form Trusthouse Forte; **trust-investment**, the investment of trust-money; a security sanctioned by law as one in which trustees may invest trust-money; †**trust-man**, a trustee; **trust-manager**, under the Education Act of 1902, one of the four managers of a voluntary elementary school appointed by the trustees; **trust officer** *N. Amer.*, an officer of a trust company or similar institution who has direct responsibility for the institution's activities as a trustee; †**trust-road**, a road administered by a turnpike trust; **trust-stock**, a high-class stock in which trust-funds are or may legally be invested; trustee-stock; **Trust Territory**, a territory administered by a nation acting on behalf of the United Nations Organization; cf. TRUSTEESHIP 2 b.

1903 *Chicago Chron.* 11 Apr. 2 Mr. Knox is surprising everybody by his zeal as a *trust-buster. **1949** *Time* 9 May 34/3 U.S. trustbusters were still locked in stalemate with the Zaibatsu. **1979** *N.Y. Times Mag.* 30 Sept. 60/2 'Fighting the oil and gas lobby'..was soon to become more fashionable among liberals than it had been since the turn of the century, when the muckrakers and the trust-busters were riding high. **1911** *Daily Colonist* (Victoria, B.C.) 22 Apr. 13/5 Clark McClercher..has been appointed special assistant to the attorney-general with '*trust-busting' duties. **1944** *Chicago Daily News* 8 May 10/1 So we have a faint revival of 'trust busting' to give color to the stuff. **1973** *Business Week* 13 Jan. 32/1 The Administrative Council for Economic Defense (ACED)..claims to be the only trustbusting agency in Latin America. **1891** *Cent. Dict.* s.v. *Trust*, *Trust certificate. **1904** *Q. Rev.* Jan. 187 The original stock-holders received trust-certificates. **1834** *Congress Debates* 14 Jan. 2392 In New York, a *trust company, incorporated only two or three years since, has now three or four millions in deposite. **1913** *Times* 9 Aug. 17/6 The movements in trust companies' stocks were in the upward direction. **1925** *Act 15 Geo. V* c. 18 §30. 422 Where there is a sole personal representative, not being a *trust corporation, it shall be obligatory on him to appoint an additional trustee. *Ibid.* §117. 491 'Trust corporation' means the Public Trustee or a corporation either appointed by the court..or entitled by rules made under..the Public Trustee Act, 1906, to act as custodian trustee. **1967** E. RUDINGER *Wills & Probate* 12 The Public Trustee is a government department which can be appointed to be your executor, as can some trust corporations. *a* **1754** P. GRANT *Decisions of Court of Session* (1813) II. 490 The Lords *nem. con.* found action competent upon the *trust-deed. **1812** *Dramatic Censor 1811* 400 The creditors on the trust deed, consisting of authors, performers, trades-people, and others, had due to them 52,611 *l.* **1880** A. MCKAY *Hist. Kilmarnock* (ed. 4) 321 Then follows a digest of the trust-deed. [**1900** EARL GREY in *Econ. Rev.* (1901) XI. 101 Arrangements have already been made for the formation of a Public-house Trust Company (Limited) for the county of Northumberland.] **1902** EARL OF CARLISLE in *Monthly Rev.* Feb. 36 This decision..may affect the reformed *trust houses. **1915** *Nineteenth Cent.* Jan. 68 The whole atmosphere of these Trust Houses..is essentially different to that of the average Trade house. **1928** *Evening News* 18 Aug. 11/7 No attempt was made to define 'disinterested management', but one gathered..that it is supposed to be found in 'trust houses'. **1942** E. WAUGH *Put out More Flags* i. 22 Basil will be covered with medals while your silly old yeomanry are still messing in a Trust House. **1972** 'M. DELVING' *Shadow of Himself* i. 17, I.. looked up hotels. There was a Trust House there, the White Swan. **1897** *Westm. Gaz.* 7 Oct. 7/3 The stock is a *trust investment stock. **1867** R. S. HAWKER *Footpr. in Far Cornw.* (1903) 151 Twenty acres of woodland copse..were bought and conveyed by..Dame Thomasine Gull, to feoffees and *trust-men. **1902** *Westm. Gaz.* 17 July 6/2 A board of management consisting of a number of *trust managers not exceeding four appointed as provided by this Act, and..two appointed [etc.]. **1905** KIRKBRIDE & STERRETT *Mod. Trust Company* iii. 41 The *trust officer must have full authority over his department. **1965** H. HOOD in R. Weaver *Canad. Short Stories* (1968) 2nd Ser. 221 You're doing splendidly. You have all your friends in the office and inside of two years you'll be a trust officer. **1976** *Globe & Mail* (Toronto) 16 Feb. 15/6 One prominent trust officer calculated that the increase would cost his company an additional $84,000 a year. **1821** GALT *Ann. Parish* x, The toll or *trust-road was set a-going. **1858** LD. ST. LEONARDS *Handy-Bk. Prop. Law* xxi. 166 One trustee sold the *trust-stock and gave the money to his co-trustee..to invest. **1898** *Daily News* 28 May 10/1 A few trust stocks have improved. **1945** *U.N. Charter* xii. §75, in *Times* 27 June 8/5 The United Nations shall establish under its authority an International Trusteeship System for the administration and supervision of..*Trust Territories. **1970** *Internat. & Compar. Law Q.* XIX. 218 New Guinea was a Mandated Territory... Its change of status in 1946 to become a Trust Territory [etc.]..have not affected section 16.

c. Passing into *adj. Soc. Psychol.* Applied to activities in which an individual is required to display trust or confidence, esp. as ***trust game***. Also with reference to techniques aimed at measuring or achieving trust.

1967 J. B. ROTTER in *Jrnl. Personality* XXXV. 653 (*heading*) Construction of the interpersonal trust scale. **1972** *Psychol. Report* XXX. 850 The authors recognize that it is inappropriate to call this particular activity a trust exercise. **1975** *Psychol. Abstr.* LIII. 1181/1 Behavior..was related to choice in the 'competition' game but not in the 'trust' game. **1978** *Peace News* 25 Aug. 10/2 As I see it, trust games (for example) don't produce trusting groups any more than brooms sweep floors.

† **trust**, *a. Obs.* Also 3–5 **trost**, 5 **truste**. See also TRAIST *a.*, TREST *a.*, TRIST *a.*[1] [Early ME. *trust* (*ū* or *ŭ*), app.:—OE. **trust* (*ū* or *ŭ*) (not recorded, evidently not WSax.), simple grade of which ON. *traustr* 'strong, firm, secure, trusty', is an ablaut grade (*trust, treust, traust*); thence ME. *trust* and *trost*; the rare *trist* was app. assimilated to TRIST *v.*]

1. Confident, safe, secure, sure.

c **1200** [implied in TRUSTLY 1]. **12..** *Ancr. R.* 66 To sum gostliche monne þat ȝe beoð strusti uppen [*MS. Titus*, þat ȝe arn trust on]. *a* **1425** *Cursor M.* 2573 (Trin.) Be trust in þis þat I þe hiȝt. *Ibid.* 11161 Be truste & in no deewrynes.

2. Faithful, trusty; reliable, sound.

c **1440** *Jacob's Well* 212 3if þou selle a crokyd hors for a clene, a ruynous hows for trust hows.

β. *c* **1330** R. BRUNNE *Chron.* (1810) 60 His sonnes boþe tille him war trost als stele. ?**13..** *Adultery* 102 in Herrig's

Archiv LXXIX. 420 Sche was..bothe trost & trewe. **1389** in *Eng. Gilds* (1870) 46 An Aldirman..; and foure skeuaynes, trost men and trewe. *c* **1425** *Cast. Persev.* 477 in *Macro Plays* 91 If he wyl be trost & trye, he schal be kyng.

trust (trʌst), *v.* Also 3-5 **trusten,** (5 **trusty**), 5-6 **truste,** 5- **trust;** *β.* 4-5 **troste(n,** (4 **trosti**). Pa. t. and pple. **trusted,** (†**trust**). See also TRAIST *v.*, TREST *v.*, TRIST *v.* [Early ME. ad. ON. *treysta*, assimilated in ME. to TRUST, *trost*, *a.* and *sb.* Cf. Sw. *tröst* comfort, *trösta* to comfort, console, Norw. *trøste sig til* to confide in; OS. *trôstan*, MLG. *trôsten*, Du. *troosten*, OHG. *trôsten*, Ger. *trösten* (with the sense to comfort (cf. L. *fortis* strong), cheer, encourage): see TRUST *a.*]

1. a. *intr.* To have faith or confidence; to place reliance; to confide. Const. *in, to* (†*of, on, upon*).

a **1225** *Leg. Kath.* 503 þeo þ[e] ham makieð..& alle þ[e] on ham trusteð [*v.r.* trusten]. *a* **1240** *Lofsong* in *Cott. Hom.* 213 þeo hwile ðet ich truste uppo mon þu..lettest me al iwurden wið þeo þet ich truste uppon. **1297** R. GLOUC. (Rolls) 9606 So muche he truste on him, þat in is warde he let do Henri is eldoste sone. *a* **1425** *Cursor M.* 4962 (Trin.) In oþere helpe me truste I nouȝt. *a* **1500** *Sir Beues* (Pynson) 3270 Moche he trusted in Arundel. **1560** ABP. PARKER *Let. to Bp. Grindal* 18 Nov., Trusting of your lordship's good diligence herein. **1638** *Hamilton Papers* (Camden) 9, I trust in God to keipe them a sunder. **1656** H. PHILLIPS *Purch. Patt.* (1676) 3 Though the man..have the repute of an honest man, yet trust not too much upon that. **1706** E. WARD *Wooden World Diss.* (1708) 50 He trusts much more to the Sun, for his Guide, than to the Creator of it. **1791** CHARLOTTE SMITH *Celestina* (ed. 2) III. 22 She trusted on the long tried, the long assured tenderness of her lover. **1860** TYNDALL *Glac.* I. xvi. 112 Each had to trust to himself.

β. *c* **1330** R. BRUNNE *Chron.* (1810) 45 Bliþely tille Inglond wild he com..If he myght on þam troste. *c* **1394** *P. Pl. Crede* 350 þei ben certayne men & syker on to trosten. *c* **1440** *Promp. Parv.* 503/1 Troston, *confido*.

b. Imperative: an instruction given to a dog, requiring it to wait for a reward, usu. in a begging position with a titbit placed on its nose. Cf. TRUST *sb.* 5 e.

1854, etc. [see PAID *ppl. a.* 4 a]. **1921** W. DE LA MARE *Mem. Midget* xlix. 331 Finger and thumb outstretched above the cringing little dog... 'Trust, Plum, trust!' **1930** M. ALLINGHAM *Mystery Mile* xiv. 132, I put a bit of sugar on his nose and said 'Trust'. **1974** G. BUTLER *Coffin for Canary* ix. 104 David was throwing him biscuits as to an old dog and saying 'trust'.

2. a. *trans.* To have faith or confidence in; to rely or depend upon.

c **1374** CHAUCER *Anel. & Arc.* 91 She him trustith aboue eche creature. **1491** *Act 7 Hen. VII*, c. 22 *Preamble*, Ye may send John Aleyne of Pole whom ye trust and y also. **1560** DAUS tr. *Sleidane's Comm.* 165 b, He woulde not retourne to his Prince, for that he trusted hym no more. **1572** *Satir. Poems Reform.* xxxiv. 24 For Lordis and Lairdes ar nather Just Nor ȝit the communis to be trust. **1687** A. LOVELL tr. *Thevenot's Trav.* I. 74 He desired the command of a Ship, but they would not trust him so much. **1756** C. SMART tr. *Horace, Sat.* II. iv. (1826) II. 133 The mushrooms, that grow in meadows, are of the best kind: all others are dangerously trusted. **1827** SCOTT *Highl. Widow* iv, He has trusted me, and I will trust him. **1874** RUSKIN *Fors Clav.* xxxvii. 17, I cannot trust other people, without perpetual looking after them.

β. **1382** WYCLIF *Isa.* xxxvi. 4 What is this trist, that thou trostest? *c* **1394** *P. Pl. Crede* 237 For sich a certeyn man syker wold y trosten. *c* **1400** *Apol. Loll.* 45 If þei lofid & trostid Him aboue þe wark of þer hondis.

b. Imperative, used sarcastically or ironically to express one's assurance that a person will or will not do something. *colloq.* (Cf. CATCH *v.* 40.)

1834 L. RITCHIE *Wand. by Seine* 67 If a woman is in danger from the rain, whose umbrella..is at her service? The Frenchman's? Trust him! **1902** R. BAGOT *Donna Diana* vi, Trust a religious old maid for scenting out love!

3. a. To have faith or confidence *that* something desired is, or will be, the case; also const. with *infin.* or *for*; to hope.

1482 *Cely Papers* (Camden) 124 Howr mother and whe ar in good heyll, thankyd be God, and so we truste that ȝe be. *c* **1500** *New Not-br. Mayd* xxxix, Trustying to shewe..That men have an yll use..women to blame. **1518** HEN. VIII in *State Papers* I. 1, I trust the Quene my Wyfe be with chylde. **1603** SHAKS. *Meas. for M.* III. i. 271, I trust it will grow to a most prosperous perfection. *a* **1648** LD. HERBERT *Hen. VIII* (1683) 466 We should not trust to obtain at their [Saints'] hands that which is to be had only of God. **1781** BURKE *Corr.* (1844) II. 445, I trust that these things are wholly repugnant to my nature, and inconsistent with my principles. **1857** T. MOORE *Handbk. Brit. Ferns* (ed. 3) Pref., The author..trusts for a continuance of similar communications. **1880** SWINBURNE *Stud. Shaks.* 307 He trusted to establish the secret history and import of each.

β. **1389** in *Eng. Gilds* (1870) 53 Oure godes [we] han dispent..; no catelle kepende,—trostende, as children, withe ȝiftes to ben amendyd. **1451** CAPGRAVE *Life St. Gilbert* 90 Trostand for þis obediens to receyue sumtyme þe mor mede.

†**b.** with simple object: To hope for, look for. *Obs. rare*$^{-1}$.

1523 LD. BERNERS *Froiss.* I. cxlvi. 174 We truste in hym somoche gentylnesse, that by the grace of god his purpose shall chaung.

4. To give credence to, believe (a statement); to rely upon the veracity or evidence of (a person, etc.).

? *a* **1366** CHAUCER *Rom. Rose* 649 So faire it was, that, trusteth wel, It semede a place espirituel. **1586** A. DAY *Eng. Secretary* II. (1625) 26 Trust me I am vnused to these deuices. **1632** LITHGOW *Trav.* III. 85 Trust me, I told..at one time, and within my sight, some 67. Villages. **1697** DRYDEN *Virg. Georg.* III. 601 'Twas thus with Fleeces milky white (if we May trust Report,) Pan God of Arcady Did bribe thee Cynthia. *a* **1806** BP. HORSLEY *Serm.* (1816) III. xlii. 262 Every man implicitly trusts his bodily senses concerning external objects placed at a convenient distance. **1871** FREEMAN *Norm. Conq.* IV. xviii. 286 If the tale is to be trusted, the ford must be looked for in the hilly country.

β. **1399** LANGL. *Rich. Redeles* I. 102 Ffor trostiþ rith treuly ..All þat þey moued..Was to be sure of hem-self. *c* **1440** *Generydes* 1624 Troste me wele it goo not as ye wene.

5. To commit the safety of (something) with confidence *to* a place, etc., *to* or *with* a person; to entrust; to place or allow (a person or thing) to be *in* a place or condition, or *to do* some action, with expectation of safety, or without fear of the consequences.

1340 *Ayenb.* 241 þanne þe angel zayde to lot..'ne trost þe naȝt ine þe stede þet þou hest ylete'. *c* **1440** *York Myst.* xxxii. 322 As touchyng þis money..Tite truste it tille oure tresorie. **1596** SHAKS. *Merch. V.* I. i. 42 My ventures are not in one bottome trusted. **1617** MORYSON *Itin.* III. 1 Neither would I aduise Angelica..to trust her self alone..to the protection of wandering Knights. **1667** MILTON *P.L.* XII. 133 Not wandring poor, but trusting all his wealth With God. **1748** *Anson's Voy.* II. xi. 254 The Spaniards never trust the silver without an armed force to protect it. **1781** GIBBON *Decl. & F.* xxii. (1869) I. 626 He trusted the event to valour and to fortune. **1819** SCOTT *Ivanhoe* xxv, The Jewish maiden will rather trust her soul with God, than her honour to the Templar! **1908** R. BAGOT *A. Cuthbert* vi, Afraid to trust herself to a retort, [she] walked out of the room.

6. To invest *with* a charge; to confide or entrust something to the care or disposal of.

1548 UDALL, etc. *Erasm. Par. Matt.* xxiv. 96 The mayster hauynge a tryall of his trustines, wyll be bolde to truste hym with greater thynges. **1598** SHAKS. *Merry W.* II. ii. 316, I will rather trust a Fleming with my butter,..then my wife with her selfe. **1651** HOBBES *Leviath.* II. xix. 98 To keep those that had trusted him with the Government [etc.]. **1718** *Free-thinker* No. 16 ¶4 They should never trust him with a Lighted Candle again. **1789** J. MOORE *Zeluco* (1797) II. lxviii. 189 She was still afraid to trust her voice with words. **1828** SCOTT *F.M. Perth* vii, Let us meet at the East Port;.. if it is your pleasure..to trust us with the matter. **1884** CHURCH *Bacon* ix. 223 English seemed to him too homely to express the hopes of the world, too unstable to be trusted with them.

7. a. To give (a person) credit *for* goods supplied; †to supply *with* goods on credit (*obs.*); also, †to supply (goods) to a person on credit (*obs.*): see CREDIT *sb.* 9 a.

1530 PALSGR. 763/2, I truste a dettoure..No man wyll trust me, except I have redy money. **1541** *Act 33 Hen. VIII*, c. 15 Straungers..vsed to credite and truste the pore inhabitauntes..which..had not redy money to pay in hand. **1648** CROMWELL *Lett.* 25 Nov., Without money the stubborn townspeople will not trust them for the worth of a penny. **1678** in Fountainhall *Decis.* (1759) I. 7 The prices of such..goods as were trusted by him. *a* **1687** PETTY *Pol. Arith.* (1690) 113 Any Tradesman of good Reputation worth 500*l.* will be trusted with above 1000*l.* worth of Commodities. **1775** *Pennsylvania Even. Post* 13 July 301/2 All persons are forbid to trust my Wife Sarah, as I will pay no debts of her contracting after this date.

b. *absol.* or *intr.*

1718 *Free-thinker* No. 152 ¶5 My Dealing being in the Retail Way, I trusted little. **1818** SCOTT *Br. Lamm.* xii, The brewster's wife—she had trusted long, and the bill was aye scored up.

†**8.** *trans.* To place (a person) in trust *with* property; to make a trustee of. *Obs. rare*$^{-1}$.

1670 *Act 22 Chas. II*, c. 12 §2 All such persons that are or shall be enfeoffed or trusted with any such Lands shall lett them to farme [etc.].

Hence **'trusted** *ppl. a.*; whence **'trustedly** *adv.* (*rare*).

1450 W. LOMNER in *Four C. Eng. Lett.* (1880) 3 The queche spynner he sente with certeyn letters to certyn of his trustid men. **1784** COWPER *Task* III. 650 Ere he gives The beds the trusted treasure of their seeds. **1816** SOUTHEY *Lay Laureate* lxxviii, Shall she not then diffuse the word of Heaven Through all the regions of her trusted reign? **1856** RUSKIN *Mod. Paint.* IV. v. xi. §9 The gateless path turns trustedly aside. **1875** JOWETT *Plato* (ed. 2) I. 467 Within the circle of his own most trusted friends.

trust, obs. f. *trussed*, pa. t. and pple. of TRUSS *v.*

trustable ('trʌstəb(ə)l), *a.* (In 7 -ible.) [f. TRUST *v.* + -ABLE.] That may be trusted, trustworthy.

1606 *Sir G. Goosecappe* I. ii. in Bullen *O. Pl.* III. 14 We might have tickled the vanity out an howre longer, if my watch be trustible. **1884** EDNA LYALL *We Two* viii, At least one trustable, sympathetic person had been with her mother at the last. *Ibid.*, Jesus Christ..is the most perfectly loveable and trustable Being I know. **1900** A. BLACK *Evening & Morn.* iii. 83 They are trusting all that men have found to be trustable.

trustee (trʌs'tiː), *sb.* Also 7 *Sc.* **trustie.** [f. TRUST *v.* + -EE[1].]

1. One who is trusted, or to whom something is entrusted; a person in whom confidence is put. *rare. Obs.*, or merged in 3.

1647 R. STAPYLTON *Juvenal* xiii. 249 It was the custome, when any person trusting would put his trustee to his oath, to bring him into the temple, and to make him sweare. **1652** J. WRIGHT tr. Camus' Nat. Paradox I. 9 It was to change her child, in case shee were brought to bed of a girle, Cleorite (her Trustee) took the business upon her. **1671** [R. MACWARD] *True Nonconf.* 132 Suppose..the exact fidelity of the one trustie, to be notourly known. **1824** BENTHAM *Bk. Fallacies* Wks. 1843 II. 413 In every public trust, the legislator should, for the purpose of prevention, suppose the trustee disposed to break the trust in every imaginable way in which it would be possible for him to reap..any personal advantage.

2. *Law. spec.* One to whom property is entrusted to be administered for the benefit of another; often *loosely*, one of a number of persons appointed to manage the affairs of an institution; also a member of the controlling body of a trust (TRUST *sb.* 7 b).

1653 W. RAMESEY *Astrol. Restored* IV. xiv. 331 Scribes and Secretaries shall suffer detriment, and..Trustees [etc.]. **1686** tr. *Chardin's Trav. Persia* 386 The fourscore Pounds have bin since converted to other uses, through the Covetousness of the Trustees. **1695-6** *Act 7 & 8 Will. III*, c. 30 §40 One Annuity..payable out of the Profittes..unto the most Noble Barbara Dutchesse of Cleveland or to her Trustees. **1782** PRIESTLEY *Corrupt. Chr.* II. x. 243 A clergyman could not..be..trustee to a child. **1818** CRUISE *Digest* (ed. 2) VI. 333 Sir R. Worsley being seised in fee of the premises in question, devised them to trustees, upon trust that they should stand seised thereof to the use of his grandson. **1846** MᶜCULLOCH *Acc. Brit. Empire* (1854) II. 53 By these Acts the administration of all matters relating to the roads is vested in trustees. **1891** E. PEACOCK *N. Brendon* I. 295, I am trustee for her property. **1902** *Fabian News* XII. 38/2 Any attempt of a trustee of a corporation or trust to make a secret profit out of his position..should be punished.

b. In *U.S.* by extension, One in whose hands the property of a debtor is attached in a *trustee process* (see 4 and quots.).

[Cf. **1758** *Stat. Massachusetts* (1814) 614 Be it..enacted, that where no goods or effects of such absent or absconding person in the hands of his attorney, factor, agent or trustee, ..can be come at so as to be attached [etc.]. **1794** *Stat. Massachusetts* c. 65 §1 The goods, effects and credits of the principal, in the hands and possession of his trustee or trustees,..shall stand bound and be held to satisfy such judgment as the plaintiff shall recover against the principal.] **1811** W. C. WHITE *Compend. Laws Massachusetts* 1268 In this state there is a process given by statute..whereby a creditor may attach any property or credits of his debtor in the hands of a third person. This third person is called in the English law, the *garnishee*: in our law he is called the *trustee*. **1864** in WEBSTER.

3. *transf.* One who is held responsible for the preservation and administration of anything.

1655 JER. TAYLOR *Unum Necess.* ix. §4. 620 The Trustees and Stewards of the mysteries of God. **1682** DRYDEN *Medal* Ep. Whigs ¶2 You are not the trustees of the public liberty. **1746-7** HERVEY *Medit.* (1767) I. 10 These dumb Monitors.. had received a Charge to preserve their Names, and were the remaining Trustees of their Memory. **1897** T. F. BAYARD in *Daily News* 3 Mar. 10/4 The recognised trustees of the world's advancement and civilization.

4. *attrib.* and *Comb.*, as ***trustee investor***, ***meeting***; also **trustee bank** (in full **trustee savings bank**): see SAVINGS BANK; so **trustee banker; trustee investment**: see *trustee stock*; **trustee process,** in *U.S.*, a judicial process by which the goods, effects, and credits (but not the real estate) of a debtor may be attached while in the hands of a third person; in Eng. Law called *foreign attachment*; **trustee security, trustee stock** = *trust-stock* (TRUST *sb.* 8 b).

1898 *Westm. Gaz.* 9 Nov. 10/1 At that time [1861] there were 638 *trustee banks in existence. **1903** *Ibid.* 11 Mar. 5/1 As for the great *trustee bankers, they are not in the least affected. **1895** *Daily News* 30 Dec. 2/2 'A gilt-edge security' or 'quite a *trustee investment'. **1906** *Westm. Gaz.* 17 Sept. 3/2 Neither of these advantages affects the private or *trustee investor. **1820** SCOTT *Monast.* Introd. Ep., The laird..had to attend *trustee meetings, and lieutenancy meetings,..and what not. **1811** W. C. WHITE *Compend. Laws Massachusetts* 1268 In what cases, and against whom, a *trustee process will lie. **18..** *Laws Massachusetts* (Bartlett), The suit may be commenced by the process of foreign attachment, or trustee process. **1860** in BARTLETT *Dict. Amer.* s.v. **1898** *Westm. Gaz.* 18 Nov. 8/1 The new capital required will be raised jointly..and will be a *trustee security. **1901** *Ibid.* 29 Aug. 7/1 The failure of the issue..to be classed as a *Trustee stock.

Hence **trus'teeism** (*nonce-wd.*), the system of vesting (church) patronage in trustees.

1889 A. H. DRYSDALE *Hist. Presbyt. Eng.* 511 The evils of both family patronage and trusteeism. **1889** *Tablet* 30 Nov. 878 A system of lay trusteeism.

trustee (trʌs'tiː), *v.* [f. prec. sb.]

1. a. *trans.* To place (a person or his property) in the hands of a trustee or trustees. **b.** *intr.* To act as a trustee. *nonce-uses.*

1818 BLACKW. MAG. III. 518 In my younger days, country gentlemen..made a shift to continue in the management of their own affairs..; but now the prevailing fashion, or rather passion is to get Trusteed with all possible expedition. **1909** *Ibid.* Sept. 413/2 Trusteeing is an unprofitable business.

2. *U.S.* **a.** To appoint (a person) trustee in the *trustee process* (see prec. 4), in order to restrain a debtor from collecting moneys due to him. **b.** To attach (effects of a debtor) in the hands of a third person.

1883 HOWELLS *Woman's Reason* I. ix. 164 You don't say you never was *trusteed* before? *Ibid.* 165 When they sent in their bill,..I didn't believe they'd really go so far as to trustee me. *Ibid.*, I presume they'll be trusteein' all of you. I shall have to pay it now. **1898** *Westm. Gaz.* 14 June 7/1 Yesterday his options were hastily closed, and his cash wheat trusteed.

Hence **trus'teed** *ppl. a.* (in quot. *absol.*), **trus'teeing** *vbl. sb.*

1818 *Blackw. Mag.* III. 518 The trusteed..secures all the pleasure, as well as the profit,..entirely to himself. **1883**

HOWELLS *Woman's Reason* I. ix. 166 Do you think she liked your coming out about that trusteeing?

trusteeship (trʌsˈtiːʃɪp). [f. TRUSTEE *sb.* + -SHIP.] **1.** The office or function of a trustee; also, a body of trustees.

1730–6 BAILEY (folio), *Trustee-ship*, the office of a trustee. **1748** RICHARDSON *Clarissa* (1811) IV. vii. 36 To settle and give up my trusteeship is one of the principal motives of my leaving these parts. **1831** DISRAELI *Yng. Duke* III. vii, I have just had a note from Challoner, preliminary, I suppose, to my trusteeship. **1883** H. P. SPOFFORD in *Harper's Mag.* Aug. 459/2 He gave his wife the trusteeship of his diet. **1885** SIR J. PEARSON in *Law Times Rep.* LI. 902/1 The will contained a direction that any vacancy in the trusteeship should be filled up within a year. **1912** *Times* 19 Dec. 16/3 Directorates and voting trusteeships of various large banks, financial institutions, and corporations.

2. a. The function of a colonial power or other dominant people as protectors of a subject people.

1936 *Internat. Labour Rev.* June 856 Something must be done at once to remedy a state of affairs which..constitutes a flagrant breach of that ideal of trusteeship of Native races not yet able to stand by themselves under the strenuous conditions of the modern world. **1943** *Ann. Reg. 1942* 88 The old ideas of exploitation [of colonial possessions] had of recent years given place to the new doctrine of trusteeship. **1944** J. C. SMUTS in H. G. Wells *'42 to '44* II. 71, I remember Cecil Rhodes used to say that the proper relation between Whites and Blacks in this country [*sc.* S. Africa] was the relation between guardian and ward. This is the basis of trusteeship. Much later, this principle of trusteeship was put into the Covenant of the League of Nations. **1946** *Ann. Reg. 1945* 9 The whole House was committed to the doctrine of trusteeship, and beyond that of partnership.

b. The administration of a territory by a nation acting on behalf of the United Nations Organization. Freq. *attrib.* Cf. *Trust Territory* s.v. TRUST *sb.* 8 b.

1945 *U.N. Charter* xii. §79, in *Times* 27 June 8/5 The terms of trusteeship for each territory..shall be agreed upon by the States directly concerned. **1946**, etc. [see MANDATE *sb.* 4 b]. **1952** *Times* 5 Aug. 3/7 The corporation is a Government-sponsored body set up by the Nigerian Government to develop 250,000 acres of plantations, formerly owned by Germans before the war, in the Cameroons territory, which was formerly under British mandate and is now under United Kingdom trusteeship. **1959** *Listener* 19 Nov. 880/1 The Belgian trusteeship territory of Ruanda-Urundi, Central Africa. **1962** *Observer* 14 Oct. 40/1 Sir Hugh Foot, Britain's representative in the United Nations on colonial and trusteeship questions, resigned.

†**trusten,** *v. Obs.* exc. *dial.* [irreg. f. TRUST *v.* + -EN[5].] = TRUST *v.* (Cf. TRISTEN.)

13.. *Metr. Hom.* (Vernon MS.) in Herrig's *Archiv* LVII. 288 Trustneþ not in ȝor wyues Ne in ȝour children. **13..** *Propr. Sanct.* ibid. LXXXI. 312/164 Tresur of seluer and of golde, He may not passe to heuene þen, Whil he trustneþ vppon hem. **1382** WYCLIF *Eph.* iii. 12 In whom we han trust and nyȝ comynge, in trustnynge [1388 tristenyng] by the feith of him. **1861** GEO. ELIOT *Silas M.* xvi, All as we've got to do is to trusten. **1895** [T. PINNOCK] *T. Brown's Black Country Ann.* (E.D.D.), If he trespasses on my ground, he knows what he's got to trusten to.

truster (ˈtrʌstə(r)). Also *technically* 7 -or. [f. TRUST *v.* + -ER[1].] One who trusts, confides, or relies; one who believes or credits; one who gives credit, a creditor.

1537 *Orig. & Sprynge Sectes* 42 Onely they y[t] be earnest trusters & beleuers in God are Christen men. **1602** SHAKS. *Ham.* I. ii. 172 Nor shall you doe mine eare that violence, To make it truster of your owne report Against your selfe. **1607** —— *Timon* IV. i. 10 Bankrupts..out with your Kniues, And cut your Trusters throates. **1649** W. BALL *Power of Kings* 5 It is against Reason..that such Trustees or Stewards should derive no Power from the People their Trustors. **1800** A. SWANSTON *Serm. & Lect.* I. 181 The trusters have been put to the severest trials. **1870** SPURGEON *Treas. Dav.* Ps. xl. 3 Through grace [they] shall receive faith and become trusters in Jehovah.

b. *Sc. Law. spec.* One who puts property in trust; correlative to TRUSTEE 2.

1675 in W. M. Morison *Dict. Decis.* (1807) 16173. **1741** *Ibid.* 16201 Where a trust does not arise from any deed or disposition of the truster, but from the voluntary interposition of the trustee [etc.]. **1838** W. BELL *Dict. Law Scot.* 1010 Where the truster had conveyed his whole estate, heritable and moveable, to trustees,..it was held [etc.]. **1885** *Law Rep. 10 App. Cas.* 452 The truster had a very large amount of personalty in Scotland.

trustful (ˈtrʌstfʊl), *a.* [f. TRUST *sb.* + -FUL I.] †**1.** Trustworthy, trusty, faithful. *Obs.*

1580 SIDNEY *Ps.* VII. i, O Lord, my God, Thou art my trustfull stay. **1582** STANYHURST *Æneis* I. (Arb.) 40 His gyde was trustful Achates. **1674** N. FAIRFAX *Bulk & Selv.* 189 The same most trustful witness that tells us when the world began [etc.].

2. Full of or exercising trust; trusting, confiding.

1832 [implied in TRUSTFULNESS]. **1834** LYTTON *Pompeii* III. iv, They went in their trustful thoughts far down the stream of time. **1850** TENNYSON *In Mem.* cix, The child would twine A trustful hand, unask'd, in thine. **1897** MARY KINGSLEY *W. Africa* xiv. 311, I am not of a trustful disposition.

Hence **ˈtrustfully** *adv.*, in a trustful manner.

1846 WORCESTER cites *Monthly Rev.* **1836** R. A. VAUGHAN *Mystics* (1860) I. VI. v. 314 *note*, Sorrow and joy, pain and pleasure, are trustfully accepted as alike coming from the hand of Love.

trustfulness (ˈtrʌstfʊlnɪs). [f. prec. + -NESS.] The quality of being trustful or confiding.

1832 LYTTON *Eugene A.* III. iii, There was a remarkable trustfulness in Madeline's disposition. **1864** DICKENS *Lett.* (1880) II. 213 Trustfulness is at the bottom of all social institutions. **1896** DK. ARGYLL *Philos. Belief* 411 A reasonable trustfulness in our fellow-men is..recognized as a virtue.

trustible, obs. form of TRUSTABLE.

trustify (ˈtrʌstɪfaɪ), *v. Commercial slang.* [f. TRUST *sb.* + -[I]FY.] *trans.* To make into a trust; to form a trust of or in (a business): see TRUST *sb.* 7 b. Only in *pa. pple.* and *ppl. a.* **ˈtrustified.** So **trustifiˈcation,** the formation of a trust.

1902 *Daily Chron.* 7 Jan. 3/1 Great American manufacturing concerns not yet trustified. **1902** *Fabian News* XII. 38/2 A somewhat novel danger in the trustification of industry. **1902** R. DONALD in *Westm. Gaz.* 12 June 1/3 Investors and speculators in the trustified interests. **1902** *Daily Record & Mail* 22 Feb. 4 More than half the capital, means of production, and distribution in the United States, are 'trustified' in one form or another. **1920** A. C. PIGOU *Econ. of Welfare* II. vii. 182 The marginal social net product of activities devoted to bringing about any widespread 'trustification' of industry is likely to be smaller than the marginal trade net product. **1922** *Encycl. Brit.* XXXII. 506/2 The large-scale and 'trustified' American capitalist system. **1938** L. HOGBEN *Science for Citizen* xiii. 653 Edison's later inventions sponsored the far-flung trustification of American industry. **1965** B. PEARCE tr. *Preobrazhensky's New Economics* 152 When there is trustification or syndication of important branches of production within a certain country, prices systematically.. deviate from value in the upward direction. **1969** P. WORSLEY in Ionescu & Gellner *Populism* 223 Petty farmers ..wanted a freer, more competitive, less trustified, market economy.

trustihood (ˈtrʌstɪhʊd). [f. TRUSTY *a.* + -HOOD; cf. *hardihood.*] The quality or condition of being trusty, trustiness.

1823 *Blackw. Mag.* XIII. 37 All are types of spotless purity, of maiden modesty, and trustyhood.

trustily (ˈtrʌstɪlɪ), *adv.* Also 5 trostili, -yly. [f. TRUSTY *a.* + -LY[2].] In a trusty manner.

†**1.** With trust or confidence; trustfully, confidently, hopefully, boldly. *Obs.*

c **1350** *Will. Palerne* 3904 þan turned þei titli aȝen & trustili gon fiȝt. **1382** WYCLIF *1 Sam.* xii. 11 He delyuerde ȝow fro the hoond of ȝoure enemyes bi enuyroun; and ȝe han dwellid trustily. *c* **1450** LOVELICH *Grail* l. 537 Trostily I beleve forsothe That God for my gilte nys not wrothe. **1485** CAXTON *Chas. Gt.* III. i. vi. 212 He shold come to hym peasybly & trustyly, with a fewe peple. **1573** TUSSER *Husb.* (1878) 17 To learne how foe to pacifie, But trust him not too trustilie. **1579** J. JONES *Preserv. Bodie & Soule* Ep. Ded. 4 Faith by the Charitie doth trustily water.

2. With fidelity or loyalty; faithfully.

c **1425** *Cast. Persev.* 635 in *Macro Plays* 96 Serue hym at honde Bothe nyth & day. *Voluptas.* Trostyly, lord, redy. **1583** GOLDING *Calvin on Deut.* Pref. 7 All such as behaue not themselues trustilie towards their neighbours. **1639** HORN & ROB. *Gate Lang. Unl.* lvi. §607 [Trustees] who, if they deale trustily.., make inventories. **1823** SCOTT *Quentin D.* xii, He would have borne a letter trustily enough.

†**3.** Truly, assuredly, certainly. *Obs.*

a **1425** *Langland's P. Pl.* C. IV. 498 (MS. F.) Trustilich [*v.r.* tristilich] a teonful text. *c* **1450** LOVELICH *Grail* liii. 262 For the I schal don More,..Trustylich, Symew, As I the Seye.

trustiness (ˈtrʌstɪnɪs). [f. as prec. + -NESS.] The quality of being trusty.

†**1.** Trustfulness, faith, confidence. *Obs.*

c **1557** ABP. PARKER *Ps.* xxxiii. 79 Extend O Lord thy gentlenesse, As we in thee have trustinesse. **1685** BAXTER *Paraphr. N.T., Gal.* v. 23 The Fruits of the Spirit..are Love to God and Men,..Trustiness and trusting God.

2. Fidelity, faithfulness, loyalty, trustworthiness.

1530 PALSGR. 283/2 Trustynesse, *fealte.* **1542** UDALL *Erasm. Apoph.* 329 b, Not so muche as any one poincte of diligence..or yet of trustynesse. **1592** tr. *Junius on Rev.* xv. 12 The girdle of gold was a sign of sincerity and trustines in taking in charge the commandments of God. **1652** LOVEDAY tr. *Calprenede's Cassandra* I. 41 Two servants, of whose trustinesse I was well assured. **1822** SCOTT *Nigel* viii, Her character for trustiness remained..unimpeached. **1868** G. STEPHENS *Runic Mon.* I. 259 Prof. Bugge was convinced of the intelligence and trustiness of the finder.

trusting (ˈtrʌstɪŋ), *vbl. sb.* [f. TRUST *v.* + -ING[1].] The action of the verb TRUST.

c **1440** *Jacob's Well* 288 Trustynge settyth a mannys herte faste in goodnes. **1526** *Pilgr. Perf.* (W. de W. 1531) 8 So moche trustynge in the cerimonyes of theyr lawe. **1573** TUSSER *Husb.* (1878) 106 Ill huswife..Through trusting of others hath this for hir fees. **1607** HIERON *Wks.* I. 301 There should be..a trusting to Him, an expecting saluation by His meanes. *a* **1771** GRAY *Dante* 17 Betray'd By trusting, and by Treachery slain. **1855** SINGLETON *Virgil* I. 22 There is no safe trusting to the bank.

ˈtrusting, *ppl. a.* [f. as prec. + -ING[2].] That trusts: see the verb.

c **1450** [implied in TRUSTINGLY]. **1545** ELYOT, *Fretus*, of *fruor*, trustyng. **1693** *Humours Town* 27 Believing Vintners, Tailors, Sempstresses, and the rest of the trusting Shopkeepers. **1707** PRIOR *Sat. Poets* 75 You've no Friend left, but trusting Landlady. **1790** HAN. MORE *Relig. Fash. World* (1791) 108 Unsuspecting goodness, and trusting honesty. **1816** BYRON *Parisina* v, She must lay her conscious head A husband's trusting heart beside. **1866** G. MACDONALD *Ann. Q. Neighb.* xxviii, He was of a kindly, gentle, trusting nature.

Hence **ˈtrustingly** *adv.*, in a trusting manner; **ˈtrustingness,** the quality of being trusting or trustful; trustfulness.

c **1450** tr. *De Imitatione* III. viii. 75 He..lasse *trustingly thynkyth or felvth of me þan it behoueþ. **1849** *Fraser's Mag.* XL. 645 Most firmly and trustingly do I believe. **1883** CON. F. WOOLSON *For the Major* iv, The person one loves becomes..trustingly dependent like a..child, upon one's.. care. **1820** L. HUNT *Indicator* No. 49 (1822) I. 386 Clearness of blood, freshness of perception, and *trustingness of heart. **1852** THACKERAY *Esmond* III. viii, Sure there is no bound to the trustingness of women.

trustle, variant of TRESTLE.

trustless (ˈtrʌstlɪs), *a.* [f. TRUST *sb.* + -LESS.]

1. Not to be trusted or relied upon; unfaithful, unreliable, treacherous, untrustworthy.

c **1530** H. RHODES *Bk. Nurture* 711 in *Babees Bk.* (1868) 101 To catche ech trustlesse traytor, see thou faythfull doe remayne. **1578** T. PROCTOR *Gorg. Gallery* B ij, A sternles ship amidst the trustles Seaes. **1603** FLORIO *Montaigne* II. xii. (1632) 320 A trustles and not to be beleeved voice. **1688–9** LADY R. RUSSELL *Lett.* (1819) II. 18 An unkind and trustless world it has been to us. **1797** ANNA SEWARD *Lett.* (1811) IV. 356 A melancholy instance of the trustless flattery of youth and prosperity. **1828** E. IRVING *Last Days* 81 Every juvenile delinquent,.. every trustless servant. **1858** H. SPENCER *Ess.* I. 308 We are constantly obliged to act out our inferences, trustless as they may be.

2. Having no trust or confidence; unbelieving, distrustful.

1598 YONG *Diana* 114, I was..so trustles and misconceiuing of my selfe, that I thought [etc.]. **1619** SIR J. SEMPILL *Sacrilege Handled* 81 Trustles Thomas must first put his finger in his side, and then beleeue. **1838** ELIZA COOK *Lines written at Midnight* x, I've learned to look With trustless eye on all and each. **1882** J. WALKER *Jaunt to Auld Reekie*, etc. 27 This trustless mammon-serving age.

Hence **ˈtrustlessness,** untrustworthy character, faithlessness; distrustfulness.

1825 LD. COCKBURN *Mem.* (1856) 324 Disclosing the trustlessness of town Councils..in their protected abuse of power. **1909** R. LAW *Tests Life* ix. 178 The sin and folly, the trustlessness and ingratitude of his children.

†**ˈtrustly,** *adv. Obs.* [f. TRUST *a.* + -LY[2].]

1. = TRUSTILY 1.

c **1200** *Trin. Coll. Hom.* 9 On swilch liflode we muȝen trustliche abiden ure louerd ihesu cristes tocume. *c* **1220** *Bestiary* 634 in *O.E. Misc.* 20 A tre he [the elephant] sekeð ..and leneð him trostlike ðer-bi. **1382** WYCLIF *Isa.* xiv. 30 And pore men trostly [Vulg. *fiducialiter*] shul resten. *a* **1400** HYLTON *Scala Perf.* (W. de W. 1494) I. xliv, Aske only salvacion bi vertue of this precious passion mekely and trustly, and wythoute dowte thou shal haue it. *c* **1440** *Promp. Parv.* 503/1 Trostly, or sekyrly, *confidenter.*

2. Certainly, surely; = TRUSTILY 3.

c **1320** R. BRUNNE *Medit.* 1107 Beeþ of gode cumfort, for trustly y say, We shullen hym se. **1426** LYDG. *De Guil. Pilgr.* 14831 And trustly..I am hys douhter.

trustor: see TRUSTER.

trustworthy (ˈtrʌstˌwɜːðɪ), *a.* [f. TRUST *sb.* + WORTHY *a.*] Worthy of trust or confidence; reliable.

1808 [implied in TRUSTWORTHINESS]. **1829** LYTTON *Devereux* VI. iii, Anselmo..was a trustworthy man. **1855** MACAULAY *Hist. Eng.* xiv. III. 442 The most trustworthy comment on the text of the Gospels and Epistles is to be found in the practice of the primitive Christians. **1874** RUSKIN *Fors Clav.* IV. xliii. 139 Whatever is set down in *Fors* for you is assuredly true,..—trustworthy to the uttermost,—however strange. **1889** GRETTON *Memory's Harkb.* 313 Because he trusted them, they proved themselves trustworthy.

Hence **ˈtrustˌworthily** *adv.*, **ˈtrustˌworthiness.**

1851–9 MALLET in *Man. Sci. Eng.* 355 Alterations of level may be *trustworthily evidenced by changes of depth or run of water. **1870** *Daily News* 14 Dec., I am trustworthily informed that [etc.]. **1893** W. C. WILKINSON in Barrows *Parl. Relig.* II. 1247 The religion that can trustworthily offer to save. **1808** *Edin. Rev.* July 478 The cardinal virtue..of historic composition,—*trustworthiness. **1879** *Cassell's Techn. Educ.* IV. 399/2 The trustworthiness of mild steel. **1885** CLODD *Myths & Dr.* I. vii. 115 Criticism is testing without fear or favour the trustworthiness of records of the past.

trusty (ˈtrʌstɪ), *a.* and *sb.* Also 3–5 trusti, 5–7 -ie, 6 -ye; 5 trosty. [f. TRUST *a.* + -Y[1].]

A. *adj.* **1.** Characterized by trust; having faith, confidence, or assurance; trustful, confident. Now *rare.*

a **1225** *Ancr. R.* 334 ȝif þu ert to trusti, & holdest God to nesche uorto awreken sunne. *c* **1230** *Hali Meid.* 45 Ne beo þu nawt tu trusti ane to þi meidenhad. *a* **1425** *Cursor M.* 3272 (Trin.) Lord..graunte me..Trusti to be of my preyere. *c* **1460** METHAM *Wks.* (E.E.T.S.) 90 Yf sqwyche lynys..pase thorw the tryangyl or by the tryangyl, yt sygnyfyith a trosty persone and a louyng. **1541** WYATT *Let.* Wks. (1861) p. xxiv, If in these matters I have presumed to be trusty more than I was trusted, surely the zeal of the King's service drove me to it. **1616** R. C. *Times' Whistle*, etc. (E.E.T.S.) 115 He wilbe..Apt to deceive even his most trusty friend. **1908** *Times* 28 July 4/1 A very intimate and trusty friendship sprang up between them.

2. a. Characterized by faithfulness or reliability; that may be trusted or relied upon; trustworthy.

In letters of the sovereign to subjects, ***Our trusty and well-beloved*** takes the place of L. *dilecto et fideli nostro*, before the names of the addressees. Privy Councillors are addressed as *Right trusty and well-beloved.*

a **1310** in Wright *Lyric P.* xv. (Percy Soc.) 47 Trusti kyng ant trewe in trone. **1432** LD. SCROPE in *Plumpton Corr.*

(Camden) p. xxxvi, Trusty & wellbeloved, I greet you wel. *c* **1440** *Promp. Parv.* 503/1 Trosty, sekyr, *fidus, fidelis.* **1511–12** *Act 3 Hen. VIII*, c. 23 §3 Billes signed..with the hande of the Kinges trusty servaunt John Heron. **1577** B. GOOGE *Heresbach's Husb.* III. (1586) 114 The Horse..the trustiest beast that we vse in our seruice. **1615** W. LAWSON *Country Housew. Gard.* (1626) 17 Euery Gardiner is not trusty to sell you good fruit. **1674** [see RIGHT *adv.* 9 c]. **1726** SWIFT *Gulliver* I. vii, A trusty servant. **1803** in *Nairne Peerage Evid.* (1874) 113 Our right trusty and wellbeloved George baron Keith. **1838** THIRLWALL *Greece* II. xvi. 369 He..sent a trusty messenger to Xerxes, to claim the merit of this service. **1877** J. D. CHAMBERS *Div. Worship* 230 It should be carried to the mill by a trusty person.

(*b*) *spec.* designating a well-conducted convict to whom special privileges are granted. orig. *U.S.*

1856 *Democratic State Jrnl.* (Sacramento, Calif.) 28 Oct. 2/3 The 'trusty guards', (commanded by Pete, Scotty acting as first lieutenant,) have recovered from the effects of their stolen debauch of Saturday. **1926** J. BLACK *You can't Win* iv. 40 A trusty prisoner appeared at my side. 'Come on, you.' **1968** *Listener* 15 Feb. 209/2 At this prison, the 200 guards are all trusty prisoners.

b. *transf.* and *fig.* of things.

1596 SPENSER *F.Q.* VI. vii. 25 His trustie sword, the servant of his might. **1697** DRYDEN *Æneid* VII. 886 The neighing steeds are to the chariots tied, The trusty weapon sits on ev'ry side. **1706** E. WARD *Wooden World Diss.* (1708) 73 One of the most trusty Timbers of the Common-wealth. **1782** COWPER *Gilpin* 63 My leathern belt..In which I bear my trusty sword. **1890** R. BRIDGES *Elegy*, Poems (1912) 239 Her trusty window open wide.

B. *sb.* **a.** One who (or that which) is trusty; a trustworthy person; *spec.* orig. in *U.S.*, a well-conducted convict to whom special privileges are granted.

1573 TUSSER *Husb.* (1878) 62 Get trustie to tend them [cattle], not lubberlie squire. *Ibid.* 124 Reape corne by the day,..By great is the cheaper, if trustie were reaper. **1756** TOLDERVY *Hist. 2 Orphans* II. 140 Why gentlemen, [answered the landlord], your old trusty there, parts with his money, and cries for it again. **1855** *San Francisco Citizen* 2 Oct. 2/3 Two 'trusties' named Scottie and Greene, escaped in a whale boat from the State Prison grounds on Sunday night. **1889** *Century Mag.* Jan. 448/1 The 'trusties' are often domesticated upon ranches near the town. **1892** *Pall Mall G.* 15 Nov. 2/3 Martin left his camp in charge of various captains—generally assisted by 'trusties', that is, well-behaved convicts, who were found to be the cruellest taskmasters. **1912** in J. SANDILANDS *Western Canad. Dict. & Phrase-Bk.* **1926** J. BLACK *You can't Win* iv. 38 He told me to stay there till he could get a 'trusty' to take me upstairs. **1958** *People* 4 May 6/4 He was a trustie working in our records office. **1963** T. & P. MORRIS *Pentonville* ii. 27 The 'outside' men who go beyond the prison walls are selected 'trusties'. **1969** *Telegraph* (Brisbane) 29 May 2/7 (*heading*) Trusties plan no trouble. **1973** R. TRAVERS *Murder in Blue Mountains* x. 100 The Chief of Police banned all general visitors to Butler's cell and a trusty was put in with him to guard against any attempt at suicide.

b. *local Irish.* A great coat.

1804 MAR. EDGEWORTH *Limerick Gloves* vii, 'There was a sort of a frieze trusty'. 'A trusty!' said Mr. Hill, 'what is that, pray?' 'A big coat, sure, plase your honour'. **1837–8** J. KEEGAN *Leg. & Poems* (1907) 4 He thrust his hands into the ample pockets of his 'trusty', which was closely buttoned round his waist. **1846** *Ibid.* 365 He opened his white frieze trusty.

†**trut**, *int. Obs.* An ejaculation of contempt.

c **1330** R. BRUNNE *Chron.* (1810) 317 A foule herlote him slowe, trut for his renoun. *c* **1440** *Promp. Parv.* 505/1 Trut, or ptrot, skornefulle word (*S.,A.*, thprut), *vath.*

truth (truːθ), *sb.* Forms: α. 1 **triewþ, treowþ, trywþ**, 2 **treothe**, 2–3 **treouþe**, 2–4 **trewþe**, 2–5 **treuthe**, 3 **treowthe, treoþe, (treweiðe)**, 3–5 **treuþe**, 4 **treuþ, (tryuþe, treweþe, -ethe, trewht,** *Sc.* **treutht, trewcht**, 4–5 *Sc.* **trewtht)**, 4–6 **trewth(e**, 4–7 **treuth**, 5 **trewþ, (treut, truyt, þreuth, treweth**, 6 **trewith, -ythe, troeuth, treugth)**. β. 3–4 **truþe**, 4 **truþ**, 4–7 **truthe**, (5 **truwþe, trwth)**, 6–7 **trueth**, 4– **truth**. [OE. *tríewþ, tréowþ, trýwþ*, ME. *trewþe, treuþ(e*, f. OE. *triewe* adj., TRUE: see -TH[1]. Cf. OHG. *triuwida*, ON. *tryggð.*

The β-forms perh. show a different ablaut grade, *u* beside *eu, eo*, whence OE. *trúwa, trúa*, faith, good faith (see TRUCE), *trúwian* to TROW, trust, confide, and ON. *trúr* true; but, as *trūþ* does not appear before the 13th c., when *u* and *eu* (*ew*) in other words had phonetically fallen together, it is possible that ME. *truthe* really comes from OE. *treowþe*. See also TROTH.]

I. The quality of being true (and allied senses).

1. a. The character of being, or disposition to be, true to a person, principle, cause, etc.; faithfulness, fidelity, loyalty, constancy, steadfast allegiance. (See also TROTH 1.) Now *rare* or *arch.*

α. *c* **893** K. ÆLFRED *Oros.* v. ii. §6 Þær dydon þeah Romane lytla triewþa. *c* **1000** ÆLFRIC *On Old Test.* (Gr.) 1 Heora ʒemynd þurhwunað..for..heora trywðe wið god. *c* **1200** *Vices & Virtues* 103 For ðare gode trewðe ðe ðu him bere. *c* **1290** *S. Eng. Leg.* I. 98/203 Bi þe treuþe þat i schal to Mahon. *c* **1390** CHAUCER *Compl. Damours* 7 On hir,..Which hath on me no mercy ne no rewthe That love hir best, but sleeth me for my trewthe. *c* **1470** HENRY *Wallace* III. 274, I knaw he will do mekill for his kyne; Gentryss and trewtht ay restis him within. *c* **1560** A. SCOTT *Poems* (S.T.S.) xxvi. 33 Thay wald be rewit, and hes no rewth;..Thay wald be trowit, and hes no trewth.

β. **1530** PALSGR. 283/2 Truthe, *uerite, loialte.* **1568** GRAFTON *Chron.* II. 729 The king had alwayes known his truth and fidelitie towarde the crowne of Fraunce. **1611** SHAKS. *Cymb.* V. v. 107 Briefely dye their ioyes, That place them on the truth of Gyrles, and Boyes. **1719** *Free-thinker* No. 137. ¶6 Lucius..preserving still his Truth to Marcia. **1800** COLERIDGE *Christabel* II. 78 Alas! they had been friends in youth; But whispering tongues can poison truth. **1860** RUSKIN *Mod. Paint.* V. IX. xii. 345 Truth to himself; that is to say, the resolution to do his duty by his art.

†**b.** *by my truth*, as an asseveration. (Cf. TROTH 1 b.) *Obs.*

13.. *Guy Warw.* (A.) 405 Bi mi trewþe y schal þe swere, Schal y mi fader þe tiding bere. **1563** in *Child-Marriages* 59 [He] promysed, bie his faith and treuth, that [etc.]. **1605** CAMDEN *Rem.* 222 By my treuth, wife (quoth he) [etc.].

†**2. a.** One's faith or loyalty as pledged in a promise or agreement; a solemn engagement or promise, a covenant: = TROTH 2. *Obs.*

α. *c* **1000** ÆLFRIC *Exod.* vi. 5 Ic ʒemunde minra treowþa þe ic Abrahame behet. **1154** *O.E. Chron.* an. 1137 Hi hadden him manred maked & athes suoren, ac hi nan treuthe ne heolden, alle he wæron forsworen & here treothes forloren. *c* **1205** LAY. 10631 Heo sworen..& treoðen heo plihten [*c* **1275** treuþe him plihte]. **1297** R. GLOUC. (Rolls) 3584 Þis luþer saxons abbeþ gret dedeyn Vor to holde me treuþe. *a* **1330** *Otuel* 311 Selpe me gode.., Eiþer oþer his trewþe pliȝte, Vppon morwen for to fiȝte. *c* **1400** *Laud Troy Bk.* 877 My trewthe .I. layd, To do al as thow hast sayd. **1460** CAPGRAVE *Chron.* (Rolls) 182 He cursed the Kyng of Scottis for brekyng of his treuth, whech he had mad to the Englisch Kyng. *a* **1572** KNOX *Hist. Ref.* Wks. 1846 I. 183 To the end, that under treuth thei mycht eyther gett the Castell betrayed, or elles some principall men..tackin at unwarres. β. *c* **1450** METHAM *Wks.* (E.E.T.S.) 42/1114 To serue yow be-ffore alle odyr my trwth I plyght. ? **16..** *Young Beichan* xiii. in Child *Ballads* II. (1884) 470 I'll give thee the truth of my right hand, The truth of it I'll freely gie.

b. *spec.* in reference to marriage; also, in quot. *a* 1300, betrothal. *Obs.*

α. *c* **1275** LAY. 2251 Locrin was on foreward Hire habbe to wife And he hire hafde treouþe i-pliȝt.

β. *a* **1300** *K. Horn* 674 Muchel was þe ruþe þat was at þare truþe. *c* **1440** *Gesta Rom.* xii. 37 (Harl. MS.) The maide saide, she wold consent; and þer they pliȝt hire truthe.

†**3. a.** Faith, trust, confidence. (Cf. TROTH 3 a.) *Obs.*

α. *a* **1300** *Cursor M.* 14072 (Cott.) Þi mikel treuth Has þe saued. **1375** BARBOUR *Bruce* IV. 223 (Cambr. MS.) He wes fule,..That gaf treuth [*Edin. MS.* throuth; *ed.* 1620 traist] to that Creature.

β. **13..** *Cursor M.* 21406 Thoru þair stedfast truth in dright. **1677** MARVELL *Corr.* Wks. (Grosart) II. 552 You shall not repent any truth you repose in me.

b. Belief; a formula of belief, a creed. (Cf. TROTH 3 b.) *Obs.*

13.. *Cursor M.* 4246 (Gött.) Putyfar..held ioseph in mensk and lare Al þou þair treuthes sundri ware. **1456** SIR G. HAYE *Law Arms* (S.T.S.) 8 The hard hertis, and untrewe treuth of the pagans. **1500–20** DUNBAR *Poems* ix. 57 The Articulis of Trewth,—in God to trow,..And in his haly blissit Sone, Jesu.

4. Disposition to speak or act truly or without deceit; truthfulness, veracity, sincerity; formerly sometimes in wider sense: Honesty, uprightness, righteousness, virtue, integrity.

α. **13..** *Cursor M.* 13891 (Cott.) Þat neuer leigh, ne neuer sale, For wijt and treuth he has ai hale. **1377** LANGL. *P. Pl.* B. XII. 284 Trewth þat trespassed neuere ne transuersed aȝeines his lawe, But lyueth as his lawe techeth. *c* **1400** *Non-Cycle Myst. Plays, Pride of Life* 330 Dred of God is al ago And treut is go to ground. *Ibid.* 334 And truyt is don of dau. **1500–20** DUNBAR *Poems* xii. 30 Fredome returnis in wrechitness, And trewth returnis in dowbilness. **1535** COVERDALE *Ps.* cxviii. [cxix.] 30, I haue chosen the waye of treuth. *a* **1657** SIR W. MURE *Sonn.* i. 12 Extold by treuth of thy most loyall word.

β. **13..** *Cursor M.* 9661 (Cott.) Dom þan com foluand in hi, And Iuged þam in sothfast truth. **1568** GRAFTON *Chron.* II. 775 [They] lacked eyther wit or truth. **1592** SHAKS. *Ven. & Ad.* 804 Loue is all truth, lust full of forged lies. **1596** — *Merch. V.* IV. i. 214 Malice beares downe truth. **1611** BIBLE *Ps.* li. 6 Thou desirest trueth in the inward parts. **1680** BURNET *Rochester* (1692) 55 Truth is a Rational Natures acting in conformity to itself in all things. **1750** GRAY *Elegy* 69 The struggling pangs of conscious truth to hide. **1802** MAR. EDGEWORTH *Moral T.* (1816) I. iii. 16 Do you doubt my truth? **1852** MRS. STOWE *Uncle Tom's C.* xx, 'La, there an't any such thing as truth in that limb', said Rosa, looking indignantly at Topsy.

II. 5. a. Conformity with fact; agreement with reality; accuracy, correctness, verity (of statement or thought).

α. **1570** LEVINS *Manip.* 96/5 Trewth, *veritas.* Vntruth, *error.*

β. **1596** DALRYMPLE tr. *Leslie's Hist. Scot.* x. (S.T.S.) II. 422 Tha declair the truth of the Catholick religioune. **1600** SHAKS. *A.Y.L.* V. iv. 124 If there be truth in sight, you are my daughter. **1628** PRYNNE *Cens. Cozens* 65, I haue here sufficiently euidenced the trueth of this Assertion. **1718** PRIOR *Solomon* Pref., In this case Probability must attone for the want of Truth. *a* **1829** J. YOUNG *Lect. Intell. Philos.* xxxviii. (1835) 382 Truth is the agreement of our ideas and words with the nature of things. **1849** JAMES *Woodman* vii, There is some truth in what you say.

b. Agreement with the thing represented, in art or literature; accuracy of delineation or representation; the quality of being 'true to life'. Also, in *Arch.*, absence of deceit, pretence, or counterfeit, e.g. of imitation of stone in paint or plaster.

1828 DUPPA *Trav. Italy*, etc. 105 The interior of the two houses of Pansa and Sallust..restored..with great apparent truth. **1840** *C. O. Müller's Hist. Lit. Greece* xi. §7. 135 These pictures..had a striking truth. **1890** C. H. MOORE *Gothic Archit.* viii. 286 In truth and skill of modelling even the sculptures of Chartres and St. Denis..surpass these of Wells.

6. Agreement with a standard or rule; accuracy, correctness; *spec.* accuracy of position or adjustment; often in phrase *out of truth.* So *out-of-truth* sb. Cf. TRUE *sb.* 3.

1669 STURMY *Mariner's Mag.* V. i. 2 This Instrument will come to the Truth, as well as a Needle of greater charge. **1707** MORTIMER *Husb.* 43 To make them [ploughs]..go true depends much upon the truth of the Iron-work. **1825** J. NICHOLSON *Operat. Mechanic* 590 Otherwise the door, when put together, will be out of truth. **1854** *Poultry Chron.* I. 609 The best fowls..as to truth of feather, condition, and general character. **1862** *Catal. Internat. Exhib., Brit.* II. No. 5831, The friction..allows the wheels to rotate with perfect truth and freedom. **1967** L. HOLMES *Odhams New Motor Man.* viii. 189/1 Out-of-truth produces irregular tyre wear.

7. Genuineness, reality, actual existence.

1599 SHAKS. *Hen. V*, IV. iii. 14 Thou art fram'd of the firme truth of valour. **1603** — *Meas. for M.* III. i. 166 She (hauing the truth of honour in her). **1842** TENNYSON *Morte D'Arthur* 291 On to dawn, when dreams Begin to feel the truth and stir of day. **1844** MRS. BROWNING *Lost Bower* xlvii, The golden-hearted daisies Witnessed..To the truth of things,..And I woke to Nature's real.

8. *Particle Physics.* = TOP *sb.*[1] 18. [An arbitrary choice of name.]

1977 *Sci. Amer.* Oct. 74/2 If the two new quarks do exist, there must also be two new properties of matter, which some physicists have taken to calling 'truth' and 'beauty'. **1978** [see TOP *sb.*[1] 18]. **1979** *Nature* 6 Dec. 546/2 They have included evidence for the 'gluon' (the photon of the quark-quark force), and excited states of the upsilon (which contains a beauty quark and its anti-particle), but 'truth' (the quark beyond and pairing with beauty) remains to be found.

III. Something that is true.

9. a. True statement or account; that which is in accordance with the fact: chiefly in phr. *to say, speak,* or *tell the truth* (also *arch.* without *the*), to speak truly, to report the matter as it really is (see also SAY *v.*[1] 11, SPEAK *v.* 23, TELL *v.* 18). Cf. sense 12, from which this is not always distinguishable.

Prov. *tell (say, speak) the truth and shame the devil*: see SHAME *v.* 4 d.

α. **1362** LANGL. *P. Pl.* A. I. 133 Þis I trouwe beo treuþe! hose con teche þe betere, Loke þou suffre him to seye. *c* **1400** *Destr. Troy* 2338 Yf ye wilne for to witte how hit worthe shulde, I shall telle you the trewthe. *c* **1440** *Jacob's Well* 152 þerfore, levyth ȝoure lesynges, & spekyth trewthe.

β. **1548** PATTEN *Exped. Scotl.* Pref. a v, An Epigram.., the whiche I had, or rather (to saie truth and shame the deuel, for out it wool) I stale.. from a frende of myne. **1576** GASCOIGNE *Philomene* xcviii, Truth is truth, and muste be tolde. **1610** SHAKS. *Temp.* II. i. 137 The truth you speake doth lacke some gentlenesse, And time to speake it in. **1610** HOLLAND *Camden's Brit.* (1637) 632 A man to say truth well skilled in antiquities. **1735–8** BOLINGBROKE *Parties* Ded. 18 Truth may sometimes offend. **1823** BYRON *Juan* XIV. ci, Truth is always strange; Stranger than fiction. **1869** LOWELL *Lett.* (1894) II. 42 Tell us the truth as much as you like,..but tell it in a friendly way.

b. *loosely.* Mental apprehension of truth (in sense 11); knowledge.

1644 MILTON *Educ.* Wks. (1847) 98/1 Assertions, the knowledge and the use of which cannot but be a great furtherance..to the enlargement of truth. **1843** LOWELL *Glance behind Curtain* Poems (1844) 176 Men..Made wiser by the steady growth of truth.

c. (Also with capital initial.) A game in which players have to answer truthfully questions put by the others or, in some forms of the game (called *truth, dare, promise*, etc., according to the rules), fulfil an alternative requirement.

1868 L. M. ALCOTT *Little Women* I. xii. 191 Do you know 'Truth'?.. The person who draws at the number has to answer truly any questions put by the rest. **1928** *Sat. Even. Post* (U.S.) 29 Sept. 7/1 The ancient game of truth had begun. 'What's your favorite color, Bill?' **1959** I. & P. OPIE *Lore & Lang. Schoolch.* xviii. 377 In 'Truth, Dare, and Promise' each player has to agree either to tell the truth, accept a dare, or promise to do as he is told. **1969** — *Children's Games* ix. 265 In Kidderminster the game is occasionally called 'Truth, Dare, Promise, or Kiss'; in Peterborough and Swansea, 'Do, Dare, Kiss, or Promise'; in Gloucester, 'Truth, Dare, Warning, Love, Kiss, or Marriage'; ..in Aberdeen, 'Truth, Dare, Force, or Promise'... At Spennymoor,..the game is called 'Truth, Dare, Will, Force, and Command'. **1970** *Times* 8 July 2/7 On one occasion she said, Carole Hanson..stripped to her panties during a game of 'truth, dare and promise'. **1980** G. M. FRASER *Mr American* xiii. 270 Playing truth or consequences in..Sir Charles's drawing-room.

10. a. True religious belief or doctrine; orthodoxy. Often with *the*, denoting a particular form of belief or teaching held by the speaker to be the true one; esp. in Quaker language. Cf. also sense 11.

α. *c* **1375** *Sc. Leg. Saints* i. (*Petrus*) 607 Twa knychttis..þe quhilk petir..Conuertit... And fra thay þe treutht had tane [etc.]. **1562** WINȜET *Cert. Tract.* iii. Wks. (S.T.S.) I. 25, I can espy na thing thairin abhorring fra the treuth. **1567** *Gude & Godlie B.* (S.T.S.) 8 Heir him that preiche the word of treuth.

β. **1387** TREVISA *Higden* (Rolls) VII. 205 Þere is no verrey martirdom bot it be by meynteninge of truþe [*v.r.* truwþe]. **1556** OLDE *Antichrist* 9 b, Fauourers of the gospelles truthe. **1655** MILTON *Sonn. Massacher Piemont* 3 Them who kept thy truth so pure of old When all our Fathers worship't Stocks and Stones. **1662** in *Extr. S.P. rel. Friends* II. (1911) 144 It is ordered that there be a Collectione this month for the seruis of the truth. **1710** O. SANSOM *Acc. Life* 40 The Friend was declaring the Truth, when the Priest..came in. **1795** MACKNIGHT *Epist.* (1820) III. 147 The inspired writers often call'd the Gospel Revelation, The Truth. **1893** A. BIRRELL *Res Judicatæ* 134 The Church became a Living Witness to the Truth.

b. Conduct in accordance with the divine standard; spirituality of life and behaviour. (Cf. sense 4.)

α. **1382** WYCLIF *John* iii. 21 He that doth treuthe, cometh to the liȝt, that his workis be schewid, for thei ben don in God. —— *1 John* i. 6 If we shulen seie, for [**1388** that] we han felauschip with him, and we wandren in derknessis, we liȝen, and we don not treuthe. —— *2 John* 4, I ioyede ful miche, for I foond of thi sones goynge in treuthe, as we receyueden maundement of the fadir.

β. **1526** TINDALE *John* iii. 21 He that doth the trueth [**1534** TINDALE, *Geneva*, doth truth; CRANMER, **1611** trueth] commeth to the light.

11. a. That which is true, real, or actual (in a general or abstract sense); reality; *spec.* in religious use, spiritual reality as the subject of revelation or object of faith (often not distinguishable from 10).

α. *c* **1380** WYCLIF *Serm.* Sel. Wks. I. 13 Crist is a corner stoon, and groundiþ al treuþe. **1382** —— *John* viii. 32 Ȝe schulen knowe the treuthe, and the treuthe schal delyuere ȝou [1388 make you fre]. *Ibid.* xiv. 6, I am weye, treuthe, and lyf. **1458** in Parker *Dom. Archit.* III. 44 Now God geve us grace to folowe treuthe even That we may have a place in the blysse of heven. **1560** DAUS tr. *Sleidane's Comm.* 31 The trewth, will, and commaundement of the heauenly father must be accomplished.

β. **1547–64** BAULDWIN *Mor. Philos.* (Palfr.) 145 Forasmuch as God is the trueth, & that truth is God, hee that departeth from the one departeth from the other. **1646** SIR T. BROWNE *Pseud. Ep.* I. v. 18 In knowledge there is no slender difficulty,.. truth.. wise men say doth lye in a well. **1785** REID *Intell. Powers* 277 The light of truth.. fills my mind. **1819** KEATS *Ode Grecian Urn* 49 Beauty is truth, truth beauty. **1855** BREWSTER *Newton* II. xxiv. 340 Truth has no greater enemy than its unwise defenders. **1895** H. R. REYNOLDS in *Expositor* Jan. 75 God's thought is our most conclusive definition of truth. **1895** VERN. LEE in *Contemp. Rev.* Mar. 346 Truth is perceived by flashes.

b. Personified; *spec.* each of the two goddesses of truth in ancient Egyptian mythology.

α. **1362** LANGL. *P. Pl.* A. I. 12 þis Tour & þis Toft.. treuþe is þer-inne,.. he is Fader of Fei, þat formed ow alle.

β. **1553** BALE *Gardiner's De vera Obed.* H j b, I.. am compelled to take my wyfe Truthe to me. **1644** MILTON *Areop.* (Arb.) 74 So Truth be in the field, we do injuriously by licencing and prohibiting to misdoubt her strength. Let her and Falshood grapple. **1858** WILKINSON in Rawlinson *Herodotus* II. lviii. II. 101 *note*, The sacred beetle of the sun, overshadowed by the wings of two figures of the goddess Thmei, or 'Truth'. **1910** MRS. H. M. TIRARD *Bk. of Dead* v. 125 The weighing of the soul takes place in the great hall of the two truths in the Heliopolis of the nether-world. The two goddesses of truth at the eastern and western ends of the hall.

12. a. The fact or facts; the actual state of the case; the matter or circumstance as it really is. (Cf. sense 9.)

α. *c* **1450** *Mankind* 831 in *Macro Plays* 31 The prowerbe seyth 'þe trewth tryith þe sylfe'.

β. **1340–70** *Alex. & Dind.* 275 Of þat þou senteste, sire king, to say þe truthe Of al þe lore of our lif.. haue vs exkused, For we ne konne þe nouht kenne our costomus alle. *c* **1537** DE BENESE *Measurynge Lande* X iv, They make the square therof muche lesse than the truthe. **1606** SHAKS. *Ant. & Cl.* IV. xiv. 126 She sent you word she was dead: But fearing since how it might worke, hath sent Me to proclaime the truth. **1691** T. H[ALE] *Acc. New Invent.* 52 The said Commissioners are to report to this Board the Truth of the Fact. **1748** HARTLEY *Observ. Man* I. ii. 202 We judge the Distances to be less than the Truth. **1908** R. BAGOT *A. Cuthbert* xxvii. 362 If he does not know, he more than suspects the truth.

b. The real thing, as distinguished from an imitation; the genuine article; the reality corresponding to a type or symbol, the antitype. Now *rare* or *Obs.*

1531 *Acc. Ld. High Treas. Scot.* VI. 20 Item, for romaney buge to lyne the samyn goune, all truth.. xiij li. ix s. *a* **1653** GOUGE *Comm. Heb.* ix. 23 (1655) 390 His body was the truth of the Tabernacle:.. His mediation the truth of the incense: .. He the truth of most types. **1774** GOLDSM. *Nat. Hist.* (1776) V. 270 [The parrot's] voice.. is more like a man's than that of any other [bird]; the raven is too hoarse, and the jay and magpie too shrill, to resemble the truth.

c. ? Actual property or nature (*of* something). *rare.*

1552 *Bk. Com. Prayer, Communion* Rubric (*ad fin.*), It is against the truthe of Christes true naturall body, to be in mo places then in one, at one tyme.

13. with *a* and *pl.* A true statement or proposition; a point of true belief, a true doctrine; a fixed or established principle; a verified fact; a reality.

α. *c* **1380** WYCLIF *Wks.* (1880) 94 Prelatis constreynen men of symple vnderstondyng.. to assente to here dampnacion of treuþes of goddis lawe.

β. *c* **1380** WYCLIF *Wks.* (1880) 293 þe creature þat tellyþ hem a truþe in name of god. **1613** JACKSON *Creed* I. 42 Some notable truth, whose beleefe did concerne vs. **1615** G. SANDYS *Trav.* 60 The truths of religion are many times above reason, but never against it. **1646** SIR T. BROWNE *Pseud. Ep.* IV. xii. 210 That women are menstruant, and men pubescent, at the year of twice seven, is accounted a punctual truth. **1758** S. HAYWARD *Serm.* i. 3 This is not a fancy,.. but is a truth built upon divine testimony. **1858** O. W. HOLMES *Aut. Breakf.-t.* iii, Leave your friend to learn unpleasant truths from his enemies. **1876** G. MACDONALD *T. Wingfold* xiii, Something at the root of all facts—namely, truths, or eternal laws of being.

IV. 14. a. Phrases. (See also 9.) ***in truth, of a truth*** (arch.), † ***of truth***, † ***for a truth*** (obs.): in fact, as a fact; truly, verily, really, indeed: mostly used to strengthen or emphasize a statement.

α. **14..** *Why I can't be a Nun* 191 in *E.E.P.* (1862) 143 Hyt was a howse of nunes in trewthe,.. But not welle gouernede, and þat was rowthe. *a* **1548** HALL *Chron., Edw. IV* 226 And for a treugth at thys season there was mortal warre betwene king Lewes and the duke of Borgoyne. *c* **1560** A. SCOTT *Poems* (S.T.S.) ii. 2 The grit Debait and Turnament Off trewth no toung can tell.

β. **1526** TINDALE *Matt.* xiv. 33 Of a truth thou arte the sonne of God. **1647** CLARENDON *Hist. Reb.* I. §67 They did in truth desire it. **1727** DE FOE *Syst. Magic* I. iii. (1840) 84 These people pretend to blame him, whereas in truth they ought only to blame themselves. **1795** BURKE *Corr.* (1844) IV. 327 In truth, all these distempers pass my skill. **1873** 'OUIDA' *Pascarèl* I. 57 Of a truth I loved you. **1884** PAE *Eustace* 6 It was in truth a scene of great beauty.

†**b.** ***of (a) truth*** (predicatively): True; actually or really so. *Obs. rare.*

c **1566** J. ALDAY tr. *Boaystuau's Theat. World* I j b, It is of a truth, that the Priests of the Heathen.. were chosen [etc.]. **1590** WEBBE *Trav.* Epist. (Arb.) 13 In this booke there is nothing mentioned.. but that which is of truth: and what mine own Eies haue perfectly seene.

c. *ellipt.* or as *int.* ***truth!*** either as an expression of assent (cf. TRUE *a.* 3 b), or as intensive (= *in truth*). Cf. TROTH *sb.* 4 c. *arch.*

1534 TINDALE *Matt.* xv. 27 She answered and sayde: truthe Lorde: neverthelesse the whelpes eate of the crommes. **1568** GRAFTON *Chron.* II. 69 Truth said he, my predecessors.. were much both better and greater than I. **1854** TENNYSON *Geraint & Enid* 289 Arms? truth! I know not.

V. 15. Combinations. **a.** attrib., as ***truth-breach, -claim, -frequency, -gold, -light, -relation, -world, -worship.*** **b.** instrumental, as ***truth-dictated, -filled, -led, -shod, -tried, -writ.*** **c.** objective and obj. gen., as ***truth-finder, -hunter, -lover, -searcher, -seeker, -speaker, -teller, -unraveller; truth-bearing, -bending, -bringing, -compelling, -denying, -desiring, -loving, -painting, -passing, -perplexing, -revealing, -saying, -seeking, -speaking, -telling,*** etc., sbs. and adjs. See also TRUTHLIKE.

1847 CDL. WISEMAN *Ess., Unreality Anglican Belief* (1853) II. 394 Such vivid, *truth-bearing phrase. **1977** P. JOHNSON *Enemies of Society* xvii. 232 The title [sc. *Travesties*] reveals the fact that the whole play is an elaborate exercise in *truth-bending and symmetrical confusion. **1979** *Tucson (Arizona) Citizen* 20 Sept. 2C/6 Tucson is.. about to have a Liar's Contest to call its very own... Big Jim Griffith, banjo plucker, anthropologist, impresario, folklorist, Ph.D and himself no slouch in the truth-bending dept., phoned with the news. **1597** BEARD *Theatre God's Judgem.* (1612) 279 A grieuous crime of disloyaltie and *truth-breach. **1895** CHURCH *Pascal Serm.* xix. 319 Imagination is at once the most misleading and the most *truth-bringing of mental powers. **1909** W. JAMES *Meaning of Truth* xiv. 273 Good consequences.. are proposed rather as the lurking *motive* inside of every *truth-claim. **1977** A. GIDDENS *Stud. in Social & Polit. Theory* i. 78 An 'empirical intersection' subject to disputation in respect of truth claims. **1925** JOYCE *Let.* 27 Sept. (1957) I. 233, I am still under the influence of the '*truthcompelling' drug, scopolamine. **1895** SAYCE *Egypt of Hebr. & Herod.* 94 Ameni the *truth-declaring name. **1850** O. WINSLOW *Inner Life* iv. 119 *Truth-denying, .. soul-destroying error. **1871** E. F. BURR *Ad Fidem* vi. 92 A *truth-desiring spirit. **1830** GEN. P. THOMPSON *Exerc.* (1842) I. 278 The noxious and *truth-destroying practice of oath-taking. *a* **1770** CHATTERTON *On Mr. Alcock* Poet. Wks. (1886) 107 In *truth-dictated lays. *a* **1847** ELIZA COOK *Poems* II. Pref. 7 Many a brave, *truth-filled mind. **1749** FIELDING *Tom Jones* VI. i, The *truth-finder, and the gold-finder. **1936** *Mind* XLV. 501 The most complete and ingenious defence of the '*truth-frequency' interpretation of probability statements. **1949** A. PAP *Elem. Analytic Philos.* ix. 169 The truth-frequency of a form of influence is the limit approached by the ratio of the number of cases making both premisses and conclusion true to the number of cases making the premisses true. **1839** BAILEY *Festus* xix. (1848) 211 Some grains of *truth-gold. **1892** A. BIRRELL *Res Judicatæ* (1893) 157 The anxious *truth-hunter. **1839** BAILEY *Festus* vi. (1848) 61 *Truth-led in Time's darkest hour. **1853** READE *Chr. Johnstone* vi, We'll fight for nature-light, *truth-light, and sun-light. **1852** TENNYSON *Ode Death Wellington* 189 *Truth-lover was our English Duke. **1828** CARLYLE in *Foreign Rev.* II. 439 He has every feature also of a just, quiet, *truth-loving man. **1856** *N. Brit. Rev.* XXVI. 16 Reasonable and truth-loving men. **1612** SELDEN *Illustr. Drayton's Poly-olb.* i. 16 *Truth-passing reports of Poeticall Bards. **1735–6** THOMSON *Liberty* v. 610 *Truth-perplexing metaphysick wits. **1947** H. REICHENBACH *Elem. Symbolic Logic* iv. §33.178 The *truth-preserving property of derivational processes. **1969** *Aristotelian Soc. Suppl. Vol.* XLIII. 77 It is tempting to generalize and actually define logical rules as truth-preserving grammatical rules. **1907** W. JAMES *Meaning of Truth* (1909) vii. 165 It is *between* the idea and the object that the *truth-relation is to be sought and it involves both terms. **1952** *Mind* LXI. 193 The truth relation is repeatedly defined by Peirce in straightforward old-fashioned correspondence terms. **1600** FAIRFAX *Tasso* v. lxvi, Ere *truth-reuealing time.. Bewraid her act. **1895** JAS. KIDD *Moral. & Relig.* x. 426 Truth-revealing teaching. **1552** HULOET, *Trought sayinge, or spekinge, or tellyng, *ueridicentia, ueriloquentia.* **1928** A. HUXLEY *Point Counter Point* xxvi. 443 *Truth-Searchers become just as silly.. as the boozers. **1864** BOWEN *Logic* vii. (1870) 225 The inductive *truth-seeker. **1828** *Truth-seeking [see *open-minded* adj. s.v. OPEN *a.* 22 c]. **1852** ROBERTSON *Serm.* Ser. III. xvi. 207 He is responsible.. for the way in which he arrived at them [opinions]—whether in a slothful and selfish, or in an honest and truth-seeking manner. **1896** W. JAMES in *New World* V. 345, I.. cannot see my way to accepting the agnostic rules for truth seeking. **1876** BLACKIE *Songs Relig. & Life* 130 A *truth-shod Christian brotherhood. **1552** HULOET, *Trought speker, *ueridicus.* **1711** POPE *Let. to Jas. Craggs* 19 July, Their Method of Revenge on the Truth-Speaker is to attack his Reputation. **1552** *Truth-speaking (*sb.*) [see *truth-saying*]. **1856** S. J. RIGAUD *Serm. Inspir. Script.* i. 20 According to that general law of truth-speaking, which exacts not that a statement should be verbally correct, but that it should convey a true impression. **1552** HULOET, *Trought speking, or sayinge, *ueridicus.* **1872** TENNYSON *Gareth & Lyn.* 415 Bounteous, merciful, Truth-speaking, brave. **1552** HULOET, *Trought teller, and trought speker. *c* **1586** C'TESS PEMBROKE *Ps.* CI. v, For truth-tellers I will search the land. **1852** TENNYSON *Ode Death Wellington* 188 Truth-teller was our England's Alfred named. **1552** *Truth-telling (*sb.*) [see *truth-saying*]. **1803** MARY CHARLTON *Wife & Mistress* IV. 278 His system of truth-telling. **1847** HELPS *Friends in C.* I. i. 8 Truth-telling in its highest sense requires a well-balanced mind. **1756** C. SMART tr. *Horace, Sat.* I. iv. (1826) II. 43 When *truth-telling Bacchus opens the secrets of his heart. **1908** R. BAGOT *A. Cuthbert* viii, Impressions.. confirmed by the truth-telling light of day. **1784** COWPER *Task* III. 56 The calm of *truth-tried love. **1850** BUSHNELL *God in Christ* 59 Whosoever.. would have the *truth-world over-hang him as an empyrean of stars. **1879** GEO. ELIOT *Theo. Such* iii. 55 This sort of *truth-worship.

d. Special Combs.: **truth-condition** (see quot. 1937); **truth drug**, any substance that is administered to a person in the supposition that it will prevent him from lying; **truth-function** (see quots.); hence **truth-functional** *a.*, **truth-functionality**; **truth-functionally** *adv.*; **truth game** = sense 9 c above; also *transf.*; **truth serum**, a truth drug in the form of an injection; **truth set** (see quot. 1966); **truth squad** *U.S. Politics*, a group of people with the task of questioning the truth of statements made by members of an opposing party; **truth-table**, a tabular representation of the truth or falsity of a complex proposition as determined by the possible combinations of truth-values of its components; also *transf.*, esp. in *Computing*; **truth-value** [ad. G. *wahrheitswert(h)*], the value of truth (or falsehood) assigned to propositions, esp. those of two-valued logic; also *transf.* and *attrib.*

1922 tr. *Wittgenstein's Tractatus* 95 The proposition is the expression of its truth-conditions. **1937** *Mind* XLVI. 191 Propositional complexes which are definable by reference to truth conditions *i.e.*, to propositions whose truth-values are logically *determined* by the truth-values of their arguments. **1978** P. PETTIT in Hookway & Pettit *Action & Interpretation* 48 Incompatible sentences have truth conditions which we cannot conceive of as being simultaneously fulfilled. **1931** 'A. ABBOT' *Murder of Geraldine Foster* xiii. 179 Neither the lie detector nor the truth drug have ever been officially adopted by the Police Department. **1947** *Lancet* 4 Jan. 39/1 If an attempt were made to use a 'truth drug' against an accused person in an English criminal court, the judge would reject its results as an involuntary confession. **1969**, **1973** [see PENTOTHAL]. **1976** T. SHARPE *Wilt* xiii. 140 You can put me on a lie detector. You can pump me full of truth drugs. **1909** W. JAMES *Meaning of Truth* i. 41 The reader will easily see how much of the account of the truth-function developed later in *Pragmatism* was already explicit in this earlier article. **1910** WHITEHEAD & RUSSELL *Principia Math.* I. i. 8 We may call a function $f(p)$ a 'truth-function' when its argument p is a proposition, and the truth-value of $f(p)$ depends only upon the truth value of p. **1967** *Encycl. Philos.* V. 76/2 *Truth-function*, a function whose arguments and values are truth-values. **1981** *Sci. Amer.* Oct. 155/1 A complete account of how the truth value of a compound sentence is determined by its constituent sentences is called a truth function, and logicians customarily display the evaluation of the truth function in an array called a truth table. **1947** *Mind* LVI. 237 A modern extensional logic containing the ordinary truth-functional modes of statement-construction. **1968** CHOMSKY & HALLE *Sound Pattern Eng.* 387 We note there that certain truth-functional conditions are required for the phonological rules. **1950** W. V. QUINE *Methods of Logic* (1952) §2.8 The property of truth-functionality.. is thus enjoyed by negation, conjunction, and alternation. **1977** *Language* LIII. 70 There was some confusion in my paper about pragmatics in philosophy and the loose way in which it is used in linguistics—unrelated, in many cases, to a semantic component based on truth-functionality. **1950** W. V. QUINE *Methods of Logic* (1952) §7.37 The one statement implies the other truth-functionally. **1935** F. SCOTT FITZGERALD *Taps at Reveille* 66, I thought you might want to know... I thought maybe you thought I liked somebody else. The truth game didn't get around to me the other night. **1941** 'N. BLAKE' *Case of Abominable Snowman* xviii. 198 Since we seem to be playing the truth game.. did you kill Elizabeth Restorick? **1980** G. MITCHELL *Whispering Knights* iv. 42 'Why don't we play the Truth Game?' 'Because nobody will tell the truth.' **1925** F. J. REYNOLDS *Marvels of 1924* 44 Dr. House believes truth serum should be a part of every court and prison equipment. **1940** [see SCOPOLAMINE]. **1977** J. CROSBY *Company of Friends* vi. 43 Acetol is the strongest truth serum there is. Do you remember talking, talking, talking? **1963** Truth set [see *solution set* s.v. SOLUTION *sb.* 12]. **1966** *Britannica Bk. of Year* 807/2 *Truth set*, a mathematical or logical set containing all the elements that may be substituted in a given statement of relationships without altering the truth of the statement (the equation $x + 7 = 11$ has as its *truth set* the single number 3). **1952** *Tuscaloosa (Alabama) News* 3 Nov. 12/5 The Republican 'Truth Squad' after trailing President Truman across the country on his campaign trips, passed down its final verdict today that the President was 'guilty of over 100 lies, half-truths and distortions.' **1980** *Washington Star* 31 Oct. B1/1 GOP leaders formed what they called a 'truth squad' to campaign this week because they said Democrats have avoided the issues. **1921** E. POST in *Amer. Jrnl. Math.* XLIII. 166 The general notion of truth-table is not introduced [in *Principia Mathematica*]. *Ibid.* 167 So corresponding to each of the 2^n possible truth-configurations of the p's a definite truth-value of f is determined. The relation thus effected we shall call the truth-table of f. **1937** *Mind* XLVI. 191 Truth-tables which analytically exhibit the logical conditions under which a given truth-function.. would be true, together with those under which it would be false. **1962** SIMPSON & RICHARDS *Physical Princ. Junction Transistors* xvi. 401 The above results may be most easily summarized for two transistors with two inputs *A* and *B* in the form of so-called truth tables, two of which are shown below. **1965** P. CAWS *Philos. of Sci.* xvi. 122 A decision procedure.. for the sentential calculus.. consists of constructing a truth-table for the *wff* in question. **1970** O. DOPPING *Computers & Data Processing* i. 26 From the truth table we can then derive a logical equation, which can be used as a basis for the program. **1977** *Sci. Amer.* Sept. 84/2 The first step in the design of the circuit is the construction of a truth table that gives the desired output for every possible combination of inputs. [**1891** G. FREGE in *Funktion, Begriff, Bedeutung* (1975) 26 Ich sage nun: 'der Wert unserer Funktion ist ein Wahrheitswert' und unterscheide den Wahrheitswert des Wahren von dem des Falschen.] **1903** B. RUSSELL *Princ. Math.* 502 There are, we are told.., three elements in judgment: (1) the recognition of truth, (2) the Gedanke, (3) the truth-value (*Wahrheitswerth*). **1932** LEWIS & LANGFORD *Symbolic Logic* vii. 215 In this calculus, it is important to distinguish the truth-*values*, 1, ?, and 0, from the truth-functions, *p*, *Mp*, and *Np*. **1936** WIRTH & SHILS tr. *Mannheim's Ideology & Utopia* 13 The truth-value of human knowledge in general. **1966** S. BEER *Decision & Control* viii. 165 Then this formulation is subjected to a truth-value analysis. **1978** J. MCDOWELL in Hookway & Pettit *Action & Interpretation* 129 Dummett's realist is attempting, with the truth-value-link manoeuvre, to respect that principle. **1981** A. BORN tr. F. Lasson in *Dinesen's Lett. from Afr.* p. xiv, The presumed documentary truth-value of the letters.

truth, *v.* [f. prec. sb., in various independent senses.]

†**1.** *trans.* To believe, trust. *Obs.*

?*a* **1300** *Prayer to Virgin* 24 in *O.E. Misc.* 196 Wil ich neuer eft more Lauedi for þine sake treuþen feondes lore.

†**2. a.** *intr.* To plight one's troth; to enter into an engagement of marriage. **b.** *trans.* To betroth, affiance: = TROTH *v. Obs.*

c **1315** SHOREHAM I. 1660 3yf an oþer treuþeþ seþe Wyþ word of þat hys nouþe. *c* **1330** *Arth. & Merl.* (Kölbing) 8639 Þer treuþed Arthour Gwenore, his quen. *c* **1412** HOCCLEVE *De Reg. Princ.* 3690 She truthede was to Indibal.

†**3.** *trans.* To name or call truly; to describe with truth as. *Obs. nonce-use.*

1638 FORD *Fancies* II. ii, The ancients Who chatted of the golden age, feign'd trifles. Had they dreamt this, they would have truth'd it heav'n.

†**4.** *intr.* with *it*: To speak or deal truly (nonce-rendering of Gr. ἀληθεύειν in Eph. iv. 15). *Obs.*

1648 T. HILL *Serm. Truth & Love* 21 Truthing it in love, which were an admirable motto for saints. **1656** S. WINTER *Serm.* Ep. Ded., I have without gall.. managed this controversie, truthing it in love.

5. *trans.* To bring to 'truth' (TRUTH *sb.* 6), adjust accurately: = TRUE *v.* 2.

1881 J. W. WARMAN in *Eng. Mechanic* No. 874. 368/1 It permits of the removal of such Rails for any truthing which they may require.

Hence '**truthing** *vbl. sb.*, †(*a*) the action of plighting troth, contract of marriage (*obs.*); (*b*) (see sense 5).

c **1315** SHOREHAM I. 1665 Bote 3ef þer fol3ede þat treuþyng A ferst flesch ymone. *Ibid.* 1759 And 3ef þer hys condicioun Yset atter treuþynge.

†'**truthable**, *a. Obs. rare*⁻¹. [f. TRUTH *sb.* + -ABLE.] = TRUE *a.* 4; correct.

a **1593** NASHE in G. Harvey *Pierce's Super.* 180 Truthable and eligible English.

truthful ('truːθfʊl), *a.* [f. TRUTH *sb.* + -FUL.]

1. Of statements, etc.: Full of truth; sincere. (Now only as *transf.* from 2.)

1596 R. L[INCHE] *Diella* xiii, My truthfull pleadings will not cause you rue. *Mod.* A perfectly honest and truthful statement.

2. Of persons (or their attributes): Disposed to tell, or habitually telling, the truth; free from deceitfulness; veracious. (In quot. 1787, Telling the truth, correct in statement.) Also *fig.* Giving true information, not deceptive (cf. 3).

1787 BERINGTON *Abeill.* Pref. 16, I profess to be as accurate as I can, and as truthful as the character of my records will allow. **1816** SCOTT *Antiq.* xx, What my poverty takes awa frae the weight o' my counsel, grey hairs and a truthfu' heart should add it twenty times. **1860** W. G. WARD *Nat. & Grace* I. 109 He has given us faculties, which are truthful and not mendacious. **1865** MAX MÜLLER *Chips* (1880) I. i. 16 In order to discover truth, we must be truthful ourselves. **1866** READE *G. Gaunt* (ed. 2) III. 39 Before he got into this mess he was a singularly truthful person; but now a lie was nothing to him.

3. Of ideas, artistic representation, etc.: Characterized by truth; corresponding with fact or reality; true, accurate, exact.

1859 [implied in TRUTHFULNESS]. **1868** E. EDWARDS *Ralegh* I. x. 163 For a long period, the truthful knowledge of what Spaniards had really achieved was slight. **1871** *Routledge's Ev. Boy's Ann., Suppl.* June 9 A beautifully executed and truthful portrait. **1885** SWINBURNE *Misc.* (1886) 294 There is none left.. whose bright and sweet invention is so fruitful, so truthful, or so delightful as Mrs. Molesworth's.

truthfully ('truːθfʊlɪ), *adv.* [f. prec. + -LY².] In a truthful manner; with truth, truly.

1846 in WORCESTER. **1871** H. AINSWORTH *Tower Hill* III. xix, One question more,.. By answering it truthfully, thou may'st escape the rack. **1892** SWINBURNE *Stud. Prose & Poetry* (1894) 226 What has been said of Lamb's or of Landor's.. briefest.. notes may as truthfully be said of Hugo's.

truthfulness ('truːθfʊlnɪs). [f. as prec. + -NESS.] The quality of being truthful.

1. Disposition to tell the truth; veracity.

1843 MIALL in *Nonconf.* III. 1 Soundness of principles, and.. truthfulness of spirit. *a* **1873** WILBERFORCE *Ch. & Empires* (1874) 110 Any.. writer.. who.. commands belief by his accuracy and truthfulness.

2. Accuracy in representing the reality; freedom from pretence or counterfeit, as in a work of art or literature.

1859 GEO. ELIOT *A. Bede* xvii, It is for this rare, precious quality of truthfulness that I delight in many Dutch paintings. **1874** GREEN *Short Hist.* vi. §5. 324 No words could paint with so terrible a truthfulness the spirit of the New Monarchy. **1886** C. E. PASCOE *Lond. of To-day* xlii. (ed. 3) 362 English work, and especially as applied to furniture, used to have a character for truthfulness, simplicity, solidity, and comfort.

†'**truthhead.** *Obs.* In 4 **treuth-hede, treuthede, truthhede, trouth-hedd,** 5 **trewþehede, trouþhede.** [f. TRUTH, TROTH + -HEAD.] Faithfulness, loyalty.

a **1300** *Cursor M.* 97 (Cott.) Of hir godnes and hir treuthede [*v.rr.* trouth-hedd, trouþhede]. *Ibid.* 4423 For þi leute and þi truthhede [*v.r.* treuth-hede]. **14..** *R. Gloucester's Chron.* (Rolls) 7370 Uor he wolde þat alle men schulde se his trewþehede [*Cott. MS.* trewehede].

'**truthify**, *v. nonce-wd.* [f. TRUTH + -(I)FY.] *intr.* To act according to truth; to deal truly. (Cf. TRUTH *v.* 4.)

1647 TRAPP *Comm. Eph.* iv. 15 Speaking the truth, or, Doing the truth, as the Vulgar hath it. Truthifying, or following the truth, as one rendereth it. **1689** M. SYLVESTER *Serm. Heb.* x. 24–5 (1690) 334 b, This is indeed.. to truthifie in Love, if I may make an English Word to express the valor of the Greek Word, ἀληθεύοντες ἐν ἀγάπῃ.

truthiness: see TRUTHY.

truthless ('truːθlɪs), *a.* Forms: see TRUTH. [f. TRUTH *sb.* + -LESS.] Destitute of truth (in various senses).

†**1.** Lacking faith; distrustful. (In quot. app. *absol.* as *sb.*) *Obs. rare*⁻¹.

c **1200** *Trin. Coll. Hom.* 73 Ten þing.. leten men of here scrifte,.. shamfestnesse, drede, ortrowe, trewðeleas [app. gloss on 'ortrowe'].

2. Faithless, unfaithful, perfidious. *Obs.* or *arch.*

1567 *Satir. Poems Reform.* iv. 84 Off Tygeris quholpis,.. Ane treuthles troup hes drewin me to this end. *a* **1600** *Flodden F.* II. (1664) 15 And turn such truthless guest to teen.

3. Untruthful, mendacious; making false statements, 'false'.

1567 *Satir. Poems Reform.* iv. 41 My truethles toung my honoure defylit. **1605** CAMDEN *Rem.* (1637) 251 He prooved a truthlesse Prophet. **1888** *Gd. Words* Oct. 682 The truthless look, the shuffling gait, The mind that darkly schemes.

4. Having no truth in it, as a statement, etc.; void of truth; untrue, false.

1610 HOLLAND *Camden's Brit.* I. 9 These opinions are altogether truthlesse. **1660** *Trial Regic.* (1679) 235, I hope.. that what I have said.. is not Truthless but of Weight. **1850** *Tait's Mag.* XVII. 715/1 Senseless and truthless clamour. **1911** *Contemp. Rev.* Nov. 666 Idolators of truthless imaginations.

Hence '**truthlessness**.

1854 *Tait's Mag.* XXI. 494 Representatives of the wit and truthlessness of our age. **1900** MORLEY *Cromwell* II. v. 184 The letters disclosed his truthlessness.

truthlike ('truːθlaɪk), *a.* [f. as prec. + -LIKE.] Like or resembling truth or the truth; †likely to be true, probable (quot. 1657).

1567 DRANT *Horace, Art Poetry* A iv, If thou feyne, feyne then the things as truthlyke as you maye. **1570** FOXE *A. & M.* (ed. 2) 124/1 They seme more legendlike, then truthlike. **1657** EARL MONM. tr. *Paruta's Pol. Disc.* 78 To seek out the truest, or at least, the most truthlike causes thereof. **1894** J. T. FOWLER *Adamnan* Introd. 25 It.. mentions certain incidents in a remarkably naïve and truthlike manner.

Hence '**truthlikeness**, likeness to truth, verisimilitude.

a **1586** SIDNEY *Arcadia* III. (1622) 241 He knew.. how few there be that can discerne betweene trueth and truthlikenesse, betweene shewes and substance. **1865** W. KAY *Crisis Hupfeldiana* 81 The results may have such simplicity, truthlikeness, and internal concinnity as may make us accept them. **1904** *Westm. Gaz.* 29 Aug. 3/1 The actor regards the part as farcical, for he pushes it.. beyond truth-likeness.

†'**truthly**, *adv. Obs. rare*⁻¹. [irreg. f. as prec. + -LY².] In accordance with truth; honestly, without deceit.

1493 *Acta Dom. Conc.* (1839) 313 Aithir of þe sadis partiis has subscriuit þis write with þar avne handis,.. leilie or trewthelie, but fraud or gile.

truth-plight: see TROTH-PLIGHT.

truthsman ('truːθsmən). *nonce-wd.* [f. *truth's*, gen. of TRUTH *sb.* + MAN *sb.*¹] A man of truth; a man characterized by or devoted to truth.

1844 MIALL *Ethics Nonconf.* (1847) 54 He stands before the world.. as a truthsman.

truthy ('truːθɪ), *a. rare* or *dial.* [f. as prec. + -Y.] Characterized by truth; truthful, true. Hence '**truthiness**, truthfulness, faithfulness.

c **1800** J. H. COLLS *Theodore* I, You.. are afraid Theodore your sweetheart shouldn't prove truthy. **1824** J. J. GURNEY in Braithwaite *Mem.* (1854) I. 242 Everyone who knows her is aware of her truthiness. **1848** *Fraser's Mag.* XXXVII. 404 Descriptions of country life and truthy touches of native manners. **1851** SIR F. PALGRAVE *Norm. & Eng.* I. 601 Regino was truthy and honest.

†'**trutinate**, *v. Obs.* [f. L. *trutināt-*, ppl. stem of *trutināre*, f. *trutina* = Gr. τρυτάνη balance, pair of scales: see -ATE³.] *trans.* To weigh in the balances; also *fig.* to weigh mentally, consider, estimate. So †'**trutinate** *ppl. a.* [ad. L. *trutinātus*, pa. pple.], weighed; *fig.* considered, estimated (usually const. as pple.); †**truti'nation**, the action of weighing; *fig.* consideration, estimation; †'**trutine** [ad. L. *trutina* = Gr. τρῦτάνη], a balance; *fig.* in ***trutine of Hermes*** (see quots.).

1528 *St. Papers Hen. VIII*, VII. 123 Howe to discerne enserche and *trutynate the true from the false. **1638** WHITING *Albino & Bellama* 10 Madam, sayes he, be pleas'd to trutinate, And wisely, weigh your servants gracefull voyce. **1657** TOMLINSON *Renou's Disp.* 136 To be trutinated by just weight and measure. **1528** *St. Papers Hen. VIII*, VII. 124 So weighty a cause well *trutinate and expended.. by the jugement of.. the most excellent clerks and doctours. **1570** FOXE *A. & M.* (ed. 2) 1127/2 Humaine fragilitie suffereth not all thinges to bee pondered, trutinate, and weyed in iust balaunce. **1610** W. FOLKINGHAM *Art of Survey* I. i. 1 The view and trutinate intimation of a subiect, from Center to Circumference. **1633** B. C. *Puritanism* I. 22 The lesser sinne, and the greatest are alike.. in Gods iust *trutination and weighing of them. **1646** SIR T. BROWNE *Pseud. Ep.* IV. vii. 196 In regard of the scale or decision of trutination. **1647** LILLY *Chr. Astrol* xcviii. 501 The first way .. of rectifying a Nativity.. was by the *Trutine or Scrutiny of Hermes. **1696** PHILLIPS (ed. 5), *Trutine of Hermes*, an artificial method of rectifying a Nativity, by finding out the Day of Conception, and the place of the Moon at that time. **1819** JAS. WILSON *Compl. Dict. Astrol.*, *Rectification*, the method of bringing a nativity to its true time... Beside the animoder of Ptolemy, we have the trutine of Hermes, the methods of Argol, Morin, Kepler, &c., &c.

truttaceous (trʌ'teɪʃəs), *a. Ichth.* [f. mod.L. *truttāceus* (Willughby *a* 1672), f. late L. *trutta* TROUT: see -ACEOUS.] Related to the trout.

1753 CHAMBERS *Cycl. Suppl.*, *Salmo*, the salmon... It is distinguished from other fish of the truttaceous kind by these characters. *Ibid.* s.v., The truttaceous fishes are divided into two tribes.

truttle, variant of TRATTLE *sb.*²

truu, obs. f. TROW *v.*

truwage, var. TREWAGE *Obs.*

truwandise, -aund, -aunt: see TRUANDISE, TRUANT.

truwe, truwes, -ys, obs. ff. TRUCE.

truwitt: see *true-wit* s.v. TRUE D. I.

trux, truxe, obs. ff. TRUCE.

truys, -yse, truyt, obs. ff. TRUCE, TRUTH.

trw, obs. f. TRUE.

trwandrye, trwandyse, trwaunt, see TRUANTRY, TRUANDISE, TRUANT.

trwce, obs. f. TRUCE.

trwcheman, obs. Sc. f. TRUCHMAN, dragoman.

trwe, trwes, trwys, obs. ff. TRUE, TRUCE.

try (traɪ), *sb.* [f. TRY *v.*]

I. An act of trying, etc.

†**1.** *Naut.* In phrase ***at try, a-try*** (see A-TRY), the position of a vessel lying-to in a storm; see TRY *v.* 17. *Obs.*

α. **1556** W. TOWRSON in Hakluyt *Voy.* (1589) 98 All the night [wee] laye at trie with much raine and foule weather. *a* **1618** RALEIGH *Royal Navy* 12 We are forced to lye at tryе with our maine Course and Missen. **1627** CAPT. SMITH *Seaman's Gram.* ix. 40 A storme let vs lie at Trie with our maine course, that is, to hale the tacke aboord, the sheat close aft, the boling set vp, and the helme tied close aboord. **1694** MOTTEUX *Rabelais* V. xviii. 80 Let us go and lye at Trie with our main Course.

β. **1558–89** A. JENKINSON *Voy. & Trav.* (Hakl. Soc.) I. 96 There arose another great storme.. and we lay a trie, being driuen farre into the sea. **1611–1867** [see A-TRY]. **1676** WOOD *Jrnl.* in *Acc. Sev. Late Voy.* I. (1694) 173 We lay a try under a Main-sail. **1729** CAPT. W. WRIGLESWORTH *MS. Log.-bk of the 'Lyell'* 22 Dec., At 5 Reefed our Courses, furled the Fore Sail, brought to, and lay a try under Main Sail.

†**2.** A trial, a test. *Obs. rare.*

1607 SHAKS. *Timon* V. i. 11 Then this breaking of his, Ha's beene but a Try for his Friends?

3. *Joinery.* The condition of being 'tried' to a perfect level; cf. TRY *v.* 8.

1678 MOXON *Mech. Exerc.* iv. 65 If your work be hollow in the middle, you must Plain both the Bearing sides thinner, till they come to a Try with the middle.

4. a. An attempt, endeavour, effort. Chiefly *colloq.*

1832 FROUDE in *Rem.* (1838) I. 322 Versification is out of my line, else I should have had a try at it. **1848** MRS. GASKELL *M. Barton* xxvii, Don't give it up..let's have a try for him. **1890** *Pall Mall G.* 30 July 2/2 The Emperor.. succeeded at the first try.

b. *Rugby Football.* The right of attempting to kick a goal, obtained by carrying the ball behind the goal-line and touching it on the ground. Cf. *touch-down* (TOUCH- 2).

1845 *Rules Footb. Rugby School* §5 *Try at goal*... The ball when punted must be within, when caught without, the line of goal. **1880** *Times* 12 Nov. 4/5 The efforts of a worsted side ..to gain the goal or the 'try' which is required to make the match a tie. **1893** *Ibid.* 18 Dec. 10/3 The North were victors by two goals and two tries to three tries.

II. An instrument for trying.

†**5.** A sieve or sifting screen. *Obs.*

c **1475** *Pict. Voc.* in Wr.-Wülcker 808/14 *Panducsator cum suis implementis*... *Hec falanga*, a try. **1603** HOLLAND *Plutarch's Mor.* 86 They will not passe thorough the holes of the sieve, ruddle, or trie, if they be narrow. **1644** G. PLATTES in *Hartlib's Legacy* (1655) 201 Mingling Corn with great Beans, exceeding hard dryed on a Kiln, which may be separated easily with a wire Trie. **1804** DUNCUMB *Hist. Hereford.* Gloss., *Try*, a wire screen for cleansing wheat from the chaff.

†**6.** = TRYSAIL. *Obs. rare*$^{-1}$.

1665–6 *Adm. Crt. Exam.* 22 Mar. 66 A maine course or try.

III. **7.** *attrib.* and *Comb.*, as (sense 4 b) ***try-getter, -getting, -scorer, -scoring.***

1954 J. B. G. THOMAS *On Tour* iv. 43 The two wings, were the try-getters. **1977** *Western Mail* (Cardiff) 5 Mar. 3/3 England could well feel the backlash of these frustrated Welsh try-getters. **1954** J. B. G. THOMAS *On Tour* 12 Without complete forward supremacy try-getting was like needle-hunting in the proverbial haystack. **1930** *Daily Express* 8 Sept. 10/5 Try-scorers for the tourists in the first half were Rew and Jones-Davies. **1976** *Scotsman* 27 Dec. 11/1 Earlier try-scorers for Gala were Gordon Dickson and George Telfer. **1974** *Times* 4 Feb. 7/2 With try-scoring so difficult, Wales missed a golden opportunity of taking a decisive lead midway through the first half.

†**try, trie,** *a. Obs.* Forms: 3–5 trie, 4 tri, triȝe, 4–6 trye, 5, 7 try. [ME. *trie*, etc., prob. a. OF. *trié*, pa. pple. of *trier* to pick out, cull, select (see TRY *v.*), or OF. *trie* sb. choice, 'élite', used attrib.]

1. Choice, excellent, good; = TRIED *ppl. a.* 2.

a **1300** *Sat. People Kildare* xiv. in *E.E.P.* (1862) 155 Worþ hit wer þat he wer king þat ditid þis trie þing. *c* **1315** SHOREHAM i. 1575 By-tuixe god and holy folk Loue hys wel trye and ryche. **1377** LANGL. *P. Pl.* B. I. 135 Treuthe is tresore þe triest [*v.rr.* trieste, tryest, triȝest] on erþe. *c* **1425** *Cast. Persev.* 536 in *Macro Plays* 93 He schal be serwaunt good & try. **1596** SPENSER *F.Q.* v. ii. 26 Those hands of gold, ..those feete of silver trye.

2. *Joinery.* Quite true, correctly wrought: cf. TRY *sb.* 3, *v.* 8.

1678 MOXON *Mech. Exerc.* vi. 101 If they can see light between the edge of the Rule and their Work: If they cannot they conclude their Work is Try, and well wrought.

Hence †'**tryly, triely** *adv. Obs.*, choicely, excellently, finely.

c **1350** *Will. Palerne* 1228 Triliche was he a-tired in ful tristy armes. *Ibid.* 3198 Tvo baþes were boun by a litel while, & a-tired tryli to trusty trewe lordes. **1377** LANGL. *P. Pl.* B. Prol. 14, I seigh a toure on a toft trielich ymaked.

try (traɪ), *v.* Forms: 4–6 tri, 4–7 trie, trye, (4 treye, trei), 5– try. Pa. t. and pple. tried (traɪd); also 4 (*pa. t.*) **triȝed**, (*pa. pple.*) **triȝede, i-triȝed, -et, ytried, ytryed,** 5 **y-tryid;** 4–5 **treid, tryyd,** 4–6 **tryede,** 4–7 **tryde,** 4–9 **tryed,** 5 (**tryude**), **triet, tryet** (also 6 *Sc.*), 5–6 **tryid,** 6–7 **tride, tryd,** *Sc.* **tryit,** 7 **tri'd,** 7–8 **try'd.** [a. OFr. *trie-r* (12th c., Benoit *Ducs de Norm.* II. 11518 Le tort del dreit Trier e conoistre e sevrer (to sift and know and sever the wrong from the right) = Pr., Cat. *triar*, also med.L. *triāre* (from Prov. or Fr.) to sift or pick out. The legal use appears to have been developed in Anglo-French, where it is known *c* 1280; there is no trace of this use in continental French. The origin of the Fr. and Prov. word is unknown.

The conjecture of Frisch, mentioned by Diez and by Skeat, that it represents a late L. **trītāre* to grind out, thresh out, freq. of *terĕre*, is incompatible with the Provençal form. Another conjecture is that it was a transposed form of *tirer* 'to draw, extract', in a specific sense; but evidence is wanting.]

1. a. *trans.* To separate (one thing) from another or others; to set apart; to distinguish. Often with *out. Obs.* or *arch.*

c **1330** R. BRUNNE *Chron. Wace* (Rolls) 13260 Þey turnde ageyn, And tryde þe Bretons fro ilk Romeyn. **1413** *26 Pol. Poems* xii. 69 Til trouþe be fro treson tryed, Shal neuere be pes in regyon. *c* **1515** *Cocke Lorells B.* 13 With this man was a lusty company, For all raskyllers fro them they dyde trye. *a* **1548** HALL *Chron., Hen. VII* 54 b, He [Henry VII] espyed and tried oute suche as he knewe..to beare no good wyll.. towarde his person. **1592** WARNER *Alb. Eng.* VII. xxxvii. (1612) 180 For what is it but reason that humaine from brutish tries? [**1847** BUSHNELL *Chr. Nurt.* I. i. (1861) 11 Human children still living a mixed life, trying out the good and evil of the world.]

†**b.** To pick out, choose, select; *pa. pple.* (quot. 1340–70), selected, choice (cf. TRIED 2).

[**1292** BRITTON II. xxvii. §5 Face le viscounte trier xii. prodeshommes.] **1340–70** *Alisaunder* 1233 For too keepe in that kith cumlich & riche All his tresour ytryed. *c* **1440** *Pallad. on Husb.* IV. 727 The kiyn also this tyme hit is to trie; Do chese hem that be chested huge & hie. *c* **1440** *Promp. Parv.* 502/2 Tryin [*v.r.* tryyn], *eligo, preeligo.* **1481** *Coventry Leet Bk.* 484 See that the seid persones so be [= by] you to be tried oute & chosen.

†**2. a.** To separate the good part of a thing from the rest, esp. by sifting or straining; hence, to sift or strain. Usually with *out. Obs.*

1382 [see TRIED 1]. *c* **1420** ? LYDG. *Assembly of Gods* 2071 Try out the corne clene from the chaff. *c* **1430** *Two Cookery-bks.* 11 Take 3olkys of eyroun y-tryid fro þe whyte. **14..** *Noble Bk. Cookry* (Napier 1882) 90 Put it to gedur with a crust of bred and try it through a strener. **1548** UDALL *Erasm. Par.* Pref. 10 The boulter tryeth out the branne. **1581** W. STAFFORD *Exam. Compl.* ii. (1876) 51 What neede they..to trie out the sandes of the ryuers of Tagus in Spaine, Pactolus in Asia, and Ganges in India, to get..small sparkes of gold. **1657** C. BECK *Univ. Char.* L viij, To trye, or fine from the dreggs. **1790** W. MARSHALL *Midl. Co.* (1796) II. Gloss. (E.D.S.), *Try*, *v.* to skreen.

b. *gen.* To take or get *out*, to extract; also, in extended sense, To put *into*, insert. *Obs. rare.*

c **1440** *Pallad. on Husb.* II. 165 Impedymentis, rootis out thou trie. *Ibid.* 263 Aysell and wyne eke oute of hem men trie, As oute of peres. *Ibid.* III. 639 Wild asperages rootes many trie Into erthe ytilde. *Ibid.* XII. 94 The boones..in askes moolde Thay mynge, and it thai into skeppes trie.

†**3.** *spec.* To separate (metal) from the ore or dross by melting; to refine, purify by fire; also, to remove (the dross or impurity) from metal by fire. Usually with *out.* Also *fig. Obs.*

13.. [see TRIED 1]. **1524** in *Acts Parlt. Scotl.* (1875) XII. 41/1 Þe gold gais furth of þe sammyn [realm] in greit quantite becaus it is tryit to ane hieare price and valoure in vþir realmis. **1535** COVERDALE *Zech.* xiii. 9, I..will clense them, as the syluer is clensed: Yee and trye them, like as golde is tryed. **1539** BIBLE (Great) *Ps.* xxvi. 2 Examen me, o Lord, & proue me: trie out my reynes and my hert. **1545** ELYOT, *Chalcites*, a stone..wherof brasse is tried. **1555** *Inv. Ch. Goods* (Surtees No. 97) 152 So moche refuse and baggaige tried out, by meane of the melting of the said plate. **1572** *Pat. Roll 14 Eliz.* XII. m. 22 (P.R.O.) Thomas Smyth ..hath..founde out and put in vse a newe and certene arte to trye out and make of yron verye true perfytt and good copper. **1596** SHAKS. *Merch. V.* II. ix. 63 The fier seauen times tried this, Seauen times tried that iud[g]ement is, That did neuer choose amis. **1686** W. HARRIS tr. *Lemery's Course Chym.* Introd. (ed. 3) 44 Coppels are porous vessels made in form of a cup to be used for the trying and purifying of Gold and Silver.

4. a. To extract (oil) from blubber or fat by heat; to melt down (blubber, etc.), to obtain the oil; to render; also, to extract (wax) from a honey-comb. Usually with *out.*

1582 in W. H. Turner *Select. Rec. Oxford* (1880) 423 No chaundeler shall..trie or melt any tallowe w[th]in the walles. **1610** BARROUGH *Meth. Physick* III. lxii. (1639) 198 Oile tried out of wooll in sheeps flanks or necks. **1630** J. LEVETT *Ord. Bees* (1634) 51 After what manner doe you deale with your Combes to try out the waxe. **1852** MUNDY *Our Antipodes* viii. (1855) 195 A dead whale was..'tried out' by some speculating fisherman. **1867** SMYTH *Sailor's Word-bk.*, *To try down*, to boil out the oil from blubber at sea in whalers. **1883** SIR A. SHEA *Newfound. Fisheries* 10 (Fish. Exhib. Publ.) The fat is then cut up,..and tried out by steam.

b. *intr.* for *pass. U.S.*

1891 *Cent. Dict.* s.v., Grease tries out of a ham in cooking; ..the perspiration is trying out of him.

5. †**a.** *trans.* To ascertain, find out (something doubtful, obscure, or secret) by search or examination; to sift out. Usually ***to try out.*** *Obs.*

[Cf. *c* **1300–25** N. BOZON *Contes Moral.* (1889) 9 La cause [of the attraction of the loadstone] ne peut estre triée.] *c* **1325** *Metr. Hom.* 56 Yef we wil the sothe treye, Gon we til dom of our Leuedye. **1430–40** LYDG. *Bochas* I. viii. (MS. Bodl. 263) lf. 36/1 But folke that list off daunger hem discharge..Til the trouthe be tried out in deed. **1567** *Satir. Poems Reform.* iii. 92 Tresoun to try sho was that tyme maist stout But sho is slak to try this tresoun out. **1584** COGAN *Haven Health* (1636) 9 By this meanes doth Galen trie out the time most fit for exercise. **1675** tr. *Camden's Hist. Eliz.* I. (1688) 129 They all agreed on this, that Lidington.. should first try the Queens mind. *a* **1761** LAW *Comf. Weary Pilgr.* (1809) 52 This therefore may serve as a touch-stone wherby every one may try the truth of his state.

†**b.** With material object. *Obs. rare*$^{-1}$.

1539 POLLARD, etc. in *St. Papers Hen. VIII* (1830) I. 619 We have dayly fownde and tryede oute bothe money and plate, hyde and muryde up in walls, vauttis and other secrette placis.

c. To ascertain the truth or right of (a matter, a quarrel, etc.) by test or endeavour; with *out*, to thrash or fight out; to determine. Now *rare.*

1542 UDALL *Erasm. Apoph.* 163 b, To trye y[e] mater w[t] dynte of swearde. **1545** ELYOT, *Disceptare armis*, to trye by battayle. **1654** R. CODRINGTON tr. *Justine* XI. 298 He was enforced by them to try it out in battel with them. **1703** POPE *Thebais* 490 The rushing winds..With equal rage their airy quarrel try, And win by turns the Kingdoms of the sky. **1857** TROLLOPE *Barchester T.* xxiii, Mr. Arabin said that he would try the question out with Mrs Bold.

d. ***to try out***: to test the advantages, possibilities, or qualities of (a material or immaterial thing); also, to test (a person). orig. *U.S.*

1888 *Judge* (N.Y.) 29 Dec. 190/1 Tried Out By Fire. **1899** *N.Y. Jrnl.* 30 July 34/6 Britain will try out heavy motor wagons. **1906** *N.Y. Evening Post* 26 Oct. 1 The new rules have been but partially tried out. **1974** A. PRICE *Other Paths to Glory* III. 254 He was being tried out on someone else's problem.

6. *Law.* To examine and determine (a cause or question) judicially; to determine the guilt or otherwise of (an accused person) by consideration of the evidence; to sit in judgement on; to judge. Also *fig.* †Also *intr.* with *of* (quot. *c* 1330). (Prob. the earliest sense recorded in English.)

a. To try a cause or question.

[**1292** BRITTON I. v. §8 Et si n'i eynt mie asez, si soint les chalengs triez. Et si les chalengs soint trovez verrays [etc.].] *a* **1300** *Cursor M.* 9686 (Cott.) Al þat þai striue a-mang þam thre, Thoru þes it agh at tried be. *c* **1330** R. BRUNNE *Chron.* (1810) 313 The wisest of þe clergie, with erles & barouns Togider went to trie of þer peticions. **1467** in *Eng. Gilds* (1870) 401 To trye it by xij. men aftur the lawe in suche case provided. **1562** *Aberdeen Kirk Sess. Rec.* (Spald. Cl.) 4 To trye, discusse, and examyn all faltis and offencis..off the haill inhabitantis off the burgh. *a* **1631** DONNE *Poems* (1650) 103 This will be tryed to morrow. **1755** W. DUNCAN *Cicero's Sel. Orations* x. (1816) 307 He..may desire to know what crime it is that is trying. **1770** C. JENNER *Placid Man* VI. iv, Whilst the..cause had been trying at Mrs. Stapleton's fire-side [etc.]. **1815** SCOTT *Guy M.* xxxiii, It was tried in the Inner-house afore the Feifteen. **1892** SIR A. KEKEWICH in *Law Times Rep.* LXVII. 139/1, I have to try the case before me according to those cases. **1895** *Daily News* 4 Nov. 4/6 Mr. Justice Mathew, who tried the action,..had granted the injunction.

b. To try a person.

1538 ELYOT, *Interrogari legibus*, to be tried by examination, that they had offended against the lawis. **1603** SHAKS. *Meas. for M.* II. i. 21 The Iury..May in the sworne-twelue haue a thiefe, or two Guiltier then him they try. **1674** in *Verney Mem.* (1907) II. 317 Judg Torner's son, who was tryed for his life last November for killing a man. **1797** MRS. RADCLIFFE *Italian* xvi, You must be tried before you are condemned. **1849** CUPPLES *Green Hand* ix, A gang o' Spanish pirates I saw tried for their lives. **1875** JOWETT *Plato* (ed. 2) V. 450 Let him who dares to smite an elder be tried for assault.

c. To submit (a case) for the judgment of a court of law. *U.S.*

1905 S. W. MITCHELL *Constance Trescot* 166 'Do you still feel that all chance of settlement is out of the question?' 'Yes; I am instructed to try the case.' **1931** *N. Amer. Rev.* Jan. 22 This is one of his jokes; he knows I can't afford to try criminal cases. It's been fifteen years since I've been in a criminal court.

7. a. To test the strength, goodness, value, truth, or other quality of; to put to the proof, test, prove.

13.. *E.E. Allit. P.* A. 311 To leue no tale be true to tryȝe, Bot þat hys one skyl may dem. **1362** LANGL. *P. Pl.* A. I. 183 Whan alle tresouris arn triȝede [83 I-triȝed] treuþ e is þe beste. **1422** tr. *Secreta Secret., Priv. Priv.* 188 No word Sholde out-Passe, but yf hit were triet wyth reyson. *a* **1536** TINDALE *Expos. Matt.* vi. (1550) 65 b, Excepte a man be proued and tried it cannot be knowen..that he is righteous. **1602** SHAKS. *Ham.* I. iii. 62 The friends thou hast, and their adoption tride, Grapple them to thy Soule, with hoopes of Steele. **1825** T. HOOK *Sayings* Ser. II. *Man of Many Fr.* (Colburn) 157 Jumping and bumping himself about in Colonel Arden's new carriage in order to try the springs. **1881** FROUDE *Short Stud.* (1883) IV. II. v. 230 He..had determined to try every fact..by the strict rules of inductive science.

b. To examine (a person) for the purpose of testing his qualifications: cf. TRIAL *sb.*[1] 6, TRIER 5. *Obs.* or *Hist.*

1636 in J. Bulloch *Pynours* (1887) 70 In cais any persone ..desyr to be admittit a laborar at the Shoir..they must first be tryit be the watter Baillie. **1654** *Clarke Papers* (Camden) III. 15 Those that sitte at Whitehall to try Ministers.

†**c.** ***to try out***: to reject after trial; in quot., to dismiss (a challenged juryman): cf. TRIER 2.

1542–3 *Act 34 & 35 Hen. VIII*, c. 26 §46 If..the residue of the sade Iurye make defaulte or be tryed out.

d. ***to try a door, window***, etc., to ascertain by attempting to open it whether it is fastened or locked.

1844 DICKENS *Chimes* I. 2 The night-wind..trying, with its unseen hand, the windows and the doors; and seeking out some crevice by which to enter. **1889** GUNTER *That Frenchman* iv, Maurice..closes the door behind him, trying it to be sure the spring lock has worked.

e. To put (a person) to the test to ascertain the truth of what is asserted or believed of him or her. Freq. in imp. ***try me.***

1970 V. CANNING *Great Affair* xi. 193 'You'll not like it.' 'Try me.' **1971** *Scope* (S. Afr.) 19 Mar. 124/2 'Miss Blandish ..ahem..I take it that you can keep a secret?' 'Try me, Mr Stone.' Her voice was like a soft caress. Her suggestion to 'try her' scared J. B. **1984** A. PRICE *Sion Crossing* vi. 106 'I think maybe you won't like it, Oliver.'..'Try me.'

8. *Joinery.* To bring (a piece of timber) to a perfectly flat surface by repeatedly testing it and planing off the projecting parts; to plane with the trying-plane; also ***to try up***; also, to test the straightness of (a planed surface) or the correspondence of (adjoining surfaces); *intr.* (of a surface) to prove accurate or straight when tested.

1593 FALE *Dialling* 2 Prepare a piece of very good wood, try it perfectly on both sides to an equall thicknesse. **1678** MOXON *Mech. Exerc.* iv. 60 To lay Boards..flat against, whiles they are Trying or Plaining. *Ibid.* v. 78 Try it again, as before, and if you find it Try all the way, you may..go over it again. **1679** *Ibid.* ix. 156 Try one side flat,..and both the edges straight. **1683** *Ibid., Printing* x. ¶2 All its Sides are tryed square to one another. **1776** G. SEMPLE *Building in Water* 85 After your Work is tried up or even put together. **1828** ADCOCK *Builders' Pocket-Bk.* 52 Swedish deals.., if tried up square at night they will be crooked in the morning.

9. ***try on***: to test the fit or style of (a garment) by putting it on. Also *absol.*

1693 CONGREVE *Old Bach.* IV. viii, The daughters only tore two pair of kid-leather gloves, with trying 'em on. **1804** MAR. EDGEWORTH *Pop. T., The Will* ii, Miss Barton was trying on her dress. **1848** THACKERAY *Van. Fair* xiii, He.. tried a new coat in Pall Mall. **1883** *Harper's Mag.* Feb. 446/1 She must go at once and 'try on!' It is a special order.

10. To subject to a severe test or strain; to strain the endurance or patience of, put to straits, afflict.

1539 BIBLE (Great) *Hebr.* xi. 36 Other were tried wt mockynges & scourgynges, moreouer, wt bondes & presonment. [Cf. 3.] **1545** ASCHAM *Toxoph.* (Arb.) 156 A syde wynde tryeth an archer and good gere verye muche. **1702** R. NELSON in *Pepys' Diary*, etc. (1879) VI. 257 If the Providence of God thinks fit to try you with the want of both. **1824** BYRON *Juan* XVI. l, Her temper had been tried So much. **1825** B'NESS BUNSEN in Hare *Life* (1879) I. vii. 248 She has been tried in life more hardly than anybody whose ..history I ever yet heard. **1859** MACAULAY in Trevelyan *Life & Lett.* (1876) II. xv. 470 This malady tries me severely. **1905** ELIN. GLYN *Viciss. Evangeline* 142 You look very pale, child—the journey has tried you probably.

11. a. To test the effect or operation of; to use, apply, or practise tentatively or by way of experiment; to experiment with. ***try an experiment***: to make an experiment; to do something in order to see what will come of it, or whether it produces the expected result.

to try conclusions, try a fall, try masteries: see the sbs.

1545 *Primer Hen. VIII* (1546) 126 Try not the lawe with thy seruaunt. **1573** TUSSER *Husb.* (1878) 24 He that of wilfulnes trieth the law, Shall striue for a coxcome, and thriue as a daw. **1625** BACON *Ess., Innovations* (Arb.) 527 It is good also, not to try Experiments in States. **1676** LADY CHAWORTH in *12th Rep. Hist. MSS. Comm.* App. v. 29 Lady Portsmouth continues sicke, and some say she will try the French ayre, others the Bath watters. **1701** in *Lett. Lit. Men* (Camden) 302, I wish you would try Smith and Walford for Cowper's Anatomy, and the Philosophical Transactions. **1702** *Eng. Theophrast.* 170 Those that will be trying masteries with their superiors. **1863** W. C. BALDWIN *Afr. Hunting* vii. 246, I have tried fishing to-day, as I dare not fire a shot for fear of frightening the elephants. **1875** JEVONS *Money* (1878) 246 The United States government tried a similar experiment.

b. To experiment upon (*with* something); to test the effect of something upon.

1784 COWPER in *Gentl. Mag.* LIV. I. 413/1 By..trying him with a variety of herbs [I] restored him to perfect health.

c. *absol.* or *intr.* To make experiment; †in quot. ? to practise.

1573 TUSSER *Husb.* (1878) 60 Dank ling forgot will quickly rot. Here learne and trie to turne it and drie.

d. ***to try (one's) hand***, to attempt to do something for the first time; to test one's ability or aptitude *at* something.

1711 SHAFTESB. *Charac.* I. i. (1737) I. 156 Who will willingly be the first to try our Hand. **1768** TUCKER *Lt. Nat.* (1834) I. 384 Why should I be debarred the liberty of trying my hand as well as another? **1809** W. IRVING *Knickerb.* v. iii. (1849) 271 He determined to try his hand at negotiation. **1896** *N. York Weekly Witness* 30 Dec. 13/1 He prayed to be permitted to try his hand at spellbinding.

e. To test the effect of (a thing) *on* (a person, thing, etc.). ***to try it on the*** (or ***a***) ***dog***: to test the effectiveness of something on someone regarded as being of lesser consequence than those for whom it is ultimately intended; *Theatr.*, to test the possibilities of a play, etc., by performing it as a matinée or before a provincial audience. *colloq.* (orig. *U.S.*).

1890 in Barrère & Leland *Dict. Slang* II. 377/1 'Bootle's Baby' will on the 7th of May be produced somewhere in the provinces. This is what the Americans call trying it on a dog. **1897** *Daily Tel.* 4 Feb. 9/1 If any enterprising person desires to make money from a play or a composition of music he does not boldly attempt the experiment upon the public. His shrewd suspicion that they would avenge the torture induces him to adopt the preliminary precaution of 'trying it on the dog'—a creature of delicate susceptibilities, and very amenable to the influences of Teutonic bands and street-corner cornet solos. **1903** [see 15 b below]. **1922** H. CRANE *Let.* 29 Sept. (1965) 101, I want to try *Dial* [a literary review] on 'F and H', before it goes anywhere else. **1941** G. HEYER *Envious Casca* xiv. 261 Mathilda had never felt less inclined to listen to a dissertation on the benefits of experience to an actress, and she very rudely told Paula to try it on the dog.

f. ***to try in*** (Dentistry): to place (a denture or prosthesis) in the patient's mouth to test the fit. [From the prepositional use illustrated in quot. 1896.]

[**1896** C. J. ESSIG *Amer. Textbk. Prosthetic Dentistry* xi. 408 After the teeth of a full upper denture have been tried in the mouth and found to be correct, a protective rim is to be made.] **1921** D. GABELL *Prosthetic Dentistry* viii. 199 The dentures should be placed in tepid water with some pleasant antiseptic, ..and then each separately tried in. **1968** NEILL & NAIRN *Compl. Denture Prosthetics* 101/2 When trying in the waxed-up dentures initially the opportunity is taken to.. check the jaw relationships.

g. ***try anything once***: a cliché indicating (often somewhat unexpected) willingness on the part of a speaker to attempt or experience something new.

1921 *Ladies' Home Jrnl.* July 20/1 This slogan runs, 'Try anything once'. **1959** N. MAILER *Advts. for Myself* (1961) 160 'I am sort of curious about the film. I've never seen one [*sc.* a pornographic film], you know.' 'Try anything once, is that it?'

h. ***try-your-strength, try-your-weight***: used *attrib.* to designate an apparatus at a fair or the like which tests or measures a person's strength or weight.

1929 J. B. PRIESTLEY *Good Companions* I. iv. 135 One o' these try-your-strength things..—down with the 'ammer and up she goes and rings the bell. **1930** R. LEHMANN *Note in Music* v. 214 A try-your-strength machine that gave him his money back. **1932** *Radio Times* 29 July 241/1 Everything to make them feel at home..try-your-weight machines, 'diddlers', peeps-at-Paris. **1963** WODEHOUSE *Stiff Upper Lip, Jeeves* iii. 24 There was plenty and to spare of the Rev. H. P. Pinker. Even as a boy..he must have burst seams and broken try-your-weight machines. **1977** 'E. CRISPIN' *Glimpses of Moon* vi. 97, I want to try the Try-Your-Strength machine.

12. To endeavour to ascertain by experiment or effort; to attempt to find out; sometimes nearly = sense 11. **a.** with simple obj. (usually *fortune, luck*, or the like.)

1573 [see FORTUNE *sb.* 3 c]. **1601** R. JOHNSON *Kingd. & Commw.* (1603) 59 If he had but thirtie thousand good footemen..he could willingly haue found in his hart to trie his fortune with this enemie. **1741** S. SPEED in *Buccleuch MSS.* (Hist. MSS. Comm.) I. 398 We shall go to Jamaica,..and try our luck once more. **1838** DE MORGAN *Ess. Probabilities* i. 21 They think they are *trying their luck*, as the phrase is. **1849** MACAULAY *Hist. Eng.* vii. II. 202 He tried the effects of frowns and menaces. **1885** 'MRS. ALEXANDER' *At Bay* x, I have not yet been accepted. I have not even tried my chance. **1902** A. E. W. MASON *Four Feathers* viii, If he tried his luck with Miss Eustace.

b. with indirect interrogative clause (*how, if, what, whether*, etc.).

1596 SHAKS. *Tam. Shr.* I. ii. 17 Ile trie how you can Sol, Fa, and sing it. *c* **1643** LD. HERBERT *Autobiog.* (1824) 20 Many ships scattering themselves to try whether they could obtain a prize. **1680** MOXON *Mech. Exerc.* xii. 208 Try how the Centers are pitcht, by Treading the Treddle lightly down. *a* **1700** in *Cath. Rec. Soc. Publ.* (1911) IX. 341 To trie what effects her Maiestys example might have on others. **1819** in *Shelley Mem.* (1859) 126 Let you and I try if we cannot be as punctual and businesslike as the best of them.

13. To show or find to be so by test or experience; to prove, demonstrate. (With simple obj., obj. cl., inf., or obj. and compl.) Now *rare* or *Obs.*

c **1412** [see TRIED 3]. *c* **1500** in I. S. Leadam *Star Chamb. Cases* (1903) 101 He wold not take oon peny of him Except his right were tryed good. *a* **1553** UDALL *Royster D.* v. i. (Arb.) 79 She may hir selfe discharge and trie hir honestie. **1589** *Whip for Ape* A 2, Sometimes his choppes doo walke in poynts too hie, Wherein the Ape himselfe a Woodcocke tries. **1592** SHAKS. *Rom. & Jul.* IV. iii. 29 He hath still beene tried a holy man. **1642** *Declar. Lords & Comm.* 2 Sept. 5 Fasting and Prayer having bin often tryed to be very effectuall. **1892** J. KENT *Racing Life Ld. G. Cavendish Bentinck* 47 Lord George Cavendish tried Godolphin to be a good horse.

†**14.** To have experience of; to undergo, go through. *Obs.*

1579 LYLY *Euphues* (Arb.) 84 The quiet life which I haue tryed being a mayden. **1625** GILL *Sacr. Philos.* Pref., That treatise tryed the common fortune of all bookes; some slighted..others condemned it. **1667** MILTON *P.L.* IX. 860 Never more Mean I to trie what rash untri'd I sought, The paine of absence from thy sight. **1738** GRAY *Propertius* II. v. 39 Or if, alas! it be my Fate to try Another Love.

15. a. To test one's ability to deal with (something); to attempt to do, perform, or accomplish (an action); to venture upon, to essay. ***to try over***, to go through (a performance, etc.) experimentally.

c **1315** SHOREHAM I. 1290 Nou ich habbe of þe ferste yteld, þat oþer wyl ich trye. **1500–20** DUNBAR *Poems* xxvii. 1 Nixt that a turnament wes tryid That lang befoir in hell wes cryid. **1607** WALKINGTON *Opt. Glass* 83 b, This little barke.., which neuer tryed the foming maine beforne. **1638** JUNIUS *Paint. Ancients* 12 All kind of worke seemeth to be hard before we doe try it. **1812** J. WILSON *Isle of Palms* II. 489 The boat hath left the lonesome rock And tries the wave again. **1870** LOWELL *Among my Bks.* Ser. I. 176 Fancy a parody of Shakespeare... You might as well try it with the Venus of Melos. *Mod.* I should like to try it over first.

b. ***try it on*** (with play on sense 9): to attempt an imposition; to endeavour to outwit or get the better of some one (usu. const. *with*); *spec.* in *Thieves Cant*, to live by thieving. *slang.*

1811 *Lex. Balatr., Try on*, to endeavour. To live by thieving. Coves who try it on; professed thieves. **1812** *Sporting Mag.* XXXIX. 284 Witness agreed to try it on again although he considered himself in danger. **1848** THACKERAY *Van. Fair* xxxiv, No jokes, old boy: no trying it on me. **1903** FARMER & HENLEY *Slang* s.v., *To try it on*, to seek to outwit, get the better of, fleece, cheat... *To try it on a dog* = to experiment at another's expense or risk. **1912** *Oxf. & Camb. Rev.* Nov. 14 If he tries it on, the audience.. is ready to convince him of his mistake.

16. a. *intr.* To make an effort, endeavour, attempt. (With *inf.*, or *absol.*)

1638 [implied in TRIAL *sb.*[1] 8]. **1697** DRYDEN *Virg. Georg.* III. 355 To repair his Strength he tries: Hardning his Limbs with painful Exercise. **1738** GRAY *Propertius* iii. 23 While to retain the envious Lawn she tries. **1847** MARRYAT *Childr. N. Forest* iv, You will have to try and try again. **1895** *Pall Mall G.* 7 Oct. 1/3 England..has tried her best to head him off the path down which he seems determined to rush. **18..** *Pop. Melody*, If at first you don't succeed, Try, try, try again.

b. Followed by *and* and a co-ordinated verb (instead of *to* with inf.) expressing the action attempted. *colloq.* Cf. AND B. 10.

1686 J. S[ERGEANT] *Hist. Monast. Convent* 9 They try and express their love to God by their thankfulness to him. **1802** H. MARTIN *Helen of Glenross* II. 143 Frances retired, to try and procure a little rest. **1819**, **1878** [see AND B. 10]. **1855** in Coleridge *Mem. Keble* (1869) II. 425, I have something to write to you on that matter, which I shall try and put on another piece of paper. **1883** L. OLIPHANT *Altiora Peto* I. 251 He had good reason to think that Sark was likely to try and back out.

c. Const. with preposition. ***try for***, to attempt to obtain or find (an object), or to reach (a place). ***try at***, to make an attempt upon, endeavour to get at; to attempt to do or accomplish.

1534 in I. S. Leadam *Sel. Cas. Crt. Requests* (Selden Soc.) 43 Your sayd humble subgett is a very powre man and nott able to trye for his sayd libertie..by the ordre of the comen lawe. **1653** *Caldwell Papers* (Maitl. Cl.) I. 108 Quhen he went to search and try for the lard's hors yt was stollen. **1763** [see FOR *prep.* 12]. **1794** CHARLOTTE SMITH *Wand. Warwick* 195 Xaviera..seemed, by an effort of resolution, to try at conquering her confusion. **1816** TUCKEY *Narr. Exped. R. Zaire* i. (1818) 10 The sea being much discoloured, we tried for soundings, but did not get bottom with 120 fathoms of line. **1913** *Illustr. Lond. News* 16 Aug. 266/2 On three occasions he made some show of trying for a degree, and between times attended as few lectures as he could.

d. *intr.* and *trans.* To search a place in order to find something, esp. game, or its scent. *colloq.*

1810 *Sporting Mag.* XXXVI. 233 He bid the other defendants try across the Six Acres. **1821** CLARE *Vill. Minstr.* I. 125 Bees in every peep did try. **1827** G. A. MCCALL *Lett. fr. Frontiers* (1868) 178 The Colonel had directed Maximo to bring..all..appliances for hunting the green turtle; and the latter..was thus early in motion to 'try' after turtle. **1909** *Toilers of Deep* Oct. 246/1 Frequently they 'try a piece', as fishing parlance has it.

e. *intr.* ***try back***: to go back (*lit.* or *fig.*) so as to cover ground afresh where something has previously been missed; to 'hark back'.

1816 KNOX & JEBB *Corr.* II. 273 At college, I was obliged to try back in mathematics. Through daily life, I am obliged to try back in minor morals. **1857** HUGHES *Tom Brown* I. vii, They tried back slowly and sorrowfully, and found the lane. **1863** WHYTE MELVILLE *Gladiators* 233 Like a hound..now trying back with untiring perseverance. **1874** R. TYRWHITT *Sketch. Club* 3 To get people to see when their work won't do, and to try back and attempt simpler things.

f. *trans.* To attempt or solicit (a woman); to endeavour to seduce; also of a stallion, to attempt to cover (a mare).

1713 LADY M. W. MONTAGU *Lady's Resolve*, In part she is to blame that has been try'd; He comes too near, that comes to be deny'd. **1811** *Sporting Mag.* XXXVIII. 212 The horse took as much pains to try the mare as any stallion.

†**17.** *Naut. intr.* Of a vessel: To lie to. (See quot. 1867.) Also, ***to try a-hull***. *Obs.*

The meaning in first quot. is doubtful.

[**1533** J. HEYWOOD *Play Wether* (1903) 572 The see.. Where shyppes by meane of wynd try from port to porte.] **1556** in Hakluyt *Voy.* (1598) I. 277 When the barke had way, we cut the hawser, and so gate the sea to our friend, and tryed out al that day with our maine corse. **1610** SHAKS. *Temp.* I. i. 37 Downe with the top-Mast: yare, lower, lower, bring her to Try with Maine-course. **1725** H. DE SAUMAREZ in *Phil. Trans.* XXXIII. 427 We had hard Gales..and a distracted Sea, insomuch that we try'd under a double reef'd Mainsail, great Part of the Time. **1773** *Life N. Frowde* 122 We were obliged..to ly too, and let the Ship drive with the Tempest, and at length, to try a Hull. **1867** SMYTH *Sailor's Word-bk., Try*, or Lie-to in a Gale, is by a judicious balance of canvas, to keep a ship's bow to the sea, and..prevent her rolling to windward in the trough of a sea.

try-, the verb-stem in combination.

1. with sbs., forming sbs. denoting appliances, etc. for trying (in various senses of the verb): **try-cock**, 'a gauge-cock' (Webster 1864); **try-gun**, a model gun with an adjustable stock (see quot.); **try-house**, a building for 'trying' or extracting oil from blubber, etc.; **try-pit**, a testing pit for trying new engines; **try-plane**, a trying-plane (Knight *Dict. Mech.* 1877); **try-pot**, a pot for 'trying' oil from blubber; **try rule** (see quot.); **try-square**, a carpenter's square for laying off short perpendiculars; **try-stick**, a stick used in fitting leather work; **try-works**, the apparatus used for 'trying' oil from blubber. See also TRYSAIL.

1892 GREENER *Breech-Loader* 95 The '*try gun'..permits of the stock being altered to any length, bend, cast-off, and shape of the butt, and is of use in fitting a sportsman who needs a gun of special build. **1891** *Cent. Dict.*, *Try-house. **1895** *Century Mag.* Aug. 575/1 To come up the crooked road ..past the try-house. **1896** KIPLING *Seven Seas, M'Andrews' Hymn* 44 Mill, forge, an' *try-pit taught them [ship's engines] that. **1795** R. MURRY *Jrnl.* 12 Oct. in R. McNab *Hist. Rec. N.Z.* (1914) II. 523 The *try pot and steam were as they were left. **1836** *Uncle Philip's Convers. Whale Fishery* 267 [They] cut the blubber, before it is thrown into the try-pots. **1875** TEMPLE & SHELDON *Hist. Northfield, Mass.* 159 In those days, no frames were set out by the square rule, but by what they called the *try rule,.. i.e. the sills, posts and beams were framed and tried, and the braces were laid on to mark their bevels and length. **1877** KNIGHT *Dict. Mech.*, **Try-square*..consists of a thin blade of steel..let into a wooden piece..and securely fastened at right angles. **1901** *J. Black's Illustr. Carp. & Build., Home Handicr.* 19 The transverse lines..drawn with the pencil.. can afterwards be corrected with the try square. **1888** FARR & THRUPP *Coach Trimming* iii. 39 He should neatly join on the back and side pieces, making use of *try-sticks..to secure their right appliance. **1792** Z. MACY *Jrnl.* 15 May in *Mass. Hist. Soc. Coll.* (1810) III. 157 The oil [was] boiled out in the *try works at sea. *c* **1825** CHOYCE *Log of Jack Tar* (1891) 198 A native trying to steal a brass cock from the try-works. **1898** F. T. BULLEN *Cruise 'Cachalot'* 11 Her deck was flush fore and aft, the only obstructions being the brick-built 'try-works' in the waist.

2. with advbs., forming sbs. derived from adverbial combinations of the verb: **try-in** *Dentistry* [TRY *v.* 11 f], the experimental trial of a denture or prosthesis in a patient's mouth as a preliminary to any further work; also, the prosthesis itself; **try-on** (TRY *v.* 15 b, 9), (*a*) (*slang*) an attempt, *esp.* an attempt at imposition or deceit; also *transf.* the subject of an attempt; (*b*) the act of trying on a garment; **try-out** *colloq.* (orig. *U.S.*), a selective trial; also, an experimental trial, a test of performance, a trial run or period, *spec.* of a play, etc., in a provincial theatre, etc.; also *attrib.*

1939 R. O. SCHLOSSER *Compl. Denture Prosthesis* xvi. 244 One of the dentures..may be completely processed, and a final *try-in made while the opposing denture is still in the wax model state. **1963** C. R. COWELL et al. *Inlays, Crowns, & Bridges* iii. 26 Immediately before the try-in the temporary dressing must be removed. **1970** J. M. BUCHANAN *Atlas Compl. Denture Prosthesis* xix. 100/2 Replace the characterized mandibular try-in in the patient's mouth. **1977** M. M. HUDIS *Dental Lab. Prosthodontics* iv. 99 The teeth are arranged on the occlusion rims so that they may be returned to the dentist for a try-in. **1823** 'J. BEE' *Slang* 181 **Try-on*,..an essay or endeavour to do a thing. **1874** *Siliad* 57 The flagitious claims—Call them, or damages, 'tries-on', or shames. **1885** *Law Times Rep.* LIII. 479/2 This was a try-on, on the part of the solicitors which ought not to be allowed. **1905** *Daily News* 28 Oct. 6 Garments must be cut to fit without successive try-ons. **1903** *Sci. Amer.* 30 May 414/1 Cup challengers in their *try-outs in British waters. **1906** *Tyer* VI. 171 One girl represented the Athena Club in the debaters' tryout, and won a place as an inter-collegiate debater. **1915** *Literary Digest* (N.Y.) 21 Aug. 361/2 The new Grinnell Sprinkler equipment..has already had its initial tryout. **1923** *N.Y. Times* 7 Oct. IX. 2/6 *Try out*, an experimental hearing of a new act, usually far away from Broadway. **1928** *Evening News* 18 Aug. 9/3 The play will not be given the provincial 'try-out'. **1933** P. GODFREY *Back-Stage* vi. 76 Had this play not first been produced at a 'try-out' theatre..its author might still be sending it round. **1941** B. SCHULBERG *What Makes Sammy Run?* i. 4 Sammy was getting a three-week tryout. **1963** A. ROSS *Australia 63* viii. 157 Davidson's final try-out in the nets was watched over.. by two selectors, Bradman and Seddon. **1970** A. GLYN *Blood of Britishman* xxi. 275 Brief try-outs of plays before they arrive in London's West End. **1976** A. DAVIS *Television* 89 It is as difficult to predict which comedy series will succeed as to forecast which records will top the hit parade charts, and that is one of the reasons for the development of try-out series. **1983** *Listener* 17 Mar. 29/3 *Gilgamesh* was chosen to give the new technology a try-out.

tryable, tryacle, obs. ff. TRIABLE, TREACLE.

tryangle, -gyl, obs. ff. TRIANGLE.

tryb, trybe, obs. ff. TRIBE.

tryce, obs. f. TRICE.

trycherye, trychor, -our: see TREACHERY, TREACHER.

tryde, obs. f. *tried*: see TRY *v.*

trydle, obs. f. TREADLE.

trye, var. TRAY *sb.*[1]; obs. f. TREY, TRY.

tryefull, tryen, tryer, tryews, obs. ff. TRIFLE, TREEN, TRIER, TRUCE.

tryfetrafe: see TRIFF-TRAFF.

tryfoly, -foyle, obs. ff. TREFOIL.

tryget, -our, var. TREGET, -OUR *Obs.*

‖**trygon** ('traɪgɒn). [L. *trȳgōn* (Pliny), a. Gr. τρυγών a dove, also the fish.] A fish with a sharp spine in its tail, a sting-ray.

[**1706** PHILLIPS (ed. Kersey), *Trygon*, the Turtle-Dove.] **1749** G. WEST tr. *Odes of Pindar* (1753) I. 258 And by my Dart the Lord of Ithaca, Not by the pois'nous Trygon's Bone expir'd. **1774** GOLDSM. *Nat. Hist.* VI. 260 Circe armed her son with a spear headed with the spine of the trygon.

trygon, tryhumphe, obs. ff. TRIGON, TRIUMPH.

trying ('traɪɪŋ), *vbl. sb.* [f. TRY *v.* + -ING[1].]

a. The action of the verb TRY, in various senses.

c **1440** *Promp. Parv.* 502/2 Tryynge, *eleccio, preeleccio, examinacio.* **1447** *Ordinaunce of Exchequer* 35 c. 62 (6) A iij, To the mayster for laboure of redynge endosynge and tryenge of peticyons and fynes. **1535** COVERDALE *Ecclus.* xvi. 22 The tryenge out of men is in the fulfillynge. **1630** *R. Johnson's Kingd. & Commw.* 216 They know not the use of trying of Mettals. **1669** STURMY *Mariner's Mag.* I. ii. 17 It is better spooning before the Sea, than trying or hulling. **1819** *Sporting Mag.* V. 123 All the frolic, fun,..gammon, and trying-it-on are depicted. **1898** F. T. BULLEN *Cruise 'Cachalot'* 95 The whole work of cutting in and trying out was got through without a single accident.

b. *attrib.*, as **trying-plane**, a long heavy plane used after the jack-plane for the accurate squaring of timber; **trying-pot**, a pot for 'trying' out oil; **trying-square** = *try-square* (see TRY- 1).

1579 [see SQUARE *sb.* 2]. **1815** J. SMITH *Panorama Sc. & Art* I. 109 The trying-plane is made use of to produce a higher degree of regularity and smoothness. **1823** P. NICHOLSON *Pract. Build.* 244 The Trying-Plane..is used to regulate and smooth, to a higher degree, the surface of a piece of stuff that has already been reduced to its intended form by means of the jack-plane. **1843** E. DIEFFENBACH *Trav. N.Z.* I. ii. 51 The blubber is..immediately put into the trying-pots. **1882** F. M. CRAWFORD *Mr. Isaacs* iii, The only way to arrive at any conclusion is by a sort of trying-on process. **1885** C. F. HOLDER *Marvels Anim. Life* 177 The trying-pots were taken to a small inlet.

trying ('traɪɪŋ), *ppl. a.* [f. TRY *v.* + -ING[2].] That tries. **1.** That tests severely; that is a trial; hard to bear or endure; severe, distressing, painful; that tries one's endurance or patience.

1718 HICKES & NELSON *J. Kettlewell* II. xv. 98 For the Security of the Church..in such a Trying Time. **1798** *Monthly Mag.* Mar. 183 Sudden vicissitudes of temperature must be exceedingly trying to delicate constitutions. **1825** HONE *Every-day Bk.* I. 652 The month of May is..a 'trying' month, to persons..ailing. **1907** J. H. PATTERSON *Man-Eaters of Tsavo* xvi. 175 She was so..exhausted by her trying march..that she was scarcely able to speak.

2. Attempting, endeavouring, striving. *rare.*

1577 GRANGE *Golden Aphrod.*, etc. O iij, This got I say my trying tongue, whiche tolde hyr many a lye. **1836** MRS. BROWNING *Poet's Vow* IV. iv, The old eyes searching..The young ones..To read their look if sound forsook The trying, trembling breath. **1841** [implied in *tryingly*].

Hence **'tryingly** *adv.*, in a trying manner or degree; in the way of attempt or endeavour (*rare*); distressingly, painfully; **'tryingness**, trying or distressing quality or character.

1841 *Tait's Mag.* VIII. 109 The small hand put out so tryingly. **1859** CORNWALLIS *New World* I. 359 The climate ..is..at times rather tryingly warm. **1885** *My Wife's Niece* II. xi, An attitude which showed so freely and tryingly the lines of her figure. **1897** MARY KINGSLEY *W. Africa* xxv. 569 To walk through, give me kokos for good all-round tryingness, particularly when they are wet.

tryist, obs. form of TRYST.

†**trylle,** *v. Obs. rare*[−1]. [app. = MDu., early mod.Du. *drillen, trillen* to tremble, shiver (Plantijn, Kilian). Cf. TRILL *v.*[4]] *intr.* To tremble.

13.. *E.E. Allit. P.* A. 78 As bornyst syluer þe lef onslydez, þat þike con trylle on vcha tynde.

‖**tryma** ('traɪmə). *Bot.* [mod.L. (Necker), ad. Gr. τρῦμα or τρύμη hole, f. τρύειν to rub down, wear out.] A fruit resembling a drupe, but formed from an originally compound ovary, and having an ultimately dehiscent fleshy or fibrous exocarp, as the walnut and coco-nut; a kind of drupaceous nut.

1857 HENFREY *Elem. Bot.* §280. **1861** BENTLEY *Man. Bot.* 321 The Tryma..differs but little from the ordinary drupe, except in being formed from an originally compound ovary. **1900** JACKSON *Gloss. Bot. Terms*, *Tryma*.., Necker's term for a drupaceous nut with dehiscent exocarp, as the walnut.

trymble, trym(m)le, etc., obs. ff. TREMBLE.

trymebote, trymle bote: see TRIMBOAT.

tryndall, -dell, -dle, etc., obs. ff. TRINDLE.

tryndle bed, -tayle, obs. ff. TRUNDLE-BED, -TAIL.

tryne, obs. f. TRAIN, TREEN, TRINE.

trynitee, -tie, trynle, trynsch, trynter, obs. ff. TRINITY, TRINDLE, TRENCH, THRINTER.

tryor, tryoumffe, obs. ff. TRIER, TRIUMPH.

tryp, var. TRIPE[2] *Obs.*, velvet.

trypaflavine (trɪpə'fleɪviːn). *Pharm.* [f. TRYPA(NOSOMA (see quot. 1954) + L. *flāv-us* yellow: see -INE[5].] = ACRIFLAVINE.

1913 *Chem. Abstr.* VII. 2944 Trypaflavine..and KCN.. give 3,6-diamino-N-methyl-ms-cyanoacridane,..partially converted back into trypaflavine by heating with conc. H_2SO_4. **1954** *Thorpe's Dict. Appl. Chem.* (ed. 4) XI. 381/2 Amongst purely organic substances, Acriflavine..was originally introduced as a trypanocide under the name *Trypaflavin.* **1975** *Biol. Abstr.* LX. 50/1 (*heading*) Investigation of the interaction between trypaflavine and nucleic acid components.

trypan ('trɪpən). [Short for TRYPANOSOMA.] In **trypan blue** [rendering G. *trypanblau*], a diazo dye used as a vital stain and in the treatment of trypanosomiasis and other protozoan infections. **trypan red** [rendering Ger. *trypanrot*], a drug used in cases of trypanosomiasis.

1905 *Brit. Med. Jrnl.* 27 May 1140 The treatment of trypan red in various trypanosomic diseases. **1907** *Daily News* 31 Aug. 4 According to 'The Hospital', the correct name for trypan red, which is now used in cases of trypanosomiasis, is 'sodium-ortho-benzidine-mono-sulphoacid-diazo-b-2-naphthylamine-3.6-sulphoacid'! [**1909** *Parasitology* II. 187 Trypanblau and Trypanrot are highly efficient remedies in the treatment of canine piroplasmosis.] **1911** *Chem. Abstr.* V. 3495 (*heading*) Tryparosan, trypan red, trypan blue and parafuchsin in immunization against rabies. **1980** *Nature* 8 May 110 (*caption*) Viable cells (trypan blue exclusion) at 16 h after infection normally contained approximately 10% bi- and multinucleated heterokaryons.

trypanocidal (ˌtrɪpənəʊ'saɪdəl), *a.* [f. TRYPANO(SOMA + -CIDE 1 + -AL.] That is fatal to trypanosomes.

1909 *Practitioner* Feb. 248 Trypanocidal substances. **1946** A. A. MORTON *Chem. Heterocyclic Compounds* xii. 339 Crude dichloro ortho-para fuchsin proved less toxic but more trypanocidal than para fuchsin, methyl violet, and like compounds. **1976** P. COLLARD *Devel. Microbiol.* v. 55 Atoxyl is a very effective trypanocidal agent.

So **try'panocide**, a trypanocidal agent; = *trypanosomacide* s.v. TRYPANOSOMA.

1917 in STEDMAN *Med. Dict.* (ed. 4) 1012/2. **1956** *Nature* 31 Mar. 604/2 Contributions on trypanocides, antimalarials, amœbicides and on the chemotherapy of virus infections. **1977** *Lancet* 8 Oct. 769/1 On its own, S.H.A.M. is ineffective as a trypanocide in vivo, but when combined with glycerol it temporarily clears bloodstream trypanosomes in rodents infected with *T. brucei.*

trypanolysis (trɪpə'nɒlɪsɪs). [f. as prec. + -LYSIS.] Destruction of trypanosomes.

1905 *Index Medicus* 2nd Ser. III. 200/1 (Index), Trypanolysis. **1936** *Ann. Trop. Med. & Parasitol.* XXX. 377 Trypanolysis by mouse immune serum is very rapidly effective in the presence of added haemolytic complement. **1979** *Infection & Immunity* XXIV. 691/1 Eleven anti-*T*[*rypanosoma*] *brucei* and five anti-*T. congolense* IIg preparations were tested in the trypanolysis assay for the presence of trypanolytic factors.

ˌ**trypano'lytic,** *a.* [f. TRYPANO(SOMA) + Gr. λυτικός loosing, dissolving.] Tending to, or connected with the destruction of trypanosomes.

1907 *Nature* 31 Oct. 680/1 The causes of trypanolytic crises and relapses. **1979** [see prec.].

‖**Trypanosoma** (ˌtrɪpənəʊ'səʊmə). *Zool.* [mod.L., f. Gr. τρύπανον borer + σῶμα body.] A genus of flagellate infusorial protozoa, species of which are parasitic in the blood of man and other animals, causing specific diseases, such as sleeping-sickness; an infusorian of this genus. Hence ˌ**trypano'somacide** [L. *-cīda*, -CIDE 1], a substance having the property of destroying trypanosomes; **trypanosomal** (-'səʊməl) *a.*, (*a*) of, pertaining to, or caused by trypanosomes; (*b*) = *trypanosomid* adj.; **trypanosomatic** (-səʊ'mætɪk), **-somatous** (-'səʊmətəs) *adjs.*, = *trypanosomal* adj. (*a*); ‖ˌ**trypanosoma'tosis** [mod.L.: see -OSIS] = *trypanosomiasis*; **'trypanosome** (-səʊm) [a. F. *trypanosome* (Gruby, 1843)], (*a*) an infusorian of the genus *Trypanosoma*; (*b*) used *attrib.* to designate trypanosomes and related hæmoflagellates at a stage in their life cycle when they have an elongated body with the flagellum arising from the posterior end; cf. TRYPOMASTIGOTE; ‖**trypanosomiasis** (-səʊ'maɪəsɪs), pl. **-ases** (-əsiːz) [mod.L., after *elephantiasis*, etc.; but the etymological pronunciation would be (-ɪ'eɪsɪs)], a disease produced by infection with trypanosomes; **trypanosomic** (-'səʊmɪk) *a.* = *trypanosomal* (in quot. 1906, infected with trypanosomes); **trypano'somid** *sb.* and *a.* [ad. mod.L. *Trypanosomidæ* (F. Doflein *Die Protozoen als Parasiten und Krankheitserreger* (1901) 57): see -ID[3]], (pertaining to or designating) a member of the family Trypanosomidæ, which comprises trypanosomes and related species of flagellate protozoans which at some stage in their life cycle have an elongated body with one nucleus and a single flagellum arising from a kinetosome; also **trypano'somatid** *sb.* and *a.* (corresponding to the synonymous family name Trypanosomatidæ).

[**1843** GRUBY in *Comptes Rendus* XVII. 1134 (*title*) Recherches et observations sur une nouvelle espèce d'hématozoaire, *Trypanosoma sanguinis.* Les travaux des physiologistes modernes ont fait connaître l'existence de parasites vivants dans le sang des animaux. *Ibid.* 1135 Je propose de nommer cet hématozoaire *Trypanosome.*] **1880** KENT *Infusoria* I. 218 **Trypanosoma*... Occurring in the blood of Amphibia, and within the intestinal viscera of domestic poultry. **1898** P. MANSON *Trop. Diseases* v. 102 [Sir David] Bruce's notable work on the tsetse fly as a medium in diffusing the trypansoma of 'fly disease'. **1903** *Daily Chron.* 20 Nov. 5/2 A fly had been found to convey the newly-discovered blood-parasite of tropical countries, called the trypanosoma. **1903** *Times* 7 Nov. 12/1 The search for what must, we suppose, be styled a *trypanosomacide. **1904** *Brit. Med. Jrnl.* 17 Sept. 644 Prowazek..finds similar *trypanosomal forms which also assume resting forms. **1908** *Lancet* 2 May 1285/2 Trypanosomal infection. **1942** D. L. BELDING *Textbk. Clin. Parasitol.* xi. 144 The species..of the genus *Herpetomonas* have four stages in their life cycle, appearing as leishmanian, leptomonad, crithidial and trypanosomal forms. **1971** MARKELL & VOGE *Med. Parasitol.* (ed. 3) vii. 115 In both the Gambian and Rhodesian forms of African trypanosomiasis, the parasites occur in the blood stream and central nervous system in the trypanosomal form. **1904** *Science* 22 July 112/2 The cultivation of the organisms causing *trypanosomatic diseases. **1962** *Jrnl. Protozool.* IX. 53/1 Because certain species of horseflies..have been incriminated in the transmission of trypanosomes of animals, a study of their own *trypanosomatid parasites has a particular interest for students of insect flagellates. **1963** F. G. WALLACE in J. Ludvík et al. *Progr. in Protozool.* 70 The criteria that have been used most in the definition of genera among the trypanosomatids of insects have been morphological. **1977** C. D. BECKER in J. P. Kreier *Parasitic Protozoa* I. x. 370 Trypanosomes of fish appear to be similar to related trypanosomatids from the blood of other vertebrates. **1903** *Lancet* 4 Apr. 945/2 [The chimpanzee] suffers from ankylostomiasis, filariasis, and *trypanosomatosis. **1891** *Cent. Dict.*, **Trypanosomatous.* **1903** *Daily Record & Mail* 16 Apr. 5 Although we found the parasite in none of the natives..we did find a *trypanasome in each of two horses belonging to the commandant. **1908** *Athenæum* 21 Nov. 651/3 Prof. E. A. Minchin exhibited a series of drawings of trypanosomes obtained from British freshwater fishes. **1924** HEGNER & TALIAFERRO *Human Protozool.* v. 151 Once these crithidial forms [of *Trypanosoma* spp.] are established in the salivary glands they probably form a permanent source for the production of the infective trypanosome forms. **1949** C. A. HOARE *Handbk. Med. Protozool.* xi. 171 The developmental stages through which trypanosomes pass in the course of their life-cycle..comprise the trypanosome, crithidial and leishmanial forms, and occasionally also the leptomonad form. **1967** A. W. JONES *Introd. Parasitol.* xxix. 412 *Trypanosoma*..may include all forms, and it parasitizes insect and vertebrate hosts. In the latter host, only the trypanosome form occurs. **1902** *Westm. Gaz.* 21 Aug. 5/2 An..expedition to West Africa..left..to-day... They go to French Senegal,..into the interior to investigate the tropical disease known as *trypanosomiasis. **1912** *Nature* 21 Nov. 338/2 The progress..of our knowledge with regard to the trypanosomiases of animals and human beings in Africa. **1905** *Brit. Med. Jrnl.* 27 May 1140 The heavy loss among horses and cattle..from various *trypanosomic diseases. *Ibid.* [see TRYPAN]. **1906** *Jrnl. Med. Research* July 125 This water is then inoculated with the otherwise sterile trypanosomic blood. **1956** *Nature* 11 Feb. 279/2 (*heading*) A synthetic growth medium for the *trypanosomid flagellate *Strigomonas* (*Herpetomonas*) *oncopelti*. *Ibid.*, This trypanosomid..is parasitic in the digestive tract of Hemiptera. **1975** *Nature* 8 May 157/1 Calcium may be responsible for the control of flagellar activity in a trypanosomid flagellate, *Crithidia oncopelti*.

tryparsamide (trɪˈpɑːsəmaɪd). *Pharm.* [f. TRYP(ANOSOMA + ARS(ENIC *sb.*[1] + AMIDE.] An arsenical organic compound, $C_8H_{10}AsN_2Na O_4.\frac{1}{2}H_2O$, used to treat trypanosomiasis and syphilis of the central nervous system.

1921 *Jrnl. Exper. Med.* XXXIII. 193 (*heading*) Therapeutic action of N-phenylglycineamide-*p*-arsonic acid (tryparsamide) upon experimental infections of *Trypanosoma rhodesiense.* **1935** *Lancet* 26 Jan. 193/2 After one injection of reduced tryparsamide the trypanocidal titre of the urine rapidly rose to an enormous level. **1974** *Trypanosomiasis & Leishmaniasis* (Ciba Foundation) 310 The problem of drug resistance has became of less importance since the discontinuance of tryparsamide for the treatment of established cases, and its replacement by melaminyl derivatives of arsenic such as melarsoprol and melarsonyl potassium.

trypet, obs. f. TRIPPET[1].

trypit: see TRIPE[2].

trypograph (ˈtrɪpəgrɑːf, -æ-). [f. Gr. τρῦπα hole, τρυπᾶν to perforate + -GRAPH.] A kind of printing done by means of a paper stencil made by writing with a stylus on paper placed over a finely roughened steel surface so as to produce minute perforations. So **trypoˈgraphic** *a.*, of the nature of, pertaining to, or made by such printing.

1883 R. HALDANE *Workshop Receipts* Ser. II. 191/2 This kind of printing is called 'trypograph'... Calico receives the trypographic impression admirably.

trypomastigote (trɪpəʊˈmæstɪgəʊt). *Zool.* [f. Gr. τρυπ-ᾶν to bore + -O + Gr. μαστῑγ-, μάστιξ whip + -ώτης (see -OT[2], -OTE).] A stage in the life cycle of trypanosomes (see quot. 1966). Cf. TRYPANOSOME b.

1966 HOARE & WALLACE in *Nature* 17 Dec. 1386/1 We have devised the following new terms... (3) Opisthomastigote.., for former 'trypanosome'..stage, represented..by forms with postnuclear kinetoplast; flagellum arising near it and emerging from its anterior end. .. (5) Trypomastigote.., for the true 'trypanosome' stage, represented by forms with postnuclear kinetoplast; flagellum arising near it and emerging from the side of the body to run along a long undulating membrane. **1980** J. N. FARMER *Protozoa* vi. 225/1 Trypomastigotes reproduce in the vertebrate host by means of longitudinal binary fission except in the case of *Trypanosoma* (*S.*) *cruzi*.

tryppe, obs. form of TRIP, TRIPE[1].

tryppgette, obs. form of TREBUCHET.

trypsin (ˈtrɪpsɪn). *Physiol. Chem.* [app. for **tripsin*, f. Gr. τρῖψις rubbing (because first obtained by rubbing down the pancreas with glycerin) + -IN[1].] The chief digestive ferment of the pancreatic juice, which converts proteins into peptones. Hence **trypˈsinogen** (-dʒən) [-GEN 1], a granular substance occurring in the pancreas, from which trypsin is formed; **ˈtrypsogen** [abbrev. of prec.], (*a*) = *trysinogen*; (*b*) a drug prepared from trypsin and other ferments with gold and arsenic bromides, used in diabetes, etc. (Dorland).

1876 FOSTER *Phys.* II. i. (1879) 233 The digestive powers of the [pancreatic] juice..depend..on the presence of a ferment, to which the name *trypsin has been given. **1907** *Westm. Gaz.* 12 Dec. 12/2 The new treatment of cancer by the pancreatic ferments, trypsin and amylopsin..suggested by Dr. Beard. **1890** BILLINGS *Med. Dict.*, *Trypsinogen. **1900** *Lancet* 27 Oct. 1187/1 The fact observed by Heidenhain of the continuous formation and storing up trypsinogen in the pancreas, and its subsequent transformation into trypsin during the culmen of gastric digestion, proved that the former substance..enjoyed an origin quite independent of all influence outside the pancreas. **1907** H. W. BETTMANN in *Med. Record* 3 Aug. 171 The intestinal juice contains two other ferments.., enterokinase, and erepsin. The former activates the pancreatic juice by transforming trypsinogen into trypsin. **1883** *Science* I. 372/1 The absence of oxygen from the blood has led to a reconversion of trypsin into *trypsogen.

trypsinize (ˈtrɪpsɪnaɪz), *v. Biochem.* [f. TRYPSIN + -IZE.] *trans.* To treat with trypsin. So **ˈtrypsinized** *ppl. a.*, **ˈtrypsinizing** *vbl. sb.*

1952 *Jrnl. Immunol.* LXIX. 688 The cultures prepared with trypsinized tissue were inoculated on the 8th day of incubation. **1959** *Virology* VIII. 396 Because these cultures sometimes contained tissue lumps which interfered with plaque production, they were usually trypsinized. **1971** *Nature* 30 July 312/2 After 10–14 days, wells containing single colonies were trypsinized. **1974** F. WARNER *Meeting Ends* I. vi. 25 Oh my head! I'm trypsinized, pepsinized, falling to bits. **1979** *Experientia* XXXV. 244/2 When the cells reached confluency standard trypsinizing procedures were used to remove them from the flask surface.

Also **trypsiniˈzation**, treatment with trypsin.

1959 *New Scientist* 19 Feb. 396/1 (*caption*) Trypsinization of monkey kidney for tissue-culture. **1980** *Parasitology* LXXX. 374 They were removed from the T-75 flask by trypsinization.

tryptamine (ˈtrɪptəmɪn). *Biochem.* [f. TRYPT(OPHAN + AMINE.] An amine, $C_8H_6N CH_2CH_2NH$, related to tryptophan, from which it is produced by decarboxylation and which itself is oxidized to indoleacetic acid.

1929 R. A. GORTNER *Outl. Biochem.* xx. 445 Tyramine, histamine, and tryptamine, all have a powerful physiological action. **1963** *Lancet* 19 Jan. 127/1 Indole and tryptamine are formed by the action of bacteria on unabsorbed tryptophan in the colonic lumen. **1980** G. GUROFF *Molecular Neurobiol.* ix. 127 An overload of tryptophan and/or an amine oxidase inhibitor is required to produce pharmacological evidence for tryptamine formation [in brain tissue].

tryptic (ˈtrɪptɪk), *a.* [f. TRYPSIN, after *pepsin, peptic.*] Pertaining to or of the nature of trypsin. So **tryptogen** (ˈtrɪptəʊdʒɛn), **-gene** (-dʒiːn) [-GEN 1], a producer of trypsin; **tryptone** (ˈtrɪptəʊn) [after *peptone*], a peptone formed by the action of trypsin upon a protein.

1888 ROLLESTON & JACKSON *Anim. Life* 196 Common Starfish... The cells in the caeca form enterochlorophyll, and *tryptic, peptic, and diastatic ferments. **1901** *Athenæum* 7 Dec. 778/3 It seems probable..that proteolytic digestion in plants is always tryptic. **1900** *Lancet* 27 Oct. 1187/1 The hypothesis of Schiff as to the manner in which the spleen acts as a *tryptogene. **1890** BILLINGS *Med. Dict.*, *Tryptone. **1901** *Athenæum* 7 Dec. 778/3 Among these final products of tryptic digestion there is a substance termed *tryptophan, which has the property of giving a pink or violet colour on the addition of chlorine-water. **1902** *Daily Chron.* 22 Nov. 6/6 Decomposing the proteid molecule into non-proteid nitrogenous substances, such as leucin and tryptophane.

tryptophan (ˈtrɪptəʊfæn). *Chem.* Also **tryptophane.** [a. G. *tryptophan* (R. Neumeister 1890, in *Zeitschr. f. Biol.* XXVI. 3), f. TRYPTIC *a.* + Gr. φαίνειν to appear.] **a.** An amino-acid essential in the diet of vertebrates; β-3-indolylalanine, $(C_8H_6N)CH_2CH(NH_2)COOH$.

1890 *Jrnl. Chem. Soc.* LVIII. 804 The term tryptophan is suggested for the substance which is formed during pancreatic digestion from proteïds, and which gives a reddish-violet coloration with bromine. **1922** *Sci. Amer.* July 42/3 Certain of the amino acids, of which about 19 have been found in proteins, are absolutely essential for growth and maintenance, among which are lysine, cystine and tryptophane. **1945**, **1949** [see CO-FACTOR 2]. **1956** *Nature* 3 Mar. 422/2 Supplementation of the [rats'] diet with either nicotinic acid or tryptophan had no effect on this depressed growth-rate. **1978** *Detroit Free Press* 5 Mar. (Parade Suppl.) 13 (Advt.), Pay less for more protein potency! A whole and complete protein derived from soybean. 0% carbohydrates, 325 mg tryptophane, 26 grams protein with lecithin and papain. **1979** *Time* 2 Apr. 42/2 Only a small dose of tryptophan—which is found in many foods, notably milk—seems to ease the insomniac to sleep.

b. Special Comb.: **tryptophan synthetase**, a bacterial enzyme that synthesizes tryptophan.

1955 C. YANOFSKY in Colowick & Kaplan *Methods in Enzymol.* II. I. 233 Tryptophan synthetase from *Neurospora*... This enzyme has also been called tryptophan desmolase... The name tryptophan synthetase was suggested by the editors of this volume. **1976** *Ann. Rev. Microbiol.* XXX. 413 Where this has been specifically tested—with tryptophan synthetase subunits in *Escherichia coli*.. homologies have not been found.

Hence **ˈtryptophanase** [a. Jap. *tryptophanase* (K. Kurono et al. 1932, in *Jrnl. Agric. Chem. Soc. Japan* VIII. 82): see -ASE], an enzyme catalysing the breakdown of tryptophan into ammonia, indole, and pyruvic acid.

1932 *Chem. Abstr.* XXVI. 5107 (*heading*) Tryptophan-decomposing enzyme, tryptophanase. **1963** *Lancet* 19 Jan. 128/1 Glucose reduces indole formation by inhibiting tryptophanase synthesis.., but does not affect the activity of tryptophanase already present. **1976** *Ann. Rev. Microbiol.* XXX. 421 Tryptophanase from *Escherichia coli* can catalyze the reversal of its normal function, forming L-tryptophan from indole, pyruvate, and ammonia.

trysail (ˈtraɪseɪl, ˈtraɪs(ə)l). *Naut.* Also 9 **trey-, tray-, trice-, tri-.** [f. TRY *sb.* + SAIL.] A small fore-and-aft sail, set with a gaff, and sometimes with a boom, on the fore- or mainmast, or on a small supplementary mast abaft either of these. Also *attrib.*, as ***trysail gaff, mast, mizen, sheet.***

1769 FALCONER *Dict. Marine* (1789) M m iv, When the sloops of war are rigged as snows, they are furnished with a horse, which answers the purpose of the try-sail-mast, the fore part of the sail being attached by rings to the said horse. **1794** *Riggings & Seamanship* I. 83 A trysail, used instead of a mizen,..is extended towards the stern, and..fastened by hoops round a small mast, called a trysail mast, fixed near the aft-side of the main-mast in a block of wood in the quarter deck. **1810** J. H. MOORE *Pract. Navigator* 290 Trey-sail. A small sail used by brigs and cutters in blowing weather. **1832** J. GUY *Pocket Cycl.* 402 A small mast, reaching up into the maintop, to which a tricesail mizen is attached. **1840** R. H. DANA *Bef. Mast* iv. 16 We..hauled up the mainsail and trysail. *Ibid.* ix. 22 Trysail gaff [see GAFF *sb.*[1] 2]. **1850** L. HUNT *Autobiog.* II. xvii. 259 We saw her..lying-to under trysails.

tryschor, variant of TREACHER *Obs.*

trysselle, obs. form of TRESTLE.

‖**tryssil, trysil.** Also trysle, trysel(l, trissle. [Said to be native name among the Arawak Indians.] Name in Guyana for a timber-tree, *Pentaclethra filamentosa*.

1862 *List Contrib. fr. Brit. Guiana to Lond. Exhib.*, Arrara, or Tryssil (*Pentaclethra filamentosa*, Benth.). Used for furniture and staves. **1878** *Woods Brit. Guiana collected by M. McTurk for local & Paris Internat. Exhib.* 1 Kooroo-balli or Trysil, from the Moraballi Creek, Essequebo River..is a dark close-grained wood suitable for making furniture. **1881** *Rep. Crown Surveyor Brit. Guiana for 1880* 24 Trysell. A beautiful light brown wood, close-grained and hard. **1912** C. W. ANDERSON *Forests Brit. Guiana* 23 Trysil or Koro-balli.

tryst (traɪst), *sb.* Chiefly *Sc.* before 19th c. Also 4–5 **triste**, 4–9 **trist**, (6 **treste**, **tryist**), 6–9 **tryste.** [Originally the same word as *triste*, TRIST *sb.*[1] (in which the *i* was in ME. long or short). The sense seems to be generalized from that of 'appointed station in hunting': cf. TRIST *sb.*[2] and the OF. and med.L. words there mentioned. The sense sometimes corresponds to some extent with that of TRUCE.]

1. A mutual appointment, agreement, engagement, covenant. Now *rare* or *Obs.* exc. as in 2.

c **1375** *Sc. Leg. Saints* xxvi. (*Nycholas*) 236 þai sailyt.. Quhare-to þare tryst wes mad[e], And þare þe quhet deliueryt hale. **1570** *Satir. Poems Reform.* xix. 90 Hudge is ȝour fais..With Ithand trystis contractand vp new bandis To bring ȝow to schame and confusioun. **1635** JACKSON *Creed* VIII. xii. §9 A captaine..being surprised by the subtilty of his enemy, whom hee had trusted too farre upon a tryste of parly. *a* **1670** SPALDING *Troub. Chas. I* (1851) II. 205 Johne Forbes of Leslie brak tryst appointit to haue satled the samen. **1715** PENNECUIK *Tweeddale* App. 36 Thus clos'd our Trist, all was Miscarried, And Bonnie Maggie's still Unmarried. **1871** WADDELL *Ps. in Scottis* lxxiv. 20 Hae min' o' the tryst ye made.

2. *spec.* An appointment or engagement to meet at a specified time and place. Chiefly in phrases, as ***to make, †set tryst; to hold, keep tryst; to break, †crack tryst; to bide tryst***, to wait at the appointed place for the person with whom the appointment is made. Also *fig.*

Only Sc. till 19th c.

1375 BARBOUR *Bruce* VII. 235 The kyng..richt toward the houss is gane Quhar he set trist to mete his men. *c* **1470** HENRY *Wallace* VI. 865 In Ruglen kyrk the tryst than haiff thai set. **1500–20** DUNBAR *Poems* lxxxiii. 13 ȝe keipit tryst so winder weill. **1546** *St. Papers Hen. VIII*, V. 561 Yar is ane trist be twin ye Lord of Loichenwer and Herell of Cassellis on Frydye nest to cum in Glasquhow. **1629** Z. BOYD *Last Battell* 1257 The Salmons..in their season returne to the place where they were spawned:..and for no rubs in the way will they be moued to cracke their tryst. **1818** SCOTT *Rob Roy* xxi, 'You walk late, sir', said I... 'I bide tryste', was the reply. **1853** C. BRONTE *Villette* xii, To keep tryste with the rising moon. **1878** SUSAN PHILLIPS *On Seaboard* 214 She stood..keeping her tryst at the stile. **1881** W. R. SMITH *Old Test. Jew. Ch.* 232 The place where Jehovah has promised to hold tryst with His people.

3. An appointed meeting or assembly: = RENDEZVOUS 5. In quot. 1681 *fig.* 'a [divinely appointed] concurrence of circumstances or events' (Jam.): cf. TRYST *v.* 4, 5.

c **1425** WYNTOUN *Cron.* IX. xvi. 1670 In Marche a day of trew was set..Schir Dauid Lorde de Lyndissay Was at þat tryst þat ilka day. **1456** SIR G. HAYE *Law Arms* (S.T.S.) 181 Ane Inglis lord..cummys till a tryst to lordis of Fraunce. **1524** *St. Papers Hen. VIII*, IV. 279 The saide Erle..hath appointed trestes and metingges with th Erle of Angwisshe and his frendes. *c* **1560** A. SCOTT *Poems* (S.T.S.) xxxiv. 75 ȝe trane þame to ane tryst. **1681** R. FLEMING *Fulfilling Script.* I. (1726) 148 Acknowledging a divine hand..where all did thus meet together in a solemn tryst to accomplish that peoples ruin. ? *a* **1700** *Lord's Marie* i. in Cromek *Rem. Nithsdale Song* (1810) 6 An' she has put on her net-silk hose, An' awa to the tryste has gane. **1859** G. MEREDITH *R. Feverel* xxi, Their tryst in the wood.

†b. An appointed journey. *Obs. rare.*

1768 Ross *Helenore* I. 65 Gin we reach na' our tryst's end gin night.

4. An appointed place of meeting: = RENDEZVOUS 2.

1375 BARBOUR *Bruce* VII. 230 And syne.. richt toward his trist is gane. *c* **1450** HOLLAND *Howlat* 307 Thai.. Walis wyslie the wayis,.. Quhill thai approche to the Pape.. At the forsaid trist quhar the trete tellis. **1844** MRS. BROWNING *Brown Rosary* I. v, 'Now where is Onora?'.. 'At the tryst with her lover'.

5. An appointed time; in quot. 1864, an appointed period or term. *rare.* ? *Obs.*

c **1470** HENRY *Wallace* IV. 731 At the set trist he entrit in the toune. **1827** HONE *Every-day Bk.* II. 164 The time agreed on.. for playing it [i.e. a curling-match] is called the *tryst.* **1864** SIR F. PALGRAVE *Norm. & Eng.* IV. 620 In the year 1100, the end of Robert's tryst, when the term would be concluded.

6. An appointed gathering for buying and selling; a market or fair, esp. for cattle. *Sc.* and *north. Eng.*

1776 NIMMO *Hist. Stirling.* iii. (1817) 62 The two great annual markets for black cattle, called the Trysts of Falkirk. ? *a* **1800** *Thomas the Rhymer* I. xviii. in Scott *Minstr. Scot. Bord.*, I neither dought to buy nor sell, At fair or tryst where I may be. **1808** SCOTT in Lockhart *Life* i, The master and servant set off to purchase a stock of sheep at Whitsun-Tryste, a fair held.. near Wooler in Northumberland. **1884** Q. VICTORIA *More Leaves* 46 We met many droves of cattle on the road, as it was the day for the tryst at Castleton.

7. *attrib.*, as **tryst-place**, a trysting-place; **tryst-stone**, 'a stone anciently erected for marking out a rendezvous' (Jam.); **tryst-word**, a password or watchword.

1795 *Statist. Acc. Scot.* XVI. 512 The tryst-stanes are commonly on high ground. They are placed perpendicularly in rows, not unfrequently in a circular direction. **1851** MRS. BROWNING *Casa Guidi Windows* I. 618 Thy favourite stone's elected right As tryst-place for thy Tuscans. **1896** R. REID in *N. York Scot. American* Oct., The tryst-word seemed 'Kirkbride'.

tryst (traɪst), *v.* Orig. and chiefly *Sc.* [f. TRYST *sb.*]

1. *intr.* To make an agreement *to do* something, *with* a person; *esp.* to fix or arrange time and place of meeting *with* some one.

c **1375** *Sc. Leg. Saints* xxx. (*Theodera*) 334 Scho kepyt þe trist.. And with hyr brocht þe man in hy, Quhare scho tristit priuely. *c* **1475** *Rauf Coilȝear* 797 To the Montane he maid hem full boun, Quhair he had trystit to meit Schir Rolland. **1678** SIR G. MACKENZIE *Crim. Laws Scot.* I. xx. §3 (1699) 108 Whosoever intercommuns with Thieves.. or Trysts with them any manner of way. **1725** RAMSAY *Gentle Sheph.* v. i, As she had trysted, I met wi'er this night. **1899** CROCKETT *Kit Kennedy* xxxiii, Kit.. had trysted with the 'Orra Man' to meet him at the smiddy.

2. *trans.* To engage (a person) to meet one at a given place and time; to appoint or agree to meet.

In quot. 1643, loosely used as = meet.

1643 *Declar. Com., Reb. Irel.* 60 It was my good fortune.. to trist a Barke come from the Isle of Man. **1766** A. NICOL *Poems* 43 He trysted me one evening fair, Among the groves to take the air. **1893** STEVENSON *Catriona* xiii, I am trysted with your cousin Charlie; I have passed my word.

b. With advb. extension: To invite or entice to a place, or to a distance.

a **1800** in Kinloch *Anc. Scott. Ballads* (1827) 157, I trysted her Unto yon shade o' broom. **1894** LATTO *Tam. Bodkin* xxiii, Trystin' me awa on that eventfu' pilgrimage.

c. To engage (a person) to do something; to appoint, agree upon, arrange, fix (a task). Only in *pa. pple.*

1897 [see *trysted* below]. **1899** CROCKETT *Kit Kennedy* viii. He was trysted to give what help he could to the herd.. in lambing time.

3. To appoint, fix (a time, occurrence, etc.).

1586 *Reg. Privy Council Scot.* IV. 63 Upoun the XI day of Marche.. as the day tryistit and appointit be the said Williame Ker. **1716** *Wodrow Corr.* (1843) II. 120 Had not God tristed the flight of the rebels just at that time.

b. To bespeak; to arrange for, or order in advance; to engage.

1825 JAMIESON s.v., 'I trystit my furniture to be hame' on such a day. **1894** LATTO *Tam. Bodkin* xxiv, I had trystit a chaise an' pair frae the Fleein' Horse.

4. To visit *with* good or evil; of an experience: to come upon, befall; 'used in relation to a divine ordination' (Jam.).

1645 R. BAILLIE *Lett.* (1841) II. 314 That this should have trysted the enemie at that tyme and place.. is evidentlie God's hand. *a* **1679** SOMERVILLE *Mem. Somervilles* (1815) II. 351 Untill Divyne Justice trysted them with some crosse dispensatione. **1681** R. FLEMING *Fulfilling Script.* Ep. to Rdr. (1726) 6 The most eminent and honourable service of the church doth usually tryst her in a low and suffering condition. **1816** SCOTT *Old Mort.* xl[i], Sair she's been trysted wi' misfortunes.

†**b.** To fix upon. *Obs. rare*$^{-1}$.

1700 SIR A. BALFOUR *Lett.* 254 They go at the Rate of an Ordinary Horse trot, & as they go will trist the stones to step upon, which lye confusedly here and there, as exactly as if they were a pair of stairs.

†**5.** *intr.* To coincide in time *with*; to fall *together*, concur. Also *trans.* in causal sense (quot. 1681). *Obs.*

1676 W. ROW *Contn. Blair's Autobiog.* ix. (1848) 134 His stroke trysting with the public burden. **1681** R. FLEMING *Fulfilling Script.* I. (1726) 148 What a marvelous concurrence of providence.. was in this judgment, the besieging of Jerusalem by the Romans, trysted with the very time of the passover [etc.]. **1730** T. BOSTON *Mem.* iv. (1899) 39 That discouragement and the spring-season trysting together, there was a notable breach made in my health.

6. *intr.* To keep tryst; to meet at the appointed time and place.

a **1842** CUNNINGHAM in *Casquet of Lit.* (1886) V. 303 There flows the stream I've trysted through, when it was wild in flood. **1898** *Westm. Gaz.* 7 Dec. 11/2 When the Cottesmore trysted at Somerby on Saturday.

†**7.** *intr.* To treat or negotiate *with*. *Obs.*

1637 RUTHERFORD *Let. to Lady Kilconquhair* 8 Aug., You came to this life about a necessary and weighty business, to tryst with Christ anent your precious soul. **1637–50** [see TRYSTING *vbl. sb.* 1]. **1639** LD. WARISTON *Diary* (S.H.S.) 351 We trysted on al day with the Commissioner, bot could settle nothing. *a* **1670** SPALDING *Troub. Chas. I* (1850) I. 176 Thay raisit ane army and cam to Innervrie, quhilk he could not resist, nor whome fra he could onnawayis flie, be sea or land, [and he] wes forsit to tryst and give his band, no doubt to thair contentment.

Hence **'trysted, 'trysting** *ppl. adjs.*

1793 BURNS *Mary Morison* i, It is the wish'd, the trysted hour! **1878** T. HARDY *Return of Native* I. ix, The conversation of the trysting pair could not be overheard. **1897** CROCKETT *Lad's Love* xxix, That his shepherd.. is shirking his trysted labour.

tryst(e, obs. f. TREST; var. TRIST *Obs.*

trystel, -ell(e, obs. forms of TRESTLE.

†**'trystell.** *Obs. rare.* [f. TRYST *sb.*] = TRYST *sb.*; *trystell-tree*, a tree where a tryst is arranged (cf. TRYSTY).

c **1500** *Gest Robyn Hode* IV. 274 in Child *Ball.* III. 69/2 Welcome be thou, gentyll knyght, Under my trystell-tre.

tryster ('traɪstə(r)). [f. TRYST *v.* + -ER[1].] One who trysts. **a.** 'A person who convenes others,.. fixing the time and place of meeting' (Jam.). **b.** One who appoints to meet another. **c.** One who attends a tryst or appointed meeting.

1655 R. BAILLIE *Lett.* (1842) III. 279 We had drawne up ane overture,.. according to the Assemblie's late overture for union, and by the hands of the trysters.. sent it into their meeting. **1810** CROMEK *Rem. Nithsdale Song* Introd. 21 The old cottars (the trysters of other years) are mostly dead in good old age. **1878** T. HARDY *Return of Native* I. ix, The expected trysters did not appear.

tryster, -ere, variants of TRISTRE *Obs.*

trysting ('traɪstɪŋ), *vbl. sb.* [f. TRYST *v.*]

1. The action of the verb TRYST, q.v.; a tryst. *under trysting* = under tryst or agreement.

1633 W. STRUTHER *True Happiness* 79 Since he keepeth both time and place of trysting, let us not be so ingrate as not to meet with him. **1637–50** ROW *Hist. Kirk* (Wodrow Soc.) 514 After some trysting, and intermediat parleying. **1640** R. BAILLIE *Lett.* (1841) I. 276 A declaration.. that our trysting there [in London] was no submission to the Inglish Parliament. *a* **1670** SPALDING *Troub. Chas. I* (1851) II. 337 The committee of Estaites.. directit him.. to hold the Marques wnder trysting whill thay sould raiss wp forces to go vpone him. **1832** MRS. CARLYLE in *Lett. & Mem.* (1903) I. 42, I was fatigued enough by the journey home; still more by the trysting that awaited me here.

2. *attrib.*, as *trysting day, ground, place, stile, thorn, tree*, etc.

1842 MACAULAY *Horatius* i, By the Nine Gods he swore it, And named a *trysting day. **1838** J. P. KENNEDY *Rob of Bowl* xx, The customary.. *trysting ground for personal combats. **1898** MAX MÜLLER *Auld Lang Syne* 195 [In] the Thirty Years' War we find Anhalt the constant trysting ground of the two parties. **1633** W. STRUTHER *True Happiness* 115 Wee come to the Sanctuarie.. the Lords *trysting place. *a* **1665** W. GUTHRIE *Chr. Gt. Interest* II. viii. (1724) 223 A fit Trysting-place for God and Men to meet into. **1805** SCOTT *Eve St. John* xliii, At our trysting place, for a certain space, I must wander to and fro. **1867** FREEMAN *Norm. Conq.* I. v. 426 Those who had horses seem to have reached the same trysting-place by land. **1858** CAPERN *Ball. & Songs* (1859) 100 Meet me.. by the *trysting stile. **1793** BURNS *Soldier's Return* iii, I pass'd the mill and *trysting thorn, Where Nancy aft I courted. **1802** SCOTT *Reiver's Wedding* 50 When he came to Falsehope glen, Beneath the *trysting-tree. **1806** *Chron.* in *Ann. Reg.* (1808) 385/2 A hurricane.. destroyed the famous elm tree, which had existed for ages, on the banks of the Teviot, and was known by the name of the *Trysting Tree.* **1872** HOLLAND *Marb. Proph.* 45, I await her in the dewy gloom Of the old trysting tree.

trystor, variant of TRISTRE *Obs.*

†**'trysty**, *a. Obs. rare.* [f. TRYST *sb.* + -Y.] Of or pertaining to a tryst: only in *trysty tree* = trysting tree: see TRYSTING *vbl. sb.* 2.

15.. *Adam Bel* 380 in Hazl. *E.P.P.* II. 154 Whan they came to Inglys wode, Under theyr trysty tre. *Ibid.* 392.

trysty, var. TRISTY *Obs.*

tryton, tryumph, -wmph, obs. ff. TRITON, TRIUMPH.

tryuþe, tryvette, trywage, trywede: see TRUTH, TRIVET, TREWAGE, TRUEHEAD.

tryys, -st, -ste, var. TRICE *sb.*[1] *Obs.*

tsabaism, tsabian, var. SABAISM, SABIAN.

Tsaconian, var. TSAKONIAN *sb.* and *a.*

tsaddik ('tsædɪk). *Judaism.* Also **tsadik, tzaddik, tzaddiq, zaddik**, etc. Pl. **-kim, -ks.** [a. Heb. *ṣaddīq* just, righteous.] A man of exemplary righteousness; a Hasidic spiritual leader or sage.

1873 *New Era* (N.Y.) III. 75 These zadiks, or leaders, have no fixed salary. **1881** [see REBBE]. **1904** *Jewish Encycl.* VI. 253/2 The Hasidim were, however, particularly noted for the exalted worship of their 'holy' zaddikim. **1907** I. ZANGWILL *Ghetto Comedies* 409 A *Tsaddik* (wonder-rabbi) was killed in the last *pogrom.* **1933** S. BIRNBAUM *Life & Sayings Baal Shem* p. iii, Chassidism.. is characterized.. by a new psychic and material organization of comprehensive scope, at whose center of crystallization stand the *tzaddikim*, the 'righteous ones', the masters of the souls of men. **1941** G. G. SCHOLEM *Major Trends in Jewish Mysticism* ix. 338 The existence of the Zaddik or saint as the actual proof of the possibility of living up to the ideal. **1964** M. WOHLGELERNTER *I. Zangwill* vii. 111 The numerous sects that mushroomed all over Europe, each with its own *Zaddik* performing untold 'miracles'. **1968** *Observer* 10 Nov. 26/5 He was bound to end up.. a great chassidic *Tsadik.* **1974** *Encycl. Brit. Micropædia* X. 225/3 In the.. movement known as Hasidism, the Jewish religious leader (*tzaddiq*) was viewed as a mediator between man and God. Since the *tzaddiq*'s life was expected to be a living expression of the Torah, his behaviour was even more important than his doctrine. **1982** *Times* 18 June 13/3 The world has much need of such *tsaddiks* (righteous men).

tsaing: see TSINE.

Tsakonian (tsə'kəʊnɪən), *sb.* and *a.* Also **-c-, Tz-.** [f. *Tsakon*, a region in the eastern Peloponnese, Greece + -IAN.] (Of or pertaining to) a modern Greek dialect spoken in an area of the south-eastern Peloponnese, containing ancient elements not derived from the koine.

1902 *Encycl. Brit.* XXIX. 102/2 Certain peculiar dialects, such as the Tzakonian in the south-eastern Morea. **1925** P. RADIN tr. *Vendryès's Language* ii. 46 For the present Tsaconian still seems to use it [*sc.* digamma]. **1933** C. D. BUCK *Compar. Gram. Gk. & Lat.* 20 The present Tsaconian dialect, spoken in a small portion of Laconia,.. is in part the offspring of ancient Laconian. **1939** A. J. TOYNBEE *Study of Hist.* VI. 71 This 'Tsakonian' *patois* is the only surviving form of spoken Greek that is not derived from the Attic κοινή. **1972** W. B. LOCKWOOD *Panorama Indo-Europ. Lang.* 7 Tsakonian is the outlandish dialect of perhaps as many as 10,000 speakers in an area difficult of access along the forbidding coast of the Peloponnese between the Parnon Range and the Gulf of Argolis.

‖**tsamba** ('tsæmbə). Also **tsampa, tsumpa.** [Tibetan.] An article of food made from barley-meal, extensively used in Tibet and adjacent parts.

1852 *Dublin Rev.* XXXIII. 12 As tsamba is not a very toothsome affair, we used to make three or four balls of it, with our tea. **1858** SIMMONDS *Dict. Trade, Tsamba*, a Tartar [properly Tibetan] name for the meal of barley. **1891** W. W. ROCKHILL *Land of Lamas* iii. 129 They cultivate the soil sufficiently to raise what barley is needed to make tsamba. **1908** *Athenæum* 13 June 721/3 The native food.. in the Tibetan districts *tsamba* (barley meal mixed with yak butter).. was plain and uninviting. **1909** *Bible in the World* Sept. 268/2 After tea and *tsamba* I retired to the roof. **1937** H. W. TILMAN *Ascent Nanda Devi* iv. 31 The Tibetan tsumpa—barley, or wheat, which has been parched and then ground into meal. **1952** MORIN & SMITH tr. *Herzog's Annapurna* v. 78 Khangsar was very poor: not a pound of tsampa to spare. **1979** P. MATTHIESSEN *Snow Leopard* ii. 86 The two outcasts dip up tsampa, the roasted maize or barley meal, ground to powder and cooked as porridge or in tea.

tsamma ('tsæmə). Also **(t)sama.** [a. Hottentot *t'sama.*] A wild water-melon, *Citrullus lanatus*, native to parts of southern Africa. Also *attrib.*

1886 G. A. FARINI *Through Kalahari Desert* vii. 106 We came across the first sama I had seen... It is the 'wild water-melon', resembling the cultivated variety in appearance, both internally and externally. **1933** *Times Lit. Suppl.* 16 Mar. 175/2 Ground melons (tsamas) provide the only water supply for the wandering tribes of bushmen. **1937** A. J. H. GOODWIN in I. Schapera *Bantu-Speaking Tribes S. Afr.* ii. 39 The tsama melon.. supplies liquid to men and beasts. **1948** L. G. GREEN *To River's End* i. 16 The dunes topped by their t'samma melons.. only form a background. **1958** L. VAN DER POST *Lost World Kalahari* ix. 212 A middle-aged woman sat diligently pounding the seeds of the tsamma. **1974** *Stand. Encycl. S. Afr.* X. 640/2 The name 'tsamma' is used mainly in the Kalahari, and is derived from a Bushman name for the plant.

tsampa, var. TSAMBA.

‖**tsantsa** ('tsantsə). Also tzantza. [Jivaro.] A human head shrunk as a trophy by the Jivaros of Ecuador.

1923 R. KARSTEN *Blood Revenge* 14 That the blood feuds which take place within the tribe have an entirely different character from the wars of extermination waged against foreign tribes also appears from the fact that only in the latter case.. the victors make trophies (*tsantsas*) of the heads of their slain enemies. **1957** *Encycl. Brit.* XIII. 70/1 The finished 'tsantsa' is about the size of the head of a small monkey, and preserves strikingly the human expression. **1966** J. M. WOODMAN in *Fodor's Guide to S. Amer.* 177 The famed Jívaro shrunken heads or *tzantzas* are extremely rare. Many good imitations are for sale in almost every gift shop in Ecuador, and a good goat-hide imitation *tzantza* usually costs around $2.60. **1977** *New Yorker* 25 July 81/2 Another is the stealthy sale by dubious chaps of shrunken heads (tsantsa), war trophies of the Jivaro head-hunters.

‖**ts'ao shu** (tsau ʃu). Also **cao shu, tsaou shoo.** [Chinese *cǎoshū*, f. *cǎo* hasty + *shū* writing.] In Chinese calligraphy, a cursive script developed during the Han dynasty (206 B.C.–A.D. 220) from the 'official' script.

1876 *Encycl. Brit.* V. 655/2 The *Tsaou shoo* or 'grass character'. **1910** *Ibid.* VI. 220/2 Out of the 'official script' two other forms were soon developed, namely the..*ts'ao shu*, or 'grass character', [etc.]. **1974** J.-F. L. CHANG in T. C. Lai *Chinese Calligraphy* (1975) p. xiii, Ts'ao Shu or Cursive Script..was originally developed as a quicker version of the Official Script during the second century A.D. **1978** *Nagel's Encycl.-Guide: China* 326 *Cao shu* is a style in which the characters are abbreviated, giving free reign to the movement. The economy of style is often such that it is hard to read for all but the initiated.

tsar, czar (tsɑː(r), zɑː(r)). Also 7 zarr, czaar, czarr, ksar, 8- tzar. [Romanized spellings of Russ. *tsarʲ*, in Bulg. *tsar* king, sovereign emperor, Serb. *tsar* emperor, Croatian, Boh., Pol. *car* (= *tsar*, *c* in the Roman Slavonic orthography = Ц in Cyrillic, being pronounced *ts* or German z). The Russian form is reduced from earlier (11th c.) *tsʲsarʲ* = OSlav. *tsêsarʲ*, in oblique cases *tsʲsar-*, 'Cæsar, emperor, βασιλεύς, king', also (in latter senses) *tsarʲ*. (In Russian, the full form *tsesarʲ* is retained in the sense 'Cæsar' and '(ancient Roman) emperor'; cf. Serb. *tsesar* applied to the German emperor, but *tsar* to the Russian tsar and the Sultan.

The Slav. word ultimately represents L. *Cæsar*, but came, according to Miklosich, through the medium of a Germanic lang. in which the word had the general sense 'emperor': cf. Goth. *kaisar*, OHG. *keisar*, OLG. *kêsar*, ON. *keysari*, whence also Finnish *keisari*, Esth. *keiser*, *keisri*. For the change of Germanic *k* to *c* = *ts* in Slav., cf. CHURCH. The spelling with *cz-* is against the usage of all Slavonic languages; the word was so spelt by Herberstein, *Rerum Moscovit. Commentarii* 1549, the chief early source of knowledge as to Russia in Western Europe, whence it passed into the Western Languages generally; in some of these it is now old-fashioned; the usual Ger. form is now *zar*; French adopted *tsar* during the 19th c. This also became frequent in English towards the end of that century, having been adopted by the *Times* newspaper as the most suitable English spelling.]

a. *Hist.* The title of the autocrat or emperor of Russia; historically, borne also by Serbian rulers of the 14th c., as the Tsar Stephen Dushan.

In Russia it was partially used by the Grand Duke Ivan III, 1462–1505, and by his son Basil or *Vasiliĭ*, but was formally assumed by Ivan IV in 1547. According to Herberstein its actual sense in Russian was 'king', but it was gradually taken as = 'emperor', a sense which it had in other Slavonic languages. Peter the Great introduced the title *imperator* 'emperor', and the official style shortly before the Revolution of 1917 was 'Emperor of all the Russias, Tsar of Poland, and Grand Duke of Finland'; but the Russian popular appellation was still *tsar*.

1555 EDEN *Decades* 290 [*tr.* Heberstein] Wheras now this prince is cauled an Emperour, I haue thought good to shewe the tytle, and the cause of this error. Note therefore that Czar in the Ruthens tounge signifieth a kynge, wheras in the language of the Slauons, Pollons, Bohemes, and other, the same woorde Czar signifieth Cesar by whiche name Themperours haue byn commonly called. **1591** G. FLETCHER *Russe Commw.* (Hakluyt Soc.) 26 Sometimes [there is a] quarrell betwixt them and the Tartar and Poland ambassadours, who refuse to call him *czar*, that is emperour. **1662** J. DAVIES *Voy. Ambass.* 95 The word *Czaar* signifies *King*, which may be seen in their Bible, where the Muscovites, speaking of David and his successors..they call them Czaars. **1667** EVELYN *Diary* 28 Aug., He [the Russian Envoy] deliver'd his speech in the Russe language aloud..half of it consisted in repetition of the Zarr's titles. **1667** MILTON *P.L.* XI. 394 The Russian Ksar In Mosco. **1756–7** tr. *Keysler's Trav.* (1760) I. 194 The czar at the commencement of the war was in the wrong. *a* **1670** [S. COLLINS] *Pres. St. Russia* (1671) 55 By the Grace of God We the Great Lord Tzar, and Great Duke Alexei, [etc.]..Tzar of Cazan, Tzar of Astrachan, Tsar of Siberia [etc.]. **1802–3** tr. *Pallas' Trav.* (1812) I. 229 Heraclius, the Tzar of Georgia. **1810** E. D. CLARKE *Trav. Russia*, etc. (1839) 29/1 The connection which subsisted between the tsars of Muscovy and the emperors of Constantinople. **1890** MORFILL *Russia* 56 Ivan assuming the cognizance of the double-headed eagle, and partially taking the title of Tsar, the complete assumption of it being the achievement of Ivan IV. **1893** *Times* (Weekly ed.) 4 Aug. 606/4 Accident to the Tsar's yacht, the Tsarevna.

b. *transf.* A person having great authority or absolute power; a tyrant, 'boss'. orig. *U.S.*

1866 in Sperber & Trittschuh *Amer. Political Terms* (1962) 111/1 There wuz an immense crowd, but the Czar uv all the Amerikas didn't get orf his speech here. **1893** *McClure's Mag.* I. 375 He was being held up as 'The Czar'—a man whose iron heels were crushing out American popular government. **1899** *Daily News* 20 Apr. 5/5 It is unlikely that any successor will be found able to dominate..as 'Czar' Reed could do. **1931** E. LINKLATER *Juan in America* IV. vii. 338 Red-eye was a czar at whose anger the household grew faint. **1959** *Listener* 5 Nov. 784/1 The Czar—as we say—or President of the Motion Picture Producers' Association. **1970** *Guardian* 18 Apr. 10/6 Many [American] Presidents..establish a staff 'Czar' to cut down on 'unnecessary' memos and contacts.

Hence **tsarlet** ('tsɑːlɪt), a petty Tsar.

1889 *Fortn. Rev.* XLVI. 285 This frightful régime of innumerable Tsarlets. **1905** DILLON in *Contemp. Rev.* Aug. 280 They are sharers of autocratic absolutism, provincial tsarlets.

'tsarate, czarate. [f. prec. + -ATE¹.] The office or position of tsar or czar.

1863 EDWARDES *Polish Captivity* I. 299 In 1611 Ladislas..was offered the Tsarate of Muscovy by the Council of Boyars. **1882** COSTELLOE in *Macm. Mag.* XLV. 414 Without really endangering the Czarate.

tsardom, 'czardom. [f. TSAR + -DOM.] The dominion, office, or power of a tsar or czar.

1841 A. C. STERLING *Russia* 158 The old czardoms of Kasan and Astrachan. **1877** D. M. WALLACE *Russia* xvii. 270 When the Grand Princes of Moscow brought the other principalities under their power, and formed them into the Tsardom of Muscovy. **1884** A. J. EVANS in *Archæol.* XLIX. 34 The palmy days of the Servian kingdom and czardom. **1901** *Fortn. Rev.* June 1034 Some..doubt as to the future of the Tzardom.

‖**tsarevich, czar-, -wi(t)ch** ('tsɑːrəvɪtʃ, 'z-, Russ. tsa'revitʃ). Also spelt (after Polish) *czarowitz*, *-witch*, etc. [a. Russ. *tsa'revich*, son of a tsar; in Pol. *carowicz*, F. *tsarowitz*, Ger. *zarewitsch*, etc. See TSAR.] A son of a tsar. (Superseded, after the time of Paul I, by *velikiĭ knyaz'* 'Grand Duke', *lit.* 'great prince'. The eldest son or hereditary prince had the differentiated title *cesa'revitch*, *-witch*, Russian *tsesarevich*, formed on *tesar'* Cæsar, emperor.)

1710 *Lond. Gaz.* No. 4688/1 The Czarowitz, his Czarish Majesty's Son, is expected here this Evening. **1712** *Ibid.* No. 4985/2 The Czarowitz..setting forwards to meet the King. **1878** G. B. MCCLELLAN in *N. Amer. Rev.* CXXVI. 151 The army of the Cesarovitch. **1906** KROPOTKIN *Mem. Revolutionist* (1908) II. ix. 143 The Tsarevich..began to scold the officer.

‖**tsarevna, czarevna** (tsa'rɛvnə). [Russ. *tsa'revna*.] A daughter of a tsar. (Not the official title in Russia; the wife of the *cesarevitch* was the *cesa'revna*. See prec.)

1880 in WEBSTER *Supp.* **1890** MORFILL *Russia* 343 The favourite of the Tsarevna Sophia. **1890** *Times* 30 Jan. 5/3 High personages—among them..the Czarevna [*meaning the* Cesarevna]. **1893** [See TSAR].

'tsarian, *a.*, **'tsaric,** *a.*, **cz-.** = TSARISH.

1710 LUTTRELL *Brief Rel.* (1857) VI. 631 His czarian majesty should look upon it as a breach of the peace. **1762** *Gentl. Mag.* 388 Her Czarian majesty's zeal for religion. **1799** W. TOOKE *View Russian Emp.* I. 10 He caused to be inserted in all the tzarian titles, the words: of all..Russia. **1905** *Daily Chron.* 21 Aug. 5/6 The ideal of Tsarian authority. **1662** J. DAVIES *Voy. Ambass.* 95 They give their Soveraign the quality of..Czaar and his Czaarick Majesty. **1843** tr. *Custine's Emp. Czar* II. 345 Czaric architecture is a descriptive term necessary to the traveller.

'tsaricide, cz-. *nonce-wd.* [f. TSAR + -CIDE.] The murder, or the murderer of a tsar.

1883 LAVROFF tr. *Stepniak's Undergr. Russia* 87 He was..a partisan of Czaricide. **1883** *St. James' Gaz.* 15 Feb. 6 The scaffold on which the Czaricides expiated their crime. **1895** *Blackw. Mag.* Feb. 312/1 The trial of those accused of Tsaricide.

tsarina, czarina (tsa'riːnə, za-). [Corresponds to It., Sp., Pg. *czarina* (*zarina*, *tzarina*), F. *czarine*, *tsarine*, all from Ger. *czarin*, *zarin* (see prec.) with conformation of the suffix to the analogies of the respective languages.] The wife of a tsar, a Russian empress.

1717 *Protestant Mercury* 18 Jan. 3 The..News, that the Czarina [*printed* -rian]..was brought to Bed of a Son. **1770** FOOTE *Lame Lover* II. Wks. 1799 II. 77 From the days of Lycurgus to the present Czarina. **1823** BYRON *Juan* X. xlix, The fair czarina's autocratic crest. **1891** *Tablet* 24 Oct. 643 The Tsarina has given 20 million roubles.

'tsarish, cz- ('tsɑːrɪʃ, 'zɑːrɪʃ), *a.* [f. TSAR + -ISH; rendering the Russian adj. *'tsarskiĭ*, for which A. Marvell used *tzarskoy*.] Of or pertaining to a tsar, *spec.* of the tsar of Russia.

[**1663–4** MARVELL *Corr.* Wks. 1872–5 II. 136 May it please Your most Potent and most Serene Tzarskoy Majesty.] **1698** J. CRULL *Muscovy* 181 His Czarish Majesty is placed in a Throne of Massie Silver. **1709** STEELE *Tatler* No. 49 ¶9 His Excellency the Czarrish Ambassador. **1833** *Fraser's Mag.* VII. 194 The czarish diplomacy. **1886** *Sat. Rev.* 777 His present Czarish Majesty..has a very ticklish temper. **1904** *Longm. Mag.* Oct. 204 If his Tsarish Grace should..find himself in danger.

'tsarism, cz-. [See -ISM.] The system of political government centering in the tsar of Russia.

1855 *Tait's Mag.* 245 The political and social results of Czarism and serfdom. **1891** *Times* 21 Oct. 5/2 Czarism is not to be destroyed, being in its essence Slavonic. **1882** C. HAMLIN in *Chicago Advance* 9 Mar., That cold-hearted cruelty which Tsarism has engendered. **1902** *Daily Chron.* 4 June 8/2 Tolstoy's last pamphlet..is hostile to Socialism, and favourable to Tsarism.

So **tsarist** ('tsɑːrɪst), an adherent or maintainer of Tsarism; **tsa'ristic** *a.*, characteristic of tsarism.

1907 *Contemp. Rev.* Feb. 202 The tide of Tsarist Power has passed over the steppes. **1883** *Harper's Mag.* Nov. 893/2 Czaristic ukases.

‖**tsaritsa, czaritza** (tsa'ritsa). Also 8 czarissa. [a. Russ. *tsa'ritsa*, fem. of *tsarʲ*.] The Russian title for which *tsarina* was in ordinary English use. (The Russian official title was *impritsa* empress.)

1698 J. CRULL *Muscovy* 187 The Dress of the Czaritza or Empress is little different. **1714** *Lond. Gaz.* No. 5268/7 The Czarissa, his Czarian Majesty's Consort, was brought to Bed of a Princess. **1833** R. PINKERTON *Russia* 300 The Tzar..performed a pilgrimage..accompanied by his Tzaritza. **1890** MORFILL *Russia* 183 The Tsaritsa Eudoxia, the first wife of Peter the Great.

tsarship, czarship ('tsɑːʃɪp, 'zɑː-). [See -SHIP.] The position or office of tsar. Also *fig.*

1851 H. MELVILLE *Whale* xxxiv. 164 A witchery of social czarship which there is no withstanding. **1852** *Tait's Mag.* XIX. 515 The pretender..obtained the Czarship.

‖**tsatlee** ('tsætliː). [Cantonese, corresp. to Pekinese *Ch'i Li* 'seven miles': named after a locality in the Chekiang province, where it is produced.] A very superior kind of white native-reeled raw silk, produced for the foreign market.

1848 S. W. WILLIAMS *Middle Kingd.* xv. II. 123 The raw silk is an article of sale; the sorts usually known in the Canton market are tsatle, taysaam, and Canton raw silk. **1858** SIMMONDS *Dict. Trade*, *Tsat-lie*, *Tseh-li*, a species of China silk obtained in Nankin and the Northern parts of the empire, superior to the Canton kinds. **1913** *Times* 27 June 24 The silk of China comprises, white, yellow, and wild silk. Of these raw white silk (the tsatlee of the European market) is the most important.

tsatske ('tsɒtskə), **tchotchke** ('tʃɒtʃkə). *U.S. colloq.* [Yiddish, f. Slavonic (cf. Russ. *tsatska*).] A trinket or gewgaw; *transf.*, a pretty girl. Also **'tsatskeleh** [Yiddish *-le* dim. suff.], an affectionate diminutive of *tsatske*.

1964 W. MARKFIELD *To Early Grave* (1965) v. 101 He was no *tsatskeleh*, Leslie, he was in certain respects far from being trustworthy. **1968** L. ROSTEN *Joys of Yiddish* 408 *Tsatske* and *tchotchke* are used interchangeably... At one time..West End Avenue in New York had an inordinately high proportion of *tchotchkies*. **1970** S. ELLIN *Man from Nowhere* (1971) xix. 94 He looked Elinor over appraisingly...'A real *tsatskeh*,' he said with approval. **1972** M. GLENNY tr. *Solzhenitsyn's August 1914* (1974) viii. 77 True, she never did anything to cross him, never even put on her expensive clothes and her *tsatski* (diamonds) at home because he disapproved of it. **1974** *N.Y. Times* 12 July 31 'Décor doesn't add to the glamour of a suit,' an owner pointed out. 'You're not buying the rugs or the lamps or the tsatskes.' **1977** *New Yorker* 1 Aug. 14/1 A..boutique, to the left of the entrance, stocked with a careful selection of New York's best tchotchkes. These include thirteen-inch-long matchbooks.

Tsaubwa, var. SAWBWA.

tsch-, German spelling of CH- (= tʃ).

‖**tschaike**, app. a form of CAÏQUE.

1790 *Naval Chron.* IV. 452 One chebec,..one tschaike,..were destroyed.

Tschaikowskian, var. TCHAIKOVSKIAN.

tschee, var. SHCHI.

tscheffkinite ('tʃɛfkɪnaɪt). *Min.* Also **tschev-**, and (after Ger. spelling) **tschewkinite**. [See quot. 1868 and -ITE¹.] A rare mineral, a silicate containing titanium, iron, and the metals of the cerium group, occurring in velvet-black masses.

1850 ANSTED *Elem. Geol., Min.* etc. 443 Tschewkinite, silicate and titanate of cerium, lanthanum, and didymium, with oxide of iron. **1868** DANA *Min.* (ed. 5) 387–8 Tscheffkinite... *Tschewkinit.* G. Rose, Reis. Ural, ii. 1839...From the Ilmen Mountains in the Urals; only a few specimens have been found... Named after the Russian general, Tschevkin [Tshefkin].

Tschermak ('tʃɜːmæk). *Min.* The name of Gustav *Tschermak* (1836–1927), Austrian mineralogist, used *attrib.* and in the possessive to designate the synthetic pyroxene $CaAl(AlSi)O_6$ as a hypothetical component of natural pyroxenes, or the part $Al(AlSi)O_6$ of this.

1943 *Amer. Mineralogist* XXVIII. 73 The substitution $Al_2/MgSi$ is that by which the 'Tschermak molecule' is derived from diopside. **1962** *Jrnl. Petrol.* III. 355 The Cs may also be traced to the Tschermak's molecule in the high-CaO titaniferous clinopyroxene. **1970** *Nature* 26 Sept. 1337/1 Omphacite (diopsidic clinopyroxene in which jadeite predominates over Tschermak's molecule). **1974** *Encycl. Brit. Macropædia* XV. 322/1 Ferric diopsides contain ferri-Tschermak's molecule ($CaFe_2SiO_6$).

Hence **'tschermakite**, an amphibole end-member of the hornblende group, $Ca_2Mg_3Al_4Si_6O_{22}(OH)_2$, that is rich in aluminium; also, any member of the series this forms with ferrotschermakite (the other end-member). Hence **tscherma'kitic** *a.*

1945 A. N. WINCHELL in *Amer. Mineralogist* XXX. 29 Hallimond notes that the second of these formulas is often called the Tschermak molecule; the writer would suggest that it be called tschermakite. **1963** W. A. DEER et al. *Rock-Forming Minerals* III. 272 Tschermakitic hornblendes. **1966** —— *Introd. Rock-Forming Minerals* II. 168 Compositions approaching those of the edenite and tschermakite end-members are rare, and the compositions of the majority of the hornblendic amphiboles are intermediate between the two end-member series, tremolite—ferroactinolite and pargasite—ferrohastingsite. **1976** *Nature* 22 Apr. 673/2 The generally tschermakitic-pargasitic nature of all the amphiboles is like that of amphiboles produced synthetically from hydrous basaltic melts.

tschermigite ('tʃɜːmɪgaɪt). *Min.* [See def. and -ITE¹.] A name for ammonia alum (see ALUM *sb.*

2), esp. as occurring native in brown coal at Tschermig in Bohemia.

1868 DANA *Min.* (ed. 5) 651–2 Tschermigite. Ammonia Alum. This salt is manufactured from the waste of gas works, and used extensively in place of potash alum.

tschernozem, var. CHERNOZEM.

‖**tschibouque**, variant of CHIBOUK.

1845 E. FITZGERALD *Lett.* (1889) I. 150 Now the bores are those who have smoked tschibouques with a Peshaw!

‖**tschoadar**, obs. variant of CHOBDAR.

1687 A. LOVELL tr. *Thevenot's Trav.* I. 25 The Tschoadar, who carries his Yagmourluk or Cloak for rain.

‖**tserin**, var. DZEREN, *dseren*.

1893 LYDEKKER *Horns & Hoofs* iv. 182 The tserin [*mispr.* tseain], or Mongolian gazelle (*Gazella* [or *Procapra*] *gutturosa*) of the desert regions of portions of Mongolia.

tsessabi, -ebe, -eby, variants of SASSABY.

‖**tsetse** ('tsɛtsɪ). Also **tzetse, tzetze,** (*erron.* **tse**). [Sechuana (i.e. Bechuana language) *tsetse.*]

1. A dipterous insect (*Glossina morsitans*, of the family *Tabanidæ*), abundant in parts of tropical and southern Africa; its bite is often fatal to horses and other domestic animals. Also applied to other species of *Glossina*. More fully ***tsetse-fly***.

1849 E. E. NAPIER *Excurs. S. Africa* II. 396 [Gordon Cumming's] horses were killed either by lions or horse sickness, and the fly called 'tzetse'. All his oxen were killed by this insect. **1850** R. G. CUMMING *Hunter's Life S. Afr.* (1902) 139/2 Four [horses] that are bitten with 'tsetse', and must die in a week or two. **1865** —— *Last Jrnls.* i. (1873) 15 The people..say there are no tsetse flies. **1889** L. V. SHELDON *S. Africa* 94 The Tse fly stings their horses. [**1895** J. BROWN *Secwana Dict.*, *Tsetse*, a fly destructive to cattle.] **1898** [see TRYPANOSOMA]. **1904** *Brit. Med. Jrnl.* 20 Aug. 368 Sleeping sickness is conveyed, at least in Uganda, by that species of tsetse fly we know as *Glossina palpalis*.

2. *attrib.* and *Comb.*, as ***tsetse-bitten***, ***-conveyed***, ***-free***, ***-infested***, ***-poisoned*** adjs.; **tsetse country, district**, an area infested by the tsetse fly; **tsetse-fly disease** = NAGANA.

1906 RIDER HAGGARD *Benita* x. 138 Meyer..had already decreed the death of the tsetse-bitten cattle. **1917** *Nature* 18 Oct. 127/2 The tsetse-conveyed sleeping sickness is being got well in hand. **1853** D. LIVINGSTONE *Jrnl.* 23 May (1960) iv. 139 There is only one small strip of Tsetse country to hinder one going westward. **1877** T. BAINES *Gold Regions S.E. Afr.* 89 Persons travelling must seek for the *latest* information..when approaching the borders of a Tsetse country. **1851** D. LIVINGSTONE *Jrnl.* 29 Aug. (1960) ii. 64 Several Englishmen have lost all their cattle horses & dogs by being led into a Tsetse district. **1895** Tsetse fly disease [see NAGANA]. **1932** C. FULLER *Louis Trigardt's Trek* ii. 28 They..were compelled to desist..on account of tsetse-fly disease among their cattle. **1948** T. A. M. NASH *Tsetse Flies in Brit. W. Afr.* I. 7/1 Inside this huge area there are only three districts which are tsetse-free. **1977** *Times* 22 Apr. 10/2 The ever-spreading erosion and desertification wreaked by over-stocking of domestic cattle in tsetse-free areas. **1948** T. A. M. NASH *Tsetse Flies in Brit. W. Afr.* I. 13/1 Should..the river flow from tsetse-infested country northwards, it would be wiser not to plant up the banks. **1977** *Times* 22 Apr. 10/4 Vast tsetse-infested tracts of Nigeria. **1906** RIDER HAGGARD *Benita* x. 138 The time was to come when she would swallow that hard, tsetse-poisoned flesh.

Tshekh (tʃɛx), variant of CZECH.

Tshi: see TWI.

T-shirt ('tiːʃɜːt). orig. *U.S.* Also **tee-shirt**. [f. the letter T (see below) + SHIRT *sb.*] A simple kind of garment, orig. a man's undershirt, typically short-sleeved, round-necked, buttonless and made from knitted cotton fabric, and forming the shape of a letter T when spread out flat; now a similar garment of various designs, widely worn as a shirt by men, women, and children for sport or as casual wear.

1920 F. SCOTT FITZGERALD *This Side of Paradise* I. i. 25 Amory, provided with 'six suits summer underwear..one sweater or T shirt..' set out for New England, the land of schools. **1944** *Survey Graphic* Aug. 368/3 We have been slow to realize that the high school crowd needs to sit in with us, with all their jive talk, their 'T' shirts and 'sloppy joes'. **1948** *Sun* (Baltimore) 2 Aug. 6/2 A ragged looking pair of trousers and as dark a shirt [as] possible or an old 'tee' shirt. **1957** J. BRAINE *Room at Top* xxv. 203 Roy..was wearing blue suède shoes, blue linen slacks, an orange T-shirt, and white sunglasses. **1958** *Daily Express* 4 Mar. 3/7 Lord M——..wore a striped tee-shirt. **1973** C. BONINGTON *Next Horizon* xiv. 202 Sebastian,..presented a sharp contrast to myself, already scruffy in T-shirt and jeans. **1980** *Times* 7 Feb. 13 There will be pop music and phone-ins, tee-shirts and car stickers.

Hence **T-shirted, tee-shirted** *adjs.*, wearing or clothed in a T-shirt.

1957 J. KEROUAC *On Road* (1958) II. vi. 134 His muscular neck, T-shirted in the winter night. **1959** *Times* 21 Oct. 11/3 T-shirted trippers perched on tubular steel chairs. **1973** *Philadelphia Inquirer* (Today Suppl.) 14 Oct. 27 (*caption*) A funeral parlor..is guarded by tee-shirted gang members outside. **1979** *Guardian* 3 Sept. 11/8 The jeaned and tee-shirted young.

†**tsia**, variant of *tcha*, CHIA *Obs.*, tea.

1662 J. DAVIES tr. *Mandelslo's Trav.* 183 A little Pot for Tsia or The..; another greater Tsia Pot. **1712** tr. *Pomet's Hist. Drugs* I. 85 The, or Tsia, is a very little Leaf, which is brought dry'd from China.

Hence **tsi'ology** (*nonce-wd.*), a scientific dissertation on tea.

1827 (*title*) Tsiology: Discourse on Tea, Tea Making, History of East India Co., &c.

tsigane, etc.: see TZIGANE.

tsimmes, -is, varr. TZIMMES.

Tsimshian ('tʃɪmʃən), *sb.* and *a.* Also **Tsimpshian**, etc. [Tsimshian self-designation *čamsián*, lit. inside of the Skeena River.]

A. *sb.* **a.** An Indian people of the north Pacific coast of N. America; also, a member of this people. **b.** Their language. **B.** *adj.* Of or pertaining to this people or their language.

1836 D. FINLAYSON *Let.* 29 Sept. in E. E. Rich *McLoughlin's Fort Vancouver Lett.* 1st Ser. (1941) 323 The Pearl Harbour, and Skeenah Indians called the Chimmesyan tribe. **1888** [see COPPER *sb.*[1] 4 b]. **1890** *Rep. Brit. Assoc. Adv. Sci. 1889* 853 The Olala is confined to the southern Tsimshian tribes. **1911, 1934** [see NASS]. **1966** [see CHILKAT]. **1972** *Language* XLVIII. 390 Geographically or genetically contiguous languages which share many features of the proposed analysis, e.g. Squamish and Tsimshian.

tsine (tsaɪn). Also **tsaing** (saɪŋ). [translit. Burmese *saing.*] A species of wild ox (*Bos banteng*) found in Burma and the Malay archipelago; = BANTENG.

1880 [see BANTENG, BANTING]. **1898** *Zoologist* Jan. 1 Tsine are certainly kittle cattle. **1900** POLLOK & THOM *Sports Burma* iii. 102 During my long residence in Lower Burma.. I killed but five tsine. *Ibid.*, Tsaing or Tsine. *Ibid.* 342 There were numerous signs of *Bos sondaicus*, the banting or tsine, as well as gaur about. **1903** *Sat. Rev.* 18 Apr. 481/1 The gaur, the gayal, the tsine or banting..might be acclimatised.

‖**tsipouro** ('tsɪpʊrəʊ). Also **tsippouro, tsipuro.** [mod.Gr., prob. a. Turk.] A rough and local kind of Greek spirituous drink.

1947 J. MULGAN *Report on Experience* viii. 98 We cheered each other in Fourna, passing *tsippouro*—a lower-class cousin of *ouzo*—across the fire. **1953** X. FIELDING *Stronghold* i. 4 [*Tsidoukhia,*] The local name for raki, similar to the *tsipouro* of Epirus, which is distilled from what is left of the grape after it has been pressed for wine. **1969** [see RAKI]. **1981** J. BOWMAN *Crete* (ed. 5) 46 On Crete the men are distinguished from the boys by drinking *raki*, a stronger unflavoured version [of ouzo] (and known in Crete as *tsipouro* or *tzikoudhia*).

tsitsith ('tsɪtsɪs, -ɪt), *sb. pl.* and *collect. sing. Judaism.* Also **tzitzit(h), zizith.** [a. Heb. *ṣīṣīṯ*.] The tassels of twisted and knotted cord worn by orthodox Jewish males on the corners of certain garments, esp. the tallith; cf. FRINGE *sb.* 1; also, a small rectangular garment, with a large hole in the middle and with tassels attached to each corner, worn over the vest but under the shirt.

Translated as 'fringes' in A.V. and R.V. and as 'tassels' in N.E.B. (see Numbers xv. 38, Deut. xxii. 12).

1675 L. ADDISON *Present State of Jews* xiii. 99 The wearing of the Zizith or Fringe, they collect from Exodus. **1738** 'GAMALIEL BEN PEDAHZUR' *Bk. Relig. of Jews* 4 The Fringe on each Corner is of eight worsted Threads double twisted [*marg.* Called Zizith]. **1816** J. ALLEN *Mod. Judaism* xvii. 305 Every male is required to have a quadrangular vestment, which they call *Talleth*... Its principal denomination, Tsitsith,..it receives from the fringes upon which all its sanctity is supposed to depend. **1854** *Asmonean* X. 198/1 In every corner is a string of plaited thread, called *zizis*, or *ziziths*. **1881** *Living Age* CIL. 418/1 The *tzitzis*, or fringes..of the boy's garment have been neglected. **1891** M. GOLDSMITH *Rabbi & Priest* 29 Shall he earn a few paltry kopecks in making tzitzith (fringes for the praying scarfs)? **1907** I. ZANGWILL *Ghetto Comedies* 389 These fellows.. wear fuses under their waistcoats instead of *Tsitsith* (ritual fringes). **1920** J. A. ROBERTSON *Hidden Romance N.T.* viii. 173, I see you are a Jew, like myself... But you don't wear the Zizith any more than I do. **1962** *New Jewish Encycl.* 475/1 The Tallit is rectangular in shape,..with *Tzitzit* (fringes) at each of its four corners. The Tzitzit is the important part of the Tallit. **1962** *Encounter* Sept. 21/2 They didn't buy ice-cream from the carts in the streets because it wasn't kosher; they never took their caps off in class..they wore *tzitzith* under their vests... They were heroic, absurd, and maddening. **1967** C. POTOK *Chosen* i. 16 They all wore the traditional undergarment beneath their shirts, and the tzitzit, the long fringes appended to the four corners of the garment, came out above their belts. **1968** L. ROSTEN *Joys of Yiddish* 418 *Tzitzit* are meant as reminders of one's duty to the laws of Judaism. **1973** *Times* 16 June 9/4 The distinctive features of Jewish dress—the *tsitsith* (tassels) [etc.].

tsk, *int.* Also **tsck**, and redupl. **tsk-tsk**. [Alveolar click formed by suction: cf. TCHICK *sb.*, TCK *int.*] A sound expressing commiseration; an exclamation of disapproval or irritation. So **tsk-tsk** *v. intr.*, to make this sound or utter this exclamation; also *trans.*, to say disapprovingly.

1947 K. L. PIKE *Phonemics* ii. 41/1 Do you get..a sound resembling the noise of commiseration which is sometimes written in literature as 'tsk-tsk', or 'tut-tut'? **1952** S. KAUFFMANN *Philanderer* (1953) xvii. 277 'When she doesn't like a writer or a composer, it sort of dampens my..activity about him. I'm henpecked.' 'Tsk, tsk,' said Ed extra clearly. **1958** L. DURRELL *Mountolive* xvi. 307 Balthazar..walked slowly..making the little clucking noise he always made with his tongue..*Tsck, tsck.* **1962** A. LURIE *Love & Friendship* xiv. 273 'Poor Carolyn Hastings is officially engaged to that dreadful Cowie boy.' 'Tsk.' **1966** M. AVALLONE *Fat Death* 47 'Mr. Noon,' he *tsk-tsked* reprovingly. 'You really pretend not to know?' **1968** *Punch* 20 Mar. 428/3 No amount of tsk-tsking indignation and bitter wit will turn a buy into a bargain. **1976** *New Yorker* 26 Apr. 102/2 She tsk-tsks over Momma. **1983** M. GEE *Sole Survivor* iv. 32 The constable went tsk, tsk and looked at us sadly. There was nothing he could do so he sent us home.

Tsonga ('tsɒŋgə), *sb.* and *a.* Also **Thonga.** [Native name: cf. TONGA[4].] **A.** *sb.* An African tribal group chiefly inhabiting the Transvaal area of the Republic of South Africa and parts of southern Mozambique; the Bantu language spoken by this people. **B.** *adj.* Of, pertaining to, or designating this people or their language.

1905 *Jrnl. Afr. Soc.* V. 12 There are three main Native languages in South Africa: Zulu, Suto and Thonga. **1907** H. A. JUNOD in C. W. Chatelain *Pocket Dict. Thonga* (*Shangaan*) (1909) 3 The Shangaan language, which would be more scientifically called the Thonga language. **1912** —— *Life S. Afr. Tribe* I. 13 The Thonga tribe is composed of a group of Bantu peoples settled on the Eastern coast of South Africa. **1933** *Bantu Stud.* VII. 4 The languages of the South-eastern [*sc.* Bantu] zone fall into four clusters, the 'Nguni', the 'Sotho', the 'Venda' and the 'Thonga'... In the Thonga cluster [are] three main groups, Ronga, Thonga and Tswa. **1937** R. H. LOWIE *Hist. Ethnological Theory* xii. 225 The Northern Thonga of Portuguese East Africa use a single word for the maternal uncle, the maternal uncle's son, and the mother's father. **1940** A. A. JAQUES in *Bantu Stud.* XIV. 259 It should be noted that it is not correct to spell the name of this people [*sc.* the Shangana-Tsonga] *Tonga* or *Thonga*... Since the recent decisions taken by the Tsonga Language Board concerning orthography, there should be no difficulty in adopting the form *Tsonga*. **1955** M. GLUCKMAN *Custom & Conflict in Afr.* iii. 63 Among the Tsonga of Mozambique..witchcraft..passes..from women to their children, so that men carry it, but not transmit it. *Ibid.* v. 116 Take this description of the Tsonga ritual which organizes the moving of a village. **1970** *Standard Encycl. S. Afr.* II. 106/2 The Tsonga group is often also called the Shangana group. These languages are spoken by the descendants of the Zulu chief Soshangana. *Ibid.* 306/1 The first portions of Scripture in Tsonga.. appeared in 1883. **1973** 'S. HARVESTER' *Corner of Playground* III. ii. 181 A Swazi king in eighteen-fiftyfour raided the Tsonga to find boys..to sell to the Boers. **1974** *Encycl. Brit. Micropædia* IX. 967/3 Although many Thonga are Christian, a substantial proportion adhere to their own traditional, highly ritualistic religion. **1979** *Jrnl. Imperial & Commonwealth Hist.* VII. 255 The provision of food, lodging and security to Tsonga migrants proved beneficial to Natal.

‖**Tsongdu** ('tsɒŋduː). Also **Tsong-du.** [ad. Tibetan *tʻsogs ḍu*, lit. 'an assembly meets'.] The Tibetan National Council or Assembly.

1905 *Spectator* 18 Feb. 243/2 When the expedition started we had two parties in Lhasa against us,—The Dalai Lama, with his adviser Dorjieff, who urged a breach in the traditional exclusiveness of the State in favour of Russia; and the Tsong-du, or Council, who were for the maintenance of the old system against Russia and Britain alike. **1970** R. D. TARING *Daughter of Tibet* vi. 68 A meeting of the *Tsongdu* (the National Assembly).

‖**tsores** ('tsɒrəs), *sb. pl.* (sometimes const. as *sing.*) *U.S. colloq.* Also **tsouris, tsuris, -us, (t)z-,** etc. [Yiddish *tsores*, pl. of *tsore* trouble, woe, a. Heb. *ṣārāh*.] Trouble(s), worries.

1901 M. WOLFENSTEIN *Idyls of Gass* viii. 143 I have other *Zores* (troubles). **1905** W. WITTIGSCHLAGER *Minna* I. i. 15 We have no money..nor do we propose ever to experience such *zorus*, (trouble). **1929** J. D. ROSENBERG *Kosher Americans* xvii. 165 Ve had plenty *tso-res* (troubles) before. **1941** B. SCHULBERG *What makes Sammy Run?* iv. 70, I had a notion that a little of Billie and Sammy Glick might not be such a bad idea, if only to get my mind off my own tsurus. **1950** *Commentary* X. 67/2 He had enough *tzores* without politics. **1956** 'T. BETTS' *Across Board* 103 During a long streak of tzuris (misery) with cards and horses. **1968** L. ROSTEN *Joys of Yiddish* 412 Oh, have I got *tsuris!* **1972** J. CAINE *Hamlet, my Boy* vi. 71 It's no *tsooras* for a child. **1975** *N.Y. Times Bk. Rev.* 16 Mar. 31 She has a bad back..and miscellaneous medical tsouris.

tsotsi ('tsɒtsɪ). *S. Afr.* [Origin uncertain: freq. said to be a corruption of *zoot suit.*] An African street thug or hoodlum, usu. from the Black townships and distinctively dressed in narrow trousers or in garments of exaggerated cut. Also in extended sense. Also *attrib.* Hence **'tsotsi-ism.**

1949 *Cape Argus* 20 July 8/9 (*heading*) Tsotsi gangs who hate Bantu students. **1949** *Cape Times* 10 Sept. 8/6 The 'Tsotsi' may be distinguished by his exceedingly narrow trousers which hardly reach his shoes, or else by his 'zoot suit'. **1952** B. DAVIDSON *Rep. Southern Afr.* II. v. 121 The conditions out of which have grown such strange and horrible manifestations of maladjustment as *tsotsi*-ism. **1956** H. BLOOM *Episode* xv. 273 One could tell they were *tsotsis* by their fancy clothes, by the way they took command... They led the mobs. **1971** *Sunday Times* (Johannesburg) *News Mag.* 28 Mar. 9/7 We do not want agitators to give hooligans and tsotsis the chance to plunder shops and businesses. **1979** A. BRINK *Dry White Season* I. vii. 70 'You may be a *lanie*' —his red tongue caressed the syllables of the taunting *tsotsi* word—'but you've got it right here.'

tsouris, var. TSORES.

T square: see T 3 b.

‖**tsu** (tsuː). *Anthrop.* [Chinese.] A patrilineal kinship group in pre-revolutionary China (see quot. 1939).

1939 H.-T. Fei *Peasant Life in China* v. 84 According to accepted principle, all the patrilineal descendants and their wives that can be traced to a common ancestor within five kinship grades consider themselves as belonging to a kinship group called Tsu. **1957** in K.-C. Chang *Archaeol. Anc. China* (1963) vi. 168 *P'i* (grandmothers and female ancestors) was partnered to *tsu* (grandfathers and male ancestors). **1966** M. Freedman *Chinese Lineage & Society* i. 5 Almost all *tsu* (lineage) relatives in the village are related through a grandfather.

‖**tsuba** ('tsuːba). Pl. tsuba, tsubas. [Jap., shortened f. *tsumiha, -ba*, f. *tsumi* to stop + *ha* (enemy's) blade, sword.] A Japanese sword-guard.

1889 J. J. Rein *Industries Japan* III. vii. 432 The sword-shell, or guard, Tsuba, is as old as the sword. It is an oval metal plate..with an opening in the middle to admit the blade of the sword. **1909** J. Masefield *Multitude & Solitude* ii. 35 Melyard collected tsuba, and fenced archæologically at the Foil Club. **1970** *Times* 11 Mar. 12/5 Sotheby's held a similar sale, mainly devoted to Japanese sword guards or tsubas. **1976** *Times Lit. Suppl.* 16 Jan. 48/4 *(caption)* Examples of the *tsuba*, or hand-guard, of Japanese swords. 'On them..may be found illustrated the whole of the mythology, customs, legends, folklore, famous scenes, characteristics and celebrated personages and events of the history of Japan.'

‖**tsubo** ('tsuːbo). Pl. tsubo, tsubos. [Jap.] A Japanese unit of area, equivalent to approximately 3.95 square yards (3.31 square metres).

1727 J. G. Scheuchzer tr. *Kæmpfer's Hist. Japan* I. IV. iii. 292 Woods and forests pay a..Ground-rent, which differs according to the number of *Tsubo's*, and the goodness and fruitfulness of the soil. **1902** *Encycl. Brit.* XXXIII. 810/1 Tsubo... Japan... 3·0306 [? *an error for* 3·306] sq. metres. **1972** P. M. Bartz *South Korea* viii. 123/2 In crowded Korea, urban land is sold by the *pyong* (35·6 square feet), the equivalent of the Japanese *tsubo* (3·3 square metres).

tsuica ('tsuːɪkə). Also tuica, ţuica, tzuica. [a. Rom. *ţuică*.] A Romanian plum brandy.

1927 *Sunday Express* 26 June 17/5 Will you come into the house and have a talk over a glass of tuica? **1938** *Times* 1 Jan. 11/1 The improvement of the facilities for the making of *ţsuica* (plum brandy, which is a national drink). **1960** O. Manning *Great Fortune* I. 52, I make my own red wine, white wine, *ţuică*, and martini. **1965** A. Sichel *Penguin Bk. Wines* III. 221 Various fruit cordials, such as plum brandy, are also exported from Rumania; there are two types, called Tzuica and Slibovitza. **1971** T. E. B. Clarke *Wrong Turning* xv. 105 She was drinking red wine with sodawater, he was having beer: there was laughter..at Jean's insistence in sticking to tuica. **1977** 'A. Stuart' *Snap Judgement* 51 She was choking—with emotion? With tuica? Both she and the room smelt strongly of plum brandy. **1981** B. de Breffny *My First Naked Lady* i. 29 Grandfather made me sip a Rumanian liqueur called Tsuica.

‖**tsukemono** (tsuːki'moːno). Also tsukimono. [Jap., f. *tsukeru* to pickle + *mono* something.] (See quots.)

1885 *Trans. Asiatic Soc. Japan* XIII. 8 *Tsukemono*, the preserved roots or leaves of certain vegetables. **1920** *Japan Advertiser* 22 Aug. 5/3 Most Japanese meals..are accompanied by vegetable dishes... Tsuki-mono stands for the pickle that accompanies the rice at the end of the meal and is made from vegetables in season, such as cucumbers, eggplant, melon, etc. **1968** P. S. Buck *People of Japan* xiv. 167 *Tsukemono*, the pickled vegetables served with any meal.

‖**tsukuri** (tsu'kuːri). [Jap.] In Judo, preparatory action taken to facilitate the breaking of one's opponent's balance. Cf. KUZUSHI.

1941 M. Feldenkrais *Judo* 25 Thus you have performed the 'fitting movement' (*Tsukuri*). **1968** [see KUZUSHI].

tsumebite ('tsuːməbaɪt). *Min.* [ad. G. *tsumebit* (K. Busz 1912, in *Festschr. gewidmet den Teilnehmern der 84. Versammlung Deutsch. Naturforscher und Ärzte in Münster von der Med.-Naturwiss. Ges. in Münster* 182), f. *Tsumeb*, name of a town in Namibia: see -ITE[1].] A basic phosphate and sulphate of lead and copper, $Pb_2Cu(PO_4)(SO_4)OH$, found as crusts of transparent green monoclinic crystals.

1913 *Mineral. Mag.* XVI. 373 Tsumebite... Hydrated basic phosphate of lead and copper..found as small, emerald-green, monoclinic crystals on white calamine at Tsumeb, Otavi, German South-West Africa. **1966** *Amer. Mineralogist* LI. 267 Due to the extreme tendency of tsumebite to occur as intimately intergrown crystals, considerable difficulty was encountered in obtaining a suitable, single crystal.

tsumpa, var. TSAMBA.

‖**tsun** (tsʊn). [Chinese.] A style of Chinese vessel, either wide-mouthed or animal-shaped (see quot. 1974). Also *attrib.*

1958 W. Willetts *Chinese Art* I. iii. 144 The Sung cataloguers proceeded to identify as *tsun* various animal-shaped vessels known to them. **1974** *Encycl. Brit. Micropædia* X. 162/3 *Tsun*,..generic term ('sacrificial vessel') for a wide range of Chinese vessel shapes, generally of the Shang (*c.* 1766–*c.* 1122 BC) and early Chou (*c.* 1122–*c.* 900 BC) dynasties, all of which have an ample interior volume probably meant for containing wine. There are two essential varieties of *tsun*: one is shaped like a much enlarged *ku*; the other consists of various animal shapes, often densely embellished with animal decoration. **1977** Kwang-Chih Chang *Archaeol. Anc. China* (ed. 3) vi. 222 Pottery *li* tripods and large-mouthed *tsun* beakers began to appear in significant numbers.

tsunami (tsuː'nɑːmɪ). Also (repr. a strict transliteration of the Jap. form) tunami. [a. Jap. *tsunami, tunami*, f. *tsu* harbour + *nami* waves.] A brief series of long, high undulations on the surface of the sea caused by an earthquake or similar underwater disturbance. These travel at great speed and often with sufficient force to inundate the land; freq. misnamed a *tidal wave* (see TIDAL *a.* 1 b). Also *fig.* and *attrib.*

1897 L. Hearn *Gleanings in Buddha-Fields* i. 24 '*Tsunami!*' shrieked the people; and then all shrieks and all sounds and all power to hear sounds were annihilated by a nameless shock..as the colossal swell smote the shore with a weight that sent a shudder through the hills. **1904** *Publ. Earthquake Investigation Comm. Foreign Lang.* (Japan) XIX. 6 Records and reports of earthquakes and '*tsunamis*'. **1938** *Nature* 12 Nov. 881/2 The authenticity of the reports of earthquakes mentioned in these catalogues is weighed.. with records of tunamis. **1956** *Jrnl. Earth Sci. Nagoya Univ.* IV. 2 The tunamis associated with strong earthquakes are frequent in Japan. **1967** *Technology Week* 23 Jan. 34/1 This system would predict..tsunami run-up floods. **1970** *Daily Tel.* 27 Nov. 11/7 A *tsunami* generated off Chile by the 1960 earthquake crashed into Japan on the other side at 400 m.p.h. **1972** *Science* 11 Aug. 502/1 The Food and Drug Administration..is currently swimming through a tsunami of comments generated by its announced intention to alter the regulations concerning the dispensation of methadone. **1981** *Monitor* (McAllen, Texas) 30 Jan. 3A/3 The National Weather Service..issued a *tsunami* warning. **1984** W. Golding *Paper Men* viii. 89 It seemed to me that I could feel the indifferent threat of the earth through the soles of my feet, the volcanoes, earthquakes, tsunamis, terrors of nature's fact.

tsuris, -us, etc., varr. TSORES.

‖**tsutsugamushi** (ˌtsuːtsugaˈmuʃi). *Path.* [Jap., f. *tsutsuga* trouble, illness + *mushi* insect.] = *scrub typhus* s.v. SCRUB sb.[1] 6. Usu. *attrib.* in *tsutsugamushi disease.*

1906 *Index Medicus* IV. Index 216/1 Tsutsugamushi disease. **1908** *Philippine Jrnl. Sci.* B. III. 1 (*heading*) A comparative study of *tsutsugamushi* disease and spotted or tick fever of Montana. **1929**, etc. [see *scrub typhus* s.v. SCRUB *sb.*[1] 6]. **1937** *Med. Jrnl. Australia* 21 Aug. 300/1 The absence of a local intradermal lesion speaks against the virus being of the spotted fever or *tsutsugamushi* types of Rickettsia. **1978** *Jrnl. R. Soc. Med.* LXXI. 507 The Japanese synonym, tsutsugamushi disease, clearly had precedence, but the name, scrub typhus, became fully established through widespread use in World War II.

‖**tsutsumu** (tsu'tsumu). [Jap., to wrap.] The Japanese art of wrapping or packaging items in an attractive and appropriate way.

1975 *N.Y. Times Mag.* 9 Feb. 56 Each of the 300 packages in the show (called 'Tsutsumu, The Art of the Japanese Package') was purchased in 1974 in Japan, where an object's wrapping can be as important as the object itself.

Tswana ('tswɑːnə), *sb.* and *a.* Also Chwana. [Native name.] **A.** *sb.* **a.** = BECHUANA (for which *Tswana* is now the usual term). **b.** The Bantu language of this people (cf. SETSWANA). **B.** *adj.* Of or pertaining to this people or their language.

1930 *Bantu Studies* IV. 211 It is therefore probable that they may still be more widespread, at least among the Sotho-Tswana tribes. **1932** D. Jones *Outl. Eng. Phonetics* xxix. 227 Strong stress without accompanying loudness is a common feature of the Chwana language of South Africa. **1937** *Bantu Studies* XI. 137 The orthography set out in the present pamphlet represents the latest result of a prolonged series of efforts made..by the Education Departments..to arrive at a uniform orthography of Tswana. **1948** M. Guthrie *Classification Bantu Lang.* iv. 68 In Tswana the verbal has the extra suffix -ŋ. **1949** I. Schapera in M. Fortes *Social Structure* 104 In contrast to most other Bantu-speaking peoples of southern Africa, the Tswana tribes of the Bechuanaland Protectorate have remarkably few marriage prohibitions. **1957** [see SOTHO]. **1973** J. J. McKelvey *Man against Tsetse* i. 16 Cumming went..down to the hunting grounds of the Limpopo against the advice of the local people, the Tswanas. **1975** 'D. Jordan' *Black Account* xviii. 96 A girl came down the steps..she was blonde, and slim and tall... 'I thought you were all Tswana here,' I said and she laughed... She explained she worked in Bantu Affairs. **1980** First & Scott *Olive Schreiner* i. 37 Basotho and Tswana refugees.

t test ('tiː tɛst). *Statistics.* [f. *t* chosen arbitrarily as a symbol.] = *Student's (t) test* s.v. STUDENT[2].

[**1924** R. A. Fisher in *Proc. Internat. Math. Congr.* (1928) II. 498 If for the accurate standard deviation we substitute an estimate based on *n* degrees of freedom we have $t = x\sqrt{n}/\sqrt{S(x^2)}$. **1925** 'Student' in *Metron* V. 105 The present tables have..at Mr. Fisher's suggestion been constructed with argument $t = z\sqrt{n}$.] **1932** R. A. Fisher *Statistical Methods for Research Workers* (ed. 4) v. 116 The validity of the *t*-test, as a test of this hypothesis, is therefore absolute. **1958** M. Argyle *Relig. Behaviour* iii. 16 The 't' test..is generally used when equal measurement units are involved, otherwise various non-parametric methods are available. **1968** *Brit. Med. Bull.* XXIV. 220/2 A selection of commonly required significance tests is available, including paired and unpaired *t* tests, correlation coefficients..and analysis of variance. **1974** *Florida FL Reporter* XIII. 73/1 Correlated one-tailed t-tests were run for both the differences between the two groups.

tu, obs. f. THOU *pers. pron.*, TO *prep.*, TWO.

tua, tuaine, obs. Sc. ff. TWO, TWAIN.

tuae, Sc. dial. form of TWAY, two.

‖**tuak** ('tuːæk). [Malay.] A locally-distilled Malaysian or Indonesian palm- or rice-wine.

[**1850** *Jrnl. Indian Archipelago* IV. 179 Liquid sugar..is obtained by boiling the juice extracted from the *loutar* or *tuak* palm.] **1852** *Ibid.* VI. 317, I could not learn that they prepared any fermented liquor, not even sago-weer or tuak. **1920** C. Lumholtz *Through Central Borneo* II. xxxi. 335 On the Upper Samba the custom still prevails of drinking tuak from human skulls. **1961** P. Kemp *Alms for Oblivion* vii. 119 *Tuak* drinking is a favourite pastime of the elderly men. *Tuak*, or toddy, is brewed from the juice of the sugar palm; it looks and tastes somewhat like farm cider,..though not so intoxicating. **1966** *Festival Malaysia 1966: Calendar of Events* 10/1 Tuak (locally distilled rice-wine) is the drink of the occasion [*sc.* a Dyak Gawai]. **1977** *Borneo Bull.* 7 May 4/5 The main cultural show was at an open night for all participants at the Rest House which would have been even more fun if the tuak had not run out early.

tualy, obs. form of TOWEL.

tuan[1] (tuː'ɑːn). Also Tuan. [Malay.] A master, a lord, formerly esp. a European as spoken to or of by Malays; freq. used as a title of respect or form of address, = 'sir', 'mister'.

1779 T. Forrest *Voy. New Guinea* I. ii. 27, I found Tuan Hadjee in high spirits. **1864** J. T. Thomson *Some Glimpses Life Far East* xxi. 106 'Why,' said he, '*tuan*, these two rows belong to the East India Company's chief official.' **1885** E. Innes *Chersonese* I. ii. 21 Before the Tuan's (master's) marriage, all his mending is cheerfully done for him by his 'boy'. **1900** Conrad *Lord Jim* i. 3 They called him Tuan Jim: as one might say—Lord Jim. **1937** G. Frankau *More of Us* xvi. 166 There is nothing frets your gent, your sahib, your tuan,..like having some old donah near his new one. **1958** J. Slimming *Temiar Jungle* ii. 25 'Greetings, Tuan!' His voice is quiet and gentle. **1978** L. Heren *Growing up on The Times* iv. 136 British conscript soldiers were expected to keep the enemy at bay in Malaya while the *tuans* made their piles.

‖**tuan**[2]. Also touan. Native name in Australia for the Flying Squirrel or Flying Phalanger (genus *Belideus*).

1846 G. H. Haydon *Five Y. Exper. Australia Felix* iii. 57 The flying squirrel, or tuan, is much sought after for its fine fur. **1859** H. Kingsley *G. Hamlyn* xxxi, The Touan, the little grey flying squirrel, only begins to fly about at night.

‖**tuant** (tyɑ̃), *a. Obs. rare.* [Fr., = killing, pres. pple. of *tuer* to slay, kill.] Of language or words: Cutting, biting, keen, trenchant.

1672 Villiers (Dk. Buckhm.) *Rehearsal* IV. i. (Arb.) 99 Ay, I gad, but is not that *tuant* now, ha? is it not *tuant*? **1672** Marvell *Reh. Transp.* I. 17 To say Mr. Bayes is more civil than to say Villain and Caitiff, though these indeed are more tuant. **1673** [R. Leigh] *Transp. Reh.* 13. **1673** Hickeringill *Greg. F. Greyb.* 142 This harangue tuant and clean. **1706** Phillips (ed. Kersey) s.v., *A Tuant Jest*, i.e. a tart, biting Jest.

Tuareg ('twɑːrɛg), *sb.* and *a.* Also 9 Tawarek, Tuari(c)k. [Native name.] **A.** *sb.* (A member of) a nomadic people of the western and central Sahara. Also, the Berber language of this people. **B.** *adj.* Of or pertaining to this people or their language.

1821 G. F. Lyon *Narr. Trav. N. Afr.* iii. 112 The nearest Tuarick to Fezzan are at Ghraat. **1826** Denham & Clapperton *Narr. Trav. & Disc. N. & Central Afr.* p. l, The greater number of Tuaricks follow the nomadic life. *Ibid.* p. lxv, They..laughed heartily at our blundering out a few Tuarick words. *Ibid.* 83 He was dressed in a light blue cotton tobe, with a white muslin turban, the shawl of which he wore over the nose and mouth, in the Tuarick fashion. *Ibid.* App. 160 Under the government of the Tawarék. **1882** [see KABYLE]. **1933** L. Bloomfield *Language* iv. 67 The *Berber* branch of Semitic-Hamitic..is represented today by various languages, such as *Tuareg* and *Kabyle.* **1955** *Sci. News Let.* 4 June 3 Called the 'People of the Veil', the Tuaregs are a nomadic people who live in the central part of the Sahara desert. **1973** *Times* 19 Mar. 6/3 The tracks..did lead to some Tuareg nomads, and to water. **1977** *Time* 3 Oct. 2/2 The peregrinations of the Tuareg in Niger, Mali and Upper Volta and the nomadic Masai in Kenya and Tanzania frighten their respective governments.

tuarn, tuart: see TEW-IRON, TOOART.

‖**tuatara** (tʊa'tara, tuːə'tɑːrə). Also (*erron.*) tuatera, -tura. [Maori, f. *tua* on the back + *tara* spine (Webster, 1911).] A large lizard, *Sphenodon punctatum* or *Hatteria punctata*, dark bronze green in colour with white or yellowish specks, and having a dorsal row of yellow spines, formerly common in New Zealand: see quot. 1911.

[**1820** *Gram. & Voc. N. Zealand* 218 (Morris) *Túa tára*, a species of lizard.] **1890** *Catal. N. Zealand Exhib.* (ibid.), The Tuatara is the largest existing New Zealand reptile. It..is placed..in a separate order (*Rhyncocephalina*). **1911** C. de Thierry in *United Empire* Mar. 183 One of the peculiar animals from which scientists have estimated the probable age of New Zealand is the tuatara, a small lizard about a foot in length and of a dark bronze colour. It is extinct on the mainland but is still to be found on the shores of the outlying islands. **1914** *Chamb. Jrnl.* Nov. 750/2 The extraordinary characteristic of the tuatara is its capacity for perfect rest, and its apparent power of existing without food or water.

‖**tuath** (ˈtuəh). *Irish Hist.* [Ir. *tūath* people, cognate with OE. *þéod*, Goth. *þiuda*, OTeut. **þeuđô*, Indo-Eur. **teutā*; ME. THEDE, q.v.] A 'tribe' or 'people' in Ireland; hence, the territory or district of a tribe, in which sense written in 16th c. *toghe*, TOUGHE, q.v.

1873 W. K. SULLIVAN in *O'Curry's Anc. Irish* I. Introd. 79 The term *Tuath* was..applied to the people occupying a district which had a complete political and legal administration, a chief or *Rig*, and could bring into the field a battalion of seven hundred men. The word was also applied however to a larger division, consisting of three or four, or even more *Tuaths*, called a *Mór Tuath*, or great *Tuath*,..associated together for certain legal and legislative purposes. **1877** W. F. SKENE *Celtic Scotl.* II. II. x. 460 Before letters were introduced..each tuath, or tribe, had probably its own variety of the common speech. **1898** J. HERON *Celtic Ch.* 14 A group of families from a common ancestry made a sept; a still larger group was called a clann ..; while a tribe or tuath consisted of several of such clanns, septs, and families. *Ibid.* 16 There were in Ireland one hundred and eighty four tuaths or tribal territories.

‖**Tuatha Dé Danann** (ˈtuəhə deː ˈdanən). Also (*erron.*) **Tuatha de Danaan**, etc. [Ir., f. *tuatha*, pl. of *tuath* TUATH + *dé* + *Danann*, name of the mother of the gods (app. formerly gen. sing. of *Danu*, but later used as nom).] In Irish mythology, a people who inhabited prehistoric Ireland.

1682 P. WALSH *Prospect State of Ireland* f. b2, He has not the least mention of Tuatha-De-Danainn, though a powerful People. **1876** [see NEMEDIAN]. **1893** W. B. YEATS in *Bookman* May 43/1 The berries were the food of the *Tuatha de Danaan*, or faeries. **1980** J. O'FAOLAIN *No Country for Young Men* ii. 41 Ever hear of the prehistoric rulers of Ireland and how they fought their wars? The Tuatha De Danaan? They wrapped themselves in a cloud and withdrew into the hills..and turned into fairies.

tuay, obs. Sc. form of TWAY, two.

tuayl, obs. form of TOWEL.

tub (tʌb), *sb.* Forms: 4–7 tubbe, 5–6 tobbe, 5–7 tob, 6 toubbe, tube, toob (also 9 *dial.*), 6–7 tubb, 6– tub. [ME. *tubbe* = MDu., MLG. *tubbe*, *tobbe*, Du. and MFl. *tobbe*, Flem. *tubbe* (*ü*), *tibbe*, WFris. *tobbe*, LG., and EFris. *tubbe*.]

1. a. An open wooden vessel, wide in proportion to its height, usually formed of staves and hoops, of cylindrical or slightly concave form, with a flat bottom.

Often with defining word indicating its special use, as ***alms-tub***, ***bath-t.***, ***butter-t.***, ***kneading-t.***, ***wash-t.***, etc.: see these words. Also loosely applied to a butt, barrel, or cask.

c **1386** CHAUCER *Miller's T.* 435 He gooth and geteth hym a knedyng trogh, And after that a tubbe and a kymelyn. **1392–3** *Early Derby's Exp.* (Camden) 224 Pro vasis ligneis.. viz. tubbes, trowes, boketes et basketes. **1481–90** *Howard Househ. Bks.* (Roxb.) 228 Item, for a lok for the almes tobbe, ij. d. **1496** *Nottingham Rec.* III. 296 For v. tobys. **1509–10** *Rec. St. Mary at Hill* 269 Paid to a Coper for hopyng of the Tobbys and þe Barelles that longith to the Chirche xvj d. **1526** *Dunmow Churchw. Acc.* lf. 5 b (MS.) Payde for a toob and ii. bokks to fett watter, vii *d.* **1531** *Lett. & Pap. Hen. VIII*, V. 180 For morter toubbis, cowlis, water bukettes,.. etc. **1557** in *Lanc. & Chesh. Wills* (1884) 64, iiij Tubbs to salte fleshe in. **1561** HOLLYBUSH *Hom. Apoth.* 3 b, Bath his fete in a depe tob. **1573** TUSSER *Husb.* (1878) 58 Take tub for a season, take sack for a shift. **1645** BP. HALL *Remedy Discontent.* xvi. 86 Here doe I see a Cynick housed in his Tub, scorning all wealth and state. **1829** LYTTON *Devereux* III. iv, Diogenes in his tub. **1838** DICKENS *Nich. Nick.* ii, A distorted fir-tree, planted..in a tub.

fig. **1693** *Humours Town* 2 Coop'd up..like a Cinic, in thy Tub of a Study.

†**b.** A sweating-tub formerly used in the treatment of venereal disease; hence, the use of this; see quots. and cf. *tub-fast* in 10; also called (***Mother***) ***Cornelius' tub***, and allusively ***powdering-tub***. *Obs.*

1594 NASHE *Unfort. Trav.* 17 Mother Cornelius tub why it was like hell, he that came into it, neuer came out of it. **1599** [see POWDERING-TUB 2]. **1603** SHAKS. *Meas. for M.* III. ii. 60 *Luc.* How doth..thy Mistris? Procures she still? Ha? *Clo.* Troth sir, shee hath eaten vp all her beefe, and she is her selfe in the tub. **1608** ARMIN *Nest Ninn.* E iv b, Where they should study in priuate with Diogenes in his Cell, they are with Cornelius in his tub. **1676** WISEMAN *Chirurg. Treat.* VIII. ii. 13 Tub and Chair were the old way of sweating, but [etc.]. **1688** R. HOLME *Armoury* III. 421/2 He beareth Argent, a Doctors Tub, (otherwise called a Cleansing Tub), Sable; Hooped, Or.

c. *Gold-mining.* A puddling tub.

1853 E. CLACY *Lady's Visit Gold Diggings Austral.* 116 Great wooden tubs are filled with the dirt and fresh water. **1859**, **1869** [see PUDDLING *vbl. sb.* 4, PUDDLE *v.* 6]. **1864** ROGERS *New Rush* II. 47 Miners' tubs and cradles, left to chance, On the resistless torrent's surface dance. **1884** T. BRACKEN *Lays of Maori* 154 The music of the puddling mill, the cradle, and the tub.

d. Used as a measure of capacity, varying with the commodity it contained: see quots.

1706 PHILLIPS (ed. Kersey), *Tub of Tea*, the Quantity of about 60 Pounds: of Camphire from 56 to 86 Pounds: of Vermilion from 3 to 4 Hundred Weight. **1858** SIMMONDS *Dict. Trade* s.v., The tub of butter must contain at least 84 lbs.; the tub of camphor is 130 Dutch lbs.

e. A small cask or keg of spirit, containing about four gallons. (A smugglers' term.)

1835 MARRYAT *Three Cutters* ii, I made three seizures, besides sweeping up those thirty-seven tubs. **1869** R. M. BALLANTYNE *Deep Down* xiv. 180 They do say that the boats-men [coast-guards] are informed about the toobs. **1884** J. C. EGERTON *Sussex Folk & Ways* v. 65 This cottage ..has..been full of tubs from top to bottom as ever it could hold.

f. *vulgar colloq.* Applied to a corpulent person.

1897 FLANDRAU *Harvard Episodes* 316 With a moon-faced tub of a woman I'd never seen before,..hanging on to me.

g. A tub-shaped carton, *spec.* one containing a portion of ice-cream; the contents of a carton.

1939 'G. ORWELL' *Coming up for Air* IV. iii. 248, I watched the floats rocking up and down among the ice-cream tubs and the paper bags. **1955** 'C. BROWN' *Lost Girls* xii. 139 You bought these ices from a fat woman holding out a podgy hand and saying, 'Two tubs, ducks?' **1981** P. VANSITTART *Death of Robin Hood* IV. i. 183 The sallow ground was strewn with..ice-cream tubs, empty tins and ruined shoes.

2. A bathing-tub, bath-tub (of any shape); *colloq.* or *jocularly*, a bath; hence, the action or practice of taking a bath, esp. on rising.

[**1594** PLAT *Jewell-ho.* III. 94 The room would be close wherin you place your bathing tub.] **1776** H. NEWDIGATE *Let.* in A. E. Newdigate-Newdegate *Cheverels* (1898) i. 11 To-night I can use my warm Bath..which I cannot at present do conveniently at home having neither Tub nor dressers. **1849** *Knife & Fork* 11 They..have an hereditary aversion for the Saturday tub. **1861** HUGHES *Tom Brown at Oxf.* iii, A great splashing in an inner room stopped..and Drysdale's voice shouted out that he was in his tub. **1865** 'C. BEDE' *Rook's Gard.*, etc. 251 I must have been prior to the date of the institution of the tub. **1893** A. LANG *St. Andrews* i. 15 *note*, George Wishart astonished his contemporaries by taking cold tubs.

3. Applied to a slow clumsy ship, esp. one which is too broad in proportion to its length; often *humorous* or *contemptuous*; also, a short, broad boat; *spec.* a stout roomy boat used for rowing practice, as distinguished from a racing-boat; cf. *tub-gig*, *tub-pair* (see 10), TUB *v.* 4.

a **1618** RALEIGH *Invent. Shipping* 9 In Cæsars time, the French Brittains..had very untoward Tubs in which they made Warre against him. **1675** HOBBES *Odyssey* (1677) 54 And now my child at sea is in a tub. **1809** W. IRVING *Knickerb.* II. iv. (1861) 52 Here the rapid tide..seizing on the gallant tub.., hurried it forward with a velocity unparalleled in a Dutch boat, navigated by Dutchmen. **1827** *Blackw. Mag.* XXI. 398 One was four feet broader, another was as much shorter than the Victory, and they were in comparison all Tubs. **1841** J. T. HEWLETT *Parish Clerk* III. 4 No lighter boat, except the little tubs used for rowing off from the beach, could be obtained. **1853** 'C. BEDE' *Verdant Green* x, He next day..made his first essay in a 'tub'. **1901** D. B. HALL & LD. A. OSBORNE *Sunshine & Surf* iv, His old tub of a vessel..was known from one end of the Pacific to the other.

4. Applied contemptuously or jocularly to a pulpit, esp. of a nonconformist preacher: cf. TUB-PREACHER, -THUMPER.

1643 OWEN *Duty of Pastors & People* viii, Must a master of a family cease praying in his family,..for fear of being counted a preacher in a tub? **1680** DRYDEN *Prol. to University of Oxford* 13 Jack Presbyter shall here erect his throne, Knock out a tub with preaching once a day. **1710** HEARNE *Collect.* (O.H.S.) II. 351 A huge Bonfire was made, and the Tub in wch he used to hold forth was plac'd on ye top of the Pile. **1728** POPE *Dunc.* II. 2 A gorgeous seat, that far out-shone Henley's gilt tub, or Fleckno's Irish throne. **1891** *Spectator* 5 Dec. 804/2 Let the pulpit speak, and the tub too —there will still be too much sleep.

5. *Coal-mining.* **a.** 'Originally a mining bucket, now specially applied to the open-topped box of wood or iron, mounted on wheels, in which coal is brought from the face to the surface. It has supplanted the old 'corf', which was a basket carried on a tram. The tram and tub are now, in most cases, a single structure' (Heslop *Northumb. Gloss.* 1894). Cf. CORF 2, TRAM *sb.*[2] 2.

1851 GREENWELL *Coal-trade Terms Northumb. & Durh.* 54 *Tub*, an open-topped box of wood or iron, attached to a tram, and used in conveying coals from the working places to the surface. **1859** R. HUNT *Guide Mus. Pract. Geol.* (ed. 2) 222 Cages [in coal mines] are attached to the wire rope, and these move in guides in the pit. The *tub* (8 cwt.) is placed in those [cages], and when drawn to the surface placed in the *teaming cradles*. **1893** *Athenæum* 21 Oct. 551/3 The old-fashioned 'tub' in the cut 'A Coal Mine' will hardly be recognized by the present generation of pit-men.., who, though they still use the word, no longer know the thing, which has been replaced by small trucks which run on rails into the cage. **1894** HESLOP (as above), The tub, containing twenty-four pecks [is] three feet in length, thirty inches in width, and twenty-six in depth.

b. The lining of a pit-shaft.

1839 [implied in *tub-plank* in 10]. **1855** *Orr's Circ. Sc., Inorg. Nat.* 237 In all cases, the foundation of a permanent tub should rest on a water-tight stratum. **1860** WEALE *Dict. Terms* (ed. 2), *Tub*, a cast-iron cylinder put in the shaft instead of bricking. **1877** KNIGHT *Dict. Mech.*, *Tub*,..a casing of wood or of cast-iron sections..lining a shaft.

6. †**a.** On the early railways vulgarly applied to an open truck or a seatless carriage. *Obs.*

1886 H. S. BROWN *Autobiog.* vii. (1887) 30 We called it a 'stand up' and it also went by the name of 'a tub'. **1890** *N. & Q.* 7th Ser. IX. 470/2 At the time when the railway between Nottingham and Grantham was opened forty years ago, carriages of the lowest class,..third or fourth, were something like [what] cattle-trucks are now, and were known colloquially as 'tubs'.

†**b.** A covered carriage or conveyance. *Obs.* **c.** ? = *tub-gig* (*a*) (see 10).

1889 *John Bull* 2 Mar. 142/2 Tubs we ca' the covered carriages, tubs wasn't known in these parts. **1911** F. HARRISON *Autobiog. Mem.* II. xxiv. 73 It was the age of 'tubs' and they often took Jane Brice, my mother and Ellinor Abraham..as sitters.

d. A fire-engine. *U.S. slang.*

1864 *Student & Schoolmate* Jan. 3 The rope was only half manned and wishing to make myself useful..I joined the party in charge of the 'tub'. **1906** J. D. LOVETT *Old Boston Boys* vii. 67 A boy without a 'tub', as they were called in the vernacular, was like a man without a country.

e. A bus; ***to work the tubs***, to pick pockets on buses or at bus-stops. *slang* (chiefly *Underworld*).

1929 G. DILNOT *Triumphs of Detection* iv. 52 Snatches of their conversation..told that they were on their way to 'work the tubs'—in other words, to pick pockets at omnibus stopping-places. **1933** C. E. LEACH *On Top of Underworld* x. 141 *Tub*, omnibus. **1974** P. WRIGHT *Lang. Brit. Industry* x. 85 Inland transport comes along with *tubs* for buses.

7. *Naut.* See quot.

1867 SMYTH *Sailor's Word-bk.*, *Tubs, Topsail-halliard*, circular framed racks in which the topsail-halliards are coiled clear for running.

8. A local name of the gurnard, esp. the sapphirine gurnard, *Trigla hirundo*. Also *tub-fish* (see 10).

Couch takes this as a contraction of Cornish *tubbot*, *-ut*.

1602 CAREW *Cornwall* 32 Of flat [fish there are] Brets, Turbets, Dories,..Tub, Breame &c. **1836** YARRELL *Brit. Fishes* I. 42 From West bay to the Land's End, where the Gurnards are called Tubs, Tubfish and, in reference to colour, Red Tubs. **1861** *Act 24 & 25 Vict.* c. 109 §4 All migratory fish of the genus salmon,..salmon,..buntling, guiniad, tubs, yellow fin, sprod, herling,..or..any other local name. **1863** *Rep. Sea Fisheries Comm.* (1865) II. 404/2 A tub..is a large specimen of the gurnet... Hake and tubs are the most we catch.

9. In proverbial phrases: †**a.** ***a tale of a tub***, an apocryphal tale; a 'cock and bull' story. *Obs.* **b.** (***to throw out***) ***a tub to the whale***, to create a diversion, esp. in order to escape a threatened danger. **c.** ***every tub must*** (or ***let every tub***) ***stand on its own bottom***: cf. BOTTOM *sb.* 11 b.

a. 1532 MORE *Confut. Tindale* Wks. 371/2 Consider the places & his wordes together, & ye shal find al his processe therin a fayre tale of a Tub. *Ibid.* [see TALE *sb.* 5 b]. **1562** J. HEYWOOD *Prov. & Epigr.* (1867) 144 A tale of a tub, thy tales taste all of ale. **1631** LENTON *Charac.* F ix b, Oft-times hee goes but to the next Tauerne, and then very discreetly brings her home a tale of a Tubbe. **1709** O. DYKES *Eng. Prov. & Refl.* (ed. 2) 57 If one talks of Chalk, another will talk of Cheese still, or tell a Tale of a Tub. **1724** [see TALE *sb.* 5 b].

b. 1704 SWIFT *T. Tub* Author's Pref. 14 Sea-men have a Custom when they meet a Whale, to fling him out an empty Tub,..to divert him from laying violent Hands upon the Ship... It was decreed, that in order to prevent these Leviathans from tossing and sporting with the Commonwealth (which of it self is too apt to fluctuate) they should be diverted..by a Tale of a Tub. **1728–31** *Lett. fr. Fog's Jrnl.* (1732) II. 73 It has been common to throw out something to divert and amuse the People, such as a Plot, a Conspiracy, or an Enquiry about Nothing,..which Method of Proceeding, by a very apt Metaphor, is call'd throwing out the Tub. **1748** RICHARDSON *Clarissa* (1810) III. vii. 54. **1768** EARL MALMESBURY *Diaries & Corr.* I. 23 We find it a mere tub to amuse the whale. **1826** J. DOYLE *Ess. Cath. Claims* 248 Some tub for a whale of prejudice to knash its teeth against. **1912** *Nation* 29 June 465/2 He throws a tub to the High Church whale.

c. *c.* **1730–6** BAILEY (folio) s.v., Every Tub must stand upon it's own Bottom. **1772** GRAVES *Spir. Quix.* (1820) I. 171. **1885** 'H. CONWAY' *Fam. Affair* xxix, I think it's better to let every tub stand on its own bottom.

10. *attrib.* and *Comb.*, as ***tub-bath***, ***-boat***, ***-ear*** (EAR *sb.*[1] 8), ***-eight*** (EIGHT B. 2 b), ***-end***, ***-hoop*** (in quot. *transf.*), ***-kennel***, ***-life***, ***-plank***, ***-plant***, ***-pulpit***, ***-timber***, ***-washing***; objective, as ***tub-buyer***, ***-carrier***, ***-filler***, ***-maker***; in sense 4, as ***tub-lecture***, ***-meeter***, ***-minister***, ***-orator***; also ***tub-bellied***, ***-brained***, ***-coopering***, ***-keeping***, ***-like***, ***-shaped*** adjs.; also **tub-bass**, a bass string instrument made from a tub; **tub-butter**, butter packed in tubs for keeping or export; **tub-camphor**, camphor imported in tubs (from Japan); **tub-cart** = *tub-gig* (*a*); **tub-chair**, a deep semicircular chair resembling a tub; **tub-dress**, a dress of washing material: cf. *tub-frock*; **tub-drubber** = TUB-THUMPER; **tub-engine**, a contrivance for raising water by means of a chain of tubs or the like; **tub-fake** (FAKE *sb.*[1]), the coiled tow-line in the line-tub of a whale-boat (*Cent. Dict.* 1891 cites J. W. Collins); †**tub-fast**, abstinence during treatment in the sweating-tub: cf. 1 b; **tub-fish** = sense 8; **tub-frock** = *tub-dress*; **tub garden**, an area containing plants grown in tubs; **tub-gardening**, cultivation of plants or trees in tubs; **tub-gig**, (*a*) a deep low-hung gig with rounded corners and seats facing inwards; a governess car; (*b*) = *tub-pair*; **tub-gin** = *tub-engine*; †**tub-hunter**, a parasite, a sponger; **tub-loader**, *Coal-mining*: see quot.; **tub-oar**, the oar next the line-tub in a whale-boat; so **tub-oarsman**, one who attends to the running of the line when in use (*Cent. Dict.* 1891); **tub-pair**, a pair-oared practice boat (*College slang*); **tub-plot**, cf. *Meal-tub Plot* (MEAL *sb.*[1] 3 b); **tub-race**, a race in which the competitors use tubs instead of boats; **tub-saw**, a cylindrical saw; **tub-size** *v.*, *trans.* to size (paper) in a tub or vat; to hand-size, as distinguished from *engine-size*; hence **tub-sized** *ppl. a.*; **tub-skirt**, **tub-suit**: cf. *tub-dress*; **tub-sugar**, sugar packed in chests and covered with fine clay (*Cent. Dict.* 1891); †**tub-tail**, a farthingale or hooped skirt; one who wears this (*contemptuous*); **tub-trimmer**, ? a cooper; in quot. *fig.*; **tub-wheel**, (*a*) the wheel of a colliery 'tub'; (*b*) a horizontal water-wheel with spiral floats; = DANAIDE; (*c*) a rotating drum in which hides are washed (*Funk's Stand. Dict.* 1895); **tub-woman**, a woman who carries a tub or tubs; also a woman suggesting a tub in figure. See also TUBMAN, TUB-PREACHER, TUB-THUMPER, etc.

1958 P. OLIVER in P. Gammond *Decca Bk. Jazz* i. 23 Parallels have been drawn between the *tub-bass and the African earth-bow, but that the former is a folk memory of the other seems unlikely. **1896** *Allbutt's Syst. Med.* I. 850 Each patient receives a *tub-bath of twenty minutes at 70° every third hour. **1846** *J. Baxter's Libr. Pract. Agric.* (ed. 4) II. 263 Before the South-down sheep were improved, they were very flat on the ribs, and *tub-bellied. **1883** *Brit. Q. Rev.* July 108 Crossing the narrow water-way in one of the heavy *tub-boats of the country. **1634** W. WOOD *New Eng. Prosp.* To Rdr., Many a *tub-brain'd Cynicke, who because any thing..is too large for the straite hoopes of his apprehension, he peremptorily concludes it is a lye. **1829** S. SHAW *Hist. Staffordsh. Potteries* iv. 105 The common people of the district at the present day, call Irish **Tub* Butter, Pot Butter. **1880** *Spons' Encycl. Manuf.* 574 Japanese camphor ..is also known as 'Dutch', or '*tub' camphor,..from its being imported to Europe in tubs covered with matting, each placed within a second tub. **1899** BARING-GOULD *Bk. of West* II. 275 The '*tub-carriers', who conveyed the kegs on their backs. **1906** *Daily Chron.* 26 Sept. 4/4 Three little girls..clambering and pushing their way into the *tub-cart. **1839** MRS. CARLYLE *Lett., to Mrs. Welsh* 7 Apr. (1903) I. 76 Carlyle in his grey plaid suit, and his *tub-chair. **1847** —— *Lett.* (1883) II. 20 In a tub-chair—a little live bundle of flannel shawls. **1818** SCOTT *Br. Lamm.* xii, The devil's in the peddling *tub-coopering carle! **1909** *Philad. Public Ledger* 24 June 5/1 (*Advt.*) Women's and Misses' Stylish *Tub Dresses. *a* **1704** T. BROWN *Wks.* (1730) IV. 199 Faith and Reason.., as has been judiciously observ'd by the fam'd *Tub-drubber of Covent Garden, can never be brought to set their Horses together. **1533** *MS. Rawl. D.* 776 lf. 170 For ij *Tubb Eares of woode sett on the same tubbe. **1901** *Daily News* 22 Feb. 5/1 The boats used in these novice races are clinker built.. They are outrigged, but have fixed seats. At Oxford and Cambridge they are generically known as '*tub' eights. **1542** *Richmond Wills* (Surtees) 30 Two trowes, and a bowtyn ton, and a *tube ende. **1702** T. SAVERY *Miner's Friend* 55 Your *Tub-Engines, or Chain-Pumps, may draw forth the Water. **1607** SHAKS. *Timon* IV. iii. 85 Bring downe Rose-cheekt youth to the *Tubfast, and the Diet. **1820** SCORESBY *Acc. Arctic Reg.* II. 176 A man, designated '*tub-filler', with a ladle of copper, was employed in filling a hogshead with chopped blubber. **1668** WILKINS *Real Char.* II. v. §3. 136 *Tub-fish, *Piper*. **1769** PENNANT *Zool.* III. 233 The Red Gurnard..agrees in its general appearance with the tub fish. **1888** GOODE *Amer. Fishes* 304 The Tub-fish, *T[rigla] hirundo*, is of frequent occurrence on the west coast of Scotland. **1909** *Westm. Gaz.* 1 Feb. 5/2 What we have for some time now called '*tub frocks' are certainly the best for the South. **1974** N. MARSH *Black as he's Painted* i. 62 She spent a good deal of time in the *tub garden at the back of the house. **1904** *Daily News* 9 Aug. 5 A most fascinating article, entitled '*Tub-Gardening'. **1836** SIR G. HEAD *Home Tour* 433, I pursued my journey to Whitehaven, in a covered car, or '*tub-gig', for which vehicle the title of the 'conveyance' is generally applied. **1884** FROUDE *Carlyle, Life in Lond.* xi. I. 316 The brothers went in a steamer from Liverpool to Bangor, and thence to Llanberis, again in a 'tub-gig', or Welsh car. **1888** WOODGATE *Boating* 72 Lessons in a tub-gig are the best remedies for this fault. **1702** T. SAVERY *Miner's Friend* 32 Others have as easily learn'd as their driving of a Horse in a *Tub-Gin. *Ibid.* 57 My Engine..will clear an old work..as readily as your Tub-Gins or Chain-Pumps. **1892** *Pall Mall G.* 24 Oct. 2/3 Hoops, or (as they were called in Queen Anne's time, when they reached their maximum proportions) *tub-hoops. **1600** *Dr. Dodypoll* III. i. in Bullen *O. Pl.* III. 125 You are a sweet smell-feast, Doctor; that I see. Ile [have] no such *tub-hunters use my house. **1900** *Speaker* 10 Feb. 506/1 The *tub-keeping philosopher..with the Psalmist crying 'All men are liars'. **1908** RHYS DAVIDS *Early Buddhism* i. 7 When he [Diogenes] lived, like a dog, in his *tub-kennel. **1709** O. DYKES *Eng. Prov. & Refl.* (ed. 2) 56 From a Pulpit-Harangue, to a *Tub-Lecture of extemporary Zeal. **1857** RUSKIN *Pol. Econ. Art* i. 2 People who..lived in tubs, and used gravely to maintain the superiority of *tub-life to town-life. **1867** *Morn. Star* 12 Apr., The miserable *pompes à incendies* that do duty in their own streets [Paris]..these weak *tublike structures. **1895** W. WRIGHT *Palmyra & Zenobia* xxix. 371 The tublike turban of the Druzes. **1891** *Labour Commission Gloss.*, **Tub Loaders*, men who hew at night-time and on other occasions, while the pit is not drawing coals, and fill the empty tubs left in the pit. **1719** D'URFEY *Pills* I. 153 The Tories, and the *Tub-meeters, That roosted near Leadenhall. **1661** GAUDEN *Hooker's Eccl. Pol.* Ded. 4 Those club-masters and *tub-ministers, who sought..to overthrow the ancient and goodly fabric of this church and kingdom. **1849** BRONTE *Shirley* viii, 'The Rev. Moses Barraclough: t' *tub orator'.. 'Ah!' said the Rector..'He's a tailor by trade'. **1845** E. J. WAKEFIELD *Adventure N.Z.* I. xi. 318 The common men have nothing to do but to ply their oars according to orders; except one, called the *tub oarsman*, who sits next to the tub containing the whale-line, and has to see that no entanglement takes place. **1870** *Daily News* 11 Feb., The president..had Messrs. Moss, Burgess, Payne, Baker, Mirehouse, and Lewis out in '*tub' pairs, a mode of improvement which had been generally found very beneficial to the individual members of the crew. **1839** URE *Dict. Arts* 973 The upper ends of the first set of *tub-planks being cut square and level all round the second spiking crib ..is fixed. **1801** JEFFERSON *Writ.* (1830) III. 455 The poor arts of *tub-plots, &c. were repeated till the designs of the party became suspected. *a* **1791** WESLEY *Wks.* (1872) VIII. 332 Let there be no..*tub-pulpit, but a square projection, with a long seat behind. **1903** SIR W. J. FARRAR in *Mem. Abp. Temple* (1906) I. vi. 86, I don't think Temple joined in the attempted *tub-race. **1874** KNIGHT *Dict. Mech.*, *Cylindrical Saw*..is variously called a *tub-saw, drum-saw, barrel-saw. **1888** F. G. LEE in *Archæologia* LI. 363 A circular *tub-shaped font. **1880** J. DUNBAR *Pract. Papermaker* 55 **Tub-sizing*, preparation of the gelatine. **1887** *Harper's Mag.* June 124/2 If paper is to be '*tub-sized' as well as 'engine-sized', an animal size..is mixed with dissolved alum and placed in a tub or vat, through which the web of paper is run after leaving the first set of driers. *a* **1912** Tub-sized [see A.T.S. s.v. A III]. **1967** E. CHAMBERS *Photolitho Offset* xvi. 250 Surfaced-sized or tub-sized paper is made by passing the moist paper (15–18% moisture) through a trough containing starch solution. **1909** *Philad. Public Ledger* 24 June 7/7 (*Advt.*) '*Tub' Skirts..Nice quality linen in white, tan & blue. **1595** GOSSON *Quippes Upst. Gentlew.* 161 in Hazl. *E.P.P.* IV. 257 Therefore *tub-tailes all may rue, That they came from so vile a crue. **1591** *Knaresb. Wills* (Surtees) I. 173 All the *tubbe tymber thatt I have hewene. **1589** *Hay any Work* Title-p., An vnskilfull and a deceytfull *tubtrimmer. **1886** C. SCOTT *Sheep-Farming* 133 *Tub-washing is sometimes more convenient for small flocks. **1851** GREENWELL *Coal-trade Terms Northumb. & Durh.* 7 The small diameter of the *tub wheels. **1858** SIMMONDS *Dict. Trade, Tub-wheel*, a peculiar kind of wheel to a water-mill. **1660** *Okie's Lament.* 33 A Fat *Tub-woman was my Goddesse great of War. **1727** CAPT. S. BRUNT *Voy. to Cackl.* 34 They carried two Pails a-piece with a Yoke, like our Tub-women. **1815–16** *Niles' Weekly Register* IX. Suppl. 182/2 Many mill owners have laid aside their tub wheels.

tub (tʌb), *v.* [f. prec. sb.]

1. *trans.* To bathe or wash in a tub or bath. *colloq.*

1610 B. JONSON *Alch.* IV. iii, In your *bathada* You shall be sok'd, and strok'd, and tub'd, and rub'd. **1883** G. H. BOUGHTON in *Harper's Mag.* Apr. 700/1 She was 'tubbing' the two babies.

b. *intr.* To wash oneself in a tub or bath; to take a tub or bath, esp. on rising. *colloq.*

1867 *Pall Mall G.* No. 708. 1722/2 Gentlemen who didn't tub of a morning. **1885** C. H. EDEN *G. Donnington* ii, It was necessary..to tub and dress by the feeble flame of a single candle.

2. *trans.* To line (a pit-shaft) with a water-tight casing of timber, masonry, or iron; to dam *back* (water) in a shaft or tunnel in this way; to shut *off* (watery strata or seams) from the shaft with tubbing.

1812 J. HODGSON in J. Raine *Mem.* (1857) I. 94 The low-main coal is kept perfectly dry by tubbing the watery seams with a circular casing of oak wood. **1839** URE *Dict. Arts* 972 When several fathoms of the strata must be tubbed, in order to stop up the water-flow. **1862** *Chamb. Jrnl.* 5 Apr. 217/1 The shaft..is built round with brick at the top and bottom, while the rest of the way is 'tubbed' with long planks placed perpendicularly round the sides. **1865** JEVONS *Coal-Question* (1866) 68 When this flood of water..had been 'tubbed back'. **1881** SANDS *Sk. Tranent* i. 17 The Coal Company offered to 'tub' or line the faulty pit with iron plates. **1884** tr. *Lotze's Logic* viii. 359 Men who are tubbing a well with masonry.

3. To put or pack in a tub; to plant in a tub.

1828 T. HOOK *Hum. Wks., Fashionable Parties* (1873) 322 Drawing rooms at ninety-six, and half-a-score sickly orange-trees tubbed on the top of a staircase. **1889** *Daily News* 29 June 6/3 As soon as the grower finds it won't pay him to send all his strawberries to market for table use, he begins to pick them and tub them, and sell them by the ton to the jam maker.

b. To soak (bricks) in a tub before setting or laying them.

1913 *Daily News* 31 Mar. 6 The walls..were built in cement mortar and the bricks properly tubbed.

4. *trans.* and *intr.* To coach (oarsmen) in a 'tub'; to practise rowing in a 'tub' (TUB *sb.* 3). *Rowing slang.*

1882 *Society* 18 Nov. 7/2 'Tubbing' vigorously, with the ..intention of putting on a boat for the Lent races. **1883** in *Standard* 17 Jan. 3/7 An hour and a half was then spent in tubbing the men. **1887** *Daily News* 28 Jan. 3/6 Proceedings commenced..by Mr. Orde tubbing the [men] in the gig pair.

Hence **tubbed** (tʌbd) *ppl. a.*

1882 SALA *Amer. Revis.* (1885) 250 Our pickled or 'tubbed' pork. **1890** J. HATTON *By Order of Czar* III. iii, A courtyard..gay with tubbed laurel and tented tables.

tuba[1] ('tju:bə). [L. and It. *tuba*.]

1. (*pl.* **tubæ**.) The straight bronze war-trumpet of the ancient Romans.

1882 *Athenæum* 8 Apr. 452/1 Two other musicians blow long straight trumpets, exactly like the Roman *tuba*. **1890** E. B. CUSTER *Following Guidon* Pref. 9 The tuba..was a kind of straight bronze clarion, about thirty-nine inches long.

2. *Mus.* **a.** (*pl.* **tubas**.) A brass wind-instrument in the bass range of the sax-horn family; a sax-tuba or bombardon; cf. SAX-HORN; also, one who plays this instrument.

1852 *Crystal Palace* 285/1 The Sax-horns in alto, soprano, tenor, tuba, bass, &c. **1888** *Pall Mall G.* 10 Dec. 4/2 Three trombones and a tuba have..a free run for their money. **1889** *Ibid.* 13 July 3/1 In 'Otello' Verdi..has written important parts for piccolo, cor anglais, bass clarinet, a third bassoon, two cornets, and a tuba. **1889** W. H. STONE in Grove *Dict. Mus.* IV. 184/1 Tubas are made in many keys, in F in Germany, in E♭ and B♭ in this country. **1909** *Punch* 20 Jan. 38/2 A..nonagenarian with a voice like a bass tuba.

b. An 8-foot high-pressure reed-stop in an organ.

1858 J. A. SYMONDS *Let.* Nov. (1967) I. 174 The stops of the organ were unusually fine—Tuba, [etc.]. **1876** HILES *Catech. Organ* x. (1878) 72 Tuba, Tuba Mirabilis, Ophicleide—a Trumpet stop (striking reed) of large scale and on a high pressure of wind. **1889** SIR J. STAINER in Grove *Dict. Mus.* IV. 184/1 The Tuba is not solely used as a Solo stop. **1907** *Westm. Gaz.* 24 Aug. 15/3 The organ.. soared and swelled.., a crash of trumpet and tuba that left a vibrant humming in the air.

‖**tuba**[2] ('tu:ba). Also **tooba**. [Arab. (in *Koran* xiii. 28) *ṭūbah*, supposed to be a. Aramaic *ṭūbā* beatitude, Heb. *ṭobah*. Some commentators suppose a tree to be meant, the opinion cited by Sale, and adopted in the quots.] A mythical tree growing in the Muslim paradise: see quots. Also *tuba-tree*.

1817 MOORE *Lalla R., Paradise & Peri* 622 My feast is now of the Tooba Tree, Whose scent is the breath of Eternity! **1833** A. CRICHTON *Hist. Arabia* I. vii. 317 The Tooba, or tree of happiness, so large that the fleetest horse could not gallop in a hundred years from one end of its shadow to the other. **1875** EMERSON *Lett. & Soc. Aims* viii. 206 In [a Persian] poem the soul is figured as the Phoenix alighting on Tuba, the tree of Life. **1894** W. R. THAYER *Poems* 26 The odors of blooming tuba-trees Thro' the gardens steal.

‖**tuba**[3] (tu:'bɑ:, 'tu:bə). [Malay *tūba*.]

1. In the Malay archipelago, the Philippines, etc., the name of species of *Derris* from the roots of which an intoxicating juice is extracted; also, the juice itself, which is used as a fish-poison. Also applied to the berry of *Anamirta Cocculus* (known as *Cocculus indicus*), and to the fruits of *Jatropha Curcas* and *Croton Tiglium*, used for the same purpose. Also *attrib.*

1839 T. J. NEWBOLD *Straits of Malacca* II. xii. 189 The Malays sometimes resort to unfair means of securing the finny tribe, by inserting at low water the roots of the Tuba ..into the holes and fissures of the coral reefs. **1890** [see DERRID, DERRIDE]. [**1894** DENNYS *Dict. Malaya* 416 *Tuba*, the name of a creeping plant (dalbergia) the root of which.. is used to stupefy fish for the purpose of capture.] **1895** SWETTENHAM *Malay Sk.* 225 The water is poisoned with the juice of the tuba root. **1898** *Blackw. Mag.* Mar. 414/1 This is how we fished with the tuba six years ago. **1899** W. H. FURNESS *Folk Lore Borneo* 27 The people go Tuba fishing, poisoning the stream with the juice of the Tuba root.

2. The fermented sap of the unopened flowerbuds of various palms, esp. the coco-nut and Palmyra palms; palm-wine; also, the alcoholic liquor distilled from this; arrack.

1704 in A. & J. Churchill *Coll. Voy.* IV. 447/2 Their Wine or Liquor is drawn from the Palm, or Coco-Tree... The Poor put into it some Bark of Trees which give it a Colour, and a hotter Tast, and then it is call'd Tuba. **1902** W. E. SAFFORD in *Amer. Anthropologist* 728 He climbed a coconut-tree..and brought in a bamboo joint full of tuba, delicious as cider just beginning to turn sharp. **1912** *Contemp. Rev.* Apr. 560 Long tumblers of pink tuba.

tubage ('tju:bɪdʒ). [= F. *tubage* (Littré, 1874), f. *tube* TUBE: see -AGE.]

1. *Surg.* The introduction of a tube into a cavity or canal; *esp.* intubation of the larynx.

1880 M. MACKENZIE *Dis. Throat & Nose* I. 181, I must here briefly refer to the subject of catheterism and 'tubage' of the larynx. **1886** in *Trans. Amer. Pediatric Soc.* (1897) IX. 29 [In 1886 O'Dwyer predicted] that at no distant day tracheotomy would be entirely superseded by 'tubage of the larynx'. **1896** [see INTUBATION].

b. *Ordnance.* The insertion of an inner tube or lining in the bore of a cannon; also, the process of shrinking an outer tube on an inner bore.

1882 *Rep. of Chief of U.S. Ordnance* 244 (Cent. D.) The present short steel tube has been the result of the essays in the tubage of guns.

2. Tubes collectively; tubing; a system of tubes; in quot., in a tubular boiler.

1896 *Daily News* 20 Apr. 5/1 When the fires are at work, the slender tubage heaves and throbs, and through it scurries the river of steam-generating water.

tubal ('tju:bəl), *a.* [f. L. *tub-us* TUBE + -AL[1].]

1. Of, pertaining to, or of the nature of a tube; consisting of tubes; tubular. *rare.*

1735–6 H. BROOKE *Univ. Beauty* IV. 126 Its wanton floods the tubal system lave. **1899** *Allbutt's Syst. Med.* VI. 46 In the early tubal form of the heart, the auricles are placed below..the ventricles.

2. *Anat.* and *Path.* Pertaining to, occurring in, or affecting the Fallopian tube, as ***tubal dropsy***, ***pregnancy***, the bronchial tubes, as ***tubal cough***, ***respiration***, or the renal tubules, as ***tubal nephritis***; ***tubal ligation***, ligation of the Fallopian tubes, esp. as a method of sterilization.

1822–34 *Good's Study Med.* (ed. 4) IV. 181 *Eccyesis Tubalis*, Tubal Exfetation. **1857** BULLOCK *Cazeaux' Midwif.* 244 Having been once deposited in the tubal canal, the ovule traverses its whole length, and falls into the uterine cavity. *Ibid.* 246 Tubal Pregnancy..is the most frequent of all the varieties of extra-uterine pregnancy. **1857** DUNGLISON *Med. Lex.* s.v. *Murmur, Respiratory*, The respiration, perceived over the trachea and bronchia in health, is called *tracheal* or *bronchial* or *tubal*,..according to the situation in which it is heard. **1860** MAYNE *Expos. Lex.*, *Tubal Cough*, see *Bronchial Cough*. **1873** T. H. GREEN *Introd. Pathol.* (ed. 2) 276 Tubal nephritis..is one of those morbid processes which constitute Bright's disease. **1890** BILLINGS *Med. Dict.* s.v., *T[ubal] dropsy*, hydrosalpinx. **1948** H. S. & R. J. CROSSEN *Operative Gynecol.* (ed. 6) 991/2 (Index), Tubal ligation. **1961** *Biol. Abstr.* XXXVI. 5391/2 (*heading*) Histological studies on the change of the adrenal cortex by means of the oophorectomy and tubal ligation in rabbits.

1975 *New Yorker* 29 Sept. 84/3 Mrs. Santana had intended to get a tubal ligation after Gabriel's birth.

tubar ('tjuːbə(r)), *a.* [f. as prec. + -AR[1]: cf. F. *tubaire*.] Of the form of a tube; tubular.

1887 SOLLAS in *Encycl. Brit.* XXII. 418/1 Articulate and inarticulate tubar skeletons of calcisponges.

tubate ('tjuːbeɪt), *a. Bot. rare.* [ad. mod.L. *tubātus*, f. L. *tubus* TUBE: see -ATE[2].] Formed into a tube; having a tube or tubes; tubal, tubular.

1866 in *Treas. Bot.*

tubbable ('tʌbəb(ə)l), *a.* [f. TUB *v.* + -ABLE.] Of garments, etc.: washable in a tub; suitable for laundering in a tub or (domestic) washing-machine.

1929 *Chicago Daily Tribune* 20 May (Advt.), Tubbable Wearable Suitable Cotton! **1960** *News Chron.* Mar. 229 Synthetic fibres..permanently pleated and tubbable. **1982** *Sunday Express* 25 July 17/1 Children's clothes this week—cute, sharp and tubbable they come in easy-care cotton.

tubbal ('tʌbəl). Also **tubble**. [? dial. var. of TWIBILL.] Local name of the common mattock, or of a special form (see quot. 1902); in Cornwall, a miner's tool of similar form (= TUBBER[2]).

1847–78 HALLIWELL, *Tubble*, a mattock. *Devon.* **1880** *W. Cornwall Gloss.*, *Tubbal*, a miner's tool. **1902** *Rep. Provinc.* Aug. (E.D.D.), *Tubbal*, usually a heavy mattock, with a small axe-head, used for grubbing or rooting. Also a very common name for the common mattock.

tubber[1] ('tʌbə(r)). [f. TUB *sb.* or *v.* + -ER[1].]

a. One who makes tubs, a cooper. **b.** One who lives in a tub, a cynic like Diogenes. **c.** A rowing man who is 'coached' in a 'tub' (*nonce-use*). **d.** One who tubs: see TUB *v.* 1 b.

1825 BROCKETT *N.C. Words*, *Tubber*, a cooper, a maker of tubs. **1883** *Almondbury & Huddersfield Gloss.*, *Tubber*, a cooper. **1891** *Blackw. Mag.* Mar. 374 A concession to Diogenes and other tubbers. **1894** *Sporting Life* 28 Feb. 6/2 Shortly after four o'clock tubbing practice was begun... Lewis and Kerrison were the third set of tubbers taken out.

'tubber[2]. *local.* [Cf. TUBBAL, TWIBILL.] A tool used in Cornish mines: = BEELE[2].

1671 *Phil. Trans.* VI. 2104 The Instruments commonly used in Mines, that serve for ripping the Loads... A Beele or Cornish Tubber (i.e. double points) of 8 l. or 10 l. weight, sharped at both ends, well steeled and holed in the middle. **1753** CHAMBERS *Cycl. Supp.*, *Tubber-Men* are the people who work with this tool,..called in other places *beel-men*.

tubbily ('tʌbɪlɪ), *adv.* [f. TUBBY *a.* + -LY[2].] In a tubby manner; with an appearance of tubbiness.

1924 D. H. LAWRENCE in M. M. *Mem. Foreign Legion* 12 He stuck his front out tubbily, like a bird. **1935** H. NICOLSON *Let.* 4 Dec. (1966) 229 Winston rose tubbily and stretched out great arms. **1957** M. SPARK *Comforters* ix. 220 He watched the movements of a young fat woman on a houseboat moored nearby... But she did emerge again, with a cup of tea. She drank it propped tubbily on the tiny bridge of the boat.

'tubbiness. [f. TUBBY + -NESS.] Tubby quality or condition.

1881 *Daily News* 29 Dec. 6/4 Fishing smacks... Stoutly built..and somewhat inclined to tubbiness. **1906** H. G. WELLS *Days of Comet* (1907) 130 Its long skirts accentuated the tubbiness of his body, the shortness of his legs. **1910** *Sat. Rev.* 18 June 785/2 Arpeggio passages..opulent and satisfying without any suspicion of tubbiness.

tubbing ('tʌbɪŋ), *vbl. sb.* [f. TUB *v.* (or *sb.*) + -ING[1].] The action of TUB *v.*

1. a. †Treatment in the sweating-tub: see TUB *sb.* 1 b. **b.** Washing or bathing in a tub or bath.

1657 G. STARKEY *Nature's Explic.* To Rdr. 9 Salivation in the Lues or Tubbing is a dotage. *a* **1845** HOOD *Black Job* xiii, In spite of all the tubbing, rubbing, scrubbing.. The blacks..were as black as ever! **1894** BOASE *Exeter Coll.* (O.H.S.) p. clxii, The quite modern institution of tubbing in the mornings.

2. The lining of a pit-shaft or tunnel with a watertight casing: see TUB *v.* 2; *concr.* the casing of timber, masonry, or metal sections used for this.

1839 URE *Dict. Arts* 969 The pit..must..be sunk through the quicksand by means of tubbing. **1851** GREENWELL *Coal-trade Terms Northumb. & Durh.* 55 At present, tubbing is put in in metal segments. **1855** *Orr's Circ. Sc., Inorg. Nat.* 237 There are several kinds of stopping out water, or tubbing, as it is called... Stone tubbing,..Plank tubbing,..Solid wood tubbing,..and Metal tubbing. **1862** SMILES *Engineers* III. 297 The skilful casing of the shaft with segments of cast-iron—a process called 'tubbing'.

b. *attrib.*, as ***tubbing-deal***, ***-plate***, ***-wedge***.

1839 URE *Dict. Arts* 973 The tubbing deals..must now be fixed. **1883** GRESLEY *Gloss. Terms Coal Mining*, *Tubbing plates*, cast-iron segments forming portion of a ring of tubbing... *Tubbing wedges*, small wooden wedges of pitch pine..hammered in between the joints of tubbing plates.., thus stopping back every drop of water from the shaft. **1886** J. BARROWMAN *Sc. Mining Terms* 68 *Tubbing-deals*, deals put behind tubbing in a shaft.

3. Rowing in a 'tub'; training for a boat-race in a 'tub': see TUB *sb.* 3, *v.* 4.

1884 *Pall Mall G.* 11 Jan. 10/2 Operations on the Cam commenced yesterday with 'tubbing'. **1904** *Daily News* 23 Mar. 11/2 The Dark Blues did some tubbing work first.

tubbish ('tʌbɪʃ), *a.* [f. TUB *sb.* + -ISH[1].] Somewhat tubby; resembling a tub.

1565 GOLDING *Ovid's Met.* IV. (1593) 91 Of tubbish timbrels..a hoarse and jarring sound. **1785** WOLCOTT (P. Pindar) *Odes Roy. Acad.* iv. 11 Men whose heads are rather tubbish, Or, drum-like, better form'd for sound than sense. **1836–7** DICKENS *Sk. Boz, Charac.* vii, He was a short, round, large-faced, tubbish sort of man.

tubble: see TUBBAL.

‖**tubboe** ('tʌbəʊ). Also **tubba**. [? native word in W. Africa.] Each of the excrescences or sores in frambœsia; also in *pl.* = FRAMBŒSIA, YAWS.

1769 E. BANCROFT *Guiana* 387 The infectious matter.. produces subcutaneous sores, which are called Tubboes. **1822–34** *Good's Study Med.* (ed. 4) II. 432 When the tumours point from the soles of the feet, they cannot press through the thickness of the skin, and hence form imperfectly, and produce highly elevated calluses, which are called tubba or crab-yaws. **1898** SIR P. MANSON *Trop. Diseases* xxvii. 428 'Tubboes', 'tubba', 'crabs', 'crappox', 'crabes' are expressions applied to the painful manifestations on the soles of the feet [in yaws]. Forms of chronic dermatitis on hands and feet are 'dartres', 'tubboe', 'crabs', dry 'tubboes'.

tubby ('tʌbɪ), *a.* [f. TUB *sb.* + -Y.] Resembling or suggesting a tub.

1. Tub-shaped, tub-like; of rounded outline, and stout or broad in proportion to the length; of a person, corpulent.

1835 ANSTER tr. *Faustus* II. v. (1887) 269 Come, short-horned, thick Devils, tubby, stubby. **1859** SALA *Tw. round Clock* (1861) 14 They are mostly square and squat in rigging, and somewhat tubby in build. **1885** *Pall Mall G.* 9 June 2/2 In 1690..he [Stradivarius] began to improve his model, bringing it flatter, the great secret of the true violin as opposed to the old tubby model. **1891** KIPLING *Plain Tales fr. Hills* vii. 54 Fat Captains and tubby Majors. **1905** *Westm. Gaz.* 21 Mar. 4/2 Driving a tubby [motor] car.

2. Sounding like a tub when struck; dull or wooden in sound. Of a sound of this quality.

1806–7 J. BERESFORD *Miseries Hum. Life* (ed. 3) XVI. 90 The dead, lumpish, tubby tones of the fourth and fifth strings of the guittar. **1883** HAWEIS *My Musical Life* (1884) I. 95 He [the violin] goes 'tubby' (a term used to express a dull vibration). **1940** *Chambers's Techn. Dict.* 869/2 *Tubby* .., characterised by reverberant booming for frequencies which are familiar when barrels are struck. **1962** A. NISBETT *Technique Sound Studio* 243 *Boomy*, subjective description of a sound quality which has resonances in the low frequencies, or a broad band of bass lift. Expressions with similar shades of meaning are tubby or, simply, bassy. **1981** *Popular Hi-Fi* Mar. 81/3 Drum sound was tubby on both decks.

tube (tjuːb), *sb.* [a. F. *tube* (1460 in Godef. *Compl.*), ad. L. *tub-us*.] **I.** Artificial.

1. a. A hollow body, usually cylindrical, and long in proportion to its diameter, of wood, metal, glass, or other material, used to convey or contain a liquid or fluid, or for other purposes; a pipe.

A more recent and more generic term than *pipe*, in which the form of the thing is chiefly considered, and thus used in reference to many things to which *pipe* is not applied, *pipe* being an older term retained for tubes used for the passage of liquids, smoke, air, or gas, while *tube* is applied to most recent inventions; but the distinction is often arbitrary, depending on the custom of the workshops.

1658 PHILLIPS, *Tube*,..any long pipe through which water or other liquid substance is conveyed. **1660** BOYLE *New Exp. Phys. Mech.* i. 33 The Mercury in the [barometric] Tube fell down lower, about three inches, at the top of the Mountain then at the bottom. **1690** LOCKE *Hum. Und.* II. iv. §3 When the Sucker in a Pump is drawn, the space it filled in the Tube is certainly the same, whether any other body follows the motion of the Sucker or no. **1837** GORING & PRITCHARD *Microgr.* 206 [In] a solar microscope ..B, the tube containing the condensing lens. **1846** GREENER *Sc. Gunnery* 288 Lateral pressure on the sides of the tube of the gun. **1861** N. A. WOODS *Pr. Wales in Canada & U.S.* 122 The whole Tube [of a tubular bridge] was first actually built in England and sent out piece meal.

b. = TUBING, material of a tubular form.

1823 J. BADCOCK *Dom. Amusem.* 78 Some feet or yards.. of that more pliable composition tube, employed by the makers of beer engines. **1893** J. A. HODGES *Elem. Photogr.* (1907) 87 A piece of india rubber tube.

2. In specific applications usually indicated by context. **a.** A glass or other tube used in chemistry; *esp.* = TEST-TUBE. ***tube of safety*** = *safety-tube* (SAFETY 11).

1800 tr. *Lagrange's Chem.* I. 60 Melt the phosphorus in boiling water, and apply to it one of the ends of the tube, while you hold the other in your mouth. **1807** T. THOMSON *Chem.* (ed. 3) II. 207 A tube of safety is a tube open at its upper end, and having its lower end plunged in water. **1827** FARADAY *Chem. Manip.* i. (1842) 21 Glass tubes of various sizes closed at one end. *Ibid.* xiv. 307 The best tubes are those made of Bohemian potash glass, and used by Liebig in his analyses of organic bodies.

b. A tubular surgical instrument; a cannula; an intubation-tube.

1803 *Med. Jrnl.* IX. 7 The tube is to be passed downwards until it again reaches the substance to be extracted. **1857** DUNGLISON *Med. Lex.*, *Tube*, *Œsophageal*, stomach tube... *Rectal tube*, defecation tube. **1877** KNIGHT *Dict. Mech.* s.v., (*Surgical tubes*) *a.* An esophageal tube, capable of being passed into the stomach. *b.* An elastic gum tube passed *per anum* into the colon... *c.* A tracheal tube. **1902** *Brit. Med. Jrnl.* 3 July, Owing to the depth of the wound two drainage tubes were introduced at the time of operation.

c. A fire-tube or water-tube in a steam-boiler; a boiler-tube.

1833 N. ARNOTT *Physics* (ed. 5) II. 32 In a long waggon-shaped boiler the tubes..should be made flat and broad enough to reach from side to side. **1903** *Daily Chron.* 7 Jan. 7/2 In the fire-tube or cylindrical boiler the fire and smoke went through the tubes, and in the water-tube the fire was outside the tubes and the water passed through them.

d. A small collapsible cylinder of tin or lead used to hold semi-liquid substances, as oil-colours.

1841 RAND *Patent Specif.* No. 8863 Their contents may easily be squeezed out by collapsing the said tubes or cases. **1877** KNIGHT *Dict. Mech.* 2643/1 Collapsible tin tubes for artists' colors. **1881** [see *tube-colour* in 12 b].

e. In wool or worsted spinning: cf. *tube yarn* in 12 b, and TUBE *v.* 2.

1884 *West. Morn. News* 5 Sept. 7/4 The foreign yarn trade keeps pretty brisk, particularly in lustre wefts, and similar yarns on the tube.

f. (See quot.)

1877 KNIGHT *Dict. Mech.*, *Tube*,..4. the barrel of a chain-pump.

g. *Electronics.* A sealed container, evacuated or gas-filled, containing two or more electrodes between which an electric current can be made to flow; *spec.* (*a*) a cathode-ray tube; (*b*) (chiefly *U.S.*) a thermionic valve. Freq. in *Comb.* with preceding sb., as ***discharge***, ***electron***, ***picture***, ***vacuum tube***, qq.v.

1859, etc. [see VACUUM TUBE 2]. **1898**, etc. [see DISCHARGE *sb.* 3 b]. **1905** *Electrician* 16 June 335/1 The phosphorescent spot on the screen of the tube follows strictly any changes which occur in the strength of the field. **1915** *Ibid.* 21 May 241/2 In the X-ray tube..the space charge effects are very much exaggerated. **1922** C. W. TAUSSIG *Bk. of Radio* ix. 111 The tubes used are 5 watt transmitting tubes. **1940** H. M. WATSON et al. *Understanding Radio* v. 223 As you experiment with this one-tube set, you will hear many stations faintly. **1947** R. LEE *Electronic Transformers & Circuits* i. 3 The limitations which inhere in transformers often influence the choice of amplifier tubes. **1973** G. J. KING *Newnes Colour Television Servicing Man.* I. i. 29/2 The output direct from the tripler is too high an impedance to accommodate the normal beam current swings of the tube without serious voltage fluctuations. **1981** NASHELSKY & BOYLESTAD *Devices* iv. 128 Production rose from about 1 million tubes in 1922 to about 100 million in 1937.

h. ***inner tube***: see INNER *a.* 1 i. Also *ellipt.*

1894 ALBEMARLE & HILLIER *Cycling* 471 The outer arch is removed, the inner tube carefully examined, the hole discovered—if necessary by inflating the tube and immersing it in water. **1904** A. B. F. YOUNG *Complete Motorist* (ed. 2) xi. 246 When the tube and cover are both in place..the air chamber is inflated by means of a pump. **1979** *United States 1980/81* (Penguin Travel Guides) 367 You can buy tubes..at gas stations and stands along the route.

i. A telephone. Cf. sense 7 a and SPEAKING-TUBE. *colloq.* or *slang.*

[**1873** C. M. YONGE *Pillars of House* II. xiii. 38 Mr. Underwood breathed through a mysterious tube, and Edgar appeared.] *c* **1899** C. H. CHAMBERS in M. R. Booth *Eng. Plays of 19th Cent.* (1973) III. 401 (*Rings off, and hangs up tube.*) That is another mistake—that telephone. **1959** *Esquire* Nov. 70 *Tube*, can be television, but usually telephone. Example: Buzz me on the tube. Call me up.

j. A type of skate (see quot.).

1923 E. JESSUP *Snow & Ice Sports* 220 The 'tubes' are a comparatively recent departure in skate design... The blade..is set in a long hollow tube. Similar but wider tubes support the heel and front plates.

k. ***the tube***, television, a television set; also, ***the boob tube*** [see BOOB *sb.* 3]; cf. *the box* s.v. BOX *sb.*[2] 3 j. *colloq.* (orig. and chiefly *U.S.*).

1959 [see sense 2 i above]. **1965** *Sunday News* (N.Y.) 4 Oct. 2 She..is making a name for herself as a singer on the tube. **1966** *Current Slang* (Univ. S. Dakota) Fall 1 Let's catch the late show on the boob tube. **1972** *Observer* 31 Dec. 24/1 Turning to the tube in order to redress the balance with a spot of the old festive vulgarity. **1977** M. FRENCH *Women's Room* (1978) ii. 115, I sit and watch the stupid boob tube. **1979** *Radio Times* 11–17 Aug. 19/1 'I see you on the tube a lot,' an American said to me recently in a pub. 'Oh really,' I replied, 'the Piccadilly line?' 'No,' he said, 'the *tube*, the dream machine.'

l. ***down the tube***(*s*), lost, finished, in trouble; freq. in ***to go down the tube***(*s*) = *to go down the drain* s.v. DRAIN *sb.* 1 e. *slang* (orig. *U.S.*).

1963 *Amer. Speech* XXXVIII. 168 To fail to pass an examination:..*go down the tubes.* **1975** *New Yorker* 5 May 32/1 It would be ludicrous to end on a note of Chris going down the tube. **1977** J. D. MACDONALD *Condominium* xii. 122 We've got too many goodies tucked into the Marliss Corporation to take a chance of it going down the tube. **1982** *Listener* 16 Dec. 35/3 The smile on Sir Freddie's face the week before it was revealed that he was down the tubes to the extent of something over £270 million was the smile of a consummate actor.

m. A bottle or can of beer. *Austral. colloq.*

1969 *Listener* 24 Apr. 588/2 This..extrovert chunders.. his way through the kangaroo valley of Earl's Court.. buoyed up by innumerable tubes (bottles) of Foster's Beer. **1980** R. HILL *Killing Kindness* xx. 187 'What do you want to do?'.. Mow my lawn and then cool off with a tube of lager, thought Pascoe.

3. An optical instrument of tubular form, *esp.* a telescope: more fully ***optic tube***. Now *arch.*

1651 [see OPTIC A. 4]. **1668** PEPYS *Diary* 4 Dec., Wrote a letter at the Board, by the help of a tube, to Lord Brouncker. **1668–9** *Ibid.* 14 Mar., My eyes being very bad, and..I forced to find a way to use by turns with my tube, one after another. *a* **1718** PRIOR *Solomon* III. 470 Of his fair Deeds a distant View I took; But turn'd the Tube upon his Faults to look. **1781** COWPER *Charity* 387 Some grave optician..finds that though his tubes assist the sight, They cannot give it. **1807** J. BARLOW *Columb.* VII. 386 On the tall decks, their curious chiefs explore, With optic tube, our camp-encumber'd shore. **1867** G. GILFILLAN *Night* iv. 116 To the silent tube in Herschel's hand A hundred suns spring up.

4. †**a.** Applied to a tobacco-pipe. *poet. Obs. rare.*

1736 I. H. BROWNE *Pipe of Tobacco* Poems (1768) 117 Little tube of mighty pow'r, Charmer of an idle hour. **1784** COWPER *Task* v. 55 With pressure of his thumb To adjust the fragrant charge of a short tube, That fumes beneath his nose.

b. A cigarette. *slang.*

1946 P. LARKIN *Jill* 16 Christopher, extending his silver cigarette[-case], said with an uneasy smile: 'Tube for anyone?' **1975** *High Times* Dec. 11/2 (Advt.), Filter tipped tubes give a smoother smoke to the very end.

5. †**a.** A cannon; also a rifle or hand-gun. *poet.*

1762 FALCONER *Ode Dk. of York* 138 The ships their horrid tubes display, Tier over tier. **1801** *Sporting Mag.* XVII. 148 With curious skill the deathful tube is made. **1816** BYRON *Siege of Cor.* iii, To point the tube, the lance to wield. **1897** KIPLING in *Times* 17 July 13/6 Heathen heart that puts her trust In reeking tube and iron shard.

b. A small pipe introduced through the vent, formerly used in firing cannon; a *friction-tube*, *quill-tube*, or *priming-tube.*

1797 *Encycl. Brit.* (ed. 3) VIII. 230/2 Firing it [gunpowder] with tubes, introduced at a vent bored through the button and breech of the gun, of different lengths, so as to reach the different parts of the powder. **1828** WEBSTER, *Tube*, in artillery, an instrument of tin, used in quick firing. **1867** SMYTH *Sailor's Word-bk., Tubes*, for guns, a kind of portable priming, for insertion into the vent,—of various patterns.

c. The inner cylinder of a built-up gun, upon which the outer case is shrunk. Cf. TUBAGE 1 b.

1895 in *Funk's Stand. Dict.*

6. a. A musical wind-instrument, a pipe. *poet. rare.* **b.** The main cylinder of a wind-instrument (*Cent. Dict.* 1891).

1820 KEATS *Hyperion* I. 206 Solemn tubes, Blown by the serious Zephyrs, gave of sweet And wandering sounds, slow-breathed melodies.

7. a. A pneumatic dispatch-tube.

1860 *Once a Week* 28 July 130/2 Written messages are sucked through tubes... We hear a whistle; this is to give notice that a despatch is about to be put into the tube at Mincing Lane, two-thirds of a mile distant. **1861, 1874** [see DISPATCH *sb.* 12]. **1866, 1894** [implied in *tube-journey, tube-room*: see 12]. **1905** *Daily Chron.* 27 May. 4/3 From Whiteley's 6,194 parcels were dispatched in five hours, of which 78 per cent. could have been sent by tube.

b. The cylindrical tunnel in which an underground electric railway runs; also short for *tube-railway*. *colloq.* Also, any tunnel or tubular bridge for a railway.

twopenny tube, the Central London Railway, opened in 1900: see TWOPENNY.

1847 QUEEN VICTORIA *Jrnl.* 15 Aug. (1868) 72 We passed the famous *Swilly Rocks*, and saw the works they are making for the tube for the railroad. **1900** H. D. BROWNE in *Londoner* 30 June (*heading*), The Twopenny Tube. **1900** *Punch* 4 July 7/1. **1901** *Lancet* 2 Nov. 1209/2 A good portion of the air must be driven backwards and forwards unchanged in the tube. **1902** *Westm. Gaz.* 24 Oct. 2/3 When the phrase 'the twopenny tube' came into existence..a similar electric 'tube' had been in regular running for close upon ten years. **1905** RIDER HAGGARD in *Gardener's Year* May 165 The first part of my journey..was by Tube.

8. *Physics.* A tubular figure conceived as being formed by lines of force or action passing through every point of a closed curve; as ***tube of flow*** (see FLOW *sb.*[1] 1 b), ***tube of force***, ***tube of induction***.

1878 W. K. CLIFFORD *Dynamic* 199 If we take a small closed curve, and draw lines of flow through all points on it, the tubular surface traced out by these lines is called a tube of flow. **1881** [see FLOW *sb.*[1] 1 b]. **1885** WATSON & BURBURY *Math. The. Electr. & Magn.* I. 104 The portions of any surfaces in an electric field intercepted by the same tube of force are called corresponding surfaces,..the algebraic sum of the electricities included in the tube in its passage from any one surface to any other. **1902** SLOANE *Stand. Electr. Dict., Tubes of Force*, aggregations of lines of force, either electrostatic or magnetic. They generally have a truncated, conical or pyramidal shape and are not hollow. Every cross-section contains the same number of lines.

II. Natural.

9. *Anat.* and *Zool.* **a.** A hollow cylindrical vessel or organ in the animal body; a canal, duct, passage, or pipe, as in the circulatory, alimentary, respiratory, reproductive, or excretory systems; often preceded by a defining word, as ***alimentary***, ***bronchial***, ***Eustachian***, ***Fallopian***, ***intestinal tube***, etc.: see these words.

[cf. **1598** FLORIO, *Tubo*,..the pipe wherethrough the marrow of the backe bone runneth. **1611** COTGR., *Tube*, a Conduit-pipe; also, the hollow of the back-bone, or the pipe through which the marrow thereof doth runne.] **1661** BLOUNT *Glossogr.* (ed. 2). **1696** PHILLIPS (ed. 5), *Fallopian Tubes*, two slender Passages proceeding from the Womb. **1741, 1755** Eustachian tube [see EUSTACHIAN]. **1809** *Med. Jrnl.* XXI. 400 The œsophagus..that animated tube. **1826** KIRBY & SP. *Entomol.* IV. xli. 128 Connected by a slender tube with each mandible in spiders is a vessel with spiral folds, which seems properly to belong to this head. **1831** J. DAVIES *Man. Mat. Med.* 374 Its passage in the intestinal tube is attended with the same phenomena. **1904** *Brit. Med. Jrnl.* 10 Sept. 584 The main depôts of lymphocytes..are round the hollow tubes of the body.

b. One of the siphons of a mollusc.

1839 DARWIN *Voy. Nat.* I. (1852) 8 It [cuttle-fish] could ..take good aim by directing the tube or siphon on the under side of its body.

c. The penis. *slang.*

1922 JOYCE *Ulysses* 750, I suppose the people gave him that nickname [*sc.* Mr de Kock] going about with his tube from one woman to another.

10. A hollow cylindrical channel in a plant; *spec.* in *Bot.* the lower united portion of a gamopetalous corolla or gamosepalous calyx; also, a united circle of stamens.

a **1704** LOCKE *Elem. Nat. Philos.* ix. (1754) 34 This [juice] is convey'd by the stalk up into the branches, and leaves, through little, and in some plants, imperceptible tubes. **1760** J. LEE *Introd. Bot.* I. iii. (1765) 7 Monopetalous [corolla]..consists of two Parts, viz. the Tube, or lower Part, which is usually Tube-shaped; and the Limb, or upper Part. **1776** WITHERING *Brit. Plants* (1796) IV. 310 Tubes white, brownish with age. **1807** J. E. SMITH *Phys. Bot.* 394 *Syngenesia*. Stamens united by their Anthers into a tube, rarely by their Filaments also. **1884** BOWER & SCOTT *De Bary's Phaner.* 187 The laticiferous tubes permeate the whole body of the plant, in most cases as a continuous system.

11. a. Applied to other tubular or cylindrical objects or formations of natural origin.

1831 *Literary Gaz.* 15 Jan. 44/2 Lightning Tubes—In the neighbourhood of the old castle of Remstein..there have been found this summer very firm and long vitreous tubes. **1860** TYNDALL *Glac.* II. xxv. 362 The tube in fact resembled a vast organ-pipe. **1865, 1884** [see FULGURITE]. **1878** HUXLEY *Physiogr.* 190 The molten matter..thus forms a hard stony tube lining the volcanic chimney.

b. *Surfing.* The hollow curve of a breaking wave.

1962 *Austral. Women's Weekly* 24 Oct. (Suppl.) 3/4 *Tube*, the area of a dumping wave between the breaking crest and the trough. **1968** *Surfer Mag.* Jan. 89/1 You get back inside the tube and the whole tunnel is glowing. **1979** *Nat. Geographic Mag.* Feb. 235 (*caption*) Shootin' the tube, a surfer threads the eye of a breaker.

III. 12. a. *attrib.* and *Comb.*, as ***tube attendant***, ***-holder***, ***-room***, ***system***, ***trade***, ***-vase***, ***-wall***, ***-work***, ***-worker***; ***tube-rolling*** sb. and adj.; ***tube-eyed***, ***-like***, ***-shaped*** adjs.; in sense 2 a, as ***tube-apparatus***, ***atmolyser***, ***-bath***, ***-chemistry***, ***-furnace***, ***-receiver***, ***-retort***; in sense 7 b, as ***tube bill*** (BILL *sb.*[3] 3), ***conductor***, ***mileage***, ***railway***, ***-route***, ***station***, ***-train***, ***traveller***, ***tunnel***.

1827 FARADAY *Chem. Manip.* xiv. (1842) 315 Sulphur may be combined with platina, and phosphorus with lime, in a *tube apparatus. **1873** WATTS *Fownes' Chem.* (ed. 11) 126 Atmolysis is best exhibited by means of an instrument called the *tube-atmolyser. **1908** *Daily Chron.* 15 Feb. 1/7 A *tube attendant at the G.P.O. **1827** FARADAY *Chem. Manip.* xvi. (1842) 400 *Tube-baths for the conveyance of limited temperatures either by the intermedium of water, solutions, or metals. **1902** *Westm. Gaz.* 5 Nov. 11/1 The County Council has found itself unable to frame a *Tube Bill. **1827** FARADAY *Chem. Manip.* vii. (1842) 225 Processes of this kind will be described and illustrated in Section xvi. on *Tube Chemistry. **1909** *Westm. Gaz.* 18 Feb. 9/4 *Tube conductor's shocking death. **1792** SOUTHEY *To Contemplation* v, I..watch'd the *tube-eyed snail Creep o'er his long moon-glittering trail. **1827** FARADAY *Chem. Manip.* xiv. (1842) 309 Placing two bricks edgeways, across a loose square grate,..makes an excellent *tube-furnace. *Ibid.* xix. 505 The tube furnace..is an excellent instrument for softening considerable lengths of tubes. **1897** *Westm. Gaz.* 16 Dec. 3/1 A cigar *tube-holder that prevents the odoriferous tube from spoiling his pocket. **1905** *Brit. Med. Jrnl.* 16 Sept. 618 The tube-holder is graduated so that the tube may be easily moved a distance of 2½ inches. **1866** GEO. ELIOT *F. Holt* Introd., The *tube-journey can never lend much to picture and narrative. **1847–9** *Todd's Cycl. Anat.* IV. 27/1 Animals whose *tube-like bodies are prolonged deeply into the common mass. **1898** P. MANSON *Trop. Diseases* xviii. 291 Sometimes tube-like pieces, evidently rings of mucous membrane..are discharged. **1902** *Westm. Gaz.* 21 Apr. 10/1 The '*tube' mileage in London. **1900** *Daily News* 3 Dec. 5/2 One of the most useful of the new *tube railways. **1906** CHARL. MANSFIELD *Girl & Gods* vi, The warm stench from the Tube railway assailed her nostrils. **1827** FARADAY *Chem. Manip.* xxiv. (1842) 644 Make some closed tubes,..some *tube receivers..and other useful apparatus. *Ibid.* xix. 510 *Tube retorts..are made by first closing the end of a piece of tube, and then [etc.]. **1908** *Westm. Gaz.* 13 Aug. 8/1 *Tube-rolling..at 1s. 6d. per 1,000. **1894** *Daily News* 22 Feb. 2/1 About 30 feet of *tube-room on ground floor and contents severely damaged by fire. **1901** *Brit. Med. Jrnl.* 9 Mar. 591/2 The lines of *tube-route being chosen with a view to supplementing and completing the means of communication from the suburbs. **1760** J. LEE *Introd. Bot.* I. iii. (1765) 7 The..lower Part..is usually *Tube-shaped. **1825** *Greenhouse Comp.* I. 56 *Erica aurea*, tube-shaped yellow flowers on plants nearly 2 feet high. **1913** *Daily News* 28 Jan. 6 The trains that roar in and out of a *tube station. **1908** *Installation News* II. 92/2 The *tube system [of electric wiring]. **1900** *Westm. Gaz.* 8 Jan. 9/1 Severe competition in the *tube trade. **1901** *Daily News* 15 June 4/7 Journeying to and from the scenes of their labour in *tube-trains. **1903** *Westm. Gaz.* 4 July 3/2 Thousands of *Tube travellers. **1910** *Daily Chron.* 19 Feb. 3/4 Macdonald ..ran to the end of the train and jumped into the *tube tunnel. **1870** MRS. WHITNEY *We Girls* iii, They were so pretty to put in..little *tube-vases. **1857** GOSSE *Creation* 226 The margin of the *tube-wall. **1890** *Daily News* 9 Jan. 2/8 The advance applies to gas, water, and steam tubes, and all the *tube works of England and Scotland are affected. **1896** *N. Brit. Daily Mail* 8 July 2 The pensioner..is a Coatbridge man, having wrought as a *tube-worker in the burgh.

b. Special Combs.: **Tube Alloys**, the code name of a section of the Department of Scientific and Industrial Research formed in 1940 and concerned with research into the production of an atomic bomb; **tube-bearing** *a.*, bearing a tube; *spec.* in *Entom.* having a tubular ovipositor, tubuliferous (*Cent. Dict.* 1891); **tube-board**, a board above the reeds in a reed-organ in which are the tubes or sound-channels to which the wind passes from the reeds; **tube-breather** (distinguished from *gill-breather*), an animal which breathes through tubes, tracheæ, or spiracles; **tube-brush**, a wire brush for cleaning out boiler-tubes or flues; also, a slender brush for cleaning the flexible tube of a feeding-bottle; **tube-budding**, budding by means of a cylindrical ring of bark; **tube-case**, in a steam-engine, the chamber containing the tubes of a surface-condenser; **tube-cast**, a cast of a kidney tubule excreted in the urine in Bright's disease; **tube-chime**, a chime of tubular 'bells'; **tube-clamp**, a grab for seizing and lifting well-tubes (Knight *Dict. Mech.* 1877); **tube-cleaner**, a tool or other device for cleaning boiler-tubes, etc. (*ibid.*); **tube-clip**, tongs for holding heated test-tubes; also a clamp or clip for gripping a pipe (*ibid.*); **tube-cock**, a valve operated by compressing an elastic tube fitted into the supply pipe (*ibid.*); **tube-colour**, paint packed in a collapsible tube; **tube-compass**, compasses with tubular telescopic legs (Knight); **tube-condenser**, (*a*) a bent glass tube with a stopper at each end through which a smaller tube is passed; (*b*) in a steam-engine, a condenser in which the cooling surface consists of tubes; **tube-coral**, organ-pipe coral (see CORAL *sb.*[1] 1 b), or its polyp; **tube counter** *Physics*, the now usual form of Geiger counter, as contrasted with the point-counter; **tube-culture**, culture of a microbe in a test-tube; **tube curare**, curare kept or transported in bamboo tubes; **tube-cutter**, a tool for cutting off metal pipes, a pipe-cutter; so **tube-cutting**; **tube-door**, a door in the smoke-box of a steam-engine, giving access to the flues (Knight); **tube-drawing**, the making of metal tubes by drawing roughly shaped cylinders through gauged holes or over a triblet; also withdrawal of boiler-tubes for inspection or repair; so **tube-drawer**; **tube-expander**, **-fastener**, a tool for fixing the ends of boiler-tubes in the *tube-plate* by expanding their ends against the holes in the plate (Knight); **tube-fed** *a.*, fed, sometimes forcibly, by passing nourishment through a tube into the stomach; so **tube-feed**, **tube-feeding** *vbl. sb.*; **tube-ferrule**, a ring or thimble forced into the end of a boiler-tube to fix it in the tube-plate (*ibid.*); **tube-filter**, in a tube-well, a strainer to prevent gravel from choking the pump (*ibid.*); **tube-firing**, ? the use of a torpedo-tube; **tube-flower**, a tropical verbenaceous plant, *Clerodendron Siphonanthus*, in which the corolla is funnel-shaped with a very long tube (*Treas. Bot.* 1866); **tube-flue**, a fire-tube in a steam-boiler; **tube-foot**, one of the numerous ambulacral tubes of an echinoderm; **tube-former**, a machine for making small tubes; **tube-frame**, a *tube roving-frame*; **tube-funnel**, a glass funnel prolonged at the bottom into a tube, a funnel-tube; **tube-germination**, the production of a germ-tube in the germination of a spore; **tube-head** = *tube-plate* (Webster, 1911); **tube-hearted** *a.*, having a series of pulsating sinuses instead of a heart, as the Amphioxus (*Cent. Dict.* 1891); **tube-ignition**, in the internal combustion engine, ignition of the charge by a hot tube; **tube journey**, a journey in a tube, *spec.* a journey by underground railway; **tube-lift**, a lift for the conveyance of passengers from street-level to an underground railway or vice versa; **tube-machine**, a tube-drawing machine; **tube-maker**, (*a*) one who makes tubing; (*b*) a tube-dwelling spider or annelid; so **tube-making**; †**tube-marine**, rendering It. *tuba* (*tromba*) *marina*, the trumpet marine: see TRUMPET *sb.* 2 b; **tube map**, a map of an underground-railway system; **tube-medusa**, a medusa with an internal system of tubes; a siphonophore; **tube-mill**, (*a*) a tube-making establishment or machine; (*b*) a mill for pulverizing ore, etc., which is placed in a revolving cylinder with loose flints or pebbles; **tube-nosed** *a.*, tubinarial (*Cent. Dict.*); **tube-packing**, packing to prevent water reaching the tube of an oil-well (Knight); **tube-plate**, the plate in which the ends of the boiler-tubes are set; **tube-plug**, a plug or stopper for boiler-tubes in case of leakage (Knight); **tube-pouch**, a pouch for priming-tubes (Webster, 1864); **tube roving-frame**,

roving-machine, a roving-frame having revolving horizontal cylinders instead of conical cans; **tube-saw**, a cylindrical saw (Webster, 1911); **tube-scaler, -scraper** = *tube-cleaner* (Knight); **tube-sheet** = *tube-plate*; **tube-shell**, a bivalve mollusc of the family *Tubicolæ* or *Gastrochænidæ*, distinguished by having a shelly tube inclosing the siphons, in addition to the ordinary valves of the shell; **tube shelter**, an underground tube station used as an air-raid shelter; also *attrib.*; **tube-shutter**, a shutter closing the outer end of a submerged torpedo-tube (Webster, 1911); **tube skate** = sense 2j above; **tube sock**, an elasticized sock with no shaping for the heel; **tube-spinner** = *tube-weaver*; **tube steak** *slang*, a hot dog, a frankfurter; **tube-stopper** = *tube-plug*; **tube-surface**, the heating or cooling surface comprised in the tubes of a boiler or condenser (*Funk's Stand. Dict.* 1895); **tube top**, a women's close-fitting elasticated top reaching from the waist to under-arm level; **tube-valve**, a tubular valve; **tube-vice (-vise)**, a pipe-vice (Knight); **tube-weaver**, a spider which spins a tubular nest or lair; **tube-well**, an iron pipe with a solid steel point, and with lateral perforations towards the point, which is driven into the earth until a water-bearing stratum is reached, when a suction pump is applied to the upper end; **tube-worm**, a tubicolous worm; a pipe-worm; **tube-wrench**, a wrench for gripping pipes or tubes, a pipe-wrench; **tube yarn**, yarn passed through a tube in the process of manufacture.

1942 J. Anderson in M. Gowing *Britain & Atomic Energy 1939–45* (1964) App. III. 437 When you asked me to take over the supervision of work on the project known as '*Tube Alloys', it was contemplated that..a full scale production would be expected in this country. **1945** W. S. Churchill *Victory* (1946) 221 Imperial Chemicals Industries Limited agreed to release Mr. W. A. Akers to take charge of this directorate, which we called, for purposes of secrecy, the Directorate of 'Tube Alloys'. **1978** R. V. Jones *Most Secret War* xxxv. 309 The British 'Tube Alloys' project, as our own nuclear bomb effort was called. **1880** A. J. Hipkins in *Encycl. Brit.* XI. 483/2 The channels, the resonators above the reeds [in the American organ] exactly correspond with the reeds, and are collectively known as the '*tube-board'. **1889** *Cent. Dict.* s.v. *Gillbreather*, *Tube-breather. **1877** Knight *Dict. Mech.* s.v., Stillwell's *tube-brush,..may be operated by pulling and pushing from the respective ends of the tubes. **1842** Loudon *Suburban Hort.* 307 Sometimes the stock is shortened, and the ring put on its upper extremity, when it is called flute-budding, or terminal *tube-budding. **1890** D. K. Clark *Steam Engine* II. 683 The water is driven through the *tube-case by two centrifugal pumps in each engine-room. **1873** T. H. Green *Introd. Pathol.* (ed. 2) 69 *Tube casts..are for the most part hyaline and finely granular. **1888** Fagge & Pye-Smith *Princ. Med.* (1891) II. 154 Tube-casts comparable with those which occur in the urine in Bright's disease. **1887** *Pall Mall G.* 20 June 3/2 *Tube chimes for church towers—an English invention. **1881** Bouvier tr. *Delamardelle & Goupil's Painting on China* 1 Thanks to the ingenious invention of *Tube Colours. **1877** Knight *Dict. Mech.*, *Tube-condenser. **1890** D. K. Clark *Steam Engine* II. 641 The exhaust steam is condensed to the extent of two-thirds in a tube-condenser overhead. **1876** Page *Adv. Text-bk. Geol.* xiv. 245 Among the zoophytes we have cup-corals, star-corals, *tube-corals. **1930** *Tube-counter [see coincidence 7a]. **1938** R. W. Lawson tr. *Hevesy & Paneth's Man. Radioactivity* (ed. 2) i. 17 We shall only discuss the two [counters] that are most important.., viz. the point-counter and the tube-counter, both of which were introduced by Geiger. **1886** H. M. Biggs tr. *Hueppe's Methods Bacteriol. Invest.* 143 The changes in such a *tube-culture after the inoculation with the bacteria vary considerably. **1898** *Jrnl. Chem. Soc.* LXXIV. i. 284 Paracurara, or *tube curara, is imported in bamboo tubes, and is the variety now usually met with in commerce. **1974** *Encycl. Brit. Micropædia* III. 300/3 Preparations have been classified according to the containers used for them: pot curare in earthenware jars; tube curare in bamboo; and calabash curare in gourds. **1901** Waterhouse *Conduit Wiring* 43 In all conduit work a certain amount of *tube cutting is necessary. **1858** Simmonds *Dict. Trade*, **Tube-drawer*, a maker of metal piping. **1897** *Daily News* 7 May 7/4 Consumers of iron—engineers' ironfounders, bridge-builders, rolling-stock manufacturers, and tube-drawers. **1835** Ure *Philos. Manuf.* 61 The foundations of kindred works, such as..*tube-drawing apparatus. **1909** *Westm. Gaz.* 23 Oct. 3/2 *Tube-fed Suffragettes. **1964** *Lancet* 26 Dec. 1349/2 Most babies were getting their first *tube-feed within 2 hours of birth. *Ibid.* 1351/1 *Tube-feeding is a very much simpler procedure. **1974** *Brit. Med. Jrnl.* 19 Jan. 108/1 The ethical problems of prolonged tube-feeding. **1980** *Ibid.* 21 June 1493/1 More work is needed to assess the relative merits of these proprietary diets compared with the tube feeds, prepared in hospitals. **1901** *Scotsman* 13 Mar. 9/8 The crews however practised *tube-firing. **1888** Rolleston & Jackson *Anim. Life* 551 The *tube feet are either partially or completely retractile. **1837** *Penny Cycl.* VIII. 96/1 The *tube frame..Instead of cans,..is provided with revolving horizontal cylinders... The rove which it produces has no twist. **1903** *Motor. Ann.* 220 *Tube-ignition is satisfactory for a fixed engine. **1866** Geo. Eliot *Felix Holt* I. 2 Posterity may be shot, like a bullet through a tube, by atmospheric pressure from Winchester to Newcastle... The *tube-journey can never lend much to picture and narrative. **1972** C. Fremlin *Appointment with Yesterday* i. 5 No one could guess..that there is one..that has left its identity behind not just for the duration of the tube journey, but for ever. **1915** E. Wallace *Man who bought London* ii. 19 The '*tube' lift was crowded. **1935** E. Farjeon *Nursery in Nineties* 428 Once she had ventured into a tube-lift—'But never again, my dear Eleanor!' **1891** *Cent. Dict.*, *Tube-machine. **1901** Waterhouse *Conduit Wiring* 8 This strip..is passed through a tube machine from which it emerges as a perfectly smooth and regular tube. **1888** *Cassell's Encycl. Dict.*, **Tube-makers*, the Tubicolæ. **1890** *Daily News* 6 Oct. 2/5 Tube makers have this week advanced their discounts 5 per cent. **1898** *Westm. Gaz.* 9 Mar. 8/2 The amalgamation of all the big *tube-making concerns in Scotland. **1962** J. Braine *Life at Top* xxiii. 256, I used to have a *Tube map on my bedroom wall when I was at College? **1977** *Times* 15 Nov. 17/8 The Bakerloo line on the tube map. **1694** W. Holder *Harmony* (1731) 152 The *Tube-Marine, or Sea-Trumpet..fully expresseth the Trumpet. **1860** Wraxall *Life in Sea* x. 243 Among the *Tube Medusæ is also classed the pleasing Velella. **1909** *Westm. Gaz.* 1 June 9/3 The addition of eighty stamps and three *tube mills at the Nourse Mines. **1864** Webster, *Tube-plate. **1875** Bedford *Sailor's Pocket Bk.* v. (ed. 2) 211 Leaks about tubes and tube-plates are most frequently caused by forced steaming. **1839** Ure *Dict. Arts* 355 The Bobbin and Fly frame is now the great roving machine of the cotton manufacture; to which may be added, for coarse spinning, the *tube roving frame. *Ibid.* 354 The cotton sliver receives a twist..in the bobbin and fly frame, or..in the *tube-roving machine. **1877** Knight *Dict. Mech.*, *Tube-sheet. **1903** *Daily Chron.* 20 Jan. 6/3 The boiler tubes getting choked up..through the tubes leaking in the back tube sheet. **1861** P. P. Carpenter in *Rep. Smithsonian Instit.* 1860, 249 Family Gastrochænidæ. (*Tube-Shells). **1942** N. Balchin *Darkness falls from Air* xi. 196 We went.. by tube... I wanted to see how the *tube shelter business was working out. **1943** C. E. Milburn *Diary* 4 Mar. (1979) 170 There was a terrible accident at a tube shelter last night after the sirens had sounded in London. **1962** *Times* 23 Jan. 13/4 Henry Moore's Tube-Shelter drawings. **1923** E. Jessup *Snow & Ice Sports* 230 '*Tube' skates. **1975** *Kingston* (Ontario) *Whig-Standard* 19 Dec. 12/3 As a reporter who has covered various classifications of professional hockey since the invention of tube skates, it is my considered opinion that Robert Earle Clarke is one of the most adept ankle-tappers in the history of the game. **1976** *N.Y. Times Mag.* 18 Jan. 4/2 Monday morning I bought a striped blue pair of training shoes,..*tube socks, a sweatband and a book called 'On the Road to Self Improvement: The Joy of Jogging'. **1963** *Amer. Speech* XXXVIII. 272 Frankfurters are **tube steaks*. **1978** *Boston Globe* 15 Aug. 1/1 The food isn't bad which is mainly tube steaks (hot dogs). **1974** *News & Reporter* (Chester, S. Carolina) 24 Apr. 4-c (Advt.), Calico-print elasticized *tube tops! **1984** *New Yorker* 23 Apr. 42/1 She was wearing khaki shorts and a lime-green tube top. **1884** Knight *Dict. Mech., Supp.*, *Tube-valve. **1899** *Daily News* 16 Jan. 7/3 The tube-valve that set those massive hydraulic triggers free. **1885** H. C. McCook *Tenants Old Farm* 233 The arbor vitæ hedge, where numbers of the speckled *Tubeweaver (*Agalena nævia*) yearly spin their broad snares. **1877** Knight *Dict. Mech.*, *Tube-well. **1885** *Daily News* 7 Feb. 3/2 Pack saddles for mules, and tube-wells. **1819** *Pantologia*, *Sipunculus*, *tube-worm. **1928** Russell & Yonge *Seas* viii. 194 The case of the concealed animals, such as the Piddock or the Tube-worm, ..presents almost equal difficulties. **1981** *Sci. Amer.* May 90/3 Occasionally a crab would climb the stalk of a tube worm, presumably to attack its plume. **1891** *Daily News* 2 Oct. 2/6 Single yarns, *tube yarns, and mohair yarns.

Hence **'tubeful**, as much as a tube will hold; **'tubeless** *a.*, having no tube or tubes.

1897 G. C. Bateman *Vivarium* vii. 292 One or more *tubefuls [*printed* tubesful] of meat can be inserted into the gullet of each Reptile. **1855** *Chamb. Jrnl.* III. 206 Huyghens made his observations with a *tubeless telescope. **1898** *Cycling* 71 The Fleuss or 'Tubeless Tyre'.

tube, *v.* [f. prec. sb.; cf. F. *tuber* (1489 in Littré).]

1. *trans.* To furnish or fit with a tube or tubes; to insert a tube in.

1828 Webster, *Tube v.*, to furnish with a tube; as, to tube a well. **1840** *Civil Eng. & Arch. Jrnl.* III. 27/1 This..shaft ..should be properly tubed with cast or sheet iron. **1867** *N. Syd. Soc. Bienn. Retrosp. Med. & Surg.* 1865–6, 247 The ease with which 'tubing' the larynx can be accomplished. **1886** H. S. Brown *Autobiog.* x. (1887) 57, I was engaged.. in tubing boilers.

2. To pass through or enclose in a tube; cf. *tube yarn* (tube *sb.* 12b).

1863–98 Luce *Seamanship* App. A. 461 A recent improvement in the spinner tubes the yarn, rendering it smoother and..leaving little to be desired in the manufacture of rope.

3. *intr.* To travel by tube railway; also *to tube it*. *colloq.*

1902 *Daily Chron.* 31 Oct. 5/1 Yet my cherished hope was this—That under our Metropolis From end to end I'd tube it. **1907** *Ibid.* 1 June 5/5 Shoppers can 'tube' to the West-end.

4. *trans.* and *intr.* To fail, to perform poorly (in). *U.S. slang.*

1966 *Current Slang* (Univ. S. Dakota) Summer 5 *Tube*, to fail; to do a poor job. College students, both sexes. Midwest. 'He tubed every test last week.' **1979** *N.Y. Times Mag.* 30 Sept. 10/3 In time, surfers used the verb 'to tube' to mean 'to do poorly'.

tubectomy (tju:'bɛktəmɪ). *Surg.* [f. tube *sb.* + -ectomy.] = *salpingectomy* s.v. salpingo-.

1925 Stedman *Med. Dict.* (ed. 8) 1057/2 *Tubectomy*, salpingectomy. **1975** *Lancet* 27 Sept. 567/1 (*heading*) Tubectomy by paraprofessional surgeons in rural Bangladesh. **1977** *Time* 7 Feb. 45/3 The government is pushing birth control programmes: 6 million people underwent vasectomies or tubectomies in six months last year.

tubed (tju:bd), *ppl. a.* [f. tube *v.* or *sb.* + -ed.]

1. Made or furnished with, consisting of, or having a tube or tubes; resembling a tube; tubular.

1816 Wordsw. *Ode Day Thanksg.* x. 12 While the tubed engine [i.e. organ] feels the inspiring blast And has begun —its clouds of sound to cast Forth. **1843** *Jrnl. R. Agric. Soc.* IX. ii. 372 The larch presents a tubed decayed heart. **1860** Wraxall *Life in Sea* x. 241 Among the strangest of existing animals are the Tubed Jelly Fish, or Siphonophoræ. **1875** Howells *Foregone Concl.* 105 Mrs. Veevain began to look at the sketch through her tubed hand.

2. Of a race-horse: having a metallic tube inserted in the air-passage.

1925 W. & A. J. Day *Racehorse in Training* 13 Tubed horses are rather a nuisance, as the tube should be taken out and disinfected occasionally. **1955** *Times* 13 May 3/3 In the absence of Defender, the tubed steeplechaser Remy was made favourite for the long-distance race, against four opponents.

‖**tuber**[1]. *Obs.* Pl. tuberes. [L. *tuber* masc. (the fruit), fem. (the tree).] A kind of apple, or the tree on which it grows.

c **1440** *Pallad. on Husb.* ii. 393 Now tuberis in quyncis me may graffe. **1546** Langley *Pol. Verg. De Invent.* iii. ii. 65 b, Zizypha and Tuberes two kyndes of apple trees. **1658** tr. *Porta's Nat. Magic* iv. vii. 124 Medlars, and the fruit Tuber may be shut up in pitchers, so to be preserved.

tuber[2] ('tju:bə(r)). [a. L. *tūber* neut., a hump, swelling, pl. *tūbera*.]

1. *Bot.* An underground structure consisting of a solid thickened portion or outgrowth of a stem or rhizome, of a more or less rounded form, and bearing 'eyes' or buds from which new plants may arise; a familiar example is the potato. Also applied to other underground structures resembling this but of different origin, as in tuberous roots.

1668 Wilkins *Real Char.* 90 Tuberous roots; consisting of one single tuber, or of several. **1704** [see b]. **1822** J. Flint *Lett. Amer.* 57 The potato crops are better.., the plants are more vigorous, and the tubers much larger. **1870** Hooker *Stud. Flora* 352 Orchis. Tubers globose ovoid or palmate. **1880** Gray *Struct. Bot.* iii. §3 (ed. 6) 59 A Tuber may be.. characterized as a short thickened rhizoma on a slender base, or a rootstock some portion of which..is thickened by the deposition of nourishing matter.

‖**b.** (With capital initial.) A genus of underground discomycetous fungi, comprising the truffles.

[**1693** *Phil. Trans.* XVII. 824 The *Tubera Terræ*.. observ'd lately at Rushton in Northamptonshire..are indeed the true French *Truffles*, the Italian *Tartuffi*. **1699** Evelyn *Acetaria* 42 Trufles, Pig-Nuts, and other subterraneous *Tubera*.] **1704** J. Harris *Lex. Techn.* I, *Tuber*, properly, is a subterraneous Mushroom, or a Truffle; but by Botanick Writers, is often used to signifie the round turgid Roots of some Plants: which they call Tuberose, or Knobby Roots.

2. A rounded swelling or protuberant part in the animal body. **a.** *Path.* A morbid swelling or enlargement, as of a gland, etc.

1706 Phillips (ed. Kersey), *Tuber*,..a Swelling or Bunch in a Man's Body. **1834** *Good's Study Med.* (ed. 4) IV. 233 Those who are constitutionally predisposed to a production of tubers and tubercles. **1888** Fagge & Pye-Smith *Princ. Med.* (ed. 2) I. 96 In a solid organ it [i.e. a tumour] may form a rounded mass, which is called a nodule or tuber.

b. *Anat.* A rounded projecting part or structure; a tuberosity.

Chiefly as Latin, with pl. *tubera*: often with defining word, as the specific name of such a structure: e.g. ***tuber cinereum***, a conical projection at the base of the brain; ***tuber cochleæ*** or ***tympani***, the promontory of the tympanum.

1741 Monro *Anat.* (ed. 3) 209 The Tuber is afterwards added in the Manner that other Epiphyses are. **1857** Dunglison *Med. Lex.*, *Tuber cinereum*, a grayish tubercle, seen at the base of the brain behind the commissure of the optic nerves. **1866** Huxley *Preh. Rem. Caithn.* 110 Norwegians are remarkable for the length of their skulls, and the very general development of an occipital tuber, or probole.

3. *gen.* A rounded projection, protuberance. *rare.*

1888 Doughty *Arabia Deserta* I. 32 We..came where in a torrent bed are laid bare certain great tubers of the lime rock underlying.

tuberaceous (tju:bə'reɪʃəs), *a. Bot.* [f. mod.L. *Tūberācei* (masc. pl.), *-āceæ* (fem. pl.), f. *Tūber*: see prec. 1b and -aceous.] Belonging to the order *Tuberaceæ* or *Tuberacei* of discomycetous fungi, typified by the genus *Tuber*.

1909 in *Cent. Dict. Suppl.*

†**'tuberant**, *a. Obs. rare*$^{-1}$. [ad. late L. *tūberānt-em* (Appuleius), f. *tūber*, tuber[2]: see -ant.] Swelling out, protruding, protuberant.

1668 Culpepper & Cole *Barthol. Anat.* i. xiv. 33 The tuberant or bossie part of the Liver.

tuberated ('tju:bəreɪtɪd), *a.* [f. L. *tūberāt-us* covered with tubers or knobs, f. *tūber*, tuber[2]: see -ed.] Having a tuber or rounded swelling; in *Her.* applied to a serpent borne with the middle part twisted in a close knot.

c **1828** Berry *Encycl. Her.* I. Gloss., *Tuberated*, gibbous, knotted, or swelled out, as the middle part of the serpent.

tuberation (tjuːbəˈreɪʃən). *rare*$^{-1}$. [f. as prec. + -ATION.] Formation or production of a tuber or tubers.

1727 BAILEY vol. II, *Tuberation*, a swelling. **1902** *Times* 19 Sept. 6/3 The excessive tuberation which potatoes brought under cultivation acquire.

tubercle (ˈtjuːbək(ə)l). [ad. L. *tūberculum* small swelling, boil, pimple, dim. of *tūber*, TUBER^{2}. Cf. obs. F. *tubercle* (Cotgr., 1611).] A small tuber or body resembling a tuber.

1. *Anat.* and *Zool.* A small rounded projection or protuberance, as on a bone, or on the surface of the body in various animals.

Often with defining word, as the specific name of such a structure: e.g. *conoid, cuneiform, genial, laminated, madreporic, optic, scalene* (etc.) *tubercle*: see the adjs.

1578 BANISTER *Hist. Man* I. 17 To this Tubercle they ['bones' of the larynx] are inarticulated and knit. **1747** *Gentl. Mag.* Mar. 122/2 These creatures have several rows of tubercles on their bodies. **1846** BRITTAN tr. *Malgaigne's Man. Oper. Surg.* 133 A more or less projecting tubercle on the first rib, which gives attachment to the anterior scalenus. **1880** BARWELL *Aneurism* iii. 29 Chassaignac's tubercle, the transverse process of the fifth cervical vertebra.

2. *Path.* A small firm rounded swelling or nodule on the surface of the body or in a part or organ; *spec.* a mass of granulation-cells characteristic of *tuberculosis*; *transf.* the disease tuberculosis.

miliary tubercle: see MILIARY I.

1661 LOVELL *Hist. Anim. & Min.* 355 The tubercles of the lungs. **1710** T. FULLER *Pharm. Extemp.* 52 A Balsamick Decoction..dissipates Crude Tubercles. **1804** ABERNETHY *Surg. Obs. Tumours* 149 The ulcerated surface may heal, and leave an indurated knob or tubercle in the affected part. **1818** *Art Preserv. Feet* 3 The corn is technically termed 'clavus pedum', and considered as a tubercle without organization, proceeding from the substance of the epidermis, and originating in the tightness of shoes or boots. **1859** J. TOMES *Dental Surg.* (1873) 51 Tubercle does not appear to interfere with the progress of dentition. **1876** BRISTOWE *The. & Pract. Med.* (1878) 67 It is a.. characteristic of tubercle that its specific cells very rapidly fall into degeneration.

3. *Bot.* **a.** A small tuber, or a root-growth resembling a tuber, as in many orchids. **b.** A small wart-like swelling or protuberance on a plant.

1727–41 CHAMBERS *Cycl.*, *Tuber*, on *Tubercle*, in botany, a kind of round turgid root. **1756–7** tr. *Keysler's Trav.* (1760) IV. 349 A particular species..has large prickles growing on round tubercles. **1807** J. E. SMITH *Phys. Bot.* 498 Fucus,.. whose seeds are collected together in tubercles or swellings, of various forms and sizes. **1880** GRAY *Struct. Bot.* iii. §3 (ed. 6) 60 Tubercles..are of a mixed..character between tubers and tuberous roots.

4. *attrib.* and *Comb.*, as ***tubercle-like***, ***-infected*** adjs.; **tubercle-bacillus**, the species of bacillus which causes tuberculosis (also *attrib.*).

1866 TATE *Brit. Mollusks* iv. 165 A tubercle-like tooth [in a shell]. **1891** *Cent. Dict.* s.v. *Tubercle*, Tubercle-bacillus. **1897** *Daily News* 1 Apr. 3/4 Both assume the so-called tubercle-bacillus tint. **1898** *Westm. Gaz.* 3 Nov. 9/2 If the Council can prevent the sale of tubercle-infected milk. **1913** *Times* 6 Aug. 8/4 Microscopical examination of milk and tubercle bacillus by analytical methods.

tubercled (ˈtjuːbək(ə)ld), *a. Nat. Hist.* and *Path.* [f. prec. + -ED^{2}.] Furnished or affected with tubercles; tuberculate.

1755 *Gentl. Mag.* Sept. 391/1 The grain..is green and tubercled. **1819** TURTON *Conchol. Dict.* 43 *Haliotis*. Sea-ear. *Haliotis tuberculata*. Tubercled Sea-ear. **1829** LOUDON *Encycl. Plants* (1836) 410 The smaller melon thistle..is tubercled all over. **1864** WEBSTER s.v., A tubercled lung.

tubercular (tjuːˈbɜːkjʊlə(r)), *a.* and *sb.* [ad. mod.L. **tūberculār-is*, f. L. *tūbercul-um* TUBERCLE + -AR.]

A. *adj.* **1.** *Nat. Hist.*, etc. **a.** Of the nature or form of a tubercle; consisting of or constituting a tubercle. **b.** Having or covered with tubercles, tuberculate.

1817 KIRBY & SP. *Entomol.* xxii. (1818) II. 279 A subcutaneous larva belonging to the same order,..moves also by tubercular legs. **1860** MAYNE *Expos. Lex.*, *Tubercular*, having tubercles; tubercled; tuberculate. **1877** HUXLEY *Anat. Inv. Anim.* v. 231 The surface of the elytron is covered with..tubercular prominences. **1880** GÜNTHER *Fishes* 176 The young are smooth and the old have a tubercular skin.

2. *Path.* **a.** Of, pertaining to, caused or characterized by, or affected with tubercles.

1799- [see b]. **1864** H. SPENCER *Princ. Biol.* II. ii. 152 Tubercular matter, making its appearance at particular points, collects more and more round those points. **1897** *Allbutt's Syst. Med.* II. 47 Symptomatology—Nodular Leprosy—'Tuberculated', 'tubercular', 'tuberculous', 'nodular-dermal', 'dermal', 'cutaneous', 'hypertrophic' leprosy. **1899** *Ibid.* VIII. 805 Tubercular syphilide... The term 'tubercular' used above refers solely to the gross infiltration of the skin causing raised nodules, and has..no relation to the tubercle bacillus.

b. *spec.* In reference to tuberculosis or the tubercle-bacillus; now technically replaced by TUBERCULOUS, q.v.

But as the discovery of the bacillus was made known only in 1882, the earlier examples of the word, though actually descriptive of results of the action of the bacillus, did not refer to it, but merely to the presence of tubercules.

1799 *Med. Jrnl.* II. 267, I have had..three cases of confirmed tubercular consumption. **1834** J. FORBES *Laennec's Dis. Chest* (ed. 4) 297 A portion of the pulmonary tissue..impregnated with grey tubercular matter. **1876** BRISTOWE *The. & Pract. Med.* (1878) 68 A..tendency of organs to become tubercular. **1898** *Westm. Gaz.* 10 Nov. 8/2 He did not recommend..the removal of every tubercular cow from our dairies and cow-sheds.

Hence **tuˈbercularize** *v.*, *trans.* to make tubercular; to infect with tubercles, *spec.* with tuberculosis, = TUBERCULIZE; whence **tuˌberculariˈzation**; **tuˈbercularly** *adv.*, by means of tubercles, in quot. *spec.* of tuberculosis.

1843 F. H. RAMADGE *Curability of Consumption* (1850) 55 The more this tissue is expanded, the less susceptibility does it retain of fresh tubercularization. **1889** *Science* 13 Sept. 177/1 Spittoons..should never be emptied on dung-heaps, [or] on garden-soil (where they may tubercularize fowl). **1889** *Pop. Sci. Monthly* Dec. 260 Having found a characteristic..bacillus in all tubercularly altered organs.

B. *sb.* A person having tuberculosis.

1952 *Sun* (Baltimore) 2 July 14/3 Maryland has three State institutions for the chronically sick, four hospitals for tuberculars, and four for the mentally ill. **1980** I. HUNTER *Malcolm Muggeridge* x. 177 In 1949 Orwell left the Isle of Jura to enter a convalescent home for tuberculars at Cranham in Gloucestershire.

tuberculate (tjuːˈbɜːkjʊlət), *a. Nat. Hist.* and *Path.* [ad. mod.L. *tūberculātus*, f. L. *tūbercul-um* TUBERCLE: see -ATE^{2}.] Furnished or affected with tubercles; tubercled.

1785 MARTIN *Rousseau's Bot.* xxxii. (1794) 497 The Tuberculate [Lichens], consisting of a crust adhering closely to the bark of trees, or stones, above which roundish tubercles rise a little. **1834** *Good's Study Med.* (ed. 4) IV. 454 A thick, rugose, livid, tuberculate..skin. **1875** C. C. BLAKE *Zool.* 27 The molar teeth are usually tuberculate. **1887** W. PHILLIPS *Brit. Discomycetes* 57 The tuberculate sporidia are frequently furnished with thread-like appendages at the extremities.

b. In comb. with another adj. (in *Bot.*), as ***tuberculate-hispid***, hispid or rough with tubercles.

1821 W. P. C. BARTON *Flora N. Amer.* I. 102 Petioles and stem tuberculate-hispid.

tuberculated (tjuːˈbɜːkjʊleɪtɪd), *a.* [f. as prec. + -ED.] = prec. **a.** *Nat. Hist.*

1771 *Pennant* in *Phil. Trans.* LXI. 272 The whole circumference of the back bounded by a tuberculated rib. **1784** ANDRÉ *ibid.* LXXIV. 274 Let us..recollect the tuberculated teeth in the thorn-back. **1845** LINDLEY *Sch. Bot.* vi. (1858) 83 Receptacle conical, toothed, tuberculated. **1861** BENTLEY *Man. Bot.* 129 When some of the divisions of a root become enlarged so as to form more or less rounded or egg-shaped expansions.., the root is said to be tuberculated, and each enlargement is called a tubercle.

b. *Path.* (also *transf.* characterized by tubercles).

1797 M. BAILLIE *Morb. Anat.* (1807) 221 The formation of the common tuberculated liver. **1804** ABERNETHY *Surg. Obs. Tumours* (1816) 51 Tuberculated Sarcoma..consists of an aggregation of small, firm, roundish tumours,.. connected together by a kind of cellular substance. **1822–7** GOOD *Study Med.* (1829) II. 489 A tuberculated state of the lungs. **1829** *Ibid.* III. 428 The palms of the hands [in leprosy] were seldom tuberculated. **1854** F. H. RAMADGE *Curability of Consumption* (1861) Pref. 11 All..might be tuberculated, and yet not one of them die of consumption.

Hence **tuˈberculatedly** *adv.*

1822 J. PARKINSON *Outl. Oryctol.* 220 With transverse tuberculatedly scabrous ribs.

tuberculation (tjuːˌbɜːkjʊˈleɪʃən). [f. L. *tūbercul-um* TUBERCLE + -ATION.]

1. *Nat. Hist.* Formation of tubercles; *concr.* a growth or set of tubercles.

1835–6 *Todd's Cycl. Anat.* I. 778/1 Branchiae..covered with a multitude of small tuberculations. **1880** HUXLEY *Crayfish* vi. 294 The tuberculation of the carapace and limbs.

2. *Path.* Formation of tubercles as a symptom of disease; tubercular or tuberculous affection.

1861 T. J. GRAHAM *Pract. Med.* 300 A confirmatory sign of tuberculation of the lungs. **1899** *Allbutt's Syst. Med.* VIII. 795 The erythematous lupus may be distinguished from lupus vulgaris..by the absence of tuberculation.

tuberculato- (tjuːˌbɜːkjʊˈleɪtəʊ), combining form of mod.L. *tūberculātus* TUBERCULATE, used in *Nat. Hist.* prefixed to adjs., expressing a form or structure with tuberculations, as ***tuberculato-gibbous***, ***-nodose***, ***-radiate***, ***-spinous***.

1822 J. PARKINSON *Outl. Oryctol.* 220 Longitudinal tuberculato-nodose ribs. **1846** DANA *Zooph.* (1848) 284 Corallum lamello-radiate above, tuberculato-radiate below. *Ibid.* 495 Lobes short,..often tuberculato-gibbous. **1852** —— *Crust.* I. 88 Carapax..sparsely tuberculato-spinous.

tubercule (ˈtjuːbəkjuːl). [a. F. *tubercule* (Paré, 16th c.), ad. L. *tūbercul-um* TUBERCLE.]

= TUBERCLE, in various senses.

1678 PHILLIPS (ed 4), *Tuberculs*, in Chiromancy are those ..protuberant parts under the Fingers,..otherwise called *Montes*. **1727–41** CHAMBERS *Cycl.*, *Tubercules, Tubercles*, little tumors which suppurate and discharge pus; often found in the lungs. **1760** J. LEE *Introd. Bot.* III. v. (1765) 183 *Scabrous, rugged*; when the Disk is covered with Tubercules. **1835** LINDLEY *Introd. Bot.* I. ii. (ed 2) 87 The roots of many plants are often fleshy, and composed of lobes, which appear to serve as reservoirs of nutriment. In Orchis the tubercules are often palmated. **1842** H. MILLER *O.R. Sandst.* viii. (ed. 2) 170 The inner sides of the pincers are armed with.. tubercules. **1901** *Scotsman* 2 Mar. 10/1 Death..of tubercule of the lungs.

Hence **ˈtuberculed** *a.*, tubercled, tuberculate.

1858 GEIKIE *Hist. Boulder* vii. 117 Ornamented by long rows of tuberculed lines.

tuberculide (tjuːˈbɜːkjʊlaɪd). *Path.* Also -id. [ad. mod.L. *tūberculīdēs*, f. L. *tūbercul-um* TUBERCLE.] A general term for any skin lesion of a tuberculous nature.

1900 *Lancet* 18 Aug. 534/1 True tuberculosis of the skin was asymmetrical, but the tuberculides were strikingly symmetrical. **1900–13** DORLAND *Med. Dict.*, Tuberculid tuberculide.

tuberculiferous (tjuːˌbɜːkjʊˈlɪfərəs), *a.* [f. L. *tūbercul-um* TUBERCLE + -I)FEROUS.] Bearing tubercles.

1822 J. PARKINSON *Outl. Oryctol.* 224 Distant tuberculiferous ribs on the larger valve; tubercles fornicated. **1846** DANA *Zooph.* (1848) 140 Sides naked above, below tuberculiferous and tubercles perforate.

tuberculiform (tjuːˈbɜːkjʊlɪˌfɔːm), *a.* [f. as prec. + -FORM.] Having the form of a tubercle.

1817 KIRBY & SP. *Entomol.* xxii. (1818) II. 277 Apodous larvæ..that move by means of fleshy tuberculiform.. prominences. **1846** DANA *Zooph.* (1848) 153 The body is covered with large tuberculiform suckers. **1885** H. O. FORBES *Nat. Wand. E. Archip.* II. App. 120 At the hinder part..are several strong tuberculiform eminences and prominences.

tuberculin (tjuːˈbɜːkjʊlɪn). *Med.* Also *erron.* -ine. [f. L. *tūberculum* TUBERCLE + -IN^{1}.]

a. A liquid prepared from cultures of tubercle-bacillus, originally by Dr. Koch of Berlin in 1890, or any one of various later modifications of this, used by hypodermic injection as a remedy, or (now esp.) as a test, for tuberculosis.

1891 *Daily News* 12 Feb. 6/5 Dr. Koch's lymph has received the name of 'tuberculine'. **1893** *Times* 19 Dec. 3/2 'Tuberculin'..has been employed as an aid to the diagnosis of tuberculosis. **1896** *Westm. Gaz.* 10 Mar. 4/1 At the Balneological Congress,..Dr. Kaatzer spoke very highly of the value of tuberculin in phthisis... Professor Liebreich asserted that the cure of lupus by tuberculin was more apparent than real. **1899** *Syd. Soc. Lex.*, *Tuberculin*, Koch's lymph..consisting of ptomaines of the tubercle bacilli.

b. *attrib.* and *Comb.*, as ***tuberculin reaction***, †***treatment***; **tuberculin test**, the injection of tuberculin, usu. intradermally, as a test for the past or present existence of tubercle bacilli in the individual; also as *vb. trans.*; hence **tuberculin-tested** *ppl. a.* (see quot. 1950).

1906 *Review of Reviews* Sept. 366 [It] showed no tuberculine reaction. **1955** *Sci. News Let.* 1 Oct. 221/1 The tuberculin test is a skin test. A tuberculin reaction means that tuberculosis germs have invaded the person's body and sensitized it to proteins of the TB germ. **1900** DORLAND *Med. Dict.* s.v. *Tests*, Tuberculin-test. **1908** *Med. Annual* 662 Tuberculin Test.—This test, prepared by the Pasteur Institute of Lille, claims to be diagnostic of tuberculosis in man. **1950** J. G. DAVIS *Dict. Dairying* 721 Three forms of tuberculin test have been evolved—the ophthalmic, the subcutaneous and the intradermal. **1966** Tuberculin test [see *intradermic* adj. s.v. INTRA- 1]. **1937** *Amer. Rev. Tuberculosis* XXXV. 598 A classification of the 56,688 persons tuberculin-tested according to age disclosed the fact that boys and girls between ten and nineteen years of age comprised almost two-thirds of the groups reported. **1936** Tuberculin-tested [see CERTIFIED *ppl. a.* d]. **1950** J. G. DAVIS *Dict. Dairying* 721 *Tuberculin-tested milk*, milk which is derived solely from a herd of tuberculin-tested cows under licence and kept pure and unmixed with other non-tuberculin-tested milk. **1982** M. YOUNG *Elmhirsts of Dartington* xi. 277 Nielsen admitted to disposing of a small quantity of milk as Tuberculin Tested when it was not. **1908** *Med. Annual* 47 Roemisch thinks that tuberculin treatment gives good results in a class of chronic phthisical patients, in whom the ordinary treatment with fresh air and rest at first gives marked improvement.., but after a time no further improvement can be obtained. **1912** *Nature* 12 Dec. 427/2 The mortality of the phthisical under sanatorium and tuberculin treatments.

Hence **tuˈberculinize** *v.*, *trans.* to treat with tuberculin; whence **tuˌberculiniˈzation** (Dorland).

1895 *Buck's Handbk. Med. Sc.* IX. 900/2 Comparing..the condition of the various organs of the tuberculinized with that of the same in healthy animals. **1899** in *Syd. Soc. Lex.*

tuberculization (tjuːˌbɜːkjʊlaɪˈzeɪʃən). [f. next + -ATION; cf. F. *tuberculisation* (Littré).] The action or process of tuberculizing; infection with or formation of tubercle.

1843 R. J. GRAVES *Syst. Clin. Med.* xxii. 277 Tuberculization commences suddenly and proceeds rapidly. **1847–9** *Todd's Cycl. Anat.* IV. 108/1 Tuberculization of the bronchial glands. **1899** *Allbutt's Syst. Med.* VI. 103 The gray pneumonia attending tuberculisation.

tuberculize (tjuːˈbɜːkjʊlaɪz), *v.* [f. L. *tūbercul-um* TUBERCLE + -IZE; cf. F. *tuberculiser* (Littré).]

a. *trans.* To affect or infect with tubercle or tuberculosis; to make tuberculous; also, 'to treat with tuberculin' (Dorland *Med. Dict.* 1913). **b.** *intr.* To become tuberculous. Hence **tuˈberculized** *ppl. a.*

1847–9 *Todd's Cycl. Anat.* IV. 106/2 Tuberculized pulmonary substance. **1863** AITKEN *Sc. & Pract. Med.* (1866) II. 191 These cells tuberculize, or undergo the tuberculous metamorphosis. **1897** D. N. KINSMAN in *Columbus* (Ohio) *Dispatch* 20 Feb., As soon as a person is known to be tuberculized. **1901** *Lancet* 9 Nov. 1252/1, I hold..that a scrofulous person is not, and need not be, a tuberculised person.

tuberculo- (tjuːˈbɜːkjʊləʊ), combining form of L. *tūbercul-um* TUBERCLE, properly used adverbially; also attrib. or objectively (instead of the regular *tuberculi-*: see -O[1]), in several technical terms, chiefly of pathology and medicine. **tuˈberculoˌcele** (-siːl) [Gr. κήλη tumour], 'tuberculous disease of the testicle' (Dorland *Med. Dict.* 1900–13). **tuˈberculoˌcide** (-saɪd) [irreg. for **tuberculicide*: see -CIDE], any preparation which destroys the tubercle-bacillus; hence **tuˌberculoˈcidin** [-IN[1]], an albumose obtained from tuberculin, used as a tuberculicide. ‖**tuˌberculoˈderma** [Gr. δέρμα skin], tuberculosis of the skin (*Cent. Dict. Suppl.* 1909). **tuˌberculo-ˈfibroid** *a.*, 'characterized by tubercle that has undergone a fibroid degeneration' (Dorland). **tuˌberculo-opˈsonic** *a.*, relating to the opsonin of the tubercle-bacillus. **tuˌberculoˈphobia** [-PHOBIA], a morbid dread of tuberculosis. **tuˌberculoˈplasmin**, a solution of the protoplasm of tubercle-bacilli. **tuˌberculo-ˈprotein**, protein from the tubercle bacillus, *Mycobacterium tuberculosis*; **tuˌberculosecˈtorial** *a.*, *Zool.* [SECTORIAL *a.*[2]], applied to a type of molar teeth having high conical tubercles or cusps adapted for cutting. **tuˌberculo-ˈsquamous** *a.* [SQUAMOUS], characterized by tubercles and scales. **tuˌberculoˈstatic** *a.* [-STATIC], inhibiting the multiplication of the tubercle bacillus, *Mycobacterium tuberculosis*. **tuˌberculoˈtherapy** [Gr. θεραπεία nurture, medical treatment], 'treatment of tuberculous patients by feeding with the raw flesh of animals affected by tuberculosis' (Dorland). **tuˌberculoˈtoxin**, 'any toxin of the tubercle bacillus' (*ibid.*). **tuˌberculoˈtropic** *a.* [? after *heliotropic*, etc.: cf. TROPIC *a.*[1] 4], having the property of combining chemically with the tubercle-bacillus.

c **1900** *Buck's Handbk. Med. Sc.* I. 461 *Tuberculocide. **1892** *Pall Mall G.* 23 July 5/1 An experiment..on twelve more or less tuberculous persons with the so-called *tuberculocidin, which is a modification of Professor Koch's remedy, invented by Professor Klebs, of Zurich. **1895** *Buck's Handbk. Med. Sc.* IX. 903/1 Tuberculin yields about two and a half per cent. of tuberculocidin. **1898** *Allbutt's Syst. Med.* V. 255 Sir A. Clark..describes two main forms [of pneumoconiosis] as..the *tuberculo-fibroid and fibro-tuberculous. **1907** *Med. Record* 14 Dec. 987 In one of these [cases] the *tuberculo-opsonic index was from normal to 0·7 below normal. **1901** *Lancet* 27 July 192/1 *Tuberculophobia must not be produced, the patient must not be made a pariah. *c* **1900** *Buck's Handbk. Med. Sc.* I. 692 *Tuberculoplasmin. **1912** HAMMAN & WOLMAN *Tuberculin in Diagnosis & Treatm.* III. 231 Tuberculocidin represents the attempts by Klebs to purify tuberculin by alcohol and bismuth precipitation... He also produced *tuberculo-protein and tuberculo-sozin. **1954** S. DUKE-ELDER *Parsons' Dis. Eye* (ed. 12) xvi. 218 In many cases the presence of sensitivity can be demonstrated by skin-reactions to tuberculo-protein or streptococci. **1893** *Proc. Zool. Soc.* 28 Feb. 197 The..*tuberculosectorial type of inferior molars. **1879** *St. George's Hosp. Rep.* IX. 592 Rupial sore; *tuberculo-squamous eruption. **1945** *Jrnl. Immunol.* L. 159 Sera, either from rabbits sensitized with a purified tuberculin protein preparation or from tuberculous rabbits, possessed *tuberculostatic activities in the chick membrane. **1971** *Nature* 4 June 301/1 We recently proposed structure (I) for the tuberculostatic antibiotic viomycin. **1909** *Cent. Dict. Suppl.*, *Tuberculotropic.

tuberculoid (tjuːˈbɜːkjʊlɔɪd), *a.* [f. L. *tūbercul-um* TUBERCLE + -OID.] **a.** *Zool.* and *Path.* = TUBERCULIFORM.

1891 in *Cent. Dict.* **1974** *Trypanosomiasis & Leishmaniasis* (Ciba Foundation Symp.) 163 In localized forms we often saw epithelioid or tuberculoid nodules, surrounded by a thick infiltration of lymphoid cells.

b. *Path.* Designating one of the two principal forms of leprosy, characterized by a few well-defined lesions similar to those of tuberculosis, often with anæsthesia.

1938 *Leprosy Rev.* IX. 20 No progress can be made..unless it is frankly admitted that at the Manila Conference [in 1931] the significance and extent of the tuberculoid phases of leprosy were not fully appreciated. *Ibid.*, Anaesthesia is by no means the sole preserve of tuberculoid leprosy. **1948** E. MUIR *Man. of Leprosy* ix. 49 The term 'tuberculoid' is given on account of the histological resemblance of this type to chronic lesions in tuberculosis. It is a somewhat unfortunate term, as it is often confused with 'tubercular', the word formerly used for the severeerl form, now called lepromatous. **1971** [see *lepromatous* adj. s.v. LEPROMA].

‖**tuberculoma** (tjuːbɜːkjʊˈləʊmə). *Path.* Pl. -omas, -omata. Also anglicized tuˈberculome. [mod.L. *tūberculōma*, f. *tūbercul-um* TUBERCLE, after *sarcoma*, etc.] A tumour or abscess caused by the tubercle-bacillus.

1897 *Lippincott's Med. Dict.* 1076/1 Tuberculoma. **1903** *Nature* 5 Mar. 431/2 If the tuberculous abscess or tuberculome is not too large, a cure may be effected by a simple washing with an antiseptic liquid. **1908** E. A. PETERS in T. N. Kelynack *Tuberculosis in Infancy & Childhood* vii. 55 Seward has collected a hundred cases of other forms of tuberculosis of the nose—*e.g.*, tuberculoma and ulcer—from a great many sources. **1954** S. DUKE-ELDER *Parsons' Dis. Eye* (ed. 12) xxx. 508 Intracranial tumours (including neoplasms and such lesions as tuberculomata) produce two sets of symptoms. **1974** J. D. MAYNARD in R. M. Kirk et al. *Surgery* x. 215/1 A tuberculoma, a round focus over 1 cm in diameter, which has failed to disappear after adequate chemotherapy.

tuberculose (tjuːˈbɜːkjʊləʊs), *a.* [f. L. type **tūberculōs-us*, f. *tūbercul-um* TUBERCLE: see -OSE.] = TUBERCULOUS 2, TUBERCULATE.

1752 J. HILL *Hist. Anim.* 249 The green Turdus..is a very beautiful fish;..it is not unfrequently..almost entire black, and sometimes spotted or tuberculose. **1854** WOODWARD *Mollusca* II. 191 Doris Bilamellata:..Back elevated, tuberculose. **1900** in B. D. JACKSON *Gloss. Bot. Terms.*

tuberculosed (tjuːˈbɜːkjʊləʊzd), *a.* *Path.* [f. TUBERCULOS-IS + -ED[2].] Affected with tuberculosis; rendered tuberculous.

1888 *Med. News* 25 Aug. 216 We must distinguish those forms in which the tuberculosed lymphatic glands are separated in chains. **1897** *Daily News* 22 Apr. 3/1 Methods ..for dealing with tuberculosed meat. **1899** H. STUART *Lochs & Loch Fishing* I. iv. 34 They contained the bacilli of consumption, and were, in a word, tuberculosed or consumptive fish.

‖**tuberculosis** (tjuːˌbɜːkjʊˈləʊsɪs). *Path.* [mod.L., f. *tūbercul-um* TUBERCLE: see -OSIS.] *Originally*, Any disease characterized by the formation of tubercles; now, since the discovery by Koch in 1882 of the tubercle-bacillus, *spec.* restricted to disease caused by this bacillus in any of the bodily tissues; examples are pulmonary consumption or phthisis (tuberculosis of the lungs), and scrofula (tuberculosis of the lymphatic glands). Also *attrib.*

1860 TANNER *Pregnancy* ii. 48 Many females with a tendency to tuberculosis having a copious watery catamenial flow. **1873** T. H. GREEN *Introd. Pathol.* (ed. 2) 203 Acute tuberculosis is..a general infective disease,..characterized ..by..numerous minute nodular lesions..in the various organs and tissues. **1877** ROBERTS *Handbk. Med.* (ed. 3) I. 267 Looking upon tuberculosis as a constitutional disease, it has almost universally been regarded as having a hereditary origin.

attrib. **1898** *Westm. Gaz.* 13 June 10/1 The provision of sanatoria for poor tuberculosis patients. **1899** Q. VICTORIA in *Daily News* 27 May 7/6, I beg your Excellency to express in my name to the Lung Tuberculosis Congress my best thanks for the good wishes tendered to me. **1913** *Times* 6 Aug. 8/4 Milk containing tuberculosis bacilli.

tubercuˈloso-, combining form of L. type **tūberculōsus* TUBERCULOUS, in combination with an adj. of form, as ***tuberculoso-subramose***.

1846 DANA *Zooph.* (1848) 497 Either convoluted-foliate, or tuberculoso-subramose.

tuberculous (tjuːˈbɜːkjʊləs), *a.* [ad. L. type **tūberculōs-us*, f. *tūbercul-um* TUBERCLE: see -OUS; cf. F. *tuberculeux* (1812 in Hatz.-Darm.).]

1. *Path.* Pertaining to or produced by tubercles; consisting or of the nature of tubercles; affected with tubercles.

1747 tr. *Astruc's Fevers* 129 Though the..tuberculous ulcers may seem to be healed, yet they frequently return. *a* **1834** R. CARSWELL *Pathol. Anat.*, *Tubercle* (1838) aiv b, I have never found these [scrofulous] glands..exempt from the presence of tuberculous matter. **1897** [see TUBERCULAR 2].

b. Since 1882, almost always used *spec.* in reference to the tubercle-bacillus or to tuberculosis, and thus technically distinguished from *tubercular* in the general sense: see TUBERCULAR 2, 2 b.

1891 *Dublin Rev.* Jan. 162 The new remedy can only act on living tuberculous tissue. **1897** *Allbutt's Syst. Med.* II. 17 Guinea-pigs inoculated subcutaneously..by virulent tuberculous material. **1899** *Ibid.* VII. 466 Tuberculous meningitis is an acute disease depending on the invasion of the cerebral pia mater by the tubercle bacillus. **1903** *Times* 7 Mar. 15/2 The eating of tuberculous pork. **1913** *Ibid.* 13 Aug. 3/2 A steady increase in the use of hospitals for the tuberculous sick.

2. *Nat. Hist.* Full of or covered with tubercles; tuberculate, tubercular. (Now disused.)

1828 WEBSTER, *Tubercular, Tuberculous*,..full of knobs or pimples. **1833** *Penny Cycl.* I. 114/2 The three first molars are pointed and trenchant, and the other four tuberculous. **1846** DANA *Zooph.* (1848) 502 Surface tuberculous, with the tubercles subconical.

‖**tuberculum** (tjuːˈbɜːkjʊləm). Pl. **tubercula**. [L. dim. of *tūber*, TUBER[2].] = TUBERCLE (in various senses).

1693 tr. *Blancard's Phys. Dict.* (ed. 2), *Tubercula*, the same that *Phymata*. **1721** BAILEY, *Tubercula*, (among Surgeons) little Swellings or Pushes. **1857** DUNGLISON *Med. Lex.*, *Tuberculum Cinereum*, 'Ash-coloured tubercle', a mass of cineritious substance at the top of the calamus scriptorius [in the medulla oblongata]. **1872** NICHOLSON *Palæont.* 350 The ribs have distinct capitula and tubercula.

tuberiferous (tjuːbəˈrɪfərəs), *a.* *Bot.* [f. L. *tūber*, TUBER[2] + -I)FEROUS.] Producing or bearing tubers.

1846 WORCESTER cites GRAY. **1847** W. E. STEELE *Field Bot.* 174 *Melantheæ*. Mostly bulbiferous or tuberiferous plants, possessing highly poisonous, acrid, and narcotic properties. **1881** BENTHAM in *Jrnl. Linn. Soc.* XVIII. 347 Their rhizome is..more or less tuberiferous.

tuberiform (ˈtjuːbərɪfɔːm), *a.* *Nat. Hist.* and *Path.* [f. L. type **tūberiform-is*: see TUBER[2] and -FORM.] Having the form of a tuber; also characterized, as a disease, by growths of this form.

1822 J. PARKINSON *Outl. Oryctol.* 61* A free, carnose, tuberiform polypifer. **1834** COOPER *Good's Study Med.* (ed. 4) II. 555 *note*, Tuberiform melanosis. **1854** JONES & SIEV. *Pathol. Anat.* (1874) 141 A globular tumour, with a smooth or somewhat tuberiform surface. **1899** *Allbutt's Syst. Med.* VI. 106 Another variety [of malignant pleural growth] is the tuberiform.

tuberin (ˈtjuːbərɪn). *Org. Chem.* [f. TUBER[2] + -IN[1].] A globulin occurring in potato-tubers.

1900 C. F. LANGWORTHY in *Year-bk. U.S. Dept. Agric.* 340 The potato contains two proteids, a globulin, to which the name 'tuberin' is given, and a proteose.

tuberless (ˈtjuːbəlɪs), *a.* [f. as prec. + -LESS.] Destitute of tubers; not bearing tubers.

1851 *B'ham & Midl. Gard. Mag.* Dec. 217 Finding..that the plant [*Tropæolum Deckerianum*] was tuberless, I came to the conclusion that it must be an annual.

ˈtubero-, combining form of TUBER[2], as in **ˈtubero-ˈcystic**, having or forming a tuberous cyst; **ˌtubero-hypophyseal, -ial** *a.* *Anat.* [for primary stress see HYPOPHYSIAL *a.*] = next; **ˌtubero-infunˈdibular** *a.* *Anat.*, relating to the tuber cinereum and the infundibulum; *spec.* applied to a tract of nerve fibres that includes those running from the infundibular and related nuclei of the hypothalamus to the infundibulum.

1879 *St. George's Hosp. Rep.* IX. 433 Tubero-cystic tumour of the ovary. **1962** Tubero-hypophyseal [see *tubero-infundibular* below]. **1969** TRUEX & CARPENTER *Human Neuroanat.* (ed. 6) xix. 494/2 The connections of the hypothalamus with the posterior lobe of the hypophysis are well established for man... A smaller bundle [of nerve fibres], the tuberohypophysial tract, is contributed by the medial cells of the tuber cinereum. **1962** J. SZENTÁGOTHAI in J. Szentágothai et al. *Hypothalamic Control of Anterior Pituitary* ii. 45 This system corresponds to the tubero-hypophyseal tract of Spatz (1951) and Nowakowski (1951). Since it terminates in the median eminence and in the proximal part of the stalk, it would be better to term it tubero-infundibular tract. **1980** *Gray's Anat.* (ed. 36) 966/1 The tuber cinereum around the base of the infundibulum is raised to form a median eminence which..is superficially marked by a shallow tubero-infundibular sulcus.

†**tuberon, -e** [ad. Pg. *tubarão*], obs. forms of TIBURON, a large shark.

[**1521** PETER MARTYR *De nuper repertis insulis* 9 Piscis vorax qui Tuberon vocatur.] **1555, 1579** [see TIBURON]. **1599** NASHE *Lenten Stuffe* (1871) 76 A shark or tuberon, that lay gaping for the flying fish. **1665** SIR T. HERBERT *Trav.* (1677) 6 When..men swim in the bearing Ocean, the greedy Hayen called Tuberon or Shark..pursue them. **1784–5** *Chron.* in *Ann. Reg.* 241/1 The dog-fish, or tuberone of Josselyn, never exceeds three feet and a half in length.

tuberose (ˈtjuːbərəʊs, *often incorrectly* ˈtjuːbrəʊz), *sb.* Also 7 tuberuse, -euse, (tuber-rose). [ad. L. *tūberōsa*, the specific name of the plant (see below), fem. of *tūberōsus* (see next); corrupted by popular etymology into a disyllable, as if f. *tube* + *rose*, and so most commonly pronounced. (In the obs. forms *tuberuse*, *-euse*, a. F. *tubéreuse*, ad. L. *tūberōsa*.)] A liliaceous plant, *Polianthes tuberosa*, with creamy white, funnel-shaped, very fragrant flowers, and a tuberous root; a native of the East Indies, cultivated in southern Europe and the southern U.S., and in northern parts as a greenhouse plant.

1664 EVELYN *Kal. Hort.* 200 Now take out your Indian Tuberoses, parting the Off-sets. *Ibid.* 208 Tuber-rose. **1691** *Lond. Gaz.* No. 2654/4 There are lately brought from Italy several Orange and Limon Trees,..Onions of Tubereuse. *a* **1718** PRIOR *Solomon* I. 80 The smelling Tub'rose and Junquele declare, The stronger Impulse of an Evening Air. *a* **1763** SHENSTONE *Ode to Sir R. Lyttelton* xiii, So would some tuberose delight, That struck the pilgrim's wondering sight. **1820** SHELLEY *Sensit. Plant* I. x, The jessamine faint, and the sweet tuberose. **1873** MRS. H. KING *Disciples, Ugo Bassi* II. (1877) 66 In the cool shadow heaps of tuberose Lay by the fountains in the market-place.

b. A perfume extracted from the flowers of this.

1682 MRS. BEHN *City Heiress* 22 Sprinkle my Handkercher with Tuberuse. **1867** AUG. J. E. WILSON *Vashti* xix, Stooping to pick it [a handkerchief] up, he inhaled the delicate, tenacious perfume of tube-rose.

tuberose (ˈtjuːbərəʊs), *a.* [ad. L. *tūberōs-us*, f. *tūber*, TUBER[2]: see -OSE[1].] = TUBEROUS; ***tuberose sclerosis*** = *tuberous sclerosis* s.v. TUBEROUS *a.* 2.

1704 [see TUBER[2] 1 b]. **1796** KIRWAN *Elem. Min.* (ed. 2) II. 259 Indurated [Calx of Arsenic]... Found Massive, or Stalactitic with a tuberose or botryoidal surface. **1815** J. SMITH *Panorama Sc. & Art* II. 670 A tuberose root, as exemplified in the turnip and carrot. **1878** H. M. STANLEY *Dark Cont.* I. xv. 381 The tuberose muscles of the flanks. **1898** SIR P. MANSON *Trop. Diseases* xxxvii. 574 Vincent.. found it [i.e. the parasite of mycetoma] in the unbroken tuberose swellings under the skin. **1933** W. R. BRAIN *Dis. Nervous Syst.* ix. 487 Beyond the fact that tuberose sclerosis is due to a congenital abnormality.. little is known about its aetiology. **1963** *Lancet* 12 Jan. 67/2 When in the Royal Air Force during the war I saw a man with tuberose sclerosis it was not unexpected to find in his son evidence of the same, genetically determined, disorder.

Comb. **1806** GALPINE *Brit. Bot.* §77 *Symphytum.. tuberosum*, tuberose-rooted.

tuberosity (tjuːbəˈrɒsɪtɪ). [a. F. *tuberosité* (Paré, *c* 1550), f. late L. *tūberōsitās*, f. *tūberōs-us* TUBEROSE + -ITY.]

1. The quality or condition of being tuberous; bulging; gibbosity. Now *rare* or *Obs.*

1541 R. COPLAND *Guydon's Quest. Chirurg.* Q iv b, Hardnes and tuberosyte of the ioyntes outwarde. **1610** GUILLIM *Heraldry* II. vi. 63 A bow, which being bent hath a moderate bowing voide of excess of tuberositie.

2. *concr.* A tuberous formation or part; a swelling, protuberance, prominence.

a. *Anat.* and *Zool.*: *esp.* a large irregular projection of a bone, usually serving for attachment of a muscle.

1611 COTGR., *Condyle*, the tuberiositie, out-swelling, roundnesse, or knots, of the thigh, knee, ankle, elbow, or knuckle-bones. **1741** MONRO *Anat.* (ed. 3) 134 The internal posterior Part of the Tuberosity and Alveoli of the Teeth. **1852** TH. ROSS *Humboldt's Trav.* I. i. 27 The brownish tuberosities of its body. **1870** ROLLESTON *Anim. Life* 13 The great triangular tuberosity of the humerus.

b. *generally.* A swelling, a swollen mass.

1611 COTGR., *Tuberositez*, tuberosities, swellings;.. knobs; knots. **1831** CARLYLE *Sart. Res.* I. v, Whether he flow gracefully out in folded mantles;.. swell-out in starched ruffs, buckram stuffings, and monstrous tuberosities; or [etc.]. *Ibid.* III. vi, I sojourned in that monstrous tuberosity of Civilised Life, the Capital of England.

tuberous (ˈtjuːbərəs), *a.* [ad. F. *tubéreux, -euse* (Paré, *c* 1550), ad. L. *tūberōsus*, f. *tūber*, TUBER[2]: see -OUS.]

1. *Anat., Zool.*, etc. Of the form of, or constituting, a tuber or rounded projection; covered with such projections; knobbed, knobby. Now *rare.*

1650 BULWER *Anthropomet.* iii. 63 This forehead is.. neither globous nor tuberous as the forehead of women. **1678** RAY *Willughby's Ornith.* II. xv. §2. 182 A broad circle of naked, tuberous, white flesh compasses the Eyes, as in the Carriers. **1804** SHAW *Gen. Zool.* V. 208 Tuberous Carp... Carp with thirteen rays in the anal fin, and slightly tuberous body.

2. *Path.* Affected with tubers or morbid swellings; of the nature of such a swelling; characterized, as a disease, by such swellings; ***tuberous sclerosis***, a rare, hereditary, usu. fatal disease in which there are hard swellings on the brain and elsewhere, with symptoms including mental deficiency and epilepsy.

1656 BLOUNT *Glossogr.*, *Tuberous*, full of bunches, swellings, wennes or knots. **1762** R. GUY *Pract. Obs. Cancers* 150 The tuberous Vessels were rather fuller than ordinary. **1834** COOPER *Goods' Study Med.* (ed. 4) I. 353 The origin of vascular tuberous growths. **1898** C. K. MILLS *Nervous Syst. & its Dis.* v. 503 Tuberous Sclerosis. An interesting form of sclerotic pseudotumor is sometimes found in the brain, especially among the idiotic.. and epileptic. **1900** J. HUTCHINSON in *Arch. Surg.* XI. 73 His face was covered with tuberous acne. **1954** S. DUKE-ELDER *Parsons' Dis. Eye* (ed. 12) xviii. 313 Tuberous Sclerosis (Bourneville's Disease), occurring in young individuals, is associated with nodular lesions in the central nervous system and the skin, particularly on the face (adenoma sebaceum). **1975** SWAIMAN & WRIGHT *Practice of Pediatric Neurol.* II. xxxii. 739/1 Tuberous sclerosis is best identified by cutaneous signs associated with neurologic deterioration and myoclonic seizures.

3. *Bot.* **a.** Of the nature of a tuber; chiefly in ***tuberous root***, (*a*) a tuber, or an underground stem bearing tubers (see TUBER[2] 1); (*b*) more strictly, a true root (usually one of a cluster) thickened so as to resemble a tuber, but bearing no buds; as in the lesser celandine and the dahlia.

1668 Tuberous roots [see TUBER[2] 1]. **1730** MARTYN in *Phil. Trans.* XXXVI. 385 Their Roots are either bulbous, tuberous, or consisting of thick, fleshy Fibres. **1776** WITHERING *Brit. Plants* (1796) IV. 346 *Peziza tuberosa*... Stem growing at the base to a blackish fungous tuberous substance. **1807** J. E. SMITH *Phys. Bot.* 140 The knobs of genuine tuberous roots, like the potatoe, are studded with them [buds]. **1872** OLIVER *Elem. Bot.* I. vii. 66 When the branches or fibres of a root become thickened in this way, as ..in the Garden Dahlia, the root is said to be tuberous.

b. Of a plant: Producing or bearing tubers; tuberous-rooted.

1664 EVELYN *Kal. Hort.* Sept. (1729) 218 Tuberous Indian Jacinth. **1786** ABERCROMBIE *Gard. Assist.* 51 Bulbous and tuberous irises. **1861** MISS PRATT *Flower. Pl.* IV. 55 Tuberous Comfrey. *Ibid.* VI. 56 Tuberous Fox-tail.

4. *Comb.* **tuberous-rooted** *a.*, having a tuberous root (in either sense: see 3 a).

1721 MORTIMER *Husb.* II. 226 Irises are both bulbous and tuberous Rooted. **1808** KNIGHT in *Phil. Trans.* XCIX. 174 Such tuberous rooted plants as the potatoe. **1914** *Daily Mail* 31 Jan. 9/2 The planting of tuberous-rooted anemones and ranunculuses.

Hence **ˈtuberously** *adv.*; **ˈtuberousness.**

1681 GREW *Musæum* III. i. i. 255 The tuberousness of the Bone in some places. **1847–9** *Todd's Cycl. Anat.* IV. 133/2 This disease produces.. irregular tuberousness of the hand. *a* **1891** *Bull. of Ill. State Laboratory* II. 28 (Cent. D.) Tuberously.

tubful (ˈtʌbfʊl). [f. TUB *sb.* + -FUL.] As much as a tub will hold.

1788 LD. AUCKLAND *Corr.* etc. (1861) II. 71 We have a large tubful brought to us every morning. **1812** SIR J. SINCLAIR *Syst. Husb. Scot.* II. 72 The rain is pouring on in tubfuls. **1894** J. MENZIES *Our Town* xx. 211 A gudewife had come to her door with a tubful of soapsuds.

tubi- (tjuːbɪ), combining form of L. *tubus* TUBE, in modern scientific terms, chiefly zoological. **tubicolar** (tjuːˈbɪkələ(r)), **tubicolous** (-ˈbɪkələs) *adjs.* [mod.L. *tubicola*, f. *colĕre* to cultivate, inhabit], inhabiting a tube; applied to annelids and rotifers that secrete tubular cases, spiders that spin tubular webs (cf. *tubitelar*), and molluscs with shelly tubes (cf. TUBE-*shell*, *tubivalve*); so **tubicole** (ˈtjuːbɪkəʊl) *a.* = prec.; *sb.* a tubicolar annelid or mollusc. **ˈtubicorn** [L. *cornū* horn], *sb.* a hollow-horned ruminant; *adj.* hollow-horned, as a ruminant; also **tubiˈcornous** *a.* **tubifacient** (-ˈfeɪʃ(ɪ)ənt) *a.* [L. *facient-em* making], making a tube for habitation, as a tubicolous annelid, etc. **ˈtubifer** [L. *-fer* bearing], an animal bearing a tube, as a tubicolous annelid; so **tuˈbiferous** (-fərəs) *a.*, bearing a tube or tubes. **ˈtubifex** [mod.L. (J. B. P. A. de M. de Lamarck *Hist. Nat. Animaux sans Vertèbres* (1816) III. 224)], a red oligochæte worm of the genus of this name, found in mud at the bottom of rivers or lakes and used as live food for aquarium animals; also *attrib.* **tuˈbificid** [mod.L. family name *Tubificidæ*: see TUBEROUS *a.*], an aquatic oligochæte worm of the family Tubificidæ; also as *adj.* **tubiflorous** (-ˈflɔərəs) *a.*, *Bot.* [L. *flōs*, *flōr-* flower], having tubular flowers or florets, as the division *Tubifloræ* of composite plants (= TUBULIFLORUS). **ˈtubiform** *a.*, having the form of a tube; tube-shaped, tubular. **tubilingual** (-ˈlɪŋgwəl) *a.* [L. *lingua* tongue], belonging to the division *Tubilingues* of passerine birds, having long extensile tubular tongues used for sucking up honey. **tubinarial** (-ˈnɛərɪəl), **tubinarine** (-ˈnɛəraɪn) *adjs.* [L. *nāris* nostril], belonging to the order *Tubinārēs* (Illiger, 1811) of water-birds, comprising the albatrosses and petrels, having nostrils of tubular form. **tubiparous** (tjuːˈbɪpərəs) *a.* [-PAROUS], producing a tube; applied to certain glands in tubicolous annelids, supposed to secrete the substance which forms the tube. **ˈtubipore** (-pɔə(r)) *sb.*, a member of the genus *Tubipora*, family *Tubiporidæ*, or order *Tubiporaceæ*, of alcyonarians (the organ-pipe corals), in which each polyp has a tubular corallet opening by a pore; *adj.* belonging to or having the characters of this genus, family, or order; in quot., containing or formed of fossil tubipores; so **ˌtubiporacean** (-pɒˈreɪʃiːən), **-poraceous** (-pɒˈreɪʃəs) *adjs.*, belonging to the order *Tubiporaceæ*; **tuˈbiporid**, a coral of the family *Tubiporidæ*; **tuˈbiporite** [-ITE[1] 2 a], a fossil tubipore; **tuˈbiporoid** *a.* [-OID], resembling or allied to the genus *Tubipora*; **tuˈbiporous** *a.* = *tubipore* adj. **tubitelar** (-ˈtiːlə(r)) *a.* [L. *tēla* web], belonging to the division *Tubitelæ or Tubitelariæ* of spiders, which spin tubular webs; so **ˌtubiteˈlarian** (-tɪːˈlɛərɪən) *a.* = prec.; *sb.* a spider of this division (*Cent. Dict.* 1891). **ˈtubivalve,** *sb.* a bivalve mollusc having a shelly tube in addition to the valves of the shell; a tube-shell; *adj.* having such a tube.

1835–6 *Todd's Cycl. Anat.* I. 619/1 A common marine *tubicolar worm. **1877** HUXLEY *Anat. Inv. Anim.* v. 238 The tubicolar Annelids possess neither proboscis nor teeth. **1842** BRANDE *Dict. Sc.* etc., **Tubicoles, Tubicola*, the name of an order of Annelidans, comprehending those which live in tubes..; also the name of a family of.. Mollusks, including those which have a tubular calcareous sheath in addition to the two shelly valves. **1864** WEBSTER, *Tubicole*,.. one of an order of annelides most of which live in shelly tubes. **1891** *Cent. Dict.*, Tubicole, *a.* and *n.* **1870** H. SPENCER *Princ. Psychol.* (ed. 2) I. I. i. 6 The *tubicolous Annelids. **1881** E. R. LANKESTER in *Jrnl. Microsc. Sc.* Jan. 123 The proximal region of the stomach.. was infested by a remarkable little free swimming, yet tubicolous Rotifer. **1842** BRANDE *Dict. Sc.* etc., **Tubicorns, Tubicornia*,.. Ruminants comprehending those in which the horns are composed of a horny axis covered with a horny sheath. **1891** *Cent. Dict.*, *Tubicorn*,.. *a.* hollow-horned, as a ruminant. **1864** WEBSTER, *Tubicornous. **1891** *Cent. Dict.*, *Tubifacient. **1899** in *Syd. Soc. Lex.* **1842** BRANDE *Dict. Sc.* etc., **Tubifers, Tubifera*, the name given by Lamarck to an order of the class *Polypi*,.. whose surface is.. covered with retractile hollow tubes. **1860** MAYNE *Expos. Lex.*, *Tubiferus*,.. bearing tubes: *tubiferous. **1952** J. CLEGG *Freshwater Life Brit. Isles* xi. 156 **Tubifex* worms lay their eggs in oval capsules and breed very rapidly. **1972** *Sci. Amer.* Oct. 115/1 Among the more commonly viewed organisms are tubifex worms. **1976** *Daily Tel.* 3 Dec. 18 The river is now almost too clean. It has led to a decrease in the tubifex worm population, on which waterfowl feed. **1950** M. GORDON in E. J. Farris et al. *Care & Breeding Lab. Animals* xiv. 382 *Tubificids are usually most plentiful about one-half mile downstream from the spot where raw pollution is dumped. **1971** *Nature* 26 Feb. 596/1 Tubificid worms.. are typical bottom dwelling animals of all fresh-water lakes and reservoirs. **1971** *Oxf. Bk. Invertebrates* 114/1 Tubificids will emerge, tail upwards, to undulate their bodies gently in the water for respiratory exchange. **1978** *Nature* 17 Aug. 644/2 Chironomid midge larvae and tubificid worms have replaced a previously rich fauna. **1888** ROLLESTON & JACKSON *Anim. Life* 246 A Cyclostomatous Polyzoan,.. which with its aggregated calcareous cells presents an appearance not unlike that of a small *tubiflorous flower belonging to a plant of the order *Compositae.* **1745** NEEDHAM *Microsc. Disc.* Introd. 6 The Barnacle.. a small *tubiform Animal,.. adhering in Clusters to Rocks. **1880** GÜNTHER *Fishes* 57 A pair of small tubiform bones, the turbinals. **1891** *Cent. Dict.*, *Tubilingual. **1882** W. A. FORBES in *Rep. Challenger Exped., Zool.* IV. 64 One branch of this stock has since become greatly modified in the *Tubinarial direction. **1895** *Funk's Stand. Dict.*, *Tubinarine. **1890** *Q. Jrnl. Microsc. Sc.* June 186 *note*, Such thoracic nephridia in other sedentary annelids have been called '*tubiparous glands' by Claparède and others. **1800** HATCHETT in *Phil. Trans.* XC. 333 In the interstices of the *Tubipore. **1846** DANA *Zooph.* iv. (1848) 68 In the Tubipores, the polyps form, by their secretions, parallel tubes. **1876** PAGE *Adv. Text-bk. Geol.* xviii. 353 The tubipore cherts and flints of the mountain limestone. **1895** *Funk's Stand. Dict.*, *Tubiporid. **1828** WEBSTER, **Tubiporite.* **1895** *Funk's Stand. Dict.*, *Tubiporoid. **1848** SMART, **Tubiporous*, pertaining to, or resembling tubipores. **1882** OGILVIE, **Tubivalve*, an annelid [*sic: read* mollusc] of the order Tubicolidæ. **1891** *Cent. Dict.*, Tubivalve *n.* and *a.*

†**tuˈbicinate,** *v.* *Obs.* *rare*$^{-0}$. [f. med.L. *tubicināt-*, ppl. stem of *tubicināre*, f. L. *tubicen* trumpeter, f. *tuba* trumpet + *canĕre* to sing, play.] (See quot.) So †**tubiciˈnation** (*obs. rare*$^{-0}$).

1656 BLOUNT *Glossogr.*, *Tubicinate*.., to sound the Trumpet. **1658** PHILLIPS, *Tubicination*,.. a sounding of a Trumpet, Pipe, or Cornet.

tubify (ˈtjuːbɪfaɪ), *v. nonce-wd.* [f. TUBE *sb.* + -IFY.] *trans.* ? To give a tubular form to.

1928 D. H. LAWRENCE *Lady Chatterley's Lover* xviii. 347 'I don't think Vulcan has a figure that interests me.' 'Not even if it was tubified and tittivated up?'

tubing (ˈtjuːbɪŋ), *vbl. sb.* [f. TUBE *v.* or *sb.* + -ING[1].] **a.** The action of furnishing with a tube or tubes; also *concr.* tubes collectively, or as a material; a length or piece of tube. Also *attrib.*

1845 I. FARRELL *Archimedean Railw.* 8 This rail is made of iron tubing. **1854** J. SCOFFERN in *Orr's Circ. Sc., Chem.* 350 India-rubber tubing can be obtained. **1881** RAYMOND *Mining Gloss.*, *Tubing*, lining a deep bore-hole by driving down iron tubes. **1886** J. BARROWMAN *Sc. Mining Terms* 69 *Tubing*, sheet-iron lining of a bore-hole. **1909** *Installation News* III. 112/1 Any carpenter could locate the weak spots in tubing work.

b. (See quot. 1976.) *U.S.*

1975 *Newsweek* 3 Feb. 69 But the big rage of the ski year —and the most painful—is a pastime called 'tubing'. For experts, the idea is to take a running start and then execute a belly-flop onto an ordinary inflated inner tube. **1976** *Webster's Sports Dict.* 464/1 *Tubing*, the sport or pastime of riding down a river or of sliding down a snow-covered slope on an inflated automobile inner tube. **1979** *United States 1980/81* (Penguin Travel Guides) 367 *Tubing*—Arizona's most popular summer sport. On any given weekend, as many as 20,000 residents strap beer-filled ice chests and their behinds to old inner tubes and float down the five or ten miles of free-flowing Salt River below Saguaro Lake.

Tubism (ˈtjuːbɪz(ə)m). [f. TUBE *sb.* + -ISM, after CUBISM.] A style of painting characterized by cylindrical and other mechanistic forms, *spec.* that developed by the French artist Fernand Léger (1881–1955). So **ˈTubist** *a.*

1923 *Weekly Dispatch* 11 Feb. 9 He [*sc.* Gregory Brown] first took up applied art, working in metal. Turning his attention to poster work, he.. became one of the pioneers of what was jocularly known as the Tubist School. **1955** *Times* 18 Aug. 13/1 'Tubism' serves well to describe the brand of Cubism that Léger made peculiarly his own. Out of the several possibilities indicated by Cézanne's famous remark about the geometrical basis of natural forms he selected the cylinder, and though he admitted other forms, a tubular tendency runs through most of his compositions. **1960** *Twentieth Cent.* Dec. 526 Léger's 'tubist' portraits. **1978** N. GOSLING *Paris 1900–1914* 165 Fernand Léger.. attracted by the Cubist experiments.. developed a variety of his own, based on interlocking cylinders—a style which was nicknamed 'Tubism'.

tubman, tub-man (ˈtʌbmən). [f. TUB *sb.* + MAN *sb.*[1]]

†**1.** = TUB-PREACHER. *Obs.*

1642 P. BLAND *Royall Position* 9 No Conventicling Tubman should have made my words his text. *a* **1643** LD. FALKLAND, etc. *Infallibility* (1646) 97 The meanest Seducer may doe mischiefe, as we finde by the effects of the Tubmen. **1651** JANE *Εικων Ακλαστος* 213 Tubmen whose prayers not only want salt, but are besmeared with prophanes.

2. †**a.** ? A maker of tubs, a cooper. *Obs.* **b.** At Christ's Hospital, formerly, one who had charge of the latrine tubs; subsequently, a lavatory attendant.

1677 (*title*) A Caution to Married Couples..how a man having beat his wife, murthered a Tub-man that endeavoured to stop him from killing her. **1723** *Lond. Gaz.* No. 6196/7 John Thumwood,..Tub-man. *c* **1865** *Skit Christ's Hospital*, Has she a round of butter'd toast to give to tubman Joe?

3. A barrister in the Court of Exchequer whose place was beside the tub used as a measure of capacity in excise cases; the position conferred the right of precedence in motions, except over the 'postman' and in Crown business. Cf. POSTMAN³. *Obs.* exc. *Hist.*

1768 BLACKSTONE *Comm.* III. iii. 28 *note*, In the court of exchequer two of the most experienced barristers called the *post*-man and the *tub*-man..have also a precedence in motions. **1841** MEESON & WELSBY *Rep.* VII. 188 The Attorney-General moved in this case. The Postman and Tubman claimed pre-audience; but upon the Attorney-General's stating that it was the Queen's business in which he moved, the Court decided that he was entitled to be heard before the Postman and Tubman. **1882** *Daily News* 15 Dec. 2/1 With the appointment of Mr. Anstie as a Queen's Counsel, the ancient office of tubman to the Exchequer disappears. **1886** [see POSTMAN³].

†**'tubnell.** *Obs. rare*⁻¹. [app. irreg. dim. of TUB *sb.*, or arbitrary alteration of TURNEL.] A small tub.

1688 R. HOLME *Armoury* III. xiv. (Roxb.) 18/1 This containeing half a Barrell of water or something lesse, is called a Tub; if lesse a Tubnell, that is vulgarly a Turnell.

tubo- (tjuːbəʊ), used in certain cases as combining form of L. *tubus* TUBE (instead of the usual Latin form TUBI-: see -O¹) in several terms of zoology, anatomy, etc. **a.** *Zool.* in adjs. denoting a combination of tubular with some other form, as ˌ*tubo-la'bellate*, -*'nariform*. **b.** *Anat.*, etc. in terms relating to the Fallopian (rarely, the Eustachian) tube in connexion with some other part; chiefly adjs., as ˌ***tubo-ab'dominal*** (pertaining to or occurring in the Fallopian tube and the abdomen), -***liga'mentous***, -***o'varian***, ***perito'neal***, -***'uterine***, -***va'ginal***; ˌ***tubo-'tympanal*** (pertaining to the Eustachian tube and the tympanum); rarely sbs. as ˌ***tubo-ovari'otomy*** (excision of the Fallopian tube and ovary).

1846 DANA *Zooph.* (1848) 432 The nariform calicle is tubular at base—tubo-nariform. *Ibid.* 444 Corallum having the calicles tubo-labellate. **1857** BULLOCK *Cazeaux' Midwif.* 245 Tubo-ovarian Pregnancy. *Ibid.* 246 Tubo-abdominal Pregnancy. **1889** J. M. DUNCAN *Lect. Dis. Woman* viii. (ed. 4) 243 An interstitial pregnancy may become tubo-uterine. **1900–13** DORLAND *Med. Dict.*, *Tuboligamentous*, pertaining to an oviduct and a broad ligament. *Tubo-ovarial*, *tubo-ovarian*,.. *Tubo-ovariotomy*,.. *Tuboperitoneal* *Tubotympanal*,.. *Tubovaginal.*

tubocurarine (tjuːbəʊ'kjʊərəriːn). *Pharm.* [ad. G. *tubocurarin*, f. *tubocurare* tube curare (see TUBO-, CURARE): see -IN¹.] An isoquinoline alkaloid that is the active ingredient of tube curare and whose chloride, $C_{37}H_{42}Cl_2N_2O_6$, is used as a muscle relaxant.

1898 *Jrnl. Chem. Soc.* LXXIV. I. 284 Paracurarine (tubocurarine). **1935** *Nature* 23 Mar. 470/1 The quaternary alkaloid tubocurarine..has now been crystallised for the first time. **1973** *Reader's Digest* Apr. 206/1 They paralysed him with 70 milligrams of tubocurarine chloride. **1977** *Lancet* 19 Mar. 650/2 Three drugs used in clinical anæsthesia consistently cause arterial hypotension in patients with essential hypertension—halothane, *d*-tubocurarine, and verapamil.

tuboplasty ('tjuːbəʊplæstɪ). *Surg.* [f. TUBO- + -PLASTY.] The surgical repair of one or both Fallopian tubes.

1961 *Obstetr. & Gynecol.* XVII. 504/2 The combination of tuboplasty and metroplasty was indicated as an attempt to overcome sterility factors and minimize the possibility of subsequent miscarriage. **1976** *Daily Colonist* (Victoria, B.C.) 14 Apr. 2/3 A few pregnancies have resulted from tuboplasty procedures—as for unblocking a tube—but generally the results here, too, have been disappointing. **1977** *Lancet* 5 Feb. 284/2 Regular ovulation and a positive postcoital test were confirmed in each patient before tuboplasty.

'tub-ˌpreacher. [See TUB *sb.* 4.] One who preaches from a 'tub' (TUB *sb.* 4); a dissenting preacher or minister (*contemptuous*). So **'tub-ˌpreaching** *sb.* and *a.*

1643 *xiv Art. of Treason exhib. I. Pennington* 5 Stephan Evans, alias Prince of Morocco, Knight of the Burning Pestle, Salter, and Tub-preacher, on Snow Hill. **1661** J. DAVIES *Civ. Warres* xxxii. 52 Tub-Preachings and Conventicle-Lectures were listened to as to Oracles. *a* **1670** HACKET *Abp. Williams* II. (1693) 165 Your lawful Ministers ..to whom..you do not resort,..but to Tub-preachers in Conventicles. **1719** D'URFEY *Pills* IV. 14 The Tub-preaching Saint was so zealous a Blade. **1899** S. R. GARDINER *Cromwell* 48 Those who looked down with scorn on the vagaries of the tub-preacher.

†**tu-brugge.** *Obs. rare.* Also 3 tobrugge, 4 tuybrugge. [The second part is the ME. *brugge*, BRIDGE; the first is uncertain; perh. a deriv. of OE. *toȝian* or *téon* to draw (see TOW *v.*¹, TEE *v.*¹): cf. Ger. *zugbrücke*, MHG. *zogebrucke*, draw-bridge.] A drawbridge.

1297 R. GLOUC. (Rolls) 11257 þe castel brugge..he barnde fram þen ende To þe tobrugge [*v.r.* tuybrugge] along. *Ibid.* 11595 þe tu brugge [*v.r.* tun brugge] hii drowe vp.

†**'tubster.** *Obs.* [f. TUB *sb.* + -STER.] A tub-preacher. (*Contemptuous.*)

1681 T. FLATMAN *Heraclitus Ridens* No. 45 (1713) II. 34 A certain Dissenting Tubster, who told his Audience, he would..divide the Observations he should make from his Text, into forty eight Particulars. **1682** *Ibid.* No. 82. 248 Why, if we should lay down,..the Tubsters would appoint a solemn Day of Thanksgiving among themselves. **1700** T. BROWN *Amusem. Ser. & Com.* 121 He, says the Tubster, that would be Rich.., must play the Thief or the Cheat.

'tub-ˌthumper.

1. A speaker or preacher who for emphasis thumps the pulpit; a violent or declamatory preacher or orator; a ranter.

1662 H. FOULIS *Hist. Plots Pretended Saints* 80 Tub-thumpers..a sort of people more antick in their Devotions than Don Buscos Fencing-Master. **1720–1** *Lett. fr. Mist's Jrnl.* (1722) II. 225 An honest Presbyterian Tub-thumper, who has lost his Voice with bawling to his Flock. **1864** *Athenæum* 27 Aug. 267/3 Preachers, humorous tub-thumpers. **1908** *Daily Chron.* 3 Nov. 5/7 It would reduce the M.P...to the position of a Temperance tub-thumper.

2. A cooper. *humorous dial.*

1872 HARTLEY *Yorks. Ditties* Ser. I. 98 At last au set up as tub-thumper. **1880** L. J. JENNINGS *Rambles* 110 'A tub-thumper?'..'Ay Mister—what you call a cooper.'

So (as a back-formation) **'tub-thump** *v. intr.*; also **'tub-ˌthumpery**; **'tub-ˌthumping** *sb.* and *a.*

1888 *Contemp. Rev.* Aug. 253 Very modest gifts, belonging to what may be called the tub-thumping school of oratory. **1894** *Westm. Gaz.* 22 Aug. 1/2 What we demand is not a display of tub-thumping at the fag-end of a Session,.. but a deliberate plan of campaign, carefully thought out and doggedly pursued. **1909** *Times* 21 Mar., A democratic election, with all its tub-thumping and unreasoning passion and sheer noise. **1920** 'SAPPER' *Bulldog Drummond* iv. 117 The sort of type one sees tub-thumping in Hyde Park. **1927** *Observer* 28 Aug. 11/4 Fanny Hawthorne's refusal to be made an honest woman..may still be regarded as advanced in ethics, even if its expression is not without a suspicion of tub-thumpery. **1933** DYLAN THOMAS *Let.* (1966) 75 And thank you for..heeding my dogmatic tub-thumpery. **1934** E. POUND *ABC of Reading* 113 A bad reader of fourteeners is almost certain to tub-thump.

tubular ('tjuːbjʊlə(r)), *a.* and *sb.* [f. L. *tubul-us* a small tube, a pipe + -AR; cf. F. *tubulaire* (1771 in *Dict. Trévoux*).]

A. *adj.* **1. a.** Having the form of a tube or pipe; constituting or consisting of a tube; cylindrical, hollow, and open at one or both ends; tube-shaped.

tubular bells, a series of tuned metal tubes of graded length vertically suspended and struck by hammers; ***tubular bridge***, a bridge formed of a great tube or hollow beam, usually of wrought iron, through which the roadway passes; ***tubular goods*** (Oil Industry) (see quot. 1922); ***tubular steel***, steel tubing, esp. as used in the manufacture of furniture; also *attrib.*

1673 GREW *Anat. Trunks* I. iv. §15 The Pins being also conceived to be Tubular. **1827** FARADAY *Chem. Manip.* xvi. (1842) 405 These tubular vessels may be supported with facility..upon the table across two or three pieces of glass. **1850** E. CLARK (*title*) The Britannia and Conway Tubular Bridges. **1872** YEATS *Techn. Hist. Comm.* 243 The idea of tubular bricks is not new, for they were used by the Romans. [**1884** J. HARRINGTON *Provisional Spec. 14,270* (Patent Office) (1885) 1 Instead of employing the costly gongs or bells hitherto employed, I employ metallic tubes which I suspend vertically by means of catgut, cord or other suitable material... I arrange the hammers so as to strike the same at their upper parts above the point of suspension thereof.] **1919** A. T. BASSETT *S. Barnabas', Oxford* iii. 25 The original bell of S. Barnabas'..did service until 1890, when a set of tubular bells was hung in the tower, and a chiming machine added. **1922** D. T. DAY *Handbk. Petroleum Industry* I. 300 The term 'tubular goods' generally covers all classes of pipe, casing and tubing used in drilling or operating oil or gas wells, and comprises the following distinct types; casing, tubing, drive pipe, line pipe and rotary drill pipe. **1930** *Melody Maker* Jan. 69/1 Tubular bells are often considered 'a bit of a bore' by drummers. **1933** *Archit. Rev.* LXXIV. 78/3 Four double tubular-steel legs shaped like hair-pins. **1946** R. GRAVES *Poems 1938–45* 35 Among box-files and tubular steel chairs. **1957** *Times* 2 July (Agric. Suppl.) p. viii/3 The gate and posts are made of tubular steel. **1962** *B.S.I. News* May 19/2 Glockenspiel, xylophone, tubular bells, celesta. **1981** *Times* 3 July 14/7 Marcel Breuer, the Hungarian-born architect..created the first tubular steel furniture..and in 1926 he equipped the new Bauhaus buildings with furniture of this type.

b. *Bot.*: *esp.* applied to a flower or floret consisting mainly of a tube, with small or inconspicuous limb; *spec.* to such florets in a composite flower (opp. to LIGULATE).

1776 J. LEE *Introd. Bot.* Explan. Terms 396 *Tubulosa*, Florets that are all tubular and equal. **1807** J. E. SMITH *Phys. Bot.* 457 Flowers..with united tubular anthers. **1877–84** F. E. HULME *Wild Fl.* p. vii, Primrose,—Calyx tubular, five-toothed. **1880** GRAY *Struct. Bot.* vi. §5 (ed. 6) 248 *Tubular*..strictly..denotes a gamophyllous perianth with limb inconspicuous..as in Trumpet Honeysuckle.

c. *Zool.* and *Anat.*

1794 SULLIVAN *View Nat.* II. 175 Those of the coral class, of a ramified and tubular form. **1802** BINGLEY *Anim. Biog.* (1813) I. 46 The tongue..in several [insects]..is fleshy and tubular. **1872** COUES *N. Amer. Birds* 29 Rounded nostrils may have a raised border or rim; when this is prolonged they are called tubular.

2. Relating to, or performed by means of, a tube.

a **1716** R. COTES *Lect.* (1738) A vj, Experiments for the most part tubular.

3. Constructed with or consisting of a number of tubes; as a ***tubular boiler*** (see also TUBULOUS 2 b and cf. *tubular-flued*).

1804 TROUGHTON in *Nicholson's Philos. Jrnl.* Dec. 225 (*title*) Description of a Tubular Pendulum. *Ibid.* 228 The first pendulum which I made of the tubular kind, had only three steel wires, and one tube above the bob. **1819** *Pantologia* s.v. *Pendulum*, We may date the invention of the tubular pendulum..about the year 1775. **1825** J. NICHOLSON *Operat. Mechanic* 527 Troughton's tubular-pendulum..is constructed of an exterior tube of brass,.. within which is another tube, and five brass wires in its belly. **1858** SIMMONDS *Dict. Trade*, *Tubular-boiler*, a boiler consisting of tubes. **1862** *Catal. Internat. Exhib.*, *Brit.* II. No. 6132 Metallic tubular bedsteads. **1877** KNIGHT *Dict. Mech.*, *Tubular Boiler*, a name properly applicable to a steam-boiler in which the water circulates in pipes,..the fire encircling them.

4. a. *Path.* (See quot.) ? *Obs.*

1822–7 GOOD *Study Med.* (1829) I. 287 Diarrhœa Tubularis. Tubular Looseness. The dejections consisting more or less of membrane-like tubes, whitish, viscous, and inodorous. *Ibid.* V. 49 Tubular diarrhœa.

b. *Phys.* and *Path.* Applied to a high-pitched respiratory murmur, like the sound made by blowing through a tube, heard normally over the trachea and bronchial tubes, and in diseased conditions over the lung.

1834 J. FORBES *Laennec's Dis. Chest* (ed. 4) 119 The stethoscope detected..no other respiratory sound, but that of a dry respiration, evidently tubular or bronchial. **1898** *Allbutt's Syst. Med.* V. 205 The breath-sounds are tubular or cavernous—the term 'tubular' is used here as synonymous with bronchial.

c. *Ophthalm.* Applied to a visual field which is restricted to a small area surrounding the fixation point; ***tubular vision*** = *tunnel vision* s.v. TUNNEL *sb.* 5.

1903 HANSELL & SWEET *Text-bk. Dis. of Eye* xviii. 488 When his sight had improved the visual fields were still contracted.., showing the so-called 'tubular' field of hysteria. **1927** H. M. TRAQUAIR *Introd. Clinical Perimetry* v. 49 A special form of concentric contraction is the 'tubular' field. The depression is severe and involves the whole field with the exception of an area surrounding the fixation point, producing a great and often extreme contraction... Such fields are obviously of functional origin. *Ibid.* xii. 222 Hysteria. The typical field change..is concentric contraction... The field is..tubular in type, a form which is necessarily of subjective origin. **1934** *Amer. Jrnl. Ophthalmol.* XVII. 384/2 (*heading*) Transient tubular vision in postencephalitic Parkinson's disease. **1956** *New Gould Med. Dict.* (ed. 2) 1319/2 *Tubular v[ision]*, a hysterical phenomenon in which the constricted visual field defies the laws of physical projection and maintains a uniform small size..; popularly called gun-barrel v[ision]; tunnel v[ision].

5. *Comb.*, as ***tubular-shaped***; *esp.* in *Bot.* with another adj., denoting a combination of tubular with another form, as ***tubular-campanulate***, ***-urceolate***; **tubular-flued**, having tubular flues.

1815 J. SMITH *Panorama Sc. & Art* II. 825 In a proper cylindrical, almost tubular-shaped vessel, two feet high. **1840** *Encycl. Brit.* (ed. 7) XX. 674/2 These tubular-flued boilers are at the present day extensively used. **1847** W. E. STEELE *Field Bot.* 118 [*Erica*] *Mediterranea.* Cor[olla] tubular-urceolate. **1870** HOOKER *Stud. Flora* 379 Polygonatum... Perianth tubular-campanulate.

B. *ellipt.* as *sb.* **1.** = *tubular bridge.*

1861 A. J. SYMONDS *Let.* 9 Aug. (1967) I. 303 We took a nice walk..to Bangor. We saw 2 trains go through the Tubular—one each way.

2. *pl.* = *tubular goods.*

1975 *North Sea Background Notes* (Brit. Petroleum Co.) 27 Most of each top deck will be occupied by a skid-mounted, electrically-driven drilling rig with appropriate storage for tubulars. **1979** *Shell Trade in Eastern Europe* (Shell Internat. Petroleum Co.) 5 Shell companies' purchases from countries in Eastern Europe include oil, chemicals and some metals and materials and equipment such as tubulars, rotary drilling hose, and items for sale in Shell filling-stations.

Hence **tubularity** (-'lærɪtɪ), the quality of being tubular, tubular form of structure; **'tubularly** *adv.*, in a tubular manner, so as to form a tube.

1746 DA COSTA in *Phil. Trans.* XLIV. 402 Such different Effects as Solidity and Tubularity. **1856** R. SHIELD *Pract. Hints Moths & Butterfl.* 74 In tubularly rolled leaves of honeysuckle we shall find the larvæ. **1890** *Manch. Exam.* 20 June, The special advantage of tubularity in bells seems to be that they are only heard in the immediate neighbourhood.

Tubularia (tjuːbjʊ'lɛərɪə). [See TUBULARIAN *a.* and *sb.*] = TUBULARIAN *sb.*

1912–13 A. S. PRINGLE-PATTISON *Idea of God* (1917) iv. 72 The Tubularia, a kind of sea-anemone, re-grows its flower-like head. **1924** *Glasgow Herald* 19 June 258/4 The tubularia and the sea-urchin. **1971** *Oxf. Bk. Invertebrates* 8/2 Tubularia, richly-coloured, with long, drooping polyps, is common locally and found at low tide under rocky overhangs.

tubularian (tjuːbjʊ'lɛərɪən), *a.* and *sb.* *Zool.* [f. mod.L. *Tubulāria* (in Linnæus, 1755, f. *tubulus*

TUBULE) + -AN.] **a.** *adj.* Belonging to the Linnæan genus *Tubularia*, the group *Tubulariæ*, or the family *Tubulariidæ*, of gymnoblastic Hydrozoa, in which the polyps are of tubular form, protected by a perisarc, with naked hydranths. **b.** *sb.* A tubularian hydroid. Also **tubularidan** (-ˈærɪdən) *a.* and *sb.* in same sense (*Cent. Dict.* 1891).

1856 GEO. ELIOT *Jrnl.* 8 May–26 June in *Lett.* (1954) II. 243 G...brought home several varieties of Polyps..—Tubularian, Plumularian and Sertularian. **1859** *Todd's Cycl. Anat.* V. 296/2 In the Tubularian Polyp the canal is modified. **1864** WEBSTER, *Tubularian*,..one of a family of polypoid acalephs, having simple or branched horny tubes, and terminating above in polyp-like extremities. **1883** *Science* I. 196/2 The Anthomedusæ (e.g., *Margelis*), from the tubularian hydroids. **1888** ROLLESTON & JACKSON *Anim. Life* 247 A Campanularian differs from a Tubularian in three important respects.

tubulary (ˈtjuːbjʊlərɪ), *sb. Zool.* [ad. mod.L. *Tubulāria*: see prec.] †**a.** ? A tubular species of coral. *Obs.* **b.** = TUBULARIAN *sb.*

1708 *Phil. Trans.* XXVI. 79 *Tubularia*, The Tubulary, or Lesser Pipe-shell. [**1753** CHAMBERS *Cycl. Supp.*, *Tubularia Fossilis*,..a species of coral found very often fossile in Germany and Italy, and composed of a great number of tubes.] **1876** *Beneden's Anim. Parasites* iv. 84 The tubulary observed by Gwyn Jeffreys..perhaps belongs to the same species.

† **ˈtubulary,** *a. Obs.* [f. as TUBULAR: see -ARY[2].] = TUBULAR.

1673 *Phil. Trans.* VIII. 6133 Lignous, consisting of Tubulary vessels. **1673** GREW *Anat. Trunks* I. iv. § 10 Sometimes the Pith is hollow or Tubulary. **1754** ELLIS in *Phil. Trans.* XLVIII. 506 That genus of corallines which I have called tubulary.

tubulate (ˈtjuːbjʊlət), *a. Nat. Hist.* [ad. L. *tubulāt-us*, f. *tubul-us* TUBULE: see -ATE[2].] Formed into or like a tube; tubular.

1753 CHAMBERS *Cycl. Supp.* App. s.v. *Petal*, The tubulate bell-fashioned flowers. **1760** J. LEE *Introd. Bot.* II. xxii. (1765) 124 Syngenesia... Characters of the Florets... Corolla..is either *tubulate*..; *ligulate* [etc.]. **1846** DANA *Zooph.* (1848) 151 A few tubulate pores over the surface. **1872** NICHOLSON *Palæont.* 74 The group of the Tubulate Corals is now much reduced in numbers.

tubulate (ˈtjuːbjʊleɪt), *v.* [f. as prec.: see -ATE[3]; cf. *tubulation*.] *trans.* **a.** To form into a tube. **b.** 'To furnish with a tube' (*Cent. D.* 1891).

1802 W. TAYLOR in *Monthly Mag.* XIII. 207 A wooden cullender..the orifices of which have in the center a wire or skewer, which tubulates the extruded dough [macaroni].

tubulated (ˈtjuːbjʊleɪtɪd), *a.* [f. L. *tubulāt-us* TUBULATE *a.* + -ED[1].]

1. Furnished with a tube; *esp.* of a retort or receiver: Having a short tube with a stopper (*tubulature* or *tubulure*), through which substances can be introduced.

1663 BOYLE *Usef. Exp. Nat. Philos.* II. v. vii. 173 This kind of Vessel is inferior to those tubulated Retorts. **1758** REID tr. *Macquer's Chym.* I. 176 Some retorts are also made with an opening on their upper side, like that of tubulated glass alembics,..closed.. with a glass stopple. **1831** BREWSTER *Nat. Magic* xiii. (1833) 343 To expose nitrate of ammonia in a tubulated glass retort to the heat of an Argand's lamp.

2. Formed into, or like, a tube; longitudinally perforated; tubular.

1713 DERHAM *Phys. Theol.* IX. i. 437 The Teeth are tubulated, for the Conveyance..of the Poyson into the Wound. **1753** CHAMBERS *Cycl. Supp.* s.v. *Tubulated Flower*, The tubulated floscules generally compose the disk [of *Compositæ*], and the ligulated ones the radius of the compound flowers. **1774** PRINGLE *Torpedo* 28 Those singular tubulated organs of the torpedo consist..of many bodies of a prismatic form. **1859** SEMPLE *Diphtheria* 96 Some slender and tubulated fragments of false members, mixed with mucus, were expelled.

So **tubulation** (-ˈeɪʃən) [ad. L. *tubulātiōn-em*, n. of action f. *tubul-us*, TUBULE, as if from **tubulāre*], the process of making or becoming tubular; **tubulature** (ˈtjuːbjʊlətjʊə(r)) [see -URE], the tube of a tubulated retort: = TUBULURE.

1656 BLOUNT *Glossogr.*, *Tubilation* [*ed.* **1674** *Tubulation*] (*tubulatio*), a making hollow like pipes. **1827** FARADAY *Chem. Manip.* vii. (1842) 201 The tubulature is safest when it is not much thicker than the retort at the part where they join, but should thicken upwards. **1855** *Q. Jrnl. Chem. Soc.* VII. 98 The liquid..was placed in a retort with a thermometer in the tubulature. **1866** *Reader* No. 163. 154/1 Pseudopodial tubulation.

tubule (ˈtjuːbjuːl). [ad. L. *tubul-us*, dim. of *tubus* TUBE; cf. F. *tubule* (Cotgr.).] A small tube; a minute tubular structure in an animal or plant body, as the *Malpighian* or *uriniferous tubules* of the kidney, the *dentinal tubules* of the teeth, etc.

1677 tr. *Groeneveldt's Treat. Stone* 19 The stone growing in the tubule or pelvis of the kidney. **1699** J. WOODWARD in *Phil. Trans.* XXI. 211 Reduced to single Corpuscles, all fit to enter the Tubules and Vessels of Plants. **1867** J. HOGG *Microsc.* II. i. 333 Contrivances to enable the tubules of the woody tissues to discharge their contents. **1869** HUXLEY *Phys.* xii. 322 The chief constituent of a tooth is dentine... It presents innumerable, minute, parallel, wavy tubules... The wider ends of these tubules open into the pulp cavity.

Hence **ˈtubulet** [-ET[1]], a minute tubule.

1826 KIRBY & SP. *Entomol.* III. xxxiii. 363 *Tubulus* (the Tubulet), The tube or retractile base of the *Rostellum*. *Siphunculus* (the Siphuncle), the real instrument of suction, which when unemployed is retracted within the tubulet.

tubuli- (ˈtjuːbjʊlɪ), combining form of mod.L. *tubulus* TUBULE, in several scientific terms. **ˈtubuliˌbranch** (-bræŋk), **ˌtubuliˈbranchian** *Zool.*, *sb.* a member of the *Tubulibranchiata*, branchiate gastropod molluscs with tubular shells, in Cuvier's classification; *adj.* = next. **ˌtubuliˈbranchiate**, *adj.* belonging to the *Tubulibranchiata*; *sb.* = prec. **ˈtubuliˌcole**, *Zool.* [L. *-cola* inhabitant], *sb.* a member of the *Tubulicolæ* in Cuvier's classification, a tubularian; *adj.* inhabiting a tubule; belonging to the *Tubulicolæ*. **ˌtubuliˈdentate** *a.*, *Zool.* [L. *dentātus* toothed], belonging to the *Tubulidentāta*, a group of edentates having compound teeth traversed by parallel vertical tubules. **tubuˈliferous** *a.*, *Nat. Hist.* [-FEROUS], bearing tubules; *spec.* having a tubular ovipositor, as the females of certain insects. **ˌtubuliˈfloral, -ˈflorous** *adjs.*, *Bot.* [L. *flōs, flōrem* flower], belonging to the division *Tubulifloræ* of Composite plants, having either all the florets, or those of the disk, tubular. **ˈtubuliˌform** *a.*, having the form of a tubule, tubular. **ˈtubuliˌpore**, *Zool.* [L. *porus* PORE], a polyzoan of the genus *Tubuˈlipora* or family *Tubuliˈporidæ*, having tubular calcareous calicles; also **tubuˈliporid** (*Funk's Stand. Dict.* 1895). **tubuˈliporoid** *a.* [see -OID], resembling, or having the characters of, the family *Tubuliporidæ* (*Cent. Dict.* 1891).

1855 T. WILLIAMS in *Ann. & Mag. Nat. Hist.* Ser. II. XVI. 408 The two preceding *Tubulibranchs. *Ibid.* 407 The *Tubulibranchiate genera. **1842** BRANDE *Dict. Sc.* etc., *Tubulibranchians... *Tubulicoles*, a name applied by Cuvier to a family of Polypes. **1822** J. PARKINSON *Outl. Oryctol.* 40 With *tubuliferous lobes. **1852** *Zoologist* X. 3405 They were certainly tubuliferous and not merely membranous appendages. **1882** M. T. MASTERS in *Jrnl. Bot.* XI. 39 The *Tubulifloral division of the Composites. **1891** *Cent. Dict.*, *Tubuliflorous. **1796** KIRWAN *Elem. Min.* (ed. 2) I. 30 **Tubuliform*, slender cylinders. **1877** HUXLEY *Anat. Inv. Anim.* vii. 381 Glands..divisible into five different kinds (aciniform, ampullate, aggregate, tubuliform, and tuberous). **1864** WEBSTER, *Tubulipore.

tubulin (ˈtjuːbjʊlɪn). *Biochem.* [f. TUBULE + -IN[1].] Either or both of two similar proteins that are the main constituent of microtubules.

1968 H. MOHRI in *Nature* 16 Mar. 1054/1 We believe that the microtubule constituent is a different protein, for which we propose the name 'tubulin'. **1977** *Jrnl. Protozool.* XXIV. 4/1 Microtubules are composed of 2 subunits, termed α and β tubulins, which form dimers and then polymers that are essentially infinitely long. **1978** *Bio Systems* X. 93/1 Tubulin..can undergo self-assembly in the absence of other macromolecules to form a microtubule. **1982** J. F. VAN PILSUM in T. M. Devlin *Textbk. Biochem.* xxi. 1042 Tubulin..comprises about 14% of the total protein found in mammalian brain.

† **ˈtubulite.** *Obs.* [ad. mod.L. *tubulītēs*, introduced by Gesner, *Tractat. Physic. de Petrificatis*, 1758.] A fossil or petrifaction of a tube or tubular shell occupied by an animal.

Gesner specified the tubular shell of the ship-worm, a lamellibranch mollusc, the coiled tube of a *Serpula*, the tubular shell of a *Dentalium*, all then regarded as 'worms'. But as these were the shells of different animals, the word was not permanently used.

1799 KIRWAN *Geol. Ess.* 236 Common marlites.. frequently [contain] shells, or petrifactions, ammonites, pectinites, tubulites. **1834** BOASE *Primary Geol.* 372 Those secondary strata, which contain tubulites and similar fossils.

tubulo- (ˈtjuːbjʊləʊ), used as combining form of mod.L. *tubulus* TUBULE, instead of the usual TUBULI-, either before a word of Greek derivation, or in adverbial relation to an adj. (see -O[1]); occurring in a few recent scientific terms. **ˈtubuloˌcyst** (-sɪst), 'any cystic dilatation of an obsolete canal or functionless duct' (Dorland *Med. Dict.* 1900–13). **ˌtubuloˈdermoid**, 'a dermoid tumor due to the persistence of a fetal tube' (*ibid.*). **ˌtubuloˈracemose** (-ˈræsiːməʊs) *a.*, 'both tubular and racemose, as, a *tuboloracemose* gland' (*ibid.*). **ˌtubuloˈsaccular** *a.*, 'both tubular and saccular' (*ibid.*). **ˌtubuloˈstriate** *a.*, 'having the surface striated with hollow ribs, as some brachiopod and molluscan shells' (*Cent. Dict. Suppl.* 1909).

c **1900** *Buck's Handbk. Med. Sc.* VII. 10 Tubulosaccular.

tubulose (ˈtjuːbjʊləʊs), *a.* [ad. mod.L. *tubulōsus*, f. L. *tubulus* TUBULE.]

1. = next, 1. Now *rare.*

1713 J. PETIVER in *Phil. Trans.* XXVIII. 203 Small tubulose Scarlet Flowers. **1752** J. HILL *Hist. Anim.* 268 The Trigla, with a bifid rostrum, and tubulose nostrils. **1826** KIRBY & SP. *Entomol.* IV. xlvi. 312 Tongue..Tubulose... When it..is long and tubular, and capable of inflation.

2. *Palæont.* Belonging to the *Tubulosa*, a group of palæozoic corals characterized by tubular thecæ.

1891 in *Cent. Dict.*

tubulous (ˈtjuːbjʊləs), *a.* [ad. mod.L. *tubulōsus*; cf. F. *tubuleux* (1771 in *Dict. Trévoux*).]

1. Having the form of a tube; = TUBULAR 1.

1664 POWER *Exp. Philos.* I. 4 The stings in all Bees are hollow and tubulous. **1755** *Gentl. Mag.* Jan. 8/2 The flower is red and tubulous. **1826** SAMOUELLE *Direct. Collect. Insects & Crust.* 23 A very short tubulous haustellum.

2. Containing or composed of tubes: = TUBULAR 3. **a.** *Bot.* (See quot.) *rare*[−0].

1864 WEBSTER, *Tubulose, Tubulous*... 2. Containing small tubes; composed wholly of tubulous florets; as, a tubulous compound flower.

b. Of a steam boiler: Having either fire-tubes or water-tubes.

1860 *Illustr. Lond. News* 5 May 422/3 Safety-boilers (Tubulous)..are now made with water fire-box. **1892** *Spectator* 19 Mar. 386/1 The tubulous boiler [for ships]..is growing in favour both in France and America.

Hence **ˈtubulously** *adv.*, in a tubulous form; **ˈtubulousness** (Bailey, 1727, vol. II).

1818 T. NUTTALL *Genera N. Amer. Plants* II. 80 Spatha tubulously cucullate.

tubulure (ˈtjuːbjʊl(j)ʊə(r)). [a. F. *tubulure* (Baumé, 1773), f. L. *tubul-us* TUBULE: see -URE.] A short tube, or projecting opening for the insertion of a tube, in a retort or receiver. (Cf. TUBULATED 1.)

1800 tr. *Lagrange's Chem.* I. 55 Put iron filings into a jar with two tubulures,..pour into the jar through the second tubulure diluted sulphuric acid. *Ibid.* 85 Fit to one of the tubulures of the bottle another tube. **1863** TYNDALL *Heat* i. 24 This glass bulb has three tubulures. **1883** R. HALDANE *Workshop Receipts* Ser. II. 46/1 The water enters the apparatus by the tubulure.

‖ **tubulus** (ˈtjuːbjʊləs). Pl. **tubuli** (-aɪ). [dim. of L. *tubus* TUBE.]

1. = TUBULE; in *Entom.* a tubular ovipositor.

[**1681** tr. *Willis' Rem. Med. Wks.* Vocab., *Tubuli*, small little pipes, the veins and very small arteries, or little hollow parts of the bowels so called. **1704** J. HARRIS *Lex. Techn.* I, *Tubuli Lactiferi*, certain Lactiferous..Pipes..through which [the milk] flows to the Nipples.] **1826** KIRBY & SP. *Entomol.* III. xxxiii. 390 *Tubulus*. A tubular ovipositor, consisting of several pieces often retractile within each other, like the tubes of a telescope. **1878** T. BRYANT *Pract. Surg.* I. 565 The tubuli serving to convey nutrition from the pulp to the periphery.

2. = TUBULURE.

c **1900** *Buck's Handbk. Med. Sc.* IV. 784 A small tubulated receiver, from the *tubulus* of which a tube..is in air-tight communication.

T.U.C. (ˌtiːjuːˈsiː). Also **TUC.** Abbrev. of *trade(s) union congress* s.v. TRADE-UNION, TRADES UNION b.

1910 W. J. DAVIS *Brit. Trades Unions Congress* I. 105 The Chairman of the Parliamentary Committee presented to the Secretary..an ornate address... The monogram 'T.U.C.'..with the motto..were..beautifully inscribed. **1926** *Manch. Guardian* 4 May 12/4 His Majesty's Government.. before it can continue negotiations, must require from the T.U.C...an immediate and unconditional withdrawal of the instructions for a general strike. **1947** *Radio Times* 2 May 16/3 George Woodcock, Assistant General Secretary of the T.U.C. **1955** *Times* 2 May 20/1 It is extraordinary that the T.U.C. should actually be advocating an increase in the tax on distributed profits. **1976** F. ZWEIG *New Acquisitive Society* II. i. 81 Three decades of incomes policies have enormously enhanced the status of the TUC and unions at large.

tuca(n: see TUSA.

tucan, var. TOUCAN.

tucatuca, -tucu: see TUCUTUCU.

† **tucet.** *Obs. rare*[−1]. [ad. L. *tūcētum*, *tuccētum* 'a kind of sausage or haggis' (Lewis and Short); cf. It. *tocchetti* 'minced meate, shread, sliced, or cut in collops' (Florio 1598), dim. f. *tocco* piece, scrap, collop.] A collop; a small piece of meat.

1653 JER. TAYLOR *Serm. for Year* I. xvi. 212 The pulse and the leeks, Lavinian sausages, and the Cisalpine tucets or gobbets of condited buls flesh [cf. *Schol. Persii* (Du Cange) Tucetum, bubula condita apud Gallos Cisalpinos condimentis crassis oblita et macerata].

tuch, obs. f. TUSH *int.*

† **tuch, tuche,** obs. ff. TOUCH (in quots. in sense 6 of TOUCH *sb.*, touchstone).

1591 HARINGTON *Orl. Fur.* XLII. lxviii, The Porch was all of Porpherie and Tuch. *a* **1647** HABINGTON *Surv. Worc.* in *Worc. Hist. Soc. Proc.* II. 410 Noble monuments..formed of Tuche, Marble, Alabaster and Rauns.

tuchas, var. TOCHUS.

tuchet, Sc. var. TEWHIT, the lapwing.

tucht, obs. Sc. f. TOUGH.

‖ **tuchun** (dudʒyn, ˈtuːtʃʊn). *Hist.* Also **Tuchun, Tu Chün.** [Chinese *dūjūn*, f. *dū* govern + *jūn* military.] In China at the time of the Three Kingdoms, the title of a military leader; later, in the early years of the Republic of China, the highest military leader in a province; a warlord.

1917 S. COULING *Encycl. Sinica* 213/2 During the disturbances of the last few years it has frequently happened that the post of Governor has been combined with that of 'Tu Chün'..or Military Governor. This latter is the principal military official of the province. **1920** *Nineteenth Cent.* Dec. 942 Nowadays, a *tuchun* or military governor,.. will address the foreigner in a patchwork of stilted literary phrases jumbled together. **1943** J. T. PRATT *War & Politics in China* xii. 194 After the death of Yuan Shih Kai China for several years presented a sorry spectacle of politicians quarrelling and Tuchuns waging civil war. **1977** J. CLEARY *High Road to China* i. 15 He was a Confucian, but he had a more immediate master, the *tuchun*, the war lord, in Hunan.

Hence **tu·chunate**, the rule of tuchuns, the office of tuchun.

1923 *Times Lit. Suppl.* 23 Aug. 558/1 At present the Tuchuns control their respective armies and are giving endless trouble. It would not, however, be sufficient to abolish the Tuchunate. A national army is necessary.

tuchus, var. TOCHUS.

tucia: see TUTTY.

tuck (tʌk), *sb.*[1] Forms: 4–7 tucke, 9 *Sc.* towk, 6– tuck. [f. TUCK *v.*[1], in various senses.]

1. A fold or pleat in drapery; †in quot. 1613, a plait of the hair (*obs.*); now *spec.* a flattened fold (or one of several parallel folds) in a garment, secured by stitching, either to shorten the article or for ornamentation. Also *fig.*

1387–8 T. USK *Test. Love* I. v. (Skeat) l. 132 That no iangling may greue the lest tucke of thy hemmes. **1591** PERCIVALL *Sp. Dict.*, *Alforza de vestido*, a plaite in a garment, a tucke. **1613** CHAPMAN *Maske Inns Court* A iv, Her tresses in tucks, braided with siluer. **1824** MACTAGGART *Gallovid. Encycl.*, *Towk*, a take up in ladies' clothing. **1861** *Gloucestershire Chron.* 21 Sept., 'What do you do when you have outgrown your clothes? You throw them aside, don't you?' 'Oh, no', replied the little girl, 'we let out the tucks'. **1878** 'MARK TWAIN' in *Atlantic* Jan. 17/2 We had an iron-clad chicken... He ought to have been put through a quartz mill until the 'tuck' was taken out of him. **1882** CAULFEILD & SAWARD *Dict. Needlework*, *Tucks*..are parallel folds of material, lying.. on any article of dress,..either for shortening a garment, or for the purpose of ornamentation. **1910** *N.Y. Evening Post* 10 Nov. 1 The sight of a wounded man lying on the pavement seemed to take the tuck out of the mob.

2. The gathering of the ends of the bottom planks of a ship under the stern; that part of the hull where the bottom planks are collected and terminated by the *tuck-rail* (see 9).

a **1625** *Nomenclator Navalis* (Harl. MS. 2301), *Ye Tuck*, the word is significant for it is (as you would saie) the verie gathering vp of the Ships quarter, vnder water. *a* **1687** PETTY *Treat. Naval Philos.* I. i, The..Stern-post, and Dead-rising up the Tuck. **1709** *Lond. Gaz.* No. 4510/7 The Hoy Burthen 9 or 10 Tun,..Moon shap'd in her Sleir, with a square Tuck. **1833** MARRYAT *P. Simple* xxvii, He's built like a Dutch schuyt, great breadth of beam, and very square tuck. *c* **1850** *Rudim. Navig.* (Weale) 157 The *tuck*, the aft-part of the ship where the ends of the planks of the bottom are terminated by the tuck-rail.

3. *Fishing.* Short for TUCK-NET.

1602 CAREW *Cornwall* I. 30 The Tucke..is narrower meashed, and..with a long bunt in the midst. **1865** COUCH *Fishes Brit. Islands* IV. 91 To take up the fish [pilchards].. the principal sean is left undisturbed, while the volyer passes within the enclosure and lays its sean, termed the Tuck, round the former on the inner side; and then the latter is drawn together so as gradually to contract the space and raise the fish to the surface.

4. A pluck, twitch, pull, tug; in quot. 1648 referring to the 'tucking' of freshmen at Oxford: see TUCK *v.*[1] 4 b. Now only *dial.*

1648 WOOD *Life* 15 Feb. (O.H.S) I. 139 Nothing was given him but salted drink..with tucks to boot. **1805** A. SCOTT *Poems* 105 (Jam.) Whan thou had fairly pass'd the clips, An' a' the taylor's tukes an' nips. **1887** *Suppl. to Jamieson*, *Took*, *touk*, *towk*, a tug, pluck, pull: 'He gied her sleeve a bit took'.

5. a. The thrusting in of the ends or edges of anything so as to secure them in position. Also with *in*.

1852 MRS. STOWE *Uncle Tom's C.* xiii, She ever and anon came to the bedside, and smoothed and arranged something about the bed-clothes, and gave a tuck here and there. **1865** DICKENS *Mut. Fr.* III. ii, The sentinel smartly giving his rolled shirt-sleeves an extra tuck on the shoulders. **1900** *Daily Mail* 5 Feb. 7/1 The guimpe or tiny tuck-in chemisette.

b. A flap on one cover of a book, which folds over and is tucked in a band or the like on the other cover, serving to keep the book closed.

1880 *Print. Trades Jrnl.* No. 32. 30 A double tuck, rendering a clasp of any description unnecessary. **1893** [see *tuck-cover* in 9].

6. a. *slang.* Usually *tuck-out* (also *tuck-in*): A hearty meal; esp. in school use, a feast of delicacies, a 'blow-out'.

1823 in *Spirit Pub. Jrnls.* 232 He, being inclined for a tuck out, repaired where he was likely to meet with oysters. **1836** E. HOWARD *R. Reefer* xxxviii, Tell my steward to give them a good tuck-out and a glass of grog. **1844** J. T. HEWLETT *Parsons & W.* xv, We meant to save all our money for the tuck. **1856** F. E. PAGET *Owlet Owlst.* 172, I was at the dessert; and a jolly good tuck I had, besides. **1886** T. HARDY *Mayor Casterbr.* ix, We will have a solid, staunch tuck-in.

b. Food, eatables; *esp.* delicacies, as sweet-stuff, pastry, jam, etc. (*school slang*). Cf. TUCKER *sb.*[1] 6.

1857 HUGHES *Tom Brown* II. v, The Slogger looks rather sodden, as if he didn't take much exercise and ate too much tuck. **1860** TYLOR *Anahuac* viii. (1861) 210 Ten or twelve of these little bowls on the table, each with a different kind of 'tuck' in it. **1899** E. PHILLPOTTS *Human Boy* IV. ii. 93 [He spoke] regretfully, as though he was being robbed of tuck.

c. A hearty appetite for food. *dial.*

1838 HOLLOWAY *Dict. Provincialisms* s.v., 'He has a pretty good Tuck of his own', means that a man is a great eater. *Hants. Sussex.* **1847–78** HALLIWELL, *Tuck* (1) to eat. Also, an appetite.

7. Phrases. **† a.** ***ducks and tucks*** (of uncertain meaning). *Obs.*

1598 BARCKLEY *Felic. Man* (1631) 621 Covet not to win estimation..by..Frierly ducks, and such like Italian and Spanish tricks and tuckes. **1609** SIR E. HOBY *Let. to T. H[iggons]* 106 *margin*, Leaue your ducks and your tuckes, and your apish toies, and serue God in spirit and truth.

b. ***nip and tuck***: see NIP *sb.*[1] 6.

8. In diving, gymnastics, etc., (the adoption of) a tuck position (see sense 9 below). Also, in downhill skiing, a squatting position (see quot. 1976).

1951 *Swimming* (Eng. Schools Swimming Assoc.) v. 81 The seat is drawn up and the head dropped slightly forward on the tuck, causing the body to spin. **1956** KUNZLE & THOMAS *Freestanding* vi. 81 The tuck and open out, as in the backward somersault, should be sharp and distinct movements. **1964** *Trampolining* ('Know the Game' Series) 31/1 It is better to learn the action slowly and then the tuck can be added later for effect and for faster rotation. **1976** *Webster's Sports Dict.* 464/1 *Tuck*.., a position in which the skier squats forward and holds his ski poles under his arms and parallel to the ground that is usually used to minimize wind resistance in downhill racing. **1981** 'E. LATHEN' *Going for Gold* xvii. 186 There was..no discontinuity between being earthborne and airborne, no jerking resolution of the hunched-over tuck into the aerial float high over the heads of the spectators. *Ibid.* xxi. 232 Tilly..hunched into the tightest tuck that Dick had ever seen, increased her speed to flat-out downhill velocity.

9. *attrib.* and *Comb.* (some f. the verb-stem): **tuck-basket**, a basket used in dipping the fish from the tuck-net; **tuck-boat**, in seine-fishing, a boat which carries the tuck-net; **tuck box**, a box for storing eatables etc., esp. at a boarding-school (see sense 6); **tuck-comb** *U.S.* = *tucking-comb* s.v. TUCKING *vbl. sb.*[1] 5; **tuck-cover** (see 5 b); **tuck-creaser**, **tuck-folder**, an attachment in a sewing-machine which marks the line of, or folds down, the next tuck in readiness for stitching (Knight *Dict. Mech.* 1877); **† tuck-hole**, a hole in a ploughshare by means of which it is hooked to the beam (cf. TUCK *v.*[1] 8, quot. 1733); **tuck-hunter**, one in search of a feast; **tuck-joint**, a joint in tuck-pointing (see TUCK-POINT); **tuck-marker** = *tuck-creaser*; **tuck-plate**, in an iron ship, a curved plate of the hull at the point where the stern-post is bolted to the transom-frame: cf. sense 2; **tuck position**, in diving, gymnastics, etc., a position in which the thighs are pulled close to the chest, the knees bent, and the hands clasped round the shins; **tuck-rail**: see quot.; **tuck-seine** = TUCK-NET; **tuck-stitch**, a stitch used in making a tuck; also *attrib.*; so **tuck-stitched** *a.* Also TUCK-MILL, -NET, -POINT, -SHOP.

1883 *Fisheries Exhib. Catal.* (ed. 4) 127 *Tuck basket for taking fish out of seine. **1855** J. R. LEIFCHILD *Cornwall Mines* 15 The '*tuck boat then makes the inner circuit of the 'seine', the smaller net being dropped overboard as she goes. **1934** I. W. HUTCHISON *North to Rime-Ringed Sun* xviii. 207 *Tuck-boxes were then opened and supper cooked and demolished. **1978** G. GREENE *Human Factor* II. ii. 70, I used to steal out at night from my dormitory and take him tins of sardines from my tuck-box. **1824** *Tuck comb [see SIDE-COMB]. **1870** E. EGGLESTON *Queer Stories* viii. 63 Sukey's way of doing up her hair in a great knot, behind, with an old-fashioned tuck comb. **1893** *Westm. Gaz.* 24 June 7/2 With *tuck cover (like pocket-book), and flap and pencil. **1805** R. W. DICKSON *Pract. Agric.* I. Pl. v. 40 Heel to *tuck hole of share—2 ft. 6½ in... Tuck hole to point of share—8¾ in. **1840** A. BUNN *Stage* I. xii. 295 Nothing can stop the mouth of a *tuck-hunter. **1879** *Cassell's Techn. Educ.* IV. 226 Rough arches..finished off with..a '*tuck joint'. This consists in marking the divisions by a neatly raised line of fine white plaster. **1877** KNIGHT *Dict. Mech.*, **Tuck-marker*,..also known as a tuck-creaser, for making a crease on goods as a guide for width in making the next fold. **1931** *Morning Post* 7 Aug. 14/2 All you have to do is hang on to your '*tuck', or 'balled-up' position a little longer. **1964** *Trampolining* ('Know the Game' Series) 32/2 Allow knees to bend to give a loose tuck position here and this helps to speed rotation. **1974** *Encycl. Brit. Macropædia* XVII. 864/1 In the tuck position, the body is gathered tightly into a ball with the hands grasping the shins firmly. *c* **1850** *Rudim. Navig.* (Weale) 157 **Tuck-rail*, the rail which..forms a rabbet for the purpose of caulking the butt ends of the planks of the bottom [see sense 2]. **1825** *Encycl. Lond.* XX. 435/1 [In pilchard fishing] three boats belong to each sean; the first and largest is called the sean-boat... The next boat is called the vollier (follower).., and carries another sean, called the *tuck-sean, which is about 100 fathoms long, and 18 deep... The third boat is called the lurker. **1874** [see SEINE *sb.*[1] β]. **1926** J. CHAMBERLAIN *Hosiery, Yarns & Fabrics* vi. 121 The *tuck-stitch is a defect in the plain fabric, but if produced systematically, forms many classes of designs. **1971** *Guardian* 7 Sept. 9/1 Tuck-stitch slipover vest in lambswool. **1922** JOYCE *Ulysses* 171 In *tuckstitched shirt sleeves.

tuck (tʌk), *sb.*[2] *arch.* and *dial.* Chiefly *Sc.* (tuk). Forms: 5 tuk, 6 tuicke, 6–9 touk, 8 tuke, 8–9 took, 6– tuck. [f. TUCK *v.*[2]: cf. Pr. *toco*, It. *tocco* 'a stroke or knock, also a stroke of a bell or clocke', f. *toccare* 'to touch, hit, to smite, strike' (Florio).]

† 1. A blast of a trumpet. *Obs. rare*[−1].

c **1400** *Destr. Troy* 7107 With the tuk of a trump, all his tore knightes He assemblit full sone.

2. A blow, a stroke, a tap; esp. in ***tuck of drum***.

a **1500** *Battle of Harlaw* xv. in *Sel. Coll. Sc. Ballads* (1790) III. 17 With trumpets and with tuicke of drum. **1513** DOUGLAS *Æneis* VIII. iv. 119 Hercules it smyttis wyth a mychty touk Apon the richt half, for to mak it jouk. **1640–1** *Kirkcudbr. War-Comm. Min. Bk.* (1855) 23 Within eight days efter intimatione be maid thairof, aither at the severall merkat crocess, or by touk of drume, or by advertisement. **1710** RUDDIMAN *Douglas' Æneis* Gloss., *Touk*, stroak, blow, ..a touch, pull; *as to take a touk of any thing*, i.e. have a touch at it. **1761** in *St. Andrews Citizen* 21 Mar. (1903), Published through the city by took of drum. **1818** SCOTT *Hrt Midl.* xii, An open convocating of the king's lieges..by touk of drum. **1891** *N.W. Devon Gloss.*, *Tuck*, a blow.

b. *fig.* or allusively.

1825 CARLYLE *Schiller* App. (1845) 259 Schubart was happy to evacuate Munich without tuck of drum. **1878** STEVENSON *Inland Voy.* 85 Wherever death..sounds his own potent tuck upon the cannons.

† 3. (?) A kiss. *Obs. rare.*

1611 COTGR., *Bouquer*, to take, or giue a tucke, or kisse.

tuck (tʌk), *sb.*[3] *arch.* Forms: 6 **toke, tocke, touke,** *Sc.* **towk, 6–7 tucke, (7 took, touk, tuke), 7– tuck.** [app. ad. F. *estoc* in same sense, in OF. and Norm. dial. *étoc* = Pr. *estoc*, It. *stocco*, ad. Ger. *stock* stick.] A slender, pointed, straight, thrusting sword; a rapier. Also *transf.* and *fig.*

1508 *Acc. Ld. High Treas. Scot.* IV. 122 Item for gilting and grathing of the lang towk,..iiij li. **1525** *Rutland MSS.* (1905) IV. 267 For the delyverance of a toke to my Lorde, xxd. *c* **1526** *Harl. MS. 4217* lf. 10 A longe Tocke iij square, the hafte of siluer. **1553** *Will of H. Cornish* (MS.), A gilte saddell..a touke, a dagger, stirropes spurres and a handgoune. **1566** DRANT *Horace, Sat.* I. A j b, The Tucke, the targe, the sheilde. **1625** DARCIE *Hist. Eliz.* III. 223 To fight..in Duels, with a Rapier called a Tucke, onely for the thrust. **1647–8** COTTERELL *Davila's Hist. Fr.* (1678) 25 Running him into the Visor with his Tuck. **1683** SIR J. TURNER *Pallas Armata* 176 Long Rapiers and Touks. **1688** R. HOLME *Armoury* III. 91/2 A Tuck [is] a four square Blade. *a* **1699** LADY HALKETT *Autobiog.* (1875) 63 Run through the body with a tuke. **1707** J. STEVENS tr. *Quevedo's Com. Wks.* (1709) 176 My Sword..was a stiff Tuck. **1770** LANGHORNE *Plutarch* (1879) II. 880/1 He appeared with a tuck, such as is used by robbers. **1826** SCOTT *Woodst.* i, He wore..a tuck, as it was then called, or rapier. **1885** *Harper's Mag.* Mar. 656/1 The..'tuck' or 'rapier' has been refined into the *épée* or duelling sword.

b. *attrib.* and *Comb.*, as ***tuck-sheath***; **tuck-cane**, a cane in which a tuck or rapier is carried, serving as a sheath; a sword-cane; **tuck-fish**: see quot.; **tuck-stick** = *tuck-cane*.

1700 S. L. tr. *Fryke's Voy. E. Ind.* 160, I had a *tuck Cane in my hand. **1785** TRUSLER *Mod. Times* II. 18, I..never went out afterwards, but with a tuck cane and a brace of pistols loaded. **1681** GREW *Musæum* I. v. i. 86 The Head of the *Tuck-Fish... The Snout is not so flat as in the Rapier-fish, but thicker and rounder, more like a Tuck, from whence I take leave to name it. **1506–7** *Acc. Ld. High Treas. Scot.* III. 250 Tua *towk schethis. **1765** *Lond. Chron.* 19 Dec. 588 The master run the apprentice through the body with a *tuck-stick, which killed him.

tuck (tʌk), *v.*[1] Forms: α. 1 **túcian, túciȝan; 3–5 tuke, 4 touk, 5 touke, 5–6 toke, 7** *Sc.* **towk.** β. **5 tokke, 5–6 tukke, tuk, 6–7 tucke, 5– tuck.** [The forms of this verb fall into two distinct groups; the development of the senses also offers difficulties. The α-forms (with long vowel or diphthong) belong to senses 1 and 2 and the earlier quots. under 3; the β-forms (with short vowel) to the rest of sense 3 and all the other senses, beginning in 14th c. in senses 4, 7, and occurring in 15th c. in sense 6 (and in one or two later instances in sense 2). The latter appear to correspond to MLG. *tucken*, *tocken* to draw, pull sharply or forcibly, MDu. *tocken*, *tucken*, OHG. *zocchôn*, *zucchen* to move or remove with a jerk, snatch away, pluck, pull, mod.Ger. *zucken* to jerk, tuck, tug, *das schwert zücken*, to draw the sword. The shortening of the *ū* in OE. *túcian*, early ME. *tuke*, etc. to *u* (ʌ) in *tuck* is notable, but is paralleled by that of OE. *súcan* to SUCK; cf. also DUCK *v.* from ME. *dūke*(*n*.]

† 1. a. *trans.* To afflict by way of punishment; to punish, chastise; to ill-treat, torment. *Obs.*

c **888** K. ÆLFRED *Boeth.* xxxviii. §7 Lustlice hi woldon lætan þa rican hi tucian æfter hiora aȝnum willan. *a* **1000** *Boeth. Metr.* xxiv. 60 Unrihtwise eorðan cyningas..ðe þis weriȝe folc wyrst tuciað. *c* **1000** ÆLFRIC *Judg.* xv. 8 He.. heora fela ofsloh and to sceame tucode. *c* **1000** —— *Saints' Lives* xxiii. 715 Swingan and to ealre sorȝe tuciȝan. *c* **1200** *Trin. Coll. Hom.* 21 His heued [was] heled mid þornene crune and on fele wise [he was] rewliche tuked. *a* **1225** *Ancr. R.* 366 He..was..so scheomeliche ituked. *c* **1230** *Hali Meid.* 17 Leccherie..tukeð hire [maidenhood] al to wundre & þreat to done hire schome.

b. *intr. Obs.*

a **1250** *Owl & Night.* 63 Þu tukest wroþe & vuele Hwar þu myht ouer smale vowele.

† 2. *fig.* To reprove, check, rebuke, find fault with; to upbraid, reproach. *Obs.*

In quot. 1584 with *up* (but sense doubtful).

a **1225** *Leg. Kath.* 550 He tukeð ure godes to balewe & to bismere. *a* **1225** *Ancr. R.* 316 Þet is tocne of hatunge þet men tukeð to wundre þet þing þet me hateð swuðe. **1584** B. R. tr. *Herodotus* II. 99 The vassals hauing ended their speeche, Protheus turned hymselfe to Alexander, and tucked hym vp with thys rounde tale. **1600** in *Maitland Club Misc.* (1843) III. 102 Towking outragious countenance. **1616** *Orkney Witch Trial* in Rogers *Soc. Life Scot.* (1886) III. 298 She haid tuckit him and given him mony injurious wordis. **1651** R. BAILLIE *Lett. & Jrnls.* (1841) III. 163 His brother Adam Wilson towks him, calling him a fool and bidding him desist.

3. To dress or finish (cloth) after it comes from the weaver, esp. to stretch on tenters; cf. TUCKER *sb.*[1] 1; also *intr.* to work as a tucker. Now *local.*

α. [**1273**: implied in TUCKER *sb.*[1] 1.] **1377** LANGL. *P. Pl.* B. XV. 447 Cloth þat cometh fro þe weuyng is nouȝt comly to were, Tyl it is fulled vnder fote or in fullyng stokkes, Wasshen wel with water and with taseles cracched, Ytouked, and ytented. **1459** in *10th Rep. Hist. MSS. Comm.* App. V. 300 It was ordayned that no woman sholde touke in no manere place aforstrete within the saide citie. **1467–8** *Rolls of Parlt.* V. 621/2 Yef..the seid Cloth [were] toked and fulled within this your Reame, your Highnes shuld have the Custume and Awnage for the same. **1513–14** *Act 5 Hen. VIII*, c. 2 Noo person make noo such Clothys..to sell without that he be whan he is rawe redy to be tokyd of the brede of a yerde and half quarter.

β. **1621** in Harding *Hist. Tiverton* (1817) II. 181 Not.. white weavers or tuckers that make white kersies, but..such as weave and tuck upon coloured mixed kerseys. **1780** A. YOUNG *Tour Irel.* II. 34 A mill for milling, tucking, &c. broad cloths. **1837** WHITTOCK, etc. *Bk. Trades* (1842) 255 After the process of fulling and dyeing, the dressed cloths are..pricked on the tenter hooks and stretched to their utmost bearing... This is considered as *tucking*, in the west of England. **1882** JAGO *Cornw. Gloss.*, *Tucking*, working in a fulling-mill.

4. a. †To tug at; to snatch, pluck, pull; to gather (herbs, fruit, etc.) (*obs.*); now *spec.* to pluck or pull the loose hay from the sides of (a new rick) (*dial.*).

13.. *K. Alis.* 2305 (Bodl. MS.), Als he hit [his weapon] tukked [*v.r.* toggid], out to habbe, Philot hym ȝaf anothere dabbe. **1625** T. GODWIN *Moses & Aaron* III. iii. 125 They held it unlawfull, to roste an apple, to tucke an herbe, to climbe a tree, to kill or catch a flea. **1658** tr. *Porta's Nat. Magic* IV. xi. 136 You must tuck them off the Tree with your hand. *Ibid.* [see TUCKER *sb.*[1] 2]. **1794** P. FOOT *Agric. Middlesex* 57 The hay-farmer pays great attention to have the stack well tucked and thatched. **1888** ELWORTHY *W. Somerset Word-bk.* s.v., Now, Bob, don't bethink thy vingers, tuck'n in tight, mind—i.e. pull it out until you get to the solid mass.

†b. See quot. 1647. *Obs.*

c **1640** SHAFTESB. in *Remin. Oxford* (O.H.S.) 37, I caused that ill custom of tucking freshmen [at Oxford] to be left off. **1647** WOOD *Life* Dec. (O.H.S.) I. 134 If any of the freshmen came off dull, or not cleverly, some of the forward or pragmatical seniors would 'tuck' them, that is, set the nail of their thumb to their chin, just under the lower lipp, and by the help of their other fingers under the chin, they would give him a mark, which sometimes would produce blood.

5. *Fishing.* To take the fish from (the seine) by means of a *tuck-net*; also with the fish as object.

1785 *Act 26 Geo. III*, c. 26 §11 (Cod fishing) It shall not be lawful.. to use..any Sean or Net..for the Purpose of catching Cod Fish by hauling such Sean or Net on Shore, or tucking such Sean or Net into any Boat or Boats, the Scale or Mesh of which said Sean or Net shall be less in Dimension than Four Inches. **1857** *Morning Chron.* 28 Aug. (Cassell's), 185 hogsheads [of pilchards] were tucked on Sunday. **1866** *Standard* 3 Oct. 3/4 All these [i.e. seines] have enclosed fish, which are being tucked, and many thousands of hogsheads are expected to be landed. **1879** *Encycl. Brit.* IX. 254/2 'Tucking' the fish..is performed with the tuck-sean,..and as it is hauled in, the foot of the bunt is raised so as to bring the fish to the surface, whence they are dipped out in large baskets and put into attendant boats to be carried on shore.

6. a. To pull or gather up in a fold or folds; to fold or turn up; *esp.* to gird up (a garment, etc.). Usually const. *up.*

c **1440** *Promp. Parv.* 504/2 Tukkyn vp, or stykkyn vp (*K.* tuckyn or stychyn up clothis),..*suffarcino.* **1513** DOUGLAS *Æneis* V. x. 21 Thair haris all war tukkit wp on thar croun. **1523** FITZHERB. *Husb.* §151 Theyr cotes be so syde [= long] that they be fayne to tucke them vp whan they ryde. **1590** SPENSER *F.Q.* III. ix. 21 Her well-plighted frock, which she did won To tucke about her short when she did ryde. **1687** A. LOVELL tr. *Thevenot's Trav.* I. 156 They are tuck'd aside, that the Diamonds may not be covered. **1756** MRS. CALDERWOOD in *Coltness Collect.* (Maitl. Cl.) 218 All the Capucines..were marching in sixes and sevens with their gowns tucked up, great fat carles. **1835–6** *Todd's Cycl. Anat.* I. 479/1 The intestines are..tucked up into folds and sacs. **1840** DICKENS *Old C. Shop* iii, He tucked up his sleeves and squared his elbows. **1880** 'OUIDA' *Moths* I. 77 The stout north countrywoman tucked up her petticoats, and began to climb up the steep path with a will. **1885** *Cornh. Mag.* Mar. 283 Priests sitting with their legs tucked up tailor-wise, in the attitude of Buddha.

b. To put a tuck or tucks in; to shorten or ornament with tucks.

1626 *Vestry Bks.* (Surtees) 181 Item for tuckeinge up the surples, xij d. **1709** [see TUCKED *ppl. a.* 1]. **1873** ELIZ. PHELPS *Trotty's Wedding Tour* 126 She tucked the pantalets, darned the stockings.

7. a. To pull or gather up and confine the loose garments of; to gird (a person) *up.* Chiefly in *pa. pple.* Now *rare.*

c **1385** CHAUCER *L.G.W.* 982 (*Dido*) Saw ȝe..Onye of myne susteryn..I-tukkid [*v.r.* Itucked] vp with arwis in hire cas? *c* **1386** —— *Sompn. T.* 29 With scrippe and tipped staf, ytukked [*v.rr.* tucked, tukked, tokked] hye In euery hous, he gan to poure and prye. *c* **1440** *Generydes* 4397 Tokkyd vppe she [the queen] was well fro the grounde. *c* **1450** in Aungier *Syon* (1840) 342 Some of the brethren tukke the mynysters..in the begynnyng of masse, and also tuk the confessour whan he taketh the cope aboute the ende of the same masse. **1483** CAXTON *Gold. Leg.* 160/2 A pylgrym tucked and made redy for to goo hastely ouer see. **1558** PHAER *Æneid* I. Bj, Tukt she was that naked was her knee. **1566** DRANT *Horace, Sat.* viii. D viij b, Bare foote, hyr lockes about her heade, ytuckde in pukishe frocke. **1727** [see TUCKED *ppl. a.* 1]. *a* **1801** BLOOMFIELD *Rural T., Rich. & Kate* xi, Who, snug tuck't up, walk'd slow behind. **1841** ORDERSON *Creol.* ix. 96 She was..'tucked up', in the indecorous manner of those days.

b. To shorten or short-coat (an infant). Usually with *up. dial.*

1888 ELWORTHY *W. Somerset Word-bk.* s.v., I was a-frightened to zee the cheel a-tuck'd up a' ready. **1901** E. PHILLPOTTS *Striking Hours* 135 Afore I was tucked-up, or, as you might say, 'short-coated', her went..down to Cornwall. *a* **1905** in *Eng. Dial. Dict.* s.v., Tuck it in May, Tuck it away.

c. *fig.* To cramp or hamper by lack of space, time, or means. See also TUCKED *ppl. a.* 2 c.

1886 *Field* 13 Feb. 179/3 They [fox-hunters] have been playing the old game of skirting, eventually to find themselves fairly tucked up by wire-fencing. **1887** [see TUCKED *ppl. a.* 2 c]. **1890** 'R. BOLDREWOOD' *Col. Reformer* xxvii, In England you have your bad seasons..; and the poor man.. gets tucked up a bit.

8. To thrust or put away (an object) into a close place where it is snugly held or concealed. Freq. with *away*; also *fig.*; esp. to hit (a ball) to the desired place.

1587 TURBERV. *Trag. T.* (1837) 195 Shee tuckt it [the head] in her apron close. **1621–3** MIDDLETON & ROWLEY *Changeling* IV. i, Folio forty-five, here 'tis, The leaf tuck'd down upon it. **1710** STEELE *Tatler* No. 164 ¶6, To carry Pistols about me, which I have always tuck'd within my Girdle. **1733** W. ELLIS *Chiltern & Vale Farm.* 321 The Sharr also is tuck'd up to the Beam by an Iron-hook. **1781** COWPER *Truth* 147 The shivering urchin..Carries her Bible tucked beneath his arm. **1861** GEO. ELIOT *Silas M.* i, Finding the well-known bag, empty, tucked behind the chest of drawers. **1874** BURNAND *My time* xxxii. 329 He tucked his wife's arm under his own. **1912** W. B. SELBIE *Nonconformity* xii. 225 The little old meeting-houses tucked away in back streets gave place to large and commodious buildings. **1936** J. BUCHAN *Island of Sheep* v. 99 My first business must be to tuck him away comfortably somewhere out of the road. **1958** *Observer* 6 July 24/4 There was greater punch in Miss Gibson's game once she had the first set safely tucked away. **1959** *Times* 29 May 4/6 His low forehand, as he tucks the ball away, is a special weapon of execution. **1966** *Listener* 12 May 702/3 What a pity that it should be tucked away into that most unlikely of all listening hours, the end of a Saturday evening. **1977** *Times* 7 Feb. 7/3 Tueart..outpaced a scattered defence and efficiently tucked away a rebound after Shilton had superbly blocked his first attempt.

9. a. To thrust in the edge or end of (anything pendent or loose) so as to retain or confine it; now *esp.* to turn in the edges of (bed-coverings or the like) under the bed or its occupant. With various advbs., esp. *in, up.*

1635 QUARLES *Embl.* III. ix. 37 Snares tuck thy bed. **1697** DAMPIER *Voy.* I. xii. 327 They gather it in their Hands,.. tucking in the twisted part between their Waste and the edge of the Petticoat, which keeps it close. **1746** JAMESON in A. McKay *Hist. Kilmarnock* (1880) 83 Tucking his shirt under the waistcoat, that it might not obstruct the blow. **1843** SIR C. SCUDAMORE *Med. Visit Gräfenberg* 102 Early in the morning, the bed-clothes were tucked up tight about him, so as to retain the animal heat. **1852** THACKERAY *Esmond* III. iii, A nymph that can tuck my bed-clothes up. **1905** ELIN. GLYN *Viciss. Evang.* 169 Mr. Carruthers..tucked his sable rug round me.

b. With the person as object. Also *fig.*

1692 LOCKE *Educ.* §22 To have his Maid tuck him in warm. **1739** 'R. BULL' tr. *Dedekindus' Grobianus* 225 The Muse would willingly..tuck you in, and then put out the Light. **1809** MALKIN *Gil Blas* VII. xvi. ¶4 The nurse forced me under the bedclothes again, and tucked me up. **1854** EMERSON *Lett. & Soc. Aims, Resources* Wks. (Bohn) III. 199 Nature keeps the lakes warm by tucking them up under a blanket of ice.

c. *intr.* To draw together, contract, pucker.

1797 *Encycl. Brit.* (ed. 3) XVIII. 102/2 When an ulcer becomes foul,..the edges of it, in process of time, tuck in. **1899** *Allbutt's Syst. Med.* VI. 834 Another symptom..is a tucking-up of one or both of the upper lids.

10. *slang.* **a.** *trans.* To consume, swallow (food or drink); to 'put away', 'put out of sight'.

1784 R. BAGE *Barham Downs* I. 191 We will dine together; tuck up a bottle or two of claret. **1833** MARRYAT *P. Simple* xi, Now that I've cured you, you'll be tucking all that into your own little breadbasket. *a* **1845** BARHAM *Ingol. Leg., House-warming*, The strawberries..Which our Grandmother's Uncle tuck'd in like a pig. **1861** HOLLAND *Less. Life* xii. 144 Let's go over and see if we can't tuck away some of that grub.

b. *intr.* To feed heartily or greedily; esp. with *in, into.*

1810 [see TUCKING *vbl. sb.*[1] 4]. **1838** DICKENS *Nich. Nick.* xxxix, If you'll just let little Wackford tuck into something fat. **1860** THACKERAY *Round. Papers* vii, There is Rasherwell 'tucking' away in the coffee-room. **1887** EDNA LYALL *Knight-Errant* xv. (1889) 129 Always in at dinner-time and to be found at odd hours tucking in.

†c. *trans.* To distend with food; to fill *out. Obs. rare*[−1].

1824 in *Spirit Pub. Jrnls.* (1825) 304 He had been 'Taking his ease in his inn',..and feeling himself comfortably tucked out, he wished to bolt.

11. a. *slang.* To hang (a criminal); usually with *up.*

a **1700** B. E. *Dict. Cant. Crew, Tuck't*, Hang'd. **1738** tr. *Guazzo's Art Conversation* 231, I expect..to see him tucked up to a Gibbet. **1755** H. WALPOLE *Lett.* (1846) III. 142 Poor Fanny! I always thought she would play till she would be forced to tuck herself up! **1825–9** MRS. SHERWOOD *Lady of Manor* V. xxix. 100, I wish some one had tucked him up before he had made acquaintance with this house.

b. To hang (a bell) high in the stock.

1860 BECKETT *Clocks, Watches*, etc. (ed. 4) 424 A large bell may be tolled easily by one man, if it is properly hung, though not if it is 'tucked up in the stock'.

12. = TUCK-POINT *v.*

1803 *Usef. Proj.* in *Ann. Reg.* 829/2 Tucking and pointing all stone and brick works that require proof against water and damp.

tuck (tʌk), *v.*[2] Now *dial.* Chiefly *Sc.* (tuk). Forms: 4–5 **tukke**, 5 **tuke**, 5–7 **touk**, 6 **tuik**, 7 **touck, -e, towke**, 9 **took, towk**, 7– **tuck.** [a. ONF. *toker, toquer, touker* (*a* 1400 in Godef. *Compl.*) to touch, strike, northern form of *toucher* to TOUCH, = Prov., Sp., Pg. *tocar*, It. *toccare* 'to touch, hit, to smite, strike' (Florio): cf. also TOCSIN.]

1. *trans.* and *intr.* To touch (*rare*); to beat the drum; also *intr.* of a drum: To sound.

13.. *E.E. Allit. P.* B. 1414, & ay þe nakeryn noyse, notes of pipes, Tymbres & tabornes, tukket [*MS.* tulket] among. *a* **1400–50** *Alexander* 2427 þe Tebies tukkid [*MSS.* tulkid, -yd] vs with tene, a-tired þam in armes. *a* **1500** *Battle of Harlaw* xviii. in *Sel. Coll. Sc. Ballads* (1790) III. 17 The trumpet sounds, The dandring drums aloud did tuik. **1629** *Reg. Privy Council Scot.* Ser. II. III. 5 The said James.. caused ring the kirk bell and towke thair drwm. **1642** *Burgh Rec. Glasgow* 12 Feb. (1876) 437 Ordains the drummers to touk throughe the toun. *a* **1670** SPALDING *Troub. Chas. I* (1850) I. 202 Trvmpettis soundis and drumis tovkis. **1887** *Suppl. to Jamieson, Took, touk, towk*, to strike, beat, blow, tuck; as, 'to took the drum'.

†2. *trans.* To sound a blast on (a trumpet); to blow *up. Obs. rare.*

a **1400–50** *Alexander* 773 With þat þai tuke vp [*v.r.* tukkyn vp] þaire trompes.

3. *intr.* Of the wind: To blow in gusts. *dial.*

1833 D. M'KAY in *Rec. & Bards Angus & Mearns* (1897) 301, I have wondered full oft as it [the hurricane] tookit and blew, If ever its sughin was leerie to you. **1893** *Wiltshire Gloss.* s.v., 'The wind is so tucking to-day', i.e. gusty, veering.

† tuck, tucka, tucke, obs. ff. TOQUE, in sense of 'a kerchief worn on the head', or 'a turban'.

1505 in *Facsimiles Nat. MSS.* I. (1865) 92 And as to hir forehed, the heighte or the breid therof, we cowde not perfectly diserne, for the maner of the wereynge of the kerches or tuckas in that contry ys suche that a man cant not welle Iuge hit. **1553** A. JENKINSON *Voy. & Trav.* (Hakl. Soc.) I. 3 Vpon his head a goodly white tuck, containing in length by estimation fifteene yards. **1582** N. LICHEFIELD tr. *Castanheda's Conq. E. Ind.* I. iv. 14 Vpon their heads they weare a certeine kinde of tucks or kerchiefe somewhat wrought with silke and gold thrid.

†'tuckage. *Obs. rare*[−1]. [f. TUCK *v.*[1] + -AGE.] Tucking, cloth-dressing.

1612 STURTEVANT *Metallica* 46 Winde water milnes..for tuckeage, and fulleage of wollen cloath.

tuckahoe ('tʌkəhəʊ). *U.S.* Forms: 7 **tockwough, tockawhough, -waugh,** 8 **tuccaho,** 8–9 **tuckahoo,** 7– **tuckahoe.** [ad. Powhatan or Virginian (N. Amer. Indian) *tockawhoughe*, app. cognate with Mohegan *tquogh*, Shawnee *tukwhah*. Webster (1911) compares Natick *petukqunneg* cake of bread, f. *petukqui* round, Cree *pitikwaw* made round.]

1. A name applied by North American Indians (esp. of Virginia) to edible roots of various plants: see *Report of Smithsonian Inst.* 1881, pp. 687–701.

1612 CAPT. SMITH *Map Virginia* 22 In Iune, Iulie, and August they feede vpon the rootes of *Tockwough* [printed *-nough*], berries, fish and greene wheat. **1612** *Proc. Virginia* 87 in *Capt. Smith's Wks.* (Arb.) 155 Others would gather as much *Tockwough* roots in a day as would make them bread a weeke. **1662** *Laws of Virginia* cxxxvi. 77 The poor Indians, whom, the seating of the English, hath forced from their wonted Conveniences of..gathering Tuckahoe, Cortenions, and other Wild-Fruits. **1671** OGILBY *Amer.* 196 Their peculiar roots are the tockawaugh, good to eat [etc.].

a. Among these are or were the thick and starchy root-stocks of certain araceous plants, particularly *Peltandra undulata* or *Virginica* (formerly *Arum Virginicum*), the Arrow Arum, and *Orontium aquaticum*, the Golden-Club.

1613 PURCHAS *Pilgrimage* VIII. v. 635 [The aborigines of Virginia] haue two rootes;..the other called Tockawhough, growing like a flagge, of the greatnesse and tast of a Potato, which passeth a fierie purgation before they may eate it, being poison whiles it is raw. **1705** BEVERLEY *Virginia* III. iv. (1722) 153 A tuberous Root they call Tuckahoe, which while crude is of a very hot and virulent Quality: But they can manage..to make Bread of it. **1770** J. R. FORSTER *Kalm's Trav. N. Amer.* (1772) I. 225 To judge by these qualities the Tuckahoo may very likely be the Arum Virginicum.

b. Now app. restricted to an underground tuber-like production (*Pachyma Cocos*, Fries, *Lycoperdon solidum*, Clayton), prob. the sclerotium of some fungus, parasitic on tree-roots in the southern parts of North America, the affinities of which are uncertain. Also called *Indian bread, Indian loaf, Indian head*, and ***tuckahoe truffle***.

1731 CATESBY *Nat. Hist. Carolina*, etc. p. x, Indians also eat the earth nuts which they call tuccaho. **1782** T. JEFFERSON *Notes State Virginia* (1787) 58 Tuckahoe. *Lycoperdon tuber.* **1816** in *Massachusetts Spy* 23 Oct.

(Thornton), The name of Tuckahoe.. has also been applied to the Troffle. **1866** *Treas. Bot.*, *Tuckahoo*,.. a curious tuberous production,.. has been referred by Fries to the genus *Pachyma*.

2. A nickname for the lowlands of Virginia; also for an inhabitant of this district. *local U.S.*

1817 J. K. Paulding *Lett. fr. South* I. x. 112 The people [west of the Blue Ridge] call those east of the mountain Tuckahoes, and their country Old Virginia. **1835** *Lett. Virginia Springs* (Philad.) 16–17 (Thornton) [The Blue Ridge] divides the Ancient Dominion into two nations, called Tuckahoes and Quo'hees; the former inhabiting the lowland. **1848–60** Bartlett *Dict. Amer.* s.v., Tuckahoe is often applied to an inhabitant of Lower Virginia, and to the poor land in that portion of the State.

ˈ**tuck-away**, *a.* [f. the vbl. phr. *to tuck away*: see tuck *v.*[1] 8.] That may be tucked away.

1935 *Sun* (Baltimore) 9 Nov. 1/3 The clipper's spick-and-span tuckaway galley producing hot bouillon, fried chicken and fruit. **1968** *Harrods Christmas Catal.* 5/3 Satin evening pochette with gilt tuck-away chain handle. **1979** *Arizona Daily Star* 1 Apr. (Advt. Section) 9/3, 1968 International 18′ high cube van trucks with tuck away tailgates.

tucked (tʌkt), *ppl. a.* [f. tuck *v.*[1] (and *sb.*[1]) in various senses + -ed.]

1. Gathered or girded *up*, arranged in tucks or folds; †of a person: having the clothes girded up (*obs.*); shortened or ornamented with tucks; thrust or doubled in; poked *in* or *away* so as to be retained in position; enveloped, covered snugly *up*.

1530 Palsgr. 327/2 Tucked up as ones clothes is, *rebroucé*. **1582** Stanyhurst *Æneis* iii. (Arb.) 75, I knew theire tuckt-locks. **1709** Steele *Tatler* No. 30 ¶9 With blue and red Stockings in Morning; tuck'd Cravats, and Nightcap Wigs. **1727** Swift *City Shower* 37 The tuck'd-up semstress walks with hasty strides. **1823** Scott *Quentin D.* xxii, The butcher.. was distinguished by his tucked-up sleeves. **1883** 'Sylvia' *Lady's Guide Dressmaking* 107, 4 tucked flannel petti-coats. **1913** *Play Pictorial* No. 131. p. vi/1 A prettily tucked chemisette of soft French net. **1963** R. N. Frye *Heritage of Persia* v. 198 The nomadic background of the Parthians may be seen in some equestrian features of dress, such as leggings *cum* boots with tucked-in trousers.

2. a. *tucked up* (of a dog or horse): having the flanks drawn in from hunger, malnutrition, or fatigue; hence, tired out, exhausted. Cf. tucker *v.*[1], *tuckered*. *slang* and *dial.*

1845 Youatt *Dog* ii. 18 They generally are very thin,.. with sharp-pointed ears, deep chest, and tucked-up flanks. **1888** Elworthy *W. Somerset Word-bk.*, *Tucked up*, applied to animals, especially horses after hard riding—looking thin. Th' old mare's a bit a-tucked up. **1891** Kipling *Light that Failed* iii. 43 'You're looking tucked up', he concluded.

b. Said of a bell that is hung high in the stock.

1874 Beckett *Clocks, Watches*, etc. (ed. 6) 366 It is difficult to set a much tucked-up bell tolling, though easy to keep it up afterwards.

c. Hampered or cramped for lack of space, time, means, etc. *colloq.*

1887 Bury & Hillier *Cycling* iv. 189 A closely built fifty-eight inch racer will be noticeably too short in the reach for him, and he will feel that he is what cyclists call 'tucked up', 'cramped', or 'going short'. **1889** *N.W. Linc. Gloss.* s.v., We're terrible tucked up e' this little hoose... Oats is ripenin that fast we shall be tucked up for time to get 'em afoore thaay begins to shak. **1891** *Cent. Dict.* s.v., At Billiards the player is said to be tucked-up when his ball lies close under the cushion.

3. *Naut.* (in combination): Having a tuck (tuck *sb.*[1] 2) of a specified shape.

1867 Smyth *Sailor's Word-bk.* s.v. *Tuck*, The fir frigates of 1812–14 had flat, square transoms similar to boats, or heart-shaped. Hence our square-tucked frigates, brigs, &c.

tucker (ˈtʌkə(r)), *sb.*[1] Forms: 4 toukere, 5 tokker, (toucher), towkere, 5–6 towker, touker, toker, (6 towcker, toukar, toocker, tooker, tukkar), 6– tucker. [f. tuck *v.*[1] + -er[1].]

1. One whose occupation is the fulling and dressing of cloth; a fuller; a cloth-finisher. *Obs.* exc. *dial.* Perh. originally one who burled or teased the cloth.

tucker's earth, fuller's earth.

[**1273** *Hundred Rolls, Dorset*, Roger le Tukere. **13..** *Fine Rolls*, Nicholas le Tokere.] **1388** Wyclif *2 Kings* xviii. 17 The water cundijt of the hiȝere cisterne,.. in the weie of the fullere, [*gloss*] ethir toukere [1382 the fullers feeld]. *c* **1475** *Pol. Poems* (Rolls) II. 285 A ordynaunce, for spynners, carders, wevers, also, Ffor toukers, dyers, and schermyn. **1496** *Somerset Medieval Wills* (1901) 344 To my wevers and tokers thorow the towne xij d a pece. **1506** *Will of Abadam* (Somerset Ho.), Tucker's schers. **1545** Elyot, *Gnafos*, a tesyll, whiche toukars do vse. **1603** Holland *Plutarch's Mor.* 1231 [Crœsus] caught one of the nobles,.. and within a fullers mill all to beclawed and mangled him with tuckers cards and burling combs. **1610** W. Folkingham *Art of Survey* i. ii. 4 Tuckers or Fullers Earth. **1615** Brathwait *Strappado* (1878) 174 Where errant pedlers, mercinarie slaues, Tinkers and Tookers and such idle knaues. **1636** in E. Owen *Catal. MSS. relating to Wales in Brit. Mus.* (1908) 724 Ground for the erection of.. tentors or tucker's rackes. **1745** *De Foe's Eng. Tradesman* xx. (1841) I. 193 Cloth-workers, tuckers, and merchants. **1837** Whittock, etc. *Bk. Trades* (1842) 253 Wool could not be spun without being combed in oil; nor would it take the dye when woven, unless divested of the oil. This is the proper business of the Fuller; ..provincially called, the *Tucker*. **1888** Elworthy *W. Somerset Word-bk.*, *Tucker*, one who mills, or fulls and finishes cloth... Probably the entire finishing of the cloth, from the time it left the weaver, was performed by the tucker at the tucking-mills.

†**2.** An instrument for tucking or plucking; *pair of tuckers*, tweezers. *Obs. rare*$^{-1}$.

1658 tr. *Porta's Nat. Magic* iv. x. 133 Tuck away the dry, and withered, and rotten grapes with a pair of tuckers.

3. A piece of lace or the like, worn by women within or around the top of the bodice in the 17–18th c.; a frill of lace worn round the neck. *best bib and tucker*: see bib *sb.*[1] b.

1688 R. Holme *Armoury* iii. 17/1 A Pinner or Tucker, is a narrow piece of Cloth.. which compasseth the top of a Womans Gown about the Neck part. **1710** Lady Grisell Baillie *Househ. Bk.* (1911) 204 For musline for night cloathes, ruffles, tuckers, etc. £3. 4. 0. **1793** J. Williams *Life Ld. Barrymore* 67 The Butcher's Lady thinks, that living in style, is manifested in putting on her best bib and tucker on holidays. **1847** C. Brontë *J. Eyre* vii, Some of the girls have two clean tuckers in the week;.. the rules limit them to one. **1875** [see bib *sb.*[1] b]. **1881** E. F. Poynter *Among Hills* I. 150 Pulling out her white tucker round her white throat.

4. One who tucks; in quot. in sense 9.

1796 *Grose's Dict. Vulg. T.* (ed. 3) s.v. *Tucked up*, A tucker up to an old bachelor or widower; a supposed mistress.

5. *Needlework.* One who makes or 'runs' tucks; the device in a sewing-machine which does this.

1905 *Daily Chron.* 11 Aug. 10/7 Machinists.., shirts and blouses; also a few vacancies for tuckers.

6. [f. tuck *sb.*[1] 6 or *v.*[1] 10.] The daily supply of food of a gold-digger or station-hand; rations, meals; also, food generally, victuals: = tuck *sb.*[1] 6 b. *to earn* or *make one's tucker*, to earn merely enough to pay for one's keep. *Australian* and *N.Z. slang.*

1858 *Morn. Chron.* 31 Aug. (Farmer), Diggers, who have great difficulty in making their tucker at digging. **1864** J. C. Richmond *Let.* 12 May in *Richmond-Atkinson Papers* (1960) II. 111 It is very hard work humping your blankets and tucker. **1874** G. Walch *Head over Heels* 73 For want of more nourishing tucker, I believe they'd have eaten him. **1883** A. Forbes in *Contemp. Rev.* Oct. 606 A peer's son who is earning his 'tucker' as a station cook in New Zealand. **1898** M. Davitt *Life & Progr. Australia* xl. 275 A pound of a week, including lodgings and 'tucker'. **1911** W. H. Koebel *In Maoriland Bush* xxi. 275 If they had obtained no wages for the first six months or so, they would have obtained their 'tucker' free. **1972** M. Shadbolt *Strangers & Journeys* iii. 43 Later Ned got the tucker cooking. It was stew and spud, like most nights.

attrib. **1870** *Append. Jrnls. House Representatives N.Z.* D. xl. 4 Tucker Flat.. has been looked upon as containing worse than 'tucker' ground. **1890** 'R. Boldrewood' *Miner's Right* iv, Cyrus and Joe will go splitting or fencing.. to pay the tucker-bill. **1902** H. Lawson *Children of Bush* 88 There's some women that can never see a tucker-bag, even if you hold it right under their noses. **1902** *Westm. Gaz.* 30 July 2/1 Weird dishes in which every ingredient in the 'tucker box' struggles for mastery. **1904** *Daily Chron.* 21 Mar. 5/5 It is no time to be mealy-mouthed when capitalists ..want slave workers at tucker wages.

Hence ˈ**tuckerless** *a.* (*Austral.* and *N.Z. slang*), without food.

1937 E. Hill *Great Austral. Loneliness* x. 82 The rind of the pods.. makes an acrid but nourishing food.. that tides over the tuckerless white man to the next out-camp. **1946** A. P. Harper *Mem. Mountains & Men* xvi. 162 We were left almost 'tuckerless' on Christmas Day.

tucker (ˈtʌkə(r)), *v.*[1] *New Eng. colloq.* [f. tuck *v.*[1]; cf. tucked *ppl. a.* 2.] *trans.* To tire, to weary; usually *tucker out*; esp. in pa. pple. *tuckered out*, worn out, exhausted. Hence ˈ**tucker** *sb.*[2], the state of being tired out (*Cent. Dict.* 1891).

c **1840** *Story of Bee Tree* (Bartlett), I'm clear tuckered out with these young ones. **1853** *Turnover* vi. 59 Set us to runnin', an' I could tucker him. **1862** Lowell *Biglow P.*, *Mason & Slidell* 12 Hard work is good an' wholesome, past all doubt; But 't ain't so, ef the mind gits tuckered out. **1879** Howells *L. Aroostook* xxiii, She's tired to death—quite tuckered, you know. **1890** S. W. Baker *Wild Beasts* I. 378 The old bear got regularly tuckered-out.

tucker (ˈtʌkə(r)), *v.*[2] *colloq.* (orig. and chiefly *Austral.* and *N.Z.*). [f. tucker *sb.*[1] 6.]

1. *trans.* To supply with food. Also *refl.*

1899 *Bulletin* (Sydney) 21 Jan. 14/3 An oldish widower with three sons.. goes out to work with Son No. 1, leaving the other two mites at home to mind the 's'lection' and tucker themselves. Old man comes home every month or so. **1920** B. Cronin *Timber Wolves* 40, I got a friend hereabouts that tuckers me when I'm along this way. **1940** E. I. Lord *Old Westland* xi. 137 He 'tuckered' many a down and out digger. **1964** B. Wannan *Fair Go, Spinner* (1965) iv. 126 In those days, the shearers had to provide their own food supplies—'to tucker themselves', as they put it.

2. *intr.* To eat, to have a meal. Also with *up*.

1903 H. B. King *Bill's Philosophy* 24 I'm sick of starving, when a cove can tucker free. **1940** F. D. Davison *Woman at Mill* 143 We were counting on it [*sc.* a money order] to tucker up with in Bairnsdale. **1959** H. P. Tritton *Time means Tucker* (1965) v. 64 We tuckered at the house and Mrs. Craig fed us till we couldn't eat another thing. **1963** *Weekly News* (Auckland, N.Z.) 5 June 37/2 The cowboy was tuckering at the cookshop on his own.

tucket[1] (ˈtʌkɪt). *arch.* Also 7 tucquet. [Connected with tuck *sb.*[2]; cf. toccata, also OF. *touchet* blow, stroke (*c* 1500 in Godef. *Compl.*).] A flourish on a trumpet; a signal for marching used by cavalry troops. (Cf. sennet[1].) Also *fig.*

1593 Shaks. *Rich. II*, i. iii. 26 (*Stage direct.*) Tucket. Enter Hereford, and Harold [Herald; the lists at Coventry]. **1599** —— *Hen. V*, iv. ii. 35 Then let the Trumpets sound The Tucket Sonuance, and the Note to mount. **1601** —— *All's Well* iii. v, (*Stage direct.*) A Tucket afarre off. Enter old Widdow of Florence [etc.]. **1605** *1st Pt. Ieronimo* i. v, (*Stage direct.*) A Tucket within. *King.* How now, what means this trumpets sound? **1623** Webster *Devil's Law-Case* v. vi, (*Stage direct.*) Two tuckets by several trumpets. **1625** Markham *Soldier's Accid.* 61 The fourth [sound or signal given by the trumpet] is, Tucquet, or March; Which being hearde simplie of it selfe.. Commands nothing but Marching after the Leader. **1889** W. B. Squire in Grove *Dict. Mus.* IV. 184. **1891** G. Meredith *One of our Conq.* 242 A tucket of herald newspapers told the world of Victor's returning to his London.

tucket[2] (ˈtʌkɪt). *local U.S.* [Origin obscure; perh. ad. F. *toquet*, dim. of *toque* cap.] A small ear of Indian corn in the unripe milky stage.

1874 J. T. Trowbridge *Coupon Bonds* etc. 253 He had made, during the day, frequent deposits of green corn, of the diminutive species called *tucket*. **1889** Farmer *Americanisms*, *Tucket*, the young green ear of Indian corn. Gathered when soft, and cooked in milk.

[**tucket**, erron. f. tucet, a steak, a collop.]

ˈ**tuck-in**, *a.* [f. the vbl. phr. *to tuck in*: see tuck *v.*[1] 9.] That may be tucked in; *spec.* of a woman's blouse, etc., designed to have its lower edge tucked into the skirt.

1929 *Daily Express* 7 Nov. 5/2 Two [blouses] are 'tuck-in', and the other comes over the skirt. **1965** *Harper's Bazaar* June 65 Slashed tuck-in top.

tuck-in, act of feasting: see tuck *sb.*[1] 6.

ˈ**tucking**, *vbl. sb.*[1] [f. tuck *v.*[1] + -ing[1].]

†**1.** The fulling and dressing of cloth. *Obs.*

1467–8 [see tucking-mill]. **1530** in Weaver *Wells Wills* (1890) 24 All that belongyth to my crafte of tokynge and sheryng. *c* **1640** J. Smyth *Lives Berkeleys* (1883) I. 167 The ..charges in the wholl manufactory.. in.. Tuckinge, shearinge, dying, dressinge and the like.

2. *Fishing.* The taking of fish from the seine with the tuck-net.

1847 *Zoologist* V. 1706 On tucking, all the fish were discovered to be dead. **1888** *Argosy* 279 To get the fish [pilchards] out of the seine is the next operation.. this is called tucking, and it is carried on by means of a small net or tuck net.

3. The gathering or girding up of one's garments; *concr.* the part or fold so gathered; also, the putting of tucks in a garment; *concr.* a tuck, or tucks collectively.

c **1440** *Promp. Parv.* 504/2 Tukkynge vp (of clothys, or stykkynge..), *suffarci(naci)o.* **1713** *Guardian* No. 10 ¶7 The taking and tucking up of gowns. **1880** *Plain Hints Needlework* 22 Tucking.. is used both as ornament, and for elongation when the material has shrunk. **1893** *Athenæum* 7 Oct. 498/1 A higher tucking of the picturesque and flowing robes.

4. The action of putting anything away so that it is snugly covered or concealed, or of thrusting in something, as a bed-covering, so as to confine it at the end or edge; hence (*slang*) *tucking in*, hearty or greedy feeding; also *concr.*

1810 *Splendid Follies* I. 186 Tom Sponge now began cramming unmercifully, exclaiming every three mouthfuls, 'Rare tucking in, Sir William'. **1833** Macaulay *Ess.*, *Walpole* (1897) 272 Whose vast volume of wig and infinite length of riband had figured at the dressing or at the tucking up of Louis the Fourteenth. **1874** J. Brown *Lett.* in *Recoll.* (1893) 65 This tucking [of the leg of a fowl under its wing] ..was due to the force automatic. **1876** Besant & Rice *Gold. Butterfly* (1877) 196 They gave themselves unreservedly to 'tucking in'. **1884** Roe *Nat. Ser. Story* vi, High winds and frosty nights prompted to careful covering and tucking away.

5. *attrib.*, as **tucking-bush**, the dwarf juniper, *Juniperus nana*; **tucking-comb**, a comb confining the hair; **tucking-gauge**: see quot.; †**tucking-girdle**, a girdle worn with the alb, which is drawn through it until the skirt is of the proper length; **tucking-maund**, a tuck-basket (tuck *sb.*[1] 9); †**tucking-shear(s**, shears used in cloth-finishing; †**tucking-stock**, a fulling-stock or fulling-mill. See also tucking-mill.

1890 W. P. Lett in *Big Game N. Amer.* 88 Large patches of '*tucking-bushes', or dwarf juniper, which grow about breast-high, with strong branches stiffly interlaced. **1822** in *Dict. Amer. Eng.* (1944) IV. 2369/1 Mr. Pettigrew Bot of D McDowell one *tucking Comb at $4.50. **1895** S. B. Kennedy in *Outing* (U.S.) XXVII. 11/2 He stopped and held up a gold-tipped tucking comb. **1877** Knight *Dict. Mech.*, * *Tucking-gage*, an attachment for marking tucks at a determinate distance ready for the next line of sewing. **1487–8** *Rec. St. Mary at Hill* 131 Item, for a dossen *tuckyng gyrdilles, x d. **1490–1** in Swayne *Sarum Churchw. Acc.* (1896) 37 For tukkynge girdillis for Awbis, iiij d. **1499–1500** *Ibid.* 51 For a dossyn Tokynggirdels for the Vestre, xij d. **1530** Palsgr. 283/2 Tuckyng gyrdell [*printed* kyrdell], *saincture a ecourter* [printed *ecourser*]. **1896** *Gd. Words* Jan. 18/1 The '*tucking-maund' is.. a somewhat shallow basket, through which water may readily escape, but mackerel cannot. **1478** *Croscombe Churchw. Acc.* (Som. Rec. Soc.) 6 A *tokyng shere. **1533** in Weaver *Wells Wills* (1890) 102 My son Thomas.. ii pere of tokyne sherys. **1778** *Eng. Gazetteer* (ed. 2) s.v. *Staverton*, Staverton, Wilts, on the Avon,.. has 4 *tucking-stocks and 2 grist-mills.

†ˈ**tucking**, *vbl. sb.*[2] *Obs.* or *arch.* [f. tuck *v.*[2] + -ing[1].] Touching; beating of a drum.

c **1485** *Digby Myst.* (1882) iii. 969 Whan he towcheyd it with his toukkyng, pey brast as ony glase, and rofe asonder, as it byn with thondor. **1632** Lithgow *Trav.* vii. 316

Singing, toucking of kettle Drummes, sounding of Trumpets, and other ostentations of ioy.

'tucking-mill. [f. TUCKING *vbl. sb.*[1] + MILL *sb.*[1]] See quot. 1888. (A West of England term.)

1467-8 *Rolls of Parlt.* V. 587/1 A Water Mille 11 Tokyng Milles and Medowes, Pastures and Wodes. **1555** *Act 2 & 3 Phil. & Mary* c. 11 §4 No.. Weaver.. shall.. kepe or have any Tucking Mill. **1617** SIR R. BOYLE *Diary* in *Lismore Papers* (1886) I. 176, I made him a new lease of thowld Tucking myll. **1796** W. MARSHALL *W. England* I. Gloss. (E.D.S.) *Tucking-mill*, fulling-mill. **1810** J. T. *Risdon's Surv. Devon* p. xxiv, The traces of ruined tucking mills, as they were provincially called,.. denote the former extent of the manufactory. **1888** ELWORTHY *W. Somerset Word-bk.*, *Tucking-mill*,.. fuller's stocks, or beaters for milling cloth. The term is also applied to the building and machinery as a whole.

tuck-mill ('tʌkmɪl). Now *rare*. [f. TUCK *v.*[1] + MILL *sb.*[1]] = prec. (Chiefly West of England.)

c **1640** J. SMYTH *Hundred of Berkeley* (1885) 4 The multitude of Tuckmills, and fullinge mills which heere abound. **1733** P. LINDSAY *Interest Scot.* 108 Where-ever there is a Conveniency of a River for Tuck-mills near the Wooll-countries, they may be made. **1780** A. YOUNG *Tour Irel.* II. 35 To this mill is since added.. two tuck-mills. **1812** J. SMYTH *Pract. of Customs* (1821) 324 All Manufactures made of Wool, which are milled in a Tuck Mill, or other machine, whether twilled or plain, as Coatings, Cassimeres, Kerseys, Druggets, German Serges, Ratteens, and such like. **1884** *St. James' Gaz.* 9 Sept. 6/2 A walk.. past the scutching-mills for flax and the old tuck-mill.

'tuck-net. [f. TUCK *v.*[1] 5.] A smaller net used within the great seine to gather and bring the fish to the surface. Also **'tuckner**, the small boat which carries the tuck-net.

1520 *Lett. & Pap. Hen. VIII*, XIX. 196 (P.R.O.) Vnum rethe vocatum a Tucknett.. de precio .xxvj. s. viij. d. **1580** in *Sussex Archæol. Collect.* (1849) II. 43 [The fishermen proceeded to set down their ancient fishing customs under certain heads, called fares,.. such as those used in] Tucknett Fare, Shotnett Fare, [etc.]. **1848** C. A. JOHNS *Week at Lizard* 52 The seine is then moored, and.. a smaller boat.. passes within the circle of floating corks and lets down a small net, called a tuck-net. **1849** *Sussex Archæol. Collect.* II. 43 The boats used in Tucknett fare were called tuckners,.. they were 'used between Februarye and Aprill to goe to sea uppon the coaste for playce', of the burden of three ton or thereabouts. **1907** *Victoria Hist. Sussex* II. 265/2 'Tucknett fare' lasted from February to April, small boats called 'tuckners' of about 3 tons plying during that season for plaice.

tuck-out (*slang*), a 'feed', feast: see TUCK *sb.*[1] 6.

'tuck-point, *v.* [f. TUCK *sb.*[1] + POINT *v.*[1]] To point or fill up the joints of (brickwork) with coloured mortar, grooved with a narrow groove, which is filled with fine white lime putty, allowed to project slightly. Hence **tuck-pointer**, **-pointing**.

1881 Tuck pointing [see POINTING *vbl. sb.*[1] 5]. **1893** *Law Times* XCV. 5/2 Any kind of brickwork, tuckpointing, or plastering that may have been contracted for.. under the original contract. **1901** *Daily Chron.* 2 Sept. 9/6 Bricklayer and tuck pointer, good, wants Work. **1902** J. HEBB in *N. & Q.* 9th Ser. X. 193/1 The brickwork.. has been coloured and tuck-pointed.

'tuck-shop. *slang.* [f. TUCK *sb.*[1] (sense 6 b).] A pastry-cook's shop for the sale of pastry, sweets, fruit, and the like, chiefly to schoolchildren.

1857 HUGHES *Tom Brown* I. vi, Come along down to Sally Harrowell's; that's our School-house tuck-shop—she bakes such stunning murphies. **1861** THACKERAY *Round. Papers* xvi. 378 We share our toffy; go halves at the tuck-shop; do each other's exercises. **1885** MOZLEY *Remin.* I. 410 The five years I was at Charterhouse [1820-5] I never once went near the tuck-shop.

‖**tucktoo** (tʌk'tuː). [Echoic: = Burmese *tokté* (Yule), *taukte*, from the animal's cry.] Name in Burma for a large house lizard.

1896 *Athenæum* 19 Dec. 870/1 The larger house lizard, which she calls the tucktoo. **1901** J. W. PAYNE in *Bulwark* Nov. 260/1 In many a village you can see and hear the children with mock gravity keeping time to the tucktoo. *Ibid.*, By day and by night he will tell you his name—'Tuck-too! Tuck-too!' And though he speaks often, it's always the same—'Tuck-too! Tuck-too!'

'tuck-up. [f. the vbl. phr. *to tuck up*: see TUCK *v.*[1] 6, 9.] †**1.** A fold or plait of hair. *Obs.*

1749 J. CLELAND *Mem. Woman Pleasure* I. 186 His hair, which was of a perfect shining black, play'd to his face in natural side-curls, and was set out with a smart tuck-up behind.

2. A boat of a particular construction (see quot. 1889).

1887 *Forest & Stream* 24 Feb. 94/1 The tuckup could swing 300 sq. ft. if desired. **1889** W. P. STEPHENS *Canoe & Boat Building* (ed. 4) 239 The peculiar name 'tuckup' is derived from the fact that in building, the flat keel is not carried out straight from the stem to sternpost.. but it.. 'tucks up'.. to the height of the waterline.

3. The action or an act of tucking someone up in bed.

1915 H. L. WILSON *Ruggles of Red Gap* iv. 81, I was strangely a little warmed at thinking I might not have seen the last of Cousin Egbert, whom I had just given a tuckup.

tucky ('tʌkɪ), *a.* *rare*$^{-1}$. [f. TUCK *sb.*[1] + -Y.] Characterized by tucks; wearing tucked garments.

1748 *Ballad* in Mitchell *Hist. Montrose* viii. (1866) 75 His curling wigs And his fine tucky lady.

tucotuco: see TUCUTUCU.

‖**tucum** ('tuːkəm). Also tocon, tocum, tokaun. [ad. Tupi *tucumá*: see next.] Name for several Brazilian palms of the genera *Astrocaryum* and *Bactris*, esp. *Astrocaryum vulgare*, from the young leaves of which the natives obtain a fibre which they make into cordage, nets, hats, etc.; also, the fibre itself. Also *attrib.*, as ***tucum-fibre***, ***-oil***, ***-thread***.

[**1658** PISO *De Ind. Re Nat. et Med.* 128.] **1810** SOUTHEY *Brazil* I. vii. 205 They used a plant called tocon for the string. **1824** tr. *Spix & Martius' Trav. Brazil* II. 248 Strings of the fibres of palm leaves (tucum). **1874** tr. *Captivity H. Stade* (Hakl. Soc.) 128 Long leaves which they call tokauns. **1901** NERY *Amazon* 180 The tucum is the fibre of a great palm, *Astrocaryum vulgare*.

‖**tucuma** ('tuːkuːmə). [Tupi *tucumá*, the native name.] A Brazilian palm, *Astrocaryum Tucuma*, which produces a fleshy fruit used by the natives as food, and a fibre like that of tucum. Also ***tucuma palm***.

1824 tr. *Spix & Martius' Trav. Brazil* II. 248 *note*, The tucuma palm and others of the same genus. **1853** WALLACE *Palm Trees Amazon* 107-8. **1901** NERY *Amazon* 363 The men wore rings of tucuma, *Astrocaryum tucuma*.

‖**tucutucu** ('tuːkuː'tuːkuː). Also tucutuco, tucotuco, tucatuca, tucatucu. [Native name, imitating the grunting sound made by the animal when in its burrow.] A rat-like burrowing rodent of the genus *Ctenomys*, esp. *C. magellanica* and *C. brasiliensis*; found in Patagonia and La Plata. Also, the sound made by this animal. Also *attrib.*

1833 DARWIN *Jrnl. Beagle* iii. (1845) 50-1 The tucutucos appear, to a certain degree, to be gregarious... They are nocturnal in their habits... This animal is universally known by a very peculiar noise which it makes when beneath the ground... The name Tucutuco is given in imitation of the sound... When angry or frightened they uttered the tucutuco. **1839** FITZ-ROY *Voy. Beagle* II. 313 The 'tucutucu', a little animal like a small rabbit. **1880** LADY F. DIXIE *Across Patagonia* ix. 112 Putting his foot in an unusually deep tuca-tuca hole, my little horse comes with a crash upon his head. **1899** *Daily News* 4 May 4/3 Patagonia was always noted for its strange ground game, as armadillos and tucotucos. **1904** *Times, Lit. Suppl.* 11 Nov. 347/2 They rode northwards towards the Andes.. knee-deep mud and tucutucu country (earth undermined by prairie rat) were common everywhere.

†**tud**, var. *tid*, obs. pa. pple. of TIDE *v.*[1]

c **1400** *Laud Troy Bk.* 3804 Off al the harme that we him dud Hadde now not this harme tud.

†**tudder, tuder.** *Obs.* [OE. *túddor*, *túdor* neut.; of uncertain origin. Cf. TIDDER *v.*[1]] Progeny, offspring.

c **897** K. ÆLFRED *Gregory's Past. C.* xv. 97 Đonne mæʒ he cennan mid ðam ðæt tuder ryhtes ʒeðohtes. *a* **1000** *Ags. Gloss.* in Wr.-Wülcker 238/5 *Foetus, i. fructus, partus, filius*, tudder, *soboles*. *c* **1000** ÆLFRIC *Saints' Lives* xxxiii. 314 He þa.. feoll and cwæð Eufrosina cristes bryd and haliʒra manna tuddor ne beo þu forgitende þinra efenþeowa. *c* **1000** *Sax. Leechd.* I. 166 Sona hyt þæt tuddur ut asendeþ. *c* **1050** *Gloss.* in Wr.-Wülcker 467/24 *Propago*, tudor oððe cyn. *c* **1200** *Trin. Coll. Hom.* 177 Deor and fishshes and fuʒeles and here tuder.

-tude (tjuːd), *suffix*, repr. L. *-tūdo*, *-tūdin-em* (F. *-tude*), a suffix of abstract nouns, chiefly from adjs., as *altitūdo* height, f. *altus* high, *fortitūdo* bravery, f. *fortis* brave, *hebetūdo* bluntness, f. *hebes* blunt, less commonly from participles, as *consuētūdo* custom, f. *consuētus* accustomed, *habitūdo* habit, f. *habitus* held, or verbs, as *valētūdo* health, f. *valēre* to be well; occurring in many words derived from Latin either directly, as *altitude*, *hebetude*, *latitude*, *longitude*, *magnitude*, or through French, as *amplitude*, *aptitude*, *attitude*, *consuetude*, *fortitude*, *habitude*, *plenitude*, *solitude*, etc., or formed (in F. or Eng.) on Latin analogies, as *debilitude*, *decrepitude*, *exactitude*, or occasionally irregularly, as *dispiritude*, *torpitude*.

Tudeh ('tuːdeɪ). [a. Pers., lit. 'mass'.] In full ***Tudeh party***. The Communist Party of Iran. Also *attrib.*

1946 *Civil & Milit. Gaz.* 16 Mar. 2/2 The Tudeh (Proletarian) Party in Azerbaijan, or what is left of it in Persia. **1966** S. ZABITH *Communist Movement in Iran* iii. 73 In its first phase the Communist movement assumed the characteristics of a democratic front... Its organizational expression was the Tudeh party of Iran, formed in early October, 1941. **1979** *Economist* 8 Sept. 60/3 There are about a dozen leftist groups (three Chinese, two Trotskyists), all in opposition except for Tudeh, the official Communist party. **1980** J. CARTWRIGHT *Horse of Darius* x. 145 They have eliminated two hundred Tudeh Communists and Russian agents in the last few months. *Ibid.* 153 Let us concentrate on the Tudeh. Does our man in Iran know what they are up to?

'tudel, *v.* *rare.* [app. repr. Ger. *dudeln*, *tudeln*, 'to perform badly on a musical instrument'; cf. also TOODLE *v.*] *intr.* A depreciative or humorous expression for 'to play on a musical instrument'. Hence **'tudeler** [cf. Ger. *dudler* bad player or singer]. So **'tudle** *adv.* or *int.*, an imitation of the sound of a flute or similar instrument (cf. *toodle-toodle* s.v. TOODLE *v.*).

1814 MME. D'ARBLAY *Wanderer* II. 109 Give her as much of your tudeling as will come to this... By then, she'll be able to twiddle over them wires by herself. *Ibid.* 110 He called her his pretty tudeler. **1834** J. DOWNING *Life & Writ.* 23 The fifes and the bugles.. went tudle, tudle, tudle, tudle.

tuder: see TIDDER *v.*[1], TUDDER.

Tudesco (tʊ'dɛskəʊ). Also Tedesco. Fem. Tudesca. [Ladino, = Sp., Pg. *tudesco* German.] A colloq. term among Sephardic Jews for an Ashkenazic Jew.

1897 I. ZANGWILL *King of Schnorrers* i. 12 You are a Tedesco. *Ibid.* v. 116 A Sephardi marry a Tedesco! Shameful. **1932** C. ROTH *Hist. of Marranos* viii. 234 They accentuated the superficial differences.. between them and the *tudescos*, from Germany and Poland, or even the *italianos* and *berberiscos* whose antecedents were nearer to their own. *Ibid.* xii. 316 Jacob Israel Bernal.. desired to marry a *tudesca*—a member of the despised German and Polish community. **1949** *Spectator* 4 Nov. 595/1 Not so long ago English Sephardic families used to sit in mourning if one of their members married, not a Goy (or non-Jew), but a Tedesco (or Ashkenazi Jew). **1964** M. WOHLGELERNTER *Israel Zangwill* II. vi. 85 The intended union of Menasseh's daughter with a Polish Jew excites.. horror in.. the *Mahamad*. A Tedesco did not pronounce Hebrew as they did, hence he was inferior.

Tudesque (tjuː'dɛsk), *a.* *rare.* [a. F. *tudesque*, It. *tedesco*:—med.L. *theotisc-us*, *theodiscus*, esp. in *lingua Theotisca*, *Theodisca*, *Theudisca* the German language: see TEDESCO, THEODISC, DUTCH, TEUTONIC.] German, esp. said of the language.

1801 RANKEN *Hist. France* I. I. iv. 409 His native tongue was the German or Tudesque. **1833** LONGF. *Outre-Mer* Prose Wks. 1886 I. 92 When at length the old Tudesque language.. had given place to the Langue d'Oil.

†**tu'diculate**, *v.* *Obs. rare*$^{-0}$. [f. L. *tudiculāre*, f. *tudicula*, dim. of *tudes* mallet, f. root *tud-* of *tundĕre* to pound: see -ATE[3].] (See quot.) So †**tudicu'lation** (*obs. rare*$^{-0}$).

1623 COCKERAM, *Tudiculate*, to pound, to bruise. **1656** BLOUNT *Glossogr.*, *Tudiculate*, to pound or bruise; to work as Smiths do with a hammer. **1658** PHILLIPS, *Tudiculation*, (Lat.) a bruising or pounding with Smiths hammers.

tudle: see TUDEL *v.*

Tudor ('tjuːdə(r)), *a.* and *sb.* [attrib. use of the surname *Tudor* (in Welsh *Tewdwr*): see below.]

A. *adj.* **1.** Belonging to the line of English sovereigns (from Henry VII to Elizabeth I) descended from Owen Tudor, who married Catherine, the widowed queen of Henry V.

1779 *Mirror* No. 18 ¶9 In England,.. the high prerogative exerted by the Princes of the Tudor race. **1906** *Q. Rev.* July 56 A Tudor dynasty held the throne.

2. Applied to the style of architecture (the latest form of Perpendicular) which prevailed in England during the reigns of the Tudors; belonging to, characteristic of, or resembling this. Also of interior decoration.

Tudor arch, the flattened form of arch characteristic of the Tudor style. ***Tudor flower***, an upright stalked trefoil ornament used in long rows on cornices, etc. in Tudor architecture. ***Tudor rose***, a conventional figure of a rose adopted as a badge by Henry VII, occurring in architectural and other decoration in the Tudor period; in *Her.* figured as a combination of a red and a white rose (either a smaller rose set upon a larger, or a single rose with the two tinctures divided quarterly). Also ***Tudor-style*** adj.

1815 J. SMITH *Panorama Sc. & Art* I. 131 [An arch] of four centres, commonly called the Tudor arch. **1842** TENNYSON *Edwin Morris* 11 A Tudor-chimnied bulk Of mellow brickwork. **1848** RICKMAN *Archit.* 212 What has been called the Tudor flower, an ornament used instead of battlement, as an upper finish. **1860** WEALE *Dict. Terms* s.v. *Tudor Badges*, [Henry VII] assumed the Tudor rose, or the red rose charged with the white, as emblematical of his united claims to the throne. **1880** MISS BRADDON *Just as I am* ii, It was a Tudor house. **1902** G. E. MITTON *Hampstead & Marylebone* 23 There is the police-station.. and adjacent an interesting Tudor house, which, though not old, is well built. **1928** KIPLING *Bk. of Words* 267, I have only to leave the Tudor grill-room, take the electric lift upstairs. **1953** R. LEHMANN *Echoing Grove* 177 A chintzy Tudor-style hotel. **1955** M. GILBERT *Sky High* viii. 116 They had a glass of sherry in the Tudor Bar, followed by a meal in the Jacobean Dining-Room. **1970** *Globe & Mail* (Toronto) 26 Sept. 42/6 (Advt.), Charming Tudor bungalow with pretty garden. **1978** J. PUDNEY *Thank Goodness for Cake* 82 Their Tudor-style manor house. **1979** R. JAFFE *Class Reunion* II. iv. 156 Would they like this Tudor house, or that Spanish one?

B. *sb.* **a.** Mock-Tudor style. **b.** *N. Amer.* A house in mock-Tudor style.

1939, etc. [see *stockbroker's Tudor* s.v. STOCK-BROKER, STOCKBROKER b]. **1961** 'J. LE CARRÉ' *Call for Dead* iv. 37 The Fountain Café.. was all Tudor and horse brasses. **1969** E. SANDON *View into Village* 93 At the Somerton corner is the Boxted and Hartest Club erected.. in 1888, in red brick Tudor, with two gigantic oriel windows. **1969** P. ZELVER *Honey Bunch* vii. 35 The Swopes lived on one side of the

McKittricks in an English Tudor. **1980** *News & Observer* (Raleigh, N. Carolina) 28 Oct. WA-5/5 This tudor is located on a circular street with many trees.

So **Tudoresque** (-'rɛsk) *a.*, characteristic of the Tudors or the Tudor period; in or resembling the Tudor style, in architecture or art.

1847 HELPS *Friends in C.* I. v. 81 Those Protestant proceedings, which we may rather hope were Tudoresque than Protestant. **1881** OAKEY *Build. Home* 101 An old sixteenth-century Tudoresque house. **1893** *Athenæum* 20 May 635/1 We have the Tudoresque, the Caroline, the Restoration, and other styles [of book-plates].

Tudorbethan (ˌtjuːdə'biːθən), *a.* (and *sb.*) [Blend of TUDOR *a.* and ELIZABETHAN *a.*] Mock Tudor; imitative of Tudor and Elizabethan styles. Also *ellipt.* as *sb.*

1933 LEAVIS & THOMPSON *Culture & Environment* 32 The outbreak of 'Tudorbethan' villas. **1958** *Spectator* 4 July 13/1 The 'mediæval character' of their 1930-Tudorbethan neighbours. **1960** *House & Garden* June 66/2 Proper treatment can make bearable the most vulgar stockbroker's 'Tudorbethan'. **1975** *Times* 13 Aug. 10/4 [Liberty's] store was rebuilt in 1924 to the Tudorbethan designs of E. T. and E. S. Hall. **1977** *Guardian Weekly* 29 July 19/2 A flash of black-and-white Tudorbethan pastiche.

Tudory ('tjuːdərɪ), *sb.* [f. TUDOR *a.* + -Y[3].] Mock-Tudor architecture or decoration.

1959 P. BULL *I know Face* viii. 144 The atmosphere of old Tudory and brass ornaments brings my bile to boiling-point. **1973** R. HILL *Ruling Passion* I. i. 11 Above the thatched roof a flock of television aerials..sang their triumph over charm and Tudory.

Tudory ('tjuːdərɪ), *a.* [f. TUDOR *a.* + -Y[1].] Imitative or suggestive of Tudor style.

1970 A. FOWLES *Dupe Negative* xi. 141 The Tudory dining room. **1974** R. INGHAM *Yoris* xiii. 41 The May Pole ..was beamy and Tudory and phony.

Tudric ('tjuːdrɪk). [App. f. TUD(OR *a.* + CYM)RIC *a.*] The proprietary designation of a type of pewter (see quots.).

1902 (*title*) 'Cymric' gold and silverwork jewellery and 'Tudric' pewter (Liberty & Co.). **1904** *Jrnl. Soc. Arts* 10 June 638/1 For pewter..only modifications of Celtic forms were used, and these were soon supplemented by floral and plant motives to which the distinguishing name of 'Tudric' was given. **1922** *Trade Marks Jrnl.* 7 Feb. 232 *Tudric*... Pewter Ware. Liberty & Co. (Cymric) Limited, 16, Hylton Street, Birmingham; manufacturers of pewter wares. **1963** *Archit. Rev.* CXXXIII. 108/2 Two or three years afterwards, he was to add the range of 'Tudric' pewter to his enterprises. **1977** FLEMING & HONOUR *Penguin Dict. Decorative Arts* 468/2 From 1894 he [*sc.* Sir Arthur Liberty] produced silver in an Art Nouveau version of the Celtic style which he termed 'Cymric' and from 1903 a new type of pewter, with a high proportion of silver in the alloy, which he called 'Tudric'.

†**tue.** *Obs.* [? a. F. *tue* kill.] A hunting cry.

1602 CAREW *Cornwall* I. 22 The Captaine hunters, discouering his sallies by their Espyals doe lay their souldier-like Hounds, his borne enemies, in ambush betweene him [the Fox] and home, and so with *Har* and *Tue* pursue him to the death.

tue, short for TUE-IRON, TEW-IRON.

1883 CRANE *Smithy & Forge* 10 In its centre a thick projecting iron nozzle, perforated to allow of the wind for the blast. This is termed the Tue.

tue, var. TEW *sb.*[1], *v.*[1], *v.*[2]

tuech(e, tueiche, obs. Sc. ff. TOUCH.

tuechit, obs. Sc. form of TEWHIT, lapwing.

Tuedian ('twiːdɪən), *a. Geol.* Also **Twedian.** [f. med.L. *Tueda* the river Tweed + -IAN.] An epithet applied by Geo. Tate in 1856 to the lowest beds of the Carboniferous series, as developed in and near the valley of the Tweed.

1856 R. EMBLETON in *Proc. Berw. Nat. Club* III. No. 7. 219 These beds form the lowest portion of the Carboniferous formation, lying below the Productal and Encrinal Mountain Limestone of Northumberland, and might properly be designated as the Tuedian group... Specimens of these fossils were exhibited by Mr. Tate. **1859** TATE *ibid.* IV. No. 3. 151 In 1856, I applied this name [Tuedian] to a series of beds, lying below the Mountain Limestone, which are largely developed on the Tweed. **1876** PAGE *Adv. Text-bk. Geol.* xiv. 240 The term Calciferous sandstones..is sometimes employed, as well as the more strictly local one of Twedian beds. **1882** G. A. LEBOUR in *Proc. Berw. Nat. Club* IX. No. 3. 527 This great division.. has been..split into two members, the *Bernician* above,.. and the *Tuedian* below, the equivalent of the Calciferous Sandstone Series and part of the Upper Old Red Sandstone of Scotland.

tuefall, -fold, erron. forms of TO-FALL *sb.*

1664 in *Northumb. Gloss.* (1894), Recd. of Mark Hobson for a year's rent for a Tuefold, 2s. 6d. **1846** WORCESTER, Tuefall; hence in later Dicts.

tuei, tueie, obs. ff. TWAY, two.

tueil, tueill, obs. ff. TOWEL, TWILL.

tue iron, var. TEW-IRON.

1862 *Catal. Internat. Exhib., Brit.* II. No. 6182, Tue irons, tin goods, wire of all kinds.

tueit, obs. Sc. f. TWIT.

tuel, tuell(e: see TEWEL, TOWEL, TWELVE.

tuelf, tuelfed, tuelft, tuelt, etc., obs. ff. TWELVE, TWELFTH.

tuen, tuene, var. TEE *v.*[1], TEEN *v.*[1] *Obs.*

tuentende, -tiand(e, -tieth, -tiþe, obs. ff. TWENTIETH.

tuenti, -tie, -ty, -tye, obs. ff. TWENTY.

tuer, obs. f. TUYERE.

Tuesday ('tjuːzdeɪ). Forms: α. 1–2 **Tiwesdæᵹ,** 3 **Tiwesday, -dai, Tywesdaiȝ,** 3–5 **Tywesday,** 4 **Tues-, Tewisdai,** 4–6 **Twysday,** 5 **Tywys-, Tyvys-, Tewys-, Towes-,** 5–6 **Tewisday,** 6 **Tewes-, Tuis-, Twis-, Teyus-, Teudins-, Tewsday,** 6–7 **Twesdaie,** 7 **Tewsday** 6– **Tuesday.** β. 3 **Tisdæi, -dei,** 4 **Tisday;** *Sc.* 4–6 **Tȳsday,** 5–9 **Tyesday,** 6–7 **Tyisday,** 8 **Tiseday.** [OE. *Tíwesdæᵹ;* = OFris. *ties-, tîsdei, -di;* OHG. *ziestag,* MHG. *zîstag* (Ger. dial. *zîstig*); ON. *týsdagr, týrsdagr* (Norw. *tys-, tisdag,* Sw. and early Da. *tisdag,* Da. *tirsdag,* ME. and Sc. *tiesdæi, tȳsday*); f. genitive of OE. *Tíw* = ON. *Týr,* OHG. *Zîo,* name of an ancient Teutonic deity, identified with the Roman Mars; whence *Tíwesdæᵹ,* etc., rendering late L. *dies Martis,* It. *martedì,* F. *Mardi. Týr, Tíw:*—OTeut. **Tîwaz* was cognate with L. *deus,* Gr. genit. διός, OIr. *dia,* cf. Skr. *dyāus.*

Another form appears in MLG. *dînstag,* whence mod.Ger. *Dienstag* (Swab. *zienstig, zeinstig*), Du. *Dinsdag,* MDu. *Ding(e)stag, dinse(n)dach,* of which the first component appears to be *ding, þing,* 'public assembly', but is thought to be *Thinxus,* a synonym of the name of the war-god preserved in a Latin inscription.]

The third day of the week.

c **1050** *Byrhtferth's Handboc* in *Anglia* VIII. 321 Tiwesdæᵹes of martie. *a* **1123** *O.E. Chron.* an. 1104 On þam Tiwæs dæᵹe þær æfter. *c* **1205** LAY. 13936 þene Sunne heo ȝiuen sonedæi, Monenen..monedæi, Tidea heo ȝeuen tisdæi [*c* **1275** (l. 13924) tisdei]. *c* **1290** *Beket* 1147 in *S. Eng. Leg.* I. 139 An alle soulene dai, þene tywesdaiȝ [*v.r.* Tuesdai]. *c* **1375** *Sc. Leg. Saints* xl. (*Ninian*) 734 Of witsone owke þe twysday. **1375** BARBOUR *Bruce* xv. 101 Quhill the tysday in pask-owk. *c* **1450** *Merlin* xiv. 205 It be-fill on a tewisday. *a* **1500** *Bale's Chron.* in *Six Town Chron.* (1911) 143þis was upon a towesday. **1530** PALSGR. 178 *Mardy,* tuesday. *a* **1572** KNOX *Hist. Ref.* II. Wks. 1846 I. 350 The nixt day..(whiche was Tyisday, the 13 of Junij). **1587** F. JAMES in *Collect.* (O.H.S.) I. 199 From Tewsdaie till Satterdaie. **1607** *Reg. Mag. Sig. Scot.* 729/1 Upon Tyisday befoir the feist of Pasche. **1691** J. WILSON *Belphegor* II. iv, I shall be married a Tuesday next. **17..** *Runaway Bride* in Herd *Coll. Sc. Poems* (1776) II. 87 The bridal-day was set, On Tiseday for to be. **1848** THACKERAY *Van. Fair* xviii, We must have a party... Shall I say Tuesday fortnight? **1912** C. MURRAY in *The Odd Volume* 21 A towmond come Tyesday, the lassies been wad.

attrib. **1473** WARKW. *Chron.* (Camden) 21 Kynge Henry ..was putt to dethe..on a tywesday nyght. **1596** SHAKS. *1 Hen. IV,* I. ii. 40 A Purse of Gold most resolutely snatch'd on Monday night, and most dissolutely spent on Tuesday morning. **1622** BOYS *Wks.* 787 A Tuesday breakfast..a Fridayes drinking.

tuesite (tjuː'iːsaɪt). *Min.* [f. L. *Tuesa* the Spey, mistaken by Camden for the Tweed + -ITE[1].] An indurated variety of lithomarge of a milk-white colour.

1837 THOMSON in *Proc. Berw. Nat. Club* I. No. 5. 157 Fracture earthy,..soiling the fingers;..tuesite and gypsum. **1868** DANA *Min.* (ed. 5) 474 *Tuesite* of Thomson is a lithomarge from Scotland, used sometimes for slate pencils; ..color milk-white.

tueþyng, obs. f. TITHING.

tuewhite, obs. Sc. f. TEWHIT, lapwing.

tuey, tueye, tueyne: see TWAY, TWIE, TWAIN.

tuf, obs. f. TOUGH; var. TUFF.

tufa ('tuːfə, 'tjuːfə). *Geol.* Also 8–9 **tuffa,** 9 **tufo, tupha.** [a. It. *tufa, tufo:*—L. *tōfus, tōphus:* see TOPHUS; cf. TUFF *sb.*]

1. A generic name for porous stones, formed of pulverulent matter consolidated and often stratified. (See Note s.v. TUFF *sb.* 1.)

1777 G. FORSTER *Voy. round World* I. 586 The stone of which the statue itself is formed..being nothing but the red tufa which covers the whole island. **1789** J. WILLIAMS *Nat. Hist. Min. Kingd.* II. 382 There are great quantities of the concreted substance called tufa in many parts of Scotland. **1849** DANA *Geol.* iii. (1850) 241 The tufa is very friable, yielding easily to the fingers.

spec. **a.** ***calcareous tufa:*** 'a porous or vesicular carbonate of lime, generally deposited near the sources and along the courses of calcareous springs' (Page *Geol. Terms,* 1865). Cf. TUFF *sb.* 1 a.

1811 PINKERTON *Petralogy* I. 518 *note,* At Bionnay there are houses built of a calcareous tufa, containing fragments of lime-spar, limestone, and slate. *Ibid.* II. 374 *note,* This [*tufo*] is the Italian and classical orthography. *Tufa* may be reserved for depositions merely aqueous. **1839** G. ROBERTS *Dict. Geol., Tufa,* or *Calcareous Tufa..,* a friable earthy deposit from calcareous springs. The more solid form is *travertin.* **1865** LIVINGSTONE *Zambesi* xi. 222 In the vicinity of the erupted rocks we usually meet soft calcareous tufa. **1867** ANSTED in Brande & Cox *Dict. Sc.* etc., *Tufa* [is] a name applied in Italy to certain porous loose rocks... Volcanic Tufa is the material under which Pompeii was buried... Calcareous Tufa when consolidated passes into Travertine.

b. ***volcanic tufa:*** see TUFF *sb.* 1 b.

1770 HAMILTON in *Phil. Trans.* LXI. 7 The Italians distinguish it by the name of tufa, and it is in general use for building. **1772** *Nat. Hist.* in *Ann. Reg.* 79/2 What is called here Tuffa..is the same that covers Herculaneum, and that composes most of the high grounds about Naples; it is..a mixture of small pumice stones, ashes, and fragments of lava,..hardened into a sort of stone. **1778** *Phil. Trans.* LXVIII. 2 The walls were..of a tuffa exactly resembling that of Naples and its environs. **1794** SULLIVAN *View Nat.* I. 84 The..mass through which the catacombs are excavated are all indurated tufa. **1811** PINKERTON *Petralogy* II. 374 Brochant..supposes that they become volcanic tufo. **1838** *Murray's Hand Bk. N. Germ.* 239/1 Composed..of tufa and scoriæ, exactly similar to that found on Vesuvius. **1862** DANA *Man. Geol.* I. 685 When rain or moisture from any source descends with the cinders, the mass forms tufa,—a stratified, somewhat earthy, granular..rock, of gray, yellowish-brown, and brownish colors. **1866** LAWRENCE tr. *Cotta's Rocks Class.* (1878) 89 Tufa is now principally used to denote an earthy compound of volcanic products of the most various kind.

2. *attrib.* and *Comb.*, as ***tufa cement, grotto, quarry, rock, stone, wall; tufa-like, -paved*** adjs.

1839 W. CHAMBERS *Tour Holland* etc. 55/1 Andernach is an ancient walled town, and the seat of a considerable export trade in oven stones and *tufa cement. **1910** *19th Cent.* Feb. 365 The piers were formed of *tufa-like Caux stone. **1905** R. BAGOT *Passport* i, The steep, *tufa-paved street. **1891** FARRAR *Darkn. & Dawn* xxiv, The overhanging sides of the *tufa quarry. **1820** T. S. HUGHES *Trav. Sicily* II. xv. 368 Some workmen were excavating a wine vault in the *tufa-rock. **1861** J. H. BENNET *Winter Medit.* I. viii. (1875) 229 The island [Capri] is of limestone—a healthier geological formation than the soft tufa rock of Naples. **1793** *Trans. Soc. Arts* (ed. 2) V. 222 A *Tufa stone, found on the rocky banks of the Rhine. **1894** *Daily News* 22 Sept. 6/2 The columns..are generally of grey tufa-stone. **1877** J. NORTHCOTE *Catacombs* I. iii. 45 He strengthened the friable *tufa walls of some of the galleries..by..arches of brick and stone work.

tufaceous (tuː-, tjuː'feɪʃəs), *a.* [f. prec. + -ACEOUS.] Having the nature or texture of tufa; consisting of tufa.

(Chiefly used of non-volcanic formations: cf. TUFFACEOUS.)

1811 PINKERTON *Petralogy* I. 518 Wallerius would perhaps have called it a tufaceous limestone. **1851** WOODWARD *Mollusca* 142 The tufaceous deposits of petrifying wells. **1876** PAGE *Adv. Text-bk. Geol.* vii. 131 The tufaceous accumulations round the craters of..volcanoes.

tufall, tufan, obs. ff. TO-FALL, TYPHOON.

tufat, dial. var. TEWHIT, lapwing.

tuff (tʌf), *sb. Geol.* Forms: 6 **tuph,** 7–8 (9 *dial.*) **tuft,** (8 **tufft**), 7– **tuff,** (9 **tuf**). [ad. 16th c. F. *tufe, tuffe,* (R. Estienne) *tuf,* Cotgr. *tuf, tuffe,* ad. It. *tufo* 'a kind of soft, crumbling, or mouldring stone to build withall' (Florio):—L. *tōfus,* TOPHUS, q.v. The change of gender in obs. F. *tuffe* (= *tufa*) has not been explained. *Tuft* follows the better known TUFT *sb.* (where also the *t* is an addition).]

1. Any light porous cellular rock; = TUFA. (But there is a recent tendency to differentiate *tuff* from TUFA, and restrict it to 'volcanic tuff'.)

a. ***calcareous*** (or ***calc***) ***tuff:*** see TUFA 1 a and quot. 1816.

1569 STOCKER tr. *Diod. Sic.* II. xliv. 99/2 With their axes and hatchets they cut thereof as a man shoulde do on a Tuph or softe Stone. **1603** [see *tuff stone* in 2]. **1744** PLATT in *Phil. Trans.* XLIII. 266 A rocky petrified Substance,..by the Miners called Tuft. **1785** BARKER *ibid.* LXXV. 353 *note,* Tuft is a stone formed by the deposit left by water passing through beds of sticks, roots, vegetables &c. of which there is a large stratum at Matlock Bath. **1816** ACCUM *Chem. Tests* (1818) 166 When these waters suddenly lose the excess of carbonic acid..essential to the solution of the lime, there is an irregular precipitation; hence those tender calcareous cellular stones, and calcareous spongy tuffs. **1839** URE *Dict. Arts* 771 Calcareous tuf consists of similar incrustations made by petrifying rivulets running over mud, sand, vegetable remains, etc. **1843** PORTLOCK *Geol.* 213 As calc tuff, it [carbonate of lime] is of very frequent occurrence throughout the primary and secondary district. **1881** RAYMOND *Mining Gloss., Tuff* or *Tufa,* a soft sandstone or calcareous deposit.

(*b*) **1893–4** HESLOP *Northumbld. Gloss., Tuft,* a bed of fine-grained, siliceous stone, like ganister, which occurs in the carboniferous series below the Great Limestone. It is also known as *water sill.*

b. ***volcanic tuff,*** a tuff produced by the consolidation of volcanic ashes and other erupted material.

1815 W. PHILLIPS *Outlines Mineralogy & Geol.* (1818) 187 Pumice, obsidian or volcanic glass, slime called volcanic tuff,..are also the products of volcanic eruptions. **1839** DARWIN *Voy. Nat.* xvii. (1852) 373 Craters, composed of the soft and yielding tuff. **1841** TRIMMER *Pract. Geol.* 173

Aqueous lavas, which, as they consolidate, form rocks of an earthy appearance, known by the name of volcanic tuff or tufa. **1850** ANSTED *Elem. Geol., Min.* etc. Gloss., *Tufa, Tuff*, an Italian name for a variety of volcanic rock of earthy texture,.. made up.. of fragments of volcanic ashes. **1881** JUDD *Volcanoes* v. 117 The tuffs covering the city of Pompeii consist of numerous thin layers of lapilli and volcanic dust. **1914** *Brit. Mus. Return* 229 Volcanic lapilli and palagonite-tuff from Monte Brazil, Terceira, Azores.

c. ***trap-tuff***: see quot.

1833-4 J. PHILLIPS *Geol.* in *Encycl. Metrop.* (1845) VI. 768/1 Aggregations of the disintegrated.. materials of trap rocks are generally known under the vague name of trap tuff and compared with volcanic tuff.

2. *attrib.* and *Comb.*, as ***tuff bed, block, cone, crater, mountain, stone*** [F. *pierre de tuffe* (Cotgr.)], ***tuff-wacke***; ***tuff-like*** adj.

1854 HOOKER *Himal. Jrnls.* I. ii. 44 Enormous *tuff beds are deposited on the sandstone. **1864** J. HUNT tr. *Vogt's Lect. Man* x. 262 In these *tuff blocks, in the vicinity of the town of Puy, are found the mammoth and the rhinoceros with a bony nasal septum. **1881** JUDD *Volcanoes* 118 Finely-stratified *tuff-cones. **1839** DARWIN *Voy. Nat.* xvii. (1845) 376 To the south of the broken *tuff-crater. **1880** *Academy* 20 Nov. 370 They [certain Chinese rocks] exhibit *tuff-like characters. **1861** E. T. HOLLAND in *Peaks, Passes & Gl.* Ser. II. I. 9 A high range of *tuff mountains. **1603** OWEN *Pembrokeshire* (1892) 80 There is *Tuff Stone found in the Mountaine over Newport. *c* **1640** J. SMYTH *Lives Berkeleys* (1883) I. 309 Fetching.. the Tuft stone from Dursley by land. **1802** *Brookes' Gazetteer* (ed. 12) s.v. *Lugano*, Most of the houses are built of tufstone. **1822-7** GOOD *Study Med.* (1829) I. 61 Tufa or *tuffwacke, as Schmeisser calls it, and tarras, which are compounds of iron, alumine, silex, and carbonate of lime. **1847** LEITCH tr. *C. O. Müller's Anc. Art* §271. (1850) 303 Pozzolana (an earthy tuff-wack).

† **tuff**, *v. Obs. rare.* [Echoic: cf. PUFF.] *intr.* To make a short explosive sound with the breath. So **tuff** *int.*, an imitation of such a sound.

1553 *Respublica* I. iii. 247 *Avarice.* What saie ye? *Inso.* Hake. *Adul.* Tuff. *Op.* Hem. *Ibid.* III. iv. 774 *Adul.* But looke, who cometh yonder, puffing and tuffing?.. *Avar*... Where have ye lost your breath? **1598** FLORIO, *Sbuffante*.. panting, breathing, tuffing as a cat, chafing. *a* **1821** KEATS in *Critic* 9 Feb. (1895) 104/1, I for a moment whiles was prisoner ta'en And rifled, tuff!

tuff, obs. form of TOUGH, TUFT.

tuffaceous (tʌˈfeɪʃəs), *a.* [f. TUFF *sb.* + -ACEOUS.] 'Having the properties of or composed of volcanic tuff' (*Cent. Dict. Suppl.* 1909); distinguished from *tufaceous* in the specific sense.

1882 GEIKIE *Textbk. Geol.* II. II. vi. 164 Tuffs passing gradually into shale, limestone, sandstone, &c. The intermediate varieties have been called *ashy shale, tuffaceous shale*, or *shaley tuff*, &c.

tuffall, tuffe, obs. ff. TO-FALL, TOUGH, TUFT.

tuffet (ˈtʌfɪt). ? *Obs.* exc. *dial.* [f. *tuff*, F. *touffe* (see TUFT *sb.*) with suffix-exchange dim. -ET[1] for -EL in OF. *touffel.*]

1. = TUFT *sb.* 1, 1 b.

1553 *Respublica* III. vi. 928 The goddesse occasyon.. weareth a greate long tuffet of heare beefore, and behinde hathe not one heare. **1578** LYTE *Dodoens* I. lxxiii. 108 At the toppe of the stalkes groweth blewish floures in thicke tuffets. *a* **1691** BOYLE *Hist. Air* (1692) 178 Emerging from the ground like tuffets of rushes. **1899** P. ROBINSON in *Contemp. Rev.* June 844 [A blackcap] standing between two 'tuffets' of bloom.

2. A hillock, mound: = TUFT *sb.* 3 b.

1877 BLACKMORE *Erema* II. xxxiv. 193 Here were six little grassy tuffets.

3. ? A hassock or footstool.

(Doubtful: perh. due to misunderstanding of the nursery rime, which may belong to sense 2.)

? **18..** *Nursery Rime*, Little Miss Muffet sat on a tuffet, Eating of curds and whey. [Cf. BUFFET[1].] **1895** BENSON in *Contemp. Rev.* July 125 Miss Moffat.. hastily got up from the tuffet—which turned out to be a three-legged stool. **1904** *Westm. Gaz.* 22 Dec. 1/3 Mamie.. gave him a tuffet for his narrow feet.

Hence † ˈ**tuffetwise** *adv.* [-WISE], in the manner or form of a tuffet or tuft.

1578 LYTE *Dodoens* II. lvi. 217 The stalke is of a foote and half long: at which groweth a great sort of floures tuffet-wise.

tuffie: see TUFTY.

tuffin, obs. f. TYPHOON.

tuffing (ˈtʌfɪŋ). *rare.* [f. *tuff*, TUFT + -ING[1].]

† **1.** Caulking material; oakum. *Obs.*

1513 DOUGLAS *Æneis* v. xii. 31 The tuffing kendillis betuixt the plankis wak.

2. *Bell-ringing* (also **tuftin**). The tufts of wool woven into a bell-rope to give a grip for the hand: = SALLY *sb.*[2] 2.

1869 TROYTE *Change Ringing* i. 2 The 'hand stroke' blow will be the one on which he pulls the 'sallie', or tuffing on the rope. **1897** F. T. JANE *Lordship* vi. 66 The tuftin being worn, she hurt a man's hands a good deal on the sally, and had mainly to be rung on the back-stroke.

tuffle (ˈtʌf(ə)l), *v. dial.* [app. onomatopœic: cf. TIFFLE *v.*[2]]

1. *trans.* To put into disorder, ruffle, rumple; to entangle, ravel; = TIFFLE *v.*[2]

1777 *Horæ Subsecivæ* 431 (E.D.D.). *a* **1810** in Cromek *Rem. Nithsdale Song* 67 An' what has tuffled yere gowden locks..?

2. To bind up (flax) in loose sheaves.

1799 A. YOUNG *Agric. Lincoln* 164 (*Flax cultivation*) Tuffle it; that is making it in a loose sheaf, open at bottom.

tuffon, -oon, obs. ff. TYPHOON.

tuff-tafata, etc.: see TUFTAFFETA.

tuff-tuff (ˈtʌfˈtʌf). Anglicized f. TEUF-TEUF.

1902 E. GLYN *Refl. Ambrosine* v. 62 The tuff-tuff-tuff of a motor car was heard, and it drew up at our gate. **1903** *Daily Chron.* 1 July 3/2 'When one has steered one's "tuff-tuff" all day,' said a Parisian.. 'or been driven through the clouds in a balloon.' **1982** N. FREELING *Wolfnight* 98 He managed.. with a tufftuff to Kehl.. and walked across the Europa Bridge.

tufit, dial. var. TEWHIT, lapwing.

tufo: see TUFA.

tuft (tʌft), *sb.* Also 5 toft, tofte, 5-7 tufft, 6 tufte; 6-7 tuffe, 7-8 tuff. [The derivation presents many difficulties. Supposed to represent F. *touffe* (in OF. also *toffe, tofe*), generally referred to L. *tūfa*, 'a kind of helmet crest', or 'a kind of military standard' (in Vegetius, 386), appearing in Byzantine Greek as τοῦφα (see Du Cange). By some held to be ult. of German origin, ? ad. OLG. *top* or OHG. *zopf.* The final *t* is evidently an Eng. addition: cf. *carafe*, vulg. *craft*; also *cliff, clift*; *draff, draft*; *graff, graft*, and vulgar *paragraft, telegraft*.

The difficulties of this derivation are that F. *touffe* is not the normal repr. of L. *tūfa*, but points to **tuffa*, whereas the long *ū* of *tūfa* is supported by the Greek and by Beda's *tuuf*; also that *tūfa, touffe*, answer phonetically neither to Low nor High German. Cf. Pr. *chuf*, It. *ciuffo*, a tuft or lock of hair, ad. Ger. *zopf.* Beside these, the final *t* in the Eng. word is of minor difficulty.]

1. A bunch (natural or artificial) of small things, usually soft and flexible, as hairs, feathers, etc., fixed or attached at the base.

[*a* **731** BEDA *Eccl. Hist.* II. xvi, Illud genus uexilli, quod Romani tufam, Angli uero appellant tuuf. (Hence in Henry of Huntingdon: see Du Cange.)]

c **1386** CHAUCER *Prol.* 555 (Harl.) Vpon þe cop right of his nose he hade A werte and þer on stood a tuft [*v.r.* toft(e) of heres. **1463** in *Bury Wills* (Camden) 36 A peyre of bedys.. with a knoppe, othir wyse callyd a tufft, of blak sylke. **1585** T. WASHINGTON tr. *Nicholay's Voy.* III. iii. 73 b, The rest of the haires.. they doe cut away.., except a tuffe of haire on the top of their head. *Ibid.* v. 78 Great tufts of feathers vpon their heads. **1664** H. MORE *Myst. Iniq.* 273 A tuft of seven bristles. **1727** [DORRINGTON] *Philip Quarll* 193 A small Tuff of Hair on each Shoulder and Hip. **1794** W. FELTON *Carriages* (1801) I. 141 The quilting of the cloth with small ornaments, called tufts, also gives a richness to the lining. **1842** TENNYSON *Lancelot & Guinevere* iii, A light-green tuft of plumes she bore Closed in a golden ring. **1845** GREGORY *Outl. Chem.* II. 345 Salicylic acid crystallises in tufts of slender prisms.

b. *Bot.*, etc. A cluster of short-stalked leaves or flowers growing from a common point, of stems growing from a common root, etc.; an umbel or fascicle; also, a clump of small herbs growing closely together.

Formerly applied more widely, e.g. to the receptacle of a composite flower, or to a compact seed-vessel.

† *London tuft*, an old name for Sweet William: see LONDON. See also CANDYTUFT.

1523 FITZHERB. *Husb.* §70 Beastes alone, nor horses aloone, nor shepe alone,.. wyll not eate a pasture euen, but leaue many tuftes and hygh grasse. **1530** PALSGR. 283/2 Tufte of grasse, *monceau de herbe.* **1578** LYTE *Dodoens* I. x. 18 The.. common Tansie hath a blackishe stalke.. diuided.. into many single braunches, at the end wherof are round tuftes, bearing yellow floures like small round buttons. **1620** VENNER *Via Recta* vii. 159 The round tufts or heads which conteine the seede. **1645-50** BOATE *Irel. Nat. Hist.* (1860) 93 Hassocky-bogs.. are very thick overspread with little Tufts or Ilets.. consisting of reeds, rushes [etc.]. **1727** P. BLAIR *Pharmaco-Bot.* v. 235 Tufts or Umbels of penta-petalous yellow Flowers. *Ibid.* 236 Dispos'd in small Umbells or Tuffs. **1824** W. IRVING *T. Trav.* IV. (1848) 278 Tom had long been picking his way cautiously through this treacherous forest; stepping from tuft to tuft of rushes and roots. **1853** MISS YONGE *Heir of Redclyffe* xxx, A tuft of deep purple, the beautiful Alpine saxifrage. **1861** BENTLEY *Man. Bot.* 137 All the leaves of that branch may be brought in contact at their base, in which case they form a tuft or fascicle. **1908** [MISS FOWLER] *Betw. Trent & Ancholme* 89 The Robin's favourite tuft on the top of the Cedar-tree.

2. A small tufted patch of hair on the head or chin; a lock; an imperial (IMPERIAL B. 8).

1601 DENT *Pathw. Heaven* (1831) 37 What say you then to these—long locks, fore tufts, shag hair, and all these new fashions? *c* **1610** *Women Saints* 160 No.. friselled tuffes, borrowed to deceiue. **1654** tr. *Martini's Conq. China* 33 In the hinder part of their Heads they leave a Tuff, which being curiously woven and plated, they let hang down. **1711** HEARNE *Collect.* (O.H.S.) III. 150 On his [Chaucer's] Chin 2 thin forked Tufts. **1831** SCOTT *Ct. Robt.* ii, One of the soldiers.. who showed the shaven head and the single tuft of a Mussulman. **1840** THACKERAY *Shabby-genteel Story* v, The stylish tuft on his chin.

3. A small group of trees or bushes; a clump. (Cf. TOFT[1] 4, which perh. belongs here.)

1555 EDEN *Decades* 352 Vppon the innermoste necke to the landewarde, is a tufte of trees. **1611** SHAKS. *Wint. T.* II. i. 34 Behind the tuft of Pines I met them. **1667** MILTON *P.L.* VII. 327 With high Woods the Hills were crownd, With tufts the vallies and each fountain side. **1778** *Eng. Gazetteer* (ed. 2) s.v. *Tottenham*, A circular tuft of elms.. called the Seven Sisters. **1879** S. C. BARTLETT *Egypt to Pal.* xi. 239 Land.. more or less sprinkled with tufts of desert shrubs.

† **b.** A grassy hillock, a small knoll or mound. (Cf. TOFT[1] 3.) *Obs. rare.*

1651 HOWELL *Venice* 32 The Adriatic Sea.. spreading himself.. towards the Continent of Italie, leaves som green tuffs or tombs of Earth uncoverd.

4. (*a*) *Anat.* A small cluster or plexus of capillary blood-vessels, as the ***Malpighian tufts*** of the kidney; a glomerule. (*b*) *Zool.* ***branchial*** or ***respiratory tuft***: a cluster of tentacles having a respiratory function, in some tubicolous worms.

1841-71 T. R. JONES *Anim. Kingd.* (ed. 4) 277 The respiratory tufts.. attached to the anterior extremity of the creature.. form most elegant arborescent appendages, generally tinted with brilliant colours. **1848** [see MALPIGHIAN 1]. **1873** T. H. GREEN *Introd. Pathol.* (ed. 2) 68 The tufts of vessels which form the Malpighian bodies.

† **5.** A crest, as of a bird. *Obs.*

1598 FLORIO, *Capelletto*, a little tuffe vpon a peacocks head. **1706** PHILLIPS (ed. Kersey), *Tuft*, a lock of Hair,.. also the Crest of a Bird.

b. *fig.* Head, chief, top. *Obs. nonce-use.*

1625 B. JONSON *Staple of N.* II. v, He is.. my Chiefe, the Point, Tip, Top, and Tuft of all our family.

† **6.** A turban. *Obs.*

1585 HIGINS *Junius' Nomencl.* 165/1 *Tiara*, a Turkish tuffe, such as the Turkes weare.. on their head. **1621** AINSWORTH *Annot. Pentat., Exod.* xxviii. 39. (1639) 117 Miter.. signifieth a thing wrapped about the head. Such as the Tuffe which.. is worne in the Easterne Countries.

7. An ornamental tassel on a cap; *spec.* the gold tassel formerly worn by titled undergraduates at Oxford and Cambridge (see quot. 1894).

Originally, at Oxford, a distinction of the sons of those peers who had a vote in the House of Lords, after 1861 of all peers and their eldest sons; after 1870 made optional.

1670 G. H. *Hist. Cardinals* I. III. 71 That invention of Bishops and Prelates to wear Green Tufts in their Caps. *a* **1704** T. BROWN *Contn. Quaker's Serm.* Wks. 1709 III. II. 3 Let not a Cap be seen among us, with an Idolatrous Tuff upon it. **1770** LANGHORNE *Plutarch* (1851) I. 336/2 As he was sacrificing the tuft of his cap fell off. **1861** HUGHES *Tom Brown at Oxf.* viii, Men.. all in tufts or gentlemen-commoners' caps. **1894** *Westm. Gaz.* 5 Mar. 3/1 Lord Rosebery.. was one of the last undergraduates of Christ Church who wore the gold tassel, known by the name of 'tuft', which was the distinguishing mark of noblemen and the sons of noblemen.

b. *transf.* in *University slang*, One who wears a tuft; a titled undergraduate.

1755 [see TUFT-HUNTER]. **1789** *Loiterer* No. 11. 6 A Tuft (when once suffered to get away from you) is scarcely ever recovered again. **1840** THACKERAY *Shabby-genteel Story* ii, The lad went to Oxford,.. frequented the best society, followed with a kind of proud obsequiousness all the tufts of the university. **1847** JOWETT *Let.* 10 Mar., in *Life & Lett.* (1897) I. 158 Dufferin of Christ Church.. seems a most excellent tuft. **1884** *Weekly Register* 18 Oct. 503/2 One don is much like another, to a lively young tuft who keeps beagles.

8. *attrib.* and *Comb.* **a.** *attrib.*: † **tuft gillyflower**, a kind of gillyflower (? = pink) growing in tufts; † **tuft mockado** (see MOCKADO 1, 1 b, and cf. TUFTAFFETA); also *attrib.*

[In both these, *tuft* may be, not the sb., but = *tuffed*, TUFTED: cf. quot. 1587 s.v. MOCKADO.]

1573 TUSSER *Husb.* (1878) 96 Herbes.. for windowes and pots..*Tuft gilleflowers. **1579** *Tuft mockado [see MOCKADO 1]. **1589** R. HARVEY *Pl. Perc.* (1590) 8, I will nickename no bodie: I am none of these tuft mockadoo mak-a-dooes. **1599** NASHE *Lenten Stuffe* 25 Penning a discourse of Tuftmockados. **1847-78** HALLIWELL, *Tuft-mockado*, a mixed stuff made to imitate tufted taffeta, or velvet.

b. *Comb.* as ***tuft-topped*** adj.; **tuft-gill**, a tuft-gilled fish, a lophobranch (*Cent. Dict.*); **tuft-gilled** *a.*, having tufted gills, as the order *Cirribranchiata* of molluscs (tooth-shells), or *Lophobranchii* of fishes (see LOPHOBRANCHIATE). See also TUFT-HUNTER.

1840 LUNDIE *Mission. Life in Samoa* xiii. (1846) 79 Tall tuft-topped cocoa-nut trees. **1861** P. P. CARPENTER in *Rep. Smithsonian Instit.* 1860, 222 Order *Cirrobranchiata.* (Tuft-gilled Crawlers).

tuft, *v.* Forms: see prec. [f. prec. sb.]

I. 1. *trans.* To furnish with a tuft or tufts.

1535 in *Archæologia* IX. 251 A pair of upper stockis of purple veluette embroidered with golde and tuffed with cameryke. **1573** in Feuillerat *Revels Q. Eliz.* (1908) 210 For Tufting vi lardge kirtells of greene Sattin with golde sarcenet. **1630** J. TAYLOR (Water P.) *Trav.* Wks. III. 98/1 She's ring'd, she's braceleted, she's richly tuff'd. **1728-46** THOMSON *Spring* 914 Solemn oaks, that tuft the swelling mounts. **1743** J. DAVIDSON *Æneid* VIII. 264 Caps tufted with wool. **1833** T. HOOK *Parson's Dau.* III. ix, The officers of a crack Hussar regiment.. tipped and tufted. **1850** TENNYSON *In Mem.* cxxviii. 20 To make old bareness picturesque And tuft with grass a feudal tower.

b. *Upholstery.* To draw together the two surfaces of (a cushion or the like) by a thread passed through at regular intervals producing depressions, which are then usually ornamented with tufts or buttons.

1884 [implied in *tufting-button*: see TUFTING *vbl. sb.* 3]. **1891** in *Cent. Dict.*

2. *intr.* To form a tuft or tufts; to grow in tufts.

1598 SYLVESTER *Du Bartas* II. i. II. *Imposture* 397 Among the dark shade of those tufting arbors. **1629** PARKINSON *Paradisus* 317 Tufting close vpon the ground, like vnto the common Thrift. **1794** G. ADAMS *Nat. & Exp. Philos.* III.

xxxiv. 408 A sea of cotton, tufting here and there by the action of the air in the undisturbed parts of the clouds.

3. *trans.* To form into a tuft. *rare*⁻¹. (Cf. TUFTED 2.)

1860 HAWTHORNE *Marb. Faun* viii, What weeds cluster and tuft themselves on the cornices of ruins.

II. 4. *trans.* To beat (a covert) in stag-hunting. Also *absol.*

1590 COKAINE *Treat. Hunting* C iv b, You may begin to tuft for a Bucke. **1612** DRAYTON *Poly-olb.* xiii. 113 When with his hounds The laboring Hunter tufts the thicke vnbarbed grounds Where harbor'd is the Hart. **1870** BLAINE *Encycl. Rur. Sports* (ed. 3) §1813 Tufting of deer. As deer frequently herd in copses, woods, and brakes, it is usual to *tuft* (hunt) a covert with a couple or two of steady old hounds, called tufters. **1908** *Q. Rev.* July 90 The lonely ridges of the Brendon hills are 'tufted' for a 'warrantable' deer.

b. To dislodge (the game) by 'tufting'; also *fig.*

a **1640** JACKSON *Creed* x. xxiv. §4 The..meaning of the learned moderator hath been by his followers..so meanly tufted, and so unskilfully hunted after. **1909** QUILLER COUCH *True Tilda* xxi, They had tufted him [a stag] out of the wood.

tuft, obs. form of TOFT¹, TUFF.

tuftaffeta, -taffety (tʌfˈtæfətə, -ˈtæfətɪ). *Obs.* or *arch.* Forms (with hyphen, or as one word, or as two words): 6–7 tuft-, tufte-; 6–9 tuf-, 7 tuffe-, 7–8 tuff-, (8 ? tiff-): see TAFFETA, TAFFETY. [f. *tuff*, TUFT *sb.* + TAFFETA, TAFFETY.]

1. A kind of taffeta with a pile or nap arranged in tufts.

1572 in *Rep. MSS. Ld. Middleton* (1911) 422 For vi yardes of tufte taffyta at xij s. the yarde. **1593** DONNE *Sat.* iv. 33 His Ierkin..had been Velvet, but 'twas now (so much ground was seen) Become tufftaffaty. **1635** CRANLEY *Amanda* 76 What shall I doe with rich Tuftafaties? **1735** POPE *Donne's Sat.* iv. 42 The suit..Was velvet in the youth of good queen Bess, But mere tuff-taffety what now remain'd. **1899** MARY JOHNSTON *By Order of Company* iii, He..hitched forward his cloak of sky-blue tuftaffeta with an air.

2. *transf.* A person wearing tuftaffeta.

1613 BEAUM. & FL. *Coxcomb* v. i, Such an old Tuff-taffity that knows not.

3. *attrib.* **a.** Made of tuftaffeta.

1587 *Lanc. Wills* (Chetham Soc.) III. 34 My blacke tuftafata hosen. **1611** MIDDLETON & DEKKER *Roaring Girle* E iij b, Any coacht veluet cappe or tuftaffety iacket. *c* **1618** MORYSON *Itin.* IV. (1903) 96, I did see her apparelled once in a Tuft taffety gowne and an other tyme in a purple Taffety gowne. **1629** B. JONSON *New Inn* II. i, I'll help to fit her With a tuft-taffeta cloak.

b. Clothed in tuftaffeta; luxuriously dressed; hence *fig.* Cf. TAFFETA B. 2.

1598 E. GILPIN *Skial.* (1878) 49, I smile at thy Atturneys silken pride, Tufttaffeta state. **1612** *Proc. Virginia* ii. 13 in *Capt. Smith's Wks.* (Arb.) 97 We daily feasted with..fish, fowle, and diverse sorts of wild beasts as fat as we could eat them: so that none of our Tuftaffaty humorists desired to goe for England. **1614** B. JONSON *Bart. Fair* IV. iii, Such as you are..with your tuft-taffata hanches. [**1829** H. MURRAY *N. Amer.* I. iv. 212 A plot which had arisen among what he [Smith] oddly calls the 'tuftaffety' part of the colony, to break up and return to England.]

c. ***tuftaffeta cream***: a very soft or smooth kind of cream; velvet cream.

1661 HAN. WOOLLEY *Ladies Direct* 98 To make the Tuff-Taffete Cream. **1773** GOLDSM. *Stoops to Conq.* II. i, A shaking pudding, and a dish of tiff—taff—taffety cream. *Hast.* Confound your made dishes.

tufted (ˈtʌftɪd), *a.* [f. TUFT *sb.* and *v.* + -ED.]

1. Having or adorned with a tuft or tufts.

a. Adorned with tufts or clumps of trees or bushes.

1606 SYLVESTER *Du Bartas* II. iv. II. *Magnif.* 1106 The tufted tops of sacred Libanon. **1779** *Mirror* No. 43 ¶3 A stream..circled round a tufted plain, and formed a little lake in front of a village. **1810** SCOTT *Lady of L.* I. xiii, Tall rocks and tufted knolls. **1883** R. BRIDGES *Prometheus* 148 The cones And needles of the fir..are strewn upon the tufted floor.

b. Adorned with tufts of some fabric, as a garment, or with a natural tuft, as the tail or other part of an animal; having or formed with tufts: *spec.* of a carpet, carpeting, etc. (see quot. 1960). Also *ellipt.* as *sb.*

1651 in *Verney Mem.* (1907) I. 480, 2 Tufted Holland Wastcoates. **1662** *Irish Stat.* (1765) II. 411 Linnen cloth or canvas called stript or tufted canvas. **1709** STEELE *Tatler* No. 45 ¶5 A young Gentleman who sat next me..in a tufted Gown. **1774** GOLDSM. *Nat. Hist.* (1776) III. 291 The tail long, and tufted at the point..like the lion. **1815** KIRBY & SP. *Entomol.* iii. (1818) I. 63 Head..adorned with elegantly tufted antennæ. **1877** KNIGHT *Dict. Mech.*, *Tufted fabric*, a fabric in which tufts are set, as in the old form of Turkish and Persian carpets. **1960** *Textile Terms & Definitions* (Textile Inst.) (ed. 4) 152 Tufted Carpet consists essentially of a pile yarn of tufts or loops which is inserted into a pre-woven backing and secured by means of a bonding material. **1963** *Which?* Mar. 70/2 Tufted carpets..are easier and cheaper to make than Wiltons or Axminsters. *Ibid.*, Tufteds may have cut or loop pile. **1965** *Guardian* 31 Mar. 14/1 Poor performance fibres..tended to give tufteds such an unwelcome reputation in the 1950s. **1970** *Which?* Sept. 265/2 There is a..labelling code..which requires that the label gives..the type of construction (eg Axminster, Wilton or tufted). **1981** *Times* 10 Aug. 16/1 The company..played the pioneering role in introducing the cheaper-to-make tufted carpet to a British market dominated by traditionally woven Axminster or Wilton.

c. *Her.* Having the tuft (of the tail) of a specified tincture.

1761 *Brit. Mag.* II. 13 An antelope,..gules;..chained, armed, crested, tufted, and hoofed, or. **1864** BOUTELL *Her. Hist. & Pop.* xvii. §3. (ed. 3) 281 An unicorn arg., armed, maned and tufted or.

d. Of a bird: Having a tuft of feathers upon the head; crested: *esp.* in *Ornith.* as the epithet of a particular species.

1768 PENNANT *Zool.* II. 458 The Tufted Duck. **1770** M. BRUCE in *Life*, etc. xii. (1914) 176 From her low nest the tufted lark upsprings. **1785** PENNANT *Arct. Zool.* II. 432 Tufted Auk. **1807** COL. HAWKER *Diary* (1893) I. 6, I saw 5 tufted ducks. **1833** TENNYSON *New-Year's Eve* v, The tufted plover [will] pipe along the fallow lea. **1883** *Fisheries Exhib. Catal.* (ed. 4) 134 Tufted Cormorant or 'Shag'.

2. Formed into or forming a tuft; growing in a tuft or tufts; clustered.

1632 MILTON *L'Allegro* 78 Towers and Battlements.. Boosom'd high in tufted Trees. **1637** —— *Lycidas* 143 The tufted Crow-toe, and pale Gessamine. **1740** SOMERVILLE *Hobbinol* I. 101 The tufted Cowslips breathe their faint Perfume. **1807** WORDSW. *Wh. Doe* VII. 142 A hut, by tufted trees defended. **1853** CHR. G. ROSSETTI *Poems* (1904) 152/2 The stream shines silver in the tufted grass.

3. *Nat. Hist.* (esp. as the epithet of a particular species or variety: see quots. See also 1 d.)

a. *Bot.* Bearing flowers in tufts or fascicles. **b.** *Bot.* and *Zool.* Growing in tufts, cæspitose.

1629 Tufted Colombines [see COLUMBINE *sb.*² 3]. **1707** MORTIMER *Husb.* (1721) II. 216 Cowslips are of various kinds..: The double green ones, the single green, the tufted, ..&c. **1805** R. W. DICKSON *Pract. Agric.* II. 895 The Tufted Vetch..might..be useful..as a green fodder. **1857** MISS PRATT *Flower. Pl.* IV. 237 *L[ysimachia] thyrsiflora* (Tufted Loosestrife). **1872** NICHOLSON *Palæont.* 95 The corallum is cæspitose, or tufted. *Mod.* Tufted violas of many colours.

4. *Comb.*, as ***tufted-eared***, ***-necked*** adjs.

1811 SHAW *Gen. Zool.* VIII. 236 Tufted Eared Creeper. *Ibid.* 345 Tufted-necked Humming-bird.

Hence **ˈtuftedness**, the quality of being tufted; in quot. *concr.* a tufted structure.

1665 HOOKE *Microgr.* xlvi. 196 A seeming tuftedness or brushy part on each side.

tufter (ˈtʌftə(r)). *Stag-hunting.* [f. TUFT *v.* 4 + -ER¹.] A hound trained to drive the deer out of cover.

1856 'STONEHENGE' *Brit. Sports* I. II. ii. §2. (ed. 2) 109 Men, called 'harbourers', with hounds trained for the purpose, called 'tufters', undertake the task. **1868** *Daily News* 2 Sept., The tufters..soon roused two fine stags. **1884** JEFFERIES *Red Deer* iii, When the tufters enter the woods —that is, the hounds detached from the pack to force the deer to break cover.

ˈtuft-ˌhunter. [f. TUFT *sb.* + HUNTER.] One who meanly or obsequiously courts the acquaintance of persons of rank and title (originally at the universities: see TUFT *sb.* 7, 7 b); a toady, sycophant.

1755 *Connoisseur* No. 97 ¶1, I remember to have heard a cousin of mine,..formerly at Cambridge,..mentioning a sect of Philosophers, distinguished by the rest of the collegians under the appellation of Tuft-Hunters. These were..the followers (literally speaking) of the fellow-commoners, noblemen, and other rich students. **1855** THACKERAY *Newcomes* xlv, Some..accused him of being a tuft-hunter, and flatterer of the aristocracy. *a* **1884** M. PATTISON *Mem.* (1885) 4 My father was too proud to be a tuft-hunter.

So **ˈtuft-ˌhunted** *a.*, sought after by tuft-hunters; **ˈtuft-ˌhunting** *sb.*, the practice of a tuft-hunter; *adj.* that is, or is characteristic of, a tuft-hunter.

1849 THACKERAY *On Friendship* Wks. 1901 VI. 625 His old acquaintances..set the *Tufthunted down as the Tuft-hunter. **1894** DU MAURIER *Trilby* II. 95 Little Billee was no tuft-hunter, he was the tuft-hunted. **1789** *Loiterer* No. 11. 6 The diversion of *tuft-hunting..has been so long.. practised in this place [Oxford]. **1848** THACKERAY *Bk. Snobs* xix, Tuft-hunting is snobbish. **1829** [H. BEST] *Pers. & Lit. Mem.* 101 He made no disgraceful *tuft-hunting distinctions in favour of noblemen or gentlemen commoners. **1856** R. A. VAUGHAN *Mystics* (1860) II. 208 A tuft-hunting sort of Quietism.

tuftily (ˈtʌftɪlɪ), *adv.* [f. TUFTY + -LY².] In a tufty manner; so as to form tufts.

1859 *Jrnl. R. Agric. Soc.* XX. I. 259 It [grass] grows tuftily.

tuftin (*Bell-ringing*): see TUFFING 2.

tufting (ˈtʌftɪŋ), *vbl. sb.* [f. TUFT *v.* + -ING¹.] The action of the verb TUFT, or the result of this.

1. a. Adornment with a tuft or tufts.

1554–5 in Feuillerat *Revels Q. Mary* (1914) 175, vj yardes of red gold sarcenet..for the tuftinge of the wemens hedpeces. **1558** *Ibid., Q. Eliz.* (1908) 24 Spente in pullinges oute, tuftinges, tyringes [etc.].

b. *concr.* Tufts collectively; a mass of tufts.

1791 GILPIN *Forest Scenery* I. 243 Sun-shine striking a wood..and reposing on the tuftings of a clump. **1894** R. BRIDGES *Shorter Poems* V. xvi. (1912) 317 The fir-trees.. wave aloft..their blue-green tuftings.

c. The process or result of using tufts in the making of carpets, etc. Also *attrib.*

1965 *Guardian* 31 Mar. 14/1 In inserting the pile vertically rather than horizontally as in weaving, tufting has been limited as to the range of effects which can be produced. *Ibid.*, Tufting machines are exclusively American and British developments. **1967** E. SHORT *Embroidery & Fabric Collage* iii. 68 There is no reason why good designs should not be carried out in candlewick cotton, using either tufting or couching and surface stitchery. **1970** *Encycl. Americana* XXIII. 763 In tufting, a preconstructed backing is used for the basic carpet structure... As the backing fabric moves through the machine, the pile yarns are stitched through it by a long bank of needles working simultaneously. **1974** J. GRAY *Canvas Work* 121 (*heading*) Turkey (Single Knot Tufting)... This stitch, like all tufting stitches, is best worked from bottom to top of the area. **1976** J. MESSENT *Designing for Embroidery from Anc. & Prim. Sources* I. 28/1 Stumpwork, raised work, high padding and quilting are among some methods of creating a protruding area of interest from an otherwise flat surface, as is a highly textured area such as a shaggy pile or tufting. **1976** *Daily Tel.* 21 Oct. 17/2 Knitting, crochet,..tufting and soft-toy making.

2. *Stag-hunting.* The action of beating a covert to dislodge the deer. Also *attrib.*

1862 C. P. COLLYNS *Chase Wild Red Deer* iv. 82 What I have said will sufficiently indicate what the object of *tufting* is. **1883** *Standard* 10 Aug. 2/1 Tufting is not a popular form of passing the time on an opening day. **1884** JEFFERIES *Red Deer* vii. 118 The hounds..are called the 'tufters';.. drawing the cover is called 'tufting'.

3. *Comb.* **tufting-button**, one of the buttons used in 'tufting' a cushion, etc. (see TUFT *v.* 1 b).

1884 FORNEY *Car-Builder's Dict.* (Cent. Dict.).

ˈtufting, *ppl. a.* [f. as prec. + -ING².] That tufts: see the vb.

1598 [see TUFT *v.* 2].

ˈtuftlet. [f. TUFT *sb.* + -LET.] A little tuft.

1892 J. MATHER *Poems* 129 Tuftlets brown Of rush and bracken.

tufty (ˈtʌftɪ), *a.* Also 7 tuffie. [f. TUFT *sb.* + -Y.]

1. Full of or abounding in tufts; covered or adorned with tufts: **a.** of hair, thread, or the like.

1641 BEST *Farm. Bks.* (Surtees) 6 Signes of a good Ewe... Her buttocke broade and large, and shewing tufty and thicke of wooll. **1716** M. DAVIES *Athen. Brit.* II. 241 His black Thread-bare Coat..of a tufty and rusty Hue. **1848** *Fraser's Mag.* XXXVII. 404 Shaven round his head, so as to leave a tufty patch at top.

b. Of foliage, herbage, or blossoms.

1638 BRATHWAIT *Barnabees Jrnl.* III. (1818) 133 Vallies.. Deckt with tufty woods. **1796** AN. SEWARD *Hoyle Lake* in *New Ann. Reg.* 158 Dry are the tufty downs, diffusive spread O'er the light surface of the sandy mound. **1869** BLACKMORE *Lorna D.* lix, Here the ground lay jagged and shaggy, wrought up with high tufts of reed... This tufty, flaggy ground..will not hold impressions. **1903** *Academy* 25 July 94/2 Yarrow and the tufty melilot.

c. Covered with tufts or clumps of trees. *rare*⁻¹.

1612 DRAYTON *Poly-olb.* xvii. 388 About the neighbouring woods..in the tufty Frith, and in the mossy Fell.

2. Forming a tuft or tufts; consisting of or growing in tufts.

1611 COTGR., *Touffu*.., tuffie [**1632** SHERWOOD, Tuftie or tuffie], thicke growing, thicke of boughs, growing close together. **1613–16** W. BROWNE *Brit. Past.* I. v. 310 An humble dale, Where tufty daizies nod at every gale. **1776** *Phil. Trans.* LXVI. 100 Islands are overspread with a short, tufty, round grass. **1889** *Standard* 24 Apr., They are all distinguished by frizzly hair, more or less tufty.

tug (tʌg), *sb.* Forms: see TUG *v.*; also 5 teug. [f. TUG *v.*]

1. An act or the action of tugging; a forcible or violent pull; a severe strain or drag.

1500–20 DUNBAR *Poems* xxxiii. 81 The tarsall gaif him tug for tug. **1635** QUARLES *Embl.* IV. iii. 28 The idle vessell slides that watry lay, Without the blast, or tug, of wind, or Oare. **1697** DRYDEN *Æneid* IX. 759 Downward by the feet he drew The trembling dastard: at the tug he falls. **1754** MRS DELANY in *Life & Corr.* (1861) III. 307 Lady Harriet had a tooth drawn by Rutter,..and he gave three tugs before he got it out! **1815** *Hist. J. Decastro* IV. 111 The door stuck to the posts so fast that I was forced to take three or four good tugs at it before it would come open. **1886** FENN *Master of Cerem.* xiv, Morton felt a tug at his line.

2. †Labour, toil (*obs. rare*); *esp.* a determined effort to accomplish or attain something; a hard try; a struggle; a 'go'.

1504 *Plumpton Corr.* (Camden) 191 It ryseth on my owne mynd to give over grett tuggs of husbandry which I had, and take me to lesse charge. **1673** LD. CONWAY in *Essex Papers* (Camden) I. 141, I shall yet have a tug for the Mʳ of the Ordnance place. **1764** *Mem. G. Psalmanazar* 84, I..found it a very hard tug to keep up my credit. **1856** BRYANT *Autumn Woods* xii, The vain low strife That makes men mad—the tug for wealth and power.

3. a. A strenuous contest between two forces or persons.

1660 GOWER in *5th Rep. Hist. MSS. Comm.* (1876) 204/1 The only tug is between Episcopacy and Presbytery. **1830** SCOTT *Demonol.* I. 11 Amid the mortal tug of combat. **1868** FREEMAN *Norm. Conq.* II. viii. 269 On this day..William began that career of..good fortune in the mere tug of battle. **1897** *Westm. Gaz.* 8 Dec. 2/3 The tug of will between the overbearing Kaiser and his hitherto subservient people.

b. ***tug of war.*** (*a*) The decisive contest; the real struggle or tussle; a severe contest for supremacy. (*b*) An athletic contest between two teams who haul at the opposite ends of a rope, each trying to drag the other over a line marked between them. Also *attrib.*

1677 N. LEE *Alex. Gt.* IV. ii, When Greeks joined Greeks, then was the tug of war. **1822** BYRON *Juan* VIII. li, At last [the mob] takes to weapons..Then comes 'the tug of war'. **1876** *World* V. No. 108. 13 The tug of war..was the most popular item in Saturday's entertainment. **1893** E. H. BARKER *Wand. Southern Waters* 263 He [the devil] therefore lost no time in entering upon a tug-of-war with the saintly interloper. **1902** *Westm. Gaz.* 6 June 7/1 Their tug-of-war team pulled over two teams of British Tommies.

c. *tug of love*, a conflict of affections; *spec.* a contest for custody of a minor; also (with hyphens) *attrib.*

Perh. infl. by the title of a comedy 'The Tug of Love' by I. Zangwill (1907).

1973 *Times* 9 Nov. 20/7 The Houghton committee was set up after some highly-publicized 'tug of love' cases, and recommended making it easier for long-term foster-parents ..to adopt. **1977** *Daily Mirror* 21 Mar. 13/1 Back home in the arms of her mother, a tiny tug-of-love girl sleeps peacefully. The girl..had been taken to California after being snatched by her father. **1984** *Times* 12 Oct. 2/2 'Tug of love' cases where a child is seized by one parent from another.

4. In harness: **a.** (Chiefly *pl.*) A pair of short chains attached to the hames, by which the collar is connected with the shafts. **b.** A trace. **c.** A short strap sewn on various parts of the harness and serving to keep it in position; also (*pl.*) the loops of the back-strap which support the shafts. **d.** A metal stud or pin on the shaft to prevent it running too far forward through the loops of the back-strap. **e.** See quot. 1844. Also *locally* applied to other parts of harness: see quot. 1888.

[*c* **1250** *MS. Barlow 49* (2) lf. 16 In carucis..emendandis. .. In iugis et tuggis ad idem emptis ix. d.] **1417–18** in *Archæol. Jrnl.* (1881) XXXVIII. 78 Item in vij Teugys, xij d. **1481–3** *Acc. Exch. K.R.* File 496 No. 26 Tuggis et hamis. **1497** *Naval Acc. Hen. VII* (1896) 96 Tugges for horsharnesse, ij baskettes. **1562** Bulleyn *Bulwark, Dial. Soarnes & Chir.* 7b, Banishe them from Chyrurgi, commende them to the Carte. To the flaile and the rake, the trace and the togge. **1589** Puttenham *Eng. Poesie* iii. xxiii. (Arb.) 281 Which word tugge..signifieth the pull or draught of the oxen or horses, and therefore the leathers that beare the chiefe stresse of the draught, the cartars call them tugges. **1786** Burns *To Auld Mare* xi, Thou was a noble fittie-lan', As e'er in tug or tow was drawn! **1794** W. Felton *Carriages* (1801) II. x. 134 Tugs to hold up the traces. *Ibid.* 135 The hipstrap..buckles to the tugs of the breeching to hold it up. *Ibid.* 147 In the middle [of each of a pair of hames] other loops are hung, to which the tugs for the draught are fixed. **1808–18** Jamieson, *Tug*, raw-hide, of which formerly plough-traces were made. **1844** Stephens *Bk. Farm* II. 695 The pace of the old horse should be subdued..by the rein and tug; which the short reins are called, that pass from the head of one horse to the collar of the other. **1862** *Catal. Internat. Exhib., Brit.* II. No. 4708, The collars, hames, and tugs are suited to give the horse the least fatigue in drawing the vehicle. **1888** Elworthy *W. Somerset Word-bk., Tug*,..the hook or other iron on the carriage, or on the whipple-tree, to which the trace is attached... The end of the leather trace at the part where it is attached to the vehicle... A loose loop buckled round the shaft, to which (when used) is fastened the kicking-strap.

f. *Mining.* The iron hoop of a corf or hoisting bucket.

1858 Simmonds *Dict. Trade, Tug*,..a hoop of iron to hold a tackle. **1877** in Knight *Dict. Mech.* **1881** Raymond *Mining Gloss., Tug* (Derb.), the iron hook of a hoisting bucket, to which the tacklers are attached.

g. A rope. *U.S.*

1805 M. Lewis *Jrnl.* in *Lewis & Clark Exped.* (1904) I. 369 The white perogue..[was] refitted in a few minutes with some tugs of raw hides and nales. **1852** H. C. Watson *Nights in Block-House* 445 They took a strong tug, made from the raw hide of the buffalo or elk. **1910** W. M. Raine *B. O'Connor* xiv. 216 He stopped as if to fasten a tug.

5. A timber-wagon. *south.* and *east. dial.*

1706 Phillips (ed. Kersey), *Tug*,..a Country-Word for a Waggon to carry Timber. **1724** De Foe *Tour Gt. Brit.* I. 59, I have seen one tree on a carriage which they call here [Lewes] a tug, drawn by two and twenty oxen. **1791** Gilpin *Forest Scenery* I. 116 A sort of wain, which in that deep country [Sussex], is expressively called a tugg. **1829** Hor. Smith *New Forest* I. i. 3 A timber-wain, in Hampshire called a tug.

6. a. A small, stoutly built, and powerful steamer used to tow other vessels; a tug-boat.

1817 *Chron.* in *Ann. Reg.* 101 This vessel,..appropriately named the Tug, is meant to track ten other vessels... The utility of the Tug is not confined to tracking. **1840** *Evid. Hull Docks Comm.* 73 You use the tug to tow them from the harbour. **1908** [Miss Fowler] *Betw. Trent & Ancholme* 12 The smoke of a tug drawing vessels.

b. Any other towing craft or vehicle, *spec.* (*a*) = *tug aircraft* below; (*b*) a tractor used to tow aircraft on the ground or unpowered road vehicles.

1942 *Jrnl. R. Aeronaut. Soc.* XLVI. 7 Aircraft towing as a method for launching high-performance gliders is a relatively recent development. Up till now, no specially designed aircraft 'tug' has become available. **1945** *Amer. Speech* XX. 227/2 *Tug*, a four- or six-wheeled tractor used for towing planes on the ground or for towing warehouse trailers. **1960** *Times Rev. Industry* Nov. 20/3 A..tractor can be a tug for two..vans. **1981** *Times* 14 Dec. 22/8 Tugs could not move the big jets because of ice.

7. Phrases. †*to hold tug*, (also *hold a tug*), *to hold one tug*, to keep one strenuously occupied, or fully engaged; *in tug*, † *upon a tug*, in conflict or contest (*with*).

1577 Grange *Golden Aphrod.* I iv, Whiche twoo pretie poyntes [for discussion] helde them tugge with hard holde vntill..aboute dinner tyme. **1659** *Burton's Diary* (1828) IV. 317 The debate held such tug that it was moved to adjourn. **1667** Wood *Life* 18 July (O.H.S.) II. 113 There was work enough..that would hold him tugg for a whole yeare. **1672** *Westminster Drollery* II. 94 No Tankerd, Flaggon, Bottle, nor Jugg..so well can hold Tugg. **1681** R. L'Estrange *Apol. Prot.* iv. i. 99 The Popes were at that time upon a Tugg with the Emperor. **1700** Motteux *Quix.* i. iv. iv. II. 398 The Barber held tugg with her till the Curate advis'd him to return it. **1791** Gouv. Morris in Sparks *Life & Writ.* (1832) I. 355 Lafayette will hold a good tug, being as cunning as any body. **1849** C. Bronte *Shirley* xx, She had seen from the window Tartar in full tug with two carriers' dogs.

8. [Perh. a different word.] *Public School slang.* At Eton College, a student on the foundation, a colleger as distinguished from an oppidan. In wider use, a studious or academic type, a swot.

1864 *Eton School Days* ii. 21 That building on the right is Tuggery, where the Tug-Muttons live; you'll hate the Tugs like anything: all the Oppidans hate the Tugs. **1922** S. Leslie *Oppidan* iv. 48 *Tugs* or Scholars were separated from Oppidans by the same gulf that lay between Professionals and Gentlemen in the world of sport. **1976** R. Pound *A. P. Herbert* i. 23 In Wykehamist parlance, he was a 'tug', a clever chap, whose achievement was held worthier than any playing-field victory. **1977** A. J. Ayer *Part of My Life* ii. 34 Traditionally, the Oppidans despised the Collegers, who tended to come from a lower social stratum, and spoke of them as Tugs, because they were believed to engage in tugs of war for the few pieces of mutton which was all that they were given to eat. **1982** Barr & York *Official Sloane Ranger Handbk.* 71/1 Swots are weeds (at Eton: 'tugs don't wash').

9. *attrib.* and *Comb.*: in sense 6, as ***tug-boat*** (whence ***tug-boatman***), ***-captain***, ***-man***, ***-master***, ***-owner***, ***-service***, ***-steamer***, ***traffic***; also ***tug-like*** adj.; **tug aircraft**, a powered aircraft used to tow a glider or train of gliders; **tug-boating** *U.S.*, working on a tug-boat; **tug-buckle**, a trace-buckle; **tug-carrier**, each of a pair of loops through which the tugs or traces pass (Knight *Dict. Mech.* 1877); **tug-chain**, a chain trace; also a short chain by which a leather trace is attached to the splinter-bar (*Funk's Stand. Dict.* 1895); **tug-hole**: cf. sense 4 f; **tug-hook**, a hook on the hame to which the trace is attached; **tug-iron**: see quot.; † **tug-mutton** = sense 8 above; **tug pilot**, the pilot of a tug aircraft; **tug-plate**: see quot.; **tug-rope**, *obs.* exc. *U.S.*, a trace of rope; **tug-slide**, a tongueless trace-buckle: cf. slide *sb.* 6; **tug-spring**, a spring connexion for traces to reduce the strain of starting a load; **tug-strap**, a leather trace; **tug-whiting**, a whiting caught by a handline (*Sc.*). See also tugwithe.

1931 *Flight* 26 June 578/2 The *tug aircraft, as it will probably be called. **1962** [see *parachute aircraft* s.v. parachute *sb.* 5]. **1976** J. Colville *Footprints in Time* xxxiii. 185 Soon there were fleets of gliders too. As each was released over the river, its tug-aircraft turned steeply away for home. **1832** Babbage *Econ. Manuf.* vi. (ed. 3) 44 A kind of *tug-boat for vessels which have occasion to ascend the rapid. **1860** *Merc. Marine Mag.* VII. 73 One ship was.. waiting to be towed out by the tugboat. **1941** E. P. O'Donnell *Great Big Doorstep* xxi. 310 If it wasn't for rain, I wooden have a job to hole down. You'd see me *tugboatin on the river or some kinda ordinary work. **1973** *Publ. Amer. Dial. Soc.* lx. 1 The coastal fringes are ideally suited to those who make their living from the sea—fishing, whaling.., boat-building, tugboating. **1891** *Daily News* 3 Feb. 3/5 The *tug-boatmen who struck on Friday at Liverpool were still out yesterday. **1851** Mayhew *Lond. Labour* I. 359 His foreman..says to me, 'Give that *tug-buckle a file'. **1862** *Catal. Internat. Exhib., Brit.* II. No. 4686 Set of carriage harness, with improved tug buckles. **1897** *Westm. Gaz.* 26 May 4/3 A *tug captain from Limehouse was called by the police. **1797** J. Curr *Coal Viewer* 18 Should the corves be made to draw by conductors, the chains..from the center of the *tug hole to the center of the ring that connects them, should measure 22½ inches. **1417–18** in *Archæol. Jrnl.* (1881) XXXVIII. 78 Item in *Teughookys. vij d. **1844** W. Barnes *Poems Rur. Life* Gloss., *Tugiron of shafts*, an iron on the shafts [of a wagon] to hitch the traces to. **1890** 'R. Boldrewood' *Col. Reformer* (1891) 155 Energetic people have certain advantages. Their *tuglike, unremitting habit of doing something keeps the machine going. **1891** *Scott. Leader* 24 Jan. 6 Over 80 per cent. of the *tugmen at Liverpool have joined the Sailors' Union. **1896** *Pall Mall Mag.* Nov. 386 The responsibilities and anxieties of a *tug-master. **1864** *Tug-mutton [see sense 8 above]. **1901** *Westm. Gaz.* 26 Aug. 5/2 They were *tug-owners, and worked the ferry between Hobbs's Point and the Neyland Ordnance Stores. **1948** Partridge *Dict. Forces' Slang* 197 **Tug pilot*, the pilot of an aeroplane towing a glider. (Colloquial.) **1978** A. Welch *Bk. of Airsports* iii. 48/2 When experienced as a tug pilot, you will probably be given the occasional cross-country retrieve from a field or private airstrip. **1794** W. Felton *Carriages* (1801) II. Gloss., **Tug Plate*, a plate, fixed on the shafts, in which the tugs of a one horse harness is placed. **1417–18** in *Archæol. Jrnl.* (1881) XXXVIII. 78 Item in cordis vocatis *Teugropis, viij^d^. **1852** J. Reynolds *Pioneer Hist. Illinois* 236 They often pack their meat..by running a tug rope through each piece. **1891** *Century Mag.* Mar. 774/2 We began by eating the rawhide tug ropes and parfleches. **1877** Knight *Dict. Mech.*, *Tug-slide..*Tug-spring. **1861** *Wheat & Tares* 252 *Tug steamers flashed hither and thither, panting and groaning with their heavy train of stone-laden barges. **1882** *Cassell's Encycl. Dict.* s.v. *Breast-strap*, The breast-collar..at its rear ends receives the *tug-straps. **1906** *Daily Tel.* 1 Feb., The Thames and London Rowing Clubs..have never complained of the general, business *tug-traffic. *a* **1670** Spalding *Troub. Chas. I* (1851) II. 174 About this tyme [1642], sum *tug-quhytinges [were] takin.

Hence ˈ**Tuggery** *Eton College slang*, the collegers' boarding-house; the position or status of a colleger.

1864 [see tug *sb.* 8]. **1883** J. Brinsley-Richards *Seven Yrs. at Eton* xii. 112 [A boy] who had come from Aberdeen 'to try for Tuggery'—that is, to try and pass on to the foundation as a King's scholar.

tug (tʌg), *v.* Forms: 3 toggen, 4–6 togge; (6 tog, toug), 4–7 tugge, 5–8 (9 *dial.*) tugg; 5– tug. [Early ME. *togg-en*, intensive from weak grade of **teuhan, tauh, tuȝum*, OE. *téo(ha)n, téah, tuȝon, toȝen*: see tee *v.*[1]]

†**1.** *intr.* To pull sportively, struggle amorously. *Obs. rare.*

a **1225** *Ancr. R.* 424 Heo ne schulen cussen nenne mon,.. ne toggen mid him, ne pleien. *a* **1225** *St. Marher.* 14 Wið plohe speche sputte to mare, swa longe þat ha tollið togederes ant toggið.

2. To contend, strive in opposition. Now *rare.*

14.. *Tourn. Tottenham* 199 in Hazl. *E.P.P.* III. 91 Thus thai tuggut and thei ruggut til hit was nyȝt. *a* **1550** *Dr. Doubble Ale* 148 ibid. III. 311 The sexton and he truly Did tog by the eares earnestly. **1598** *Mucedorus* Epil. 28 Let us tugge, till one the mastrie winne. **1657** *Burton's Diary* (1828) II. 255, I..came away, and left them tugging upon that debate. **1693** Dryden *Love Triumph.* i. i, Fierce Ramirez, the Castilian king, Who tugged for empire with our warlike son. **1701** J. Sage *Vind. Cyprianic Age* Wks. 1847 II. 45, I have dared to tug a little with Gilbert Rule. **1807** J. Barlow *Columb.* iii. 602 Man tugs with man, and clubs with axes play. **1872** Le Fanu *In a Glass Darkly* III. 116 All her energies seemed strained to suppress a fit, with which she was then breathlessly tugging.

†**b.** *tug it out*, to decide a matter by contest or debate; to 'have it out'; also, to go through with a thing to the end. *Obs.*

1624 Heywood *Captives* i. ii. in Bullen *O. Pl.* IV, We'll tugge it out by the teeth. **1648** in *Verney Mem.* (1907) I. 411 My Lord is resolved to go aboard this night and to tugge it out with any wind. **1655** Fuller *Ch. Hist.* ii. iii. §1 This tough old man, being 70. years of age, took a Journey to Rome, there to tugg it out with his Adversaries. **1673** Hickeringill *Greg. F. Greyb.* 319 The great courage of Cæsar reviv'd the poor spirited man and made him tug it out.

3. *intr.* To toil, labour, struggle; to go toilsomely, advance laboriously.

1619 Visct. Doncaster in *Eng. & Germ.* (Camden) 46, I came..to Cologne.. put myselfe into the boate..tugged up the river in five days to Francfort. **1634** Rainbow *Labour* 40 All for which you tugge thus diligently, shall perish. **1691** Wood *Ath. Oxon.* II. 238 He was..deprived of all the Church lands..notwithstanding he tugged hard to keep some. **1719** Watts *Hymn*, '*My drowsy pow'rs, why sleep ye so*' ii, The little ants for one poor grain Labour, and tug, and strive. **1860** Holland *Miss Gilbert* vi, To tug and tug all their lives to get money together. **1911** E. Sidgwick *Le Gentleman* x, He had..tugged up one great boulevard..and down another.

†**b.** *trans.* To acquire by toil or exertion. *rare.*

1649 G. Daniel *Trinarch., Hen. V* cccxciii, The Soldier tumbles what the owner Tugg'd.

c. To carry or convey (something ponderous) with difficulty or exertion; to lug, drag. *colloq.*

1710 Steele *Tatler* No. 231 ¶2 [He] then says to his Wife, Child, prithee take up the Saddle; which she readily did, and tugged it Home.

4. *trans.* To pull at with force; to strain or haul at.

13.. *K. Alis.* 2305 He hit toggid [*Bodl. MS.* tukked] out to habbe. *a* **1375** *Lay Folk's Mass Bk.* App. iv. 314 Wiþ his teeþ he gon hit togge. *c* **1440** *Promp. Parv.* 495/2 Toggyn, or drawyn.., *tractulo.* **1513** More *Rich. III* (1883) 85 His here in despite torn and togged lyke a cur dogge. **1671** Milton *Samson* 1650 Those two massie Pillars..He tugg'd, he shook, till down they came. **1697** Dryden *Virg. Past.* iii. 153 In vain the Milk-maid tugs an empty Teat. **1711** Gay *Rural Sports* i. 154 He greedily sucks in the twining bait, And tugs and nibbles the fallacious meat. **1855** Macaulay *Hist. Eng.* xvi. III. 649 Each oar was tugged by five or six slaves.

†**b.** To pull about roughly; to touse, to maul.

1493 *Festivall* (W. de W. 1515) 102 b, His neyghbours.. all to-bette this man & drewe hym and tugged hym in the worst maner that they coude. **1577–87** Holinshed *Chron.* III. 1029/1 He himselfe was cruellie tugged and cast into a dich. **1600** Holland *Livy* vi. xvi. 227 Suffer ye your Knight and Defender, to be thus tugged, misused, and evill entreated by his adversaries? **1605** Shaks. *Macb.* iii. i. 112 And I..So wearie with Disasters, tugg'd with Fortune. **1611** Speed *Hist. Gt. Brit.* ix. xix. §59 The slaine body of the vsurping Tyrant, all tugged, and torne.

c. To get into some condition by tugging. *rare.*

1548 Udall, etc. *Erasm. Par. Mark* i. 15 Tugged and haled into sondrye pieces.

†**d.** *intr.* for *pass. Obs. rare.*

1568 *Satir. Poems Reform.* xlviii. 40 It [cloth] tuggis in hoilis, and gais abbreid.

†**e.** *fig. tug out*, to go through with a struggle to the end; to drag out. *Obs. rare*[−1].

1631 Weever *Anc. Fun. Mon.* 617 Hauing beene Earle of Oxford full fifty yeares; a long time to tugge out, in the troublesome raignes of so many kings.

5. To move by pulling forcibly; to pull with great exertion or difficulty; to drag, haul. Also *fig.*

c **1320** R. Brunne *Medit.* 441 Some tugge [*v.r.* tugge him], sum drawe [*v.r.* drawe him] fro ce to ce. **1406** Hoccleve *Misrule* 197 Ther the bootmen took vp-on me keep..With hem was I I-tugged to and fro. **1526** *Pilgr. Perf.* (W. de W. 1531) 97 b, With all abieccyon haled and tugged from place to place. **1659** *Burton's Diary* (1828) IV. 308 The debate was thus tugged to and again till one o'clock. **1715** J. Chappelow *Rt. way Rich* (1717) 142 Often sin tuggs him down. **1730** Pope *Let. to Gay* 11 Sept., I am tugg'd back to the world and its regards too often. **1840** Macaulay *Ess., Clive* (1887) 547 Fifty pieces of ordnance of the largest size, each tugged by a long team of white oxen. **1877** W. R. Cooper *Egypt. Obelisks* viii. (1878) 35 Three hundred rowers tugged the huge trireme with its ponderous burden across the waters of the Mediterranean.

6. *intr.* To pull with great effort or force; to drag, haul. Often with *at*.

1303 R. BRUNNE *Handl. Synne* 9286 With hys teþe he gan to drawe, And harde for to tugge and gnawe. **1500-20** DUNBAR *Poems* xxxiii. 69 And evir the cuschettis at him tuggit, The rukis him rent, the ravynis him druggit. *c* **1613** MIDDLETON *No Wit like Woman's* II. iii, The streams of fortune, 'gainst which he tugs in vain. **1698** FRYER *Acc. E. India & P.* 51 The Men tugged stoutly at their Paddles. *a* **1721** PRIOR *Dial. betw. Locke & Montaigne* 381 If you are always tugging at your Purse Strings, you may chance to break them. **1791** COWPER *Iliad* XII. 485 Sarpedon.. with both hands Tugg'd, and down fell the battlement entire. **1852** MRS. STOWE *Uncle Tom's C.* xvii, Tugging at her pocket to get out the package.

b. In phrase *to tug at the (an) oar*, to row as a galley-slave; hence *fig.* to toil unremittingly; to labour in a subordinate capacity; to do the drudgery. Cf. OAR *sb.* 1 b.

1612 DEKKER *If it be not good* Wks. 1873 III. 265 Hels drudge, her Gally-slaue. I ha' wore My flesh to th' bones.. at the Oare Tugging. *a* **1680** BUTLER *Rem.* (1759) I. 295 We must sit here.. and tug at the Oar, while they steer which way they please. *a* **1764** LLOYD *Author's Apol.* 21 Oh! 'Tis a service irksome more Than tugging at the slavish oar. **1875** MCLAREN *Serm.* Ser. II. viii. 145 Kept him tugging away all his life at the oar, administering the affairs of a Kingdom.

c. *transf.* and *fig.*

1706 E. WARD *Wooden World Diss.* (1708) 103 Tugging at a large Rummer of Rhenish and Sugar. **1833** L. RITCHIE *Wand. by Loire* 79 How many recollections tugged at his heart as he went on! **1860** EMERSON *Cond. Life, Consid.* Wks. (Bohn) II. 426 All sensible people are selfish, and nature is tugging at every contract to make the terms of it fair.

d. The verb-stem used adverbially.

1849 CUPPLES *Green Hand* viii, Tug came both Mrs. Brady's hands through the hair.

7. *trans.* [f. TUG *sb.* 6.] To tow by means of a steam-tug.

1839 J. M. W. TURNER (*title of painting*), The Fighting Téméraire Tugged to her Last Berth to be Broken Up.

b. To tow (a glider) by means of a powered aircraft.

1942 W. S. CHURCHILL *Second World War* (1951) IV. 800 The Whitley aircraft.. is unsuitable for tugging gliders.

tug (tʌg), *a.* *Public School slang.* [Origin uncertain: cf. TUG *sb.* 8.] (Esp. at Winchester College) ordinary, commonplace.

1890 BARRÈRE & LELAND *Dict. Slang* II. 378/2 *Tug* (Winchester College), usual, ordinary, common, stale, as tug-clothes, every-day clothes. **1907** *Wykehamist* Mar. 387/1 Accounts of events, 'tug' to the average reader, but recorded in print for the sake of the past and the future. **1951** C. P. SNOW *Masters* vi. 53 No one on earth could call Jago tug... He's the least commonplace of men.

tugged (tʌgd), *ppl. a.* [f. TUG *v.* + -ED[1].] *tugged-at*: pulled at.

1930 AUDEN *Poems* 25 The tugged-at teat. **1962** I. MURDOCH *Unofficial Rose* xxxiv. 320 Tugged-at leaves and whirling branches knew that summer was defeated and departing.

tugger ('tʌgə(r)). [f. TUG *v.* + -ER[1].] One who tugs or pulls with force; *spec.* one who pulls in a tug-of-war (*colloq.*).

1611 COTGR., *Tireur*, a drawer, puller,.. tugger. *a* **1624** BP. M. SMITH *Serm.* (1632) 243 Being vnequally yoked with a tugger. **1909** *Athenæum* 13 Mar. 315/1 The strain from without slackened, and.. the victorious tuggers fell on their backs.

tugging ('tʌgɪŋ), *vbl. sb.* [f. TUG *v.* + -ING[1].] The action of TUG *v.* in various senses.

a **1225** *Ancr. R.* 204 Hwonne þe schil & te heorte.. hunten þer efter, mid wouhinge, mid togginge, oðer mid eni tollunge. *c* **1440** *Promp. Parv.* 495/2 Toggynge, or strogelynge.., *colluctacio*. ? *a* **1500** *Chester Pl.* vii. 210 For thy teeth here is good tugging. **1551** T. WILSON *Logike* (1580) 60 In all whiche matchyng and touggyng together, this would bee obserued, that [etc.]. **1660** MILTON *Free Commw.* Wks. 1851 V. 441 An endless tugging between Petition of Right and Royal Prerogative. **1742** FIELDING *Jos. Andrews* III. vi, Being roused by these Tuggings, he constantly awaked. **1866** MRS. GASKELL *Wives & Dau.* i, After some tugging, she opened the casement.

'tugging, *ppl. a.* [f. as prec. + -ING[2].] That tugs, in various senses.

c **1440** *Promp. Parv.* 495/2 Toggynge (*A.* or) drawynge, *attractulus*. **1611** COTGR., *Roulier*,.. a lustie, tugging Iade. **1642** ROGERS *Naaman* 149 Oh! it is a tugging crying sinne. **1657** *Burton's Diary* (1828) II. 270 The Bill for the Excise was read the third time, and after.. a great and tugging debate thereupon, the Bill passed. **1865** *Cornh. Mag.* May 584, I should like a little more quiet talk with you, without this tugging brute for a third.

Hence **'tuggingly** *adv.*, with tugging.

1731 BAILEY, *Tuggingly*, difficulty.

† **'tuggle,** *v.* *Obs.* Forms: 5 tuggel, tugle, *Sc.* tuggill, 6 tuggle. [app. a freq. of TUG *v.*; see -LE 3; cf. FORTOGGLE *v.*, TOGGLE *v.*[2], also Du. *tokkelen* from *tokken*.]

1. *trans.* To pull about roughly; to drag about. Cf. TUG *v.* 4 b.

[Cf. *a* **1225** *Ancr. R.* 424 Heo ne schulen.. toggen [*v.r.* toggle] mid him, ne pleien. *a* **1300** *Cursor M.* 24606 (Edin.) Fortuglid [*Cott.* Fortoglid, *Gött.* Fortugild] þus wit trai and ten.] *c* **1440** *Bone Flor.* 1938 He was so tuggelde in a toyle. *c* **1470** *Golagros & Gaw.* 34 Tuglit and travalit thus trew men can tyre. *c* **1475** *Rauf Coilzear* 521 Thair is mony toun man to tuggill is full teuch. *a* **1585** MONTGOMERIE *Flyting* 362 Tousled and tuggled with towne tykes.

2. *intr.* To struggle, labour: = TUG *v.* 3.

1650 TRAPP *Comm. Num.* vi. 4 He that would not toll the bell, must not tuggle with the rope. **1768** ROSS *Helenore* I. 38 Tuggling an' struggling how to get him free.

† **tugh,** obs. variant of TOUGH.

a **1660** *Contemp. Hist. Irel.* (Ir. Archæol. Soc.) I. 151 The waies from thence to Sligo 20 miles, verie roughe, sliperie and tugh for artilerie or wagons.

tughra, tuğra, varr. TOUGHRA.

† **tug-net.** *Sc. Obs.* [? f. TUG *sb.* or *v.* + NET.] ? A fishing-net that is drawn or tugged, not fixed; a drag-net. (Cf. also *draw-net*.)

1584 *Reg. Mag. Sig. Scot.* 232/1 Ad locum et aquam de Spay ubi rete piscationis vulgo tugnettis fisching dicti Rob. solebant piscare. **1607** *Ibid.* 686/1 Salmonum piscariam et lie tug-net tam rubrorum piscium et lie scaill-fische quam aliorum. **1611** *Ibid.* 170/1. **1603** in *Inform. Dk. Gordon* v. *Earls Murray & Fife* 2 The said Marquis's tugnet to be used by him within the bounds used and wont. **1760** *Ibid.* 1 A tugnet-fishing in the mouth of the river, or a fishing with a larger kind of net, such as is used for fishing in the sea and mouths of rivers.

tugrik ('tu:gri:k). Also **tukhrik.** [Mongolian.] A monetary unit of Mongolia, equal to one hundred mongos.

1935, etc. [see MONGO[2]]. **1978** *Financial Times* 10 Jan. 21/2 The Mongolian tugrik has lately been reported to stand at an official commercial rate of 0·225 Russian roubles.

tugtupite ('tʌgtʌpaɪt). *Min.* [f. the name of *Tugtup* agtakôrfia in southern Greenland, where it was first found + -ITE[1].] A tetragonal aluminosilicate and chloride of sodium and beryllium, $Na_4AlBeSi_4O_{12}Cl$.

1962 H. SØRENSEN in *Meddelelser om Grønland* CLXVII. I. 219 At the oral presentation of the mineral, it was suggested that it should be termed tugtupite, because it clearly differs from sodalite. **1977** *Mineral. Mag.* XLI. 130 Tugtupite.. has a distorted sodalite type of structure.

† **'tugury, 'tigurye.** *Obs. rare.* Also 5 tygurie, -ye, te-, tugurry. [ad. L. *tugurium, tigurium* a hut, cot, peasant's cottage. Cf. F. *tugure, tugurion* (Cotgr.).] A hut, cot, cell.

1412-20 LYDG. *Chron. Troy* II. 8660 From storm & reyn hem silf[e] for to saue, þei deuised oþer habitacles, Tegurries [*ed.* **1555** tiguryes] & smale receptacles To schroude hem in. *c* **1440** *Promp. Parv.* 505/1 Tugurry, schudde, *tugurrium*. **1483** CAXTON *Gold. Leg.* (1498) 11 b/1 O blessyd tygurie or lytyl hous. **1491** —— *Vitas Patr.* (1495) 11 They [hermits] were unyed in charytee in theyr tyguryes or celles.

† **'tugwithe, 'tugwithy.** *Obs.* In 6 togwith, -whythe, -wethe, togewith, 6-8 tugwith; 6 tugwithie, -wydie, -wedie, tough wethie. [f. TUG *sb.* or *v.* + WITHE, WITHY.] A withe formerly used to attach the swingle-tree to the head of the plough or to the harrow or cart.

1523 FITZHERB. *Husb.* §15 A swyngletre to holde the tresses abrode, and a togewith to be bytwene the swyngletre and the harowe. **1536** in *Archæologia* XLIII. 240 Temys and togwhythys of ij horses. **1565** *Richmond Wills* (Surtees) 169 Inventory.. a tugwydie. **1572** *Ibid.* 152, ij payre of clammers, one foit eche, with togwethes, xx[d]. **1570** LEVINS *Manip.* 150/33 Y[e] Tugwith, *traha, helcinum*. **1747** HOOSON *Miner's Dict.*, *Tugwith*, a writhen Hassel Rod.. fastened with the small end to the Spindle, then brought over the Turntree at one end of it, and made fast to the Spindle again.

tuh (təh), *int. rare.* An ejaculation expressing disgust or disdain. Cf. POOH.

1607 *Puritan* II. i. 179 Purgatory? tuh; that word deserues to bee spit vpon.

tuhseel, var. TAHSIL.

tuhseeldar, var. TAHSILDAR.

† **tuht** (*ü*), obs. form of TIGHT *sb.*[1] (OE. *tyht*), discipline, training, breeding; conduct; usage. Also † **tuhtle** in same sense.

c **1205** LAY. 2419 To Corinee hine sende.. þat he hine sculde wel i-teon & tuhten [*printed* tuhlen; *c* **1275** manscipe] him teachen. *Ibid.* 2720 Hire tuhtlen weren gode. *Ibid.* 24675 For þere ilke tuhtle Cnihtes weoren ohte.

tuhte (pa. t.), **tuhten**: see TIGHT *v.*[1] *Obs.*

‖ **tui** ('tu:i:). [Maori name.] A New Zealand bird, *Prosthematodera novæ-zelandiæ*: = PARSON-BIRD 1, MOCKING-BIRD 2 f.

1832 A. EARLE *Narr. Residence in N.Z.* 174 The only sounds which broke the calm were the wild notes of the tooe (or New Zealand blackbird). **1835** [see MOCKING-BIRD 2 f]. **1857, 1866** [see PARSON-BIRD 1]. **1869** G. H. KINGSLEY *Sport & Trav.* iv. (1900) 64 Singing birds, some like the New Zealand tui. **1884** BRACKEN *Lays Maori* 101, I hear the swell Of Nature's psalms through tree and bush, From tui, blackbird, finch and thrush. **1908** *Auckland Weekly News* 17 Dec. 50/1 It is only occasionally that the silence is broken by the liquid notes of the tui and the bell-bird.

tuica, ţuica, varr. TSUICA.

tuicche, obs. f. TWITCH.

tuich, tuiche, obs. Sc. ff. TOUCH, TOUGH.

tuig, obs. Sc. f. TWIG.

tuik, Sc. f. *took*, pa. t. of TAKE *v.*

tuil, -ll, obs. ff. TEWEL, TUILYIE, TWILL.

Tuileries ('twi:ləri:, ‖tɥilri). *Hist.* [Fr., so called because built on the site of an ancient tile-works: see TUILLE, TUILE.] A palace in Paris begun by Catherine de Medici in 1564 and destroyed by fire in 1871. It stood on the site between the Champs Elysées and the Louvre, now occupied by the Jardin des Tuileries, and was a residence of the court in royal and imperial France: hence, the royal or imperial family, the court, the administration.

1814 M. BIRKBECK *Journey through France* 81 Every paragraph in the public journals is modelled and pared down to suit the temper of the Tuilleries. **1863** [see POLITESSE]. **1885** H. JAMES *Little Tour in France* xi. 80 The gardens.. are the promenade—the Tuileries—of the town [*sc.* Bourges]. **1967** *Listener* 25 May 678/1 By the end of the next decade, [Victor] Hugo.. had become.. the tame poet of the Tuileries. **1972** T. ARONSON *Queen Victoria & Bonapartes* x. 126 The coolness between Windsor and the Tuileries.

tuille, tuile (twi:l; in sense 2 usu. ‖ tɥil). Forms: 5-7 toile, 7 toyle, 9 tuille, tuile. [a. F. *tuile*, OF. *tieule*, in 15th c. *teuille*, L. *tēgula* TILE, plaque.]

1. In mediæval armour, One of two or more plates of steel hanging below, or forming the lowest part of, the tasses, and covering the front of the thighs.

c **1400** *Destr. Troy* 6420 Ector.. come.. þere the corse lay, Wold haue Robbit the Renke of his riche wede With the ton hond in the toile tyrnyt it offe. *a* **1470** TIPTOFT in Segar *Hon. Mil. & Civ.* III. li. (1602) 189 Who so hitteth the Toyle three times, shall haue no prize. **1688** R. HOLME *Armoury* III. xix. (Roxb.) 180/2. **1834** PLANCHÉ *Brit. Costume* 195 *Tuiles*, plates depending from the taces or skirt of the armour in front, over an apron of chain-mail, are first visible at this period [that of Henry VI]. **1869** BOUTELL *Arms & Arm.* viii. (1874) 147 Over the flanks, on each side of the figure, to the faudes or taces was appended a plate, or small shield, or *gardefaude* (in England called a *tuille*), which would cover the front of the thigh.

‖ **2.** As **tuile.** A thin curved biscuit, usu. made with almonds. Also *attrib.* and with defining addition.

1943 A. L. SIMON *Conc. Encycl. Gastron.* IV. 133/1 *Tuiles d'oranges.* Cream 1 oz. butter, add 1½ oz. castor sugar and cream together. Add 1½ oz. chopped blanched almonds, 1½ oz. chopped candied peel, dessertspoonful flour, dessertspoonful milk. **1966** *Observer* (Colour Suppl.) 3 Apr. 41 In France the biscuits shown below are called 'tuiles'—which is French for roof tiles. These thin, crisp biscuits contain chips of almond. **1972** P. V. PRICE *Eating & Drinking in France Today* II. 276 *Tuiles* from Amiens (thin chocolate and orange biscuits). **1976** *Times* 2 Oct. 10/3 The coffee ice was served in a tuile basket. **1979** *Harper's & Queen* Apr. 42/1 Sorbets.. in a fragile basket of crisp, sweet, *tuiles*, made without almonds.

† **tuillet,** obs. form of TOILET.

1673 *Lady's Call.* II. i. §15 For more worthy uses then those of the comb, the tuillets, and the glass.

tuillette, tuilette (twi:'lɛt). [dim. of TUILLE: see -ETTE.] A small tuille.

1869 BOUTELL *Arms & Arm.* x. (1874) 205 [In the effigy of Richard Beauchamp, Earl of Warwick] besides two large tuilles, there are two smaller ones or *tuillettes*. **1882** *Athenæum* 26 Aug. 278/3 Tuilettes are.. generally later than 1406.

tuilyie, tulyie, tulie ('tøl(j)ɪ, 'tʏlɪ), *sb.* *Sc.* Forms: 4-6 tulȝe, tolȝe, 5 tuyl, toilȝe, (tulyhe, tohile, tohyle), 5-6 tulye, 6 tulȝe (-ze), tuylȝe, -ȝhe, tuill, tule, toulȝe, 6-7 tuilye; 5-6 tuilyie, 6-9 tulyie, -ȝie (-zie), 8 tuilie, toolie, 7-9 tuilȝie (-zie), 8-9 tooly, 9 tully. [ad. OF. *tooil, touil, tueil*, contention, f. OF. *toillier*: see next and TOIL *v.*[1] For the forms cf. *brulyie, fulȝie, spulȝe, ulye*. The forms in *-ie, -ye* are app. taken from the vb.] A quarrel, brawl, fight; a noisy contest, dispute: = TOIL *sb.*[1] 1.

(In quot. *c* 1425 vaguely used. In Hawick it was formerly usual in time of frost to have a slide of a quarter of a mile long down the centre of the steep street called the Loan, on which long files of sliders came down at a thundering pace: this was famous as the '*Yokit tuilie*' or '*Yoke o' tuilie*'.)

c **1425** WYNTOUN *Cron.* v. xii. 3943 (Wemyss MS.) It may be callit vnhonest tulȝe [*v. rr.* tuyl, tohyle, tolȝe, tule, tuylȝe, tuylȝhe] To se þe quyk þe dede dispulȝe Quhen he is woundit in his schete. *a* **1500** *Peebles to Play* xix, Sevin-sum, that the tulye maid, Lay gruffling in the stokks. **1557** *Peebles Burgh Rec.* (1872) 242 Gif ony suddand tulye happyng within the tovne. **1609** SKENE *Reg. Maj.* I. 142 Na man quha is given to tuilzies or strife, sall presume to beare ane knife with ane poynt, within the Portes.. of our Gild. **1728** RAMSAY *Advice to Mr.* —— 38 And, smiling, ca' her little foolie, Syne with a kiss evite a toolie. **1814** SCOTT *Wav.* lxiii, Killed that same night in the tuilzie. **1886** MASSON *Edinb. Sk.* 25 Edinburgh was famous for its tulzies or causeway fights between noblemen and lairds.

b. without article: Quarrelling, contention, strife; trouble, turmoil.

1550 *Records of Elgin* (New Spald. Cl. 1903) I. 106 Burges that beis convict for tuilze sall pay for the first tuilze viii s. **1572** *Satir. Poems Reform.* xxxiv. 59 In Scotland had not bene sic tuill, Gif this had bene þe common reull. **1785** BURNS *To W. Simpson* xxxi, But tho' dull-prose folk Latin splatter In logic tulzie, I hope we Bardies ken some better Than mind sic brulzie.

c. Also **tulyie-mulyie.**

1819 W. TENNANT *Papistry Storm'd* (1827) 4 In mony a fecht and tulzie-mulzie. *Ibid.* 196 In hideous tulyie-mulyie.

'tuilyie, 'tulyie, 'tulie, *v. Sc.* Forms: see prec. sb.; also 6 teulie. [a. OF. *tooillier, toillier, touillier*: see prec. and TOIL *v.*¹]

†**1.** *trans.* To harass; to quarrel with, assail contentiously, assault. *Obs.*

1375 (MS. 1487) BARBOUR *Bruce* IV. 152 (Camb. MS.) þai on twa halfis war assalit; Within with fyre, þat þame sa brulȝeit, Without with folk þat þaim sa tulȝeit [*Edinb. MS.* (1489) broilȝit, toilȝit]. *c* **1425** WYNTOUN *Cron.* VI. xv. 1477 (Wemyss MS.) Fell tyrandis, þat had delite Possessionis and pilgrymage to tulȝe. **1595** in *Maitl. Cl. Misc.* I. 70 To have followit Thomas McNair, and to have teuliit him in the porche of Govane kirk.

2. *intr.* To quarrel, fight, contend. Hence **'tuilyieing** *vbl. sb.* and *ppl. a.*

1444 *Aberdeen Regr.* (1844) I. 12 Conuicte thrise for barganyng and tulyheing. **1565** *Reg. Privy Council Scot.* I. 333 Ony Scottismen that fechtis, tulyeis, or drawis bluid. **1725** RAMSAY *Gentle Sheph.* I. ii, Sic wee tots toolying at your knee;..to be made o', and obtain a kiss. **1818** SCOTT *Rob Roy* xxvi, That they suld let folk tuilzie in their yards. **1862** HISLOP *Prov. Scot.* 27 A toolying tike comes limping hame. **1895** CROCKETT *Men of Moss-Hags* 55 Let there be no more tullying and brawling.

tuilyier ('tøl(j)ɪər). *Sc.* Forms: 5 tuilyeour, -your, (tulyhour), 6 tulȝear, -ȝeour (-zeour), -yeour, tuilyair, -ȝour, -ȝeour (7 -zeour), 7 tuilȝier. [ME. *tuilȝeour*, agent-n. from *tuilȝie* TUILYIE *v.*: see -OUR.] A quarrelsome person, a brawler. Also in comb. **tuilyier-like** *a.*, quarrelsome.

1444 *Aberdeen Regr.* (1844) I. 12 A common tulyhour and rebellour. *c* **1480** HENRYSON *Test. Cres.* 194 Lyk to ane bair quhetting his tuskis kene Richt tuilyour-lyk. **1535** STEWART *Cron. Scot.* (Rolls) III. 440 Semdill[is]..Ane mydding tulzear in ane battell bydar. **1583** *Burgh. Rec. Edinb.* (1882) IV. 295 Tuilyairs and trubleris of the quyett estaitt of this burgh. **1650** in Butler *Ch. & Parish Abernethy* xxv. (1897) 389 Fighters and tuilȝiers to satisfy publicly by siting on a seat in face of the congregation.

'tuilyiesome, *a. Sc.* [f. TUILYIE + -SOME.] Quarrelsome, contentious. Hence **'tuilȝiesomeness.**

1599 JAS. I. *Βασιλ. Δωρον* (1682) 84 Tuilyesome weapons in the Court, betokens confusion in the Countrey. **1808** JAMIESON s.v., 'Tuilyiesum dogs cum happing hame'. S. Prov.

tuim (tøm), Sc. var. TOOM *a.*, empty.

tuin, tuine, tuinne, obs. ff. TUNE, TWIN.

Tuinal ('tju:ɪnəl). *Pharm.* [f. *tuin-*, of unkn. origin + *-al* in AMYTAL, SECONAL.] A proprietary name for a combination of the two barbiturates quinalbarbitone and amylobarbitone, used as a sedative-hypnotic.

1949 *Trade Marks Jrnl.* 25 May 453/2 *Tuinal*... Medicinal preparations composed of sodium propylmethylcarbinyl allyl barbiturate and sodium isoamyl ethyl barbiturate. Eli Lilly and company,.. Indianapolis,.. United States of America. **1952** *Martindale's Extra Pharmacopœia* (ed. 23) I. 259 Tuinal (*Lilly*). 1½ or 3 gr. capsules containing equal parts of Seconal Sodium and Sodium Amytal. **1980** *Daily Tel.* 5 Nov. 3/1 She was drunk and they went on to a party at a friend's house. He saw her take two Tuinal tablets during the night.

tuiron, tuis, tuise: see TEW-IRON, TWICE.

Tuisday, obs. form of TUESDAY.

tuism ('tju:ɪz(ə)m). *rare.* [f. L. *tū* thou + -ISM, after *egoism, egotism.*] A form of expression involving the use of the pronoun *thou*, or implying reference to a second person; also, in *Ethics*, primary regard to the interests of another person or persons (opp. to EGOISM 2, EGOTISM 2); in *Philos.*, 'the doctrine that all thought is addressed to a second person, or to one's future self as a second person' (*Cent. Dict.* 1891; cf. EGOISM 1).

1796 COLERIDGE *Watchman* 9 Mar. 38 Omitting the long preambles..and the whole parade of egotisms and tuisms: we shall select from each speech [etc.]. **1809–10** —— *Friend* (1818) I. iv. 36 For one piece of egotism that presents itself under its own honest bare face of 'I myself I', there are fifty that steal out in the mask of tuisms and ille-isms. **1824** BYRON *Juan* XVI. xiii, To hail her with the apostrophe—'O thou!' Of amatory egotism the Tuism. **1884** J. RAE *Contemp. Socialism* 124 Feuerbach's peculiar ethical principle..has been well termed Tuism, to distinguish it from Egoism.

Hence **'tuistic** *a.* [see -ISTIC], of the nature of tuism.

1880 H. BRADSHAW in *Life* (1888) 292 You should..avoid ..the tuistic form of letter.

†**tuit,** obs. form of TEWHIT.

1570 LEVINS *Manip.* 149/35 A Tuit, lapwing, *vpupa.*

tuitch, obs. Sc. form of TOUCH.

tuition (tju:'ɪʃən). Forms: 5–6 tuicion, tuission, etc. (with *y* for either *i*, and *-one, -oun(e,* for *-on*), 6 tuytion, -tyon, tuityon, 6–7 -tione, 5– tuition. [a. AF. *tuycioun*, obs. F. *tuition* (Cotgr., 1611), OF. *tuicion, -ssion, -tion* (1335 in Godef.), ad. L. *tuitio* guard, guardianship, n. of action from L. *tuērī* to look to, look after.]

†**1. a.** The action of looking after or taking care of, or condition of being taken care of; safe-keeping, protection, defence, custody, care, tutelage. *Obs.*

[**1292** BRITTON I. xvii. §2 Et si il reconusent felonie..et prient tuycioun del eglise [*transl.* and beg the protection of the church].] **1436** *Libel Eng. Policy* in *Pol. Poems* (Rolls) II. 204 There glorified in reste wyth his tuicione, The deité to see wyth fulle fruicione. **1462** EDW. IV in Ellis *Orig. Lett.* Ser. II. I. 129 For the tuicion and defence of this owr Realme. **1557** *Order of Hospitalls* F vij, Which [copy] he shall haue vnder the Auditors hands, in his own tuition. *c* **1575** J. HOOKER *Life Sir P. Carew* (1857) 276, I commit your Lordeship to the tuission of the Almightie. **1611** BROUGHTON *Require Agreeement* 53 A jest..that Diana.. was so busie about Alexanders birth, that she forgot the tuition of her owne Temple. **1693** STAIR *Inst. Law Scot.* (ed. 2) I. vi. §1 There is a Duty of Tuition, and Protection of Orphans. **1790** BURKE *Fr. Rev.* 352 Liberty without wisdom, and without virtue..is folly, vice, and madness, without tuition or restraint.

b. *spec.* The position of a guardian or TUTOR in relation to a ward; guardianship. *Obs.*

1494 FABYAN *Chron.* v. ci. 75 Clodomyrus was slayne, leuyng..iii. sonnes..whiche .iii. sonnes Clotilde toke to her tuyssion & guydynge. **1568** *Hist. Jacob & Esau* I. ii. A iv, They were brought vp bothe vnder one tuition. **1643** PRYNNE *Sov. Power Parl.* App. 21 They chose Eudo,..to be King..till Charles should come to his lawfull age, whom they put under Eudo his tuition. **1690** LOCKE *Govt.* II. vi. §67 That [power] which the Father hath, in the Right of Tuition, during Minority.

c. *concr.* A defence, fortification. *Obs. rare*⁻¹.

1513 *Life Hen. V* (1911) 109 This Towne was fortified wth innumerable tuytions and defences.

2. a. The action or business of teaching a pupil or pupils; the function of a tutor or instructor (see TUTOR); teaching, instruction.

1582 in *Campion's Wks.* (1909) Introd. 26 Allowance for Thomas Sisley and Thomas Campion at Cambridge beginning at cristmas 1582. First, eche of them for thir diete weakely ijs. vjd.: in the whole yere..xiij. li. Item, thir tuition yerely xlv.s. for eche. **1619** SIR R. BOYLE *Diary* in *Lismore Papers* (1886) I. 235, vli that he gave the ffrenchman and his wyffe for their first quarters tuicon of my children. **1781** GIBBON *Decl. & F.* xix. II. 129 They pursued their studies..under the tuition of the most skilful masters. **1807** SOUTHEY *H. K. White* 3 One of the ushers, when he came to receive the money due for tuition. **1845** E. HOLMES *Mozart* 7 Obliged to devote every hour that he could spare..to tuition on the violin and clavier.

b. *attrib.*, as ***tuition-fee, -money.***

1867 AUG. J. E. WILSON *Vashti* viii, In future I shall not advance one cent of my tuition-money.

c. = *tuition-fee. U.S.*

1828 WEBSTER, s.v., In our colleges, the tuition is from thirty to forty dollars a year. **1940** W. FAULKNER *Hamlet* II. i. 101 Your tuition will be paid. **1979** *Arizona Daily Sun* 19 Apr. 1/6 Wettaw..was given the award for his opposition to increases in university tuitions.

Hence **tu'itional** *a.*, pertaining or relating to tuition; of a school, supported by tuition-fees; **tu'itionary** *a.*, pertaining to tuition.

1847 BUSHNELL *Chr. Nurt.* II. i. (1861) 229 *Tuitional and regulative influences that come after. **1892** E. F. WILLIAMS in *Chicago Advance* 24 Nov., What are called 'Daughter Schools', or the 'Higher Girls' Schools' [in Germany],..are for the most part tuitional schools. **1906** *United Free Ch. Mag.* July 6/1 The tuitional side of missionary work. **1816** J. B. GILCHRIST (*title*) The orienti-occidental *tuitionary pioneer to literary pursuits [etc.]. **1879** M. C. TYLER *Hist. Amer. Lit.* xiii. II. 93 The clerical profession..to develop the other learned professions—the legal, medical, and tuitionary.

tuitive ('tju:ɪtɪv), *a. rare.* [f. L. *tuit-*, ppl. stem of *tu-ērī*: see prec.]

1. Giving tuition or instruction.

1776 *Adv. Corkscrew* ii. 17 His tutor resolved not to swerve from the general rule of these tuitive companions, but let his pupil indulge in every extravagance.

2. Acquired by instruction as opposed to *intuitive* or innate (INTUITIVE 3 c). *rare.*

1784 *New Spectator* No. 22. 1 A man without an innate idea would be incapable of acquiring any.—Without intuitive knowledge he could have no tuitive.

tuix, obs. form of TWIXT.

tuk, obs. pa. t. of TAKE *v.*; obs. f. TUCK.

tukal, var. TUKUL.

†**tuke, tewke.** *Obs.* Also 6 tuyke. [Etymology uncertain. (See Prof. Weekley in *N. & Q.* 11th Ser. III. 130.) Connexion suggested with F. *teugue, tuque*, in Boyer *Fr.-Eng. Dict.* 1702 '*tuque*, a tarpaulin, or tarpawling', Lescallier *Vocab. des Termes de Marine* 1777 has '*toile de tugue*, a canvas covering for the poop of a frigate'. According to Jal *Gloss. Nautique*, related to L. *tēgula* tiling, subseq. a canvas awning: but in Eng. applied to the material.] Canvas, such as is used for an awning or canopy; but also applied to a finer fabric.

1477 *Lanc. Wills* (1884) 2, vij yardes Cane Tuke price the yarde vd...iiij yardes of fustian Tuke, price ye yarde xijd. **1481–90** *Howard Househ. Bks.* (Roxb.) 416 Item, iiij. yardes of tewke rossett, price vj. s. viij. d. **1494** in Rogers *Agric. & Prices* (1882) III. 560 (Oxford), 1 piece of Tewke for Tergates..@1/3. **1496** *Ibid.*, 3 yds Tewke 3/4. **1521** *MS. Will*, A gowne watteryd tuyke. **1527** *MS. Inv. Goods T. Cromwell* (P.R.O.), ij jerkyns of blacke saten lyned with tuke. **1530** PALSGR. 280/1 Tewke to make purses of, *trelis.* **1552–3** *Inv. Ch. Goods Staffs.* in *Ann. Lichfield* (1863) IV. 75 One canopye of tewke,..iij crosse clothes, ij of sarsnet, and the other of tewke. **1586** *Rates of Custome* F j, Tukes the peece viij. s.

tuke, obs. pa. t. of TAKE *v.*; obs. Sc. f. TUCK.

tukhrik, var. TUGRIK.

tukkar, tukne, obs. ff. TUCKER, TOKEN.

tukul ('tʊkəl). Also tukal, tukl. [Native name.] In Ethiopia and some adjacent regions: a dwelling shaped like a beehive, and constructed with a thatched roof.

1901 H. VIVIAN *Abyssinia* vii. 174 The capital is rather a camp than a town, and there is no particular trouble in rooting up a tukul and planting it elsewhere. **1920** *Blackw. Mag.* Nov. 675/2 The tukls were strongly built of rough stone. **1936** E. WAUGH *Waugh in Abyssinia* v. 188 The office was a small, lightless *tukal* a hundred yards or so off the road. **1958** *Spectator* 18 July 111/1, I would not like my daughter to become the mistress of a *kraal* or a *tukl.* **1971** *Daily Tel.* 12 June 11/1 Rough compounds of mushroom-like *tukals* —round, mud-walled thatched peasant huts. **1981** E. NORTH *Dames* i. 5 Thatched huts known as *tukuls*, some now with corrugated roofs.

tuku-tuku ('tʊkʊ'tʊkʊ). *N.Z.* Also (as one word) tukutuku, tuku tuku. [Maori.] (See quots. 1946 and 1958.)

1936 [see KAKAHO]. **1946** *Jrnl. Polynesian Soc.* June 160 *Tukutuku*, ornamental lattice-work of toetoe-reeds (kakaho) cross-laced in various patterns with narrow strips of flax and pingao: a panel of tukutuku was placed between every pair of poupou on the whare walls. **1950** *N.Z. Jrnl. Agric.* Aug. 187/3 The tuku tuku (decorative reed panels) [on the meeting house] are admirable examples of Maori art. **1958** *Listener* 20 Nov. 825/2 The tuku-tuku, a weaving of a wall-covering with split, or rather halved, bamboo as the warp. **1977** *N.Z. Herald* 5 Jan. 1-4/7 The old tukutuku or woven panel walls will in most cases be restored and cleaned.

tul, obs. or dial. f. TILL *prep.* and *conj.*

tula ('tu:lə). In full **tula metal**: Niello made at Tula in Russia. Also *attrib.*, as ***tula-work.***

1839 URE *Dict. Arts* 1259 Tula Metal, is an alloy of silver, copper, and lead. **1884** KNIGHT *Dict. Mech., Suppl.*, *Tula*, the Russian niello silver. **1891** *Cent. Dict.*, *Tula-work.*

tuladi ('tu:lədi:). Also toledi, touladi. [a. Canad. Fr., f. Algonquin, Micmac.] = NAMAYCUSH.

1846 C. L. HATHEWAY *Hist. New Brunswick* 61 The Toledi..weighs from five to twenty-five pounds,..and is a very voracious fish. **1856** C. LANMAN *Adv. Wilds U.S.* II. 79 The principal fish which it yields are the common trout, tuladi or great gray trout, and a small species of white fish. **1896** *Trans. R. Soc. Canada* II. 135 The Mackinaw trout of the great lakes [is] ..the touladi of the country of the Micmacs. **1957** *Field & Stream* (N.Y.) May 90/2 A fourth kind of trout called touladi..the French-Canadians say, is a natural cross between the lake trout and the brook trout.

tularæmia (tju:lə'ri:mɪə). *Path.* Also (chiefly *U.S.*) -emia. [f. mod.L. *tular-ensis*, specific epithet of the causative organism (f. the name of *Tulare* Co., California) + Gr. *αἷμα* blood + -IA¹.] An acute infectious febrile disease of man and domestic animals caused by the bacterium *Francisella tularensis*, endemic among wild rodents in N. America and elsewhere, and transmitted to man by biting insects and by other means, producing very variable symptoms.

1921 E. FRANCIS in *Public Health Rep.* (U.S.) 29 July 1731 The names thus far used for this disease are strictly vernacular and do not lend themselves to international usage as easily as a name in Latin form. Accordingly, the name tularæmia is proposed as a technical international name. **1925**, etc. [see *rabbit fever* s.v. RABBIT *sb.*¹ 4]. **1949** A. HUXLEY *Ape & Essence* 30 On the pressure-tanks of one army are painted the words *super tularemia*; on those of their opponents, *improved glanders.* **1961** R. D. BAKER *Essent. Path.* ix. 183 Tularemia is acquired, usually, from the handling of infected rabbits.

tulasi: see TULSI.

tulat, obs. Sc. f. TOILET.

tulban, -bent, obs. ff. TURBAN.

tulce, obs. form of TULSI.

tulchan ('tʌlxən). *Sc.* Forms: 6 tulchen, 6–9 -in, 9 -ane, 8– tulchan. [a. Gaelic *tulchan*, app. local variant of *tulachan* 'little hillock', applied locally to a device used to induce a cow to give her milk: still so called in the Outer Hebrides, and in Moidart in Inverness-shire, and prob. more widely in the 16th c.

The cow is allowed to sniff at the skin of her own calf, which may be stuffed with straw or hay, but is often merely spread over the bottom of a creel or a small heap or hump of earth or turf, whence app. the name 'little hillock'. The etymology given in Highland Society's Dict., 1828, is erroneous.]

1. *lit.* A calf's skin set under a cow to make her yield her milk freely: see above.

a **1578**–*a* **1651** [see 2]. **1785** *Jrnl. fr. London to Portsmouth* 2 Flae him belly-flaught, his skin wad mak' a gallant tulchin for you. **1808–18** JAMIESON, *Tulchane, -in*...2. A bag or budget, generally of the skin of an animal. **1866** LIVINGSTONE *Last Jrnls.* (1873) I. ii. 51 The cattle of Africa ..never give their milk without the presence of the calf or its stuffed skin, the 'tulchan'.

2. *Hist.* Hence *attrib.*, applied in derision to the titular bishops appointed in Scotland immediately after the Reformation, in whose names the revenues of the sees were drawn by the lay barons.

a **1578** LINDESAY (Pitscottie) *Chron. Scot.* (S.T.S.) II. 282 The tulchen, to wit ane feinȝeit counterfeitt bischope... The kingis lordis that obtenit thair beneficeis culd find na way to have proffeit thairof without thay had ane tulchen lyk as the kow had or scho wald gif milk, ane calfis skin stoppit with stra. **1583** *Leg. Bp. St. Androis* Pref. 61 Albeit they be now Tulchin bischops stylit. *a* **1651** CALDERWOOD *Hist. Kirk* (1678) 55 The Bishops, admitted according to this new order, were called in jest, Tulchane Bishops. A Tulchane is a calf's skin stuffed full with straw, to cause the cow give milk. **1703** D. WILLIAMSON *Serm. bef. Gen. Assemb. Edin.* 43 Then were imposed the Tulchan, or meer nominal Bishops, who by simoniacal Contracts allowed the great men to enjoy the Revenues of the Church. **1859** J. J. MARSHALL *Hist. Scott. Eccles. & Civ. Affairs* x. 211 The Episcopacy thus introduced has always gone under the name of the Tulchan or Titular Episcopacy.

transf. **1884** DUNCKLEY in *Contemp. Rev.* July 7 Henceforth the Khedive was to be a mere 'tulchan' ruler.

‖**tule** ('tuːleɪ). *U.S.* Also **tula, toolie, tulé, tuley.** [ad. Aztec *tullin*, the final *n* being dropped by the Spaniards as in *Guatemala, Jalapa*, etc.]

a. Either of two species of bulrush (*Scirpus lacustris* var. *occidentalis*, and *S. Tatora*) abundant in low lands along riversides in California; hence, a thicket of this, or a flat tract of land in which it grows.

1837 P. L. EDWARDS *Jrnl.* 20 July (1932) 26 Driving her along the margin of a bulrush or Tule pond she turned about. **1845** J. C. FRÉMONT *Rep. Exploring Expedition* 252 They.. live principally on acorns and roots of the tulé, of which also their huts are made. **1850** W. R. RYAN *Personal Adv. Upper & Lower Calif.* I. 298 The Indians of the party were despatched to hunt up the banks of the river for toolies. **1856** OLMSTED *Journ. Texas* iii. 149 Windowless cabins of stakes, plastered with mud and roofed with river-grass or 'tula'. **1882** *Harper's Mag.* Nov. 876 The tules or rushes rise high above our heads, and.. are infested with a dangerous breed of wild hogs. **1892** *Outing* Jan. 329/2 Arriving at a small patch of tuleys about the middle of the lake. **1893** A. F. BATTELLE in *Chicago Advance* 2 Feb., Because of the tall rushes that grow there the land is called the tule. The tule is always low and level. **1894** O. WISTER in *Harper's Mag.* Sept. 520 That dug-out with side-thatch and roofing of tule.

b. *attrib.*, as *tule-farm, hut, land, marsh, root, swamp*; **tule fog** *U.S.*, fog over low-lying ground; **tule wren**, a kind of marsh wren (*Telmatodytes* or *Cistothorus palustris*, var. *paludicola*) which frequents the tules of California.

1850 B. TAYLOR *Eldorado* vii. (1862) 73 The hazy air, made more dense by the smoke of the burning tule marshes. **1883** STEVENSON *Silverado Sq.* 2 Across the cornlands and thick tule swamps of Sacramento Valley. **1890** GUNTER *Miss Nobody* iv, The baked leaves of century plant, acorns, and tule roots. **1891** A. WELCKER *Wild West* 64 A cabin on a swampy tule farm. **1899** *Monthly Weather Rev.* Dec. 536/2 Connected with this pressure distribution was the prevalence of tule fog in the great valleys of California... This ground or tule fog was so dense as to seriously inconvenience farming operations. **1934** S. E. WHITE *Folded Hills* 340 A *tule* fog lay thick over the bottomlands. **1980** M. G. EBERHART *Casa Madrone* vi. 81 The evening breeze freshened, yet was still moist... Scott said.. 'The tule fog is coming in.'

tule, obs. f. TOOL, TUILYIE; var. TULY *Obs.*

†**tulet**, obs. Sc. f. TOILET, wrapper.

1541 *Acc. Ld. High Treas. Scot.* VIII. 22 For ane tulet to thir clathis quhilkis wer deliverit be Thomas Arthuir to the Kingis grace.

tulgey ('tʌldʒɪ), *a.* Also (*erron.*) **tulgy.** A factitious word introduced by 'Lewis Carroll' applied to a wood; (usu. interpreted as) thick, dense, and dark; also *fig.*

1871 'L. CARROLL' *Through Looking-Glass* i. 22 The Jabberwock, with eyes of flame, Came whiffling through the tulgey wood. **1936** J. R. R. TOLKIEN in *Proc. Brit. Acad.* XXII. 250 The jabberwocks of historical and antiquarian research burble in the tulgy wood of conjecture, flitting from one tum-tum tree to another. **1949** E. TAYLOR *Wreath of Roses* xiv. 216 You came out of that tulgy wood? **1972** K. BONFIGLIOLI *Don't point that Thing at Me* viii. 71, I battled .. with Professor Aschloch's tulgey prose—only German poets have ever written lucid German prose. **1976** *Times Lit. Suppl.* 23 Jan. 71/5 A suitable backcloth to the dark, thick gothic forest of his own tulgey forebodings. **1982** *Ibid.* 10 Dec. 1352/4 The tulgey wood of semiotics.

tuliban, tulie, obs. ff. TURBAN, TILL *v.*[1]

tulip ('tjuːlɪp). [Formerly *tulipa, tulippa*, also *tulipant, -pan* = F. *tulipan, tulipe*, It. *tulipano*, Sp. *tulipan*, Pg. *tulipa, -ippa*, mod.L. *tulipa*; early mod.Du. and Ger. *tulpe*, Du. *tulp*, Da. *tulipan*, Sw. *tulpan*; all from *tul(i)band*, vulgar Turkish pronunciation of Persian *dulband* 'turban', which the expanded flower of the tulip is thought to resemble: cf. TURBAN.]

1. a. A bulbous plant of the genus *Tulipa* (NO. *Liliaceæ*), esp. the species *T. Gesneriana*, introduced from Turkey into Western Europe in the 16th c., and since extensively cultivated in very numerous varieties, blooming in spring, with broad bell-shaped or cup-shaped, usually erect, showy flowers, of various colours and markings; also, the flower itself.

The first mention of it by a Western European is by Busbek (*c* 1554), the Emperor's ambassador, on the way from Adrianople to Constantinople, where 'ingens ubique florum copia offerebatur, narcissorum, hyacinthorum, et eorum quos Turcae tulipan vocant'. It was grown by the Fuggers at Augsburg, where it was seen and described by Gesner in 1561. It was introduced successively in Vienna, Mechlin, France, and England; it is mentioned by Lyte in his transl. of Dodoneus.

α. **1578** LYTE *Dodoens* II. lii. 212 Of Tulpia, or Tulipa... The great Tulpia, or rather Tulipa. *Ibid.* 213 The greater Tulpia is brought from Grece, and the Countrie about Constantinople... The greater is called both *Tulpia*, and *Tulpian*, and of some *Tulipa*, which is a Turkie name or worde, we may call it Lillynarcissus. **1582** in Hakluyt *Voy.* (1599) II. 165 Now within these foure yeeres there haue bene brought into England from Vienna.. diuers kinds of flowers called Tulipas. **1597** GERARDE *Herbal* I. lxxvii. 116 Tulipa, or the Dalmatian cap, is a strang and forraine flower. [*Ibid.* 117 After [the Tulipa of Bolonia] hath beene some fewe daies floured, the points and brims of the flower turne backward, like a Dalmatian or Turkes cap, called *Tulipan, Tolepan, Turban*, and *Turfan*, whereof it tooke his name.] **1621** BURTON *Anat. Mel.* III. ii. IV. i, As a tulipant to the sun (which our herbalists call Narcissus) when it shines is.. a glorious flower exposing itself. **1629** PARKINSON *Paradisus* II. viii. 46 The early Tulipa (and so all other Tulipas) springeth out of the ground with his leaues folded one within another. *Ibid.* 66 We call it in English the Turkes Cap, but most vsually Tulipa.

β. **1615** G. SANDYS *Trav.* I. 57 You cannot stirre abroad but you shall be presented by the Deruises and Ianizaries, with tulips and trifles. **1633** JOHNSON *Gerarde's Herbal* I. lxxxvii. 139 The bloud-red Tulip with a yellow bottome. *Ibid.* 140 *Tulipa purpurea*. The purple Tulip. *Tulipa rubra amethistina*. The bright red Tulip. **1758** JOHNSON *Idler* No. 30 ⁋5 Another searches the world for tulips. **1842** TENNYSON *Gard. Dau.* 189 A Dutch love For tulips. **1872** YEATS *Techn. Hist. Comm.* 228 Tulips were introduced from Constantinople, and first bloomed in the beautiful grounds of Heinrich Herwart, in 1559.

b. Applied, usually with defining word, to species of this, and various plants more or less resembling it, or their flowers; also to the flowers of the TULIP-TREE; in S. Africa, to a poisonous herb also called *tulip-grass* (see 5).

African tulip, the genus *Hæmanthus* (N.O. *Amaryllidaceæ*). **butterfly tulip**, the genus *Calochortus* of California, also called *mariposa lily*. **Cape tulip**, name for several S. African plants: (*a*) various species of *Homeria* (= *tulip-grass*: see 5); (*b*) *Melanthium uniflorum* (*Bæometra columellaris*); (*c*) Red Cape tulip, *Hæmanthus coccineus*. **chequered tulip, drooping tulip** = *wild tulip*, (*b*). **native tulip**, of Australia (see quot. 1898, and TULIP-TREE 2 a). **parrot tulip** (see PARROT *sb.* 4). **wild tulip**, (*a*) *Tulipa sylvestris*, a rare and doubtful native of Britain, with fragrant yellow flowers; (*b*) a name for the wild fritillary, *Fritillaria Meleagris*; (*c*) in California, = *butterfly tulip*.

1759 MILLER *Gard. Dict.* (ed. 7) s.v. *Tulip-tree*, The Flowers..[have] six Petals,..which form a Sort of Bellshaped Flower, from whence the Inhabitants of North America gave it the Title of Tulip. **1760** J. LEE *Introd. Bot.* App. 330 African Tulip, *Hæmanthus*... Chequer'd Tulip, *Fritillaria*. **1850** PAPPE *Floræ Capensis Med. Prodr.* 26 *Moræa collina*, Thbg. (known to almost every child in the colony as the *Cape Tulip*), not for its therapeutical use, but for its obnoxiousness. **1861** MISS PRATT *Flower. Pl.* V. 276 Wild Tulip.. has a much smaller blossom than the cultivated species,.. its colour within is bright yellow, and externally yellowish-green. [**1863** W. C. BALDWIN *Afr. Hunting* vi. 144 Donker, my best ox is dead, having got at a poisonous kind of grass, called by the Dutch tulp.] **1884** MILLER *Plant-n.*, Cape Tulip, *Melanthium uniflorum* (*Tulipa Breyiana*). ——, Red Cape, *Hæmanthus coccineus*... Drooping T., *Fritillaria Meleagris*. *Ibid.*, *Calochortus*, Butterfly-Tulip,.. Mariposa Lily,.. Wild Tulip, of California. **1885** RIDER HAGGARD *K. Solomon's Mines* iv, The other three [oxen] died from eating the poisonous herb called 'tulip'. **1898** MORRIS *Austral Eng.*, *Telopea*,.. the genus containing.. the *Waratah*... The name has been corrupted popularly into *Tulip*, and the flower is often called the *Native Tulip*. **1908** *Westm. Gaz.* 14 May 12/1 A field.. covered with the purple blossoms of the 'tulip', as the villagers call it [the fritillary].

2. *fig.* **a.** A showy person or thing, or one greatly admired.

1647 COWLEY *Mistress, Beauty* iii, Beauty, thou active passive Ill!.. Thou Tulip, who thy Stock in Paint dost waste. **1672** *Mede's Wks.* Life p. xlii, Such Fellow-commoners who came to the University only to see it and to be seen.. he call'd The University-Tulips, that made a Gaudy shew for a while. **1701** CIBBER *Love makes Man* V. ii, My little Blossom! my Gilliflower! my Rose! my Pink! my Tulip! **1837** THACKERAY *Ravenswing* i, Morgiana was a tulip among women, and the tulip fanciers all came flocking round her.

b. *slang.* **my tulip**, 'my fine fellow'.

1847 *Punch* 16 Oct. 148/1 This, my tulip, is a *salle de danse*. **1895** 'G. MORTIMER' *Tales from Western Moors* iii. 67 'Cos for this, my tulip,.. work and me fell out a long time back.

3. a. A bell-shaped outward swell in the muzzle of a gun, now generally disused.

1884 [implied in *tulip choke*]. **1889** *Engineer* Oct. 314 Breech-loading guns,.. gradually tapering from a diameter of 4 ft. 7 in. at the breech to 17 in. near the muzzle, which possesses what artillerists call a tulip or 'swell'.

b. An explosive charge used to destroy a length of railway track. Now *Hist.*

1918 T. E. LAWRENCE in *Lett.* (1938) 250 A gang of four men can lay twenty 'tulips' in an hour on easy ballast, and for each two slabs (and single fuse) you ruin a sleeper, a yard of bank and two rails. **1920** *Blackw. Mag.* May 599/2 J. and I tried our prentice hands at the new game of 'planting tulips'. **1956** *Railway Mag.* Mar. 167/1 'Tulips', so called because of the appearance of the track after they had 'flowered', were the most effective means of derailing a train.

4. *slang.* A bishop's mitre, or a figure of one.

1879 A. R. ASHWELL *Bp. Wilberforce* I. iii. 66 *note*, I heard one of the fellows.. say 'No, It's not a Tulip', meaning that there was no mitre on the panel [of the carriage].

5. *attrib.* and *Comb.*, as ***tulip-bed, -bulb, -fancier, -field, -glass, -grower, -leaf, -mania, -time***; ***tulip-fancying, -like, -shaped, -tinted*** adjs.; **tulip-apple**, a variety of apple with bright-coloured fruit; **tulip break(ing)**, the variegated colouring of certain tulip flowers, caused by a virus infection; **tulip choke** (cf. sense 3 and CHOKE *sb.*[1] 4); **tulip ear**, of a dog: see quot. 1877; so **tulip-eared** *a.*; **tulip fire**, a fungus disease of tulips, caused by *Botrytis tulipæ* and producing speckled, discoloured leaves and flowers; **tulip-grass**, a name for several S. African poisonous herbs of the genus *Homeria* (N.O. *Iridaceæ*); **tulip-laurel**, ? a species of *Magnolia*; **tulip poplar** = TULIP-TREE 1 (see POPLAR 2); **tulip-poppy**, a Mexican papaveraceous plant, *Hunnemannia fumariæfolia*, with flowers like those of *Eschscholtzia*; **tulip-root**, (*a*) the 'root' or bulb of a tulip; (*b*) a disease of oats, characterized by a swelling at the base of the stem, caused by a minute nematoid worm; **tulip-shell**, (*a*) a bivalve of the genus *Tellina*; (*b*) any gastropod of the family *Fasciolariadæ*, as *Fasciolaria tulipa*. Also TULIP-TREE, -WOOD.

1842 LOUDON *Suburban Hort.* 529 The tree is still more beautiful when covered with fruit, especially with such as are highly-coloured, such as the red Astrachan, the *tulipapple, &c. **1822** T. G. WAINEWRIGHT in *London Mag.* June 552/2 A delicate Schiavone, various as a *tulip bed with rich broken tints. **1939** JOYCE *Finnegans Wake* 526 Or tulipbeds of Rush below. **1958** *Manch. Guardian* 28 May 6/3 These changes of colour are symptoms of the virus disease known as *tulip break. **1929** *U.S. Dept. Agric. Yearbk. 1928* 596 (*heading*) Tulip '*breaking' is proved to be caused by mosaic infection. **1664** EVELYN *Kal. Hort.* June (1729) 208 Take up your *Tulip Bulbs. **1884** BURGESS *Sporting Fire Arms* 4 The sketches show the ordinary choke and the *tulip choke. **1877** G. STABLES *Pract. Kennel Guide* iii. (ed. 3) 36 *Tulip-ear.—Partly pricked, and drooping at the tip. *Ibid.* vii. §3 81 [Ears of Skye Terrier] may be pricked, or tulip. **1837** *Tulip fanciers [see 2]. **1826** SCOTT *Woodst.* xxxiii, A *tulip-fancying fellow,.. intended for a Dutch gardener. **1969** G. LYALL *Venus with Pistol* vii. 38 Amsterdam was cold... Carlos told me.. not [to] stop off to look at any *tulip fields. **1931** *Pamphl. Seale-Hayne Agric. Coll.* XXXVI. 27 Several suggestions have been made as possible methods for the control of *Tulip Fire. **1976** *Homes & Gardens* June 131/2 Tulips are particularly susceptible to tulip fire; this produces malformed leaves and shoots, which wither and stop growing. **1760** J. LEE *Introd. Bot.* App. 330 *Tulip-flower, *Bignonia*. **1755** *Gentl. Mag.* Sept. 416/1 Several lacrymatories have also been dug up, some are of glass,.. and some are of burnt earth, like our *tulip-glasses. **1952** M. ALLINGHAM *Tiger in Smoke* ii. 49 He was carrying two large tulip glasses which he had overfilled. **1976** D. FRANCIS *In Frame* v. 83 When Jik opened the champagne he poured it into shining tulip glasses. **1900** *Blackw. Mag.* Apr. 574/1 He has eaten *tulip-grass. **1882** *Pall Mall G.* 18 Oct. 4 A Dutch *tulip-grower. **1766** W. STORK *Acc. East Florida* 47 The magnolia, *tulip-laurel, tupelow-tree, are all beautiful. *a* **1718** PRIOR *Alma* I. 381 But *Tulip-leaves, and Limon-peel Help only to adorn the meal. *c* **1711** PETIVER *Gazophyl.* IX. Tab. 85 Red *Tulip-like Flowers. **1839** *Penny Cycl.* XIV. 314/1 The extravagances of those visited by the *tulip mania. **1683** *Lond. Gaz.* No. 1810/4 Lost.., a Gold Pendulum Watch,.. with.. a Steel Chain, and *Tulip Pillars. **1868** *Rep. U.S. Comm. Agric.* (1869) 99 *Endecatomus rugosus*.. has been also taken under the bark of *tulip poplars. **1909** *Cent. Dict. Suppl.*, *Hunnemannia*.. contains a single Mexican species, *H. fumariæfolia*, now somewhat cultivated under the name *tulip-poppy. **1728–46** THOMSON *Spring* 538 Then comes the *tulip race, where Beauty plays Her idle freaks. **1711** ADDISON *Spect.* No. 108 ⁋3 He carries a *Tulip-root in his Pocket. **1875** *Encycl. Brit.* I. 360/2 The oat frequently suffers much from a disease called 'segging' or 'tulip root'. **1833** LOUDON *Encycl. Archit.* §190 Ornamental *tulip-shaped chimney-pots. **1835** KIRBY *Hab. & Inst. Anim.* I. viii. 265 The *tulip-shell (Tellina) when it walks,.. opens and shuts its valves. **1861** P. P. CARPENTER in *Rep. Smithsonian Instit.* 1860, 180 Family *Fasciolariadæ*. (Tulip-shells and Mitres). **1954** L. MACNEICE *Autumn Sequel* 41 Its *tuliptime and playtime.

Hence (or from mod.L. *tulipa*) **tuli'piferous** *a.* [-FEROUS], bearing flowers like tulips, as the tulip-tree; **'tulipine**, *Chem.*, a poisonous stimulant alkaloid obtained from the garden tulip; **'tulipist**, a person devoted to the cultivation of tulips; **ˌtulipo'mania** [-MANIA], a craze for tulips, as that which prevailed in Holland in the 17th c.; **ˌtulipo'maniac**, one affected with tulipomania; **'tulipy** *a.*, abounding in tulips; †*sb.* a tulip.

1786 J. ABERCROMBIE *Arrangem.* in *Gard. Assist.* 38/1 *Tulipiferous, or common tulip bearing [Tulip tree]. **1909** *Cent. Dict. Suppl.*, *Tulipine. **1913** DORLAND *Med. Dict.*, Tulipin. **1658** SIR T. BROWNE *Hydriot.* Ded., The Ingenuous delight of *Tulipists. **1710** ADDISON *Tatler* No. 218 ⁋7 A Person of good Sense, had not his Head been touched with.. the.. Tulippomania. **1842** *Chamb. Jrnl.* 12 Feb. 32/3 When the Tulipomania infected Holland, and single roots were sold for many hundred pounds. **1842** *Blackw. Mag.* LI. 426 The prices of these roots.. are enough .. to delight the cupidity of a Dutch *tulipo-maniac. *a* **1849** J. C. MANGAN *Poems* (1859) 322 Shaarmal's *tulipy dell. *c* **1626** W. BOSWORTH *Arcadius & Sepha* I. 882 That blood with wat'ry eye Which leaves her breast to turn t' a *tulippy.

tulipan, -pant, obs. ff. TULIP, TURBAN.

† **tuli'panted**, *a. Obs. rare.* [f. *tulipant*, early form of TURBAN + -ED².] = TURBANED.

1634 SIR T. HERBERT *Trav.* 206 They [Chinese] are tulipanted about their heads.

'tulip-tree.

1. A large N. American tree, *Liriodendron Tulipifera* (N.O. *Magnoliaceæ*), bearing flowers resembling large tulips of a greenish colour variegated with yellow and orange; also called *tulip poplar*, *saddle-tree* (from the shape of its peculiar truncated leaves), and *whitewood*.

1705 BEVERLEY *Virginia* II. iv. §18 (1722) 123 The large Tulip-Tree, which we call a Poplar. **1800** *Med. Jrnl.* IV. 376 The leaves and roots of the tulip tree,.. recommended as an useful bitter. **1857** GOSSE *Omphalos* vii. 165 This noble Tulip-tree.., a giant of this primeval forest.

b. Applied to other trees with tulip-like flowers, as species of *Magnolia*, and the mountain mahoe (*Paritium elatum* or *Hibiscus elatus*, N.O. *Malvaceæ*) of the West Indies.

1751 J. HILL *Hist. Plants* 487 The great-flowered Magnolia, the Laurel-leaved Tulip-tree. **1884** MILLER *Plant-n.*, Tulip-tree, Chinese, *Magnolia fuscata*.

2. Applied in Australia to two proteaceous trees with brilliantly coloured flowers: **a.** A Victorian and Tasmanian species of Waratah, *Telopea orcades*, also called *native tulip* (see TULIP 1 b); **b.** *Stenocarpus cunninghami*, of Queensland.

1830 *Hobart Town Almanack* 66 (Morris) That magnificent shrub called warratah or tulip-tree, and its beautiful scarlet flowers. **1835** ROSS *Hobart Town Almanack* 110 The generic name [*Telopea*].. has been corrupted into tulip tree, to which it bears not the least resemblance. **1866** *Treas. Bot.*, Tulip-tree, Queensland, *Stenocarpus Cunninghami*. **1898** MORRIS *Austral English*, *Tulip-tree*. The name is given, in Australia, to *Stenocarpus cunninghamii*,.. on account of the brilliancy of its bright-red flowers.

'tulip-wood.

a. The wood of the tulip-tree (see prec. 1), a light ornamental wood used by cabinet-makers, etc. **b.** A name for various coloured and striped woods, or the trees producing them, as *Physocalymma floribundum* of Brazil, *Homoiceltis* (*Aphananthe*) *philippinensis*, and species of *Owenia* and *Harpullia*, of Australia. (Also *attrib.*)

1843 HOLTZAPFFEL *Turning* I. ii. 20 Some of the hardest foreign woods, as king-wood, tulip-wood,.. are rarely sound in the center. **1845** J. O. BALFOUR *Sketch N.S. Wales* ii. 39 The tulip wood, with its variegated flowers, and delightful perfume, grows in abundance. **1866** *Treas. Bot.* 882 The beautifully striped rose-coloured wood imported from Brazil, and called Tulip-wood by our cabinet-makers,.. is the produce of *P[hysocalymma] floribundum*. **1884** MILLER *Plant-n.*, *Harpulia Hillii* and *H. pendula*, Tulip-wood, of Queensland. **1891** *Cent. Dict.* s.v. *Owenia*, *O[wenia] cerasifera* and *O. venosa* are in Queensland called respectively *sweet* and *sour plum*. Both have hard wood, that of the latter highly coloured.., used in cabinet-making and wheel-wrights' work. *O. venosa* is called *tulip-wood*. **1898** MORRIS *Austral Eng.*, *Tulip-wood*. The name is given, in Australia, to *Aphnanthe philipinensis*, Planch., N.O. *Urticaceæ*, and to the timber of *Harpullia pendula*, Planch. [Moreton Bay tulip-wood], N.O. *Sapindaceæ*. It is, further, a synonym for the Emu-Apple [*Owenia acidula*, called also Native Nectarine and Native Quince]. **1906** *Times* 8 Feb. 7/6 A Dutch kingwood and tulipwood secretaire cabinet.

† **tulk, tolk**, *sb. Obs.* [Generally identified with ON. *túlkr* interpreter, spokesman (cf. ON. *túlka* vb.: see next), Da., Sw. *tolk* = MLG. *tolk*, *tollik*, Du. *tolk* translator, MHG. *tolc*, *tolke*, ad. Lith. *tulkas*, Lett. *tulks*, OSl. *tlᵘkᵘ* interpreter: cf. Russ. *tolkᵘ* sense, meaning, talk. But nothing has been found to connect the ME. sense, common in alliterative verse, with these.]

A man.

13.. *E.E. Allit. P.* B. 498 Tyl þay had typyng fro þe tolke þat tyned hem þer-inne. *Ibid.* 1262 Er he to þe tempple tee wyth his tulkkes alle. **13..** *Gaw. & Gr. Knt.* 3 þe tulk þat þe trammes of tresoun þer wroȝt, Watz tried for his tricherie. *a* **1400-50** *Alexander* 752 Alexander.. turnyd hym þan to þis tulke & talkez þir wordez. *c* **1400** *Destr. Troy* 5790 Prothenor, the prise kyng, & proud Archelaus, Mony tolke of þe Troiens tyrnyt to dethe. *Ibid.* 6115 Mony abill knyghtes,.. Of þe tulkys of troy, tidé men all.

† **tulk**, *v. Obs. rare*⁻¹. [app. a. ON. *túlka* to interpret, plead one's cause, be the spokesman: cf. prec.] *intr.* To utter sound, to sound.

13.. *E.E. Allit. P.* B. 1414 And ay þe nakeryn noyse, notes of pipes, Tymbres & tabornes, tulket among.

tull, obs. or dial. f. TILL *prep.* and *conj.*

‖ **tulle** (tyl, tu:l). [F. *tulle* (1812 in Hatz.-Darm.), 'named from Tulle, chief town of the department of Corrèze, where the fabric was first manufactured' (Littré).] **a.** A fine silk bobbin-net used for women's dresses, veils, hats, etc.

c **1818** MRS. CAREY *Tour France* xv. (1823) 310 This imitation is of silk, called tulle, from the name of the town where it is principally made. **1868** *Morn. Star* 7 Mar., Her Royal Highness.. wore.. a petticoat of white tulle over rich glacé silk. **1888** 'J. S. WINTER' *Bootle's Childr.* ix, The effect of the sweeping train, the shower of *tulle* which fell from the golden coronet of her hair.

attrib. **1859** *Habits Gd. Society* iv. (new ed.) 183 A beautiful tulle dress. **1900** EL. GLYN *Visits Eliz.* (1906) 54, I wore the white silk and my pink tulle hat.

b. *tulle gras* (gra) [F. *gras* fatty], a gauze dressing for the skin impregnated with petroleum jelly.

1933 *Jrnl. R. Army Medical Corps* XL. 353 The 'Tulle Gras' dressing.. was first placed on the market.. by a French firm some years ago. It consists.. of a fairly large-mesh gauze net, impregnated with vaseline containing 1 per cent. of balsam of Peru, supplied in sections of about four inches by five inches in size. **1974** R. M. KIRK et al. *Surgery* v. 75 A partial thickness burn, or one that is of doubtful nature, is treated by removing debris, pricking and emptying the blisters, and covering the area with tulle gras .. which is non-adherent.

tulle, var. TILL *v.*³ *Obs.*; obs. f. TOLL *v.*¹

tullibee ('tʌlɪbi:). Also **tulibbi**. [ad. N. Amer. Indian (Cree and Odjibway) *too-nie-bee*.] A species of whitefish (*Coregonus tullibee*) found in the Great Lakes of N. America.

1789 A. SHAW *Let.* 16 Dec. in L. F. R. Masson *Bourgeois de la Compagnie du Nord-Ouest* (1889) I. 33, I take a walk to my traps, return to the house, eat *Tollibees* about nine. **1823** J. FRANKLIN *Narr. Journey to Shores of Polar Sea* II. 711 The Cree name of this fish, ottonneebees, has been corrupted by the traders into tullibee. **1888** GOODE *Amer. Fishes* 93 Tautog, chogset,.. tullibee.. are among the best. **1906** *Blackw. Mag.* Mar. 394/1 The tulibbis.. often sold as fresh water herring.. are only fit to eat in winter.

tullipant, obs. form of TURBAN.

tulp (tœlp). *S. Afr.* Also **tulpe**. [a. Du. *tulp* tulip.] Any of several bulbous plants of the genus *Homeria* or *Moræa* of the family Iridaceæ, esp. *Homeria breyniana* or *Moræa polystachya*, which are native to southern Africa, bear yellow, pink, or blue flowers, and are extremely poisonous to cattle.

[**1795**: see SUIKERBOS.] **1835** T. H. BOWKER *Jrnl.* 10 May (MS.), Lots of Bullocks sick with eating Tulp. **1844** J. BACKHOUSE *Narr. Visit Mauritius & S. Afr.* xviii. 276 Among the grass, on the south side, there was an abundance of the species of *Moræa*, known in the country by the name of Tulip or Tulpe, which is very destructive to cattle. **1871** T. BAINES *Diary* 28 May (1946) III. 601 Tulp, a plant poisonous to cattle, grew at Blauwe Krantz. **1896** R. WALLACE *Farming Industries Cape Colony* iv. 96 Cattle bred on the ground do not eat tulp unless they are very hungry. **1958** *Cape Times* 23 Aug. 11/6 Poisonous plants, such as tulp,.. led to illness among animals. **1973** *Grocott's Mail* (Grahamstown, S. Afr.) 19 June 3 An abundance of the highly poisonous tulp plant.. could mean stock losses for unsuspecting farmers.

‖ **tulsi** ('tu:lsi:). *E. Ind.* Also 7 **tulce**, 9 **tulsee**, **toolsee**, **-si**, **-sy**. [Hindī *tūlsī*:—Skr. *tulasī*.] A species of basil (*Ocimum sanctum*), sacred to Vishnu, cultivated by the Hindus as a sacred plant. Also *attrib.*

1698 FRYER *Acc. E. India & P.* 199 Having a little place or two built up a Foot Square of Mud, where they plant Calaminth, or (by them called) Tulce, which they worship every Morning. **1813** J. FORBES *Oriental Mem.* III. 62 A garden and fountain with an altar of Tulsee, the sacred plant of the Brahmins. **1834** [A. PRINSEP] *Baboo* II. iii. 44 They.. would laugh at the holy Toolsee-leaf, and Ganges water. **1866** *Treas. Bot.*, *Toolsi*, *Tulasi*, Indian names for species of Basil. **1895** R. W. FRAZER *Silent Gods, Pearl of Temple* (1896) 46 The short square pillar.. with sacred Tulsī plant growing on its summit.

‖ **tulwar** ('tʌlwɑ:(r)). Also **talwar**. [Hindī *talwār* (also *tarwār*).] An (Indian) sabre.

c **1810** W. HICKEY *Mem.* (1960) xv. 252 In about half an hour after the first grand attack had thus been made, an alarm was given that the mob armed with *tulwars* (scimitars) had forced the sentries. **1834** [A. PRINSEP] *Baboo* I. viii. 125 With my tulwar unsheathed on my arm, I moved to the edge of the tope. **1861** HUGHES *Tom Brown at Oxf.* xliv, I just caught the flash of his tulwar, and thought it was all up. **1892** J. PAYN *Mod. Whittington* I. 195 The tulwar of the Rajah of Bundlecumbad: the scabbard he described as a triumph of Eastern decoration.

† **'tuly**, *a.* (*sb.*) *Obs.* Forms: 4 **tuli**, **tule**, **tuely**, **twily**, 4-5 **tuly**, 4-6 **tewly**, 5 **toly**. [app. from a place-name. The quots. from *Gaw. & Gr. Knt.* suggest connexion with Toulouse.] An attribute of silk, tapestry, etc. of a rich red colour; perh. orig. applied to such fabrics imported from Toulouse. Also *absol.* Any fabric described as 'tuly'.

1321 in Legg & Hope *Inv. Ch. Ch. Canterb.* (1902) 52 Casula.. de rubeo sindone de tuly cum rosis brudato. *Ibid.* 55 Capa.. de Rubeo panno de Tuly. **13..** *Coer de L.* 67 Her ropes wer off tuely sylk, Al so whyt as ony mylk. **13..** *Gaw. & Gr. Knt.* 568 Fryst a tule tapit, tyȝt ouer þe flet. *Ibid.* 858 Tapytez tyȝt to þe woȝe, of tuly & tars. [Cf. 77 A selure.. Of tryed Tolouse, of Tars tapites.] **1523** SKELTON *Garl. Laurel* 798 Reche me that skane of tewly sylk.

b. *transf.* Of a deep red colour, like that of 'tuly' silk; *absol.* or as *sb.* the red colour of this.

1398 TREVISA *Barth. De. P.R.* XVI. lxxxi. (Tollem. MS.) Ofte it gendreþ semely colour and feyre, as tewly reed and stibium. *a* **1400-50** *Alexander* 4335 Nouthire to toly ne to taunde transmitte we na vebbis, To vermylion ne violett ne variant littis. **14..** *MS. Sloane 73* lf. 200 Resseit.. for to make bokerham tuly or tuly þred. *c* **1440** *Promp. Parv.* 505/2 Tuly, colowre, *puniceus*.

tuly, obs. f. TEWLY *a.*, sickly.

tulye, obs. f. TILL *v.*¹

tulye, -yie, -ȝe, -ȝie: see TUILYIE.

tulyhour, obs. f. TUILYIER.

tum (tʌm), *v.*¹ *north. dial.* [Origin not ascertained.] *trans.* To card (wool), esp. for the first time, in preparation for the finer cards. Also, to mix wool of different colours. Hence **'tumming** *vbl. sb.*, the action or process of doing this; *concr.* coarse cardings of wool; also **'tummer**: see quots. 1877, 1884.

1615 MARKHAM *Eng. Housew.* iii. 88 After your wooll is oild.. you shall then tumme it; which is, you shall.. card it ouer againe vpon your Stocke cards: And then those cardings which you strike off are called tummings. *Ibid.*, After your Wooll is thus mixed oiled and tummed, you shall then Spinne it vpon great Wooll wheeles. **1691** RAY *N.C. Words* 77 To *Tum* Wooll; to mix Wool of divers colours. **1703** THORESBY *Let. to Ray* Gloss. (E.D.S.) *Tooming*, wool taken off the cards. **1788** W. MARSHALL *Yorksh.* II. Gloss. (E.D.S.) *Tum*, *v.*, to card wool roughly, to prepare it for the finer cards. **1822** *Lonsdale Mag.* Jan. 13/1, I thought my father had a neater method of mixing the black and white wool, in tumming. **1877** *Encycl. Brit.* VI. 494/2 The carding engines [in cotton-manufacture] are often made with two main cylinders and a connecting cylinder called the tummer. **1878-81** *Cumberld. Gloss.*, *Tummins*, rough cardings of wool. **1879** *Ibid.* Suppl., *Toom*, *tum*, to tease wool. **1884** R. MARSDEN *Cotton Spinning* (1891) 129 In these cards there are two large cylinders, the first being stripped by a doffer cylinder called a slow tummer.

tum (tʌm), *sb.*¹ and *v.*² [Echoic; more usual in reduplicated form TUM-TUM.] An imitation of the sound made by plucking a tense string, as in a musical instrument, or by striking a drum, or the like. also as vb. *trans.* and *intr.* to produce this sound; hence **'tumming** *vbl. sb.*

c **1830** *Negro Song*, Don't ye 'ear de banjo tum? **1882** ELWES tr. *Capello & Ivens' Benguella to Yacca* II. iv. 77 The echoes.. repeating the tumming of the drums. **1911** *Daily News* 23 June 3 The monotonous tum to which the dancers keep time for weeks together.

tum (tʌm), *sb.*² *joc.* Short for TUMMY. Cf. TUM-TUM *sb.*⁴

1869 W. S. GILBERT *Bab Ballads* 121 They can reduce a bulging tum To measures fair By taking air And exercise in plenty. **1890** A. JAMES *Diary* 18 July (1965) 129 That dissipated organ known in the family as 'Alice's tum'. **1937** G. FRANKAU *More of Us* xiv. 153 Chilled all those suns for which we oiled the raw tum Or boracized the blistering shoulder blade. **1977** *Time* 14 Feb. 33/2 To re-establish old wisdom and simple certitudes: hot chestnuts in the hand, calories in the tum.

tum, obs. form of TOOM *a.*

tumain, obs. form of TOMAN¹, Persian coin.

tuman (tʊ'mɑ:n). [Var. TOMAN¹.] A tribe of Baluchis or Pathans.

[**1816** H. POTTINGER *Trav. Beloochistan* iv. 62 An assemblage of these Ghedans [*sc.* tents] constitute a Toomun, or village, and the inhabitants of it a Kheil, or society.] **1907** *Baluchistan District Gazetteer Ser.* III. 372 A tribe is not responsible for the actions of any person who takes up his abode temporarily with it for purposes of cultivation or for grazing. In this case his heirs and his own *tuman* is responsible for his acts. **1950** *R. Central Asian Jrnl.* XXXVII. 284 There are nine Baloch tumans (tribes) of Dera Ghazi Khan. **1974** *Encycl. Brit. Micropædia* I. 773/3 Each tribe (*tuman*) consists of several clans and acknowledges one chief, even though in some *tuman* there are clans in habitual opposition to the chief.

So **tuman'dar**, a Baluchi or Pathan chief.

1907 *Baluchistan District Gazetteer Ser.* III. i. 78 Among the Baloch.. a chief or *tumandār* may invite contributions on the occasion of a marriage. **1932** *Cambr. Hist. India* VI. xxv. 455 Casting all fear on one side, he boldly advanced into their mountain retreats and made friends with the tribal chiefs or tumandars. **1979** *Indo-British Rev.* (Madras) VIII. I-II. 52/2 The Tumandars, or chiefs of the unadministered territory, had come in for their annual reunion with.. the political Agent.

tumângong, var. TEMENGGONG.

tumasha, var. TAMASHA.

‖ **tumata-kuru** ('tu:mata,kʊrʊ). Also **tumatu-**, **tomata-kuru**, **-guru**, **tumatagowry**, **toomatoo-gooroo**. [Maori.] A spiny, spreading New Zealand shrub, *Discaria Toumatou*, N.O. *Rhamnaceæ*, the thorns of which were used by the Maori in tattooing. Also called New Zealand Hawthorn, Wild Irishman, and corruptly MATAGOURI.

1859 J. T. THOMSON in *Otago Gaz.* 22 Sept. 264 (Morris) Much over-run with the scrub called 'tomata-guru'. **1883** J. HECTOR *Handbk. N. Zealand* 131 Tumatakuru, Wild Irishman. A bush or small tree with spreading branches.. The spines were used by the Maoris for tatooing. **1898** MORRIS *Austral Eng.*, *Tumata-kuru*.. Tumatagowry, or Matagory is the Southern corruption of contractors, labourers, and others.

† **tumb**, *v. Obs. rare.* Also 4 **tombe**. [OE. *tumbian* (see TUMBLE *v.*) = ON. *tumba*, OHG. *tūmôn* (from OLG.).] *intr.* To tumble, to perform saltatory feats; to dance.

c **1000** *Ags. Gosp.* Matt. xiv. 6 Ða on herodes ȝebyrd-dæȝe tumbude [*Hatton MS.* tumbede; Vulg. *saltavit*] þære herodiadiscean dohtur beforan him. —— Mark vi. 22 þa ð a þære herodiadiscan dohtor inneode & tumbode [*Hatt. MS.* tumbede; Vulg. *saltasset*]. **1387** TREVISA *Higden* (Rolls) IV. 365 þe eorþe swelowede þe wenche þat tomblede [*MSS. α and γ* tombede (which represents Trevisa's own s.w. form)].

tumb, obs. f. TOMB.

tumbaga, var. TOMBAC.

‖**tumbak, tumbaki** (tuːm'bɑːk, -'bɑːkiː). Also **tumbek, -i, toumbeki, toombak, (tumbki).** [a. Arabic *tun'bāk*, ad. F. *tabac* tobacco.] Name in Turkey for a coarse kind of tobacco imported from Persia; Shiraz tobacco.

1836 LANE *Mod. Egypt.* I. v. 167 A particular kind of tobacco, called *toombák*, from Persia, is used in the water-pipe. **1858** SIMMONDS *Dict. Trade*, *Toumbeki*, a Turkish name for Schiraz tobacco. **1882** O'DONOVAN *Merv Oasis* I. v. 80 A handful of *tumbaki*, a coarse kind of tobacco used in these regions, is thrown in, and the smoker..inhales the fumes of the tobacco, mingled with air. **1891** *Kew Bulletin* 77 Tumbeki. **1897** *Daily News* 31 Dec. 3/6 Lazily smoking a narghilé charged with fragrant Persian tumbki.

tumbe, obs. form of TOMB.

†**tumbester.** *Obs.* Also 4–5 **tombester(e, tumbestere, 5 -istere.** [Feminine of OE. *tumbere* tumbler, dancer, acrobat: see -STER. Cf. OF. *tumberesse, tumeresse* (f. *tomber* to fall), in same sense (13th c. in Godef.).] A female tumbler or dancer. See also TUMBLESTER.

c **1386** CHAUCER *Pard. T.* 15 (Ellesm.) And right anon thanne comen Tombesteres [*Cambr.* Tumbesteris; *Corp., Petw., Lansd.* tombl.] Fetys and smale and yonge frutesteres. **1387** TREVISA *Higden* (Rolls) IV. 15 In Grees was no man grettre þan Alisaundre; noþeles Perdica, a tombester [*MS. β and Caxton* tomblestres; HIGDEN *saltatricis*] sone, was his successour, and nouȝt his owne sone. **1387–8** T. USK *Test. Love* II. ii. (Skeat) l. 118 Perdicas ..was of no kinges blod, his dame was a tombystere. **14..** *MS. Harl. 2398* lf. 8 Herodias douȝ ter, þat was a tumbestere, and tumblede by fore him and oþer grete lordes. *c* **1430** *Pilgr. Lyf Manhode* IV. ix. (1869) 180, I hatte jolyfnesse, þe lyghte, þe tumbistere, þe rennere, þe fonne, þe lepere.

tumble ('tʌmb(ə)l), *sb.* [f. next.] An act of tumbling; the condition of being tumbled.

1. An act of acrobatic tumbling; an acrobatic feat. *rare.*

1824 LANDOR *Imag. Conv., Gen. Lascy & Curate Merino* II. 75 A tumble of heels over head, a feat performed by beggar-boys on the roads. **1825** J. NEAL *Bro. Jonathan* I. ii. 28 A few hearty tumbles, all alone.

2. a. An accidental fall; also, the falling of a stream.

1716 LADY M. W. MONTAGU *Let. to C'tess Mar* 21 Nov., In case of a tumble, it was utterly impossible to come alive to the bottom. **1749** FIELDING *Tom Jones* XII. viii, The landlord..became perfectly well acquainted with the tumble of Sophia from her horse. **1860** TYNDALL *Glac.* I. xvi. 116 The end..was always a plunge and tumble in the deeper snow. **1871** R. ELLIS *Catullus* lxviii. 60 As hill-born brook..O'er his moss-grown crags leaps with a tumble a-down. **1880** MISS BIRD *Japan* I. 101 Mountains..noisy with the dash and tumble of a thousand streams.

b. *fig.* A fall, downfall.

1728 VANBR. & CIB. *Prov. Husb.* II. i, The Demoivre Baronet had a bloody Tumble [at cards]. **1765** G. WILLIAMS in Jesse *Selwyn & Contemp.* (1843) I. 404 Pembroke gave him such a tumble the other night, by telling him Mr. Pitt would no more trust him than his postilion, that [etc.]. **1833** T. HOOK *Parson's Dau.* III. x, Our unlooked-for tumble [from high estate]. **1886** *Pall Mall G.* 8 Oct. 11/2 There will be a terrible tumble in the price of American oil in Europe. **1893** STEVENSON *Catriona* xxvi, Here were all my dreams come to a sad tumble.

c. In phrase ROUGH-AND-TUMBLE, q.v.

d. ***to take a tumble*** (***to oneself***): to realize the facts of one's situation; to wake up *to* something, to tumble. *slang* (orig. *U.S.*).

1877 [see ON TO, ONTO *prep.* 2]. **1928** F. HURST *President is Born* xiv. 182 An iron negro boy, with a hitching ring in his fist, stood..at the curb... Once, some town-wag..had hung a pasteboard tag about his neck, 'Take a tumble to yourself, Joe.' **1944** *Living off Land* v. 106 At one goldfield where malaria broke out virulently no one took a tumble why for a long time. **1949** J. R. COLE *It was so Late* 65 The woman, taking a tumble to our set up, gave me the come on. **1959** M. GEE in C. K. Stead *N.Z. Short Stories* (1966) 267 After a while I give up, and I take a tumble to what's happening. I'm getting the bum's rush. **1973** 'J. PATRICK' *Glasgow Gang Observed* viii. 79 Ma wee brother will learn sense; he'll take a tumble tae hissel'.

e. A sign of recognition or acknowledgement, a response; chiefly in phr. ***to give a tumble.*** *U.S. slang.*

1921 H. C. WITWER *Leather Pushers* xi. 282 Neither of 'em give him a tumble. **1934** J. O'HARA *Appointment in Samarra* (1935) vii. 208, I went in his office and started kidding around... I noticed I wasn't getting a tumble from him, so I finally broke down and asked him, I said what was the matter. **1935** D. RUNYON in *Cosmopolitan* Jan. 160/3 He never lets on he knows me, and naturally I do not give Mr. Labez any tumble whatever. **1953** *N.Y. Times Book Rev.* 8 Feb. 17 If the right boy won't give you [*sc.* a girl] a tumble, you've got a problem. **1976** *Washington Post* 19 Apr. c3/6 Der Bingle took a subway ride in New York over the weekend and not a soul gave him a tumble. Bing Crosby said he knew what it meant to be just another straphanger.

3. Tumbled condition; disorder, confusion, disturbance; a confused or tangled heap.

1634 JACKSON *Creed* VII. xxxii. §4 Some authority in all this tumble did still remain in the tribe of Judah. **1641** LAUD *Wks.* (1853) VI. 88 After much tumble, a major part of the votes made choice of me. **1755** H. WALPOLE *Lett.* (1846) III. 129, I could not expect that any drawing could give a full idea of the..masterly tumble of the feathers [of Walpole's eagle]. **1762–71** —— *Vertue's Anecd. Paint.* (1786) I. x. 138 Rubens was never greater than in landscape; the tumble of his rocks and trees [etc.] show a variety of genius. **1869** BLACKMORE *Lorna D.* xxxi, Glad..that his story might get out of the tumble which all our talk had made in it. **1903** *Westm. Gaz.* 21 Mar. 5/1 The moorhen..swimming out from the overhanging tumble of bush and bramble.

4. *slang.* An act of sexual intercourse; a woman giving opportunity for this; chiefly in phr. ***to give*** (or ***get***) ***a tumble.***

1903 FARMER & HENLEY *Slang* VII. 224/2 *To do a tumble* (of women) = to lie down to a man. **1934** H. MILLER *Tropic of Cancer* 297 She's a big, healthy bitch... I wouldn't mind giving her a tumble. **1954** J. TRENCH *Dishonoured Bones* iii. 110 He was..giving la Vitrey a tumble somewhere. **1970** 'J. & E. BONETT' *Sound of Murder* xiii. 172 Most men think that a woman who has been loved by a married man is an easy tumble. **1976** P. CAVE *High Flying Birds* iii. 45 'Back-pay', he said, 'plus an advance on a quick tumble tomorrow night.'

tumble ('tʌmb(ə)l), *v.* Also 4–5 **tumbel**, 4–6 **tumbil**, 4–7 **tomble**, 5 **towmble, tumbell, -bill** (also 6 *Sc.*), 5–6 **tombel, toumble**, 6 **toomble**; *Sc.* 4 **twmmyll**, 4–6 **tummyll, tumle**, 6 **tummill**, *north. dial.* **tomyll**, 8–9 **tummle.** [ME. *tumbel*, etc. = MLG., LG., mod.Ger. (*sich*) *tummeln*, EFris. *tummeln*, early mod.Du. (Kilian) *tommelen, tummelen*, Fris. *tommelje*, Da. *tumle*, Sw. *tumla* to tumble down, (*refl.*) to roll oneself, turn round, also OHG. *tumalôn*, mod.Ger. *tummeln* to bustle, hurry, make haste. By the side of these, OHG. had, with long *ū*, *tûmalôn*, mod.Ger. *taumeln* to be giddy, reel, stagger, tumble, Du. *tuimelen*, earlier *tuymelen* (Kilian), to tumble, fall. The forms with short and long *u* were originally variants, formed as frequentatives or diminutives of OHG. *tumôn*, OE. *tumbian*, TUMB; in mod.Ger. they have become differentiated in sense as well as in form. From an OLG. *tumben, tummen*, came OF. *tumer, tumber, tomber* to fall, which has prob. influenced the Eng. sense of *tumble*. The ME. spelling *tomb-* was merely graphic: see O (the letter).]

I. 1. *intr.* †To dance with posturing, balancing, contortions, and the like (*obs.*); to perform as an acrobat; *esp.* to execute leaps, springs, somersaults, and similar feats.

a **1300** *Cursor M.* 13140 (Gött.) His broþer doghtir..Balid wele and tumblid [*v.rr.* tumbel, tumble, tomblyng] wid al. **1303** R. BRUNNE *Handl. Synne* 2820 Eroud swore To here þat tumbled yn þe flore, þat [etc.]. *a* **1350** *St. Thomas* 40 in Horstm. *Altengl. Leg.* (1881) 20 A woman was þore in þe hall þat tumbild fast bifor þam all. **1530** PALSGR. 763/2, I tumble, as a tombler dothe, *je tumbe*... This felowe can tomble well. **1604** E. G[RIMSTONE] *D'Acosta's Hist. Indies* VI. xxviii. 493 Their great agilitie, in leaping, vaulting and tumbling. **1768** JOHNSON in *Boswell* (1906) I. 343 A man who is paid for tumbling upon his hands. **1840** DICKENS *Old C. Shop* v, The boy..having a natural taste for tumbling, was now standing on his head.

2. a. *intr.* To roll about on the ground, or in the water or air; to wallow; also to throw oneself about in a restless way on a bed or couch; to toss. Also *fig.*

14.. *26 Pol. Poems* xxv. 223 The pyt of hell..Where synful soules tumble and raue. **1549** COVERDALE, etc. *Erasm. Par. Eph.* Prol., Yf thou..wylt tomble and walowe styll in wylful ignoraunce, and errour. **1606** SHAKS. *Ant. & Cl.* I. iv. 17 Let us grant it is not Amisse to tumble on the bed of Ptolomy. **1608** —— *Per.* II. i. 27, I saw the Porpas how he bounst and tumbled. *a* **1684** LEIGHTON *Wks.* (1835) I. 116 Shall they then, who are purified..return to live among the swine, and tumble with them in the puddle? **1745** P. THOMAS *Jrnl. Anson's Voy.* 20 Seals..leaping and tumbling in the Water. **1819** BYRON *Juan* II. cxxxviii, Haidée..sadly toss'd and tumbled, And started from her sleep. **1840** DICKENS *Barn. Rudge* v, He was very restless.., and for some hours tossed and tumbled.

†**b.** *refl.* in same sense. *Obs.*

1577 B. GOOGE *Heresbach's Husb.* III. (1586) 122 A place meete for their wallowing, wherein..they may tumble themselues. **1616** SURFL. & MARKH. *Country Farme* 75 The Goose..doth loue to swim, and to coole, plunge, and tumble her selfe euerie day. **1661** LOVELL *Hist. Anim. & Min.* 95 When hungry they tumble themselves in red earth, and so lie as if dead.., and when the birds of prey come to feed on them, they suddainly take them.

c. *intr. spec.* of a pigeon: To throw itself over backwards during its flight; cf. TUMBLER 4; in gunnery, of a projectile, to turn end over end in its flight.

1698 FRYER *Acc. E. India & P.* 116 Pigeons tumbling in the Air. **1735** J. MOORE *Columbarium* 40 When they are up at their Pitch, the better Sort seldom or never tumble. **1868** DARWIN *Anim. & Pl.* I. v. 151 The Common English Tumblers have exactly the same habits as the Persian Tumbler, but tumble better. **1906** *Westm. Gaz.* 4 Oct. 5/3 Erosion..not sufficiently serious to..affect the flight of the projectiles, none of which were observed to 'tumble'.

II. 3. a. *intr.* To fall; *esp.* to fall in a helpless way, as from stumbling or violence; to be precipitated, fall headlong; also said of a stream falling in a cataract.

13.. *K. Alis.* 2465 (Bodl. MS.) Men miȝtten sen.. Heuedes tumblen guttes drawe Many body ouerþrowe. *c* **1330** R. BRUNNE *Chron.* (1810) 70 He stombled at a nayle, Into þe waise..he tombled top ouer taile. **1470–85** MALORY *Arthur* x. lvi. 507 He tombled doune of his hors in a swoune. **1560** DAUS tr. *Sleidane's Comm.* 323 b, They..tomble of the bridge into the Rhine. **1610** G. FLETCHER *Christ's Tri.* I. xlix, From heav'n it tombled to the deep. **1687** A. LOVELL tr. *Thevenot's Trav.* II. 74 One of the gang tumbled off of his Mule, and had almost broken his Neck. **1697** DRYDEN *Æneid* VIII. 317 The fix'd foundations of the rock Gave way; ..Tumbling it chok'd the flood. **1796** MORSE *Amer. Geog.* I. 449 In passing through this hilly country, it tumbles over many falls. **1855** MACAULAY *Hist. Eng.* xiv. III. 401 He opened the barrel; and from among a heap of shells out tumbled a stout halter. **1878** HUXLEY *Physiogr.* 132 Fragments of rock..tumble down into the stream.

b. *intr.* To fall prone, fall to the ground; often const. *down, over*. Also, to stumble by tripping *over* an object.

c **1350** *Will. Palerne* 3388 But our on [= unless one of us] titly tumbel trowe me neuer after. *Ibid.* 3866 He tit ouer his hors tayl tombled ded to þerþe. **1375** BARBOUR *Bruce* XIII. 29 Thar mycht man..se tummyll knychtis and stedis. *c* **1489** CAXTON *Sonnes of Aymon* xxii. 478 Suche a stroke..that he made him tomble over & over at his fete. **1732** LEDIARD *Sethos* II. IX. 325 The force..only made him tumble the sooner. **1843** BORROW *Bible in Spain* xxiv. (Pelh. Libr.) 167 The mule of the peasant tumbled prostrate.

c. *intr.* Of a building or structure: To fall in ruins or fragments; to collapse. Also *fig.*

a **1400–50** *Alexander* 552 All þe erd euyn ouer sa egirly schakis, þat teldis, templis, & touris tomble on hepis. *a* **1539** *Cartular. Abb. de Rievalle* (Surtees) 337 A steple tomylled down The tymber all to brokyn. *a* **1682** SIR T. BROWNE *Tracts* ix. (1683) 156 Obelisks have their term, and Pyramids will tumble. **1820** BELZONI *Egypt & Nubia* III. 385 There are a great number of houses, half tumbled down. **1880** MISS BRADDON *Just as I am* xix, We should tumble to pieces without you.

d. *intr.* To fall rapidly in value, amount, or price: said esp. of stocks. *Commercial slang.*

1886 *Pall Mall G.* 8 Nov. 2/1 Rents had tumbled from 18 to 30 per cent., were likely to tumble still more. **1895** *Daily News* 21 Dec. 5/4 As stock after stock tumbled the shouting became a prolonged roar.

e. Of laundry: to be tossed about in the revolving drum of a tumble-drier (or washing-machine).

1970 *Which?* Aug. 240/1 Too much foam will certainly stop your clothes from tumbling freely and so getting clean. **1975** C. WESTON *Susannah Screaming* (1976) i. 9 Rees.. watched his laundry tumbling inside the barrel of the dryer.

4. a. *trans.* To cause to fall suddenly or violently; to throw or cast down.

1375 BARBOUR *Bruce* VI. 255 He tumlit doun on þaim þe stane. *c* **1489** CAXTON *Sonnes of Aymon* xxiii. 496 Whan bayarde was thus tombled in the ryver, he sanke vnto the botome of it. *a* **1533** LD. BERNERS *Huon* clix. 611 With all his strengthe he tombelyd Barnarde ouer the bourde into the water. **1588** SHAKS. *Tit. A.* II. iii. 176 Oh..tumble me into some loathsome pit. **1623** R. CARPENTER *Conscionable Christian* 72 Let Romish Jezebel..not be spared, tumble her out at window. **1774** GOLDSM. *Nat. Hist.* (1776) III. 68 It [the chamois] drives at the hunter with its head, and often tumbles him down the neighbouring precipice. **1889** GRETTON *Memory's Harkb.* 36 He collared one of the men, and tumbled him over the balusters.

fig. **1549** COVERDALE, etc. *Erasm. Par. 1 Pet.* 11 God forbydde that I..shoulde be tombled backe agayne to this worlds delices. **1663** BP. PATRICK *Parab. Pilgr.* xi. (1687) 65 They tumbled themselves into an Abysse of misery and woe irrecoverable. **1812** BYRON *Ch. Har.* I. lii, He whose nod Has tumbled feebler despots from their sway. **1848** THACKERAY *Van. Fair* xxxv, It is she who has tumbled my hopes and all my pride down.

b. To cause to fall prostrate; to overthrow.

c **1400** *Destr. Troy* 7243 Achilles..Mony Troiens ouer-tyrnyt, tumblit to dethe. **1534** MORE *Treat. Passion* Wks. 1294/2 Thys fierce furious kynge..was with the waues of the water..ouer throwen and tumbled downe..and wretchedlye drowned. **1625** T. GODWIN *Moses & Aaron* v. vii. 246 One of the witnesses tumbled him by a stroke vpon the loynes. **1700** DRYDEN *Pal. & Arc.* III. 653 King Lycurgus..was tumbled on the plain. **1837–8** J. KEEGAN *Leg. & Poems* (1907) 59 Come boys, have at him,..now's the time to tumble him. **1895** *Outing* (U.S.) XXVII. 219/2, I now had him [the bull] in plain view, broadside on, and tumbled him in his tracks.

c. To throw down and destroy (a structure); to overthrow, demolish, reduce to ruins. Also *fig.*

1375 BARBOUR *Bruce* IX. 452 Þe towris euerilkane And vallis gert he tummyll doune. *c* **1400** *Destr. Troy* 4877, I put not vnpossible ȝon place for to take..And all the toures of the toun tumbell to ground. **1596** SHAKS. *1 Hen. IV*, III. i. 32 Vnruly Winde..which..tombles downe Steeples, and mosse-growne Towers. **1696** BROOKHOUSE *Temple Open.* Pref. A iv, To undermine the Foundation, and to tumble down the whole Frame. **1809** W. IRVING *Knickerb.* VI. ix. (1849) 375 The noblest monuments which pride has ever reared..the hand of time will shortly tumble into ruins. **1875** WHITNEY *Life Lang.* ii. 30 Some antagonist or successor, perhaps,..tumbles into ruins the whole magnificent structure of fancied truth.

5. To cause to fall in a confused heap; to throw *down, in, out*, etc. without order or regularity; to mix *up* in confusion, jumble *together*. Also *fig.*

1562 in W. H. Turner *Select. Rec. Oxford* (1880) 291 To be shaked and tombled together [in balloting]. **1601** ? MARSTON *Pasquil & Kath.* (1878) I. 133 And after death.. We all together shall be tumbled vp, into one bagge. **1663** GERBIER *Counsel* 26 Car-men turne or tumble down their Bricks. **1787** SIR J. HAWKINS *Life Johnson* 99 He would not suffer any one to approach, except the compositor or Cave's boy for matter, which, as fast as he composed it, he tumbled out at the door. **1821** LAMB *Elia* Ser. I. *Mackery End*, She was tumbled early..into a spacious closet of good old

English reading. **1869** TOZER *Highl. Turkey* I. 312 He tumbled on to my plate..half a dishful of mulberries.

6. To propel or drive headlong, or with a falling, stumbling, or rolling movement; to precipitate; to throw or thrust roughly or forcibly; to toss, pitch, bundle. Also *fig.*

1509 HAWES *Past. Pleas.* xiv. (Percy Soc.) 52 O thoughtful herte, tombled all about Upon the se of stormy ignoraunce. **1553** T. WILSON *Rhet.* (1580) 109 We..tell one thyng after an other, from tyme to tyme, not tomblyng one tale in an others necke. **1595** SHAKS. *John* III. iv. 176 A little snow, tumbled about, Anon becomes a Mountaine. **1684** BUNYAN *Pilgr.* II. 23 They were greatly tumbled up and down in their minds, and knew not what to do. **1757** SMOLLETT *Reprisal* I. i, To be tossed and tumbled about like a football. **1760–72** H. BROOKE *Fool of Qual.* (1809) III. 87, I was bound.., and then tumbled with kicks..along the deck. **1818** SCOTT *Hrt. Midl.* v, Effie used to help me to tumble the bundles o' barkened leather up and down. **1840** CARLYLE *Heroes* iii. 171 He [Shakspere]..tumbles and tosses him [his butt] in all sorts of horse-play.

refl. **1548** UDALL *Erasm. Par. Luke* iii. 47 No manne should presse or toumble himselfe into such an high office. **1884** TENNYSON *Becket* I. i, The hog hath tumbled himself into some corner.

7. a. *intr.* To move or pass with a motion as if falling or stumbling; to move precipitately; to proceed hastily, without order or premeditation; to bowl, bundle, roll, rush. Also *fig.* Now *colloq.*

1590 GREENE *Orl. Fur.* Wks. (Rtldg.) 92 When I take my truncheon in my fist, A sceptre then comes tumbling in my thoughts. **1590** SPENSER *F.Q.* II. xi. 18 A great water flood, ..tombling low From the high mountaines. **1683** BUNYAN *Greatness of Soul* Wks. (ed. Offor) I. 141 What was the cause ..? Why, their profits came tumbling in. **1712** STEELE *Spect.* No. 552 ¶1, I was tumbling about the town the other day in a hackney-coach. **1798** *Hull Advertiser* 10 Nov. 1/4 We.. have been tumbling about in very bad weather. **1843** LEVER *J. Hinton* xiii, Tumble into bed, and go to sleep as fast as you can. **1850** SMEDLEY *F. Fairlegh* i, Hastily tumbling into my clothes,.. I rushed down-stairs.

b. ***to tumble up***: to make haste, orig. (*Naut.*) from below deck. *slang.*

1826 W. N. GLASCOCK *Naval Sketch-Bk.* I. 8 The command was repeated by the boatswain and his mates, who were piping and roaring down the hatchways—'Tumble up, tumble up from below.' **1832** MARRYAT *N. Forster* xxii, Tumble up smartly, my lads. **1838** DICKENS *Nicholas Nickleby* (1839) viii. 65 'Now, Nickleby, come; tumble up, will you?' Nicholas..'tumbled up' at once, and proceeded to dress himself. **1842** J. F. COOPER *Wing-and-Wing* I. viii. 125 This sight produced a great commotion in the ship, even the watch below 'tumbling up', to get another sight of a craft so renowned. **1858** TROLLOPE *Three Clerks* II. ii. 40 'Mr. Tudor to attend in the board-room immediately,' said a fat messenger... 'All right,' said Charley—'I'll tumble up and be with them in ten seconds.'

8. *trans.* To turn over as in examination or search; hence *fig.* to examine cursorily. Now *rare.*

1597 MORLEY *Introd. Mus.* Pref., What labour it was to tomble, tosse, and search so manie bookes. **1633** G. HERBERT *Temple Ch. Porch* xxv, Look in thy chest;..And tumble up and down what thou find'st there. **1652** COTTERELL *Cassandra* III. (1676) 49 Tumbling over a thousand several designs in his head. **1737** [S. BERINGTON] *G. di Lucca's Mem.* To Rdr. (1738) 12 The Custom-House Officers at Marseilles..tumbled over his Effects at a very rude Rate. **1823** BYRON *Juan* XIII. cii, The elderly walk'd through the library, And tumbled books.

9. a. To have sexual intercourse with. *slang.*

1602 SHAKS. *Ham.* IV. v. 62 Quoth she before you tumbled me. You promis'd me to Wed. **1698** VANBRUGH *Prov. Wife* v. iii, To deliver up her fair body, to be tumbled and mumbled by..Heartfree. **1772** T. BRIDGES *Burlesque Transl. Homer* I. 4 What priest beside thyself e'er grumbl'd To have his daughter tightly tumbl'd? **1922** JOYCE *Ulysses* 502 Beware of the flapper and bogus mournful... Tumble her. **1971** 'R. MACDONALD' *Underground Man* xxxii. 225 He had tumbled the prettiest girl, and got her with child, and Albert and Fritz had taken the rap for it. **1973** *Guardian* 21 June 10/1 A hip young girl who tumbles him when his wife is away. **1976** R. LEWIS *Witness my Death* v. 166 Tommy Elias had tumbled the schoolgirl in the ferns.

b. To handle roughly or indelicately; to touse, tousle; to upset the arrangement of (anything neat or orderly); to disorder, rumple; to disarrange by tossing: e.g. to tumble bedclothes, a bed, or dress.

1715 LADY M. W. MONTAGU *Town Eclogues, Tuesday*, Her night-cloaths tumbled with resistless grace. **1716** B. CHURCH *Hist. Philip's War* (1867) II. 24 The ground being much tumbled with them. *a* **1732** GAY *Rehearsal at Goatham* I, How frightfully he hath tumbled me. **1825** SCOTT *Talism.* ix, Lay me the couch more fairly, it is tumbled like a stormy sea.

10. a. *intr. fig.* or in *fig.* context; *esp.* To come by chance, stumble, blunder *into, on, upon.*

1565 T. STAPLETON *Fortr. Faith* 56b, A sorte of Christians, called papistes, which were tombled themselues in idolatry, blindnesse, and superstition. **1632** LITHGOW *Trav.* I. 38 [We] tumbled in by chance, *Alla capello Ruosso.* **1706** E. WARD *Wooden World Diss.* (1708) 90 If he had not tumbl'd into a Ship, he had long ago dropt from the Gallows. **1874** LISLE CARR *Jud. Gwynne* I. ii. 47 After hunting for you everywhere..here I tumble on you amidst the howling wilderness of Furrowshire. **1903** MORLEY *Gladstone* I. 428 The impossible parliament had tumbled into a great war.

b. *fig.* To understand something not clearly expressed; to perceive or apprehend a hidden design or signal. Const. *to, that. slang.* Also *trans.*, to detect, see through.

1846 *Swell's Night Guide* 58, I..officed Bet, she tumbled to the fake, and stalled off to the dossery. **1851** MAYHEW *Lond. Labour* I. 15/1 The high words in a tragedy we call jaw-breakers, and say we can't tumble to that barrikin. **1889** *Opelousas* (Louisiana) *Democrat* 4 Feb. 3/4 The clerk smiled rather wickedly..but I didn't tumble worth a cent. **1889** H. O'REILLY *50 Yrs. on Trail* 375, I didn't tumble to this for a long time. **1901** 'J. FLYNT' *World of Graft* iii. 104 Women.. tumble more guns 'n all the coppers in existence. **1926** *Variety* 29 Dec. 7/4 The pincher would never tumble that 'nice people' meant an act that kicked in more than the usual vaudeville agent's legitimate commission. **1936** G. INGRAM *Muffled Man* iii. 49 You can't go on for ever at any game, and not get tumbled some time or other. **1938** F. D. SHARPE *Sharpe of Flying Squad* xxvi. 262 We thought you wouldn't tumble us, Guv'nor. **1962** *New Statesman* 21 Dec. 899/1 By the time you tumble that your drum has been turned over, we're miles away. **1974** *Times* 7 Feb. 3/7 John Rodger.. heard the radio and said: 'They have tumbled us.' **1981** J. BARNETT *Firing Squad* vi. 57 Have to have words with Simonson, in case he has tumbled the tattoo.

c. To fall in with, agree *to*; to take a liking or fancy *to. slang.*

1887 E. J. GOODMAN *Too Curious* xvii, He did not like the idea at first; but..he tumbled to it at last. **1892** *Daily News* 21 Apr. 2/1 But the British public, in the slang of the day, 'tumbles' to a man who refuses anything good.

III. 11. *intr.* Of the sides of a ship: To incline or slope inwards, to contract above the point of extreme breadth; to batter. Usually ***tumble home.*** Opposed to FLARE *v.* 4a. Also *transf.*

a **1687** PETTY *Treat. Naval Philos.* I. ii, Let the supernatant sides of a Ship so much tumble..as that the said sides may remain perpendicular when the Ship stoops. **1711** W. SUTHERLAND *Shipbuild. Assist.* 165 Tumbling home; when the Ship-side declines from a Perpendicular upwards, or, as some call it, houses in. **1761** H. WALPOLE *Let. to G. Montagu* 28 Apr., Old Newcastle, whose teeth are tumbled out, and his mouth tumbled in. **1848** T. WHITE *Ship Build.* 39 The upper works usually incline towards the middle line, or as it is termed 'tumble home'.

12. *trans. Carpentry.* See quot.

1823 P. NICHOLSON *Pract. Build.* 120 Tumbling in a Joist, is to frame a joist between two timbers, of which the sides, which ought to be vertical or square to the upper edges, are oblique to these edges. **1856** BREES *Gloss. Terms* s.v., The purlines are sometimes tumbled in..between the sides of the principals of a roof.

13. *Mech.* To mix, cleanse, or polish in a tumbling-box. Cf. TUMBLER 13e.

1884 WAHL *Galvanoplastic Manip.* 529 (Cent. D.) Small castings can be tumbled and thus deprived of much of their adhering scale and sand.

tumble-, the verb-stem in combination:

1. with substantives: **tumble-action**, the tumbling action of a tumble-drier; **tumble-bug** = *tumble-dung*; **tumble-car, -cart**: see quots.; **tumble-dung**, name in *U.S.* for a scarabæid beetle which rolls up balls of dung, in which it deposits its eggs and in which the larvæ go through their transformations; a dung-beetle; also *attrib.*; **tumble fruit**, fallen fruit, windfalls; **tumble-rose**, a species of the parrot-fish, *Scarus cæruleus*, found on the Atlantic coast from southern U.S. to Brazil (*Cent. Dict. Suppl.* 1909); †**tumble-turd** = *tumble-dung*; **tumble-weed**, name in *U.S.* for various plants which form a globular bush which in late summer is broken off and rolled about by the wind; a rolling weed (ROLLING *ppl. a.* 6).

1958 *Sunday Times* 9 Mar. 22/6 Here [in an electric washing machine] *tumble-action replaces a wringer. **1976** *National Observer* (U.S.) 11 Dec. 9/1 Do not use tumble-action dryer. **1805** R. PARKINSON *Tour Amer.* 362 A kind of beetle, called a *tumble-bug,..in the summer forms a cave in the earth. **1848** LOWELL *Biglow Papers* Ser. I. II. 62 *note*, Tumblebug. **1868** *Rep. U.S. Commissioner Agric.* (1869) 86 The best known and most common beetle of this family in this country is the Canton lævis, usually termed the tumble-bug. **1794** BAILEY & CULLEY *Agric. Cumberld.* 31 We suppose they had the name of *tumble carrs, from the axle being made fast in the wheels, and the whole turning or tumbling round together. **1887** *Suppl. to Jamieson* s.v., The *tumble-cart, tumbler, or car, continued in use in the upland districts till the beginning of the present century. **1775** R. TWISS *Trav. Portugal & Sp.* 247 The beetle, known by the name of *tumble-dung. **1798** in *Spirit Pub. Jrnls.* (1799) II. 355 The *scarabæus carnifex*, or tumble-dung-beetle. **1880** *New Virginians* I. 103 The humble rusty-black 'tumbledung'. **1891** *B'ham Weekly Post* 8 Aug. 4/7 Babies, like *tumble fruit, everywhere. **1754** CATESBY *Carolina* II. App., The *Tumble Turds. *Scarabæus pillularis Americanus. Scarabæus carnifex*, L. **1887** *Amer. Nat.* Oct. 930 *Amarantus albus*, the common *tumble-weed.

2. with adverbs: **tumble home**, in a ship, = *tumbling home* (TUMBLING *vbl. sb.* b); also *transf.* of a motor vehicle; **tumble-over**, *sb.* an act of falling over; *concr.* a toy so weighted that it always takes a position of equilibrium; also *attrib.* inclined to fall down, rickety, tottering; **tumble-up**, a tumbler designed to be placed upside down on the neck of a carafe. See also TUMBLE-DOWN.

1833 T. RICHARDSON *Merc. Marine Archit.* 13 Giving only six inches *tumble home of the topside. **1874** THEARLE *Naval Archit.* 60 When the ship has considerable beam, the breadth of the channel is kept within reasonable limits by giving a 'tumble home' to the top-sides. **1924** *Motor* 7 Oct. 450/2 The body is of particularly pleasing lines, with a V windscreen and tumble-home stern. **1968** *Motor Industry Res. Rep.* IX. 25/1 Decreases due to increasing the canopy tumble-home. **1883** BLACK *Shandon Bells* xxx, But the gable of the house is a *leetle* *tumble-over, isn't it? **1895** *Outing* (U.S.) XXVI. 380/1 Those lead-weighted, pith 'tumble-overs', with which we played when children. **1899** *Allbutt's Syst. Med.* VI. 51 He was suddenly seized with intense darting pain in the region of the heart..accompanied by a sensation of 'tumble over' of the organ. **1891** *Sale Catal. Glass Wks. Stourbridge*, Seventy-one *tumble-ups.

tumbled ('tʌmb(ə)ld), *ppl. a.* [f. TUMBLE *v.* + -ED[1].] That has tumbled or fallen; that has been thrown, tossed, or pitched *down, together*, etc.; also, tousled, disordered, rumpled.

1649 G. DANIEL *Trinarch., Hen. V* cclxxxvii, Stand Harrie,..Whose tumbled Character, tooke from the Life, Has but resemblance. **1727** POPE, etc. *Art of Sinking* 79 If he looks upon a tempest, he shall have an image of a tumbled bed. **1815** SCOTT *Guy M.* xxxvii, [A preacher with] no gown, not even that of Geneva, a tumbled band [etc.]. **1857** DUFFERIN *Lett. High Lat.* (ed. 3) 7 An amphitheatre of tumbled porphyry hills. **1872** BLACK *Adv. Phaeton* xiv, Bell was seated on a bit of tumbled pillar. **1891** tr. *Didon's Jesus Christ* I. III. vii. 388 The old basalt walls of the tumbled-down houses..are still to be distinguished. **1895** ZANGWILL *Master* 443 Poets with lack-lustre visages and tumbled hair. **1907** *Daily Chron.* 11 Nov. 4/4 We read in these tumbled-together books the progress of a nation through all its stages.

'tumble-down, *a.* (*sb.*) [the phrase *tumble down* used attrib. or as sb.] †**a.** Of a horse: That falls down habitually. *Obs. rare*$^{-1}$.

1791 'G. GAMBADO' *Ann. Horsem.* i. (1809) 67 The Noble Puzzle for Tumble down Horses.

b. That is in a tumbling condition; falling or fallen into ruin; dilapidated, ruinous.

1818 SCOTT *Br. Lamm.* xxi, His old tumble-down tower yonder. **1859** GEO. ELIOT *A. Bede* ii, The parsonage here's a tumble-down place, sir, not fit for gentry to live in. **1898** *N. & Q.* 9th Ser. II. 124 One of the grimiest and most tumbledown of the many dilapidated craft.

c. *absol.* as *sb.* A tumble-down house. *rare.*

1866 HOWELLS *Venet. Life* vii, The tumble-down is patched up and sold at rates astonishing to innocent strangers who come from countries in good repair, where the tumble-down is worth nothing.

tumble-'drier. Also **-dryer.** [f. TUMBLE *v.* + DRIER, DRYER.] A machine for drying washing in a heated drum that turns about a horizontal axis. So **tumble-dry** *v. trans.* (also *absol.*), **tumble-'dried, -'drying** *ppl. adjs.*

[**1952** *Gas Age* 8 May 62/1 The tumbler-type of clothes dryer.] **1962** J. T. MARSH *Self-Smoothing Fabrics* xiv. 228 Different results may be obtained according to whether the fabric is dried on a line or on one of the tumble-drying machines. *Ibid.* xx. 347 Fabrics with wet recovery only cannot be tumble-dried with satisfaction but need line-drying. **1969** *Which?* Nov. 372/2 (*caption*) Line dry or Tumble dry. **1972** J. MCCLURE *Caterpillar Cop* vi. 98 The lady next door has a tumble drier so you put your clothes outside and I'll take them round. **1976** *Ilkeston Advertiser* 10 Dec. 12/1 (Advt.), Don't have wet clothes hanging around, buy a Tumbledryer. **1977** 'M. YORKE' *Cost of Silence* v. 36 Mrs Costello hung her tumble-dried washing round the kitchen. **1982** A. PRICE *Old Vengeful* vi. 86 We can do your things... Clarkie can wash them, and tumble dry them, and iron them.

tumbler ('tʌmblə(r)). [f. TUMBLE *v.* + -ER[1].]

1. One who performs feats of agility and strength, somersaults, leaps, and gymnastics; an acrobat.

a **1340** HAMPOLE *Psalter* xxxix. 6 Hoppynge & daunceynge of tumblers and herlotis. *c* **1380** WYCLIF *Sel. Wks.* III. 352 Mynystrel or joȝelour, tumbler and harlot. *c* **1440** *Promp. Parv.* 506/1 Tumlare (*P.* tumblar), *volutator* (S. *volutatrix*). **1581** PETTIE *Guazzo's Civ. Conv.* II. (1586) 57b, Certaine vearses like us verie well,..when we heare some tumbler or dauncer sing them to the Harpe. **1614** RALEIGH *Hist. World* v. vi. §7 A tricke of climing vpon mens heads, somewhat after the manner of our tumblers. **1840** DICKENS *Old C. Shop* xl, Kit faced about on the ladder like some dexterous tumbler. **1874** BLACKIE *Self-Cult.* 16 Dexterous riders and expert tumblers in the circus.

2. a. A dog like a small greyhound, formerly used to catch rabbits; a lurcher. So called from its action in taking its quarry: see quots. *Obs.* exc. *Hist.*

1519 HORMAN *Vulg.* 277 Tumblers, houndes, that can goo an huntynge by them selfe: brynge home theyr praye. **1576** FLEMING tr. *Caius' Dogs* (1880) 11 This sorte of Dogges.. we..call Tvmblers, because in hunting they turne and tumble, winding their bodyes about in circle wise... He.. so prouideth..that the selly simple Conny is debarred quite from his hole. **1646** SIR T. BROWNE *Pseud. Ep.* IV. v. 187 Men observe that the eye of a Tumbler is biggest not constantly in one, but in the bearing side. **1688** R. HOLME *Armoury* II. 185/1 The Tumbler, or Lurcher is..in shape like the Grey-hound. **1766** PENNANT *Zool.* (1768) I. 54 The *Vertagus*, or Tumbler,..took its prey by mere subtility. **1847–78** HALLIWELL, *Tumbler*, a dog formerly employed for taking rabbits. This it effected by tumbling itself about in a careless manner till within reach of the prey, and then seizing it by a sudden spring. **1897** *Q. Rev.* Jan. 141 Dogs are no longer trained as 'Norfolk tumblers', to attract the rabbits on the warrens by their quaint antics.

†**b.** *transf.* applied to a person; *spec.* one who allures or inveigles persons into the hands of swindlers (*slang*). *Obs.*

1601 B. JONSON *Poetaster* I. ii, Away, setter, away. Yet, stay, my little tumbler. *a* **1700** B. E. *Dict. Cant. Crew*, *Tumbler*,..one that Decoys, or draws others into Play. **1785** GROSE *Dict. Vulg. T.*, *Tumbler*,..a sharper employed to draw in pigeons to game.

†**c.** The six of trumps in the game of gleek. *Obs.*

1680 [see TOWSER *sb.* b]. **1688** R. HOLME *Armoury* III. xvi. (Roxb.) 73/2 Tumbler, is the sixth of the trumps.

†**3.** A name of the porpoise. *Obs.*

1671 MARTEN *Voy. Spitzbergen* in *Acc. Sev. Late Voy.* II. (1694) 125 They are not Sword-fish, nor of the same kind we call Tumblers. **1808-12** J. WALKER *Ess. Nat. Hist.* 532 *Delphinus Phocaena*... Porpesse... Scot. Pellock. Tumbler.

4. A variety of domestic pigeon characterized by the habit or faculty of turning over and over backwards during its flight.

1678 RAY *Willughby's Ornith.* II. xv. §2. 182 Pigeons... *Tumblers*..are small, and of divers colours. They have strange motions, turning themselves backward over their Heads, and shew like footbals in the Air. **1859** DARWIN *Orig. Spec.* i. (1878) 16 The common tumbler has the singular inherited habit of flying at a great height in a compact flock, and tumbling in the air head over heels.

5. a. One who tumbles or falls. *nonce-use.*

1904 *Daily Chron.* 1 Mar. 6/3 It was real hockey..; when a collision brought a tumble, the tumbler took the accident like a lady.

b. An inexperienced window-cleaner.

1960 'A. BURGESS' *Doctor is Sick* i. 8 Me, I clean windows. .. I've seen these young ones just starting—'tumblers' we call them—get froze stuck up there on a ladder. **1972** *Times* 20 Sept. 3/2 Forty years ago..novice window cleaners starting at the bottom of the ladder were known in the cold-blooded jargon of the trade as tumblers.

6. a. A drinking cup, originally having a rounded or pointed bottom, so that it could not be set down until emptied; often of silver or gold; now, a tapering cylindrical, or barrel-shaped, glass cup without a handle or foot, having a heavy flat bottom.

1664 PEPYS *Diary* 20 Oct., Thence home, taking two silver tumblers home, which I have bought. **1689** *Lond. Gaz.* No. 2485/4 A Gold Tumbler of 100 l. value. **1698** B. BULLIVANT in *Phil. Trans.* XX. 168, I put a Straw for a Perch into a Venice Glass Tumbler. **1779** BLACK in *Phil. Trans.* LXXIII. *305 A common tumbler or water-glass. **1842** S. LOVER *Handy Andy* iii, I thought there was no tumbler but a tumbler for punch. **1865** LUBBOCK *Preh. Times* 136 Rings of pottery..evidently intended to serve as supports for these earthenware tumblers. **1876** W. F. COLLIER *Tales O. Eng. Life* 79 The guests were supplied with tumblers, or glass vessels, which, being rounded at the base, could not stand upright, and must, therefore, be emptied at a draught. **1886** G. R. SIMS *Ring o' Bells*, etc. I. Introd. 1 The tumblers were rattled upon the table.

b. The contents of a tumbler; a tumblerful.

1831 J. DAVIES *Manual Mat. Med.* 150 From two to five tumblers, pure or mixed with any other drink, every morning. **1873** BLACK *Pr. Thule* v, Mackenzie mixed another tumbler of toddy.

c. A toy, usually representing a grotesque squatting figure, having the centre of gravity low and the base rounded so as to continue rocking when touched; cf. MANDARIN 1 b. *rare.*

1850 DICKENS in *Househ. Words* 21 Dec. 289/2 The Tumbler with his hands in his pockets, who wouldn't lie down. **1851** MAYHEW *Lond. Labour* (1861) II. 504/1 Her legs tucked up mysteriously under her gown into a round ball, so that her figure resembled in shape the plaster tumblers sold by the Italians.

7. = TUMBREL[1] 3, 3 b; cf. *tumbler-cart* in 14. *slang* and *dial.*

1673 R. HEAD *Canting Acad.* 16 (Flaugg'd at the Tumbler) whipt at the Carts-arse. **1692** LUTTRELL *Brief Rel.* (1857) II. 534 They had on board 200 horses for the artillery,..40 feild pieces, 80 tumblers. *a* **1700** [see SHOVE *v.*[1] 10]. **1757** WASHINGTON *Lett.* Writ. 1889 I. 490 Choose me.. as much thread as is necessary,..and send them up by John who comes down with a Tumbler for that purpose. **1799** ROBERTSON *Agric. Perth* 92 The shafts had two pins that embraced the axle and made these awkward wheels tumble along; from which circumstance they were named tumblers. *a* **1814** RAMSAY *Scot. & Scotsm. in 18th C.* (1888) II. x. 199 Tumblers, a trifling species of carts which have for ages been used about Alloa for transporting coals to the shore. **1815** SCOTT *Guy M.* viii, Small carts of tumblers, as they were called in that country.

8. *Geol.* A detached mass of rock; a rolled stone or boulder. Now only *dial.*

1789 MILLS in *Phil. Trans.* LXXX. 77 On the surface are tumblers of red granite, and some few of lava. *Ibid.* 80 The bottom of the glen is covered with large tumblers of lava. **1799** KIRWAN *Geol. Ess.* i. 209 That [sandstone]..must also be primary, though it contains tumblers (*caillous roulés*). **1876** H. B. WOODWARD *Geol. Eng. & Wales* x. 305 *note*, In the eastern part of North Wales the boulders are called 'Granite tumblers'. **1894** *Northumbld. Gloss.*, *Tumbler*, *Tumler*, a boulder, a detached block of stone.

9. With capital *T*: A *Dunker* or *Tunker* (see DUNKER[1]): in allusion to their method of baptism. *U.S.*

1796 MORSE *Amer. Geog.* I. 281 They are also called Tumblers, from the manner in which they perform baptism, which is by putting the person, while kneeling, head first under water, so as to resemble the motion of the body in the action of tumbling.

†**10.** One who tumbles or tosses things into confusion or disorder; a muddler; one who turns something over confusedly. *Obs. rare.*

1580 HOLLYBAND *Treas. Fr. Tong*, *Brouilleur, ou qui Brouille*, a tumbler togither, a slubberer. **1694** MOTTEUX *Rabelais* IV. lxiv. (1737) 260 Tumblers of Beads, Mumblers of *Ave Marias*.

†**11.** A class of street ruffians; see quot., and cf. MOHOCK. *Obs.*

1712 STEELE *Spect.* No. 324 ¶1 The Mohock Club... A third sort are the Tumblers, whose office it is to set Women on their Heads. **1878** LECKY *Eng. in 18th C.* (1883) I. 482.

12. a. = *tumble-dung* (see TUMBLE-). **b.** The aquatic larva of the mosquito or other species of the *Culicidæ*: see quot. 1858-63. *U.S.*

1807-8 W. IRVING *Salmag.* xv. (1824) 282 The aspiring politician may be compared to that indefatigable insect, called the tumbler,..which..forms a little ball, which it rolls laboriously along. **1858-63** RIPLEY & DANA *Amer. Cycl.* VIII. 51 (Cassell's) They are..called tumblers from the manner in which they roll over and over in the water.

13. In mechanical applications.

a. In a gun-lock, a pivoted plate through which the mainspring acts on the hammer, and in the notches of which the sear engages.

1624 *Althorp MS.* in Simpkinson *Washingtons* (1860) App. 58 For a new tumbler for a muskit locke 00 00 06. **1688** R. HOLME *Armoury* III. xviii. (Roxb.) 135/1 The seuerall parts of a Fire lock and a match lock, and wheele lock... The Tumbler. **1833** J. HOLLAND *Manuf. Metal* II. 117 In consequence of the firm locking of the sear in the Tumbler, the gun cannot possibly go off. **1862** *Catal. Internat. Exhib.* II. XI. 24 The cock works in a slot in the middle of the stock; there is no tumbler. **1871** 'STONEHENGE' *Brit. Sports* I. I. ii. §1 Occasionally, in central-fire guns, the tumbler itself is made to propel the striker.

b. In a roasting-jack, a pawl or catch which allows a barrel to revolve in one direction independently of a wheel centred on the same axle, but which takes the wheel with it when it revolves in the other direction.

1677 MOXON *Mech. Exerc.* iii. 47 The Tumbler is so placed..that while the Jack line is winding up upon the Barrel its round britch passes forwards by all the Crosses of the Main wheel,..But when the Barrel is turned the contrary way,..the Tumbler..thrusts the Main Wheel about with [it]. **1688** R. HOLME *Armoury* III. 323/1 [Of a jack] The Tumbler, the Center whereof moveth upon the Center Pin.

c. In a lock: †A pivoted piece through which the pressure of a spring was transmitted to the tail of the bolt, tending to keep it pushed forwards (*obs.*); now, a pivoted piece kept in position by a spring, with projections which drop into notches in the bolt and hold it until lifted by the proper key.

1677 MOXON *Mech. Exerc.* ii. 28 The Tumbler..is a long piece of Iron,..and it hath an Hook returning at the other end of it, to fall into the breech of the Bolt, and by the spring H forces the Bolt forwards. **1792** *Trans. Soc. Arts* (ed. 2) III. 166 The tumbler and tail of the latch or spring bolt. **1833** J. HOLLAND *Manuf. Metal* II. 277 Mr. Kemp..published in 1816, a lock, the interior security of which consists in the adaptation of tumblers or sliders. **1911** J. WARD *Roman Era in Brit.* xiii. 238 The lock had both wards and tumblers.

d. *Naut.* App. a sleeve or cap fitted on a mast, with a hook, ring, or swivel to afford means of attachment, etc.; see also quot. 1877.

1867 SMYTH *Sailor's Word-bk.*, *Tumbler*,..a contrivance to avoid the necessity of having copper nailed on the mast to prevent a gaff from chafing it. **1877** KNIGHT *Dict. Mech.*, *Tumbler* (Nautical), one of the movable pins with which the cathead-stopper and shank-painter are respectively engaged. **1882** NARES *Seamanship* (ed. 6) 9 There is a tumbler on each cap to connect the conductors of the two masts together. *Ibid.* 121 A..derrick..working on a swivel tumbler on the mast.

e. A revolving barrel, or a barrel with a rotating paddle, used in tanning skins; also, a tumbling-box.

1857 *Encycl. Brit.* (ed. 8) XIII. 310/2 They [lamb-skins] are first fed with alum and salt in a drum or tumbler made like a huge churn. **1877** KNIGHT *Dict. Mech.*, *Tumbler*,..a vertically rotating case for cleaning castings placed within it. **1883** R. HALDANE *Workshop Receipts* Ser. II. 367/2 After leaving the press, they [the skins] are put into a 'tumbler', or revolving barrel. **1891** SADTLER *Hand-bk. Industr. Org. Chem.* x. (1900) 329 The tanning was formerly done with sumach and gambier, either in revolving paddle 'tumblers' ..or according to the English method.

f. Each of the stickers of a *tumbler-coupler* in an organ (see 14).

1881 W. E. DICKSON *Organ-Build.* xii. 154 A slender bridge, having as many notches as keys in the manual, and fitted with short stickers called tumblers.

g. *Coal-mining.* A tipper; cf. *tumbling tom* (TUMBLING-).

1883 GRESLEY *Coal-mining Gloss.*, *Tumbler*, (S[cotland]), see *Tipper*. **1886** J. BARROWMAN *Sc. Mining Terms* 69 *Tumbler*, tipping apparatus for tubs or waggons.

h. In a clock or watch: see quot.

1884 F. J. BRITTEN *Watch & Clockm.* 110 [A] Tumbler [is] a revolving finger that in striking clocks and repeating watches moves the rack one tooth for each blow struck.

i. In some looms, each of the levers from which the heddles are suspended.

1891 in *Cent. Dict.*

j. *ellipt.* for *tumbler-drier* below.

1947 W. L. CARMICHAEL et al. *Callaway Textile Dict.* 360/1 *Tumbler*, a clothes-drying device consisting of a revolving cage in which hot air is circulated. **1961** *Listener* 30 Nov. 951/2 The most trouble-free and quick-to-use kind of dryer, the electric 'tumbler'.

14. *attrib.* and *Comb.*, as ***tumbler bitch, -brush*** (sense 6), ***fancier, -glass, lock, -maker, movement*** (cf. *tumbler-coupler*), ***pigeon, -pin, -pivot, -screw; tumbler-shaped*** adj.; **tumbler-bearing,** a bearing which automatically falls out of position to make way for a gear travelling upon the shaft which it supports; **tumbler-beds,** *pl.*, a local name for the loose crumbly upper portion of the carboniferous limestone; **tumbler-cart** = sense 7; **tumbler closet**: see quot.; **tumbler-coupler,** a unison manual coupler in an organ in which the connexion between each two keys is made by a short sticker (see 13 f) which turns over at an angle when not in use; **tumbler-cup,** a cup with a rounded bottom: cf. sense 6; **tumbler dog** = sense 2 (*obs.*); also, a catch or detent in a padlock which retains the hasp (Forney *Car-Builder's Dict.* 1884); **tumbler-drier, -dryer** = TUMBLE-DRIER; **tumbler-drum,** = sense 13 e; **tumbler-holder,** a metal frame in which a tumbler of drink is served (Knight *Dict. Mech.* 1877); **tumbler-music,** music produced with tumblers or 'musical glasses'; **tumbler-punch**: see quot.; **tumbler-stand,** a tray on which tumblers are automatically rinsed (Knight); **tumbler switch,** an electric switch operated by pushing over a small spring tumbler or thumb-piece; **tumbler-tank,** a flushing cistern having two compartments, one of which when filled tilts the other into the position for filling and empties itself (*Cent. Dict.* 1891); **tumbler-washer,** a stand with jets of water for rinsing tumblers (Knight).

1901 *J. Black's Carp. & Build.*, *Scaffolding* 60 We have power transmitted with square shaft, with *tumbler bearings bolted to the walls of a building. **1821** W. FORSTER *Section of Strata* (ed. 2) 103 About sixteen feet of the upper part of [the Great Limestone] is called the *Tumbler Beds. **1680** *Lond. Gaz.* No. 1481/4 Lost..a white *Tumbler Bitch with yellow ears. **1877** KNIGHT *Dict. Mech.*, *Tumbler-brush. **1880** D. MURRAY *Old Cardross* 38 The only wheeled vehicles known prior to that time [*c* 1763] were *tumbler carts, which were simply sledges mounted on small wheels ..made solid.. united by a wooden axle, and all turning round together. **1888** *Q. Rev.* July 38 Sledges were used.., more recently tumbler carts with solid wheels, mere slabs of timber. **1870** CORFIELD *Treatm. Sewage* 123 The '*Tumbler' closet... In this there is..a trough running under the privy-seats..; the water trickles into a swinging basin at the upper end, which is so constructed that it capsizes when full and washes out the contents of the trough into the drain. **1876-98** STAINER & BARRETT *Dict. Mus. Terms* 342/2 The *tumbler coupler is now almost obsolete. **1900** *Westm. Gaz.* 7 Mar. 1/3 A pair of *tumbler cups, 1698, 10 oz. **1908** *Ibid.* 27 Mar. 8/1 A Georgian plain tumbler-cup, ..weighing 4oz. 13dwt. **1675** *Lond. Gaz.* No. 1022/4 Lost.. a white *Tumbler Dog, both Ears spotted with red. **1956** *Good Housek. Home Encycl.* 13/2 Electric *Tumbler Dryers dry by means of a revolving drum in a heated cabinet. **1969** *Which?* Nov. 352/2 Generally all the tumbler driers were easy to use. **1883** R. HALDANE *Workshop Receipts* Ser. II. 373/1 The skins are either trodden in it with the feet, or put into a *tumbler-drum. **1854** *Poultry Chron.* II. 276/1 The Almond *Tumbler fancier, whose 'little wonders' cannot feed their own young! **1795** J. WOODFORDE *Diary* 14 Oct. (1929) IV. 234 The third [remarkable fact] was, of a Man drinking half Pint *Tumbler Glass of Beer and eat the Glass after it. **1831** BREWSTER *Nat. Magic* viii. (1833) 194 Stretch a thin sheet of wet paper..over the mouth of a tumbler-glass with a footstalk. **1844** J. T. HEWLETT *Parsons & W.* xi, A tumbler-glass of iced punch. **1833** LOUDON *Encycl. Archit.* §1585, 3-inch brass *tumbler lock and key on each door. **1881** YOUNG *Ev. Man his own Mechanic* §1488 A lock of better and more complicated construction..called a tumbler lock. **1902** *Westm. Gaz.* 29 Mar. 9/1 Under the present rule the *tumbler-makers must keep on working just as long as the fancy glass makers continue to work. **1881** C. A. EDWARDS *Organs* 112 The means provided to effect this coupling was called the '*tumbler' movement. **1893** F. F. MOORE *I Forbid Banns* (1899) 150 She thought the *tumbler-music very interesting. **1688** R. HOLME *Armoury* II. 244/2 The *Tumbler Pigeon is small and of diverse colours. **1890** *Science-Gossip* XXVI. 215/2 A tumbler-pigeon hatched out a Minorca chicken, a hen having laid in the pigeon-box. **1853** URE *Dict. Arts* II. 251 The lock outside,..*a*, the plate; *b*, the cock; *c*, the *tumbler-pin. **1881** GREENER *Gun* 264 The tumbler-pin is first turned out, and by means of a wire punch inserted in the hole, the tumbler is knocked away from both hammers and lock-plate. **1892** —— *Breech Loader* 116 Knock in the *tumbler-pivot half-way. **1843** *Act relating Militia State of Vermont 1842* 80 Each squad of ten men, a wire and *tumbler punch. **1877** KNIGHT *Dict. Mech.*, *Tumbler-punch*.., a small two-bladed punch used for pushing the arbor of the tumbler, the band-springs, etc., from their seats, in taking a gun apart. **1843** *Act relating Militia State of Vermont 1842* 80, Order in which the lock is taken apart... 9. The *tumbler screw. **1856** 'STONEHENGE' *Brit. Sports* I. I. ii. (ed. 2) 19/1 The various parts of the lock [of a gun] are..5th, the tumbler-screw, which fastens the tumbler and cock together. **1862** *Catal. Internat. Exhib.* II. XI. 16 The loop upon each barrel receiving the end of a steel *tumbler-shaped bolt. **1907** *Installation News* Apr. 16/1 A new form of *Tumbler Switch.

tumblerful ('tʌmbləfʊl). [f. prec. + -FUL.] The quantity that fills a tumbler.

1831 J. DAVIES *Manual Mat. Med.* 94 From four to five tumblerfulls every morning. **1857** *G. Bird's Urin. Deposits* (ed. 5) 171 The use of a small tumblerful of this water on rising in the morning. **1897** *Allbutt's Syst. Med.* III. 419 Several tumblerfuls of lukewarm or warm water.

†'**tumblester.** *Obs.* Forms: 4-5 tomblester, -stre, tomblister(e, 5 tumbelyster. [Feminine of TUMBLER: see -STER, and the parallel form TUMBESTER.] A female tumbler or dancer; a dancing-girl.

c **1386** CHAUCER *Pard. T.* 15 (Lansd. MS.) And riht anone þan come tomblesters [so *Petw.*; *Corpus* tomblisteres] Fetis and smal and ȝonge fruytsters. **14..** *Voc.* in Wr.-Wülcker 616/47 *Tornatrix*, a tumbelyster. **1844** JAMES *Agincourt* I. 233 Who ever heard of King before who troubled his nobility about minstrels and tomblesteres? **1850** —— *Old Oak Chest* I. 125 To make the contortions of their 'saltimbanks' and 'tomblesteres' act as a sort of argument or introduction to what was to follow.

tumblification (ˌtʌmblɪfɪˈkeɪʃən). *humorous.* [irreg. f. TUMBLE *v.* + -FICATION.] Tumbling, falling, or tossing; *esp.* the pitching and rolling of a ship in a storm.

1833 M. SCOTT *Tom Cringle* xi. (1859) 250 Then another Tumblification of the whole party. **1881** CLARK RUSSELL *Ocean Free Lance* II. iv. 169 The tumblification was sometimes so furious that we had to hold on with our hands to save ourselves. **1890** *Chamb. Jrnl.* 14 June 371 The jerky, feverish, staggering, tumblification of the wreck.

tumbling (ˈtʌmblɪŋ), *vbl. sb.* [f. as prec. + -ING[1].] The action of TUMBLE *v.* in various senses.

a **1425** *Cursor M.* 13195 (Trin.) In euel tyme bigan she tomblyng To make his heed of be brouȝt. *c* **1440** *Promp. Parv.* 506/1 Tumlynge, *volutacio.* **1523** FITZHERB. *Husb.* § 102 It apperethe by stampynge of the horse or tomblynge. *c* **1580** JEFFERIE *Bugbears* Epil., Song ii. in *Archiv Stud. Neu. Apr.* (1897), With joomblynges, with foomblynges, with toomblynges. **1611** COTGR., *Basteleuse*, a woman that makes a profession of Jugling, Tumbling, and such other idle, or base exercises. **1660** BURNEY *Κέρδ. Δῶρον* (1661) 30 The tumblings of the Leviathan in the Seas. **1687** FOUNTAINHALL *Decis.* (1759) I. 440 Physicians attested the employment of tumbling would kill her. *a* **1774** TUCKER *Lt. Nat.* (1834) II. 456 Lucretius..granted that the atoms,.. after infinite tumblings and tossings about, would fall into their former situation. **1870** LOWELL *Study Wind.* 2 We can explain the odd tumbling of rooks in the air.

b. *tumbling home*: the inward inclination of the upper part of a ship's sides; opposed to FLARE *sb.*[1] 4: see TUMBLE *v.* 11. Also *tumbling-in.*

1664 E. BUSHNELL *Compl. Shipwright* 11 Then set off the Tumbling Home, at the Height of the two first Haanses. **1769** FALCONER *Dict. Marine* (1789), *Encabanement*, the tumbling-home of a ship's side from the lower-deck-beam upwards, to the gunnel. **1832** *Encycl. Amer.* XI. 367/2 Nothing can be urged in favor of tumbling in..but that it brings the guns nearer the centre. *c* **1850** *Rudim. Navig.* (Weale) 157 The topsides of three-decked ships have the greatest tumbling-home, for the purpose of clearing the upper works from the wind and fire of the lower guns.

ˈ**tumbling**, *ppl. a.* [f. as prec. + -ING[2].] That tumbles, in various senses of the verb; falling; tossing; rolling headlong; also *fig.*

c **1374** CHAUCER *Boeth.* III. pr. ix. 67 (Camb. MS.) Trowesthow þat ther be any thing in thise erthely mortal towmblynge thinges? **1509** HAWES *Past. Pleas.* (Percy Soc.) 131 Stere well the frayle tombling barge. *c* **1620** Z. BOYD *Zion's Flowers* (1855) 109 Where tumbling billowes bath the very sky. **1638** JUNIUS *Paint. Ancients* 306 A tumbling and wallowing horse. **1760–72** H. BROOKE *Fool of Qual.* (1809) II. 128 All that I owed came like a tumbling house upon me. **1837** W. IRVING *Capt. Bonneville* II. ix. 130 Down the ravine of a tumbling stream, the commencement of some future river. **1873** BLACK *Pr. Thule* vi, This tumbling mass of dark stones standing high over the green hollows.

Hence ˈ**tumblingly** *adv.*, in a tumbling manner.

1620 THOMAS *Lat. Dict.*, *Volutatim*,..rollingly, tumblingly, tossingly.

tumbling-. The vbl. sb. and ppl. adj. in combinations and special collocations, as *tumbling boy, girl, -ground, lass, -trick*; also **tumbling-barrel** = *tumbling-box*; **tumbling-bay**, an outfall from a river, canal, or reservoir; a weir; also, the pool into which the water falls from this; **tumbling bob**, a weighted lever or arm in machinery, which when moved to a certain point falls and produces some motion; **tumbling-box**, a rotating drum in which small articles (usually of metal) are cleaned and polished by attrition; also used in dissolving and mixing paints, varnishes, etc.; **tumbling car**, a tumbrel; †**tumbling cast**, a somersault; a fall, overthrow; **tumbling crank**: see quot.; **tumbling gear**, a gear with one or more idle wheels on a swinging frame for producing reverse motion; †**tumbling glass**, a tumbler; **tumbling joint**: see quot.; **tumbling metre**, cf. *tumbling verse*; **tumbling-mill**, a tumbling-box or set of these (*Cent. Dict. Supp.* 1909); **tumbling-room**, space for tumbling; *spec.* a room in which a tumbling-box is set up; **tumbling shaft**, a revolving shaft carrying cams producing intermittent motion; **tumbling-star**, an iron ball with projecting spikes which is put into the tumbling-box to stir up the polishing or abrading medium (*Cent. Dict. Supp.* 1909); **tumbling stone**, a loose stone embedded in clay; a boulder: = TUMBLER 8; **tumbling tom**, in Coal-mining: see quot. 1883; also *Sc.* (*tumbling Tam*), a thick heavy halfpenny of George III's reign; **tumbling-trough**, in sulphuric acid manufacture, a receptacle which pours nitric acid from each of its two balancing chambers in turn (*Cent. Dict.* 1891); **tumbling verse**, a kind of irregular anapæstic verse: see quot.; **tumbling water-cracker**, a kind of aquatic firework; **tumbling weight** = *tumbling bob*; **tumbling-wheel**, a revolving chamber in which small wooden objects are smoothed by attrition; cf. *tumbling-box.*

1724 *Jrnl. Ho. Comm.* XX. 382 The water is to be divided by an overfall or *tumbling bay. **1795** J. PHILLIPS *Hist. Inland Navig.* Add. 90 To preserve the water of the same river, a tumbling bay is to be erected. **1847** ADDISON *Law of Contracts* II. i. § 1. (1883) 244 The lessee of a water-mill..has no right to alter the height of the tumbling-bay. **1891** A. J. FOSTER *Ouse* 136 A fine large 'tumbling bay', as the pools below the sluices are sometimes called. **1824** R. STUART *Hist. Steam Engine* 73 A weight or *tumbling bob, or Y piece, to give the necessary momentum to the movement of the injection-cock lever. **1877** KNIGHT *Dict. Mech.*, **Tumbling-box*,..a cylindrical or barrel-shaped vessel.. mounted on an axis so as to be revolved by a winch or pulley. Called also *rumble, rolling barrel.* **1840** DICKENS *Old C. Shop* xi, He sent an express to the wharf for the *tumbling boy. **1881** *Daily News* 2 June 5 The little tumbling boy and his oppressors. **1811** in *Chamb. Jrnl.* 11 Jan. (1845) 31/2 The chief part..was brought from the sand-beds of Esk in *tumbling cars. **1530** PALSGR. 179 *Sombresault*, a *tumblyng caste. **1677** NEEDHAM *2nd Pacquet Adv.* 31 They are for a Tumbling-Cast to the present rulers of Church and State. **1886** J. BARROWMAN *Sc. Mining Terms* 69 **Tumbling-crank*, a crank on the end of the pumping shaft for giving reciprocating motion. **1793** *Trans. Soc. Arts* (ed. 2) V. 202 The common *Tumbling Geer, as used in the Fire Engine. **1854** DICKENS *Hard Times* vii. 52 Tom Gradgrind's whim, ma'am, of bringing up the *tumbling-girl. **1896** K. LEASK *H. Miller* ii. 39 A tumbling-girl who had been sold by her parents to a travelling mountebank. **1803** *MS. Diary* in *N. & Q.* 8th Ser. (1893) III. 168/1 Had a few friends to dine, tried my new *tumbling-glasses; very successful, all got drunk early. **1861** *Sat. Rev.* 14 Dec. 604 A field is lent for a circus or a *tumbling-ground for an acrobat. **1844** STEPHENS *Bk. Farm* III. 981 The English hay-tedding machine.. having a series of revolving rakes... The rakes are attached to the wheels by a *tumbling-joint,..when any undue resistance is opposed to a rake..the rake falls back till the obstruction has been passed. **1687** FOUNTAINHALL *Decis.* (1759) I. 439 Reid the Mountebank pursues Scot of Harden ..for stealing away from him a little girl, called the *Tumbling-Lassie, that danced upon his stage. **1847** *Proc. Philol. Soc.* III. 103 When this licence is taken frequently the metre becomes of that species..called..'*tumbling metres'. **1860** G. MEREDITH *Evan Harrington* viii, No *tumbling-room for the wine, eh? **1901** *Trans. Amer. Inst. Electr. Engin.* 562 (Cent. Supp.). *c* **1790** IMISON *Sch. Art* I. 36 It [the universal joint] is of great use in cotton mills, where the *tumbling shafts are continued to a great distance from the moving power. **1857** J. ROBERTSON in Charteris *Life* xii. (1863) 338 There are many sloughs and *tumbling stones on the road. **1881** *Borrings & Sinkings* II. 2 (E.D.D.) Strong blue clay with large tumbling stones. **1826** GALT *Last of Lairds* iv, I gave him a whole penny—twa new bawbees, gude weight, for it was then the days o' the *tumbling Tams. **1883** GRESLEY *Coal-Mining Gloss.*, *Tumbling Toms*, tippers that turn completely over. **1596** SHAKS. *Tam. Shr.* Induct. ii. 140 Is it not a Comontie, a Christmas gambold, or a *tumbling tricke? **1673** HICKERINGILL *Greg. F. Greyb.* 302 They coming not to church to see tumbling tricks and hocus juglings. **1585** JAS. I *Ess. Poesie* (Arb.) 63 Thir hes twa sort, and ane lang throuch all the lyne, quhen they keip ordour: albeit the maist pairt of thame be out of ordour, and keipis na kynde nor reule of Flowing, and for that cause are callit *Tumbling verse. **1799** G. SMITH *Laboratory* I. 24 Charges for *Tumbling Water-crackers. Mealed powder.., nitre.., and charcoal. [Cf. 21 Water-crackers, which turn in the water.] **1903** *Nature* 19 Nov. 68/1 Barney's illustration of the Dudley Castle engine (erected in 1712) was made in 1719, and contains the plug-frame and *tumbling-weight device... It is possible that the tumbling-weight had just been added for actuating the steam-valve.

tumbly (ˈtʌmblɪ), *a. rare.* [f. TUMBLE *v.* + -Y.] Ready to tumble; tumble-down, ruinous.

c **1855** SIR E. BURNE-JONES in Mackail *Life Morris* (1899) I. 51 They were tumbly old buildings.

‖**tumbok lada** (ˈtumbok ˈlada). [Malay, lit. 'pepper-crusher', f. *tumbok* to thump, pound + *lada* pepper.] A small Malayan dagger.

1839 T. J. NEWBOLD *Straits of Malacca* II. xii. 212 The Battas of Sumatra, wear..knives called tombak lada. **1911** *Encycl. Brit.* XVII. 477/1 The Malays use..short stabbing daggers called *tumbok lada.* **1936** G. B. GARDNER *Keris* viii. 113 A nasty ripping knife is sometimes made by fixing an old razor blade into a *tumbok lada* hilt. **1967** J. CLEARY *Long Pursuit* i. 25 He..took from his belt the *tumbok lada*, the small Malayan knife.

tumboora, var. TAMBOURA, musical instrument.

tumbrel[1], **tumbril** (ˈtʌmbrəl, -ɪl). Forms: 4 tombrel, 4–5 tumberell, tumrelle, 5 tomberel, tomerel, tumrel, 5–7 tumbrell, 6 -e, tumrell, tomberell, -brill, 6–8 -brell, 7 -bril, 8 tumbral, 9 *dial.* tumril, 6– tumbrel, -il; also 6–7 timbrell. [ad. med.L. *tumb(e)rellum* (Du Cange), *-ellus*, OF. *tumb-, tomberel, tummerel, tumerel, -il*, etc., fall, chute, tip-cart, dung-cart, trebuchet (13th c. in Godef.), mod.F. *tombereau* 'a Tumbrell or Dung-cart' (Cotgr.), a tipcart for carting and shooting dung, sand, stones, etc., f. *tomber* to let fall, tumble out. (No record in French of its use in punishment.)]

1. An instrument of punishment, the nature and operation of which in early times is uncertain; from 16th c. usually identified with CUCKING-STOOL, q.v. See also THEW *sb.*[2], TREBUCHET 4.

For full account of the word, with additional quots., see Dr. Brushfield's article quoted below.

[**1223** *Bracton's Note Bk.* (1887) III. 504 Et Radulfus quesitus quando leuauit tumberellum et per quod warantum, dicit quod de nouo et ea occasione quod habet tumberellum in quodam manerio suo in comitatu Essexie, et bene putauit quod per libertatem illam illum leuare potuit. Et quia nulla fuit mencio in carta Dom. Regis de tali libertate, consideratum est quod tumberellus prosternatur et Radulfus in misericordia. **1266–7** *Judicium Pillorie* in *Stat. Realm* (1810) I. 201/1 Si aliquis senescallus vel ballivus ..remiserit judicium pillorie vel tumbrelli adjudicatum.] **1313–14** *Eyre of Kent* (Selden Soc.) III. 182 Cely qvad amendes dassisse de payn et de servoise il ad pillori et tombrel [*v.rr.* turmberell, turmelle]. **1494** FABYAN *Chron.* VII. 345 Syr Hughe..punysshed the bakers for lacke of syze by the tumberell [**1568** GRAFTON tomberell] where before tymes they were punysshed by the pyllery. *Ibid.* 385 Myllers for stelyng of corne to be chastysed by yᵉ tumbrell. **1538** ELYOT, *Numellæ*, a tumbrelle, wherein menne be punysshed, hauyng their heedes and fete put into it. **1581** LAMBARDE *Eiren.* I. xii. (1588) 67 Setting on the Pillorie or Cucking stoole, which in old time was called the Tumbrell. **1607** COWELL *Interpr.*, *Cucking stoole*..is an engine inuented for the punishment of scolds and vnquiet women, called in auncient time a tumbrell... Kitchin, where he saith, that euery one hauing view of Frankpledge, ought to haue a pillorie and a tumbrell, seemeth by a tumbrell to meane the same thing [i.e. a cucking-stool]. *a* **1634** COKE *On Litt.* III. ci. (1648) 219 Those that have been adjudged to the Pillory, or Tumbrell, are so infamous [as not to be admitted to give evidence]. **1688** Ducking Tumbrel [see DUCKING-STOOL]. **1857–9** T. N. BRUSHFIELD *Obs. Punishments* II. *Cucking Stool* (1861) 5 In the Statutes, manorial claims, and law books, [the cucking stool] is usually alluded to as a *tumbrel* or *tre-buchet. Ibid.* 9 From the 15th c., the identity of the meaning of the two terms [*cucking stool* and *tumbrel*] is easily proved.

†**2.** A counterpoise beam for raising a well-bucket. *Obs. rare.*

c **1475** *Pict. Voc.* in Wr.-Wülcker 799/36 *Nomina Aquarum... Hoc tolumen*, a tumrelle. **1483** *Cath. Angl.* 396/1 A Tumrelle of A wele,..*ciconia, tollinum.*

3. A cart so constructed that the body tilts backwards to empty out the load; *esp.* a dung-cart.

c **1440** *Promp. Parv.* 496/2 Tomerel, donge cart. *Ibid.* 506/1 Tumrel, donge carte, *fimaria, titubatorium.* **1481–90** *Howard Househ. Bks.* (Roxb.) 174 Item, Gante is owing for another day with his tomberel. **1494** FABYAN *Chron.* VII. 495 He was..sette in a tumbrell, & therunto fastenyd with chaynes of iren, and so conueyed, bareheded, with dynne and crye, thorough the hyghe stretes of Parys tyll he came vnto the bysshoppes palays. **1620** MARKHAM *Farew. Husb.* (1625) 69 Any clay earth..you shall carry it in tumbrels or carriages to the new plowed ground. **1632** *Foxe's A. & M.* III. *Contin.* 69/1 The dead bodies..were conueyed in tumbrils out of the citie. **1700** DRYDEN *Cock & Fox* 251 My corps is in a tumbril laid; among The filth and ordure, and enclos'd with dung. **1856** R. A. VAUGHAN *Mystics* (1860) I. 281 He sees..the emissaries of the Pope..dragged through the streets in a scavenger's tumbril. **1901** *Essex Weekly News* 8 Mar. 3/3 The frequent tipping of the tumbril.

†**b.** app. *transf.* to a lumbering cart. *Obs.*

Cf. also TUMBLER 7.

1597–8 BP. HALL *Sat.* V. iv. 14 A Friezeland trotter halfe-yarde deepe To drag his tumbrell through the staring Cheape. **1699** GARTH *Dispens.* V. 57 Haspt in a Tombril, awkwardly you've shin'd With one fat Slave before, and none behind. **1709** STEELE *Tatler* No. 51 ¶ 1 He sometimes rode in an open Tumbril, of less Size than ordinary, to show the Largeness of his Limbs. **1800** WEEMS *Washington* vi. (1877) 44 And he assisted him in a tumbril or little cart.

c. *fig.* Applied to a person or his gorge.

1601 WEEVER *Mirr. Mart.* E iij b, But by misfortune t'was the Abbots land Whereas we lay; so by his priuie spies The fat-backt tumbrell soone did vnderstand. **1630** J. TAYLOR (Water P.) *Laugh & be fat* Wks. II. 72/1 Thou mightst relate At thy returne, their manners liues and law, Belcht from the tumbrell of thy gorged maw.

†**4.** *transf.* A flat-bottomed boat or barge; cf. *tumbrel boat* in 7; also *fig.* applied to a person loaded with drink. *Obs.*

1468 *Medulla Gram.* in *Cath. Angl.* 396 *note, Cimbula*, a tomerel [cf. *c* 1050 *Gloss.* in Wr.-Wülcker 379/16 *Cimbula*, lytlum scipe]. *a* **1625** FLETCHER *Woman's Prize* III. ii, There rid (like a Dutch hoy) the Tumbrel. When she had got her Ballast..How fain [etc.]. **1676** ETHEREDGE *Man of Mode* III. ii, Have you taken notice of the gallegh I brought over?.. 'Tis as easily known from an English Tumbril, as an Inns of Court-man is from one of us. **1700** CONGREVE *Way of World* IV. ii, Good lack! what shall I do with this beastly tumbril [a drunken man]?

5. *Mil.* A two-wheeled covered cart which carries ammunition, tools, or sometimes money for an army.

1715 *Lond. Gaz.* No. 5383/3 We have..carried off.. Tombrells with Ammunition. **1803** WELLESLEY in Owen *Desp.* (1877) 393 Sixty-four tumbrils, completely laden with ammunition, together with three tumbrils of money. **1859** JEPHSON *Brittany* xvi. 267 In our Artillery the guns are.. drawn by horses, and the men sit on the ammunition-tumbrels.

6. A square rack for holding fodder in the open field or yard. *dial.*

1635 BP. J. WILLIAMS *Articles Enq. Linc.* A iv, Tumbrels, or other things in your church-yard, to fodder cattell in. **1840** *Boston Advert.* 30 June 3/4 We went together into the crew, and found some eggs under a tumbril. **1870** *Daily News* 6 Dec., A small quantity of linseed cake, crushed fine, scattered upon the top of the provender, as it is placed in the tumbrils.

7. *attrib.* and *Comb.*, as *tumbrel boat, cart, load, post* (sense 6), *-slop* (cf. 3 b); *tumbrel-shaped* adj.

1688 R. HOLME *Armoury* III. xv. (Roxb.) 26/1 A *Tumbrell boate, or flat bottomed boate or Turnell boate.

1852 WIGGINS *Embanking* 101 The application of chalk rubbish, i.e. soft chalk, to the land, after the rate of at least ten *tumbril cart-loads per acre. **1764** *Museum Rust.* III. lxiii. 292, I have mentioned a *tumbrel-load to be thirty bushels, and a waggon-load to be but two tumbrels. **1821** *Bill* in *N.W. Linc. Gloss.* (1877) s.v., 12 *tumprill posts at 1s. 3d. **1598** B. JONSON *Ev. Man in Hum.* II. ii, I'le goe neere to fill that huge *tumbrell-slop of yours, with somewhat, an I have good luck. **1826** HOR. SMITH *Tor Hill* (1838) II. 279 That French tumbril-slop is transcendant. **1776** *Evelyn's Sylva* I. ii. 43 The water might fall..like drops of rain; which I should much prefer before the barrels and *tumbral way.

†**tumbrel**². *Obs. rare*⁻¹. In 3 tumberel. [app. deriv. of OF. *tumber*, *tomber* to tumble; cf. TUMBLER 3, the porpoise (*obs.*), the young codfish (*Eng. Dial. Dict.*).] A kind of fish.

c **1300** *Havelok* 757 Keling he tok, and tumberel, Hering, and þe makerel, þe butte, þe schulle, þe þornbake.

tumbrel(le, obs. forms of TIMBREL *sb.*¹

tumbu fly (ˈtʊmbuː flaɪ). [f. Bantu name of the insect + FLY *sb.*¹] A yellow fly with grey markings, *Cordylobia anthropophaga*, found in sub-Saharan Africa, where its larva is a parasite of man and other animals.

1911 A. ALCOCK *Entomol. for Med. Officers* x. 155 The notorious species is..the Tumbu-fly, the larva of which is a subcutaneous parasite of man and other animals. **1930** *Discovery* Aug. 265/1 Wild beasts..and tumbu flies abound. **1979** C. ALLEN *Tales from Dark Continent* i. 5 There was the *tumbo* [sic] fly..whose worm manifested itself as a large boil.

tume, obs. Sc. form of TOOM, empty.

tumefacient (tjuːmɪˈfeɪʃ(ɪ)ənt), *a. rare*⁻¹. [ad. L. *tumefacient-em*, pr. pple. of *tumefac-ĕre* to tumefy.] Tumefying, swelling. (In quot. *humorously pedantic.*)

1885 B. HARTE *By Shore & Sedge, Sarah Walker* 45 The infant..had grown unctuous and tumefacient under the kisses.

†**tumeˈfacted**, *a. Obs. rare.* [f. L. *tumefact-us*, pa. pple. of *tumefac-ĕre* to tumefy + -ED¹.] = TUMEFIED, swollen.

1597 A. M. tr. *Guillemeau's Fr. Chirurg.* 44b/2 This ligature is very commodiouse in tumefacted Legges. **1599** —— tr. *Gabelhouer's Bk. Physicke* 238/2 When as the privityes..are tumefactede, or swollene.

tumefaction (tjuːmɪˈfækʃən). [a. F. *tumefaction* (16th c. in Godef. *Compl.*), f. L. *tumefac-ĕre* to tumefy: see -TION.]

1. The action or process of tumefying, or state of being tumefied; swelling; swollen condition: **a.** as a morbid affection of some part of the body.

1597 A. M. tr. *Guillemeau's Fr. Chirurg.* 14/2 Throughe the tumefactione which therof ensueth. **1689** MOYLE *Sea Chyrurg.* III. iv. 108 A Tumifaction of the inward Tunicle of the Ribbs, called Plura. **1737** BRACKEN *Farriery Impr.* (1757) II. 268 An Inflammation and Tumefaction of these Kernels. **1872** COHEN *Dis. Throat* 93 Tumefaction of the tonsils.

b. in general. *rare.*

1665–6 *Phil. Trans.* I. 287 The Progressive motion, which he fansieth to follow upon this Tumefaction. **1686** GOAD *Celest. Bodies* II. vii. 249 Tumefaction is inseparable from a troubled Sea. **1837** HERSCHEL in Babbage *Bridgew. Treat.* App. I. 237 Granting the heat, there is no difficulty in deducing expansions, disruptions, tumefactions, &c.

2. *concr.* A swollen part; a swelling, a tumour.

1802 PALEY *Nat. Theol.* ix. §4 (ed. 2) 138 The muscles which move the toes..gracefully..disposed in the calf of the leg, instead of forming an unwieldy tumefaction in the foot itself. **1854** MARION HARLAND *Alone* xiv, She beheld reflected in the mirror, a tumefaction of the cheek, nearly closing one eye.

tumefied (ˈtjuːmɪfaɪd), *ppl. a.* (erron. tumi-.) [f. next + -ED¹, repr. L. *tumefactus*, pa. pple. of *tumefacĕre.*] Caused to swell, swollen. (Const. as *pa. pple.* or *ppl. adj.*) **a.** said of a bodily part thus morbidly affected.

1597 LOWE *Chirurg.* (1634) 71 The signes of resolution are lightnesse or ease of the member tumified, diminution of dolour [etc.]. **1691** HOWE *Carnality Relig. Contention* Wks. (1846) 211 This angry, tumefied, proud flesh. **1748** *Phil. Trans.* XLV. 412 The Eye was inflamed, and the Lids tumefied. **1762** *Gentl. Mag.* 250 A tumefied tendon. **1847** YOUATT *Horse* xii. 258 The parotids are a little tumefied.

b. generally. *rare.*

1651 BIGGS *New Disp.* ¶248 Tumified gumme. **1796** KIRWAN *Elem. Min.* (ed. 2) I. 314 Melted..into a spongy,.. tumefied semitransparent mass. **1815** J. SMITH *Panorama Sc. & Art* II. 726 Where a figure..is fore-shortened, the drapery must appear more tumefied.

c. *fig.* 'Inflated' or 'puffed up' with pride or the like. *rare.*

1677 GILPIN *Demonol.* (1867) 114 Yet were they so tumefied with the apprehensions of their privileges. **1680** BAXTER *Cath. Commun.* Pref. Aiij, The Crimes of a few tumified Sectarian Soldiers. **1892** G. HAKE *Mem. Eighty Y.* 118 Tumid young men rigged out in newest apparel... None of these tumefied gentlemen ever walked in a hurry.

tumefy (ˈtjuːmɪfaɪ), *v.* (erron. tumi-). [= F. *tuméfi-er*, ad. L. type **tumeficāre* (cf. L. *tumefacĕre*), f. L. *tumē-re* to swell: see -FY, and cf. *stupefy*, *rubefy*.]

1. *trans.* To cause to swell; to swell, make tumid.

1597 [see prec. a]. **1656** BLOUNT *Glossogr.*, *Tumefie*.., to make to swell, or puff up. **1686** [see *tumefying* below]. **1718** J. CHAMBERLAYNE *Relig. Philos.* (1730) I. xi. §15 The Sucker, tumified with Water, is thrust into the Tube. **1822–7** GOOD *Study Med.* (1829) III. 132 Like the Athenian plague..it commenced in the head, inflamed the eyes, and tumefied the face.

b. *fig.* To 'swell'; to make too bulky; to 'puff up', as with pride; to make turgid or bombastic.

1674 JEAKE *Arith.* (1696) 89 Being not willing to spare so much time, or tumefie these Papers. **1677** [see prec. c]. **1837** J. MORIER *A. Allnutt* iv. 21 Having tumefied himself and his possessions by all the pomp and circumstance of two shields, and..a variety of heraldic insignia. **18..** DE QUINCEY (Webster 1864), To swell, tumefy, stiffen, not the diction only, but the tenor of the thought.

2. *intr.* To swell, swell up, become tumid.

1615 [see *tumefying* below]. **1689** MOYLE *Sea Chyrurg.* II. vii. 51 The wound..will be apt to Tumifie. **1811** PINKERTON *Petralogy* II. 286 Where the air..has most liberty to escape, it will tumify, burst through the liquid mass, and form cellular lava. **1822–7** GOOD *Study Med.* (1829) I. 102 The tongue tumefies; the throat becomes sore. **1883** R. HALDANE *Workshop Receipts* Ser. II. 304/2 The solid sheet glue, while drying.., tumefied and became very porous.

Hence **ˈtumefying** *vbl. sb.* and *ppl. a.*

1615 CROOKE *Body of Man* 79 Although there be no outward tumifying..to be seene. **1686** GOAD *Celest. Bodies* II. vii. 249 Its tumefying influence.

tumeler, var. TUMMLER.

tumen, obs. form of TOMAN¹.

tumerous, obs. f. TIMOROUS, TUMOROUS.

tumesce (tjuːˈmɛs), *v.* [Back-formation from TUMESCENCE or f. L. *tumēscere* (see TUMESCENT *a.*).] *intr.* = TUMEFY *v.* 2. Also *fig.* Hence **tuˈmescing** *ppl. a.*

1966 *New Statesman* 10 June 853/3 Forming open alliances which were secret before, exposing sexual and ethical weaknesses as they tumesce under the threat of death. **1976** *Theriogenology* V. 261 Those [monkeys] that tumesced before they were 3 years old tended to be heavier than their peers, but were not necessarily heavier than older, nonswelling females. **1976** *New Scientist* 9 Sept. 528/2 Other aids to prediction [of eruptions]... As a volcano tumesces the distance between fixed points increases, and these distances can be measured accurately with optical instruments using laser beams. **1980** *Sci. Amer.* Feb. 86/1 In a tumescing system such as the Yellowstone one the ring fractures could propagate downward, eventually penetrating the main magma chamber.

tumescence (tjuːˈmɛsəns). [f. next, corresp. to a Latin type **tumēscentia.*] A becoming tumid, swelling up; a tendency to tumidity; *spec.* the swelling of a volcano as a result of increasing pressure of magma inside it. Also *concr.* a tumid part, a swelling.

1859 R. F. BURTON *Centr. Afr.* in *Jrnl. Geog. Soc.* XXIX. 321 Tumescence..appears to characterize the human as it does the vegetable productions of Inner Africa. **1874** NASMYTH & CARPENTER *Moon* Contents p. xiii, Scrope's Hypothesis of Terrestrial Tumescences. **1901–6** H. ELLIS in Westermarck *Orig. & Devel. Moral Ideas* xl. (1908) II. 374 Erethistic excitement which produces sexual tumescence. **1943** *Amer. Jrnl. Sci.* CCXLI. 243 Easterly tilt has long been known to indicate tumescence of Mauna Loa accompanying the rise of magma pressure preceding eruption. **1976** P. FRANCIS *Volcanoes* x. 310 The tumescence of the Hawaiian volcanoes, however, is slight, only one metre or so at the summit.

tumescent (tjuːˈmɛsənt), *a.* [f. L. *tumēscent-em*, pr. pple. of *tumēscĕre* to begin to swell, become tumid, inceptive of *tumēre* to swell.] Becoming tumid, swelling; somewhat tumid; also *fig.*

1882 ADAMSON in *Mind* Apr. 281 The style is of a vapid and somewhat tumescent character. **1899** *Allbutt's Syst. Med.* VIII. 479 Heat..will make the lesions red and tumescent. **1899** BARING-GOULD *Bk. of West* v, Tumescent undergarments.

tumfie, var. TUMPHY.

tumid (ˈtjuːmɪd), *a.* Also 6 -yde. [ad. L. *tumid-us*, f. *tumē-re* to swell: see -ID¹.]

1. Swollen; characterized by swelling.

a. Morbidly affected with swelling, as a part of the body.

1541 R. COPLAND *Galyen's Terap.* 2 F j, Varyce (that is to say a tumyde vayne). **1650** BULWER *Anthropomet.* 178 Making..the Belly tumid. **1784** JOHNSON *Let. to Mrs. Thrale* 12 Jan., My thighs grow very tumid. **1878** T. BRYANT *Pract. Surg.* I. 32 Ulcers..distinguished by their livid colour and irregular tumid border.

b. Of a swollen or protuberant form; swelling, bulging; in quot. 1659, swollen or puffed out with the wind. In later use chiefly *Nat. Hist.*

1621 G. SANDYS *Ovid's Met.* XI. (1626) 221 Who, with the Father of the tumid Maine, Indues a mortall shape. **1659** T. PECKE *Parnassi Puerp.* 132 Tumid Sail-cloths gratifi'd our Sight. **1819** STEPHENS in Shaw *Gen. Zool.* XI. I. 1 The upper mandible with a soft and tumid membrane at its base. **1828** J. E. SMITH *Eng. Flora* II. 97 Styles short and close in the flower;..their bases tumid.

2. *fig.* esp. of language or literary style: 'Swelling', inflated, turgid, bombastic.

1648 BOYLE *Seraph. Love* xx. (1700) 126 Such expressions may seem somewhat tumid and aspiring. **1760** JORTIN *Erasmus* II. 200 A puerile performance, in a poetical, tumid, and idolatrous style. **1809** BYRON *Bards & Rev.* xiv, Turgid ode and tumid stanza. **1877** SYMONDS *Renaissance in Italy* v. 272 His Greek style is at the same time tame and tumid.

b. 'Big', pregnant, teeming. *rare.*

1840 DE QUINCEY *Style* III. Wks. 1860 XI. 252 It is tumid with revolutionary life. **1850** BLACKIE *Æschylus* I. Pref. 6 Greek..is a language..tumid with luxuriant growth and overgrowth.

Hence **ˈtumidly** *adv.*, in a tumid manner (*lit.* and *fig.*); **ˈtumidness**, tumidity.

1688 BOYLE *Final Causes Nat. Things, Vitiated Sight* 259 Her eyes did not always retain the same measure of tumidness. **1822** J. PARKINSON *Outl. Oryctol.* 164 A multilocular, tumidly discoidal and elliptically spiral shell. **1864** CARLYLE *Fredk. Gt.* XVI. v. (1872) VI. 184 Remarks.. of dim tumidly insignificant character.

tumidity (tjuːˈmɪdɪtɪ). [ad. late L. *tumiditās*, f. *tumidus* TUMID.] The quality or condition of being tumid; swollenness. **a.** *lit.*; also *concr.* a swelling.

1721 BAILEY, *Tumidity*, swelling. **1828** MACAULAY *Dryden* Wks. 1898 VII. 152 No more than the tumidity of a muscle resembles the tumidity of a boil. **1873** A. W. WARD tr. *Curtius' Hist. Greece* I. I. i. 24 Every muscle, every sinew, is developed into full play,..there is no trace of tumidity or of inert matter. **1897** *Allbutt's Syst. Med.* III. 476 Windy tumidities and occasionally phantom tumours arise.

b. *fig.* in reference to language: see TUMID 2.

1791 BOSWELL *Johnson* an. 1784 (1816) IV. 433 [A passage] blown up into such tumidity, as to be truly ludicrous. **1883** R. BROWN in *Fortn. Rev.* 1 Sept. 380 Their periods turned with Johnsonian tumidity. **1895** *Q. Rev.* Oct. 336 Aeschylus, grandiose at times almost to tumidity.

tummer: see TUM *v.*¹

tummied (ˈtʌmɪd), *a.* [f. TUMMY + -ED².] In parasynthetic combs., having a stomach (of a specified kind).

1975 T. HEALD *Deadline* iv. 72 He..wondered if she had to wear a corset. She was remarkably flat tummied. **1975** *Times* 5 July 10/5 A carved, fat tummied elephant.

tummler (ˈtʊmlə(r)). *colloq.* (orig. and chiefly *U.S.*). Also **toomler**, **tumeler.** [Yiddish, f. G. *tummeln* stir.] Someone who acts the clown, a prankster; *spec.* a professional maker of amusement and jollity at a hotel or the like.

1966 ADAMS & TOBIAS *Borscht Belt* iv. 41 If Mrs. Rappaport complained about not getting her third portion of blueberries or Mrs. Davidoff was scrounging fruitlessly for a dancing partner..it was the Toomler to the rescue. **1968** L. ROSTEN *Joys of Yiddish* 413 It is the *tummler's* job to guarantee, to the blasé (but insatiable) patrons of a summer resort, that most dubious of vacation boons: 'Never a dull moment!' **1970** L. M. FEINSILVER *Taste of Yiddish* iii. 345 Danny Kaye and other entertainers got their starts as tumelers in the Catskills. **1977** *New Yorker* 12 Sept. 86/3 A summer job as part-time social director and tummler at a hotel in Lake Hopatcong, New Jersey. **1984** *Times* 20 Mar. 12/3 Why should she not believe the agents and promoters, the spivs and *tummlers*?

tummock (ˈtʌmək). *dial.* Also (*Sc.*) **tammock, tummack.** [app. f. Gaelic *tom* hillock + -OCK; cf. TUMP *sb.*] A hillock, mound, knoll.

1789 D. DAVIDSON *Seasons* 5 Twa 'herds..straught down on tammocks clap Their nether ends, and talk their unco's o'er. **1855** KINGSLEY *Westw. Ho.* xiv, Your ghost may sit there on a grass tummock, and tell your beads. **1901** A. TROTTER *E. Galloway Sk.* 32/1 Wandering among its hills and 'tummacks', its singing spouts and burns.

tummon, obs. form of TOMAN¹.

tummy (ˈtʌmɪ). *colloq.* [Repr. a childish alteration of *stomach*: see -Y⁶.] The stomach or intestine.

1869 W. S. GILBERT *Bab Ballads* 200 Why should I hesitate to own That pain was in his little tummy? **1884** KIPLING *Let.* ? Sept. in Ld. Birkenhead *Rudyard Kipling* (1978) vi. 74, I felt the cramps in my legs dying out and my tummy more settled. **1922** JOYCE *Ulysses* 356 Cissy poked him..out of fun in his wee fat tummy. **1936** N. STREATFEILD *Ballet Shoes* iii. 40 Laughing so much that they fell on the floor, and their tummies ached. **1962** V. NABOKOV *Pale Fire* 191 That was Dad's tummy, I think—not a spook. **1979** *Beautiful British Columbia* Fall 14 The bucks..lie napping with heads tucked against tummies like so many dogs.

2. An abdominal pain or complaint. Freq. with preceding place-name: diarrhœa suffered by visitors there.

1888 KIPLING *Story of Gadsbys* (1889) 21 He has nothing more than a wet weather tummy. **1937** F. STARK *Let.* 25 Oct. in *Coast of Incense* (1953) 177, I am spending these five days rather tiresomely in hospital with a *tummy*. **1939** R. GODDEN *Black Narcissus* vi. 77 'Sister Briony..thinks it must be some local infection, as we all have it.'.. 'Darjeeling tummy,' said Mr. Dean. **1943**, etc. [see GIPPY 1 c]. **1959** L. DURRELL *Spirit of Place* (1969) 423 The Mediterranean affliction of high summer known to us all as 'tummy' (Egyptian, Greek or Naples tummy). **1970** N. MARSH *When in Rome* iv. 97 A sudden onslaught of the affliction known to tourists as Roman Tummy..necessitated an immediate withdrawal. **1979** A. V. BADGLEY *Rembrandt Decisions* (1980) ix. 119 He's sick... Says he's got 'Bombay Tummy'.

3. *attrib.* as ***tummy muscle, pain, rumble, trouble, upset***; **tummy ache**, an abdominal pain; **tummy bug**, (a germ causing) a disorder of the stomach; **tummy-button** = NAVEL *sb.* 1.

1926 GALSWORTHY *Silver Spoon* III. viii. 284 Kit had tummyache this morning. **1979** L. & J. BROWN *Our Miracle* *called Louise* iii. 35 'I've got a tummy ache,' I told her. 'It will be gone in the morning,' she said. **1969** M. Pugh *Last Place Left* xvii. 121 We're rather below strength... Some sort of tummy bug. **1945** A. Huxley *Time must have a Stop* ii. 13 Everybody's tummy-button grew inwards like that. **1974** G. Butler *Coffin for Canary* x. 133 My waist and tummy muscles are really taut. **1924** J. Buchan *Three Hostages* xvi. 238 He really has had a bad tummy pain. **1947** G. Greene *Nineteen Stories* 192 It was the doctors who called his complaint Borborygmi: in England we usually call it just 'tummy rumbles'. **1982** N. Marsh *Light Thickens* iii. 91 His tummy rumbles are positively deafening. **1937** W. H. S. Smith *Let.* 12 Jan. in *Young Man's Country* (1977) ii. 51 My tummy trouble persisted for several days after my return to Madaripur. **1926** A. Huxley *Let.* 21 Oct. (1969) 274 Matthew meanwhile flourishes.. in spite of a tummy upset.

‖**tu-mo** (dumo). Also Tu Mu. [Chinese *dū mài*.] In Chinese medical theory, the chief passage through which the vital energy circulates, located within the spine; *spec.* in acupuncture.

1972 Da Liu *T'ai Chi Ch'uan & I Ching* (1974) i. 9 In meditation one learns to focus and direct energies which are usually squandered in the mundane perceptions of the five senses. In Taoist meditation these energies are directed through two main channels: *Tu Mu*, a channel along the spinal column.. and *Jen Mu*, a channel which passes down the front of the body to the genital region. **1974** *Barefoot Doctor's Man.* iv. 105 The governing 'tu-mo' meridian.

tumorigenic (tjuːmərɪˈdʒɛnɪk), *a. Med.* Also tumo(u)r(o)-. [f. tumour, tumor + -i-, -o + -genic.] Capable of causing tumours.

1948 *Cancer Res.* VIII. 410/1 It is thought that they [*sc.* these observations] afford an example of the tumorigenic action of.. follicle-stimulating hormone. **1965** *Dissertation Abstr.* XXVI. 1300/2 (*heading*) The salivary gland chromosomes of a tumorgenic strain of *Drosophila melanogaster*. **1971** *New Scientist* 24 June 732/2 Tumourigenic hybrids had 80 chromosomes instead of the expected 116. **1979** *Nature* 11 Oct. 486/1 The significance of EBV [*sc.* a virus] as a tumorigenic agent in humans could be finally established if it were possible to prevent tumours by vaccination. **1980** *Ibid.* 21 Feb. 777/1 The present experiments show that human diploid cells can be transformed *in vitro* into tumorogenic cells by X-ray-irradiation.

So **ˈtumorigen** (and varr.), a tumorigenic agent; **tumoriˈgenesis**, the production or formation of a tumour; **ˌtumorigeˈnicity**, tumorigenic property.

1948 *Cancer Res.* VIII. 397 (*heading*) Hormonal imbalances in tumorigenesis. **1952** J. E. Gregory *Pathogenesis of Cancer* (ed. 2) xii. 147 These elements [*sc.* coal tar, etc.] are called carcinogens. We now know that if the virus was present cancer would develop, but if it was not present only benign tumors and hyperplasia would develop as a result of the irritation. This latter fact makes it appear that a better name for these substances might have been tumorgens, instead of carcinogens. **1967** *New Scientist* 25 May 478/2 More than 50 per cent of the tumorigenicity of 24-hour condensate.. was due to stable, non-volatile carcinogens. **1970** *McGraw-Hill Yearbk. Sci. & Technol.* 217/2 Other studies have shown.. the dominance of tumorogenicity, and the characteristics of polyoma transformation in hybrids between transformed and nontransformed cells. **1971** *Nature* 17 Sept. 195/1 Irradiated hamster foetal cells protect male hamsters against SV40 tumorigenesis. **1978** *Brit. Med. Jrnl.* 11 Mar. 649/2 It would be a disservice to the public to allow marketing of a compound which is a demonstrated tumorigen. **1980** *European Jrnl. Cell Biol.* XXII. 491 The tumorgenicities of RBCF-1 cells.

tumorous (ˈtjuːmərəs), *a.* Also 7 tumerous, -ourous. [ad. L. *tumōrōsus*, f. *tumor* tumour: cf. OF. *tumoreux* (*c* 1400 in Godef.).]

†**1.** Characterized by tumour or swelling; swollen, protuberant, bulging, tumid. *Obs.* exc. as in b.

1547 Boorde *Brev. Health* cccxliv. 111 b, A venemous humour which is tumorous. **1601** B. Jonson *Poetaster* v. iii, That should purge His braine, and stomack of those tumorous heates. **1678** Cudworth *Intell. Syst.* i. v. §3. 30 Besides this Outside Bulky Extension, and Tumourous Magnitude, there must be another kind of Entity [cf. quot. 1678 s.v. tumour 2].

b. Pertaining to or of the nature of a (morbid) tumour: affected with tumours.

1863 Sala *Capt. Dangerous* II. ii. 78 It began to swell.. to a most alarming size and tumorous discoloration. **1884** J. Tait *Mind in Matter* (1892) 80 Other influences.. may produce tumourous growths. **1890** H. M. Stanley in *Times* 6 May, There are trees prematurely aged and blanched, others were tumorous.

†**2.** *fig.* **a.** Swelling with pride or passion; vainglorious, puffed up, haughty. *Obs.*

1603 Drayton *Bar. Wars* iii. lxxxi, To ease the anguish of her tumorous Spleene. *a* **1639** Wotton *Panegyrick Chas. I* in *Reliq.* (1652) 147 He had no austerity of behaviour, nothing outwardly tumerous. **1676** Sparrow *Caution agst. False Doctr.* 8 The same tumorous vain-glory.

†**b.** Of language, style, or demeanour: Inflated, bombastic, turgid: = tumid 2. *Obs.*

1636 B. Jonson *Discov.* Wks. (Rtldg.) 759/1 These styles vary..: for that which is high and lofty, declaring excellent matter, becomes vast and tumorous, speaking of petty and inferior things. *a* **1639** Wotton *Charac. Will. I*, Sublime and almost Tumorous in His Looks and Gestures. *a* **1652** A. Wilson *Jas. I* (1653) 285 Some tumorous Discourses.

tumour, tumor (ˈtjuːmə(r)). [a. L. *tumor*, *-ōrem*, swollen state, a swelling, f. *tum-ēre* to swell; cf. OF. *tumour* (14th c. in Godef. *Compl.*).]

†**1.** The action, or an act, of swelling; distension, increase of bulk; swollen condition. *Obs.*

1541 R. Copland *Galyen's Terap.* 2 A iv, The.. flesshe.. whan with the euyl qualyte it hath tumour agaynst nature. **1609** Holland *Amm. Marcell.* xxv. iv. 267 The tumor of his veines and arteries stopped his spirits. **1671** R. Bohun *Wind* (Contents), The suddain tumours in the Lake of Geneva. **1693** Evelyn *De la Quint. Compl. Gard., Refl. Agric.* xix. 72 This Distension or Tumor of such typed Branches.

2. *concr.* A part rising above or projecting beyond the general level or surface; a swollen part or object; a swelling. Now *rare* or *Obs.* exc. as in 3.

In quot. 1678 applied to anything having bulk, i.e. occupying space.

1601 Holland *Pliny* viii. xlv. I. 225 [The cattle] of Caria.. are illfavoured to be seen, having between their necks & shoulders a tumor or swelling hanging over. **1647** H. More *Song of Soul* Notes 151/2 The tumour [of water] at B is bigger then that at A. **1678** Cudworth *Intell. Syst.* i. v. §3. 780 There are.. two kinds of Substances in the universe; the first corporeal,.. are nothing but ὄγκοι, bulks, or tumours, devoid of all self-active power; the second incorporeal.. are ἄογκοι δυνάμεις, substantial powers. **1692** Bentley *Boyle Lect.* 111 A like ferment makes notable tumours and ventricles. **1847** W. E. Steele *Field Bot.* 13 Style.. thickened beneath its branches, and often fringed at the tumour.

3. a. An abnormal or morbid swelling or enlargement in any part of the body of an animal or plant; an excrescence; a tumefaction. Now usually in restricted sense: see b.

[**1541**: cf. 1.] **1597** Hooker *Eccl. Pol.* v. lxxii. §18 To helpe the tumors which alwaies fulnes breedeth. *a* **1601** ? Marston *Pasquil & Kath.* ii. 61 The gowt causeth a great tumour in a mans legs. **1692** Bentley *Boyle Lect.* iv. 136 Tumors and Excrescences of Plants.. made by such Insects. **1758** Gooch *Cases Surg.* 17 A Species of tumor called by the common people the Mumps. **1874** Lubbock *Orig. & Met. Ins.* i. 10 To produce a tumour or gall.

b. *spec.* A permanent circumscribed morbid swelling, consisting in a new growth of tissue, without inflammation.

phantom tumour: see phantom 8.

1804 Abernethy *Surg. Obs.* 6, I shall restrict the surgical signification of the word 'Tumour' to such swellings as arise from some new production. **1807–26** S. Cooper *First Lines Surg.* (ed. 5) 428 The tumour being removed, the surgeon should examine the interior of the wound... He should also examine the surface of every scirrhous tumour, immediately it is taken out. **1870** Maudsley *Body & Mind* 184 Certain colloid tumours have the structure of the umbilical cord. **1878** T. Bryant *Pract. Surg.* (1879) II. 28 Tumours of the pharynx or tonsils are occasionally met with.

†**4.** *fig.* **a.** 'Swelling' of passion, pride, or the like; the condition of being 'puffed up'; haughtiness, arrogance, vain-glory; inflated pride or conceit. *Obs.*

1600 Heywood *1st Pt. Edw. IV* Wks. 1874 I. 5 If you resist this tumour of her will. **1636** Wotton *Let. to Q. of Bohemia* in *Reliq.* (1651) 394 There is in him no tumour, no sowrenesse,.. but a quiet mind. **1751** Johnson *Rambler* No. 98 ⁋11 The tumour of insolence, or petulance of contempt. **1778** Sir J. Reynolds *Disc.* viii. (1876) 444 The tumour of this presumptuous loftiness.

b. Turgidity of language, style, or deportment; affected grandeur; bombast: = tumidity b. *Obs.*

a **1639** Wotton *Parallel Essex & Buckhm.* (1641) 8 His Stile was.. rich of praise [**1651** phrase],.. and so farre from Tumor that it rather wanted a little Elevation. **1652** J. Hall *Height of Eloquence* p. v, It appears one of the nicest cautions in all Speech to beware of Tumour. **1751** Johnson *Rambler* No. 105 ⁋4 A slow pace, and tumour of dignity. **1840** De Quincey *Style* i. Wks. 1860 XI. 204 Better to be flippant, than by a revolting habit of tumour and perplexity [etc.].

c. Something vain or empty; a 'bubble'. *Obs.*

1629 Massinger *Picture* i. i, Nor is it in me mere desire of fame.. that puts on my armour: Such airy tumours take not me. **1662** *Royal Trade of Fishing* 15, I present you with no Chimeraes or tumors, toyes to please Children.

5. *attrib.* and *Comb.*, as ***tumour-cell***, ***-formation***, ***growth***, ***-mass***, ***symptom***, etc.; ***tumour-like*** adj.; **tumour virus**, a virus that causes tumours.

1880 Barwell *Aneurism* 116 Tumor symptoms on the left side of the chest. **1889** J. M. Duncan *Clin. Lect. Dis. Women* ii. (ed. 4) 5 A rounded soft, tumour-like mass. **1898** J. Hutchinson in *Arch. Surg.* IX. No. 36. 295 Multiple Fractures.. with Tumour Growths. [**1934** *Lancet* 21 July 117/2 Neutralising antibodies can be shown to be formed against fowl-tumour viruses.] **1950** *Amer. Jrnl. Med.* VIII. 495/2 There is no proof that tumor viruses are of a different nature from other viruses. **1982** *Sci. Amer.* Mar. 69/3 Some tumor viruses are oncogenic (that is, they induce tumors) only in animals that are not their host in nature, whereas other tumor viruses are oncogenic in their natural host.

Hence †**tumoured, tumored** (ˈtjuːməd) *a.*, *obs.*, affected with tumour or swelling, swollen (*lit.* and *fig.*): const. as *adj.* or *pa. pple.*

1635 Heywood *Hierarch.* vi. 362 By his poys'nous draught which life expel'd I might behold his legs tumor'd and swell'd. **1639** Junius *Sin Stigm.* 50 Such an one.. seldome unbuttons his tumored breast. **1647** Trapp *Comm. Matt.* xix. 23 The greatest wealth.. tumoured up with the greatest swelth of rebellion.

tump (tʌmp), *sb.* Also 6 tumpe, 7 toompe, tomp. [Not found before end of 16th c.; chiefly a western and w. midl. word; see *Eng. Dial. Dict.*; origin obscure.

Also in Welsh *twmp* (cf. Buttington Tump in Montgomeryshire); but this may be from English. Welsh has also *Twmpath* (in Mabinogion *twympath*), 'a clump or tuft of rough grass, a barrow or tumulus', etc., with which cf. *tumpet* in *Eng. Dial. Dict.*]

1. A hillock, mound, a mole-hill, or ant-hill; a barrow, tumulus. *local.*

1589 Nashe *Martins Months M.* 53 They brought him vnawares to a dunghill, taking it for a tumpe, since a Tombe might not be had. **1603** Owen *Pembrokeshire* (1892) 84 *note*, No traces remained.. but highe and rounde toompes of earth. *Ibid.* 283 Tomps of erth. **1664** Evelyn *Pomona* vi. (1729) 71 To raise Tumps, or temporary Banks in the midst of an Inclosure. **1763** J. Hutchins in *Mem. W. Stukeley* (Surtees) II. 133 On the top of the hill.. are small tumps. **1829** E. Jesse *Jrnl. Nat.* 313 Cutting up anthills, or tumps, as we call them. **1881** Freeman in *Life & Lett.* (1895) II. 245 A few tumps so old that you can tell nothing about them. **1891** *Kelly's P.O. Guide Herefordsh.* 1 Tump is a peculiar term for barrow hills in the western shires.. the Tumps at Bolston, Horne Lacy, and Hope Mansel.

2. A clump of trees or shrubs; a clump of grass, esp. one forming a dry spot in a bog or fen. *local.*

1802 G. Montagu *Ornith. Dict.* N iij, The nest.. is placed on a tump or dry spot. **1869** Blackmore *Lorna D.* xxxi, He.. looked ahead of him, from behind a tump of whortles. **1880** —— *Mary Anerley* xvii, Every tump of wiry grass.

3. A heap of anything; a hay-cock or rick; a heap of stones. *local.*

Also a store-heap of potatoes, turnips, etc., covered with straw and earth (*Eng. Dial. Dict.*).

1892 *Stratford-on-Avon Herald* 5 Aug. 4/2 To sell by Auction,.. Tump of Old Hay about 2 tons. **1905** *Daily News* 24 Jan. 6 A tump of rubbish.

4. *fig.* Trivial writing, bad prose.

1917 Kipling *Divers. Creatures* 172 It's the most vital, arresting and dynamic bit of tump I've done up to date. **1933** D. L. Murray *Eng. Family Robinson* ii. 36 Did you ever read such tump as our parish magazine?

Hence **ˈtumpy** *a.*, of ground: humpy, hummocky.

1825 in *Eng. Dial. Dict.* **1847–78** in Halliwell.

tump, *v.*[1] *local* [f. prec. sb.] To make a 'tump' or mound about the root of a tree. Also, to store roots in a tump (*E.D.D.*). Hence **ˈtumping** *vbl. sb.*

1721 Bailey, *Tumping*, a sort of Fencing for Trees. **1725** *Bradley's Fam. Dict.* s.v. *Paling*, This Method is.. more chargeable than Tumping.., but much more durable. *Ibid.*, *Tumping*, a sort of Fencing in Fields, when a Tree is set.. no deeper than to make it stand, tho' all the Roots be not cover'd, till the Tump or Mould be raised about it. **1727** Bailey vol. II, To *Tump*, to fence trees.

tump, *v.*[2] *U.S.* [Origin obscure: cf. tump-line.] *trans.* To drag or carry by means of a tump-line.

1855 Haliburton *Nat. & Hum. Nat.* I. 268 A man passed the.. barrack-gate, tumping (which means.. hauling) an immense bull-moose on a sled. **1860** Bartlett *Dict. Amer.*, *To Tump*. Probably an Indian word... 'We tumped the deer to our cabin'. (Maine.)

tumphy (ˈtʌmfɪ). *Sc.* Also tumfie. [Cf. sumph, in same sense.] **a.** A stupid person, a blockhead. **b.** *Coal-mining.* (See quot. 1886.)

1795 A. Wilson *The Spouter* in *Poems & Lit. Prose* (1876) II. 331 The puir unfort'nate tumphy. **1823** Galt *Entail* III. iv. 41 Neither you nor that unreverent and misleart tumphy your wife. **1886** J. Barrowman *Sc. Mining Terms* 69 *Tumphy*, coaly fire-clay. **1890** J. Service *Thir Notandums* i. 3, I hear that tumfie o' a lassock nicherin' an' lauchin' in the kitchen.

ˈtump-line. *local U.S.* [Origin obscure: cf. tump *v.*[2]] See quots.

1860 Bartlett *Dict. Amer.*, *Tumpline*, a strap placed across the forehead to assist a man in carrying a pack on his back. Used in Maine, where the custom was borrowed from the Indians. **1890** W. J. Gordon *Foundry* 114 Bundles.. secured by the leather strap or 'tump' line, are slung across the chest or forehead. **1904** S. E. White *Forest* xiii, The carrying we did with the universal tump-line. It passes across the top of the head. The weight should rest on the small of the back just above the hips.

tump-tump (ˈtʌmpˈtʌmp). [Echoic.] A short sound as of water slopping without splashing, or a large ball being kicked.

1917 [see punt-about]. **1983** *Listener* 20 Oct. 26/3 The one creation that is seen in innumerable moods is the Fenland water—rising to the tump-tump of the water-pumps.

tum-tum (ˈtʌmˈtʌm), *sb.*[1] and *adv.* Also in various extended forms, as **tum-a-tum, tum-ti-tum**, etc. An imitation of the sound of a stringed instrument or instruments, esp. when monotonously played; strumming; a monotonous air. Also *attrib.*

1859 *Habits Gd. Society* xiii. 344 A.. nightmare of 'tum-tum-tiddy-tum', and waltzes *à deux temps*. **1884** *Pall Mall G.* 4 July 4/1 The thrum-thrum, ting-ting, tum-a-tum-tum of their banjoes. **1886** *Overland Monthly* Dec. 612/2 Tum! tum-ti-tum! tum! went the guitar. **1887** *Pall Mall G.* 31 Oct. 5/1 'Florid' accompaniments consisting of tum tum in the bass and scales like pianoforte finger studies in the treble. **1894** Baring-Gould *Kitty Alone* III. 79 All the harmonies in thirds and fifths, and a solemn tum-tum bass.

So **tum-tum** *v.*, *intr.* to play monotonously (or make a similar sound), to strum; hence

tum-'tummer, tum-'tumming *vbl. sb.* and *ppl. a.*

1866 A. G. MIDDLETON *Earnest* (1867) 5 The lubras.. tum-tummed on bits of stick. **1879** BARING-GOULD *Germany* II. 87 Nothing better in the musical line than pretty tum-tumming. **1892** D. SLADEN *Japs at Home* ii, A 'tum-tumming' noise is kept up. **1898** *Westm. Gaz.* 20 Apr. 3/2 Mr. Cookson..the tootler and tumtummer on old themes.

tum-tum, *sb.*[2] *Anglo-Indian.* [Derivation unascertained.] A dog-cart.

1863 TREVELYAN *Compet. Wallah* vi. (1864) 139 We.. started off..in two tumtums, or dog-carts. **1908** *Ch. Mission. Gleaner* 1 Oct. 150/1 Our low two-wheeled tum-tum..bumping and jolting along the track of dry grass.

tum-tum, *sb.*[3] *W. Indies.* [Derivation uncertain; perh. from the thumping sound made.] A West-Indian dish: see quot.

1833 CARMICHAEL *W. Indies* I. vii. 183 They often have tum-tum—made of plantains boiled quite soft, and beat in a wooden mortar,—it is eaten like a potatoe pudding. **1860** in BARTLETT *Dict. Amer.*

tum-tum ('tʌmtʌm), *sb.*[4] *joc.* [Redupl. TUM *sb.*[2]] = TUMMY.

1864 G. MEREDITH *Let.* 1 Mar. (1970) I. 245, I hope hope your tum-tum is stronger, old boy? **1894** G. DU MAURIER *Trilby* II. IV. 6 Many other unaccustomed good things, so bad for their little French tumtums. **1930** [see *icky-boo* adj. s.v. ICKY *a.* and *sb.*]. **1981** P. MALLORY *Killing Matter* ii. 22 Make some toast and coffee. My tum-tum's empty.

tumular ('tjuːmjʊlə(r)), *a.* [f. L. *tumul-us* (see TUMULUS) + -AR[1].] Pertaining to or consisting of a mound or tumulus.

1828 WEBSTER, *Tumular*, consisting in a heap; formed or being in a heap or hillock. **1851** D. WILSON *Preh. Ann.* (1863) II. IV. iv. 306 The disturbance of this tumular cemetery.

tumulary ('tjuːmjʊlərɪ), *a.* [f. as prec. + -ARY[2]; cf. F. *tumulaire* (1835 in *Dict. Acad.*).]

1. Pertaining to or placed over a tomb; sepulchral.

1758 *Monthly Rev.* 160 Adapted to the..tumulary style. **1834** L. RITCHIE *Wand. by Seine* 97 On some prostrate tumulary stone. **1869** MRS. PALLISER *Brittany* 194 The pavement [of the church] is covered with tumulary stones.

2. = TUMULAR.

18.. W. H. RUSSELL (Ogilvie), Bounded by red tumulary cliffs.

†**'tumulate,** *ppl. a. Obs.* Also 5 -ylat, 6 -ylate, -ulat. [f. L. *tumulāt-us*, pa. pple. of *tumulāre* to bury, f. *tumulus*: see TUMULUS and -ATE[2].] Buried, entombed. (Const. as *pa. pple.*)

1455 *Rolls of Parlt.* V. 308/1 The..Erle,..is..tumylat and restyng within the Priory. **1513** BRADSHAW *St. Werburge* II. 659 The body of Saynt Oswalde..she translate ..to Gloucetur, there to be tumulate. *c* **1536** in Ellis *Orig. Lett.* Ser. III. III. 18 Many of them be there tumulate and buryed.

tumulate ('tjuːmjʊleɪt), *v. rare.* [f. ppl. stem. of L. *tumulāre* to bury: see prec. and -ATE[3].] *trans.* To bury, entomb.

1623 COCKERAM, *Tumulate*, to enterre, to bury. **1656** in BLOUNT *Glossogr.* **1866** J. B. ROSE tr. *Ovid's Fasti* III. 592 Dido despondent, on the funeral pyre,..Consumed, inurned, and tumulated.

[**tumulate,** *v.* (in J. with quot. from Boyle, and in Richardson and later Dicts. with quot. from Wilkins), error for TUMULTUATE.]

tumulation (tjuːmjʊ'leɪʃən). *rare.* [f. L. *tumulā-re* to bury + -TION.] Burying, interment; *spec.* interment in a tumulus or grave-mound.

1623 COCKERAM, *Tumulation*, a burying or enterring. **1827** J. ANDERSON *Ess. St. Soc. & Knowl. Highl.* 138 Burning before tumulation seems to have succeeded simple interment.

tumuli, pl. of TUMULUS.

†**'tumulose,** *a. Obs. rare*[−0]. [ad. L. *tumulōs-us* (Sallust), f. *tumulus*, TUMULUS: see -OSE.] (See quot.) Hence †**tumu'losity** (*obs. rare*[−0]).

1727 BAILEY vol. II, *Tumulose* (*tumulōsus*, L.), full of little Hills or Knops. *Tumulosity* (*tumulōsitās*), Hilliness.

tumulous ('tjuːmjʊləs), *a. rare.* [f. L. *tumul-us*, TUMULUS + -OUS: cf. prec.] **a.** = prec. (*rare*[−0]). **b.** Forming a tumulus; tumular.

1828 WEBSTER, *Tumulous*, full of hills. **1897** *Daily News* 21 Sept. 8/3 Parcels built up in tumulous columns, which rise from the floor nearly up to the ceiling.

tumult ('tjuːmʌlt), *sb.* Also 5-6 -te. [ad. L. *tumultus* (*u*-stem), f. *tumēre* to swell: cf. F. *tumulte* (12th c. in Godef. *Compl.*; in OF. also *temulte*, 1201 in Hatz.-Darm).]

1. Commotion of a multitude, usually with confused speech or uproar; public disturbance; disorderly or riotous proceeding.

1412-20 LYDG. *Chron. Troy* II. 5235 Al tumulte stinted, and silence Was þoruȝ þe pres, to ȝif hym audyence. **1562** *Reg. Privy Council Scot.* I. 209 Ane seditious persone and rasar of tumult. **1615** G. SANDYS *Trav.* 8 To avoid occasions of tumult. *a* **1718** PRIOR *Henry & Emma* 332 When the loud Tumult speaks the Battel nigh. **1838** LYTTON *Leila* II. i, The tumult of the Camp was to him but a holiday exhibition.

b. (with *pl.*) An instance of this; a popular commotion or disturbance; a riot, an insurrection.

1560 DAUS tr. *Sleidane's Comm.* 22 b, It is like to styre vp such tumultes in Germany. **1641** EVELYN *Diary* 8 Oct., The late tumults in Belgia. **1775** JOHNSON *Tax. no Tyr.* 68 The tumults of a conflagration. **1838** THIRLWALL *Greece* II. xii. 155 A tumult..in which the populace set fire to Milo's house.

†**c.** *transf.* A disorderly crowd, a mob. *rare.*

1628 GAULE *Pract. The.* (1629) 189 The Tumult shall know [that, etc.]. **1648** *Eikon Bas.* vi. 38 To see the barbarous rudenesse of those Tumults who resolved they would take the boldnesse to demand any thing.

2. *gen.* Commotion, agitation, disturbance; disorderly or noisy movement or action. Also *pl.*

1580 SIDNEY *Ps.* XXXV. viii, Oh! on my soul let not these tumults hitt. **1591** SHAKS. *1 Hen. VI*, I. iv. 98 It Thunders and Lightens... What tumult's in the Heauens? **1662** CHARLETON *Myst. Vintners* (1675) 178 The tumult will..be recomposed, the liquor refined. **1781** COWPER *Retirement* 176 Some..are averse to noise And hate the tumult half the world enjoys. **1844** DISRAELI *Coningsby* I. iii, His heart beat with tumult. **1846** TRENCH *Mirac.* vi. (1862) 190 The fiercest tumult of the elements allays itself at last.

3. *fig.* Great disturbance or agitation of mind or feeling; confused and violent emotion.

[**1595** SHAKS. *John* IV. ii. 247 Hostilitie, and ciuill tumult reignes Betweene my conscience and my Cosins death.] **1663** BP. PATRICK *Parab. Pilgr.* xxxi. (1687) 378 Such contrary passions..I cannot overcome..without suffering a great tumult and disorder. **1711** ADDISON *Spect.* No. 164 ¶1 A long Tumult of Passions which naturally rise in a Lover's Heart. **1777** BURKE *Corr.* (1844) II. 199 The wild tumult of joy that the news..caused. **1844** THIRLWALL *Greece* VIII. lx. 31 A tumult of grief and indignation.

'tumult, *v.* [f. prec.]

1. *intr.* To make a tumult, commotion, or disturbance; to raise an insurrection, to riot. ? *Obs.*

1570 LEVINS *Manip.* 187/42 To Tumulte, *tumultuare.* **1616** HAYWARD *Sanct. Troub. Soul* II. To Rdr. ¶2 The sensuall powers did tumult, and breake loose. **1653** MILTON *Paraphr. Ps. ii.* 1 Why do the Gentiles tumult..? **1699** R. L'ESTRANGE *Erasm. Colloq.* (1725) 248 Monks run up and down,..the Rabble tumult; Erasmus writes Colloquies. **1864** [see *tumulting* below].

2. *trans.* To put into tumult; to agitate violently.

1819 'B. CORNWALL' *Dram. Scenes, Rape Proserpine* i, My heart..seems tumulted By some delicious passion. *a* **1851** MOIR *To wounded Ptarmigan* iv, The snortng whale..In its anger tumults ocean.

Hence **'tumulting** *vbl. sb.*; also †**'tumulter**, one who stirs up a tumult, a rioter (*obs.*).

1584 HORSEY *Trav.* (Hakl. Soc.) App. 270 To subdue the *tumulters and mainteine quietnes. **1670** MILTON *Hist. Eng.* II. Wks. (1847) 497/1 He..punished the tumulters. **1658** CROMWELL *Sp.* 4 Feb. in Carlyle *Lett. & Sp.* (1871) V. 130 To stir up the people of this town into a *tumulting. **1864** CARLYLE *Fredk. Gt.* XVII. ii. IV. 519 Tired of..fighting and tumulting.

tumultuarily (tjuː'mʌltjuːərɪlɪ), *adv.* [f. TUMULTUARY + -LY[2].] In a tumultuary manner.

1. Hastily and without order; irregularly, confusedly, unsystematically, at random.

1590 SIR J. SMYTH *Disc. Weapons* Ded. 5 Ciuill warres,.. maintained..tumultuarilie..by spoyle, sedition, passion, and faction. **1613-18** DANIEL *Coll. Hist. Eng.* (1626) 5 The ..souldiers..tumultuarilie proclaimed Emperour one Marcus. **1676** EVELYN in Aubrey *Nat. Hist. Surrey* (1719) I. Pref. 9, I have set things down tumultuarily, as they came into my..thoughts. **1695** H. DODWELL *Def. Vind. Deprived Bps.* 1 More hastily and tumultuarily laid together.

2. With tumult or disturbance; tumultuously.

1609 DANIEL *Civ. Wars* I. xii. *margin*, Stephen.. contendes with Maude the Empresse for the succession, and raigned tumultuarily 18 yeares and 10 monethes. **1647** JER. TAYLOR *Lib. Proph.* Ep. Ded. 20 Arrius behav'd himselfe so seditiously and tumultuarily. **1682** T. FLATMAN *Heraclitus Ridens* No. 74 (1713) II. 203 Those so tumultuarily assembled and so outragious.

So **tu'multuariness**, the quality of being tumultuary; in quots., disposition to tumult.

1648 *Eikon Bas.* xvii. 148 The tumultuariness of People. **1653** GAUDEN *Hierasp.* 24 Tumultuariness, faction, and sedition.

tumultuarious (tjuːmʌltjuː'ɛərɪəs), *a. rare*[−1]. [f. as next + -OUS.] = next, 2.

1895 E. F. M. BENECKE tr. *Comparetti's Virgil in Mid. Ages* xiv, Neither a tumultuarious improvisation nor a frigid versification.

tumultuary (tjuː'mʌltjuːərɪ), *a.* (*sb.*) [ad. L. *tumultuāri-us* of or belonging to hurry or tumult, raised hastily (as troops), f. *tumultus* TUMULT: see -ARY[1]; cf. F. *tumultuaire.*]

1. Of troops: Gathered hastily and promiscuously, without order or system; irregular, undisciplined. Also of warfare, etc. carried on by such troops, or in an irregular way.

1590 SIR J. SMYTH *Disc. Weapons* Ded. 2 b, The tumultuarie and disordered wars of the Lowe Countries. **1600** HOLLAND *Livy* VIII. ii. 289 A tumultuarie armie in great hast levied..out of all quarters. **1759** ROBERTSON *Hist. Scot.* (1817) I. II. 396 With tumultuary..violence, they fell upon the churches. **1841** ELPHINSTONE *Hist. Ind.* II. VII. iv. 165 A tumultuary attack, which was repelled by the garrison.

2. Hurriedly done; irregular, disorderly, confused; haphazard, unsystematic, random.

1609 HOLLAND *Amm. Marcell.* 245 In hast and in tumultuarie manner. **1613-18** DANIEL *Coll. Hist. Eng.* (1626) 22 Content with a tumultuarie learning. *a* **1638** MEDE *Wks.* (1672) 772 So tumultuary and confused a Discourse. **1771** MACPHERSON *Introd. Hist. Gt. Brit.* 235 Their resolutions must..have been tumultuary and precipitate. **1843** CHURCH *St. Anselm & Hen. I*, ¶4 The tumultuary beginnings of society. **1879** FARRAR *St. Paul* I. 501 Ashamed of their tumultuary injustice.

†**b.** Of a person: Acting, writing, or speaking hastily and at random; unsystematic, disorderly. *Obs.*

1618 BOLTON *Florus* To Rdr., With mathematicall Stadius, Florus is but a tumultuary author. **1644** BULWER *Chiron.* Prælud., Those upstart and tumultuarie Oratours. **1648** *Eikon Bas.* vi. 40 Whatever tumultuary Patrons shall project.

3. Disposed to, marked by, or of the nature of tumult; tumultuous, turbulent.

1650 HOWELL *Giraffi's Rev. Naples* I. 42 Against the will of a tumultuary people. **1661** GLANVILL *Van. Dogm.* 13 The tumultuary disorders of our passions. **1664** POWER *Exp. Philos.* Pref., The..tumultuary motion of the Atoms. **1705** tr. *Bosman's Guinea* 229 This confused Tumultuary Noise. **1834** *Tait's Mag.* I. 404/1 The reign of Governor King.. was a tumultuary period. **1876** GEO. ELIOT *Dan. Der.* VIII. lviii, Struggling with a tumultuary crowd of thoughts.

B. *sb.* in *pl.* Tumultuary forces: see 1.

1654 EARL MONM. tr. *Bentivoglio's Warrs Flanders* 76 The Tumultuaries expecting..better progress. **1830** JAMES DARNLEY xxxiv, The leader of the tumultuaries.

tumultuate (tjuː'mʌltjuːeɪt), *v.* Now *rare.* [f. ppl. stem of L. *tumultuārī* to make a bustle or disturbance: see -ATE[3].]

1. *intr.* To stir up a tumult; to make a disturbance or commotion; to become or be tumultuous, turbulent, agitated, or restless.

1611 [see *tumultuating* below]. **1616** JAS. I *Sp. Star-Chamb.* 20 June 35 Acquiesce in the Iudgement, and doe not tumultuate against it. **1671** R. BOHUN *Wind* 27 Noise of Winds, that..tumultuate. *a* **1734** NORTH *Exam.* I. ii. §44. (1740) 51 To afflict the poor People..to make them restless and apt to tumultuate. **1860** W. ARNOT *Laws fr. Heaven* 268 The dread of evil and the desire of good tumultuate and struggle for the mastery in a human breast.

2. *trans.* To excite to tumult, put into a state of tumult, make tumultuous; to disorder or disturb violently.

1616 JAS. I *Sp. Star-Cham.* 20 June 44 Tumultuating the countrey. **1661** R. L'ESTRANGE *Interest Mistaken* Ded. 2 Their Ayme being to Tumultuate the People. **1768** [W. DONALDSON] *Life Sir B. Sapskull* II. Ded. 3 The street.. was tumultuated with the loud roar of.. raps, perpetually thundering at my..door! **1820** *Blackw. Mag.* VII. 316 The feelings that tumultuate the heart of a father.

Hence **tu'multuating** *vbl. sb.* and *ppl. a.*

1611 SPEED *Hist. Gt. Brit.* IX. viii. (1623) 574 Hauing let loose many tumultuating Spirits. **1642** HALES *Gold. Rem.*, *Tract on Schism* (1673) 5 Ecclesiastical stories.., of which the greatest [part] consists of factionating and tumultuating of great and potent Bishops. **1815** J. LOVE *Lett.* (1840) 367 Whatever be the tumultuating of flesh and blood. **1854** MAR. HARLAND *Alone* xxxi, Tumultuating passions were stilled into a calm, delicious ecstasy.

tumultuation (tjuːmʌltjuː'eɪʃən), Now *rare.* [ad. L. *tumultuātiōn-e*, n. of action from *tumultuārī*: see prec. and -ATION. Cf. OF. *tumultuation* (13th c.).] The action of making a tumult; a condition of tumult; commotion, disturbance, agitation.

c **1475** *Harl. Contn. Higden* (Rolls) VIII. 454 A grete tumultuacion and murmur..amonge the peple. **1559** KENNEDY *Let. to Willock* in *Wodrow Soc. Misc.* (1844) 270. I desire nolder tumultuatioun, cummyr, nor stryfe. **1631** R. H. *Arraignm. Whole Creature* xviii. 326 The tumultuations ..of our inordinate affections. **1786** G. FRAZER *Dove's Flight to Thicket* 71 The wicked have great tumultuations in their minds. **1883** J. PARKER *Tyne Ch.* 109 The tumultuations of His tabernacle.

tumultuous (tjuː'mʌltjuːəs), *a.* Also 6 -eous, 7 -ious. [ad. OF. *tumultuous*, F. *tumultueux*, ad. L. *tumultuōs-us* full of tumult, bustle, or confusion: f. *tumultu-s* TUMULT: see -OUS.]

1. Full of tumult or commotion; marked by confusion and uproar; disorderly and noisy; violent and clamorous; turbulent.

a **1548** HALL *Chron., Edw. IV* 223 Suche, as in the last tumulteous busines, toke part with..Fauconbrige. **1553** BRENDE *Q. Curtius* x. 210 b, They..disturbed his tale with their tumultuous crye. **1638** SIR T. HERBERT *Trav.* (ed. 2) 274 After 30 yeeres tumultuous reigne. **1739** WESLEY *Wks.* (1830) I. 214, I do indeed go out into the highways and hedges, but not in a tumultuous manner. **1807** WORDSW. *White Doe* II. 62 Tumultuous noises filled the hall. **1840** HAWTHORNE *Biog. Sk. Sir W. Pepperrell* (1879) 193 The tumultuous advance of the conquering army. **1881** JOWETT *Thucyd.* I. 160 Embarking in tumultuous haste.

†**b.** Tending to excite tumult; seditious. *Obs.*

1619 [implied in TUMULTUOUSNESS]. **1623** COCKERAM, *Tumultuous*, seditious, full of trouble. **1651** HOBBES *Leviath.* II. xxii. 122 An unlawfull, and tumultuous designe. **1679** LUTTRELL *Brief Rel.* (1857) I. 27 Tumultuous and seditious petitions.

†**c.** Causing tumult; disturbing, disquieting. *Obs. rare.*

1604 R. Cawdrey *Table Alph.*, *Tumultuous*, troublous, disturbing or disquieting. **1614** Raleigh *Hist. World* iv. vi. §3 The tumultuous newes of Lysimachus his victories.

2. Making a tumult or commotion; acting in a disorderly and noisy way; turbulent, riotous.

1576 Fleming *Panopl. Epist.* 49 He might..fortifie, with his ayde,..those tumultuous villaines. **1635** Jackson *Creed* viii. xvii. §6 The promised Prince of peace..should not be sought amongst the tumultuous hosts of warre. *a* **1718** Prior *1st Hymn Callimachus* 59 The fierce Curetes..trod tumultuous Their Mystic Dance. **1868** E. Edwards *Ralegh* I. xxi. 471 His house was beset by a tumultuous crowd.

3. Of physical actions or agents: Marked by disorderly commotion; acting or moving irregularly and violently; confusedly agitated; tempestuous.

1667 Milton *P. L.* ii. 936 The strong rebuff of som tumultuous cloud Instinct with Fire. **1794** G. Adams *Nat. & Exp. Philos.* I. ix. 335 A sudden and very tumultuous ebullition ensued. **1843** R. J. Graves *Syst. Clin. Med.* ix. 104 The action of the heart tumultuous. **1856** Kane *Arct. Expl.* I. ix. 97 A roaring and tumultuous river. **1870** Morris *Earthly Par.* (1871) IV. 124 The far-off rooks' sweet tumultuous voice.

4. *fig.* of, or in reference to, emotion or thought.

1667 Milton *P. L.* iv. 16 His dire attempt, which nigh the birth Now rowling, boiles in his tumultuous brest. **1719** De Foe *Crusoe* (1840) II. iii. 57 He..found his thoughts tumultuous. **1772** Priestley *Inst. Relig.* (1782) II. 102 Tumultuous joy. **1822–56** De Quincey *Confess.* Wks. 1897 III. 446 A tumultuous dream.

tu'multuously, *adv.* [f. prec. + -ly[2].] In a tumultuous manner; with tumult or commotion; with confusion and uproar; riotously.

1548 Udall, etc. *Erasm. Par. Matt.* xii. 53 b, He shall not do this tumultuously or violently. For he shall not chide, nor ..crye oute. **1617** Moryson *Itin.* iii. 27 If they tumultiously revenge thy wrong. *a* **1768** Abp. Secker *Serm.* (1771) V. xviii. 431 Death..suddenly and tumultuously inflicted. **1834** L. Ritchie *Wand. by Seine* 166 The clang of innumerable church-bells comes tumultuously on the breeze. **1857** Miller *Elem. Chem.* (1862) III. 118 The reaction..is apt to become and tumultuously violent.

†**b.** Seditiously: cf. prec. 1 b. *Obs.*

1682 *Addr. Lond. Freemen* in *Lond. Gaz.* No. 1738/2 Being Popishly and Tumultuously Inclined.

†**c.** Hurriedly and irregularly; in a hurry, without order or system: cf. tumultuarily 1. *Obs.*

1597 Hooker *Eccl. Pol.* v. lxxvi. §6 They attempted tumultuously they saw not what. **1726** Leoni tr. *Alberti's Archit.* II. 8/2 The Wall of Athens..was built so tumultuously that they even threw into it some of the Statues.

tu'multuousness. [f. as prec. + -ness.] The quality or state of being tumultuous or disturbed; †in quot. 1619, seditiousness (*obs.*).

1619 Hieron *Wks.* II. 442 Swaggering, and tumultuousnesse, and carelesnesse. **1647** Trapp *Comm. Matt.* iv. 19 The world is compared to the sea, for its.. tumultuousness. **1822** De Quincey *Confess.* 39 The tumultuousness of my dreams. **1899** *Allbutt's Syst. Med.* VII. 159 The tumultuousness of the movements.

‖**tumulus** ('tju:mjʊləs). Pl. tumuli (-laɪ). [Derivative (? dim.) from root *tum-* of *tumē-re* to swell, *tumor*, etc.] An ancient sepulchral mound, a barrow (barrow *sb.*[1] 3).

[**1398** Trevisa *Barth. De P.R.* xiv. xlv. (Bodl. MS.), A downe [is] lower þan an hille..and hatte *tumulus*, as it were swelling londe.] **1686** Plot *Staffordsh.* 403 Not the only signe of Roman tumuli. **1765** J. Bartram *Jrnl.* 26 Dec., in W. Stork *Acc. E. Florida* (1766) 7 A middling sized Indian tumulus. **1794** Sullivan *View Nat.* IV. 393 The tumuli, and the other repositories of the dead,..discovered in the.. deserts of the north. **1853** Felton *Fam. Lett.* xxx. (1865) 264 Leonidas and his Three Hundred..lie beneath yonder tumulus. **1863** Lyell *Antiq. Man* 15 Tumuli of the stone period.

tumyde, obs. form of tumid.

tun (tʌn), *sb.* Forms: α. 1–7 tunne, 4 toun, 4–5 towne, 4–6 toune, 4, 7–8 tunn, 5–6 towne, 5–7 tune, *Sc.* tonn(e, 6 tonne, 4– tun. β. 3–7 tonne, 5–6 tonn, tone, 5–8 ton, 6 toon. See also ton[1]. [OE. *tunne*, wk. fem., ME. *tunne*, later *tonne*; cogn. with OFris. *tunne*, *tonne*, OLG. **tunna* (MLG., LG. *tunne* (*tünne*)), MDu. *tonne* (Du. *ton*), OHG. *tunna* (MHG. *tunne*, Ger. *tonne*); late ON. *tunna* (Sw. *tunna*, mod.Norw. *tunna*, *tynna*, MDu. *tunde*, Da. *tønde*); also med.L. *tunna* (9th c. in Cassel Gloss.), OF. *tonne*, Pr. *tona* (in other Rom. langs. only in derivative forms: see tonnel, tunnel); also MIr., Ir. and Gael. *tunna*. Origin uncertain; app. not orig. Latin or Romanic.

As the OHG. retains initial *t* it must have been adopted (from LG. or med.L.) after the HG. sound shifting, i.e. after 700. Some suggest a Celtic source, viz. OIr. *toun* hide, skin, so that the original sense would be 'wine-skin'; but the MIr. *tunna* looks like an adopted word. At present it can only be said that the word appears to be as old or older in the LG. group of langs., including OE., than anywhere else; its occurrence in the Corpus Gloss *c* 725 is app. the earliest trace of the word in any lang. The later ME. spelling *tonne* was perh. after F., but prob. largely due to the scribal fashion of writing *o* for *u*, in contiguity to *m*, *n*, *v*, etc., as in *son*, *tongue*, *honey*, *come*, *some*, *above*, *love* etc. From *c* 1688 the two forms *tun* and *ton* have been differentiated in use: see ton[1].]

1. A large cask or barrel, usually for liquids, esp. wine, ale, or beer, or for various provisions. Now less common than *cask*.

α. *c* **725** *Corpus Gloss.* (Hessels) C 945 *Cuba*, tunne. **791–6** in Birch *Cart. Sax.* I. 380 Twa tunnan fulle hlutres aloð. *c* **1205** Lay. 14957 Rouuenne eode to are tunne þer wes idon in þes kinges deoreste win. *c* **1325** *Gloss. W. de Bibbesw.* in Wright *Voc.* 160 Cerveyse en tonne [*gloss* a toune]. **1387** Trevisa *Higden* (Rolls) III. 309 He [Diogenes] torned þe mouth of his toun toward þe souþ in colde tyme and toward þe norþ in somer tyme. *c* **1425** *Voc.* in Wr.-Wülcker 658/20 *Hoc dolium*, towne. *c* **1475** *Pict. Voc.* ibid. 770/36 *Hoc dolium*, a tune. *a* **1529** Skelton *El. Rummyng* 194 In the ale tunnes. **1644** Evelyn *Diary* 6 June, The Abbot's Palace, where we were shew'd a vast Tun (as big as that at Heidelberg). **1717** Prior *Alma* iii. 426 L'Avare..Strikes not the present Tun, for fear The Vintage should be bad next Year. **1819** Keats *Lamia* ii. 188 Wine Came from the gloomy tun.

β. **1340** *Ayenb.* 35 Tonnen mid wyn. *c* **1400** *Laud Troy Bk.* 4677 Grete tonnes ful of flour. *c* **1440** *Gesta Rom.* lxi. 252 (Harl. MS.) Do gete me..a ler tonne. **1562** J. Heywood *Prov. & Epigr.* (1867) 158 He hath fed till he is as full as a toon. **1577** B. Googe *Heresbach's Husb.* 11 Tonnes..for Wine; Beere..and suche like.

†**b.** A large vessel in general; a tub or vat; a chest. *Obs.*

α. *c* **1205** Lay. 6079 Heo makeden ane tunne of golde and of ȝimme. *a* **1225** *St. Marher.* 17 Salomon the wise.. bitunde us in ane tunne. *a* **1300** *Cursor M.* 21042 (Cott.) Þat Imperur wend [John] to mat In a tun was welland hat. *a* **1400–50** *Alexander* 1807 He tellis quyche a tunne of tresoure he hauys. **1577** B. Googe *Heresbach's Husb.* 11 Wherefore serueth that great Tounne? To water the Barly in. **1599** Shaks. *Hen. V*, i. ii. 255. **1601** Holland *Pliny* iii. vi. I. 61 Earthen vessels, as tunnes and such like.

β. *c* **1290** *S. Eng. Leg.* I. 401/315 Þis tormentores nomen þis guode kniȝht and is sones and is wif, And duden heom is ane tonne of bras,..Gret fuyr huy þare-aboute maden. *c* **1330** R. Brunne *Chron. Wace* (Rolls) 2246 Tonnes of bras wiþ queynte þynges þat make þe water euere hot. *a* **1450** Myrc *Festial* 31 Domician..send aftyr Ion, and made put hym yn a brasyn tonne full of oyle. *c* **1450** *Brut* ccxliv. 374 Yn scorne & despite he [the Dauphin] sent to hym [Henry V] a tonne fulle of teneys-ballis. **1567** *Wills & Inv. N.C.* (Surtees) I. 266 A tonning tubb, a tonn for bread.

c. *Brewing.* A mashing-vat (*mash-tun*) or fermenting-vat (*gyle-tun*).

1713 [see *mash-tun* s.v. mash *sb.*[1] 5]. **1743** [see *gyle-tun* s.v. gyle 4]. **1815** J. Smith *Panorama Sc. & Art* II. 569 The mash-tun is shallow in proportion to its diameter... When the mashing is completed, the tun is covered, to prevent the escape of heat. **1830** M. Donovan *Dom. Econ.* I. 221 He urges it to a tumultuous effervescence,..threatening the overflow of the tun.

d. *fig.* or in figurative allusion.

α. **1447** Bokenham *Seyntys* (Roxb.) 58 Of annes wombe sprange ye oyle tunne Of gracyous helthe to alle that beth seke. **1596** Shaks. *1 Hen. IV*, ii. iv. 493 A Deuill..in the likenesse of a fat old Man; a Tunne of Man is thy Companion. **1603** Knolles *Hist. Turks* (1638) 148 In Iupiter's court no man might drinke of the tun of blisse, but that he must taste also of the tun of wo. *a* **1704** T. Brown *Walk round London* (1709) 25 Such a Tun of Female Fat [a very fat woman]. **1909** *Remin. Lady Wake* xv. 168 His enormous tun of a body.

β. **1340** *Ayenb.* 247 In-to þe greate tauerne, huer þe tonne is betake, þet is ine þe liue eurelestinde. *c* **1485** *Digby Myst.* (1882) i. 515 Tonne of tranquylyte, to yeve hem drynke that han thrustyd sore. **1513** Douglas *Æneis* i. Prol. 59 All man purches drink at thi sugurat tone.

2. A cask of definite capacity; hence, a measure of capacity for wine and other liquids (formerly also for other commodities), usually equivalent to 2 pipes or 4 hogsheads, containing 252 old wine-gallons.

α. *c* **1440** *Jacob's Well* 47 He hadde a vyneȝerd, þe whiche, ȝere be ȝere, bare hym x. tunne of wyn. and euery ȝere he payed þe tenthe tunne of wyn to tythe. **1504** *Acc. Ld. High Treas. Scot.* II. 277 For xx twn of plaistir. **1535** in Weaver *Wells Wills* (1890) 90 A tunne of leade or the value thereof. **1583** *Rates of Custome Ho.* Hj, What number of all kinde of dry French wares make a Tun..Wol cardes,..Two C. dosen. Playing cardes,..Fiftie groce. Canuas..ii. M. vi. c. elles. **1655** *Acts Parlt. Scotl.* VI. ii. 829/1 Two Buts, two Pipes, four Hogsheads..., six Tierces, three Punchions.., and eight Quarter-Casks, shal be accounted..for a Tun. **1674** *Reg. Privy Council Scot.* Ser. iii. IV. 275 Importation of brandie upon payment of ten lib. sterling per tune for custome. **1778** Pennant *Tour Wales* (1883) I. 54 The well ..is found to fling out about twenty one tuns of water in a minute. **1898** F. T. Bullen *Cruise Cachalot* 33 At the rate of £40 per tun or £4 per barrel.

β. *c* **1400** *Gamelyn* 316 Fyue tonne of wyn. **1526** Tindale *Luke* xvi. 6 A hondred tonnes of oyle. **1654** Graham *Glencairn's Exp.* in *Misc. Scot.* (1819) IV. 69 She was loaded with near forty tons of French wine. **1793** Nelson in Nicolas *Disp.* (1845) I. 352 Five hundred tons of Wine.

†**b.** *tun of gold*: 100,000 guilders, florins, etc. [transl. the corresponding use of *tonne* in G., obs. Du., etc.] *Obs.*

1603 Knolles *Hist. Turks* (1621) 1052 Promising..to lend him a tunne of gold to pay them their wages. **1666** *Lond. Gaz.* No. 28/2 Holland and Zealand..are like to carry it in favour to the East-India Company, upon payment to be made by them of 12 Tuns of Gold, as they count here, that is, about 120000 *l.* sterling. **1680** C. Nesse *Church Hist.* 501 To let about nine tun of gold go yearly hence to Rome. **1683** *Lond. Gaz.* No. 1789/1 The King [of Sweden]..demanded of them a Supply of 16 Tun of Gold, that is 16 hundred thousand Florins.

3. A measure of capacity or weight: see ton[1] 3, 4.

4. 'A chimney, esp. the upper part above the roof of a house; a chimney-pot' (*Eng. Dial. Dict.*). Now *dial.*

1463 *Bury Wills* (Camden) 20 My newe hous with the iij. tunnys of chemeneyis. **1596** Harington *Metam. Ajax* 89 The tuns..drawing up the aire as a chimney doth smoke. **1859** Parker *Dom. Archit.* III. ii. 37 *note*, Chimney shafts are still called tuns in some districts. **1905** in *Eng. Dial. Dict.* in various dialects of south and S.W.

†**5.** Name of a prison in Cornhill, London. *Obs.*

a **1500** in Arnolde *Chron.* (1811) 92 Sette in the tonne in Cornhyll for his dishoneste. **1533** *Fabyan's Chron.* vii. 64 b/2 This yere..certayne persones of London brake vp the tunne [*so edd.* 1542, 1559; *ed.* 1516 towre] in the warde of Cornhyll. **1598** Stow *Surv.* (1603) 189 The Tunne upon Cornehill, because the same was builded somewhat in fashion of a Tunne standing on the one ende.

6. A kind of cup or small drinking vessel.

1555 in Hakluyt *Voy.* (1599) I. 263 A great chamber, where stood many small tunnes, pailes, bowles, and pots of siluer,..all parsel gilt. **1634** Brereton *Trav.* (Chetham Soc.) 6 The young children, girls, walked all the Sabbath in the afternoon, with cups or tuns in their hands. [The name is still applied at Magdalen College, Oxford, to silver drinking cups, holding a third of a quart, some of which are dated 1657 and 1663.]

7. †**a.** *sea tun*, a name for a seal (the animal). *Obs.*

1601 Holland *Pliny* xxxii. xi. II. 451 Sea Men and Women,..Sea Tuns or Pipes. **1672** Josselyn *New Eng. Rarities* 31 A Catalogue of Fish,..Sea Tun.

b. *Conch.* = *tun-shell*: see 8.

1837 [see *partridge-tun* s.v. partridge 5]. **1861** P. P. Carpenter in *Rep. Smithsonian Instit.* 1860, 184 The Tuns are nearly related to the Helmets, both in animal and shell.

8. *attrib.* and *Comb.*, as *tun* †*board*, *hole*, *hoop*, *stave*; *tun-like*; **tun-back**, name of a breed of pigs; **tun-butt** (in quot. applied *fig.* to a very corpulent person); † **tun form**, *Geom.* the form of a tun; an ellipsoid or similar figure; **tun-glass**, ? a barrel-shaped drinking-glass; † **tun-great** *a.*, as thick as a tun or cask; † **tun-grown** *a.*, grown as big as a tun, very corpulent; † **tun-gutted** *a.* = tunbellied; **tun liquor** (see quot.); **tun-man**, a man who attends to a tun (1 c) in brewing; **tun-pail**, a kind of funnel used in brewing (cf. tun-dish); **tun-room**, a room in a brewery in which a tun (1 c) is kept; **tun-shell**, *Conch.* a shell of the genus *Dolium* (*Cent. Dict.* 1891); † **tun-silver** (*Sc. Obs.*), a duty levied upon casks of merchandise; **tun-tub**, = sense 1 c. See also tun-bellied, etc.; also *tun tight* (*ton tight*) s.v. tight *a.* 14.

1778 [W. Marshall] *Minutes Agric.* 15 Oct. an. 1776, A fine farrow of the large black-spotted *tun-backs. **1558** in Feuillerat *Revels Q. Eliz.* (1908) 99 For furnysshinge of *tunbborde and other parties of the banketinge howse at westmynster. **1829** Clapperton *Jrnl. Africa* iv. 112 A walking *tun-butt for a queen! **1551** Recorde *Pathw. Knowl.* i. Defin., If it be lyke..a circle pressed in length, and bothe endes lyke bygge, then is it called a *tunne forme. *a* **1843** Southey *Comm.-pl. Bk.* IV. 575 Always a *tun-glass standing by him. *c* **1386** Chaucer *Knt.'s T.* 1136 Euery pyler..Was *tonne greet. **1628** Prynne *Brief Survay* 71 Like so many Epicures, or *Tonne growne Abbylubbers. **1607** *Lingua* iii. ii. E iv, *Tun-gutted drones. **1657** Austen *Fruit Trees* i. 77 Take Clay and lay it round about the *Tunne hole. **1510** in *10th Rep. Hist. MSS. Comm.* App. v. 394 Towe *toune hopis for a penye. **1498** *Aberdeen Regr.* (1844) 426 Tunnys and vyther gudis *tunlyk. *a* **1813** A. Wilson *Prayer to Love* Poet. Wks. (1846) 168 Cits with tun-like bellies, Melted down almost to jellies. **1853** Ure *Dict. Arts* i. 57 The mother liquor of the 'rock alum' is called '*tun liquor'. **1743** *Lond. & Country Brew.* iii. (ed. 2) 221 The *Tun-man..ambitious to supplant the Workman Brewer. **1833** Loudon *Encycl. Archit.* §1318 Racking-can, *tun-pail. **1870** J. Fleet in *Eng. Mech.* 18 Feb. 561/1 Insert a tunpail and strainer. **1826** *Art Brewing* (ed. 2) 40 In cold weather keep the *tun-room closed. **1600** *Reg. Mag. Sig. Scot.* 377/2 Levare..doliorum pecunias (*lie *tun-silver*). **1398** Trevisa *Barth. De P.R.* xix. cxxviii. (1495) 934 Bordes and *tonne staues. **1842** J. Aiton *Domest. Econ.* (1857) 330 A *tun-tub..to put the ale into to work, the mash-tub, as we shall see, serving as a tun-tub for the small beer.

tun, *v.* Forms: see prec. sb. [f. prec.]

1. *trans.* To put into or store in a tun or tuns. Often with *up*, more rarely *in*; also *absol.*

α. *c* **1430** *Pilgr. Lyf Manhode* iii. xliii. (1869) 158 Þe fonelle ..aualeth and tunneth þe wyn. *c* **1440** *Promp. Parv.* 506/1 Tunnon, or put drynke or other thynge yn a tunne. *a* **1533** Ld. Berners *Gold. Bk. M. Aurel.* (1546) C cij, Whan the newe wine is tunned. **1638** *MS. Min. Archdeaconry of Essex* lf. 18 b, He did brew on a Satterday and tunne vpon the Sunday morneing. **1696** *Phil. Trans.* XIX. 274 When they [Figs] were pulled off and Tunned up, to be sent beyond Seas. **1766** Entick *London* (1776) I. 410 Merchandize.., to be packed, tunned, piped, barrelled. **1843** *Jrnl. R. Agric. Soc.* IV. ii. 489 To carry and tun the cider.

β. **1426** Lydg. *De Guil. Pilgr.* 12987 Thys phonel Wyth wych my wynes I vp tonne. **1477** J. Paston in *P. Lett.* III. 175, I shall do tonnen in to your place a doseyn ale. **1580** Hollyband *Treas. Fr. Tong*, *Entonner*, to tonne wine, or poure it into tonnes.

b. *fig.* To put or store as in a cask; *spec.* to drink to excess, to swill oneself with. Also *absol.*

α. **1589** Nashe *Anat. Absurd.* 20 These Bussards thinke knowledge a burthen, tapping it before they haue halfe tunde it. **1595** R. Hasleton *Strange & Wonderf. Things* in Arb. *Garner* VIII. 384 Pouring water through a cane which was in my mouth..until they had tunned in such quantity as was not tolerable. **1628** Feltham *Resolves* ii. [i.] lxxxiv. 241

Whose delights are only to tunne in. **1761** STERNE *Tr. Shandy* III. xx, They [brain-cells] might continue to be injected and tunn'd into. **1841** *Fraser's Mag.* XXV. 514 He used to tun down beer.. during dinner.

β. **1597–8** BP. HALL *Sat.* V. ii. 101 The swolne bezell.. That tonnes in gallons to his bursten panch.

c. (See quot.)

1781 P. BECKFORD *Hunting* (1802) 337 Poachers.. catch the young foxes in trenches dug at the mouth of the hole, which I believe they call tunning them.

2. To fill as, or like, a tun or cask. ? *Obs.*

1635 QUARLES *Embl.* II. x. 6 A Cask, that seems as full, as faire; But meerely tunn'd with Ayre. **1664** COTTON *Scarron.* I. 104 Tunning themselves with Ale, and Beer.

3. app. *intr.* Of young rabbits: To become corpulent or 'pot-bellied'.

1741 *Compl. Fam.-Piece* III. 510 Ground Malt helps to recover the young ones when tunned. [Cf. TUNNING 2.]

Hence **tunned** (tʌnd) *ppl. a.*

1671 GREW *Anat. Plants* i. §32 The said Aperture being that.. to the Sap, which.. the Bung-hole of the Barrel, is to the new tunn'd Liquor.

tun, obs. form of TON[1], TOWN.

‖**tuna**[1] ('tuna). Also 7–8 in anglicized form **tune**. [According to Humboldt, taken from Haitian into Spanish: see quot. 1852.] = INDIAN FIG 1, PRICKLY PEAR; esp. ***opuntia tuna***, a tall-growing species found in Central America and the West Indies, and introduced elsewhere.

1555 EDEN *Decades* (Arb.) 228 Wyld plantes.. which I haue not seene but in the Ilande of Hispaniola... These they caule *Tunas.* They growe of a thistle full of thornes, and brynge foorth a frute muche lyke vnto great fygges. **1614** PURCHAS *Pilgrimage* VIII. vii. (ed. 2) 774 A kind of fruit called Tune, of the bignes of an egge, black and of good tast. *a* **1715** TATE tr. *Cowley's Plants* v. C.'s Wks. 1721 III. 411 The Tuna to the Indian-Fig a kin, (The Glory of Tlascalla) next came in. **1760–72** tr. *Juan & Ulloa's Voy.* (ed. 3) I. 325 The leaf of the tuna being broad, flat, and prickly. [**1852** TH. ROSS *Humboldt's Trav.* I. 328 The following are Haytian words, in their real form, which have passed into the Castilian language since the end of the 15th century... *Tuna.*] **1866** *Treas. Bot.* 818 Tuna is a Spanish-American name given to several Opuntias, but botanists have adopted it as the.. name of a single species, *O. Tuna*, a native.. from Quito to Mexico and the West Indies.

attrib. **1911** *Dundee Advertiser* 12 Apr. 12/1 San Luis Potosi had long been the great *tuna cheese market of Mexico... The cheese is made by simply boiling and straining the tuna pulp until the proper consistency is reached. **1748** *Earthquake of Peru* iii. 210 These they call Higas de Tuna, or *Tuna Figs. **1912** R. B. C. GRAHAM in *Eng. Rev.* May 229 The great trumpet-shaped and dark red fleshy *tuna flowers.

tuna[2] ('tju:nə, ‖tuna). [Spanish American: perh. related to L. *thunnus, tunnus*, tunny, cf. med.L. *tunnina* 'thunnus falsus' false tunny (Du Cange).] **a.** Any of several large marine food and game fishes of the family Scombridæ, belonging to the genus *Thunnus, Euthynnus, Katsuwonus*, or a closely related genus and found in Atlantic, Pacific, and Mediterranean seas. Cf. SKIPJACK *sb.*[4], TON[4], and TUNNY.

1881 *Proc. U.S. Nat. Mus.* IV. 45 Another *Orcynus*, known as the 'tuna', exists about Santa Cruz Island. **1900** *Westm. Gaz.* 29 June 8/1 The tuna, one of the gamest fighting fish for its size in the sea. **1901** *Field* 23 Nov. 812/2 There is no doubt whatever as to the identity of the horse mackerel of the Gulf of St. Lawrence, the tuna of Catalina, and the thon, thuna, or tunny of the Mediterranean. **1911** *Chambers's Jrnl.* Jan. 63/2 My Californian friends might well possess their disappointed souls in patience if there were any promise of such compensation.. for the loss of the tuna. **1949** *Manch. Guardian Weekly* 24 Mar. 11/2 Water you can't swim in, and good tuna and jacks you can't eat. **1970** *Nature* 19 Dec. 1141/2 Tuna is a fisheries term for the larger tunny species.

b. *attrib.*, as ***tuna bait, boat, fisherman, fishing, fleet, meat, packer, packing, salad, sandwich, school***; **tuna clipper** *U.S.*, a powered fishing boat with facilities for catching and storing small fish; **tuna fish**, the flesh of the tunny as food.

1901 *McClure's Mag.* Feb. 370/1 Vincente.. is just taking the *tuna bait from his gill-nets. **1968** *National Fisherman* July 18-C/2 Much squid was used for tuna bait. **1903** C. F. HOLDER *Big Game Fishes* iv. 59 The *tuna boats of Catalina Island are designed for the purpose. **1956** *Fishery Bull.* LVII. 195/1 (*heading*) Grounds fished by tuna boats operating in the Inner South Seas. **1929** *Pacific Fisherman* Sept. 39/1 The 100-ft *tuna clipper 'Enterprise' was driven ashore. **1970** *National Fisherman* Sept. 1-B/2 A tuna clipper is a vessel equipped to carry small fish alive for use as bait; capable of being trimmed in such a way as to bring her stern rail as low as possible in the water; and fitted with a system which permits her to hold her catch for long periods of time. **1917** M. GREEN *Better Meals for Less Money* xvi. 130 (*heading*) *Tuna fish salad. **1922** *Guardian* 27 June 6/2 Tinned goods.. are the most suitable for storing... 1 tin 'tuna' fish or crayfish. **1978** *Amer. Poetry Rev.* Nov./Dec. 16/3 To a tunafish gray on a bruised, greenish blue. **1982** J. GARDNER *For Special Services* viii. 64 Tuna fish sandwiches were hardly Bond's style. **1919** *Pacific Fisherman Yearbk.* 64/2 The *tuna fishermen return to port each evening. **1901** *McClure's Mag.* Feb. 370/1 The rods and reels in *tuna fishing are of the finest description. **1926** G. FRANKAU *My Unsentimental Journey* xvii. 222 His hobby—he told me at once—is tuna-fishing. **1980** *Times* 4 Nov. 18/4 [In Peru] tuna fishing.. has now virtually ended. **1932** M. MILLER *I cover Waterfront* xvii. 97 The only people who know of him are the two men who live on the island and the crews and skippers of the *tuna fleet. **1968** *National Fisherman* Apr. 2-A/2 Commander, a steel hulled, 20-year-old veteran of the Southern California tuna fleet, sank off Mexico. **1923** A. WARD *Encycl. Food* 537 Very little *tuna meat is sold fresh in our markets. **1951** TRESSLER & LEMON *Marine Products of Commerce* (ed. 2) xx. 448 A machine for molding blocks of tuna meat the exact size for the can is in operation in some canneries. **1922** *Pacific Fisherman* May 43/1 Prominent *tuna packers. *Ibid.*, Mr. Ambrose was one of the organizers of the first tuna packing plant in California. **1967** *Commerical Fisheries Rev.* Nov. 64/2 Japanese tuna packers.. switched from fruit canning to tuna packing in September. **1953** *Special Sci. Rep.* (U.S. Fish & Wildlife Service, Fisheries) No. 104. 32 [Chunk tuna] was especially suited to the preparation of *tuna salads. **1977** C. McFADDEN *Serial* (1978) xiii. 32/2 He left Fred's, absent-mindedly leaving her to pay for his tuna salad special. **1957** HESELTINE & DOW *New Basic Cook Bk.* 718 (*heading*) *Tuna sandwiches. **1977** C. MCCARRY *Secret Lovers* iii. 42 The passenger compartment of the BMW smelled.. of bay rum, Brylcreem, tuna sandwiches. **1930** *Pacific Fisherman* Apr. 41/1 In search of distant *tuna schools. **1967** *Trans. Amer. Fisheries Soc.* XCVI. 127/1 Purse seines capture only about half the number of tuna schools upon which they are set.

‖**tuna**[3] ('tʊna). [Maori name.] Either of two freshwater eels, *Anguilla dieffenbachii* or *A. australis schmidtii*, found in New Zealand.

1843 E. DIEFFENBACH *Trav. N.Z.* II. III. 389/2 *Tuna*, eel. **1851** J. C. RICHMOND *Let.* 25 Mar. in *Richmond-Atkinson Papers* (1960) I. ii. 79 They set off.. to catch crawfish & tuna, the eels of the country. **1895** *Funk's Standard Dict.*, *Tuna*, the common eel.. of New Zealand. **1898** MORRIS *Austral Eng.* s.v. *Eel*, New Zealand Eels... Tuna E[el], *Anguilla aucklandii.* **1966** *Encycl. N.Z.* I. 565/1 These are the common freshwater eels called tuna by the Maoris.

tunability (tju:nə'bɪlɪtɪ). [f. next: see -BILITY.] The capability of being varied in frequency and wavelength.

1969 *Sci. Jrnl.* Apr. 57/3 Spectroscopy is one of the most obvious fields for exploitation of laser tunability. **1977** *Jrnl. R. Soc. Arts* CXXV. 766/2 Tunability and the time-compression of laser energy into very short pulses.. represent considerable technological achievements.

tunable, tuneable ('tju:nəb(ə)l), *a.* [f. TUNE *sb.* or *v.* + -ABLE: cf. *comfortable.*]

1. Tuneful, musical, melodious, harmonious, sweet-sounding. *arch.* **a.** Of music, musical instruments, the singing voice, etc.

c **1500** *Proverbs* in *Antiq. Rep.* (1809) IV. 407 In tunabill tewnys he hathe non experyment. *c* **1525** in Herrig *Archiv Neu. Spr.* (1908) CXX. 423 The songe of hym selff, yet nevyrtheles, Ys trew and tvnabyle, & syng yt as yt ys. *c* **1581** LODGE *Repl. Gosson's Sch. Abuse* (Shaks. Soc.) 20 The tunable voyces of men. **1598** FLORIO, *Simphonia*,.. a tunable singing without iarring. **1658** R. FRANCK *North. Mem.* (1821) 250 The birds.. beat the ambient air with their tunable notes. **1700** J. BROME *Trav. Eng.* etc. ii. (1707) 52 A Chapel.. in which there is placed a tunable Organ. **1820** H. MATTHEWS *Diary of Invalid* (ed. 2) 34 Airs not at all tuneable to an English ear. **1890** W. MORRIS in *Eng. Illustr. Mag.* July 757 The noise though it was great was tuneable.

b. *spec.* Of a peal of bells: in first 2 quots., well-tuned, in tune.

1510–11 *Rec. St. Mary at Hill* 274 To go and see wheþer Smythes bell wer Tewneabill or nat. **1581** in *Rep. Hist. MSS Comm., Var. Coll.* (1907) IV. 91 Such of the sayd bells as be not tuneable at this present. **1631** WEEVER *Anc. Fun. Mon.* 226 A tunable ring of fiue bels vpon the same. **1778** G. WHITE *Selborne* lxxx, The notes of a hunting horn, a tunable ring of bells. **1844** PALEY *Church Restorers* 33 The Tower contained a tunable ring of eight new bells.

c. Of speech or the speaking voice, or other sounds.

1579 FULKE *Heskins' Parl.* 21 A well tunable sound of the waues reboundeth. **1589** PUTTENHAM *Eng. Poesie* I. v. (Arb.) 26 Without any rime or tunable concord in th'end of their verses. **1661** H. D. *Disc. Liturgies* 82 A tunable and distinct pronouncing of the words. **1709** STEELE & SWIFT *Tatler* No. 70 ⁋7 What a secret Force there is in the Accents of a tunable Voice! **1836** S. ROGERS *From Euripides* 7 As tuneable as harp of many strings.

d. *fig.* Harmonious, concordant; pleasant-sounding (quot. 1639); well-strung (quot. 1691).

1561 DAUS tr. *Bullinger on Apoc.* (1573) 68 b, A continuall holdyng on and tunable agrement in praysing God. **1639** FULLER *Holy War* v. vii. (1840) 253 This counsel, harsh at first, grew tunable in the ears of the Hospitallers. **1691** NORRIS *Pract. Disc.* 327 He that is blessed with the strongest and most tunable Constitution. **1854** EMERSON *Lett. & Soc. Aims, Quot. & Orig.* Wks. (Bohn) III. 214 It [the Bible] has been played upon by the devotion of thousands of years until every word and particle is.. tunable.

†**e.** with *to*: In tune with, accordant to (*lit.* and *fig.*). *Obs.*

1584 LODGE *Hist. Forbonius & Prisc.* (Shaks. Soc.) 85 Making his lute tunable to the straine of his voice. **1688** W. BATES *Harm. Div. Attrib.* v. (ed. 3) 87 His Heart might be made tunable to the Hearts of the afflicted.

2. Capable of being tuned; *spec.* capable of having its operating frequency and wavelength varied.

1706 PHILLIPS (ed. Kersey), *Tunable*, that may be tuned, or put in Tune; agreeable to the Rules of Musick. **1828** in WEBSTER. [Hence in later Dicts.] **1934** E. LITTLE *Mod. Rhythmic Drumming* (rev. ed.) 26 No outfit is complete without at least one tomtom. The 'tuneable' models are the best, because any dampness in the atmosphere can be counteracted by the use of the tensioning handles. **1943** C. L. BOLTZ *Basic Radio* xii. 195 It is seen that the aerial is not tunable. **1957** *Proc. IRE* XLV. 1467/2 The system [*sc.* for a maser] is 'tunable'; i.e., the useful frequency can be adjusted. **1969** R. B. FULLER *Operating Man. Spaceship Earth* v. 67 The macrocosmic irrelevancies are all the events too large and too infrequent to be synchronizably tuneable in any possible way with our consideration. **1969** *Sci. Jrnl.* Apr. 53/3 Lasers capable of producing megawatts of power and tunable right through the visible spectrum. **1971** *Daily Tel.* (Colour Suppl.) 22 Oct. 57 (Advt.), The VHF radio has pushbutton programme selection and each programme is separately tunable. **1979** *Jrnl. R. Soc. Arts* Jan. 106/2 In conjunction with a tunable x-ray monochromator, anomalous scattering experiments can be performed close to absorption edges.

tunableness, tune- ('tju:nəb(ə)lnɪs). [f. prec. + -NESS.] The quality of being tunable; tunefulness, harmoniousness, sweetness of sound.

1561 T. HOBY tr. *Castiglione's Courtyer* I. I iij, The tunablenes of musicke is a very great refreshing of.. griefs. **1694** W. WOTTON *Anc. & Mod. Learn.* (1697) 27 That derived Language actually has a Sweetness and Tunableness in its Composition. **1727** J. SPENCE *Ess. on Pope's Odyss.* 15 A general tunableness in the Verse will carry a Man on strangely. **1887** *Athenæum* 26 Mar. 411/2 There is a certain lilt and tuneableness about some of these songs.

b. *fig.* Harmony, concord.

1569 GOLDING *Heminges Post.* Ded. 21 All the degrees of the realme being setled in a most sweete tunablenesse.

tunably, tuneably ('tju:nəblɪ), *adv.* [f. as prec. + -LY[2].] In a tunable manner; tunefully, musically, harmoniously.

1586 W. WEBBE *Eng. Poetrie* (Arb.) 38 He sang fine ditties.. tunably to their Musick notes. **1644** FEATLY *Gentle Lash* 9 The more to praise God, and sing more tuneably and delightfully. *a* **1668** LASSELS *Voy. Italy* (1698) II. 199 Pan also plays on his mouth-organ tuneably. **1834** H. AINSWORTH *Rookwood* III. iv, They can sing.. most tuneably.

tunack, tunake, obs. forms of TUNIC.

‖**tunal** (tu'nal). [Sp., f. TUNA[1] + -AL (cf. CHAPARRAL).] A grove or thicket of tunas: see TUNA[1]. (Also erron. used for *tuna.*)

1613 PURCHAS *Pilgrimage* VIII. x. 661 That they should goe seeke out a Tunal in the Lake, which grew out of a stone. **1666** J. DAVIES *Hist. Caribby Isles* 62 A kind of Tunal, on which there have been seen certain little Worms in colour like a Ruby, which dye Linen.. a very fair and lively Scarlet-colour. **1722** D. COXE *Descr. Carolina* 85 This noble ingredient for dying is produc'd by a tree or shrub call'd the tunal or tuna. **1857** KINGSLEY *Two Y. Ago* II. 104 Mexicans among tunals of cactus and agave.

tun-bellied ('tʌn,bɛlɪd), *a.* Having a belly rounded like a tun; pot-bellied, corpulent.

1550 LEVER *Serm.* (Arb.) 119 Fyfty tunne belyed Monckes geuen to glotony fylled theyr pawnches. **1683** KENNETT tr. *Erasm. on Folly* 134, I prefer the opinion of the good old tun-bellied Divines. **1760** FAWKES tr. *Anacreon, Ode* xxxviii. 17 *note*, Silenus was.. represented by a little, flat-nosed, bald, fat, tun-bellied, old drunken Fellow. **1866** *Cornh. Mag.* May 636 A crew of useless tunbellied gourmands.

So **'tun-belly**, a belly like a tun, a big round belly.

a **1704** T. BROWN *Lett. Ser. & Com., To Men* Wks. 1709 III. 120 The presumptuous Wretch that should think irreverently of a double Chin, and a Tun-Belly.

Tunbridge ('tʌnbrɪdʒ). **a.** Used *attrib.* to designate water from the chalybeate spring at Royal Tunbridge Wells in Kent.

a **1661** FULLER *Worthies* (1662) Kent 62 Tunbridgewater... Good for Splenitick distempers. **1678** T. BROWNE *Let.* 1 May (1946) 92 He may hopefully drink Tunbridge waters.. if they passe well. *c* **1702** C. FIENNES *Journeys* (1947) 125 Tunbridge waters whose property is to retrieve lost limbs that are benumbed. **1967** E. S. TURNER *Taking Cure* iii. 46 Nothing was to be gained from the Tunbridge waters unless the person who drank them was facetious, merry.. and jovial.

b. Also **Tonbridge**. Used *attrib.* (rarely *absol.*) to designate wooden articles with a characteristic mosaic decoration, made in and about Royal Tunbridge Wells and nearby Tonbridge by slicing cross-sections from a bundle of thin strips of differently coloured wood glued together, to obtain identical copies of the pattern for sticking on the article to be decorated; chiefly in ***Tunbridge ware***.

1773 R. GRAVES *Spiritual Quixote* I. II. xiii. 101 His Tunbridge-ware tobacco-dish. *c* **1795** *Advt. C. Fellows's Circul. Library, Salisbury*, With various Articles in Tunbridge, Ivory, and Morocco. **1816** JANE AUSTEN *Emma* III. iv. 50 A pretty little Tunbridge-ware box. **1842** MARRYAT *Perc. Keene* I. ix. 98 In the front windows.. were.. prints, caricatures, and Tonbridge ware. **1888** *Encycl. Brit.* XXIII. 607/1 Tunbridge ware.. includes work tables, boxes, toys, &c. **1901** J. BLACK *Illustr. Carpenter & Builder Ser.: Home Handicrafts* 61 Developments of the art of what may be termed 'wood mosaic', and amongst these may be reckoned 'Tarsia work' and 'Tonbridge work'. **1934** N. MARSH *Man lay Dead* xiii. 237, I suddenly remembered.. a funny Victorian casket made out of inlaid wood... Antique dealers call those caskets.. Tunbridge boxes. **1973** *Times* 25 Aug. 11/5 It has a Tunbridge-ware change-tray and an Edward VII crown set into the base.

‖**tunc, tunk.** *Welsh Hist.* Also 4 tung, 7–8 tuncke. [ad. Welsh *twng, twnc* (pl. *ty(n)geu*); perh. connected with *tyng-u* to swear.] A kind of customary rent or payment (analogous to the 'chief-rents' or 'quit-rents' of English Real Property Law), issuing out of certain lands in

North Wales, and still until recently payable in respect of Crown Lands.

Commonly explained as the money-commutation paid in lieu of the *gwestva* (in Latin *cena*), an entertainment due or tribute-in-kind rendered to the lord of the cymwd or prince, in respect of the free maenols of the cymwds (see COMMOT). Hence translated by Seebohm as 'food-rent'. As to the derivation, the conjecture has been offered that an oath was originally required of inability to render the *gwestva* in kind, before the tunc-pound was accepted instead.

1311 *Inq. P.M.* (*C.*) *Edw. II*, File 22. m. 23 (P.R.O.) Idem Comes.. habuit lx.s., tam de liberis quam de natiuis, pro quadam custuma que vocatur Tung. **1334** in Vinogradoff *Survey of Denbigh* (1914) 7 Quelibet istarum xj. gavellarum reddit de Tung' per annum xij d. et pro pastu familie Principis per annum ij. s. v. d. q. **1658** in W. M. Myddelton *Chirk Castle Acc.* (1908) 73 Tuncke rent for the same lands for yeare ended at Michelmas 1657. **1793** *Jrnls. Ho. Comm.* 28 Mar. 558/2 The Sheriffs of the County of Flint.. are charged with an Annual Rent called The Tuncke Rent, payable in small Sums, or Rents, for diver Tenures.. in the said County. *Ibid.* 560/1 The Nature and Original of the Tunck Rent, called also *Porthan Keys*, cannot now be traced or explained. **1895** SEEBOHM *Tribal Syst. Wales* vi. §4 (1904) 154 In the Extents the food-rents of the free tribesmen were found to be commuted into definite money payments made under the name of *tunc*. **1914** MISS M. NEILSON in Vinogradoff *Survey of Denbigh* Introd. 59 The tunk-pound in the Venedotian code is due from the maenol. *Ibid.*, In the Denbigh Survey the tunk is a definite money charge on all Welsh customary tenants, free and *nativi*.

tund (tʌnd), *v.* [ad. L. *tund-ĕre* to beat.]

1. *Winchester School slang. trans.* To beat with a stick, esp. an ash rod, by way of punishment. Hence **'tunded** *ppl. a.*, **'tunding** *vbl. sb.*; also **'tunder**, one who 'tunds'.

1866 *School Life at Winchester Coll.* iii. 38 When I was a big Inferior, I have more than once received.. a 'Tunding' (thrashing with a stick). **1871** *Echo* 11 Apr. 1 He may be 'tunded', in which case he has to stand upon a table, that the præfect may the more conveniently cut into the calves of his legs with an apple twig. **1872** *Punch* 23 Nov. 210/1 'Tunding'.. is a brutality, in the way of chastisement, inflicted by the big lads on the little ones at Winchester School. **1876** LD. SHERBROOKE in *Life & Lett.* (1893) I. 12 To put a stick into the hand of a boy of sixteen and allow him to use it upon his schoolfellows.. is neither fair on the tunder nor the tunded. **1884** *Times* 13 Feb. 11/4 The clamour aroused by the celebrated 'tunding' case [at Winchester].

2. *gen.* To beat, thump (*trans.* and *intr.*).

1885 BURTON *Arab. Nts.* (1887) III. 44 All the apes were wroth with the plucked ape.. and tunded him the more. **1895** *Brit. Weekly* 29 June 131 If he had.. but command of the racial tom-tom, it seems to him that he would tund upon it in honour of that great man. **1904** *Speaker* 28 May 206 Louder than the Sea-surge tunds the Harbour-bar.

†**'tunder**[1]. *Obs. rare.* Also **tundor.** (app.) A funnel: cf. TUNNEL *sb.* 3, TUNNER 1.

1343–4 *Pipe Roll 18 Edw. III*, m. 45 (P.R.O.), j tunder et j skopa pro aqua in eisdem doliis infundenda. **1344** *Acc. Exch. K.R.* 492/26. m. 2 Pro uno Tundor et uno skopo pro aqua infundenda in dolia.

tunder[2]: see TUND *v.* 1.

tunder, -dyr, obs. or dial. ff. TINDER.

tun-dish, tundish ('tʌndɪʃ). [f. TUN *sb.* + DISH *sb.*] A wooden dish or shallow vessel with a tube at the bottom fitting into the bung-hole of a tun or cask, forming a kind of funnel used in brewing; hence *gen.* = FUNNEL *sb.*[1] 1 (now *local*). In mod. use, a broad, open container with one or more holes in the bottom, used in various industrial processes, e.g. to feed molten metal into an ingot mould so as to avoid splashing and give a smoother flow.

1388–9 *Abingdon Acc.* (Camden) 57, iij scale, j tundys. **1573** in *Rep. MSS. Ld. Middleton* (1911) 437 Making.. a forme and a tundishe for the buttrye. **1603** SHAKS. *Meas. for M.* III. ii. 182 For filling a bottle with a Tunne-dish. **1756** MATTHEWS in *Phil. Trans.* XLIX. 549 These pits.. growing gradually narrower to a center, in shape of a funnel or tundish. **1795** SIR J. DALRYMPLE *Let. to Admiralty* 3 The froth, that is, the Yeast, is prevented by a tun-dish from running over. **1892** GREENER *Breech-Loader* 176 The shot must be poured in through a tundish, and preferably counted with the 'Greener Shot Counter', or weighed to measure. **1926** *Jrnl. Iron & Steel Inst.* CXIV. 74 This tun-dish is provided with one large hole or several smaller holes, dividing the stream of metal into several smaller streams. **1957** *Technology* Aug. 223/1 Plugged into the base of a fireclay tundish.. fed with liquid metal from an electric furnace, is a vertical die of.. graphite. **1965** *Economist* 25 Dec. 1437/2 In the new [spray steelmaking] process, the liquid iron flows from the bottom of a tundish (a container used to keep a constant head of metal). **1975** *Petroleum Rev.* XXIX. 118/1 The tank vent pipes have now been fitted with tundishes to collect condensate.

‖**tundra** ('tʌndrə, 'tʊn-). Also **toondra, toundra.** [a. Lap. *tundra.*] One of the vast, nearly level, treeless regions which make up the greater part of the north of Russia, resembling the *steppes* farther south, but with arctic climate and vegetation. Also applied to similar regions in Siberia and Alaska.

1841 *Penny Cycl.* XXI. 458/1 The most northern part of Siberia is a low plain, called the Tundra. The surface is nearly a dead level, and quite destitute of trees. **1861** H. MACMILLAN *Footnotes fr. Page Nat.* 93 In the vast sandy plains called by the Laplanders tundra, which border on the Arctic ocean. **1889** G. F. WRIGHT *Ice Age in N. Amer.* 32 Much of the region north of St. Elias, Alaska, is now covered with tundra.

attrib. **1894** *Outing* (U.S.) XXIII. 388/1 In the far north-west, the vast tundra plains, bordering upon the Arctic Ocean. **1894** *Daily News* 24 July 5/4 Russian traders and inhabitants of the polar tundra zone. **1901** H. SEEBOHM *Birds Siberia* xiv. 119 A swampy, hummocky strip of tundra land.

tundrite ('tʌndraɪt). *Min.* [ad. Russ. *tundrít* (E. I. Semenov *Mineralogiya Redkikh Zemel'* (1963) 209), f. Russ. *túndra* tundra (from its being first found on the Lovozero tundra near Murmansk): see -ITE[1].] A silicate and carbonate (essentially) of cerium (normal tundrite, tundrite-(Ce)) or neodymium (tundrite-(Nd)), sodium, and titanium found as triclinic brownish- or greenish-yellow crystals.

1965 *Amer. Mineralogist* L. 2098 Tundrite occurs in 3 nepheline syenite pegmatites of Mt. Nepkha, Lovozero tundra, Kola Peninsula. **1974** *Ibid.* LIX. 633/2 Infra-red study of tundrite from a new locality in the Khibina massif showed bands of carbonate; this was confirmed by spectra of the Greenland mineral.

tundun: see TURNDUN.

tune (tju:n), *sb.* Forms: (4 tun), 4– tune; also 5 **tuyn(e, (tyune, teone), twn(e, 5–6 tewne, toyn(e,** 6 *Sc.* **tuin, tone, toon,** 6–7 *Sc.* **toone;** cf. also TONE *sb.* [A peculiar phonetic variant of TONE *sb.*, appearing first in 14th c.: the Sc. *toon, tuin* (= tøn, tʏn) show the normal Sc. representative of ME. *ō*, as in *muin, suin, duin, shuin* (shoes).]

†**1. a.** A (musical) sound or tone; *esp.* the sound of the voice: = TONE *sb.* 1. *Obs.*

1387 TREVISA *Higden* (Rolls) I. 355 þey makeþ wel mery armonye and melody wiþ wel þicke tunes [CAXTON tewnes], werbeles, and nootes. *c* **1400** *Laud Troy Bk.* 14292 He tolde him of the deth of Brunes; Then were mad hidus tuynes Off many a gentil damysel. **1413** *Pilgr. Sowle* (Caxton) v. i. (1859) 72 There was no tune of musik that ther was forgeten. **1435** MISYN *Fire of Love* II. iii. 73 Emonge aungels twnys it has a acceptabyll melody. *c* **1450** *Songs & Carols* (E.E.T.S.) 89/53 Thus seyth þis byrde, in tyunes gay. **1508** FISHER *Penit. Ps.* xxxviii. Wks. (E.E.T.S.) I. 71 In the whiche swete soundes we shall here so grete plente & dyuersite of tunes as euer was herde before. **1560** INGELEND *Disob. Child* C ij, Her tonge and her tune is very shryll. **1573–80** BARET *Alv.* T 415 The tune of the Harpe, *canor lyræ.* Ouid. **1592** SHAKS. *Ven. & Ad.* 431 Melodious discord, heauenly tune harsh sounding. *a* **1600** MONTGOMERIE *Misc. Poems* vi. 31 Lamenting toons best lyks me for relief. *c* **1600** SHAKS. *Sonn.* cxli, Nor are mine ears with thy toungs tune delighted. *c* **1614** SIR W. MURE *Dido & Æneas* III. 20 And als the light-envying owl, alone, With tragick toones her smarte and sorrow shew. **1706** PRIOR *Ode to Queen* 9 High as their Trumpets Tune His Lyre he strung. **1819** KEATS *Isabella* iv, Lorenzo, if thy lips breathe not love's tune. *a* **1849** HOR. SMITH *Addr. Mummy* ii, Thou hast a tongue: come, let us hear its tune.

b. Applied to a special affected or peculiar intonation in speaking: cf. 2, and TONE *sb.* 5 c.

1783 BLAIR *Lect. Rhet.* xxxiii. II. 214 If any one, in Public Speaking, shall have formed to himself a certain melody or tune, which requires rest and pauses of its own, distinct from those of the sense, he has.. contracted one of the worst habits into which a Public Speaker can fall.

2. a. A rhythmical succession of musical tones produced by (or composed for) an instrument or voice; an air, melody (with or without the harmony which accompanies it). Now the leading sense. (Not in TONE *sb.*)

1387 TREVISA *Higden* (Rolls) III. 207 By the sleuþe of þe manere of tunes [*orig.* modorum tarditate]. **1491** *Cartular. St. Nicholai Aberdon.* (New Spald. Cl.) I. 256 Chaplannis yat kepis nocht ye Seculorum and twne gewin yame be ye chantour. **1500–20** DUNBAR *Poems* lxxxii. 29 Ȝour commone menstrallis hes no tone, Bot 'Now the day dawis', and 'Into Joun'. **1535** COVERDALE *Ezek.* xxxiii. 32 As a balet y^t hath a swete tune, and is pleasaunt to synge. **1591** SHAKS. *Two Gent.* I. ii. 82 Best sing it to the tune of *Light o' Loue.* *a* **1600** MONTGOMERIE *Misc. Poems* xlviii. 94 Vp uent our saillis, tauntit to the huins; The trumpets soundit tuentie mirrie tuins. **1697** DRYDEN *Virg. Past* IX. 62 The Tune I still retain, but not the Words. **1717** LADY M. W. MONTAGU *Let. to Pope* 1 Apr., The tunes are extremely gay and lively. **1798** COLERIDGE *Anc. Mar.* v. 81 A hidden brook In the leafy month of June, That to the sleeping woods all night Singeth a quiet tune. **1828** SCOTT *F.M. Perth* x, The tune,.. played upon a viol, was gay and sprightly in the commencement.

(*b*) *Proverb.* (See quot. *a* 1915.) Hence, ***to call the tune***, to hold the initiative, to have control of events.

a **1915** *Proverb.* He who pays the piper, calls the tune. **1928** A. HUXLEY *Point Counter Point* xii. 211 Lucy insisted, when she was with men, on doing as much of the paying as possible. Paying, she was independent, she could call her own tune. **1948** W. S. CHURCHILL *Second World War* I. I. x. 182 If Britain had used her naval power, closed the Suez Canal, and defeated the Italian Navy in a general engagement, she would have had the right to call the tune in Europe. **1963** A. ROSS *Australia 63* iii. 92 A match throughout which, despite frequent fluctuation, England had called the tune. **1978** *Lancashire Life* Nov. 70/1 The Listers had called the local tune ever since the reign of Henry IV, although it was not until 1797 that the head of the family was ennobled.

b. *spec.* A musical setting of a hymn or psalm, usually in four-part harmony, intended for use in public worship; a hymn-tune.

c **1450** CAPGRAVE *Life St. Aug.* xix. 27 Ambrose mad hem to be sunge delectabily with consent of dyuers tewnys whech had not be used þere be-for. **1567** *Gude & Godlie B.* (S.T.S.) 7 Heir followis the Catechisme put in meter, to be sung with the tone [*edd.* **1578**, *etc.* tune]. **1795** MASON *Ch. Mus.* iii. 195 Adapted, if not originally written, to one particular Melody or Tune. **1833** T. HOOK *Parson's Dau.* I. i, Which [house-clock] strikes every hour, chimes the quarters, and plays Rule Britannia and the Hundreth Psalm tune two hundred and fifty times in the four and twenty hours. **1908** [MISS FOWLER] *Betw. Trent & Ancholme* 50 The tune ('Oxford') was brought by our grandfather from thence.

†**c.** Applied to the mediæval ecclesiastical modes (***the eight tunes***): see MODE *sb.* 1 a (*b*), and cf. TONE *sb.* 3 b. *Obs.*

1597 MORLEY *Introd. Mus.* 147 The churchmen for keeping their Keyes haue deuised certaine notes commonlie called the eight tunes, so that according to the tune which is to be obserued,.. if it beginne in such a key, it may end in such and such others. *Annot., The eight tunes...* The tunes (which are also called *modi musici*) the practitioners do define, to be a rule whereby the melodie of euerie song is directed.

d. (In full, ***act-tune.***) A piece of music played between the acts of a play. Cf. ENTR'ACTE b.

1889 W. H. HUSK in Grove *Dict. Mus.* s.v. *Tune*, In the latter half of the 17th century and first quarter of the 18th century act-tunes were composed specially for every play... But act-tunes, now styled 'Entr'actes', have been occasionally composed in modern times. **1891** *Cent. Dict.*, *Tune...* 4. Same as *entr'acte.* Sometimes called *act-tune.*

e. ***the tune the*** (***old***) ***cow died of***: humorously applied to a grotesque or unmusical succession of sounds, or a tedious ill-played piece of music. Also ***the tune the cat died of.***

Supposed to refer to an 'old ballad' in which a piper who had nothing else to give his cow 'took his pipe and played a tune, and bade the cow consider'. See *N. & Q.* 11th Ser. XI. 309.

1820 M. WILMOT *Let.* 4 May (1935) 60, I am made laugh heartily three times a week.. when they cut capers in the air with solemn faces, to the tune which *the old Cow died of.* **1836** LADY GRANVILLE *Lett.* (1894) II. 218 The tune the old cow died of throughout, grunts and groans of instruments. **1943** H. C. BAILEY *Mr. Fortune finds Pig* xxxvi. 140 What are they singing?.. It sounds like the tune the cat died of.

3. a. The state of being in the proper pitch; correct intonation in singing, or in instrumental music; agreement in pitch, unison, or harmony (*with* something): mostly in phr. ***in*** or ***out of tune***; cf. TONE *sb.* 2 b, c. Also, simply, the pitch of a musical note (quot. 1694, *obs.*).

c **1440** *Jacob's Well* 82 Whanne an harpe is weel sett in tewne. **1450–1530** *Myrr. our Ladye* 56 That all the notes be songe, as they are in youre bokes, eche of them in theyr owne tewne. **1483** *Cath. Angl.* 396/1 Oute of Tune, *dissonus,.. discors.* **1530** RASTELL *Bk. Purgat.* II. xviii, When hys harpe is out of tune. *a* **1548** HALL *Chron., Hen. VII* 3 To set all the strynges in a monacorde and tune. **1602** SHAKS. *Ham.* III. i. 166 Like sweet Bels iangled out of tune [*2nd Qo.* time], and harsh. **1617–18** in Swayne *Sarum Churchw. Acc.* (1896) 167 For keeping the Organ in tune. **1694** W. HOLDER *Harmony* ii. (1731) 5 The Tune of a Note.. is constituted by the Measure and Proportion of Vibrations of the sonorous Body. **1707** WATTS *Hymn*, '*Let others boast how strong they be*' iii, Strange that a harp of thousand strings Should keep in tune so long! **1773** *Phil. Trans.* LXIII. 268 The B flat of the spinnet.. was perfectly in tune with the great bell of St. Paul's. **1884** TENNYSON *Becket* Prol. 16 My voice is harsh here, not in tune.

b. *fig.* in phr. ***in tune, out of tune***, in or out of order or proper condition; in or out of harmony *with* some person or thing. (See also 4, and cf. TONE *sb.* 2 c.)

1535 STEWART *Cron. Scot.* (Rolls) II. 390 On euerie syde thair wes richt mony slane, Or tha culd weill be put in tune agane. **1579** TOMSON *Calvin's Serm. Tim.* 280/2 How many occasions are there to bring vs out of tune? **1605** ROWLANDS *Hell's Broke Loose* 21 If Siluer in my Pockets do not ring, All's out of tune with mee in eu'ry thing. **1638** W. MOUNTAGU in *Buccleuch MSS.* (Hist. MSS. Comm.) I. 282 Fire-locks.. are not mendable when out of tune. *c* **1680** BEVERIDGE *Serm.* (1729) I. 332 If our bodies be out of tune so are our minds too. **1737** BRACKEN *Farriery Impr.* (1757) II. 100 If you have a Horse in good Tune and Order. **1887** RIDER HAGGARD *Jess* xi, Bessie's mind was not quite in tune with the profundities of that learned journal.

c. *Phren.* The faculty of perception of musical pitch, and thus of melody and harmony.

1860 MAYNE *Expos. Lex.*, *Tune. Phrenol.*, a faculty (its organ at the lateral part of the forehead immediately above Number and Order) giving the perception of harmony and melody.

d. *transf.* Harmony or accordance in respect of vibrations other than those of sound; *spec.* between the transmitter and receiver in wireless telegraphy.

1909 *Westm. Gaz.* 29 Apr. 5/3 You see, we must have a commercial or general 'tune', and when that is known any person installing the same 'tune' can intercept the messages... No one could intercept messages in such a case unless they had instruments of the same 'tune'. **1911** WEBSTER s.v., To place the receiver of a system of wireless telegraphy in tune with the transmitter so as to respond to impulses given out by the latter.

†**4. a.** Style, manner, or 'tone' (of discourse or writing). *Obs.* (Cf. TONE 5 d.)

1537 CROMWELL in Merriman *Life & Lett.* (1902) II. 74, I must nedes now.. write unto you in an other tune. **1610** HOLLAND *Camden's Brit.* (1637) 107 Missive letters.. in this tune; To Ætius thrice Consul, the grones of Britans.

b. ***to change one's tune, sing another tune*** (etc.): *fig.* to change one's tone, speak in a different strain. (Often directly *fig.* from 1 or 2.)

1524 *St. Papers Hen. VIII*, VI. 349 Percace the said Frenche King wolde by this tyme have spoken of an other toyne. ?*a* 1800 *Wedding Robin Hood & Lit. John* ii. in Child *Ballads* (1886) IV. 422 O gin I live and bruik my life, I'll gar ye change your tune. 1890 [see SING *v.*[1] 10 a].

5. *fig.* Frame of mind, temper, mood, disposition, humour: cf. TONE 8.

1599 SHAKS. *Much Ado* III. iv. 41 *Hero.* How now? do you speake in the sick tune? *Beat.* I am out of all other tune, me thinkes. 1605 —— *Lear* IV. iii. 41 (Qo.) [Lear] some time in his better tune remembers, What we are come about. 1647 T. CALVERT *Heart Salve for Wounded Soul* 33 This is the tone and tune of men in distress. *a* 1691 FLAVEL *Sea Deliverances* (1754) 165 Our fancies were out of tune to be pleasant with anything. 1785 BURNS *Holy Fair* xxvi, They're a' in famous tune For crack that day. 1833 MOORE *Mem.* (1854) VI. 335 Being in but bad tune for a fête.

6. *Phrases. to the tune of* (*fig.* from 2):

†**a.** According to the gist of, in accordance with (*obs.*). **b.** To the amount or sum of. So *to some tune* (to a considerable extent), etc.

1607 HIERON *Wks.* I. 405 Singing nothing but to the tune of Judas 'What will ye give me?' 1692 R. L'ESTRANGE *Fables* ccclvi. (1694) 372 This came to the Bishop's Ear, who presently sent for the Curate, Rattled him to some Tune. 1714 R. FIDDES *Pract. Disc.* II. 95 This is exactly to the tune of the old popular objection. 1716 M. DAVIES *Athen. Brit.* II. 296 To Libel the Bishop..by exhibiting Articles against him to the Tune of 56. 1722 DE FOE *Col. Jack* (1840) 113 To go over..into Flanders, to be knocked on the head at the tune of 3s. 6d. a week. 1797 *Wonderf. Advant. Lottery* (Cheap Repos. Tr.) 8, I had demands on me yesterday to the tune of 300 l. 1809 MALKIN *Gil Blas* VII. xvi. ¶13 Other articles were much to the same tune. 1874 *Punch* 22 Aug. 76/2 A defaulter to the imposing tune of £10,000. 1883 *Manch. Exam.* 24 Nov. 5/1 His peasant countrymen..have been spoiled and pilled, and whipt to every tune.

7. *Comb.*, as ***tune-grinder, -hummer, -maker, -phrase, -tinkler, -weaving; tune-composed, -led, -skilled*** adjs.

1606 SYLVESTER *Du Bartas* II. iv. II. *Magnif.* 898 Their Tune-skill'd feet in so true Time doe fall. 1756 COWPER *Connoisseur* No. 138 ¶4 The Whistlers or Tune-hummers, who never articulate at all. 1795 WOLCOTT (P. Pindar) *Frogmore Fête* Wks. 1812 III. 315 Musicians and racers, tunegrinders and dancers. 1816 J. GILCHRIST *Philos. Etym.* 234 A tune-composed style. 1898 T. HARDY *Wessex Poems* 118 She trod the flags with tune-led feet. 1901 *Palestine Exploration Fund Q. Statem.* Oct. 420 One tune-phrase, repeated to every line, serves for a whole song.

tune, *v.* [f. TUNE *sb.*]

I. 1. a. *trans.* To adjust the tones of (a musical instrument) to a standard of pitch; to bring into condition for producing the required sounds correctly; to put in tune. Also *absol.*

1505 *Tower of Doctrine* xxvi. in *Percy's Reliq.*, With goodly pypes, in their mouthes ituned. 1513 BRADSHAW *St. Werburge* I. 1696 A synguler mynstrell..Toyned his instrument in pleasaunte armony. 1530 PALSGR. 763/2, I pray you, tune my virgynalles. 1567 *Triall Treas.* (1850) 16, I must tune my pipes first of all by drinking. 1584 GREENE *Anat. Fort.* Wks. (Grosart) III. 187, I thought..that where fortune once tuned, in the strings could neuer be found anie discord. 1597 *1st Pt. Return fr. Parnass.* v. i. 1978 Letts tune our instruments. 1638 in Willis & Clark *Cambridge* (1886) II. 142 Mr Dallam for tuneing the Organ. 1681 DRYDEN *Span. Friar* II. i. 21 Tune your Harps Ye Angels to that sound. 1871 TYNDALL *Fragm. Sc.* (1879) I. iii. 81 These two tuning-forks are tuned absolutely alike.

b. To adapt (the voice, song, etc.) to a particular tone, or to the expression of a particular feeling or subject; to modify or modulate the tones of, according to the purpose in view.

†In 1688, to adapt (a song) to a particular instrument (*obs.*).

1596 SPENSER *F.Q.* VI. x. 7 Nymphes and Faeries..to the waters fall tuning their accents fit. *c* 1630 MILTON *Passion* 8 For now to sorrow must I tune my song. 1688 R. HOLME *Armoury* III. 201/2 Odes [are] Songs Tuned to the Lute, or other Instrument. 1702 POPE *Sappho* 8 Love..tun'd my heart to Elegies of woe. 1751 *Transl. & Paraphr. Ch. Scot.* XLIII. iv, His presence fills each heart with joy: tunes every mouth to sing. 1852 MISS YONGE *Cameos* I. xxxiii. 282 The bards tuned their songs to recall the indignities of Islington.

c. *transf.* To adapt, put into accordance, or make responsive, in respect of some physical quality or condition; e.g. an organ or organism in relation to a particular stimulus, or the transmitter and receiver in wireless telegraphy. *spec.* To make (a radio or television) sensitive *to* a chosen signal frequency or wavelength; to adjust (any device or component) by varying its operational frequency. Also *absol.*

1887 LOCKYER *Chem. Sun* vii. 87 Ears are tuned to hear different sounds. 1899 *Notices Proc. R. Inst.* XV. 475 It is easy to transmit many messages in any direction at the same time. It is only necessary to tune the transmitters and receivers to the same frequency or 'note'... Tuning is very easy. 1900 *Daily News* 6 Sept. 2/4 'Tapping' the messages is quite impossible, the transmitter and receiver being so 'tuned' or synchronized to each other that no message can be received except by the instrument for which it is intended. 1904 *Electr. World & Engin.* 11 June 1120 The distance between the transmitter and receiver was varied from two meters to twenty meters. No effort was made to 'tune' the circuits. 1915 W. H. ECCLES *Wireless Telegr.* 304 The primary—*i.e.*, the antenna—is tuned to the incoming waves. 1943 C. L. BOLTZ *Basic Radio* xii. 192 At the transmitter.. the LC circuit is tuned to produce free oscillations at a chosen frequency. 1972 *Daily Tel.* (Colour Suppl.) 3 Mar. 17 For several months an 85 foot radio telescope, tuned to 21 centimetres, was aimed at the stars *Tau Ceti* and *Epsilon Eridani*. 1974 *Guardian* 23 Mar. 10/1 The kind of programme listeners tune to, broadcasters respect, and disc critics certainly rarely miss. 1975 D. G. FINK *Electronics Engineers' Handbk.* XIII. 74 Solid-state microwave masers can be tuned over a wide range of frequencies by adjustment of an external magnetic field.

d. *transf.* To set (a machine, etc.) in order for accurate working (*local*); to adjust. In mod. use, to adjust (an engine or part) to improve its efficiency or some other attribute; also with the vehicle or craft as obj. (Cf. TUNER 2 b.) See also 10 c, and TUNING 1 c.

1814 W. NICHOLSON in Trotter *E. Galloway Sk.* (1901) 44/1, I wot a pleugh he weel could tune. 1891 [see TUNING *vbl. sb.* 1 c]. *c* 1904 in *Eng. Dial. Dict.* s.v., He tunes his own loom (w. Yks.). 1916 R. T. NICHOLSON *Bk. of Ford* 151 You know now how to 'tune' your carburetter for the best results. 1931 T. E. LAWRENCE *Let.* 10 June (1938) 724 The R.A.F. detached me to Hythe on special duty, to test and tune their new-type speed-boats for the Schneider Cup. 1955 *Times* 23 Aug. 7/6 The Rootes Group have chosen..an engine..and have tuned it for economy and longevity rather than maximum efficiency. 1978 R. WESTALL *Devil on Road* i. 3, I can strip her [*sc.* a motor-bike] in a day *and* put it all back. Tuned her like Yehudi Menuhin's violin.

2. *fig.* To 'put in tune' (with various shades of meaning). **a.** To bring into a proper or desirable condition; to give a special tone or character (esp. of a good kind) to.

1530 RASTELL *Bk. Purgat.* II. xviii, Curyng & tunyng his body. 1639 FULLER *Holy War* II. xviii. (1647) 68 All his life was religiously tuned. *c* 1811 FUSELI in *Lect. Paint.* v. (1848) 461 Violent foreshortening, set off and tuned by magic light and shade. 1866 G. MACDONALD *Ann. Q. Neighb.* xiii, The place.. tuned me to a solemn mood.

b. To bring into accord or harmony; to attune. Also *intr.* for *refl.* to attune itself, to harmonize (quot. 1653).

1590 MARLOWE *Edw. II*, IV. ii, Thou art deceiv'd,..To think that we can yet be tun'd together. 1653 HOLCROFT *Procopius* IV. 137 Mens judgements ever thus tune to that which pleases their wills. *a* 1711 KEN *Hymnotheo* Poet. Wks. 1721 III. 310 They both were tun'd with equal Sympathy.

c. To put into a proper condition for producing some effect; to adapt to a particular purpose; *esp.* to make subservient to one's own ends.

1581 PETTIE *Guazzo's Civ. Conv.* III. (1586) 168 b, The maister is troubled to tune his new seruaunts to his fancie. 1636 W. SCOT *Apol. Narr.* (1846) 93 Mr. Thomas Buchanan tuned and tutored him as he saw it fitting. *a* 1722 FOUNTAINHALL *Decis.* (1759) I. 184 A Scots Council is instantly called, who..fly very high, as they had been tuned. 1868 J. H. BLUNT *Ref. Ch. Eng.* I. 161 The most effective way, except the pulpit, of tuning public opinion. 1882 *Ibid.* II. 483 The pulpits were industriously tuned by means of lecturers.

3. a. *intr.* To give forth a musical sound; to sound; to sing.

c 1500 *Proverbs in Antiq. Rep.* (1809) IV. 407 A Shawme makithe a swete sounde, for he tunythe the basse. *c* 1580–1627 [implied in TUNER 1]. 1760–72 [see TUNING *vbl. sb.* 2]. 1906 *Westm. Gaz.* 10 Nov. 14/2 Last week..I heard a blackbird tuning. 1907 GALSWORTHY *Country Ho.* I. i, Like a breeze tuning through the frigid silence of a fog.

b. with *to*: To sing or sound in tune with (*intr.* of 1 b).

1627 DRAYTON *Quest of Cynthia* xxxiv, Tuning to the waters fall, The small Birds sang to her. 1755 JOHNSON, *Tune*, to form one sound to another.

c. To utter inarticulate musical notes or melody; to hum. *dial.*

1755 JOHNSON, *To Tune*, v.n...2. To utter with the voice inarticulate harmony. 1848 A. B. EVANS *Leicester. Words* s.v., My children could tune before they could speak. 1882 in OGILVIE.

4. a. *trans.* To utter or express (something) musically, to sing; to celebrate in music. *poet.* or *arch.*

1593 SHAKS. *Lucr.* 1107 The little birds that tune their mornings ioy. 1667 MILTON *P.L.* v. 196 Fountains and yee that warble, as ye flow, Melodious murmurs, warbling tune his praise. 1678 DRYDEN & LEE *Œdipus* I. i, Rouze up ye Thebans; tune your Io Pæans! 1697 DRYDEN *Virg. Georg.* II. 542 To Bacchus..let us tune our Lays. 1791 BURNS *Lament for Glencairn* ii, As he tuned his doleful sang. *a* 1814 A. BURN in *Mem.* iii. (1816) 135 Tuning a hymn of thanksgiving to her praise.

†**b.** To set or start the tune for (a hymn, etc. in public worship), as a precentor. *Obs.*

1667 PEPYS *Diary* 21 Apr., The organ, which is handsome, and tunes the psalm. 1679 *Marriage Chas. II* 10 The Cardinal tun'd the *Te deum*, which was sung with musick. 1895 J. BROWN *Pilgr. Fathers* xi. 349 The 'tuning the psalm' as it was called was left to some member of the congregation who volunteered the performance.

5. To produce music from, to play upon (an instrument), esp. the lyre. *poet.*

1701 ADDISON *Epil. to Granville's Brit. Enchant.* Wks. 1721 I. 142 When Orpheus tun'd his lyre..Rivers forgot to run, and winds to blow. 1746 FRANCIS tr. *Horace, Epist.* I. iii. 16 To tune to Theban Sounds the Roman Lyres.

6. *intr.* Of a radio, etc.: to be capable of being tuned.

1922 *Wireless World* 1 July 435/1 Will the Reinartz Tuner tune to any wavelength by means of external coils? 1930 J. H. REYNER *Testing Radio Sets* iv. 55 It may be found that the circuit does not tune correctly when the aerial is connected to its proper terminal. 1970 J. EARL *Tuners & Amplifiers* i. 23 The f.m. section will..tune over Band II, usually from about 88 to 108MHz.

II. With adverbs.

7. tune in. a. *intr.* To strike into a chorus; to interpose in a conversation.

1912 *World* 7 May 680/1 The..Passenger is preparing to continue the cross-examination, when an old lady carrying a long broom tunes in.

b. *trans.* and *intr.* To tune a radio or television to (a particular station or transmission, or a particular frequency). Freq. ***to tune in on*** or ***in to.*** Also *transf.*

1913 *Wireless World* Apr. p. xxxviii/1 It is possible to tune out one ship or station and tune in others. 1919 *Ibid.* May 105/2 Operators at the various Government wireless stations in and about town, who promptly 'tuned in' and listened. 1922 *Westm. Gaz.* 12 Dec., While listening-in on a Lincoln wireless company's apparatus..Mr. H. Mawer was successful in tuning in to an American broadcasting station. 1929 S. CHENEY *Theatre* xxiv. 536 A million or so people may..sit in their parlors and 'tune in' on a song by Al Jolson or a scene from *Twelfth Night.* 1935 S. LEWIS *It can't happen Here* 52 He tuned in on a program of old songs. 1936 AUDEN & ISHERWOOD *Ascent of F6* (1937) II. iii. 102 Turn off the wireless. Tune in to another station. 1956 R. M. LESTER *Towards Hereafter* 18 This higher range of inspirational thought is constantly being radiated, and each one of us in his own capacity can tune into it. 1957 A. C. CLARKE *Deep Range* xii. 104 This was a simple enough task for the sub's frequency converters; if he wished, Franklin could tune in to any sounds from almost a million cycles a second down to vibrations as sluggish as the slow opening of an ancient, rusty door. 1964 MRS. L. B. JOHNSON *White House Diary* 12 Jan. (1970) 42 We tuned in on my TV appearance in '*The Week That Was*'. 1976 *Shooting Times & Country Mag.* 16–22 Dec. 30/3 The Indians when on a hunt think of anything but their quarry, as they believe that the hunted can 'tune in' on their thoughts. 1977 'J. FRASER' *Hearts Ease in Death* vii. 61 You make it sound like a radio serial. Tune in next week for the latest episode.

c. *fig.* To become mentally receptive to, or aware of; to comprehend. Const. as prec. sense.

1926 *Variety* 29 Dec. 5/4 Those fortunate individuals who can tune in on the conversation of a flock of cannons and follow it without the aid of a central office dick or an interpreter. 1961 A. MILLER *Misfits* ii. 18 His mind is constantly trying to tune in on the world, but the message is never clear. 1977 R. GADNEY *Champagne Marxist* xiii. 84 He'd been so slow in tuning in to the presence of an intruder.

d. *fig.* To harmonize *with.*

1938 L. MACNEICE *I crossed Minch* ii. 25, I had a passion for the wild... This tuned in with my other passions for the antique, the fantastic,..and the Irish.

8. tune off. a. *intr.* To get out of 'tune' or adjustment.

1703 T. N. *City & C. Purchaser* (1736), *Raking-Work*, that which (..in Mouldings, etc.) is to be join'd by Mitering exactly, to prevent the Work tuneing off, as Workmen call it, after 'tis put together.

b. *trans.* and *intr.* = *tune out* (sense 9 below). Also *fig. rare.*

1926 MAINES & GRANT *Wise-Crack Dict.* 14/1 *Tune off that station*, change the conversation. 1931 F. A. ARNOLD *Broadcast Advertising* 140 The public has its own method of self protection. The listener may..tune off and find some program less offensive. 1957 *Practical Wireless* XXXIII. 721/1 When the input signal decreases, as one tunes off the station, the valve will conduct.

9. tune out. a. *trans.* To eliminate reception of (a radio signal of a particular frequency) by tuning.

1908 *Rep. Brit. Assoc. Adv. Sci. 1907* 621 It is easy to hear the ships in the Channel, but it is also easy to tune everything out and listen to the desired station alone. 1913 [see sense 7 b above]. 1957 *Practical Wireless* XXXIII. 722/1 When..the signal is tuned out, the voltage at point A drops. 1970 J. EARL *Tuners & Amplifiers* ii. 47 The filter tunes out the 19kHz pilot carrier. 1981 G. MACBETH *Kind of Treason* xiii. 124 Strand was kneeling at the radio. He found the station and tuned the static out.

b. *fig.* To disregard; to cease listening to.

1928 T. E. LAWRENCE *Let.* 1 May (1938) 599 In the East ..you hear everything that's happening, and a great deal more. The selective ear tunes out the false news. 1969 *Sat. Rev.* (U.S.) 5 July 28 If you don't like what I say, you can tune me out. 1970 E. G. OLIM in S. Rogers *Children & Language* (1975) v. 322 He learns, as a result of failure and frustration in school, either to tune out the school or to adopt a defiant, rebellious attitude towards it. 1978 G. A. SHEEHAN *Running & Being* iii. 38, I have the ability to tune out what is going on around me.

10. tune up. a. *trans.* and *intr.* To raise one's voice (in song or otherwise), to sing out (cf. 3).

1701 STANHOPE *St. Aug. Medit.* xxvi. 54 Let us tune our Voices up with theirs. 1763 T. SMITH *Jrnl.* (1849) 274 The robin and spring birds begin to tune up. 1895 J. G. MILLAIS *Breath fr. Veldt* (1899) 202, I have heard an old cow tune up in like manner.

b. *trans.* To bring (an instrument) up to the proper pitch, to put in tune (= 1); also *fig.* (cf. 2). Now usu. *absol.*

a 1718 PENN *Maxims* Wks. 1726 I. 830 We are too apt to awaken and tune up their [Children's] Passions by the Example of our own. 1776 GRAVES *Euphrosyne* I. 224 Each Cockney that tunes up his lyre. 1869 W. S. GILBERT *Bab Ballads* 182 He requested them to tune up and begin. 1902 VIOLET JACOB *Sheep-Stealers* x, The band began to tune up, and a general feeling of expectation pervaded the building. 1929 W. FAULKNER *Sound & Fury* 31 'Now you got to tune up.' Dilsey said. 1981 A. SCHLEE *Rhine Journey* xii. 154 Already the orchestra was tuning up for the next waltz.

c. To put (a machine, a racing vessel, etc.) into the most efficient working order (cf. 1 d).

1901 *Daily Chron.* 24 Aug. 5/7 The..captain will keep all hands at work tuning her [a yacht] up until she is able to show all the speed she has in her. 1908 *Westm. Gaz.* 31 Dec. 4/2 The art of tuning up a car is understood by very few amateurs, who..are satisfied with results which could be improved upon.

† **tune** (tyn), early ME. form of *tyne*, TINE *v.*[1] (OE. *týnan*), to close, shut; to fence or enclose. *c* **1175** *Lamb. Hom.* 49 þe mon þe tuneð his eren in halie chirche toȝeines godes laȝe. *Ibid.*, þe put ne tuneð noht..his muð ouer us bute we tunen ure muð. *a* **1225** *Ancr. R.* 80 Vuel speche; þat ȝe þertoȝeines tunen ower earen. **1605** VERSTEGAN *Dec. Intell.* ix. (1628) 295 His Cote or house was fenced or tuned about.

tune, anglicized form of TUNA[1].

tuneable, etc.: see TUNABLE, etc.

tuned (tju:nd, *poet.* 'tju:nɪd), *ppl. a.* [f. TUNE *v.* (and *sb.*) + -ED.] **1.** Put in tune, sounded musically, etc. (see the verb): usually with qualifying word (in which case sometimes from the sb. = having a specified 'tune' or tone); also with adv.

1579 W. WILKINSON *Confut. Familye of Loue* 26 b, Straunge doctrine and new tuned opinions. *c* **1586** C'TESS PEMBROKE *Ps.* LVII. vi, To spread thy praise With tuned laies. **1598** *Mucedorus* Induct. 6 Sound foorth Bellonas siluer tuned strings. **1662** PLAYFORD *Skill Mus.* (1674) 58 The Dorick Mood consisted of sober slow Tun'd Notes. **1746–7** HERVEY *Medit.*, *Tombs* (1767) I. 37 Their Inclinations were nicely-tuned Unisons, and all their conversation was Harmony. **1908** *Daily Report* 31 Aug. 9/1 The professional rider on a specially tuned-up machine [motor].

2. a. *Electronics.* Adjusted so as to resonate at a particular frequency; forming part of a circuit so adjusted. Also *transf.*

1899 J. J. FAHIE *Hist. Wireless Telegr.* 182 The circuits are said to be in resonance, or to be electrically tuned. **1928**, etc. [see LITZ]. **1936** *Discovery* June 197/2 This is of importance in short-wave technique, seeing that condensation is constantly varying the capacity of the tuned circuit. **1962** SIMPSON & RICHARDS *Physical Princ. Junction Transistors* xiv. 328 Two types of high-frequency amplifiers are in general use, tuned amplifiers and untuned wide-band or video amplifiers. **1971** *Nature* 3 Dec. 256/1 In *Diptera*, the antennae are the principal organs of hearing and are tuned and directional. **1980** K. J. BOHLMAN *Colour & Mono Television* I. viii. 97 At Band 4 and 5 frequencies, conventional *L, C* tuning circuits are not practical... Fortunately..it is possible to use tuned transmission lines.

b. Having one's radio or television tuned (*in*) to a particular station; esp. in imp. phr. ***stay tuned***, go on listening to this station.

1956 *Amer. Speech* XXXI. 258 Stay tuned for Roy Neal and his program. **1970** *Wall St. Jrnl.* 15 June 1/1, 13 million American homes are tuned in via ABC-TV to a previously taped episode of Mr Welk's 15-year-old show. **1972** *Guardian* 8 Jan. 8/3 Our own Keith Dewhurst..had stayed tuned for this unique blend. **1977** 'E. CRISPIN' *Glimpses of Moon* viii. 152 She fiddled with volume control in order to get him satisfactorily tuned in.

c. ***tuned in*** (fig.): (*a*) in rapport with, in harmony with; const. *to*, *on*; (*b*) (*slang*) = *switched on* s.v. SWITCHED *a.* and *ppl. a.* 3 b.

1958 *Oxf. Mag.* 1 May 398/1 It took us some time to get tuned in... Everyone was saying how much better the second half was than the first... Had we just begun to get the wave-length?.. A minor triumph in the difficult art of getting acquainted. **1963** N. MARSH *Dead Water* (1964) i. 29, I miss..the way people think. All the same, it's fun trying to get tuned-in. **1968** P. BROOK *Empty Space* iii. 85 It is perhaps for this reason that..the pop tradition in England has such wide appeal: non-political, unaligned, it is none the less tuned in on a fragmented world in which bombs, drugs, God, parents, sex, and private anxieties, are inseparable. **1972** D. HASTON *In High Places* xii. 143 I'd walk alone, slowly shaking off the delights of civilization and getting completely tuned in once again to a mountain environment. **1976** *National Observer* (U.S.) 14 Aug. 12/2 This is a regional museum tuned in to the story of man's relationship to the wilderness. **1977** *Hudson Rev.* Spring 69, I thought he'd be some kind of *creep*, instead I meet this really sweet cat... He's really tuned in.

tuneful ('tju:nfʊl), *a.* [f. TUNE *sb.* + -FUL.] **1.** Full of 'tune' or musical sound; musical, sweet-sounding.

1598 MARSTON *Sco. Villanie*, *Ad rithmum* (1599) 194 In tunefull numbers keeping musicks time. **1697** PRIOR *Sat. Mod. Translators* 120 The just Measure of a tuneful Dance. *a* **1764** LLOYD *Actor* Poet. Wks. 1774 I. 22 The tuneful voice, the eye that spoke the mind. **1814** SCOTT *Ld. of Isles* IV. xi, His bright and brief career is o'er, And mute his tuneful strains. **1843** JAMES *Forest Days* iii, It was a time of year when the whole world was tuneful.

2. Producing or yielding musical sounds; making melody; performing or skilled in music; musical (as a person, instrument, etc.).

1591 SPENSER *Teares of Muses* 27 The trembling streames ..were by them right tunefull taught to beare A Bases part amongst their consorts oft. **1606** SYLVESTER *Du Bartas* II. iv. I. *Trophies* 416 With his tunefull Lyre, Expels th' ill Spirit which doth the body tyre. **1671** MILTON *P.R.* II. 290 With chaunt of tuneful Birds resounding loud. **1693** YALDEN *Ode to Congreve* v, From tuneful Chaucer's down to thy own Dryden's Muse. **1704** PRIOR *Let. to Despreaux* 18 When thy young Muse invok'd the tuneful Nine. **1805** SCOTT *Last Minstr.* I. Introd. i, For, well-a-day! their date was fled, His tuneful brethren all were dead. **1878** H. S. LEIGH *Town Garland* 10, I listen, contented and calm, to a band Of the tuneful Teutonics who favour the Strand.

3. Relating or adapted to music.

1697 DRYDEN *Virg. Past.* IX. 44 A Member of the tuneful trade. **1762–77** SIR W. JONES *Arcadia* Poems (1777) 105 Ev'n Pan thy tuneful skill confess'd. **1842** WHITTIER *Raphael* xviii, Think ye the notes of holy song On Milton's tuneful ear have died?

Hence **'tunefully** *adv.*, in a tuneful manner, with sweet sound, musically; **'tunefulness**, tuneful or musical quality.

1638–56 COWLEY *Davideis* I. 476 Storehouse of all Proportions! single Quire! Which first God's Breath did tunefully inspire! **1798** WORDSW. *Peter Bell* Prol. xv, How tunefully the forests ring! **1882** OGILVIE, Tunefulness. **1893** L. S. KEYSER in *Chicago Advance* 3 Aug., A song sparrow.. taking the bays for real tunefulness from every rival.

tune-in ('tju:nɪn). *U.S.* [f. vbl. phr. *to tune in*: see TUNE *v.* 7 b.] **a.** The state of being tuned to a particular station or channel. **b.** The size of the audience for a station or channel.

1931 in F. A. Arnold *Fourth Dimension* 141, I hit the high spots between 7:00 and 10:00 p.m. four evenings a week with a tune-in on the biggest features that come occasionally. **1951** *Sun* (Baltimore) (B ed.) 20 Mar. 1/7 No figures were available for the afternoon telecasts, but..the average tune-in from 12 noon to 6 P.M. here is about twelve per cent. **1970** *T.V. Guide* (N.Y. Metro ed.) 8 Aug. A1/1 The network is abandoning..long familiar Sabbath half hours..in favor of occasional hour-long specials to be scheduled late Sunday afternoon when tune-in is higher than it is at midday.

tuneless ('tju:nlɪs), *a.* [f. TUNE *sb.* + -LESS.] **1.** Having no sweetness of tone; untuneful, unmusical, unmelodious, harsh-sounding.

1594 SPENSER *Amoretti* xliv, Then Orpheus with his harp theyr strife did bar..But, when in hand my tunelesse harp I take, Then doe I more augment my foes despight. **1656** COWLEY *Misc.*, *Swallow* 3 Foolish Prater, what dost thou.. With thy tuneless Serenade? **1759** [H. DALRYMPLE] *Woodstock: an Elegy* (1761) 16 His tuneless numbers hardly now survive. **1870** MORRIS *Earthly Par.* II. III. 47 The music of her voice Made the birds' song seem tuneless noise.

2. Giving no 'tune' or sound; not making music; songless; silent.

1728 W. STARRAT *Epist.* 48 in *Ramsay's Poems* (1877) II. 275 What tuneless heart-strings wadna twang, When love and beauty animate the sang? **1774** GOLDSM. *Nat. Hist.* IV. ii. (1824) II. 337 The Field-fare and the Red-wing..With us..are insipid tuneless birds, flying in flocks. **1821** BYRON *Juan* III. *Isles of Greece* v, The heroic lay is tuneless now. **1868** GEO. ELIOT *Sp. Gipsy* 227 As tuneless as a bag of wool.

3. Without musical knowledge or skill. *rare.*

1821 BYRON *Juan* IV. lxxxvii, An ignorant, noteless, timeless, tuneless fellow.

Hence **'tunelessly** *adv.*, **'tunelessness**.

1881 M. ARNOLD in *Macm. Mag.* Mar. 370 The slovenliness and tunelessness of much of Byron's production. **1905** Q. COUCH *Shining Ferry* II. xii, Mr. Sam spoke tunelessly.

tunellite (tʌ'nɛlaɪt). *Min.* [f. the name of George *Tunell* (b. 1900), U.S. geologist + -ITE[1].] A hydrated borate of strontium, $SrB_6O_{10}.4H_2O$, found as colourless or white monoclinic crystals.

1961 R. C. ERD et al. in *Prof. Papers U.S. Geol. Survey* No. 424-C 294/1 Tunellite was first noted..in some samples collected in 1957 from a ventilating shaft in the Jenifer mine, Kramer borate district, California. **1964**, **1968** [see NOBLEITE]. **1978** *Mercian Geologist* VI. 263 Tunellite..has been found only in the lower part of the borate zone in the Emet deposits in the clay layers in the Kirka deposits [in Turkey].

tuner ('tju:nə(r)). [f. TUNE *v.* + -ER[1].] One who or that which tunes.

1. a. One who produces or utters musical sounds; a player or singer. *arch.*

c **1580** LODGE *Reply Gosson's Sch. Abuse* (Hunter. Cl.) 26 A doleful tuner. **1627** DRAYTON *Sheph. Sirena* 200 Our mournefull Philomell, that rarest Tuner.

b. One who gives a particular (vocal) tone to something. *rare*$^{-1}$.

1592 SHAKS. *Rom. & Jul.* II. iv. 30 The Pox of such antique lisping affecting phantacies, these new tuners of accent.

2. a. One who tunes a musical instrument; *spec.* whose occupation is to tune pianos or organs. Also *fig.*

1801 BUSBY *Dict. Mus.*, *Tuner*, one whose profession it is to rectify the false sounds of musical instruments. **1842** MRS. BROWNING *Grk. Chr. Poets* etc. 128 Lord Surrey passes as the tuner of our English. **1872** SPURGEON *Treas. Dav.* Ps. lix. Introd. III. 74 Affliction is the tuner of the harps of sanctified songsters. **1883** GODDEN in *Knowledge* 25 May 315/2 This [interval] is so equally dispersed by good tuners as to be almost imperceptible.

b. A workman employed to 'tune' a loom: see TUNE *v.* 1 d.

1885 *Scotsman* 26 Aug. 3/6 Tweed Trade—Wanted..An assistant power-loom tuner. **1888** *Engineering* 20 Jan. 69 Mules and looms..in the charge of men known as 'tuners'.

c. An adjustable flap or opening in a flue-pipe of an organ, by means of which it is tuned (cf. *tuning-hole* s.v. TUNING 4).

1891 in *Cent. Dict.*

3. Any device for varying the frequency to which a radio or television is tuned; *spec.* a separate unit for detecting and preamplifying the programme signal and supplying it to an audio amplifier. Also ***tuner unit***.

1909 J. ERSKINE-MURRAY *Handbk. Wireless Telegr.* (ed. 2) 148 Another instrument..has been designed quite recently (1908). It is called the tuner and contains the inductances, capacities, and coupling arrangements required in a tuned receiving station. **1925** W. GREENWOOD *Text-bk. Wireless Telegr. & Telephony* vi. 122 (*heading*) The tuner portion of a receiving circuit. *Ibid.* 124 The various tuning inductances and condensers are often assembled in a separate box called the 'tuner'. **1953** E. T. CANBY *Home Music Syst.* iii. 37 There are separate units that combine numerous functions: AM-FM radio tuners;..separate AM tuners and FM tuners; [etc.]. **1959** *Listener* 26 Mar. 541/2 There is no substitute for a high-quality FM tuner unit. **1967** *Ibid.* 30 Mar. 424/1 Some parts of the [television] receiver, such as.. the tuner unit, and the box, will cost no more than in a black-and-white receiver. **1970** *Which?* Apr. 115/1 Most of the tuners had a device to show when you were exactly tuned to a station. **1976** K. THACKERAY *Crownbird* vi. 127 Priest rotated the tuner on his receiver until he was listening to the police frequency.

4. Special Comb.: **tuner-amplifier**, a combined radio tuner and amplifier; cf. RECEIVER[1] 7 c; also abbrev. **tuner-amp**.

1970 J. EARL *Tuners & Amplifiers* i. 21 The tuner-amplifier is a new breed of hi-fi equipment. **1975** *Hi-Fi Answers* Feb. 49/1 Your choice of possible tuner-amps is limited by your requirement for an MW section. **1979** J. GARDNER *Nostradamus Traitor* xi. 37 A big reel-to-reel tape machine..was linked to a tuner/amplifier set to a pre-selected clear channel.

Tunesin(e), obs. var. TUNISINE *sb.* and *a.*

tunesmith ('tju:nsmɪθ). *colloq.* (orig. *U.S.*). [f. TUNE *sb.* + SMITH *sb.*] A composer of popular music or songs; *derog.*, a composer of unoriginal or trifling music.

1926 WHITEMAN & MCBRIDE *Jazz* viii. 171 Jazz..is the hardest of all to write, the tunesmiths say. **1959** E. S. TURNER *Court of St. James's* xxiii. 256 A modern lyric writer and tunesmith in Tin Pan Alley. **1962** *Times* 24 Aug. 11/6 How else does it happen that Bellini, dismissed for years as a vapid tunesmith, has become admired in our own day as a master of poised classical music-drama. **1976** *Gramophone* Nov. 843/3 How dare he dismiss Duke Ellington as a mere 'tunesmith'!

tunesome ('tju:nsəm), *a. rare.* [f. TUNE *sb.* + -SOME.] Having 'tune' or melody; tuneful.

1890 *Sat. Rev.* 26 Apr. 514/2 These pieces are..tunesome and original. **1921** W. DE LA MARE *Crossings* iii. 82 As neat a brace of nightingales as ever I heard. Shy, but tunesome.

tunester ('tju:nstə(r)). Chiefly *U.S.* [f. TUNE *sb.* + -STER.] A song-writer or singer; a musician, composer.

1903 R. HUGHES *Love Affairs of Great Musicians* I. xii. 126 (*heading*) A few tunesters of France and Italy—Peri, Monteverdi, et al. **1935** *Amer. Speech* X. 154/2 Singers are now tunesters to advertisement writers for vaudeville and other entertainments. **1936** *N.Y. World-Telegram* 22 Aug. 14/4 At that studio, too, are Mack Gordon and Harry Revell, best known of all movie tunesters. **1983** *Washington Post* 9 May B11/1 Luigi Proietti as a tour guide is pretty lively and alert, like a merry tunester at a funeral.

tune-up ('tju:nʌp). orig. *U.S.* [f. vbl. phr. *to tune up*: see TUNE *v.* 8.]

1. The action, or an act, of tuning up (*lit.* and *fig.*).

1933 *Automotive Electrician* Nov. 16 (*heading*) Analyzing the need for winter tune-up. **1959** [see HOT ROD]. **1962** *Daily Tel.* 17 Jan. 20/5 Parties begin on election tune-up... Preliminary moves to 'tune-up' the Conservative and Labour party machines for the next general election have already begun. **1968** 'E. LATHEN' *Stitch in Time* viii. 71 He always does the tune-ups on Dr Neverson's sports cars. **1977** *Rolling Stone* 16 June 12/1 They still take ten-minute tuneups between songs.

2. *Sport* (chiefly *U.S.*). An event that serves as a practice for a subsequent one.

1934 *Collier's* 11 Aug. 48/3 Webb..intended starting Black Gold in a few tune-up races. **1940** *Sun* (Baltimore) 19 Aug. 20/5 The rain..spoiled several attempts to stage an informal flying exhibit as a tuneup for the annual meet. **1946** *Richmond* (Va.) *Times-Dispatch* 10 Apr. 16/3 A couple of Purple Heart fighters..went along fine in easy tuneups. **1962** *Times* 25 Apr. 4/5 Warburg, who must have benefited from his thorough tune-up against Hughes. **1979** E. NEWMAN *Sunday Punch* xx. 181 'When's Turner?' 'In about four months. I have a tune-up in Pittsburgh first.'

tuney, tune-y, var. TUNY *a.*

tunful ('tʌnfʊl). [f. TUN *sb.* + -FUL 2.] As much as fills a tun.

1562 TURNER *Baths* 4 Manye..carye great tunnfulls of it awaye, and drinke it in theyr houses. *a* **1592** GREENE *Vision* Wks. (Grosart) XII. 203 But for euery dram of mirth, they leaue behinde..a Tunfull of infecting mischiefs. **1819** SHELLEY *Cyclops* 197 You may drink a tunful if you will.

tung (tʌŋ). [a. Chinese *tóng*.] **1. a.** Any of three trees of the genus *Aleurites* or *Vernicia* (family Euphorbiaceæ), *A. fordii*, *A. cordata*, and *A. montana*, which are native to China and Japan and are cultivated there and elsewhere for the oil from their seeds. So ***tung tree***.

1889 *Cent. Dict.*, Tung-tree. **1914** N. SHAW *Chinese Forest Trees* I. ii. 70 Tallow, tea-oil trees, and tung grow wild in these hills. **1921** *Outward Bound* Jan. 42/1 The *tung* tree was the abode of the phoenix. **1959** E. POUND *Thrones* xcix. 52 Phoenix to *t'ung* tree A mirrour to flowers, as water is to the moon. **1965** J. CH'ÊN *Mao & Chinese Revolution* (1967) I. vii. 138 The mountains are covered..with *t'ung*-trees. **1974** *Tropical Agriculture* LI. 10 This series of trials has shown that nitrogen is the most important nutrient for tung in Malawi.

b. The oil extracted from seeds of the tung tree, used chiefly in the manufacture of inks, paints, and varnishes; = WOOD-OIL (*c*).

1911 *Encycl. Brit.* XX. 46/1 (*table*) Name of oil... Tung. **1950** *Caribbean Q.* I. III. 42 A trial should be made with a settlement of 200 families, beginning with pigs and poultry and proceeding to tree crops (coffee, cocoa, citrus, tung). **1962** H. G. CHAMPION *Streets's Exotic Forest Trees Brit. Commonw.* II. 173 The oil [of *Aleurites montana*] is known commercially as Tung.

2. *attrib.*, as ***tung nut***; **tung oil**, a drying oil obtained from the seeds of tung trees and used in varnishes, paints, and inks; so ***tung oil tree***; cf. WOOD-OIL.

1937 R. FROST *Let.* 5 Jan. (1964) 287 We will probably end our days growing *Tung nuts in northern Florida. **1881** *Tung-oil [see WOOD-OIL]. **1913** E. H. WILSON *Naturalist in W. China* II. vii. 64 'T'ung Oil tree'..produces this valuable oil. **1937** A. F. HILL *Econ. Bot.* ix. 213 The United States uses so much tung oil that trees of the latter species have been introduced. **1951** R. MAYER *Artist's Handbk.* iii. 112 Tung Oil..is highly valued as an ingredient of industrial paints and varnishes. **1972** *Guardian* 16 Feb. 15/3 American businessmen..are confronted with increasing difficulties in obtaining soya beans, bristles, tung-oil and egg products from China. **1973** *Times* 21 Mar. (China Trade Suppl.) p. xiv/5 Huge tracts of hillside had only recently been terraced for planting with..tung oil trees.

Also **tung-yu** [Chinese *yóu* oil], tung oil.

1788 tr. *Groiser's Gen. Descr. China* I. IV. vi. 449 The work is..daubed over with a kind of oil, which the Chinese call *tong-yeou*. **1913** E. H. WILSON *Naturalist in W. China* II. vii. 66 'T'ung-yu' is the chief paint oil throughout the Chinese Empire. **1973** T. R. TREGEAR *Chinese* iv. 89 The Yangtze valley is noted for its production of..*tung yu* (wood oil), which forms the basis of paints and varnish.

tung: see TUNC.

tung, tunge, obs. ff. TONGUE.

tungah, var. TANGA[1], an Indian (etc.) coin.

Tungan ('tʌ-, 'tʊŋgən; dʌ-, 'dʊŋgən), *sb.* and *a.* Also †**Tungani** *sing.* and *pl.*; **Dungan.** [ad. Jagatai *Döngan*.] **A.** *sb.* A member of a Muslim people in China and in Russian Central Asia of Chinese descent. **B.** *adj.* Of or pertaining to the Tungans.

1875 BELLEW & CHAPMAN in T. D. Forsyth *Report Mission Yarkund* ii. 81 The Kara Khitay, the Khitay, and the Tungani. **1908** LADY MACARTNEY *Diary* 12 July in *Eng. Lady in Chinese Turkestan* (1931) xi. 166 Tunganis and Kirghiz, noticeable by reason of their big fur hats. **1927** CABLE & FRENCH *Through Jade Gate* xxxvii. 221 A stranger on first seeing a Tungan youth would probably say: 'What a handsome Arab boy.' *Ibid.*, Whereas the Tungan speaks Chinese, the Turki has his own tongue. **1965** K. P. S. MENON *Many Worlds* xiv. 201 A young Tungan General. **1974** *Encycl. Brit. Micropædia* V. 190/3 Some Chinese Muslims, called Dungans, have settled in the Soviet Union in the villages and towns of the Uzbek Soviet Socialist Republic, and the Alma-Ata *oblast* (region) of the Kazakh S.S.R.

Tungar ('tʌŋgɑː(r)). *Electronics.* [f. TUNG(STEN + AR(GON.] A type of low-voltage discharge tube filled with argon and having a heated cathode of thoriated tungsten, used as a rectifier for currents of a few amperes. (A proprietary name in the U.S.)

1917 *Official Gaz.* (U.S. Patent office) 4 Dec. 270/1 General Electric Company... *Tungar*... Rectifying apparatus. Claims use since October, 1916. **1935** NILSON & HORNUNG *Practical Radio Communication* xv. 710 The Tungar battery charger..is a device for charging storage batteries from an alternating-current line. **1966** *McGraw-Hill Encycl. Sci. & Technol.* VI. 61/1 Hot-cathode gas tubes. .. Three representative types may be distinguished, (1) the Tunger..; (2) the phanotron; and (3) the thyratron.

Tungkingese, -quinese, obs. varr. TONKINESE *sb.* and *a.*

tungstate ('tʌŋstət). *Chem.* [f. TUNGST(IC + -ATE[4].] A salt of tungstic acid.

1800 tr. *Lagrange's Chem.* I. 371 The other is known by mineralogists, under the name of *wolfram*..this is the tungstate of iron. **1839** DE LA BECHE *Rep. Geol. Cornwall*, etc. xv. 584 Except when mixed with wolfram, or the tungstate of iron and manganese. **1897** *Allbutt's Syst. Med.* IV. 596 One patient..recovered..while taking tungstate of soda.

tungsten ('tʌŋstɛn, -ən). [a. Sw. *tungsten*, f. *tung* heavy + *sten* stone.]

†**1.** *Min.* = SCHEELITE, native calcium tungstate. *Obs.*

1770 ENGESTROM tr. *Cronstedt's Syst. Min.* 201 *Ferrum calciforme terrâ quâdam incognitâ intimè mixtum.* The Tungsten of the Swedes. **1786** BEDDOES *Chem. Ess. Scheele* 285 Lapis Ponderosus, or Tungsten... It is probable that the constituent parts of this..have been hitherto unknown. **1799** *Med. Jrnl.* I. 239 Tungsten... Scheele..affirmed that it consisted of calcareous earth, united to a peculiar acid. **1822** IMISON *Sc. & Art* II. 120 A mineral called *Tungsten* or ponderous stone, affords a peculiar metal.

2. *Chem.* (Formerly also in L. form **tungstenum**, as in other names of metals.) A heavy, steel-grey, ductile, very infusible metal, contained in the above mineral and in WOLFRAM (iron and manganese tungstate) and other minerals; used for wire in incandescent electric lamps. Symbol W (= *wolframium*); atomic weight 184 (O = 16).

1796 HATCHETT in *Phil. Trans.* LXXXVI. 291 The yellow oxyde of tungsten by ignition becomes blue or black. **1812** DAVY *Chem. Philos.* 427 Tungstenum is obtained from a mineral known by the name of *wolfram*. **1836-41** BRANDE *Man. Chem.* (ed. 5) 921 Tungsten..which has also been called *Scheelium* and *Wolframium*, was first obtained by Messrs. de Luyart [in 1783], from the *tungstic acid* previously discovered by Scheele, in 1781. **1862** *London Rev.* 16 Aug. 154 Tungsten added to steel communicates a most intense hardness to it, and renders it also very fine-grained. **1911** *Daily News* 22 Aug. 2 Tungsten may be converted into strong ductile form and drawn into a wire only one thousandth of an inch in diameter. **1912** *Ann. Rep. Chem. Soc.* IX. 69 Tungsten melts at 3100° ± 60°.

3. *attrib.*, as ***tungsten filament, lamp, -steel, wire.*** **tungsten carbide**, either of two compounds of tungsten and carbon, WC and W_2C, that are very hard and are used for cutting tools and abrasives.

1899 *Jrnl. Chem. Soc.* LXXVI. II. 104 On heating a mixture of tungstic anhydride.., iron.., and petroleum coke.., an iron *tungsten carbide..is obtained. **1930** *Engineering* 14 Nov. 634/2 The enhanced cutting properties of the newer cutting steels, such as the tungsten-carbide tools. **1963** C. R. COWELL et al. *Inlays, Crowns, & Bridges* iii. 12 Penetrate to just within the dentine, using a small round tungsten-carbide bur. **1973** *Sci. Amer.* July 42/1 Tungsten carbide, a cermet, has long been used as a cutting tool. **1922** GLAZEBROOK *Dict. Appl. Physics* II. 379/2 From 1904..it became obvious that the future of the incandescent lamp for some time to come would be with the *tungsten filament lamp. **1962** V. NABOKOV *Pale Fire* 192 The dead, the gentle dead—who knows?—In tungsten filaments abide. **1909** *Installation News* II. 171/2 The *Tungsten lamp will not withstand over running to any great extent. **1862** *London Rev.* 16 Aug. 154 The alloy..is now becoming rather celebrated under the name of wolfram- or *tungsten-steel. **1911** *Encycl. Brit.* XVI. 669/2 The zirconium and *tungsten wire lamps are equal to or surpass the tantalum lamp.

Hence †'**tungstenane**, Davy's proposed name for a chloride of tungsten: see -ANE[2]; **tung'stenic**, †**tung'stenical, tungste'nitic**, *adjs.*, of, pertaining to, or containing tungsten, tungstic; **tungste'niferous** *a.* [-FEROUS], yielding tungsten.

1812 DAVY *Chem. Philos.* 429 *Tungstenane. **1796** KIRWAN *Elem. Min.* (ed. 2) I. 131 The *tungstenic acid.. assumes a blue colour when heated to redness. *Ibid.* 133 An ore of *tungstenical substance. *Ibid.* II. 316 *Tungstenitic Calx, with Iron and Manganese, or Iron singly. Wolfram.

tungstenite ('tʌŋstənaɪt). *Min.* [f. TUNGSTEN + -ITE[1].]

†**1.** = TUNGSTEN 2. *Obs.*

1796 KIRWAN *Elem. Min.* (ed. 2) II. 308 Tungstenite... This substance is capable of existing in three states. That of a Regulus, which I call Tungstenite. *Ibid.*, Tungstenite... Hitherto it has been produced only in very minute Globules, being more difficulty reducible to a Metallic State than Manganese or Uranite.

2. = TUNGSTEN 1.

1894 MUIR & MORLEY *Watts' Dict. Chem.* IV. 797 *Tungstenite*, or *scheelite* (tungstate of Ca[lcium])..occur in various localities.

3. A tungsten sulphide, probably WS_2, that occurs as both hexagonal and rhombohedral polytypes in dark grey scaly aggregates that mark the fingers.

1917 WELLS & BUTLER in *Jrnl. Washington Acad. Sci.* VII. 596 It is..a pleasure to announce the discovery of tungsten sulphide..from..Utah... On account of the apparent resemblance to molybdenite in formula and some of its properties the new mineral has been named tungstenite. **1970** *Canad. Mineralogist* X. 731 It is virtually impossible to distinguish the *x*-ray powder pattern of a given polytype of molybdenite from the same polytype of tungstenite... Consequently it is quite possible that tungstenite is more widespread than the literature indicates.

tungstic ('tʌŋstɪk), *a. Chem.* [f. TUNGST(EN + -IC 1 b.] Pertaining to or formed from tungsten; applied to compounds in which tungsten combines as a hexad (see -IC 1 b), as ***tungstic acid***, $H_2O.WO_3$ (formerly = *t. oxide*), ***tungstic chloride***, WCl_6, ***tungstic oxide***, WO_3; also to minerals containing tungsten, as ***tungstic ochre*** (see OCHRE *sb.* 2), native tungstic oxide, also called '**tungstite**.

1796 HATCHETT in *Phil. Trans.* LXXXVI. 286 In 1790, Mr. Heyer..made some experiments on this ore [molybdate of lead], from which he inferred that it was composed of lead, combined with the tungstic acid. **1836-41** BRANDE *Man. Chem.* (ed. 5) 923 The *Nitro-tungstate of Potassa* is the salt originally described by Scheele [1781] as tungstic acid. **1868** WATTS *Dict. Chem.* V. 915 *Tungstic compounds*,..in which tungsten is hexatomic. **1868** DANA *Min.* (ed. 5) 186 Tungstite.

'**tungsto-**, combining form from TUNGSTEN, used in the names of compound acids (and their salts) containing the oxides of tungsten and another element, as ***tungsto'boric*** and ***tungsto-si'licic acids***, whose salts are ***tungsto'borates*** and ***tungsto'silicates***.

1868 WATTS *Dict. Chem.* V. 915 Tungstosilicic acids. *Ibid.* 917 The tungstosilicates are obtained by saturating the acid with carbonates. **1883** *Science* I. 489/2 Tungstoboric acid proves to be a convenient reagent for characterizing the alkaloids and peptones. *Ibid.*, Cadmic tungstoborate.

tungstous ('tʌŋstəs), *a. Chem.* [f. TUNGST(EN + -OUS c.] Applied to compounds in which tungsten combines as a tetrad, as ***tungstous chloride***, WCl_4, ***tungstous oxide***, WO_2. (Cf. TUNGSTIC.)

1860 in MAYNE *Expos. Lex.* **1868** WATTS *Dict. Chem.* V. 898 Tungsten forms two classes of compounds, in one of which it is tetratomic, and in the other hexatomic: Tungstous Chloride, WCl^4; Tungstous Oxide, WO^2.

‖'**tungua**, a West Indian name of the CHIGOE.

1815 KIRBY & SP. *Entomol.* iv. (1818) I. 103 The celebrated Chigoe or Jiggers, called also..Tungua. **1861** MAYHEW *Lond. Labour* III. 35 The most annoying species, however, is..a native of the tropical latitudes, variously named in the West Indies, chigoe, jigger, nigua, tungua, pique.

Tungus ('tʊŋʊs, tʊŋ'uːs). Forms: 6 **Tingus**, 6-7 **Tongu(e)se**, 8 **Toongus.** [Yakut name of a people called by themselves Evenki.] **a.** (A member of) a people of eastern Siberia. Also *attrib.*

1625 PURCHAS *Pilgrimes* III. III. vii. 527 The people.. signified.. that they were called *Tingoesi*, and that their dwelling was vpon the banke of the great Riuer Ienisce. *Ibid.* x. 543 These *Tingusses* report, that there is another huge Riuer. **1698** tr. *A. Brand's Embassy Muscovy into China* 48 The Tongueses..have of late years been conquered by the Victorious Arms of the Czars of Muscovy, unto whom they pay a yearly Tribute. **1698** [see SHAMAN *sb.*]. **1763** J. BELL *Trav. from St. Petersburg* I. iii. 225 The Tongusy, so called from the name of the river, who live along its banks, are the posterity of the ancient inhabitants of Siberia. *Ibid.* 229 When a Tonguse kills an elk or deer, he never moves from the place, till he has eat it up. **1799** W. TOOKE *View Russian Empire* II. 98 That the Tunguses originally composed one people with the Mandshee, is apparent not only from the resemblance of features..but also chiefly from the agreement of their languages. **1841** *Penny Cycl.* XXI. 459/2 The whole region..has been abandoned to the Toonguses, who get their subsistence by the chace. **1882** A. H. KEANE *Asia* 478 Conterminous on the north with the Buriats are the Tunguses. *Ibid.* 479 The Tungus race. **1914** M. A. CZAPLICKA *Aborig. Siberia* 52 The Nomadic Tungus are cattle-breeders. **1931** M. BURR *Bolshevik Siberia* 154 When a Tungus hits off the spoor of one of these grand beasts. **1948** A. L. KROEBER *Anthropol.* (rev. ed.) x. 429 The Manchu, the Mongols, and the still earlier Tungus conquerors of China lost their own cultures there. **1974** J. R. BAKER *Race* x. 174 The Tungus and Kalmuks (Tungid subrace of Mongolids) are said to be devoid of axillary smell.

b. An Altaic language or group of languages related to Manchu, spoken in parts of Siberia, and since 1931 set down in an alphabet based on the Russian alphabet. Also *attrib.* Cf. MANCHU-TUNGUS.

1822 tr. *Malte-Brun's Universal Geogr.* I. xxiii. 571 The Tunguse is a dialect of the Mantchou. **1888** *Encycl. Brit.* XXIV. 1/2 An exuberance..of verbal forms, which in Osmanli, Finnish, Magyar, Tungas, and Mordvinian may be said to run riot. **1961** L. F. BROSNAHAN *Sounds of Language* viii. 177 The area of the simple stress accent.. includes..the Mongolian, Tungus and Paleosiberian languages of eastern Asia. **1977** C. F. & F. M. VOEGELIN *Classification & Index World's Languages* 335 The Tungus languages are bifurcated into two groups... Northern Tungus..= Evenki... Southern Tungus.

Hence **Tun'gusian** *a.*, of or pertaining to this people or language; *sb.*, a Tungus; also, the Tungus language; **Tun'gusic** *a.*, Tungusian; *sb.*, the Tungus language.

1706 tr. *E. Y. Ides's Trav.* 27 Subject to the Jurisdiction of this City are several Tunguzian Heathens. **1706** [see SHAMAN *sb.*]. **1763** J. BELL *Trav. from St. Petersburg* I. iii. 231 From all the accounts I have heard..of the natives of Canada..they..resemble..the Tongusians. **1799** W. TOOKE *View Russian Empire* II. 100 At that time [*sc.* 1607] many tungusian stems owned the paramount supremacy of the Buriats who had shortly before been expelled from Mongolia. **1839** *Jrnl. R. Geogr. Soc.* IX. 198 The Tungusian, though confined to the eastern extreme of the ancient continent, contains some words common to it with languages spoken in Europe. **1854** MAX MÜLLER in C. Bunsen *Christianity & Mankind* III. 277 Some of them are certainly widely distant; as, for instance, the dialects of the Finnic nations in the west, and of the Mongolic and Tungusic tribes in the east. **1855** H. D. SEYMOUR *Russia on Black Sea & Sea of Azof* v. 49 The Tungusians extend on the east from the Yenisei to the Sea of Okhotsk. **1864** *Ann. Rep. Smithsonian Inst. 1863* 111 The rank of the Scythian languages..is but an inferior one... They diminish in value eastward, the Tungusic being the poorest of all. **1885** J. BYRNE *Struct. Lang.* I. 391 The Tungusian dialect. *Ibid.* 398 The verb *bi*, which in Tungusian takes *hi* in the present. **1888** *Encycl. Brit.* XXIV. 2/2 Turkic lies much closer to Mongolic than it does to Samoyedic and Tungusic. **1890** [see GILYAK]. **1914** [see PALÆO-SIBERIAN *sb.*]. **1951** W. K. MATTHEWS *Languages U.S.S.R.* iv. 54 Of the three branches of Altaic the easternmost and least significant numerically is the Manchurian or Tungusic. This comprises two subdivisions, viz. the declining Manchu of Northern Manchuria (Manchukuo), with the related languages..and the more primitive and vigorous Tungus (Evenki) and its cognates. **1956** J. WHATMOUGH *Language* ii. 32 The great belt of Mongolian and Tungusian..is connected with the Turkic languages further west, and with Yakut to the North, reaching through Siberia to the Arctic. **1977** *N.Y. Rev. Books* 14 Apr. 3/1 Founded in 947 as a capital of the Khitan Mongols' Liao dynasty, it [*sc.* Peking] had been used similarly by the Tungusic Chin dynasty 1122–1234.

tunhoof ('tʌnhuːf). Now *dial.* Forms: 1 **tunhófe**, 4 **tunhowe, -hoo**, 5-6 **tunhove**, 6 **tune-**, 7 **tunnehoofe**, 8- **tunhoof.** [f. TUN *sb.* + OE. *hófe*, HOVE *sb.*[1]: see ALE-HOOF.] The herb Ground Ivy (*Nepeta Glechoma*).

c **1000** *Sax. Leechd.* II. 344 Wyrc gode earsealfe..tunhofe nioþoweard, celeþonian leaf garleac, cropleac, do on win. **14** .. *Stockh. Med. MS.* II. 406 in *Anglia* XVIII. 317 Anoþer herbe is callyd soo [ground-ivy] þat we callyn tunhoo. *c* **1440**

Promp. Parv. 506/1 Tunhove, herbe (*K.* tunhowe, *S.* thomyhow, *A.* thonnhowe), *edera terrestris.* **1597** GERARDE *Herbal* I. ccc. 705 In English ground Iuie, Alehoof,.. Tunehoofe, and Cats foote. **1640** PARKINSON *Theatr. Bot.* v. xciii. 677 Gill creepe by the ground, Catsfoote, Haymaides, and Alehoofe most generally, or Tunnehoofe, because the countrey people use it much in their Ale. **1869** *Gd. Words* Mar. Supp. 4, I used to gather in armfuls primroses,.. and strong-scented tunhoof.

tunic (ˈtjuːnɪk). Forms: 1 tunece, (tonica), 1–2 tunice, 2 tuneke; 6 tunake, 7 -ike, 7–8 tunick, tunique (also 9 as Fr.), 7– tunic. [ad. F. *tunique* or its source L. *tunica* (whence also Pr., Sp., Pg. *tunica*, It. *tonica, tonaca, tunica*, OE. *tunece*, OHG. *tûnihha*).]

1. A garment resembling a shirt or gown, worn by both sexes among the Greeks and Romans; in OE. and mediæval times, a body-garment or coat over which a loose mantle or cloak was worn.

Now worn on ceremonial occasions by princes and nobles.

[*c*893 K. ÆLFRED *Oros.* v. x. §3 Eft hie him sendon ane tunecan ongean. *c*975 *Rushw. Gosp.* Matt. xxiv. 18 Seþe on londæ sy ne cerraþ he eft to nimene his tunican [*c* **1000** *Ags. Gosp.* tunecan, *c* **1160** *Hatton* tuneken; Vulg. *tunicam*]. **1603** *Cerem. Coronat. Jas I* (1685) 3 There is then also to be delivered to his Majesty the *Tunica*, or Shirt of red Silk.] **1609** BIBLE (Douay) *Lev.* viii. 7 (*Comm.*) A Tunike, or long robe downe to the foote. **1666** EVELYN *Diary* 30 Oct., To London to our office, and now had I on the vest and surcoat and tunic as 'twas call'd, after his Maᵗʸ had brought the whole Court to it. *a* **1678** MARVELL *Royal Resolutions* Wks. (Grosart) I. 434 I'll have a fine tunick, a sash, and a vest. **1725** POPE *Odyss.* x. 647 The goddess with a radiant tunick drest My limbs. **1768** STERNE *Sent. Journ., The Monk, Calais*, He [a Franciscan] gave a slight glance with his eye downwards upon the sleeve of his tunick. **1835** LYTTON *Rienzi* i, His garb.. consisted of the long loose gown and the plain tunic, both of dark-grey serge.

2. *Eccl.* = TUNICLE 2. Only *Hist.*

1696 PHILLIPS (ed. 5), *Tunic*,.. a Church Ornament among the Romanists, worn by the Deacons that serve the Priest or Bishop at the Altar. **1764** in J. H. Harting *Hist. Sardinian Chapel* (1905) 23 Two tunics, with a stole, two maniples of taffeta. **1844** [see DALMATIC B.]. **1877** J. D. CHAMBERS *Div. Worship* 54 The Subdeacon was invested with the Tunic by the Bishop at his ordination.

3. In modern costume. **a.** A close, usually plain body-coat; now *spec.* that forming part of the uniform of soldiers and policemen.

1667 PEPYS *Diary* 20 Oct., Put on my new tunique of velvett; which is very plain, but good. **1668** *Ibid.* 17 May, Put on my new stuff-suit,.. the bands of my vest and tunique laced with silk lace, of the colour of my suit. **1868** *Regul. & Ord. Army* §607 Medals are only to be worn with the tunic.

b. A garment worn by women, consisting of a bodice and an upper skirt, belted or drawn in at (or fitted to) the waist, worn over and displaying a longer skirt. (In very recent use, applied to the upper skirt alone.) Also, a kind of belted frock or smock worn by children.

Now often in Fr. form *tunique* (tynik).

1762 STERNE *Tr. Shandy* VI. xviii, The child looks extremely well.. in his vests and tunicks. **1800** *Hull Advertiser* 4 Oct. 3/3 Paris fashions.. tuniques of black crape are coming into wear. **1803** *Times* 15 Jan., The short tunics of last year, which were called Mamelukes, are in great esteem this year under the name of Jewess Tunics. ? **1838** *First Year of Silken Reign* 230 (Cent. D.) Her Majesty wore a white satin petticoat, over which was a silver llama tunic, trimmed with silver and white blonde lace. **1883** *Truth* 31 May 768/2 Tabs.. appear on tunics, polonaises, bodices, and sleeves. **1899** *Westm. Gaz.* 19 Jan. 3/2 It has consented to sport something tapering away over the back, which it has called its tunique. **1909** *Daily Graphic* 20 Oct. 13/1 A noticeable feature in these dresses is the tight-fitting tunic which runs to the knees.

4. *transf.* **a.** *Anat.* A membranous sheath enveloping or lining an organ of the body; a 'coat'.

1661 BLOUNT *Glossogr.* (ed. 2), *Tunick*.. a skin or coat that covers the eye, whereof there are four sorts. **1678** *Phil. Trans.* XII. 976 The inner Tunick of the Nose. **1725** *Bradley's Fam. Dict.* s.v. *Appetite*, When the Stomach proves empty, the acid Liquor begins to work upon its internal Tunick. **1826** KIRBY & SP. *Entomol.* IV. xxxvii. 7 Besides these is an exterior and an interior tunic. **1880** M. C. DRYSDALE in *Med. Temp. Jrnl.* Oct. 9 The tunics of the capillaries.

b. The integument of a part or organ in a plant; *spec.* in *Bot.* any loose membranous skin not formed from the epidermis; also, each layer or coating of a tunicate bulb.

1760 J. LEE *Introd. Bot.* I. vi. (1765) 14 A Seed.. is a Rudiment of a new Vegetable.. covered with a bladdery Coat or Tunic. **1830** LINDLEY *Nat. Syst. Bot.* 155 The long loose tunic of the seed is intended to act at first as a buoy, to float the seed upon the surface of the water. **1832** *Veg. Subst. Food* 295 The tunics of the onion.

5. *attrib.* and *Comb.* Also **tunic shirt**, a long loose-fitting shirt worn outside the trousers; cf. CAFTAN, CAFTAN.

1828 *Souvenir* II. 79/2 A Tunique pelisse robe of white jaconet muslin. **1832** G. CLARKE *Pompeii* II. xiii. 317 Tunic-pallium displayed. **1835** *Court Mag.* VI. p. i/1 The shirt is trimmed in the tunic style. **1860** RUSSELL *Diary India* II. ix. 174 Thus, with an able-bodied aborigen holding on by my tunic-tails behind, I parachuted down. **1900** *Daily News* 12 Dec. 7/3 The skirt is in the tunic form now fashionable. **1918** G. FRANKAU *One of Them* xxx. 234 Smart bosom itch in horsehair tunic-shirts. **1930** *Daily Express* 6 Oct. 5/1 (Advt.), Men's tunic shirts made of the balloon fabric. **1971** 'D. HALLIDAY' *Dolly & Doctor Bird* viii. 104 Mr Tiko, in a blue tunic shirt and blue trousers.

Hence **ˈtunic-hood** (*nonce-wd.*), the condition of one who wears a tunic; **tunicked** (ˈtjuːnɪkt) *a.*, wearing a tunic: usually as second element in a compound; **ˈtunicless** *a.*, without a tunic.

1756 C. SMART tr. *Horace, Epist.* I. vii. (1826) II. 211 Vulteius.. selling brokery-goods to the tuniced populace. **1859** SALA *Tw. round Clock* (1861) 155 Still in a state of tunic-hood, I remember a very tall, handsome gentleman, with a crimson velvet under-waistcoat. **1876** A. J. EVANS *Through Bosnia* ii. 77 Croat men, white tunicked and white breeked. **1893** R. K. DOUGLAS *Chinese Stories* 218 A larger band of red-tunicked men. **1899** *Westm. Gaz.* 21 Sept. 2/1 The King wears a long tunic-like garment.. and a cloak. **1904** *Daily News* 30 Sept. 7 He pulled me, tunicless, out, giving me my sword and revolver.

tunica[1] (ˈtjuːnɪkə). *Anat.* [L.: see TUNIC.] = TUNIC 4 a in various mod.L. collocations, as ***tunica adventitia*** [see ADVENTITIOUS *a.*], an outer sheath, esp. of a blood-vessel; ***tunica albuginea*** [L. *albūgin-is* white spot], a white fibrous layer, esp. of the penis or testes; ***tunica vaginalis***, a serous membrane covering much of the testis.

1698 W. COWPER *Anat. Humane Bodies* sig. Aa, The tunica albuginea, or proper membrane of the testes. **1828** J. QUAIN *Elem. Anat.* 530 The tunica vaginalis, or serous covering derived from the peritonæum. **1890** *Gray's Anat.* (ed. 12) 48 The arteries are composed of three coats: internal or endothelial coat (tunica intima of Kölliker); middle muscular coat (tunica media); and external cellular coat (tunica adventitia). **1963** *Lancet* 5 Jan. 19/2 The two layers of the tunica vaginalis, which normally invest the testis alone, extend upwards to cover the whole epididymis and the cord, sometimes as high as the inguinal canal. **1977** *Proc. R. Soc. Med.* LXX. 645/1 They observed degenerative changes mainly in the progressive thickening of the tunica adventitia. **1980** *Gray's Anat.* (ed. 36) 1152/1 The fibrous layer of the eyeball.. consists of an opaque, posterior part, the tunica sclera, and a transparent, anterior part, the tunica cornea.

Tunica[2] (ˈtjuːnɪkə). Also †**Tonica, Tonika.** [ad. F. *Tonika, Tounika*, perh. ad. Tunica *tóniku* the man.] (A member of) an American Indian people of the lower Mississippi valley; their language, now extinct. Hence **ˈTunican**, †**ˈTonikan**, a postulated linguistic family of which Tunica was the chief member.

1806 J. SIBLEY in *Message from President of U.S., communicating Discoveries made in exploring Missouri by Capts. Lewis & Clark* 83 Tunicas. These people lived formerly on the Bayan Tunica.. on the Mississippi, east side... Their native language is peculiar to themselves. **1891** D. G. BRINTON *Amer. Race* I. v. 91 The Tonicas are frequently mentioned in early French accounts of the colony of Louisiana. **1891** J. W. POWELL *Indian Linguistic Families* 125 The distinctness of the Tonika language, has long been suspected, and was indeed distinctly stated by Dr. Sibley in 1806. *Ibid.*, The Tonika are known to have occupied three localities. **1902** *Encycl. Brit.* XXV. 374/1 [Linguistic families of North America] Tonikan, Miss. **1911** J. R. SWANTON *Indian Tribes Lower Miss. Valley* 19 The method of distinguishing masculine and feminine pronominal forms is also decidedly unlike, Taënsa employing a suffix while Tunica uses entirely distinct forms. **1947** *Romance Philol.* I. 145 (*title*) Some French loan-words in Tunica. **1965** *Canad. Jrnl. Linguistics* Spring 100 Tunican (comprising Tunica, Atakapa, and Chitimacha).

†**ˈtunical**, *a. Obs. rare.* [f. L. *tunica* TUNIC + -AL[1].] Of, pertaining to, or of the nature of a tunic.

1805 *Med. Jrnl.* XIV. 299 Different from pericardium, dura mater, or any other yielding tunical covering.

tunicary (ˈtjuːnɪkərɪ), *a.* and *sb.* [f. as prec. + -ARY[1].]

A. *adj.* Of or pertaining to a tunic or membrane.

1900–13 in DORLAND *Med. Dict.* **1901** *Jrnl. Exper. Med.* 15 Jan. 343 (Cent. D. Suppl.) The tunicary hernia of the jejunum.. still lay entirely on one side of the mesentery.

B. *sb. Zool.* A member of the *Tunicata*; a tunicated mollusc.

1835 KIRBY *Hab. & Inst. Anim.* I. vii. 218 The Tunicaries.. form part of the headless Molluscans of Cuvier and belong to the section of them that have no shells. **1851** WOODWARD *Mollusca* I. iii. 11 The tunicary cements itself to rock or sea-weed. **1872** NICHOLSON *Palæont.* 30 The entire class of the Tunicaries presents no hard structures.

‖**Tunicata** (tjuːnɪˈkeɪtə), *sb. pl. Zool.* [mod.L., neut. pl. of *tunicātus* (sc. *animālia*) coated, TUNICATE.] A division of animals, now regarded as a sub-phylum of the *Chordata*; also called *Urochorda*: see next, B.

1828 STARK *Elem. Nat. Hist.* II. 115 Class III.—Tunicata. Gelatinous or coriaceous biforous, bitunicated animals, isolated, in groups, or often joined together in a common mass. **1851** RICHARDSON *Geol.* viii. (1855) 230 The Tunicata have no shell, and are enclosed in an elastic muscular sac, with two openings. **1855** H. SPENCER *Princ. Psychol.* (1872) I. I. i. 10 Humble Mollusks, like the fixed Tunicata.

tunicate (ˈtjuːnɪkeɪt), *a.* and *sb.* [ad. L. *tunicāt-us*, pa. pple. of *tunicāre*: see next.]

A. *adj.* Having or enclosed in a tunic or covering; *spec. Bot.* having or consisting of a series of concentric layers, as a bulb; *Entom.* sheathed in or issuing from one another, as the joints of antennæ; *Zool.* having a tunic or mantle; belonging to the *Tunicata*.

1760 J. LEE *Introd. Bot.* III. ix. (1765) 195 A tunicate Bulb, when it consists of many Tunics or Coats. **1825** *Greenhouse Comp.* I. 237 Tunicate bulbs.. may be increased by cutting off the upper part of the bulb horizontally. **1826** KIRBY & SP. *Entomol.* IV. xlvi. 323 Tunicate Knob (*Capitulum tunicatum*). When the laminæ, at least on one side, appear to inosculate or to be imbedded in each other. **1847** *Nat. Encycl.* I. 752 It embraces.. the conchiferous and tunicate mollusks. **1875** *Zoologist* X. 4313 Sponges, Anemones, and Tunicate Mollusca.

B. *sb.* One of a class of marine animals, formerly regarded as molluscs, but now classified as a degenerate branch of *Chordata*, comprising the ascidians and allied forms, characterized by a pouch-like body enclosed in a tough leathery integument, with a single or double aperture through which the water enters and leaves the pharynx.

1848 SMART Suppl., *Tunicates*, or *Tunicaries*, an order of acephalous mollusks having a soft outer covering or mantle; otherwise called Ascidians. **1863** E. V. NEALE *Anal. Th. & Nat.* 177 The Tunicates, a class of creatures with a fleshy centre and tough leathery skin. **1877** HUXLEY *Anat. Inv. Anim.* x. 600 All the fixed Tunicates present two, more or less closely approximated, apertures. **1889** GEDDES & THOMSON *Evol. Sex* v. §2 Among the sea-squirts or tunicates, the reproductive organs are frequently ductless.

†**ˈtunicate**, *v. Obs. rare*[−0]. [f. L. *tunicāt-*, ppl. stem of *tunicāre* to clothe with a tunic, cover with a skin, peel, etc., f. *tunica* TUNIC.]

1623 COCKERAM, *Tunicate*, to cloake or hide a thing.

tunicated (ˈtjuːnɪkeɪtɪd), *a.* [f. as TUNICATE *a.* + -ED[1].] †**a.** Clad in a coat or tunic (*obs. rare*[−0]). **b.** = TUNICATE *a.*

1623 COCKERAM II, One Wearing a Coate, *tunicated.* **1744** J. WILSON *Synopsis Brit. Pl.* 256 Garlick.. hath a bulbous tunicated root. **1760** J. LEE *Introd. Bot.* II. xxxi. (1765) 152 *Iris*, with a tunicated Bulb. **1828** J. E. SMITH *Eng. Flora* II. 1 Chenopodium. Seed lenticular, tunicated, superior. **1840** F. D. BENNETT *Whaling Voy.* II. 322 Fishes, shell-fish, and tunicated molluscs have their luminous matter deposited beneath a dense integument. **1861** BENTLEY *Man. Bot.* (1870) 110 There are two kinds of bulbs commonly distinguished by botanists, the tunicated, and the scaly.

tunicin (ˈtjuːnɪsɪn). *Chem.* [f. TUNIC + -IN[1].] A kind of animal cellulose, $C_6H_{10}O_5$, or chitin, occurring in the mantles of tunicates.

1862 MILLER *Elem. Chem.* (ed. 2) III. 781 Berthelot calls it [chitin] tunicin, from its entering into the composition of the envelope of some of the tunicate mollusks. **1876** tr. *Schützenberger's Ferment.* 147 Derived.. from the decomposition of a substance analogous to tunicin or chitin.

tunicle (ˈtjuːnɪk(ə)l). Forms: 4– tunicle, 4–6 -ycle, 5–7 -acle, (5–6 -akyl, -ekil, -ek(k)el(l), -yk(k)il(l), -ycale, tuinicle, twynykil, tunnycall); 4–5 tonacle, (5 -ecle, -icle, -ycle, -ykyl, -ykle, -akle, -ucle, 6 -aculle); (5 tenekylle, -ucle, 6 -acull, tin-, tynacle, -akle, tynnacle, *Sc.* -akil, -akyl, -akel). [ad. L. *tunicula* dim. of *tunica* TUNIC.

But it may also represent OF. *tunikle* for *tunike* (cf. *bouticle, dalmaticle, triacle*: see M. Antoine Thomas in *Romania* XXXIX. 231.]

†**1.** A small tunic; also *fig.* a wrapping, covering, integument. *Obs.*

1377 LANGL. *P. Pl.* B. xv. 163 As gladde of a goune of a graye russet As of a tunicle of tarse or of a trye scarlet. *a* **1400–50** *Alexander* 1547 Doctours & deuynours.. tyrett all in tonacles of tartaren webbys. **14..** *Nom.* in Wr.-Wülcker 721/28 *Hec tunicula*, a tunakyl. **1656** BLOUNT *Glossogr., Tunicle*.., a little jacket or coat. **1678** CUDWORTH *Intell. Syst.* I. v. 789 The Chaldaick Philosophers bestow upon the Soul, Two Interiour Tunicles or Vestments. **1744** BERKELEY *Siris* §171 This tunicle of the soul, whether it be called pure æther, or luciform vehicle, or animal spirit.

2. *Eccl.* A vestment resembling the dalmatic, worn by subdeacons over the alb (and also by bishops between the alb and the dalmatic) at celebrations of the Eucharist.

c **1425** WYNTOUN *Cron.* IX. v. 595 A prestis westment alhaille, Withe tunakyl [*v. r.* tynnakyllis] and dalmatyk. **1495** in *Somerset Medieval Wills* (1901) 330, 2 Tenucles with the hole appurtenances. **1502** *Acc. Ld. High Treas. Scot.* II. 288 To the woman that maid the frenȝeis for tunycales.., xs. **1536** *Reg. Riches in Antiq. Sarisb.* (1771) 197 Ten Chesibles.. with dyvers Albs and Tunicles. **1548–9** (Mar.) *Bk. Com. Prayer, Communion* (Rubric), Albes with tunacles. **1583** FULKE *Defence* iv. 132 If the word Deacon, be taken for such an one, as at a popish masse standeth in a disguised tunicle, holding a patten. **1849** ROCK *Ch. of Fathers* I. v. (1903) I. 315 The sleeves of the tunicle were neither so wide nor so long, nor did its skirts reach quite so far down as those of the dalmatic. **1877** J. D. CHAMBERS *Div. Worship* 54 The Tunicle of the Subdeacon and Dalmatic of the Deacon are nearly identical.

†**b.** One vested in a tunicle; a subdeacon or 'clerk'. *Obs.*

1554 *Ludlow Churchw. Acc.* (Camden) 56 Item, paid for a tonacule to cary hally water.

†**3.** A membrane enclosing a bodily organ, part of a plant, etc.; = TUNIC 4. *Obs.* (or *rare arch.*)

1398 TREVISA *Barth. De P. R.* v. v. (1495) g iv/2, The glasy humour.. kepyth the humour cristalyn [of the eye] fro touchyng and sharpnes of tunycles. **1543** TRAHERON *Vigo's Chirurg.* I. ix. 8 The tunicles or rymes of the arteries ben of harder substaunce than the tunicles proceeding from the veynes. **1601** HOLLAND *Pliny* XIII. iv. I. 387 Some of these stones be.. covered with many skins or pellicles, and others with fewer: ye shall have in this Date, those tunicles thicke and grosse; in that, thinner and more fine. **1725** SLOANE *Jamaica* II. 313 The stomach had a very thick inward tunicle. **1912** *Nation* 5 Oct. 13/1 Our modern doctors apparently leave the tunicles of the brain unpurged.

Hence **'tunicled** *a. nonce-wd.*, enclosed in or as in a tunicle.

1652 A. WILSON *Pref. Verses* in Benlowes *Theoph.*, The distances of every Sphere Which in full Orbs do move, tunicled so That the lesse Spheres within the greater go.

tunie, tunill, obs. ff. TUNNY, TUNNEL.

tuning ('tjuːnɪŋ), *vbl. sb.* [f. TUNE *v.* + -ING[1].] The action of the verb TUNE.

1. a. The action or process of putting an instrument in tune; a system according to which this is done (cf. TEMPERAMENT 10).

1554-5 *Burgh Rec. Edinb.* (1871) II. 358 Item, to Sir Johne Fietie,.. for tonying of the organis at Sanct Geillis day,.. xxiiij[s]. **1615** G. SANDYS *Trav.* 72 The foolish Musitians.. spent so much time in unseasonable tuning. **1655** in *12th Rep. Hist. MSS. Comm.* App. v. 5 The polyphon is an instrument of so different a stringing and tuning that [etc.]. **1787** *Thompson's Pat.* in *6th Rep. Dep. Kpr. Pub. Rec.* II. 176 A perfect and compleat Machine or Instrument.. for the more easy and expeditious tuning of Harpsichords, Piano Forts, Spinnets [etc.]. **1910** TOVEY in *Encycl. Brit.* III. 129/2 (*Bach*) With the object of stimulating tuning by 'equal temperament' instead of sacrificing the euphony of remoter keys to that of the more usual ones.

b. *fig.*: see TUNE *v.* 2.

1654 WHITLOCK *Zootomia* 342 The Soule needs not more a well organiz'd Body, to exercise it Functions with spritely Vigor,.. than that Soule, and those Organs need the Tuneings of Education. **1711** SHAFTESB. *Charac.* (1737) II. 95 It might be agreeable.. to enquire thus into the different tunings of the passions. **1868** J. H. BLUNT *Ref. Ch. Eng.* I. 273 Such a 'tuning' of pulpits and official houses.. has been succeeded.. by the influence of the press.

c. *transf.*: see TUNE *v.* 1 c, d. Also, the process of making adjustments to the engine of a motor vehicle so as to improve its performance.

1863 E. FITZGERALD *Lett.* (1889) I. 290 Yesterday we gave her what they call 'a tuning' in a rather heavy swell round Orford Ness. **1891** *Labour Commission Gloss., Tuning*, a term used in Yorkshire synonymous with the term 'tackling' ..; it means repairing, &c. a loom when it breaks down and keeping it generally in order. **1916** R. T. NICHOLSON *Bk. Ford* 151 With proper 'tuning', you ought.. to get from 25 to 30 miles per gallon on give-and-take roads. **1939** W. HASSAN in Earl Howe et al. *Motor Racing* (Lonsdale Libr. XXVII) xv. 181 One of the most important items in the tuning of a racing car is the correct interpretation and application of the rules of the race for which it is being prepared. **1971** C. WILLIAMS *Car Conversions for Power & Speed* v. 127 The most advanced tuning of all is found on racing engines, where the average small capacity unit may be producing more than twice the power of an equivalent engine in a road car.

d. The adjustment of a transmitter or receiver to a particular signal frequency or wavelength; variation of the resonant frequency of an oscillatory circuit. Also *tuning in*, the action of adjusting a radio set to a desired frequency; the selection (of a frequency) by this process; also *transf.*; *tuning out*, the cutting out (of a radio transmission) by tuning.

1899 [see TUNE *v.* 1 c]. **1908** *Rep. Brit. Assoc. Adv. Sci. 1907* 622 The various self-inductions and other arrangements for effecting tuning are similarly wound. **1927** W. E. COLLINSON *Contemp. Eng.* 113 If they have heard through a friend's set they.. will have some inkling of the mysteries of tuning in and tuning out. **1929** *Radio Times* 8 Nov. 386/1 Only three knobs.. one for tuning, one for volume and one for wavelengths. **1934** H. JACKSON *Maxims Bks. & Reading* 9 Reading is nothing but tuning oneself in to a book in a spirit of reverential subjection. **1940** *Amer. Speech* XV. 247 He allows nobody else to have anything to do with the *tuning-in* and the *tuning-out* (or the *turning-off*) of the radio programs. **1970** J. EARL *Tuners & Amplifiers* iii. 73 Very accurate tuning is essential for good stereo reception. **1975** D. G. FINK *Electronics Engineers' Handbk.* XXI. 11 The transmitter is designed for a minimum of tuning adjustment, and.. all tuning can be performed from the front panel using only two controls. **1977** *Listener* 17 Mar. 344/1 A furtive tuning-in to Radio 3.

2. a. The action of uttering musical sounds.

1609 DOULAND *Ornith. Microl.* B ij b, Musicke.. is a knowledge of Tuning, which consists in sound and Song. **1610** ATTERSOLL *Hist. Balak* (*N. & Q.* 9th Ser. IV. 104/1) Many vse in their teaching.. knocking of the Pulpit.. fidling with the fingers, tuning with the voice. **1760-72** H. BROOKE *Fool of Qual.* (1809) III. 158 Sentimental and rapturous tunings that rise up.. from eternity to eternity.

†**b.** The setting or determination of pitch in singing; the exercising of the voice in the correct pitch of the notes of the scale. *Obs.*

1597 MORLEY *Introd. Mus.* Pref., Any of but meane capacitie, so they can but truely sing their tunings, which we commonly call the sixe notes. **1662** PLAYFORD *Skill Mus.* I. xi. (1674) 42 The Tuning of the Voice in all the Notes.

3. With *up*: see TUNE *v.* 8.

1902 *Westm. Gaz.* 24 Oct. 3/1 These chapters, however, form but a preliminary tuning-up,.. and the first vigorous note is struck in the fourth chapter, 'Dissent and Defoe'. **1908** *Ibid.* 14 May 10/1 A new place had been provided for 'tuning-up'.. a long way from plaintiffs' houses.

4. *attrib.* and *Comb.* (sense 1 d) *tuning circuit*, *coil*, *condenser*, *indicator*, *inductance*, *knob*, *meter*; (all in sense 1): **tuning-board,** in the organ, a piece of wood screwed to one side of the top of an open wood pipe for tuning it; **tuning-cone,** a hollow cone of wood or metal used for tuning the metal flue-pipes of an organ; **tuning-crook,** (*a*) an implement used in tuning the reed-pipes of an organ; (*b*) in brass wind-instruments, = CROOK *sb.* 8 a; **tuning-funnel,** = *tuning-cone*; **tuning-hammer,** a tuning-key for a piano, properly one with a double wooden head like that of a hammer, used for driving in the wrest-pins when new strings are fitted in; **tuning-hole,** in the organ, an opening near the top of a flue-pipe, adjustable by a flap (see TUNER 2 c) so as to alter the pitch; **tuning-horn,** = *tuning-cone*; **tuning-key,** a key (KEY *sb.*[1] 13 (*b*)) used for turning the wrest-pins in tuning a stringed instrument, as a piano or harp; **tuning-knife,** a long piece of steel used in tuning the reed-pipes of an organ (also called *reed-knife*); **tuning-lever,** = *tuning-key*; **tuning-peg, -pin,** one of the pegs round which the strings of a stringed instrument are passed, and by turning which they are tuned; a wrest-pin; **tuning-screw,** a screw used in tuning a musical instrument; **tuning-slide,** a slide in a metal wind-instrument, used to bring it into tune with other instruments in an orchestra; **tuning-wire,** in the organ, a bent wire in a reed-pipe, used in tuning; **tuning-wrench,** = *tuning-key*.

1852 SEIDEL *Organ* 149 Open wood pipes have at their aperture a small board, called a *tuning-board. **1943** C. L. BOLTZ *Basic Radio* xii. 195 We then put a coil in the aerial to earth circuit, and couple this inductively to the coil of the *tuning circuit. **1923** *Popular Wireless* 13 Oct. (Suppl.) 1 Many wireless amateurs experience considerable difficulty in estimating the maximum wavelengths of their *tuning coils. **1978** F. MACLEAN *Take Nine Spies* iv. 148 The copper wire needed for the tuning coils he managed.. to buy in Tokyo. **1913** *Wireless World* Apr. p. xxix, If the aerial *tuning condenser was set to its previous value and the tuning-switch (not the aerial tuning inductance) put to the second stop, the maximum signals were again obtained. **1881** BROADHOUSE *Mus. Acoustics* 405 An organ-pipe is.. slightly sharpened by pressing out the edges of its open end, as by the '*tuning cone'. **1852** SEIDEL *Organ* 28 The screw-key (now used in tuning the reed-pipes instead of the *tuning-crook) is an invention of our own time. *Ibid.* 149 With some open pewter pipes the *tuning-funnels cannot be used. **1801** BUSBY *Dict. Mus.*, *Tuning-hammer. **1805** E. THUNDER *Specif. Patent* No. 2811. 2 The top.. is flattened to receive the tuning hammer. **1937** F. E. TERMAN *Radio Engin.* (ed. 2) xiii. 559 A more recent development in *tuning indicators is a special miniature cathode-ray tube. **1913** *Tuning inductance [see *tuning condenser* above]. **1860** *All Year Round* No. 68. 430 The *tuning-key of David's harp, which was shown at Erfurt. **1981** *Sunday Express* (Colour Suppl.) 12 July 33/4 For a monthly subscription fee the *tuning knob of a British domestic TV set could then offer a dozen or more channels. **1889** A. J. HIPKINS in Grove *Dict. Mus.* IV. 189/2 The old way of tuning pianos by the Tuning Hammer (or a *Tuning Lever) remains in vogue. **1978** *N.Y. Times* 30 Mar. B11/1 (Advt.), Model STA-52.. includes.. *tuning meter and a cabinet that's made of genuine walnut veneer. **1842** S. LOVER *Handy Andy* xv, Having adjusted the blue ribbon over her shoulder, and twisted the *tuning-pegs, and thrummed upon the wires for some time. **1877** KNIGHT *Dict. Mech.*, *Tuning-pin. **1896** A. J. HIPKINS *Pianoforte* 13 The Wrest-plank.. is the plank or block in which the wrest or tuning-pins are inserted. **1872** ELLACOMBE *Ch. Bells Devon* 208 There was in the *tuning room a peal of eight bells. **1852** SEIDEL *Organ* 153 Some organ-builders provide reed-pipes with a *tuning-screw instead of a tuning-crook. **1885** *Tuning-slide [see SHANK *sb.* 5 w]. **1961** A. BAINES *Mus. Instruments* 358 *Tuning slide*, in wind instruments, a part of the tubing that is made extensible for the purposes of tuning. **1876-98** STAINER & BARRETT *Dict. Mus. Terms* 345/1 A reed-pipe consists of a *boot, block, reed, tongue, wedge,* **tuning wire*, and *tube.*

'tuning-fork.

1. A small steel instrument (invented in 1711 by John Shore) consisting of a stem with two stout flat prongs which on being caused to vibrate produce a definite musical note of constant pitch, thus serving as a standard for tuning musical instruments and in acoustical investigations, etc.

1799 YOUNG in *Phil. Trans.* XC. 134 The fundamental note was found to be one-sixth of a tone higher than the respective octave of a tuning-fork marked C. **1862** *Catal. Internat. Exhib., Brit.* II. No. 3403 Chromatic tuning-forks. **1878** G. B. PRESCOTT *Sp. Telephone* (1879) 51 Vibrating a tuning fork in front of the mouth.

2. An instrument used for turning the pins in tuning a pianoforte.

1877 in KNIGHT *Dict. Mech.*

tunique, obs. and Fr. form of TUNIC.

Tunisian (tjuː'nɪzɪən), *sb.* and *a.* [f. *Tunis* + -IAN, or *Tunisia* + -AN (see below): cf. the earlier TUNISINE *sb.* and *a.*] **A.** *sb.* **a.** A native or inhabitant of the country of Tunisia in North Africa (or of its capital Tunis), or of the former Barbary state of Tunis which preceded it. **b.** The demotic speech of the Tunisians. **B.** *adj.* Of, pertaining to, or belonging to Tunisia, or Tunis.

1825 J. C. LOUDON *Encycl. Agric.* I. vi. 175 The Tunisians are much more agriculturists than their neighbors either of Tripoli or Algiers. **1843** *Penny Cycl.* XXV. 361/1 Grain is frequently imported into the Tunisian territory. **1891** O. WILDE *Pict. Dorian Gray* xi. 199 Yellow-shawled Tunisians plucked at the strained strings of monstrous lutes. **1902** *Encycl. Brit.* XXXIII. 483/2 No doubt in vulgar Tunisian a good many Berber words remain. **1926** A. HUXLEY *Let.* 31 Dec. (1969) 279, I hope the children's Tunisian dates will arrive fairly soon. **1958** *Ann. Reg. 1957* 325 The Franco-Tunisian customs union. **1973** 'A. HALL' *Tango Briefing* xvii. 217 There was a police guard.. a young Tunisian with a peaked cap.

Tunisine ('tjuːnɪsiːn), *sb.* and *a.* ? *Obs.* Also **Tunesin(e), Tunis(s)een.** [f. *Tunis* + -INE[1]: see prec.] **A.** *sb.* A native of Tunis, a city and former Barbary state in North Africa; esp. a pirate from Tunis. **B.** *adj.* Of or belonging to Tunis.

c **1670** J. VERNEY *Let.* in M. M. Verney *Mem.* (1899) IV. v. 159 [The ship was taken] by the Tunisseens. **1738** T. SHAW *Trav. Barbary & Levant* 155 The Tuniseens, are the most civilized Nation of Barbary. **1764** A. ANDERSON *Origin Commerce* I. III. 126 The Genoese grew very uneasy, lest the Tunesins.. should seize on all their effects. **1843** *Penny Cycl.* XXV. 360/1 Susa.. is.. one of the wealthy cities of the Tunisine state. *Ibid.* 364/2 The Tunisines in general, like the Algerines, are a mixed race of Turks, Moors and Jews. *Ibid.* 366/2 The Tunesine corsairs continued their excursions at sea until 1655.

tunist ('tjuːnɪst). *rare.* [f. TUNE *v.* + -IST.] = TUNER 2.

18.. SEDLEY TAYLOR *Science of Music* 132 (Cent. Dict.).

tunk: see TUNC.

tunker: see DUNKER[1].

tunket ('tʊŋkɪt). *U.S. dial.* or *colloq.* Sometimes with initial capital. Also **tunkett.** [Origin doubtful.] Euphem. for *hell*; chiefly ***who*** (***what, why,*** etc.) ***in tunket.***

1871 *Scribner's Monthly* II. 630 What in tunket are you making such a to-do about it for? **1894** *Life* 4 Jan. 13/2 What in the name o' Tunkett makes all boys so crazy to leave the old farm? **1905** G. S. WASSON *Green Shay* iii. 37 'Who in tunket is it backs up the old creetur', anyways?' asked Master Fairway. **1922** JOYCE *Ulysses* 420 Golly, whatten tunket's yon guy in the mackintosh? **1951** E. GRAHAM *My Window looks down East* vii. 59 'And why not, in tunket?' she says. **1971** H. A. SMITH *View from Chivo* xix. 192, I cannot forego the use of harsh language when I think of him; he makes me madder'n tunket.

tunku ('tʊŋkuː). Also ‖**tengku** ('tɛŋkuː). [Malay.] A title of rank in certain states of Western Malaysia; = 'prince'.

1879 in C. W. Harrison *Council Minutes, Perak, 1877-79* (1907) 63 Toh Puan, the chief wife of the former Tengku Mentri. **1897** D. C. BOULGER *Life Sir Stamford Raffles* x. 314 He also goes on to say that Tunku Long, a native rajah, arrived from Rhio, and that Raffles thereupon acknowledged him as Sultan of Johore. **1911** R. J. WILKINSON *Papers Malay Subjects*: *Malay Hist.* v. xi. 34 His son, Tengku Antah, on claiming the throne, was opposed by a Sumatran prince. **1956** *Britannica Bk. of Year* 283/2 Tengku Abdul Rahman was to head a delegation to London early in 1956. *Ibid.* 284/1 On Dec. 28-29, less than a week before he left for the London talks, the Tengku.. met Chin Peng, secretary of the Malayan Communist Party. **1961** *Listener* 23 Nov. 866/2 The Tunku is in this country to discuss with the British Government proposals for a Federation of Malaysia. **1977** P. THEROUX *Consul's File* vi. 48 A boy vaguely related to the Sultan.. known locally (but inaccurately) as 'Tunku', The Prince. **1977** *Times* 31 Aug. (Malaysia Suppl.) p. viii/8 When someone is a Tengku or Tunku.. his blood is very blue indeed, or very white, as the Malays put it; unless.. he comes from Perak where a Raja is usually higher.

tun-moot. *Hist.* [repr. OE. *túngemót*, f. *tún*, TOWN + *gemót* meeting: see MOOT *sb.*[1]] A public meeting of the town or village community.

1881 GREEN *Making of Eng.* iv. 193 *note*, There is no ground for believing that the 'tun-moot' was a judicial court. Its work was the ordering of the village life and the village industry.

tunn(e, tunnage, obs. ff. TON, TUN, TONNAGE.

tunnel ('tʌnəl), *sb.* Forms: 5-7 **tonel,** 6 **-ell,** 6-7 **tonnel, -ell, tunell,** 6-8 **tunnell,** (7 **tunill**), 6- **tunnel**; see also TONNEL. [a. OF. *tonel* masc., in mod.F. *tonneau* tun, cask, and the fem. derivative *tonnelle*, to which the early Eng. in sense 1 corresponds. The sense of 'tube, pipe, opening' and its extensions are of Eng. development, and for that of 'subterranean passage' *tunnel* has been adopted in mod.F. (in *Dict. Acad.* 1878) from English.]

1. a. A net for catching partridges or water-fowl, having a pipe-like passage with a wide opening, and narrowing towards the end; a tunnel-net. ? *Obs.*

c **1440** *Promp. Parv.* 496/2 Tonel, to take byrdys, *obvolutorium*. **1538** *York Wills* (Surtees) VI. 85 To Brian Lelome all my partrike nettes called a tonnell. **1611** COTGR., *Tonnelle*, a Tunnell, or staulking horse for Partridges. **1616** SURFL. & MARKH. *Country Farme* 731 To take Partridges with the Tonnell, or Tombrell, there must a man be placed behind a Cow or a Horse, of wood, or of osier, painted in.. the fashion of a Cow or a Horse. **1710** *Act 9 Anne* c. 27 §5 The pernicious Practice of driving and taking [Wild Fowl] with Hayes Tunnells and other Nets in the Fens. **1822** *Sporting Mag.* IX. 177 A tunnel.. (a net used in taking game).

b. 'The funnel-shaped conductor leading from the *heart* to the pound in a pound-net' (Knight *Dict. Mech.* Suppl. 1884).

1873 [see CRIB *sb.* 10 b].

†**2. a.** The shaft or flue of a chimney. *Obs.*

1508 STANBRIDGE *Vulgaria* (W. de W.) A vj b, *Infumibulum*, the tonell [*printed* towell] of the chymnaye. **1510** —— *Vocab.* (W. de W.) B ij b, *Infunibulum*, a tunnell of a chymney. **1530** PALSGR. 282/1 Tonnell [283/2 Tunnell] of a chymney, *tuyau*. **1595** in *Archæologia* LXIV. 374 Opening yᵉ tunnel in yᵉ low bakt mete house. **1680** AUBREY *Lives, Bacon* (1898) I. 78 The tunnells of the chimneys were carried into the middle of the howse. *c* **1710** CELIA FIENNES *Diary* (1888) 4 The Chimney is just under the window and the Tunnells runnes upon each side. **1818** SCOTT *Rob Roy* v, The fire..roared, blazed, and ascended, half in smoke, half in flame, up a huge tunnel, with an opening wide enough to accomodate a stone seat within its ample vault.

†**b.** A pipe or tube in general. Now *rare*.

1545 RAYNOLD *Byrth Mankynde* 144 Let the woman set her selfe..on a couar made for the nonce with a tunnel or cundyte. **1601** HOLLAND *Pliny* XVII. xxi. I. 528 Let them passe..through..an earthen pipe or tunnell. **1615** G. SANDYS *Trav.* 248 It [the island Volcano] had three tunnels whereat it evaporated fire. **1642** ROGERS *Naaman* (1662) 3 By and with them [miracles] as by Tunnels, the influence, power and authority of truth might enter and prevaile. **1890** [see TUNNELLED 1 b].

†**c.** *fig. pl.* Applied to the nostrils (as a passage for tobacco-smoke). *Obs. humorous nonce-use.*

1598 B. JONSON *Ev. Man in Hum.* I. iii, He dos take this same filthy roguish tabacco,..it would doe a man good to see the fume come forth at 's tonnells!

3. A funnel. *Obs.* exc. *dial.*

a **1529** SKELTON *El. Rummyng* 403 Another..brought a pottel pycher, A tonnel, and a bottell. **1530** PALSGR. 282/1 Tonnell to fyll wyne with, *antonnoyr*. **1601** HOLLAND *Pliny* XXX. vi. II. 381 Given in drink and swallowed downe by a pipe or tunill. **1662** R. MATHEW *Unl. Alch.* lxxxix. 157 Be careful that..it fit thy Funnel or Tunnel. **1719** D'URFEY *Pills* (1872) III. 251 For the Bottle, you cannot well fill it, Without a Tunnel. **1802** PALEY *Nat. Theol.* xv. (ed. 2) 286 Cocks, pipes, tunnels, for transferring the cyder from one vessel to another. *a* **1825** FORBY *Voc. E. Anglia*, *Tunnel*, s. a funnel,..in constant use. **1863** MRS. TOOGOOD *Yorks. Dial.* (MS.), Pour the wine thro the tunnel into the bottle.

4. a. A subterranean passage; a road-way excavated under ground, esp. under a hill or mountain, or beneath the bed of a river: now most commonly on a railway; also in earliest use on a canal, in a mine, etc. (The chief current sense.)

1765 T. LOWNDES *Let.* 1 July in *Hist. Inland Navigations* (1766) I. 41 Mr. Brindley..is driving a large tunnel through the center of this hill. **1782** PENNANT *Journey* 52 The most southern tunnel, as it is called, is at Hermitage. **1790** JANE SNOW in *A. C. Bower's Diaries & Corr.* (1903) 105 We went through what they call a Tunnel—a passage through the Earth for the convenience of carrying Coals by Water: it is two miles and a half long, fifteen feet wide, the same high. **1792** A. YOUNG *Trav. France* 366 At Orgon the canal de Boisgelin..is a noble work, but unfinished; it passes here in a tunnel four hundred and forty yards through a mountain. **1792** J. PHILLIPS *Hist. Inland Navig.* xiv. 363 The celebrated tunnel through Harecastle-hill, Staffordshire, was cut under the direction of..Mr. Brindley [in 1766]. **1798** *Monthly Mag.* July 74 A cylindrical tunnel under the Thames from Gravesend to Tilbury. **1861** *Sat. Rev.* 23 Nov. 540 The projectors of a tunnel thirty miles long under the Channel. **1872** RAYMOND *Statist. Mines & Mining* 15 The vein has been attacked by various tunnels and shafts.

b. An arched drain. *dial.*

1828 *Craven Gloss.*, *Tunnel*, an arched drain.

c. A working-hole in the wall of a glass-furnace.

1839 URE *Dict. Arts* 587 Two principal openings of the furnace... These are called tunnels. They are destined for the introduction of the pots and the fuel.

d. *transf.* The burrow of an animal.

1873 TRISTRAM *Moab* vii. 124 The burrows of the mole-rat, which does duty, in the making of runs and molehills, for the common mole, but excavates much larger tunnels. **1886** BURROUGHS *Signs & Seasons* (1895) 179 Through the tunnel of the meadow mouse the water rushes as through a pipe.

e. A canal in an animal body resembling a tunnel, as that of the organ of Corti in the internal ear.

1882 *Syd. Soc. Lex.*, *Corti, organ of*, a papillary-looking structure, stretching along the whole length of the canalis cochlearis... It is a sort of tunnel, composed of closely lying arches, the arches of Corti. **1898** P. MANSON *Trop. Diseases* xxxiv. 525 The septa between the tunnels may break down and a considerable cavity be thus produced.

f. Applied fig. to a prolonged period of difficulty, suffering, etc. Freq. in phr. ***light at the end of the tunnel*** and the like: a long-awaited sign that a period of hardship or adversity is nearing an end. *colloq.*

1879 GEO. ELIOT *Let.* 7 July (1956) VII. 178 Though I am getting out of the tunnel into daylight, this renewal of weakness..makes it seem as if we should be wiser to defer the visit. **1899** H. JAMES *Awkward Age* x. xxxvii. 437 We've worked through the dark tunnel of artificial reserves. **1922** J. M. MURRY *Let.* in A. Alpers *Life K. Mansfield* (1980) xx. 359, I begin to feel that the horror may move away and that there is a big round spot of real daylight at the end of the tunnel. **1943** J. B. PRIESTLEY *Daylight on Saturday* xxxv. 283 The work..seemed to him a long way off,..seen at the end of a tunnel. It had retreated from him. **1971** *Guardian* 6 Sept. 2/5 The world has reached a crucial point in its drive to reduce illiteracy, UNESCO reports today. There is now 'light at the end of the tunnel'. **1975** LD. ROBBINS *Against Inflation* (1979) xviii. 89, I confess I do not understand the suggestion..that there is any strong light at the end of the tunnel, the way we are going now.

g. *Aeronaut.* A wind tunnel (WIND *sb.*¹ 32).

1911 A. P. THURSTON *Elem. Aeronautics* viii. 84 The *wind tunnel* consists of a tube, passage or tunnel, through which air may be forced or drawn by means of rotating fans, steam jets, or the like. The tunnel may be vertical or horizontal. Sir Hiram Maxim used a horizontal tunnel... Dr Stanton used a wind tunnel..in which the current was vertical and downwards. **1930** NAYLER & OWER *Aviation* 116 Essentially, the tunnel consists of a large tube..along which the air is drawn by means of a motor driving a fan. **1972** *Nature* 18 Aug. 379/2 A low density tunnel for simulating supersonic and hypersonic flight at altitudes of 20 to 70 miles.

h. *Sport.* A subway or covered passage by which players pass to or from the field of play.

1950 *Sport* 24–30 Mar. 3/3 He..made for the tunnel under the impression that the game was over. **1976** *S. Wales Echo* 22 Nov., He..threw it towards the players' tunnel where the police were escorting the referee.

5. *attrib.* and *Comb.*, as ***tunnel-borer***, ***-boring***, ***darkness***, ***-drain***, ***excavation***, ***-maker***, ***-making***, ***-mouth***, ***-passage***, ***-way***, ***-worker***, ***-workman***; ***tunnel-like***, ***-shaped*** adjs.; **tunnel-anæmia**, = *tunnel-disease* (*a*) (Dorland *Med. Dict.* 1900–13); **tunnel-back** *local*, the rear extension of a house, containing the scullery and other functional rooms; a house built in this style; **tunnel diode** *Electronics*, a two-terminal semiconductor device, consisting of a heavily doped *p-n* junction, which has negative resistance at low voltage due to quantum-mechanical tunnelling and is principally used as a high-speed switching device; **tunnel-disease**, a disease incident to workers in tunnels, mines, etc.; *spec.* (*a*) a form of anæmia caused by an intestinal parasite, the *tunnel-worm* (*Dochmius duodenalis* or *Ankylostoma duodenale*); (*b*) = CAISSON-*disease*; †**tunnel dish**, ? a funnel (= sense 3; cf. TUN-DISH); **tunnel effect** *Physics* = TUNNELLING *vbl. sb.* 3; **tunnel-head**, (*a*) the top of a shaft- or blast-furnace; (*b*) the point to which the construction of a tunnel has progressed; **tunnel-hole**, 'the throat of a blast-furnace' (*Cent. Dict.* 1891); **tunnel-kiln** (see quot.); **tunnel-man**, a workman employed in making a tunnel; **tunnel-net**, = sense 1; also a similar net for fishing; **tunnel of love**, a fairground amusement involving a train- or boat-ride through a darkened tunnel, intended for courting couples; **tunnel-pit**, **-shaft**, a shaft sunk to the level of a tunnel; **tunnel-sickness**, = *tunnel-disease*; **tunnel-vault**, = *barrel-vault* (see BARREL *sb.* 11); **tunnel vision**, a condition in which there is a major loss of peripheral vision; also, one in which anything away from the centre of one's field of view escapes attention; also *fig.*, inability to see more than a single or limited point of view; hence **tunnel-visioned** *a.*; **tunnel-weaver**, a spider that weaves a tunnel-like underground web; **tunnel-worm**, the parasitic nematode worm (see *tunnel-disease*) which causes *tunnel-anæmia*.

1957 R. HOGGART *Uses of Literacy* i. 20 They have, almost city by city, their own recognizable styles of housing—back-to-backs here or *tunnel-backs there. **1981** C. DEXTER *Dead of Jericho* vi. 52 No tunnel-backs to the houses, and so the bicycles had to be left outside. **1877** KNIGHT *Dict. Mech.*, **Tunnel-borer*, a ram, operated by compressed air, for making excavations through rock. **1899** CAGNEY tr. *Jaksch's Clin. Diagn.* vi. (ed. 4) 228 Where a severe form of anæmia occurs in labourers..especially.. brick-burners, miners, and tunnel-borers. **1909** *Westm. Gaz.* 29 Dec. 5/4 No Swiss are employed..because they have enough other work and do not care particularly for such employment as *tunnel-boring. **1877** RAYMOND *Statist. Mines & Mining* 123 Rich placer-mines formerly existed in many of the gulches, and several *tunnel-claims in the gravel-hills gave excellent profits. **1839–48** BAILEY *Festus* xxi. 273 Without God all things are in *tunnel darkness. **1959** *Proc. IRE* XLVII. 1204/1 The *tunnel diode has a very high admittance. **1982** J. E. UFFENBECK *Introd. Electronics* i. 24 This switching property of the tunnel diode makes it suitable for digital applications. **1887** *19th Cent.* Aug. 149 Italians who died from cholera in digging the Suez Canal, or from '*tunnel-disease' in the St. Gothard Tunnel. **1898** P. MANSON *Trop. Diseases* xxxvi. 537 In Europe it [i.e. ankylostomiasis] is sometimes known as 'miner's anæmia' or 'tunnel disease',..in allusion to the notorious Saint Gothard epidemic. **1610** *Althorp MS.* in Simpkinson *Washingtons* (1860) App. p. vii, Itm *tunnell dishes. **1840** MARRYAT *Olla Podr.* III. 317 A long *tunnel drain. **1877** RAYMOND *Statist. Mines & Mining* 190 A *tunnel drive at the Dutchman Mine, to reach the ledge about 225 feet below the outcrop. **1932** J. FRENKEL *Wave Mech.* iii. 111 (*heading*) Transition through a potential energy mountain (*tunnel effect). **1974** G. REECE tr. *Hund's Hist. Quantum Theory* xiv. 187 A barrier is not completely impenetrable. In fact it allows..the 'tunnel effect'. **1843** HT. MARTINEAU *Hill & Valley* 79 They saw the filler at the *tunnel-head pouring in at the doors the materials that were furnished by the kilns. **1905** *Daily News* 24 Feb. 6 In the St. Gothard Tunnel there was much disease due to the imperfect sanitation and ventilation at the tunnel-head. **1889** H. DRUMMOND *Trop. Africa* vi. 133 As the Esquimaux heap up snow, building it into the low *tunnel-huts in which they live. **1828** WEBSTER, **Tunnel-kiln*, a lime-kiln in which coal is burnt, as distinguished from a flame-kiln, in which wood or peat is used. **1901** Tunnel kiln [see *continuous kiln* s.v. CONTINUOUS 3]. **1961** M. KELLY *Spoilt Kill* I. 11 We have gas-fired tunnel kilns now... There's very little coal firing left in the [pottery] industry. **1880** 'MARK TWAIN' *Tramp Abr.* xlvi. 530 One of the shows of the place was a *tunnel-like cavern, which had been hewn in the glacier. **1885** *Fortnight in Waggonette* 51, I know no part of our complex system that requires more constant and careful attention than the tunnel-like way to the machinery within us. **1894** SMILES *J. Wedgwood* x. 95 He had known him as a ..*tunnel-maker. **1910** *Tunnel-making [see *road-building* s.v. ROAD *sb.* 11 a]. **1954** J. R. R. TOLKIEN *Fellowship of Ring* 31, I know of no tunnel-making. **1897** *Daily News* 25 Sept. 7/1 Average daily wages earned.., *tunnel-men, 9s. 10d. **1877** RAYMOND *Statist. Mines & Mining* 125 The scenes of extensive *tunnel-mining. **1908** *Daily Chron.* 19 Aug. 1/7 Turning his head towards the *tunnel-mouth. **1721** BRADLEY *Philos. Acc. Wks. Nat.* 131 The Figure of a *Tunnel-Net, disposed for catching all kind of Flies that come into it. **1828** WEBSTER, *Tunnel-net*, a net with a wide mouth at one end and narrow at the other. **1840** [see TUNNEL *v.* 1 b]. **1883** G. C. DAVIES *Norfolk Broads* xxii. (1884) 165 The 'tunnel net'..is a bow-net 8 or 10 feet long, the extreme end of which is stretched out and tied to a stake. **1954** *New Yorker* 8 May 100/2 'And the lights!.. There are thirty-eight hundred on that ride alone. Why, even the World's Fair in its heyday—' he cried, and then for a moment, words failed him. 'And yet it's only a *Tunnel of Love!' **1968** [see *loop-the-loop* sb. s.v. LOOP *v.*¹ 6]. **1976** 'W. TREVOR' *Children of Dynmouth* i. 13 The Hall of a Million Mirrors and the Tunnel of Love and Alfonso's and Annabella's Wall of Death were in the process of erection. **1908** SIR H. JOHNSTON *Grenfell & Congo* II. xxvi. 746 The *tunnel-passage goes straight to the river. **1688** R. HOLME *Armoury* III. xx. (Roxb.) 232 The *Tunell pipe by which the water may be poured in. **1828** WEBSTER, **Tunnel-pit*, a shaft sunk from the top of the ground to the level of an intended tunnel, for drawing up the earth and stones. **1882** *Rep. to Ho. Repr. Prec. Met. U.S.* 638 *Tunnel-running is expensive, and where the depth..is not supposed to exceed 150 feet, a vertical prospect shaft is often sunk. **1858** SIMMONDS *Dict. Trade.*, **Tunnel-shaft*. **1826** KIRBY & SP. *Entomol.* III. xxx. 147 When retracted, they form a *tunnel-shaped cavity, varying in depth. **1903** *Strand Mag.* July 98/2 Hundreds.. had perished in the darkness and heat of the terrible '*tunnel sickness'. **1870** MRS. WHITNEY *We Girls* ix, Gathers and gores, *tunnel-skirts and barrel-skirts and paniers. **1949** SNYGG & COMBS *Individ. Behav.* vi. 110 It has often been observed that in emotional experiences there exists a very high degree of attention sometimes referred to as '*tunnel vision'. *Ibid.* vii. 125 This narrowing of the field is particularly likely to occur when the individual feels he is threatened. The effect has sometimes been called 'tunnel vision'. **1962** *Times* 3 Apr. 17/2 One of the dangers of 'tunnel vision' in driving was brought home to a motorist who recently took the test of the Institute of Advanced Motorists. **1967** *Freedomways* VII. 137 The confused black college graduate, thrust out into a hostile racist society and handicapped by tunnel vision and a self-negating perspective. **1968** *New Scientist* 29 Aug. 449/3 The alternative theory, that of 'Tunnel Vision'. The idea here is that a high level of arousal causes the brain to select very narrowly from among the signals reaching the eyes. **1979** *Daily Tel.* 7 Apr. 3/2 He was now registered as blind. He had tunnel vision, but even this was imperfect... There was some brain damage. **1980** T. BARLING *Goodbye Piccadilly* viii. 169 Prebble had the ghetto mind and the tunnel-vision of a committed social climber. **1985** *Observer* 10 Mar. 5/1 Only someone with Tony Benn's tunnel vision could see the strike as 'a turning point in the battle against monetarism'. **1968** J. LOCK *Lady Policeman* vi. 50 What happened to the juvenile after the Court's decision was not really in our province but we would have been *tunnel-visioned indeed if we had never felt any concern. **1883** *Century Mag.* Oct. 823/2 A *tunnel-way for passengers connects the whole. **1903** *Tunnel worker [see *sand-hog* s.v. SAND *sb.*² 10 a]. **1911** *Daily News* 1 Apr. 4 All tunnel-workers in Switzerland being of this nationality [Italian]. **1843** HT. MARTINEAU *Hill & Valley* 36 The *tunnel-workmen were..going to dinner. **1895** *Funk's Standard Dict.*, **Tunnel-worm*, an anchylostome. **1906** *Scott. Rev.* 29 Mar. 338/1 Acute anæmia due to the bite of the so-called tunnel-worm.

Hence **'tunnelism**, the theory or practice of tunnelling; **'tunnelist**, one who constructs a tunnel (in quot. 1871 *transf.* a burrowing animal); **'tunnellite**, one in favour of a proposed submarine tunnel between England and France; **'tunnelly** *a.*, resembling a tunnel.

1799 C. CLARKE *Obs. Tunnel Thames* 23 *note*, A complete system of Tunnellism. *Ibid.* 14 The Tunnelist and his Friends. **1871** A. STEWART *Nether Lochaber* xxiii. (1883) 138 The velvet coated tunnelists live on worms and insect larvae. **1874** LADY HERBERT tr. *Hübner's Ramble* I. xi. (1878) 169 Having passed through the tunnelly trunk of one of these trees and the interior of the other [Big Trees of Mariposa]. **1882** *Sat. Rev.* 4 Mar. 261/1 The Tunnellites..can say nothing but that their opponents are panic-mongers.

'tunnel, *v.* [f. prec. sb. Cf. F. *tonneler* to net partridges.]

1. †**a.** *trans.* ? To furnish with a tunnel-net, or a tubular passage resembling one. *Obs. rare*⁻¹.

1577 B. GOOGE *Heresbach's Husb.* IV. (1586) 169 b, The windowes must be so placed..hauing a hole of sufficient widenesse ouer against them, well netted and tunnelled, in such sort as the Pigions may easely flee out and in at.

b. To catch (partridges) with a tunnel-net. Also *absol.*

1687 [see TUNNELLING *vbl. sb.* 1]. **1718** *Free-thinker* No. 49 ¶8 A Poacher..has writ to a Friend to send him a Dozen of Second-hand Hoops into the Countrey, which by the Addition of a Cabbage-Net, will serve to Tunnel Partridges. **1840** BLAINE *Encycl. Rur. Sports* VII. iv. §2623 By tunnelling them [partridges], that is, by taking them in what is called a tunnel net.

†**2.** To pour *in* through a funnel. *Obs.*

1664 POWER *Exp. Philos.* I. 94 You may alter the height of the Mercurial Cylinder, as you do rudely or cautiously tunnel in the Quicksilver into the Tube.

†**3. a.** To form into, or like, a tube or pipe. *Obs.*

1713 Derham *Phys.-Theol.* iv. xiii. (1727) 232 With what prodigious Subtilty do some foreign Birds.. plat and weave the fibrous Parts of Vegetables together, and curiously tunnel them, and commodiously form them into Nests. *Ibid.* 235 *note*, These little Houses look coarse, and shew no great Artifice outwardly; but are well tunnelled, and made within with a hard tough Paste.

†**b.** (In earlier use.) To line a shaft or pit with tubbing: see tub *v.* 2. *Obs.*

1686 [see tunnelling 2 b].

4. a. *intr.* To make a tunnel; to excavate a passage under ground, or through some body or substance.

1795 [see tunnelling *vbl. sb.* 4]. **1839** J. Sterling *Ess.*, etc. (1848) I. 322 As some great earth-monster, Johnson tunnels under ground, and heaves out rocks and tons of soil. **1887** *Century Mag.* Dec. 250/1 Then [I] began to tunnel into the huge bank of snow. **1889** *Nature* 11 Apr. 600/2 This had to be tunnelled through before an inch of progress could be made. **1897** *Allbutt's Syst. Med.* IV. 418 Below, the abscess has.. tunnelled along the psoas muscle.

b. *trans.* To excavate, as a tunnel; to make (one's way) by boring or excavating. Also *fig.*

1856 Kane *Arct. Expl.* II. xxi. 208 The stream, which tunnels its way out near the glacier-foot. **1856–1898** [see tunnelled 3]. **1884** J. Tait *Mind in Matter* (1892) 114 In tunnelling out a theory of thought-production Mr. Spencer's light grows dim and expires.

c. To make a tunnel through; to perforate with or as with a tunnel.

1865 Ruskin *Sesame* i. §35 You have tunnelled the cliffs of Lucerne by Tell's chapel. **1910** *Blackw. Mag.* Jan. 33/2 The cover warped and tunnelled by white ants. **1913** *Times* 6 Aug. 7/4 A more formidable rival to the plan of tunnelling the Channel is that of instituting a ferry service from Dover to Calais.

d. *intr.* Physics. Of a sub-atomic particle: to pass *through* a potential barrier by tunnelling (tunnelling *vbl. sb.* 3).

1938 S. Dushman *Elem. Quantum Mech.* iii. 66 The probability that a particle coming up to the boundary at $x = 0$ shall 'tunnel' through the barrier. **1966** D. G. Brandon *Mod. Techniques Metallogr.* iv. 181 Electrons may be able to 'tunnel' through to the far side. **1978** P. W. Atkins *Physical Chem.* xiii. 402 An electron is able to tunnel through even quite high potential barriers (for example, they can escape from the powerful forces inside nuclei, and emerge as β-rays).

tunnelled, -eled ('tʌnəld), *ppl. a.* [f. tunnel *v.* (and *sb.*) + -ed.]

†**1.** Formed like a pipe or tube. *Obs.*

1713 Derham *Phys.-Theol.* iv. xiii. (1727) 234 *note*, The Phalænæ-Tribe.. inhabit the tunnelled, convolved Leaves.

b. Perforated with a tube.

1890 Billings *Nat. Med. Dict.*, *Tunnelled*, term applied to sounds or other instruments having a short tube or tunnel, through which a fine bougie.. passes.

c. Enclosed in a tunnel-like cavity.

1901 *Westm. Gaz.* 13 May 5/3 A double-funnelled lifeboat, with a tunnelled screw, which will enable her to go in safety into shallow waters and amongst rocks, was launched at Harwich on Saturday.

†**2.** Having a tunnel (sense 2), as a chimney.

1818 Scott *Br. Lamm.* x, The soot.. showered down the huge tunnelled chimneys.

3. Excavated as, or by, a tunnel; formed by tunnelling.

1856 Kane *Arct. Expl.* I. xxix. 380 An expansion of the tunnelled entrance made an appendage of.. two feet more. **1861** Wilson & Geikie *Mem. E. Forbes* viii. 206 The caves and tunnelled caverns worn out by the Atlantic breakers. **1879** Jas. Grant in *Cassell's Techn. Educ.* v. 286 A tunnelled staircase led to the roof. **1898** P. Manson *Trop. Diseases* xxxiv. 525 In the latter [the brain]it [the distomum Ringesi]forms a sort of tunnelled tumour.

tunneller, -eler ('tʌnələ(r)). [f. tunnel *v.* + -er[1].]

1. One who catches birds with a tunnel-net. ?*Obs.*

1611 Cotgr., *Tonnelleur*, a Tunneller; a Taker of Partridges with a tunnell. **1706** Phillips (ed. Kersey), *Tunnel*.., a sort of Net to catch Partridges. *Tunneller*, one that goes a Fowling with such a Net.

2. One who excavates a tunnel; *transf.* a burrowing animal.

1860 P. P. Carpenter in *Rep. Smithsonian Instit.* 1859, 213 Our little tunneler [*Gastrochæna*, a bivalve mollusc] sets to work with all the ardor of youth. **1871** Proctor *Light Sc.* 153 Tunnellers from one end have sometimes.. failed to meet those from the other.

tunnelling, -eling ('tʌnəlɪŋ), *vbl. sb.* [f. tunnel *v.* (and *sb.*) + -ing[1].]

I. The action of tunnel *v.*

1. The use of a tunnel-net to catch birds.

1687 *Roy. Proclam.* 30 July in *Lond. Gaz.* No. 2267/1 That henceforward none presume,.. to Kill or Destroy any Hare, Partridge [etc.] by Hunting, Hawking,.. Tunnelling, Gins, or any way whatsoever. **1796** Anstey *Pleader's Guide* (1803) 129 Acts 'gainst tunneling and snaring. **1819** *Sporting Mag.* IV. 208 It is neither very dark nor very light, in tunnelling for partridges.

2. a. The work or process of making a tunnel; excavation of, or by, a tunnel.

1810 J. T. in *Risdon's Surv. Devon* p. xxix, This is the Tavistock canal, which is.. attended with the grand operations of tunnelling. **1871** Proctor *Light Sc.* 153 Any inaccuracy in the direction of the two tunnellings would have been fatal to the success of the work.

attrib. **1812** Sir R. Wilson *Diary* in *Life* (1862) I. 377 The excavations are certainly some of nature's most surprising tunnelling achievements. **1871** *Daily News* 25 Apr., A new tunnelling machine.. was exhibited at the meeting of the British Association last year.

†**b.** The lining of a shaft or pit with tubbing.

1686 Plot *Staffordsh.* ii. 98 The Art of tunnelling much used in Cheshire to keep out the freshes.

3. *Physics.* The quantum-mechanical process whereby a particle has a non-zero probability of penetrating a finite potential barrier even if it has less energy than the height of the barrier.

1938 S. Dushman *Elem. Quantum Mech.* iii. 68 The 'tunneling effect'.. is one of the most important deductions contributed by the new quantum mechanics. **1970** *New Scientist* 1 Oct. 38/2 Tunnelling is a phenomenon particular to quantum mechanics. **1978** P. W. Atkins *Physical Chem.* xiii. 402 The particle might be found on the outside of a container, even though according to classical physics it has insufficient energy to escape. This passage through classically forbidden zones is called tunnelling.

II. 4. *concr.* Work of the nature of a tunnel; subterranean excavation for a canal, road, or railway; a tunnel, or tunnels collectively.

1795 J. Phillips *Hist. Inland Navig.* Add. 131 Another navigable cut.., principally tunneling, will shorten the line four miles. **1798** *Monthly Mag.* July 74, 900 yards of tunneling. **1894** *Daily News* 22 Jan. 4/8 One of the fat, pink, repulsive-looking grubs, coiled up in one of the wide tunnellings that have ruined the tree.

†**tunner** ('tʌnə(r)). *Obs.* exc. *dial.* Forms: 4 tonour, 5 -owre, tunnowre, 6 tuner, 6– tunner. [f. tun *sb.* or *v.* + -er[1].]

1. An instrument for tunning liquor; a funnel.

1337 in Riley *Memorials* (1868) 200 [One iron spit, 3*d*,; one frying-pan, 1*d*. one] tonour, 1*d*. *c* **1440** *Promp. Parv.* 496/2 Tonowre, or fonel, *infusorium*. *Ibid.*, Tunnowre, *idem quod* tonowre. **1552–3** in *Midl. Counties Hist. Coll.* I. 233 A cherne a tuner a hopp iiij kytts. **1888** Elworthy *W. Somerset Word-bk.*, *Tunner*, a wooden funnel. 'Urn down, Jack, to farm' Perry's and borry he's tunner.'

†**2.** One who tuns liquor. *Obs.*

1598 Stow *Surv.* 192 The successors of those Vintners.. were all incorporated by the name of wine tunners.

So **'tunnery**, a place in which liquor is tunned.

1796 Morse *Amer. Geog.* II. 444 The tunnery, fishery, and salt produce a good revenue. **1869** W. Molyneux *Burton on Trent* 250 [The cask] is thence transmitted to the tunnery to be refilled.

tunnified ('tʌnɪfaɪd), *ppl. a. humorous nonce-wd.* [f. tun *sb.* + -i)fy + -ed[1].] Grown as big as a tun; very corpulent. (Cf. tun-bellied.)

1806 R. Cumberland *Memoirs* (1807) II. 72 Scarcely able to support himself on his tottering legs, now miserably tunnified.

tunning ('tʌnɪŋ), *vbl. sb.* [f. tun *v.* + -ing[1].] The action of the verb tun.

1. Putting into or storing in a tun or tuns. Also with *up*.

14.. [see *tunning-dish* in 3]. *a* **1529** Skelton *El. Rummyng* 130 Wyth all theyr myght runnynge.. To haue of her tunnynge. **1577** Harrison *England* ii. vi. in *Holinshed* I. 95/1 The bere.. is commonlye of a yeare olde (or.. of two yeres tunning or more). **1669** Worlidge *Syst. Agric.* vii. §12. 120 The best Vessels for the tunning up of Cider. **1766** *Compl. Farmer* s.v. *Cyder*, At first tunning they do not fill their hogsheads to the bung, but leave an empty space to receive a pailful of fresh cyder from the press. **1822** Imison *Sc. & Art* II. 159 It is mixed with yeast.. in order to excite the vinous fermentation. This process is called tunning.

2. Of rabbits: see tun *v.* 3.

1741 *Compl. Fam.-Piece* iii. 510 The main Art of keeping these Creatures, is to preserve them from Tunning, or being Pot-belly'd.

3. *attrib.* Used in or for tunning liquor, as ***tunning cask, tub, vessel***; †**tunning dish**, = tundish; †**tunning mell**, ? a 'mell' or mallet used to knock in the bung of a tun or cask.

1891 *Cent. Dict.*, **Tunning-cask*, a cask in which fermented ale is stored when racked off. **14..** *Voc.* in Wr.-Wülcker 574/15 *Colum*, a colyndore, or a *tunnyng dysch. **1611** Cotgr., *Sibille*, a tunning and tasting dish in the time of Vintage. **1688** R. Holme *Armoury* iii. 320/1 A Tunning Dish, some term it a Fulling or Filling Dish; for by the help of it Liquor is poured into Vessels with small holes. **1362–3** *Durham Acc. Rolls* (Surtees) 565 In j *Tunnyngmell et ij duzayns de ciphis ligneis empt. ij d. ob. **1567** *Wills & Inv. N.C.* (Surtees) I. 266 A *tonning tubb, a tonn for bread. **1504** *Bury Wills* (Camden) 101 All brewyng ledys,.. brasse bruyng vessells, *tonnyng vessells.

†**tunnis**, *a. Her. Obs.* = tenné. (? error.)

1625 Markham *Souldiers Accid.* 31 Proper Colours, as Blacke, Blew, Red, Greene, Purple, Tunnis, and Ermine. *Ibid.* 32 Tunnis, or Tawnie, signifieth Merit, or desert, and a foe to Ingratitude. **1661** Peacham *Compl. Gent.* (ed. 3) 156.

†**'tunnish**, *a. Obs. rare*[−1]. In 6 tonnish. [f. tun *sb.* + -ish[1].] Somewhat like a tun or cask; very corpulent.

a **1529** Skelton *El. Rummyng* 99 She is a tonnish gyb.

tunny ('tʌnɪ). Forms: 6 tuny(e, thunie, tunnye, 6–7 tony, tonny, tunnie, 7 tonnie, tunie, tunney, thinnye, 8–9 thunny, 7– tunny. [ad. F. *thon* (14th c.), ad. Pr. *ton*, or It. *tonno*, L. *thunnus* (*thynnus*), ad. Gr. *θύννος*, in same sense; the termination *-ie*, *-y* seems to be only English, perh. orig. diminutive, as in *Johnnie*.] **a.** A scombroid fish of the genus *Orcynus*, esp. the common tunny, *O. thynnus*, which has been fished from ancient times in the Mediterranean and Atlantic; it is one of the largest of food-fishes, often reaching a length of ten feet.

1530 Palsgr. 282/1 Tonny. **1555** Eden *Decades* 202 The Tunnye which is a great and good fysshe. **1556** Withals *Dict.* (1568) 8 b/2 A tony, *thinnus*. **1565–73** Cooper *Thesaurus*, *Auxumae*, the yong fish, comming of the spawne of Thunie. **1591** Harington *Orl. Fur.* vi. xxxvi, The Dolphin strong, the Tunny good of tast, The Mullet, Sturgeon, Samon (princely fish). **1601** Holland *Pliny* ix. xv. I. 242 The Tunies are exceeding great fishes: we have seene some of them to weigh fifteen talents, and the taile to be two cubits broad and a span. **1617** Moryson *Itin.* iii. 47 The fish called a Thinnye of Calcedonia. **1760–72** tr. *Juan & Ulloa's Voy.* (ed. 3) II. 308 We now.. saw the Tunny and a great many flying-fish. **1781** Gibbon *Decl. & F.* xvii. II. 10 *note*, Among a variety of different species, the Pelamides, a sort of Thunnies, were the most celebrated. **1834** *Nat. Philos.* III. *Phys. Geog.* 50/2 (U.K.S.) Tunnies.. migrate.. every year from the Atlantic Ocean to the Mediterranean.

b. *attrib.* and *Comb.*, as ***tunny boat, fish*** (= tunny), ***-fisher, -fishery, fishing*** (hence ***-fish*** vb. intr.); ***net; tunny-faced*** adj.; **tunnyman**, a boat engaged in tunny fishing.

1934 *Yachting Monthly* LVII. 24/1 An ever-interesting panorama is provided by the sardiniers and *tunny boats [at Concarneau]. **1974** 'J. Graham' *Bloody Passage* xiii. 173 There are a hell of a lot of tunny boats scattered around. **1901** *19th Cent.* Oct. 641 The stupid or *tunny-faced man. **1552** Huloet, *Tunye fyshe when it exceadeth not a foote in length, *limaria*. **1620** J. Mason *New-found-land* 5, I haue also seene Tonnie fish in Newland. **1796** Morse *Amer. Geog.* II. 428 The fisheries on the coast of Sardinia produce upwards of 60000 scudi in the article of tunny-fish. **1977** C. Watson *One Man's Meat* viii. 78 He was with me, *tunny-fishing off Scarborough. **1889** C. Edwardes *Sardinia* 350 A veteran *tunny-fisher. **1765** Smollett *Trav.* (1766) II. xxxix. 225 Pliny says it [Antibes] was famous for its *tunny-fishery. **1971** 'D. Halliday' *Dolly & Doctor Bird* v. 66 Between its [*sc.* a bridge's] arches *tunny-fishing boats were constantly sprinting. **1930** *Sea Breezes* Dec. 94 Whilst the motor is making rapid headway amongst the sardine luggers and crabbers, at present the *tunnymen are unaffected. **1961** A. J. R. Fraser Taylor *Diary* 13 Aug. in *Roving Commissions 1962* (1963) 123 The following day a slow passage to Bermeo, tying up late in the evening alongside a tunnyman. **1901** *19th Cent.* Oct. 645 Steaming out in our little launch to the fixed *tunny-nets.

Hence **'tunnyhood** (*nonce-wd.* after *manhood*), the state of a full-grown tunny.

1853 Badham *Halieut.* 193 An unfortunate habit of squinting acquired by the young cordylas, and not corrected by the parents as their offspring advanced to thunnyhood.

tuno, variant of tunu.

†**'tunsion.** *Obs.* Also 6 tonsion. [n. of action on L. type **tunsio*, from *tundĕre* to beat.] The action, or an act, of beating or striking.

c **1440** *Alphabet of Tales* 390 þan þe monkis with all þer hertis prayed for hym, & did of þer clothis & bete þer selfe for hym, & made tunsions on þer breste. **1526** *Pilgr. Perf.* (W. de W. 1531) 60 b, But if thou fynde the gylty, gyue a tonsion on thy brest. **1532** More *Confut. Tindale* Wks. 350/1 He diuers times repeted those wordes with tunsions and knockinges vppon his brest.

†**'tunster.** *Sc. Obs. rare.* [f. tun *v.* + -ster.] ? An officer who superintended the tunning of liquor.

1610 in J. Davidson *Inverurie* vi. (1878) 195 Appointit taisters tunsters of aill within the bruch. *Ibid.*, Who evere refuses to gif lawful obedience to the tunsters or Bailis.

‖**tunu** ('tuːnuː). Also tuno, toonu. [Carib name in Honduras.] A Central American tree, *Castilloa Tunu*, Hemsley (N.O. *Artocarpaceæ*), which yields a non-elastic caoutchouc called ***tunu gum*** (or *tunu*). (Other species produce rubber.)

1883 D. Morris *Colony Brit. Honduras* 74 Next to cacao, the most interesting plant found wild in the forests of British Honduras is the indiarubber-tree, called by the natives 'Toonu'. **1886** Sir J. D. Hooker in *Trans. Linnean Soc.* Ser. ii. II. 209 Three forms or species of Castilloa.. two of these are named Ule.., the third is named Tunu, and said to yield a gutta-percha. **1894** *Outing* (U.S.) XXIII. 354/1 On the smooth bamboo lie thick piles of tuno-bark blankets. *Ibid.* 356/2 Tuno gum, with which wicked huleros are wont to adulterate their rubber.

tuny ('tjuːnɪ), *a. colloq.* Also tuney. [f. tune *sb.* + -y.] Characterized by 'tune' or melody; melodious: sometimes depreciative.

1885 *Graphic* 21 Feb. 190/3 Oh, Mozart!.. So very tune-y, isn't he? **1887** *Twin Soul* vii, Music that is not 'tuny' is not to my taste.

Hence **'tuniness.**

1905 *Athenæum* 5 Aug. 169/3 Patrick Hannay.. has a pretty, if thin, tunefulness (we might rather say tuniness). **1909** *Daily Chron.* 8 June 4/7 Italian music.. has shape, form, symmetry, in its tuniness.

tuo, obs. form of two.

tuoche, tuouche, obs. ff. touch.

tuo-name: see to-name.

tup (tʌp), *sb.* Forms: 4 tope, *Sc.* toupe, 4–6 tupe, 5–7 tuppe, (6 tuepe, touppe, towpe), 6–7 tupp, 6, 8–9 *Sc.* tip, 6– tup; 8–9 *Sc.* and *north.*

dial. tuip (tʏp), teep, teap, toop. [Origin unknown; chiefly Sc. and north. Eng. App. etymologically *tōp*, which would regularly give *toop* (tuːp) in north. Eng., and (tʏp) or (tøp) in Sc.: cf. *bóc*, *bōk*, *book*, Sc. *buik*. (Skeat suggests that it may be a transferred use of Norw. and Sw. *tupp* 'cock', said to be the same word as TOP *sb.*[1])]

1. A male sheep; a ram.

13.. *Ballad Scot. Wars* xxvii. in Ritson *Anc. Songs & Ball.* (1877) 38 A Toupe sal stande agayn ay Bare. *c* **1340** [see *tup-head* in 2]. *a* **1400–50** *Alexander* 5566 Þai ware hedously hoge & horned as Tupis. *c* **1440** *Pallad. on Husb.* VIII. 77 The tuppe is chosun fair of altitude Ywombe[d] side. **1510** STANBRIDGE *Vocab.* (W. de W.) C v b, *Aries*, a tup or a ram. **1570** LEVINS *Manip.* 140/18 A Tip, shepe, *aries.* **1590** *Shuttleworths' Acc.* (Chetham Soc.) 58 A touppe iij[s] viij[d]. *Ibid.* 61 Seven towpes. **1594** *Ibid.* 118 Three tupes. **1600** *Ibid.* 123 Towe old tupps. **1653** GATAKER *Vind. Annot. Jer.* 61 To run ful but, as rams, or tups, use to do, one against another. **1771** *Usef. Proj.* in *Ann. Reg.* 107/1 He sells no tups, but lets them at from 5 guineas to 30 guineas for the season. **1804** SCOTT *Let. to Ellis* 19 May, in *Lockhart*, Long sheep, and short sheep, and tups, and gimmers, and hogs, and dinmonts, had made a perfect sheepfold of my understanding. **1903** *Times* 12 Feb. 12/4 Heavy sheep 7½d. to 8d.; ewes and tups 6d. to 7d.

b. *transf.* Applied to a person.

1652 SHIRLEY *Honoria & Mam.* III. i, Cuckolds' sconce, Or haven, to which all the tups strike sail. **1694** MOTTEUX *Rabelais* IV. viii, The Ship being clear'd of Dingdong and his Tups. **1785** GROSE *Dict. Vulg. T.*, *Tup*, a ram; figuratively a cuckold. **1815** SCOTT *Guy M.* xxxvi, 'He'll be a Teviotdale tup, tat ane', said the chairman, 'tat's for keeping ta crown o' ta causeway tat gate'. **1880** EBEN. SMITH *Verses* 68 Douce old tups.

c. *transf.* (*a*) A pavier's mallet. (*b*) The head of a forge-hammer or steam-hammer. (*c*) The falling weight of a pile-engine.

1848 'TOM TREDDLEHOYLE' *Bairnsla Foak's Ann.* 46 (E.D.D.) Little undersized munkeys, not much heigher than tups at thay knock boolders daan we i't street. **1873** *Iron* 5 Apr. 356/1 A 45-cwt. double-acting Nasmyth's steam hammer, with wrought iron tup. **1884** *Building News* 15 Aug. 242/3 Ram, tup, monkey, are names variously given by workmen to the block..which is let fall upon the head of the pile. **1907** *Daily Chron.* 22 Mar. 9/5 The heavy 'tup' comes down smack! on the bar.

2. *attrib.* and *Comb.*, as ***tup-breeder***, ***-head***, ***-horn*** (in quot. *attrib.*), ***-mutton***, ***-seller***; ***tup-headed***, adj.; also **tup-eild**, **-eill** *a. Sc.* [EILD, GELD, YELD *adjs.*], of a ewe: barren; **tup fair**, a fair or annual market mainly for the sale of rams; **tup-hog**, a male lamb from its weaning till its first shearing; **tup-lamb**, a he-lamb; **tup-man**, one who keeps and supplies rams for breeding purposes; **tup running**: see quot.; **tup society**, a sheep-breeding association; **tup-yeld**, **-yield** *a.* = *tup-eild*.

1831 *Sutherland Farm Rep.* 82 in *Libr. Usef. Knowl., Husb.* III, In order to suit the market, the *tup-breeders preserved only the finest of their young store. **1823** *Farmer's Mag.* 278 At the lambing time..there were found 99 *tup-eild ewes and gimmers. **1844** STEPHENS *Bk. Farm* II. 38 If she has failed being in lamb she is said to be a tup-eill gimmer. *c* **1340** *Peter & Paul* 248 in Horstm. *Altengl. Leg.* (1881) 79/1 When þe heuede was smiten awaie, A *tope-heued on þe erde laie. **1816** SCOTT *Antiq.* vi, Did you ever hear such an old *tup-headed ass? **1591** *Vestry Bks.* (Surtees) 30 Shepe remainynge in this parishe... At North Pittington a *tuppe hogge. **1844** STEPHENS *Bk. Farm* II. 38 After a lamb has been weaned, until the first fleece is shorn from its back..a female is called a *ewe-hogg*, a male a *tup-hogg*. **1718** RAMSAY *Christ's Kirk Gr.* III. iii, Twa *toop-horn-spoons down Maggie lays. *a* **1772** LISLE *Husb.* (1757) 313 They used..to cut their *tup-lambs early within six weeks old. **1782** BURNS *Death Poor Mailie* 43 My poor toop-lamb, my son an' heir. **1844** STEPHENS *Bk. Farm* II. 613 Tup-lambs are allowed to retain their full tails until a year old, in order to strengthen the back. **1790** W. MARSHALL *Midl. C.* I. 429 Getting Rams, to be let out again to inferior *tupmen, as ram-getters. **1844** STEPHENS *Bk. Farm* II. 100 *Tup-mutton..is always hard, of disagreeable flavour, and in autumn not eatable. **1785** GROSE *Dict. Vulg. T.*, **Tup running*,..in Derbyshire, a ram whose tail is well soaped and greased is turned out to the multitude, any one that can take him by the tail and hold him fast is to have him for his own. **1831** *Sutherland Farm Rep.* 82 in *Libr. Usef. Knowl., Husb.* III, To the surprise of the *tup-sellers..nothing could be sold [at the fair] but tups of coarse quality. **1799** A. YOUNG *Agric. Lincoln.* 309 In 1796 there was a new *Tup Society established at Lincoln, for the encouragement of breeding. **1825** JAMIESON, **Tup-yield*, *tup-eild*, adj.

tup (tʌp), *v.* [f. prec. sb.]

1. a. *trans.* Of the ram: To copulate with (the ewe); also *transf.* (*coarse slang*), of a man: to copulate with (a woman).

1604 SHAKS. *Oth.* I. i. 89 An old blacke Ram Is tupping your white Ewe. **1641** BEST *Farm. Bks.* (Surtees) 28 Those that have theire ewes tupped betimes. **1694** MOTTEUX *Rabelais* v. (1737) 222 They will not be ridden, tupp'd, and ramm'd. **1844** STEPHENS *Bk. Farm* III. 1108 Most of the ewes will be tupped during the second week the tup is amongst them. **1861** *Times* 16 Oct., Ewes are tupped on grass, have hay on the winter pasture in case of deep snow, lamb in the same field, and are also fattened off on grass. **1970** B. W. ALDISS *Hand-Reared Boy* 96 In Derbyshire's dull dorms... When lesser souls abused themselves, out-classed, Our Dancer, saint and patron, he upped and tupped the matron. **1976** R. JEFFRIES *Two-Faced Death* xviii. 210 You wouldn't tup her?.. Neither of us cut out for adultery.

b. To beget (a lamb); in quot. *pass.*

1721 KELLY *Scot. Prov.* 307 The Lamb where it's tipped, and the Ewe where she's clipped. A proverbial Rule about Tythes; signifying that the Lamb shall pay Tythes in the Place where the Ewe was when she took the Ram, but the old Sheep where they were shorn.

c. To put (ewes) to the ram. *dial.*

1799 A. YOUNG *Agric. Lincoln.* 318 Mr. Skipwith of Alesby tups 1400 ewes. *Ibid.* 337 Little farmers, who tup under 60 ewes.

2. *intr.* **a.** Of the ewe: To admit the ram. **b.** Of the ram: To copulate. Also *transf.*

1549 CHALONER *Erasm. Praise Folly* F ij b, These old women..will euer yet haue this prouerbe (lyfe is lyfe) in their mouthes, still plaie the wantons, and still be tuppyng. **1614** C. BROOKE *Eglogues* F vj b, Whiles thy Rams do Tup, thy Ewes do twyn. **1641** BEST *Farm. Bks.* (Surtees) 3 The tuppes goinge allwayes with them, some of the ewes will tuppe sooner, and some later. **1721** KELLY *Scot. Prov.* 306 Tip when you will, you shall Lamb with the Leave [= lave].

†**3.** *trans.* To furnish with horns like a ram's; cf. HORN *v.* 2. *Obs. rare*[−1].

1608 DAY *Law Trickes* I. i. A iv, She was my wife and by her meanes, my head Was fayrely tupt, and you will buy a Lanthorne: Bespeake my sconce, tis ready hornd and all.

4. *trans.* and *intr.* 'To but like a ram' (J.).

1654 [see *tupping* vbl. sb. below]. **1847–78** in HALLIWELL. **1876** *Mid-Yorks. Gloss.*, *Tup*,..to butt.

Hence **tupped** (tʌpt) *ppl. a.*, **'tupping** *vbl. sb.* (also *attrib.*).

1654 GAYTON *Pleas. Notes* III. iv. 89 Ramms taken for Gyants,..the Wethers bels for Drumms, and their taile clouts, their colours, their tupping and rutting for the maine Battalia. **1799** A. YOUNG *Agric. Lincoln.* 318 Never give turnips to tupped ewes. **1844** STEPHENS *Bk. Farm* II. 599 A shepherd..has attentively observed the tupping, and marked the reckoning of every ewe. **1886** C. SCOTT *Sheep-Farming* 80 The ewes will have been marked at tupping-time for each week's lambing.

‖**Tupaia** (tuːˈpaɪə). *Zool.* [mod.L., ad. Malay *tūpai* squirrel, in *tūpai tāna* ground-squirrel.] A genus of insectivorous mammals, typical of the family *Tupaiidæ*, including the Banxring, *Tupaia peguana*, of Burma and Pegu, and the Tana tupai, *Tupaia tana*, of Borneo, etc. (sometimes erroneously called the *Tana*).

1820 SIR T. S. RAFFLES in *Linnæan Trans.* (1822) XIII. 256 Tupaia... Snout elongated... Habit and tail of a Squirrel. *Ibid.* 257 Tupaia Tana. **1824** HORSFIELD *Zool. Res. Java* s.v. *Tupaia*, The Bangsring fell under my observation during an early period of my researches in Java. **1847** CARPENTER *Zool.* §179 The last family..*Tupaidae*, at present contains only one genus, the *Tupaia* or *Banxring*.. of which only three species are known. **1868** OWEN *Vertebr. Anim.* III. xxx. 428 The Tupaias and some of the snouted-shrews.

tupaiid (tʊˈpaɪɪd). [a. mod.L. family name *Tupaiidæ*, f. TUPAIA + -ID[3].] A tree-shrew of the family Tupaiidæ.

1885 T. GILL in J. S. Kingsley *Riverside Nat. Hist.* (1888) V. 141 The proper diet of the Tupaiids is small insects. **1972** T. A. VAUGHAN *Mammalogy* vi. 70/1 Paleontological evidence indicates that tupaiids were derived from the Insectivora and not from the Primates.

tupaioid (tʊˈpaɪɔɪd), *a.* (*sb.*) [a. mod.L. superfamily name *Tupaioidea*, f. TUPAIA + -OID.] Of or pertaining to the superfamily Tupaioidea, or resembling a member of this group. Also as *sb.*, an arboreal mammal of the superfamily Tupaioidea.

1912 *Rep. Brit. Assoc. Adv. Sci.* 583 Its Tupaioid ancestor took to an arboreal life. **1972** W. C. O. HILL *Evolutionary Biol. Primates* ii. 18 The order is remarkable for the persistence..of living forms that illustrate several successive evolutionary steps..from tupaioids to man.

‖**tupak-grass** (ˈtuːpək grɑːs, -æ-). [f. the Maori name + GRASS *sb.*[1]] A New Zealand grassy sedge, *Carex appressa*.

1884 MILLER *Plant-n.*, *Carex appressa*, Otago Tupak-grass. **1901** A. TROTTER *E. Galloway Sk.* 319/2 He advocated a plan for making tracts of sand productive by planting them with Tupac grass.

‖**tupakihi.** [Maori.] A small tree of New Zealand, *Coriaria ruscifolia*; = TOOT *sb.*[5]

1867 E. SAUTER tr. *Hochstetter's N. Zealand* vii. 139 *note*, The Toot-plant, Tutu or Tupakihi of the Maoris (*Coriaria sarmentosa*, Forst. = *C. ruscifolia*, L.). **1883** J. HECTOR *Handbk. N. Zealand* 131 Tupakihi, Tree Tutu.

Tupamaro (tuːpəˈmɑːrəʊ). [f. the names of the Inca leaders *Tupac Amaru* I (d. 1571) and *Tupac Amaru* II (d. 1781).] A member of a left-wing guerrilla organization in Uruguay. Also *attrib.*

1969 *N.Y. Times* 23 Jan. 12/2 The Tupamaros represent a new approach to guerrilla warfare in Latin America. *Ibid.* 12/4 Tupamaro intelligence sources. **1970** *Guardian* 11 Aug. 11/3 The Tupamaros..would like to see a Cuban-style revolution in Uruguay. **1973** G. JACKSON *People's Prison* xxiv. 194 Tupamaro hideouts were even then notoriously subterranean. **1977** *Time* 31 Jan. 54/3 Urban guerrilla movements, such as the extinct Tupamaros of Uruguay, may have seen their day.

‖**tupan** (ˈtuːpæn). [Chinese.] The civil governor of a Chinese province under the Republican regime.

1925 *Glasgow Herald* 31 Aug. 9 Another mandate appoints General Feng's associate, Sun Yueh, Tupan of Shensi. **1928** T. F. MILLARD *China* 28 That process grew the crop of tuchuns, tupans, field marshals, and what not, so much heard of in these times. As originally used, the word 'tuchun' was distinctly a military term, and 'tupan' meant an officer who exercised civil authority; but in late years the terms are used indiscriminately. **1936** P. FLEMING *News from Tartary* VI. ii. 250 Chin Shu-Jen was succeeded by the present *tupan*, General Sheng Shih-tsai. **1949** F. MACLEAN *Eastern Approaches* (1951) I. v. 98 The intention was that I should go to Urumchi, the capital of Sinkiang, to contact the Tupan, or Provincial Governor.

tupe, obs. form of TUP.

†**tupee**, obs. var. TOUPEE.

1751 ELIZA HEYWOOD *Betsy Thoughtless* II. 163 A fine fellow, with his tupee wig, and laced waistcoat.

‖**tupelo** (ˈtuːpɪləʊ). Also 8 **tupelow**, 9 **tupeloo**, **tupola**. [N. Amer. Ind.] Native name of trees of the North American genus *Nyssa* (N.O. *Alangiaceæ* or *Nyssaceæ*), large trees growing in swamps or on river banks in the southern states; esp. *N. villosa* or *multiflora* (also called Black or Sour Gum, and Pepperidge), and the large tupelo or tupelo gum (*N. uniflora*), which produces a light tough timber. Also *attrib.*, as ***tupelo-gum***, ***-swamp***, ***-tree***; **tupelo-tent**, a surgical tent made of the spongy wood of the root of the tupelo.

1730 MORTIMER in *Phil. Trans.* XXXVI. 431 The Tupelo Tree. *Ibid.* 434 The Water Tupelo. **1756** P. COLLINSON in Darlington *Mem.* (1849) 202 Billy's drawing and painting of the Tupelo, is fine. **1765** in W. Stork *Acc. East Florida* (1766) 79 The low lands are partly cypress and tupelow swamps. **1816** W. DARBY *Descr. Louisiana* iv. 62 The tupeloo is known in Louisiana by the popular name of olive. **1864** LOWELL *Fireside Trav.* 42 Maple, and the rarer tupelo with downward limbs. **1865** PARKMAN *Champlain* ix. (1875) 305 The garnet hue of the young oaks, the bonfire blaze of the tupelo at the water's edge. **1885** in *Milnor* (Dakota) *Free Press* 25 Apr. 5/5 The tupelo-gum and the willow-oak are timbers that are destined to a commercial value never until recently dreamed of. **1900** W. D. HOWELLS in *Scribner's Mag.* Sept. 367/2 He wished to show me a tupelo-tree.

tuph, **tupha**, obs. ff. TUFF, TUFA.

tuphan, obs. var. TYPHOON.

tuphlo-: see TYPHLO-.

tuphramancy, error for TEPHROMANCY.

‖**Tupi** (ˈtuːpɪ, tuːˈpiː). **a.** A native language widely spoken in Brazil, which has yielded various names of animals, plants, etc.; the group of tribes speaking this language; a person belonging to one of these tribes. Also *attrib.*

1842 [see THE *dem. adj.* and *pron.* B. 3 b]. **1863** [see JACITARA]. **1882** *Athenæum* 9 Sept. 341/2 The widely diffused Tupi language, spoken throughout a great part of Brazil. **1911** *Encycl. Brit.* XXVII. 410/2 Latham makes the Tupis members of the Guarani stock. **1950** C. LÉVI-STRAUSS in J. H. Steward *Handbk. S. Amer. Indians* VI. 475 The fruit of a Bignoniaceae..was used as a comb by the *Tupí* and other tribes. **1950** C. O. SAUER in *Ibid.* 499 The peanut was..important in Tupí economy.

b. ***Tupi-Guarani*** (gwɑːrəˈniː), also unhyphened: a South American linguistic and ethnic stock of which Tupi and Guarani are the most prominent members; a person belonging to this ethnic stock. Also *attrib.* Cf. GUARANI 1.

1850 R. G. LATHAM *Nat. Hist. Varieties of Man* 443 The Guarani. Synonyms.—Tupi, Brazilian, Guarani-Brazilian, Tupi-Guarani. **1876** *Encycl. Brit.* IV. 235/1 They [*sc.* the tribes of Brazil] belong..to one original stock, called by ethnographers, the Tupi-Guarani. **1901** *O.E.D.* s.v. *Jaguar*, According to writers on Tupi-Guarani, *jaguara* or *jagua* is orig. a class-name for all carnivorous beasts. **1933** L. BLOOMFIELD *Language* iv. 73 In South America, we note.. the Tupi-Guarani [family of languages], stretched along the coast of Brazil. **1956** E. HAUGEN *Bilingualism in Americas* ii. 15 Tupí-Guaraní is taught in some Brazilian schools. **1968** M. GILBERT *Cork in Bottle* in *Ellery Queen's Christmas Hamper* (1975) 231 The three mestizos..were Tupi-Guaranis, half Indian, half Spanish. **1977** G. CLARK *World Prehistory* (ed. 3) x. 449 Polychrome pottery closely resembling the Tupi-guarani ware of East Brazil.

Also **Tupian** *sb.* and *a.*

1902 *Encycl. Brit.* XXV. 374/1 [Linguistic families of America] Tupian, Amazon R. **1948** A. L. KROEBER *Anthropology* (rev. ed.) xviii. 833 A Tupian tribe, the Chiriguano, having conquered an Arawakan one, the Chané, pushed on westward. **1974** *Encycl. Brit. Micropædia* X. 187/1 *Tupians*, South American Indians who speak languages of the Tupian linguistic group. Tupian-speaking peoples were widespread south of the Amazon.

‖**tupik** (ˈtuːpɪk). Also 9 **toupik**, **tupic**; **topek**, **tubik**. [Eskimo of Alaska.] A hut or tent of skins used by Eskimo as a summer residence.

1864 C. F. HALL *Life with Esquimaux* I. ix. 176 On my way,..just outside the angeko's tupic, I noticed an oar of a kia[k] stuck upright in a drift of frozen snow. **1878** C. HALLOCK *Sportsman's Gazetteer* (ed. 4) 700 *Toupik*, an Esquimaux summer lodge of poles covered with seal-skins. **1895** KIPLING *Second Jungle Bk.* 152 One of their hunters came across a *tupik*, a skin-tent. **1898** *Geogr. Jrnl.* Nov. 499 These people [Eskimo], who live in *tupiks* (tents or huts of skin) in summer, and in *igloos*, partly excavated, partly stone-built dwellings, in winter. **1900** *Scribner's Mag.* Sept. 297/2 There were three or four tupiks, or sealskin tents, pitched upon the turf at the foot of the talus. **1920** W. T. GRENFELL *Labrador Doctor* vi. 129 Wooden huts had largely replaced the former 'tubiks', or skin tents.

Tupinamba (tuːpɪˈnæmbə, *prop.* tupinamˈbɑː). Also †**Tupinambo.** [Native name; cf. F. *Topinambou* (1578 in form *Tououpinambaoults*) and TUPI.] A group of extinct tribes on the coast of Brazil; a person belonging to one of these tribes. Also *attrib.*

1810 SOUTHEY *Hist. Brazil* I. viii. 229 Nobrega learnt from the Tupinambas that two persons..taught them the use of the mandioc. **1819** SHELLEY *Let.* 3 Nov. (1964) II. 140 An Otaheitan or a Tupinambo. **1863** H. W. BATES *Naturalist on River Amazons* I. vii. 285 The old historians relate that the island of Tupinambarána was colonised by a portion of the great Tupí or Tupinámba nation, who were driven from the sea-coast near Pernambuco, by the early Portuguese settlers in the 16th century. **1949** WAGLEY & GALVÃO *Tenetehara Indians of Brazil* i. 5 The Portuguese.. found the Island of Maranhão inhabited by the Tupí-Guaraní Tupinambá. **1974** *Encycl. Brit. Macropædia* XVII. 124/1 The Tupinamba shaman fumigates his rattle with tobacco.

‖**Tupiˈnambis.** [mod.L., said to have been coined by Lamarck, perh. f. TUPI.] A genus of South American lizards.

Misapplied by Geoffrey to the Egyptian Monitor (*Varanus Niloticus*), whence app. Lytton's use, quot. 1863.

1839 *Penny Cycl.* XV. 332/1 Cuvier divides them [the Monitors] into two groups, and Fitzinger into three, under the names of *Tupinambis*, *Varanus*, and *Psammosaurus*. **1863** LD. LYTTON *Ring Amasis* II. II. i, The museum..presented a very respectable arrangement of gems, scarabaei, sphinxes, stuffed crocodiles, and tupinambes.

-tuple (ˈtjuːp(ə)l), *a.* and *sb.* Chiefly *Math.* [The ending of QUINTUPLE *a.* and *sb.*, etc.] With preceding algebraic symbol: (an entity or set) consisting of as many parts or elements as indicated by the symbol.

1863 *Phil. Trans. R. Soc.* CLIII. 457 The curve *m* is a $(m-1)n$-tuple line on the scroll $S(m^2, n)$. **1910** *Encycl. Brit.* I. 615/2 We may regard it as a (2^n-1)-tuple linear algebra. **1938** *Jrnl. Symbolic Logic* III. 151 Each function is defined over a subset..of the *n*-tuples of natural numbers. **1963** J. LYONS *Structural Semantics* ii. 12 In so far as words can be segmented into morphemes, the lexeme can be defined extensionally as the set of all the ordered *n*-tuples ($n \geqq 1$) of morphemes (each *n*-tuple being a word) which are grouped together in setting up the paradigm. **1972** *Computer Jrnl.* XV. 232/1 A structure of a string *A* is an ordered *n*-tuple *T*.

tuppat, obs. Sc. f. TIPPET.

†**tuppee**, obs. var. TOUPEE.

1778 B'NESS DE BODE *Lett.* 27 Jan. (1900) 10 A dwarf man with an immense *tuppée*.

tuppence, -pens: see TWOPENCE.

Tuˈpperian, *a.* and *sb.* **a.** *adj.* Of, belonging to, or in the style of Martin F. Tupper's Proverbial Philosophy (1838–42). **b.** *sb.* An admirer of Tupper. So **ˈTupperish** *a.*, **ˈTupperism, ˈTupperize** *v.*

1858 O. W. HOLMES *Aut. Breakf.-t.* xi. (1891) 271 Whether I dipped them from the ocean of Tupperian wisdom,..I cannot say. **1866** *Reader* No. 168. 271/3 Tupperian pretentiousness and moralizations. **1869** BARING-GOULD *Orig. Relig. Belief* (1878) II. xx. 380 Truth must be Tupperish—allow me the word,—or public opinion will not tolerate it. **1870** J. R. LOWELL *Among my Books* 114 The gradual degeneration of a poetic faith into the ritual of unimaginative Tupperism. **1870** *Observer* 13 Nov., Tupperising in deerskin breeches is not an intellectual frolic that we can contemplate with patience. **1905** *Daily Chron.* 20 June 3/3 Our fathers found entertainment and even worldly wisdom in the Tupperisms of yesterday.

Tupperware (ˈtʌpəwɛə(r)). [Trade name, f. Earl S. *Tupper*, President of the Tupper Corporation + WARE *sb.*[3]] The proprietary name of a range of plastic vessels, containers, etc., sold exclusively at 'parties' in private homes to which potential purchasers are invited. Freq. *attrib.*; also in allusive use.

1956 *Official Gaz.* (U.S. Patent Office) 12 June TM 53 Tupperware... For Molded Plastic Tumblers, Canisters, Pitchers, Dispensers; Empty Condiment Holders... Empty Soap, Hair Massage and Tooth Brush Boxes [etc.]. First use Mar. 3, 1950. **1961** *Trade Marks Jrnl.* 23 Aug. 1162/1 Tupperware... Small domestic utensils and containers..; combs and sponges; brushes...; Rexall Drug and Chemical Company.., City of Los Angeles, State of California, United States of America; manufacturers. **1965** *Which?* Dec. 373/1 Are more expensive brands [of food container], in particular Tupperware, better than cheaper brands at storing foods? *Ibid.*, You can't buy Tupperware in the shops. It is sold through local 'dealers'... The dealer gets a housewife to be the hostess at a party. **1966** T. PYNCHON *Crying of Lot 49* i. 9 Mrs Oedipa Maas came home from a Tupperware party whose hostess had perhaps put too much kirsch in the fondue. **1971** N. STACEY *Who Cares?* viii. 131 We were not training a group of people to give Tupperware parties or sell cosmetics to housewives. **1979** T. BARLING *Olympic Sleeper* i. 15 There were too many cowboys on the Thames nowadays, playing sailors in their Tupperware boats.

‖**tupsee** (ˈtʌpsiː). *E. Indies.* Also **tupsy, -ey,** and more etymologically spelt *tăpsī*. [a. Hindī *tapsī*, more fully *tapsī machh*:—Skr. *tapasya matsya*, i.e. fish produced from heat, or in the spring season *Phalguna* (Feb. and March) when the mango blossoms.] A fish of the genus *Polynemus*, allied to the mullet, 8 or 9 inches long, found in the Ganges and Irrawaddy; a variety from the estuaries of the Hooghly is considered a great delicacy at Calcutta. Also called MANGO-*fish*.

1839 CANTOR in *Proc. Zool. Soc.* July 116 The species best known is the *Polynemus risua*, Hamilton; *Pol. longifilis*, Cuvier; the Tupsee or Mango Fish of the Anglo-Indians. **1858** SIMMONDS *Dict. Trade*, *Mango-fish*,..esteemed as a delicacy in India, where it is also called the Tupsee. *Ibid.*, Tupsee, Tupsey.

tupsiturvie, obs. form of TOPSY-TURVY.

tupto-ing (ˈtjuːptəʊɪŋ), *pres. pple. nonce-wd.* In quot. tuptowing. [f. Gr. τύπτω, 1st pers. pres. ind. of τύπτειν (as the verb commonly learned first) + -ING[2].] Conjugating τύπτω; 'grinding' at Greek (and Latin) verbs.

[**1762** STERNE *Tr. Shandy* V. xlii, Seven long years ..τυπτω-ing it, at Greek and Latin.] **1824** SCOTT *Redgauntlet* ch. xiv, Jack Hadaway..was 'tuptowing' away with a dozen of wretched boys.

tuque (tjuːk, tyk). *Canadian.* [a. Canadian Fr., f. F. *toque*, TOQUE.] A knitted stocking-cap tapered and closed at both ends, one end being tucked into the other to form the cap; formerly the characteristic winter head-dress of the Canadian 'habitant'; now chiefly worn as part of a toboggan or snow-shoe club costume.

1871 W. G. BEERS in *Scribner's Monthly* Sept. 454/2 The snow-shoe clubs have adopted the tuque. **1887** *Cornh. Mag.* Mar. 267 The real head-dress of the snowshoer being the knitted woollen *tuque*, a bag-shaped cap,..suggesting..the headgear of the Royal Artillery. **1894** *Outing* (U.S.) XXIII. 358 The Snow Shoer's Song. Tighten the tuque, and girdle the sash, Lads and lasses, the snow shoes lash. **1909** *Westm. Gaz.* 23 Feb. 8/3 Their uniforms were blanket costumes, with tuques, mocassins and snowshoes.

tuquheit, Sc. dial. var. TEWHIT, lapwing.

1553 *Burgh Rec. Edinb.* II. 185 The best tuquheit iij.d.

‖**tu quoque** (t(j)uː ˈkwəʊkwiː). [L., lit. 'thou also', = Eng. slang 'you're another!'] An argument which consists in retorting a charge upon one's accuser. Also *attrib.*

[**1614** J. COOKE (*title*) Greenes Tu quoque, Or, The Cittie Gallant. *Ibid.* E ij b, *Rash*... M. Bubble, God saue you. *Bub.* Tu quoque Sir. *Ibid.* G j b, *Bub*... I want the *Bone Ioure*, and the *Tu quoques*, Which yonder Gentleman has.] **1671** SHADWELL *Humorist* II. 28 Nay Sir, I say nothing, Mum is the Italian *tu quoque* word. **1838** LYTTON *Alice* III. iv, No man knew better the rhetorical effect of the *tu quoque* form of argument. **1874** J. O. DYKES *Relations Kingd. to World* II. 107 The tu quoque rejoinder, 'Physician heal thyself', is in its place here. *a* **1903** 'MERRIMAN' *Last Hope* v, I leave myself open to a *tu quoque*, I know.

tur (tʊə(r)). [a. Russ.] A greyish-brown wild goat, *Capra caucasica*, native to south-eastern Russia.

1894 C. PHILLIPPS-WOLLEY *Big Game Shooting* II. iii. 51 The tûr is the mountain beast, *par excellence*, of the Caucasus. **1894** R. LYDEKKER *Royal Nat. Hist.* II. 235 There occur in the Caucasus range..wild goats, known locally as tur. **1925** G. BURRARD *Big Game Hunting* 87 The East Caucasian tur..is an undoubted goat. **1965** D. MORRIS *Mammals* 428 There are several other species which are also called Ibex. These include the Tur, or Caucasian Ibex.

turacin (ˈtjʊərəsɪn). *Chem.* [f. mod.L. *Turac-us* TURACO + -IN[1].] A crimson animal pigment, found by Professor A. H. Church in the wing-feathers of about 26 species of birds of the genera *Turacus*, *Gallirex*, and *Musophaga*, confined to the Æthiopic region of Central Africa; closely allied to hæmoglobin, but free from iron, and containing over 7 per cent. of copper.

1868 A. H. CHURCH in *Student & Intell. Observ.* I. 161 Turacine, a new animal pigment containing copper. **1869** —— in *Phil. Trans.* CLIX. 627 Researches on Turacin. **1885** *Riverside Nat. Hist.* (1888) IV. 5 Another red [pigment], turacin, causes the magnificent red on the wings of the Musophagidæ.

turaco (ˈtʊərəkəʊ). Also touraco, -cou, -caw, turako, -koo. [= F. *touraco*, Du. *toerako*: native name in W. Africa of *Turacus persa*.

Buffon, *Hist. Nat. Oiseaux* (1783), calls it *tourocco*, which name he claims to have invented from the first part of *tourterelle* turtle-dove + *hocco*, Fr. name of the curassow; but the bird was known to G. Edwards 40 years earlier as *touraco*.]

Any bird of the family *Musophagidæ* (plantain-eaters), natives of southern, west, and central Africa, and esp. of the genus *Turacus* (or *Corythaix*), large birds with brilliant purple, green, and crimson plumage and prominent crest (hence formerly called *crown-birds*); also of the genus *Schizorrhis*, with plumage of a plainer character.

1743 G. EDWARDS *Hist. Birds* I. 7 The Touraco. This Bird is about the Bigness of a Magpye or Jay; the Make of its Body is rather long than round; the Head of a moderate Size. **1840** *Penny Cycl.* XVI. 29/2 The Touracos..feed principally on soft fruits. **1861** DU CHAILLU *Equat. Afr.* vii. 77 (*Among the Fans*) His head was..decorated with the red feathers of a touracaw. **1863** R. F. BURTON *Abeokuta* I. 38 The gay crested touraco (*Corythaix*), with its jay-like manner, beautiful and harsh-voiced as the Maids of Athens, aired its gorgeous coat in the sunbeams upon the tree-top. **1896** *List Anim. Zool. Soc.* 321 *Turacus persa*..Senegal Touracou... West Africa... *T. livingstonii*..Livingstone's Touracou... British Central Africa... *T. corythaix*.. White-crested Touracou... South Africa. *Ibid.* 322 *Gallirex chlorochlamys*..Green-necked Touracou... *Schizorhis africana*..Variegated Touracou. **1932** *Discovery* Jan. 25/1 Colies, turacos, various doves and barbets..throng to the Amani plantations. **1965** G. B. SCHALLER *Year of Gorilla* ii. 69 A black-billed turaco flew up, flashing its brilliant crimson wings. Then this crow-sized bird hopped along a branch, chattering like a squirrel. **1977** *Daily Colonist* (Victoria, B.C.) 9 Oct. 23/4 You will see..exotic birds—bee-eaters, love-birds, sun-birds and turacos.

turacoverdin (ˌtjʊərəkəʊˈvɜːdɪn). *Chem.* [f. as TURACIN; cf. *biliverdin*.] A green colouring-matter occurring in the feathers of some Touracos.

1885 *Riverside Nat. Hist.* (1888) IV. 5 A really green pigment has only been found in the touracos—hence the name turacoverdin. **1892** A. H. CHURCH in *Phil. Trans.* CLXXXIII. 512 Dr. C. F. W. Krukenberg..has described a green colouring matter obtained from the green feathers of *Turacus corythaix*, and of other plantain-eaters, by the employment of a 2 per cent, caustic soda-solution as the solvent. He calls this pigment 'turacoverdin', and..states that it contains 'much iron, but no great quantity of copper and manganese'.

Turanian (tjʊˈreɪnɪən), *sb.* and *a.* [f. Pers. *Tūrān*, name of the realm beyond the Oxus, used by Firdusi *c* 1000 in opposition to *Irān* or Persia.

In 1840 Pott (Ersch & Gruber II. xviii. 1) contrasts *Turan* with *arisch* (Aryn).]

A. *sb.* **1.** A member of any of the races speaking the 'Turanian' or Ural-Altaic languages: see B.

1777 J. RICHARDSON *Dict. Persian*, etc., Dissert. p. xxx/2 The Tartars, Scythians, or Turanians. **1788** *Asiatick Researches* I. 7 A Turanian pronunciation. **1841** J. C. PRICHARD *Res. Physical Hist. Mankind* (ed. 3) III. i. 16 A great number of roots are thus to be traced in several of the Turanian languages. **1854** BUNSEN *Christianity* IV. 26 The native religion of the Turanian is Shamanism. **1861** HULME tr. *Moquin-Tandon* I. v. 32 Turanians: Physiognomy: Mongol. Language: Agglutinate. Area: Mongolia, Mantshuria. **1888** G. SMITH *S. Hislop* vii. (1889) 182 Brahmanism assimilated to itself the cults of the Turanians and Sudras.

2. The so-called Turanian languages collectively.

1836 J. C. PRICHARD *Res. Physical Hist. Mankind* (ed. 3) I. iv. 267 The skulls of the Esquimaux..bring them into the same class of human races with the Kalmuk and other Turanian nations. **1908** *Christian Express* 1 Apr. 59/1 He states that in Bantu, as in Turanian (by-the-bye, we would be thankful to know what is Turanian) there is a regular phonetic interchange k = p = b = f = d!

B. *adj.*

1. Applied loosely to a group or supposed 'family' of languages, originally applied to all or nearly all of Asiatic origin that are neither Aryan nor Semitic; in later use nearly = URAL-ALTAIC.

1854 BUNSEN *Christianity* VI. 64 All the languages of Asia and Europe which are neither Semitic nor Arian. I ventured in 1847 to write all these under the name Turanian. **1860** FARRAR *Orig. Lang.* 199 Languages which belong to neither of these two..families have been classed together under the name of the Turanian, Nomadic, or Allophylian family. **1865** —— *Chapt. Lang.* 29 Various sporadic families, which some would call Turanian. **1892** WHITNEY *Max Müller* 49 The old 'Turanian' aggregation, which..has for a generation been a stumbling-block in the way of science.

2. Applied to the peoples speaking these languages.

1859 MAX MÜLLER *Sc. Lang.* (1861) I. 276 The name Turanian is used in opposition to Aryan and is applied to the nomadic races of Asia as opposed to the agricultural or Aryan races. **1874** BANCROFT *Footpr. Time* i. 30 Turanian means 'outside', or 'barbarian'. **1890** J. G. FRAZER *Gold. Bough* (1913) I. iv. 179 The Magyars belong to the great Turanian family of mankind.

Hence **Tuˈranianism**, the principle of uniting speakers of Turanian or Ural-Altaic languages (esp. Turkish); cf. *pan-Turanianism* s.v. PAN- I.

1922 *19th Cent.* Nov. 835 The seeming paradox of the Bolshevist *régime* cementing Islamism and Turanianism in a widespread brotherhood.

‖**turaˈnira, touraˈnero.** [Native name in Guyana.] A small tree of Brazil and Guyana, *Humirium floribundum*, the wood of which, **turanira-wood**, is used for rafters; its bark is greatly esteemed as a perfume, and when wounded a fragrant yellow balsam, termed in Brazil balsam of Umiri, flows from it. See also quot. 1884.

1862 *List Contrib. Brit. Guiana to Lond. Exhib.* in Veness *El Dorado* (1866) App. 136 Turanira, Touranero, or Bastard Bully-tree (*Humirium floribundum*, Mart.). Used for framing timber, spokes, &c. **1884** MILLER *Plant-n.*, *Turanira-wood*, the wood of *Bumelia retusa*.

turanose (ˈtjʊərənəʊz). *Chem.* [ad. Russ. *turanoza* (A. Alekhina 1889, in *Zhurnal Russkago fiziko-khim. Obshchestva* XXI. 418), after Pers. *Tūrān* Turkistan, place of origin of the manna used to prepare this: see -OSE[2].] The reducing disaccharide sugar $C_{12}H_{22}O_{11}$, formed by partial hydrolysis of melezitose; 3-α-D-glucopyranosyl-D-fructose.

1890 *Jrnl. Chem. Soc.* LVIII. 733 Melezitose, on inversion with dilute mineral acids, yields at first turanose and dextrose; the former is a new saccharose of the formula $C_{12}H_{22}O_{11}$. **1927** M. BODANSKY *Introd. Physiol. Chem.* ii. 43 Turanose (fructose + glucose) is obtained by hydrolyzing the trisaccharide melicitose. **1975** *Nature* 10 July 128/1 Maltose was slightly more effective, and sucrose, turanose, kojibiose, trehalose and melezitose all inhibited binding at significantly lower concentrations than glucose.

turat, obs. Sc. form of TURRET.

turb (tɜːb). *Obs.* exc. *Hist.* Forms: 4–6 turbe, 5–6, 9 tourbe, 7–9 turb. [a. F. *tourbe*, OF. *torbe* (11th c. in Hatz.-Darm.) also *turbe*, ad. L. *turba* crowd.] A crowd, swarm, heap; a troop; also, a group or clump of trees.

c **1330** R. BRUNNE *Chron.* (1810) 188 In þe secund turbe was maister Coradyn. *c* **1480** *St. Ursula* vii, This holy turbe to Colen made theyr retourne. *c* **1489** CAXTON *Blanchardyn* xlix. 191 They came so fast by and by, And by so grete tourbes and hepes, that [etc.]. **1509** WATSON *Ship of Fools* xx. (1517) F ij, A grete turbe of foles fleeth to our shyppe. **1618** DEKKER *Owles Almanack* 21 Every heddge and quick-set, every knot, and turb of trees. **1694** MOTTEUX *Rabelais* v. (1737) 230 When the Turb is once accumulate. [**1886** *Punch* 20 Mar. 144 His front by nasiterge occult To serve from muscan turb his vult.] **1900** A. LANG *Hist. Scot.* I. vi. 149 John Knox or Bothwell would come to his trial at the head of an armed tourbe, or gathering of partisans.

‖**turba** (ˈtʊəbə). *Mus.* [L., = crowd.] A name given to the chorus in Passions and other religious oratorios in which crowds participate in the action. (See also quot. 1889.)

1876 STAINER & BARRETT *Dict. Mus. Terms* 443/1 *Turbæ* (*Lat.*), the chorus part or voice of the multitude in a Passion-music. **1889** *Cent. Dict.* s.v., *Turba*, the chorus in mediaeval passion-plays, representing the Jewish populace. **1947** A. EINSTEIN *Music in Romantic Era* xiii. 173 It is a work with fanatic *turbae*, the 'crowds', as in the Passions. **1962** *Listener* 15 Feb. 317/3 The Roman Church's dramatic Passions now come into view with Victoria's and Byrd's settings of the *turba*.

turban (ˈtɜːbən), *sb.* Forms: α. 6 **tolipane, -epan, tolliban, tulbant, (tal-), 6–7 tuliban, tolibant, -e, tulipan, 7 tulipant, -e, tullipant, -band, tul-, (tel-)-bent, dulipan, tulban**; β. 6 **torbant, turribant, turbanto, 6–9 turbant, -band, 6–7 -bante, -bent, 7 -bond, -bat**); γ. 7 **turben, -bine, -bane, 6– turban**. [Altered form of Pers. *dulbănd* or *dōlbănd*, in vulgar Turkish pronounced *tulbant*, *tul(i)pant*, *toli-*, whence OIt. *tolipante*, *tolipano*, mod.It., Sp., Pg. *turbante*; obs. F. *tolliban* (15th c.), *tulban*, *turbant* (Cotgr.), F. *turban*; early mod.Du. *turbant* (Kilian), Du. *tulband*, Ger., Da., Sw. *turban*. It is not clear in which language the change of *tul-* to *tur-* took place; it may have been in S.W. India, or in Portuguese; we find it first in Hickock's translation of Cesar Frederick, who cites it from the Portuguese Indies. *Tulipant*, *turbant*, were the most usual English forms in 17th c.; *turban* was used by Johnson and Gibbon. See also TULIP, which goes back to the same word.]

1. a. A head-dress of Muslim origin worn by men of Eastern nations, consisting of a cap round which is wound a long piece of linen, cotton, or silk.

(In quot. 1561, the tarboosh or fez as distinct from its wrapping.)

α. **1561** A. JENKINSON *Voy.* (Hakl. Soc.) I. 132 Upon his head was a tolipane with a sharpe end standing upwards halfe a yard long, of riche cloth of golde, wrapped about with a piece of India silke of twentie yards long, wrought with golde, and on the left side of his tolipane stood a plume of feathers. **1585** T. WASHINGTON tr. *Nicholay's Voy.* III. xx. 108 Kinsemen of Mahomet..doe weare a green Tulbant. *Ibid.* IV. iv. 116 Their custome is to weare a Talbant high topped before. **1588** in Hakluyt *Voy.* (1600) III. 821 Died linen cloth folded vp like vnto a Turkes Tuliban. **1589** PUTTENHAM *Eng. Poesie* III. xxiv. (Arb.) 291 The Turke and Persian to weare great tolibants of ten, fifteene, and twentie elles of linnen a peece vpon their heads. **1596** DANETT tr. *Comines* (1614) 296 They were not vppon their head such a great roule of linnen as the Turkes doe, called Tolliban. **1597** GERARDE *Herbal* 117 Tulipan, Tolepan [see TULIP 1]. **1600** J. PORY tr. *Leo's Africa* III. 160 On their heads they weare a blacke dulipan. **1603** KNOLLES *Hist. Turks* (1621) 201 Upon his tombe lieth..a little Turkish tulipant, much differing from those great turbants which the Turks now weare. **1613** PURCHAS *Pilgrimage* III. xi. 255 With a great Tullipant on his head. *Ibid.* xiv. 267 These weare greene Tulipans, which colour none else may weare, and that onely on their head. **1617** MORYSON *Itin.* III. 174 A round globe, which in their tongue is called a Tulbent. **1652** H. L'ESTRANGE *Amer. no Jewes* 57 A Cap of linnen somewhat full like a Turk's Turband or Tulliband. **1653** GREAVES *Seraglio* 129 The name of the stuff (as we call ours lawn, cambrick, holland, &c.) is *Telbent*; whence we (falsly) call that which a Turk wears a Turbant, using the name of the stuff for the thing made up. **1662** J. DAVIES tr. *Olearius' Voy. Ambass.* 314 The Coeffure of the Men, which they call Mendils, and the Turks, Tulbans, or Turbants, is made of Cotton cloath, or some silk Stuff,..of several Colours. [**1686** tr. *Chardin's Coronat. Solyman* 40 A *Dhul-bandt* (which our Writers..erroneously call a Turbant).] **1688** R. HOLME *Armoury* IV. xi. (Roxb.) 440/2 In Egypt the great Sultan used a Tulipant or Turbat made of three score or more elles of thin stuffe diuersely folded.

β. **1588** T. HICKOCK tr. *Frederick's Voy.* 5 The *Torbants* are made in Diu. **1596** SPENSER *F.Q.* IV. xi. 28 Old Cybele, ..Wearing a Diademe embattild wide With hundred turrets, like a Turribant. **1598** R. HAYDOCKE tr. *Lomazzo* II. 124 Some of them beare blewe turbantes;..the Iewes beare them yeallow. **1599** HAKLUYT *Voy.* II. 168 With their turbents very white and cleane. **1607** R. C[AREW] tr. *Estienne's World of Wonders* 235 A Turkish turbant [*margin* or tolibante]. **1611** SHAKS. *Cymb.* III. iii. 6 The Gates of Monarches Are Arch'd so high, that Giants may iet through And keepe their impious Turbonds on. **1652** Turband, **1653–86** Turbant, **1688** Turbat [see α]. **1697** DAMPIER *Voy.* I. xv. 427 They wear no Hat, Cap, nor Turbat, nor any thing to keep off the Sun. **1710** ADDISON *Tatler* No. 161 ¶9 Ignorance with a Turband upon her Head. **1735** JOHNSON *Lobo's Abyssinia*, *Voy.* v. 30 He [the King]..with a Turbant on his Head, to which were fastned some Rings. **1839** MONTEITH in *Madras Jrnl. Lit. & Sc.* X. 162 Dressed in their blue clothes and white turbands.

γ. **1597** GERARDE *Herbal* 117 Turban, Turfan [see TULIP 1]. **1623** COCKERAM, *Turbine*, a thing of linnen which the Turks weare on their heads. **1624** BEDELL *Lett.* iii. 78 There were also Turkish Turbanes, and Diadems of diuers fashions. **1687** A. LOVELL tr. *Thevenot's Trav.* III. 37 The turban worn in the Indies is commonly little. **1755** JOHNSON, Turban, turbant, turband. **1774** GOLDSM. *Nat. Hist.* (1776) II. 77 The size of the head is encreased by a great variety of bandages, formed into a turban. **1788** GIBBON *Decl. & F.* lvii. V. 667 His ample turban was fashioned in the shape of a crown. **1803** *Med. Jrnl.* X. 281 Oriental travellers, who exchange their hat for the turban, experience it to be a much cooler and more agreeable covering.

b. As the symbol of Islam, or of those who profess it.

1610 MARCELLINE *Triumphs Jas. I* 74 Go generous Race, go gather Laurels..chase the Turbants from those Provinces. **1660** INGELO *Bentiv. & Ur.* II. (1682) 55 Their Emperour commanded only the Turbants to be beaten. **1693** *Mem. Cnt. Teckely* I. 13 The Turk..does not force the Transylvanians to take up the Turban. **1753** HANWAY *Trav.* (1762) II. v. iii. 139 As he refused to wear the turbant, his younger brother..offered himself in his stead. **1812** BYRON *Ch. Har.* II. lxxix, Though turbans now pollute Sophia's shrine, And Greece her very altars eyes in vain. **1878** VILLARI *Machiavelli* (1898) I. iii. 160, I was better fitted for the turban than the cowl.

c. A figure or representation of a turban, e.g. on Muslim funeral monuments. Also in *Her.*

1687 A. LOVELL tr. *Thevenot's Trav.* I. 224 Five great Sepulchres, in one whereof a Basha is Interred, having his Turban cut in Marble, at one end of his Tomb. **1717** LADY M. W. MONTAGU *Let. to Abbé Conti* 29 May, They set up a pillar with a carved turbant on the top of it. **1720** STRYPE *Stow's Surv.* (1754) II. v. xiv. 320/2 A Turk..upon his Head a Turbant, Argent..with a Tassel upon the Top, Gules. **1766** PORNY *Elem. Her.* (1787) 214 The Great-Turk bears over his arms a Turband..under two Coronets,..and the uppermost is surmounted with Crescents. **1844** E. WARBURTON *Crescent & Cross* (1846) II. xvii. 249 A cemetery, whose sculptured turbans showed that the neighbouring village was Moslem. **1876** [see TURBANED b].

d. Applied to the head-dress of the ancient Jewish high priest.

1624 BP. HALL *Imprese of God* I. Wks. 442 An honourable Motto; such as was written vpon the מצנפת, the Turbant, of the High priest; Holinesse to the Lord. **1885** BIBLE (R.V.) *Exod.* xxviii. 37 Upon the forefront of the mitre [*marg.* turban].

e. *transf.* and *fig.* Applied to a head-dress, or a head of hair, likened to a turban.

1609 B. JONSON *Sil. Wom.* I. i, A huge turbant of night-caps on his head, buckled over his eares. **1609** BP. W. BARLOW *Answ. Nameless Cath.* 161 Obedience to Princes makes not for the Popes Triple Turbant. **1727** A. HAMILTON *New Acc. E. Ind.* I. xiii. 152 A sanctified Rascal of 7 Foot high,..with a large Turband of his own Hair wreathed about his Head. **1827** STEUART *Planter's G.* (1828) 429 The woolly head of the Negro; who, without that light and natural turban, would [etc.].

f. Erroneously supposed to be worn by women of Eastern nations and Jewesses.

1805–6 CAMPBELL *Turkish Lady* vii, 'Captive! could the brightest jewel From my turban set thee free?' 'Lady, no!' **1819** SCOTT *Ivanhoe* viii, Her [Rebecca's] form..was shewn to advantage by a sort of Eastern dress,..Her turban of yellow silk suited well with the darkness of her complexion. **1835** *Ladies' Cabinet* Nov. 337 The Jewish style of *coiffure*, as copied from the daughters of Israel in their days of splendour, will be decidedly fashionable. We have seen already some turbans *á l'Israelite*,..that have been ordered by *élegantes* of high fashion.

g. *Cookery.* (See quot. 1911: perh. only as Fr.)

1846 SOYER *Cookery* 514 *Turban de Meringues glacé.* Make a turban as directed in the last..fill the turban, at the moment of serving [etc.]. **1911** WEBSTER, *Turban*..5. *Cookery.* A drum-shaped case for entrées, fillets, etc.

2. a. A head-dress made to resemble or suggest the oriental turban, worn by ladies in Europe and America during the late 18th and the earlier part of the 19th c., and temporarily revived in 1908. Cf. *turban-fold* in 8.

1776 *Lady's Mag.* Mar. 118/1 Ladies'..Hair..very.. high..Turbans more the taste than caps. **1796** MME. D'ARBLAY *Camilla* III. 325 Assuring her [the cap] was grown so old-fashioned, that not a lady's maid..would now be seen in it, she offered to pin her up a turban. **1823** LADY BLESSINGTON *Sk. & Fragm.* 59 Went to the Opera: wore my tissue turban. **1835** *Ladies' Cabinet* Mar. 199 Hats and turbans are equally fashionable for ladies who do not dance. **1838** DISRAELI *Corr. w. Sister* (1886) 96 She was most becomingly dressed in a white turban of a very *recherché* construction. **1908** *Paris Fashions* 15 Feb. 6/2 The large 'de Stael' turbans, such as are seen in old pictures, are being worn at the theatre.

b. A style of hair-dressing for women.

1909 *Daily Graphic* 13 Oct. 13/3 The up-to-date turban.. is in a loose wave wound round with a plain strand of smooth hair. *Ibid.*, The turban coiffure. *Ibid.* 25 Oct. 13/3 The Revived Turban. Hair draped round head in turban fashion.

3. A bright-coloured cloth worn as a head-dress by Blacks (esp. women) in the West Indies and southern U.S.

1839 DARWIN *Voy. Nat.* i. (1879) 4 Their black skins and snow-white linen being set off by coloured turbans and large shawls. **1852** MRS. STOWE *Uncle Tom's C.* xx, Miss Ophelia found Topsy with her very best scarlet India Canton crape shawl wound round her head for a turban. **1852** THACKERAY *Esmond* III. iii, A..negro..with a bird of paradise in his turbant.

4. Name for a small brimless hat, or round cap with closely turned up brim, worn, chiefly by women and children, since about 1850.

1862 [implied in *turban-hat* in 8]. **1865** MELTON *Hints on Hats* 53 The boating-hat of straw; the 'turban', or 'pork-pie'; the fishing-cap, [etc.].

5. *Zool.* A name for certain species of echinoderms, esp. the genus *Cidaris*.

1713 PETIVER *Aquat. Anim. Amboinæ* Tab. viii, *Echinus S. Diadema Turcarum*... Turks Turband. **1837** *Penny Cycl.* IX. 262/1 Fossil Echini... Subspheroidal species, more elevated than wide..(The Turbans). Example, *Cidaris imperialis*.

6. a. The spire or whorl of a twisted univalve shell. *rare.* **b.** A mollusc of the genus *Turbo*.

Taken to represent L. *turbo*; but confounded with *turban*.

1681 GREW *Musæum* I. VI. i. 125 A Shell like the Oriental, with a Knobed Turban or Whirle. **1685** *Phil. Trans.* XV. 1019 Fig. 3[d]. Represents the Shell in its true bigness,..there are six or seven spiral lines or Rounds in the Turban. **1815** W. WOOD *Gen. Conchol.* I. *Dict. Terms* 60 All the whirls, or spires, of a Univalve, taken collectively, are called the turban. **1819** W. TURTON *Conchol. Dict.* 198 *Turbo petræus.* Rock Turban.

7. Florist's name for cultivated varieties of *Ranunculus*; more fully ***Turk's turban***.

1760 J. LEE *Introd. Bot.* App. 330 Turk's Turban, *Ranunculus*. **1882** *Standard* 6 Nov. 1/8, 25 Ranunculi, scarlet turban. 25 Ranunculi, mixed turban.

8. *attrib.* and *Comb.*, as ***turban-cap***, ***-cloth***, ***encrinite***, ***-flower***, ***-fold***, † ***grout-head***, ***hat***, ***-roll***, ***style***, ***-wisp***; ***turban-crested***, ***-crowned***, ***-like***, ***-shaped***, adjs.; **turban-eye**, a pillared eye, found in the males of some May-flies; **turban gourd**, a variety of *Cucurbita maxima*: cf. *turban squash*; **turban-lily**, the Siberian *Lilium Pomponium*, bearing deep-red spotted flowers and edible bulbs; **turban-shell** = 5, 6 b; **turban squash**, a variety of squash or pumpkin in which the fleshy receptacle does not extend over the ovary, which therefore protrudes so as to resemble a turban (Webster, 1911); **turban-stone**, a Muslim tombstone, a pillar having at the head the carved representation of a turban: cf. 1 c; **turban swathe**, in hair-dressing: cf. 2 b; **turban-top**, ? the Bishop's Mitre mushroom, *Helvella Mitra*; **turban toque**: see quot.; **turban tumour** *Path.*, a rare benign tumour, probably of sweat glands, that spreads over the scalp or thorax in grape-like clusters.

1900 *Westm. Gaz.* 15 Feb. 3/2 All toques, and especially those of tulle, had more or less the *turban build. **1881** 'RITA' *Lady Coquette* iii, She's got a *turban-cap to match it. **1900** S. WEYMAN *Sophia* x, Sir Hervey's turban-cap and embroidered gown. **1877** J. T. BEER *Proph. Nineveh* i. 17 My leather wallet and best *turban cloth. **1894** MRS. DYAN *All in a Man's K.* i, The General's carriage, with its *turban-crested servants. **1822** J. PARKINSON *Outl. Oryctol.* 174 The vertebral column of the *turban Encrinite. **1907** *Nature* 4 Apr. 541/2 These *turban-eyes are restricted to the males of these may-flies, which seek the females during flight in the gloaming. **1841** BROWNING *Pippa Passes* Introd. 93 Fairies watch unroll Such *turban-flowers. **1898** *Daily News* 31 May 6/4 *Turban folds of tulle are worn in the evening..at the opera. In one instance the turban was in palest blue. **1884** *De Candolle's Orig. Cultiv. Pl.* 250 The principal varieties of *Cucurbita maxima* are the great yellow gourd,.. the Spanish, the *turban gourd. **1599** NASHE *Lenten Stuffe* 39 Those *Turbanto grout-heads, that hang all men by the throates on Iron hookes. **1862** *Eng. Wom. Dom. Mag.* IV. 237/1 The velvet *Turban Hats that are being worn by little boys. **1862** MISS YONGE *C'tess Kate* ix, Sylvia's face was exposed by a little turban hat. **1909** *Daily Graphic* 20 Oct. 13/3 A swathed turban hat of pale blue velvet. **1900** *Dundee Advertiser* 16 Apr. 4 Stalwart Zouaves..in their richly embroidered jackets, wide trousers, and quaint *turban-like headgear. **1884** MILLER *Plant-n.* 78 *Turban Lily, *Lilium Pomponium*. **1762** *Lond. Chron.* XI. 167/3 The present *Turband Roll, which is now wore round the Mecklenburgh caps. **1776** WITHERING *Brit. Plants* (1796) IV. 181 Fungi. Agaricus..convex hemispherical,..at length *turban-shaped and viscid. **1897** *Allbutt's Syst. Med.* IV. 738 The epiglottis..becoming enormously swollen and turban-shaped. **1753** CHAMBERS *Cycl. Supp.*, *Turban-Shell, *Cidaris*,..the name of a genus of the echinodermata. **1895** *Funk's Stand. Dict.*, *Turban-shell*, a gastropod of the genus *Turbo*, or its shell. **1902** L. H. BAILEY *Cycl. Amer. Hort.* IV. 1713/1 The *Turban Squashes..have a 'Squash within a Squash'. **1949** *Nat. Geogr. Mag.* Aug. 162/2 Several years ago a North Dakota horticulturist bred a small variety of turban squash. **1981** *Farmstead Mag.* Winter 38/3 The last of the six types to be mentioned is the turban squash. **1872** J. FERGUSSON *Rude Stone Mon.* x. 404 A headstone which, if it is not the *turban-stone that is usually found in Turkish tombs of modern date, is most singularly like it. **1909** *Punch* 10 Nov. 326/1 Women are in revolt against the '*turban' style of coiffure. **1912** *Daily News* 13 Aug. 5 The imported '*Turban swathe' has had a very short run. **1828** WEBSTER, **Turban-top*, a plant of the genus Helvella; a kind of fungus or mushroom. *Cyc.* **1897** *Westm.*

Gaz. 18 Feb. 3/1 The *turban toque,..in form pertaining to the fez, is just encircled with twisted tulles and finished by some one note of height. **1903** H. RADCLIFFE-CROCKER *Dis. of Skin* (ed. 3) II. viii. 961 Sarcoma Capitis, or Endothelioma Capitis (*Turban tumours). A peculiar form of tumour, in rare instances attacks, and is limited to the hairy scalp; in extreme cases, covering the whole scalp like a wig. **1974** J. D. MAYNARD in R. M. Kirk et al. *Surgery* ix. 196 Turban tumour... These rare tumours are sub-epithelial basal cell carcinomas, usually of sweat-gland origin which grow steadily and slowly, without ulceration or metastasis, on the scalp, face and thorax. **1899** *Westm. Gaz.* 2 Dec. 2/1 He..could doze in a tree like a crow (the *turban-wisp passed round his body and tied to a branch steadied him from falling).

Hence **turba'nesque** *a.*, having the appearance of a turban; **turba'nette**, a diminutive turban; **'turbanless** *a.*, without or destitute of a turban; **turban(n)y** *a.*, resembling or suggestive of a turban; **'turbanwise** *adv.*, in the manner of a turban.

1840 BROWNING *Sordello* I. 708 He Partook the poppy's red effrontery, Till Autumn spoiled their fleering quite with rain, And, turbanless, a coarse, brown, rattling crane Lay bare. **1882** O'DONOVAN *Merv Oasis* xiii. (1884) 142 Not turban-wise, but rather as if it were applied as a bandage for some cranial injury. **1890** JESSOPP *Trials Country Parson* 64 Do you mean..that you will persist in sporting that emasculated felt turbanette? **1891** STEVENSON *South Seas* (1908) III. iii. 221 The hair is worn turban-wise in a frizzled bush. **1893** *Nat. Observer* 25 Feb. 361/1 Caps, too—Greek, Byzantine, turbanesque—are popular vanities. **1912** A. HUXLEY *Let.* 13 May (1969) 42 The banner bearers..wear marvellous uniforms—usually consisting of a..sort of turbanny object or a cocked hat..white breeches and highly polished top-boots. **1924** E. BOWEN in *Spectator* 5 July 11/1 Yes, but haven't you got *any* goldish sort of turbany thing?

turban ('tɜːbən), *v.* [f. prec. sb.]

a. *trans.* To envelop as or with a turban; also, to wind a cloth round (a cap).

1822 MILMAN *Belshazzar* 108 The wreaths, like mist, That turban thy dusk brow. **1851** G. W. CURTIS *Nile Notes* xxv. 111 Long men and short, bald and grisly, capped and turbaned variously. **1860** TYNDALL *Glac.* I. xvi. 109 Clouds turbaned the head of the giant [mountain], and hid it from our view. **1876** A. ARNOLD in *Contemp. Rev.* June 48 They wear skull-caps of felt, turbaned with cotton.

b. To wind in the form of a turban.

a **1861** T. WINTHROP *John Brent* (1883) xvi. 151 A strip of old white blanket..was turbaned askew about his head. **1969** *Daily Tel.* 20 Jan. 11 A long white and cream silk scarf turbanned round the head and floating free.

turbaned ('tɜːbənd), *a.* Also **turbanned.** [f. TURBAN *sb.* + -ED².] **a.** Wearing a turban.

1591 JAS. I *Lepanto* 10 Circumsised Turband Turkes. **1604** SHAKS. *Oth.* v. ii. 353 A malignant, and a Turbond-Turke Beate a Venetian. *a* **1649** DRUMM. OF HAWTH. *Poems* 170 Though turban'd Princes for a Badge her weare. **1802** SOUTHEY *La Caba* 67 Moor! turbaned misbeliever! renegade! Circumcised traitor! **1817** SCOTT *Harold* III. vi, The turban'd race of Termagaunt. **1895** W. WRIGHT *Palmyra & Zenobia* xxv. 296 The old green-turbaned keeper of the Mosque. **1968** T. STOPPARD *Real Inspector Hound* (1970) 12 Mrs. Drudge is the char, middle-aged, turbanned. **1976** G. S. COX in M. Drabble *Genius of Thomas Hardy* III. 172 A turbanned Indian.

b. Of a Muslim tombstone: Surmounted by a carved turban.

1835 WILLIS *Pencillings* II. xlvi. 60 Its small dark cemetery of cypressed and turbaned head-stones. **1876** A. J. EVANS *Through Bosnia* iii. 93 A Turkish graveyard, with the usual turbaned tombstones—some of the turbans of majestic height.

c. Arranged to form a turban. (In quot., *transf.*) *poet. rare.*

1924 E. SITWELL *Sleeping Beauty* vi. 28 The..shore Where curled and turbanned waves sigh 'Nevermore'.

turbarian (tɜː'bɛərɪən), *a. Geol.* [f. med.L. *turbāria* peat-bog + -AN.] Of or pertaining to peat-bogs; denoting a subdivision of the Pleistocene or glacial period, during which extensive deposits of peat were formed in Northern Europe and Asia.

1895 J. GEIKIE in *Jrnl. Geol.* (Chicago) III. 251 'Lower Turbarian' Fifth glacial epoch. *Ibid.* 252 'Upper Turbarian' Sixth glacial epoch.

turbary ('tɜːbərɪ). Forms: 4-6 **turbarye**, (5 **turbere**), 5-7 **turbarie**, (6 **to(u)rberie**), 8 **turbery**, 6- **turbary**. [a. AF. *turberie* (Britton), a. OF. *turb-*, *torb-*, *tourberie* (12-13th c. in Godef.), med.L. *turbāria*, f. OF. *tourbe* (Swiss *turbe*), med.L. *turba*, ad. LG. *turf* or *turv*: see TURF.]

1. a. Land, or a piece of land, where turf or peat may be dug for fuel; a peat-bog or peat-moss.

[**1292** BRITTON II. xxix. §3 Mes si turberie, ou bruere, ou herbage, ou pesson,..soit tenu en commun par entre parceners ou veisins, et acun face exces [etc.]. **1314-15** *Rolls of Parlt.* I. 313/2 A fower tourbes en la tourberie denz lour Commune pasture.] **1363** *Cockersand Chartul.* (Chetham Soc.) I. 64 They may..delfe theyr turves in yᵉ mosse and turbarye in Gayrstang. **1455** *Rolls of Parlt.* V. 311/2, cc acres of Turbarie in the marshe of Holand. **1571** *Lanc. Wills* (Chetham Soc.) II. 244 My mosse and turbarie commonly called Toft Mosse. **1583** *Shuttleworths' Acc.* (ibid.) 15 For turbery and paustere. *Ibid.*, For his tourberie and pausture. *Ibid.*, For his torberie and pastre. **1607** NORDEN *Surv. Dial.* II. 66 Woodsales, sales of heath, flags, and Turbarie. **1765** *Acts 5 Geo. III* c. 26 *Preamble*, Moors, marshes, turbarys, waters,..commons, and other commodities. **1832** LYELL *Princ. Geol.* II. 215 In a turbary on the estate of the Earl of Moira, in Ireland, a human body was dug up,..covered with eleven feet of moss. **1865** LUBBOCK *Preh. Times* i. (1869) 19 This sword was discovered in a turbary..in a large boat, which had evidently been sunk.

†**b.** *transf.* The substance obtained from or forming a turbary; peat. *Obs.*

c **1440** *Jacob's Well* 38 In tythyng of wyn,..of flex, of hemp, of turbarye & fewall, of frute of treen. **1798** *Trans. Soc. Arts* XVI. 241 The soil consists chiefly of about twelve inches of turbary, and under that, gravel or stone.

2. *Law.* In full ***common of turbary***: The right to cut turf or peat for fuel on a common or on another person's land.

1567 *Lanc. Wills* (Chetham Soc.) II. 84 Concerning turbarye and sute of Court. **1622** CALLIS *Stat. Sewers* (1647) 106 Common of Pischary, Turbary, or of Pasture in great Fens, Marishes and Wastes, may be charged..for their Commons. **1641** *Termes de la Ley* 209 Turbary is an interest of digging turfes upon a common. **1798** J. MIDDLETON *View Agric. Middlesex* 103 The value of the commons..including ..pasturage, locality of situation, and the barbarous custom of turbary. **1807** VANCOUVER *Agric. Devon* (1813) 294 The parishioners have a right of turbary on these moors, by which they have been much injured. **1884** *Times* (weekly ed.) 19 Sept. 6/4 Each infinitesimal right of grazing or turbary had to be surveyed, examined into.

3. a. *attrib.* and *Comb.*

1850 MANTELL in *Q. Jrnl. Geol. Soc.* VI. 327 The so-called 'turbary deposit', whence bones of the Moa..have been obtained. **1896** *N. Brit. Daily Mail* 8 June 4 The clauses relating to purchase, turbary rights, and other matters. **1896** *Speaker* 18 July 58/2 The turbary and sea-wrack clause will have the most important effects.

b. [tr. G. *torf-*.] Applied to kinds of domesticated sheep and pig of prehistoric times that were first found in turbaries in Swiss lake-dwellings.

1908 R. PUMPELLY *Explorations Turkestan* I. I. v. 67 The turbary sheep (Torfschaf) and..the turbary pig (Torfschwein)..appear towards the end of the neolithic period. **1912** R. LYDEKKER *Sheep & its Cousins* vii. 150 An apparently pure-blooded breed of small sheep inhabiting Crete..is identified by Dr. Keller with the turbary sheep. **1920** J. RITCHIE *Animal Life Scotl.* 40 Even in Neolithic times the Turbary or Peat Sheep..was widely distributed in Scotland. **1936** *Antiquity* X. 203 We find a small sheep with erect horns,..the so-called 'goat-horned' or turbary sheep. **1963** F. E. ZEUNER *Hist. Domesticated Animals* x. 257 In the earlier group of Neolithic lake-dwellings the small turbary pig (*Sus palustris* Rütimeyer) occurs beside the ordinary European wild pig. There is no doubt that this turbary pig was introduced into Switzerland by Neolithic man from the East. *Ibid.* 258 According to Kuhn, the turbary pig has survived to the present day in some of the Alpine valleys. **1972** *Science* 12 May 656/2 With regard to sheep and pig, he believes that the well-known turbary type..is a natural product of malnutrition and poor care.

turbat, -batt, obs. ff. TURBAN, TURBOT.

†**turbation** (tɜː'beɪʃən). *Obs.* [a. OF. *turbacioun* (14th c. in Godef.), ad. L. *turbātio, -ōnem*, from *turbāre* to disturb.] Confusion, disorder, disturbance; perturbation, agitation of mind.

c **1400** *Sc. Trojan War* II. 117 In the tyme of turbacions. *c* **1450** tr. *De Imitatione* III. xxv. 96 A liȝt turbacion shuld not so sone springe in me. **1480** CAXTON *Chron. Eng.* v. (1520) 61 b/2 There was then turbacyon in the chyrche for stryfe and heretykes. *c* **1530** *Judic. Urines* II. ii. 12 b, Turbacyon and distemperaunse of the humours in the body. **1642** T. HODGES *Glimpse Gods Glory* 38 It intimates a turbation of minde.

‖**turbeh** ('turbe(θ)). Also **turbé.** [Turkish, a. Arab. *turbah* tomb, sepulchre.] A small mosque-like building erected over the tomb of a Muslim, esp. a person of sanctity or rank.

1687 A. LOVELL tr. *Thevenot's Trav.* I. 22 At the back of this Mosque there is a Turbe, where are the bodies of Sultan Achmet and his children. **1853** LAYARD *Nineveh & Babylon* ii. 24 In the midst..rose here and there a conical *turbeh* of beautiful shape, covered with exquisite tracery. **1906** W. M. RAMSAY in *Expositor* Nov. 463 When it [the building] is little more than a mausoleum, it is called a turbe.

turbel, obs. form of TROUBLE.

turbellarian (tɜːbɛ'lɛərɪən), *a.* and *sb. Zool.* [f. mod.L. *Turbellāria*, neuter pl. (f. L. *turbella* a little crowd, a bustle, stir, dim. of *turba* crowd) + -AN.] **a.** *adj.* Of or belonging to the *Turbellaria*, a class of worms inhabiting fresh or salt water or damp earth, having the body covered with vibratile cilia producing minute whirls in the water. **b.** *sb.* A worm of this class; a whirl-worm.

1879 E. P. WRIGHT *Anim. Life* 580 Rhynchocœla. These are the flat worms. To one section thereof would belong the Turbellarian and Nemertean worms. **1883** *Science* I. 433/1 The form and armature of the tail resemble those of many turbellarians.

So **turbellariform** (-'ɛərɪfɔːm) *a.*, having the form of a turbellarian.

1877 HUXLEY *Anat. Inv. Anim.* xii. 675 The Tunicate *Pharyngopneusta*, with their caudate larvæ, may be supposed to stand in the same relation to the Turbellariform *Pharyngopneusta*, as the *Trematoda*, with their cercariform larvæ, to the *Turbellaria*.

‖**turben.** *Obs. rare.* [L. *turben*, by-form of *turbo, turbin-em*: see TURBO.] The spire or whorl of a twisted shell.

1669 *Phil. Trans.* IV. 1012 This Turben or Conical figure [of a snail shell] is well neare a quarter of an inch.

turben, turbentyne, obs. ff. TURBAN, TURPENTINE.

turbescency (tɜː'bɛsənsɪ). *rare.* [f. assumed L. **turbescĕre* to grow turbid: see -ENCY. Cf. *putrescency*.] The condition of becoming turbid.

1834 *Fraser's Mag.* X. 569 The sudden turbescency of water is generally attributed to rains.

turbet, obs. form of TURBIT, TURBOT.

turbeth: see TURPETH.

turbid ('tɜːbɪd), *a.* [ad. L. *turbid-us* full of confusion or disorder; troubled, muddy; perplexed, violent, etc.; f. *turba* crowd, disturbance.]

1. Of liquid: Thick or opaque with suspended matter; not clear; cloudy, muddy.

1626 BACON *Sylva* §306 Though the Lees doe make the Liquour turbide, yet they refine the Spirits. *a* **1701** MAUNDRELL *Journ. Jerus.* (1732) 4 It's Waters are turbid and very unwholesome. **1800** tr. *Lagrange's Chem.* II. 375 At the end of some time this water becomes turbid, putrifies, and emits an ammoniacal odour. **1896** *Q. Rev.* Apr. 498 Gases.. acted upon them [the X rays] as turbid media, stopping them by vague diffusion, as milky water stops light.

b. Of air, smoke, clouds, etc.: Thick, dense; dark.

1705 J. PHILIPS *Blenheim* 145 Horrible Flames, and turbid streaming Clouds Of Smoak sulphureous. **1807** J. BARLOW *Columb.* III. 21 The nations, temper'd to the turbid air, Breathe deadly strife. **1811** PINKERTON *Petralogy* II. 330 The sun rose above the horizon, turbid at first and dimmed by mists. **1829** *Chapters Phys. Sc.* 267 Whether the sky be clear and serene, or cloudy and turbid, whether it snows or rains. *a* **1831** A. KNOX *Rem.* I. 7 Turbid wreaths, Sullying joy's gilded ceilings.

c. *fig.* or in figurative language.

1752 WARBURTON *Serm. 1 John iv. 20* Wks. 1788 V. 45 Benevolence, arising from this source, at first runs thick and turbid. **1800** WELLESLEY in Owen *Desp.* (1877) 732 It is not the nature of these inestimable blessings to spring from a turbid source. **1810** CRABBE *Borough* xxiii. 144 Each feature in the face, Pinched through neglect or turbid by disgrace. **1876** MERIVALE *Rom. Triumvirates* vi. 121 The readers and thinkers of the day..withdrew more and more from the turbid sphere of political action.

2. *fig.* Characterized by or producing confusion or obscurity of thought, feeling, etc.; mentally confused, perplexed, muddled; disturbed, troubled.

c **1645** HOWELL *Lett.* (1650) II. xxx. 44, I had divers fits of melancholy, and such turbid intervalls that use to attend close prisoners, who for the most part have no other companions, but confus'd troops of wandring cogitations. **1663** COWLEY *Ess. in Verse & Prose, Of Greatness*, Senecio was a man of a turbid and confused wit. **1684** HOWE *Redeemer's Tears* Wks. 1862 II. 316 No grief, sorrow or sighing, which are all fled away; as there can be no other turbid passion of anykind. *a* **1688** CUDWORTH *Immut. Mor.* (1731) 90 The Perceptions of which..are confused, indistinct, turbid and encumbered Cogitations. **1744** HARRIS *Three Treat.* III. II. (1765) 245 This turbid, this fickle, fleeting Period. **1820** BYRON *Mar. Fal.* II. i. 487 Your sleep for many nights has been so turbid. **1839** STONEHOUSE *Axholme* 207 Wesley's mind seems at this time to have been in a turbid and restless state. **1866** GEO. ELIOT *F. Holt* xxx, A grimy man in a flannel shirt, hatless and with turbid red hair. **1896** *Edin. Rev.* Apr. 332 The turbid utterances and twisted language of Carlyle.

3. *Comb.*, as ***turbid-looking***.

1899 *Allbutt's Syst. Med.* VI. 911 The latter membrane is turbid-looking and thickened.

turbidimeter (tɜːbɪ'dɪmɪtə(r)). *Chem.* and *Biol.* [f. TURBID *a.* + -I- + -METER.] An instrument for determining the turbidity of a liquid from the decrease in the intensity of a beam of light passing through it.

1905 *Water Supply & Irrigation Papers* (U.S. Geol. Survey) No. 151. 26 The needs of the Survey were found to be met in a satisfactory manner by the use of a turbidimeter devised by Mr. Daniel D. Jackson. **1920** *Jrnl. Biol. Chem.* XLII. 191 Turbidimeters and nephelometers are instruments designed for practically the same purpose. **1973** *Sci. Amer.* June 112/1 Extinction turbidimeters are doubtless the simplest instruments that have been devised for measuring the concentration of solids in suspension. They are based on the principle that turbidity is inversely proportional to the minimum length that a column of fluid must have in order to extinguish at one end of the column a source of light at the other end.

Hence (all also turbido-) **turbidi'metric** *a.*, obtained with or employing a turbidimeter; **turbidi'metrically** *adv.*; **turbi'dimetry**, the use of a turbidimeter, esp. for the quantitative analysis of turbid solutions.

1911 *Jrnl. Industr. & Engin. Chem.* III. 554/1 The discrepancies between the turbidimetric and gravimetric results..were..thought to be caused by the presence of nitrates in the solutions examined. **1918** *Jrnl. Biol. Chem.* XXXVI. 33 This reagent gives quite good results used either turbidometrically or nephelometrically. **1920** *Ibid.* XLII. 196 With several of the substances which have already been standardized for turbidimetry we can multiply the accuracy. **1943** *Jrnl. Bacteriol.* XLVI. 377 Applications of turbidimetry to the study of *in vitro* penicillin effects. **1971** Turbidimetric [see *nephelometric* adj. s.v. NEPHELO-]. **1975** D. H. BURRIN in Williams & Wilson *Biologist's Guide to Princ. & Techniques Pract. Biochem.* v. 145 Very dilute suspensions may be assayed by turbidometry. **1981** *Jrnl. Protozool.* XXVIII. 371/2 Growth was determined turbidimetrically.

turbidite ('tɜːbɪdaɪt). *Geol.* [f. TURBID(ITY + -ITE[1].] A sediment or rock deposited, or presumed to have been deposited, by a turbidity current. Hence **turbi'ditic** *a.*

1957 P. H. KUENEN in *Jrnl. Geol.* LXV. 231/1 The term 'turbidite' for all deposits of turbidity currents is more appropriate, and the writer accepts this verbal suggestion of C. P. M. Frijlinck. **1973** *Nature* 9 Feb. 389/2 The lowest (Unit I)..has at the base a phyllitic formation..followed by turbiditic sandstones. **1977** A. HALLAM *Planet Earth* 204/1 The thick clastics and turbidites of the upper Devonian of the Yukon seem to be derived from an oceanic zone of uplift.

turbidity (tɜː'bɪdɪtɪ). [ad. med.L. *turbiditās* (Albertus Magnus, *c* 1255), f. L. *turbidus* TURBID: see -ITY.]

1. = TURBIDNESS.

1782 KIRWAN in *Phil. Trans.* LXXX. 215 Dr. Priestley, in a similar experiment, did not observe this turbidity. **1845** G. E. DAY tr. *Simon's Anim. Chem.* I. 323 The serum.. exhibited a remarkable milk-white turbidity. **1862** TYNDALL *Mountaineer.* iii. 25 No mist or turbidity interferes with the sharpness of the outlines. **1868** VISCT. STRANGFORD *Select.* (1869) II. 306 A dense circumfluous atmosphere of intellectual turbidity, of ignorance, of gross superstition. **1888** RUTLEY *Rock-Forming Min.* 127 Any turbidity or milkiness which a crystal may exhibit.

2. Special Comb.: **turbidity current**, an underwater current flowing swiftly downslope owing to the weight of sediment it carries.

1939 D. W. JOHNSON *Origin of Submarine Canyons* iii. 27 By analogy those [currents] due to turbidity will here be called *turbidity currents.* **1950** *Jrnl. Geol.* LVIII. 91/1 The most important types of graded bedding appear to have been produced by the action of turbidity currents of high density on the sea floor. **1977** A. HALLAM *Planet Earth* 54/2 An unusual but geologically very important type of suspension deposit is that produced by a turbidity current.

turbidly ('tɜːbɪdlɪ), *adv. rare.* [f. TURBID + -LY[2].] In a turbid or troubled manner.

1728 YOUNG *Vind. Providence* 21 A Person of small Merit is anxiously jealous of Imputations on his Honour, because he knows his Title is weak; one of great Merit turbidly resents them, because he knows his Title is strong. *a* **1861** MRS. BROWNING *Musical Instr.* ii, The limpid water turbidly ran. **1874** SYMONDS *Italy & Gr.* (1898) I. xiv. 305 The gondolas moved turbidly upon the face of the waters.

turbidness ('tɜːbɪdnɪs). [f. as prec. + -NESS.] The quality or condition of being turbid; thickness of a fluid; cloudiness; also *fig.*

1676 *Phil. Trans.* XI. 614 It will mixe..without turbidness and without coagulation. **1772** JACKSON *ibid.* LXIII. 5 Instead of clarifying beer, [it] increased both its tenacity and turbidness. **1800** W. SAUNDERS *Min. Waters* iv. 278 Lime water produces a turbidness when added to the fresh water. **1807** *Med. Jrnl.* XVII. 194 On examining the anterior chamber [of the eye], all the turbidness had disappeared. **1906** E. A. ABBOTT *Silanus* xxxv. 352 Trouble of soul does not mean confusion or turbidness of soul.

turbidometric, etc., varr. TURBIDIMETRIC *a.*, etc.

† **'turbidous**, *a. Obs. rare.* [f. L. *turbid-us* TURBID + -OUS.] = TURBID.

1628 HOBBES *Thucyd.* (1822) 130 The stream of the river is swift, broad and turbidous.

turbill, turbillion, -billoun, obs. forms of TROUBLE, TOURBILLION.

turbinaceous (tɜːbɪ'neɪʃəs), *a.*[1] *rare.* [f. L. *turbo, turbin-em*: see TURBO and -ACEOUS.] Resembling the gastropod genus *Turbo*; top-shaped.

1842 *Penny Cycl.* XXII. 53/1 *Siphonostomata.. Turbinella*... Turbinaceous and spiny species.

† **turbi'naceous**, *a.*[2] *Obs.* [Erroneous formation for **turbaceous* f. med.L. *turba* turf, peat, as if f. L. *turbo, turbin-* (cf. prec.).] Pertaining to peat; peaty; flavoured with peat-smoke.

1824 SCOTT *St. Ronan's* xiii, The real turbinacious flavour [of the whisky] no sooner reached the nose of the Captain than the beverage was turned down his throat.

‖ **turbinage** (tyrbinaʒ). *Sugar manuf.* [F. (Littré), f. *turbine*, TURBINE: see -AGE.] Separation of the sugar crystals from the molasses by centrifugal filters or turbines. Cf. TURBINE 1 c.

1911 in WEBSTER.

turbinal ('tɜːbɪnəl), *a.* and *sb.* [f. L. *turbo, turbin-em* (see TURBO) + -AL[1].]

A. *adj.* Turbinated, top-shaped; in *Anat.* = TURBINATE *a.*: cf. B.

1584 R. SCOT *Discov. Witchcr.* XIII. xix. (1886) 258 Experiments..in diverse sorts of glasses;..the columnarie, the pyramidate or piked, the turbinall. **1883** *Science* I. 233/1 The arrangement of the turbinal bones in the fissiped carnivores. **1903** *Brit. Med. Jrnl.* 18 Apr. 910 No swelling as yet of turbinal bodies or septal mucous membrane.

B. *sb. Anat.* A turbinal or turbinate bone; the ethmo-, the maxillo-, or the spheno-turbinal.

1848 OWEN *Archetype & Homol. Vertebr. Skel.* i. 13 'Turbinal'..is a substitute for the phrase 'os turbinatum inferius' and its synonym 'os spongiosum inferius'. *Ibid.* ii. 114 The Turbinal or nose-capsule. **1854** —— *Skel. & Teeth* in *Orr's Circ. Sc.* I. *Org. Nat.* 179 An ossified part of the capsule of the organ of smell, 'turbinal'. *Ibid.* 251 The superior turbinals extend..below into the presphenoidal sinus. **1871** HUXLEY *Anat. Vertebr. Anim.* v. 237 Forming the floor of the front part of the nasal chamber, on each side, is a large concavo-convex bone, which..protects the nasal gland, and is commonly termed a turbinal, though, if it be a membrane bone, it does not truly correspond with the turbinals of the higher Vertebrata.

turbinate ('tɜːbɪnət), *a.* and *sb.* [ad. L. *turbināt-us*, f. *turbo, turbin-*: see TURBO and -ATE[2].]

A. *adj. Nat. Hist.* Resembling a spinning-top in shape; of a mollusc, having a spiral shell; in *Bot. spec.* inversely conical; having a narrow tapering base and broad rounded apex; in *Anat.* applied to the scroll-like spongy bones of the nasal fossæ in the higher vertebrates.

1661 LOVELL *Hist. Anim. & Min.* Introd., Fishes, which are..testaceous, and..turbinate, which are either involute, as the Nautilus,..murex,..or orbicular, as the Welke. *a* **1706** EVELYN *Sylva* (1776) II. i. §1 [The larch tribe] Easily raised of the kernels and nuts, which may be gotten out of their polysperm and turbinate cones. **1750** G. HUGHES *Barbadoes* 283 The largest, as well as the most beautiful of the turbinate kind. **1760** J. LEE *Introd. Bot.* III. xxii. (1765) 229 The *Pericarpium* is.. turbinate, Top-shaped, when it tapers towards the Base. **1828** STARK *Elem. Nat. Hist.* II. 24 *C[onus] Hebræus*, Lin. Shell turbinate, coronate, white..the spire convex, obtuse. **1840** G. V. ELLIS *Anat.* 244 Three convoluted portions of bone named spongy or turbinate bones, which project into the cavity. **1870** HOOKER *Stud. Flora* 366 *Leucojum æstivum*.. Fruit turbinate.

b. In combination, modifying another adj., as ***turbinate-lentiform, -truncate.***

1887 W. PHILLIPS *Brit. Discomycetes* 355 *Tympanis Fraxini*,..cups subsessile, turbinate-truncate, shining, black.

B. *sb.* **a.** A turbinate shell. **b.** A turbinate bone.

1802–3 tr. *Pallas' Trav.* (1812) I. 70 A multitude of turbinates of the large kind, and especially whole strata, full of small striped turbinates. **1872** MIVART *Elem. Anat.* 84 That part of it immediately below the cribriform plate is called the upper spongy bone, or superior turbinate, or turbinal. **1903** *Detroit Med. Jrnl.* 733 (Cent. D. Suppl.) Cases of asthma treated by removal of the middle turbinate.

† **'turbinate**, *v. Obs. rare.* [f. L. *turbo, turbin-* (see TURBO) + -ATE[3].] **a.** *trans.* To fashion like a top; to make top-shaped. **b.** *intr.* To turn or whirl like a top or a whirlwind.

1721 BAILEY, *Turbinate*, to fashion like a Top, to sharpen at one End. **1791** BURKE *French Affairs* Wks. VII. 41 The Russian Government is..liable to be subverted by military seditions,..and sometimes by headlong rebellions of the people, such as the turbinating movement of Pugatchef.

turbinated ('tɜːbɪneɪtɪd), *a.* [f. as TURBINATE *a.* + -ED[1].]

1. Top-shaped, top-like; *spec.* in *Nat. Hist.* whorled, = TURBINATE *a.*

1615 CROOKE *Body of Man* 215 It is equall, smooth, and turbinated, that is, broad at the basis or bottom, and growing smaller. **1668** WILKINS *Real Char.* 122 Turbinated; consisting of a cone-like cavity, rouled up in a spiral. *a* **1706** EVELYN *Sylva* II. i. (1776) 274 The Wild or Bastard-Pine and Teda..bearing a turbinated cone. **1759** JOHNSON *Idler* No. 56 ¶6 An irregular contortion of a turbinated shell. **1800** *Phil. Trans.* XC. 434 The turbinated bones are in the same relative situation to the other parts of the skull as in quadrupeds. **1835** LINDLEY *Introd. Bot.* (1848) I. 387 [The placenta] its form is now turbinated. **1840** E. WILSON *Anat. Vade M.* (1842) 38 The inferior Turbinated or spongy Bone is a thin layer of loose and spongy bone, slightly curled upon itself, and projected inwards from the inner wall of the Nares. **1884** M. MACKENZIE *Dis. Throat & Nose* II. 233 There are always three turbinated bones, and frequently a fourth.

† **2.** Of motion: Like that of a top; gyrating, rotary, whirling. *Obs.*

1665 HOOKE *Microgr.* lx. 246 [Gravitation] does not depend upon the diurnal or turbinated motion of the Earth. **1692** BENTLEY *Boyle Lect.* iv. 125 Let Mechanism here.. produce a spiral and turbinated motion of the whole moved Body without an external director.

turbination (tɜːbɪ'neɪʃən). [ad. L. *turbinātiōn-em* a pointing in the form of a cone, f. *turbināt-us* TURBINATE *a.*: see -ATION.]

1. †The action of making top-shaped (*obs.*); top-like or turbinate form; formation of a whorl.

1623 COCKERAM, *Turbination*, the fashioning of a thing like a top or gigge. **1656** in BLOUNT *Glossogr.* **1834** McMURTRIE *Cuvier's Anim. Kingd.* 257 Their shells are very open,..most of them without the slightest turbination.

† **2.** The action of spinning or whirling round like a top. *Obs.*

1665 HOOKE *Microgr.* lx. 246 Then certainly the turbination cannot be the cause of the attraction of the Earth. *a* **1680** ALLESTREE *Serm., Matt. xi. 28* (1684) II. 124 They have a most perfect acquiescency in that their turbination.

turbinato- (tɜːbɪ'neɪtəʊ), combining form from L. *turbinātus* TURBINATE *a.*; qualifying adjs. used in natural history, as ***turbinato-concave, -cylindrical, -globose, -stipitate.***

1846 DANA *Zooph.* (1848) 384 Turbinato-cylindrical, four and a half lines broad at top. **1846** BERKELEY in *Proc. Berw. Nat. Club* II. No. 14. 190 Cup..turbinato-stipitate. **1887** W. PHILLIPS *Brit. Discomycetes* 195 *Mollisia versicolor*..at first globose, then turbinato-concave. *Ibid.* 236 *Lachnella caulicola*... Cups gregarious, stipitate, turbinato-globose, then hemispherical.

turbine ('tɜːbaɪn, -ɪn). [a. F. *turbine*, ad. L. *turbo, turbin-em*: see TURBO.]

1. a. Originally applied to a wheel revolving on a vertical axis, and driven by a column of water falling into its interior, and escaping by pipes, channels, or apertures, so arranged as to press by reaction on the periphery of the wheel, and cause it to revolve in the direction opposite to that of the escaping water. Now applied to any kind of machine in which this principle (sometimes combined with that of direct impact) is used or developed; the modifications and developments are very numerous, many of these being of highly complicated structure, in which neither the horizontality of the wheel nor the motive power is retained.

[**1824** BURDIN in *Bull. Soc. Encouragem.* July 256 Machines rotatoires à grande vitesse nommées turbines hydrauliques.] **1838** *Railway Mag.* IV. 51 Turbine.—An instrument under this name has lately been invented by M. Fourneyron, worked by water-pressure, which is said to have made a great sensation in Germany. *Ibid.*, It is said that a turbine, only thirteen inches diameter,..under a vertical pressure of water of 118 yards, revolved 2,300 times in a minute, and..realized a power, which estimated in steam, would be equal to that of sixty horses. **1842** *Civil Eng. & Arch. Jrnl.* V. 266/1 The mechanical construction of the Turbine is..given, and its action..described. **1861** O. W. HOLMES *Voice of Loyal North* 33 'Tis hard..To see the rusting turbines stand Before the emptied flumes. **1861** RANKINE *Steam Engine* 189. **1881** W. C. UNWIN in *Encycl. Brit.* XII. 524/2 The Scotch turbine..differs in no essential respect from the older form of reaction wheel. **1884** *Athenæum* 16 Aug. 212/2 A well-constructed water-wheel or turbine can..be worked with far greater economy than steam. **1897** *Spectator* 4 Sept., There are at Niagara single turbines which produce 5000 horse-power.

b. More fully ***steam-turbine***: A steam motor in which rotatory motion is produced by steam impinging directly upon a series of vanes upon the circumference of a revolving cylinder or disk (or, in some types, acting and reacting alternately on moving and stationary elements).

1900 *Engineer* 2 Feb. 127/3 The main applications of the De Laval steam turbine are:—(1) Turbine motors, driving machinery direct by means of belts or ropes; (2) Turbine dynamos, the dynamos being placed on the second motion shafts or a prolongation of the same; (3) turbine pumps.. and (4) turbine exhaust and pressure fans or ventilators. **1900** *N. Brit. Daily Mail* 30 Jan. 4 That is the whole secret of the turbine. In the modern application of it the steam blows upon the shaft and the shaft turns, and by an ingenious application of blades the steam which enters the first turbine when it leaves the boiler at a pressure of 225 lbs. to the square inch is utilised till the value of the last pound is all used up. **1905** *Westm. Gaz.* 16 Mar. 10/1 The dynamo is coupled directly to a Parsons turbine, which has introduced great changes and great economies in the driving of huge electrical plants.

c. A centrifugal separator used in sugar manufacture.

1873 BESANT & RICE *Little Girl* II. x. 116 The sweet, rich smell of the sugar; the huge vats of seething, foaming juice, and the whirling turbines.

d. = *gas-turbine* s.v. GAS *sb.*[1] 7.

1904 *Proc. Inst. Mech. Engineers* Oct. 1078 Some or all of the available heat energy of the gas can be converted into kinetic energy before causing it to act on the turbine. **1940** A. W. JUDGE *Aircraft Engines* I. vii. 231 An alternative method of driving the supercharger is to couple it directly to an exhaust turbine of the de Laval type. **1950** E. T. VINCENT *Theory & Design Gas Turbines & Jet Engines* vi. 161 The power-plant turbine can be divided into the following units: (1) compressor, (2) combustion chamber, (3) turbine, and (4) regenerator. **1971** B. SCHARF *Engin. & its Lang.* xv. 215 After expansion in the turbine, the combustion gases escape at high velocity through the jet pipe, thus providing the forward thrust for the aeroplane.

2. *attrib.* and *Comb.*, as ***turbine blade, dynamo, dynamometer, engine, machinery, mill, motor, shaft, top, (water) wheel; turbine-driven, -engined, -like, -propelled***, adjs.; driven by a steam-turbine, as ***turbine boat, destroyer, steamer, yacht***, etc.; **turbine-alternator, -generator**: see TURBO-; **turbine-pump**, a turbine water wheel used to raise water by being driven by external power in the direction opposite to that in which it turns when used as a motor.

1911 *Encycl. Brit.* XXV. 843/2 The general arrangement of the steam nozzle and *turbine blades is illustrated. **1977** *R.A.F. News* 11–24 May 18/2 A pair of turbine blades from an Orpheus jet engine. **1904** *Longm. Mag.* Jan. 215 The *Revolution*..the first American-built *turbine boat. **1900** *Engineer* 8 June 595/3 The Elswick *turbine destroyer, which made 36·88 knots on trial. *Ibid.* 22 June 645/2 This will be the largest *turbine-driven generating set ever built. **1901** *Westm. Gaz.* 19 June 4/3 The adaptability of the turbine-driven steamship for passenger traffic was tested on the Clyde yesterday. **1900** *Turbine dynamo [see 1 b]. **1900** *Engineer* 16 Feb. 170/1 The *turbine engines are similar to those of the Turbinia. **1901** *Scotsman* 20 Sept. 4/4 The new turbine engines..were built to secure a speed of 35 knots. **1902** *Daily Chron.* 12 Nov. 7/2 At the present time there is only one *turbine-engined war-vessel in the world. This is H.M.S. Velox. **1904** *Longm. Mag.* Jan. 214 Two new cross-channel steamers..are turbine-engined. **1906** J. W. THURSO *Mod. Turbine Pract.* etc. 147 Of great importance in connection with *turbine governors is the time of closing. **1907** *Westm. Gaz.* 11 Nov. 6/3 The many advantages of this special type of engine [six-cylinder motor] are its smooth, *turbine-like motion. **1900** *Engineer* 2 Nov. 444/3 *Turbine machinery occupying less space than the present cramped-up reciprocating engines. **1904** *Daily Chron.* 3 June 6/6 It has yet to be proved that turbine machinery is suitable for the propulsion of cargo vessels where speed is not a great requisite. **1900** *Engineer* 2 Feb. 127/3 A steam consumption as low as 13·9 lb. of steam per brake horse-power on a 300 horse-power steam *turbine motor. **1901** *Ibid.* 11 Jan. 45/1 The first absolute decision to adopt the *turbine principle in a large passenger vessel. **1906** *Westm. Gaz.* 3 May 6/3 Only their fast vessels would be *turbine-propelled. **1901** *Engineer* 11 Jan. 45/1 *Turbine propulsion for a new Clyde passenger steamer. **1900** *Turbine pump [see 1 b]. **1887** D. A. LOW *Machine Draw.* (1892) 120 Bearing for a *turbine shaft. **1900** *Engineer* 2 Feb. 127/3 The pinion on the turbine shaft gears into two wheels on opposite sides. **1904** *Longm. Mag.* Jan. 214 The first Transatlantic *turbine steamer. **1906** STEVENS & HOBART *Steam Turbine Engin.* 12 At high speeds the *turbine vessels excel in economy. **1860** EMERSON *Cond. Life, Worship* Wks. (Bohn) II. 396 There is faith in chemistry, in meat and wine, in..*turbine-wheels, ..but not in divine causes.

Hence **'turbined** *a.*, having or propelled by a turbine or turbines (Webster, 1911); **'turbiner**, a turbine-driven vessel.

1905 *St. John (N. Brunswick) Daily Sun* 3 Apr. 1/1 Turbiner Victorian will dock this morning.

turbinectomy (tɜːbɪ'nɛktəmɪ). *Surg.* [f. TURBIN(AL + Gr. ἐκτομή excision.] Excision of a turbinal bone or bones.

1900–13 in DORLAND *Med. Dict.* **1901** *Lancet* 16 Nov. 1321/2 For short operations, such as..turbinectomy,..gas is sometimes sufficient.

turbinelloid (tɜːbɪ'nɛlɔɪd), *a. Zool.* [f. mod.L. *Turbinella* (f. *turbin-em*: see TURBO) + -OID.] Resembling or having the characters of the *Turbinellidæ*, a family of large marine gastropods having a pyriform shell with transverse columellar folds.

In recent Dicts.

†**turbineous** (tɜː'bɪniːəs), *a. Obs. rare.* [f. L. *turbine-us* (f. *turbo*: see TURBO) + -OUS.] Of the nature of a whirlwind.

1656 BLOUNT *Glossogr.*, *Turbineous* (*turbineus*), of or belonging to a storm and blustering winde, whirling round. **1675** E. WILSON *Spadacrene Dunelm.* 26 The mighty Tempests and turbinious Winds.

turbiner: see after TURBINE.

‖**turbines** ('tɜːbɪniːz), pl. of TURBO, a genus of gastropod molluscs, q.v.

Perh. sometimes used as pl. of **turbine*, in sense of TURBO.

turbiniform (tɜː'bɪnɪfɔːm), *a. Nat. Hist.* [ad. mod.L. *turbiniform-is*, f. L. *turbin-em*: see TURBO and -FORM.] Top-shaped, turbinate; also, having the form of the genus *Turbo* of gastropods; turbinoid, spiral.

1826 KIRBY & SP. *Entomol.* IV. xlvi. 265 Turbiniform (*Turbiniformis*). Whose vertical section is turbinate, and horizontal circular. Ex. *Antennæ* of *Aleochara socialis*. **1856** WOODWARD *Mollusca* III. 463 Vitrinella... Shell minute, hyaline, turbiniform, umbilicated.

turbinite ('tɜːbɪnaɪt). [ad. mod.L. *turbinīt-ēs*, or a. F. *turbinite*, f. L. *turbin-em*: see TURBO and -ITE[1].] A fossil turbinate shell. Also **turbite**.

1828 WEBSTER, *Turbinite, Turbite.* **1852** TH. ROSS *Humboldt's Trav.* I. vi. 204 Some beds are almost unmixed with petrifactions, but..the cardites, the turbinites, the ostracites, and shells of small dimension, are found.

turbinoid ('tɜːbɪnɔɪd), *a. Zool.* [f. L. *turbin-em* (see TURBO) + -OID.] Resembling the genus *Turbo* or family *Turbinidæ* of gastropod molluscs (esp. those of tropical and subtropical seas) characterized by a thick top-shaped shell with a rounded opening closed by a calcareous operculum.

1861 P. P. CARPENTER in *Rep. Smithsonian Instit.* 1860, 213 Fossils of Turbinoid form. **1879** W. B. CARPENTER in *Encycl. Brit.* IX. 379/2 The type of the second group is the almost universally diffused *Rotalia*, in which the chambers are disposed in a turbinoid spire.

turbinotomy (tɜːbɪ'nɒtəmɪ). *Surg.* [f. TURBIN(AL + Gr. τομή cutting.] Incision of the turbinal bone. So **turbinotome** (tɜː'bɪnətəʊm), an instrument for performing this operation (Dorland *Med. Dict.* 1900–13).

1895 T. C. JONES in *Brit. Med. Jrnl.* II. 1289 Turbinotomy in cases of deafness and tinnitus aurium.

turbit ('tɜːbɪt). Also 8 -et. [app. f. L. *turbo* a top, from its figure; cf. TURBOT.] A small fancy variety of the domestic pigeon, distinguished by its stout rounded build, a short beak, the ruffle or frill on its neck and breast, and a small crest. Also *attrib.*

1688 R. HOLME *Armoury* II. 244/2 The Turbit Pigeon, or Cortbeck. **1725** *Bradley's Fam. Dict.* s.v. *Pigeon*, Many Sorts of Pigeons, such as Carriers,..Jacobins, Turbits, Helmets, [etc.]. **1859** DARWIN *Orig. Spec.* i. (1878) 16 The turbit has a short and conical beak, with a line of reversed feathers down the breast. **1896** *Westm. Gaz.* 17 Feb. 2/1 He has a strain of the turbit pigeon in him, while all the rest are just the common wild Blue Rock sort.

Hence **turbiteen** (tɜːbɪ'tiːn), an oriental frilled variety of domestic pigeon resembling the turbit, and said to be derived from it. Also *attrib.*

1876 H. P. CARIDIA in R. Fulton *Bk. Pigeons* 317 The Turbiteens. These are the present Oriental Turbits, which twenty-five years ago were marked as the present British Turbits. **1885** *Bazaar* 30 Mar. 1265/1 Handsome chequered turbiteen cock.

turbite: see under TURBINITE.

turbith: see TURPETH.

turblaunce, var. TROUBLANCE *Obs.*

turble, obs. f. TROUBLE.

turble, var. TURRIBLE.

turbo ('tɜːbəʊ). [a. L. *turbo* (also *turben*), *turbin-em* a whirlwind or tornado, a spinning-top, a reel or spindle, a whirl, twirl, twist, revolution.]

†**1.** A whirlwind, a tornado. *Obs. rare.*

1677 PLOT *Oxfordsh.* 5 Those that have sailed to the Indies can inform them what force Hurricane's and Turbo's have.

‖**2.** (mod.L., pl. *turbines* (-niːz).) A genus of gastropod molluscs, typical of the family *Turbinidæ*, having a regularly turbinate or whorled shell, with a rounded aperture and a calcareous operculum; also loosely, any member of the *Turbinidæ*; any turbinate or wreathed shell.

1661 LOVELL *Hist. Anim. & Min.* Introd., The turbines are great, eared, tuberous. **1760–72** tr. *Juan & Ulloa's Voy.* (ed. 3) I. 168 This species of turbines, the juice of which is also used in dying cotton threads. **1779** MRS. DELANY in *Life & Corr.* Ser. II. (1862) II. 475 She has found at her grotto some shells,..and found on Bunster a left-handed tooth'd turbo. **1837** *Encycl. Brit.* (ed. 7) XV. 347/2 A rigorous examination of the turbines of British writers. **1884** G. ALLEN in *Pall Mall G.* 26 Sept. 4/1 The objects inside the bower [of the Australian bower-bird] comprise a large and very handsome marine shell,..a pale blue turbo; a purplish pink cowrie.

3. *Mech.* **a.** = TURBINE: cf. next. *colloq.*

1904 *Electr. World & Engin.* 30 July 165/1 Oil coolers are erected in the basement below the turbos, through which the lubricating oil is passed, and cooled by means of a cold water circulation.

b. = TURBOCHARGER; also, a motor vehicle equipped with this device. Also *attrib.*

1957 *Motor* 6 Mar. 168/1 General Motors have built four turbo vehicles. The 370 b.h.p. Firebird I..had single-stage centrifugal compressor and two-stage turbine layout. **1978** *Country Life* 17 Aug. 460/1 While turbo is a term associated with power, the Saab 99 Turbo has no shortcomings in terms of comfort. **1980** *Daily Tel.* 23 Jan. 14/4 Driving it in Portugal last week, I found it impressively smooth and quiet, with a quicker throttle response from low speeds than usual with a turbo.

turbo- ('tɜːbəʊ), a verbal element repr. TURBINE, in compounds forming the names of various machines driven by and directly coupled to a turbine, or which are themselves turbines, the second element being the name of the machine so driven or coupled; thus = TURBINE in comb.; as ***turbo-alternator, -blower, -compressor, -dynamo, -generator, -machine, -motor, -pump, -unit, -ventilator***; **'turbocar**, a motor car powered by a gas-turbine engine; **turbo-'compound** *a.*, applied to a piston engine in which the exhaust gases drive a turbine coupled to the crankshaft; hence **turbo-com'pounded** *a.*, **-com'pounding** *vbl. sb.*; **'turbodrill** *Oil Industry*, a drill in which the drilling bit is rotated by a turbine situated next to it in the drilling string and driven by the upflow of mud; also as *v. trans.*; hence **'turbodrilled** *ppl. a.*, **'turbodrilling** *vbl. sb.*; **turbo-e'lectric** *a. Engin.*, involving or employing electricity generated by means of a turbine; **turbomo'lecular** *a. Physics*, applied to a type of high-vacuum pump in which momentum is imparted to molecules by a high-speed rotor inside a stator, both of which possess inclined slots or blades designed so as to cause the molecules to move axially towards the outlet; **'turbopump**, a pump that incorporates a small turbine to provide the necessary mechanical power, used esp. in aircraft and rockets; **turbo'ramjet** *Aeronaut.*, any of a class of jet engines combining the operations of a turbojet and a ramjet, either as a turbo-jet with provision for afterburning, or as a ramjet containing a turbojet which is shut down at high velocities; **'turboshaft** *Engin.*, used *attrib.* and *absol.* to designate a gas turbine engine in which the turbine drives a shaft other than a propeller shaft; **,turbo'supercharger** *Engin.* = TURBOCHARGER; hence **,turbo'supercharged** *ppl. a.*, **-'supercharging** *vbl. sb.*; **'turbotrain**, a train powered by a gas-turbine engine.

1900 *Engineer* 2 Nov. 444/3 Tests..on two *turbo alternators of 1000 kilowatts per hour nominal output. **1902** SLOANE *Stand. Electr. Dict.* App., *Turbo-alternator*, an alternating current dynamo coupled direct to a high-speed steam turbine. **1911** *Trans. Inst. Mining Engineers* XL. 580 (*heading*) *Turbo-blowers and turbo-compressors. **1947** *Jrnl. R. Aeronaut. Soc.* LI. 95/1 For high altitude cruising the application of turbo-blowers has received much consideration. **1979** *Truck & Bus Transportation* (Austral.) Feb. 41/2 With a turboblower, you literally shovel the air in. [**1950** *Motor* 15 Mar. 183/1 (*caption*) The Rover turbine car easily reached 90 m.p.h.] **1956** *Times* 3 July 4/6 The Rover *turbocar..was timed at 152 m.p.h. **1974** D. NYE *Motor Racing Mavericks* xix. 190 This turbine car sparked off a terrific controversy... Wallis was taken on..to build two cars similar to his 'STP Turbocar'. **1954** *Economist* 11 Sept. 11/3 *Turbo-compound; piston compound. A combination of gas turbine and reciprocating engine. **1955** C. E. CHAPEL et al. *Aircraft Power Plants* (ed. 2) xvii. 339/2 Aircraft powered by the Wright turbo-compound engine are the Douglas DC-7, the Lockheed Super Constellation, [etc.]. **1983** *Truck & Bus Transportation* (Austral.) July 60/2 Whilst the turbocompound diesel has progressed to the operational stage..the benefits of this concept can be more fully realised and cost justified when used in conjunction with an adiabatic or insulated engine. **1978** *Automotive Engin.* Aug. 85/1 In a *turbocompounded engine..the exhaust gases are expanded in a turbine and the power generated is transmitted back to the crankshaft. *Turbocompounding can be incorporated in naturally aspirated, as well as turbocharged engines. **1911** *Turbo-compressor [see *turbo-blower* above]. **1922** *Daily Mail Year Bk. 1923* 75/1 By the development of a mechanism known as a 'turbo-compressor', he has enabled aero-engines to maintain their power in the thin air of upper altitudes. **1979** A. L. LYDERSEN *Fluid Flow & Heat Transfer* xi. 327 Turbo-compressors are used for vapour recompression of large vapour volumes..while steam ejectors are used in many smaller installations. **1948** *Oil & Gas Jrnl.* 3 June 58/3 During initial field tests conducted in May.., the new Edco *Turbodrill penetrated 950 ft. of shallow section in a wildcat test drilling. *Ibid.* 61/1 Photoclinometer and hole-section surveys showed a total drift of 3 ft. or 10½ minutes from vertical through the section *turbo-drilled. **1949** *World Oil* 1 July 88/1 Electric logs..were run after the *turbodrilled section was completed. **1955** *World Petroleum* XXVI. 84/3 The advantages of *turbodrilling stem from the fact that only the bit is actually involved in the rotating effort. **1977** *Offshore Engineer* May 20/1 (Advt.), Our turbodrilling and directional drilling engineers and equipment are at your service. **1981** 'D. RUTHERFORD' *Porcupine Basin* iv. 66 We're developing a new turbo-drill on a flexible string which can be reeled out on a drum. **1904** *Electr. World & Engin.* 19 Mar. 558 Electrical and mechanical difficulties which arise in the design of *turbo-dynamos (dynamo-electric generators directly connected to steam-turbines). **1904** *Ibid.* 21 May 945 Each of the..*turbo-electric units is of the vertical type. **1930** *Engineering* 18 Apr. 513/3 Turbo-electric propulsion must exhibit an overwhelming superiority in reliability and maintenance cost to overcome the disadvantages. **1974** *Encycl. Brit. Macropædia* XVII. 752/2 On most nuclear submarines reduction gears are used between the turbines and the propeller shaft; however, a few incorporate turbo-electric drive. **1903** *Electr. World & Engin.* 25 July 147 Two groups of *turbo-exciters, of 110 h.p. each. **1902** SLOANE *Stand. Electr. Dict.* App., **Turbo-generator*, a generator coupled or geared to a high-speed steam turbine, and on the same base with it. **1911** *Evolution of Parsons Steam Turbine* 30 This turbo-generator worked for many years. **1903** *Sci. Amer., Supp.* 26 Sept. 23185 Steam-turbines are..analogous to hydraulic turbines, and form part of the general class which the author [Professor Rateau] will call '*turbo-machines'. **1969** *Gloss. Terms Vacuum Technol.* (*B.S.I.*) 17 **Turbo-molecular pump*, a molecular drag pump in which the rotor has inclined slots or blades moving between corresponding slots or blades in a stator. **1976** *Physics Bull.* Nov. 499/2 The vacuum system is kept at 10^{-7} Torr by about 650 sputter ion pumps and 80 turbomolecular pumps. **1900** *Westm. Gaz.* 7 Sept. 6/1 A torpedo-destroyer..driven through the water at the rate of forty-three miles an hour by the use of the *turbo-motor instead of reciprocating engines. **1903** *Turbo-pump [see *turbo-ventilator* below]. **1947** *Aircraft Engin.* Aug. 254/2 The turbo-pump assembly consists of a shaft carrying a single stage impulse steam turbine, on each side of which is a centrifugal pump. **1962** F. I. ORDWAY *Basic Astronautics* x. 411 The turbopump proves to be the best means of pressurizing the propellants for large liquid rocket engines. The bipropellant turbopump consists of two centrifugal pumps and a gas turbine that supplies the driving power for the pumps. **1979** *Nature* 11 Jan. 84/1 A fire in the high pressure turbo-pump that feeds oxygen into the combustion chamber caused the engine to explode. **1948** *Aviation Week* 23 Feb. 36/2 *Turboramjet—A conventional turbojet engine with provision for reheating the gas between the turbine discharge and the exhaust nozzle. **1971** P. J. MCMAHON *Aircraft Propulsion* iii. 119 At the moment the most promising fields of use for the turboramjet would seem to be those in air-breathing boosters for the launching of space vehicles. **1958** P. H. WILKINSON *Aircraft Engines of World 1958/59* 31 Bristol-Siddeley Engines Ltd...is specializing in advanced turbojets, turboprops, *turboshafts, [etc.]. **1967** *Jane's Surface Skimmer Systems 1967–68* 130/2 The GE LM1500 turboshaft engine is the result of a company investment in a programme to adapt the J79 jet engine to a free power turbine for commercial use. **1977** I. M. CAMPBELL *Energy & Atmosphere* vi. 127 The gas turbine engine used in aircraft under the names of turbojet, turboprop or turbofan, or in industrial or marine settings as a turboshaft engine. **1944** P. H. WILKINSON *Aircraft Engines of World 1944* 34 The Boeing Flying Fortress B-17 (powered with a *turbo-supercharged engine). **1978** *Financial Times* 20 Dec. 21/5 At the moment, Mercedes is unique in marketing a turbo-supercharged diesel car. **1938** A. SWAN *Handbk. Aeronaut.* (ed. 3) II. IV. 206 The inherent advantages of the *turbo supercharger are mainly centred around the fact that it possesses remarkable flexibility of speed control. **1971** P. J. MCMAHON *Aircraft Propulsion* xi. 319 From the turbo-supercharger, it is a logical step to develop the fully compound engine. **1979** *Financial Rev.* 14 June 29/1 *Turbosupercharging is very much in as far as motoring is concerned these days. **1966** *Time* 27 May 52/3 Canadian National Railways..has now ordered five of the *turbotrains developed by the U.S.'s United Aircraft Corp. .. These light-weight, low-slung, turbojet-powered whiz-bangs should be able to clip nearly an hour off the present five-hour Montreal–Toronto run. **1978** *Times* 9 June 1/8 The turbo-train between Strasbourg and Lyons. **1903** *Electr. World & Engin.* 4 July 17 Prof. Rateau has installed *turbo-ventilators giving a pressure of half an atmosphere, and turbo-pumps with a lift of several hundred metres.

turbocharger (ˈtɜːbəʊˌtʃɑːdʒə(r)). *Engin.* Also **turbo charger.** [f. *turbo(super)charger* s.v. TURBO-.] A supercharger driven by a turbine powered by the engine's exhaust gases.

1934 *Jrnl. R. Aeronaut. Soc.* XXXVIII. 182 After explosion, the first exhaust valve which is connected to the turbo charger, opens. **1961** *Engineering* 9 June 786/1 The advantages obtained by applying turbochargers to diesel engines are well known. **1980** 'D. RUTHERFORD' *Turbo* viii. 107, I gently depressed the accelerator. The turbocharger came in with its characteristic whine and the Saab swept quickly to 120 m.p.h.

Hence (as a back-formation) **ˈturbocharge** *v. trans.*, to equip with a turbocharger; **ˈturbocharged** *ppl. a.*, **ˈturbocharging** *vbl. sb.*

1961 *Engineering* 10 Mar. 370/1 The cycle for the Ford 704 engine of 300 hp rating may be described as a turbocharged gas turbine. *Ibid.* 9 June 786/1 Turbocharging has brought with it the reduced weight and space requirements. **1970** *Commercial Motor* 25 Sept. 97 Ford offers a turbocharged version of its 360 cu. in. engine, ..while Perkins has turbocharged the 6·354. **1971** *Farmer & Stockbreeder* 23 Feb. 21/3 The combination of air cooling and turbocharging is said to reduce engine noise and smoke emission. **1981** *Sci. Amer.* May 41/2 Turbocharging automotive diesels has made possible fuel-economy advances of between 10 and 15 percent. **1981** D. BOGGIS *Time to Betray* x. 54 The Skylane..was turbocharged, with retractable gear.

turbofan (ˈtɜːbəʊfæn). *Aeronaut.* Also with hyphen. [f. TURBO- + FAN *sb.*[1]]

a. A fan connected to or driven by a turbine. **b.** Used *attrib.* and *absol.* to designate a jet engine employing such a fan for additional thrust; = *fan-jet* (*engine*) s.v. FAN *sb.*[1] 11.

1911 *Trans. Inst. Mining Engineers* XL. 580 The smaller efficiency of the turbo-fan. **1949** *Gloss. Aeronaut. Terms (B.S.I.)* II. 17 *Ducted-fan turbine engine, turbo-fan,* a gas turbine engine in which a portion of the net energy is used to drive a ducted fan. **1959** *Wall St. Jrnl.* 7 July 10/1 The turbofan engine is the latest in the family of jet power plants. **1961** [see *double-flow* s.v. DOUBLE *a.* C. 2 a]. **1970** *Daily Tel.* (Colour Suppl.) 13 Nov. 14/4 Large turbofan engines of the Spey type tend to expel ingested objects along the cold fan duct, so that they do not enter the engine core. **1980** R. L. DUNCAN *Brimstone* x. 261 A cruise missile..propelled by a jet turbofan.

turbojet (ˈtɜːbəʊdʒɛt). *Aeronaut.* Also with hyphen. [f. TURBO- + JET *sb.*[3] 5 c.] Used *attrib.* and *absol.* to designate (an aircraft having) a type of jet engine in which the jet gases also power a turbine-driven compressor for compressing the air drawn into the engine.

1945 *Aeronautics* Mar. 28/2 The turbo-jet shows definite advantages in comparatively light aircraft designed to operate at high speeds. **1950** *Ann. Reg. 1949* 424 Propelled by..turbo-jet engines,..the Comet flew at an altitude of 35,000 feet. **1958** *Times Rev. Industry* Dec. 50/2 Within five years it is probable that over 1,300 turbo-jet and turbo-prop aircraft will be in service. **1962** E. SNOW *Other Side of River* (1963) i. 17, I had flown half-way around the world and landed at Peking in a Soviet turbojet manned by a Chinese crew. **1977** *Sci. Amer.* Feb. 23/2 A turbojet engine exhausts its gases at 1,450 degrees, whereas a turbofan engine, because of turbulent mixing at the outlet, exhausts them at 600 degrees.

turbopause (ˈtɜːbəʊpɔːz). *Meteorol.* [f. TURB(ULENCE + -O + PAUSE *sb.*] The outer limit of a turbosphere, where the distribution of constituents is due equally to diffusion and turbulent mixing.

1951 S. CHAPMAN in *Jrnl. Atmospheric & Terrestrial Physics* I. 201 The diffusive tendency becomes increasingly effective at greater heights, and it may be (but it is not certain) that at some level diffusion becomes dominant over the turbulent mixing. The name turbopause is suggested for this level. **1967** R. W. FAIRBRIDGE *Encycl. Atmospheric Sci. & Astrogeol.* 5/1 Above the turbopause, which [on earth] lies between 100 and 130 km, diffusion is more important than turbulent mixing in distributing the constituents. **1979** *Nature* 17 May 221/1 The δ-bands, present in the Earth's twilight and night time airglow spectra,..indicate a significant population of atomic nitrogen at or below the Venus turbopause.

turboprop (ˈtɜːbəʊprɒp). *Aeronaut.* Also **turbo-prop.** [f. TURBO- + PROP *sb.*[6]] Used *attrib.* and *absol.* to designate (an aircraft having) a jet engine in which a turbine is used as in a turbojet and also to drive a propeller; = *prop-jet* s.v. PROP *sb.*[6] 2 b. Also **ˌturbopro'peller.**

1945 H. H. ARNOLD *Third Rep. Commanding General U.S. Army Air Forces* in *War Reports* (1947) 464 This war has evolved six distinct methods of utilizing atmospheric oxygen for propulsion, such as:..*turboprop*—a gas turbine plus propeller. **1946** *Shell Aviation News* No. 102. 5/2 The following..types of planes will be..powered by turbo props. **1947** *Aircraft Engin.* Mar. 79/1 The question can turbo-jets or turbo-propellers be used in transport is timely. **1957** *Times* 17 Dec. 13/2 There has been an increasing demand for equipment for civil aircraft, particularly those employing turbo-propeller engines. **1958** *Daily Mail* 3 Mar. 5/2 The more economical turbo-props could be used to force down the price of air travel. **1958** [see TURBOJET]. **1968** MILLER & SAWERS *Technical Developments Mod. Aviation* vi. 205 A turbopropeller-driven airliner will have an advantage over a jet if they both seat significantly fewer than 50 passengers on stage lengths exceeding 200 miles. **1972** *Physics Bull.* Oct. 580/3 The four turboprops which will power the biggest ship at speeds up to 120 mph are located on the tail spars. **1978** *N.Y. Times* 30 March B19/1 (Advt.), Mechanics... Exp on..air research turboprop engines.

turbosphere (ˈtɜːbəʊsfɪə(r)). *Meteorol.* [f. TURB(ULENCE + -O + SPHERE *sb.*] A region of a planetary atmosphere in which mixing occurs predominantly through turbulence.

1951 S. CHAPMAN in *Jrnl. Atmospheric & Terrestrial Physics* I. 201 Throughout the lower atmosphere, and up to at least 60 km height, turbulence suffices to mix the permanent constituents effectively, overcoming the diffusive tendency for each to distribute itself independently of the others, according to its molecular weight... It is suggested that this whole region be called the turbosphere. **1979** J. K. HARGREAVES *Upper Atmosphere & Solar-Terrestrial Relations* iv. 52 The well mixed part of the atmosphere, in which composition does not change with height, can be called the turbosphere.

turbostratic (tɜːbəʊˈstrætɪk), *a. Physics.* [f. L. *turb-ātus*, pa. pple of *turbāre* to disturb, disorder + -O + STRAT(UM + -IC.] Of or pertaining to a material (esp. one allotrope of carbon) having a structure intermediate between amorphous and crystalline, consisting of stacked disordered layers.

1942 BISCOE & WARREN in *Jrnl. Appl. Physics* XIII. 370/1 Carbon black is a simple and definite example of an intermediate form of matter, which is distinctly different from both the crystalline and the amorphous states. The term 'turbostratic' (unordered layers) is suggested as a name of this particular class of mesomorphic solids. **1966** *R. Inst. Chem. Lect. Ser.* V. 12 The so-called 'turbostratic' boron nitride is still basically the hexagonal form. **1975** *Physics Bull.* June 260/1 This model is distinctly different from the traditional, 'turbostratic' model..in which crystallites comprise flat, graphite layer planes in disordered stacking.

turbot (ˈtɜːbət). Forms: 3–8 turbut, 4–5 -bote, 4–7 -butt, 5 -bott, 6 -butte, 6–7 -bat, 7 *Sc.* -batt, 6–8 -bet, 7, 9 -bit, 4– turbot. [a. OF. *tourbout* (12th c. in Hatz.-Darm.), *torbout*, AF. *turbut*, MDu. *turbot, terbot, tarbot*; of uncertain origin; perh. a deriv. of L. *turbo* spinning top (also in med.L. 'turbot'), referring to its shape; but the termination of the F. word is unexplained.]

1. A large flat fish (*Rhombus maximus* or *Psetta maxima*), having a wide scaleless body covered with conical bony tubercles, with the eyes normally on the left side, found on the European coasts and much esteemed as food.

c **1300** *Havelok* 754 He tok þe sturgiun, and þe qual, And þe turbut, and lax with-al. **1307–8** *Durham Acc. Rolls* (Surtees) 4 In j turbote, iiij s. ij d. **1377** *Ibid.* 46 In j Turbutt et j leyng emp. in villa, xs. vj d. **14..** *Nom.* in Wr.-Wülcker 704/36 (*Nomina piscium*) *Hic turbo*, -[*i*]*nis*, a turbott. *c* **1450** *Two Cookery-bks.* 112 Nym luys, turbot, and elys & gobete hem in mosselys. **1502–3** *Rec. St. Mary at Hill* 248 Payd for di. a turbutt xx d. **1570** LEVINS *Manip.* 93/24 A Turbet, fish, *rhombus, i. Ibid.* 195/28 Turbutte, fish, *chalchis, rhombus, i.* **1596** DALRYMPLE tr. *Leslie's Hist. Scot.* (S.T.S.) I. 41 Turbat, ffluik, and plase fluik. **1655** MOUFET & BENNET *Health's Improv.* (1746) 266 Turbots..were in old time counted so good and delicate, that this Proverb grew upon them, *Nihil ad Rhombum*; that is to say, *What is all this in comparison of a Turbot.* **1728** YOUNG *Love Fame* III. 74 The salmon is refus'd, the turbot bought. **1771** SMOLLETT *Humph. Cl.* 5 June, My uncle..asked him to dinner, and treated him with a fine turbot. **1836** YARRELL *Brit. Fishes* II. 238 Reversed Turbots..that is, Turbots having the eyes and dark colour on the right side instead of the left, are also occasionally brought to market. **1870** YEATS *Nat. Hist. Comm.* 324 The English markets..are supplied chiefly with Dutch turbot.

2. Applied to other fish more or less resembling the turbot.

a. In north of Eng. and parts of Scotland, the halibut. **b.** In U.S., any of various large flat fishes, as the diamond flounder of California (*Hypopsetta guttulata*), or the spotted flounder of the Pacific coast (*Bothus maculatus*). **c.** In New Zealand, *Ammotretis guntheri*, also called *lemon-sole* (Morris). **d.** Locally, any of various species of *Balistes*, the file-fishes and trigger-fishes (*Cent. Dict.* 1891).

1555 EDEN *Decades* 200 Certeyne other fysshes: as soles, mackerelles, turbuttes [in W. Indies]. **1598** HAKLUYT *Voy.* I. 104 They gaue vnto vs a great fresh turbut. **1601** HOLLAND *Pliny* IX. xx. I. 247 In a Turbot the right side turneth upward, and in a Plaice the left. **1674** RAY *Collect. Words, Fishes* s.v., What in the [South] they call the Halibut in the North they call the Turbot;..in some parts of the West of England they call the Turbot Bret and the Halibut Turbot. **1794** *Statist. Acc. Scot.* XII. 171 *note,* The fish.. are cod, ling, skate, mackerel, hollybut, here called turbot. **1810** P. NEILL *List Fishes* 11 (Jam.) Holibut... In our [Edinburgh] market..named the turbot; the proper turbot ..getting another name, that of rawnfleuk. **1883** *Chambers' Encycl.* IX. 581/2 The American or Spotted Turbot (*Rhombus maculatus*)..is common on the coasts of New England and New York. **1885** LADY BRASSEY *The Trades* 302 There were fish here [Jamaica] called turbot—not the least like our turbot, but of bright ultramarine and azure blue.

3. *attrib.* and *Comb.*, as ***turbot-boat, -fish, -fisher, -fishery, -kettle, -line,*** †***-sprout*** (SPROUT *sb.*[2]); ***turbot-like*** adj.

1845 GOSSE *Ocean* ii. (1849) 82 *Turbot-boat off Scarborough. **1611** COTGR., *Turbot,* the *Turbot fish. **1845** GOSSE *Ocean* ii. (1849) 82 Even the practised eye of the *turbot-fisher..fails to detect a fish when thus concealed. **1765** *Museum Rust.* IV. 238 The *turbot-fishery off the British coasts. **1846** SOYER *Cookery* 85 Put the whole of the turtle..into a large *turbot kettle. **1611** COTGR., *Barbue,*.. a kind of lesse Turbot, or *Turbot-like fish, called by some, a Dab, or Sandling. **1763** *Chron.* in *Ann. Reg.* 162/1 A complete sett of *turbot-lines. **1324–5** *Durham Acc. Rolls* (Surtees) 14 In..xij *torbotes sproutes, xvj Lopsters. **1430** *Ibid.* 61 In..j Turbotspreute [*printed* -sprente].

†**turbulacioun, -aunce,** obs. var. TRIBULATION, TROUBLANCE.

c **1430** LYDG. *Min. Poems* (Percy Soc.) 251 My socoure and refuge, Geyn every tempest and turbulacioun.

turbulence (ˈtɜːbjʊləns). Also 7 **-ance.** [ad. L. *turbulentia*, f. *turbulentus* TURBULENT: see -ENCE: cf. F. *turbulance, -ence* (14th c. in Hatz.-Darm.), perh. the immediate source.] **a.** The state or quality of being turbulent; violent commotion, agitation, or disturbance; disorderly or tumultuous character or conduct; with *a* and *pl.*, an instance of this.

1598 FLORIO, *Torbolenza,* turbulence, disturbance. **1606** SHAKS. *Tr. & Cr.* v. iii. 11, I haue dreampt Of bloudy turbulence. **1639** in *Kirkcudbr. War-Comm. Min. Bk.* etc. (1855) 231 Whatsomever tumilts and turbulances that shall happen to fall out. **1777** ROBERTSON *Hist. Amer.* II. v. 4 The turbulence of youth..gradually subsided. **1845** M. PATTISON *Ess.* (1889) I. 18 It required all the personal influence of the king to check the turbulence of his irritated followers. **1853** J. H. NEWMAN *Hist. Sk.* (1873) III. I. i. 5 A temporary retreat from the turbulence of ecclesiastical politics.

b. Of natural conditions: Stormy or tempestuous state or action; violence.

1726–46 THOMSON *Winter* 56 Congregated clouds, And all the vapoury turbulence of heaven. **1748** *Anson's Voy.* I. viii. 82 The turbulence of the weather. **1820** SCORESBY *Acc. Arctic Reg.* I. 301 Capable of resisting the turbulence of the ocean. **1862** GOULBURN *Pers. Relig.* III. vii. 205 Think of Him as calm..amidst the most furious agitations and turbulences of nature.

c. Of fluid flow (see TURBULENT *a.* 2 c).

1907 F. W. LANCHESTER *Aerodynamics* ii. 53 When a certain critical velocity is exceeded the continuity is broken and the phenomenon of turbulence manifests itself. **1922** GLAZEBROOK *Dict. Appl. Physics* I. 299/2 The important part played by turbulence in reducing the time of explosion in actual engines, and thus rendering high revolution speeds practicable. **1928** N. SHAW *Man. Meteorol.* II. vi. 284 The variation of wind with height is now treated as the effect of turbulence or eddy-motion in the moving air. **1935** *Discovery* Oct. 390/2 This is remedied either by small fans or, automatically, by injecting some cold air from the dehumidifier with the heated air, causing a form of turbulence in the enclosure. **1980** R. P. BENEDICT *Fund. Pipe Flow* iv. 141 A stability theory has been given that explains the origin of turbulence in terms of arbitrary small disturbances which initiate instabilities in the laminar boundary layer.

turbulency (ˈtɜːbjʊlənsɪ). Now *rare.* [f. as prec.: see next and -ENCY.] Turbulent state, disturbed condition.

1607 *Puritan* I. ii. 61, I..for my part wish a Turbulency in the world. *c* **1645** HOWELL *Lett.* vi. 80 Since the turbulency of these times, the same moderation shines in you. **1671** MILTON *P.R.* IV. 462 Like turbulencies in the affairs of men,.. They oft fore-signifie and threaten ill. **1694** SALMON *Bate's Dispens.* (1713) 512/1 Where there is need of quieting the Turbulency and Effervescency of the Humours. **1734** tr. *Rollin's Anc. Hist.* XVI. ii. (1827) VI. 349 Endeavour to calm the turbulency of their minds. **1831** POE *Bells* iii, What a tale of terror their turbulency tells!

turbulent (ˈtɜːbjʊlənt), *a.* [ad. L. *turbulent-us* full of disturbance or commotion, restless, f. *turba* crowd, *turbāre* to disturb, agitate: cf. *corpulent, truculent.* So F. *turbulent* (12–13th c.).]

1. a. Of persons, their attributes and actions: Causing disturbance or commotion; disposed or inclined to disorder; tumultuous; unruly; violent.

1538 COVERDALE *N.T.* Ded., These turbulent and stormy assaultes of the wicked. **1593** G. HARVEY *Pierce's Super.* 98 That execrable Seruetus, or other turbulent rebells in Religion. **1602** SHAKS. *Ham.* III. i. 4 Grating so harshly all his dayes of quiet With turbulent and dangerous Lunacy. *a* **1780** WATSON *Philip III*, III. (1793) I. 289 The danger to which he was exposed from their turbulent ambition. **1846** TRENCH *Mirac.* vi. (1862) 188 He expelled from the house the crowd of turbulent mourners. **1856** EMERSON *Eng. Traits, Char.* Wks. (Bohn) II. 59 They stoutly carry into every nook and corner of the earth their turbulent sense.

†**b.** Of things: Having a disturbing effect; tending to produce disturbance or trouble. *Obs.*

1625 BACON *Ess., Innovations* (Arb.) 527 A Froward Retention of Custome, is as turbulent a Thing, as an Innouation. **1625** K. LONG tr. *Barclay's Argenis* II. xvii. 121 Such, whose angry and turbulent Planets have indued them with a more violent disposition. **1671** MILTON *Samson* 522 Nor envied them the grape Whose heads that turbulent liquor fills with fumes.

c. Violent in action or effect.

1656 RIDGLEY *Pract. Physick* 65 The cause is a Narcotick vapour, but it is turbulent also. **1874** GARROD & BAXTER *Mat. Med.* (1880) 440 When the heart is turbulent in its action, then the sedative remedies which act upon this organ are indicated;..a turbulent cardiac condition is often combined with a very imperfect flow of blood through its cavities.

2. Characterized by violent disturbance or commotion; violently disturbed or agitated; disorderly, troubled.

a. Of weather, the sea, etc.: Stormy, tempestuous.

1573 G. HARVEY *Letter-bk.* (Camden) 34 After thes turbulent raging tempests I hope verrely for caulm and faier wether. **1608** SHAKS. *Per.* III. ii. 4 T'as been a turbulent and stormie night. *a* **1687** PETTY *Pol. Arith.* (1690) 20 One sort of Vessels for the turbulent Sea, another for Inland Waters. **1770** G. WHITE *Selborne* xxix. 80 Last month we had such a series of cold turbulent weather. **1860** TYNDALL *Glac.* I. xiv. 94 Our way sometimes lay..across turbulent brooks. **1864** A. McKAY *Hist. Kilmarnock* 261 The swollen waters bore upon their turbulent bosoms planks, trees, [etc.].

b. Of a state of mind or thought, social or political affairs, etc.

1609 DANIEL *Civ. Wars* I. 9 [He] making the succession doubtfull, rent This new-got State, and left it turbulent. **1667** MILTON *P.L.* IX. 1126 Thir inward State of Mind, calme Region once And full of Peace, now tost and turbulent. **1788** GIBBON *Decl. & F.* xxxix. (1869) II. 433 The reign of the usurper was short and turbulent. **1848** DICKENS *Dombey* lix, However turbulent his thoughts,.. that was all past now. **1849** MACAULAY *Hist. Eng.* iv. I. 455 In the City of London, lately so turbulent, scarcely a murmur was heard.

c. Of, pertaining to, or designating flow of a fluid in which the velocity at any point fluctuates irregularly and there is continual mixing rather than a steady flow pattern.

Turbulent flow was earlier called *sinuous* or *eddying flow*.

1895 H. LAMB *Hydrodynamics* xi. 574 The resistance, in the case of turbulent flow, is found to be sensibly independent..of the viscosity of the fluid. **1907** F. W. LANCHESTER *Aerodynamics* ii. 53 When this critical velocity is reached the parallel flow breaks up, and is replaced by an irregular turbulent motion. **1926** H. R. RICARDO *Engines of High Output* 63 In the actual engine cylinder..the mixture ..is being whirled about very rapidly; it is, in fact, in a highly turbulent condition. **1930** *Engineering* 7 Mar. 319/3 Hence, when viscous flow changes to turbulent flow the dissipation of energy is increased. **1947** [see *Reynolds stress* s.v. REYNOLDS]. **1956** A. A. TOWNSEND *Struct. Turbulent Shear Flow* i. 3 In turbulent motion..the motion at any point influences the motion at other distant points. **1968** [see LAMINAR *a.* 2 a]. **1982** *Sci. Amer.* July 99/1 When the bore of a tube flares gradually (as the aortic lumen does in an incipient aneurysm), the fluid near the wall slows down, generating turbulent flow.

Hence **'turbulently** *adv.*, in a turbulent manner; with much commotion, tumultuously, violently; **'turbulentness**, *rare* = TURBULENCE.

1602 WARNER *Alb. Eng.* Epit. (1612) 392 The aforesaid intermitted Controuersie..hence-forth turbulently and Tragically proceeded. **1609** W. SCLATER *Threefold Preserv.* (1610) Ep. Ded., I know not what show of turbulentnesse they can accuse me of. **1655** FULLER *Ch. Hist.* XI. i. §11 This meeting..proceeded turbulently, and suspiciously. **1746** SMART *Ode St. Cecilia's Day* vi, In sorrow's tempest turbulently tost. **1863** W. C. BALDWIN *Afr. Hunting* ix. 397 The gorge [at Victoria Falls] cannot be more than a hundred yards wide, and at the bottom the river rolls turbulently boiling.

† **'turbulous**, *a. Obs. rare.* Also 6 tourbulus. [f. L. *turbul-entus* TURBULENT + -OUS: cf. OF. *torbleus* TROUBLOUS.] = TURBULENT, TROUBLOUS 2.

1527 HACKET *Let. to Wolsey* (MS. Cott. Galba B. xiv. 91), That [we] may cheyse the best for owr own parte and for t[he] welt and comodyte of all the tourbulus Cristynd[om]. **1579** J. STUBBES in *Harington's Nugæ Ant.* (1804) I. 151 A miserable turbulous wretch, seekinge to interrupt her peace. **1676** W. ROW *Contn. Blair's Autobiog.* xii. (1848) 582 Turbulous and seditious.

turbyll, obs. form of TROUBLE.

Turc, obs. f. TURK.

turcais, -cas, -e, -casse, turches, -is, -ois: see TURKIS, TURQUOISE.

turchine, var. TURKIN *Obs.*, blue cloth.

† **'Turcian**, *a. Obs.* = next.

1576 FOXE *A. & M.* 3/1 Ottomannus the first Turcian Emperour.

† **'Turcic**, *a. Obs. rare.* [f. med.L. *Turc-us* TURK *sb.*[1] + -IC.] Of Turkey, Turkish. So † **'Turcical** *a. Obs. rare*, Turkish, Turk-like.

1600 W. WATSON *Decacordon* (1602) 331 Their [the Jesuits'] intended gouernment is most Antichristian, Tartarian, Turcicall and Tyrannicall. **1661** LOVELL *Hist. Anim. & Min.* Introd., Pulveratricious domestick, as the Cock and hen, Patavine, Turcick, Persick,..Indian, and Guinie.

Turcification: see TURKIFICATION.

† **turciman**, obs. var. TRUCHMAN.

1562 J. SHUTE tr. *Cambini's Turk. Wars* 68 b, A notable matter, which was declared vnto me..(by a Persian..) hauing for my turciman a citizen of ours named Iohn Cerini.

† **Turcism** ('tɜːsɪz(ə)m). *Obs.* See also TURKISM. [f. med.L. *Turc-us* TURK *sb.*[1] + -ISM.] The religion or system of the Turks; Islam.

1566 in Neal *Hist. Purit.* (1732) I. 233 Turcism stood upon as good ground as Popery. **1582** MUNDAY *Breefe & True Rep. Exec. Traytours* 122, I think..if any Prince fal by infidelity into Turscisme, Atheisme, Paganisme or any such lyke, that the Pope hath auctthoritie to depose such a Prince. **1607** R. C[AREW] tr. *Estienne's World of Wonders* 75 If a man would haue a perfect..religion.., he must compound it of Christian religion, Iudaizm, and Turcizm. **1621-31** LAUD *Sev. Serm.* (1847) 13 Heathenism, and Turcism, and Judaism, and Heresy, and Superstition, and Schism. **1721** STRYPE *Eccl. Mem.* I. xxxv. 271 He grounds his..discourse upon the probability of the fall of Turcism.

b. Turkish principles and practice.

1581 ALLEN *Apol.* 29 b, Greekes and Hungarians infected with Turcisme. **1613** ZOUCH *Dove* 29 Illyricum whilst Turcisme it oreflowes, Feeles not her billowes, nor respects her blowes. *a* **1643** LD. FALKLAND, etc. *Infallibility* (1646) 109 The very using of this violence is a prime piece of Turcisme. **1705** STANHOPE *Paraphr.* III. 324 The Parts of the Christian Church once most conspicuous and flourishing..have long since been overrun with Turcism and Barbarity.

Turcize: see TURKIZE.

turco ('tɜːkəʊ). [a. Sp., Pg., and It. *turco* TURK.]

1. A Chilean bird, *Hylactes megapodius*, related to and resembling the TAPACULO.

1839 DARWIN *Voy. Nat.* xii. (1873) 270 The former, called by the Chilenos 'el Turco', is as large as a fieldfare... The Turco is not uncommon. **1896** NEWTON *Dict. Birds* 947 The 'Turco',..*Hylactes megapodius*, is larger, with greatly developed feet and claws.

2. A Turk or Moor (in S. America).

1909 *Bible in World* Aug. 242/2 The Arabic Version is needed by the so-called Turcos, who settle chiefly in North Brazil.

3. One of a body of native Algerian light infantry in the French army; a Zouave soldier. Also *attrib.* or *adj.*

1860 CAPT. S. OSBORN in *Once a Week* 7 July 35/1 A small breadth of blue water stayed the charge of the Tartar cut-throat of the olden day, as we trust it may do the *pas accéléré* of the more modern Zouaves or Turcos. **1898** *Edin. Rev.* Apr. 344 The Turco battalion was constantly engaged. *Ibid.* 345 A battalion of Turcos. **1902** R. W. CHAMBERS *Maids of Paradise* v, A Turco soldier came into the room.

Turco-, Turko- ('tɜːkəʊ), combining form repr. med.L. *Turcus* or TURK. **a.** Used with adjs. or sbs. denoting other peoples or countries, signifying 'Turkish and..' or 'Turkishly..', as ***Turco-Bulgarian, -German, -Italian, -Persian, -Russian, -Tartar, -Tatar, -Tataric***, etc.

1813 A. BRUCE *Life Alex. Morus* ii. 27 The iniquity of that Turcopopish government. **1813** *Q. Rev.* Oct. 256/2 Turcotartarian. **1854** MAX MÜLLER in C. Bunsen *Christianity & Mankind* III. 279 The still undivided 'Turko-Tataric' speech. **1854** J. H. NEWMAN *Lect. Hist. Turks* 62 The ancient Turco-Tartar empire..extended to the Caspian and towards the Indus. **1865** *Reader* No. 107. 33/3 Hungarian and Turco-tartaric dialects. **1880** A. H. SAYCE *Introd. Sci. Lang.* II. viii. 190 The whole Turanian family..may be divided into five branches, the Finno-Ugric, the Turko-Tatar, the Samoyedic, the Mongolian, and the Tungusian. **1884** *Graphic* 4 Oct. 360/3 The style is Turco-Byzantine—the beginning of the end. **1897** *Westm. Gaz.* 25 Sept. 2/2 Other Greek statesmen..were also enamoured of the idea of a Turko-Greek alliance. **1903** *Daily Chron.* 28 May 6/1 On my arrival I found the Turkish and Turco-Albanian population of the town calm. **1909** *Westm. Gaz.* 13 July 1/3 In order to gain the confidence of the Turco-Cretans. **1909** G. DRAGE in *Cambr. Mod. Hist.* (1921) XI. ix. 276 The settlement of the Turco-Persian frontier question. **1915** W. S. CHURCHILL in M. Gilbert *Winston S. Churchill* (1972) III. Compan. I. 421 The Turco-German fleet. **1923** G. BUCHANAN *My Mission to Russia* I. vi. 64 The Turco-Bulgarian agreement. **1948** D. DIRINGER *Alphabet* 567 Turco-Tatar and Caucasian languages. **1969** V. N. DATTA *Jallianwala Bagh* 5 The Turco-German organisation at Berne. **1982** M. BINGHAM *Princess Lieven* xiii. 189 The Turco-Russian conflict rumbled on.

b. in other derivatives, as **Turco'centric** *a.*, centred round Turkey or the Turks; hence **,Turcocen'tricity; Tur'cologist**, one who is versed in Turkish history, literature, language, or art; also **Turco'logical** *a.*, **Tur'cology; Turco'mania**, a rage for Turkish manners or customs; excessive favour for Turkish policy, etc.; **'Turcophil, -e** *a.*, tending to favour Turkey or the Turks; *sb.* one who favours Turkey; hence **Tur'cophilism, -'philia; 'Turcophobe**, one who has a morbid fear or dislike of the Turks; so **Tur'cophobist**.

1964 *Jrnl. R. Central Asian Soc.* LI. 72 A *Turco-centric history. **1969** *Middle Eastern Studies* May 173 The passage is worth noting for Gökalp's *turcocentricity: 'Europeans committed an historical sin by translating Attila's title..as "Scourge of God".' **1952** *Round Table* Dec. 25 The well of *Turcological study. **1881** A. VÁMBÉRY in *Athenæum* 31 Dec. 888/2 *Turcologists will be always thankful for his edition of the Cumanian glossary. **1951** W. K. MATTHEWS *Languages U.S.S.R.* iv. 63 Gyula Németh, the Hungarian turcologist. **1976** *Times Lit. Suppl.* 3 Sept. 1077/3 The Russians..began to produce excellent Persianists, Turcologists, Mongolists. **1918** *Q. Rev.* Apr. 513 The transformation of the *Medresses*..into 'National' schools for the teaching of *Turkology. **1951** W. K. MATTHEWS *Languages U.S.S.R.* iv. 64 This uses phonetic as well as morphological data, and has received the sanction of Soviet turcology. **1834** *Ayesha* I. i. 9 He had been bitten by the **turcomania* to such a degree, that [etc.]. **1876** *Times* 16 June, *Turcophile. **1880** *Manch. Guard.* 3 Nov., They are Turcophiles, but they would very much like to see a sequestration of Turkish revenues for their own advantage. **1895** *Eclectic Mag.* Oct. 566 A Turkophil Bulgaria might come..to mean a great autonomous..Balkan Kingdom. **1903** *Speaker* 10 Oct. 28/2 His wonderful achievement in destroying the great Turcophil tradition. **1908** J. MORLEY *Recoll.* (1917) II. 245 Am I quite wrong in suspecting a degree of *Turcophilia in you? **1967** C. SETON-WATSON *Italy from Liberalism to Fascism* x. 376 William II was impressed. His Turcophilia of the previous autumn had by now quite vanished. **1880** *Daily News* 7 Oct. 4/6 Their conduct is not to be ascribed to what they call *Turcophilism—meaning..affection for the Turk. **1896** *Westm. Gaz.* 14 May 2/2 His kindness..should convince the sternest *Turkophobe. **1877** J. BAKER *Turkey* Pref. 4 Another resident of..long standing, but a *Turcophobist.

turcois, obs. form of TURQUOISE.

Turcoman ('tɜːkəʊmən). Also 7 Turcomane, Turkeman, 9 Toorkoman, Turkoman; *β.* 7 Turcman, 7- Turkman. See also TURKMAN. [a. Pers. *turkumān* 'one like or resembling a Turk', f. TURK *sb.*[1] + *mān-dan* to resemble: applied to the Turkish nomads. Hence med.L. *Turcomannus*, F. *tourcouman*. In English sometimes made into *Turkman*, and the second element treated as MAN, as in *Chinaman*, etc., with pl. *Turkmen*: cf. *Mussulman*.]

1. a. A member of a branch of the Turkish race, consisting of a number of tribes inhabiting the region lying east of the Caspian Sea and about the Sea of Aral, formerly known as Turkestan or Independent Tartary (now Turkmenistan, a constituent republic of the U.S.S.R.) and parts of Persia (Iran) and Afghanistan; mainly nomadic and pastoral, and once notorious for their predatory habits.

1600 J. PORY tr. *Leo's Africa* IX. 337 Camels are gentle and domesticall beasts, and..are vsed in Asia by the Tartars, the Curdians, the Dalemians, and the Turcomans. **1625** PURCHAS *Pilgrims* II. IX. iv. §2. 1427 The noble Kingdome of Armenia, called now Turcomania, because of the Turcomanes a people that came out of Scythia..who live as Shepheards in their Tents. **1632** LITHGOW *Trav.* v. 196 Poore miserable people called Turcomani, liuing in Tents. **1854** CHURCH *Misc. Writ.* (1891) I. 288 The traveller in Asia Minor comes from time to time upon encampments of Turkomans.

β. **1683** T. SMITH *Acc. Prusa* in *Misc. Cur.* (1708) III. 73 The Turkmans, (for so they are peculiarly called, as if they were the true Descendents of the Old Turks or Scythians,) ..have no fixt Residence any where, but Travel with their Families and Cattle from Place to Place, carrying their Wives and Children upon Camels. **1686** tr. *Chardin's Coronat. Solyman* 123 A great number of Turkmans or Shepherds. *Ibid.* 124 These People our Modern Authors call Turcomans, which are properly Turks. **1823** BYRON *Island* II. xix, Sublime tobacco! which from east to west Cheers the tar's labour or the Turkman's rest. **1897** RAMSAY *Every Day Life Turkey* iii. 96 These people are Turkmans and their customs are different from those of other Moslems. **1906** —— in *Contemp. Rev.* July 11 The Byzantine historians, who distinguish these Turkmen or Nomads..from the Turks.

b. The Turkish language of this people. Cf. TURKMEN, TÜRKMEN.

1798 *Brit. Critic* XI. 37 The Turkish language,..that corrupt jargon; a strange harsh mixture of the vernacular Turcoman, Arabic, and Persian. **1888** *Encycl. Brit.* XXIV. 1/1 Ural-Altaic Languages..*Turkoman* (*Turkmenian*), west Turkestan, north Persia, and Asia Minor. **1908** [see JAGATAI]. **1954** PEI & GAYNOR *Dict. Ling.* 222 *Turkoman*, a Near-Eastern language; it belongs to the Southern Turkic group of the Altaic subfamily of the Ural-Altaic family of languages.

2. A Turcoman horse: see quot. 1831.

1831 YOUATT *Horse* ii. 17 The Toorkoman horse. Turkistan..has been celebrated from very early times, for producing a pure and valuable breed of horses. They are called Toorkomans. They are said to be preferable even to the pure Persians, for service. **1884** O'DONOVAN *Merv* xxiv. 270 They are generally..a mixture of Arab and Turcoman blood, but thoroughbred Turcomans are also..for sale. **1905** *Statesman* (Calcutta) 23 Aug. 2/3 For Sale—Pair of Handsome Red spotted Cream Turcomans (ponies).

3. A kind of textile material; cf. *Turcoman carpet* in 4. Also, a Turcoman carpet or rug.

1881 C. C. HARRISON *Woman's Handiwork in Mod. Homes* I. 57 Turcoman, when ravelled, produces a superb fringe, like soft chenille. **1885** E. W. LIGHTNER in *Harper's Mag.* Mar. 531/2 An autograph *portière* with alternate stripes of 'crazy patch-work' embroidered on crimson turcoman. **1962** C. W. JACOBSEN *Oriental Rugs* I. vi. 63 Up until 1940, all rugs known as Turkomans or Bokharas..came from Turkestan. **1975** P. SOMERVILLE-LARGE *Couch of Earth* iv. 54 On the floor..were good carpets, mostly small Turcomans.

4. *attrib.* or as *adj.* Of or pertaining to this people, their language, or the region they inhabit. **Turcoman carpet, rug**, a soft, rich-coloured carpet made by the Turcomans.

1613 PURCHAS *Pilgrimage* (1614) 44 Some also attribute the Turkes or Turkeman Nation to this name and Authour. **1687** A. LOVELL tr. *Thevenot's Trav.* II. 44 A score of Turcoman Horsemen, armed with Muskets and Lances. **1798** *Brit. Critic* XI. 34 The Turcoman nymphs there spoken of, are not, by any means, the damsels of the country we now denominate Turkey. **1842** J. B. FRASER *Mesopot. & Assyria* xv. 366 Of hares there are two kinds; the Turkoman variety, which haunts the plains, and that of the desert, with long hair and ears. **1859** *Blackw. Mag.* Oct. 428/1 The Arab and Turcoman women go unveiled. **1901** SKRINE *Sir W. W. Hunter* xxi. 450 The feats of Alexander are still told with bated breath in the Turkoman nomad's tent. **1901** J. K. MUMFORD *Oriental Rugs* xii. 235 One division of these Turkoman carpets, which avoids on the one hand close adherence to the Bokhara device, and on the other the latch-hook style of the Yomuds, is called Beshir. **1911** B. HOLLAND *Life Dk. Devonshire* I. xiv. 321 Some new advance across the Turcoman steppes. **1922** H. CLARK (*title*) Bokkara, Turkoman and Afghan rugs. **1975** *Oxf. Compan. Decorative Arts* 791/1 A design peculiar to Turcoman rugs is that known as katchli.

turcopole ('tɜːkəʊpəʊl). *Hist.* [ad. med.L. *Turcopōlus* (Orderic. Vital.) *-pūlus* (Matt. Paris),

Turcoplus (Roger Hoveden), in Byzantine Gr. *Τουρκόπουλοι* or *-πουλα*, according to Albert Aq. (in Du Cange) f. *Τουρκο-* TURK + *πῶλος* foal, young animal, in late Gr. 'child', L. *pullus* young animal, applied to children of a Turkish or Saracen father and Greek mother. So OF. *turcople*.] A light-armed soldier of the Order of St. John of Jerusalem.

[**1852** SIR J. TAAFFE *Hist. Order St. John* I. I. iii. 191 Of *Turcopili* we read in old chronicles they were light cavalry, but on other occasions they had cuirasses. There were a corps of them kept by the Emperor of Constantinople.] **1896** *Dict. Nat. Biog.* XLVII. 336/2 He [John Rawson] was appointed [in 1527] turcopolier or commander of the turcopoles or light infantry of the order.

turcopolier ('tɜːkəpəˌlɪə(r)). *Hist.* Forms: 5 **turkepler, twrkepler,** 6 **turkeplyer, Turkeiplier, Turcuplyar,** 6–7 **Turcoplier,** 8– **Turcopolier.** [ad. med.L. *turcopolerius* (Statutes of Order Hospitallers, xix. 7), also *-ārius*, f. *Turcopolus*: see prec. In F. *Turcopolier*, OF. *turcoplier*, *Turcupler*: see -IER 2.] The commander of the turcopoles or light-armed soldiers of the order of St. John of Jerusalem (later of Rhodes, and Malta).

1481 *Cely Papers* (Camden) 60 My loorde and the turkepler goys to the Rodys togyddyr. *Ibid.* 63 Twrkepler. **1527** SIR R. WESTON *Let. to Wolsey* 12 Apr., The Turkeplyer hath evermore bene wont to succede the master of Sainct Johns in his rome. *a* **1548** HALL *Chron., Hen. VIII* 204 The Lorde Master appoynted the Prior of Rome and the Turcuplyar of England to be Capitaynes of this enterprise. *Ibid.*, The Turkeiplier with .vi. English knyghtes were appoynted to defende the Molle or Peere at the hauen mouthe. **1599** HAKLUYT *Voy.* II. I. 83 Sir Iohn Bourgh Turcoplier of England, chiefe captaine of the succours of the sayd posterne of England. *a* **1648** LD. HERBERT *Hen. VIII* (1649) 461 They never attained higher dignity then the Turcoplier or Captains place. **1709** STRYPE *Ann. Ref.* I. xxii. 231 Shelly..went..to Malta, to establish his office and dignity of Turcopolier for the English nation. **1788** tr. *Bisani's Pict. Tour Europe*, etc. 20 The different Nations of which the Order is composed..have each of them chiefs, who are here called Piliers... The Pilier of Germany is Grand Chancellor; and that of England, Turcopolier, or General of Infantry. **1887** DOWDEN *Shelley* I. 1 Sir Richard as English Grand Prior enjoying the eminent title of Turcopolier.

turd (tɜːd). Not now in polite use. Forms: 1, 3–6 **tord,** (3 **tort**), 4–6 **toord,** 6 **toorde,** 5–6 **torde,** 5–7 **turde,** 6 **tourd, -e, towrde,** *Sc.* **tuird,** 5– **turd.** [OE. *tord*, = MDu., MFl. *torde, tort*, (whence also early mod.Du. *tort-wevel* (Kilian), OE. *tord-wifel*, ON. *tord-ýfill*, OSw. *tord-öfvil*, Sw. *tordyfvel*, Norw. *tordivel*, *-yvel*, dung-beetle, sharn-bug), prob.:—IndoEur. **drtó-*, pa. pple. of **der-* to tear, split. See Falk and Torp *Etymol. Wbch.* s.v. *Torbist*. Cf. also *tirdle, trottle*, TRATTLE, TREDDLE.]

1. a. A lump or piece of excrement; also, excrement, ordure.

c **1000** *Sax. Leechd.* II. 62 Swines tord. *Ibid.* 322 Culfran tord. *Ibid.* 330 Niwe horses tord. *a* **1250, 13..** [see b]. **1382** WYCLIF *Zeph.* i. 17 The blood of hem shal be shed out as erthe, and the bodyes of hem as tordis. **1388** —— *Isa.* v. 25 The deed bodies of hem weren maad as a toord [**1382** drit] in the myddis of stretis. *c* **1400** *Lanfranc's Cyrurg.* 194 Sprynge þeron poudre maad of tapsia,..& tordis of a culuere. **1483** *Cath. Angl.* 189/2 An Horse turde, *donarium*. **1553** BALE *Vocacyon* 45 Yet will a toorde be but a stinkinge toorde, both in smele and syght, pepper him and bawme him ..as wele as they can. **1651** C. CARTWRIGHT *Cert. Relig.* I. 91 No marvel that he [Luther] is so taxed for his stincking repetition of turds and dunghils. *c* **1720** W. GIBSON *Farrier's Dispens.* ix. (1734) 232 Turd and all manner of filth. **1761** *Brit. Mag.* II. 63 Thatch your house with t——d, and you'll have more teachers than reachers. **1922** JOYCE *Ulysses* 649 The horse..added his quota by letting fall on the floor.. three smoking globes of turds. **1928** in A. W. Read *Class. Amer. Graffiti* (1935) 81 Now and then a fart is heard Mingling with a dropping turd. **1968** *Listener* 1 Aug. 152/2 His protest at the killing in Vietnam is at least original: he parcels up a rich turd and mails it to the White House. **1981** N. GORDIMER *July's People* 35 It was true that it was difficult to get the children to remember to bury the paper along with the turd.

b. As a type of worthlessness or vileness.

a **1250** *Owl & Night.* 1686 A tord [*v.r.* tort] ne yeue ic for eu alle. **13..** *Guy Warw.* (A.) 3704 þou nart nouȝt worþ a tord. **1382** WYCLIF *Phil.* iii. 8 Alle thingis..I deme as toordis, that I wynne Crist. *c* **1450** *Debate Carpenter's Tools* 110 in Hazlitt *E.P.P.* I. 83 Thou arte not worth a tord. **1619–20** *Archdeaconry of Essex Minutes* lf. 265 (MS.) He did demaunde rent of one who holdeth some land which was given..for the poore of the same parishe, who bid a turde for him and a turde for them.

c. In coarse abuse; also applied to a person as a term of execration or contempt. Cf. SHIT *sb.* 1 b.

c **1450** *Mankind* 127 in *Macro Plays* 6. *a* **1518** SKELTON *Magnyf.* 397 Do away, I say, the deuylles torde! **1598** E. GILPIN *Skial.* (1878) 37 The foul-mouthd knave wil call thee goodman Tord. **1614** B. JONSON *Bart. Fair* I. iv, Good Master Hornet, turd i' your teeth, hold you your tongue. **1936** A. HUXLEY *Eyeless in Gaza* xxii. 315 'But why not?' the poor old turd kept asking. **1944** D. WELCH *In Youth is Pleasure* viii. 152 Somebody called Woods a dirty old sod, another called him a great turd. **1965** HOWARD & WEST *Making of Prime Minister* xiii. 204 A purple-faced steward walked up to a scrawny, pale heckler and yelled, 'Shut up, you ignorant turd!' **1978** B. FREEMANTLE *Clap Hands* ix. 66 The man..could make everyone else feel a turd.

2. *attrib.* and *Comb.*, as ***turd-monger***; also ***turd-coloured, -eating, -faced*** adjs; **turd-bird**, local name for species of Skua (*Stercorarius*).

1550 BALE *Apol.* 112 That torde monger, whych dysdaynynge my preciouse preceptes, presenteth me with his vile dirty donge. *a* **1585** POLWART *Flyting w. Montgomerie* 787 Tuirdfacit, ay chaisit, almaist fyld for ane theif! *a* **1704** T. BROWN *Walk round Lond., Thames* Wks. 1709 III. III. 59 Out you nasty T——d colour'd dog. **18..** ATKINSON *Provinc. Names Birds* (MS.), *Turd-bird*, a provincial name for Richardson's Skua. **1969** Turdeating [see *cock-sucking* ppl. adj. s.v. COCK *sb.*[1] 23]. **1978** in R. Quirk *Style & Communication in Eng. Lang.* (1982) ii. 33 Lofty structures of turd-coloured brick..seemed to be deserted. **1978** J. KRANTZ *Scruples* x. 295 Those turd-eating Mexican border guards'll put you away.

Hence **'turdish** *a.*, characteristic of a 'turd' or contemptible person.

1936 A. HUXLEY *Eyeless in Gaza* xxii. 315 'Turds to the core,' he said. 'So they can't think anything but turdish thoughts.' **1966** *Punch* 12 Jan. 64/2 An aristocratic, even Byronic work which finds strident anti-communism turdish.

turdiform ('tɜːdɪfɔːm), *a. Ornith.* [ad. mod.L. *turdiform-is*, f. L. *turdus* thrush: see -FORM.] Having the form or appearance of a thrush; thrush-like. So **turdine** ('tɜːdaɪn) *a.* [-INE[1]], belonging to the sub-family *Turdinæ* of true thrushes; **'turdoid** *a.* [ad. F. *turdoïde* (Temminck, 1823)], akin to a thrush; *spec.* belonging to the family *Turdidæ*.

1874 A. R. WALLACE in *Ibis* Oct. 409 Typical or Turdoid Passeres. Wing with 10 primaries. **1890** *Field* 12 Apr. 517/3 The three leading forms of Turdine families, viz., Thrushes, Warblers, and Flycatchers, are well characterized.

turdion, var. of TORDION.

turdy ('tɜːdɪ), *a.* [f. TURD + -Y.] Full of, befouled, or defiled with ordure; †of or pertaining to excrement, fæcal (*obs.*).

c **1600** *Timon* I. iv. 11 *G.* Bloudy. *P.* Nay, rather, turdy. **1605** B. JONSON *Volpone* II. ii. **1611** COTGR., *Stercorin*.. Excrementall, turdie. **1668** CULPEPPER & COLE *Barthol. Anat.* I. ii. 26 The *Fermentum stercoreum* or turdie Leaven, which turns the Excrements of the Chyle into plain Turds.

ture, obs. or dial. form of TURF *sb.*[1]

tureen (tə'riːn, tjʊ'riːn). Forms: *α.* 8 **terrene, terene,** 8–9 **terrine,** 9 **tereen;** *β.* 8 **turen(n)e, -ein, turrene,** 8– **tureen.** [a. F. *terrine* a large circular flat-bottomed earthenware dish, as a milk-pan, in OF. *therine* (1412 in Godef. *Compl.*), fem. of OF. *terrin* of earth, earthen:—pop.L. **terrin-us*, f. *terra* earth. In English first spelt etymologically *terrene, terrine*, and later corrupted to *turein, tureen*, from phonetic equivalence of *terr-* and *tur-*, and then perh. conformed to the place-name *Turin*.] A deep earthenware or plated vessel (usually oval) with a lid, from which soup is served. Also a smaller vessel of similar shape for sauce or gravy.

α. **1706** PHILLIPS (ed. Kersey), *Terrine* (Fr.), an Earthen Pan. **1708** W. KING *Cookery* 298 In their gilt plate all delicates were seen And what was earth before became a rich terrene. **1745–6** MRS. DELANY in *Life & Corr.* (1861) II. 416 Did I write you word we had got a new terene? The.. chasing is mighty well done: it holds six quarts, and has a very light look. **1760** H. WALPOLE *Lett. to Montagu* cxx, The house is..loaded with terreens, philigree, figures, and every thing upon earth. **1779** FORREST *Voy. N. Guinea* 244 The contents of the small terrenes were put into eight large ones, consequently jumbled together; but, fish with fish, and fowl with fowl. **1865** ELIZA METEYARD *J. Wedgwood* I. 227 Ordinary jugs, globular teapots, circular terrines, and other articles. [*Note.*] The old term..the one preferred and always used by Josiah Wedgwood.

β. **1752** G. WHITE *Acc. Bk.* in *Selborne* etc. (1877) II. 323 A round China-turene. **1761** *Ann. Reg.* 242 First service,.. turrenes, fish, venison, etc. **1769** *De Foe's Tour Gt. Brit.* (ed. 7) I. i. 2 They have already made large Quantities of Tea-Cups, Saucers, Plates, Dishes, Tureins. **1771** GOLDSM. *Haunch of Venison* 82 At the bottom was tripe, in a swinging tureen. **1776** *Pennsylvania Even. Post* 27 Apr. 212/1 Blue and white and enamelled sauce Turennes, 2 sizes. **1910** *Civ. Serv. Supply Assoc. Catal.* 1427 Dinner Services, 61 pieces, ..2 Sauce Tureens and Stands, 1 Soup Tureen and Stand.

Hence †**tu'reener**, a dish of various meats, etc. baked in a closed pot or tureen; cf. HOT-POT 2; **tu'reenful**, as much as a tureen contains.

1728 E. SMITH *Compl. Housewife* 101 To make a Tureiner. Take a China Pot or Bowl, and fill it [with]..Beef steaks.. Veal steaks..Forc'd meat..Chickens, Pigeons,.. Rabbets ..; Season..every Thing as you put it in..: Then put in a quart of Gravy,..and cover it close with a Lid of Puff-paste. .. Eight hours will bake it. **1883** 'ANNIE THOMAS' *Mod. Housewife* 58 The making of one tureenful of soup. **1895** KIPLING *Wee Willie Winkie* (1896) 3 Shovelling down his ice by tureenfuls.

tureile, turel, var. TOURELLE *Obs.*

turet, -ette, obs. forms of TURRET.

turf (tɜːf), *sb.*[1] Forms: 1– **turf;** also 4–7 **turfe,** 4–5 **torf,** 4 (8–9 *dial.*) **turff,** 6–7 **turffe,** (5 **turfh,** 6 **turph, tourffe, torve, towrve,** 6–7 **turue,** 7 **turfth, terf, turph**); 6 **toure,** *Sc.* 6– **turr,** (8–9 **toor, ture,** 9 **tour, -e,** etc.). *Pl.* 1 **tyrf;** 3–6 **turues** (v), (4–5 **-uys,** 6 *Sc.* **-uis**), 4–7 **torues** (v), (4–5 **toruys**), 6– **turves** (*Sc.* 6 **tirvis**); 5– **turfs** (6 **tyrfes,** 6–7 *Sc.* **turreffis, turres, -is**). *β.* 6 **troffe,** 7 **truffe,** 7–9 **truff;** *pl. Sc.* 6–7 **truiffis,** 6–8 **troves, -is.** [OE. *turf* fem. cons. stem (gen.-dat. sing. and nom.-acc. pl. *tyrf*): Common Teut. (with variation of gender and declension); cf. OFris. *turf* (EFris. *turf*); OS. *turf*, (MDu. *torf, turf*, Du. *turf*), MLG., LG. *torf* (whence mod.Ger. *torf* peat); OHG. *zurba*, *zurf* 'terra avulsa, cespes', sod; ON. *torf* (Norw. *torv*, Sw. *torf*, Da. *tørv*):—OTeut. **turb-*, from Indo Eur. **drbh*: cf. Skr. *darbhá* tuft of grass, f. *drbh* to make into tufts, string together. From the Teut. came also med.L. *turba* (cf. TURBARY), F. *tourbe* (1200), It. *torba*, Sp. *turba*.]

1. a. A slab pared from the surface of the soil with the grass and herbage growing on it; a sod of grass, with the roots and earth adhering. Also, in early quots., a small portion of the sward *in situ*.

c **725** *Corpus Gloss.* (O.E.T.) 452 *Cespites* (pl.), tyrb. *a* **1000** *Prose Life Guthlac* xv. (1848) 64 Hi þa [flaxan] ȝehyddon under anre tyrf. *c* **1000** *Sax. Leechd.* I. 290 Ðeos wyrt..of anre tyrf maneȝa boȝas asendeþ. *c* **1122** *O.E. Chron.* an. 189 þa ȝewrohte he [Seuerus] weall mid turfum, & bred weall ðær on ufon fram sæ to sæ. *c* **1205** LAY. 15395 Vortigerne þe king Bi-tæhte heom al þis lond þ ne bilæfde him an heonde a turf of londe. *a* **1250** *Owl & Night.* 1167 Hervore hit is þat me þe suneþ & þe totoreuþ & tobuneþ Mid staue & stone & turf & clute. *a* **1300** *Cursor M.* 16762 + 120 (Cott.) War-on he miȝt dee fayre, Ne a torf of herd erth. *c* **1386** CHAUCER *Merch. T.* 991 A bench of turues [*v.rr.* turves, torues] fressh and grene. *c* **1482** J. KAY tr. *Caoursin's Siege of Rhodes* (1870) ¶ i 1 They made certayn dyches..and couered theym with grene bowes, and afterward they putted erthe and turues uppon the same. **1550** BALE *Eng. Votaries* II. 57 b, His owne clergye wold scarsely suffer hym to be buryed about the church vnder turfes or soddes of the grasse. **1551** ROBINSON tr. *More's Utop.* I. (1895) 29 Vpon a benche couueryd wyth grene torues, we satte downe. **1691** NORRIS *Pract. Disc.* 252 There are some..that..will readily part with the great Reversion of another World for a Turf of Ground in present Possession. **1776** WITHERING *Brit. Plants* (1796) II. 509 In a turf containing 6 plants the roots were all distinct. **1832** *Planting* 53 in *Libr. Usef. Knowl., Husb.* III, The coping consisted of a row of turfs laid with the grass side upwards. **1851** GLENNY *Handbk. Fl. Gard.* 40 The compost in which it should be grown is loam from rotted turves.

b. *collect.*, as a substance or material.

1565 STAPLETON tr. *Bede's Hist. Ch. Eng.* 16 A trench and a rampaire of turue and timber, thyck fenced with bulwarkes and turrets. **1598** BARRET *Theor. Warres* III. ii. 132 A number of other places fortified with earth and turfe onely. **1774** M. MACKENZIE *Maritime Surv.* 66 Cause Turrets, or Signals, of Stone or Turf, to be built. **1821** BYRON *Cain* III. i, They to me are so much turf And stone.

†**c.** A clod of earth. Also *fig.* cf. CLOD *sb.* 4. *Obs.*

1607 MARSTON *What you will* II. i, He is a turfe that will be slave to man. **1674** ABP. LEIGHTON in *Lauderdale Papers* (Camden) III. 76 Those pains and distempers that hang about this litle crazy turf of earth y^t I carry.

†**d.** A sod cut from the turf of an estate, etc., as a token or symbol of possession. Also in phrase ***turf and twig***. *Obs.*

1585 in H. Hall *Soc. Eliz. Age* (1886) 239 Delyvered lyke possession..by a turffe cutt there. **1613** R. HARCOURT *Voy. Guiana* 42, I tooke possession of the land, by turfe and twig. **1643** TRAPP *Comm. Gen.* xiv. 23 The most High God, possessour of heaven and earth, who hath sent me with this bread and wine, as by turfe and twig, as by an earnest, and a little for the whole, to give thee possession of both.

2. a. *collect. sing.* The covering of grass and other plants, with its matted roots, forming the surface of grassland; the greensward; growing grass. Also *fig.*

c **890** tr. *Bæda's Hist.* v. vi. (1890) 400 Sum stan ðære eorðan ȝelic mid ðinre tyrf bewriȝen. *a* **1000** *Gloss.* in Wr.-Wülcker 236/18 *Feraces glebas*, þa wæstmbære tyrf. *Ibid.* 240/27 *Florei cespitis*, blowendre tyrf. **1387** TREVISA *Higden* (Rolls) II. 15 Vnder þe torf of þe lond is good marl i-founde. **1600** SHAKS. *A.Y.L.* III. iv. 52 The Shepheard..Who you saw sitting by me on the Turph. **1634** MILTON *Comus* 280 They left me weary on a grassie terf. **1721** BRADLEY *Philos. Acc. Wks. Nat.* 4 The first Stratum immediately under the Turff, a yellowish Clay. **1838** LYTTON *Alice* I. i, The first few flowers and fresh turf of the reviving Spring. **1895** G. W. SMALLEY *Stud. Men* 144 Sunny glades clothed in rough turf.

b. as a substance or material.

1601 HOLLAND *Pliny* XVII. xiv. 518 To preserve it [the graft] with turfe and mosse against the injurie of rain and cold. **1632** LITHGOW *Trav.* x. 429 These Fabrickes are.. erected in a singular Frame of Smoake-torne straw, greene long prick'd truff [*ed.* **1682** turff], and Raine-dropping watles. **1706** HEARNE *Collect.* 12 Apr. (O.H.S.) I. 223 The.. Garden..he order'd to be cover'd with Green Turff. **1874** J. D. HEATH *Croquet Player* 87 If the subsoil be poor, the turf should not be placed directly on it, but on a layer of good earth some inches thick.

3. a. A slab or block of peat dug for use as fuel.

But in many districts *turfs* are distinguished from *peats*, as being pared from a dry surface, containing roots of grass and recent herbage, and being lighter coloured, while *peats* are usually dug from a 'moss' or bog, and consist chiefly of long-decayed and compressed vegetable matter, black or dark brown, formed from Sphagnum and other mosses.

c **1300** *Havelok* 939 He bar þe turues, he bar þe star, þe wode fro the brigge he bar. **1363** *Cockersand Chartul.* (Chetham Soc.) I. 64 To delfe turvez and carye at theyr wylle in ye mosse of Gayrstang. **1398** TREVISA *Barth. De P.R.* XV. lviii. (Bodl. MS.) Myres and mores in þe whiche þei diggeþ turues and makeþ fuyre þereof in stede of wode. **1506**

Reg. Mag. Sig. Scot. I. 623/2 Licentiam ad capiendum genestam, petas et glebas, viz. *le hadir, petis et turffis.* **1536** *Act 28 Hen. VIII* in Bolton *Stat. Irel.* (1621) 77 The third part of all the tythe torves. **1557** *Peebles Burgh Rec.* (1872) 235 Castand tirvis..without licence. **1592** *Reg. Mag. Sig. Scot.* 755/1 Turris. **1604** *Urie Court-bk.* (1892) 4 Fewaill..syik as petteis, turris, or haidder. **1637** *Reg. Mag. Sig. Scot.* 237/2 Cum..libertate lucrandi *lie peittis plodis* et *truffis* in maresia sua. **1709** Lady Grisell Baillie *Househ. Bk.* (1911) 77 For 8 darg troves casting at 6 pence per day. **17..** *Old Song* in Jamieson s.v. *Tour*, O! is my corn a' shorn, he said, Or is my toors a' won? **1809** *Med. Jrnl.* XXI. 7 Turfs or peat, dug for fuel in the fenny parts of Cambridgeshire. **1822** C. W. Wynn in Dk. Buckhm. *Mem. Crt. Geo. IV* (1859) I. 275 There are considerable apprehension in Ireland of distress from the utter failure of the potatoes,..and of the turves which they were prevented by the wet from cutting.

b. *collect.* as a substance; peat.

1510 in *10th Rep. Hist. MSS. Comm.* App. v. 394 Anny man to bring in wode, troffe, or vattil. **1573** Tusser *Husb.* (1878) 133 Er winter preuenteth,..get home with thy wood, ..both timber and furzen, the turfe and the cole. **1610** Holland *Camden's Brit.* (1637) 500 Abundance of turfe gotten for fewell. **1725** *Bradley's Fam. Dict.* s.v. *Turfing Spade*, In some Counties they call that *Turf*, which in others they name *Peat*, which is dug out of Fenny and Moorish Grounds. **1796** Morse *Amer. Geog.* I. 523 There is said to be coal on Raritan river,..and turf in Bethlehem. **1818** Scott *Rob Roy* xxvii, Swamps, green with treacherous verdure, or sable with turf, or, as they call them in Scotland, peat-bogs. **1866** Rogers *Agric. & Prices* I. ii. 12 All tenants had right of pasture, and sometimes of turf. **1878** Huxley *Physiogr.* 233 Accumulations of partially decomposed vegetable matter form the substance known as peat or turf.

4. ***the turf*** (often with capital T).

a. The grassy track or course over which horse-racing takes place; hence, the institution, action, or practice of horse-racing; the racing world.

1755 *Gentl. Mag.* Apr. 153/1 If you are a true sportsman, and have the honour of the turf at heart. **1771** P. Parsons *Newmarket* I. p. ii, The heroes of the Turf. **1785** Grose *Dict. Vulg. Tongue*, *Man of the turf*, a horse racer, or jockey. **1803–5** W. Pick *Turf Reg.* (title-p.), All the Horses..that have appeared on the British and Irish Turfs as Racers. **1838** Lytton *Alice* III. v, Have you any horses on the turf? **1849** Macaulay *Hist. Eng.* iii. I. 315 Already..there was among our nobility and gentry a passion for the amusements of the turf.

b. *transf.* The road or street as the milieu of prostitutes, tramps, etc.; esp. ***on the turf***, engaged in prostitution. *slang.*

1860 Hotten *Dict. Slang* (ed. 2) 241 *On the turf*, one who occupies himself with race course business; said also of a street-walker. **1899** 'J. Flynt' *Tramping* I. ii. 28 The road proper, or 'the turf', as the people who toil along its stretches sometimes prefer to call it, is low life in general. **1936** H. Asbury *French Quarter* xii. 369 During [Kate Townsend's] early years 'on the turf', as the saying went, she was..thrifty and ambitious. **1962** Parker & Allerton *Courage of his Convictions* v. 179, I wouldn't let her go out on the turf, because of this thing I've got about not poncing. **1984** J. O'Donoghue *Sergeant Horn's Murder Trap* vi. 41 'I might have been one of Ma Dolma's brasses for all you know.' ..'Come off it. You've never been on the turf.'

5. Usu. with substantive in possessive case or with possessive adj. orig. and chiefly *U.S.*

a. The streets controlled by a juvenile street-gang and regarded by them as their territory.

1953 Cramer & Karr *Teen-Age Gangs* i. 4 He had looked forward to drifting pleasantly through the Emerald turf—the term currently used in Brooklyn instead of territory. *Ibid.* 6 No War Hawk was safe if caught on the turf of the Emeralds. And no Emerald was safe on the turf of the War Hawks. **1959** H. Salisbury *Shook-Up Generation* i. 19 These blocks constituted the 'turf' of a well-known street-gang. **1964** [see chippy *sb.* 4]. **1973** 'J. Patrick' *Glasgow Gang Observed* xx. 189 Like most American adolescent gangs..the Young Team attached enormous importance to territory and used the same word 'turf' for it.

b. The part of a city or other area within which a criminal, detective, etc., operates. Cf. patch *sb.*[1] 3 e.

1962 *Sat. Even. Post* 28 Apr. 30/2 Her [*sc.* a social worker's] turf: the lower Bronx. **1966** 'J. Ashford' *Consider Evidence* iii. 23 She [*sc.* a prostitute] claimed she could make a hundred quid a week on her turf. **1971** *N.Y. Times* 10 Jan. xx-1/1, I came to Beverly Hills..to see the stars' home turf. **1976** D. Bennett *Jigsaw Man* (1977) viii. 153 Special Branch would not want to be involved in a killing so far from their own turf. **1978** S. Brill *Teamsters* ii. 48 As both men sat in prison, they were dividing up Teamsters turf.

c. *transf.* and *fig.* A person's sphere of influence or activity.

1970 *Sat. Rev.* (U.S.) 17 Oct. 67/3 The lives of all our children and the very mindedness of society itself cannot be made whole as long as educators are obsessed by indecent needs to defend their own turfs. **1973** *Family Circle* Apr. 120/1 Male occupations are a turf from which women are excluded. **1977** J. F. Fixx *Compl. Bk. Running* xiii. 157 Dogs, he explained, are assiduous defenders of turf. **1982** 'E. Lathen' *Green grow Dollars* vii. 55 They think that, on their own turf, they can overawe Ackerman and Werzel.

6. *attrib.* and *Comb.* **a.** simple attrib., as ***turf-ashes, -back*** (back *sb.*[2]), ***-barge, -bed, -bog, -cart, -charcoal, -fire, -fuel, -ground, -heap, -hole, -house, -land, -moor, -moss, -nook, -pit, -pool, -rick, -shears, -shed, -smoke, -stack, -wain***; made, built, or consisting of turf, as ***turf-cabin, -dike, -hedge*** (Webster, 1828), ***-hut, -monument, -roof, -seat, -walk, -wall***; also in sense 4, as ***turf affair, -associate, -guide, horse, -market, parlance, phrase, -racing, -writer***; **b.** obj. and obj. gen., as ***turf-digger, -getter, -graver, -worker; turf-boring, -cutting, -forming, -getting, -graving*** sbs. and adjs.; **c.** instrumental, etc., as ***turf-bound, -built, -clad, -coloured, -covered, -grown, -laid, -like, -roofed, -spread, -theekit*** (*Sc.*, = thatched) adjs.

1825 T. Hook *Sayings* Ser. II. *Man of Many Fr.* (Colburn) 195 The man to whose guidance I have committed all my *turf affairs. **1763** *Museum Rust.* I. 221 One sort of ashes, which are on all accounts valuable; I mean peat or *turf-ashes. **1818** Scott *Rob Roy* xxviii, I boldly entered the house;..narrowly escaping breaking my shins over a *turf-back and a salting-tub. **1922** Joyce *Ulysses* 218 Father Conmee saw a *turf-barge... Father Conmee reflected on the providence of the Creator who had made turf to be in bogs where men might dig it out and bring it to town. **1811** W. R. Spencer *Poems* 137 This *turf-bed with flow'rs Ever crown'd. **1685** W. King in *Phil. Trans.* XV. 950, I chiefly impute the red, or *turf Bog to it [moss, called in the north of Ireland *old wives' tow*]. **1767** Bush *Hibernia Cur.* (1769) 76 By the natives it [peat] is called turf..and from thence they are usually called turf bogs. **1816** Kirby & Sp. *Entomol.* xxiii. (1818) II. 368 The common *turf-boring crane-fly (*T*[*ipula*] *oleracea*, L.)..moves over the grass with her body in a vertical position. **1787** Winter *Syst. Husb.* 219 Harrowing loosens the hardened, *turf-bound soil. *a* **1748** J. Warton *Ode to Fancy* 5 My footsteps to thy temple guide, To offer at thy *turf-built shrine. **1803** Leyden *Scenes of Inf.* III. 364 On Yeta's banks the vagrant gypsies place Their turf-built cots; a sun-burnt swarthy race. **1865** Alex. Smith *Summ. Skye* v. 103 His school-house was a *turf-cabin. **1557** in *Lanc. & Chesh. Wills* (1884) 61 Implements of husbandrye..ij *torve cartes. **1839** *Civil Eng. & Arch. Jrnl.* II. 145/2 The iron founders..might probably..be supplied with *turf-charcoal. **1782** V. Knox *Ess.* xciii. II. 45 The *turf-clad heap of mould which covers the poor man's grave. **1916** Joyce *Portrait of Artist* (1969) i. 54 He had skin the same colour as the *turf-coloured bogwater in the..bath. **1828** Webster, *Turf-covered. **1898** F. Davis *Rom.-Brit. City Silchester* 21 Over the turf-covered area, denudation is not inoperative. **1868** *Rep. U.S. Commissioner Agric.* (1869) 154 *Turf-cutting field. **1882** F. Pollock in *Macm. Mag.* XLVI. 362 It is subject..to rights of turf-cutting. **1851** Mantell *Petrifact.* iii. §5. 308 A spade used by *turf diggers. **1863** Kingsley *Water Bab.* v. 193 They liked better to brew potheen..shoot each other from behind *turf-dykes. **1818** Lady Morgan *Autobiog.* (1859) 88 All my Irish *turf-fire habits came strong upon me. **1880** Haughton *Phys. Geog.* vi. 301 Its meadows are clothed with *turf-forming grasses. **1838** *Civil Eng. & Arch. Jrnl.* I. 383/2 *Turf fuel is also used most extensively in working the steam engine in many districts of Ireland. **1751** *Phil. Trans.* XLVII. 221, I..have made all possible inquiry from the shepherds, *turf-getters, &c. **1884** *Cheshire Gloss.* s.v. *Turf*, *Turf-getting is a peculiar industry carried on at most of the larger peat bogs, and notably at Lindow Common near Wilmslow. **1483** *Cath. Angl.* 397/1 A *Turfe grauer, *glebarius, turbarius.* *a* **1905** in *Eng. Dial. Dict.* s.v., (N. Yorks.) We cut turves wiv a turf-greeaver. **1411** *Rolls of Parlt.* III. 650/1 Certein Commune of Pasture, and *Turf-gravyng, the whiche the said Lord the Roos claymes. **1599** Nashe *Lenten Stuffe* 8 As stable as clod-mould, or *turffe ground. **1867** J. G. Whittier *Tent Beach* 10 Above..*turf-grown wall They saw the fort flag rise and fall. **1893** Pater *Wks.* (1901) VIII. 147 They went through the endless, lonely, turf-grown tracts. **1868** Yates *Rock Ahead* I. vi, Ruff, Bell, Bailey, and other leading *turf-guides. **1862** Borrow *Wild Wales* lxxxviii. (1911) 453 *Turf-heaps..are in abundance in the vicinity. **1851** —— *Lavengro* xii, He had some difficulty in getting there on account of the *turf-holes in the bog. *c* **1802** S. Chifney *Genius Genuine* (title-p.), Why the *Turf Horses Degenerate. **1569** in *Lanc. & Chesh. Wills* (1884) 35 The haybarne and two bayes of the *turfehowse next the halle. **1789** J. Wesley *Jrnl.* 26 May (1916) VII. 502 Part of them [*sc.* his congregation] were sheltered by a spacious turf-house, and the rest little regarded the rain. **1967** H. Harrison *Technicolor Time Machine* (1968) v. 50 Smoke still drifted down from the chimney hole of the squat, turf house. **1865** Alex. Smith *Summ. Skye* v. 101 We passed a colony of *turf-huts. **1806** J. Grahame *Birds Scot.*, etc. 141 Still shall the *turf-laid seat invite Thy weary limbs. *a* **1625** Sir H. Finch *Law* (1636) 286 Likewise an assise is giuen for common of *Turue land, fishing, and such like. **1756–7** tr. *Keysler's Trav.* (1760) III. 315 That ashes, coals, bones, potsherds, trees, &c. are frequently found in the turf-lands or marshes in Holland and Friesland. **1910** *Westm. Gaz.* 19 Mar. 10/2 Hard at work in converting the barren surface into turf-land. **1841** Lever *C. O'Malley* xxx, A brown, scruffy, *turf-like face. **1884** H. Smart *From Post to Finish* ix, One of the wiliest speculators in the *turf market. **1695** J. Edwards *Perfect. Script.* 286 There are many of these *turf-monuments on Salisbury plain. **1834–5** J. Phillips *Geol.* in *Encycl. Metrop.* VI. 595/2 The *turf or peat moors,..which occur in low ground toward the estuaries of rivers. **1583–4** *Shuttleworths' Acc.* (Chetham Soc.) 17 For workinge at the *tourffe mosse [= bog] nene dayes xiij[d] ob. **1840** A. Laing *Wayside Flowers* (1878) 37 The *truff neuk is toom o' its eenin' supply. **1884** *Marshall's Tennis Cuts* 148 It is only played by what in *Turf-parlance we should call 'crocks', or gentlemen who are not physically capable of taking part in any other outdoor amusement. *Ibid.* 141 From first to last Owen à Biscoe simply cantered away (to use a *turf phrase) from his antagonist. **1678** *Massacre in Ireland* 4 Thousands..were drowned, cast into Ditches, Bogs, and *Turf-pits. **1764** *Museum Rust.* II. cvi. 355 The pits, or *turf-pools as they are commonly called. **1828** *Sporting Mag.* XXII. 235 His happiness was road-racing, as it is now *turf-racing. **1869** Blackmore *Lorna D.* iv, A dozen men, who seemed to come out of a *turf-rick. **1871** W. Morris in Mackail *Life* (1899) I. 247 Close by the sea lay the many gables (black wood with green *turf-roofs). **1842** I. Williams *Baptistery* II. xxxii. (1874) 188 With each her Saviour deigns to dwell E'en in the *turf-roof'd cell. **1818** Scott *Hrt. Midl.* xviii, The old man was seated on the deas, or *turf-seat, at the end of his cottage. **1822** Loudon *Encycl. Gard.* §617 *Turf-Shears.., for cutting the tops of box-edgings and the tufts of grass at the roots of shrubs. **1912** *Daily News* 4 Oct. 6 The peat..has been stacked by now in rick or *turf-shed ready for the winter's burning. **1815** Scott *Guy M.* xxvi, Fish, dried in the *turf smoke of their cabins, or shealings. **1743** Lady Grisell Baillie *Househ. Bk.* (1911) 279 That the *Turf Stack be not tred down. **1881** *Mod. Scott. Poets* III. 75 Thy *turf-theekit roof. **1589** *Shuttleworths' Acc.* (Chetham Soc.) 52 For dryvinge a *turffe-wane a fortenyghte, xvj[d]. **1902** Cornish *Naturalist Thames* 181 Half wild banks, and *turfwalk stretches for nearly a mile among the fields. **1849** Thoreau *Week Concord Riv.* 168 But as it were, by a *turf wall this valley was concealed. **1911** J. Ward *Rom. Era in Brit.* iii. 70 No trace of a turf-wall has been found. **1865** *Daily Tel.* 1 Nov. 5/1 'Warning off' intruders, whether defaulting betters, or *turf-writers whose criticisms were displeasing.

d. Special combs: **turf-accountant**, a bookmaker in horse-racing; **turf-ant**, a small yellow European ant (*Formica flava*, or *Lasius flavus*), living in dry heathy turf; **turf-boy** (see quots.); **turf-cake**, a tea-cake baked in a covered pan among the ashes of a peat-fire; **turf-cutter**, one who is employed in cutting or digging peat; also, a *turf-spade*; also, a paring-plough or *turf-plough*; **turf-drain**, a drain in which the channel is covered by turves placed over it; a sod-drain; so **turf-draining**; † **turf-graft** [graft *sb.*[3]], the right to dig turf for fuel; also, a place where turf is dug, a turbary; **turf-hog**: see quot.; **turf-knife**, a cutting blade set upright in a curved handle, which is pushed along to mark out turves, lines of ditches, etc. (Ogilvie, 1882); **turf-line**, a line formed from turf; *spec.* in an archæological excavation, a layer of soil representing former grassland; **turf-man**, a devotee of the turf, a racing man; † **turf-penny**, a rent or due paid for turbary; **turf-plough**, a plough for paring off the surface to destroy weeds and grubs preparatory to deep ploughing (Knight *Dict. Mech.* (1877); **turf-spade**, a spade for cutting turf or peats; also, a turfing-iron; **turf-spanker**, name for a kind of croquet mallet: see quot.; **turf-stick**, a stick from a turbary or peat-bog; **turf-tie**: see tye; **turf-time**, the season for digging turf, usually between hay-time and harvest; **turf-worm**, the sod-worm (sod *sb.*[1] 5).

1915 *Scots Pictorial* 27 Mar. p. iv, The time when the standing and stability of all *turf accountants are put to the test. **1816** Kirby & Sp. *Entomol.* (1818) II. 94 The little *turf-ants (*F*[*ormica*] *cæspitum*, L.) carry their recruits uncoiled. **1905** *Blackw. Mag.* Jan. 58 There was the *turf boy whose duty it was to fill the turf-boxes. **1906** Somerville & Ross *Irish Yesterdays* 71 In those days the turf-boy was an institution... All day they plied bare-foot between the turf-house and the various fuel-depôts of the house with baskets. **1863** Mrs. Gaskell *Sylvia's L.* iii, Neither cream nor finest wheaten flour was wanting for '*turf-cakes' and 'singing-hinnies'. **1817–18** Cobbett *Resid. U.S.* (1822) 129 The surface of the land is taken off to a depth of two or three inches... In England, this operation is performed with a *turf-cutter, and by hand. **1844** in Whitelaw *Bk. Scot. Song* (1875) 228, I promised to rove With the turf-cutter's daughter. **1860** G. H. K. in *Vac. Tour.* 164 The turf-cutter left her divots unturned. **1805** R. W. Dickson *Pract. Agric.* I. Plate xlviii. 332 Fig. 1. Represents a shouldered *turf-drain. *c* **1830** *Glouc. Farm Rep.* 26 in *Libr. Usef. Knowl., Husb.* III. *Turf-draining answers well, where the turf is strong enough to bear ramming. **1313** *Yorkshire Deeds* (Yorks. Archæol. Soc.) II. 18 [His common of pasture with] le *turff graft [from either moor]. **1483** *Cath. Angl.* 396/2 Turfe grafte, *turbarium.* **1773** *Holme-on-Sp. Moor Inclos. Act* 2 Which privilege of selling turves is called Turf-Graft. **1880** Dawkins *Early Man* viii. 261 The third group consists of the short-horned ox, the *turf-hog, and the goat, which escaped from the servitude of man and reverted to a wild state. **1841** Thoreau *Jrnl.* 20 Apr. in *Coll. Wks.* (1906) VII. 251 The ditching spade and *turf knife may be engraved on the coat-of-arms of his posterity. **1935** E. H. W. Meyerstein *Verse Lett. to Five Friends* (1954) 11 One joy..To take the *turf-line of the Pilgrim Road. **1936** *Proc. Prehist. Soc.* II. 214 Well marked turf lines isolated these ditches from the Iron Age above them. **1957** V. G. Childe *Dawn Europ. Civilization* (ed. 6) i. 3 Fossil turf-lines of Atlantic age. **1975** J. G. Evans *Environment Early Man Brit. Isles* vi. 119 At the surface of the buried soil is a thin stone-free horizon or turf line... This is caused by earthworm sorting. **1818** *Sporting Mag.* II. 214, I never was a *turfman, and am only a spectator. **1881** *Scribner's Mag.* XXII. 642 The form which turfmen love to see in a horse which they have backed heavily. **1282** *Inquis. P.M.* (*C.*) *Edw. I*, File 31. m. 3 (P.R.O.) Coterii et bondi reddunt per annum de consuetudine que vocatur *Turfpeny et grundpeni xlviij s. x d. **1477–8** *Durham Acc. Rolls* (Surtees) 95 Pro j *Turfspade, viijd. **1824** Loudon *Encycl. Gard.* 2101 The turf-spade or turfing iron is employed to separate the individual turves. **1868** Atkinson *Cleveland Gloss.*, *Turf-spade, turf-spit*, the implement or tool used in graving Turves,..a triangular cutting instrument with one upright side, to sever the Turf sideways as well as from the subsoil. **1874** J. D. Heath *Croquet-Player* 25 The bottom of the cylindrical head..is sliced off, so that the part of the mallet that rests on the ground is quite flat. This '*turf-spanker'..met with some opposition at first. **1843** *Florist's Jrnl.* (1846) IV. 86 A mixture of loam and peat, with all the *turf-sticks, etc. contained in it, should be well chopped with the spade and mixed with some rich garden mould. **1912** *Daily News* 28 Feb. 4 Every Dartmoor farmer has his *turf-tie lying somewhere near his farm in a hollow between the tors. **1594** *Shuttleworth's Acc.* (Chetham Soc.) 90 He is to be hired for haytyme, *turvetyme and harvest.

† **turf, tyrf,** *sb.*[2] Forms: 5–6 tyrf(e, turfe, turff(e; *pl.* 6 **turves**: see also tarf, tarve. [f. root of tirve *v.*[2] to turn, roll back.] The turn-over, turn-up, or facing of a cap, hood, sleeve, etc.; a cock (of a

cap, etc.). Also *attrib.*

c **1440** *Promp. Parv.* 494/2 Tyrf, or tyrvynge vp on an hoode or sleue (*K.* tyrfe or turnynge vp aȝen, *S.* tyrwynge of an hoode, *A.* tyrvyng of an hood, etc., *P.* tyrfte or turnynge vp agayne), *resolucio* (H., S. *revolucio*). **1522** in *Archæologia* XXV. 460 Item.. for a black bonett wt a dobill turffe yt was dressyd wt velvett vj s. viij d. **1530** PALSGR. 281/2 Tyrfe of a cappe or suche lyke, *rebras. Ibid.* 284/1 Turfe. **1546–7** in Feuillerat *Revels Edw. VI* (1914) 6 For making of one doble turff Cappe of vellett. **1547** *Ibid.* 10, xij hedpeces to the same Rounde of clothe of Syluer the Turffes of Crymsin Tilsent bownde with yolowe Satten. *a* **1548** HALL *Chron., Hen. VIII* 235 Euery man.. garnyshed their bassenetes with torues lyke cappes of sylke. **1587** FLEMING *Contn. Holinshed* III. 947/1.

turf, *v.*[1] Also 5–7 turve. [f. TURF *sb.*[1]]

1. a. *trans.* To cover with turf; to lay with turf.

c **1430** LYDG. *Min. Poems* (Percy Soc.) 181 Alle the aleis were made playne with sond, The benches torued with newe turvis grene. *a* **1500** *Flower & Leaf* 51 A plesaunt herber.. That benched was, and [al] with turves new Freshly turved. **1644** G. PLATTES in *Hartlib's Legacy* (1655) 187 Barley.. had cover'd the ground so full, that it was as if it were even turfed with the Corn. *a* **1774** TUCKER *Lt. Nat.* (1834) I. 299 After you have new turfed the banks. **1882** CON. F. WOOLSON *Anne* 118 Graves are made and turfed over.

b. *transf.* To place or lay under the turf; to cover with turf, or as turf does; to bury; also *intr.* with *it*, to die and be buried.

1628 [see TURFED *ppl. a.*]. **1763** COWPER *Let.* in Nichols *Lit. Anecd. 18th C.* (1814) VIII. 563 That you may not think I have turfed it, to speak in the Newmarket phrase.. I send you this letter. **1844** J. T. HEWLETT *Parsons & W.* xxxii, Until the governor was turfed. **1859** TENNYSON *Merl. & Vivien* 655 As vast a mound As after furious battle turfs the slain. **1888** G. MEREDITH *Question Whither* i, You who sadly turf us, Believe not that all living seed Must flower above the surface.

2. To dig up or excavate for turf or peat.

1780 INGENHOUSZ in *Phil. Trans.* LXX. 372 Draining a large meer.. which was turfed out in former ages. **1878** J. DAVIDSON *Inverurie* 352 They protected the burgh muir from being indiscriminately turfed.

3. *intr.* To get turf or peat for fuel. *dial.*

1876 *Whitby Gloss.* s.v. *Turf-spit*, 'We're turfing', getting our turves for a winter supply. **1896** BARING-GOULD *Dartmoor Idylls* v. 131 Her wants to take the washing.. and the turving out o' my hands.

4. *trans.* To throw or kick (a person, etc.) forcibly *out* (occas. *off*); also *transf. colloq.* Without const. (*Public School slang*), to kick.

1888 KIPLING *Only Subaltern* in *Under Deodars* 97 The Colonel will turf you out of that in double quick time. **1905** H. A. VACHELL *Hill* ii. 32 Sorry I turfed that little ass so hard... [*Note*] To 'turf', *i.e.* to kick—*Harroviana.* **1925** WODEHOUSE *Carry on, Jeeves!* 90 The old boy turfed me out, Bertie, because he said I was a brainless nincompoop. **1930** J. B. PRIESTLEY *Angel Pavement* viii. 410 She'd bought hundreds of them [*sc.* magazines]. I've just had them turfed out. **1957** C. MACINNES *City of Spades* II. iv. 128 The guv'nor tried turfing them all out at first.. but he's given up the struggle. **1976** J. I. M. STEWART *Memorial Service* iv. 58 These people have become my colleagues. If you use that sort of language about them I'll have to turf you out myself. **1977** 'O. JACKS' *Autumn Heroes* iv. 60 The plane's loaded... I can't turf off passengers.

†**turf,** *v.*[2] Variant of TIRVE *v.*[2] (sense 2 c): cf. TURF *sb.*[2] *Obs.*

1592 GREENE *Def. Conny Catch.* (1859) 60 A beaver hatte turft with velvet, so quaintly as if he had been some Espagnolo trickt up. **1611** BEAUM. & FL. *Philaster* IV. i, Marry, the steward would have had the velvet head [of the deer].. to turf his hat withal.

'turfage. *rare.* [f. TURF *sb.*[1] + -AGE; cf. *herbage, leafage.*] Turf collectively, sward.

1899 CROCKETT *Kit Kennedy* liii, A little short slope of bare gray turfage.

Turfanian (tɜː'feɪnɪən). [f. *Turfan* in Chinese Turkestan + -IAN.] A name given to the western dialect of Tocharian, otherwise known as Tocharian A. Also **'Turfan, Turfa'nese.**

1939 Turfanese [see KUCHAEAN, KUCHEAN]. **1958** PRIEBSCH & COLLINSON *German Lang.* (ed. 4) I. i. 6 Another extinct group of I.E. dialects is.. Turfan (Turfanian, W. Tocharian or Toch. B). **1972** W. B. LOCKWOOD *Panorama Indo-Europ. Lang.* 254 Tocharian A was spoken at Karashahr and Turfan; it is sometimes called Turfanian.

'turfdom. *rare.* [f. TURF *sb.*[1] 4 + -DOM.] The votaries of the turf; the racing community.

1864 *Daily Tel.* 20 Sept., Gentlemen of high standing who are very useful to the rising turfdom of this country.

†**'turfed,** *a. Obs.* Also 6 turft. [f. TURF *sb.*[2] + -ED[2]. See also *tarfed* s.v. TARF.] Provided, adorned, or turned up with a facing, as a cap, a sleeve, etc.

1526 *Lett. & Pap. Hen. VIII*, IV. 846 A black Milan bonnet, double turfed,.. A black single turfed bonnet, with 11½ pair of small aglets. **1547** in Feuillerat *Revels Edw. VI* (1914) 21 One Capp doble turft of grene satten. **1586** *Rates of Customs* Bj, Caps double turfed called cockred caps the dosen xxxiiij .s.

turfed (tɜːft), *ppl. a.* [f. TURF *v.*[1] + -ED[1].] Overlaid or covered with turf.

1628 FELTHAM *Resolves* II. [I.] xxv. 81 Degenerate Man! that hauing so often experimented his Iugling, wilt yet beleeue his fictions, and his turfed Mines. **1649** BLITHE *Eng. Improv. Impr.* (1653) 61 For although I differ from many.. about this denshiring their thin turved Lands, that are pure from roots, twitch, or moss. **1741** RICHARDSON *Pamela* I. 157 The turfed Slope of the fine Fish-pond. **1862** M. HOPKINS *Hawaii* 152 Between the parallel walls, there are turfed spaces terminating suddenly in faults or breaks of some thirty feet depth. **1896** *Edin. Rev.* July 166 Turfed seats with brick fronts appear to be usual.

†**turfel,** *a. Obs. rare*[−1]. In 6 turfill. [Deriv. of TIRVE *v.*[2]; cf. TURFED *a.*] Of a hat: Furnished with a turn or cock.

1558 *Richmond Wills* (Surtees) 126 Inventory 21 January, 1 Mary. In ye Shoppe. Inprimis, xxxj feltts, ij turfill hatts, ij ruggid hatts.

turfen ('tɜːf(ə)n), *a.* [f. TURF *sb.*[1] + -EN[4].] Made of or covered with turf; turfy.

1778 [W. MARSHALL] *Minutes Agric., Digest* 115 A turfen hut might screen us from the tempest. **1824** *Blackw. Mag.* XVI. 582 He pluck'd them from the branches, scattering them Wide o'er the turfen floor. **1849** *Zoologist* VII. 2338 A kind of earthen or turfen wall. **1903** N. MUNRO in *Blackw. Mag.* Jan. 87/2 Sea scents and the odours of turfen fires.

†**'turfer.** *Obs. rare*[−0]. [f. TURF *sb.*[1] + -ER: cf. med.L. *turbārius.*] One who enjoys common of turbary. So †**'turfery** *dial.* = TURBARY.

c **1440** *Promp. Parv.* 507/2 Turvare, *glebarius.* **1769** *Public Advertiser* 2 June 3/4 Right of Pasturage and Turfery on the .. Commons of Sunning-Hill and Wingfield.

turfing ('tɜːfɪŋ), *vbl. sb.* [f. TURF *v.*[1] or *sb.*[1] + -ING[1].] The action of TURF *v.*[1] Also *attrib.* **turfing-iron**, a tool for raising turf; **turfing-spade**, a spade used in digging peat, a peat-spade.

1649 BLITHE *Eng. Improv. Impr.* (1653) 69 [Figure of] The Turving Spade. **1677** PLOT *Oxfordsh.* 249 To be pared off the ground with a turfing Spade. **1725** *Bradley's Fam. Dict., Turf*, or *Green Turf*, Earth cover'd with small and very short Grass; its done two ways either by sowing or Turfing. **1842** LOUDON *Suburban Hort.* 173 Take a piece of turf four feet by four feet, shaped out with the edging-iron, and taken up with the turfing or floating spade. **1852** G. W. JOHNSON *Gard. Dict.* 898/1 The Turfing Iron is for raising or peeling off the turves from the soil. **1896** [see TURF *v.*[1] 3].

turfite ('tɜːfaɪt). [f. TURF *sb.*[1] + -ITE[1] 1 b.] A votary or frequenter of the turf; a racing man. Also *attrib.*

1836 [see BOOK-MAKING 3]. **1846** G. J. DOW (*title*) Calculus, the turfite's computer. **1847** *Illustr. Lond. News* 2 Oct. 219/2 Mr. Pedley, a professional turfite, won the Derby. **1870** *Sat. Rev.* 26 Feb. 275/1 Bankrupt Dukes, spendthrift and profligate Lordlings, turfite peers. **1910** GOLDW. SMITH *Remin.* xi. 180 A patron.. with a good deal of the turfite in his character.

turfless ('tɜːflɪs), *a.* [f. TURF *sb.*[1] + -LESS.] Devoid of turf, bare.

a **1743** SAVAGE *Public Spirit* 44 Turfless, leafless, and uncultur'd plains. **1816** BYRON *Pr. of Chitlon* vii, The flat and turfless earth above The being we so much did love. **1897** *Blackw. Mag.* Mar. 338 The graveyard with its turfless mounds of red earth.

turfy ('tɜːfɪ), *a.* Forms: see TURF *sb.*[1] [f. TURF *sb.*[1] + -Y.]

1. Covered with or consisting of turf; grassy; turfen; in quot. 1733, of arable land: full of weeds and roots, not 'clean'.

1552 HULOET, Turffie, or of turfe, *cespitius, a.* **1610** SHAKS. *Temp.* IV. i. 62 Thy Turphie-Mountaines, where liue nibling Sheepe. **1685** POMFRET *Cruelty & Lust* 149 When Charion saw me from his turfy bed. **1718** ROWE tr. *Lucan* 137 Each to his turphy Table bids his Guest. **1733** TULL *Horse-Hoeing Husb.* xi. 136 The Third Crop made that Land so Foul and Turffy, that 'twas forc'd to lie for a Fallow. **1818** MISS MITFORD in L'Estrange *Life* (1870) II. ii. 23 A turfy, almost inaccessible hill, called Finchamstead Ridges. **1869** TOZER *Highl. Turkey* II. 185 We made our way along a turfy level to the city.

2. Of the nature of or abounding in turf or peat; peaty.

1660 H. MORE *Myst. Godl.* VI. vii. 231 For what of the Earth is not combustible? The exteriour turfy part is ordinary fewel. *a* **1661** FULLER *Worthies, Lanc.* (1662) II. 107 They pierce the Turffie ground, and under it meet with a black and deadish water. **1776** WITHERING *Brit. Plants* (1796) II. 362 *Alisma ranunculoides*.. Lesser Thrumwort Wet turfy bogs... Boggy meadows, common. Bungay, Suffolk. **1842** LOUDON *Suburban Hort.* 509 He uses turfy loam two parts, thoroughly decomposed dung two parts, leaf mould two parts, and very sandy turfy peat two parts. **1870** HOOKER *Stud. Flora* 302 *Centunculus minimus*... Wet turfy and sandy places, local.

3. Pertaining to or characteristic of the turf; suggestive of horse-racing; horsy.

1844 DICKENS *Mart. Chuz.* xxvi, It was an easy, horse-fleshy, turfy sort of thing to do. **1868** YATES *Rock Ahead* II. vii, The man has an air of turfey, horsey life. **1885** 'MRS. ALEXANDER' *At Bay* ii, The talk became.. of the Turf—turfy.

Hence **'turfiness**, turfy character, horsiness.

1905 *Daily Chron.* 22 June 4/4 Each American newcomer feels.. at first horribly out of it in this world of universal turfyness.

†**turgeman**, obs. f. TRUCHMAN, an interpreter: cf. METURGEMAN.

1670 COVEL in *Early Voy. Levant* (Hakl. Soc.) 109 A Greek (who had been in England some time to learn our language, in order to be a Turgeman). **1864** PUSEY *Lect. Daniel* i. 41 The Turgeman was not to be under 50; his was one of the most honourable offices in the Synagogue.

†**'turgence.** *Obs.* [f. TURGENT: see -ENCE.] The action of swelling or becoming swollen.

1671 R. BOHUN *Wind* 34 Suddain turgences of the river Severn.

turgency ('tɜːdʒənsɪ). Now *rare* or *Obs.* [f. TURGENT: see -ENCY.]

1. The condition or quality of swelling or being turgent; a swollen or turgid state.

1650 H. BROOKE *Conserv. Health* 49 A Turgency of Humors. **1684** tr. *Bonet's Merc. Compit.* XIX. 776 The Patients feel a certain sense of turgency in that part. **1713** DERHAM *Phys.-Theol.* IV. ii. 108 Nature repaired the watery Humour again, the Eyes returned to their former Turgency. **1794** G. ADAMS *Nat. & Exp. Philos.* (1806) IV. xlix. 349 This excessive mobility of parts.. of the most rigid bodies.. implies a great turgency of their substance with some very active fluid.

2. *fig.* **a.** An inflated or bombastic style of language.

1654 HAMMOND *Answ. Animadv. Ignat.* iii. §2. 54 This double objection against turgencie of style and barbarousnesse of words. **1660** H. MORE *Myst. Godl.* I. v. 14 Their Tongues are swelled with greater tumor and turgency of speech.

b. An insurrectionary condition or movement.

1660 T. M. *C. Walker's Hist. Independ.* IV. Ded., Yet is it necessary that the history of such turgencies in the State should be communicated, that posterity may hereafter see.. the certain punishment of Treason.

turgent ('tɜːdʒənt), *a.* Now *rare* or *Obs.* [ad. L. *turgent-em*, pr. pple. of *turgēre* to swell out, be swollen or inflated: see -ENT.]

1. Physically swelling or swollen; distended, turgid.

c **1440** *Pallad. on Husb.* IV. 601 The turgent trunke let scarifie, That humour effluent out of it hie. **1657** *Physical Dict., Turgent*,.. usually spoken of the humors of the body when they are in combustion and violent motion. **1664** POWER *Exp. Philos.* I. 59 When [the eyes] are preternaturally distended in an Ophthalmia, and so grow turgent and conspicuous. **1684** tr. *Bonet's Merc. Compit.* XIV. 478 An Asthmatical Woman, whose Lungs [were] turgent with Serum. *a* **1722** LISLE *Husb.* (1752) 332 The cow's.. teats will be turgent and spring forth. **1730–46** THOMSON *Autumn* 693 While Perfection breathes White o'er the turgent film [of the grape] the living dew.

2. *fig.* Swollen or inflated with pride or conceit; bumptious; also, using inflated language.

1621 BURTON *Anat. Mel.* II. iii. VII, Good men doe not alwaies finde grace and favour, least they should be puffed vp with turgent titles, growe insolent and prowd. **1654** HAMMOND *Answ. Animadv. Ignat.* iii. §2. 54 All must be rejected.. which hath any of this turgent style, or these barbarous words in it. **1681** H. MORE *Exp. Dan.* App. iii. 303 This Title were too big and turgent for any private Church.

turgesce (tɜː'dʒɛs), *v. rare.* [ad. L. *turgēscĕre*, inceptive of *turgēre*: see prec. and -ESCE.] *intr.* To begin to swell, to become turgid or inflated.

1864 in WEBSTER; and in later Dicts.

turgescence (tɜː'dʒɛsəns). [ad. med. or mod.L. *turgēscentia*: see next and -ENCE. So mod.F. *turgescence* (1752).]

1. The action or condition of swelling up; the fact or state of being swollen.

1631 JORDEN *Nat. Bathes* xiv. (1632) 106 Animals haue their set times when their spermatick spirits are in turgescence. **1737** BRACKEN *Farriery Impr.* (1763) 47 Any Turgescence or Swelling of the Blood-Vessels. **1843** R. J. GRAVES *Syst. Clin. Med.* ix. 98 That turgescence of the cerebral vessels which precedes apoplectic seizures. **1875** BENNETT & DYER *Sachs' Bot.* 634 The pressure caused by the tension and turgescence of the tissues.

2. *fig.* **a.** Progressive swelling or increase. **b.** Inflation, pomposity, bombast.

1806 W. TAYLOR in *Ann. Rev.* IV. 244 The turgescence of effort travelling at every hitch from head to tail. **1813** —— in *Monthly Rev.* LXX. 451 A marked tendency to affectation, to turgescence.

turgescency (tɜː'dʒɛsənsɪ). [ad. med. or mod.L. *turgēscentia* (Blancard *a* 1693), f. *turgēscent-em*, pr. pple. of *turgēscĕre*: see above and -ENCY.] The quality or state of being turgescent; swelling or swollen condition.

1666 J. SMITH *Old Age* (1676) 117 Inflation, and Turgescency of the Seminary vessels. **1721** QUINCY *Hodges' Hist. Acc. Plague Lond.* 157 A Turgescency or Distemperature of Humours. **1860** *Encycl. Brit.* (ed. 8) XXI. 973/2 The turgescency and relaxation of the organs that perform the offices of feet.

fig. **1710** *Brit. Apollo* II. No. 109. 2/2 It.. proceeds from a certain Turgescency of Soul.

turgescent (tɜː'dʒɛsənt), *a.* [ad. L. *turgēscent-em*: see prec. and -ENT.] Becoming swollen; swelling, growing bigger.

1727 BAILEY vol. II, *Turgescent*, swelling or growing big. **1755** in JOHNSON. **1822–7** GOOD *Study Med.* (1829) I. 378 A turgescent, and especially a varicose state of the internal hemorrhoidal vessels. **1831** T. L. PEACOCK *Crotchet Castle* 6 Arms, three empty bladders, turgescent, to show how opinions are formed. **1857** BULLOCK *Cazeaux' Midwif.* 83 The nipple is more projecting, turgescent, and sensitive. **1891** F. DARWIN in *Nature* 27 Aug. 408/1 In a growing shoot the turgescent pith stretches the cortex.

turgescible (tɜːˈdʒɛsɪb(ə)l), *a.* [f. L. *turgēsc-ĕre*: see above and -IBLE.] Capable of swelling up.
1886 *Med. News* 21 Aug. 214 Similar but less extensive turgescible tissue exists in other portions of the nasal mucous membrane.

turgid (ˈtɜːdʒɪd), *a.* [ad. L. *turgid-us* swollen, inflated, f. *turgēre* to swell: see -ID[1].]
1. Swollen, distended, puffed out.
1620 VENNER *Via Recta* iv. 82 You shall commonly see them..to haue turgid, and strouting-out bellies. **1660** BOYLE *New Exp. Phys. Mech.* v. 52 A Bladder, but moderately fill'd with Air and strongly ty'd, being..held near the Fire,..grew exceedingly turgid and hard. **1669** J. ROSE *Eng. Vineyard* (1675) 33 Proud and turgid buds. **1674** GREW *Anat. Trunks* II. i. §15 The Bladders..being swelled up and turgid with Sap. **1776** WITHERING *Brit. Plants* (1796) III. 618 *Anthyllis*. Cup swoln and turgid; inclosing the legumen. **1797** M. BAILLIE *Morb. Anat.* (1807) 456 The veins of the pia mater have been found turgid with blood. **1846** ELLIS *Elgin Marb.* I. 102 Turgid muscles of the breast. **1860** MAURY *Phys. Geog. Sea* (Low) xi. §523 This condensation is followed by a turgid intumescence.
fig. **1692** BENTLEY *Boyle Lect.* ix. 329 Their Imaginations turgid and pregnant with the glorious Ideas. **1697** EVELYN *Numism.* iii. 82 That turgid Vanity and gross Adulation.
2. *fig.* in reference to language: Inflated, grandiloquent, pompous, bombastic.
1725 WATTS *Logic* II. iii. III. §6 Some..have a violent and turgid manner both of talking and thinking. **1762** FOOTE *Orators* II. Wks. 1799 I. 219 The frothy, the turgid, the calm, and the clamorous [declaimers]. **1781** GIBBON *Decl. & F.* xvii. II. 40 The advocates, who filled the Forum with the sound of their turgid and loquacious rhetoric. **1856** R. A. VAUGHAN *Mystics* (1860) I. 97 His verbose and turgid style, too, is destitute of all genuine feeling.

turgidity (tɜːˈdʒɪdɪtɪ). [f. L. *turgid-us* (see prec.) + -ITY.]
1. The state of being turgid or swollen.
1732 ARBUTHNOT *Rules of Diet* iii. in *Aliments*, etc. 363 Weakness, Wateryness and Turgidity of the eyes. **1820** JEFFERSON *Writ.* (1830) IV. 323 The tendency to turgidity may proceed from debility alone. **1854** JONES & SIEV. *Pathol. Anat.* (1874) 255 Turgidity of the blood-vessels. **1875** BENNETT & DYER *Sachs' Bot.* 700 By *Turgidity* we understand the hydrostatic pressure which the water absorbed by endosmose exercises equally on all sides on the cell-wall.
2. *fig.* Inflation of language; grandiloquence, pomposity, bombast; also with *a* and *pl.* an example of this.
1756–82 J. WARTON *Ess. Pope* (ed. 4) I. iii. 103 Obscurity or turgidity, and a false grandeur of diction. **1788** *Lond. Mag.* 247 They appear to abound with turgidities, and, if they can be called splendid, to dazzle by their splendour. **1827** HARE *Guesses* Ser. I. (1847) 62 The empty turgidity of Dryden. **1903** *Edin. Rev.* Apr. 320 We are willing to forget the latter turgidities [of a poem].

turgidly (tɜːdʒɪdlɪ), *adv.* [f. TURGID + -LY[2].] In a turgid, inflated, or swollen manner; in turgid style or language.
1668 H. MORE *Div. Dial.* II. xviii. 282 A kind of Lunacy ..that reigns thus turgidly in Cuphophron's copious Harangue. **1846** DANA *Zooph.* (1848) 344 Interstices.. usually throughout turgidly elevated. **1910** *Spectator* 29 Oct. 696/2 He..puts turgidly and obscurely what could far better have been expressed in homely idioms.

ˈturgidness. [f. as prec. + -NESS.] The quality of being turgid; = TURGIDITY.
1757 WARBURTON *Lett. to Hurd* 15 Jan. (1809) 227 The turgidness of a young scribbler. **1817** COLERIDGE *Biog. Lit.* i. 2 A general turgidness of diction, and a profusion of new-coined double epithets. **1864** BURTON *Scot Abr.* II. i. 43 That strange flighty turgidness of style which Urquhart had caught by working so much on Rabelais.

†**ˈturgidous,** *a. Obs. rare.* [f. as TURGID + -OUS.] = TURGID.
1601 B. JONSON *Poetaster* v. iii, Barmy froth, puffy, inflate, turgidous, and ventositous are come vp.

turgion: see TORDION.

turgite (ˈtɜːdʒaɪt). *Min.* [Named by Hermann 1845, from the Turginsk mine, Ural Mtns., where found: see -ITE[1].] A hydrous sesquioxide of iron, allied to limonite but containing less water.
1850 ANSTED *Elem. Geol., Min.* etc. §454 Brown hæmatite. Under this..we include..Limonite,..Turgite, Iron ochre, and others. **1888** RUTLEY *Rock-Forming Min.* 122 Turgite.. also gives a red streak.

†**turgman,** obs. f. TRUCHMAN, interpreter.
1615 BEDWELL *Arab. Trudg.* O j, *Tvrgman*, Trudgman, ταργούμενος, δραγούμενος, in the latter Greeke writers, signifieth, an interpretor.

turˈgometer. [irreg. f. L. *turgēre* to swell + -[O]METER.] A measurer of turgidity.
1885 W. GARDINER in *Proc. Roy. Soc.* XXXIX. 232 The plastoid may be regarded as a turgometer, since it indicates the state of turgidity of the cell.

turgor (ˈtɜːgə(r)). *Physiol.* and *Bot.* [a. post-cl. L. *turgor* (Martianus Capella), f. *turgēre* to swell: cf. *horror*, *terror*, etc.] **a.** The normal swollen condition of the capillaries and smaller blood-vessels. **b.** A state of turgidity and consequent rigidity in a cell, as that caused by the absorption of fluid.
1876 tr. *Wagner's Gen. Pathol.* 178 Lymphatics are the chief regulators of the turgor of the tissues. **1882** *Nature* 12 Jan. 258/2 The second phase of the..variation is probably dependent on the diminution of turgor of the excited cells. **1882** *Quain's Med. Dict.* 328/1 With the cessation of the circulation and vital turgor, the skin becomes ashy pale, and the tissues lose their elasticity.

†**turify,** obs. f. THURIFY.
c **1400** MAUNDEV. (Roxb.) xix. 87 Þai bring..incense and oþer thinges swete smelland for to turify þat ymage.

Turinese, var. TORINESE.

Turing machine (ˈtjʊərɪŋ). [Named after A. M. *Turing* (1912–54), English mathematician, who described such a machine in 1936.] A notional computing machine for performing simple reading, writing, and shifting operations in accordance with a prescribed set of rules, invoked in theories of computability and automata.
It is represented as a scanner that has a number of internal states and moves left or right along a tape on which is a sequence of symbols. The symbol read and the state of the scanner determine (in accordance with the rules) what replacement symbol is written, what new state the scanner enters, and what move it makes along the tape before the cycle is repeated.
1937 A. CHURCH in *Jrnl. Symbolic Logic* II. 43 [Abstract of Turing's paper.] Certain further restrictions are imposed on the character of the machine, but these are of such a nature as obviously to cause no loss of generality—in particular, a human calculator, provided with pencil and paper and explicit instructions, can be regarded as a kind of Turing machine. **1955** *Sci. Amer.* Apr. 62/1 To understand a Turing machine we need only know its table of commands. **1961** *Proc. Symposium Appl. Math.* XII. 39 A Turing machine plus random elements is a reasonable model for the human brain. **1969** P. B. JORDAIN *Condensed Computer Encycl.* 550 No Turing machine has ever been physically constructed or realized in hardware as a device for its own sake, but general-purpose digital computers have been programmed to simulate Turing machines. **1984** *Sci. Amer.* May 70/1 Beginning with the intuitive idea that a method is an algorithm—a procedure that can be mechanically carried out without creative intervention—he [*sc.* A. M. Turing] showed how the idea can be refined into a detailed model of the process of computation in which any algorithm is broken down into a sequence of simple, atomic steps. The resulting model of computation is the logical construct called a Turing machine.

turion (ˈtjʊərɪən). *Bot.* [= F. *turion* (15th c.), ad. L. *turio*, pl. *turiōnēs*, formerly also in Eng. use.] A young shoot rising from the ground, produced from a subterranean bud: see quot. 1894.
[**1693** tr. *Blancard's Phys. Dict.* (ed. 2), *Turiones*, the tender Tops of Trees, that grow yearly. **1704** J. HARRIS *Lex. Techn.* I, *Turiones*, amongst Botanick Writers, are the first young tender shoots or tops which any Plants do annually put forth of the Ground.] **1725** *Bradley's Fam. Dict.* s.v. *Sallet*, The gentle Turiones and Tops [of Blite] may be eaten like Asparagus. **1880** GRAY *Struct. Bot.* iii. §2. (ed. 6) 41 In the Turions, or subterranean budding shoots of.. perennial herbs. **1894** OLIVER tr. *Kerner's Nat. Hist. Plants* I. 624 The scale-leaves..developed on subterranean shoots, especially on bulbs, rhizomes, and turions, differ considerably... By turion..is meant a bud originating laterally on underground stem-structures and developing in the summer into a shoot which rises above the ground.
Hence **turioˈniferous** *a.*, producing turions.
1828 in WEBSTER (citing BARTON). **1900** in B. D. JACKSON *Gloss. Bot. Terms.*

‖**turismo** (tuˈrizmo). [Sp., It.] Tourism as an industry or dedicated pursuit (in the Latin countries of Europe).
1926 R. MACAULAY *Crewe Train* I. v. 29 Poor Humphrey is looking quite sick and wan, either with turismo, the motion of the Andorran diligences, or *l'amour*. **1959** *Times Lit. Suppl.* 20 Nov. 679/4 His descriptions of the countries he collected on his speedometer seem more often to be drawn from the handbooks of *Turismo* than from fresh observation. **1977** J. I. M. STEWART *Madonna of Astrolabe* xii. 179 Ravello hadn't changed much... *Turismo* hadn't gained its hoped-for grip.

‖**turista** (tuˈrista). [Sp., lit. = tourist.] A name for a form of traveller's diarrhœa affecting visitors to Mexico.
1970 *New Scientist* 8 Jan. 47/1 An intestinal attack known as gyppy tummy..in the Middle East;..Montezuma's revenge..and turista in Mexico. **1976** M. MILLAR *Ask for me Tomorrow* v. 40 *Turista* is bad enough..but infectious hepatitis is worse. **1980** *Jrnl. R. Soc. Arts* Jan. 90/1 Even avoiding water does not entirely protect me against turista.

turit, obs. Sc. form of TURRET.

Turk (tɜːk), *sb.*[1] Also 4–7 **Turke**, 5 **turque**, 7 **Turc**; 9 **Toork** (sense 1). [= F. *Turc*, fem. *turque*, It., Sp., Pg. *Turco*, *-a*, med.L. *Turcus*, *-a*, Byz. Gr. Τοῦρκος, Pers. (and Arab.) *turk*. A national name of unknown origin. Possibly the same as the Chinese equivalent *Tu-kin*, applied to a division of the Hiong-nu (identified by Deguigne with the Huns), who occupied the country south of the Altaian mountains *c* 177 B.C. (In Persian dicts. *turk* is explained as 'A Turk, a beautiful youth, a barbarian, a robber', but the last three definitions are only applications of the national name, not explanations of its original meaning.)]
1. *Ethnology.* Pl. *Turks.* The name of a numerous and widely spread family of the human race, occupying from prehistoric times large parts of Central Asia, and speaking a language and dialects belonging to the TURKIC branch of the Ural-Altaic (Finno-Tartar, or Turanian) linguistic family (a primary family of co-ordinate rank with the Indo-European or Aryan, and Semitic). Within this linguistic family the Turks are usually held to stand between the Ugrians and Mongols, having closest relationship to the latter group. The form *Toork* or *Tourk* (after Persian) has been used by some (esp. in India) in this wide sense.
From their original home in Central Asia, chiefly from Turkestan, hordes of Turks at various times assailed and conquered other lands. Of these, the best known in the West were those calling themselves, after famous leaders, Seljúk and Osmânli respectively. The former overthrew the Abbasides, or first Muslim caliphs of Baghdad, and founded the Seljúk dynasty in their room; the latter, after embracing Islām, and receiving much Persian and Arab culture, arose on the ruins of the Seljúk empire in A.D. 1300 and became the ancestors of the Osmanli or Ottoman Turks in Asia and south-eastern Europe (see sense 2).
Probably the name *Turk* appears in English first in connexion with the Third Crusade, 1187–1192. The Turks of that date were Seljúks, not Ottomans. Saladin, the antagonist of Richard I, was a Kurd, originally in the service of the Seljúks. In the wider sense 1, the name is of comparatively late use in English and the European langs. generally, the Turks of Central Asia being unknown in Western Europe.
1500–20 DUNBAR *Poems* xxxiii. 5 Me thocht a Turk of Tartary Come throw the boundis of Barbary And lay for-loppin in Lumbardy. **1545** ASCHAM *Toxoph.* I. (Arb.) 80 After them the Turkes hauing an other name, but yet the same people, borne in Scythia. **1815** ELPHINSTONE *Acc. Caubul* (1842) I. 417 The Kuzzilbaushes are members of that colony of Toorks which now predominates in Persia. I call them by this name (which is usually given them at Caubul)... They speak Persian, and among themselves Toorkee. *Ibid.* II. 185 That great division of the human race which is known in Asia by the name of Toork, and which, with the Moguls and Manshoors, compose what we call the Tartar nation. Each of these divisions has its separate language, and that of the Toorks is widely diffused throughout the west of Asia. *a* **1833** SIR J. MALCOLM *Life & Corr.* (1856) I. vi. 91 We were now threatened with an invasion of Toorks and Tartars. **1843** *Penny Cycl.* XXV. 395/1 The Turks-Osmanlis are a branch of the Turks in the larger meaning of the word. *Ibid.*, We cannot precisely ascertain when the Turks (..in the larger meaning of the word) first appeared in Europe. *Ibid.*, The Káyi,..the most illustrious of all [the Turkish tribes], because the Turks-Osmanlis descend from them. **1877** FREEMAN *Ottoman Power in Europe* vii. 286 It is..in the Anatolian peninsula only, that the Turk is really at home. The Ottoman is hardly at home even there; but the Turk, the representative of the earlier and better Turkish races, is at home. **1888** *Encycl. Brit.* XXIII. 658/2 The use of the name 'Turks' has never been limited in a clear and definite way from the time of the Byzantine authors to the present day. To the former, as also to the Arabs, it has a collective sense like Scythians or Huns. *Ibid.*, The Kirghiz..are considered as the typical Turks of the present day, and are described..as being midway between the Mongol and the Caucasian. **1899** J. T. BEALBY in *Times Gazetteer* 1613/2 Thirty years later [than 1017] the Turks—not the Ottomans (Osmanlis), but their predecessors, the Seljuks—invaded the Byzantine Empire for the first time.
2. a. A native or inhabitant of Turkey; formerly, a member of the dominant race of the Ottoman empire; sometimes extended to any subject of the Grand Turk or Turkish Sultan, but usually restricted to Muslims; in earlier times, a Seljúk; from 1300, an Osmanli or Ottoman; one who was, or considered himself, a descendant of the Osmanlis or other Turks. Pl. ***the Turks***, the Turkish people; (now *Hist.*) the Ottomans.
13.. *Coer de L.* 5003 Thre thousand Turkes com, with bost, Betwen Jakes and his hoost. *c* **1375** *Sc. Leg. Saints* xxvi. (*Nycholas*) 591 Lang tyme eftyre with gret were, þe turkis thru iniquite distroyt þe towne of myrre [Myra]. *c* **1400** MAUNDEV. (1839) iv. 26 [Rodes] was wont to be clept Collos; and so callen it the Turkes ȝit. *Ibid.* xiii. 145 But a gret man þat he [the Greek Emperour] sente for to kepe the contree aȝenst the Turkes vsurped the lond & helde it to him self, & cleped him Emperour of Trapazond. *c* **1489** CAXTON *Sonnes of Aymon* xiv. 348 We shall werre styll on goddys enmyes as ben turques & sarrasins. **1517** TORKINGTON *Pilgr.* (1884) 23 We war receyvyd by the Turkys and Sarrasyns. **1547** in Feuillerat *Revels Edw. VI* (1914) 11 Hedpeces to the same, turkes ffasshyon of blewe Red & yolowe sarcenet. **1599** DALLAM in *Early Voy. Levant* (Hakl. Soc.) 79 My drugaman.. was a Turke, but a Cornish man borne. **1634** *Cal. St. Papers, Dom.* 31 May (1864) 44 Complaints out of the west country of divers outrages lately committed in those parts by Turks and pirates. **1644** EVELYN *Diary* 7 Oct., One Turke he much favor'd, who waited on him in his cabin. *a* **1658** J. DURHAM *Exp. Rev.* v. ii. (1680) 275 To redeem so many of them from the bondage of the Turks. **1673** RAY *Journ. Low C.* 140 The Turcs at our being there [Vienna] having taken Neuhausel. **1696** PHILLIPS (ed. 5), *Turk*, a Subject of the Grand Signiors, who is also call'd the Great Turk. **1801** *Med. Jrnl.* V. 352 The debt which England and all Europe had contracted with the Turks for the inoculation of the Small-pox. **1847** MRS. A. KERR tr. *Ranke's Hist. Servia* 24 The Servians, the Bosnians..and the Albanians, once more stood united against the Osmanlis. But the Turks were stronger than all these nations

combined. **1888** *Encycl. Brit.* XXIII. 658/2 At the present day we are wont to restrict the name to the Osmanli Turks, though they themselves refuse to be called Turks, having.. ceased to be such in becoming imbued with Arabo-Persian culture. On the other hand when we speak of Uigurs and Tatars, we mean tribes who style themselves Turks and really are such.

b. ***the Turk***, comprehensively or collectively: the Turks; the Turkish power; also (*Hist.*), the Turkish Sultan, the Grand Turk.

c **1482** J. Kay tr. *Caoursin's Siege of Rhodes* ¶3 In what tyme that thees thynges were thought and counseyled in Constantynople among the turke and his counseyle. **1561** *New Calendar* 17 Jan. in *Prayer-bk. Q. Eliz.* (1890) 194 The good Prince Scanderberg.., a scourge to the Turke. **1581** Allen *Apol.* 18b, Christians of al sortes,..and al other vnder the Turke. **1591** Shaks. *1 Hen. VI*, iv. vii. 73 The Turke that two and fiftie Kingdomes hath, Writes not so tedious a Stile as this. **1605** —— *Lear* iii. iv. 94. **1735** Pope *Prol. Sat.* 198 Should such a man, too fond to rule alone, Bear, like the Turk, no brother near the throne. **1896** *N. Brit. Daily Mail* 17 June 4 The unfortunate lands over which the Turk now exercises his baleful sway. **1898** *Daily News* 7 Sept. 5/4 The Dervishes..animated by an implacable hatred of 'The Turk', which is a comprehensive phrase applied to Egyptians and Englishmen alike.

c. ***the Grand*** or ***Great Turk***, the Ottoman Sultan. Cf. *the Great Khan*, *the Great Mogul*. Now only *Hist.*

c **1482** J. Kay tr. *Caoursin's Siege of Rhodes* ¶6 The turkes ..saydyn that theyr lord the gret Turke was dede. **1503** *Lett. Rich. III & Hen. VII* (Rolls) I. 210 He said that the Grete Turke feared not the pope. **1563** *Homilies* ii. *Place of Prayer* ii. (1859) 348 The Enemie of our Lord Christ, the great Turke. **1615** Bedwell *Arab. Trudg.* N iv. s.v. *Sultan*, For thus they now call the Great Turke,..The Souldan of Stamboli. **1689** *Andros Tracts* I. 165 They were as Arbitrary as the great Turk. **1846** Huxley in *Life* (1900) I. ii. 26, I am in a very fair way, and would snap my fingers at the Grand Turk. **1853** C. Bronte *Villette* iii, He was more than the Grand Turk in her estimation.

†**d.** Applied vaguely to Saracens. *Obs.*

13.. *Coer de L.* 4971 Thre thousand Turkes com at the last, With bowe Turkeys, and arweblaste.

e. ***Young Turks***, a name given in the 20th century to the Ottomans who tried to rejuvenate the Turkish empire, and bring it more into line with European ideas: opposed to ***Old Turks*** who were against such ideals. (See also sense 4.) Also *transf.* (sometimes with lower-case initials): any group of young or relatively young men full of new ideas and impatient for change; esp. a radical or 'progressive' element in a political party. Occas. *sing.*

1908 *Daily News* 5 Aug. 4/7 Will the glorification of the 'Young Turk' kill this expression as one of reproach to be used in the nursery? **1909** [see *Turkdom* below]. *c* **1929** in W. Safire *New Lang. Politics* (1968) 496/2 These new Republican warriors were called the Young Turks, a band of about 20 who had mutinied against the feeble leadership of the Old Guard. For Senators they were young men (average age: 56). **1953** W. S. Churchill in *Ibid.* 497/2 You're just like the Young Turks in my government. **1963** D. Ogilvy *Confessions Advert. Man* (1964) ii. 24 In hiring, the emphasis will be on *youth*. We are looking for young turks. **1971** A. Mizener *Saddest Story* 331 E. E. Cummings and Pound..were writers little calculated to attract the Young Turks, for whom they would seem elder statesmen of the modern movement. **1981** J. Dunning *Deadline* (1982) xvii. 160 Malcolm Dawes had been a career man. He was a young turk, graduating from the FBI Academy in 1952.

3. a. Often used as = Muslim.

(The Turks being to Christian nations the typical Muslim power from *c* 1300.)

a **1548** Hall *Chron., Edw. IV* 233 He..hated hym more then a Panym or a Turke. **1548–9** (Mar.) *Bk. Com. Prayer, Collect Gd. Friday*, Haue mercy upon all Jewes, Turkes, Infidels, and heretikes. *c* **1645** Howell *Lett.* (1650) II. 16 No Jew is capable to be a Turk but he must be first an Abdula a Christian. **1697** Collier *Ess. Mor. Subj.* ii. 137 He is a Christian at Rome, a Heathen at Japan, and a Turk at Constantinople. **1725** Watts *Logic* i. vi. §10 A divine distributes [mankind] into Turks, Heathens, Jews, or Christians.

b. In *to turn Turk*, *become Turk*, and similar phrases. (But also used in senses 2 and 4.)

1592 Kyd *Sol. & Pers.* iii. v, What say these prisoners? will they turne Turke, or no? **1602** Shaks. *Ham.* iii. ii. 287 If the rest of my Fortunes turne Turke with me. **1615** G. Sandys *Trav.* i. 54 No Iew can turne Turke, untill he first turne Christian. **1629** J. M. tr. *Fonseca's Dev. Contempl.* 403 The Souldier, he will turne Turke vpon point either of profit, or of honor. **1632** Lithgow *Trav.* iv. 141 [He] turnd Turke, and was circumcised. **1687** A. Lovell tr. *Thevenot's Trav.* i. 42 Many are perswaded, that when a Jew turns Turk, he must first become Christian, which is very false. **1737** [S. Berington] *G. di Lucca's Mem.* (1738) 282 He offered to turn Turk if they would spare him.

4. *transf.* **a.** Applied to any one having qualities attributed to the Turks; a cruel, rigorous, or tyrannical man; any one behaving as a barbarian or savage; one who treats his wife hardly; a bad-tempered or unmanageable man. Often, with alliterative qualification, ***terrible Turk***; ***young*** or ***little Turk***, an unmanageable or violent child or youth.

1536 *Exhort. North* 56 in Furniv. *Ballads fr. MSS.* I. 306 Thes Sothorne turkes pervertyng owre lawe. **1579** Lyly *Euphues* (Arb.) 42 Was neuer any Impe so wicked and barbarous, any Turke so vyle and brutishe. *a* **1700** B. E. *Dict. Cant. Crew*, *Turk*, any cruel hard-hearted Man. *a* **1845** Hood *Lay Real Life* v, Who said my mother was a Turk, And took me home—and made me work, But managed half my meals to shirk? My Aunt. **1847** Helps *Friends in C.* Ser. i. vii. 114 Why you Mahometan, you Turk of a lawyer—would you do away with all the higher things of courtesy, tenderness for the weaker [etc.]? **1854** *N. & Q.* 1st Ser. IX. 451/1 We often hear of people bad to manage being 'regular Turks'. **1862** *Spectator* 6 Dec. 1363/1 The new generation of Greeks have a real passion for education; without it they say a man is a 'Turk', that last epithet of opprobrium. **1863** Frith in *Autobiog. & Remin.* (1887) I. xxiv. 351 As to Prince William of Prussia, of all the little Turks he is one of the worst. **1874** Sir W. W. Hunter in *Life* xiii. (1901) 228 Mr. Lyall is a terrible Turk at keeping his wife up to her social duties. **1875** Anne Mozley *Ess. fr. Blackwood* 217 A bad temper does seem often favourable to health. The man who has been a Turk all his life lives long to plague all about him. **1891** G. Meredith *One of our Conq.* xxix, The tastes of the civilized man—a creature that is not clean-washed of the Turk in him. **1904** *Police Magistrate* in *Daily News* 26 Nov. 9/2 'You are a young Turk, and a bad Turk, too;..I think I ought to send you to a reformatory school.' **1908** [see 2 e].

b. A person of Irish birth or descent. *slang* (usu. *depreciatory*). Chiefly *U.S.*

In this sense perh. really a derivative of Ir. *torc* boar, hog, as suggested by W. A. McLaughlin (*Dialect Notes* (1914) IV. 147–8); but cf. turkey *sb.*[2] 6b.

1914 in *Dialect Notes* IV. 148 You Italians have the votes, but it takes us Turks to run the government. **1945** Mencken *Amer. Lang.* Suppl. I. 603 *Turk* is used among Roman Catholic priests in the United States to designate a colleague of Irish birth. **1959** *Observer* 1 Mar. 10/1 Their backs are to the wall in a desperate tyre-chain feudal war to protect the integrity of their declining manor against the invasion of 'bubbles and squeaks' (Greeks and Cypriots), 'turks' (Irish) and 'spades' (coloureds). **1971** S. Houghton *Current Prison Slang* (MS.) 17 *Turk*, Paddy, Irishman.

†**5. a.** A human figure at which to practise shooting. **b.** A hideous image to frighten children; a bugbear. *Obs.*

1569 in *Camden's Hist. Eliz.* (1717) Pref. 29 The shotinge with the brode arrowe, the shotinge at the twelve skore prick, the shotinge at the Turke. **1598** Florio, *Manduco*, a disguised or vglie picture vsed in shewes to make children afraid,..a turke, or a bug-beare. **1608** [see prick *sb.* 10b]. **1616** *Manifest. Abp. Spalato's Motives* App. iii. 7 All the rest were but painted posts, and Turkes of ten pence, to fill and adorne the shooting-field. **1631** J. Burges *Answ. Rejoined* 182 The Replier hath set vp a man of cloutes of his owne making, and then shootes at a Turke, as boyes doe.

6. a. A Turkish or Turkey horse. †**b.** A Turkish sword or sabre, a scimitar (*obs.*).

1623 Markham *Cheap Husb.* i. iii. (ed. 3) 42 The best Stallion to beget horses for the warres is the Courser, the Iennet, or the Turke. **1638** Whiting *Hist. Albino & B.* 108 He forthwith unsheathd his trusty Turke, Cald forth that blood which in his veines did lurk. **1831** Youatt *Horse* iii. 29 Charles II sent his master of the horse to the Levant, to purchase brood mares and stallions. These were principally Barbs and Turks.

c. A Turkish cigarette.

1926 'Sapper' *Final Count* iii. 65 Why the devil don't you smoke a Corona Corona, you fool! Put out that Turk. **1935** N. Marsh *Enter Murderer* vi. 71 Cigarette? These are Turks. **1965** 'R. Erskine' *Passion Flowers in Business* v. 60 Fat, oval Turks in a Wedgwood box.

7. *attrib.* or *adj.* = Turkish; also in *comb.*, as ***Turk-like*** adj. and adv., ***-ruled***, ***-worked*** adjs. Also in possessive in names of plants, etc., as Turk's cap, Turk's head, ***Turk's knife***, ***Turk's turban***.

?*a* **1366** Chaucer *Rom. Rose* 923 In his honde holdyng Turke bowes two, fulle wel deuysed had he. **1534** *Acc. Ld. High Treas. Scot.* VI. 193, iij quarteris of taphety turke, price of the elne xiiij s. **1688** R. Holme *Armoury* iii. xiv. (Roxb.) 3/2 These are called Turks knives because they turne vpward in the back towards the end, or point of the blade. **1708** *Lond. Gaz.* No. 4435/4 To be sold.., a true Turk Stalion about 15 Hands high. **1760** J. Lee *Introd. Bot.* App. (1788) 353 Turk's Turban, *Ranunculus*. *a* **1791** Grose *Olio*, *Grumbler* xi. (1796) 44 The best parlour..was furnished with Turk-worked chairs. **1850** Browning *Christmas Eve* xviii, Or Turk-like brandishing a scimetar. **1857** Livingstone *Trav.* Introd. 5 Adopting the Turk-like philosophy of this Scotchman! **1873** W. Cory *Lett. & Jrnls.* (1897) 328 Frankified Turk-ruled Egyptians.

Hence **'Turkdom**, the realm or domain of the Turks; Turkey. ***Young T.***, the party of Young Turks.

1900 *Eng. Hist. Rev.* Jan. 150 For fifty years the whole of Turkdom was then more or less effectively administered by Chinese proconsuls. **1909** Vambéry in *19th Cent.* Mar. 371 The whole Turkish nation, with very few exceptions, belongs to Young Turkdom. Every one who feels Turkish and speaks Turkish is a Young Turk.

turk, *sb.*[2] [ad. F. *turc*; origin and history uncertain. As early as 1688 associated in French with the national name *turc* Turk; but Littré and Hatz.-Darm. treat it as a distinct word.

Boyceau de la Baraudière *Tr. du Jardin* 58 (1688) has 'Les poiriers de bon chrestien en sont sur tous autres endommagez, et c'est pourquoy on a nommé ce ver Turc.' But the American *Little Turk* is said to be named from the crescent-shaped punctures made in the fruit by the female.]

The larva of an insect (perh. of the fruit-bark beetle, *Scolytus rugulosus*) dreaded for the destruction it does to pear-trees by mining under the bark; also, the larva of the cockchafer (Littré). According to *Century Dict.*, the plum-weevil or plum-curculio, *Conotrachelus nenuphar*, which is very destructive to fruit-trees generally, is known as the *Turk* or *Little Turk*.

1712 J. James tr. *Le Blond's Gardening* 173 The great Enemies to Trees, are..Snails, Tons, Turks, and abundance of Worms. *Ibid.* 176 Turks are certain white Worms that get into Trees and eat Holes in them, running betwixt the Bark and the Stem. **1815** Kirby & Sp. *Entomol.* vi. (1818) I. 213 Their ravages have long been known in Germany under the name of Wurm trökniss (decay caused by worms); and in the old liturgies of that country the animal itself is formally mentioned under its vulgar appellation, 'The Turk'.

Turkana (tɜː'kɑːnə). [Native name.] (A member of) an East African tribe living between Lake Rudolph and the Nile; their language. Also *attrib.*

1902 H. Johnston *Uganda Protectorate* II. xx. 887 Turkana has a few more words in it betraying Hamitic.. affinities. **1911** [see Karamojo]. **1930** C. G. Seligman *Races of Africa* vii. 161 The Masai and Turkana are nomadic herdsmen. **1959** A. Moorehead *No Room in Ark* vii. 137 The local tribesmen—people like the Karamojong and the Turkana—have not taken to western civilization in the way nearly all other Africans are doing. **1963** *Times* 7 June 12/3 Thirty-two Turkana tribesmen and women have been killed in inter-tribal fighting in Kenya's Eastern Region. **1977** H. Innes *Big Footprints* i. i. 26 He's a Turkana. He was born up there and he's been back to Lake Rudolph many times. *Ibid.* 27 'Is that Turkana you're talking?'.. 'No. A mixture of Samburu and Swahili.'

turkas, -ass, -eis(e. see turkess(e, turkis, turquoise.

†**turkein.** *Obs. rare.* Also tour-. [a. OF. **turcain*:—L. type *Turcān-us*, f. *Turcus* Turk.] = Turk *sb.*[1]

a **1330** *Otuel* 1380 A turkein þat was ful of prude. *Ibid.* 1392 He smot þe tourkein oppon þe hood.

†**'turken**, *v. Obs. rare.* Also 6 turquen, turkin. [Etymology uncertain. Taken by Skeat as a deriv. of F. *torquer* to twist, 'to writhe, wreath, wind in, wrap about' (Cotgr.), ad. L. *torquēre* to twist; but there are difficulties both of form and of sense; see turkess(e, turkish *v.*

Possibly f. Turk *sb.*[1] + -en[5], referring to the action of the Turks in transforming Christian churches into mosques, or from the Koran being regarded as a transformation or perversion of the Bible.)]

trans. = turkess(e *v.* 2.

1575 Gascoigne *Making of Verse* in *Steele Gl.* etc. (Arb.) 37 This poeticall licence is a shrewde fellow,..it maketh wordes longer, shorter, of mo sillables, of fewer, newer, older..and to conclude it turkeneth all things at pleasure, for example, *ydone* for *done*. **1575** —— *Poesies, Ep. to Rev. Divines* Wks. 1907 I. 7 You shall find it now in this second imprinting so turquened and turned, so clensed from all unclenly wordes. **1587** Golding *De Mornay* xxiii. (1592) 353 They turkining themselues as much as they can into Gods, that is to say into Angels of light, to beguile our sence and imagination with strange vanities. *Ibid.* xxiv. 368 If they chaunce to stumble vpon some good saying for maners or for the life of man, they turkin it a thousand waies to make it seem good for thir purpose. **1607** T. Rogers *39 Art.* Pref. §28 Not either Articles of his owne, lately deuised; or the old newly turkened: but the very Articles agreed vpon by the Archbishops and Bishops.

Turkery ('tɜːkərɪ). [f. Turk *sb.*[1] + -ery: cf. *popery*, *foolery*.] †**a.** The Turkish religion or practice; Islam (*obs.*). **b.** 'Turks' collectively.

1585 W. Whitaker *Answ. Rainolds* 360, I thinke it flat Atheisme and Turkery to denie that Christ was borne of a virgine. **1678** Marvell *Growth Popery* 4 Either open Judaism, or plain Turkery, or honest Paganism. **1709** Strype *Ann. Ref.* I. lvi. 576 A religion of their devising worse than Turkery. **1878** Freeman in *Life & Lett.* (1895) II. 164 The whole accursed den of Jewry and Turkery, clubs, rookeries, and all.

turkes, -ese, -esse, var. turkis, turquoise.

†**Tur'kesco**, *a. Obs. rare.* [a. It. *turchesco*, = obs. F. *turquesque* (Cotgr.).] = Turkish.

1584 W. Barret in Hakluyt *Voy.* (1599) II. i. 272 The said danine is of siluer, hauing the Turkesco stampe on both sides, and 2 and a halfe of these make a Saie,..in value as the Saie of Aleppo.

turkese, var. Turkeys *Obs.*

Turkess ('tɜːkɛs), *sb. nonce-wd.* [f. Turk *sb.*[1] + -ess.] A female Turk; the consort of the Turkish Sultan.

1586 Marlowe *1st Pt. Tamburl.* iii. iii, Disdainful Turkess, and unreverend boss. *Ibid.*, Bind them both, and one lead in the Turk; The Turkess let my love's maid lead away.

†**turkess(e, -eis(e, -is(s**, *v. Obs.* Forms: 6 torcasse, torkes, -esse, turkiss, -ise, 6–7 turkess(e, 7 turkeise, turquese, turkis(s, turkize, turcase, turches. [Derivation uncertain: evidently related to turken, and, like that verb, referred by some to F. *torquer*, ad. L. *torquēre* to twist; but there are difficulties both of form and sense, and possibly both *turken* and *turkesse* were Eng. formations from Turk and Turkeys, Turkish; at least, they were often associated with these words, this verb being actually in 17th c. spelt *turkize*; cf. also turkish *v.* in same sense. (There is no trace of any OF. verb *torquir*, *torquiss-ant.*)]

1. *trans.* To transform or alter for the worse; to wrest, twist, distort, pervert.

1521 FISHER *Serm. agst. Luther* Wks. (E.E.T.S.) I. 341 Many of [these heretics]..had the propre fayth [*ed.* 1556 feate] to wrye and to torcasse the scryptures. *a* **1603** T. CARTWRIGHT *Confut. Rhem. N.T.* (1618) 245 The body of Christ is a more pretious thing then hee will suffer to be turkessed and transformed after that sort. **1612** SIR R. NAUNTON in *Buccleuch MSS.* (Hist. MSS. Comm.) I. 118 My mediation..was, I know not how, turquesed into a reprobate sense with Sir H. Nevill. **1612** T. TAYLOR *Comm. Titus* ii. 1. 159 (1619) 336 Some sentence of Scripture.. must be turkist, and mishapen out of his natiue simplicitie. **1648** *Petit. Eastern Assoc.* 5 Those..which are so audacious as to turcase the revealed, and sealed Standard of our salvation..to the mishapen models of their intoxicated phansies.

2. To alter the form or appearance of; to change, modify, refashion (not necessarily for the worse).

1530 PALSGR. 759/1, I torkes, I alter the shappe of a thyng, *je contourne*, and *je transmue*. He hath torkessed his house quyte a newe. *c* **1577** G. HARVEY *Marginalia* (1913) 141 Erasmus three cheefist Paper bookes..His Similes.. Apothegges..Prouerbs, newly turkissed by diuers. **1593** ABP. BANCROFT *Surv. Discipl.* i. 6 He taketh the said sentence out of Esay (somewhat turkised) for his poesie as-well as the rest. *a* **1610** HEALEY *Theophrastus* (1636) 21 Hee trimmeth himselfe often: he..changeth and Turkizeth his cloathes. **1613** PURCHAS *Pilgrimage* I. iii. (1614) 298 The Turkes, when they turkeised it [St. Sophia], threw downe the Altars, turned the Bells into great Ordinance [etc.]. **1639** HORN & ROB. *Gate Lang. Unl.* xlvii. §505 He that makes cast-cloathes new of old (trimmeth up, new turkizeth), and exposeth them to sale, is a broker. *a* **1650** P. FLETCHER *Father's Test.* (1670) 108 So curiously painted..and turchest in new fashions.

Hence †**turkessing, -ising,** *vbl. sb. Obs.*

1612 T. TAYLOR *Comm. Titus* i. 5 (1619) 84 Adding, detracting, or depraving his institutions by a restless turkising of them. **1673** *Jackson's Wks.* III. *Creed* x. xxxi. Notes 133 An Alteration, Change, or Turning. Or if these be thought Terms too good, Let it be called a Turkizing of Sensitives.

Turkey[1] ('tɜːkɪ). Also 5 torke, 6–7 Turkie, 6–8 Turky, (5–7 Turkye, 6 torkey, Turquey, Turkeye, 7 Tyrkye). [= F. *Turquie*, med.L. *Turchia*, *Turquia*, f. *Turc*, *Turc-us*, TURK *sb.*[1]: cf. *Germān-us*, *Germānia*, *Germany*; *Indus*, *India*.]

1. The land of the Turks, 'Turkey in Asia' and 'Turkey in Europe'; formerly sometimes Turkestan or Tartary.

c **1369** CHAUCER *Dethe Blaunche* 1026 Ne sende men in-to Walakye,..To Alisaundre, ne in-to Turkye. *c* **1485** *Digby Myst.* (1882) III. 1435 þer is þe lond of torke. **1500–20** DUNBAR *Poems* xxxiii. 61 A fedrem on he tuke..in Turky for to fle. **1570** LEVINS *Manip.* 98/45 Turkie, *Tartaria*. **1626** BACON *Sylva* §49 Rice is in Turky..most fed upon. **1719** W. WOOD *Surv. Trade* 180 The Turkey Company..have Factories and Houses in Turkey. **1892** *Chamb. Encycl.* X. 329 Turkey or the Ottoman Empire comprises the wide but heterogeneous territories really or nominally subject to the Osmânlî sultan, in Europe, Asia, and Africa.

†**2.** Short for **a.** TURKEY STONE, the turquoise; **b.** *Turkey horse* (cf. TURKI); **c.** *Turkey leather*.

a. 1487 *Ann. Barber-Surgeons Lond.* (1890) 530, I bequeath to my mother my golde ringe which hath in it a stone called a Turkey. **1509** HAWES *Past. Pleas.* xxxviii. (Percy Soc.) 197 Of the mervaylous rofe set full of rubyes, And tynst with saphers and many turkeys. **1577** E. HOGAN in Hakluyt *Voy.* (1589) 158 A short dagger set with 200 stones, rubies, and turkies. **1587** GREENE *Tritameron* Wks. (Grosart) III. 59 The Turkie hauing lost his color is of no value. **1592** *Wills & Inv. N.C.* (Surtees) II. 204 To my daughter Gee my Turkey ringe. **1595** *Ibid.* 168 My goulde ringe wherein my turkie is. **1615** G. SANDYS *Trav.* 221 They haue [in Cyprus]..diuerse kinds of precious stones of inferiour value, amongst which the emerald, and the turky. *c* **1618** MORYSON *Itin.* IV. IV. i. (1903) 335 Three ringes on his fingers, a Dyamond, a Turky, and a Ruby. **1680** MORDEN *Geog. Rect.* (1685) 358 There are Mines of..divers Kinds of precious Stones, viz. the Emerald and the Turky.

b. 1678 *Extracts Govt. Rec. Fort St. George* 6 Mar. (Yule), Four horses bought for the Company—One young Arab, One old Turkey [etc.].

c. 1715 *Hearne's Collect.* (O.H.S.) V. 66 One in large paper, bound in Turkey. **1721** RAMSAY *Conclusion* 4 Dear, vent'rous book..In gilded Turkey clad. **1835** *J. R. Smith's Catal. Bks.* Nov. 8/2 Life of the Famous Comedian, Joe Hayns,..in old turkey, very scarce.

3. *attrib.* and *Comb.* **a.** Simple *attrib.*; now mostly superseded by TURKISH, except in particular connexions, as in ***Turkey Company, merchant***.

a **1518** SKELTON *Magnyf.* 1480 Porcenya, the prowde prouoste of Turky lande. **1543** *Rutland MSS.* (1905) IV. 346, v long table carpettes of Turky makyng, j fote carpet of Turky makyng. *a* **1548** HALL *Chron.*, *Hen. VIII* 6 b, Appareled after Turkey fashion. **1585** T. WASHINGTON tr. *Nicholay's Voy.* IV. xiii. 126 b, A fair Turkie horse. *Ibid.* xvi. 130 b, [They] are not permitted to print the Turkie or Arabian tongue. **1651** HOWELL *Venice* 134 They had taken some Turky Vessells in the Venetian Seas. **1690** CHILD *Disc. Trade* (1698) 118 The Turkey-Company do maintain an Ambassador and two Consuls. **1817** BYRON *Beppo* xcvii, He ..pass'd for a true Turkey-merchant. **1845** DISRAELI *Sybil* II. vi. A couple of centuries ago, a Turkey Merchant was the great creator of wealth.

b. In names of things of actual or supposed Turkish or Levantine origin, as ***Turkey apricot, gall, myrrh, parsley, plum, sponge, tobacco, wood***; of Turkish workmanship or manufacture, or made in imitation of this, as ***Turkey bow, coverlet, cushion, garter, grogram, morocco, opium, satin, slipper, tapestry, towel***.

1696 LANGFORD *Fruit Trees* 140 Amongst Apricocks..the *Turkey is much commended. **1731–59** MILLER *Gard. Dict.* s.v. *Armeniaca*, The Turkey Apricot is yet larger..and of a globular Figure; the Fruit turns to a deeper Colour. **1572** in Feuillerat *Revels Q. Eliz.* (1908) 157 One *Turky Bowe and iii arrowes. **1578** *Ibid.* 292, vii Turkie Bowes at XII[d] the peece. **1585** T. WASHINGTON tr. *Nicholay's Voy.* II. v. 35 *Turkie couerlettes. **1596** SHAKS. *Tam. Shr.* II. i. 355 Fine Linnen, *Turky cushions bost with pearle. **1684** in *Archæol. Cambr., Orig. Doc.* (1877) 8 Turky cushions. **1874** FLÜCKIGER & HANBURY *Pharmacographia* 536 *Gallæ Halepenses, Gallæ Turcicæ*; Galls, Nutgalls, Oak Galls, Aleppo or *Turkey Galls. **1650** in *Verney Mem.* (1907) I. 469 A paire of Scarletsilk stockings, with a paire of *Turkey garters to them. **1603–4** BP. W. BARLOW *Confer. Hampton Crt.* P ij, These are Cartwrightes Schollers, Scismatikes,..; you may know them by their Turkie gownes, and silke *Turky Grogorum. **1819** REES *Cycl.*, *Turkey Opium. **1890** BILLINGS *Med. Dict.*, *Turkey opium*, the official opium of the pharmacopœias, produced in Asia Minor, and shipped from Turkish ports. **1690** in *Thanes of Cawdor* (Spald. Club) 353 Ane unce of *Turkie persell. **1577** B. GOOGE *Heresbach's Husb.* II. (1586) 88 Quinces, Pomegranates, and *Turkie Plomes. **1664** EVELYN *Kal. Hort.* (1729) 214 Plums..Great Anthony, Turkey-Plum [etc.]. **1545** *Rates of Customs* C viij, *Turky satten the pece. **1551** SIR J. WILLIAMS *Accompte* (Abbotsf. Cl. 1836) 51 A cope..with an orpheres of redde Turquey satten. **1760** W. J. MICKLE *Song*, '*There's nae Luck aboot the House*' iv, My *Turkey slippers maun gae on, My stockings pearly blue. *c* **1645** HOWELL *Lett.* vi. 41 The wrong-side of a *Turky Tapistry. **1812** J. SMYTH *Pract. of Customs* (1821) 260 *Turkey Tobacco may be imported in small packages within any hogshead. **1545** ASCHAM *Toxoph.* (Arb.) 123 Steles be made of dyuerse woodes, as Brasell, *Turkie wood, Fusticke, Sugercheste, Hardbeame, Byrche.

c. Special combs., as **Turkey alder**, *Alnus oblongata* Willd.; †**Turkey balm**, *Dracocephalum Moldavica* Linn.; **Turkeybean**, ? the scarlet runner, *Phaseolus multiflorus*; **Turkey berry**, the fruit of species of *Rhamnus*, used in dyeing; cf. *Persian berries*; see also TURKEY[2] 7; **Turkey blue**, a dye: see quot.; **Turkey chair**, (*a*) a chair of Turkish make; (*b*) the sphenoid bone (of the horse); also ***Turkey-chair bone***; **Turkey colour**: see quot.; **Turkey corn**, an old name for Indian corn; **Turkey cress, earth**: see quots.; **Turkey fig**, the common fig, *Ficus carica*; in Australia, the Indian fig or prickly pear, *Opuntia*; **Turkey gilliflower**, the French and the African marigold; †**Turkey gown**; †**Turkey gruel**, app. a contemptuous description of coffee; **Turkey gum**: see quot.; †**Turkey hirse** = *Turkey millet*; **Turkey hone** = TURKEY STONE 2; **Turkey leather**, leather tawed with oil, the hair side not being removed until after the tawing; hence **Turkey-leathered** *a.*, bound in Turkey leather; **Turkey †mill, millet**, *Sorghum vulgare*: see MILLET[1] 2; **Turkey oak**, the mossy-cup oak of southern Europe, *Quercus Cerris*; **Turkey rhubarb**, medicinal RHUBARB *sb.* (1): see quot. 1866; **Turkey rug** = *Turkish rug* s.v. TURKISH *a.* 2 b; **Turkey slate** = TURKEY STONE 2 (Ogilvie 1882); **Turkey sponge**, a superior grade of commercial sponge from the Mediterranean and Adriatic. †**Turkey stool**: cf. *Turkey chair* (*a*); **Turkey twill**: see quot. 1904. See also TURKEY CARPET, T. RED, T. STONE, T. WHEAT, T. WORK.

1822 *Hortus Angl.* II. 468 *A*[*lnus*] *Oblongata*. *Turkey Alder. Leaves elliptic, bluntish, glutinous. **1688** R. HOLME *Armoury* II. 72/1 The *Turky Balm have the flowers growing on the top of the branch spire-like. **1690** in *Thanes of Cawdor* (Spald. Club) 353 Half pd. of *Turkie benes. **1806** SOUTHEY *Let. to W. Taylor* (*Pearson's Catal.* (1900) 76) My acorn will continue to grow when his Turkey bean shall have withered. **1841** *Penny Cycl.* XIX. 445/1 The berries of several species of Rhamnus..under the name of French, *Turkey, and Persian berries. **1815** J. SMITH *Panorama Sc. & Art* II. 541 To dye Silk Blue... For the *Turkey blue, which is the deepest, a very strong archil bath is first used. **1683** SNAPE *Anat. Horse* III. viii. 122 The Bone called the *Turkey chair. [Cf. *Ibid.* v. iv. 204 The Sphenoides, or Wedge-like Bone..hath several Processes, of which..the internal are four, standing out like four feet of a Table or Chair, which..form the *Sella Turcica*.] *Ibid.* III. ix. 124 Near the side of the Turky-chair-bone they are inoculated with the second or greater branches of the fifth pair. **1684** in *Archæol. Cambr., Orig. Doc.* (1877) 7 In the greate Parlour ..twelve turky chaires one table and Carpett. **1661** PEACHAM *Compl. Gent* (ed. 3) 156 *Turkie colour, *i.e.* Venice blew, or as others will have it, red. [Cf. **1611** COTGR., *Couleur Turquine*, a right blue, or Venice blue. *Ibid.* s.v. *Turc, Couleur Turque*, azure.] **1597** GERARDE *Herbal* I. liv. 74 Of *Turkie cornes there be diuers sorts. **1611** COTGR., *Mays*,..Turkie corne, Turkie wheat. **1865** WEDGWOOD *Dict. Eng. Etymol.* s.v., It is singular that a bird which came from America should have been considered as a Turkey fowl, but the same is the case with maize, which was called Turkey corn or Turkey wheat, Fr. *bled de Turquie*. **1633** *Gerarde's Herbal* II. xxiv. 274 *Turkie cresses..is iudged to be the *Arabis* or *Draba* of the Ancients. **1748** J. HILL *Hist. Fossils* 14 Friable greyish red Bole, called *Turky Earth. **1866** *Treas. Bot.* 492/1 *Turkey figs are imported from Smyrna. **1888** *Antipodean Notes* 12 The 'Turkey fig' [in Adelaide] is about four times the size of a well-grown English fig. **1578** LYTE *Dodoens* II. xxv. 176 Of *Turkie or Aphrican Gilofers. We do call this floure Turkie Gillofers, and French Marygoldes. **1558** in Feuillerat *Revels Q. Eliz.* (1908) 20, vi longe streighte *turkye gounes of redd cloth. **1603–4** BP. W. BARLOW *Confer. Hampton Crt.* ii. 27 They [Puritan divines] appeared before his Maiestie in Turky gownes, not in their Scholastical habites, sorting to their degrees. **1705** E. WARD *Hud. Rediv.* II. III. 54 Some sucking Smoak from Indian Fuel, And others sipping *Turky Gruel. **1890** BILLINGS *Med. Dict.*, **Turkey gum*, the generic name applied to the various species of Egyptian gums. **1597** GERARDE *Herbal* I. lv. 77 [Millet] is called..Turkie Mill or *Turkie Hirsse. **1796** KIRWAN *Elem. Min.* (ed. 2) I. 238 Novaculite. *Turkey hone. **1839** URE *Dict. Arts* 1141 Whet-slate, or Turkey hone, is a slaty rock, containing a great proportion of quartz. **1843** *Penny Cycl.* XXV. 410/2 Turkey-hone..was first brought to Europe from the Levant. **1655–6** WOOD *Life* Mar. (O.H.S.) I. 200 A very fair copie of them [sermons] bound in blew *Turkey-leather. **1821** SCOTT *Kenilw.* v, A small dagger..which hung in his turkey-leather sword-belt. **1843** *Penny Cycl.* XXV. 408/1 The so-called Turkey leather is made in England. **1710** *Lond. Gaz.* No. 4521/4 A small *Turkey Leather'd Bible. **1597** *Turkey mill [see *Turkey hirse*]. **1597** GERARDE *Herbal* I. lv. 77 *Tvrkie Millet is a stranger in England. **1640** PARKINSON *Theat. Bot.* 1137. **1819** *Pantologia*, *Quercus cerris*, *Turkey oak.. South of Europe. **1842** J. B. FRASER *Mesopot. & Assyria* xv. 353 The forest-trees are for the most part the following:—..*Quercus cerris*..Turkey oak. **1789** *Trans. Soc. Arts* I. 94 Commonly sold in the shops under the name of *Turkey or Russian Rhubarb. **1866** *Treas. Bot.* 971/2 What is known..as the best Turkey Rhubarb in reality comes from China through Russia... It was formerly imported from Natolia, whence the name Turkey Rhubarb. **1881** C. C. HARRISON *Woman's Handiwork in Mod. Homes* III. 143 The hardwood floors are stained dark, with *Turkey rugs. **1920** F. G. ELLERTON *Let.* 25 Feb. in J. Bailey *Lett. & Diaries* (1935) 201 Now stamp up and down your Turkey rugs. **1902** D. SALOMONS in A. C. Harmsworth *Motors* vi. 94 A large *Turkey sponge is best for cleaning the body and wheels of the car. **1968** *Canad. Antiques Collector* Nov. 21/1 A fine piece of Turkey sponge was soaked in this mixture [*sc.* aromatic vinegar] and enclosed in a small container called a vinegar box or vinaigrette. **1640** *Inv.* in Nicholson *Hist. & Trad. Tales* (1843) 267 A *Turky stule and a rich work stule. **1904** *Woollen Draper's Terms* in *Tailor & Cutter* 480/1 **Turkey Twill*, a soft make of cotton twill, usually red, but by no means confined to that colour. **1912** D. CRAWFORD *Thinking Black* xiv. 271 Four cut-throats, with red turkey-twill turbans.

Hence (*nonce-words*) '**Turkeydom, the realm** or empire of the Turks; †**Turkeyed** ('tɜːkɪd), *a.* [-ED[2]], Turkish, Turk-like, Turkified; '**Turkeyism**, belief in Turkey, Turkish political sympathies.

1849 THACKERAY *Pendennis* liii, We will cut off all the heads in Christendom or *Turkeydom rather than that. **1600** O. E. *Repl. Libel* III. Pref. 1 His owne friendes charge him with *Turkeied machiauelisme. **1877** GLADSTONE in *Daily News* 13 Nov. 6 This distinguished man, who represents what I have called *Turkeyism, in his speech at the Guildhall drops entirely the 'integrity' of the Turkish empire.

turkey[2] ('tɜːkɪ). Also 6–7 **turkie**, 6–8 **turky**. Pl. **turkeys**, formerly **turkies**. [Short for TURKEY-COCK, -HEN, app. applied orig. to the Guinea-fowl, a native of Africa, with which the American turkey was at first confounded: see TURKEY-COCK.]

†**1.** The Guinea-fowl. *Obs.*

[**1552–1601**: see TURKEY-COCK 2, TURKEY-HEN 1.] **1655** MOUFET & BENNET *Health's Improv.* (1746) 166 They were first brought from Numidia into Turky, and thence to Europe, whereupon they were called Turkies.

2. a. In current use: A well-known large gallinaceous bird of the Linnæan genus *Meleagris*, the species of which are all American; esp. *M. gallopāvo*, which was found domesticated in Mexico at the discovery of that country in 1518, and was soon after introduced into Europe, and is now valued as a table fowl in numerous countries.

Two races of this, which have been variously regarded as sub-species or species, are found wild, of which one, the Northern wild turkey, which has been variously distinguished as *americana*, *sylvestris*, and *fera*, is a native of the eastern half of the continent, from parts of Canada and the Missouri region to Texas, where it is succeeded by *M. mexicana*, the Mexican wild turkey. As in the case of many long-domesticated animals, it is doubtful from which of these wild types the domestic turkey has arisen, but the fact that the latter was domesticated in Mexico, and that the northern race shows less adaptability to domestication, favours the opinion that *M. mexicana* was the source. Some however hold that there may have been two domestic breeds, represented in England by the Norfolk and the Cambridgeshire breeds, or that at least mixture with *americana* has taken place. Another species, *M. ocellata*, which inhabits Guatemala, is smaller and much more beautiful; it has not been tamed.

(The first two quotations app. belong to this sense.)

1555 in Dugdale *Orig. Jurid.* xlviii. (1666) 135 Turkies 2. rated at 4[s]. a piece..00. 08. 00. **1573** TUSSER *Husb.* (1878) 89 Runciuall pease..more tender and greater they wex, If peacock and turkey leaue iobbing their bex. **1596** SHAKS. *1 Hen. IV*, II. i. 29 The Turkies in my Pannier are quite starued. **1616** CAPT. SMITH *Descr. New Eng.* 29 Teale, Meawes, Guls, Turkies, Diue-doppers. **1634** W. WOOD *New Eng. Prosp.* (1865) 32 The Turkey is a very large Bird, of a blacke colour, yet white in flesh. **1643** BAKER *Chron.* (1660) 317 About [1524], it happened that divers things were newly brought into England, whereupon this Rhyme was made: 'Turkeys, Carps, Hoppes, Piccarell, and Beer, Came into England all in one year'. **1698** FRYER *Acc. E. India & P.* 116 Others [Pigeons] walked on the Ground, with their Breasts bearing out, and the Feathers of their Tails spreading like Turkies. *a* **1705** PRIOR *Ladle* 74 Fat Turkeys gobbling at the Door. **1766** PENNANT *Zool.* (1768) I. 213 The Turky was unknown to the antient naturalists, and even to the old world before the discovery of America. **1805** SOUTHEY *Madoc* II. xi, The loud turkey's voice Is heralding the dawn. **1860** TYLOR *Anahuac* ix. (1861) 228 The turkey, which was introduced into Europe from Mexico, was called 'huexolotl' from the gobbling noise it makes. **1886** RUSKIN *Præterita* I. iv. 115 Civilities at Christmas, in the way of turkeys and boxes of raisins.

b. ***wild turkey***, the wild original of the domestic fowl; commonly applied to the North American bird: see above and sense 3.

1613 PURCHAS *Pilgrimage* (1614) 762 They haue Eagles, Haukes, wilde Turkeys and other Fowle. **1624** CAPT. SMITH *Virginia* II. 27 Wild Turkies are as bigge as our tame. **1707** MORTIMER *Husb.* (1721) I. 260, I knew a Gentleman that had a Hen-Turkey of the wild kind from Virginia; of which, and an English Cock, he raised a very fine Breed. **1830** 'B. MOUBRAY' *Domest. Poultry* x. (ed. 6) 81 There is a sameness of colour in the wild turkey, and the original stock seems to have been black, domestication generally inducing a variety of colours. **1849** D. J. BROWNE *Amer. Poultry Yd.* (1855) 138 Two species only are known to naturalists, namely, the common wild turkey, (*Meleagris gallopavo*,) of North America, the origin of our domestic stock, and the Honduras turkey, (*M. ocellata*).

c. The flesh of this bird, esp. the domestic turkey, as food.

1573 TUSSER *Husb.* (1878) 70 Christmas husbandlie fare.. shred pies of the best,..and turkey well drest. **1840** BARHAM *Ingol. Leg., St. Nicholas*, The lay-brothers bring To the board a magnificent turkey and chine. The turkey and chine ..are done to a nicety. **1886** W. J. TUCKER *E. Europe* 122 Cold turkey and ham, or roast chicken. How I hate that turkey! It's so vulgar too; almost as vulgar as goose.

d. *U.S.* and *Canada*. Allusively, in colloquial or dialect phrases, etc.

to say or *talk turkey*, to talk agreeably or affably, to say pleasant things; now usu. (in this sense also ***to talk cold turkey***) to speak frankly and without reserve; to talk hard facts, get down to business; (no longer restricted to N. Amer.); ***to talk turkey***, to use high-flown language; hence *absol.* language of this character; ***not to say (pea-) turkey***, to say nothing at all, 'not to say a word' (about something); ***to walk turkey***, to strut or swagger; of a ship, to pitch and roll. (See Bartlett *Dict. Amer.*, and Thornton *American Glossary*.)

1824 *Little Bit of Tid-Re-I* II. 109 So that, all things considered, I hope neither the Indian, whom the Yankee could not cheat in the division of their game (a turkey and a buzzard,)..will accuse me of *not talking Turkey* to them in this article. **1846** J. W. ABERT in *Congress Documents* XXX. 502 The Indian replied, 'You never once said turkey to me'. **1851** *Adv. Capt. Suggs* 122 (Thornton) He won't get a chance to say turkey to a good lookin gall to-day. *a* **1860** MCCLINTOCK *Beedle's Marriage* (Bartlett), I was plaguy apt to talk turkey always when I got sociable, if it was only out of politeness. **1888** *San Francisco Weekly Examiner* 22 Mar. (Farmer *Amer.*), The north wind commenced to make the Yaquina walk turkey, standing her up on either end alternately. **1888** *Washington Critic* (ibid.), 'What..does locum tenens mean, Tim?'.. 'Why, that's turkey for *pro tem.*, of course'. **1903** *Dialect Notes* II. 333 *Talk turkey*, v.phr., to talk plainly: 'I'm going to *talk turkey* with him and see if I can't get him to mend his ways.' **1909** *Ibid.* (U.S.) III. 356 (Thornton) She never said pea-turkey to me about it. **1919** E. HOUGH *Sagebrusher* xiv. 125 Do you know when he got rattled he began to talk Dutch to me? Well, I talked turkey to him. **1928** *Daily Express* 4 Jan. 11/5 She talked cold turkey about sex. 'Cold turkey' means plain truth in America. **1939** A. HUXLEY *After Many a Summer* II. x. 279 'I'll make it worth your while,' he said. 'You can have anything you care to ask for.'.. 'Ah,' said Dr. Obispo, 'now you're talking turkey.' **1946** E. HODGINS *Mr. Blandings builds his Dream House* (1947) xv. 196 The boss painter.. wanted to talk turkey about..the final colours. **1967** A. CHRISTIE *Endless Night* ix. 67 Send for a high powered lawyer and tell him you're willing to talk turkey. Then he fixes..the amount of alimony. **1982** T. BERGER *Reinhart's Women* xix. 270 Maybe I'll be in a position to talk turkey about an arrangement that would work out for us both.

e. ***cold turkey***: a method of treating drug addicts by sudden and complete withdrawal of the drug, instead of by a gradual process. Also *attrib.* and as *advb. phr.*; also *transf.* Hence ***cold-turkey*** vb. trans., to cure of drug addiction by 'cold turkey' treatment. *slang* (orig. *N. Amer.*).

1921 *Daily Colonist* (Victoria, B.C.) 13 Oct. 15/6 Perhaps the most pitiful figures who have appeared before Dr. Carleton Simon..are those who voluntarily surrender themselves. When they go before him, they [*sc.* drug addicts] are given what is called the 'cold turkey' treatment. **1936** *Amer. Speech* XI. 120/1 *Cold turkey*, treatment of addicts in institutions where they are taken off drugs suddenly without the 'tapering off' which the addict always desires. **1941** W. C. HANDY *Father of Blues* xviii. 243 We went on 'cold turkey' that morning without a rehearsal. **1951** *N.Y. Times* 27 June 19 She tried it 'cold turkey' once, which she explained meant merely stopping completely, without any attendant medication. **1960** *Times Lit. Suppl.* 16 Sept. 589/4 *The Scene* is written by a junkie..who was snitched by a flip, busted by the nailers and after a stretch in the pen cold turkeyed..that is to say, was once a dope addict; he was arrested and..managed to break himself of his addiction. **1962** 'K. ORVIS' *Damned & Destroyed* xi. 72, I made one cold-turkey cure and it near killed me. **1976** S. GEORGE *Fatal Shadows* 154 She took a cold turkey, no methedrine, no sedatives, nothing, just off.

3. a. Applied with qualification to other birds: A local name of the Bustard; now usually applied to the Australian Bustard, also called ***native, plain,*** or ***wild turkey*** (*Eupodotis* (*Otis*) *australis*); in Australia also, the ***brush-*** or ***wattled turkey*** and the ***scrub-turkey***: see these words; in America, ***Colorado*** or ***water-turkey***, names for native species of Ibis; ***water-turkey***, the Darter or Snake-bird (*Plotus anhinga*); in South Africa, the Bald Ibis (*Gerontius calvus*).

1847, 1852 Brush-turkey [see BRUSH *sb.*[1] 4]. **1848** Native turkey [see NATIVE *a.* 13 c]. *c* **1868** G. PRYME in *Autobiog. Recoll.* xxvi. (1870) 386, I have seen Bustards,..which the natives called *Wild Turkey*,..flying over the Gogmagog Hills. **1872** C. H. EDEN *Queensland* iv. 122 The plain turkey or bustard (*Otis Australasianus*),..the male weighing from eighteen to twenty-five pounds. **1872** Scrub-turkey [see SCRUB *sb.*[1] 6 c]. *a* **1889** RIPLEY & DANA *Amer. Cycl.* V. 692 This bird [*Plotus anhinga*] is a constant resident in Florida, and the lower parts of Louisiana, Alabama, and Georgia... In these localities it bears the various names of water crow, Grecian lady, water turkey, and cormorant.

b. ***plain turkey, scrub turkey***: humorous names for swagmen who haunt, respectively, the Australian plains and the bush [perhaps with partial allusion to the 'turkey' (sense 5 below) which they carry]. *Austral. slang.*

1955 A. MARSHALL *I can jump Puddles* 152 Father..was familiar with the ways of swagmen... The bearded men who kept to the bush he called 'Scrub Turkeys' and those who came down from the plains he called 'Plain Turkeys'. **1973** F. HUELIN *Keep Moving* 178 *Scrub Turkey*, bagman who has gone Bush. Usually slightly mental or eccentric.

†**4.** *Angling.* Short for *turkey-fly* (see 7). *Obs.*

1799 G. SMITH *Laboratory* II. 301 The Turkey, or March-fly. Body, brown foal's hair [etc.].

5. *transf.* in lumbering: see quots. 1893, 1905; applied more generally to bundles or hold-alls carried by other itinerant workers, vagrants, etc. *N.Amer.* and *Austral.*

1893 *Scribner's Mag.* June 715/2 With his 'time' in his pocket and his 'turkey', a two-bushel bag in which he carries his belongings, strung over his shoulder, the shanty boy starts..for town. **1905** *Logging Terms* (U.S. Dept. Agric., Forestry, Bulletin lxi.), *Turkey*, a bag containing a lumberjack's outfit. To 'histe the turkey' is to take one's personal belongings and leave camp. **1909** *Outlook* 2 Jan. 19/1 A [Colorado] desert miner calls his valise a 'turkey'. **1912** G. H. GIBSON *Ironbark Splinters* 6 So you 'pack' your bloomin' turkey, and you take the northern train. **1931** 'D. STIFF' *Milk & Honey Route* 216 *Turkey*, a bundle, a suitcase or a canvas bag. **1945** BAKER *Austral. Lang.* v. 104 Expressions to describe being on the tramp...[*to*] *coil one's turkey* (strictly this applies to the rolling of a swag) [etc.]. **1963** R. SYMONS *Many Trails* v. 54 The cowboys' 'turkeys' —as they called their bedrolls, in which were wrapped their personal possessions such as tobacco—when the outfit was on the move. **1973** in B. Broadfoot *Ten Lost Years* ii. 19, I took to the road with..my poor clothes tied together with two leather thongs, and that is what they call a turkey.

6. *U.S. slang.* **a.** An inferior or unsuccessful cinematographic or theatrical production, a flop; hence, anything disappointing or of little value.

1927 *Vanity Fair* (N.Y.) XXIX. 132/3 'A turkey' is a third rate production. **1939** G. MARX *Let.* 27 Oct. (1967) 21 The boys at the studio have lined up another turkey for us... I saw the present one the other day and didn't care much for it. **1941** J. M. CAIN *Mildred Pierce* 176 The beach..was studded with rocks and was therefore unsuitable to swimming. For all ordinary purposes it was simply a turkey. **1962** *Movie* June 18/1 With *The Four Horsemen*, Minnelli was once more landed with a turkey, an old one, too. **1977** H. FAST *Immigrants* III. 201 'Have you ever thought of selling the place?' Jake asked... 'Oh? And who the hell would buy this turkey?'

b. = TURK *sb.*[1] 4 b; *spec.* an Irish immigrant in the U.S.

1932 J. T. FARRELL *Young Lonigan* i. 31 Dooley was one comical turkey, funnier than anything you'd find in real life. **1966** [see SALT WATER B. c].

c. A stupid, slow, inept, or otherwise worthless person.

1951 in Wentworth & Flexner *Dict. Amer. Slang* (1960) 556/2 So, if you got a collector [of internal revenue] through the civil service system who was a real turkey, you'd be stuck with that turkey practically until he died. **1969** C. BURKE *God is Beautiful, Man* (1970) 105 You better get real strong like so that you won't be a turkey. **1978** *Time* 3 July 13/3 'Come on, you turkeys! Let's speed this show up!' cries an irreverent observer. **1984** *Tampa* (Florida) *Tribune* 5 Apr. 4D/3, I decided I had had enough of that turkey.

7. *attrib.* and *Comb.*, as ***turkey-butcher, -chick*** (also fig.), ***-coop, dinner, -drumstick*** (in quot. *attrib.*), ***farm, farmer, -feather, -gobbler, -hunt, -hunter, meat, -pie, -poult, -shooter, -tail, -wing***; ***turkey-like*** adj.; **turkey-apple**, local name of *Cratægus induta*, a small tree of Arkansas, bearing small reddish berries (*Cent. Dict. Supp.* 1909); **turkey-back**, a large variety of the yellowshank, *Totanus melanoleucus*; **turkey-beard**, also **turkey's beard**, a North American herb, *Xerophyllum asphodeloides*, N.O. *Liliaceæ*, having a tuft of wiry root-leaves, and an erect stem with a raceme of white flowers; **turkey-berry**, (*a*) *Solanum mammosum* and *S. torvum* of the West Indies; (*b*) the fruit of a W. Indian tree, *Cordia Collococca* (***turkey-berry tree***); see also TURKEY[1] 3 c; **turkey-bird**, local name of the wryneck, and of the turnstone; **turkey-blossom**, W. Indian name of *Tribulus cistoides*; **turkey-bush**, an evergreen shrub, *Myoporum deserti*, native to Australia and bearing white flowers followed by purple berries; **turkey-buzzard**, an American carrion vulture, *Cathartes aura*, so called from its bare reddish head and neck and dark plumage; the John Crow of Jamaica; also *fig.*; in W. Africa, the Vulturine Pie, *Picathartes gymnocephalus*; **turkey-call**, (*a*) the gobbling sound characteristic of the turkey-cock; also (*b*) an instrument for imitating this, used to decoy the wild turkey; **turkey-corn**, *Dicentra* (*Dielytra*) *canadensis* of eastern N. America, having yellow tubers like grains of maize; also called *squirrel-corn*; see also TURKEY[1] 3 c; **turkey-dog**, a dog trained to hunt the wild turkey; **turkey-egg**, the egg of the turkey; also (*pl.*) the common fritillary (*local*); **turkey-fat ore**, local name for a variety of smithsonite (carbonate of zinc) coloured yellow by greenockite (*Cent. Dict.* 1891); **turkey-feather fucus, laver**, peacock's-tail seaweed, *Padina pavonia*; **turkey-flower** = *turkey-blossom*; †**turkey-fly**, a kind of angler's fly: cf. sense 4; **turkey-foot**, (*a*) [from the shape of the spike], local name for North American grasses of the genus *Andropogon*; (*b*) applied to other things resembling a turkey's foot (in quot. 1957, a weaving pattern); **turkey-gnat**, a small black fly of the genus *Simulium* which infests poultry in southern and western N. America; **turkey-grass**, goose-grass or cleavers (*Galium Aparine*); **turkey-louse**, a feather-eating parasite, as *Goniodes stylifer*, infesting turkeys (*Cent. Dict.*, and *Supp.*); **turkey-merchant** (*slang*): see quots.; cf. TURKEY[1] 3 a; **turkey-oak**, *Quercus Catesbæi*, of south-eastern N. America; also, the American 'Spanish' oak, *Q. falcata*; **turkey-pea** (***wild-turkey pea***) = *turkey-corn*; also applied to the hoary pea, *Tephrosia virginiana*; **turkey-pen** (*U.S.*), a pen for trapping wild turkeys; **turkey-shoot**, a shooting-match in which the mark is a live turkey, or its head only; †**turkey-tomb**, a turkey-pie (*humorous*); **turkey-trot**, a kind of ball-room dance introduced from U.S.; also, a fast jogging trot like that of a turkey; hence **turkey-trotting** *a.*; **turkey vulture** = *turkey-buzzard*; **turkey-yelper**, a decoy call: = *turkey-call* (*b*). See also TURKEY-COCK, -HEN.

1888 G. TRUMBULL *Names Birds* 168 At Salem, Mass., the larger birds of the species [*Totanus melanoleucus*] have long been distinguished from the others under the name of **Turkey-back.* **1884** MILLER *Plant-n.*, *Turkey's-beard, *Xerophyllum asphodeloides*. *Ibid.*, *Turkey-berry, *Solanum mammosum* and *S. torvum*. **1819** *Pantologia* s.v. *Cordia*,.. *C. collococca*,..of Jamaica..the clammy-cherry, or *turky-berry tree. **1858** HOGG *Veg. Kingd.* 538 Turkey and other poultry feed on the fruit of *C*[*ordia*] *collococca*, called Turkey-berry Tree and..Clammy Cherry. **1885** SWAINSON *Provinc. Names Birds* 104 Wryneck (*Jynx torquilla*), ..*Turkey bird. Because it erects and ruffles the feathers of its neck when disturbed. **1894** SCOTT WILLCOX *Egg Collector's Handy Dict.*, *Turkey-bird*,..Turnstone, *Strepsilas interpres*. **1849** CRAIG, **Turkey-blossom*, the name given in Jamaica to the plant *Tribulus terrestris*. **1911** W. R. GUILFOYLE *Austral. Plants* 265 '*Turkey-bush'..evergreen shrub..reputed poisonous and injurious to stock. **1936** F. CLUNE *Roaming round Darling* xvii. 163 Shrubs..mingled with turkey-bush flower—white and small, having five petals to each bloom, like an English daisy. **1965** *Austral. Encycl.* IX. 59/2 Turkey-bush, one of several names applied to the inland shrub *Myoporum deserti* because wild turkeys or native bustards have been observed to eat the berried fruits. **1849** D. J. BROWNE *Amer. Poultry Yd.* (1858) 165 There are *turkey butchers of whom you may buy the half or a quarter of a bird. **1672** JOSSELYN *New Eng. Rarities* 12 The *Turkie Buzzard, a kind of Kite, but as big as a Turkie, brown of colour, and very good meat. **1839** DARWIN *Voy. Nat.* iii. 68 The turkey-buzzard (*Vultur aura*)..is found wherever the country is moderately damp, from Cape Horn to North America. **1897** MARY KINGSLEY *W. Africa* 23 One of the chief features of Free Town are the jack crows... *Picathartes gymnocephalus*. To the white people who live in daily contact with them they are turkey-buzzards; to the natives, Yubu. **1873** *Forest & Stream* 2 Oct. 123/1 A *turkey-call is easily imitated by using the hollow bone of the leg or wing of the same. **1555** in Dugdale *Orig. Jurid.* xlviii. (1666) 135 *Turkey-Chicks 4. rated at iiij[s] a piece. oo. 16. oo. **1664** BUTLER *Hud.* II. III. 150 Putting Knavish tricks Upon Green-Geese, and Turkey-Chicks. **1833** MARRYAT *P. Simple* xxvii, The geese and *turkey-coops are divided off into apartments for four sows. **1884** MILLER *Plant-n.*, *Turkey-corn, *Corydalis formosa*. **1953** G. W. BRACE *Spire* xiii. 125 '*Turkey dinner, eh?' 'With gravy,' Sylvia said. **1977** 'W. TREVOR' in D. Marcus *Best Irish Stories* II. 78 The Bulrush Café has a turkey dinner advertised. **1895** *Outing* (U.S.) XXVII. 231/1 This setter..was an excellent *turkey dog. **1860** O. W. HOLMES *Prof. Breakf.-t.* ii, The *turkey-drumstick style of organization. **1718** LADY M. W. MONTAGU *Let. to C'tess of Mar* 10 Mar., A fine coloured emerald, as big as a *turkey-egg. **1952** *Turkeys* Nov. p. ix. (Advt.), Beale's *turkey farm. **1959** *Ibid.* July–Aug. 29 (Advt.), One of Norfolk's leading *turkey farmers. **1972** K. BONFIGLIOLI *Don't point that Thing at Me* iv. 40 A rich turkey-farmer in Suffolk. **1624** CAPT. SMITH *Virginia* II. 30 We haue seene some vse mantels made of *Turky feathers. **1767** ELLIS in *Phil. Trans.* LVII. 407 It is well known by the name of *Turky-feather Fucus,.. *Fucus Pavonius*. **1866** *Treas. Bot.*, **Turkey-feather laver*, the common name of *Padina pavonia*. **1843** *Penny Cycl.* XXVII. 830/2 *T*[*ribulus*] *cistoides*..is abundant about Kingston in Jamaica, where it is called *turkey-flower... Fowls are said to be fond of this plant. **1676** COTTON *Angler* II. vii. 63 The first flie we take notice of..is call'd the *Turky-flie. **1932** SIMPSON & WEIR *Weaver's Craft* xii. 126 **Turkey Foot* (24 threads).—Each pedal should be used six times in the following order: 4, 2, 3, 1; repeat. **1935** M. MOORE *Sel. Poems* 71 The firs stand in a procession, each with an emerald turkey-foot at the top. **1899** D. SHARP in *Cambr. Nat. Hist.* VI. vii. 477 In North America the..*Turkey-gnats attack a variety of mammals and birds. **1836** W. T. PORTER in *Spirit of Times* 9 July 162/1 They seemed to me about the size of a big Christmas *turkey gobbler. **1879** J. BURROUGHS *Locusts & W. Honey* 46 The turkey-gobbler and the rooster. **1874** EDITH WADDY *Year*

Wild Fl. 62 Goosegrass, *Turkey-grass, Cleavers,..names ..familiar to all..for the Bedstraw. **1827** J. F. Cooper *Prairie* I. iii. 46 Dreaming of a *turkey hunt. **1895** *Outing* (U.S.) XXVII. 231/1 Nearly every negro man and boy on the plantation came up to have a look at the famous *turkey hunter. **1855** *Poultry Chron.* III. 67 Large *turkey-like bird, native of Mexico. **1901** A. H. Rice *Mrs. Wiggs of Cabbage Patch* ii. 24 If you ain't never et *turkey meat you don't know how good it is. **1972** *Country Life* 30 Nov. 1507/1 The promoters of turkey-meat sales. *a* **1700** B. E. *Dict. Cant. Crew*, **Turky-Merchants*, drivers of Turkies. **1785** Grose *Dict. Vulg. T.*, *Turkey merchant*, a poulterer. **1717** *Petiveriana* III. 206 *Turkey Oak. From a small Acorn it bears which the Wild Turkeys feed on. **1884** Miller *Plant-n.*, *Turkey-pea, Wild, *Corydalis formosa*. **1602** *2nd Pt. Return fr. Parnass.* II. vi. 982, I inuited the hungry slaue.. to the canuasing of a *Turkey Pye. **1694** *Turkey-poots [see turkey-cock 3]. **1769** Mrs. Raffald *Eng. Housekpr.* (1778) 373 Ducklings, Turkey Poults, Plovers. *a* **1809** Anna Seward *Lett.* (1811) I. 113 A Turkey-poot casting about with a pitiful poked-out neck, for its lost companion. **1849** D. J. Browne *Amer. Poultry Yd.* (1855) 165 To eat turkey poults is a wasteful piece of luxury. **1845** S. Judd *Margaret* I. 62 Its succedanea..were a *turkey shoot the next day, and a ball. **1898** H. Frederic *Deserter* 81 The farther of the two was now so far away that he seemed a mere dark speck, like the object seen from the gun-line of a turkey-shoot. **1980** *Outdoor Life* (U.S.) (Northeast ed.) Oct. 92/2 Saturday afternoon turkey shoots used to be popular in my community. **1869** T. W. Higginson *Army Life* 11 Some steady old *turkey-shooter hit the mark. **1851** J. J. Hooper *Widow Rugby's Husband* 84 Betsy dodged behind the wild *turkey-tail which she carried by way of a fan. **1936** M. Mitchell *Gone with Wind* xviii. 318 Girls who laughed from behind turkey-tail fans. **1622** Fletcher *Beggar's Bush* IV. iv, Fat capons..And *turkey-tombs, such honourable monuments. **1839** *Southern Lit. Messenger* V. 337/1 May-be I didn't set up a high *turkey-trot, and peeled it like thunder. **1895** F. Remington *Pony Tracks* 187 He would run me off the plantation at a turkey trot if I did shoot. **1908** W. G. Davenport *Butte & Montana beneath X-Ray* 42 The light fantastic, the turkey trot and the pazamala were indulged in by all to a late hour. **1912** *Nation* 22 June 427/1 The Lord's prayer, followed by the 'Turkey trot'. **1913** G. Grossmith in *Daily Graphic* 12 May 9/1 Adventurous persons will see the Turkey trot or Tango as they are danced in a cabaret, but not as danced in a Paris ball-room. **1859** H. E. Taliaferro *Fisher's River Scenes & Characters* 36 You're a purty set uv ill-begotten, *turkey-trottin' pukes, to raise a quarrel with a peaceubble man, and then run like a gang uv geese. **1823** E. James *Acct. Exped. Rocky Mts.* I. 4 At evening we..saw..several *turkey vultures. **1846** in *Congress Documents* XLI. 405 Amongst the birds [we have] the turkey vulture. **1908** *Daily Chron.* 18 Aug. 5/4 They are about the size of large barn-door fowls, with red heads (hence their name 'turkey vultures'). **1872** Mrs. Stowe *Sam Lawson's Oldtown Fireside Stories* 4 'I'll sweep up the coals now,' he added, vigorously applying a *turkey-wing to the purpose. **1888** *Century Mag.* XXXVI. 769/2 Turkey-wing fans and fans of peacock feathers. **1895** *Outing* (U.S.) XXVII. 231/2 Matt drew from his pocket a '*turkey-yelper' and began to call.

'Turkey 'carpet. [f. Turkey[1] + carpet.] A carpet manufactured in or imported from Turkey, or of a style in imitation of this; made in one piece of richly-coloured wools, without any imitative pattern, on a foundation of flax, hemp, or other material, and having a deep pile, cut so as to resemble velvet.

1546 *Acts Privy Council* 9 Oct. (1890) I. 537, vij chestes of Spanisshe velvettes, one fardell of Turkey carpettes. **1552** in J. O. Payne *St. Paul's Cathedr. time Edw. VI* (1893) 24 One Turkeye carpett for the Communyon table. **1688** in Willis & Clark *Cambridge* (1886) II. 219 A long Turkey Carpet in the Meeting roome. **1751** Johnson *Rambler* No. 112 ¶10 She spilt her coffee on a Turkey carpet. **1836** W. Irving *Astoria* I. xviii. 305 The prairies..were gaily painted with innumerable flowers, exhibiting the motley confusion of colours of a Turkey carpet. **1894** Fenn *In Alpine Valley* I. 3 The thick Turkey carpet.

Hence **Turkey-'carpeted** *a.*, furnished with a Turkey carpet; **Turkey carpeting**, the material of Turkey carpets.

1831 M. Edgeworth *Let.* 29 Mar. (1971) 505 The library at Eton College is the most *comfortable* I ever was in—turkey carpetted. **1843** *Penny Cycl.* XXVII. 181/1 Fustians are..a kind of cotton velvet, as Turkey carpeting is a woollen velvet. **1849** Dickens *Dav. Copp.* xx, A snug private apartment, red-curtained and Turkey-carpeted.

turkey-cock ('tɜːkɪ,kɒk). Also 6–7 Turkicock(e. [f. Turkey[1] + cock *sb.*[1] In the 16th c. synonymous with *Guinea-cock* or *Guinea-fowl*, an African bird known to the ancients (the μελεαγρίς of Aristotle, *meleagris* of Varro and Pliny), the American bird being at first identified with or treated as a species of this. The African bird is believed to have been so called as originally imported through the Turkish dominions; it was called *Guinea-fowl* when brought by the Portuguese from Guinea in West Africa. After the two birds were distinguished and the names differentiated, *turkey* was erroneously retained for the American bird, instead of the African. From the same imperfect knowledge and confusion *Meleagris*, the ancient name of the African fowl, was unfortunately adopted by Linnæus as the generic name of the American bird.]

†**1.** Of doubtful meaning (? = sense 2 or 3): in quot. 1555 perh. the Curassow. *Obs.*

1541 *Constitutio T. Cranmeri* in Wilkins *Concilia* (1737) III. 862 It was also provided, that of the greater fyshes or fowles there should be but one in a dishe, as crane, swan, turkeycocke, hadocke, pyke, tench. **1555** Eden *Decades* 79 The inhabitantes of Paria..gaue them also a greate multitude of theyr peacockes [L. *pavones*]. [*margin*] Paria. Peacockes whiche wee caule Turkye cockes. **1561** in Rogers *Agric. & Prices* III. 195/4 Oxford..Turkey Cocks 2@5/-. **1579** E. Hake *Newes Powles Churchyarde* iv. D ij b, He must prouide..Both Peacock, Crane, and Turkicock. **1599** Hakluyt *Voy.* II. 165 In time of Memory things haue bene brought in that were not here before, as..the Turky cocks and hennes about fifty yeres past.

†**2.** The male of the Guinea-fowl, *Numida meleagris*: cf. turkey[2] 1, turkey-hen 1. *Obs.*

1577 B. Googe tr. *Heresbach's Husb.* (1586) 12 b, Here I keepe Geese, Duckes, Peacocks, Turkicockes, and other poultry. **1601** Holland *Pliny* XI. xxxvii. I. 331 The Ginnie or Turkie Cockes and Hens.

3. The male of the turkey.

1578 T. N[icholas] tr. *Conq. W. India* 38 They..brought bread and fruite and eyght Turkie Cockes. **1588** Parke tr. *Mendoza's Hist. China* vi. 322 You shall buy there [in Mexico]..a whole sheepe for foure rials, and two hennes, such as you haue in Spaine for one riall, and of Ginny hennes, otherwise called Turkey cockes, and in Spanish *Pauos*, you shall haue an hundred thousande..for a rial and a halfe of plate a peece. **1592** *Shuttleworths' Acc.* (Chetham) 73 A turkye coke and a hene iij*. **1599** Shaks. *Hen. V*, v. i. 15 *Gower.* Why heere hee comes, swelling like a Turky-cock. *Flu.* 'Tis no matter for his swellings, nor his Turky-cocks, God plesse you aunchient Pistoll. **1616** R. C. *Times' Whistle* iii. 1095 And swell in big lookes like some turkie cocke. **1668** Charleton *Onomast.* 72 *Gallopavo*..the Turky-Cock. **1694** Motteux *Rabelais* IV. lix. (1737) 243 Hortolans. Turkey-Cocks, Hen-Turkeys, and Turkey-poots. **1727** Somerville *Bowling-green* 58 No turkey-cock appears with better grace, His garments black, vermilion paints his face. **1727** Swift *Country Post* Wks. 1755 III. I. 176 An old turkey-cock attacked a maid in a red petticoat, and she retired with great precipitation. **1760** Edwards in *Phil. Trans.* LI. 836 Whether this bird be produced from a turkey-hen and a cock-pheasant, or from a turkey-cock and hen-pheasant, no one knows. **1833** Marryat *P. Simple* xxxiv, The idea..mantled the blood in my cheeks till I was as red as a turkey-cock. **1855** *Poultry Chron.* III. 149/2 Turkey Cock and one Hen.

b. *fig.* and *allusively*. Also *attrib.*

1601 Shaks. *Twel. N.* II. v. 36 Contemplation makes a rare Turkey Cocke of him, how he iets vnder his aduanc'd plumes. **1650** B. *Discolliminium* 2 Which makes him write with such a Turky-cocks quill, too..censoriously. *a* **1849** J. C. Mangan *Poems* (1859) 428 Thy snub nose..And thy turkey-cock air.

turkey-hen. [Cf. turkey-cock.]

†**1.** The guinea-hen. *Obs.*

1552 Elyot, *Meleagrides*, byrdes, whiche we doo call hennes of Genny, or Turkie hennes. **1578** Lyte *Dodoens* II. lii. 214 Called..*Flos Meleagris*..from a kinde of birde.. whose feathers be speckled..not with Violet speckes, but with white and blacke spots, lyke to the feathers of the Turkie or Ginny hen, which is called *Meleagris auis*: some do also cal this flower *Fritillaria*. **1601** Holland *Pliny* I. 296 The Ginnie or Turkey hens in a part of Africke called Numidia, be in great request.

2. The female of the turkey.

1555 Eden *Decades* 158 They [of Yucatan] brought.. eyght of their hennes beynge as bygge as peacockes, of brownyshe coloure, and not inferiour to peacockes in pleasaunte tast. [*margin*] Turky hens. **1580** Hollyband *Treas. Fr. Tong*, *Poule d'Inde*, a Turkie henne. **1592** *Shuttleworths' Acc.* (Chetham) 72 Towe turkes and onne turkie henne vij*. **1760** [see turkey-cock 3]. **1844** Stephens *Bk. Farm* II. 710 When a turkey-hen is seen disposed to lay, a nest should be made for her in the hatching-house.

Turkey red. [Turkey[1].] **a.** A brilliant and permanent red colour produced on cotton goods, essentially a madder red in combination with oil or fat, with an aluminous mordant. Also called *Adrianople* or *Levant red*. Also *attrib.*

1789 *Trans. Soc. Arts* I. 19 Dying Turkey red. **1799** *Med. Jrnl.* I. 168 A whole month's labour is scarcely sufficient to terminate the different operations thought necessary to obtain the fine Turkey red, called Adrianople. **1799** *Monthly Rev.* XXX. 561 The art of dyeing cotton scarlet, or turkey-red, was imported into France by Greek families. **1801** *Encycl. Brit.* Suppl. II. 393/2 Turkey-Red, Levant-Red and Adrianople-Red, the names indifferently given to that beautiful red dye which distinguishes the cotton manufactured in the Ottoman empire. **1815** J. Smith *Panorama Sc. & Art* II. 545 P. J. Papillon established a dyehouse at Glasgow, for giving to cotton-yarn that beautiful colour known by the name of Turkey or Adrianople red. **1838** T. Thomson *Chem. Org. Bodies* 396 The first Turkey-red work in Great Britain was established about 50 years ago in Glasgow by M. Papillon. **1844** G. Dodd *Textile Manuf.* ii. 74 About a century ago some Greek dyers were invited to settle in France, where they introduced the art of Turkey-red dyeing. **1862** *Catal. Internat. Exhib., Brit.* II. No. 4329 Turkey red goods. *Ibid.* No. 4340 Turkey red plain and printed cottons. **1877** O'Neill in *Encycl. Brit.* VII. 576/1. **1899** *Westm. Gaz.* 10 Aug. 2/1 Before the days of Turkey-red-dyeing and calico-printing. *Ibid.* 2 Dec. 9/1 It is a turkey-red dyeing firm.

b. Cotton cloth of this colour.

1880 J. Dunbar *Pract. Papermaker* 72 For pink blottings furnish two thirds of white cottons and one third of turkey reds. **1882** Caulfeild & Saward *Dict. Needlework* 503 *Turkey Red*, a cotton cambric, of a bright scarlet colour of indelible dye,..originally imported from Turkey.

c. Turkey red oil (also **Turkey-red, turkey Red Oil**), sulphonated castor oil, principally used with alizarin to produce the colour Turkey red.

1879 *Jrnl. Chem. Soc.* XXXVI. 187 This 'Turkey-red oil' is a mixture of sulpho-ricinoleate and sulpho-pyroterebate of sodium. **1903** [see *oil tanning* s.v. oil *sb.*[1] 6 c]. **1980** K. G. Ponting *Dict. Dyes & Dyeing* (1981) 172/2 John Mercer did a great deal of research on the production of the necessary turkey red oil produced by the action of sulphuric acid on castor oil.

†**Turkeys, Turkese,** *a. Obs.* Also 5–6 Turkes, 6 Turcas, Turkys. [a. OF. *turqueis*, *-queze*, mod.F. *turquois* Turkish (= It. *turchese*, Pr., OSp. *turques*): see -ese.] = Turkish.

13.. *Coer de L.* 4972 Thre thousand Turkes com at the last, With bowe Turkeys, and arweblaste. **14..** *Sir Beues* (M.) 767 With Bowes turkes and arablaste. *Ibid.* 3706 They shott dartys with bows turkeys. **1513** Douglas *Æneis* XI. xiii. 11 Apon hir schulder the gyltin bow Turcas. **1517** Torkington *Pilgr.* (1884) 23 Jherusalem—And Rama thane beyng turkys. **1530** Palsgr. 284/1 Turkes bowe, *arc turquoys*.

turkeys, obs. form of turquoise.

Turkey stone. [Turkey[1].]

1. = turquoise.

1607 Topsell *Four-f. Beasts* (1658) 5 Mammonets are lesse than an Ape:..his stones greenish blew, like a Turkey stone. **1611** Cotgr., *Couleur Turquine*,..the colour of the Turkie stone. **1667–8** Pepys *Diary* 18 Feb., She shows me her ring of a Turky-stone, set with little sparks of dyamonds. *a* **1668** Lassels *Voy. Italy* (1698) II. 239 They shewed us a cup or dish..all of one Turky-stone entire. **1710** Steele *Tatler* No. 245 ¶2 Another [ring] of Turkey Stone. **1820** Lady Granville *Lett.* (1894) I. 188 A beautiful ring, a turkey stone set in gold. **1877** W. Jones *Finger-ring* 158 The turquoise, turkise, or turkey-stone having, from remote periods, been supposed to possess talismanic properties.

2. A hard, fine-grained, siliceous rock imported from the Levant for whetstones; novaculite; a whetstone made of this. Also *attrib.*

1816 Cleaveland *Min.* 364 The Novaculite is employed in the arts under the names of hone, oil-stone, Turkey stone, and whetstone. **1840** *Civil Eng. & Arch. Jrnl.* III. 421/1 A scraping tool..carefully sharpened on a Turkey stone. **1867** J. Hogg *Microsc.* I. iii. 210 Polish..on a hone of Turkey-stone kept wet with water. **1875** Sir T. Seaton *Fret Cutting* 3 Oil-stones are sold by weight, Turkey-stone being the dearest, and also by far the best. *Ibid.* 117 A Turkey-stone slip will polish them.

turkey wheat. [Turkey[1].] The cereal Maize, called also †*Guinea corn* and *Indian corn*.

1598 Florio, *Brena*, a kind of ginnie or turkie wheate. **1611** Cotgr., *Mays*, Turkie corne, Turkie wheat. **1674** Josselyn *Voy. New Eng.* 73 Maze, otherwise called Turkie-wheat, or rather Indian-wheat, because it came first from thence. **1704** tr. *Lemery's Treat. Foods* 71 (D.) There grows in several parts of Africa, Asia, and America, a kind of corn called Mays, and such as we commonly name Turkey wheat. **1777** Robertson *Hist. Amer.* (1796) II. IV. 102 Maize, well-known in Europe by the name of Turkey or Indian Wheat. **1883** Parkman *Discov. Gt. West* ii. 13 The ordinary food is Indian corn, or Turkey wheat as they call it in France.

'Turkey work. [Turkey[1].] Turkish tapestry work, or an imitation of this. Also *attrib.* Hence **Turkey-worked** *a.*

1537 *Wills & Inv. N.C.* (Surtees) 101 The carpet of turkey warke. **1608** [Tofte] *Ariosto's Sat.* III. (1611) 30, I.. vnder rugs, as much safe quiet hold, As vnder Turky workes, Arras or gold. **1687** A. Lovell tr. *Thevenot's Trav.* I. 143 Fine ones are made at Caire, and are called Turkie-work Carpets. **1697** Vanbrugh *Relapse* III. iii, Set all the Turkey-work chairs in their places. **1714** *Fr. Bk. of Rates* 83 Turkey-work English, for Chairs. **1748** Richardson *Clarissa* VI. 157 Four old turkey-worked chairs, bursten-bottomed, the stuffing staring out. **1751** Johnson *Rambler* No. 84 ¶8 A large screen, which I had undertaken to adorn with turkey-work against winter, made very slow advances.

Turki ('tuːrkiː), *a.* (*sb.*) Also 8 toorkay, 8–9 toorkee, toorky. [a. Pers. *turkī*, deriv. of *turk* Turk, applied to language and race: cf. *Shīrāzī*, *Panjābī*, *Hindūstānī*, etc.] Turkish; belonging to the typical Turkic languages, *East* and *West Turki*, and to the peoples speaking them. **b.** *sb.* A member of the Turkish race; also, a Turkish horse.

1782 *India Gaz.* 2 Mar. (Y.), To be disposed of..a Buggy, ..a pair of uncommonly beautiful spotted Toorkays. **1800** *Misc. Tr.* in *Asiat. Ann. Reg.* 189/1 A Toorky horse which I generally rode. **1841** Elphinstone *Hist. Ind.* II. i, The Túrki slaves, who rose to sovereignty throughout Asia, and ..furnished a succession of rulers to India. **1888** *Encycl. Brit.* XXIV. 1/2 Corrupt Turki dialects spoken by Tatarized Finn populations from the Altai to the Urals. **1907** *Blackw. Mag.* May 661/2 The Turki can holloa. *Ibid.* June 807/1 He had a Turki interpreter.

Turkic ('tɜːkɪk), *a.* [f. Turk *sb.*[1] + -ic.] Name of one of the branches of the Ural-Altaic or Turanian family of languages, which comprises the Samoyedic, Finnic, Ugric, Turkic, Mongolic, and Tungusic; the Turkic branch comprises Eastern Turki or Uigur (including Jagatai and Turconian), West Turki or Seljúk and Osmanli, Kazan Tartar, Kirghiz, Nogai, Yakut, etc., the languages of the Turks (in the wide sense); also applied to the peoples using these: cf. Turkish, Tartar *sb.*[2], and Turcic.

1859 Dwight *Mod. Philol.* 124 The Turkic [languages]. **1863** C. L. Brace *Races Old World* xi. 86 Another Turanian tribe are the Khazars, probably Finnic, though with Turkic mixture. They appear in Europe between the seventh and tenth century,..between the Caspian and the Dnieper. They are followed by the Pechenegs, a Turkic tribe, who occupy Bessarabia, Cherson, and part of Taurida, in the tenth and eleventh centuries. **1875–6** RAWLINSON *Orig. Nat.* I. i. (1878) 4 The Muscovite and Turkic hordes are becoming scarce distinguishable from other Europeans. **1878** *N. Amer. Rev.* CXXVI. 557 The Magyars received the knowledge of southern products and of agriculture from their Turkic neighbors. **1892** S. LAING *Hum. Orig.* iii. (1894) 86 Various Turkic and Mongolian dialects.

Turkicize ('tɜːkɪsaɪz), *v.* Also **turkicize.** [f. TURKIC *a.* + -IZE.] *trans.* To render Turkic or Turkish. Hence ˌ**Turkiciˈzation**; **Turkicized** *ppl. a.*

1939 C. S. COON *Races of Europe* vii. 233 The Magyars were Ugrians from the region between the Volga and the Urals, who had been partially Turkicized by the Petchenegs and others. **1951** W. K. MATTHEWS *Languages U.S.S.R.* iii. 17 A tiny remnant of a mostly turkicised tribe living in the Turkic-speaking country north of the Altai range. **1964** *Language* XL. 301 It was long believed..that Chuvash was a Turkicized Finnic language. **1964** G. WHEELER *Mod. Hist. Sov. Central Asia* ii. 24 The Turkicization of the Mongol rulers appears to have started very early after the Mongol state was established.

turkies, obs. pl. of TURKEY; obs. f. TURQUOISE.

Turkify ('tɜːkɪfaɪ), *v.* In 7 Turkefy. [f. TURK *sb.*[1] + -I)FY.] *trans.* To render Turkish. Hence **Turkifiˈcation, Turcification,** a rendering Turkish.

1682 MRS. BEHN *False Count* Wks. 1724 III. 150, I hope the Jade will be Turkefied with a vengeance. **1813** T. MOORE *Interc. Lett.* ii. (ed. 2) 9 With sashes, turbans, and paboucheṣ..And all things fitting and expedient To turkify our gracious R—g—nt. **1911** *Contemp. Rev.* July 11 They believed that every institution ought to be Turkified. *Ibid.* 12 The desire for Turkification. **1922** BUXTON & CONWIL-EVANS *Oppressed Peoples & League of Nations* v. 132 The Armenians..resisted all attempts at 'turcification'. **1949** J. PARKES *Hist. Palestine* xii. 241 Unhappily at this point the new policy of Turcification caused the government to maintain the deposition [of the Patriarch Damianus], as they had no intention of supporting what appeared—and was—an Arab demonstration. **1976** *Economist* 4 Sept. 45/1 The demographic Turkification of the north will soon be complete.

†**turkin,** *a.* and *sb. Obs.* In 5 -kyn, 7 -chine. [a. F. *turquin, turquine* (1471 in Hatz.-Darm.), = It. *turchino, -ina,* 'blue, azure, watchet' (Florio), dim. of *turco* Turk. See TURQUIN.] **a.** *adj.* Light blue. **b.** *sb.* A kind of light blue cloth.

1483 *Act 1 Rich. III* c. 8 § 18 Provided alwey that this Acte ..extende not..to the makynge..of eny clothe called Vervise, otherwise called Plounkettes Turkyns or Celestrines, with broade Lists. [Cf. **1611** COTGR., *Couleur Turquine,* a right blue, or Venice blue; the colour of the Turkie stone. *Ibid.* s.v. *Turc, Couleur Turque,* Azure, Sky-colour, the colour of a Turkeis-stone (betweene a blue, and an Azure).] *c* **1618** MORYSON *Itin.* (1903) 441 The Dukes [= doge's] officers,..50 in nomber, attyred in Turchine gownes.

turkin, var. TURKEN *v. Obs.*

turkis, turkes, -esse ('tɜːkɪs). Chiefly, now only, *Sc. dial.* Forms: 4 **thourkeys,** *Sc.* 5–6 **turkas,** 6 **turkass, turkes, turcase, turcas,** 7 **turkesse,** 9 **turkis.** [ad. OF. *turcaise, -quaise, -queise, turquoise* (14–15th c.), *terquoise, truquaise, trucoise,* mod.F. *tricoises,* fem. pl. of *turcois, -queis, -quois* Turkish; prop. *tenailles turquoises,* Turkish nippers.] A pair of smith's pincers; pincers or nippers generally; forceps.

1390–1 *Earl Derby's Exped.* (Camden) 35 Pro j pare de thourkeys, xij d. *c* **1470** HENRY *Wallace* VI. 411 He gert a smyth, with his turkas rycht thar, Pow out his eyne. **1503–4** *Acc. Ld. High Treas. Scot.* II. 419 Ane turcas to tak out teith. **1513** DOUGLAS *Æneis* VIII. vii. 185 Wyth the grippand turkas [*v.r.* turkes] oft also The glowand lump thai turnit to and fro. **1591** *News fr. Scot.* (1820) 33 His nailes upon all his fingers were riven and pulled off with an instrument called in Scottich a Turkas, which in England we call a pair of pincers. **1629** Z. BOYD *Last Battle* 534 Like a tooth in the jaw, the deeper roote it hath, the more paine it causeth, when it is drawing out with the Turkesse. **1871** W. ALEXANDER *Johnny Gibb* xxvii. (1873) 162 There's yersel', 't kens nae mair aboot the prenciples o' the struggle nor that turkis i' the smith's sheein [= shoeing] box.

turkis(e, obs. or arch. ff. TURQUOISE.

turkise, var. TURKESS(E *v. Obs.*

Turkish ('tɜːkɪʃ), *a.* (*sb.*) [f. TURK *sb.*[1] + -ISH[1]; the usual adj. from *Turk, Turkey,* taking the place of the earlier TURKEYS from French.]

A. *adj.* **1. a.** Of, pertaining or belonging to the Turks or to Turkey; commonly (now *Hist.*) = Ottoman.

1545 ASCHAM *Toxoph.* I. (Arb.) 81 Surely no Turkyshe power can ouerthrowe vs, if Turkysshe lyfe do not cast vs downe before. **1546** P. ASHTON tr. *Jovius* (*title*) A shorte treatise vpon the Turkes Chronicles;..The begynnyng of the turkysshe empyre. The lyues of al the Turkyshe Emperours. **1552–3** *Inv. Ch. Goods, Staffs.* in *Ann. Lichfield* (1863) IV. 44 Itm: a cope of turkishe saten. *a* **1568** ASCHAM *Scholem.* I. (Arb.) 61 This opinion is not French, but plaine Turckishe. **1585** T. WASHINGTON tr. *Nicholay's Voy.* I. xvii. 19 b, To weare armes against the Turkish nation. *Ibid.* III. ii. 71 To learne the turkish language. **1604** SHAKS. *Oth.* I. iii. 8 Yet do they all confirme A Turkish Fleete, and bearing vp to Cyprus. *a* **1658** J. DURHAM *Exp. Rev.* IX. ii. (1680) 385 The first Turkish Government being by four Souldans. **1732** BERKELEY *Alciphr.* v. § 18 Free-thinkers, who at present applaud Turkish maxims and manners. **1842** PRICHARD *Nat. Hist. Man* 209 The Turkish tribes have been often erroneously termed Tartars. **1870** DICKENS *E. Drood* iii, 'I want to go to the Lumps-of-Delight shop.' 'To the ——?' 'A Turkish sweetmeat, sir.' **1896** A. MACKAY *Hist. Fife & Kinross* ii. 32 His Arab charger with his Turkish trappings was led to the high altar.

b. Like or resembling the Turks, their character, or that attributed to them; cruel, savage, barbarous.

1600 W. WATSON *Decacordon* (1602) 242 Turkish, Iesuitish, Puritanian, and barbarous designements. *Ibid.* 246 There is no mischiefe or villany, which they [Jesuits] will not attempt, to further their most sauage and Turkish designements. **1603** DEKKER *Wonderfull Yeare* F iij b, They seeme by their turkish and barberous actions to beleeue that there is no felicitie after this life. **1648** LD. ORMOND in Milton *Observ. Art. Peace* Wks. (1847) 259/1 To constitute an elective kingdom..then..to establish a perfect Turkish tyranny. *a* **1700** B. E. *Dict. Cant. Crew, Turkish Treatment,* very sharp or ill dealing in Business.

2. In special collocations. **a. Turkish bath**: a hot bath introduced from the East and once extensively used, inducing copious perspiration, followed by soaping, washing, shampooing, massage, and cooling. Also *attrib.*

1644 DIGBY *Nat. Bodies* xxvii. § 2. 243 The Turkish bathes ..that seemeth chilly cold att his returne; which appeared melting hoat att his going in. **1867** F. W. NEWMAN in *Mem.* ix. (1909) 200 Turkish-bath keepers find it [smallpox] a most tractable disease. **1876** BRISTOWE *The. & Pract. Med.* (1878) 745 For diaphoretic purposes we must not forget the value of the hot bath, the vapour bath, and the Turkish bath. **1908** *Daily Chron.* 5 Oct. 5/7 The Turkish bath conditions in which London has been living for the past few days were not so pronounced, and a drier heat seems to have taken the place of the vapour.

b. ***Turkish bean, cock, hen, horse, red, stone, wheat***: see TURKEY[1] 3 a, 3 c, TURKEY-COCK, etc.; ***Turkish cigarette*** (or *cig*), ***tobacco***; **Turkish carpet** = TURKEY CARPET; **Turkish coffee,** the strong (usu. sweet) black coffee commonly drunk in the East, in which the ground beans are boiled thrice over and the liquid is served with the grounds; a cup of such coffee; **Turkish crescent** *Mus.* = *Chinese pavilion* s.v. CHINESE *a.* 2; cf. *jingling Johnny* (*a*) s.v. JINGLING *ppl. a.*; **Turkish delight,** a sweetmeat consisting of gelatine boiled, cubed, and dusted with sugar, RAHAT LOKUM; cf. DELIGHT *sb.* 4; **Turkish music, rug**: see quots.; **Turkish slipper,** a soft heelless slipper with turned-up toe, a babouche; **Turkish stitch,** a kind of stitch used in Turkish and other Oriental embroideries; **Turkish towel**: see quot. 1882; **Turkish trousers,** baggy oriental pantaloons.

1894 E. EGGLESTON in *Century Mag.* Apr. 849 The beans ..found here were called '*Turkish-beans' by the first Dutch and Swedish writers on America. **1886** S. W. MITCHELL *Roland Blake* v. 42 The room..was luxuriously comfortable with a heavy-piled *Turkish carpet and easy-chairs. **1977** FLEMING & HONOUR *Penguin Dict. Decorative Arts* 805/2 Turkish carpets..differ from Persian carpets.. stylistically in that their design seems invariably to have been created by weavers rather than painters. **1897** KIPLING *Captains Courageous* i. 6 Any gen'elman got a real *Turkish cig on him? **1903** A. BENNETT *Truth about Author* xiii. 172 The aroma of coffee, the odour of *Turkish cigarettes. **1950** G. GREENE *Third Man* vii. 56 The Turkish cigarettes that Harry always smoked. **1982** T. KENEALLY *Schindler's Ark* ix. 102 Oskar Schindler—in his coat with the fur lapels.. reaching for another Turkish cigarette. **1849** D. J. BROWNE *Amer. Poultry Yd.* (1855) 51 Aldrovandi [1599–1603] in describing a *Turkish cock and two *Turkish hens, says: 'The cock, whose likeness we now give, is called the Turkish cock'. **1854** F. DUBERLY *Let.* 17 Aug. in E. E. P. Tisdall *Mrs. Duberly's Campaigns* (1963) ii. 54 Rum and water till bedtime, or the very strongest *Turkish coffee. **1898** G. B. SHAW *Arms & Man* II. 22 (*stage direction*), A small table.. is laid for breakfast with Turkish coffee pot, cups, rolls, etc. **1958** L. DURRELL *Mountolive* xiv. 267 She was sitting in the lounge of Shepheards Hotel under the clock with an untouched Turkish coffee before her. **1978** H. KAPLAN *Damascus Cover* xv. 155 Ari ordered a second cup of thick Turkish coffee. **1891** C. R. DAY *Descr. Catal. Mus. Instruments R. Military Exhib., London, 1890* XII. 233 There were specimens of the old *Turkish Crescent (*chapeau chinois*), once a favourite adjunct to military bands, and known in former years by the familiar nick-name of 'Jingling Johnny'. They consisted of brass hoops, hung with little bells.., and ornamented with gilded crescents and long streaming tails of horse-hair. They were carried upon poles. **1938** *Oxf. Compan. Mus.* 965/1 *Turkish crescent* or *Turkish jingle*.., a noise maker introduced into military bands..at a time when there was a craze for 'Turkish music'. **1961** J. BLADES in A. Baines *Mus. Instruments through Ages* xiv. 338 The middle of the eighteenth century when European military bands were being increased to include percussion instruments on the lines of the Turkish military music—bass drum, cymbals, triangle, and sometimes also tambourine and the Jingling Johnny or Turkish Crescent. [**1870** Turkish delight [cf. quot. from Dickens in 1].] **1877** *Porcupine* 31 Mar. 843/2 Arabs and Greeks vended *Turkish delight (horrible compound). **1888** *Boy's Own Paper* Summer 38/1 Instead of the usual boxes of ..Turkish delight,..there was little to tempt the youthful appetite but piles of fruit. **1901** F. HUME *Golden Wang-ho* x, The thrusting forward of the Turkish delight box. *a* **1648** LD. HERBERT *Henry VIII* (1683) 184 He got hastily upon a *Turkish and swift Horse. **1889** GROVE *Dict. Mus.* IV. 191 **Turkish Music*.., the accepted name for the noisy percussion instruments—big-drum, cymbals, triangle—in the orchestra. **1900** *Jrnl. Soc. Dyers* XVI. 4 Dyeing in Adrianople or *Turkish Red. **1901** ROSA B. HOLT *Rugs* ii. (Chicago) 52 *Turkish Rugs includes all those rugs that are manufactured within the Turkish Empire, whether [by] Kurds or Circassians or Christians;..Turkish rugs are not so finely woven as Persian. **1865** DICKENS *Our Mutual Friend* II. III. i. 3 Mr. Fledgeby's appearing erect at the foot of the bed in *Turkish slippers, rose-coloured Turkish trousers..and a gown and cap to correspond. **1971** 'D. HALLIDAY' *Dolly & Doctor Bird* v. 65 He [*sc.* a Turkish dancer] wore a cinnamon tunic and trousers with gold Turkish slippers. *c* **1890** TH. DE DILLMONT *Encycl. Needlewk.* 94 Triangular two-sided *Turkish stitch worked diagonally. *Ibid.* 96 Triangular two-sided Turkish stitch worked horizontally. *Ibid.* 115 The triangular Turkish stitch..is particularly effective when combined with other kinds of embroidery. **1577** tr. *Bullinger's Decades* (1592) 737 His bodie..was like the *Turkish or Iasper stone. **1827** M. WILMOT *Let.* 10 Oct. (1935) 305 If you add a *pipe* and some *turkish tobacco..you will have the portrait of most of our beaux. **1981** A. MACKAY *Death on Eno* 68 The Turkish tobacco is added for aroma. **1862** *Catal. Internat. Exhib., Brit.* II. No. 3648 Royal *Turkish towels. **1882** CAULFEILD & SAWARD *Dict. Needlework* 504 *Turkish Towels*..are cotton cloths, having a long nap, cut or uncut. [**1612** W. STRACHEY *Trav. Virginia* (1849) v. 66 A kynd of leather breeches and stockings, all fastened together..which they tye and wrappe about the loynes after the fashion of the Turkes or Irish Trouses.] **1821** BYRON *Don Juan* III. lxxii. 39 Her orange silk full *Turkish trowsers furl'd About the prettiest ankle in the world. **1865** [see *Turkish slipper* above]. **1928** V. WOOLF *Orlando* iv. 140 The Turkish trousers which she had hitherto worn. **1973** *Guardian* 10 Apr. 13/2 Twinsets.. allied to jersey wrapover skirts, loose lopped-off pants, Turkish trousers. **1670** COVEL in *Early Voy. Levant* (Hakl. Soc.) 120 They make some [bread] of pure good wheat,.. some of what we call *Turkish wheat. **1894** *Century Mag.* Apr. 849 Henry Hudson..called the maize 'Turkish wheat'.

B. *sb.* **1.** The Turkish or Turk's language.

1718 LADY M. W. MONTAGU *Let. to Lady Rich* 16 Mar., In Pera they speak Turkish, Greek, Hebrew, Armenian, Arabic, Persian, Russian [etc.]. **1753** [see RUSS *sb.* 2]. **1888** *Encycl. Brit.* XXIII. 662/1 The relative pronoun has been borrowed from the Persian in many dialects; it is absent in the original Turkish.

2. *ellipt.* for *Turkish fashion, people,* etc.; also *colloq.* for *Turkish delight, Turkish tobacco,* etc.

a **1674** MILTON *Hist. Mosc.* i. Wks. 1738 II. 132 The rest ..ride with a short Stirrup after the Turkish. **1859** A. J. MUNBY *Diary* 2 Mar. in D. Hudson *Munby* (1972) 24 Long clays also, & a tall jar..of real Turkish. **1898** *Century Mag.* Feb. 558/1 The best 'Turkish' [*sc.* tobacco] the town provided. **1901** F. HUME *Golden Wang-ho* x, Feeling for another lump of 'Turkish' [*sc.* delight].

Hence †ˈ**Turkisher,** a Turk; cf. *Britisher. Obs.*

1607 R. C[AREW] tr. *Estienne's World of Wonders* 13, I soone perceiued that it was my onely course to preuent these turkishers, by being mine owne interpreter.

†ˈ**turkish,** *v. Obs.* [app. f. TURKISH *a.*: cf. TURKESS(E *v.*] *trans.* To transform, esp. for the worse; to pervert; to turn into something different.

1560 DAUS tr. *Sleidane's Comm.* 142 b, He [Cardinal Poole] sayeth how the Turkyshed seede is sowen abroade in England and in Germany, signifiyng the doctrine that is contrary to the byshop of Rome. **1596** HARINGTON *Ulysses upon Ajax* (1814) 62 Away with this serious talk, let us turkish this text into a merrier colour. **1607** R. C[AREW] tr. *Estienne's World of Wonders* 19 Turkishing the storie, or (to speak more properly) turning it into a meere fable.

ˈ**Turkishly,** *adv.* [f. TURKISH *a.* + -LY[2].] In a Turkish way or manner.

1611 SPEED *Hist. Gt. Brit.* IX. ix. § 29 Seeing the Great Emperour Fredericke..so Turkishly in his absence deposed from his owne Empire by the Pope. **1662** J. SPARROW tr. *Behme's Rem. Wks., 2nd Apol. Tylcken* 56 They live Turkishly, and more then Turkishly or Heathenishly. **1828** SOUTHEY in *Q. Rev.* Oct. 556 The Pope himself, if he were Turkishly inclined.

So ˈ**Turkishness,** Turkish quality or conduct; addiction to what is Turkish.

1545 ASCHAM *Toxoph.* I. (Arb.) 81 A more Turkishnesse and more beastlye blynde barbarousnesse. **1701** J. SAGE *Wks.* (1847) II. 52 The Turkishness of the Government whether in Church or State I do confess. **1814** SOUTHEY *Lett.* (1856) II. 382 The Turkishness of the writer is sometimes very comical. **1897** *Westm. Gaz.* 24 Aug. 1/3 The Turkishness of the Turk might make him restive under England's controlling advice.

Turkism ('tɜːkɪz(ə)m). [f. TURK *sb.*[1] + -ISM.] †**1.** Islam; = TURCISM. *Obs.*

1595 J. KING *Queen's Day Serm.* in *On Jonas* (1618) 704 So much of Christendom at this day buried in the very bowels of Turkisme & infidelity. **1645** E. CALAMY *Indictment agst. Eng.* 33 An illimited toleration of all Religions, even of Turkisme, Iudaisme, &c. **1660** F. BROOKE tr. *Le Blanc's Trav.* 8 Resolved to leave Turkisme, and become a Christian again.

2. = TURCISM b.

1877 GLADSTONE in *Echo* 28 Sept., The professors of Turkism..declared that the people of England had changed their minds.

Turkize ('tɜːkaɪz), *v.* Also 6–9 **turkise,** 7 **turkeise;** 9 **turcise** ('tɜːsaɪz). [f. TURK *sb.*[1] + -IZE.]

1. *trans.* To render Turkish.

1599 in *Archpriest Controv.* (Camden) I. 220 All three words of one significacion, viz. turkized atheism. **1625** PURCHAS *Pilgrims* II. vi. Pref. 1464 A halfe-turkised Christian with divers Turkes following immediatly after. **1911** *Q. Rev.* Apr. 471 The 'Turcising' of the Ottoman Empire which is one of the objects of the Young Turk party.

2. *intr.* To play the Turk; †to tyrannize *over.*

1599 in *Archpriest Controv.* (Camden) I. 97 Blackwell, y[t] will turkise over vs to vrge our consent by violent force. **1600** W. WATSON *Decacordon* (1602) 169 The Iesuits..would Turkize ouer vs in that shamelesse manner. **1612** T. JAMES *Jesuits' Downf.* 2 They vse to turkize over men in a shameful maner, nay, it were better to liue vnder the Turke. **1862**

CUNNINGHAM *Hist. Theol.* (1864) I. xx. 629 A book..called 'Calvinus Turcisans' or Calvin Turkising,—that is teaching the doctrine of the Turks or Mohometans.

turkize, var. TURKESS(E *v. Obs.*

turkle ('tɜːk(ə)l), U.S. dial. var. TURTLE *sb.*[1] and *sb.*[2] Hence '**turkling** = TURTLING.

1861 O. W. HOLMES *Elsie Venner* 384 Don' wan' no snappin'-turkles in my stable. **1893** H. A. SHANDS *Some Peculiarities of Speech in Mississippi* 65 *Turkle*, Negro for *turtle*. *Turkle-dove* is the common name given by negroes to the *turtle-dove*. **1929** W. FAULKNER *Sartoris* ii. 64 It wuz jes' like shootin' turkles in a slough. **1941** J. STILL *Proud Walkers* in *Sat. Even. Post* 10 May 112/3 The hours crawled turkle-slow. **1978** J. A. MICHENER *Chesapeake* p. ix, *Turkling*: State Senator Frederick C. Malkus, the region's premier turtle trapper, took me turkling, as that sport is called.

'Turkman. [Altered from TURCOMAN.]

†**1.** = TURK *sb.*[1] *Obs. rare.*

1481 CAXTON *Godeffroy* cl. 222 They sente to the admyrals of the turkes... The turkmans acorded wel to this werk.

2. = TURCOMAN, q.v.

Türkmen. Also Turkmen. Pl. -mens. A more accurate form of the name rendered as TURCOMAN.

1927 W. M. RAMSAY *Asianic Elements Gk. Civilization* viii. 86 The Turkish term *ova* and the Turkmen *oba*... The distinction between the Turks and the Turkmens or Nomads. **1953** O. CAROE *Soviet Empire* xiv. 235 Yet Uzbeks, Kazaks and Turkmens persist in abstract praises of their 'motherlands'. One Turkmen even had the insolence to write a poem 'My Turkmenistan'. **1962** A. TIETZE in Householder & Saporta *Probl. Lexicogr.* 267 Other languages of the Southern Turkic or Oghuz subgroup, as Azerbaijani or Türkmen. **1978** *Times* 18 Oct. 16/8 [In] Uzbekistan..many..speak Tadzhik, Turkmen and other Asian languages.

Turko-: see TURCO-.

turkois, obs. f. TURQUOISE.

Turkoman: see TURCOMAN.

Turk's cap. [TURK *sb.*[1]]

†**1.** Early name for the tulip. *Obs.*

1597 GERARDE *Herbal* I. lxxvii. §14. 120 It is called..after the Turkish name Tulipa, or it may be called Dalmatian Cap, or the Turkes Cap. **1629** PARKINSON *Paradisus* Table 12 The Turkes Cap, that is, the *Tulipa*.

2. The Martagon lily; also ***Turk's-cap lily***. **American Turk's-cap lily**, *Lilium superbum*.

1672 JOSSELYN *New Eng. Rarities* 54 Turning up their Leaves like the Martigon, or Turks Cap. **1778** MILNE *Bot. Dict.* (ed. 2) 130 Martagon lilly..having its petals rowled or turned backwards in form of a Turkish turbant; from which ..the flower is generally known by the name of Turk's-cap. **1791** *Gentl. Mag.* July 619/1 The Martagon or Turk's-cap Lily. **1884** MILLER *Plant-n.*, *Lilium superbum*, Great American Turk's-Cap Lily, Swamp Lily. **1899** WARNER *Capt. Locusts* 5 A couple of blossoms of the crimson Turk's-cap lily. **1906** EARL SELBORNE *Pers. & Pol. Mem.* II. xxxii. 268 A cream-coloured Turk's-cap and several kinds of white lilies.

3. The Melon-thistle, *Cactus Melocactus*: see quot. 1866; also ***Turk's cap cactus***, ***Turk's head***. Also, any of several other members of the genus *Cactus*.

1731 P. MILLER *Gardeners Dict.* s.v. *Melocactus*, The common or large Melon-Thistle, commonly call'd Turk-cap or Pope's-Head in the West-Indies. **1829** LOUDON *Encycl. Plants* (1836) 410 C[actus] melocactus, the great melon thistle or Turk's cap. **1866** *Treas. Bot.* 733/2 *Melocactus communis*, the Turk's-cap Cactus, so called from the flowering portion on the top of the plant being of a cylindrical form and red colour like a fez cap. **1926** FAWCETT & RENDLE *Flora of Jamaica* V. 283 Turk's Head, Turk's Cap, Pope's Head, Melon Thistle. **1951** *Dict. Gardening* (R. Hort. Soc.) I. 345/2 The Turk's Cap. The species [of *Cactus*] are characterized by the formation of a woolly cap or cephalium when the plants reach flowering size.

4. A local name for the common aconite (*Aconitum Napellus*).

1854 MISS BAKER *Northampt. Gloss.*, Turk's cap. *Ibid.* 129 *Pope's-Ode*, the garden Monk's-hood or Turk's-cap. *Aconitum napellus*.

5. A variety of the great pumpkin, *Cucurbita maxima*.

1891 in *Cent. Dict.*

6. *Cookery.* A form of mould. Cf. TURBAN *sb.* 1 g.

1859 F. S. COOPER *Ironmongers' Catal.* 178 Jelly and Cake Moulds... Turk's Cap.

Turk's head. [TURK *sb.*[1]]

†**1.** The Melon-thistle; = TURK'S CAP 3; also called *Englishman's head*, *pope's head*. *Obs.*

1725 SLOANE *Jamaica* II. 159 Turks head. This has a great many..roots,..which send up a very strange plant, or masse. **1760** J. LEE *Introd. Bot.* App. 330 Turk's Head, *Cactus*.

2. *Naut.* An ornamental knot resembling a turban.

1833 MARRYAT *P. Simple* vi, Whether something should not be fitted with a *mouse* or only a *Turk's head*. *c* **1860** H. STUART *Seaman's Catech.* 5 The train tackles are fitted with a Turk's head on the standing part. **1909** *Blackw. Mag.* Apr. 536/2 He could work a Turk's head, cover a manrope, or point a lashing for the cable table.

3. A round long-handled broom or brush; also called *pope's head*.

1859 F. S. COOPER *Ironmongers' Catal.* 34 Turks' Heads. **1889** HUXLEY in *19th Cent.* XX. 102 Phyllis, gracefully wielding her long-handled 'Turk's head'.

4. (See quot.) ? *Obs.*

1853 URE *Dict. Arts* I. 345 This colour is generally known by the name of *solitaire bistre*, and sometimes turks-head.

5. A round pan for baking cake, having a conical core in the centre.

1891 in *Cent. Dict.*

6. *attrib.* and *Comb.*, as ***Turk's-head besom***, ***broom***, ***brush*** (= 3); **Turk's-head grass**, *Lagurus ovatus*, having a rounded inflorescence; hare's-tail grass.

1851 *Regul. R. Engineers* xix. 95 The bore must be well brushed out..with a Turks-head brush. **1853** LYTTON *My Novel* x. xx, Dick was all for sweeping away other cobwebs, ..he saw a great Turk's-head besom poked up at his own. **1882** *Garden* 14 Jan. 28/3 *Lagurus ovatus* (the Turk's-head Grass) is one of the most distinct kinds, as well as one of the best for keeping purposes. **1910** *Chron. Lond. Mission. Soc.* Mar. 44/1 What looks more like a turks-head broom than anything else.

turky, turkyn: see TURKEY, TURKIN.

turle, obs. form of TIRL *sb.*[1] and *v.*[3]

†**turlehyde**, var. THURLHEAD (= THIRLEPOLL).

1766 W. HARRIS *Hist. Dublin* xi. 265 About the 24th of June [1331] a prodigious number of large sea fish, called Turlehydes, were brought into the bay of Dublin, and cast on Shore at the Mouth of the river Dodder.

†**turlery, turlery ginke**: see TERLERIE.

1593 G. HARVEY *Pierce's Super.* 158 Where [can be found] such a Turlery-ginkes of conceit, or such a gibbihorse of pastime as Straunge Newes?

turlough ('tuːrləʊx). [ad. Ir., Gael. *turloch* a brook, ground covered with water in winter and dry in summer, f. *tur* whole, absolute, entire + *loch* lake, pool.] (See quots.)

1685 *Phil. Trans.* XV. 958 As to those places we call Turloughs, *quasi Terreni lacus*, or land-lakes; they answer the name very well, being lakes one part of the year of considerable depth; and very smooth fields the rest. **1861** *Zoologist* XIX. 7617 Serving..as water-courses for the 'buried' rivers which give rise to the sink-holes and turloughs for which the district of the Burren is famous. **1878** KINAHAN *Geol. Irel.* xix. 325 When the water during floods rises in the [shallow hollows], it overflows the adjoining lands, forming the turloughs, which are usually lakes in winter and callows in summer.

†**'Turlupin.** *Obs. rare.* [In sense 1, = OF. *turlupin*, in med.L. *turlupin-us* (14th c., Du Cange), of unknown origin. In later F. in other senses: see below, also Littré and Hatz.-Darm.]

1. A name given to a sect of heretics in the 14th c., who are said to have maintained that one ought not to be ashamed of anything that is natural.

1639 FULLER *Holy War* III. xix. (1840) 149 Turlupins; that is, dwellers with wolves..being forced to flee into woods. **1804** RANKEN *Hist. France* III. ii. §1. 198 We shall not trace their [the Waldenses'] progress under the new names of Wickliffites, Lollards, Turlupins, Bohemians, etc. in other countries. **1882-3** *Schaff's Encycl. Relig. Knowl.* III. 2407/2 Gregory XI in 1373 urged the king of France to support the Dominicans against the Turlupins. **1910** *Encycl. Brit.* XIV. 592/2 [A woman, Jeanne Daubenton] being the head of a sect called the Turlupins. The Turlupins reappeared in 1421 at Arras and Douai and were persecuted in a similar way.

¶**2.** By Urquhart taken to render F. *tirelupin* in Rabelais, said by Duchat to be a name given in 1372 to a certain people who imitated Cynics, and lived on *lupins* which they gathered (*tiraient*) in the fields.

Cotgrave and Littré (who spells *tirelopin*) treat this as a separate word. Cotgr. has '*Tirelupin*, a catch-bit, or captious companion; a scowndrell, or scuruie fellow'; '*Turlupin*, a grub, mushrome, start-up, new-nothing, man of no value'. Urquhart applied Cotgrave's explanation of *turlupin* to *tirelupin*.

1653 URQUHART *Rabelais* I. Prol., So saith a Turlupin or a new start-up grub of my books, but a turd for him. [RABELAIS Aultant en dict ung Tirelupin de mes livres: mais bren pour luy.]

[Mod.F. has *turlupin* in the sense 'buffoon, merry-andrew' (from the name assumed by an actor in French farce *a* 1630), hence 'a sorry jester, a low punster', and *turlupinade* a low pun or word-play. Cf. obs. Ital. *turlupino* (Douce) = '*turluru* a foole, a gull, a ninnie, a patch' (Florio).]

turm (tɜːm). [a. OF. *turme*, *torme* (15th c. in Godef.), ad. L. *turma* a troop, squadron.] A body or band of people, *esp.* a troop of horsemen; *spec.* a troop of thirty or thirty-two horsemen (= L. *turma*).

1483 CAXTON *Gold. Leg.* 47b/1 Iacob was sore aferde thenne and devyded his companye in to tweyne turmes. *c* **1520** BARCLAY *Jugurth* (1557) 41 One bande or cohorte of Lumbardes and two turmes, that is to saye three score Thraciens. **1533** BELLENDEN *Livy* II. xx (S.T.S.) I. 210 But dout þai had gevin bakkis, war nocht marcus fabius..come on ane spedy horss, with ane certane turmys of horsmen. **1671** MILTON *P.R.* IV. 66 Legions and Cohorts, turmes of horse and wings. **1800-24** CAMPBELL *Dead Eagle* 18 Rome array'd her turms And cohorts for the conquest of the world.

turmagant, turmalin(e, turmat: see TERMAGANT, TOURMALINE, TURNIP.

†**turmatur.** *Obs. rare.* App. corruption of TORMENTOR.

c **1440** *Alphabet of Tales* 404 We rede of Saynt Pawle þat ..when þe turmaturs smate of his head [etc.]... When þe turmatur was gone, þis Ploattyll mett hym & axkid hym whare he had done hur maister Pawle.

turment, etc., obs. ff. TORMENT, etc.

turmeric ('tɜːmərɪk), *sb.* (*a.*) Forms: 6 **tarmaret**, **tormarith**, **-marthe**, **tormerik**, **-yke**, **turmirick**, 6-7 **turmericke** (7 **turn-merick**, **turmerocke**, **-ack**, **termarcke**, **tarmanick**, **tarmaluk**), 7-9 **turmerick**, 8- **turmeric**. [Origin obscure. The English forms vary greatly, but *tarmaret*, *tormarith* resemble a recorded F. *terre mérite* and med. or mod.L. *terra merita* 'deserving or deserved earth', a name which the powder is said by Littré to have borne in commerce. The reason and origin of this L. and F. appellation are obscure; but in English the final *t* appears (by scribal error, or phonetic differentiation, or influence of such words as *arsenic*) to have become *c* or *k*, with the second *r* sometimes changed to *l* or *n*. Some have suggested a corruption of the Persian-Arabic name *kurkum* 'saffron', whence L., F., and Sp. *curcuma*; but the change seems too unlikely. The application of the name in Eng. to Tormentil arose apparently from some real or fancied similarity of properties or uses.

(Littré has s.v. *Curcuma* 'safran des Indes et curcuma, dite *terre-mérite*, quand elle est réduite en poudre'. Hatz.-Darm. have also, s.v. *Curcuma*, Du Pinet, 16th c. in Delbœuf *Recueil* 'La curcuma ou terra merita des apothicaires'.)]

1. The aromatic and pungent root-stock of an East Indian plant (see 2), or the powder made of this, the chief ingredient in curry powder, used also in dyeing yellow, and as a chemical test, and in the East as a condiment and medicinally; also called *curcuma* (CURCUMA b).

1545 *Rates of Custome* c vj b, Tarmaret the C. pounde xl s. **1577** *Richmond Wills* (Surtees) 269 Spicknell, turmirick, and galingall ijᵈ. **1586** *Rates of Custome* F j, Tormarith the c, contayning v. xx. xii. pound, iij. l. vj. s. viij. d. **1607** TOPSELL *Four-f. Beasts* (1658) 300 Take..of Ale a quart, and put thereunto of Saffron, Turmerick, of each half an ounce [for the Yellows (Jaundice) in the horse]. **1614** MARKHAM *Cheap Husb.* I. (1668) Table, *Turn-merick* is a yellow Simple, of strong savour, to be bought at the Apothecaries. **1621** *Shuttleworths' Acc.* (Chetham Soc.) 248 Longe peper graines and turmerocke. **1685** *Minute Bk. New Mills Cloth Manuf.* (S.H.S.) 97 Dye stuffs..tarmanick, logwood, woad. **1694** in Dunbar *Soc. Life Moray* (1865) 148 Ane kinkine tarmaluk, for dying. **1791** HAMILTON *Berthollet's Dyeing* II. II. III. iv. 185 Neither fustic nor turmeric gives a permanent colour. **1805** W. SAUNDERS *Min. Waters* iv. 117 The yellow of turmeric is not altered, shewing therefore the absence of an alkali. **1812** J. SMYTH *Pract. of Customs* (1821) 264 Turmerick..with alum, communicates a beautiful but perishable yellow dye to woollen cloth, cotton, or linen. It is also used as a drug. **1851** RICHARDSON *Geol.* v. (1855) 84 Alkalis..change to a reddish brown the yellow colour of paper stained with turmeric.

b. applied to other products: †by English herbalists to the root of Tormentil (in obs. F. *souchet de bois*, as distinct from *souchet d'Inde*, Indian galingale, curcuma) (Cotgr.); also, the root-stock of *Sanguinaria canadensis*, having medicinal qualities.

African turmeric, the fleshy underground stems of a species of *Canna*, cultivated in Sierra Leone and used for dyeing yellow. ***Indian turmeric*** (of N. America), the yellow root of *Hydrastis canadensis*, occasionally used in dyeing and medicinally. See also quot. 1898.

1538 TURNER *Libellus*, *Heptaphillon*, officinis bistorta, & tormentilla, nostratibus Tormentyll & Tormeryke dicitur. **1548** —— *Names of Herbes* 87 *Tormentilla*,..in englishe Tormentil, or Tomerik. **1857** DUNGLISON *Med. Lex.*, Turmeric, *Curcuma longa*, *Sanguinaria Canadensis*. **1888** *Encycl. Brit.* XXIII. 662/2 In Sierra Leone a kind of turmeric is obtained from a species of *Canna*. **1890** BILLINGS *Med. Dict.*, Indian turmeric, *Hydrastis canadensis*. **1898** MORRIS *Austral Eng.*, *Turmeric*, i.q. *Stinkwood* (q.v.); also applied occasionally to *Hakea dactyloides*, N.O. *Proteaceæ*. [*Ibid.*, *Stinkwood*,..in Tasmania,..the timber of *Zieria smithii*, Andr., N.O. *Rutaceæ*.]

2. The plant *Curcuma longa*, N.O. *Zingiberaceæ*.

1601 HOLLAND *Pliny* XXI. xviii. II. 101 Cyperus..is counted to have a depilatorie vertue for to fech off haire. [*Margin*] This Cyperis is taken to be Curcuma, or Terramerita, called therupon corruptly, Turmericke. **1671** SALMON *Syn. Med.* III. xxii. 397 Curcuma, κυπάρισσος ἰνδικός, Turmerick, the root opens the Gall,.. cures the Jaundies. **1785** MARTYN *Rousseau's Bot.* xi. (1794) 118 This order contains several interesting plants, such as..turmerick. **1840** F. D. BENNETT *Whaling Voy.* I. 42 Tobacco and turmeric grow wild in great abundance.

3. *attrib.* and *Comb.*, as ***turmeric crop***, ***plant***, ***powder***, ***root***, ***test-paper***, ***water***; ***turmeric-faced*** adj.; **turmeric-oil** = TURMEROL; **turmeric paper**, unsized paper tinged with a solution of turmeric, used as a test for alkalis; **turmeric pudding**, a pudding coloured with turmeric; **turmeric-tree**, *Zieria Smithii* (*Acronychia Baueri*), the stinkwood of Tasmania, a tree having bright yellow inner bark.

1912 Thurston *Omens & Superst. S. India* vii. 206 A human sacrifice, which was intended to give a rich colour to the *turmeric crop. **1840** Hood *Up the Rhine* 48 That *turmeric-faced Yankee is my evil genius. **1809** Pearson in *Phil. Trans.* XCIX. 316 The presence of an alkali I could in no instance perceive, by means of the usual tests, namely, *turmeric paper, litmus paper [etc.]. **1826** Henry *Elem. Chem.* II. 522 Turmeric paper and tincture are changed to a reddish brown by alkalis... Turmeric paper.. however.. is turned brown by muriatic acid gas and strong acids in general. **1857** *G. Bird's Urin. Deposits* (ed. 5) 288 The urine was clear, alkaline, turning turmeric paper brown. **1837** *Penny Cycl.* VIII. 233/2 *Curcuma longa*, the *Turmerick plant. **1866** *Treas. Bot.* 1250/2 The ground ginger of the shops is adulterated with sago-meal,.. mustard husks, and *turmeric powder. *a* **1704** T. Brown *Walk round Lond., Thames* Wks. 1709 III. iii. 59 To make his Countenance shine like a *Turmerick Pudding. **1843** *Penny Cycl.* XXV. 416/2 *Turmeric root. **1868** Watts *Dict. Chem.* V. 919 The root of *Canna speciosa*,.. in West Africa, is said to be exactly similar to East Indian turmeric-root, in taste, smell, and chemical reactions. **1880** J. Dunbar *Pract. Papermaker* 70 *Turmeric test paper. **1866** *Treas. Bot.* 1249/2 One [species of Zieria] common at Illawarra, and there called *Turmeric-tree, has a very yellow inner bark, suitable for dyeing. **1913** Frazer *Gold. Bough* I. ii. vi. 68 Smeared with *turmeric water, they all bathe and return home.

B. *adj. Chem.* Obtained from turmeric: in ***turmeric acid***, an acid, $C_{11}H_{14}O_2$, formed by the oxidation of turmerol.

turmerol (ˈtɜːmərɒl). *Chem.* [f. turmer-ic + -ol 3.] (See quot.)

1890 Billings *Med. Dict.*, *Turmerol*, $C_{19}H_{28}O$, an aromatic volatile product obtained by Jackson and Menke (1882–83) from turmeric.

turmoil (ˈtɜːmɔɪl), *sb.* Forms: see turmoil *v.* [See turmoil *v.*] A state of agitation or commotion; disturbance, tumult; trouble, disquiet.

1526 *Pilgr. Perf.* (W. de W. 1531) 75 Where.. the mynde is full of vayne cogitacyons and turmoyle of worldly desyres. **1555** Eden *Decades* 144 In all the turmoyles and tragicall affayres of the Ocean, nothynge hath so muche displeased me as the couetousnes of this man. **1596** Dalrymple tr. *Leslie's Hist. Scot.* ii. (S.T.S.) I. 138 Nathir in al this truble and Tormoyle of the Scottis was the Pechtis frie of truble. **1698** Fryer *Acc. E. India & P.* 2 What makes these Seas in such a constant Turmoil? **1792** V. Knox *Serm.* xix. 412 The noise of business, as it is called, or the jarring turmoil which avarice occasions. **1838** Thirlwall *Greece* II. xv. 251 For four years longer Asia was still kept in restless turmoil. **1872** Jenkinson *Guide Eng. Lakes* (1879) 259 Relics of bygone ages of turmoil and border warfare. **1888** Bryce *Amer. Commw.* I. vii. 90 The presidential election.. throws the country for several months into a state of turmoil.

†**b.** Harassing labour, toil. *Obs. rare.*

1568 Grafton *Chron.* II. 915 Myning and digging tynne and mettall oute of the grounde both daye and night with great turmoile and laboure. **1591** Shaks. *Two Gent.* ii. vii. 37 And there Ile rest, as after much turmoile, A blessed soule doth in Elizium.

turmoil (ˈtɜːmɔɪl), *v.* Also 6 tour-, tor-, 6–7 -moile, -moyle, 7 -moyl. [Found along with turmoil *sb.* early in 16th c.; origin unascertained. There is no corresp. word in French, but some have conjectured a connexion with OF. *tremouille* (Cotgr.), in 17th c. *tremuye*, mod.F. *trémie de moulin* mill-hopper, in reference to its constant motion to and fro. The sb. is app. from the verb. In sense 3 app. associated with *moil*.]

1. a. *trans.* To agitate, disquiet, disturb; to throw into commotion and confusion; to trouble, harass, worry, torment. Often ***to toss and turmoil***. Now somewhat *rare*.

1530 Tindale *Gen.* Pref. A iij, I was so turmoyled in the contre where I was that I coude no lenger there dwell. **1530** —— *Answ. to More* iii. xiii, The matter in the meane tyme is turmoyled and tossed among them-selues. **1552** Latimer *Serm.*, *Luke ii. 6, 7* (1584) 279 b, Heritickes do wrongfully violate, tosse, and turmoyle the scriptures of God. *a* **1586** Sidney *Arcadia* (1622) 372 Yet of all other were Zelmanes braines most turmoyled, troubled with loue both actiue and passiue. **1610** Holland *Camden's Brit.* ii. 39 After he had beene tormoiled with many troubles. **1697** Dryden *Æneid* i. 381 Haughty Juno, who, with endless broils Earth, seas, and heav'n, and Jove himself, turmoils. **1746–7** Mrs. Delany in *Life & Corr.* (1862) II. 454 Mr. Stanley and twenty fiddle faddles have turmoiled me all the morning. **1862** *Zoologist* XX. 8151 Mr. Beilby.. could not be turmoiled with disputes of any kind. **1894** W. Walker *Hist. Congregat. Ch. U.S.* 53 The quarrel which was to turmoil the early Amsterdam life of this little communion had its beginnings in London.

b. To disorder or distress physically. *arch.*

1542 *Lam. & Piteous Treat.* in *Harl. Misc.* (Malh.) I. 241 Our shippes of warre, rydyng alongest the coste, were woondrefully turmoyled. **1561** T. Hoby tr. *Castiglione's Courtyer* ii. (1577) M vij b, A great throng of people caryed him to the ynne aboue grounde, all tourmoyled and without his cappe. **1601** Dolman *La Primaud. Fr. Acad.* (1618) III. 746 The seas are much turmoiled with tempests. *a* **1610** Healey *Theophrastus* (1636) 41 Hee will tosse, turmoile, and ransacke euery corner of the house. **1657** Trapp *Comm. Ps.* lxxvii. 17 The Lord.. so troubled and turmoiled them with stormy tempests. **1867** J. B. Rose tr. *Virgil's Æneid* 145 Aeolus.. let loose his slaves And on your ocean empire turmoiled waves.

†**c.** *refl. Obs.*

c **1511** Colet *Serm. Conf. & Ref.* B viij, Religious men.. nat to turmoile them selfe in busynes, nother secular nor other. **1530** *Proper Dyaloge* 194 in Roy *Rede me*, etc. (Arb.) 139 We tourmoyle oure selfes nyght and daye.. For to maynteyne the clargyes facciones. **1611** A. Stafford *Niobe* 202 Hee hath turmoiled himselfe through-out all the six Ages of the world. **1651** *C. Love's Case* 53 How doth he here toyl and turmoyl himself to salve the honor of his Conscience. **1720** Mrs. Manley *Power of Love* (1741) 76 After turmoiling himself for some Hours, he saw the Stone was cast, and that it was in vain now to repine.

†**d.** With advb. extension: *fig.* To drive or throw roughly or without ceremony. *Obs.*

1588 G. D. *Brief Discov. Dr. Allen's Sedit. Drifts* 112 They were imprisoned, tossed, and turmoyled from place to place. **1596** Spenser *F.Q.* iv. ix. 39 But thus turmoild from one to other stowre I wast my life. **1602** *Contention betw. Liberality & Prodigality* iv. i. D iij b, I haue bin turmoyled From post to piller.

2. *intr.* To be or live in turmoil, agitation, or commotion; to move agitatedly or restlessly; (in quot. 1900 in humorous mock-solemn use). Now *rare*.

c **1540** tr. *Pol. Verg. Eng. Hist.* (Camden) I. 186 Then Eugenius the viij. Fergusius the iij. bothe continuallie weltered and turmoyled in fillthie vices. **1548** Recorde *Urin. Physick* ii. (1651) 4 If the way by any means be stopped, then the water turmoileth and laboureth. **1560** Daus tr. *Sleidane's Comm.* 134 Nowe that God hathe made a restraynte, he rageth and tourmoyleth. **1618** G. Strode *Anat. Mortalitie* 9 Sicke men which turmoile and tosse from one side of the bed vnto the other. **1681** in *Lond. Gaz.* No. 1640/6 Continual overflows of violent Misrule.. turmoiling to a common Chaos. **1900** W. Sewell in W. Tuckwell *Reminisc. Oxford* xiii. 237 Garlic, deadlier without question E'en than hemlock: oh digestion... What is this, that still so deep here, Keeps turmoiling in my chest? **1981** T. Holme *Funeral of Gondolas* v. 216 The noise of the storm receded. Outside, where it still turmoiled, was a long way away.

3. *intr.* To toil, drudge; cf. moil *v.* 3. Now *dial.*

a **1548** Hall *Chron., Hen. VII* 41 Cornyshmen.. gate their lyuyng hardly.. bothe daye and night labouryng and turmoylyng. **1598** Barckley *Felic. Man* vi. (1603) 574 What doe men but digge and turmoile in the earth? **1652** C. B. Stapylton *Herodian* xx. 171 To stop the flame both Rich and poor Turmoile, Some carry hooks, some water Conduits turne. **1684** N. S. *Crit. Enq. Edit. Bible* iv. 22 A person that had very much and long turmoil'd in these studies. *c* **1755** Murphy *Apprentice* i. i, I have been turmoiling for the fellow all the days of my life. **1759** Sarah Fielding *C'tess of Dellwyn* I. 53 That [mind] which is burthened with many Griefs, and at the same time is turmoiling and bustling. **1840** Pusey tr. *Confess. August.* iii. vi. 11 Toiling and turmoiling through want of Truth. **1901** F. E. Taylor *Folk-Sp. S. Lanc.* s.v., He has for t' turmoil hard for his bread.

Hence **ˈturmoiled, ˈturmoiling** *ppl. adjs.*

1550 Bale *Apol.* 33 A doctryne.. for turmoylynge Thomistes. *c* **1555** Harpsfield *Divorce Hen. VIII* (Camden) 221 The tossing, turmoyling, tempestuous sea. **1570–6** Lambarde *Peramb. Kent* (1596) 429 In the time of the turmoiled King Ethelred, the whole fleete of the Danish army lay at roade.. before Greenewiche. **1671** F. Phillips *Reg. Necess.* 141 A turmoiled impoverished, and over burdened Debtor. **1676** E. Bury *Medit.* 322 Turmoiling thoughts, how he shall pay his rent, discharge his debts. **1735** Sewel *Dutch Dict.*, *Raasbol*, a Turmoiling fellow. **1823** Scott *Quentin D.* v, Quentin.. endeavoured to compose his turmoiled and scattered thoughts. **1866** J. B. Rose tr. *Ovid's Met.* 332 The turmoiled waters gurgitate the crew.

turmoiler (ˈtɜːmɔɪlə(r)). *rare.* [f. turmoil *v.* + -er[1].] One who turmoils; a disquieter.

1591 Percivall *Sp. Dict.*, *Rebolvedor*, an ouerturner, a turmoiler, a disquieter. **1906** W. Walker *Calvin* xii. 335 He was an intentional turmoiler of the public peace.

turmoiling (ˈtɜːmɔɪlɪŋ), *vbl. sb.* [f. turmoil *v.* + -ing[1].] The action of the verb turmoil; commotion, agitation, disquietude; also, toiling, severe labour.

1550 Latimer *Serm. Stamford* (1562) 102 b, I was once in examination before fiue or sixe Bishops, where I had much turmoyling. **1550** Bale *Eng. Votaries* ii. M iv, To rehearce yᵉ turmoilinges of Pope Calixte yᵉ second. **1578** Lyte *Dodoens* iii. xxxiv. 365 It rayseth vp great windinesse, blastinges, tormoyling and ouerturning the whole body. **1691** Wood *Ath. Oxon.* II. 205 After a great deal of moyling, turmoyling, perfidiousness, and I know not what, he laid down his head and died. **1863** Cowden Clarke *Shaks. Char.* xi. 291 Amidst the turmoiling and common-places of every-day action.

†**turmoilous**, *a. Obs. rare.* [f. turmoil *sb.* + -ous.] Full of turmoil or tumult; disturbed, troublous. So **ˈturmoily** *a. rare*, in same sense.

1553 Eden *Treat. Newe Ind.* (Arb.) 10 Settynge forth Christes true Relygion in those turmoylous dayes. **1877** Mary Mohl in Simpson *Lett. & Recoll.* (1887) 360 This country is in a great turmoily state.

turmyntyne, obs. corrupt f. turpentine.

turn (tɜːn), *sb.* Forms: 3– turn; also 3–7 turne, 4–6 torn, torne, 4–7 tourne, 5–7 tourn, 6 terne. [Partly a. AF. **torn, turn, tourn*, = OF. *tor, tour*, F. *tour* (= Pr. *torn, tor*, Cat. *torn*, Sp., Pg., It. *torno*):—L. *torn-us* (acc. *-um*), a. Gr. τόρνος turning-lathe. Cf. for the form, F. *jour*, AF. *jorn*:—L. *diurn-um*. In English, partly treated as n. of action from turn *v.* (So OF. *torne, tourne*, fr. *tourner* vb.) See also tour *sb.* from the later French form.]

I. Rotation, and connected senses. (Cf. turn *v.* I, II.)

1. The action of turning about an axis or centre, as a wheel; rotation, revolution. Now *rare*.

c **1250** *Gen. & Ex.* 79 On walkenes turn wid dai and niȝt Of foure and twenti time riȝt. *c* **1400** *Rom. Rose* 5470 Froward Fortune.., Whanne high estatis she doth reverse, And maketh hem to tumble doune Off hir whele, with sodeyn tourne. **1500–20** Dunbar *Poems* xxiv. 8 Fortoun sa fast hir quheill dois cary; Na tyme bot turne can [*v.r.* in turning can it] tak rest. *c* **1680** Hickeringill *Hist. Whiggism* ii. Wks. 1716 I. 111 Fortune's-wheel.. is always.. upon the Turn. **1879** J. Martineau *Hours Th.* (1880) II. i. 6 You may expect a prize from the turn of a lottery.

2. a. An act of turning; a movement of rotation (total or partial); *esp.* a single revolution, as of a wheel.

1481 Caxton *Myrr.* iii. viii. 148 The sonne.. gooth euery yere aboute the heuen one torne. **1596** Davies *Orchestra* lxxi, A gallant daunce,.. With loftie turnes and capriols. **1665** Boyle *Occas. Refl.* i. vi, The Giddy turns of Fortune's Wheel. **1687** A. Lovell tr. *Thevenot's Trav.* i. 35 He darts his Zagaye.. with a turn of hand that doubles the force of it. **1759** Smeaton in *Phil. Trans.* LI. 157 The turns of the sails in a given time will be as the square of the velocity of the wind. **1849** Clough *Dipsychus* ii. ii. 32 And hear the soft turns of the oar! **1872** Ruskin *Fors Clav.* (1896) I. xix. 370 In a few turns of the hands of the.. clock.

b. (*roasted, done*, etc.) ***to a turn***, i.e. exactly to the proper degree, precisely right: orig. in reference to the turns of the spit.

1780 Mackenzie *Mirror* No. 93 ¶ 12 The beef was roasted to a turn. **1864** D. G. Mitchell *Sev. Stor.* 11 The chops were done to a turn.

c. ***turn of the scale***(*s*, the slight advantage given to the buyer by which the article sold overbalances the weight and brings down the scale-pan. Hence, a very slight degree or amount, a very little (just enough to ***turn the scale***: see turn *v.* 58).

In quot. 1888 ***the turn of a hair*** = a close chance, a 'narrow shave'. But cf. *not to turn a hair*, in hair *sb.* 8 n.

1888 *Century Mag.* May 127/1 It was the turn of a hair that they hadn't buried him alive. **1890** 'R. Boldrewood' *Col. Reformer* (1891) 218 All that's a turn too good for making slaughter-yard bacon, does for the Chinamen.

d. ***turn of the screw***: an additional twist to tighten up the hold; an extra twist given to a thumbscrew by way of increasing the torture (in quots. *fig.*).

1796 [see screw *sb.*[1] 2 a]. **1853** Dickens *Bleak House* xxiv. 331 (*heading*) A turn of the screw. **1898** H. James *Turn of Screw* 4 If the child [in a ghost story] gives the effect another turn of the screw, what do you say to *two* children? **1940** *Manch. Guardian Weekly* 1 Mar. 175 Even more far-reaching schemes of increasing direct taxation.. are certain to be realised.. whenever the psychological ground is favourable for this further turn of the screw. **1973** *Listener* 14 June 785/2 The first turns of the screw on the car commuter are already being prepared. The GLC wants to put up parking fines from £4 to £20.

3. A brain-disease of sheep and cattle, caused by a hydatid, and characterized by giddiness: = gid[1]. Also *transf.* a beast affected with this (quot. 1658).

1523 Fitzherb. *Husb.* §62 *heading*, The turne, and remedy therfore. **1651** *Manchester Crt. Leet Rec.* (1887) IV. 51 Sellinge a beast.. yett had the turne. **1658** *Ibid.* 243 Sellinge parte of a Turne which was not Markettable. **1718** Bp. Hutchinson *Witchcraft* ix. (1720) 162 Twirl like a Calf that hath the Turn. **1805** R. W. Dickson *Pract. Agric.* II. 1168 The Turn or Giddy is a disorder with which these animals [sheep] are often seized.

4. A movement round something, a twist; *spec. Naut.* an act of passing a rope once round a mast or other object.

1743 Bulkeley & Cummins *Voy. S. Seas* 115 All Hands haul'd, took a Turn round the Main-Mast, and went aft. **1881** Whitehead *Hops* 35 The young bines only take short turns, and cannot lay hold of supports which are stout at the base. **1882** Nares *Seamanship* (ed. 6) 256 The blocks.. act like a sailor's 'turn and a half'.

5. *Mus.* A melodic ornament consisting of a group of three (four, or five) notes, viz. the principal note (*on* which it is performed) and the notes one degree above and below it.

In the ***common*** or ***direct turn***, the note above precedes, and that below follows, the principal note; in the ***inverted turn*** or ***back-turn***, the note below precedes and that above follows; in either case, the principal note is repeated at the end, and sometimes also precedes. ***turn of a shake***: see quot. 1881 s.v. shake *sb.*[1] 5.

1801 Busby *Dict. Mus.* **1818** —— *Gram. Mus.* 143 Full, or Double Turn. Partial Turn. Inverted Turn. **1868** Browning *Ring & Bk.* i. 1210 Clavecinist debarred his instrument, He yet thrums—shirking neither turn nor trill, ..on dumb table-edge.

6. The condition of being, or direction in which something is, twisted or convoluted; hence, a portion or 'length' of something of a convoluted or twisted form, corresponding to one whole revolution; a (single) coil or twist; a round (of coiled rope, etc.); (*Naut.*) a twist of rope round a mast, etc.

1669 Ray in *Phil. Trans.* IV. 1011 Observations Concerning the odd Turn of some Shell-snailes... The Turn of the wreaths is from the right hand to the left. **1678** *Lond. Gaz.* No. 1269/4 A dapple gray Mare,.. a feather under the mane, two turns in the forehead. **1774** Goldsm. *Nat. Hist.* (1776) VII. 32 Its convolutions are more numerous. The garden snail has but five turns at the most; in the sea snail the convolutions are sometimes.. ten. **1827** D. Johnson *Ind. Field Sports* 83 Wound round with a few turns of fine silk.

1884 Higgs *Magn. & Dynamo Electr. Machines* 214 We can ..calculate the length..of the turns wound on a magnetic core, if we divide the length of the coil by the number of turns. **1886** R. Brown *Spunyarn & Spindrift* vii. 91, I.. jumped to let go of the main-sheet. But Lord! we was in the white water almost before I could cast the turns off. **1930** *Sea Breezes* 74 Brushing off the snow and hammering gasket turns warmed my hands.

7. Something that turns or spins round; a rotatory apparatus or contrivance. **a.** A lathe; now only applied to a watchmaker's lathe, also called ***a pair of turns***. **b.** A spinning-wheel, windlass, or the like; in quot. 1578, a top. ? *Obs.* exc. *dial.* **c.** = turntable 2.

a. 1483 *Cath. Angl.* 397/2 A Turne of a turnour, *tornus.* **1580** Hollyband *Treas. Fr. Tong, Vu tour*.., a turne, as *boule faite au tour*, a boule made at the turne. **1668** *Phil. Trans.* III. 795 An Artist, that polishes Optick-Glasses on a Turn. **1884** F. J. Britten *Watch & Clockm.* 202 The wheel ..is put in a pair of turns. *Ibid.* 205 The hollows of small pinions are often polished in the turns.

b. *c* **1564** in Noake *Worc. Relics* (1877) 10 A spynynge turne and a spolynge turne. **1578** Lyte *Dodoens* vi. vi. 664 Almost like to a little Turne or Peare, brode beneath, and narrow aboue. **1675** *Phil. Trans.* X. 452 It shot off the Turne at the mouth of the Pit. **1688** R. Holme *Armoury* iii. 342/1 An Engine called a Turne, or the Turne Engine..by which great Weights are lifted up. **1870** R. S. Hawker *Footpr. Far Cornw.* 88 The mother stood by her turn or wheel, and span.

c. *a* **1668** Lassels *Voy. Italy* (1670) II. 71 A grate..where ..infants are put into a squar hole of a Turne, and so turned in by night. **1808** Lady Jerningham *Lett.* (1896) I. 321 Her victuals were put in a turn, like at a Convent. **1932** G. F.-H. Berkeley *Italy in Making* I. xviii. 268 At suitable points were inset 'turns', similar to those used in convents, so as to enable the servants to hand in food for both the cardinals and their attendants, without themselves entering the isolated wing. **1966** M. C. Lorang *Footloose Scientist in Mayan America* 90 Food was passed into the dining room through a '*turn*'..—a hollow roller set into the wall so that when one side is open, the other side is closed.

II. Change of direction or course, and connected senses. (Cf. turn *v.* III, IV, V.)

8. a. An act of turning or facing another way; a change of direction or posture.

1412–20 Lydg. *Chron. Troy* iv. 3273 Fortnys variaunce, ..And sodeyn torn of hir false visage. **1606** Shaks. *Ant. & Cl.* ii. v. 59 He's bound vnto Octauia. *Cleo.* For what good turne? *Mes.* For the best turne i' th' bed. **1754** Richardson *Grandison* (1810) IV. xxxii. 237 Her..half-saucy turns upon him. **1827** Scott *Surg. Dau.* xiv, Shooting a glance at his.. companion by a turn of the eye. **1847** Tennyson *Princess* iv. 375 She..made a sudden turn As if to speak.

b. 'A step off the ladder at the gallows' (J.); hanging. Cf. turn *v.* 74 d. Now *rare* or *Obs.*

1631 Weever *Anc. Fun. Mon.* 49 What man will venture a turne at the Gallows, for a little small siluer chalice?

c. Change of position (by a rotatory movement) of something inanimate, as a die when thrown.

1801 Strutt *Sports & Past.* Introd. iii. 4 Stake their liberty upon the turn of the dice. **1802** Mar. Edgeworth *Moral T.* (1816) I. xi. 89 Few people choose to venture a hundred guineas upon the turn of a straw. **1809** Malkin *Gil Blas* v. i. ¶29 Florence and her dowry therefore were lost.. by a turn of the dice.

d. *Cards.* The dealing or inversion of two cards in faro; hence ***to call the turn***, to guess the order of the last three cards in the pack. Also *fig.*

1864 W. B. Dick *Amer. Hoyle* 207 The two cards drawn from the dealer's box—one for the bank and the other for the player..constitute a turn. **1889** *Cent. Dict.* s.v. *faro*, The showing of two cards constitutes a 'turn'. After each turn new bets are made for another, down to the last three cards of the pack; the only betting allowed after this is on 'calling the turn', or guessing which will show first. **1901** H. James *Sacred Fount* 44 The face of Guy Brissenden, as recognizable at a distance as the numbered card of a 'turn'. **1908** *Sat. Even. Post* 5 Dec. 18/2 Ye-e-s, but this Wallingford person called the turn. **1940** D. W. Maurer *Big Con* viii. 257 The odds are always greater on the last turn, and anyone who wins on that play may make a young fortune. **1964** A. Wykes *Gambling* vii. 169 When three [cards] are left (the 'last turn'), players bet on the order of their appearance.

e. *Cricket.* A deviation of the ball's course after pitching; = break *sb.*[1] 5.

1900 P. F. Warner *Cricket in Many Climes* 190 The Newlands ground is the most difficult to make runs on in the whole of South Africa, the bowlers always being able to get considerable turn on the ball. **1977** *Observer* 30 Jan. 23/8 A deficit of even 50 runs..could pose problems for England because the spinners have already begun to extract a lot of turn.

9. *Printing.* A reversal of type in composing; also *concr.* a type turned face downwards so as to produce a square black mark on the proof, in place of a missing letter.

1888 J. H. Hessels in *Encycl. Brit.* XXIII. 693/1 The whole of the last reference-line is put in upside down... A 'turn' of this magnitude could hardly have occurred [etc.].

10. a. An act (or, rarely, the action) of turning aside from one's course; deflection, deviation; a round-about course, a detour. Also *fig.*

a **1300** *Cursor M.* 4323 (Cott.) Qua folus lang, wit-outen turn, Oft his fote sal find a spurn. *c* **1410** *Master of Game* (MS. Digby 182) xxx, þen he shulde make a longe turne and vmbicaste aboute by somme wayes, or by pathes. *c* **1530** Ld. Berners *Arth. Lyt. Bryt.* (1814) 327 And some behelde the hye tournes & tournynges of the sakers & gerfawcons. **1685–6** Stillingfl. *Serm.* (1698) III. i. 13 True Repentance is the turn of the whole Soul from the Love, as well as the Practice of Sin. **1689–90** Temple *Ess. Heroic Virt.* Wks. 1731 I. 222 The Arians..made easy Turns to the Mahometan Doctrines, that professed Christ to have been so great and so divine a Prophet. **1874** Whyte Melville *Uncle John* xxiii, To follow him through the many turns and windings of his wearisome..chase. **1892** Greener *Breech Loader* 231 The woodcock..is one of the most difficult birds to bag;..its turn to right and left being most erratic.

b. in phr. ***at every turn***: usually *fig.* at every change of circumstance (cf. 18); hence, on every occasion, constantly, continually.

(Cf. quot. 1579 in turning *vbl. sb.* 4 b.)

1590 Shaks. *Mids. N.* iii. i. 114 Ile leade you about a Round, Through bogge, through bush, through brake,.. And neigh, and barke, and grunt,..Like horse, hound, hog, ..at euery turne. *c* **1685** South *Serm., Will for Deed* (1715) 377 One or both..being used by Men, almost at every Turn, to elude the Precept. **1735** Berkeley *Reasons* etc. §2 Wks. 1871 III. 340 Should he at every turn say such uncouth things. **1876** Trevelyan *Life & Lett. Macaulay* II. ix. 131 Compelled to disgust his supporters at every turn. **1907** *Blackw. Mag.* Apr. 48 Palaces of rusticated stone meet us at every turn.

11. a. A place or point at which a road, river, or the like turns, or turns off; a curved or bent part of anything; a bend, curve, or angle.

1412–20 Lydg. *Chron. Troy* i. 1367 Thoruȝ many halle and many riche tour, By many tourn and many diuerse way. **1513** Douglas *Æneis* ix. vii. 26 The horsmen than prekis, and fast furth sprentis To weil beknawin pethis, and turnys [and] wentis. **1688** R. Holme *Armoury* iv. xi. (Roxb.) 438/2 Annoynted..in..the breast, betweene the shoulders, in the Joynts, and turne of the Armes. **1768** Sterne *Sent. Journ., Pulse* (1778) I. 163 There are two turns; and be so good as to take the second. **1816** Byron *Ch. Har.* iii. lv. Song iv, The river nobly..flows,..And all its thousand turns disclose Some fresher beauty. **1856** Kane *Arct. Expl.* I. xxiii. 286 They..walked around the turn of the cape.

b., c. *Mining.* (See quots.)

b. 1681 T. Houghton *Rara Avis* Gloss. (E.D.S.), *Turn*, a pit sunk in some part of a drift; if the mine be deep, there is many of these turns, one below another. **1824** Mander *Derbysh. Miner's Gloss.* s.v., Eight, ten, or twelve fathoms is [a depth] common for a Turn; and note, that a vein which is wrought ninety or a hundred fathoms must have divers Turns.

c. 1851 Greenwell *Coal-trade Terms Northumb. & Durh.* 55 *Turns*, curved plates, made of cast metal, used at a branch-off tramway in the workings. **1886** J. Barrowman *Sc. Mining Terms* 69 *Turn*,..the arrangement of rails, sleepers and pulleys at a curve on a haulage road.

d. *Golf.* The point in the course (after the ninth hole) at which the players begin the return journey.

1899 *Golf Illustrated* 1 Sept. 336/2 The hole was halved, as were also the eighth and ninth... The match..was all square at the turn. **1930** *Cambridge Daily News* 24 Sept. 7/3 Compston, who went out in 37 and was five up at the turn, won by seven and five.

12. *Arch.* The curved flank or haunch of an arch, between the key-stone and the foot. ? *Obs.*

1726 Leoni tr. *Alberti's Archit.* I. 53/2 An Arch is..a conjunction..of wedges, whereof some..are call'd the foot .., those in the middle above, the Key.., and those on the sides.., the Turn, or Ribs of the Arch.

13. The act of turning so as to face about or go in the opposite direction; reversal of position or course; turning back. ***on the turn***, in or close upon the act of turning, at the turning-point. Also *fig.* esp. in ***turn of the tide***, etc. (cf. tide *sb.* 9).

1669 R. Fleming *Fulfill. Script.* (1801) I. 302 Antichrist should be at his height and his kingdom upon the turn. **1690** C. Nesse *O. & N. Test.* I. 271 The half-turn, from West to North. *Ibid.*, The whole turn from West to East. *Ibid.*, The round turn from sin to Christ. **1782** Miss Burney *Cecilia* vii. v, Whether we shall go on, or take a turn back? **1796** —— *Camilla* V. 540 Such turns in the tide of fortune. **1862** R. H. Patterson *Ess. Hist. & Art* 329 Fine Art is at a low ebb. But ..the tide is on the turn.

14. *Coursing.* The act of suddenly turning, as a hare when closely pursued, and making off more or less in the opposite direction, or at least at a considerable angle from the direction of pursuit. Usually in phr. ***to give the hare*** (etc.) ***a turn***, said of the hound.

1575 Turberv. *Venerie* 246 A Cote is when a Greyhounde goeth endways by his fellow and giueth the Hare a turne (which is called setting a Hare aboute). **1670** Narborough *Jrnl.* in *Acc. Sev. Late Voy.* i. (1694) 30 A Greyhound..gave Chase to one of them, and at last gave her a turn. **1834** T. Thacker *Courser's Comp.* I. 183 A turn to be reckoned one point; but if the hare turn not, as it were round, she only wrenches... A wrench is when she strikes off..at about a right angle. **1856** 'Stonehenge' *Brit. Sports* i. iii. viii. 212/1 It is a Turn if the hare is forced more than 45 degrees, and one point is to be scored.

†**15. a.** A journey, expedition, tour, course. *Obs.*

c **1400** *St. Alexius* (Laud 622) 341 He took his tourne From Rome. **1570** Levins *Manip.* 191/13 Turne,..*cursus.* **1665** Chas. II in Julia Cartwright *Henrietta of Orleans* (1894) 224, I am goeing to make a little turne into dorset sheere for 8 or 9 dayes. **1734** H. Walpole *Let.* Oct., in *10th Rep. Hist. MSS. Comm.* App. i. 254 His design to take a turn into England.

b. A sheriff's tour, or court: see tourn.

†**c.** *Venery.* Pairing of roe-deer. *Obs.*

1486 *Bk. St. Albans* E iv b, Then shall the Roobucke gendre with the Roo..Then is he calde a Roobucke goyng in his turne. **1610** Guillim *Heraldry* iii. xiv. (1660) 166 You shall sey Roe goeth to his Tourne.

16. a. An act of walking or pacing around or about a limited area, as a park, garden, or sequence of streets; a short walk (or ride) forth and back, esp. by a different route; a stroll.

a **1591** H. Smith *Wks.* (1866) I. 185 Go now and walk in thy galleries, fetch one turn more before thou be turned out of door. **1610** Shaks. *Temp.* iv. i. 162 A turne or two Ile walke To still my beating minde. **1710** Steele *Tatler* No. 160 ¶2, I took several Turns about my Chamber. **1715** *Lond. Gaz.* No. 5336/1 He..has..taken a Turn on Horse-back on the Isle. **1823** Scott *Quentin D.* Introd., This circumstance of explanation and remark..occupied us during two or three turns upon the long terrace. **1867** Trollope *Chron. Barset* xlvii, I will take a turn round the garden.

b. *Knitting.* See quot.

1893 Eliz. Rosevear *Text-bk. Needlework*, etc. 406 A Turn is used for two rows in the same stitches backwards and forwards.

III. Change in general. (See also sense 36.) Cf. turn *v.* VI.

17. The action, or an act, of turning or changing; change, alteration, modification; in quot. 1901, change of colour. *rare* exc. as in next sense. ***on the turn***, turning sour, as food; of the weather or the season, changing.

1597 Hooker *Eccl. Pol.* v. xxxviii. §1 An admirable facilitie which musique hath to expresse..the turnes and varieties of all passions. **1726** Leoni tr. *Alberti's Archit.* I. 3/2 Sudden Turns and Changes in the Air, from Hot to Cold, and from Cold to Hot. *c* **1850** *Arab. Nights* (Rtldg.) 251 One..would fain have given a turn to these melancholy ideas by singing a little air to her lute. **1901** L. Malet *Sir R. Calmady* iii. ii, The turn of the leaf was very brilliant.

18. *spec.* **a.** A change in affairs, conditions, or circumstances; vicissitude; revolution; *esp.* a change for better or worse, or the like, at a crisis; hence, sometimes, the time at which such a change takes place. (Often *fig.* from or associated with 10.)

1607 Shaks. *Cor.* iv. iv. 12 Oh World, thy slippery turnes! Friends now fast sworn..shall within this houre..breake out To bitterest Enmity. **1622** Bacon *Hen. VII* 217 The State of Christendome might by this late Accident haue a turne. **1725** B. Higgons *Rem. Burnet* i. Hist. Wks. 1736 II. 71 Why the Republicans..made so little Opposition to a Turn of State [the Restoration] which must infallibly be their Ruin. **1781** Gibbon *Decl. & F.* xviii. II. 120 The engagement..was maintained with various and singular turns of fortune. **1842** Tennyson *Two Voices* 55 Some turn this sickness yet might take. **1892** W. Ramage *Last Words* 65 Two turns are possible in a crisis: the issue may be favourable or fatal.

b. ***turn of life***: a name for the time, or symptoms, of cessation of menstruation: = *change of life* (change *sb.* 3 d).

1834 Cooper *Good's Study Med.* (ed. 4) IV. 54 *note*, When menstruation is about to cease, the period is called 'the change or turn of life'. **1860** Mayne *Expos. Lex., Turn of Life*, popular term for the constitutional disturbance frequently attendant on the cessation of the catamenia.

c. The point at which one named period of time gives way to the next; the beginning or end *of* a named period of time, regarded in relation to the transition point between it and the preceding or following period; *spec.* (*a*) ***turn of the century***, the beginning or end of the century under consideration; also (usu. with hyphens) *attrib.* or as *adj.*; (*b*) ***turn of the year***, the end of winter and the beginning of spring; also, the beginning of the calendar year.

1853 R. S. Surtees *Mr Sponge's Sporting Tour* lxxi. 395 Who doesn't know the chilling feel of an English spring, or rather of a day at the turn of the year before there is any spring? **1859** G. Meredith *R. Feverel* xxv, In the turn of the year. **1926** O. Barfield *Hist. in Eng. Words* xi. 195 Just before the turn of the century there burst..upon England that strange explosion..the Romantic Movement. **1934** J. C. Powys *Autobiogr.* vii. 300 How well I remember watching out the turn of the centuries—the nineteenth becoming the twentieth—in the little dining-room at Court House. **1935** *Discovery* Oct. 310/2 It is interesting to compare Dr Burr's notes, dating back to the turn of the century, with present conditions. **1947** R. Church in M. Balcon et al. *Eng. Lang. & Lit.* xii. 200/2 Blatant imperialism shouted with a loud voice round the turn of the last Victorian years. **1947** W. H. Lewis in *Ess. presented to C. Williams* 140 If they reached the port at the turn of the year,..the galleys, stripped to their hulls, would be emerging from their winter hibernation. **1952** G. Sarton *Hist. Sci.* I. xx. 512 We know that Autolycos was the teacher of..Arcesilaos of Pitane (315–240)... This suggests that he resided in Pitane and fixes the date approximately, the turn of the century. **1955** E. Blishen *Roaring Boys* iv. 251 The school lavatories..were a product of turn-of-the-century parsimony. **1955** I. & P. Opie *Oxford Dict. Nursery Rhymes* 4 Romantic lyrics of a decidedly free nature..which were carefully rewritten to suit the new discrimination at the turn of the last century. **1955** *Time & Tide* 19 Nov. 1503/1 Can those who were young in the nineteen-twenties..remember the favourites as vividly as their elders recollect the tunes of the century's turn? **1961** I. Murdoch *Severed Head* xiii. 120, I brought to mind that it was New Year's eve. Some nearer bells took up the peal... Soon it would be the turn of the year. **1961** *Times* 29 Dec. 11/7 Mr. William Brodie's sets, vaguely turn-of-the-century. **1965** C. E. Pocknee *Parson's Handbk.* (ed. 13) p. xiv, At the turn of this century there were many who were in that state. **1968** A. M. Farrer *Interpretation & Belief* (1976) 190 It was as a doctrine of free will that Neo-Platonism was embraced by St Augustine at the turn of the fourth to the fifth century. **1970** *New Scientist* 17 Sept. 563/1 The latest estimates suggest that the area will be short of..1 270 000 cu.m. a day in 1981, and more than three million cu.m. a day by the turn of the century. **1970** H. Braun *Parish Churches* i. 22 At the turn of the millennium the monastic churches were quite enormous. **1970** *Daily Tel.* 26 Feb. 6/2 It was inevitable that at the turn of the decade there should appear yet more 'condition of Britain' analyses. **1971** *Ibid.* 23 Aug. 8 At the turn of the year, Kuala

Lumpur officials talked confidently of reduced Communist terrorism along the Thai-Malaysia border. 1976 *National Observer* (U.S.) 29 May 9/1 Her modest, turn-of-the-century home on a quiet street in Indianapolis. 1976 *Church Times* 9 July 6/2 He begins with a splendid assembly of Church of England men all earnestly proclaiming, at the turn of the eighteenth and nineteenth centuries, doctrines then trendy. 1977 K. M. E. MURRAY *Caught in Web of Words* xv. 282 In 1897 James had set himself the target of completing half the letters of the alphabet by the turn of the century. 1979 *Sci. Amer.* Dec. 96/1 The evolutionary significance of the original Neanderthal discovery and of other human remains uncovered at Paleolithic sites was not apparent until the turn of the 20th century. 1981 'W. HAGGARD' *Money Men* xi. 122 What was still called the parlour..was vintage turn of the century.

19. A momentary shock caused by sudden alarm, fright, or the like. *colloq.* (Cf. 25 b.)

1846 DICKENS *Cricket on Hearth* ii, What a hard-hearted monster you must be, John, not to have said so, at once, and saved me such a turn! 1860 GEO. ELIOT *Mill on Fl.* I. vii, Mrs. Tulliver gave a little scream as she saw her, and felt such a 'turn' that she dropt the large gravy-spoon into the dish. 1886 BESANT *Children of Gibeon* II. xix, It was only a dream... But it gave me a terrible turn.

IV. Senses denoting actions of various kinds.

†**20.** A movement, device, or trick, by which a wrestler attempts to throw his antagonist: = F. *tour*.

a 1225 *Ancr. R.* 280 He iseih hu ueole þe grimme wrastlare of helle breid up on his hupe, & werp, mid þe haunche turn, into golnesse. *c* 1325 *Metr. Hom.* 83 Bot sinful man gers him [the devil] oft schurne, And castis him wit his awen turne. *c* 1400 *Gamelyn* 244 Of all the tornes that he cowthe he schewed him but oon, And caste him on the lefte syde that three ribbes to-brak. 1562 J. HEYWOOD *Prov. & Epigr.* (1867) 162 He is cast in his owne turne, that is likly And yet in all turnes he turnth wonders quikly.

21. A subtle device of any kind; a trick, wile, artifice, stratagem. ? *Obs.*

a 1225 *Ancr. R.* 78 Vre strencðe..aȝein þes deofles turnes & his fondunges. *c* 1380 *Sir Ferumb.* 796 Y warne þe of a torn ..Y leuede ȝond on a buchyment sarasyns wonder fale. *a* 1533 LD. BERNERS *Huon* lxiv. 221, I thynke to playe hym a tourne. 1697 VANBRUGH *Relapse* v. iii, Come, no equivocations, no Roman turns upon us. 1720 WATERLAND *Eight Serm.* Pref. 30 The unlearned Reader..may be easily imposed upon by little Turns, and Fallacies. 1735 H. WALPOLE *Let.* 9 Sept., in *10th Rep. Hist. MSS. Comm.* App. I. 259 A variety of artifices and turns.

†**22.** An act, deed, proceeding; a deed of valour, feat, exploit. *Obs.*

13.. *E.E. Allit. P.* B. 192 In þe creatores cort com neuer more, Ne neuer see hym with syȝt for such sour tournez. 1415 HOCCLEVE *To Sir J. Oldcastle* ii, Was no knyghtly turn no where, Ne no manhode shewid in no wyse, But Oldcastel wolde, his thankes, be there. 1590 *Reg. Privy Council Scot.* IV. 560 He had done greitar turnis nor to ding oute all thair harnis.

23. An act of good or ill will, or that does good or harm to another; a service: almost always with qualifying word, as ***good turn***, a benefit; ***bad***, ***evil***, ***ill***, †***shrewd turn***, an injury. Cf. *to do the turn* in 30 b (*c*).

13.. *Cursor M.* 4330 (Cott.) Sco [Potiphar's wife] waited him wit a werr turn. *c* 1386 CHAUCER *Pard. T.* 487 Hadde I nat doon a freendes torn to thee? *c* 1440 *Alphabet of Tales* lviii. 43, I hafe yit in my mynde a little gude turn at þou did me. *Ibid.* xcvii. 72 Thow hase done me ane ill turn. 1526 *Pilgr. Perf.* (W. de W. 1531) 98 Wysshe hym a shrewde turne, or saye, I wolde the deuyll had hym. 1546 J. HEYWOOD *Prov.* (1867) 34 One good tourne askth an other. 1647 H. MORE *Cupid's Conflict* xlv, He..Requiteth evil turns with hearty love. 1654 H. L'ESTRANGE *Chas. I* (1655) 15 One good turn deserves another. 1724 DE FOE *Mem. Cavalier* (1840) 242 Ready..to do us any ill turn. 1886 G. R. SIMS *Ring o' Bells*, etc. vii. 198, I did the lass a bad turn when I took her away.

24. A stroke or spell of work; a piece of work; a task, job. *Sc.* ? *Obs.* exc. in ***hand's turn*** (see HAND *sb.* 59).

c 1375 *Sc. Leg. Saints* xxx. (*Theodera*) 121 Of sorcery scho cuth do, And as scho mycht did turne and chare. 1572 *Satir. Poems Reform.* xxxii. 35 Thay..brocht thair butter and egges To Edinburgh Croce, and did na vther turne. 1609 SKENE *Reg. Maj.* II. xli. 36 b, The over-lord sall doe all the turnis and affairs perteining to the heire. 1791 J. LEARMONT *Poems* 331 My turns are lying to do.

25. a. A spell or bout of action, a 'go'; *spec.* a spell of wrestling; hence, a contest (quot. 1829). Now often associated with sense 28.

c 1380 *Sir Ferumb.* 335 Þov hast y dremed of venesoun; þov mostest drynke a torn. *a* 1400–50 *Alexander* 2276, I walde..now wrastyll a turne. ? *a* 1500 *Chester Pl.* vii. 246 A turne to take have I tight with my maistores. 1653 *Clarke Papers* (Camden) III. 9 Yesterday wee had another turne in the House. 1829 SCOTT *Anne of G.* xxv, We have seen..so many turns betwixt York and Lancaster. 1877 SPURGEON *Serm.* XXIII. 643 You young people, I like to see you run, and I am glad to take a turn at it myself. 1882 FURNIVALL in *E.E. Wills* Ded. 8 Since I first saw the Boxes and their contents at Doctors' Commons,..I always meant to have a turn at them.

b. An attack of illness, faintness, or the like; also, a fit of passion or excitement. (Cf. 19.)

1775 ABIGAIL ADAMS in *Fam. Lett.* (1876) 97 Jonathan is the only one..in the family who has not had a turn of the disorder. 1859 TENNYSON *Merl. & Vivien* 519 Not so much from wickedness, As some wild turn of anger, or a mood Of overstrain'd affection. 1913 EDITH WHARTON *Custom of Country* I. ii, Her mother..sat in a drooping attitude, her head sunk on her breast, as she did when she had one of her 'turns' [of palpitation].

c. *pl.* A name for monthly courses or catamenia.

1857 DUNGLISON *Med. Lex.*, *Turns*, menses.

†**26.** An event, circumstance, occurrence, hap. (Not always clearly distinguishable from 18.) In quot. 1719, a series or course of events (cf. 25). *Obs.* or merged in other senses.

1579 TOMSON *Calvin's Serm. Tim.* 853/1 Beside the losse of our time, there is a worse turne followeth it, and more deadly. 1596 SPENSER *F.Q.* VI. x. 18 The shepheard..broke his bag-pipe quight, And made great mone for that unhappy turne. 1708 MRS. CENTLIVRE *Busie Body* v. i, Pox on 't, this is an unlucky turn. What shall I say? 1719 DE FOE *Crusoe* (1840) II. xiii. 268 To bring this long turn of our affairs to a conclusion.

V. Occasion, etc.

†**27.** The occasion or time at which something happens. (Cf. 18, 26.) *Obs.*

13.. *Cursor M.* 19445 (Cott.) He sagh him croised þat ilk turn þat he for staning suld not skurn. *c* 1330 R. BRUNNE *Chron.* (1810) 154 Richard at þat turne gaf him a faire Juelle.

28. a. The time for action or proceeding of any kind which comes round to each individual of a series in succession; (each or any one's) recurring occasion of action, etc. in a series of acts done, or to be done, by (or to) a number in rotation. (Often in adverbial phrases: see below.)

c 1393 CHAUCER *Scogan* 42 Tak euery man his torn as for his tyme. 1586 B. YOUNG *Guazzo's Civ. Conv.* IV. 188 It came to L. Iohns turne to drinke. 1593 SHAKS. *3 Hen. VI*, II. ii. 105 Then 'twas my turne to fly, and now 'tis thine. 1642 DENHAM *Sophy* Prol. 10 His turne will come, to laugh at you agen. 1697 COLLIER *Ess.* II. *Envy* 113 Every one has a fair Turn to be as Great as he pleases. 1719 YOUNG *Paraphr. Job* 5 Wks. 1757 I. 204 At length misfortunes take their turn to reign, And ills on ills succeed. 1778 C. JONES *Hoyle's Games Impr.* 79 If..the last Player plays out of his Turn. 1849 MACAULAY *Hist. Eng.* ix. II. 553 It was Northumberland's turn to perform this duty. 1885 *Manch. Exam.* 12 Feb. 5/3 The manufacturers have had their share [of protection]; now it is the turn of the corn growers and cattle breeders.

b. Phrases. (*a*) ***by turns*** (also †***by turn***), one after another in regular succession; successively, in rotation. (*b*) ***in turn***, ***in turns***, each in due succession: = (*a*). (*in turn* is also used rhetorically like *in one's turn*: see next.) (*c*) ***in one's turn***, in one's due order in the series. (Often also used rhetorically to indicate an act duly or naturally following a similar act on the part of another, but without the notion of pre-arranged succession.) (*d*) ***turn about***, ***turn and turn about*** (also rarely ***turn and turn***): *advb.* in turn, by turns, alternately (†sometimes preceded by possessive: cf. *c*); *adj.* performed in turn, mutual, reciprocal (*rare*); *sb.* the action of doing something in turn; alternate or successive turns at doing something. (*e*) ***out of*** (***one's***) ***turn***: out of one's due order or place in a series; ***to talk*** or ***speak out of*** (***one's***) ***turn***: to say more than one ought to say, to speak inadvisedly or tactlessly.

(*a*) 1538 ELYOT, *Vicissatim*, by tymes, by tournes. *Vicissim*, by tourne, nowe one, nowe an nother. 1585 T. WASHINGTON tr. *Nicholay's Voy.* III. iv. 76 [They] by change and turnes..keepe watch. 1667 MILTON *P.L.* II. 598 The damn'd..feel by turns the bitter change Of fierce extreams. 1712 STEELE *Spect.* No. 508 ¶3 He is by turns outrageous, peevish, froward and jovial. *a* 1839 PRAED *Poems* (1864) II. 13 He aped each folly of the throng, Was all by turns and nothing long. *c* 1850 *Arab. Nights* (Rtldg.) 326 They slept only by turns, in order to guard against wild beasts.

(*b*) 1586 A. DAY *Eng. Secretary* II. (1625) 59 The next and last in turne, are those letters familiar. 1688 PRIOR *Ode* v, Why does each consenting Sign With prudent Harmony combine In Turns to move? 1832 TENNYSON *Palace of Art*, '*I send you here a sort of allegory*' 14 He that shuts Love out, in turn shall be Shut out from Love. 1883 FENN *Middy & Ensign* xxxv, They would take it in turns to sleep. 1908 [MISS FOWLER] *Betw. Trent & Ancholme* 303 The daughters in turn riding on pillion-seat.

(*c*) 1573–80 BARET *Alv.* T 430 By course, or euerie man in his turne, *alternis*. 1710 W. KING *Heathen Gods & Heroes* xi. (1722) 44 Argus..had a hundred Eyes, two of which sleeping in their Turns, the rest continu'd waking. 1781 COWPER *Charity* 74 To see the oppressor in his turn oppressed. 1861 M. PATTISON *Ess.* (1889) I. 47 A committee ..in which every Hanse town was in its turn represented, according to a fixed cycle. 1864 BRYCE *Holy Rom. Emp.* viii. (1875) 143 Germany became in her turn the instructress of the neighbouring tribes.

(*d*) 1650 EARL MONM. tr. *Senault's Man bec. Guilty* 357 Being weary of obeying, they fain would command their turn about. 1709 T. ROBINSON *Vind. Mosaick Syst.* 94 The Cock..Sitting upon the Eggs his turn about. 1802 H. MARTIN *Helen of Glenross* II. 14 To complete the turn-about good offices, Frances can marry your cast-off Sedley. 1821 SCOTT *Kenilw.* xv, Fit to sit low at the board, carve turn about with the chaplain. 1833 T. HOOK *Widow & Marquess* vii, Turn-about is all fair play. 1834 [S. SMITH] *Lett. J. Downing* xxvii. (1835) 176 When one gets drunk, tother keeps sober, and so they take turn and turn about. 1840 E. E. NAPIER *Scenes & Sports For. Lands* II. v. 174 We took it turn and turn to send out [etc.]. 1848 MRS. GASKELL *M. Barton* ix. (1882) 23/2 We took it turn and turn about to sit up and rock th' babby.

(*e*) 1888 *Rules of Golf* 5 Playing out of turn. 1930 'SAPPER' *Finger of Fate* 186 Well, old boy, our Lady Carrington was talking a little out of her turn. I don't blame her—it's a bit disconcerting to lose a thing like that. 1939 I. BAIRD *Waste Heritage* vi. 79 Easy, Eddy, I shouldn't have spoken out of turn there. 1945 J. B. PRIESTLEY *Three Men in New Suits* i. 7 I'm talking out of my turn, I expect—as usual. 1969 P. ROTH *Portnoy's Complaint* 14, I voluntarily and out of my turn set the table. 1978 P. VAN GREENAWAY *Man called Scavener* ix. 123 I'm going to talk out of turn and you'll be welcome to tell me I should mind my own business.

29. *spec.* **a.** The time during which one workman or body of workmen is at work in alternation with another or others; a shift. (Cf. 24.)

1793 SMEATON *Edystone L.* §230, I proposed to visit each company..once in each company's turn, if wind and weather should permit. 1883 GRESLEY *Gloss. Coal-mining*, *Turn*, the hours during which coals, &c., are being raised from the mine. 1897 *Worc. County Express* 3 Apr., In the turn's work, six hours, Potts would have been able to make 1½ dozen shades.

b. *Theatr.* 'A public appearance on the stage, preceding or following others' (Farmer *Slang*); an item in a variety entertainment; also *transf.* applied to the performer.

1715 D. RYDER *Diary* 19 Sept. (1939) 101 There was rope dancing and tumbling... There were now and then some good humorous turns came in that made us laugh with a just pleasure. 1861 E. COWELL *Diary* 16 Apr. in M. W. Disher *Cowells in America* (1934) 293 Mr. Odgen, not appreciated and evidently uncomfortable, would not sing a second 'turn'. 1889 G. B. SHAW *London Music in 1888–89* (1937) 234 Five out of six of the 'turns' are of the deadliest dulness. 1890 *Even. News & Post* 9 June 1/7 The wire-walking of Mme. Zuila and her little girl..furnishes a clever and interesting turn. 1905 *Daily News* 15 July 8 An animal 'turn' new to England will be seen at the Palace Theatre... Kern and his Mimic Dog have been drawing crowded houses..in Paris. 1907 *Times* 30 Jan 6/6 Under the barring clause the gentleman, who is not a big turn, did not appear.

30. a. Requirement, need, exigency; purpose, use, convenience. *arch.* (Chiefly in special phrases; see below.)

1573 TUSSER *Husb.* (1878) 33/1 To serue to burne for many a turne. 1602 *Life T. Cromwell* II. iii, We hardly shall finde such a one as he, To fit our turnes. 1659 HAMMOND *On Ps.* xviii. 5 Annot. 99 Ropes or cords are proper for that turne. 1788 JEFFERSON *Writ.* (1859) II. 354 Such persons as his turn and time might render desirable. 1881 MRS. RIDDELL *A. Spenceley* I. 285 You will answer my turn..as well as another.

b. Phrases. (*a*) ***to serve one's turn***: to answer one's purpose or requirement; to suffice for or satisfy a need; to be useful or helpful in an emergency; to suit, answer, serve, avail, 'do'. Also in passive. So: †(*b*) ***to serve a*** (***this, that,*** etc.) ***turn*** (*obs.*). (*c*) ***to serve the turn***; also † ***to do the turn*** (cf. 23). †(*d*) ***to serve turn***; also with inf. = to serve *to do* something (*obs.*). †(*e*) ***to serve*** or ***do the turn of***, to serve the purpose of, do instead of (*obs.*). (*f*) ***to serve one's*** (***one's own***, or ***a***) ***turn*** (said of the person): to compass one's own purpose; to consult one's own need. (Cf. (*a*).) †Also with *by, on, upon*: to operate by or upon another in order to gain one's end; to make use of for one's own purposes. †(*g*) ***for one's turn***: (suitable) for one's requirement or purpose (*obs.*).

(*a*) 1540 PALSGR. *Acolastus* II. iii. L iij b, Loke thou serue my tourne, what so euer I saye [orig. *Fac uerbis meis subseruias*]. 1576 GASCOIGNE *Steel Gl.* Wks. 1910 II. 159 Let not the Mercer pul thee by the sleeve For sutes of silke, when cloth may serve thy turne. 1647 N. BACON *Disc. Govt. Eng.* I. xvi. (1739) 32 The turns both of Pope and King were competently served. 1742 FIELDING *Jos. Andrews* I. xiv, Nothing would serve the fellow's turn but tea. *a* 1859 MACAULAY *Hist. Eng.* xxiii. V. 72 Pipes he could not obtain; but a cow's horn perforated served his turn.

(*b*) 1577 B. GOOGE *Heresbach's Husb.* I. (1586) 10 It serueth other turnes beside. 1586 in *Eng. Hist. Rev.* Jan. (1914) 117 The lord chauncellor should have a serjant at armes..and hathe none,..his gentleman ussher sarvethe that torne. *a* 1628 PRESTON *New Covt.* (1634) 17 All the fish in the Sea should be..little enough to serve such a turne. 1687 DRYDEN *Hind & P.* III. 65, I serv'd a turn, and then was cast away.

(*c*) 1551 in Feuillerat *Revels Edw. VI* (1914) 57 Furnysshed of suche thinges..as yourself shall thyncke convenient to serue the turne. 1591 SHAKS. *Two Gent.* III. i. 131 A cloake as long as thine will serue the turne? 1594 J. MELVILL *Diary* (Wodrow Soc.) 318 The forces that war reposit on to do the turn. 1669 STURMY *Mariner's Mag.* Advt. C iij b, Where the Fear of God is not, no Art can serve the turn. 1731 MILLER *Gard. Dict.* s.v. *Wine*, A little Yeast, ..or even a little new Wine may serve the Turn. 1768 ROSS *Helenore* II. 79 Nor will sick aff setts do the turn wi' me.

(*d*) *a* 1638 MEDE *Wks.* (1672) 68 To say the Ark was brought thither upon this occasion, will not serve turn. 1667 POOLE *Dial. betw. Protest. & Papist* (1735) 91 This may serve Turn, to let you see, that I had Warrant to say, that [etc.]. 1700 TYRRELL *Hist. Eng.* II. 847 When the Lyon's Skin alone would not serve turn, he knew how to make it out with that of the Fox.

(*e*) 1577 B. GOOGE *Heresbach's Husb.* II. 49 b, Some Pompe is to be made, or Kettell, Myll, or such like, as may serve the turne of a naturall streame. *a* 1653 BINNING *Serm.* (1845) 605 Imputed righteousness comes in as a covering over the man's nakedness, and doth the turn of perfect inherent holiness. 1818 SCOTT *Br. Lamm.* ix, As if there werena men eneugh in the castle, or as if I couldna serve the turn of ony o' them that are out o' the gate.

(*f*) 1581 MULCASTER *Positions* v. (1887) 32 Necessitie caught hold of it, to serue her owne tourne. 1583 GOLDING *Calvin on Deut.* iii. 13 Although Iethro was an heathen man: yet did God serue his owne turne by him [orig. *Dieu s'est servi de luy*] in this behalfe. 1604 SHAKS. *Oth.* I. i. 42, I follow him to serue my turne vpon him. 1664 BUTLER *Hud.* II. II. 123 If the Dev'l, to serve his turn, Can tell Truth. 1697 BENTLEY *Phal.* (1699) 114 Changing a plain Reading against the Authority of three MSS,..purely to serve a turn. 1759 BP. HURD *Moral Dial.* iv. 154 A parade of courage, put on to serve a turn, and keep her people in spirits. **1855** MACAULAY *Hist. Eng.* xii. III. 208 Those slanderers who had accused him of affecting zeal for religious liberty merely in order to serve a turn.

(*g*) **1579** W. WILKINSON *Confut. Familye of Loue* 38 b, To judge, if that.. shalbe for their turne or no. **1625** USSHER in *Lett. Lit. Men* (Camden) 132 For my turne he is altogether unfit. **1719** DE FOE *Crusoe* (1840) II. xii. 256 When.. I could find a ship for my turn. **1773** *Life N. Frowde* 25, I am not a Man for their turn.

VI. Various other abstract senses, of later development.

31. Style, character, quality; *esp.* style of language, arrangement of words in a sentence. (Cf. TURN *v.* 5 b.)

1601 B. JONSON *Poetaster* III. i, Doubtlesse this gallants tongue has a good turne when hee sleeps. **1692** DRYDEN *St. Euremont's Ess.* Pref. 6 A Purity of Language, and a beautiful turn of Words, so little understood by modern Writers. **1697** BENTLEY *Phal.* (1699) 158 It has not the Turn and Composition of a Greek Name. **1718** *Free thinker* No. 80 ¶3 Her Turn of Wit was gentle, polite, and insinuating. **1825** MRS. SHERWOOD *Yng. Forester* I. 5 Such a turn of behaviour as enabled him to conceal much roguery under a smooth appearance. **1869** GLADSTONE *Juv. Mundi* i. 15 A careful comparison.. between the Odyssey and Iliad, and of a number of particulars of turn and manner.

32. (with *a* and *pl.*) A modification of phraseology for a particular effect, or as a grace or embellishment; a special point or detail of style or expression (in literary work, or *transf.* in art, etc.).

1693 DRYDEN *Juvenal* Ded. (1697) 84 Had I time, I cou'd enlarge on the beautiful Turns of Words and Thoughts; which are as requisite in this, as in Heroique Poetry. **1705** ADDISON *Italy, Ferrara* 121 There is a Turn in the Third Verse that we lose by not knowing the Circumstances. **1738** EARL OF OXFORD in *Portland Papers* (Hist. MSS. Comm.) VI. 178 The dress of this person.. gives a turn and life to the other figures... He is leading her up and has one foot upon the step, which gives a fine turn. **1868** M. E. G. DUFF *Pol. Surv.* 4 His felicitous turns of expression.

33. Form, make, mould, cast (of a material object). Cf. TURN *v.* 5 a. ? *Obs.*

1702 ADDISON *Dial. Medals* ii. (1726) 84 The Roman poets, in their descriptions of a beautiful man, so often mentioning the Turn of his Neck and Arms. **1709** STEELE *Tatler* No. 75 ¶8 The Turn of Faces he meets as soon as he passes Cheapside-Conduit. **1748** *Anson's Voy.* III. iii. 325 For.. rollers.. the body of the coco-nut tree was.. useful;.. its smoothness and circular turn.. fitted it for the purpose.

34. a. Natural inclination, disposition, bent; aptitude, capacity for something. Usually const. *for* (rarely *to*), or with defining adj. (Cf. TURN *v.* 5 c.)

1702 ROWE *Tamerl.* Ded., That happy Turn which your Lordship has to Business. **1736** BUTLER *Anal.* Introd. 6 A person of such a Turn of Mind. **1749** WESLEY *Acc. School at Kingswood* 3 They.. learn, (those who have a Turn for it) to make Verses. *a* **1763** W. KING *Lit. & Polit. Anecd.* (1819) 67 Ladies.. who have a fine understanding and a turn to poetry. **1812** SIR H. DAVY *Chem. Philos.* 15 He [Roger Bacon] was a man of a truly philosophical turn, desirous of investigating nature. **1821** SCOTT *Kenilw.* xi, But Flibbertigibbet.. hath that about him which may redeem his turn for mischievous frolic. **1844** ALB. SMITH *Adv. Mr. Ledbury* i, Mr. Ledbury was of an inquiring turn of mind. **1854** MILMAN *Lat. Chr.* IV. i. (1864) II. 190 The rude and simple Arab had.. no turn to or comprehension of metaphysical subtlety. **1871** NAPHEYS *Prev. & Cure Dis.* I. ii. 58 Persons of a dyspeptic turn.

b. *transf.* That to which (the age or time) is disposed. (Cf. *the fashion, the rage.*) *rare*$^{-1}$.

1709 SWIFT *Advanc. Relig.* Wks. 1755 II. I. 114 This is not to be accomplished [but] by introducing religion as much as possible to be the turn and fashion of the age.

†**c.** ? Aptitude, talent. *Obs. rare*$^{-1}$.

1721 CIBBER *Refusal* I. (1777) 19 Honest Witling is not to be put out of humour, I see. *Gran.* No, faith, nor out of countenance. *Wit.* Not I, faith..; and a man of turn may say any thing to me.

†**d.** A particular element of the disposition; a characteristic; in quot. 1745, a characteristic act.

1729 LAW *Serious C.* vi. (1732) 84 Some turn of mind, which every good Christian is called upon to renounce. **1745** P. THOMAS *Jrnl. Anson's Voy.* 313 A true French turn, and not unlike old Lewis le Grand's singing Te Deum for being defeated. **1764** STERNE in Traill *Life* (1882) 85 This amiable turn of his character.

e. *turn of speed*, capacity for speed, ability to run or go fast.

1867 in Sir M. G. Gerard *Leaves fr. Diaries* iii. 65 Showing an unexpected turn of speed. **1894** ASTLEY *50 Y. my Life* I. 35, I discovered that I possessed a fair turn of speed.

35. Direction, tendency, drift, trend. (Cf. TURN *v.* 26, 28.)

1704 M. HENRY *Commun. Comp.* iv. Wks. 1853 I. 312/1 If this blessed turn be given to the bent of my soul. **1719** DE FOE *Crusoe* (1840) II. vi. 143 Providence gave a.. happy turn to all this. **1736** BUTLER *Anal.* II. vii. 355, I know no pretence for saying the general turn of them [prophecies] is capable of any other [application]. **1815** SCOTT *Guy M.* xxxii, 'What turn did your conversation take?' said Glossin. **1845** J. COULTER *Adv. in Pacific* xiii. 180 Four days after, I discovered what gave my thoughts a new turn.

36. A change from the original intention; a particular construction or interpretation put upon something: usually with *give.*

1710 PALMER *Proverbs* 141 His best actions [are] thrown by and lessen'd by false turns. **1749** FIELDING *Tom Jones* VII. v, For heaven's sake, sir,.. do not give so cruel a turn to my silence. **1796** JANE AUSTEN *Pride & Prej.* x, You are giving it a turn which that gentleman did by no means intend. **1850** MRS. JAMESON *Leg. Monast. Ord.* (1863) 85 The turn which they have given to the story differs altogether from what I conceive to be the real significance.

VII. Various technical senses.

37. A measure of various commodities, etc. (? the quantity dealt with at one 'turn' or stroke of work: cf. 24).

a. A quantity or measure by which some fish are sold: of loose haddocks it is ten stone or 140 lbs.: see also quot. 1674. **b.** (See quot. 1805.) **c.** A load of wood or other commodity; also in *Logging*: see quot. 1905. **d.** *Fur trade.* A bundle of sixty skins. **e.** *Mining.* The number of cars filled by a miner during his turn or shift (cf. 29 a).

a. 1674 JEAKE *Arith.* (1696) 66 Soles. In 1 Turn 4. **1882** *Daily News* 9 Mar. 2/8 Plaice, 30s. per turn. **1895** *Times* 7 Jan. 3/5 Haddocks,.. 25s. to 30s. per turn.

b. 1805 R. W. DICKSON *Pract. Agric.* II. 923 Turn of Water.—As much as can be distributed at a single operation by the management of the hatches within the reach of the labourers employed. **1862** M. D. COLT *Went to Kansas* 99 Have just been to the spring for my turn of water. **1981** *Publ. Amer. Dial. Soc.* LXVIII. 48 *Turn of water*.., a container in each hand.

c. 1792 G. CARTWRIGHT *Jrnl. Coast of Labrador* I. p. xvi, *Turn of timber*, So much as a man can carry on his shoulders. **1888** J. C. HARRIS in *Harper's Mag.* Apr. 704/2 Sometimes he would bring a 'turn' of wood, sometimes a bag of meal or potatoes. **1893** *Daily News* 9 Jan. 5/7 Another has slipped while carrying a 'turn' of deal upon his shoulders. **1905** *Terms Forestry & Logging* (U.S. Dep. Agric., Forestry, Bulletin No. 61), *Turn*,.. two or more logs coupled together end to end for hauling.

d. 1891 in *Cent. Dict.* **1897** *19th Cent.* Nov. 737 A turn means sixty skins and the rate of pay is 11^{d} per turn.

38. The amount of some commodity turned out or produced: = TURN-OUT 9.

1875 R. F. MARTIN tr. *Havrez' Winding Mach.* 9 The steel cages.. had worked for four years, with a daily 'turn' of 637 tons (coal and dirt together).

39. *Comm.* (in full, ***turn of the market***): A change in price, or the difference between the buying and selling prices, of a stock or commodity; the profit made by this.

1857 *Sat. Rev.* 18 Apr. 348/2 Nobody understands the turn of the market better than Tomkins. **1870** J. K. MEDBERY *Man & Mysteries Wall Street* 78 This neat profit is called a 'turn'. **1882** BITHELL *Counting-Ho. Dict., Turn of the Market.* The 'turn of the market', or the 'jobbers' turn', is the difference between the two prices quoted in the official lists for stocks, shares, &c... Consols are quoted 99$\frac{3}{8}$ to $\frac{5}{8}$, and it means that the jobber, when asked the price of Consols at that moment, was prepared to give 99$\frac{3}{8}$ for them, or to sell them at 99$\frac{5}{8}$. The difference between the two is the compensation to the jobber. **1885** *Pall Mall G.* 23 May 5/2 Brokers coming together without paying exorbitant 'turns' to the middleman—that is, the jobber. **1897** *Daily News* 28 June 2/7 Tows, hemps, and flaxes are also the turn dearer. **1913** EDITH WHARTON *Custom of Country* II. xi, In consequence of a lucky 'turn' in the Street.

VIII. Collocations and Combinations.

40. With adverbs, forming sb. phrases corresponding to the adverbial combinations of the verb (see TURN *v.* VIII): as ***turn in***, an act of turning in. (Most commonly with hyphen or as one word; see TURN-, TURNABOUT, etc.)

1833 T. HOOK *Parson's Dau.* III. i, Now for.. a glass of grog, and then for a turn in.

41. *attrib.* and *Comb.*, as ***turn-claimer*** (see quot.), †***turn-keeping*** sb. and adj., ***turn movement***. ***turn toll***: see TOLL *sb.*^{1} 2 g. See also TURN-SERVING. **turns** (*rarely* **turn**) **ratio** *Electr.*, the ratio of the number of turns on the primary of a transformer to the number on the secondary, or vice versa.

1610 HOLLAND *Camden's Brit.* I. 195 A rocke about whose foote the tides turne-keeping play. **1708** *Constit. Watermen's Co.* xxxiii. 38 The Country-Watermen shall have equal Privilege and Turn keeping with the Towns-men. **1892** *Labour Commission* Gloss., *Turn-claimers*, the persons occupied in a coal-mine who possess the privilege of claiming a 'ben'..., that is a tub to fill in turn. **1908** *Installation News* II. 14 The switch has a turn movement worked from the outside. **1927** R. E. BROWN *Alternating-Current Machinery* iii. 66 The turn ratio of a transformer may be obtained from the designer or may be approximately measured by determining the ratio of the indications of two voltmeters. **1965** *Wireless World* Sept. 431/2 The number of turns on each coil, the turns ratio and the inductances are in no sense critical. **1976** RYDER & THOMSON *Electronic Circuits & Systems* xii. 286 A loudspeaker of 4 Ω can be made to appear as 400 Ω on the primary side if we use a transformer with the turns ratio $a = \sqrt{(\frac{400}{4})} = ..10$.

turn (tɜːn), *v.* Forms: α. 1 tyrnan, 3 tuyrne; 3 teorne, 3–5 terne, 5 tern. β. 1 turnian, 3 (*Orm.*) turrnenn, (3–4 teurne), 3–7 turne, 4–6 *Sc.* twrn(e, 4– turn; 3–6 torne, 4–6 tourne, 4–7 torn. [OE. *tyrnan* and *turnian*, both ad. L. *tornāre* to turn in a lathe, round off, f. *torn-us* a lathe, a turner's wheel = Gr. τόρνος a carpenter's tool to draw circles with, compasses, whence τορνεύειν to turn, work with a lathe; perhaps reinforced in ME. by OF. *torner, turner, tourner*, F. *tourner*, Pic. *torner*, Prov., Sp. *tornar*, It. *tornare*, all:—L. *tornāre*; cf. OHG. *turnen*, Icel. *turna* to turn (*turnera* to tilt, joust, Norw. dial. *tunna* to swing, whirl), ad. F. *tourner*.

On the twofold representation of L. *tornāre* in OE. see Pogatscher *Latein. u. Roman. Lehnworte im Altenglischen*, §§9, 159, 271; he shows that the umlauted *tyrnan* must have already existed *c* 600.

The pa. pple. in Southern Eng. in the 12–13th c. had commonly the prefix *i-*, *y-*, *i-tyrnd*, *i-turned*, and the pa. t. was freq. *i-turnde*; there is also one instance of the infinitive *i-turnen* in the earlier text of Layamon, but no known instance in OE. of a compound **ȝetyrnan* or **ȝeturnian*; these ME. forms with *i-*, *y-* have therefore been included here.]

General arrangement of senses. I. To rotate or revolve, and derived uses: 1–3. II. To form or shape by rotation, and derived uses: 4–5. III. To change or reverse position: *Senses denoting change of position: 6–9; **Senses denoting reversal of position: 10–12. IV. To change or reverse course or direction: *denoting change of course or direction: 13–18; **denoting reversal of course or direction: 19–21. V. Senses allied to III and IV, but referring specially to direction or destination: 22–34. VI. To change, alter: *general senses: 35–43; **specific senses: 44–47. VII. Phrases, *with sb.: 48–60; **with adj. or advb. phrase: 61–63; ***with another verb: 64. VIII. In comb. with adverbs (*turn about, again, aside, in, out, up*, etc.): 65–81. (Combinations formed on the vb.-stem are given in a separate article, TURN-, or as Main words.)

I. To rotate or revolve, and derived senses.

1. *trans.* To cause to move round on an axis or about a centre; to cause to rotate or revolve, as a wheel.

See also *turn about*, 65 c; *turn round*, 79 d.

c **1000** ÆLFRIC *Saints' Lives* xiv. 93 þa tyrndon þa hæðenan hetelice þæt hweowl. *a* **1300** *Cursor M.* 23719 (Cott.) Dame fortune turnes [*Gött.* ternes] þan hir quele And castes vs dun vntil a wele. *c* **1440** *Promp. Parv.* 507/2 Turnon forthe, *idem quod* trolle [502/2 Tryllyn, or trollyn, *volvo*]. **1599** SHAKS. *Much Ado* II. i. 261 She would haue made Hercules haue turnd spit. **1687** A. LOVELL tr. *Thevenot's Trav.* II. 38 There were two Boys.., one turning a wheel by the handle, to grind the Coffee, and the other boyling it. **1781** COWPER *Retirement* 334 Waters turning busy mills. **1852** THACKERAY *Esmond* III. ix, Preparing paste, and turning rolling-pins.

b. To cause to move round, or (usually) partly round, in this way, esp. for opening or closing something: as a key, tap, door-handle, screw, etc.

a **1300** *Cursor M.* 16906 (Cott.) Þe prince o preistes.. sperd it wit a mikel stan, To turn i-nogh had tuent [? twenty]. **1382** WYCLIF *Prov.* xxvi. 14 As a dore is turned in his heeng. **1593** SHAKS. *Rich. II*, V. iii. 36 Giue me leaue, that I may turne the key, That no man enter. **1655** [see COCK *sb.*^{1} 12]. *a* **1715** BURNET *Own Time* (1823) I. 401 He.. turned all the cocks that were then open, and stopped the water. **1880** P. GREG *Errant* III. xi. 158 The lamp was turned very low. [Cf. 72 g.] **1890** FENN *Double Knot* III. xiv. 192 She softly turned the handle of the door.

c. To perform by revolving, as a somersault.

1860 [see SOMERSAULT]. **1863** [see COACH-WHEEL 3]. **1864** [see CART-WHEEL *sb.* 3]. **1881** [see CATHERINE WHEEL 4].

2. *intr.* To move round on an axis or about a centre; to rotate, revolve, whirl, spin, as a wheel; to move partly round in this way, as a door or the like upon hinges, a key, a weathercock, etc.

See also *turn about*, 65 a; *t. round*, 79 a.

c **1000** *Sax. Leechd.* III. 270 Se firmamentum went on ðam twam steorran, swa swa hweoȝel tyrnð on eaxe. *c* **1330** R. BRUNNE *Chron. Wace* (Rolls) 1453 Nykeres.. brynge schipmen.. To som swelw to turne or steke. *c* **1435** *Torr. Portugal* 188 They tornyd xxxii tymys, In armys walloyng fast. **1560** BIBLE (Genev.) *Prov.* xxvi. 14 As the dore turneth vpon his henges. **1589** PUTTENHAM *Eng. Poesie* II. xi. (Arb.) 111 The Roundell or Spheare is.. most voluble and apt to turne. **1698** KEILL *Exam. Th. Earth* (1734) 109 Jupiter.. turns round his own Axis in.. ten hours. **1796** MME. D'ARBLAY *Camilla* I. 259 A little boy.. turning head over heels. **1843** MACAULAY *Horatius* lxix, The kid turns on the spit. **1890** MRS. LAFFAN *Louis Draycott* III. ii, The key turned and grated in the lock.

b. *fig.* To revolve (as time, etc.). In later use said chiefly of the head or brain: To have a sensation as of whirling; to be affected with giddiness; to reel, swim, be in a whirl. (Cf. 45 c, 79 a.)

c **1000** ÆLFRIC *Hom.* (Th.) I. 514 þa arleasan turniað on ymbhwyrfte. *c* **1200** ORMIN 3641 All þiss middellærdess þing Aȝȝ turrneþþ her & wharrfeþþ.. swa summ þe wheol. *c* **1230**, **1398** [see TURNING *vbl. sb.* 1 b]. *c* **1400** *Destr. Troy* 9400 The tyme of the tru turnyde to end. **1605** SHAKS. *Lear* IV. vi. 23 How fearefull.. And dizie 'tis, to cast ones eyes so low... Ile looke no more, Least my braine turne. **1853** M. ARNOLD *Requiescat* 9 Her life was turning, turning, In mazes of heat and sound. **1892** STEVENSON & L. OSBOURNE *Wrecker* vi. 93, I looked at the handbill and my head turned.

3. ***turn on*** or ***upon*** (fig.): **a.** To hinge upon, depend on, have as the centre or pivot of movement or action.

1661 J. STEPHENS *Procurations* 26 They that turn upon this hinge, I mean that receive Procurations upon the ground of Custome. **1712** SWIFT *Conduct of Allies* ¶35 Great Events often turn upon very small Circumstances. **1823** *Examiner* 268/2 The plot.. turns upon the secret marriage of Claudio. **1892** *Sat. Rev.* 2 Jan. 2/2 The contest .. is to turn on Home Rule.

b. To have as its subject, be about or concerned with, relate to: usually said of conversation or debate.

App. orig. a development of prec. sense, but often associated with other senses: cf. 28.

1711 ADDISON *Spect.* No. 119 ¶7 As the two Points of Good Breeding, which I have..insisted upon, regard Behaviour and Conversation, there is a third which turns upon Dress. **1729** BUTLER *Serm.* Wks. 1874 II. 49 That the conversation might turn upon somewhat instructive. **1879** M. PATTISON *Milton* xiii. 203 The Dutch drama turns entirely on the revolt of the angels. **1884** *Manch. Exam.* 26 May 4/7 The debate..did not turn upon any..practical proposition.

II. To form or shape by rotation, and derived senses.

4. *trans.* To shape, esp. into a rounded form, by cutting with a chisel or similar tool while rotating in a lathe; to form, work, or make by means of a lathe. Also *absol.* to work with a lathe.

c **1305** *Land Cockayne* 68 in *E.E.P.* (1862) 158 Þe pilers of þat cloistre alle Beþ i-turned of cristale. **1341–2** *Ely Sacr. Rolls* (1907) II. 117 In le turning xxx bases pro columpnis. *c* **1440** *Promp. Parv.* 507/2 Turnon, or throwe treyne [*S.* trene] vessel, *torno.* **1504** in *Bury Wills* (Camden) 101, I wyll that my sonne..shall haue..also ij cheyres, on turnyd and the other closse. **1600** J. PORY tr. *Leo's Africa* v. 253 Such as turne wooden vessels. **1756** MRS. CALDERWOOD in *Coltness Collect.* (Maitl. Club) 212 A famous turner.., he turns things in ivory that would exceed beleif. **1796** JANE AUSTEN *Let.* 1 Sept. (1952) 8 Frank..enjoys himself here very much, for he has just learnt to turn. **1833** J. HOLLAND *Manuf. Metal* II. 140 In turning..metals..and even wood, much depends upon the proper management of the tools. **1858** RAMSAY *Remin.* iv. (1870) 80 He..taught us to saw, and to plane, and to turn.

b. *Building.* To form, construct, build (an arched or vaulted structure).

1703 MOXON *Mech. Exerc.* 256 You may turn Arches over those insufficient places,..and..Arches inversed, or upside down. **1720** W. STUKELEY *Mem. & Corr.* (Surtees) I. 32 At this time [1706–7]..the great arch of boards was made to turn the Cupola of St. Pauls. **1828** ELMES *Metrop. Improv.* 88 The arches for the coal-cellars [were] turned.

c. *Cookery.* To pare off the rind or peel of (an orange, lemon, etc.) round and round in a long narrow thin strip; to stone (an olive) in this way.

1706 PHILLIPS (ed. Kersey), *Turning* (among Confectioners) a..manner of paring..Oranges and Lemons when the..Rind..is par'd off very thin and narrow..; turning it [the knife] round about the Fruit, so as the Peel may be extended to a very great length. **1846** SOYER *Cookery* 43 Turning or peeling mushrooms is an art that practice alone can attain. **1904** *Daily Chron.* 6 June 8/5 Soak the olives in cold water.., drain thoroughly and proceed to 'turn' them... This means to peel them very evenly..so that it unfolds..in one strip, which will close up again..without the stone in the centre when done.

d. *Knitting* and *Lace-making.* To make in a curved form: see quots.

1882 CAULFEILD & SAWARD *Dict. Needlework* 504/1 *Turn Heel*—See Knitting Stockings. *Ibid.* 504/2 *To Turn a Scallop*: work across to the inside..but instead of completing the edge, work back with the same pair of Bobbins [etc.]... Repeat until the scallop has been rounded. **1902** R. BAGOT *Donna Diana* viii. 93 She was always knitting, and appeared to be in a perpetual state of turning the heel of a stocking.

5. *fig.* To shape, form, or fashion artistically or gracefully: **a.** a material object: usually into a rounded form, as if shaped on a lathe. Chiefly in *pa. pple.*

1616 B. JONSON *Devil an Ass* II. vi, This smooth, round, And well torn'd chin. **1695** BLACKMORE *Pr. Arthur* IV. 88 He turn'd their Orbs, and polish'd all the Stars. **1711** STEELE *Spect.* No. 2 ¶5 His Person is well turn'd. **1847** L. HUNT *Men, Women, & B.* I. xiv. 273 The hand long, delicate, and well turned. **1855** THACKERAY in *Yates' Recoll.* (1884) I. 280 The T of the signature..is [not] near so elegant as my ordinary T's are;..my attention was drawn off just as I was turning it.

b. a piece of literary work, a tune, a compliment, etc.

1636 B. JONSON *Discov.* Wks. (Rtldg.) 762/2 Cast not away the quills..; but bring all to the forge and file again; torn it anew. **1687** A. LOVELL tr. *Thevenot's Trav.* I. Cj b, The Reader..is not to expect that the Language should be so Accurate, nor the Style so well turned, as [etc.]. **1791** BOSWELL *Johnson* an. 1754, Some studied compliments, so finely turned, that [etc.]. **1849** THACKERAY *Pendennis* ix, If I could turn a tune,..I should sing. **1850** W. IRVING *Goldsmith* xv. 178 Turning a couplet.

†**c.** *pa. pple.* Of a person (or the mind, etc.): Naturally adapted, fitted, or 'cut out' for some pursuit. *Obs.*

1671 TEMPLE *Let. to de Witt* Wks. 1731 II. 247, I find I am better turned for making a good Gard'ner. **1723** in *Eng. Hist. Rev.* Jan. (1912) 56 *note*, A head the most turned for business of any I have known. **1728** SWIFT *Jrnl. Mod. Lady* 36 By nature turn'd to play the rake. **1767** *Woman of Fashion* I. 41 A Genius like her's, is little turn'd to Business.

d. ***to turn a profit*** (U.S.): to earn or make a profit.

1969 *Time* 21 Jan. 44 Partly because of the competition from IBM it is unlikely to turn a profit before 1970. **1976** *National Observer* (U.S.) 14 Aug. 4/1 The iron rule of business dictates staying open anytime there's a decent chance to turn a profit.

III. To change or reverse position.

* *Senses denoting change of position.*

6. *intr.* To move or shift (by a rotary motion, or through an angle) so as to change one's posture or position; *esp.* to shift the body (as on an axis) from side to side; to twist or writhe about.

to make a person turn in his grave: see GRAVE *sb.*[1] 1 d.

c **1000** ÆLFRIC *Hom.* (Th.) II. 508 He ealle ȝefæstnode heora fet to eorðan... Hi tyrndon mid bodiȝe, ȝebiȝedum sceancum. *c* **1205** LAY. 4586 Scipen þer sunken... In þa teonfulle sæ Torneden sæiles. *c* **1394** *P. Pl. Crede* 543 But he lepe vp on heiȝ,..& þi name lakke Wiþ proude wordes... And turne as a tyrant þat turmenteþ him-selue [etc.]. **1500–20** DUNBAR *Poems* lxix. 11, I walk [= wake], I turne, sleip may I nocht. *a* **1700** DRYDEN (J.), I turn'd, and try'd each corner of my bed, To find if sleep were there, but sleep was lost. **1827** SCOTT *Chron. Canongate* v, Turning to the other side to enjoy his slumbers. **1881** MRS. LYNN LINTON *My Love* II. v. 92 It is enough to make your poor father turn in his grave. **1888** [see GRAVE *sb.*[1] 1 d].

b. To move circularly or as on a pivot, so as to face all ways successively, or so as ultimately to face in the opposite direction. (Cf. 2, 10.)

1500–20 DUNBAR *Poems* lxvi. 43 On thair conscience.. May turne aucht oxin and ane wane. **1644** EVELYN *Diary* 8 Feb., Capable of containing an hundred coaches to turne commodiously. **1893** *Chamb. Jrnl.* 28 Jan. 50/2 She veered as if she would turn within her own length.

c. Said of the scale or beam of a balance, or of the balance itself: To move up or down from the horizontal position. (Cf. 49, 58.)

1596 SHAKS. *Merch. V.* IV. i. 330 If the scale doe turne But in the estimation of a hayre. **1654** tr. *Scudery's Curia Pol.* 59 To weigh in the Scales and not discern how the Beam turnes. **1827** FARADAY *Chem. Manip.* ii. (1842) 25 Another balance..turning with about one-half or one-third of a grain.

7. *trans.* To alter the position or posture of (an object) by moving it through an angle; to move (a thing or person) into a different posture.

1377 LANGL. *P. Pl.* B. XVII. 183 Vnfolden or folden, my fuste & myn paume, Al is but an hande [= one hand] how so I torne it. *c* **1440** *Promp. Parv.* 507/1 Turnon a thynge, *verto, verso.* **1578** BANISTER *Hist. Man* v. 65 Some partes of the skinne are wholly immouable, and resistant to turne. **1644** S. KEM *Messengers Prepar.* 22 He speaks too late..for a reprieve, when the ladder is turned. **1711** ADDISON *Spect.* No. 120 ¶14 When she [a hen] has laid her Eggs.., what Care does she take in turning them frequently! **1720** WATTS *Moral Songs, Sluggard* i, As the door on its hinges, so he on his bed Turns his sides, and his shoulders, and his heavy head. **1843** R. J. GRAVES *Syst. Clin. Med.* ix. 100 He cannot be lifted up or even turned in bed, without having a tendency to faint. **1885** 'MRS. ALEXANDER' *At Bay* iv, He took up a paper-knife, which he turned restlessly to and fro.

b. *refl.* = senses 6, 6 b. *Obs.* or *arch.*

13.. *Sir Beues* (A.) 4414 Þat lane was so narw..He ne Arondel, is stede, Ne miȝte him terne. *c* **1385** CHAUCER *L.G.W.* Prol. 144 Vpon the braunches..In hire delyt, they turned hem ful ofte. **1509** HAWES *Past. Pleas.* xvi. (Percy Soc.) 75, I myght not lye styll; On every syde I tourned me ful ofte.

8. *fig.* To consider in different aspects; to revolve in the mind. (See also *turn over*, 78 e.)

1725 [see *turn about*, 65 e]. **1825** T. HOOK *Sayings* Ser. II. *Sutherl.* (Colburn) 54 Turn these things in your mind. **1891** *Strand Mag.* II. 483/2, I pondered over it, and turned it every way in my mind.

9. To give a curved or crooked form to; to bend or twist; †to fold (quot. 1303); †to form by twisting, to plait (quot. 1665); to bend or twist *round* something so as to encircle it (quot. 1821); to form by bending (quot. 1827[2]). (Cf. *turn down*, 72 a.)

1303 R. BRUNNE *Handl. Synne* 1153 [He] bade hym take A sak..And..turne hyt tweyfolde..And ley hyt on hys fadyr for colde. **14..** *Sloane MS. 1986* lf. 19 b, Wyspes drawen out at fote and syde, Wele wrethyn and turnyd. **1665** HOOKE *Microgr.* xxvii. 149 Let all the sides of this Box be turned of Basket-work. **1821** SCOTT *Kenilw.* xiv, A bonnet..encircled with a gold chain turned three times round it. **1827** —— *Surg. Dau.* xiv, His mustaches were turned and curled. **1827** FARADAY *Chem. Manip.* xiv. (1842) 307 Those [tubes] which are turned or bent, and soldered with gold, will not bear the high temperature.

b. *spec.* To bend back (the edge of a sharp instrument) so as to make it useless for cutting; to blunt in this way. ***to turn edge***, to have the edge thus bent, to become blunt. Also *fig.*

a **1568** ASCHAM *Scholem.* (Arb.) 32 Quicke wittes are..like ouer sharpe tooles, whose edges be verie soone turned. **1593** SHAKS. *2 Hen. VI*, II. i. 180 This Newes I thinke hath turn'd your Weapons edge. **1639** FULLER *Holy War* v. iii. (1647) 234 However at this time they might turn edge, they had formerly been true blades for his Holinesse. **1673–4** GREW *Anat. Trunks* II. vii. §3 It turns not the edge of their Knives. **1714** FIDDES *Pract. Disc.* II. 82 A difficulty sufficient to turn the edge of the finest wit. **1879** J. C. SHAIRP *Burns* viii. 193 When the caustic wit is beginning to get too biting, the edge of it is turned by a touch of kindlier humour.

c. ***to turn*** (a person) ***round one's*** (***little***) ***finger***, a proverbial phrase denoting that one can 'do what one likes' with him. (Cf. *turn and wind*, 64 b.)

1855 [see FINGER *sb.* 3 a]. **1861** HUGHES *Tom Brown at Oxf.* xxv. (1889) 244, I am sure one could turn him round one's finger.

d. *intr.* for *pass.* To assume a curved form, to bend; to become blunted by bending. (See also *turn again*, 66 e.)

[**1579**: see *turn again*, 66 e.] **1815** J. SMITH *Panorama Sc. & Art* I. 4 If..it be too soft,..the edge will turn or bend.

** *Senses denoting reversal of position.*

10. *trans.* To reverse the position or posture of; to move into the contrary position, so that the upper side becomes the under (= *turn* UPSIDE DOWN), or the front the back; to invert.

See also *turn about*, 65 d; *turn over*, 78 a; *turn round*, 79 e. ***to turn turtle***: see TURTLE *sb.*[2] 2.

c **1200** *Trin. Coll. Hom.* 103 Wi list þu turnd [orig. L. *pronus*] on þe eorðe? aris. *c* **1440** *Douce MS.* 55 lf. 15 b, Folde vppe the cake..& turne it onys in the panne. **1533** J. HEYWOOD *Johan* A iv b, It were tyme for to tourne The pye, for ywys it doth borne. **1577** B. GOOGE tr. *Heresbach's Husb.* 46 The grasse being cutte, must be well tedded and turned. **1687** A. LOVELL tr. *Thevenot's Trav.* I. 268 They turn a half minute Sand-Glass. **1706** PHILLIPS s.v. *Literal Fault*, When a Letter is..transpos'd or turn'd. **1773** BOSWELL *Tour Hebrides* 3 Oct., When he turned his cup at Aberbrothick, where we drank tea. **1868** MISS YONGE *Pupils of St. John* vii. 97 He turned his horse, and was about to flee. **1875** RUSKIN *Fors Clav.* V. liii. 117 Her..fine legerdemain in turning pancakes.

†**b.** *fig.* To invert the order of, to reverse; to convert (a proposition). *Obs.*

a **1569** KINGESMYLL *Godly Advise* (1580) 20 Christe tourned Water into Wine. Turne not his miracle, make not, I meane, water of wine. **1654** Z. COKE *Logick* 114 These.. are not to be turned; Christ is a vine; Bread is Christs body.

11. *spec.* **a.** To reverse (a leaf of a book) in order to read (or write) on the other side (or on the next leaf); to do this with the leaves of (a book) in succession, to read or search through. (See also *turn over*, 78 b, and LEAF *sb.*[1] 7 b.)

In quot. *c* 1830, to find and open at the place in (the service-books) for the organist and choir; cf. *turn up*, 81 h.

c **1275** LAY. 46 Laweman þes bokes bi[h]eolde An þe leues tornde [*c* 1205 wende]. **1377** LANGL. *P. Pl.* B. III. 337 Had she loked þat oþer half and þe lef torned. **1526** *Pilgr. Perf.* (W. de W. 1531) 167 Handes..redy to turne theyr boke. **1599** DAVIES *Immort. Soul* Introd. xiv, When we have all the learned Volumes turn'd. **1688** PENTON *Guard. Instruct.* (1877) 67 Able to read Greek, and turn the Lexicon upon occasion. *c* **1830** G. ELVEY in *Bumpus's Cathedrals, Canterbury* (1906) 36 Going down..to turn the books for the service one morning. *Mod.* I had just turned the leaf of my diary and begun to write on the other side.

b. To reverse the position of the turf, or of the soil, in ploughing or digging, so as to bring the under parts to the surface. Also *absol.*

In quot. 1844, to bring (seed) *under* by doing this. See also *turn in*, 73 b; *turn over*, 78 c; *turn up*, 81 f.

c **1477** CAXTON *Jason* 81 Thou shalt yoke hem and make hem to tourne foure rodd of londe. **1523** FITZHERB. *Husb.* §4 Howe these plowes shulde be tempered, to plowe and turne clene. **1697** DRYDEN *Virg. Georg.* III. 138 Starting, with a bound He turns the Turf, and shakes the solid Ground. **1799** HT. LEE *Canterb. T., Old Woman's T.* (ed. 2) I. 392 The earth has been newly turned. **1825** *Mirror* V. 278/2 He ..when turning peats walked..fearlessly among the Hags of Lochar Moss. **1844** *Jrnl. R. Agric. Soc.* V. I. 62 The seed being sown on the surface, and turned under by a shallow furrow with the plough. **1892** *Sat. Rev.* 11 June 671/1 The first sod of the..Railway was turned on Tuesday.

c. To reverse (a garment, etc.) so that the inner side becomes the outer, to turn inside out; hence, to alter or remake by putting the inner side outward.

1483, 1552 [implied in TURNED *ppl. a.* 6 c]. **1557** [implied in TURNCOAT]. **1576–** [see COAT *sb.* 13]. **1596** SHAKS. *Tam. Shr.* III. ii. 44 A paire of olde breeches thrice turn'd. **1680** V. ALSOP *Mischief Impos.* Ep. Ded., Like an old Livery new turn'd and fresh trim'd up. **1834** MRS. CARLYLE *Lett.* (1883) I. 10, I am now turning my pelisse. **1893** *Illustr. Sport. & Dram. News* 11 Feb. 774/2 A way of turning an old frock. (See also *turn one's coat* 51.)

12. To cause (the stomach) to reject or revolt against the food (also *transf.* and *fig.*, as in quots. 1749, 1818); ***to turn the stomach of***, to nauseate, to disgust extremely.

1622 MABBE tr. *Aleman's Guzman d'Alf.* II. 355, I may not giue it a worse word, for feare of turning thy stomake. **1738** POPE *Epil. Sat.* II. 182 This filthy simile..Quite turns my stomach. **1749** FIELDING *Tom Jones* I. i, The one provokes.. the most languid appetite, the other turns and palls that which is..keenest. **1818** BYRON *Ch. Har.* IV. lxxvi, The daily drug which turn'd My sickening memory. **1892** *Temple Bar Mag.* Sept. 35 Questions that would turn the stomach of a school inspector.

b. *intr.* Of the stomach: To be affected with nausea.

1719 DE FOE *Crusoe* (1840) II. iv. 78 Their stomachs turned at this sight. *c* **1850** *Arab. Nts.* (Rtldg.) 159 He was obliged to take it out of his mouth again, for his stomach turned against it.

IV. To change or reverse course.

* *Senses denoting change of course or direction.*

13. *trans.* To alter the course of; to cause to go another way; to divert, deflect. (In quot. *c* 1200 *refl.* = 16.)

See also *turn aside*, 67 a; *turn off*, 74 f. ***turn house*** (Mining): see quot. 1778, and cf. HOUSE *sb.*[1] 7 c.

c **1200** ORMIN 6568 Þatt ta þreo kingess turrndenn hemm Ut off þe rihhte weȝȝe, & forenn till Herode. *c* **1205** LAY. 4092 He turnde his fare & ferd feorh riht to Wales. **1303** R. BRUNNE *Handl. Synne* 4624 As a shyppe þat ys turned with þe roþer. *c* **1330** —— *Chron. Wace* (Rolls) 8165 Do scope þis water, & turn þe borne. **1596** SHAKS. *1 Hen. IV*, III. i. 136 You shall haue Trent turn'd. *a* **1648** LD. HERBERT *Autobiog.* (1824) 66 His Rod over the left Ear of his Horse, which he is to use for turning him every way. *a* **1680** CHARNOCK *Attrib. God* (1834) II. 67 You..see a..flight of birds..turn wing another way. **1778** PRYCE *Min. Cornub.* 99 If they are working or driving from east to west,..and perceive the Lode is gone,..they..turn house as they call it, or, in other words, they drive north or south. **1794** *Act for inclosing South Kelsey* 12 Such..Path so stopped up or turned. **1821** CLARE *Vill. Minstr.* II. 48 They turn'd the winding rivulet's course.

b. To check the course of; to cause to go aside or retreat (cf. 19); to throw off, keep out (wet).

c **1620** SANDERSON *Serm.* (1689) 204 Like an unruly colt..; no ground will hold him, no fence turn him. *a* **1658** CLEVELAND *Inund. Trent* 60 We whose unliquor'd Hides will turn no wet. **1821** CLARE *Vill. Minstr.* I. 51 Spreading thorns that turn'd a summer shower. **1843** MACAULAY *Horatius* xliv, With shield and blade Horatius Right deftly turned the blow. **1891** *Eng. Illustr. Mag.* IX. 153 The snapping of a dry stick is not sufficient to turn the tiger.

c. *Cricket.* Of the bowler: to cause the ball to 'break' (BREAK *v.* 32 b). Also *intr.* of the ball: to break or turn in its course after pitching.

1898 G. GIFFEN *With Bat & Ball* iii. 47 There are very few men bowling at Mac's pace who can turn the ball on the Adelaide Oval. **1909** W. G. GRACE *W. G.'s Little Book* iii. 33, I don't know the moment he delivers the ball which way it will turn on pitching. **1928** *Morning Post* 2 July 15/1 Garland-Wells is slow right, and can turn the ball both ways. **1930** *Ibid.* 16 July 11/6 The bowlers were making the ball turn more than before luncheon. **1955** [see FLIGHT *v.* 7].

14. *fig.* To divert or deflect from a course of action, purpose, thought, etc.; to alter the course of (something immaterial); †sometimes (with mixture of sense 34), to pervert, misapply (*obs.*).

See also *turn aside*, 67 a; *turn off*, 74 f.

c **1200** ORMIN 14240 Swa to turrnenn all þe boc Till þeȝȝre grediȝnesse. *a* **1225** *Leg. Kath.* 1514 Ne mei me nowðer teone ne tintreohe turnen From mi leofmonnes luue. *a* **1340** HAMPOLE *Psalter* xvii. 41, I sall noght be turnyd fra þat entent. **1474** CAXTON *Chesse* III. iii. (1883) 95 How torne they the lawe and statutes at their pleasir. **1591** SHAKS. *1 Hen. VI*, v. iv. 59 Will nothing turne your vnrelenting hearts? **1622** FLETCHER & MASSINGER *Prophetess* III. iii, It is not in thy power to turn this destiny. **1687** DRYDEN *Hind & P.* III. 34 She turn'd the talk. **1766** GOLDSM. *Vic. W.* xxviii, No submission can turn our severe master. **1859** JEPHSON *Brittany* xvi. 273, I..turned the conversation to something else. **1888** BRYCE *Amer. Commw.* I. v. 55 These thirty six votes turned the election. [Cf. 49, 58.]

†**b.** To mislead, beguile, cheat. *Obs. rare*$^{-1}$.

c **1386** CHAUCER *Can. Yeom. Prol. & T.* 618 Hym to bigile he thoghte..Til he had terned hym, he koude nat blynne.

†**c.** *refl.* To change one's course of action. *Obs.*

1535 COVERDALE *Josh.* xxiv. 20 Yf ye forsake the Lorde,.. then shall the Lorde turne him, and do you euell. —— *Ps.* xc. 13 Turne the agayne (o Lorde) at the last, and be gracious vnto thy seruauntes.

15. †**a.** To transfer, hand over. (Cf. *turn over*, 78 h.) Also *intr.* in passive sense. *Obs.*

c **1200** *Trin. Coll. Hom.* 185 He dude his wille þar-offe, swo ich wile mine, nu hit [property] is to me iturnd. *c* **1290** *Beket* 243 in *S. Eng. Leg.* I. 113 Þis holi Man was i-torned fram þe office of holi churche To a gret office of þe worlde. **1387** TREVISA *Higden* (Rolls) VII. 301 Þe abbot was i-chaunged and i-torned [orig. L. *translatus est*] to his owne abbay in Normandie. **1400** in *Ancestor* July (1904) 14 Yef it so be that Sir Nicholl deye..I wil that the fornseyd place wyth alle the portenans torne to Anneys Nook myn servant. **1535** COVERDALE *1 Chron.* xi. [x.] 14 Therfore slewe he him, & turned the kyngdome vnto Dauid. —— *Lam.* v. 2 Oure enheritaunce is turned to the straungers.

b. 'To keep passing in a course of exchange or traffick' (J.); to cause (money or commodities) to circulate.

See also *turn over*, 78 i. ***to turn the penny, to turn an honest penny***: see PENNY 9 k, HONEST *a.* 4 b.

1605 B. JONSON *Volpone* I. i, I turne no moneys, in the publike banke. **1673** TEMPLE *Ess. Adv. Trade Irel.* in *Misc.* (1680) 119 Hide, Tallow, Butter..yield the readiest Money of any [commodities] that are turned in this Kingdom. **1863** D. G. MITCHELL *Farm Edgewood* 214 The shopkeeper, who turns his capital three or four times in a year.

16. *intr.* To change one's course, so as to go in a different direction; to deviate.

See also *turn aside*, 67 b; *t. away*, 69 f; *t. down*, 72 i; *t. in*, 73 e; *t. off*, 74 k; *t. up*, 81 u.

13.. *Sir Beues* (A.) 3669 Out of þe way ȝhe gan terne Ase ȝhe wolde do hire dedes derne. **1375** BARBOUR *Bruce* III. 106 Quhen þai þe king..Saw sua behind his mengne rid, And saw him torne sa mony tid. **1579** GOSSON *Sch. Abuse* (Arb.) 41 Hee runnes farre that neuer turnes. **1645** EVELYN *Diary* 21 Feb., Turning a little down we came to another piazza. **1797** MRS. RADCLIFFE *Italian* i, As they turned into the Strada di Toledo he had nearly lost them. **1827** SCOTT *Highl. Widow* v, He..turned from the road, and descended the path towards the hut. **1894** BARING-GOULD *Kitty Alone* II. 164, I shall turn to the left, and leave the road.

fig. **1613** PURCHAS *Pilgrimage* (1614) 292 Imminent miserie,..(they say) together with the almes, turneth from them to the poore man. **1697** DRYDEN *Æneid* Ded., Ess. (ed. Ker) II. 202 Virgil..turns short on the sudden into some similitude, which diverts..your attention from the main subject.

b. *Naut.* To beat to windward; to tack.

1569 SIR J. HAWKINS *Voy.* (Hakl. Soc.) 37 With contrary windes blowing, whereby for feare of the shore we were faine to hale off to haue ankerhold, sometimes a whole day and a night turning vp and downe. **1633** T. JAMES *Voy.* 93 We turned amongst this Ice, staying the Ship. **1706** *Lond. Gaz.* No. 4215/3 The Wind being at North-East, they turned all that day.., but could not fetch Torbay. **1835** MARRYAT *Pirate* xvi, The sloop of war..continued to turn to wind-ward. **1867** SMYTH *Sailor's Word-bk.*, *Turn to windward, to*, to gain on the wind by alternate tacking.

†**c.** ***turn about*** (something); to walk or travel round, circumambulate. *Obs.*

1585 T. WASHINGTON tr. *Nicholay's Voy.* III. xxi. 110 b, They goe turning seuen times about a fouresquare towre. **1642** TASMAN *Jrnl.* in *Acc. Sev. Late Voy.* I. (1694) 135 In turning about this Island there appeared very few Men.

d. Of the wind: To shift, so as to blow from a different quarter.

1610 HOLLAND *Camden's Brit.* (1637) 587 Unlesse the winde turne from West into the South. **1702** MARWOOD *Diary* in *Cath. Rec. Soc. Publ.* VII. 121 After Noon the Wind turned, and it rayned a little.

e. Of a road, path, line, etc.: To change direction, as at a bend or curve; also, to branch off at an angle from the main road or line.

1535 COVERDALE *Josh.* xix. 34 Their border..goeth out vnto Iordane, and turneth westwarde to Asnoth Thabor. **1821** SCOTT *Kenilw.* xiii, Following the smith down a lane which turned to the left hand towards the river. **1892** *Harper's Mag.* May 907/2 Railways turn and curve through the valleys.

17. *trans.* To bend one's course so as to get to the other side of; to go or pass round (a corner, etc.). See also CORNER *sb.*[1] 2 b.

1687–1877 [see CORNER *sb.*[1] 2 b]. **1743** P. FRANCIS tr. *Hor. Odes* I. i. 6 To turn with kindling wheels the goal. **1820** BELZONI *Egypt & Nubia* III. 318 With the expectation, that on turning the next angle, I should have the glorious sight. **1855** MACAULAY *Hist. Eng.* xx. IV. 493 Before Columbus had crossed the Atlantic, before Gama had turned the Cape.

b. *Mil.* To get round (an enemy's position, etc.); also *fig.* See also *turn flank*, 55.

1845–6 TRENCH *Huls. Lect.* Ser. II. i. 152 Not so much anxiously defending our own position as confidently turning theirs. **1861** MILL *Utilit.* v. 84 These are difficulties;..and many devices have been invented to turn rather than to overcome them. **1892** *Black & White* 19 Mar. 371/2 The skill of the attack in turning the Russian defences.

c. In *Assoc. Football*, etc., to get round (an opponent at close quarters) by making it necessary for him to change direction.

1976 E. DUNPHY *Only a Game?* (1977) iv. 121 He turns full backs, he does unusual things on the ball, he creates unusual situations. **1980** *Times* 3 Apr. 13/2 Francis..turned Buchan and sent in a stinging shot.

18. To pass, get beyond (a particular age, time, or amount).

1789 MRS. PIOZZI *Journ. France* I. 90 Let a man once turn sixty..and his natural heirs are sure of him. **1844** W. H. MAXWELL *Sports & Adv. Scotl.* xxxvii. (1855) 290, I had turned my fourteenth year. **1893** *Illustr. Sport. & Dram. News* 10 June 524/3 It had turned a quarter past one. **1899** *Q. Rev.* Jan. 194 The vast 'Coleccion de documentos inéditos' is turning the hundred in the numbering of its volumes.

b. *pa. pple.* (in active sense) with or (now more usually in England) without *of*: Having passed (a particular age or time); more than, past.

1700 CONGREVE *Way of World* III. viii, I hear he is turn'd of forty. **1703** FARQUHAR *Inconstant* I. i, *D.* Sirrah, What's a Clock? *P.* Turn'd of Eleven, Sir. **1789** MRS. PIOZZI *Journ. France* I. 21 The little knot of unmarried females turned fifty. **1890** FENN *Double Knot* I. i. 84 I'm nineteen,..and you are turned twenty. **1892** *Harper's Mag.* Aug. 450/2, I was young then—only just turned of two-and-twenty. And now,..I am turned of forty-five!

*** Senses denoting reversal of course or direction.*

19. *trans.* To reverse the course of; to cause to go in the opposite direction: = *turn back*, 70 a. Also *fig.*

turn the dice (quot. *a* 1700), to reverse the luck.

13.. *Cursor M.* 20713 (Cott.) Feres, gon we son onan, And turn we þis processiun. **1664** HOWARD & DRYDEN *Ind. Queen* II. ii, Till this strange man had power to turn the tide, And carry conquest unto any side. *a* **1700** DRYDEN *Cock & Fox* 754 But see how Fortune can confound the Wise, And when they least expect it, turn the Dice.

20. *intr.* To reverse one's, or its, course; to begin to go, or to tend, in the opposite direction; to be reversed: = *turn back*, 70 e. (*lit.* and *fig.*)

c **1205** LAY. 7547 He..turnde to flæme [*c* **1275** tornde to flende]. *a* **1400** *Cato's Morals* 170 in *Cursor M.* p. 1671 Quen þi hap turnis baft, and logh þou lise. **1593** SHAKS. *Lucr.* 646 My vncontrolled tide Turnes not, but swels the higher by this let. **1689** *Lond. Gaz.* No. 2518/3 About four in the Afternoon the Tide turn'd. **1827** DISRAELI *Viv. Grey* v. xiv, Stocks fell.., the exchange turned, money became scarce. **1867** J. B. ROSE tr. *Virgil's Æneid* 337 Before a woman do ye turn and flee? **1885** MALET *Col. Enderby's Wife* III. iv, I fancied..the luck would turn.

†**21.** *intr.* To go or come back; to return. (See also *turn again*, 66 b.) *Obs.*

a **1300** *Cursor M.* 11526 (Cott.) Þai had in wil þat ilk night To torn be herods. *c* **1385** CHAUCER *L.G.W.* 1619 (*Hypsipyle & Medea*) So that ȝe schal nat die But turnyn sound hom to ȝoure tessalye. *c* **1420** *Anturs of Arth.* 284 Turne þou to tuskayne. **1594** SHAKS. *Rich. III*, IV. iv. 184 Ere from this warre thou turne a Conqueror.

†**b.** Of property: To return *to* the former possessor; to revert. (See also *turn again*, 66 c.) *Obs.*

1500 *Reg. Mag. Sig. Scot.* 537 Landis..To be haldin to the said Patrik and hys airis maill.., the quhilkis failyeand turnand to me..and my airis.

†**c.** *trans.* To give or send back; to return. *Obs.*

1593 SHAKS. *Rich. II*, IV. i. 39, I will turne thy falshood to thy hart, Where it was forged, with my Rapiers point. **1637** B. JONSON *Sad Sheph.* I. ii, She'll turn us thanks.

V. Senses allied to III and IV, but referring specially to direction or destination.

22. a. *trans.* To change the direction of; to direct another way, or different ways alternately (esp. the eyes or face); sometimes, to avert (= *turn away*, 69 a); also, to cause to face in the opposite direction (= *turn round*, 79 e).

a **1300** *Cursor M.* 4311 (Cott.) Fleand turn þou noght þin ei. *c* **1300** *St. Margarete* 128 Þe justise..nolde loke þerto Ac bihuld abac & tournde his eȝen. *c* **1450** MYRC *Par. Pr.* 63 Tuynde [*v.r.* Turne] þyn ȝe þat thow ne se The cursede worldes vanyte. *c* **1460** *Towneley Myst.* iii. 336 For lak nor for gille wille I turne my face Tille I haue..spon a space on my rok. **1697** DRYDEN *Virg. Georg.* III. 353 Often he turns his Eyes, and..Surveys the pleasing Kingdoms. **1842** TENNYSON *Walking to Mail* 38 Jack, turn the horses' heads and home again. **1842** —— *Day Dream* Prol. 17 Turn your face, Nor look with that too-earnest eye.

b. *refl.* To change one's position (or course) so as to face (or go) another way: = c. *arch.*

13.. *Cursor M.* 17288 + 224 (Cott.) Scho tourned hir and saȝe our lord stand nere. *c* **1400** *Destr. Troy* 11000 Turnes yow full tyte, & taries a while. **1592** SHAKS. *Rom. & Jul.* I. i. 74 Turne thee Benuolio, looke vpon thy death. **1849** M. ARNOLD *Sick King in Bokhara* 127 Turning him quickly to go in.

c. *intr.* To change one's position so as to face in the contrary, or a different, direction; to face about.

right turn!, left turn!, as military words of command = turn (through a right angle) to the right, to the left; ***right about turn!*** = turn (by a movement to the right) so as to face in the opposite direction (see RIGHT ABOUT).

c **1275** LAY. 26576 Þo tornden hii sone..And ech his sweord swipe droh. **1388** WYCLIF *John* i. 38 Jhesu turnede, and say hem suynge hym. *a* **1533** LD. BERNERS *Huon* lix. 205 Whan they aprochyd nere, Huon sodenly tournyd. **1606** SHAKS. *Tr. & Cr.* v. vii. 33 Turne slaue and fight. **1667** MILTON *P.L.* VIII. 507 Seeing me, she turn'd. **1780** C. SIMEON in Carus *Life* (1847) 19 Turning at the Creed, [I] saw the table covered. **1844** DICKENS *Mart. Chuz.* ii, He..turned upon his heel, and walked out. **1890** A. GISSING *Vill. Hampden* II. iv. 72 He recognised her figure, but never turned to look behind.

23. With reference chiefly to the new direction taken. (See also uses with adverbs in VIII.)

a. *trans.* To direct, present, point (towards or away from some specified person or thing, or in some specified direction).

c **1205** LAY. 20658 Turnden [*c* **1275** tornde] heo heore ordes, Stikeden & sloȝen Al þat heo neh comen. *c* **1230** *Hali Meid.* 17 Þu most turne þe rug [= back]. *a* **1330** *Roland & V.* 341 An image..Stode on a roche..Þe face of him was turned souþe riȝt. *c* **1425** WYNTOUN *Cron.* v. xiv. 5608 Be þe takyn þat þat ymage Had turnyt fra Romule his wissage. *a* **1533** LD. BERNERS *Huon* lxxxii. 254 He tournyd his face to her warde. **1583** MELBANCKE *Philotimus* H j b, You are so wetherwise, turninge your tayle into euery wynde. **1667** MILTON *P.L.* IX. 527 His gentle dumb expression turn'd at length The Eye of Eve to mark his play. *a* **1700** DRYDEN *Ovid's Met.* XIII. *Acis, Pol. & Galatea* 111 Plums, to tempt you, turn their glossy side. **1756** MRS. CALDERWOOD in *Coltness Collect.* (Maitl. Cl.) 205 The armies upon which the eyes of all Europe are turned. **1823** SCOTT *Quentin D.* xxxvi, D'Hymbercourt turned two culverins on the gate. **1880** L. STEPHEN *Pope* vi. 157 A soured man prefers to turn his worst side outwards.

b. *refl.* = next sense. *arch.* (See also e.)

c **1375** *Sc. Leg. Saints* xviii. (*Egipciane*) 265, I ma nocht me turne to þe. *c* **1400** MAUNDEV. (Roxb.) xvi. 72 When a man turnez him to þe este. **1548–9** (Mar.) *Bk. Com. Prayer, Communion* (Rubric), Then the priest shall turne hym to the people. **1596** SHAKS. *Merch. V.* III. ii. 138 Turne you where your Lady is. **1725** POPE *Odyss.* III. 603 The Monarch turns him to his royal guest. **1812** CARY *Dante, Paradise* XXII. 2 To the guardian of my steps I turn'd me.

c. *intr.* To change one's position so as to face towards or away from some specified person or thing; to direct oneself; to face (with implied change of direction). See also e.

c **1325** *Spec. Gy Warw.* 435 For toward hem he wole turne Boþe wrapful and eke sterne. *c* **1425** *Cursor M.* 11711 (Trin.) Iesu turned to þat tre. **1593** SHAKS. *3 Hen. VI*, I. i. 189 Turne this way Henry, and regard them not. **1602** HARINGTON *Nugæ Ant.* (ed. Park 1804) I. 321 To turne askante from her condition withe tearlesse eyes. **1754** GRAY *Poesy* 37 Where'er she turns the Graces homage pay. **18..** T. MOORE *Irish Melodies*, '*She is far from the land*' i, But coldly she turns from their gaze, and weeps. **1890** A. GISSING *Vill. Hampden* II. xiii. 273 All faces turned towards him as he rose.

†**d.** (without the notion of change.) To have a specified direction or aspect; to face. *Obs. rare.*

1535 COVERDALE *Ezek.* xliii. 1 He brought me to yͤ dore, that turneth towarde the east. **1604** E. G[RIMSTONE] *D'Acosta's Hist. Indies* III. xxi. 188 In places whereas the land..turnes from the shadow of the mountaines.

e. In ***not to know which way to turn*** (or ***turn oneself*** arch.), and similar phrases, the sense is partly *lit.* and partly *fig.* (= what course to take, what to do: cf. 28 c).

c **1400** *Brut* xxxix. 146 He hade so miche to done wiþ þe Erl Randulf..& wiþ Hugh Bigot..þat he ne wist whider to turne. **1526** TINDALE *Luke* xxi. 25 They shall not tell which waye to turne them selves. **1669** STURMY *Mariner's Mag.* Advt. C iij b, We have been at our wits end, and knew not which way in the World to turn our selves. **1719** DE FOE *Crusoe* (1840) II. x. 219 They knew not which way to turn themselves. **1825** WATERTON *Wand. S. Amer.* III. iii. 270 There is a vast deal of knowledge to be picked up.. whichever way we turn ourselves. **1885** SIR W. V. FIELD in *Law Times Rep.* LII. 651/1 She did not know which way to turn to find means.

24. a. *trans.* To direct in the way of movement; to set going in a particular direction; to bend the course of.

a **1300** *Cursor M.* 13476 (Cott.) If þai..turn ham [= home] þair wai, Bi þe wai son faile sal þai. *a* **1548** HALL *Chron., Hen. V* 49 In whiche..just quarel al good persons shal rather set bothe theyr feete forwarde, then once to turne theyr one heale backward. **1692** PRIOR *Ode in Imit. Horace* x, Where-e'er old Rhine his fruitful Water turns. **1891** *New Rev.* Oct. 347 He then turned his steps towards the south.

b. *refl.* = next sense. *arch.*

a **1240** *Sawles Warde* in *Cott. Hom.* 257 Al þat hird.. turneð ham treowliliche to wit hare lauerd. *a* **1300** *Cursor M.* 2391 (Cott.) Abram turned him to þe south. *c* **1482** J. KAY tr. *Caoursin's Siege of Rhodes* ⁋7 And thenne they tourned theyme in the see toward Rhodes. **1700** S. L. tr. *Fryke's*

Voy. E. Ind. 306 We turned our selves to a River. **1867** J. B. Rose tr. *Virgil's Æneid* 342 Turn thee hither, turn thee.

c. *intr.* To direct one's course; to set oneself to go in a particular direction: usually with implied change of course (cf. 16); sometimes almost synonymous with 'go' or 'come', with special reference to destination.

c **1200** Ormin 6596, & tatt te kingess turrndenn efft Till þeȝȝre rihhte weȝȝe. *c* **1290** *S. Eng. Leg.* I. 25/54 þat he scholde after þis lijf tuyrne into þulke blis. *c* **1380** *Sir Ferumb.* 3545 þay..in-to þe paleys þan tornde. *c* **1470** *Golagros & Gaw.* 2 The king turnit on ane tyde towart Tuskane. *a* **1631** Donne *Poems* (1650) 58 Turne thou ghost that way, and let me turne this. **1653** Walton *Angler* i. 38, I thought we had wanted three miles of the thatcht House.. but now we are at it, we'l turn into it. **1893** *Cornh. Mag.* Nov. 474 Thither their footsteps turn.

25. *trans.* To cause or command to go; to send, drive; *esp.* (with qualifying adv. or advb. phrase) to send or order away, dismiss.

See also *turn away*, 69 c; *t. off*, 74 b; *t. out*, 76 c, e. In quot. 1903 app. short for *turn loose* (61 b).

1526 Tindale *Heb.* xi. 34 [They] turned to flyght the armees of the alientes. **1545** Ascham *Toxoph.* i. (Arb.) 88 Where they turned with so fewe Archers so many Frenchemen to flight. **1586** A. Day *Eng. Secretary* ii. (1625) 118 They are turned at the last quite forth by the elbowes. **1600** Shaks. *A. Y. L.* iii. i. 18 Push him out of dores..turne him going. *a* **1649** Winthrop *New Eng.* (1853) II. 267 A vessel ..was fallen into the hands of D'Aulnay, who had made prize of her, and turned the men upon an island. **1782** Miss Burney *Cecilia* vii. ix, You will not..turn me from your door. **1891** L. Keith *Halletts* II. ii. 37 He would turn me adrift without the smallest consideration. **1903** A. Adams *Log Cowboy* xiii, Five six-shooters were turned into the ceiling.

b. *spec.* To drive or put forth (beasts) to pasture. (See also *t. out*, 76 d.) Also in *fig.* or *allusive* use (= prec. sense).

1602 *2nd Pt. Return fr. Parnass.* i. ii. 268 Clap a lock on their feete, and turne them to commons. **1646** J. Lilburne *Unhappy Game Scotch & Eng.* 12 When the King hath got all, he'll turne our brethren to grasse. **1765** *Museum Rust.* IV. 183 Let the grass take head for about..three weeks, before you turn your sheep upon it. **1825** Scott *Betrothed* x, It's like old Raoul and I will be turned to grass with the lord's old chargers. **1847** *Jrnl. R. Agric. Soc.* VIII. i. 35 The privilege of turning stock into the park.

c. To put, cast, or convey into a receptacle or the like; now esp. by inverting the containing vessel (cf. 10), or diverting into a new channel (cf. 13).

In quot. 1598 *turn into* = 'put into' (a different dress), with mixture of sense 'change' (branch VI).

1594 Shaks. *Rich. III*, i. ii. 261 But first Ile turne yon Fellow in [= into] his Graue. **1598** —— *Merry W.* v. v. 214, I knew of your purpose: turn'd my daughter into white. **1844** *Jrnl. R. Agric. Soc.* V. i. 107 The sewers..may be cleansed by turning some water into them out of a large pond. **1901** Alldridge *Sherbro* ii. 15 A common method to detect bad kernels is to turn them into great casks containing water.

d. *intr.* for *pass.*

1801 *Naval Chron.* VI. 76 At the top of the tide she turned off the stocks.

26. *fig. trans.* To direct or set (thought, desire, speech, action, etc.) towards (or away from) something. Usually const. *to*, rarely *on*, *upon*.

†In quot. 1659, to direct, refer (a person) *to* something (cf. 28 d).

c **1200** *Trin. Coll. Hom.* 59 We and ure heldrene habbæð ben turnd fro him [God] eure siððen þe deuel com on neddre liche to adam. *a* **1225** *Ancr. R.* 52 Eue biheold o þen uorbodene eppele,..& turnde hire lust þer toward, & nom & et þerof. **1297** R. Glouc. (Rolls) 6824 þe luþer men of denemarch..To hor olde luþerhede iturnd adde hor þoȝt. *c* **1325** *Metr. Hom.* Prol. 32 An unkind man es he, That turnes alle his thoht fra the. *c* **1386** Chaucer *Miller's T.* 6 Al his fantasye Was turned for to lerne Astrologye. **1483** Caxton *G. de la Tour* F ij b, Moche meruelled the neyghbours how she had tourned her herte to loue suche a pryour. **1560** Daus tr. *Sleidane's Comm.* 420 b, Turning his talke to him. **1659** H. Thorndike *Wks.* (1846) II. 504 Those who..turn simple..Christians to that translation. **1727** Swift *What passed in Lond.* Wks. 1755 III. i. 183 His mind was wholly turned upon spiritual matters. **1823** Scott *Quentin D.* xi, He turned his thoughts from this subject of reflection. **1863** A. Blomfield *Mem. Bp. Blomfield* II. iii. 90 He could turn the whole force of his mind at a moment's notice on any subject. **1883** Stevenson *Treas. Isl.* iv. xviii, We..turned our attention to poor Tom.

b. To cause or induce (a person, etc.) to take a particular course; to direct the course of (events, etc.) *arch.*

c **1386** Chaucer *Knt.'s T.* 380 Wel hath ffortune y-turned thee the dys. **1390** Gower *Conf.* III. 73 The kinge he torneth at his wille, And makth him forto dreme. *c* **1400** *Destr. Troy* 2943 Throgh which treason betydes, & ternes vmqwhile Bolde men to batell and biker with hond. **1611** Shaks. *Wint. T.* iii. i. 15 Great Apollo Turne all to th' best.

27. *refl.* To direct one's mind, will, attention, etc. to or from a person or thing: = 28, 28 b, 28 c. Now *rare* or *arch.*

c **1200** *Trin. Coll. Hom.* 61 Turneð ȝiu to me, and ich wile turnen me to ȝiu. *c* **1200** *Ormin* 6586 He þatt turrneþþ himm fra Crist..Forrleoseþþ sawless soþe lihht. *c* **1375** *Sc. Leg. Saints* xli. (*Agnes*) 242 Men sal..twrne þaim to þe cristine fay. **1535** Coverdale *Exod.* xxxii. 12 O turne the from the fearcenesse of thy wrath. **1539** Bible (Great) *Ps.* xxv. 16 Turne the vnto me, and haue mercy vpon me. **1551** Robinson tr. *More's Utop.* i. (1895) 87 Ynough for hym, yea, and more then he can well turne hym to. **1832** *Examiner* 92/1 They were compelled to turn themselves to other employments.

28. *intr.* To direct one's mind, desire, or will to or from some person, thing, or action.

c **1200** *Trin. Coll. Hom.* 61 We turnen ofte to him, and fro him. *c* **1315** Shoreham *Poems* i. 122 þaȝ he torni to senne aȝen. *c* **1475** *Partenay* 518 Vnto my purpos torn shall I therfore. **1539** Bible (Great) *Exod.* xxxii. 12 Turne from thy fearse wrath. **1567** *Gude & Godlie B.* (S.T.S.) 173 Turnand till Goddis infinite. **1690** Locke *Hum. Und.* ii. i. §8 Ideas.. make not deep Impressions..till the Understanding turn inwards upon it self, and reflect on its own Operations. **1764** Goldsm. *Trav.* 8 Where'er I roam,..My heart untravell'd fondly turns to thee. **1891** M. Maartens *Old Maid's Love* II. iii. 46 She turned from the thought of scandal with impatience.

b. *spec.* To direct one's attention *to* a different subject; to begin to speak or think of something else.

c **1374** Chaucer *Troylus* ii. 639 (688) Now lat vs stynte of Troylus.., and late vs tourne [*v.rr.* torne, turne] faste Vnto Criseyde. *c* **1375** *Sc. Leg. Saints* xxi. (*Clement*) 622 Off þis matere now no mare I tel, Bot to þe story twrne I sel Of sancte clement. **1836** W. Irving *Astoria* III. lvi. 188 It is with a feeling of momentary relief we turn to something of a more pleasing complexion. **1880** L. Stephen *Pope* ii. 43 Let us now turn from the poems to the author's personal career.

c. To direct one's attention *to* something practically; to apply oneself *to* or take up an occupation or pursuit.

1667 Milton *P.L.* v. 630 Forthwith from dance to sweet repast they turn. **1842** Tennyson *Locksley Hall* 99 What is that which I should turn to..? Every door is barr'd with gold, and opens but to golden keys. **1891** *Sat. Rev.* 26 Dec. 730/1 He turned next to log-splitting.

d. ***turn to***: to refer to, look up, consult (a book, list, table, etc.).

1631 Cotton (*title*) A Complete Concordance..By helpe whereof any passage of holy Scripture may be readily turned unto. **1693** Locke *Educ.* §172 Helvicus's Tables may be..turned to on all occasions. **1850** *Jrnl. R. Agric. Soc.* XI. ii. 400 To their reports the reader must turn for accurate information. **1886** K. S. Macquoid *Sir J. Appleby* II. viii. 111 He took up a local paper and turned to the list of visitors.

e. To resort, betake oneself, have recourse *to* (a person, etc.); to appeal *to* for help or support.

1821 Clare *Vill. Minstr.* II. 80 He turns to heaven to witness what he feels. **1869** A. W. Ward tr. *Curtius' Hist. Greece* II. iii. iii. 472 The Milesians were unable to maintain themselves in Priene and turned to Athens. **1890** Clark Russell *Ocean Trag.* I. i. 20 You are the one man..that I should turn to in such a time. **1912** *Jrnl. Friends' Hist. Soc.* IX. 204 Once more we have to turn to a German writer for information.

†f. To tend, have a tendency *to* something. *Obs.*

1340–70 *Alex. & Dind.* 365 Tale tende we non þat turneþ to harme. *Ibid.* 469 When we tenden any tale þat turneþ to bourde. **1583** *Leg. Bp. St. Androis* 976 Whairto it turnes I can no' tell.

29. *trans.* To induce or persuade to adopt a (different) religious faith (usually with implication of its truth or excellence), or a religious or godly (instead of an irreligious or ungodly) life; to convert; less commonly in bad sense, to pervert (cf. 14). *Obs.* or merged in other senses, except as in c. **†a.** Const. *to*, *into*; *from*. *Obs.*

c **1200** Ormin 169 He shall turrnenn mikell flocc..till þe rihhte læfe. *c* **1205** Lay. 12734 Heo þencheð..to..turne to heðenesse þa hæȝe & þa læsse. **1297** R. Glouc. (Rolls) 4956 Seint birin þe bissop..þat in to þis lond..ysend was. To turne þe king of west sex, kingilf, to cristendom. *a* **1375** *Joseph Arim.* 11 In þe nome of þe fader Ioseph him folewede, And hedde I-turned to þe feyþ fifti with him-seluen. *c* **1380** *Antecrist* in Todd *3 Treat. Wyclif* 122 þei shal..bowe a wey from trewþe and ben turned in to fables. *c* **1380** Wyclif *Sel. Wks.* III. 107 We scholde nouȝt tarye to be yturned to God. *c* **1440** *Promp. Parv.* 507/2 Turne, to badnesse, *perverto*. **1513** More *Rich. III* (1641) 14 But if grace turne him to wisedome. **1579** W. Wilkinson *Confut. Familye of Loue, Brief Descr.* iij b, Who sought to peruert and turne from the truth xii godly Christians.

†b. *simply*. *Obs.*

c **1305** *St. Swithin* 10 in *E.E.P.* (1862) 43 Seint berin her bi weste wende And turnde þe king kenewold as oure louerd him grace sende. **1377** Langl. *P. Pl.* B. xv. 540 Many miracles he wrouȝte man for to turne. **1539** Bible (Great) *Jer.* xxxi. 19 As soone as thou turnest me, I shall refourme my selfe. *c* **1592** Marlowe *Jew of Malta* iv. i, Why, brother, you converted Abigail..One [friar] turn'd my daughter, therefore he shall die. **1692** Locke *Toleration* ii. Wks. 1727 II. 266 The two Reynold's (..one a Protestant, the other a Papist) who upon the exchange of Papers between them, were both turn'd.

c. To induce or persuade (a person) to act against his country, former associates, etc., esp. as a spy.

1971 C. Egleton *Last Post for Partisan* xvi. 162 'How did they turn you?' 'I was shopped... They said I could save my neck if I helped them, and so I agreed.' **1973** T. Allbeury *Choice of Enemies* vii. 32 It's my assessment that this officer gave no information to the Russians and was not turned by them. **1979** A. Boyle *Climate of Treason* ix. 309 The process of cornering and 'turning' the Fifth Man made such limited sharing of the secret almost inevitable. **1982** *Times* 27 Aug. 2/4 Several have been 'turned' only after being shown evidence from another 'supergrass'.

30. *intr.* To adopt a different (esp. the true) religion, or a godly life; to be converted.

a. Const. *to*. (Now merged in sense 28.)

a **1225** *St. Marher.* 22 Turnden þa þurh þis to criste swiðe monie. *c* **1300** *Cursor M.* 22119 (Edinb.) If þai wil noȝte turne til his lare, He sal taim sla wiþoutin spare. **1387** Trevisa *Higden* (Rolls) VI. 335 þe kyng of Bulgares and his men tornede to Cristes fey and bileve. [*c* **1410** *Hampole's Psalter* lxxxvi. 3 (MS. U²) þai resceyf sinfull men that will torune [? tourne] to me. *c* **1590** Marlowe *Faust.* v. 8 Abjure this magic, turn to God again. **1891** *Temple Bar* Dec. 599 It is never too late to turn to God.]

b. *simply*. To be converted; to repent. *arch.*

c **1300** *Cursor M.* 19013 (Edinb.) þis wordis herd, þair hertis gan turne, alsua for þaire misdedis murne. **13..** *Ibid.* 16762 + 148 (Cott.) Mony þat stode & saȝe..Torned & wore baptized. **1526** Tindale *Matt.* xviii. 3 Except ye tourne and become as children. **1679** *Establ. Test* 45 So would they say to all Protestants,..Turn, or burn. **1876** W. Arnot *Anchor of Soul* 333 If..the lost shall turn, they will get life in the Lord.

c. To go over to another side or party; to revolt, desert. Const. *to*. *arch.* (*b*) Now, of a criminal, to become an informer, to 'grass'.

1297 R. Glouc. (Rolls) 9891 Richard þe kinges sone,.. Aȝen is fader turnde to þe king of france alas! **13..** *Cursor M.* 15137 (Cott.) All þis werld es turnand Til him. *c* **1470** Henry *Wallace* i. 110 Erle Patrik than..Till our fa turnd, and harmyng did ws mast. **1593** Shaks. *3 Hen. VI*, i. i. 151 All will reuolt from me, and turne to him. **18..** J. Forbes *Battle of Corichie* ix. in A. Whitwell *Bk. Sc. Ball.* (1857) 556 Whan the haf o' the Gordones desertit, An' turnit wi' Murray in a crack.

(*b*) **1977** *Chicago Tribune* 2 Oct. i. 24/3 Like many other informants, Bompensiero 'turned' in order to avoid jail. **1982** *Times* 27 Aug. 2 (*heading*) Pressures that lead a man to 'turn'.

31. *trans.* To direct or bring to bear in the way of (active) opposition; to retort or cause to recoil *upon*; to proceed to use *against*.

1297 [see *turn one's hand*, 56 a]. **1538** Cromwell in Merriman *Life & Lett.* (1902) II. 125 By this meane their owne craft..shalbe torned into their owne neckes. *a* **1641** Bp. Mountagu *Acts & Mon.* iii. (1642) 184 To wrest his weapon out of his hands, and turne it upon himselfe. **1687** Atterbury *Answ. Consid. Spirit Luther* 48 Luther's Conscience..turn's these very reasonings upon him. **1839** Yeowell *Anc. Brit. Ch.* x. (1847) 107 Her cruel masters turned their ruthless hands against every thing and person that had a religious character. **1855** *Jrnl. R. Agric. Soc.* XVI. ii. 569 He has sufficient security that the disclosure will not be turned against himself.

b. To direct *against* in feeling; to make antagonistic; to imbue with hatred or dislike.

1831 *Examiner* 722/2 The hearts of the poor were turned in bitterness against the rich. **1881** Mrs. Lynn Linton *My Love* xi, Not even Papa could turn me against Cyril.

32. *intr.* To recoil *upon*; to fall *upon* with disastrous effect; to have an adverse tendency or result. Now *rare* or *Obs.*, or merged in next.

1377 Langl. *P. Pl.* B. xviii. 359 Now bygynneth þi gyle ageyne þe to tourne. *c* **1380** Wyclif *Sel. Wks.* III. 351 Certis synne of siche children turneþ into heed of þer fadir. **1550** J. Coke *Eng. & Fr. Heralds* §71 (1877) 80 Thus your bostes, syr heralde, turne upon your heles. **1625** Bacon *Ess.*, *Empire* (Arb.) 305 The destruction of Demetrius, Sonne to Philip the Second of Macedon, turned vpon the Father, who died of Repentance. **1660** *Trial Regic.* 24 *Court.* There is nothing you can say, but Guilty, or Not guilty. All other discourses turn upon your self. *a* **1715** Burnet *Own Time* (1823) I. ii. 430 (an. 1667) The Dutch war had turned so fatally on the king. **1881** Gardiner & Mullinger *Stud. Eng. Hist.* i. viii. 153 It turns upon those who attempt it, as the Florentine people turned upon Savonarola.

33. *intr.* To change one's position in order to attack or resist someone; to take up an attitude of opposition; to oppose oneself; with *on* or *upon*, to assail suddenly or violently (in act or word); with *against*, usually implying a change from previous friendliness.

See also *turn again*, 66 d; *turn round*, 79 c.

13.. in *Pol. Songs* (Camden) 189 Hue turnden hem aȝeynes with suerd ant with launce. **1477** Earl Rivers (Caxton) *Dictes* 72 Be not gladde of the euill fortune of another, for thou knowest not howe the worlde may tourne ayenst the. **1596** Shaks. *1 Hen. IV*, ii. iv. 297 Should I turne vpon the true Prince? **1625** Bacon *Ess.*, *Friendship* (Arb.) 169 Pompey turned vpon him againe, and..bad him be quiet. **1804** A. Duncan *Mariner's Chron.* II. 241 At this place, Mr. Hamilton met with a large seal, or sea-lion, and fired a brace of balls into him, upon which the animal turned upon him open-mouthed. **1854** Thackeray *Rose & Ring* iii, These people who are following you will be the first to turn against you. **1865** Kingsley *Herew.* xxxii, The king turned on his courtiers, glad to ease his own conscience by cursing them. **1887** F. W. Robinson *In Bad Hands* I. 33 The impudence of some people..would make a worm turn. **1892** *Black & White* 12 Mar. 327/2 His adulators of yesterday are prepared to turn and rend him.

34. *trans.* To apply *to* some use or purpose; to make use of, employ.

See also *turn one's hand to*, 56 b; *turn to account*, 62 b. †In quot. *a* 1225, to dedicate *to* a saint.

a **1225** *Ancr. R.* 18 To þeo halewen þet ȝe habbeð to þurh luue iturnd ower weouedes. **1398** *Munim. de Melros* (Bann. Cl.) 489 To be distreignede..and in[to] þaire profite to be turnide. **1445** in *Charters rel. Glasgow* (1906) 440 A certane sowm..beforehand..payit be the said Davy and in myne use turnit. **1605** Bacon *Adv. Learn.* i. ii. §1 Virgil, turning his pen to the advantage of his country. **1711** Addison *Spect.* No. 251 ¶2, I..would willingly turn my Head to any thing for an honest Livelihood. **1821** Scott *Kenilw.* vi, I trust that what I have spoken..will not be turned to my ruin. **1873** Mrs. Oliphant *Innocent* II. iii. 33 An old house ..which she had turned to a great many uses.

b. To set (a person) to some work or employment; in quot. 1781 *Naut.* = *turn up*, 81 r.

1781 Archer in *Naval Chron.* XI. 283 Turn all hands! make sail! **1869** Hughes *Alfred Gt.* xii. 139 The whole manhood of the kingdom might have been..turned upon this work. **1892** *Blackw. Mag.* CLI. 204/2 To turn the whole country on a deserter, and so take him dead or alive.

VI. To change, alter.

* *General senses.*

35. *trans.* To change, transmute; to alter, make different, or substitute something else (of the same kind) for. Now *rare* or *Obs.* exc. as in 37, 40 or associated with other senses: cf. *turn colour*, 52.

†*turn sides* (quot. 1736), to change sides, go over from one side to the other.

c1230 *Hali Meid.* 9 Godd ne schop hit neauer swuch, Ah Adam & eue turnden hit to beo swuch þurh hare sunne. a1300 *Cursor M.* 10434 (Cott.) Mend þi mode and turn þi chere. c1400 Maundev. (1839) viii. 86 An Aungel helde Jacob stille, & turned his name, & cleped him Israel. c1470 *Golagros & Gaw.* 1066 Schir Gawane tretit the knight to turn his entent. c1489 Caxton *Sonnes of Aymon* vii. 170 Whan the barons sawe reynawde & bayarde so torned, they began to laughe. 1566 Drant *Horace, Sat.* viii. F vj b, But pleasure hath lyke Circes cuppes yturnde them from their Kynde. 1596 Shaks. *Merch. V.* iii. ii. 249 Some deere friend dead, else nothing in the world Could turne so much the constitution Of any constant man. 1607 Topsell *Four-f. Beasts* (1658) 340 Orus writeth, that there is a Fish of this name which turneth sex. 1736 Lediard *Life Marlborough* II. 524 Their good Fortune..may, hereafter, turn Sides. 1892 *Temple Bar Mag.* Jan. 144 Suddenly she turned the subject. *Ibid.* Apr. 485 They..turned their dresses and their opinions.

36. *intr.* To undergo change or alteration; to become different, to change; in quot. 1599, to be fickle or inconstant. *rare* (exc. as in 38, 39).

c1175 *Lamb. Hom.* 91 þa þet folc þis iherde, þa iturn[d]e heore mod. c1275 Lay. 3069 His euhe [= hue] torne[d] and ..Bicom alse a blac cloþ. 14.. *Sir Beues* (MS. C.) 1283 + 47 Al his þouȝt bygan to tern. 1474 Caxton *Chesse* iii. iii. (1883) 98 Whan fortune torneth and perishith ther abideth not to hym one frende. 1599 Shaks. *Passionate Pilgr.* vii, She bad loue last, and yet she fell a turning. 1732 Pope *Ep. Bathurst* 379 Things change their titles, as our manners turn. 1894 Parry *Stud. Gt. Composers, Schubert* 226 How to make the form turn and vary.

37. *trans.* with *into* or *to*: To change, transform, or convert into; to cause to become (something else).

c1175 *Lamb. Hom.* 97 Petrus wes fixere [= fisher] þene iturnde þe ilcan godes gast to apostle. c1200 *Trin. Coll. Hom.* 45 þanne is here foshipe turnd al to frendshipe. c1275 *Passion of our Lord* 10 in *O.E. Misc.* 37 He..turnde water to wyne. a1350 Hampole *Poems* Wks. 1895 I. 78 Ihesu es lufe þat lastes ay:..Ihesu þe nyght turnes to þe day, þe dawyng in til spryng. 1413 *Pilgr. Sowle* (Caxton 1483) iv. xxviii. 73 The floure is forfaded and al the beaute therof torned to nouȝt. 1484 Caxton *Fables of Alfonce* xi, The goddes..haue torned my daughter in to this catte. a1569 [see 10 b]. 1631 Weever *Anc. Fun. Mon.* 433 This religious house is now turned into an Hospitall. 1765 Gray *Shakespeare* 11 May not honey's self be turn'd to gall? 1853 J. H. Newman *Hist. Sk.* (1873) II. i. ii. 63 A river overflows and turns a fruitful plain into a marsh.

b. To change into, cause to become of (a specified nature, form, or aspect).

1390 Gower *Conf.* II. 326 Echon of hem..Was torned into a briddes kinde. c1400 Maundev. (Roxb.) iv. 13 He schall turne þat damysell in to hir riȝt schappe. 1644 Milton *Areop.* (Arb.) 75 She turns herself into all shapes. 1651 Hobbes *Leviath.* ii. xxv. 132 Then is the Counsell turned into the nature of a Command.

c. *transf.* To exchange for; to get something else instead of; also, to substitute something else for. Cf. convert *v.* 15.

c1449 Pecock *Repr.* v. xiv. (Rolls) 557 Eer than he haue turnede or chaungid the iewelis into money. c1537 De Benese *Measurynge Lande* F iv b, Ye must turne the perches in to pence. c1593 *Trag. Rich. II*, ii. iii. 23 My iewells and my plaite are turnd to coyne. 1697 Dryden *Virg. Past.* vii. 51 Thy Marble Statue shall be turn'd to Gold. 1827 Jarman *Powell's Devises* (ed. 3) II. 97 He laid some stress upon the fact of the real estate being turned into personal. 1855 *Jrnl. R. Agric. Soc.* XVI. ii. 557 [They] turned their little stock into Cash.

†**d.** With inverse construction: To form by change *out of*. *Obs. nonce-use.*

1526 *Pilgr. Perf.* (W. de W. 1531) 180 Whiche worde Aue was turned out of Eua, & made Aue, & that not without great mistery.

38. *intr.* with *into* or *to*: To change into; to be changed, transformed, or converted into; to become.

c1250 *Long Life* 3 in *O.E. Misc.* 156 Fair weder turneð ofte into reine. 1393 Langl. *P. Pl.* C. xiv. 19 Al hus sorwe to solas þorgh þat songe turnede. c1400 *Brut* cc. 228 þe sonne þo turnede into blode. 1526 *Pilgr. Perf.* (W. de W. 1531) 93 Lest our Ire turne to enuy, and our enuy to hate. 1660 Boyle *New Exp. Phys. Mech.* xxxvii. 312 Water turning from perspicuous to white. 1764 Goldsm. *Trav.* 86 These rocks, by custom, turn to beds of down. 1892 *Monthly Packet* May 532 The monkeys did not turn into men, the men turned into monkeys.

b. To change into, become of (a specified nature, form, or aspect).

1678 J. Phillips *Tavernier's Trav.* ii. xxii. 155 The milk will turn to the colour of an Apostemated matter. 1856 *Jrnl. R. Agric. Soc.* XVII. ii. 482 Black cattle have been observed to turn..to a dun colour.

39. *intr.* with *compl.* To change so as to be, to become. **a.** with *adj. compl.* (in quot. 1303 with *advb. phr.*).

1303 R. Brunne *Handl. Synne* 6584 With wykked man, þou turnest as he. 1450 *Paston Lett.* I. 158 Therwith he turned pale colour. a1548 Hall *Chron., Hen. VI* 103 Saiyng: that God was turned Englishe, and the devill would not helpe Fraunce. 1592 Shaks. *Rom. & Jul.* i. ii. 48 Turne giddie, and be holpe by backward turning. 1626 Bacon *Sylva* §851 Cygnets from Gray turne White. 1758 R. Brown *Compl. Farmer* (1759) 111 When..the stalk begins to die, and to turn brown. 1818 Scott *Br. Lamm.* xxii, 'It is my mother!' said Lucy, turning as pale as ashes, and clasping her hands together. 1861 *Jrnl. R. Agric. Soc.* XXII. i. 48 The milk is apt to turn sour. 1888 'J. S. Winter' *Bootle's Childr.* viii, Lassie turned very white, and gasped for breath.

b. with *sb. compl.* (most commonly without article). Freq. as *pa. pple.* modifying a sb.

1596 Shaks. *Merch. V.* iii. i. 82 Vnlesse the diuell himselfe turne Iew. 1660 Fuller *Mixt Contempl.* (1841) 172 The remedy turned the malady of the land. 1758 S. Hayward *Serm.* xvii. 531 A mother must turn monster if she does not love her babe. 1853 Lytton *My Novel* v. ix, Did not you turn..a common stage-player, sir? 1879 Dowden *Southey* vi. 178 Under such strokes a courageous heart may turn coward. 1879 Minto *Defoe* x. 170 He had seen Whig turn Tory and Tory turn Whig. 1945, etc. [see poacher¹ 1 b]. 1964 *Eng. Studies* XLV. 382 Their Scandinavian conquerors-turned-neighbors. 1973 E. Schumacher *Small is Beautiful* i. iii. 44 The economist-turned-econometrician is unwilling..to face the question. 1982 *Times Lit. Suppl.* 10 Sept. 968/3 Jerome's father was a Nonconformist preacher, turned architect, turned mine-owner.

c. *turn after* (of offspring): to become or grow like, to 'take after' (the parent).

1848 *Jrnl. R. Agric. Soc.* IX. ii. 256 Where one parent is sound and the other diseased the progeny may turn after the former; but then it is just as likely to turn after the latter.

40. *trans.* with *compl.* (usually *adj.*) To change so as to make...; to make (so) by alteration; to render.

1607 Shaks. *Timon* iv. iii. 499 It almost turnes my dangerous Nature wilde. 1732 Pope *Ep. Cobham* 163 That gay Free-thinker,..What turns him now a stupid silent dunce? 1821 Clare *Vill. Minstr.* I. 23 His fears would turn him chill. 1849 *Jrnl. R. Agric. Soc.* X. i. 177 It turns the fibre black. 1904 Weyman *Abbess of Vlaye* xiv, With a..shock of the mind that turned her hot.

†**41. a.** *trans.* To change so as to bring *into* some specified condition: e.g. *to turn into madness* = to cause to become mad, to make mad. *Obs.*

In quot. c 1400, to set *on fire*; in quot. 1470-85 *torned vnto helpyng* (?) = brought into a condition of recovery, 'getting better'.

1382 Wyclif *Mark* iii. 21 Thei seiden, for he is turnyd in to wodenesse. c1400 *Destr. Troy* 7112 The Troiens þaire tore shippis hade turnyt on fyre. 1470-85 Malory *Arthur* xiii. xiii. 631 He asked syr Melyas how it stood with him. Thenne he sayd he was torned vnto helpyng, god be thanked. 1608 Topsell *Serpents* (1658) 701 Dionysius,..being turned by Juno into madnesse.

†**b.** *intr.* To get *into* some specified condition: e.g. *to turn into ire* = to become angry. *Obs.*

c1400 *Destr. Troy* 12252 þen Thelamon was tenfull, & turnyt into yre.

42. *trans.* with *into* or *to*: To make the subject of (praise, mockery, etc.); now chiefly in phr. *to turn* (a thing) *into ridicule* (see ridicule *sb.*¹ 3 b).

1387 Trevisa *Higden* (Rolls) IV. 143 He wolde torne [*v.r.* teurne] hit to bourde and to lawȝhynge. 1533 Gau *Richt Vay* (S.T.S.) 13 Thay that..twrnis the halie writ to lichtlines and scorne. 1601 Shaks. *Twel. N.* ii. v. 223 It cannot but turn him into a notable contempt. 1611 —— *Cymb.* iv. i. 23 Her Father..may..be a little angry..: but my Mother..shall turne all into my commendations. 1673-1784 [see ridicule *sb.*¹ 3 b]. 1891 E. & D. Gerard *Sensitive Pl.* I. ii. vii. 276 Does any one turn the true poet..into ridicule?

†**43.** *intr.* with *to*: To lead to as a consequence; to become the cause or occasion of; to result in, bring about. (See also *turn to account*, 62 a.) *Obs.* or merged in other senses.

c1200 Ormin Ded. 18 þu þohhtesst tatt itt mihhte wel Till mikell frame turrnenn. c1205 Lay. 25574 Let þu mi sweuen To selþen iturnen. 1297 R. Glouc. (Rolls) 7711 þe vnriȝt ido to poueremen to such mesaunture turnde. c1350 *Will. Palerne* 254 Perauenture þurth goddis grace to gode may it turne. 1422 tr. *Secreta Secret., Priv. Priv.* xxxvii. 194 Yef hit shold torn to pereill of the child. 1560 Daus tr. *Sleidane's Comm.* 42 Fearynge lest this broile..would tourne to his vtter destruction. 1631 Gouge *God's Arrows* iii. § 93. 355 Their plots turned to their owne damage. a1774 Goldsm. *Surv. Exp. Philos.* (1776) II. 147 To deduce any general theory that shall turn to public benefit.

†**b.** *to turn* (a person) *to* (something): to result in or bring about for the person; to put him to (trouble, etc.); to be for his (advantage, etc.). *Obs.*

Orig. *intr.* with dative of person; afterwards taken as *trans.* with the person as direct object.

c1200 Ormin Ded. 150 ȝiff þeȝȝ all forrwerrpenn itt, Itt turrneþþ hemm till sinne. c1230 *Hali Meid.* 7 Serue Godd ane, & alle þinge schulen þe turnen to gode. 13.. *Guy Warw.* (A.) 898 Wiþ him he wald iusti, It turned him to vilani [*Caius MS.* And therof hym befelle grete vilanye]. 1463 in *Acts Parlt. Scotl.* (1874) XII. 28/2 That occupatioun & vse þat I sal haue of þe said landis..sal turn ȝou na ȝoure successowris in na preiudice. 1523 Ld. Berners *Froiss.* I. cccxlii. 537 It shall tourne hym to moche blame. *Ibid.* ccccxxxvi. 767 He was as thanne xl. dayes iourney from thens, but..he rode it in fourtene dayes..whiche tourned to hym [*prob.* = hym to] a great valyantnesse. [*Orig.* On luy doit tourner a bonne voulenté et vaillance.] 1593 Shaks. *3 Hen. VI*, v. v. 16 All the trouble thou hast turn'd me to. 1607 —— *Cor.* iii. i. 284 A word or two, The which shall turne you to no further harme, Then so much losse of time. 1610 —— *Temp.* i. ii. 64 O my heart bleedes To thinke oth' teene that I haue turn'd you to.

** *Specific senses.*

44. *trans.* To change from one language or form of expression to another; to translate or paraphrase; to render. Also *absol.*

c1200 Ormin Ded. 129, & tærfore hafe icc turrnedd itt Inntill Ennglisshe spæche. a1225 *Juliana* 2 þat is of latin iturnd into englisch. a1300 *Cursor M.* 21108 (Cott.) Godspell he turnd in tung of ind. 14.. *Minor Poems fr. Vernon MS.* (E.E.T.S.) I. App. 407 This romance turned [a] Munk of sallay out of a frenche romance. 1548 Turner *Names of Herbes* (1881) 62 Picea is called in greeke as Theodore Gaza turneth, pitys. 1605 Camden *Rem.* (1637) 86 Others untruely turne it [Robert] Red-beard. 1700 Dryden *Fables* Pref., Ess. (ed. Ker) II. 248, I..resolved to put their merits to the trial, by turning some of the *Canterbury Tales* into our language, as it is now refined. 1711 Addison *Spect.* No. 39 ¶6 If the Writer laid down the whole Contexture of his Dialogue in plain English, before he turned it into Blank Verse. 1735 Pope *Prol. Sat.* 180 The Bard..Who turns a Persian tale for half a Crown. 1879 M. Pattison *Milton* vii. 90 In 1648 he turned nine psalms, and..in 1653, 'did into verse' eight more.

b. To alter the phrasing of (a sentence); to word differently, give another turn to.

1593 Shaks. *Lucr.* 1539 She..turn'd it thus, it cannot be, I find, But such a face should beare a wicked mind. 1869 Browning *Ring & Bk.* xii. 651 How he dares reprehend both high and low! Else had he turned the sentence 'God is true And every man a liar—save the Pope'. 1895 North & Hillard *Latin Prose Comp.* (1901) 24 The English has to be turned; *e.g.* 'The Greeks, having captured Troy, burnt it', cannot go straight into Latin, because Latin has no Perfect Participle Active.

45. To disturb or overthrow the mental balance of; to impair the power of judgement of; to make mad or crazy, distract, dement, infatuate.

a. with the brain or head as obj.

c1340 Hampole *Prose Tr.* 17 He..ouertrauells by ymaginacions his wittes, and by vndiscrete trauellynge turnes þe braynes in his heuede. 1601 R. Johnson *Kingd. & Commw.* (1603) 167 The Arabians..delight in sower milke, or Cosmus, a kind of charmed-sower-mares milke verie forcible to turne the braine. 1683 *Apol. Prot. France* iv. 40 The Prince's head was a little turned. 1719 De Foe *Crusoe* (1840) II. i. 8 My head was..turned with..whimsies. 1816 Scott *Bl. Dwarf* v, Your plays and romances have positively turned your brain. 1861 Hughes *Tom Brown at Oxf.* xxxv, You have been making serious love to Patty, and have turned the poor girl's head.

†**b.** with the person as obj. *Obs.*

c1400 *Destr. Troy* 3272 All tourniet with tene,..Wailyng & weping. 1560 Daus tr. *Sleidane's Comm.* 136 b, Albeit they did not chaunge him wholy,..yet did they turne him & confounde him. 1709 Hearne *Collect.* (O.H.S.) II. 300 It quite turn'd him, and destroy'd his Memory.

c. *intr.* for *pass.* of the head. *rare.* (Cf. 2 b.)

1852 M. Arnold *Second Best* 8 So many books thou readest,..That thy poor head almost turns. 1885 'Mrs. Alexander' *At Bay* xi, I trust the poor man's head hasn't turned with all his troubles.

46. *trans.* To make sour, taint (milk or fermented liquor); †in early use, to coagulate, curdle. Also *fig.*

1548 Elyot, *Coagulum*..a courde or creame, the ruen of a beaste, wherewith mylke is tourned. 1563 Hyll *Art Garden.* (1593) 164 A Hogshead..of white wine Lees, not yet turned and sowr. 1670 Dryden *2nd Pt. Conq. of Granada* iii. i, Love..'Tis soon made sour, and turn'd by jealousy. 1722 De Foe *Col. Jack* (1840) 138 This..turned the very blood within my veins. 1887 M. B. Edwards *Next of Kin Wanted* II. x. 130 A thunderstorm to-night might turn the syllabub.

b. *intr.* To become sour or tainted, as milk or fermented liquor; †in early use, To become curdled. Also *transf.* and *fig.*

1577 B. Googe *Heresbach's Husb.* 147 Some vse to put into the bottome of the payles, the greene kernelles of the Pine apple, and milking into them, doo cause it so to turne. 1594 Lyly *Moth. Bomb.* ii. v, If it thunder, though all the Ale and Beere in the towne turne, it will be constant. 1623 Massinger *Bondman* i. iii, The blood turns! 1727 *Bradley's Fam. Dict.* s.v. *Chocolate*, If you would have Milk Chocolate, take as much Milk as you do Water,..and take care it does not turn. 1839 Ure *Dict. Arts* 602 A thunder-storm sometimes destroys the coagulating power in the whole laminæ at once; or causes the glue to turn on the nets, in the language of the manufacturer.

47. *intr.* To change colour, become of a different colour (as ripening fruit, fading leaves, hair in old age): = *turn colour*, 52.

†*turn upon*, to verge upon or shade off into (a different colour). *Obs.*

1578 Lyte *Dodoens* iii. lxxix. 428 In the middle of the sayde flowers are many smal hearie thredes..turning vpon yellowe. 1888 Howells *Annie Kilburn* iv, When her hair had begun to turn. 1892 *Daily News* 8 Nov. 6/2 No two trees turn alike; in every group each member wears his own livery. 1893 *Argosy* Jan. 71 Really some ripe strawberries?.. Ours are not turning yet.

b. *trans.* To change the colour of.

1791 Hamilton *Berthollet's Dyeing* II. ii. iii. ix. 233 The silk being distributed on the rods..., lemon-juice..is poured into the bath, till it is of a fine cherry colour. This is called turning (*virer*) the bath. 1867 Adelaide Sartoris *Week Fr. Country Ho.* i. 17 Poplars, already turned by the season.

VII. Phrases.

Phrases. * *with sb. obj.*

(For *turn* cat *in pan*, *t. the* (*other*) cheek, *t. a* hair, *t. the* (or *a new*) leaf, *t. the* penny, *t. the* tables, *t.* tippet, *t.* turtle, *t.* wind, see the sbs.)

48. turn the (or **one's**) **back**: to turn away, go away; ***turn the back upon***, to depart from, abandon: see back *sb.*¹ 24 g.

c1330 R. Brunne *Chron. Wace* (Rolls) 8486 When þey wer sondred, þey tur[n]d þe bak. c1400–1866 [see back *sb.*¹

24 g]. **1581** EARL MORTON in *Calr. Scott. Pap.* VI. 14, I was purposed to have .. turned my backe upon Scotland while I had sene further.

49. turn the balance or **beam**: to preponderate: = *turn the scale*, 58.

1590 SHAKS. *Mids. N.* v. i. 324 A Mote [ed. 1623 Moth] wil turne the ballance, which Piramus which Thisby is the better. **1602** —— *Ham.* IV. v. 157 Thy madnesse shall be payed by waight, Till our Scale turnes the beame. **1722** WOLLASTON *Relig. Nat.* iii. 59 When there is nothing in the opposite Scale .. this [probability] in the course of nature must turn the beam. **1892** *Eng. Illustr. Mag.* X. 36 A straw will often suffice to turn the balance.

50. turn bridle: to turn one's horse and ride back; to retreat, as a rider. (In first quot. *fig.*)

1579 TOMSON *Calvin's Serm. Tim.* 731/2 If there bee but one man that turneth backe the bridle [orig. *qui aura tourné bride*], wee seeme to seeke such occasions to become wicked and lewde. **1653** HOLCROFT *Procopius, Pers. Wars* II. 60 The Persians .. drave them out of the fastnesses, and then turn'd bridle. **1825** SCOTT *Betrothed* xiii, Were I you, my Lady Eveline, .. I would turn bridle yet; for this old dungeon seems little likely to afford food or shelter to Christian folk. **1892** *Black & White* 9 Jan. 47/1 We turned bridle and trotted back.

51. turn one's coat: to change one's principles or party: see COAT *sb.* 13, and cf. TURNCOAT.

1565 SHACKLOCK *Hatchet of Heresyes* 74 Howe many tymes Melancthon hath turned his cote in this one opinion. **1577** GRANGE *Golden Aphrod.*, etc. O iij b, Now must I turne my coate and cleaue vnto my God, Desiring pardon for my crime. **1655** FULLER *Ch. Hist* IX. vii. §24 That all the Protestants would either turn their Coats, Copies, arms, or fly away. **1819** SCOTT *Leg. Montrose* xvii, Sir John Urrie, a soldier .., who had already changed sides twice during the Civil War, and was destined to turn his coat a third time before it was ended. **1946** G. MILLAR *Horned Pigeon* ix. 130 Like good policemen all over the world, they were only too willing to turn their coats (to keep law and order, of course). **1981** *Times Lit. Suppl.* 2 Jan. 7/5 What prompted Sohō, Japanese intellectuals have endlessly debated, to 'turn his coat' in the 1890s?

52. turn (one's) colour: to change colour, become of a different colour; of a person, to become pale or red in the face (now *rare*).

[**1450**: cf. 39 a.] **1602** SHAKS. *Ham.* II. ii. 542 Looke where he ha's not turn'd his colour, and ha's teares in's eyes. **1720** MRS. MANLEY *Power of Love* (1741) VI. 346 She turned colour, and was much surprized to see so great a Company. **1899** *Tit-Bits* 19 Aug. 420/2 [These] buttons .. do not turn colour. *Mod.* The fruit is beginning to turn colour.

53. turn a deaf ear: to refuse to listen: cf. EAR *sb.*[1] 3 d.

1663 BP. PATRICK *Parab. Pilgr.* xviii. (1687) 176 Turn a deaf ear to him, and do not go along with him. **1793** R. HALL *Apol. Freed. Press* 45 They .. turn a deaf ear to their complaints. **1855** DICKENS *Dorrit* II. xxiii, Affery .. turned a deaf ear to all adjuration.

54. turn edge: see 9 b.

55. turn .. flank: *Mil.* to get round an enemy's flank so as to make an attack in flank or in rear (cf. 17 b); hence *fig.* to 'get round', circumvent, or outwit a person.

1813 WELLINGTON in Gurw. *Desp.* (1839) X. 596 Sir Lowry Cole .. retired .. because his right flank was turned. **1841-4** EMERSON *Ess., Circles* Wks. (Bohn) I. 128 There is not a piece of science, but its flank may be turned to-morrow. **1844** H. H. WILSON *Brit. India* II. ii. II. 45 Detaching .. seven companies to turn the left flank of the position.

56. turn one's hand. a. To make an attack *upon*: cf. 31. *arch.*

1297 R. GLOUC. (Rolls) 6070 Suan þe duc of denemarch, bigan to turne is hond. & after þat he adde destrued þe souþhalf of þis lond, He wende & robbede al þis lond al þe norþ side. **1382** WYCLIF *2 Sam.* xxiv. 17, I biseche, be thin hoond turned aȝens me, and aȝens the hows of my fader. **1839** [see sense 31]. **1877** *Queen's Printers' Bible-Aids* 134 David .. entreating him [God] to spare the innocent people, and to turn his hand upon himself.

b. with *to*: To apply oneself to, set to work at, take up as an occupation: cf. 34.

1703 STEELE *Tender Husb.* II. i, A good Servant should turn his Hand to every thing in a Family. **1856** *Jrnl. R. Agric. Soc.* XVII. II. 358 [He] can turn his own hand to the plough when wanted. **1867** SMILES *Huguenots Eng.* ii. (1880) 22 [He] was ready to turn his hand to anything that might enable him to earn a living.

57. turn head: to turn and face an enemy; to show a bold opposing front: the opposite of *turn tail*. Cf. HEAD *sb.*[1] 29. ? *Obs.*

1596 SHAKS. *1 Hen. IV*, III. ii. 102 He .. Turnes head against the Lyons armed Iawes. **1677** N. COX *Gentl. Recreat.* (ed. 2) 17 When Deer .. turn head against the Hounds, we say, they Bay. **1724** DE FOE *Mem. Cavalier* I. 125 Twas to no Purpose to turn Head, no Man would stand by us.

58. turn the scale: to cause one scale of a balance to descend: said of an additional weight, usually a slight or just sufficient one; hence *fig.* to preponderate so as to determine the success or superiority of one of two opposing parties or sides.

1603 SHAKS. *Meas. for M.* IV. ii. 32 You waigh equallie: a feather will turne the Scale. **1697** DRYDEN *Æneid* x. 736 A single Soul's too light to turn the Scale. **1814** [see SCALE *sb.*[1] 4]. **1874** STUBBS *Const. Hist.* I. x. 311 The scale was turned in favour of strong measures by the voice of the native troops.

b. with *at*, in lit. sense: To weigh slightly more than.

1889 J. K. JEROME *Three Men in Boat* 283 He had weighed it carefully .. and it turned the scale at thirty-four pounds. **1892** *Photogr. Ann.* II. 883 A case containing a ¼-plate camera .. turning the scale at 6 lbs.

59. turn tail. a. (orig. in *Falconry*) To turn the back and flee; to run away, retreat: see TAIL *sb.*[1] 11 d.

1575 TURBERV. *Flaconrie* 126 Most commonly if a yong hawke be let flee at olde game shee will turne tayle. *a* **1586-1719** [see TAIL *sb.*[1] 11 d]. **1841** CAPT. B. HALL *Patchwork* II. vii. 139 As soon as my companion turned tail .. I was compelled .. to run for it likewise. **1891** GWEN. D. GALTON *La Fenton* v, He turned tail and fled.

b. with *on* or *upon*: To abandon, forsake.

1624 QUARLES *Job* v. 4 As a Truant-Scholler .. turnes speedy tayle Upon his tedious booke. **1807** [see TAIL *sb.*[1] 11 d]. **1852** JAMES *Agnes Sorel* (1860) I. 14 [They] have turned tail upon their former faith.

†**c.** To turn in opposition or defiance: in proverbial phrase (see quots., and cf. 33, 66 d). *Obs.*

1611 MIDDLETON & DEKKER *Roaring Girle* D.'s Wks. 1873 III. 158 Tread vpon a worme they say twill turne taile. **1641** G. RALEIGH *Albania* 28 There is not the least Worme, but being trodden upon will turne taile.

†**60. turn one's tale**: to tell a different story, 'change one's tune'. *Obs.*

1535 COVERDALE *Ecclus.* xxvii. 23 Whan thou art present, he shal .. prayse thy wordes: but at the last he shall turne his tayle [**1560** tale] and slaunder thy sayenge. **1678** BUNYAN *Pilgr.* I. 13 Then they all turned their tales, and began to deride poor Christian behind his back.

** *with compl. adj. or adv. phr. (prep. + sb., etc.)*

(See also IN AND OUT 2, *inside out* (INSIDE A. 4), *top over tail* (TOP *sb.*[1] 25 d), TOPSY-TURVY, UPSIDE DOWN, *out of* (or *at*) WINDOW, *the* WRONG *side out*.)

61. turn loose. *trans.* To set free (an animal) and allow to go loose; *transf.* and *fig.* to free from restraint and allow to go where, or do as, one will; to leave to oneself or one's own devices.

1598 SHAKS. *Merry W.* II. i. 190 If hee should intend this voyage toward my wife, I would turne her loose to him. **1679** DRYDEN *Tr. & Cr.* I. ii, He's the ablest man for judgment in all Troy; you may turn him loose, i' faith. **1765** *Treat. Dom. Pigeons* 77 He braces a letter under the wings of a Pigeon, .. and .. turns it loose. **1892** *Sat. Rev.* 9 Jan. 40/2 They are turned loose to graze on the succulent grasses.

b. To discharge, fire off (a bullet, or a firearm); also (*humorously*) *fig. intr.* with *on*, to speak to, address (cf. *open fire*, FIRE *sb.* 14). *U.S.*

1874 J. W. LONG *Amer. Wild Fowl* xxvi. 269 When they are coming to your decoys down-wind .. as they double back to alight, 'turn it loose' at the middle of the cluster. **1903** A. ADAMS *Log Cowboy* x, The chief could not speak a word of English ..; when I turned loose on him in Spanish, he .. signed back to his band. *Ibid.* xiii, Somebody .. turned his gun loose into the air.

c. *trans.* and *intr.* Also *turn aloose*. To let go (of), to leave hold (of). *U.S. dial.*

1906 *Dialect Notes* III. 162 *Turn loose*, .. to get rid of, let go. **1910** *Ibid.* 457 *Turn it loose*, .. let go of it. **1929** W. FAULKNER *Sound & Fury* 199 He turned my hands loose. **1934** C. CARMER *Stars fell on Alabama* 139, I jus' *got* to hold you now. I *can't* turn you aloose. **1935** T. WOLFE *Of Time & River* III. xlii. 376 You git his other hand, Jim, an' try to make him turn a-loose. *a* **1938** —— *Web & Rock* (1947) 34 'You turn loose of me,' the captive panted, 'I'll show you who's the cry-baby!' **1966** R. PRICE *Generous Man* (1967) i. 63 'Safe! We're in awful danger. Turn loose, old fool!' He turned loose and lay flat, small on the ground.

62. turn to account. †**a.** *intr.* To result in profit or advantage (cf. 43 and ACCOUNT *sb.* 5); to be profitable, to 'pay'; also with dat. of person (prob. often taken as direct object: cf. 43 b). *Obs.*

1675 G. R. tr. *Le Grand's Man without Passion* 227 Sometimes troubles turn us to account. *a* **1677** BARROW *Serm.* Wks. 1716 I. 10 Any of us may .. throughly compass and carry it on; which will exceedingly turn to accompt. *a* **1692** POLLEXFEN *Disc. Trade* (1697) 20 Bullion or Coyn will turn them to a better Account. **1700** WALLIS in *Collect.* (O.H.S.) I. 326 It may turn to good account. **1727** SWIFT *Modest Prop.* Wks. 1755 II. II. 61 They will not yield above three pounds .. which cannot turn to account either to the parents or kingdom. **1743** POCOCKE *Descr. East* I. 134 Of late the West India coffee .. has sold so cheap, that it does not turn to account to send it to England.

b. *trans.* To make use of for one's advantage or profit (cf. 34); to employ profitably.

1826 B'NESS BUNSEN in Hare *Life* (1879) I. vii. 267 Whether I shall ever find time .. to turn to account the instructions of Neukomm. **1870** TYNDALL *Notes Lect. Electr.* §20 Others have turned to account mechanically the attraction exerted by electro-magnetic cores on bars of iron. **1878** L. STEPHEN *Johnson* i. 11 He could at least turn his talents to account.

63. turn to bay: to turn and defend oneself, as a hunted animal at bay (see BAY *sb.*[4] 3); also *fig.*

1810 SCOTT *Lady of L.* I. viii, The Stag must turn to bay, Where that rude rampart barred the way. **1832** MACAULAY *Armada* 25 So glared he when at Agincourt in wrath he turned to bay. **1849** —— *Hist. Eng.* vi. II. 137 The colonists turned to bay with the stubborn hardihood of their race.

*** *with another verb.*

†**64. turn and wind** (in specific uses). *Obs.*

a. *intr.* and *refl.* To turn this way and that; to go or move in a winding course.

a **1300** *Cursor M.* 6540 (Cott.) He ne wist queþer it bettur war To turn or winde him forþar mare. **1634** SIR T. HERBERT *Trav.* 20 In Mæanders [the dancers] turne and winde themselues. **1676** D'URFEY *Mad. Fickle* IV. ii, Turn and wind Like Foxes in a storme. *c* **1680** BEVERIDGE *Serm.* (1729) I. 462 We see how all things wind and turn and work together, till they accomplish the end for which they were designed. **1824** SCOTT *Redgauntlet* Let. iv, A tall man, well mounted on a strong black horse, which he caused to turn and wind like a bird in the air.

†**b.** *trans.* To turn this way and that, as a rider his horse; *fig.* to manage according to one's pleasure, to do what one will with. (Cf. 9 c.)

1596 SHAKS. *1 Hen. IV*, IV. i. 109 To turne and winde a fierie Pegasus. **1606** *Sir G. Goosecappe* I. iv. in Bullen *O. Pl.* III. 26 Wee will turne her, and winde her, and make her so plyant, that we will drawe her thorugh a wedding ring yfaith. **1673** MILTON *True Relig.* Wks. 1851 V. 414 An ordinary Protestant, well read in the Bible, may turn and wind their Doctors.

†**c.** To put in circulation, circulate, cause to pass in exchange: = *turn over*, 78 i. (Cf. 15 b.) *Obs.*

1598 GRENEWEY *Tacitus' Ann.* IV. iv. (1622) 93 By turning and winding base merchandise in Affrica and Sicilia, he gayned his liuing. **1686** tr. *Chardin's Coronat. Solyman* 92 All the money that we turn and wind is the Kings.

VIII. In combination with adverbs.

65. turn about. (See also simple senses and ABOUT *adv.*)

* *intr.* †**a.** To move circularly on an axis; to rotate, revolve: = *turn round*, 79 a. *Obs.*

c **1000** *Sax. Leechd.* III. 254 Seo firmamentum tyrnþ symle onbutan us under þyssere eorðan & bufan .. & ealle ða steorran þe hyre on fæste synd turniað onbutan mid hyre. *a* **1300** *Holy Rode* 379 in *Leg. Rood* 48 þer-aboute he let do þe fourme of sonne and mone and of sterres also Scyne as it hem-sulf were and turne aboute vaste. **1539** BIBLE (Great) *Prov.* xxvi. 14 Lyke as the dore turneth aboute vpon the thresholde. **1609** BIBLE (Douay) *Numb.* xxviii. 14 Through al monethes, that succede one another as the yeare turneth about.

b. To reverse one's position or course; to turn so as to face or go in the opposite direction: = *turn round*, 79 b. Now *rare*.

1303 [see TURNING *vbl. sb.* 4]. **13..** *Sir Beues* (A.) 4070 'Fro whanne komeþ þis fair deistrer?.. Which is þe kroupe? terne about!' Aboute he ternde þe deistrer. **1526** TINDALE *John* i. 38 Jesus turned about, and sawe them folowe. **1676** DRYDEN *Aureng-z.* v. i, The Morning, as mistaken, turns about, And all her early fires again go out. **1719** DE FOE *Crusoe* (1840) I. xx. 358 They began to retire, and turn about. **1804** *Man in Moon* 191, I turned about and went to sleep again. **1868** MORRIS *Earthly Par., Man born to be King* 250 He .. turned about and left him there.

** *trans.* †**c.** To cause to rotate or revolve: = sense 1. *Obs.*

1483 CAXTON *G. de la Tour* F viij, [They] made hym to tourne aboute a mylle as a blynde hors. **1579** TOMSON *Calvin's Serm. Tim.* 348/1 They .. doe but turne about the pot. **1669** STURMY *Mariner's Mag.* I. 34 The other Foot [of the compasses] being turned about, will .. touch the Line AG.

d. To alter or reverse the position of; to put into a different, or the opposite, position (by a rotatory motion): = *turn round*, 79 e; *refl.* = b. Now *rare* or *Obs.*

a **1300** *Cursor M.* 15951 (Cott.) Jesus þan turnd him abute. *c* **1300** *Ibid.* 23223 (Edinb.) Quil þou moht turn þin hand about. **13..** [see b]. *c* **1550** *Song Sir A. Barton* iii. in *Surtees Misc.* (1888) 65 King Henry was stout, and turnd hime about. **1590** SPENSER *F.Q.* II. iii. 42 So [she] turned her about, and fled. **1826** F. REYNOLDS *Life & Times* I. 174 Give me only time to turn myself about, and something must soon turn up trumps. [Cf. 79 b, note.]

e. To turn this way and that; to move or push about; also *fig.* = *turn over*, 78 e.

1598 SHAKS. *Merry W.* v. v. 108 Pinch him, and burne him, and turne him about. **1610** —— *Temp.* II. ii. 118 'Prethee doe not turne me about, my stomacke is not constant. **1725** WATTS *Logic* II. iv. §3 Turn these Ideas about in your Mind.

66. turn again. (See also simple senses and AGAIN *adv.*)

* *intr.* †**a.** To face round the other way (usually in order to go back): = *turn back*, 70 e. *arch.*

a **1300** *Cursor M.* 12594 (Cott.) At þe vte-cuming o þe yatte He turnd again. *c* **1400** MAUNDEV. (Roxb.) iv. 13 Scho turned agayne with a hidous crie. **1678** [See AGAIN A. 1 b]. **1818** SCOTT *Rob Roy* xxi, Few turned again to take some minutes' voluntary exercise.

†**b.** To return, go back (= sense 21). *Obs.*

c **1200** *Trin. Coll. Hom.* 87 Ihc wile turnen agen to mine huse. **1340** HAMPOLE *Pr. Consc.* 7241 Alle þase þat tylle helle wendes .. Salle never after turne ogayne. *c* **1386** CHAUCER *Clerk's T.* 872 Naked out of my fadres hous, quod she, I cam and naked moot I turne agayn. *c* **1420** *Anturs of Arth.* 292 Ther salle .. Ane torne home a-ȝayne [*v.r.* ye shullene turne ayene] for that tydynge. *c* **1511** *1st Eng. Bk. Amer.* (Arb.) Introd. 33/1 To tourne ageyne unto there owne lande. **1535** COVERDALE *Ruth* i. 11 But Naemi sayde: Turne agayne my doughters, why wolde ye go with me? **1612** R. JOHNSON *Song Sir Richard Whittington* v. in *Crown-Garl. Gould. Roses* B v b, London bells sweetly rung... Euermore sounding so, turne againe Whittington: For thou in time shalt grow, Lord Maior of London. **1640** SHIRLEY *Constant Maid* II. ii, Six bells in every steeple, And let them all go to the city tune,—*Turn again, Whittington.* **1667** PEPYS *Diary* 2 Sept., I took a coach and went home-wards; but then turned again, and to White Hall.

†**c.** *fig.* To return to a former condition (or possessor: cf. 21 b); to revert. *Obs.* (or merged in other senses).

1303 R. BRUNNE *Handl. Synne* 5232 To leue hys synne .. And turne aȝen to lyfe and grace. *c* **1400** MAUNDEV. (Roxb.) iv. 12 þan sall scho turne agayne to hir awen kynde and be a womman. *c* **1450** *Godstow Reg.* 198 Aftur þ[e] deceasse of þ[e] foreseyde .. þ[e] foreseyde mansyon with hys pertinences shulde turne holly & fully a-geyne to þ[e] foreseyde abbas & couent. **1600** SHAKS. *A.Y.L.* II. vii. 162 His bigge manly voice, Turning againe toward childish trebble, pipes And whistles in his sound. 1697 DRYDEN *Virg. Georg.* IV. 597 Till ..he turns agen To his true Shape.

†**d.** To turn in opposition or defiance; in quot. 1393, to recoil *on*; cf. 32, 33. *Obs.*

c1330 *Arth. & Merl.* (Kölbing) 6871 þe Sarrazins turned oȝen On king Vrien. 1393 LANGL. *P. Pl.* C. XXI. 402 Now by-gynneþ thi gyle a-gayn on þe turne. a1548 HALL *Chron., Edw. IV* 199 What worme is touched, and will not once turne again? 1641 in *Verney Mem.* (1907) I. 199 A worme will turne agayne if it be trod on.

†**e.** Of an edge: To bend back so as to become blunted: = sense 9d. *Obs.*

1579 SPENSER *Sheph. Cal.* Feb. 203 The Axes edge did oft turne againe.

** *trans.* †**f.** *refl.* = a, b. *Obs.*

c1275 *Passion of our Lord* 653 in *O.E. Misc.* 55 Hi turnden heom ayeyn..to iherusalem. 13.. *Cursor M.* 12608 (Gött.) Ioseph and mari þaim turned againe To sek him. c1420 *Chron. Vilod.* 1739 When þe messagers seyen herre so stedfaste..þey tur[n]den hem aȝeyne. 1539 BIBLE (Great) *Ps.* xc. 13 Turne the agayne (O Lorde) at the last, and be gracious.

†**g.** *trans.* To cause to turn back (in various senses); to avert (cf. 13b); to drive back, repel (cf. 19, 25); to convert (= 29). *Obs.*

c1380 WYCLIF *Wks.* (1880) 288 To turnen aȝen þis þondir þat it persiþ noȝt. 1387 TREVISA *Higden* (Rolls) V. 233 By his witte and sleiþe þe Hunnes were i-torned aȝen. 1483 *Cath. Angl.* 397/1 To Turne agayn to gudnes,..*conuertere*.

67. turn around. (See simple senses and AROUND *adv.*) = *turn round*, sense 79. orig. *U.S.*

1880 'MARK TWAIN' *Tramp Abroad* xiii. 119, I could see the dim blur of the windows, but in my turned-around condition they were exactly where they ought not to be. 1919 E. O'NEILL *Moon of Caribbees* 114 Smitty does not turn around. 1925 F. SCOTT FITZGERALD *Great Gatsby* i. 9 Turning me around by one arm. *Ibid.* ix. 208 He opened it at the back cover and turned it around for me to see. 1932 W. FAULKNER *Light in August* xiv. 315 When he sat up he found that the sun..now shone upon him from the opposite direction. At first he believed that he was merely turned around. Then he realised that it was now evening. 1945 DYLAN THOMAS in *Horizon* Feb. 83 The weather turned around. 1963 J. JOESTEN *They call it Intelligence* I. iv. 45 A spy..caught..usually is given a chance to switch sides.. such a helpless foreign agent is being 'turned around'. 1967 V. C. WELBURN *Johnny So Long* II. ii. 63 He shakes his hands high at the crowd, then turns around and does it to Judy. 1971 *Sci. News* 13 Feb. 108 Children..with severe behavioral problems..are treated in a 'family' situation... An innovative school program helps 'turn youngsters around'. 1971 *Black World* Mar. 54/1, I felt so sorry for them and they wuz so turned around that one day over to Tony's crib I got high wid em. 1972 B. MOORE *Catholics* i. 21 Order them to turn that boat around and send it back for him. 1976 *National Observer* (U.S.) 29 May 3/4 This thing is so close, so fragile, that anything could happen tomorrow to turn it around. 1977 J. D. MACDONALD *Condominium* xxxiii. 322 We're past our marker... More than a mile. We can turn around. 1978 *Globe & Mail* (Toronto) 16 May 5/1 The Ontario Government has announced a..campaign to turn around the image Ontarians have gained as boorish and unfriendly hosts to foreign visitors.

68. turn aside: see simple senses and ASIDE *adv.*

a. *trans.*: cf. 13, 14. In quot. 13.. *refl.* (= b); cf. 7b.

13.. *Coer de L.* 355 The baroun turnyd hym asyde. 1535 COVERDALE *Isa.* xliv. 20 Folishnesse of herte hath turned them a syde. a1648 LD. HERBERT *Autobiog.* (1824) 114 Lieutenant Prichard..taking me by the shoulder, turned me aside. 1718 *Free-thinker* No. 62 ¶14 The Gods were beseeched to turn aside the Event. 1892 *Cornh. Mag.* May 478 He had never been turned aside from the execution of his purpose.

b. *intr.*: cf. 6, 16, 28.

1535 COVERDALE *Deut.* v. 32 Turne not asyde nether to yᵉ right hande ner to the lefte. 1560 BIBLE (Genev.) *Exod.* iii. 3, I wil turne aside now, and se this great sight. —— *Ps.* xl. 4 Blessed is the man, that..regardeth not the proude, nor suche as turne aside to lies. 1606 SHAKS. *Ant. & Cl.* I. iii. 76, I prythee turne aside, and weepe for her. 1844 LD. BROUGHAM *A. Lunel* (1872) I. xiv. 282 The Baron turned not aside from his argument. 1891 *Temple Bar Mag.* Dec. 581 He turned aside and crept in at the open door.

69. turn away. (See simple senses and AWAY *adv.*)

* *trans.* **a.** To avert (one's face, etc.); in quot. 1827, to place so as to be directed away from something (cf. 23d).

c1175 *Lamb. Hom.* 53 Swa sone se hi beoð iturnd awey from heom. c1380 WYCLIF *Wks.* (1880) 8 His preiere is cursid..þat turneþ a-wey his eris. 1382 —— *Ps.* xii[i]. 1 Lord..hou longe thou turnest awei thi face fro me? 1588 SHAKS. *L.L.L.* v. ii. 148 Each turne away his face. 1782 COWPER *Anti-thelyphthora* 87 She saw,—and turn'd her rosy cheek away. 1827 FARADAY *Chem. Manip.* xv. (1842) 327 In filling the fresh jar with water, its mouth is to be turned away from the gas jars. 1889 FRANCES M. PEARD *Paul's Sister* v, She..turned away her head.

b. *fig.* To divert; to avert (calamity, etc.): cf. 14, 26; in quot. 1848 = *turn off*, 74g.

1382 WYCLIF *Ps.* liii[i]. 7 [5] Turne awei euelis to myn enemys. —— *Isa.* xliii. 13, I shal werchen, and who shal turnen awei it? c1591 in *Lett. Lit. Men* (Camden) 79 To turne awaie the peoples likinge from him. 1658 *Whole Duty Man* v. 112 Deprecation,..when we pray to God to turn away some evil from us. 1848 THACKERAY *Bk. Snobs* xxvi, Which question Lady Hawbuck turned away with a sudden query regarding her..daughters.

c. To send away, dismiss; *spec.* to dismiss from service; †in quot. c 1400, ? to take away, carry off. (Cf. 25.)

c1400 *Destr. Troy* 8553 He was takon full tite & turnyt away. 1598 SHAKS. *Merry W.* I. iii. 4, I must turne away some of my followers. a1654 SELDEN *Table-T.* (Arb.) 63 The Master of the House may turn away all his Servants. 1793 *Regal Rambler* 17 The footman..was turned away without wages or warning. 1866 MRS. GASKELL *Wives & Dau.* xxiii, He has turned away all the men off the new works. 1901 W. R. H. TROWBRIDGE *Lett. Mother to Eliz.* vii, We were lucky to get rooms.., for they are turning people away.

d. *refl.* = e, f. *Obs.* or *arch.*

1375 BARBOUR *Bruce* I. 167 [He] turnyt him in wreth away. 1382 WYCLIF *Ezek.* xviii. 24 If a iust man shal turne hym awei fro his riȝtwisness.

** *intr.* **e.** To turn so as to face away from some person or thing; to avert one's face; also *fig.*: cf. 22c, 23c, 28.

a1300 *Floriz & Bl.* 744 Al wepinge he turnde away. 1470–85 MALORY *Arthur* XIII. viii. 623 The kyng tourned awey and myghte not speke for wepynge. 1593 SHAKS. *2 Hen. VI*, III. ii. 74 What, dost thou turne away, and hide thy face? 1840 DICKENS *Barn. Rudge* xxii, 'Oh, very well—if you're in a huff', cried Miggs, turning away. 1865 RUSKIN *Sesame* ii. §91 Instead of trying to do this, you turn away from it.

f. To leave the straight course, deviate; to be averted: cf. 16. *Obs.* or *arch.*

1535 COVERDALE *Ezek.* xviii. 24 Yf the rightuous turne awaye from his rightuousnes. 1611 BIBLE *Gen.* xxvii. 45 Vntill thy brothers anger turne away from thee.

†**g.** To go away, depart; to vanish. (Cf. 24c.) *Obs. rare.*

1340 HAMPOLE *Pr. Consc.* 516 Naked,..I cam Hyder,.. And naked I sal turne away. c1425 *Cursor M.* 22472 (Trin.) Whenne alle þinge shul turne away.

70. turn back. (See simple senses and BACK *adv.*)

* *trans.* **a.** To reverse the course of, drive back, cause to retreat: cf. 19.

1535 COVERDALE *Jer.* xxi. 4, I will turne backe the weapens ..wherwith ye fight agaynst the kinge of Babilon. 1872 MORLEY *Voltaire* vi. (1886) 314 The man who turned the tide back. 1880 R. MACKENZIE *19th Cent.* III. ix. 448 To arrest and turn back the mightiest power.

b. To send or give back, return: cf. 21c. *Obs.* exc. *U.S.*

1597 SHAKS. *2 Hen. IV*, I. i. 34 Sir Iohn Vmfreuill turn'd me backe With ioyfull tydings. 1606 —— *Tr. & Cr.* II. ii. 69 We turne not backe the Silkes vpon the Merchant When we haue spoyl'd them. 1672 VILLIERS (Dk. Buckhm.) *Rehearsal* II. iii. (Arb.) 55 These insolent Raskals have turn'd 'em all back upon my hands again. 1927 *Publishers' Weekly* 12 Feb. 610 We felt that the only course open to us in view of the authors' feelings in the matter was to offer to turn back the book to them, subject to their disposal.

c. To reverse the direction of; to direct backwards: cf. 22a, 23a.

In quot. 1845, to expose by reversing: = *turn over*, 78c. 1663 BP. PATRICK *Parab. Pilgr.* xxxiv. (1687) 417 They heard the noise of an horses heels behind them. Which causing them to turn their eyes back [etc.]. 1825 SCOTT *Talism.* ii, It were better..to turn back thy horse's head towards the camp of thy people. 1845 *Jrnl. R. Agric. Soc.* VI. II. 344 Both heaps [of potatoes] have now been turned back, and none are diseased.

d. To fold or double back or over (part of a garment, etc.) Also in *pa. pple.* with *with* = *turned up with*: see 81e.

1869 H. S. LEIGH *Carols of Cockayne* 166 He turn'd back his cuffs, and he put back his hair. 1913 *Play Pictorial* No. 130. 18/2 A gown of green paon broché crêpe de chine, draped..with tulle,..turned back with handsome cream guipure.

** *intr.* **e.** To reverse one's position so as to face (and, usually, go) in the opposite direction; to turn and go back: cf. 20, 22c, 23c, 24c.

1535 COVERDALE *Ps.* cxiii[i]. 5 Whatayled the..thou Iordan that thou turnedst backe? 1592 SHAKS. *Rom. & Jul.* II. i. 2 Can I goe forward when my heart is here? Turne backe dull earth, and find thy Center out. 1816 SCOTT *Antiq.* vii, 'Turn back! turn back!' exclaimed the vagrant. 1843 MACAULAY *Horatius* lii, He..thrice came on in fury, And thrice turned back in dread. 1886 MRS. LYNN LINTON *P. Carew* xxv, He had put his hand to the plough, and he was not the man to turn back.

†**f.** To come or go back, return: cf. 21. *Obs.*

c1600 SHAKS. *Sonn.* cxliii. 11 Turne back to me. 1611 BIBLE *2 Kings* i. 5 When the messengers turned backe vnto him, he said.., Why are ye now turned backe? 1660 F. BROOKE tr. *Le Blanc's Trav.* 37 We turned back again into Persia.

†**71. turn by.** *trans.* To set aside, reject (a candidate): cf. BY *adv.* 2. (Also with *by* as prep.: cf. BY *prep.* 16c.) *Obs.*

1705 HEARNE *Collect.* 7 Dec. (O.H.S.) I. 119 When he stood for orders [he] was turn'd by for Deficiency. [1709 *Ibid.* II. 294 Reasons..not reckon'd as sufficient for turning Mr. Littleton by his Degree.] 1803 J. ADAMS in *Harvard Grad. Mag.* IX. 349, I was in a great fright, and expected to be turned by.

72. turn down. (See simple senses and DOWN *adv.*)

* *trans.* **a.** To fold or double down; to bend downwards: cf. 9.

1601 SHAKS. *Jul. C.* IV. iii. 273 Is not the Leafe turn'd downe Where I left reading? 1793 SMEATON *Edystone L.* §273 The cramps..were turned down at each end. 1828 [H. BEST] *Italy as it is* 128 The beds..were all, in the housewife's phrase, turned down. 1841 THACKERAY *Gt. Hoggarty Diam.* vii, Nothing could make him..refrain from wearing his collars turned down.

b. To turn upside down, to invert; to turn (a card) face downwards: cf. 10.

1763 *Brit. Mag.* IV. 117 Sometimes she turns down my cup herself, after the first dish, because..tea is nervous. 1859 FITZGERALD *Omar* lxxv, Turn down an empty Glass! 1890 FENN *Double Knot* III. viii. 115 The played cards were solemnly turned down.

c. To put down, send to a lower position (as in a class at school; also *fig.*): cf. 25. *Obs.* exc. *U.S.*

1581 J. BELL *Haddon's Answ. Osor.* 69 You beyng ignoraunt what difference is betwixt an affirmative, & a negative proposition, must be turned doune agayne behinde the Schoolehouse doore. 1693 DRYDEN *Examen Poeticum* Ded., Ess. (Ker) II. 3 Julius Scaliger would needs turn down Homer and abdicate him. 1876 'MARK TWAIN' *Tom Sawyer* vi. 71 He took his place...in the spelling class, and got 'turned down', by a succession of mere baby words. 1946 G. WILSON *Fidelity Folks* 136 We had regular places in the line and turned down those who could not spell a word.

d. orig. *U.S. slang.* To rebuke, snub, 'put down'; to reject, refuse to accept.

1891 *Cent. Dict.* s.v., *To turn down*..(*c*) to snub; suppress. (Slang, U.S.) 1897 *Boston* (Mass.) *Jrnl.* 14 Jan. 7/6 Secretary Olney was turned down by the Senate..in his effort to have the vote on the extradition treaties.. reconsidered. 1900 *Montreal Gaz.* 3 Mar. 2/7 [Denmark] turns down America's offer. 1913 EDITH WHARTON *Custom of Country* II. xvi, The Ararat investigation had been.. quashed,..and Elmer Moffatt 'turned down'. 1915 J. CHURCHILL *Let.* 11 Aug. in M. Gilbert *Winston S. Churchill* (1972) III. Compan. II. 1128 Everybody seemed to have 'turned it down'. 1927 A. CONAN DOYLE *Case-Bk. Sherlock Holmes* x. 261 A quarter's rent..in advance and no arguing about terms. In these times a poor woman like me can't afford to turn down a chance like that. 1951 *Sport* 7–13 Jan. 17/1 Many of our suggestions are turned down. 1956 A. H. COMPTON *Atomic Quest* iii. 202, I had been approached with regard to college and university presidencies... I had.. turned them down. 1958 P. GIBBS *Curtains of Yesterday* xxvii. 214 Many nations..put forward plans for a gradual process of disarmament, and each plan was turned down by the other delegations. 1979 R. JAFFE *Class Reunion* I. vii. 70 A lot of attractive, eligible men kept asking Annabel for dates, and she didn't like having to turn them down.

e. *colloq.* To drink down, 'toss off' (? *obs.*); also in *Brewing*, to put (liquor) into a vat to ferment. (Cf. 25c.)

1760–72 H. BROOKE *Fool of Qual.* (1809) III. 150 Asking for a flask of champaign, [he] turned it down without taking it once from his head. 1826 *Art Brewing* (ed. 2) 109 Turned down 28 barrels of liquor, at 158 deg. 1844 W. H. MAXWELL *Sports & Adv. Scotl.* xxxvi. (1855) 289 We turned down a second tumbler.

f. *Sporting*, etc. To put (game, etc.) in a place to stock it.

1891 *Field* 26 Dec. 963/3 Foxes..are turned down in order that the supply may be kept up. 1892 *Ibid.* 19 Nov. 793/3, I would urge all farmers to turn down some Indian game cocks in their yards.

g. To lower (a lamp, gas) by turning the handle or stop-cock: cf. 1b; to lower the temperature of (an electrical appliance, heating system, etc., and *transf.*, that which it heats or cooks), orig. by turning a knob or switch; to reduce the volume of sound from (a radio, record-player, etc.), usu. by turning a knob or switch; to turn (a knob or switch) in order to reduce the temperature, volume of sound, etc. Cf. sense 81m below.

1868 MISS BRADDON *Dead Sea Fr.* xix, Love's torch.. flames anew before we turn it down for ever. 1892 *Harper's Mag.* LXXXIV. 283/2 She..turned the lamps down low. 1941 N. MARSH *Death & Dancing Footman* (1942) xv. 277 'To get back to the wireless.'..'I turned it down.'..'You turned it *down*... Not off. Down.'..'I turned it down, and five minutes later somebody turned it up.' 1950 B. PYM *Some Tame Gazelle* x. 111 The beef..would be roasted to a cinder by now, unless Emily had had the sense to turn down the oven. 1961 J. STROUD *Touch & Go* v. 48 'Excuse me if I just turn my liver down?'.. She hustled back into the kitchen. 1966 P. WILLMOTT *Adolescent Boys* ix. 170 He was alone, playing records... He said, 'Just a minute, I'll turn this down.' 1969 'D. RUTHERFORD' *Gilt-Edged Cockpit* vi. 93 Could you turn that transistor down a bit? 1970 'A. GILBERT' *Death wears Mask* ix. 138 Miss Buxton's client.. began to fidget under her drier and call out something about it being too hot. 'Turn it down, dear,' said Miss Buxton crisply. 1970 J. PORTER *Dover strikes Again* ii. 30 Old Mr Revel..switched on the television set. Miss Kettering.. turned the volume control right down. 1975 *Guardian* 21 Jan. 5/1 Turn down your heating a couple of degrees. 1975 'M. SINCLAIR' *Long Time Sleeping* xii. 143 He stopped to turn down the potatoes.

h. To let down with a winch or the like.

1929 [see sense 81s below].

** *intr.* **i.** To bend one's course downwards (with change of direction); to turn aside and go down: cf. 16.

c1595 CAPT. WYATT *R. Dudley's Voy. W. Ind.* (Hakl. Soc.) 29 Commaundinge him that they shoulde..turne downe unto the other carvell. 1833 T. HOOK *Parson's Dau.* I. i, Opposite the limekilns, as you turn down to the Duke's Head, near the turnpike. 1887 P. M'NEILL *Blawearie* 88 Long before the men in general began to turn down, he had every box in the pit-bottom filled.

j. To bend downwards: cf. 9d.

1885 MALET *Col. Enderby's Wife* III. ii, The corners of his mouth began to turn down in an ominous fashion.

k. Of business or economic activity or fortune; to decline, worsen.

1960 *Economist* 8 Oct. 261/1 Wall Street has shown an impressive record of moving ahead of business activity. In the recession of 1957–58..it turned down in July, one month before the index of industrial production; and turned up again in December, four months before production did. 1980 *Daily Tel.* 23 July 19 Unemployment is rising fast in all the major economies, partly because the economic cycle is turning down.

73. turn in. (See simple senses and IN *adv.*) * *trans.* **a.** To send, drive, put, or take in: cf. 25, 25 b, 25 c. Also, to hand in or over; *spec.* to betray or surrender to the police; to trade in; to give up, to stop (freq. with *it*). Also, to register, to produce (a result or performance, etc., of a specified kind). †In quot. *c* 1300 *refl.* = e below.

c **1300** *St. Brandan* 472 Ther cam out a grislich wiȝt.. Thurf suart and berning al his eȝen upe hem he caste, And turnde him in anon. **1607** TOPSELL *Four-f. Beasts* (1658) 373 He turned in amongst them some of his foresaid children. **1762** in W. Wing *Ann. Steeple Aston* (1875) 63 No horse or sheep to be turn'd in under the penalty of twenty shillings.. for each offence. **1830** R. DAWSON *Present State of Australia* v. 201, I asked him..the reason of his having been 'turned in', as they call it, to government. **1891** F. W. ROBINSON *Her Love & His Life* IV. x, You will turn in the cash by wholesale. **1912** *Technical World Mag.* June 403/1 When they discover any part of the track..which they cannot readily repair they turn in a signal that summons the roadmaster. **1919** in F. A. Pottle *Stretchers* (1930) 359 Tomorrow we will turn in what few articles of equipment we have not left at Merritt. **1926** J. BLACK *You can't Win* vii. 85 If either of you gets grabbed ..and thinks he can get a light jolt by turning me in, he's wrong. **1931** H. CRANE *Let.* 15 July (1965) 376 I'm very glad that you spoke about the check... I couldn't figure it out any other way than that you had waited until the following month before turning it in. **1938** F. A. POTTLE *Boswell & Girl from Botany Bay* 17 Bligh published a book..and Edwards turned in a report to the Admiralty. **1947** A. HUXLEY *Let.* 27 July (1969) 573 Jessica Tandy..is a first-rate actress and seems to be likely to turn in a performance which will make most of the more celebrated Hollywood stars look merely silly. **1948** C. DAY LEWIS *Otterbury Incident* iii. 23 'I'll kill myself, then.' 'Turn it in, Nick!' Ted punched him in a friendly way. **1952** L. DURRELL *Let.* 4 Nov. in *Spirit of Place* (1969) 114 I've turned in my resignation and we are clearing off in December. **1958** *Listener* 23 Oct. 632/2 This company, in common with many others, turned in a sizeable loss. *Ibid.* 13 Nov. 777/1 They didn't have to pay anything really [*sc.* for a new car];.. they've turned in their old one..and that only left a £50 balance. **1968** *Globe & Mail* (Toronto) 13 Jan. 39/5 Doug Acomb and Frank Hamill scored two goals each as their line turned in one of its best performances of the season. **1971** *Sci. Amer.* July 5 It turns in the kind of performance that delivers up to 25 miles per gallon. **1973** L. MEYNELL *Thirteen Trumpeters* iv. 66 'Turn it in, Hooky,' he advised himself. 'Go while the going's good.' **1977** M. SOKOLINSKY tr. *Merle's Virility Factor* xii. 236 If she'd gone to bed with you, she would have enjoyed it—and then she'd have turned you in. **1978** 'M. YORKE' *Point of Murder* iii. 35 His Ford Escort..was being turned in for an older car with a higher mileage on the clock. **1979** *SLR Camera* Mar. 53/3 At full aperture the 75mm f2.8 optic turned in a surprisingly good performance. **1982** *Sunday Tel.* 1 Aug. 5/3 It [*sc.* the year 1981–82] has seen Sotheby's turn in its first loss in over 20 years.

b. *Agric.* To bury or cover (weeds, stubble, manure) by turning the soil over them in digging or ploughing; to dig or plough into the ground. Also with the ground as obj. (Cf. 11 b, 25 c.)

1563 HYLL *Art Garden.* (1593) 3 The Gardens..should be..both well digged and turned in with dung. **1577** B. GOOGE *Heresbach's Husb.* 22 In the Spring the ground being mellowe..the weedes are then best turned in. **1864** *Jrnl. R. Agric. Soc.* XXV. II. 526 Not to turn in the wheat-stubble much before Christmas. *Ibid.* 528 The clover-lands that I have just turned in for roots. **1866** *Ibid.* Ser. II. II. I. 170 Loamy land is ploughed a second time before winter, and the manure turned in.

c. To bend or fold inwards: cf. 9. Also *Naut.*: see quot. 1867.

1572 in Feuillerat *Revels Q. Eliz.* (1908) 159 White Rownde plates turnde in with a crest. **1721** SWIFT *George-Nim-Dan-Dean's Answ.* 18 Thus a wise tailor is not pinching, But turns at every seam an inch in. **1776** WITHERING *Brit. Plants* (1796) IV. 201 Pileus pale yellow,.. edge turned in, 1 ½ to 2 inches over. **1867** SMYTH *Sailor's Word-bk.*, *Turn in a dead eye* or *heart, to*, to seize the end of a shroud or stay, &c., securely round it.

d. To cause to point or face inwards: cf. 7, 23 a.

1851 MAYHEW *Lond. Labour* (1861) III. 200/2, I gives 'em ..the bandy jig, that's dancing with my toes turned in. **1865** *Morn. Star* 27 Jan., To turn the tallies in. That is to put the tallies against the wall, so that they should not be seen. **1870** *Daily News* 19 July 6 Go-ahead, a good mare..turns in her toes a little.

** *intr.* **e.** To turn aside and go in (to a place, house, room, etc.): cf. 16, 24 c.

1535 COVERDALE *Judg.* iv. 18 Iael wente forth to mete Sissera, & sayde..: Turne in my lorde. **1658** GURNALL *Chr. in Arm.* verse 14. III. ix. 257 Even they sometimes turne in at the fairest signe. **1888** MISS TYTLER *Blackhall Ghosts* II xv. 23 Hearing your stable clock strike as I turned in at your gate.

f. (orig. *Naut.*) To go to bed. *colloq.*

1695 CONGREVE *Love for L.* III. xv, *Mrs. F.* I believe it's late. *B.*.. An you think so, you had best go to Bed... I mean to toss a Can..afore I turn in. **1837** T. HOOK *Jack Brag* xiii, Jack 'turned in', as the sailors say. **1891** N. GOULD *Double Event* 218 It's late..and quite time we turned in.

g. To change its course and go inwards; †of an eruption, to disappear (opp. to *break out*).

a **1776** R. JAMES *Dissert. Fevers* (1778) 29 Small-pox.. which turned in the seventh day of the eruption and went off in the most desirable manner. **1862** PYCROFT *Cricket Tutor* 35 Spinning bowling is always liable to turn in or break away contrary to all expectation.

h. To have an inward direction, point inwards: as, 'his toes turn in'. (Cf. 23 c, d.)

74. turn off. (See simple senses and OFF *adv.*) * *trans.* **a.** To strip off, peel off. Also *intr.* for *pass.* (Cf. 4 c.) ? *Obs.*

1737 BRACKEN *Farriery Impr.* (1756) I. 108 The Crystalline..becomes White, and turns off in..Laminae.. like unto the Coats of an Onion. *Ibid.* 109 We cut this..thin Membrane, and turn off..one or more of the Laminae of the Crystalline Humour.

b. To dismiss, send away; *spec.* to discharge from service or employment: cf. *turn away*, 69 c.

In quot. 1841, = *turn loose* (61).

1564 HARDING *Answ. Welles Chalenge* xi. 128 If any deuout person require to be partetaker with the priest,..he is not tourned of, but with all gentlenes admitted. **1601** SHAKS. *All's Well* v. iii. 220 You that haue turn'd off a first so noble wife. **1676** EARL ESSEX in *Essex Papers* (Camden) II. 73 It not being reasonable to turne off an old servant without some provision. **1768** GOLDSM. *Good-n. Man* I, Pay him his wages and turn him off. **1841** *Jrnl. R. Agric. Soc.* II. II. 152 His unshod cattle..were turned off to regale themselves upon the neighbouring waste. **1892** *Temple Bar Mag.* Mar. 321 A packer had been turned off for carelessness.

†**c.** To give over, resign, consign (*to*). *Obs.*

1667 *Decay Chr. Piety* (J.), We are not so wholly turned off to that reversion, as to have no supplies for the present. **1674** *Govt. Tongue* x. 185 The murmurer seems to be turn'd off to the company of those doleful Creatures..which were to inhabit the ruines of Babylon.

d. To hang (on a gallows): orig. ***to turn off the ladder*** (cf. 7, and LADDER *sb.* 1 b). Now *rare* or *Obs.*

[**1594** NASHE *Unfort. Trav.* Wks. (Grosart) V. 185 A fidler cannot turne his pin so soone, as he would turn a man of the ladder.] **1680** C. NESSE *Church Hist.* 143 His own mule..as it were, turns him off the ladder..he turns himself off when he had tyed his halter. **1715** J. CHAPPELOW *Right Way Rich* (1717) 64 The executioner has him upon the ladder..and turns him off in an instant. **1840** THACKERAY *Catherine* viii, I've seen a many men turned off. **1888** 'R. BOLDREWOOD' *Robbery under Arms* I. i. 8 You can have..anything you like ..you unfortunate young beggar, until you're turned off.

e. *humorously* (? *fig.* from prec.). To marry, join in marriage. (Cf. *to tie the knot.*)

1759 H. WALPOLE *Let. to G. Montagu* 16 May, Lord Weymouth is to be married on Tuesday, or, as he said himself, to be turned off. **1833** MARRYAT *P. Simple* xxxix, They will be turned off next Friday, and I only wish you were here to dance at the weddings. **1891** S. MOSTYN *Curatica* 157, I sent a reply..wishing her every happiness and consenting 'to turn her off'.

f. To deflect, divert (*lit.* and *fig.*): cf. 13, 14.

1716 ADDISON *Freeholder* No. 34 ¶6 To turn off the Thoughts of the People from busying themselves in Matters of State. **1719** DE FOE *Crusoe* (1840) II. vi. 151 He turned off the discourse to the rest. **1736** LEDIARD *Life Marlborough* III. 75 To turn off the Waters of the River..which made the Inundations. **1846** H. G. ROBINSON *Odes Horace* II. xvii, Had Faunus not turn'd off the stroke.

g. *spec.* To give a different turn to; to divert attention from, or alter the effect of (a remark, etc.).

1744 OZELL tr. *Brantome's Sp. Rhodomontades* 18 He turn'd it off with a Laugh, which was only Teeth out-wards. **1886** G. GISSING *Isabel Clarendon* viii, Ada seemed about to rise, but turned it off in an arrangement of her dress. **1892** *Blackw. Mag.* CLI. 88/2 That's all very fine;..you may turn it off in that way, but the fact remains.

h. To stop the flow of (water, gas, electric current, etc.) by turning a tap or the like (cf. 1 b), or by closing a sluice; to shut off; to turn out (a light). Also with the tap, etc. or *transf.* an electrical appliance, a recording or broadcast, etc. as obj. Also *fig.*, esp. (*colloq.*) to put (a person) off, to repel, to disillusion, to cause to lose interest.

1850 *Jrnl. R. Agric. Soc.* XI. I. 199 The waste steam..may be..turned on or off by a cock. **1886** *Law Times Rep.* LIII. 676/1 The gas is turned off at eleven o'clock. **1891** L. KEITH *Lost Illusion* II. xiv. 101 She did not turn the gas off at the meter. **1892** *Black & White* 23 Jan. 116/2 The electric lights ..were turned off. **1892** *Monthly Packet* Dec. 656 When the water is running away one must hurry up and turn off the tap. **1965** *Harper's Bazaar* Apr. 173 *Turned off*: Humperdinck turns me off. **1966** P. WILLMOTT *Adolescent Boys* iii. 51 You can always get a bit if you want it, with the girls with the big mouths... But that sort of thing turns you off after a while. **1967** B. PATTEN *Little Johnny's Confession* 33 Until death comes and turns me off. **1968** J. HUDSON *Case of Need* II. vi. 128, I was just turned off, I wasn't paying attention. **1969** J. GASKELL *Sweet Sweet Summer* 70 Or for the water and electric to stay on all the time, instead of being turned off after midnight. **1971** *Radio Times* 18 Nov. 80, I wonder how many viewers turned off the play, as we did. **1972** *Daily Tel.* 5 Feb. 14 [He] is kinky for short-back-and-sides and turned off by long-haired television performers. **1973** *Sci. Amer.* Dec. 14/2 Having become 'turned off' by economics, I was not sure what I wanted to be. **1975** *Nature* 20 Nov. 228/1 The male [cichlid fish] has bright colour patterns which he can turn on and off quickly. **1977** I. SHAW *Beggarman, Thief* I. viii. 101 School was a big part of his life and he couldn't just turn it off because it would be unimportant to grown-ups at this time. **1979** *Financial Rev.* 24 Oct. 10/1 Many voters were turned off by a strike in the last moment of the campaign. **1982** *Times* 21 Oct. 3, I had three frigates badly turned off in terms of capability. We were running out of steam.

i. To complete and get off one's hands; to produce (with skill or facility): = *turn out*, 76 j.

In quot. 1897, to accomplish (a distance) swiftly.

[**1684** *New Hampshire Prov. Papers* (1867) I. 521 The actions go on, and are turned off hand apace, twelve at a clap.] **1840** DICKENS *Barn. Rudge* xxxix, 'When I [the hangman] look at that hand and remember the helegant bits of work it has turned off.' [With play on sense d.] **1855** *Poultry Chron.* III. 160 The hens were..square short-legged birds, likely to turn off some good chickens. **1879** M. PATTISON *Milton* ix. 108 Turning off 300 pages of fluent Latin. **1897** *Outing* (U.S.) XXX. 242/2 We [cyclists] rode on through Harrisonburg and turned off the twenty-five miles to..Staunton.

j. To turn the soil so as to form (a furrow); in quot. 1858, to round off (a corner) in ploughing.

1842 *Jrnl. R. Agric. Soc.* III. I. 11 Admiring..its [the Scotch plough's] apparent facility in cleaving and turning off the furrow. **1858** *Ibid.* XIX. II. 277 One plough goes and turns off the corners.

** *intr.* (See also a.) **k.** To turn away or aside from the direct road; to deviate; also *transf.* of a road or path, to branch off: cf. 16, 16 e.

1687 NORRIS *Misc.*, *To his Muse* iv, Where with noise the waters creep Turn off with Care, for treacherous rocks are nigh. **1742** POPE *Dunc.* IV. 525 The vulgar herd turn off to roll with Hogs. **1776** *Pennsylv. Even. Post* 27 June 320/2 A road that turns off on the left hand. **1820** W. IRVING *Sketch Bk.* (1859) 11 He turned off, through a gate, into some ornamented grounds. **1892** *Leisure Hour* Jan. 188/1, I took a wrong turning, or kept straight on when I ought to have turned off.

l. To fall off in quality, 'go off', change for the worse; to wither and fall off; also, of food, etc.: to become sour or bad. Also with *compl. adj.*

1797 *Monthly Mag.* III. 489 The Rye-Grass and Clovers are expected..to turn off light. **1813** JANE AUSTEN *Lett.* (1884) II. 202 The day turned off..and we came home in some rain. **1846** *Jrnl. R. Agric. Soc.* VII. II. 380 My ash-leaf potatoes..looked healthy; they, however, turned off sickly in June... The Shaw[s]..were short in the haulm, and turned off by the middle of July. **1889** *Devonsh. Provinc.* in *Eng. Dial. Dict.* s.v., I think the chutney's turned off, sir.

75. turn on. a. *trans.* To induce a flow of (water, steam, gas, electric current) by turning a tap or stop-cock (cf. 1 b), or by opening a sluice; also with the tap, etc. or *transf.* an electrical appliance, a recording or broadcast, etc. as obj.; also *intr.* for *pass.* (quot. 1890); also *fig.* ***to turn the tap(s) on***, to start weeping; ***to turn it on***, to make a particular effort, esp. to be charming; ***to turn on the heat***: see HEAT *sb.* 12 b.

In quot. 1877 of piped music.

1833 HT. MARTINEAU *Loom & Lugger* I. i. 10 He turned on the gas in his back room to an unusual brightness. **1846** *Jrnl. R. Agric. Soc.* VII. II. 403 The steam being turned on. **1866** 'MARK TWAIN' *Screamers* (1871) xxix. 149 There was a good deal of honest snickering turned on this time. **1874** MICKLETHWAITE *Mod. Par. Churches* 186 Having certain jets [of gas] turned on at full. **1877** *Punch's Almanack for 1878* 14 Dec. 3/1 Now, recollect, Robert, at a quarter to nine turn on 'Voi che sapete' from Covent Garden. **1883** *Daily Tel.* 8 Feb. 3/2 When she had finished her song she fell a crying... She can turn the taps on at a moment's notice. **1890** MRS. HUNGERFORD *Born Coquette* xiii, A moon.. warranted to last for eight hours and to turn on at any moment. **1891** *Review of Rev.* 14 Nov. 523/2 The electric lamp that glows..when the current is turned on. **1892** *Blackw. Mag.* CLI. 79/2 A sluice might be turned on to flood a certain meadow. **1892** *Black & White* 21 May 674/2 A woman who turned on her smiles as we do the electric light. **1930** A. P. HERBERT *Water Gipsies* iii. 23 They had the wireless, which they turned on often for the 'jazz' bands. **1930** R. MACAULAY *Staying with Relations* iii. 43 They turned on a gramophone and danced. **1948** M. LASKI *Tory Heaven* i. 7 'Don't turn it on till the eleven o'clock news,' Janice called out. **1966** *Listener* 24 Nov. 779/1 Thomas could turn it on and brilliantly, when he wanted to. **1976** E. DUNPHY *Only a Game?* (1977) ii. 52 But Preston, who knows? They could turn it on under the floodlights. **1981** T. HEALD *Murder at Moose Jaw* xii. 144 She used to be some looker... And she could turn it on. But not any more.

b. To set (a person) *to do* something; to employ: cf. 34 b. *colloq.*

1893 *Chamb. Jrnl.* 8 July 419/2 Ainsworth had turned him on to assist him in 'doing' the theatres.

c. To excite, interest, fill with enthusiasm; to intoxicate with drugs, to introduce to drugs; to arouse sexually. Also const. *to* the object of interest, etc. *slang* (orig. *U.S.*).

1903 H. JAMES *Ambassadors* xxii. 291 One of his sisters.. had observed her somewhere with me. She had spoken to her brother—turned him on. **1953** W. BURROUGHS *Junkie* ii. 31 We kept the weed in Marian's apartment, turned her on for all she could use, and gave her a 50 per cent commission on sales. **1965** *Harper's Bazaar* Apr. 173 Bach really turns me on. **1966** *Current Slang* (Univ. S. Dakota) Winter 8 *Turn on*,..to excite sexually. **1966** *Guardian* 18 Apr. 13/4 Police in New York said that they had seized enough of the drug LSD to 'turn on' the entire population of New York if it was put in the water supply. **1967** J. HAYES *Deep End* 16 The excitement in her eyes deepened. 'You turn me on, man.' **1967** *Melody Maker* 29 July 10/6 There is a compulsive beat so maybe even the nation's half-wits may be turned on to Lloyd. **1972** J. BROWN *Chancer* iv. 53 It must be about this time he turns her on too—onto heroin. **1975** J. I. M. STEWART *Gaudy* ix. 173 It's a funny thing..how quite sure I was she wasn't going to turn me on. **1976** *News of World* 14 Mar. 5/3 Dinner jacket, wing collar, and bow tie may not sound the sort of gear to turn on a teeny bopper. **1976** *National Observer* (U.S.) 10 Apr. 14/5 My work is important. When I can turn on a student or write a good paper, I'm really happy, I'm elated. **1979** S. WILSON *Glad Hand* I. v. 30 Well..it's probably God's way of saying He takes a rather dim view of what turns you on.

d. *intr.* To become intoxicated; to take drugs. Also with *to*, to become interested in. *slang* (orig. *U.S.*).

1955 [see POD *sb.*[2] 1 c]. **1967** *Sunday Truth* (Brisbane) 2 Apr. 63/2 According to Dr. Timothy Leary, the avowed leader of the LSD set, you can turn-on without using drugs. **1969** *Gandalf's Garden* IV. 9/1 It was about this time I had turned on to Zen. **1970** *New Scientist* 12 Nov. 314/1 Young people who turn on by sniffing the vapour of airplane glue.. sometimes..drop dead. **1971** *Nature* 12 Feb. 462/2 Increasingly scientists are 'turning on' to the human environment. **1976** *Maclean's Mag.* 17 May 22/3 More and more teen-agers..are turning on with alcohol. **1979** R. JAFFE *Class Reunion* III. iii. 242 She walked in while I was turning on so I offered her some [marijuana].

76. turn out. (See simple senses and OUT *adv.*)
* *trans.* †**a.** ? To change from one's normal condition, to 'put out'; or ? to divert from one's course. *Obs. rare*$^{-1}$.

c **1320** *Cast. Love* 1211 In wonhope weore his disciples.. Ac þou weore studefast..Ne miȝte þe no þing tornen out.

b. To put or take out by a rotary movement (in quot. 1892, on a lathe); †to bore or gouge out.

13.. *Erasmus* in Horstm. *Altengl. Leg.* (1878) 202 Þe turmentours..turnyng oute his ien withe wymbles. **1892** *Photogr. Ann.* II. 286 Extending frame and reversing back mitred, keyed and glued up; the front turned out for circular disc.

c. To cause to go or come out; to drive out or forth, to expel; also (*trans.* of o), to fetch or summon out (quots. 1867, 1903). Cf. 25.

1546 J. HEYWOOD *Prov.* (1867) 82 He turnde hir out at doores. **1611** BEAUM. & FL. *Knt. Burning Pest.* III. v, Open the doore, and turne me out those mangy companions. **1672** VILLIERS (Dk. Buckhm.) *Rehearsal* II. iv. (Arb.) 61 If they heard us whisper, they'l turn us out. **1832** *Examiner* 418/1 If he ever turned out a tenant for voting against him. **1867** SMYTH *Sailor's Word-bk., Turn out the guard!* the order for the marines of the guard to fall in, on the quarter-deck, in order to receive a superior officer. **1894** BARING-GOULD *Queen of L.* I. viii. 86 'Turn him out!' was shouted from the further side of the hall. **1903** BOSW. SMITH in *19th Cent.* Mar. 436 One raven..managed more than once to 'turn out' the guard, who thought they were summoned by the sentinel.

d. To drive or put out (beasts) to pasture or to the open, or (pheasants, etc.) into a covert: cf. 25 b.

1560 DAUS tr. *Sleidane's Comm.* 360 b, The cattel which the townes men daily turned out into the pasture. **1679** J. GOODMAN *Penit. Pard.* II. iv. (1713) 229 He hath now, like Nebuchadnezzar, been turned out to grass. **1802** G. MONTAGU *Ornith. Dict.* (1831) 424 Lord Caernarvon.. turned out several [ring pheasants] at his seat at Highclere. **1853** *Jrnl. R. Agric. Soc.* XIV. I. 64 The colts were turned out on the open commons.

e. To dismiss or eject from office or employment.

1588 J. UDALL *Diotrephes* (Arb.) 16 Neither will the Churche euer be in quiet vntill you be all turned out. **1667** in *10th Rep. Hist. MSS. Comm.* App. v. 41 The..Captain hath..turned out some of his said Company that have refused to compound for lesse than the King's pay. **1708** *Constit. Watermen's Co.* xviii, If any..of the Rulers or Auditors shall happen to dye, or be turned out for Corruption. **1885** 'MRS. ALEXANDER' *At Bay* ii, I am very sorry he lost the election.. It was the radical mining people that turned him out. **1892** *Sat. Rev.* 17 Dec. 705/2 They will seize 'the first occasion' to turn the Government out.

f. To put (things) out of a house, room, or receptacle; to empty out by sloping or inverting the containing vessel.

1666 in *Verney Mem.* (1907) II. 255 My hous is not yet burnt, but all I have turn'd out. **1827** FARADAY *Chem. Manip.* xvi. (1842) 420 The small quantity of fluid remaining..is to be turned out, by inclining the tube. **1892** *Blackw. Mag.* CLI. 190/1, I shall turn out all your furniture.

g. (*transf.* from f.) To clear (a receptacle or room) of its contents; to empty (usually for the sake of examining or re-arranging the contents).

1809 MALKIN *Gil Blas* VII. xi. ¶6 The enraged marquis.. turning her whole house out at window. **1862** MRS. H. WOOD *Mrs. Hallib.* I. xxi, She turned out his pockets. **1887** E. F. BYRRNE *Heir without Heritage* III. iii. 66, I will go to my room..and turn my drawers out. **1894** HALL CAINE *Manxman* 211 She overhauled the linen; turned out every room twice a week.

h. To put or throw (land) out of cultivation.

1813 J. TAYLOR *Arator* 117 The phrase 'the land is killed and must be turned out', has become common over a great portion of the United States. **1856** OLMSTED *Slave States* 373 The greater part, even of these once rich low lands, that had been in cultivation, were now 'turned out', and covered ..with..broom-sedge and brushwood.

i. To put out, extinguish (a lamp, gas) by turning a tap or the like.

1884 *Punch* 27 Dec. 310/2 Then the gas was turned out. **1905** ELIN. GLYN *Viciss. Evangeline* 237 She..was turning out the light.

j. To finish making and get off one's hands; to dispose of as a finished product; to produce (usually implying rapidity, facility, or skill): = 74 i.

[**1757** W. THOMPSON *R.N. Advoc.* 47 Casks would..be turn'd out of their Hands, fit for the several Purposes.] **1847** L. HUNT *Men, Women, & B.* II. vi. 86 Books were books in those days, not batches, by the baker's dozen, turned out every morning. **1878** BESANT & RICE *Celia's Arb.* xv, No place..could..turn out more splendid ships' figure-heads. **1878** L. STEPHEN *Johnson* ii. 16 A man who turned out books as a bricklayer turns out houses or a tailor coats. **1913** E. H. D. SEWELL in *Daily Graphic* 26 Mar. 14/2 La Touche..is one of the best half-backs Sedbergh has ever turned out.

k. To equip, 'rig out', 'get up'.

1812 [implied in TURN-OUT *sb.* 7]. **1833** [see TURNED *ppl. a.* 8]. **1886** C. E. PASCOE *Lond. of To-day* xli. (ed. 3) 354 At either of these places the visitor may be sure of being turned out 'one of the best-dressed men in London'. **1892** *Pictorial World* 4 June 12/1 Coaches were fewer..but they were better 'turned out'.

l. To refer to, look up: = *turn up*, 81 h. *rare.*

1834 *Tracts for Times* No. 29. 8 To turn out for him the texts he had referred to. **1895** RASHDALL *Universities* II. 329 Turning out the word..in the indices of..chroniclers.

m. To alter the position of so as to bring it to the outside. (In quot. with figurative allusion.)

1605 SHAKS. *Lear* IV. ii. 9 He..told me I had turn'd the wrong side out.

n. To direct or cause to point outwards.

1697 J. LEWIS *Mem. Dk. Glocester* (1789) 12 Turning out his toes. **1813** PRICHARD *Phys. Hist. Man.* (1837) II. 138 The lips are thick without being turned out. **1892** *Illustr. Sport. & Dram. News* 5 Nov. 270/3 Do not reject a nag, though he may turn out his toes a little.

** *intr.* **o.** To turn aside and go out; to go away, depart, 'clear out'; to go forth, sally forth (usually with the notion of some compelling force, or of leaving a place of safety or comfort for one of danger or discomfort).

1473 WARKW. *Chron.* (Camden) 18 A prest that turnyd oute at his messe and the sacrament in his handys, whanne Kynge Edwarde came with his swerde into the chirche. **1649** BAXTER *Saints' R.* III. x. §4 If there be but one gap open ..how ready are we to..turn out at it? **1700** T. BROWN *Amusem. Ser. & Com.* 21 Turn out there you Country Put, says a Bully with a Sword two Yards long. **1763** C. JOHNSTON *Reverie* II. 9 To run into danger with delight, turning out to a man, at the first mention of the matter. **1811** *Regul. & Ord. Army* 15 The Line turns out without arms whenever any part of the Royal Family..comes along the Front of the Camp. **1889** JESSOPP *Coming of Friars* ii. 86 When the Friars came into a village,..the whole population would turn out to listen.

p. To get out of bed. (Cf. 73 f.) *colloq.*

1805 W. IRVING in *Life & Lett.* (1864) I. 154 The next morning on turning out, I had the first glimpse of old England. **1837** MARRYAT *Dog-fiend* vi, 'Turn out', said Dick. *c* **1847** in R. C. Winthrop *Rem. For. Trav.* (1894) 14 (*attributed to Dk. Wellington*) When a man begins to turn at all in bed, it is time for him to turn out.

q. To leave one's abode and betake oneself to some outside occupation. *spec.* (*Austral. slang*) to become a bush-ranger.

1793 [EARL DUNDONALD] *Descr. Estate of Culross* 42 He had two sons..ready to turn out in the sea line. **1862** *Western Post* 24 Sept. 2/2 He was immediately told by the robber they ought to turn out. **1888** 'R. BOLDREWOOD' *Robbery Under Arms* xxii, What lay we're going upon and whether we're all greed in our mind to turn out. **1891** L. KEITH *Halletts* x, She may have to turn out and be a governess. **1910** J. CAMERON *Spell of Bush* 131 [The bush] had been his home; for even before he had 'turned out', four walls had never held Michael Moran for long.

r. To abandon one's work; to go out on strike.

1806 [implied in TURN-OUT *sb.* 2]. **1825** *Examiner* 79/1 The journeymen spinners..have turned out for an advance of wages. **1871** W. PHILLIPS *Labor Question* 17 He becomes a railway conductor. If that doesn't suit him, he turns out, and becomes the agent of an insurance office. **1885** *Manch. Exam.* 23 June 5/1 It is expected that the whole of the operatives will turn out against the reduction.

s. To bend or be directed outwards. (*intr.* of n.)

1676 WISEMAN *Chirurg. Treat.* VII. x. 498 The Ancle-bone is apt to turn out on either side, by..Relaxation of the Tendons. **1807–26** [see TURNING *vbl. sb.* 12]. *Mod.* His toes turn out.

t. (*a*) To come about in the end or issue; to result, eventuate.

Now always with adv., advb. phr., or *as*; †also *absol.* (*obs. rare*: nearly = *turn up*, 81 w).

1735 WALPOLE *Let.* 19 Oct. in *10th Rep. Hist. MSS. Comm.* App. I. 264 As things have fortunately turn'd out. **1786** MRS. A. M. BENNETT *Juvenile Indiscr.* III. 85 Who knows what may turn out? **1830** B'NESS BUNSEN in Hare *Life* (1879) I. ix. 353 Our expedition up Vesuvius turned out very well. **1891** *Law Times* XC. 460/2 A speculator..whose transactions..had turned out disastrously to himself.

(*b*) with *compl.* To come to be, become ultimately (and so be found or known to be).

1744 M. BISHOP *Life & Adv.* 98 She has turned out a very undutiful Child. **1769** LADY MARY COKE *Jrnl.* 13 May (1892) III. 70 The day has turned out better then I expected it. **1875** JOWETT *Plato* (ed. 2) I. 140 Why then do the sons of good fathers often turn out ill? **1883** W. E. NORRIS *No New Thing* vii, What a pretty girl Nellie..has turned out!

(*c*) To be ultimately found or known, to prove *to be* (without implication of becoming).

Const. usually with inf.; also with simple compl. (cf. *b*).

1790 PALEY *Horæ Paul.* ii. §1 We have that time turning out, upon examination, to be in all the same. *a* **1859** DE QUINCEY *Autobiog. Sk.* vii. Wks. 1863 XIV. 205 *note*, These propositions, not..seeming to be true and turning out false, but..wearing an air of falsehood and turning out true. **1859** THACKERAY *Virgin.* xxi, That he should turn out to be the son of my old schoolfellow. **1893** SIR R. BALL *Story of Sun* 81 The result turns out to be considerably less. **1907** J. H. PATTERSON *Man-Eaters of Tsavo* App. I. 331 His photograph..unfortunately turned out a failure. *Mod.* He pretended to be destitute, but turns out to have had £200 in the bank.

77. turn out of. (See simple senses and OUT OF.)

a. *trans.* To drive, send, or put out of (a place), or dismiss from (a position or office), forcibly or peremptorily; to expel or eject from; †formerly more widely, to put or take out of in any way; *fig.* to bring out of, deliver from; to dissuade from.

c **1300** *Havelok* 154 He [= they]..preyden cristes hore, þat he wolde turnen him [Athelwold] Vt of þat yuel. *c* **1430** in *Hymns Virg.* 108 Ȝif þei talke of tales vn-trewe, þou torn hem out of þat entent. **1562** *Child-Marriages* 104 The said Roger turnid the said mare out of the Close. **1610** HOLLAND *Camden's Brit.* (1637) 518 His dead Corps was..turned out of his grave. **1690** E. GEE *Jesuit's Memorial* Introd. 2 He was ..turned out of his Fellowship. **1818** SCOTT *Hrt. Midl.* viii, The tenants..were not actually turned out of doors among the snow wreaths. **1890** F. M. CRAWFORD *Cigarette-maker's Rom.* v, He turned me out of the house.

†**b.** To do out of, deprive or strip of. *Obs.*

1545 ASCHAM *Toxoph.* I. (Arb.) 88 They..turned so many out of theyr Iackes. **1560** DAUS tr. *Sleidane's Comm.* 56 To torne you out of your weapons.

c. To put or empty out of (a vessel) by inverting it.

1791 *Gentl. Mag.* Jan. 25/1 Like a pudding turned out of a bason.

d. *intr.* To get out of, leave, quit. (Cf. 76 o, p.)

1860 DICKENS *Uncomm. Trav.* x, My last special feat was turning out of bed at two, after a hard day. **1892** *Chamb. Jrnl.* 1 Oct. 638/1 Five is an early hour to turn out of bed.

78. turn over. (See simple senses and OVER *adv.*)

* *trans.* **a.** To turn (something) from its position on to one side, or from one side to the other, or upside down; to invert, reverse; to knock over, overturn, upset; *refl.* (now *rare*) = j below. Cf. senses 7, 10, and OVER *adv.* 4 b, c.

c **1375** *Cursor M.* 8611 (Fairf.) Þe toþer womman childe ho hent..Ho turned hir ouer wiþ hit in arme. *a* **1635** SIBBES *Confer. Christ & Mary* (1656) 12 We must..turn over every stone,—use all kind of means, till we find him. **1710** ADDISON *Tatler* No. 243 ¶3 He turned himself over hastily in his Bed. **1897** *Boston* (Mass.) *Jrnl.* 4 Jan. 1/2 The 'Blue Goose' saloon, which is situated in the middle of the river, was turned over by the flood. *Mod.* Turn the patient over on his right side (or, on his face).

b. To reverse (a leaf, or the successive leaves, of a book) in order to read (or write) on further; to read or search through, peruse (a book) by doing this. Cf. 11 a.

to turn over a new leaf (fig.): see LEAF *sb.*[1] 7 b.

1551 ROBINSON tr. *More's Utop.* I. (1895) 84 If I, sely man, should..wylle them to turne ouer the leafe, and learne a newe lesson. **1635** in Foster *Crt. Min. E. India Co.* (1907) 16 The Company were surprized..when the Voyages were turned over. **1711** STEELE *Spect.* No. 75 ¶2 Turning over the Leaves, she reads alternately, and speaks. **1821** SCOTT *Kenilw.* xxii, The countess..turning over such rare volumes as would now make the fortune of twenty retail booksellers. **1885** 'MRS. ALEXANDER' *At Bay* ii, 'I must read it again,' said Glynn,..as he turned over the pages.

c. To reverse or shift (soil, hay, etc.) so as to expose the under parts, or different parts successively: cf. 11 b.

1737 BRACKEN *Farriery Impr.* (1756) I. 25 The same ground has not been turned over for a Hundred Years. **1842** *Jrnl. R. Agric. Soc.* III. I. 43 The trench-plough..turns over from 10 to 18 inches of clean soil. **1862** *Ibid.* XXIII. 51 Turn over and lighten up the hay.

d. To reverse and shift successively (papers or other articles lying flat in a heap) for the purpose of examining those that are beneath.

1798 S. & HT. LEE *Canterb. T., Yng. Lady's T.* II. 405 In turning over his papers.., Sir Edward laid his hand on the will. **1887** E. F. BYRRNE *Heir without Heritage* III. iii. 66 She ..began to turn over the linen and examine it.

e. *fig.* To agitate or revolve *in the mind*, go through and examine mentally, consider and reconsider: cf. 8.

1821 W. IRVING *Sketch Bk., Royal Poet*, After closing the volume, he turns its contents over in his mind. **1850** *Tait's Mag.* XVII. 118/1 The rumour induces us to turn over again this question. **1902** VIOLET JACOB *Sheep-Stealers* x, Turning over in his mind what possible pretext he could invent for an early visit.

f. To turn off the ladder in hanging: = 74 d.

1678 BUTLER *Hud.* III. II. 598 As Criminals condemn'd to suffer, Are blinded first, and then turn'd over. **1702** [see TURNING *vbl. sb.* 12]. **1882** J. TAYLOR *Sc. Covenanters* 37 Just before he was turned over, the..intrepid sufferer lifted the napkin from his face and exclaimed, [etc.].

†**g.** To drink off, swallow at one draught: cf. 72 e. *Obs.*

1796 *Hist. Ned Evans* I. 115 He turned over a full bumper to the toast.

h. To transfer, hand over, make over, deliver, commit (*to*); *spec.* to transfer (an apprentice) to another master, (a sailor) to another ship (cf. TURN-OVER *sb.* 2); in quot. 1632[2], to convert to a different use.

1552 HULOET, Turne ouer, *transuerto.* *a* **1586** SIDNEY *Arcadia* I. (1629) 63 He excusing himselfe, and turning ouer the fault to fortune. **1632** LITHGOW *Trav.* III. 91 [He] was turned ouer to the new Captaine for fiue yeares more. *Ibid.* VI. 273 That house..is turned ouer for a shelterage to sheepe. **1744** M. BISHOP *Life & Adv.* 41 Our Ship was condemned, and the Men turned over, some on board the *Breda*, and some to the *Ipswich*. **1795** *Lupton's Thous. Notable Th.* XIV. 254 The chamberlain of London attends.. to enrol and turn over apprentices. **1890** MRS. H. WOOD *House of Halliwell* i, She would..turn over to her all the sewing. **1925** W. L. CROSS *Life Sterne* I. 175 Robert Dodsley had just turned over the management of his business to his brother. **1930** *Publishers' Weekly* 5 Apr. 1896 By retiring and turning the business over to his son. *Ibid.* 1917 Columbia University has just come into possession of the famous collection of works on economics which Professor E. R. A. Seligman..has turned over..for a price of one-half, or less. **1930** *Harper's Mag.* July 196 My German instinct to care for my own child kept me from turning her over to someone else.

i. *Comm.* To pass or hand over in the way of exchange; to employ in business, to invest and realize; to sell or dispose of goods to the amount of (a specified sum). Cf. 15 b. Also in extended sense.

1611 L. BARRY *Ram-Alley* I. B iv b, Some hundred bookes ..I haue Turnd ouer..But that is nothing for a studient. Or a Stationer: they turne them ouer too. **1863** FAWCETT *Pol. Econ.* II. (1876) 260 Their capital is not unfrequently turned over ten times in the course of the year. **1890** *Spectator* 6 Sept., His land can produce corn but once a year, and he cannot 'turn over' his capital so invested. **1893** *Gd. Words* Mar. 187/1 Thousands of dollars were being turned over hourly. **1971** *Nature* 24 Dec. 483/2 *Sminthopsis crassicaudata* turns over water at about three times the rate of *Dasycercus cristicauda*. **1976** *Ibid.* 22 July 280/1 This indicates that the bulk of dentinal protein is not turned over.

j. To search; to ransack (usu. in order to commit robbery). *Criminals' slang.*

1859 HOTTEN *Dict Slang*, *Turned over*, to be stopped and searched by the police. **1925** [see DRUM *v.* 9 b]. **1960** *Observer* 25 Dec. 7/6 The drummers, those squalid day-time operators who turn over empty semi-detached villas while the housewives are out shopping. **1971** [see GOON 2]. **1981** L. MEYNELL *Hooky goes to Blazes* vi. 83 What about that girl's bedroom that got turned over?

k. To distress, upset, affect with nausea. Cf. sense 81 k. *colloq.*

1865 DICKENS in *All Year Round* 7 Dec. 47/2 The discovery turned me over. **1962** N. STREATFEILD *Apple Bough* ix. 126 Proper turned me over, you did. I don't want to lose my old man yet. **1972** *New Society* 11 May 302/1 Escalope I had, though what they do to those calves turns me over.

l. To cause (an engine, propeller, etc.) to revolve.

1913 *Autocar Handbk.* (ed. 5) vii. 143 The motor should be able to turn the engine over at not less than 150 r.p.m. **1927** C. A. LINDBERGH *We* v. 75 Learning how to turn the propellers over in starting the engine. **1976** P. ALEXANDER *Death of Thin-Skinned Animal* xx. 209 He..pulled the wires away from the ignition switch and tied them together. This turned the [car] engine over but she wouldn't start without the choke. She was..cold.

m. *Printing.* To carry over (a letter, part of a word, etc.) to the next line.

1925 *Hart's Rules for Compositors & Readers* (ed. 27) 64 In most divisions it is the consonantal letter that should be turned over. **1981** I. A. GORDON in *N.Z. Listener* 14–20 Feb., The fragmented word is 'turned over' into the following line.

n. *U.S. Sport.* To lose possession of (the ball) to the opposing team.

1971 *Tuscaloosa* (Ala.) *News* 29 Jan. 8/5 We knew we could force Kentucky to turn the ball over and we did. **1979** *Honolulu Advertiser* 8 Jan. C-4/1 We turned over the ball and we just didn't score.

*** intr.* **o.** To turn on to one side, or from one side to the other, or upside down; to reverse itself; to be upset, fall over, capsize; to roll about. Cf. a, and sense 6.

1660 [implied in TURN-OVER *sb.* 1]. **1845** J. COULTER *Adv. in Pacific* vii. 87 [The whale] died, and turned over in a few minutes. **1892** *Illustr. Sport & Dram. News* 17 Dec. 486/1 They cannot turn over if pushed, but must right themselves immediately. **1895** MRS. B. M. CROKER *Village T.* (1896) 88, I had watched the big rohu turning lazily over in the river. **1899** *Tit-Bits* 28 Oct. 97/3 Turn over and go to sleep.

p. To be transferred, to shift. (Cf. h.) *rare.*

1851 *Jrnl. R. Agric. Soc.* XII. I. 287 The embankment has been made on that portion which is not liable to 'turn over' [*i.e.* be shifted by the tide].

q. Of a body or part of a body or any collective whole: to replace or renew its constituent parts, to renew itself or be replaced.

1956 *Planning* XXII. 155 The entire research staff has turned over on an average about every three years as the various studies have been completed. **1971** J. Z. YOUNG *Introd. Study Man* xii. 151 The body..has some parts that turn over very little..while others turn over so efficiently that we do not normally think of them as suffering wear. **1973** *Times* 17 Apr. 4/7 Nearly three-quarters of the men.. have stayed. The other 27 per cent have 'turned over' several times.

r. Of an engine, etc.: to revolve.

1978 T. GIFFORD *Glendower Legacy* (1979) 281 He.. heard the engine turning over;..the boat quivered.

79. turn round. (See simple senses and ROUND *adv.*)

** intr.* **a.** To move round on an axis or centre; to revolve, rotate. Also *fig.* of the brain or head, to be affected with giddiness. Cf. 2, 2 b.

*c*1400 *Destr. Troy* 453 Hir Ene as a trendull turned full rounde, First on hir fader,..And sethyn on þat semely. *c*1500 [see ROUND *adv.* 6]. **1596** SHAKS. *Tam. Shr.* v. ii. 20 He that is giddie thinks the world turns round. **1676** MARVELL *Mr. Smirke* 11 As it fares with those whose Brain turnes round. **1687** A. LOVELL tr. *Thevenot's Trav.* I. 54 Making a leap,..they fall a turning round with their naked feet. **1710** SWIFT *Jrnl. to Stella* 31 Oct., I had a fit of giddiness: the room turned round for about a minute. **1824** SCOTT *St. Ronan's* xxxvi, The strangeness of the news..made Mowbray's head turn round.

b. To turn so as to face in the opposite direction; to reverse one's position or course; to face about; to turn from one side to the other. Cf. 6, 22 c.

Also *fig.* in such phrases as *to give one time to turn round*, i.e. to get into the proper position or condition for doing something required.

1591 [see TURNING *vbl. sb.* 12]. **1787** 'G. GAMBADO' *Acad. Horsemen* (1809) 38 If his horse has stopt and turned round five thousand times with him. **1802** F. BURDETT *Let.* 18 Aug. in H. Maxwell *Creevey Papers* (1903) I. i. 3, I have scarcely time to turn round, but will not defer sending a line in answer to your very kind letter. **1830** *Debates in Congress* 29 Mar. App. 105 Payment is..suffered to lie occasionally until the bank can turn round. **1856** SIR B. BRODIE *Psychol. Inq.* I. iv. 137 We see persons turn round in their sleep. **1886** *Lesterre Durant* vi, She turned round to where her brother stood. **1911** A. BENNETT *Hilda Lessways* (ed. 2) III. ii. 226 He simply walked out of the office!.. Didn't give me time to turn round. **1969** *Listener* 14 Aug. 217/2 Before my parents could turn round and ask what I was going to do for a living, I went back and announced I'd already got a job as a ship's musician.

c. *fig.* To change to the opposite opinion, state of mind, etc.; *esp.* to change from a friendly to a hostile attitude; with *on* or *upon*, to assail suddenly, esp. in words (cf. 33).

1822 *Examiner* 427/1 The Alderman being absent, our schemer turns round, and personates the Alderman. **1846** DICKENS *Dombey & Son* (1848) v. 38 You're a good little thing..; and yet you turn round on me, because there's nobody else. **1863** KINGSLEY *Water Bab.* v, Now he turned round and abused it. **1891** *Law Times* XCI. 405/2 [They] cannot turn round on the executors and blame them.

*** trans.* **d.** To cause to revolve or rotate (cf. 1); also, to cause to face in all directions successively.

*c*1633 MILTON *Arcades* 66 Those that hold the vital shears, And turn the Adamantine spindle round. **1731** POPE *Ep. Burlington* 135 In Books, not Authors, curious is my Lord; To all their dated Backs he turns you round. **1823** H. J. BROOKE *Introd. Crystallogr.* 28 If we now turn round the circle with its attached crystal. **1857** TENNYSON *Geraint & Enid* 740 The maiden..robed herself, Helped by the mother's careful hand and eye,..Who, after, turn'd her daughter round, and said, She never yet had seen her half so fair.

e. To put into the opposite position or direction, to reverse (*lit.* and *fig.*): cf. 10, 10 b.

1858 J. MARTINEAU *Stud. Chr.* 40 The Prophets, whom we shall very imperfectly understand, if we suppose them mere historians, for whom God had turned round time the other way. **1887** *Times* (weekly ed.) 11 Nov. 4/3 He has.. turned it right round and made it say exactly the opposite of what it does say.

f. To cause to face in a different direction; *refl.* = b above (*arch.*). Also *fig.* to induce (a person) to take an opposite course or view (quot. 1860).

1628 FELTHAM *Resolves* II. [I.] xxxii. 101 That Philosopher ..turn'd him round, and vanisht. *a*1765 [see ROUND *adv.* 8]. **1782** COWPER *Gilpin* 51 Turning round his head, he saw Three customers come in. **1850** TENNYSON *In Mem.* xliv. 14 If such a dreamy touch should fall, O turn thee round, resolve the doubt. **1860** GEO. ELIOT *Mill on Fl.* III. viii, The utter impossibility of ever turning Mr. Tulliver round.., or getting him to hear reason.

g. In *pa. pple.* Confused, disorientated. *U.S. dial.*

1877 R. I. DODGE *Plains Great West* 46 To me, Detroit is always in Canada, and New Orleans always on the right bank of the Mississippi, because I happened to be 'turned round' when I first arrived in those cities.

h. To prepare (a ship, aircraft, etc.) for its return journey. Cf. TURN-ROUND 1.

1942 *R.A.F. Jrnl.* 16 May 13 Cleanliness also shortens the time it takes to turn a ship round. **1972** *Nature* 21 Apr. 363/1 Is there..a chance that supersonic aircraft can be turned round at international airports with the speed that will be necessary if operators are to make..the fullest use of their capital investment?

i. = sense 29 c above.

1966 *New Statesman* 6 May 657/2 SOE's intrigues included..'turning round' captured agents. **1974** 'J. LE CARRÉ' *Tinker, Tailor* xxi. 180 All right. The Russians have turned Tarr round... What sort of plant can he be when we don't believe a word he says?

80. turn to. a. *intr.* To apply oneself to some task or occupation; to set to work. Cf. 28 c.

1813 SOUTHEY *March to Moscow* vi, But the Russians stoutly they turned-to Upon the road to Moscow. **1840** R. H. DANA *Bef. Mast* iii, The watch..'turning to' at daybreak and washing down, scrubbing, and swabbing the decks. **1893** *Chamb. Jrnl.* 8 July 421/1 She..would turn to again and earn a living.

b. *trans.* To set (a person) to work. Cf. 34 b.

1840 R. H. DANA *Bef. Mast* xii. 27 We were turned-to upon the rigging.

81. turn up. (See simple senses and UP *adv.*)

** trans.* **a.** To direct or bend upwards (also *fig.*); in *pa. pple.* often denoting the form of a projecting part or border of something; in quot. 1707, to have (such a part) bent or directed upwards. Cf. 9.

In *Bookbinding*, to flatten the back of (a book) with trindles, in preparation for cutting the front edge: see TRINDLE *sb.* 4.

*c*1510 MORE *Picus* B v, He exhorted them to turne vp theyr myndes to loue God. *a*1548 HALL *Chron., Hen. VIII* 6 b, Bootes with pykes turned vp. **1607** SHARPHAM *Fleire* v. (1610) H ij, A Puritane [damn'd] for saying Grace without turning vp the white of his eyes. **1623** GOUGE *Serm. Extent God's Provid.* §15 A red cap, over a white linnen one turned up about the brimmes. **1707** MORTIMER *Husb.* (1721) I. 259 A sort of Duck that turns up the Bill more than the common kind. **1819** SCOTT *Leg. Montrose* Introd., The right side of his head a little turned up, the better to catch..the clergyman's voice. **1877** [see TURNING *vbl. sb.* 12]. **1888** MISS TYTLER *Blackhall Ghosts* II. xv. 12 He even..turned up the collar of his morning coat.

b. esp. in phr. *to turn up one's nose* (as an expression of contempt): usually *fig.* (*turn up one's nose at* = despise, scorn).

1779 MME. D'ARBLAY *Diary* 20 Oct., Mr. Thrale.. turned up his nose with an expression of contempt. **1836** MARRYAT *Midsh. Easy* xxiv, Miss Julia, who turned up her nose at a midshipman.

c. To turn upside down, invert (now esp. in order to examine what is beneath); †to overthrow, demolish; *fig.* to upset, throw into disorder (*obs.*). Cf. 10.

*a*1548 HALL *Chron., Hen. VI* 137 b, No doubt, but kyng Charles, and the whole publique wealthe of Fraunce, had been turned vp, and cleane ouerthrowen. **1581** A. HALL *Iliad* IV. 71 You should haue seene them [the walls of Thebes] torne, & turned vp from the rout. **1592** SHAKS. *Rom. & Jul.* I. v. 29 Turne the Tables vp. **1664** EVELYN *Kal. Hort.* (1729) 191 Turn up your Bee-hives, and sprinkle them. **1843** MIALL in *Nonconf.* III. 209 Men who turn up words that they may see the ideas that lie under them. **1848** THACKERAY *Van. Fair* vii, The chairs are turned up heads and tails along the walls.

d. To fold over (a garment or part of one) so as to shorten it; to shorten (a garment or part of one) by increasing the width of the hem or by making a hem; to increase the width of (a hem); also *transf.* with the person as obj.

1611 COTGR., *Rebrasser*, to turne, fould, or tucke vp, the sleeues, &c. **1662** J. DAVIES tr. *Olearius' Voy. Ambass.* 375 They turn up their sleeves above the Elbow. **1836** [see TURNED 8]. **1896** HARE *Story my Life* I. ii. 136 If any of the children behaved ill during the service, they were turned up and soundly whipped then and there. **1918** E. & M. WALLBANK *Dress-Cutting & Making* xiv. 89 To turn up the skirt to the required length, a skirt gauge..may be used. *Ibid.* xxi. 126 Turn up the hem, fell down the pleats. **1958** M. JOHNSON *Sewing the Easy Way* (1960) 127 Turn up the hem, matching seam upon seam. **1976** J. TATE tr. *Bodelsen's Operation Cobra* xi. 54 Margrethe had borrowed a skirt from her mother and was busy turning it up. **1979** R. RENDELL *Make Death love Me* iii. 29 Pam turned up the hem of an evening skirt.

e. In *pa. pple.* of a garment: Having the border turned or folded over and covered *with* some ornamental material. †In quot. 1573 app. *transf.* to decorate, adorn.

1537 *Test. Ebor.* (Surtees) VI. 72 My mariage gowne of russet damaske, with the sleves turne[d] upe with russet velvet. **1573** TUSSER *Husb.* (1878) 100 [Plants] to turn vp their house, and to furnish their pot. **1714** *Lond. Gaz.* No. 5270/7 A..Cap of Crimson Velvet, turn'd up with Ermine. **1850** *Tait's Mag.* XVII. 749/1 A green blouse up with red.

f. To turn (soil, etc.) so as to bring up the under parts to the surface, as by digging or ploughing, or with the snout or paws, as an animal (cf. 11 b); to dig or plough up; also, to bring to the surface (something buried) by digging, etc.

1563 *Homilies* II. *Rogation Week* IV. (1640) 235 They doe wickedly, which doe turne up the ancient terris of the fields. **1577** B. GOOGE *Heresbach's Husb.* 44 Take heede of Swyne, that spoyle and turne vp the grounde ilfauoredly. *a*1613 J. DENNYS *Secr. Angling* II. xlvii, Yealow bobs turnd vp before the Plough. **1667** MILTON *P.L.* VII. 213 The vast..Abyss Outrageous as a Sea,..Up from the bottom turn'd by furious windes. **1774** GOLDSM. *Nat. Hist.* (1776) VI. 226 The neck is furnished with very strong muscles, which enable it the readier to turn up the sand. **1833** JAS. DAVIDSON *Brit. & Rom. Rem. Axminster* 27 A man digging a hole for a gate-post,..turned up a golden ornament. **1843** *Jrnl. R. Agric. Soc.* IV. II. 116 Turn up the earth with a trowel.

g. To turn (a card) face upwards; *esp.* to do this in dealing to determine the trump suit (cf. TURN-UP *sb.* 3).

1611 SHAKS. *Cymb.* II. iii. 2 The most coldest that euer turn'd vp Ace. **1709** *Brit. Apollo* II. No. 18. 2/2 D...turns up the last Card for Trump. **1891** *Field* 28 Nov. 842/3 The card turned up by the second hand is the king.

h. To find in a book, a set of papers, etc. some passage or document; to look up, refer to. (With the book, etc., or the passage, as obj.) Cf. 11 a, 78 b.

'In the Durham Cathedral Choir *to turn up* means to look out and place ready the music for the organist and singers' (Canon J.T. Fowler).

1710 STEELE *Tatler* No. 179 ¶11 When I turn up some Masterly Writer to my Imagination. **1818** SCOTT *Hrt. Midl.* xxxi, She then turned up the ritual. **1892** *Illustr. Sport. & Dram. News* 7 May 267/2, I have not time now to turn up my old notes on the subject. *Mod.* Turn up the article in the Encyclopædia.

i. To lay (a person or animal) on the back; to turn belly upwards; hence, to kill.

In quot. 1850 causal of y below.

1740 tr. *De Mouhy's Fort. Country-Maid* (1741) I. 62 Go your ways, or I'll turn you up as I would a Hare. **1832** COL. HAWKER *Diary* (1893) II. 46, I turned up two [geese] with the first barrel, and the other with the second. **1844** STEPHENS *Bk. Farm* II. 95 You will have to turn him up, as it is termed; that is, the sheep is set upon his rump with his back down and his hind-feet pointing upwards and outwards. **1850** SCORESBY *Cheever's Whalem. Adv.* xiv. (1859) 212 After Captain Hosmer had succeeded in 'turning up' his whale.

j. *to turn up one's heels* (or *toes*), to die; *to turn up* (a person's) *heels*, to lay low, kill: see HEEL *sb.*[1] 24, TOE *sb.* 5 j.

k. To turn the stomach of (see 12); to nauseate; also *fig.*

1892 *Chamb. Jrnl.* 11 June 375/2 Men who have never known what sea-sickness is..get thoroughly 'turned up' with the awful motion and vibration. **1932** S. GIBBONS *Cold Comfort Farm* xii. 178 Turns you up, don't it, seein' terday's dinner come in 'anging round someone's neck? **1968** M. WOODHOUSE *Rock Baby* i. 11 You don't like the rules. Well, well, Giles. Do you know, sometimes you science boys turn me up.

†**l.** To roll up, twist up in a wrapper. *Obs. rare.*

1701 *Lond. Gaz.* No. 3741/4 A painted Fan..turned up in a white Paper.

m. To turn the handle or tap of (a lamp or gas-jet) so as to raise the wick, or increase the flow of gas, and thus make it burn more brightly; to raise the temperature of (an electrical appliance, heating system, etc., and *transf.*, that which it heats or cooks), orig. by turning a knob or switch; to increase the volume of sound from (a radio, record-player, etc.), usu. by turning a knob or switch; to turn (a knob or switch) in order to increase the temperature, volume of sound, etc. Cf. sense 72 g above.

1889 *Repent. P. Wentworth* II. v. 105 He..turned up his reading lamp. **1893** KIPLING *Many Invent.* 102 Turn up the gas a little, I want to go on reading. **1941** [see sense 72 g above]. **1962** A. NISBETT *Technique Sound Studio* 259 The volume can be turned up louder. **1967** 'E. LINDALL' *Time too Soon* v. 57 Put on your hi-fi... Just turn it up a bit more. **1971** M. LEE *Dying for Fun* ix. 53 The producer of the radio magazine programme turned up his loudspeaker. **1976** W. CORLETT *Dark Side of Moon* II. 85 It *is* colder... I must turn up the central heating. **1978** *Sci. Amer.* Apr. 67/1 The microscope [operating] is then turned up to high magnification (25 or 40 diameters).

†**n.** ? To excite, rouse. *Obs. rare.*

1579 GOSSON *Sch. Abuse* (Arb.) 63, I shall please the wise, though the malicious turne vpp their gall.

o. To set free, turn loose; to discharge or release (a prisoner). Cf. 25. Now only *slang*.

1653 H. MORE *Antid. Ath.* III. ii. §2 The Horse..for his unserviceableness..was fain to be turned up loose in the pasture. **1715** *Lond. Gaz.* No. 5368/4 Which said..Gelding was turned up by the said Rogues. **1812** J. H. VAUX *Flash Dict.* s.v., A person acquitted by a jury, or discharged by a magistrate..is said to be turned up. **1904** MAJ. A. GRIFFITHS *50 Y. Public Service* xxiii. 354 They are not brothers, only brother convicts, who 'did time' together.., were 'turned up' together.

p. To give up, renounce, abandon, cast off, discard, 'throw up'. Now only *slang*. Also *imp.* with *it*, stop it!

1621 BURTON *Anat. Mel.* III. iv. II. i. (1651) 685 He..married wives, and turned them up as he thought fit. **1643** TRAPP *Comm. Gen.* xii. 1 Many follow God..as a dog doth his master, till he meet with carrion; and then turn him up. **1885** *Punch* 13 June, So turn up the job,..And leave it to me! **1893** *Illustr. Sport. & Dram. News* 10 June 532/3 After one disastrous round..I intimated to the champion my intention to turn it up. **1945** J. B. PRIESTLEY *Three Men in New Suits* i. 6 Turn it up, will you... You're arguing with yourself. **1948** M. ALLINGHAM *More Work for Undertaker* (1949) x. 127 Turn it up... Keep it for your reminiscences. **1961** J. B. PRIESTLEY *Saturn over Water* xvii. 240 'Are you sure you can trust her?' 'Yes, Joe. So turn it up.'

q. *Naut.* To cause to appear above the horizon; to come in sight of: = RAISE *v.*[1] 24 a. Also *transf.*

1698 FRYER *Acc. E. India & P.* 82, I was sent to Surat. In a week's time we turned it up. **1859** SALA *Tw. round Clock* (1861) 25 Keep struggling; and..you will eventually turn up Printing House Square.

r. *Naut.* To summon (the crew) on deck.

1782 in *Ann. Reg. 1783* (1785) 122/2 The main-sail aback; all hands turned up; the main-clue garnets manned. **1805** in Nicolas *Nelson's Disp.* (1846) VII. 164 *note*, Ceased firing and turned the hands up to clear the wreck. **1835** MARRYAT *Pirate* ix, 'Turn the hands up',..said the captain.

s. To draw up with a winch or the like.

1911 D. H. LAWRENCE *Prussian Officer* (1914) 282 The winding-engine rapped out its little spasms. The miners were being turned up. **1929** —— *Pansies* 82 My father was a working man And a collier was he, At six in the morning they turned him down And they turned him up for tea.

** *intr.* **t.** To bend or point upwards; to have an upward direction: cf. 9 d. Also *fig.*

1608 TOPSELL *Serpents* (1658) 675 The tail is very long, at the end and turning up like a Vipers tail. **1710** STEELE *Tatler* No. 245 ⁋2 Nose very broad at bottom, and turning up at the end. **1827** FARADAY *Chem. Manip.* xvi. (1842) 417 The apparatus delivering gas should always be made to turn up at the end. **1974** *Nature* 22 Feb. 514/2 Lillie presented preliminary evidence that the zodiacal light spectrum turns up below 2,500 Å. **1977** *Evening Post* (Nottingham) 27 Jan. 4/5 The rate of inflation has turned up again and we must expect to see some further deterioration in the next few months.

u. To turn aside and go up; to make one's way up: cf. 16.

c **1350** *Will. Palerne* 2906 Sche went..to þe castel, & turned vp to þe heiȝest tour. *c* **1450** in Aungier *Syon* (1840) 334 Alle seruyse ended..they schal echone turne up in to ther stalles, and say..knelynge fyftene Aues. **1760–72** H. BROOKE *Fool of Qual.* (1809) III. 60, I turned up to a sorry kind of inn.

v. *Naut.* To beat up to windward; to tack. Also with *it*. Cf. 16 b.

1569 [see 16 b]. *a* **1647** PETT in *Archæologia* (1796) XII. 227 We weighed and turned up with the wind at South-west as high as Lambeth. **1682** W. HEDGES *Diary* (Hakl. Soc.) I. 31 We..bore down about 2 or 3 miles to 2 sloops which could not turn it up to us. **1701** CUNNINGHAM in *Phil. Trans.* XXIII. 1201 We were forced to turn it up against Wind and Current all the way. **1711** LITTLETON *Let.* 13 Aug. in *Lond. Gaz.* No. 4906/3 We turn'd up to Windward as far as Donna Maria Bay. **1745** P. THOMAS *Jrnl. Anson's Voy.* 178 We had run three or four Leagues too far to Lee-ward, which we now had to turn up.

w. (often *intr.* for *refl.* or *pass.* of various *trans.* senses.) To make its (or one's) appearance; to present itself (or oneself) casually or unexpectedly; to occur, appear, be discovered or encountered (as if exposed by turning something over, by turning face upwards, by turning the leaves of a book, etc.); to arrive or present oneself (with no connotation of unexpectedness or casualness); freq. *neg.*, to fail to arrive when expected (*colloq.*).

1704 N. N. tr. *Boccalini's Advts. fr. Parnass.* I. 255 Hoping a Card might turn up to better their Fortunes. **1715** M. DAVIES *Athen. Brit.* I. 202 He open'd the New Testament at a venture, and pray'd that such a Place might turn up as might comfort him in his last moments. **1755** *Monitor* No. 10. I. 82 They must watch..the..occasions, which in the whirl of time will turn up. **1809** MALKIN *Gil Blas* x. vi. ⁋2 It seems incredible that Raphael should turn up in such a guise! **1824** WHEWELL in *Life* (1881) 97 Leaving directions to have the thing sent after me if it should turn up. **1827** *Examiner* 731/2 When..a flat cries 'head'.., a 'tail' is sure to turn up. **1849** DICKENS *Dav. Copp.* xi, 'And then', said Mr. Micawber,..'I shall, please Heaven, begin to be beforehand with the world,..if—in short, if anything turns up'. **1889** W. E. NORRIS *Miss Shafto* 170 You didn't expect me to turn up here, did you? **1903** SOMERVILLE & 'ROSS' *All on Irish Shore* i. 18 And if you'll believe me, the two chaps there had never turned up at all. **1939** G. B. SHAW *Geneva* III. 52 The judge himself hasnt turned up. **1977** *Arab Times* 14 Dec. 2/5 Let women everywhere from this day on encourage men to have the courage not to turn up for war. **1979** J. COOPER *Class* iv. 84 At prep schools they insist you turn up [at sports days] and then ignore you. **1981** R. HAYMAN *K* iv. 38 They..turned up in large numbers to the general meetings.

x. with *compl.* To appear or present itself in a specified character; to be found to be: nearly = *turn out*, 76 t (*b*), (*c*).

to turn up rough, to become angry or quarrelsome (cf. *cut up rough*, CUT *v.* 60 l). *to turn up trumps*, to turn out favourably (see TRUMP *sb.*[2] 2).

1756 *Monitor* No. 39. I. 374 A great deal of waste land and timber.., which by care and cultivation, must in time turn up a great thing. **1831** *Examiner* 534/1 A lottery ticket which has turned up a prize. **1872** *Judy* 29 May 59/2 (Farmer) Have the ornaments [= handcuffs] handy, in case he should turn up rough.

y. Of soil (*intr.* for *pass.* of f, with qualifying phr. or compl.).

1855 *Jrnl. R. Agric. Soc.* XVI. I. 176 Such soils turn up as a fine mould. *Ibid.* 197 The soil..will turn up raw and stubborn. **1858** *Ibid.* XIX. I. 186 It [a soil] is all exceedingly sticky when wet, and, if ploughed in that state, turns up in large masses, which as they dry become hard as rock.

z. 'To turn belly upward: said of a dying whale' (*Cent. Dict.* 1891). Cf. quots. 1850 in i, and 1845 in 78 o (*turn over*).

aa. *slang.* To throw up or abandon one's work. (Cf. o, p.)

1904 MAJ. A. GRIFFITHS *50 Y. Public Service* xiii. 173 Smith..'turned up' one day, in other words refused to labour on the works.

*** *trans.*, and *intr.* (for *refl.*) **bb.** Of doubtful sense: app. to prostitute; to prostitute oneself. *Obs.*

1670 DRYDEN *1st Pt. Conq. Granada* Epil. 12 Fame is false to all that keep her long; And turns up to the fop that's brisk and young. **1678** BUTLER *Hud.* III. i. 824 Prepost'rously would have all women Turn'd up to all the world in common. **1682** DRYDEN *Abs. & Achit.* II. 383 'Tis a leading card to make a whore To prove her mother had turned up before. [Cf. TURN-UP *sb.* 1.]

turn-, the verb-stem in combination with a sb., adv., or adj., forming sbs. and adjs., in the sense 'that turns or is turned', 'for turning', in various uses of the verb. The more important compounds are entered as Main words: see TURNCOAT, TURNKEY, TURN-OUT, TURNPIKE, TURNSPIT, TURNSTONE, etc.; those of less importance follow here. **turn-and-bank**, **turn-and-slip** *Aeronaut.*, used *attrib.* and *absol.* to designate an indicator which shows the pilot his rate of turn and correctness or error in banking; **turn-away**, †(*a*) one who turns away; a deserter, forsaker (*obs.*); (*b*) the act of turning people away from a place of assembly already full; also *transf.*; **turn-bat**, in *Metallurgy*: see quot.; **turn-beam**, the drum of a windlass; **turn-bench**, a small portable lathe used by watchmakers, etc.; **turn-bolt**, †(*a*) a wrench or spanner; (*b*) a bolt that rotates, as to unlock a mechanism; **turn-boat**, a boat used as a turn-mark in yacht-racing; †**turn-bout** [BOUT *adv.*[2]] = TURN-BUCKLE 1; **turn-bridge**, a bridge turning horizontally on a pivot; a swing-bridge; **turn-button**, a small bar pivoted near its centre, so that when turned its end engages with a catch, the edge of a door, or the like; **turn-cap**, (*a*) (also **turn-cap lily**), *Lilium Martagon*; (*b*) a revolving cowl; **turn-crowned** *a.*, having the feathers on the crown reversed, as some varieties of the domestic pigeon: cf. *turn-pate*; **turn-file**: see quot.; †**turn-frame** = TURNTABLE 1; **turn-furrow**, the mould-board of a plough; **turn-gate** = TURNSTILE; **turn-hole**, an eddy or whirlpool; **turn-in** *a. rare*, that turns or folds in; **turn indicator**, (*a*) *Aeronaut.* (see quot. 1930); (*b*) = INDICATOR 3 g; **turn-lathe**, a turning-lathe; **turn-mark**, a buoy or boat round which yachts turn in racing; **turn-net**: see quot.; **turn-off** *a.*, that is turned off, or turns off; that is taken or got off by turning or screwing; *sb.* that which is turned off; in quot., the quantity of any product finished and disposed of; †**turn-pate**, a crested pigeon: cf. *turn-crowned*; **turn-penny**, a person who is intent on profit (cf. TURN *v.* 15 b); **turn-pin**, (*a*) a pin that turns, or on which something turns; a pivot; (*b*) a conical plug for stopping or enlarging the end of a pipe; **turn-plate**, †(*a*) a curved plate-rail; (*b*) = TURNTABLE 1; **turn-plough**, a plough with a mould-board, which turns over the furrow-slice, as distinct from a shovel-plough (*Cent. Dict.*, *Supp.* 1909); †**turn-point**, turning-point; in quot., the sun's 'turning-point': see TROPIC *sb.* 1 a; †**turn-poke**, in cock-fighting, a game-cock of the largest breed; = SHAKE-BAG 1; **turn-rail** = TURNTABLE 1; also, a point or switch for directing railway vehicles from one line to another; **turn-row**, the space at the side of a field in which the horses turn in ploughing, used as a path (*U.S.*); **turn-saw**, a narrow saw for cutting curves (= *turning-saw*, TURNING *vbl. sb.* 13); **turn-scale** *a.*, that (merely) turns the scale: cf. MAKE-WEIGHT 2; **turn-screw**, a screw-driver; also, a wrench; **turn-shoe**, a shoe that is made inside out and then turned: see quots.; a pump; **turn-side**, a disease of cattle, also affecting the dog, resembling the gid in sheep: cf. TURN-SICK *sb.*, TURNABOUT b; **turn signal** *U.S.* = INDICATOR 3 g; **turn-skin** (rendering L. *versipellis*), one who turns or changes his skin; *spec.* one who can turn into a wolf at will, a were-wolf; †**turn-stair**, a winding staircase; **turn-stick**, a tourniquet consisting of a bandage tightened by twisting a stick or bar passed through it; **turn-stitch**, in knitting, = *purl-stitch* (PURL *sb.*[1] 5); in lace-making: see quot. 1882[2]; **turn-stool**, a stool with a revolving seat; †**turn-tale** *Rhet.* = APOSTROPHE[1] 1; †**turn-tippet**, a turncoat, a renegade: see TIPPET *sb.* 1 e; **turn-to**, a tussle, a set-to; also, a beginning or setting to work (in quot. *attrib.*); †**turn-tool**, a turning lathe; **turn-tree** = *turn-beam*; **turn-trencher**, a game of forfeits in which a trencher or the like is spun; more commonly *turn the trencher*; **turn-turtle** *a.* (*nonce-wd.*), in which one turns turtle and dies; **turn-under**, the curving in of a carriage-body towards the bottom; †**turn-wheel**, ? a boy employed to turn a lathe or rope-wheel; †**turn-wicket**, a kissing-gate.

1933 *Jrnl. R. Aeronaut. Soc.* XXXVII. 930 If operating in daylight, they must have a complete set of instruments including duplicate *turn and bank indicators, compass, air speed indicator, [etc.]. **1981** *Pilot* Jan. 45/1 A Motorola low-frequency transceiver with..altimeter, turn-and-bank and a clock. **1955** LIPTROT & WOODS *Rotorcraft* iii. 25 Further instruments include..*turn-and-slip indicator. **1978** A. WELCH *Bk. of Airsports* ii. 36/2 The instruments used to cope with cloud flying are either a turn-and-slip indicator or an artificial horizon, or both. **1688** BUNYAN *Jerus. Sinner Saved* (1886) 42 Witness those *turn-aways from God that you also read of in Jeremiah. **1858** DICKENS *Let.* 11 Aug., Wherever I read twice the turn-away is invariably on the second occasion. **1867** *Ibid.* (1880) II. 277 We had an enormous turn-away last night, and do not doubt about having a cram to-night. **1881** RAYMOND *Mining Gloss.*, **Turn-bat*, a wooden stick used in turning the tongs which hold a bloom under the hammer. **1909** in *Cent. Dict. Suppl.* **1679** *Phil. Collect.* XII. 7 The *turn-beam which hangs over the shaft has been thrown off its frame by the force of it [explosion]. **1828** WEBSTER s.v. *Jig-pin*, A pin used by miners to hold the turn-beams, and prevent them from turning. **1680** MOXON *Mech. Exerc.* xiii. 225 An Iron Lathe called a *Turn-Bench..When they use it they screw it in the Chaps of a Vice. **1688** R. HOLME *Armoury* III. 359/2 To work small work in Metal..a Turn-Bench. **1895** *Model Steam Engine* 94 Turn Bench..a miniature lathe, used for small turning, and to which the..circular motion is imparted by a catgut bow. **1896** *Daily News* 29 June 7/1 Ailsa rapidly gained.., and at the *turn-boat she had reduced the gap between her and Britannia to five minutes. **1596** in *Richmond Wills* (Surtees) 226 Inventorium..a *torne boltte: a peate sledd..etc. **1898** *Daily News* 9 May 3/1 The Lee Turnbolt Rifle..is easily kept in order by a soldier or sportsman. **1703** T. N. *City & C. Purchaser* 100 Smiths..ask'd me 6*d.* per Pound for Casements..with *Turn-bouts (or Turn-buckles, as some call'd 'em) or Cock-spurs, and Pull-backs at the Hind-side to pull them to with. **1767** S. PATERSON *Another Trav.* I. 109 Their draw bridges, ..*turn-bridges, as the bars of turnpikes. **1861** SMILES *Engineers* II. 361 The turnbridges which he introduced upon his canals, instead of the old drawbridges. **1849** NOAD *Electricity* ix. (ed. 3) 419 The rings are secured in the circular rabbett of the square piece of wood..by small *turn buttons. **1893** J. A. HODGES *Elem. Photogr.* (1907) 33 Two turn-buttons, screwed to the window frame, will keep the frame in position. **1688** R. HOLME *Armoury* II. 65/2 The Mountain Lilly Imperial,..by Florists called Martagon Imperial, but by common People the *Turn-Cap. **1842** G. FRANCIS *Dict. Arts, Turn-Cap*, a chimney top, which turns round with the wind. **1908** [MISS FOWLER] *Betw. Trent & Ancholme* 14 The little bright scarlet or 'Turn-cap' Lily. **1765** *Treat. Dom. Pigeons* 134 The Trumpeter..very feather-footed and leg'd, *turn-crown'd like the nun. **1859** DARWIN *Orig. Spec.* v. (1872) 127 The parent rock-pigeon was not feather-footed or turn-crowned. **1877** KNIGHT *Dict. Mech.*, **Turn-file*, a burnisher used in throwing up slight burs on the edges of the comb-maker's files, the teeth of which are originally made by the file and not by the chisel. **1789** BRAND *Hist. Newcastle* II. 256 *note*, Waggons, after being emptied, are brought round into the road or waggon-way by a *turn-frame. **1810** in Thirsk & Imray *Suffolk Farming 19th Cent.* (1958) ii. 77 Various sorts of mould boards, *turn furrows or breast plates. **1837** *Flemish Husb.* 15 in *Libr. Usef. Knowl., Husb.* III, The sole is a kind of sledge, formed by the end of the share towards the heel, and the lower edge of the turn-furrow. **1905** *Pall Mall G.* 29 May 2/2 Some belated visitor hurrying to leave the gardens by one of the *turngates. **1851** NEWLAND *The Erne* 352, I.. gaffed him out of the great boiling *turnhole below. **1894** *Outing* (U.S.) XXIV. 249/2 Under the seat..of the car was a sort of turn-up or *turn-in bunk, with a comfortable hair-mattress. **1919** *Nature* CIV. 183/2 A trustworthy *turn-indicator and improved compass made accurate navigation through clouds possible. **1930** P. M. HENSHAW *Air Questions & Answers* 180 A Turn Indicator is an instrument that warns a pilot when the machine is turning right or left in circumstances (at night or in a cloud) when he would not be aware of it. **1953** C. A. LINDBERGH *Spirit of St. Louis* II. vi. 303, I glance at the turn indicator, kicking rudder slightly as I do so. The needle jumps over to the side. Yes, it's working properly. **1959** *Motor Manual* (ed. 36) vi. 183 Flashing turn indicators are operated either by a switch.. mounted on the steering column, or by an independent switch mounted within easy reach of the driver. **1970** *Motoring Which?* July 88/2 All had warning lights for ignition, turn indicators and headlamp main beam. **1665–6** *Phil. Trans.* I. 71 The contrivance of Signor Campani for making Great Optick-Glasses, by the means of a *Turn-lath. **1896** *Daily News* 29 June 7/1 Britannia closed on the leaders and had the *turn mark first. **1883** G. C. DAVIES *Norfolk Broads* xxxvi. (1884) 278 The '*turn-net'... This was a long drag-net, having a pocket at one end. This end was fixed to the bank, and the other paid out so as to enclose a space of water, and then drawn ashore, when the fish were driven into the pocket. **1688** R. HOLME *Armoury* III. xviii. (Roxb.) 135/1 A *Turn off screwed barrell is a barrell of two peeces and screwed together iust at the height of the charge. *Ibid.*, Turn off vnscrewed, is when the barrell is in two peeces as foresaid and the top part bored round. **1889** *Daily News* 5 Aug. 11/3 The turnoff from looms is very limited, prices very steady. Bleached and finished stocks are very small. **1611** COTGR. s.v. *Hupé, Pigeons hupez*, copped, or crested Pigeons, called about London, *Turn-pats. [**1824** SCOTT *Redgauntlet* xii, That's always the way with old *Turnpenny,..he cares for nothing of the trade but the profit.] **1872** DE MORGAN *Budget of Paradoxes* 83 Some observant turn-penny might construct such a treatise as this from the third book. **1862** *Catal. Internat. Exhib.* II. xi. 16 The centre of the breech-piece being cut away, all the strain acts upon the attaching of the *turnpin. **1877** KNIGHT *Dict. Mech., Turn-pin*, a plug for stopping the flow from the open end of a pipe. A tube-stopper. **1797** J. CURR *Coal Viewer* 25 Plain *turn plates. Used for going round a turn. **1838** *Civil Eng. & Arch. Jrnl.* I. 164/2 The shed for the engines and the coaches is erected—the necessary turnplates fixed. **1854** G. N. JONES *Florida Plantation Rec.* (1927) 104, I think you will nead about 10 *turnplowes. **1907** T. F. HUNT *Forage & Fiber Crops* 352 The land having been plowed with an ordinary mold board or turn plow. **1587** GOLDING *De Mornay* vii. (1592) 86 The Sunne maketh there his naturall course in the Zodiacke between the two Tropickes or *Turnepointes. **1615** MARKHAM *Pleas. Princes* (1635) 42 The huge Cocke (which we call the *turne-Pocke). **1773** PEGGE in *Archæologia* (1775) III. 142 What our sports-men call Shakebags, or Turn-pokes. **1793** SMEATON *Edystone L.* §167 *note*, The carriage being turned a quarter round upon the Turnpike, or *Turnrail. **1801** W. COXE *Monmouthshire* xxiv. II. 231 At the junction of two roads.., moveable rails, called turn rails, are occasionally used, which are fastened with screws.., and may be pushed sideways. **1838** SIMMS *Publ. Wks. Gt. Brit.* 49 The turn-rails to be twelve feet diameter..the table to be hung on a centre pivot. **1885** 'C. E. CRADDOCK' *Prophet Gt. Smoky Mts.* 3 A young man.. came to a meditative halt in the *turn-row. **1888** *Atlantic Monthly* May 677/1 All adown the turn-row between the ranks of corn. **1875** *Carpentry & Join.* 16 For cutting out curved or circular pieces,..the sweep saw or *turn saw.. comes into..use. **1841** *L'pool Mercury* 11 June 196/2 The majority..was only a *turn-scale one; but it was expected to be on the other side. **1778** J. WOODFORDE *Diary* 4 June (1924) I. 226 For a *turn screw and picker for a gun pd 0. 1. 0. **1801** *Sporting Mag.* XVII. 148 Be the spare flint, and ready turn-screw there. **1837** *Civil Eng. & Architect's Jrnl.* I. 29/1 The fourth was screwed into the bed of the river.. by a curious windlass, and lengthening turn-screw, worked by forty men. **1889** HENTY *With Lee in Virginia* (1890) 176 By a strong turn-screw a bar could be removed in five minutes. **1886** *Encycl. Brit.* XXI. 830/2 The making of '*turn shoes' embraces all work in which there is only one thin flexible sole which is sewed to the upper while outside in and turned over when completed. *Mod. Advt.*, The shoe is made inside out and then turned. 'Turn shoes' they are called in some parts of the country. **1845** YOUATT *Dog* vi. 118 *Turnside, or Giddiness..a singular disease prevalent among cattle, but only occasionally seen in the dog. **1949** *N.Y. Times* 20 Mar. II. 19/5 Mechanical *turn signals must be standard equipment on all new motor vehicles sold in Minnesota after July 1. **1977** J. WAMBAUGH *Black Marble* (1978) vi. 79 He started the Plymouth, flicked on his turn signal,..then pulled into traffic. **1831** A. H. in *Will. & Werwolf* (1832) 6 That notion has become so inveterate, that a *turnskin (*versipellis*) is become a common term of reproach. **1861** T. L. PEACOCK *Gryll Gr.* xxxiv, I felt that he was a turnskin, and I could never after taste bread with him. **1871** TYLOR *Prim. Cult.* I. iii. 77 Men who are versipelles or turnskins have the actual faculty of jumping out of their skins, to become for a time wolves. **1616** SURFL. & MARKH. *Country Farme* 17 Vnder, or vpon the side of your *turne-stayres,..your Farmer shall haue a way into the Gardens. **1813** J. THOMSON *Lect. Inflam.* 259 The *turn-stick is still a very useful instrument,..but its place in operation is now generally supplied by the screw tourniquet. **1882** CAULFEILD & SAWARD *Dict. Needlework* 286/2 *Turn-Stitch*, another name for Purl. *Ibid.* 504/2 *Turn Stitch.* Also known as Turning Stitch, used [in lace-making]..at the end of a row ..is made with a Cloth Stitch and a half-Cloth Stitch as follows: Work a Cloth Stitch, give each pair of Bobbins one Twist to the left, put the middle left hand Bobbin over the middle right; lift the two pairs with each hand. **1893** ELIZ. ROSEVEAR *Text-bk. Needlework*, etc. 405 Purl, Pearl, Seam, Rib, and Turn Stitch all mean the same thing. **1890** S. W. BAKER *Wild Beasts* I. 153 The watcher will sit upon a low *turn stool, that will enable him to rest in comfort. **1589** PUTTENHAM *Eng. Poesie* III. xix. (Arb.) 244 *Apostrophe*, or the *turnetale. **1558** CRANMER *Confut. Unwritten Verities* Pref. C ij *margin*, The priestes for the most part wer double faced, *turne tippettes and flattere[r]s. **1562** PILKINGTON *Expos. Abdyas* Pref. 14 All turntippets that turn with the worlde, and kepe their livings still, should have no office in Christs Church. **1893** HUXLEY *Evol. & Ethics* 7 A *turn-to with a giant. **1909** *Chron. Lond. Mission. Soc.* Aug. 150/2 This nine o'clock 'turn-to' whistle is also the signal for a girls' muster. **1665** *Phil. Trans.* I. 2 Campani..pretends to have found a way to work great Optick Glasses with a *Turne-tool, without any mould. **1653** MANLOVE *Lead-mines* 268 (E.D.S.) Crosses, Holes, Hange-benches, *Turntree, and Coes. **1747** HOOSON *Miner's Dict.* E ij, If he once set on his Stoce and Turn-tree, and falls to drawing. **1829** *Glover's Hist. Derby* I. 74 The spindles of a turn-tree, or rope-barrel, for winding up ore in small tubs. **1837** HOWITT *Rur. Life* II. ii. (1862) 101 The old games of blindman's-buff, *turn-trencher and forfeits..pursued in the evening firelight. **1951** DYLAN THOMAS in *World Rev.* Oct. 66 Dolphins dive in their *turnturtle dust. **1891** *Cent. Dict.*, *Turn-under. **1908** *Westm. Gaz.* 16 Nov. 4/2 The back panel in particular is conspicuously attractive, by reason of..the 'big turn-under' from top to bottom, the very large side-sweep. **1672–3** in Welch *Hist. Pewterers' Co.* (1902) II. 145 [Richard Heath was summoned..for setting his] *Turn Wheel to work on yᵉ mistery [by employing him to pour saudware and open a mould. A 'turn-wheel' was an unskilled labourer, usually a lad]. **1816** T. PARKER *Ess. Turnpike Gate* 18 The three posts in front of the *turn-wicket should be sawed into octagons.

turnable (ˈtɜːnəb(ə)l), *a. rare.* [f. TURN *v.* + -ABLE.] That may be turned.

1483 *Cath. Angl.* 397/1 Turneabylle, *conuertibilis, tropicus, versilis, versatilis.* **1603** FLORIO *Montaigne* III. iii. (1632) 458 A wit so turneable for all things alike. **1611** COTGR. s.v. *Flechir, Facile à flechir*, gentle, pliant, flexible, tractable, turnable. **1820** *Examiner* No. 612. 1/2 Some-thing laudable, or at least complimentable,—something turnable into a little grace and acknowledgment. **1935** E. R. EDDISON *Mistress* xiii. 262 What's good in Lessingham is right sense ..and a wit so turnable for all things alike. **1972** C. MUDIE *Motor Boats & Boating* 37 This grill in some units is turnable to direct the jet in any required direction.

turnabout (ˈtɜːnəbaʊt). Also with hyphen. [f. the verbal phr. *turn about* (TURN *v.* 65). See also TURN *sb.* 40, and *turn-bout* (TURN-).] The action or an act of turning about; one who or that which does this. **a.** The act of turning so as to face the other way. Also *fig.*

1833 *Regul. Instr. Cavalry* I. 48 By a turn-about the dressing is changed. **1878** BROWNING *Poets Croisic* cxxxviii, A moment's horror; then quick turn-about On high-heeled shoe. **1897** *Westm. Gaz.* 25 Mar. 1/2 The strange turn-about in the attitude of some zealous people towards Russia.

†**b.** A disease causing cattle to turn round and round; gid. Also *turn-about sickness*, vertigo. *Obs.*

1598 SYLVESTER *Du Bartas* II. i. III. *Furies* 610 The Turn-about and Murrain trouble Cattell. **1611** COTGR., s.v. *Tournement, Tournement de teste*, the turne-about sicknesse; a giddinesse, or dizzinesse.

†**c.** A winding; a 'maze'. *Obs.*

a **1603** T. CARTWRIGHT *Confut. Rhem. N.T.* (1618) 604 The Iesuites ignorant of their owne mystery of iniquity, and strangers as it were in the giddy turn-about of their owne Cloisters.

†**d.** One who turns about or alters things; an innovator. *Obs.*

a **1670** HACKET *Abp. Williams* II. (1693) 36 Our modern Turn-abouts cannot evince us, but that we feel we are best affected, when the great Mysteries of Christ are celebrated upon Anniversary Festivals.

†**e.** A double-barrelled gun. *Obs.* †**f.** A turnstile. *Obs.* **g.** A small steamer having the deadwood cut away astern, and an additional rudder fitted in the space thus made, to facilitate quick turning; also *attrib.* **h.** *U.S.* A 'giant's stride' or merry-go-round.

1789 J. BYNG *Torrington Diaries* 1 June (1938) IV. 109 There was (today) a little Fair, and a Stall, and a Turnabout to make the children sick after their Gingerbread. **1801** *Sporting Mag.* XVII. 159 A kind of double gun, known by the name of Turnabout. **1805** R. W. DICKSON *Pract. Agric.* I. 144 The *turn-about* or w[h]irlout gate is only necessary where a frequency of passage is required. **1885** *Pall Mall G.* 22 June 3/1 The folly which led them [the Admiralty] to use a swift and finely lined turnabout, built by White, of Cowes, to carry cabbages and potatoes on board the vessels lying in Portsmouth Harbour. **1889** *Harper's Mag.* Sept. 560/1 The high swings and the turnabouts; the tests of the strength of limb and lung. **1894** W. H. WHITE *Man. Nav. Archit.* xviii. (ed. 3) 652 In a considerable number of small vessels and torpedo-boats an arrangement of balanced rudders has been fitted... This arrangement..is known as the 'turn-about' system. *Ibid.* 699 A second [gun-boat]..identical..except that the after deadwood had been cut away, and the 'turn-about' system applied.

turnado, obs. form of TORNADO.

turnagain (ˈtɜːnəgɛn, -əgeɪn), *sb.* (*a.*) [f. the verbal phr. *turn again* (TURN *v.* 66).]

†**1.** A turning again or about; a revolution; a winding or deviation. *Obs.*

1545 RAYNOLD *Byrth Mankynde* I. x. (1634) 34 The.. vaines infinitely intricate and writhed with a thousand revolutions or turnagaines. **1587** GOLDING *De Mornay* xxv. (1592) 380 Moyses in leading the people of Israell through so many turnagaines.

†**b.** That which turns back an advance. *Obs.*

1630 *R. Johnson's Kingd. & Commw.* 43 Mountaines are natures bulwarkes..; the Retreats they are of the oppressed, the scornes and turne-againes of victorious Armies. **1642** ROGERS *Naaman* 252 Why then fall there out so many turnagaines in the lives of the best?

2. A device in the bobbin-net machine.

1832 BABBAGE *Econ. Manuf.* xxxiii. (ed. 3) 349 An improvement in a particular part of such machines, called a turn-again.

3. = ANTISTROPHE.

1871 BROWNING *Balaust.* 214 Sing them a strophe, with the turn-again, Down to the verse that ends all, proverb-like.

†**4.** *attrib.* or as *adj.* in **turn-again alley, lane,** a blind alley, a cul-de-sac; also, a winding or crooked lane. *Obs.*

1531 TINDALE *Expos. 1 John* Prol. (1537) 5 It is become a turne-agayne lane unto them, which they can not go thorow. **1624** HEYWOOD *Gunaik.* v. 256 A turne-againe-lane, that had no passage through. *c* **1730** BURT *Lett. N. Scotl.* (1818) I. 56 [In Scotland] A little court or turn-again alley, is a closs. **1807** *Antiq. Rep.* I. 346 It was Friar Richard's ill fate to take into a turn-again lane, that had no passage through.

turnament, obs. f. TOURNAMENT, TORMENT.

turnaround (ˈtɜːnəraʊnd). orig. and chiefly *U.S.* Also **turn-around.** [f. the verbal phr. *turn around* (TURN *v.* 67).] **1.** = TURN-ROUND 1.

1936 *Sun* (Baltimore) 20 Aug. 11/6 The dirigible Hindenburg landed..at the Naval Air Station tonight for what was expected to be the quickest turn-around in transatlantic airship service. **1946** *Ibid.* 9 Apr. 17/6 Another feature of the day's market was the turn-around of two loads of 100-pound Iowa wooled lambs which brought $18.55. **1952** *Ibid.* 9 Oct. 5/4 At present the two queens have a 48-hour turnaround at Southampton. **1971** D. BAGLEY *Freedom Trap* ix. 202 The skipper was returning in the tender. It seemed as though they intended a faster turnaround than Gibralter. **1974** T. P. WHITNEY tr. *Solzhenitsyn's Gulag Archipelago* I. II. i. 497 So that the prisoner shouldn't attempt to escape during the moment he was in the toilet, and also for a faster turn-around, the door to the toilet was not closed. **1977** *Sci. Amer.* Jan. 127/1 Ships designed to carry a unitized cargo, for ease of transshipment, quick turnaround, low damage and low longshore labor costs.

2. = TURN-ROUND 2.

1941 *Sun* (Baltimore) 30 Dec. 15/1 Many [railroad bonds] had been depressed to the lowest level since 1938 prior to the turn-around late last week. **1961** *N.Y. World-Telegram* 15 Mar. 31/2 Yet this would mean a turn-around in the trend of residential construction. **1972** M. WILLIAMS *Inside Number 10* iv. 82 He was found an office and in the general turnaround the Private Secretary..was shifted from the study..to a large room on the first floor. **1975** *N.Y. Times* 19 May 18/4 The migration to the Arkansas countryside is part of a national turnaround in population. **1984** *Times* 13 Jan. 13/1 Associated Newspapers..yesterday disclosed a £5m turnaround from loss to profit.

3. A space for vehicles to turn round in, often at the end of a drive or cul-de-sac.

1954 C. ARMSTRONG *Better to eat You* vi. 63 He..ran across the turn-around and the parking apron. **1969** 'F. RICHARDS' *Risky Way to Kill* (1970) vi. 68 She swung the Volks in the graveled turnaround, so that it headed back the way it had come. **1975** *New Yorker* 31 Mar. 29/3 Then they ..got into the truck, circled the turnaround, and drove straight off. **1984** *Ibid.* 7 May 57/3, I turned up my driveway and parked in the turnaround.

4. The action or fact of turning round; a point in a team-game at which the teams change ends to play in the opposite directions.

1959 I. & P. OPIE *Lore & Lang. Schoolch.* vii. 116, I can do the splits, I can do the turn-arounds, I can do the kicks. **1960** T. MCLEAN *Kings of Rugby* 212 Then, at the turnaround, when the Lions now had the northerly wind at their backs, the change which came over the game was remarkable. **1962** A. SHEPARD in *Into Orbit* 108, I could feel the capsule begin its slow, lazy turnaround to get into position for the rest of the flight.

5. *attrib.*

1944 *Sun* (Baltimore) 15 Aug. 12/5 The 'Big Inch' line.. has done the work of 23,000 tank cars operating on an 18-day turn-around schedule. **1946** *Ibid.* 27 Dec. 6/1 Ease of maintenance and servicing will cut costs and turn-around time. **1950** *Ibid.* 14 Aug. 10/6 The harbor to be built at Lake Washington will consist of a turn-around area 1,000 feet square. **1959** *Wall St. Jrnl.* 29 July 6/3 He described the current period as a 'turn-around year' leading to higher sales and earnings next year. **1976** *National Observer* (U.S.) 17 July 7/3 There ought to be some turnaround time to get into a system different than the one that has existed for nearly 40 years.

†**turnas**, obs. var. TOURNOIS, coin of Tours.

1617 MORYSON *Itin.* I. 292 At Naples..ten quatrines make one sequin, three quatrines one turnas.

turnaway (ˈtɜːnəweɪ), *sb.* and *a.* Also **turn-away.** [f. the verbal phr. *turn away* (TURN *v.* 69).] **A.** *sb.* The action or an act of turning away or deviating (from a course, etc.).

1922 *Encycl. Brit.* XXXI. 666/1 The British battle fleet turned away two points to port... This was the 'turn-away' which has given rise to considerable controversy. **1976** *Nature* 27 May 278/2 The complete turn-away from crop uniformity by employing mixed varieties or multi-lines, which are heterogeneous for disease resistance and other characters, may be of advantage only where there is severe and continuous disease present.

B. *adj.* Of a crowd: so large that part of it has to be turned away. Also *transf.*, of business, trade, etc.

1943 *Life* 1 Nov. 76 Since the beginning of her radio show she has enlarged her audience 34%, business at the Persian room is turnaway. **1950** *Richmond* (Va.) *News-Leader* 27 Oct. 11/2 In death, as in life, Al Jolson drew a turnaway crowd. **1968** *Punch* 18 Sept. 395/2 Sunday evensong—a service that always did turn-away business. **1977** *Oxford*

Times 22 July 16/5 A French restaurant.. opened at the end of June, and has been enjoying a turn-away trade ever since.

turnay: see TOURNEY.

turnback ('tɜːnbæk), *sb.* and *a.* [f. the verbal phr. *turn back* (TURN *v.* 70).] One who or that which turns back or is turned back; an act of turning back. **a.** *sb.* (*a*) One who faint-heartedly retreats, or gives up an enterprise. (*b*) That part of anything which is folded back. (*c*) The return of something borrowed or rented. (*d*) A reduction in price; a reversal.

1843 *Vermont Militia Act 1842* 61 *Coat*—dark blue, double breasted;.. the skirts to reach to the bend of the knee, with buff kerseymere turnbacks. **1847–78** HALLIWELL, *Turnback*, a coward. **1879** *Unif. Regul.* in *Navy List* July (1882) 489/2 Stand-up collar, with a white turn-back on each side of the collar. **1881** A. C. GRANT *Bush-Life Queensland* II. 232 The unfavourable reports of these turnbacks were.. little heeded. **1943** *Daily Progress* (Charlottesville, Va.) 19 Nov. 4/1 (*heading*) 13 billion dollar turnback... The War Department is returning to the Budget Bureau more than 13 billion dollars.. from its 1943 appropriation. **1949** *Sun* (Baltimore) 18 Mar. 1/2 (*heading*) Second auto turnback. **1967** *Electronics* 6 Mar. 351/2 A rise in turnbacks of rented machines in recent years has Japanese computer makers uneasy. **1977** *Sunday Times Mag.* (Perth, Austral.) 16 Jan. 6/5 When the turn back came on the last three days of trading, it was the farm leaders in particular that held their gains.

b. *attrib.* or *adj.* That is folded back.

1900 *Westm. Gaz.* 29 Nov. 2/2 A little more protection round the throat than a turn-back collar can afford. **1909** *Daily Graphic* 19 Oct. 17/3 The little turn-back brim in a Dutch baby bonnet. *Ibid.* 20 Oct. 13/1 The tight-fitting tunic.. ends in a turnback fold of the material.

turnbroach ('tɜːnbrəʊtʃ). *arch.* [f. TURN *v.* + BROACH *sb.*[1]] = TURNSPIT 2, 3. Also *attrib.* or *adj.*

14.. *Voc.* in Wr.-Wülcker 619/1 *Verugirus*, a turnebroche. *c* **1430** LYDG. *Min. Poems* (Percy Soc.) 52 A turne-broche, a boy for hogge at Ware, With loury face, noddyng and slombryng. *a* **1548** HALL *Chron., Hen. VII* 10 b, This Lambert.. was made the kynges faulkener, after that he had been a turne broche.. in the kynges kytchyn. **1596** NASHE *Saffron Walden* 127 Downe his throate I will thrust this turn-broach comparison. **1610** W. FOLKINGHAM *Art of Survey* I. xiii. 45 Fulling-mils, Shere-mils, Turne-broach-milles, Oyle-mills, Barke-mills. **1682** N. O. *Boileau's Lutrin* II. 112 A Bastard-brat rather of some Turn-broch. **1795** *Commons Jrnls.* L. 525, 5 Boys in the Kitchen. Scowerer.. Soil Carrier.. 3 Turnbroaches. **1822** SCOTT *Nigel* xxxi, A turn-broche, or deputy scullion.

turn-broacher, erroneous f. TURNBROACH.

'turn-ˌbuckle. [f. TURN *v.* + BUCKLE *sb.*]

1. A catch or fastening for window casements, shutters, etc., consisting of a thin flat bar pivoted so that it falls by its weight into a slit or groove.

1703 Turn-buckle [see *turn-bout*, TURN-]. **1717** *Inventory of Goods* (MS.), One Glass Window, One Casem[t] with a Turnbuckle. **1859** F. A. GRIFFITHS *Artill. Man.* (1862) 184 Turnbuckles, small.. 6.

2. A coupling with internal screw threads for connecting metal rods lengthwise or for regulating their length or tension; *transf.* a device for coupling electric wires (*Funk's Stand. Dict.*, 1895).

1877 KNIGHT *Dict. Mech.*, *Turn-buckle*,.. (*Nautical*), a link used for setting up and tightening the iron rods employed as stays for the smoke-stack. **1895** *Outing* (U.S.) XXVI. 44 Deadeyes and lanyards are fast giving way before the advance of the turnbuckle.

turncoat ('tɜːnkəʊt), *sb.* and *a.* [f. TURN *v.* + COAT *sb.* lit. one who turns his coat; cf. TURN *v.* 51.]

A. *sb.* **a.** One who changes his principles or party; a renegade; an apostate.

1557 WOODMAN in Foxe *A. & M.* (1570) 2193/2, I will beleue none of you all, for you be turne coates, and chaungelinges, and be wauering minded. **1579** FULKE *Confut. Sanders* 688 It sheweth what turne coates they were, which changed as euerie prince was affected. *a* **1632** G. HERBERT *Outlandish Prov.* §929 Wine is a turne-coate (first a friend, then an enemy). **1777** MME. D'ARBLAY *Early Diary*, I am afraid Mrs. Wall is a turn-coat. **1855** MACAULAY *Hist. Eng.* xv. III. 567 The Tory who voted for those motions would run a great risk of being pointed at as a turncoat by the.. Cavaliers.

†**b.** *transf.* applied to anything that changes in appearance or colour. Also *turn-coat-coloured.*

1567 MAPLET *Gr. Forest* 11 This is a maruellous turncote, for that it doth conforme it self to all settes and dispositions of the Ayre. *Ibid.* 12 b, Kaman the stone may well be called a turncote, for that it is now blacke, now white, now shamefast & blushing. **1608** TOPSELL *Serpents* (1658) 672 Of a changeable colour, betwixt white, green, brown and yellow, for which occasion some have called it *versicolor Chamæleon*, that is, a turn-coat-coloured Chamæleon.

c. A coat renovated by being turned; in quot. 1726 *fig.* Also, a reversible coat.

1726 GAY in *Swift's Lett.* (1766) II. 65 Next week I shall have a new coat, and new buttons, for the birth-day, though.. a turn-coat might have been more for my advantage. **1958** *Vogue* Oct. 163 Givenchy's barrelled and narrowing turn-coat, in pearl grey wool reversing to off-white.

B. *adj.* Of, pertaining to, or that is a turncoat.

1571 GOLDING *Calvin on Ps.* lviii. 5 Hee peynteth out more expressely theire turnecote craftynesse. **1624** MIDDLETON *Game at Chess* II. ii, Yond greasy turncoat gormandising prelate. **1706** HEARNE *Collect.* 3 Nov. (O.H.S.) I. 302 An old, rich,.. turn-coat D[r]. **1796** WOLCOTT (P. Pindar) *Satire* Wks. 1812 III. 400 Turncoat Windham to no party true. **1876** LOWELL *Among my Bks.* Ser. II. 40 We have heard that the Commedia was.. the revengeful satire of a disappointed Ghibelline, nay, worse, of a turncoat Guelph.

Hence (*nonce-wds.*) **'turncoat** *v., intr.* to play the turncoat, to change sides; **'turncoated** *a.*, having the coat turned; **'turncoatery, 'turncoating** *vbl. sb.*, **'turncoatism**, the action or practice of a turncoat.

1892 *Pall Mall G.* 4 July 3/1 Whichever way I've voted, One or the other's sure to swear that I've *turn-coated. *c* **1645** HOWELL *Lett.* (1650) III. xxi. 33 Translations are but as *turn-coated things at best, specially among languages that have advantages one of the other. **1841** HAMPDEN in *Some Mem.* (1871) 132 Apologising for his *turn-coaterie, saying, that those who now brought in the new Government would as soon turn them out if they came forward with the proposal of a fixed duty. **1624** BP. MOUNTAGU *Immed. Addr.* A j b, To take notice of his dealing,.. in his *turne-coating from side to side. **1965** *National Observer* (U.S.) 11 Jan. 2 He told Mr. Watson he didn't 'think much of turncoating' when Mr. Watson announced for the House in 1962. **1889** W. ROBERTS in *N. & Q.* 7th Ser. VII. 41/1 The most barefaced and flagrant *turncoatism.

'turncock. [f. TURN *v.* + COCK *sb.*[1]]

†**1.** A stop-cock of which the plug is turned to open or close it. *Obs.*

1702 SAVERY *Miner's Friend* 42 At every Floor there may be a turn-cock with a Skrew. **1755** HALES in *Phil. Trans.* XLIX. 320 When, by means of a turn-cock, a gallon of water was two minutes in running, then the heat was 140.

2. A water-works official entrusted with the turning on of the water from the mains to supply-pipes, etc.

1711 in Halliwell *Acc. Collect. Bills*, etc. (1852) 27 Christmas Boxes,.. Turncock, 2s. 6d. **1791** 'G. GAMBADO' *Ann. Horsem.* xvii. (1809) 139 No Turncocks to be found—all the Water at a stop. **1863** DICKENS *Uncomm. Trav.* xxi, A meditative turncock.. gives the fire-plug a disparaging wrench. **1875** RUSKIN *Fors Clav.* V. 56 The turncock.. turned and turned till a fountain sprang up in the middle of the street.

'turn-down, *a.* and *sb.* Also **turndown.** [f. the verbal phr. *turn down* (TURN *v.* 72).]

A. *adj.* **1.** That turns down or may be turned down; esp. said of a collar worn with the upper part turned down over the neck-band; ***turn-down bed***, a folding bed.

1840 MARRYAT *Poor Jack* xlvi, He wore.. a turn-down collar. *a* **1860** ALB. SMITH *Lond. Med. Student* (1861) 86 The faithful Mary.. has long since retired to rest in the turn-down bedstead of the back kitchen. **1884** *Marshall's Tennis Cuts* 104 A pretty shape which.. admits of a tie being passed under the turn-down corners.

2. *Electr. spec.* designating an incandescent lamp of which one small filament only is used when little light is wanted.

1911 in WEBSTER.

B. *sb.* **1.** The turned-down part of anything; also, an article of dress that is worn turned down; *spec.* a turn-down collar (see A. 1).

1849 ALB. SMITH *Pottleton Leg.* iv, Her other hand.. hidden beneath the turn-down of the thin worn sheet. **1865** LEVER *Luttrell* xxxii. 232, I showed him the turn-down, only the turn-down, of your note. **1896** *Punch* 8 Aug. 64/1 When he's out of Jackets and Turn-downs, and gets into Tails and Stick-ups! **1903** *Blackw. Mag.* Mar. 372/1 Heather stockings with loud-patterned 'turn-downs'.

2. a. The action of turning down (see TURN *v.* 72 d).

1902 *Speaker* 23 Aug. 550/2, I look back on that period of sour welcome and curt turn-down with feelings I cannot express.

b. *U.S.* A person who is 'turned down' or rejected, esp. as unfit for military service.

1945 *Daily Progress* (Charlottesville, Va.) 30 Jan. 4/1 The high proportion of turndowns among Negro registrants. **1977** *Sat. Rev.* (U.S.) 23 July 14/1 We've gotten a lot of turndowns, yeah; but we've gotten guys who're willing, too.

3. = DOWN-TURN, DOWNTURN *sb.*

1957 *Economist* 26 Oct. 283 This slow-down in expansion is not the same thing as a turn-down in activity. **1960** V. PACKARD *Waste Makers* (1961) xiv. 153 How far Americans could continue running up debts.. during an economic turndown was not clear. **1979** *Daily Tel.* 5 May 23/2 Shares in EMI were sent reeling yesterday after a warning by the company of likely.. losses.. following an unforeseen and severe turndown in its music division. **1980** *Jrnl. R. Soc. Arts* Mar. 208/2 The industry.. is fearful of a turn down in the volume of work.

‖**'turndun, 'tundun.** [Native Australian of the Kurnai tribe in Gippsland.

Originally written *tŭrndŭn* by Howitt (see quot. 1880), who however employs the spelling *tundun* in his *Native Tribes S.E. Austr.* (1904) 493.]

A flattish, fish-shaped piece of wood fastened by one end to a thong, which when whirled round makes a peculiar penetrating roaring sound; a bull-roarer.

1880 FISON & HOWITT *Kamilaroi & Kurnai* 197 About a week after the boys have run away.., the old men go out and make certain wooden instruments called tŭrndŭn. **1883** *Cornh. Mag.* Jan. 84 This object, called Turndun by the Australians, is a very early savage invention, probably discovered and applied to religious purposes in various.. centres, and retained from the age of savagery in the mystic rites of Greeks and perhaps of Romans. **1887** *Athenæum* 1 Oct. 430 The living Australian savage as he twirls the turndun, bedaubs himself with clay. **1898** A. LANG *Making Relig.* v. 91 Many other races use the bull-roarer, turndun, or *rhombos*.

†**turne,** *a. Obs. rare*[−1]. [Cf. OE. *torn* anger.] ? Hot-tempered, irritable.

c **1375** *Sc. Leg. Saints* xl. (*Ninian*) 1242 For men hurt communly Ar mar turne & mare angry.. þane he þat has his lymmys al.

turned (tɜːnd), *ppl. a.* [f. TURN *v.* + -ED[1].] In various senses corresponding to those of the verb, q.v.; those chiefly in use are given here.

1. Moved round on an axis, rotated: see TURN *v.* 1.

1552 HULOET, Turned, or dryuen aboute wyth the handes as a mustarde querne is, *trusatilis.* **1606** MARSTON *Parasit.* II. D iv, Beware legge-ringes And the turnd key on thee.

2. a. Wrought in a lathe; shaped or rounded with a lathe: see TURN *v.* 4.

c **1440** *Promp. Parv.* 507/1 Turnyd vessel, or other thynge, ..*toreuma.* **1501** *Maldon, Essex, Crt. Rolls* Bundle 60, No. 7, I tabill, ii trestellis,.. a turned cheyr. **1556** in Willis & Clark *Cambridge* (1886) II. 564 Thende of the partitions to be with turned pillers. **1681** GREW *Musæum* III. I. ii. 271 It looks like some sort of Turn'd-Work. *c* **1790** IMISON *Sch. Art* I. 221 A small turn'd handle.. to screw on or off at pleasure. **1792** BELKNAP *Hist. New Hampsh.* III. 112 [Poplar] is used.. for some kinds of turned work. **1838** DICKENS *Nich. Nick.* x, Chairs, with turned legs.

b. ***turned shells*** (Zool.), a name for the family *Actæonidæ* or *Tornatellidæ* of gastropods.

1891 in *Cent. Dict.*

3. (With advs., as *well*, etc.) **a.** Shaped, formed, fashioned: see TURN *v.* 5.

a **1637** B. JONSON *Underwoods* xii. 68 The race Of Shakespeare's mind and manners brightly shines In his well torned, and true filed lines. **1699** VANBRUGH *False Friend* II. i, See, here he comes.. a pretty turn'd fellow. **1710** *Lond. Gaz.* No. 4689/4 A strong well turned little Mare. **1837** CARLYLE *Fr. Rev.* III. III. iv, In sweetly turned periods. **1874** L. STEPHEN *Hours in Libr.* (1892) I. iii. 123 So many exquisitely turned compliments.

b. *U.S. colloq.* Of a person: disposed, natured. Cf. TURN *sb.* 34 a.

1931 *Amer. Speech* VII. 94 *Quar-turned*, droll-natured. **1949** H. HORNSBY *Lonesome Valley* 334 She's the best turned girl I ever talked to. She's as friendly turned as anybody! **1951** L. CRAIG *Singing Hills* 70 A nicer-turned man you never saw when he ain't in liquor. **1972** J. S. HALL *Sayings from Old Smoky* 138 Turned, etc. Having a disposition (of a certain kind)... 'She's a mild-turned girl.' She has a mild disposition.

4. Bent or twisted: see TURN *v.* 9.

1585 *Durham Wills* (Surtees) II. 111 A eireon wayne, a turned teame. **1703** T. N. *City & C. Purchaser* 193 They call it Turn'd-lead, when the Came has pass'd through the Vice, and is thereby made with a Groove on each side to go on upon the Glass. *Mod.* The knife has a turned edge, and won't cut.

5. a. Moved into a different posture or direction (*lit.* or *fig.*); diverted, deflected, etc.: see TURN *v.* 7, 13, 14, 22, etc.

c **1586** C'TESS PEMBROKE *Ps.* LXXVII. iv, With turned thought, A new I fell to thinck Upon the auncient tymes. **1621** BP. HALL *Heaven upon Earth* §4 The galled soule.. after many tossed and turned sides, complaines of.. vnabated torment. **1847** TENNYSON *Princ.* I. 65 He chew'd The thrice-turn'd cud of wrath.

b. ***turned of*** (an age, etc.): see TURN *v.* 18 b.

6. †**a.** Opposite, contrary, adverse. *Obs. rare*[−1].

a **1325** *MS. Rawl. B.* 520 lf. 64 For partie torned [*MS. Rawl. B.* 820 lf. 139 Pro parte aduerssa].

b. Reversed so as to be upside down; inverted (see TURN *v.* 10); *spec.* in *Printing*, of a type placed or letter printed upside down.

1513 DOUGLAS *Æneis* VIII. vi. 114 The housis war lik a turnit barge. **1638–56** COWLEY *Davideis* I. lix, Numbers which still encrease more high and wide From One, the root of their turn'd Pyramide. **1771** LUCKOMBE *Hist. Print.* 443 The Article of marking turned letters tries a Corrector's skill. **1826** WELLINGTON in *Croker Papers* (1884) I. xi. 330 They.. lay sprawling and kicking like.. turned turtles. **1877** SWEET *Handbk. Phonetics* §45 The narrow back unrounded vowels are indicated by the 'turned' letters of the corresponding wides.. (ɔ) is assumed to be a turned (o).

c. Reversed or altered so as to be inside out, as a garment (see TURN *v.* 11 c); also of a shoe (see quot. 1882).

1483 *Cath. Angl.* 397/2 A Turnyd cloth, *interpola.* **1552** HULOET, Turned garmente whose wronge side is turned vpwarde, *tra[n]slata uestis.* *a* **1643** CARTWRIGHT *On Dram. Poems Fletcher* in *Comedies*, etc. (1651) 8 Old fashioned wit! which walked.. In turned hose. **1766** W. GORDON *Gen. Counting-ho.* 317, 12 doz. turned pumps for men [cf. *turnshoe*, TURN-]. **1819** *Metropolis* I. 120 A turned coat,.. and a wig turned inside out, were spoken of. **1837** THACKERAY *Ravenswing* iv, Professionals with turned frocks. **1882** *Worc. Exhib. Catal.* iii. 30 Turned work [in shoemaking] (so called from being made inside out and afterwards turned).

7. That has turned sour or become tainted, as milk; †curdled (*obs.*): see TURN *v.* 46.

1548 UDALL *Erasm. Par. Luke* vi. 72 b, The olde soure turned wine of Moses lawe. **1556** WITHALS *Dict.* (1568) 49 b/1 Turned milke or sower, *oxia gala.* **1665** NEEDHAM *Med. Medicinæ* 408 Curded or Turnd Milk. **1903** N. MUNRO in *Blackw. Mag.* 237/1 Curdling like turned cream.

8. With adverbs, as ***turned-around, -back, -down, -in, -off, -on, -out, -up***: see TURN *v.* VIII.

1880 *Turned-around [see TURN *v.* 67]. **1958** T. STANWELL-FLETCHER *Clear Lands* 156 The two missionaries, each in black clerical garb and turned-around collars. **1966** T. PYNCHON *Crying of Lot 49* v. 117 She thought she saw a turned-around collar but took no chances. **1861** *Eng. Wom. Dom. Mag.* III. 263 A..crêpe sleeve, with a *turned-back cuff in Brussels lace. **1889** HENTY *With Lee in Virginia* (1890) 17 There was no mistaking the expression of its [the horse's] turned-back eye. **1840** THACKERAY *Shabby-genteel Story* ii, A dirty *turned-down shirt-collar. **1900** *Law Rep.* App. Cas. 404 At the *turned-in end of the hook. **1911** 'O. ONIONS' *Widdershins* iv. 35 The dripping of water from an imperfectly *turned-off tap. **1972** D. E. WESTLAKE *Bank Shot* xiii. 97 [He] stared moodily at the turned-off television set. **1976** *Washington Post* 19 Apr. A 3/2 Camejo hopes to capture votes of turned-off blacks and blue-collar workers. **1967** *Wall St. Jrnl.* 9 Feb. 1/4 The *turned-on generation..will beat a path to your door. **1971** *Guardian* 25 May 8/1 Is it merely a difference in style between Huxley's experience and that of the turned-on teenager? **1977** E. J. TRIMMER et al. *Visual Dict. Sex* (1978) vi. 62 The most obvious change in the turned on male is erection of the penis. **1722** DEFOE *Plague* 272 Some of the Dissenting *turn'd out Ministers staid, and their Courage is to be commended. **1833** T. HOOK *Widow & Marquess* xii, The best turned-out equipage that rattled through its streets. **1621** G. SANDYS *Ovid's Met.* v. (1626) 92 As he did roule His *turn'd-vp eyes. **1686** *Lond. Gaz.* No. 2131/4 A little..white Bitch, with a turned-up Nose. **1836** *Penny Cycl.* VI. 444/1 The turned-up edges of the mantle. **1904** BUDGE *3rd & 4th Egypt. Rooms Brit. Mus.* 226 A pair of gazelle skin sandals, with turned up toes.

turneke, obs. f. TOURNIQUET.

turnel^1 ('tɜːnəl). *Obs.* exc. *dial.* Also 5 -elle, 6 -yll(e, 6–7 -ell, 7 tournell, 7–9 turnil. [Derivative of TURN *v.*: cf. OF. *tornel, tournel*, that which turns, in various spec. applications.]

1. A ring turning on a swivel, a terret.

1469 in *Househ. Ord.* (1790) 97 The maister of the horses ..for sadelles, harnesse, horse-houses, wateringe-bridles, halters, turnelles, pastrons. **1607** MARKHAM *Caval.* IV. ix. 41 This peece of leather you shall buckle about your horses farre fore-leg,..also when it is buckled on you must so place it, that a strong tournell of iron being cunningly fastned within the leather, may stand iust behind his leg.

2. The windlass over a well.

1578 *Nottingham Rec.* IV. 179 Mendyng of the turnyll of the welle. **1599** *Ibid.* 251 One bucket, one turnell, and a rope.

3. The catch or fastening of a casement: = TURNBUCKLE 1.

1696 *Rector's Bk. Clayworth* (1910) 118 The Thief came in at y^e Casem^t window, in wch he broke a Quarry to get in his hand to turn y^e Turnil.

4. (See quots.)

1621 MARKHAM *Prev. Hunger* xi. 115 Certaine toyes made of long Goose feathers in the manner of shettlecocks and with little small turnells of wood running in broad and flat Swan quilles made round like a small hoope, and so with longer strings fastened to the Poale will with any small winde or ayre whatsoeuer, twirle and flicker in the ayre. **1905** *Eng. Dial. Dict.*, *Turnil*, a small, round lump of coal.

turnel^2 ('tɜːnəl). *Obs.* exc. *dial.* [Etymology doubtful.] A tub; *esp.* a shallow oval tub. Also *attrib.* **turnel boat**: see quot. 1688^2.

1688 R. HOLME *Armoury* III. xiv. (Roxb.) 11/2 He beareth Gules, a Tub, or Turnell, with handles Argent, Hooped.. also termed a Netting or washing Turnell, because in such washer women and Laundresses use to wash their linnens. *Ibid.* xv. 26/1 A Tumbrell boate, or flat bottomed boate, or Turnell boate... This kind of boate is for the conveying of cowes or horses. **1875** *Auctioneer's Catal.* in Miss Jackson *Shropsh. Word-bk.* (1879), Salting turnel. **1886** *Cheshire Gloss.*, *Turnel*... Large ones are used for scalding pigs and are called 'pig turnels'. Smaller ones are used for various purposes, such as putting under a cheese press; kneading bread, salting meat, etc.

turnell, -elle, var. TOURNELLE, *Obs.*, turret.

turnement, obs. f. TORMENT, TOURNAMENT.

turnep, obs. f. TURNIP.

turner^1 ('tɜːnə(r)). Forms: 4 tourner(e, 4–5 tornere, 5 turnere; 5 turnor, -owre, 5–6 -our, tornour; 5 tornar, 5–6 torner, 6 -ar, turnar, 5– turner. [a. OF. *tornere* (nom.):—L. *tornātor*, and *torneor* (acc.), F. *tourneur*:—L. *tornatōr-em*, agent-n. from *tornāre* to turn in a lathe; in later senses f. TURN *v.* + -ER^1.]

I. 1. a. One who turns or fashions objects of wood, metal, bone, etc., on a lathe. Also *fig.*

c **1400** *Destr. Troy* 1586 Taliours, Telers, Turners of vessells. **1415** in *York Myst.* Introd. 25 Tielmakers, Milners,..Turnours,..Bollers. *c* **1440** *Promp. Parv.* 507/2 Turnowre, *tornator*. **1485** *Naval Acc. Hen. VII* (1896) 22 William Parken of London Turnor for iij dd shodde shovilles..xv^s. **1507–8** *Durham Acc. Rolls* (Surtees) 104 Le Tornour pro CCC parapsidum et CCC discorum ligneorum, vijs. **1530** PALSGR. 284/1 Turnar a maker of bolles and dysshes, *torneur*. **1551** RECORDE *Cast. Knowl.* (1556) 111 Euery common turner can..know y^t a little altering of the one side, maketh the boul to run biasse waies. **1552** HULOET, Turnours whele or instrument, *tornus*. **1578** LYTE *Dodoens* I. lxviii. 99 Horse tayle..stemmes..their roughnesse is such, that Turners..do vse them to polish.. and smoth their workes. **1685** BOYLE *Effects of Mot.* ii. 7, I have caused a skilfull Turner to turn for me an oblong piece of Iron. **1709** STEELE *Tatler* No. 3 ¶5 Advice to the Poets; that is to say, to the Turners of Verse, as he calls 'em. **1776** *Pennsylvania Even. Post* 23 Mar. 149/1 A Turner of Brass is likewise wanted. **1838** DICKENS *Nich. Nick.* xiv, One Mr. Kenwigs, a turner in ivory. **1892** *Labour Commission Gloss.* s.v., When a turner himself holds the tool which cuts the iron or other material he is turning, he is termed a hand tool turner.

b. A potter; *esp.* one who finishes and smooths the ware before it is fired.

1601 HOLLAND *Pliny* XXXV. xii. II. 553 That kind [of earthenware] that is wrought by turners craft with the wheele. *Ibid.* XXXVI. xxii. 592 A stone, which they use to hew hollow, and by turners craft make vessels for the kitchin. **1790** in *Guide Mus. Pract. Geol.* (1859) 98 About 90 painters ..and about 200 throwers, turners, &c., were employed. **1853** URE *Dict. Arts* II. 455 When the 'thrown ware' is sufficiently dry, it is transferred to the hands of the 'turner'. **1881** *Porcelain Works, Worcester* 20 The turner..finishes the edge and foot, and if necessary the outside surface. **1892** *Labour Commission Gloss.*, *Turners*, potters who shape pottery ware upon a lathe.

II. One who or that which turns, in various other senses of the verb.

2. a. In general senses: see TURN *v.*

c **1440** *Promp. Parv.* 507/1 Turnare, or he that turnythe a spete or other lyke, *versor*. **1491** in *York Myst.* Introd. 39 Tixt-wryters, luminers, noters, turners, and florisschers. **1527** *Luton Trin. Guild* (1906) 188 Item payd to a xj^{tis} turners of spyttis xvij d. **1546** BP. GARDINER *Declar. Art. Joye* 55 b, I affirme ye same iustification that was then taught, and yow be the turners. **1552** HULOET, Turnour of one out of the ryght waye, *obuaricator*. **1593** *Rites of Durham* (Surtees 1903) 3 Which wheele did burst in peices and caught the turners of the said wheele and..rent them in peices. **1697** BENTLEY *Phal.* (1699) 422 If I really were such a Turner of Index's and Lexicons. **1702** DENNIS *Monument* xxxiii, Nor sordid Turner of his Gold for Gain. **1730** SAVERY in *Phil. Trans.* XXXVI. 338 The whole may be made to turn with one's Hand, either with a Crank.., or with a Turner like that of a Grinding-stone. **1861** *Times* 1 June, Several winnowing machines and one hay turner are damaged. **1868** MORRIS *Earthly Par.* (1870) I. II. 588 An accursed race, Who with the turner of all hearts once strove. **1878** *N. Amer. Rev.* CXXVII. 490 He is a turner of night into day. **1893** W. B. YEATS *Celtic Twilight* (1902) 24 Villages of fishermen and turners of the earth.

b. With adverbs: cf. TURN *v.* VIII.

1653 WATERHOUSE *Apol. Learn.* 245 Perswaders, and turners away of the people from obedience. **1681** MACWARD *Contendings* (1723) 89 Such Backdrawers, and Turners-aside with the Workers of Iniquity. **1892** *Sat. Rev.* 13 Aug. 205/2 To the idle turner-over, perhaps the most remarkable thing is the frequency of the phrase 'no information'.

†**3.** A translator. *Obs. rare.*

1387 TREVISA *Higden* (Rolls) II. 237 Þe seuenty torneres [CAXTON turneres] and Isidre also..seiþ two þowsand ȝere seuen hondred and two and fourty. *Ibid.* 245 Þey beeþ specialliche i-cleped þe Seuenty tourneris [*v.r.* turneres], for þey torned Holy Writte out of Ebrew in to Grewe. *c* **1425** *Saints' Lives, Apol.* in *Anglia* VIII. 195/31 Þe turner of þis englysshe.

4. In shirt-making: see quot.

1884 E. SIMCOX in *19th Cent.* June 1041 A preparer of collars and wristbands, known as a 'tacker and turner'.

†**5.** A variety of fancy pigeon. See quot. 1735. *Obs.*

1688 R. HOLME *Armoury* II. 244/2 Of Pigeons... Turners having a tuft turning down backwards from the Head. **1735** MOORE *Columbarium* 50 *Columba Circumagens*, The Turner ..in many Respects like the Finnikin, except that when it.. plays to the Female it turns only one Way, whereas the other turns both. [**1854** MEALL *Moubray's Poultry* 280 The *Turner* is also mentioned... However, if they ever existed, there are certainly none such known now. **1867** TEGETMEIER *Pigeons* xxii. 175.]

6. In the Newfoundland seal-fishery, a seal which is between the immature and mature stages of development; a three-year old seal. Also attrib. ***turner-harp, -hood*** (see HARP *sb.*^{1} 7, HOOD *sb.*^{1} 6).

1891 in *Cent. Dict.*

7. A small piece of fire-clay on which a watch-dial is held and turned while in the enamelling oven.

1891 in *Cent. Dict.*

III. 8. A member of one of the gymnastic societies instituted in Germany by F. L. Jahn (1778–1852); cf. TURNING *vbl. sb.* 4 d. Also, a member of a TURNVEREIN.

[In this sense a. G. *turner*, f. *turnen* to perform gymnastic exercises, an adoption (by Jahn) of F. *tourner*.]

1854 *Calif. Chron.* 16 May 7/3 We..paid a hasty visit to Russ' Gardens, where the Turners and their compatriots had resumed the sports of the previous day. **1860** in WORCESTER citing ADLER. **1860** BARTLETT *Dict. Amer.*, *Turner* (Germ.), a gymnast. **1865** *Pall Mall G.* 31 May 9 The late meeting of German turners in Paris. *Ibid.*, The turners who had come from Germany. **1888** *U.S. Newspaper* 17 Aug., The red and white flags of the turners may be seen. **1913** *N.Y. Times* 13 Oct. 12/4 There was a big gathering of Turners and guests at the North German Lloyd Line Pier.

'turner^2. *Hist.* Also 7 turno(u)r. [Etymology not ascertained: perh. an alteration of TOURNOIS, as the coin has considerable resemblance to the double tournois of copper current in France in the 17th cent.; cf. the Irish TURNEYS.] A small copper coin, current in Scotland in the 17th c., called also a twopenny piece or bodle, valued (when pure) at one-sixth of an English penny. See also TURNOVER.

They were originally coined by the Earl of Stirling *c* 1623. Counterfeits were also fabricated by gipsies: see quots.

1631 *Act Privy Council* in Cochran-Patrick *Rec. Coinage Scot.* (1876) II. 28 It is our pleasure that yow giue order.. for calling in of the copper money callit Turnours. **1635** BRERETON *Trav.* (Chetham Soc.) 188 Coins current in Scotland—In Copper, Turners 6 to one penny English or 12 Scottish. **1640** *Records of Elgin* (New Spald. Cl.) I. 266 Geving..thrie dolloris in siluer and receaving back..sex dolloris in turnoris for the samyn. **1642** in Row *Hist. Kirk* (Wodrow Soc.) p. xviii, Four pund weght of turnoris. *Ibid.* p. xix, Four markis of turnouris quhilk was gottin out of the Coinze-house. *a* **1670** SPALDING *Troub. Chas. I* (1850) I. 235 King Charles turnouris, stricken be the Erll of Striviling,.. wes, be proclamatioun..cryit doun fra tua penneis to ane penny; King James turnouris to pas for tua penneis, becauss thay war no less worth; and the kaird turnouris simpliciter dischargeit as falss cungzie. **1786** CARDONNEL *Numism. Scot.* 34 After 1660, we hear of two pennies, bodles, and turners. **1842** *Penny Cycl.* XXIII. 60/1 s.v. *Stirling, Wm. Earl of*, He obtained the privilege of coining for Scotland a sort of base copper-money, called 'turners'. **1882** FRANCISQUE-MICHEL *Scot. Lang.* vi. 123 Charles I..continued the coinage of the turner. The name was revived and applied to a similar piece coined after the Restoration, in the beginning of Charles II's reign. **1893** *Antiquary* Mar. 105 Coins found in St. Queran's Well 1869. Scottish..Charles II., Turners and Half Turners.

'Turner^3 ('tɜːnə(r)). The name of James *Turner*, eighteenth-century London colour-maker, used *attrib.* and in the possessive to designate a yellow pigment patented by him in 1781; = *mineral yellow* s.v. MINERAL *a.* 5 b.

[**1792** *Act 32 Geo. III.* c. 73 The yellow colour invented by the said James Turner, and which is composed of British materials only, has been found to be far superior to the foreign.] **1835** [see *Montpellier yellow* s.v. MONTPELLIER]. **1886** H. C. STANDAGE *Artists' Man. Pigments* iv. 46 Turner Yellow, Cassel Yellow,..Mineral Yellow. **1951** R. MAYER *Artist's Handbk. Materials & Techniques* ii. 63 *Turner's yellow*, lead oxychloride... Patented by James Turner, England, 1781. **1970** R. D. HARLEY *Artists' Pigments* viii. 92 Accounts of the legal proceedings give no indication of the place where Turner's yellow was made, although, according to one authority the pigment was manufactured at.. Walker-upon-Tyne where it was sold as Turner's Patent Yellow.

Turner^4 ('tɜːnə(r)). *Med.* The name of Henry Hubert *Turner* (b. 1892) U.S. physician, used in the possessive (less commonly *attrib.*) to designate a syndrome he described in 1938 which affects females and is characterized by developmental abnormalities including an absence of ovaries, underdeveloped breasts and womb, and shortness of stature, and is usu. caused by a missing X chromosome in normally XX cells.

1942 *Amer. Jrnl. Med. Sci.* CCIV. 641 Dr. Lawson Wilkins..showed one of the authors a patient who..has both coarctation of the aorta and webbing of the neck. He called the authors' attention to 'Turner's syndrome'. **1961** *Lancet* 23 Sept. 711/2 It had taken more than 50 years from the recognition of the sex chromosome to the discovery that children with Turner's syndrome had just one X chromosome, and Klinefelter's syndrome 2Xs and a Y. **1970** [see KLINEFELTER]. **1977** *Lancet* 19 Mar. 649/2 There have been conflicting reports about the level of amniotic-fluid α-fetoprotein (A.F.T.) when a fetus has Turner syndrome.

turneraceous (tɜːnə'reɪʃəs), *a. Bot.* [f. mod.L. *Turnerăce-æ* (f. *Turnera*, the typical genus, named after William Turner, the herbalist) + -OUS.] Of or pertaining to the *Turneraceæ*, a small order of tropical herbs and undershrubs, mainly American and African, having yellowish or blue axillary flowers and alternate leaves.

1895 in *Funk's Standard Dict.*

'turnerad. *Bot.* [f. mod.L. *Turner-a*: see prec.] *pl.* Lindley's name for the *Turneraceæ*.

1846 LINDLEY *Veget. Kingd.* 347 The forked styles of Turnerads are very peculiar.

Turneresque (-'ɛsk), *a.* [f. the name of J. M. W. *Turner* (1775–1851), landscape painter + -ESQUE.] Partaking of the character of the pictures of Turner.

1846 LADY TREVELYAN *Let.* 7 Oct. in J. Brown *Lett.* (1912) 417 It is in his boundless prodigality of thought that Turner differs from other painters, and that the more Turneresque he was..the more full of meaning every bit of his work became. **1851** RUSKIN *Stones Ven.* I. App. xi. 369 The peculiarly Turneresque characters of the earlier pictures. **1862** MISS BRADDON *Lady Audley* xv, A water-coloured sketch of an impossibly beautiful Italian peasant, in an impossibly Turneresque atmosphere. **1877** *Contemp. Rev.* Feb. 351 The Turneresque splendour of sunset in a great city.

So **Tur'nerian** *a.*, characteristic of or resembling the work of Turner; **'Turnerism**, the manner or school of Turner; **'Turnerize** *v.*, *trans.* to render Turnerian.

1851 Turnerism [see RAPHAELITE]. **1857** GEO. ELIOT *Scenes Clerical Life* (1858) II. 87 Her cheeks..loomed through a Turnerian haze of net-work. **1889** RUSKIN *Præterita* III. ii. 90 Turnerian mist effects of morning, and Turnerian sunsets at evening. **1893** W. G. COLLINGWOOD *Ruskin* (1911) II. I. 79 The father was more or less converted to Turnerism and lined his walls with Turner drawings. **1903** *Daily Chron.* 3 July 3/2 'Blackwood'..foretold that the pictorial world would never be Turnerised.

turnerite ('tɜːnəraɪt). *Min.* [f. the name of C. H. Turner + -ITE^1.] A variety of monazite, occurring in yellow or brown crystals.

1823 A. LEVY in *Ann. Philos.* V. 242 Mr. Heuland has proposed to me to call it *Turnerite*, from the name of the gentleman in whose collection it was first noticed as a distinct species. **1850** ANSTED *Elem. Geol., Min.* etc. §441 Turnerite; Aluminate of lime and magnesia. **1868** DANA *Min.* (ed. 5) 540 Turnerite is isomorphous with monazite, and like it in cleavage and color... It is known only in rare crystals... Lustre adamantine; color yellow or brown.

turnery (ˈtɜːnərɪ). Also 7 tourn-. [f. TURNER¹ + -Y.]

1. The art of the turner; the fashioning of objects or designs by means of a lathe.

1662 J. BARGRAVE *Pope Alex. VII* (1867) 126 A very artificial anatomy of a human eye, with all its films or tunicles, by way of turnery in ivory and horn. **1783** JUSTAMOND tr. *Raynal's Hist. Indies* IV. 449 This wood is very fit for works of turnery. **1842** LOUDON *Suburban Hort.* 545 The wood [of the pear] is light, smooth, and compact, and much used in turnery. **1882** HASLUCK in *Mechanical World* 4 Mar. 138/1 Numerous objects of turnery lying on the bench.

2. Collectively: Turner's work; objects fashioned on the lathe; turnery ware. †Also with *a* and *pl.*

1644 EVELYN *Diary* 22 Oct., In another roome are such rare tourneries in ivory as are not to be described for their curiosity. **1761** H. WALPOLE *Let. to G. Montagu* 20 Aug., [Some old chairs] the backs, arms, and legs loaded with turnery. **1881** YOUNG *Ev. Man his own Mechanic* §41 The Birch..is used..for making wheels, casks, tubs, and turnery.

3. A place where turning is done; a turner's workshop.

1863 P. BARRY *Dockyard Econ.* 271 Boiler shop, erecting shop, turnery, foundry, forge, &c. **1878** F. S. WILLIAMS *Midl. Railw.* 649 The light turnery or fitting shop. **1888** *Pall Mall G.* 6 June 2/1 In the shell turnery, shrapnel, Palliser, and other projectiles of divers weight and pattern, were shown us.

4. *attrib.* and *Comb.*, as ***turnery-room, ware, warehouse, work.***

1895 *Jrnl. R. Instit. Brit. Archit.* May 490 The shaft may in itself be elaborately enriched with *turnery forms. **1756–7** tr. *Keysler's Trav.* (1760) III. 294 In the *turnery-room are all kinds of lathes and instruments for turning. **1670** CAPT. J. SMITH *Eng. Improv. Reviv'd* 195 This Timber is..very good for Hoops and Hoppoles, *Turnery ware and Joyners. **1717** *Petiveriana* III. 218 They make Mortars, Pestles, and other Turnery Ware of it. **1788** AIKIN *Eng. Delineated* 269 Tunbridge..is famous for its elegant turnery ware. **1815** *Times* in *N. & Q.* 11th Ser. XI. 325/2 To be seen at Wyatt's toy and *turnery warehouse. *a* **1734** NORTH *Lives* (1826) II. 336 Ivory wrought most exquisitely;..for *turnery work there is of it so small and crooked as is admirable. **1859** W. S. COLEMAN *Woodlands* (1862) 81 The heart-wood of the Yew is..the finest of all native woods for purposes of cabinet-making and turnery-work.

turnesall, obs. form of TURNSOLE.

†**turnet.** *Obs. rare.* [var. of, or error for, *turret* TORRET; cf. obs. F. *tournet* 'a small turning rundle, or ring, in the mouth of a Bit' (Cotgr.).] = TORRET c.

1543 *Act 1 Rich. III* 1483. c. 12 §2 Laton nayles with yron chaunkes, turnettes [*so in some later edd.; Record ed. and Anglo-F.* turrettes], hangyng candelstyckes.

turney, dial. var. TORNEY, attorney.

1807 R. ANDERSON *Cumbld. Ball., Kit Craffet* v, When onie neybor was fash'd by the turnies. **1886, 1895** in *Eng. Dial. Dict.* s.v. *Torney.*

turney, obs. f. TOURNEY *sb.* and *v.*

†ˈ**turneys.** *Obs. rare*⁻¹. [Prob. the same as TOURNOIS. Cf. TURNER².] A 'black money' or base coin, made in Ireland in the 14th c.

1339 in Rymer *Foedera* (1708) V. 113 Dato nobis intelligi quod quidam, Homines Hibernici, quandam Nigram Monetam, vocatam Turneys, in partibus Hiberniæ fabricari fecerunt.

turneys, obs. var. TOURNOIS.

†**turnˈgiddy**, *a.* and *sb. Obs. rare.* [f. TURN *v.* to rotate + GIDDY *a.* Cf. TURN-SICK *a.*] **a.** *adj.* Giddy as from turning round; dizzy; affected with vertigo. **b.** *sb.* Giddiness, dizziness. Hence †**turnˈgiddiness** *Obs. rare.* = b.

Perh. a western dial. word, as the first quot. is from the work of Nicholas of Hereford.

1382 *Wycliffite Bible* Isa. xix. 14 The Lord mengde in his myddel the spirit of turnegidy [Vulg. *vertiginis*]. **1398** TREVISA *Barth. De P.R.* XVII. cviii. (Tollem. MS.), Yf he eteþ many þerof, it bredeþ heedache and makeþ hem turnegedy [orig. *capiti vertiginem inferunt*]. *Ibid.* VII. xl. (Add. MS. 27944 lf. 90 b/2) Þe mouþ is soure with mystringe of yȝen and tur[n]gidinesse [orig. *vertigine*] & wiþ oþir wel yuel signes.

†**turngrece, turngree.** Chiefly *Sc. Obs.* [f. TURN *v.* + GRECE, GREE *sb.*¹] A winding stair, as in a turret, etc. Also *attrib.*

c **1470** HENRY *Wallace* IX. 511 Richard Wallace the turngreys [*ed.* **1570** Turngrece] weill has seyn; He folowit fast apon the portar keyn,..Tuk wp the port, and leit in all the layff. **1483** *Cath. Angl.* 397/2 A Turne grece, *troclea.* **1506–7** *Acc. Ld. High Treas. Scot.* III. 366 Item for ane lok to the turngree dur in the Abbay, xiiij d. **1535** COVERDALE *1 Kings* vi. 8 They might go vp to the myddest stacion by a turne grese. **1554** *Burgh Rec. Edinb.* (1871) II. 296 To Thomas Hallis servand for paittelling and deichting of all the steppis of the turngryss of the tolbuith, viij^d^. **1600** *Reg. Mag. Sig. Scot.* 353/1 De cellario sub inferiore gradu lie turnegres tenementi quondam M. Thome Marjoribankis.

turnicimorphic (tɜːnɪsɪˈmɔːfɪk), *a. Ornith.* [f. mod.L. *Turnicimorphæ* (f. *Turnix* + Gr. μορφή form) + -IC.] Resembling, or having the structure or characters of, the *Turnicimorphæ*, in Huxley's classification the group of birds akin in form to the genus *Turnix.*

In recent Dicts.

turnicine (ˈtɜːnɪsaɪn), *a. Ornith.* [f. mod.L. *Turnic-, Turnix,* TURNIX + -INE¹.] Belonging to the *Turnicidæ*, a family of birds of which the turnix or hemipod is the type.

1891 in *Cent. Dict.*

turn-in (ˈtɜːnɪn), *sb.* (*a.*) [f. the verbal phr. *turn in* (TURN *v.* 73).] **1.** An edge of material that is folded inwards, as at a seam; *spec.* in *Bookbinding* (see quot. 1952).

1873 *Young Englishwoman* Mar. 147/2 Pin the edge.. allowing an inch and a half for the turn in. **1901** [see JOINT *sb.* 4 c]. **1931** *N. & Q.* 28 Feb. 146/1 Showing the price on the 'spine' of the jacket instead of at the foot of the front turn-in. **1933** J. E. LIBERTY *Practical Tailoring* v. 52 It should be remembered that the first turn in is not as an ordinary *turned-in* edge, the turn being on the top and not underneath. **1952** J. B. OLDHAM *English Blind-Stamped Bindings* 66 *Turn-in*, the portion of leather that shows along the edges on the inside of the covers.

2. An entrance, a way by which one may turn in, a road or passage leading off another road.

1959 *Cape Times* 7 July 9/2 What could be more pleasant than the old 'leafy lane' road..to the left of the High Constantia gateway? One wonders what this new and awkward turn-in is going to cost. *Ibid.* 26 Oct. 6/4 The accident..occurred on the Port Elizabeth-Uitenhage road at the Despatch turn-in. **1973** E. LEMARCHAND *Let or Hindrance* xiii. 157 'Look, there's a turn-in at the side of the office.'.. Toye negotiated the narrow entry.

3. *attrib.* or as *adj.*

1955 J. E. LIBERTY *Practical Tailoring* (ed. 2) v. 66 Baste the silesia edge to the turn-in edge across the top, and sew it. **1973** S. JENNETT *Making of Books* (ed. 5) xii. 195 It [*sc.* the leather] must be pared thin on all turn-in edges.

turning (ˈtɜːnɪŋ), *vbl. sb.* [f. TURN *v.* + -ING¹.] The action of the verb TURN, in various senses (also concretely).

The earliest examples occur in senses 1 b (*c* 1230) and 4 (1303).

1. a. Movement about an axis or centre; rotation, revolution.

1387–8 T. USK *Test. Love* I. v. (Skeat) I. 64 Olde doinges and by many turninges of yeres used. **1390** GOWER *Conf.* I. 8 After the tornynge of the whiel. **1538** ELYOT, *Reuolutio,*.. a reuolucion or tournynge of celestiall bodyes or spheres. **1615** G. SANDYS *Trav.* 55 An Order of Monkes,..called Dervises, whom I haue often seene to dance..; dances that consist of continuall turnings. **1802** PALEY *Nat. Theol.* xx. (ed. 2) 376 As the turning of a weather-board or tin cap upon the top of a chimney. **1821** SCOTT *Kenilw.* xxix, I mind it not the turning of a key. **1868** MISS BRADDON *Dead Sea Fr.* viii, An earthly river..instrumental in the turning of paper-mills.

b. A sensation as of rotation; 'whirling', giddiness, vertigo.

c **1230** *Hali Meid.* 35 Of breines turnunge þin heaued [schal] ake. **1398** TREVISA *Barth De P.R.* XVI. lxii. (Add. MS. 27944) lf. 202/2 It schal seme..þat þe hous schulde falle anone and þat semynge is by moeuynge þat comeþ by tornynge of þe brayne.

2. a. The action of shaping or working something on a lathe; the art of shaping things by means of a lathe; the work of a turner.

c **1440** *Promp. Parv.* 507/1 Turnynge, or throwynge of treyn vessel..*tornatura.* **1620** in Swayne *Sarum Churchw. Acc.* (1896) 171 Turninge of Banisters and pendantes. **1680** MOXON *Mech. Exerc.* xi. 194 In Turning, all Irregularities must be wrought smooth down. **1726** LEONI tr. *Alberti's Archit.* I. 25/1 Workmen lay their Timber under water.., especially such as they design for turning. **1873** J. RICHARDS *Wood-working Factories* 158 Turning is an..important branch of wood work.

b. *pl.* (*concr.*) Chips or shavings *of* some substance produced by turning in a lathe.

1800 HENRY *Epit. Chem.* (1808) 64 A small ball formed of turnings of zinc. **1812** SIR H. DAVY *Chem. Philos.* 322 If iron turnings be heated to whiteness in a curved gun-barrel, and potash be melted and made slowly to come in contact with the turnings,..potassium will be formed. **1868** JOYNSON *Metals* 115 To make an iron cement..mix..112 lbs. of clean cast-iron borings or turnings, with 8 oz. of sal ammoniac.

3. *fig.* Shaping, moulding, fashioning (of literary work, etc.).

1586 W. WEBBE *Eng. Poetrie* (Arb.) 65 Such are the turning of verses: the infolding of wordes. **1858** LONGF. *M. Standish* II. 90 You are an elegant scholar, Having..skill in the turning of phrases.

4. a. The action, or an act, of changing posture or direction by moving as on a pivot; movement so as to face or point in a different, or in some particular, direction. Also *fig.*

1303 R. BRUNNE *Handl. Synne* 8875 Whan we turnede aboute On a womman myn yȝe ys y-caste... Þe dekene loked at þe nexte turnyng, She was a-wey, he sagh no þyng. *c* **1489** CAXTON *Sonnes of Aymon* iii. 114, & at this tornyng that he thus made he slewe Esmenfray. **1545** ASCHAM *Toxoph.* I. (Arb.) 89 A weake smithe..wyl wyth a lipe and turnyng of his arme, take vp a barre of yron. *c* **1618** MORYSON *Itin.* IV. v. i. (1903) 440 The Crossings, Bowings, turnings of the body to the Alter. **1631** WIDDOWES *Nat. Philos.* 53 Griefe is his [Delight's] contrary, which is a turning from the hurtfull object. **1738** SWIFT *Pol. Conversat.* Introd. 17 Turnings of the Head, and motions of the Hands. **1825** COLERIDGE *Aids Refl.* (1884) 271 A turning of the thoughts exclusively to the so-called physical attributes. **1845** J. COULTER *Adv. Pacific* ix. 116 The seal cannot quickly turn, so you may..finish him..with a..sharp axe..; but be careful to watch his turning on you.

†**b.** Phr. ***turning of a hand*** = moment, instant (see HAND *sb.* 60 f). So ***turning of a straw.*** *Obs.*

(Cf. quot. *c* 1425 for *turning about*, in 12 below.)

1579 TOMSON *Calvin's Serm. Tim.* 239/1 Y^e^ Christians are at euery turning of an hand, at the pits side. **1600** HOLLAND *Livy* XXI. xiv. 401 Anniball..assailed the cittie, and wan it in the turning of an hand. **1679** J. GOODMAN *Penit. Pard.* II. v. (1713) 236 In the turning of an hand a lewd and flagitious person starts up a great saint. **1755** SMOLLETT *Quix.* (1803) IV. 224 Two thousand copies, that will fetch six rials a-piece in the turning of a straw.

c. *Obstet.* (See quot. 1857.)

1857 DUNGLISON *Med. Lex., Turning..Versio Fœtûs*, the operation of bringing down the feet, or some part of the lower extremity, when the presentation of the child is such that it cannot be delivered by the natural efforts. **1899** *Allbutt's Syst. Med.* VII. 737 A labour necessitating the use of instruments or of turning.

d. The practice of gymnastics according to the system of F. L. Jahn: cf. TURNER¹ 8.

1888 *U.S. Newspaper* 17 Aug., Turning began at 10 o'clock.

5. a. Reversal, inversion: as of soil, or other substance or object, for exposure to air; of a leaf of a book in reading; of an hour-glass; of a garment; of words in a sentence.

1536 *MS. Rawl. D.* 780 lf. 73 In the turnyng of tymbre in the tymber yard. **1538** ELYOT Addit. Gg iij b/1 *Anastrophe*, a tournynge out of a commune order, as, *Italiam contra*, for *contra Italiam.* **1551** in Feuillerat *Revels Edw. VI* (1914) 53 The layenge abroade eyringe turnynge soinge mendinge.. foldinge and layeng vp of the same. **1551** T. WILSON *Logike* (1580) 29 When I intreated of the conversion, or tournyng of Propositions. **1562** J. HEYWOOD *Prov. & Epigr.* (1867) 137 He hath turned his typpet an honest turnyng. **1573** TUSSER *Husb.* (1878) 56 By oft turning [of wheat] ye seeme to refresh it. **1581** *Confer.* III. (1584) Pj, After a little turning, he sayde, This is not the booke that I meant. **1726** SHELVOCKE *Voy. round World* 137 At the turning of every glass..we beat 3 ruffs on the drum. *c* **1830** *Glouc. Farm. Rep.* 14 in *Libr. Usef. Knowl., Husb.* III, It will be ready to carry in four or five days, with one turning. **1842** LOUDON *Suburban Hort.* 57 Peat..reduced..to a fine mould..by exposure to the air, and repeated turnings. **1844** MRS. BROWNING *Wine of Cyprus* ix, Betwixt the folio's turnings, Solemn flowed the rhythmic Greek.

b. A row of hay turned with the rake; a windrow. *local.*

1795 *Scots Mag.* LVII. 304/2 [The hay] is again made into small rows called turnings. **1834** *Brit. Husb.* I. 491 It is turned with the rake-head, and is before noon raked into small rows, called 'turnings';..and in the evening of the same day, the rows are made into small 'hay-cocks'.

6. The action of bending or folding over, or condition of being folded over; a part of something folded over, a fold; in quot. 1660, a curl, a volute.

1631 WEEVER *Anc. Fun. Mon.* 581 The forme of a Rose..: and in the turnings of the leaues this Inscription. **1660** BLOOME *Archit.* Ej, The middle Voluta hath a Circle..of one part, but the corner turning hath two parts. **1886** *Girl's Own Paper* 25 Dec. 202/3 All paper patterns..are of medium size... No turnings are allowed. **1894** *Daily News* 18 Sept. 6/4 Providing deep hems and turnings..for the days when the garments will be all too short.

7. a. A change in the direction of movement or course; deflection, deviation; winding, tortuous course. Also *fig.*

1426 LYDG. *De Guil. Pilgr.* 8666 Lyk a corde..Wythinne yt tourneth ofte aboute,..For cordys be sayd..Off offte tournynges in an herte. **1585** T. WASHINGTON tr. *Nicholay's Voy.* IV. xxv. 140 b, [The] riuers by the turning in their course haue made..many..yles. **1587** HARMAR tr. *Beza's Serm.* i. 11 The diuers turnings and windings, by the which men wander and goe astray. **1617** MORYSON *Itin.* I. 244 The Mountaine..was very high, but the way easie, with many turnings about the Mountaine. **1719** D'URFEY *Pills* (1872) VI. 102 For 'tis of the making of Dunstable way, Plain without turning. **1751** LABELYE *Westm. Br.* 25 This Bridge was built without turning of..the River.

b. *fig.* of verse or melody; in quot. *a* 1830, a refrain.

1579 SPENSER *Sheph. Cal., Aug.* 194 How I admire ech turning of thy verse. **1662** PLAYFORD *Skill Mus.* I. xi. (1674) 39 Those long Windings and Turnings of the Voice. *a* **1830** *Yng. Musgrave* xi. in Child *Ballads* II. 249/2 And aye the turning o the tune 'Away, Musgrave, awa!'

8. A place or point where a road, path, etc. turns, or turns off. Also *fig.*

c **1384** CHAUCER *H. Fame* I. 182 In a forest..At a turnynge of a went How Creusa was y-loste allas. *c* **1440** *Promp. Parv.* 507/1 Turnynge, of dyuerse weyys, *diverticulum.* **1596** SHAKS. *Merch. V.* II. ii. 43 Turne vpon your right hand at the next turning, but at the next turning of all on your left. **1600** HAKLUYT *Voy.* III. 300 We discouered 32 Islands..hauing many turnings and windings betweene them, making many faire harboroughs and chanels. **1624** BP. MOUNTAGU *Immed. Addr.* 125 God..knoweth the secrets, discouereth the boughts and turnings of the heart. **1771** SMOLLETT *Humph. Cl.* 26 June, At the turning of a lane, that led to a village,.. a couple of robbers a-horseback suddenly appeared. **1778–** [see LANE *sb.* 1 b]. **1864** BURTON *Scot Abr.* II. i. 110 About the turning of the 17th into the 18th century. **1866** G. MACDONALD *Ann. Quiet Neighb.* vii. (1878) 121, I had not gone down more than three turnings [of the stairs].

9. Reversal of movement or course; †return, going back (*obs.*).

c **1440** *Gesta Rom.* lxiv. 276 (Harl. MS.) In hire turnyng hom fro chirch. **1806** SCOTT *Let. to Earl Dalkeith* 11 Feb. in *Lockhart*, I abhor even the shadow of changing or turning with the tide. **1857** J. W. CROKER in *C. Papers* 1 Feb. (1884) I. 83, I..never saw..so..complete a turning of the tide of victory.

10. *fig.* Conversion; perversion; desertion to another side (quot. 1665). *arch.*

1340 HAMPOLE *Pr. Consc.* 4111 Thurgh his turnyng fra gode til ille. 1434 MISYN *Mending Life* 105 Of conuersyon or holy turnynge. 1532 MORE *Confut. Tindale* Wks. 819/2 The turnyng to them selfe or to Lucifer was in it selfe a tourning from God. *a*1555 BRADFORD in Coverdale *Lett. Mart.* (1564) 262 [The Lord] hath no pleasure in the death of a sinner: he rather wold our conversion and turning. 1665 MANLEY *Grotius' Low C. Warres* 544 More..that among all these turnings, would yet remain faithful to their Parties.

11. Change; vicissitude; alteration.

1548 ELYOT, *Volubilitas*...the turnyng of any thyng. 1617 HIERON *Wks.* II. 264 An abuse of Gods goodnesse, and a turning of His graces into wantonnesse. 1659 HAMMOND *On Ps.* lxix. 22 Annot. 342 Safe from the turnings of the World. 1689 in *Acts Parlt. Scotl.* (1875) XII. 71/1 The clause anent the turneing of this meetting into a parliament.

12. With adverbs, corresponding to adverbial combinations of the verb in various senses (see TURN *v.* VIII), as ***turning about***, ***again***, ***away***, ***back***, ***down***, ***in*** (also *attrib.*), ***off***, ***out*** (also *attrib.*), ***over***, ***round***, ***up*** (also *concr.* a part turned up).

*c*1425 *Cursor M.* 23223 (Trin.) In *turnyng of þin honde aboute. 1570 DEE *Math. Pref.* C iv b, Two Wheles.., whose turnynges about in one and the same tyme [etc.]. 1663 BP. PATRICK *Parab. Pilgr.* xvii. (1687) 150 The converting and turning about of our minds and hearts to the original of our Being. *c*1400 *Brut* clxiii. 182 þere was so miche presse of peple at the *turnyng aȝeyne. 1382 WYCLIF *Prov.* i. 32 The *turning awei of litle childer [1611 the turning away of the simple] shal slen hem. 1552 HULOET, *Turnyng backe, *vide in* reuolucion. 1703 MOXON *Mech. Exerc.* 233 The end of an Iron Axis turned Square down, and again turned Square to the first *turning down. 1837 MRS. SHERWOOD *H. Milner* III. xv, A turning-down which contained the signature..of the epistle. 1808 *Lady's Econ. Assist.* 5 The patterns are drawn, allowing for *turning in. 1877 KNIGHT *Dict. Mech.*, *Turning-in*, the process of strapping a dead-eye, that is, bending a rope tightly around it in the score. 1901 *Daily Express* 21 Mar. 6/5 The crew had gathered about the forecastle to smoke their turning-in pipe. 1940 *Amer. Speech* XV. 247 He allows nobody else to have anything to do with the..*tuning out* (or the **turning-off*) of the radio programs. 1973 *Black Panther* 5 May 2/1 It is hard to understand how any Oakland residents could have missed some exposure to the..campaign... But turning off can be a total thing. 1976 'W. TREVOR' *Children of Dynmouth* iv. 84 The abrupt turning-off of the kitchen radio, and the bang of the door. 1711 SWIFT *Jrnl. to Stella* 22 May, This man has grown by persecutions, *turnings out, and stabbing. 1807–26 S. COOPER *First Lines Surg.* (ed. 8) 325 Ectropium. A turning out of the eyelids is so named. 1894 ELIZ. L. BANKS *Camp. Curiosity* 29 You must turn out a room... On turning-out day, you must shake the rug, and scrub up the floor. 1702 C. MATHER *Magn. Chr.* VI. v. App. 38 It prov'd her own Father that was to be hang'd, at whose *Turning over, she thus cry'd out. 1842 LOUDON *Suburban Hort.* 131 Picks..combine the operation of perforating with that of separating, breaking, loosening, and turning over. 1856 *Jrnl. R. Agric. Soc.* XVII. I. 119 There is a quicker turning over of the farmer's capital. 1899 *Allbutt's Syst. Med.* VIII. 173 The heart executes an asymmetry of movement which gives rise to a sensation popularly known as turning over. 1591 PERCIVALL *Sp. Dict.*, *Buelta*, a returne, turning away, *turning round, *reditus*, *conuersio*, *auersio*. 1690 NORRIS *Beatitudes* (1692) 159 The swiftest turnings round of a Globe look like standing still. 1966 M. R. D. FOOT *SOE in France* viii. 190 Among [Pierre] de Vomécourt's achievements, this successful turning round again of Mme Carré stands second only to his indispensable contribution towards getting organized resistance going at all. 1628 EARLE *Microcosm.*, *Shee Precise Hypocrite* (Arb.) 63 Her deuotion at the Church is much in the *turning vp of her eye. 1648 HEXHAM *Dutch Dict.* 11 *Schoenen met tuyten*, Shoes with turnings up. 1683 MOXON *Mech. Exerc.*, *Printing* xxii. ¶1 He leaves no wrinckles in the turnings up [of the paper lining] against the sides of the Box. 1712 J. JAMES tr. *Le Blond's Gardening* 166 Tillings, or second Turnings up of the Ground. 1844 STEPHENS *Bk. Farm* II. 95 The turning up of a fat sheep. 1877 KNIGHT *Dict. Mech.*, *Turning-up* (*Bookbinding*), taking the round out of the back, while the fore edge is cut.

13. *attrib.* and *Comb.*, as (in sense 2) ***turning-carrier***, ***-chisel***, ***-gauge***, ***-gouge***, ***-lathe***, ***-tool***; also **turning circle**, the smallest circle within which a ship, motor vehicle, etc., can be turned round completely; **turning-engine**, (*a*) a lathe (Knight *Dict. Mech.* 1877); (*b*) a small engine for turning over a large one slowly for inspection or adjustment (*Cent. Dict.* Suppl. 1909); **turning-glass** (see quot.); **turning-loom**, a lathe; **turning-machine**, **-mill**, **-piece** (see quots.); **turning-pin** = *turn-pin* (*a*) (see TURN-); also *attrib.*; **turning-plate**, (*a*) = *turn-plate* (*a*): see TURN-; (*b*) (see quot. 1877); **turning radius**, the radius of a turning circle; **turning-rest**, a rest for a turning-tool, attached to a lathe, as a slide-rest (*Cent. Dict.* 1891); **turning-saw**, a saw with a narrow blade adapted for cutting in a curve, as a bow-saw, compass-saw, keyhole-saw, etc.; **turning-steel**, a smooth round bar of steel used to turn the edge of a cutting instrument so as to give it a flanged form (*Cent. Dict.* 1891); †**turning-tree**, a gallows (cf. TURN *v.* 74 d, 78 f). See also next, 7, and TURNING-EVIL, -POINT.

1877 KNIGHT *Dict. Mech.*, **Turning-carrier*, a device for holding metallic work while being turned in the foot-lathe. *Ibid.*, **Turning-chisel*, a chisel used by turners for finishing work after being roughed out by the gouge. 1881 DICKSON *Organ Build.* i. 6 The usual turning-chisels and gouges. 1903 KIPLING *Traffics & Discoveries* (1904) 39 The endurance, armament, *turning-circle, and inner gear of every ship in the British Navy. 1928 *Motor Man.* (ed. 27) 219 *Turning circle*, the minimum diameter of circle within which a car can be turned round completely. 1959 [see LOCK *sb.*[2] 15 b]. 1963 *Listener* 21 Feb. 339/2, I cannot myself.. accept the suggestion..that Admiral Tryon confused radius and diameter of the ship's turning circle... Diameter is so inseparable in the mind of a seaman with 'turning circle' that the phrase 'turning circle' is commonly and loosely used to mean its diameter. 1980 *Jrnl. R. Soc. Arts* July 513/2 The dimensions of a ship's turning circle vary approximately in proportion to ship's length. 1983 *Sunday Tel.* (Colour Suppl.) 20 Mar. 18 Although over three feet longer than the Golf, the Volvo's turning circle is seven inches smaller. 1877 KNIGHT *Dict. Mech.*, **Turning-gage*, an instrument to assist in setting over the tail-stock of the lathe, so that a given taper in a given length of work may be obtained. 1902 *Census Bulletin* 216, 28 June 64 (Cent. Dict. Suppl.) After the negative [in half-tone engraving] is developed the film is stripped from the plate, reversed, and placed on another, called a *turning-glass, thus becoming a positive. 1877 KNIGHT *Dict. Mech.* s.v. *Turning-tools*, [description of figure] *n*, *turning-gouge. 1794 *Rigging & Seamanship* I. 152 **Turning-lathe*, a well known machine for turning. 1840 *Civil Eng. & Arch. Jrnl.* III. 175/2 An improved expanding mandrel for turning-lathes. 1879 R. S. BALL in *Cassell's Techn. Educ.* VII. 60 The turning-lathe..enables us to produce with perfect accuracy any surface of revolution. *a*1805 A. CARLYLE *Autobiog.* (1860) 96 He said he would order his son.., who was a more powerful master of the *turning-loom than he was, to turn me a nice snuff-box or egg-cup. 1849 E. CHAMBERLAIN *Indiana Gazetteer* 429 There are..one foundry and several *turning and carding machines, all driven by water. 1877 KNIGHT *Dict. Mech.*, *Turning-machine*, one for turning boot-legs after the seams have been sewn and rolled. 1844 *Knickerbocker* XXIV. 184 The uplifted arm of Labor..meets his eye everywhere, in the paper-mill and grist-mill, and..*turning-mill. 1877 KNIGHT *Dict. Mech.*, *Turning-mill*, a form of horizontal lathe or boring-mill. 1823 P. NICHOLSON *Pract. Build.* 595 **Turning-piece*, a board with a circular edge, for turning a thin brick arch upon. 1591 PERCIVALL *Sp. Dict.*, *Vira*, a *turning pin, a shaft, *verticulum*, *subscus*, *sagitta*. 1875 W. MCILWRAITH *Guide Wigtownshire* 43 This quern-stone.. has three turning-pin holes in it. 1797 CURR *Coal Viewer* 28 These *turning plates [in a cast iron rail road]. 1877 KNIGHT *Dict. Mech.*, *Turning-plate*, a circular plate above the front axle, where the bed moves upon it as the carriage turns from its direct course; a *fifth-wheel*. 1967 *Jane's Surface Skimmer Systems 1967–68* 79/1 Characteristics... *Turning radius at cruising speed 1,640 ft (500 m). 1973 T. PYNCHON *Gravity's Rainbow* I. 105 She's fed back who knows how many reams' worth of Most Secret flimsies.., squadron numbers, fueling stops, spin-recovery techniques and turning radii. 1725 W. HALFPENNY *Sound Building* 24 With a narrow *Turning-Saw cut directly thro' the Arch-Line. 1825 J. NICHOLSON *Operat. Mechanic* 584 A compass-saw,..a key-hole-saw. Both of these..are called turning-saws, and have their plates thin and narrow towards their bottoms, and each succeeding tooth finer. 1680 MOXON *Mech. Exerc.* x. 192 These Gouges (and..other *Turning Tools). *a*1548 HALL *Chron.*, *Hen. VIII*, 224 b, She and her husband..were.. hanged at the foresayd *turnyng tree.

'turning, *ppl. a.* [f. as prec. + -ING[2].] That turns, in various senses of the verb.

1. That moves round, or so as to face another way; rotating, revolving, etc. (See also 7.)

1558 KNOX *First Blast* (Arb.) 19 The turning wether cocke. 1629 MILTON *Ode Nativity*, *Hymn* iii, Peace..came softly sliding Down through the turning sphear. 1700 PRIOR *Carmen Seculare* xxxiii, Practise them now to curb the turning Steed.

2. Changing direction of movement or course; winding, sinuous; branching off, as a road or path.

1495 *Trevisa's Barth. De P.R.* XVII. clxxiii. (W. de W.) 715 Of Thus set a fyr comyth a good smellynge smoke:..full meuable and tornynge and crokyd wyth many bendynges and wrynklynges. 1552 HULOET, Turnyng or wyndyng manye wayes lyke an eale, or snake, *tortuosus*. 1573–80 BARET *Alv.* T 439 A little lane, or turning path going out of the great or high waie, *diuerticulum*. 1590 GREENE *Orl. Fur.* Wks. (Rtldg.) 96/2 And Rhodanus..flew with calm alongst his turning bounds. 1867 TROLLOPE *Chron. Barset* II. liii. 98 Near a corner, where a turning path made an angle in the iron rails. 1879 STEVENSON *Trav. Cevennes* (1892) 163 A deep turning gully in the hills.

3. *Mil.* That turns an enemy's position.

1877 *Daily News* 30 Nov. 5/7 The cavalry of the turning column had captured their whole camp. 1912 COL. H. S. MASSY in *Standard* 20 Sept. 7/2 Direct general attacks are not anticipated, but wide turning movements..will be the chief aim.

4. Reversing its course; beginning to go back.

In quot. 1601 as rendering of Gr. τροπικός (see TROPIC).

1601 DOLMAN *La Primaud. Fr. Acad.* (1618) III. 686 These circles are nominated Tropickes, that is, turning or conuertiue. 1857 W. A. BUTLER *Serm.* iv. 98 Turning with the turning tide.

5. Changing, changeful, variable. *Obs.* or *arch.*

*c*1450 *Songs, Carols*, etc. (E.E.T.S.) 78/202 Love..vertu, ..Which dowble Fortune may neuer tak þe fro: Than mayst þou boldly desire her tornyng chance. 1599 SHAKS. *Hen. V*, III. vi. 35 Fortune..is painted..with a Wheele, to signifie.. that shee is turning and inconstant.

6. With adverb (cf. TURN *v.* VIII), as ***turning-up***.

1591 PERCIVALL *Sp. Dict.*, *Tornatiles*, turning vp, *aduncus*. 1841 MRS. GREY *Lit. Wife* xxix, I won't let them come into this room, with all their sneers, and turning-up noses.

7. In combinations or special collocations: **turning-beam**, an axle-tree (cf. *turn-beam*, TURN-); **turning-box**, a kind of turn-table; **turning bridge**, = *turn-bridge* (see TURN-); **turning pitch** *Cricket*, a pitch on which the ball turns or deviates on delivery; †**turning platform**, = TURNTABLE 1; **turning plough**, = *turn-plough* (see TURN-); †**turning-stile** = TURNSTILE; **turning-table** = TURNTABLE; †**turning-wheel**, (*a*) a turnstile or similar device; (*b*) an apparatus consisting of a rapidly revolving wheel (see quot.).

1766 *Compl. Farmer* s.v. *Madder*, Another axle-tree, or *turning-beam,..ten inches square near the trundle-head, and fourteen inches diameter in its octogonal part. 1611 COTGR., *Tour*,..the open *turning box in the wall of a Nunnerie, whereby the sisters..receiue in, and deliuer out, commodities. 1809 MALKIN *Gil Blas* I. xiv. ¶2, I besought the attendant at the turning-box to tell the lady. 1840 *Evid. Hull Docks Comm.* 39 *Q.* Are those bridges all draw-bridges? *A.* Yes, draw or *turning bridges. 1956 N. CARDUS *Close of Play* 31 Parkin had no superior at off-breaks on a *turning pitch. 1959 *Listener* 19 Mar. 516/1 Slow and turning pitches. 1825 TREDGOLD *Railroads & Carriages* 121 *Turning platforms for changing the direction of a carriage. 1850 in J. A. Turner *Cotton Planter's Man.* (1865) 118 Many planters here say they scrape with the *turning-plough as well. 1868 *Rep. U.S. Commissioner Agric.* (1869) 414 The field was plowed with a turning plow, followed in the same furrow with a long bull-tongue plow. 1611 COTGR., *Tour*,.. a Turnepike, or *Turning-stile. 1839 *Civil Eng. & Arch. Jrnl.* II. 202/2 Some method of turning..trains more efficiently than the common *turning-table. 1843 BORROW *Bible in Spain* vi. 39 A kind of window occupied by a turning table, at which articles were received into the convent, and delivered out. 1671 WOODHEAD *St. Teresa* II. 274 [Knocks] given by some Body at the *turning-wheel of the Vestry. 1734 tr. *Rollin's Anc. Hist.* (1827) VI. xv. vi. 91 They warded off..the darts..by the assistance of turning-wheels.

Hence **'turningness**, *rare* (in quot. *fig.* tortuous character, as opp. to 'straightforwardness').

*a*1586 SIDNEY *Arcadia* II. (1622) 135 So had nature formed him, and the exercise of craft conformed him to all turningnesse of sleights.

†**'turning-evil.** *Obs.* [f. TURNING *vbl. sb.* + EVIL *sb.*[1] 7.] = TURN-SICK *sb.* 2.

1614 MARKHAM *Cheap Husb.* 47 Of the diseases in the head, as the Sturdie, or turning-euill. 1663 BOYLE *Usef. Exp. Nat. Philos.* II. v. xii. 234 Oxen, and such-like Cattle, are troubled with that Disease..called The turning Evil, or Sturdy. [1704 *Dict. Rust.* s.v. 1725 *Family Dict.* s.v.]

'turning-point. [f. TURNING *vbl. sb.* + POINT *sb.*]

1. *lit.* A point at which something turns, or changes its direction of motion, etc.; *spec.* a maximum or minimum point on a graph, where it begins to tend downwards or upwards.

1856 STANLEY *Sinai & Pal.* xii. 400 Near what may be called the turning-point of its course, where its spacious stream is diverted..by the chain of Amanus. 1956 *Railway Mag.* Mar. 165/2 Katrane..is the only turning point (a triangle) for engines between Amman and Ma'an. 1977 *Wandsworth Borough News* 16 Sept. 9/3 London Transport should be asked to stop using Medfield-street as a turning-point for their buses.

2. *fig.* A point at which a decisive change of any kind takes place; a critical point, crisis. (The usual sense.)

1836 J. KEBLE *Wks. R. Hooker* I. p. li, In the annals of the Church,..we may from time to time mark out what may be called *turning points*. 1851 RUSKIN *Arrows of Chace* (1880) I. 86, I believe these young artists to be..at a turning-point, from which they may either sink into nothingness or rise to very real greatness. 1874 PARKER *Illustr. Goth. Archit.* I. iii. 92 At this principal turning-point in the history of architecture. 1885 *Athenæum* 23 May 669/1 The turning-point from summer to autumnal weather. 1887 J. C. MORISON *Service of Man* 8 One of those turning-points in the evolution of thought which mark the close of an old epoch.

3. *Surveying.* A subsidiary bench-mark whose height above datum is determined during the operation of finding, by differential levelling, the difference of level of two permanent bench-marks.

So called because the graduated staff on which the height is read off is at this point turned round so as to be read from the permanent (or the next subsidiary) bench-mark.

1891 in *Cent. Dict.*

turnip ('tɜːnɪp), *sb.* Also 6–7 **turnepe**, **(-eppe**, **-op)**, 6–9 **turnep**, (7 **turnepp**, **turnup**, **turneupp**, **turneip**, **turnoop**); *dial.* **turmit**, **-at**, **-ut**, **tormit**, **tummit**, etc. [In 16–17th c. *turnepe*, in 16–19th c. *turnep*, from *c*1782 *turnip*; the second element being NEEP, *nepe*, or *nep*, OE. *nǽp*, ad. L. *nāpus* navew, turnip (mentioned by Columella and Pliny); the first element is uncertain, but is generally supposed to be F. *tour* or Eng. TURN, referring to its rounded shape. There is no kindred name in other langs., except when evidently from Eng., as in Welsh and Irish.]

1. a. The fleshy, globular or spheroidal root of a biennial cruciferous plant, *Brassica Rapa*, var. *depressa*, having toothed, somewhat hairy leaves, and yellow flowers, cultivated from ancient times as a culinary vegetable, and for feeding sheep and cattle; also, the plant itself, of which the young shoots (***turnip-tops***) are frequently boiled as greens.

1533 ELYOT *Cast. Helthe* (1539) 25 Turnepes beinge welle boyled in water, and after with fatte fleshe, norysheth moche. 1562 TURNER *Herbal* II. 113 The great round rape, called commonly a turnepe, groweth in very great plenty in all Germany. 1601 HOLLAND *Pliny* XVIII. xiii. I. 571 The best Husbandmen..give order, That the ground for Turneps [L. *napum*] should have five tilthes. 1629

PARKINSON *Paradisus* 508 There are diuers sorts of Turneps, as white, yellow, and red. **1672** *Court-bk. Barony of Urie* (1892) 92 Some people..did steall furth thereof turnepes and carrottis and uther rootis. **1759** in *Q. Jrnl. Economics* (1907) Nov. 78 In case of Wet Weather while the Sheep are at turneps they are to have the Liberty of Great Oxenden. **1764** in W. Wing *Ann. Steeple Aston* (1875) 63 Agreed at vestry to sow Sandhill turnoops this next year. **1782** BARKER in *Phil. Trans.* LXXII. 282 A wet week in the middle did not greatly hurt the hay, and was very good for the turnips. **1839** COL. HAWKER *Diary* (1893) II. 168, I brought home 18 prime partridges and I lost another in the high turnips. **1863** ROBSON *Bards of Tyne* 315 We hev taties and turmits like Rosemary toppin.

†**b.** *spec.* The spheroidal root itself. *Obs. rare.*

1578 LYTE *Dodoens* v. xxxiii. 593 There is another kinde of Turnep or Rape... His rootes or Turneppes are not white but red. **1765** J. W. BAKER in *Museum Rust.* V. 265 When the sheep have eaten all the leaves, and begin to eat the butts or turneps of this plant [turnip-cabbage], they will not rot as turnips do, when wounded.

c. app. = *turnip-lantern*: see 4 b.

1766 LADY MARY COKE *Jrnl.* 30 Sept. (1889) I. 64, I told Lucy unless She cou'd produce more light I must go. She said She wou'd send for two turnips; 'twas all She cou'd do.

2. a. Applied, usually with defining word, to other species or varieties of *Brassica*; as **cabbage-t.** or **Hungarian t.**, the turnip-rooted Cabbage or Kohlrabi (*B. oleracea gongylodes*); **French t.** (*a*) the rape, *B. Napus* or *B. campestris*; (*b*) a variety of *B. Napus*, extensively cultivated in France and Germany, and much used as a flavouring for soups; **Swedish t.**, *B. campestris Rutabaga*; **teltow t.** = *French t.* (*b*); **wild t.**, the rape; see also b; **yellow t.**, a yellow variety of the common turnip.

1548 TURNER *Names Herbs* (E.D.S.) 55 Napus... I haue hearde sume cal it in englishe a turnepe, and other some a naued or nauet. **1562** —— *Herbal* II. 112b, Rapum..is called in English of them of the South countre, turnepe, of other countre men a rape. **1597** GERARDE *Herbal* II. ii. 179 There be three sorts of wilde Turneps. *Ibid.*, Wilde Turneps or Rapes, haue long, broad, and rough leaues like those of Turneps. *Ibid.* 180 Wilde Turneps or Rapes, do grow of themselues in fallow fields. **1600** HAKLUYT *Voy.* (1810) III. 288 We sowed it part with Naueaus or small Turneps. **1707** MORTIMER *Husb.* (1721) I. 157 Yellow Turneps..are commonly sown in Gardens, but are of very great advantage to be sown in Fields, not only for the use of the Kitchen, but for Food for Cattle in Winter. **1731–3** MILLER *Gard. Dict.* (ed. 2), *Napus*, the Navew or French Turnip. **1760** J. LEE *Introd. Bot.* App. 330 Turnep, French, *Brassica*. *c* **1791** *Encycl. Brit.* (ed. 3) VIII. 761/1 The ruta baga, or Swedish turnip, is a plant from which great expectations have been formed. **1796** C. MARSHALL *Garden.* xv. (1813) 261 The most common [turneps] are the white sorts; but the yellow and red are worthy of trial. *Ibid.* 262 The cabbage turnep is of two kinds: one apples above ground, and the other in it. **1858** HOGG *Veg. Kingd.* 67 *B. napus* is the..Rape or Cole-seed... There is a variety of this, called by the French *Chou Navette*, and by us French Turnip (*B. n. esculenta*), which is employed in flavouring all foreign soups. **1866** *Treas. Bot.* 167/2 The Teltow Turnip, or 'Navet de Berlin petit' of the French (*B. Napus var.*), is very different from any of our cultivated varieties of Turnip, its root being long and spindle-shaped.

b. Applied to plants of other genera having roots or tubers like those of the turnip, as *Indian t.*, *lion's t.*, *prairie t.*: see these words; also *St. Anthony's t.*, the bulbous buttercup, *Ranunculus bulbosus*; *wild t.* = *Indian t.* (in both uses).

1597 GERARDE *Herbal* II. iv. 182 Lyons turnep [*Leontice Leontopetalum*] is of force to digest. **1856** A. GRAY *Man. Bot.* (1860) 94 *Psoralea esculenta*,..the Indian Turnip,..used as food by the aborigines. *Ibid.* 427 *Arisæma triphyllum*, Indian Turnip. **1866** *Treas. Bot.* 176/1 *B*[*ryonia*] *dioica*, the Common Bryony... The root is used..as a purgative; but it is unsafe from its uncertain and sometimes violent action, whence the French call it Devil's-turnip. **1894** GIBSON in *Harper's Mag.* 565 The wild arum of Great Britain..the foreign counterpart of our well known jack-in-the-pulpit, or Indian turnip.

3. a. In slang phrases, sometimes with pun on *turn-up*. See quots.

a **1596** *Sir T. More* II. ii, Come, come; wele tickle ther turnips, wele butter ther boxes. Shall strangers rule the roste? **1812** J. H. VAUX *Flash Dict.*, *Turnips*, to give any body turnips signifies to turn him or her up, and the party so turned up, is said to have knap'd turnips. **1845** FORD *Handbk. Spain* I. 27 *note*, This gourd forms a favourite metaphor in common parlance: '*le ha dado Calabazas*', she has refused him; it is the 'giving cold turnips' of Suffolk.

b. Slang term for an old-fashioned thick silver watch.

1840 E. FITZGERALD *Lett.* (1889) I. 59 An old turnip of a watch..on the table beside her. **1853** 'C. BEDE' *Verdant Green* I. vi, His mechanical turnip showed him that he had no time to lose. **1903** A. ADAMS *Log Cowboy* xv. 234 My turnip says it's eight o'clock now.

c. Humorously applied to a person: cf. *turnip-head*, *-headed* in 4.

1837 DICKENS *Pickw.* xxxiii, 'But now', continued Sam, 'now I find what a reg'lar soft-headed, inkred'lous turnip I must ha been'.

4. *attrib.* and *Comb.* **a.** simple attrib., as ***turnip-cart***, ***crop***, ***-culture***, ***-drill***, ***-farmer***, ***-field***, ***-husbandry***, ***-leaf***, ***-pit***, ***plot***, ***-root***, ***-seed***, ***-trough***, etc.; also allusively, ***turnip-head***, ***-heart***, ***-pate***, ***-watch***; in names of things made of turnips, or in which the turnip is a principal ingredient, as ***turnip-bread***, ***pasty***, ***pie***, ***poultice***; objective and obj. genitive, as ***turnip-chopper***, ***-cutter***, ***-grower***, ***-hoer***, ***-picker***, ***-puller***, ***-pulper***, ***-slicer***, ***-sower***, ***-thinner*** (freq. as names of machines); ***turnip-bearing***, ***-cutting***, ***-eating***, ***-hacking***, ***-sowing***, ***-thinning***, sbs. and adjs.; instrumental, parasynthetic, similative, etc., as ***turnip-feeding***; ***turnip-faced*** (cf. sense 3 b), ***-fed***, ***-headed***, ***-leaved***, ***-like***, ***-pointed***, ***-rooted***, ***-shaped***, ***-stalked***, ***-stemmed***, ***-tailed*** adjs.

1812 W. TENNANT *Anster F.* I. viii, Anster's *turnip-bearing vales. **1693** S. DALE in *Phil. Trans.* XVII. 970 Of this *Turnep-Bread (for so they call it) I have both seen and tasted. **1763** *Museum Rust.* (ed. 2) I. 106, I baked my turnep-bread rather longer than the other. **1832** *Veg. Subst. Food* 236 In..1629 and 1630..good..wholesome bread was made of boiled turnips,..kneaded with..wheaten flour,.. called turnip-bread. **1664** BUTLER *Hud.* II. *Heroic. Ep. Sidrophel* 20 A Wheel-barrow, or *Turnip Cart. **1837** *Brit. Husb.* II. 246 The roots are commonly cut into pieces by an instrument called the '*turnip-chopper'. **1844** STEPHENS *Bk. Farm* II. 119 Much better instruments will be found in the two hand turnip-choppers. **1801** *Farmer's Mag.* Jan. 107 The *turnip crop is probably the best..ever remembered. *Ibid.* Aug. 279 The soil..is not..of that stiff sort adapted to beans or wheat, but abundantly free, so as to be well adapted to *turnip-culture. **1837** *Flemish Husb.* 89 in *Libr. Usef. Knowl.*, *Husb.* III, The roots were cut by a machine something like our *turnip-cutters. **1879** J. WRIGHTSON in *Cassell's Techn. Educ.* IV. 108/2, 1 bushel of swedes, cut small in a..turnip-cutter. **1854** MARY HOWITT *Pict. Calend. Seasons* 17 There was a noise of straw-cutting and *turnip-cutting. **1733** TULL *Horse-Hoeing Husb.* xxii. 328 The spring of the *Turnep-Drill being so very thin [etc.]. **1805** R. W. DICKSON *Pract. Agric.* I. 17 Turnip-Drill..for sowing turnips on the tops of one-bout ridges. **1856** MORTON *Cycl. Agric.* II. 1026 The proper width of a turnip drill in Scotland seems..to be..twenty-seven inches. *a* **1668** DAVENANT *Vacation in Lond.* Wks. (1673) 291 All these on hoof now trudge from Town, To cheat poor *Turnip-eating Clown. **1939** F. THOMPSON *Lark Rise* iii. 49 The old *turnip-faced watches which descended from father to son. **1733** TULL *Horse-Hoeing Husb.* x. 103 If Turneps be sown in June,..the most experienc'd *Turnep-Farmers, will have no more than Thirty to a square Perch left in Hand-hoeing. **1805** R. W. DICKSON *Pract. Agric.* I. Plate x. 40 A Scuffler employed..in putting in grain crops on *turnip-fed lands after one ploughing. **1812** SIR J. SINCLAIR *Syst. Husb. Scot.* I. 354 If straw be economically applied in littering turnip-fed stock [etc.]. *a* **1722** LISLE *Husb.* (1757) 329 *Turnip-feeding was apt to breed wind in the sheep. **1773** *Gentl. Mag.* Dec. 618/2 In his distress he frequented a *turnep-field. **1812** SIR J. SINCLAIR *Syst. Husb. Scot.* I. 39 Sheep-flakes, or hurdles, a sort of portable fence, well known to every *turnip grower. **1883** T. HARDY in *Longm. Mag.* July 267 A farm-woman's occupation is often '*turnip-hacking'—that is, picking out from the land the stumps of turnips which have been eaten off by the sheep. **1869** D. G. ROSSETTI *Let.* 1 Mar. (1965) II. 689 The *turnip-head falls off the broomstick. **1931** S. KAYE-SMITH *Susan Spray* III. 281 He..saw her standing there..fooling all those turnip-heads, who wanted to be fooled. **1962** *Spectator* 2 Nov. 684 Pop..has become the divisive symbol between the turnip-heads and the giant intellects. **1898** J. ARCH *Story of Life* xiii. 322 The *turnip-headed farmer turned his back upon us. *c* **1620** FLETCHER & MASSINGER *Trag. Barnavelt* II. ii, We are strong enough to curb 'em. But we have *turnop hearts. **1791** W. H. MARSHALL *W. England* (1796) II. 283 Any woman..will, in one full season become a sufficient *Turnep hoer. **1886** T. HARDY *Mayor of Casterbr.* i, A turnip-hoer with his hoe on his shoulder. **1733** TULL *Horse-Hoeing Husb.* x. 102 The greatest Inconvenience, which has been observ'd in the *Turnep-Husbandry, is when they are Fed off late in the Spring. **1848** HEPBURN in *Proc. Berw. Nat. Club* II. No. 6. 272 Turnip husbandry, and the cultivation of red clover, were introduced about 1740. **1766** J. W. BAKER in *Compl. Farmer* s.v. *Turnep*, The upper side of the *turnip leaf, in its infant state, is very smooth, and on that part the flies always lodge. *c* **1711** PETIVER *Gazophyl.* Dec. ix. Tab. 81 *Turnep-leaved Cape Dandelion. **1766** *Museum Rust.* VI. 46 By this ..production of the *turnep-like knob, together with its being perennial, this species of cabbage is distinguished from all others. **1905** *Daily Chron.* 14 July 4/7 In Cornwall the fisherman home from sea, in the intervals of blowing the fire, blows himself out with *turnip pasty. **1813** *Columbian Centinel* (Boston) 1 Sept. 1/2, I cannot protect every man's *turnip patch. *a* **1700** B. E. *Dict. Cant. Crew*, **Turnep-pate*, White or Fair-hair'd. **1844** STEPHENS *Bk. Farm* II. 40 The shells..were picked out of the ground with..a *turnip-picker. **1835** W. HOWITT in L'Estrange *Friendships Miss Mitford* (1882) I. 267 A *turnip-pie fit in size to set on Arthur's own round table. **1899** CROCKETT *Kit Kennedy* xxx, Kit only lifted the lantern and made for the *turnip-pits. **1670** WOOD *Life* 2 June (O.H.S.) II. 194 Buried..in her garden..under a *turnip plot. **1887** *Amer. Naturalist* XXI. 435 *Turnip-pointed red [beet]. **1735** BURDON *Pocket Farrier* 29 The *Turnip Poultice will infallibly cure it. **1606** G. W[OODCOCKE] *Lives Emperors* in *Hist. Ivstine* L l v b, It rained wheat, *Turnup-rootes, and pease in Slesia, which much comforted the poore people, in the extreamity of famine. **1733** TULL *Horse-Hoeing Husb.* I. 5 A large Root.. which..might have..extended near as far as the Turnep Roots did. **1727** *Bradley's Fam. Dict.* s.v. *Cyclamen*, The German Cyclamens are rather *Turnep-rooted Plants than Bulbs. **1769** *Chron.* in *Ann. Reg.* 65/2 A premium for the cultivating..of..the turnip-rooted cabbage. **1842** LOUDON *Suburban Hort.* 651 The Red Beet... The turnip-rooted is an early variety with the roots round. **1580** HOLLYBAND *Treas. Fr. Tong*, *De la Navette*, *turnop seed. **1621** *Shuttleworths' Acc.* (Chetham Soc.) 250 Turneppe seede, iiij[d]. **1833** *Ridgemont Farm Rep.* 155 in *Libr. Usef. Knowl.*, *Husb.* III, It was drilled with turnip-seed upon a limestone soil. **1788** *Trans. Soc. Arts* VI. 231 A Model of a Cabbage and *Turnep Slicer. **1844** STEPHENS *Bk. Farm* II. 41 The.. better plan of serving turnips to sheep..is to cut them into small pieces with a turnip-slicer into troughs conveniently placed for use. **1889** H. M. B. REID *Galloway Folk* 42 A brand-new gaudily painted *turnip-sower. **1765** J. W. BAKER in *Museum Rust.* V. 270, I could not accomplish my *turnip-sowing earlier. **1786** ABERCROMBIE *Arr.* in *Gard. Assist.* p. vi, *Turnep-stalked, with the turnep above ground. **1844** STEPHENS *Bk. Farm* II. 29 The *turnip-stemmed cabbage or kholrabi. *Ibid.* 11 Fig. 213 represents the form of the *turnip-store. **1875** *Encycl. Brit.* I. 321/2 *Turnip-Thinners... A class of machines has been brought out, of which Huckvale's turnip-thinner may be named as a type. **1905** *Contemp. Rev.* July 97, [I] went down the cart-track to the *turnip-thinning. **1844** STEPHENS *Bk. Farm* II. 41 A simple form of *turnip-trough. **1898** *Tit-Bits* 25 June 245/2 Consulting his..*turnip watch to see if his daughters' train was due. **1886** C. SCOTT *Sheep-Farming* 77 A bad *turnip year.

b. Special combinations: **turnip-aphid**, **-aphis**, the plant-louse of the turnip, *Aphis rapæ*; **turnip-beetle**, the *turnip-flea*; **turnip-cabbage**, the turnip-stemmed cabbage or KOHLRABI; **turnip-flea** (also **turnip flea-beetle**), a minute shiny black leaping beetle, *Haltica nemorum*, which feeds on the young leaves of the turnip and other crucifers; its larva mines in the full-grown leaf; **turnip-flower beetle**: see quot.; **turnip-fly**, (*a*) = *turnip-flea*; (*b*) the turnip-sawfly, a hymenopterous insect, *Athalia centifoliæ*, the larva of which (*turnip-nigger*) feeds on turnip-leaves; (*c*) a dipterous insect, *Anthomyia radicum*, whose larva lives in the root of the turnip; **turnip-gall weevil**: see quot.; **turnip-ghost**, a simulated ghost or apparition of which the head is formed by a turnip-lantern; **turnip-grass**, *Panicum bulbosum*, used as hay in Texas, Arizona, and Mexico, the stems of which have a bulbous base (*Cent. Dict. Supp.* 1909); **turnip greens** = *turnip-tops*; **turnip-jack** = *turnip-flea*; **turnip-land** = *turnip-soil*; **turnip-lantern**, the hollowed rind of a turnip employed as a lantern; also as a term of abuse (*Eng. Dial. Dict.*); **turnip leaf-miner**, ? the larva of the turnip-flea; **turnip-louse** = *turnip-aphis* (*Cent. Dict. Supp.*); **turnip-maggot**, the larva of *Anthomyia radicum* (*turnip-fly* c) (*Cent. Dict.*); **turnip-mutton**, the flesh of *turnip-sheep*; **turnip-nigger**, the black larva of *Athalia centifoliæ* (*turnip-fly* b); **turnip-oats**, a crop of oats succeeding turnips; **turnip-parsnip**, a turnip-rooted parsnip; so **turnip-radish**; **turnip-saw-fly** = *turnip-fly* b; **turnip-sheep**, sheep that have been fed on turnips; **turnip-shell**, a shell of the family *Turbinellidæ*, esp. of the genus *Rapa* (*Cent. Dict.*): **turnip-sick** *a.*, of land: exhausted by successive crops of turnips; **turnip-soil**, soil suitable or used for turnip-culture; **turnip-system**, a system of crop-rotation based on turnip-culture; **turnip-top** (usu. *pl.*), the sprouting leaves of the second year's growth of the turnip, used as a vegetable; **turnip-tray**, a hurdle used for penning sheep on turnip-land; **turnip-wheat**, cf. *turnip-oats*; **turnip-wood**, Australian rosewood, *Synoum glandulosum* (N.O. *Meliaceæ*), or its timber, which smells like turnips; see also quot. 1898.

1891 *Cent. Dict.*, *Turnip-aphid... Also *turnip-aphis. **1908** *Westm. Gaz.* 30 May 7/3 The corn-aphis, hop-aphis, turnip-aphis, bean-aphis. **1816** KIRBY & SP. *Entomol.* xxiii. (1818) II. 312 When the *turnip-beetle (*Haltica oleracea*, F.) walks, its antennæ are alternately elevated and depressed. **1882** *Garden* 25 Mar. 198/1 The Turnip fly (or, as the well-known insect should more properly be called, the Turnip beetle or flea). **1765** *Ann. Reg.* II. 146/2 The *turnep-cabbage is so called, because the stalk, after rising to some distance from the ground..swells suddenly into a roundish knob. **1842** LOUDON *Suburban Hort.* 627 The Turnip-cabbage, or turnip borecole,..is a dwarf-growing plant, with the stem swelled out so as to resemble a turnip above ground, but of a delicate green colour. **1867** BRANDE & COX *Dict. Sc.*, etc. III. 881/2 The *turnip-flea belongs to a genus..of minute Coleopterous insects, of the section Tetramera, and family Galerucidæ. **1843** *Zoologist* I. 371 The valuable Sweedish turnip [has] put forth its second pair of leaves, and just escaped the ravages of the turnip flea beetle. **1882** *Garden* 25 Mar. 198/2 The *Turnip flower beetle..a very small, flat, bronzy green beetle. **1733** TULL *Horse-Hoeing Husb.* xxiv. 391 By the shallow or deep [seed sown], the *Turnep-Fly is generally disappointed. **1765** J. W. BAKER in *Museum Rust.* V. 277, I discovered last season three distinct species of the turnip fly..one of them is black; it seems to hop like a flea. **1771** [see DOLPHIN 7]. **1813** SIR H. DAVY *Agric. Chem.* (1814) 217 The turnip fly..fixes itself upon the seed leaves of the turnip at the time that they are beginning to perform their functions. **1879** E. P. WRIGHT *Anim. Life* 498 One of the best-known species [of *Tetramera*] is the so-called Turnip-fly (*Haltica nemorum*). **1844** STEPHENS *Bk. Farm* III. 781 The *Curculio plurostigma*, the *Turnip-gall weevil. **1863** KINGSLEY *Water-Bab.* viii. (1864) 349 Out popped *turnip-ghosts and magic-lanthorns and paste-board bogies. **1796** J. WOODFORDE *Diary* 9 Feb. (1929) IV. 262 Dinner to day, fryed Pork & *Turnip Green. **1858** GLENNY *Gard. Every-day Bk.* 247/2 They may give a few Turnip-greens when they are very useful. **1873** *Routledge's Yng. Gentl. Mag.* Mar. 229/1 The young and tender leaves, which are popularly called 'turnip-greens'. **1801** *Farmer's Mag.* Apr. 238 Almost every acre of *turnip-land has been sown with wheat, as fast as the grounds were cleared. **1844** E. FITZGERALD *Lett.* (1894) I. 163 You have seen a *turnip-lantern, perhaps. **1844** STEPHENS *Bk. Farm* III. 778 A class of insects called *turnip-leaf miners. *a* **1722** LISLE *Husb.* (1757) 335 Several butchers..agreed..that *turnip-mutton would be waterish. **1893** *Daily News* 20 Apr. 6/2 The sparrow,..that brazen little thief who affects to despise wireworm, *turnip nigger, and gooseberry grub, but has the keenest of keen eyes for blossoming peas and delicate young wheat. *c* **1800** T. BLACKADDER in *Proc. Berw. Nat. Club* II. No. 12. 101 Your queys and stots, Hae trampled a' my *turnip oats. **1786** ABERCROMBIE *Gard. Assist.* 81 *Turnep-radish—sow the small white Italian sort. **1844** STEPHENS *Bk. Farm* III. 772 The *turnip saw-fly, *Athalia spinarum*,..is denominated a *saw*-fly, from the use and appearance of the instrument with which it deposits its eggs. *Ibid.* II. 48 *Turnip-sheep are thus easily obtained at fairs in autumn. **1880** JEFFERIES *Gt. Estate* i. 6 Some of the land is getting '*turnip-sick', the roots come stringy and small and useless. **1812** SIR J. SINCLAIR *Syst. Husb. Scot.* I. 34 This ought more especially to be attended to upon all *turnip soils. **1844** STEPHENS *Bk. Farm* I. 330 No kind of soil affords so dry and comfortable a lair to sheep on turnips, and on this account it is distinguished as 'turnip-soil'. **1805** R. W. DICKSON *Pract. Agric.* I. 540 Another sort of this grain that may probably be cultivated to advantage in particular cases, as where the *turnip system is much practised. **1710** SWIFT *City Shower* 63 Dead Cats and *Turnip-Tops come tumbling down the Flood. **1848** C. C. CLIFFORD *Aristoph., Frogs* 22 Don't beat him with a leek or turnip-top. **1886** C. SCOTT *Sheep-Farming* 44 Turnip-tops contain a considerable amount of nutritive matter. **1805** R. W. DICKSON *Pract. Agric.* II. 672 Sheep-penns or *turnip-trays made and fixed in such a way as to constitute a sort of moveable trough. **1807** VANCOUVER *Agric. Devon* (1813) 164 This stubble as well as that of the lay and *turnip wheat is frequently refreshed with..dung. **1891** *Cent. Dict.*, *Turnip-wood,..*Synoum glandulosum*. **1898** MORRIS *Austral Eng.*, *Turnip-wood*, the timbers of the trees *Akania hillii*,..N.O. *Sapindaceæ*, and *Dysoxylon Muelleri*.. N.O. *Meliaceæ*, from their white and red colours respectively.

Hence **turni'pology** (*nonce-wd.*), contemptuous term for phrenology; whence **turni'pologist**; **'turnipy** *a.*, like, or like that of, a turnip; pertaining to or connected with turnips; tasting of turnips.

1824 J. WILSON in *Blackw. Mag.* XV. 711 Bad novels, which no human creature above the calibre of a *Turnipologist would now endure three pages of. *Ibid.* 150 The system..I mean *Turnipology. **1826** SCOTT *Jrnl.* 29 Dec., The son..tampers with phrenology... There is a certain kind of cleverish men..who are attached to that same turnipology. **1792–5** AIKIN *Even. at Home* xxiii. (1805) V. 70 The reason why *turnip milk and butter have such a strong taste. **1818** *Sporting Mag.* II. 229 His constitution is inclined to the turnippy sort, and..he will not stand through those lengthened..combats. **1853** *Jrnl. R. Agric. Soc.* XIV. I. 72 Disagreeable turnipy flavour. **1873** MISS BROUGHTON *Nancy* I. 70 My acquaintance is confined to half-a-dozen turnipy squires and their wives.

'turnip, *v.* [f. prec. sb.]

1. *trans.* To plant or crop (land) with turnips.

1789 *Trans. Soc. Arts* (ed. 2) II. 63 Was the ground turneped three years? **1854** *Jrnl. R. Agric. Soc.* XV. II. 420 The land is given to couch if not turniped often.

2. To feed or fatten (sheep) on turnips.

1799 A. YOUNG *Agric. Lincoln* 320 Shearling wethers; turniped by many, and sold in the wool. **1847** *Jrnl. R. Agric. Soc.* VIII. II. 430 Those [sheep] in good condition, and off the best farms, are bought for turniping. **1868** *Ibid.* Ser. II. IV. II. 350 Not a few 'Penrith hoggs' are turniped in Dumfries.

‖**Turnix** ('tɜːnɪks). *Ornith.* [mod.L. (Bonnaterre, 1790), app. shortened from L. *coturnix* quail.] A genus of quail-like birds (also called *Hemipodius*: see HEMIPOD); the bush-quails.

1819 STEPHENS in Shaw *Gen. Zool.* XI. 388 Black-fronted Turnix... Turnix with the forehead with three fasciæ. *Ibid.* 389 Black-necked Turnix. **1869** GILLMORE tr. *Figuier's Rept. & Birds* (1870) 392 The Turnix are [*sic*] closely allied to the Quails.

turnkey ('tɜːnkiː). [f. TURN *v.* + KEY *sb.*]

1. One who has charge of the keys of a prison; a jailer, *esp.* a subordinate; also *transf.*

1654 H. L'ESTRANGE *Chas. I* (1655) 106 Mr. Atturney was turn-key, *pro tempore*, and let them in single at one door. **1680** C. NESSE *Church Hist.* 31 God..vouchsaf'd to be Noah's turnkey. **1791** BOSWELL *Johnson* an. 1780 (1848) 649/1 Mr. Akerman..ordered the outer turnkey upon no account to open the gate. **1864** MRS. CARLYLE *Lett.* (1883) III. 232 He bowed to the judge, and walked away with the turnkey. **1878** SPURGEON *Treas. Dav.* Ps. cv. 20 When God means to enlarge his prisoners, kings become his turnkeys.

2. a. ? A burglar's implement for turning from the outside a key left in the door. ? *Obs.* **b.** A tooth-key, formerly used in dentistry; a tooth-wrest.

1803 *Sporting Mag.* XXII. 126 A Bow-street officer found a little loose powder, a turnkey, and some other trifling articles. **1855** P. T. BARNUM *Life* vi. 91 The pseudo-dentist went to work, and by dint of hammer, pincers, and 'turnkeys', he extracted the twenty teeth. **1877** KNIGHT *Dict. Mech.*, *Turnkey*, an instrument to extract teeth; not much used now.

3. Used *attrib.* to designate a contract, system, etc., whereby the contractor undertakes to supply or install a complete product or service that is ready for immediate use.

1934 WEBSTER, Turn-key job. **1958** *Times* 16 Dec. 6/5 The station, which is to supply the colony's rapidly growing needs, is being built on a 'turnkey' contract by the English Electric Company, which is supplying all the electrical plant. **1964** *Times Rev. Industry* Feb. 48/2 It now has a reputation for successful completion of contracts on a 'turnkey' basis, starting from a survey of the geology of the country concerned and ending with the handing over of a complete factory with trained staff. **1966** *Economist* 5 Mar. 925/1 The so-called 'turnkey' factories, bought ready to go into production and wholly on credit. **1979** *Personal Computer World* Nov. 32 (Advt.), We offer a variety of turnkey systems. **1980** *Nature* 24 Apr. 657/2 A standard PWR reactor of the type sold by Westinghouse all over the world under turn-key contract. **1984** *Christian Science Monitor* 2 Mar. 17/1 One likely institutional change is the construction of 'turnkey' nuclear power plants.

†**'turnkind**, *sb.* and *v.* *Obs.* In 6 tornekynde. [f. TURN *v.* 35 + KIND *sb.* 3.] A nonce rendering of *transubstantiation*, *transubstantiate*.

1548 GESTE *Pr. Masse* B ij, Nowe to transubstantiatyon, or tornekynde. *Ibid.* B v b, What can be more effectually & expresselye spoken agaynste tornekynde, then thys the rehersed Englysshed sentence of Augustyne? *Ibid.* B vij b, Yf say they yᵉ bred nature were not tornekynded vnto christes body: why dyd he name it hys bodye? *Ibid.* C j b, Some of our catholiques do contend yᵗ the sayd tornekinding must be nedes granted as right certayn & godly.

turn-off ('tɜːnɒf). Also turnoff. [f. the verbal phr. *turn off* (TURN *v.* 74).] **1.** A turning off a main road; a side road; a junction where a track or road branches off a main road.

1881 'R. BOLDREWOOD' *Robbery under Arms* (1888) III. xvii. 255 It's the wrong turn-off that makes a man lose his way. **1894** J. WINSOR *Cartier to Frontenac* 151 The turn off at Lake Athabasca..would have conducted him to the northern tributaries of the Columbia. **1949** F. SARGESON *I saw it in my Dream* xv. 237 The boss managed to keep the sheep nicely bunched together until he'd pushed them past the turn-off. **1955** E. BOWEN *World of Love* xi. 221 The road due soon to go on without them to Galway, for soon would be coming the Turn Off. **1977** *Times of Zambia* 7 Sept. 5/5 The premises situate at Lukashya turn-off, Mungwi Road. **1980** *Beautiful British Columbia* Summer 20 Access to Golden Ears Park is from a turnoff at Haney.

2. Disposal (of cattle) at market; the number or quantity marketed.

1960 *Times* 1 Oct. 7/7 The Territory's annual turn-off of 150,000 cattle. **1961** in *Webster* s.v. *turnoff*, Average annual turnoff of fat bullocks. **1969** *Northern Territory News* (Darwin) *Focus '69* 30/3 Last year the turn-off from the Alice Springs pastoral district was more than 20,500 head, earning more than $2,750,000.

3. The action or an instance of turning (something) off, stopping, or causing to cease functioning.

1967 *Technology Week* 23 Jan. 52/1 (Advt.), Each satellite was cycled through turn-off, cold soak, and restart during approximately 53 eclipses of the sun. **1970** *Globe & Mail* (Toronto) 25 Sept. 1/1 'It's inconvenient, but it's bearable,' she said of the electricity turnoffs. **1974** R. S. BRAY in *Ciba Symposium* No. 20. 97 Another possible mechanism for the 'turn off' of the cellular immune system is a viraemia. **1978** S. BRILL *Teamsters* iii. 104 Hicks attributed Kleindienst's unusual turnoff of the investigation to 'the love affair between Fitzsimmons and Nixon'.

4. Something that repels, disgusts, or 'turns one off' (see TURN *v.* 74 h). *colloq.*

1975 *N.Y. Times* 1 Nov. 18/1 Patrons dined on cervelle Grenobloise. 'Sounds better in French,' said the chef... 'Brains is a turn-off.' **1976** *National Observer* (U.S.) 13 Mar. 6/6 Should it become unpleasant or prove a turn-off to either, they stop the game. **1982** *Listener* 23 & 30 Dec. 48/1 At first impression, this uneasy blend of piano quintet and violin sonata..was a gigantic, four-square turn-off.

turn-on ('tɜːnɒn). [f. the verbal phr. *turn on* (TURN *v.* 75).] **1.** The action or an instance of turning something on; activation.

1962 SIMPSON & RICHARDS *Physical Princ. Junction Transistors* vii. 145 It thus produces a further delay in the turn-on of the transistor. **1967** *Technology Week* 23 Jan. 12/2 Availability of the eight new satellites in orbit, assuming proper operation after turn-on..should provide the U.S. with an estimated 95% certainty of continuous service for shorter path lengths and about 89% for longer-haul traffic. **1969** A. M. CAMPBELL *Episomes* ii. 19 Gene *Q* is not required for DNA synthesis, but is necessary for normal turn-on of late phage genes.

2. The action or an instance of turning somebody on; a drug-taker's 'trip'; something which or someone who arouses interest, enthusiasm, or sexual response. *slang.*

1969 FABIAN & BYRNE *Groupie* (1970) xxi. 138 There is enough in one bottle for two turn-ons. **1969** *Telegraph* (Brisbane) 3 June 12/2, I think I'm more of a turn-on now than I ever was when I was trying to conform to that curvy image. **1969** *Sunday Mail Mag.* (Brisbane) 22 June 11/5 Other turn-ons are music.., qualities of appearance or character.., and straight-out sex. **1975** *N.Y. Times* 1 Nov. 15/3 A museum spokesman said nearly 50,000 people visited the galleries during the first 25 days. 'It's been a real turn-on,' she said. **1978** J. KRANTZ *Scruples* iii. 81 Masturbation isn't a great big turn-on in my life. **1982** D. HOCKNEY in S. Spender *China Diary* 189 A medieval city is unstimulating to me, whereas to others it might be a great turn-on.

3. *attrib.*

1967 *Electronics* 6 Mar. 133/2 A desirable feature of this circuit is that the turn-on time of the relay is very sharp. **1972** G. S. HOLT in T. Kochman *Rappin' & Stylin' Out* 204 This 'turn-on' ability in terms of communication style.

turnor, -our, obs. ff. TURNER, TOURNEYER.

†**turnour.** *Obs. rare*⁻¹. [irreg. ad. OF. *tourneure* TOURNURE.] A piece of turned work.

1382 WYCLIF *1 Kings* vi. 18 With cedre al the hows with ynforth was clothid, hauynge his turnours, and his iunctions forgid.

turn-out ('tɜːnaʊt), *sb.* (*a.*) Also turnout. [f. the verbal phr. *turn out* (TURN *v.* 76).]

A. *sb.* **1.** A turning out or getting out (of bed, etc.); hence, a call to duty, esp. during one's period of rest; *spec. Mil.* a signal to rise (? *obs.*).

1688 R. HOLME *Armoury* III. xix. (Roxb.) 154/2 The seuerall Beates or points of warre are these...13. A Turn out. **1815** SCOTT *Guy M.* xxxix, Is he always fit for duty upon a sudden turn-out? **1848** THACKERAY *Van. Fair* xxx, The bugles were sounding the turn-out. **1873** *Routledge's Yng. Gentl. Mag.* July 482/1 A sudden turn-out during his watch below.

2. a. A withdrawal of workmen from their place of employment by common consent; a strike.

1806 *Docum. Hist. Amer. Industr. Soc.* (1910) III. 74 In a little time there came a turn-out to raise the wages... They would grant me no quarters at all, but I must turn out. **1834** HT. MARTINEAU *Moral* II. 55 To show how tremendous is the waste of capital in a turn-out. **1835** URE *Philos. Manuf.* 283, I have had several turn-outs, and have heard of many more, but never heard of a turn-out for short time. **1837** WHITTOCK, etc. *Bk. Trades* (1842) 430 A..turn out which proved instructively unavailing, and was utterly disastrous to their funds. **1898** W. WHITE *Jrnls.* 15 Much discussion in shop, relative to the turn-out; refused to join.

b. One of a body of strikers.

1826 *Examiner* 663/2 Skirmishes..between the turn-outs and those whom they call 'knobsticks'. **1842** R. OASTLER *Fleet Papers* II. 286 The failure of 'the Strike' will be attributable..to divisions in the camp of the 'turn-outs'. **1848** MRS. GASKELL *M. Barton* xxi, One of the poor, maddened turn-outs.

3. Those who turn out or assemble for any purpose; an assemblage, muster; also, a turning out or assembling of persons; *spec.* (the number of) those who turn out to vote in an election.

1816 CHALMERS *Let.* in *Life* (1851) II. 78, I met with several people here, and had a turn out of population from several of the houses. **1819** *Sporting Mag.* V. 54 The circumstances..account..for the small turn-out of sportsmen. **1843** LE FEVRE *Life Trav. Phys.* III. II. x. 5 Compared with the turn-out in Hyde Park in the season, it sinks into insignificance. **1880** *Antrim & Down Gloss.*, *The Hurries*, a term for the Irish Rebellion of 1798. Called also the *Turn-out.* **1901** *Scotsman* 1 Mar. 8/1 The turnout was much larger than might have been expected. **1970** *Guardian* 20 June 15/5 Only one of the five polls gave full weighting..to differential turnout—the question of how many Labour or Conservative supporters will in fact bother to vote. **1976** *New Yorker* 15 Nov. 204/2 Only eighty per cent of the Democratic turnout voted for Carter. **1976** *Honolulu Star-Bull.* 21 Dec. A-2/4 He called his committeemen into party headquarters on the day after elections and made them account for the turnout in their wards.

4. A loop-line or siding in a railway or tramway; also, in a narrow road, a part wider than the rest, or a short side road, to enable vehicles to pass one another; a similar place in a canal.

1824 T. G. CUMMING *Rail & Tram Roads* 16 A pointer, fixed at the intersection between the principal rail and the turn out,..to open the way into the turn out, and shut that along the road. **1826** *Act 7 Geo. IV*, c. 49 §38 Passing-places or turn-outs, for the purpose of enabling waggons, carts, and other carriages drawn along the said [L'pool and Manch.] railway or tram road to pass each other. **1898** *Westm. Gaz.* 31 May 6/3 A canal..with locks at each end, and suitable turnouts.

5. A place where animals may be turned out to graze.

1895 *Queenslander* 7 Dec. 1090 There was not a turnout for a carrier from Westwood to Tambo, a distance of fully 300 miles,..the marsupials having cleared the pasture off the face of the country. **1901** *19th Cent.* July 59 The cottager could get fuel..with a turn-out for a cow, pig,.. donkey and geese.

6. A turning or clearing out; a clearance, emptying.

1856 MISS YONGE *Daisy Chain* xiv, You must make interest with Margaret for the turn-out of my pocket tomorrow. **1857** HUGHES *Tom Brown* II. iii, A regular turn-out of the den.

7. a. The manner in which anything is turned out or equipped; style of equipment; 'get-up'; also *concr.* equipment, outfit, array.

1812 COL. HAWKER *Diary* (1893) I. 46 Their 'turns-out' of horses and harness are beggarly. **1825** *Sporting Mag.* XV. 355 The turn-out of himself and his horse is 'quite the thing'. **1859** JEPHSON *Brittany* x. 171 On a holiday..the whole turn-out would be much more dressy. **1883** *Harper's Mag.* Aug. 378/2 The parishioners coming to mass in their best turn-outs. **1901** *Scotsman* 1 Mar. 8/1 The significant feature of their turn out, however, was that they carried, not the cavalry carbine, but the infantry service rifle.

b. *tea and turn out* (cf. TEA *sb.* 4), tea and something with it; tea and accompaniments.

1806 *Francis Lett.* (1901) II. 638 We brought the Irish custom of suppers into fashion,..for last year they only gave tea and turn out. **1830** H. ANGELO *Remin.* II. 184 This was not tea and turn out, but tea and walk up stairs. **1858** RAMSAY *Remin.* v. (1870) 120, I hope you will sport it..at your first tea and turn out.

8. A driving equipage; a carriage with its horse or horses, and other adjuncts. Also *transf.*

1817 LADY MORGAN *France* (1818) I. 258 No man.. founds his celebrity..upon the superior excellence and appointment of his turn-out. **1842** THACKERAY *Sultan Stork* Wks. 1900 V. 750 Egad! what a neat turn-out of a barge! **1856** KANE *Arct. Expl.* I. xvii. 211 Quite a neat turn-out of sledge and dogs. **1891** 'J. S. WINTER' *Mrs. Bob* 19 The sort of coach-man that you get in London with a turn-out from the job-master's. **1895** *Daily News* 13 July 5/4 A special prize will be given for the best turn-out of donkey and barrow.

9. The quantity of anything turned out or produced in an industry, etc.; the total product; output.

1879 *Spons' Encycl. Manuf.* I. 10 If a large turn-out is necessary, carbonization may be effected in twelve or thirteen hours. **1884** LD. BRAMWELL in *Law Rep.* 9 *App. Cases* 203 The actual turnout was over one million a year.

B. *attrib.* or as *adj.* That turns out, or is turned out, in various senses.

1899 *Westm. Gaz.* 11 Feb. 7/1 A slashed velvet jacket with a Manx turn-out collar. **1908** *Daily Chron.* 9 Jan. 7/2 The 'turn-out' switch rings electric bells in every room in the building [fire station]. **1909** *Toilers of Deep* Sept. 225/1 As we are working on 'turn out' tides, we must be up betimes to embark on the outward turn... The men turn out..at one o'clock in the morning.

turn-over ('tɜːn,əʊvə(r)), *sb.* and *a.* Also **turnover.** [f. the verbal phr. *turn over* (TURN *v.* 78).]

A. *sb.* **1. a.** The action of turning over, in various senses: see quots.; *spec.* in *Polit. slang*, a transference of votes from one party to another.

1660 F. BROOKE tr. *Le Blanc's Trav.* 365 Dancers on the rope, standing with their head down, and feet up, with a thousand Turn-overs, and Gamboles. **1825** J. NEAL *Bro. Jonathan* II. 62 The turn-over proved quite a relief to the company. **1868** A. K. H. BOYD *Less. Mid. Age* 279 The music was good, after the choir got themselves settled to their work. But if I were Dean of Wells, there should be a thorough turn-over. **1895** G. W. E. RUSSELL in *Forum* (N.Y.) Oct. 160 No very sweeping change of opinion—no very considerable turnover of votes.

b. The point at which it is necessary to turn over a gramophone record; a break in play at the end of a side of a record.

1931 *Times Educ. Suppl.* 12 Dec. 1/3 With almost incredible perversity the engineers have made the turn-over not at the beginning of the Scherzo, but at the *piu mosso.* **1976** *Gramophone* Apr. 1603/3 Now that DG have put the whole work on to one disc,..there is a turn-over in the 'Gretchen' movement (it comes at the beginning of the fourth bar after letter G).

2. An apprentice whose indentures are transferred to another master on the retirement or failure of his original one; also, the action or process of turning over an apprentice. Now *dial.*

1631 HEYWOOD *1st Pt. Fair Maid of West* II. i. Wks. 1874 II. 276 *Bess.* Your olde Master..hath turn'd over your yeares to me. *Clem.* Right forsooth: before he was a Vintner, hee was a shoo-maker, and left two or three turne-overs more besides my selfe. **1666** in *Eng. Gilds* (1870) Introd. 161 *note*, Supernumerary Apprentices and Turn-overs, which have increased the number [of printers] almost to twice as many. **1708** *Constit. Waterman's Co.* xii. 24 Every Apprentice, whose Master and Mistress shall happen to dye ..shall..apply himself to the Rulers,..and..be by them.. turned over to some other able and fit Master or Mistress,.. by Indorsing such Turn-over upon his Indenture of Apprentiship. **1886** T. FROST *Remin. Country Journalist* v. (1888) 52 A 'turn-over', that is, an apprentice who, after serving a portion of his term, is transferred to another employer.

3. Any thing or part which is turned or folded over. †**a.** ? In a cork shoe, a welt which is turned over the insole; also a shoe with such a welt. *Obs.* **b.** The flap of an envelope; a leaf of a book, etc. **c.** An article that begins in the last column of a newspaper page and continues overleaf. **d.** *Printing.* (See quots. 1938, 1956.)

1611 COTGR., *Bord*,..the welt, or turneouer of a corke shoe. **1630** in Welford *Hist. Newcastle* (1887) III. 298 Stall rooms—of Mark Milbank, for himself for a turnover, 3[s]. **1829** *Yng. Lady's Bk.* 338 A very small bit of wax may be dropped beneath the turn-over of the letter. *Ibid.* 340 These envelopes..resemble a sort of pocket; the ends are closed, and the turn-over is sealed in the usual way, after the enclosure is inserted. **1842** S. LOVER *Handy Andy* ii, He caught some words that were on the last turn-over of the sheet. **1883** (*title*) 'Turnovers' from 'The Globe'. **1899** ROBERTON *Kipling Guide Bk.* 52 'Turn-overs', so called from the sketch ('turning over' to the second page) by Mr. Kipling. **1938** L. M. HARROD *Librarians' Gloss.* 652 *Turn-over*, an extension of printed matter, beyond the space allotted. **1956** *Bookman's Conc. Dict.* 44/1 *Break line*, the last line of a paragraph not spaced full out to the measure; also known as..Turn Over. **1981** I. A. GORDON in *N.Z. Listener* 14–20 Feb., I am well aware that newspaper columns are narrow and that words must consequently be broken up into two bits, joined by a hyphen at the end of the first line. This necessity is known by printers as the 'turn-over'.

4. a. A linen band or the like worn round the neck and turned down; a turn-down collar or neck-band.

1716–20 *Lett. fr. Mist's Jrnl.* (1722) I. 204 Curious Linnen, made up into very fine Turnovers, Necks, and Ruffles. **1802** JAMES *Milit. Dict.*, *Turnover*, a piece of white linen which is worn by the soldiers belonging to the British cavalry over their stocks, about half an inch deep. Three turnovers per annum are ordered to be provided. **1825** HONE *Every-day Bk.* I. 158 The 'turnovers' worn by the beaus of those days [1770] with 'ruffles'.

b. *local.* A small shawl worn by women.

1891 QUILLER COUCH *Noughts & Crosses, Gifts F. Himkoff* 206 She wore a violet turnover.

5. A kind of tart in which the fruit is laid on one half of the rolled out paste, and the other half turned over it; a child's sweetmeat resembling this. Also *attrib.* as *turn-over shop.*

1798 *Sporting Mag.* XI. 176 An old woman..preparing her turnovers, commonly called apple-pies. **1825** S. R. in Hone *Every-day Bk.* I. 1291 Our 'tart' and 'turn-over' shop. **1847** in HALLIWELL. **1882** *Gd. Words* 606 Venison pasties and apple turnovers and runlets of ale. **1892** *Star* 24 Dec. 3/2 There were sweets called turnovers, in which were coins of various values.

6. a. The total amount of business done in a given time; also, the amount of goods produced and disposed of by a manufacturer; also, the 'turning over' of the capital involved in a business; also, the net profit derived from a business in a given time; in extended sense, the amount or number of anything (or of persons) dealt with, processed, etc.; the throughput; ***turnover tax***, a tax on the turnover of a business.

1879 ESCOTT *England* I. 391 On this large turn-over the gross profit averages 8¼ per cent. **1880** *Daily News* 10 Dec. 5/7 The Blarney mills make a great 'turn over' of tweed. **1883** BLOOMFIELD *Fisheries Irel.* 13 (Fish. Exhib. Publ.) The great trading motto of low price and large and quick turn overs. **1894** *Brit. Jrnl. Photogr.* XLI. 5 The cost of production, unless very carefully managed, runs the turnover very close. **1911** G. B. SHAW *Doctor's Dilemma* Pref. p. xxvi, The sixpenny doctor, with his low prices and quick turnover of patients,..makes much more than you do. **1920** *Manch. Guardian* 28 Dec. 11/5 A turnover tax operates whether the transaction is a profit or a loss. **1938** *Sun* (Baltimore) 13 Sept. 3/1 Under the old paper-ballot system the turnover was many times faster. **1944** *Ibid.* 15 June 20/8 It is only by speeding up the rate of turn-over that, with our depleted staff, we are able to deliver practically as many babies as in [a] normal period. **1973** E. OSERS tr. *Waldheim's Austrian Example* ii. 30 Economic recovery required..the application of a severe austerity programme which involved ..the introduction of a turn-over tax. **1976** *Howard Jrnl.* XV. I. 43 The subject-matter is the frequency of remands for medical reports..in relation to the total turnover of magistrates' courts.

b. The simultaneous synthesis and degradation of a substance in a living organism; ***turnover rate, time*** (see quot. 1943).

1943 *Jrnl. Gen. Physiol.* XXVI. 326 *Turnover.*—This term refers to the process of renewal of a given substance... *Turnover rate*..is the amount of the substance that is turned over by that tissue per unit of time... *Turnover time*..is the time required for the appearance or disappearance of an amount of that substance equal to the amount of that substance present in the tissue. **1961** *Times* 3 Feb. 19/7 In health the myelin sheath is a stable tissue element with little or no evidence of metabolic turnover. **1967** M. E. HALE *Biol. Lichens* iv. 58 Slow rates of protein turnover might well be a characteristic of all lichens. **1977** P. B. & J. S. MEDAWAR *Life Sci.* x. 84 The turnover rate of bodily constituents varies widely from tissue to tissue. **1982** S. G. CHANEY in T. M. Devlin *Textbk. Biochem.* xxv. 1180 The turnover of body protein is a normal process.

c. The number of employees leaving a workforce and being replaced, change of staff.

1955 *Times* 7 June 7/3 The plan was also expected to reduce labour turnover since a qualifying period would be —or should be —needed to secure the guarantee. **1956** W. H. WHYTE *Organization Man* I. v. 58 Employees like it and absence and turnover are low. **1963** E. P. THOMPSON *Making of Eng. Working Class* viii. 246 The labour turnover in the early engineering workshops was prodigious; Galloway, who employed eighty or ninety men in 1824, claimed to have had between 1,000 and 1,500 men pass through his works in the previous twelve years; that is more than a total turnover of the labour force *per annum.* **1977** W. B. EBERHARD in Bond & McLeod *Newslett. to Newspapers* II. 149 Postal rates soared..and personnel turnovers were unusually high.

7. *U.S. Sport.* The (unintended) loss of possession of the ball to the opposing team.

1969 *Eugene* (Oregon) *Register-Guard* 3 Dec. 1 D/3 Not often does a team commit 27 turnovers and win, but South Eugene did just that. **1975** *New Yorker* 7 Apr. 108/2 Similarly, in their other defensive ploys the Knicks' object was to harass their opponents into committing turnovers —that is, losing the ball by making wayward passes or committing technical infractions. **1979** *Tucson* (Arizona) *Citizen* 20 Sept. 11D/2 Four turnovers took the Ducks out of the contest.

B. *adj.* That turns or is turned over, as ***turnover apprentice, collar, hand, lip, majority***: cf. senses above; **turnover article** = sense 3 c; **turnover board** *Founding*, a flat board on which a flat-bottomed pattern or half-pattern may be stood for sand to be rammed round it; **turnover boiler**: see quot. 1877; **turnover cartridge**, a gramophone cartridge with a pivoted mounting for two styluses for use at different speeds; **turnover concern, gear**: see quots.; **turnover rake**, a hay-rake which, when full, turns over and deposits its collection; **turnover-table**, a table with hinged top: see quot.; also a table with a sliding panel prepared for use as a draught-board or the like when reversed (*Cent. Dict.* 1891).

1605 P. ERONDELLE *French Garden* i. sig. D 8[v], Send for the shoomaker that he may haue againe these turn-ouer shooes, for they be too high. **1747** H. GLASSE *Art of Cookery* ii. 25 Close the two Ends of your Paper as you do a Turnover Tart. **1836** DICKENS *Sk. Boz* 1st Ser. I. 238 Soiled buff boots with turnover red tops. **1849** CRAIG, *Turnover-table*, a sort of small table, the top of which..may be turned over perpendicularly when out of use, thus occupying less room. **1859** *Autobiog. Beggar Boy* 113 There was no opening for a turnover apprentice. *a* **1861** T. WINTHROP *Life in Open Air* (1863) 318 In jacket and turn-over collar. **1864** WEBSTER s.v., A turn-over collar. **1874** F. G. LEE *Man. Cleric.* 7 The Chalice should never have turn-over lips. **1877** KNIGHT *Dict. Mech.*, *Turn-over Boiler*, a form of boiler in which the flues were turned over the fire-box or furnace. *Ibid.*, *Turn-over Gear*,..an application of machinery for hauling up logs from the saw-mill to the log-carriage, or turning the log on the carriage after slabbing one side. **1883** *Daily News* 20 July 6/1 Messrs. Riches and Watts's turn-over gathering rake. **1888** *Lockwood's Dict. Mech. Engin.* 391 *Turn over board*, a board used for ramming a pattern upon. **1892** *Labour Commission Gloss.*, *Turn-over Concerns*, mills and machinery..turned over to a limited liability company. **1913** *Daily Graphic* 24 Mar. 13/1 Nearly all the women were wearing low turn-over collars in colour, with flowing Quartier Latin ties. **1928** W. RAWLINSON *Mod. Foundry Operations & Equipment* xiii. 168 A method adopted in certain instances of repetition work..is that of a 'turnover board', also termed 'bottom board' or 'joint board'. **1944** *Penguin New Writing* XXII. 142 *Moby Dick* marks the turnover point where balance was perhaps precariously achieved. **1952** H. HERD *March of Journalism* vi. 82 The third column had a turnover article giving a retrospect of political events since the beginning of the year. **1958** *Spectator* 20 June 795/1, I was glad to see *The Times* coming out so strongly, in Monday's 'turnover' article, against recent abuses by the courts of their Contempt powers. **1958** *Practical Wireless* XXXIV. 57/2 (Advt.), Latest type lightweight crystal pick-ups with turn-over cartridge. **1962** A. NISBETT *Technique Sound Studio* 264 The pick-up head may consist of a turnover cartridge having styli for coarse and fine groove records on the two sides. **1964** S. CRAWFORD *Basic Engin. Processes* (1969) x. 238 The flat face of the pattern is placed on a turnover board and a suitable size moulding box..is placed over it. **1978** *Rugby World* Apr. 59/2 (Advt.), Best quality stretch nylon socks in plain colours and turn-over tops.

†**turnover**, erroneous for *turnour*, TURNER[2].

1640 *Burgh Rec. Glasgow* (1876) I. 422 Thretie dollours and ane halfe of good dollours, and alevine and ane halfe of turnovers, quhilk sall be put in the touns commoune chist to bee applayed *ad pios usus.* **1679** R. CAMERON in Herkless *Life* (1896) 111 For suffering, that man will confine in the breadth of a turnover that that he will suffer for.

turnpike ('tɜːnpaɪk), *sb.* Forms: see TURN *v.* and PICK *sb.*[1], PIKE *sb.*[1]; also 5–7 *Sc.* **-pik**, 6 *Sc.* **-pek**, 7 *Sc.* **-pecke, -pyck**; 7–8 **turn(e)-peg.** [f. TURN- + PICK *sb.*[1], PIKE *sb.*[1]]

I. 1. *Hist.* A spiked barrier fixed in or across a road or passage, as a defence against sudden attack, esp. of men on horseback.

It does not appear certain how this was originally constructed, or how it acted; later writers identify it with the CHEVAL DE FRISE (see quotations 1704–1716), but the other senses suggest that in older use the axis was vertical.

c **1420** *Siege of Rouen* in *Collect. Lond. Cit.* (Camden) 17 He made a dyche of grete coste, Pyght with stakys that wolde perysce, With turnepykys, and with many an hers. *c* **1425** WYNTOUN *Cron.* VIII. 5716 Þan a staf tuk Wate of Curry, And set vndyr þe portculyce, þat cum down it mycht on na wise. Syne þe crelis and colis wiþe all Apon þe turn-pik [*v. rr.* turnepike, -pyk] let he fal. And ane þan blew a horne in hy. **1477** *Paston Lett.* III. 203 My lord hath do brokyn all the passages excep Newham bryge, weche is wached, and the turne pyke shette every nyght. **1543** WALLOP in *St. Papers Hen. VIII*, IX. 454 There was 2 horsemen of Mr. Bowlmers companey taken, which went over at Marguyson, notwithstanding the turnpike, being then there sett on with certen horsemen of Bullen, were constrayned to take the ryver, where as it is saied never any hath passed. **1545** ASCHAM *Toxoph.* (Arb.) 88 At the Turne pike besyde Hammes where they turned with so fewe Archers, so many Frenchemen to flight. **1577–87** HOLINSHED *Chron.* (1807) III. 103 A large trench..pight full of sharpe stakes, with a great rampire fensed with bulworks, and turnepikes. **1642** *Relat. Action bef. Cirencester* 4 Each end of the high street.. was secured against Horse with strong slaght-boomes which our men call Turne-pikes. **1644** in Rushw. *Hist. Coll.* III. II. 739 They had no Drawbridge but only a Turnpyke. **1704** J. HARRIS *Lex. Techn.* I, *Turn-Pikes* in the Art of War, are Spars of Wood of 12 or 14 Foot long, and about 6 Inches diameter in a sexangular Form: They are bored with holes.. six Inches one from another, but to go by turns from each side, the Pickets that are driven into the hole[s], are 6 or 5 Foot long, pointed with Iron. **1711** *Milit. & Sea Dict.* (ed. 4), *Chevaux de Frise*,..the same as Turnpikes,..one being the French, the other the English Name, yet both indifferently now used in England, and the French rather the most. **1716** PERRY *St. Russia* 47 The Czar having disposed his Army behind a Line of Chevaux de Frize, or Turn-pikes shod with Iron,..maintain'd so regular and strong a fire, that [etc.]. **1724** DE FOE *Mem. Cavalier* I. 108 Coming up to the Turn-pike, I found it defended by 200 Musqueteers.

†**b.** *transf.* and *fig.* in various applications. *Obs.*

a **1616** BEAUMONT *Antiplatonic* v, Love stormes his lips, and takes the fortresse in, For all the bristled turn-pikes of his chin. **1641** G. H. *Wit's Recreat.* X vj, He hath such subtile turnes and nookes, Such turne-pegs, mazes, tenter-hookes. **1661** FELTHAM *Resolves* II. xxix. (ed. 8) 241 It makes a man a Turn-pike, that will be sure to prick you, which side soever you come on. **1661** K. W. *Conf. Charac.*, *Covetous Usurer* (1860) 74 That Fryday face of his, whose rowsey whiskers and brischy turn-pikes make him resemble some shaggy meteor, or some borish Turk. **1665** HOOKE *Microgr.* l. 205 Each of these legs were bestuck..with multitudes of small hairs, or (if we respect the proportion they bore to the bigness of the leg) turnpikes. **1679** V. ALSOP *Melius Inquir.* I. i. 77 He that..shall thrust other men upon the turn-pikes of sin, and force them to act against their light.

†**2.** A horizontal cross of timber turning on a vertical pin, set up to exclude horse-traffic from a foot-way: a turnstile. *Obs.*

1547 in J. R. Boyle *Hedon* (1875) App. 135 For makynge on hoppe to the tornepyke, iiij.d. **1600** W. KEMP *Nine Days' Wonder* D j, The Cittizens [of Norwich] had caused all the turne-pikes to be taken vp..that I might not be hindred. **1626** B. JONSON *Staple of N.* III. i, I moue vpon my axell, like a turne-pike. **1684–5** in Willis & Clark *Cambridge* (1886) II. 642 Painting the bears and Turnepikes in the entrance to the New walke. **1755** JOHNSON, *Turnpike*,..a cross of two bars armed with pikes at the end, and turning on a pin, fixed to hinder horses from entering.

†**3.** A barrier across a water-course or stream; a water-gate, allowing the water to flow, but

obstructing cattle; also, a lock on a navigable stream. Also ***turnpike-lock*** (see 9). *Obs.*

1623-4 *Act 21 Jas. I*, c. 32 §1 To open prepare or make all Weares and Lockes or Turnepickes fitt for the said Passage. *Ibid.*, To make and erect any Wharfes Lockes or Turnepickes or Pennes for Water. **1677** PLOT *Oxfordsh.* 233 Where the declivity of the Channel, and fall of water is so great, that few barges could live in the passage of them, there we have Turn-pikes. **1702** *Act 1 Anne* St. II. c. 11 §2 Altering the said Wharfs Sluces Wears Sasses Locks Turnpikes or Pens for Water or Passages. **1751** *Act 24 Geo. II*, c. 8 §2 Tenants or Occupiers of all Locks, Weirs, Bucks, Winches, Turnpikes, Dams, Flood-Gates.

4. a. A barrier (orig. of the nature of a turnpike in sense 2, later a gate or gates) placed across a road to stop passage till the toll is paid; a toll-gate. Cf. TURNSTILE. Now chiefly *Hist.*

a **1678** [see b]. **1695-6** *Act 7 & 8 Will. III*, c. 9 §4 The Place for collecting the said Toll to be in some convenient Place upon the said Highway..by setting up a Turnpike or otherwise. **1705** *Lond. Gaz.* No. 4125/4 Whoever..gives Notice to Mr. John Baker, Keeper of the Turn-Pipe [*sic*] aforesaid,..shall have a Guinea Reward. **1723** MANDEVILLE *Fab. Bees* (1725) I. 365 A poor Traveller that at every Ten Miles end is stop'd by a Turnpike. **1771** SMOLLETT *Humph. Cl.* 26 June, Considering the tax we pay for turnpikes, the roads of this country constitute a most intolerable grievance. **1806** *Chron.* 23 Feb., in *Ann. Reg.* (1808) 375/2 Close to Oxford-street turnpike. **1829** *Chapters Phys. Sc.* 58 The weighing-machine is formed of a combination of levers.. and is commonly used at turnpikes in weighing waggons, to ascertain that they are not loaded beyond what is allowed by law to the breadth of their wheels. **1845** MᶜCULLOCH *Taxation* Introd. (1852) 33 Turnpikes being erected only on the principal roads, the old plan for keeping up cross or parish roads [by statute labour, or at the cost of the parish] was not affected by their institution. **1885** *Act 48 & 49 Vict.* c. 37 §5 The provisions now in force respecting turnpikes and tolls [etc.]..shall continue in force until Parliament otherwise provides.

b. *transf.* and *fig.*

a **1678** MARVELL *Growth Popery* 11 It will suffer no man to pass without paying at their Turn-pikes. **1730** FIELDING *Rape upon Rape* II. ii. 16 The Laws are Turnpikes, only made to stop People who walk on Foot. **1745** *Season. Adv. Protest.* 38 A Tax to the Priests, for suffering them to pass the Turnpike of Purgatory. **1765** FOOTE *Commissary* II. i, He capers through a whole region of turnpegs. **1807** OPIE in *Lect. Paint.* ii. (1848) 271 The possessors..had..been often denied the usual road to eminence:..they defrauded the turnpike, and conducted their silent march another way.

c. *dial.* A wire snare set by a poacher across a hare's or rabbit's run.

1879 JEFFERIES *Amateur Poacher* ii. 29 The blacksmith started the idea of putting up a 'turnpike',—i.e. a wire.

5. a. Elliptical for TURNPIKE ROAD; also *fig.* Now *Hist.* exc. *U.S.*

1748 DE FOE *Tour Gt. Brit.* II. 178 The Road is by this means so continually torn, that it is one of the worst Turnpikes round about London. **1756** *Demi-Rep* 10 You may ride the turnpike to her heart. **1796** BURKE *Regic. Peace* i. Wks. VIII. 124 There is a Minister from Denmark at Paris... We sent through this turnpike to demand a passport. **1802** *Debates in U.S. Congress* 25 Feb. (1850) 759 As plain as a turnpike. **1861** GEO. ELIOT *Silas M.* i, [Raveloe] was nestled in a snug well-wooded hollow, quite an hour's journey on horseback from any turnpike. **1875** W. MCILWRAITH *Guide Wigtownshire* 77 Here the turnpike winds along a terrace hewn from the hillside. **1950** *Sun* (Baltimore) 2 June 10/5 One route will be recommended for the turnpike. **1965** *New Statesman* 5 Nov. 713/1 The good, fast, safe roads are toll roads, called in New England by the old name of turnpikes. **1977** *New Yorker* 3 Oct. 43/1 Halfway up the Connecticut Turnpike, I slowed the car.

b. Short for *turnpike trust* (see 9) or the like.

1728 VANBR. & CIB. *Prov. Husb.* I. i, He won't sit long enough to give his Vote for a Turn-pike. **1773** *Observ. State Poor* 105 The roads of our nation are its standing opprobrium, the complaint and the jest of foreigners. The few, which under the direction of turnpikes, are justly exempted from this general censure or ridicule, only serve to facilitate the conveyance of provision to the capital.

†**6.** A turn-table on a railway. *Obs.*

1793 SMEATON *Edystone L.* §167 *note*, The carriage being turned a quarter round upon the Turnpike, or Turnrail.

7. *U.S.* A small cake used to raise bread: see quots. ? *local.*

1850 SUSAN WARNER *Wide, Wide World* xiv, I am scalding this meal with it to make turnpikes. **1850** *Knickerbocker Mag.* (N.Y.) July 83 (Thornton) Some little yellow cakes, called turnpikes, and used, I believe, for some purpose or other in baking bread.

II. 8. *Sc.* A staircase which winds round a central axis; a spiral or winding stair; later applied to other forms of staircase: cf. *turnpike stair, staircase* in 9.

1501 DOUGLAS *Pal. Hon.* III. xvii, A palice..with mony royall towris,..Pinnakillis, fyellis, turnpekkis mony one, Gilt birneist torris,..Skarsment, reprise, corbell, and battellingis. **1516** *Acc. Ld. High Treas. Scot.* V. 78 For the makin of ane turnpek in the palis of the Abbay Halyrudhous. **1546** LYNDESAY in *St. Papers Hen. VIII*, V. 560 Normond Leslie and his cumpanye met hym [Cdl. Beaton] in þe turnpyk þer off, and slew hym. **1552** *Acc. Ld. High Treas. Scot.* X. 91 Item, foure lokkis put in the ȝett, ȝard ȝett, and durris of the tway turnpykis of my lord governouris lugeing of the Kirk of Feild..iij li. *c* **1590** J. STEWART *Poems* (S.T.S.) II. 55/93 Butt and ben he bends from bour to bour, Vp turnpyks, turats, And from tour to tour. **1600** *Gowrie Conspir.* in *Harl. Misc.* (Malh.) II. 343 The Earle of Gowrie and his seruants made them for another way vp a quyet turnpyke, which..was onlie then left open, as appeared for that purpose. **1643** in A. Maxwell *Hist. Old Dundee* (1884) 213 [The Council] concludit that the turne-pyk upon the steeple be presently repaired. **1730** *Mem. Capt. Creichton* in *Swift's Wks.* (1869) 534/2 Steele suddenly opening the door, fired a blunderbuss down at the two dragoons as they were coming up the stairs; but the bullets, grazing against the side of the turnpike, only wounded and did not kill them. **1818** SCOTT *Rob Roy* xxii, The turnkey, who..led me up a 'turnpike' (so the Scotch call a winding stair). **1899** CROCKETT *Black Douglas* (1900) 106 He was upon the last step of the turnpike and at the entrance of the corridor.

III. 9. *attrib.* and *Comb.* (chiefly in sense 4), as ***turnpike act, bridge, -house, -keeper, -man, -people, -system, trust***; in sense 8, as ***turnpike foot, head, stair, staircase***; also **turnpike cake**: see sense 7; **turnpike-free** *a.*, free from tolls for passage; **turnpike gate**, †(*a*) a gate or door at the foot of a turnpike stair (*Sc.*); †(*b*) = sense 1; (*c*) = sense 4; †**turnpike-lock** = sense 3; **turnpike meeting**, a meeting of a turnpike trust; **turnpike sailor**, a beggar in the guise of a distressed sailor. See also TURNPIKE ROAD.

1794 DONALDSON *Agric. Carse of Gowrie* 32 Making another application to parliament, and in a short time a *turnpike act was procured, in which these, and other particular roads in the county, were included. **1841** *Penny Cycl.* XX. 29/1 The inefficiency of the system of maintenance by parish and statute labour was proved before the passing of the first Turnpike Act in 1653. **1903** *Law Rep.* 1 *K.B.* 407 A bicycle is not a carriage for the purposes of a turnpike Act. **1840** *Act 3 & 4 Vict.* c. 88 §1 That no Toll shall be demanded or taken on any *Turnpike..Bridge for any Horse, or Police Van, Carriage or Cart,..in the Service of the Police. **1850** SUSAN WARNER *Wide, Wide World* xiv, Cakes, child, cakes!—*turnpike cakes—what I raise the bread with. **1565** in Hay Fleming *Reform. in Scot.* (1910) Append. M. 610 In the chalmer at the *turne pyk fuit. **1903** J. K. JEROME *Tea T. Talk* (ed Tauchn.) 112 The world's highroads run *turnpike-free from pole to pole. **1513** *Acc. Ld. High Treas. Scot.* IV. 526 To the..smyth for viij score of square hedit nalis to the *turnepyk yett of the nethir toure. **1688** R. HOLME *Armoury* III. xvi. (Roxb.) 88/1 A Turne pike... Some terme it a Turnepike Gate. **1793** J. WOODFORDE *Diary* 21 July (1929) IV. 45 We got to Bruton Turnpike Gate. **1806** *Chron.* 19 Feb., in *Ann. Reg.* (1808) 371/2 A boy riding on a cart, drove against a turnpike-gate. **1840** DICKENS *Barn. Rudge* iii, The horse stopped until the turnpike gate was opened. **1889** GRETTON *Memory's Harkb.* 115 The wheelers..knocked against the turnpike-gate-post in passing through. **1623** *Reg. Mag. Sig. Scot.* 151/1 Infra *lie turnpyke* ejusdem cameram *lie *turnpyke-heid*, occidentalem ..et mediam cameram. **1774** NICHOLSON in *Phil. Trans.* LXIV. 351 These appearances continued till I reached the *turnpike-house. **1806** *Chron.* 15 May, in *Ann. Reg.* (1808) 405/1 The toll-table, against the turnpike house, at Whalley. **1863** DICKENS *Uncomm. Trav.* xxii, The Turnpike-house was all overgrown with ivy; and the Turnpike-keeper, unable to get a living out of the tolls, plied the trade of a cobbler. **1738** *Gentl. Mag.* May 247/2 From the Respect he was treated with by the *Turnpike-keeper, I perceived.. that he was..some Person of Distinction. **1771** *Act 11 Geo. III*, c. 45 §8 Making *Turnpike Locks on the Sides of the present Locks. **1769** EARL MARCH in Jesse *Selwyn & Contemp.* (1843) II. 366, I wrote you a note with a pencil upon the road, which a *turnpike-man promised to send to you. **1782** COWPER *Gilpin* 119 In a trice the turnpike-men Their gates wide open threw. **1876** BLACKMORE *Cripps* xxxii, He would rather have a row with three turnpike-men than presume to speak to a gentleman. **1764** FOOTE *Mayor of G.* I. i, After twenty years attendance at *turnpike-meetings. **1858** DICKENS *Holly Tree Inn* i, Even *turnpike people have children. **1839** H. BRANDON *Poverty, Mendicity & Crime* 165/1 *Turnpike sailors. **1851** MAYHEW *Lond. Labour* I. 415/2, I became a turnpike sailor,..and went out as one of the Shallow Brigade. **1884** CLARK RUSSELL in *Longm. Mag.* III. 563 The roadway was filled with a crowd of grimy fellows, turnpike sailors, loafing scarecrows. **1730** *Mem. Capt. Creichton* in *Swift's Wks.* (1869) 534/1 The dragoons ..went up a pair of *turnpike stairs. **1779** ARNOT *Hist. Edin.* 246 *note*, A turnpike stair is the term used..over all Scotland, to denote a stair, of which the steps are built in a spiral form, like a screen winding round the same axis. **1805** FORSYTH *Beauties Scotl.* II. 309 A small turnpike-stair, built in the wall. **1818** SCOTT *Hrt. Midl.* xxvi, A half-circular turret,..bartizan'd on the top, served as a case for a narrow turnpike-stair. **1888** STEVENSON *Black Arrow* IV. iv, The authors..had clattered down a turnpike stair and decamped. **1800** W. F. BAYLAY *Northern Tour* 267 (MS.) A beautiful *turnpike staircase here..the roof of it winding like a snail cap. **1801** *Farmer's Mag.* Apr. 158 The defective principles, adopted when the *turnpike system was first introduced, are completely avoided. **1895** *Westm. Gaz.* 28 Oct., The last of the turnpike system... The turnpike gates, which will enjoy the honour of thus being last in the field, belong to that portion of the Shrewsbury and Holyhead-road which traverses the island of Anglesea, the trust for which was continued by a special Act of Parliament until November 1, 1895. **1843** *Penny Cycl.* XXV. 429/1 *Turnpike trusts. Turnpike-roads are..highways placed.. under the management of trustees or commissioners.

Hence **'turnpike** *v.*, *trans.* to erect turnpikes on (a road); to make into a turnpike road; **turnpiker**, one who frequents the turnpike or turnpike road; hence (*a*) a foot-traveller; (*b*) = *turnpike sailor* (see 9 above).

1791 J. HILTZHEIMER *Diary* 17 Sept. (1893) 172, I took Mr. Francis..to view the road, from Vine Street to Vanderen's Mill, six miles, which it is proposed to *turnpike. **1806** WEBSTER, *Turnpike*,..to form or erect a turnpike. **1825** *Amer. St. Papers, Post-office* (1834) 137 The road from Elkton to Staunton has been turnpiked. **1903** H. T. CROFTON *Old Moss Side* 6 The lane was but little altered even after Acts are passed in 1749 and 1793 for turnpiking and improving it. **1812** *Boston Gaz.* 27 Aug. (Thornton), The heroes, who were to have mounted the heights of Abram, are yet in the garb of *turnpikers, unaccoutred and undisciplined. **1896** CLARK RUSSELL *What Cheer!* xi. 189 When it came to lee shores and frightful cliffs resounding the thunder of the tempest of the Atlantic..the turnpikers bent their backs and pulled with a will.

'turnpike road. A road on which turnpikes are or were erected for the collection of tolls; hence, a main road or highway, formerly maintained by a toll levied on cattle and wheeled vehicles. Also *fig.*

1745 WESLEY *Wks.* (1830) I. 485 Turnpike roads were not known in that part of England till some years after. **1776** ADAM SMITH *W.N.* I. xi. I. (1869) I. 156 Some of the counties in the neighbourhood of London petitioned the Parliament against the extension of the turnpike roads into the remoter counties. **1845** MᶜCULLOCH *Taxation* Introd. (1852) 33 It was not..till after the peace of Paris, in 1763, that turnpike-roads began to be extended to all parts of the kingdom. *Ibid.* II. x. 377 It has..been proposed to abolish tolls, as being essentially partial and unfair, and to raise a fund for constructing and repairing turnpike roads by a tax on property assessed and collected in the same way..as the rate for cross and parish roads. **1875** W. S. HAYWARD *Love agst. World* 16 After an hour's ride, by cross-country lanes and by-paths, they struck into the turnpike road.

turn-rice, -rise, var. TURNWREST.

turn-round ('tɜːnraʊnd). [f. the verbal phr. *turn round* (TURN *v.* 79).]

1. The arrival, unloading, and preparation for the return journey of a ship, aircraft, goods vehicle, etc.; the time taken for this. Also *gen.*, the course of receiving, processing, and sending out again; progress through a system.

1913 A. BENNETT *Regent* x. 291 She's going to do the quickest turn-round that any ship ever did... She'll leave at noon to-morrow. **1929** *Evening News* 18 Nov. 5/5 In these cabin ships the engines do not take up nearly as much space ..nor is it necessary to provide for such a rapid turn-round at the terminal ports. **1951** *Engineering* 1 June 658/1 An exceptional amount of sickness among the key and other operative staff, resulting in a slower turn-round of wagons. **1958** *Daily Mail* 3 July 4/3 An efficiency service that is.. capable of..achieving a quicker turn-round in the hospitals. **1963** *Times* 9 Feb. 9/4 The campaign for quicker 'turnround'..is being conducted jointly by the Road Haulage Association and British Road Services. **1972** L. LAMB *Picture Frame* xiv. 125 The expertness of the waiters in getting a quick turn-round of occupants at their tables. **1974** *Physics Bull.* Apr. 142/2 The total time which the material spends in the office including editing time, turn-round of proofs and any waiting time is usually not more than a month. **1976** *Southern Even. Echo* (Southampton) 12 Nov. 3/4 Heavy demands were made on her [*sc.* QE2], particularly with the short turn-rounds which were the pattern today. **1976** P. R. WHITE *Planning for Public Transport* viii. 156 On the railways,..increases in average speed..coupled with much quicker turnround of stock, have improved utilization of rolling stock on all-year service, by about 100 per cent. **1979** *Dan-Air In-flight Mag.* Winter 15 His [*sc.* the captain's] is the responsibility for the proper turn-round of an aircraft at its outward destination.

2. The reversal of a trend, a change to an opposite direction, opinion, etc.

1963 *Times* 29 Jan. 14/5 There is a growing feeling in market quarters that..the end of the upswing is in sight and a turnround may be near. **1976** *Listener* 22 Jan. 86/4 Critics in Britain are much more often attacked these days for their indiscriminate praise of everything new than for their obscurantism. To be fair, there is some perception of this turn-round. **1981** *Times* 22 May 19/2 Associated Engineering's £12.2m turnround from first half profits of £10.5m last year to a loss of £1.7m this time shows how bad conditions are in engineering. **1984** *Daily Tel.* 1 Feb. 18/5 There was a notable turn-round in leading engineers. GKN, down to 201p at the opening, were finally a shade better at 208p.

3. *attrib.*

1920 *Glasgow Herald* 16 Aug. 8 The strike has arisen from a dispute about special payment for quick turn-round voyages. **1969** *Times* 5 Nov. 23/6 Turnround time on orders has been cut from 15 to six days. **1977** *Modern Railways* Dec. 462/1 A turnround time of about 5min would permit the running of a half-hourly service with only the barest of margins.

turn-serving ('tɜːnˌsɜːvɪŋ), *sb.* and *a.* [f. TURN *sb.* 30 + SERVING *vbl. sb.* and *ppl. a.*] **a.** *sb.* The action or practice of serving one's own turn; the promotion of one's private interest; self-seeking; an instance of this. **b.** *adj.* That serves its own turn; promoting one's own ends. So †**'turn-served** *a.*, that has served his own turn (*obs.*); **'turn-ˌserver**, one whose motive is his own interest. Cf. TIME-SERVER, etc.

1613 CHAPMAN *Masque Inns of Court* Plays 1873 III. 109 The sight of an attendant for reward is abominable in the eyes of a *turne-seru'd Politician. **1611** SPEED *Hist. Gt. Brit.* IX. xvi. (1623) 839 A deceitfull man, a *turn-server. **1710** *Answ. to Bp. of Oxford's Sp.* 18 The Memory of all Time and Turn-Servers will be forgotten. **1611** SPEED *Hist. Gt. Brit.* IX. xi. §62 His name was abased to all sorts of *turne-seruings. **1616** BACON *Let. to Sir G. Villiers* 12 Aug., Though now, since Choice goeth better both in Church and Common-wealth, yet Money, and Turn-Serving, and Cunning Canvises, and Importunity, prevail too much. **1584** POWEL *Lloyd's Cambria* 278 Let people take heede how they build upon *turne-seruing freendship. **1842** G. S. FABER *Prov. Lett.* (1844) II. 189 A mere temporary and turn-serving appeal to Antiquity.

turn-sick ('tɜːnsɪk), *a.* and *sb.* *Obs.* exc. *dial.* Also 5-6 **-seke, -sycke, -sicke.** [f. TURN *v.* + SICK *a.*]

†**A.** *adj.* Affected with vertigo; giddy; dizzy.

c **1440** *Promp. Parv.* 507/1 Turnseke, *vertiginosus.* **1534** WHITINTON *Tullyes Offices* I. (1540) 49 We here tell of Lysander of Lacedemony, a turnesycke person and a man that myght abyde all paynes. **1626** BACON *Sylva* §795 If a Man see another turn swiftly, and long; Or if he look upon Wheeles that turne, Himselfe waxeth Turne-sick. **1657** J.

WATTS *Dipper Sprinkled* 6 Running round in a ring until you be turn-sick and giddy-headed.
fig. a **1603** T. CARTWRIGHT *Confut. Rhem. N.T.* (1618) 179 You are fallen out with your selues, and turne-sick with the maze of your own inuentions. *Ibid.* 382 These turnesick Iesuites make their note cleane contrary to the text. a **1617** BAYNE *On Eph.* (1658) 104 An escape of a turn-sick brain blinded with wilfulness. **1664** J. C. *Praxis Lat. Syntax* 130 Divers teachers, so giddy turn-sick.

†**b.** ***turn-sick giddiness***, vertigo. *Obs.*
1577 B. GOOGE *Heresbach's Husb.* IV. (1586) 192 The water of this hearbe..helpeth the turnesicke giddinesse of the heade.

B. *sb.* †**1. a.** Vertigo, swimming in the head; also, staggers in the horse. *Obs.*
c **1450** in *Vicary's Anat.* (1888) App. ix. 229 Be-hynde þe eres er twa vayns þat er gude to be opynd for turnseke and for scall, & alsso for euyll sight. **1565** BLUNDEVIL *Horsemanship* IV. xvi. (1580) 8 In the ventricles or celles of the braine..do breede the turnesicke, or staggers. **1592** in *Vicary's Anat.* (1888) App. ix. 228 If thowe lett blode of thoo, His syght shall neuer fale, And heles of torne-seke, and of scale.

2. A disease caused by an encysted worm in the brain of the sheep; the gid or sturdy. *dial.* Cf. TURN *sb.* 3.
1834 YOUATT *Cattle* 294 The sheep is subject to a disease strangely termed *turnsick*, in which the animal goes round and round. **1837** —— *Sheep* 391 The turnsick is not so frequent as it used to be thirty or forty years ago. **1844** STEPHENS *Bk. Farm* III. 877 There is a disease in sheep called sturdy or turnsick. **1870** ROLLESTON *Anim. Life* 136 The cause of the disease commonly known as the 'sturdy', 'gid', 'staggers', or 'turn-sick'.

Hence †**turnsickness** = B. 1. *Obs.*
1559 MORWYNG *Evonym.* 137 The headache, fallinge sicknesse, swindle or turnsicknes.

†**turnsilver.** *Obs. rare*$^{-1}$. [? f. TURN *sb.* or *v.* + SILVER *sb.*] A local payment of uncertain nature.
1578 in Whellan *Hist. Cumb. & Westm.* (1860) 208/2 [From the inquisition taken in 1578, we learn the following particulars... The tenants of Ulterside pay yearly]..for cornage, 4 s. 6 d.; for seawake, 7 d.; for turnsilver, 1 s. 3 d.

turnsole ('tɜːnsəʊl). Forms: 4 turnisoll, 4–8 turnesole, (5–6 turne-, 7 turnsoyle, turn(e)soil(e), 6 turnesoll, -sell, -sall, -saule, turnsale, -sowell, tornsole, -sell, -salle, tornesall(e, -sol(e, -solt, tournesoll, -sole, -soule, 6–7 turnsall, 7 -soll, -soule, 7–8 turnesol, 8 tournsol, 6–9 turnsol, 5– turnsole. [a. F. *tournesol* (14th c. in Littré), prob. ad. older Prov. *tournasol* (now *tournosol*) = Sp. and Pg. *tornasol*, It. *tornasole*, f. Romanic *tornare* to TURN + L. *sōl* the sun.
In F., as in Eng., first recorded as the name of the colouring matter derived from one of the plants bearing the name. In mod. Sp., Pg., and It. chiefly used in sense 2 b.]

1. A violet-blue or purple colouring matter, obtained from the plant *Crozophora tinctoria* (see 2 a), formerly much used for colouring jellies, confectionery, wines, etc., and later as a pigment. (See also quots. 1712 and 1830.)
Coarse linen rags are steeped in the juice, and then dried and exposed in vats over an ammoniacal mixture; hence the designation †*turnsole in rags* = F. *tournesol en drapeau.*
1375 *Exch. Rolls Scotl.* II. 507 Computat per empcionem de iij libris alkynet, j libra de turnisoll, et j libra de savndre. **1392** *Earl Derby's Exp.* (Camden) 154 Pro iij lb. turnesole ad xiiij d. c **1440** *Anc. Cookery* in *Househ. Ord.* (1790) 437 Colour hit with turnesole, or with ynde, or with alkenet, or saunders, or saffron. **1513** *Bk. Keruynge* in *Babees Bk.* (1868) 268 Tornsole is holsome for reed wyne colourynge. **1573** *Art of Limming* 4 To make azure and bize sadder, take good blewe tournesoll and wet it in gumme water. **1606** PEACHAM *Art of Drawing* I. xxiii. (1612) 86 The sorts of Red are these. Vermilion. Synaper lake... Red lead. Roset. Turnsoile [etc.]. *Ibid.* 88 Turnesoile is made of old linnen ragges died:..it is good to shadow carnations, and all yealowes. **1615** MARKHAM *Eng. Housew.* II. ii. 70 If you will haue [the jelly] coloured, then put in a little Tournesall. **1616–61** HOLYDAY *Persius* 308 The armorists indeed slight your common purple made of grocer's turnesol, a mixture of vermilion and blew bysse, or cynnaber, or the colour of violets. **1688** [see 2 a]. **1712** tr. *Pomet's Hist. Drugs* v. 93/2 Tornesol or Turnsole in Rags, is made of Linnen Cloth dyed at Constantinople, with Cocheneal and some Acids. The Cotton Turnsole, call'd Portugal or Spanish Wool, is made from Cotton that is..dyed in Spain or Portugal with Mestich Cochineal. Both Sorts are made use of to colour Liquors, Fruits and Gellies. There is another Kind of Turnsole that is made with Rags dipp'd in a red Tincture, prepar'd with the Juice of the Berry, and a little acid Liquor. **1783** *Phil. Trans.* LXXIII. 39 Acids possess the property of changing the juice of turnsol, or infusion of litmus, red. **1830** LINDLEY *Nat. Syst. Bot.* 103 The preparation called Turnsol,..chiefly obtained from Crozophora (Croton) tinctoria, is to be procured equally abundantly from many other plants of the order [Euphorbiaceæ]. **1866** *Treas. Bot.* 352/1 *C[rozophora] tinctoria*..is cultivated in the South of France for the sake of a dye which is obtained from it. This dye is called Turnsole, and is obtained by grinding the plants..to a pulp in a mill, when they yield about half their weight of a dark green coloured juice, which becomes purple by exposure to the air or under the influence of ammonia.
fig. **1599** *Broughton's Let.* xi. 38 Coloured with the Turnsalue of your Phantasticall braine.

b. *transf.* = LITMUS.
So F. *tournesol* and *tournesol en pain.*
1839 URE *Dict. Arts* 53 The lichen which produces archil is subjected to another preparation, to make turnsole (litmus). This article is made in Holland. **1842** BRANDE *Dict. Sc.* etc. 671/1 *Litmus*..a blue pigment obtained from the lichen *Rocella*..it is often called *turnsol*, and yields the dye called *archil.*

2. A plant of which the flowers or leaves turn so as to follow the sun; a heliotrope. **a.** An annual euphorbiaceous plant, *Crozophora tinctoria*, the ***small tornesol*** of Lyte's Herbal, found wild by the Mediterranean, and cultivated in the south of France for its colouring juice (see 1).
In earlier botanical use called *Croton tinctorium* (or *-ius*), *Ricinoides* (Tournefort), and (after Pliny) *Heliotropium tricoccum.*
1578 LYTE *Dodoens* I. xli. 61 With the seede of the smal Tornesoll..they die and stayne old linnen cloutes and ragges into a purple colour,..wherewithall in this countrey men vse to colour gellies, wynes, fine Confections, and Comfittes. **1688** R. HOLME *Armoury* II. 91/1 Turnsole, at the leaves comes forth three berries..which have within them a juice, or moisture of a purple colour of which that Turn-sole is made; sold by the Drugists. **1728** CHAMBERS *Cycl.*, *Tornesol, Tournesol*, or *Turnsol*, called also *Heliotrope*, and *Sunflower*, and by the Botanists *Ricinoides. Ibid.*, The *tournsol* being no Plant of their [i.e. Dutch] Growth. **1756** C. LUCAS *Ess. Waters* I. 21 Blews obtained from..archil, tournsol, &c. have their colors exalted or preserved by alcalies.

b. The plant *Heliotropium europæum*, the ***great tornesol*** of Lyte's Herbal; sometimes used by modern botanists as a name for the genus *Heliotropium.*
1578 LYTE *Dodoens* I. xli. 60 The great Tornesol hath straight round stalkes, couered with a white hearie cotton... The floures be white, at the toppe of the stalke, growing thicke togither in rewes. **1603** B. JONSON *Jas. I's Entertainm.* Wks. (Rtldg.) 528/2 Agrypnia, or Vigilance, in yellow,..her chaplet of Heliotropium, or turnsole. **1707** *Curios. in Husb. & Gard.* 142 The Famous Plant, call'd Heliotrope, Turn-Sole, or Sun-Flower. **1731** MILLER *Gard. Dict.* s.v. *Heliotropium*, The great Turnsole of Dioscorides. *Ibid.*, Blue American Turnsole, with Clary Leaves. a **1832** BENTHAM *Deontol.* i. (1834) I. 20 Let the moralist regard the great Deontological law, as steadily as the Turnsole looks upon the sun. **1866** *Treas. Bot.* 576/2 The Heliotrope or Turnsole, is a large genus of *Ehretiaceæ*... They are herbs or undershrubs found chiefly in tropical and subtropical regions, but a few species reach Europe, and one, *H[eliotropium] europæum*, is distributed over..southern and central Europe. **1887** MOLONEY *Forestry W. Afr.* 388 Indian Turnsole (*Heliotropium indicum*, L.).—Small annual.

c. Formerly applied to the Sunflower; also to the Sun-spurge or Wartwort, *Euphorbia helioscopia.*
1725 *Family Dict.* s.v. *Sunflower*, It's named *Turn-Sol* by the Italians and French. *Ibid.*, Between which [trees], at three Foot distance one from the other, our Turn-Sols may be planted. **1804** MALKIN *Scen. etc. S. Wales* 606 Turnsoles, ..though beautiful, are never planted on graves, because they are not sweet-scented. **1863–79** PRIOR *Pop. Names Brit. Plants*, *Turnsole* or *Tornsole*, a name erroneously given in some old works to the wartwort.

3. *attrib.*, as ***turnsole paper***, ***rag***, ***tincture.***
1733 SHAW *Chem. Lect.* xi. (1755) 210 We put four Ounces of what is commonly called Turnsol Rags into an earthen Vessel. **1753** *Chambers' Cycl.* Supp. s.v. *Turnesol*, The plant that afforded the Turnesol colour. *Ibid.*, The true Turnesol plant here described. **1797** PEARSON in *Phil. Trans.* LXXXVIII. 35 It reddened turnsole paper and tincture. **1836** J. M. GULLY *Magendie's Formul.* (ed. 2) 191 The solution in question reddened turnsol paper.

turnspit ('tɜːnspɪt). [f. TURN *v.* + SPIT *sb.*; cf. TURNBROACH.]

1. A dog kept to turn the roasting-spit by running within a kind of tread-wheel connected with it; a ***turnspit dog.*** Also *fig.*
1576 FLEMING tr. *Caius' Dogs* (1880) 35 A certaine dogge ..when any meate is to bee roasted they go into a wheele.. turning rounde about with the waight of their bodies... Whom the popular sort herevpon call Turnespets. a **1619** FLETCHER *Mad Lover* III. ii, Get thee to school again, and talk of turnspits. **1793** [E. D. CLARKE] *Tour S. Eng.* iv. 215 Dogs are universally used, in this part of the world, as turnspits. **1801** COL. G. HANGER *Life* II. 246 These turnspits, who, in the metaphysical wheel, turn the spit of conjecture. **1863** JESSE in Chambers *Bk. Days* 8 Apr. I. 490/1 His two turn-spits..were long-bodied, crook-legged, and ugly dogs.

2. A boy or man whose office was to turn the spit. Also used as a term of contempt.
1607 *Puritan* I. ii. 3 As hot as a turn-spit. **1683** *Roxb. Ball.* (1885) V. 455 Fat Turnspit Frank,..Whom we despise, in time may rise to be Jester to King Perkin. **1723** SWIFT *French Dog* Wks. 1755 IV. I. 36 A turn-spit in the royal kitchen. **1802–12** BENTHAM *Ration. Judic. Evid.* (1827) II. 139 The King's turnspit used to be a member of parliament. **1809** MALKIN *Gil Blas* II. i. ¶5 Leonarda..passed for a very decent plain cook; but a mere turnspit to dame Jacintha. **1869** BLACKMORE *Lorna D.* v, All good people..knowing his kitchen range to be cold, no longer would play turnspit.

3. A roasting-jack. *rare.*
1606 CHAPMAN *Gent. Usher* III. i, Euen as in a turne-spit calld a Iacke..the great wheeles, Turning but softly, make the lesse to whirre. **1858** SIMMONDS *Dict. Trade*, *Turn-spit*, a clock-work machine for cooking.

4. *attrib.*, as ***turnspit-boy***, ***cur***, ***dog***, ***-jack***, ***terrier.***
1820 SCOTT *Monast.* xiv, A little dirty *turnspit-boy. **1603** HARSNET *Pop. Impost.* xxii. 145 Moved..as a Wheele is by a *turnspit curre, that is put into it. **1625** N. CARPENTER *Geog. Del.* I. iv. (1635) 81 *Turne-spit-dogs labouring in their wheeles. a **1704** T. BROWN *Laconics* Wks. 1711 IV. 14 Seeing one of the Turn-spit Dogs bask himself in the Sun. **1845** YOUATT *Dog* ii. 18 Colonel Sykes says..among the pariahs is frequently found the turnspit-dog. **1674** PETTY *Disc. Dupl. Proportion* 39 In any good *Turnspit-Jack,..a quadruple weight makes double Velocity. **1857** HUGHES *Tom Brown* I. iii, Toby the *turnspit terrier.

turnstile ('tɜːnstaɪl). [f. TURN *v.* + STILE *sb.*]

a. A gateway formed of four radiating arms of timber or iron at right angles to each other, revolving horizontally on a fixed vertical post, set up in a passage or entrance, originally to exclude any but foot-passengers; now often to prevent the passage of more than one person at a time at a place where fees, fares, or tickets are collected, or where it is desired to count those passing.
a **1643** CARTWRIGHT *Lady Errant* I. v, Double forked Like a turn-stile, or some such engin. **1650** B. *Discolliminium* 48, I can devise none fitter then Weather-cocks and a Turne-stile. **1716** GAY *Trivia* III. 108 Where twirling turnstiles intercept the way, The thwarting passenger shall force them round. **1818** LEIGH *New Pict. Lond.* 313 The kind of iron turn-stiles, which admit of only one person passing at a time. **1861** *All Year Round* 29 June 324 The railway station is full, the voluminous gowns are jamming up the ticket collectors' turnstiles. **1890** *Spectator* 31 May 756 Sixty thousand passed the turnstiles of the Zoological Gardens.
fig. **1852** JERDAN *Autobiog.* II. xxi. 296 Bills..were frequently only turnstiles opening into paths of difficulty.

b. *attrib.*
1688 R. HOLME *Armoury* III. 336/2 A Turning Hatch, or Turnstyle gate. **1877** KNIGHT *Dict. Mech.* s.v., A turnstile counter for omnibuses and cars is described in English patent No. 2189, of 1854. *Turnstile-register*,..for registering the number of persons who pass through a turnstile. **1896** *Daily News* 21 Aug. 3/5 Turnstile attendant at the Crystal Palace. **1952** D. G. FINK *Television Engin.* (ed. 2) vii. 367 Decoupling in the antenna itself is accomplished by separating the elements of the turnstile antenna..into two orthogonal groups and connecting these groups in a bridge circuit. *Ibid.* 371 The appearance of two horizontal dipoles at right angles has given rise to the descriptive term turnstile radiator. **1959** K. HENNEY *Radio Engin. Handbk.* (ed. 5) xx. 76 Many forms of vertical arrays have already been evolved using magnetic dipoles, turnstile elements, or current sheets. **1971** *Gloss. Electrotechnical Power Terms (B.S.I.)* III. vii. 16 *Turnstile aerial*, aerial consisting of one or more tiers, each tier being a combination of two horizontal dipoles arranged in the form of a right angled cross. **1978** *Nature* 5 Oct. 375/2 The VHF system consists of duplicate transponders and a four-element turnstile antenna.

turnstone ('tɜːnstəʊn). [f. TURN *v.* + STONE *sb.*] A limicoline bird (*Strepsilas interpres*) of about the size of the snipe, widely distributed in the Old and New Worlds, which turns over stones to get at the crustacea and other small animals to be found under them.
1674 RAY *Words, Water Fowl* 91 *The Turn-stone*:.. Cinclus Turneri. This bird we observed on the coast of Cornwall: it is lesser then a Plover, and somewhat bigger then a Black-bird. **1678** RAY *Willughby's Ornith.* III. v. 311 The Turn-stone, or Sea-Dottrel. **1731** MORTIMER in *Phil. Trans.* XXXVII. 176 The Turn-Stone or Sea-Dottrel..is a Native both of England and America. **1802** MONTAGU *Ornith. Dict.* s.v., The Turnstone is subject to great variety in respect to the markings about the head and neck. **1862** ANSTED *Channel Isl.* 207 The turnstone is found about the neighbourhood of Herm throughout the year. **1904** *Blackw. Mag.* Feb. 250/2 The turnstones..breed in Alaska.

turntable ('tɜːnteɪb(ə)l). Also **turn-table.** [f. TURN *v.* + TABLE *sb.*]

1. On a railway: A revolving platform turning on a central pivot, laid with rails connecting with adjacent tracks, for turning railway vehicles; a turn-plate.
1835 *Massachusetts Stat.* 4 Apr., To unite any rail-road or rail-roads..by turn-tables or otherwise. **1838** N. WOOD *Railroads* (ed. 3) 186 On each of these lines..circular turn-tables are placed, upon which the carriages are run. **1854** *John Bull* 2 Sept. 558/2 An engine having been accidentally put in motion while on the turn table, ran over a side wall, and rested on end in the street below.

2. A revolving platform, table, stand, or disk of various kinds: see quots.; *spec.* (*a*) a rotating disk on which microscope slides are held for tracing the circular cement cells in which specimens are placed for examination; (*b*) see quot. 1889; (*c*) a turning device allowing a photographic camera to rotate on the stand or tripod; (*d*) a rotating plate-glass show stand used in shop-windows (*Funk's Stand. Dict.* 1895); (*e*) the rotating plate on which a gramophone record is placed to be played; the unit housing this plate.
1865 *Morn. Star* 2 Sept., The burial board..determined on placing a stand, or what is called a 'turn-table', in the church, and also one in the chapel [for use at funerals]. **1867** J. HOGG *Microsc.* I. iii. 254 The little box contains:—Shadbolts turn-table, brass table [etc.]. **1887** T. A. TROLLOPE *What I remember* II. xv. 279 His food..is passed in to him by a little turntable made in the wall. **1889** WELCH *Text Bk. Naval Archit.* v. 79 The four heavy guns are carried on revolving turntables in two fixed armoured redoubts or barbettes. **1892** *Photogr. Ann.* II. p. cxci, A special form of Turntable is fixed to the Camera, to which the legs may be quickly attached... The centre of the Turntable is cut away. **1908** *Sears, Roebuck Catal.* 195/2 The Type FH Harvard Disc Talking Machine... The turntable, of a special composition metal, is 10 inches in diameter. **1921** P. A. SCHOLES *Learning to Listen by Means of Gramophone* 157 The motor should be wound up fully for each record played, in order that the turntable can rotate at its normal and even speed. **1960** *Practical Wireless* XXXVI. 421/2 Wedge the turntable so that it does not move. **1962** *Times* 5 July 15/7 The disc had been standing on the turntable for a few minutes before playing. **1979** L. KALLEN *Introducing C. B. Greenfield* xiii. 166 An old armoire..held his recordings and the turntable.

3. *attrib.*, as ***turn-table ladder, stack.***
1893 *Nation* (N.Y.) 13 July 28/3 At the Columbian Fair there is a turn-table stack of official publications. **1912** *Times* 19 Dec. 12/6 A horsed escape, a fire engine, a turn-table ladder, and ten men turned out from the Theobald's-road fire station.

ˈturn-tail, *sb.* and *a.* [f. the verbal phr. *turn tail* (TURN *v.* 59).]

A. *sb.* **1.** One who turns tail; one who abandons or forsakes his former associates or principles; also, a coward. Now *rare*.
1621 BRATHWAIT *Nat. Embassie*, etc. (1877) 301 Thou art the rich mans claw-backe,..Go turne-taile go. *a* **1670** SPALDING *Troub. Chas. I* (1850) I. 206 Mony covenanteris proveit turne-taillis throw plane feir, and cam most willinglie into him. **1819** LINGARD *Hist. Eng.* I. xix. III. 136 *note*, Under the penalty of culvertage (culvert, a turn-tail) that is perpetual slavery.

†**2.** A variety of domestic pigeon. *Obs.*
1741 *Compl. Fam.-Piece* III. 512 The Croppers are valuable for their Swell... The Turn-tails for their turning them up almost to their Back.

B. *adj.* That turns tail.
1861 GEO. ELIOT *Silas M.* vi, I aren't a turn-tail cur.

turn-up (ˈtɜːnʌp), *sb.* and *a.* [f. the verbal phr. *turn up* (TURN *v.* 81).]

A. *sb.* †**1.** See quot., and cf. *turn up*, TURN *v.* 81 ***. *Obs. rare*⁻¹.
1612 *Benvenuto's Passenger* I. iv. 315 They are whores, harlots, trulls, baggages, bayards, turne-vps, curtesanes.

2. The turned up part of anything, esp. of a garment. *spec.* The turned-up cuff of a trouser-leg.
1688 R. HOLME *Armoury* IV. iv. (Roxb.) 295/2 A pilgrims hat of St. James,..on the turne-vp, two staves in salter debrused with an Escalop shell Or. *Ibid.* vi. 307/1, I haue obserued that sleeues both in coates and crests haue had their Turn-vps of diuerse fashions. **1764** FOOTE *Patron* I. 5 He found the turn-up of her nose too exactly resemble the bust of the princess Popæa. **1901** *Daily Record* 21 Dec. 4 They..have velvet collars, narrow turn-ups at the cuffs, and are well shaped to the waist. **1902** ELIZ. L. BANKS *Newspaper Girl* 230 A hat..that'd suit you to a T! It's exactly made for you, turn-up on the side and all! **1925** *Minister's Rep. of Fashion for Gentlemen* Feb. 8/2 Permanent turn-ups are still worn for outdoor wear. **1933** J. E. LIBERTY *Practical Tailoring* vi. 77 For turned-up bottoms, called permanent turn-ups, go down on the seam from the mark the width of turn-up required..and make a straight line across the bottom. *a* **1944** K. DOUGLAS *Alamein to Zem Zem* (1946) xiii. 81 He had..beautifully cut narrow trousers of fawn cavalry twill, without turn ups. **1969** B. MALAMUD *Pictures of Fidelman* (U.K. ed.) i. 25 His blue gabardine suit—a one-button jacket affair, the trousers a little frayed at the turn-ups. **1972** G. DURRELL *Catch me a Colobus* vii. 142 She..nosed round our legs eagerly, searching in our turn-ups to see whether she could find anything to eat.

3. a. The turning up of a particular card or die in games of chance; the card or die turned up; hence *fig.*, a mere chance, a 'toss-up'; a result which is purely a matter of chance; also, an unexpected appearance or phenomenon; an unexpected occurrence, a surprise. Cf. sense 3b.
1810 *Sporting Mag.* XXXVI. 265 He..recorded turns up of all the chances. **1820** W. IRVING *Sketch Bk., Stratford* (1865) 327 It is often a turn-up of a die, in the gambling freaks of fate, whether a natural genius shall turn out a great rogue or a great poet. **1844** J. T. HEWLETT *Parsons & W.* vi, What the 'turn-up' would be I knew no more than a card-player, who has just had the pack cut to him. **1870** HARDY & WARE *Mod. Hoyle, Cribbage* 79 If the turn up should also be of the same suit, you count one extra. **1884** J. BURROUGHS in *Century Mag.* XXVII. 926 The type of men of which Emerson and Carlyle are the most pronounced..examples ..are comparatively a new turn-up in literature. **1942** BERREY & VAN DEN BARK *Amer. Thes. Slang* §178/1 *Surprise* ..bob-up, springer, turn-up. **1961** R. PARK *Hole in Hill* (1962) x. 79 'Well, this is a turn-up,' said Dunk in disgust. 'How do we get out?' **1972** *Jazz & Blues* Oct. 26/3 What a turn-up then to find there's another version.

b. *spec.* in Racing: see quot. 1873. Freq. in phr. ***a turn-up for the book(s)***; also in *gen.* use (*colloq.*), an unexpected turn of fortune, a surprise.
1873 *Slang Dict., Turn up*,..an unexpected slice of luck. Among sporting men bookmakers are said to have a turn up when an unbacked horse wins. **1895** *Westm. Gaz.* 10 Sept. 7/2 With such a moderate field nobody will be surprised if the result is a 'turn-up' as astonishing as was the victory of Throstle last year. **1900** *Ibid.* 15 May 8/1 The Jubilee Handicap on Saturday ended in a tremendous turn-up for the fielders. **1948** 'J. TEY' *Franchise Affair* xviii. 209 Won by a length and a half on a tight rein; and was that a turn up for the book! **1951** *People* 3 June 2/2 What a Derby Day it was! And what a turn up for the books! **1959** P. BULL *I know Face* ii. 35, I reported my findings to Mr Huth, who said.. perhaps I would like to write the script. Now this was quite a turn-up for the book, as very few people..are allowed to say what they write. **1968** 'C. FRANKLIN' *Escape* viii. 104 This was indeed a turn up for the book. 'Penelope!' he exclaimed. **1978** J. WAINWRIGHT *Jury People* v. 16 A bit of a turn up for the book, isn't it? Murder, I mean. **1983** *Daily Tel.* 13 Oct. 8/7 Even..the Labour group's spokesman.. could not hide his surprise... 'This is a real turnup for the books. I am quite amazed by it..,' he said.

4. A boxing contest; hence, *loosely*, a fight, a set-to, esp. with the fists; also, a tussle, struggle; a disturbance, row.
1810 *Sporting Mag.* XXXVI. 195 The next amusement was a turn-up betwixt Crib and Richman. **1827** SCOTT *Two Drovers* ii, We must have a turn-up, or we shall be the talk of the countryside... Come, stand forward like a man. *c* **1874** G. H. KINGSLEY *Sport & Trav.* vi. (1900) 160 Campbell, however, had a turn-up with a grizzly. **1891** SARAH J. DUNCAN *Amer. Girl in Lond.* 78 The why and the wherefore of all this turn-up.

5. The curve of the projecting lower jaw of a bull-dog.
1905 [see LAY-BACK 1]. **1922** R. LEIGHTON *Compl. Bk. Dog* v. 64 It [*sc.* a type of bulldog] has certain well-defined characteristics, notably the extreme width and turn-up of underjaw. **1973** J. F. GORDON *Bulldog* (rev. ed.) iv. 53 (*caption*) Nice head and skull, good 'turn-up'.

B. *attrib.* or *adj.* That is turned up, or turns up, in various senses.
1685 *Lond. Gaz.* No. 2032/4 A small Spaniel Lap Dog.., with..a short turn-up Nose. *c* **1690** *Roxb. Ball.* (1895) VIII. 17 Turn-up stockings they constantly wear. **1767** in *Daily Chron.* 19 Nov. (1908) 4/7 You may sit in their Royal presence, not in pews, but in turn-up seats on the side of them. **1800** *Hull Advertiser* 19 Apr. 3/2 An infant..was smothered..with the bed-clothes of a turn-up bedstead. **1809** MALKIN *Gil Blas* XI. ii. (Rtldg.) 397 The sharp-pointed, turn-up chin of a pantaloon. **1821** LAMB *Elia* Ser. I. *Mrs. Battle on Whist*, She would not take advantage of the turn-up knave. **1848** RICKMAN *Archit.* 211 Stalls with turn-up seats and benches. **1874** BURNAND *My Time* xix. 166 It was neatly furnished, with a small table, a turn-up bedstead, etc. **1909** *Daily Graphic* 20 Oct. 13/1 The hat with the turn-up brim.

turnverein (ˈtɜːnvəraɪn). [Ger., f. *turnen* to do gymnastic exercises + *verein* society, club.] In the United States, a gymnastic society, orig. for German immigrants, on the model of those instituted by Jahn (see TURNER¹ 8). Also *attrib.*
1852 *San Francisco Herald* 1 Nov. 2/2 The Turnverein Society held another of their fetes yesterday. **1949** *Minnesota Hist.* Mar. 26 The Cincinnati Turnverein built the first Turner Hall in the United States in 1850. **1959** R. CONDON *Manchurian Candidate* (1960) xxvii. 267 Petitions and documentations were submitted to the Resolutions Committee by farm lobbies, labour unions,..and national manufacturers' Turnvereins. **1974** *Encycl. Brit. Micropædia* X. 202/1 Turnvereins continue to foster citizenship and cultural programs together with health and physical-education activities, particularly gymnastics.

†**turnway¹.** *Rhet. Obs. rare*⁻¹. [f. TURN *v.* + WAY *adv.* away, after Gr. ἀποστροφή.] = APOSTROPHE¹ 1.
1589 PUTTENHAM *Eng. Poesie* III. xix. (Arb.) 245 When we haue runne a long race in our tale..we do sodainly flye out and either speake or exclaime at some other person or thing, and therefore the Greekes call such figure (as we do) the turnway or turnetale.

turnway² (ˈtɜːnweɪ). [f. TURN *sb.* + WAY *sb.*] A system or method of turns; in quot. *attrib.*
1897 WEBB *Indust. Democ.* I. II. ix. 437 The 'turnway' societies of the Thames watermen, for regulating the 'turns', or order in which the men plying at any particular 'stairs' serve the passengers who present themselves.

turnwrest (ˈtɜːnrɛst), *a.* (*sb.*) Also 8–9 **turnwrist, -rise,** 9 **-rice.** [f. TURN- + WREST *sb.* (See also REEST *sb.*)] ***turnwrest plough***, a plough in which the mould-board may be shifted from one side to the other at the end of each furrow, so that the furrow-slice is always thrown the same way; a one-way plough.
In the 18th cent. freq. called the *Kentish plough*.
1653 BLITHE *Eng. Improv. Impr.* II. xxix. (ed. 3) 203 There is another double Wheeled-plough, & it is called the Turn wrest plough, which of all ploughs that ever I saw, surpasseth for weight and clumsiness. **1766** *Museum Rust.* VI. 129 He had made one, which he called a turn-rise plough. **1794** A. PRINGLE *Agric. Westmorland* 34 The turnwrist plough is about to be introduced into the county. **1812** SIR J. SINCLAIR *Syst. Husb. Scot.* I. 156 A plough with a shifting mould-board, usually called a turn-wrest plough, admits of ploughing both backwards and forwards. **1846** DAVIS in *Jrnl. R. Agric. Soc.* VII. II. 526 This I accomplished with a monster turn-rice plough made for the purpose. **1856** MORTON *Cyclop. Agric.* II. 628–30 [Various forms described]. **1884** *W. Sussex Gaz.* 25 Sept., Strong turnwrist, round, snap, and strike furrow ploughs.
transf. **1844** STEPHENS *Bk. Farm* II. 624 The mountain turn-wrist snow-plough.

b. *ellipt.* as *sb.* Also *attrib.*
1778 [W. MARSHALL] *Minutes Agric.* 25 Oct. an. 1775, A Turn-wrist is obviously preferable to a fixed-wrist, for cross-plowing. **1846** CLARKE in *Jrnl. R. Agric. Soc.* VII. II. 512 The old Kentish turn-wrest. **1902** *Westm. Gaz.* 7 Nov. 7/2 In the North Kent Agricultural Association's ploughing match..the variety of ploughs to be seen was surprising. The old wooden turnrise type was well to the fore.

†**turny** (ˈtɜːnɪ), *a. Obs. rare.* [f. TURN *sb.* 3 + -Y.] Of an ox, etc.: Affected with the turn.
1651 *Manch. Crt. Leet Rec.* (1887) IV. 51 Thomas Peele [presented] for sellinge a leane turney beast.

†**Turon.** *Obs. rare.* [ad. med.L. *Turonia* or *Turonī*: see next.] The city of Tours; used *attrib.* = next, b.
Freq. in Trevisa's *Higden* as the name of the city.
1568 GRAFTON *Chron.* II. 136 He..solde him his title that he had in Normandy, Gascoyne and Guyan... Taking for the same title three hundreth thousande of small Turon money.

†**Turoneis, Turoneys,** *sb.* and *a. Obs.* [ad. med.L. *Turonensis* (f. *Turonēs*, later *Turonī*, *Turonii*, a people of ancient Gaul, whence Tours on the Loire took its name), with ending assimilated to OF. *torneis* (F. *tournois* TOURNOIS *a.*).] **a.** *sb. pl.* The people or citizens of Tours. **b.** *adj.* Of or pertaining to Tours; = TOURNOIS.
The sing. form *Turoney* employed by Trevisa is irregular. Both Trevisa and the anonymous translator of Higden also employ the Latin ending *-ens(e*.
1387 TREVISA *Higden* (Rolls) VI. 259 He sette and pighte a lettre of gold of þe wight of an hondred pound of Turoneys [*v. rr.* Turoneyes, -eies]. *Ibid.*, He schal not spende at his comencement passynge þre þowsand of grootes turonens [*v.r.* turoneies]. Þe groot turoney is somwhat lasse worþy þan an Englische groote, ffor..I have i-fonge in chaunge enlevene grotes turoneys for a duket... But þere is double manere of money of turoneis [*v.r.* turoneies], more and lasse [etc.].

Turonian (tjʊˈrəʊnɪən), *a. Geol.* [= F. *turonien*, f. L. *Turonēs*: see prec. and -IAN.] Denoting a subdivision of the Cretaceous or Chalk period and series of strata, answering to the 'Lower White Chalk without flints' of English geologists.
1850 ANSTED *Elem. Geol., Min.* etc., Index, Turonian formation. [*Ibid.* §792 These beds are represented in France by the lower members of the 'Terrain turonien', which exhibit nearly the same peculiarities as in England, though to a somewhat greater extent.] **1885** GEIKIE *Text Bk. Geol.* VI. II. iii. §2 (ed. 2) 820 The Cretaceous system of Europe has been subdivided as follows:—Upper..Danian, Senonian, Turonian, Cenomanian, Gault. Lower..Neocomian.

†**turow,** ? var. of *thorow*, THROUGH *sb.*¹ 2.
1533 in Weaver *Wells Wills* (1890) 139 To be buryd in holy turow.

turpel, -pele, -pell, var. TIRPEIL *Obs.*

turpentine (ˈtɜːpəntaɪn), *sb.* Forms: α. 5–6 **terebentine, -yne** (see also TEREBINTHINE); β. 4–5 **terb-,** 5 **turbentyne;** γ. 5–6 **terpentin, turpentyne,** 6 **-tyn,** 7 **terpentine,** 6– **turpentine;** δ. 5 **turmyntyne,** 6 **termenteyne.** [In 14–15th c. *terebentyne, terbentyne*, a. OF. *tere-, terbentine*, ad. L. *terebintina* or *terebinthina* (*rēsīna*): see TEREBINTHINA, -INE. Already *a* 1400, OF. had *tourbentine* (in R. Estienne 1550, *turbentine*); so Eng. *turbentyn* and *turpentine*. The 15–16th c. variant *termenteyne* curiously approaches the earlier Gr. τερμινθίνη (ῥητίνη) terebinthine resin, turpentine.]

1. a. A term applied originally (as in Gr. and Lat.) to the semifluid resin of the terebinth tree, *Pistacia Terebinthus* (Chian or Cyprian turpentine); now chiefly to the various oleoresins which exude from coniferous trees, consisting of more or less viscid solutions of resin in a volatile oil.
α. [**1398** TREVISA *Barth. De P.R.* XVII. clxiv. (Bodl. MS.) lf. 232/1 Therebintus..is a tre þat sweteþ rosine..and þe rosine þereof hatte Therebentina.] *c* **1425** tr. *Arderne's Treat. Fistula* 31 Putte to of terebentyne als moche as sufficeþ..moue it strongly wiþ a spature vnto þat þe terebentyne be dronken in. **1541** R. COPLAND *Guydon's Formul.* Xj b, Fomentacyon with oyle and terebentyne medled & warmed. **1597** A. M. tr. *Guillemeau's Fr. Chirurg.* 42 b/2 Made of Oyle of Egges and of Venetiane Terebentine.
β. **1322** in *Wardr. Acc. 16 Edw. II* 23/20 Terbentyn 7ᵈ þe lb. *c* **1400** MAUNDEV. (1839) v. 51 A gome, þat men clepen Turbentyne. *c* **1425** tr. *Arderne's Treat. Fistula* 32 Terbentyne. **1460–70** *Bk. Quintessence* II. 25 Wiþ frank-encense, mirre, and rosyn, terbentyn and rewe.
γ. *c* **1400** MAUNDEV. (Roxb.) vii. 26 A maner of gumme, þat es called Turpentyne. **1576** BAKER *Jewell of Health* 128 Turpentine, which is a lycour dystilled and gotten of the Fyrre tree. **1580** HOLLYBAND *Treas. Fr. Tong, Térébinthine*, turpentyne. **1601** HOLLAND *Pliny* xv. xii. I. 465 In Syria they use to plucke the barke from the Terebinth, yea, and they pill the boughs and roots too for Terpentine. **1673** GREW *Anat. Trunks* I. ii. §18 Out of these Vessels all the clear Turpentine, that drops from the Tree, doth issue. **1718** QUINCY *Compl. Disp.* 125 Common Turpentine..is procured from the Larch-Tree. **1813** SIR H. DAVY *Agric. Chem.* iii. (1814) 97 When a portion of the bark is removed from a fir tree in Spring a matter exudes which is called turpentine. **1875** H. C. WOOD *Therap.* (1879) 131 Turpentine is remarkable for having the property of absorbing oxygen and converting it into ozone.
δ. **1448–9** in Willis & Clark *Cambridge* (1886) I. 403, j lb et di. de Turmyntyne. **1502** ARNOLDE *Chron.* 35/2 Kark of termenteyne, xij d.

b. With qualification, indicating different varieties. See quot. 1831.
1577 FRAMPTON *Joyful News* 45 Adde therto three Ounces of Venise Turpentine. **1634** PEACHAM *Gentl. Exerc.* I. xxvii. 98 Temper it with Spanish Turpentine. **1728** CHAMBERS *Cycl.* s.v. [Various kinds described.] **1744** BERKELEY *Siris* §20 The Strasburgh turpentine..is procured from the knots of the silver fir. *Ibid.*, Venice turpentine, which is got by piercing the larch tree. **1831** J. DAVIES *Manual Mat. Med.* 191 The principal kinds of turpentine are—the American Turpentine, furnished abundantly by the *Pinus palustris*, Lin., *P. australis*, Michaux, a tree growing principally in the southern states; the Common Turpentine, *Terebinthina communis*, obtained from the *Pinus sylvestris* and *P. rubra*, Lin.;..the Bordeaux Turpentine, *Terebinthina picea*, from the *P. maritima*, Lin., Bordeaux pine; the Strasbourg Turpentine, *Terebinthina abietina*, from the *P. picea*,..silver fir tree; the Venice Turpentine, *Terebinthina laricea*, from ..*P. larix*, Lin., white larch; and..Canada or Fir Balsam, *Terebinthina canadensis*,..furnished by the *P. balsamea*, American silver fir. *c* **1865** LETHEBY in *Circ. Sc.* I. 106/1 The oleo-resin is imported into this country under the names of common turpentine, Bordeaux t..., Strasburg t..., and Venice t.

c. *pl.* Varieties of turpentine.

1605 TIMME *Quersit.* III. 184 After one manner, hony,.. after another, turpentines and gummes (as mastic, euphorb[i]um, styrax, and such like).. are to be distilled. **1718** QUINCY *Compl. Disp.* 7 Of Turpentines, Gums, and all of that Tribe. **1843** *Penny Cycl.* XXV. 432/1 As turpentines have a very disagreeable taste, it is customary to form them into pills or boluses. **1874** GARROD & BAXTER *Mat. Med.* (1880) 366 Canada balsam resembles the other turpentines in its action, but it is not often given as a medicine.

d. = *oil of turpentine*: see 3. ***to talk turpentine*** (colloq.), to discuss painting.

1876 BRISTOWE *The. & Pract. Med.* (1878) 607 Among the remedies.. recommended [for scurvy] are perchloride of iron, acetate of lead, arsenic, digitalis, turpentine. **1891** KIPLING *Light that Failed* vii. 118, I was told that all the world was interested in my work, and everybody at Kami's talked turpentine.

2. †**a.** The fruit of the terebinth tree. *Obs.* **b.** A terebinth tree; = TEREBINTHINE B. 1, TURPENTINE TREE 1. Also, any tree that yields turpentine, as the larch.

1562 TURNER *Herbal* II. 115 The fruite [of Sumach] is lyke vnto small clusters of grapes of the bignes of a turpentine. **1577** B. GOOGE *Heresbach's Husb.* (1586) 72 b, The cherie refuseth not the companie of the Peach, nor the Turpentine, nor they his. **1601** CHESTER *Love's Mart.* (N. Shaks. Soc.) 96 The Turpentine that sweet iuyce doth deplore. **1615** G. SANDYS *Trav.* 90 Cypresse trees and Turpentine, with divers others. **1885** 'WANDERER' *Beauteous Terrorist* 29 There 'mid giant turpentines Groups of climbing, clustering vines. **1898** MORRIS *Austral Eng.*, *Turpentine, Brush*, name given to two trees—*Metrosideros leptopetala*,.. and *Rhodamnia trinervia*,.. both N.O. *Myrtaceæ*.

3. oil of turpentine (also vulgarly known as ***spirit of t.***), a volatile oil, contained in the wood, bark, leaves, and other parts of coniferous trees, and usually prepared by distilling crude turpentine. There are many varieties according to the source, which, though all having the same formula, $C_{10}H_{16}$, vary in their physical and, more especially, their optical properties.

1597 A. M. tr. *Guillemeau's Fr. Chirurg.* 30/2 Hott oyle of Terpentin. **1660** BOYLE *New Exp. Phys. Mech.* xxiv. 188 Common Oyl or Spirit (for in the Shops.. the same Liquor is promiscuously call'd by either name) of Turpentine. **1728** CHAMBERS *Cycl.* s.v. *Turpentine*, What is commonly sold under the name of Oil of Turpentine, or Etherial Oil, is only a Distillation of the Rosin called Galipot, fresh from the Tree. **1791** HAMILTON tr. *Berthollet's Dyeing* I. I. I. i. 6 The oil of turpentine.. has a considerable refracting power. **1859** GULLICK & TIMBS *Paint.* 208 The rectified oil, improperly called Spirit of turpentine, is now most commonly employed. Its great use among house painters, under the cant name of 'turps', is to thin and assist the drying of oil paints. **1875** H. C. WOOD *Therap.* (1879) 501 Oil of turpentine is never employed to increase the flow of urine.

4. *attrib.* and *Comb.*, as ***turpentine ball, business, clyster, distiller, epithem, fomentation, liniment, odour, pill, smell, stupe, varnish***; 'pertaining to the production of turpentine or the cultivation of turpentine trees', as ***turpentine camp, district, farm, farmer, orchard, region, wood***; instrumental, as ***turpentine-anointed, -filled*** adjs.; **turpentine bucket**: see quot.; **turpentine camphor**, a name sometimes given to the solid monohydrochlorate, sometimes to the solid hydrates of turpentine oil; **turpentine gall-nut**, an excrescence formed on the branches of the terebinth-tree by the puncture of an insect; **turpentine gum**, American THUS (*sb.*) (*Cent. Dict. Supp.* 1909); **turpentine hack**, a tool for hacking the bark of pine trees, to cause the turpentine to exude (Knight *Dict. Mech.* 1877); **turpentine moth**, any of several leaf-roller moths of the family Tortricidæ of which the larvæ bore into the twigs of conifers (*Cent. Dict.* 1891); **turpentine oil** = *oil of turpentine*; **turpentine ointment**, an ointment of which turpentine oil is a principal ingredient (*ibid.*); †**turpentine rod**, a rod of a terebinth tree; **turpentine shrub**, a name of the Prairie Burdock, *Silphium terebinthinaceum*, a tall herbaceous plant with bright yellow flowers, a native of North America cultivated in European gardens since 1765 (*Cassell's Encycl. Dict.* 1888); **Turpentine State** (U.S.): see quot. 1859; **turpentine still**, an apparatus for distilling turpentine from pine wood or spirit from turpentine (Knight *Dict. Mech.* 1877); **turpentine vessel**, in a coniferous tree, one of the tubes formed in the interstices of tissue, into which turpentine or like secretion naturally drains during the growth of the plant; **turpentine weed** = *turpentine shrub*; also, any of several other herbs containing an aromatic sap. See also TURPENTINE TREE.

1861 KNIGHT *Pop. Hist. Eng.* VII. xvii. 309 Robespierre.. sets fire to the *turpentine-anointed images. **1844** A. PAGE *Suppl. to Kirby's Suffolk Trav.* 141 A *turpentine ball.. which they set on fire. **1877** KNIGHT *Dict. Mech.*, **Turpentine-bucket*, a cup or vessel to catch crude turpentine as it exudes from the tree. **1856** OLMSTED *Slave States* 338 There are very large forests of [*Pinus Palustris*] in North and South Carolina, Georgia, and Alabama; and the *turpentine business is carried on.. in all these States. **1901** *Westm. Gaz.* 16 Mar. 4/1 A *turpentine camp in Baldwin County, Alabama. **1857** MILLER *Elem. Chem.* III. 452 *Turpentine camphor.. ($C_{20}H_{16}$, 4HO). **1694** SALMON *Bate's Dispens.* III. viii. (1713) 708/2 *Enema Terebinthinatum*, A *Turpentine Clyster. **1858** SIMMONDS *Dict. Trade*, **Turpentine and Tar Distiller*, a refiner of these substances. **1901** *Westm. Gaz.* 4 May 5/2 The *turpentine district along the St. John's River has been completely wiped out. **1843** R. J. GRAVES *Syst. Clin. Med.* x. 107 *note*, A warm *turpentine epithem should be placed upon this region. **1867** H. LATHAM *Black & White* 124 The paths which lead among the *turpentine farms. **1856** OLMSTED *Slave States* 350 The majority of what I have termed *turpentine-farmers—.. the small proprietors of the long-leafed pine forest land. **1887** FENN *Dick o' the Fens* ii, They were the roots of *turpentine-filled pines. **1879** *St. George's Hosp. Rep.* IX. 319 Great tenderness over the lower half of the abdomen. *Turpentine fomentations were applied. **1860** MAYNE *Expos. Lex.*, **Turpentine Liniment*,.. a preparation.. of yellow basilicon ointment diluted with turpentine. **1842** T. W. HARRIS *Insects Injurious to Vegetation* 350 *Turpentine-moths.. injure pines and firs. **1830** LINDLEY *Nat. Syst. Bot.* 127 A copious flow of limpid oil of a pungent *turpentine odour. **1868** WATTS *Dict. Chem.* V. 920 The diversities of character exhibited by *turpentine-oils.. relate chiefly to the specific gravity, boiling-point, and optical rotatory power. **1884** C. S. SARGENT *Rep. Forests N. Amer.* 518 Their owners oftener.. employing them [negroes in N. Carolina] in *turpentine orchards than in the cotton-fields. **1622** DEKKER & MASSINGER *Virgin Mart.* III. Wks. 1873 IV. 52 One gave me *turpentine pils. **1856** OLMSTED *Slave States* 325, I was now .. in the *Turpentine region of North Carolina. **1632** LITHGOW *Trav.* (1906) 230 A *Turpentine rod brought from Jordan and given to King James. **1887** MOLONEY *Forestry W. Afr.* 372 The plant has a strong *turpentine smell. **1850** MAYNE REID *Rifle Rangers* I. v. 46 The danger is, we may stick in the *Turpentine State. **1859** BARTLETT *Dict. Amer.*, *Turpentine State*, the State of North Carolina, so called from the quantity of turpentine obtained from its pine forests. **1799** *Wilmington* (N. Carolina) *Gaz.* 12 Dec. 2/1 Will be sold.. at Public Sale... Two *turpentine stills. **1935** Z. N. HURSTON *Mules & Men* I. iv. 86 One woman had killed five [men] when I left that turpentine still where she lived. **1877** ROBERTS *Handbk. Med.* (ed. 3) I. 130 Occasionally *turpentine-stupes or sinapisms are needed in order to give relief. **1815** J. SMITH *Panorama Sc. & Art* II. 791 It dries as well as any other *turpentine-varnish, and when dry it appears to be as durable as any other solution of copal. **1868** WATTS *Dict. Chem.* V. 925 *Turpentine-varnishes*, solutions of resins in oil of turpentine. **1673–4** GREW *Anat. Trunks* I. ii. §20 The.. *Turpentine-Vessels of Pine are likewise remarkably bigger.. than the Milk-Vessels themselves. **1861** BENTLEY *Man. Bot.* 55 In the Coniferæ they.. have.. been termed turpentine vessels. **1819** *Western Rev.* I. 95 Among the most remarkable and singular [plants of Kentucky is].. *Silphium therebinthaceum*, *Turpentine weed. **1866** *Treas. Bot.* 1059/1 The plant [*Silphium laciniatum*] is also known as the.. Turpentine-weed. **1885** F. WHYMPER in *Girl's Own Paper* Jan. 171/1 The compass plant—.. known, also, as the.. turpentine weed—is a vigorous perennial. **1913** W. C. BARNES *Western Grazing Grounds* 236 There is a little green weed (*Gutierrezia*) known locally as snakeweed, fireweed, turpentine weed. **1931** G. H. VANSELL *Nectar & Pollen Plants Calif.* 14 Turpentine weed.. is also visited freely by bees for nectar. **1890** *Philadelphia Inquirer* 1 June 1/4 He would find there every interest and every occupation of the period fully depicted, from the forests of Maine to the *turpentine woods of North Carolina. **1892** *Pall Mall G.* 15 Nov. 2/3 The Florida convicts.. were mostly put to work in the turpentine woods.

'turpentine, *v.* [f. prec. sb.] *trans.* To treat, rub, or smear with turpentine or turpentine oil. Hence **'turpentined** *ppl. a.* So **'turpentining** *vbl. sb.*, the process of obtaining crude turpentine from living pine-trees (*Cent. Dict. Supp.* 1909).

1759 *N. Jersey Archives* XX. 374 Stolen.. A Battoe.. painted with Spanish Brown in the Inside, and the Outsides turpentined. **1789** WOLCOTT (P. Pindar) *Subj. for Painters* 110 Fir'd like turpentin'd poor roasting rats. **1836** DICKENS *Sk. Boz, Old Lady*, The table-covers are never taken off, except when the leaves are turpentined and bees'-waxed. **1893** *Spons' Mechanics' Own Bk.* (ed. 4) 433 Put in others with the second marbling colour, also on a turpentined feather. **1910** C. VAN HISE *Conservation Natural Resources of U.S.* iii. 229 (*heading*) Reduction of loss in turpentining. **1971** *Forest Products Jrnl.* Feb. 53/2 The Southeastern Forest Experiment Station conducted a.. study to determine the effect of turpentining on.. yields of butt peeler blocks.

'turpentine tree.

1. *orig.* The Terebinth, *Pistacia Terebinthus* (N.O. *Anacardiaceæ*), the source of Chian or Cyprian turpentine.

1562 TURNER *Herbal* II. 29 Amongest other rosynes, it of ye turpentinetre is best. *Ibid.* 151, I call it Turpentine tre, because Turpentine cometh oute of it. **1615** G. SANDYS *Trav.* 176 Some two miles from the City.. there groweth a Turpentine-tree yet flourishing. **1726** LEONI *Alberti's Archit.* II. 6/2 The Turpentine-tree near Hebron, which was reported to have stood from the creation of the world to the days of Josephus. **1728** BRADLEY *Dict. Bot.* s.v. *Terebinthus*, The Broader-leav'd Turpentine-Tree. *Ibid.*, The Narrow-leav'd Turpentine-Tree. **1869** H. SNOW *Theocritus, Epigr.* i. Notes (1873) 214 The terebinth or turpentine-tree (*Pistachia Terebinthus*), is often mentioned in the Bible, under the names of oak or terebinth.

2. Any tree yielding turpentine, esp. species of pine and fir, as the Larch, *Abies Larix*, which yields Venice turpentine; *Bursera gummifera* (N.O. *Amyridaceæ*), of the West Indies; in Australia, species of *Eucalyptus, Syncarpia*, and *Tristania*; in New Zealand, the Tarata (Morris).

1726 LEONI *Alberti's Archit.* I. 26/2, I do not know any Wood that is to be preferr'd to the Larch, or Turpentine Tree. **1818** OXLEY *Jrnls. Two Exped. N.S. Wales* (1820) 331 The timber was chiefly.. stringy bark, turpentine tree, and forest oak. **1866** *Treas. Bot.*, Turpentine-tree, *Pistacia Terebinthus*; also *Bursera gummifera*. ——, Australian, *Tristania albicans*. **1889** J. H. MAIDEN *Usef. Native Plants Australia* 493 *Eucalyptus microcorys*.. North of Port Jackson it bears the name of 'Turpentine Tree', and 'Forest Mahogany'. *Ibid.* 523 *Eucalyptus Stuartiana*.. frequently called 'Turpentine Tree', or 'Peppermint Tree'.

turpentinic (-'tɪnɪk), *a. Chem.* [f. TURPENTINE *sb.* + -IC.] In ***turpentinic acid***, a synonym of TEREBIC *acid*.

1868 WATTS *Dict. Chem.* V. 724 Discovered by Bromeis, who called it turpentinic acid.

'turpentinous, *a. rare.* [f. TURPENTINE *sb.* + -OUS.] Of the nature of turpentine.

1909 *Eng. Rev.* Jan. 311 Powder 'em and get a little tar and turpentinous smell in.. woodpacking for hot baths.

'turpentiny, *a.* [f. as prec. + -Y.] Containing turpentine; having the smell or other properties of turpentine; smeared with turpentine.

1735 *Dict. Polygraph.* I. S ij, The best wood for this purpose,.. provided it be not turpentiny. **1866** *Treas. Bot.* 718/2 Manna of Briançon, a turpentiny saccharine exudation from the larch. **1894** DU MAURIER *Trilby* III. (1901) 44/2 Clasping his pointy turpentiny hand. **1906** *Macm. Mag.* Sept. 809, I should have.. got my fingers all sticky and turpentiney.

turpeth, turbith ('tɜːpɪθ, -bɪθ). Forms: *α.* 5 turbyte, 5–8 -bit, 6 torbith, turbythe, *pl.* -bithes, 7–9 turbeth, 6– turbith; *β.* 7– turpith, -peth. [a. OF. *turbit, -ith, turpet* (F. *turbith*) or ad. med.L. *turbith(um, turpethum, turpetum*, ad. Pers. and Arab. *turbid, -bed*, whence also Pg., Sp. *turbit*. *Turbith* was the preponderant Eng. form to the 18th c., till assimilated to med.L. *turpethum*.]

1. A cathartic drug prepared from the root of East Indian jalap, *Ipomœa Turpethum*, an Indian and Australian plant; also, the plant itself, or its root.

† ***Garganic turbith***: see quot. 1760.

α. *c*1400 *Lanfranc's Cirurg.* 180 He mote ofte purge fleume with turbit. **1460–70** *Bk. Quintessence* 16 þo laxatyues þat purgen flewme & viscous humouris, as a litil of euforbie, or turbit, or sambucy. **1545** *Rates of Custom-ho.* C vj b, Torbith the pounde, xij d. **1567** MAPLET *Gr. Forest* 63 Tvrbit whose Leafe is like the Laurell, groweth in Ægypt .. It is giuen to purge fleume. **1652** CULPEPPER *Eng. Physic.* (1809) 261 For choler, rhubarb; for phlegm, turbith; for watery humours, scammony. **1760** J. LEE *Introd. Bot.* App. 330 Garganic Turbith, *Thapsia*. *Ibid.*, Indian Turbith, or of the Shops, *Convolvulus*. **1785** MARTYN *Rousseau's Bot.* xvi. (1794) 185 This genus contains several remarkable plants; as .. Turpethum or Turbith.

β. **1658** ROWLAND *Moufet's Theat. Ins.* 1119 The Turpeth drives them from their nests. **1758** J. S. *Le Dran's Observ. Surg.* (1771) A a iv b, Turpeth, Hermodactyles, Polypody of the Oak. **1905** H. D. ROLLESTON *Dis. Liver* 262 Turpeth, the Ipomœa turpethum of the Colonial and Indian Pharmacopœias, is recommended in 20 grain doses.

b. ***Montpellier turpeth***, common name for *Globularia alypum*, the decoction of the leaves of which acts as an active but gentle purgative.

1860 in MAYNE *Expos. Lex.*

2. ***turpeth*** or ***turbith mineral*** (MINERAL *a.* 4): basic sulphate of mercury ($HgSO_4 \cdot 2HgO$), obtained as a lemon-yellow powder from the normal sulphate by washing with hot water.

It has emetic, cathartic, and sternutatory properties, but is no longer used internally.

α. **1616** BULLOKAR *Eng. Expos.*, *Turbith minerall*, a certaine red powder.. which is vsed against the French disease. **1669** W. SIMPSON *Hydrol. Chym.* 60 Dissolving quicksilver in oyl of vitriol, according to what is done in making turbith mineral. **1685** BOYLE *Enq. Notion Nat.* vi. 233 A patient, who.. could not be brought to salivate, neither by the gentler ways, nor by turbith-mineral and other harsher medicines. **1758** REID tr. *Macquer's Chym.* I. 402 Wash this yellow matter in five or six warm waters, and it will be what is called in medicine Turbith mineral; that is, a combination of the Vitriolic Acid with Mercury, five or six grains whereof is a violent purgative, and also an emetic; qualities which it possesses in common with the vegetable Turbith, whose name it hath therefore taken. **1849** D. CAMPBELL *Inorg. Chem.* 236 This yellow powder is a subsulphate [of mercury] ($3HgO,SO_3$), and is known as turbeth mineral. **1874** GARROD & BAXTER *Mat. Med.* (1880) 110 The yellow subsulphate above mentioned, under the name of Turbith Mineral, has been employed as an errhine.

β. **1716** M. DAVIES *Athen. Brit.* II. 352 Turpith Mineral, made of Hydrargyry and Oyl of Vitriol. **1815** J. SMITH *Panorama Sc. & Art* II. 795 King's yellow, turpith mineral, and Dutch pink, all form very bright yellows. **1868** WATTS *Dict. Chem.* V. 925 *Turpeth* or *turbith mineral*, an old name for basic mercuric sulphate, $HgSO_4 \cdot 2HgO$. **1899** *Allbutt's Syst. Med.* VIII. 516 Native mercurous sulphate (turpeth mineral) is much used in France.

†**3.** *ellipt.* = prec. sense. *Obs.*

black turpeth: see quot. 1895.

α. **1658** PHILLIPS, *Turbith*,.. a red Mineral, which being beaten to powder, is used in physick. **1675** *Phil. Trans.* X. 299 Mercury.. having been.. reduced into water, turbith and ashes. **1707** *Curios. in Husb. & Gard.* 325 Olaus.. tormented some Quicksilver.. into Water, Turbith and Ashes.

β. **1678** PHILLIPS (ed. 4), *Turpith*, a Chymical preparation of Mercury, and the Oyl of Vitriol, whereby the Mercury is precipitated into a sweetnesse. **1800** *Phil. Trans.* XC. 215 Not only the pure red oxide, but the red nitrous oxide, and turpeth, may be substituted. **1895** *Funk's Standard Dict.* s.v., *Black turpeth*, black mercurous acid: old name.

4. *attrib.*, as *t. plant, root, vomit.*
1773 T. PERCIVAL *Ess.* II. 163 The powerful effects of Turpeth vomits in white swellings of the joints. **1860** MAYNE *Expos. Lex.*, *Turbeth Plant*, common name for the *Convolvulus turpethum.* **1868** WATTS *Dict. Chem.* V. 925 *Turpeth* or *turbith root.*

turpethic (tɜːˈpɛθɪk), *a. Chem.* [f. mod.L. *turpeth-um* TURPETH + -IC.] Of or pertaining to turpeth or turbith; in ***turpethic acid***, $C_{34}H_{60}O_{18}$, produced by the action of bases on turpethin. So **turpethin** (ˈtɜːpɪθɪn), *Chem.* [see -IN[1]], a brownish-yellow purgative resin, $C_{34}H_{56}O_{16}$, obtained from turpeth- or turbith-root; **turpeˈtholic** *a.*, in ***turpetholic acid***, $C_{16}H_{32}O_4$, a derivative of turpethin, crystallizing in a mass of slender microscopic needles having an irritant taste; hence **turˈpetholate**, a salt of turpetholic acid.
1868 WATTS *Dict. Chem.* V. 926 When turpethin is dissolved in warm baryta-water, the baryta removed [etc.], turpethic acid remains as an amorphous yellowish mass. *Ibid.*, Under the influence of mineral acids, it [turpethin] is re-dissolved into glucose and turpetholic acid. *Ibid.*, Turpetholate of Sodium, $C_{16}H_{31}NaO_4$.

turpeyl, var. TIRPEIL *Obs.*, fear.

turph, -y, obs. ff. TURF, TURFY.

ˈturpid, *a. rare.* [irreg. f. L. *turp-is* ugly, unsightly, foul, disgraceful + -ID, after *torpid*, etc.] Base, filthy, worthless. Hence **ˈturpidly** *adv.*
1623 COCKERAM, *Turpid*, filthy. **1866** J. B. ROSE tr. *Virg. Georg.* II. 60 But fruit degenerates,—its flavour lost, The turpid grapes are left to birds or frost. **1867** —— *Æneid* 44 Smitten with turpid fear. **1866** —— tr. *Ovid's Fasti* VI. 623 The female crew..Turned turpidly and fled.

†**ˈturpie**, *a. Obs. rare.* [f. L. *turpi-s* ugly, foul; in quot. after the L. phrase *turpe lucrum* (see FILTHY *a.* 4b).] Filthy.
1632 NASHE *Quaternio* 90 How the nostrils savour nothing more than turpie lucre.

ˈturpify, *v. rare.* [ad. L. *turpificāre* (recorded only in pa. pple. *turpificātus*) to make filthy, foul, or bad, f. L. *turpi-s* + *-ficāre*: see prec. and -FY.] *trans.* To make foul or filthy; to befoul, besmirch.
a **1586** SIDNEY *Wanstead Play* Wks. (1629) 620 O [that] a woman..should thus turpifie the reputation of my doctrine, with the superscription of a foole.

†**turpin**[1]. *Obs. rare.* A fanciful name for, or appellation of, the hare.
a **1325** *Names of Hare* in *Rel. Ant.* I. 133 He shal saien on oreisoun In þe worshipe of þe hare..The scotewine, the skikart, The turpin, the tirart.

†**turpin**[2], obs. abbreviated f. TURPENTINE.
1688 R. HOLME *Armoury* II. 80/1 The Turpin, or Turpentine Tree [hath] the leaves smooth, four on a side.

turpinite (ˈtɜːpɪnaɪt). [a. F. *turpinite*, f. Turpin, name of the inventor + -ITE[1].] An explosive, used in making shells.
1895 *Daily Chron.* 6 Dec. 6/1 'Turpinite', a comprehensive word coined in honour of a string of episodes bearing upon the new methods of putting a stop to war by the prospective destruction of all cities.

turpith: see TURPETH.

turpitude (ˈtɜːpɪtjuːd). Also 5 **turpytude**. [a. F. *turpitude* (*a* 1417 in Godef. *Compl.*), or directly ad. L. *turpitūdo*, f. *turpi-s* base: see -TUDE.]
1. Base or shameful character; baseness, vileness; depravity, wickedness.
1490 CAXTON *Eneydos* xxii. 83 In sygne of vengaunce of the dethe of hys fader, And turpytude dyshonest of clytemnestra his moder. **1589** PUTTENHAM *Eng. Poesie* III. xxiv. (Arb.) 295 All maner of conceites that stirre vp any vehement passion in a man, doo it by some turpitude or euill and vndecency that is in them. **1606** SHAKS. *Ant. & Cl.* IV. vi. 33 How would'st thou haue payed My better seruice, when my turpitude Thou dost so Crowne with Gold. **1659** HAMMOND *On Ps.* cxix. 137–8 Paraphr. 609 Those which have a natural turpitude and indispensable sinfulnesse in them! *a* **1711** KEN *Preparatives* Poet. Wks. 1721 III. 25 Some for their Turpitude had Shame, And Terrors of infernal Flame. **1794** LD. AUCKLAND *Corr.* (1862) III. 261 Indignation and horror at the infatuated turpitude of some of the allied powers. **1849** MACAULAY *Hist. Eng.* iii. I. 402 The artists corrupted the spectators, and the spectators the artists, till the turpitude of the drama became such as must astonish all who are not aware that extreme relaxation is the natural effect of extreme restraint. **1879** *Temple Bar Mag.* Oct. 172 A career great from the historical importance of the period..but inglorious and almost without a parallel in recent times for moral turpitude and unscrupulous self-seeking.
b. With *a* and *pl.* An instance of this.
1597 J. PAYNE *Royal Exch.* 28 Every Christian ought..to lament to se suche turpitudes. **1607** COKE *Charge at Norwich Assizes* 5 Partialitie in a Judge is a Turpitude, which doth soyle and stayne all the Actions done by him. **1810** BENTHAM *Packing* (1821) 71 A picture in which all deformities and turpitudes are plaistered over with the most brilliant colours. **1833** CHALMERS *Const. Man* (1835) I. iii. 157 Temptation to a turpitude or a crime. **1913** *19th Cent.* Aug. 393 The minor offences and turpitudes which are condemned in the court of conscience.

†**c.** Rendering L. *turpitudo* of the Vulgate: 'nakedness'; 'shame'. *Obs. rare.*
1570 FOXE *A. & M.* 157/2 The holy lawe of God forbiddeth to reueale the turpitude of thy blood or kyndred. *Ibid.*, Thou shalt not reueale the turpitude of thy father.
†**2.** in *lit.* sense: Foulness, offensiveness, unsightliness. *Obs. rare.*
1684 tr. *Bonet's Merc. Compit.* XIX. 719 This Medicin helps notably any cutaneous turpitude whatsoever.

turple, var. TORPLE.

turps (tɜːps). [Colloq. (workmen's or painters') abbreviation of TURPENTINE; the final *-s* appears to be collective.]
1. Oil of turpentine.
1823 P. NICHOLSON *Pract. Build.* 411 Oil of Turpentine, or Turps, is made from the resin of that name, which is obtained from all larch and fir-trees. **1867** F. FRANCIS *Angling* xiv. (1880) 506 Cut up some white indiarubber..dissolve it in turps. **1894** *Brit. Jrnl. Photogr.* XLI. 5 Not soluble in either benzole, turps, or xylol.
2. *Austral. slang.* Intoxicating liquor, esp. beer.
1945 BAKER *Austral. English* 168 Australians have a fair selection of terms to describe drinking and drinking bouts, such as *a beer-up*,..and to *bash the turps*. **1962** MARSHALL & DRYSDALE *Journey among Men* 84 The Sergeant alleged that Ah Fong was a notorious drunkard, forever on the 'turps'. **1973** J. O'GRADY *Survival in Doghouse* 57 He's humping a dozen cans with him. Ice cold. And he gets a great welcome. Not only because of the turps, but because with him there we can have a four-handed game.

Turque, obs. f. TURK.

turquen, var. TURKEN *v. Obs.*

turques, var. TURKIS *v. Obs.*

†**turˈquesque**. *Obs. rare.* [a. obs. F. *turquesque* (= It. *turchesco*) Turkish.] *pl.* ? Turkish cloths or carpets.
1594 BLUNDEVIL *Exerc.* v. IV. (1597) 259b, The chiefe marchandizes that come from this countrie [Turkey] to other Prouinces are..Veluets, Damaske, Grograins, Turquesques and Wood.

†**turquet**[1]. *Obs. rare*[−1]. [app. f. *Turque*, TURK + -ET[1]; cf. F. *turquet* 'petit chien, d'origine turque, à nez camus et à poil ras' (16–17th c. in Hatz.-Darm.). But *Turquets* may be a misprint for *Turques*.] A player dressed up to resemble a Turk.
1625 BACON *Ess., Masques* (Arb.) 540 Anti-masques..haue been commonly of Fooles, Satyres, Baboones, Wilde-Men, Antiques, Beasts, Sprites, Witches, Ethiopes, Pigmies, Turquets,..and the like.

†**turquet**[2]. *Obs. rare*[−1]. [a. F. *turquet*, now = maize, but given by Cotgr. as a var. of *turguet* spelt.] ? Spelt.
The passage is translated from a French source, and the rendering *starch-corn* is perh. derived from Cotgrave.
1725 *Family Dict.* II. s.v. *Stone*, A Remedy for the Stone and Gravel is, to take the Herb Turquet or Storch-Corn [*sic*], dry it and reduce it to Powder.

†**turquin**. *Obs. rare.* [a. F. *turquin* (= Sp. and Pg. *turqui*), ad. It. *turchino* (med.L. *turchīnus*) blue, f. *Turco* Turk.
Different reasons are assigned for the use of the adj. to designate 'blue'. In sense 1 the meaning of 'Turkish' may be preserved.]
1. A dark-green pumpkin.
After obs. F. *pompon Turquin* (Cotgr.).
1616 SURFL. & MARKH. *Country Farme* 193 Some of them are called Turquins, as those which haue a verie greene colour, and drawing somewhat toward a blacke.
2. A bluish-grey or slate-coloured marble.
1811 PINKERTON *Petralogy* I. 412 A singular marble is still known to be found at Sitifi, in the north of Africa, being the proper turquin, because, like the turquois, it is supposed to be brought from a country subject to the Turks. It is of a bluish grey, or slate colour, with spots of siderite or hornblende.

turquoise (ˈtɜːkwɔɪz, -kɔɪz, təˈkɔɪz, *arch.* təˈkiːz, ˈtɜːkɪz), *sb.* (*a.*) Forms: see below. [In 15–16th c. *turkeis, -keys*, a. OF. *turqueise, -quaise*, later *turquoise*, fem. of *turqueis, -quais, turquois* adj. Turkish, in full *pierre turquoise*, i.e. 'Turkish stone' (cf. Marco Polo c. xxxiv 'pierres qui s'appellent *turquesses*') = Pr., Sp. *turquesa*, Pg. *turqueza*, It. *turchese*, med.L. (*lapis*) *turchēsius* or *turkēsius*; = MDu. *turcoys, turckois*, Du. *turkoois*, MHG. *turkīs, -koys*, etc., mod.Ger. *türkis, türkiss*, Da. *turkis, tyrkis*, Sw. *turkos*. So named as coming from Turkestan, where first found, or through the Turkish dominions: cf. also med.L. *turchīnus*, It. *turchino*, F. *turquin* blue, azure. The earliest Eng. form was the OF. and AF. *turkeis*; this by vowel-progression became *turˈkēse, -ˈīse*, and by stress-shift, as in other Teutonic languages, *ˈturkes, -as, -is*; but these forms began before 1600 to be displaced by adoption of the French spelling *turquoise, turkois*. Ben Jonson stresses *ˈturkise*, Dr. Johnson *ˈturkois, -koise*, Milton and Tennyson *ˈturkis*. Walker and Smart (1846) pronounce *turˈkīz*, Cent. Dict. and Funk's Stand. *tərˈkoiz, tərˈkīz*, Webster 1911 *turˈkoiz* or *ˈturkwoiz*.]
I. 1. a. A precious stone found in Persia (***the true*** or ***oriental turquoise***), much prized as a gem, of a sky-blue to apple-green colour, almost opaque or sometimes translucent, consisting of hydrous phosphate of aluminium.
α. 4–7 **turkeis**, 5–7 **turkeys**, 6 **turkeies, turquays, turkese, turkies**, 7 **turcais, torqueis, turquies, -quize, turchis**; 6– **turkis**, 7– **turkise** (both now *archaic*).
1398 TREVISA *Barth. De P.R.* XVI. xcvi. (Bodl. MS.) lf. 183b/2 De Turtogis. Turtogis that hatte Turkeis also is a ȝelow white stone and haþ þat name of the contrey of Turkeis. þis stone kepeþ and saueþ þe siȝt and bredeþ gladnes and comforte. **1463** in *Bury Wills* (Camden) 36, I beqwethe to the said Dame Margarete a doubyl ryng departyd of gold with a ruby and a turkeys. **1503** HAWES *Examp. Virt.* iv. 5 Of vertuous turkeys there was a cheyr. *c* **1530** *Crt. of Love* xii, There lacked than, nor emerald so grene, Balais, Turkeis, ne thing to my devise. **1545** *Test. Ebor.* (Surtees) VI. 226 A rynge of golde with a turquays. **1596** SHAKS. *Merch. V.* III. i. 126 Out vpon her,..it was my Turkies, I had it of Leah when I was a Batcheler. **1599** HAKLUYT *Voy.* II. I. 306 Orient perles & great Turkeses. **1603** B. JONSON *Sejanus* I. i, True as turkise in the deare lords ring. **1608** WILLET *Hexapla Exod.* 642 It is more like to be the turkeis..the turcais is of a blewish metalline colour. **1616** BULLOKAR *Eng. Expos.*, *Turkise*, a precious stone of a silke blew colour. **1634** MILTON *Comus* 894 The azurn sheen Of Turkis blew and Emrauld green. **1648** GAGE *West Ind.* 71 Bracelets of Turkises and of gold likewise. **1688** R. HOLME *Armoury* II. 40/2 The Turches or Turky stone..some call it Eranus, others Turcois or Torqueis. **1694** STRYPE *Abp. Cranmer* III. i. 308 They seized..a good Turkeys and a Diamond. **1857** TENNYSON *Geraint & Enid* 661 The turf was rich in plots that look'd Each like a garnet or a turkis in it. **1877** W. JONES *Finger-ring* 158 The turquoise, turkise, or turkey-stone having..been supposed to possess talismanic properties. *a* **1913** S. VINES *Hotel* 16 in *Oxford Poetry* 154 Sapphires and amethysts and wicked Turkises.
β. 5–6 **turkes**, 5–7 **turques**, (5 **torcas**, 5–6 *Sc.* **turcas**, 6 **turkas, torchas, turcasse, tourques, turquez, toorkes, turquesse, turkesse**), 6–7 **turches**.
1478 *Croscombe Churchw. Acc.* (Som. Rec. Soc.) 6 A ryng gold with a torcas. **1488** *Acc. Ld. High Treas. Scot.* I. 81 Item, a ryng with a turcas. **1511–12** *Ibid.* IV. 331 Ane ruby, ane turkas. **1501** *Bury Wills* (Camden) 91 A ryng of gold w[t] a toorkes set in. *a* **1512** FABYAN *Will* in *Chron.* Pref. 7 A ryng of gold, sett w[t] a turques, a dyamaunt, and a ruby. **1518** *Test. Ebor.* (Surtees) V. 8 A rynge of golde with a stone in hit callede a turkes. **1527** *Ibid.* 244 Unum annulum cum le torchas. **1530** PALSGR. 282/1 Tourques a precious stone, *tourquois*. **1551** T. WILSON *Logike* (1580) 4 *Lapis*, a stone, comprehendeth in it self, a Saphire, a Rubbie, a Christall, a Turkas. **1553** —— *Rhet.* 209 No Diamonde, no Saphire, no Rubie, no Christall: no Turcasse, no Emerode. **1555** EDEN *Decades* 235 Turquesses are founde in Exer a place of Siech Ismael. **1567** MAPLET *Gr. Forest* 23 The Turches or Turcois, is of the common sort called Eranus... It is called a Turches for that it is onely found in Turkland or amongst the Turkes. **1599** *Warn. Faire Wom.* I. 217 You wear a pretty turkesse there, methinks. **1601** CHESTER *Love's Mart.* (N. Shaks. Soc.) 107 The Turches being worne in a Ring. **1653** GREAVES *Seraglio* 15 A Basen and Ewer of massive gold, set with Rubies and Turkesses. **1688** [see α].
γ. 6 **turkoise**, 6–7 **turquoys, turcoyse, turquoies**, 6–8 **turcois**, 7–8 **turcoise**, (**turchois**), 7–9 **turkois**, (8 **torquois, turkquoise**, 9 **tourquois**), 6– **turquoise, -ois**.
1567 Turcois [see β]. **1601** HOLLAND *Pliny* XXXVII. viii. II. 619 The best Turquois is that which approcheth nearest to the grasse green of an Emeraud. **1607** Turchois, **1631** Turcois [see b]. **1646** SIR T. BROWNE *Pseud. Ep.* II. i. (1686) 42 Crystall..will receive impression from Steel, in a manner like the Turchois. *a* **1658** CLEVELAND *Common Place* Wks. (1677) 166 The Compassionate Turcoise confesseth the Sickness of his Wearer by changing colour. **1668** WILKINS *Real Char.* II. iii. 63 Turkois. **1676** *Phil. Trans.* XI. 755 Turkoises are no where found but in Persia. **1679** *Lond. Gaz.* No. 1418/4 Lost..a Ring with a large Turquoies of the Old Rock, very good colour. **1747** MORTIMER in *Phil. Trans.* XLIV. 429 This Stone has received its..Name of Turchesia, and Turquoise, from its being most commonly brought from Turky. **1859** GEO. ELIOT *A. Bede* v, The small brown hand..is laden with pearls, diamonds, and turquoises.
b. In *collect. sing.*, esp. as a substance.
1607 *Lingua* IV. iv, Orient Pearles, and sparkling Diamonds: Beset at the end with Emeraulds and Turchois. **1631** WIDDOWES *Nat. Philos.* 28 Turcois is darke, of a skie colour, and greenish. **1836** T. THOMSON *Min., Geol.* etc. I. 230 Tourquois seems to have been known to the ancients. **1857** WOOD *Comm. Objects Sea Shore* 64 They..are blue and bright as turquoise, to which jewel they bear some resemblance. **1882** 'OUIDA' *Maremma* I. 62 The Ligurian sea, blue as turquoise. **1884** BROWNING *Ferishtah, Melon-seller* 35 Ferishtah..passed..To Nishapur, that Elburz looks above—Where they dig turquoise.
2. More fully **turquoise stone**: see also TURKEY STONE, *Turkish stone* (TURKISH *a.* 2b). Now *rare*.
1556 *N. C. Wills* (Surtees 1908) 240 One ring of golde with a turkeys stone in it. **1600** HAKLUYT *Voy.* (1810) III. 440 In the gates..there are many Turques-stones. *c* **1610** in *Heriot's Mem.* App. VII. (1822) 215 A ring sett with 5 little Turkis stones. **1673** RAY *Journ. Low C., Florence* 333 An entire image made of one Turchois stone. **1796** MORSE *Amer. Geog.* II. 568 Persia contains mines of..above all, turquoise stones. **1831** LD. HOUGHTON *Mem. Many Scenes* (1844) 75 This heaven..With richer, but less brilliant, hue, Built up of turkis-stone.

3. As name for a colour (short for *turquoise blue*): see 6 b.

1853 KANE *Grinnell Exp.* viii. (1856) 61 The blue and white were mixed in a pale turkois. **1860** W. G. CLARK in *Vac. Tour.* 42 A cave with a floor of liquid turquoise. **1876** MISS BROUGHTON *Joan* I. xix, Looking out through the open windows at the absolute turquoise of the heavens. **1878** MISS J. J. YOUNG *Ceram. Art* (1879) 41 The Chinese value one piece..for the depth of its turquoise. **1881** *Porcelain Works, Worcester* 35 To the admirers of colour, the Persian turquoise, Imperial yellow,..and other enamels present an interesting series.

4. a. Lapidaries' name for odontolite: see quot. 1839; also called ***bone-turquoise*** and ***occidental turquoise***.

1796 KIRWAN *Elem. Min.* (ed. 2) II. 154 Turquoise is ivory tinged by the blue Calx of Copper. **1819** Odontolite Turquoise [see *odontolite* (ODONTO-)]. **1839** URE *Dict. Arts,* etc. 744 A totally different kind of turquois, called *bone turquois*, which seems to be phosphate of lime coloured with oxide of copper. **1868** DANA *Min.* (ed. 5) 580 *Turquoise de vieille roche* (in distinction from Odontolite, or *T. de nouvelle roche*, called also Occidental Turquois).

b. (See quot.)

1840 *Penny Cycl.* XVIII. 472/2 s.v. *Pottery*, These mixtures give a fine white body for ornaments... A body called turquoise has been manufactured to a great extent for a few years past... When glazed, it has the peculiar milky tint of the gem after which it has been named.

II. *attrib.* and *Comb.*

5. a. Simple attrib. 'of turquoise': as ***turquoise bead, colour, enamel, gem, mine, miner, treasure, work, working***.

1662 MERRETT tr. *Neri's Art of Glass* 56 This [sea] salt so calcin'd, keep to make a Blew or Turcois colour. **1753** *Chambers' Cycl.* App. s.v. *Turcois*, The pale blue of the natural turcois gem. *Ibid.*, Turcois enamel. **1765** *Phil. Trans.* LV. 21 Copper..gives the torquois colour to white glass. **1826** KIRBY & SP. *Entomol.* III. xxx. 177 Three blue tubercles, like..little turquois beads. **1849** M. ARNOLD *Strayed Reveller* 195 Their wealth..Of gold and ivory, Of turquoise-earth and amethyst. **1876** BIRCH *Rede Lect. Egypt* 20 Magarah and its turquoise treasures had been lost. **1877** W. R. COOPER *Egypt. Obelisks* iv. (1878) 16 The copper and turquoise miners of the Wady Magari. **1882** *Rep. to Ho. Repr. Prec. Met. U.S.* 323 Many ancient turquois workings are found in the neighborhood. **1896** GEORG. M. STISTED *True Life of Sir R. F. Burton* xv. 377 The Land of Midian is still wealthy; turquoise mines exist. [**1906** *Outlook* 30 June 881/2 In common, doubtless, with the Sinai Bedawys, the Egyptians worshipped the Goddess of the Turquoise.] *Ibid.* That..the worship of the Turquoise goddess [was] non-Egyptian in nature. **1908** *Ch. Times* 20 Mar. 392/2 Turquoise and Indian Work for..Zenana Mission.

b. In sense 'set or adorned with a turquoise or turquoises, or composed of turquoises', as ***turquoise ear-ring, locket, ring***.

1808 SCOTT *Marm.* v. x, The fair Queen of France Sent him a Turquois ring. **1868** LD. HOUGHTON *Select. fr. Wks.* 60 And turkis-lockets, that no churl Hath fashioned out mechanic-wise. **1896** GEORG. M. STISTED *True Life Sir R. F. Burton* vii. 164 A red sausage-shaped cushion strung with turquoise rings. **1901** *Westm. Gaz.* 28 Dec. 1/3 The girl with turquoise eyes and turquoise earrings.

c. Instrumental, similative, etc., as ***turquoise-coloured, -encrusted, -gemmed, -hued, -like, -studded, -tinted*** adjs.; **turquoise-berry**, a liliaceous Tasmanian herb, *Drymophila cyanocarpa*, bearing white flowers and blue pendulous berries.

1823 C. J. MATHEWS *Jrnl.* 13 Nov. in Dickens *Life Charles J. Mathews* (1879) I. iv. 93 The beautiful turquoise-coloured bay. **1862** G. M. HOPKINS *Poems* (1967) 9 One bound o'er dripping gold a turquoise-gemm'd Circlet of astral flowerets. **1864** *Daily Tel.* 26 Sept., The turquoise-like water, too, sparkled in the light of the declining day. **1881** *Athenæum* 4 June 754 A pure turquoise-coloured sky. **1893** J. ASHBY-STERRY *Naughty Girl* xii, A coquettish turquoise-hued tea-gown. **1898** MORRIS *Austral Eng.* 426/2 *Solomon's Seal*,..the Tasmanian name for *Drymophila cyanocarpa*,..also called Turquoise Berry. **1899** *Edin. Rev.* Jan. 35 The turquoise-tinted feathers of the Kingfisher. **1901** KIPLING *Kim* xiv. 361 A fair-coloured woman with turquoise-studded headgear. **1906** *Daily Chron.* 23 Mar. 8/1 Her strings of Orient pearls, her turquoise-encrusted heart-lockets. **1906** *Westm. Gaz.* 24 Nov. 7/2 A gossamer turquoise-coloured scarf, lightly thrown across her shoulders. **1909** *Daily Chron.* 15 July 4/5 Neck ornament in the form of a turquoise studded serpent.

6. a. As *adj.* Of the colour of the turquoise; turquoise-blue.

1573 G. HARVEY *Letter-bk.* (Camden) 125 An alabaster neck, a turcois eie. **1844** LADY G. FULLERTON *Ellen Middleton* (1854) II. xiv. 149 The cordon bleu [bird], with his turquoise breast. **1882** MRS. B. M. CROKER *Proper Pride* xi, Rising here and there against the turquoise sky were palms. **1891** E. ROPER *By Track & Trail* x. 138 Pools of lovely turquoise water. **1901** [see 5 b]. **1909** LE QUEUX *House of Shadows* xviii, Her pretty gown of turquoise chiffon.

b. With adj. or sb. of colour.

1799 G. SMITH *Laboratory* I. 122 A Turcoise blue enamel. **1828** STARK *Elem. Nat. Hist.* I. 279 Wings with from 8 to 10 spots of turquoise blue, bordered with orange. **1863** MISS BRADDON *Eleanor's Vict.* III. viii. 108 The turquoise-blue eyes shone with a feverish light. **1877** BLACK *Green Past.* xii, Beds of turquoise-blue forget-me-nots. **1883** *Truth* 31 May 769/2 A train and corsage of turquoise blue satin. **1886** KIPLING *Departm. Ditties, Delilah* viii, The wasteful sunset faded out in turkis-green and gold. **1890** *Daily News* 15 July 5/6 One of the..ladies who wore the beautiful turquoise blue that has been a specialty of this season.

turr, *v.* *Obs.* or *dial.* Also 5 turre. [Origin unascertained.] *intr.* and *trans.* To butt, as a ram; to push *down* by butting. Hence **turr** *sb. dial.*

a **1400–50** *Alexander* 5567 Neddirs..hedously hoge & horned as Tupis þai turred doun of his tulkis & with þar tyndis sloȝe. **1483** *Cath. Angl.* 398/1 To Turre, *arietare, est enim Arietum & aliorum animalium.* **1886** CUNLIFFE *Rochdale Gloss.* 93 *Turr*, to butt with the head. A beast possessing this vicious habit is said to have 'th turr ith head'.

turr (tɜː(r)), *sb.* *Newfoundland.* Also †tuir, turrh. [Prob. imit.] = MURRE.

1794 A. THOMAS *Newfoundland Jrnl.* (1968) x. 144 Here are..Penguins, Hegdowns, Muirs and Tuirs, Ice Birds..and a number of other Sea Fowl. **1853** *Trans. Lit. & Hist. Soc. Quebec* IV. 334 Among the sea birds are *Mernettes*, Moyocks, Gulls,..Turrhs, Paraquets, Penguins, and divers others. **1960** L. M. TUCK *Murres* 34 A common vernacular name for the murre in Newfoundland is 'turr'. **1974** *Nat. Geographic* Jan. 122/2 The seabirds here called stearin, turr, and tickle-ace are the birds known elsewhere as tern, murre, and kittiwake.

turr, Sc. form of TURF.

†**turrell.** *Obs.* [Derivation uncertain: perh. ad. OF. **tourel* (not recorded, but cf. *touret* 'instrument servant à percer', 15th c. in Godef.), or obs. F. *tarelle, terelle* auger (Cotgr.), surviving in Picard *térelle*.] A cooper's auger.

1611 COTGR., *Barroir*, a Turrell; th' Oager wherewith Coopers make holes for the barre-pinnes of a peece of caske. *Ibid.*, *Tirefond de tonnelier*, a Coopers Turrell; the Auger wherewith he boreth holes. *Ibid.*, *Ville*..the long oagar tearmed by our Coopers, a Turrell. [Hence in Sherwood, Littleton, Kersey, Bailey, etc.]

turrene, obs. form of TUREEN.

turret (ˈtʌrɪt), *sb.*[1] Forms: α. 4–6 turet, 5 -ete (6 *pl.* -ettes, *Sc.* -ettis, -etis), 5–6 *Sc.* -at(e (*pl.* -atis, -attis), 6 turryt, -ite, *Sc.* turit, turrat, 6–8 turrit, 7 *Sc.* turrett, 5– turret (*pl.* 4–6 -ettes, *Sc.* 5 -ettis, 6 -etis). β. 4–5 (7–8 *Hist.*) touret, 5–6 -ette (*pl. Sc.* -ettis), tourrett (*pl.* -ettes), towrette (*pl.* -ettis, -ys), 6–7 towret, 8 tourett. γ. 4–5 toret, 5–8 torret (5 *pl.* torettes, -is, torrettes). δ. 6 territ, 6–7 -et, -ett (*pl.* -ettes), 7 tirritt. [ME. *turet, toret, tourette*, a. OF. *torete, tourete* (12th c. in Godef.), later *tourette* (still in 17th c.), dim. of *tur, tor, tour* fem., TOWER; cf. mod.It. *torretta*, dim. of *torre*:—L. *turris* (to the influence of which the current spelling *turret* may be due).

The slightly earlier *toret, torret*, occurring in the *S. Eng. Leg.* I. 300/15 and in R. Glouc. (Rolls) 3625 in the sense of 'summit' of a hill, is app. not identical with this word, but ad. OF. *turet* (still in Artois dial.), var. of *turel* (later and now dial. *tureau*) eminence, hill.]

1. a. A small or subordinate tower, usually one forming part of a larger structure; *esp.* a rounded addition to an angle of a building, sometimes commencing at some height above the ground, and freq. containing a spiral staircase.

α. **13..** *Guy Warw.* (A.) 7306 + xxi. 1 To a turet sir Gij is went, And biheld þat firmament. *c* **1470** *Golagros & Gaw.* 42 Ane ciete..With torris and turatis. *c* **1470** HENRY *Wallace* VIII. 1014 A ryoll sted..With turrettis fayr. **1555** WATREMAN *Fardle of Facions* I. vi. 89 The gentlemen..haue neither cities nor townes, but Turrettes builte vpon the waters side. **1610** HOLLAND *Camden's Brit.* (1637) 37 An Elephant with a turret upon his backe. *Ibid.* 40 He raised an high turret, out of which..there might blaze all night long, lights and fires for the better direction of ships at sea. **1644** EVELYN *Diary* 17 Nov., Another wall full of small turrets. **1765** FOOTE *Commissary* III. (1782) 48 The large brick house ..with a turrit at top. **1824** W. IRVING *T. Trav.* I. iii. 17 He perceived the turrets of an ancient chateau rising out of the trees of its walled park. **1861** M. PATTISON *Ess.* (1889) I. 45 Thick walls and turrets at the angles gave the whole the aspect..of a fortress.

transf. **1671** *Phil. Trans.* VI. 2265 By a new Earth-quake the Top or Turret of Mount Ætna..fell in.

β. **13..** *Coer de L.* 3969 The Sarezynes, armyd, forth lepe Upon the walles the toun to kepe, Stout in touret, and in hurdys. *c* **1400** *Rom. Rose* 4164 He hired hem to make a tour. .. And rounde environ eek were set Ful many a riche and fair touret. **1481** CAXTON *Godeffroy* ccvii. 303 They were so pour and so greued of tayllages and excises, that vnnethe they had among them alle wherof to repayre two towrettys. **1545** JOYE *Exp. Dan.* i. 13 It was dowble walled with many highe and strong towrets. **1633** *Stow's Surv.* 7/1 The wals of [London], which were sore decayed, and destitute of Towres and Towrets, to be repaired. **1736** MCURE *Hist. Glasgow* 256 The Town-house or Tolbooth..has Four large Touretts on the Corners thereof.

γ. *a* **1400–50** *Alexander* 1418 (Ashm.) Sum..Tilt torettis [*v.r.* torrettes] doun, toures on hepis. *c* **1400** *Gamelyn* 329 In a litel toret his brother lay i-steke. *c* **1440** *Promp. Parv.* 497/1 Toret, lytylle towre, *turricula.* **1648** J. RAYMOND *Il Mercurio Italico* 129 An ancient Torret, built halfe of solid Marble.

δ. *a* **1600** *Hymn, 'Hierusalem my happie home'* viii. in Julian *Dict. Hymnology* (1907) 580/2 Thy terrettes and thy pinacles. *c* **1618** MORYSON *Itin.* (1903) 335 Germany aboundes with Copper, wherewith many Cittyes have Terretts steeples and whole Churches Covered. **1643** MRS. THORNTON *Autobiog.* (Surtees) 33 The window sudainly shutt with such a force the whole tirritt shooke.

b. In *Heraldry*: see quots.

1766–87 PORNY *Heraldry* Gloss., *Turret*, a small Tower. *Turreted*, having Turrets on the top. *c* **1828** BERRY *Encycl. Her.* I. Gloss., *Turret*, a small tower on the top of another. **1868** CUSSANS *Her.* vii. (1882) 123 *Turret*: a small tower commonly set upon a Castle. **1894** *Parker's Gloss. Her.* s.v. *Tower*, The tower is..frequently represented as bearing three smaller towers or turrets, and then it is blazoned *triple towered*, or triple turretted... The..turret is sometimes used alone, separate from the tower, and can only be represented as a smaller tower.

†**c.** *fig.* Highest point or position, height, acme. *Obs.*

1593 *Tell-Troth's N.Y. Gift* (1876) 36 We thinke we are neuer at the territ of delight. **1614** RALEIGH *Hist. World* I. (1634) 111 Jupiter, whom the Greekes have seated in the top and highest Turret of their Divinitie. **1680** T. LAWSON *Mite into Treasury* 11 Mounted to the Terret of Philosophick Elevations, and to the Zenith of Scholastick Notions.

2. *Mil.* †**a.** = TOWER *sb.*[1] 5 a. *Obs. rare*$^{-1}$.

1563 GOLDING *Cæsar* II. (1565) 62 Then they saw..the mount raysed and a turret a buylding a farre of,..they began to laugh at it.

b. A low flat armour-plated tower, commonly cylindrical or conical, on a ship of war or a fort, made to contain a gun and gunners, and usually to revolve horizontally; a similar structure on a tank, armoured car, or aircraft.

1862 CAPT. P. COLES in *Times* 5 Nov., I obtained permission..to substitute in the 'Prince Albert' three turrets, each carrying one 300-pounder. **1869** SIR E. J. REED *Iron-Clad Ships* Introd. 16 The 'Monarch'..with 25-ton guns mounted in turrets. **1887** *Spectator* 30 July 1019/1 The 'Inflexible'..with four 80-ton guns in her turrets. **1889** WELCH *Text Bk. Naval Archit.* xiv. 143 The plan of placing the guns in revolving towers or turrets. **1897** H. W. WILSON in *United Service Mag.* July 351 The distinction between turret and barbette is this; the turret is an armoured shelter revolving with the gun; the barbette an armoured shelter inside which the gun revolves on a turn-table. **1914** E. A. POWELL *Fighting in Flanders* iii. 70 The earlier armoured cars used by the Belgians..consisted of a circular turret, high enough so that only the head and shoulders of the man operating the machine-gun were exposed, covered with half-inch steel plates and mounted on an ordinary chassis. **1933** *Gloss. Aeronaut. Terms (B.S.I.)* IV. 27 *Turret*, a form of cockpit primarily intended for the use of a gunner. **1942** *Tee Emm* (Air Ministry) II. 140 Give yourself a few minutes each day in the training turrets so that your turret manipulation is absolutely one hundred per cent. *Ibid.* 141 For most of the trip your hands will be on the turret controls. **1969** G. MACBETH *War Quartet* 26, I stretched Across my turret, thinking. **1978** J. IRVING *World according to Garp* i. 15 This ball turret was a metal sphere with a glass porthole; it was set into the fuselage of a B-17 like a distended navel—like a nipple on the bomber's belly.

3. Applied to various things resembling a small tower. †**a.** A high head-dress formerly worn by women (*obs.*). †**b.** A tall chimney on a lamp (*obs.*). **c.** A raised central portion in the roof of a railway passenger carriage (*U.S.*).

1473–4 *Acc. Ld. High Treas. Scot.* I. 29, j½ elne of satyne for turatis to the Quene. **1578** *Inv. Roy. Wardr.* (1815) 231 Ane hude and ane turit of quheit velvot. **1626** BACON *Sylva* §373 Take a Turreted Lampe of Tinne,..The Height of the Turret being thrice as much, as the length of the lower part, whereupon the Lampe standeth. **1875** KNIGHT *Dict. Mech.*, *Turret*..3. (*Railway*.) The elevated central portion of a passenger-car, whose top forms an upper story of the roof, and whose sides are glazed for light and pierced for ventilation.

4. a. An attachment to a lathe, drill, or similar machine, consisting of a round or polygonal block with sockets for various dies or cutting tools, and capable of being rotated (cf. 2 b) so as to present the required tool to the work.

1875 [see *turret-lathe* in 5]. **1898** H. S. WILSON *Pract. Tool-Maker & Designer* vi. 58 Knurling fixtures for both the slide and turret. **1963** [see SEMI-AUTOMATIC *sb.* 1]. **1975** BRAM & DOWNS *Manuf. Technol.* vii. 200 The turret is then indexed to perform a number of drilling, reaming, tapping and counter-sinking operations.

b. *Cinematogr.* and *Television.* = *lens turret* s.v. LENS *sb.* 4.

1951 R. SPOTTISWOODE *Film & its Techniques* iii. 64 On almost all cameras..the lenses are mounted in clusters of three or four on a turret, a revolving device which serves to bring the wanted lens in front of the aperture. **1960** O. SKILBECK *ABC of Film & TV* 138 *Turret*, a circular mounting of several lenses held in readiness for use on the front of a camera. **1961** G. MILLERSON *Telev. Production* iii. 34 The internal complexity of a zoom lens makes it bulkier than a turret assembly. **1965** J. VON STERNBERG *Fun in Chinese Laundry* (1966) vii. 184 We illuminated every possible retreat he might find, and more cameras, turrets, and various lenses were employed. **1976** A. DAVIS *Television* 27 The turret camera with a revolving disc offering the choice of several lenses of different focal lengths, and the single zoom lens of variable focal length..were still to come.

5. *attrib.* and *Comb.*, as (sense 1) ***turret-bell, -bridge, -chamber, -clock, -door, -roof, -room, -stair, -top***; ***turret-like, -shaped, -topped*** adjs.; (sense 2 b) ***turret armour, -gun, -gunner***; (senses 2 and 4 b) ***turret-mounted*** adj.; (sense 4 b) ***turret-mounting***; ***turret-turning*** adj.; also **turret-crown**, a turreted crown (see TURRETED 2 a); **turret-deck**: see quot. 1909 (also *attrib.*); **turret head** = sense 4; **turret-lathe**, a lathe fitted with a turret (sense 4); **turret-light**, a light on top of a police car, ambulance, etc., which flashes to signal an emergency; **turret-shell** = TURRITELLID; **turret-ship**, a ship of war with a turret (sense 2 b); **turret-spider**, a spider that constructs a turret-like nest, as the N. American *Lycosa arenaria*; **turret-vessel** = *turret-ship*; **turret window** = *tower-window* (TOWER *sb.*[1] 10).

1889 WELCH *Text Bk. Naval Archit.* xiv. 144 The side and *turret armour was made up of two thicknesses. *c* **1800** R. CUMBERLAND *John De Lancaster* (1809) III. 3 The *turret-bell gave the signal of an arrival. *c* **1470** HENRY *Wallace* VII. 990 Schir Jhon the Grayme, and Ramsay..The *turat bryg segyt. **1819** SCOTT *Ivanhoe* xx[i]v, A step was heard on the stair, and the door of the *turret chamber slowly opened. **1821** —— *Kenilw.* xviii, Immured for day and night in a desolate turret-chamber. *c* **1820** S. ROGERS *Italy* (1839) 52 An hour and more, by the old *turret-clock. **1884** F. J. BRITTEN *Watch & Clockm.* 84 De Vick..made for Charles V of France the first turret clock of which we have reliable record. **1667** MILTON *P.L.* IX. 525 Oft he [the serpent] bowd His *turret Crest. **1886** CONDER *Syrian Stone-Lore* vii. (1896) 235 Jerusalem herself, with *turret-crown, appears on another [coin]. **1904** *Westm. Gaz.* 10 Oct. 9/1 Rules for the construction of *turret-deck steamers. **1909** *Cent. Dict. Supp.* s.v. *Deck*, In a special British design of cargo-steamer, ..the side, instead of meeting the main deck rectangularly, is rounded off so as to make a continuous curved surface with the deck. Inboard of this the side is again curved up. The space between the sides at the top is covered by a narrow deck called the turret-deck. **1825** SCOTT *Betrothed* iii, The form of the huge and substantial Fleming at length issued from the *turret-door. **1875** KNIGHT *Dict. Mech.*, **Turret-gun*, one specially adapted for use in revolving turrets of vessels. **1870** *Daily News* 27 Sept., The *turret-gunner stands with his head through a hole in the roof of the turret. **1884** KNIGHT *Dict. Mech.* Supp., **Turret Head*, the revolving head of a bolt cutter. **1875** *Ibid.*, **Turret-lathe*.., a screw-cutting lathe having a slide provided with a polygonal block or turret, having apertures in each face for receiving dies which are secured therein by set-screws. **1898** H. S. WILSON *Pract. Tool-Maker & Designer* vi. 58 The variety of work that may be executed on a screw machine or turret lathe. **1939** *Daily Tel.* 18 Dec. 12/3 (Advt.), Experience should include the setting up and tooling of automatic and turret lathes. **1975** BRAM & DOWNS *Manuf. Technol.* v. 129 The vertical turret-lathe is a chucking machine only. **1972** 'G. NORTH' *Sergeant Cluff rings True* i. 14 A small van..carried a *turret-light on its roof and had, 'Police,' lettered on its sidepanels. **1711** SHAFTESB. *Charac.* (1738) II. 253 Like..old reverend Cybele,..on her head a *turret-like attire. **1961** *Observer* 21 May 5/1 (Advt.), Twin lenses, standard and telephoto, *turret mounted to whisk you smoothly from close-up to long shot. **1963** *Times Lit. Suppl.* 31 May 394/5 The loss of the Captain..marked the end of the attempt to combine a full set of sails with steam propulsion and turret-mounted guns. **1923** F. A. TALBOT *Moving Pictures* 86 Behind this turret-plate is a second and fixed disk or '*turret-mounting' of identical diameter, but having only two openings, corresponding to the photographing and focussing apertures respectively. **1966** 'A. HALL' *9th Directive* ix. 83, I set it [*sc.* a camera] up on a tripod with a turret-mounting that was rigid enough for the weight. **1813** SCOTT *Rokeby* I. i, The warder..Hears, upon *turret-roof and wall, By fits the plashing rain-drop fall. **1803** *Lett. Miss Riversdale* III. 368, I have been removed from the *turret room I occupied, to a bed room on the ground floor. **1822** SCOTT *Pirate* xxxi, A great banqueting-hall, communicating with several large rounds, or projecting turret-rooms. **1844** MARG. FULLER *Wom. 19th C.* (1862) 362 Two vast towers of rock with *turret-shaped tops. **1859–62** SIR J. RICHARDSON, etc. *Mus. Nat. Hist.* (1868) II. 339 The family of *Turret or Screw shells (*Turritellidæ*). **1862** CAPT. P. COLES in *Times* 22 Nov., [The idea] that broadside ships can..effectively work these ponderous guns against *turret ships. **1880** *Daily News* 18 Dec., The trials of the eighty-ton guns on board the turret ship *Inflexible*. **1883** *Science* 13 July 43/2 A species of ground spider..known as the *turret spider. **1819** SCOTT *Ivanhoe* xx[i]v, Slowly and with difficulty she descended the *turret stair. **1886** WILLIS & CLARK *Cambridge* II. 573 An external turret-stair on the north side. **1866** *Capt. Coles & the Admiralty* 9 Captain Coles is not the inventor of the *turret system at all..the turret itself belongs to Ericsson. *c* **1800** R. CUMBERLAND *John De Lancaster* (1809) III. 115 The whole Castle garrison [turned out] from their sky-chambers on the *turret tops. **1892** E. REEVES *Homeward Bound* 271 The outside walls..are of the plain, one story, level, *turret-topped..style. **1889** WELCH *Text Bk. Naval Archit.* xiv. 143 The parts immediately underneath turrets must be protected by armour in order to shield the *turret-turning gear. **1862** CAPT. P. COLES in *Times* 5 Nov., A sea-going *turret vessel. **1870** O. H. STOKES in *Eng. Mech.* 7 Jan. 396/3 In a turret vessel, the whole of the deck, 'exclusive of that part which is occupied by the turrets', is exposed to the fire of the enemy. **1603** *Rites of Durham* (Surtees 1903) App. 110, 3 white *turret wyndowes. **1823** SCOTT *Quentin D.* iv, Little turret-windows,..the lattice..half open to admit the air.

turret, *sb.*² var. TORRET.

'turret, *v.* [f. TURRET *sb.*¹] *trans.* To furnish, fortify, or adorn with or as with a turret or turrets. Usually in *pa. pple.*: see also next.

1450 in *Charters &c. Edinb.* (1871) 71 To..wall, toure, turate, and uther wais to strengthen oure foresaid Burgh. *a* **1548** HALL *Chron., Hen. VIII*, 36 The citee..was strong, wel walled, and turryted with good Bulwarkes & defenses. **1636** DAVENANT *Platonick Lovers* I, Since yonder building on the Mount, And that large Marble square was turretted, The house lookes pleasant. **1818** SCOTT *Hrt. Midl.* xxxvi, The Thames, here turreted with villas and there garlanded with forests. **1843** S. C. HALL *Ireland* III. 180 A keep or castle turreted at the angles.

turreted ('tʌrɪtɪd), *a.* [f. TURRET *sb.*¹ or *v.*]

1. Furnished with or having a turret or turrets.

a **1550** [see TRIPLE *a.* C. a]. **1552** HULOET, Turretted or made full of turrettes, *turritus*. **1794** MRS. RADCLIFFE *Myst. Udolpho* vi, The one [avenue] leading to the turreted chateau. **1826** DISRAELI *Viv. Grey* II. iv, Over the gateway there rose a turreted tower. **1863** GEO. ELIOT *Romola* xxvi, It was a grand moment for those who were stationed on turreted roofs.

2. Furnished with something resembling a turret: cf. TURRET *sb.*¹ 2, 3. **a.** Of artificial things; *spec.* applied to a figure of a crown with battlements, or of a head (or person) wearing such a crown.

1610 HOLLAND *Camden's Brit.* (1637) 801 The Goddesse Svria..with a turreted crown on her head. **1626** [see TURRET *sb.*¹ 3]. **1824** MISS MITFORD *Village* Ser. I. (1863) 120 No bonnet could hold the turreted cap. **1837** WHEWELL *Hist. Induct. Sc.* (1857) I. 189 Turretted ships. **1872** HEAD *Sel. Grk. Coins in Electrotype Brit. Mus.* 37 Head of Kybele.., wearing turreted crown. *Ibid.* 42 Turreted female figure, city of Antioch, seated..on rock.

b. Of natural objects; *spec.* of a shell with a long spire: = TURRITED.

1826 KIRBY & SP. *Entomol.* IV. xlvi. 306 Turreted... When the head is producted into a kind of columnar re-curved turret or rostrum, in the sides of which, towards the end, the eyes are fixed. **1828** STARK *Elem. Nat. Hist.* II. 30 Terebra,..Shell elongated, turreted, acuminate. **1872** NICHOLSON *Palæont.* 62 In other cases, the shell becomes turreted or top-shaped, in consequence of the coils of the spiral passing obliquely round a central axis. **1875** C. C. BLAKE *Zool.* 254 In the Pyramidellidæ the shell is spiral and turreted.

'turreting, *vbl. sb.* [f. as prec. + -ING¹.] The action of furnishing with turrets; *concr.* turrets collectively.

1847 CHR. G. ROSSETTI *Dead City* xxiv, Where..Rose a palace for a king; Golden was the turreting.

'turretry. *nonce-wd.* [f. TURRET *sb.*¹ + -RY.] Turrets collectively.

1824 GALT *Rothelan* II. xv, All the mysterious castles and turretry of Christendom.

turribant, obs. form of TURBAN.

turrible, turble, dial. (chiefly U.S.) varr. TERRIBLE *a.*, esp. in sense 3.

1893 H. A. SHANDS *Some Peculiarities of Speech in Mississippi* 65 *Turrible*... A pronunciation of *terrible* very common among the illiterate, and sometimes heard in the conversation of the educated. **1897** KIPLING *Captains Courageous* vii. 148 Jason was tur'ble praoud of his boy. **1903** K. D. WIGGIN *Rebecca of Sunnybrook Farm* xxviii. 305 It's a turrible risk splittin' up families. **1912** J. MASEFIELD *Everlasting Mercy* 20 You must be turble strong. **1929** H. W. ODUM in A. Dundes *Mother Wit* (1973) 183 Had some turrible times in France. **1966** J. AIKEN *Trouble with Product X* vii. 123 'Tis a long pull up from the village and turble weather. **1971** *Black World* Apr. 67 You musta done somethin turble to aggravate me like that.

turricle ('tʌrɪk(ə)l). *rare*⁻¹. [ad. L. *turricula*, dim. of *turris* tower.] A small tower, turret.

1884 J. PAYNE *Tales fr. Arabic* II. 36 *note*, *Nawous*, a sort of overground well or turricle of masonry.

turricular (tʌ'rɪkjʊlə(r)), *a.* *rare*⁻¹. [f. L. *turricula* (see prec.) + -AR.] Having the form of or resembling a turret.

1661 FELTHAM *Resolves* II. liii. (ed. 8) 293 In their Turricular Chariots.

turriculated (tʌ'rɪkjʊleɪtɪd), *ppl. a.* [f. as prec. + -ATE + -ED.] Furnished with a turret or turrets, turreted: *spec.* in *Conch.* = TURRETED 2 b, TURRITED. Also **turriculate** (tʌ'rɪkjʊlət) *a.*

1822 J. PARKINSON *Outl. Oryctol.* 155 A longish turriculated univalve. *Ibid.* 250 The multilocular turriculated shells of the genus *Turriculites*. **1834** MCMURTRIE *Cuvier's Anim. Kingd.* 255 A shell with a turriculated spire. **1843** *Penny Cycl.* XXVI. 444/2 *Mitra*... Turriculate species, with large spiral whorls, the aperture effuse anteriorly.

tu'rriferous, *a.* *rare*⁻⁰. [f. L. *turrifer* (Ovid) + -OUS.] = TURRIGEROUS.

1656 BLOUNT *Glossogr.* [copying Cooper], *Turriferous*.., that beares a Tower.

turriform ('tʌrɪfɔːm), *a.* *rare* [f. L. *turri-s* tower + -FORM.] Tower-shaped.

1875 C. C. BLAKE *Zool.* 254 The Staircase Shell has a spiral turriform operculum. **1959** E. A. FISHER *Anglo-Saxon Archit. & Sculpture* 57 Turriform churches. These were not uncommon and are so-called as they were built in the form of towers. **1970** H. BRAUN *Parish Churches* iii. 33 The structural nucleus of every Byzantine church is a central turriform structure with four..arches rising from four tall and massive piers.

tu'rrigerous, *a.* *rare*⁻¹. [f. L. *turriger*, f. *turris* tower: see -GEROUS.] Carrying a tower or 'castle'.

1713 DERHAM *Phys.-Theol.* 398 We admire, saith he [*sc.* Pliny *Nat. Hist.* XI. 2], the turrigerous Shoulders of Elephants.

turrilite ('tʌrɪlaɪt). *Palæont.* [ad. mod.L. *Turrilitēs* (Lamarck, 1801), f. L. *turris* tower + Gr. λίθος stone: see -LITE.] A fossil cephalopod belonging or related to the genus *Turrilites*, allied to the ammonites, but having a long spiral (turreted) shell, found in the Cretaceous formations.

1828 WEBSTER, *Turrilite*, the fossil remains of a spiral multilocular shell. **1842** H. MILLER *O.R. Sandst.* viii. (ed. 2) 187 The..turrilites and sea-urchins of the Cretaceous group. **1850** ANSTED *Elem. Geol., Min.* etc., Gloss., *Turrilite*, an extinct genus of chambered shells, resembling an Ammonite wound into a turbinated form.

Hence **turriliticone** (tʌrɪ'lɪtɪkəʊn) [CONE *sb.*¹], a fossil shell resembling and allied to the turrilites, found in the Upper Cretaceous formations (*Cent. Dict. Suppl.* 1909).

†**turrion**, var. TORRION *Obs.*, a large tower.

1599 HAKLUYT *Voy.* II. 108 Foure principall bulwarkes, and bitweene them turrions. *Ibid.* 123 The Turrion of the Arsenall.

turrited ('tʌraɪtɪd), *a.* [f. L. *turrīt-us* towered (f. *turris* tower) + -ED.] = TURRETED 2; *spec.* of a shell, having a long spire resembling a tower or turret: = TURRETED 2 b. Also **'turrite** *a.*

1758 SWINTON in *Phil. Trans.* L. 794 All these coins present..a turrited head and a branch of palm. **1835** KIRBY *Hab. & Inst. Anim.* I. ix. 276 The shells of some [Trachelipods] are what are called turrited or long and slender, with spiral whorls. **1856** W. CLARK *Van der Hoeven's Zool.* I. 798 Pyramidella... Shell turrite. **1863** P. P. CARPENTER in *Rep. Brit. Assoc.* I. 662 '*Columbella*' *carinata*... Small, turrited, smooth, with stout posterior keel.

turritellid (tʌrɪ'telɪd). *Zool.* [ad. mod.L. *Turritellid-æ* pl., f. *Turritella* (Lamarck, 1799), name of the typical genus, f. *turris* tower; see -ID³.] A gastropod of the family *Turritellidæ*, characterized by long turreted shells with spiral striations; a screw-shell. So **turri'telloid** *a.* [-OID], resembling a screw-shell; having the characters of the *Turritellidæ*.

1860 P. P. CARPENTER in *Rep. Smithsonian Instit.* 1859, 206 The Turritelloid worm-shells. **1861** *Ibid.* 1860, 210 The shells of *Siphonium*, though spiral at birth, have no Turritelloid portion. **1895** *Funk's Standard Dict.*, Turritellid.

‖**turron** (tu'ron). Pl. **turrones, turrons**. [Sp. *turrón*.] A Spanish sweetmeat resembling nougat, made from almonds and honey; a piece of this.

1918 *Chambers's Jrnl.* Jan. 33 The best hams of Montanchez, the finest turron from Jijona. **1950** E. DAVID *Bk. Mediterranean Food* 153 In the winter there are..the sugar-plums of Nice; Spanish nougats and *turrons*; *pralines* from Aix-en-Provence. **1976** E. P. BENSON *Bulls of Ronda* xvi. 100 Their desserts were to his taste... 'You can bring me some *turrones*.' He selected two of the creamiest.

†**'turrulet.** *Obs.* *rare*⁻¹. [dim. formation from L. *turris* tower; cf. *rivulet*.] = TURRET *sb.*¹ 1.

c **1620** T. ROBINSON *Mary Magd.* 49 A turrulet tooke vp each angles shade,..The battelments of smoothest Iett were made.

turs, turse, turss, obs. Sc. ff. TRUSS.

†**tursable**, *a.* *Sc.* *Obs.* [f. *turs*, TRUSS *v.* + -ABLE.] Capable of being packed up and carried off; portable; see TRUSS *v.* 2.

a **1670** SPALDING *Troub. Chas. I* (1850) I. 283 The laird..displenishis the place, left nothing tursabill within. [**1897** RAMPINI *Hist. Moray & Nairn* iv. 186.]

†**'tursion.** *Obs.* *rare*. [ad. L. *tursio*, *-ōnem* (Pliny).] A porpoise.

1655 MOUFET & BENNET *Health's Improv.* (1746) 257 Porpoises, Tursions, or Sea-hogs, are..never good till they be fat. **1661** LOVELL *Hist. Anim. & Min.* 217 Porpaise... Tursions, or Sea-hoggs are fatter than Dolphins. [**1706** PHILLIPS (ed. Kersey), *Tursio* or *Tyrsio*, a Sea-fish like a Dolphin, which some take for a Sturgeon, and others for a Porpoise.]

tursk, var. TUSK *sb.*³, fish.

turskill. *Sc. dial.* [var. of TUSKAR, prob. after Gael. *tairisgil*.] A kind of spade for cutting peat.

1812 J. HENDERSON *Agric. Surv. Caithn.* xv. 234 When the peat-moss is not more than from one to two feet deep, the peat is cut perpendicularly, by a spade, called a *turskill*.

turtle ('tɜːt(ə)l), *sb.*¹ Now *rare* or *arch.* Forms: 1 turtla, 1– turtle, 3 (*Orm.*) turrtle, 3–5 turtul, 4 tortle, 4–5 turtill, 4–6 -il, (5 -yl, -yle, -ylle, 5–6 -yll), (5 turckell), 5 tyrtle, 6 tyrtyll, turtell. [OE. *turtla* masc., *turtle* fem. = OHG. *turtulo* masc., *turtula* fem. (Du. *tortel* fem.): either dim. or dissimilated form of L. *turtur* TURTUR with *r–l* for *r–r* (cf. Sp. and It. *tortola*, It. *tortora*). For other Germanic forms see TURTLE-DOVE.]

1. a. = TURTLE-DOVE 1. (Often mentioned as a type of conjugal affection and constancy: cf. 2.)

c **1000** *Ags. Ps.* (Th.) lxxxiii[i]. 3 Him eac spedlice spearuwa hus begyteð, and tidlice turtle nistlað. *c* **1000** *Ags. Gosp.* Luke ii. 24 Twa turtlan oððe twegen culfran briddas. *c* **1200** *Trin. Coll. Hom.* 49 Turtle ne wile habbe no make bute on and after þat non..þe bitocninge þat is imene turtlen and duues... Eiðer turtles and duues habbet sorinesse for song. *c* **1200** ORMIN 7588 Twezzenn cullfre briddess..Oþþr..twezzen turrtless. **1382** WYCLIF *Ps.* lxxxiii. 4 [lxxxiv. 3] Forsothe the sparowe fonde to hym an hous; and the turtil a nest. *c* **1400** tr. *Secreta Secret., Gov. Lordsh.* ciii. 104 Pytous as turtyll. **1483** CAXTON *Gold. Leg.* 373/2 Lyke a turtle that allone without make waylleth and wepeth. *a* **1548** HALL *Chron., Hen. VI* 118 As louyng to him, as the Turtle to her make. **1611** SHAKS. *Wint. T.* IV. iv. 154 Your hand (my Perdita:) so Turtles paire That neuer meane to part. **1670** G. H. *Hist. Cardinals* I. III. 91 A Mass is sung, and his Holiness presented with two young Turtles. **1713** STEELE *Guard.* No. 22. ¶2 [She] kept a pair of turtles cooing in her chamber. **1802** MONTAGU *Ornith. Dict.* s.v. *Dove-turtle*, The Turtle visits the southern parts of England in the spring. **1851** MAYHEW *Lond. Labour* (1861) III. 64 His pigeon-cote..is no longer stocked with carriers,..jacobins, ..turtles. **1860** CHR. G. ROSSETTI *O. & N. Year Ditties* iii, Turtle calleth turtle in Heaven's May.

b. ***Greenland turtle, sea-turtle***, names for the Black Guillemot: see GREENLAND 1, SEA-TURTLE¹.

c. *Rhyming slang.* = TURTLE-DOVE 3. (Usu. in *pl.*)

1893 P. H. EMERSON *Signor Lippo* xiv. 55 A long sleeve cadi on his napper, and a pair of turtles on his martins finished him. **1936** 'J. CURTIS' *Gilt Kid* 24 Got any turtles? The Gilt Kid, having no gloves, answered: 'No, but I'll buy a pair.' **1962** *John o' London's* 25 Jan. 82/1 Of course he [*sc.* the criminal] takes the precaution of wearing *turtles* (short for *turtle-doves*, rhyming slang for gloves).

2. *fig.* Applied to a person, as a term of endearment, etc. (cf. DOVE *sb.* 2 d), or (esp.) to lovers or married folk, in allusion to the turtle-dove's affection for its mate.

14.. LYDG. *Balade Commend. Our Lady* 78 O trusty turtle, trewest of al trewe. *c* **1440** *Gesta Rom.* lxix. 312 (Harl. MS.), I shal be turtill in your absence þat hadde lost hire make. *a* **1548** HALL *Chron., Hen. VII* 20 b, Hym that.. watched, howe to..steale thys turtle oute of her mewe and lodgynge. **1588** SHAKS. *L.L.L.* IV. iii. 211 *Berow.* Will these Turtles be gone? *Kin.* Hence sirs, away. **1693** *Humours Town* 24 The Fool..concludes her the most constant pretty cooing Turtle in the Nation. **1717** LADY M. W. MONTAGU *Let. to Pope* 1 Apr., Several couple of true turtles..saying soft things to one another. **1865** E. W. BENSON in *Life* (1899) I. vi. 232, I am a solitary Turtle (Dove, not Reptile) just now, my wife being at Rugby.

3. *attrib.* and *Comb.*, as ***turtle love***, ***pigeon***, ***wing***; ***turtle-billing***, ***-footed***, ***-haunted***, ***-like***, ***-winged*** adjs.; † **turtle-bird**, the young of the turtle-dove.

1598 B. JONSON *Ev. Man in Hum.* I. iv, The happy state of *Turtle-billing lovers. *c* **1200** *Trin. Coll. Hom.* 47 Gif hie was riche wimman, a lomb, gif hie was bitwene two, two *turtle briddes, gif hie was poure, two duue briddes. **1599** B. JONSON *Ev. Man out of Hum.* Epil., Let..The throat of War be stopt.., And *turtle-footed Peace dance fairy rings About her court. **1624** —— *Sun's Darling* v. i. **1873** T. L. KINGSBURY *Comm. Song Sol.* iii, The *turtle-haunted groves. *a* **1586** SIDNEY *Arcadia* IV. (1629) 415 Lamenting.. such as the *turtle-like loue is wont to make for the euer ouer-soone losse of her onely loued make. **1669** DRYDEN *Tyrannic Love* III. i, Then, turtle-like, I'll to my mate repair. **1608** TOPSELL *Serpents* (1658) 784 Such faithfull dealing, uprightnesse of conscience, and *Turtle love. **1819** STEPHENS in Shaw *Gen. Zool.* XI. 72 *Turtle Pigeon, *Columba Turtur*... Pigeon with the tail-feathers white at their tips, the back griseous, the breast vinaceous, a black spot on the sides of the neck, with white stripes, the abdomen white. **1629** MILTON *Nativity, Hymn* iii, Peace.. With *Turtle wing the amorous clouds dividing. **1821** R. S. HAWKER *Cornish Ballads*, etc. (1908) 249 As on turtle-wings the moments fleet. **1745** AKENSIDE *Ode on Lyric Poetry* 18 While *turtle-wing'd the laughing hours..Lead youth, and love, and harmless joy.

Hence (*nonce-wds.*) '**turtlish** ('**turtleish**) *a.*, having the character or qualities of a turtle-dove; '**turtlize** ('**turtleize**) *v.*, *trans.* to turn into or make like a turtle-dove.

1855 *Fraser's Mag.* LI. 229 The most *turtleish of doves. **1798** SOUTHEY *Lett.* (1856) I. 59, I am softened, *turtleised, yea, a very lamb!

turtle ('tɜːt(ə)l), *sb.*[2] Also 7 tortel. [app. a corruption, by English sailors, of the earlier *tortue*, or the French original of this (see TORTOISE), assimilated to the known word TURTLE *sb.*[1]]

1. **a.** Any species of marine tortoise; also extended to various other tortoises. (Pl. *turtles*, collectively usually *turtle*.)

As to the varying application of the names *tortoise* and *turtle*, see the note to sense 1 of the former word.

With defining words, applied to various species, as *box-turtle* (BOX *sb.*[2] 24), DIAMOND-BACKED *t.*, HAWK'S-BILL *t.*, LAND *t.*, LEATHER-*t.*, *loggerhead t.* (LOGGERHEAD 6 a), MUD *t.*, PAINTED *t.*, SEA-TURTLE[2], SNAPPING-*t.*, SOFT-SHELLED *t.*, TRUNK-*t.* (see these words); **alligator-turtle**, the snapping-turtle, also called *alligator tortoise* (ALLIGATOR 4); **bastard turtle**, *Thalassochelys kempi*; **chicken-turtle**, *Chrysemys reticulata*, also called *chicken-tortoise*; **greaved turtle**, any species of the genus *Podocnemis*; **green turtle**, various species of *Chelonia*, having green shells, as *C. midas* of the W. Indies and *C. virgata* of the Pacific, both much esteemed as food; **horned turtle**, an extinct turtle of the genus *Miolania*, having projections at the back of the skull like the 'horned toad'.

1657 *North's Plutarch, Add. Lives* 90 He took a Ship-board..fourty Parrots, many Tortels, and many other Animals strange to our World. **1657** R. LIGON *Barbadoes* (1673) 4 The Loggerhead Turtle,..the Hawks bill Turtle. .. A third kind called the Green Turtle,..far excelling the other two, in wholesomness, and Rareness of taste. **1689** *Relat. Sufferings H. Pitman* 22 We walked along the sea shore to watch for tortoise or turtle. **1712** E. COOKE *Voy. S. Sea* 13 Sea Tortoises, or, as the Sea-men call them, Turtle. **1719** DE FOE *Crusoe* I. 101, June 17. I spent in cooking the Turtle; I found in her threescore Eggs. **1745** P. THOMAS *Jrnl. Anson's Voy.* 105 Great Quantity of Tortoises, or, as the Seamen call them, Turtles. **1785** *Jackson's Oxford Jrnl.* 16 July, Dressing a very fine lively Chicken Turtle.. supplied..at 6/- per quart or 10/6 the Tureen. **1792** MAR. RIDDELL *Voy. Madeira* 63 Four species of turtle are found on the shores of this island—the green-turtle, the hawk's-bill,..the logger-head, and the land-tortoise. **1839–40** W. IRVING *Wolfert's R.* v. (1855) 75 The island abounded with turtle, and great quantities of their eggs were to be found among the rocks. **1870** YEATS *Nat. Hist. Comm.* 114 Turtles abound in the enclosed seas of Central America.

b. The flesh of various species of turtle used as food; also short for *turtle-soup*. (See also MOCK TURTLE.)

Often mentioned or alluded to as a feature of civic banquets.

1755 *World* No. 123 ¶3 Of all the improvements in the modern kitchen, there are none that can bear a comparison with the introduction of Turtle. **1780** T. DAVIES *Mem. Garrick* (1781) II. xxxviii. 122 High seasoned venison, delicious turtle, and excellent claret. **1848** THACKERAY *Van. Fair* xxvii, He..had dined on horse-flesh and turtle with equal relish. **1859** *Habits Gd. Society* xi. 310 A light soup is better than a thick one,..turtle is only fit for an alderman.

†**c.** Short for *turtle-dinner* or *turtle-feast*. *Obs.*

1771 SMOLLETT *Humph. Cl.* 30 Apr., I..have almost prevailed upon uncle to give him a small turtle at the Bear. **1785** A. C. BOWER *Diaries & Corr.* 16 Sept. (1903) 29 Tuesday next the good people at Dulish intend giving a Turtle and the Misses have prevailed on their Mother to add a little Hop in the Evening by way of helping Digestion. **1788** *Ibid.* 49 We were at Whatcombe Tuesday—a large party and a turtle.

2. *to turn turtle*. **a.** *lit.* To catch turtle by throwing them on their backs.

1689 *Relat. Sufferings H. Pitman* 20 They going ashore on the Main to turn Turtle, were set upon by the Indians. **1861** DU CHAILLU *Equat. Afr.* iv. 25 Turtle frequent the shores, and are 'turned' in considerable numbers. **1867** SMYTH *Sailor's Word-bk.*, *To turn a turtle*, to take the animal by seizing a flipper, and throwing him on his back, which renders him quite helpless.

b. *fig.* (in earlier use *to turn the turtle*.) To turn over, capsize, be upset. (See also quot. 1818.)

1818 'A. BURTON' *Johnny Newcome* II. 69 John..in the next week..would take Twice calling, to be once awake; They turned the turtle, cut him down. *Ibid.* 254 *Turn the turtle*, to get under a hammock, and lift it up in the middle, thus pitching the sleeper out on one side of it. **1830** *United Service Jrnl.* June 709 The chance on some equally squally night of 'turning the turtle', as Jack facetiously calls upsetting. **1842** MARRYAT *Perc. Keene* xxiii, But 'turning the turtle' is not making a quick passage, except to the other world. **1843** —— *M. Violet* xli, The canoe turned the turtle with them. **1860** *All Year Round* No. 66. 384 If the wind catches that 'ere, she'll turn turtle at once. **1896** *Daily News* 2 July 9/1 An engine and two trucks had turned turtle on the embankment.

†**3.** *American turtle*: = TORPEDO *sb.* 2. *Obs.*

1775–83 THACHER *Milit. Jrnl.* (1823) 75 A singular machine invented for destroying the British Shipping by explosion... American Turtle or Torpedo.

4. *Typog.* A curved bed in which types or stereo-types are secured, and which is mounted on one of the cylinders of a rotary printing-press: so called from a fancied resemblance of the bed to the back of a turtle.

1860 *Ure's Dict. Arts* (ed. 5) III. 540 An American [printing] machine, the invention of R. Hoe and Company. .. Each page is locked up upon a detached segment of the large cylinder, called by the compositors a 'turtle'. **1875** KNIGHT *Dict. Mech.* 1797/2 The type is secured in *turtles*, or the stereotype is bent to the curve of the cylinder.

5. *attrib.* and *Comb.*, as ***turtle-catcher***, ***-chase***, ***-dinner***, ***-eater***, ***-egg***, ***-feast***, ***-fishery***, ***-fishing***, ***-skeleton***, ***-soup***; **turtleburger**, a kind of hamburger made from turtle; **turtle-corral** = *turtle-crawl (a)*; **turtle cowry**, a large species of cowry, *Cypræa testudinaria*; **turtle-crab**, a minute species of crab parasitic upon turtles and other marine animals; **turtle-crawl**, (*a*) [CRAWL *sb.*[2]] an enclosure in which turtles are kept; (*b*) [CRAWL *sb.*[1]] 'the track of a turtle to and from its nest' (*Cent. Dict.* 1891); **turtle-deck**, (*a*) = TURTLE-BACK 1 a; also applied to a similar structure on an aircraft; (*b*) = TURTLE-BACK 1 b; **turtle-egging**, the gathering of turtles' eggs (*Cent. Dict.* 1891); **turtle-frolic** (*colloq.*), a turtle-feast; **turtle-grass**, name for two marine plants with long narrow grass-like leaves: (*a*) *Thalassia testudinum*, of the W. Indies, etc.; (*b*) the grass-wrack, *Zostera marina*; **turtle-head**, a N. American scrophulariaceous plant, *Chelone glabra*, allied to *Pentstemon*, so called from the shape of the flower; **turtle-insect**, a widely-distributed species of scale-insect, *Coccus* (*Lecanium*) *hesperidum*; **turtle-kraal** = *turtle-crawl (a)*; **turtle-net**, a net for catching turtle; **turtle-peg**, a prong fastened to a pole or cord used for harpooning turtles (= PEG *sb.*[1] 8 a); hence **turtle-pegger**, one who uses a turtle-peg to catch turtles; **turtle-pegging**, the catching of turtles with a turtle-peg; **turtle-press**, a printing-press in which a 'turtle' (sense 4) is (or was) used; **turtle-shell**, (*a*) the shell of a turtle; the material of this, tortoise-shell; (*b*) = *turtle-cowry*; **turtle-stone** = SEPTARIUM 2 (from the markings on section resembling those of a tortoise-shell); **turtle-twine**, twine for making turtle-nets.

1946 *Amer. Speech* XXI. 67/1 While in Florida Keys in the service in the Spring of 1940 I came across a road stand selling *turtleburgers. **1979** *Daily Tel.* 29 Nov. 18 It must be admitted that the meat can be tasteless and fibrous, but its strength is its versatility: 'turtleburgers', for example, are delicious. **1726** G. ROBERTS *Four Yrs. Voy.* 5 There might be some *Turtle-catchers here since the last Turtle Season. **1815** J. CAMPBELL *Trav. S. Afr.* xlii. 501 We were detained till noon next day..for the turtle catchers. **1860** WRAXALL *Life in Sea* iv. 90 A picturesque description of such a *Turtle-chase on Ascension Island. **1838** *Penny Cycl.* XI. 362/1 *Nantilograpsus minutus*..*Turtle-Crab, Browne;.. M. Milne Edwards..sees no sufficient reason for distinguishing this species from *Grapsus testudinum*, Roux. **1833** M. SCOTT *Tom Cringle* xvi. (1859) 420 The *Turtle Crawls filled with beautiful clear water. **1903** *Daily Mail* 9 Sept. 5/3 A turtle crawl in Kingston, where over two hundred turtles were confined awaiting shipment,..was broken up by the force of the sea during the cyclone in Jamaica. **1889** *Cent. Dict.* s.v. *Deck*, The *turtle-deck* or *turtle-backed deck*..is a convex deck extending a short distance aft from the stem of an ocean steamer to shed the water in a head sea; in many..steamships..there is a similar arrangement on the stern. **1908** *Daily Chron.* 15 May 8/6 The engines of the launch were not running... Mr. Moody and Mr. Smith stood on the turtle deck at the bow. [**1912** *Flight* 26 Oct. 966/2 The fabric is..stretched over light formers above the girder so as to provide a kind of turtle-back deck.] **1913** *Flight* 31 May 586/2 The comfort of the pilot has been carefully studied and he is well sheltered behind an aluminium turtle deck. **1937** *Jrnl. R. Aeronaut. Soc.* XLI. 7 It was customary for the pilot to carry the parachute in the cockpit with the cable laid along the turtle deck and fastened securely with adhesive tape. **1954** *Amer. Speech* XXIX. 103 *Turtledeck*, the trunk or turtleback of a roadster. **1967** A. SHENNAN *Sopwith Snipe Described* 17 To this basic structure was affixed a turtledeck structure of plywood formers and stringers. **1805** in *Edin. Rev.* July 357 Who freely give two guineas for a *turtle dinner at the tavern. *a* **1774** TUCKER *Lt. Nat.* (1834) II. 430 Your *turtle eaters, city feast hunters, and persons who live in a continual round of pleasures. **1760** GARRICK *Prol. to Murphy's Desert Isl.* 22 Keep *turtle-eating Aldermen awake. **1860** WRAXALL *Life in Sea* iv. 87 Our two soldiers..stopped..to dig *turtle eggs out of the sand. **1753** H. WALPOLE *Lett.* (1846) III. 12 Knightly..has been entertaining all the parishes round with a *turtle-feast. **1760** LYTTELTON *Dial. Dead* xix. 204 A Turtle feast is a Novelty to me. **1767** GOLDSM. *Ess., Let. Common-council-man*, The mayor and aldermen.. celebrating the royal nuptials by a magnificent turtle feast. **1793** LD. H. SPENCER in *Ld. Auckland's Corr.* (1862) III. 112 Count Bernstorff gave us a turtle-feast at his château. **1848** THACKERAY *Van. Fair* xli, An alderman coming from a turtle feast will not step out of his carriage to steal a leg of mutton. *Ibid.* xx, A parcel of *turtle-fed tradesmen. **1834** *Tait's Mag.* I. 390/2 Your *turtle-feeding Aldermen. **1707** SLOANE *Jamaica* I. Introd. 87 The *Turtle-fishery.. thought..to be ours by right... The *Turtle-fishing.. pretended to by the French of the Island Tortugas. **1904** *Westm. Gaz.* 12 Apr. 9/2 The crews of the six Caymans turtle-fishing vessels..were seized..by the Nicaraguan Government for alleged fishing in territorial waters. **1750** F. GOELET *Jrnl.* 2 Oct. in *New-England Hist. & Geneal. Reg.* (1870) XXIV. 53 Had an Invitation to day to Go to a Turtle *Frolick. **1787** M. CUTLER in *Life*, etc. (1888) I. 205, I received a polite invitation from Governor Brown..to join them in a Turtle frolic. **1886** BYNNER *A. Surriage* xv, There was a turtle-frolic at Cambridge. **1735** MORTIMER in *Phil. Trans.* XXXIX. 116 *Alga marina, gramineo angustissimo folio*... *Turtle-Grass: It grows at the Bottom of the Sea in shallow Water. **1756** P. BROWNE *Jamaica* 71 The small grassy-leaf'd Alga or Turtle-grass. **1871** KINGSLEY *At Last* vi, Manatis..coming in..to browse on mangrove shoots and turtle-grass. **1884** MILLER *Plant-n.*, *Thalassia testudinum*, Manatee-grass, Turtle-grass. *Ibid.*, *Zostera marina*, Bell-ware,..Grass Wrack.., Turtle-grass. **1857** GRAY *First Less. Bot.* (1866) 94 The fifth stamen..appears in the..*Turtlehead as a sort of filament without any anther. **1896** E. G. LODEMAN *Spraying of Plants* I. i. 10 Corrosive sublimate..dissolved in..spirits, and..added to the water..possesses the power of destroying the brown *turtle (scale) insect, white scaly coccus, pine bug [etc.]. **1885** LADY BRASSEY *The Trades* 353 What they call a '*turtle-kraal', consisting of a large tank, in which were a number of turtle. **1898** *Allbutt's Syst. Med.* V. 295 He sits ..*turtle-like, with his neck dropped into his chest. **1906** *Westm. Gaz.* 20 June 8/2 A great turtle-like head, with large eyes. **1794** *Turtle-nets [see *turtle-twine*]. **1839** CAPT. WILSON in *Mag. Nat. Hist.* Oct. 519 They had got a large saw-fish entangled in their turtle-net. **1828** WEBSTER, **Turtle-shell*, a shell, a beautiful species of Murex; also, tortoise-shell. **1845** J. COULTER *Adv. Pacific* x. 126 Round it [*sc.* the hut] were scattered a number of terrapin and turtle shells. **1860** WRAXALL *Life in Sea* iv. 88 Hundreds of *Turtle skeletons lying about. **1763** SMOLLETT *Trav.* xi. (1766) I. 190 As for the *turtle-soupe, it is a good restorative. **1846** A. SOYER *Syst. Cookery* 85 Turtle Soup. This soup, the delight of civic corporations,..has been, and perhaps ever will be, the leading article of English cookery. *Ibid.* 87 Clear Turtle Soup. **1851** DE LA BECHE *Geol. Observer* 687 Those commonly known as septaria and *turtle stones. **1859** R. HUNT *Guide Mus. Pract. Geol.* (ed. 2) 32 Good specimens of septaria or turtle stone from the Oxford clay. **1766** W. GORDON *Gen. Counting-ho.* 386, 3 cwt. 2 qrs. 18 lb. *turtle twine. **1794** *Rigging & Seamanship* I. 65 Turtle-twine, for turtle-nets, is made of good bar hemp.

Hence '**turtledom**, a collective name for those who eat turtle (i.e. *spec.* London aldermen), or for their practices, methods, etc.; '**turtly** *a.*, addicted to or habitually eating turtle. (Cf. 1 b.)

1893 *Punch* 4 Mar. 102/1 *Turtledom feareth what Turtledom deems The perils of—Unification! **1894** WOOLACOTT (*title*) The Curse of Turtledom: an Exposé of the Methods and Extravagant Expenditure of the Livery Companies. **1900** *Daily News* 26 Nov. 4/1 They appeal as much to the epicure of turtledom as to the vegetarian. **1868** *Cosmopolitan* 25 July 334 We doubt..if the most *turtly Alderman out can beat in legal acumen Monsieur le Juge de Paix de la Nièvre.

†'**turtle**, *v.*[1] *Obs.* [f. TURTLE *sb.*[1]] *intr.* To play the turtle, behave like a turtle-dove (cf. TURTLE *sb.*[1], 1, 2). Also with *it*.

1701 J. PRINCE *Worthies of Devon* 338 He left..a Widow ..to Turtle it after him, as he had done before. **1754** SHEBBEARE *Marriage Act* xxv. I. 148, I..am convinced how foolish all this Stuff called Love, Fidelity, Billing and Turtling in England is.

'**turtle**, *v.*[2] Chiefly *nonce-wd.* [f. TURTLE *sb.*[2]; in sense 2 a back-formation (or inference) from TURTLER, TURTLING.]

1. *trans.* To make mock turtle of.

a **1756** MRS. HAYWOOD *New Present* (1771) 149 To turtle a Calf's Head.

2. *intr.* To catch or 'fish' for turtle.

1838 in G. C. Anderson *Laws of Bahamas* (1843) 119 If any person..be found turtling, or fishing, against the provisions of this Act. **1952** E. HEMINGWAY *Old Man & Sea* 15 He never went turtle-ing. That is what kills the eyes.

3. *trans.* To turn over: cf. *to turn turtle* (TURTLE *sb.*[2] 2 b). Also *intr.*

1896 *Daily News* 3 Aug. 4/7 She [the boat] turtled herself right again. **1920** [see CAREEN *v.* 4 b].

4. a. To stretch (the neck) forward like a turtle.

1909 *Daily Chron.* 30 Dec. 9/5 Nothing makes a woman look more awkward than to 'turtle' the neck.

b. *intr.* To act in a manner characteristic of a turtle (perh. *spec.* to bridle or show indignation.) Also with *up.* ? *nonce-wd.*

1914 D. H. LAWRENCE *Widowing of Mrs. Holroyd* I. ii. 28 *Clara*: Turning-out time, Laura. *Laura* (*turtling*): I'm sorry, I'm sure. **1920** —— *Lost Girl* v. 64 It was most curious to see Miss Pinnegar turtle up at the mention of this scheme. .. She blurted, bridling and ducking her head..like a indignant turkey.

turtle-back. [TURTLE *sb.*[2]]

1. a. An arched structure over the deck of a steamer at the bow, and often also at the stern, to protect it from damage by a heavy sea.

1881 *Standard* 30 Aug. 2/3 Erections for the purposes of shelter, such as turtle-backs, open at one end. **1882** *Ibid.* 14 Aug. 2/4 Covering these are a fine promenade deck amidships and a turtle-back forward. **1886** *Times* 20 Apr. 10/2 He went beneath the turtle-back. **1897** KIPLING *Captains Courageous* i, The second-saloon deck at the stern ..was finished in a turtle-back.

b. A rounded projecting boot on a motor vehicle; the lid of this. *N. Amer.*

1941 'A. A. FAIR' *Double or Quits* iii. 33 He raised up the turtleback in the car. **1971** D. CONOVER *One Man's Island* 23 The right fender fell off and rolled into a ditch. I stuck it disgustedly in the turtleback and in the village asked Lloyd at the garage to put it back on.

2. *Archæol.* A roughly chipped stone implement, having one or both faces slightly convex. Also *attrib.*

1890 W. H. HOLMES in *Amer. Anthrop.* Jan. 14 The familiar turtle-back or one-faced stone, the double turtle-back or two-faced stone. **1912** S. H. WARREN in *Man* XII. 205 The present writer also has a Levallois, or 'turtle-back' core, which he found in the Lea Valley in 1896.

3. The back of a turtle.

1898 G. B. SHAW *Let.* 18 Oct. (1972) II. 68 They all.. betrayed gross ignorance on the points they were most cocksure about, such as riding on turtleback and the like follies. **1905** *Westm. Gaz.* 4 Apr. 3/2 The legends of the peopling of the islands are interesting... Some make the passage on turtle-back; others go afloat on rafts of cocoa-nut shells.

4. A land form likened to the shell of a turtle.

1913 *Geogr. Jrnl.* XLII. 149 Thick forests..alternate with tall grassland and bare and rocky turtlebacks. **1928** *Amer. Speech* IV. 126 'Hog-back' and 'turtle-back' are common names for hills or ridges suggesting those forms. **1938** *Bull. Geol. Soc. Amer.* XLIX. 1875 Three turtleback areas have been recognized in the Black Mountains [of Death Valley, California]. They prove to be structural as well as topographic features.

5. *attrib.*, as *turtle-back core* (see 2); **turtle-back scale** = *turtle-insect* (see TURTLE *sb.*[2] 5).

1909 in *Cent. Dict. Suppl.* s.v. *Scale.*

Hence **'turtle-,backed** *a.*, having a back like a turtle's; furnished with a turtle-back (sense 1).

1889 [see *turtle-deck*, TURTLE *sb.*[2] 5]. **1891** *Chambers' Encycl.* VII. 421/2 An armoured turtle-backed deck which extends throughout the length of the ship. **1908** *Blackw. Mag.* Jan. 51/1, I can see..a turtle-backed affair pushing out from the advanced trench.

turtle-dove ('tɜːt(ə)ldʌv). Forms: see TURTLE *sb.*[1] and DOVE. [f. TURTLE *sb.*[1] + DOVE: cf. Da. *turteldue* (Sw. *turturdufva*), Du. *tortelduyf* (Kilian *-duyve*), MLG. *torteldûve*, G. *turteltaube* (MHG. *turtel-*, *türteltûbe*, OHG. *turtel-*, *turtil(i)-*, *turtula-tûba*).]

1. a. A dove of the genus *Turtur*, esp. the common European species *T. communis*, noted for its graceful form, harmonious colouring, and affection for its mate: = TURTLE *sb.*[1] 1.

Also applied to *T. risorius*, the Barbary dove, and locally to doves of other genera, as the N. American *Zenaidura carolinensis*, and the Australian *Stictopelia cuneata*.

a **1300** *Cursor M.* 11304 (Cott.) To offer turtuls douues [*v.rr.* turtill dovis, turtil douues, turtur doufes] tua. *c* **1420** ? LYDG. *Assembly of Gods* 820 A turtyldoue he bare an hygh for hys crest. *c* **1530** *Crt. of Love* 234 Anelida, true as turtill-dove. **1616** SURFL. & MARKH. *Country Farme* 83 Of all these fore-named kinds of Birds, there is none more apt to tame than the Turtle doues. **1742** BLAIR *Grave* 532 The shrill-tongu'd Shrew, Meek as the Turtle-Dove, forgets her Chiding. **1802** MONTAGU *Ornith. Dict.* G 6 b, Spotted-necked Turtle-dove. **1834** PRINGLE *Afr. Sk.* ix. 308 The turtle dove (*Columba risoria*) cooing amorously in every mimosa brake. **1909** *Westm. Gaz.* 17 July 14/3 The turtle-dove, which we see so frequently in the fanciers' shops,..is not the common turtle-dove of this country, but the Collared or Barbary dove.

†**b.** *sea turtle-dove*, the Black Guillemot or Dovekie: = SEA-TURTLE[1]. *Obs.*

1753 [see DOVE *sb.* 1 c].

2. *fig.* applied to a person: cf. TURTLE *sb.*[1] 2.

1535 COVERDALE *Ps.* lxxiii[i]. 19 O delyuer not the soule of thy turtle doue vnto the beestes. **1575** JUD. SMITH *Misticall Deuise* A iij b, My darling and my harts desyre, my onely Turtle Doue. *a* **1800** *Fause Foodrage* xxii. in Child *Ballads* II. 299, I shall learn your turtle-dow As well to write and read. **1856** MISS MULOCK *J. Halifax* xix, I am not interested in old turtle-doves.

3. *Rhyming slang.* A glove. (Usu. in *pl.*) Cf. TURTLE *sb.*[1] 1 c.

1857 'DUCANGE ANGLICUS' *Vulgar Tongue* 23 *Turtle doves*, ..gloves. **1935** A. J. POLLOCK *Underworld Speaks* 127/1 *Turtle doves*, a pair of gloves. **1959** I. & P. OPIE *Lore & Lang. Schoolch.* xiv. 320 'Turtle doves' for gloves, and so on, normally associated with cockneys, is neither confined to the metropolis, nor to the shift-for-a-living class. **1972** *Lebende Sprachen* XVII. 8/4 *Turtle dove*, glove.

Hence as *v. trans.*, ? to show affection for (another), like a turtle-dove for its mate. *nonce-use.* Also **'turtle-'doveism, 'turtle-'dovery,** *nonce-wds.*

1850 LD. LYTTON in *Life* (1906) I. ii. 25 Only just married, and in a state of turtle-doveism. **1886** K. S. MACQUOID *Sir J. Appleby* iii, Half afraid I might be considered an intruder in such a turtle-dovery [the abode of a newly married couple]. **1922** JOYCE *Ulysses* 196 Take her for me... Jove, a cool ruttime send them. Yea, turtledove her.

'turtle-neck, *sb.* (and *a.*) orig. *U.S.* [TURTLE *sb.*[2]]

1. a. A close-fitting roll or band collar, now usu. one intermediate in height between a crew-neck and a polo-neck; formerly also = *polo-neck* (*a*) s.v. POLO[1] 4. **b.** A shirt or jersey with such a collar.

1897 *Sears, Roebuck Catal.* 217/3 Turtle Neck Sweater. Extra heavy knit, all wool, turtle neck. **1939** M. B. PICKEN *Lang. Fashion* 102/3 (*caption*) Turtle Neck. **1957** *New Yorker* 5 Oct. 112/2 The roll at the round neck suggests a turtleneck, and little inverted tucks do nice things for the bosom. **1960** *Daily Express* 30 Aug. 5/3 Back buttoning turtle necks of matching fabric. **1970** E. TIDYMAN *Shaft* xiii. 170 Tall, young men in..turtlenecks, leatherjackets. **1977** *New Yorker* 3 Oct. 40/2 Dr. Sayles..asks me to take off my shirt, a turtleneck. **1982** J. GARDNER *For Special Services* xvi. 174 Bond, clad now in dark slacks, a black turtle-neck and short jacket.

2. *attrib.* or as *adj.*, esp. as ***turtle-neck sweater.***

1895 *Montgomery Ward Catal.* Spring & Summer 483/1 The Turtle Neck Shirt or Sweater, double from waist up, one of the most desirable garments ever invented for cold-weather shooting. **1896** F. D. ROOSEVELT *Let.* 14 Oct. (1947) 47, I should very much like a red turtle neck sweater for skating and coasting. **1905** *Outing* Mar. 743/1 Shape the coat like a turtle-neck sweater. **1926** *Daily Colonist* (Victoria, B.C.) 7 Jan. 18/4 (Advt.), Balbriggan Turtle-Neck Pull-Overs of fine quality, finished with ribbed band at the waist. **1938** J. STEINBECK *Long Valley* 95 The younger wore a blue turtle-neck sweater. **1946** WODEHOUSE *Joy in Morning* vi. 42 He dresses like a tramp-cyclist, affecting turtle-neck sweaters and grey flannel bags. **1952** M. MCCARTHY *Groves of Academe* (1953) xiii. 266 He.. signalled to a tall blonde girl in a tight turtle-neck sweater. **1964** *McCall's Sewing* xi. 182/2 Turtle-neck collar. A wide true bias band that stands up from the neck edge and then rolls back over the neckline seam. **1978** G. GREENE *Human Factor* II. i. 53 She wore brown trousers and a turtle-neck sweater.

Hence **'turtle-necked** *a.*

1931 G. S. CHAPPELL *Gardener's Friend* 7 When long-haired athletes in turtle-necked sweaters were the idols of the hour. **1954** *Encounter* Feb. 47/1 Long-haired men in turtle-necked sweaters marched into the room. **1978** J. WAINWRIGHT *Jury People* iii. 13 He wore a cheap wind-cheater over a turtle-necked sweater.

turtler ('tɜːtlə(r)). [f. TURTLE *sb.*[2] + -ER[1].]

1. A person, or a vessel, engaged in turtling; a turtle-catcher.

1697 DAMPIER *Voy.* (1729) I. 395 The Jamaica Turtlers have such [nets]. **1707** SLOANE *Jamaica* I. p. lvi, The Turtlers who furnish the island with Turtle, may be reckoned among the trading ships. **1831** JANE PORTER *Sir E. Seaward's Narr.* II. 91 The turtlers returned with twenty-six. **1898** *Blackw. Mag.* July 62/2 He had made acquaintance..with Florida wreckers, Tortuga turtlers, and Labrador eggers.

2. A seller of turtle.

1740 *New Hist. Jamaica* vii. 180 No Butcher or Turtler shall sell any Meat or Turtle by Retail.

turtlet ('tɜːtlɪt). [dim. of TURTLE *sb.*[2]: see -ET[1], -LET.] A small or young turtle.

1831 TRELAWNY *Adv. Younger Son* II. 31 When, off Ceylon, I picked up that pretty little turtlet. **1899** *Nat. Science* Sept. 224 The turtlets show a greater percentage of abnormalities in the carapace than the older individuals.

turtling ('tɜːtlɪŋ). [f. TURTLE *sb.*[2] + -ING[1].] The action or occupation of 'fishing' for or catching turtle. Also *attrib.*, and as *pres. pple.* (as if from TURTLE *v.*[2]).

1669 *Admiralty Crt. Exam.* 77 19 Aug., Intended to goe.. with the ship to the island of Kiamanas to make a turtling voyage. **1726** G. ROBERTS *Four Yrs. Voy.* 19, I sent my Boat ashore, to see..if any People were there a Turtling. **1810** *Sporting Mag.* XXXV. 287 The French fishermen come there turtling. **1889** H. H. ROMILLY *Verandah N. Guinea* 184 A turtling trip. *Ibid.* 189 The turtling was not very successful.

turtois, turtu, obs. forms of TORTOISE.

†**turtur.** *Obs.* Forms: 1, 4–5 turtur, (3 *gen.* turtres), 4–7 turture, 5–6 -our, 6 -or. [In OE. direct from L.; cf. OHG. *turtur* (Notker), OIcel. *turturi*. In ME. partly a. OF. *turtre*, *tortre*, *tourtre*, *tourte*, mod.F. *tourtre*; = Pr. *tortre*, It. *tortore*, *-ora*, OSp. *tortora* (Sp. *tortola*); all representing L. *turtur-em*, *turtur*, app. an echoic name, imitating the cooing of the dove.] = TURTLE *sb.*[1]

c **825** *Vesp. Psalter* lxxxiii. 4 [lxxxiv. 3] Speara ȝemoeted him hus & turtur nest hwer ȝesettað briddas his. *c* **950** *Lindisf. Gosp.* Luke ii. 24 þætte sealdon..tuoe turturas *vel* tuoȝe birdas culfras. **971** *Blickl. Hom.* 23 Tweȝen culfran briddas..& tweȝen turturan ȝemæccan. *c* **1220** *Bestiary* 694 In boke is ðe turtres lif Writen o rime. *c* **1375** *Sc. Leg. Saints* xxiv. (*Alexis*) 231 þane scho sad,..þat but mak ay sulд scho dwel As turtur. **1382** WYCLIF *Luke* ii. 24 A peyre of turtris [**1388** turturis]. **1398** TREVISA *Barth. De P.R.* XII. xxxv. (Bodl. MS.), The Turture is a semple bridde. *c* **1440** *Pallad. on Husb.* I. 556 With whete & milk in this thi turturs fede. *c* **1450** HOLLAND *Howlat* 127 The Turtour trewest, Ferme, faithfull and fast. **1500–20** DUNBAR *Poems* lxxiv. 37 Swete gentill turtour, quhair is ȝour pete went? **1508** —— *Tua Mariit Wemen* 262 And be as turtoris in your talk,..Be dragonis baith and dowis, ay in double forme. **1649** JER. TAYLOR *Gt. Exemp.* I. Ad Sect. v. 81 The turtures..being an oblation.

attrib. *c* **1425** *Cursor M.* 11304 (Trin.) And elles who þat myȝte not so Shulde offer turtur doufes two.

'tur-'turring, *vbl. sb.* [Echoic.] An imitation of the cooing of a dove, used to designate the action or sound.

1896 *Q. Rev.* July 73 The 'tur-turring' of the turtledove, the 'coo' of the queest..tell of the shade.

†**'turvary.** *Obs.*[−1] [ad. med.L. *turvāria*, var. of *turbāria*.] = TURBARY 2.

1651 G. W. tr. *Cowel's Inst.* II. ii. 72 Fishing, digging of Turfes,..called Piscaryes, Turvaryes [orig. *turuariam*].

turve, turved, turves, turving: see TURF *sb.*[1] and [2], *v.*[1], TURFING.

†**turver.** *Obs.*[−1] In 5 -are. [f. *turv-* TURF *sb.*[1] or *turve* TURF *v.*[1]] A turf-cutter.

c **1440** *Promp. Parv.* 507/2 Turvare, *glebarius.*

Turveydrop ('tɜːvɪdrɒp). The surname of a character in Dickens's *Bleak House* (1852), who poses as a perfect model of deportment; allusively, a person who does this. Hence (*colloq.* and *journalistic*) **'Turveydropdom; Turvey'dropian** *a.*

1876 J. WEISS *Wit, Hum. & Shaks.* iii. 101 Malvolio's conceit is Turveydropian and runs to deportment. **1877** W. H. RUSSELL *Prince of Wales' Tour* iv. 117 The maintenance of that staid deportment which the Oriental Turveydrop considers the best proof of high State and regal dignity. **1889** *Catholic News* 3 Aug. 5/1 She..deported herself so as to delight a Turveydrop's heart. **1892** *Pall Mall G.* 21 June 2/1 He showed himself a past master in deportment and might be envied by Court Chamberlains, Gold Sticks, Masters of Ceremonies, and the whole of Turveydropdom. **1897** *N.B. Daily Mail* 31 May 4 They pose in the deprecatory attitude, and become [a] sort of 'Turveydrops' in Church politics. **1899** *Longm. Mag.* Apr. 337 Those Turveydropian maxims on deportment and dress.

tusa: see TUZA.

Tuscan ('tʌskən), *a.* and *sb.* Also 6 **Tuskan(e, Thuscane,** 6–7 **Tuscane,** 6–8 **Thuscan;** 6 **Toscane, Thoscan, -kan,** 7 **Toscan.** [= F. *Tuscan*, *-ane*, It. *Toscano*, ad. late L. *Tuscān-us* of or belonging to the *Tuscī* or *Thuscī*, a people of ancient Italy (called also *Etruscī* Etruscans), pl. of *Tuscus* adj. and sb., an ethnic name.]

A. *adj.* **a.** In reference to ancient times = ETRUSCAN *a.* **b.** Of or pertaining to Tuscany, formerly a grand duchy, having Florence as its capital; now a region of the Italian Republic, nearly corresponding to the ancient Etruria.

a. 1513 DOUGLAS *Æneis* XI. xii. 3 The Tuscane Dukis and horsmen. **1552** HULOET, Tuskan tongue or language. **1587** W. FOWLER *Wks.* (S.T.S.) I. 100 Also Horatius that did alone defend the bridge aganis the Thoskan force. **1600** HOLLAND *Pliny* IX. 340 He was taught the Tuscane learning and knowledge. **1649** OGILBY *Virg. Georg.* I. (1684) 72 Great Vesta, Romulus, and Patriot Gods, Who guard Imperial Rome, and Tuscan Floods. **1706** SMITH in Hearne *Collect.* 14 Dec. (O.H.S.) I. 312 The old Thuscan language. **1843** MACAULAY *Horatius* xxxv, The Tuscan army, Right glorious to behold.

b. 1588 KYD *Househ. Phil.* Wks. (1901) 263 Therefore was it well sayde of that Thoscan Poet [Petrarch]. **1728** CHAMBERS *Cycl.* s.v. *Italian*, The Tuscan is usually preferred to the other Dialects. **1841** W. SPALDING *Italy & It. Isl.* II. 171 All the Tuscan towns yield in interest to the classic city [Florence] which became their chief. **1841–4** EMERSON *Ess.*, *Art* Wks. (Bohn) I. 149 The pictures of the Tuscan and Venetian Masters. **1886** PATER *Appreciations* (1890) 158 The delicate..sculpture of the early Tuscan school.

c. *Arch.* Name of the simplest and rudest of the five classical orders of architecture; allied to the Doric (of which it is by many considered a simpler form), but devoid of all ornament; belonging to this order, as ***a Tuscan pillar.***

1563 SHUTE *Archit.* C iv, I haue more at large spoken of this matter in the ending of the Tuscan piller. **1624** WOTTON *Archit.* I. in *Reliq.* (1651) 228 The Tuscan is a plain, massie, rurall Pillar, resembling some sturdy well-limb'd Labourer, homely clad. *Ibid.* 230 The Tuscan is of all the rudest Pillar, and his Principall Character Simplicity. **1728** CHAMBERS *Cycl.* s.v., Of all the Orders, the Tuscan is the most easily executed; as having neither Triglyphs nor Dentils, nor Modillions to confine its Intercolumns. **1801** RANKEN *Hist. France* I. I. v. 446 The Tuscan was more robust and unadorned than any of these orders [Doric, Ionian, and Corinthian]. **1851** RUSKIN *Stones Venice* I. App. vii. 359 Another order, called Tuscan (which is no order at all, but a spoiled Doric).

d. Applied to a method of plaiting the fine wheaten straw grown in Tuscany for hats, bonnets, etc.; also to the golden yellow colour of this (see sense B. d below). Cf. LEGHORN 1. Also ***Tuscan grass, hat.***

1830 in A. Adburgham *Shops & Shopping* (1964) iv. 38 Chip and Tuscan Hats. **1833** in *Ibid.* 40 A new bonnet, composed of Tuscan Grass and prepared whalebone. **1834** McCulloch *Dict. Comm.* (ed. 2) 629 The Tuscan plait.. largely imported, and made up into bonnets in this country. **1842** *Penny Cycl.* XXIII. 222/2 Men..employed in drabbets and Tuscan plait at Haverhill [Suffolk]. **1882** Caulfeild & Saward *Dict. Needlework* 504 *Tuscan straw work*, finely plaited straw of wheat, having a delicate and slender stalk, and golden hue; growing in Tuscany, and manufactured into circular 'flats', for hat and bonnet.

B. *sb.* **a.** = ETRUSCAN *sb.* **b.** A native or inhabitant of mediæval or modern Tuscany.

a. 1387 Trevisa *Higden* (Rolls) II. 435 Eneas afterward was kyng of eiþer kyngdom of Latyns and of Tuscans. *Ibid.* III. 159 He ouercame þe Vulces..and made pees wiþ Tuscans. *c* **1425** Wyntoun *Cron.* iv. 149 He knyt hym to þe Tuskanys, And warrayide wiþe þaim þe Romanys. **1533** Bellenden *Livy* i. xx. (S.T.S.) 117 King tarquyne.. renewit þe bond of confederacion with tuskanis. **1600** Holland *Livy* ix. 340 The Romanes having slaine many thousands of the Tuscanes, gained thirtie eight ensignes of the field. **1770** Langhorne *Plutarch* (1851) I. 158/2 The Gauls expelled the Tuscans. **1843** Macaulay *Horatius* xliii, He eyed the flinching Tuscans, And scorn was in his eye.

b. 1633 Massinger *Guardian* ii. v, The lusty girl of France, the sober German,..The Roman libertine, and sprightful Tuscan. **1857** J. F. Maguire *Rome* xxi. 245 Tuscans only, or their descendants to the third generation, are received into the society. **1901** M. Carmichael *In Tuscany* i. 9 Certainly the Tuscan has some real love of the Englishman.

c. The language of Tuscany, regarded as the classical form of Italian.

1568 (*title*) The Fearfull Fansies of the Florentine Couper: Written in Toscane, by Iohn Baptista Gelli..and ..translated into English by W. B[arker]. **1671** J. Gailhard *Pres. St. Italy* (ed. 2) 173 The right Italian language, or Toscan, as they usually call it, is very Sententious. **1817** Byron *Beppo* xxxi, He knew..French and Tuscan. **1906** *Hibbert Jrnl.* Apr. 583 Their language is the purest Tuscan of the golden age of the Italian Vernacular.

d. The golden-yellow colour of Tuscan straw.

1887 *Daily News* 11 Jan. 3/1 Tiring of that novelty the public called for other colours, and tuscan, apricot, coffee, and beige followed in quick succession. **1912** *T. Eaton & Co. Catal.* Spring & Summer 3/3 Draped Toque..Colors Black, Navy or Tuscan, with corded silk in colors to harmonize. **1923** *Daily Mail* 16 Apr. 1 Colours:..Old Gold, Tuscan, Mastic.

C. *Comb.*, as ***Tuscan-coloured*** adj. (of the colour of Tuscan straw, ***-like*** adj. or adv.; **Tuscan lamb**, a variety of processed lambskin, used mainly to make headwear; †**Tuscan-top**, applied sarcastically to a style of hair-dressing.

1581 Pettie *Guazzo's Civ. Conv.* ii. (1586) 65 If it be lawfull for me to write Tuscane like, why..not..likewise.. to speake Tuscane like? **1601** B. Jonson *Poetaster* iii. i, These high gable-ends, these tuscane-tops. **1905** *Westm. Gaz.* 8 Mar. 8/2 Such a hat would be very dainty in a.. Tuscan-coloured straw with Saxe blue ribbon velvet. **1956**, **1962** [see Lucca]. **1970** *Guardian* 24 Nov. 9/4 A Tuscan Lamb Hat (in black or white) complete with ear muffs.

Hence †**Tu'scanic** *a.* [ad. L. *Tuscānic-us*] = sense A. c; **'Tuscanish** *a.* = sense A. b; **'Tuscanism**, Tuscan style or character; a Tuscan idiom or phrase; **'Tuscanize** *v.*, (*a*) *intr.* to become Tuscan; (*b*) *trans.* to make Tuscan; (*c*) *intr.* to speak in the Italian of Florence or Tuscany.

1601 Holland *Pliny* xxxvi. xxiii. II. 595 Such pillars as beare in compasse.., as much as..the sixt part of the height, be called Dorique:.. such as have a seventh part, be *Tuscanique. **1580** G. Harvey *Let. to Spenser* Wks. (Grosart) I. 84 Not a looke but [is] *Tuscanish alwayes. *Ibid.*, Since Galateo came in, and *Tuscanisme gan vsurpe. **1593** —— *Pierce's Super.* ibid. II. 19 The glory of our English Eloquence, and our vulgar Tuscanisme (if I may so terme it). **1596** Nashe *Saffron Walden* Wks. (Grosart) III. 90 He would needs crosse the seas to fetch home two penniworth of Tuscanisme. **1906** *Athenæum* 2 June 664/3 The Tuscanism 'si domanda'. *a* **1618** Sylvester *Epistles* vii. 13 When every thing now *Tuskanizeth so, That nothing is the same it is in show. **1768** Baretti *Mann. & Cust. Italy* I. 161 His language is the most nauseous medley..taken from several of the Italian dialects, and tuscanized in a most ridiculous manner. **1905** *Athenæum* 8 Apr. 431/1 The Genoese who blames his Tuscanizing friend for saying 'arimmetica' in place of *aritemetica*.

Tuscarora (tʌskə'rɔːrə). [Iroquois, = hemp-gatherer.] An Iroquoian people, originally inhabiting Carolina, which, after moving to upper New York State, joined the Iroquois Confederacy of North American Indians, commonly called the Five Nations (thereafter Six Nations), in 1722; a member of this people; their language. Also *attrib.*

1650 E. Bland *Jrnl.* 28 Aug. in *Discovery New Britaine* (1651) 3 An Englishman, a Cockarous hard by Captaine Floods, gave this Indian Bells..to lay downe to the Tuskarood King. **1713** in *N. Carolina Colonial Rec.* (1886) II. 2 An order from ye Government of New Yorke to Caution ye Tuscaroras against going to warr with ye English here. **1785** T. Jefferson *Notes Virginia* 390 The Monacans or Tuscaroras..were taken into the confederacy.., making the sixth [nation]. **1878** *Jrnl. R. Soc. Arts* 10 May 537/2 He wants one of my improved phonographs to preserve the accents of the..Tuscaroras, who are dying out. **1910** F. W. Hodge et al. *Handbk. Amer. Indians N. of Mexico* II. 842 The Tuscarora..possessed in early times the 'country lying between the sea shores and the mountains, which divide the Atlantic States'. **1915** J. Buchan *Salute to Adventurers* ix. 137 All this land..is Sioux country... But cheek by jowl is a long strip held by the Tuscaroras. **1933** L. Bloomfield *Language* iv. 72 The Iroquoian family was spoken in a district surrounded by Algonquian; it includes..the languages of the Iroquois type (Mohawk, Oneida,.. Tuscarora). **1976** W. L. Chafe in T. A. Sebeok *Native Languages of Americas* I. 532 The Northern Iroquoian languages which are still spoken are six in number. They include the very closely related languages of the original Five Nations of the Iroquois..plus Tuscarora, now the Sixth Nation, a language somewhat more divergent. **1979** *United States 1980/81* (Penguin Travel Guides) 654 The Tuscarora Indian Reservation is nearby.

tusche ('tʊʃə). orig. *U.S.* Also **tushe**. [Ger., back-formation from *tuschen*, f. F. *toucher* to touch.] A greasy black liquid composition used in lithography and other printing techniques; lithographic drawing ink. Also *attrib.*

1885 *Lithographer & Printer* 24 Jan. 114/1 By the term autography we designate..everything that is written with lithographic tushe on transfer paper in order to enable it to be transferred to the lithographic stone. We use the word 'tushe', for though specially coined, it has been adopted by the entire craft of lithographers in this country. **1912** W. C. Brown *Practical Textbk. Lithography* iii. 26 The most useful of all inks for writing or drawing on stone come under the name tusche. **1940** R. Mayer *Artist's Hand-bk.* xii. 440 Lithographic crayons and tusche are always black, regardless of the color in which the final proof is to be printed. *Ibid.* 460 (*heading*) Tusche-wash-out method. **1965** Zigrosser & Gaehde *Guide Coll. Orig. Prints* iv. 49 The crayons used [in lithography]—and their liquid equivalent, tusche or lithographic ink—are made of a mixture of grease, wax, soap, and lampblack... Many technical manipulations are possible:..tusche effects with pen, brush, drybrush or spatterwork, [etc.]. **1967** V. Strauss *Printing Industry* v. 274/2 If lithographic tusche is used as a painting medium [in serigraphy], glue can serve as blocking medium as it will be repelled by the fatty lithographic tusche which is, of course, water-repellent.

tusche, obs. Sc. f. TISSUE; obs. f. TUSH.

†**tuscle.** *Obs.* Forms: 1, 4 tuxl, 6 tussle, tuscle. [OE. **tuscel*, *tuxl*, derivative of *tusc*, *tux*, TUSK *sb.*[1]] = TUSK *sb.*[1] 1.

c **1000** *Sax. Leechd.* II. 104 Wið onfealle ȝefoh fox asleah of cucum þone tuxl. *a* **1400** *Octouian* 929 Twey tuxlys out of hys mouth set, As of a bore. **1600** F. Walker *Sp. Mandeville* 10 b, This man..was borne..with all the teeth and tussles which he nowe hath. *Ibid.* 25 b, Her teeth and tussles.. began to bud and growe out anew. *Ibid.* 149 A wilde Boare, with two great tuscles shooting aboue foure spans out of his mouth.

tush (tʌʃ), *sb.*[1] Forms: *α.* 1 tusc, 4 tussche, 4–6 tusche, 5 tusshe, 6– tush. *β.* 4 tossche, 5 tosch(e, toyssh, 6 (9 *dial.*) tosh. [ME. *tus(s)ch*, *tos(s)ch*, normal representatives of OE. *tusc* (see TUSK *sb.*[1]); partly specialized in use.]

1. = TUSK *sb.*[1] 1. Now chiefly *arch.* or *dial.*

α. *c* **725** *Corpus Gloss.* G. 62 *Genuino*, tusc. *c* **1050** in Wr.-Wülcker 489 *Genuinis*, tuscum. **13..** *Seuyn Sages* (W.) 914 The tusches in the tre he smit. **13..** *Gaw. & Gr. Knt.* 1573 [The boar] Whettez his whyte tuschez. **1398** Trevisa *Barth. De P.R.* xviii. xxxi. (Bodl. MS.), Beestes wiþ teeþ and tussches in aiþer iowe haue none hornes. *c* **1410** *Master of Game* (MS. Digby 82) v, Men beyonde þe see calleth þe neither tusshes of þe boore his armes, or elles his files,..also þei calleth his tusshes aboue gres. **1576** Turberv. *Venerie* 150 Amonge the reste they have foure [teeth],..and we call them Tuskes or Tusches. **1621** G. Sandys *Ovid's Met.* viii. (1626) 157 His tushes equall those Of Indian Elephants. **1672** Josselyn *New Eng. Rarities* 97 Morse, or Sea Horse, having a great Head,..armed with Tushes as white as Ivory. **1737** Stackhouse *Hist. Bible* (1767) VI. vi. iii. 77 The whale has neither teeth nor tushes. **1848** Kingsley *Saint's Trag.* ii. viii. 299 He is an old boar, and honest; he wears his tushes outside, for a warning to all men.

β. **13..** *Seuyn Sages* (W.) 911 The bor..wette his tossches and his fet. *c* **1440** *Promp. Parv.* 497/2 Tosche, longe tothe (*Winch. MS.* tosch; *Pynson* toyssh), *colomellus, culmus.* *a* **1563** Becon *Humble Supplic.* Wks. iii. 22 Whose teeth ar like to ye venomous toshes of ye rampyng lyon. **1823–78** in dial. glossaries (E. Anglia, Northumb., Cumb.).

b. *spec.* A canine tooth, esp. of a horse: cf. TUSK *sb.*[1] 1 b.

1607 Markham *Caval.* i. iv. (1617) 28 At fiue yeares olde he changes his tushes. **1610** —— *Masterp.* ii. clxvii. 477 The [horse's] tush will be white, small, short, and sharp. *c* **1720** W. Gibson *Farrier's Guide* i. vi. (1738) 86 The canini or Dog teeth, which in Horses are called the Tushes. **1766** Pennant *Zool.* (1768) I. 107 The Hedge hog... In each jaw are two sharp pointed cutting teeth: in the upper jaw are on each side four tushes, and five grinders: in the lower..three tushes.. and..four grinders. **1850** Smedley *F. Fairlegh* xl, Rising five and six..tush well up in one, and nicely through in the other.

c. A stunted tusk in some Indian elephants.

1859 Tennent *Ceylon* II. viii. i. 274 Not one elephant in a hundred is found with tusks in Ceylon... Nearly all, however, have those stunted processes which are called tushes, about ten or twelve inches in length and one or two in diameter. **1859** *All Year Round* No. 32. 129 All the untusked elephants of Ceylon have 'tushes',..which they use in snapping off small branches. **1878** J. Gibson in *Encycl. Brit.* VIII. 125/1 The male [Ceylon elephant].. generally has a pair of upper incisors, known as 'tushes', about a foot long, and one or two inches in diameter. **1900** Pollok & Thom *Sports Burma* ii. 35 The result of the cross-breed is that you get large males with very poor tusks, but still tusks, as distinct from tushes.

2. In a plough: = FIN *sb.*[1] 3 b. *Obs.* exc. *dial.*

1649 Blithe *Eng. Improv. Impr.* (1653) 193 The Tush or Phin of the Share will whelm the more being set down to the work which is the Levell or bottom of the head. **1787** Grose *Provinc. Gloss.*, *Tush*, the wing of a ploughshare. *Glouc.* **1894** *S.E. Worc. Gloss.*, *Tush*, (1) the broad part of a plough-share.

3. *Arch.* (See quot. and cf. TUSS.)

1905 Bond *Gothic Archit.* 366 There may still be seen the 'tushes'; i.e. the projecting courses on which the heads of the flying buttresses were to rest.

Hence **tushed** (tʌʃt) *a.*, having a tush or tushes; tusked.

c **1440** *Promp. Parv.* 497/2 Toschyd, or tuskyd (*P.* toysshyd), *colomellatus.* **1649** Blithe *Eng. Improv. Impr.* (1653) 29 Plow thy Land a thin broad furrow,..or rather flay it, or take off thy Skin or Turf with a very broad whinged or tushed share. *c* **1828** [see TUSKED *a.* b].

†**tush,** *sb.*[2] *Obs. rare.* [Variant of TUSK *sb.*[2]; for the form cf. prec.] A tuft.

1570 Levins *Manip.* 193/39–41 A Tushe of heyres, *crinetum.* A Tushe of thornes, *dumetum.* A Tushe of trees, *arboretum.*

tush, *sb.*[3]: see TUSH *int.*

tush (tʊʃ), *sb.*[4] *slang* (chiefly *N. Amer.*). Also **tushie, -y.** [Abbrev. or dim. of TOCHUS.] = BACKSIDE 3.

1962 *Amer. Speech* XXXVII. 205 Another bilingual children's diminutive, *tushie*—from Yiddish *toches* or *tuches* 'rump'—has appeared in phrases like *tushie slide* 'a slide down a slope on one's bottom', the delights of which a group of Midwestern Jewish children have, I am told, expressed to their Gentile social workers. **1969** P. Roth *Portnoy's Complaint* 47 You'd think I was a twenty-one-year-old girl; you'd think I hadn't wiped your backside and kissed your little tushy for you all those years. **1970** *Pix* (Austral.) 26 Dec. 11/4 Pretty young girls who walk around with..their tushes out there asking for it. **1973** *N.Y. Times* 10 June ii. 1/3, I felt a fork hanging from the seat of my pants. I threw it off, just like Stanley would, and the audience went wild. I mean, there were 1,100 people there, looking at me with a fork up my tush! **1977** *Detroit Free Press* 11 Dec. 23-A/1 Eight hundred guests danced their tushies off on the world's largest discotheque floor. **1981** G. V. Higgins *Rat on Fire* xxviii. 170 Her tush is tight and she's got great boobs. **1984** *Miami* (Florida) *Herald* 6 Apr. 4B/6 (*caption*) So what's a damp tush between good friends?

tush (tʌʃ), *int.* (*sb.*[3]) *arch.* Forms: 5 tussch, tysche, 6 tusche, tusshe, tushe, tuch, 6– tush. [A natural utterance: cf. TWISH.] An exclamation of impatient contempt or disparagement.

c **1440** *York Myst.* xxxiii. 121 3a, tussch! for youre tales, þai touche not entente. *c* **1450** *Mankind* 783 in *Macro Plays* 29 Tysche! a flyes weynge! *c* **1520** Skelton *Magnyf.* 591 Tushe! holde your pece. **1535** Coverdale *Jer.* v. 11 Tush, there shall no miszfortune come vpon vs. **1602** Shaks. *Ham.* i. i. 29 Tush, tush, 'twill not appeare. **1678** Bunyan *Pilgr.* i. 251 Tush, said Obstinate, away with your book. **1791** Cowper *Iliad* ii. 290 But tush,—Achilles lacks Himself the spirit of a man. **1837** Hawthorne *Twice-told T.* (1851) II. i. 16 Tush! we have nothing to fear. **1891** Farrar *Darkn. & Dawn* xlv, Tush, Cæsar! be a man. Sweep aside these flies. Poison them both.

B. *sb.* as a name for this utterance: esp. in phr. †*to make a tush at* (or *of*), to scoff at, to pooh-pooh (*obs.*).

1600 Holland *Livy* vi. xxxviii. 244 When the Tribunes.. made but a tush therat. **1628** Earle *Microcosm.*, *Worlds wise Man* (Arb.) 61 His tush is greatest at Religion. **1632** Lithgow *Trav.* (1906) p. xxii, A tush for that snarling Crew. *a* **1643** J. Shute *Judgement & Mercy* (1645) 128 People..that make a tush of the Devills power. **1883** R. L. Stevenson *Lett.* (1901) I. vi. 272 These tushes Are wearisome.

Hence **tush** *v.*[1], *intr.* to say 'tush!', to scoff or express impatience *at*: also *trans.* to dismiss with 'tush!' (*nonce-use*); whence **'tushing** *vbl. sb.*; also **'tusher**, one who 'tushes'; **'tushery**, used by R. L. Stevenson for a conventional style of romance characterized by excessive use of affected archaisms such as 'tush!'; *gen.*, sentimental or romanticizing writing.

1548 Udall *Erasm. Par. Luke* vi. 78 Thou makest muche tushyng, and many exceptions. **1555** Harpsfield in Bonner *Homilies* 30 b, [He] doth thou hym or tushe at hym. **1597** J. Payne *Royal Exch.* 11 To make men laughe at there tushinge and scoffinge of religiouse matters. **1679** J. Brown *Life of Faith* (1824) II. xxii. 428 People become hardened in their sins..tushing at all threatenings. **1819** Scott *Ivanhoe* xl[i]v, Cedric tushed and pshawed more than once at the message. **1883** R. L. Stevenson *Lett.* (1901) I. vi. 270 Every tusher tushes me so free that may I be tushed if the whole thing be worth a tush. **1883** —— *Let. to Colvin* Oct. (1899) I. 285 It's great sport to write tushery. **1907** *Academy* 26 Jan. 96/1 This is what R. L. S. called 'tushery'. Luckily.. for those who write tushery there is an enormous reading public that does not care a fig for Life. **1908** *Times* 9 Dec. 14/4 We overheard..an occasional pishing and tushing. **1921** H. S. Walpole *Young Enchanted* i. ii. 42 In literature her great period had been during the Romantic Tushery of 1895 to 1905. **1932** *Times Lit. Suppl.* 21 Apr. 292/4 Unlike many novelists who set their scene in Japan, Mr. John Paris indulges in no sentimental tushery about the Japanese. **1967** *Guardian* 16 May 7/5 What a wonderful vanished world of tushery is brought back by 'The Desert Song'. **1981** *Times* 14 Oct. 13/4 The *Idylls* wound their endless way... Such Arthurian tushery seems far removed from..*In Memoriam*.

tush (tʊʃ, tʌʃ), *v.*[2] orig. *dial.* [Origin unknown.] *trans.* To pull or drag (a heavy object, esp. a log) along the ground.

1841 C. H. Hartshorne *Salopia Antiqua* 602 *Tush*,..to draw a heavy weight, as *tushing* timber. **1879** G. F. Jackson *Shropshire Word-bk.* 458 'Can yo' carry them faggits to the 'ŏŏd-pil?' 'I dunna know, but if I canna carry 'em, be'appen I can *tush* 'em alung.' **1953** H. L. Edlin *Forester's Handbk.* xv. 238 Felled logs are *tushed*, or drawn over the ground, butt-end foremost, by hauling chains attached to a tractor, a horse-team or a winch, until the nearest hard road is reached. **1963** *Times* 12 Feb. 12/7 Dolgelly's eight oak pillars had originally been snaked or tushed by oxen 10 miles over the mountains from Dinas Mawddwy, where they had been grown.

tushwe, obs. form of TISSUE.

†**'tushy**, *a. Obs.* [f. TUSH *sb.*^{1} + -Y.] Having tushes; = TUSKY.
1430-40 LYDG. *Bochas* I. i. (MS. Bodl. 263) 10 Thei stood ..in daunger and in dreed Off cruel beestis, tigres and leouns, Off tusshi booris. *c* **1557** ABP. PARKER *Ps.* lxxx. 233 The tushy bore..doth route it up to stoure.

tusk (tʌsk), *sb.*^{1} Forms: α. 1-4 **tux** (1 **twux**), 3-7 **tuske**, 7- **tusk**. β. 4-5 **tosk**, *pl.* **toskes**. [OE. *tux* (whence by metathesis ME. *tusk, tosk*), normal and common variant of the rare OE. *tusc* (whence TUSH *sb.*^{1}), = OFris. *tusk, tusch, tosch* (mod. WFris. *tosk*, NFris. *tosk, toske*, LG. of East Friesland *tûsk*); in OEFris. the mutated plural form *tesch* also occurs. There are no certain cognates outside of the Anglo-Frisian area; in mod. WFris. *tosk* has entirely displaced the OFris. *tôth* tooth.
On the supposition that the stem is that of Goth. *tunþ-us* tooth (with *-sko* suffix), it has been assumed that the OE. forms had a long vowel (*túsc, túx*), but of this there is no clear evidence. It is also very doubtful whether the second element in the ON. mythical name *Rata-toskr* or *-tǫskr* (a squirrel) can be definitely identified with this word.]

1. A long pointed tooth; *esp.* a tooth specially developed so as to project beyond the mouth, as in the elephant, wild boar, and various other animals.
A tusk is most frequently a development of a canine tooth, as in the boar and walrus; but it may be an incisor, as in the elephant and narwhal.
a **900** *Laws Ælfred* c. 49 Monnes tux bið xv. scill. weorð. ?*a* **950** *Prose Guthlac* v (Vercelli MS.), Heora teð wæron horses tuxum [*v.r.* twuxan] ȝelice. *c* **1000** *Sax. Leechd.* I. 370 Hundes tux ȝebærned & smale ȝegniden. *a* **1225** *Ancr. R.* 280 þe wilde bor..is al kareleas of his tuxes. *a* **1225** *Juliana* 68 As an burst bar þat grunde his tuskes. *a* **1300** *E.E. Psalter* lvii. 6 [lviii. 6] Toskes of liouns lauerd breke sal ma. **13..** *Sir Beues* (A.) 742 A wilde bor..Wiþ his toskes he al to-schok. *a* **1340** HAMPOLE *Psalter* lvii. 6 Tuskis of lyons breke sall lord. *a* **1400-50** *Alexander* 4114 þai..Tuke out þe tuskis & þe tethe [of elephants]. *c* **1470** HENRYSON *Mor. Fab.* 1184 Wks. (S.T.S.) II. 88 3e, Schir Wolf,..with 3our Tuskis rauenous Hes slane [etc.]. **1555** EDEN *Decades* 354 These great teeth or tuskes [of the elephant] growe in the vpper iaw downewarde. **1601** R. JOHNSON *Kingd. & Commw.* (1603) 203 To their tusks were fastened long and broad swords, to cut in sunder whatsoeuer stoode in their way. **1697** DRYDEN *Virg. Georg.* III. 387 Boars whet their Tusks. **1841-71** T. R. JONES *Anim. Kingd.* (ed. 4) 828 In the Male Narwal..from the intermaxillary bone of the left side of the face there projects a single tusk of great strength, which sometimes attains the length of eight or ten feet. **1851** D. WILSON *Preh. Ann.* (1863) II. III. iii. 101 Several very large tusks of boars or wolves. **1868** OWEN *Vertebr. Anim.* III. xxix. 369 Teeth ..of uninterrupted growth, are called 'tusks'; such..are the incisors of the elephant, narwhal, dinotherium, and dugong, the canines of the boar, walrus, and hippopotamus. **1907** J. H. PATTERSON *Man-Eaters of Tsavo* ii. 23 The unfortunate jemadar's head had been left intact, save for the holes made by the lion's tusks on seizing him.

b. Applied *spec.* to the permanent canine teeth of a horse. More commonly called *tush*.
1808 *Compl. Grazier* Introd. (ed. 3) 19 Twenty-four grinders,..four tushes or tusks, and twelve foreteeth. **1854** OWEN *Skel. & Teeth* in *Orr's Circ. Sc.* I. *Org. Nat.* 285 The permanent canine, or 'tusk', next follows; its appearance indicates the age of four years.

c. Used in contempt for human teeth.
[Cf. quot. 1614 s.v. TUSK *v.*^{1} 2.] **1632** LITHGOW *Trav.* x. 446 He hath the longest Tuskes that euer stroke at Table.

2. A projecting part or object resembling the tusk of an animal. **a.** *Carpentry.* A bevel or sloping shoulder on a tenon, for additional strength.
1679 MOXON *Mech. Exerc.* viii. 140 They cut a Tusk on the upper side of the Tennant, and let that Tusk into the upper side of the Girders. **1688** R. HOLME *Armoury* III. 110/2 *Tusk*, is a Bevel shoulder made to strengthen the Tennant of a Joyst. **1825** J. NICHOLSON *Operat. Mechanic* 566 In introducing binding joists,..it is necessary, in order to make the tenons sufficiently strong, to have a shorter bearing tenon attached to the principal tenon, with a sloping shoulder above, called a tusk, which term is likewise applied to this tenon, called the tusk tenon.

b. In miscellaneous uses.
1823 BYRON *Juan* VII. lxiii, I've vow'd..that shortly plough or harrow Shall pass o'er what was Ismail, and its tusk Be unimpeded by the proudest mosque. **1871** G. MACDONALD *Songs Days & Nights, Winter Days* IV. ii, Down tusks of ice one drop will go. **1908** *19th Cent.* Jan. 128 From the base of this tusk of land the grand river front of new Khartoum stretches.

c. In a lock, 'A sharp projecting point or claw which forms a means of engagement or attachment' (Knight *Dict. Mech.* 1875).

d. Short for *tusk-shell*: see 3.
In recent Dicts.

3. *attrib.* and *Comb.*, as **tusk hunter**, **-mark**: **tusk-carrying**, **-like** adjs.; **tusk-shell** = TOOTH-SHELL; **tusk tenon**, a tenon made with a tusk (see 2 a); **tusk vase**, a vase made of an elephant's tusk, or in imitation of one so made.
1898 *Daily News* 28 Apr. 6/1 Mr. Neumann brought many a procession of *tusk-carrying Zanzibaris to Mombasa... Carriers of the heaviest tusks are given the post of honour—the van. **1902** *Q. Rev.* Oct. 418 The *tusk-hunter will not be able to shoot his two elephants in.. Kassola. **1876** HUXLEY in *Nature* 11 May 33/2 The male horse has a *tusk-like tooth, or canine. **1909** STACPOOLE *Pools of Silence* xvii, Above the *tusk marks..could be seen the rubbing mark where great shoulders had scratched themselves. **1861** P. P. CARPENTER in *Rep. Smithsonian Instit.* 1860, 222 Family *Dentaliadæ*. (*Tusk-Shells.) **1825** *Tusk tenon [see 2 a].

Hence **'tuskish** *a.*, resembling a tusk; **'tuskwise** *adv.*, in the manner of a tusk.
1653 R. SANDERS *Physiogn.* 253 The teeth tuskish-like long. **1844** MRS. BROWNING *Drama of Exile* Wks. 1850 I. 72 Ye would perish,—beast by beast Devouring,—tree by tree, with strangling roots And trunks set tuskwise.

tusk, *sb.*^{2} *Obs.* exc. *dial.* [Of obscure origin; agrees in sense with TUSSOCK, which is found in use 20 years later. The variant *tush* (see TUSH *sb.*^{2}) is common to this and TUSK *sb.*^{1}, but it is doubtful if there is any real connexion between the words.] A tuft (of hair); also, of rushes, grass, etc.
1530 PALSGR. 284/1 Tuske of heer, *monceau de cheueulx*. **1565-73** COOPER *Thesaurus* s.v. *Cirrus, Cirratus*, that hath his heare..growing in tuskes and lockes. **1577** B. GOOGE *Heresbach's Husb.* II. (1586) 67 b, With a yellow hearie tuske in the midst. **1598** W. PHILLIP *Linschoten* xxxix. (Hakl. Soc.) I. 262 They weare onely a tuske of haire on the toppes of their heades. **1611** MARKHAM *Country Content.* I. iv. (1668) 26 Grounds that are all tusks of rushes, short ling, bramble bushes, or such like. **1851** STERNBERG *Dial. Northampt.*, *Tusk*, a tuft of grass or weeds.

tusk (tʌsk), *sb.*^{3} Also locally **tursk**, **torsk** (tɔːsk), **tosk**. [a. Norw. *torsk, tosk*, Sw., Da. *torsk*:—ON. *þorskr, þoskr*; prob. f. root of ON. *þurr*, Sw. *torr*, Gothic *þaurs-us* dry. Cf. LG. (and Ger.) *dorsch*.] A gadoid fish, *Brosmius brosme*, abundant in the northern seas, especially about the Shetland Islands, and much used for food in the dried form of *stockfish*. Also *attrib.*
1707 MIEGE *St. Gt. Brit.* ii. 14 They have abundance of Fish on that Coast call'd Tusk, as big as Ling. **1776** PENNANT *Zool.* III. 179 The Torsk, or as it is called in the Shetlands, Tusk and Brismak is a northern fish; and as yet undiscovered lower than about the Orknies. **1822** SCOTT *Pirate* xxii, There is torsk for the gentle, and skate for the carle, And there's wealth for bold Magnus, the son of the earl. **1837** M. DONOVAN *Dom. Econ.* II. 179 The Torsk is not so slender as the ling, and is altogether a smaller fish. As food it is considered more delicate than ling. **1864** COUCH *Brit. Fishes* III. 96. **1875** W. A. SMITH *Lewsiana* 237 The tursk or tosk..is perhaps the finest of the *Gadidæ* when fresh. **1883** *Fisheries Exhib. Catal.* 72 Dried Salted Tusk-fish,..mostly consumed in Scotch Markets. **1925** J. T. JENKINS *Fishes Brit. Isles* 164 The Torsk or tusk..is moderately elongate and covered with very small scales. **1926** *Glasgow Herald* 19 Oct. 3 The inhabitants fit out boats for the..tusk fishing. **1935** *Fisheries Notice* (Min. Agric. & Fisheries) XXIII. 6 Suggested Trade Name. Tusk. **1977** *Grimsby Even. Tel.* 26 May 18/5 Principal sorts were..monk 28, tusk 20.

tusk, *v.*^{1} [f. TUSK *sb.*^{1}]
†**1.** *trans.* The technical expression for: To carve (a barbel). *Obs.*
Perh. suggested by the tusk-like appearance of the two pairs of cirri depending from the upper jaw.
1486 *Bk. St. Albans* F vij b, A Barbill tuskyd. **1513** *Bk. Keruynge* in *Babees Bk.* (1868) 265 Tuske that barbell. [**1787** BEST *Angling* (ed. 2) 169 *Tusk a barbel*, cut him up. **1853** *Fraser's Mag.* XLVIII. 694 The reader will remember when he puts the slice into a fish, that he gobbets trout, truncheons eel, fins chub, tusks barbel (etc.).]

2. *intr.* †**a.** ? To show the teeth. *Obs.*
1614 B. JONSON *Bart. Fair* II. iii, Vapours? Neuer tuske, nor twirle your dibble... You shall not fright me with your Lyon-chap, Sir, nor your tuskes. **1616** —— *Epigr.* cvii, Nay, now you puffe, tuske, and draw vp your chin, Twirle the poore chain you run a feasting in.

b. To use, or thrust with, the tusks; of a horse, to pull roughly with the teeth *at*.
1825 JAMIESON, *To Tusk at*, to pluck or pull roughly; as when a horse tears hay from a stack, *Fife*. **1893** KIPLING *Many Invent.* 204 They were rooting and tusking among the young Sal.

3. *trans.* To root or dig *up*, or to tear *off* with the tusks; to wound with the tusk.
1629 DEKKER *Londons Tempe* Wks. 1873 IV. 120, I could (to swell my trayne) beckon the Rhine, (But the wilde boare has tusked up his vine). **1818** KEATS *Endym.* II. 474 My poor mistress went..mad, When the boar tusked him. **1909** STACPOOLE *Pools of Silence* xvii, A tree..showed half its bark ripped off, tusked off by some old bull elephant. *Ibid.* xix, The screams of men trodden under foot or tusked to pieces.

4. To furnish with tusks; to project from or adorn like tusks.
1896 KIPLING *Seven Seas, Merchantmen*, We've ratched beyond the Crossets That tusk the Southern Pole.

†**tusk**, *v.*^{2} *Obs. rare*$^{-1}$. [app. f. TUSK *sb.*^{2}: cf. in the same sense TUFT *v.* 4.] *trans.* ? To beat the bushes in (a wood) in order to rouse the game.
1592 LYLY *Gallathea* II. i, You were best..make them tuske these Woodes, whilst we stande with our bowes.

Tuskan, obs. f. TUSCAN.

tuskar ('tʌskə(r)). Also tusker; tuysker, twiscar. [ad. ON. *torfskeri* (Fær. *torvskeri*), f. *torf* turf + *skera* to cut, shear. Hence also Sc. Gael. *toirsgein* (*-sgian*, assimilated to *sgian* knife), *tairisgein*, *tairisgil* (cf. TURSKILL).] An implement for cutting peats used in Orkney and Shetland: see quots.
1808-18 JAMIESON, *Tusker*, an instrument made of iron, with a wooden handle, for casting peats, *Orkn.* **1809** EDMONDSTON *Zetl. Isl.* I. v. 177 The peats are cut with an instrument called a tuysker, which resembles a narrow spade, having a sharp plate of iron, called the feather, about seven inches long, projecting from the bottom on its left hand side, and it determines the form and size of the peat. **1822** HIBBERT *Shetl. Isl.* 430 An ancient Scandinavian implement of husbandry is used for casting the peats, named a tuskar. **1822** SCOTT *Pirate* xii, His thoughts were.. engrossed in the deficiencies of the one-stilted plough; of the 'twiscar', with which they dig peats. **1883** *Chamb. Jrnl.* 211 Here he cuts his peats.., using..a spadelike instrument called a tusker. **1884** RAMPINI *Shetl. & Shetlanders* ii. 86 His archaic implements of agriculture—his tuskar or peat spade. **1900** J. GUNN *Orkney Bk.* 297 The flaying-spade and the tuskar are not mere toys, nor is 'taking out' the newly-cut peats a holiday task.

tusked (tʌskt, *poet.* 'tʌskɪd), *a.* [f. TUSK *sb.*^{1} + -ED^2.] Having tusks; armed with tusks.
c **1386** CHAUCER *Frankl. T.* 526 Biforn hym stant brawen of the tusked [*v.r.* tuxed] swyn. **1513** DOUGLAS *Æneis* VII. Prol. 82 Fed tuskit baris, and fat swyne. **1555** EDEN *Decades* 355 Of the Indian elephantes, only the males haue tuskes. But of them of Ethiopia and Lybia, both kyndes are tusked. **1656** COWLEY *Anacreontiques, Beauty*, Some with hard Hoofs, or forked claws, And some with Horns, or tusked jaws. **1681** GREW *Musæum* I. 27 As to those Beasts [wild boar] no one was horned and tusked too. **1860** WRAXALL *Life in Sea* ii. 44 A young animal [walrus], not yet tusked,.. continued the attack. **1906** A. NOYES *Drake* III. in *Blackw. Mag.* May 622 Weird troops of tusked sea-lions.

b. *Her.* Having the tusks of a specified tincture different from that of the rest of the body.
1766-87 PORNY *Heraldry* v. (ed. 4) 162 Gules, an Elephant statant Argent, tusked Or. *c* **1828** BERRY *Encycl. Her.* I. Gloss., *Tusked*, or *Tushed*,..is said of a boar, tyger, or elephant, when their tusks are borne of a different tincture to that of the body. **1864** BOUTELL *Her. Hist. & Pop.* xvii. §3 (ed. 3) 281 Two boars arg., bristled, tusked, and unguled or.

tusker ('tʌskə(r)). [f. as prec. + -ER^1.] A beast having tusks, esp. an elephant or wild boar.
1859 TENNENT *Ceylon* II. VIII. i. 280 Some natives,.. attracted by a noise in the jungle, witnessed a combat between a tusker and one without tusks. **1865** LIVINGSTONE *Zambesi* ix. 188 The tusker, fearing less, keeps his trunk down. **1887** E. GILLIAT *Forest Outlaws* 238 He..would fare forth in quest of a stag, a fox, or even a tusker [wild boar]. **1893** SELOUS *Trav. S.E. Africa* 372 About twenty elephants .., but no good tuskers.

tusker, var. TUSKAR.

†**'tusking.** *Obs. rare.* [f. TUSK *sb.*^{2} + -ING^1.] = TUFTING *vbl. sb.* 1.
1558 in Feuillerat *Revels Q. Eliz.* (1908) 93 Spente in attyres of hedpeces gerdells tuskynges pullinges owte and other garniture.

tuskless ('tʌsklɪs), *a.* [f. TUSK *sb.*^{1} + -LESS.] Having no tusks.
1859 TENNENT *Ceylon* II. VIII. i. 281 The tuskless elephant. **1879** PRYER *Let.* 22 Nov. in J. Hatton *New Ceylon* iii. (1881) 72 Two of the elephants (tuskless) ran off, but the third faced about. **1895** *Chamb. Jrnl.* XII. 726/2 Apparently it is the male elephant that is usually found tuskless in Ceylon. **1907** *Spectator* 5 Jan. 11/1 Tuskless swine will grout up ground, if it be not too hard, almost as fast as the tusked boar.

tusky ('tʌskɪ), *a.* [f. as prec. + -Y.] Characterized by tusks; tusked: chiefly as a poetic epithet of the wild boar.
1620 SHELTON *Quix.* II. xxxiv. 228 The Tuskie Boare was laid along, with many iauelins points. **1697** DRYDEN *Virg. Past.* x. 89 On Mountain tops to chace the tusky Boar. *a* **1763** SHENSTONE *Elegies* xx. 61 For them our tusky elephant expires. **1853** KANE *Grinnell Exp.* xx. (1856) 160 That marine pachyderm, the tusky walrus.

b. Having projections like tusks.
1830 GALT *Lawrie T.* VI. x, The banks, ragged and tusky with fallen trees, were in few places accessible.

tusmose, tussemose: see TUZZY-MUZZY.

tuss. *dial.* or *Obs.* [Northern var. of TUSK *sb.*^{1}] *Arch.* One of a series of stones or bricks forming a projecting course for the attachment of an additional structure. Cf. TUSH *sb.*^{1} 3 and TOOTHING *vbl. sb.* 2 b.
1412 in Raine *Catterick Church, Yorks.* (1834) 9 And the forsaide Richarde sall putte oute tusses for the makyng of a Reuestery. *Ibid.* 10 And also forsaide Richarde salle schote out tusses in the west ende for makyng of a stepill. **1834** RAINE *note*, This..term..implies the projecting stones left in..masonry..by which a contemplated building might in due time be attached... Such..stones..are still in the north of England not unfrequently called *tusses*, a corruption of *tusks*.

tussac, -ack: see TUSSOCK.

tussah, -eh, var. TUSSER, TUSSORE.

tussal ('tʌsəl), *a. rare*$^{-0}$. [f. L. *tuss-is* cough + -AL^1.] Of or pertaining to a cough.
1890 BILLINGS *Med. Dict.*, *Tussal*, pertaining to cough. **1900-13** in DORLAND *Med. Dict.*

tusseeldar, var. TAHSILDAR.

tusser ('tʌsə(r)), **tussore** ('tʌsɔə(r)). Also 7 **tussre, tessar, tessur,** 9 **tasar, tassar, tussar, tussur;** 8–9 **tusseh, tussah, tusha.** [ad. Hindī (and Urdū) *tasar* ('tʌsʌr):—Skr. *tasara* (also *trasara*) shuttle, 'perhaps from the form of the cocoon' (Yule & Burnell).

Of the various spellings of this word the type *tussar, -er, -ur* represents most exactly the Hindī original. The forms *tussah, -eh,* though frequently employed in works dealing specially with India, are erroneous and due to some misunderstanding. The prevailing form in ordinary use is now *tussore* (prob. after Indian place-names such as *Mysore*), to which the incorrect pronunciation (tə'sɔə(r)) is frequently given.]

1. A coarse brown silk (furnished by *Antheræa mylitta* and other species of silkworm) made in and imported from India. Also *ellipt.* a dress made of this.

α. **1619** in Foster *Eng. Factories Ind.* (1906) 112 A kind of Bengala stuff of silke..called tessar. **1620** *Ibid.* 198 Quilts of 'Sutgonge'..lined..partly with taffeta and partly with 'tessur'. **1620** (Oct. 6) *Factory Rec., Patna* I. (India Office MS. Rec.), Wee have finished our provisiones for this yeare ..12 courge of Tussres. **1810** in Milburn *Oriental Comm.* (1825) 263 Duty on..Tusha, 5 annas per seer of 80 Sic. wt. **1827** D. Johnson *Ind. Field Sports* 165 A coarse kind of silk known by the name of tussar, is produced there in large quantities. **1845** Stocqueler *Handbk. Brit. India* (1854) 196 A lighter silk, termed tusser, much used..for room-punkahs,..gentlemen's blouses and ladies' morning-dresses. **1873** Blochmann tr. *Āīn-i-Akbarī* I. 94 (Y.) Tassar, per piece..½ to 2 Rupees. **1876** Cobb *Silk* in *Brit. Manuf. Industr.* V. 171 The silks now generally recognized as tussahs,..are a description of wild silk [etc.]. **1884** *Health Exhib. Catal.* p. xliii, Illustrations of silk culture, especially tussur.

β. **1876** Besant & Rice *Gold. Butterfly* III. 132 You think it is silk,..and I believe they call it Indian tussore. **1884** G. Allen *Philistia* I. 58 A perfect fright in my shabby old Indian tussore. **1893** F. F. Moore *I Forbid Banns* (1899) 120 Wearing a costume that..must have cost fifty guineas, while my daughters..are compelled to put up with the plainest of Tussores!

b. More fully ***tusser*** or ***tussore silk.***

α. **1796** M. Atkinson in *Trans. Linn. Soc.* (1804) VII. 41 A specimen of Bughy Tusseh silk. **1838** M. Martin *East India* II. I. iv. 157 The chief use to which the tree..is..applied is to rear the Tasar silk. **1867** Pitt-Rivers *Evol. Culture, Prim. Warfare* I. (1906) 62 *note,* The *Saturnia mylitta* is the caterpillar from which the Tusseh-silk is obtained. **1884** *Health Exhib. Catal.* 148/2 Tussah Silk, Corah Silk, Chuddahs.

β. **1882** Caulfeild & Saward *Dict. Needlework* 504 Tussore silks..are of Indian manufacture. **1896** *Daily News* 26 May 6/4 The wild silks of India, known in commerce as 'Tussore silk', of which ladies' dresses and various articles are made.

2. A silkworm which yields tusser silk: = *tusser-worm* (see 3).

1796 M. Atkinson in *Trans. Linn. Soc.* (1804) VII. 41 There are none of the Palma Christi species of Tusseh to be had here.

3. *attrib.* and *Comb.*, as ***tusser cloth, dress, parasol, stuff; tusser-coloured*** adj.; **tusser-moth,** any moth of which the larva (*tusser-worm*) yields tusser, as the Indian *Antheræa mylitta* and the Chinese *A. pernyi;* **tusser-(silk)worm,** any silkworm yielding tusser; the larva of a tussermoth.

α. **1908** *New Reformer* I. 414 The varieties are that of the well-known Tassar..woven into the common *Tassar cloth, so highly esteemed all over the world for light clothing. **1802** Roxburgh in *Trans. Linn. Soc.* (1804) VII. 34 A most durable, coarse, dark-coloured silk, commonly called Tusseh-silk, which is woven into a kind of cloth called *Tusseh doot'hies [Dhoti]. **1834** T. Brown *Bk. Butterfl. & Moths* (ed. 2) I. Pref., That splendid insect, the *Tusseh Moth of Bengal. **1876** *Sat. Rev.* 14 Oct. 468/1 The work of the *Tussur silk-weavers. **1796** M. Atkinson in *Trans. Linn. Soc.* (1804) VII. 41 There is another variation of the *Tusseh silk-worm in the hills near Bauglipore. **1837** Helfer in *Jrnl. Asiatic Soc. Bengal* VI. 42 The Tusseh Silkworm..is the most common in use of the native silkworms. **1620** in Foster *Eng. Factories India* (1906) 197 *Tusser stufes of Bengala, of halfe silke, halfe cotten. **1813** W. Milburn *Oriental Comm.* (1825) 303 There are two other kinds of worms which produce silk in Bengal, viz. the *Tusseh and Arrindy worms. **1878** T. Wardle *Monogr. on Tusser & other Silks India* 3 Silk produced by the Tasar, Tusser or Tussore worm. **1890** 'R. Boldrewood' *Col. Reformer* (1891) 336 Augusta's dust-coloured *tusser wrap.

β. **1887** *Daily News* 20 July 6/1 A *tussore-coloured lace dress. **1896** 'H. S. Merriman' *Flotsam* iv. 46 Cool brown *tussore dresses, embroidered in white. **1881** Miss Braddon *Asphodel* I. 54 Under her big *tussore parasol.

† **tusserd(e.** *Obs. rare.* (?)

1496 *Naval Acc. Hen. VII* (1896) 164, iij quarters of a c of Tusserdes iij[s] & a lode of grenewode xvj[d].

tusshe, obs. form of tush.

† '**tussicate,** *v. Obs. rare*⁻¹. [f. L. *tussic-us* afflicted with *tussis* a cough: see -ate³.] *intr.* To cough. Also **tussicular** (tʌ'sɪkjʊlə(r)) *a.* [ad. L. *tussiculāris,* f. *tussicula,* dim. of *tussis* cough]; **tussicu'lation**: see quots.

1598 Bastard *Chrestol.* I. xv. 11 Phisition Mirus talkes of saliuation,..Who doth ingurgitate, who tussicate. **1857** Dunglison *Med. Lex., Tussicular,* relating to a cough, or to a slight cough. **1890** Billings *Med. Dict., Tussiculation,* slight, frequent, dry cough.

tussie-mussie: see tuzzy-muzzy.

‖**Tussilago** (tʌsɪ'leɪgəʊ). *Bot.* Also formerly, in French and anglicized form, 6 **tussyllage,** 7 **tussilage.** [L. (Pliny), f. *tussis* cough, from its use for curing coughs.] A genus of composite plants, including the coltsfoot, *T. Farfara.*

Formerly also including the butterbur (*T. Petasites,* now *Petasites vulgaris*).

1510 Stanbridge *Vocabula* (W. de W.) D ij b, *Tussilego,* tussyllage. **1657** Tomlinson *Renou's Disp.* 499 This syrupe is denominated from Tussilage. **1706** Phillips (ed. Kersey), *Tussilago,* the Herb Foal's-foot, or Colts-foot, good for a Cough. **1712** in *Roses of Kilravoch* (Spald. Cl.) 399 Debtor to A. Paterson, chyr-apothecarie..for tussilago-flower, maidenhair,..etc. **1741** *Compl. Fam.-Piece* I. i. 70 Put to it 3 Leaves of good Tussilago. **1786** Abercrombie *Arr.* in *Gard. Assist.* 68 (Petasites) butterburr, or greater tussilago.

tussimussie, obs. f. tuzzy-muzzy, nosegay.

tussive ('tʌsɪv), *a.* [f. L. *tussi-s* cough + -ive.] Pertaining to or caused by cough.

1857 Dunglison *Med. Lex., Tussive,* belonging or relating to cough:—as tussive vibration; the vibration of the parietes of the chest, caused by coughing. **1862** H. W. Fuller *Dis. Lungs* 22 Tussive fremitus and rhonchal fremitus..possess little value as indications of disease. **1899** *Allbutt's Syst. Med.* VI. 87 Vocal or tussive vibrations and sounds from the main air-tubes.

tussle ('tʌs(ə)l), *sb.* Forms: see tussle *v.* [f. tussle *v.* Rare in literary use before 19th c.] A vigorous or disorderly conflict; a severe struggle, a hard contest; a scuffle. **a.** in physical sense; †in quot. 1629, an assault (*obs.*).

1629 in Picton *L'pool Munic. Rec.* (1883) I. 232 Wee present Hugh Houghton for a tussle vpon Mr. Ballive Chantrell. **1749** Fielding *Tom Jones* ix. iv, I hate to see two people bear ill-will to one another, after they have had a tussel. **1818** Scott *Hrt. Midl.* li, It is some comfort, when one has had a sair tussle..that it is in a fair leddy's service. **1848** Clough *Bothie* I. 146 Where the life and the strength came out in the tug and the tussle. **1851** Borrow *Lavengro* lxxxii. (1893) 318, I put myself into a posture which I deemed the best both for offence and defence, and the tuzzle commenced. **1862** Smiles *Engineers* III. 31 There was a terrible tussle and worrying between the dogs.

b. in figurative sense: *esp.* a sharp and determined contention or dispute.

1857 Dickens *Lett.* (1880) II. 23, I hope you have seen my tussle with the 'Edinburgh' [Review]. **1883** C. F. Adams *College Fetich* 11 An experience in the tussle of life. **1884** *Pall Mall G.* 17 July 2/1 The prospect of a tussle with the Peers.

tussle ('tʌs(ə)l), *v.* Forms: 5 **tussill,** 6–7 **tusle,** 6–9 **tussel,** 8–9 **tustle,** 9 **tussell, tussle, tuzzle.** [Orig. app. Sc. and northern; prob. dim. or freq. of touse *v.*: cf. tousle, in north. dial. *toozle.*]

1. *trans.* To pull or push about roughly, to hustle; to struggle or contend roughly with, to engage in a tussle with. Now *rare.*

c **1470** Henryson *Mor. Fab.* ix. (*Wolf & Fox*) xvii, I trow, ye haif bene tussillit with sum tyke. **1573** G. Harvey *Letter-bk.* (Camden) 18 Sum of them..hath baitid and tuslid and chasid me. **1706** Phillips (ed. Kersey), To *Tustle,* to rumple, ruffle, or touze. **1775** S. J. Pratt *Liberal Opin.* lxxii. (1783) III. 34 The maid opened the door..and then we tussel'd her against the door-post. **1858** Carlyle *Fredk. Gt.* vii. vi. (1872) II. 318 His Majesty hustled and tussled the unfortunate Crown-Prince.

2. *intr.* To struggle or contend in a vigorous and determined way; to wrestle confusedly; to scuffle. **a.** in physical sense.

1638 in Picton *L'pool Munic. Rec.* (1883) I. 232 Wee present..Iane Ireland and Elizabeth Ireland for tusling and scolding one uppon another. **1719** D'Urfey *Pills* III. 322 These sons of him That hurls the bolt trisulcate..Did tustle with red-ey'd pole-cat. **1836** Marryat *Japhet* xxvi, I tussled with the man until my coat and shirt were torn. **1852** *Fraser's Mag.* XLVI. 95 When..fairly hooked, he shakes his head, tuzzles a little at the line, and..slips away.

b. in fig. use.

1862 H. Marryat *Year in Sweden* I. 425 The Catholics tustled with the Reformed clergy for the pulpit. **1864** *John Greswold* I. 187 That..bitter thought..tussles hard with ones fortitude. **1897** *N.Y. Voice* 18 Mar. 8/2 The new tariff bill with which the extra session of Congress will tussle and pass, is said to be in the main a restoration of the McKinley tariff of 1890.

Hence '**tussling** *vbl. sb.* and *ppl. a.*; also †'**tusslement,** an act of tussling, an assault (*obs.*).

1597 *Salford Portmote Rec.* (1902) 3 Adam Pilkington and Isabell Traves made an affraye or tusselment. **1844** Kinglake *Eöthen* xxvii. (1878) 352 Forest trees, tall and stately..yet lead a tussling life of it below. **1858** Carlyle *Fredk. Gt.* iii. xvi. (1872) I. 240 The innumerable sanguinary tussellings of this War.

tussle, var. tuscle *Obs.*, tusk.

tussock ('tʌsək), *sb.* Forms: 6–7 **tussocke,** (6 **thussocke**), 7–9 **tussuck,** 8– **tussock,** (9 **-ack, -ac, -ick**). [perh. an altered form of tusk *sb.*² (which is known in 1530), assimilated to diminutives in -ock; but the actual relation of the two forms, as well as their ulterior history, is obscure.]

1. A tuft or bunch of hair. Now *rare* (cf. sense 3).

1550 Latimer *Last Serm. bef. Edw. VI* (1584) 107 b, If they would keepe it [hair]..as they ought to doe, there should not any such Thussockes nor Tuftes be seene. *Ibid.*, These Thussockes that are layd out now a dayes, there is no mention made in Scriptures, because they were not vsed in scripture tyme. They were not yet come to be so farre out of order, as to lay out suche Thussockes and Tuftes. **1550** Crowley *Epigr.* 1303 If theyr hayre wyl not take colour, then must they by newe, And laye it oute in tussockis: this thynge is to true. **1893** Crockett *Stickit Minister* (1894) 10 Bushy tussocks of grey eyebrow.

2. A tuft, clump, or matted growth, forming a small hillock, of grass, sedge, or the like; formerly also, a tuft or bunch of leaves, thorns, etc.

1607 Markham *Caval.* vi. iv. (1617) 12 If there bee any tussockes of long grasse, rushes, or dead fogge. **1681** Grew *Musæum* ii. i. ii. 186 The Fruit [Prickle Apple] is remarkable for the several Tussucks or Bunches of Thorns where-with it is armed. **1783** C. Bryant *Flora Diæt.* (1787) 84 It hath a creeping root, from which comes forth a tussuck of long slender leaves. **1829** Loudon *Encycl. Plants* (1836) 59 A[ira] cæspitosa is common in marsh-meadows, and occasions those excrescences called tussocks or hassocks which interrupt the progress of the scythe. **1883** *Century Mag.* XXVI. 925 Obliged to pick his way through an unusually soft marsh, springing from tussock to tussock. **1898** *Dublin Rev.* Jan. 166 Hills..overgrown with prickly plants forming rounded tussocks.

3. Short for *tussock-moth* or *caterpillar*: see 5.

1819 G. Samouelle *Entomol. Compend.* 247 Lar[ia] pudibunda (pale tussock)... Lar. fascelina (dark tussock). **1911** G. H. Carpenter in *Encycl. Brit.* XVI. 472/2 The larvae..are very hairy, and often carry dense tufts on some of their segments; hence the name of 'tussocks' frequently applied to them.

4. Short for tussock-grass. Also in *pl.*

1832 C. M. Goodridge *Voy. South Seas* 34 The Johnnys build their nests..among the long grass, generally termed Tussick. **1869** Lady Barker *Station Life N. Zealand* iv. (1874) 25 Tussocks, the tall native grass, has the colour and appearance of hay. **1886** Britten & Holland *Eng. Plant-n.*, Tussocks, *Agrostis vulgaris,* and *A. alba.*—Glou[cester].

5. *attrib.* and *Comb.*, as (in sense 'covered with or consisting of tussock-grass') ***tussock-bog, ground, mound;*** **tussock-caterpillar,** the larva of the *tussock-moth;* **tussock land** *Austral.* and *N.Z.*, uncultivated grassland used for sheep-grazing; **tussock-moth,** one of various kinds of moth, as those of the genus *Orgyia,* the larvæ of which have long tufts of hairs; **tussock-sedge,** a species of sedge, *Carex stricta,* growing in thick clumps. See also tussock-grass.

1847 Sir J. C. Ross *Voy. S. Seas* II. 262 A *Tussock-bog (for so a tract of land covered with this grass is called). **1843** J. D. Hooker in *Gard. Chron.* 4 Mar. 131/1 These heaps, or tussacks, grow generally apart, but within a few feet of one another,..so that, in walking among them, you are quite hidden from view, and the whole *Tussac ground is a perfect labyrinth. **1881** W. Bateman *Colonists* x. 186 The *tussock land abounds in the Middle Island..Prior to breaking up the tussock land the native grass is first burnt. **1928** 'Brent of Bin Bin' *Up Country* ii. 17 The journey started across tussock land alive with purling streams. **1941** Baker *N.Z. Slang* v. 41 The tussock lands are a peculiar feature of this country. **1826** Kirby & Sp. *Entomol.* III. xxx. 176 In the larva of *Tussock moths (*Laria pudibunda, fascelina,* etc.) the hairs are collected into tufts. **1887** *Amer. Naturalist* XXI. 581 The white-marked tussock-moth, and the fall web-worm are the insects discussed. **1901** *Westm. Gaz.* 6 Sept. 10/2 The New York city parks have lately been invaded by a great army of caterpillars. The cause of all the trouble is the tussock moth. **1825** Waddell *Voy.* 57 They differ from the king penguin..in having nests, which are sometimes in the sides of *tussac mounds. **1884** Miller *Plant-n., Carex stricta,* Greater Tufted Sedge, *Tussock Sedge.

Hence '**tussocked** (-əkt) *a.*, covered with or formed into tussocks; planted, covered, etc. with tussock-grass; '**tussocker** (*slang*): see quot.; '**tussocky** *a.*, abounding in or forming tussocks.

1796 Morse *Amer. Geog.* I. 540 The marshes..are banked, drained, *tussocked, ploughed, and harrowed. **1832** C. M. Goodridge *Voy. South Seas* 29 Our domicile..comfortable, in comparison to our boat tussicked up. **1892** *Times* 27 Dec. 10/1 Sunlight filters through..to promote the growth of the tussocked grass. **1889** V. Pyke *Wild Will Enderby* x. 148 A 'sun-downer' or '*tussocker'..is..one who loiters about till dusk, and then makes for the nearest station or hut, to beg for shelter and food. **1805** R. W. Dickson *Pract. Agric.* II. 920 The grass [is liable]..to become *tussocky, or rise in large tufts. **1863** *Spring Lapl.* 54 We saw..rough tussocky meadows. **1880** Seebohm *Siberia in Europe* 180 The tussocky ridges between the little bogs. **1908** *Daily Chron.* 24 Dec. 1/3 A girl who has..a piece of his tussocky brown hair in a little locket on her breast.

'**tussock-,grass.** Also tussac, -ack.

1. One or other of several grasses of the Southern Hemisphere; esp. (*a*) *Poa flabellata* (formerly *Dactylis cæspitosa*), a tall-growing valuable grass of the Falkland Islands and Patagonia; (*b*) *Lomandra longifolia* of Australia (N.O. *Juncaceæ*); (*c*) various New Zealand species of *Arundo* and *Poa.* Freq. in *Comb.*, as ***tussock-grassland.***

1842 *Guernsey Star* Sept., The splendid Tussack Grass is the..glory of the Falkland Islands. Every animal there feeds upon it..and fattens in a short time... The blades are about six foot long, and from 200 to 300 shoots spring from one plant. **1845** Lindley *Veg. Kingd.* (1846) 113 Attention has lately been directed to the Tussac-grass of the Falklands, *Festuca flabellata,* a species forming tufts 5 or 6 feet high. **1848** J. White *Jrnl.* 13 Mar. 266 (MS.), The top [of the house] is of the nikau leaf and tussock grass. **1866** *Treas. Bot.* 550 Tussac or Tussock [Grass], *Dactylis* *cæspitosa.* **1867** J. T. THOMSON *Rambles with Philosopher* v. 25 The natural tussock-grass lands.. stretched beyond the narrow precincts of incipient colonization. **1878** J. BULLER *N. Zealand* I. Introd. 9 It is generally.. covered with either forest, tall fern or tussock-grass. **1880** BUCHANAN *Grasses N. Zealand* Tab. xxvii & xxviii, *Arundo conspicua*.. *A. fulvida*, plumed tussac grass. **1884** 'R. BOLDREWOOD' *Melbourne Mem.* v. 38 The roof was neatly thatched with the tall, strong tussock-grass. **1906** CHEESMAN *N. Zealand Flora* 908 *Poa caespitosa*, Tussock grass. **1959** A. H. MCLINTOCK *Descr. Atlas N.Z.* p. xiv, Some pockets of beech forest still survive .. along with a depleted tussock grassland.

2. The tufted hair-grass, *Aira cæspitosa*, or other native grass growing in tussocks.

1860 G. H. K. in *Vac. Tour.* 117 Her cozy lair, amongst the sweet bog myrtle and warm tussock grass. *Ibid.* 134 The splashy moor, too wet to grow heather,.. covered with tufts of coarse tussock grass. **1861** MISS PRATT *Flower. Pl.* VI. 73 Tufted Hair-grass.. is commonly known.. by the name of Hassock or Tussack-grass.

tussore, tussur: see TUSSER.

† **'tussy.** *Obs. rare.* [? Derivative of a simple **tus* or **tusse*, in *tus(se)mose*: see TUZZY-MUZZY.] A cluster, posy, or knot of flowers or leaves; an ornament of silver or gold of this form, forming a buckle or the like.

1541 *Will E. Myllar* (Somerset Ho.), My blacke rybbonde with the hookes & a Tussy of syluer. **1633** J. DONE *Hist. Septuagint* 49 The Master Goldsmiths had laboured a Girdle of Flowers, and Tussies of all Fruits.

tussyllage, tustle: see TUSSILAGO, TUSSLE.

tut (tʌt), *sb.*^{1} Also 6, 8 **tutt**, 7 **tit, toyte**, 8–9 **toit.** [There is perh. more than one word here. Of the origin nothing has been ascertained.]

1. Each of a number of objects set up as 'bases' in rounders or similar games; also (in *pl.*), a kind of stool-ball in which the player at each base must move to the next base each time the ball is struck; also called ***tut-ball***; also the game of rounders. *local.*

1519 in *Priory of Hexham* (Surtees) II. 157 Ludi inhonesti, prout pili-ludus pedalis, et manualis, viz. tuttes, et handballac Pennyston. *c* **1572** GASCOIGNE *Fruites of Warre* xciv, Yet haue I shot at maister Bellums butte And throwen his ball although I toucht no tutte, I haue percase as deeply dealt the dole As he that hit the marke and gat the gole. **1655** CLARKE *Phraseol. Puerilis* 141 (Halliw.). **1777** *Horæ Subsecivæ* (MS.) 443 (E.D.D.) *Tut*, a sort of stool ball much practised about the Easter holidays, particularly at Exeter. **1877** *Holderness Gloss., Tut-ball*,.. a very ancient game,.. elsewhere called stool-ball. **1883** JACKSON & BURNE *Shropsh. Folk-Lore* 524 Tut-ball... One of the players in the den.. hit back the ball with the palm of the hand, and immediately ran to one of three brick-bats, called 'tuts'— which were set up at equal distances.

2. *western dial.* 'A small seat or hassock made of straw; a cushion or hassock for kneeling upon' (*Eng. Dial. Dict.*).

1553 BRADFORD *Serm. Repent.* (1574) Fj, Oh hard harts that we haue, which make tuts for syn. **1637** *Churchw. Acc. Cheddle* (Davies), Paid for a tut for him that drawes the bellowes of the organes to sit upon. **1637–8** *Hartland (Devon) Church Acc.* in Chope *Hartland Gloss.* s.v. *Toyte*, Paid John Couch for a toyte for Mr. Churton to kneele upon 4 d. **1647–8** *Ibid.*, Paid for a tit for the minister 2 d. **1751–2** *E. Budleigh Churchw. Acc.* in *Rep. Devonsh. Provinc.* July (1902) (E.D.D.), For three tutts for the parson, 1 s. **1786** *Pilton Churchw. Acc.* in *Notes & Gleanings* (Exeter) II. 37/2 Pd for a Toit for the Minister's Dusk [*sic*].

b. *transf.* as a butchers' term: = CUSHION *sb.* 4 a.

1856 *Farmer's Mag.* Jan. 55 Wide fore-quarter.. not quite matched by.. the hind-quarters, the flank and tut being rather deficient.

† **3.** The orb borne as an emblem of sovereignty. *Obs. rare*$^{-0}$.

1674 BLOUNT *Glossogr.* (ed. 4), *Tut*,.. a globe or ball, with a golden cross on it, anciently carried by Emperours and Kings. **1706** PHILLIPS (ed. Kersey), *Tut*, or *Mound*, an Imperial Ensign of a Golden Globe, with a Cross on it.

tut (tʌt), *sb.*^{2} *local.* Also 8 **tote, tet-.** [Origin unascertained.] Orig. in the Cornish tin-mines, now also in Derbysh. lead-mining: in the phrase ***upon tut*** (also ***by the tut***), and *attrib.* as ***tut-bargain, -man, -work*** (also as vb.), ***-worker, -working, -workman***: denoting a system of payment by measurement or by the piece, adopted in paying for work which brings no immediate returns, as distinct from TRIBUTE 3; hence, work of this character; dead-work.

1778 PRYCE *Min. Cornub.* 180 [Under certain conditions] they set it to be sunk, driven, stoped, or cut down upon Tut; and in such case the Miners take what they term a Tut-bargain; that is, a piece or part of unmeasured ground, by the lump, for such price as can be agreed upon. *Ibid.* 184 The great inconvenience that attends this Tut-work or bargains by the lump or by the fathom, is, that if the ground proves hard and chargeable in the working, the labourer has no ability to go through with it. **1790** GROSE *Provinc. Gloss.* (ed. 2) s.v., To do work by the tut, or tote; to undertake it by the great. *West.* **1832** BABBAGE *Econ. Manuf.* xxvi. (ed. 3) 252 Tutwork.. consists in sinking shafts, driving levels, and making excavations. **1839** DE LA BECHE *Rep. Geol. Cornw.* etc. xv. 567 Persons performing the work under the captains in the various parts of mines may.. be divided into tributers, tutworkmen, and labourers. **1855** J. R. LEIFCHILD *Cornwall Mines* 147 The tutworkers, or tutmen, can readily judge of the hardness of the ground to be excavated. *Ibid.* 152 Dolcoath miners,.. blasting and breaking, tut-working and tributing. *Ibid.* 175 Details of Expenses... Tutwork Bargains. **1874** J. H. COLLINS *Metal Mining* 40 Shafts are sunk and levels driven, in Cornwall and elsewhere, at a fixed rate per lineal fathom... This form of bargain is called tutwork. **1906** G. R. LEWIS in *Victoria Co. Hist., Cornw.* I. 568/2 The workmen.. are, either tribute, tut, or daymen,.. the tut worker contracting, at a certain rate for the sinking of shafts and.. driving of levels.

b. Also in agricultural work (in s.w. counties).

1800 SIR J. CALL in *Commun. to Board of Agric.* II. 482 Labourers and mechanics, who, instead of living with their employers,.. have.. undertaken tet-work, or worked for daily hire. **1854** *Jrnl. R. Agric. Soc.* XV. II. 401 The [Dorset] labourers are paid by 'tut' work, the dung-put fillers being paid by the square yard, and the spreaders and ploughmen by the acre. **1865** *Daily Tel.* 16 Nov. 3/5 He had had only one week of tut-work since harvest, when he earned 1s. extra. Mr. Bartlett.. admitted that,.. when he worked by the day, he gave him only 8s. a week, but he let him have his thatching and other tut-work, including hedging.

tut (tʌt), *int.* (*sb.*^{3}). Also 6 **tutt, -e**, 9 *Sc.* **tuts.** *β.* 9 *Sc.* **toot, tout; toots.** [A natural utterance; the spelling *tut* sometimes represents the palatal click (also spelt TCHICK, TCK). Cf. also *hut tut, hoot toot, hout tout* s.v. HOOT *int.*] An ejaculation (often reduplicated) expressing impatience or dissatisfaction with a statement, notion, or proceeding, or contemptuously dismissing it. (The Sc. *toot, toots*, expresses mild expostulation.)

a **1529** SKELTON *Caudatos Anglos* 27 Shake thy tayle, Scot, lyke a cur, For thou beggest at euery mannes dur: Tut, Scot, I sey, Go shake thy dog, hey! **1536** in Strype *Eccl. Mem.* (1721) I. xxxvi. 282 [He said, to what she had spoken, as it seems, in her own defence] Tut, tut, tut [and shaking his head three or four times]. *a* **1553** UDALL *Royster D.* I. ii. (Arb.) 14 Tut I owe nought. **1580** LUPTON *Sivqila* 18 Alteration (quoth you) tutte, it is wonderful. **1591** *Troub. Raigne K. John* (1611) 67 Tut, tut, my mercie serues to maime my selfe. **1599** PORTER *Angry Wom. Abingd.* (Percy Soc.) 57 Tut, tell not me of your impatience. **1601** SHAKS. *Jul. C.* v. i. 7 Tut, I am in their bosomes, and I know Wherefore they do it. **1773** GOLDSM. *Stoops to Conq.* v. i, I come,.. once more, to ask pardon... Tut, boy, a trifle. **1826** J. WILSON *Noct. Ambr.* Wks. 1855 I. 200 *North.* I wish you would review these four volumes... *Shepherd.* Tuts! What's the use o' reviewin? **1859** THACKERAY *Virgin.* xc, Tut, tut!.. let us hear no more of this nonsense! **1865** 'LEWIS CARROLL' *Alice's Adv.* ix, 'Tut, tut, child!' said the Duchess. 'Everything's got a moral, if only you can find it.'

β. **1805** MCINDOE *Poems* 71 Guillie said, toots, We'll have that there's no doubts. **1818** (Oct.) SCOTT in Lockhart *Life* xlii, He.. rebuked the Captain with 'Toots, Adam! toots, Adam!' **1835** CARRICK *Laird of Logan* (1841) 137 Toot, man, haud your tongue. **1896–99** in *Eng. Dial. Dict.*

b. *sb.* The (or an) utterance of this exclamation, or a sound resembling this.

1676 MACE *Musicks Mon.* 109 The Tut, is a Grace,.. is a sudden taking away the Sound of any Note.. in such a manner, as it will seem to cry Tut. **1894** DONOVAN *With Wilson in Matabeleland* 229 The incessant 'tut-tut tut' of the Maxims. *Ibid.* 232 Each 'tut-tut' represents a bullet, at the rate of two to three hundred a minute. **1906** *Daily Chron.* 16 Jan. 6/7 There should be fixed stopping places [for motor-busses]... They would save many Balfourian 'Tut-tuts'.

† **tut,** *sb.*^{4} obs. var. *tit*, TEAT.

1702 S. PARKER tr. *Cicero's De Finibus* III. 168 Parts of the Body.. such as have no manifest Use, but serve only to beautifie, as the Peacock's Tail,.. the Tuts and Beard of a Man [orig. *viris mammæ atque barba*].

† **tut,** *sb.*^{5} app. a var. of TOUTE *Obs.*, buttocks.

13.. *Cursor M.* 28003 (Cott.) If þou.. has bituix hir scankes gan, Or tirid or [? *read* hir] tut or skirt uptan.

tut, *v.* Freq. reduplicated as **tut-tut**, etc. [f. TUT *sb.*^{3}]

1. *intr.* To utter the exclamation 'tut'.

1832 CARRICK in *Whistlebinkie* (1890) I. 99 Toots, sic nonsense. You may toots awa, but it's true sense, Mem. **1849** LYTTON *Caxtons* VIII. iii, In another moment the member of Parliament had forgotten the statist, and was pishing and tutting over the *Globe* or the *Sun.* **1873** MISS BRADDON *Str. & Pilgr.* III. x, The doctors had simpered at her, and tut-tuted, and patted her gently on the head. **1894** HALL CAINE *Manxman* v. ii, He laughed and tut-tutted.

2. *trans.* To express disapproval of by the exclamation 'tut'; to say disapprovingly.

1972 *Times* 10 Nov. 7/2 He [*sc.* President Nixon] felt sure some of his ideas would be 'tut-tutted' by 'the Georgetown cocktail set'. **1975** *Nature* 3 Jan. 1/2 The authors never address the problem, instead tut-tutting that university geology courses are unsuited to the demands of petroleum geology. **1984** A. CARTER *Nights at Circus* III. vii. 239 But when he embarrassedly confessed there'd been no bang nor damage because the dynamite was damp, I'd 'tut-tutted' his inefficiency.

Hence **'tutting** *vbl. sb.* and *ppl. a.*

1929 J. B. PRIESTLEY *Good Companions* I. i. 25 Ted.. was shaking his head and.. making a loud tut-tutting noise. **1947** *Manch. Guardian Weekly* 30 Oct. 8/3 Great and glossy cars rolled up in smooth procession. Into this a taxi-cab had strayed, to be hurriedly diverted with much tutt-tutting by police officers into the unimportant wastes of Millbank. **1962** *John o' London's* 19 Apr. 386/2, I simply could not see what all the tutting was about. **1976** T. HEALD *Let Sleeping Dogs Die* ix. 183 She sucked her teeth and made little tutting noises. **1984** *Times* 11 June 6/6 There was much tut-tutting and an agreement that something should be done.

† **'tutage.** *Obs. rare*$^{-1}$. [f. L. *tūt-*, ppl. stem of *tuērī* to protect: see -AGE.] An object of protection or tutelage; (one's) care or charge.

1593 DRAYTON *Eclogues* iii. 74 Apollo.. Whose Tutage and especiall care I wish her still to bee.

† **'tutament.** *Obs. rare*$^{-1}$. [ad. L. *tūtāmentum* defence, protection, f. *tūtārī* to protect: see -MENT.] A means of defence; a safeguard.

1609 J. DAVIES *Holy Roode* (1878) 19 This holy Crosse is the true Tutament, Protecting all ensheltered by the same.

tutaneg: see TUTENAG.

‖ **tutang.** Also 7 **tutan.** [Chinese, f. *tu* to direct + *t'ang* hall; the latter is used as a kind of suffix in many Chinese titles.] One of several designations applied familiarly to a Chinese viceroy.

1613 PURCHAS *Pilgrimage* IV. xvi. 369 These all are in subiection vnto the Tutan or Vice-roy of the Prouince. **1638** SIR T. HERBERT *Trav.* (ed. 2) 337 The whole Empire [China] is divided into fifteene great Provinces: governed by so many Quon-fu and Lausiæ; who have their Tutans, and Chyans, or Deputies under them. **1705** ROWE *Biter* II. i, I will put you into the Hands of the *Tutang*, which is,.. according to English Expression, the Constable of Croydon.

tutania (tjuːˈteɪnɪə). [f. *Tutin*, name of the inventor or maker.] An earlier name for Britannia-metal.

1790 RICHARDSON *Chem. Princ. Metallic Arts* 168 Tutania —8 oz brass; 2 lbs regulus of antimony, and 7 oz tin. **1825** J. NICHOLSON *Operat. Mechanic* 708 Tutania, or Britannia Metal... 4 oz. of plate brass, and 4 oz. of tin; when in fusion, add 4 oz. of bismuth, and 4 oz. of regulus of antimony. **1842** G. FRANCIS *Dict. Arts*, etc., *Tutania*, or *Britannia Metal*... For the German tutania take 2 drachms of copper, 1 ounce regulus of antimony, and 12 ounces of tin. **1875** KNIGHT *Dict. Mech., Spanish Tutania*, an alloy composed of 24 parts tin, 2 antimony, and 1 steel.

† **tutch.** *Sc. Obs. rare*$^{-1}$. See quot.

Perhaps an error for *cutches* (COACH *sb.*).

1643 *Sc. Act Chas. I* (1870) VI. 16/2 That the parliament wald appoynt tuo pinnaces or tutches for convyeing diligence betuixt them & this Kingdome.

tutch, tutche, -ie, obs. ff. TOUCH, TOUCHY.

tute (tjuːt). Colloq. abbrev. of TUTOR *sb.* and *v.* or TUTORIAL *sb.*

1895 W. C. GORE in *Inlander* Nov. 65 *Tute*, tutor. **1934** WEBSTER, *Tute*, v.t. & i. **1942** BERREY & VAN DEN BARK *Amer. Thes. Slang* §197/9 *Tute*, tutor, to give private instruction. **1955** J. I. M. STEWART *Guardians* III. ii. 217 Jones is my tutor, and this happened at my first tute this term. **1957** D. BALSDON *Oxford Life* 169 But the College tutor's public lecture is an interruption in a week otherwise devoted to teaching pupils in his rooms, listening to their essays and talking about them. These are 'private hours' —'tutes', as undergraduates call them, or tutorials. **1982** T. HEALD *Masterstroke* iii. 64 We did political theory tutes together.

tute, obs. form of TEAT, TOOT *v.*^{2}

tutee (tjuːˈtiː). orig. *U.S.* [f. TUT(OR *v.* + -EE^{1}.] A university student (in relation to his tutor); a pupil of a private tutor.

1927 *Amer. Speech* II. 214/1 *Tutee*, English 'pupil'. I met this queer coinage in two academic publications. **1937** *Life* 7 June 58/2 Wolff at work is a two-hour torrent of words covering the high spots of a whole college course. Tutees take hasty notes, try to remember what he says overnight. **1952** M. MCCARTHY *Groves of Academe* (1953) i. 6 He was feeling more than half tempted to take the letter over to the main hall and post it on the faculty bulletin board, before the arrival of the eleven-o'clock tutee. **1975** D. LODGE *Changing Places* i. 19 His girl tutees suddenly began to dress like prostitutes.

† **'tutel,** *sb. Obs. rare.* [app. a derivative (with -EL^{1}) of *tūte*, not recorded in Eng. but occurring in MDu. and MLG. and surviving as Du. *tuit*, WFris. *tute, tût*, LG. *tûte, tüte*, etc., spout, lip (of a can), pouting or protruding mouth, etc. (Sw. and Norw. *tut*, Da. *tud*, spout, are from LG.) The equivalent formation *tutel, tûtel* occurs in WFris. in transferred senses.] The mouth with the lips protruded in the act of whispering. (Cf. next.)

a **1225** *Ancr. R.* 74 þe veond of helle mid his ferd went þurh þe tutel þ is euer open into þe heorte. *Ibid.* 80 Ne blowe ȝe hire [*sc.* hope] nout ut mid maðelinde muðe, ne mid ȝeoniinde tuteles. *Ibid.*, 212, & te deouel leieð his tutel adun to his earen, & tuteleð him al þet he euer wule.

† **tutel, totel,** *v. Obs.* Forms: 3–5 **tutel**, 5 **totel, -il, -yl, -ul.** [ME. *tutel* (from early 13th c.), *totel* (*c* 1400), app. from the variant stems *tūt-* (see prec.) and *tōt-* (see TOOT *v.*^{1}), the former of which occurs in the same sense in older Flemish *tuyten* (*in de oore*, Kilian), Du. dial. *tuiten*, WFris. *tûtsje* to whisper.] *intr.* and *trans.* To whisper. Hence † **tutelinde** *ppl. a.*, † **tuteling, toteling** *vbl. sb.*, whispering. (See also TUTELER.)

a **1225** *Ancr. R.* 106 þu, uor þe luue of him.. dute [= close] þinne tutelinde muð mit þine lippen. *Ibid.* 212 [see TUTEL *sb.*]. *Ibid.* 422 þe ueond beot hire his werc þet ine Godes werke ne wurcheð: and he tuteleð anonrihtes touward hire. *c* **1440** *Promp. Parv.* 498/1 Totelon talys (.. *S.* totylyn tale in onys ere), *susurro.* Totelynge, *susurrium.*

tutel, obs. var. TOOTLE *v.*

tutelage ('tjuːtəlɪdʒ). Also 7 tutillage, 8 tutilage. [f. L. *tūtēla* watching, keeping, guardianship (f. *tūt-*, ppl. stem of *tuērī* to watch) + -AGE.]

1. The office or function of a guardian; protection, care, guardianship, patronage; governorship of a ward. Also *fig.*

1605 SYLVESTER *Du Bartas* II. i. IV. *Handie-crafts* Ded., To beare againe.. The noble Pasport of thy Tutelage, To salue her still from sullen Enuies wound. **1612** DRAYTON *Poly-olb.* iii. 217 That Citie.. The Tutilage whereof.. Some to Minerua gane, and some to Hercules. **1689** *Def. Liberty agst. Tyrants* 29 A slave, or one that is under tutillage. **1777** PRIESTLEY *Disc. Philos. Necess.* 205 It came forth under my tutilage and kind protection. **1832** tr. *Sismondi's Ital. Rep.* iii. 60 Reigning under the pope's tutelage over the Two Sicilies only. **1879** DIXON *Windsor* I. xviii. 187 Under the tutelage of a patron saint.

b. Instruction, tuition.

1857 H. MILLER *Test. Rocks* vi. 221 The dog acquires, under his tutelage, the virtues of fidelity.. and affection. **1857** KINGSLEY *Two Y. Ago* (1877) 243 Under whose tutelage he had learnt to smoke.. assiduously. **1863** HOLLAND *Lett. Joneses* xvii. 447 Under the tutelage of several different masters.

2. The condition of being under protection or guardianship.

1650 R. STAPYLTON *Strada's Low C. Warres* IV. 87 On his Christening day they delivered him in tutelage to the Prince Electour Augustus. **1792** V. KNOX *Serm.* xiv. 309 Pleasure .. during the period of tutelage, engaged only a part of her votary's attention. **1878** MISS BRADDON *Open Verd.* ii, At seventeen, when he was in his state of tutelage.

tutelar ('tjuːtɪlə(r)), *a.* and *sb.* Also 7 tutelare. [ad. L. *tūtēlār-is*, f. *tūtēla*: see prec. and -AR[1].]

A. *adj.* = TUTELARY *a.*

1600 E. BLOUNT *Hosp. Incur. Fooles* A iv, I coniure.. the Gods Tutelar, that they will vndertake the tuition.. of this new Hospitall. **1606** HOLLAND *Sueton.* 51 The Tutelare Images of crosse-wayes called *Lares Compitales*. *a* **1661** FULLER *Worthies, Surrey* (1840) III. 215 He [Hammond] was the tutelar angel, to keep many a poor royalist from famishing. **1777** G. FORSTER *Voy. round World* I. 3 Reflecting on the tutelar guidance of Divine Providence. **1884** TENNYSON *Becket* v. iii, All the tutelar Saints of Canterbury.

B. *sb.* One who is tutelar; a tutelar deity, angel, or saint. Also *transf.* and *fig.*

1603 HOLLAND *Plutarch's Mor.* 1232 Minerva Poliuchos, that is to say, Tutelar and protectresse of the city. **1648** tr. *Senault's Paraphr. Job* 319 That Angel which hath been chosen out of a thousand to be their Tutelar. **1655** FULLER *Ch. Hist.* VI. iv. §13 Were Judgment consulted with, Luke should be Tutelar to Physicians as his proper calling. *a* **1680** BUTLER *Rem.* (1759) I. 238 Dame Fortune some Men's tutelar Takes charge of them without their Care. **1702** H. DODWELL *Apol.* §22 in S. Parker *Cicero's De Finibus*, Those who had brought themselves under the Dominion of ill Spirits by deserting their good Tutelars. *a* **1849** H. COLERIDGE *Ess.* (1851) II. 87 Ringlets that have been twisted with irons—to be the tutelars of hoops and earrings. **1890** E. JOHNSON *Rise of Christendom* 361 A religious congregation settled there to honour him as tutelar.

Hence **'tutelarship** (*nonce-wd.*), the position or function of a tutelar.

1875 J. HAWTHORNE in *Contemp. Rev.* Nov. 925, I resigned my deputy-tutelarship perforce, and retired.

tutelary ('tjuːtɪlərɪ), *a.* and *sb.* Also 7 tutilary. [ad. L. *tūtēlāri-us* a guardian, f. as prec: see -ARY[1]. So F. *tutélaire.*]

A. *adj.* **1.** Of supernatural powers: Having the position of protector, guardian, or patron; *esp.* protecting or watching over a particular person, place, or thing.

1611 in *10th Rep. Hist. MSS. Comm.* App. I. 529 A Spanish governor, who adoreth them [Jesuits] as his tutelary gods. **1643** SIR T. BROWNE *Relig. Med.* I. §33, I could easily beleeve, that.. particular persons have their Tutelary and Guardian Angels. **1741** MIDDLETON *Cicero* I. v. 400 That tutelary Minerva. **1794** SULLIVAN *View Nat.* I. xxiii. 316 Fountains and springs.. watched over and guarded by tutelary divinities. **1806** R. FELLOWES tr. *Milton's 2nd Defence* 290 The patron and tutelary genius of liberty. **1860** MOTLEY *Netherl.* (1868) I. vi. 314 A little republic.. suddenly bereft of its tutelary saint. **1908** BIGG *Orig. Chr.* i. (1909) 14 The Lares,.. the little tutelary gods, who watched over the prosperity of the home.

2. *transf.* Of or pertaining to protection or a protector or guardian; protective.

1651 G. W. tr. *Cowel's Inst.* 203 Obligations.. arise from implyed Contracts many wayes: As for transacting businesse Tutelary. **1692** DRYDEN *St. Euremont's Ess.* 2 They acknowledged a particular Care and Protection from its Tutelary Vertue. **1721** PRIOR *Predestination* 306 My Voice and heart I lift To ask th' Almighty's Tutelary Care. **1853** GROTE *Greece* II. lxxxv. XI. 198 The conduct of Timoleon and Æschylus.. was in the highest degree tutelary to Corinth. **1879** GLADSTONE *Glean.* I. i. 30 Great acts of tutelary friendship.

B. *sb.* = TUTELAR *sb.*

(In quot. 1866 used as almost = tutor; cf. TUTELAGE 1 b.)

1652 GAULE *Magastrom.* 177 The tutilaries of kingdoms, nations, &c. **1654** Z. COKE *Logick* aj, It is Janitrix Scientiarum; the Tutelary and Guardian of all. **1657–83** EVELYN *Hist. Relig.* (1850) II. 279 They have tutelaries for every trade. **1866** DE MORGAN in *Athenæum* 27 Oct. 535/1 My spiritual tutelary.. referred the difficulty to the Almighty. **1908** S. A. COOK *Relig. Anc. Palestine* vi. 67 The status of a local tutelary was affected when commercial intercourse widened the horizon of both the traveller and the native.

† **tutele.** *Obs.* Also 6 tutell, 6–7 tutle, 7 *Sc.* tutill. [a. OF. (also mod.F.) *tutelle* protection (14th c. in Godef. = Pr., Sp., It. *tutela*), or ad. L. *tūtēla*: see TUTELAGE.] Guardianship, protection; care of a ward; = TUTELAGE.

c **1420** LYDG. *Ball. our Lady* 57 in *Minor P.* (1911) I. 257 Of alle Cristen protectrix and tutele.. To hem þat erryn, the path of her sequele. **1517** in *Acts Parlt. Scotl.* (1875) XII. 38/1 ȝe have sa usit ȝoure self tuiching the said tutele and regiment of oure soveran Lorde [etc.]. **1528** ROY *Rede Me* (Arb.) 24 The preservacion and tutell of the innocent and simple. **1579** *Sc. Acts Jas. VI* (1814) III. 158/2 Nwrist and brocht vp within our said Castell of striueling vndir his tutele and gouuernance. **1602** E. BRUCE in *Corr. Jas. VI* (Camden) 46 Her nerrast kinsman.. sould be inwest in the tutill and administration of her state. **1622** in *Buccleuch MSS.* (Hist. MSS. Comm.) I. 210 He seeks not that the children should remain under the tutle of women. **1651** HOWELL *Venice* 20 They have the tutele of Pupills and Orphans when ther is no Gardian nominated in the Will of the Testator.

Hence † **tuteleship** *Obs.*, the office or function of a guardian.

1557 N. T. (Genev.) *Gal.* iv. 1 *note*, The Churche of Israel was vnder the Lawe as the pupil subiect to his tutor, euen vnto the tyme of Christ.., and then her tutelshyp ended. **1580** HOLLYBAND *Treas. Fr. Tong, Clientelle*, tutleship or custodie, keping. *a* **1656** USSHER *Ann.* VI. (1658) 377 The patronage and tutele-ship of the Minor.

† **tuteler, toteler.** *Obs.* Forms: see TUTEL *v.*; also 5 tutlar, -er. [f. TUTEL *v.* + -ER[1].] A whisperer, gossip, tale-bearer.

c **1385** CHAUCER *L.G.W.* 353 (*Balade*) Ffor in ȝoure court is manye a losenger And manye a queynte totulour [*v.rr.* totelere, toteler, tutelere] acusour. *a* **1400** *Langland's P. Pl.* B. xx. 297 (MS. Camb. Dd. I. 17) Alle taletellers and tutelers. *c* **1400** *MS. Bibl. Reg. 17 B. xvii.* lf. 100 b, Be rightful. Be no totiler. *c* **1400** *Song Roland* 226 Yet will tutlers in toun talk bound [etc.]. *c* **1440** *Promp. Parv.* 498/1 Totelare, *susurro*. *c* **1470** HENRYSON *Poems* (S.T.S.) III. 142 (Maitl. MS.) Fals Tutlaris [*Bann. MS.* titlaris] now growis vp full rank. *Ibid.* 143 Giff þe tutelar [*Bann. MS.* tittillaris] so in his eir do roun. *a* **1500** *Colkelbie Sow* 128 (Bann. MS.) A tuttivillus, a tutlar, And a fanyeit flatterar.

tute-mowitt: see TUT-MOUTHED.

tutenag ('tjuːtənæg). Forms: 7 (tintenagall), tutunaga; tutunac, tutanag, -eg, tuthinag(e, 8 tutanague; (tuten-, tutanaque), tutteneg, 9 tuthenag, tutenage, 7– tutenag, tutenague; also 7 (teutenage), totaneg, 8 tootanag, toothenague, -aque, toothanegg (tooth and egg), tootnague (Yule). [a. Marāṭhī *tuttināg* (Tamil *tuttunāgam*, Telugu *tuttunāgamu*), derived (according to native writers) fr. Skr. *tuttha-* blue vitriol, sulphate of copper + *nāga* tin or lead. Hence also Pg. *tutanaga, tutenaga*, F. *toutenague* (1723 in Hatz.-Darm.). The early forms in *tint-* used by Eng., Du., and French writers are difficult to account for.] A whitish alloy of copper, zinc, and nickel, with a little iron, silver, or arsenic, resembling German silver; said to have been originally imported from China; also used loosely in the Indian trade for zinc.

1622 in Foster *Eng. Factories in India* (1908) II. 135 Tintenagall [*sic*] not yet paid for. **1668** in J. F. Davis *Chinese* ii. (1836) I. 47 China commodities, as tutanag, silk, raw and wrought. **1679** in *Notes & Extr. Govt. Rec. Fort St. George* 31 Oct. (Y.), Dacca is not a good market for Gold, Copper, Lead, Tin, or Tutenague. **1681** GREW *Musæum* App. 386 *Teutenage*. A sort of Speltar... Hereof.. Vessels are made in Japan, wherein their Thea is brought over. **1684** W. HEDGES *Diary* (Hakl. Soc.) I. 148 All the Copper and Tutenag which he sold them. **1687** A. LOVELL tr. *Thevenot's Trav.* III. 46 A certain Metal called *Tutunac*, that looks like Tin, but is much more lovely and fine, and is often taken for Silver. **1698** FRYER *Acc. E. India & P.* 86 To China for Sugar, Tea, Porcelane, Laccared Ware, Quick-silver, Tuthinag and Copper. *Ibid.* 264 Tuthinage brought from the South-Seas answers in all respects. **1699** DAMPIER *Voy.* II. I. 173 The product of the Country.., besides Rice and other eatables, is Tutaneg, a sort of Tin. **1711** C. LOCKYER *Trade in India* v. 129 Tutanaque is a kind of course Tin in Oblong Pieces five or six to a Pecull. **1727** A. HAMILTON *New Acc. E. Ind.* II. l. 223 The subterraneous Grounds were stored with Minerals, as Copper, Quick-silver, Allom, Toothenague, &c. *Ibid.* 233, 80 Chests of Japon Copper, and some Toothenague that I had weighed off at Canton. **1751** *Narr. Trans. Brit. Squadrons E. Indies* 20 From Malacca they bring a Metal very like Tin, call'd Toothanegg, and made much Use of for Alloy with Silver in Coining at all the European Settlements. **1754** SMEATON in *Phil. Trans.* XLVIII. 613 The semi-metallic substance call'd Zink, spelter, or tootanag. **1773** JOS. WRIGHT *Let.* in Bemrose *Life* iv. (1885) 27 Four pillar Candlesticks called Tooth & Egg, to be cleaned as silver. **1782–3** W. F. MARTYN *Geog. Mag.* I. 459 Tin, thus hardened, is the metal now well known in Europe by the name of tutanaque. **1806** *Naval Chron.* XV. 465 Ballasted with tuthenag or zinc. **1815** W. PHILLIPS *Outl. Min. & Geol.* (1818) 46 With zinc and iron, copper forms tutenag. **1836** J. F. DAVIS *Chinese* I. viii. 316 Teapots.. made of tutenague externally, covering earthenware on the inside. **1843** *Penny Cycl.* XXV. 446/1 *Tutenag*.. is white, resembling silver... Dr. Fyfe found it to consist of—Copper 40·4, Zinc 25·4, Nickel 31·6, Iron 2·6. **1885** *Horological Jrnl.* Nov. 45/1 *note*, Tutenage, called Chinese copper..; in India, a name given to pure zinc or spelter.

attrib. **1699** J. OVINGTON *Ess. Tea* 11 Tea is brought over in round totaneg canisters. **1715** *Lond. Gaz.* No. 5394/4 Spanish Snuff, in Tutteneg Pots.

† **tuther**, obs. Sc. f. TOTHER, the other.

1539 in *Abst. Protocols Town Clerks of Glasgow* (1897) IV. 113 The messis to be said.. the tane half.. the tane day, and the remanent of thame the tuther day.

tuþing, early ME. f. TITHING.

tut-hoo, var. of TATTOO *sb.*[3], Indian pony.

tutia, tutie: see TUTTY[1].

tutill, -age: see TUTELE, TUTELAGE.

tutiorist ('tjuːʃɪərɪst). *R.C. Theol.* [f. L. *tūtior* safer, comp. of *tūtus* safe + -IST.] One who holds that in cases of conscience the course of greater moral safety should be chosen. Cf. RIGORIST 2 and LAXIST. Also *attrib.* So **'tutiorism**, the doctrine of the tutiorists; a less strict form of RIGORISM.

1845 GLADSTONE *Glean.* (1879) VII. 192 There is also in the Latin Church a rigid school of those who pass by the name of Tutiorists. These hold that even such likelihood is insufficient, and that certainty is required as a warrant for our acts. **1885** *Catholic Dict.* (ed. 3) 602/2 The Rigorists, or Tutiorists.. held that we must always take the safer way, always sacrifice our freedom, however small the probability that our freedom is restrained by the law. *Ibid.* 603/2 We cannot see that Probabiliorism is logical and consistent,.. the arguments adduced by its advocates really tend to Tutiorism. **1906** *Ch. Times* 2 Mar. 291 Hence the prevailing 'tutiorist' tone [in the Lower House of Convocation].

tutivillar, -villus, tutlar, -er, tutle: see TITIVILLER, TITIVIL, TUTELER, TUTELE.

† **'tutlyng**, *vbl. sb. Obs. rare*[−1]. Also 5 tutilling. [f. OF. *tuteler, tutuler* (Godef.; Walloon *tûteler*), freq. of *tuter* to blow a horn, related to the Germanic forms cited s.v. TOOT *v.*[2]] A blowing (of a horn).

1375 BARBOUR *Bruce* XIX. 604 A tutlyng [*MS. E.* tutilling, *ed. Hart* (1616) towting] of his horne herd thai.

tut-mouthed, *a. rare.* Now *Sc. dial.* Also 6 *Sc.* tute-mowitt, 9 tuit-moot. [f. *tute*, TOOT *v.*[1] to protrude, stick out + MOUTH *sb.* + -ED[2]. Cf. older Flem. *tuyt-muyl* 'broncus, brochus' (Kilian).] Having protruding lips; also, having a projecting under jaw. So **tut-mouth** (*Sc.* **tuit mow**).

α. **1500–20** DUNBAR *Poems* liv. 6 Quhou fain wald I descrywe perfytt, My ladye with the mekle lippis. Quhou scho is tute mowitt lyk an aip. *a* **1585** POLWART *Flyting w. Montgomerie* 755 (Harl. MS.) Tout mowe [*v.rr.* tait, tuit mow, cruik mow] woodie sow, sone bowe, or I wand thee. **1893** W. GREGOR in *Dunbar's Poems* (S.T.S.) III. 286 *Tute mowitt*.. still in use in parts of the North as a word of contempt, as, 'He's a tuit-moot smatchit'.

β. **1538** ELYOT, *Bronchi*, they whyche haue their mouthe and tethe standyng farre out, tut mouthed. **1601** HOLLAND *Pliny* XI. xxxvii. I. 336 The Lips: some men there be that put them far out, by reason that they are gag-toothed or tut-mouthed. **1616** BULLOKAR *Eng. Exp.*, *Tutmouthed*, he that hath the chin and nether iaw sticking out farther than the vpper.

tutoiement: see under TUTOYER.

tutor ('tjuːtə(r)), *sb.* Also 4–7 tutour, 5–6 -oure, (5 -owre, 5–7 -ur, 6 *Sc.* toutour); 6 tutar, *Sc.* tuttar, 6–8 tuter). [a. OF., AF. *tutour* (mod.F. *tuteur* = Sp., Pg. *tutor*, It. *tutore*), or a. L. *tūtor* watcher, protector, f. *tuērī* to watch, guard.]

† **1.** A guardian, custodian, keeper; a protector, defender. *Obs.*

1377 LANGL. *P. Pl.* B. I. 56 Kynde witte be wardeyne ȝowre welthe to kepe, And tutour of ȝoure tresore and take it ȝow at nede. **1425** *Ord. Whittington's Alms-house* in Entick *London* (1766) IV. 354 To be one principal, which shal pas al other in power.. and be called tutor. *Ibid.*, The seid tutour. *c* **1425** *Found. St. Bartholomews* (E.E.T.S.) 16 The kynge.. behestid hym-self to be a tutur and defensur of hym and of hys. *c* **1440** *Promp. Parv.* 507/2 Tutowre, *tutor*. **1530** PALSGR. 284/1 Tutar, *tuteur*. **1562** PILKINGTON *Expos. Abdyas* 85 The poore oppressed people, whom God takes in to his custodie to be their tutor. **1570** LEVINS *Manip.* 77/14 A Tûter, *tutor*. **1602** *Narcissus* (1893) 276 O thou which hast thy staffe to bee thy tutor.

2. One who has the custody of a ward; a guardian. † **a.** in *gen.* sense. *Obs.*

1382 WYCLIF *Gal.* iv. 2 How moche tyme the eyr is litil.. he is vndir tutouris and actouris. **1413** *Pilgr. Sowle* (Caxton) IV. xxxviii. (1859) 64 They leden the kynge at theyr owne lust,.. as tutours, and couratours. **1526** TINDALE *Gal.* iv. 2 The heyre as longe as he ys a chylde.. is vnder tuters and governers. *c* **1550** BECON *Catech.* VI. Wks. 1564 I. 533 b, The honor that the chyldren owe to their parents and tutors. **1560** DAUS tr. *Sleidane's Comm.* 175 The tutours.. sent ambassadours to the Turke to commend the childe vnto hym. **1615** *North Riding Rec.* (1884) II. 109 [Taking away] a woman childe under eleven yeares of age from.. her grandfather and lawfull tutor. **1616** BULLOKAR *Eng. Expos.*, *Tutour*, a defender, he that hath charge to bring vp a childe. **1642** FULLER *Holy & Prof. St.* v. xviii. 432 That interest which carefull tutours claim in those whose protection they tender. **1690** LOCKE *Govt.* II. vi. §59 If the Father.. hath not provided a Tutor, to govern his Son, during his Minority.. the Law takes care to do it.

b. *spec.* in *Rom.* and *Sc. Law*: The guardian and representative, and administrator of the estate, of a person legally incapable, failing the father.

tutor dative, t. nominate, t. optive, t. testamentar: see these adjs. ***tutor-at-law, of law***, or ***-legitim***, the nearest male relative on the father's side, who becomes guardian in the absence or failure of the tutor nominate.

1387 TREVISA *Higden* (Rolls) IV. 197 Pompeus.. hymself fleigh to þe.. kyng of Egipt, and axede help of hym, for he was assigned hym by þe senatoures to be his tutor and his wardeyn. **1432-50** tr. *Higden* (Rolls) IV. 75 Ptholomeus begynnenge to reigne the vthe yere of his age, legates of Alexandrye preyede the Romanes thei wolde be tutores of þat childe, and defende the realme of Egipte. **1521** in *Acts Parlt. Scot.* (1875) XII. 39/1 Þe Richt Illustre prince Duke of Albany Tutoure of Law to our said Soverane Lord [James V]. **1536** BELLENDEN *Cron. Scot.* (1821) I. 34 He was left tutour-testamenter be thair fader. **1546** [see TESTAMENTAR]. **1575** [see DATIVE *a.* 4]. **1597** HOOKER *Eccl. Pol.* v. lxxiii. §5 In ancient times all women which had not Husbands or Fathers to gouerne them, had their Tutors. **1681** [see NOMINATE B. 2]. **1765** BLACKSTONE *Comm.* I. xvii. 448 The guardian with us performs the office both of the *tutor* and *curator* of the Roman laws;.. according to the language of the court of chancery, the *tutor* was the committee of the person, the *curator* the committee of the estate. *a* **1768** ERSKINE *Inst. Law Scot.* I. vii. §8 (1773) 117 In default of tutors-legitim, there is place for tutors-dative. **1826** G. J. BELL *Comm. Laws Scot.* (ed. 5) I. 133 Tutors may effectually grant deeds of ordinary administration of their pupil's estate. **1880** MUIRHEAD *Ulpian* xi. §3 Those are tutors-at-law, *legitimi*, who derive their office from some *lex*.

c. Formerly in Scotland used as a designation with the name of the estate of which the 'tutor' had charge. Now *Hist.*

1529 *Reg. Privy Seal Scot.* II. 53/1 Ane lettre maid to William Makclellane, tutour of Bomby, his airis and assignais [etc.]. *a* **1578** LINDESAY (Pitscottie) *Chron. Scot.* (S.T.S.) I. 89 Ane callit Makclalene.. quha was tutour of bombie for the tyme [in 1452]. *a* **1670** SPALDING *Troub. Chas. I* (1850) I. 27 The Erll of Sutherland.. with the tutour of Duffus and some seruandis followit. **1808** SCOTT *Autobiog.* in *Lockhart* i, Beardie became.. Tutor of Raeburn .. that is, guardian to his infant nephew.

3. One employed in the supervision and instruction of a youth in a private household. Also, one engaged to travel abroad with one or more pupils, a ***travelling*** or ***foreign tutor***.

1398 TREVISA *Barth. De P.R.* VI. v. (Bodl. MS.) lf. 36/2 Þe child [that] knowith goode and yuel is.. isette to lore vndur tutours. **1494** FABYAN *Chron.* cxxvii. 107 Clothayre, consyderynge the frowardnesse of.. his sone Dagobert, assigned to hym a tutoure or lerner of worldlye and knyghtlye maners. **1531** ELYOT *Gov.* I. xvi, Diuers maners of exercises... All these ought he that is a tutor to a noble man to haue in remembrance. **1622** GATAKER *Spirituall Watch* (ed. 2) 74 Two home-bred Tutors.. that God hath set ouer each of vs, Shame and Feare, the shame of sinne, and the feare of wrath. **1699** LOCKE *Educ.* (ed. 4) §167 Passionate words or blows from the Tutor fill the Child's Mind with Terror and Affrightment. **1701** tr. *Le Clerc's Prim. Fathers* (1702) 22 Aristobulus, a Peripatetick, who is said to have been Tutor to Ptolemy Philometer. *a* **1743** SAVAGE *Author to Let* Wks. 1777 II. 274 Few foreign tutors understand the dead languages. **1815** ELPHINSTONE *Acc. Caubul* (1842) I. 285 Some subsist by teaching and practising the law; others teach schools, or are tutors to the sons of rich men. **1822** SHELLEY *Triumph of Life* 261 The tutor and his pupil, whom Dominion Followed as tame as vulture in a chain.

4. a. In the Universities of Oxford, Cambridge, and Dublin: A graduate (most often the fellow of a college), to whom the special supervision of an undergraduate (called his pupil) is assigned. Subsequently also used in other British universities and other further education establishments. Also, in Cambridge and some other universities and colleges, a member of the teaching staff assigned responsibility for the general well-being of a student (cf. *moral tutor* s.v. MORAL *a.* 3 d).

The word was first used of those who stood in a supervisory relation to undergraduate members of colleges or halls, not on the foundation, and were responsible to the hall or college for their pupils' payments (= *creancers*: cf. CREANCER 2.) By Wykeham's Statutes for New Coll., Oxf., imitated at King's Coll., Camb., and Magdalen Coll., Oxf., each junior foundationer was assigned to the special charge of a senior called his *informator*. Both these offices appear to have been merged later in the tutor. Naturally the tutor looked after his pupils' studies also, and this came to be the main part of his duties, esp. at Oxford. *Tutores* are also found at Louvain in 1476 supervising the studies of the *scholares* (Rashdall *Universities of Eur.* (1895) II. 766).

c **1610** in *Brasenose Coll. Quatercent. Monogr.* (1909) II. II. xi. 14 Tradesmen.. inveagle young Gentlemen into new and chargeable fashions contrary to the desires of their parents and the directions of their Tutors. *a* **1648** LD. HERBERT *Autobiog.* (1824) 42 As if they meant to proceed Masters of Art and Doctors in some Science, for which purpose their tutors commonly spend much time in teaching them the subtilities of Logic. **1653** *Register of Visitors Univ. Oxford* (1881) 359 That noe man be admitted to the office of a Tutor in any Colledge or Hall that is not first approved of by the respective Head of such Colledge or Hall and the Visitors of the University. *Ibid.* 360 That all persons of whatever quality soever, untill they be admitted to the Degree of Bachelor of Arts.. doe live under the care, tuition, and instruction of approved Tutors. **1696** PHILLIPS (ed. 5) s.v., A Tutour in the University, is one that takes care to teach and instruct the Youth that are sent thither from inferior Schools; and the Scholar so taught, is call'd the Tutour's Pupil. **1864** J. H. NEWMAN *Apol.* i. (1904) 7/2, I gave up that office in 1826, when I became Tutor of my College. **1884** C. DICKENS *Dict. Cambr.* 124/2 The Tutor.. generally acts as agent for the College in all business transactions with its members... The Tutor himself does not necessarily lecture or teach. Private Tutors are called Coaches. **1884** J. B. MULLINGER *Univ. Cambr. from 1535*, 396 The Cambridge system by which the expenditure of the student is supervised to a certain extent by the tutor was in operation as early as the sixteenth century. **1886** WILLIS & CLARK *Cambridge* I. Introd. 91 In the [Latin] statutes of.. Clare Hall [1551].. we meet for the first time at Cambridge with the term *tutor*, in the modern sense, namely, a fellow of the college who is to be responsible for his pupil's expenses, to explain to him what he has to do and to learn, and.. is to be treated by him with filial obedience and respect. **1887** *Q. Rev.* Oct. 403 By the middle of the sixteenth century, the modern system of admitting students not on the foundation was fully established; and, as a natural result, the office of 'tutor' in the present meaning of the term then first appears. **1895** RASHDALL *Universities of Eur.* II. 515 It seems probable that before the middle of the fifteenth century the teaching of Undergraduates.. was mainly in the hands of Tutors in the Colleges, or Principals and their assistant Regents or non-graduate Lectors in the Halls. *Note*, The word used both at New College [*c* 1400] and Magdalen [1479] is *Informator*. At Brasenose College [founded 1509] the word *Tutor* occurs for the first time, but only in reference to the Fellow who is to be responsible for a Commoner. **1933** *Times Lit. Suppl.* 14 Dec. 889/3 He [*sc.* Sir John Sandys] was for long Senior Tutor of his college, a different thing in Cambridge from Oxford. **1980** L. P. WILKINSON *Century of King's* p. xiv, *Tutor*, a Fellow responsible for a student's general welfare. Every student has one.

b. In U.S. universities and colleges: 'A teacher subordinate to a professor, usually appointed for a year or a term of years' (*Cent. Dict.*).

1828 WEBSTER s.v., Tutors are graduates selected by the governors or trustees, for the instruction of undergraduates. .. They are usually officers of the institution, who have a share, with the president and professors, in the government of the students.

c. ***private tutor*** (at the English Universities): A person engaged by students to assist them in their studies and preparation for the examinations, but not appointed or recognized by the University or College. Also, a person who makes it his business to prepare students for professional examinations apart from the universities, as *an army tutor*, *a law tutor*.

1827 LYTTON *Falkland* I. 15, I was sent to a private tutor. **1840** *Encycl. Brit.* (ed. 7) XXI. 498/1 Although recognised neither by the universities, nor by any particular college, a very numerous class has long existed both at Oxford and Cambridge, who, under the denomination of *Private Tutors*, superintend and assist the studies of individuals. **1884** C. DICKENS [see 4 a].

5. In some English public schools: **a.** A senior boy appointed to help a junior in his studies.

1689 A. HILL *Life Barrow* B.'s Wks. 1687 I. a 2, Removing [from the Charterhouse] to Felsted.. he quickly made so great a progress in Learning.. that his Master appointed him a little Tutour to the Lord Viscount Fairfax. **1898** SARGEAUNT *Ann. Westminster* vii. 123 The very name of 'little tutor' familiar in the schools of the seventeenth century is now wholly forgotten... The 'little tutor' was paid for his services and might thus gather a small purse against the time when he should go to the University. **1901** *Winchester Coll. Notions* 130 The ten Senior Praefects in College are called Tutors.

b. A master charged with the special supervision of a particular boy.

1861 J. T. COLERIDGE *Publ. Sch. Educ.* 37 [At Eton] Every Master therefore but the Head Master is also a Tutor and every boy must have his Tutor... Every exercise the pupil does is first submitted to the Tutor for inspection and correction and then carried into school. **1901** *Winchester Coll. Notions* 130 College Tutor formerly had to correct the composition of College men, but now he helps College Juniors with their work.

6. *transf.* As the name of an instruction book in any subject. Now chiefly applied to books of instruction in playing a musical instrument.

1665 MOXON (*title*) A Tutor to Astronomy and Geography. **1776** *Pennsylvania Even. Post* 15 June 299/2 Just published,.. a complete Tutor for the Fife. *a* **1916** *Mod.* An Easy French Tutor. Hémy's Pianoforte Tutor. **1918-19** *T. Eaton & Co. Catal.* Fall & Winter 383/6 Bellak Piano Tutor.. one of the best tutors in use. **1956** F. REIDY in S. Traill *Play that Music* 108 Any tutor I have ever read says that the tip of the reed should be struck with the tip of the tongue. **1981** LD. HAREWOOD *Tongs & Bones* iii. 60, I wanted to learn the clarinet... A beautiful Boehm arrived together with an English 'tutor'.

7. *attrib.* and *Comb.*, as ***tutor-companion***, ***-confessor***, ***-farmer***, ***-room***; ***tutor-sick*** adj.

1771 SMOLLETT *Humph. Clinker* 8 Aug., I was tutor-sick at Alma Mater. **1844** STEPHENS *Bk. Farm* I. 96 The tutor-farmer should be provided with such a plan to give to each of his pupils. **1899** C. K. PAUL *Mem.* 247 My tutor days are not satisfactory in the retrospect. **1901** *Westm. Gaz.* 8 May 2/1 The tutor-confessor was instantly turned out. **1903** *Daily Chron.* 20 Mar. 6/1 Dr. Jüttner, the tutor-companion, who holds that youth should be allowed to revel in the sunshine. **1906** *Mem. Abp. Temple* I. 155 The power of the tutor-rooms had over-asserted itself.

tutor ('tju:tə(r)), *v.* [f. TUTOR *sb.*]

1. a. *trans.* To act the part of a tutor towards; to give special or individual instruction to; to teach, instruct (*in* a subject).

1592 WARNER *Alb. Eng.* VII. xxxvii. (1612) 186 The last of our three Phaetons was tuter'd of a Fryer. **1621** in Foster *Eng. Factories Ind.* (1906) 241 [An accusation of having said] that our hopefull Prince Charles was tutored in the Papist religion. **1740** J. DUPRÉ *Conform. Anc. & Mod. Cerem.* 39 An Old Capuchin tutoring a Novice. **1814** CHALMERS *Evid. Chr. Revel.* x. 292 His mind is not yet tutored to the philosophy of the subject. **1867** MACFARREN *Harmony* vi. (1876) 221 Their ear being thus tutored. **1903** *Times, Lit. Suppl.* 2 Oct. 280/1 He was sent away to be tutored in English rectories, whence he proceeded to University College, London.

absol. **1892** *Nation* (N.Y.) 11 Aug. 116/2 Graduate.. of experience wishes to tutor for the September examinations.

b. With extension: To get (a quality or the like) *out* or *in* by instruction or discipline. *rare.*

1646 J. HALL *Poems* 64 Let not wealth tutor out Our spirits with her gout.

2. To instruct under discipline; to subject to discipline, control, or correction; to school; also to admonish or reprove.

1592 SHAKS. *Rom. & Jul.* III. i. 33 Didst thou not fall out with a taylor for wearing his new doublet before Easter, with another for tying his new shoes with olde riband, and yet thou wilt tuter me from quarelling? **1641** MILTON *Ch. Govt.* i. Wks. 1851 III. 100 If men were but as good to discipline themselves, as some are to tutor their Horses and Hawks. **1645** —— *Tetrach.* Wks. 1738 I. 240 The Fanatic boldness of this age, that dares tutor Christ to be more strict than he thought fit. **1667** DRYDEN & DK. NEWCASTLE *Sir Martin Mar-all* I. i, Saucy rascal, avoid my sight; must you tutor me? **1711** SHAFTESB. *Charac., Wit & Hum.* I. iii, The World however it may be taught will not be tutor'd. **1837** CARLYLE *Fr. Rev.* III. I. i, France is roused! Long have ye been lecturing and tutoring this poor Nation. **1850** MAURICE *Mor. & Met. Philos.* (1854) I. 9 Seneca.. had tutored himself to endure personal injuries without indulging in anger. **1882** STEVENSON *Fam. Stud. Men & B.*, *Thoreau* (1905) 115 Thoreau had plenty of humour till he tutored himself out of it.

3. To instruct (a person) in a course of action, to tell (one) what to do or say; often in sinister sense: to sophisticate or tamper with (a witness or his evidence).

1757 J. LIND *Lett. Navy* ii. 77 Notwithstanding all the care that had been taken to manage and tutor his evidence. **1767** J. WINGRAVE *Narr. Cruelties Eliz. Brownrigg* 6 After tutoring the girl.. what answer to make, and what behaviour to follow. **1826** C. BUTLER *Vind. Rom. Cath. Ch.* 126 Emissaries were employed, witnesses tutored,.. and even torture applied to procure evidence. **1850** MERIVALE *Rom. Emp.* (1865) III. xxiii. 67 The populace, tutored.. or bribed for the purpose, offered him the high priesthood.

†**4.** To take care or charge of. *Obs. rare.*

1682 A. PEDEN in *Life* x. (1902) 209 Our blessed second Adam hath our Stock in guiding and he tutors it better.

5. *intr.* To study under a tutor. *U.S.*

1900 C. C. MUNN *Uncle Terry* 55, I tutored some, read law, and was admitted to the bar. **1920** [see FLUNK *v.* 1 b].

Hence **'tutored** *ppl. a.*, **'tutoring** *vbl. sb.*

1589 R. HARVEY *Pl. Perc.* (1860) 25 A little tutoring in Diuinitie, and the reuersion of a benefice,.. where his godfathers commendatorie letters may preuaile. **1601** WEEVER *Mirr. Mart.* F ij b, His Tutor'd pen.. would.. still repaire the ruin of my name. **1707** in Hearne *Collect.* 13 June (O.H.S.) II. 20 They must by the Tutoring of Plato maintain the same Doctrine. **1805** *Chron.* in *Ann. Reg.* (1807) XLVII. 475/2 His exhibition consisted of tutored birds. A number of little birds.. formed themselves into ranks, like a company of soldiers. **1887** SAINTSBURY *Hist. Elizab. Lit.* viii. (1890) 299 [He] died possessed of landed property.. (an unusual result of tutoring). **1889** Bosw. SMITH *Life Ld. Lawrence* viii. (1911) 124 The little prince.. flung himself back.. with a tutored obstinacy which was not to be shaken.

tutorage ('tju:tərɪdʒ). Also 7 tutridge, tutaradge. [f. TUTOR *sb.* + -AGE.]

1. The office, authority, or action of a tutor or guardian; tutorship, guardianship, custody; tutorial control, direction, or supervision; instruction.

1617 MORYSON *Itin.* III. 217 By the Law of Saxony, Tutorage belongs onely to the Kinsmen, by the Fathers side. **1657** R. LIGON *Barbadoes* 23, I wanted no tutridge, in the learning this mystery. **1711** SHAFTESB. *Charac., Misc.* IV. i, The Tutorage of Fancy and Pleasure. **1716** PRIDEAUX *Connex. O. & N. Test.* I. iv. (1718) 168 Under the discipline and tutorage of that prophet. **1801** STRUTT *Sports & Past.* I. i. §2 These qualities.. were natural to them, and not the effect of tutorage. **1837** LOCKHART *Scott* I. iii. 91 He was placed.. under the domestic tutorage of Mr. James French.

b. *spec.* at a university; also, the charge for or cost of this.

1638 EARL OF CORK *Diary* in *Lismore Papers* Ser. I. (1886) V. 64 Whose expences.. for three yeares, for diett, and tutaradge, and aparell, I paid. **1721** AMHERST *Terræ Fil.* App. (1726) 322 He has, ever since his admission into Baliol, constantly paid the same tutorage, which other scholars do. **1733** *Oxford Act* I. 7 Fifty Pounds with which I should have paid off my old Score, my Battles, my Tutorage, my Taylor [etc.]. **1775** A. BURNABY *Trav.* 55 The expence to a student for room-rent, commons, and tutorage. **1835** DE QUINCEY in *Tait's Mag.* II. 367 The next item.. is that which in college bills is expressed by the word Tutorage.

c. A tutor's post, a tutorship.

1796 LAMB *Let. to Coleridge* in *Mem.* i, Concerning the tutorage, is not the salary low? **1833** CARLYLE *Misc. Ess.*, *Diderot* (1872) V. 40 He has reconciled Brothers, sought out Tutorages.

†**2.** The condition of being under authority or control; = TUTELAGE 2. *Obs. rare.*

1651 BAXTER *Inf. Bapt.* 28 He hath redeemed us from our bondage and tutorage. **1751** JOHNSON *Rambler* No. 147 ¶4 Banqueting upon my own perfections, and longing in secret to escape from tutorage. **1768** TUCKER *Lt. Nat.* (1834) I. 596 Conceited pertness teaches the new-loosened school-boy.. thy scorn of tutorage and control.

'tutordom. *rare.* [f. TUTOR *sb.* + -DOM.] The occupation of a tutor; tutorship.

1840 *Blackw. Mag.* XLVIII. 124 He then betook himself .. to tutordom and secretaryship. **1957** G. AVERY *Warden's Niece* xi. 214 There will be a storm to-night, a very suitable end to my tutordom.

tutorer (ˈtjuːtərə(r)). *rare.* Also 8 **tuterour.** [f. TUTOR *v.* + -ER¹.] One who tutors; an instructor, tutor.

1702 BLACKWELL *Compleat Tutor* 1 The English Fencing-Master: or, the Compleat Tuterour of the Small Sword. **1824** in *Spirit Pub. Jrnls.* (1825) 213 Of these patriarchal tutorers was Mr. Larry O'Larrop. **1841** J. T. HEWLETT *Parish Clerk* I. 144 The next time the tutorer went out for a drive.

tutoress (ˈtjuːtərɪs). Also 7 **tutoresse.** [f. TUTOR *sb.* + -ESS; cf. TUTRESS.] A female tutor.

a. An instructress, a governess. Also *fig.*

1614 RALEIGH *Hist. World* II. (1634) 456 Jezebel had cunning enough to be his Tutoresse. **1675** HAN. WOOLLEY *Gentlewom. Comp.* 4 A Gentlewoman every way accomplisht for a Tutoress to young Ladies. **1741** RICHARDSON *Pamela* II. 125, I hope, from her good Example, and your friendship,.. in time to be half as good as my Tutoress. **1781** H. DOWNMAN tr. *Voltaire's Dram. Wks.* I. 238 School'd by adversity, Great tutoress of mankind. **1830** *Examiner* 822/1 Let her trust to these, and not to any tutoress in acting. **1848** THACKERAY *Van. Fair* xii, Love was Miss Amelia Sedley's last tutoress, and it was amazing what progress our young lady made under that popular teacher. **1888** *Pall Mall Gaz.* 20 Jan. 14/1 University tutoresses promise to be numerous within the next few years.

b. A female guardian.

1759 *Chron.* in *Ann. Reg.* 59/1 The king.. and the Princess.. are appointed honorary tutor and tutoress to her children.

tutorhood (ˈtjuːtəhʊd). *rare.* [f. TUTOR *sb.* + -HOOD.] The condition or office of a tutor, tutorship; also, †a society or body of tutors.

1752 H. WALPOLE *Lett.* (1845) II. 455 Storms gathering in the tutorhood [of Prince George]. *a* **1797** —— *Mem. Geo. II* (1847) I. x. 298 The dissensions in the tutorhood had been carried so high. **1882** H. C. MERIVALE *Faucit of B.* I. I. v. 91 Faucit.., after six years of tutorhood,.. had made up his mind to leave the place and the life.

tutorial (tjuːˈtɔərɪəl), *a.* and *sb.* [f. L. *tūtōri-us* (f. *tūtor*, TUTOR) + -AL¹.] Of or pertaining to a tutor.

A. *adj.* **1. a.** *Rom.* and *Sc. Law.* Of or pertaining to a legal guardian; cf. TUTOR 2 b.

1742 KAMES *Decis. Crt. Sess. 1730–52* (1799) 44 After the Major's death, tutorial inventories were made up of his estate. *a* **1768** ERSKINE *Inst. Law Scot.* I. vii. §32 (1773) 131 The defender does not.. insist for any balance that may be due by the tutor upon his tutorial accounts. **1880** MUIRHEAD *Gaius* III. §107 Provided that, where tutorial authorization is required, his tutor has intervened.

b. Protecting, defensive. *nonce-use.*

1898 *Blackw. Mag.* Oct. 536/2 Stones.. held in their place by diverse-running lines of Bricks.. tutorial bricks till the adobe coping is reached.

2. Of or pertaining to a teacher or instructor; *esp.* pertaining to a college tutor.

1822 MACAULAY in *Life & Lett.* (1883) I. ii. 110, I begin my tutorial labours to-morrow. **1858** GOLDW. SMITH in *Oxford Ess.* 265 The tutorial system was aroused from its lethargy, and the number of tutors and lectures was increased. **1881** *Nature* 28 Apr. 614/1 Their tutorial and laboratory courses of instruction. **1886** F. POLLARD in *Antiquary* Feb. 53/2 Colleges to be closed, and professorial and tutorial duties to be entirely suspended. **1906** *Times* 23 June 6/3 A tutorial Fellow will be appointed at Pembroke College early in Michaelmas term.

B. *sb.* **a.** A period of individual instruction given by a college or university tutor to pupils, either singly or in small groups.

1923 G. SAINTSBURY *Second Scrap Bk.* 27 For 'Mods' Logic one went to Professor Wall's University lectures and Mr. Sidgwick's tutorials. **1927** W. E. COLLINSON *Contemp. Eng.* 124 In regard to teaching within the University the only terms worthy of notice are the use of Oral (where some universities use Viva..) and tutorials (practical classes for recapitulating the formal lectures). **1932** C. BAILEY in *Handbk. Univ. Oxford* 128 During term each man will attend a 'tutorial', as post-war Oxford has agreed to name it, at least once a week. **1953** A. MOOREHEAD *Rum Jungle* i. 19 Old Jack or Geoff with whom I had attended tutorials at the university. **1966** *Rep. Comm. Inquiry Univ. Oxf.* II. 450 A 'tutorial' is to be taken to mean teaching of not more than three people at one time. **1979** *Washington Post* 26 Oct. B4/1 Windt did not show up for her 11:15 math tutorial that day.

b. Any period of tuition or training; a printed account or explanation of a subject intended for private study.

1978 *Sci. Amer.* Feb. 99/1 (Advt.), You'll find our tutorials on hardware and software invaluable reading, also our reports on home applications and evaluative reviews based on experiences with home computer products. **1980** *Amer. Banker* 15 Jan. 6/1 The 1980 conference will feature state-of-the-art developments to help assure the integrity of information systems. The schedule includes 10 tutorials, three general sessions, [etc.]. **1980** *Washington Post* 5 July B2/1 Sonny Stitt, that world-traveling, one man be-bop workshop, is holding tutorials at the One Step Down through tonight.

Hence **tuˈtorially** *adv.*, in a tutorial manner; as or by a tutor; by way of tuition.

1818–60 WHATELY *Commpl. Bk.* (1864) 34 Rough and awkward,.. and of course tutorially pedantic. **1891** *Academy* 31 Jan. 102/2 (Advert.) His duties will be to assist the Professor.. and to direct tutorially the English work of the Normal Students.

tutoriate (tjuːˈtɔərɪət). *rare.* [f. L. *tūtōri-us* (see prec.) + -ATE¹: cf. *professoriate.*] A body of tutors; the tutorial staff of a college.

1858 GOLDW. SMITH in *Oxford Ess.* 281 The tutoriate will also be generally feeble in lay subjects, because the rule of celibacy will continue to drive from College all but clerical fellows.

tutorify (ˈtjuːtərɪfaɪ), *v. nonce-wd.* [f. TUTOR *sb.* + -(I)FY.] *trans.* To make or render tutorial.

1826 WHEWELL in Todhunter *Acc. Writ.* (1876) II. 77, I do not see why you should suppose I am so thoroughly tutorified.

ˈtutorism. [f. as prec. + -ISM.] The sphere or duty of a tutor.

1855 CLOUGH *Poems*, etc. (1869) I. 94 Working away in the thoroughly terrestrial element of College tutorism.

tutorize (ˈtjuːtəraɪz), *v.* [f. as prec. + -IZE.]

a. *intr.* To act as a tutor; to play the tutor. (Also with *it.*) **b.** *trans.* To be tutor to; to instruct as a tutor.

1611 COTGR., *Preceptorizer*, to teach, instruct, tutorize it. **1839** F. W. FABER *Lett.* (1869) 77, I have been tutorized in the Breviary by a very nice priest. **1861** *Wheat & Tares* 3 You are coming with us to Westborough,.. to tutorise Robert? **1873** HELPS *Anim. & Mast.* vi. (1875) 145 He would tutorize a poor Sizar without receiving any payment. **1899** H. G. GRAHAM *Soc. Life Scotl. in 18th C.* IX. §5. II. 116 For £5 a year, 'with board and washing', they tutorised the children.

Hence **ˈtutorizing** *vbl. sb.*; also **tutoriˈzation**, tutoring, tuition.

1837 WHEWELL in Todhunter *Acc. Writ.* (1876) II. 263 Operations in the way of tutorizing and the like. **1842** G. S. FABER *Prov. Lett.* (1844) I. 18 He.. will not be long in perceiving, under good Romish Tutorisation, that [etc.]. **1844** *Q. Rev.* June 78 Mr. Wm. Scott.. was very willing to have his brother's assistance in the tutorizing at University, for which John no doubt had remuneration.

tutorless (ˈtjuːtəlɪs), *a.* [f. as prec. + -LESS.] Having no tutor or guardian.

1618 J. RAWLINSON in Spurgeon *Treas. Dav.* Ps. lv. 6 As a husbandless widow, as a tutorless orphan. **1896** HARE *Story my Life* I. v. 397 Left tutorless just when I was going up to Oxford.

tutorly (ˈtjuːtəlɪ), *a. rare.* [f. as prec. + -LY¹: cf. *fatherly.*] Befitting or pertaining properly to a tutor; like a tutor; dictatorial, pedagogic.

1611 COTGR. s.v. *Bonnet, Prendre le bonnet*,.. to take on him the gouernment of himselfe; to waiue all tutorly Iurisdiction. *a* **1734** NORTH *Exam.* III. vi. §42. (1740) 453 The Earl.. was grown so infirm, peevish and forgetful, as also not a little tutorly, in his Majesty's Affairs. **1879** G. MEREDITH *Egoist* I. vi. 88 He was.. indulgent, almost frolicsome, in contradistinction to Mr. Whitford's tutorly sharpness.

tutorship (ˈtjuːtəʃɪp). [f. as prec. + -SHIP.]

†**1.** The office of guardian or protector; guardianship. *Obs.*

1559 AYLMER *Harborowe* L j, In the ciuill lawe, the tutorshippe endith in the males at .14. yeares of age. **1579** J. STUBBES *Gaping Gulf* D j, Putting it in the hands of the father, who vnder colour of some tutorship to hys daughter, will haue her into Fraunce. **1586** *Acts Privy Counc.* (N.S.) 66 Douglas.. desireth to haue the tutorshippe and keeping of the idiot with the goodes, leases [etc.]. **1629** WADSWORTH *Pilgr.* vi. 52 My Father continued in his tutorship of the Infant vntill he.. dyed. **1665** SIR T. HERBERT *Trav.* (1677) 75 Anno 1610... The Prince (under tutorship of Mortesachan) was sent Viceroy to Guzurat.

2. a. The position or office of an instructor or teacher.

1581 MULCASTER *Positions* xxxvii. (1887) 155 So long as the child shalbe either vnder maistership in schole, or tutorship in colledge. **1796** MME. D'ARBLAY *Camilla* I. 105 An entire discontinuance of all pupilage and tutorship. **1841** W. SPALDING *Italy & It. Isl.* I. 140 Seneca, whose tutorship of Nero, and his murder by that wicked prince, are familiar to every one. **1856** MISS YONGE *Daisy Chain* xxi, Norman.. had undertaken the tutorship of two school-boys for the holidays. **1893** W. G. COLLINGWOOD *Ruskin* iii. 34 He was now growing out of his mother's tutorship.

b. A post as a tutor, *spec.* in a university.

1925 C. CONNOLLY *Let.* 9 Mar. in *Romantic Friendship* (1975) 62, I don't expect your tutorship will be till April. **1929** S. LESLIE *Anglo-Catholic* xviii. 262 Colley had taken a travelling tutorship in Switzerland. **1980** *Daily Tel.* 19 Feb. 14/2 The following elections have been made: Magdalen: Official Tutorship as Tutor in Law, [etc.].

tutory (ˈtjuːtərɪ). Also 5 **tutry**, 6 **tutoury.** [f. TUTOR: see -ORY¹. The form *tutry* is ad. OF. *tutrie, tuterie*, from *tuteur.*]

1. Guardianship, charge, protection; *spec.* the custody of a ward. *Obs.* exc. in *Law.*

tutory-at-law, tutory dative, etc.: cf. *tutor-at-law*, etc. (TUTOR *sb.* 2 b).

c **1400** *Sc. Trojan War* II. 1624 Þir two sonnes, quhen þai war ȝing, War gevin in tutory and keping To king Teuteus. **1456** SIR G. HAYE *Law Arms* (S.T.S.) 264 Gif a man war our ȝong, within elde of tutry. **1596** DALRYMPLE tr. *Leslie's Hist. Scot.* VIII. (S.T.S.) II. 65 Alexander Ogiluie,.. in quhais tutorie was Johne Ogiluie, his oy. **1614** in Ramsay *Bamff Charters* (1915) 175 To exerce the said office of tutorie to the weill of the saidis bairnis. **1643** *Ibid.* 262 Borrowing of money.. be the tutour befoir the expyreing of his tutorie. **1754** Tutory dative [see DATIVE *a.* 4 c]. *a* **1768** ERSKINE *Inst. Law Scot.* I. vii. §1 Tutory.. is a power and faculty to govern the person, and to manage the estate, of a pupil. **1838** W. BELL *Dict. Law Scot.* 1018 The tutory may.. expire by the tutor's renunciation made on reasonable cause. **1880** MUIRHEAD *Ulpian* xi. §9 A tutory-at-law is lost by *capitis deminutio.*

attrib. a **1768** ERSKINE *Inst. Law Scot.* I. vii. §32 (1773) 131 All purchases made by the tutor,.. till settling the tutory-accounts.

†**2.** Tuition, instruction. *Obs. rare.*

1692 A. PITCAIRN *Assembly* V. i. (1766) 62 The Tutory of Mr. Salathiel, who is as profess'd an Enemy to poor Priscian.. as he is to King James. **1764** REID *Inquiry* vi. §24 Reason and reflection must superadd their tutory in order to produce a Rousseau, a Bacon, or a Newton.

‖**tutoyant** (tytwajɑ̃), *a. rare.* [a. F. *tutoyant*, pres. pple. of *tutoyer* TUTOYER *v.*] Intimate, affectionate; suggesting a degree of familiarity sufficient to 'tutoyer'.

1899 'A. LESLIE' *Some Players* 110 He turns facile and covert scorn upon the pretty tutoyant affection of happily wedded woman and man. **1975** *Times Lit. Suppl.* 14 Mar. 274/4 Many of her [*sc.* Lady Tennyson's] letters to her fiancé and husband have been destroyed, but there are enough affectionately *tutoyant* letters to her 'Ally' to show the nature of their correspondence.

‖**tuˈtoyer**, *v.* Also 7 **tutay**, 9 **tutoy**, (9 **tutoyé**). [a. and ad. F. *tutoyer* (tytwaye), f. the sing. pronoun *tu, toi, te*, as used in speaking to a person instead of the pl. *vous*: see Littré.] *trans.* To use the singular pronoun *tu, toi, te* ('thou' and 'thee') to; to 'thou' (any one); to treat as an intimate; to address with familiarity, or as an inferior in rank or order. Also *intr.*

1697 J. DENNIS *Plot & no Plot* II. 24 There is an air of greatness in Tutaying men. **1819** *Hermit in London* III. 159 They [nobles] often tutoyered the leading favourite. **1840** CAROLINE FOX *Jrnls. & Lett.* vi. (1882) 53 He.. promised to *tutoyer* us as long as we liked, but not to answer to *thee.* **1852** MRS. BROWNING *Lett.* 7 Apr. (1897) II. 63 The Greek in Greek costume who tutoyéd her, and kissed her. **1861** T. HEYWOOD *S. Lancs. Dial.* in *Chetham Misc.* III. 9 Tutoying still pervades South Lancashire. **1865** KINGSLEY *Herew.* xvi, He was growing warm, and began to tutoyer Hereward. **1895** *Edin. Rev.* Oct. 386 Freron thought he perceived.. that 'tutoying' might be displeasing to him,.. so he instantly substituted 'vous'.

Hence ‖**tutoiement** (tytwamɑ̃), the action of addressing in this way; 'thouing'.

1817 LADY MORGAN *France* I. (1818) I. 72 The *tutoiement* universal in France, in all the intercourse of friendship and intimacy, is always used among the peasants, except to their superiors. **1879** *Scribner's Mag.* XIX. 97/1 It was not merely the *tutoiement* that struck him as saucy. **1898** *Daily News* 18 Apr. 4/5 M. Aulard and M. Sigismond Lacroix read.. papers, the one on the 'tutoiement', or use of the pronouns 'thee' and 'thou' during the Revolution.

tutress (ˈtjuːtrɪs). Also 6–7 **tutresse**, 7 **tuteresse**, 8–9 **tut'ress.** [ad. OF. *tutreisse, tuteresse* (14th c. in Godef.), or f. L. *tūtrix* TUTRIX by change of ending.] **a.** = TUTORESS a.

1599 *Warn. Faire Wom.* I. 317 My tutress, Drury, gave me charge to speak. **1624** HEYWOOD *Gunaik.* VII. 344 A fit tuteresse for such an apt and forward pupill. **1664** BUTLER *Hud.* II. i. 812 Whipping, that's Virtues Governess, Tutress of Arts and Sciences. **1751** *Female Foundling* I. 20 Ah my dear Tutress, my dear Tutress, I cried out. **1796** MME. D'ARBLAY *Camilla* I. 98 To [her], however, she was but nominally a tutress. **1801** *Sporting Mag.* XVII. 42 Not many months since She was thought a fit Tut'ress for Statesman or Prince. **1871** M. COLLINS *Mrq. & Merch.* iv, Amy Gray became tutress to Mowbray's unmanageable daughter. **1886** *Pall Mall G.* 10 Feb. 4/2 Rouen, Geneva, and Pisa.. have been tutresses of all I know.

b. = TUTORESS b.

1653 H. COGAN tr. *Pinto's Trav.* liii. (1663) 209, I.., a poor woman, Governess, and Tutress of my Son, an Orphan. *a* **1693** *Urquhart's Rabelais* III. xxxi. 262 The Goddess of Wisdom, Tutress, and Guardianess of such as are.. studious. **1747** R. KEITH in *Buccleuch MSS.* (Hist. MSS. Comm.) I. 413 If the Prince should die.., the Princess his spouse should be tutress to the child.. during the nonage.

†**tutrice.** *Obs. rare.* [a. OF. *tutrice* (14th c. in Littré), or ad. L. *tūtrīcem*, acc. of *tūtrix* (see next).] A tutoress.

1490 CAXTON *Eneydos* xxiii. 85 Theire maistres, theire tutryce and techer. **1514** JAS. V *Let* in *Munim. Burgh Irvine* i. (1890) 33 Oure dearest moder, tutrice testamentar & governour.

†**tutrix** (ˈtjuːtrɪks). *Obs.* [a. L. *tūtrix*, fem. of *tūtor* TUTOR. Cf. prec. and TUTRESS, TUTORESS.] A female tutor. **a.** A female guardian. **b.** An instructress, a governess. *rare.*

1515 in *Archæologia* XLVII. 303 Suffre me as tutrix of the yong king. **1546** *Reg. Privy Council Scot.* I. 50 Tutrix testamentar to hir barnes and said umquhile Hew. **1590** SWINBURNE *Testaments* 97 By the ciuill lawe a woman (the mother and grand-mother excepted) can not bee assigned tutrix. **1652** W. HARTLEY *Infant-Baptism* 10 Those pupils she became tutrix to. **1659** A. HAY *Diary* (S.H.S. 1901) 209 That the Lady subscryve her renunciation.. in her name as tutrix. **1680** DALGARNO *Deaf & Dumb Man's Tutor* v. 49 A pratling Nurse is a better Tutrix to her foster-child. **1702–3** in Tindal tr. *Rapin's Hist. Eng.* (1745) IV. XXVI. 596/1 A Tutrix or Regent, during the minority of her supposed brother.

Hence †**ˈtutrixship**, the office of tutrix. *Obs. rare*⁻¹.

1520 Q. MARGARET in Ellis *Orig. Lett.* Ser. II. I. 276 The recoveryng of my.. Turixship of the Kyng my Soon.

tutsan (ˈtʌtsən). Forms: *α.* 5 **totsane, toutsayne**, 6 **totsan, tutsane**, 6– **tutsan**, 7 **tutesain**; *β.* 6 **tutson, -sone, -som, -some.** [app. of F. or Anglo-F. origin. But the mod.F. *toute-saine* is not in Cotgr. (who gives *tutsan*, perh. from Lyte), and is known to Hatz.-Darm. only from 1762, when it appears in the Dict. of the Académie, whereas the name is found in Eng. *c* 1400–50.]

A name applied to various plants on account of their alleged healing virtues; formerly to Agnus Castus, and, in French, to Sanicle (Hatz.-Darm.); now, in Eng., to a shrubby species of St. John's-wort, *Hypericum Androsæmum*, with strongly aromatic foliage and berry-like fruit; formerly esteemed as a vulnerary. Also called PARK-LEAVES.

α. *a* **1400–50** *Stockh. Med. MS.* 157 Totsane or parkleuys: *agnus castus.* **14..** *Voc.* in Wr.-Wülcker 562/24 *Agnus castus*,.. toutsayne. **1548** TURNER *Names of Herbes* 13 *Androsaemon.* Androsaemon is the herbe (as I dooe gesse) whiche we call totsan, and the Poticaries falsly cal *Agnus castus.* **1552** ELYOT (ed. Cooper), *Androsæmon*, an hearbe called sainct Johns woort, or rather Tutsane, and groweth in gardeyns, and no where els. **1578** LYTE *Dodoens* I. xlv. 66 Tutsan so called in French and in English. **1597** GERARDE *Herbal* II. clii. 435 The leaues laide vpon broken shins,.. healeth them, and many other hurtes and griefes, whereof it tooke his name Tout saine, or Tutsane,.. healing all things. **1612** DRAYTON *Poly-olb.* xiii. 206 The yarrow,.. The healing Tutsan then and Plantan for a sore. **1614** MARKHAM *Cheap Husb.* I. Table A v, *Agnus Castus*, of some called *Tutesaine*, is an hearbe with reddish leaues, and sinewie like Plantaine. **1640** PARKINSON *Theat. Bot.* v. lii. 575 *Androsæmum Matthioli.* Matthiolus his Tutsan. This Tutsan (for other English name I know not well, what it may haue, unlesse you would call it a great S. Iohns wort, because it is so like it). **1731** MILLER *Gard. Dict.* s.v. *Androsæmum*, Tutsan or Park-leaves. This Plant grows wild in many Parts of England. **1785** MARTYN *Rousseau's Bot.* xxv. (1794) 374 Garden Tutsan is evidently of this genus (*Hypericum*). **1859** R. THOMPSON *Gard. Assist.* (1878) 649 Hypericum Androsæmum, tutsan, sweet amber.

β. **1552** ELYOT (ed. Cooper), *Ascyrum*, the herbe, which of some is called Peter worte: other would haue it to be Tutson. *Ibid.*, *Cruciata*, of some is taken for the herbe called Tutsome. **1575** TURBERVILE *Venerie* 232 Take a handfull of Tutsome, a handfull of Rewe [etc.].

b. *attrib.* and *Comb.*

1804 CHARLOTTE SMITH *Conversations*, etc. I. 172 The Apocynum, or tutsan leaved dog's bane. **1872** H. KINGSLEY *Hornby Mills* I. 6 The golden Tutsan St John's wort lit up the darkness of the shrubbery.

Tutsi ('tʊtsɪ). [Native name.] = WATUSI 1.

1950 HUNTINGFORD & BELL *E. Afr. Background* (ed. 2) 123/2 (Index), Tutsi. **1965**, etc. [see HUTU]. **1972** *Times* 8 May 13/2 The Tutsi feudal regime was destroyed in massacres in Rwanda. **1976** *Daily Times* (Lagos) 3 Nov. 1/2 At the heart of the conflict and Burundi's general political malaise lay the fact that the Tutsi, tall cattle herders who make up only 14 per cent of the population, politically and economically dominate the Hutu who number 85 per cent of the population. **1979** 'D. GRANT' *Olympic 5000* i. 27 Ochengwe was a Tutsi... In 1964.. the Hutu massacred several thousand Tutsis, the traditional ruling caste of Rwanda.

‖**tutti** ('tutti). *Mus.* [It. *tutto* sing., *tutti* pl. all:—L. *tōtus*, *tōtī*.] In concerted music, a direction that all the performers are to take part; also, a passage or movement rendered by all the performers together; also *attrib.*

1724 *Short Explic. For. Wds. in Mus. Bks.*, *Tutti*, or *Tutto*, .. signifies All, or All together,.. in Musick of several Parts, .. signifying that.. all the several Parts are to perform together. **1816** G. F. GRAHAM *Acct. First Edin. Festival* 105 The flowing and cantabile style of the subject is well contrasted with the spirited *tutti* beginning at the 28th bar. **1833** *Penny Cycl.* I. 74/1 Except in the *tutti* parts (*i.e.*, those portions of the concerto in which the principal instrument rests). **1839** LONGF. *Hyperion* IV. iv, A surfeit of music; tuttis, finales, choruses, must be performed. **1884** *Leeds Mercury* Weekly Supp. 15 Nov. 1/6 Her solo passages were very pleasing, but the tutti music was wanting in tone and point.

tutti-frutti (ˌtuːtɪ'fruːtɪ). [It., = all fruits.]

a. A confection of mixed fruits; *spec.* a mixture of chopped preserved fruits, nuts, etc., used to flavour ice-cream; ice-cream so flavoured. **b.** (**Tutti Frutti, Tutti-frutti.**) A proprietary name for a chewing-gum with a mixed fruit flavouring. **c.** *attrib.* and *transf.*

1834 *Knickerbocker* IV. Sept. 232 *Tutti Frutti*, (all fruits) is the cognomen of an Italian ice, composed of, or rather flavored with, various fruits. **1876** M. J. HENDERSON *Cooking* 313 *Tutti Frutti.* When a rich vanilla cream is partly frozen, candied cherries, English currants, chopped raisins, .. or any other candied fruits chopped rather fine, are added. **1885** *Official Gaz.* (U.S. Patent Office) 30 June 1564/1 *Chewing-gum.*—Adams and Sons, New York, N.Y. .. The words '*Tutti Frutti*'. **1888** A. RANDALL-DIEHL *Two Thousand Words* 210 *Tutti-frutti*, a compound of many kinds of sliced fruits mixed with sugar and alcohol, also the name of a chewing gum. **1898** A. M. BINSTEAD *Pink 'Un & Pelican* v. 125 Most of my readers will very well remember old Bob Bignell, who kept the Argyll rooms, and, after the powers put a stop to the dancing and tutti-frutti business, turned the place into the cheery old Trocadero. **1916** *Daily Colonist* (Victoria, B.C.) 4 July 9/1 The pleasing tang of its mellow fruit flavors alone was always sufficient for you to prefer Adams Tutti frutti gum. **1924** *Official Gaz.* (U.S. Patent Office) 21 Oct. 478/1 *American Chicle Company*, Long Island City, N.Y... *Tutti-frutti.* Particular description of goods.—Chewing gum. Claims use since October 1882. **1951** *Good Housek. Home Encycl.* 516/1 *Tutti Frutti*: Add chopped pistachio nuts, cherries and angelica. **1974** D. CHANTLER *Man who followed in Front* II. 60 'And look at them fuckin' ice cream machines,' he said. 'Tell the waiters.. the Tutti-Frutti is off.' **1976** *Listener* 29 Jan. 121/3 Felix Mendelssohn and his Hawaiian Serenaders, and all those kitsch tutti-fruttis which drop like coconuts from a set of plastic palm trees.

‖**tutti quanti** ('tutti'kwanti). [It.] Everyone, everything, all (of this, that, kind).

[**1671** MME DE SÉVIGNÉ *Let.* 1 Apr. (1862) II. 135 M. et Mme de Duras, a qui j'ai fait vos compliments, MM. de Charost et de Montausier, et *tutti quanti*, vous les rendent au centuple. **1676** —— *Ibid.* 29 July IV. 545 Enfin *tutti quanti*: vous savez ce que c'est que de recevoir un mot de tout ce qu'on trouve en chemin.] **1772** LD. CHESTERFIELD *Let.* 10 Sept. (1932) VI. 2937, I hope you and *tutti quanti* are in a better plight. **1814** *Edin. Rev.* Jan. 403 All the heretical sects are active partisans of Passion, and furiously inimical to Reason, and to all his adherents, *tutti quanti.* **1864** J. A. SYMONDS *Let.* 6 July (1967) I. 488 If you come with Green & me you will have all the published Dramatists, tutti quanti, to read at pleasure. **1934** H. JAMES *Art of Novel* xv. 274 Whether 'Daisy Miller',.. 'Julia Bride' and *tutti quanti* do in fact conform to any such admonition would be an issue by itself. **1948** J. FLANNER in *New Yorker* 8 May 43/1 The idea.. was to bring over from New York.. Barrymore, Bankhead, Hayes, *e tutti quanti.*

tutty ('tʌtɪ), *sb.*[1] Forms: α. 4–7 **tutie**, (6 **thutie**), 5–8 **tuty**, (5 **tutye**, **tuthye**); β. in Latinized form 6–9 **tutia**, (6 **tucia**, 7 **tussia**); γ. 6– **tutty**, (7 **tuttie**, **tutti**). [a. F. *tutie* 13th c. in Wr.-Wülcker 559/13) = Sp. *tutia*, *atutia*, Pg. and med.L. *tutia* (erron. *tucia*); a. Arab. *tūtiyā* oxide of zinc (marked as a foreign word in Arabic lists, perh. Persian). Vullers compares the Sanskrit *tuttha* blue vitriol, used as an eye-ointment, and this is favoured by the statement of Ibn Baitar that the best *tūtiyā* comes from India.] A crude oxide of zinc found adhering in grey or brownish flakes to the flues of furnaces in which brass is melted (cf. POMPHOLYX); also occurring in some countries as a native mineral; formerly used medically, chiefly in astringent ointments and lotions, and now as a polishing powder. Also *attrib.* as ***tutty ointment***, ***powder***.

α. *c* **1400** *Lanfranc's Cirurg.* 95 Anoynte þe wounde.. with þis oynement of rasis & tutie [*v.rr.* tutye, tuthye]. *c* **1400** tr. *Secreta Secret., Gov. Lordsh.* lxxxvii. 95 Stones, Margarites, Corale, Tuty, and alany, and swylk lyk. **1541** R. COPLAND *Galyen's Terap.* 2 H j b, Pampholix commonly called thutie. *c* **1550** H. LLOYD *Treas. Health* (1585) ℭij, Tuty doth dry and clear the eyes, more than all medycynes. **1601** HOLLAND *Pliny* XXX. viii. II. 384 The tried grease of unwashed wooll, (whereunto some adde Tutie and oile of Roses). **1610** B. JONSON *Alch.* II. iii. 398 Your marchesite, your tutie, your magnesia. [**1656–1706** in BLOUNT and PHILLIPS.]

β. **1543** TRAHERON *Vigo's Chirurg.* 107 b/1 Let the sayd thynges be boyled togyther, excepte the tutia. **1581** STYWARD *Mart. Discipl.* I. 12 They ought to haue.. greate store of.. Tarre, Campher, Waxe, Tucia, Ars-nicke. **1615** MARKHAM *Eng. Housew.* (1660) 17 Take two drams of prepared Tussia. **1652** CULPEPPER *Eng. Physic* (1656) 308 For Distillations of Rhewms in the Eyes, especially if it be used with Tutia. **1678** R. R[USSELL] *Geber* III. II. I. iv. 149 Tutia is the fume of White Bodies. **1727–41** [see γ].

γ. **1547** BOORDE *Brev. Health* ccv. 71 To bedwarde anoynt the eyes divers tymes with Tutty. **1605** TIMME *Quersit.* III. 179 Infuse tuttie and lytharge, of each two ounces. **1682** WHELER *Journ. Greece* III. 223, I was shewed a dried Herb.. whereof the Powder is made, we commonly call Tutti. **1727–41** CHAMBERS *Cycl.*, *Tutty*, *Tutia*, or *Lapis Tutiæ*... Tutty is now brought chiefly from Germany. Anciently it came from Alexandria. **1731** FIELDING *Grubstreet Opera* II. iv, Your bills for tutty and rotten-stone, when you us'd nothing but poor whiting. **1812** J. SMYTH *Pract. of Customs* (1821) 119 The better sorts of Tutty.. are in semi-cylindrical concave pieces, like the bark of a tree; ponderous, and somewhat sonorous. **1868** WATTS *Dict. Chem.* V. 1073 An impure oxide, sold under the name of *tutty*, is obtained from the furnaces in which brass is melted. **1883** *Chambers' Encycl.*, Tutty-powder. **1890** *Cent. Dict.* s.v. *Ointment*, Tutty ointment.

tutty ('tʌtɪ), *sb.*[2] Now *dial.* Forms: 6 **tuttay**, **-ey**, 7 **-ie**, **titty**, 9 *dial.* **totty**, **tutto**, 7– **tutty** (also in comb. 9 **tutti-**). [Origin obscure: perh. orig. a nursery or children's word. Cf. TUSSY, TUZZY-MUZZY.] A nosegay, a posy; a tuft or bunch of flowers.

1578 LYTE *Dodoens* III. xxii. 344 At the highest of the stalkes groweth white flowers.. ioyning one to another lyke a tuttay, or little nosegaye. *Ibid.* VI. xvi. 677 Two kindes of Heath, one.. bearing his flowers in tutteys or tuftes. **1599** MINSHEU *Span. Dict.*, A Tuttie, nosegay, or poesie, *ramillète de florés.* *c* **1613** T. CAMPION *Bk. Ayres* I. I. '*Jack & Joan they think no ill*' iii, She can wreathes and tuttyes make. **1664** [see TUZZY-MUZZY]. **1706** PHILLIPS (ed. Kersey), *Tutty* or *Tuzzimuzzy*, an old Word for a Nosegay. *a* **1800** PEGGE *Suppl. Grose*, *Tutty*, and *Titty*, a nosegay. *Somersetsh.* **1825** J. JENNINGS *Obs. Dial. W. Eng.* 128 When spreng, adresst in tutties, Calls all tha birds abroad. **1904** *19th Cent.* Sept. 233, I had a tutty—a nosegay,.. zix times zo big as the biggest picklen cabbage.

b. *Comb.*: **tutty men**, **tuttimen** *pl.*, at Hungerford, tithingmen who collect contributions on Hock Tuesday, carrying a **tutty-pole**, wreathed with flowers and ribbons; **tutty-more**: see quot. 1873.

1873 WILLIAMS & JONES *Somerset Gloss.*, *Tutty*, flower. *Tutty-more*, flower-root. **1893** *Wilts. Gloss.* s.v. *Totty*, At Hungerford the tything-men are known as Tutti-men, and carry Tutti-poles, or wands wreathed with flowers. **1904** *Daily News* 13 Apr. 11 The tutti-men sallied forth, armed with staves, adorned with handsome bouquets.

†'**tutty**, *a.*[1] *Obs. rare.* [Of obscure origin; cf. the dial. verb *tut*, to be uneven in length or height.] Of ground: Uneven, hummocky. Also in comb. ***tutty-nosed***, ? snub-nosed.

1607 MARKHAM *Caval.* III. (1617) 29 If the ground bee tuttie, and full of false treading (which we call broken swarth).. then he must gather vp his body round and close. **1681** T. FLATMAN *Heraclitus Ridens* No. 39 (1713) I. 255 It is a little Tutty-nos'd yappeting Sprite; the Good Old Cause's Lap-Dog.

tutty ('tʌtɪ), *a.*[2] *dial.* [Of obscure origin: cf. TEETY, TETTY.] Irritable, testy, peevish.

1809 T. BATCHELOR *Anal. Eng. Lang.* 145 *Tutty*, ill-tempered, sullen. **1848** A. B. EVANS *Leicestersh. Words*, *Tutty*, touchy. **1855** [see TEETY]. **1902** BARING-GOULD *Nebo the Nailer* vii, He's that tutty, if not minded at wunce.

‖**tutu**[1] ('tuːtuː). [Maori.]

a. A New Zealand shrub yielding shining black juicy berries, containing poisonous seeds; = TOOT *sb.*[5] Also *attrib.*

1845 E. MEURANT *Diary* 4 Oct. (typescript, Alex. Turnbull Library, Wellington) 24 Bullocks.. had been eating the tutu bush wich [*sic*] is poisonous to cattle. **1849** [see SLASH *v.* 1 c]. **1857** [see TOOT *sb.*[5]]. **1861** C. C. BOWEN *Poems* 57 And flax and fern and tutu grew In wild luxuriance round. **1867** [see TUPAKIHI]. **1884** A. COX *Recoll.* 258 Footpaths.. fringed with tutu bushes.

b. Phr. ***to eat (one's) tutu*** or ***toot***, to become acclimatized, *spec.* to colonial life in New Zealand (see quots.). *N.Z. slang* (now *Obs.* exc. *Hist.*).

1857 R. B. PAUL *Lett. from Canterbury* ii. 26 [The newly arrived settlers] passed.. through the crisis of unreasonableness, false pride, and grumbling, which old settlers call 'eating their tutu'... The tutu, or 'toot',.. is a native shrub the leaves of which may be eaten with safety by cattle gradually accumstomed to its use, but are often fatal to newly-landed animals. **1889** G. P. WILLIAMS & W. P. REEVES *Colonial Couplets* 20 (Morris) The troublesome process.. Which old settlers are wont to call 'eating your tutu'. **1941** BAKER *N.Z. Slang* iii. 27 *To eat toot* was the pioneer way of describing the period during which new immigrants settled down to the cold facts of New Zealand life. More correctly the expression was *to eat tutu*.. the poisonous plant. **1966** G. W. TURNER *Eng. Lang. in Austral. & N.Z.* viii. 165 The early colonial phrase 'to eat one's tutu' meaning 'to be acclimatized to colonial life'.

Hence '**tutued** *a.*, poisoned by eating tutu.

1874 A. BATHGATE *Colonial Experiences* xv. 211 Flock-owners have sometimes to contend with a poisonous plant called the tutu (*Coriaria ruscifolia*), commonly pronounced toot... Those [sheep] feeding amongst it.. are apt to be affected by it, or be, as the phrase is, 'tutued'. **1878** E. S. ELWELL *Boy Colonists* 34 When they [*sc.* bullocks] were 'tutu'd' the only cures were either to bleed them or to put ammonia on the tip of the tongue.

tutu[2] ('tuːtuː). Also **tu-tu**. [a. F. *tutu*, childish alteration of *cucu*, dim. of *cul* CUL.] A ballet skirt made up of layers of stiff frills, reaching halfway between the knee and the ankle (***romantic tutu***) or very short and standing out from the legs (***classic tutu***). Also *attrib.*

1910 E. F. SPENCE *Our Stage & its Critics* ix. 196 She wished to exhibit what in technical slang is called *le tutu*, a term descriptive of the abbreviated costume and possessed also of a secondary meaning. **1913** A. E. JOHNSON *Russian Ballet* 56 Columbine.. attired in a scanty *tu-tu.* **1934** A. L. HASKELL *Balletomania* 26 An old-fashioned ballet for this old-fashioned tragedy of naked footlights and a dancer's *tutus.* **1947** N. NICOLAEVA-LEGAT *Ballet Educ.* III. 49 To make a tutu skirt, the basque should first be cut. **1949** CHUJOY & MANCHESTER *Dance Encycl.* 486/1 The classic tutu reaches to a little above the knee, the romantic to the ankle. **1958** L. GIBBS *Gowns & Satyr's Legs* xii. 82 Four miniature ballet-girls, each poised gracefully on one toe and wearing a diminutive *tutu.* **1970** B. CARTLAND *We danced All Night* vii. 196 A snow-white figure in a fluffy *tutu.* **1980** 'M. FONTEYN' *Magic of Dance* 239 The soft, full ballet skirt Marie Taglioni had introduced climbed to just below the knee, then to mid-thigh. As it was shortened, it was made fuller and stood out more and more stiffly until it became the modern tutu.

‖**tutulus** ('tjuːtjʊləs). *Archæol.* [L. *tutulus.*] A Roman head-dress formed by plaiting the hair in a cone above the forehead, worn esp. by the Flamen and his wife.

1753 CHAMBERS *Cycl. Supp.*, *Tutulus*, among the Romans, a manner of dressing the hair, by gathering it up on the forehead into the form of a tower... *Tutulus* likewise signified a woollen cap with a high top. **1816** J. DALLAWAY *Statuary & Sculpt.* vi. 321 The head-dress is that of the wife of a pontifex,.. the tutulus or top of the hair is rolled with a lace round the crown of the head. **1891** FARRAR *Darkn. & Dawn* xxvi, Domitia Lepida, whose *tutulus*, or conical head-dress, it was the exclusive task of a slave-maiden to adorn.

tutunac, tuty, -ye, obs. ff. TUTENAG, TUTTY.

tuuei, tuueine, tuuelf, tuuiȝes, obs. ff. TWAY, TWAIN, TWELVE, TWICE.

tuum, 'thine': see phr. *meum and tuum* s.v. MEUM[1].

Tuvaluan (tuːvə'luːən, tuː'vɑːluːən), *sb.* and *a.* [f. *Tuvalu* (see def.) + -AN.] **A.** *sb.* A native or inhabitant of the Commonwealth State of Tuvalu, formerly the Ellice Islands, in the south Pacific. **B.** *adj.* Of or pertaining to Tuvalu.

1975 *Pacific Islands Monthly* Dec. 15/2 The Tuvaluans, known before October 1 as the Ellice Islanders. **1978** *Daily Mirror* 20 Feb. 6/4 In 1975 the Polynesian Ellice Islanders voted to part peacefully from the Micronesians on the

Gilberts... Today the Tuvaluans rely on coconuts for food and exports. **1978** *Daily Tel.* 30 Sept. 17/6 On Sunday, Tuvalu will become a constitutional monarchy, with the Queen as Head of State represented by a Tuvaluan Governor-General.

tuwel, obs. form of TEWEL.

tu-whit (tuːˈhwɪt), *v.* [See next.] *intr.* To hoot as an owl.

1902 A. LANG in *Longm. Mag.* Dec. 99 He heard the owls towhitting and towhooing from the wood.

tu-whit, tu-whoo (tuːˈhwɪt tuːˈhwuː), *int.* (*sb.*). Also 6–9 to-, too-, -who, -hoo; 9 towhoo towhoo; etc. [Imitative.] An imitation of the call of an owl. See also prec. and next.

1588 SHAKS. *L.L.L.* v. ii. 928 Then nightly sings the staring Owle Tu-whit to-who. A merrie note. **1594** LYLY *Moth. Bomb.* III. iv, To whit to whoo, the Owle does cry. **1607** *Barley-Breake* (1877) 9 Too whit, too whoo, cries out the broad-fac'd Owle. **1797** COLERIDGE *Christabel* I. 3 The owls have awakened the crowing cock; Tu—whit!—— Tu—whoo!

b. *sb.* The utterance of this cry; the hoot of an owl; also, the use of the expression in literature.

1830 TENNYSON *2nd Song to Owl* i, Thy tuwhits are lull'd I wot, Thy tuwhoos of yesternight. *Ibid.* ii, With a lengthen'd loud halloo, Tuwhoo, tuwhit, tuwhit, tuwhoo-o-o. **1862** BORROW *Wild Wales* liii, What resemblance does Shakespear's to-whit-to-whoo bear to the cry of the owl? none whatever.

c. Hence as a name for the owl. *nonce-use.*

1604 TERILO *Fr. Bacon's Proph.* (Percy Soc.) 8 And olde to whit to whoo Did watch the winter night.

tu-whoo (tʊˈhwuː), *int.* (*sb.*). Also to-who(o, too-hoo. [Cf. prec.] Imitation of the call of an owl.

1797 COLERIDGE *Christabel* I. Concl. 31–2 From cliff and tower, tu—whoo! tu—whoo! Tu—whoo! tu—whoo! from wood and fell! **1853** HICKIE tr. *Aristoph.* (1872) II. 425 The owls, which are constantly crying 'to-who'. **1862** BORROW *Wild Wales* liii, The owl..who cried Too-hoo-hoo. **1868** TENNYSON *Last Tourn.* 346 Tuwhoo! do ye see it? do ye see the star? **1899** E. J. CHAPMAN *Drama Two Lives, Canadian Summer-night* 69 The owl's weird cry..With its long too-hoo! too-hoo! **1906** *Essex Rev.* XV. 54 The White or Barn owl cries 'Tu-which', and the Brown owl 'Tu-whoo', or 'Hoohoo; hoo, hoo, hoo, Hoo-hoo'.

b. *sb.* The owl's cry.

1830 [see prec. b]. **1889** *Hilman's Handbk. Chepstow & Wye* (ed. 4) App. 125 Unless fair Philomel is silenced by the too-whoo of the prowling owl.

Hence **tu-ˈwhoo** *v. intr.*, to utter the cry *tu-whoo*; to hoot as an owl. Hence **tu-ˈwhooing** *vbl. sb.* Also **tu-whoot** *v.*

1843 THACKERAY *Bluebeard's Ghost* Wks. 1908 VI. 363 An owl was too-whooing from the church tower. *Ibid.*, The toowhooing of the owl. **1893** BARING-GOULD *Cheap Jack Z.* xxxvii, A barn-owl..to-whooed in its terror. **1912** *Blackw. Mag.* Mar. 374/1 An owl tu-whooted to us from the trefoiled arch.

tuwyte, obs. dial. form of TEWHIT, the lapwing.

tux (tʌks). Also Tux. *U.S.* colloq. abbrev. of TUXEDO.

1922 S. LEWIS *Babbitt* i. 11 Everyone knows I can put on as expensive a Tux. as anybody else. **1951** W. C. WILLIAMS *Autobiogr.* xii. 61, I agreed to take her to a dance and showed up in a tux. **1974** K. MILLETT *Flying* (1975) III. 322 Daddy doing his tux. First the black tie. Next the studs.

tuxedo (tʌkˈsiːdəʊ). orig. and chiefly *U.S.* Also Tuxedo. [Named from *Tuxedo* Park, N.Y., where the jacket was first introduced at the country club in 1886.]

1. In full *tuxedo coat, jacket.* A short jacket without tails, for formal wear; a dinner-jacket.

1889 *Sartorial Art Jrnl.* Aug. 18/1 The low-roll, silk-faced sack, variously called the 'Cowes' coat, the 'Tuxedo' coat, and the Dress Sack, is undoubtedly popular. *Ibid.* Dec. 97/1 The 'Tuxedo' or dress sack is steadily growing in favor for dress negligee purposes. **1900** ADE *Fables in Slang* 130 A jimmy little tuxedo. **1925** H. L. FOSTER *Trop. Tramp with Tourists* 333 Dress coats and tuxedo jackets were removed. **1931** *Times Lit. Suppl.* 12 Nov. 888/4 Bert..is to pose in public as a successful lover,..in the traditional Tuxedo, with the ribbon of the Garter pinned across his bosom as a Right Honourable. *a* **1944** K. DOUGLAS *Alamein to Zem Zem* (1946) vi. 47 Beneath the oil stains their white tuxedos and seductive dresses shone. **1950** J. VEDEY *Band Leaders* p. xiii, The budding maestro must make up his mind whether he will present his band in orthodox tuxedos or in some distinctive style of uniform. **1971** 'A. BURGESS' *MF* viii. 93 He was in a white tuxedo with black floppy tie.

2. Special combinations. †**tuxedo net**, a kind of net veiling (*obs.*); **tuxedo sofa**, a sofa of a style having back and arms the same height; also *tuxedo-style sofa*; **tuxedo (trade) unionism** (see quot. 1965).

1895 *Montgomery Ward Catal.* Spring & Summer 79/1 Black silk tuxedo net veiling, 13 inches wide. *c* **1900** in *Amer. Mail Order Fashions* (1961) 19, 28 in. tuxedo net. Entirely new pattern in black, white and navy. **1961** WEBSTER, tuxedo sofa. **1965** *Economist* 6 Feb. 537/2 Critics accuse him of having become aloof from the rank and file of his union and of practising what they call 'tuxedo trade unionism'... As a 'labour statesman' he associates freely with leading officials in both the government and the steel companies. **1965** *Amer. Home* Mar. 43/1 (*caption*) Curved Tuxedo sofa..illustrates the graceful, softer look for 1965 Modern. **1972** *N.Y. Times* 29 Oct. 85/5 (Advt.), Tuxedo-style sofa. **1977** *Time* 17 Jan. 48/2 Sadlowski calls McBride's style 'tuxedo unionism'. **1977** *Chicago Tribune* 2 Oct. I. 45 (Advt.), An elegant and timeless tuxedo sofa with loose pillows and arm bolsters in a rich champagne beige velvet.

Hence **tuˈxedoed** *a.*, wearing a tuxedo.

1934 J. T. FARRELL *Young Manhood Studs Lonigan* xviii. 284 They..passed the tuxedoed orchestra, which was playing wildly on a dais. **1973** E. MCGIRR *Bardel's Murder* ii. 45 Near him was Jack Prat, tuxedoed, urbane.

tuxl: see TUSCLE.

tuycion, -oun, obs. ff. TUITION.

tuye, var. TWIE *adv. Obs.*, twice.

tuyegge, obs. f. TWIG *sb.*

tuyere (twɪə(r), twaɪə(r), ‖tɥijɛr, tyjɛr). Forms: (4 tuer, toyer, toyere). *α.* 7 twire-, 9 twyer(e, twyére, twyeer. *β.* 8–9 tweer, 9 twear. *γ.* 9 tuyer(e, tuyère; tewer, tewyre. [The common current spelling of the word already entered in the forms TEW-IRON and TOW-IREN, and taken as ad. OF. *toiere* (1389 in Godef. *Compl.*), *tuyere, tuhiere, touyere* (1459), mod.F. *tuyère*. The remarkable gap between the 14th cent. instances and modern usage is partly filled by the occurrence of TWIRE-PIPE in the 17th cent.]

The nozzle through which the blast is forced into a forge or furnace.

[**1350–1** in *Archæologia* LXIV. 158 Item in ij tuers ferri emptis ij.s. viij.d. *Ibid.* 159 Item in xxvj egyn faciendis pro tuers vj s. vj d., pro ege iij d. **1354** *Ibid.* 150 Liberabuntur.. in fabrica predicta..unum angire [? andire = and-iron] precii viij d. duo toyers precii xij d. *Ibid.* 163 In emendacione iij toyeres xij d.]

1781 MORE *Iron Scoria* in *Phil. Trans.* LXXII. 51 *note*, The Tweer is that opening through which the air is driven by the bellows into the body of the furnace. **1839** *Civil Eng. & Arch. Jrnl.* II. 233/2 The 'Twyer' (or aperture by which the blast is admitted) of a cupola or furnace for melting cast iron. **1839** *Penny Cycl.* XIII. 33/1 The three tubes leading to this hearth..which are called *tuyeres*, are used for introducing the blast of air. **1859** R. HUNT *Guide Mus. Pract. Geol.* (ed. 2) 229 The use of hot blast at the tuyères. **1862** *Catal. Internat. Exhib.* II. x. 1 The horizontality of the lines of equal temperature from the tuyères upwards. **1864** *Q. Jrnl. Sc.* I. 492 The twyers are in the upper part of the boshes, and the blast is directed downwards. **1877** RAYMOND *Statist. Mines & Mining* p. viii, With the view of diminishing the waste of heat, it is customary to run the water through tuyeres and jacket just fast enough to keep it almost boiling. **1881** YOUNG *Ev. Man his own Mechanic* §1419 A short pipe or tuyere..acting as the nozzle of an ordinary pair of bellows. **1892** *Labour Commission Gloss.*, *Twear*, the pipe which conveys the hot blast into the furnace ..surrounded by a large pipe, through which passes a constant flow of cold water to keep the twear cool. **1900** *Archæologia* LVII. 119 A blast of air from a bellows was admitted to the furnace through a pipe or twyer.

b. *attrib.* and *Comb.*, as ***tuyere hole, opening, -pipe***; **tuyere arch**, in a blast furnace, an arch through which a tuyere is admitted (*Cent. Dict.* 1891); **tuyere box**, in a converter or the like, a detachable chamber with a number of tuyeres; **tuyere coil**, a water-pipe coiled about the tuyere for cooling (Knight *Dict. Mech.*, *Suppl.* 1884); **tuyere-house**, ? a recess in the wall of a furnace where the blast is admitted: cf. HOUSE *sb.* 7c; **tuyere-plate**: see quot.

1861 FAIRBAIRN *Iron* 155 The *tuyere-box..is so arranged as to be easily detached. Two or more of these tuyere-boxes are provided, so that on the removal of one set of tuyeres, another box and tuyeres may be in readiness. **1836–41** BRANDE *Chem.* (ed. 5) 762 The expansion of the boshes; but as this is more than four feet above the *tuyere hole, the blast must be delivered with great velocity. **1879** G. GLADSTONE in *Cassell's Techn. Educ.* IV. 145/1 The blast ..is let on through the twyer-hole. **1861** FAIRBAIRN *Iron* 50 The number of blowpipe nozzles to each furnace varies..; the usual number is three, one for each of the *tuyere-houses. **1882** *Rep. to Ho. Repr. Prec. Met. U.S.* 580 Water ..flows also around the *tuyere openings. **1674** *Twire-pipe [see TWIRE-PIPE 2]. **1840** *Civil Eng. & Arch. Jrnl.* III. 297/2 A second layer of charcoal..is thereafter laid..under the twyére pipe. **1881** RAYMOND *Mining Gloss.*, *Bloomary*, a forge for making wrought iron... The sides are iron plated, ..the *tuyere-plate (through which the tuyere passes) at one side.

tuyis, obs. Sc. f. TWICE.

tuyke, var. TUKE, *Obs.*

tuyl, tuylʒe, obs. ff. TUILYIE.

tuyn, tuyne, tuynne, obs. ff. TWIN, TWINE.

tuynde, tuyne, obs. ff. TINE *v.*[1]

† **tuyre**, app. erron. f. TIRVE *v.*[2]

13.. *E.E. Allit. P.* B. 1234 ȝet nolde neuer Nabugo þis ilke note leue, Er he hade tuyred þis toun & torne hit to grounde.

tuyrne, obs. f. TEW-IRON: cf. TUYERE.

tuys, tuyse, tuyss, tuyssion, -yon, tuyx, obs. ff. TWICE, TUITION, TWIXT.

tuz, tuzz (tʌz). [Perhaps identical with **tus* in TUSSY and *tus(se)mose*: see TUZZY-MUZZY. But it may be related to TOUSE *sb.* 2, a tousled mass (of hair).] A tuft of hair; in quot. applied to whiskers: *dial.* a knot of wool or hair.

1693 DRYDEN *Persius* iv. 90 With odorous Oyl thy head and hair are sleek; And then thou kemb'st the Tuzzes on thy Cheek. **1847–78** HALLIWELL, *Tuz*, a knot of wool or hair. *Leic.*

tuza (ˈtuːzə). Also tuça (*erron.* tuca). [a. Sp. *tuza*, ad. Mexican *tuçan* or *tozan*, the native name.] A Mexican pocket-gopher or pouched rat: a rodent, formerly supposed to be a kind of mole.

[**1651** HERNANDEZ *Hist. Anim. & Min. Novae Hisp.* I. xxiv. 7 De Tucan, seu Talparum Indicarum quodam genere.] **1787** CULLEN tr. *Clavigero's Mexico* II. 321 Tuza, not Tucan as Count de Buffon writes, in Mexican tozan, a quadruped of Mexico of the mole kind but larger and more beautiful. **1895** C. H. MERRIAM in *U.S. Dept. Agric., N. Amer. Fauna* No. 8. 112 The *tuza* series [of *Geomys*] inhabits the South Atlantic and Gulf States south of the Savannah River and east of the Mississippi... The members of the *tuza* series agree among themselves and differ from the remaining forms of the genus *Geomys* in having longer and more naked tails, and in numerous cranial characters.

tuzzle, variant of TUSSLE.

tuzzy (ˈtʌzɪ). [See TUZ and next, and cf. TUSSY.] (See quot.)

1890 *Sci. Amer.* 1 Mar. 131/3 A ball of horsehair, such as is used by copper plate printers to assist in freeing their hands from ink (they call it a 'tuzzy').

tuzzy-muzzy (ˈtʌzɪˌmʌzɪ), *sb.* (*a.*) Forms: *α.* 5 tusmose, tussemose, 7 tussimussie; *β.* 7 tuzzimussie, 6–8 tuzzie-, tuzzi-, -muzzie, -muzzy, 8–9 tuzzy-muzzy, 20— tussie-mussie. [app. a kind of reduplicated or riming jingle on TUSSY. The early form *tus-* or *tussemose*, with the transitional *tussimussie*, suggest the existence of **tus* or **tusse* in the sense 'cluster or knot of flowers', whence TUSSY.]

A. *sb.* **a.** A bunch or posy of flowers, a nosegay; a garland of flowers. Also *fig.* Revived in 20th cent., usu. in form *tussie-mussie*.

α. *c* **1440** *Promp. Parv.* 494/2 Tyte tust, or tusmose of flowrys or othyr herbys (*S.* tytetuste or tussemose), *olfactorium*. **1629** PARKINSON *Paradisus* 281 A delicate Tussi-mussie, as they call it, or Nosegay.

β. **1585** J. HIGINS *Junius' Nomencl.* 113/2 *Seruia*, a nosegay: a tuzziemuzzie: a sweete posie. **1587** GOLDING *De Mornay* xxiii. (1592) 342 [Apollo] commaunded..to remoue the tuzzimuzzies of flowers from his feete. **1598** FLORIO, *Serta*..a circlet or garland or wreath, a tuzzie-muzzie. **1620** THOMAS *Lat. Dict.*, *Sertum*,..a nosegay, a tuzzimussie. **1629** SYMMER *Spir. Posie* Ep. A ij b, Then shall this Tuzzi-muzzie have its wished and expected smell. **1664** GOULDMAN *Copious Dictionary* (1669) s.v. *Tuttie*, A Tuttie, nosegay, posie or tuzziemuzzie, *fasciculus*. **1706** [see TUTTY *sb.*[2]]. **1958** J. G. CONWAY *Encycl. Flower Arrangement* vi. 104 Tuzzy-muzzy, a small, neat arrangement with flowers in repeated circular lines, edged with foliage or lace. **1960** V. WILLIAMS *Walk Egypt* 180 He gave her a hand bouquet of lemon-colored roses which smelled like lemon too, a sour-sweetness that matched the morning. He said, 'A tussie-mussie... I figured you belonged to have something, a day like this.' **1968** *Herb Grower Mag.* XXI. 1. 1 From a little Tussie-mussie to a formal garden at the White House, the warmth of herbs reaches across the miles. **1973** *New Yorker* 7 Apr. 126/3 (Advt.), Tussie-mussies... Delightful bouquets of fragrance herbs, cooking herbs,..and medicinal herbs. A full-color limited edition portfolio.

b. *dial.* As popular name of particular plants or flowers (see quots.); also, a bur.

1842 PHELPS *Collect. Glouc.* 281 *Tuzzy muzzy*, a burr. **1886** BRITTEN & HOLLAND *Eng. Plant-n.*, Tuzzy muzzy, *Muscari comosum*... *Norf*[*olk*]. **1890** *Gloucester Gloss.* Supp., *Tuzzy-muzzy*, old man's beard; Clematis Vitalba.

†**c.** *transf.* See quots. *slang. Obs.*

1711 E. WARD *Quix.* I. 70 And Salt as Lot's Wife's Tuzzy-muzzy. **1721** BAILEY, *Tuzzimuzzy*,..a jocular Name for the *Pudendum Muliebre*. [Hence in HALLIWELL, and in later Dicts.]

B. *adj.* Dishevelled, ragged, fuzzy. *dial.*

1847–78 HALLIWELL, *Tuzzimuzzy*, rough; ragged; dishevelled.

TV (tiːˈviː). Abbrev. of TELEVISION.

1948 *Fortune* May 82/1 It is not where TV has gone,..but the pace at which it is going that causes all the excitement. **1948** *Time* 25 Oct. 82/2 TV is not only color-blind; its eye is astigmatic. **1957** *Times Lit. Suppl.* 29 Nov. 722/3 He knows 'most of the tricks of popular journalism, films, radio, TV'. **1962** V. NABOKOV *Pale Fire* 35 The gauzy mockingbird.. Returning to her perch—the new TV. **1964** M. ARGYLE *Psychol. & Social Probl.* iv. 47 Is the effect of showing violence in films or on TV to arouse or to satiate aggressive feelings? **1977** *R.A.F. News* 22 June–5 July 2/3 (*heading*) TVs for hospital.

b. Freq. *attrib.* and *Comb.* **TV dinner**, a prepared frozen meal that needs only to be heated and is suitable for eating while watching television (formerly a proprietary name in the U.S.); **TV evangelist** orig. *U.S.* = TELEVANGELIST; also **TV evangelism**.

1948 *Fortune* May 83/1 The average capital investment for a TV station is about $375,000. **1950** 'A. GILBERT' *Is She Dead Too?* vii. 135 That's the best of livin' in a village. It's like livin' on a TV screen. **1953** A. HUXLEY *Let.* 25 Jan. (1969) 663 One must read 100% in order to be able to leave out 99%, as has to be done in this medium and for a TV audience. **1954** TV aerial [see SHOW-OFF *sb.* (*a.*) d]. **1954** *Official Gaz.* (U.S. Patent Office) 27 July 735/2 C. A. Swanson & Sons, Omaha, Nebr... TV Dinner... For frozen Turkey Dinner, Including Turkey, Dressing, Giblet Gravy, Sweet Potatoes, and Green Peas. **1955** *Radio Times* 22 Apr. 39/3 Gilbert Harding's outspoken autobiography.. the frank, personal story of the popular Radio and T.V. personality. **1955** *Times* 9 Aug. 4/5 Mr. Leon Goodman, chairman of T.V. Commercials, Ltd. **1955** H. KURNITZ *Invasion of Privacy* (1956) iii. 26 He's been in two flops on Broadway and in five T.V. shows. **1958** *New Statesman* 5 July 1/2 The argument about the third TV network. **1961** P. FRANKAU *Pen to Paper* 21 '*That's it!*' as the T.V. announcer snaps at the winning point of the tennis match. **1961** *Times* 18 May 9/7 One TV antenna. **1962** L. DEIGHTON *Ipcress File* xvi. 92 A girl featured weekly in a badly made TV series. **1962** N. STREATFEILD *Apple Bough* xv. 216 They went all the way to the T/V studio on a bus. **1963** H. A. HARGREAVES in *New Worlds Science Fiction* Dec. 62 It would have to be a TV satellite. **1964** L. DEIGHTON *Funeral in Berlin* vii. 51 Spectacles swung the TV receiver around so that I couldn't see it. *Ibid.* x. 66 The very same people who made the great little TV film.. paid for by the TV company, N.B.C. **1964** J. MASTERS *Trial at Monomoy* x. 292 TV dinners, and everything quick frozen, dehydrated and prepacked. **1964** M. MCLUHAN *Understanding Media* (1967) I. i. 19 If the TV tube fires the right ammunition at the right people it is good. *Ibid.* II. xiii. 140 The combined radio and TV channels in the United States. *Ibid.* II. xvii. 176 The cartoon is clue to understanding the TV image. *Ibid.* II. xxxi. 334 The TV camera does not have a built-in angle of vision like the movie camera. **1969** TV licence [see *radio licence* s.v. RADIO *sb.* 7]. **1970** KOENIG & DIXON *Children are Watching* (1971) i. 6 Inside the stove glinted four TV dinners.. nested in silver-aluminum trays,.. identical portions of gray pot roast, dinner roll, wrinkled peas and rigid mashed potatoes under foil. *Ibid.* 7 These dinners.. she wheeled across the hall into the TV room. **1974** *Guardian* 23 Mar. 10/6 It was dense, thick, primeval onion soup. But it was not a TV play. **1974** *Broadcast* 11 Nov. 16/3 The bulk of the population.. needs effortless entertainment... The theatre mogul, the film-maker, and now the TV programme producer, have found the truth of this platitude. **1975** D. LODGE *Changing Places* ii. 49 He filled the micro-refrigerator with TV dinners. **1976** B. BOVA *Multiple Man* xix. 209 TV crews were rolling their cameras in. **1976** *Liverpool Echo* 7 Dec. 3/1 The Wirral TV mast saga. For more than two years the B.B.C. have been seeking to erect a 200 ft. mast on Wirral. **1977** *Washington Post* 25 July B1/ Rev. M.G. 'Pat' Robertson has changed the style of TV evangelism. *Ibid.* 29 Apr. B11/3 'Rev. Ike', New York radio and TV evangelist. **1981** HADDEN & SWANN *Prime Time Preachers* i. 5 Jerry Falwell, another TV evangelist, and his Moral Majority showed up in force at the Republican National Convention. **1986** *Time* 17 Feb. 63/3 Powered by TV evangelism, the Christian right 'is destined to become the major social movement in America' during the late 20th century.

tvorog ('tvɔːrɔk). [a. Russ. *tvórog.*] A soft Russian cheese similar to cottage or curd cheese.

1918 DOANE & LAWSON *Varieties of Cheese* (U.S. Dept. Agric. Bull. No. 608) 59 Tworog. This is a sour-milk cheese made in Russia.. on a large scale by Russian farmers. **1960** K. DAVYDOVA *Good Food from Russia* 107 The following recipes have as their main ingredient, tvorog, the Russian version of cottage cheese. *Ibid.* 109 Tvorog Pudding with candied peel. **1973** S. SKIPWITH *Eat Russian* i. 16 Cottage cheese and curd cheese are the nearest equivalent to the Russian Tvorog which is dry but not 'cheesy'. **1981** J. TRENHAILE *Kyril* xxiv. 180 He ate only a biscuit smothered with *tvorog*, the stodgy cottage cheese of the peasants. **1982** L. CHAMBERLAIN *Food & Cooking of Russia* (1983) 245 By Good Friday several pounds of *tvorog* (curd cheese) would have been sitting for at least 24 hours under a wooden press to extract.. the last drops of whey.

twa, OE. and Sc. form of TWO.

twa(a)-gras(s) ('twɑːgrɑːs, -æ-). Also **dwa-, toa-grass.** [f. *umTwa* name used by Bushmen + GRASS *sb.*^{1}] Any of several species of the genus *Aristida*, which includes several tall feathery grasses native to southern Africa.

1857 A. WYLEY *Rep. Min. Struct. Namaqualand* 44 Twa-grass.. grows from two to three feet in height, from a small bushy base... When it is green, oxen, horses, and sheep all thrive upon it. **1896** R. WALLACE *Farming Industries Cape Colony* v. 100 'Twa-gras' is the most abundant grass.. in the Kalahari region. **1897** EDMONDS & MARLOTH *Elem. Bot. S. Afr.* xvii. 185 The Dwa-grass or Toa-grass. **1920** F. C. CORNELL *Glamour of Prospecting* xv. 246 We lit fires of dry *toa* grass. **1946** L. G. GREEN *So Few are Free* I. x. 137, I can hear the 'twaa grass' crackling in the wind. **1949** K. L. SIMMS *Sun-Drenched Veld* i. 10 Because they [*sc.* plains] are thickly peppered with drought-resisting bushes and tufts of toa grass, they constitute wonderful ranching country. **1974** *Stand. Encycl. S. Afr.* X. 367/1 In the times of occasional rain Bushman grass and twa grass.. will spring up.

twachel, var. TWATCHEL.

twachylle, obs. f. TWITCHEL^1, passage.

Twaddell ('twɒd(ə)l). Also **Twaddel, Twaddle.** [Short for *Twaddell's hydrometer*, from the name of the inventor.] A form of hydrometer or hydrometric scale in which 200 degrees correspond to a unit of specific gravity, that of distilled water being denoted by zero. Also *attrib.*

1853 URE *Dict. Arts* (ed. 4) II. 828 The patentee employs diluted sulphuric acid, at 105° Twaddle. **1860** O'NEILL *Chem. Calico Print.* etc. 11 To obtain the value of any degree of Twaddle, it must be multiplied by five, and the product added to 1,000. *Ibid.* 12 The specific gravity and the Twaddle value of a degree of Beaumé. **1873** E. SPON *Workshop Receipts* Ser. I. 30/1 A hot solution of nitro-sulphate of iron, 5° Twaddle, 150° Fahrenheit.

†'**twadding,** *adv. Obs. rare*$^{-1}$. [Of obscure origin: cf. TWAGGER.] Abundantly (fat).

1657 G. THORNLEY *Daphnis & Chloe* 175 Nor had the Wolf raven'd away so much as one [goat], and they were all more twadding fat then the very sheep.

twaddle ('twɒd(ə)l), *sb.* (*a.*) [Origin obscure: not found *a* 1780; perh. an alteration of the earlier TWATTLE (known as *vb.* from 1573, as *sb.* from 1639; in *twittle-twattle* from *c* 1550).]

1. Senseless, silly, or trifling talk or writing; empty verbosity; dull and trashy statement or discourse; empty commonplace; prosy nonsense.

1782 in *Mrs. Delany's Life & Corr.* Ser. II. (1862) III. 125 Fanny Burney has taken possession of the ear of those who found their amusement in reading her twaddle (that piece of old fashioned slang I should not have dared to write or utter, within hearing of my dear mother). **1825** SCOTT *Jrnl.* 29 Nov., A letter.. quoting the twaddle of some old woman. **1851** THACKERAY *Eng. Hum.* v, Pouring out endless volumes of sentimental twaddle. **1878** M. C. JACKSON *Chaperon's Cares* II. xii. 145 The odious small-talk and twaddle he was compelled to hear. *Ibid.* xx. 243 No need to talk a lot of twaddle and nonsense to a woman with brains. **1906** SIR F. TREVES *Highways Dorset* xviii. 291 He was guided by personal.. experience, and not by the twaddle of theorists.

b. In extended sense: Something trashy or worthless; rubbish.

1786 *Lounger* (1787) II. 197 The Ton of London is mere Twaddle,.. the only right Ton is to be found in Paris. **1842** BARHAM *Ingol. Leg.* Ser. II. *Babes in Wood*, Greek and Latin old twaddle I call!

†**2.** (See quots. and BORE *sb.*^{2} I.) *Obs. slang.*

1785 *European Mag.* Dec. 473/2 The favourite phrases fall, and are no more, The Rage, the Thing, the Twaddle, and the Bore. **1785** GROSE *Dict. Vulg. Tongue* Pref. 2 The fashionable words, or favourite expressions of the day,.. vanish without leaving a trace behind, such were the late fashionable words, a Bore and a Twaddle, among the great vulgar. **1796** *Ibid.* (ed. 3), *Twaddle*, perplexity, confusion, or anything else: a fashionable term that for a while succeeded that of *bore*.

†**3.** A person who talks or writes twaddle; a twaddler. *Obs.*

1802 MRS. J. WEST *Infidel Father* II. 100 [He] acknowledged himself to be.. bored by detestable twaddles. **1813** MOORE *Post-bag* ii. 29 He thinks.. the imagination.. Could only enter in the noddles Of dull and ledger-keeping twaddles. **1830** MACAULAY *Ess., R. Montgomery's Poems* (1887) 142 A respectable and pious gentleman, whose principal fault is that he is something of a twaddle. *a* **1838** C. MORRIS *Lyra Urban.* (1840) II. 187, I fear I'm becoming a twaddle.

4. *attrib.* or *adj.* Of the nature of twaddle; empty and prosy; in quot. 1830, feeble.

1830 COL. HAWKER *Diary* (1893) II. 20 The difference between the twaddle and the vigorous in shooting. **1845** CARLYLE *Cromwell* (1871) V. 114 High Art paintings, gilt frames, and twaddle criticisms. **1865** TROLLOPE *Belton Est.* v, I hate the twaddle talk of love. **1889** GRETTON *Memory's Harkb.* 219 Twaddle truisms instead of vital truths.

Hence '**twaddlesome** *a.*, full of or addicted to twaddle; also (*nonce-wds.*) '**twaddledom**, the realm of twaddle, the habit of uttering twaddle; '**twaddleize** *v.*, *trans.* to reduce to twaddle.

1837 *Tait's Mag.* IV. 454 The *twaddledom of old age. **1850** *Ibid.* XVII. 547/1 Dulling his [Burns's] humour, prosefying his poetry, and *twaddleising his vigour. **1865** *Pall Mall G.* 11 Nov. 10 A grim villain immensely stupid, and.. a virtuous duke immensely *twaddlesome. **1892** G. MEREDITH *Let.* 25 Apr. (1970) II. 1080 *Dorothy Penrose*, an enormous bulk, is uninterruptedly twaddlesome. **1966** K. S. SORABJI in 'H. MacDiarmid' *Company I've Kept* ii. 65 The twaddlesome sentimentalities about trusting the ultimate judgement and good sense of the public.

Twaddle, var. TWADDELL.

'**twaddle,** *v.*^{1} [f. TWADDLE *sb.*; or perh. altered, like it, from TWATTLE *v.*]

1. *intr.* To utter twaddle; to talk or write in a silly, empty, or trashy style.

1825 J. WILSON *Noct. Ambr.* Wks. 1855 I. 15 Pope.. beats them hollow. Catch him twaddling. **1831** SCOTT *Jrnl.* 14 Feb., I am afraid I am twaddling. **1862** THACKERAY *Round. Papers, Dessein's*, 'What is that old fellow twaddlin' about?' cries Brummel.

2. *trans.* To utter as twaddle, or in a trashy and prosy way.

1837 PRESCOTT in Ticknor *Life* (1864) 271 *note*, They twaddle out their humour as if they were afraid of its biting too hard. **1850** CARLYLE *Latter-d. Pamph.* viii. (1872) 273 You are not bound to.. twaddle pretended raptures. **1900** *Westm. Gaz.* 19 Jan. 7/1 Instead of twaddling out platitudes.

b. with *away*: To spend or pass in empty talk.

1826 SCOTT *Jrnl.* 11 Apr., We twaddled away the evening well enough.

†'**twaddle,** *v.*^{2} *Obs. rare*$^{-1}$. [Cf. prec. and TWIDDLE *v.*^{1}] *intr.* To trifle or play *with.*

1797 MRS. M. ROBINSON *Walsingham* IV. 3, I hate twaddling with other people's happiness.

'**twaddle,** *v.*^{3} Chiefly *dial.* [Cf. WADDLE *v.*, and dial. *quaddle* in similar sense.] *intr.* 'To walk with a feeble, uncertain gait' (*E.D.D.*). So **twaddle-toed** *a.*

1823 in *Spirit Pub. Jrnls.* 43 The unfortunate gentleman had walked, or rather twaddled to the office in a pair of loose slippers. **1907** *Daily News* 20 Mar. 6 Greenfinches.. have an unmistakable twaddle-toed walk that.. makes them look like parrots.

twaddler ('twɒdlə(r)). Also **twadler.** [f. TWADDLE *sb.* or *v.*^{1} + -ER^1.] One who twaddles; one who talks or writes twaddle.

1787 DUKE OF RUTLAND in *14th Rep. Hist. MSS. Comm.* App. I. 395 Pray be particularly attentive to them (even tho' they be twaddlers). **1837** DICKENS *Pickw.* li, A laugh at the style of this ungrammatical twaddler. **1882** MISS BRADDON *Mt. Royal* x, One of your sickly, sentimental twaddlers.

twaddling ('twɒdlɪŋ), *ppl. a.* [f. TWADDLE *sb.* or *v.*^{1} + -ING^2.]

1. Having the character of twaddle; empty and prosy; rubbishy.

1804 *Edin. Rev.* Jan. 448 And this *twaddling* stuff is supposed to be spoken by John of Gaunt! **1832** LADY GRANVILLE *Lett.* 8 Sept. (1894) II. 132 Dearest sis, what a twaddling letter this is. **1858** *Ecclesiologist* XIX. 38 The twaddling derivation of Pointed architecture from interlacing boughs. **1859** GEO. ELIOT *A. Bede* v, It's a volume of poems,.. most of them seem to be twaddling stuff.

b. Petty, paltry, trifling, insignificant: = TWATTLING *ppl. a.* 3. *rare*$^{-1}$.

1852 W. C. BALDWIN *Afr. Hunting* 12 Jan. (1863) 8 A little twaddling weapon.

2. Uttering or addicted to talking twaddle.

1826 F. REYNOLDS *Life & Times* II. 92 [I] heard an old twaddling special pleader. **1862** SHIRLEY *Nugæ Crit.* xi. 470 The position.. assumed.. by twaddling doctrinaires, and political pedants.

twaddly ('twɒdlɪ), *a.* [f. TWADDLE *sb.* + -Y.] Characterized by, or of the nature of, twaddle.

1841 *Fraser's Mag.* XXIII. 273 [The dialogue] sounds rather twaddly. **1879** MISS BRADDON *Clov. Foot* xxx, When a mother gets to the elderly and twaddly age,.. one can't feel poetical about her.

twae, Sc. dial. form of TWO.

twafald, twae-, obs. and Sc. ff. TWOFOLD.

†**twag.** *Cant. Obs.* (See quot.)

1592 GREENE *Conny-Catching* III. C, Their word for knowing ech other, as is said, was *Quest*, and this villaines comfortable newes to them, was *Twag*, signifying he had sped.

twagger ('twægə(r)). *dial.* [Cf. QUAG *v.*^{1} and TWADDING *adv.*] A (? big or fat) lamb.

1599 PEELE *Arraignm. Paris* I. i, I have brought a twagger for the nones, A bunting lamb;.. my cunning much I miss, If ever Pan felt fatter lamb than this. *c* **1900** in *Eng. Dial. Dict.* (West Sussex).

†**twail, twayle.** *Obs. rare*$^{-1}$. [app. a. F. *toile* (*d'araignée*) spider's web:—L. *tēla* web, cloth.] A spider's web.

1608 TOPSELL *Serpents* 273 They [spiders] labour to, and doe prouide Gainst winds and things that break their twayles [*ed.* **1658** twails] That bands from tacklings may not slyde When greater strength doth them assayle.

twaile, obs. form of TOWEL.

twain (tweɪn), *numeral a.* and *sb. arch.* Forms: 1 **twœȝen, tueȝen,** 1–2 **tweȝen, twæȝen,** 2 **tweiȝen,** 2–3 **tweien,** 3 **tweyen;** 2–5 **twein,** 3–5 **tweyne, tweine, twene,** (4 **tweiyne, tuueine**), 4–5 **tweyn,** 5 **twayne;** 4 **tuayn, tuain,** 4–6 **twayne** (5 **tueyne, thwayne**), 5–6 **twayn,** 6 *Sc.* **twane,** 6–7 **twaine,** (7 *Sc.* **tuaine**), 6– **twain.** [The modern representative of OE. *twéȝen*, the nom. and acc. masc. of the numeral of which the fem. and neuter *twá, tú*, remain as TWO (q.v.). It corresponds to OFris. *twêne, twên* (mod. Fris. dial. *tween, twein, twain*), OS. *twêna, twêne*, OHG. and MHG. *zwêne* (archaic Ger. *zween*). In ME. *twain* ceased to be confined to the masc., and became merely a secondary form of *two*, used esp. when the numeral followed the sb. Its use in the Bible of 1611 and in the Marriage Service, and its value as a rime-word, have contributed to its retention as an archaic and poetic synonym of *two*. See also the apocopate form TWAY; and, for the inflexions, TWO.]

A. Illustration of Forms.

c **725** *Corpus Gloss.* (O.E.T.) 1510 *Passus*, faeðm *vel* tueȝen stridi. *a* **800** *Casket* I in *O.E. Texts* 127 Twœȝen ȝibro-þæra, fœddæ hiæ uylif in Romæcæstri. *a* **900** *O.E. Chron.* an. 822 Her tueȝen [*Laud MS.* twæȝen] aldormen wurdon ofslæȝene. *c* **1000** ÆLFRIC *Gen.* xlii. 37 Ic hæbbe tweȝen suna. *c* **1160** *Hatton Gosp.* Matt. xviii. 20 Ðær tweiȝen [*Ags. G.* tweȝen] oððe þreo synden on minen namen ȝegadered. *c* **1175** *12th c. Hom.* (Bodley) 86 Tweȝen þisseræ dæle habbæð deor & nyten. *c* **1175** *Lamb. Hom.* 41 Heo tweien eoden et sume time in to helle. *Ibid.* 85 He haueð.. þa twein peneȝes. *c* **1200** *Trin. Coll. Hom.* 5 Tweien oðer tocumes of ure helende. *c* **1290** *S. Eng. Leg.* I. 276/168 Tweyen faire wommen. *a* **1325** *MS. Rawl. B.* 520 lf. 81 Noȝt.. bi tuueine assoines a sullen sollemnen suuche ane assoine. *c* **1380** WYCLIF *Sel. Wks.* III. 194 And þei schullen be tweiyne in o flesch. *c* **1385** CHAUCER *L.G.W.* 1963 (*Ariadne*) It was longynge to the doughteren tweyne. **1387** TREVISA *Higden* (Rolls) VIII. 151 By twene [*v.r.* tweye] burgeys of Londoun. *c* **1400** *Gamelyn* 734 (Harl. MS.) To his tweyne bretheren anon-right he cam. **1423** JAS. I *Kingis Q.* xlii, With.. wommen tueyne. *c* **1425** *Cursor M.* 523 (Trin.) [Þe] heed wiþynne haþ eȝen tweyn [*Cott., Gött.* tuin; *F.* twyn; *rime* certeyn]. *c* **1440** *Generydes* 155 It was be twix them thwayne. *c* **1450** *Godstow Reg.* 193 Rent, to be paid.. at twayne termes in the yere. **1503** DUNBAR *Thistle & Rose* 172 Haill, Roiss, both reid and quhyt,.. of michty cullouris twane. **1511–12**

Act 3 Hen. VIII, c. 23 §5 Lettres..to twayn of his honourable Conseillours. **1542** UDALL *Erasm. Apoph.* 165 The vertues..of bothe twain. **1548** FORREST *Pleas. Poesye* 61 b, Wee shall deuyde it into lessons twayne. **1675** HOBBES *Odyssey* IV. 470 But of the Princes lost are only twain. **1784** COWPER *Task* I. 77 The soft settee..received, United yet divided, twain at once. **1897** MAY KENDALL in *Longm. Mag.* Aug. 340 Forth went..Soldiers twain.

β. Abnormal genitive pl.: ***her tweyners*** = of them two. (After *alleris, altheris, botheris*: see ALL D. 4, BOTH A. 4 b.)

c **1450** *Cov. Myst.* (Shaks. Soc.) 125 And of her tweyners metyng Here gynnyth the proces.

B. Signification. = TWO. **I.** *adj.*

1. In concord with a sb., etc. **a.** Preceding the sb. Now *rare*.

c **725**- [see A.]. *c* **1205** LAY. 8144 þeos tweien cnihtes. *Ibid.* 12255 Twene ibroðeren. *c* **1380** WYCLIF *Sel. Wks.* III. 310 Whanne tweyne horis stryvede whos was þe child. **1382** *Ibid.* 512 A þousand and tweyn hundrid ȝeer. **1432–50** tr. *Higden* (Rolls) I. 167 There be tweyne Mauritanyes, that firste is Mauritany Cesariense, whiche hathe at the este of hit Numidia. *a* **1450** *Knt. de la Tour* (1906) 162 It might be proued..by tweyn witnessis. *c* **1460** *Wisdom* 1077 in *Macro Plays* 71 In twayn myghtys of my soule I the offendyde. **1554** CDL. POLE in *Eng. Hist. Rev.* July (1913) 528, I have recevyd twayne yowr lettres. **1870** R. BUCHANAN *Bk. Orm* IV. 89 Thy blue eyes twain stars. **1871** F. W. NEWMAN *Iliad* XIII. 201 The twain full arm'd Aiantes.

b. *poet.* Following the sb.

Chiefly for the sake of a rime.

13.. *Cursor M.* 4032 þir breþer tuain þam tok to red. *c* **1330** R. BRUNNE *Chron.* (1810) 106 Godefrey of Louayn,.. Bi messengers tuayn sent to kyng Henry, For his douhter Adelayn. *c* **1386** CHAUCER *Frankl. T.* 334 Let this flod enduren yeres twaine. *c* **1440** *R. Gloucester's Chron.* 1099 þo adde king lud..ȝonge sones tueie [*MS.* δ tweyne]. *c* **1440** *Pallad. on Husb.* I. 671 On cok for hennys tweyne. **1513** BRADSHAW *St. Werburge* I. 174 Whylom dyuyded in sondry kyngdomes twayne. *c* **1560** A. SCOTT *Poems* (S.T.S.) xxiii. 26 Hir bricht fair ene twane. **1700** DRYDEN *Cock & Fox* 717 The trembling widow, and her daughters twain. **1724** SWIFT *To Delany* Wks. 1755 IV. I. 46 Where we find the members twain. **1782** COWPER *Gilpin* 123 The bottles twain ..Were shatter'd at a blow. **1843** NEALE *Hymns for Sick* (1863) 42 He loved the sisters twain. **1846** KEBLE *Lyra Innoc.* (1873) 147 Five loaves hath he, And fishes twain. **1860** LONGF. *Wayside Inn, Saga K. Olaf* IV. 23 She had given the ring to her goldsmiths twain, Who smiled, as they handed it back again. **1871** R. ELLIS *Catullus* lxxviii. 1, Brothers twain has Gallus.

2. a. Absolutely with ellipsis of sb., or following a pronoun or pronominal adjective.

c **1000** *Ags. Gosp.* Matt. xviii. 20 ȝyf tweȝen of eow ȝeþwæriað..be ælcum þinge. *c* **1160**, *c* **1175** [see A.]. *c* **1275** *Passion of Our Lord* 243 in *O.E. Misc.* 44 þer arysen tweyne and bigunne to speke. *c* **1350** *Will. Palerne* 2507 Se what sorwe he suffres to saue vs tweine! **1401** *Pol. Poems* (Rolls) II. 27 What betokeneth that ye goe tweine and tweine togither? **1470–85** MALORY *Arthur* II. x. 87 Of the tweyne he had leuer kyng Lotte had be slayne than kynge Arthur. **1526** *Pilgr. Perf.* (W. de W. 1531) 143, I shall wryte a worde or twayne. **1596** *Edward III*, IV. v. 82 Which of these twaine is greater infamie? **1610** SHAKS. *Temp.* I. ii. 438 All his Lords, the Duke of Millaine And his braue sonne, being twaine. **1657** HOWELL *Londinop.* 322 They had six.. Meeting places,..twain in Bridge Street,..twain in Old Fish Street, and twain in Stock-Fishmonger Row. **1824** SCOTT *Redgauntlet* Let. vii, We will pray him..to tarry a day or twain. **1847** TENNYSON *Princ.* VII. 271 These twain..Sit side by side. **1881** —— *Cup* II. i. 37 That the world may know You twain are reconciled.

b. ***in (†on) twain***: into two parts or pieces, in two, asunder.

1398 TREVISA *Barth. De P.R.* III. ix. (1495) 54 The vertue of apprehendynge..is departed in tweyne. **1415** *E.E. Wills* (1882) 23 Y wolle hit be parted on tweyne. *c* **1430** *Hymns Virg.* (1867) 58 Or þei be fulli partide on tweyne. *c* **1440** *Generydes* 2632 With that stroke he brake his sheld on twayn. **1509** HAWES *Past. Pleas.* xxxviii. (Percy Soc.) 197, I have thought long Sithen the time that we parted in twayne. **1598** *Mucedorus* II. iv. 77 To cut in twaine the twisted thread. **1697** DRYDEN *Virg. Georg.* IV. 202 Cold Winter split the Rocks in twain. **1798** SOPH. LEE *Canterb. T., Yng. Lady's T.* II. 145 The marble fountain..was cloven in twain. *a* **1862** BUCKLE *Misc. Wks.* (1872) I. 84 The nation was..severed in twain by..religious faction.

†c. *U.S. Naut.* Two fathoms. Esp. in phr. ***mark twain***, the two fathom mark on a sounding-line. Cf. MARK *sb.*[1] 12 b. *Obs.*

1799 J. W. RUSSELL in R. D. Paine *Romance Old Time Shipmaster* (1907) iii. 43 The man in the chains suddenly sung out 'quarter less twain', and we instantly struck. **1863** 'MARK TWAIN' in A. B. Paine *Mark Twain* (1912) I. xl. 221, I want to sign my articles..'Mark Twain'. It is an old river term, a leads-man's call, signifying two fathoms—twelve feet. **1947** E. M. MACK *Mark Twain in Nevada* xv. 228 How many times when he was on the River had he heard the leadsman..call out, 'By the mark, twain!'

3. With special connotations. (Cf. ONE III.) **a.** Separate, parted asunder; disunited, estranged, at variance. (Only in predicate.)

c **1600** SHAKS. *Sonn.* xxxvi, We two must be twaine, Although our vndeuided loues are one. **1611** SIR W. MURE *Misc. Poems* iv. 28 ȝit in a breist sall both our herts no more at all be tuaine. **1619** DRAYTON *Idea* ix, Reason and I (you must conceive) are twaine. **1671** MILTON *Samson* 929 Thou and I long since are twain. **1844** TALFOURD *Athenian Capt.* IV. i, Henceforth we are twain.

b. Consisting of two parts or elements; double, twofold. *rare.*

1398 TREVISA *Barth. De P.R.* V. i. (1495) f viij/2 A chylde borne, y[t] was tweyne in y[e] ouer partye & one in the nether partye. **1870** MORRIS *Earthly Par.* III. IV. 132 Hope and shame, Twain help,..unto her spirit came.

II. *sb.*

†1. The abstract number two. *Obs.*

1398 TREVISA *Barth. De P.R.* XIX. cxxiii. (1495) mm iij b/1 Superfluus is the nombre y[t] hath partyes that maketh a greter nombre than itself:..one, tweyne, thre [etc.]. *c* **1425** *Craft of Nombrynge* (E.E.T.S.) 9 þou maynst not draw sex out of 2. But þou mayst draw 2 out of sex. And þou maiste draw twene out of twene. *c* **1483** CAXTON *Dialogues* x. 51/6 *Ung, deux, trois*, one, tweyne, thre.

2. A group of two; a pair, couple.

1607 TOPSELL *Four-f. Beasts* (1658) 555 Horns which some men guess to be of the Unicorns..because they are found several, never by twains. **1610** SHAKS. *Temp.* IV. i. 104 To blesse this twaine, that they may prosperous be. **1816** BYRON *Let. to Moore* 24 Dec., You received my other twain of letters. **1843** S. BAMFORD *Homely Rhymes* etc. (1864) 71 The twain of young lovers have tarried behind.

3. *pl.* Twins. *dial.*

1580 HOLLYBAND *Treas. Fr. Tong, Besson*, twaines. **1897** J. HAMMOND *Cornish Parish* ix. 199, I remark in 1699 three entries of 'twains' out of 76 births. *Ibid.* xix. 344 Instead of 'twins', [we say] 'two twains'.

III. *Comb.*: **twain-cloud**, a name for the cumulostratus; **† twain-edged** *a.* = TWO-EDGED.

1382 WYCLIF *Heb.* iv. 12 The word of God is..more able for to perse than al tweyne eggid swerd. **1823** T. FORSTER *Res. Atmospheric Phenomena* i. §7. (ed. 3) 20 Of the Cumulostratus or Twaincloud. **1844** STEPHENS *Bk. Farm* I. 246 Why..the heaped stratus [should be called] the twain-cloud is by no means obvious, unless..[as] being composed of two clouds,..but, on the same principle, the cirro-cumulus, and the cirro-stratus and the cumulo-stratus may be termed twain-clouds.

† twain, *v. Obs.* [f. TWAIN *a.* or *sb.*] *trans.* To part or divide in twain; to put apart, separate.

13.. *E.E. Allit. P.* A. 251 Fro we in twynne wern towen & twayned, I haf ben a Ioylez Iuelere. **15..** *Chester Pl.* (Shaks. Soc.) I. 20 (Add. MS.) Nowe will I make the firmamente,..For to be a devidente To twayne [*Harl. MS. 2124* twyne] the watters. *Ibid.* II. 151 My people of Jewes he wulde twayne. ?**17..** *Clerk Saunders* xii. in Child *Ballads* (1886) II. 159 It wear great sin this twa to twain. **1878** B. TAYLOR *Deukalion* III. vi, Who twains What once was one. **1900** CROCKETT *Joan Sw. Hand* xxxix, You may slay my husband, but he is mine still. You cannot twain our souls.

b. *intr.* for *refl.* or *pass.* To separate.

15.. *Chester Pl.* (Shaks. Soc.) I. 18 (Add. MS.) Lightnes and darcknes, I byde you tweyne [*Harl. MS. 2124* twyn; *rimes* begin, myn, in].

Twainian ('tweɪnɪən), *a.* [f. the name of 'Mark *Twain*' (S. L. Clemens), American writer (1835–1910) + -IAN.] Of, pertaining to, or characteristic of 'Mark Twain' or his work.

1938 *Times Lit. Suppl.* 27 Aug. 551/4 When stimulated by the potentialities of human sacrifice or the vapourings of a politician, it [*sc.* the pen] moves to a Twainian climax. **1968** *Word Study* Feb. 2/1 Here is such a Twainian reference, appearing in the late novel *The American Claimant*. **1977** *Time* 28 Feb. 53/1 They contain their share of Twainian 'stretchers', or exaggerations.

twait, var. of THWAIT(E; obs. f. TWAT.

twait, twaite (tweɪt). *local.* Forms: 7 **tweat, thwait**, 9 **twayt, thwaite**, 8- **twait, twaite.** [Origin not ascertained.] A European species of shad, *Alosa finta*. Also attrib. ***twait shad.***

1613 J. DENNYS *Secr. Angling* II. xlii, The Shad..The Bocher sweet, the pleasant Flounder thin, The Peele, the Tweat, the Botling, and the rest. *c* **1640** J. SMYTH *Lives Berkeleys* (1885) III. 319, 53. sorts of sea fish... The turbut, Lamprey, Lamperne, Shad, tweat. **1688** R. HOLME *Armoury* II. 325/1 The Shad, Thwait, Plaice, and Flou[n]der have the greatest love for Salt, or Brackish Waters, which ebb and flow. **1769** PENNANT *Zool.* III. 298 The variety [of the Shad] called near Gloucester the Twaite. **1882** *Standard* 2 Mar. 2/8 Two species which ascend certain streams..about the month of May—..the Twait shad and the Allice shad. **1904** GALLICHAN *Fishing Spain* 168 The two kinds of shad of our coast are known as the twaite and the allice.

twal(l, twalf, Sc. and obs. ff. TWELVE.

twalicht, obs. Sc. f. TWILIGHT.

twalt, twalue: see TWELFTH, TWELVE.

Twana ('twɑːnə). [ad. Twana *tuwáduxq*, in an earlier pronunciation that had *n* for *d*.] **1.** A Salishan people of western Washington; a member of this people. Also *attrib.* Cf. SALISH, SALISHAN.

1838 J. DOUGLAS *Let.* 18 Oct. in E. E. Rich *McLoughlin's Fort Vancouver Lett. 1825–38* (1941) 262 [*in a list*] Too a nook. **1889** M. EELLS in *Ann. Rep. Board of Regents Smithsonian Inst. 1887* 605 The name of the Twanas is spelled Too-au-hooch, in their treaty. The Klallams pronounce it Tu-an'-hu. The Twanas say Tu-ád-hu... These various pronunciations have been shortened into Twana, now used in all governmental reports. It is said to mean a portage, and to be derived from the portage between the head of Hood's Canal and the main waters of the Sound, where the Indian, by carrying his canoe 3 miles, avoids rowing around a peninsula 50 miles long. **1960** W. W. ELMENDORF in *Research Stud.* (Washington State Univ.) Sept. Monogr. Suppl. No. 2. 281 Few non-Twana cared to learn the Twana language. **1978** *Amer. Poetry Rev.* Sept./Oct. 19/1 The Twana of Puget Sound maintained that if a woman in seclusion touched her head with her fingers, it would at once rot away.

2. The language of this people. Also *attrib.*

1886 M. EELLS *Ten Yrs. Missionary Work* vi. 34 The Twana language..is said to be so difficult to learn that no intelligent Indian advised me to learn it. *Ibid.* 37 We have often sung in English, Chinook jargon, Twana, and Nisgually, on the same Sabbath. **1960** W. W. ELMENDORF in *Research Stud.* (Washington State Univ.) Sept. Monogr. Suppl. No. 2. 280 Twana seems a unique case among all Coast Salishan tongues in its features of areally simple distribution restricted to a single inlet and its fresh-water drainage, and very slight heterogeneity of dialects. **1971** *Language* XLVII. 844 Twana (Salish, Puget Sound area) uses duplication of the root vowel.

twancle, obs. f. TWANGLE *v.*

twane, obs. Sc. pa. t. of TWINE *v.*[1]; obs. f. TWAIN.

twang (twæŋ), *sb.*[1] Also 6 **twange, twangue.** [Echoic: the *tw-* element expresses the sound or noise of the twitching or plucking, the *-ang* element the ringing or resonance.]

1. A vocal imitation of the resonant sound produced when a tense string is sharply plucked or suddenly released; used as interjection or adverb, e.g. ***to cry twang, twang goes the bow.*** Also extended, ***† twangledom twang*** (*obs.*). Cf. TANG *sb.*[2] b.

a **1553** UDALL *Royster D.* II. i. (Arb.) 32 Then vp to our lute at midnight, twangledome twang, Then twang with our sonets, and twang with our dumps. **1596** NASHE *Saffron-Walden* Wks. (Grosart) III. 101 He..made Powles Church-yard resound, or crie twang againe, with foure notable famous Letters. **1600** DEKKER *Shoemaker's Holiday* III. iv, Ile fill your bellies with good cheare til they crie twang. *c* **1720** PRIOR *Advice of Venus* 4 Twang goes the bow, my Girls, have at your hearts. *a* **1741** *Robin Hood & Ranger* ix. in Child *Ballads* (1888) III. 153/1 He made his broad weapon cry twang. **1881** BESANT & RICE *Chapl. of Fleet* II. 80 Twang, twang, twang, went the fiddles.

b. A sound of the above character; also, any sharp ringing sound resembling this. In quot. 1565 *fig.*

1565 T. STAPLETON *Fortr. Faith* 8 To go to the matter alleaged directly without idle twanges. **1567** DRANT *Horace, Art Poetry* B iij, With twang of harp to stir the stones. **1594** NASHE *Unfort. Trav.* Wks. (Grosart) V. 159 None of them could make the cord come aloft with a twange halfe like him. *c* **1611** CHAPMAN *Iliad* IV. 143 The sinew forged string Did giue a mightie twang; and forth, the eager shaft did sing. **1728** POPE *Dunc.* II. 254 So swells each wind-pipe; ass intones to ass, Harmonic twang of leather, horn, and brass. **1779** WARNER in Jesse *Selwyn & Contemp.* (1844) IV. 133 The last twang of the postman's bell. **1804** J. GRAHAME *Sabbath* (1808) 65 The buzz..of moss-entangled bee, That, soon as loosed, booms with full twang away. **1853** KANE *Grinnell Exp.* xxiv. (1856) 196 The twang of a bow-string. **1858** R. S. SURTEES *Ask Mamma* li, A twang of the horn. *fig.* **1663** COWLEY *Cutter Coleman St.* V. xiii, There should ha' been..a lusty Cudgeling [at the end of the farce] to make it come off smartly, with a Twang at the Tail.

c. *transf.* and *fig.* Ringing sound or tone.

1646 G. DANIEL *Poems* Wks. (Grosart) I. 89 When to the Twang of meeter, Poesie Shall fall to Sordid Groomes. *a* **1680** BUTLER *Elephant in Moon* II. 181 Transported with the Twang Of his own Elocution. **1714** R. FIDDES *Pract. Disc.* II. 345 Great things have been done by the mere twang of two or three good words. **1825** T. HOOK *Sayings* Ser. II. *Passion & Princ.* ix. III. 168 His father-in-law..had just pitched his voice to the true poetical twang.

2. a. The modification of vocal sound by its passage through the nose; nasal intonation, as formerly attributed to the Puritans; now esp. as characterizing the pronunciation of an individual, a country, or locality. More fully ***nasal twang, twang of the nose.***

1661 SOUTH *Serm., Tit.* ii. 15 (1715) I. 201 To make.. incoherent Stuff (seasoned with Twang and Tautology) pass for high Rhetorick, and moving Preaching. **1663** BUTLER *Hud.* I. III. 1157 To find in lines of Beard and Face, The Physiognomy of Grace; And by the sound and twang of Nose, If all be sound within disclose. **1704** SWIFT *Mech. Operat. Spirit* Misc. (1711) 300 By this Method the Twang of the Nose becomes perfectly to resemble the Snuffle of the Bag-pipe. **1784** COWPER *Task* II. 436 Odious as the nasal twang Heard at conventicle. **1839** SYD. SMITH *Mem. & Lett.* (1855) II. ccccxv, She..has the true Kentucky twang through the nose, converting that promontory into an organ of speech. **1877** SWEET *Handbk. Phonetics* 8 Many speakers pronounce all their vowels with imperfect closure of the nose passage, which gives their pronunciation the so-called 'nasal twang'. **1902** R. BAGOT *Donna Diana* ii, A wealthy American widow, the owner of a pronounced twang.

b. A distinctive manner of pronunciation or intonation differing from that usual, or regarded as the standard, in a country; esp. one associated with a particular district or locality.

In some of the earlier instances the fig. notion of 'a smack' is perhaps intended: cf. TWANG *sb.*[2] 2.

1697 BENTLEY *Phal.* (1699) 313 Phalaris..must needs, for that reason, have a twang of their Dialect. **1705** ELSTOB in Hearne *Collect.* 30 Nov. (O.H.S.) I. 109 I'll make you Master of ye Gallick Twang. **1706** PHILLIPS (ed. Kersey), *Twang*,..an ill sound in one's Pronunciation. **1707** FARQUHAR *Beaux Strat.* III. ii, You talk very good English, but you have a mighty Twang of the Foreigner. **1725** tr. *Dupin's Eccl. Hist. 17th C.* I. II. iii. 35 His Italian has a twang of the Country in which he liv'd. **1736** DRAKE *Eboracum* I. vii. 242 The broad open accent, and twang, of the more northern [people]. **1781** MME. D'ARBLAY *Diary* Aug., The Hibernian twang of his pronunciation. **1822** SCOTT *Nigel* ii, His voice had a twang in it. **1852** THACKERAY *Esmond* III. v, A grating voice that had an Irish twang. *Ibid.* viii, This family..spoke French with the twang which the Flemings use. **1855** BAIN *Senses & Int.* III. ii. §19 (1864) 485 By 'accent' I understand that indescribable accompaniment with the voice, termed also 'twang' or 'brogue'..which constitutes the indelible distinction between English, Irish, Scotch, Americans, French, &c. **1867** MISS BRADDON *Aur. Floyd* xxx, They talked with an honest northern twang.

1883 *Gd. Words* 12 You must not be too near them, or you will hear the Cockney twang.

3. *transf.* A ringing or resounding blow. Cf. TWANK *v. rare.*

1712 STEELE *Spect.* No. 504 ¶ 1 These can slap you on the back unawares,.. ask you how you do with a twang on your shoulders. **1843** LYTTON *Last Bar.* I. i, The leathern gauntlet that protected the arm from the painful twang of the string.

4. *transf.* A sharp pluck or twitch; a tweak; also, the effect of this: a twinge, a sharp pang. Now *dial.*

1720 *Lett. Lond. Jrnl.* (1721) 29 A Kick in the Breech, or a Twang by the Nose. **1723** RAMSAY *Fair Assembly* xvi, 'T wad gi'e your hearts a twang! **1728** —— *To G. Drummond* ix, Few twangs of guilt they feel. **1789** BURNS *To the Toothache* i, Your venom'd stang, That shoots my tortur'd gums alang; And thro' my lugs gies monie a twang. **1825** BROCKETT *N.C. Words*, *Twang*, a quick pull, a tweak—also pain. **1852** *Tomlinson's Cycl. Usef. Arts* (1866) I. 836/1 He then.. gives repeated and sudden twangs to the string [in bowing furs for hats].

twang, *sb.*^{2} [Alteration of TANG *sb.*^{1}; but often confused or associated with TWANG *sb.*^{1}]

1. A penetrating or persisting taste, flavour, or odour, usually disagreeable: = TANG *sb.*^{1} 5.

1611 COTGR., *Deboire*, an after taste, ill smacke, or twang, which an vnsauorie thing leaues behind in the mouth. **1670** W. SIMPSON *Hydrol. Ess.* 69 The brackishness and sulphureous twang of the lee of kelp. **1768** TUCKER *Lt. Nat.* (1834) I. 468 Though the liquor was not at all impaired thereby.. it might get some twang of the vessel. **1809** *Med. Jrnl.* XXI. 476 Its smell is alliaceous, mixed with another twang.. still less grateful. **1859** F. E. PAGET *Curate of Cumberworth* 242, I particularly dislike a twang of onion. **1891** T. HARDY *Tess* xxii, A customer.. complained that the butter had a twang.

b. ***a tongue with a twang***: see TANG *sb.*^{1} 5 c.

1667 DRYDEN & DAVENANT *Tempest* II. i, She had a tongue with a twang.

2. *fig.* A trace or suggestion of some specified origin, quality, or the like; a 'smack', touch, tinge; a taint; = TANG *sb.*^{1} 6.

1633 MASSINGER *Guardian* V. iv, This is neither begging, borrowing, nor robbery; Yet it hath a twang of all of them. **1678** DRYDEN *Limberham* II. i, A twang of the mother; but I love to graff on such a crab-tree. **1702** *Eng. Theophrast.* 331 The Fondness or Indifference that Philosophers express'd for Life, was but a particular Twang of the Love of themselves. **1826** SCOTT *Jrnl.* 2 May, Yesterday had a twang of frost in it. **1855** HAWTHORNE *Eng. Note-bks.* (1870) I. 284 This position of tutor to a young Englishman.. has an ugly twang of upper servitude.

†**3.** A tooth; *esp.* a canine tooth, a fang. Cf. TANG *sb.*^{1} 2 b. *Obs.*

1677 PLOT *Oxfordsh.* 276 Rapine with her fiery eyes, grinning teeth, sharp twangs, her hand imbrewed in blood. **1682** *Lond. Gaz.* No. 1782/4 Lost.., two Land Spaniels, a Dog and Bitch,.. the ends of the two upper Twangs of the Dog cut off.

†**twang**, *sb.*^{3} *Obs.* [Of obscure origin.] ***huddle and twang***, a term of contempt for a person. Cf. CUM-TWANG, HUDDLE *sb.* 3.

Differently, and perh. improperly, applied in quot. 1591.

1579 LYLY *Euphues* (Arb.) 106 Though Curio be olde huddle and twang, *ipse*, he, yet Euphues had rather shrinke in the wetting than wast in the wearing. **1591** FLORIO *2nd Fruites* 41 Who lets his wife goe to euerie feaste.. Shall haue .. of his best wife a twang with a huddle. **1600** *1st Pt. Sir J. Oldcastle* I. ii. 161 If euer woolfe were cloathed in sheepes coate, Then I am he,—olde huddle and twang, yfaith.

†**twang** (twæŋ), *sb.*^{4} *Austral. slang. Obs.* [perh. back-formation from TWANKAY.] Opium.

1898 *Bulletin* (Sydney) 1 Oct. 14/3 A few more W.Q. [*sc.* West Queensland] slang words... Opium 'twang', a Chinaman a 'canary' [etc.]. **1910** O'BRIEN & STEPHENS *Material for Dict. Austral. Slang 1900–10* (typescript), *Twang*, opium. **1945** T. RONAN *Strangers on Ophir* (1966) 68 The honest Chinese limits himself to his one pipe of 'Twang' per night. **1966** BAKER *Austral. Lang.* (ed. 2) 157 Opium was once known as *twang* in bush slang (the later use of *treacle* was noted earlier).

twang, *v.*^{1} [Echoic. Goes with TWANG *sb.*^{1}]

I. Of sound.

1. *intr.* To give forth a ringing note, as a tense string or a stringed instrument when plucked; to clang. Said also of the sound produced. Also *fig.*

† *to go off twanging*, to be a great success. *Obs.*

1567 [see TWANGING *ppl. a.*]. **1570** LEVINS *Manip.* 23/47 To Twangue, *resonare.* **1607** R. TURNER *Nosce Te* F iij, Now noses twang, guts grone. **1621** G. SANDYS *Ovid's Met.* VI. (1626) 114 This said, the bow-string twangs. **1626** MASSINGER *Rom. Actor* II. i, Had he died, As I resolve to do, .. It [a play] had gone off twanging. *a* **1700** DRYDEN *Iliad* I. 70 His bow twanged, and his arrows rattled as they flew. **1728** W. STARRAT *Epist.* 48 in *Ramsay's Poems* (1877) II. 275 What tuneless heart-strings wadna twang When love and beauty animate the sang? **1812** H. & J. SMITH *Rej. Addr.*, *Theatre* 27 Winds the French-horn, and twangs the tingling harp. **1840** R. H. DANA *Bef. Mast* xviii. 50 We found the violin and guitar screaming and twanging away under the piazza. **1862** MRS. H. WOOD *Mrs. Hallib.* II. v, [She] burst in at the door, with a violence that made its bell twang and tinkle.

2. *trans.* To cause to make a ringing note, as by plucking or twitching a tense string or strings of a bow or of a musical instrument; hence, to play on (an instrument). Also *fig.*

1579–80 NORTH *Plutarch* (1595) 949 The Scythians, when they are disposed to drink drunk together, do diuerse times twang the strings of their bowes. **1652** BENLOWES *Theoph.* III. i, Muse, twang the powerful harp, and brush each String. **1788** R. CUMBERLAND *Aristoph.*, *Clouds* viii, He would not sit twanging the lute, not he. **1855** THACKERAY *Newcomes* xxxi, Musicians came and twanged guitars to her. **1864** ENGEL *Mus. Anc. Nat.* 45 The strings are of lamb's gut, and are twanged with two small plectra. **1910** J. MACINTOSH in *Ayrshire Poets* 139 Hoar Winter twangs his trump in vain.

†**b.** ***to twang one's nose***, to blow the nose loudly (see also 6). *Obs.*

1748 RICHARDSON *Clarissa* V. 343 The mother twang'd her damn'd nose. **1810** S. GREEN *Reformist* I. 202 Percival felt for his handkerchief, twanged his nose.

3. *intr.* To produce a ringing note by or as by plucking a string or stringed instrument; hence (in depreciative sense) to play *on* a stringed instrument. ***to twang (all) upon one string, the same string***: cf. HARP *v.* 2.

1594 LYLY *Moth. Bomb.* III. iv, I wish'd for a noyse Of crack-halter Boyes, On those hempen strings to be twanging. **1624** GEE *New Shreds O. Snare* 18 The plots of their Comedies twang all vpon one string. **1671** H. FOULIS *Hist. Rom. Treasons* (1681) 88 Both twang upon the same string. **1840** R. H. DANA *Bef. Mast* xxvii. 92 The musicians were still there,.. scraping and twanging away. **1885** *Chr. World* 15 Jan. 38/5 They took to twanging away on what seemed an inferior kind of guitar.

†**b.** In the phrases ***the worst that, as good as, ever twanged.*** *Obs.*

1542 UDALL *Erasm. Apoph.* 110 b, A minstrel.. ye wurste that euer twanged. **1579** GOSSON *Sch. Abuse* (Arb.) 24 His skill is showne too make his Scholer as good as euer twangde. **1678** RAY *Prov.* (ed. 2) 285 As good as ever twang'd. **1681** W. ROBERTSON *Phraseol. Gen.* (1693) 486 The worst that ever twang'd; He has all the ill qualities that you can name.

4. *trans.* To play (a melody or the like) on a stringed instrument; to sound forth on a twanging instrument. Also said of the instrument or its strings.

1542 UDALL *Erasm. Apoph.* 207 Paris with his harpe did nothyng but twang fonde fansies of daliaunce and lasciuiousnesse. **1577** STANYHURST *Descr. Irel.* viii. in *Holinshed* I. 28/2 When the harper twangeth or singeth a song, all the company must be whist, or else he chafeth like a cutpurse, by reason his harmony is not had in better price. **1582** —— *Æneis* I. (Arb.) 41 Curled Iöppas Twanged on his harp golden, what he whillon learned of Atlas. **1809** W. IRVING *Knickerb.* IV. iii. (1820) 240 His sturdy trumpeter.. twanging his trumpet in the face of the whole world. **1842** THACKERAY *Fitz-Boodle's Conf.*, *Ottilia* ii, She twanged off a rattling piece of Liszt. **1851** H. D. WOLFF *Madrilenia* (1853) 111 Three guitar players, hired for the occasion, twanged a variety of airs. **1872** BLACK *Adv. Phaeton* xiv, The cords of the guitar twanged out a few notes.

†**5.** Of a speaker: **a.** *trans.* To utter with a sharp ringing tone; = TANG *v.*^{2} 2. *Obs. rare.*

1601 SHAKS. *Twel. N.* III. iv. 198 A terrible oath, with a swaggering accent sharpely twang'd off.

†**b.** *intr.* To speak. *Obs. rare.*

1601 B. JONSON *Poetaster* I. ii, The tongue of the oracle neuer twang'd truer. *Ibid.* V. iii, Thou twang'st right, little Horace.

6. *intr.* To speak with a nasal intonation or twang. Also *trans.* with *nose* (cf. 2 b). *rare.*

1615 [see TWANGING *vbl. sb.*]. **1826** SCOTT *Woodst.* v, With yonder Puritanic, Round-headed soldiers.. I.. twanged my nose and turned up my eyes. **1844** WILLIS *Lady Jane* I. 238 Nasal Smith and Jones Will twang as usual in 'the better sphere'.

b. *trans.* To utter or pronounce with a nasal or other twang.

1748 RICHARDSON *Clarissa* (1810) IV. xxviii. 154 [She] Twanged out a heigh-ho through her nose. **1754** J. SHEBBEARE *Matrimony* (1766) I. 17 The Master of the Family.. twangs the Dictates of the Gospel through his Nose all Sunday. **1836** T. HOOK *G. Gurney* I. 155 Hearing Miss Crab.. twang out the following. **1851** THACKERAY *Eng. Hum.* ii. (1858) 69 The Cicerone twangs his moral. **1864** *Daily Tel.* 29 July, A purer Whitechapel accent.. than that with which a damsel with a dulcimer twanged out a nasal-guttural lyric. **1893** SALTUS *Madam Sapphira* 191 'Now Becky,' twanged the ponderous person, 'what is your name?'

II. Of the action (without special reference to the sound).

7. *trans.* To pull or pluck (the string of a bow), so as to shoot.

1600 FAIRFAX *Tasso* VII. ciii, But from his quiuer huge a shaft he hent, And set it in his mightie bowe new bent, Twanged the string, out flew the quarell long. **1715–20** POPE *Iliad* I. 67 He twang'd his deadly bow, And hissing fly the feather'd fates below. **1890** C. MARTYN *W. Phillips* 236 Those [wits] twanged their bow-strings and sped their arrows of ridicule at so plain a target. **1891** E. FIELD *Bk. Western Verse* 25 He twanged his bow.

b. Used with reference to the bow (see BOW *sb.*^{1} 13) employed in hat-making; also with the material as obj.

1882 FLOYER *Unexpl. Baluchistan* 326 A boy 'twanging' wool with a bow, and reducing it to a coarse fluff. **1886** *Cheshire Gloss.* s.v. *Bow*, To 'twang the bow' was formerly considered a very skilful branch of hat manufacturing.

8. *trans.* To discharge (an arrow) with a twang of the bow-string; to let fly (an arrow). In quot. 1751 *absol.* Also *fig.*

1751 SMOLLETT *Per. Pic.* lxxxvii, She.. twanged off with the appellations of b—— and w——. **1807** W. IRVING *Salmag.* viii. (1824) 124 To be shot by the first lady's eye that can twang an arrow. **1833** MRS. BROWNING *Prometh. Bound* Poems 1850 I. 172 Where Scythia's shepherd peoples dwell aloft,.. And twang the rapid arrow past the bow. **1847** TENNYSON *Princ.* II. 380 A thousand baby loves Fly twanging headless arrows at the hearts. **1862** THACKERAY *Philip* xi, This.. may not have been the precise long bow which George Firmin.. pulled; but.. he twanged a famous lie out. **1863** *Reader* 31 Oct. 502 An athletic man.. has twanged an arrow from his box against some object.

b. *intr.* Of an arrow: To leave the bow-string with a twang.

1795 COLERIDGE *Lines in Manner of Spenser* iv, When twanged an arrow from Love's mystic string. **1831** JAMES *Phil. Augustus* I. v. The missile twanged away from the string.

†**9.** *intr.* To pluck, twitch *at. Obs. rare*$^{-1}$.

a **1678** MARVELL *Appleton House* 648 At my lines the fishes twang.

twang, *v.*^{2} [f. TWANG *sb.*^{2}, or alternation of TANG *v.*^{1}]

†**1.** *trans.* To furnish with a tang or point; in quot. *fig.*; cf. TANG *v.*^{1} 2. *Obs. rare.*

1678 DRYDEN & LEE *Œdipus* V. i, With her thundring Voice she menac'd high, And every Accent twang'd with smarting Sorrow.

2. To cause (a sharp object) to pierce through something; to thrust *through. rare.*

1821 CLARE *Vill. Minstr.* I. 155 How deep was the sorrow .., Like a bramble-thorn twang'd through her heart!

3. *intr.* To have a twang or 'smack' of something specified; to savour *of. rare*$^{-1}$.

1821 SCOTT *Kenilw.* iv, Your speech twangs too much of the old stamp.

†**twang'dillo.** *Obs. rare.* Also **twangdillow.** [f. TWANG *sb.*^{1} or *v.*^{1} with a Sp. or It. adjunct; a more correct form than TRANGDILLIO.] The twanging of a stringed musical instrument.

1762 COLLINS *Misc.* viii. (Farmer) The twangdillows of poor Crowdero in a country fair. **1794** J. COURTENAY *Manners*, etc. *France & Italy* 89 Music.. the seed of the plague, by twang-dillo destroys.

twanger ('twæŋə(r)). [f. TWANG *v.*^{1} + -ER^1.] One who or that which twangs. **a.** One who plays a twanging instrument. **b.** Anything very large or fine of its kind; a whacker. *slang.*

1598 FLORIO, *Tempélla*, a fiddle, a croud, or kit. Also a great swaggring twanger. **1631** HAUSTED *Rival Friends* I. iii, You euerlasting Twanger [boy with a lute]—Auoyd. **1677** W. HUGHES *Man of Sin* III. iii. 59 Well,.. Doth it not ring aloud like a Twanger, that the Angels should ring Bells in Heaven unto the honour of the Trinity? **1877** *N.W. Linc. Gloss.*, *Twanger*, a barefaced lie. **1889** *Ibid.* (ed. 2) s.v., Them to'nups e' th' foherteen aacre is twangers.

'twanging, *vbl. sb.* [f. TWANG *v.*^{1} + -ING^1.] The action of TWANG *v.*^{1} in various senses.

1615 BRATHWAIT *Strappado, Poem to Cottoneers* 204 Bradford.. Stile it I might Banberry of the North.. Famous for twanging, Ale, Zeale, Cakes and Cheese. **1788** GIBBON *Decl. & F.* xli. (1869) II. 505 *note*, The twanging of the bow. **1831** CARLYLE *Misc.* (1857) II. 284 Twanging of the true Poetic Lyre. **1832** TENNYSON *Kate* i, Kate hath an unbridled tongue, Clear as the twanging of a harp. **1836** T. HOOK *G. Gurney* I. 81 The loud twanging of an elderly gentleman's nose, who was fast asleep. **1904** *19th Cent.* Apr. 633 The drawn, nasal twangings of the Samisen.

'twanging, *ppl. a.* [f. as prec. + -ING^2.] That twangs, in senses of the verb.

1567 DRANT *Horace, Art Poet.* A vij, With the twanginge instrumente the singers voyce did matche. **1697** DRYDEN *Æneid* V. 688 To shew An archer's art, and boast his twanging bow. **1784** COWPER *Task* IV. 1 Hark! 'tis the twanging horn. **1856** KANE *Arct. Expl.* I. vii. 69 The sharp twanging snap of a cord. **1905** G. THORNE *Lost Cause* xi, The twanging accent of the United States, the guttural German, the purring, spitting Russian.

†**b.** *colloq.* Exceptionally fine or good. Cf. *stunning*, *ripping*, etc. *Obs.*

1609 B. JONSON *Sil. Wom.* V. iii, O 'twill be full and twanging!

Hence **'twangingly** *adv.*, in a twanging manner, with a twang; *fig.* successfully, with éclat (*arch.*).

1825 SCOTT *Jrnl.* 22 Dec., I wrote six of my close pages [of the *Life of Napoleon*] yesterday,.. I think it comes off twangingly. The story is so very interesting in itself. **1825** —— *Talism.* xxvi, I like these rattling rolling Alexandrines; methinks they come more twangingly off to the music than that briefer measure.

twangle ('twæŋg(ə)l), *sb.* [Cf. TWANGLE *v.*] A twangling sound; a continuous or repeated resonant sound, usually lighter or thinner than a twang; a jingle.

1812 COLMAN *Lady of Wreck* II. xxvi, Loud, on the heath, a twangle rush'd That rung out Supper.. From the crack'd bell. **1873** *All Year Round* 18 Oct. 590/1 What gives that thin twangle to the sound? **1883** G. W. CABLE in *Century Mag.* XXVII. 55 That sight touched the pathetic chord of his heart with a rude twangle.

twangle ('twæŋg(ə)l), *v.* Also 6 **twancle**, 9 *dial.* **twankle** (*Eng. Dial. Dict.*). [dim. and freq. of TWANG *v.*^{1} (see -LE), describing a resonant sound of the nature of a twang, but thinner and continuous or repeated. Used with contemptuous force.]

1. *intr.* Of a stringed instrument or one who plays it: To twang lightly and continuously or frequently; to jingle.

1558 PHAER *Æneid* VI. R ij b, Rimes thei sown And Orpheus among them stands, as priest in trayling gown. And twancling makes them tune. **1576–1610** [see TWANGLING *ppl. a.*]. **1823** SCOTT *Peveril* xxii, The coxcomb is twangling it on the lute. **1824** *Blackw. Mag.* XV. 160 The guitar..is twangling on every side. **1868** TENNYSON *Last Tourn.* 251 He twangled on his harp.

2. *trans.* To twang (a stringed instrument) lightly; to play upon in a petty or trifling manner. Also to play (a melody) in this way. Also *fig.*

1607 [see *twangling* vbl. sb.]. **1829** SCOTT *Anne of G.* xxx, The King looked after him, with some wonder at this want of breeding,..and then again began to twangle his viol. **1840** THACKERAY *Shabby Genteel Story* ii, The young Andrea bears up gaily..; twangles his guitar. **1874** RUSKIN *Fors Clav.* xlvii. 259 To..find you a barrel-organ, or a harmonium, to twangle psalm-tunes on.

Hence **'twangling** *vbl. sb.*; also **'twangler**, one who twangles.

1594 LYLY *Moth. Bomb.* v. iii, What a mischiefe make the twanglers [fiddlers] here? **1607** HIERON *Wks.* I. 104 Not the twangling of religion vpon the tongue, but the practise of holinesse in the life. **1825** SCOTT *Betrothed* xxi, Such twangling of harps as would be enough to frighten our walls from their foundations. **1871** RUSKIN *Fors Clav.* vi. 17 He supposed David's 'twangling upon the harp' would have been unsatisfactory to modern taste. **1879** E. ARNOLD *Lt. Asia* I. (1881) 7 Beaters of drum, and twanglers of the wire. **1881** RUSKIN in Mather *Life* (1897) 102 A twangler or scratcher on keys or cat-gut. **1891** FARRAR *Darkn. & Dawn* lxiii, Vindex..described Nero as a wretched twangler on the harp.

'twangling, *ppl. a.* [f. TWANGLE *v.* + -ING[2].] That twangles.

1576 FLEMING *Panopl. Epist.* 239 A tuneable sounde vpon twangling strings. **1596** SHAKS. *Tam. Shr.* II. i. 159 While she did call me Rascall, Fidler, And twangling Iacke. **1610** —— *Temp.* III. ii. 146 Sometimes a thousand twangling Instruments Will hum about mine eares. **1831** SCOTT *Cast. Dang.* viii, Far less has it [my life] allowed me leisure for such twangling follies. **1831** —— *Ct. Robt.* iii, Some one.. who could contribute to his pleasure, instead of a twangling, squalling infant. **1867** *Athenæum* No. 2062. 587/2 Little twangling musical-box.

†**'twango**, *int. Obs. nonce-wd.* [An affected form of TWANG *sb.*[1]; app. after It. or Sp. words in -*o*.] = TWANG *sb.*[1] 1.

1617 RICH *Irish Hubbub* (1623) 24 Hee..giues the cup a phillip, to make it cry *Twango*.

twangy ('twæŋɪ), *a.* [f. TWANG *sb.*[1] and [2] + -Y.] Having a twang (in various senses). In quot. 1887, having a tang (TANG *sb.*[1] 5).

1887 *Sat. Rev.* 8 Jan. 48 Worse..than any other cheese, being, as a rule, either tasteless or else twangy. **1893** E. H. BARKER *Wand. Southern Waters* 126 It [the American voice] becomes less twangy and harsh a little farther South. **1905** *Blackw. Mag.* Mar. 387/2 Hendriks showed off..on the twangy piano.

Hence **'twanginess**, twanging quality. *rare.*

1870 BLACK *Kilmeny* xxvi, The twanginess of the guitar.

twank (twæŋk), *v. dial.* [Echoic; expressing a sound that begins like a twang, but is abruptly cut short, such as is produced by striking a body with small resonance.] **a.** *intr.* To twang with short and sharp effect. **b.** *trans.* To strike with the open palm, to spank. Hence **'twanking** *vbl. sb.* and *ppl. a.*; also **'twanker** = TWANGER b.

1711 ADDISON *Spect.* No. 251 ¶4 Disturbing a whole Street for an Hour together, with the Twanking of a Brass-Kettle or a Frying-Pan. **1821** CLARE *Vill. Minstr.* I. 90 While distant thresher's swingle drops With sharp and hollow-twanking raps. *a* **1825** FORBY *Voc. E. Anglia*, *Twank*, *v.*..2. To give a smart slap with the flat of the hand, on the breech, or other fleshy part. **1828** *Craven Gloss.*, *Twanker*, a large bulky person; any thing large. **1905** *Daily Chron.* 16 June 6/5 When she tried to escape Mrs. Lewthwaite gave her a 'twanking'.

twanka-pang, twank-a-pank. An imitation of the sound of a banjo or guitar.

1929 J. B. PRIESTLEY *Good Companions* I. vi. 201 This banjo..was being *played*. The night retreated hastily before its impudent twanka-pang, twanka-pang. **1980** M. GILBERT *Death of Favourite Girl* i. 6 Twank-a-pank... The guitar quickened to a livelier tempo.

Twankay ('twæŋkeɪ). Also **twanky**. [ad. Chinese *Tong* (or *Taung*) *-ké* (or *-kei*), dialect form of *Tun-ki* or *Tun-chi*, the name of two streams (and a town) in An-hui and Chi-kiang, China. Authorities differ as to which of these is the real source of the tea; S. Ball refers it generally to the 'district' of Tuon Ky (Twankay) in the province of Kiang Nan.] A variety of green tea (in full *Twankay tea*), properly that from the place so called (see above), but also applied to blends of this with other growths.

A full account is given by S. Ball (1848) in the work cited below, pp. 235–240.

1840 J. T. HEWLETT *P. Priggins* xiv, Our conversation over the twanky and brown Georges..chiefly related to college and university matters. **1843** THACKERAY *Wks.* (1886) XXIII. 60 We'll have a roaring pot of twankay. **1857** A. MAYHEW *Paved with Gold* III. xviii, He didn't want to sit drinking hot grog with the old boy. He infinitely preferred cold Twankay, with the young damsel. **1864** W. WOOD *Few Words about Tea* 7 The Green Tea-leaf is made up into six different shapes, called by us..Twankay, Hyson-Skin, Hyson, Young Hyson, Imperial and Gunpowder.

attrib. **1848** S. BALL *Cultiv. & Manuf. Tea in China* 235 A tendency to Twankay flavour. *Ibid.* 240 The first gathering of common Twankay shrubs.

b. *slang.* (See quot.)

1900 F. ADAMS in *N. & Q.* 9th Ser. VI. 163/1 A friend mentions 'twankay', properly denoting a kind of green tea, as a name by which gin is frequently called.

twankle, dial. var. or parallel f. TWANGLE.

twantie, obs. Sc. form of TWENTY.

tward, obs. form of TOWARD.

twart(e, obs. ff. THWART.

'twas (twɒz), abbreviation of *it was*, formerly common colloquially and in literature, now poetic or archaic, and dialectal. Cf. 'TIS, and see IT A. γ.

1604 SHAKS. *Oth.* III. iii. 158 'Twas mine, 'tis his, and has bin slaue to thousands. **1693** J. BYROM *Let. to Aubrey* 15 Nov., in *Lett. Eminent Persons* (1813) II. I. 167 'Twas then commonly said. **1741** RICHARDSON *Pamela* I. 175 'Twas a Thing to be lamented. **1859** FITZGERALD *Omar* xlii, He bid me taste of it; and 'twas—the Grape!

twat (twɒt). *low slang.* Also 8 **twait**, 20 **twot(t**. [Of obscure origin.]

1. (See quot. 1727.)

Erroneously used (after quot. 1660) by Browning *Pippa Passes* IV. ii. 96 under the impression that it denoted some part of a nun's attire.

1656 R. FLETCHER tr. *Martial* II. xliv. 104. **1660** *Vanity of Vanities* 50 They talk't of his having a Cardinalls Hat, They'd send him as soon an Old Nuns Twat. *a* **1704** T. BROWN *Sober Slip in Dark* Wks. 1711 IV. 182 A dang'rous Street, Where Stones and Twaits in frosty Winters meet. **1719** D'URFEY *Pills* III. 307. **1727** BAILEY vol. II, Twat, *pudendum muliebre. Twat-scowerer*, a Surgeon or Doctor. *E. Ward.* **1919** E. E. CUMMINGS *Let.* 18 Aug. (1969) 61 On Tuesday an Uhlan To her twat put his tool in. **1934** H. MILLER *Tropic of Cancer* 55 A man with something between his legs that could..make her grab that bushy twat of hers with both hands and rub it joyfully. **1959** N. MAILER *Advts. for Myself* (1961) 101 The clothes off, the guards are driving them into the other room, and smack their hands on skinny flesh and bony flesh, it's bag a tittie and snatch a twot. **1970** G. GREER *Female Eunuch* 39 No woman wants to find out that she has a twat like a horse-collar. **1973** P. WHITE *Eye of Storm* iii. 137 This young thing with the swinging hair and partially revealed twat.

2. A term of vulgar abuse. Cf. TWIT *sb.*[1] 2 b and CUNT 2.

1929 F. MANNING *Middle Parts of Fortune* II. xv. 383 Yes, they let a bloody twat like 'im off. **1933** M. LOWRY *Ultramarine* i. 16 He can't help it if you're just a bloody, senseless twat. **1958** H. WILLIAMSON *Love & Loveless* i. 27 Looked a proper twott to me. **1969** P. ROTH *Portnoy's Complaint* 211 Here comes another dumb and stupid remark out of that brainless twat. **1978** J. UPDIKE *Coup* (1979) iii. 123 Divorce me and you'll have a slot for this new twat, what's her name. **1979** R. FIENNES *Hell on Ice* ix. 134 Sterns not prows, you twot.

3. *U.S. dial.* The buttocks.

1950 *Publ. Amer. Dial. Soc.* XIII. 20 *Twat*,..the buttocks. **1964** M. KELLY *March to Gallows* xii. 132, I could tell her what to do with her twat if she's frightened to sit on it.

†**twat**, an error for TROAT *v.*

1686 BLOME *Gentl. Recr.* II. 76 A Hart Belloweth, a Buck Groaneth or Twateth.

twatchel ('twætʃəl). *arch.* Also 7–8 **twachel**. [Related to *twæcce* in OE. *angol-twæcce*, ANGLE-TWITCH, -TOUCH, earthworm. Cf. TOUCHANGLE, TWEYANGLE.] A name for the earthworm.

Added in the 3rd ed. of Walton's Angler, and thence in subsequent books on fishing.

1661 WALTON *Angler* v. (ed. 3) 92 The twachel or lob-worm, (which of all other is the most excellent bait for a Salmon). **1681** CHETHAM *Angler's Vade-m.* iv. §2 (1689) 30 Dew-worm, Garden-worm, Lob-worm or Twatchel are all but one Worm, although called in different Places by all the said Names. **1787** BEST *Angling* (ed. 2) 16 The Lob-worm, Dew-worm, Garden-worm, Twatchel or Treachet. **1865** A. S. MOFFAT *Secr. Angling* viii. 164 The Lob, Dew, Twatchel, or Garden Worm.

†**'twatter-light.** *Obs. rare.* [Cf. TWITTER-LIGHT.] Twilight.

1606 *Wily Beguiled* (1623) E iij, *Mother Midnight*. What mak'st thou heere this twatter light?

twattle ('twɒt(ə)l), *sb.*[1] Now *dial.* [The vb. and sb. (known in 1573 and *a* 1639 respectively) were perh. altered from TATTLE; the earliest appearance of *twattle* yet recorded being in the reduplicated TWITTLE-TWATTLE (1556), app. from TITTLE-TATTLE (evidenced *a* 1529).

The group of words *tittle*, *tittle-tattle*, *twittle*, *twattle*, *twittle-twattle*, and *twaddle*, being primarily colloquial and largely echoic, is prob. far from fully represented in written remains, so that dated evidence for the chronological order of these shows many lacunæ; the important data are that *tittle*, to whisper, is known from 1399, and *tattle* (in *tattler*) from *c* 1450, and that *tittle-tattle*, *twittle-twattle*, *twattle*, and *twaddle*, and their derivatives, appear successively later. No reason for the suggested change of *tattle* to *twattle* has been found, but the passage of *twattle* into *twaddle* seems certain.]

Idle talk, chatter, babble. Also in comb. **twattle-basket**, a chatterbox.

Passing in later use into the sense of TWADDLE *sb.*

a **1639** W. WHATELEY *Prototypes* I. xix. (1640) 234 Being men of tongue,..their chiefe employment is twattle. **1650** B. *Discolliminium* 47 It is pity any honest man should lose his life for want of a game at Twattle. [*Cf. above* I cannot hold my tongue for my life.] **1687** MIÈGE *Gt. Fr. Dict.* II, Twattle-basket,..*un caseur*. **1699** T. BROWN *Let. to Dr. Brown at Tunbridge* Wks. 1711 IV. 133 The empty Twattle of these silly..Country Projectors. **1715** tr. *C'tess D'Aunoy's Wks.* 462 Hold thy Peace, Twattle-basket. **1720** DE FOE *Apparition in 1665* Wks. 1841 XIX. 259 In the midst of our twattle. **1824** COBBETT *Weekly Reg.* L. 12 June 674 Men who have no cant, no evangelical twattle. **1876–** in dialect glossaries (Yorksh., E. Anglia).

†**twattle** ('twɒt(ə)l), *sb.*[2] *(a.) Obs.* [Origin obscure. The sb. can hardly be related to TWATTLE *v.* or *sb.*[1]] A pygmy, a dwarf. Also *attrib.* or as *adj.*

1598 FLORIO, *Pigméo*, a pigmey, a kinde of little man like a dwarfe, a dandiprat, a twattle, or an elfe. **1611** COTGR., *Nain*, a dwarfe, or dandiprat, an elfe, or twattle; one thats no higher then three horse-loaues. *a* **1693** *Urquhart's Rabelais* III. xviii. 144 They shew him the short and twattle [F. *petits*] Verses that were written [lines of 4 syllables].

'twattle, *v. Obs.* exc. *dial.* [See TWATTLE *sb.*[1]]

1. *intr.* To talk idly or trivially; to chatter, babble, tattle, prate.

In later use passing into sense of TWADDLE *v.*[1]

1573, **1586** [see TWATTLING *ppl. a.* 1, *vbl. sb.*]. **1596** NASHE *Saffron-Walden* Wks. (Grosart) III. 204 In that he twatleth, it had bin better to haue confuted Martin by Reuerend Cooper than such leuitie. *a* **1620** J. DYKE *Sel. Serm.* (1640) 34 Talking and twatling with other idle persons. **1685** J. DUNTON *Lett. fr. New-Eng.* (1867) 7 By that time I could move my Tongue, it would be twattling of Forreign Countrys. *a* **1800** PEGGE *Suppl. Grose*, *Twattle*, to prattle and tell idle tales. *Lanc.* **1833** SARAH AUSTIN *Charac. Goethe* I. 118 He [Mephistopheles] argues, dogmatizes, and twattles right and left. **1845** S. JUDD *Margaret* II. ii, How I twattled, skurried! **1877–** in dialect glossaries (Yorksh., E. Anglia, Cornw.).

b. *trans.* To utter or tell idly.

1577 STANYHURST *Descr. Irel.* vi. in *Holinshed* I. 20/2 Such fables [are] twitled, such vntrue reportes twatled. **1582** —— *Æneis* II. (Arb.) 46 No gloasing fabil I twattle. *Ibid.* IV. 101 As true tales vaynelye toe twattle. **1660** *Charac. Italy* 10 He [the Pope]..causeth whatsoever he parrot[s], or if you will have it Anagrammatically praterlike twattles, to pass for Bullion, and current. *a* **1688** VILLIERS (Dk. Buckhm.) *Chances* Wks. (1714) 149, I heard her grave Conductress twattle something as they went along.

c. with *prep.* To bring or get by chattering or gossiping.

1692 R. L'ESTRANGE *Fables* cclxxvii. (1715) II. 266 Are you not a fine Gossiping Lady..to twattle your Husband thus out of his Life and Fortune?

2. *intr.* To sound, make a noise. (See also TWATTLING *ppl. a.* 2.) *vulgar.*

1664 COTTON *Scarron.* I. 15 The Winds burst out with such a rattle, As he had broke the strings that twattle.

3. *trans.* To pat, fondle, make much of. *dial.*

Perh. not the same word.

1790 GROSE *Provinc. Gloss.* (ed. 2), *Twattle*, to pat, to make much of, as horses, cows, dogs. *North.* **1825** BROCKETT *N.C. Words*, *Twattle*, to pat, to make much of, to fondle.

twattler ('twɒtlə(r)). *Obs.* exc. *dial.* [f. prec. + -ER[1].] One who 'twattles'; a chatterer, babbler, tattler.

1577 STANYHURST *Descr. Irel.* vi. in *Holinshed* I. 22/1 Let vs..leaue lying for varlettes,..chatting for twatlers. **1679** J. SMITH *Narr. Pop. Plot* 21 Aspersed by..publick Scriblers, as well as by Coffee-house Twatlers. **1685** BAXTER *Paraphr. N.T.*, *1 Tim.* v. 14, 15 To speak evil of the Church, as if it were a Society of idle twatlers. **1818** COBBETT *Pol. Reg.* XXXIII. 515 As to the resources of the nation, what do these twatlers mean?

'twattling, *vbl. sb. Obs.* exc. *dial.* [f. as prec. + -ING[1].] The action of the verb TWATTLE; idle talking, chattering.

1586 J. HOOKER *Hist. Irel.* in *Holinshed* II. 83/1 The continuall twatling of fliring clawbacks in their eares. **1634** W. WHATELEY *Redempt. Time* 15 When one talkes toyes or trifles,..such twatling cuts out the heart of good time. **1653** W. RAMESEY *Astrol. Rej.* 176 Addicted to twatling and prating. *a* **1745** SWIFT *To Dr. Sheridan* 14 Dec., You keep such a twattling with you and your bottling.

'twattling, *ppl. a. Obs.* exc. *dial.* [f. as prec. + -ING[2].]

1. That 'twattles'; chattering, babbling, prating. (Said of the person, or of the talk.)

1573 TWYNE *Æneid* XI. H h iv, Persist, And thoundre out thy twatling talke, as longe as thou shalt list. **1647** LILLY *Chr. Astrol.* cxxxiv. 594 She is..a twatling huswife, making discord where-ever she comes. **1702** *Eng. Theophrast.* 165 It is not for every Twatling Gossip.

2. Sounding, making a noise. *vulgar.*

twattling strings, a vulgar expression for the *sphincter ani.* **1611** FLORIO, *Naccare*, drom-slades... And vsed for twatling fartes. **1654** GAYTON *Pleas. Notes* III. iii. 83 Her Base Violl went..with great danger of breaking her twatling-strings. **1739** 'R. BULL' tr. *Dedekindus' Grobianus* 268 Her twattling Strings, with Laughter overcome, No more contract the Passage of the Bum.

†**3.** Petty, trifling, paltry: = TWADDLING *a.* 1 b. *Obs. rare*[−1]. [Perh. related to TWATTLE *sb.*[2]]

1651 *Miller of Mansf.* 20 You feed us with twatling dishes so small.

tway (tweɪ), *numeral a.* Now *arch.* Forms: see below. [Apocopate form of OE. *twéᵹen*, ME. *tweyen*, TWAIN, the final *n* being normally dropped. OE. *twéᵹe* seems not to be recorded in WSax., but it occurs in Anglian in Rushw. Gospel Gl., and in the late Hatton Gosp. before a consonant, and is the ordinary form in Old Northumbrian (varying in Lindisfarne Gl. as *twoeᵹe*, *tuoᵹe*, *tueᵹ*, *tuoe*, *twoe*, *tue*; Rit. Dunelm.

has *tvoeȝi, twoeȝo*). These forms are not rigidly confined to the masc. From the OE. *twéȝe* (or by similar apocopation of ME. *tweyen, tweien*) came ME. *tweye, twei(e, twey* in Midld. and South Eng., *twai, tway* in North. and North-Midld. But *tway* in Scotch from *c* 1500 may also be only a variant spelling of the later *twae* from *twā*, TWO: the Sc. forms have therefore been separated as γ. Even as an archaism the form is now rarely employed.]

A. Illustration of Forms.

α. 1 **twóeȝe, tuéȝe** (**tuóȝ, tuéȝ, twé, tué**), 1-2 **twéȝe, twǽȝe**, 3 **tueye, tueie, tuei**, 2-5 **twei**, 3-5 **tweie, tweye**, 3-7 **twey**, 4 **tweiȝe, tweyȝe, tuuei**; 3 **twie**, 4-5 **twy**.

a950 *Rituale Dunelm.* (Surtees) 113 Ðerh hvnd seofontiȝ tvoeȝi boec aldes & nives ȝicyðnisses. **c950** *Lindisf. Gosp.* Mark vi. 41 Fif hlafo & tue fiscas. —— Luke ii. 24 Tuoe turturas *vel* tuoȝe birdas culfras [*Rushw.* twoeȝe t. *vel* twoeȝe birdas culfra]. **c975** *Rushw. Gosp.* John ii. 6 Nimende syndriȝe sestras twoeȝe *vel* ðria. **c1160** *Hatton Gosp.* Matt. xxvi. 37 He ȝenam petrum & zebedeus tweȝe sunes [*Ags. G.* tweȝen suna]. **c1175** *12th c. Hom.* (Bodley) 98 Twæȝe men herbiforen þis festen festen. **c1200** *Trin. Coll. Hom.* 207 Þe gostliche rode..haueð twei names, *cordis contritio et proximi compassio*. **c1275** *Passion of Our Lord* 43 in *O.E. Misc.* 49 Hi nome twey þeoues. **c1275** LAY. 10670 Hii..sende twie [*c* 1205 tweien] eorles. **c1290** *S. Eng. Leg.* I. 10/317 Þe tweie croiz..þat þe þeoues on i-hanguede were. **1297** R. GLOUC. (Rolls) 731 And ȝef is tueie doȝtren half, & half him sulf nom. *Ibid.* 6322 Bi tuene þis tueye kinges. **a1325** *MS. Rawl. B.* 520 lf. 65b, Tuuei writes of wuche comez tuueine assoines. **c1325** *Spec. Gy Warw.* 785 Tweye manere shame ..þat on goþ to dampnacioun; þat oþer, to sauuacioun. **1387** TREVISA *Higden* (Rolls) VI. 5 Bytwene þe tweie [*MS.* γ twy] riveres. **c1400** *R. Gloucester's Chron.* 754 (MS. α) Þeos tweiȝe kinges. **c1449** PECOCK *Repr.* I. ii. (Rolls) 8 A sillogisme is mad of twey proposiciouns dryuyng out of hem the thridde proposicioun.

β. *north.* and *midl. Eng.* 3-4 **tuai**, 4 **tuay**, 4-7 (8-*arch.*) **tway** (6 **twaye**),

a1300 *Cursor M.* 12699 (Cott.) Of hir war born god childer tuai [*rime* sai; *F.* tway; *Tr.* twey, *rime* sey]. **c1330** *Arth. & Merl.* (Kölbing) 4788 He hadde strengþe of kniȝtes tvay. **13..** *Cursor M.* 21756 (Gött.) Þe bodi [is] of element[s] tuis tuay [*Cott.* tuai; *F.* twies tway, *rime* I say]. **1559** *Mirr. Mag., Ld. Hastings* li, Vniudgd hangth yet the case betwixt them twaye [*rime* saye]. **1579** SPENSER *Sheph. Cal.* May 18 We tway bene men of elder witt. **1611** *Coryat's Crudities, Panegyr. Verses* d viij b, Tom is..the Greeker of the tway [*rime* say]. **1742** SHENSTONE *Schoolmistress* 51 For sceptre she does wield Tway birchen sprays. **1865** Tway [see B. 1 b].

γ. *Sc.* 4-7 **tway**, 6-7 **tuay**.

c1375 *Sc. Leg. Saints* xxii. (*Laurentius*) 512 Þai tuk þe cors ..þai tway it bare. **c1470** HENRY *Wallace* IX. 801 Mycht we get ane or tway [*rime* way]. **1513** DOUGLAS *Æneis* I. vi. 17 Amyd the wod his modir met thame tway [*rime* array]. **1537** *Registr. Aberdon.* (Maitl. Cl.) I 413 Tway pennies for ilk barne absent. **1549** *Ibid.* 438 For þe tuay part of þe mylne. **1570** *Satir. Poems Reform.* xvi. 105 That schot, allace! yis realme hes shot in tway [*rime* away]. **a1584** MONTGOMERIE *Cherrie & Slae* 460 Ane foule in hand, or tway [*rime* day]. **a1600** —— *Misc. Poems* (S.T.S. 1887) i. 12 A turne in tyme is ay worth other tuay [*rime* auay.] **1615** SIR W. MURE *Misc. Poems* viii. 44 Reflecting only on ws tuay [*rime* away].

B. Signification. = TWO.

1. In concord with a sb. **a.** Preceding the sb.

a950 Tvoeȝi boec; **c950** Tuoȝe birdas; **c1160** Tweȝe sunes; **c1200** Twei names [see A. α above]. **c1275** *Passion of Our Lord* 645 in *O.E. Misc.* 55 Þer stoden twei veyre men. **1297** R. GLOUC. (Rolls) 312 Tweie dawes hii wende in þe see. *Ibid.* 1806 Tueie [*v.r.* twei] emperours of rome, Dioclician & ..maximian. **1303** R. BRUNNE *Handl. Synne* 11264 To pray ..saueþ man on twey partys. **1362** LANGL. *P. Pl.* A. v. 109 He was bitel-brouwed, with twei blered eiȝen. **c1380** WYCLIF *Sel. Wks.* III. 188 Oure Lord..spekiþ..of tweie matrimoneys. **c1394** *P. Pl. Crede* 439 A litell childe..And tweyne of tweie ȝeres olde. **a1425** *Cursor M.* 19419 (Trin.) Tweye witenes had þei hem purueide. **c1450** *Godstow Reg.* 191 An hundred shillyngis..at twey termes in the yere. **c1570** *Marr. Wit & Science* IV. iv. D ivb, *Ignoraunce.* Choulde geue twaye pence to see it and tway pence moore. **1573** TYRIE *Refut.* in *Cath. Tractates* (S.T.S.) 17 The kirk is vniuersall, and..it hes continewall successioun of pastoures: quhilk tuay markis did neuer..aggrie to onie.. congregatioun of heretikes. **a1586** SIDNEY *Arcadia, Geron & Mastix* 20 'Tis now full tway score Of yeares..since I good Mastix knew. **1712** PRIOR *Erle Robert's Mice* 1 Tway Mice..Batten beside Erle Robert's Table.

b. Following the sb. *poet.*

c1205 LAY. 26235 Þa cleopede he eorles tweie. **c1275** *Moral Ode* 225 in *O.E. Misc.* 66 Hunger and þurst, vuele tweye [*earlier MSS.* twa, two] ivere. **13..** *K. Alis.* 7254 (Laud MS.) He knew þoo barouns tweye [*rime* cuntreye]. **c1320** R. BRUNNE *Medit.* 50 Þe soper was dyȝt..By dyscyplys seuenty and twey. **c1400** *Rom. Rose* 1744 Thanne toke I with myn hondis tweie The arowe. **c1440** *Pallad. on Husb.* VIII. 161 Vppon feet but tway. **1543** GRAFTON *Harding's Chron.* Ded. xii, The Scottish kyng, sending foorth heraldes tway. **1559** *Mirr. Mag., Dk. Buckhm.* xxviii, Downthrow we strayt his sellie nephewes twaye. **1865** S. EVANS *Bro. Fabian* 58 Now..shut mine eyen tway.

†**c.** *tway part* (Sc.), two-thirds (= *twa part*: see TWO B. I. 1 c). *Obs.*

1531 *Acc. Ld. High Treas. Scotl.* (1905) VI. 18 For tway elnis and ane tway-part elne gray weluet. **1549** *Registr. Aberdon.* (Maitl. Cl.) I. 438 With brew hous and tuay part of þe myln of þe said toune.

2. Absolutely with ellipsis of sb., or following a pronoun or pronominal adj.

1297 R. GLOUC. (Rolls) 4071 Sibile þe sage sede..þat þer ssolde of brutayne þre men be ybore þat ssolde winne þe aumperye of rome; of þe tueye ydo it is,..& þou art þe þridde. **13..** *Cursor M.* 635 (Gött.) Naked war þai bath tway [*Tr.* þei boþe tweyn]. **c1350** *Will. Palerne* 2147 To take hem tweie. **a1450** *Knt. de la Tour* (1906) 153 Y shalle saie of euery astate an ensaumple or twey. **a1553** UDALL *Royster D.* IV. i. (Arb.) 59, I haue a message or tway. **a1586** SIDNEY *Arcadia* III. *Geron & Histor* 91 Betwixt vs tway We beare our double yoke. **1642** H. MORE *Song of Soul* I. I. xxxiii, When Hattubus old..did tie them tway With nuptiall charm.

b. In genitive after possess. pron.

1476 J. PASTON in *P. Lett.* III. 155 Ther tweys dysposysyon [= the disposition of them two].

c. as *sb.* A pair, couple.

?**a1800** *Lord Livingston* ix. in Child *Ballads* (1892) VIII. 432 They were a comely tway.

3. *in* (*into*) *tway*: into two parts or pieces, in two.

c1375 *Cursor M.* 20556 (Fairf.) For ferde hir hert sulde brast in-twai. **1558** *Lydgate's Bochas* IX. xxxv. 36b, The lyues threde for to breke in tway [*Bodl. MS.* tweyne]. **1567** *Gude & Godlie B.* (S.T.S.) 195 Cut ȝour typpet in to tway. **1590** SPENSER *F.Q.* I. vii. 27 Which..almost rent her tender hart in tway.

4. *Comb.* as *tway-coned, -edged, -footed, -handed* adjs.; †**tway-biting** *a.*, 'biting' or cutting two ways, two-edged; †**tway-fold** *adv.* = TWIFOLD, TWOFOLD; †**tway-like** *a.*: see quot. and cf. TWILEKE; †**tway-toothed** *a.*, having two rows of teeth. See also TWAYBLADE.

1382 WYCLIF *Prov.* v. 4 The tunge of hir sharp as a *twei bitende swerd. **1872** BLACKIE *Lays Highl.* 105 Fare-thee-well, thou *tway coned Cruachan. **1545** JOYE *Exp. Dan.* i. Biij b, With the *twei edged swearde. **1303** R. BRUNNE *Handl. Synne* 1153 Þys olde man..bade hym take A sak.. And ..turne hyt *tweyfolde. **c1386** CHAUCER *Can. Yeom. Prol. & T.* 13 (Ellesm.) A male tweyfoold [*v.r.* twyfold] vp on his croper lay. **1398** TREVISA *Barth. De P.R.* v. liv. (Bodl. MS.) lf. 28/1 þe feete of foules and of *twey footed beestes. **1552** *Acc. Ld. High Treas. Scotl.* X. 82 *Tway handit sword. **1551** RECORDE *Pathw. Knowl.* I. Defin. Biij, An other distinction of the names of triangles, according to their sides, whiche other be all equal..other els two sydes bee equall and the thyrd vnequall, which the Greekes call *Isosceles*,..and in english *tweyleke may they be called. **1387** TREVISA *Higden* (Rolls) VI. 405 Wormes þat were *twweie [*v.r.* twy] toþed [L. *bidentati*] and i-liche to wontes.. ete þe brede corne.

twayblade ('tweɪbleɪd). Also 8 **twyblade**. [f. TWAY two + BLADE *sb.* leaf. Cf. *twa-, two-blade(s)*, s.v. TWO *a.* IV. 2.] **a.** An orchidaceous plant of the genus *Listera*, characterized by two nearly opposite broad leaves springing from the stem; esp. the Common Twayblade, *L. ovata*, and Mountain or Heart-leaved T., *L. cordata*. **b.** Applied to N. American species of another orchidaceous genus *Liparis*, with two leaves springing from the root.

a. **1578** LYTE *Dodoens* II. lvii. 224 The Twayblade or Double-leaf delighteth..in moyst..places. **1597** GERARDE *Herbal* II. lxxxiii. 326 Of Twayblade, or herbe Bifoile. **1668** WILKINS *Real Char.* II. iv. 78 That [herb] which hath only two leaves...Tway-blade. **1728** BRADLEY *Dict. Bot., Ophris*, sive *Bifolium*, in English, Twyblade. **1778** LIGHTFOOT *Flora Scot.* (1789) I. 524 *Ophrys ovata.* Great Twayblade... *Ophrys cordata.* Little Twayblade. **1785** MARTYN *Rousseau's Bot.* xxvii. (1794) 419 Common Twayblade, or Twyblade,..is frequent in woods. **1859** MISS YONGE *Hist. Sir Thos. Thumb* iv. 21 He was no larger than the green lip of the tway-blade blossom. **1882** *Cornh. Mag.* Jan. 33 The twayblade and the parsley-piert are..descended from bright-hued ancestors. **1884** MILLER *Plant-n.*, Tway-blade, American, *Listera convallarioides*. **1905** *Longm. Mag.* Jan. 253 The rare mountain twayblade.

b. **1846-50** A. WOOD *Class-bk. Bot.* 530 *Liparis lilifolia*... Tway-blade. **1884** MILLER *Plant-n.*, Tway-blade, Green-flowered, *Liparis Loeselii*. ——, Purple-flowered, *Liparis liliifolia*.

twayle, twaylle, obs. ff. TOWEL; var. TWAIL.

twayn, twayne, obs. ff. TWAIN.

twch, obs. Sc. f. TOUGH.

tweag, tweague, obs. or dial. ff. TWEAK *sb.*[1], *v.*

tweak (twiːk), *sb.*[1] Also 8 **tweague**, 8-9 **tweag**. [f. TWEAK *v.*]

1. An act of tweaking; a sharp wringing pull; a twitch, a pluck.

1609 B. JONSON *Sil. Wom.* IV. v, Hee will..make you beare a blow, ouer the mouth,..tweakes by the nose, *sans numbre*. **1716** ADDISON *Drummer* v. i, He has given my shoulder such a cursed tweak. **1738** *Common Sense* II. 106 They may be drawn out of their Sockets with a moderate Tweag. **1809** W. IRVING *Knickerb.* VI. vii. (1861) 216 [He] was courteously dismissed with a tweak of the nose, to assist him in recollecting his message. **1847** C. BRONTE *J. Eyre* xxiv, A severe tweak of the ear. **1883** *Mag. of Art* June 309/2 Tweaks and slaps and pinches.

†**2.** *fig.* **a.** In phrase *in a tweak*, in a state of excitement or agitation, in a 'taking'. *Obs.*

a1700 B. E. *Dict. Cant. Crew, Tweak, in a Tweak*, in a heavy taking,..very angry. **1706** PHILLIPS (ed. Kersey), *Tweag* or *Tweak*, Perplexity, Trouble; as To be in a sad Tweak. **1712** ARBUTHNOT *John Bull* III. vi, This put the old fellow in a rare tweag [*ed.* **1755** tweague]! **1755** JOHNSON, *Tweague, Tweak*, perplexity; ludicrous distress. A low word. **1779** WARNER in Jesse *Selwyn & Contemp.* (1844) IV. 12 What a tweague and a taking you would be in. **1841** HARTSHORNE *Salopia Antiqua* 602 'To be in a tweag' is a phrase of long standing, and not peculiarly dialectical.

b. *dial.* See quots.

1881 MISS JACKSON *Shropsh. Word-bd.*, *Tweak*, a sharp, severe attack of illness—'a pinch'. **1886** DARLINGTON *S. Chesh. Gloss.*, *Tweak*,..a sharp, severe pain.

†**tweak**, *sb.*[2] *Obs. slang.* Also 7 **tweake**. [? from TWEAK *sb.*[1] or *v.*] A harlot; 'also, a whoremonger' (Halliwell).

1617 MIDDLETON & ROWLEY *Fair Quarrel* IV. iv, Your tweaks are like your mermaids, they have sweet voices to entice the passengers. **1631** BRATHWAIT *Whimzies, Char. Painter* 134 Hee sometimes playes the witty satyrist, and displayes light tweakes in loose roabes. **1638** —— *Barnabees Jrnl.* I. D v, An apt one To be Tweake unto a Captaine. *Ibid.* III. R vij, From the bushes neare the Lane there Rush'd a Tweake in gesture flanting. **1719** D'URFEY *Pills* (1872) III. 146 If any man here be in bodily fear, Of a Wolf, a Wife, or a Tweak.

tweak (twiːk), *v.* Also 7 **tweake**; β. 7-8 (9 *dial.*) **tweag**, 8 **tweague**. [Of obscure origin: cf. TWICK *v.*]

1. *trans.* To seize and pull sharply with a twisting movement; to pull at with a jerk; to twitch, wring, pluck; *esp.* to pull (a person) *by* the nose (or a person's nose) as a mark of contempt or insult; †to press (the lips) *together* so as to pinch.

α. **1601** HOLLAND *Pliny* XI. xxiv. I. 324 These Spiders hunt also after the yong Lizards:..they catch hold and tweake both their lips together, and so bite and pinch them. **1602** SHAKS. *Ham.* II. ii. 601 Who calles me Villaine?.. Tweakes me by th' Nose? giues me the Lye i' th' Throate..? **1663** BUTLER *Hud.* I. II. 974 To rouze him..He tweak'd his Nose, with gentle Thump Knock'd on his Breast. **1748** SMOLLETT *R. Random* xxvi, He seized me by the nose, which he tweaked so unmercifully, that I roared with anguish. **1795** WOLCOT (P. Pindar) *Hair Powder* Wks. 1812 III. 305 With hot pincers tweak each nose and ear! **1816** SCOTT *Old Mort.* iv, I will tweak thy proboscis or nose. **1826** F. REYNOLDS *Life & Times* I. 111 [He] tweaked our crabbed oppressor by the nose. **1858** BAILEY *Age* 148 He'd have tweaked your head clean off your shoulders. **1913** *Blackw. Mag.* June 796/1 She tweaked the coiffure of her much-enduring parent into position.

β. **1685** CROWNE *Sir C. Nice* III. Dram. Wks. 1874 III. 296 I'll not only libel him, but tweag him by the nose, kick him, cudgel him. **1738** *Common Sense* II. 106 They are all tweag'd into a Degree of Insensibility, which may incapacitate them for smelling a Fox. **1755** J. SHEBBEARE *Lydia* (1769) II. 139 Sweetwood stretched forth his hand and tweaged his nose. **1841** HARTSHORNE *Salopia Antiqua* 602. **1876** *Mid-Yorks. Gloss.*, *Tweag*.., to tweak.

†**2.** *fig.* (See quot., and cf. TWEAK *sb.*[1] 2 a.) *Obs.*

1721 BAILEY, *To Tweag, to Tweak* (*tweken*, Du. to pinch), to put into a Fret or Perplexity. [Not in Johnson.]

3. *slang.* To hit with a missile from a catapult. Cf. TWEAKER.

1898 KIPLING *Stalky* in *Windsor Mag.* Dec. 35 Corkran, through the roof, scientifically 'tweaked' a frisky heifer on the nose.

4. *Cricket. colloq.* Of a bowler: to impart spin to (the ball).

1958 D. BRADMAN *Art of Cricket* 94/1 My pal..R. W. V. Robins, tweaked his leg breaks so hard that he left the ground altogether with both feet.

5. To make fine adjustments to (a mechanism).

1966 *Punch* 16 Feb. 233/1 He has been running a Morris 1100 'tweaked so it'll do nearly 100'. **1971** *Daily Tel.* 13 Oct. 11/1 The three-litre V6 engines..have been 'tweaked' to produce eight per cent. more power. **1978** *Gramophone* May 1960/1 It was possible to improve its performance very considerably by 'tweaking' the internal pre-set controls.

Hence **tweaked** *ppl. a.*, **'tweaking** *vbl. sb.*

1609 B. JONSON *Sil. Wom.* IV. v, Good, Sir John, leaue tweaking, you'll blow his nose off. **1894** H. SPENCER in *Life Mrs. Lynn Linton* xxi. (1901) 311 To return to the tweaking of the nose above indicated. **1900** *Daily News* 15 Nov. 6/1 This tweaked-up eyebrow..carries the idea of evil to the modern audience. **1949** E. M. WELLINGS in *Boys' Bk. of Cricket* 78/1 Most right-handed off-break bowlers do their spinning largely with the forefinger. Personally I do not even have that finger resting on the ball when bowling an off-break. My 'tweaking' is done by the middle finger. **1975** *Drive* Nov.-Dec. 90/3 These engine hiccups are the result of carburettor tweaking that has been necessary to bring cars in line with current exhaust emission regulations. **1983** *Australian Personal Computer* Sept. 123/1 Most parallel [daisy-wheel] printers should work with a little tweaking.

tweaker ('twiːkə(r)). *slang.* Also **tweeker**. [f. TWEAK *v.* + -ER[1].]

1. A catapult.

1884 C. H. *Her World* vii. 39 Every now and then taking aim with his 'tweeker'..at the said person below. **1897** *Badminton Mag.* Apr. 459 A few shot from a 'tweaker,' commonly called a catapult.

2. *Cricket. colloq.* **a.** A bowler who spins or 'tweaks' the ball, esp. a left-arm leg-spinner. **b.** A ball bowled with spin.

1948 C. SLY *How to bowl them Out* ii. 17 The slow bowler should have great patience... There should also be an element of precision in his brain—a slapdash fellow will never make a good 'tweaker'. **1956** R. ALSTON *Test Commentary* 12 Johnson's insidious 'floaters' were likely to be more penetrative than Ring's 'tweakers'. **1961** *Times* 12 June 3/6 Lancing's leg tweaker came on too late. **1976** J. SNOW *Cricket Rebel* 40 When I came into the side Ron Bell, a left-arm spinner, was the only genuine tweaker of the ball on the staff. **1982** *Guardian* 26 July 19/3 The fragile left-arm tweakers of Steele.

tweamen, variant of TWEME *v. Obs.*

twear, var. of TUYERE.

tweaser-, tweat, obs. ff. TWEEZER-, TWAIT, shad.

twech, tweche, obs. Sc. ff. TOUCH.

twechell, obs. f. TWITCHEL[1], narrow passage.

† **'tweddle**, *v. Sc. Obs.* [app. a back-formation from next.] (See quot.)

1808 JAMIESON, *To tweddle, tweel*, to work cloth in such a manner, that the woof appears to cross the warp vertically.

† **'tweddling.** *Sc. Obs. rare.* Forms: 6 **twedlyne**, 6–7 **tuidling**, 8 **tweedling**, 9 **tweddlin, -len.** [Of obscure origin: not a normal variant of Sc. *tweeling*, but app. a parallel formation to it.] = TWILLING.

1541 *Aberdeen Regr.* XVII. (Jam.), Ane sark of small twedlyne. **1596** *Compt Bk. D. Wedderburne* (S.H.S.) 47 Item..xxvj ellis tuidling. **1658** *Records of Elgin* (1903) I. 305 Tailyors within the said burghe shall neither buy nor sell any merchandice except so much plaiding, harne, lining, tuidling, stenting, bleached or unbleached. **1747** in *Nairne Peerage Evid.* (1874) 80 Sixteen pair tweedling sheets att one pound three shillings four pence. **1808** JAMIESON, *Tweddlin*, cloth that is tweeled, used also as an adj., as *tweddlen sheets*, sheets of cloth wrought as described above.

twedian, var. TUEDIAN.

† **twee**, *sb.*[1] *Obs.* Also 8 **twey-**; 7 *pl.* **tweeze.** [Aphetic f. *etwee* ETUI.] = TWEEZE *sb.*

1690 *Songs Costume* (Percy Soc.) 196 [We also see] Tweeze As rich and costly as all these. **1747** HOADLY *Susp. Husb.* II. ii, Sure I have not dropt my Twee. **1749** in *6th Rep. Dep. Kpr.* App. II. 123 Small perspective Glasses with Mathematical and other Instruments and Twees, in one and the same case. **1767** *Poetry* in *Ann. Reg.* 236 Seals, rings, 'twees, bodkins.

attrib. **1782** MISS BURNEY *Cecilia* v. ix, What has he left behind him? a twey-case, I suppose, and a bit of a hat won't go on a man's head.

twee (twiː), *sb.*[2] (*int.*) Variously extended, as **twee-we-we, twee-twee-twee, twee-ee.** [Echoic.] An imitation of the sound of a horn, and also of the notes of some birds: see quots.

1708 MOTTEUX in *Muses Mercury* Jan. 11 With a Twee-we-we, Twee-we-we, think it no Scorn, Cits, Souldiers, and Courtiers, give way to the Horn. **1880** A. B. TODD *Poet. Wks.* (1907) 258 A little wren its twee-twee-twee let fall. **1909** *Daily News* 21 June 4 Only the greenfinch's tireless 'twee-ee' was to be heard.

twee (twiː), *a.* (and *sb.*[3]) *colloq.* [f. *tweet*, an infantile pronunciation of *sweet*.]

1. Originally: 'sweet', dainty, chic. Now only in depreciatory use: affectedly dainty or quaint; over-nice, over-refined, precious, mawkish.

1905 *Punch* 8 Mar. 178/1, '*I* call him perfectly twee!' persisted Phyllis. **1917** M. T. HAINSSELIN *Grand Fleet Days* xv. 91 *Girl*: Oh, here's another little gun; isn't it a darling! Isn't it just too twee for words! **1947** E. HYAMS *William Medium* viii. 164 'Isn't he *twee*!' said Mary, and pinched his cheek. **1956** G. DURRELL *Drunken Forest* x. 193 'What twee individuals?' 'Those knowledgeable sentimentalists who are forever telling me that it's cruel to lock up the poor wild creatures in little wooden boxes.' **1962** *Observer* 25 Mar. 25/3 She has a small and, it must be said, pretty twee cottage. **1967** E. SHORT *Embroidery & Fabric Collage* iv. 102 The best of our designers who have abandoned the rather 'twee' decorative type of embroidered picture. **1973** G. ROBYNS *Wimbledon* xxix. 192 There is..a twee Arcadian outdoor studio complete with white trellis and plastic flowers. **1983** *Listener* 21 July 33/1 Mike Nichols's thriller-fantasy about dolphins should be as nauseatingly twee as the worst Disney—but it isn't.

2. *ellipt.* as *sb.*

1957 *Daily Mail* 29 Oct. 12/8, I cannot understand why television's handling of fashion in evening programmes has never got past the twee.

Hence **'tweely** *adv.*, in a twee manner; **'tweeness.**

1958 *Spectator* 2 May 565/3 He manages..to resist the temptation to play up the tweeness and tell the English what they expect to hear. **1962** *Guardian* 12 July 7/1 The..highly commendable idea of importing bulk grains..and passing them, tweely packaged, to cage-bird fanciers. **1973** *Observer* 18 Nov. 36/2 'And no doubt, if the bride is awake and has peeped out through the curtains..,' he speculated tweely. **1981** *Radio Times* 7–13 Nov. 21/2 The word 'herbs'..seems to have become associated with tweeness.

tweed (twiːd). [A trade name originating in an accidental misreading of *tweel*, Sc. form of TWILL (or a misunderstanding of an abbreviated *tweeled* TWILLED *a.*[1]), helped by association with the River Tweed.

The form appears to have originated in or about 1831, but published statements are not quite in accord as to the circumstances which gave rise to it. The more important of these accounts are to be found in Jas. Locke's *Tweed & Don* (1860) 37, in a paper by D. Watson in *Trans. Hawick Archæol. Soc.* (1868) 14, and in A. Barlow's *Weaving* (1878) 49. Barlow and others attribute the misreading of the word to Jas. Locke himself (who was a London merchant), but Locke in his own book does not claim to have been the originator of the name, which had become fully current by 1850.]

a. A twilled woollen cloth of somewhat rough surface, and of great variety of texture, originally and still chiefly made in the south of Scotland (usually of two or more colours combined in the same yarn); inferior kinds are made of wool with a mixture of shoddy or cotton. In *pl.*, cloths or garments of this kind.

1847 MᶜCULLOCH *Acc. Brit. Empire* (ed. 3) I. 667 Narrow cloths, of various kinds, known by the name of Tweeds,.. are extensively produced at Galashiels and Jedburgh, but especially at the former. They used, also, to be produced in considerable quantities at Hawick. **1859** JEPHSON *Brittany* i. 5 A suit of stout grey tweed. **1859** SALA *Tw. round Clock* (1861) 91 Lank office-boys, in..corduroys and tweeds too short, and jackets..too short for them. **1869** C. GIBBON *R. Gray* iv, Garments of rough home-spun tweed. **1882** CAULFEILD & SAWARD *Dict. Needlework* 505 *Tweed*, a woollen cloth woven of short lengths of wool, and lightly felted and milled, the yarn being dyed before woven. It is soft, durable, and flexible. **1894** FENN *In Alpine Valley* I. 186 We do look disreputable enough in our rough tweeds.

b. *attrib.* and *Comb.*, as ***tweed cap, cloth, clothes, finisher, mill, suit, trousering, -weaving***; ***tweed-clad, -covered, -jacketed, -skirted, -suited*** adjs.

1851 *Catal. Gt. Exhib.* III. 495/1 Specimens of Scotch tweed trouserings. *Ibid.* 497/2 Striped and Tweed cloth. **1864** *Fraser's Mag.* Apr. 494 A young gentleman in tweed suit and wideawake. **1865** ALEX. SMITH *Summ. Skye* i. 37 Tweed-clad tourists are everywhere. **1877** MAR. M. GRANT *Sun-Maid* i, His tweed-stalking-cap was drawn over his eyes. **1888** *Daily News* 26 Sept. 7/1 A tweed finisher, employed at Dunsdale mill. **1890** E. WARREN *Laughing Eyes* 61 Tweed-suited monthly-return-ticket visitors. **1928** A. HUXLEY *Point Counter Point* iii. 46 This huge bent old man, pipe-smoking and tweed-jacketed. **1949** C. GRAVES *Ireland Revisited* x. 156 The only really interesting person..was Robert Miller, to whose tweed mill he directed us. **1957** C. MACINNES *City of Spades* II. v. 138 The recalcitrant bowler-hatted or tweed-skirted natives.

tweeded ('twiːdɪd), *a.* [f. TWEED + -ED[2].] Clad in tweed.

1921 G. B. SHAW *Back to Methuselah* II. 38 *The tweeded gentleman.* (Coming in very slowly.) I have something on my mind. **1949** N. MITFORD *Love in Cold Climate* II. v. 241 Why are the English roads always so covered with these tweeded stumpers? **1979** M. RUSSELL *Touchdown* i. 14 Her companion..was nursing on a tweeded lap..a Thermos flask.

‖**Tweede Nuwejaar** ('tvɪədə nyːvə'jaːr). Also **Tweede Nuwe Jaar, Tweedenuwejaar.** [Afrikaans, lit. = second New Year.] The second of January, a public holiday in Cape Province, celebrated especially by the Black population.

1947 *Cape Times* 30 Dec. 14 The Coons are ready for the New Year—and tweede nuwejaar—that extra holiday which is taken only in the Cape. **1953** *Ibid.* 1 Jan. 1/6 There will be no issue of the *Cape Times* to-morrow, January 2 (*Tweedenuwejaar*). **1959** *Ibid.* 3 Jan. 7/3 The coons have enjoyed fine weather for New Year and the Tweede Nuwe Jaar and we have enjoyed them too. **1978** *Argus* (Cape Town) 29 Dec. 3 Normal editions of The Argus will be published on Tuesday January 2, Tweede Nuwejaar.

tweedle ('twiːd(ə)l), *v.*[1] [app. echoic: cf. TEEDLE, TOODLE, TWIDDLE *v.*[2] In sense 2, app. influenced by WHEEDLE.]

1. *intr.* Of a musical instrument or one who plays it: To produce a succession of shrill modulated sounds; also, to play triflingly or carelessly *upon* an instrument; of a bird, etc., to whistle or pipe with modulations of tone.

1684 'PHILO PATER' *Observ. Reproved* 2 The Replyer is only an Instrument of the Faction, the Club blows the Bagpipes, and he Tweedles. **1728** MRS. DELANY in *Life & Corr.* (1861) I. 182 Yesterday I dined at the Percivals, and tweedled away upon a lovely harpsichord. **1795** COWPER *Pairing Time Anticipated* 38 Dick heard, and tweedling, ogling, bridling,..Attested, glad, his approbation. **1835** BECKFORD *Recoll.* vii. 107 A pair of flutes most nauseously tweedled upon by two..young monks.

2. *trans.* To bring into some place or condition by or as by playing on an instrument in this way; to entice by or as by music; to wheedle, cajole.

a **1719** ADDISON (J.), A fiddler brought in with him a body of lusty young fellows, whom he had tweedled into the service. **1740** SOMERVILLE *Hobbinol* I. 149 Touch The trembling chords,..and the fond yielding Maid Is tweedled into Love. *a* **1763** SHENSTONE *Ess.* (1765) 216 Why should he be esteemed devout..when he is tweedled into zeal by the dron pipe of an organ? **1896** OLIVE SCHREINER *Afr. Farm* I. xii, Wheedle her, tweedle her, teedle her, but don't let her make sure of you.

tweedle, *v.*[2] *Criminals' slang.* [prob. f. *tweedle*, var. TWIDDLE *v.*[1], in sense 2 b of the latter.] *trans.* To counterfeit, swindle, practise a confidence trick on. Hence **'tweedler**, one who tweedles; **'tweedling** *vbl. sb.*

1925 E. JERVIS *Twenty-Five Years in Six Prisons* i. 17 Some of the boys go 'tweedling'. I am afraid that the knowing author of the 'cracking-a-crib' book would be flummoxed by 'tweedling'. *Ibid.* 18 The chain is handed over in tissue-paper, and the 'tweedler' departs. **1959** J. GOSLING *Ghost Squad* ix. 114 The tweedler will flog you sawdust cigarettes or dummy diamond rings. **1975** P. G. WINSLOW *Death of Angel* iv. 94 'Tweedling'—small con jobs, mostly against the old and weak. *Ibid.* ix. 195 He was always blubbing to Joss, a tweedler like that has to make himself big to a woman. **1980** 'D. KAVANAGH' *Duffy* ii. 30 Big bad villain. Girls, smokes, bit of smack, mossing, tweedling.

tweedle ('twiːd(ə)l), *sb. Criminals' slang.* [See TWEEDLE *v.*[2]] A counterfeit ring; hence, a swindle (involving counterfeit goods); a 'fiddle', 'racket'.

1890 BARRÈRE & LELAND *Dict. Slang* II. 383/2 *Tweedle* (thieves), a spurious ring, used to swindle jewellers and pawn brokers. **1938** F. D. SHARPE *Sharpe of Flying Squad* xxvii. 275 One of the oldest methods of crime is the Tweedle... The Tweedler spots a ring worth a lot of money in a jeweller's shop and goes..to have an exact..replica made. He goes in..and when the assistant isn't looking very carefully substitutes the fake for the real thing. **1959** J. GOSLING *Ghost Squad* ix. 122 A bloke's tried to pull a tweedle on me with a load of jargoons. **1963** H. SLESAR *Bridge of Lions* (1964) 2 'What's 'is tweedle?' the youth asked suspiciously. **1982** *New Society* 2 Dec. 382/3 Then it was back to the shop for the 'tweedle'—for the switch.

tweedle- ('twiːd(ə)l), the stem of TWEEDLE *v.*[1], employed in combination with other elements (see below) to denote the action of the verb, or a high-pitched musical sound; chiefly in the humorous phrase **tweedledum and tweedledee**, in the earliest example used in reference to two rival musicians (whence the *fig.* sense: see b); ***tweedledee and tweedledum*** (also ***tweedle-dum***), used to suggest the contrast or combination of the sounds of high- and low-pitched musical instruments; hence in quot. 1792 *attrib.* = musical (*obs.*); ***tweedle-dee, tweedle-dum***, a high-, or a low-pitched instrument, or one who plays it; in quots. 1785, 1806, 1826, a fiddler (*obs.*); ***tweedle-tweedle***, the action or practice of tweedling; music, harmony (*obs.*).

1725 BYROM *Handel & Bononcini* Poems 1773 I. 344 Strange all this Difference should be, 'Twixt Tweedle-dum and Tweedle-dee! **1769** *Trinculo's Trip* 47 Squeeking fife and rumbling drum, Tweedle dee—and tweedle dum. **1785** BURNS *Jolly Beggars* Recit. vi, He taks the fiddler by the beard, And draws a roosty rapier—..Wi' ghastly ee, poor tweedle-dee Upon his hunkers bended. **1786** WOLCOTT (P. Pindar) *Bozzy & Piozzi* 70 Great in the noble art of tweedle-tweedle. **1792** —— *Odes Condol.* i. 61 No longer on the tweedle-dum account..Those Men of Taste and Music joyful greet. **1804** J. COLLINS (*title*) Scripscrapologia; or Collins's Doggerel Dish of All Sorts. Consisting of Songs.. which may be sung without..the ravishing Accompaniments of Tweedle-dum or Tweedle-dee. **1805** MRS. GRANT in Campbell *Mem. & Corr.* (1844) I. 59 Two hours of tweedle-dum and tweedle-dee were too much for me. **1806** LAMB *Let. to Manning* 5 Dec., Mary and I are to sit next the orchestra in the pit, next the tweedledees. **1826** F. REYNOLDS *Life & Times* II. 288 Two ordinary violin players..quarrelled..to such a pitch, that each tweedle-dum offered the opposing tweedle-dee, to play him for his whole year's salary.

b. *fig.*, usually in phrase ***tweedledee and tweedledum***, two things or parties the difference between which is held to be insignificant. Also *attrib.*

1851 THACKERAY *Eng. Hum.* v. (1876) 304 Swift could not see the difference between tweedle-dee and tweedle-dum. **1871** MRS. BROOKFIELD *Influence* I. 76 Do you believe in tweedledee or in tweedledum? **1882** MISS BRADDON *Mt. Royal* II. x. 218 To the ears of Mopsy and Dopsy it was all tweedledum, and tweedledee. **1885** *Spectator* 24 Jan. 119/2 By no effort of the mind can we separate tweedle-dum and tweedle-dee. **1886** *Pall Mall G.* 29 Sept. 2/2 The general public need have no special objection to half-pay officers and local Bumbles spending their superfluous time and money in Tweedledum and Tweedledee quarrels. **1889** *Spectator* 14 Dec. 850 The political instinct..which leads Lord Randolph..to discover a Tory Tweedledee for the Radical Tweedle-dum. **1911** *Chr. Endeavour Times* 10 Aug. 724/1 A ..war of words over tweedledees of subtle doctrinal differences and tweedledums of Church polity.

Hence **tweedle-'dee** *v. intr.*, to play or sing in a high-pitched tone; also, to play idly; to tweedle.

1837 CARLYLE *Fr. Rev.* III. I. vi, While right-arms here grew weary of slaying, right-arms there were twiddledeeing on melodious catgut. **1873** W. MORRIS in Mackail *Life* (1899) I. 299 A sandy-haired German tenor tweedledeeing over the unspeakable woes of Sigurd!

tweedle, var. TWIDDLE *v.*[1]

tweedling, var. TWEDDLING *Obs.*

tweedy ('twiːdɪ), *a.* [f. TWEED + -Y[1].]

a. Consisting of or relating to tweed cloth. **b.** Characterized by or given to wearing tweeds. **c.** *fig.* Characteristic of those (e.g. the country gentry) who wear tweeds; heartily informal, exclusively clannish, etc.

1912 R. BROUGHTON *Between Two Stools* xiv. 107 Iris stood before them in tweedy brevity of skirt and pertness of tam-o-shanter. **1928** *Sunday Dispatch* 5 Aug. 17/3 In Scottish country houses you rarely get away from the tweedy atmosphere until the afternoon has worn on. **1930** J. B. PRIESTLEY *Good Companions* II. vii. 445 An angel of a woman, very erect, y'know, and tweedy, and straight out of the Old Moated Grange. **1946** G. D. KLINGOPULOS in *Scrutiny* XIV. II. 144 The only excuse for noticing this tweedy sequel [*sc.* V. Sackville-West's *The Garden*]..is that we need to be reminded..that, in Courses of English, 'The Land' is still too often the substitute for modern poetry. **1949** L. P. HARTLEY *Boat* 80 She nodded very perceptibly in the direction of the tweedy group who were talking to each other as members of the same family do. **1978** I. MURDOCH *Sea* 164 He is a big stout man, always dressed..in tweedy suits with waistcoats. **1980** *Daily Tel.* 20 Mar. 14/5 Miss

Foster, who seems to have been a perfectly splendid, large and tweedy lady.

Hence **'tweedily** *adv.*, **'tweediness.**

1964 C. P. SNOW *Corridors of Power* xxiv. 195 Roger.. lolloped tweedily along between them. **1965** *Listener* 27 May 788/1 The exotic tweediness of little Phyllis Benton, so despised by Mr Amis. **1978** R. HILL *Pinch of Snuff* x. 100 He would have classified her as genuine English county with a good seat but not erring on the side of tweediness. **1980** 'A. SKINNER' *Mind's Eye* i. 10 An old James Bond movie relayed rather tweedily from the mainland.

tweek (twiːk). *Radio.* [Echoic.] A type of whistler which is heard as a short, high-pitched chirruping noise.

1933 BURTON & BOARDMAN in *Proc. IRE* XXI. 1479 Two varieties of distinct musical atmospherics have been observed and given the onomatopœic names 'swish' and 'tweek'. **1953** *Phil. Trans. R. Soc.* A. CCXLVI. 114 The 'short whistler', 'tweek', or 'chink'..is the short (about 20 ms) musical tone produced by repeated reflexion between the earth and the ionosphere of the waves from a distant lightning flash. **1981** *Jrnl. Atmospheric & Terrestrial Physics* XLIII. 1271 The appearance of tweeks on whistler sonograms has been discussed in terms of VLF wave propagation through the land-sea and ionospheric waveguide.

tweel, etc.: see TWILL, etc.

tweely, tweeness: see TWEE *a.*

'tween, † tween (twiːn), *prep.* Forms: 4 **tuene,** 5 **twene, twen, twyn,** 6 **tweene,** 7 **'tweene,** 8– **'tween.** Aphetic form of ATWEEN, BETWEEN.

13.. *Cursor M.* 9363 (Gött.) Tuene þaim fayre acord es nane. **13..** *Guy Warw.* (A.) 4482 Þemperour cleped Herhaud him to, & aresound him tvene hem tvo. **c 1420** ? LYDG. *Assembly of Gods* 16 Twene slepyng and wakyng he bad me aryse. **1430-40** —— *Bochas* I. xiv. (MS. Bodl. 263) 62/1 Thus atwen yre and twen affeccion She heeld hir longe. **1443** *Pol. Poems* (Rolls) II. 214 God send us pees twen Ynglond and Ffraunce! **1447** BOKENHAM *Seyntys* (Roxb.) 20 Of alle thyngys lord thou art juge Twyn hym and me. **1581** A. HALL *Iliad* x. 178 Hie noise tweene them is trold. **1605** SHAKS. *Lear* I. ii. 12 A whole tribe of Fops Got 'tweene a sleepe, and wake. **1783** BURNS *Rigs o' Barley* i, The time flew by, wi' tentless heed, Till 'tween the late and early. **1806** SCOTT *Wandering Willie* vii, But oh, how we doubt when there's distance 'tween lovers.

b. In Combinations (cf. BETWEEN *adv.* 4): **'tween-brain**: see quot.; **'tween doffer**, a doffer intermediate between two others; **'tween-watch**, ? = DOG-WATCH. Also 'TWEEN-DECKS.

1821 CLARE *Vill. Minstr.* etc. (1823) I. 205 As 'tween-light hangs the eve. **1825** J. NICHOLSON *Operat. Mechanic* 391 A small intervening cylinder, called the 'tween doffer, which carries it to the third main cylinder. **1890** BILLINGS *Nat. Med. Dict.*, *'Tween-brain*, portion of brain between the hemispheres and the corpora quadrigemina:..proposed as an equivalent for the German Zwischen-hirn, the second of the five vesicles of the embryonic brain. **1899** W. CHURCHILL *R. Carvel* xx, Many and many the 'tween-watch have I passed in a coil of rope in the tops.

'tween-decks ('twiːndɛks). The usual sailors' abbreviation of BETWEEN-DECKS *sb.*

1816 TUCKEY *Narr. Exped. R. Zaire* ii. (1818) 64 At night our visitors were satisfied with a sail in the 'tween-decks. **1829** MARRYAT *F. Mildmay* ii, Another ladder..brought us to the 'tween-decks. **1892** *Labour Commission Gloss.*, *'Tween Decks*,..used to denote the inside deck immediately below the main or upper deck.

tweeny ('twiːnɪ). *local.* Also **tweeney, -ie.** [f. 'TWEEN + -Y.] A maid-servant who assists both the cook and the housemaid; a between-maid. Also *tweeny girl, -maid.*

1888 in *N. & Q.* 7th ser. VI. 458/1 A few years back.. Being in want of a girl to ease both the cook and the housemaid..[a] neighbour..replied..'You want a tweenie'. **1904** *Daily News* 18 Apr. 8 A certain useful section of the servant class, who..were known as 'tweenies'. **1906** *Daily Record & Mail* 17 Dec. 4 We may learn tone from our valets, courtesy from our cooks, and tact from our tweeny girls.

tweer, var. TUYERE, TWIRE.

twees, -e, -es: see TWEEZE *sb.*

tweet (twiːt), *sb.* and *int.* [Echoic.] An imitation of the note of a small bird. Also repeated.

Cf. *tueit* in the *Compl. Scot.* (1549) vi. 39.

1845 *Zoologist* III. 1063 Its usual note is monosyllabic, and like tweet, tweet, tweet. **1851** G. MEREDITH *S.-W.-Wind in Woodland* 8 A chirp or tweet, That utters fear or anxious love. **1897** A. H. REA in *Bards Angus & Mearns* 378, I heard the skylark singing gay, The tweet o' tiny wren. **1900** *Westm. Gaz.* 3 Dec. 10/1 'Wheet, tweet, tweet',..they [quails] called in the meadows. **1910** *Blackw. Mag.* Feb. 286/1 The 'tweet tweet' of the snipe.

Hence **tweet** *v. trans.*, to utter in this way, to twitter; also *transf.*

1851 G. MEREDITH *Pastorals* v, The little bird..Tweets to its mate a tiny loving note. **1891** S. MOSTYN *Curatica* 63 'Oh', tweet-tweets a diaconal pullet, 'how splendid!' **1902** *Westm. Gaz.* 8 Oct. 8/2 The tweet-tweeting chicks make as much noise in their way as the crowing cockerels.

tweet, dial. var. THWITE *v.*, to cut.

tweeter ('twiːtə(r)). [f. *tweet* vb. s.v. TWEET *sb.* and *int.* + -ER¹.] A small loudspeaker designed to reproduce accurately high-frequency sounds whilst being relatively unresponsive to those of lower frequency. Cf. SQUAWKER, WOOFER.

1934 *Nature* 25 Aug. 294/1 The extension of the range of acoustic fidelity permitted by the 'tweeter'—the high frequency auxiliary speaker—is a boon. **1952** *Electronic Engin.* XXIV. 583/3 The..Tweeter Unit is of the moving coil pressure type and is similar to that used in the 10in. and 12in. concentric Duplex loudspeakers. **1957** *Times* 3 May 13/4 Bearded young men talk of Beethoven in terms of baffles and tweeters. **1959, 1975** [see SQUAWKER 3]. **1982** *Hi-Fi Answers* Oct. 77/1 These drive units are pretty unusual beasts, and the NS1000M sports two: a 30mm dome tweeter and a 8·8cm dome midrange unit.

† tweetle, *v.* By-form or altered form of TWEEDLE. Hence **'tweetling** *vbl. sb.*, fiddling.

1749 J. COLLIER in Bamford *Dial. S. Lanc.* (1854) 72 He's gone Who lov'd the tweetling-trade. **1912** C. MURRAY *Hamewith* 5 He wheepled on 't at morning an' he tweetled on 't at nicht.

† tweeze, *sb. Obs.* Also *pl.* **tweeses, twizes, twises**; rare in *sing.* [Aphetic f. *etweese* (1657) = *etuys, etuis*, pl. of ETUI, ETWEE. See also TWEE¹.

The form-history in Eng. is not quite clear, but app. the plural form *etuis, etwees* was taken also as sing. and spelt *etweese*, and this aphetized to *tweese*.]

A case of small instruments, an etui; also *pl.* instruments kept or carried about in a small case. Occas. *a pair* (= set) *of tweezes.*

1622 MABBE tr. *Aleman's Guzman d'Alf.* II. (1623) 130 Whether shee would buy a very fine paire of twizes which we ..had cut from another gentlewomans girdle..having ground and whet them..and fitted them with a case. **1623-4** MIDDLETON & ROWLEY *Span. Gipsy* II. i, Take anything.., purses, knives, handkerchers, rosaries, tweezes, any toy. **1632** SHERWOOD s.v. *Tweese*, A Surgeons tweese (or box of instruments). [cf. **1611** COTGR., *Pennarol de Chirurgien*, a Chirurgians Case or Ettuy; the box wherein he carries his Instruments.] **1638** FORD *Fancies* I. ii, I will..break the teeth of thy combs, poison thy camphire-balls,..be-tallow thy tweezes. **c 1645** HOWELL *Lett.* I. xvii. 32, I send you.. the French Bever and Tweeses you writ for. **1665** BOYLE *Occas. Refl.* IV. xv. (1848) 255 Drawing a little Penknife out of a pair of Twises I then chanced to have about me. **1672** *Descr. Lake Geneva* in *Misc. Cur.* (1708) III. 409 There are found..Knives, and Needles as thick as Bodkins of tweeses. **1681** W. ROBERTSON *Phraseol. Gen.* (1693) 206 A barber's tweese, or case of instruments.

tweeze (twiːz), *v.* [Back-formation from TWEEZERS *sb. pl.*] *trans.* To pull out (hair) with tweezers. Also, to pull as with tweezers. Hence **'tweezing** *vbl. sb.*

1932 V. WOOLF *Common Reader* 2nd Ser. 153 He.. tweezed out hairs with a silver tweezer. **1956** *Sun* (Baltimore) 13 June B 12/4 Before tweezing, apply to brow area a soft cloth wrung out in hot water. **1968** B. HINES *Kestrel for Knave* 29 So he tweezed the lashes between his finger and thumb and drew the lid down. **1979** M. MCMULLEN *But Nellie was so Nice* I. i. 9 The mouth was scarlet, the brows tweezed to an almost invisible line. **1982** *Chicago Sun-Times* 20 Nov. 19 When Gordon finished, makeup artist Gloria Percival tweezed Schaefer's brows.

'tweezer, *sb.* Also 8 **tweeser.** [f. TWEEZE *sb.*, or *twees, tweeze* pl. of TWEE¹. Also, in mod. use, a back-formation from TWEEZERS.]

† 1. A case of small instruments; an etui, a tweezer-case. *Obs.*

1654 GAYTON *Pleas. Notes* III. vii. 111 His signe..is as attractive as..his Plaister-box (if he be a Chyron too) or if not, as his Tweezer. **1745** *Gentl. Mag.* Jan. 34/2 They admired my tweeser, and the trinkets in it. **1746** ELIZA HEYWOOD *Female Spect.* No. 22. (1748) IV. 187 Her maid.. went privately away in the night, taking with her..her watch, tweezer, a diamond solitaire, and several other trinkets.

2. = TWEEZERS 2; also *attrib.* formed like tweezers.

1904 H. G. WELLS *Food of Gods* I. iv. 105 His hand upon the tweezer of his balance weights. **1909** *Westm. Gaz.* 18 Nov. 4/2 Vertical springs in front and half-'tweezer' cross-springs in the rear.

'tweezer, *v.* [f. TWEEZERS: cf. prec. 2.] *intr.* To use tweezers; *trans.* to pull out with tweezers; also to pinch or pluck with or as with tweezers. Hence **'tweezering** *vbl. sb.*

1806 W. TAYLOR in Robberds *Mem.* (1843) II. 146 There is less micrology, less tweezering at trifles, in his erudition. **1848** in *Q. Rev.* Mar. 446 A hero..who when he has '*tweezered* out the slender blossom of manhood that lives on his lip and cheek', passes well for a tall young lady. **1911** *Blackw. Mag.* July 48/2 If he halted he was tweezered into activity again.

'tweezer-case. Also 7 **tueser-,** 8 **tweaser-, twiser-, twitzer-.** [f. TWEEZER(S) + CASE *sb.*²] A case in which tweezers and other small instruments are carried; an etui or 'tweeze'.

1686 *Lond. Gaz.* No. 2122/4 A round Tueser Case of Tortoise-shell. **1707** J. STEVENS tr. *Quevedo's Com. Wks.* (1709) 229 We..lay as close..as Herrings in a Barrel, or Tools in a Tweezer-Case. **1709-10** STEELE *Tatler* No. 142 ¶5 His Tweezer-Cases are incomparable: You shall have one not much bigger than your Finger, with 17 several Instruments in it. **1712** ARBUTHNOT *John Bull* III. i, Ladies, hung about with toys and trinkets, twiser cases [etc.]. **1755** SMOLLETT *Quix.* (1803) IV. 85 My lady..pulled out a large pin, or rather,..a bodkin, from her tweezer-case. **1899** R. WHITEING *5 John St.* xvii. 177 Writing pads, tweezer cases, shaving sets.

tweezers ('twiːzəz), *sb. pl.* Also 7 **twizers, twezers, tweesers.** [An extended form of *tweezes*, pl. of TWEEZE *sb.* (cf. TROUSE *sb.*² and TROUSERS). See also TWEEZER *sb.*]

† 1. A set or case of small instruments. Also *a pair* (= set) *of tweezers. Obs. rare.*

1654 DOROTHY OSBORNE *Lett. to Sir W. Temple* (1888) 223 Did not you say once you knew where good French tweezers were to be had? Pray send me a pair; they shall cut no love. **1662** PEPYS *Diary* 20 June, Bought me a pair of tweezers, cost me 14/-. **1686** tr. *Chardin's Trav. Persia* 122 Ribbands, Paper, Needles, Twizers, Knives and Scissars. **1688** R. L'ESTRANGE *Brief Hist. Times* III. 121 A Present of Twezers, and a Case of Knives to Father Sweetman at Madrid. **1742** MRS. DELANY in *Life & Corr.* (1861) II. 173 They much admired my tweezers and the trinkets that were in them.

2. Small pincers or nippers (orig. as included in the contents of an etui) used for plucking out hairs from the face or for grasping minute objects. Also *a pair of tweezers.*

1654 GAYTON *Pleas. Notes* III. vii. 110 If he had but spirit enough to have drawne, the very sight of his Tweezers would have put the Don to the Roares. *Ibid.* III. xii. 156 Mr. Barber with his Razor or his Tweezers, could not be so expeditious. **a 1704** T. BROWN *Lett. to Gent. & Ladies* Wks. 1709 III. II. 122 His Eye-brows are fair, but over large,..I mean, when the Tweezers have not play'd their Part. **1796** MORSE *Amer. Geog.* II. 489 They pluck up the hairs..by the roots with tweezers. **1821** BYRON *Juan* v. lxxx, With some small aid from scissars, paint, and tweezers, He look'd in almost all respects a maid. **1863** LYELL *Antiq. Man* ii. 28 In it were found..a pair of tweezers in bronze. **1904** *Mission Field* June 71 Tweezers were used by the Indian men to pull out every hair that grew on their faces.

b. *transf.* in various senses.

1654 GAYTON *Pleas. Notes* II. ii. 40 Until these unpar'd nailes, these sharp and tearing tweesers I fasten on his face. **1889** *Science-Gossip* XXV. 118 That the use of the 'tweezers', borne by the ear-wig at the end of the abdomen, was considered somewhat obscure.

twei, tweie, obs. ff. TWAY.

tweich, obs. Sc. form of TOUCH.

tweien, twein, tweine, obs. ff. TWAIN.

tweies, tweis, obs. ff. TWICE.

twelf, twelfe, twelff, obs. ff. TWELFTH, TWELVE.

twelfth (twɛlfθ), *a.* and *sb.* Forms: see below. [OE. *twelfta*, = OFris. *twilifta, twel(e)fta* (WFris. *toalfte, -de*), MDu. *twal(e)fde, twael(e)fde, twel(e)fde* (Du. *twaalfde*), OS. **twelifto* (MLG. *twelf-, twalf-, twolfde*, LG. *twölfte*, etc.), OHG. *zwelifto, -lefto* (MHG. *zwelfte*, Ger. *zwölfte*), ON. *tólfti, -te*, (Norw. *tolvte*, dial. *tolte*, Sw. *tolfte*, Da. *tolvte*), Goth. **twalifta*: f. OE. *twelf* TWELVE. In southern ME. (14th c.), *twelft* became *twelfth*, after *fourth*, etc., but *twelft, twelt, twalt* remain in various dialects: see -TH² and Note to TENTH.]

A. *adj.*

1. The ordinal numeral corresponding to the cardinal TWELVE; last of twelve; that comes next after the eleventh. **a.** In concord with a sb. expressed.

α. 1 **twelfta,** 1–6 **-te,** 2–3 (*Orm.*) **twellfte,** 3 **tweolfte, tuelfte,** (4 **tuelfd, -fed**), 4 (*Sc.* -6) **tuelft,** 4–7 (9 *dial.*) **twelft,** (4–5 **tuelfete**), 6 *Sc.* **tuelfet, tuelt,** 6 *Sc.* (9 *dial.*) **twelt, twalt.**

a 900 *O.E. Martyrol.* Dec. 216 On þam twelftan monðe. **c 1000** *Sax. Leechd.* III. 190 Mona se twelfta on eallum weorcum nytlic ys. **c 1200** ORMIN 11063 Þe twellfte daȝȝ. **1297** R. GLOUC. (Rolls) 8606 Þe tuelfte [*v.r.* (a 1400) tuelf] ȝer temese moni toun aseincte. **a 1300** *Cursor M.* 22653 (Cott.) Þe twelft [*v.rr.* tuelft, twelþe] signe. **c 1400** *Rule St. Benet* vii. 15 Saint benet spekis in þis sentence Of þe telfete [? tuelfete] maner o mekenes. **1513** DOUGLAS *Æneis* XII. Prol. 306, I..my pen furth tuike, Syne thus begouth of Virgill the twelt buike. **1535** STEWART *Cron. Scot.* (Rolls) III. 16 The tuelt ȝeir..of his ring. **1596** DALRYMPLE tr. *Leslie's Hist. Scot.* III. xxix. (S.T.S.) I. 180 The twelfte ȝeir of his regne. *Ibid.* VI. xcii. 332 The tuelfet ȝeir of his rigne. **1621** *N. Riding Rec.* (1894) 87 The twelft day of February.

β. 4 **twelfþe, tuelfthe,** 5 **twellifth, -yfth,** 6 **twelfyth, -veth,** 6– **twelfth,** (9 **twelvth**); also 4 **tweolthe,** 4–5 **twelþe,** 5 **twelthe, twolthe.**

13.. *K. Alis.* 6403 On tweolthe nyght. **c 1380** Twelþe [see b]. **1387** TREVISA *Higden* (Rolls) V. 145 Þe twelfþe [*ed. Caxton* twellyfth] ȝere he was i-made cathecuminus. **c 1420** *Chron. Vilod.* 4451 In þe twolthe ȝere of his regnynge. **1530** PALSGR. 372/1 *Douziesme*, twelfyth. **1564** HARDING *Answ. to Jewel's Challenge* (1565) 180b, The twelfth councell of Toledo. **1820** CHALMERS *Congregat. Serm.* (1838) II. 189 The 31st verse of the 12th chapter. **1830** W. TAYLOR *Hist. Surv. Germ. Poetry* II. 4 The twelvth section. **1884** *Athenæum* 10 May, A star of the twelfth magnitude.

γ. (Chiefly *Sc.*) 4–5 **tuelf,** 4–7 **twelf,** 5–7 **twelfe,** 7 **twelff.**

c 1375 Twelf [see b]. **a 1400** Tuelf [see quot. 1297 in a]. **1587** FLEMING *Contn. Holinshed* III. 1369/1 On the twelfe daie of Februarie. **1640** in P. H. Waddell *Old Kirk Chron.* (1893) 16 The twelff day of October. **1653** W. RAMESEY *Astrol. Restored* 4 His twelfe chapter.

b. With sb. understood, usually from context; also *spec.* with ellipsis of *day* (of the month), or *chapter* (of a book of Scripture).

a 1000 *Andreas* 665 (Gr.) He wæs twelfta sylf. **c 1200** ORMIN 11063 Itt iss þe þrittennde daȝȝ Fra ȝoldaȝȝ, nohht te twellfte. ? **a 1300** *Shires & Hundreds Eng.* in *O.E. Misc.* 146 þe teonþe on wirecestre, þe eollefte on hereforde, þe tweolfte on lycchesfeld..Her beoþ xv. bispryche. *c*1375 *Sc. Leg. Saints* xii. (*Mathias*) 355 Sa tuk þai hyme for þe twelf to be. *c*1380 *Sir Ferumb.* 2846, Y me self was þe twelþe. 1558 *Lydgate's Bochas* IX. xiv. 26 The twelft [*Bodl. MS.* twelue] in nombre. 1562 WINȜET *Last Blast* Wks. (S.T.S.) I. 39 Sen the twelft of Marche. 1600 ABP. ABBOT *Exp. Jonah* 176 In the twelfth of the Revelation. 1611 BIBLE *1 Kings* xix. 19 Elisha..was plowing with twelue yoke of oxen before him, and hee with the twelfth. 1867 'OUIDA' *Cecil Castlemaine's Gage*, etc. 345 We soon made up..to the Norwich girls for the loss of the Twelfth [Lancers]. 1887 BOWEN *Virg. Eclogues* VIII. 39 Years I had finished eleven, the twelfth was beginning.

c. *ellipt.* (*a*) The 12th of August, on which grouse-shooting legally begins.

1816 SCOTT *Antiquary* III. ix. 196 'I must be prepared for Lord Glenallan's moors on the twelfth, sir,' said M'Intyre. 'Ah, Hector! Thy great *chasse*, as the French call it.' 1868 *Field* 8 Aug. 105/3 Many seasons have come and gone since the first Twelfth that I remember. 1895 *Times* (Weekly ed.) 16 Aug. 657/2 In Derbyshire the 'Twelfth' opened delightfully.

(*b*) The 12th of July, celebrated by Protestants in Northern Ireland as the anniversary of the Battle of the Boyne (1 July (Old Style) 1690) at which William III defeated James II.

1896 M. HAMILTON *Across an Ulster Bog* vi. 57 The greatest excitements of her life—next always to 'the twelfth'—had been occasional Methodist or Plymouth Brethren meetings. 1936 *Ann. Reg. 1935* 115 The Orange celebrations of 'The Twelfth' were on a bigger scale than ever, but the atmosphere was highly charged, and in the evening there were serious riots. 1957 *Belfast News-Letter* 2 July 6 (*heading*) Record 'Twelfth' parades expected. 1978 D. MURPHY *Place Apart* xiii. 269 The Twelfth festivities commemorate the victory at the Boyne.

2. ***twelfth part***, any one of twelve equal parts into which a whole may be divided.

1590 in *Reg. Mag. Sig. Scot. 1595*, 120/1 Reddendo 2 bollas 2 firlotas 2 peccas 2 mensuras vocatas twelf-pairtis farine avenatice. 1724 SWIFT *Drapier's Lett.* i. Wks. 1755 V. II. 23 The twelfth part of a half-penny will do him no more service. 1878 J. DAVIDSON *Inverurie* v. 184 The owners of Twelfth Parts had their lands divided..periodically by lot.

†**3.** ***twelfth whist***, whist with only twelve cards in each hand. *Obs.*

1752 H. WALPOLE *Let. to R. Nugent* (in *N. & Q.* 9th Ser. IV. 538/2), Amusing my selfe..at a game of 12th whist.

4. ***twelfth man*** (Cricket), a twelfth player selected as reserve to the team of eleven.

1876 *Haygarth's Scores* VI. 20 Mr. E. Arkwright..was first choice out of the [Harrow] Eleven, or 'twelfth man' in 1858. 1928 J. BUCHAN *Runagates Club* vii. 195, I saw you play at Lord's. I was twelfth man for Harrow that year. 1976 J. SNOW *Cricket Rebel* 26 There were just a couple of minutes to the off when the two twelfth men appeared on the field, the horses lined up as we gathered round the radio.

B. *sb.*

1. a. A twelfth part: see A. 2.

1557 RECORDE *Whetst.* B ij b, *Sesquiduodecima*, 13 to 12.. a tweleuth more. 1696 LOCKE *Lower. Interest* (ed. 2) 136 Supposing..5*s.* or a Crown, were to weigh an Ounce.. whereof one twelfth were Copper, and eleven twelfths Silver. 1712 J. JAMES tr. *Le Blond's Gardening* 197 Five Twelfths of an Inch thick. 1792 A. YOUNG *Trav. France* 537 No such thing was ever known in any part of France..as a tenth: it was always a twelfth, or a thirteenth, or even a twentieth of the produce. 1812 SIR H. DAVY *Chem. Philos.* 419 From a third to a twelfth of zinc is used. 1812 WOODHOUSE *Astron.* xxxv. 347 Expressed in twelvths of that diameter. 1897 *Westm. Gaz.* 20 Apr. 3/1 A decrease of a twelfth since 1894.

b. *spec.* A twelfth part of rents or movables granted or levied by way of tax.

1884 DOWALL *Hist. Taxation* I. IV. iv. 77 The use of grants of fractional parts of moveables was continued..in 1296 a twelfth and eighth..were granted. *Ibid.* 81 The grants made ..were..in 1318 a twelfth from demesne.

2. *Mus.* **a.** A note twelve diatonic degrees above or below a given note (both notes being counted); the octave of a fifth; hence (usually) the interval, or consonance, between two such notes. **b.** An organ-stop sounding a twelfth above the normal pitch.

1597 MORLEY *Introd. Mus.* 70 Those notes which are distant from them eight notes, as from a fift, a twelfe..from Gamvt to D la sol re is a twelfe. 1613 *Organ Specif. Worcester Cathedral*, The particulars of the great organ..1 twelfth of mettal. 1797 *Encycl. Brit.* (ed. 3) XII. 511 Note E, The chord formed with the twelfth and seventeenth major united with the principal sound. 1891 PROUT *Counterpoint* (ed. 2) 74 The thirds above it now give the inversion in the twelfth.

†**3.** Short for TWELFTH-DAY. (Cf. TWELFTH-EVE(N.) *Obs.*

1472 SIR J. PASTON in *P. Lett.* III. 33, I have my pardon, ..for comffort whereoffe I have been the marier thys Crystmesse,..be ffor Twelthe I come to my Lorde Archebysshope.

C. *Comb.*: **twelfth-century** *a.*, of or belonging to the century from 1101 to 1200.

1867 FURNIVALL in *Percy Folio* I. 403 A twelfth-century writer.

Twelfth-cake. [Short for *Twelfth-night* or *Twelfth-tide cake*: cf. TWELFTH B. 3.] A large cake used at the festivities of Twelfth-night, usually frosted and otherwise ornamented, and with a bean (see BEAN *sb.* 6 b) or coin introduced to determine the 'king' or 'queen' of the feast.

1774 in Brand *Pop. Antiq.* (1777) 206, I did not return till I had been present at drawing King and Queen, and eaten a Slice of the Twelfth Cake. 1826 HONE *Every-Day Bk.* [55 A citation by Brand represents the..Twelfth-night-cake to have been composed of flour, honey, ginger, and pepper.] 56 In France, the Twelfth-cake is plain, with a bean; the drawer of the slice containing the bean is king or queen. 1876 G. MEREDITH *Beauch. Career* xxix, A ricketty ornament like that you see on a confectioner's twelfth-cake.

attrib. 1837 [MISS MAITLAND] *Lett. fr. Madras* (1843) 54 A queer kind of sprig made of rice and beads, like a twelfth-cake ornament. 1838 *Civil Eng. & Arch. Jrnl.* I. 337/1 The house at Kenwood is quite in the twelfth-cake style—patched all over with panels of filagree work.

Twelfth-day. Forms: see TWELFTH and DAY. The twelfth day after Christmas; the sixth of January, on which the festival of the Epiphany is celebrated; formerly observed as the closing day of the Christmas festivities. (Cf. *the twelve days* s.v. TWELVE *adj.* 1 c.)

[*c*900 tr. *Bæda's Hist.* IV. xix. 318 Æt Pentecosten & þy twelftan deȝe ofer ðeochol.] *c*1000 *Ags. Gosp.* Matt. ii. 1 *rubric*, Ðys sceal on twelftan dæȝ. *a*1100 [see TWELFTH-EVE(N]. *c*1200 ORMIN 11047 Jesu Crist wass fullhtnedd Rihht o þatt daȝȝ..þatt twellfte daȝȝ iss nemmnedd. 1389 in *Eng. Gilds* (1870) 117 Ye sonunday next after ye twelft day. 1455 E. CLERE in *Paston Lett.* I. 315 On the morow after Twelftheday. 1553 BECON *Reliques of Rome* (1563) 75 b, The feastful day of the Epiphanye commonly called Twelf-day. 1585 T. WASHINGTON tr. *Nicholay's Voy.* IV. xix. 133 b, They do not celebrate the natiuitie of..Christ, but on the twelfth day, vse great feasts and solemnitie. 1662 J. DAVIES tr. *Olearius' Voy. Ambass.* 211 *margin*, The Armenians blesse the Water on Twelf-day. 1689–90 WOOD *Life* Jan. (O.H.S.) III. 320 A great flood about Oxon before 12th day. 1725 H. BOURNE *Antiq. Vulg.* xvii, The Twelfth-Day it self is one of the greatest of the Twelve. 1863 *Chambers' Bk. Days* I. 61/1 January 6. This day, called Twelfth-day..and Epiphany..is a festival of the Church.

attrib. 1913 *19th Cent.* Aug. 320 He had promised the children a twelfth-day cake.

†**Twelfth-eve(n.** *Obs.* The eve of Twelfth-day; Twelfth-night.

*c*1000 *Ags. Gosp.* Matt. ii. 19 *rubric*, Ðys sceal on twelftan æfen. *a*1100 *O.E. Chron.* an. 1065 (MS. C.) Eadward.. forðferde on twelftan æfen, & hyne man bebyriȝde on twelftan dæiȝ. 1538 *MS. Acc. St. John's Hosp., Canterb.*, Rec. vpon twelfte euen iij s v d. 1582 in Feuillerat *Revels Q. Eliz.* (1908) 349 At wyndesor at Twelf Eve at night. 1634–5 LAUD *Diary* 5 Jan., Monday night, being Twelfth-eve.

'twelfthic. *Math.* [f. TWELFTH + -IC, after *quartic*, etc.] A quantic of the twelfth degree.

1882 DURFEE in *Amer. Jrnl. Math.* V. 45 (*heading*) Tables of the Symmetric Functions of the Twelfthic.

twelfthly ('twɛlfθlɪ), *adv.* [f. TWELFTH *a.*] In the twelfth place; as the twelfth in a series.

*c*1532 DU WES *Introd. Fr.* in *Palsgr.* 929. *a*1642 SIR W. MONSON *Naval Tracts* III. (1704) 322/1 Twelfthly, They should make quarterly Payments. 1644 PRYNNE & WALKER *Fiennes's Trial* 82 Twelfely, Might not every Governour and Generall upon this pretence deliver up any Fort? 1693 J. EDWARDS *Author. O. & N. Test.* 181 Twelfthly, we read in several authors [etc.].

'Twelfth-night. Forms: see TWELFTH and NIGHT. The evening before Twelfth-day, formerly observed as a time of merry-making. Also *attrib.*

*c*900 *O.E. Chron.* an. 878 Her hiene bestæl se here on midne winter ofer tuelftan niht to Cippanhamme. 13.. *K. Alis.* (Laud MS.) 6388 Of þat cite comen..þe kynges thre, þat foloweden goddis sterre..In cristemasse, on þe tweleuþ niȝth. 1601 SHAKS. (*title*) Twelfe Night, Or what you will. 1649 MILTON *Eikon.* Pref., Wks. 1851 III. 333 Quaint Emblems..begg'd from the olde Pageantry of some Twelfe-nights entertainment. 1764 *Chron.* in *Ann. Reg.* 45/1 The ancient custom of public hazard playing at court on twelfth night. 1826 Twelfth-night-cake [see TWELFTH-CAKE]. 1854 THACKERAY *Rose & Ring* Prel. (1866) 3 Twelfth-Night characters—those funny painted pictures of the King, the Queen, the Lover, the Lady, the Dandy, the Captain, and so on—with which our young ones are wont to recreate themselves at this festive time. 1863 *Chambers' Bk. Days* I. 64/1 In the last century, Twelfth-Night cards represented ministers, maids of honour, and other attendants of a court.

†**'Twelfthtide.** *Obs.* Forms: 6 twelfe tyde, 6–7 twelftide, twelfetide (in 7 also with hyphen), 6–8 twelftyde, (7 twelvetide). (*Twelfth-tide* occurs app. only in modernized editions.) [See TIDE *sb.* 4 b, 6.] The season including Twelfth-night and Twelfth-day; the season of Epiphany: formerly the concluding part of the Christmas holidays.

1530 PALSGR. 283/2 Twelftyde, *la typhayne*. 1561 T. NORTON *Calvin's Inst.* IV. xix. 159 That there be no mariages celebrate..from Aduent to Twelftide. 1632 MASSINGER & FIELD *Fatal Dowry* II. ii, As if he had come this Christmas ..To see his friends, and returned after twelf-tide. 1656 FINETT *For. Ambass.* 48 A mask prepared for twelftyde. 1687 *Lond. Gaz.* No. 2301/3 It will not be before Twelvetide.

attrib. 1639 S. DU VERGER tr. *Camus' Admir. Events* 64 Like a right Twelfetide King. 1648 HERRICK *New-yeares Gift to Sir S. Steward* 17 Of twelf-tide cakes, of pease, and beanes, Wherewith ye make those merry sceanes, When as ye chuse your king and queen.

twell (twɛl), *prep.* and *conj.* Also **twel.** U.S. dial. and Black English var. of TILL *prep.*, *conj.*, *adv.*

1837 A. SHERWOOD *Gazetteer Georgia* (ed. 3) 72 *Twell*, for till;—twell night—twell next week. 1893 H. A. SHANDS *Some Peculiarities of Speech in Mississippi* 65 *Twel* (twell). Negro for *till*. 1901 W. CHURCHILL *Crisis* I. iv. 38 Dis ole woman'll wuk fo' you twell de flesh drops off'n her fingers, suh. 1938 W. FAULKNER *Unvanquished* vi. 229 Uncle Cash that druv the Benbow carriage twell he run off with the Yankees two years ago.

†**twell,** obs. form of TOWEL.

1422–3 *Abingdon Rolls* (Camden) 92 In twellis emptis pro Refectorio xj s.

twell, obs. form of TWELVE.

twelt, twelth, obs. or dial. Sc. ff. TWELFTH.

†**'twelter aithe.** *Orkney* and *Shetland.* [ad. (after Sc. *twelt* TWELFTH *a.*) ON. *tylftar-eiðr*, f. *tylft* a body of twelve, a dozen + *eiðr* oath: cf. SAXTER AITHE.] An oath of twelve compurgators.

1603 *Lawting Court* 21 July, in Peterkin *Notes Orkney & Zetl.* (1822) App. 35 Ordained to quit himsel of theft by the twelter-aith, because the stowth is great.

twelve (twɛlv), *numeral a.* and *sb.* Forms: see below. [Comm. Teutonic: OE. *twelf*, (also *tuelf*, and in Lindisf. gl. *tuoelf*), = OFris. *twelef*, *twilif*, *twelf* (OWFris. *tolef*, WFris. *toalf*); MDu. *twalef*, *twaelf*, *twelef*, *twelf* (Du. *twaalf*); OS. *twelif*, *twilif*, *twulif* (MLG. *twelf*, *twolf*, *twalf*, LG. *twölf*); OHG. *zwelif*, MHG. *zwelif*, *zwelf*, Ger. *zwölf*, ON. *tólf*, (Sw. *tolf*, Norw., Da. *tolv*), Goth. *twalif*:—OTeut. **twalibi-*, f. *twa* two + *lib-* or *lif-*, of uncertain origin, but generally considered to belong to the same root as OTeut. **liban* to LEAVE (q.v.), and thus to denote 'two left or remaining over (ten)'; cf. ELEVEN. Analogous formations to *eleven* and *twelve* are the Lith. *vênů'lika* 11, *dvýlika* 12, in which the second element, Lith. *-lika*, has also the meaning of 'left over'. All other Indo-Eur. langs. have or had forms composed of 'two' + 'ten', like the numbers 13 to 19; cf. L. *duōdecim*, Gr. δώδεκα, Skr. *dwādaçan*.

As an adj. standing before a sb. OE. *twelf* was as a rule indeclinable; in other positions it was usually declined, nom.-acc. *twelfe*, gen. *twelfa*, dat. & prep. *twelfum*, but exceptions on both sides are found in OE., esp. in Northumbrian, and in ME. *twelfe*, and at length *twelve*, became the form in all positions. Reduction to *tuoel* occurs once in Lindisf. Gl., and in ME. and mod. dialects *twell*, *twall* are frequent.]

A. Illustration of Forms.

α. 1–7 **twelf,** (1–6 **tuelf,** 1 **tuoelf**) 2–3 **tweolf,** (*Orm.*) **twellf,** 3 **tueolf, twælf, twealf, twalf,** 3–4 **twolf,** 5 **twellif, -yf,** *Sc.* **tuelff** (6 **twelef**), 6–7 *Sc.* **twelff.**

*c*888 K. ÆLFRED *Boeth.* xxxiv. § 10 Ðe..on twelf monðum ȝewexð. 971 *Blickl. Hom.* 15 Hælend ȝenam his twelf þeȝnas. *c*1000 *Ags. Gosp.* Matt. x. 5 Ðas twelf se hælynd sende. *c*1020 *Rule St. Benet* (Logeman) 40 þæt ne siȝ læs twelf sealma. *c*1175 *Lamb. Hom.* 141 þa fouwer [walmes] weren ideled a twelue, for þa twelf kunreden sculden þer mide heore þurst kelen. *c*1200 ORMIN 8900 Off twellf winnterr elde. *c*1205 LAY. 1617 His tueolf iferen [*c* 1275 his twelue iueres]. *Ibid.* 25441 þer comen þa twalf [*c* 1275 twealf] iueren. *Ibid.* 25971 Twælf [*c* 1275 twealf] swine. *c*1330 R. BRUNNE *Chron. Wace* (Rolls) 8232 Twolf ȝer old. 1375 BARBOUR *Bruce* x. 547 A schort leddir..I trow of tuelf fut. *c*1470 *Golagros & Gaw.* 411 Tuelf crovnit kingis. 1567 *Gude & Godlie B.* (S.T.S.) 3 The twelf Articklis of our Faith. 1588 A. KING tr. *Canisius' Catech.* I. G vij, The cowrse of the moone, quhilk do change twelff tymes in the yere.

β. 1 **twelfe** (**tuelfe**, etc.), 2–3 (*Orm.*) **twellfe,** 3–7 **twelfe,** 5 **tuelfe.**

*a*900 *Fate Apostles* 4 Twelfe wæron dædum domfæste. *c*950 *Lindisf. Gosp.* Matt. x. 5 Ðas tuelfe [*Rushw.* twælfe] sende ðe hælend. *c*1200 ORMIN 956, & off þa twellfe namess ec þatt wærenn don þæronne. *a*1400–50 *Alexander* 1079 Fyftene Burghes, And..xij grym waters [*Dubl. MS.* twelfe gret waters]. 1483 *Cath. Angl.* 398/2 Twelfe, *duodecim*. *Ibid.*, Twelfe ȝere space. 1552 HULOET, Twelfe together, *duodeni*. 1603 OWEN *Pembrokeshire* v. (1892) 42 Ten or twelfe yeeres of age.

γ. 2–7 **twelue,** 3 **twælue, twalue,** 3–5 **twelwe,** 3–6 **twolue,** 4 **tuelue** (7 **twellue**), 4– **twelve.**

*c*1175 Twelue [see α]. *c*1250 *Gen. & Ex.* 663 Twelwe and sexti men. *c*1275 *Passion our Lord* 42 in *O.E. Misc.* 38 He ches hym twolue yuere myd him vor to lede. *c*1275 Twelue [see quot. *c* 1205 in α]. 1387 TREVISA *Higden* (Rolls) III. 401 Whanne Alisaundre was twelve ȝere olde. *c*1440 *Promp. Parv.* 504/2 Twelwe, *duodecim*. 1535 COVERD. *Matt.* xix. 28 Ye..shal syt also vpon twolue seates. 1607 SHAKS. *Cor.* IV. v. 128 Thou hast beate mee out Twelue seuerall times.

δ. 4 **tuel,** 4–7 **twel;** *Sc.* 6 **twoll,** 6–7 **twell,** 6–9 **twall,** 7 **tuel(l,** 8–9 **twal.**

*c*1400 *Trevisa's Higden* (Rolls) III. 23 He regned in al twelve [*MS.* γ twel] ȝere. 1500–20 DUNBAR *Poems* xxviii. 1 Betuix twell houris and ellevin. 1588 A. KING tr. *Canisius' Catech.* II. 3 The somme off our faith..quhilk ye twoll apostlis compylit..callit the creid, quhilk yai..dewyddit in twoll articlis. 1599 in *Maitl. Cl. Misc.* III. 341 The space of twell dayis. 1639 LD. WARISTON *Diary* (S.H.S.) 329 At tuel hours. 1785 Twal [see B. I. 2 b]. 1837 R. NICOLL *Poems* (1843) 106 Twal corporation feasts within the year.

B. Signification.

The cardinal number composed of ten and two; represented by the symbols 12 or XII.

I. *adj.* **1. a.** In concord with a sb. expressed. (*a*) Preceding the sb.

Beowulf (Z.) 147, .xii. wintra tid. 971 [see A. α]. *c*1050 *Byrhtferth's Handboc* in *Anglia* (1885) VIII. 298 On þisum daȝum beoð ȝesette twelf monðas. 1297 R. GLOUC. (Rolls) 431 þis folc..departede hor ost in tuelf [*v.rr.* twolf, twelue] parties. *c* **1330** R. BRUNNE *Chron. Wace* (Rolls) 13534 þey were..set In twolue batailles. **1420–2** LYDG. *Siege Thebes* 3540 I-braunched out vpon twelue trees. **1526** TINDALE *Acts* vii. 8 And Isaac begat Iacob, and Iacob the twelve patriarkes. **1584** POWEL *Lloyd's Cambria* 53 He choose out of that companie..twelue men. **1638** BROME *Antipodes* III. ii, Twelve Hymnes, For the twelve Sessions. **1750** tr. *Leonardus's Mirr. Stones* 80 There are twelve species of it. *a* **1774** GOLDSM. *Hist. Greece* I. 30 At twelve years old the boys were removed into another class. **1847** GROTE *Greece* II. xix. III. 390 The division of the day into twelve parts.

(*b*) Following the sb. (Chiefly for rime.)

a **1000** *Sal. & Sat.* 15 (Gr.) Mine suna twelfe. *a* **1300** *Cursor M.* 174 (Cott.) Iesu crist him selue Ches til him apostels tuelue. *Ibid.* 29063 Crist..Spekand to his aposteles tueluen. *c* **1374** CHAUCER *Troylus* II. 59 (108) Herof ben þere maked bokes twelue. *c* **1386** —— *Prol.* 527 But cristes lore, and hise Apostles twelue He taughte, but first he folwed it hym selue. **1390** GOWER *Conf.* I. 181 The Souldan hise hostages sende..of Princes Sones tuelve.

b. As multiplier before a higher numeral (*hundred, thousand*, etc.). ***twelve score***, twelve twenties, two hundred and forty; †also *ellipt.* for *twelve score yards*, a common range for a shot in archery; hence *attrib.* in ***twelve score prick*** (see PRICK *sb.* 10 b).

c **1205** LAY. 25443 Twelf [*c* **1275** Twealf] þusend cnihtes. *c* **1290** *S. Eng. Leg.* I. 66/450 He deide tweolf hundred ȝer.. Aftur ore louerdes burtyme. **1297** R. GLOUC. (Rolls) 10121 In tuelf hundred ȝer of grace & þe secunde ȝere. *c* **1425** WYNTOUN *Cron.* VIII. 2011 Twelf hundir nynti ȝhere and sewyn Fra Crist was borne. [*c* **1470** HENRY *Wallace* VI. 107 Tuelff hundreth ȝeer, tharto nynte and sewyn.] **1552** HULOET, Twelue hundreth thousande *sestertia.* **1653** H. COGAN tr. *Pinto's Trav.* ix. 28 Eleven or twelve thousand staves hardened in the fire. **1726** SWIFT *Gulliver* II. vii, A gallery of twelve hundred feet long.

a **1300** *Cursor M.* 2168 (Cott.) Ragan..[lived] Twelue scor o yeires. **1550–3** *Decaye of Eng.* A v, Twelf score persons in Oxfordshire. **1569–1620** [see PRICK *sb.* 10 b]. **1597** SHAKS. *2 Hen. IV*, III. ii. 52 Hee would haue clapt in the Clowt at Twelue-score. *a* **1700** DRYDEN *Theocritus, Epithal. Helen & Menelaus* 39 Twelvescore viragos of the Spartan race. **1753** CHAMBERS *Cycl. Supp.* s.v. *Coursing*, When a hare is put up,..let her run twelve-score yards or thereabouts, before the greyhounds are slip'd at her.

c. In special collocations, as *the twelve* APOSTLES, *twelve labours* (of HERCULES, q.v.), *twelve* SIGNS (of the zodiac, also †TOKENS), *Twelve* TABLES, *twelve* TRIBES (of Israel): see these words; also †***the twelve days***, i.e. those immediately following Christmas (cf. TWELFTH-DAY); †***the twelve men***, a body of twelve men having some special function, as a jury, a select vestry, etc.

c **975** *Rushw. Gosp.* Matt. x. 2 þara *twelf apostola noma [*Ags. Gosp.* naman] sindun þas. *c* **1175** *Lamb. Hom.* 75 þet rihte ileue setten þe twelue apostles on write. **1377** LANGL. *P. Pl.* A. XI. 25 He þat..con tellen of Tobie and þe Twelue Apostles. **1890** *Science-Gossip* XXVI. 10/2 Among the most curious birds of Queensland are those known familiarly as the 'Twelve Apostles', from the circumstance that they are always seen in flocks of exactly twelve. [**1600** NASHE *Summer's Last Will* Wks. (Grosart) VI. 156 To feede the poore twelue dayes, & let them starue all the yeare after.] **1693** SIR T. P. BLOUNT *Nat. Hist.* 132 Tobacco. In the *Twelve-Days they begin to Sow their Seed. **1725** H. BOURNE *Antiq. Vulg.* xvii. (*heading*), The Wickedness of observing the Twelve Days after the common Way. *a* **1577** SIR T. SMITH *Commw. Eng.* (1633) 110 They which either condemne or acquite the man..are not called Judges but the *twelve men. **1607** *Henley-in-Arden Rolls* (MS.) 22 Oct., Henleye. Agreementes & paines bie the Tweluemenne as followeth made at the Couurte holden ther the 22 daye of october. **1608** in *N. & Q.* 8th Ser. XI. 201/1 Paines laid at the great courte at Sheffelde..by the twelue men of the sooke of Ecclesfelde. **1672** *Cowell's Interpr., Twelve Men*,.. otherwise called the Jury or Enquest, is a number of twelve persons [etc.]. **1744** in J. Hammond *Cornw. Parish* (1897) vi. 80 [It was resolved] that every Principall Inhabitant..under the denomination of a twelve-man shall be an acting Manager and Trustee [of the Workhouse]. **1886** *Johns Hopkins Univ. Stud.* Ser. IV. i. 55 The patentees are said to have been called the 'Twelve Men' or Duzine, and to have had both legislative and judicial powers in town affairs. **1390** GOWER *Conf.* III. 108 Ther ben *signes tuelve, Whiche have her cercles be hemselve Compassed in the zodiaque. **1509** HAWES *Past. Pleas.* XXII. (Percy Soc.) 105 In the xii. signes them selfe to domify. *a* **1585** MONTGOMERIE *Flyting* 421 Be the poles, and the planets, and the signes all twell. *c* **1000** *Ags. Man. Astron.* in *Pop. Treat. Sc.* (1841) 7 Under ælc þæra *twelf tacna. **1535** COVERDALE *2 Kings* xxiii. 5 Them that brent incense..to the Sonne, and the Mone, and the twolue tokens.

2. *absol.* **a.** with ellipsis of sb., preceded by a pronoun or demonstrative, or as predicate.

a **900**, *c* **950** [see A. *β*]. *c* **1000** [see A. *α*]. *c* **1000** *Ags. Gosp.* Mark xiv. 20 þa sæde he him, An of eow twelfum me sylð. *c* **1205** LAY. 25275 þas twælfe heore wai ferden. *Ibid.* 26206 For aȝan þine tweie Heo habbeoð twælue [*c* **1275** twalue]. **1382** WYCLIF *Gen.* xxxv. 22 The sones of Jacob weren twelue. —— *2 Sam.* ii. 15 Twelue of the children of Dauid. **1535** COVERDALE *Josh.* xxi. 40 All the cities of the children of Merari..were twolue. **1646** J. BENBRIGGE *Vsura Accom.* 5 A Banke of Recovery..herein Twelve were given for the use of an Hundred per annum.

spec. **b.** with ellipsis of *hours* (of the day: cf. *twelve hours* in III. c.); also ***twelve o'clock***.

to strike twelve the first time (or ***all at once***), *fig.* to display all one's capacities in one's first performance.

c **1482** J. KAY tr. *Caoursin's Siege of Rhodes* (1870) ¶ 11 All the nyght frou twelfe the clocke unto v in the daye. **1605** SHAKS. *Macb.* II. i. 3 *Fleance.* The Moone is downe: I have not heard the Clock. *Banq.* And she goes downe at Twelve. **1638** SANDERSON *Serm.* (1681) II. 129 If a man should vow he would never eat till all the clocks in the city should strike twelve together. **1665** in *Extr. S.P. rel. Friends* III. (1912) 237 Betweene eleauen and twelue A clocke. **1709** PRIOR *Hans Carvel* 33 She..was wak'd at Ten;..At Twelve She rose. **1785** BURNS *Dr. Hornbook* xxxi, Some wee, short hour ayont the twal. **1818** SCOTT *Rob Roy* xxii, D'ye think I wad hae comed out at twal o'clock at night? **1832** TENNYSON *Death Old Year* v, The light burns low: 'Tis nearly twelve o'clock. **1847** EMERSON *Eng. Traits* xix. (1856) 310 Their best parts were slowly revealed;..they did not strike twelve the first time. **1862** MISS BRADDON *Lady Audley* xxiii, The clock struck twelve. **1894** J. A. NOBLE in *Academy* 10 Feb. 119/3 There are some writers who, to use a homely colloquialism, strike twelve all at once: their first achievement..tells us all about them.

c. with ellipsis of *years* (of age).

1607 SHAKS. *Cor.* IV. v. 135 We would muster all From twelue, to seuentie. **1646** J. HALL *Horæ Vac.* 75 Unlesse an inclination be very discoverable [in a child], it cannot be perceived till after Twelve. **1818** BYRON *Juan* I. l, At twelve he was a..quiet boy.

d. ***the twelve*** (spec.): applied to various bodies of twelve men having some special office, as the twelve apostles, a select vestry consisting of twelve parishioners, etc.; also, the books of the twelve 'minor prophets' in the Old Testament.

c **950** *Lindisf. Gosp.* John vi. 71 An of ðæm tuelfum. **1382** WYCLIF *John* xx. 24 Thomas, oon of the twelue..was not with hem. **1526** TINDALE *Luke* ix. 1 Then called he the xij. to-gether, and gave them power and auctorite over all devyls. *c* **1605** *Acc. Bk. W. Wray* in *Antiquary* XXXII. 213 A great contention betwixt the xij as they tearmed theymselves and the commonaltie of Rippon about the election of the wakeman. **1635** *Vestry Bks.* (Surtees) 97 It was agreed by the twell of the parish of Pettingtone there should be a ceasment of sex penns a pound. **1843** MACAULAY *Regillus* xxxvii, Manlius, eldest of the Twelve Who kept the Golden Shield. **1882** FARRAR *Early Chr.* II. 484 St. John was the last survivor of the Twelve. **1898** J. ROBERTSON *Poetry & Relig. Ps.* iii. 52 The Twelve minor prophets..perhaps the very first notice we have of them in history is a reference to them as a collection, known as 'the twelve'. **1909** SIR W. M. RAMSAY in *Expositor* July 14 The duties..discharged by the Twelve in the original congregation.

3. Used for the ordinal TWELFTH; in quot. 1682 ***Twelve eve*** = TWELFTH-EVE(N. *Obs.* (exc. after the sb. in such expressions as *page twelve, chapter twelve*, etc.).

See also TWELFTH A. 1 *γ*; some of the quots. there may properly belong here.

1430–40 LYDG. *Bochas* IX. xiv. (MS. Bodl. 263) 419/2 The twelue in noumbre Callid Pope Iohn. **1586** W. WEBBE *Eng. Poetrie* (Arb.) 62 Transpose anie of those feete..and make short either the two, foure, sixe, eight, tenne, twelue sillable, and it will..fall out very absurdly. **1660** BLOOME *Archit.* B c, Within that twelve part. **1682** PIERS *Descr. W. Meath* (1770) 124 On Twelve Eve in Christmas.

II. *sb.* (with plural *twelves*).

1. The abstract number.

c **1425** *Craft of Nombrynge* (E.E.T.S.) 9 Cast 6 to 6, & þere-of wil arise twelue. **1571** DIGGES *Pantom.* I. xii, Multiplie the distance..by 12. **1875** TODHUNTER *Algebra* (ed. 7) xxix. §440 The number ten has only two divisors.., the number twelve has four... On this account twelve would have been more convenient than ten as a radix. *Mod.* Five twelves make sixty.

2. A set or group of twelve persons or things; *esp.* a company of twelve players forming a 'side' at some game.

1573 *Satir. Poems Reform.* xlii. 289 Amang Christis awin twelf..Ane tratour was. **1887** *Cornh. Mag.* Mar. 258 A 'twelve' of Irish players [at Lacrosse]. **1898** G. MEREDITH *Odes Fr. Hist.* 70 The rosed and starred Revolving Twelves [i.e. hours of the days and nights]. **1910** *Westm. Gaz.* 28 June 12/2 Both the University twelves were playing last week.

3. a. A thing or person distinguished by the number twelve, usually as being the twelfth in a series; also ***number twelve*** (see NUMBER *sb.* 5). **b.** A shoe, glove, etc. of size twelve (in quot. 1607 allusively).

1607 TOURNEUR *Rev. Trag.* V. i, Courtiers haue feete a' th' nines and tongues a' th' twellues. **1652** *Proposals for regul. Law* in *Harl. Misc.* VI. 294 That there may be a distinction made between clerks of the children's threes, and stagers of the long twelves. **1855** BROWNING *Master Hugues of Saxe-Gotha* vii, Your masterpiece, hard number twelve.

c. A flower-pot eleven inches in width, of which there were twelve in a cast.

1802, etc. [see SIXTEEN *sb.* 5]. **1852** G. W. JOHNSON *Cottage Gardeners' Dict.* 392/2 Eleven-inch..[Old name] 12s.

4. A thing characterized in some way by the number twelve; *e.g.* a twelve-pounder, or a twelve-bore, gun (see III.), a candle weighing twelve to the pound, etc.

1804 CAPT. MAITLAND in *Naval Chron.* XI. 409 A Ship Privateer, carrying sixteen twelves and sixes. **1895** *Outing* (U.S.) XXVII. 64/1 The opinion of sportsmen has changed during recent years, and twelves have steadily grown in favor.

5. (Only in *pl.*) **a.** A sheet of a book folded into twelve leaves (usually in phr. ***in twelves***). (Cf. TWELVEMO.)

1670 in S. Lennard tr. *Charron's Wisd.* Advert. Bks., Ovid Metamorphosis, in Verse, by George Sandys, in twelves. **1675** *Clavel's Gen. Catal. Bks.* 19 Divinity in large Twelves. *Ibid.* 30 Physick in small Twelves. **1683** MOXON *Mech. Exerc., Printing* xxii. ¶ 4 If the Form be..Twelves, he sets also under the Fifth Page Signature 3, and under the Seventh Page Signature 4. **1766** *Public Advertiser* 20 May, Saturday will be published..in two volumes in twelves,.. the second edition of The Vicar of Wakefield. **1792** *Advt. Perry's New Fr. Eng. Dict.*, To be comprised in 750 Pages, in large Pocket Twelves. **1882** J. SOUTHWARD *Pract. Printing* xiii. 121 Twelves, or duodecimo, is a sheet folded into twelve leaves, making twenty-four pages. It is written 12 mo. *Ibid.* 124 Long Twelves is a twelvemo the pages of which read across the broad way.

b. *transf.* A book (or books) of which each sheet is folded into twelve leaves.

1683 MOXON *Mech. Exerc., Printing* xxii. ¶ 7 There are four Volumns in use that are differently Imposed, viz. Folio, Quarto, Octavo and Twelves. *Ibid.*, The other Volumns, viz. Sixteens, Twenty-fours, Thirty-two's, are but the Octavo's and Twelves doubled, or twice doubled. **1716** M. DAVIES *Athen. Brit.* III. 9 In a very small twelves of 36 sides in Print, call'd, *The Marrow of Prayer.* **1786** COWPER *Gratitude* 27 This moveable structure of shelves,..charged with octavos and twelves. **1809** BYRON *Bards & Rev.* viii, And Little's lyrics shine in hot-press'd twelves. *c* **1888** A. LANG *Rowfant Books* ii, 'Dear, dumpy twelves', to fill the nooks.

c. *attrib.*

1755 *Connoisseur* No. 71 ¶ 6 Though contracted into the small space of a twelves volume. *Ibid.* No. 93 ¶ 10 The Twelves edition of the Connoisseur will be published on Tuesday the 25th of this instant November. **1771** LUCKOMBE *Hist. Printing* 110 He printed a small twelves volume with the following title.

III. Combinations:

a. with sbs. forming adjs. in sense 'of, pertaining to, having, containing, measuring, weighing, costing, or in some way connected with, twelve of the things named', as ***twelve-button, -candle, -feet, -foot, -head, -hole, -horse (-power), -inch, -mile, -pint, -pound, -shilling, -stone, -thread.*** **b.** with sbs. + -ED², forming parasynthetic adjs. in sense 'having or characterized by twelve of the things named', as ***twelve-banded, -footed, -fruited, -gated, -legged, -oared, -rayed, -sided, -starred, -stranded, -towered.*** **c.** Special Combs.: **twelve-bore** *a.* (of a gun), having a bore corresponding to the diameter of spherical bullets of twelve to the pound; *sb.*, a twelve-bore gun; **twelve-divided** *a.*, divided into twelve parts; **twelve-eight** (usually $\frac{12}{8}$), *Mus.*, denoting a 'time' or rhythm with twelve quavers in a bar, distributed in threes, the bar thus containing four beats; **twelve-gauge** = *twelve-bore*; **twelve-hour** *a.*, (*a*) *Sc.* (*twal-hour*) of or pertaining to twelve o'clock (noon); (*b*) turning once in twelve hours, as a wheel in a clock or watch; (*c*) consisting of twelve hours, as a working day; **twelve hours** (*Sc.*), twelve o'clock in the day, midday (also *attrib.*); a meal or refreshment taken at noon; **twelve-note, -tone** *attrib. Mus.*, of the technique of musical composition developed by Arnold Schoenberg (1874–1951): using the twelve notes of the chromatic scale so that none is dominant, as opposed to basing composition on the seven notes of the diatonic scale; cf. *note-row, -series* s.v. NOTE *sb.*² 21, SERIAL *a.* h, *tone-row* s.v. TONE *sb.* 11; hence **twelve-toner**, a composer employing the twelve-tone technique; **twelve-point sphere**, *Geom.*, a sphere passing through twelve special points in connexion with a tetrahedron, analogous to the *nine-point circle* of a triangle; **twelve-pounder**, a cannon which discharges shot weighing twelve pounds; †**twelve-tide** = TWELFTHTIDE (*obs.*); **twelve-yearly** *a.*, occurring every twelve years.

1781 PENNANT *Hist. Quad.* II. 501 *Twelve-banded A[rmadillo]. **1859** 'STONEHENGE' *Shot-gun* 243 A good muzzle-loading gun of *twelve-bore, with a charge of..$1\frac{1}{4}$ ounces of shot. **1892** GREENER *Breech-Loader* 132 The best all-round gun for sporting purposes is the 12-bore with 30-inch barrels. **1886** KIPLING *Departm. Ditties* (1888) 42 *Twelve-button gloves. *c* **1865** LETHEBY in *Circ. Sc.* I. 124/2, 26,000 cubic feet of *twelve-candle gas. **1904** *Westm. Gaz.* 15 Dec. 12/1 The Japanese material consists of a sharp strong warp of *twelve-cut yarn, with soft weft. **1864** TENNYSON *Aylmer's F.* 759 Sent like the *twelve-divided concubine To inflame the tribes. **1884** *Pall Mall G.* 8 Sept. 4/1 A..prelude in the key of A major, *twelve-eight time. **1792** in Picton *L'pool Munic. Rec.* (1886) II. 267 A *twelve feet figure executed in..green Bronze. **1898** *Review of Rev.* Feb. 178/2 A twelve-foot basswood Canadian Canoe. **1611** COTGR., *Charrée*,.. a little *twelue-footed water-worme, much hunted after by Trowtes. **1872** O. W. HOLMES *Poet Breakf.-t.* i. (1885) 34 Yon *twelve-fruited tree. **1911** RAMSAY in *Expositor* Mar. 224 The *twelve-gated celestial city with its twelve-towered gates. **1859** 'STONEHENGE' *Shot-gun* 173 A gun of *12 gauge carries a ball weighing the twelfth part of a pound avoirdupois. **1894** *Outing* (U.S.) XXIII. 393/2, I carried a twelve-gauge and Srû his nondescript weapon. **1891** FARRAR *Darkn. & Dawn* li, Ishmael ben Phabi, High Priest of the Jews, on whose ephod has hung the *twelve-gemmed oracle. **1798** *Hull Advertiser* 6 Oct. 2/1 Damaged St. Petersburg *Twelve-Head Flax. [**1834** MCCULLOCH *Dict. Commerce* 581 The Petersburgh and Narva flax..come to us in bundles of 12, 9, and 6 heads.] *Ibid.* Charges at Petersburgh on 12 Head Flax, per ton. **1765** *Museum Rust.* IV. xxiii. 107 Cloth..made..of Narva *twelve-headed flax. **1903** *Westm. Gaz.* 16 Jan. 2/1 The wall that used to be the confine of the old *twelve-hole green. *Ibid.* 16 May 7/2 The car..was a *twelve-horse-power Gladiator. **1791** J. LEARMONT *Poems* 67 The Sun now frae the *twal hour point Had nearly skifftit twa hours yont. **1825** J. NICHOLSON *Operat. Mechanic* 491 The twelve-hour wheel turns the minute index. **1909** *Westm. Gaz.* 12 Aug. 6/3 The employers refuse to grant them the twelve-hour day. **1500–20** DUNBAR *Poems* xxviii. 1 Betuix *twell houris and ellevin. **1599** in *Spottisw. Miscell.* (1845) II. 279 She furnished drink to him until twelve hours (at noon). **1637**

Rutherford *Letters* 14 Mar. (1664) cxvii. 224 Our moon-light is better then their twelve-hours-sun. **1844** Jas. Ballantine *Miller of Deanhaugh* ii. 30 Was it to be expected ..that such friends could meet..in the middle of a winter day, and separate without their 'twal hours'? **1876** S. R. Whitehead *Daft Davie* 189 She sat down and took her twal-hours (noon meal). **1611** Cotgr. s.v. *Royal, Pied Royal*.. the ordinarie *twelue-ynch foot. **1882** *Rep. to Ho. Repr. Prec. Met. U.S.* 275 A 12-inch vein of high-grade ore was met in a cross-cut. **1839** T. Mitchell *Aristoph., Frogs* 42 *note*, A laugh, such as the *twelve-labour demigod alone could give. **1656** *New Almanack* (ed. 2) 7 That triple-headed and so consequently *twelve legged curre. **1896** Baden-Powell *Matabele Campaign* xv. 116 A *twelve-mile ride next morning. **1928** C. Gray *Hist. Music* vi. 96 A reaching out towards the chromatic or *twelve-note scale of to-day. **1959** *Times Lit. Suppl.* 16 Oct. 588/5 The most interesting letters are those in which Schoenberg speaks about his own work and his theory of composition. There is one to the Viennese composer Josef Hauer, in December, 1923, in which are discussed the rival claims of the two composers to have invented the twelve-note system. **1975** *Gramophone* Jan. 1329/3 Moses is an uncompromisingly twelve-note composition. **1815** Scott *Guy M.* xvi, I saw his boat..fly across the lake like a *twelve-oared barge. **1891** *Daily News* 17 Nov. 3/7 The pulling race for 12-oared cutters. **1785** Burns *Address to Deil* x, An' dawtit, *twal-pint Hawkie's gaen As yell's the Bill. **1670** Eachard *Cont. Clergy* 107 The service..is read by some ten or *twelve-pound-man [who] has but just skil enough to reade the lessons with twice conning over. **1862** *Catal. Internat. Exhib., Brit. Div.* II. No. 2612 The average ranges obtained..with a 12-lb. shot. **1800** *Misc. Tr.* in *Asiat. Ann. Reg.* 24/2 A lucky ball from a *twelve-pounder. **1876** Bancroft *Hist. U.S.* III. ix. 425 The 'Inflexible'..carried eighteen or twenty twelve-pounders and ten smaller guns. **1855** Kingsley *Glaucus* (1878) 167 The *twelve-rayed sun-star (Solaster papposa) with his rich scarlet armour. **1811** *Regul. & Ord. Army* 153 Good marketable Wheat, and well dressed through a *Twelve-Shilling seamed Cloth. **1831** Brewster *Optics* xxx. (1838) 250 This mineral, which crystallises in six and *twelve-sided prisms [etc.]. **1876** Ruskin *St. Mark's Rest* ii. §19 A twelve-sided figure. **1839** Bailey *Festus* xix. (1848) 216 Like her who wears in Heaven the *twelve-starred crown. **1882** F. M. Crawford *Mr. Isaacs* ii, Able to carry a *twelve-stone man. **1890** 'R. Boldrewood' *Col. Reformer* (1891) 243 The properly-wielded *twelve-stranded intimidator [*i.e.* whip]. **1797** *Encycl. Brit.* (ed. 3) XVII. 433/2 Reef and head holes of large sails have grommets of *twelve thread line. **1557** Tusser *100 Points Husb.* xlv, While *twelue tide doe last. **1568–70** *Darrell Papers* in H. Hall *Soc. Eliz. Age* (1886) App. ii. 242 Seven night at the lest after twelve-tide last. **[1923** A. Schoenberg *Let.* 1 Dec. in *Briefe* (1958) 108 Mir handelt es sich ausgesprochen dabei um gar keine anderen Theorien, als um die Methoden der 'Komposition mit 12 Tönen', wie ich das—nach vielen Irrtümern und Abschweifungen—heute (hoffentlich endgültig) nenne.] **1926** *Mod. Music* Mar.–Apr. 6 He (*sc.* Schoenberg), too, is convinced that no tone of the *twelve tone system should dominate and that the new structural elements should be sought in sequence of twelve tones. **1956** Auden & Kallman *Magic Flute* (1957) 58 A *Geist* whose music was composed from *Angst*, at International Festivals enjoys An equal status with the Twelve-Tone Boys. **1980** *Times* 4 Sept. 12/5 There was an almost missionary zeal in the Schoenberg circle to spread the Twelve-Tone gospel of the master. **1966** N. Rorem *Paris Diary* ii. 215, I despair of *twelve-toners: they have lost the need for pleasure. **1977** Y. Menuhin *Unfinished Journey* viii. 165 Bartók pours them [*sc.* chromatic sequences] out with a lavishness of invention which the twelve-toner, working away with his slide rule, will never know. **1911** *Twelve-towered [see *twelve-gated*]. **1906** C. A. Sherring *West. Tibet* xiv. 283 Every twelfth year, when there is a..*twelve-yearly fair.

twelvefold ('twɛlvfəʊld), *a.* and *adv.* [f. twelve + -fold. Cf. OE. *twelf-feald* adj.]

A. *adj.* **a.** Twelve times as great or as much. **b.** Composed of twelve parts or divisions, or (in quot. 1854) of twelve kinds.

1557 Recorde *Whetst.* Bij, *Duodecupla*, 12 to 1:.. Twelue-fold. *c* **1586** C'tess Pembroke *Ps.* lxxviii. xxii, The twelve-fold race of godly Israell. **1854** Chr. G. Rossetti *Paradise* iv, The Tree of Life..with its twelvefold fruits.

B. *adv.* Twelve times in amount.

1660 R. Coke *Power & Subj.* 150 First fruits shall be paid upon the mass of S. Martin; he who shall not then pay them, shall forfeit forty shillings, and pay twelvefold the value of the fruits. **1910** *19th Cent.* Feb. 373 In Queensland the amount of sugar grown by white labour has increased twelvefold.

twelvemo ('twɛlvməʊ), English reading of the abbreviation 12mo or xiimo for duodecimo. Also *attrib.*

1819 'R. Rabelais' *Abeillard & Heloisa* 56 We stew them down for twelvemo use. **1835** J. Hannett *Bibliopegia* i. 12 The twelvemo also presents us with the eighteens, after the sheet is cut into three divisions. **1888** Jacobi *Printers' Vocab., Twelvemo*, a sheet of paper folded into twelve leaves, written thus—12 mo. Also called 'duodecimo'. **1914** *Chambers' Jrnl.* Jan. 7/2 Another French book..is a twelvemo volume.

twelvemonth ('twɛlvmʌnθ). Forms: see twelve and month; also 4 **tuelfmoth**; *β.* 4 **tuelmoneth, -monþ, -moth, twelmoneþ**, 4–6 **twelmunth**, 5 **-monyth, twolmonthe**, 5–6 **twelmoneth(e, -month(e, -mond(e, (6 -motte)**; *γ.* 5 **towlmonyth**, 6 **tolmonth, -mont**, *Sc.* **-mount, -mond, -mowth, towmound**, 8 *Sc.* **towmond, -month**, 8–9 *Sc.* **towmont**. [f. OE. *twelf* twelve + *mónað* pl., month. The *γ*-forms, however, are app. ad. ON. *tólfmánuðr*, of similar formation.]

1. A period of twelve months; a year.

[**1038** *Charter of Harold Harefoot* in Kemble *Cod. Dipl.* IV. 56 Wel neh twelf monað. *a* **1131** *O.E. Chron.* an. 1128 Wær it tweolf monð oððe mare. *a* **1225** *Ancr. R.* 218 Iðe uormeste tweolf moneð þet heo bigon ancre lif.] *c* **1275** *Passion our Lord* 86 in *O.E. Misc.* 39 Heore muchele feste Of alle þe twelfmoneþ þat wes þe alre meste. *a* **1300** *Cursor M.* 1917 A tuelfmoth [*v.rr.* twelf-monþe, tuelmoneth, tweluemoneþ] was gan. **1377** Langl. *P. Pl.* B. xiii. 337 A feure, þat taketh me al a twelf-moneth. **1470–85** Malory *Arthur* vii. xix. 242 A twelue moneth will soone be done. **1588** Shaks. *L.L.L.* v. ii. 837 A tweluemonth and a day. **1640** Brome *Antipodes* i. vii, He has not drunke so deepe a draught this twelvmonth. **1766** Blackstone *Comm.* II. ix. 141 A lease for 'twelve months' is only for forty eight weeks; but if it be for '*a* twelvemonth' in the singular number, it is good for the whole year. **1876** Bancroft *Hist. U.S.* IV. xv. 420 Not a twelve-month passed away without a massacre of the pioneers.

β. [*c* **1305** *11000 Virgins* in *E.E.P.* (1862) 68 Tuelmonþ & elleue wyke.] **13..** *Cursor M.* 1919 (Gött.) A tuelmoneth was gan. *c* **1400** *Destr. Troy* 13230 A twelmond & two wekes. [*c* **1420** *Chron. Vilod.* 3148 þe whyche was twol-monthe seke in þe palsy.] **1421** *Coventry Leet Bk.* 24 At the fourthe trespas to forswer the fredom of this Cite a twelmonyth & a day. **1573** G. Harvey *Letter-bk.* (Camden) 12 The putting on of mi hat at problem, which I did not twelmunth nethir.

γ. **1477** Marg. Paston in *P. Lett.* III. 215 He was not gladder of no thyng that he harde thys towlmonyth. **1535** *St. Papers Hen. VIII*, II. 287 He would not haue come in this tolmont, at the least. **1596** in *Spalding Club Misc.* I. 85, I sall giwe breid to my bairnis this towmound. **1726** Ramsay *Verses on Last Leaf* ii, Thrice fifty and sax tow-monds neat. *a* **1774** Fergusson *Election* Poems (1845) 42 For towmonths twa their saul is lent. **1785** Burns *Cottar's Sat. Night* xi, 'Twas a towmond auld, sin' lint was i' the bell. **1818** Scott *Hrt. Midl.* xxxix. [xl], There will be less scathe amang us; mine owsen hae been reckan this towmont.

b. Following and qualifying a date, in such phrases as ***that day*** **(†*a*)** ***twelvemonth, Michaelmas was a twelvemonth, Easter come twelvemonth***: = a year before or after... (see be *v.* 20, come *v.* 36 b).

c **1290** *S. Eng. Leg.* I. 178/15 In þat dai a twelf monþe ore louerd..turnde water to win. *c* **1400** tr. *Higden* (Rolls) VII. 521 (MS. *β*) This day a twelve monthe the same houre whanne y schal dye, he schal dye. **1430–1** *Rolls of Parlt.* IV. 368 To been arezed and paied be the Fest of Ester come tuelfemonethe the next. **1473–4** *Acc. Ld. High Treas. Scot.* I. 63 For schone..fra Michelmes wes a tuelfmoneth to the xxiiij day of Nouember last bipast. **1545** in Leadam *Court Requests* (Seldon Soc.) 187 Abowte our Ladys day in Lent was a Twelmonethe. **1586** *Burgh Rec. Edinb.* (1882) IV. 464 The pest wer in the town as it wes this tyme tolmowth. **1667** in *Verney Mem.* (1907) II. 260 [They will pay no rent] till Christmas come twelvemonth. **1674** *Essex Papers* (Camden) I. 182 Discharging yᵉ Twelvemonths Arrear..yᵉ paymᵗ of wᶜʰ ought to have begun at Christmass last was twelve-month. **1712** Addison *Spect.* No. 435 ¶3 When I was at my Friend Sir Roger de Coverley's about this time Twelve-month. **1715** Ramsay *Christ's Kirk Gr.* ii. iii, Till this time towmond. **1802** Anna Seward *Lett.* (1811) VI. 22 The added weakness entailed upon me by the yet unrecovered accident of spring-twelvemonth.

2. ***twelvemonth('s mind***: a commemoration of a deceased person by celebration of masses, etc. a year after (or annually on the anniversary of) the day of his death or funeral. Cf. month's mind. *Obs.* exc. *Hist.*

1428 *E.E. Wills* (1882) 82 Y wolle þat myne executours, vij yere after my decesse, holdyn twelf monthes mynde. **1538** *MS. Acc. St. John's Hosp., Canterb.*, For wast of tapers att ye twelmonths mynde iiij d. **1572** R. H. tr. *Lauaterus' Ghostes* (1596) 211 Rites instituted by the Commandement of wandring soules, as Masses for the dead, vigils, prayers, and twelvemonths minds. **1829** Heath *Grocers' Comp.* (1869) 232 A solemn obiit anniversary, or twelve months mind.

3. *attrib.* (In quot. 1536 referring to the 'twelvemonth's mind': see 2.)

a **1300** *Cursor M.* 7339 (Cott.) Þai wit-in a tuel-moth stage, War put vte o þair heritage. **13..** *Ibid.* 21038 (Gött.) Þar he was in a tuelfmoth quile. **1536** *Test. Ebor.* (Surtees) VI. 53 At the daye of my berelay, at my vij daye, and at my twelve moneth daye. **1897** Mary Kingsley *W. Africa* 649 Engaging for twelve-month terms of work.

Hence **†'twelvemonthing**, *a.* (of a beast) twelve months old; *sb.* a beast, as a calf or colt, twelve months old; = yearling; **'twelve-monthly** *adv.*, every twelve months, yearly, annually.

1551 in *Longm. Mag.* Apr. (1905) 531, viii twelmonthyng bullocks..a twelmonting maire colt. **1600** in W. F. Shaw *Mem. Eastry* (1870) 226 Item vij kine iij towyering beasts and fower twelve monthings. **1686** Plot *Staffordsh.* 261 A Cow-calf..had another..3 weeks and some odd days, before she was a Twelve-monthing. **1847–8** H. Miller *First Impr.* x. (1857) 167 Six thousand loads of the young pole-wood..being used twelvemonthly.

twelvepence ('twɛlvpəns). **a.** A sum of money equal to twelve pennies (now *rare*). **†b.** A coin of this value, a shilling (*obs.*). Also formerly abbreviated xij d.

c **1380** Wyclif *Sel. Wks.* III. 301 Men of lawe and jurours han non conscience to forswere hem for twel pens and her dyner. **1563** *Child-Marriages* 60 Apon Midsomer even last, the said Thomas send a Token, videlicet a xijᵈ. to the said Eleine. **1568** *Satir. Poems Reform.* xlviii. 58 3our court-men heir hes maid my claith deir, And raisd it twell-pennis of the ell. **1622** Bacon *Hen. VII* 216 The Recoinage of Groats and Halfe-groats now Twelve-pences and Six-pences. **1665** in De Foe *Plague* (1840) 41 Every of the said chirurgeons shall have twelvepence a body searched by them. **1864** Burton *Scot Abr.* II. ii. 183 We..dined..very well for twelvepence a man.

twelvepenny ('twɛlvpənɪ), *a.* (*sb.*) Now *rare*.

1. Of the value of, or amounting to, twelvepence. **†*twelvepenny piece***, a shilling (*obs.*).

1594 Blundevil *Exerc.* i. vii. (1636) 21, 7 twelue-penny peeces of silver. **1710** Addison *Tatler* No. 249 ¶1 The Adventures that this Twelvepenny-Piece has been engaged in. **1712** Prideaux *Direct. Ch.-wardens* (ed. 4) 99 Done for the base Lucre of a Six-penny or Twelve-penny Fee.

2. Costing or priced at twelvepence; for or in connexion with which a shilling is paid or payable.

1609 Dekker *Gvlls Horne-bk.* Proœm Bj b, When at a new play you take vp the twelue-penny roome, next the stage. **1609** B. Jonson *Sil. Wom.* ii. v, At the tweluepeny ordinary. **1678** Dryden *All for Love* Pref. b iv, This Rhyming Judge of the Twelve-penny Gallery. **1712** *Lond. Gaz.* No. 4988/3 The Twelvepeny Stamps prescrib'd by Law for Ale-house-Licenses. **1726** Swift *Gulliver* ii. iii, A bit of bread..as big as two twelve-penny loaves. **1728** Morgan *Algiers* I. Pref. 15 A twelve-penny Pamphlet would contain full as much. **1814** Shirreff *Agric. Shetl. Isl.* 21 Rent is paid by the merk of land,..an indefinite quantity..of ground; merks being divided into different classes, such as sixpenny, ninepenny, and twelvepenny merks.

3. That may be hired for twelvepence; paying, or receiving, twelvepence.

1614 B. Jonson *Bart. Fair* v. vi, Thou Esquire of Dames, Madams and twelue-penny Ladies. **1620** Melton *Astrolog.* 31 The twelve-penny Hirelings made artificiall Lightning. **1683** Bunyan *Greatn. Soul* Wks. 1853 I. 132 More vigilant in dealing with a twelvepenny customer than they will be with Christ. **1707** *Lond. Gaz.* No. 4296/3 The Out-Pensioners (commonly called the Twelve-Penny Pensioners).

4. *fig.* Of small value, paltry, insignificant.

1603 in Fuller *Ch. Hist.* (1655) x. i. §24 *ad fin.*, That men be not excommunicated for trifles, and twelve-peny matters.

B. *sb. Sc.* (in form *twalpenny*). A twelvepenny piece, a shilling (Scots): see shilling 1 b. Hence ***twalpenny worth*** = twelve pennyworth.

1786 Burns *Twa Dogs* 115 An' whyles twalpennie worth o' nappy Can mak the bodies unco happy. **1816** Scott *Antiq.* Advt., Perhaps a Scottish 'twalpenny', or English penny, which was expended in snuff or whisky.

†'twelver[1]. *Obs. slang.* [f. twelve + -er[1].] A coin worth twelve pence.

a **1700** B. E. *Dict. Cant. Crew, Twelver*, a Shilling. **1725** in *New Cant. Dict.* **1732** *Tricks of Town* 15 Coachmen.. demanding t'other Twelver or Tester above their Fare.

Twelver[2] ('twɛlvə(r)). *Islam.* [f. twelve + -er[1].] A member of the larger of the two Shiah sects (the 'Twelvers' and the 'Seveners'), a follower of the twelve Imams or prophets (cf. imam 2 b, Shiah).

1876 R. D. Osborn *Islam under Arabs* ii. i. 167 The Ismailiens, like the Twelvers, make profession of an exclusive attachment to Ali and his descendants. **1934** R. Strothmann in *Encycl. Islām* IV. 353/2 We shall consider the main branch somewhat more fully, the Imāmīs or 'Twelvers'. **1979** *Sunday Tel.* (Colour Suppl.) 27 May 25/4 In Iran the Shias are divided essentially into two sects, the Twelvers and the Seveners.

twelvetide, obs. var. Twelfthtide.

twelye, obs. form of twilly *sb.*[1]

†tweme, *v. Obs.* Forms: 1 **twǽman**, 3 **twemen, tweamin, tweamen**. [OE. *twǽman*, f. an extension of the stem of *twá*, two.] *trans.* To divide into two parts, separate (*lit.* and *fig.*).

[*c* **893**, *a* **1225**: see to-tweme.] *a* **1023** Wulfstan *Hom.* l. (Napier) 272 þæt we..ne lætan us deofol dwelian ne twæman. *c* **1050** *Byrhtferth's Handboc* in *Anglia* VIII. 334 Þys taken [dyple] ȝesetton þa ealdan writeras on ciriclicum bocum, þæt hiȝ twæmdon oððe ætywdon þa ȝewitnyssa haliȝra ȝewrita. *c* **1205** Lay. 2948 Ic wlle..twemen mine bearnen. *a* **1225** *St. Marher.* 5 Ne mei unc nowðer lif ne deað tweamin atwa. *a* **1240** *Sawles Warde* in *Cott. Hom.* 265 Hwet mei tweamen us from godd ant halden us þeonne.

†twen, obs. form of towen *a.*

1612 in *Antiquary* Jan. (1906) 28/1 Thirtie paire of Twen Sheets,..sixe dozen of table napkins, thone halfe flexen, and thother halfe Twen.

twen, twene, obs. ff. twain, 'tween, twin *v.*[1]

twenter, obs. form of twinter.

twentieth ('twɛntɪɪθ), *a.* and *sb.* Forms: 1 **twentiȝoþa** (-teoȝoþa, -tuȝoþa), **twentiȝþa** (-teȝþa), 3 **tuentiþe, twentide**, 3–4 **twentiþe**, 4 **tuuentiþe**, 5 **twentythe, (-tyd**, 6 **tuentieth)**, 6–7 **twentith, -teth**, 6– **twentieth**; *β.* 4 **tuentende, tuentiand(e**; *γ.* 4 **twentiest**, 5 **twentyest**. [OE. *twentiȝoða*, etc. (see above), f. *twentiȝ* twenty + *-oða* (see -th[2]); becoming in ME. *twentiþe, -ythe*, from 16th c. *twentieth*. Northern ME. had also *twentende, twentiand(e*, with the Norse ordinal suffix *-andi, -ende*; cf. ON. *tuttugandi*, Norw. *tjugande*, Sw. *tjugonde*, MDa. *tjugende*, Da. *tyvende*. The other WGer. langs. have forms with the superlative suffix *-ōst-*, as OFris. *twinti-, twintegosta* (WFris. *twintichste*), MDu. *twintechste*, Du., MLG., LG. *twintigste*, OHG. *zweinzugôsto*, (MHG. *zweinzigeste*, Ger. *zwanzigste*), also mod.Icel. *tuttugasti*; a similar form *twentiest* appears in 14–15th c. southern Eng.: cf. Caxton's *thirtiest* for THIRTIETH.]

A. *adj.*

1. The ordinal numeral corresponding to the cardinal TWENTY; last of twenty; next after the nineteenth. **a.** in concord with a sb. expressed.

† ***twentieth penny***, one penny in every twenty: cf. THIRD B. I. 4, and sense 2 below.

a **900** *O.E. Martyrol.* 20 Mar., On þone twenteȝðan dæȝ þæs monðes bið se þridda worolde dæȝ. *c* **1000** *Sax. Leechd.* III. 194 Mona se twentiȝoþa. *c* **1250** *Gen. & Ex.* 3641 On ðat oðer twentide dai, of ðe oðer moned taȝte he wei. **1297** R. GLOUC. (Rolls) 9036 In þe tuentiþe ȝer of is kinedom. **1387** TREVISA *Higden* (Rolls) VIII. 255 Kyng Henry hadde þe twentiþe peny of lewed men['s] catel. *c* **1470** HENRY *Wallace* XI. 376 Xix thai war, and Craufurd,.. The twentyd man, the nowmer to fullfill. **1530** PALSGR. 372/2 *Vingtiesme*, twenteth. **1564** HARDING *Answ. Jewell's Chalenge* (1565) 96 b, [This] Origen sheweth.. in the twentith homilie vpon Josue. **1643** BAKER *Chron.* (1653) 395 In this twentieth yeer.. Sir Piers Butler.. was created Earle of Osory. **1779** *Mirror* No. 57. ¶6 Soon after my twentieth year my father died. **1818** FRERE *Monks & Giants* III. xi, The festivals.. That every twentieth century come in season. **1894** S. WEYMAN *Under Red Robe* vii, I was pondering for the twentieth time what step I should take next.

β. *c* **1330** R. BRUNNE *Chron.* (1810) 309 Whan it wer.. stabled & sette, To gyue þe penie tuentende þe Kyng. **13..** *Cursor M.* 10999 (Cott.) þe four and teuntiand night.

γ. **1398** TREVISA *Barth De P.R.* XIX. cxxxi. (1495) nn iij/2 Siliqua is the twentiest parte of Solidus. **1480** CAXTON *Contn. Higden* (Rolls) VIII. 523 The two and twentyest day. **1483** —— *Gold. Leg.* 334 b/1 The one and twentyest Chapytre.

b. with ellipsis of sb., usually to be supplied from context; also *spec.* of *day* (of the month), occas. of *year*.

1643 BAKER *Chron.* (1653) 533 The twentieth of September, seven of the.. Conspirators.. were condemned. *a* **1700** in *Cath. Rec. Soc. Publ.* IX. 337 In the 20th of her age. **1704** N. N. tr. *Boccalini's Advts. fr. Parnass.* III. 157 Yesterday.. being the Twentieth of this Instant. **1749** F. SMITH *Voy. Disc.* II. 31 The Interim, between the twentieth and twenty-eighth was filled. **1782** in J. H. Harting *Hist. Sardin. Chapel* (1905) 25 On the 20th of April, 1782, on Easter Eve, this year. **1902** J. K. MANN *Hist. Popes* I. I. 245 In the sixth century, as in the twentieth.

c. with numerals below ten, forming ordinals of those between twenty and thirty: ***one-and-twentieth, two-and-twentieth***, etc. (also † ***twentieth (and) one***, etc., obs. rare); now mostly superseded by ***twenty-first, twenty-second***, etc.

a **900** *O.E. Martyrol.* 22 Jan., On þone twa & twentiȝðan dæȝ þæs monðes. *c* **1000** *Sax. Leechd.* III. 194 Mona se an & twentiȝoða. *c* **1290** *S. Eng. Leg.* I. 53/221 In þe on an twentiþe ȝere. *a* **1325** *MS. Rawl. B.* 520 lf. 50 b, þe ȝere of his regne þe ȝette ant tuuentiþe. *c* **1420** *Chron. Vilod.* 3086 In Septembre þe won & twentythe day. **1536** WRIOTHESLEY *Chron.* (Camden) I. 53 The twentith tow daie of Julie. **1596** DALRYMPLE tr. *Leslie's Hist. Scot.* II. xviii. (S.T.S.) I. 157 The tuentieth and ane ȝeir eftir the deith of his vnkle. **1631** MILTON *Sonn., On having arrived at Age of 23*, 2 How soon hath Time.. Stoln on his wing my three and twentith yeer! **1719** DE FOE *Crusoe* I. 231 The four and twentieth Year.

d. *Comb.*

1888 E. BELLAMY *Looking Backwards* xxvii. 432 My thoughts made better music than even twentieth century orchestras discourse. **1898** *(title)* The Twentieth Century New Testament. Part I. **1903** G. MATHESON *Repr. Men Bible* 201 Our interest in the narrative is a twentieth-century interest.

e. Special Comb.: **twentieth century cut** *Diamond-cutting* (see quots.); **Twentieth Century (Limited)** the name of an express train running between Chicago and New York from 1902 to 1967.

1903 W. R. CATTELLE *Precious Stones* 63 The 'twentieth century' is a new form of cutting lately introduced. The number of facets is greater than in the brilliant-cut and they are differently shaped and arranged. **1925** KRAUS & HOLDEN *Gems & Gem Materials* vii. 77 The '*twentieth century*' *cut* has eighty or eighty-eight facets. **1970** E. BRUTON *Diamonds* x. 164 Jubilee or twentieth century cut (40 + 40 = 80 facets). **1902** *N.Y. World* 16 June 7/2 The 'Twentieth Century Limited', the new fast train,.. yesterday afternoon at 2.45 o'clock pulled out of the Grand Central Station. **1913** E. WHARTON *Custom of Country* III. xxii. 332 The Twentieth Century's generally considered the best route to Dakota. **1980** M. G. EBERHART *Casa Madrone* iii. 39 The Twentieth Century made a record run of eighteen hours from New York to Chicago... It is a very good train.

2. ***twentieth part***: any one of twenty equal parts into which a whole may be divided.

c **1350** *Will. Palerne* 5354 No tong miȝt telle þe twentiþe parte. **1611** COTGR., *Vintain*, a twentieth; or a twentieth part of. **1710** SWIFT *Mem. to Mr. Harley* ¶7 The twentieth parts are 12*d.* in 1*l.* paid annually out of all ecclesiastical benefices. **1848** DICKENS *Dombey* xxxvii, Not a twentieth part of the affection that you have for Florence. **1911** *Act 1 & 2 Geo. V*, c. 16 §2 (1) *(a)* The yearly value.. being taken to be one-twentieth part of the capital value.

B. *sb.*

1. A twentieth part: see A. 2.

c **1330** R. BRUNNE *Chron.* (1810) 145 þe tende suld be nouht, no þe tuen[ten]de non make. **1611** [see A. 2]. **1719** W. WOOD *Surv. Trade* 345 Crown Pieces.. one Twentieth lighter. *Ibid.*, Nineteen twentieths of a Crown. **1792** A. YOUNG *Trav. France* 537 No such thing was known in any part of France.. as a tenth: it was always a twelfth, or a thirteenth, or even a twentieth of the produce. **1815** J. SMITH *Panorama Sc. & Art* II. 218 The balls should not be more than one-twentieth of an inch in diameter.

2. *Mus.* A note twenty diatonic degrees above or below a given note (both notes being reckoned), or the interval between two such notes (equal to two octaves and a sixth). So ***two and twentieth***: see TWO.

1609 DOULAND *Ornith. Microl.* 79 Others are tripled, to wit,.. a twentieth, which is equall to a sixt, and a thirteenth, and so forth.

twenty ('twɛntɪ), *numeral a.* and *sb.* Forms: 1 **twentiȝ, (tuentiȝ, tuoentiȝ, twoeȝentiȝ)**, 2–6 **twenti**, 3 (*Orm.*) **twenntiȝ**, 3–6 **tuenty**, 4–5 **tuenti**, (4 **tuent**), 5–7 **twentie**, 6 **tuentie, twentye**, (*Sc.* **twantie**, *Sc. dial.* **twinti, twenti, tuonti, toontie**) 4– **twenty**. [OE. *twentiȝ*, f. *twen-* two + *tiȝ* (= Goth. *tigus*, ON. *tigr* decade: see -TY²): = OFris. *twintich, -ech, tweintich, -tig* (WFris. *tweintich*, NFris. *twuntich*), OS. *twentig* or *twēntig*, MDu. *twintich* (Du. *twintig*), MLG. *twentig, twintig* (LG. *twintig*); OHG. *zweinzug, -uc, -och* (MHG. *zweinzec, -ic, zwênzic, -ig*, Ger. *zwanzig*); the first element is variously explained as a nom. plur. (OE. *twéȝen*) and as a dative form. Cf. also ON. *tuttugu, -ogu* (Norw. *tjuge, tjug*, Sw. *tjugo*, MDa. *tiuge*, Da. *tyve*), and Goth. *twai-tigjus* (two decades).

Like the other cardinals in -TY, in OE. orig. a neuter sb. followed by a genitive plural: e.g.

c **893** K. ÆLFRED *Oros.* I. i. 18 Næfde he þeah ma ðonne twentiȝ hryðera, & twentiȝ sceapa, & twentiȝ swyna. **971** *Blickl. Hom.* 231 Onbid her seofon & twentiȝ nihta. *c* **1000** ÆLFRIC *Gen.* xxxi. 38 Wæs ic.. mid þe nu twentiȝ wintra. *Ibid.* xxxii. 14 Twentiȝ buccena.. and twentiȝ rammena.]

The cardinal number equal to twice ten: represented by the symbols 20 or xx (formerly sometimes xxti = L. *viginti*).

A. *adj.* **1. a.** In concord with a sb. expressed (or in OE. in plural form with implied sb.).

a **900** *Elene* 830 (Gr.) On twentiȝum [*MS.* xx] fotmælum. *c* **1000** ÆLFRIC *Numb.* xi. 19 Næs to anum dæȝe, ne to twam, .. ne to tynum, ne to twentiȝum [daȝum]. *a* **1225** *Leg. Kath.* 2502 Twenti dahene ȝong [= journey]. *c* **1330** R. BRUNNE *Chron.* (1810) 282 Wele tuenti ȝere. **1478** W. PASTON in *P. Lett.* III. 237 He seythe ye be xxtis. in hys dette. **1583** STOCKER *Civ. Warres Lowe C.* II. 48 A great multitude of people, who come twentie mile of to this goodly feast. **1637** *Decree Star Chamb.* § 15 in Milton *Areop.* (Arb.) 16 There shall be but Twentie Master Printers allowed to haue the vse of one Presse. **1758** R. BROWN *Compl. Farmer* (1759) 71 A hen sits twenty days. **1853** J. H. NEWMAN *Hist. Sk.* (1873) II. I. ii. 75 In the course of twenty years a new generation would arise.

b. Combined with the numerals below ten (*one* to *nine*) to express the numbers between twenty and thirty; formerly (and still occasionally) ***one and twenty, two and twenty***, etc. (rarely ***twenty and one***, etc.); now commonly ***twenty-one, twenty-two***, etc.; similarly with the ordinals from *first* to *ninth*, forming the ordinals corresponding to the above (***twenty-first, twenty-second***, etc.), in modern use substituted for the earlier *one-and-twentieth, two-and-twentieth*, etc. (see TWENTIETH A. 1 c).

c **893** K. ÆLFRED *Oros.* VI. ii. 256 þara twa & twentiȝra monna þe he him to fultume hæfde acoren. *a* **1131** *O.E. Chron.* an. 1124 þes kinges cnihtes.. namen.. fif and twenti oðre cnihtes. **1297** R. GLOUC. (Rolls) 1532 Vif & twenti ȝer. *a* **1400–50** *Alexander* 3930 Aȝt & tuenti men of armes. **1526** *Proclam.* 5 Nov. (*Pat. Roll 18 Hen. VIII*, II. m. 2 d), The Soueraygne.. shalbe curraunt.. for twenty two shillynges and sixe pens. **1596** DALRYMPLE tr. *Leslie's Hist. Scot.* II. xvi. (S.T.S.) I. 150 Four and tuentie cubites hich. **1604** E. G[RIMSTONE] *D'Acosta's Hist. Indies* III. xviii. 177, I haue gone ouer twenty and seauen riuers vpon that coast. **1777** ROBERTSON *Hist. Amer.* (1783) I. II. 163 In the parallel of twenty-two degrees of latitude. **1794** STEDMAN *Surinam* (1813) II. xxv. 224 What he called his Silver-feast, being the twenty-fifth anniversary of his marriage. **1820** SOUTHEY *Wesley* I. 53 More than four-and-twenty pounds. **1857** MILLER *Elem. Chem.* (1862) III. 204 Allowing the.. mixture to stand for twenty-four hours.

c. As multiplier before a numeral, usually a higher one, as † ***twenty hundred*** obs. (= two thousand), ***twenty thousand***, etc. (often hyperbolically: cf. d). So ***twenty-one thousand***, etc.

c **950** *Lindisf. Gosp.* Luke xiv. 31 Mið tuoentiȝum ðusendum [*Rushw.* twoeȝentiȝum ðusenda] cymeð to him. *c* **1000** *Ags. Gosp.* ibid., Aȝen þone þe him aȝen cymð mid twentiȝum þusendum. *c* **1205** LAY. 26824 Twenti hundred cnihten. **1377** LANGL. *P. Pl.* B. XVI. 10, I wolde trauaille .. þis tree to se twenty hundreth myle. *c* **1386** CHAUCER *Manciple's T.* 65 Yet hath this brid by twenty thousand foold Leuere in a fforest.. Goon ete wormes. **1500–20** DUNBAR *Poems* l. 16 Off the Glen Quhettane twenti scoir He drawe as oxin him befoir. **1592** SHAKS. *Ven. & Ad.* 775 If loue haue lent you twentie thousand tongues. **1847** TENNYSON *Princess* IV. 83, I would pipe and trill, And cheep and twitter twenty million loves. *Mod.* Twenty thousand pounds sterling. Twenty million dollars.

d. Used vaguely or hyperbolically for a large number.

† ***a twenty devil way***: see DEVIL *sb.* 19.

c **1470** *Golagros & Gaw.* 970 His scheild he chopit hym fra In tuenty pecis and ma. **1513** DOUGLAS *Æneis* I. Prol. 260 A twenty devill mot fall his werk at anis. **1592** SHAKS. *Ven. & Ad.* 575 Were beautie vnder twentie locks kept fast. **1622** BACON *Hen. VII* 228 Vpon Twentie respects hee could not haue beene the Man. **1748** RICHARDSON *Clarissa* II. xxviii. 164, I only came.. to sit and talk of twenty and twenty fond things, as I used to do. **1848** BUCKLEY *Iliad* 412 Not even if they should place ten-fold and twenty-times such ransoms.

e. Phr. ***twenty-four hours a day***, all the time, incessantly.

1914 G. B. SHAW *Misalliance* p. xl, If we were habitually underworked and overfed, our notion of heaven would be a place where everybody worked strenuously for twenty four hours a day and never got anything to eat. **1942** *R.A.F. Jrnl.* 13 June 15 The least useful man.. is the.. type, who is belligerent 24 hours a day. **1951** W. FAULKNER *Requiem for Nun* II. i. 143 Shut up in that room twenty-four hours a day. **1980** J. BARNETT *Palmprint* xiv. 149 There are American military planes over the Caribbean twenty-four hours a day.

2. a. With ellipsis of sb. (which may usually be supplied from the context). So ***twenty-one, twenty-first***, etc. † ***and twenty***, used as an intensive.

c **961** ÆTHELWOLD *Rule St. Benet* xxii. 47 (Gr.) [Let them sleep] tynum and twentiȝum on anum inne ætgædere. [*c* **1000** ÆLFRIC *Gen.* xviii. 31 God cwæð: Ne do ic hit, ȝif þær beoð twentiȝ.] *c* **1205** LAY. 3387 We mine fader habbet vnderfon mid þirtti cnihten,.. Do we awai þane twenti. **13..** *Cursor M.* 16906 (Cott.) A mikel stan, to turn i-nogh had tuent [*rime* monument]. **1535** COVERD. *Gen.* xviii. 31 Peraduenture there might be twentie founde therin. **1601** SHAKS. *Twel. N.* II. iii. 52 In delay there lies no plentie, Then come kisse me sweet and twentie: Youths a stuffe will not endure. **1605** ROWLEY *When you see me*, etc. D ij, Godyegodnight and twentie syr. **1607** MIDDLETON *Five Gallants* I. i, As in one pie twenty may dip their sippits. **1735** JOHNSON *Lobo's Abyssinia, Descr.* xii. 115 The ordinary Dose is six of these Rinds, and I had devour'd twenty. **1897** MARY KINGSLEY *W. Africa* 550 The first man to reach the summit was Sir Richard Burton... He went up, as did the succeeding twenty-five (mostly Germans) from Babundi. **1902** O. WISTER *Virginian* xxiii, His thermometer.. registered twenty below zero.

b. *spec.* with ellipsis of *years* (of age); so ***twenty-one***, etc.

1773 GOLDSM. *Stoops to Conq.* III, What will repair beauty at forty, will certainly improve it at twenty. **1836–9** DICKENS *Sk. Boz, Steam Excursion*, He.. was smart, spoffish, and eight-and-twenty. **1849** E. B. EASTWICK *Dry Leaves* 83 A young man of twenty. **1898** MRS. B. M. CROKER *Peggy of Bartons* xxix, I shall be twenty-one in April.

c. The ordinals ***twenty-first, twenty-second***, etc. are ordinarily used with ellipsis of *day* (of the month), also *year* (of a reign). Also ***twenty-first*** with ellipsis of *birthday*; cf. TWENTY-FIRSTER.

1669 F. VERNON *Let.* 19 June in Lang *Valet's Trag.*, etc. (1903) 51 My last of the 26th Currt. **1711** *Lond. Gaz.* No. 4902/2 The King.. was to embark on the Twenty-seventh. **1777** ROBERTSON *Hist. Amer.* (1783) I. II. 141 He set sail.. on the twenty-fifth of September. **1873** C. M. YONGE *Pillars of House* I. xi. 229 Here was his twenty-first not very far off. **1879** E. WATERTON *Pietas Mariana Brit.* 78 In the twenty-second of Henry the Seventh. **1886** STEVENSON *Kidnapped* xxvi, The house.. where we slept the twenty-first of the month. **1937** 'M. INNES' *Hamlet, Revenge!* I. i. 23 Celebrating a daughter's twenty-first by dressing her in white satin. **1975** 'J. LYMINGTON' *Spider in Bath* vii. 121 My daughter's twenty-first tomorrow. I should have collected a watch from the jeweller.

d. ***the twenty*** (at Rugby School): see quot. *a* 1894. ***the twenty-four***, a body of 24 men having some special office (at various times and places: see quots.).

1440 in Glew *Hist. Walsall* (1856) 105 The Masters.. shall not make gift or graunt of eny donacion of eny Chantrey.. withoute the assent of the xxiiij. **1736** DRAKE *Eboracum* I. vi. 184 These citizens are commonly called by the name of the twenty four; though they may be more or less than that number. **1857** HUGHES *Tom Brown* II. viii, How well I remember the day we were put out of the twenty [into the sixth form]. **1890** GROSS *Gild Merch.* II. 347 The governing body is no longer [after 1622] called 'the twenty-four'.. but simply the 'probi homines'. *a* **1894** C. H. PEARSON in Stebbing *Life* (1900) 23 Scholarship at Rugby was picked up in the Twenty, a sort of lower sixth.

e. Phr. † ***twenty in the hundred***, a 20 per cent. rate of interest on loans; *transf.* a usurer. ***twenty to one***, twenty chances to one; an expression of very strong probability.

1591 SHAKS. *Two Gent.* I. i. 72 Twenty to one then, he is ship'd already. **1602** B. JONSON *Poetaster* (Qo.) III. i, Thou art an honest twenty in the hundred. *Mod.* Ellington won the Derby in 1856 at 20 to 1.

3. Used for the ordinal TWENTIETH; so ***twenty-one (one and twenty)*** for *twenty-first*, etc. Now only after a sb. in such collocations as *chapter twenty, verse twenty-one*, etc.

a **1100** *O.E. Chron.* (Laud MS.) an. 1086 On þam an & twentiȝan ȝeare þæs þe Willelm weolde & stihte Engle land. **1297** R. GLOUC. (Rolls) 7105 In þe ȝer of is kinedom tuenty & tuo. *c* **1375** *Sc. Leg. Saints* xviii. (*Egipciane*) 208 One [= on] þe twenty day At þe sexte oure. *c* **1380** WYCLIF *Last Age Ch.* in Todd *3 Treat.* p. xxxv, As Dauiþ seiþ, þe on and twenty Salme. **1544** tr. *Littleton's Tenures* (1574) 73 Thoughe the horse.. bee not the twentye parte woorth in value of the summe of money. **1567** *Gude & Godlie B.* 2 The ten commandementis.. in Exodus the twentie Chapter.

B. *sb.* (with plural *twenties*).

1. a. The abstract number 20; a symbol representing this. So ***twenty-one***, etc.

c **1425** *Craft of Nombryng* (E.E.T.S.) 22 Take 12 out of twenty, and þere schal leue 8. **1688** R. HOLME *Armoury* III. 141/1 Country People.. reckon.. their numbers.. by.. Scores or Twenty's. **1725** WATTS *Logic* II. v. §5 Some Things.. almost as certain.. as that.. five Twenties make a Hundred. **1845** *Encycl. Metrop.* I. 384 The numeral language is constructed in conformity with the Phœnician numerals, proceeding by twenties as far as 100. *Mod.* Twenty is an even number. A twenty is printed thus: xx, 20.

b. A person or thing distinguished by this number, usually as the twentieth in a series; so *twenty-one*, *twenty-two*, etc.

1888 H. Mortem *Sk. Hospital Life* 18, I..heard her ask ..'Who is "Twenty-two"?'—one of the detestable habits of the place being to call you by the number of your bed.

2. a. A group or set of twenty persons or things. So (rarely) ***a twenty-five***, etc.

1637 Gillespie *Eng. Pop. Cerem.* IV. vi. 26 Many societies conveened to the eating of the Paschall Supper by Twenties. **1725** Swift *Upright Judge* iii. Wks. 1755 IV. I. 64 My grand-dame had gallants by twenties. **1878** *Athletic World* 6 Dec. 430/1 The game lasting two twenties. **1879** Browning *Ned Bratts* 34 A twenty-five were tried, rank puritans caught at prayer In a cow-house.

b. Something equivalent to twenty of some unit, *e.g.* a twenty-pound bank-note.

1839 *Spirit of Times* 8 June 162/2 We had the gratification of seeing it [*sc.* his jockeyship] rewarded by more presents of odd fifties and twenties than probably Daniel ever saw in his lifetime. **1850** *Househ. Words* 21 Sept. 620/1 There were two twenties, were there not? **1977** *Transatlantic Rev.* LX. 140 'God knows neither of you can call me ungrateful.' He put a twenty in front of each of them.

c. A sheet (of a book) folded into 20 leaves (4 × 5), or each leaf of such a sheet. (Cf. TWENTYMO.)

1771 Luckombe *Hist. Printing* 418 A Sheet of Twenties. **1824** J. Johnson *Typogr.* II. vi. 172 [*headed* *28] A Half Sheet of Twenties.

3. Something characterized in some way by the number twenty. So the compound numerals, as ***twenty-four*** (a flower-pot of which there are 24 in a cast, etc.) See also (in special senses) TWENTY-FIVE, TWENTY-FOUR.

1842 Loudon *Suburban Hort.* 515 Those that have the strongest roots re-pot into twenty-fours. **1851** Glenny *Handbk. Fl. Gard.* 251 In June, the potted ones will bear shifting to a size twenty-four. **1895** *Daily News* 22 Feb. 4/6 From twenties to twenty-fours, that is, from cotton with twenty hanks in the pound to the finer sort of cotton with twenty-four hanks in the pound.

4. *pl.* The numbers from 20 to 29; the years in a century or of one's life, or the degrees of any scale (e.g. of a thermometer) so numbered.

1874 Miss Mulock *My Mother & I* xiv. 301 In their twenties girls feel differently from what they do in their teens. **1886** *Athenæum* 16 Oct. 495/2 Little Claude Ramsay ..in his twenties is always thinking about 'the draught'. **1886** Seeley *Short Hist. Napoleon* 262 Had Louis XV died in childhood..there would certainly have been in the twenties a war of the French Succession. **1893** Louisa Twining *Recoll.* 242 A temperature in the twenties for some days. **1893** Georgiana Hill *Hist. Eng. Dress* II. 235 Arrayed in the costume of the twenties. **1894** *Voice* (N.Y.) 22 Feb., In age I judged them to be near the middle of the twenties. **1898** Kipling in W. Nicholson *Almanac of Twelve Sports* July, The child of the Nineties..in pursuit of a girl whom The Twenties will dub a 'last-century heirloom'. **1930**, etc. [see *roaring twenties* s.v. ROARING *ppl. a.* 4]. **1956** A. S. C. Ross in M. Black *Importance of Lang.* (1962) 97 At Oxford in the late twenties the use of the surname..was a known *gaucherie*. **1969** *Listener* 26 June 903/1 A scandalous title, or course, for a book which was, in the Twenties manner, meant to scandalise. **1976** J. Grenfell *Joyce Grenfell requests Pleasure* (1977) i. 21, I see us now,..our peculiar Twenties figures forced flat by bust-bodices.

5. *attrib.* (and *ellipt.*) as in ***twenty (twenty-two,*** etc.) ***port***, port wine of the year 1820 (1822, etc.).

1860 *All Year Round* No. 54. 87 Acquainted with 'Twenty port, and comet vintages. **1891** S. Mostyn *Curatica* 10 Mostyn likes the 22 Port very much.

C. Combinations.

a. Adjs. or attrib. phrases formed by *twenty* with a sb. (= measuring, containing, weighing, etc. twenty of the things named), as ***twenty-centimetre, -cubit, -foot*** († ***twenty-foot worm***, a centipede), ***-grain, -gun, -inch, -knot, -man, -mark, -mile, -minute, -penny, -plume*** (applied to a small species of moth, *Alucita polydactyla*), ***-pound, -round, -shilling, -yard, -year***; so with compound numerals, as ***twenty-five-foot***; ***twenty-four-feet, -thread***; ***twenty-one-inch***; ***twenty-thousand-ton***; ***twenty-two-mile***, etc. Also ***twenty-bore, twenty-two-gauge***, etc. (of a gun: cf *twelve-bore* s.v. TWELVE III. c). **b.** Parasynthetic sbs. (see -ER[1] 1), as ***twenty-footer, -knotter, -pointer, -pounder***; so with the compound numerals, as ***twenty-eight (-four, -five, -six, -thousand,*** etc.) ***-pounder, twenty-one-gunner***, etc. **c.** Parasynthetic adjs., as ***twenty-breeched, -coloured***.

1892 Greener *Breech-Loader* 43 The *20-bore has been strenuously advocated by writers in the sporting papers, but there are very few sold. **1908** *Outlook* 29 Aug. 280/1 The light twelve-bores now built especially for ladies' use.. weigh no more than sixteen- or even twenty-bore guns of average weight. **1819** Scott *Leg. Montrose* ii, A soldier of honour shall be dragged..before a base mechanical burgomaster,..as if he were one of their own mean, amphibious, *twenty-breeched boors. **1904** *Daily Chron.* 28 May 5/4, *20-centimetre guns. **1600** Fairfax *Tasso* XVI. xxiv, Nor golden Iris so bendes in the aire Her *twentie colour'd bow. **1877** Tennyson *Harold* III. i, Golden cherubim With *twenty-cubit wings. **1684** J. Peter *Siege Vienna* 109 *Twenty eight pounders. **1897** *Outing* (U.S.) XXX. 355/2 Two twenty-seven-footers,..*Rocky John*, as the Commodore's *twenty-five-foot craft was dubbed. *a* **1944** K. Douglas *Alamein to Zem Zem* (1946) 10, *25-pounders and quads, Bofors guns in pits with their crews lying beside them. **1983** J. Masters *Man of War* xx. 264 Now came the first shell from the 25-pounders. *c* **1475** *Pict. Voc.* in Wr.-Wülcker 766/28 *Hic multipes*, a *tuentifot-wurme. **1910** *Encycl. Brit.* X. 258/1 Several large feeding-drains were dug, including the Forty Foot,..the Sixteen Foot river,..and the Twenty Foot river. **1899** *Daily News* 18 Nov. 4/5 A twenty-foot snake..had a quarrel with a fourteen-foot snake. The fourteen-footer was eating a chicken, which the *twenty-footer coveted. **1825** J. Nicholson *Operat. Mechanic* 82 The superior velocity of the *24 feet wheel. *c* **1850** *Rudim. Navig.* (Weale) 135, *24, 30, and 40-penny nails. **1825** J. Neal *Bro. Jonathan* III. 380 A few *twenty four pound shot. **1684** J. Peter *Siege Vienna* 108 *Twenty four pounder. **1769** Falconer *Dict. Marine* (1789) I iv, A piece that discharges a ball of twenty-four pounds, is called a twenty-four-pounder. **1903** *Daily Chron.* 30 May 5/1 A light rod and *24-thread line. **1890** *Anthony's Photogr. Bull.* III. 40 A *twenty-grain solution of gelatine. **1757** J. Lind *Lett. Navy* i. 34 Captains of *20, 40, and 50 gun ships. **1849** Noad *Electricty* 92 A *twenty-inch cylinder electrical machine. **1903** *Daily Chron.* 3 July 8/2 The *twenty-knot wind blowing here to-day. **1898** *Harper's Mag.* XCVI. 830 They [ships] are to be *twenty-knotters. **1905** *Daily Chron.* 24 July 7/1 A member of the English *twenty-man team. **1788** J. Skinner *Eccl. Hist. Scot.* II. 588 These itinerant preachers were..called the '*Twenty Merk Men'. **1908** *Daily Chron.* 4 Aug. 1/2 The Kaiser..rewarded him with a twenty mark piece. **1902** *Ibid.* 10 May 10/1 Come down to the country and take *twenty-mile walks. **1905** *Westm. Gaz.* 4 Aug. 6/3 Districts within the twenty-mile radius of London. **1898** *Ibid.* 27 July 1/1 The *twenty-minute sitting [of the House of Lords]. **1939** Wodehouse *Uncle Fred in Springtime* xi. 150 No matter how suave her manner for the nonce, she is at heart a twenty-minute egg. **1900** *Daily Chron.* 31 Aug. 5/1 The Gaekwar is a '*twenty-one gunner'—one of the three Indian Princes who alone are entitled to the royal salute. **1794** W. Hutchinson *Hist. Cumberld.* I. 175 *note*, 3l. a year customary rent..with a *twenty-penny fine. **1908** *Westm. Gaz.* 11 Sept. 10/1 Some remarkably fine heads have been secured in Highland deer forests... A *twenty-pointer was killed by Lord Burton.. fifteen years ago. **1761–2** Hume *Hist. Eng.* (1806) III. 800 The small proprietors, or *twenty-pound men. **1822** Galt *Provost* xxx, I received a twenty-pound note. **1861** W. F. Collier *Hist. Eng. Lit.* 403 A silver-scaled *twenty-pounder [salmon]. **1891** S. C. Scrivener *Our Fields & Cities* 39 Persons paying rates on twenty pounds... These twenty-pounders. **1899** *Daily News* 12 Jan. 7/5 A *twenty-round glove fight. **1797** *Chron.* 4 Mar., in *Ann. Reg.* 14/1 *Twenty shilling Notes were issued by the Bank of England. **1855** Macaulay *Hist. Eng.* xxii. IV. 698 The ministers at one time resolved to issue twentyshilling bills..for the payment of the troops. **1684** J. Peter *Siege Vienna* 109 *Twenty six pounders. **1756** *Connoisseur* No. 121 ¶6 A careful old gentleman came..to marry his son, and was recommended..to a *twenty thousand pounder. **1909** *Daily Chron.* 25 Sept. 5/5 The nineteen or *twenty-thousand ton Dreadnoughts. **1840** Blaine *Encycl. Rur. Sports* §2430 The higher the number of bullets [to the pound], the smaller is the caliber... Mr. Joseph Manton..recommends two-feet-eight and *twenty-two gauge as a general sporting length and bore of gun-barrel. **1902** *Westm. Gaz.* 7 Nov. 2/1 A *twenty-two-mile bridge across the Great Salt Lake. **1903** *Ibid.* 23 Oct. 3/1 You practically never see a *twenty-yard putt go ten yards off the line of the hole. **1902** *Ibid.* 2 Sept. 8/2 Rated..heavily upon the *twenty-year endowment plan.

d. Special Comb.: **twenty-first century** *attrib.* or as *adj.*, living in the twenty-first century; characteristic of the imagined conditions of the twenty-first century; **twenty-four carat** *a. colloq.*, (*a*) thoroughgoing, unalloyed, out-and-out; (*b*) genuine, flawless, trustworthy; **twenty-four-hour** *attrib.*, (*a*) lasting twenty-four hours; (*b*) of or pertaining to a system of reckoning the time whereby the hours of the day are numbered from one to twenty-four; (*c*) operating all day and all night, round-the-clock; **twenty questions**, a parlour game in which one party is allowed twenty questions (answered by either 'yes' or 'no') to discover the object of the other's thoughts; *spec.* the name of a popular radio panel game; **Twenty-six Counties**, the counties which by the Irish peace agreement of 1921–2 formed the Irish Free State, now the Republic of Ireland; cf. *Six Counties* s.v. SIX *a.* 1 d; **twenty-twenty** (also **20/20**) *Ophthalm.*, the Snellen fraction for normal visual acuity, expressed in feet; *colloq.* used to denote good eyesight; also *fig.*; **twenty-two carat** *a. colloq.* = *twenty-four carat* (*b*) above; also *ellipt.* as ***twenty-two***.

1964 D. Francis *Nerve* iii. 37 He was what I pictured *twenty-first century man should be—intensely alive, curiously innocent. **1979** D. Brierley *Cold War* v. 49 The computer...it's very big, very expensive, very twenty-first century. **1980** *Jrnl. R. Soc. Arts* July 467/2 Everyone in the country must adapt to twentyfirst-century living and working patterns. **1900** Sarah Grand *Babs* lxxxi, A regular *twenty-four carat cad—without alloy. **1965** D. Francis *Odds Against* iii. 40 It is you..who is the dyed-in-the-wool, twenty-four carat, unmitigated bastard. **1968** *Times* 21 Dec. 2/3 The legs in thigh-length boots are still lissom, 24 carat. **1974** G. Jenkins *Bridge of Magpies* v. 71 I'd accepted her story as 24-carat. **1984** *Times* 7 Mar. 28 The rest..had to work up real 24-carat grins. **1908** *Westm. Gaz.* 25 May 5/2 The *twenty-four-hour trip across the country. **1919** in *Cook's Continental Time-Table* (1973) Mar. p. vi/2 Cook's Continental Time-Table...Based on the 24-Hour System. **1947** Crowther & Whittington *Science at War* 7 A continuous twenty-four-hour watch for strange aircraft started. **1975** C. Egleton *Skirmish* xvii. 169 He had located a twenty-four hour service station and had had the tyre repaired. **1978** H. Kemelman *Thursday the Rabbi walked Out* (1979) xxix. 141, I got sick. It was this twenty-four-hour bug. **1978** G. Vaughan *Belgrade Drop* i. 11 A clipboard..contained dates, 24-hour clock times, and a short, neatly typed entry against each. **1786** H. More *Lett.* (1925) 107 Mrs Fielding and I..diverted ourselves with teaching Sir Joshua and Lord Palmerston the play of *twenty questions. **1846** R. Bell *Life of Rt. Hon. George Canning* x. 255 Canning proposed that they should play at 'Twenty Questions'. They had never heard of this game. **1930** 'Hay' & Wodehouse *Baa, Baa, Black Sheep* I. ii. 21 All right, a vicarage garden. What are we playing at? Twenty Questions, or something? **1979** E. H. Gombrich *Sense of Order* iv. 104 This can be done by a simple series of yes or no answers which allows a questioner to locate an item on a given grid as in the game of Twenty Questions. **1922** *Times* 6 June 16/2 The requirement that Ulster shall deliberately 'contract out' of the arrangements made between Great Britain and the *twenty-six Southern counties. *Ibid.*, If Mr. Griffith is right in claiming all but two per cent. of the population in the twenty-six counties as supporters of the Treaty. **1949** C. Graves *Ireland Revisited* viii. 102 The Bantrymen have always provided a strong contingent in the Government of the Twenty-six Counties ever since 1922. **1978** [see SOUTH *sb.* 2 a]. **1979** W. Nelson *Minstrel Code* vi. 45 The garage..belonged to a brother-in-law of one of the Sinn Fein leaders in the Twenty-Six Counties... O'Hagan explained that, within the IRA, no one talked of the 'Irish Republic' by any term other than this. **1875** T. Longmore *Man. Instructions Army testing Vision* (ed. 2) iii. 46 The 20-feet types are read at 20 feet, the 30-feet types at 30 feet; then V. = *20/20 or 30/30, and the acuteness of vision is normal. **1945** L. Shelly *Jive Talk Dict.* 35 *Twenty twenty*, excellent. **1951** E. F. Tait *Textbk. Refraction* ii. 16 The visual acuity of healthy corrected eyes may be much better or considerably worse than that represented by the 6/6 or 20/20 standard. **1956** 'E. McBain' *Cop Hater* (1958) iii. 21 Having 20/20 vision without glasses..he..had been appointed a patrolman. **1962** *Flight International* LXXXI. 426/2 Perfect eyesight is denoted as 20/20 vision, and the newest expression in the US air transport business—ruefully coined, we believe, by somebody in Convair—is 20/20 hindsight. Hindsight, of the 20/20 kind, abounds in plenty. But the aviation business is more interested in 20/20 foresight, because it can prevent people from losing a lot of money. **1977** H. Greene *FSO-1* ix. 83 We're looking back with twenty-twenty hindsight, now. **1981** P. Turnbull *Deep & Crisp & Even* ix. 162 He had 20:20 vision... He glimpsed a black shape. **1962** R. Cook *Crust on its Uppers* iv. 45 You come out *twenty-two carat. *Ibid.* 47, I tell you they're absolutely twenty-two. **1974** W. J. Burley *Death in Stanley Street* ii. 46 I've got a twenty-two carat alibi. **1981** J. Barnett *Firing Squad* vi. 61 Lady Lowderton was no nutter and her title was twenty-two carat.

twenty-eight. [TWENTY A. 1 b, 2.]

twenty-eight parrakeet, a name for the yellow-collared Parrakeet of Australia (*Platycercus semitorquatus*), from its note.

1848 J. Gould *Birds Australia* V. pl. 19 Yellow-collared Parrakeet... It often utters a note, which from its resemblance to those words has procured for it the appellation of 'twenty-eight' Parrakeet from the colonists.

See also TWENTY C.

twenty-firster (-ˈfɜːstə(r)). *slang.* [f. *twenty-first* (sc. *birthday*) + -ER[6].] A twenty-first birthday party (until 1970 in the U.K. celebrating the coming-of-age), or one who celebrates this. Also, a twenty-first birthday present.

1912 *Isis* 17 Feb. 204/1 There always are, or seem to be, celebrations of a sort on a twenty-firster. **1930** R. Lehmann *Note in Music* IV. 129 'What a lovely case!' 'Yes, it was a twenty-firster.' **1964** C. Mackenzie *My Life & Times* III. 166 The conventional Twenty-Firster at one of the Oxford hotels or clubs. *Ibid.* 214 Our rendez-vous with the rest of the Twenty-firsters was for supper. **1975** J. I. M. Stewart *Young Pattullo* iii. 69 The contraption itself was familiar to me, Ninian once having brought one home from the twenty-firster of an older friend.

twenty-five. [TWENTY A. 1 b.]

1. *Hockey* and *Rugby Football.* The line drawn across the ground twenty-five yards from each goal; also, the space enclosed by this.

1877 *Field* 24 Feb. 220/2 They were completely penned in their own twenty-five. **1889** *Pauline* VIII. 36 The play was constantly in our opponents' twenty-five. **1895** [see BULLY *sb.*[2] 2]. **1930** *Times* 14 Mar. 7/4 With 12 minutes to go, Home worked his way to the German '25' and then suddenly sent in another long shot.

2. *Cards* (also ***twenty-fives***): A variety of SPOIL-FIVE, in which the 'game' or winning score is twenty-five: cf. FORTY-FIVE b, JINK *sb.*[1] 2.

1870 'Cavendish' (*title*) The Pocket Guide to Spoil-Five, Twenty-Five and Forty-Five. **1894** 'Hoffmann' *Card & Table Games* (1898) 248 A player making all five tricks is said to make a 'jink', and wins the game, whether at twenty-five or forty-five. **1904** *Longm. Mag.* June 142 They produced an old pack of cards and played twentyfives.

See also TWENTY C.

twentyfold (ˈtwentɪfəʊld), *a.*, *adv.*, and *v.* [f. TWENTY + -FOLD. Cf. OE. *twentiȝfeald*.]

A. *adj.* Twenty times as many or as great; multiplied by twenty; twenty times repeated.

1610 Holland *Camden's Brit.* (1637) 679 Rye with twenty fold encrease. **1653** T. C. in Blithe *Eng. Improv. Impr.* To Capt. W. B. C vj, To raise from one to ten, yea Twentyfold. **1855** Milman *Lat. Chr.* XIV. iii. (1864) IX. 160 The interminable process of twentyfold assertion, twentyfold objection, twentyfold conclusion. **1897** P. Warung *Tales Old Regime* 207 Even in the twenty-fold perjurer and the thrice condemned murderer.

B. *adv.* Twenty times (in amount); twenty times as much.

1872 Tennyson *Gareth & Lyn.* 970 The savour of thy kitchen came upon me A little faintlier: but the wind hath changed: I scent it twentyfold. **1905** *Standard* 3 Mar. 2/5

After..heavy rains,..the volume of water..was twentyfold as great.

†**C.** *vb.* To multiply by twenty. *Obs. rare*⁻⁰. **1611** FLORIO, *Ventiplicare*, to twentyfold.

twenty-four. [TWENTY A. 1 b.]

1. A sheet folded into 24 leaves; a form of type for printing a sheet to be so folded (quot. 1683); a book in which the sheets are thus folded. (Always in *pl.*; usually in phr. ***in twenty-fours***.)

1673 *Term Catal.* 6 May, Valerii Maximi dictorum factorumque memorabilium Libri IX. In Twenty-fours. **1683** MOXON *Mech. Exerc., Printing* xxiv. ¶15 Any Form Imposed like Twelves, as Twenty fours. **1688** R. HOLME *Armoury* III. xv. (Roxb.) 23/2 Other bookes..whether they be..octavo's, sixteens or twentyfoures. **1715** M. DAVIES *Athen. Brit.* I. 11 Bound in Twelves, Sixteens, or Twenty-fours. **1771** LUCKOMBE *Hist. Print.* 419 A Sheet of Twenty-fours, with Two Signatures. *Ibid.* 420 A Half Sheet of Long Twenty-fours.

2. A period of 24 hours; a day. *nonce-use.*

1735 BERKELEY *Querist* §125 To pass the twenty-fours with tolerable ease.

See also TWENTY A. 2 d, B. 3, C.

twenty'fourmo. [English reading of 24mo or xxivmo, used as abbreviation of L. *vicesimo quarto*, after 12mo = *duodecimo*, etc.] The size of a book in which each sheet is folded into 24 leaves. So **'twentymo** [= 20mo or xxmo, for L. *vicesimo*], the size of a book in which each sheet is folded into 20 leaves.

1841 SAVAGE *Dict. Print.* 798 *Twenty-Fourmo*, a sheet of paper folded into twenty-four leaves, forty-eight pages, is termed twenty-fourmo. *Twentymo*, a sheet of paper folded into twenty leaves, forty pages, is termed twentymo. **1901** EGGLESTON *Transit Civiliz.* iii. 128 The sizes and shapes.. running all the way to twenty-fourmos.

twentyish ('twɛntɪɪʃ), *a.* [f. TWENTY + -ISH¹.] **a.** Of a person, (looking) approximately twenty years old. **b.** Characteristic of the 1920s.

1928 *Daily Express* 20 July 4 On the other hand, her blazer-clad, twentyish escort was impressed. **1940** GRAVES & HODGE *Long Week-End* viii. 125 The discovery..of the unrifled tomb of the Pharaoh Tutankhamen was given typical Twentyish publicity. Ancient Egypt suddenly became the vogue. **1975** L. DICKSON *Radclyffe Hall at Well of Loneliness* 9, I try to show her as the unique personality she was, part of a 'twentyish scene now vanished in the clearer if harsher light of our times. **1981** 'J. ROSS' *Dark Blue & Dangerous* viii. 43 The woman..wasn't twenty-ish..or startlingly beautiful.

twenty-one. [TWENTY A. 1 b.] = VINGT-ET-UN, VINGT-UN. Cf. BLACK JACK, BLACK-JACK 10; PONTOON *sb.*²

1790 E. WYNNE *Diary* 11 Mar. (1952) 30 My aunt winned 80 livers in playing at twentyone. **1917** [see PONTOON *sb.*² a]. **1977** *Time* 21 Nov. 44/2 New croupiers are taught the 'theory of craps', while Twenty-One dealers are told to slap their hands and hold them upward when they leave their posts to show that they are not concealing any chips.

twenty-second. *Mus.* [TWENTY A. 1 b.] A note 22 diatonic degrees distant from a given note, or the interval between two such notes (equal to three octaves); hence, an organ-stop formerly used, sounding three octaves above the normal pitch (more commonly called *two-and-twentieth*: see TWO B. I. 3 a).

*c***1700** in Grove *Dict. Mus.* II. 595/1 Great Organ. 1. Open Diapason... 13. Tierce. 14. Larigot. 15. Twenty-second.

twentysome: see -SOME *suffix*².

twenty-three. [TWENTY A. 1 b.] Ellipt. for *twenty-three skidoo*: see SKIDOO *v.* 2 b.

1930 J. DOS PASSOS *42nd Parallel* 72 We want to take a look at this burg an then twentythree. **1933** L. BLOOMFIELD *Language* xxiv. 443 One suspects that the queer slang use, a quarter of a century ago, of *twenty-three* for 'get out' arose in a chance situation of sportsmanship, gambling, crime, or some other rakish environment.

twenty-two. [TWENTY A. 1 b.] A twenty-two calibre rifle; = *two-two* (a) s.v. TWO IV. 2. Also *attrib.*, as ***twenty-two rifle***.

*a***1930** D. H. LAWRENCE *Phoenix II* (1968) 464, I went back to the house, and got the little twenty-two rifle. **1937** J. STEINBECK *Red Pony* 13 Jody took his twenty-two rifle up to the cold spring at the brush line. **1958** 'E. MCBAIN' *Killer's Payoff* (1960) xiii. 134 I've got three guns. A shotgun, a twenty-two, and a big-game rifle. **1967** K. S. PRICHARD in *Coast to Coast 1965–66* 182 Quick as light, Mac swung his twenty-two.

†**tweon,** *v. Obs.* [OE. *twéonian* (with variant *twýnian*), f. *twéon* doubt, a derivative from the same root as TWO.] *intr.* To be doubtful, to doubt; to debate.

*c***897** K. ÆLFRED *Gregory's Past. C.* xvi. 102 ȝif hie ðonne ȝit ðær tweonað, gongen ðonne to ðæm halȝum ȝewritum. *c***1000** *Ags. Gosp.* Matt. xxviii. 17 Witodlice sume hiȝ tweonedon. *c***1160** *Hatton Gosp.* Mark xi. 23 Swa hwilc swa ..on his heorte ne tweoneð. *c***1175** *Lamb. Hom.* 109 ȝunge monnan mei tweonian hweðer hi moten alibban. *c***1205** LAY. 907 þa wile þe heo tweoneden þus Clepede Membricius. *Ibid.* 25741 þæ cnihtes þa tweoneden To whaþere heo faren mihten.

twere, variant of TUYERE.

'twere (twɛə(r), twə(r)), also **twer**, abbreviation of *it were* (= it would be), formerly common, now poetic or archaic: see IT.

1605 SHAKS. *Macb.* I. vii. 1 If it were done,..then 'twer well, It were done quickly. **1607** —— *Cor.* IV. iv. 15 Friends ..who Twin (as 'twere) in Loue, Vnseparable. **1614** GORGES *Lucan* x. 448 Thus doubtfull musing whether tweare Fitter to die or basely feare. **1808** [see IT A. γ]. **1832** TENNYSON *To J. S.* 66 'Twere better I should cease.

twerle, obs. f. TWIRL *sb.*

twerp (twɜːp). *slang.* Also **twirp.** [Of uncertain origin. See quots. 1944, 1957; T. W. Earp of Exeter College, Oxford, matriculated in Michaelmas Term, 1911.] A despicable or objectionable person; an insignificant person, a nobody; a nincompoop.

1925 FRASER & GIBBONS *Soldier & Sailor Words* 292 *Twerp*, an unpleasant person. **1934** J. O'HARA *Appointment in Samarra* iv. 87 'And what a husband.' 'Exactly!.. That little twirp.' **1936** WODEHOUSE *Laughing Gas* xxv. 265 You're simply a lot of low twerps who kidnapped me in order to cash in. **1944** J. R. R. TOLKIEN *Let.* 6 Oct. (1981) 94 He lived in O[xford] at the time when we lived in Pusey Street (rooming with Walton, the composer, and going about with T. W. Earp, the original twerp). **1945** [see RAT *sb.*¹ 3 a]. **1955** E. POUND *Section: Rock-Drill* xcv. 105 Among all these twerps and Pullizer sponges no voice for the Constitution, No objection to the historic blackout. **1957** R. CAMPBELL *Portugal* 87 T. W. Earp (who gave the English language the word twirp, really twearp, because of the Goering-like wrath he kindled in the hearts of the rugger-playing stalwarts at Oxford, when he was president of the Union, by being the last, most charming, and wittiest of the 'decadents'). **1960** S. BARSTOW *Kind of Loving* I. iv. 91 If she turns me down I'll look more of a twerp than ever. **1973** B. BROADFOOT *Ten Lost Years* xxvii. 309 The R. B. Bennetts of Canada and that despicable little twerp Mac. **1980** *National Times* (Austral.) 21 Dec. 30/3 Kendig's former boss..is a twerp. His offices contain a gallery of framed photographs of [himself]: there he is with John Wayne, with Nixon, [etc.].

Twesdaie, -day, obs. ff. TUESDAY.

twesel, var. TWISEL *v. Obs.*

twey, tweye: see TWAY, TWIE.

†**tweyangle.** *Obs. rare*⁻¹. App. synonym (or error) for TOUCHANGLE, ANGLE-TWITCH.

14.. *Stockh. Med. MS.* II. 409 in *Anglia* XVIII. 317 [If] wermys, tweyanglys be name, [be] Mad to powdyr.

twey-case: see TWEE¹.

tweyen, tweyn, tweyne, obs. ff. TWAIN, TWINE.

tweyfold, tweyleke: see TWAY 4.

tweys, tweyss, obs. ff. TWICE.

tweyst, obs. dial. f. TWIST.

twezers, obs. f. TWEEZERS.

twhart, twhert, obs. ff. THWART.

twhite, twhyte, obs. ff. THWITE.

Twi (twiː, tʃwiː). Also **Tshi** (tʃiː). **a.** The chief language spoken in Ghana, consisting of several mutually intelligible dialects. **b.** The speakers of Twi. Also *attrib.*

1874 J. G. CHRISTALLER *Dict. Eng., Tshi-Asàntè-Akra* p. iv, Tshi is the prevailing language of the Gold Coast. *Ibid.* p. ix, In the publications of the Basel missionaries, the language is called Tw̌i, pronounced as *Chwee* would be in English. **1887** A. B. ELLIS (*title*) The Tshi-speaking peoples of the Gold Coast. **1920** A. W. CARDINALL *Natives N. Territories Gold Coast* 113 There are in the Gold Coast and its dependencies..two great languages: Twi,..and a language which in its simplest form is spoken by the Moshi. **1931** *Times Lit. Suppl.* 17 Sept. 692/3 The author's argument that the Twi people originally came from the grass country. **1955** [see FANTI *sb.* and *a.*]. **1972** *Bk. Thousand Tongues* (rev. ed.) 441/1 The administrative term 'Akan' is used to denote all forms of Twi (Fante, Asante, and Akuapem)... In the 1850's, when Johannes Christaller translated the Bible into 'Twi', he chose..a form of the language which fell phonetically between the linguistic extremes of Fante and Asante-Akyem... Thus Scriptures were finally provided for the Twi. **1978** *Language* LIV. 458, I would like to enumerate the contributions in terms of the languages treated:..one paper each on Bambara (David Dwyer), Twi (Lynette Nyaggah), Nupe (Isaac George), [etc.].

twi-, twy- (twaɪ), *prefix.* [OE. *twi-* = OFris. *twi-*, MLG. *twi-*, MDu. *twe-*, Du. *twee-*, OHG. *zwi-*, Ger. *zwie-*, ON. *tví-*, Norw., Sw., Da. *tve-*; cognate with Skr. *dvi-*, Gr. δι-, L. *bi-*, Lith. *dvi-*, from root akin to Skr. *dwau*, *dwē*, Gr. δύο, L. *duo*, TWO. In OE. the regular comb. form expressing *two*, sometimes *twice*.]

a. In parasynthetic comb. with sb. + -ED², forming adjs. with the sense 'having two..', 'two..-ed', as ***twi-*** (or ***twy-***)***arched***, ***-clustered***, ***-coloured***, ***-eared***, ***-faced***, ***-flamed***, ***-gated***, ***-headed***, ***-linked***, ***-mouthed***, ***-natured***, ***-necked***, ***-peaked***, ***-pointed***, ***-shaped*** (see also *twi-banked*, etc. in e); also with sb. simply, in the same sense, as ***twi-top*** adj. (see also *twiform* in e). **b.** With adj. or pple. in sense 'in two ways or respects, doubly', as ***twi-*** (***twy-***)***streaming***, ***-yoked***. **c.** With sb. in sense 'twofold, double', as ***twi-circle***, ***-nature***, ***-reason*** (see also *twi-car*, etc. in e). **d.** In sense 'twice' or 'a second time', as ***twi-*** (***twy-***)***born*** adj. (see also *twichild* in e). **e.** Special Combs.: **twi-banked** *a.*, having two banks of oars; **twi-car**, used by W. Morris to represent Gr. δίφρος chariot (properly 'the chariot-board, on which two could stand', L. & Sc.); **twichild** (**twy-**) (*obs.* exc. *dial.*), one who is 'twice a child', an old man in his second childhood; also, (one's) second childhood; also as *adj.*; **twifoil** (**twy-**) *Her.* = DUFOIL; **twi-forked** (**twy-**) *a.*, divided in two like a fork, bifurcate; **twiform, -formed** (**twy-**) *adjs.*, having a double form; formed of two (esp. different or incongruous) parts (in quot. 1703, having some part double); **twi-life** (*nonce-wd.* after *twilight*), a life marked by indistinct perception or consciousness; **twi-minded** *a.*, having two minds or thoughts (about something); considering (it) in two ways or aspects; **twy-prong**, a two-pronged fork; **twi-thought** (*nonce-wd.* after *twilight*), an indistinct or vague thought; †**twi-wifing**, bigamy. See also TWIBILL, TWIBIT, TWIFALLOW, TWIFOLD, TWILIGHT, TWIREDE, TWISPECHE.

1903 *Westm. Gaz.* 22 Aug. 2/1 A *twi-arched bridge of stone. **1875** MORRIS *Æneid* VIII. 79 Two *twi-banked keels. **1908** G. MURRAY *Euripides' Hippolytus* 30 That Mother fair Of *Twy-born Bacchus. **1887** MORRIS *Odyss.* XV. 75 But abide till I bring to thy *twi-car the gifts. *c***1580** JEFFERIE *Bugbears* I. iii. 69 in *Archiv. Stud. Neu. Spr.* (1897) XCVIII. 313 O my *twichild and my babye! **1656** W. D. tr. *Comenius' Gate Lat. Unl.* §199 Old men are said to grow children again, and to bee twichilde. **1829** SOUTHEY *Oliver Newman* vi, Encumber'd with a twichild man. **1889** GISSING *Both of this Parish* xxiii. II. 175, I thought it was but a deception o' my twichild, for I be getting aged. **1895** F. THOMPSON *Sister Songs* 13 In *twi-circle o'er the grass. *a***1834** COLERIDGE *The Pang more sharp* ii, Babe..From its *twy-cluster'd hiding-place of snow. **1903** *Academy* 18 July 56/1 A *twi-coloured thread, red and white. **1904** FARRER *Garden Asia* 270 Little twy-coloured bubbles. **1879** BUTCHER & LANG *Odyssey* 359 A..*twy-eared chalice of gold. **1635** QUARLES *Embl.* V. xiv. 40 Wry-mouth'd disdaine,..And *twy-fac'd Fraud. **1875** MORRIS *Æneid* XII. 198 Twi-faced Janus. **1822** T. G. WAINEWRIGHT *Ess. & Crit.* (1880) 298 The *twi-flamed torch. **1688** *Twyfoile [see DUFOIL]. *c***1828** BERRY *Encycl. Her.* I. Gloss., Twyfoil or Dufoil. **1891** *Cent. Dict.*, Twifoil. **1635** QUARLES *Embl.* II. xiii. 10 Her flaming head, *Twy-forked with death. **1639** G. DANIEL *Ecclus.* xxvii. 60 A Twi-forkt Iavelin doth divide his heart. **1658** BROMHALL *Treat. Specters* IV. 258 Ioves twy-forked lightning. **1738** *Gentl. Mag.* VIII. 375/1 Twi-fork'd Malvern with his tow'ring height. **1812** CARY *Dante, Purg.* XXXII. 95 The wain..Bound to the *twyform beast. **1907** F. THOMPSON *Ode Setting Sun*, Thou twi-form deity. **1607** J. DAVIES *Summa Totalis* H iij, This huge *twy-form'd Fabrick. **1703** T. N. *City & C. Purchaser* 7 Twiform'd Creatures, as..a Serpent with a Head at each end; the Spread Eagle with 2 Heads. **1852** KINGSLEY *Andromeda* 58 Twyformed, many-handed, terrible, shapeless. **1887** BOWEN *Æneid* VI. 25 Twiformed Minotaur, two bodies combined. **1573** TWYNE *Æneid* X. D d j, In parliment house they sat *twigated wyde. **1895** *Month* June 237 Illustrations of the eagle both single and *twi-headed. **1889** LOWELL in *Atlantic Monthly* LXIV. 146 This illusion..That witches us to hear and see As in a *twi-life what it will. **1875** MORRIS *Æneid* XII. 375 His *twilinked coat of mail. **1883** G. MEREDITH *Earth & Man* xliv, *Twi-minded of him, as the waxing tree, Or dated leaf. **1886** E. DOWDEN *Let.* Jan. in *Fragments from Old Lett.* (1914) I. 176 You raise..a difficult general question concerning the destruction of old letters. As usual, *I* am twi-minded. **1932** V. WOOLF *Common Reader* 2nd Ser. 174 From the first he [*sc.* Hazlitt] was a twy-minded man. **1875** MORRIS *Æneid* IX. 617 To hear the flute's *twi-mouthed song. **1897** W. B. YEATS *Secret Rose* 178 Then the *twy-nature faded. **1868** TENNYSON *Lucretius* 194 A satyr,..but him I proved impossible; *Twy-natured is no nature. **1879** F. W. H. MYERS in *19th Cent.* June 959 That strange antithesis in the 'twy-natured' French. **1916** G. SAINTSBURY *Peace of Augustans* viii. 287 The cat was a nymph and the nymph was a cat; the two lines fit the twynatured creature in both its natures. **1840** BROWNING *Sordello* IV. 388 The Kaiser's ominous sign-mark..The crowned, grim, *twy-necked eagle. **1906** *Edin. Rev.* Apr. 319 A *twy-peaked monticule. **1623** LISLE *Ælfric on O. & N. Test.* Ded. 1 *Twi-pointed Pernas hill. **1840** BROWNING *Sordello* III. 1019 That's no *twy-prong, but a pastoral cross. **1884** —— *Ferishtah, Camel-Driver* 51 This red-hot twy-prong. **1632** B. JONSON *Magn. Lady* III. v, You shall pardon me For a *twi-reason of State. **1907** F. THOMPSON *New Poems, Hermes* 188 Behold, with rod *twy-serpented Hermes, the prophet. **1875** MORRIS *Æneid* VI. 286 *Twi-shaped Scyllas. **1794** COLERIDGE *Relig. Musings* 204 Property..*twy-streaming fount, Whence Vice and Virtue flow, honey and gall. **1885** G. MEREDITH *Diana* xxiv, Diana saw herself through the haze she conjured up. 'Am I worse than other women?' was a piercing *twi-thought. **1622** WITHER *Fair Virtue* E ij, The *twy-top Hill, Where the Poets learne their skill. *c***1250** *Gen. & Ex.* 450 Bigamie..On engleis tale, *twie-wifing. **1875** MORRIS *Æneid* XII. 164 With *twiyoked horses white.

twibill, twybill ('twaɪbɪl, †'twɪb(ə)l). *arch.* and *dial.* Forms: 1 twibile, 1–4 **twybile** (4 -byle); 1, 4– twibil, 1, 6– twibill (6 -bylle); 1, 4– twybill, 4–6 -bil, -byl(l(e, 6 -bille; 4 twybel(l, 5–6 twyble, 6 twible, *Sc.* twibbil, 7 twibble; 6–7 twyvel(l, 8 twivil(l: see also TUBBAL, TUBBER², and *two-bill*

(TWO B. IV. 2). [OE. *twibil*, *-bill* neut., and *twibile* masc., f. TWI- + BILL *sb.*[1] and *sb.*[2]]

†**1.** A kind of axe with two cutting edges; formerly used for cutting mortises. *Obs.*

a **1000** *Prose Life Guthlac* xii. (1848) 56 He..ʒenam sum twibil, and mid þan þry men to deaðe ofsloh. *a* **1000** *Ags. Gloss.* in Wr.-Wülcker 194/35 *Bipennis securis*, twilafte æx, *uel* twibile. **1295** *Acc. Exch. K.R.* 5/8 m. 9 (P.R.O.) Et iiij.d. ..in .j. Twybile emendando. *a* **1310** in Wright *Lyric P.* xxxix. 110 He mot myd is twybyl other trous make. *a* **1340** HAMPOLE *Psalter* lxxiii. 7 Wiþ bradaxis þai share down þe ʒates of it..in brade axe and twybile [Vulg. *in securi et ascia*] þai kest it down. **14..** *Tundale's Vis.* (Wagner) 722 Summe had twybyll, brodax and nawger. *c* **1440** *Promp. Parv.* 505/1 Twybyl, wryhtys instrument..*bisacuta, biceps.* **1500** *Ortus Vocab.*, *Bisacuta*, a twybyll. *c* **1500** *Debate Carpenter's Tools* 13 in Hazl. *E.P.P.* I. 80 Ʒe, ʒe, seyd the twybylle, Thou spekes euer ageyne skylle. **1548** *Elyot's Dict.*, *Bipennis*, a twybill, wherwith carpenters doo make their mortayses. **1587** *Will of Arraie* (Somerset Ho.), Two wombells and a Twyvell. **1656** BLOUNT *Glossogr.*, *Twibil* (Belg. *Tweebill*), an instrument used by Carpenters to make mortise-holes. **1686** PLOT *Staffordsh.* 168 Grinding-stones..for thicker edg'd tooles, such as Axes, Hatchets, Chisells, Adds, Twy-bills, &c.

attrib. **1641** *Wit's Recreat.* §583 'Twill make a good ship-anchor, when he lackes. It is his gimlet, and his twibill axe.

2. A mattock; also a similar tool used in mining, a tubbal. Now *local.*

c **1440** *Pallad. on Husb.* I. 1153 The mattok, twyble [*v.r.* twibil], picoys. *c* **1440** *Promp. Parv.* 505/1 Twybyl, or mattoke, *marra*,..*ligo.* **1555** PHAER *Æneid* II. E iv, The plowmen with their axes strong..and twibles tall. **1577** B. GOOGE *Heresbach's Husb.* (1586) 11 b, Iron hookes, Iron forkes, Twybilles, Dongforkes. **1612** DRAYTON *Poly-olb.* XVIII. 77 She learn'd the churlish ax and twybill to prepare, To steel the coulter's edge. **1687** TAUBMAN *London's Tri.* 7 Miners..bearing Spades, Pickaxes, Twibbles and Crows, fit to sink Shafts, and make Addits. **1898** *N. & Q.* 9th Ser. I. 243/2 [Given as a Devonshire name for 'a two-billed pick'.]

b. A reaping-hook used in cutting beans and peas; a pea-hook. *dial.*

1763 *Museum Rust.* I. lxii. 263 The regularity with which these beans are sown, makes it much easier to cut them with the twibil and hink, than if they were sown at random. *Ibid.* lxiii. 266 Each labourer had in his right hand a cutting instrument called a twibil, and in his left a sort of hook called a hink. **1796** J. BOYS *Agric. Kent* 91 It [canary seed] is cut in the harvest..with a hook, called a twibil, and a hink. **1887** *Kentish Gloss.*, *Twibil* (twei·bil), a hook for cutting beans.

†**c.** See quot. *Obs. rare*$^{-0}$.

1706 PHILLIPS (ed. Kersey), *Twivill*, an Iron-Tool us'd by Paviers.

3. A double-bladed battle-axe or bill. *poet. arch.*

In quot. 1678 app. a halberd carried by a constable of the watch.

1558 PHAER *Æneid* II. E ij, Him self in hand..a twyble great doth bryng. **1565** GOLDING *Ovid's Met.* IV. 28 Lycurgus with his twibill sharpe. *c* **1611** CHAPMAN *Iliad* XV. 656 Sharpe axes, twibils, two-hand swords, and speares with two heads borne, Were then the weapons. **1678** *Jovialists Coronat.* 3 in *Loyal Garland* D viij, If..a Halberdly train, Or a Constable chance to rebel, And would with his twyvels maliciously swell And against the Kings party raise Arms. **1834** PLANCHÉ *Brit. Costume* 31 They [Anglo-Saxons] had also axes with long handles which they called bills,..and the double-axe or *bipennis* (twy-bill). **1865** KINGSLEY *Herew.* xix, A little fair-haired man..who heaved up a long twybill, or double axe. **1876** MORRIS *Sigurd* I. 68 He bore a mighty twi-bill as he waded the fight-sheaves through.

†**twibit.** *Obs. rare.* In 5 **twybyte**, 6 **-byt**, **twibytte.** [f. TWI- + BIT *sb.*[1] 5.] = TWIBILL.

14.. *MS. Lansd.* 560 fol. 45 *Bipennis*, twybyte. **1510** STANBRIDGE *Vocabula* (W. de W.) B iv b, *Bipennis*, a twybyt. **1560** BECON *Jewel of Joy* Wks. II. 26 b, Is not my word lyke fire,..and lyke a twibytte cleauynge the rocke of stonne?

twice (twaɪs), *adv.* (*sb.*, *a.*) Forms: 2 **twiȝes**, 3 (*Orm.*) **twiȝȝess**, **twiȝess**, 4 **twiȝes**, **tuuiȝes**; 2–5 **twies**, 4 **twyese**, **tweis**, 4–5 **twyys**, **tweies**, 4–6 **twyes**, **twys**, *Sc.* **twyss**, 4 (7 *Sc.*) **tuis**, 4–7 **twyse**, **twise**, 5 **tweys**, 5 (6 *Sc.*) **twyis**, **tuyse**, 5–6 **twis**, *Sc.* **tuys(s**, 6 *Sc.* **twyiss**, **tweyss**, **tuyss**, **tuise**, 7 **twyce**, 5– **twice**; 6 **twyst**, 7 **twist**, 9 *dial.* **twyste**, **twiste**, 9– *dial.* **twicet**, **twict.** [Late OE. *twiȝes*, f. *twiȝe*, TWIE + advb. genitive ending *-es*; cf. *ǽnes*, *ānes* ONCE, *þriȝes* THRICE.

Twees, given by Kilian as a Du. and Fris. word, may be a similar formation, but Da. dial. *tøs*, *tøse* is a reduced form of MDa. *tøsser*, ON. *tvisvar*.]

In all senses now the regular substitute for the phrase *two times*: see TWO B. I. 1 d.

1. a. Two (successive) times; on two occasions.

c **1122** *O.E. Chron.* (Laud MS.) an. 1120 Ðises ȝeares com þet leoht to Sepulchrum Dni..twiȝes. *a* **1175** *Cott. Hom.* 227 Þat cild his twies acenned. *c* **1200** ORMIN Ded. 104, & tatt he loke wel þatt he An bocstaff write twiȝȝess, Eȝȝwhær þær itt uppo þiss boc Iss writenn o þatt wise. *Ibid.* 16635 Niss nan mann..þatt muȝhe Godess riche sen Butt he be borenn twiȝess. **13..** *Cursor M.* 27912 (Cott. Galba) Als gude war men to ett twise. *a* **1325** *MS. Rawl. B.* 520 lf. 54 Tuuiȝes in þe ȝere. *c* **1330** R. BRUNNE *Chron. Wace* (Rolls) 4704 Þe Bretons..had wonnen of Cesar twys. *c* **1350** *Will. Palerne* 3721 It a-louted lowe to vs twiȝes. *c* **1375** *Lay Folks Mass Bk.* (MS. B.) 309 In excelsis he neuens twyese. **1377** LANGL. *P. Pl.* B. v. 421, I nam nouȝte shryuen..tweies in two ȝere. *a* **1400–50** *Alexander* 1605 'Ay mott he leue, ay mot he leue', quod ilke a lede twyse. **14..** *R. Gloucester's Chron.* (Rolls) 9018 (MS. β) He smote him tweys on þe heuede. *c* **1449** PECOCK *Repr.* IV. vii. (Rolls) 462 If he hadde be twies weddid..Eny man tweies weddid. **1473–4** *Acc. Ld. High Treas. Scot.* I. 47 Passand twis to Sanctandrois and anys to Dunbare. **1508** DUNBAR *Tua Mariit Wemen* 303, I wes tuyse maryit. **1526** TINDALE *Luke* xviii. 12, I fast twyse in the weke. **1549** *Acc. Ld. High Treas. Scot.* IX. 280 To the furroure for tuys lynyng of ane goun. **1563–7** BUCHANAN *Reform. St. Andros* Wks. (1892) 11 At iij howris ryng twyiss. **1596** SHAKS. *Merch. V.* IV. i. 69 Wouldst thou haue a Serpent sting thee twice? **1612** in *2nd Rep. Rec. Irel.* 264 Twist or thrist a week. **1774** GOLDSM. *Nat. Hist.* (1776) V. 350 The swallow..sometimes breeds twice a year. **1789, 1867** Twicet [see ONCE *adv.* A. γ]. **1839** T. MITCHELL *Aristoph.*, *Frogs* 145 *note*, [Cinesias] is alluded to twice more in the present play. **1868** LOCKYER *Elem. Astron.* III. xxxiii. (1879) 195 The sun crosses the equator twice a year at the equinoxes. **1888** EGGLESTON *Graysons* i. 15, I wouldn't look at her twiste. **1895** *Dialect Notes* I. 375 Some other words reported indiviually are...onct, twict. **1922** JOYCE *Ulysses* 453 And he interfered twict with my clothing. **1958** E. BIRNEY *Turvey* v. 48, I los all my good time for climbin the fence twicet.

b. Strengthened by *over* (OVER *adv.* 13 a).

1648 BP. HALL *Serm. Higham* Rem. Wks. (1660) Z j b, The justice of God never punished the same sin twise over. **1711** ADDISON *Spect.* No. 72 ¶ 11 The Senior Member has outlived the whole Club twice over. **1721** RAMSAY *Richy & Sandy* 6 This aught days twice o'er tell'd. **1893** *Times* 29 Apr. 11/3 To tax the owners of property twice over in respect of the same thing.

c. Contextually: A second time; for the second time.

13.. *Sir Beues* (A.) 4256 Now is ȝhe þer twies quene. **1382** WYCLIF *Phil.* iv. 16 To Tessalonyk ȝe senten oonis and twyes [TINDALE, CRANMER, *Geneva*, once and afterwarde agayne]. *a* **1450** *Knt. de la Tour* (1906) 85 The kynge sente vnto her onis, tuyes, thries. *c* **1475** *Rauf Coilȝear* 148 Now is twyse..me think thow hes forȝet. **1501** DOUGLAS *Pal. Hon.* I. 388 And now this time is twyis. **1582** T. WATSON *Centurie of Loue* lxxxv, I at last, Am now twise free. **1602** SHAKS. *Ham.* II. ii. 403 That great Baby..is not yet out of his swathing clouts. *Rosin.* Happily he's the second time come to them: for they say, an old man is twice a childe. **1633** BP. HALL *Occas. Medit.* (1851) 112 The old word is, that 'An old man is twice a child'; but I say, happy is he, that is thus a child always.

d. In phr. ***once or twice***, ***twice or thrice***, used indefinitely: a few times.

a **1225**–*c* **1450** [see ONCE 8 a]. *c* **1440** MAUNDEV. (1839) xxv. 261 Ones or twyes in the Woke. *c* **1400** tr. *Secreta Secret.*, *Gov. Lordsh.* xix. 58 Do noght þat ofte, but twyes or thryes yn þe ȝeer. **1526** *Pilgr. Perf.* (W. de W. 1531) 173 b, Not onely ones or twyse he hath hurted me. **1711** ADDISON *Spect.* No. 120 ¶ 1 He has caught me twice or thrice looking after a Bird's Nest. **1750** GRAY *Long Story* 125 He once or twice had pen'd a sonnet.

e. ***to think twice***: to consider a matter a second time (before deciding or acting); to deliberate.

1623 W. PAINTER in *Oxf. Dict. Eng. Proverbs* (1970) 263/1 Thinke twise, then speak, the old Prouerbe doth say. **1640** R. BRATHWAIT *Ar't Asleepe Husband?* vii. 277 You thinke twice before you speake, and may be demanded twice before you answer. **1818** SCOTT *Heart Midl.* in *Tales my Landlord* 2nd Ser. IV. viii. 180 If a fule may gie a wise man a counsel, I wad hae him think twice or he mells wi' Knockdunder. **1853** C. BRONTË *Villette* I. viii. 147, I saw in her countenance a something that made me think twice ere I decided. **1877** SPURGEON *Serm.* XXIII. 56 Do not think twice about it.. but say 'No'. **1890** *Spectator* 27 Dec. 932/1 He may..think twice before he formally undertakes so unremunerative a struggle. **1910** [see THINK *v.* 5 b]. **1934** [see ONCE *adv.* A. γ]. **1940** H. G. WELLS *Babes in Darkling Wood* II. i. 137 'Seems like Hitler's thinking twicet,' said a gentleman behind him.

2. Expressing multiplication by two: Two times in number, amount, or value.

a. with a numeral, or a sb. or sb. phr. expressing quantity: Two times as much as; double of.

1308 *Song* in Ritson *Anc. Songs & Ball.* (1877) 61 Tak twies ten ifere That wol be tuenti fulle. **1377** LANGL. *P. Pl.* B. XIII. 270 In þe date of owre dryȝte..A þousande and thre hondreth tweis thretty & ten. *c* **1425** *Craft of Nombrynge* (E.E.T.S.) 28 Yf þat þou wold wete qwat is twyes 40. **1593** in T. Morris *Provosts of Methven* (1875) 82 For the haill space of twyss nynetene ȝeiris. **1697** DAMPIER *Voy.* I. xv. 408 Any Stranger..must be a great Favourite to get a pair of Shoes of them [Chinese women], tho he give twice their value. **1743** FRANCIS tr. *Hor.*, *Odes* V. ix. 19 Twice a thousand Gauls aloud proclaim..great Cæsar's name. **1824** ARNOLD *Let.* in Stanley *Life & Corr.* (1844) I. 69, I am twice the man for labour that I have been..for the last year or two. **1826** HENRY *Elem. Chem.* II. 373 These crystals..require.. between twice and three times their weight of water at 60°. **1875** JOWETT *Plato* (ed. 2) I. 475 Two is twice one. **1926** R. HUGHES in *Hearst's Internat.* Feb. 44/2 Wha'd' you say, Kid, if I'd 'a' matched Coily up wit' some old vet'ran twicet his weight wit' twicet his ring-gener'lship.

b. In a twofold degree; two times as much; doubly.

Usually with *as* (†*so* obs.); more rarely with comparative, or (rhetorically) with an adj. of quality.

[*c* **1394** *P. Pl. Crede* 178 Mo þan twenty and two twyes y-noumbred.] **1398** TREVISA *Barth. De P.R.* XIX. cxxv. (1495) mm iv/1 A nombre that hyght Multiplex conteyneth yᵉ lesse nombre twyes or thryes or foure tymes. *c* **1460** *Towneley Myst.* viii. 320 We shall þem bond twyse as fast. **1500–20** DUNBAR *Poems* xvi. 9 Sum gevis for twyiss als gud agane. **1542** UDALL *Erasm. Apoph.* 303 A newe hous..twys so good & double so faire. **1583** STUBBES *Anat. Abus.* II. (1882) 63 Twise vnhappy be those parents that thinke any moneth, day or houre, infortunate for their children to be borne in. **1601** DOLMAN *La Primaud. Fr. Acad.* (1618) III. 728 The fire is twise more subtile then the aire. *a* **1774** GOLDSM. *Surv. Exp. Philos.* (1776) I. 238 If..the wedge be twice as long..the driver will cleave his wood with twice greater force. **1825** T. HOOK *Sayings* Ser. II. *Sutherl.* (Colburn) 9 Which..makes beauty doubly winning, and talent twice bewitching. **1885** 'MRS. ALEXANDER' *Valerie's Fate* iv, I am nearly as old as you are, and I know twice as much of the world.

3. quasi-*sb.*, preceded by a preposition or demonstrative: Two times. (Cf. ONCE 9.) **a.** with preposition; esp. ***at twice***, on two occasions, in two distinct operations (somewhat *rare*); † ***by twice***, twofold, doubly (*obs. Sc.*).

1494 *Acc. Ld. High Treas. Scot.* I. 248 For a rape to the locke at twys,..brokyne wyth towen of the tymmyr.

?*a* **1500** *Wycket* (1828) p. xii, Whether is the body of the lorde made at once or at twyse. **1560** WHITEHORNE *Ord. Souldiours* (1573) 33 b, A ladle..that will take so muche pouder up at twise or thrise. *a* **1600** MONTGOMERIE *Sonn.* lxii. 5 My trumpets tone is terribler be tuyis [*rimes* wyse, lyis] Nor ȝon couhorne. **1664** J. WILSON *Projectors* IV, As many Citizens and their Wives at once, as the great Bed at Ware, will hold at twice. **1791** H. WALPOLE *Let. to Miss Berry* 29 Jan., I have written this at twice. **1860** GEO. ELIOT *Mill on Fl.* III. iii, 'Did Mr. Tulliver let you have the money all at once?'..'No; at twice.'

b. with demonstrative word or phrase. *rare.*

1872 BAGEHOT *Eng. Constit.* (1878) 100 We reject your Bill for this once or these twice, or even these thrice. **1907** T. COBB in *Story-Teller* 93/1 Judging by Lady Kitty's demeanour the last twice they had met.

4. quasi-*adj.* Performed, occurring, given, etc. twice; doing something (implied by the sb.) twice.

Chiefly with verbal sb. or agent-n., the vb. in which is implicitly qualified by *twice*.

1577 B. GOOGE *Heresbach's Husb.* 28 Sommer Barley [is to be sowed] in March or April, after twyse plowing. **1624** CAPT. SMITH *Virginia* 239 We heard of the twice returne of the Paragon. **1683** *Life & Death Ld. Shaftesbury* in *Select fr. Harl. Misc.* (1793) 458 His twice Imprisonment in the Tower. **1876** FREEMAN *Hist. Sk.* 83 The twice pilgrim. **1894** MRS. H. WARD *Marcella* I. i. 6 Twice meat was forbidden and twice pudding allowed.

5. a. In combination with pples., forming compound adjs., as ***twice-baked***, ***-bearing***, ***-blowing***, ***-boiled***, ***-conquered***, ***-dipped***, ***-dyed***, ***-given***, ***-married***, ***-refined***, ***-roasted***, ***-shelled***, ***-sworn***, ***-turned*** (see also TWICE-BORN, -LAID, -TOLD); rarely with other adjs., as ***twice-foul***, ***-mortal***; also † **twice-childish** *a.* in one's 'second childhood' (cf. quot. 1602 in 1 c); **twice-stabbed** *a. Entom.*, having two red marks suggesting stabs on the wing-cases, as the twice-stabbed ladybird, *Chilocorus bivulnerus* (*Cent. Dict.* 1891); † **twice-writhen**, Turner's rendering of med.L. *bistorta*, BISTORT.

1542 *Reg. Mag. Sig. Scot.* 616/2 Tuyse schelit meill. **1568** TURNER *Herbal* III. 12 It [Bistort] may be called..twise-writhen. **1591** SYLVESTER *Du Bartas* I. iv. 304 The twice-foul Raven. **1592** HOOKER *Eccl. Pol.* Pref. ii. §5 These twice-sworne men. **1598** SYLVESTER *Du Bartas* II. i. I. *Eden* 224 The passage of twice-childish age. **1642** FULLER *Holy & Prof. St.* V. xi. 405 Such as take themselves to be twice-refined. **1700** T. BROWN *Amusem. Ser. & Com.* x. 125 That unpalatable Ragoust, called in Latin *Cramben Biscoctum*, and in plain English, Twice-boil'd Cabbage. **1705** POPE *Jan. & May* 110 Twicemarry'd dames. **1742** YOUNG *Nt. Th.* IV. 765 Faith..dying, tenfold terror gives to death, And dips in venom his twice-mortal sting. **1743** FRANCIS tr. *Hor.*, *Odes* II. xvi. 42 The twice-dyed purple. *c* **1820** S. ROGERS *Italy*, *Paestum* 89 Paestum's twice-blowing roses. **1842** LOUDON *Suburban Hort.* 568 The twice-bearing red [raspberry]. **1846** H. G. ROBINSON *Odes of Horace* II. xvi, And wool with Afric's dye..Twice-dipp'd. **1851** H. MELVILLE *Whale* xxvi. 125 As hard as twice-baked biscuits.

b. In combination with advbs., forming compound advbs. or adjs. (and sbs.), as ***twice-nightly***, ***-weekly***, ***-yearly***.

1929 D. H. LAWRENCE *Pansies* 133 And let the nodding tempests of verbosity Weekly or twice-weekly whistle round your bottles. **1949** M. STEEN *Twilight on Floods* IV. vi. 611 There was English's.., the first of the twice-nightlies, down in Hackney. **1976** 'W. TREVOR' *Children of Dynmouth* v. 102 The cartoonist responsible..was now, in the sunset of his life, himself the recipient of twice-weekly Meals on Wheels. **1980** M. BABSON *Queue here for Murder* iv. 30 The twice-yearly Sales.

Hence **twice** *v.* (*nonce-wd.* or *slang*), *trans.* to make twice as much, to double; to do twice as much as.

a **1636** FITZ-GEFFRAY *Compassion towards Capt.* ii. (1637) 33 Twice your gift by timely giving it. **1890** 'R. BOLDREWOOD' *Col. Reformer* (1891) 304 We can 'twice' you over and over.

'twice-born, *a.*

1. Born twice: esp. in classical mythology as an epithet of Bacchus (also *absol.*).

14.. W. PARIS *Cristine* 323 in Horstm. *Altengl. Leg.* (1878) 187 As twys borne childe that were righte yonge, Twys in credelle rokkede to be. **1608** SYLVESTER *Du Bartas* II. iv. III. *Schisme* 909 The twice-born Preacher to the Ninivite. **1697** CREECH *Manilius* II. 49 How twice-born Bacchus burst the Thunderer's Thigh. **1866** J. B. ROSE tr. *Ovid's Met.* 78 The twice-born whom with milk they feed.

2. An epithet of the three higher castes of Hindus: see CASTE 2. Also *absol.*

1794 SIR W. JONES *Inst. Hindu Law* ii. §169 The first birth is from a natural mother; the second, from the ligation of the zone; the third, from the due performance of the sacrifice; such are the births of him, who is usually called twice-born, according to the text of the Véda. **1841** ELPHINSTONE *Hist. Ind.* I. I. iv. 79 Every Bramin, and, perhaps, every twice-born man, must bathe daily. **1877** J. E. CARPENTER tr. *Tiele's Outl. Hist. Relig.* iv. §75. 120 The members of the three highest castes are all..*dvijâ's*, or twice-born. **1908** *Westm. Gaz.* 7 Dec. 11/1 He was a Hindu of the caste of 'The Twice Born', or 'Regenerates'.

3. *Theol.* That has experienced the second birth; born again, regenerate. Also *absol.*

1849 F. W. NEWMAN *The Soul* iii. §2 (ed. 2) 140 God has two families of children on this earth; the once born and the twice born. **1875** E. WHITE *Life in Christ* II. xi. (1878) 122

Regeneration, and..the spiritual union of the twice-born with the..Lord. **1902** W. JAMES *Varieties Relig. Exper.* viii. 166 The sick souls, who must be twice-born in order to be happy.

twice-laid, *a.* [See LAY *v.*[1] 37.]

a. Of rope: Made from the yarns of old rope. Also *absol.* = twice-laid rope.

1592–3 *Act 35 Eliz.* c. 8 (*heading*) An Acte for the auoiding of deceite vsed in making and selling of twicelayed Cordage. **1669** *St. Papers, Dom.* 280 A cable, and some twice-laid stuff. **1748** *Anson's Voy.* II. ii. 135 Working up all our junk and old shrouds, to make twice-laid cordage. **1796** NELSON in Nicolas *Disp.* (1846) VII. p. lxix, What [rope] is sent us is the worst I ever saw. The twice-laid we make on board is far preferable. *c* **1860** H. STUART *Seaman's Catech.* 56 Nippers are usually made of twice-laid rope.

b. *Naut. slang.* (See quots.)

1777 P. THICKNESSE *Year's Journey* II. xlvi. 110 My entertainment..was half a second-hand roasted turkey, or, what the sailors call, a *twice-laid* dish, i.e. one which is *done over* a second time. **1867** SMYTH *Sailor's Word-bk., Twice-laid*.., a sea-dish made of the salt-fish left from yesterday's dinner, and beaten up with potatoes or yams. **1937** G. P. LOW *Sea made Men* ii. 35 Bread that had been on one long voyage and had been baked over again. It was called by sailors 'twice laid bread', and poor at that.

twicer (ˈtwaɪsə(r)). *colloq.* or *slang.* [f. TWICE.]

1. a. One who does something twice; *esp.* one who attends church (in quot. 1679, one who conducts public worship) twice on a Sunday.

1679 V. ALSOP *Mel. Inquirend.* II. i. 170 What if a thousand or two more of Ministers were silenced..? What is Lectures were proscribed, private Conferences interdicted, and your Twicers suspended? **1902** *Onlooker's Note-Bk.* xxiii. 180 In his [Gladstone's] view every respectable person should be a 'Twice-er'. **1904** *Times, Lit. Supp.* 4 Mar. 68/1 The prodigious proportion of absentees from church or chapel and the small number of 'twicers'.

b. *Printers' slang.* (See quot.)

1888 JACOBI *Printers' Vocab., Twicer*, a term of contempt for a man who professes to work both at case and press.

2. Something of twice the usual force or value.

1857 A. MAYHEW *Paved w. Gold* III. xiv, He expressed his delight by exclaiming, 'Here's a start! a reg'lar twicer!'

3. A crook, liar, cheat; a deceitful or cunning individual.

1924 *Truth* (Sydney) 27 Apr. 6 *Twicer*, a deceitful fellow. **1925** FRASER & GIBBONS *Soldier & Sailor Words & Phrases* 292 *Twicer*, a cunning fellow. **1949** E. WINGFIELD-STRATFORD *King Charles & King Pym* IV. ix. 262 The recent dismissal..of that elderly twicer, Sir Harry Vane.

twice-told, *a.* (*adv.*) [See TELL *v.* 21, 2.]

1. Counted or reckoned twice; twice as much as, twice (in amount). (Usually following the word or phrase qualified.) †In quot. 1579 advb. = in a twofold degree, doubly.

1430–40 LYDG. *Bochas* I. xiv. (MS. Bodl. 263) 64/1 Vpon my fyngirs fyue twies told I hadde ryngis. **1579** TOMSON *Calvin's Serm. Tim.* 472/2 We see also yᵗ we are guiltie twise tolde. **1678** BUNYAN *Pilgr.* I. 195 An hundred times, twice told. **1742** YOUNG *Nt. Th.* IV. 66 Twice-told the period spent on stubborn Troy, Court-favour, yet untaken, I besiege.

2. Narrated or related twice.

1595 SHAKS. *John* III. iv. 108 Life is as tedious as a twice-told tale. **1725** POPE *Odyssey* XII. 538 What so tedious as a twice-told tale? **1826** F. REYNOLDS *Life & Times* I. 94, I will now merely state, (to avoid a twice told tale,) that we arrived. **1837** HAWTHORNE (*title*) Twice-Told Tales.

twich, twiche, obs. ff. TOUCH, TOUGH, TWITCH.

twicher, obs. f. TWITCHER.

twick (twɪk), *v. Obs.* exc. *dial.* Also 5 **twyk** (**twykkyn**). [OE. *twiccian* = OHG. *zwĕcchôn* (rare). In ME. almost entirely displaced by the related *twicchen* TWITCH *v.*[1], but still surviving in south-western dial.] *trans.* and *absol.* To pull sharply or suddenly; to twitch.

a **1000** *Lat. & Ags. Gloss.* in Wr.-Wülcker 199/38 *Carpere, arripere*, twiccian. *c* **1000** *Sax. Leechd.* II. 196/13 Teoh him þa loccas & wringe þa earan & þone wangbeard twiccige. *c* **1000** *Malchus* in *Shrine* (Cockayne) 41 þa geseah ic micelne æmetena heap..& sume hio twiccedan þa grasu mid hiora muðe. *c* **1440** *Promp. Parv.* 505/1 Twykkyn, or sum-what drawyn (*K.* twychyn), *tractulo*. *c* **1440** *Pallad. on Husb.* VI. 26 Whil that me may..With fyngres lightly twyk hem [leaves] from the tre. **1825** JENNINGS *Obs. Dial. W. Eng.* 78 *To Twick*, to twist or jerk suddenly. **1837–91** in Somerset and Devon glossaries.

twiddle (ˈtwɪd(ə)l), *sb.* [f. TWIDDLE *v.*[1]] An act of twiddling; a twirl or twist; also, a curl, a twirled mark or sign; a 'grace' in music.

1774 T. TWINING in *Recreat. & Stud.* (1882) 30 Purcell, with all his old curls and twiddles, is perfection to him. **1849** THACKERAY *Dinners* Wks. 1901 VI. 646 The coaxing twiddle which they give to the ties of their white chokers. **1893** *Spectator* 28 Jan. 101/2, 'e' for 'æ' is just as much a contraction as 'r' with a twiddle for 'rum'. **1903** *Daily Chron.* 11 Dec. 7/2 A curious-looking diagram..with a few spots or twiddles on the light part of it. **1908** [see DYNAMICS 3]. **1975** *New Yorker* 21 Apr. 115/1 She adds to Rossini's tense exclamations a cascade of pretty twiddles.

twiddle (ˈtwɪd(ə)l), *v.*[1] Also 6 **twydle**, 9 **tweedle.** [App. onomatopœic, intended to combine the idea of *twirl* or *twist* with that of trifling action, as in *fiddle, piddle*. Both verb and sb. (see prec.) are very rare before the 19th c.]

1. *intr.* To be busy about trifles; to trifle; also ***to twiddle with*** or ***at*** = sense 2.

c **1540** J. REDFORD *Mor. Play Wit & Sc.* (Shaks. Soc.) 18 As for her syngyng, pypyng, and fydlyng, what unthryftynes therin is twydlyng? *a* **1825** FORBY *Voc. E. Anglia, Twiddle*,..to be busy and bestow seeming pains about the merest trifles... 'What are you twiddling about there?' **1848** THACKERAY *Van. Fair* xxxii, Even in the midst of his terror he began mechanically to twiddle with his hair. **1865** LE FANU *Guy Dev.* ii, The Baronet twiddled at his whisker..in the glass. **1874** CARPENTER *Ment. Phys.* I. viii. (1879) 373 The hands..may often be seen unconsciously stealing upwards to 'twiddle' with their watch-keys.

2. *trans.* To cause to rotate lightly or delicately; to turn (anything) about, esp. with the fingers; to twirl; to play with idly or absently; also, to adjust or bring into some place or condition by twirling or handling lightly.

1676 WISEMAN *Chirurg. Treat.* III. ii. 220 With my fingers upon the Stupe I pressed close upon it, and twiddled it in first one side, then the other. **1814** L. HUNT *Feast of Poets* 6 He fell twiddling a sunbeam as I may my pen. **1824** BEDDOES *Let.* Feb., in *Poems* (1851) p. xxx, The sign of a fellow tweedling a mask in his fingers. **1840** MRS. F. TROLLOPE *Widow Married* xiv, The quilling of her tulle..twiddling it into becoming shape. **1851** D. JERROLD *St. Giles* xvii. 182 He twiddled the reins between his fingers. **1860** THACKERAY *Round. Papers, Tunbridge Toys* 62, I..amused myself with twiddling round the moveable calendar. **1886** G. ALLEN *Maimie's Sake* xii, With one hand twiddling his watch-chain nervously.

b. *fig.* To twist, twirl, in various senses. Also *Sc.*, to diddle or do (one) *out of* something.

1825 JAMIESON s.v., 'He tried to twiddle me out of my money.' **1885** *Times* 12 Dec. 5 After being twiddled between the thumbs of two Conferences. **1891** *Sheffield Gloss.* Supp. s.v. *Tweedle*, 'I can tweedle him round my thumb.' **1898** *Daily News* 11 Nov. 3/4 They can twiddle the facts about so that you don't know where you are. **1901** 'R. CONNOR' *Man fr. Glengarry* xi, Bella just twiddled her father round her finger.

c. ***to twiddle one's thumbs,*** or ***fingers***, to keep turning them idly around each other; *fig.* to have nothing to do, to be idle.

1846 D. JERROLD *Mrs. Caudle* xxii, You'd have all the world do nothing half its time but twiddle its thumbs. **1849** CUPPLES *Green Hand* ii, The..cotton-grower twiddled his thumbs and looked modestly down on the deck. **1883** STEVENSON *Lett.* (1901) I. vi. 284, I have to twiddle my fingers and play patience. **1904** *Times* 15 June 4/1 We didn't twiddle our thumbs much that week.

3. *intr.* To move in a twirling manner; to turn about in a light or trifling way.

1812 W. TENNANT *Anster F.* IV. lv, Five hundred fingers ..Play twiddling up and down on hole and bore. **1844** THACKERAY *Contrib. to Punch* Wks. 1901 VI. 56 A few wretched little vessels are twiddling up and down. **1848** —— *Bk. Snobs* xxiv, She..made a majestic curtesy, during which all the bugles in her awful head-dress began to twiddle and quiver. **1876** SMILES *Sc. Natur.* xiii. (ed. 4) 261 Away went the bird, twiddling and straddling. **1887** *Suppl. to Jamieson, Tweedle*, to work in a trifling, careless, or slovenly manner. **1907** MRS. FR. CAMPBELL *Sheph. of Stars* 146 [The donkey's] very ears twiddled with laughter.

Hence **ˈtwiddling** *ppl. a.*, that twiddles; twirling; also, trifling, paltry; also **ˈtwiddler**, one who or that which twiddles; in quot. 1904, a twirling delivery of the ball at Cricket, a 'twister'.

1844 THACKERAY *Little Trav.* i, A lady in a little twiddling Parisian hat and feather. **1848** Mustachio-twiddler [see MUSTACHIO 3]. **1851** J. COLQUHOUN *Moor & Loch* (1880) I. 70 There is..the uncertainty whether the next point may be the red, or the 'jetty, heath-cock', or whether a twiddling snipe may spring. **1862** H. MARRYAT *Year in Sweden* I. 81 The wishiwashy lady with little twiddling curls round her face. **1862** G. MEREDITH *Modern Love* xxxiv, Time leers between, above his twiddling thumbs. **1904** *Daily Chron.* 29 June 4/1 Reputable batsmen going out to Jephson's twiddlers.

ˈtwiddle, *v.*[2] [Imitative, or modification of TWEEDLE *v.*[1] after prec.] *intr.* To twitter or warble; to play triflingly on an instrument; to talk in a trifling or inept manner.

1863 J. R. WISE *New Forest* App. I. 287/2 The robins are twiddling,..which fact is said to be a sign of rain. **1873** C. KEENE *Let.* in G. S. Layard *Life* vii. (1892) 150 You have the great advantage of having already twiddled on the flute. **1893** *Nat. Observer* 4 Mar. 386/2 The mob that twiddles of Ibsen will to-morrow shout of the morals of sculpture.

ˈtwiddle-ˈtwaddle. [Reduplication of TWADDLE *sb.*: cf. TWITTLE-TWATTLE.] Mere twaddle or foolish chatter. Also *attrib.*

1798 CHARLOTTE SMITH *Yng. Philos.* I. 164 Then my Aunt will come with her tendernesses, and her tears, and twiddle twaddle ways of dear niecing and sweet girling me. **1868** J. GREENWOOD in *Morn. Star* 8 June, His schoolmaster ..gave him to learn twiddle-twaddle rubbish, without the least flavour in it! **1886** *Pall Mall G.* 31 Aug. 11/2 Mann.. reserved the hottest passages of his fiery speech for denunciations of the 'twiddle-twaddle of trade unionism'.

Hence as *v. intr.*, to chatter foolishly (*nonce-wd.*).

a **1930** D. H. LAWRENCE *Phoenix II* (1968) 480 All you can do now is to twiddle-twaddle about golden boughs.

twiddling (ˈtwɪdlɪŋ), *vbl. sb.* [f. TWIDDLE *v.*[1] + -ING[1].] The action of the verb TWIDDLE; twirling; trifling.

twiddling line (*Naut.*), a light line formerly used to steady or secure the wheel; now, a line attached to the compass-box, by which the card may be jerked free when caught.

1847 THACKERAY *Sk. Lond.* (1891) 166 A chin-tuft is a cheap enjoyment.., and the twiddling it about..a harmless amusement. **1867** SMYTH *Sailor's Word-bk., Twiddling-line*, a piece of small rope ornamentally fitted and used for steadying the steering-wheel when required: no longer used. **1882** NARES *Seamanship* (ed. 6) 195 The rudder..must be secured..with the twiddling lines. **1890** *Daily News* 3 Nov. 3/1 Jerry builders and draughtsmen, with their mindless twiddlings in stone and brick. **1906** *Spectator* 6 Jan. 10/2 That dance..interspersed with meaningless bowings, scrapings, and twiddlings in odd corners.

† twiddling string. *Obs. rare*[−1]. Cf. *twattling string*, TWATTLING *ppl. a.* 2.

1594 GREENE & LODGE *Looking-gl.* I. iii, For indeed, sir, she is a woman that hath her twidling strings broke.

twiddly, *a.* Also **twiddley.** [f. TWIDDLE *v.*[1]] Characterized by twiddling; freq. in Comb. ***twiddly bit***, a fancy or intricate embellishment; a detail.

1906 *Westm. Gaz.* 19 Apr. 4/2 In your cradle safely nestling,..All your twiddly fingers wrestling With the toe-toes on your feet. **1912** C. MACKENZIE *Carnival* viii. 83 That's no tune to dance to. You want something to show off the twiddly-bits. **1922** H. JENKINS *Mrs Bindle* ii. 52, I like them little twiddley bits wot you been puttin' into that 'ymn. **1935** 'G. ORWELL' *Let.* Sept. in *Coll. Ess.* (1968) I. 152, I have three more chapters and an epilogue to do, and then I shall spend about two months putting on the twiddly bits. **1964** V. S. NAIPAUL *Area of Darkness* x. 255 He was tall and thin,..and had a brisk, twiddly walk. **1974** *Guardian* 23 Mar. 14/4, I was..enchanted by the dining car, all wood panelling and twiddly bits. **1982** BARR & YORK *Official Sloane Ranger Handbk.* 148/1 Sloane windows need curtains with a capital C: with pelmets, twiddly bits, bands, tassels, tie-backs, edging.

† twie, twye, *adv. Obs.* Forms: 1 **twiʒea, twiʒa** (**tuiʒa, -ʒo**), **twia,** 1–2 **twiʒe,** 3 **tuye, tweiȝe, tueie, twi,** 3–5 **twie,** 4 **twiȝe, twyȝe, tueye, tuey, twy,** 4–5 **tweye,** 5 **twey, twye.** *β.* 2 **twiȝen,** 3 **twien, tweien.** [OE. *twiʒa*, etc. (also *twiwa, tuwa*, etc.) = OFris. *twîa, tuiia*, OS. *tuuio* (MLG. *twie, twige*), adv. f. stem *twi-*, TWI-: cf. the etym. note to THRIE, THRYE *adv.*] = TWICE.

a **900** tr. *Bæda's Eccl. Hist.* IV. iv. 278 (Tanner MS.), þætte twiʒea on ʒere seonoð ʒesomnode. *c* **950** *Lindisf. Gosp.* Lk. xviii. 12 Ic fæsto tuiʒo [*Rushw.* twiʒe] in wico. *c* **1000** *Sax. Leechd.* I. 320 Eac, ys..sæd, þæt heo on ʒeare twiʒea blowe. *c* **1050** *Byrhtferth's Handboc* in *Anglia* (1885) VIII. 303 Twia seofon beoð feowertyne. *c* **1160** *Hatton Gosp.* Mk. xiv. 72 Ær se coc creowe twiʒe. *a* **1225** *Ancr. R.* 34 And so al þene psalm vt, mid Gloria Patri,..twie. *c* **1275** LAY. 8325 Twi þou hauest beon ouer-come. **1297** R. GLOUC. (Rolls) 4556 King arþure was anguisous..þat þe luþer traytour adde ofscaped so tuye [*v.rr.* twyȝe, tweye]. *Ibid.* 6646 Is [= his] stepmoder ..þat quene adde ybe tueie [*v.r.* twyȝe]. *a* **1325** *Adam & Eve* 272 in Horstm. *Altengl. Leg.* (1878) 142 Now he haþ ygiled þe tvie. *c* **1375** *Cursor M.* 13627 (Fairf.) Quy quarto sulde I tel ȝou mare Twy or thry I talde ȝou are. *a* **1450** MYRC *Par. Pr.* 119 Folowe thow not þe chylde twye.

β. c **1175** *Lamb. Hom.* 37 Mon scal beon twiȝen awesscen of his sunne. *c* **1205** LAY. 8325 Twien [*c* 1275 Twi] þu hafuest ibeon ouer-cummen.

twies, obs. form of TWICE.

† twiˈfallow, twy-, *v. Obs.* [f. TWI- + FALLOW *v.*[2]] *trans.* To fallow twice; to fallow a second time; to plough up (land) a second time in the course of its lying fallow. Hence **† twifallowing** *vbl. sb.*; also **twifallow** *sb.*

1557 TUSSER *100 Points Husb.* lxxviii, In May at the furdest, twy fallow thy lande. **1573** —— *Husb.* (1878) 114 Twifallow once ended, get tumbrell and man, And compas that fallow as soone as ye can. **1577** B. GOOGE *Heresbach's Husb.* I. (1586) 22 b, For some seede, you must not only twyfallowe and threefallowe your ground, but also fourefallow it. **1610** FOLKINGHAM *Art of Survey* I. xi. 43 Orders and seasons for fallowing, twifallowing, trifallowing and seed-furre. **1707** MORTIMER *Husb.* (1721) I. 155 The Land being fallowed in May, must be twy-fallowed in June. **1725** *Bradley's Fam. Dict.* s.v. *Plough*, The Times of the second plowing is about June, it bears the Name of Twy-fallowing. *Ibid.* s.v. *Barley*, Some at the Time of Twy-fallowing in June make the Land very fine. **1733** MILLER *Gard. Dict.* s.v. *Rapa*, The Land..should be ploughed in May, and twy-fallow'd in June. **1890** *Glouc. Gloss., Twy-fallow*, the second ploughing.

twifold, twyfold (ˈtwaɪfəʊld), *a.* and *adv. arch.* Forms: 1 **twyfeald,** (**twiefeald, -fald, twiʒfeald, tweofeald**), 1–3 **twifeald,** 3 **twifald, -feld,** 4–5 **tweyfold(e,** 5–6 **twifolde,** 3– **twifold,** 5– **twyfold,** 7, 9 **twy-fold.** [OE. *twifeald, twyfeald*: = OFris. *twifald*, OHG. *zwifalt* (MHG. *zwivalt*), ON. *tvifaldr* (Norw. dial. *tvifald*): see TWI- and -FOLD, and cf. TWOFOLD.]

A. *adj.*

1. Twofold, double.

c **890** tr. *Bæda's Hist.* I. x. [xiii.] (1890) 48 Betwih him twam we þus tweofealdne deað þrowiað, oððe sticode beoð oððe on sæ adruncene. *c* **897** K. ÆLFRED *Gregory's Past. C.* xxxv. 238 Hu hefiʒ ðæt twyfealde [*v.r.* twiefalde] ʒeswinc bið. *c* **1200** ORMIN 4997 þatt fulle lufe..birrþ ben..Twifald ..; Forr þe birrþ lufenn Godd & mann. *c* **1220** *Bestiary* 424 in *O.E. Misc.* 14 Twifold forbisne in ðis der..we muȝen finden her. **1583** MELBANCKE *Philotimus* Q j, Her twifolde murther committed on her selfe and Telamon. **1623** LISLE *Ælfric on O. & N. Test.* Gen. B ij, Adam..begat of his wife a twifold race of children. **1812** CARY *Dante, Purg.* XXXI. 122 Within those orbs the twyfold being shone. **1912** *Eng. Rev.* Apr. 1 Queen of the Shadows, Maid and Wife, Twifold in essence, as in life.

†**2.** *fig.* **a.** Double-dealing, deceitful, insincere: = DOUBLE *a.* 5. **b.** Double-minded, irresolute. *Obs.*

c **897** K. ÆLFRED *Gregory's Past. C.* xxxv. 244 Hwæt tacniað ðonne ða hean hwammas buton unclænu & twyfeald [*v.r.* twiefeald] mod? *c* **1200** *Vices & Virt.* 15 Bute he bie rihtwis and naht twifeald. *c* **1200** *Trin. Coll. Hom.* 187 Ðe twifealde man is unstedefast on alle his spechen, twifold oðer manifold is þe man þe nis stedefast.

B. *adv.*

1. In two parts or divisions; (folded) double.

1591 PERCIVALL *Sp. Dict., Doblegar* to double, to bend twifold.

2. In two ways or respects, doubly.

a **1619** FLETCHER, etc. *Q. Corinth* IV. i, Your T beard.. twifold doth express the enamour'd Courtier.

twifold, *v. rare. arch.* [f. TWI- + FOLD *v.*[1]; cf. OE. *twifildan* to double.] *trans.* To fold in two; to bend double.

1875 MORRIS *Æneid* XII. 927 Then falleth.. Turnus with his hampered knee twifolded with the wound.

¶ *trans.* and *intr.* [perh. f. TWIFOLD *a.*] (Sense uncertain; rendering L. *distinguĕre*, itself app. a mistranslation, in two passages of the Vulgate.) *Obs.*

a **1300** *E.E. Psalter* lxv[i]. 14 Mi hotes.. Whilk twi-falded mi lippes. *Ibid.* cv[i]. 33 For þai gremed gast of him swa, And he twi-falded [*v.r.* twifolded] in his lippes.

†**twifoldly,** *adv. Obs.* [OE. *twyfealdlíce*, f. *twifeald*, TWIFOLD *a.* + *-líce*, -LY[2].] Twofold, doubly, to twice the amount.

c **1000** *Ags. Gosp.* Matt. xxiii. 15 ðe ȝedoð hyne helle bearn twyfealdlicor þonne eow. *c* **1000** ÆLFRIC *Exod.* xvi. 22 On þam sixtum dæȝe hiȝ gaderodon twyfealdlice. *c* **1200** *Trin. Coll. Hom.* 169 Ure drihten ȝiald twifoldliche iob, þat þe deuel him hadde binumen.

twig (twɪg), *sb.*[1] Forms: 1–2, 4–7 **twigge** (1 tuigge, tuicg-), 4–6 **twygge** (4 *pl.* tuygges, tuyegges); 2, 4 **twige**, 4 **tvige**, 6 **twike**; 4–5 **tuyg**, 4–6 **twyg**, 6–7 **twygg**, 5– **twig** (6 *Sc.* tuig, 7 twigg). [Northern OE. *twigge* fem. (pl. *twiggo*), obscurely related to OE. *twiȝ* neut. (pl. *twiȝu*), later also *twí*. Neither *twigge* nor *twiȝ* correspond exactly to the usual Continental forms having the same sense, viz. WFris. *twiich*, *twige* (NFris. *twich*), Du. *twijg* (Kilian *twijgh*), MLG. *twîch* (LG. *twîg*), OHG. *zwîg* (MHG. *zwîg-*, *zwîc*, G. *zweig*), but the Da. dial. forms *tveg*, *tvege*, may be more closely akin to *twigge* or to the ME. variant *twige*. All the types appear to be variant formations from the stem TWI-.]

1. a. A slender shoot issuing from a branch or stem.

c **950** *Lindisf. Gosp.* Mk. xi. 8 Oðero.. ða twiggo *vel* ða telȝo.. rendon of ðæm trewum. *Ibid.* xiii. 28 Mið-ðy.. telȝe *vel* twigge his.. nesc bið. *c* **1175** *Lamb. Hom.* 5 Heo stiȝen uppe on þe godes cunnes treowe & nomen þa twigga & þa blostme. *Ibid.* 149 Hwenne he.. for his sunne swingeð him mið smele twige. **13..** *Guy Warw.* (A.) 2542 Wiþ þat come Gij.., a smal tvige in his hond bereinde Of oliue. **1340** [see b]. *c* **1384** CHAUCER *H. Fame* III. 846 Al thys hous.. Was made of twigges [*v.rr.* twygges, twigys] falwe, rede, And grene eke. **1398** TREVISA *Barth. De P.R.* XVII. i. (Bodl. MS.) A tre haþ.. outeward.. þerinde twigges leues blossomes and fruyte. **1415** HOCCLEVE *To Sir J. Oldcastle* 471 A smal twig or rod. **1509** BARCLAY *Shyp of Folys* (1570) 13 A little twygge plyaunt is by kinde, A bigger branche is harde to bowe or winde. *a* **1552** LELAND *Itin.* (1711) V. 75 Hole Trees.. without Twike or Bow. **1596** DALRYMPLE tr. *Leslie's Hist. Scot.* (S.T.S.) I. 39 Capercalȝe.. lyues of only the tuigs or tendir branches of this [fir] trie. **1637** J. TAYLOR (Water P.) *Drinke & Welcome* D j b, My Muse doth.. like a Squirrell skip, from twigge to twigge. **1732** POPE *Ep. Cobham* 150 Just as the Twig is bent, the Tree's inclin'd. **1784** COWPER *Task* I. 484 These.. love life, and cling to it, as he That overhangs a torrent, to a twig. **1851** CARPENTER *Man. Phys.* (ed. 2) 107 Fibrine.. may be obtained.. by whipping fresh blood with a bundle of twigs. **1906** *Times, Lit. Supp.* 23 Mar. 99/2 The snap of a twig.. gave the alarm.

b. *transf.* and *fig.*, and in fig. context.

to hop the twig (slang): see HOP *v.* 6 a.

c **950** *Lindisf. Gosp.* John xv. 5 Ic am þe wintreo, ȝie ða tuiggo [L. *palmites*] sint. **1340** *Ayenb.* 22 Þe uerþe tuyg of þe ilke boȝe [of pride].. is yelpinge. *Ibid.* 41 Þe zixte boȝ of auarice is symonye.. And þes boȝ heþ manie tuygges. *c* **1386** CHAUCER *Pars. T.* ¶ 315 Euerich of thise chief synnes hath hise braunches and hise twigges. **1535** COVERDALE *Isa.* ix. 14 The Lorde shal rote out of Israel both heade and tale, braunch and twygge in one daye. **1553** *Respublica* I. iii. 339 *Adul.* Doe but whistle for me, and I comme foorth with-all. *Avar*... I love suche a towarde twygg. *a* **1623** FLETCHER *Love's Cure* II. ii, Traiterous brat,.. impious twig Of that old stock, dew'd with my kinsman's gore. **1678** in *Trial E. Coleman* 100 They would not you should have any Twigg to hold by to deceive you. **1764** LD. HALIFAX *Let.* 11 Mar., in *10th Rep. Hist. MSS. Comm.* App. I. 363, I was willing to keep Hold of any Twig of Hope that was left me. **1827** G. HIGGINS *Celtic Druids* 24 [The Irish] characters were called twigs and branch-letters.. from their shape.

†**c.** *collect.* as the material for basket-making. *Obs. rare.*

c **1440** *Pallad. on Husb.* III. 209 Let make a skeppe of twygge. **1661** *Rec. Basketmakers Co.* (1911) 114 Paid an officer for seizing 10,000 of twigg at Bull Wharfe. 00. 05. 00.

2. *spec.* **a.** Short for LIME-TWIG (*obs.*); also, in *pl.*, the twigs forming a birch-rod.

1601 SHAKS. *All's Well* III. vi. 115, I must go looke my twigges, He shall be caught. [**1603** —— *Meas. for M.* I. iii. 24 Fond Fathers, Hauing bound vp the threatning twigs of birch, Onely to sticke it in their childrens sight, For terror, not to vse.] **1622** BP. HALL *Contempl.*, *O.T.* XVII. iii, Wise Salomon.. laies insensible twigs for so foule an offender. **1736** *Gentl. Mag.* Nov. 679/2 Ye awful twigs!.. Long may ye.. far from my posteriors keep your sway! **1896** MAX PEMBERTON *Purit. Wife* iii, I had smarted often at the switch of his twigs.

b. *dial.* (*a*) A stout stick. (*b*) A divining-rod (cf. ROD *sb.*[1] 3 c). ***to work the twig***, to use the divining-rod.

1842 B. BRIERLEY *Lanc. Tales & Sk.* 87 [He] could not see that his 'twig' would stand any chance against a bayonet. **18..** in T. Allan *Tyneside Songs* (1872) 201 Aw danced a jig an' swung my twig. **1883** *Folk-Lore Jrnl.* I. 28 At one spot the 'twig' was so violently affected that it flew out of his hands. **1883** A. LANG *Custom & Myth* (1884) 180 'To work the twig' is rural English for the craft of Dousterswivel in the *Antiquary*. **1894** [see DOWSE *v.*].

3. *transf. Anat.* A small ramification of a blood-vessel or nerve.

1683 A. SNAPE *Anat. Horse* I. ix. (1686) 18 The Stomachal Arteries are twigs from the Coeliacal branch of the *Arteria magna*. *Ibid.* xvi. 33 A Twig of the Splenic Artery opens into this Vein. **1691** RAY *Creation* II. (1692) 14 Particular Branches send forth some twigs to the neighbouring Muscles. **1741** MONRO *Anat. Nerves* (ed. 3) 80 A Twig of the Ophthalmick Branch of the fifth Pair of Nerves. **1831** R. KNOX *Cloquet's Anat.* 684 This artery gives numerous twigs to the pectoralis major. **1875** HUXLEY in *Encycl. Brit.* I. 766/1 The pulmonary artery gives twigs to the stomach.

4. *Pottery.* 'A thin strip of plastic clay used in modelling a pottery vessel, especially in the imitation basketwork common in Leeds pottery' (*Cent. Dict.* 1891).

5. *attrib.* and *Comb.* **a.** attrib. (usually = 'made of twigs'), as ***twig-basket***, ***-broom***, ***charcoal***, ***corf***, ***-cutter***, †***head***, (? HEAD *sb.*[1] 5), ***-hurdle***, ***ware***. **b.** instrumental, similative, etc., as ***twig-formed***, ***-green***, ***-like***, ***-limed***, ***-strewn***, ***-suspended***, ***-wrought***, adjs. **c.** Spec. Comb.: **twig-ait**: see quot.; **twig-beetle**, **-borer** (*U.S.*), names for various small beetles which bore into the twigs of trees (*Cent. Dict.* & *Supp.* 1891–1909); **twig-blight** (*U.S.*), a disease of the apple and quince, caused by *Micrococcus amylovorus*: see *pear-blight* a, PEAR *sb.* 5 (*Cent. Dict.* 1889); †**twig-bottle**, a bottle with a wicker envelope; **twig-bug** (*U.S.*) = *twig insect*; **twig-climber**: see quot.; **twig-gall**, an abnormal enlargement of a twig, due to the action of insects, fungi, or bacteria; **twig girdler** (*U.S.*), an American beetle, *Oncideres cingulatus*, which deposits its eggs in the tips of twigs, which it then girdles below the eggs (*Cent. Dict.* 1891); **twig insect**, the stick-insect or 'walking-stick'; **twig-pruner** (*U.S.*) = *oak pruner* s.v. OAK 9; **twig-rune**, a runic inscription with characters of twig-like form; **twig-rush**, a tall marsh-plant, *Cladium Mariscus*, N.O. *Cyperaceæ*, having very long narrow rigid leaves.

1867 SMYTH *Sailor's Word-bk.*, **Twig-ait*, a river island where osiers grow. **1748** tr. *Vegetius' Distemp. Horses* 173 A close-wrought *Twig-basket must be put upon him. **1695** *Lond. Gaz.* No. 3085/3 Captain Bonnamy.. took a French Ship of 40 Tuns, laden with Burstones and *Twig Bottles. **1863** HAWTHORNE *Our Old Home* (1879) 187 *Twig-brooms, beehives,.. things that are commonly sold at a rural fair. **1895** *Westm. Gaz.* 31 Aug. 3/2 These latter doors are over a foot in thickness, each bearing a lining of twelve inches of '*twig charcoal'. **1900** B. D. JACKSON *Gloss. Bot. Terms*, **Twig Climbers*, Schenck's term for certain Brazilian lianes, the young leafy lateral branches being sensitive.. in contact with their supports. **1797** J. CURR *Coal Viewer* 8 The basket or *twig corf.. cannot.. be introduced in the southern parts. **1911** *Contemp. Rev., Lit. Suppl.* June 9 The chisel, the gouge.. the sickle, the *twig-cutter, the scythe. **1806** J. GRAHAME *Birds Scot.*, etc. 75 The Raven's *twig-formed house. **1900** B. D. JACKSON *Gloss. Bot. Terms*, **Twig-Gall*, a morbid growth ascribed to the action of bacteria. **1874** *Rep. U.S. Dept. Agric. 1873* 153 The *twig girdler, *Oncideres cingulatus*... The insects girdle the twig before depositing their eggs. **1972** SWAN & PAPP *Common Insects N. Amer.* xx. 452 The Twig Girdler.. is rough-surfaced, grayish brown or yellowish brown. **1974** *Ridge Citizen* (Johnston, S. Carolina) 18 Apr. 6/3 The twig girdlers deposit their eggs in the portions of the branches that fall to the ground. **1892** *Daily News* 17 Dec. 5/7 The material is *twig-green velvet shot with gold. **1572** in Feuillerat *Revels Q. Eliz.* (1908) 156 Strigges of bay Leaves for *twigg heades. **1726** S. LOWE *Lat. Gram.* Suppl. 15 *Gerrae*, *twig-hurdles, gabions. **1882** A. WILSON in *Nature Stud.* 37 The so-called 'stick insects', or 'walking twigs',.. the *Phasmidæ* of the naturalist... The bodies of these '*twig insects'.. are represented by mere lines. **1898** *Pop. Sc. Monthly* LIII. 762 Curious plants with *twiglike leaves seem.. provided against too great loss by transpiration. **1905** *Westm. Gaz.* 23 June 4/1 The twig-like attitudes assumed by some caterpillars and other insects. **1657** BILLINGSLY *Brachy-Martyrol.* xvi. 55 A third Is taken captive like a *twiglim'd bird. **1928** METCALF & FLINT *Destructive & Useful Insects* xix. 664 Maple and oak *twig pruner. **1972** SWAN & PAPP *Common Insects N. Amer.* xx. 446 Twig Pruner.. Brown, clothed with irregular patches of grayish yellow pubescence. **1868** G. STEPHENS *Runic Mon.* I. 84 *Twig-runes occur on both Old-Northern and Scandinavian.. runic monuments. **1836** J. T. MACKAY *Flora Hibern.* I. 324 *Cladium Mariscus*, Br. Prickly *Twig-rush. **1848** C. A. JOHNS *Week at Lizard* 311 *Cladium Mariscus*, Twig-rush, abounds in the higher parts of the stream. **1900** *Blackw. Mag.* Mar. 392/1 Bare and *twig-strewn circles in which the argus-pheasants strut. **1826** KIRBY & SP. *Entomol.* III. xxix. 96 The eggs of the tailor bird in its *twig-suspended nest. **1829** S. SHAW *Stafford. Potteries* vii. 173 A Lady's work-basket, which he was led to consider.. as *twig or willow ware, and was.. surprised, to find it of cane coloured pottery. **1855** SINGLETON *Virgil* I. 80 Celeus' furniture, *twig-wrought And mean.

Hence **'twigless** *a.*, destitute of twigs; **'twiglet**, (*a*) a little twig; (*b*) (with capital initial) the proprietary name of a crisp, savoury snack in the shape of a twig; **twigling** = *twiglet* (*a*); **'twigsome** *a.*, twiggy.

1839 *Fraser's Mag.* XX. 345 A birch-tree, entirely boughless, branchless, and twigless. **1849** J. A. CARLYLE tr. *Dante's Inferno* 146 If thou breakest off any twiglet from one of these plants. **1860** DICKENS in *All Year Round* No. 50. 558 The twigsome trees by the wayside (which, I suppose, never will grow leafy, for they never did). **1882** *Garden* 18 Mar. 181/2 Slender twiglets of this semi-weeping Spruce. **1907** *Westm. Gaz* 19 Oct. 6/1 As pliant twigling to the rigid oak. **1932** *Trade Marks Jrnl.* 15 June 766 *Twiglets*... Biscuits. Peek, Frean & Company, Limited,.. London, S.E. 16; manufacturers. **1962** M. FRAYN *Day of Dog* 57 A cheese twiglet slips from my fingers. **1980** J. MELVILLE *Chrysanthemum Chain* 103 Walker set out a.. drinks tray.. and opened a tin of imported Twiglets.

twig, *sb.*[2] Now *dial.* [f. TWIG *v.*[3] 2.] A pull; a twitch; a tug; a draught.

a **1800** *Laird of Wariston* vi. in Child *Ballads* VII. (1890) 31/2 The nurice she knet the knot,.. The lady did gie it a twig, Till it began to wicker. **1808** JAMIESON, *Twig*, a quick pull, a twitch. **1818** *Naval Chron.* XXXIX. 65 He was taken in tow by *A Friend*,.. which twig to windward.. will.. enable him to round the Cape. **1825** J. NEAL *Bro. Jonathan* I. 54 A 'twig o' cider' a piece.

twig, *sb.*[3] *slang.* ? *Obs.* [Origin unascertained.] Style, fashion; also condition, state, fettle; esp. in the phrases ***in*** (***prime, good***) ***twig***. **b.** ***out of twig*** [cf. TWIG *v.*[4]], out of knowledge or recognition: see quot. 1812.

1811 *Lexicon Balatr.* s.v., *In twig*, handsome; stilish. The cove is togged in twig; the fellow is dressed in the fashion. **1812** J. H. VAUX *Flash Dict.* s.v., Any thing accomplished cleverly, or as it should be, is said to be done in twig, in good twig, or in prime twig. *Ibid.*, *Out of twig*, to put yourself out of twig is to disguise your dress and appearance, to avoid being recognised..; a man reduced by poverty to wear a shabby dress is said by his acquaintance to be out of twig; to put any article out of twig, as a stolen coat, cloak, &c. is to alter it in such a way that it cannot be identified. **1828** *Sporting Mag.* XXII. 77 Palemon was not in the twig I should like to see a horse of mine if about to start for such a stake. **1834** H. AINSWORTH *Rookwood* III. v, With my strummel faked in the newest twig. **1840** DICKENS *Barn. Rudge* xi, You're in twig to-night I see. **1842** S. LOVER *Handy Andy* xvii, Going to the ball in proper twig.

twig, *v.*[1] *Obs.* or *dial.* [f. TWIG *sb.*[1]]

1. *trans.* To beat with or as with a twig; *fig.* to reprove. ? *Obs.*

1550 BALE *Apol.* 142 Not one kynge hath bene in Englande sens the conquest, but they haue twygged hym one way or other, and had theyr false flynges at him. **1553** *Respublica* v. viii. 1630 *Insol.* I will whippe youe for this, ye peasaunte lowte. *Adul.* And twygge youe. **1570** LEVINS *Manip.* 119/4 To Twig, *verberare*. *a* **1825** FORBY *Voc. E. Anglia*, *Twig*, to give such.. correction as may be inflicted with a twig... To give somewhat sharp, but not angry and severe reproof. **1826** MOORE *Mem.* (1854) V. 118 Only for my knowing Lord Holland (said Southey) I would have twigged him for that.

†**2.** To trim, prune (a tree). *Obs. rare.*

1570 LEVINS *Manip.* 119/5 To Twygge, *putare viburna*.

†**3.** To bind with twigs or withes. *Obs. rare.*

1688 R. HOLME *Armoury* III. 108/1 Twigging a Hoop [of a barrel], is binding the two ends together with cloven Twiggs of Withy, or Osier Twiggs.

Hence **'twigging** *vbl. sb.*[1]

1916 JOYCE *Portrait of Artist* iv. 174 To flee from noise which caused him painful nervous irritation such as the sharpening of knives.. and the twigging of the carpet.

twig, *v.*[2] *Obs.* or *dial.* [Of obscure origin: cf. next.] *intr.* To do anything vigorously or strenuously. Hence **'twigging** *vbl. sb.*[2] and *ppl. a.*[1]

1573 TWYNE *Æneid* XI. I i iv b, Lyke a fawcon that.. at a twyggynge doue vnto the cloudes swyft winge doth make. *Ibid.* XII. L l iij, The bird of mightie Ioue.. a shole of foules she did pursue And twigginge forth apace fast on her flight the Egle flue. **1573** TUSSER *Husb.* (1878) 81 The lamb of such twinners for breeders go take, For twinlings be twiggers, encrease for to bring, Though som for their twigging Peccantem may sing. **1828** *Craven Gloss.*, *Twig*,.. to do any thing strenuously, to work with might and main.

twig, *v.*[3] Now *dial.* [Of obscure origin; perh. merely an imitative word of the same type as TWICK, *tweag* TWEAK, and TUG.]

†**1.** *trans.* See quot. *Obs. slang.*

1725 *New Cant. Dict.*, *To Twig*, to disingage, to sunder, to snap, to break off. *To twig the Darbies*, to knock off the Irons.

2. To pull, pluck, twitch.

1755 J. SHEBBEARE *Lydia* (1769) II. 49 Write,.. or Frank shall twig your nose from your face. **1790** D. MORISON *Poems* 78 Let rantin billys twig the string, An' for the tither mutchkin ring. **1864** *Reader* 23 Jan. 105 To stretch strings on pegs and to twig them with thumb or with plectrum was one of the earliest of human amusements. **1867** SMYTH *Sailor's Work-bk.*, *Twig, to*, to pull upon a bowline.

Hence **'twigging** *ppl. a.*[2]

1864 *Reader* 23 Jan. 105 The genus stringed-instrument consists of three species, which may be defined, to use the vernacular, as the twigging, the hammering, and the scraping.

twig, *v.*[4] *slang* or *colloq.* [Origin unascertained.]

1. *trans.* **a.** To watch; to look at; to inspect.

1764 FOOTE *Mayor of G.* II. Wks. 1799 I. 180 Now, twig him; now, mind him: mark how he hawls his muscles about. **1824** SCOTT *St. Ronan's* iv, 'Twig the old connoisseur', said the squire to the knight. **1837** DICKENS *Pickw.* xx, 'They're a twiggin' of you, sir', whispered Mr. Weller. **1841** J. T. HEWLETT *Parish Clerk* I. 173 Oblige me by twigging that trio. **1876** A. J. EVANS *Through Bosnia* iii. 89 A motley assemblage..'twigged us' at their leisure.

b. To become aware of by seeing; to perceive, discern, catch sight of; to recognize.

1796 J. G. HOLMAN *Abroad & at Home* III. ii, He twigs me. He knows Dicky here in his real and masquerade character both. **1801** M. G. LEWIS *Tales Wonder, Sailor's T.* ii, With strange surprise and fear, Jack Tackle's ghost I twigg'd. **1825** LADY GRANVILLE *Lett.* 30 Jan. (1894) I. 339 They have twigged me. **1860** *Hunting Grounds Old World* Ser. I. xii. (ed. 2) 189 The leader, whom at last I twigged lying down and chewing the cud. **1879** F. POLLOK *Sport Brit. Burmah* I. 191, I twigged the tigress creeping away in front of us.

2. *fig.* To understand, comprehend.

1815 *Zeluca* III. 144 You twig me—eh? **1821** LADY GRANVILLE *Lett.* (1894) I. 208 York roared again [at the jokes], Clarence was dull and did not twig them. **1852** R. S. SURTEES *Sponge's Sp. Tour* xxvii. 166, I twigged what you were after, and kept him up in talk. **1897** 'TIVOLI' (H. W. Bleakley) *Short Innings* ix, Make a howler or two, or else he'll twig you've cribbed.

b. *intr.*

1833 M. SCOTT *Tom Cringle* xiii. (1859) 311 The Captain twigged and smiled. **1845** DISRAELI *Sybil* III. x, 'I twig', said Mick. **1893** LELAND *Mem.* I. 197, I twig; it's all right; I'll keep your secret.

twig(g)age (ˈtwɪgɪdʒ). *Literary. rare.* [f. TWIG *sb.*[1] + -AGE.] Twigs collectively.

1923 *Glasgow Herald* 11 Dec. 6/8 Even the umbered purple loom of the birch twigage and its stem washes of amethystine-cream were but enhanced. **1964** *Listener* 16 Apr. 633/3 The dry stuff's best To start with, twiggage and haulm and herby tops.

twigged (twɪgd), *a.* [f. TWIG *sb.*[1] or *v.*[1]]

1. Furnished with or bearing twigs.

1640 PARKINSON *Theatr. Bot.* 483 Hard and hoary twigged stalks. **1725** *Family Dict.*, *Ivy*,..a Shrub or Tree whose twigged Branches raise and extend themselves by creeping and sticking to Walls and Trees.

†**2.** Made of twigs or wickerwork. *Obs. rare*$^{-1}$.

1643 *Farington Papers* (Chetham Soc.) 99 One twiged cheare.

twiggen (ˈtwɪg(ə)n), *a. arch.* [f. TWIG *sb.*[1] + -EN.] **a.** Made of twigs or wickerwork; also, having a wickerwork covering. **b.** Arising from burning twigs or brushwood.

1549 COVERDALE, etc. *Erasm. Par. Acts* vii. 29 A twiggen basket or hamper. **1588** *Lanc. Wills* (Chetham Soc.) III. 136 A twiggen cheare xij[d]. **1604** SHAKS. *Oth.* II. iii. 152 Ile beate the Knaue into a Twiggen-Bottle [*Qq.* wicker bottle]. **1681** GREW *Musæum* IV. iii. 372 The Sides and Rim sewed together after the manner of Twiggen-Work. **1747** CARTE *Hist. Eng.* I. 44 Those twiggen machines..filled in every part or member with the miserable wretches destined to be burnt by way of sacrifice. **1826** HOR. SMITH *Tor Hill* (1838) I. 94 What, neighbour Stiles, pawn thy wedding ring to fill the twiggen-bottle! **1875** MORRIS *Æneid* VII. 463 When with a mighty roar the twiggen flame [*L. flamma virgea*] goes up about the hollow side of brass.

†**ˈtwigger.** *Obs.* [app. f. TWIG *v.*[2] + -ER[1].] A vigorous prolific breeder: orig. said of a ewe; hence *slang*, an unchaste or lascivious person; *esp.* a strumpet, a harlot.

1573 [see TWIG *v.*[2]]. **1594** MARLOWE & NASHE *Dido* IV. v, Go, you wag! You'll be a twigger when you come to age. *c* **1613** MIDDLETON *No Wit like Wom.* IV. i, The mother of her was a good twigger. **1694** MOTTEUX *Rabelais* v. *Pantagr. Prognost.* v, Those whom Venus is said to Rule, as Punks, Jills, Flirts,..Whipsters, Twiggers, Harlots, Kept-wenches ..will be famous this Year.

twiggery (ˈtwɪgəri). [f. TWIG *sb.*[1] + -ERY.] Twigs collectively. Also *fig.*

1909 in WEBSTER. **1922** *Contemp. Rev.* Feb. 255 Something that was not merely discursive wooden twiggery. **1931** *Observer* 11 Oct. 26 In the winter of 1929 it was only the twiggery that was killed. The main stems broke out into bud... The numerous end-twigs do habitually suffer in winter. **1980** *Washington Post* 6 July K2/3, I would walk into the apartment..warm myself at the fire, admire my twiggery, [etc.].

twiggy (ˈtwɪgɪ), *a.* [f. TWIG *sb.*[1] + -Y.]

1. Like a twig; slender, as a shoot or branch; also, †made of twigs or wickerwork (*obs.*).

1562 TURNER *Herbal* II. 40b, Lithospermon..hath.. diuerse twyggy braunches. **1597** GERARDE *Herbal* III. cxxix. 1330 These [trees]..do cast their branches and twiggie tendrels vnto the earth, where they likewise take hold and roote. **1664** EVELYN *Sylva* xix. 42 Oziers..yielding more limber, and flexible twigs for Baskets, Flaskets, Hampers, Chairs, Hurdles, Stages, Bands, &c...; In fine, for all Wicker and Twiggy Works. **1713** J. PETIVER in *Phil. Trans.* XXVIII. 35 This seems to differ..in having more twiggy Branches. **1721** BAILEY, *Wanded Chair*, a Wicker or Twiggy-Chair. **1800** *Misc. Tr.* in *Asiat. Ann. Reg.* 267/2 A slender twiggy climbing plant on the mountains. **1896** G. ALLEN in *Longm. Mag.* Nov. 45 The netted willow..sends up twiggy shoots from a prostrate stem.

2. Full of or abounding in twigs; bushy, shrubby.

1600 SURFLET *Countrie Farme* VII. xxiv. 844 A hart passing through a thick and twiggie woode. **1728** CHAMBERS *Cycl.* s.v. *Root*, *Sarmentous*, i.e. twiggy, or branching. **1881** *Encycl. Brit.* XII. 274/2 For the slender twiggy sorts [of pear-trees] the fan form is to be preferred. **1882** *Garden* 14 Jan. 19/3 Masses of twiggy growth at the bottom.

Hence **ˈtwigginess**, the condition or quality of being twiggy.

1927 *Smallholder* 26 Mar. 105/1 Pea sticks ought to last through two seasons. Of course, in the second year they lose most of their twigginess. **1981** *Country Life* 1 Jan. 39/2 *Potentilla fruticosa*... Its winter-brown twigginess should match the tawny beech.

†**twight**, obs. variant of QUITE *adv.*

c **1400** *Song Roland* 40 Mahoun And margat he will forsak twight.

†**twight**, obs. pa. t. and pple. of TWITCH *v.*[1]

In the following quots. the form appears to be erroneously used for *touched* (pa. t.) and for *touch* or *twitch* (inf.).

1558 PHAER *Æneid* IV. Kjb, Whan first the bowres of Affrike land with wingid feete he twight [L. *tetigit*]. **1559** *Mirr. Mag.*, *Collingbourne* xxiv, No bit nor reyne his tender iawes may twight. **1573** TWYNE *Æneid* XI. Kkijb, Arowehead doth twight The bowhand.

twight, obs. form of TWIT *v.*

twik, obs. f. TWICK *v.*; obs. Sc. pa. t. of TAKE *v.*

twike, obs. f. TWIG *sb.*[1]

twile, obs. form of TWILL *sb.*[1]

†**twile**, obs. abbreviation of *it will*.

a **1660** *Contemp. Hist. Irel.* (Ir. Archæol. Soc.) I. 274, I beleeue twile be otherwise don.

†**ˈtwileke**, var. *twey-leke*: see TWAY 4. *Obs.*

1551 RECORDE *Pathw. Knowl.* I. Def., Further more it may be y[t] they haue neuer a one syde equall to another, and they be in iij kyndes also distinct lyke the twilekes.

twilet, twilight, obs. ff. TOILET.

twilight (ˈtwaɪlaɪt), *sb.* Forms: 5 twyliȝt, -lyghte, twye lyghte, 6 twie light, twylyght, *Sc.* twa licht, lycht, 6–8 twylight, 6– twilight; also 6–8 with hyphen. [ME., f. TWI- + LIGHT *sb.*, corresponding to WFris. *twieljocht*, Du. *tweelicht* (from 16th c.), LG. *twilecht*, G. *zwielicht*. The rare form TWILIGHTING is recorded a little earlier. The exact force of *twi-* here is doubtful: cf. in same sense MHG. *zwischenliecht* "tweenlight', and LG. *twêdustern*, *twêdunkern*, lit. 'twi-dark'.]

1. The light diffused by the reflection of the sun's rays from the atmosphere before sunrise, and after sunset; the period during which this prevails between daylight and darkness. **a.** Generally.

c **1440** *Promp. Parv.* 505/1 Twylyghte, be-twyx þe day and þe nyghte, or nyghte and þe day, *hesperus*. **1555** EDEN *Decades* 32 At the beginnynge of the euenyng twilight..in the morninge twylight. *a* **1600** HOOKER *2nd Serm. upon Jude* §33 He must haue darknes for a vision, hee must stumble at noone daies, as at the twi-light. **1617** MORYSON *Itin.* I. 113 It [the grotto of Posilippo] hath no light in the middest, but like twilight,..in the twilight of morning and euening passengers vse torches. **1661** BOYLE *Style of Script.* (1675) 99 Faith and the Twilight seeming to agree in this Property, that a mixture of Darkness is requisite to both. **1698** FRYER *Acc. E. India & P.* 55 There is little or no Twilight, as there is nearer the Poles. **1796** MORSE *Amer. Geog.* I. 52 The twilight is that faint light which opens the morning by little and little in the east, before the sun rises; and gradually shuts in the evening in the west, after the sun is set. **1815** J. SMITH *Panorama Sc. & Art* I. 544 The atmosphere reflecting and refracting the sun's light, forms a twilight at the distance of even 18 degrees.

b. *spec.* Most commonly applied to the evening twilight, from sunset to dark night. ***second twilight***: see quot. 1883.

1412–20 LYDG. *Chron. Troy* I. 2733 In þe twyliȝt whan þe day gan fade. **1509** HAWES *Past. Pleas.* ii. (Percy Soc.) 14 In the fayre twylight, I sate me downe for to rest me all nyght. **1588** A. KING tr. *Canisius' Catech.* i vij, Ye quantitie of ye day brake and twa licht (for ye ane is æquall to ye vther) of euerie day. **1667** MILTON *P.L.* IV. 598 Now came still Eevning on, and Twilight gray Had in her sober Liverie all things clad. *a* **1700** DRYDEN *Cock & Fox* 214 When the sun was down, They just arrived by twilight at a town. **1793–6** COLERIDGE *Lines on Autumnal Evening* 63 When Twilight stole across the fading vale. **1836** W. IRVING *Astoria* xlviii. III. 99 A chasm that looked dark and frightful in the gathering twilight. **1883** *Chambers' Encycl.* IX. 604/1 A curious phenomenon, known as the afterglow, or second twilight, often seen in the Nubian desert, is referred by Sir John Herschel to a second reflection of solar light in the atmosphere.

c. Morning twilight, which lasts from daybreak to sunrise.

c **1440** *Promp. Parv.* 505/1 Twye lyghte, be-fore the day, *diluculum*. **1609** DANIEL *Civ. Wars* VIII. xiv, Upon the twi-light of that day..ere they had full light. **1617** MORYSON *Itin.* I. 240 By twilight of the morning we set sayle from Joppa. **1709** STANHOPE *Paraphr.* IV. 349 The Law and the Prophets, like the Glimmerings of the Twi-light, dawned first. **1727–46** THOMSON *Summer* 637 At once the bright-effulgent sun, Rising direct, swift chases from the sky The short-lived twilight. **1845** BROWNING *How they brought the Good News* iii, 'Twas moonset at starting; but while we drew near Lokeren, the cocks crew and twilight dawned clear. **1863** GEO. ELIOT *Romola* ii, [She] was weary after her labour in the morning twilight.

2. *transf.* A dim light resembling twilight; partial illumination.

1667 MILTON *P.L.* I. 597 As when the Sun..In dim Eclips disastrous twilight sheds. **1709** STEELE *Tatler* No. 8 ¶6 A Sable Cloud over-shadowed the whole Land... A Twilight began by Degrees to enlighten the Hemisphere. **1768** STERNE *Sent. Journ.*, *Captive*, I..look'd through the twilight of his grated door. **1819** KEATS *Eve St. Agnes* xxix, The faded moon Made a dim, silver twilight. **1858** HAWTHORNE *Fr. & It. Note-Bks.* I. 264 The church..had a grand effect in its tinted twilight. **1872** BLACK *Adv. Phaeton* xxx, The soft green twilight of an avenue of trees.

3. *fig.* **a.** An intermediate condition or period; a condition before or after full development.

twilight of the gods [transl. of Icel. *ragna rökkr*, altered from the original *ragna rök*, the history or judgement of the gods], in *Scandinavian mythol.* the destruction of the gods and of the world in conflict with the powers of evil; also *transf.* Cf. GÖTTERDÄMMERUNG, RAGNARÖK.

c **1600** SHAKS. *Sonn.* lxxiii, In me thou seest the twi-light of such day, As after Sun-set fadeth in the West. **1679** C. NESSE *Antichrist* 144 As if the twilight of the church in her minority and nonage..exceeded the noon-day of the gospel-church. **1682** DRYDEN *Relig. Laici* Pref., Wks. (Globe) 186 The twilight of Revelation, after the sun of it was set in the race of Noah. **1768** GRAY *Desc. Odin* (note), Lok is the evil Being, who continues in chains till the Twilight of the Gods approaches. **1820** BYRON *Mar. Fal.* I. ii. 315 At my hour Of twilight little light of life remains. **1821** SCOTT *Kenilw.* xii, He is ever in a sort of twilight, that is neither sleeping nor waking. **1877** SPARROW *Serm.* xix. 251 Voltaire was..in the habit of saying that he lived in the twilight of Christianity; meaning thereby, that its sun would soon go down. **1888** R. GARNETT (*title*) The twilight of the gods and other tales. **1944** *Sun* (Baltimore) 22 July 2/1 The German nation is split wide open... The twilight of the gods has begun. **1979** A. R. PEACOCKE *Creation & World of Science* ii. 55 Under the pressure of experimental facts and the bold and convincing analyses of Planck and Einstein, there was, as Karl Heim puts it, a 'twilight of the gods' of absolute space, time, object, and determinism.

b. esp. in reference to imperfect mental illumination or perception.

1610 HOLLAND *Camden's Brit.*, *Irel.* II. 89, I am out of all hope in so great darknesse to discover any twy-light of the truth. **1648** BOYLE *Seraph. Love* (1700) 167 The dim Twilight of Human Intellects in this Life. **1722** WOLLASTON *Relig. Nat.* iii. 54 Thus blind ignorance was succeeded by a twilight of 'Sense'. **1838** PRESCOTT *Ferd. & Is.* (1846) III. xiv. 127 A shadowy twilight of romance enveloped every object. **1869** TOZER *Highl. Turkey* II. 307 The minor deities ..live in a dim twilight of popular belief.

4. *attrib.* or as *adj.* **a.** Of, pertaining to, or resembling twilight; seen or done in the twilight.

twilight arc, arch, or ***curve***, the outline of the earth's shadow, which rises in the east as the sun sets, forming an arch which divides the twilight or shaded portion of the sky from that which is lighted by the direct rays of the sun. ***twilight glow***, a diffuse glow in the sky at twilight; *spec.* in *Meteorol.*, that caused by spectroscopic emission in the upper atmosphere from atoms excited by solar radiation. ***twilight parallel***, the small circle of the celestial sphere, parallel to and 18 degrees below the horizon, at the sun's crossing which evening twilight ceases or morning twilight begins (Webster, 1911). ***twilight vision***, vision in which colours are hardly perceptible owing to the dimness of the light; scotopic vision.

c **1633** MILTON *Arcades* 99 Nymphs and Shepherds.. Trip no more in twilight ranks. **1754** GRAY *Poesy* 56 The muse has broke the twilight-gloom. **1762–9** FALCONER *Shipwr.* I. 721 Now Morn advanced Whitening with orient beam the twilight sky. **1794** MRS. RADCLIFFE *Myst. Udolpho* xxxiv, Twilight shade and darkness veil the scene. **1812** BYRON *Ch. Har.* II. lx, When the lingering twilight hour was past. **1819** —— *Don Juan* II. clxxxviii. 213 The twilight glow, which momently grew less. **1837** LYTTON *E. Maltrav.* I. viii, That twilight shower had given a racy and vigorous sweetness to the air. **1855** BAIN *Senses & Int.* III. ii. §10 (1864) 472 There is a point of twilight dimness when objects begin to be doubtful. **1856** KANE *Arct. Expl.* I. xv. 169 It is either all day here, or all night, or a twilight mixture of both. **1921** Twilight vision [see *rod vision* s.v. ROD *sb.*[1] 11 c]. **1924**, etc. [see SCOTOPIC *a.*]. **1950** *Sci. News* XV. 17 It has been suspected for many years that the coloured pigment 'visual purple', found in the retinas of such animals as frogs, is associated with twilight vision. This supposition has recently become a certainty. **1955** *Sci. Amer.* Sept. 150/3 There is also a twilight glow, about 100 times as intense as the nightglow but not detectable by the eye because of the brighter sky. **1972** *Ibid.* Jan. 80/3 The spectrum of the twilightglow differs from the nightglow spectrum in that certain features disappear shortly after the end of twilight and others are markedly stronger in twilight than they are during the night. **1980** F. H. LUDLAM *Clouds & Storms* iv. 77/1 The twilight glow continues to fade and its upper border to descend more rapidly than the sun, but it does not disappear below the horizon until the sun's depression exceeds about 16°, and astronomical twilight ends.

b. *fig.* Having an intermediate character.

1730 T. BOSTON *Mem.* vii. (1899) 136 The two days before I had a twilight frame, it being neither day nor night with me. **1825** WATERTON *Wand. S. Amer.* III. i. 211 A kind of twilight state of health, neither ill nor..well.

c. Lighted as by twilight; dim, obscure, shadowy; also *fig.* of early times.

1629 MILTON *Hymn Nativity* xx, The Nimphs in twilight shade of tangled thickets mourn. **1632** —— *Il Penseroso* 133 Arched walks of twilight groves And shadows brown..Of pine. **1810** SCOTT *Lady of Lake* VI. Concl., In twilight copse the glow-worm lights her spark. **1863** HAWTHORNE *Our Old Home* (1879) 77 Warwick,..founded by King Cymbeline in the twilight ages. **1873** BLACK *Pr. Thule* viii, Some dim twilight recess—far in among the perilous rocks.

d. *fig.* Of the nature of or pertaining to imperfect mental light.

a **1677** BARROW *Serm. Acts ii. 38* Wks. 1686 III. 531 Philosophy may yield some twilight glimmerings thereof.

1774 FLETCHER *Salvation by Grace* Wks. 1795 IV. 65 Our short-sightedness and twilight knowledge do not alter the nature of things. **1818** SCOTT *Hrt. Midl.* xxix. [xxx], A doubtful, uncertain, and twilight sort of rationality.

e. Special Combs.: **twilight area** = *twilight zone* (*a*) below; **twilight home,** (*a*) a home (see HOME *sb.* 8) for old people or animals; (*b*) = *twilight house*; **twilight house,** a house in a twilight zone (see *twilight zone* (*a*) below); hence **twilight housing; twilight night** *Baseball* = TWI-NIGHT; **twilight shift,** a shift worked between the day shift and the night shift; **twilight sleep** [tr. G. *dämmerschlaf* (C. J. Gauss, *c* 1905)], a state of amnesia and partial analgesia induced by the administration of morphine and scopolamine (hyoscine), esp. to lessen the pains of childbirth; **twilight world,** (*a*) a shadowy region; (*b*) a world characterized by uncertainty, obscurity, or decline; (*c*) the world which comes to life after sunset, characterized by merry-making or criminal activities; **twilight zone,** (*a*) *spec.*, an urban area in which housing is becoming decrepit; (*b*) *gen.*, an indistinct boundary area combining some of the characteristics of the two areas between which it falls (cf. sense 4 b); (*c*) occas., a dimly illuminated region.

1960 *Daily Tel.* 18 June 8/3 Where debate begins and should be encouraged is over the question whether redevelopment of what Sir Keith Joseph called the 'twilight areas' must wait entirely on these other two housing operations. *a* **1974** R. CROSSMAN *Diaries* (1975) I. 44 A Labour Minister should impose central leadership, large-scale state intervention, in these blighted areas of cities, the twilight areas, which were once genteelly respectable and are now rotting away. **1934** WEBSTER, *Twilight home*, a charitable institution providing a home for aged people. *Colloq., Australia.* **1966** 'K. A. SADDLER' *Gilt Edge* v. 74 Twilight homes for retired beach donkeys. **1968** *Guardian* 5 Apr. 1/6 A plan to modernise Britain's four million twilight homes has been agreed by the Cabinet. **1978** I. MURDOCH *Sea* 493 [I] arranged for her mother to be packed off to a comfortable and expensive 'twilight home'. **1971** *New Society* 1 July 20/2 There were 600,000 'slums' and about two million 'twilight' houses. *Ibid.*, A current comparison of slum and twilight housing. **1971** *Mod. Law Rev.* XXXI. VI. 698 He has sections on.. houses in disrepair, on planning blight and on twilight housing areas. **1949** P. CUMMINGS *Dict. Sports* 478/1 *Twilight-night. Baseball.* A double-header, the first game played late in the afternoon, the second in the evening under lights. **1953** *Sun* (Baltimore) 28 Oct. (B ed.) 21/2 There can be none of those frisky twilight-night double headers. **1970** 'C. AIRD' *Late Phoenix* x. 115 He didn't come home last night after the twilight shift at his factory. **1977** *Wandsworth Borough News* 7 Oct. 18/2 (Advt.), Laundry workers evening shift, 5.30–9.30 p.m. We require a number of part-time workers for clean and simple work on our twilight shift, Monday–Friday. **1912** F. W. HEWITT *Anæsthetics & Administration* (ed. 4) ix. 278 As a matter of actual experience in hospital practice by no means all patients achieve the state of *dammerschlaf*, or 'twilight sleep', which foreign authors advocate. **1922** JOYCE *Ulysses* 159 Twilightsleep idea: queen Victoria was given that. **1971** D. D. MOIR *Pain Relief in Labour* i. 5 Twilight sleep is seldom used today because it causes respiratory depression in the new-born and tends to cause delirium and restlessness in the mother. **1981** J. GARDNER *License Renewed* xiv. 161 A nice mix—Scopolamine with morphine: twilight sleep, like having a baby. **1887** BOWEN *Virg. Æneid* IV. 25 Down to the twilight world and the gloom where the buried rest. **1954** KOESTLER *Invisible Writing* xxvi. 281, I mention this episode as one example of the ambiguities of the twilight world in which we lived. **1963** *Times* 8 May 6/7 But in this unhappy twilight world in which we live in a state of truce—neither peace nor war. **1970** C. MAJOR *Dict. Afro-Amer. Slang* 117 *Twilight world*, the world of all-night parties. **1977** D. SEAMAN *Committee* 116 The twilight world of the mentally ill. **1977** 'J. D. WHITE' *Salzburg Affair* v. 45 The twilight world that exists in every city.. the doctor who will tend a bullet wound, the hotel that will provide accommodation without papers. **1909** *Arena* XLI. Mar. 273/2 Such organization will leave no 'twilight zone', no 'no man's land', for railway corporation dodgers. **1918** *Policeman's Monthly* June 30/1 There still remain twilight zones in most centers of population. **1920** J. G. FREDERICK *Great Game of Business* iii. 23 Be aware that the test of real 'honesty' comes in the 'twilight zone' between what is quite clearly honest and dishonest. **1938** *Jrnl. Royal Aeronaut. Soc.* XLII. 492 The twilight zone extends to about 20° either side of the equi-signal zone centre. **1960** *Daily Tel.* 20 June 17/6 There are many towns with 'twilight zones' of shabby and out-dated houses. **1969** *Times* 29 Jan. 10/7 It lives between 300 and 500 metres below the surface of the ocean, in the region to which light penetrates with such difficulty that it may be considered as a kind of twilight zone. **1981** *Washington Post* 26 Apr. A1/1 Several key officials charged with formulating foreign policy remain in a bureaucratic twilight zone almost 100 days after Reagan's inauguration.

5. In combination with participle or adj., as *twilight-enfolded, -hidden, -like, -loving, -seeming, -tinctured* adjs.

1891 C. JAMES *Rom. Rigmarole* 88 Looking out at the soft *twilight-enfolded square. *a* **1882** ROSSETTI *Ho. Life* iv, Thy *twilight-hidden glimmering visage lies. **1839** BAILEY *Festus* xix. (1848) 202 A state Of *twilight-like existence. **1745** WARTON *Pleas. Melanch.* 267 The *twilight-loving bat. **1821** SCOTT *Kenilw.* vi, Two silver lamps.. diffused a ..*twilight-seeming shimmer. **1777** WARTON *Ode Hamlet* 5 Morning's *twilight-tinctur'd beam.

Hence **'twilight** *v. trans.*, to light imperfectly or dimly; **'twilighted** *a.*, partly illuminated; = TWILIT; **'twilightless** *a.*, having no twilight; **'twilighty** *a.*, resembling twilight.

1819 KEATS *Song of Four Fairies* in R. M. Milnes *Life, Lett. & Lit. Remains J. Keats* (1848) II. 275 And the beams of still Vesper.. Are shed thro' the rain.. And *twilight your floating bowers. **1866** HOWELLS *Venet. Life* 149 Cavernous recesses.. twilighted by twinkling altar-lamps. **1880** P. GREG *Errant* I. xvi. 245 A room.. lighted or rather twilighted by a window looking out on a back court. **1865** ALEX. SMITH *Summ. Skye* I. 314 A *twilighted shepherd at watch. **1868** MRS. WHITNEY *P. Strong* xvi, Warm twilighted evenings. **1886** MRS. F. CADDY *Footsteps Jeanne D'Arc* 226 Centuries, which.. we have been until lately accustomed to consider as twilighted ages. **1892** M. DODS *Gosp. John* II. 94 The sudden night of the Eastern *twilightless sunset had fallen. **1856** MAYHEW *Rhine* 250 The soft *twilighty tone of more ancient piles. **1894** E. F. BENSON *Rubicon* I. 69 That grey shawl is very twilighty.

† **twilighting.** *Obs. rare.* In 4 twyliȝtynge, 5 -light-. [f. TWI- + LIGHTING *vbl. sb.*[2]] = TWILIGHT *sb.* 1 b.

1387 TREVISA *Higden* (Rolls) VII. 97 In þe twyliȝtynge of þe nyȝt he deide. **1483** *Cath. Angl.* 398/2 Þe Twylightynge, *vespere*.

twilit ('twaɪlɪt), *ppl. a.* [pa. pple. of TWILIGHT *v.*] Lit by or as by twilight.

1869 MISS BRADDON *Lady's Mile* xviii, Within the twilit painting-room. **1887** STEVENSON *Merry Men, Will o' Mill* 79 He was like someone lying in twilit, formless, preëxistence. **1900** 'H. S. MERRIMAN' *Isle of Unrest* xvi, In the gloom of the twilit church.

twill (twɪl), **tweel** (twiːl), *sb.*[1] Forms: α. 4 twyle, 6 twile; 4–5 twyll (6 tywell), 4–6 twylle (6 tywlle, tylle), 5– twill (7 tuill). β. 4 twel, 6 tweal-, 7 *Sc.* tueill, tueile, 8– (orig. *Sc.*) tweel. [Northern and Sc. forms of *twīle* TWILLY *sb.*[1], with normal dropping of the final *-e*, and (esp. in Sc.) lengthening of original *ĭ* to *ē* in the stem-syllable: cf. the Sc. forms of the verbs *swill, till.*] A woven fabric characterized by parallel diagonal ridges or ribs, produced by causing the weft threads to pass over one and under two or more threads of the warp, instead of over and under in regular succession, as in plain weaving.

In quot. 1670, a twilled cloth used as a covering for a bed or mattress.

α. **1329** *Acc. Chamberl. Scotl.* (1771) 7 Sexaginta et decem ulnarum de twyll. **1330** in Dalrymple *Ann. Scot.* (1797) III. 356 De 70 ulnis de twylle. *c* **1330** *Durham Acc. Rolls* (Surtees) 519 In ij pec. de Twyle pro saccis faciendis. **1335–6** *Ibid.* 529 In ij peciis panni de Twyll pro saccis. **1465** *Reg. Gild Co. Chr. York* (1872) 294 Una mappa de twill, cont. viij ulnas. **1511** *Knaresborough Wills* (Surtees) I. 2, j mensale de le twile. **1552** *Inv. Ch. Goods* (Surtees No. 97) 10 One vestment of read twill. **1583** *Shuttleworths' Acc.* (Chetham Soc.) 12 Fivffe and tynty yardes of tywlle to be sakes. **1586** *Ibid.* 29 Sixtene yardes of tylle to be scakes. *Ibid.* 34 Sixtene yardes of tywell for to be sackes. **1670** COVEL in *Early Voy. Levant* (Hakl. Soc.) 115 All that lay on twills and bedsteads were sorely bitten with little bugs. **1674** JEAKE *Arith.* (1696) 65 In 1 Hundred of Tiking and Twill of Scotland, 120 Ells. *a* **1825** FORBY *Voc. E. Anglia*, *Twill*, a sort of coarse linen cloth, of which loose frocks, trowsers, &c. are made for working men. **1851–4** *Tomlinson's Cycl. Usef. Arts* (1867) II. 856/1 Twills are distinguished by the number of leaves required in weaving them, as a three-leaf twill. **1889** *Anthony's Photogr. Bull.* II. 310 A large piece of black twill, or other opaque material.

β. **1371** *Durham Acc. Rolls* (Surtees) 130, iiij manutergia de Twel. [**1571**: see TWILLED *a.*[1]] **1647** *Caldwell Pap.* (Maitl. Cl.) I. 99, 4 elnes of Northland tueill at 14 ss ye elne. *a* **1724** in Ramsay *Tea-t. Misc.* (1733) I. 29 (*Maggie's Tocher*) Ye shall hae twa good pocks That anes were o' the tweel. **1815** SCOTT *Guy M.* xxvi, As gude a tweel as ever cam aff a pirn. **1824** *Blackw. Mag.* XV. 220 Manchester tweel, or by whatever more proper denomination.. a white waistcoat may be characterized.

b. The, or a, method or process of weaving this fabric (also *fig.*); also the ribbed appearance or diagonal pattern of the material so woven.

c **1779** in J. Skinner *Misc. Poet.* (1809) 185 Some pawky chiel, That.. seems to understand the tweel O' rustic rhyme. **1839** URE *Dict. Arts* 373 Crape.. is woven with any crossing or tweel. *Ibid.* 1231 The first is the regular or run tweel, which.. interweaves the warp and woof only at every fifth interval. **1843** *Penny Cycl.* XXVII. 178/1 When.. in addition to a twill, the weaver has to produce.. any kind of figure. **1892** *Labour Commission Gloss.*, *Twill*, the pattern of a piece running diagonally from left to right.

c. *attrib.* and *Comb.*, as *twill bolster, calico, cloth, -heddle, hem, overall; twill-wove* adj.; **twill set**: see quot.

1656 *Melrose Regality Rec.* (S.H.S.) 185 A *tueile bolster. **1904** *Woollen Draper's Terms* in *Tailor & Cutt.* 4 Aug. 480/1 **Twill Calico*, a rather heavy calico with a twill pattern on it. **1839** URE *Dict. Arts* 1236 For such a pattern.., two sets of common *tweel-heddles, moved in the ordinary way,.. are sufficient. **1897** MARY KINGSLEY *W. Africa* 420 My favourite coloured cloth, bright pink, with a cardinal *twill hem round it. **1909** *Cent. Dict.* Supp. s.v. *Set*[1], **Twill set*, one of the three methods of inserting wire into the foundation of card-clothing. **1880** *Plain Hints Needlework* 109 Strong twilled flannel with closely *twill-wove self-edge .. used for petticoats.

twill (twɪl), *sb.*[2], dial. var. QUILL *sb.*[1]

1664 POWER *Exp. Philos.* I. 8 You may plainly see the twills by which they [feathers] stick to the wings. **1691** RAY *N.C. Words* (E.D.S.), *Twill*,.. a spoole... In the South they call it winding of quills. **1788** W. MARSHALL *Yorksh.* II. Gloss. (E.D.S.), *Twill*, a quill. **1825** BROCKETT *N.C. Words*, *Twill*, a quill; either for a pen, or on which to wind yarn. **1855** ROBINSON *Whitby Gloss.*

twill (twɪl), **tweel** (twiːl), *v.*[1] [f. TWILL *sb.*[1] or TWILLED *a.*[1]] *trans.* To weave so as to produce diagonal ridges on the surface of the cloth.

1808–18 JAMIESON, *To.. tweel*, v.a., to work cloth in such a manner, that the woof appears to cross the warp vertically. **1828** *Craven Gloss.*, *Twill*, to weave in a particular manner. **1839** URE *Dict. Arts* 1231 Florentine silks are tweeled with sixteen leaves. **1870** ROCK *Text. Fabr.* vii. (1876) 73 Fustian .. with a warp of linen thread and a woof of thick cotton, so twilled and cut that it showed on one side a thick but low pile.

twill, *v.*[2], dial. var. QUILL *v.*; cf. TWILL *sb.*[2]

1848 THACKERAY *Van. Fair* xvi, The great fat pin-cushion lined with pink inside, and twilled like a lady's night-cap.

† **twill,** obs. form of TEWEL.

1611 FLORIO, *Budello dritto*, the twill, the longaon or straight gut. **1659** in TORRIANO.

twilled (twɪld), **tweeled** (twiːld), *a.*[1] [f. TWILL *sb.*[1] and *v.*[1] + -ED.] Woven with a twill; having diagonal lines or ridges on the surface.

c **1423** in Raine *Abps. York* (Rolls) III. 306, j fethirbed de panno vocato twylled. **1536** *Test. Ebor.* (Surtees) VI. 53 A long twilte towell. **1536** *Wills & Inv. N.C.* (Surtees) III. 141 Two dossyn napkyns, one twilled towell. **1571** *Ibid.* I. 360, vj twealed bord clothes short and long. **1666** in *Maitl. Club Misc.* (1840) II. 539 Another greene tuilled night cap. **1805** *Trans. Soc. Arts* XXIII. 249 Any web, twilled, striped, checked or plain. **1824** HOGG *Tales & Sk.* (1837) V. 206 (*Mem. Fanatic*) His coat.. is tweeled, milled, and thicker than a carpet. **1831** G. R. PORTER *Silk Manuf.* 236 Tweeled or twilled cloth is a description of figure weaving. **1857** MILLER *Elem. Chem.* (1862) III. 87 A filtering apparatus consisting of tubes of twilled cotton.

† **twilled,** *a.*[2] *Obs.*

Origin and meaning uncertain: numerous conjectures have been offered by commentators, but none has met with general acceptance. Cf. PIONED.

1610 SHAKS. *Temp.* IV. i. 64 Thy bankes with pioned, and twilled brims Which spungie Aprill at thy hest betrims.

twillet, obs. form of TOILET.

twilley: see TWILLY *sb.*[2]

twilling ('twɪlɪŋ), **tweeling** ('twiːlɪŋ). [f. TWILL *sb.*[1] or *v.*[1] + -ING[1].] A twilled fabric or texture; also, the process of producing this. Also, *attrib.* **twilling-bar,** a device in the twilling-machine; **twilling-hook,** one of the hooks for lifting the warp-threads in a twilling-machine; **twilling-machine,** a modification of the Jacquard loom.

1839 URE *Dict. Arts* 385 Damask belongs to that species of texture which is distinguished by practical men by the name of tweeling. **1880** *Plain Hints Needlework* 122 The regularity of the parallel lines is broken in various ways, in fanciful twillings. **1894** T. W. FOX *Mechanism Weaving* VI. 168 The advantage of a twilling machine over an ordinary Jacquard. *Ibid.* 171 When [the] barrel is pegged to produce the desired pattern, twilling bars.. will turn two or more griffe blades vertical, and push corresponding twilling hooks over slanting blades.

† **twillock,** obs. var. WILLOCK.

1620 J. MASON *New-found-land* 4 Teales, Twillockes, excellent wilde Duckes.

twilly ('twɪlɪ), *a.* and *sb.*[1] Also 4 tywele, twyle, 7 twylle; 5 twelye, 6 twyley, 7 twylly(e. [OE. *twili* (= OHG. *zwilîh*), formed after L. *bilix* from *twi-* TWI-: cf. THRILI *a.* The ME. var. *twile* is parallel to *thrile*, the reduced form of *thrili*, and is the source of the northern TWILL *sb.*[1]]

†**a.** *adj.* Twilled. *Obs.* **b.** *sb.* †(*a*) A twilled cloth; also *attrib.* (*Obs.*); (*b*) (see quot. 1948); so *twill(e)y hole*, a hole left in the centre of a wattle hurdle for the insertion of a pole on which several hurdles may be carried simultaneously.

c **875** *Erfurt Gloss.* (Sweet) 1151 Biplex, duplex, tuili. *a* **900** *Leiden Gloss.* 157 *Bilex*, t[u]ili.

1310 *Acc. Exors. of Bp. of Exeter* (1874) 4, j capa de samitrico tywele linita sindone yndico. **1375** in Boys *Hist. Sandwich* (1792) 556/2 De chescun twylecloth de la lb... ij d. **1440** in G. P. Scrope *Castle Combe* (1852) 230, ij. borde cloths, one of twelye. **1552** *Berksh. Ch. Goods* (1879) 11 One other Coope lyke unto twillye the border of woursted. **1560** *Will of Salmon* (Somerset Ho.) A Twyley cloth to lay upon her bed. **1600** HOLLAND *Livy* VII. xiv. 258 The mules sumpters should bee taken off their backes, leaving onely two course twillies or coverings upon them. **1601** —— *Pliny* IX. lix. I. 269 His companion.. latcheth them in a course twillie or couering. **1602** *Inv.* in *Collect. Archæol.* (1863) II. 98 Twyllye canvasses. *Ibid.*, One twylle. *Ibid.* 101 A doble twyllye. **1631** *Patent Specif.* No. 54. 2 All such kersy seves, otherwise twilly seves or haire seves. **1714** *Fr. Bk. of Rates* 152 Four Livres.. for every Piece of Boucassines, Twillis, Fustians, Bazins, and Bombasins. **1893** A. KENNARD *Diogenes' Sandals* vi. 90 A 'twilley' hole, is left in the centre of each hurdle for the insertion of the.. pole, on which the shepherds carry them. **1948** E. J. STOWE *Crafts of Countryside* iii. 24 About two-thirds of the way up from the bottom of the hurdle there are two important rods. They are known as 'twillies' (a country name for twisted rods), and are twisted about each other and around the upright sails one by one across the hurdle. *Ibid.* 128 *Twillies*, two twisted rods woven across wattle hurdles just above the twilly hole. **1959** *Times* 2 June 12/7 The split rods are twisted until the complete hurdle is ready with the twilly hole in the middle. **1971** *Country Life* 25 Feb. 424/1 These hurdles differ slightly from sheep hurdles which had a gap or twilly hole in their middle through which a shepherd put his stick to carry a load to the next enclosure.

twilly ('twɪlɪ), *sb.*[2] Also **twilley**. [Altered f. *willy*, WILLOW.] A willowing machine: = DEVIL *sb.* 8 a; also called ***twilly-devil***. Hence '**twilly** *v. trans.* to willow.

1858 SIMMONDS *Dict. Trade*, *Twilly*, a common name for the willying machine. **1859** TOMLINSON *Illustr. Usef. Arts* 19/1 Supposing the wool to be dyed, it is passed through the willy, or twilly—resembling the willow of the cotton manufacture. **1860** —— *Usef. Arts* Ser. I. 37 The *willy*, or *shakewilly*, as it is called in Yorkshire, and *twilly* in Gloucestershire. **1869** *Eng. Mech.* 19 Nov. 240/2 The best machine for pulling flocks is called a 'twilly'. **1894** C. VICKERMAN *Woollen Spinning* viii. 117 This is the first operation after the wool is dyed, and is known by a variety of names, as teasing, willeying, willowing, and twilleying.

twilt (also 6 **twylt**), obs. and dial. f. QUILT *sb.*[1], *v.*[1] and *v.*[3] (See also TWILLED *a.*[1])

1477 [see QUILT *sb.*[1] 1]. **1538** in *Bury Wills* (Camden) 134, I wyll the bed, and the twylt couerlyt..be solde. **1593** [see QUILT *v.*[1] 2 *transf.*]. **1594** [see QUILTED *ppl. a.* 1]. **1715** PENNECUIK *City & Country Mouse* 34 The City-Mouse then plac't his Country-Guest, On a Rich Purple-Twilt to grace his Feast. **1790** GROSE *Provinc. Gloss.* (ed. 2), *Twilt*, a quilt or bed-cover. *North.* **1813** DUFF *Poems* (1816) 56 Blankets, sheets, and stripit tykin'; Twilts an' cov'rins to your likin'. **1818** SCOTT *Br. Lamm.* xxv[i], Beds of state, twilts, pands and testors, napery and broidered wark. *a* **1825** FORBY *Voc. E. Anglia*, *Twilt*,..a quilt; here as well as in the North. *Twilt*... 1. To quilt... 2. To beat. An expressive word, inasmuch as it is implied that weals are left, like the stripes or ridges in quilted work.

twin (twɪn), *a.* and *sb.* Forms: 1 *adj.* **twinn**, (*sb. pl.* **ȝetwinnas**, 3 **itwinnes**), 3–6 **twynne**, 3–7 **twinne**, 4 **tuine**, *Sc.* **twene**, 4–5 **tuynne**, 4–5 (6 *Sc.*) **twyne**, 4 (6 *Sc.*) **tuin**, **tuinne**, **tuyne**, 4–7 **twyn**, 5–7 **twine**, 6 **twynn**, 7 **twinn**, 3– **twin**. [OE. *twinn* adj. (rare), *ȝetwinn* adj. and sb., f. the stem of TWI-. Cf. OFris. *twina*, *twine* (NFris. *twĕne*, *twăne*) two together, ON. *tvinnr*, *tvennr* double, (pl.) two, two pairs of, Norw. *tvinne*, *tvenne*, Da. *tvende* two. In northern ME. perhaps partly or mainly from ON.: cf. THRIN *a.*]

A. *adj.*

† **1.** Consisting of two; twofold, double. *Obs.* (exc. as in 4).

c **1000** in Napier *O.E. Glosses* I. 1836 *Gemina*, .i. *duppla*, twinnum. *Ibid.* 2605–6 *Geminis concentibus*, twinnum sangum. *c* **1200** ORMIN 7737–9 Ȝho brohhte twinne lac, Forr ..her iss twinne lufe sett Bitwenenn menn onn eorþe; Forr uss birrþ lufenn Godd & mann. *c* **1250** *Gen. & Ex.* 485 [Lamech sinned in] Twin-wifing ant twin manslaȝt. **1357** *Lay Folks Catech.* 508 This is principaly done opon twyn wise. *c* **1400** *Rule St. Benet* (Prose) 5 Of twine maner at lere his discipilis..at serue god: baþe in word and dede.

† **2.** Two; a pair of...; the two, both. *Obs.*

c **1250** *Gen. & Ex.* 3248 Ðe water up-stod..On twinne half. *Ibid.* 4020 Heft haueð he mad her .vii. alter, And on ilc brend eft twin der. *a* **1300** *Cursor M.* 523 (Cott.) His heued with in has eien tuin. *Ibid.* 5235 Ioseph had þan suns tuin, Manassen and effraim. *Ibid.* 9136 His eild was fourti yeir and tuin. *Ibid.* 21750 þe laghes tuin sal þou find sua.

3. (attrib. use of B. 1.) Born at the same birth, as two children or animals, or one of such. See also TWIN-BROTHER, -SISTER.

1590 SHAKS. *Com. Err.* v. i. 350 He, and I, And the twin Dromio. *a* **1722** LISLE *Husb.* (1757) 313 A..twin-lamb. **1751** WARBURTON *Pope's Ep. Burlington* 117 *note*, These groves..can express themselves only like twin-ideots by nods. **1822** T. MITCHELL *Aristoph.* II. 191 By the twin-gods I vow. **1847** W. C. L. MARTIN *The Ox* 40/2 Every twin female..is not necessarily barren, even when the other calf is a male.

4. a. Forming a pair or couple; two closely associated, connected, or related, and (usually) alike or equal. (In quot. 1601 said of one thing cut in half; in quot. 1776 *loosely* of more than two.)

In this sense, and in senses b, d, and 5, often hyphened to the noun (cf. the combinations under C), or occasionally written as one word with it.

1591 SYLVESTER *Du Bartas* I. ii. 64 Th' Elements, twin-twins (two sons, two daughters) To wit, the Fire, the Aire; the Earth, and Waters. **1601** SHAKS. *Twel. N.* v. i. 230 An apple cleft in two, is not more twin Then these two creatures. **1614** SYLVESTER *Litt. Bartas* 617 Those twin-Princes [the sun and moon]..Began their Kingdoms over day and night. **1673** [R. LEIGH] *Transp. Reh.* 131 Therefore are the twin-diseases deservedly associated. **1743** FRANCIS tr. *Hor., Odes* III. xxix. 96 Perhaps some kinder gale, While the twin stars appear, shall fill my joyful sail. **1765** *Museum Rust.* IV. 20 When you meet with twin fruit, take off the least of them with all possible care not to shake the other. **1776** MICKLE tr. *Camoens' Lusiad* 163 The seven twin-mountains tremble at the sound. **1809–10** COLERIDGE *Friend* I. xv. (1865) 207 These twin truths, or rather..this one great truth considered in its two principal bearings. **1835** URE *Philos. Manuf.* 117 The leather must..be pierced with twin holes for each double tooth. **1875** KNIGHT *Dict. Mech.*, *Twin-screws*, a pair of screw-propellers on separate shaft[s], and having right-handed and left-handed twists respectively. **1898** J. T. FOWLER *Durham Cath.* 38 Twin shafts of Purbeck marble.

b. Composed of, or having, two similar and equal (or closely connected or related) parts or constituents; consisting of two joined in one.

twin boat, *steam-engine*, *valve*: see quots. *c* 1816, 1875. *twin crystal*: = B. 3 b. *twin earthquake*: see quot. 1906.

1585 JAS. I *Ess. Poesie* (Arb.) 35 Let Christ both God and man your Twinrock [orig. *croupe iumelle*] be. *a* **1661** FULLER *Worthies, Kent* (1662) II. 86 An Ingenuous Yeoman in this County..hath two Ploughs fastened together so finely, that he plougheth two furrows at once, one under another,..this device of a Twinne-Plough. **1805–16** R. JAMESON *Char. Min.* (ed. 2) 220 A crystal..composed of two halves of one ..crystal, of which the one-half appears to be turned round. Example, Twin-crystal of felspar. *c* **1816** REES *Cycl.* s.v. *Steam-Engine*, In 1811 and 1812 two steam-boats were built ..as ferry-boats for crossing the Hudson river. These boats are what are called twin-boats; each of them being two complete hulls united by a deck or bridge. **1826** KIRBY & SP. *Entomol.* IV. xlvi. 288 Double Ocellus (*Ocellus geminatus*). When two ocelli are included in the same circle or spot... Twin Ocellus (*Ocellus didymus*). When such ocelli join each other. **1848** RICKMAN *Archit.* 152 They may be called twin-windows, consisting of two single lights coupled together. **1875** KNIGHT *Dict. Mech.* 2667 A large twin channel steamer ..has lately been put upon the Dover and Calais ferry. *Ibid.* 2668 *Twin Steam-engine*,..a duplex engine; one in which two engines, complete in their parts, are associated in a single effort. *Ibid.*, *Twin-valve*, a form of valve attached to the discharge outlet of a pump..used for making a double connection, one with the steam-boiler..and the other..for conducting water wherever desired. **1906** *19th Cent.* Mar. 465 To earthquakes of this description the name of 'twin' has been given, because the double shock is due to two distinct impulses resulting from a single generative effort. **1910** THOMPSON tr. *Aristotle's Hist. Anim.* 562 In some twin eggs a thin partition of white intervenes to prevent the yolks mixing.

c. *Nat. Hist.* Growing or occurring in pairs; geminate.

1812 *New Bot. Gard.* I. 26 The anthers twin and erect. **1830** LINDLEY *Nat. Syst. Bot.* 130 Seeds solitary or twin. **1891** *Cent. Dict.*, *Twin*..I. *a*...6. In *entom.*, geminate: applied to spots, punctures, spines, etc., which are close together in pairs.

d. Pertaining to two (persons or things) in close connexion.

1827 SOUTHEY *Devil's Walk* v, Such a twin-likeness there was in the pair. **1870** MORRIS *Earthly Par.* II. III. 174 Their twinlife seemed so piteous.

5. Forming one of a pair or couple; closely associated with or related to another.

1605 CHAPMAN *All Fools* III. i, Here comes the twyn-Courtier his companion. **1781** COWPER *Hope* 102 Yesterday's face twin image of to-day. **1835** LYTTON *Rienzi* III. iii, True sentiment..is twin with melancholy. **1842** LOUDON *Suburban Hort.* Introd. 1 Having in a twin volume treated of Gardening as an Art of Design and Taste.

B. *sb.*

1. a. *pl.* Two children or young brought forth at one birth.

[*a* **900** *O.E. Martyrol.* 17 Jan. 24 Seo cierece..is neah Lingona byriȝ, þa man nemneð æt *sanctos geminos*, æt þæm halȝum ȝetwinnum. *a* **1000** in Cockayne *Shrine* (1864) 92 Hi wæron ȝetwinnas. *c* **1205** LAY. 12256 Twene ibroðeren itwinnes heo weoren.] *c* **1290** *S. Eng. Leg.* I. 322/5 Twynnes boþe huy were. **1388** WYCLIF *Song Sol.* vii. 3 Thi twei teetis ben as twei kidis, twynnes of a capret. **1514** BARCLAY *Cyt. & Uplondyshm.* (Percy Soc.) 10 So yere by yere two twynnes forthe she brought. **1573** TUSSER *Husb.* (1878) 74 Keepe twinnes for breed. **1607** TOPSELL *Four-f. Beasts* (1658) 86 They conceive and bring forth for the most part twins, or two at a time. **1793** HOLCROFT *Lavater's Physiogn.* xxix. 140, I have known twins not to be distinguished from each other, between whose minds there was not the least similarity. **1847** W. C. L. MARTIN *The Ox* 40/2 The cow..produces.. sometimes..twins, and very rarely three. **1852** MRS. STOWE *Uncle Tom's C.* xix, My brother and I were twins.

b. *sing.* One of two children or young brought forth at a birth; with possessive or *of* = twin brother or sister.

c **1440** *Promp. Parv.* 505/2 Twynne, or twynlynge.., *gemellus*,..*geminus*. **1530** PALSGR. 283/2 Twyn, *jumeau*. *a* **1658** CLEVELAND *King's Ret. fr. Scotl.* 19 The divided Dam Runs to the Summons of her hungry Lamb; But when the Twin cryes halves, she quits the first. **1824** BYRON *Def. Transf.* I. ii. 81, I saw your Romulus..Slay his own twin. **1899** *Westm. Gaz.* 4 Mar. 2/1 It's not me..but Hilda, and she's my twin. **1912** KEITH *Human Body* viii. 116 All of these 'acardiac' or 'parasitic' fœtuses are never born alone; they are the twin of a normal child.

c. *Astron.* (*pl.*) The zodiacal constellation and sign GEMINI.

1413 *Pilgr. Sowle* (Caxton 1483) v. x. 100 The signe of gemini that been cleped twynnes or doubles. **1561** B. GOOGE *Palingenius' Zodiac of Life* Pref. ¶j b, Saturne..with a backward course he ranne from out the twinnes apace. **1669** STURMY *Mariner's Mag.* VI. 95 Here in the zodiack begins The Ram, the Bull, the loving Twins. **1727–46** THOMSON *Summer* 43 When now no more the alternate Twins are fired, And Cancer reddens with the solar blaze. **1868** LOCKYER *Guillemin's Heavens* II. i. (ed. 3) 315 Part of the constellation of the Twins.

d. *dial.* (*pl.*) Applied to three children born at one birth; triplets.

1606 *Transcr. Regrs. Cosmus Bleane in Kent* (MS.), Was Baptyzed three Twines, John, Sara, and Margeret, the sonne and daughters of Liby Strydwicke. **1631–2** *Canterbury Transcr., Kingsdown* (MS.), Two (of three twinnes) to wit daughters of Christopher Bacheler..were buried. **1646** *Inscr. Blyton Church, Lincs*, Hadassah Tabitha Cephas Twins of Robt. and Elizabeth Drury.

e. ***with twins*** (strengthening of *with child*, CHILD *sb.* 17 c (*b*)). *fig.* greatly longing. *rare*$^{-1}$.

1768 GARRICK *Let.* June in *Burke's Corr.* (1844) I. 156 Hearing what a sweet place you have,..I am with twins till I am well delivered at Gregories.

2. *fig.* **a.** *pl.* Two persons or things intimately associated, connected, or related (esp. in origin, or from the beginning), or, as in quot. 1784, closely resembling or agreeing with each other; two forming a pair or couple. (In quot. *a* 1600 *loosely* applied to more than two.)

Applied by Puttenham (quot. 1589) to the figure HENDIADYS.

1589 PUTTENHAM *Eng. Poesie* III. xvi. (Arb.) 188 Another manner of speach when ye will seeme to make two of one.., which therefore we call the figure of Twynnes, the Greekes *Endiadis*. *a* **1591** H. SMITH *Serm.* (1637) 395 Sinnes and excuses are twinnes born at a birth. *a* **1600** MONTGOMERIE *Sonn.* viii. 9 Come, troup of tuinis, about his temple tuyn Ȝour laurell leivis. **1612** *Two Noble K.* II. ii. 21 Never Shall we two exercise, like Twyns of honour, Our Armes again. **1784** COWPER *Task* IV. 738 Two were never found Twins at all points. **1820** SHELLEY *Ode to Liberty* xiii, Twins of a single destiny!

b. *sing.* One of two thus related; in early use sometimes = mate, companion; now usually with *of*, *to*, or possessive: something closely connected with or resembling the other thing mentioned; a fellow, counterpart.

1540 HYRDE tr. *Vives' Instr. Chr. Wom.* (1592) N iij, A woman..with whom he shall live a twin. **1616** LANE *Contn. Sqr.'s T.* XI. 190 Hee..shall have his landes, and her to wifelie twinn. **1697** BENTLEY *Phal.* (1699) 249 Another consequence the very twin to that which went before. **1819** BYRON *Juan* II. clxxii, All who joy would win Must share it —Happiness was born a twin. **1822–7** GOOD *Study Med.* (1829) IV. 11 The great sympathetic..nerve..meets its twin from the opposite side. **1867** MAURICE *Patriarchs & Lawg.* viii. (1877) 168 Love would be seen to be the eternal twin of Truth. **1908** O. SEAMAN *Salvage, Sweet Uses Obesity* vii, Her bed, as a matter of course, is A twin of the wonder of Ware.

3. a. A pair of twin children or young; also *fig.* or *gen.* a pair, couple, brace. *Obs.* exc. *dial.*

1569 in *Spenser's Poet. Wks.* (1910) I. 494, I saw the roote in his disdaine Sende forth againe a twinne of forked trees. **1607** TOPSELL *Four-f. Beasts* (1658) 195 Commonly they are brought forth in twins. **1635** A. STAFFORD *Fem. Glory* (1869) 80 Her Soul was delivered of a twinne of Vows. **1817** J. NICHOLS *Illustr. Lit. Hist. 18th C.* II. 657 [He] was born in December, 1744..and was one of a twin. **1901** M. E. FRANCIS *Past. Dorset* 142 'The twin', a fine healthy pair of four-year-old boys.

b. *Cryst.* A composite crystal consisting of two (usually equal and similar) crystals united in reversed positions with respect to each other, either by juxtaposition, embedding, or interpenetration. (Also extended to composite crystals consisting of more than two.)

1845 *Encycl. Metrop.* XVI. 364/2 Twinning on an octahedral face is seen in the apposition twin of Spinel. **1868** DANA *Min.* (ed. 5) 354 Orthoclase... Twins..right- or left-handed... A twin of 4 crystals... A twin of 3 crystals. **1895** STORY-MASKELYNE *Crystallogr.* vi. §156 The two individuals may present a mere contact at a common surface .., the juxtaposed twin..: or there may be an interlocking of the crystals,..as in the..embedded twin of orthoclase..: or again, there may be a complete mutual interpenetration.., as in..an interpenetrant twin of galena... In the case of polysynthetic twins several or almost innumerable hemi-tropic individual crystals may be combined. *Ibid.* vii. §193 Simple twins composed of two individuals, and..complex twins formed by repeated twinning.

c. *local.* An agricultural implement with two rows of teeth, for breaking up ploughed land and clearing it of weeds.

1847 in HALLIWELL. **1859** *Jrnl. R. Agric. Soc.* XX. I. 216 A pair of 'twins', or heavy drag-harrows. **1881** MISS JACKSON *Shropsh. Word-bk.*, *Twins*,..for breaking the clods and uprooting the weeds of ploughed land, preparatory to the harrows going on... The implement..is either single or double, and in the latter case is spoken of as 'a pair of twins', the several parts being coupled together.

d. *ellipt.* for *twin aerial*, *bed*, *-city*, *-cylinder car*, *-cylinder engine*, *-engined aeroplane*, *-town*, etc. (see C.).

1928 [see *sun arc* s.v. SUN *sb.* 13 a]. **1930** *Times* 14 Mar. 12/3 As soon as the B.B.C. 'twins' came into use and two wave-lengths were available. **1938** O. NASH *I'm a Stranger here Myself* 85 A double bed or twins. **1944** G. L. NUTE *Lake Superior* III. xii. 277 Superior had hoped to be the terminus of the first railroad to the head of the lake, but when one came, in 1870, its terminal was Duluth rather than the other twin. **1955**, **1963** [see SINGLE *sb.* 3 o]. **1975** B. MEGGS *Matter of Paradise* VI. ii. 167 Nice..room, double bed... Should have made a point to ask for twins. **1976** R. BARNARD *Little Local Murder* i. 11 They've done one before—for a town in Essex with a twin in Canada. **1976** B. LECOMBER *Dead Weight* iii. 45 If I was going into the charter business I had to have a twin—and she was..the only twin on the whole airport that I could afford.

† **4. a.** ***in twin*** (also contr. ***itwin***), ***on twin***: in or into two parts or divisions; in twain, in two, apart, asunder. (Cf. ATWIN *advb. phr.*[1]) Chiefly *northern*. *Obs.*

a **1300** *Cursor M.* 3968 (Cott.) For doute he delt þam in tuin. *Ibid.* 6269 He sagh þe see it drau in tuin. **13..** *E.E. Allit. P.* A. 251 Fro we in twynne wern towen & twayned, I haf ben a Ioylez Iuelere. *Ibid.* B. 1047 Quen hit is brused oþer broken, oþer byten in twynne. **1375** BARBOUR *Bruce* VIII. 175 Sa fer..that thai War in-twyn a bow-draucht & mar. *c* **1400** *Gamelyn* 317, I wil not þis companye parten on twyne. *c* **1400** *Destr. Troy* 6581 Anoþer..he nolpit to ground, Shent of þo shalkes, shudrit hom itwyn. *c* **1450** *Bk. Curtasye* 735 in *Babees Bk.* (1868) 324 þe smalle lofe he cuttis euen in twynne. *c* **1480** *Lyt. Childr. Lyt. Bk.* 24 ibid. 18 Kerue not thy brede to thynne, Ne breke hit not on twynne. **1535** STEWART *Cron. Scot.* (Rolls) III. 226 Quhilk causit him stand..fra him..rycht far in tuyn.

† **b.** Hence (or from TWIN *v.*[1]) *twin* is used for 'parting, separation'. *Obs. rare*$^{-1}$.

a **1300** *Cursor M.* 24285 (Edin.) Ik am wit þe With outen twin [*Cott., Gött.* tuin] and ai sal be Fra nu for euirmar.

C. Combinations. **a.** with sbs., forming adjs. in sense 'having or characterized by twin...s, i.e. a pair of (the things named)', as ***twin-burner***, ***-cylinder***, ***-engine***, ***-float***, ***-fuselage***, ***-light***, ***-power***, ***-roller***, ***-track***, ***-wire***. **b.** with sb. + -ED[2], forming parasynthetic adjs. in same sense, as ***twin-balled***, ***-engined***, ***-forked***, ***-headed***, ***-hued***, ***-leaved***, ***-named***, ***-peaked***, ***-spiked***, ***-striped***, ***-towered***, ***-towned***, ***-tyred***, ***-walled***, ***-wheeled***. **c.** objective, etc., as ***twin-bearing*** adj., ***-getter***, ***-killing***; ***twin-like*** adj. and adv. **d.** adverbial ('as a twin or twins'), as ***twin-begot***, ***-existent*** adjs.; ***twin-slumber*** vb. **e.** Special Combs.: **twin aerial** (*temporary*), a twin-wire aerial; **twin-axis** *Cryst.*, the axis of twinning in a twin crystal, i.e. the line about which either of the constituent crystals would have to revolve to come into the position of the other; **twin-barren**, a barren female calf twin with a male, a freemartin; **twin bed**, one of a pair of matching single beds; hence **twin-bedded** *a.* (*a*) tucked up in a twin-bed (*nonce use*); (*b*) furnished wth twin beds; **twin bedstead**, one of a pair of matching single bedsteads; **twinberry**, *U.S.*, a name for *Gaultheria procumbens* (also called *checkerberry*, *partridge-berry*, or *wintergreen*), or its fruit; **twin-bill** *Baseball* = DOUBLE-HEADER c; **twin-birth**, the birth of twins; a pair born or produced as twins, or one of such in relation to the other (usually *fig.*); **twin carburettor**, one of a pair of carburettors in the same engine; so **twin carb.**; **twin city**, (*a*) *N. Amer.*, either of two cities that are very close neighbours; *spec.* in *pl.* (*U.S.*) St. Paul and Minneapolis, (*Canad.*) Fort William and Port Arthur; (*b*) occas. used of a city in the sense of *twin town* below; **twin double**, a system of betting (on horse-races, etc.) in which the winners of four successive races must be selected (i.e. two *doubles* in sequence); **twin-face** *Cryst.*, a face in a twin crystal perpendicular to the *twin-axis*; **twin floats**, a pair of floats (FLOAT *sb.* 8 e) on a seaplane; **twinflower**, an American name for *Linnæa*, from the flowers being produced in pairs; **twin-jet** *a. Aeronaut.*, having two jet engines; also *ellipt.* as *sb.*, a twin-jet aircraft; †**twin-kin** *a.* [KIN *sb.*[1] 6 b], of two kinds, twofold, double; **twin lamb disease**, a pregnancy toxæmia in sheep, apparently caused by malnutrition; **twin-law** *Cryst.*, the law or principle of twinning of a twin crystal; **twin-leaf**, a name for the N. American herb *Jeffersonia diphylla*, the leaves being divided each into two leaflets; **twin-lens** *a.*, designating a camera with two identical sets of lenses, either for taking stereoscopic pictures, or (more commonly) with one forming an image for viewing and the other an image to be photographed; **twin-pair**, a pair of things precisely similar and equal; *attrib.* in **twin-pair sheet** *Geom.*, that part of the surface of a cone of the third or higher degree which meets the concentric sphere in two equal and similar closed curves; **twin paradox** *Physics*, in relativity theory, the conclusion that if one of a pair of twins makes a long journey at high speed and then returns, he will have aged less than the twin who remains behind; **twin-plane** *Cryst.*, a plane perpendicular to the *twin-axis* of a twin crystal; **twin plate** *Glass Manufacture*, plate glass which is ground and polished on both sides at once; also *attrib.*; **twin prime** *Math.*, each of a pair of prime numbers whose difference is 2; **twin-screw**, *a.* having twin screws; *spec.* of a steamer, having two screw propellers on separate shafts, which turn in opposite directions so as to counteract the tendency to lateral vibration; also *ellipt.* as *sb.* a twin-screw steamer; **twin set** (also with hyphen and as one word), a woman's matching jumper and cardigan; **twin soul**, a kindred spirit; also as *attrib. phr.*; **twin species** *Biol.* [tr. F. *espèce jumelle* (L. Cuenot 1929, in *Reunion Plénière de la Soc. de Biol. et de ses Filiales, 17–18 Mai* 85], two species which are morphologically identical but which are separated by reproductive isolation; cf. *sibling species* s.v. SIBLING 3; **twin-spot** *a.*, having twin spots; used in collectors' names of various moths having pairs of spots upon the wings; **twin-stock**, a beehive containing two colonies; **twin town**, one of a pair of towns (usu. in different countries) that have established official links; **twin-tub** *a.*, (of a washing machine) having two separate top-loading drums, one for washing and the other for spin-drying; also *ellipt.* as *sb.*

1913 *Wireless World* June 211/2 The ordinary '*twin' aerial used by the Marconi Company on most of their ship-stations. **1928** J. FROST *Wireless Man.* iv. 17 A twin aerial, or aerial of two wires. **1855** *Orr's Circle Sci., Crystall.* 469 The axis about which the crystals are supposed to revolve is called the *twin axis, and the plane to which it is perpendicular the twin plane. **1608** SYLVESTER *Du Bartas* II. IV. IV. *Decay* 1165 With sharp bodkins bore they out his eyes: ..an end-less night Be-clouds for ever his *twin-balled sight. **1778** [W. MARSHALL] *Minutes Agric., Digest* 40 English Beasts of Agricultural Labour..*Twin-Barrens. **1788** BURNS *Let.* 25 May, Wks. 1879 V. 125 A certain girl's prolific, *twin-bearing merit. **1919** G. B. SHAW *Heartbreak House* p. xxxviii, If the twin flats and *twin beds produce a guinea more than Shakespear, out goes Shakespear. **1940** GRAVES & HODGE *Long Week-End* xi. 181 Twin-beds replaced the old..double-bed for married couples. **1973** E.-J. BAHR *Nice Neighbourhood* i. 8, I pictured her..slipping into bed beside her husband... Of course, they may have had twin beds. **1937** G. FRANKAU *More of Us* xiii. 138 O happy nests (nest's best!) where Bob and Bill Sleep (sleep?) *twin-bedded by their spawn-glad spouses. **1960** *News Chron.* 27 July 4/3 The writer asked for the best twin-bedded room, with private bathroom. **1981** 'E. LATHEN' *Going for Gold* iii. 29 The twin-bedded cubicle. **1900** *Heal & Son Catal.: Guest's Room: Paris Exhib.* 4 *Twin bedsteads. Each 3 feet by 6 feet 6 inches. **1930** *Heal & Son Catal.: Matter of Taste in Furnit.* 17 Twin bedsteads in limed oak. **1939** in E. J. Nichols *Hist. Dict. Baseball Terminol.* (Ph.D. thesis, Pennsylvania State Coll.) 81 *Twin bill. **1974** *Anderson* (S. Carolina) *Independent* 19 Apr. 5B/1 Virginia's Cavaliers invade Clemson Friday afternoon for a 1:30 Atlantic Coast Conference twin-bill. **1865** SWINBURNE *Atalanta* 1261 Jason, and Dryas *twin-begot with war. **1836** MRS. TRAILL *Backw. Canada* xiv. 248 This plant is also called winter-green, or *twin-berry. **1868** *Rep. U.S. Comm. Agric.* (1869) 178 Among them [small fruits] may be noted red and black currants,..twin-berries [etc.]. **1807** COLERIDGE *To Wordsworth* 13 Of smiles spontaneous, and mysterious fear, The first-born they of Reason and *twin-birth. **1837** LOCKHART *Scott* xxv, The quarto of Rokeby was followed..by the small volume which had been designed for a twin-birth. **1850** MRS. JAMESON *Leg. Monast. Ord.* (1863) 227 The portentous twin-birth of the two great mendicant communities. **1912** KEITH *Human Body* viii. 113 Twins are common; in Ireland a twin birth has a frequency of one in seventy-two, in England about one in seventy-five. **1907** *Yesterday's Shopping* (1969) 219/2 A *twin-burner Stove, strongly recommended as a boiler and heater. **1974** *Country Life* 5 Dec. 1772/1 Refrigerator, twin-burner stove.. stainless-steel sink. **1967** *Autocar* 5 Oct. 47/1 New car called TC (for *Twin Carb.), retaining all the special equipment of the basic model. **1973** 'R. MACLEOD' *Burial in Portugal* v. 93 The Lancia had..a high compression alloy engine which sucked fuel through twin carburettors. **1856** *Rock Island* (Illinois) *Argus* 23 Apr., The church bells of the *twin-cities [*sc.* Rock Island, Ill. and Davenport, Iowa] rang out their joyous notes in honor of the achievement [*sc.* bridging the Mississippi]. **1883** *Harper's Mag.* June 73/2 The twin cities [*sc.* St. Paul and Minneapolis, Minn.]..emulate each other in metropolitan airs. **1912** J. SANDILANDS *Western Canad. Dict. & Phrase Bk.*, *Twin Cities*, when spoken of in Canada, usually refer to Port Arthur and Fort William, neighboring cities and ports in Ontario. **1949** *St. Paul Pioneer-Press* 12 Aug. 1/3 Fog and clouds gave the Twin Cities respite from the hot weather for a few hours Thursday morning. **1968** A. HAILEY *Airport* (1969) III. iii. 319 Detroit and Windsor, the twin cities straddling the [U.S.-Canada] border. **1973** *Guardian* 13 Apr. 10/5 Manchester..is what they, laughingly I trust, call the 'twin city' of Leningrad. **1980** *Quilt World* Sept./Oct. 28/3 A learning-packed three-day seminar..will be held at a camp on the shores of Silver Lake in the Twin Cities. **1846** T. CRADDOCK *Chemistry of Steam-Engine* 91 The loss..as that shown by the expansive curve, induced me to devise the arrangement I have designated the *Twin-Cylinder Engine. **1884** KNIGHT *Dict. Mech.* Suppl., Twin Cylinder Steam Engine. **1907** *Daily Chron.* 24 May 9/3 The International Motor Cycle Tourist Trophy Race... Twenty-two single-cylinder and seven twin-cylinder machines have been entered. **1960** *N.Y. Times* 25 Oct. 43/7 The new method, called the *twin double, requires a fan to pick four consecutive winners from the sixth through the ninth races. **1979** *Internat. Herald Tribune* 31 Oct. 23/4 There were seven more races, four more swingers, two daily doubles and a jackpot, or twin double, still to come. Plenty of chances to get well. **1931** *19th Cent.* Feb. 155 *Twin-engine Farman 'Goliath' seaplanes. **1916** *War Illustr.* 1 Jan. 474/1 The *twin-engined Caudron biplane. **1942** *R.A.F. Jrnl.* 27 June 1 The aircraft employed..were..twin-engined Handley-Page bombers. **1974** E. AMBLER *Dr. Frigo* III. 190 There was a small twin-engined plane waiting. **1860** DORA GREENWELL *Patience of Hope* 75 Two principles.. within contrariety, *twin-existent,..the desire for unity, and the..love of truth. **1878** GURNEY *Crystallogr.* 99 When the twin axis is perpendicular to a possible face this is called the *twin face. **1913** *Flight* 19 Apr. 436 (*caption*) One of the floats on the *twin-float Breguet. **1942** E. SARGENT *Every Boy's Bk. Aircraft* viii. 39 A good example of a military seaplane..is the Fairey Seafox... It has twin floats. **1977** G. R. DUVAL *World Float Planes* (*caption*), The Fairey Fly-catcher was the standard Fleet Air Arm fighter from 1923 to 1934... The land undercarriage was readily interchangeable with twin floats. **1980** P. LEWIS *Brit. Bomber since 1914* v. 204 During 1933 another Fairey twin-float biplane made its appearance as the Fox Mk. IVM. **1836** MRS. TRAILL *Backw. Canada* xiv. 238 The Americans call this honeysuckle '*twinflower'. **1845** S. JUDD *Margaret* I. xiv, Beds of purple twin-flower. **1776** WITHERING *Brit. Plants* (1796) II. 441 Ceratophyllum submersum... Leaves forked... Specimens from Paris had the leaves *twin-forked. **1931** *19th Cent.* Feb. 159 The *twin-fuselage Blériot 125 mono-plane. **1980** *Jane's Encycl. Aviation* II. 305/1 *Blackburn T.B. Twin* (*UK*), large twin-fuselage twin-engined seaplane designed to attack Zeppelin airships with incendiary steel darts. **1837** YOUATT *Sheep* xv. 508 Certain rams..have the credit of being *twin-getters. **1872** BROWNING *Fifine* xi, The *Twin-headed Babe, and Human Nondescript! **1906** G. G. COULTON *Pearl* 43 *Twin-hued topaz. **1946** *Jrnl. R. Aeronaut. Soc.* L. 348/1 It may therefore be possible to make more advanced explorations into the transonic region with similar *twin-jet installations. **1953** *Ann. Reg. 1952* 405 An English Electric Canberra B5 twin-jet bomber made history on 26 August by completing a double crossing of the Atlantic in a single day. **1961** E. BROWN *Wings on my Sleeve* 85 We had a standing date to go back to Grove and pick up the first of the Arado 234 B twin jets. **1895** *Pall Mall G.* 13 Nov. 2/3 If *twin-killing is more reprehensible than drunkenness. **1897** MARY KINGSLEY *W. Africa* 473 This twin-killing is a widely diffused custom among the Negro tribes. **13..** *Cursor M.* 512 (Cott.) Þat kyng of craft Wald mensked be wyth *tuinkyn scaft. *Ibid.* 27677 Þaa dedes þat man mai Vnderstand on tuin-kyn wai. **1945** J. F. H. THOMAS *Sheep* v. 93 When in-lamb ewes have a diet which is protein-adequate,..*twin lamb disease is never a serious cause of loss. **1974** *Country Life* 28 Mar. 740/1 Twin-lamb disease..is often fatal. **1895** STORY-MASKELYNE *Crystallogr.* vi. §162 The *twin-law..appears to permit of considerable divergence from precision in the relative orientation of the crystals subject to it. *Ibid.* vii. §281 The twin-laws governing the union of rhombohedral crystals. **1912** *Return Brit. Museum* 196 Quartz, group of twinned crystals (Japanese twin-law) from New Mexico. **1845–50** MRS. LINCOLN *Lect. Bot.* App. 115/2 *Twin-leaf. **1857** GRAY *First Less. Bot.* (1866) 133 In Jeffersonia or Twin-leaf. **1861** MISS PRATT *Flower. Pl.* V. 272 *Scilla bifolia* (*Twin-leaved Squill). **1894** *Country Gentlemen's Catal.* 158/3 Hand-Cameras... The 5 × 4 *Twin Lens Artist Magazine or dark slides—£15 15s. od. **1911** *Encycl. Brit.* XXI. 505/1 (*heading*) Twin-lens and reflex cameras. *Ibid.* 505/2 Stereoscopic cameras are another form of twin-lens cameras. **1977** J. HEDGECOE *Photographer's Handbk.* 19 The twin lens reflex design is much older than the SLR and was one of the most popular 'advanced' types of camera prior to World War II. **1862** *Catal. Internat. Exhib., Brit.* II. No. 6720, *Twin-light window, with tracery. **1599** NASHE *Lenten Stuffe* Wks. (Grosart) V. 226 A *twinlike image of it. **1631** BRATHWAIT *Whimzies, Ballad-monger* 18 It would doe a mans heart good to see how twinne-like hee and his songman couple. **1816** SOUTHEY *Poet's Pilgr.* Proem ix, The playmate of her infancy, Her twin-like comrade. **1614** SYLVESTER *Bethulia's Rescue* VI. 48 *Twin-nam'd Ister, and Seaven-mouthed Nile. **1820** BYRON *Mar. Fal.* I. ii. 574 Twin-named from the apostles John and Paul. **1957** *Nature* 5 Jan. 35/2 The '*twin paradox' is not even qualitatively discernible in any experiment that does not involve relative accelerations. **1982** W. R. RINDLER *Introd. Special Relativity* iii. 51 If the twins A and B, in the twin-paradox 'experiment'.., visually observe the regular ticking of each other's standard clocks, describe quantitatively what each sees as B travels to a distant point Q and back. **1904** W. M. RAMSAY *Lett. to Seven Ch.* xvii. 213 A large..part of ancient Ephesus..can be seen only by ascending to the top of the *twin-peaked Pion. **1855** *Twin-plane [see *twin-axis* above]. **1939** *Archit. Rev.* LXXXV. 104 *Twin-plate has arrived to supersede ordinary plate glass. **1962** *Gloss. Terms Glass Industry* (*B.S.I.*) 28 *Twin-plate process*, a process for making polished plate glass in which rolling, annealing and grinding are carried out on a continuously produced ribbon of glass without first cutting it into sections and in which top and bottom surfaces are ground simultaneously. **1875** KNIGHT *Dict. Mech.*, **Twin-power Press*, one in which the power is brought upon two objects in alternation, as in some machines where the punch and shears are in the same frame. **1930** T. DANTZIG *Number* iii. 49 It has been shown that the so-called *twin-primes, such as (3,5), (5,7),..(41,43), etc., become rarer and rarer as the numbers increase. **1981** *Sci. Amer.* Feb. 19/2 The largest pair of twin primes given in the December column has now been surpassed by an even larger pair discovered in 1980. **1835** URE *Philos. Manuf.* 118 The *twin-roller mechanism, which was perfected..by Arkwright. **1864** *Athenæum* 24 Sept. 410/3 Small *twin screw boats. **1884** *Health Exhib. Catal.* 94/1 Patent Twin-screw Bath Fittings. **1891** KIPLING *Light that Failed* vii. 123 'It's a steamer', he said,—'a twin-screw steamer, by the beat'. **1897** *Daily News* 17 Feb. 2/7 They had increased their staff of steamboats by adding the twin-screw Connemara. **1937** *New Yorker* 9 Jan. 62 Here you will find sweater classics—*twin sets of the conventional type. **1944** M. LASKI *Love on Supertax* iii. 35 I've got a Worth frock..I swopped ..for my cashmere twin-set. **1970** *Listener* 27 Aug. 289/2 Sophia Loren wandering in a tidy twinset across the USSR. **1850** S. DOBELL *Roman* vii, The foemen, Good and Ill, *twin-slumber in the womb of Fate. **1868** HELPS *Realmah* viii. (1869) 217 Her soul was a *twin-soul to his. **1927** WODEHOUSE *Meet Mr Mulliner* vi. 172 It seemed to him so plain a proof that they were twin souls that he decided to offer her his hand and heart without delay. *a* **1930** D. H. LAWRENCE *Mod. Lover* (1934) v. 37 You know, love isn't the twin-soul business. **1931** *Archivio Zool.* XV. 289 During his studies upon evolution the A. has been led to propose some neologisms that seemed to him useful and he reunites in this study, defining precisely the sense of them. Those neologisms are: statistic adaptation, homochromy, preadaptation, differentative death, differentative fecundity, *twin species. **1971** *Biol. Abstr.* LII. 11353/2 (*heading*) Study of 2 twin species of parasitic copepods. **1861** MISS PRATT *Flower. Pl.* VI. 133 *Twin-spiked Cord-grass. **1819** G. SAMOUELLE *Entomol. Compend.* 423 *Geometra quadrifasciaria.* The large *Twin-spot. —— *didymaria.* The Twin-spot Carpet. **1884** PHIN *Dict. Apiculture* 73 **Twin-stock*, a word that has been borrowed from the German. It signifies a hive containing two colonies. **1819** SAMOUELLE *Entomol. Compend.* 423 *Geometra costostrigata.* The *twin-striped Pinion. **1886** MRS. F. CADDY *Footsteps Jeanne D'Arc* 108 A *twin-towered church. **1955** *Harrogate Advertiser* 18 June 8/3 In the afternoon they met in the Council Chamber to discuss Le Monde Bilingue *Twin Town Scheme. **1976** *Southern Even. Echo* (Southampton) 2 Nov. 2/2 Wickham entertained 11 French visitors from their proposed twin town of Villers-Sur-Mer at the Kings Head. **1878** *Archæol. Cantiana* XII. 331 The port for London was the *twin-towned port of Rutupiae. **1916** *Chambers's Jrnl.* Dec. 829/1 The *twin-tired commercial vehicle. **1960** *Twin-track [see *Speed-walk* s.v. SPEED *sb.* 11 c]. **1983** *Listener* 13 Oct. 3/2 When the 'twin-track' approach to European nuclear weapons was devised by NATO (make preparations to deploy, but hold arms control talks at the same time) no one seems to have remembered Euclid's principle that parallel lines can never meet. **1962** *Which?* May 139/1 We carried out washing tests..in a *twin-tub washing machine. **1970** *New Scientist* 15 Oct. 134/1 An overnight soak and a wash (in a twin-tub), did remove some..stains. **1913** D. H. LAWRENCE *Love Poems & Others* 26 As if..the twin-walled darkness had bled In one great spasm of birth. **1904** *Windsor Mag.* Jan. 245/1 A *twin-wheeled machine like the tricycle. **1892** *Daily News* 26 May 6/5 The New Telephone Company... The new exchange will be on the *twin-wire or metallic circuit system.

Hence (*nonce-wds.*) **'twinfold** *a.*, twofold, with the two parts or elements in close connexion; **'twinhood**, **'twinism**, **'twinness** = TWINSHIP;

ˈ**twinity** [after *trinity*], a group of two in intimate union, two in one; ˈ**twinly** *a.*, characteristic of or befitting a twin (brother or sister).

1842 TENNYSON in *Mem.* (1897) I. viii. 200 Its [the heart's] *twinfold necessity, Capacious both of Friendship and of Love. **1871** BP. WILBERFORCE *Let.* in *Life* (1882) III. xiv. 387 That mystery of *twin-hood which seems to reach into the spirit world. **1796** BURNEY *Mem. Metastasio* III. 92 My fond *twinism has suggested to me, that you pass the chief part of your time in the open air. **1879** BARING-GOULD *Germany Past & Present* I. 201 [tr. Schiller] Herder and his wife..form together a sort of sacred *twinity. **1889** J. VEITCH *Knowing & Being* i. 22 This may be called a unity; it is rather, if we might invent a term suited to the new and marvellous conception,..an unparalleled and unbegotten twinity. **1796** BURNEY *Mem. Metastasio* III. 98 Accepting of your *twinly offer. *Ibid.* 259, I am, with usual twinly kindness, yours most faithfully. **1909** *Mod. Lang. Rev.* Jan. 197 The resemblance of the scheme of the play [*Twelfth Night*], with the wonderful likeness of Viola and Sebastian, to that of the *Comedy of Errors*, with the *twinness of the Antipholi.

twin, *v.*[1] *Obs.* exc. *Sc.* Forms: see prec.; cf. also TWINE *v.*[2] [ME. *twinnen*, f. TWIN *a.* or *sb.* For the development of the senses cf. TWIN *sb.* 4.]

1. *trans.* To put asunder (*properly* two things or persons, or one *from* the other); to separate, disjoin, disunite, sunder, sever, part, divide; †to deliver, set free; *fig.* to distinguish.

a **1225** *Ancr. R.* 254 Euerichon to dealed [*MS. T.* itwinned] from oðer. *c* **1230** *Hali Meid.* 13 Engel & meiden beon euening in uertu of meidenhades mihte þah eadinesse ham twinni 3ette & to-tweame. *a* **1300** *Cursor M.* 390 (Cott.) For to tuin dai fra night. *Ibid.* 7948 Þi hus..Sal neuer tuind [*v.rr.* tuinned, twynned] be fra suord. *Ibid.* 22912 Nan es ..þat can Tuin þat erth þat com o man Fra þat erth þat es bredd o best. *c* **1400** LOVE *Bonavent. Mirr.* (1907) 252 Our bodily felauschip is twynned, and now moste I nedes be departed fro the. *c* **1450** *St. Cuthbert* (Surtees) 6704 Twede fra scotlande bernyce twynnes. *c* **1460** *Towneley Myst.* i. 11 Oone god in persons thre, Which may neuer twynnyd be. *Ibid.* ii. 325 With cheke bon,..Shal I the and thi life twyn. *Ibid.* vii. 12 From hell he will theym twyn. **1513** DOUGLAS *Æneis* VI. vii. 11 From the sweit lyf twynnit vntymusly. **1637** [see 2 a]. **1686** G. STUART *Joco-Serious Disc.* 58 Then out he drew a gully knife With that he twinned me and my life. **1826-** in dial. glossaries (Chesh., Lanc., Northumb.). **1832** MOTHERWELL *Poems* 184 The waves and cruel wars hae twinn'd My winsome luve frae me. **1855** *Fraser's Mag.* LI. 95 Ah, my cruel cruel step-dame, who hath twinn'd our love for aye.

†**b.** To divide or share; to part with. *Obs. rare.*

c **1330** R. BRUNNE *Chron.* (1810) 86 þing þat a man wynnes, It is told purchase, whedir he it hold or tuynnes. **1790** SHIRREFS *Poems* 74 Narrow's the saul wha winna twin his gear To..help the poor!

c. To deprive *of*.

1722 RAMSAY *Three Bonnets* I. 180 His [Samson's] strength, O' which she twinn'd him at the length. *a* **1800** *Fine Flowers in Valley* in Child *Ballads* (1882) I. 220/1 She's taen out her little pen-knife, And twinnd the sweet babe o its life. **1887** SERVICE *Dr. Duguid* xvi. 103 It was just like the twinnin' him o' his vera life to part wi a plack.

2. *intr.* **a.** Of two persons or things: To go asunder; to separate, part.

a **1225** *Ancr. R.* 396 Leoue ureond beoð sorie hwon heo schulen twinnen. **1340** HAMPOLE *Pr. Consc.* 1823 When þe body and þe saule salle twyn. *c* **1410** *Master of Game* (MS. Digby 182) xxv, And or þei twynne þei moste acorde where þe metynge shall be on þe morowe. ? *a* **1500** *Chester Pl.* (E.E.T.S.) i. 271 Lightenes, darkenes, I byd yow twyn. **1567** *Gude & Godlie B.* (S.T.S.) 60 How suld we twin [*ed.* 1621 twine] that na man can depart? **1637** RUTHERFORD *Lett.* (1862) I. 209 We should never twin again, except heaven twinned and sundered us. **1790** *Scots Songs* I. 77 We twa will never twin.

†**b.** To depart, go away (also in weakened sense, to go, proceed); to escape, get free. *Obs.*

c **1375** *Sc. Leg. Saints* iv. (*Jacobus*) 375 Out of þis warld þat we ma twene But schame, det, or dedly syne. *c* **1386** CHAUCER *Prol.* 835 Now draweth cut er þat we ferrer twynne He which þat hath the shorteste shal bigynne. —— *Monk's T.* 15 O Lucifer..Now artow sathanas, þat mayst nat twynne Out of miserie, in which þat thou art falle. *c* **1400** LYDG. *Flour of Curtesye* 256 And if you liste I dyed, I wolde assente, As ever twinne I quik out of this lynde! *c* **1422** HOCCLEVE *Learn to Die* 183, I keepe nat þat y shal hennes twyne [*rime* synne]. *a* **1600** MONTGOMERIE *Devot. Poems* v. 22 Or thou be sommound by vncerten death,..Sen tym is precious tak it or 3e tuin.

†**c.** With *from*: To separate oneself from; to part from, take leave of; to depart from, leave, forsake, renounce. *Obs.*

a **1300** *Cursor M.* 23182 (Edin.) Fra þat dai forþe..Sal neuir fra bodi sauil tuin. *c* **1375** *Sc. Leg. Saints* xxxiv. (*Pelagia*) 182 Men but nombre..haf I Gert..fra god twyn. *c* **1386** CHAUCER *Pard. Prol.* 102 Yet kan I maken oother folk to twynne From Auarice. **1406** HOCCLEVE *Misrule* 42 Whan fro thee twynned shee. *c* **1430** LYDG. *Min. Poems* (Percy Soc.) 247 Thy feet embracyng fro whiche I shal nat twynne, Mercy requeryng. **1430-40** —— *Bochas* I. xiv. (MS. Bodl. 263) 62/1 Whan the sperit shal fro the bodi twynne.

d. With *with*: To part with; to take leave of; to deprive oneself of, give up.

a **1400-50** *Alexander* 2750 He..takis þam of his tresoure & twynnes with þaim faire. **1486** *Bk. St. Albans* E iij b, When he [the hare] is female and kyndelis hym with in In .iij. degrees he hem berith or he with hem twyn. **1591** R. BRUCE *Serm.* (Wodrow Soc.) 207 No heart..can twin with the thing that it loveth, without exceeding sorrow. **1629** SIR W. MURE *True Crucifixe* Introd. 38 As crucified to sinne Readie for Him, with each thing els to twinne Wee labour should. **1721** RAMSAY *Katy's Answer* iii, He's unco sweer To twin wi' his gear.

†**e.** To break asunder; to burst or cleave in twain. *Obs.*

c **1450** *Cov. Myst.* (Shaks. Soc.) 326 Myn herte with peyn is pressyd, For sorwe myn hert doth twynne. **1513** BRADSHAW *St. Werburge* II. 706 For whiche the citezens.. Were sore disconsolate, like for to twyn.

twin, *v.*[2] [f. TWIN *a.* and *sb.*]

1. a. *intr.* To bring forth two children or young at a birth; to bear twins.

1573 [see TWINNING *vbl. sb.*[2] 1]. **1587** HARRISON *England* III. i. in *Holinshed* I. 219/2 Kine..now and then twin. **1614** C. BROOKE *Eglogues* (1772) 99 Whiles thy rams do tup, thy ewes do twyn. **1659** HEYLIN *Examen Hist.* I. 108 The world had..never increased to such vast multitudes in so short a time, if Eve had not twinned at least at every birth. **1817** KEATINGE *Trav.* II. 187 The ewes of this country rarely twin. **1874** T. HARDY *Madding Crowd* xv. (1889) 111 Two more ewes have twinned.

b. *trans.* To conceive or bring forth as twins, or as a twin *with* another.

1607 [see TWINNED *ppl. a.* 1]. **1621** G. SANDYS *Ovid's Met.* IX. (1626) 176 From each seuer'd head Each of her hundred necks two fiercer bred: More strong by twinning heires. **1760-72** H. BROOKE *Fool of Qual.* (1809) IV. 138, I have.. a sister, twinned with me in the womb.

c. *intr.* in passive sense: To be born at the same birth *with*; to be the twin brother or sister of another. ? *Obs.*

1604 SHAKS. *Oth.* II. iii. 212 Though he had twinn'd with me, both at a birth. **1701** WATTS *Horæ Lyr.*, *Indian Philos.* ix, Might I but see That gentle nymph that twinn'd with me. **1790** *Bystander* 308 If a brother..who had twinned with him should dare [etc.].

2. a. *trans.* To couple, join, unite, combine (two things or persons) closely or intimately. *lit.* and *fig.* Also *spec.* to cause (towns) to be twinned (chiefly in *pass.*): see TWINNED *ppl. a.* 2 c.

c **1394** *P. Pl. Crede* 496 Here y touche þis two, twynnen hem I þenke. **1611** BIBLE *Exod.* xxvi. 24 They shall be coupled [*marg.* twinned] together beneath. **1616** B. JONSON *Masque Ld. Haddington* Wks. 941 That twins their hearts; and doth, of two, make one. **1667** MILTON *P.L.* XII. 85 True Libertie..alwayes with right Reason dwells Twinn'd, and from her hath no dividual being. **1725** W. HALFPENNY *Sound Building* 22 To form a Centre so, that the Mason.. shall twin their Arches thereon. **1847** TENNYSON *Princ.* I. 56 Still we moved Together, twinn'd as horse's ear and eye. **1957** *Harrogate Advertiser* 16 Mar. 13/5 Harrogate was the first town in the country to be twinned with a French town —Luchon. **1983** *Guardian Weekly* 6 Feb. 13/5 One thousand towns and villages from each country have been twinned.

b. *intr.* To be coupled; to join, combine, unite; to be parallel or equal, to agree. *spec.* Of a town or city: to become twinned *with* (another).

1621 [see TWINNING *ppl. a.*]. **1638** G. SANDYS *Paraphr. Div. Poems*, *Job* xxxvii. 48 O how inscrutable! his equitie Twins with his Power. **1652** BENLOWES *Theoph.* x. lxxvi, Wealth twins with fear. **1973** *Daily Tel.* 1 Feb. 1/4 Liverpool is to go ahead with a plan to 'twin' with the port of Haiphong in North Vietnam. **1977** *Cornish Times* 19 Aug. 15/5 Pleyber-Christ, the Breton town with which it is proposed that Lostwithiel should 'twin'.

c. *Cryst.* (*trans.*) To unite (two crystals) according to some definite law so as to form a twin crystal (see TWIN *sb.* 3 b). Only in passive, and in vbl. sb. (TWINNING *vbl. sb.*[2] 2).

1845 [see TWIN *sb.* 3 b]. **1883** *Encycl. Brit.* XVI. 363/2 Occasionally a simple form is twinned with a more complex one, as in chabasite. **1895** STORY-MASKELYNE *Crystallogr.* vii. §193 Crystals twinned on an octahedron-face. *Ibid.* §194 Two crystals twinned round an axis.

3. *trans.* To be, or furnish, a 'twin' or counterpart to; to match, parallel.

1605 *1st Pt. Ieronimo* II. ii. 14 A suit iust of Andreas cullers, Proportiond in all parts—nay, twins his own. **1869** *Good Words* 1 Mar. 176 Thou hast no mate To..twin those matchless heights. **1873** LOWELL *Graves Eng. Soldiers Concord* 32 O'erhead the balanced hen-hawk slides, Twinned in the river's heaven below.

4. *Agric.* To break up or clear (land) with a 'twin' (TWIN *sb.* 3 c). *local.*

1841 HARTSHORNE *Salopia Antiq.* Gloss., Twinning to tak away the scutch. **1859** *Jrnl. R. Agric. Soc.* XX. I. 217 Some of the turnip-soil, broken up and then 'twinned'.

twin-born, *a.* Born a twin or twins; born at the same birth, as two, or one of two. Usually *fig.*

1599 SHAKS. *Hen. V*, IV. i. 251 Let vs our Liues, our Soules,..our Sinnes, lay on the King:..O hard Condition, Twin-borne with Greatnesse. **1610** HEALEY *St. Aug. Citie of God* 122 Him that misliked the fellowship of his owne twin-borne brother. *c* **1647** MILTON *Sonnet* xii. 6 As when those Hinds..Raild at Latona's twin-born progenie. **1753** HANWAY *Trav.* (1762) I. III. xxx. 134 Ingratitude..is twin-born with pride. **1781** COWPER *Expost.* 634 Wisdom and Goodness are twin-born. **1855** BAILEY *Mystic*, etc. (ed. 2) 103 Twin-born passions.

twin-brother. (Now usu. as two words.) [TWIN *a.* 3.] A brother born at the same birth, as one of twins. Also *fig.* something closely related to or resembling the other thing mentioned.

1598 SHAKS. *Merry W.* II. i. 74 Heere's the twyn-brother of thy Letter: but let thine inherit first, for I protest mine neuer shall. **1727** SWIFT *Wonder of Wonders* Wks. 1755 II. II. 51 He hath..a twin-brother, who lives over against him. **1829** LYTTON *Devereux* I. iii, My twin brother, Gerald, was a tall, strong, handsome boy. **1850** TENNYSON *In Mem.* lxviii, Sleep, Death's twin-brother.

twinch, twinck(e, obs. forms of TWINK.

†**twind** (twaɪnd), *v. Obs.* Also **twinde, twynd**; *pa. t.* and *pple.* **twound.** [Variant of TWINE *v.*[1], perh. after the pa. t. and pple. *twined*, or by assimilation to WIND *v.*]

1. *trans.* To twist, twine, wind, turn.

1548 THOMAS *Ital. Dict.* (1550), *Imbarbugliare*, to tangle, twynde, encombre. *a* **1562** G. CAVENDISH *Poems*, etc. (1825) II. 93 The spyndells end alredy is at the ground, The thred ontwynned cannot more be twound. **1590** FENNE *Fruits* F fj, In token of her last farewell her head towards me she twound [*rime* bound]. **1606** MARSTON *Sophonisba* III. i, Syphax with his dagger twound about her haire, drags in Sophonisba. **1610** MARKHAM *Masterp.* II. clvii. 464 Take a tampin of horse haire twound together. **1616** SURFL. & MARKH. *Country Farme* 130 The Rider euer obseruing..to make the Colt goe straight forth-right, and by no meanes to turne or twynd him about anie way. *Ibid.* 154 When the Brambles begin to shoot forth, to interlace them and twynd them bought-wise about the blacke Thornes. **1659** TORRIANO, *Torcere*, to wrap, to twinde in [**1598** FLORIO, winde in].

2. *intr.* To become entangled or knotted; to twist, twine, wind.

1575 TURBERV. *Falconrie* 175 The falcon bating this way and that way she shall neuer twinde nor tangle bicause the ring followeth hir still. **1575** GASCOIGNE *Flowers*, *Dan Barth.* Tri. i. 19 The gentle slippe, which could both twist and twind. *c* **1626** W. BOSWORTH *Arcadius & Sepha* I. 955 She turn'd To Ivy, whence it still is twinding found.

3. Of an arrow: To part *from* the bow. *rare*[−1]. (Cf. TWINE *v.*[1] 7 b.)

1592 WYRLEY *Armorie*, *Ld. Chandos* 50 As the arrow from the bow doth twind [*rime* behind] He flieth towards the enimies field.

Hence ˈ**twinding** *vbl. sb.*, **twound** *ppl. a.*

1600 W. WATSON *Decacordon* (1602) 35 Their dissimulation,..sophistication, winding, twinding, and doubling. *Ibid.* 335 [The hawk] flew a foule flight in windings, twindings, and girdings ouer all. **1610** MARKHAM *Masterp.* II. xviii. 245 Hard new twound hemp. **1616** SURFL. & MARKH. *Country Farme* 663 The making of naues for waggons or cart-wheeles, for which..the more knottie and twound they are, a great deale the fitter they are for that purpose.

twindle (ˈtwɪnd(ə)l), *sb.* Now *dial.* Also 6 **twyndle, -del,** 9 **twinnel.** [app. for **twinnle*, dim. of TWIN *sb.*: see -LE. Cf. OHG. *zwinal*, *-el*, *zwenel* (adj.), twin.] = TWIN *sb.* 1.

1526 R. WHYTFORD *Martiloge* 45 A woman..with her two chylder twyndles. **1529** RASTELL *Pastyme* (1811) 12 Romulus and Remus, bredyrne and twyndels. **1642** in Collins *Kirkburton Regrs.* (1887) I. 237 Thomas and Elizabeth children of Thomas Hepworth beinge twindles. **1674** LOWE *Lanc. Diary* (1876) 43 Ffriday was buried a twindle of John Leyland...lordsday was buryed the other twindle of John Leylands. *a* **1800** PEGGE *Suppl. Grose*, *Twindles*, twins. Lanc. **1882** *Lanc. Gloss.*, *Twindles*, twins.

b. *attrib.* = TWIN *a.* 4 b.

1636 W. SAMPSON *Vow-Breaker* H ij, I dream'd my husband, when he came first a woing, cam i' the liknes of a Kentish twindle Pippen; that is, just as if two stones grew together.

Hence **twindle (twinnel)** *v.*, *intr.* to bring forth twins: = TWIN *v.*[2] 1.

1845 THORNBER *Penny Stone* (1886) 14 Mother Cowburne has twinnelled.

twindle (ˈtwɪnd(ə)l), *v.*[2] *intr. nonce-wd.* Used by G. M. Hopkins: prob. a blend of TWIST *v.* and DWINDLE *v.*

1881 G. M. HOPKINS *Poems* (1967) 89 A windpuff-bonnet of fáwn-fróth Turns and twindles over the broth Of a pool so pitchblack, féll-frówning.

twine (twaɪn), *sb.*[1] (*a.*) Forms: 1 **tuiȝin, tuuin, tuin,** 1–3 **twin,** 4–5, (7) **twyn,** 4–7 **twyne,** (5 **tuyne,** 6 **twhyne, twind),** 6– **twine.** [OE. *twín* (also early *twiȝin*) = Du. and Flem. *twijn* (in Kilian also *tweyn*), related to TWINE *v.*[1], and ultimately from the stem of TWI-. Cf. ON. and Icel. *tvinni* (Norw. dial. *tvinne*, Da. *tvinde*, dial. *twin*, *twen*, NFris. *twin*), Du. *tweern*, MLG. *twern*, MHG. and G. *zwirn* in the same sense.]

1. Thread or string composed of two or more yarns or strands twisted together; now *spec.* string or strong thread, made of hemp, cotton, or other fibre, used for sewing coarse materials (as canvas or sacking), tying packages, netting, and the like; with *a* and *pl.* a piece or kind of this.

In OE. found only as a rendering of L. *byssus*, *bissus*, prob. through association of this with *bis* twice. In mod. English use chiefly technical or commercial, but in Scotland and U.S. common as a general synonym of *string*.

c **725** *Corpus Gloss.* (O.E.T.) 343 *Byssum*, tuin. *a* **800** *Erfurt Gloss.* 138 *Byssum*, tuiȝin. *c* **897** K. ÆLFRED *Gregory's Past. C.* xiv. 83 Ðæt hræȝl..of twispunnenum twine linenum. *Ibid.* 87 Ðæt scyle beon twiðræwen twin on ðæm masseȝierelan. *c* **1000** *Ags. Gosp.* Luke xvi. 19 He wæs ȝescrydd mid purpuran & mid twine. *c* **1205** LAY. 14220 Nes þe þwong noht swiðe bræd, Buten swulc a twines þræd. *c* **1385** CHAUCER *L.G.W.* 2016 (*Ariadne*), By a clewe of twyn [*v.r.* twyne] as he hath gon..he may returne a-non. **14..** HOCCLEVE *Ad beatam Virginem* 71 His sotil snares, and cacchynge twyn. *c* **1425** tr. *Arderne's Treat. Fistula* 23 A fourfold þrede of silk white or of strong lyne or tuyne. **1481-90** *Howard Househ. Bks.* (Roxb.) 63 Paid for marlyn twyn xvj. d. *c* **1500** *New Not-br. Mayd* 297 in Hazl. *E.P.P.* II. 284 Shetis clene, to lye betwene, made of thred and twyne. **1512-13** *Durham Acc. Rolls* (Surtees) 106 Pro vj li. lez sayll twyne..xviij[d]. **1592** R. D. *Hypnerotom.* 17 b, A spindle ful of twind. **1614** GORGES *Lucan* VIII. 346 A twine,

That strangle may this throate of mine. **1692** *Capt. Smith's Seaman's Gram.* II. xxxi. 150 The Cases..must be Armed about with strong Twine or Cord. **1719** De Foe *Crusoe* (Globe) 20 A Parcel of Twine or Thread. *Ibid.* 578 We had Twine or Packthread. **1791** Cowper *Odyss.* x. 30 The winds,..so bound With silver twine that not a breath escaped. **1806–7** J. Beresford *Miseries Hum. Life* (1826) III. xii, No garters, except twine, which you are at last obliged to use. **1827** D. Johnson *Ind. Field Sports* 42 To these cords a small twine or silk thread is fixed. **1862** *Catal. Internat. Exhib., Brit.* II. No. 3659, Cotton twines run 30 per cent. longer length than hemp, same weight. **1867** Smyth *Sailor's Word-bk.* s.v., Irish twine or thumb-line, like nettles, is worked by the fingers from fine yarns drawn from bolt-rope. **1871** C. Gibbon *Lack of Gold* vi, He had a bundle of twine between his teeth.

b. *transf.* and *fig.* in various applications.

1557 *Tottell's Misc.* (Arb.) 165 Of her vntrue professed loue so feble is the twine. **1567** Drant *Horace, Epistles* II. i. G vij, Our toyle..in making of our poems..By drawing them so featly forth and with so cleane a twyne. **1595** Markham *Sir R. Grinvile* cxxiii, Behold a goddesse shall my lifes twine breake. **1614** Sylvester *Bethulia's Rescue* II. 279 That sacred Twine Which Man to Man, and Man to God doth joyn. **1615** Hieron *Wks.* I. 595 An holy twine, artificially made vp..of three seuerall threeds..for the fastning of the soule of a Christian to his God. **1667** Dryden *Secret Love* III. i, Destiny..Spinn's all their fortunes in a silken twine. **1728–46** Thomson *Spring* 210 The dissolving clouds Form..thy showery prism; And..unfold The various twine of light. *a* **1763** Shenstone *Elegies* xviii. 58 Rob'd in the Gallic loom's extraneous twine. **1895** Crockett *Men of Moss-Hags* xxv. 187 It liketh us to go to our King's court through the crash of battle rather than through the hank of the hangman's twine.

2. A twined or twisted object or part. **a.** A twining or trailing stem or spray of a plant.

1579 Spenser *Sheph. Cal.* Oct. 111 My temples..girt in girlonds of wild Yuie twine. **1590** —— *F.Q.* I. vi. 14 With an yuie twine his waste is girt about. **1652** Culpepper *Eng. Physic.* 35 The root..with many long twines or branches growing from it. *a* **1678** Marvell *Appleton Ho.* 609 Bind me, ye woodbines, in your 'twines. **1908** *Blackw. Mag.* Oct. 536 Golden clusters from the twine depend.

b. A fold; a coil; a convolution; a twist or turn in the course of anything.

1600 Fairfax *Tasso* XVIII. c, That glorious ensigne, with a thousand twines. **1629** Milton *Nativity* 226 Typhon huge ending in snaky twine. **1649** G. Daniel *Trinarch.* To Rdr. 191 A trayterous spider in the Twine Of her owne Thred. **1814** Scott *Ld. of Isles* VI. xiii, A diadem of gold..And clasp'd within its glittering twine Was seen the glove of Argentine. **1870** E. Peacock *Ralf Skirl.* I. 22 As full of twines as a sheep-track.

c. A tangle, knot, snarl. In quots. *fig.*

1865 J. Thomson *Art* I. i, Such subtle knots and twines! **1869** Browning *Ring & Bk.* VIII. 778 So multiplied were reasons *pro* and *con*, Delicate, intertwisted and obscure, That Law refused loan of a finger-tip To unravel, re-adjust the hopeless twine.

3. The action or an act of twining. **a.** An embrace, a clasping. Now *rare* or *Obs.*

1602 Marston *Antonio's Rev.* I. iv. Wks. 1856 I. 84 Clipping the strumpet with luxurious twines. **1607** Beaumont *Woman Hater* II. i, The twyns of Adders, and of Scorpions..will seem to me More tickling than those claspes, which men adore. **1697** Dryden *Virg. Georg.* II. 301 Aspiring Vines, Embracing Husband Elms in am'rous twines. **1759** W. Mason *Caractacus* Poems 1830 II. 78 In undulating twine, The foaming snakes prolific join. *a* **1839** L. E. Landon *Poems* (1844) I. 34 The lattice..Half hidden by a bridal twine Of jasmine with the emerald vine.

b. *poet.* in various applications: see quots.

1615 Chapman *Odyss.* x. 306 As she some web wrought; or her spindles twine She cherisht with her song. **1652** J. Ramsey in *Fletcher's Wild Goose Chase* Pref. Verses a ij, Till to his watry Center he [*sc.* the river] hath got By wrigling twines, subtile as Fletcher's plot. **1880** Browning *Dram. Idyls, Pan & Luna* 51 Vain each twist and twine Those lithe limbs try.

c. A turn of fortune, a vicissitude.

1768 Ross *Helenore* III. 124 A' that's past By unko twines, has fa'en sae well.

†**4.** as *adj.* Made by twining or twisting; twisted; spun. *Obs. rare.* (See also twine thread.)

1513 Douglas *Æneis* IV. x. 102 The god..biddis smyte the twyne cabill in tuay. **1583** *Durham Wills* (Surtees) II. 78, ij paire of twine roppes.

†**b.** Of a line: Forming a spiral; helical. *Obs. rare*$^{-1}$.

1551 Recorde *Pathw. Knowl.* I. Defin., A twine or twist line..goeth as a wreyth about some other bodie.

5. *attrib.* and *Comb.*, as ***twine-ball*** (ball *sb.*[1] 10 c), ***-box, colour, -cord, -maker, net, netting, -reel, -tone***; ***twine-coloured, -like, -toned*** adjs.; ***twine-making, -twisting*** adjs. and sbs.; also **twine-binder**, a binder which ties the sheaves with twine (cf. *wire-binder*); so **twine-binding** *a.*; **twine-bush**, an Australian shrub, *Hakea flexilis*, N.O. *Proteaceæ* (*Cent. Dict.* 1889, s.v. *Hakea*); **twine cloth**, fine cotton shirting, calico; **twine-cutter**: see quot.; **twine-grass**, the Tufted Vetch (*Vicia Cracca*), or the Hairy Vetch (*V. hirsuta*); **twine-holder, twine-machine**, †**twine-masking** [cf. mask *sb.*[1]], **twine-reeler**: see quots.; **twine-spinner**, one who spins twine; so **twine-spinning**; **twine-wheel**, in a spinning-machine, a wheel through which the twisting motion is given. See also twine thread.

1889 *Pall Mall G.* 26 Dec. 5/3 Freethinkers who imagine themselves able to sound with their penny *twine-balls the ocean of immensity. **1902** *Sci. Amer. Supp.* 20 Dec. 22546/3 A practical *twine binder. *Ibid.*, He established *twine binding machines as the grain harvesters of the time. **1907** *Westm. Gaz.* 1 Aug. 2/1 In the tinsmiths' shop..*twine-boxes, boxes for stamping-pads, and similar articles, are turned out. **1815** *Roy. Milit. Chron.* June Advt., The New Imperial *Twine Cloth..for family use and for Sheeting. **1882** *Daily News* 3 June 3/1 Lace in the prevalent *twine colour. **1897** *Westm. Gaz.* 25 Mar. 3/2 Nile green and *twine-coloured lace. **1712** Steele *Spect.* No. 444 ¶4 A *Twine-Cord, strained with two Nails at each End, over his Window. **1862** *Catal. Internat. Exhib., Brit.* II. No. 3800 Twine cord and line. **1875** Knight *Dict. Mech.*, **Twine-cutter*, a blade or knife on a table, stand, or counter, to cut twine when tying packages. **1744–50** W. Ellis *Mod. Husbandm.* VI. II. 48 (E.D.S.) Wild thetch or *twine-grass. **1875** Knight *Dict. Mech.*, **Twine-holder*, a box or case to hold a ball of twine on a counter. **1817** Coleridge *Biog. Lit.* 82 Lank, black, *twine-like hair. **1875** Knight *Dict. Mech.*, **Twine-machine*, a spinning-machine for small hempen or cotton string. **1815** Simond *Tour Gt. Brit.* II. 79 A number of *twine-makers. **1904** *Daily News* 18 May 5 At eleven I started *twine-making. **1615** E. S. *Britain's Buss* B iij, The 7 deepinges of each net are to be sowed, each to other, altogether, with a small thred called, *Twine Masking. **1855** *Poultry Chron.* II. 574 One tarred *Twine Net, 9 feet long, by 9 wide. **1854** *Ibid.* I. 228 New *twine netting..one yard wide, 1½d. per yard. **1858** Simmonds *Dict. Trade*, **Twine-reel*, a shop reel or box for holding string. *Ibid.*, **Twine-reeler*, a mule-doubler; a string-twister. **1723** *Lond. Gaz.* No. 6128/4 Foulk Wyatt,..*Twine-spinner or Ropemaker. **1896** *Daily News* 14 Nov. 7/6 A retired twine spinner. **1808** *Pict. London* 235 Rope-making and *twine-spinning. **1900** *Westm. Gaz.* 22 Mar. 3/1 *Twine-toned lawn... To get that *twine-tone,..one must either tint one's white collar with tea or coffee or [etc.]. **1897** *Daily News* 1 June 1/1 *Twine twisting and polishing mills for making the yarns into twines and thread. **1884** W. S. B. McLaren *Spinning* viii. 159 The driving power comes..through all the *twine wheels, to the front roller.

Hence **'twineless** *a.*, destitute of twine.

1909 A. Reid *Kirriemuir* ii. 12 They were the laddies' 'strings' in an almost twineless age.

†**twine**, *sb.*[2] *Obs. nonce-wd.* [app. f. twi- after trine (cf. *twinity*, s.v. twin *a.* and *sb.*).] Division, separation, disunion.

1606 Sylvester *Du Bartas* II. iv. II. *Magnif.* 1338 Th' Vnity dwels in God, i' th' Fiend the Twine.

†**twine**, app. an error for tunny.

The form is prob. due to mere copying of a misprint.

1601 Chester *Love's M.* (1878) 100 Here swimmes the Shad..The Twine, the Trout, the Scallop, and the Whiting. [Cf. 1589 Rider *Bibl. Schol.* 1724 A fish called a Twinne..*Pelamys*; *ed.* 1617 II. Thinnie; *ed.* 1640 Thunny.]

twine (twaɪn), *v.*[1] Forms: 4–7 **twyne**, 4 (9 *dial.*) **tweyne**, 4–5 **twyn**, 6 *Sc.* **tuyn**, 6– **twine**. *Pa. t.* and *pple.* **twined**; also *pa. t.* 6 *Sc.* **twane**; *pa. pple.* 4 **twynnen**, 6 **twon**, 7 **twone**. See also twind *v.* [ME. *twīnen*, = WFris. *twine*, *twynje*, Du. *twijnen* (in Kilian also *tweynen*), related to twine *sb.*[1] Cf. Icel., Norw., Sw. *tvinna*, Da. *tvinde* (NFris. *twinne*, etc.), and Du. *tweernen*, MLG. *twernen*, MHG. and G. *zwirnen* (OHG. *zwirnên*), to twist (thread).]

I. *trans.* **1.** To twist (two or more strands or filaments) together so as to form a thread or cord; to twist (one thread, etc.) *with* another; to form (thread or cord) by twisting or spinning; to spin (yarn, etc.) into thread or cord; also generally, to combine or make compact by twisting.

c **1275** Lay. 14220 Nas þe þwang noht brod Bote ase hit were a twined þred [*c* 1205 a twines þræd]. **13..** *Gaw. & Gr. Knt.* 191 Þe tayl & his toppyng [were] twynnen of a sute & bounden boþe wyth a bande. **1377** Langl. *P. Pl.* B. XVII. 204 To a torche or a tapre þe trinitee is lykned; As wex and a weke were twyned [*v.rr.* tweyned, twynnyd] togideres. **14..** *Tundale's Vis.* (Wagner) 1885 The cordes..were alle wyth silver twynned [*rime* shynned]. **1447** Bokenham *Seyntys* (Roxb.) 8 My fatal threed..Wych lachesys hath twynyd ful yerys fyfty. *c* **1470** Henryson *Mor. Fab.* VIII. (*Preach. Swallow*) xxx, His wyfe it span, and twynit [*Bann. MS.* twane] it in to threid. **1523** Fitzherb. *Husb.* §25 Make a lyttell rope..and twyne it as harde together bytwen your handes as ye canne, and soo beynge hard twon,..cut it. **1599** Hakluyt *Voy.* II. II. 91 They..do curiously keame their dainty locks..and, hauing twined and bound them vp, they couer them with calles. **1681** in *New Mills Cloth Manuf.* (S.H.S.) Introd. 86 [Wool] to be carded spunn twisted and twyned for listing to the cloaths made. **1697** Dryden *Virg. Georg.* I. 357 Let him..twine The Sallow Twigs to tye the stragling Vine. **1803** R. Anderson *Cumberld. Ball.* 55, I mind..at her wheel, How she'd tweyne the slow thread. **1855** Kingsley *Westw. Ho!* xxv, We'll twine a double strong halter for the Captain. **1899** Rider Haggard *Swallow* xi, To twine little threads into a rope.

b. *fig.*

14.. *Beryn* 686 Þe Nyȝtyngale, His amerous notis, lo, how he twyneth smale! [Cf. out-twine *v.*, quot. *a* 1400]. **1430–40** Lydg. *Bochas* I. xi. (MS. Bodl. 263) 52/2 Whan Antropos our lyuys threed hath twyned. **1612** *Two Noble K.* II. ii. 70 Our fortunes Were twyn'd together. **1651** N. Bacon *Disc. Govt. Eng.* II. xxvii. (1739) 128 By Oath, which to make sure, was treble twined. **1670** Dryden *1st Pt. Conq. Granada* IV. ii, My clue of Life is twin'd with Ozmyn's Thred. **1827** Scott *Highl. Widow* i, If I persisted in twisting the discourse one way while Donald was twining it another, I should make his objection, like a hempen-cord,..the tougher. **1833** Lamb *Elia* Ser. II. Pref. (1865) 236 To imply and twine with his own identity the griefs and affections of another. **1871** R. H. Hutton *Ess.* (1877) I. 77 So closely twined are the threads of human faith and scepticism.

c. *transf.* To form by interlacing; to weave, to wreathe.

1612 Drayton *Poly-olb.* XV. 139 The Naiads..some dainty Chaplets twine. **1697** Dryden *Virg. Æneid* VIII. 365 A double wreath Evander twin'd. **1709** Prior *Love & Friendship* 51 I'll twine fresh Garlands for Alexis' Brows. **1817** Moore *Lalla R.* (1824) 311 Oh! twine that wreath for me tonight. **1858** W. T. Matson *Armiger* iv. Poems 59 Mourning garlands twined of many a bloom Of doleful hue.

d. *transf.* To interlace, entwine.

1679 S. Lee in *Row's 'Emmanuel'* Pref., Pray for the mantle..of Elijah, for the love of John, and the zeal of Paul, to twine hands together. *a* **1701** Maundrell *Journ. Jerus., Euphrates* (1732) 2 Two Syrens..twining their fishy Tails together. **1870** Mrs. Riddell *Austin Friars* ii, She only sat still, with her fingers twined together. **1880** *Blackw. Mag.* Feb. 218 Reata..sat twining her fingers together in silence.

2. To cause (one thing) to encircle or embrace another; to twist, wreathe, clasp, or wrap (a thing) *about* or *around* another; also, to insert (one thing) *in* or *into* another with a twisting or sinuous movement (also *fig.*).

c **1585** Montgomerie *Sonn.* viii. 9 About his temple tuyn ȝour laurell leivis with palmis perfytly plet. **1602** Marston *Antonio's Rev.* II. i. Wks. 1856 I. 89, I have but newly twone my arme in the curld locks Of snakie vengeance. **1607** Shaks. *Cor.* IV. v. 112 Let me twine Mine armes about that body. **1613** Purchas *Pilgrimage* (1614) 513 In many places he insinuates himselfe within the Land by Gulfes or Bayes, twining his louing armes about some whole countries. **1617** Moryson *Itin.* I. 239 Long bracelets of peeces of gold twined about his arme. **1789** E. Darwin *Bot. Gard., Loves Plants* II. 180 Round the white circlet in relievo bold, A Serpent twines his scaly length. **1820** W. Irving *Sketch Bk.* I. 38 (*The Wife*) The vine, which has long twined its graceful foliage about the oak. **1838** Sparks *Biog.* IX. 27 The only garment they possess is a blanket elegantly twined about them. **1853** Rock *Ch. of Fathers* III. II. 25 'Tropes'..twined and threaded into the words of the daily service. **1862** Miss Braddon *Lady Audley* xxxii, My lady twined her fingers in her amber curls. **1890** R. Bridges *Shorter Poems* (1912) 298, I feel thy being twine Her graces over me. **1901** Alldridge *Sherbro* xxi. 220 The stem [of the pipe]..formed separately by twining a strip of clay round a thin stick of palm cane.

b. *refl.*

1543 Traheron *Vigo's Chirurg.* Interpr., *Vitis alba*.. twyneth it self aboute brambles, wyth hys tendrelles, as a vine byndeth it selfe to trees. **1662** J. Davies tr. *Olearius' Voy. Ambass.* 10 One end of the rope..twin'd itself about one of the Rocks. **1796** Morse *Amer. Geog.* I. 220 They [Snakes] have sometimes twined themselves round the bodies of children, squeezing them till they die. **1823** Lamb *Elia* Ser. I. *Poor Relations*, Awful ideas..twined themselves about his presence. **1852** Robertson *Serm.* Ser. III. xvii. 216 Round which the heart's best affections have twined themselves.

3. To enfold, wreathe, or encircle (one thing) *with* another; also of a plant, wreath, etc.: to clasp, encircle, enwrap. Also *fig.*

1602 Marston *Antonio's Rev.* III. iii. Wks. 1856 I. 111 Maist thou be twined with the softst embrace Of clere eternitie. **1712–14** Pope *Rape Lock* III. 161 Let wreaths of triumph now my temples twine. **1790** W. Wrighte *Grotesque Archit.* 3 Branches of trees twined round with ivy. **1819** Wiffen *Aonian Hours* (1820) 102 The weed of ruin darkly twines Her marble walls. **1848** Lytton *Harold* I. i, Boys, with their May-gads (peeled willow wands twined with cowslips). **1876** Lowell *Among my Bks.* Ser. II. 127 Twining the bare stem of old tradition with graceful sentiment.

4. a. To turn (something) *about*, *away*, *round*, etc.; to twist or wring. Now *dial.*

1598 B. Jonson *Ev. Man in Hum.* I. v, O, twine your body more about, that you may fall to a more sweet, comely, gentleman-like guard. **1600** Fairfax *Tasso* XVII. lvii, From the waste shore their steps at last they twinde. *Ibid.* XX. cxxviii, She shrikes, and twines away her sdeignefull eies, From his sweete face. *a* **1655** J. Naylor *Answ. Perfect Pharisee* 12 You wrest and twine the Scriptures. **1901** F. E. Taylor *Folk-Speech S. Lanc.* s.v. (E.D.D.), Iv aw catch him, aw'll twoine his neck reawnd.

b. To get *off*, or *out*, by twisting. Now *dial.*

1600 Fairfax *Tasso* XI. xliii, He..from the wound the reed out twinde, But left the iron in his flesh behinde. **1705** S. Wesley in Quiller Couch *Hetty Wesley* (1913) I. ix. 87 The iron latch of my door was twined off. **1885** *Ballads & Poems Glasgow Club* 213 Twine out his lugs, root out his tongue.

II. *intr.* **5.** To wind or twist (*about*, *over*, or *round* something); almost always of a plant: to grow in a twisting or spiral manner; *spec.* to become twisted or wreathed together in growing; to grow in spiral convolutions. Also *fig.*

13.. *E.E. Allit. P.* B. 1691 Faxe fyltered,..þat schad fro his schulderes..& twenty-folde twynande hit to his tos raȝt. **1567** Maplet *Gr. Forest* 64 b, It [woodbine] twineth like a threede or line, about other herbes and fruits. **1592** Shaks. *Ven. & Ad.* 873 Some [bushes] twin'd about her thigh to make her stay. **1647** Crashaw *Panegyr. Dk. York's Birth* 38 For whose manly brow Both laurels twine into one wreath. *a* **1652** J. Smith *Sel. Disc.* i. 7 Like the wanton ivy..it will twine about our judgments and understandings. **1697** Dryden *Virg. Past.* VIII. 17 Amidst thy Laurels let this Ivy twine. *a* **1748** Thomson *Happy Man* 9 For whom the cooling shade in summer twines. **1810** Scott *Lady of L.* I. xxvi, Where Ellen's hand had taught to twine The ivy and Idæan vine. **1831** James *Phil. Augustus* I. ii, A thousand shrubs and flowers twined..over them. **1875** McLaren *Serm.* Ser. II. viii. 136 His heart and will twined..round the fragments. **1875** Bennett & Dyer *Sachs' Bot.* 772 Only a few plants twine to the right..the greater number twine to the left. **1879** Tennyson *Lover's T.* I. 128 The light soul twines and mingles with the growths Of vigorous early days.

†**b.** To become entangled or complicated. *Obs. rare.*

1658 OSBORN *Adv. Son* Wks. (1673) 220 Whilst one is unraveling, another twines.

†**6. a.** Of a weapon: To twist or turn aside. *Obs.*

c **1400** *Rowland & Otuel* 557 þe Sarazene.. hit hym on þe hede.. And nere þe swerde twynede hade, His life þer hade he lefede.

†**b.** Of timber: To be contorted or irregular in formation. *Obs. rare.*

1601 HOLLAND *Pliny* XVI. xxxviii. I. 486 If a man lay his eare close to one end of a beame or peece of timber, he shall heare the knocke or pricke that is made but with a penknife at the other end... By this meanes also a man shall find when the timber doth twine. *Ibid.* XVI. xl. 490 Because it twineth and casteth not, it is passing good for hinges and hookes, for sawne bords, for ledges in dores and gates.

7. To extend or proceed in a winding manner; to bend, incline circuitously; to wind about, meander; of a serpent, etc., to crawl sinuously (also *refl.*).

1553 [see TWINING *vbl. sb.*]. **1601** HOLLAND *Pliny* VI. xvii. I. 124 Streight forth, as farre as to that place where India beginneth to twine and bend toward the Indian sea. **1610** HOLLAND *Camden's Brit., Irel.* II. 117 The shore, as it twineth backe from hence Southerly. **1674** JOSSELYN *Voy. New Eng.* 2 The 28th we twined into the Downs. *c* **1710** CELIA FIENNES *Diary* (1888) 291 The river runns twineing about. *a* **1774** TUCKER *Lt. Nat.* (1834) II. 464, I have been forced to twist and twine over a great deal more ground than had otherwise been needful. **1831** SCOTT *Ct. Robt.* ix, The snake.. twines himself through the grass. **1857** GOSSE *Omphalos* ii. 40 Sea-worms twined over the mud. **1902** BUCHAN *Watcher by Threshold* 267 The little brown river.. twined to the sea. **1913** *Daily News* 28 Mar. 6 A highway.. twining through a wilderness.

†**b.** To turn away. *Obs. rare.*

1600 FAIRFAX *Tasso* XVIII. xxxiii, But yet the knight, wise, warie, not vnkind, Drew foorth his sword and from her carelesse twind. **1614** W. BROWNE *Shepherd's Pipe* B vj b, He twyned thence, and home to his countree.

†**c.** To bend, bow, or sink *down.* *Obs.*$^{-1}$

1600 FAIRFAX *Tasso* XX. xliii, Right on the front he gaue that Ladie kinde A blow, so huge,.. That out of sense and feeling, downe she twinde.

8. To contort the body; to writhe, wriggle, squirm. Now *dial.*

1666 BUNYAN *Grace Abounding* § 166 Thus did I wind, and twine, and shrink under the burthen that was upon me. **1680** V. ALSOP *Mischief Impos.* iii. 19 When men are pincht with plain Scripture, they use to twist and twine and turn themselves into all shapes to get out of their streights. **1734** tr. *Rollin's Anc. Hist.* (1827) I. 75 The antagonists tumbling and twining with each other. **1837** MRS. PALMER *Devonshire Dial.* II. 17 I'd twack thee till I made thee twine like an angletwitch. **1877** MRS. M. TROTTER *Gall. Gossip* 290 The wean twining and kicking.

twine, *v.*[2] *Sc.* [Later form of TWIN *v.*[1], prob. by misunderstanding of ambiguous spellings under the influence of TWINE *v.*[1]] *intr.* and *trans.* To separate, part, etc.; = TWIN *v.*[1] in various uses.

It is doubtful whether an inf. *twyne* is to be assumed for the ME. examples of the pa. t. *twynde* cited below; in other cases the form is shown by rimes or other evidence to be a mere variant of TWIN *v.*[1] The spelling *twin'd* is ambiguous, and may represent either *twined* or *twinned.*

[*c* **1450** *St. Cuthbert* (Surtees) 6305 In partyes he it twynde, ȝit sulde he.. within a while Aboute his nek it fynde. *a* **1500** *New Nut-brown Maid* 303 in Hazlitt *E.P.P.* III. 13 And I am twynde Out of his mynde, Ryght as a banysshed man.]

1621 [see quot. 1567 s.v. TWIN *v.*[1] 2 a]. **1728** RAMSAY *Robt., Richy, & Sandy* 57 Twin'd of its nourishment it lifeless lay. **1795** BURNS *Destr. Woods Drumlanrig* v, What ruefu' chance Has twin'd ye o' your stately trees? ? *a* **1800** *Bob Norice* vi. in Child *Ballads* (1886) II. 267/2 To twyne him o his wife. **1886** STEVENSON *Kidnapped* xviii, 'You and me must twine', I said... 'I will hardly twine from ye, David, without some kind of reason for the same', said Alan. **1894** R. REID in *Poets of Dumfriesshire* x. (1910) 303 Cauld maun his heart be, twined o' its joys. **1895** CROCKETT *Men of Moss-Hags* 31 What cause is guid that twines a woman frae her ain man?

twined (twaɪnd), *ppl. a.* [f. TWINE *v.*[1] + -ED[1].] That has been twined, in various senses of the verb; twisted, plaited, curled, coiled, wreathed, etc.

c **1275** [see TWINE *v.*[1] I]. **1510** STANBRIDGE *Vocabula* (W. de W.) C ij, *Filum contortum*, twyned threde. **1513** DOUGLAS *Æneis* VII. vii. 88 The round top of tre, Hit with the twynit quhyp, dois quherle. **1535** COVERDALE *Judg.* xvi. 9 He brake the roapes in sunder, euen as a twyned threde breaketh, when it hath catched the heate of the fyre. **1539** BIBLE (Great) *Exod.* xxvi. 36 An hangynge.. of yelow sylke, purple, scarlet, & white twined silk. **1565** JEWEL *Repl. Harding* (1611) 66 The substance of all that he hath alleged hitherto, hangeth only by a twined thread. **1568** *Satir. Poems Reform.* xlviii. 35 Off all thir thre hewis I haif left clewis,.. Tuynit and small. **1576** FLEMING *Panopl. Epist.* 310 One hanges himselfe.. with a twyned haulter. **1611** COTGR., *Espée Romaine*, certaine twined, and retorted haires on a horse;.. by some called, a feather. **1668** CULPEPPER & COLE *Barthol. Anat.* I. xi. 25 [It] spreds it self upon the Colon like a twined worm. **1799** *Hull Advertiser* 23 Feb. 3/2, 500 millfuls of twined yarn. **1851** MRS. BROWNING *Casa Guidi Wind.* II. 509 Priestcraft burns out, the twinèd linen blazes. **1900** CROCKETT *Black Douglas* I The twined May-pole had not yet been taken down.

twiner ('twaɪnə(r)). [f. TWINE *v.*[1] + -ER[1].]

1. One who or that which twines; *esp.* one who or a machine which twines or spins thread: see quot. 1891.

1611 COTGR., *Retordeur*, a twister, twiner; a wrester, a retorter. **1708** SEWELL II, *Twynder*, a twiner, throster. **1864** JEFFREY *Hist. Roxburghshire* IV. ii. 117 In 1810 the twiner was invented by William Johnstone, Galashiels. **1885** *Pall Mall G.* 7 Oct. 7/2 The Huddersfield operative cotton twiners, after being out on strike.. resumed work yesterday. **1891** *Labour Commission Gloss.*, *Twiners*, operative spinners who double yarn which has been spun by the common spinners.

2. A plant of twining habit.

1830 LINDLEY *Nat. Syst. Bot.* 32 Schizandra is scarcely a twiner. **1859** DARWIN *Orig. Spec.* vii. (1880) 198 Plants became twiners.. by the increase of a tendency to slight and irregular revolving movements. **1885** GOODALE *Physiol. Bot.* (1892) 405 Twiners are distinguished from proper climbers by the absence of any special organs, other than the stem itself for grasping supports.

†**twine thread.** *Obs.* [f. TWINE *sb.*[1] + THREAD *sb.* Cf. Flem. *twijndraad* (in Kilian *tweyndraed*).] A twisted or double-spun thread; also *collectively*, cord, twine.

1530 PALSGR. 283/2 Twynethrede, *fil reteurs.* **1560** DAUS tr. *Sleidane's Comm.* 63 b, A sworde dependynge ouer your neckes by a twhyne threde. **1607** TOPSELL *Four-f. Beasts* (1658) 488 A twine thread will not hold stretching in the presence (I mean in comparison) of a silk thread. **1654** FULLER *Comm. Ruth* (1868) 169, I have seen the twine-thread of a cordial friend hold. **1706** E. WARD *Wooden World Diss.* (1708) 76 The Boatswain... His Bamboo,.. tip'd with simple Twine-thread.

twing, *sb.* Now *dial.* Also 7 **twyng.** [Of obscure origin.] A small red spider supposed to be injurious to cattle; cf. TAINT *sb.* C. 3.

1608 TOPSELL *Serpents* (1658) 770 There is to be found in Harvest-time amongst Pease, Beans, and other sorts of pulse,.. certain small Spiders called *Kantharidessi Eikela*.. of a very red and fiery colour, such as we Englishmen call Twinges, by eating or licking up of which, both Oxen and other Beasts do many times die. **1658** ROWLAND *Moufet's Theat. Ins.* 1060 Small Phalangia.. like to beetles, of a flame-red colour; such are those the English call Twyngs. **1878** *Cumberland Gloss.*, *Twing*, a small scarlet-coloured insect, said by the superstitious to occasion fatal illness to cattle.

†**twing,** *v.*: see TWINGE *v.*[2]

twinge (twɪndʒ), *sb.* Forms: 6 **twynge, twynche,** 7 **twindge, (twing),** 7- **twinge.** [f. TWINGE *v.*[1]]

†**1.** An act of tweaking or pinching; a tweak or pinch. Also *fig.* *Obs.*

1548 UDALL *Erasm. Par. Luke* Prol. 15 Nipped my hert also with a litell twynge. *c* **1550** *Pryde & Abuse Women* 200 in Hazl. *E.P.P.* IV. 243 Rubbe a galde horse on thee backe, And he wyll kicke and wynse; And so wyll wanton wylyons When they have anye snaper or twynche. **1611** COTGR., *Strette*, a pinch, nip, wrinche, twindge. *Ibid.*, *Tire*, a.. ierke, twang, twing. *a* **1625** FLETCHER *Nice Valour* III. ii, For the twindge by th' nose, 'Tis certainly unsightly. **1692** R. L'ESTRANGE *Fables* ccxciii. I. 255, I wonder.. how you can Fawn thus upon a Master that gives you so many Blows, and Twinges by the Ears. [**1869** BROWNING *Ring & Bk.* IX. 146 Gently thou joggest by a twinge the wit.]

2. A sharp pinching or wringing pain; often, a momentary local pain; esp. applied to that of gout and rheumatism.

1608 MIDDLETON *Mad World* II. vii, You feel as it were a twinge? **1639** in *Verney Mem.* (1907) I. 220 Crewell twinges [of gout]. **1787** WOLCOTT (P. Pindar) *Instr. Laureat* Wks. 1812 I. 497 They've felt a pain in all their Toes And often at the twinges started. **1824** LADY GRANVILLE *Lett.* 21 Mar. (1894) I. 267 Your.. letter.. soothed and comforted me during my sharpest twinges [of toothache]. **1827** *Edin. Weekly Jrnl.* 28 Feb., I can agree with Lord Ogleby as to his rheumatism, and say, 'There's a twinge'. **1831** BREWSTER *Nat. Magic* iii. (1833) 48 The account of any person having suffered severe pain.. produces acute twinges of pain in the corresponding parts of her person. *a* **1839** PRAED *Poems* (1864) II. 77 When the twinge comes shooting through you. **1863** GEO. ELIOT *Romola* vii, The gout.. gave him such severe twinges. **1880** L. STEPHEN *Pope* iv. 88 Philosophers capable of rheumatic twinges.

b. *transf.* A 'nip' of cold, etc.

1888 E. GERARD *Land beyond Forest* lv. 360 Alternate twinges of cold and heat.

3. *fig.* A sharp mental pain; a pang of shame, remorse, sorrow, or the like; a prick of conscience; in quot. *a* 1745, a stimulating prick.

1622 MABBE tr. *Aleman's Guzman d'Alf.* I. 19 Her feigned pangs cease[d], and those truer ones of loue beganne to manifest themselues, giuing other kinde of twinges. **1681** DRYDEN *Spanish Fryar* IV. i, The Wickedness of this old Villain.. gives me a twinge for my own Sin. *a* **1745** SWIFT *Serm.* viii. Wks. 1841 II. 157/2 The poorer sort.. have no twinges of ambition. **1780** COWPER *Table Talk* 425 Conscience will have twinges now and then. **1800** WEEMS *Washington* xv. (1877) 223 This could not save poor Jack from the twinges of envy. **1834** L. RITCHIE *Wand. by Seine* 168 The sudden clang of a church-bell arrests us, like a twinge of remorse. **1861** HUGHES *Tom Brown at Oxf.* viii. (1889) 69 It cost the Vicar some twinges of conscience to persuade him. **1874** L. STEPHEN *Hours in Library* (1892) II. iii. 91 Burke's politics gave him some severe twinges.

4. A twist, a turn. *lit.* and *fig.* *rare.*

1860 HOLLAND *Miss Gilbert* ii. 38 'Easy!' exclaimed Arthur, a half-contemptuous twinge in his lip. **1875** J. MORISON in *Expositor* I. 124 Grotius gave the expression a most unnatural twinge.

5. *dial.* An earwig.

1790 GROSE *Provinc. Gloss.* (ed. 2), *Twinge*, or *Twitch*, an earwig. *North.* **1828** *Craven Gloss.* **1863** MRS. TOOGOOD *Yorks. Dial.* (MS.).

twinge (twɪndʒ), *v.*[1] Forms: 1 **twengan** (twæng-), 3 **twenge,** 3-4 **tuenge,** 5 **twynch,** 7 **twindge,** 7- **twinge.** [OE. *twengan*, of obscure etymology; there is no evidence of connexion with Continental forms from the stem *þwing-* denoting 'to constrain, oppress, etc.']

1. *trans.* To pinch, wring, tweak, twitch. Also *intr.* (quot. 1858). *Obs.* exc. *dial.*

c **1000** in *Techmer's Internat. Zeitschr.* II. 124/23 Twenge hine siððan mid þara swiþran hande. *Ibid.* 125/19 Wænd þinne scytefinger adune and twængc hine mid þinum twam fingrum. *a* **1250** *Owl & Night.* 156 þu hauest clyures swiþe stronge þu twengest þar mid so doþ a tonge. *Ibid.* 1114 An holeh stoc hwar þu þe mist hude þat me ne twenge þine hude. *c* **1305** *St. Dunstan* 81 in *E.E.P.* (1862) 36 þe deuel he hente bi þe nose: He tuengde and schok hire bi þe nose. **1440** J. SHIRLEY *Dethe K. James* (1818) 26 The tourmentours.. withe hookid ynstrumentes of yryne,.. pynchid and twynchid his theghis, his legges,.. and over all his body. **1607** BEAUMONT *Woman Hater* II. i, I doe use to tear their hair, to kick them, and twindge their noses, if they be not carefull in avoiding me. **1611** BEAUM. & FL. *King & no K.* V. i, Thus twinge your nose, thus kick, thus tread upon you. **1628** A. LEIGHTON *Zion's Plea* x. (1842) 195 There are too many flesh-flies, who.. twinge and bite such as do deal faithfully with Princes. **1630** B. JONSON *New Inn* I. i, To.. twinge three or four buttons From off my lady's gown. **1678** BUTLER *Hud.* III. I. 1155 Twindging him by th' Ears or Nose. **1858** KINGSLEY *Winter-Gard.* in *Misc.* I. 146 That flock of long-tailed tit-mice, which were twinging and pecking about the fir-cones.

2. †To cause to smart or tingle; to irritate (*obs.*); to affect (the body or mind) with a twinge or sharp pain; to prick (the conscience).

1647 [see *twinging* below.] **1666** BUNYAN *Grace Ab.* § 184 Nothing did twinge my Conscience like this. **1674** N. FAIRFAX *Bulk & Selv.* 114 A willingness to be rid of those gallers that twinge the brain of the stiff maintainer of this. **1686** F. SPENCE tr. *Varillas' Ho. Medicis* 431 Leo.. twing'd him sometimes with severe corrections. **1727** GAY *Fables* I. xxxi. 7 As, twing'd with pain, he pensive sits, And raves, and prays, and swears by fits. **1780** S. J. PRATT *Emma Corbett* (ed. 4) II. 71 His old aches would twinge him a little. **1785** E. PERRONET *Occas. Verses, Acrostic* 203 His mission.. Like that dumb brute's, that twing'd a prophet's ear. **1801** MAR. EDGEWORTH *Out of Debt* i, If any of his father's old notions of economy by chance twinged his conscience. **1815** SCOTT *Paul's Lett.* (1839) 173 The Bishop of Ghent.. has found his conscience alarmingly twinged. **1893** D. C. MURRAY *Time's Revenges* II. xxviii. 208 The old wound twinged him.

b. *intr.* To experience a twinge or smart.

1640 GLAPTHORNE *Wit in Constable* IV, To have your nose Twinge if ours' chance to itch. **1757** E. PERRONET *Mitre* IV. xiii, Shudder ye sires—twinge ev'ry ear. **1850** SIR A. AGNEW in McCrie *Mem.* viii. (1852) 199 Reflection arising and conscience twinging. **1868** [see *twinging* below].

Hence **twinging** ('twɪndʒɪŋ) *vbl. sb.*[1] and *ppl. a.*; also **twinger** ('twɪndʒə(r)), one who or that which twinges.

1608 DAY *Law Trickes* II. C ij, One Tristella.. a twindger, a meere Horsleach, one that will suck out the braines of his treasurie. **1621** B. JONSON *Gipsies Metam.* Wks. (Rtldg.) 625/2 There's an old twinger Can shew ye the ginger. **1647** SPRIGGE *Anglia Rediv.* Address (1854) p. vii, Twinging convulsions. **1659** TATHAM *London's Triumph* 14 Ginger, That Nose tosting twinger. **1682** BUNYAN *Greatness of Soul* Wks. (ed. Offor) I. 120 Despair, which is the most twinging stripe of hell. **1816** J. WILSON *City of Plague* II. iii. 219 Felt you no little twinging of remorse? **1868** GEO. ELIOT *Sp. Gipsy* I. (1908) 27, I've a twinging knee. **1906** *Daily Chron.* 29 Mar. 6/4 How would he wear.. with a twingeing tooth and an influenza cold?

†**twinge,** *v.*[2] *Obs. rare.* [Perh. intended as a fig. use of prec., but prob. originating in some misunderstanding of earlier glosses. The strong pa. pple. *twungen* is app. less original than the weak form *twinged.*] *trans.* To oppress, afflict, persecute. Hence **twinging** *vbl. sb.*[2]

a **1300** *E.E. Psalter* xvi. 10 [xvii. 9] Hile me.. Fra face ofe wicked þat twinged me swa. *Ibid.* xvii. 21 [xviii. 18] þai forcome me in daie of twinginge. *Ibid.* xxxvii[i]. 8, I am twinged, and meked for vnquerte [*MS. H.* I am meked and twungen smert]. *Ibid.* xli. 13 [xlii. 9] Wharfore murned in I go, Whil þat twinges me þe fo?

twingle ('twɪŋg(ə)l), *v.* *rare.* Now *dial.* [Prob. imitative.] *intr.* To twist, twine, wriggle, writhe.

c **1645** HOWELL *Lett.* II. lv, German mothers.. put.. into a cup of Rhenish.. somtimes a little living Eel, which twingling in the wine while the child is drinking so scares him, that many com to abhor.. wine all their lives after. **1813** W. BEATTIE *Fruits Time Parings* (1873) 4 A lingle, To swing the roast; They had nae jack, but this could twingle Wi' little cost. **1880** *W. Cornw. Gloss.*, *Twingle*, to wriggle; to writhe.

twingle, obs. variant of TWINKLE.

twingle-twangle (twɪŋg(ə)l'twæŋg(ə)l). [Reduplication of TWANGLE.] A representation of the continuous sounds of a harp or the like. Also as *vb.*

1634 FORD *Perkin Warbeck* III. ii, Discord of bells pipes and tabours Hodgepodge of Scotch and Irish twingle twangles. **1791** BURNS *Let. to A. Alison* 14 Feb., The twingle twangle of a Jew's harp. **1900** CROCKETT *Black Douglas* 327 When he had.. finished cocking his viol and twingle-twangling it to his satisfaction.

twing twang ('twɪŋ 'twæŋ). *rare.* [Reduplication of TWANG.] A representation of the sound of the harp, or other such instrument.

1761 H. WALPOLE *Let. to C'tess Ailesbury* 20 July, All the guitars are untuned;.. she must take some David or other to teach her the new twing twang, twing twing twang. **1762** STERNE *Tr. Shandy* V. xv, Ptr... r.. r.. ing,—twing,—twang,—prut,—trut; 'tis a cursed bad fiddle. **1800-1**

SOUTHEY *Thalaba* Pref. to ed. 4, The regular Jew's harp twing-twang, of what has been foolishly called heroic measure. **1922** JOYCE *Ulysses* 436 Their paler smaller negroid hands jingle the twingtwang wires. **1953** *John o' London's* 23 Jan. 75/3 Central in the 'orchestra' was a guitar making a lazy twing-twang of sound.

twingy (ˈtwɪndʒɪ), *a. rare.* Also **twingey.** [f. TWINGE *sb.* or *v.*[1] + -Y[1].] Experiencing twinges of pain.

1865 N. HOGG *Poet. Lett. tu es Brither Jan* (ed. 5) 52 And then tha litt'l pigs wid zook, an twinjy in tha jaw wis took. **1915** V. WOOLF *Voyage Out* ix. 120 Aunt E. cheerful, though twingy, she says. **1974** D. SEARS *Lark in Clear Air* (1976) xv. 187 Hearing that song made me feel twingey and kind of lonesome.

twi-night (ˈtwaɪnaɪt). *Baseball.* [Blend of TWILIGHT *sb.* and NIGHT *sb.*] (See quot. 1955.) Freq. *attrib.*, as ***twi-night double-header*** (cf. DOUBLE-HEADER c). Hence **ˈtwi-nighter,** in same sense.

1939 *Amer. Speech* XIV. 5 Blending..has proved practical in the formation of useful compounds where a combination of ideas is desired; as in..'brunch', 'twinight', 'Anglamerican'. **1953** *Sun* (Baltimore) 28 Oct. (B ed.) 21/2 (*heading*) Twi-nighters? **1955** M. REIFER *Dict. New Words* 214/2 *Twinight, n. Baseball*, a double-header game which begins in the afternoon and continues into the night with artificial illumination. **1975** *New Yorker* 17 Nov. 148/2 The pitching left something to be desired, but the next afternoon, in the opener of a twi-night doubleheader, Frank Tanana struck out seventeen Texas batters. **1980** *N.Y. Post* 4 Aug. 56 The Mets are still—again—two games under .500 and twi-night double-header here tonight..opens another five-game series against the division-leading Expos.

twining (ˈtwaɪnɪŋ), *vbl. sb.* [f. TWINE *v.*[1] + -ING[1].] The action of the verb TWINE; twisting, spinning, winding, embracing, writhing.

1398 TREVISA *Barth. De P.R.* XVII. cxlii[i]. (Bodl. MS.) lf. 227 b/1 Smal [weþies]..beþ made stronge wiþ..windinge as þrede is wᵗ twynynge. *c* **1440** *Promp. Parv.* 505/1 Twynynge (or wyn(d)ynge, of threde..), *tortura.* **1553** T. WILSON *Rhet.* (1580) 101 A priuie twinyng, or close crepyng in, to win fauour.., called insinuation. *a* **1639** WEBSTER *Appius & Virginia* IV. ii, The rude twinings of a lecherous judge. *a* **1703** POMFRET *Poet. Wks.* (1833) 21 Love to one centre every twining brought. **1841** EMERSON *Lect., Man the Reformer* Wks. (Bohn) II. 238 Inextricable seem to be the twinings and tendrils of this evil. **1872** G. B. CHEEVER *Lect. Pilgr. Progr.* ii. 44 The twinings and wrestlings, the strivings and agonies of Bunyan's spirit. **1875** BENNETT & DYER *Sachs's Bot.* 772 The Twining of Climbing Plants... Twining is a consequence of unequal growth, of a revolving nutation.

attrib. **1648** HEXHAM II, *Een Twern ofte twijn-molen*, a Twinning-mill.

twining (ˈtwaɪnɪŋ), *ppl. a.* [f. as prec. + -ING[2].] That twines, in various senses; twisting, winding, coiling, writhing, etc.; *spec.* of a plant: growing spirally round a support.

a **1593** MARLOWE in *Eng. Parnassus* (1600) 480 The Eglantine and Rose..As kind companions in one union grows, Folding their twining armes. **1664** POWER *Exp. Philos.* I. 8 The twining tendrils of the Vine. **1669** PENN *No Cross* vii. §4 A Crooked, Twining, Twisting Serpent. **1735** SOMERVILLE *Chase* IV. 153 Spare not thou The twining whip, but ply his bleeding Sides. **1824** MISS L. M. HAWKINS *Annaline* II. 213 The thick forest [was] decorated with twining plants. **1861** BENTLEY *Man. Bot.* (1870) 100 If such stems twist round other bodies in a spiral manner they are said to be twining.

Hence **ˈtwiningly** *adv.*, in a twining manner.

1731 BAILEY, *Twiningly*, twistingly.

twink (twɪŋk), *sb.*[1] Forms: 5 **twynk,** 5–6 **twynke,** 6–7 **twinke,** 7 **twinck(e,** 7 **twinch,** 6– **twink.** [f. TWINK *v.*[1]]

1. A winking of the eye; *transf.* the time taken by this; a twinkling; now always in phrase ***in a twink***; formerly ***at, in, with*** (***a*** or ***the***) ***twink of an eye***; also ***with a twink***; ***in the twink of a bedstick***: cf. BEDSTAFF.

14.. *Cov. Corp. Chr. Plays* I. 506 Myne enmyis to vanquese.. And with a twynke of myn iee not won to be lafte alyve. **1471** RIPLEY *Comp. Alch.* Pref. ii. in Ashm. *Theatr. Chem. Brit.* (1652) 127 In twynke of an Eye most sodenly. **1556** J. HEYWOOD *Spider & F.* lii. A a iv. (*heading*), Wherat with twynke of an iye (as it were) the head spider.. hath builded a strong castell in that copweb. *Ibid.* xci. Oo iv b, Change (by chance) brought him (at twinke of an iye) From twig top of the tree, at the rote to lie. **1561** NORTON & SACKV. *Gorboduc* IV. ii. (Shaks. Soc.) 142 A pereles prince.. Euen with a twinke a censeles stocke I sawe. **1596** SHAKS. *Tam. Shr.* II. i. 312 Kisse on kisse Shee vi'd so fast, protesting oath on oath, That in a twinke she won me to her loue. **1607** R. C[AREW] TR. *Estienne's World of Wonders* I. xxiv. 194 The poore gentlewoman..speaking not a word, gaue him a twinch with a weeping eye. **1715** NELSON tr. *à Kempis' Chr. Exerc.* III. xxv. 173 As lightning in the Twink of an eye, so do all the Kingdoms and Times of the World pass away. **1754** SHEBBEARE *Matrimony* (1766) II. 121 I'll cut it less in a Twink. **1756** TOLDERVY *Hist. 2 Orphans* I. 71, I can tell you in the twink of a bedstick. **1833** NYREN *Yng. Cricketer's Tutor* (1902) 93 The confident old bowler..thought to settle his business in a twink. **1898** WATTS-DUNTON *Aylwin* III. i, She's got the real witch's eye, and can do you a mischief in a twink, if she likes. **1902** BARRIE *Little White Bird* xiii. 135 Night passes in a twink.

transf. **1904** R. J. FARRER *Garden Asia* 276 With the merest twink of some nerve, sending prone his brawny opponent.

2. A twinkle or sparkle. *rare.*

1830 [implied in *twinkless*: see below]. **1870** J. W. BOULDING *Catalina* 8 Saw ye not a strange twink in her eye?

Hence **ˈtwinkless** *a.*, without a twink or twinkle.

1830 R. MONTGOMERY *Satan* II. 121 When weary stars grow twinkless, and depart.

twink (twɪŋk), *sb.*[2] [Echoic; cf. PINK *sb.*[6], SPINK *sb.*[1] I.] A local name for the chaffinch.

1816 STEPHENS in Shaw *Gen. Zool.* IX. II. 444 It [Chaffinch] is called by various names in this country, such as..Horse-finch, Pink, Twink, Spink, &c. **1829** [see PINK *sb.*[6]]. **1881** MISS JACKSON *Shropsh. Word-bk.*, *Twink*, the Chaffinch.

twink (twɪŋk), *v.*[1] Forms: see TWINK *sb.*[1] [ME. *twinken* (= MHG. and G. *zwinken* to wink), repr. the simple stem from which TWINKLE *v.*[1] is formed.]

†**1.** *intr.* To wink, to blink. *Obs.*

c **1400** *Gamelyn* 453 Whan I twynke [*v.r.* twynk] on the, loke for to goon. *c* **1440** *Promp. Parv.* 505/2 Twynkyn, wythe the eye.., *conniveo.* **1600** J. LANE *Tom Tel-troth* 262 Some winke, some twinke, some blinke, some stare. *a* **1652** BROME *Covent-Garden* III. i. Wks. 1873 II. 47, I will..set mine eye against his, that he shall not twink, but I'le perceive it. **1681** W. ROBERTSON *Phraseol. Gen.* (1693) 567 To wink or twink with the eye, *nictare.*

2. To twinkle, sparkle.

1637 N. WHITING *Albino & Bellama* 3 The curled tapers of the Firmament Did cease to twinke. **1795** *Cicely of Raby* I. 195 The last star had twinked in the west, ere we had gone half our journey. **1856** AIRD *Poet. Wks.* 194 The wings of birds Twink with illumination. **1884** BROWNING *Ferishtah, Cherries* 80 Like yon blue twinkle, twinks thine eye, my Love. **1896** C. K. PAUL tr. *Huysman's En Route* iv. 54 Durtal faintly saw..stars twinking in the air.

Hence **ˈtwinking** *vbl. sb.*

1519 HORMAN *Vulg.* 27 Ouermoche twyngynge [*sic*] of the yie betoketh vnstedfastnesse. **1627** MAY *Lucan* VI. 863 The eyes with twincking hard Are op'd.

twink (twɪŋk), *v.*[2] ? *Obs. rare.* [Echoic; cf. TINK, TWANK.] *intr.* To make a light clear abrupt ringing sound; to clink, chink. Also of a bird (*intr.* and *trans.*), to utter, or utter with, a shrill metallic note.

a **1529** SKELTON *Col. Cloute* 493 And wrest vp my harpe With sharpe twynkyng trebelles, Agaynst all suche rebelles. **1615** CHAPMAN *Odyss.* XXI. 548 A swallow..Twinks out her scatter'd voice in accents shrill. **1674** FLAVEL *Medit. Birds* ii. in *Husb. Spiritualized* App. 238 A whole quire of Birds chirping and twinking together.

twink, *v.*[3] Now *dial.* [Of obscure origin: cf. TWANK *v.*] *trans.* To chastise. Hence **twinˈkation** (*nonce-wd.*).

1747 ELIZ. CARTER *Lett.* (1808) 132, I have been called away ten times, and shall be twinked if I do not leave you. **1748** *Ibid.* 164, I..wrote a twinkation to Mr. Richardson about it, to which I received so civil an answer that I knew not how to be angry. **1892** HEWETT *Peas. Sp. Devon* 138 I'll twink thee purty tight vur that, sure's a gun!

twinkle (ˈtwɪŋk(ə)l), *sb.* Forms: see TWINKLE *v.*[1] [f. TWINKLE *v.*[1]]

1. a. A winking of the eye; a wink, blink; also, a momentary glance (in quot. 1593, of the mind); cf. BLINK *sb.*[2] 2. ? *Obs.*

1548 THOMAS *Ital. Gram.* (1567), *Cennare*, a nodde or twyncle with the eye. **1593** Q. ELIZ. tr. *Boethius* v. pr. iv, 112 Vnderstanding..orderly by one twynkell of the mynde, all ouerlookith. **1594** SPENSER *Amoretti* xvi, One of those archers..Ayming his arrow..suddenly, with twincle of her eye, The Damzell broke his misintended dart. **1660** tr. *Amyraldus' Treat. conc. Relig.* II. i. 143, I do not conceive an honest man can consent so much as with one twinkle of his eye to such abominations. **1709** STEELE *Tatler* No. 22 ¶1 Her true Lover,..his Heart..waiting for a second Twincle of her Eye. **1818** SCOTT *Hrt. Midl.* xiv, An occasional convulsive sigh, or twinkle of the eyelid.

b. *transf.* A slight tremulous movement; a twitch, a flicker, a quiver.

1733 CHEYNE *Eng. Malady* II. xiii. §1 (1734) 246 Now and then an uncertain Twitch or Twinkle in the Pulse. **1862** CARLYLE *Fredk. Gt.* XI. ix. (1872) IV. 106 The slightest twinkle of Fleury's eyelashes would be duly speeded to Voltaire.

2. The time it takes to wink; = TWINKLING *vbl. sb.*[1] 3; now only in phrase ***in a twinkle, in the twinkle of an eye.***

c **1592** MARLOWE *Jew of Malta* IV. iv, Vanish, and return in a twinkle. **1644** DIGBY *Nat. Soul* x. §8. 429 That twinkle or moment, in which she becometh an.. inhabitant of the next world. **1679** DRYDEN *Troilus & Cr.* III. ii, Hast not slept to night? wou'd a not (a naughty Man) let it sleep one twinkle? **1681** OTWAY *Soldier's Fort.* IV. i, I'll..be with you in a Twinkle. **1903** *Pilot* 17 Oct. 373/1 The reduction of the military service to two years..ought to be done in a twinkle. **1905** ELINOR GLYN *Viciss. Evangeline* 166 In the twinkle of an eye we were rolling..to Willis's.

3. a. An intermittent or transient shining; a sparkle, a scintillation; also, a faint or momentary gleam; a glimmer.

1663 J. HEATH *Eng. Chron.* (1691) 76 The King..caused the Twinkles of his Eyes to be put out..by burning Glasses. **1718** POPE *Let. to Lady M. W. Montagu* 1 Sept., In the very twinkle of one eye of it [your body] there is more wit,..than [etc.]. **1748** THOMSON *Cast. Indol.* I. 617 He had a roguish twinkle in his eye. **1818** SCOTT *Rob Roy* xvii, As the benighted sailor descries the first distant twinkle of the lighthouse which marks his course. **1825** —— *Talism.* iii, A twinkle in the star of thy nativity, which promises for thee something that is good and gracious. **1858** CARLYLE *Fredk. Gt.* III. i. (1872) I. 141 A certain twinkle of mirth in the serious eyes. **1860** MAYHEW *Upper Rhine* i. §1. 15 Nor is it possible to catch sight of even so much as a twinkle of the fire.

b. *transf.* and *fig.*

1864 BURTON *Scot Abr.* II. ii. 169 The broad accent..and its sly twinkles of humour. **1885** G. MEREDITH *Diana* xxxiii, Was there a twinkle of probability in the story? **1893** L. S. KEYSER in *Chicago Advance* 3 Aug., The twinkle of wings, the twitter of voices.

4. A ballroom dance (step), danced to slow Blues music. Also ***twinkle step.***

1920 A. E. W. MASON *Summons* xxi. 220 'Do you know the fox-trot?' 'A little.' 'The twinkle step?' 'Not at all.' **1936** A. MOORE *Ballroom Dancing* v. 214 A Twinkle is a figure of three steps. The feet are closed..on the 2nd step and the weight is changed, and the 1st and 3rd steps are both taken in a forward direction or both in a backward direction. **1962** L. K. ENGEL *Fred Astaire Dance Bk.* xv. 47 The Open Twinkle is a slight variation of the basic One Step. **1975** G. HOWELL *In Vogue* 9/2 We got syncopated music and what to do to it—the Baleta, the Maxina, the Twinkle, the Jog Trot, the Vampire, [etc.].

5. *Comb.*, as **twinkle-dress** *poet. nonce-wd.*, a sparkling party dress; **twinkle roll** *Aeronautics*, an aerobatic stunt (see quot. 1962); **twinkle-toed** *a.*, light-footed, nimble; (of a dance) quick, requiring agility.

1960 S. PLATH *Colossus* 59 When on tiptoe the school-girls danced, Blinking flashlights like fireflies And singing the glowworm song, I could Not lift a foot in the twinkle-dress. **1962** *Flight International* LXXXII. 269/2 Highlights of an outstanding presentation by the Lightnings were the 'twinkle roll' in which the two wingmen of a three-aircraft formation rolled individually on either side of their leader as they passed low and fast in front of the crowd. **1978** R. JANSSON *News Caper* 7 The fighter..slid over our port wing and did a twinkle roll in front of our nose. **1960** *Farmer & Stockbreeder* 29 Mar. (Suppl.) 10/2 Hand-in-hand with about six other youngsters she was scampering through a twinkle-toed dance which she later informed me is called 'the shuffle'. **1961** *Sunday Express* 7 May 14/3 Abandoned, twinkle-toed dancers leaping about. **1978** *Lancashire Life* Nov. 129/1 John Travolta doesn't have the monopoly of twinkle toed addicts.

twinkle (ˈtwɪŋk(ə)l), *v.*[1] Forms: 1 **twinclian,** 4–6 **twinkel, twynkle, twyncle,** (4 **twyngle,** *Sc.* **twinkil,** 4–5 **twynkel,** 5 **-kele, -kyl,** 5–6 *Sc.* **-kil,** 6 **-kell, twinckel),** 4–8 **twincle,** 6–8 **twinckle,** (**twingle**), 4– **twinkle.** [OE. *twinclian*, freq. of ***twincan*:** see TWINK *v.*[1] and -LE 3.]

1. a. *intr.* To shine with rapidly intermittent light; to emit tremulous radiance; to sparkle; to glitter; †to shine dimly, to glimmer; to flicker (*obs.*).

c **888** K. ÆLFRED *Boeth.* xxxv. §3 Ic hire [the door] grapode ymbutan þæt ðe ic þæt lytle leoht ȝeseah twinclian. *c* **897** —— *Gregory's Past. C.* xiv. 86 Se spearca ðara godra weorca, þe her twinclað [*v.r.* tuinclað] beforan monnum. *c* **1386** CHAUCER *Prol.* 267 Hise eyen twynkled..As doon the sterres in the frosty nyght. **1423** JAS. I *Kingis Q.* i, Heigh In the hevynnis figure circulere The rody sterres twynklyng as the fyre. **1551** RECORDE *Cast. Knowl.* (1556) 8 The Fixed starres doo twinkle, and not the Planetes. **1582** STANYHURST *Æneis* II. (Arb.) 69 Thee twylight twinckled [L. *consumta nocte*]. **1658** tr. *Porta's Nat. Magic* XIII. 306 When the Iron is sparkling red hot..that it twinkles. **1678** CUDWORTH *Intell. Syst.* I. i. §37. 46 The Flame of a new lighted Candle is [not] the same with that Flame that twinkles last in the socket. **1740** SOMERVILLE *Hobbinol* I. 145 His single Eye Twinkles with Joy. **1784** COWPER *Task* VI. 251 The green blade that twinkles in the sun. **1818** SCOTT *Rob Roy* i, The tear twinkled in his dark eye. **1855** MACAULAY *Hist. Eng.* xiii. III. 364 A solitary light which twinkled through the darkness. **1863** W. C. BALDWIN *Afr. Hunting* vii. 283 His large black diamond eyes..used to twinkle like stars.

transf. **1850** KINGSLEY *Alt. Locke* xxiv, He twinkled, and winked, and chuckled. **1871** 'M. LEGRAND' *Cambr. Freshm.* xvii, A smile twinkled in his eyes. **1889** BARRIE *Window in Thrums* xix. 177 Jess twinkled gleefully over tales of sweethearting.

b. *trans.* To emit (radiance, flashes, or beams) rapidly and intermittently; to communicate (a message or signal) in this way.

a **1547** SURREY *Paraphr. Ps.* viii. Wks. (1815) 85 Thou mad'st..each one of the wand'ring stars to twinkle sparkles bright. **1632** J. HAYWARD tr. *Biondi's Eromena* 185 The minde..twinkled forth sparkles that argued great flames of excellencies. **1857** G. MEREDITH *Farina* viii. 134 A broad fire that twinkled branchy beams through an east hill-orchard. **1894** MRS. DYAN *All in a Man's K.* (1899) 162 Not one bright star to twinkle hope and light to him. **1899** *Westm. Gaz.* 4 Aug. 7/3 The challenge-word..was twinkled ..by the luminous dots and dashes from her masthead.

†**c.** To vary in twinkling. *Obs. rare*[−1].

1665 HOOKE *Microgr.* lviii. 218 The Starrs neer the Horizon, are twinkled with several colours.

d. *poet.* To guide or light *to* some place by twinkling.

1690 DRYDEN *Don Sebastian* IV. i, The star of love That twinkles you to fair Almeyda's bed. **1818** KEATS *Endymion* IV. 719 Those eyes..Shall be my grief, or twinkle me to pleasure.

2. a. *intr.* To close and open the eye or eyes quickly (voluntarily or involuntarily); to make a signal by this means; to wink, blink; also said of the eye or eyes. *Obs.* or *arch.*

a **1300** [see TWINKLING *vbl. sb.*[1] 2]. *c* **1374** CHAUCER *Boeth.* II. pr. iii. 26 (Camb. MS.) She hath now twyncled [*v.r.* twynkeled] fyrst vp on the with wyckede eye. *c* **1375** *Sc. Leg. Saints* xxviii. (*Margarete*) 595, & þis merwale alsone cane be As man mycht twinkil with his e. **1382** WYCLIF *Prov.* vi. 13 He twinclith [1388 bekeneth] with the eȝen. *c* **1440** *Bone Flor.* 1750 He twynkylde wyth hys eye, As who seyth, holde the stylle. **1513** DOUGLAS *Æneis* IV. xii. 96 With ene rolling, and twynkilling wp full fane, Assayis scho to spy the hevinis lycht. **1608** Topsell *Serpents* (1653) 684 They have but one eye-lid, and that groweth from the neather part of the cheek, which by reason of their eyes never twinckleth. *a* **1625** Fletcher *Woman Pleas'd* iv. i, I saw the wench that twir'd and twinkled at thee The other day. **1653** R. Sanders *Physiogn.* 173 Beware of those who, when they speak to thee, twinkle. **1686** *Lond. Gaz.* No. 2103/4 He is about 17 years old,..near sighted, twinkling with his eyes. **1753** Richardson *Grandison* (1754) II. x. 64 We hemm'd, handkerchief'd, twinkled. **1772** *Test Filial Duty* I. 128 He did so simper and twinckle, and was so gallant, that [etc.]. **1784** R. Bage *Barham Downs* II. 309 The old Justice twinkles, hems, coughs, and chuckles. **1815** Scott *Guy M.* lv, He was observed to twinkle with his eyelids. **1825** —— *Betrothed* xxxi, Ere an eye could twinkle, his right knee was on the croupe of the Constable's horse.

b. *trans.* with the eyes, eyelids, etc., as obj.

1591 Percivall *Sp. Dict.*, *Parpadear*, to twinkle the eies. **1846** Landor *Imag. Conv.*, *Pope Leo xii & Gigi* Wks. I. 347/1 Her little kid ran after the soldier..twinkling its ears and rubbing them between its legs. **1851** Hawthorne *Ho. Sev. Gables* xiv, Phœbe took leave of the desolate couple;.. twinkling her eyelids to shake off a dewdrop.

3. *intr.* To move to and fro, or in and out, with rapid alternation; to appear and disappear in quick succession; to flutter, flit, flicker.

In quot. 1799–1805 said of a space filled with moving objects; in quot. 1849 *trans.* (cf. 2 b).

1616 [see twinkling *ppl. a.* 2]. **1642** in P. H. Hore *Hist. Wexford* (1900) I. 303 A man might see them through the smoake of the gunpowder run twinckling like the moates in the sun. **1799–1805** Wordsw. *Prelude* vii. 691 The open space..twinkles, is alive With heads. **1849** Saxe *Poems, Rape Lock* xix, [She] twinkled a foot in the polka's twirl. **1852** M. W. Savage *R. Medlicott* v. ii, I love to see the fans fluttering, the ankles twinkling, the bouquets waving. **1863** Kingsley *Water Bab.* i. 39 Her feet twinkled past each other so fast, that you could not see which was foremost.

4. *intr. Dancing.* To perform the twinkle step. *temporary.*

1920 *Punch* 10 Nov. 366/2 *Chassée* to the left, two steps forward, two steps back, twinkle each way. *Ibid.*, I quite enjoyed that twinkling business. **1928** *B.B.C. Handbk. 1929* 201 Wireless dance music is often heard from houses where no one has ever 'twinkled' or 'hesitated' or 'glided' or 'dragged'.

twinkle ('twɪŋk(ə)l), *v.*[2] *rare.* Forms: 4 **twynkel**, 6 **twynkle**, 6– **twinkle**. [Echoic; cf. tinkle *v.*[1]] *intr.* = tinkle *v.*[1] 2, 3. Hence '**twinkling** *vbl. sb.*

13.. *K. Alis.* 2572 Mury is the twynkelyng [*Laud MS.* touchyng] of the harpour. **1523** Skelton *Garl. Laurel* 687 There Cintheus sat twynklyng vpon his harpe stringis. **1575** Laneham *Let.* (1871) 61 My wanton warblz, my running, my tyming, my tuning, and my twynkling. **1683** Pettus *Fleta Min.* i. (1686) 48 When the Grains of such two tryals have twinkled, fresh and clean, then take the Copper out of the oven. **1907** H. Wyndham *Flare of Footlights* i, An electric bell twinkled warningly.., and there was a general move towards the stalls and circle.

twinkledum ('twɪŋk(ə)ldəm). An imitation of the sound of the guitar.

1681 Dryden *Spanish Fryar* i. ii, A Serenade of Twinckledum Twinckledum under my Windows.

twinkler ('twɪŋklə(r)). [f. twinkle *v.*[1] + -er[1].] One who or that which twinkles.

†**1.** One who winks; a winker. *Obs. rare*[−1].

1382 Wyclif *Ecclus.* xxvii. 25 The twynclere with the eȝe forgeth wicke thingus.

2. Anything which emits intermittent, transient, or faint radiance; sometimes applied to eyes.

1591 Sylvester *Du Bartas* i. iv. 574 The Hoasts of th'upper Twinklers bright. **1654** Gayton *Pleas. Notes* ii. v. 56 His Dulcinea's twinclers enlarged to the full breadth of Queen Proserpines sawcers. **1708** Mrs. Centlivre *Busie Body* v. i, A consenting Look with those pretty Twinklers. **1747** Richardson *Clarissa* I. xxvii. 170 Such a sun in a family where there are none but faint twinklers. **1802** Mrs. E. Parsons *Myst. Visit* I. 18 The small twinkler held by the servant..is perfectly sufficient. **1813** Shelley *Q. Mab* ix. 223 Such tiny twinklers as the planet orbs. **1837** Marryat *Dog-fiend* xvii, Be plased..and not be staring at me, following me up and down..with those twinklers of yours. **1868** Lockyer *Guillemin's Heavens* xvii. 244 Enceladus, and coy Mimas, faintest of twinklers, are caught by Herschel's giant mirrors.

twinkling ('twɪŋklɪŋ), *vbl. sb.*[1] [f. twinkle *v.*[1] + -ing[1].] The action of twinkle *v.*[1]

1. The action of shining with tremulous or faint radiance; scintillation; †glimmering. Also *transf.* and *fig.*

1398 Trevisa *Barth. De P.R.* xvi. xxxvii. (Bodl. MS.) lf. 174 b/2 In twinkelinge and in liȝt [electrum] schyneþ more clere þan oþer metal. **1477** Norton *Ord. Alch.* v. in Ashm. *Theatr. Chem. Brit.* (1652) 64 Twinckling and glittering as in *Magnetia* is. **1551** Recorde *Cast. Knowl.* (1556) 8 Many men do make a difference of them by twinkelinge, affirming that the Fixed starres doo twinkle, and not the Planetes. **1635** Swan *Spec. M.* vii. §3 (1643) 325 The twinkling of the starres is the vibration or trembling of their light. **1796** Morse *Amer. Geog.* I. 36 There is only a dim twinkling of twilight for an hour or two in the middle of the day. **1806** Wordsw. *Sonn., To Sleep*, O gentle Sleep! do they belong to thee, These twinklings of oblivion? **1815** Scott *Guy M.* xxvi, These [salmon] the party in the boat detected by the slightest indications; the twinkling of a fin, the rising of an air-bell. **1853** Herschel *Pop. Lect. Sc.* vii. §117 (1873) 336 The twinkling or scintillation of the stars partakes..of the nature of a phænomenon of diffraction. **1879** Butcher & Lang *Odyssey* viii. 123 Odysseus gazed at the twinklings of the feet.

2. The action or an act of winking; nictitation; also *fig. Obs.* exc. as in 3.

a **1300** in *Minor Poems fr. Vernon MS.* (E.E.T.S.) 519/1 þoruȝ twinklingues of heore eyȝen Heore soules been alle for lore. **1398** Trevisa *Barth. De P.R.* xi. xv. (Bodl. MS.) lf. 111 b/2 Liȝtnynge..comeþ oute of his moder as þe twinkelinge of an yȝe. *c* **1440** *Promp. Parv.* 505/2 Twynkelynge, of the eye, *conniventia.* **1530** Palsgr. 283/2 Twynclyng of an eye, *cilement, clin doeil.* **1601** Holland *Pliny* xxxii. x, An ague..accompanied with head-ach and much twinkling or inordinat palpitation of the eyes. **1609** Bible (Douay) *Isa.* iii. 16 The daughters of Sion..have walked with stretched out necke, and went with twinglings of eies. **1632** Lithgow *Trav.* x. 458 Being euery second or third day attended with the twinckling of an eye, and my sustenance agreeable to my attendance, my body grew exceeding debile and infirme. **1649** Jer. Taylor *Gt. Exemp.* ii. Disc. ix. 122 The first motions,..the twincklings of the eye as the Philosophers call them. **1691** Ray *Creation* ii. (1692) 145 The Eyes in squinting, the Eye-lids in twinkling. **1800** Wellington in Gurw. *Desp.* (1837) I. 252 He can extricate himself by the twinkling of an eye if he wishes it. **1822–7** Good *Study Med.* (1829) IV. 462 Twinkling or winking of the eyes is performed every minute without our thinking of it.

3. The time taken in winking the eye; a very brief period; a moment, an instant. Chiefly in phrases: see b, c, d.

1303 [see b.]. *c* **1374** Chaucer *Compl. Mars* 222 Her Ioy.. Ne lasteth not the twynkelyng of an eye. **1535** Coverdale *Ps.* xxix. [xxx.] 5 His wrath endureth but the twincklinge of an eye. **1557** Traheron *Expos. John* i. Hj b, He shewed not him selfe the twinckling of an eye, and so vanished awaie. **1644** Digby *Nat. Soul* ix. §10. 421 He scorneth for this litle twinckling of his life, to take any present paines..to auoyde being ill. **1841** Lane *Arab. Nts.* I. ii. 114, I will never quit thee for the twinkling of an eye.

b. ***in the twinkling of an eye***, in an instant; formerly also † ***in (a), with (a or the) twinkling of an eye*** (in quot. 1390 ***of a look***) (*obs.*).

1303 R. Brunne *Handl. Synne* 9179 Yn twynkelyng of an ye, Yn-to þe cherche gun þey flye. *a* **1310** in Wright *Lyric P.* xxxvii. 106 In a twynglyng of an eȝe. *a* **1340** Hampole *Psalter* lxxii. 19 In þe twinkeling of an eigh þai fal downe. *a* **1380** *Minor Poems fr. Vernon MS.* (E.E.T.S.) 673 Wiþ a twynklyng of an eiȝe. **1390** Gower *Conf.* I. 144 In a twinklinge of a lok His mannes forme aȝein he tok. **1483** Caxton *Cato* E v b, In the twynklyng of an eye. *c* **1489** —— *Sonnes of Aymon* xxviii. 588 The corps..was broughte in to the carte agayne wyth the twynkelyng of an eye. **1508** Dunbar *Gold. Targe* 235 In twynkling of ane eye to schip thai went. **1567** *Gude & Godlie B.* (S.T.S.) 27 With twingling [*v.r.* twinkling] of ane eye anone, God sall the tak. **1599** Hakluyt *Voy.* (1903) IV. 250 In the very twinckling of an eye, both shippe and men were all cast away. **1792** Burke *Corr.* (1844) IV. 11 This clergy would lose,..in the twinkling of an eye, the little remains of influence which they yet retain. **1847** L. Hunt *Men, Women, & B.* II. iv. 52 A book, a picture, a memory, puts us, in the twinkling of an eye, in the midst of the most enchanting solitudes. **1904** *Times* 7 Sept. 7/4 Events..transformed Japan..in the twinkling of an eye..into a modern State.

c. ***in a twinkling*** (†***at a, in the twinkling***).

1582 Stanyhurst *Æneis* i. (Arb.) 22 At a twinckling thee swelling surges he calmed. **1609** *Ev. Woman in Hum.* i. i. in Bullen *O. Pl.* IV, Heere and there in the twinckling. **1610** B. Jonson *Alch.* v. v, An old Hargubuzier..Could prime his poulder, and give fire and hit, All in a twinckling. **1673** Dryden *Marr. à la Mode* ii. i, I'll..be with you again in a twinkling. **1760–72** H. Brooke *Fool of Qual.* (1809) III. 151 The liquor was out of sight in a twinkling. **1807** W. Irving *Salmag.* xiii. (1824) 224 The stoutest line-of-battle ship.. may be..decomposed in a twinkling. **1883** E. Pennell-Elmhirst *Cream Leicestersh.* 182 In a twinkling the pack is half a field away.

d. With (usually humorous) substitution: see quots.

1660, 1676 [see bedstaff]. **1681** T. Flatman *Heraclitus Ridens* No. 40 (1713) II. 9 This Letter would alone have done it in the twinkling of a Broomstick. **1695** Congreve *Love for L.* ii. v, I have known an astrologer made a cuckold in the twinkling of a star. *a* **1704** T. Brown *Declam. Adverts* Wks. 1730 I. 40 All Thessaly had in the twinkling of a Shoeing-horn been certainly undermin'd by Lobsters. **1709** *Brit. Apollo* II. No. 57. 2/2 I'll do it in the twinkling of a Bedstaff. **1819** *Blackw. Mag.* V. 718 He went off in the twinkling of a bed post. **1821** *Ibid.* IX. 134 In the twinkling of a fan. **1853** Reade *Peg Woff.* iv. 106 You can..master a play in the twinkling of a tea-cup.

4. *attrib.*

c **1620** Z. Boyd *Zion's Flowers* (1855) 68 In a twinkling trice To goe to work.

twinkling, *vbl. sb.*[2]: see twinkle *v.*[2]

twinkling ('twɪŋklɪŋ), *ppl. a.* [f. twinkle *v.*[1] + -ing[2].] That twinkles.

1. Shining tremulously (or †faintly); sparkling, scintillating; †glimmering; flickering (*obs.*).

1508 Dunbar *Gold. Targe* 31 All the lake as lamp did leme of licht, Quhilk schadovit all about wyth twynkling glemis. **1567** *Satir. Poems Reform.* iii. 58 Browis brent and twinkland Cristell eine. **1591** Shaks. *Two Gent.* ii. vi. 9 At first I did adore a twinkling Starre. **1683** Norris *Poems* (ed. Grosart) 58 Some twinkling stars give feeble light. **1765** Beattie *Judgm. Paris* cxvi, Till the morn Spangle with twinkling dew the flowery waste. **1821–30** Ld. Cockburn *Mem.* iv. (1874) 191 A bulky man with..twinkling eyes. **1829** Scott *Anne of G.* xviii, The windows exhibited here and there a twinkling gleam.

2. *transf.* Appearing and disappearing with rapid alternation; producing an effect as of tremulous light by rapid vibratory movement; tremulous, fluttering, quivering. Also *fig.*

1616 Capt. Smith *Descr. New Eng.* 29 The twinkling mountaine of Aucociso. **1791** Cowper *Odyss.* viii. 324 Ulysses wonder-fixt, The ceaseless play of twinkling feet admired. **1814** Southey *Roderick* xvi. 11 The lark..On twinkling pinions poised. **1816** Chalmers *Let.* in *Life* (1851) II. 41 We were looking back on the twinkling rapidity of the months and the weeks which have already gone. **1889** Gregory Smith *Fra Angelico*, etc. (ed. 2) 90 The little twinkling feet which sped so fast and free.

†**3.** Winking, blinking. *Obs.*

1740 Somerville *Hobbinol* iii. 201 To point the holy Leer, by just Degrees To close the twingling Eye. **1742** Richardson *Pamela* III. 332, I often endeavoured, by a twinkling Motion, to disperse the gathering Water, before it had formed itself into Drops too big to be restrained.

4. *Comb.*, as ***twinkling-eyed, -footed*** adjs.

1871 Howells *Wedd. Journ.* (1892) 308 Devotees of the twinkling-footed burlesque..living the life of strolling players. **1904** *Daily Chron.* 13 July 8/2 A sunburnt, healthy-looking twinkling-eyed scamp of thirteen years.

Hence '**twinklingly** *adv.*, in a twinkling manner.

1561 T. Norton *Calvin's Inst.* ii. 143 They shewed it.. twincklingly shining a farre of. **1657** J. Sergeant *Schism Dispach't* 528 This Authority of the Pope in England twinklingly went out and in againe. **1850** *Chamb. Jrnl.* XIV. 16 The glittering grains..leapt twinklingly.

twinkly ('twɪŋklɪ), *a.* [f. twinkle *sb.* or *v.*[1] + -y.]

1. Characterized by twinkling.

1884 *St. James's Gaz.* 21 June 5/1 The most twinkly star of contemporary journalism. **1903** *Daily Record & Mail* 5 Aug. 4 A twinkly humour about the lips.

2. *Comb.*, as ***twinkly-eyed*** adj.

1926 G. Frankau *My Unsentimental Journey* x. 135 A very self-possessed if somewhat twinkly-eyed young woman. **1974** P. Gzowski *Bk. about this Country* 11/2 Professor Hiebert..made twinkly-eyed, flirtatious remarks to Edith.

†'**twinkum 'twankum.** *Obs. rare.* A refrain of a song, expressing careless jollity.

1728 Gay *Polly* i. Air x. (1777) 23 Old oaks can defy the thunder's roar, And I can stand woman's tongue—that's more. With a twinkum, twankum, &c.

†**twinlepi**, *a. Obs. rare*[−1]. [f. twin *a.*, after onlepy.] Twofold, double.

a **1400–50** *Alexander* 5013 Þus be twinlepi tongis [*sc.* Greek and Indian] tell þai oure wirdis.

†**twinlight**, obs. pseudo-archaism for twilight.

c **1532** *Remedie of Love* xliv, The night approched in the twinlight.

twinling ('twɪnlɪŋ). Now *dial.* Forms: see twin; also 4–6 **-lyng(e**, **-linge**, 5 **-lenge**, 8 **-lin**; 5 **twyndyllyng.** [ME., f. twin *a.* and *sb.* + -ling[1]. Cf. in the same sense Norw. dial. *tvinnling*, MSw. and MDa. *tvinling*, NFris. *twen-*, *twanling*, MLG. *twenneling*, MHG. *zwinlinch*, *zwineling*, (OHG. *zwiniling*); also the reduced or variant forms Da., Sw., Norw. *tvilling*, WFris. *twielling* (*twilling*), MDu. *twilinc*, *twēlinc* (Du. *tweeling*), MLG. *twēlinc*, MHG. *zwillinc* (G. *zwilling*).] = twin *sb.* 1.

a **1300** *Cursor M.* 3445 (Cott.) Now sco bredes tua for ane, Tuinlinges [*v.rr.* tuynlinges, twynlynges, twinlinges]. **1382** Wyclif *Song Sol.* iv. 5 Thi two tetes as two ȝunge capretes, twynlingus of the capret. *c* **1430** *Chev. Assigne* 27 Se ȝe þe ȝonder pore womman, how þat she is pyned With twynlenges two. **1483** *Cath. Angl.* 399/1 A Twynlynge (*A.* Twyndyllyng), *gemellus.* **1573** Tusser *Husb.* (1878) 81 Twinlings be twiggers. *a* **1625** Sir H. Finch *Law* (1636) 334 Two being found heires by one and the same title, whether twinlings..or diuerse men..found heires to the same auncestour. **1710** Hilman *Tusser Redivivus* (1744) 8 In some part of Norfolk and Lincolnshire they will keep none but Twinlins.

b. *attrib.* = twin *a.* 3.

1573 Twyne *Æneid.* xii. Llij, A priest..A younglings yelt or brestled sow, and twynlinge sheepe vntwight Bringes forth, and hales the beastes vnto the altars.

twinly ('twɪnlɪ), *adv. rare.* [f. twin *a.* and *sb.* + -ly[2].] To an equal extent, doubly; in an identical degree.

1913 A. O'Connor *Poems* 50 A spot for man, bearing his cross, to seek, Where night and day are healers twinly bright. **1981** C. Dexter *Dead of Jericho* xxii. 123 Even if, in his boyhood, Sergeant Lewis's parents had been twinly blessed with privilege and wealth, it seems unlikely that their son would have won a scholarship to Winchester.

twinned (twɪnd, *poet.* 'twɪnɪd), *ppl. a.* [f. twin *sb.* or *v.*[2] + -ed[1].]

1. Born two at one birth; twin.

1607 Shaks. *Timon* iv. iii. 3 Twin'd Brothers of one wombe. **1611** —— *Wint. T.* i. ii. 67 We were as twyn'd lambs, that did frisk i' th' sun. **1621** G. Sandys *Ovid's Met.* viii. (1626) 157 The twin'd Tyndarides. [**1905** Garnett *Shaks.* 33.]

2. a. Intimately joined or united, as two things; coupled (usually also implying close similarity).

1611 Shaks. *Cymb.* i. vi. 35 The twinn'd Stones Vpon the number'd Beach. **1641** Sir E. Dering *4 Sp. conc. Laud*, etc. i. 2 Two twinned Nations, united together under one regall head. **1872** Sir A. de Vere *Leg. St. Patrick* (Cassell) 26 The sun had set; But still those summits twinned,..Laughed with his latest beam.

b. *Cryst.* United, as two crystals, or consisting of two crystals united, so as to form a 'twin': see twin *sb.* 3 b.

1879 Rutley *Study Rocks* x. 98 A group of three twinned crystals of triclinic felspar. **1895** Story-Maskelyne

Crystallogr. vii. §192 Cubic System. Twinned Forms. **1912** *Brit. Museum Return* 194 Tilasite, a large twinned crystal.

c. Of a city, town, etc.: linked *with* another (in a different country) for the purpose of friendship and cultural exchange. Usu. *predic.* Cf. *twin town* s.v. TWIN *a.* and *sb.* C. e.

[**1923** E. CONYBEARE *Highways & Byways Cambr. & Ely* iii. 51 William of Wykeham..first conceived the idea of twinned colleges, in the provinces and at the University.] **1957** *Harrogate Advertiser* 16 Mar. 13/5 The congress is to talk about problems facing twinned towns, and report on the progress of the twinning. **1960** *Guardian* 25 Feb. 5/5 About 68 towns in Britain are now 'twinned' with towns abroad. **1976** *Times* 5 July 13/6 Leicester city is twinned with Krefeld and a most encouraging friendship has grown up between the two cities. **1980** *Times* 11 July 14/8 Delegates pay visits to twinned cities.

twinner (ˈtwɪnə(r)). *rare.* [f. TWIN *v.*[2] + -ER[1].] An animal that brings forth twins.

1573 TUSSER *Husb.* (1878) 81 The lamb of such twinners for breeders go take.

twinning (ˈtwɪnɪŋ), *vbl. sb.*[1] *Obs.* exc. *Sc.* [f. TWIN *v.*[1] + -ING[1].] The action of TWIN *v.*[1]; parting, separation.

a **1225** *Ancr. R.* 396 Þe soule lueð þet bodi..& þet is eðcene iðe twinnunge. *c* **1374** CHAUCER *Troylus* IV. 1303 Þe twynnynge of vs twayne Wol vs dishese and cruwellyche anoye. *c* **1425** tr. *Arderne's Treat. Fistula* 58 Cleuyng or twynnyng, þat is called rixis. **1591** R. BRUCE *Serm.* (Wodrow Soc.) 206 Death is a violent twinning and rugging sundrie of ..the soul and the bodie.

ˈ**twinning**, *vbl. sb.*[2] [f. TWIN *v.*[2] + -ING[1].] The action of TWIN *v.*[2]

1. Production of two children or young at a birth; bearing of twins.

1573 TUSSER *Husb.* (1878) 81 Ewes yeerly by twinning rich maisters doo make. **1822–9** GOOD *Study Med.* (ed. 3) V. 226 In Congruous Twinning, or ordinary twin cases, in which there is no disparity of size between the two. **1883** DUNCAN in *Brit. Med. Jrnl.* I. 497 In the mare, twinning is a far rarer event than in woman and the cow.

2. Coupling, close union or combination; *spec.* in *Cryst.* the union of two crystals so as to form a twin crystal (see TWIN *sb.* 3 b).

1845 [see TWIN *sb.* 3 b]. **1879** RUTLEY *Study Rocks* x. 87 This twinning is frequently..many times repeated in the felspars. **1898** *Naturalist* 176 A zonal structure as well as twinning—both on the pericline and albite plans.

b. The linking (of two towns or of one town *with* another) for the purpose of friendship and cultural exchange. Cf. TWINNED *ppl. a.* 2 c.

Occas. (as in quot. 1975) used of similar links between institutions such as schools.

1956 *Harrogate Advertiser* 9 June 8/3 French week celebrates the town's pioneer contribution to Le Monde Bilingue in its 'twinning' with Luchon, the spa town in the Pyrenees. **1962** *Guardian* 10 Mar. 16/3 The British Bi-Lingual Association..exists to promote the 'twinning' of towns in Britain with towns abroad. **1973** *New Society* 8 Feb. 284/2 Twinning [of towns]—a translation of the French term *jumelage*—became popular after the second world war, and reached a zenith of municipal goodwill in the late 1950s. **1975** *Globe & Mail* (Toronto) 12 Sept. 5/2 Students in Ontario and nine Caribbean countries and the Bahamas will have a chance to learn more about one another's lives through a new twinning program launched by the Ontario Ministry of Education. **1983** *Listener* 6 Jan. 4/1 There is the twinning of cities.

3. *attrib.*, as **twinning-axis, -law, -plane,** *Cryst.* = *twin-axis, -law, -plane* (see TWIN C.); **twinning-machine, -saw,** names of apparatus for cutting two combs from a single piece of material.

1875 KNIGHT *Dict. Mech.*, *Twinning-machine*, a machine for cutting two combs (twins) from the single piece... *Twinning-saw*. **1883** *Science* I. 331/2 The twinning plane is parallel to the ortho-pinacoid.

ˈ**twinning**, *ppl. a. rare.* [f. as prec. + -ING[2].] That twins (see TWIN *v.*[2]); in quot., joining, becoming united.

1621 G. SANDYS *Ovid's Met.* XI. (1626) 218 Her twinning legs in timber meet.

†**twinny.** *Obs. rare*$^{-1}$. [f. TWIN B. 4; cf. *a twyn(n)y*, variant of ATWIN *advb. phr.*[1]] In phr. ***in twinny***, asunder, apart.

c **1380** WYCLIF *Wks.* (1880) 318 Many men when þey ben gederid preyen more plesingliche to god þen wen þei ben scaterid in twynny.

†**twinse,** *v. Obs. rare*$^{-1}$. (Meaning uncertain.)

c **1205** LAY. 4236 Þa kingges weoren deædde Heore duȝeðe to-dealde Twinseden cnihtes, here tir wes at-fallen.

twinship (ˈtwɪnʃɪp). [f. TWIN *a.* or *sb.* + -SHIP.] The condition of being twin, or a twin; the relation of a twin or twins. *lit.* and *fig.*

1674 N. FAIRFAX *Bulk & Selv.* 107 It [an atome or leasting] has neither East side nor West side;..top nor bottom,..nor any thing that speaks twinship to any thing else. **1796** BURNEY *Mem. Metastasio* I. 378 With all the tenderness of twinship. **1899** GRIFFITH JONES *Ascent through Christ* II. ii. 28 The two streams of mental and organic life coalesce..and begin that marvellous twinship which ends only at death.

twin-sister. (Now usu. as two words.) [TWIN *a.* 3.] A sister born at the same birth, as one of twins. Also *fig.* (Cf. TWIN-BROTHER.)

1707 NORRIS *Treat. Humility* v. 213 Humility..with its twin-sister meekness. *a* **1721** PRIOR *Colin's Mistakes* x, Twin Sisters still were Ignorance and Pride. **1798** WORDSW. *Peter Bell* Prol. xvi, A Boat twin-sister of the crescent-moon. **1884** W. G. HORDER in *Chr. World Pulpit* 12 Nov. 311/1 Music is twin-sister to poetry. **1885** MISS BRADDON *Wyllard's Weird* i, Twin sisters who had loved each other with more than common love.

Hence **twin-sisterhood**, the relation of twin sisters.

1824 MISS MITFORD *Village* Ser. I. (1863) 164 Never was the..tie of twin-sisterhood more closely knit than in these two charming young women.

twinter (ˈtwɪntə(r)), *a.* and *sb.* Chiefly *north.* and *Sc.* Forms: 5–6 **twynter,** (5 **twyntour,** 6 **twintter, twyntter, tynter, twenter**), 6– **twinter;** also 6 **qwintter,** 9 *Sc.* **quinter.** [Reduced f. OE. *twi-wintre, -winter* of two winters: see TWI- and WINTER, and cf. THRINTER. So WFris. *twinter-* two years old (of horses or cows; known to Kilian in *tweenter-, twinterdier*), and *twinter* (also *twainter*) a two-year-old horse or cow, NFris. *twenter* an ox of this age.]

A. *adj.* Of two winters; two years old: said of cattle and sheep (also of colts).

1537 *N.C. Wills* (Surtees 1908) 103 To every oon..of my kynde servauntes..oon twynter calf. **1540** *Test. Ebor.* (Surtees) VI. 94, ij twintter bolokes..one twyntter heffer. **1582** *Shuttleworths' Acc.* (Chetham Soc.) 1 A twinter kowlt. **1620** *Ibid.* 245 A twinter steere. **1638** *Will E. Burton* in *Reliquary* VIII. 221 One twinter bay filly with a whyte foote. **1844** STEPHENS *Bk. Farm* II. 38 After a ewe has been shorn three times she is called a twinter ewe, that is, a two-winter ewe. **1876** *Whitby Gloss.*, *Twinter*, 'a twinter stot', an ox of two winters old.

B. *sb.* A two-year-old cow, ox, horse, or sheep.

1404 *Durham Acc. Rolls* (Surtees) 399 Item xiiij twynterys. **1408** *Hist. MSS. Comm., Var. Coll.* II. 16 Vnum twyntour. **1513** DOUGLAS *Æneis* v. ii. 105 Five twinteris britnit he,..and tydy quyis. **1536** *Durham Acc. Rolls* 419, 4 Trynters, 7 Twynters, 9 Stirks. **1567** *Richmond. Wills* (Surtees) 204 One yonge colte beinge a twinter. **1570** *Wills & Inv. N.C.* (Surtees) I. 341, xxiij twenters, stotts and whies. **1674** BLOUNT *Glossogr.*, *Twinters*, Cattle of two Winters old, so called in Bedford-shire. *c* **1720** RAMSAY *Ram & Buck* 22 When sleet Made twinters and hog-wedders bleet. **1777** *Antiq.* in *Ann. Reg.* II. 149/1 Twinter, a calf two winters or two years old: Derbyshire. **1808** *Compl. Grazier* (ed. 3) 97 The name of the female neat cattle is for the first year, cow-calf, then a..twinter. **1868** *Jrnl. R. Agric. Soc.* Ser. II. IV. II. 428, I turned 20 yearly calves and 'twinters'—as two-year-old animals are locally termed—into a 6-acre field. *a* **1898** [see THRINTER].

b. *transf.* Applied to pasture for, or the right to pasture, a two-year-old sheep, in a common or jointly-held field.

1846 *Award* cited in *High Crt. of Justice* (1892), *Chanc. Div.* (Coulston *v.* Harvey), Four gaits, two twinters, in Bolton Highfield. **1892** *Ibid.*, The Plaintiffs are entitled to 11 gaits 2 twinters and 2 claws or..22 A. 1 R. 35 P. And the Defendants to 2 gaits and 1 claw or..3 A. 2 R. 5 P.

twiny (ˈtwaɪnɪ), *a. rare.* Also 9 **twiney.** [f. TWINE *sb.*[1] or *v.*[1] + -Y.] **a.** Of the nature of, or resembling, twine. **b.** Characterized by, or suggestive of, twining.

1620 QUARLES *Jonah* (1638) 12 Arise O Sleeper,..Theres not a twiny thred 'twixt death and thee. **1771** J. FOOT *Penseroso* v. 203 Whilst swelling nets Their twiny bondage spread. *c* **1868** G. H. KINGSLEY *Sport & Trav.* iii. (1900) 56 Wait till you feel a twiney and twisty sensation which informs you of uneasiness at the other end [of the fishing-line]. *c* **1870** *Ibid.* v. 133 His subtle, twisty and twiny mind. **1902** *Westm. Gaz.* 20 Mar. 3/2 The fichu should be of Alençon lace in the cream or twiny tones.

†**twire,** *sb.*[1] *Obs. slang.* Also 7 **tweer.** [f. TWIRE *v.*[1]] A glance, a leer.

1676 ETHEREDGE *Man of Mode* III. iii, The affected smiles, the silly by-words, and Amorous Tweers, in passing. **1679** MRS. BEHN *Feigned Courtezans* I. ii, Such an Eye, so sparkling, with an amorous Twire. **1682** —— *False Count* I. ii, Winks, and nods, and signes, and twires. **1719** D'URFEY *Pills* V. 74 You toss a twire, a grin.

†**twire,** *sb.*[2] *Obs. rare*$^{-1}$. (See quot.; but perhaps only a misprint for *twirl.*)

1679 LOCKE *Obs. Silk* (1766) 71 They put the cocons in hot water, and so stirring them about with a kind of rod, the ends of the silk twires of the cocons stick to it.

twire (twaɪə(r)), *v.*[1] *arch.* and *dial.* Forms: 7 **twyre,** 7– **tweer, twire.** [Of obscure origin, but corresponding in form to MHG. *zwieren* (now Bavarian dial.) to blink, to peer. There is prob. no connexion with the cant word *tower, towre, toure*, given by Harman (1567) in his *Caveat* (1869) 84–6, and copied by Dekker and later writers.]

1. *intr.* To look narrowly or covertly; to peer; to peep. Also *fig.* of a light, etc.

c **1600** SHAKS. *Sonn.* xxviii, When sparkling stars twire not thou guil[d]'st th' eauen. **1602** MARSTON *Ant. & Mel.* IV. Wks. 1856 I. 52, I saw a thing stir under a hedge, and I peep't, and I spyed a thing: and I peer'd, and I tweerd underneath. *a* **1625** FLETCHER *Women Pleased* IV. i, I saw the wench that twir'd and twinkled at thee The other day. **1637** B. JONSON *Sad Sheph.* II. ii, The common Parent of us all! Which Maids will twire at, 'tween their fingers. **1723** STEELE *Consc. Lovers* I. i, If I was rich, I could twire and loll as well as the best of them. **1874** SWINBURNE *Midsummer Holiday*, etc. (1889) 19 Star by star on the unsunned waters twiring down. **1893** *Wiltshire Gloss.* s.v., 'How he did twire an' twire at she, an' her wouldn't so much as gie 'un a look!'

†**2.** *intr.* Used in sense 'to wink'. *Obs. rare*$^{-1}$.

1601 HOLLAND *Pliny* XI. xxxvii. I. 334 So hard a matter is it for a man to keepe his eies from twiring. And many men naturally cannot chuse but be evermore winking and twinckling with their eies.

Hence ˈ**twiring** *vbl. sb.* and *ppl. a.*

1604 MIDDLETON *Father Hubburd's T.* Wks. (Bullen) VIII. 99 The tweering constable of Finsbury with his bench of brown bill-men. **1612** DRAYTON *Poly-olb.* xiii. 169 The Sunne..with a fervent eye lookes through the twyring glades. **1638** LISLE *Heliodorus* x. 172 The Wiseman lookt on King with twiring eyes. **1728** MRS. DELANY *Life & Corr.* (1861) I. 175 We had ogling and tweering [*printed* tweezing], and whispering and glancing. **1738** *The Briton Described* 13 And then for her Eyes, they are excellent at twiring. *a* **1832** MOTHERWELL *Facts fr. Fairyland* ii, By the winking light of the tweering star.

†**twire,** *v.*[2] *Obs. rare*$^{-1}$. (Perh. a misprint for TWIRL *v.*[1] 3.)

1628 BURTON *Anat. Mel.* III. ii. III. i. (ed. 3) 490 No sooner doth a young man see his sweetheart coming, but he.. slickes his haire, twires his beard, &c.

twire, obs. form of TUYERE.

†**twirede,** *a. Obs.* [OE. *twirǽde*, f. *twi-*, TWI- + *rǽd*, REDE *sb.*[1]] Of two minds or counsels; undecided, irresolute; divided in mind, not unanimous.

c **888** K. ÆLFRED *Boeth.* xli. §3 Hwæðer þu eft on ænȝum ȝeþeahte swa twioræde sie þæt þe helpe hwæðer hit ȝeweorðe, ðe hit no ne ȝeweorðe. *c* **1000** *Ags. Gosp.* Matt. xii. 25 Ælc rice þe byð twyræde on him sylfum byþ toworpen. *c* **1205** LAY. 19416 Bruttes hafden muchel mode & vnimete prute... And weoren alle twiræde. *c* **1250** *Gen. & Ex.* 3271 Egipcienes woren in twired wen Queðer he sulden folȝen or flen.

†**twire-pipe.** *Obs. rare.* [In sense 2 f. *twire* TUYERE. Sense 1 may have the same origin.]

1. App. a contemptuous name for a musical pipe; in quots. applied to persons.

1619 FLETCHER *Mons. Thomas* III. i, Ye are an Ass, a twirepipe, A Jeffery John bo peepe. *a* **1634** CHAPMAN (Webster), I have said..that you looked like Twire-pipe, the taborer.

2. A tuyere-pipe: see TUYERE b.

1674 PETTY *Disc. Dupl. Proportion* 105 The Bellows.. rising in double Quickness admits double air..the whole passing through the same Twire-pipe in half the time.

†**twirk,** *v. Obs. rare*$^{-1}$. [App. from the same stem as *twirl*, with different suffix, but possibly a misprint.] *trans.* = TWIRL *v.*[1] 3.

1599 BRETON *Praise of Vertuous Ladies* (Grosart) 57/2 If shee have her hand on the pette in her cheeke, he is twyrking of his mustachios.

twirl (twɜːl), *sb.* Also 6, 8 **twirle,** 7 **twerle.** [f. TWIRL *v.*[1]] **a.** The action or an act of twirling, or the condition of being twirled; a rapid whirling or spinning; a twist; a spin; a whirl; also *fig.*

1598 FLORIO, *Giro*,..a twirle. **1700** T. BROWN *Amusem. Ser. & Com.*, *City Circle* 136 A Grave Old Gentleman.. gave his Whiskers a Twirl. **1709–10** STEELE *Tatler* No. 128 ¶4 The dextrous Twirl of your Mop. **1775** ADAIR *Amer. Ind.* 400 He commonly sends it [ball] the right course, by an artful sharp twirl. **1818** MOORE *Fudge Fam. Paris* v. 2 Like a tee-totum, I'm all in a twirl. **1827** SOUTHEY *Devil's Walk* x, Satan gave thereat his tail A twirl of admiration. **1840** DICKENS *Old C. Shop* viii, He performed..such spins and twirls as filled the company with astonishment. **1853** KANE *Grinnell Exp.* xiv. (1856) 106 A ballet-dancer in full twirl.

b. Anything that twirls or is twirled; †a reel, winch (*obs.*); each of the whorls of a shell; a curved line. Also *fig.*

steam twirl, a revolving steam-heated cylinder for mixing materials in soap-making (*Cent. Dict.*, *Supp.* 1909).

1688 R. HOLME *Armoury* III. xxii. (Roxb.) 277/2 An Instrument called a Twerle, or Line Reeles: It is to wind a long line of a fishing Rod vpon. **1696** *Phil. Trans.* XIX. 188 The inner Twirls of which Shell were preserved entire. **1716** M. DAVIES *Athen. Brit.* III. *Arianism* 12 Athanasius's Creed is a Twirle of Words. *a* **1728** WOODWARD *Nat. Hist. Fossils* II. (1729) 37 The Twirl in this is different from that of the others;..the Twirls turning from the Right-hand to the left. **1841** CARLYLE *Misc.*, *Baillie* (1857) IV. 230 Not a twirl in that cramp penmanship.

c. *Criminals' slang.* A skeleton key. Cf. TWIRLER b.

1879 *Autobiogr. of Thief* in *Macmillan's Mag.* Oct. 502/2 It was now that I got acquainted with the use of twirls (skeleton-keys). **1923** J. C. GOODWIN *Sidelights* xxvi. 165 In the room Bill cracked with his twirls we piped a pater. **1980** P. KINSLEY *Vatchman Switch* x. 82 She scarcely heard him open the old lock..with the set of 'twirls'.

d. *slang.* A prison warder.

1891 J. BENT *Criminal Life* 272 Will you go and tell Dutch Doll to come up to try and get me a right twirl (good warder)... There is a twirl here from another stir. **1933** G. INGRAM *Stir* xi. 160 I'm standing orderly on this landing and the twirl'll do anything for me. **1962** *John o' London's* 25 Jan. 82/2 Prison officers..are sometimes referred to as *twirls*.

e. A cake in the shape of a twirl.

1973 E.-J. BAHR *Nice Neighbourhood* ii. 20 My Viennese aunt's recipe for butter twirls. **1979** M. INGATE *Tomb of Flowers* i. 8 All kinds of rolls and buns..twirls that went round and round with currants in between.

twirl (twɜːl), *v.*1 Forms: 6 **twyrle**, 6–8 **twirle**, 7 **twurl**, 7–8 **twerle**, 7– **twirl**. [Of obscure origin: perh. merely imitative (or an alteration of *turl* TIRL *v.*3) after *whirl*. The initial *t*- and late appearance of the word are against direct connexion with Continental synonyms from the stem *þwer*-: cf. THWERL *v.*]

1. *intr.* To rotate rapidly, to spin; to be whirled round or about; also to turn *round* quickly so as to face or point the other way; also *fig.* of the mind or head: to be in a whirl, be confused or giddy.

1598 FLORIO, *Girare*,..to twirle about, to wander. *Ibid.*, *Girellare*, to twirle or gire about. **1611** COTGR., *Pirouetter*, to whirle, twirle, turne swiftly about. **1621** MARKHAM *Hunger's Prev.* 117 Vpon the least touch it will twerle and tourne as round as any Scopperill. **1639** S. DU VERGER tr. *Camus' Admir. Events* 307 A Labyrinth where mens spirits twirle about and stray into acts so unreasonable, that they end in folly. **1712** STEELE *Spect.* No. 466 ¶6 Such Impertinents as fly, hop, caper, tumble, twirl,..and..play a thousand Pranks. **1791** COWPER *Iliad* XXIII. 1047 His staff That twirling flies. **1792** MME. D'ARBLAY *Diary* V. VII. 299 A grave man's voice behind me said, 'Is not that Miss Burney?' I twirled round and saw the Bishop of Dromore. **1830** SCOTT *Demonol.* viii. 235 Dost thou not twirl like a calf that hath the turn? **1860** TYNDALL *Glac.* I. xx. 142 The [compass] needle..sometimes twirling swiftly round. **1879** G. MEREDITH *Egoist* III. xi. 240 My head twirls; I did unwisely to come out.

b. The verb-stem used adverbially.

1806 BLOOMFIELD *Wild Flowers* Poems (1845) 190 Twirl went his stick.

2. *trans.* To cause to rotate or spin; to turn (an object) round rapidly; to turn about in the hands; to spin between the finger and thumb, etc.; to twiddle idly or playfully.

a **1623** FLETCHER *Love's Cure* III. iii, Her sighs, powerful as the violent North, Like a light feather twirl me round about. **1647** H. MORE *Poems* 196 'Bout which are hurld [the planets]..round on their own axes twurld. **1664** POWER *Exp. Philos.* I. 55 Hairs..are..angular and corner'd, which you may even perceive by your fingers, by twirling a Horse-hair in them. **1716** GAY *Trivia* II. 422 When..dexterous Damsels twirle the sprinkling Mop. **1797** COLERIDGE *Christabel* I. 48 There is not wind enough to twirl The one red leaf. **1812** H. & J. SMITH *Rej. Addr.* ix. (1873) 85 Roll thy hoop, and twirl thy tops. **1832** G. R. PORTER *Porcelain & Gl.* 184 The workman then dexterously twirls the punt.., the glass yields to the centrifugal impulse. **1871** TYNDALL *Fragm. Sc.* (1879) II. v. 57 A boy twirls round his head a bullet at the end of a string.

b. *fig. to twirl* (a person) ***round one's finger***: cf. TURN *v.* 9 c, TWIDDLE *v.*1 2 b.

1748 RICHARDSON *Clarissa* (1811) III. ix. 64 Who would not wish to outwit such girls, and to be able to twirl them round his finger?

c. To turn (one's fingers or thumbs) rapidly about one another; spec. ***to twirl one's thumbs***, as an idle occupation when one has nothing to do. Cf. TWIDDLE *v.*1 2 c.

1777 MME. D'ARBLAY *Early Diary, Lett.* 27 Mar., Dr. Johnson..has a strange method of frequently twirling his fingers, and twisting his hands. **1816** *Remarks Eng. Mann.* 26 'What can I say?' 'Oh! any thing is better than sitting twirling your thumbs like a fool.' **1833** HT. MARTINEAU *Manch. Strike* vii. 77 Sitting down demurely..and twirling his thumbs. **1864** MISS BRADDON *Henry Dunbar* iii. 23 Bad thoughts..come fastest when a fellow sits twirling his thumbs.

d. *transf.* To shake out or sprinkle by or as by twirling a mop.

1762 CHURCHILL *Ghost* IV. 49 Those, who Physic twirl, Full fraught with death, from ev'ry Curl. **1842** MOTLEY *Corr.* (1889) I. iv. 117 The archbishop with a little mop or swab twirling water on all the dignitaries.

3. To twist spirally (threads, etc.); now *esp.* to twist (the moustache).

1614 B. JONSON *Bart. Fair* II. iii, Neuer tuske, nor twirle your dibble. *a* **1619** FLETCHER *Mad Lover* II. i, I'll take him And twirl his neck about. **1728** MORGAN *Algiers* II. iv. 271 Sir, said he,..twirling his starched Mustachio, I am the Cavallero [etc.]. **1791** COWPER *Odyss.* VI. 379 Twirling her fleecy threads Tinged with sea-purple. **1882** OUIDA *Maremma* I. 169 Joconda was silent, as she twirled her flax. **1894** MRS. F. ELLIOT *Roman Gossip* iv. 121 He twirled his long moustache.

4. To move or cast with a rapid or violent turning motion; to whirl. Now *rare*.

1646 LILBURNE *Unhappy Game Scotch & Eng.* 10 Twerle up your Blew caps, and hurle them up at the Moone. **1648** HERRICK *Hesper.*, *N.-y. Gift to Sir S. Steward* 42 Carouse, Till Liber Pater twirles the house About your eares. **1695** ADDISON *Poems, King* 157 Misc. Wks. 1726 I. 13 Crags of broken Rocks are twirl'd on high. **1742** RICHARDSON *Pamela* III. 392 The Knight following him with Outrage to the Top of a Pair of Stairs, he twirled him from Top to Bottom almost. **1848** THACKERAY *Van. Fair* xl, She would..twirl away his chair from the fire which he loved to look at.

5. *intr.* To twine, coil, curl. *rare*.

1706, *a* **1719** [see *twirled*, *twirling* below]. **1725** *Family Dict.* s.v. *Melon*, The Sun will soon draw the Heat of so fresh a Bed to that Degree, that..the two first Leaves..of the Plant will twirl or coffer. **1840** THACKERAY *Shabby-genteel Story* iv, His great Spanish cloak..of so prodigious a size that the tail of it, as it twirled over his shoulder, whisked away a lodging-card from the door of the house opposite. **1848** —— *Van. Fair* lxiv, The monster's hideous tail.. writhing and twirling.

Hence **twirled** *ppl. a.*, **'twirling** *ppl. a.*

1611 COTGR., *Giré*, veered, or turned..; twirled, whirled, or twyned about. *Ibid.*, *Pirouetteux*, whirling, twirling, trilling, turning swiftly about. **1706** in *Hearne's Collect.* 19 Mar. (O.H.S.) I. 205 Fifty to one yᵉ twirl'd tail'd Cur does win. *a* **1719** ADDISON *Ovid's Metam.* IV. 97 The wriggling snake is snatcht on high In eagle's claws,..Around the foe his twirling tail he flings. **1794** G. ADAMS *Nat. & Exp. Philos.* IV. xlvi. 291 [Electric] boats, with each of them a twirling fly..fixed to the top of the mast. **1871** TYNDALL *Fragm. Sc.* (1879) II. xiii. 307 The retention of the retinal impression transforms the little living rod into a twirling wheel. **1897** *Q. Rev.* July 230 Trying to unravel the twisted and twirled tangle of philosophies of life.

† **twirl**, *v.*2 *Obs. rare.* [Cf. prec. and TIRL *v.*2 and *v.*3] *trans.* To lay *open* by rolling or turning back the covering. Also *intr.* for *refl.*

1523 FITZHERB. *Husb.* §55 Take bothe your handes, and twyrle vpon [*read* open] his [the sheep's] eye, and if he be ruddy, and haue reed stryndes, in the white of the eye, than he is sounde. *Ibid.* §68 Her shap..wyll twyrle open, and close agayne.

twirl- [TWIRL *sb.* or *v.*1 in comb.]: **twirlblast, -wind**, a whirlwind; **twirl-mop** *a.*, that twirls a mop.

1865 *Morn. Star* 22 July, This rock [Hoonister Crag, Rosthwaite] and its neighbourhood is famous for what is called hereabouts '*twirlblasts'—that is, in our southern dialect, 'whirlwinds'. **1765** E. THOMPSON *Meretriciad* 27 A venal trick..practis'd now by all the *twirl-mop maids. **1764** T. BRYDGES *Homer Travest.* (1797) II. 305 Have you not seen a sort of *twirlwind, Which country people call a whirlwind, Whip up a haycock from the ground?

twirler ('twɜːlə(r)). [f. TWIRL *v.*1 + -ER1.]

a. One who or that which twirls. *spec.* (*N. Amer.*), one who leads a marching band; a drum-major or drum-majorette. Cf. TWIRLING *vbl. sb.*

In quot. 1827, a decoy for larks, consisting of a curved piece of wood set with small mirrors, mounted on a spindle and turned by a string.

1808 *Sporting Mag.* XXXII. 134 The twirler is usually some gay youth..he whirls his cane in the air by means of a ribbon. **1827** J. H. H. in *Hone's Every-day Bk.* II. 93/1 The fascination of the twirler is so strong..After being fired at several times they [larks] return to the twirler. **1828** MISS MITFORD *Village* Ser. III. 214 An household..that should shame all the twirlers of mops and brandishers of brooms in the county. *a* **1891** *Tribune Bk. of Sports* 81 (Cent.) Critics [in base-ball] are still looking for the pitcher par excellence. .. Their ideal twirler of the diminutive globe has not yet made his appearance. **1949** R. L. LEE *Baton* 2 A twirler must 'sell' himself to the audience..having..a big natural smile. **1965** *Daily Progress* (Charlottesville, Va.) 21 May 9/2 Twirlers from Maryland, Ohio, Pennsylvania, [etc.] will compete in the individual events [in a baton-twirling competition]. **1980** *Times* 7 Aug. 12/7 British twirlers tend to call themselves Majorettes.

b. *Criminals' slang.* = TWIRL *sb.* c.

1921 J. C. GOODWIN in *Chambers's Jrnl.* 24 Sept. 680/1 Skeleton-keys, or 'twirlers', as the thieving fraternity call them. **1935** R. T. HOPKINS *Life & Death at Old Bailey* ii. 64 In a burglar's kit of tools will be found a jemmy, a bunch of skeleton keys, known as 'twirlers',..wedges, glass-workers' diamond, and a 'treacle plaster'. **1974** 'J. ASHFORD' *Colour of Violence* iv. 34 Weir, who was an expert with the twirlers, forced the lock in six seconds.

twirlification (ˌtwɜːlɪfɪ'keɪʃən). *nonce-wd.* [f. TWIRL: see -FICATION.] Twirling, gyrating.

1834 M. SCOTT *Cruise Midge* (1859) 300 He again floundered past me with his partner..contriving in their complex twirlifications..to tread heavily on my toes.

twirligig ('twɜːlɪgɪg). [f. TWIRL *v.*1 after *whirligig*.] A twirly pattern; a whirligig.

1902 H. BELLOC *Path to Rome* 58 Investigating the twirligigs of the brain to find out where the soul is. **1903** *19th Cent.* June 950 A lumpish, putty-coloured object.. embossed all over with serpentine flourishes and twirligigs. **1942** R. KNOX *In Soft Garments* ii. 11 Take those twirligigs in our brains which are concomitant..of our thoughts. **1980** *Washington Post Bk. World* 2 Nov. 9/4 The dress with an orange twirligig pattern worn by Mrs Umphelby.

twirling, *vbl. sb.* [f. TWIRL *v.*1] In senses of the verb; *spec.* manipulating a baton as the leader of a marching band.

1598 FLORIO, *Girata*,..a twirling of anything. **1623** FLETCHER *Rule a Wife* II. iii, Leave twirling of your hat, and hold your head up, And speak to th' lady. **1626** BACON *Sylva* §845 The Twisting of Thred; And the Practice of Twirling about of Spindles. **1822–9** GOOD *Study Med.* (ed. 3) V. 200 The sudden twirlings of the mouth..the jactitating struggle of the limbs. **1938** BENNER & PAINTER *Art of Baton Spinning* I. ii. 4/1 All actions of baton spinning may be divided into four categories: Looping, Twirling, Spinning and Throwing. **1945** F. H. RODGERS *Keokuk High School Marching Band Student's Handbk.* II. 11 It is not necessary that the drum major do any twirling. **1974** *Cleveland* (Ohio) *Plain Dealer* 26 Oct. 6-D/3 They got fancier with their twirling and began to do tricks. **1980** *Times* 7 Aug. 12/7 The United States Twirling Association..[wants] to have twirling recognized as a full Olympic sport.

twirly ('twɜːlɪ), *a.* [f. TWIRL *sb.* + -Y.] Full of or characterized by twirls or curves.

1887 *Story of a Kiss* I. iv. 56, I can never make out those twirly monograms. **1906** N. MUNRO in *Blackw. Mag.* July 18/1 A curious twirly wooden candlestick.

twirp, var. TWERP.

twiscar, var. TUSKAR, peat-cutting implement.

Twisday, twise, obs. ff. TUESDAY, TWICE.

twisel, twissel ('twɪs(ə)l, 'twɪz(ə)l), *sb.* (*a.*) *Obs.* exc. *dial.* Forms: 1 **twisla, twisel-**; 4 **twisil**, 6 **twisel, twissell**, 9 **twissel**, (**twistle, twizzle**). [OE. *twisla* = OHG. *zwisila* (MHG. *zwisel*, G. *zwiesel*), f. *twi*- TWI-; cf. also ON. *kvísl*.]

1. A point or part at which anything divides into branches; a fork. Now *dial.*

931 *Chart. Æðelstan* 21 June in Birch *Cart. Sax.* II. 360 Of þam mere on þan lace þær þa brocas twisliað; þanne of ðæm twislan on mær beorh. **1586** J. HOOKER *Hist. Irel.* in *Holinshed* II. 43/1 The same were so soft, that with the weight of their bodies they sunke downe vp to the hard knees or twisels. **1847–78** HALLIWELL, *Twissel, Twistle*, that part of a tree where the branches divide from the stock. *West.* **1888** ELWORTHY *W. Somerset Word-bk.* 784 In the twizzle of that there pollard.

†**2.** A double twig or shoot. *Obs. rare.*

1567 TURBERV. *Poems*, '*The Lover wisheth*' 34 As from a tree we sundrie times espie A twissell grow by Natures subtile might, And being two..For one are tane.

3. *attrib.* or as *adj.* Double, twofold (in comb.). *Obs.* exc. *poet.*

c **1000** *Ælfric's Voc.* in Wr.-Wülcker 108/15 *Scinodens*, twiseltoðe. **1382** WYCLIF *Prov.* viii. 13 The mouth of the twisil tunge I wlate. —— *Ecclus.* v. 16 Be thou not clepid a twisil tunge, or a priue bacbiter. *Ibid.* vi. 1 Eche synnere enuyous and twisil tungid. **1956** [see PENELOPIZE *v.*].

† **'twisel**, *v. Obs.* Forms: 1 **twislian**, 3 **twiselen**, 4 **twesel**, 5 **twysle**. [f. prec.; cf. MHG. *zwiselen* and ON. *kvísla*.] *intr.* To separate into two or more branches; to fork; to bifurcate. Hence † **'twisled** *ppl. a.*, † **'twisling** *vbl. sb.* and *ppl. a.*

931 [see TWISEL *sb.*]. **967** *Charter of Eadgar* in Kemble *Cod. Dipl.* III. 14 On ðone twisledan beam. *a* **1000** *Sax. Leechd.* III. 436 Æfter his forðsiþe Eadgar..þæs rices twislunge eft to annesse brohte. *c* **1000** in Wr.-Wülcker 148/25 *Scandula*, twisld corn. **1042** *Charter of Hardacnut* in Kemble *Cod. Dipl.* IV. 66 Ðær ða weȝes twisliȝað. *c* **1200** *Trin. Coll. Hom.* 117 Ðo openede þe holi gost him seluen to isende bi þan þe hem þuhte shapen alse tunge fele twiselende and on fires hewe. **1398** TREVISA *Barth. De P.R.* V. xxvi. (Bodl. MS.), þe tweseled [*ed.* **1495** twyslyd] forkes ben nedeful.

twiser case, obs. f. TWEEZER-CASE.

† **twish**, *int. Obs. rare.* [A natural utterance: cf. TUSH *int.*] An exclamation of contempt or vexation.

1577 STANYHURST *Descr. Ireland* viii. in Holinshed *Chron.* (1587) II. 13/1 There is a cholerike or disdainfull interiection vsed in the Irish language called Boagh, which is as much in English as twish. **1583** —— *Æneis* etc. (Arb.) 144 Twish, what woonder is yt, quod one of the coompanye, If [etc.].

† **twisk**, obs. var. TUSK *sb.*2

1611 CORYAT *Crudities* 247 They wore double maskes upon their faces..with twiskes of downy or woolly stuffe covering their noses.

† **twispeche**. *Obs.* [OE. *twispræc*, f. *twi*-, TWI- + *spræc* (later *spæc*): see SPEECH *sb.*1] Double or deceitful speech.

a **950** *Rituale Dunelm.* (Surtees) 25 Facon and eswico and aefisto and allo tuispreco. *c* **1200** *Trin. Coll. Hom.* 163 Ðe defles sed is hoker and scorn..cheast and twispeche.

twissel, twissle: see TWISEL, TWISTLE.

twist (twɪst), *sb.*1 Forms: 4–6 **twyst, -e**, 4–7 **twiste**, (5 **twest, tweeste**, 5–6 **twys**, 6 **tweyste**, *Sc.* **tuist**), 4– **twist**. [Related to TWIST *v.*, and presenting similar obscurities of history (except in senses directly derived from the verb). Sense 1 may be related to the OE. *-twist* which appears in *candel-twist* glossing L. *emunctoria*, and *mæst-twist* glossing L. *parastates*. Sense 2 corresponds to ON. *kvistr* (Norw. and Da. *kvist*, Sw. *qvist*), which may ultimately be from the same stem: Kilian also gives a Flemish *twist* 'rami abscissi, ramalia'. To sense 4 the only parallel appears to be Kilian's '*twist* i. *twijn*, filum duplex, retortum', the genuineness of which as a Flemish word is doubtful. (G. *twist*, cotton-twist, is from English.) In English there is no sense corresponding to MDu. and Du., MLG. and LG. *twist* (hence Da. and Sw. *tvist*), MHG. and G. *zwist* discord, dissension.]

I. A divided object or part.

†**1.** The flat part of a hinge, fastened on a door or gate, and turning on a hook or pintle fixed in the post: = BAND *sb.*1 3. *Obs.*

1350–1 in J. R. Magrath *Obituary Bk. Queen's Coll., Oxf.* 67 Recepta de dono Willelmi Muscham xvijˢ pro twystes portarum. **1388** WYCLIF *Amos* viii. 3 And the herris [*gloss* ether twistis; Vulg. *cardines*] of the temple schulen greetli sowne in that dai. **1388–9** *Abingdon Rolls* (Camden) 54 In hokis, twystis, et clauis, xij d. **1405–5** *Ibid.* 69 In j hacche cum j twyste et opere ij s. **14..** *Beryn* 478 The Pardonere.. went to have fond þe dor vp by þe haspe; & eke þe twist Held hym out a whils, & þe lok also. **1491–2** in Swayne *Sarum Churchw. Acc.* (1896) 40 Twistes and hokes necessary vnto the Wedyr Dorys. **1529** *Yatton Churchw. Acc.* (Som. Rec. Soc.) 145 Yᵉ levys of yᵉ wyndowes in yᵉ Church-howse, with hookys, twystys, and haspys. **1545** *Croscombe Churchw. Acc.* (Som. Rec. Soc.) 44 Paid for a tweyste and naylys and greffe, iiiᵈ. Paid for greffe thred and silke, iiiᵈ. *c* **1568** in Swayne *Sarum Churchw. Acc.* (1896) 114, iiij pere of twysse and ij pere of hookes. **1805** R. W. DICKSON *Pract. Agric.* I. 71 Smith, for locks, hooks, and twists, latches, etc.

†**2.** A twig; a branch. *Obs.*

c **1374** CHAUCER *Troylus* III. 1181 (1230) As a-bowte a tre with many a twyste [*v.rr.* twist, -e] Bytrent and wryþe the soote wode bynde. **1375** BARBOUR *Bruce* VII. 188 The kyng ..had drede of thai thre men... Tharfor he slepit as foul on twist. *c* **1386** CHAUCER *Merch. T.* 1905 On his bak she stood And caughte hire by a twiste, and vp she gooth. **1423** JAS. I *Kingis Q.* xxxiii, On the small[e] grene twistis sat The lytill suete nyghtingale. *c* **1440** *Alph. Tales* 360/2 þis man happend to be smyten in þe ee with a twyste, so þat he mot not se. **1513** DOUGLAS *Æneis* III. i. 58 Ane vthir smale twist of a tree I chesit. **1583** STUBBES *Anat. Abus.* I. (1879) 76 So long as a sprigge, twist, or braunche, is yong, it is flexible and bowable. **1622** W. WHATELEY *God's Husb.* II. 2 The cutting off from the branches such vnprofitable and ouergrowing twists,..as doe no way benefit the branch.

3. a. The part of anything at which it divides or branches; *spec.* the junction of the thighs, the fork; now (exc. *arch.*) only that of sheep and cattle.

1398 TREVISA *Barth. De P.R.* v. xxxi. (Bodl. MS.), þe boones of the rybbes..beth ybounde togedres in þe twiste of þe breest. *c* **1440** *Promp. Parv.* 504/2 Twest, or twyste, of þe eye (*H., P.* tweeste of the iye), *hirquus* [cf. **1677** COLES *Lat. Dict.*, *Hirquus*, the corner of the eye]. **1572** J. JONES *Bathes Buckstone* 13 b, The one apply vnder the arme holes, and the other in the twyste. **1575** TURBERV. *Venerie* 36 Split one of his forefeete from the twiste of the cleas unto the ioynte of the foote. **1607** TOPSELL *Four-f. Beasts* (1658) 509 Bowes are requisite to remove them [squirrels] when they rest in the twists of trees. **1611** COTGR., *Fourcheure*..that part of the bodie from whence the thighes doe part; I thinke we call it the Twist. *a* **1668** DAVENANT *Siege* III. i, If thou dost grin I'll cleave thee from the Scalp, unto the Twist. **1719** DE FOE *Crusoe* (1840) I. ii. 25, I took him by surprise with my arm under his twist. **1799** A. YOUNG *Agric. Lincoln* 359 The gambrels of the hind legs rather inclining inwards, and the twist fat. **1831** *Sutherland Farm Rep.* 82 in *Libr. Usef. Knowl., Husb.* III, The breast and twist much narrower than to all appearance was compatible with so broad a carcase. **1882** STEVENSON *New Arab. Nts.* (1901) 97/2 If I had my hand under your twist I would send you flying. **1899** *Jrnl. R. Agric. Soc.* Mar. 7 The breast, flank, and twist [of a bull] of great size.

†**b.** *transf.* See quot. *Obs.*

1706 PHILLIPS (ed. Kersey), *Twist*,..the Hollow on the inside of the Thigh;..among Carpenters it is taken for a piece of Timber otherwise call'd *the Girder*. **1823** CRABB *Technol. Dict.*, *Twist*, another name for a girder.

II. The twisting of threads into a cord, and derived senses.

4. a. Thread or cord composed of two or more fibres or filaments of hemp, silk, wool, cotton, or the like, wound round one another; often with defining word, as ***silk, woollen, cotton, gold*** or ***silver twist.***

1555 EDEN *Decades* 200 The other [cord] is grosser lyke the wycke or twyste of hempe. **1558** in Feuillerat *Revels Q. Eliz.* (1908) 93, iiiior oz. di. silke twyste. **1591** SPENSER *M. Hubberd* 461 Ne to weare garments base of wollen twist, But with the finest silkes us to aray. **1601** J. WHEELER *Treat. Comm.* 110 White veluet ierkins cut, imbroidered with siluer twist. **1674** *Essex Papers* (Camden) I. 277 Rolling up Wooll into great Twist, & so passing it as Yarne. **1762** GOLDSM. *Cit. W.* liv, His coat was trimmed with tarnished twist. *c* **1850** *Arab. Nights* (Rtldg.) 306 A small silk purse..tied with a piece of twist.

b. *spec.* (*a*) in *Cotton-spinning*, warp yarn, which is more twisted in spinning, and stronger than weft; (*b*) fine silk thread used by tailors, hatters, etc. With *pl.*, a kind of this.

1805 EAST *Rep.* V. 175 The Battiers received orders from abroad for cotton twist. **1825** C. M. WESTMACOTT *Eng. Spy* I. 265 Buttons, twist, and small ware. **1851** L. D. B. GORDON *Art Jrnl. Illustr. Catal.* p. vi**/2 Twist is the term usually applied to the kind of yarn used for cotton warp; organzine to that for silk warp. **1890** 'R. BOLDREWOOD' *Miner's Right* xxxi, A small piece of silk thread, known by tailors as 'twist'. **1891** *Daily News* 18 Nov. 2/7 Wefts are still more pressed for sale than twists.

5. a. A cord, thread, or the like, formed by twisting, spinning, or plaiting; in quot. 1872, a conical bag or wrapper made by twisting a piece of paper, a 'cornet' or 'screw'.

1598 SYLVESTER *Du Bartas* II. i. IV. *Handie-crafts* 293 On either horn a three-fold twist he ty'd Of Osiar twigs. **1603** B. JONSON *Jas. I's Entertainm.* Wks. (Rtldg.) 529/1 She..sits weaving certain small silver twists. **1607** SHAKS. *Cor.* v. vi. 96 Breaking his Oath and Resolution, like A twist of rotten Silke. **1662** GERBIER *Princ.* 5 Twists of Hair on both sides of their Cheeks. **1700** DRYDEN *Ovid's Met.* XII. 198 About his chin the twist He ty'd, and soon the strangl'd soul dismiss'd. **1740** CHEYNE *Regimen* 151 To suppose the Nerves to be.. membranous Tubes, Twists or Ropes. **1791** COWPER *Odyss.* XVII. 238 His tatter'd wallet o'er his back.., suspended by a leathern twist. **1859** TENNYSON *Vivien* 70 A twist of gold was round her hair. **1872** *Routledge's Ev. Boy's Ann.* 127/2 A twist of newspaper, holding salt, was next placed on the table. **1906** ALICE WERNER *Natives Brit. Centr. Afr.* viii. 206 A few leaves, or a twist of grass, are put on the top to keep the water from spilling.

b. *Naut.* Each of the strands of which a rope consists. Also ***to spin a twist*** (*fig.*): see quot. 1867.

c **1635** CAPT. N. BOTELER *Dial. Sea Services* (1685) 192 The ends of the Strands or several Twists, are with a Fidd drawn into the ends of the other Ropes Strands, and this is called a Splice. **1769** FALCONER *Dict. Marine* (1789) Bb ij b, The twists or strands of a rope. **1867** SMYTH *Sailor's Word-bk.*, *Spin a Twist* or *a Yarn*, to tell a long story; much prized in a dreary watch, if not tedious.

†**6.** *fig.* The continuation or course of life figured as a thread; cf. THREAD *sb.* 6 a. *Obs.*

1568 T. HOWELL *Arb. Amitie* (1879) 25 For thin is twist or fatall threed, on mortall wheele so spun. **1581** —— *Deuises* (1879) 197 But when the twyste of this our tyme is wownde, No meanes by man may serue the same to stretch. **1596** SPENSER *F.Q.* IV. ii. 48 Cruell Atropos..cutting the twist in twaine. **1614** GORGES *Lucan* VI. 254 The Fatall sisters three, ..their spinning twists did guide. **1638** FORD *Fancies* IV. i, 'Tis in my power to cut off The twist thy life is spun by.

7. In other figurative applications, e.g. a slight or weak support upon which something depends; a means of tracing one's way in a labyrinth; an intimate union or connexion; the composition or substance of something figured as being spun.

1580 LYLY *Euphues* (Arb.) 458 Vpon what a twist they hang that now are in honour. **1633** G. HERBERT *Temple, Pearl* iv, Through the labyrinths..thy silk twist let down from heav'n to me, Did both conduct and teach me. **1660** *Charac. Italy* 90 Nor doth her incolumity depend upon the slender twist of the life of one single person. **1675** BAXTER *Cath. Theol.* I. 54 Here is a wonderful inseparable twist; and in the main an Identity. *a* **1734** NORTH *Exam.* II. v. §151 (1740) 410 We must necessarily have to do with him, because the Author has so taken him into his Twist, that we cannot baulk him.

8. A beverage consisting of a mixture of two liquors or ingredients, as tea and coffee, gin and brandy, etc.: see quots. *slang.*

a **1700** B. E. *Dict. Cant. Crew*, *Twist*, half Tea, half Coffee. **1712** ADDISON *Spect.* No. 317 ¶19 Coffee-house. Read the News. A Dish of Twist. **1725** *New Cant. Dict.*, *Twist*,.. Likewise Brandy and Eggs mixed. Hot-pot. **1823** JON BEE *Slang, Gin-twist*, hot water and gin, with sugar and lemon-juice, or orange ditto. **1826**, **1849** [see GIN *sb.*[2] 2].

9. Tobacco made into a thick cord; a piece or 'length' of this. Cf. PIGTAIL 1 a.

1791 W. BARTRAM *Carolina* 499, I distributed my presents, giving him a very fine hankerchief and a twist of choice Tobacco. **1808** PIKE *Sources Mississ.* (1810) II. 121 The prize offered to the successful person was a jacket and a twist of tobacco. **1809** A. HENRY *Trav.* 315 Tobacco.. fetched one beaver-skin per foot of Spencer's twist. **1818** SCOTT *Hrt. Midl.* xl[i]v, Gang down to the Clachan and bring me up a pennyworth of twist. **1849** CUPPLES *Green Hand* iii, Cakes of cavendish, twists of negrohead, and coils of pigtail. **1886** HALL CAINE *Son of Hagar* III. i, Wot's to prevent me having a screw of twist on the strength of it? **1909** J. STARK *Priest Gordon of Aberdeen* ii. 22, I tried the daily use of small twist.

10. A small loaf made of one or more twisted rolls of dough; a small twisted roll of bread.

1830 G. COLMAN *Random Rec.* II. iii. 78 But plague upon their *bapps*..a doughy sort of something, between a roll and a *twist*. *a* **1845** HOOD *Love has not Eyes* iv, Though she's all so much awry, she can only eat a twist! **1852** DICKENS *Bleak Ho.* xix, Dainty new bread, crusty twists, cool fresh butter. **1893** EARL DUNMORE *Pamirs* I. 274 Three or four different sorts of bread, round balls, chupatties, twists [etc.].

11. Stringy india-rubber in the crude state made up in lumps like balls of cord.

1909 in *Cent. Dict. Supp.*

12. A curled piece *of* lemon (or other citrus) peel used to flavour a drink. Also (colloq.) *ellipt.*

1958 A. L. SIMON *Dict. Wines* 58/1 *Merry Widow*, 50 per cent Byrrh Wine; 50 per cent Dry Gin. Fill glass with ice; stir and strain in cocktail glass; twist of orange peel and serve. **1968** *Spirits* ('Know the Drink' Series) 36/1 *Cuba Libre*, 2 oz. light rum, 1 tablespoon unsweetened lime juice. Pour over ice in glass, top up with Coca-Cola, add a twist of lime or lemon rind. **1971** G. V. HIGGINS *Friends of Eddie Coyle* (1972) viii. 55 He ordered a vodka martini on the rocks with a twist. **1973** [see LILLET]. **1981** W. SAFIRE in *N.Y. Times Mag.* 2 May 18/3 A *twist* is of course a twist of lemon skin.

III. Senses denoting chiefly the action of the verb.

13. a. An act or the action of turning on or as on an axis; a turn; a twirl; the condition of being twisted or turned in this way; rotary motion, spin.

1576 GASCOIGNE *Grief of Joye* i. Wks. (Roxb.) II. 265 The strongest thryd yt ever yet was sponne..Is nockthrowen yet even with ye spindles twyst. **1762** STERNE *Tr. Shandy* V. v, Bending her head a little downwards, with a twist of her neck. **1799** A. YOUNG *Agric. Lincoln.* 151 It is gathered by hand, grasping the leaves of the plants, and taking them off with a twist. **1826** SAMOUELLE *Direct. Collect. Insects & Crust.* 63 The net should be of such a length, that, upon a slight twist, it may fall against one side of the hoop, and prevent the escape of the insect. **1840** THACKERAY *Shabby-genteel Story* ix, Mr. Fitch..gave a twist of the curling-tongs to his beard. **1849** H. MILLER *Footpr. Creat.* ix. (1874) 161 In order to accommodate it to the general twist, which rendered lateral what in other fishes is dorsal and abdominal. **1855** BROWNING *A Light Woman* x, [A pear] 'Twas quenching a dozen blue-flies' thirst When I gave its stalk a twist. **1906** *Daily Chron.* 7 June 4/7 We have to allow for the twist of the earth,..mid-Europe time and Eastern Europe time..are ahead of Greenwich.

b. *spec.* in *Arch.*: see quot. 1875.

1840 *Civil Eng. & Arch. Jrnl.* III. 232/2 A short portion of a course, or a single arch-stone, is very nearly contained between two planes slightly inclined to each other; and..the loss of material arising from the *twist* of the stone must always be insignificant. **1875** KNIGHT *Dict. Mech.*, *Twist* (3), *Archit.*, the wind of the bed-joint of each course of voussoirs in a skew arch.

c. A dance in which the body is twisted from side to side; *spec.* a dance of this kind popular in the early 1960s. Also, music for such a dance.

1894 in *Sunday Times* (1962) 11 Mar. 42/5 They're ready an' willin', An' fair at Kadrillin', But my little Flo does the twist. **1898** J. D. BRAYSHAW *Slum Silhouettes* 239 An' there's no kid abaht it, they can both on 'em darnce. Kitty took fust prize..at the contest at that there 'all in Bow. You orter see 'er do the twist. **1928** *Daily Tel.* 11 May 11/1 'The Twist', created by M. Camille de Rhynal..is designed to cultivate gliding and swaying movements. **1961** *Guardian* 4 Nov. 6/3, I have read recently that a new dance has been introduced in America called 'The Twist'. **1965** M. SPARK *Mandelbaum Gate* iv. 116 My mother makes a party for the girls to do the Twist. **1966** *Crescendo* Nov. 6/1 'Manchild'..is an exciting, driving twist. **1978** S. NAIPAUL *North of South* I. iv. 102 Modishly dressed African men and women dancing what I assumed to be the twist.

14. a. In *Tennis, Cricket, Billiards*, etc.: Lateral spin imparted to a ball in striking or delivery, causing it to diverge on rebounding; 'screw'; a stroke by which such spin is given; the action or knack of giving this spin to a ball; also, a ball having such spin.

1699 E. S——CY *Country Gentl. Vade M.* 54 The Players [at Tennis]..talking of *Cuts* and *Twists*, and *Forces*. **1833** NYREN *Yng. Cricketer's Tutor* 68 The ball was delivered quite low, and with a twist. **1856** [see SCREW *sb.*[1] 11 b]. **1884** I. BLIGH in *Lillywhite's Cricket Ann.* 3 W. H. Cooper, as to whose powers of twist and singularity of method so much has been heard. **1889** S. GIBNEY in *Boys' Own Paper* 4 May 496/1 The way well pitched up balls to crump, And how the twists should smothered be.

b. *Physics.* Movement parallel to, combined with rotation about, an axis (as in the motion of a screw); also, the velocity of such movement (= *twist-velocity*).

1891 in *Cent. Dict.*

15. The amount or direction of twisting given to the strands of a rope (*rare*); also, the twisting given to yarn in spinning.

1712 ARBUTHNOT *John Bull* III. iii, Habbakuk brought him a smooth strong tough rope... Jack..found fault with the length, the thickness, and the twist. **1810** J. T. in *Risdon's Surv. Devon* p. xxv, The other yarn, of a softer twist, is called the abb or shoot. **1825** J. NICHOLSON *Operat. Mechanic* 383 When the spindles have given the requisite degree of twist to the yarn. **1831** G. R. PORTER *Silk Manuf.* 205 The action of steam..is found effectually and permanently to set the twist. **1839** URE *Dict. Arts* 983 The flat band, made of four ropes placed horizontally together, the ropes being laid alternately right and left... The ropes counter-act one another in the twist. *c* **1905** in *Eng. Dial. Dict.* (W. Yks.), *Twist*,..the turns put into the end of thread by the rotation of the spindle.

16. a. The condition of being twisted spirally; the amount or degree of this; *spec.* the angle of torsion; also, a spirally twisted object or figure; a spiral line or pattern; *spec.* the rifling in the bore of a gun, etc. (Knight *Dict. Mech.* 1875).

Damascus twist: see DAMASCUS.

1711 ADDISON *Spect.* No. 120 ¶3 There is not the least Turn in the Muscles or Twist in the Fibres of any one [animal], which does not render them more proper for that particular Animal's Way of Life than any other Cast or Texture of them would have been. **1774** GOLDSM. *Nat. Hist.* (1776) IV. 283 The tusks [of this elephant]..have a larger twist, or spiral curve, towards the smaller end. **1833** J. HOLLAND *Manuf. Metal* II. 100 The experience of the workmen [gun-making] enables them to produce any intricacy of twist by this drawing out, doubling and twisting. **1846** GREENER *Sc. Gunnery* 114 It is then twisted like a rope, or..wrung as wet clothes are, until it has from twelve to fourteen complete turns in the inch... Three of these rods are then placed together, with the inclinations of the twists running in opposite directions; they are then welded. *Ibid.* 368 The twist of the spirals..being one turn in four feet. **1858** —— *Gunnery* 218 Drop a few drops of muriatic acid in a basin of water, and wash the barrel slightly, to brighten the twists. **1859** *Handbk. Turning* 113 Examine your work, and see whether the twists begin to appear... As the ivory twists are, of course, very delicate,..employ the screw guides, as directed for the spiral turning. **1867** THOMSON & TAIT *Nat. Phil.* §120 The whole twist of any length of a straight rod is the angle between the transverses of its ends. **1885** WATSON & BURBURY *Math. Th. Electr. & Magn.* I. 81 The suspending wire or fibre will be perfectly free from any twist or torsion.

(*b*) *concr.* A spiral ornament in the stem of a wine-glass. Usu. with defining word, as ***air-twist, colour twist*** (see under the first elements), ***enamel twist***, and freq. *attrib.*; also *transf.*, a glass with this kind of stem.

1897 A. HARTSHORNE *Old Eng. Glasses* 275 The stems are of opaque-white twists of many threads. **1923** H. J. POWELL *Glass-Making in Eng.* iv. 61 A goblet with enamel-twist stem. **1927** W. A. THORPE *English & Irish Glass* 18 Enamel-twists in white or coloured enamels. **1930** T. ROHAN *Old Glass Beautiful* 72 A Norwich twist glass. **1961** C. M. ELVILLE *Collector's Dict. Glass* 81 Those glasses in white monochrome included ales and glasses with straight-sided and bucket-shaped bowls, most of which had enamel-twist stems. **1965** P. M. HUBBARD *Hive of Glass* iv. 42 Have you anything in the way of drinking glasses?.. A twist for choice. **1973** *Guardian* 17 Mar. 18/6 A wine glass with an opaque twist might be worth £25, but with a blue spiral as well £200. A goblet with coloured twists would be worth upwards of £500. **1979** *Radio Times* 7–13 Apr. 25/2 We don't normally touch chipped [glass] items—though we did have a very fine colour twist with a slight chip which went for £800... You can still get a little opaque twist of the 1750s for £20–£30.

b. *Dynamics.* Twisting strain or force; torque.

1891 in *Cent. Dict.*

c. *fig.* A means or opportunity of twisting; a hold. Cf. SCREW *sb.*[1] 2. *slang.*

1880 E. W. HAMILTON *Diary* 30 Nov. (1972) I. 83 The Irish land question evidently weighs heavily on Mr. G... He is afraid of Forster 'getting a twist'. Forster is evidently in favor of very strong measures. **1881** *Home Missionary* (N.Y.) Feb. 386 An artful scheme by which to get a twist on them for the extortion of money.

d. ***the twist***: cheating, dishonesty; treachery; also in phrs. ***on, at the twist.*** *Criminals' slang.*

1933 C. E. LEACH *On Top of Underworld* x. 141 *Twist, at the*, double-crossing. **1938** F. D. SHARPE *Sharpe of Flying Squad* 334 *Twist* (*the*), to change something written or said from right to wrong. Sometimes called 'the Oliver Twist'... A dishonest bookmaker..would say: 'Put the Oliver on it', instead of..'Put the Twist on it'—which might be understood by the 'Mug'. **1977** J. WAINWRIGHT *Day of Peppercorn Kill* 29 Silver-smiths,..one of 'em on the twist. **1979** —— *Duty Elsewhere* x. 36 If I'd wanted you picked up —if I'd wanted to work a twist—would I be here, now? *Ibid.* xxv. 67 Who the hell's poor? *Really* poor? Poor enough to merit going on the twist?

e. Slang phr. ***to get one's knickers in a twist***: to become unduly agitated or angry (*joc.*).

1971 *Morning Star* 26 June 2/1 Britain's Foreign Office mandarins have had their knickers in a twist for the past fortnight. **1982** *Brand New York* (Lit. Rev. special issue) 118/3 There is no reason to get one's knickers in a twist and believe the revolution is nigh.

17. a. ***out of twist***, free from twisting or torsion.

1854 H. MILLER *Sch. & Schm.* x. (1858) 216 If their [the plants'] plane be, as a workman would say, out of twist, their lines will seem parallel. **1901** *J. Black's Illustr. Carp. & Build., Scaffolding* 34 As on the way the holes are bored will depend in a great measure whether the ladder is out of twist or not when finished, they should be made as true as possible.

b. A twisting or screwing of the body or features; a contortion or screw.

1865 DICKENS *Mut. Fr.* III. i, Another dry twist in place of a smile. **1896** *Pall Mall Mag.* Sept. 5 'Indeed!' said Mr. Paget, with an upward twist of his grizzled brows.

c. A strain or wrench (of a limb or joint).

1865 DICKENS *Mut. Fr.* I. vii, You have got a twist in that bone. **1868** ATKINSON *Cleveland Gloss.*, *Twist*, a strain, or wrench; of a joint.

18. A hearty appetite. Cf. TWIST *v.* 13. *slang.*

1785 GROSE *Dict. Vulg. T.* s.v., A good twist, a good appetite. ?*a* **1830** in Norman *London Signs & Inscript.* iii. (1893) 63 Milo the Crotonian an ox slew with his fist, And ate it up at one meal, ye Gods what a glorious twist. **1834** W. H. AINSWORTH *Rookwood* IV. viii, What a devil of a twist he has got! **1861** HUGHES *Tom Brown at Oxf.* vi, You talking of my twist, indeed; you ate four chops and a whole chicken to-day, at dinner. **1890** 'R. BOLDREWOOD' *Miner's Right* iv, 'Cyrus has such a tremendous appetite...' 'If I've got a good twist, I can do a day's work.'

19. An irregular bend; a crook, a kink; also, a confused intertwining, as of a yarn or thread; a tangle. Chiefly *fig.*

a twist in one's tongue, inability to articulate or pronounce clearly.

1776 FOOTE *Capuchin* III. Wks. 1799 II. 401, I am told I have a small twist in my tongue. **1806–7** J. BERESFORD *Miseries Hum. Life* (1826) III. v, Some plaguy twist in our horoscope. **1858** LONGF. *M. Standish* VIII. 75 She disentangled expertly Twist or knot in the yarn. **1897** *19th Cent.* Nov. 786 A twist in the language, an intricate turn, an idiomatic knot. **1903** *Westm. Gaz.* 23 Dec. 9/2 The twists into which some consciences have got tangled.

20. A turning aside, a deviation; also *fig.* a change of circumstances, vicissitude; in quot. 1884, the twisting flight of a snipe; also, a point or place at which a road alters its direction; a bend, turn (also *fig.*); often in phrase ***twists and turns***, intricate windings, ins and outs.

1798 SOPHIA LEE *Canterb. T.*, *Yng. Lady's T.* II. 6 Anxiously did she..form to every fantastic twist of fashion, Miss Arden's rich profusion of auburn hair. **1806–7** J. BERESFORD *Miseries Hum. Life* (1826) VI. Introd., A hot sun ..to stare in upon me all day..at every twist of the road. **1853** JERDAN *Autobiog.* IV. xvii. 330 After all his twists and turns of fortune. **1875** JOWETT *Plato* (ed. 2) III. 38 When men have learned to take a pleasure and pride in the twists and turns of the law. **1884** *St. James's Gaz.* 19 Dec. 6/2 Before the snipe got into his twist..the single-barrel seemed to drop the shot with certainty. **1884** TENNYSON *Becket* v. ii, He knows the twists and turnings of the place. **1897** G. ALLEN *Type-writer Girl* v, After various intricate twists and turns,..I found myself at last by the side of a pond.

21. *fig.* **a.** An eccentric or perverted inclination or attitude; *esp.* a peculiar mental turn or bent; an intellectual or moral bias or obliquity; a craze, whim, crotchet.

1811 BYRON *Hints fr. Hor.* 734 *note*, If she don't take a poetical twist, and come forth as a shoe-making Sappho. **1813** SIR R. WILSON *Diary* in *Life* (1862) II. 204 He has a twist, or, as the Scotch say, a 'craze' on the subject of dress. **1840** DICKENS *Old C. Shop* xxxvi, If in a mind so beautiful any moral twist or bandiness could be found. **1842** L. HUNT *Men, Women, & B.* (1847) II. xii. 305 It took a twist of intrigue and worldliness. **1872** MORLEY *Voltaire* vi. (ed. 2) 311 The twist which polemical fury may give to the most acute intelligence. **1885** DUNCKLEY in *Manch. Exam.* 20 July 6/1 Attendance at Government night schools might easily give them a pauper twist for the rest of their lives.

b. A wresting, perversion, distortion.

1862 GOULBURN *Pers. Relig.* IV. vii. (1873) 304 What twists has the mind of man contrived to give it [the Gospel]. **1875** WHITNEY *Life, &c. of Lang.* v. 96 The most curious twist of meaning. **1876** DOUSE *Grimm's L.* §34. 71 Minute phonetic twists in the several adopting dialects..might still wrench the sound on to widely divergent lines of debilitation.

c. An unexpected development of events, esp. in a work of fiction; a change from usual procedure.

1941 B. SCHULBERG *What makes Sammy Run?* ii. 31 It's a comedy with a helluva twist in it... *she* kidnaps *him*. **1943** B. SMITH *Tree grows in Brooklyn* (1947) xxvi. 145 She did not report happenings truthfully, but gave them colour, excitement and dramatic twists. **1962** [see SNAPPER *sb.*[1] 2 d]. **1974** 'E. LATHEN' *Sweet & Low* xii. 125 Well, there's a new twist for you... I wonder how much it's costing Dreyer to go on network TV and remind us all that they specialize in murder, as well as chocolate. **1978** *Navy News* Oct. 3/1 Portraying a sailor came almost naturally to Peter O'Toole when he played Robinson Crusoe in 'Man Friday', which provides a new twist to the Daniel Defoe classic. **1982** M. YOUNG *Elmhirsts of Dartington* ix. 227 The fact that he was nephew to..a staunch opponent of theirs was a twist that.. appealed to them both. He got the job.

d. ***round the twist*** = *round the bend* s.v. BEND *sb.*[4] 10 c. *slang.*

1960 D. ABSE *House of Cowards* in *Plays of Year 1960–61* XXIII. 190, I knew he was barmy. I knew that man was round the twist, sayin' things like that. **1971** 'F. CLIFFORD' *Blind Side* IV. iii. 178, I ask you. Enough to send you round the twist. **1977** D. BAGLEY *Enemy* v. 38, I swear Ogilvie thought I was going round the twist.

22. *Anglo-Irish.* A spell or turn; a bout; a contest. Cf. TURN *sb.* 25. *rare.*

1846 J. KEEGAN *Leg. & Poems* (1907) 430 The great Queen's County bruiser..to take a twist with Davy Fetherstone.

IV. 23. *attrib.* and *Comb.*, as ***twist-cop***, ***hand***, ***-loaf***, ***manufacturer***, ***service*** (sense 14), ***-spinning***, ***tobacco***; **twist barrel**, a gun-barrel formed of a spirally twisted strip or strips of iron; hence **twist-barrelled** *a.*; **twist-bit**, = *twisted bit* (TWISTED 4); **twist-drill**: see quot.; **twist-frame**, a throstle for spinning cotton; **twist-gear**, a gear in which the teeth are helices (*Cent. Dict. Supp.* 1909); **twist grip**, a control operated manually by twisting, *spec.* one which serves as a hand-grip, and alters the throttle on a motor cycle or scooter, or the gears on a bicycle; **twist-joint**, *Telegraphy*, a joint made by placing the ends of two wires side by side and coiling each round the other for a few turns (*Cent. Dict.* 1891); **twist knot**, a figure-of-eight knot, repeated or continued so as to form a kind of plait; **twist-lace** = BOBBIN-NET; †**twist line**: see TWINE *sb.*[1] 4 b; **twist-lock**, a locking device for securing large containers to the trailers on which they are transported; **twist-machine**: see quot.; also a machine for cutting spiral mouldings in wood-work (*Funk's Stand. Dict.* 1895); **twist-off**, (*a*) *Oil Industry* (see quot. 1932); (*b*) *attrib.*, that may be removed manually by twisting; **twist-pinion** = *twist-wheel*; **twist-rail**, a banister-rail characterized by a twisted or curved end or part; **twist-shaft**, the shaft of the *twist-wheel*; **twist-stitch**, an embroidery stitch: see quot.; **twist-wheel**, in a spinning-machine, a wheel by which the number of turns put into the yarn is determined; **twist-yarn** = sense 4 b (*a*).

1833 J. HOLLAND *Manuf. Metal* II. 98 The *twist barrels ..are used for the most curious and expensive kinds of guns and pistols. **1881** GREENER *Gun* 81 The great step to the success of the double fowling-piece was the employment of twist barrels. **1858** —— *Gunnery* 189 A *twist barrelled gun. **1901** *J. Black's Illustr. Carp. & Build., Scaffolding* 34 They must now be bored..with brace and *twist-bit. **1881** *Manch. Guard.* 12 Jan., Medium counts of *twist and weft cops. **1875** KNIGHT *Dict. Mech.*, **Twist-drill*, (Metalworking) a drill having a twisted body like that of an auger. **1888** HASLUCK *Model Engin. Handybk.* (1900) 66 A twist-drill will run through easily and will leave two holes. **1819** *Encycl. Brit.* Suppl. III. 396/2 The mule..contains a system of rollers like that belonging to the *twist frame. **1590** *Acc. Bk. W. Wray* in *Antiquary* XXXII. 371 Cre[mosin] and black *twiste fringe..twiste blacke fringe. **1954** J. MASTERS *Bhowani Junction* I. 13, I was bending over the handlebars, turning the *twist-grip throttle. **1962** *Engineering* 2 Nov. 584 Travel controls consist of a twist-grip (the amount of twist governing the speed of travel) and a steering wheel. **1975** *Which?* May 143/4 Twistgrip gear change. **1980** *Outdoor Life* (U.S.) (Northeast ed.) Oct. 26/1 Several times I've bumped that twist grip accidentally, turning the motor on. **1886** *Daily News* 20 Oct. 6/2 The *twist hands or workmen who have charge of a machine earned their..seven pounds a week. **1871** *Routledge's Ev. Boy's Ann.* 246 The *twist knot is by no means so generally known. Dissected it is an ordinary 'three plait', though formed of one piece... If well done it forms a hard, tight, and compact long knot. **1840** *Civil Eng. & Arch. Jrnl.* III. 432/1 Improvements in machinery, for..making figured or ornamental bobbin-net or *twist-lace. **1856** KANE *Arct. Expl.* II. x. 100, I made my meat-ball like a *twist-loaf. **1969** *Jane's Freight Containers 1968–69* 137/2 'Tie-down' devices ..are designed to mate with the bottom corners of the containers, which are fitted with *twist-locks. **1977** *Grimsby Even. Tel.* 26 May 4/8 (Advt.), One new Crane Freuhauf 40 ft PSK twistlock trailer, available for hire, £35 per week. **1875** KNIGHT *Dict. Mech.*, **Twist-machine*, one form of lace-making machine. **1800** *New Ann. Direct.* 235 *Twist Manufacturers. **1932** *Amer. Speech* VII. 271 **Twist-off*.., a breaking off of the rotary drill pipe in the hole by torsional stress. **1964** *Supermarket & Self-Service* May/June 19/2 The new twist-off cap. **1970** W. SMITH *Gold Mine* xiii. 38 The whole rig was seconds away from a twist-off. **1974** P. L. MOORE et al. *Drilling Practices Manual* ii. 14 Other limitations have to be considered such as..pipe wear and the danger of twist-offs. **1981** A. LOPEZ *Compl. Course in Canning* (ed. 11) I. viii. 183 (*caption*) 'Twist-off' or Lug cap. **1879** J. ROBERTSON in *Cassell's Techn. Educ.* IV. 397/2 The *twist-pinion requires to be changed when any material alteration is made in the count of the yarn. **1778** *Encycl. Brit.* (ed. 2) I. 618/1 Plate xxxviii. Shews the manner of squaring *twist-rails. **1901** *Munsey's Mag.* XXV. 657/1 Mahony was beaten at Newport..chiefly through the *twist service. **1884** W. S. B. MCLAREN *Spinning* (ed. 2) 139 The crown wheel.. appears at first sight as if it were driven by the *twist shaft. **1825** J. NICHOLSON *Operat. Mechanic* 387 In water *twist-spinning, the operation of stretching is not introduced. **1882** CAULFEILD & SAWARD *Dict. Needlework* 180/1 *Cord Stitch*, a stitch used in Embroidery to cover straight threads thrown across spaces, and not run into the material; also known as *Twist Stitch... Throw a line of thread across a space and fasten it firmly. Return the thread to where it first started from by twisting it over and over the straight and tight line first made. **1894** H. NISBET *Bush Girl's Rom.* 63 He would be reduced once more to the old patched suit and station *twist tobacco. **1851** L. D. B. GORDON *Art Jrnl. Illustr. Catal.* p. vi**/2 The requisite quantity of twist..is regulated by the *twist-wheel. **1835** URE *Philos. Manuf.* 413 Spinning of *twist yarn is the sole business of the establishment. **1891** *Labour Commission Gloss.* s.v., Twist yarn is used for the warps which run lengthwise in a piece of cloth... Twist yarn is always made much stronger than weft, and is so called because more twists per inch are put into the yarn while being spun.

†**twist**, ? *sb.*[2] *Obs. rare.* In 4 **twyst-**. [Perhaps identical with the second element of OE. *mæst-twist* (glossing L. *parastates*), which may be connected with TWIST *sb.*[1] 1–3.] Used with *line* and *rope* to designate some part of the tackle of a vessel.

1336 *Acc. Exch. K.R.* 20/20 (P.R.O.) De .xj. petris cordarum de Canabo..emptis..pro vno Twystrop inde faciendo. **1336–7** *Ibid.* 19/31 m. 5 In vj. petris corde de canabo..pro vno boltrope vno Twystrope et j. lychrop. **1356** in *Pipe Roll 32 Edw. III*, m. 34/2 (P.R.O.), xj. forloks. iij toppelynes, v. twystlyne [*sic*], vj tregetropes.

twist (twist), *sb.*[3] *slang* (chiefly *U.S.*). [short for *twist-and-twirl* (also used), rhyming slang for *girl*.] A girl, a young woman (freq. depreciatory).

1924 *Truth* (Sydney) 27 Apr. 6 *Twist and twirl*, a girl. **1926** *Clues* Nov. 162/2 *Twist*, a girl. **1927** *Dialect Notes* V. 466 *Twist*, n., a loose woman. **1932** [see DOG-HOUSE b]. **1953** 'R. MACDONALD' in H. Waugh *Merchants of Menace* (1969) 93, I hate to see it happen to a pretty little twist like Fern. **1956** H. GOLD *Man who was not with It* (1965) xvii. 154 I'm just as good as any of those Pittsburgh twist-and-twirls. **1979** [see PROPOSITION *sb.* 7 b].

twist (twist), *v.* Forms: 4–5 **twiste**, 4–6 **twyst**, 5 **twyste**, (4 **tuyst**), 6– **twist**. *Pa. t.* and *pple.* **twisted**; also 4–5 **twyst(e**, **twist(e**; (*pa. t.* 5 **tueste**, 7 *Sc.* **twust**; *pa. pple.* 6–7 **twist**). [Evidently (like TWINE *v.*[1]) a deriv. from the stem TWI-, denoting either division in two (Branch I) or combination of two (threads, etc.) into one (Branch II). With the former cf. Flem., Du., and LG. *twisten* to disagree, quarrel (hence Da. *tviste*, Sw. *tvista*), Icel. *tvistra* or *tvístra* to scatter (also *á tvist*, OIcel. *tvistróttr* scattered); with the latter cf. older Flem. (Kilian) *twisten* to twine (thread), Da. dial. *tviste*, *tweste*. Branch III would be a natural development of II, though actually recorded a century earlier.

The meaning of *twisteð* in *Trin. Coll. Hom.* 213 is obscure, and the passage appears to be in some way corrupt.]

I. To divide, separate.

†**1.** *intr.* To divide into branches; to branch. *Obs. rare.*

1340 *Ayenb.* 159 Yef þe onderstondingge is wrong, oþer yef huy tuysteþ..al þe inwyt ssel by þiestre... He tuysteþ ine tuo, huanne me wylneþ of one half to god, and of oþer-half to þe worlde. **1398** TREVISA *Barth. De P.R.* v. xxi. (Bodl. MS.) lf. 12/1 The tunges of addres bene blacke..swifte in meuyng..þat meueþ þe tunge so swiftelich so þat on tunge semeþ iforked and twisted [*orig.* Qui tam velociter linguas agitat vt vna numero bifurcari videatur lingua].

2. *trans.* **a.** To prune, clip. *Obs.* or *dial.*

1483 *Cath. Angl.* 399/2 To Twyste, *defrondare*. **1535** COVERDALE *Isa.* v. 6, I will laye it waist, that it shall nether be twysted nor cut, but beare thornes and breares. —— *2 Esdras* xvi. 43 He that twysteth the vynyarde, as he that shal not gather the grapes. **1672** in W. Grainge *Nidderdale* (1863) 137 *note*, [The tenant also agrees] not to cut, fell, or twist the wood standing and growing thereon.

†**b.** *fig.* To detach, separate, take away. *Obs.*

c **1440** CAPGRAVE *St. Kath.* I. 103 He prechyd so ther þat [he] hem alle twyst [*v.r.* twyste] Fro all her maumentrye & fals be-leue. *Ibid.* II. 866, I haue ȝit no list þat ony man my maydynhod schuld twyst.

II. To combine, unite, and derived senses.

3. a. *trans.* To combine two or more yarns or fibres of (any suitable material) into a thread or cord by spinning; to form (a thread or cord) by spinning the yarns or strands. Also *absol.*

1471 *Mann. & Househ. Exp.* (Roxb.) 551 Alys Haweryng hat spowne and cardyd and twystyd tweyntey pownde of ȝerne. **1530** PALSGR. 764/2, I twyst threde, I twyne threde. This terme is northren; declared in 'I twyne'. **1595** SHAKS. *John* IV. iii. 128 The smallest thred That euer Spider twisted from her wombe Will serue to strangle thee. **1599** T. M[OUFET] *Silkwormes* 73 Man and maide Whilst winding, twisting, and in weauing, thay Now laugh, now chide. **1650** W. BROUGH *Sacr. Princ.* (1659) 458 Cords..if well twist and made will bind and hold any though never so strong. **1690** LUTTRELL *Brief Rel.* (1857) II. 3, 6000 *l.* worth of hay is already bought on the river Severn and ordered to be twisted and sent on board. **1725** DE FOE *Voy. round World* (1840) 347 Tow-lines..they supplied by twisting a strong tough kind of flag or rush. **1796** MORSE *Amer. Geog.* I. 557 Manufactory for spinning and twisting cotton. **1844** G. DODD *Textile Manuf.* vi. 184 Organzine, besides being wound, cleaned, and doubled, is twisted or thrown twice.

b. *fig.* or in fig. context.

1599 SHAKS. *Much Ado* I. i. 313 Was't not to this end, That thou beganst to twist so fine a story? **1643** HERLE *David's Song* 5 A double string,..twisted of two parts into a kind of discordant concord. **1663** BUTLER *Hud.* I. I. 157 He a rope of sand could twist As tough as learned Sorbonist. **1760–72** H. Brooke *Fool of Qual.* (1809) III. 18 It twists the sacred and endearing cord of society. **1872** Bagehot *Physics & Pol.* (1876) 120 His life is twisted into a thousand curious habits. **1884** F. M. Crawford *Rom. Singer* I. 17, I am trying hard to twist a rope of which I never held the other end.

c. *transf.* To plait, weave, twine, wreathe.

a **1592** T. Watson *Poems* (Arb.) 15 Where Lawrell wreath's are twist for them alone, Whose gals are burst with often tasted sowre. **1693** *Patent Specif.* No. 313 A certaine Engine or Machine for the Makeing or Twisting of Whips. **1760–72** H. Brooke *Fool of Qual.* (1809) III. 6 To twist the garland of your blessedness. **1878** M. A. Brown *Nadeschda* 20 Of straw a girdle twisted up.

4. To join or unite by twining or interlacing; to twine *together*; to entwine (one thing) *with* or †*to* another; to intertwine, interweave.

1563 Golding *Cæsar* vii. (1565) 225 Fyue rowes of them ioyned and twysted one wythin another, so that whosoeuer ventured in, must nedes gore them selues vppon the sharpe pointes of the stakes. **1601** Holland *Pliny* xvii. xxiii. I. 537 These meet one with another in the space betweene, and are interlaced, twisted, and tied together. **1634** Sir T. Herbert *Trav.* 94 The people..thought to forbid..his desired entrance, by twisting one tree to another. **1687** A. Lovell tr. *Thevenot's Trav.* i. 22 A Pillar made of three brazen Serpents twisted together. **1756–7** tr. *Keysler's Trav.* (1760) I. 234 The seat..is made of bark and ropes twisted together. **1825** Scott *Talism.* viii, A small silken bag made of net-work, twisted with silver. *Ibid.* xxvii, The sashes were twisted with silk and gold. **1827** Faraday *Chem. Manip.* xxiv. (1842) 632 Twist together five or six folds of steel harpsichord wire.

5. *fig.* **a.** To unite, combine, connect, associate intimately, like strands in a cord.

1573–80 Baret *Alv.* T 460 To bind, or twist hard together, to mingle so together that one cannot tell what the thing meaneth. **1639** Fuller *Holy War* iii. xxiv. (1840) 160 John de Bren..to twist his title with another string, married Maria Jole. **1646–8** G. Daniel *Tomb Earl Strafford* ii, Our Monarch's Fate Was twist in his. **1652** Benlowes *Theoph.* i. xcvi, Make arts thy tributaries, twist heart, tongue and pen. **1697** Dryden *Æneid* xi. 561 Pity your own, or pity our Estate; Nor twist our Fortunes with your sinking Fate. **1712** M. Henry *Commun. w. God* i. Wks. 1853 I. 205/1 God has been pleased therein to twist interests with us. **1731** W. Bowman *Serm. Vers.* 24 The church then with the state was twisted.

b. ***twist in***, to initiate or swear in as a member or associate of the Luddites. ***twist out***: see quot. 1883; also *lit.*, to get out (a strand) from a cord by unravelling it.

1812 *Chron.* in *Ann. Reg.* 63/1 Offering five guineas bounty, and 15*s.* per week to all that would be twisted in. **1813** B. Walker in *Examiner* 11 Jan. 21/2 The murder was well known amongst those twisted in. **1883** *Almondbury & Huddersfield Gloss.*, *Twisted out*, after the trials at York, an order in Council directed that..the Luddites..should go before a magistrate, and be twisted out, as it was called; that is, they took the Oath of Allegiance. **1887** J. Hutchison *Lect. Philippians* iv. 35 The whole cordage..has a red thread moving throughout it, which cannot be twisted out without undoing it all.

c. *fig.* To entangle or mix *up with* something; to get into a tangled or confused state; to confuse, confound.

1863 Susan Warner *Old Helmet* 179 The question..was inextricably twisted up with the other question. **1908** Rider Haggard *Ghost Kings* viii, They had twisted up the story..into that [story] which they had narrated to her.

6. To wind or coil (a thread or the like) *on* or *round* something; to attach in this way; to encircle (an object) *with* or as with a thread, etc.; to entwine *in* something else.

1582 Stanyhurst *Æneis* ii. (Arb.) 66, I twisted a wallet On my broad shoulders. **16..** in Burton *Scot Abroad* I. iii. 150 He had long hair platt over his neck, whilk David Home ..twust to his saddle-bow. **1710** W. King *Heathen Gods & Heroes* x. (1722) 34 His Thighs were all twisted round with Folds of Vipers. **1820** W. Irving *Sketch Bk.* I. 51 A few wild flowers were twisted in her fine hair. **1825** T. Hook *Sayings* Ser. ii. *Sutherl.* I. 21 Jane ran to a looking-glass and.. twisted her limp ringlets round her long pale fingers into apologies for curls. *Ibid.*, *Passion & Princ.* xii. III. 268 Twisting silk on bits of cards cut star-wise. **1870** J. Hamilton *Moses* v. 99 A sinful habit entwined and twisted round your souls. **1885** 'Mrs. Alexander' *At Bay* x, Lambert twisted the comforter round his throat and face.

7. *intr.* and *refl.* To pass or move in a tortuous manner; to coil or twine *about* or *round*; to penetrate *into* something with a tortuous movement or action.

1635 Quarles *Embl.* iv. xii. 43 O how these Armes..did twine, And strongly twist about his yeelding wast! **1644** Evelyn *Diary* 7 Mar., A fountaine of serpents twisting about a globe. *a* **1652** J. Smith *Sel. Disc.* i. (1821) 7 Any filthy vice..perpetually twisting itself into the thread of our finest spun speculations. **1705** Addison *Italy* 391 (*Sienna*) Great Columns..finely engraven with Fruits and Foliage that run twisting about 'em from the very Top to the Bottom. **1774** Goldsm. *Nat. Hist.* (1776) VII. 227 They [boas]..will dart down upon travellers, and twist themselves so closely round their bodies, as to dispatch them in a very few minutes. **1849** Cupples *Green Hand* xvi, Flowers, trailing and twisting in thick snaky coils close up the stems. **1850** Hawthorne *Scarlet L.* iii, A writhing horror twisted itself across his face. **1851** Ruskin *Stones Ven.* I. App. viii. 364 The weeds..have twisted themselves into its crannies.

III. To wring, wrench.

†**8.** *trans.* To compress with a turning movement; to wring; also *fig.* to torment, harass. *Obs.*

Cf. *tuaste* pa. t. (*c* 1325) in Ritson *Metr. Rom.* II. 272. *c* **1374** Chaucer *Troylus* iv. 226 (254) Þe furye and þe rage Whiche þat his herte twyste & faste þreste. *c* **1384** —— *H. Fame* ii. 267 For whan a pipe is blowen sharpe The aire ys twyst with violence And rent. *c* **1386** —— *Wife's Prol.* 494 Ther was no wight saue god and he þat wiste In many wise how soore I hym twiste. —— *Merch. T.* 761 She taketh hym by the hand and harde hym twiste.

9. a. To wring out of place or shape, or so as to change the shape; *esp.* to force (a limb, etc.) round so as to sprain it; to wrench. ***to twist up***, to screw up into a rounded form. Also *refl.*

c **1530** *Hickscorner* B ij, *Imag.*.. At tyburne..Some there taketh a fall that maketh theyr necke lame. *Frewyll.* Ye but can they go no more? *Imag.* Oh no man. The wrest is twyst so sore. **1655** Fuller *Ch. Hist.* ix. vii. §36 The Doctor fairly twisted his wrists almost to the breaking thereof. *c* **1803** C. K. Sharpe *New Oxford Guide* ii, I twisted my ancle—foment it with grease. **1827** Carlyle *Misc.*, *Richter* (1857) I. 2 This mirror is so twisted with convexities. **1844** W. H. Maxwell *Wand. Highl.* II. xxi. 249 Twisting the neck of a skoray, or young kittiwake. **1857** Hughes *Tom Brown* i. viii, [He] seized him [Tom] and twisted his arm. **1865** Dickens *Mut. Fr.* i. vi, It seemed to twist itself into some likeness of boughs.

†**b.** *spec.* ***to twist a horse***: see quot. *Obs.*

1727–41 Chambers *Cycl.* s.v., To twist a horse, is violently to wring or twist his testicles twice about, which causes them to dry up, and deprives them of nourishment.

c. *pass.* To be hanged. *slang.*

1725 *New Cant. Dict.*, *Twisted*, executed, hanged. **1811** *Lexicon Balatr.* s.v. *Nose*, His pall nosed, and he was twisted for a crack,..was hanged for burglary.

d. ***to twist the tail*** (of a person): to annoy, to coerce (someone). ***to twist the lion's tail*** (*U.S.*): to provoke the resentment of British people.

1895 *Lit. Digest* 25 May 112/2 Papers in the U.S. take to shouting 'Hands off!' to England... Twisting the lion's tail is a regular electioneering maneuver. **1909** 'O. Henry' *Roads of Destiny* xvi. 259 [He] twisted the tail of a Connecticut insurance company that was trying to do business contrary to the edicts of the great Lone Star State. **1926** E. L. Abbey *Twist of Lion's Tail* 9 John Bull takes the lion for his emblem... Twist the lion's tail and how he hollers! **1935** 'N. Blake' *Question of Proof* v. 91 Revenge seems to me least likely. Grown men don't kill boys just because they've had their tails twisted by them. **1956** A. Wilson *Anglo-Saxon Attitudes* i. iv. 173 I get a good deal of amusement twisting both their 'advanced' tails, particularly the egregious parson's. **1965** P. O'Donnell *Modesty Blaise* vi. 72 So they were going to twist his tail for a while. Well, ..the side-effects would have to be accepted stoically. **1979** E. Newman *Sunday Punch* vii. 58, I took a silent vow never again to twist the lion's tail editorially.

e. ***to twist*** (someone's) ***arm***: to force or persuade someone to do something. Also used *joc.* when no coercion is needed, esp. with reference to drinking.

1953 *Word for Word* (Whitbread & Co.) 36/2 *Twist one's arm*, to 'persuade' one to have a drink, when no persuasion is needed. **1953** Berrey & Van den Bark *Amer. Thes. Slang* (1954) §221/2 *Force; compel*.. twist one's arm. *Ibid.* §223/5 *Induce; persuade*..twist one's arm. **1968** C. Cooper *Thunder & Lightning Man* iv. 65 The National Trust, in their genteel fashion, are beginning to twist my arm. The property must be made to pay its way. **1972** G. Bell *Villains Galore* v. 57 'That looks a very nice little pub over there.'.. 'All right —you've twisted my arm enough,' admitted Boote. **1977** G. Scott *Hot Pursuit* xii. 108 If you'd twisted my arm I would have had to admit that it was even important enough to justify the risks. **1982** H. Engel *Ransom Game* xxv. 154, I let him twist my arm into taking a Scotch with water.

10. a. To turn awry; to screw up or contract (the features, etc.); to contort, distort.

1789 W. Buchan *Dom. Med.* (1790) 433 In the fit..his extremities are bent or twisted various ways. **1818** Scott *Hrt. Midl.* xlvi, Sorely did he twist about his physiognomy, and much did he stumble in his speech, before he could express his idea. **1859** Tennyson *Lancelot & Elaine* 1139 The dumb old servitor..Winking his eyes, and twisted all his face. **1867** Aug. J. E. Wilson *Vashti* xxx, A bitter smile twisted the muscles about Mrs. Gerome's mouth. **1898** 'H. S. Merriman' *Roden's Corner* viii, At times he twisted his lips, moistening them with his tongue.

b. *fig.* To wrest the form or meaning of; to pervert; to distort; to force a meaning from.

1821 Scott *Kenilw.* xiv, Twisting into all manner of uncouth and incomprehensible forms of speech the honest plain English phrase which God gave us to express our meaning withal. **1829** Lytton *Disowned* xlviii, I tried to twist her words into a hundred meanings. **1853** Kingsley *Hypatia* viii, A mere logician, twisting Aristotle to mean what she knew..Aristotle never meant. **1871** Palgrave *Lyr. Poems* 120 A law no guile can twist to harm. **1883** *19th Cent.* May 730 Twisting my opinions into accordance with a party.

11. To force *down*, pull *off* or *out* with a turning strain; to wrench or wring *off*, etc. Also *fig.*

1784 Cowper *Task* iv. 62 A demagogue..with a dexterous jerk soon twists him down [from the summit of ambition]. **1804** C. B. Brown tr. *Volney's View Soil U.S.* (Philad. ed.) 140 They [whirlwinds] twist off and lay level the largest trees. **1823** Scott *Quentin D.* v, Untwining his gold chain from his neck, Balafré twisted off, with his firm and strong-set teeth, about four inches from the one end of it. **1838** James *Robber* vi, These foxes have almost twisted my thumbs off. **1890** Gunter *Miss Nobody* xiii, A summons or writ or some other cursed legal thumb-screw to twist the dollars out of my pocket!

12. a. To form into a spiral; to bend, curve, or coil spirally; to screw *up*.

a **1744** Pope (J.), Either double it into a pyramidical, or twist it into a serpentine form. **1765** Sterne *Tr. Shandy* VIII. xi, By all that is hirsute and gashly! I cry, taking off my furred cap, and twisting it round my finger. **1818** Scott *Br. Lamm.* xxi, A cow chased by a whole nest of hornets, and her tail twisted over her rump like a corkscrew. *a* **1839** Praed *Poems* (1864) I. 326 Twisting up his songs Into the sweetest candlepapers. **1843** Holtzapffel *Turning* I. 207 Some twist the iron before hammering to prevent it from becoming 'spilly'. **1858** Greener *Gunnery* 195, I found that the inside was entirely composed of iron, over which the covering of Damascus had been twisted. **1861** Bentley *Man. Bot.* 512 Flowers usually symmetrical... Petals twisted in æstivation. **1875** Bennett & Dyer *Sachs' Bot.* 838 When the tendrils have fixed themselves by their extremities, they draw the stem towards the support by twisting themselves spirally. **1906** Marj. Bowen *Viper of Milan* x, He turned back into the corridor, twisting the ends of his scarlet robe between his fingers.

b. ***to twist*** (a person) ***round one's finger***, to have completely under one's influence; so ***to turn, twist, and wind*** (one): cf. turn *v.* 64.

1780 *Mirror* No. 95 ¶7 At the first glance I saw into him, and could now twist him round my finger. **1787** Mme. D'Arblay *Diary* Aug., You turn, twist, and wind me just as you like. **1840** Dickens *Barn. Rudge* vi, Women may twist me round their fingers at their pleasure. **1855** Kingsley *Westw. Ho!* xxix, The man has twisted the whole council round his finger.

c. *intr.* for *refl.* or *pass.*

1881 Greener *Gun* 224 The rod is carefully watched while twisting, and should one part commence to twist more rapidly than another [etc.]. *a* **1886** in C. E. Pascoe *Lond. of To-day* xl. (ed. 3) 337 Seams are crooked and wrinkle, sleeves twist, the chest is tight,..&c. &c. The arrival of a new dress brings with it agonies.

d. *trans.* To cheat, to defraud. *slang.*

1914 Jackson & Hellyer *Vocab. Criminal Slang* 95 They had to learn awareness in the school of cold, hard facts, having been..'twisted'..times innumerable. **1956** *People* 13 May 2/3 Don't imagine that all the boys in the trade are out to twist you. **1967** P. Ryan *How I became Yorkshireman* xv. 95 He were..content to be twisted daft wi'out mekking a mouse-squeak after value for his brass.

e. *trans.* and *intr.* *Insurance.* To induce someone to change a policy from one company to another. Cf. twisting *vbl. sb.* 5.

1924 Webster Add., *Twist, v.t. Life Insurance.* To induce (a person) to drop a policy already in force in a company other than that of the twisting agent for one in the agent's company.—*twister, n.* **1936** *Sun* (Baltimore) 29 July 16/2 He expressed the hope that any agent found 'twisting' or attempting to discourage policyholders in the Pacific Mutual not to retain their insurance would be reported to the Insurance Division.

13. *intr.* and *trans.* To eat heartily; also ***to twist*** (food) ***down***. *slang.*

1694 Motteux *Rabelais* v. v. 17 Twist like Plough-jobbers, and Swill like Tinkers. *Ibid.* xxvii. 132 They us'd to twist store of Holy-bread, Cakes, Buns, Puffs, Lenten-Loaves, Jumbals and Biscuits. *a* **1700** B. E. *Dict. Cant. Crew*, *Twist*, to Eat. *To Twist lustily*, to Feed like a Farmer. **1785** Grose *Dict. Vulg. T.* s.v. *Twist*, To twist it down apace, to eat heartily. **1817–18** Cobbett *Resid. U.S.* (1822) 165 She will twist down a half pound of beef with her 'potatoe', and has twisted down half a pound of buttered toast in the morning.

IV. To rotate, etc.

14. a. *trans.* To cause to rotate as on an axis; to turn (anything) round so as to alter its position or aspect. ***to twist one's fingers***, to turn one's fingers about nervously.

1789 W. Buchan *Dom. Med.* (1790) 589 He must pull the head with considerable force, gently twisting it at the same time, if the face be turned to one side, till he perceives that the joint is replaced. **1796** Mme. D'Arblay *Camilla* IV. 80 She twisted it..hastily round, to hide the hand-writing of the direction. **1827** Scott *Surg. Dau.* vi, I will twist your head round till your eyes look at the drummer's hand-writing on your back. **1864** Lowell *Fireside Trav.* 264 Blocks of stone,..lowered, tipped, twisted, undermined, and generally capsized by the rains and frosts of centuries. **1885** 'Mrs. Alexander' *Valerie's Fate* vi, Speak then, you stupid child, and don't stop short to twist your fingers.

b. *Cricket.* In bowling, to give a lateral spin to (the ball), so that it 'breaks' or turns aside on rebounding.

1816 W. Lambert *Instructions & Rules for playing Cricket* 20 The Ball may be twisted by the usual mode of under-armed Bowling. **1833** Nyren *Yng. Cricketer's Tutor* 118 If either of your bowlers twist his balls, favour such twist as much as possible.

c. *intr.* To dance the twist (twist *sb.*[1] 13 c).

1961 *Guardian* 30 Dec. 5/3 It is a week with only one new film, a small loud monstrosity called 'Hey, Let's Twist'. **1968** J. Updike *Couples* ii. 166 Frank was grotesquely Twisting..opposite Carol Constantine.

15. a. *intr.* To rotate, revolve; also, to turn so as to face another way.

1680 Moxon *Mech. Exerc.* x. 177 A strong Iron Screw.. with a square Shank near the Head, that..it may not twist about. **1850** Tennyson *In Mem.* ci. 12 When the lesser wain Is twisting round the polar star. **1857** Hughes *Tom Brown* ii. viii, The ball comes skimming and twisting along about three feet from the ground. **1907** J. H. Patterson *Man-Eaters of Tsavo* xviii. 199 As we moved, the lion also twisted round and so always kept his head full on us.

b. In Vingt-et-un, to receive a card dealt face upwards; also, to deal a card in this manner. Occas. *trans.* and as *imp.* Also *fig.* Cf. stick *v.*[1] 6 e.

1921 P. Alston *Card Games* 121 If it is not desired to buy, the usual expression is to say 'Twist'. *Ibid.* 122 Having bought a player can then twist; but once having twisted, a card cannot be bought. **1939** Phillips & Westall *Compl. Bk. Card Games* 194 The player can either buy cards or can have them 'twisted'..; a card twisted is turned face upwards. *Ibid.*, B has a 9 and a 5; he says 'twist me one'. **1963** G. F. Hervey *Handbk. Card Games* 285 He can twist: that is to say he elects to receive a card face upwards. **1972** *Guardian* 12 Oct. 1/3 Every pontoon player will understand the dilemma of the Tory chiefs. They are undecided whether to stick or twist on a relatively modest hand of cards. **1976** J. ARCHER *Not a Penny More, Not a Penny Less* xii. 136 The young man on Harvey's left also drew a ten and asked the dealer to twist again.

16. *intr.* To turn aside and proceed in a new direction; *spec.* of a ball (at cricket, etc.): to turn aside or 'break' on rebounding; also, to proceed with frequent turns (often associated with *turn*); to follow a circuitous route; to wind, meander.

1800 T. BOXALL *Rules & Instructions for Playing Cricket* 18 When the ball goes out of a bowler's hand he must endeavour to make it twist a little. **1833** NYREN *Yng. Cricketer's Tutor* 45 If the ball be struck to his right hand, he will surely find it twist to his left. **1851** LILLYWHITE *Guide Cricketers* 15 Try every manœuvre to make the ball twist and shoot after it touches the ground. **1852** DICKENS *Bleak Ho.* iv, We just twist up Chancery Lane. **1863** W. C. BALDWIN *Afr. Hunting* vii. 257 He turned, dodged, and twisted from side to side, with amazing quickness. **1879** S. C. BARTLETT *Egypt to Pal.* xiii. 289 The valley or ravine twisted this way and that. **1895** *Review of Rev.* Aug. 168 The stream twists down through the valley. **1906** MARJ. BOWEN *Viper of Milan* x, The steps were few in number, before they twisted abruptly out of sight.

twistable ('twɪstəb(ə)l), *a.* [f. TWIST *v.* + -ABLE.] That may be twisted.

1853 LYNCH *Chr. Practicaln.* in *Lett. to Scattered* (1872) 364 Take the solemnity out of religion, and you do as if you should take the hardening element out of human bones. The bones would then become all soft and twistable. **1901** *N. & Q.* 9th Ser. VII. 468/2 Shades of meaning more or less twistable into that attributed to *-itis*.

'twisted, *ppl. a.* [f. as prec. + -ED[1].]

†**1.** Divided, branching. *Obs. rare*[−1].

1398 [see TWIST *v.* 1].

2. a. Consisting of two or more threads, strands, or the like twined together; (of a thread or strand) formed into a cord by being intertwined with another or others; made of spun or doubled thread, or by spinning; also *transf.* wreathed, plaited, interwoven.

a **1548** HALL *Chron., Hen. VI*, 135 An indissoluble knot, like the twisted tree, whiche cannot seuer. **1573–80** BARET *Alv.* T 456 Twined or twisted thred, *filum retortum*. **1590** SPENSER *F.Q.* II. xi. 22 In a canvas thin he was bedight, And girded with a belt of twisted brake. *a* **1603** *Council Order* in *Antiq. Rep.* (1807) I. 23 Twisted with two rows of twisted lace russet..the clothe itself set with the said twisted lace. **1609** BIBLE (Douay) *Exod.* xxxvi. 8 Ten curtines of twisted silke, and hyacinth, and purple, and scarlet twise died. **1718** BLACKMORE *Alfred* III. (1723) 92 Cables in Rings,..Their twisted Lengths voluminous enfold. **1718** LADY M. W. MONTAGU *Let. to Mrs. Thistlethwayte* 25 Sept., We began to ascend Mount Cenis, being carried in little seats of twisted osiers. **1757** GRAY *Bard* 5 Helm, nor Hauberk's twisted mail. **1791** COWPER *Iliad* v. 135 Blood spouted through his twisted mail. **1794** SOUTHEY *Slave Trade* iv. 7 No tear escaped him, not one suffering groan Beneath the twisted thong. **1825** SCOTT *Talism.* iii, Mattresses, wrought of twisted flags, lay by the side of the cell. **1835** T. MITCHELL *Acharn. of Aristoph.* 400 *note*, A round twisted basket, in which any thing was carried. **1895** SCULLY *Kafir Stories* 24 A musical instrument..consisted of a stick about three feet long, bent into a bow by a string made of twisted sinews.

†**b.** *fig.* Intimately associated or connected; united; combined; also, consisting of two elements united. *Obs.*

1573–80 BARET *Alv.* T 460 Twisted together, hard to be loosed, intricate, doubtfull. **1642** GAUDEN *Three Serm.* 29 Hypocrisie is a double and twisted impiety. **1655** W. HAMMOND *Poems* (1906) 500 Our twisted lives must be cut both Together. **1665** GLANVILL *Scepsis Sci.* Addr. A iv, Their..deep Sagacity, twisted Endeavours, ample Fortunes, and all other advantages.

c. Of the stem of a wine-glass: having a spiral ornament inside. Cf. TWIST *sb.*[1] 16 a (*b*).

1897 [see *air-twisted* s.v. AIR *sb.*[1] II]. **1897** A. HARTSHORNE *Old Eng. Glasses* 61 The glasses which we know generically as those with 'twisted stems', that is, with thin air-threads, and opaque white spiral lines in their standards. **1929** W. A. THORPE *Hist. English & Irish Glass* I. 199 Between 1714 and 1745..twisted stems are rare. **1970** G. GROS-GALLINER *Glass* iv. 108 A twisted stem decoration could be achieved by rib-moulding and rib-twisting.

3. a. Wrung out of shape; distorted; contorted; turned or bent awry; *spec.* in *Bot.* = CONTORTED 2; crooked, tortuous, winding; turned or wrung spirally, of coiled or screw-like form, spiral or helical; in *Geom.* applied to curves in space, as ***twisted Cartesian, t. cubic***, etc. (see CURVATURE 1 b); also, involved, tangled, confused.

1725 W. HALFPENNY *Sound Building* 13 The two different Edges of a Twisted Schofeet. **1776** WITHERING *Brit. Plants* (1796) II. 319 Parnassia... Stem somewhat twisted. **1782** A. MONRO *Compar. Anat.* 167 The eight upper ribs were formerly classed into pairs,..to wit, the *crooked*, the *solid*, the *pectoral*, the *twisted*. **1828** STARK *Elem. Nat. Hist.* II. 135 *Siliquaria*, Lam.—*Serpula*, Lin. Shell tubular, irregularly twisted. **1830** CARLYLE *Richter Again* Ess. 1840 II. 297 Abounding..in the most twisted phraseology. **1831** SCOTT *Cast. Dang.* xvii, A clear fountain of living water bubbled forth from under the twisted roots of one of those trees. **1842** BISCHOFF *Woollen Manuf.* II. 355 They [horns] protrude nearly at right angles from the head, and then become twisted in a singular way. **1854** MURCHISON *Siluria* v. 93 Highly twisted micaceous schists. *a* **1861** T. WOOLNER *My Beautiful Lady, Her Gard.* iv, The mad gale had.. fiercely blown The stalks [of the lilies] in twisted heaps. **1876** HOOKER *Bot. Primer* 68 *Twisted*, when each overlaps by one margin the contiguous margin of that next to it. **1894** H. NISBET *Bush Girl's Rom.* 240 Worrogonga handed to her a small twisted note.

b. Of a person: neurotic, emotionally unbalanced; perverted. Also *transf.* and with *up*.

1900 *Dialect Notes* II. 68 [College words.] *Twisted*, pp. as adj. 1. Wrong. 2. Crazy. 3. Confused. **1956** R. M. LESTER *Towards Hereafter* xiv. 165 Those who had held to the twisted idea that all psychical phenomena and spirit communication was 'the work of the devil' began to think again. **1963** *Times Lit. Suppl.* 25 Jan. 64/3 Alan..who is as extroverted as Paul is twisted up. **1963** A. HERON *Towards Quaker View of Sex* iii. 34 The emotional strains..produce the twisted embittered woman, only too familiar to psychiatrists. **1971** A. MORICE *Death of Gay Dog* v. 72 Old Roger..does so enjoy having lots of money; not like that twisted-up Nancy. **1978** S. SHELDON *Bloodline* xlii. 360 Snuff films..would have been made to be shown privately to wealthy individuals who got their pleasure in twisted, sadistic ways.

4. In special collocations: **twisted bit**, a bit of which the mouthpiece consists of a square bar spirally twisted; also in *Carpentry*: see quot.; **twisted drill** = *twist-drill* (TWIST *sb.*[1] 23); **twisted flower**, rendering of *Strophanthus*, name of a genus of tropical shrubs, natives of Asia and Africa, esp. applied to those species cultivated for the singularity of their flowers (*Cent. Dict.* 1891); **twisted horn** = TWISTY *sb.*; **twisted mouth**: see quot.; **twisted pair** *Teleph.*, a pair of insulated conductors twisted about each other, as in a flex or by alternating their positions on successive telegraph poles; **twisted pillar**, a pillar having the appearance of being spirally twisted, or apparently consisting of two shafts intertwined; **twisted pine**, *Pinus contorta*, a small pine of the Pacific coast of North America, the twisted-branched pine; also *P. Teocote* of Mexico; **twisted stalk**, rendering of *Streptopus*, name of a genus of perennial herbaceous plants bearing bell-shaped flowers with curious bent stalks; **twisted stick** = ***twisted horn***; **twisted suture**: see quot.; † **twisted tree**, ? a branch of willow or other tree formerly used in connexion with Easter celebrations.

1875 KNIGHT *Dict. Mech.*, **Twisted bit*.., a wood-boring tool adapted to be used in a brace. It is a..flat bar twisted into a spiral form and provided..with a cutter and a routing-table. **1884** F. J. BRITTEN *Watch & Clockm.* 95 For long holes of small diameter a *twisted drill is desirable. **1866** *Twisted horn [see TWISTY *sb.*]. **1875** KNIGHT *Dict. Mech.*, **Twisted mouth* (Manège), a bit whose mouthpiece has been twisted, to make it more severe than it otherwise would be. **1923** T. E. HERBERT *Telephony* xxiii. 651 The disturbing effect of a *twisted pair in good condition is relatively minute when compared with a single wire. **1979** *Sci. Amer.* Aug. 9/2 (Advt.), Each link can be up to five miles long, and uses a single, shielded, twisted pair cable. **1717** BERKELEY *Tour in Italy* Wks. 1871 IV. 550 The altars generally adorned with *twisted pillars. **1756–7** tr. *Keysler's Trav.* (1760) IV. 77 The great altar has sixteen twisted pillars of white and green marble. **1869** TOZER *Highl. Turkey* I. 238 Balustrades and windows with twisted pillars. **1866** *Treas. Bot.* s.v. *Pine*, *Twisted pine, *Pinus Teocote*. **1884** MILLER *Plant-n.*, Pine-tree, Twisted Mexican, *Pinus Teocote*. **1856** A. GRAY *Man. Bot.* (1860) 474 *Streptopus*, *Twisted-stalk. **1866** *Twisted stick [see TWISTY *sb.*]. **1767** GOOCH *Treat. Wounds* I. 154 The *twisted-suture..is performed by introducing one, two or more, needles or pins through the whole substance of the lips of the wound, twisting a waxed thread neatly about them, in the form of a figure of 8. **1598** STOW *Surv.* 72 In the weeke before Easter had yee great shewes made for the fetching in of a *twisted Tree, or With, as they termed it, out of the woodes into the kinges house, and the like into euery mans house of honor or worship.

5. Comb., as ***twisted-branched, -convolute, -locked***.

1830 LINDLEY *Nat. Syst. Bot.* 131 Æstivation for the most part twisted-convolute. **1862** *Eng. Wom. Dom. Mag.* IV. 218 Those frizzly-haired, lank-haired, twisted-locked, top-knotted foreigners. **1884** MILLER *Plant-n.*, *Pinus contorta*, twisted-branched pine.

Hence **'twistedly** *adv.*, in a twisted manner.

1910 *Westm. Gaz.* 2 Feb. 8/2 Every single strand of the tobacco smokes perpendicularly downwards instead of horizontally across, or twistedly diagonal. **1915** *Blackw. Mag.* May 590/1 A twistedly pathetic thing a battery team and limber is without a gun.

twister ('twɪstə(r)), *sb.* [f. TWIST *v.* + -ER[1].] One who or that which twists.

†**1.** One who prunes or clips trees. *Obs. rare*[−0].

1483 *Cath. Angl.* 399/2 A Twyster of trees, *defrondator*.

2. A girder. Cf. TWIST *sb.*[1] 3 b.

1875 KNIGHT *Dict. Mech.*, *Twister*..2, a girder.

3. a. One who (or that which) spins thread, cord, or the like; *spec.* one whose occupation is to twist together the ends of the yarns of the new warp to those of that already woven. Also ***twister-in***.

1579 J. STUBBES *Gaping Gulf* B iv b, Which strong cord.. the Lorde..turned to the strangling of the twisters thereof. **1599** T. M[OUFET] *Silkwormes* 69 How many winders liue, How many twisters eke, and weauers thriue Vppon this trade? **1611** COTGR., *Retordeur*, a twister, twiner. **1723** *Lond. Gaz.* No. 6172/8 Samuel Brooke.., Twister. *Ibid.*, Nicholas Gudgeon.., Silver-Twister. **1799** *Hull Advertiser* 2 Mar. 4/4 The Man of the People..at a rope-maker's shop ..besought..his interest..when the twister replied [etc.]. **1815** G. BEATTIE *John o' Arnha'* (1826) 36 Elspet, Mausie, fatal sisters, Of the thread of life the twisters. **1878** A. BARLOW *Hist. & Princ. Weaving* xxx. 311 The 'twister-in' has no difficulty in finding the proper threads to twist together. **1895** *Daily News* 3 July 7/5 The threatened lock-out..at Burnley has been averted by the settlement of the twisters' dispute.

b. A mechanical device for spinning yarns, etc.; *spec.* a throw-crook (*dial.*).

a **1703** WALLIS in J. Greenwood *Eng. Gram.* (1711) 283 He [a rope-maker], twerling his twister, makes a twist of the twine. **1875** KNIGHT *Dict. Mech.*, *Twister*, a reel used in twisting yarns or threads. **1890** *Gloucester. Gloss.*, *Twister*, an implement used for twisting straw ropes for thatching, resembling a brace and bit, except that the bit has a hooked end. **1903** *Dundee Advertiser* 25 July 9 This machine..does more work in a given time than any other type of twister.

c. A wheel, tourniquet, or other device by which torsional force is applied.

1833 LOUDON *Encycl. Archit.* §2075 The Wringing-Machine..for small laundries. The articles to be wrung, when large, are taken out of the washing-tub, and, being passed over the pin,..the two ends are put through the hole of the twister,..which is turned round by the spokes. **1892** *Columbus* (Ohio) *Dispatch* 24 May, One of the highwaymen ..confessed his guilt after being tortured with 'twisters' and hot coals.

4. One who or that which turns about, turns from side to side, rotates, etc. † **a.** A twisting or twining shoot. *Obs. rare.*

1799 G. SMITH *Laboratory* I. 431 Fill a bag..of leaves and twisters of vine.

b. One who turns this way and that; *fig.* one who shuffles or prevaricates; a dishonest person, a crook. *slang.*

1834 BECKFORD *Italy*, etc. II. xvi. 359 The ambassador is ..no commonplace twister and turner in the paths of diplomacy. **1863** *Once a Week* IX. 568/2 One swags all that the palmer purchases, and stays outside to render the 'twister' any assistance he may need. **1897** BLACKMORE in *Blackw. Mag.* July 61/2, I have handled a good many twisters and skippers in the way of savages. **1915** *Film Flashes* 4 Dec. 1 'Twisters'..endeavour to put German films in the picture houses, under the pretext that they were made in a neutral, Continental country. **1930** J. B. PRIESTLEY *Angel Pavement* vii. 367 If you ask me, he looks a rotten twister—bit of a crook or something. **1937** [see SPIV *sb.*]. **1940** E. POUND *Cantos* lv. 53 And Liu-hoei said Ngan was a twister. **1966** [see KNUCK 3]. **1976** *Milton Keynes Express* 23 July 7/3 He was said to have called two women teachers 'cheats and twisters' and had refused to apologise for his remarks.

c. *Cricket.* A delivery in which the ball twists or 'breaks'; a break; *transf.* in *Tennis* and other ball-games, a 'screw'.

1832 P. EGAN *Bk. Sports* I. 348/2 The batsman now his weapon rais'd To meet a puzzling twister. **1857** HUGHES *Tom Brown* II. vi, To come out..to Tom's wicket, and bowl slow twisters to him. **1862** CALVERLEY *Verses & Tr.* '*Hic vir, hic est*' viii, I have stood serene..While the Buttress of the period Bowled me his peculiar twisters. **1884** MARSHALL *Tennis Cuts* 202 T was the Twister, that settled the rest.

d. *U.S.* A whirling wind-storm: a cyclone, tornado.

1897 *Strand Mag.* Sept. 266/1 Kansas..is a favourite spot of the 'twisters' as the Westerns playfully term their windy enemy (the tornado). **1902** W. M. DAVIS *Elem. Phys. Geog.* ii. 67 Violent local storms..are often called cyclones, or prairie twisters, in the Mississippi valley, but the name tornado is to be preferred. **1903** G. S. WASSON *Cap'n Simeon's Store* vi. 108 He see in his paper where the English ship Falls of Ettrick was plunked on the Diamond Shoal and had went to pieces in that ole twister of a breeze there was a spell ago. **1930** NEFF & HENRY *Folk-Say Regional Misc.* 48, I never did see so many of them little twisters all a-goin' at one and the same time. **1955** *Sci. News Let.* 18 June 388/2 A Weather Bureau meteorologist is making miniature tornadoes in a small box in the hope of learning more about what causes 'twisters'. **1967** *Boston Sunday Globe* 23 Apr. 1/2 The most vicious twisters in the history of the Midwest, striking heavily-populated sections of Northern Illinois and Western Michigan, left 53 dead. **1974** V. NABOKOV *Look at Harlequins* (1975) IV. ii. 162 A group of fifteen schoolchildren..were safe in the sudden darkness of that sturdy building when the twister struck. **1977** J. CLEARY *Vortex* iv. 93 You hear the twister warnings, too?

e. A handle operated by twisting or rotating it.

1902 F. T. BIDLAKE in *Cycl. Tour. Cl. Gaz.* Aug. 359/2 The..machine with the compound brake application, i.e., the combination of the lever and the twister.

f. A grossly exaggerated tale; a lie. *Naut. slang.* ? *Obs.*

1834 W. N. GLASCOCK *Naval Sketch-Bk.* 2nd Ser. I. 235 I'm an even-minded man..that's providin' I wasn't provok'd by lying lip,—but if the best man in the sarvus was to come up to me,..to tell *me* such a thund'ring twister.. why I'd just..floor the feller as flat as a flounder. **1850** H. MELVILLE *White Jacket* II. xxviii. 184 Among innumerable 'yarns and twisters' reeled off in our maintop during our pleasant run to the north, none could match those of Jack Chase. **1873** *Routledge's Yng. Gentl. Mag.* May 358/1 'Twister', broke in the petty officer; 'I tell you it's as true as gospel'.

g. A type of handcuff (see quot. 1939).

1910 [see NIPPER *sb.*[1] 4 c]. **1939** *Fortune* July 104/1 A style of handcuff, sometimes called 'twisters', used by the New York police instead of the old bracelet type. It consists of a short length of chain with a T-bar at each end. The policeman wraps it around the prisoner's wrist, twists the two T's like a tourniquet as tightly as necessary to make the prisoners come along like a lamb.

h. A key. ***twister to the slammer***: (see quot. 1940). *U.S. slang.*

1940 *Music Makers* May 37/3 *Twister to the slammer*, the key to the door. **1941** J. SMILEY *Hash House Lingo* 55 *Twister*, key. **1944** D. BURLEY in A. Dundes *Mother Wit* (1973) 208 Give the jivers a break and substitute the phrase, 'twister to the slammer', for the word 'key'. **1970** C. MAJOR *Dict. Afro-Amer. Slang* 117 *Twister*, doorkey.

i. = TWITCH *sb.*[1] 3 b (*spec.* sense). *U.S.*
1940 W. FAULKNER *Hamlet* III. ii. 223 He..reached down from its nail in the wall a short, smooth white-oak stick eyed at the end with a loop of hemp rope—a twister which Houston had used with his stallion. **1948** *Richmond* (Va.) *Times-Dispatch* 23 Aug. 4/4 A mean horse may take up to eight hours to shoe, using rope harnesses to tie up the leg being worked on, or even a 'twister' for the horse's nose. **1968** R. F. ADAMS *Western Words* (ed. 2) 334/1 *Twitch*, a small loop of cord with a stick through it used to punish a held horse. The loop is placed vertically around the animal's upper lip and then tightened by twisting the stick. Also called *twister*.

j. One who dances the twist (TWIST *sb.*[1] 13 c).
[**1942** BERREY & VAN DEN BARK *Amer. Thes. Slang* §583/27 *Hip dancer*...twister, wiggle dancer, wiggler.] **1966** 'K. NICHOLSON' *Hook, Line & Sinker* viii. 97 'I just go on Twist nights, don't I, Di?' 'She's a jolly good twister too.' **1977** J. WILSON *Making Hate* ii. 21 He'd been the runner-up in the Champion Twister competition at the Palais.

5. One who curves, bends, or rolls something.
1879 *Cassell's Tech. Educ.* III. 158 The leaves are..placed over charcoal fires... The twisters roll them over with their hands until twisted.

6. That which (or one who) wrings or causes contortion; *esp. fig.* something that confounds, non-plusses, or 'doubles up', a 'staggerer' (*slang*). Also (*dial.*), a blow which makes the victim twist or writhe; also *fig.* in U.S. colloq. phr. ***to knock*** **one *the*** (or ***a***) ***twister***.
1835 in *Amer. Speech* (1965) XL. 133 So, low each pill was a twister. I swallow'd about three Doctor's shops. **1843** J. R. PLANCHÉ *Fortunio* I. ii. 9 Ha, ha! I think that was a twister! **1879** BLACK *Macleod of D.* xl, Well, you have had a twister; but you'll come through it. **1884** CLARK RUSSELL *Jack's Courtship* xvi, She had a letter from you this morning—a regular twister. **1886** F. T. ELWORTHY *W. Somerset Word-bk.* 783 *Twister*.., a blow with a whip or other instrument. **1893** *Daily Tel.* 1 May 5/1 This was evidently a twister for the beggar-boy. **1896** G. ADE *Artie* vi. 55 That's what knocked me the twister. I thought this fellow was all right. **1908** G. SANGER *70 Yrs. a Showman* xvii. 59, I got a twister well home under his ribs that sent him grunting and staggering. **1934** G. ADE *Let.* 15 Mar. (1973) 181, I was, to use an old slang phrase, 'knocked a twister' when I received your letter [etc.].

7. A voracious feeder. *slang.* ? *Obs.*
1694 MOTTEUX *Rabelais* v. Prol. A vj b, What Swillers, what Twisters will there be!

8. *Insurance.* An insurance salesman or agent who unscrupulously induces a holder to switch his policy from one company to another. orig. *U.S.*
1924 [see TWIST *v.* 12 e]. **1979** *Telegraph* (Brisbane) 24 Sept. 24/2 The industry calls it twisting. Presumably its practitioners are called twisters. The industry says that life insurance consumers are being ripped off by its practice.

9. *U.S. slang.* In various senses with reference to the taking of drugs (see quots.).
1936 [see *marijuana addict* s.v. MARIJUANA 3]. **1936** *Amer. Speech* XI. 127/1 *Twister*. 1. A feigned spasm. **1938** *Ibid.* XIII. 192/1 *Twister*. 3. A speed-ball or whiz-bang [vein-shot of mixed drugs]. 4. A bit of violent retching or vomiting of blood or mucus during withdrawal distress. 5. A ration of narcotics. **1951** *Even. Sun* (Baltimore) 27 Mar. 4/1 A powerful combination of 'bernice snorting' and heroin 'shooting' was called 'blowing speed balls' or 'twisters' or 'whiz bangs'. **1959** J. E. SCHMIDT *Narcotics* 185 *Twister*, an intravenous injection of a potent narcotic taken by a drug addict, esp. a dose composed of heroin or morphine and cocaine.

10. Var. TWISTOR 1.

11. Comb. **twister's cramp** *Path.*, pain in the hands or fingers produced by twisting or wringing.
1923 E. W. HOPE *Industr. Hygiene & Med.* viii. 516 This process of knotting [the warp threads] is done by a peculiar rolling motion of the fingers. The constant repetition of the movement..gives rise in certain operatives to a peculiar trade affection known as 'twister's cramp', the symptoms of which are pain, usually referred to the base of the thumb, tenderness of the muscles, and sometimes swelling at the base of the thumb. **1967** *Punch* 29 Mar. 458/3 Twister's Cramp can still be acquired by any housewife who is eccentric enough to wring clothes by hand.

twister ('twɪstə(r)), *v.* Now *dial.* [f. TWIST *v.* + -ER[5].]

† **1.** *trans.* and *intr.* To twist, spin thread. *Obs.*
c **1605** *Alleg. Worsted Weavers* (B.M. Add. MS. 12504, art. 64), Twistering one thridd of one coullour with another of another coullour. *Ibid.*, To twister a thridd of one colour with a thridd of another. **1687** R. FERRIER in *Camden Misc.* IX. VII. 30 Many..as they grow up, do work, some of whom twister, others net.

2. *intr.* To wind, meander. *dial.*
1872 [J. SPILLING] *Giles' Trip to Lond.* ii. 17 Straight on as ever yow can go in these twistering straats. **1895** *E. Anglian Gloss.*, *Twister*, to twist or turn.

Hence **'twistering** *ppl. a.*, winding, twisting; also † **'twisterer** *Obs.*, a twister or spinner.
1725 *Lond. Gaz.* No. 6380/13 Charles Scot,..Twisterer. **1872** Twistering [see 2 above].

twisteroo (ˌtwɪstə'ruː). *colloq.* [f. TWIST *sb.*[1] 21 c; cf. -EROO.] (A narrative with) an unexpected twist.
1963 *Punch* 13 Feb. 237/1 The story was a twisteroo, a variation, of the legend of King Midas. **1965** J. P. CARSTAIRS *Concrete Kimono* xxx. 251, I think when you hear me out the twisteroo will appeal to you. **1970** M. PEI *Words in Sheep's Clothing* iii. 23 There is in the field [of 'weasel' words used on the screen] one suffix which may be described as derogatory, and that is the -eroo of 'twisteroo'.

twist-foot. *rare*[−1]. [Translation of the generic name *Streptopus*.] = *twisted stalk*, TWISTED 4.
1846–50 A. WOOD *Class-Bk. Bot.* 554 *Streptopus roseus*... Rose Twist-foot.

twistical ('twɪstɪkəl), *a. colloq.* [irreg. f. TWIST + -ICAL.] Somewhat twisted or crooked; *fig.* not straight or plain in character; morally or mentally tortuous.
1805 T. G. FESSENDEN *Democracy Unveiled* v. 158 *Certain* sages, learn'd and *twistical*... Have prov'd what's wonderful. **1815** D. HUMPHREYS *Yankee in Eng.* 43 In his dealings with t'other sex, he is a leetle twistical. **1852** A. BALLOU *Spirit Manifest.* Pref. 9 They are..prejudiced, captious, twistical. **1890** *Harper's Mag.* Feb. 449/1 It lay on the route to Edinburgh, at a rather twistical sort of corner.

twistification (ˌtwɪstɪfɪ'keɪʃən). *nonce-wd.* [f. as prec.: see -FICATION.] A twisting; a twisted object or part.
1835 BECKFORD *Recoll.* 137 To entertain any doubts of the supreme excellence of Don Emanuel's scollops and twistifications amounted to heresy. **1841** HAWTHORNE *Amer. Note-Bks.* (1883) 230 Dry jokes, the humor of which is so incorporated with the strange twistifications of his physiognomy, that [etc.].

twistify ('twɪstɪfaɪ), *v. U.S. dial.* and *colloq.* ? *Obs.* [f. TWISTY *a.* + -FY. Cf. TWISTIFICATION.] *trans.* To make twisty (*lit.* and *fig.*); to twist. Hence **'twistified**, **'twistifying** *ppl. adjs.*
1835 R. M. BIRD *Hawks of Hawk Hollow* I. xix. 254 The path is astonishing twistified, and not fit for horse. **1843** 'J. SLICK' *High Life in N.Y.* I. 148 There was the fat nigger a twistifying his whip-lash round the horses' heads. **1845** in C. Cist *Cincinnati Misc.* I. 167, I knew..an individual.. who possessed this twistifying talent in high perfection... Many amusing stories of his faculty of shifting have been told me. **1872** *Newton Kansan* 17 Oct. 4/3 [The Republicans] repudiate his twistified explanations now.

twisting ('twɪstɪŋ), *vbl. sb.* [f. TWIST *v.* + -ING[1].] The action of the verb TWIST.

† **1.** Pruning, clipping. (In quot. *attrib.*) *rare.*
1535 COVERDALE *Song Sol.* ii. 12 The floures are come vp in the felde, the twystinge tyme is come [*Vulg.* Tempus putationis advenit].

2. The spinning of thread, etc.; twining, wreathing, plaiting; also with *in* (in quot. 1812 *fig.* the swearing in of a Luddite), and *attrib.* In quot. *a* 1673 app. *concr.*
1552 HULOET, Twystyng wande, as wyker or osyer, *uimen, inis, uimineus, a, um*, of twystyng roddes. **1577** B. GOOGE *Heresbach's Husb.* 38 b, Flaxe and Hempe..serueth for webbes of Linnen, and twysting of Cordes. **1599** in *Archæologia* LXIV. 382 For mending the twisting wheele. **1649** MILTON *Eikon.* vi. Wks. 1851 III. 386 They..have to our Saviours crown of thorns no right at all. Thornes they may find anow of thir own gathering, and thir own twisting. **1668** WILKINS *Real Char.* 247 Making several vegetable or animal substances into Thred. Twisting,..Spinning. *a* **1673** T. HORTON *Serm.* xxii. (1679) 160/1 He can gather a Rod of these boughes, and make a scourge of these twistings. **1688** R. HOLME *Armoury* III. xxi. (Roxb.) 253/2 A Twisting wheele... This is an engine wherewith 2, 3 or more silk thrids are twisted, or turned all together into one entire double thrid. **1812** *Chron.* in *Ann. Reg.* 86/2 Thirty-eight were committed to Lancaster gaol, to take their trials for having administered the abominable and unlawful oath, known by the term of twisting-in. **1825** J. NICHOLSON *Operat. Mechanic* 421 The motions of both machines, excepting those of that set of twisting-spindles facing the opposite company, are then struck into geer. **1844** G. DODD *Textile Manuf.* vi. 188 There does not seem to be any definite distinction among silk-throwsters, between spinning, twisting, and throwing. **1878** A. BARLOW *Hist. & Princ. Weaving* xxx. 312 It is not to be wondered at that attempts should be made to perform twisting-in by mechanical means.

3. Wringing, screwing; spiral turning; contortion, distortion; *fig.* perversion or wresting of sense; *slang*, a scolding; a trouncing.
1725 W. HALFPENNY *Sound Building* 29 The Angles..in the Figure, do represent the Twisting of each Piece. **1738** SWIFT *Pol. Conversat.* Introd. 16 The Twistings and Movements, and different Postures of the Body. **1776** DA COSTA *Elem. Conchol.* vii. 148 The Vermiculi in general are of no determinate or fixed regular shape, from their windings and twistings. **1808** LADY SARAH LYTTELTON *Corr.* (1913) 14 A few pretty distortions of the features or graceful twistings of the body. **1818–20** E. THOMPSON tr. *Cullen's Nosol. Method.* (ed. 3) 224 Pain in the belly with a sense of twisting. **1827** FARADAY *Chem. Manip.* xix. (1842) 523 This should be done without any twisting or distortion of the glass. **1833** MARRYAT *P. Simple* xvi, I say, Bill, if them were we, what a precious twisting we should get to-morrow at six bells! **1890** *Daily News* 1 Dec. 6/2 Telling me that it [the letter] is being twisted this way and that, and asking me to put a stop to the twisting process.

4. Tortuous course; intricate winding; turning this way and that; *fig.* evasion, prevarication; also turning aside, or about; rotation.
1768 TUCKER *Lt. Nat.* (1834) I. 76 To follow..all the twistings and crossings, and entanglements in those intricate subjects that have hitherto perplexed the learned world. **1856** F. PERTHES *Mem.* II. vi. 94 What toil and trouble, what twisting and turning this undertaking has cost me. **1872** LIDDON *Elem. Relig.* iv. 154 A second regards sin as a twisting or perversion of the will from the right way. **1875** BENNETT & DYER *Sachs' Bot.* 188 A useful arrangement is..that all the parts..by a single twisting of the axis..assume those positions which are most favourable for the functions of the leaves... In the terminal buds of such shoots this twisting is no longer necessary. **1886** *Athenæum* 10 July 39/1 The twistings and eddyings of the political current.

5. *Insurance.* (See quots.) Cf. TWISTER *sb.* 8. orig. *U.S.*
1906 *Even. Post* (N.Y.) 20 Jan. (Financial Section) 7/1 By 'twisting' is meant the persuading of policyholders in one company to transfer their insurance to another. **1962** L. E. DAVIDS *Dict. Insurance* 205/2 *Twisting*, practice of inducing any policyholder to lapse or cancel a policy for the purpose of replacing such policy with another to the detriment of the policyholder. The practice is considered to be unethical as well as illegal. **1979** *Telegraph* (Brisbane) 24 Sept. 24/2 In simple terms twisting works like this. A life insurance agent sells you a policy when he is working for company X... Three years later he switches allegiance to company Y. To make life easier he retraces his steps..to tell you that the policy from company X is outdated.

'twisting, *ppl. a.* [f. as prec. + -ING[2].] That twists, in various senses of the verb; turning; wringing or wrenching; curving, winding, crooked; †interlacing (*obs.*); involved.
1683 MOXON *Mech. Exerc., Printing* xxiv. ¶ 1 [To] hinder the Press from working into a twisting Position. **1712** J. JAMES tr. *Le Blond's Gardening* 156 Borders that are twisting and circular. **1761** YOUNG *Resignation* I. xxx, The twisting strings Of ardent hearts combin'd. **1835** R. WILLIS *Archit. Mid. Ages* vii. 74 The twisting form of the groin is disagreeable to the eye. **1872** H. W. BEECHER *Lect. Preaching* ix. 178 Some long sentences are good, but not twisting ones. **1882** *Daily Tel.* 4 May, The longitudinal or twisting strain, such..as a ship receives when she is struck at the same moment by a heavy sea on the starboard quarter and a heavy sea on the port bow. **1899** *Allbutt's Syst. Med.* VI. 676 They [pains] may be aching, burning, twisting or shooting in character. **1902** F. T. BIDLAKE in *Cycl. Tour. Cl. Gaz.* Aug. 360/1 Any further brake pressure put on by the lever will remain locked on by the twisting handle.

Hence **'twistingly** *adv.*, in a twisting manner.
1731 in BAILEY.

† **twistkey.** *Obs.*[−1] [f. TWIST *v.*] A turnkey.
1617 EARL OF CORK *Diary* in *Lismore Papers* Ser. I. (1886) I. 178 John geffreys my twistekey died.

twistle ('twɪs(ə)l), *sb. Sc.* Also **twissle.** [Cf. next.] A twist, a wrench (also *fig.*).
1785 BURNS *Twa Herds* iii, The Lord's cause ne'er gat sic a twistle, Sin' I hae min'. **1871** J. MILNE *Sel. Poems*, etc. 58 If he but aince come through thy twissle He'll rue sic gamin'. **1882** J. WALKER *Jaunt to Auld Reekie*, etc. 29 Screw the pegs wi cheepin twistle And strum the thairms. *Ibid.* 211 The deil gae a' their necks a twistle.

'twistle, *v. dial.* Forms: 8 *Sc.* **twisle**, 8–9 **twistle**, 9 **twissle** (*Sc.* **twussle**). [app. f. TWIST *v.* + -LE.] *trans.* To twist, twirl; to screw.
1788 PICKEN *Poems* Gloss., *Twisle*, to twist, fold. **1819** RENNIE *St. Patrick* II. 191 (Jam.) I'll twussle your thrapple in a jiffy. **1826–** in various Eng. dial. glossaries (E.D.D.). **1886** COLE *S.W. Linc. Gloss.* 157 The wind seems to twistle the straw. **1890** *Anthony's Photogr. Bull.* III. 151 A tuft of clean cotton, formed into a ball and twistled on one side.

twistle, variant of TWISEL.

twistor ('twɪstə(r)). [f. TWIST *v.* + -OR.]

1. *Computers.* Also -er. A non-volatile memory element consisting of an insulated copper wire wound helically round with a wire of readily magnetized material. Freq. *attrib.*
1957 A. H. BOBECK in *Bell Syst. Technical Jrnl.* XXXVI. 1319 Three methods have been developed for storing information in a coincident-current manner on magnetic wire. The resulting memory cells have been collectively named the 'twistor'. **1962** *Flight Internat.* LXXXII. 170/1 A permanent twistor memory and a ferrite-core scratch-pad memory are vital to reliability, assuring continuous operation until an attacking missile is intercepted and destroyed. **1975** D. G. FINK *Electronics Engineers' Handbk.* XXII. 19 A twister memory is used as the semipermanent memory constituting a major portion of the program store in central control.

2. *Physics.* A type of spinor used in some descriptions of space-time (see quots. 1967, 1973).
1967 R. PENROSE in *Jrnl. Math. Physics* VIII. 346 Twistors are..the 'spinors' which are relevant to the six-dimensional space whose (pseudo-) rotation group is isomorphic with the conformal group of ordinary Minkowski space-time. The simplest (non-scalar) twistors constitute a four-dimensional, four-valued representation of the restricted conformal group... The general twistor is then a many-index quantity constructible from the above basic twistors by means of the usual 'tensor type' rules. **1973** —— & MACCALLUM in *Physics Rep.* VI. 244 Twistors (that is to say, the original flat-space twistors about which these notes are mainly concerned) are actually the reduced spinors for the proper pseudo-orthogonal group SO(2,4) which is locally isomorphic with, and 2-1 homomorphic with, the restricted conformal group of flat space-time. *Ibid.*, A twistor (of the simplest type) can be pictured 'classically' as effectively a zero rest-mass particle in free motion, where the particle may possess an intrinsic spin. **1979** *New Scientist* 31 May 737 Twistor theory is incomplete, but it offers considerable hope for a quite new approach to the basic problems of theoretical physics.

twisty ('twɪstɪ), *a.* (*sb.*) [f. TWIST *sb.*[1] or *v.* + -Y.]

A. *adj.* **1.** Full of twists or turns; characterized by twisting or winding; also *fig.* dishonest, not straightforward. (Cf. *twistical*.)
1857 W. ARNOT *Let.* in *Life* vi. (1877) 330 It [a valley] was narrow and hilly and woody and beautiful and twisty. **1869** E. W. BENSON in *Life* (1900) I. ix. 309 Neither olive nor vine, only the poor twisty bramble. **1894** BLACKMORE *Perlycross* xxxviii, I just chucked 'un into a pool of watter, for to kape

'un out o' sight of twisty volk. **1905** *Daily Chron.* 21 July 4/7 A somewhat twisty redistribution of seats. **1912** D. CRAWFORD *Thinking Black* i. 7 This Africa for thousands of twisty miles ahead is..wholly innocent of roads.

2. = TWISTED *ppl. a.* 2c.

1929 L. P. HARTLEY in *Mercury Story Bk.* 206 The glasses with twisty stems were there.

B. *sb.* The fruit of the screw-tree, *Helicteres Isora*, of Southern India; see quot.

1866 *Treas. Bot.* 576/1 *H[elicteres] Isora* is a native of Southern India, where its singular twisted screw-like fruit, about two inches in length, is called 'twisted stick', 'twisted horn', or 'twisty', and..is supposed to be a sovereign remedy against colic or twistings of the bowels.

Hence **'twistiness**, the condition or quality of being twisty; **'twistiways, 'twistiwise** *advbs.*, in a twisty manner. So **'twisty-'wisty** *a. nonce-wd.*

1904 *Daily News* 16 July 4/2 As Miss Morison went upstream her progress was very tardy, a fact partly owing to the curious *twistiness of the river. **1903** *Speaker* 9 May 135/1 To drift *twistiways on the variant currents of men's thoughts. **1907** *Westm. Gaz.* 13 Sept. 2/1 Pace it [a 'magic' ring] three times round, '*twisty-wise', with face against the sun. **1892** KIPLING *Barrack-r. Ballads* 33 A single man gets bottled on them *twisty-wisty stairs.

twit (twɪt), *sb.*[1] Also 6 **twyte**. [f. TWIT *v.*]

1. a. An act of twitting; a (light) censure or reproach; a taunt.

1528 in Strype *Eccl. Mem.* (1721) I. App. xvii. 38 Which bookes the sayd Frear dyd litle regard, and made a twyte of it. **1664** ETHEREDGE *Love in Tub* v. v, Upon Condition that there be no Twits of the Good Man departed. **1847** L. HUNT *Men, Women & B.* II. x. 224 An occasional twit at him for disappointing her.

b. *dial.* (See quot.)

*a***1825** FORBY *Voc. E. Anglia*, *Twit*, a fit of hasty ill-humour; snappishness.

2. a. ? A person given to twitting; *dial.* a tale-bearer.

1719 D'URFEY *Pills* (1872) VI. 241 A silly, peevish Twit. **1896** *Warwick Gloss.* s.v., 'You are a twit'.

b. A fool; a stupid or ineffectual person. *slang.*

1934 E. LINKLATER *Magnus Merriman* xvi. 178 He was..a false hero who flaunted himself in fine colours when he was drunk and dwindled to a shabby twit when sober. **1960** F. RAPHAEL *Limits of Love* I. iii. 34 Don't be a twit, Sid. **1964** *Spectator* 10 Apr. 493/1 By making his psychologists a dim bunch of twits he weakens his statements. **1970** N. FLEMING *Czech Point* i. 20 No one but a prize twit or Captain Oates would have ventured out in this weather. **1977** C. MCCULLOUGH *Thorn Birds* xviii. 467 There's no need to get so worked up about it, you twit. **1984** *Observer* 4 Mar. 7/7, I hear and read such phrases as 'geriatric old twit': an expression which would hardly have sprung to the lips of the pious Aeneas.

twit, *sb.*[2] [Of obscure origin.] A fault or entanglement in a thread, which hinders the process of spinning or weaving.

1819 THOMSON *Poems* 27 (E.D.D.) Is 't a cursed wab o' yarn That winna work, for knots and twits? **1884** W. S. B. MCLAREN *Spinning* vii. (ed. 2) 131 Freedom from twits.

twit, *sb.*[3]: see TWIT *int.*

twit (twɪt), *v.* Forms: α. 6 **twyte, (twhyte)**, 6–7 (9 *dial.*) **twite, (twight)**. β. 6– **twit**, (7 **twitt, twytt**); 6 *pa. pple.* **twyte, twit**. [Orig. *twite* (with long *i*), aphetic form of ATWITE, q.v.]

1. *trans.* To blame, find fault with, censure, reproach, upbraid (a person), esp. in a light or annoying way; to cast an imputation upon; to taunt.

1530 PALSGR. 764/2, I twhyte one, I caste hym in the tethe or in the nose, *je luy reprouche*. This terme is also northren. *a***1553** UDALL *Royster D.* II. iii. (Arb.) 36 No man for despite, By worde or by write His felowe to twite. **1573** G. HARVEY *Letter-bk.* (Camden) 127, I take him very..simpely wittid, That may the second tyme be iustly twittid. **1593** SHAKS. *2 Hen. VI*, III. i. 178 Hath he not twit our Soueraigne Lady here With ignominious words..? As if she had suborned some to sweare False allegations. **1633** T. ADAMS *Exp. 2 Peter* ii. 22 An Egyptian priest thus twitted Solon, You Grecians are ever Children. **1814** D'ISRAELI *Quarrels Auth.* (1867) 364 The Antiquarian Society were twitted as medal-scrapers. **1865** TROLLOPE *Belton Est.* viii, Anything would be better than being twitted in this way. How can I help it that I am not a man..?

b. Const. most usually *with*; also *about* (rare), *for*, *of* (now rare or obs.), *on*; †also with clause or infin. (*obs. rare*).

1563 HARDING *Answ. Welles Challenge* (1565) 6 The woont of some feastemakers, who of their neighbours twited with nyggardnes [etc.]. **1569** J. SANFORD tr. *Agrippa's Van. Artes* 116 b, And twite their husbandes with the courtly excesse. **1581** J. BELL *Haddon's Answ. Osor.* 374 Ill may the Snight the Woodcock twight for his long bill. **1586** A. DAY *Eng. Secretary* II. (1625) 80 To twit him, That he had like to haue knockt his hand against the gallowes. **1593** T. WATSON *Tears of Fancie* lviii, Yet still I twit my selfe of Surcuidrie. **1593** DRAYTON *Eclogues* ii. 14 Nor twit me so, my senses to haue lost. **1612** BEAUM. & FL. *Cupid's Rev.* IV. iii, You do not twit me with my calling, neighbor? **1613** T. ADAMS *Heav. & Earth Reconciled* Wks. 1861 I. 469 Shall they twit us, that our *Our Father* hath taken from the church what their *Paternoster* bestowed on it? **1650** FULLER *Pisgah* II. ix. 186 Hannah though silent when twitted by Peninnah of barrenness, found her tongue when..taxed by Eli of drunkenness. **1664** H. MORE *Myst. Iniq.* vi. 19 Twitting them..for their Idolatry. **1743** FIELDING *Journey* I. xv, My friend..now twitting me with all his kindness,..discarded me for ever. **1791** BOSWELL *Johnson* Dec. an. 1775 (1831) III. 295 He was twitted by Mrs. Thrale for being very late. **1855** MACAULAY *Hist. Eng.* xix. IV. 308 Those who held this language were twitted with their inconsistency. **1870** *Lit. World* 16 Dec. 387 When twitted for his inconsistency. **1871** TYNDALL *Fragm. Sc.* (1879) II. xv. 381 The opponent of the undulatory theory might effectually twit the holder of it on his change of front. **1877** WHITTIER in Pickard *Life* (1894) II. 635 It is bad enough to be old, without being twitted of it. **1882** L'ESTRANGE *Friendships Miss Mitford* I. vii. 176 She was sometimes twitted about partialities for her cousin.

c. Also *to twit* (a person) *in the teeth*. *Obs.* or *arch.*

1579–80 NORTH *Plutarch* (1676) 386 In his youth he was fain to hire another mans house,..at a small rent, as afterwards he was twitted in the teeth withall. **1651** *Fuller's Abel Rediv., Bradford* (1867) I. 218 They twitted him in the teeth with heresy. **1729** GAY in *Swift's Lett.* (1766) II. 103 You have often twitted me in the teeth for hankering after the court. **1835** LYTTON *Rienzi* IV. i, They twit me in the teeth, because I cannot say who my father and mother were.

2. To condemn as a fault, blame, reprove, rebuke (an act, etc.); to cavil at, to disparage. Now *rare*.

1571 CAMPION *Hist. Irel.* II. viii. (1633) 105 Thus was Perkins bragge twighted. **1580** STANYHURST *Æneis*, etc. (Arb.) 152 Percase carpers wyl twight his iollitye youthful. **1592** GREENE *Upst. Courtier* To Rdrs. A iv, Though he speakes againste Veluet breeches..yet hee twits not the weede but the vice. **1673** HICKERINGILL *Greg. F. Greyb.* 214 Endeavouring to foyl and always twitting a good cause. **1675** tr. *Camden's Hist. Eliz.* I. 84 Others..twitted the Authority of the Queen's Majesty too much. **1876** J. WEISS *Wit, Hum. & Shaks.* iii. 87 The clown..remembers how the steward used to twit Olivia's contentment at his sallies.

†**b.** *twit it*: to phrase it tauntingly; to utter a taunt or reproach. *Obs. rare.*

1570–6 LAMBARDE *Peramb. Kent* (1826) 276 This Archbishop..suffered the King to hold his stirup twise in one day in Normandie, but in *Prato proditorum*, as Mathew Parise very pretily twiteth it. **1673** HICKERINGILL *Greg. F. Greyb.* 24 To twit it home as wittily and effectually as he can.

3. *intr.* To tell tales; to blab. Now *dial.*

*a***1643** [see TWITTING *vbl. sb.* 2]. **1854** MISS BAKER *Northampt. Gloss.* s.v., 'If he knows he'll twit'.

twit, *int.* and *sb.*[3] Also 6 **twyt**.

†**1.** An imitation of the cry of an owl. Cf. TU-WHIT. *Obs. rare*$^{-1}$.

1591 LYLY *Endym.* III. iii, A goodly Owle..sitting vpon my shoulder, cryed twyt, twyt... I meruailed what the Owle said, til at the last, I perceiued twyt twyt, to it, to it.

2. An imitation of the shrill chirp of a small bird; hence as *sb.* a name for this. Cf. TWEET.

1820 CLARE *Rural Life* (ed. 3) 147 The flap of a leaf, and the twit of a bird. **1828** *Lights & Shades* II. 130 A fat chirping sparrow gave you a twit, twit, twit, that kept you awake. **1922** T. S. ELIOT *Waste Land* (1923) iii. 15 Twit twit twit Jug jug jug jug jug jug So rudely forc'd. Tereu.

twitch (twɪtʃ), *sb.*[1] Also 6 **twycche, twytch-, twitche**, 6–8 **twich**. [f. TWITCH *v.*[1]]

1. An act of twitching; a sudden sharp pull or tug; a jerk; a pluck; a snatch.

1523 FITZHERB. *Husb.* §15 'The oxe is neuer wo, tyll he to the harowe goo', And it is bycause it goeth by twytches. **1567** GOLDING *Ovid's Met.* IX. (1593) 211 Three times a twich Gaue Hercules, and could not wrinch my leaning breast him fro. **1607** HIERON *Wks.* I. 431 A single twine, which is snapt in sunder with a twitch. **1688** R. HOLME *Armoury* III. xv. (Roxb.) 27/1 The bowes of the boat..would else be torne out with the twitches which the ship vnder saile would giue it. **1728–46** THOMSON *Spring* 412 Then fix, with gentle twitch, the barbed hook. **1821** CLARE *Vill. Minstr.* I. 154 A twitch at her sleeve!..a bramble had caught at her gown passing by. **1851** D. JERROLD *St. Giles* xvi. 169 He felt a twitch at his pocket, and..saw a child..carrying away a silk handkerchief.

b. *transf.* and *fig.* or in fig. context. *at a twitch*, in a moment, without delay.

1528 *Impeachm. Wolsey* 174 in Furnivall *Ball. fr. MSS.* I. 357 They wold from þer bodyes þer hedis devyde, or hang them at A twycche. **1599** NASHE *Lenten Stuffe* (1871) 27 The city of Norwich, as in the *Præludium* hereof I had a twitch at. **1633** G. HERBERT *Temple, Church Porch* xxxvii, Think not thy fame at ev'ry twitch will break. **1649** MILTON *Eikon.* xxvii. Wks. 1851 III. 514 His Noose, which when he pleases to draw together with one twitch of his Negative, shall throttle a whole Nation.

c. *twitch-up*, a pegged-down snare attached to an elastic sapling or the like, which springs up and strangles the game when sprung.

1885 HORNADAY *2 Yrs. in Jungle* xxxvi. 428 A fine, large porcupine..caught by a hind foot in a twitch-up.

2. A sharp pain; a pinch, pang, twinge. Freq. of mental pain.

1532 MORE *Confut. Tindale* Wks. 440/1 We sustayn..euery man for himself the paynefull twitche of bodely death. **1573** TUSSER *Husb.* (1878) 118 Reward not thy sheepe (when ye take off his cote) with twitchis and patches. **1612** T. TAYLOR *Comm. Titus* ii. 11 (1619) 441 The smarting twitches of our consciences. **1688** WOOD *Life* 14 Nov. (O.H.S.) III. 282 A twich and paine in the instep. **1717** PRIOR *Alma* I. 458 Their Heart, descending to their Breeches, Must give their Stomach cruel twitches. **1796** MME. D'ARBLAY *Camilla* II. 421 [It] had caused his conscience to give him so many twitches, that it never let him rest a moment. **1821** LAMB *Elia* Ser. I. *Imperfect Sympathies*, My conscience..beginning to give some twitches. **1867** G. EASTON *Autobiog.* xiii. 178 Sensations very similar to a twitch of toothache.

3. †**a.** Forceps, tweezers. *Obs. rare*$^{-1}$. (Cf. QUITCH *sb.*[2])

1596 BARROUGH *Meth. Physick* I. xxxvi. (ed. 3) 59 Take therfore a twich of siluer, & therewith lift up subtilly the vngle from the tunicle.

b. A noose or loop; *spec.* a noose which may be tightened by twisting the stick to the end of which it is attached, used to compress the lip or muzzle of a horse to restrain him during a painful operation.

(Quot. 1623 is doubtful: cf. TWITCH *v.*[1] 3 b.)

1623 MIDDLETON *More Dissemblers* III. i. (1657) 34 Oh those dear Gipseys, they..eat sweet stoln Hens, pluckt over Pales or Hedges by a twitch. **1831** [YOUATT] *Horse* xviii. 321 Among the minor methods of restraint..are the twitch and the barnacles. **1894** ASTLEY *50 Years Life* II. 297 That horribly cruel invention, the twitch, is..twisted..tightly round the poor brute's tender upper lip. **1910** T. SHEPPARD in *Trans. E. Riding Antiq. Soc.* XVI. 41 Two holes have been pierced on each side of the projecting portion of the stern, evidently to receive a lashing or twitch which would pass to and from the sides, thus holding them firmly against the stern-board. **1910** *Times* 19 Mar. 4/2 Twitches were used for holding vicious or nervous horses for veterinary purposes or shoeing, or washing the legs.

4. *Mining.* A place in, or part of, a vein where it is compressed and narrowed.

1653 MANLOVE *Lead-Mines* 265 (E.D.S.) Cauke, Sparr, Lid-Stones, Twitches, Daulings, and Pees. **1747** HOOSON *Miner's Dict.* s.v. *Brassil*, Some Veins that are Caukey are very subject to it; but more especially in Twitches, and hard Places. **1789** J. WILLIAMS *Min. Kingd.* I. 256, I saw coal..in the checks or twitches of those veins between the open bellies, not above one inch in thickness. **1821** W. FORSTER *Section Strata Newcastle-on-Tyne, etc.* (ed. 2) 236 Some..twitches carry a small rib of solid ore quite through.

5. A quick, involuntary, usually slight movement of a muscle, etc., esp. of nervous origin; a convulsive or spasmodic jerk or quiver.

1718 QUINCY *Compl. Disp.* 173 Any Medicine which so far vellicates the..Stomach and Bowels, as to draw them into convulsive Twitches. **1774** GOLDSM. *Nat. Hist.* (1776) II. 44 It is owing to these alterations that the mother so frequently feels those twitches, which are usually attended with pain. **1804** *Med. Jrnl.* XII. 112 Considerable pain in the head usually accompanied the convulsive twitches in the face. **1825** SCOTT *Talism.* xvii, Mark me the smallest twitch of the features, or wink of the eyelid. **1836** *Random Recoll. Ho. Lords* xiv. 315 A hasty scratch at the back of his head, accompanied with two or three twitches of his nose. **1897** MRS. E. L. VOYNICH *Gadfly* (1904) 47/1 That side of his face was affected with a nervous twitch.

6. A small lock of wool or flax twisted round the forefinger of the left hand in spinning.

*a***1801** BLOOMFIELD *Rural T., Rich. & Kate* viii, She..laid aside her Lucks and Twitches.

twitch (twɪtʃ), *sb.*[2] [Altered form of QUITCH *sb.*[1]] Couch-grass, *Triticum repens*; = COUCH *sb.*[2]

1595 LODGE *Fig for Momus* III. 48 If thou espie within thy curious knot, Some tangling twitch, that doth thy flowers rot. **1620** MARKHAM *Farew. Husb.* (1625) 48 The sand that bringeth forth nothing but wyld Twitch, Bryars, Thornbush, and such like vndergrowth. **1733** W. ELLIS *Chiltern & Vale Farm.* 264 Lands which are over-run with Twitch or Couch-grass. **1816** G. SINCLAIR *Hort. Gram. Woburn.* (1825) 222 The *Trifolium medium* is inadmissible [in alternate husbandry] on account of its creeping roots constituting what in arable lands is termed *twitch*. **1821** CLARE *Vill. Ministr.* I. 202 The big clod..a hiding-place Breaking off the scorching sun Where the matted twitches run. **1827** —— *Sheph. Cal.* 29 From teazing twitch, that in the spongy soil, Clings round the coulter. **1884** F. J. LLOYD *Science Agric.* 256 Of the weeds..none is more common or more troublesome than twitch, or couch grass.

b. *attrib.* and *Comb.*: **twitch-drag** (DRAG *sb.* 2e), a drag or rake for clearing land of twitch; **twitch-fire**, a fire for burning twitch or other weeds; **twitch-grass**, (*a*) *Triticum repens*; (*b*) a species of fox-tail grass, *Alopecurus agrestis* (Britten and Holland, 1886); **twitch-rake** = *twitch-drag*.

1799 A. YOUNG *Agric. Lincoln.* 69 A *twitch drag..for tearing out twitch. **1905** *Eng. Dial. Dict.*, **Twitch-fire*. **1908** [MISS FOWLER] *Betw. Trent & Ancholme* 81 The sweet-smelling twitch..fire. **1707** MORTIMER *Husb.* (1721) I. 312 *Twitch-grass is a very pernicious Weed to some Land. **1792** *Trans. Soc. Arts* X. 109, I sowed twitch-grass and rye-grass. **1805** R. W. DICKSON *Pract. Agric.* I. 8 The want of proper management..has suffered twitch-grass to become abundant. **1884** *St. James's Gaz.* 19 Sept. 6/1 In some wonderful way, twitch-grass sows itself on fields that were apparently clean. **1799** A. YOUNG *Agric. Lincoln.* 73 A *twitch rake, containing a double row of teeth. **1805** R. W. DICKSON *Pract. Agric.* I. 33 The Twitch-Rake..necessary for the clearing of certain descriptions of land from these, as well as other kinds of weeds.

twitch (twɪtʃ), *v.*[1] Forms: 4 **tuicche**, 5 **twych**, 5–6 **twycche**, 6 **twyche, twytche, twitche**, 6–9 **twich**, 5– **twitch**. *Pa. t.* and *pple.* 5 **twychyde**, 5– **twitched**, etc.; also 4 **twiȝt, -e**, *Sc.* **tuiȝt**, 4–5 **twyȝt, -e, twyght, -e, twyte, twite**, 4–7 **twight**. [ME. *twicchen* (found earliest in the comb. *to-twicchen*), = LG. *twikken*, MHG. and G. *zwicken* (OHG. **zwicjan*, pa. t. *kizwicta*), prob. representing and OE. **twiccan* related to *twiccian*, TWICK *v.*]

1. *trans.* To give a sudden abrupt pull at; to pluck; to jerk; to pluck (a person) *by* some part of the body or dress; also, to pluck (the strings of a musical instrument, etc.).

[*c* 1175–*c* 1350: see TO-TWITCH.] *c* **1450** *Mankind* 608 in *Macro Plays* 23, I was twychyde by þe neke; þe game was begunne; A grace was, þe halter brast asondur. **1587** GOLDING *De Mornay* xxii. (1592) 341 Notwithstanding that our Lawe in euery line..doe reproue vs for it, and after a sort twich vs euery howre by the Cote, to pull vs from it. **1658** BROMHALL *Treat. Specters* I. 44 This foul spirit often twitched and pulled them by the hair. **1704** SWIFT *T. Tub* xi, Providence either forgot or did not think it convenient to twitch me by the Elbow. **1715** S. CROXALL *Vision* 15 His fellow Bard..

twitch'd the sounding Chords in solemn State. **1791** COWPER *Iliad* III. 458 She..twitch'd her fragrant robe. **1802** MAR. EDGEWORTH *Moral T.* (1816) I. xiii. 107 Their master twitched the rope, that was fastened round their necks. **1821** CLARE *Vill. Minstr.* I. 47 Such strength had they to twitch the thrumming string. **1849** J. FORBES *Physic. Holiday* ix. (1850) 90 The driver hardly twitched the reins or used the whip from first to last. **1889** GRETTON *Memory's Harkb.* 88 The rector went and twitched him by the sleeve.

2. *intr.* To pull or pluck sharply or forcibly; to give a sharp pull or jerk (*at* something); to tug. Also *fig.*

c **1305** *St. Lucy* 131 in *E.E.P.* (1862) 105 Hi gonne to drawe & tuicche And euere lai þis maide stille, hi ne miȝte hire enes icche. *c* **1386** CHAUCER *Friar's T.* 265 That was wel twight [*v.rr.* twyȝt, twite] myn owene lyard boy. *c* **1460** *Play Sacrament* 512 Now set on, felouse,.. and pluke hys armes awey..; wat, y se he [? *read* y seye,] twycche felovse, a ryght. **1575** TURBERV. *Falconrie* 210 When she sitteth always.. twitching at hir feathers with hir beake. **1824** W. IRVING *T. Trav.* I. 63 It seemed as if a legion of imps were twiching at him. **1829** LANDOR *Imag. Conv., Diog. & Plato* Wks. 1846 I. 455/1 Try to barter one with the other, amicably; and not to twitch and carp. **1871** B. TAYLOR *Faust* (1875) II. III. 222 The garment let not go. Already twitch The Demons at its skirts. **1913** EDITH WHARTON *Custom of Country* I. ii, Fidgeting, twitching at her draperies,.. when people were noticing her.

3. a. *trans.* (With various advs. and preps.) To pull, draw, or take suddenly or with a jerk; to pull sharply or forcibly; to pluck, snatch. *to twitch up* (the strings of an instrument), to sound by plucking.

c **1320** *Sir Tristrem* 1952 Þe bord he fond of tviȝt. *c* **1374** CHAUCER *Troylus* IV. 1157 (1185) His swerde anon out of his shethe he twyghte. *c* **1380** *Sir Ferumb.* 1596 Hure swerdes out þay twyȝte. *a* **1450** *Le Morte Arth.* 1038 That purs..in hond he hente, A letter there-of than oute he twight. **1530** PALSGR. 764/2, I twytche, I pull a thynge sodaynely or hastely, *je happe*... He twitched it out of my handes or I was ware. **1549** COVERDALE, etc. *Erasm. Par. Jas.* v. 38 b, Those riches wherin now you most folishly put your confidence, being twitched awaye. **1575** TURBERV. *Falconrie* 141 Your hande being twitched away fearefully would make hir proceed the more eagerly. **1658** GURNALL *Chr. in Arm.* verse 14. III. xv. §2. 302 Their fellows that were twitcht up by their gills from them even now with the anglers hook. **1674** BUNYAN *Light in Darkness* Wks. (ed. Offor) I. 412 He is mocked, spit upon, His beard is twitched from His cheeks. **1784** COWPER *Task* IV. 448 Twitched from the perch, He gives the princely bird..to his voracious bag. **1791** A. WILSON in *Poems & Lit. Prose* (1876) II. 77 Come twitch up the strings to great 'John Barleycorn'. **1833** MARRYAT *P. Simple* xxi, One of the strings..catching the lock of the musket carried by one of the sentries..and twitching it out of his hand. **1865** SWINBURNE *Atalanta* 2010 The King twitched his reins in and leapt down. **1876** *Trans. Clinical Soc.* IX. 5 In this eye I had afterwards to twitch away the partially detached piece. **1934** T. S. ELIOT *Rock* i. 28 As he names them they twitch off their caps and kneel.

fig. **1578** *Chr. Prayers* in *Priv. Prayers* (Parker Soc.) 557 Twitch our minds from time to time to the remembrance of so great happiness. **1653** J. OWEN *Dissert. Div. Just.* Wks. 1852 X. 600 He twitches the argument various ways.

b. To snatch by way of robbery or theft.

1607 DEKKER & WILKINS *Jests*, etc. 39 He..gaue him a little Justle: and withall, twicht 3 l. out of his pocket. **1655** tr. *Com. Hist. Francion* II. 33 To wander about the streets.. purposely to try if they could handsomely twich a Cloak. **1849** MRS. CARLYLE *Let. to Dr. Carlyle* Dec. in *New Lett. & Mem.* (1903) II. 10 Mercifully it was near home that he [a small dog] was twitched up [by a dog-stealer].

†**c.** *to twitch up*, to hang. *Obs.*

1611 R. BRADLEY in *Coryat's Crudities* kij, The Ducall Gallowes..Which twich him vp, when he offends their law. **1625** SANDERSON *Serm. Ps. cvi. 30* §22 To twitch up a poor sheep-stealer.

d. *Lumbering.* See quots.

1835–40 HALIBURTON *Clockm.* (1862) 262 He is a giant,.. and can twitch a mill-log as easy as a yoke of oxen can. **1848** BARTLETT *Dict. Amer.*, *To Twitch*, to draw timber along the ground by a chain. Used by lumbermen in Maine. **1905** *Terms Forestry & Logging* (*U.S. Dept. Agric., Forestry* Bulletin lxi.), *Skid*, to draw logs from the stump to the skidway, landing, or mill... *Syn.* snake, twitch.

4. To pinch and pull at with or as with pincers or the like; to nip; to hurt or pain, as by doing this. Also *fig.*

c **1374** CHAUCER *Troylus* IV. 544 (572) Thus am I with desir and reson twyght. *c* **1412** HOCCLEVE *De Reg. Princ.* 5058 A wight..who is with greuous þoughtes twight. **1440** J. SHIRLEY *Dethe K. James* (1818) 22 A paire sharpe tangis, with the which he twitched and all to tare thare skynne and flessh. **1577–87** HOLINSHED *Chron.* (1807) III. 184 To twitch a quareller with such pinsars as wherewith afore he had nipt an other. *a* **1652** BROME *Eng. Moor* v. i, Had..both been kil'd indeed, as you in jest, Where had been then your witty subtilty..? Ha! have I twight ye there? *a* **1680** CHARNOCK *Attrib. God* (1834) I. 19 Something in him twitching him upon the pursuit of uncomely actions. **1737** BRACKEN *Farriery Impr.* (1757) II. 174 Such Purges as vellicate and twitch the Nerves. **1760–72** H. BROOKE *Fool of Qual.* (1809) III. 144 His heart twitched him with a kind of compunction. **1851** D. JERROLD *St. Giles* iv. 31 [He] was twitched by a momentary surprise, but directly recovered himself. **1865** DICKENS *Mut. Fr.* I. xiii, I am tickled and twitched all over.

5. *intr. Mining.* Of a vein of ore: To contract; with *out*, to come to an end; = PINCH *v.* 14; also *trans.* of the containing rock: to converge upon and contract or close (a vein of ore); cf. PINCH *v.* 11.

1709 T. ROBINSON *Nat. Hist. Westmld. & Cumbld.* xiv. 80 When the Vein opens wide in some place, and again closeth, or as the Miners speak, Twitcheth at both Ends, this is called a Belly of Ore, or Pipe-Ore. **1747** HOOSON *Miner's Dict.* Vj, The Vein keeping a reasonable Compass, and cannot be said to be Twitched. **1789** J. WILLIAMS *Min. Kingd.* I. 255 The coal..grew thinner towards the ends of the belly or concavity of the vein, and it soon dwindled away to nothing, and twitched out entirely. **1836** R. FURNESS *Medicus-Magus* 17 Where wough or rider twitch'd a leading fast.

6. a. *trans.* To draw tight by means of a cord or the like; to tie, fasten, secure tightly or firmly. Also with the cord as object. Now *dial.*

1615 G. SANDYS *Trav.* 63 They twitch the offender about the waist with a towell,..pricking him in the body, until they have drawn him within the compass of a span. **1634** T. JOHNSON tr. *Parey's Chirurg.* VII. xxii. (1678) 186 Ganglia.. must be tied with a string at the root, and every day twitched harder and harder. **1641** BEST *Farm. Bks.* (Surtees) 66 Twitch the other cooarde a little below the mouth of the newe hive. **1729** LAW *Serious C.* xix. (1732) 354 Her Stays which her Mother had ordered to be twitch'd so strait [etc.]. **1809** T. DONALDSON *Poems* 191 The Shoon indeed did leuk fu' weel,..Ye'd twitcht them weel thegither. **1877** *Holderness Gloss.* s.v., Twitch thi shavs (sheaves) tighther.

b. To castrate by means of a cord looped over the testicles and drawn tight; see also quot. 1841.

1831 [YOUATT] *Horse* xii. 227 To the practice of some farmers, of twitching their colts at an early period, sometimes even so early as a month, we have stronger objection. **1841** HARTSHORNE *Salopia Antiq.* s.v. *Twitchel*, To twitch a horse, or apply to him a twitchel or twitch. **1877** in *N.W. Linc. Gloss.*

7. a. To draw *up* (a limb, etc.) sharply or with a jerk; to move (the skin, etc.) spasmodically or convulsively.

1523 FITZHERB. *Husb.* §108 The stryng halte..maketh him to twyche vp his legge sodeynly, and maketh hym to halte. **1616** SURFL. & MARKH. *Country Farme* 132 Ride him vpon new-plowed Lands, or in Wayes that are deepe and heauie, for that will make him twitch vp his legges, and strike them cleane and high. **1821** CLARE *Vill. Minstr.* I. 203 The cows..Twitching slow their fly-bit hides. **1863** GEO. ELIOT *Romola* xviii, A white rabbit..was twitching its nose with much content on a box full of bran. **1897** W. C. HAZLITT *Four Gen. Lit. Fam.* I. III. i. 239 As a young man [he] had a way of twitching his ears. **1899** *Allbutt's Syst. Med.* VII. 512 He rolled his eyes, clenched his hands, and twitched both arms and legs.

b. *intr.* Of a nerve, etc.: To twinge, 'shoot'.

a **1845** HOOD *True Story* ii, Why then they [teeth] only twitch'd the quicker.

8. a. *intr.* To proceed in a jerking or irregular way (*obs. rare*); now always in reference to involuntary bodily movements: to move in a jerky, spasmodic, or convulsive manner; to jerk, jump, start. Also *refl.* (const. *into*).

1592 NASHE *Strange News* G iij, The Hexamiter verse.. goes twitching and hopping in our language like a man running vpon quagmiers vp the hill in one Syllable and downe the dale in another. **1832** HT. MARTINEAU *Weal & Woe* vii, His bony fingers sometimes twitching, sometimes drooping with an appearance of utter helplessness. **1839–40** W. IRVING *Wolfert's R.* (1855) 217, I tried to keep my countenance,..but it would not do. My muscles began to twitch. **1848** THACKERAY *Van. Fair* lviii, If the Major had twitched before, he started now. **1870** MORRIS *Earthly Par.* II. III. 513 His mouth twitched, though his eyes gazed steadily. **1871** B. TAYLOR *Faust* (1875) I. v. 87 In the last convulsion twitching. **1885** HOWELLS *Silas Lapham* (1891) I. 15 Some of the younger children had twitched themselves into wavering shadows [in a photograph]. **1899** *Allbutt's Syst. Med.* VII. 519 In 2 [cases] the eyes 'had been rolled about', and in 2 others they had twitched. **1930** 'SAPPER' *Finger of Fate* 31 The faintest suspicion of a smile would twitch round his lips.

b. *intr.* To go with a sudden swift motion; to dart, shoot.

1836 PARTINGTON *Brit. Cycl. Nat. Hist.* II. 139/2 It [the shag] floats with wonderful buoyancy in the air, twitches down to the water with the rapidity of lightning.

9. *Comb.*: **twitch-ballock**, an earwig; also, a large black beetle; **twitch-bell**, an earwig; **twitch-clock, -clog**, a cockroach. All *dial.*

1658 ROWLAND *Moufet's Theat. Ins.* 1023 The Northern English by an obscene name call it [the earwig] *Twitch-ballock. *a* **1800** PEGGE *Suppl. Grose*, *Twitch-ballock*, the large black beetle. *Lanc.* **1790** GROSE *Provinc. Gloss.* (ed. 2), **Twitchbell*, an earwig. *North.* **1825** in BROCKETT *N.C. Words.* **1863** in Robson *Bards of Tyne* 237 Nee spiders an twitchbells to 'larm ye. **1876** J. HARTLEY *Yorksher Puddin'* 187 Boxes full o' butterflies, an buzzards, an *twitchclocks.

Hence **twitched** *ppl. a.* (*a*) *gen.*; (*b*) *spec.*, twitchy, irritable, 'rattled'. *slang.*; **'twitching** *ppl. a.*

1567 DRANT *Horace, Epist.* vi. D j, If that thy sydes, or Renes became With twitchinge stitche attainted. **1580** BABINGTON *Exp. Lord's Prayer* (1596) 274 His heart smote him,..and the woorde importeth a twitching smart. **1700** DRYDEN *Fables, Theod. & Hon.* 372 She..fear'd at ev'ry step a twitching spright behind. **1821** CLARE *Vill. Minstr.* I. 5 The spinning-top whirl'd from the twitching string. **1881** MIVART *Cat* 137 The muscle by its contraction effects those twitching movements of which the cat's skin is capable. **1883** G. MEREDITH *Day Dau. Hades* vii, His twitched lips puffing to tell In music his tears and his need. **1959** P. TOWNEND *Died o' Wednesday* xii. 216 He or she is likely to be..worried..'twitched to the eyebrows' as the flying boys have it. **1981** S. JACKMAN *Game of Soldiers* I. i. 16 The C.O.'s in there and he's a bit twitched.

†**twitch**, *v.*² *Obs. rare.* [Alteration of *quitch*, QUETCH *v.*, perhaps partly after prec.] *intr.* To move, stir.

1543 BECON *Policy of War* Wks. 1564 I. 143 b, God wyll so watche the borders..of our Realmes that no Tyraunte shoulde..once be able to twytche agaynst vs. **1674** N. FAIRFAX *Bulk & Selv.* 127 Springs, some shaping or plastick, some bigning or growing, others barely stirring or twitching.

twitch (twɪtʃ), *v.*³ *dial.* [f. TWITCH *sb.*²] *intr.* To gather and destroy twitch or couch-grass; also *trans.* to clean (land) from twitch. Hence **'twitching** *vbl. sb.*²

1795 *Gentl. Mag.* Aug. 695/1 At Beighton, Derbyshire,.. a respectable farmer was killed by lightning, as he was twitching in his land. **1799** A. YOUNG *Agric. Lincoln.* 398 Women..are employed in..picking up twitch to burn,..for twitching and weeding, they have, upon an average, 9*d.* per day. **1865** *Pall Mall G.* 13 May 2 They are employed in weeding, twitching, hoeing, and various other kinds of agricultural labour. **1886** *S.-W. Linc. Gloss.* s.v., I must twitch and do my land for wheat.

twitch, obs. form of TOUCH.

twitchel¹ ('twɪtʃ(ə)l). *dial.* Forms: 5 **twe-, twychel(l, twachylle**, 8–9 **twitchel, -ell.** [An alteration, or a variant with different suffix, of ME. *twychen*, late OE. *twichene*, OE. *twycene*, *twicen* a fork in a road, a forked way.

The form *twychen* survived in ME. times in Oxford in the names of special passages or lanes: see Wood *City of Oxford* (O.H.S.) I. viii. 187, 199, 223, etc., and Hurst *Oxford Topogr.* (O.H.S.) 186, 197. In Lanc. and Yorksh. the reduced form *twitch* is still in use. Cf. also TWITTEN.]

A narrow passage between walls or hedges. In quot. *c* 1460 *transf.*

1435 *Nottingham Rec.* (1883) II. 357 Ye comon twechell yat lyges on ye northe syd ye Fleshusse. *Ibid.*, Twychel. *c* **1460** *MS. Laud* 416 lf. 54 in *Rel. Ant.* II. 28 She..wyth her twachylle wille encrece and multeply. **1484** *Nottingham Rec.* (1883) III. 229 þe dore..þat gothe into the twychell betwix þe Shaumelles and þe Draperie. *a* **1800** PEGGE *Suppl. Grose*, *Twitchell*, a narrow passage, or alley, not a thoroughfare. Derb. **1848** A. B. EVANS *Leicester. Words, Phrases*, etc., *Twitchell*, a narrow passage or alley between houses. *a* **1889** *Notice* (Bedford) in *N. & Q.* 7th Ser. VII. 275/2 All persons passing by this twitchel are requested to go up or down directly.

'twitchel². *dial.* [f. TWITCH *sb.*¹ or *v.*¹] A noose; *spec.* = TWITCH *sb.*¹ 3 b. *dial.*

1688 [implied in *twitchelling* below]. **1841** [see TWITCH *v.*¹ 6 b]. **1882** *Lanc. Gloss.*, *Twitchel*, a short wooden lever with a loop of rope fastened to one end; the rope is put round the lower jaw of an unruly horse, and the stick is twisted round.

Hence **'twitchelled** (**'twichelt**) *a.*, noosed, held in a noose; **'twitchelling**, the taking of fish with a noose.

1688 CHETHAM *Angler's Vade-m.* Pref., The unlawful practice..of Damming, Groping, Spearing, Hanging, Twitchelling, [etc.]. **1855** E. WAUGH *Lanc. Life* (1857) 31 He wacker't an' stare't like a twichelt dog. **1865** B. BRIERLEY *Irkdale* II. 128 He geet how'd o' th' young womman, an' made her squeeal as leawd as a twitchelt gonner wi' th' squeeze he gan her.

twitcher ('twɪtʃə(r)). [f. TWITCH *v.*¹ + -ER¹.] One who or that which twitches.

1. An instrument for plucking or pinching something. †**a.** An instrument for clinching hog-rings; cf. *hog-ringer* (HOG *sb.*¹ 13). *Obs.* †**b.** = TWITCH *sb.*¹ 3 b. *Obs.* †**c.** Tweezers for extracting superfluous hairs. *Obs.* †**d.** Tweezers or nippers used in cookery for trimming or ornamenting pastry, etc. *Obs.*

1573 TUSSER *Husb.* (1878) 38 Strong yoke for a hog, with a twicher and rings. **1688** R. HOLME *Armoury* III. 244/1 Yoke for Swine, Twitchers or Rings. *Ibid.* 302/2 Horse Twichers, or Bracks..to put on Horses Noses, when they will not stand quietly to be Shooed [etc.]. *Ibid.* 427/1 A Twitcher, or Twitchers; by them Hair superfluously growing in any part is pulled up by the Roots. *Ibid.* xxii. (Roxb.) 274/2 Instruments belonging to the Cook. The first is termed a Runner with Twichers. Some Cooks call these Iging [? edging] Irons.

2. One who or that which moves jerkily or spasmodically. *rare.*

1793 MARY WOLLSTONECR. *Lett. to Imlay* viii. (1879) 19 Where shall I find a word to express the relationship which subsists between us? Shall I ask the little twitcher?

3. That which causes twitching; a severe blow; acute pain. *dial.*

1828 *Craven Gloss.*, *Twitcher*, a severe blow. **1877** *Sunday Mag.* 182 'The rheumatis' had, in his own phrase, 'caught him on the hop and given him a twitcher'.

4. A bird-watcher whose main aim is to collect sightings of rare birds.

1977 *Birds* Summer 59/3 Twitchers are difficult to identify because they are polymorphic. Best clues are behavioural including carrying Zeiss binoculars and *Where to Watch Birds*... Known to have nested in Wandsworth and possess a sense of humour. **1978** *Sunday Times* 19 Feb. 5/1 (*caption*) The people in the picture are 'twitchers'— birdwatchers. **1980** [see TICKER² 2]. **1980** L. BROWN in Howard & Moore *Compl. Checklist Birds of World* p. vii, Certainly, knowing what a bird is and where it occurs is the first step towards the wider interest that may stem from merely ticking a bird off on a list—twitching, as the vulgar parlance has it. **1982** *Times* 15 June 10/4 Twitchers are only interested in spotting rarities to claim they have seen them. Ornithologists are serious students, who despise and distrust twitchers. **1982** *Brit. Birds* LXXV. 537 The word 'twitcher' has, over the last decade, gained widespread use, meaning a person who 'chases' rare birds... I first heard the term from Bob Emmett at Beachy Head in 1968, when it was used to mean anyone who got 'twitchy' when southeast winds blew and headlands bristled with Pied Flycatchers and Redstarts.

twitchety ('twɪtʃɪtɪ), *a.* Also **twitchetty**. [f. TWITCH *v.*[1] or *sb.*[1] + *-et* + -Y[1], perh. after *crotchety*, *fidgety*, etc.] Twitchy, nervous; of things, moving back and forth.

1859 HOTTEN *Dict. Slang*, *Twitchetty*, nervous, fidgetty. **1936** W. GREENE *Death in Deep South* III. 214 When I heard the buzzer, I wuz' mos' asleep and I wait two three minutes. .. It didn't ring again, but I git up anyways and look at the elevator and see where Number One gone twitchety. **1973** *Nature* 28 Sept. 225/3 Variables are, apparently, pulsating, eruptive, symbiotic, eclipsing or twitchety.

'twitchily, *adv.* [f. TWITCHY *a.*[1] + -LY[2].] Nervously, in a twitchy manner; displaying nervous energy.

1934 in WEBSTER. **1964** J. BRAINE *Jealous God* iii. 70 A girl ..who was pretty in an acceptable way, not tartish, not twitchily refined. **1978** J. UPDIKE *Coup* (1979) iii. 108 She no longer moved like the great-granddaughter of a leopard, but more electrically, twitchily, like a modern woman connected to a variety of energy-sources.

twitching ('twɪtʃɪŋ), *vbl. sb.*[1] [f. TWITCH *v.*[1] + -ING[1].] The action of the verb TWITCH; jerking, plucking; nipping; convulsive or spasmodic movement; (see also quot. 1980). *attrib.*

1607 MARKHAM *Caval.* I. xviii. (1617) 75 Let them which haue hold vpon the halter, with twitchings and strainings torment him. **1626** BACON *Sylva* §37 Almost all Purgers have a kind of Twitching and vellication besides the griping which commeth of winde. **1768** TUCKER *Lt. Nat.* I. xxxiii. (1834) I. 241 A man, who should find a troublesome twitching in his muscles, would do very wrong to destroy the tone of them. **1789** *Trans. Soc. Arts* VII. 189 Model of a machine for twitching of wool. **1799** *Med. Jrnl.* I. 480 Starting tremors, convulsive twitchings are frequent. **1831** CARLYLE in Froude *Life* (1882) II. 189 An occasional twitching up of the corners of the upper lip, and point of the nose. **1872** M. CREIGHTON *Hist. Ess.* ii. (1902) 101 His suffering was known only by..the twitching of his lips. **1881** *Trans. Obstet. Soc. Lond.* XXII. 20 The twitching attacks do not recur periodically and their duration is variable. **1899** *Allbutt's Syst. Med.* VIII. 589 The patient complains of.. twitching of the extremities. **1980** [see TWITCHER 4].

†**b.** *concr.* See quot. *Obs. rare.*

1688 R. HOLME *Armoury* III. 300/1 *Twitchings*, the ends of Nails cut off, as of Horse-shooe Nails.

twitching, *vbl. sb.*[2]: see TWITCH *v.*[3]

†**twitchmill**. A nonce-rendering of G. *zwickmühle*, a certain advantage in the game of merels.

c **1640** H. BELL *Luther's Colloq. Mens.* (1652) 307 The Pope..maketh between the Emperor and French King a Twittchmill, without which two hee cannot subsist. *Ibid.*, Hee forsaketh not that Twittchmill with the Emperor and French King.

twitchy ('twɪtʃɪ), *a.*[1] [f. TWITCH *v.*[1] + -Y.]

1. Characterized by twitching; having a tendency to twitch; also, nervous, fidgety, irritable; also said of a smile.

1839 *Fraser's Mag.* XX. 671 Her lips were long, loose, and twitchy. **1861** DICKENS in *All Year Round* IV. 457 Faces peculiarly swollen, and twitchy about the nose. **1874** A. J. C. HARE *Story of my Life* (1900) IV. xvii. 245 An excellent person, but very nervous and twitchy. **1898** TALMAGE *Serm.* in *N.Y. Chr. Herald* 27 Apr. 368/3 Your nerves will become more twitchy and your dyspepsia more aggravated. **1924** W. M. RAINE *Troubled Waters* xx. 221 When she said goodbye to him it was with a wan twitchy little smile on her face.

2. *Mining.* Cf. TWITCH *sb.*[1] 4, *v.*[1] 5.

1747 HOOSON *Miner's Dict.* Rij b, Many good Veins that ..have been wrought to a vast Depth, yet it is found in the end to grow hard and Twitchey on the Soles.

Hence **'twitchiness**, the state or condition of being twitchy; nervousness, fidgetiness, irritability.

1933 J. THURBER *My Life & Hard Times* p. xv, This type of writing is..the manifestation of a twitchiness at once cosmic and mundane. **1984** *Times* 23 Mar. 12/6 (*heading*) Twitchiness in the president's camp.

twitchy ('twɪtʃɪ), *a.*[2] [f. TWITCH *sb.*[2] + -Y.] Full of or infested with twitch; made of twitch.

1653 BLITHE *Eng. Improv. Impr.* xxviii. (ed. 3) 193 If upon a stony land, or twichy woody Land, it must be narrower. *Ibid.* 196 Lands..hard rooty, rushy, twichy, or any way unfeacible. **1829** *Glover's Hist. Derby* I. 195 He ploughs twitchy lands but once. *c* **1837** CLARE *To the Lark* iii. in *Life & Rem.* (1873) 137 How beautiful to see thee..Winnowing thy russet wings above thy twitchy nest.

twite (twaɪt). [Imitative, from the note of the bird.] A species of linnet, *Linota flavirostris* or *L. montium*, found in hilly and moorland districts in the northern parts of Britain and in Scandinavia, and elsewhere as a winter visitant; also called Mountain Linnet or **twite-finch**.

1562 TURNER *Baths* Pref., Flockinge byrdes..linnettes, goldfinches, sparrowes and twyes [? twytes]. **1676** GREW *Musæum, Anat. Stomach & Guts* viii. 36 The Twite or Avicula Anadavadensis. **1773** BARRINGTON in *Phil. Trans.* LXIII. 282 *note*, The London bird-catchers also sell..the yellow hammer, twite and brambling as singing birds. **1815** STEPHENS in Shaw *Gen. Zool.* IX. 521 Twite Finch. **1876** SMILES *Sc. Natur.* xiii. (ed. 4) 260 The Twite..bred in suitable localities round the loch. **1894** R. B. SHARPE *Handbk. Birds Gt. Brit.* I. 43 The Twite is a moorland species... In winter it migrates south in large flocks, which frequent the neighbourhood of the coast, and enliven the marshes with their twittering song.

twite, obs. or dial. form of TWIT *v.*

twithe, obs. Sc. form of TOOTH.

twitten ('twɪt(ə)n), *Sussex dial.* Also **twitting**. [Perh. related to LG. *twiete* alley, land; but cf. also OE. *twicen* and TWITCHEL[1].] A narrow path or passage between two walls or hedges.

1801 PENNANT *Journ. fr. Lond. to Isle of Wight* II. 77 Alleys, or, as they are called here [at Brighton] twittings, narrow passages, often not three feet wide. **1860** W. H. AINSWORTH *Ovingdean Grange* 334 Having tracked a series of 'twittens'..they issued forth into West-street. **1904** *Sat. Rev.* 2 Apr. 424/1 Along the bostals of the Downs and through the village twittens.

twitter ('twɪtə(r)), *sb.*[1] [f. TWITTER *v.*[1]]

1. A condition of twittering or tremulous excitement (from eager desire, fear, etc.); a state of agitation; a flutter, a tremble. Now chiefly *dial.*

1678 BUTLER *Hud.* III. i. 83 The ancient errant knights Won all their ladies' hearts in fights, And cut whole giants into fritters, To put them into amorous twitters. *a* **1734** NORTH *Exam.* I. iii. §31 (1740) 141 The Attorney-General.. was in a Twitter; for some of his Friends told him he would certainly be questioned for it in Parliament. **1802** G. COLMAN *Poor Gentleman* I. i, If I ben't all of a twitter to see my old John Harrowby again! **1825** J. NEAL *Bro. Jonathan* II. 151 A leap of the heart..and a sort of tingling twitter through all his blood. **1861** THACKERAY *Four Georges* iv. (1862) 198 In a twitter of indignation. **1869** TROLLOPE *He knew*, etc. xxxi, [She] was in a twitter, partly of expectation, and partly..of fear. **1869** LOUISA M. ALCOTT *Little Women* vi, Beth hurried on in a twitter of suspense.

b. A suppressed laugh, a titter; a fit of laughter. *dial.*

1736 LEWIS *Isle of Tenet* Gloss. s.v. (E.D.S.), He is in a mighty twitter. **1847–78** HALLIWELL, *Twitter*,..(2) A fit of laughter. *Kent.*

2. An act or the action of twittering, as a bird; light tremulous chirping. Also *transf.* a sound resembling this.

1842 BROWNING *Waring* I. vi. 35 As pours some pigeon.. her melodious cry Amid their [swallows'] barbarous twitter! **1849** W. S. MAYO *Kaloolah* v. (1850) 40 The hesitating twitter of the sleepy birds. **1871** BLACKIE *Four Phases* i. 43 A mere swallow-twitter of inarticulate jargon. **1902** SNAITH *Wayfarers* xvi, The ceaseless twitter of the rain on the road.

'twitter, *sb.*[2] [Dial. var. QUITTER *sb.*[1]]

1. *Farriery.* = QUITTER *sb.*[1] 2. Cf. TWITTER-BONE.

1892 *Lincolnsh. N. & Q.* Apr. 45 *Twitter*, a tumour or gathering on a horse's foot, just above the hoof.

2. *Whaling.* The refuse of the case of the sperm-whale, consisting of a gummy and thready substance (*Cent. Dict.* 1891).

'twitter, *sb.*[3] *Sc.* and *north. dial.* [Cf. TWIT *sb.*[2] and TWITTER *v.*[2]] **a.** A thin part in a thread that is unequally spun. Also *transf.* **b.** A shred, a fragment. **c.** An entanglement; a complication.

1721 KELLY *Sc. Prov.* 395 You are as small as the Twitter of a twin'd Rusky, a Taunt to a Maid, that would gladly be esteem'd neat, and small. **1825** JAMIESON s.v., Yarn is said to be twined to twitters, when twined too small... It is said of a lank delicate girl; 'She's a mere twitter'. **1847–78** HALLIWELL, *Twitters*, shreds; fragments. *North.* **1876** *Whitby Gloss.*, *Twitters*, entangled threads; complications of all sorts.

'twitter, *sb.*[4] *rare.* [f. TWIT *v.* + -ER[1].] One who twits; *dial.* a tale-bearer.

1854 MISS BAKER *Northampt. Gloss.* s.v., 'Don't tell him anything, he's a twitter.' **1882** in OGILVIE.

twitter ('twɪtə(r)), *v.*[1] Forms: 4 **twyter**, **twiter**, 5– **twitter**. [Of imitative origin: cf. OHG. *zwizirôn*, *-erôn* (MHG. *zwitzern*, G. *zwitschern*), Du. *kwetteren*, and Sw. *qvittra*, Norw. dial. *kvittra*, *kvitra*, Da. *kvidre* (see QUITTER *v.*[2]), in sense 1.]

1. *intr.* Of a bird: To utter a succession of light tremulous notes; to chirp continuously with a tremulous effect.

c **1374** CHAUCER *Boeth.* III. met. ii. 54 (Camb. MS.) The Iangelynge bryd..enclosed in a streyht cage..twiterith desyrynge the wode with her swete voys. **1387** TREVISA *Higden* (Rolls) I. 237 þe nyȝtyngale in his note Twytereþ wel fawnyng Wiþ full swete song. **1697** DRYDEN *Virg. Georg.* IV. 434 Swallows twitter on the Chimney Tops. **1750** GRAY *Elegy* v, The swallow twittring from the straw-built shed. **1840** DICKENS *Barn. Rudge* i, Colonies of sparrows chirped and twittered in the eaves.

b. *transf.* Of a person: To sing after the above manner; also (esp. of a woman), to talk or chatter rapidly in a small or tremulous voice.

1829 LADY GRANVILLE *Lett.* 22 Nov. (1894) II. 49 They.. are enchanted, twittering like hedge-sparrows. **1875** JOWETT *Plato* (ed. 2) III. 40 While a man is singing and twittering and pouring music like water through the funnel of his ears, the edge of his soul gradually wears away. **1879** K. S. MACQUOID *Berkshire Lady* 178 The old lady twittered and fluttered.

2. *trans.* Of a bird: To utter or express by twittering.

1387 TREVISA *Higden* (Rolls) I. 237 þe osul twytereþ mery songes. **1645** G. DANIEL *Poems* Wks. (Grosart) II. 70 The Squallid owle Twitters a midnight note. **1821** CLARE *Vill. Minstr.* II. 105 Linnets,..twittering their welcomes to the day's return. **1884** W. C. SMITH *Kildrostan* I. iii. 14 The swifts and swallows..Twitter their gossip in the evening light. **1891** FARRAR *Darkn. & Dawn* xxxvii, The very birds of the air seemed to flit away from him [Nero], twittering 'Matricide! matricide!'

b. *transf.* Of a person: cf. 1 b.

1864 BROWNING *Youth & Art* iii, I..trilled and twittered, 'Kate Brown's on the boards ere long'. **1878** —— *Poets Croisic* lxxi, These [lines], brisk as any finch, He twittered. **1900** SARAH GRAND *Babs* xvii, 'Really, Mrs. Kingconstance,' Miss Spice twittered excitedly, 'you are too kind!'

3. *intr.* To move tremulously, tremble, shake, quiver, shiver; *esp.* to tremble with excitement, eagerness, fear, etc.; to be in a flutter; hence, †to long eagerly, to hanker (*after*, or *to do* something). Now *dial.*

a **1616** BEAUM. & FL. *Scornf. Lady* IV. i, When it twitter'd to be at me. **1629** GAULE *Holy Madn.* 206 Hands clap, Fingers twitter. **1635** BROME *Sparagus Gard.* III. v, How the slave twitters. **1675** BUNYAN *Saved by Grace* Wks. (ed. Offor) I. 342 Doth not thy mouth water, doth not thy heart twitter at being saved? **1684** SOUTHERNE *Disappointm.* II. i, Her eyes and lips, see how they blubb and pout, and twitter and swell at you. *a* **1688** BUNYAN *Israel's Hope Encouraged* Wks. (ed. Offor) I. 620 Doth not all this discourse make thy heart twitter after the mercy that is with God? **1821** CLARE *Vill. Minstr.* I. 46 Where the sunbeam twitter'd on the walls. *Ibid.* II. 92, I twitter'd like a leaf. **1861** THACKERAY *Four Georges* iv. (1876) 115 The bigness, boisterousness..appear to have..set all the teacups twittering on the tray. **1878** STEVENSON *Inland Voy.* 114, I was..twittering with cold.

b. *trans.* To move (something) tremulously; to twiddle (the fingers). *rare*$^{-1}$.

1855 THACKERAY *Newcomes* vii, Mademoiselle..was twittering her fingers.

4. *intr.* To laugh in a suppressed way, titter, giggle. *dial.*

1687 MIÉGE *Gt. Fr. Dict.* II, To twitter, or snear at one, to laugh at him with some contempt, *se moquer de quêcun.* **1694** MOTTEUX *Rabelais* IV. lii. 204 The Maidens began to snicker,..giggling and twittering among themselves. *a* **1700** B. E. *Dict. Cant. Crew*, *Twitter*, to Laugh much with little Noise. **1901** 'ZACK' *Dunstable Weir* II Folks would have twittered louder had they known whose fancy he was like to take.

5. *trans.* To bring *into* a specified condition by twittering. *rare*$^{-1}$.

1861 T. L. PEACOCK *Gryll Gr.* xiv, The pianoforte is not much to my mind... Its incapability of sustaining a note has led..to those infinitesimal subdivisions of sound, in which all sentiment and expression are twittered and frittered into nothingness.

'twitter, *v.*[2] *Sc.* and *north. dial.* [Of obscure origin: cf. TWIT *sb.*[2] and TWITTER *sb.*[3]] *trans.* To spin or twist unevenly, to make 'twitty'.

1674 RAY *N.C. Words* 50 To Twitter Thread or Yarn, is to Spin it uneven. **1828** *Craven Gloss.*, *Twitter*, to entangle, as thread which is too hard twisted. **1843** *Whistlebinkie* (1890) II. 165 Baith twittered and knotty's the thread o' our life.

'twitter, *v.*[3] Now *dial.* [f. TWIT *v.* + -ER[5].] *trans.* = TWIT *v.* 1; *dial.* to tease.

1749 FIELDING *Tom Jones* VIII. vii, It doth not become such a one as you to twitter me. **1800** BROWNE *Poems* 155 (E.D.D.) She twitters me out of my life.

twitte'ration. *Obs. rare.* [f. TWITTER *v.*[1] 3 + -ATION.] = TWITTER *sb.*[1] 1.

1820 G. COLMAN *X.Y.Z.* I. iii. 26 A female hand! bless me, I'm all over in a twitteration! **1835–40** HALIBURTON *Clockm.* 373 (Cassell) When they struck up our blood-stirrin' national air, it made me feel all over in a twitteration. **1855** —— *Nat. & Hum. Nat.* xiv. II. 50, I am so skared, Sam, I feel all over of a twitteration.

twitter-bit. (See quot.)

1875 KNIGHT *Dict. Mech.*, *Twitter-bit*, the bottom of the countersink which receives the head of the screw, uniting the halves of a pair of scissors.

twitter-bone. *dial.* or *Obs.* [var. of *quitter-bone*, QUITTER *sb.*[1] 4.] A suppurating tumour on a horse's foot. Hence **twitter-boned** *a.*, affected with a twitter-bone.

1688 *Lond. Gaz.* No. 2395/4 A yellowish bay Horse,..a Twitterbone taken out of each hind Foot. **1759** STERNE *Tr. Shandy* I. x, His horse was either clapp'd, or..twitter-bon'd, or broken-winded. **1828** *Craven Gloss.*, *Twitter-bone*, an excrescence on a horse's hoof.

twitterer ('twɪtərə(r)). [f. TWITTER *v.*[1] + -ER[1].] A bird that twitters; also *transf.* of a person (cf. TWITTER *v.*[1] 2 b).

1834 R. MUDIE *Feathered Tribes Brit. Isles* (1841) I. 2 When the forest howls to its fury, driving the twitterers from the spray. **1890** O. CRAWFURD *Round Calendar in Portugal* 178 Several feeble-winged twitterers. **1895** J. G. WOOLLEY in *Voice* (N.Y.) 17 Oct. 2/1 A mere twitterer of lackadaisical platitudes.

twittering ('twɪtərɪŋ), *vbl. sb.* [f. TWITTER *v.*[1] + -ING[1].] The action of TWITTER *v.*[1]

1. Light tremulous chirping of a bird or birds; a sound resembling or likened to this.

1781 COWPER *Conversation* 448 Will the sweet warbler of the livelong night..Forget his harmony, with rapture heard, To learn the twittering of a meaner bird? **1824** LAMB *Elia* Ser. II. *Captain Jackson* (1833) 87 Chords responsive to the twitterings of that slender image of a voice. **1877** BARING-GOULD *Myst. Suffering* 87 The twanging of fiddles and twittering of flutes. **1877** BLACK *Green Past.* ii, The twittering of the young starlings in their nests.

2. Trembling; tremulous excitement; †eager desire or longing, hankering (*obs.*).

1668 SEDLEY *Mulberry Gard.* v. i, Though you had a twittering to Althea, you will make ne'er the worse husband to Victoria. **1692** L'ESTRANGE *Fables* I. cccxxxii. 289 A Widow that had a Twittering toward a second Husband.

'twittering, *ppl. a.* [f. as prec. + -ING^2.] That twitters.

1. Chirping lightly and tremulously, as a bird.

1827 HOOD *Mids. Fairies* xxxi, We gather in loud choirs the twittering race. **1857** J. HAMILTON *Less. fr. Gt. Biog.* (1859) 172 New leaves are on the trees and twittering broods are in the nest.

2. Trembling, quivering; trembling with excitement or the like, in a flutter. Now *dial.*

1681 W. ROBERTSON *Phraseol. Gen.* (1693) 1257, I am in a twittering case, *inter sacrum saxumque sto.* **1821** CLARE *Vill. Minstr.* II. 75 The sun now sinks behind the woodland green, And twittering spangles glow the leaves between. **1884** STEVENSON *Let. to Henley* Nov. (1899) I. 335 Hardly able to come downstairs for twittering knees. **1936** T. S. ELIOT *Coll. Poems 1909–35* 189 Not here Not here the darkness, in this twittering world.

Hence **'twitteringly** *adv.*

1860 RUSSELL *Diary India* I. xvi. 255 A large zigzag fire of musketry goes twitteringly along the lines of the trenches.

† twitter-light. *Obs. rare.* [? f. TWITTER *v.*^{1} 3 + LIGHT *sb.* Cf. TWATTER-LIGHT.] Twilight.

1607 MIDDLETON *Your Five Gallants* v. i, You can steale secretly hether.. at twylight, twitterlights! *a* **1626** —— *More Dissemblers* III. i, Come not till twitter light.

'twitterly, *a. rare*$^{-1}$. [f. TWITTER *sb.*^{1} 1 or *v.*^{1} 3 + -LY^1.] = next.

1896 KIPLING *Seven Seas, Cholera Camp* (1897) 188 Our Colonel's white an' twitterly—'e gets no sleep nor food.

twittery ('twɪtərɪ), *a.*^{1} [f. TWITTER *sb.*^{1} 1 or *v.*^{1} + -Y.] Apt to twitter or tremble; feeble, shaky; also *fig.*

1883 L. WINGFIELD *A. Rowe* II. iv. 92 Olivia was.. twittery, nervous and sensitive. **1889** *Cornh. Mag.* July 69 A feeble, twittery tale of love. **1907** UNA L. SILBERRAD *Gd. Comrade* ii, The Captain was rather twittery at lunch.

'twittery, *a.*^{2} *Sc.* [f. TWITTER *sb.*^{3} or *v.*^{2}] 'Slender; properly, spun very small' (Jam.).

1819 *Edinb. Even. Cour.* 1 July (Jam.), Clothing.. far afore the twittery worn-wabs made now-a-days.

twitting ('twɪtɪŋ), *vbl. sb.* [f. TWIT *v.* + -ING^1.] The action of the verb TWIT.

1. (Light) reproach or censure; taunting.

1580 HOLLYBAND *Treas. Fr. Tong, Exprobation*, or *reproche*, a reproch, a twiting. **1586** A. DAY *Eng. Secretary* II. (1625) 48 Tush, pedegree, pedegree, here is nothing with you in hand but twitting with pedegree. **1611** COTGR., *Reproche*, an vpbraiding, twitting, or casting in the teeth. **1647** HEXHAM I, A twiting, *een verwijting*. **1891** E. W. GOSSE *Gossip in Library* xiv. 175 The only rough thing he ever did was the result of one such twitting.

2. Tale-telling, blabbing. Now *dial.*

a **1643** CARTWRIGHT *Ordinary* IV. iv, D' y' think I would undo me self by twitting?.. I'm faithfull, And secret, though a Barber.

So **'twitting** *ppl. a.*, that twits; whence **'twittingly** *adv.*, in the way of twitting, tauntingly.

1675 tr. *Camden's Hist. Eliz.* I. 125 Having reckoned all his Civilities to the English Nation, he twittingly upbraided them therewith. **1838** B. CORNEY *Controversy* 20 The points whereon you may have been criticised rather twittingly.

twitting, variant of TWITTEN.

† 'twittle, *v. Obs.* [app. altered from TITTLE *v.*^{1}; cf. TWITTLE-TWATTLE.] *trans.* To utter idly, chatter, babble: = TITTLE *v.*^{1}

1577 STANYHURST *Descr. Irel.* Ep. to Sir H. Sidney, in Holinshed *Chron.* (1587) II. 6 His hystorie.. twitled more tales out of schoole, and drowned weightyer matters in silence, then the Autor vpon better view.. woulde haue permitted. *Ibid.* vi. 34/2 Such rumors noised, such tales bruted, such fables twitled, such vntrue reports twatled.

† 'twittle-,twat. *Obs. rare*$^{-1}$. [app. shortened from next.] A tattler, babbler.

1662 *Rump Songs* I. 52 Next come those idle Twittle-twats, Which calls me many God-knows-whats.

† 'twittle-,twattle. *Obs.* Also 6 **twitle twattle, twitell-twaytel.** [app. altered from TITTLE-TATTLE: see TWATTLE *sb.*^{1}] Idle talk, tittle-tattle. Also *attrib.*

1556 OLDE *Antichrist* 7 b, Suche a kynde of religioun, as hath more twitle twattle toyes in it, then the Leuitical lawe. **1565** ABP. PARKER *Corr.* (Parker Soc.) 237 My lord of Leicester, they say, shall move.. the Queen's Majesty,.. and Mr. Cole is now at the Court.., which will overthrow all this attempt: and such twitell-twaytel there is much. *a* **1578** W. ROPER *Life Sir T. More* (1729) 89 She.. not likinge suche talke, answered, twittle, twattle, twittle, twattle. **1668** R. L'ESTRANGE *Vis. Quev.* (1708) 244 The squalling of the Child, and the Twittle-Twattle-Gossipings of the Nurse and Midwife. **1719** D'URFEY *Pills* III. 250 Leave your twittle twattle.

† twit-twat. *Obs. rare.* Also **twit twot.** [app. shortened from prec.]

† **1.** = prec. Also *attrib. Obs.*

1677 YARRANTON *Eng. Improv.* 46 This way of ordering the young Women in Germany is one great cause that the German Women have so little of the twit twat. *Ibid.* 101 The strange News you hear at Coffee-houses.. is generally idle Twit twot Discourse. *Ibid.* 170 Command Silence; Suffer not your Wives to use any Twit-twat.

2. A name for the house-sparrow.

1891 in *Cent. Dict.*

twitty ('twɪtɪ), *a.*^{1} *dial.* [f. TWIT *sb.*^{1} + -Y.] See quots.

a **1825** FORBY *Voc. E. Anglia, Twitty, adj.* cross; snappish. **1893** ZINCKE *Wherstead* xxvi. (ed. 2) 251 (E. Anglian Dial.) 'Trunch' for short and thick; 'twitty' for snappish.

'twitty, *a.*^{2} [f. TWIT *sb.*^{2} + -Y.] Full of or containing 'twits': see TWIT *sb.*^{2}

1884 W. S. B. MCLAREN *Spinning* (ed. 2) 119 Such a draft would.. be too much for any wool and would make the sliver twitty. *Ibid.* 131 No yarn can spin well when it is twitty.

twitzer-case, obs. f. TWEEZER-CASE.

† twive, *v. Naut. Obs. rare.* Also **twyve.** [Of obscure origin.] *intr.* Of a ship at anchor: To swing up or down with the tide.

1576 *Admir. Crt. Exam.* 22, 30 Aug., The Salamon twyved to the Southwarde upp with the flud and when the water turned she twivid downe agaGeneral with the ebb. *Ibid.*, She twived upwards agaGeneral and therewith twyved uppon an anchor.

'twixt, † twixt (twɪkst), *prep.* Forms: 4 **twix, tuyx,** 4, 6–7 *Sc.* **tuix,** 6–7 **twixt,** 7– **'twixt.** Aphetic form of ATWIXT, BETWIXT.

13.. *Cursor M.* 3179 (Cott.) [Abraham] loked bi him tuyx þe thorns. *Ibid.* 22028 O fader and moder he sal be born.. Bituix a man and a womman.. Noght tuix a biscop and a nun. **1570** *Satir. Poems Reform.* xx. 51 This I will say tuix sport and play. **1578** LYTE *Dodoens* II. xlviii. 206 The seede [of hyacinth] is drie in the thirde degree, yet temperate twixt heate and colde. **1611** SIR W. MURE *Misc. Poems* i. (*title*) Ane Conflict tuix Love and Ressoun. **1611** SHAKS. *Wint. T.* v. ii. 79 But, Oh the Noble Combat, that 'twixt Ioy and Sorrow, was fought in Paulina. **1634** SIR T. HERBERT *Trav.* 146 All the difference.. twixt him and others. **1742** YOUNG *Nt. Th.* IX. 673 In thy nocturnal rove, one moment halt, 'Twixt stage and stage. **1885–94** R. BRIDGES *Eros & Psyche* May xxxi, He fondly kisst her.., And peace was 'twixt them.

†**b.** *twixt and*, until (see BETWIXT A. 3), before. *Sc.* and *north. dial. Obs.*

13.. *Cursor M.* 927 (Gött.) Þu sal bi þi bred ful dere, Tuix and þu again be gan. **1689** in *Acts Parlt. Scotl.* (1875) XII. 59/1 To compeir before the meetting twixt and þe 9th day of Apryle.

c. *Comb.*: **'twixt-brain** = *'tween-brain*: see 'TWEEN b.

1878 BELL & LANKESTER tr. *Gegenbaur's Comp. Anat.* 503 These primitive cerebral vesicles give rise to new segments. .. The first is known as the Fore-brain or Prosencephalon; the next as the Twixt-brain or Thalamencephalon.

Also **†'twixten (twyxten)** *prep. Obs.* (Cf. BETWIXEN.)

c **1330** R. BRUNNE *Chron. Wace* (Rolls) 2282 [Lear] þoughte his doughtres gyue hosebandes, & twyxten hem parten his landes.

† twizeled, *a. Obs. rare*$^{-1}$. [Perh. a survival of OE. *twisled* forked; but cf. TWIZZLE *v.*] (Meaning uncertain.)

1685 *Lond. Gaz.* No. 2070/4 An Iron grey Gelding,.. having upon each shoulder a twizeled Flower.

twizers, obs. f. TWEEZERS.

'twizzle, *sb.* Chiefly *dial.* [Cf. next]

1. A twist or turn; a change of direction.

1848 A. B. EVANS *Leicestersh. Words*, etc. s.v. *Twizzle*, There be so many turns and twizzles. **1876–** in dial. glossaries (Chesh., Shropsh., Warw., etc.).

2. In a spinning-machine, the eye of a flyer.

1884 W. S. B. MCLAREN *Spinning* (ed. 2) 153 The flyer.. revolves 'the way the sun goes', the yarn is hooked into the flyer-eye, or twizzle, at its lower extremity.

'twizzle, *v. dial.* and *colloq.* [app. an imitative formation suggested by TWIST *v.*: cf. TWISTLE *v.*]

1. *intr.* To rotate rapidly, spin, twirl.

a **1825** FORBY *Voc. E. Anglia* s.v., He came twizzling down. **1886** P. ROBINSON *Valley Teet. Trees* 126 But those on the more exposed spots were fairly 'twizzling' like tops. **1898** KIPLING in *Morn. Post* 11 Nov. 5/2 From 6 to 10 p.m. one screw twizzled for the most part in the circumambient ether. **1908** W. W. JACOBS *Salthaven* ii, I suppose you never twizzle round on your chair.

2. *trans.* To twirl, twist; to turn round; to form by twisting.

1788 E. PICKEN *Poems & Epistles* Gloss. 248/1 Twisle, to twist, fold. *c* **1840** LADY WILTON *Art of Needle-Work* xvi. 255 In vain she cut and screwed the thread, she burnt it in the candle.. she twizled it between her finger and thumb.. but enter the eye of the needle it would not. **1854** BAKER *Northampt. Gloss., Twizzle*, to twist, to twirl. Variously applied... Corn that is beat about by the wind in different directions, till it is twisted and entangled, is said to be *twizzled*. **1866** BROGDEN *Linc. Gloss.*, I have twizzled all the cotton. **1887** C. KEENE *Let.* in *Life* xii. (1892) 391 My friends directly after breakfast began twizzling up cigarettes. **1888** F. BARRETT *Recoiling Vengeance* vi, The girl he loved was being hugged and twizzled round by his rival. **1890** *N. & Q.* 7th Ser. IX. 138/1 If a couple of waxed-ends became twizzled [in the game of 'cob-nut']. **1905** *Longm. Mag.* June 134 'Shall us come and twizzle th' old churn?'

twizzle, variant of TWISEL.

twke, obs. Sc. pa. t. of TAKE *v.*

twm, twme, twn, obs. Sc. ff. TOOM, TON, TUN.

twne, obs. Sc. f. TIN, TUN.

two (tuː), *numeral a., sb.* (*adv.*) Forms: see below; also TWAIN, TWAY. [OE. *twá* fem. and neut., *tú* neut., of the numeral of which the masc. *twéȝen* survives as TWAIN and TWAY. The forms in the cognate languages which more or less closely correspond to OE. *twá* and *tú* are OFris. *twâ* fem. and neut. (WFris. *twa*, EFris. *twô*, NFris. *tâw, tau, tô, tû*), MDu. and Du. *twee*, OS. *twâ, twô* fem., *twê* neut. (MLG. *twô, twu* fem., *twê* neut.; LG. *twê, twe*), OHG. *zwâ, zwô* fem., *zwei* neut. (MHG. *zwô, zwei*, G. *zwei*), ON. and Icel. *tveir* masc., *tvær* fem., *tvau* (*tvö*) neut. (Norw. dial. *tvei, tvæ, tvo, tvau*, etc.; Sw. *två*, Da. *to*), Goth. *twai* masc., *twōs* fem., *twa* neut. (For the forms corresponding to the OE. masc. *twéȝen* see TWAIN.) The word is common to all the Indo-European languages, as Skr. *dwau* masc., *dwē* fem. and neut., Gr. δύο, L. *duo*, OIr. *dá*, Lith. *du, dvi*, etc.

The genitive and dative forms (see A. 2 and A. 3) did not survive beyond the 13th century.

The pronunc. (tuː), like that of *who* (huː) from OE. *hwá*, is due to labialization of the vowel by the *w* (cf. *womb*), which then disappeared before the related sound. The successive stages would thus be (twaː, twɔː, twoː, twuː, tuː).]

A. Illustration of Forms.

1. *nom.* and *acc.* α. 1, 4–5, *Sc.* 6 **tua,** 1–5, *dial.* -9, *Sc.* 5– **twa** (6 *Sc.* **thwa**), 8–9 *dial.* **twaa;** 7 *Sc.* **tuae,** 8– *Sc.* **twae,** 9 *north. dial.* **tweae, twea, tweea, twee.** (See also TWAY.)

The later Sc., and rare northern Eng., *twa* (twaː, twɔː) in place of *twae, twea*, etc., is abnormal, but has parallels in *wha* WHO, and NA *adv.*^{2} Examples are given under (*b*) below.

Beowulf 1194 Earmhreade twa. *a* **831** in *O.E. Texts* 444 An hriðer.. & tua flicca. *Ibid.*, Fore Osuulfes sawle twa messan. *c* **893** K. ÆLFRED *Oros.* III. ii. §1 Tua byriȝ.. on eorþan besuncon. *c* **1000** *Ags. Gosp.* Luke xvii. 35 Twa beoð ætgædere grindende. *c* **1000** ÆLFRIC *Gen.* xxv. 23 Twa þeoda.. and twa folc. *Ibid.* xxvii. 9 Bring me twa þa betstan tyccenu. **1154** *O.E. Chron.* an. 1137 ðif twa men oþer III coman ridend to an tun. *c* **1230** *Hali Meid.* 35 Gulteð o twa half. *a* **1300** Tua [see B. I. 5 a]. **1340** HAMPOLE *Pr. Consc.* 987 Þe tother world.. In twa partes divised may be. **1375** BARBOUR *Bruce* II. 234 Twa Erlis alsua with him war. *c* **1470** [see B. I. 2]. **1483** *Cath. Angl.* 398/2 Twa,.. *duo*. **1513** DOUGLAS *Æneis* v. Prol. 17 Tua appetitis vneith accordis with vther. **1540** *Registr. Aberdon.* (Maitl. Cl.) I. 416 Mortificatioun.. of thwa merkis ȝerelie. **1596** DALRYMPLE tr. *Leslie's Hist. Scot.* (S.T.S.) I. 3 The tua partes.. ar called ..from.. the first tua sones. *c* **1620** HUME *Brit. Tongue* (1865) 8 Of this letter the latines them-selfs had tuae other sounds. **1721** RAMSAY *Bessy Bell & Mary Gray* 27 Our fancies jee between you twae [*rime* Gray]. **1789** BURNS *Five Carlins* vii, But nae ane could their fancy please, O ne'er a ane but twae. **1802** ANDERSON *Cumbld. Ball., Nichol the Newsmonger* vii, I've twee, nit aw England can bang them. **1825** BROCKETT *N.C. Words*, Twea, twee, two. **1851** *Cumberld. Gloss., Twea*, two. **1901** W. LAIDLAW *Poetry & Prose* 34 Twae windows. *Ibid.* 35 The twae were kind to ane an' a'.

(*b*) **1721** RAMSAY *Lucky Spence* xiii, I.. whistl'd ben whiles ane, whiles twa. **1780** J. MAYNE *Siller Gun* I. xxvii, His Craft, the Hammermen, fu' braw, Led the Procession, twa and twa. **1815** SCOTT *Guy M.* xxii, I have six terriers at hame, forbye twa couple of slowhunds. **1828** *Craven Gloss., Twaa*, two.

β. 3– **two,** 4–7 **tuo, twoo,** (5 **thwo**); *pl.* 7 **twoes,** 7–8 **two's,** 9 **twos.**

c **1200** *Trin. Coll. Hom.* 47 Two turtle briddes, ȝif hie was poure two duue briddes. ? *a* **1300** *Shires & Hundreds Eng.* in *O.E. Misc.* 145 Þis bis[co]pryche wes hwylen two bispriche. **13..** *Cursor M.* 16814 + 18 Vnto þe theues twoo [*rime* froo]. *c* **1330** R. BRUNNE *Chron.* (1810) 282 Tuo watres þer er togidir gon. *c* **1400** *Apol. Loll.* 38 Boþ thwo are dedly synne. *c* **1400** *Laud Troy-bk.* 18599 That the traytoures bothe two [*rime* so]. *c* **1420** *Chron. Vilod.* 3769 He hadde y-fedryde to-gedur his leygus two [*rime* þo]. **1447** BOKENHAM *Seyntys* (Roxb.) 75 For victory of tuo mo she must have. *a* **1548** Twoo [see B. I. 3 b]. **1560** DAUS tr. *Sleidane's Comm.* Pref. 4 It is set-forth.. by mo than one or two. **1605** CAMDEN *Rem.* 191 Twoo Monkes. **1611** Twoes [see B. II. 2]. *c* **1620** A. HUME *Brit. Tongue* (1865) 16 At one consonant,.. or at tuo consonantes. *c* **1659** *Roxb. Ball.* (1887) VI. 324 Here's a health to the Figure of Two [*rime* adieu]. **1697** [see B. I. 2 d]. **1845** BROWNING *Time's Revenges* 22, I am as sure that this he would do, As that Saint Paul's is striking two.

γ. 1 **tuu,** 1, 4 **tu,** 4–7 **tow** (5 **thow,** 6–7 **towe).**

Tu, tuu, was only neuter in OE., in ME. *tow* was general in some dialects.

c **825** *Vesp. Psalter* lxi. 12 Tu [*L. duo*] ðas ic ȝeherde. *c* **887** *O.E. Chron.* an. 887 (Parker MS.) And tu [*Laud MS.* twa] folc-ȝefeoht ȝefuhton. *c* **890** tr. *Bæda's Hist.* III. xv. [xxi.] (1890) 222 Aan biscop sceolde beon ofer tuu folc. *a* **950** *Rituale Dunelm.* (Surtees) 106 Voeron.. tvv in lichome anvm. *c* **950** *Lindisf. Gosp.* Matt. xxiv. 41 Tuu wif ȝegrundon on coernae. **13..** *Cursor M.* 16786 (Gött.) Þe stanes brast, þe temple clef in tu [*Trin.* in two]. **13..** *E.E. Allit. P.* B. 866, I haf a tresor in my telde of tow my fayre deȝter. **1422** tr. *Secreta Secret., Priv. Priv.* 164 The thow Sharpe eggis of youre Swerde. *c* **1440** *York Myst.* xix. 86 Tow townes betwene. **1510** in *10th Rep. Hist. MSS. Comm.* App. v. 394 Every couper shall gyve towe toune hopis for a penye. **1536** *Exhort. to North* 64 in Furnivall *Ball. fr. MSS.* I. 306 Bothe nowghty cromwell and the chancelleres towe [*rime* knowe]. **1597** *Vestry Bks.* (Surtees) 127 Paid.. for mending of tow baudrigs to the bells, xv d. **1602** CAREW *Eng. Tongue* ¶ 19 Yf, like towe Turkeyes,.. wee match it with our neighboures. **1666** WOOD *Life* 11 Dec. (O.H.S.) II. 95, I walked tow dayes before in the garden.

δ. 2–6 to, 4–6 too, 5–6 toe (6 tooe).

1154 *O.E. Chron.* an. 1137 To munekes him namen and bebyried him. **1297** R. GLOUC. (Rolls) 11150 Wiþoute þe toun to mile. **c 1330** R. BRUNNE *Chron. Wace* (Rolls) 330 Com of hym to noble sones. **c 1400** Too [see B. I. 3 a]. **c 1420** *Anturs of Arth.* xl. (Ireland MS.) Syxti maylis and moe, The squrd squappes in toe, His canel-bone allsoe. **c 1440** *Promp. Parv.* 495/1 To, or tweyne (*K.* to, nowmere), *duo.* **c 1460** J. METHAM *Wks.* (E.E.T.S.) 61/1625 Amoryus and Cleopes must dye ther with both to [*rime* so]. **a 1500** *Brome Bk.* 17 Ȝe that haue sys, dewes, and too [*rime* goo]. **a 1552** LELAND *Itin.* (1907) II. 141, I saw to antique heddes. **1552–3** *Inv. Ch. Goods, Staffs.* in *Ann. Lichfield* IV. 85 Tooe ornaments of dornex. **1558** in Feuillerat *Revels Q. Eliz.* (1908) 88 Syse, toe pannes—iiij[d]. **1567** DRANT *Horace, Epist.* II. ii. H iv, Too Orators..th' one was to the other..a faste ytrothed brother.

2. *genitive.* **1 tweᵹa (twoeᵹa), tweᵹea, tweaᵹea, tueᵹa; tweᵹra (twoeᵹra, tuoeᵹara), 2 tweiȝre, 2–3 tweire, 3 tweyre, twere.**

Beowulf 2531 Uncer tweᵹa. **c 825** *Vesp. Hymns* vi. 2 In midle twoeᵹa netna [*duorum animalium*] cuðas. **c 890** tr. *Bæda's Hist.* I. xvi. [xxvii.] (1890) 70 Tweᵹra ᵹebroðra bearn oððe tweᵹea ᵹesweostra sunu & dohtor. **c 897** K. ÆLFRED *Gregory's Past. C.* xiv. 86 Ðæt tweaᵹea [*Hatton* tweᵹea] bleo godweb. **c 950** *Lindisf. Gosp.* John viii. 17 Tuoeᵹara monna uittnesa. **c 1000** *Ags. Gosp.* Matt. xviii. 16 On tweᵹra oððe þreora ᵹewittnesse [*Hatton* tweiȝre]. **c 1200** *Trin. Coll. Hom.* 95 Tweire kinne. **a 1250** *Owl & Night.* 991 Weþer is betere of twere [*v.r.* tweyre] twom.

b. *possessive genitive.* **6 twoos, twooes, 7 twoes, 7– two's.**

1510–20 Twoos [see B. I. 2]. **1587** Twooes [see B. I. 5 a]. **1619** HIERON *Wks.* I. 34 After a yeare or twoes nursing. **1676** RAY *Corr.* (1848) 126 A year or two's time. **1773** Two's [see B. I. 5 a].

3. *dative.* **1 twæm, tuæm, 1–3 twam, 3 twom.**

Beowulf 1191 Be þæm ᵹebroðrum twæm. **c 890** tr. *Bæda's Hist.* I. x. [xiii.] (1890) 48 Betwih him twam. **c 1000** *Ags. Gosp.* Matt. xxii. 40 On þysum twam [*Lindisf.* tuæm; *Rushw.* twæm] bebodum. **c 1175** *Lamb. Hom.* 133 Of twam þingen. **a 1250** Twom [see 2 above]. **c 1275** *Woman of Samaria* 40 in *O.E. Misc.* 85 Bi-twene þis twam volke.

B. Signification.

The cardinal number next after one; one added to one: denoted by the symbols 2 or II.

I. *adj.*

1. In concord with a sb. expressed.

Frequent in proverbial expressions, as ***to make two bites of a cherry*** (BITE *sb.* 4, CHERRY *sb.* 1 b); ***to have two strings to one's bow*** (BOW *sb.*[1] 4 c); ***of two evils (or ills) choose the less*** (EVIL *sb.* 4, ILL *sb.* 5 b); ***between two fires*** (FIRE *sb.* 14); ***two heads are better than one*** (HEAD *sb.*[1] 69); ***as like as two peas*** (PEA[1] 1 c); ***two cents' worth*** (U.S.): = TWO PENNYWORTH (fig.); cf. *two-cent* adj. in sense IV. 2 below; ***no two ways about it***: see WAY *sb.*[1] 14 j; etc.

two men (quot. 1533), the *duumviri*: see DUUMVIR.

Beowulf 1095 Ða hie ᵹetruwedon on twa healfe fæste frioðuwære. **a 900** *O.E. Martyrol.* 21 Sept. 172 Æfter Cristes upastignesse he ᵹelærde twa [*v.r.* twua] mæᵹða to godes ᵹeleafan. **c 1000** *Ags. Gosp.* Luke ii. 24 Twa turtlan, oððe tweᵹen culfran briddas. **c 1175** *Lamb. Hom.* 7 Þe castel þe wes aȝeines drih[t]nes twa leornikenehtes; he bitacnet þeos world. **a 1225** *Ancr. R.* 10 Þer beoð two dolen to two manere of men. **13..** *Coer de L.* 504 Hys schelde in twoo peces off. **c 1400** *Destr. Troy* 310 Tow pyllers he pight.. Vppon Gades groundes. **c 1485** *Digby Myst.* I. 240 To sle all the children..within to yeer of age. **1530** PALSGR. 594/1 Two wyttes be farre better than one. **1533** BELLENDEN *Livy* III. v. (S.T.S.) I. 256 The solempne preistis, namyt the two men, war commandit to serche þe werkis of Cibil. **1611** [TARLTON] *Jests* (1844) 21 Two tailors goe to a man. **1671** MILTON *P.R.* I. 159 To conquer Sin and Death the two grand foes. **c 1765** GRAY *Satire* 16 As like as two beans. **1850** MCCOSH *Div. Govt.* III. ii. (1874) 335 The two inductive methods of acquiring knowledge..are observation and experiment. **1875** T. W. HIGGINSON *U.S. Hist.* vii. 49 No two explorers agreed about the actual shape of the coast. **1942** *Short Guide Gt. Brit.* (U.S. War Dept.) 18 You will hear..Britons openly criticizing their government... That isn't an occasion for you to put in your two-cents worth. **1954** *Sun* (Baltimore) 20 Dec. (B ed.) 14/7 The discussion concerning writers about old age in your column..impels me to add my 2 cents' worth.

b. With a superlative, either following (***the two best, eldest, first, last, next***, etc.; †formerly sometimes ***two the first***), or in later use preceding (***the first two***, etc.): the latter is now more usual. Cf. FIRST *a.* 2 e, LAST *a.* 1 b. So with *former, latter.* (Also *absol.*, as in 2.)

c 1330 R. BRUNNE *Chron.* (1810) 52 Emme þe quene..of þe whilk was born Alfred & Edward, Hardknoute þe þrid, þe tuo first of Eilred, of Knoute Hardknoute tid. **c 1350** *Will. Palerne* 2162 Tvo þe bremest white beres þat euer burn on loked. **c 1471** FORTESCUE *Wks.* (1869) 459 Than nedith it, that the Kyngs Lyvelood..be gretter than the Lyvelood of two the grettest Lords in Englond. **1556** OLDE *Antichrist* 70, I haue..expounded two the furst. **1560** DAUS tr. *Sleidane's Comm.* 44 b, Which two last were not agreed vpon. **1626** BACON *Sylva* §249 [The echo] will..report you the whole three Words; And then the two latter Words..; and then the last Word alone. **1635** J. HAYWARD tr. *Biondi's Banish'd Virg.* Ep. Ded., The translation of the two first bookes of.. Sir Phillip Sydney's Arcadia. **1669–** The last two [see LAST *a.* 1 b (*b*)]. **1688** DRYDEN *Lines on Milton*, To make a third, she joined the former two. **1692** BP. PATRICK *Answ. Touchstone* xiv. 100 The two first of them. *Ibid.*, The two next. **1704–** The first two [see FIRST *a.* 2 e (*c*)]. **1805** SOUTHEY *Let.* 15 Nov., in *Life* (1850) II. 353 The two best ships in the navy. **1829** JAS. MILL *Hum. Mind* (1869) II. 329 The association theory may account for the two last, but not for the former.

c. ***two parts***: two out of three equal parts (cf. PART *sb.* 5), two thirds (see 3 c). Chiefly *Sc.*, usually in form ***the twa part*** (sometimes as one word ***twapart***). So ***twa daill*** (DEAL *sb.*[1] 1).

1375 BARBOUR *Bruce* v. 47 Mair than twa part [*v.r.* partis] of his rout. *Ibid.* 369 In schort tym men mycht se ly þe twapart ded, or þan deand. **c 1475** *Rauf Coilȝear* 123 He tyt the King be the nek, twa part in tene. **1535** STEWART *Cron. Scot.* (Rolls) II. 21 He loissit be Storme of the Se the Tua Part of his Schippis. **1565** *Reg. Privy Council Scot.* I. 334 To confisk thair gudis, the twa daill to the Quenis Majesteis behuif, and the thrid to the conservatour. **c 1611** CHAPMAN *Iliad* x. 223 Two parts of night are past, the third is left. **1637–50** Row *Hist. Kirk* (Wodrow Soc.) 36 Shall Papists peaceablie possess a twa-part of the patrimonie of the Kirk.., and shall Christ's Ministers..not have a thirde? **1678** SIR G. MACKENZIE *Crim. Laws Scot.* I. xxiii. §7 (1699) 118 The two part thereof belongs to the King, and the third to the Sheriffs. **1808–25** JAMIESON, *Twa part, twaparte*, two thirds... This mode of expression is still quite common... *The twa part and third*, i.e., two thirds, and the remaining one.

d. ***two times*** as advb. phr. (expressing repetition or multiplication) is now used only with a demonstrative or defining word; otherwise *twice* is substituted: see TWICE.

a 1450 *Knt. de la Tour* (1906) 43 The auicion come to hem bi two tymes. **c 1489** CAXTON *Sonnes of Aymon* iii. 67 He was discomfyted two tymes. **1535** COVERDALE *Ecclus.* xlv. 14 Daylie perfourmed he his burntofferinges two tymes. **1574** HELLOWES *Gueuara's Fam. Ep.* (1577) 112 Two times I haue moued the Cardinal Tortosa in your businés. *Mod.* I have known it happen two separate times. I called upon him three times, but saw him only once; the other two times he was away.

e. As ordinal: = SECOND *a.* 1. Now only after the sb. (also ***number two***); cf. II. 1 c.

1586 W. WEBBE *Eng. Poetrie* (Arb.) 62 Make short either the two, foure, sixe, eight, tenne, twelue sillable. **1824** DE QUINCEY *Templars' Dial. Pol. Econ.* vi. §2 in *Misc.* (1854) 251 Column two. **1911** *Act 1 & 2 Geo. V*, c. 14 §1 The additional duty..imposed by the second paragraph of section two of that Act. *Mod.* Hymn number two.

2. *absol.* with ellipsis of sb. (which may usually be supplied from context; also often = 'two persons'), or after a pronoun or demonstrative, or as predicate. (For *both two* see BOTH A. 7.)

Also in proverbial expressions, as ***two can play at that game***; ***two's company, three's none*** (COMPANY *sb.* 1 d). Phr. ***that makes two of us***, colloq. formula of agreement: the same is true of me, I am in the same position, I agree.

c 882 *O.E. Chron.* an. 882 (Parker MS.) Ælfred..þara scipa tu [*Laud MS.* twa] ᵹenam. **c 890** tr. *Bæda's Hist.* I. xvi. [xxvii.] (1890) 70 Wer & wiif, heo tu beoð in anum lichoman. **c 1175** *Lamb. Hom.* 31 He wule..eaten..et ane mele swa muchel swa et twam. **c 1200** ORMIN 429 Swa ne didenn nohht ta twa. **a 1225** *Ancr. R.* 202 Uor monie reisuns... Two ich chulle siggen. *Ibid.* 406, I þisse tweire monglunge. **a 1300** *Cursor M.* 308 (Cott.) Þe hali gost comms of hem tua. **a 1375** *Joseph Arim.* 184 Þe bark of þat on semede dimmore þen ouþer of þe oþer two. **c 1425** *Cast. Persev.* 679 in *Macro Plays* 97 To may not to-gedyr stonde, but I, Bakbyter, be þe thyrde. **c 1470** HENRY *Wallace* IV. 781 Twa him beheld, and said: 'We will go se'. **1510–20** *Compl. too late maryed* (1862) 3, I wyll..a wyfe to me take For to increase both our twoos lynage. **1535** COVERDALE *Eccl.* iv. 9 Two are better then one. **1556** *Chron. Gr. Friars* (Camden) 55 Too of the men that labord at yt. **1560** BIBLE (Genev.) *Amos* iii. 3 Can two walke together except thei be agreed? **1596** DALRYMPLE tr. *Leslie's Hist. Scot.* v. (S.T.S.) I. 298 Ilk of the tua slayis othir. **c 1610** *Women Saints* 166 Committed to our twoes knowledge onelie. **1612** COLSON *Gen. Tresury* A j b, The generall parts ..are only two, or of two sorts. **c 1620** A. HUME *Brit. Tongue* (1865) 1 Nae tuae of the tuentie..wald agree. **1653** W. RAMESEY *Astrol. Restored* 335 Here is two to two,..we stand upon equal terms. **1768** PENNANT *Zool.* II. 363 The males, or Ruffs, assume such variety of colors..that it is scarce possible to see two alike. **1779** WARNER in Jesse *Selwyn & Contemp.* (1844) IV. 101 The Ministry carried it two to one. **1820** KEATS *Hyperion* I. 85 These two were postured motionless. **1847** HELPS *Friends in C.* I. vi. 94 What do you two..think about representative government? **18..** FLOR. MARRYAT (Dixon), Now, don't you call me any names, or you will find that two can play at that game. **1875** TENNYSON *Q. Mary* I. iv, The two were fellow-prisoners. **1956** H. KURNITZ *Invasion of Privacy* x. 71 'He was an amnesia victim.' 'That makes two of us,' said Zorn bitterly. **1974** P. DICKINSON *Poison Oracle* ii. 37 She wanted reassurance. That makes two of us, he thought. **1980** A. E. FISHER *Midnight Men* ix. 116 'She barely understands anything that is g-going on.' 'That makes two of us,' he said.

b. With ellipsis of *hours*, in stating the time of day; also ***two o'clock***. Also with ellipsis of *years* (of age), as ***a child of two***.

c 1485 in *Digby Myst.* (1882) 167 At the parvyse I wyll be .., be-twyn two and three. **1510** *Sel. Cases Star Chamb.* (Selden) II. 72 Abowt twoo of the Clok in the nyght. **1600** SHAKS. *A.Y.L.* IV. i. 183 By two a clock I will be with thee againe. **1795** MACNEILL *Will & Jean* xlvi, Now that nightly meetings Sat and drank frae sax till twa. **1799** WORDSW. *Lucy Gray* v, The minster-clock has just struck two. **1884** A. WAINWRIGHT in *Harper's Mag.* July 272/1 From two o'clock ..until 'two-fifteen', the 'two-twenty' train gradually fills.

c. ***in*** **(†** ***on*****)** ***two*** (after vbs. expressing division or the like): into or in two parts or pieces. (See also A-TWO.)

c 890 *O.E. Chron.* an. 885 (Parker MS.) Her to dælde se fore sprecena here on tu [*v.r.* twa]. **c 1000** *Ags. Gosp.* Mark xv. 38 Þæs temples wah-rift wæs tosliten on twa [*Lindisf.* & *Rushw.* in tuu]. **c 1275** *Passion of our Lord* 448 in *O.E. Misc.* 50 Hi nolden hyne nouht delen a to ne a þreo. **a 1300** *Cursor M.* 1957 (Cott.) O beist has clouen fote in tua [*v.rr.* to, two]. **c 1400** *Laud Troy Bk.* 5942 Ther he smot on-two his polle. **1535** COVERDALE *1 Sam.* ii. 31, I wyll breake thyne arme in two. **1623** GOUGE *Serm. Extent God's Provid.* §15 The massy timber shivered in two. **1794–5** in B. Ward *Dawn Cath. Revival* (1909) II. 119 A Collier's vessel fell foul of ours, and broke the cable in two. **1805** MCINDOE *Poems* 107 This trout ..Was faulded in twa like a speldin.

†(*b*) So as to be separate the one from the other; asunder, apart. *Obs.*

c 897 K. ÆLFRED *Gregory's Past. C.* vii. 49 Ðeah heo an tu tefleowe, ðeah wæs sio æsprync sio soðe lufu. **c 1000** ÆLFRIC *Hom.* I. 388 Ða..wearð him [*sc.* Paul and Barnabas] ᵹeþuht þæt hi on-twa ferdon. **c 1430** *Syr Tryam.* 60 Betwene the quene and the kyng Was grete sorowe..When they schulde parte in twoo.

d. ***two and two, two by two***, formerly also ***by two and two***: in groups or sets of two; two at a time; by twos.

c 1000 ÆLFRIC *Hom.* II. 528 He sende hi twam and twam ætforan him. **c 1290** *S. Eng. Leg.* I. 281/109 He saiȝ þe freres go þoruȝ þe londe, two and two. **13..** *Cursor M.* 1713 Ȝee sal ..tak..Beist and fouxul..Þe meke be þam ai tua and tua, þe wild do be þam-self al-sua. **c 1400** MAUNDEV. (Roxb.) xix. 87 Before þe chariot gase..all þe maydens of þe cuntree, twa and twa togyder. **c 1440** CAPGRAVE *St. Kath.* IV. 1264 The clerkis eke were sette be too and too. **a 1533** LD. BERNERS *Huon* lxii. 216 Guyer held his brother Gerames by the hande, and so all the other .ii. and .ii. **c 1575** J. HOOKER *Life Sir P. Carew* in *Archæologia* XXVIII. 144 Foremoste wente all the soylders..by tooe and tooe. **1604** E. G[RIMSTONE] *D'Acosta's Hist. Indies* VI. xxviii. 494 They daunced two and two. **1697** DRYDEN *Virg. Georg.* III. 270 Join'd with his School-Fellows by two and two [*rime* pursue]. **1709–10** ADDISON *Tatler* No. 120 ¶3 Coming out Two by Two, and marching up in Pairs. **1863** STANLEY *Serm. in East* App. I. 153 We started on foot, two and two, between two files of soldiers.

†**e.** ***rule of two*** (Arith.): an inclusive name for the ordinary rules for finding a third number from two given numbers, viz. those of addition, subtraction, multiplication, and division. (Cf. *rule of three*, RULE *sb.* 8 b.) *Obs. rare.*

1612 COLSON *Gen. Tresury* A j b, The..Rules of two, of three, of Reduction. *Ibid.* B bb j/1 The Rule of Two is by two numbers knowne to finde out the third.., and is generally of two sorts, Rationall, and Proportionall. The Rule of Two Rationall..is of two sorts,..Addition.. Substraction.

3. Forming compound numerals.

a. Added to multiples of ten, as ***two-and-thirty***, now usually ***thirty-two***; ***a hundred and two***. So formerly (now rarely) with the ordinals, as ***two-and-fiftieth*** (now almost always ***fifty-second***).

† ***two-and-thirty, a pip out*** see PIP *sb.*[2] 1 b.

two-and-twentieth (*Mus.*), a note 22 diatonic degrees (= 3 octaves) above or below a given note (both notes being reckoned); hence, an interval of 3 octaves; *spec.* an organ-stop formerly used, sounding 3 octaves above the normal pitch. (Now TWENTY-SECOND.)

c 893 K. ÆLFRED *Oros.* VI. ii. §1 Þara twa & twentiᵹra monna. **a 900** *O.E. Martyrol.* 29 On þone twa & twentiᵹðan dæᵹ. **c 961** ÆTHELWOLD *Rule St. Benet* xiii. (1885) 37 Se twa and feowertiᵹeða sealm. **c 1200** *Trin. Coll. Hom.* 47 On þe two and þrittuðe dai. **1297** R. GLOUC. (Rolls) 11861 To & tuenti kniȝtes. **c 1380** *Antecrist* in Todd *3 Treat. Wyclif* 121 In þe two and þritti boke. **c 1400** *Destr. Troy* 2747 There were twenty and too. **1488–92** *Acc. Ld. High Treas. Scot.* I. 80 Sex score twa bedis and a knop. **1579** FULKE *Heskins' Parl.* 201 The two and twentieth Chapter. **1613** *Organ Specif. Worcester Cathedral*, In the chaire organ 1 flute of wood, 1 two and twentith of mettal. **1768** FOOTE *Devil on 2 Sticks* III. Wks. 1799 II. 276 The two-and-fiftieth part of a scruple. **1896** MRS. CAFFYN *Quaker Grandmother* 137 Two-and-thirty last March.

b. As multiplier before *dozen, score*, or before *hundred, thousand, million*, etc., or the ordinals of these.

Also in comb., as ***two-hundred-mile-long*** adj.; ***two-hundred-pound*** adj. (weighing, or costing, two hundred pounds).

a 900 *Cædmon's Exod.* 184 (Gr.) Hæfde him alesen leoda duᵹeðe tireadiᵹra twa þusendo. **c 1000** *Ags. Gosp.* John vi. 7 On tweᵹera hundred peneᵹa wurþe. **c 1205** LAY. 1556 Þa he hefde twa [**c 1275** two] hundred mid sweorde to-hewen. **c 1290** *S. Eng. Leg.* I. 91/145 In þe to hondrede ȝere. **a 1548** HALL *Chron., Hen. VIII*, 147 b, Twoo hundred thousande Crounes. **1807** HERSCHEL in *Phil. Trans.* XCVII. 228 Its thickness at one end was 33, and at the other 31 two-hundredths of an inch. **1867** THIRLWALL *Lett.* (1881) II. 118 The two hundred mile long iceberg is still afloat. **1895** MRS. B. M. CROKER *Village Tales* (1896) 122 Tall and erect, ..carrying his two-score years with grace. **1897** *Outing* (U.S.) XXIX. 439/1 A two-hundred-pound buck.

c. As multiplier before an ordinal expressing an aliquot part (i.e. as numerator of a fraction), as ***two-thirds***; *spec.* in *Fashion*, applied to a garment that is shorter than the standard full length by about a third; also *attrib.* as ***a two-thirds majority***.

[**c 1643** LD. HERBERT *Autobiog.* (1824) 64 The other two third parts.] **1776** ADAM SMITH *W.N.* I. xi. III. (1869) I. 241 In the Saxon times the fleece was estimated at two-fifths of the value of the whole sheep. **1777** ROBERTSON *Hist. Amer.* (1783) III. 263 All laws..must be approved of by two-thirds of the members. **1888** RUTLEY *Rock-Forming Min.* 3 The wire is then bent to about two-thirds of a circle. **1910** H. W. STEED in *Encycl. Brit.* III. 38/2 The German parties.. stipulated that a two-thirds majority should be necessary for any alteration of the law. **1963** *Harper's Bazaar* Oct. 56/2 This dreamy two-thirds coat. **1980** *Washington Post* 4 Dec. D3 The writers are really more interested in who's being reassigned to the Ottawa bureau than in whether two-thirds stockings are a trend or not.

4. In pregnant sense: = Two different, two distinct.

to be in two minds: see MIND *sb.*[1] 11 e.

1570 T. WILSON *Demosthenes* 42 *margin*, To say and to do are two things. **1603** SHAKS. *Meas. for M.* II. iv. 112 Ignomie in ransome, and free pardon Are of two houses. **1754** RICHARDSON *Grandison* (1811) I. xii. 71 A learned man and a linguist may very well be two persons. **1797** BURKE *Regic. Peace* iii. Wks. VIII. 273 But reason of state and common sense are two things. **1865** RUSKIN *Sesame* i. §25 There need be no two opinions about these proceedings. **1895** G. S. STREET *Episodes* 134 Gerald in town and Gerald in the country were two people.

†**b.** *predicatively*: Discordant, disagreeing, at variance. (Cf. ONE 14, TWAIN B. 3 a.) *Obs.*

c **1645** HOWELL *Lett.* (1892) II. 547 The Author thereof and I are two in point of opinion. **1738** SWIFT *Pol. Conversat.* 105 When did you see your old Acquaintance, Mrs. Cloudy? You and She are Two, I hear.

5. a. ***a . . . or two***: an indefinite small number of (the things denoted by the sb.); one or two of . . . ; a few . . . (For *one or two* see ONE B. I. 2 c.)

The whole phrase may take the possessive inflexion, as ***a year or two's experience*** = the experience of a year or two.

a **1300** *Cursor M.* 4342 (Cott.) Spek wit me a word or tua. **1543** *Sel. Cases Star Chamb.* (Selden) II. 267 A moneth or Towe before the said Faire. **1587** FLEMING *Contn. Holinshed* III. 1419/1 After a daie or twooes tariance. **1615–16** in J. C. Jeaffreson *Middlesex Co. Rec.* (1886) II. 113 To answere the causing of a tumult . . , a poore man or two being much hurt. **1773** GOLDSM. *Stoops to Conq.* v. i, An hour or two's laughing with my daughter. **1861** M. PATTISON *Ess.* (1889) I. 45 The garden, where a vine or two and some of the finer sorts of fruit were trained.

b. ***two or three*** (chiefly dial. and U.S. ***two-three***, Sc. ***twa-three***): an indefinite (small or inconsiderable) number (of); a few.

1500–20 DUNBAR *Poems* lxxi. 4 3eiris and dayis mo than two or thre. **1557** *Peebles Burgh Rec.* (1872) 240 The baillies, accumpanit with the thesaurare and tua thre honest men. **1669** *Extr. S.P. rel. Friends* IV. (1913) 296 Here is many theeues and two Three murtherers and aboue thirty quakers in the Castle. **1670** LADY MARY BERTIE in *12th Rep. Hist. MSS. Comm.* App. v. 21 The under pettycoatt very richly laced with two or three sorts of lace. **1785** BURNS *Death & Dr. Hornbk.* xxiv, In twa-three year. **1843** BORROW *Bible in Spain* xxviii. (Pelh. Libr.) 198 The walls being covered with books except in two or three places. **1893** STEVENSON *Catriona* xv. 166 She was daundering on the craigs wi' twa-three sodgers. **1930** W. FAULKNER *As I lay Dying* 83 It'd taken them two-three days to get her to town in the wagon. **1949** L. HUGHES *One-Way Ticket* 40, I knock on your door About two-three A.M. **1962** J. F. STRAKER *Coil of Rope* ii. 13 You'll have to wait two-three days if you don't go now. **1976** A. PRICE *War Game* I. viii. 159 The last two-three years he's been working on a post-graduate thesis.

c. So rarely *two* simply.

1661 in *Extr. S.P. rel. Friends* II. (1911) 136 We humbly intreate two lynes from your hands. **1818** SCOTT *Heart Midl.* III. ix. 229, I will explain to you in two words the connection betwixt this young woman and me. *a* **1845** S. SMITH *Sk. Moral Philos.* (1850) Lect. xix. 280, I never could find any man who could think for two minutes together. **1956** N. MARSH *Off with his Head* (1957) v. 92, I wonder if I may have two words with Dame Alice Mardian?

II. *sb.*

1. The abstract number equal to one and one. Also in phrases, as *two and two make four*, used as a typically obvious or undeniable statement; ***to put two and two together***, to consider two or several facts together and draw an inference; to reason about something and come to a conclusion (cf. PUT *v.* 52 e).

1697 COLLIER *Ess. Mor. Subj.* II. (1703) 85 The . . notion . . is as clear as that two and two makes four. **1848** THACKERAY *Bk. Snobs* xvii, When will you acknowledge that two and two make four, and call a pikestaff a pikestaff? **1849** LYTTON *Caxtons* II. XII. i. 254 If they saw that, in proportion to their civility to me, they were depopulated by you, they would put two and two together and renounce my acquaintance. **1855** THACKERAY *Newcomes* xlix, Putting two and two together . . it was not difficult . . to guess who the expected Marquis was. **1875** WHITNEY *Life Lang.* 279 Mathematics began with the apprehension that one and one are two. **1898** W. W. JACOBS *Sea Urchins, Disbursem. Sheet* (1906) 138 Twenty-eight twos equals fifty-six.

b. The figure (2) denoting this number.

1877 *Daily News* 21 Nov. 5/5 Two and two don't always make four, but sometimes 22. **1886** *Punch* 23 Feb. 84/2 '2222'. Four twos!

c. A person or thing denoted by this number, usually as being the second in a series. Also ***number two***.

1890 [see NUMBER *sb.* 5]. **1890** *Eng. Illustr. Mag.* Apr. 499 Smith who rowed two in the last University race.

2. A group or set of two persons or things; a pair, couple. Usually in *pl.*

a **1585** POLWART *Flyting w. Montgomerie* 208 In anes and twaes. **1611** SHAKS. *Wint. T.* I. ii. 438 By twoes, and threes. **1625** in Rymer *Foedera* (1726) XVIII. 237/1 Eighte greate Rocke Rubies and twenty greate Pearles sett in twoes. *a* **1758** RAMSAY *Fables* xvii. 20 Pike out joys by twas and threes. **1865** KINGSLEY *Herew.* xxxiv, They would lodge by twos and threes . . in the lonely farmhouse. **1902** VIOLET JACOB *Sheep-Stealers* ix, The people dispersed in twos and threes.

b. A card or domino, or the side of a die, marked with two pips or spots.

a **1500** *Brome Bk.* 17 3e that haue sys, dewes, and too. **1680** COTTON *Compl. Gamester* (ed. 2) 12 You have . . turn'd up two two's, or two treys. *Mod.* He took the trick with the two of trumps.

c. In military drill, A set of two men forming a unit in wheeling.

1796 *Instr. & Reg. Cavalry* (1813) 106 The two's must first wheel up, and then break into three's, and close up. **1833** *Regul. Instr. Cavalry* I. Plate 16 Twos from the Right at three horses length distance.

d. *Cricket.* A hit for which two runs are scored.

1881 *Daily News* 21 June 3/7 A capital innings, which included seven fours, a three, and four twos.

e. *slang* or *colloq.* Two pennyworth (of spirits).

1894 HENTY *Dorothy's Double* i, I don't mind if I do take a two of gin with you. **1896** *Daily News* 23 Sept. 3/5 He had had six twos of whiskey.

f. ***two-at-length***, a tandem.

1823 E. NARES *Heraldic Anomalies* (1824) I. 355 Driving their fours-in-hand, and twos-at-length.

g. ***in two twos***: in a very short time; directly, immediately. *slang* or *colloq.* Also ***in two ups*** (Austral. colloq.) = *in two shakes* s.v. SHAKE *sb.*[1] 2 h.

1838 HALIBURTON *Clockm.* Ser. II. xiv. 211 The press can lash us up to a fury here in two twos any day. *Ibid.* xxi. 315 They'd soon set these matters right in two twos. **1882** STEVENSON *New Arab. Nts.* II. 112 The business was over in two twos. **1934** T. WOOD *Cobbers* iii. 25 He said we'd be there in two ups. **1941** BAKER *Dict. Austral. Slang* 79 *Two ups, in*, in a brief space of time. **1967** J. MORRISON in *Coast to Coast 1965–6* 133 Too close to dark now, Mister, but we'll have you out of that in two ups in the morning.

†**III.** *adv.* = TWICE 2; followed by *so* and a word expressing quantity = twice as (much, etc.). *Obs.*

c **900** *O.E. Chron.* an. 897 Lang scipu . . þa wæron fulneah tu swa lange swa þa oðru. **13 . .** *Coer de L.* 3128 The hethenes wer twoo so fele. *c* **1350** *Lybeaus Disc.* 1446 Now am y two so lyght. *c* **1420** *Sir Amadace* (Camden) l, He wold gif hom toe so muche . . As any lord.

IV. Combinations (unlimited in number; the following are examples).

1. a. Adjectives formed of *two* with a sb. in sense 'of, pertaining to, consisting of, having, containing, measuring, etc. two of the things named', as ***two-anna*** (of the value of two annas), ***-bar, -base, -bearing, -beat*** (also *ellipt.* as *sb.*), ***-bed, -berth, -blade, -bond, -bout*** (formed by two bouts of the plough), ***-bushel, -car, -centre, -chamber, -channel, -colour*** (also *fig.*), ***-column, -component, -cultures*** (cf. CULTURE *sb.* 5 c), ***-cylinder, -day, -deck, -digit, -dollar*** (also *fig.*), ***-door, -drift*** (DRIFT *sb.* 2 f), ***-electrode, -figure, -floor, -fluid, -front, -gallon, -groove, -guinea, -hour, -inch, -income,*** †***-kind, -lane*** (LANE *sb.* 2 d), ***-level, -light*** (LIGHT *sb.* 10), ***-man, -mast, -member, -mile, -minute, -needle(s), -ounce, -pack, -part, -party, -pedal, -person, -phase*** (PHASE *sb.* 3; cf. THREE-*phase*), ***-piano, -pin, -place, -ply*** (PLY *sb.* 1), ***-point, -position, -pound, -quart, -rail, -reel, -room, -row, -seat, -sex, -shilling, -speed, -stage, -stall, -story*** (also ***-storey***), ***-stripe, -syllable, -term, -tier*** (usu. *fig.*), ***-topsail, -track*** (also *fig.*), ***-volume, -wheel, -wire, -word.*** **b.** Parasynthetic adjectives formed on similar collocations, usually with -ED[2], in sense 'having or characterized by two of the things named', as ***two-arched, -armed, -banked, -barred, -barrelled, -bedded, -bristled, -capsuled, -celled, -chambered, -coloured, -columned, -decked, -dimensioned, -engined, -fingered, -flowered, -forked, -formed, -framed, -fronted, -grained, -grooved, -gunned, -handled, -horned, -horsed, -humped, -lobed, -masted, -membered, -named, -necked, -nerved, -oared, -peaked, -petaled, -pronged*** (also *fig.*), ***-ranked, -roomed, -rowed, -seated, -seeded, -shanked, -shaped, -spined, -spotted, -stalled, -storied*** (also ***-storeyed***), ***-stranded, -stringed, -sworded, -termed, -tiered, -tined, -toed, -toothed, -topped, -valved, -wheeled, -winged***; also with other endings, as ***two-handy*** (see TWO-HANDED), ***-monthly*** (see 2). **c.** Parasynthetic sbs. in -ER[1], as ***two-feeder, -hitter*** (*U.S.*), ***-master*** (a two-masted vessel), ***-mover*** (MOVER[1] 7), ***-parter, -pounder, -reeler, -striper*** (see STRIPER 1), ***-wheeler***; see also *two-yearer* in 2, TWO-DECKER, TWO-HANDER. **d.** Adjectives formed of *two* in adverbial relation to an adj. or pple. (= in two, doubly), as ***two-cleft, -ploughed, -soused, -twisted***: see also *two-high* in 2, TWO-FORKED, TWO-PARTED. **e.** Adjs. and sbs. formed from phrases, as ***two-and-a-half-inch, two-days-old, two-feet-nine*** adjs.; ***two-and-a-half striper*** (see STRIPER 1), ***two-and-two*** (cf. sense I. 2 d); †***two-face-bearer*** (cf. TWO-FACED), ***two-in-oneness, two-plus-two, two-pound-tenner, two-to-one.***

1899 *Westm. Gaz.* 9 Feb. 4/2 That hatch was of *two-and-a-half inch teak. **1861** 'R. HARRINGTON' *Swimming* p. iii, They [*sc.* school children] often passed a river when out for a miserable *two-and-two walk. **1882** F. M. CRAWFORD *Mr. Isaacs* xi, A *two-anna bit. **1897** W. C. HAZLITT 4 *Generations* II. 183 The *two-arched bridge at Rugby. **1725** RAMSAY *Gentle Sheph.* v. iii. Prol., Sir William fills the *twa-arm'd chair. **1957** J. S. BRUNER *Beyond Information Given* (1974) i. 35 The experiment is done on a conventional two-armed bandit, the subject having the task of betting on whether a light will appear on the left or on the right. **1935** L. MACNEICE *Poems* 25 Poetry is not only the bridging of *two-banked rivers. **1967** 'M. HUNTER' *Cambridgeshire Disaster* x. 65 He warmed his hands briefly at the two-bar fire. **1894** R. B. SHARPE *Handbk. Birds Gt. Brit.* I. 59 The *two-barred Crossbill. *Loxia bifasciata.* **1852** MUNDY *Our Antipodes* (1857) 114 *Two-barrelled guns. **1880** N. BROOKS *Fairport Nine* 184 Ned made a fine *two base hit which brought Watson home amidst great excitement. **1974** J. H. SUBAK-SHARPE et al. in Carlile & Skehol *Evolution in Microbial World* 132 Correlations exist between three-base sequences (that is codons) in messenger RNA and two-base sequences in the DNA coding for that Messenger RNA. **1922** *Times* 20 June 8/5 A short *two-bearing auxiliary shaft. **1960** E. L. DELMAR-MORGAN *Cruising Yacht Equipment & Navigation* i. 20 The principle . . , as with all two-bearing fixes, attains its best accuracy when the position lines are 90 deg. to each other. **1938** *Swing* July 18/2 **Two-beat swing* . . , swing in which the accent is on the second or fourth beats. **1978** *Detroit Free Press* 16 Apr. 11 c/2 Chet Bogan plays two-beat, Dixiebelle sing same. **1792** H. NEWDIGATE *Let.* Feb. in A. E. Newdigate-Newdegate *Cheverels* (1898) viii. 110 She . . shew'd me a neat *2 bed Garret where I dare say we shall sleep as well as in a Palace. **1962** E. SNOW *Other Side of River* (1963) lx. 461 Bachelor quarters varied from small two-bed to larger four-bed and six-bed rooms. **1784** H. NEWDIGATE *Let.* in A. E. Newdigate-Newdegate *Cheverels* (1898) iv. 59 We have obtained to Sleep to-night in a tollerable *two bedded Room. **1788** J. WOODFORDE *Diary* 19 May (1927) III. 26, I slept at the Kings Head, in a two bedded Room. **1843** BORROW *Bible in Spain* vii. 42 A large two-bedded room. **1969** M. PUGH *Last Place Left* xxi. 164 He made out sleeper tickets for us . . and we shared a *two-berth compartment. **1967** *Jane's Surface Skimmer Systems 1967–68* 9/1 Propulsion is provided by two *two-blade metal variable pitch propellers. **1983** *Flight Internat.* 10 Sept. 703/1 A pair of two-blade teetering rotors are mounted 50° apart. **1900** *Daily News* 13 Oct. 6/4 The propeller is *two-bladed. **1674** RAY *Collect. Words, Mann. Wire Work* 133 A *two-bond wire as big as a great pack-thread. **1805** R. W. DICKSON *Pract. Agric.* I. 409 The *two-bout ridges, as they are called, may be the most advantageous. **1681** GREW *Musæum* I. VII. i. 156 The *Two-Bristled-Fly. **1796** W. H. MARSHALL *W. England* II. 61 The Corn Market well filled with long *two-bushel bags; chiefly of wheat. **1793** MARTYN *Lang. Bot.*, *Two-capsuled. **1927** *Sat. Even. Post* 9 Apr. 89 This is a *two-car country. **1961** M. BEADLE *These Ruins are Inhabited* (1963) viii. 105 Two-car families are rare in England. **1793** MARTYN *Lang. Bot.*, *Bilocular* pericarp . . *two-celled, divided into two cells internally. . . Some seeds are also two-celled. **1964** J. W. LINNETT *Electronic Struct. Molecules* ix. 152 Sovers showed that a very good description of the excited states could also be achieved by employing *two-centre bonding and anti-bonding orbitals only. **1898** *Daily News* 16 Feb. 7/6 The advantages or disadvantages of a bi-cameral system, . . a *two-Chamber system. **1851** RICHARDSON *Geol.* viii. (1855) 229 A *two-chambered heart. **1888** BRYCE *Amer. Commw.* II. II. xl. 86 Its two-chambered legislature. **1939** *Florida* (Federal Writers' Project) I. 75 *Two-channel highways divided by a parkway to reduce the menaces of bright lights and head-on collisions. **1973** G. TALBOT *Ten Seconds from Now* (1974) xvi. 203 A blaring juke-box and two-channel television. **1979** H. KISSINGER *White House Years* xx. 827 The two-channel system and its significance. **1793** MARTYN *Lang. Bot.*, **Two-cleft*, or *Bifid.* . . *Utricularia* is an instance of the two-cleft perianth. **1907** *T. Eaton & Co. Catal.* Spring & Summer 43/1 Men's fancy Sweaters, . . medium weight, *two color effect. **1925** I. A. RICHARDS *Princ. Lit. Crit.* xxvii. 211 *Macbeth* . . is a highly successful, easily apprehended, two-colour melodrama. **1967** E. CHAMBERS *Photolitho-Offset* xv. 236 The wide use of lithography for colour work has resulted in the development of two-colour machines. **1648** HEXHAM II, *Twee-verwigh*, *Two-coloured, or Partie-coloured. **1827** GRIFFITH *Cuvier's Anim. Kingd.* V. 251 *Sciurus Bicolor* (Two-coloured Squirrel). **1885** W. PATER *Marius* II. xx, A two-sided or two-coloured thing. **1916** E. WALLACE *Let.* 13 Nov. in M. Gilbert *Winston S. Churchill* (1972) III. Compan. II. 1583 Do a *two column story. **1922** JOYCE *Ulysses* 465 Tom Rochford . . jumps from his *two-columned machine. **1956** *Nature* 18 Feb. 328/2 Only *two-component solvent systems were investigated. **1966** *Listener* 1 Sept. 297/1 As Margaret Mead puts it: 'The recent *two-cultures discussion is essentially a lament about . . lack of communication.' **1901** *Westm. Gaz.* 9 Dec. 8/2 Rigal, on his *two-cylinder, 12-h.p. tricycle. **1898** *Harper's Mag.* XCVI. 829 They . . can only make *two-day . . cruises. **1868** SWINBURNE *Blake* 9 The *two-days-old baby. **1797** *Encycl. Brit.* (ed. 3) XVII. 403/2 In all *two-deck ships it [the fire hearth] is placed under the forecastle. **1960** *Farmer & Stockbreeder* 29 Mar. 93/1 Sending the farm two-deck lorry to the south-west and back. **1883** *Man. Seamanship for Boys' Training Ships* (Admiralty) (1886) 2 A *two-decked ship. So named from having two gun decks below the upper deck. **1963** *Rep. Comm. Inquiry Decimal Currency* 9 in *Parl. Papers 1962–3* (Cmnd. 2145) XI. 195 People find considerably greater difficulty in remembering and manipulating three-digit numbers than *two-digit numbers. **1885** W. K. CLIFFORD *Common Sense Exact Sc.* 223 *Two-dimensioned space. **1793** *Deb. Congr. U.S.* 3 Jan. (1849) 788 The miserable *two-dollar men who were raised for a six months' service. **1873** T. B. HAZARD *Nailer Tom's Diary* (1930) 414/2 Went to Thomas Rodmans Store to get a two dollar bill changed. **1929** *Century Mag.* Autumn 68 He hated what he called 'two-dollar words' and 'high hat' manners. **1908** *Sears, Roebuck Catal.* 61/1 The *two-door automatic Model 'A' desk cabinet. **1982** *Sunday Tel.* 1 Aug. 6/2 You can get a 1.8 litre, two-door, four-seat sports saloon for £5,950. **1926** H. MACPHERSON *Mod. Astron.* 156 The results of this study of stars of very large proper motion, scattered all over the sky, were strongly in support of the *two-drift hypothesis. **1921** *Wireless World* IX. 187/1 The *two-electrode Fleming valve. **1931** *19th Cent.* Feb. 154 The standard *two-engined type. **1966** D. FRANCIS *Flying Finish* v. 64 Small two-engined job . . cost nearly thirty-five pounds per flying hour to hire. *c* **1515** *Cocke Lorell's B.* 11 Flaterers, and *two face berers. **1886** *Daily News* 18 Oct. 7/2 News Machine Wanted, fast *two-feeder. **1905** *Daily Chron.* 13 July 5/1 What is known as the *two-feet-nine seam. **1890** W. J. GORDON *Foundry* 223 The percentage of profit . . may be a fraction with a *two-figure denominator. **1898** F. M. HUEFFER in *Contemp. Rev.* Aug. 182 A two-figure sketch by Burne-Jones. **1910** W. DE LA MARE *Three Mulla-Mulgars* 47 A behemothian bull-Ephelanto . . wound his long, *two-fingered trunk round Nod's belly. **1978** *Church Times* 27 Jan. 5/3 What she was doing was making a kind of 'I'm as good as you, see if I'm not' two-fingered gesture of defiance at society. **1981** H. CARPENTER *W. H. Auden* (1983) II. iv. 341 He was an adequate two-fingered typist. **1900** *Daily News* 11 July 7/5 A . . *two-floor building. **1793** MARTYN *Lang. Bot.*, *Two-flowered peduncle. **1909**

Daily Chron. 20 Mar. 3/5 Here you first find the two-flowered yellow violet..3,500 feet above the level of the sea. **1866** R. M. Ferguson *Electr.* (1870) §31 The *two-fluid theory of Dufay and Symmers, and the one-fluid theory of Franklin. **1876** Preece & Sivewright *Telegraphy* 244 Two-fluid batteries. **1743** Francis tr. *Hor., Odes* II. xx. 2 A *two-form'd poet. **1934** Dylan Thomas in *Criterion* Oct. 28 The *two framed globe that spun into a score. **1946** *New Yorker* 23 Mar. 74/2 One of those *two-front wars which 'Mein Kampf' had sensibly argued couldn't be won. **1856** J. G. Whittier *Panorama* 12 The *two-fronted Future... To-day, your servant, subject to your will; To-morrow, master, or for good or ill. **1693** T. Power in *Dryden's Juvenal* XII. (1697) 307 A *two Gallon Draught. **1793** Martyn *Lang. Bot., Dicoccous* or *two-grained* capsule... Consisting of two cohering grains or cells, with one seed in each. **1846** Greener *Sc. Gunnery* 357 A *two-grooved rifle. **1803** Hatchett in *Phil. Trans.* XCIII. 137 A *two-guinea piece. **1818** Cobbett *Pol. Reg.* XXXIII. 368 A man, who, bred to the bar, had never had a two-guinea fee in his life. **1936** Dylan Thomas *Twenty-Five Poems* 44 And from the windy West came *two-gunned Gabriel. **1949** *Time* 10 Oct. 47/2 Accompanied by a grim, 200-lb., two-gunned Big Spring sheriff. **1839** Ure *Dict. Arts* 764 The fleshing knife; a large *two-handled implement [with] which the hide is scraped. **1877** J. D. Chambers *Div. Worship* 258 A two-handled Chalice. **1974** *State* (Columbia, S. Carolina) 26 Apr. 4-B/3 Paul Splittorff pitched a *two-hitter for seven innings. **1561** Daus tr. *Bullinger on Apoc.* (1573) 5 b, The old seuen-headed, and the new *twohorned beast. **1628** A. Leighton *Zion's Plea agst. Prelacy* ix. (1842) 121 A two-horned idol, pushing both the Church and Commonwealth. **1781** Pennant *Hist. Quad.* I. 136 Two-horned Rhinoceros. **1793** Martyn *Lang. Bot., Bicornes* (two-horned). Plants with anthers having two horns. **1848** Mill *Pol. Econ.* II. viii. §3 (1876) 189 A cowhouse for two-horned cattle. **1939** W. B. Yeats *On Boiler* 31 There in a *two horsed carriage..Great bladdered Emer sat. **1880** 'Mark Twain' *Tramp Abr.* xix. 171 A *two-hour pedestrian excursion. **1900** *Westm. Gaz.* 15 Nov. 2/1 We..did not dismount except for a two-hour halt till three p.m. **1834** *Nat. Philos.* III. *Phys. Geog.* 55/2 (Usef. Knowl. Soc.) The *two-humped or Bactrian camel. **1639** *Crabtree Lect.* 184, I will make you looke through a *two inch boord [*i.e.* pillory]. **1748** *Anson's Voy.* III. viii. 380 A strong net-work of two inch rope. **1859** F. A. Griffiths *Artil. Man.* (1862) 309 A two-inch rope means a rope two inches in circumference. **1868** *Rep. U.S. Commissioner Agric.* (1869) 328 A fountain capable of filling..a two-inch pipe. **1969** *Guardian* 31 Mar. 2/1 The *two-income family spends 15 per cent more on alcohol. **1895** Hardy *Jude* VI. ii. 404 O my comrade, our perfect union—our *two-in-oneness—is now stained with blood! **1613** W. Browne *Brit. Past.* I. iv, The *two-kinde Bat. **1957** J. Kerouac *On Road* (1958) II. viii. 156 On a *two-lane highway to Baton Rouge in purple darkness. **1882** Vines *Sachs' Bot.* 466 Divisions take place in the epidermal cells by..which the wall becomes *two-layered. **1957** H. Whitehall in N. Frye *Sound & Poetry* II. 142 Metrical patterns..based on the *two-level contrast of stressed versus unstressed syllables. **1981** *Beautiful Brit. Columbia* Summer 23/1 A glassed-in two-level public seating area provides a view of busy False Creek. **1845** S. R. Glynne *Notes Churches of Cheshire* (Chetham Soc.) (1894) 56 There are large gargoyles at the angles..; in the second stage a *two-light window. **1859** Cornwallis *Panorama New World* I. 221 The sunshine glancing through a two-light window. **1793** Martyn *Lang. Bot.*, *Two-lobed leaf. **1847** W. E. Steele *Field Bot.* 167 *Neottia*,..lip dependant, 2-lobed. **1895** *Outing* (U.S.) XXVI. 399/1 A *two-man balloon. **1911** *Q. Rev.* Jan. 215 The two-man Government ..becomes one-man Government. **1775** Dalrymple in *Phil. Trans.* LXVIII. 400 A small *two-mast vessel. **1774** *Hull Deck Act* 33 *Two-masted vessels. **1899** Quiller-Couch *Ship of Stars* xiv, That there *two-master's got a fool for skipper. **1924** O. Jespersen *Philos. Gram.* xxii. 306 Every sentence is said to be composed of two parts, Subject and Predicate... Besides such *two-member sentences..we may have one-member sentences. **1967** R. S. Churchill *Winston S. Churchill* II. viii. 261 The city of Dundee in 1908 ..was, like Oldham, a two-member, primarily working-class, constituency. **1905** *Westm. Gaz.* 29 Nov. 2/2 A *two-membered constituency. **1909** R. Law *Tests of Life* i. 2 Two-membered sentences. **1875** W. S. Hayward *Love agst. World* 117 A *two-mile spin. **1895** *Outing* (U.S.) XXVII. 48/1 A *two-minute gait [*i.e.* at the rate of a mile in 2 minutes; cf. *two-forty* in 2]. **1905** *Westm. Gaz.* 23 Dec. 2/3 There were two-minute intervals between the start of each bob. **1868** *Westm. Chess Club Papers* I. 47 A *two-mover now knocks me down. **1891** *Athenæum* 31 Jan. 148/1 Thirty-six two-movers. **1661** T. Ross *Silius Italicus* I. 13 By the Banks of *two-nam'd Ister. **1931** R. Graves *To Whom Else?* 17 Two-named one, how shall I call you without duplicity? **1854** J. Scoffern in *Orr's Circ. Sc., Chem.* 14 The mouths of a *two-necked bottle. **1890** Billings *Med. Dict.*, **Two-needles operation*, tearing through a secondary cataract by two needles introduced from opposite sides. **1891** *Cent. Dict.*, Two-needle operation. **1833** Hooker in Smith *Eng. Flora* V. I. 85 Leaves..*two-nerved at the base. **1899** Doyle *Duet* Ded., The little *two-oared boats. **1838** Dickens *O. Twist* xxiii, A *two-ounce tin tea-caddy. **1952** V. Wilkins *King Reluctant* I. ix. 131 The involved *two-pack patience game known as 'Maréchal Saxe'. **1977** *Listener* 10 Mar. 295/2 He is a two-pack smoker, drinks on occasion to keep going. **1928** *Daily Tel.* 11 Dec. 17/4 '*Two-part tariffs' will be introduced by the County of London Electric Supply Co. Ltd. from Jan. 1 for domestic and business consumers. **1939** F. Scott Fitzgerald *Let.* 8 June (1964) 106, I have..over half-finished what will be a *two-parter for *The Saturday Evening Post*. **1984** J. Wain in *Listener* 28 June 30/2 They are making two plays out of it, or, perhaps more exactly, a three-hour two-parter. **1901** *Edin. Rev.* Oct. 506 It is..premature to suppose..that the *two-party system has..broken up. **1861** Paley *Æschylus* (ed. 2) *Chœroph.* 1026 *note*, The *two-peaked hill of Parnassus. **1961** *New Scientist* 5 Jan. 50/3 Mr. Saunders's *two-pedal system..interested me, so I tried it on my car. **1920** D. H. Lawrence *Lost Girl* vii. 134 Madame and the German did a screaming *two-person farce. **1977** *New Yorker* 17 Oct. 93/1 A new playwright..made a pleasing début on Broadway..with a harsh little two-person comedy. **1793** Martyn *Lang. Bot.*, *Two-petalled corolla. **1909** *Cent. Dict. Suppl.*, *Two-phase circuit..Two-phase generator.. Two-phase system. **1952** S. Kauffmann *Philanderer* xv. 242 Turning the phonograph very low, he played the Mozart *two-piano concerto. **1978** Ld. Drogheda *Double Harness* x. 92 During the two years that she had been in America, Joan had become a very active pianist, giving a considerable number of two-piano concerts with her partner Harold Triggs. **1894** D. Salomons *Electr. Light Installations* (ed. 7) II. vi. 233 The plug to be used with this connector is of the *two-pin type. **1962** *B.S.I. News* Feb. 24/1 Three proposals were considered for a standard two-pin plug for use with all-insulated and double-insulated appliances. **1948** H. Reichenbach *Elem. Symbolic Logic* §17. 83 Both functions are *two-place functions; i.e. they possess two arguments. **1963** W. V. Quine *Set Theory* §1. 13 Suppose the only primitive predicate of some theory is a two-place predicate. **1856** *Farmer's Mag.* Jan. 20 *Two-plowed furrows (that is, one plowed under another). **1966** *Publ. Amer. Dial. Soc.* 1964 XLII. 10 **Two-plus-two*,..two-seater with capacity to hold two additional passengers in back. **1977** *Lancashire Life* Mar. 118/3 The 104ZS is cramped in the back and is more of a two-plus-two than a proper four seater. **1847** Webster, **Two-ply*..double; consisting of two thicknesses, as cloth. **1960** *Farmer & Stockbreeder* 1 Mar. 131/1 Experience has proved this *two-point system. **1972** J. Potter *Going West* 180 The plane made a jerky two-point landing. **1951** *Two-position [see bistable *a.*]. **1960** *Farmer & Stockbreeder* 8 Mar. 108/2 Two-position Hitch. Easy for field or transport. **1552** Huloet, *Two pounde weight, *dipondium*. **1887** *Roy. Proclam.* in *Standard* 18 May 3/2 Every Two Pound Piece should have the same obverse and reverse impression..as the Five Pound Piece. **1771** tr. *Pernety's Voy. Malouine Isl.* in *Ann. Reg.* (1771) II. 15/1 Round stones, of the size of a *two-pounder ball. **1836–9** Dickens *Sk. Boz, Dancing Acad.*, Mr. Augustus Cooper had ordered a new coat..a *two-pound-tenner. **1825** T. Hook *Sayings* Ser. II. *Man of Many Fr.* (Colburn) 104 *Two-pronged forks. **1919** W. S. Churchill in M. Gilbert *Winston S. Churchill* (1977) IV. Compan. I. 535 With Mr Balfour's approval, I made the following two-pronged proposals. **1958** O. Caroe *Pathans* xxiii. 375 The success of the two-pronged advance by the Khaibar and the Kurram. **1727** *Fam. Dict.* s.v. *Fryars Balsam*, Put..into a *Two-quart-Bottle. **1844** *Port Phillip Patriot* 25 July 3/6 A *two rail fence. **1793** Martyn *Lang. Bot.* s.v. *Distichus*, A distich or *two-ranked stem or stalk. **1857** T. Moore *Handbk. Brit. Ferns* (ed. 3) 38 Fructification forming two-ranked simple spikes. **1929** Wodehouse *Mr. Mulliner Speaking* ix. 301 Come on, let's beef in or we'll be missing the educational *two-reel comic. **1978** *Radio Times* 18–24 Mar. 15/1 Within the next couple of years he made over 20 two-reel Westerns. **1928** *Sunday Express* 3 June 4 The British Screen *two-reeler 'Homes of Our King'. **1979** *Guardian* 4 Aug. 9/2 He had made a few modest pictures, two-reelers mostly. **1897** Hughes *Medit. Malta* etc. *Fever* ii. 62 The staff-sergeant..occupied a *two-room quarter. **1897** *Daily News* 14 Apr. 5/1 A *two-roomed home. **1868** *Rep. U.S. Commissioner Agric.* (1869) 251 The Strength of *Two-Row Hedges when Pleached. **1793** Martyn *Lang. Bot.*, Two-ranked or *Two-rowed. **1812** Sir J. Sinclair *Syst. Husb. Scot.* I. 247 Two-rowed barley. **1868** *Rep. U.S. Commissioner Agric.* (1869) 249 Two-rowed hedges. **1895** *Montgomery Ward Catal.* Spring & Summer 580/2 *Two-seat business wagons. **1880** W. Whitman *Daybks. & Notebks.* (1978) III. 642 Heavy *two-seated covered voitures. **1936** G. B. Shaw *Six of Calais* 89 Between them, near the King's pavilion, is a two-seated chair of state for public audiences. **1793** Martyn *Lang. Bot.*, *Two-seeded fruit. **1933** O. Jespersen *Essent. Eng. Gram.* xix. 192 When a special indication of sex is wanted with one of the *two-sex words, this can always be done by the addition of the adjectives *male* and *female*, respectively: *a male reader, a female cousin*,..etc. **1973** Talamini & Page *Sport & Society* v. 271 To note [sport's] emergence as a two-sex activity.. should not obscure the persistence in sport of male domination, male prejudice, and discrimination against girls and women. **1621** G. Sandys *Ovid's Met.* VIII. (1626) 156 *Two-shankt Compasses. **1756** P. Browne *Jamaica* 328 The larger Passion-flower with two-shanked leaves. **1613** Heywood *Silver Age* III. Wks. 1874 III. 143 The *two-shap't Centaurs. **1717** Addison tr. *Ovid* II. *Coronis* 29 The two-shap'd Ericthonius. **1789** J. Woodforde *Diary* 11 June (1927) III. 112 Briton also went into the *2 Shilling Gallery. **1880** *Sat. Rev.* 2 Oct. 424/1 Our two-shilling dinner. **1882** A. Somerville in G. Smith *Mod. Apostle* x. (1891) 240 Some two-shilling pieces. *a* **1625** Fletcher *Bloody Bro.* IV. ii, Wholsom *two-sous'd petitoes. **1875** Knight *Dict. Mech.*, **Two-speed Pulley*, a variable speed arrangement consisting of two fast pulleys, the shaft of one being tubular and sleeved upon that of the other. **1888** *Encycl. Brit.* XXIII. 560 Two-speed gears. **1785** Pennant *Arct. Zool.* II. Suppl. 132 Stickleback. *Two-spined. **1803** Shaw *Gen. Zool.* IV. 476 Two-spined Sparus. *Ibid.* 608 Two-spined Stickleback. **1802** Bingley *Anim. Biog.* (1813) III. 130 The seven-spotted and *two-spotted lady-bug. **1944** R. V. Jones *Most Secret War* (1978) xlv. 460 A *two-stage rocket of about 150 tons starting weight could deliver a 1 ton warhead to nearly 3,000 miles range. **1963** *Ann. Reg. 1962* 183 The Skybolt was a two-stage solid fuel missile. **1979** *Dædalus* Summer 50 'Hypocrisy displayed', then, is a two-stage process, a masking followed by an unmasking. **1859** W. Collins *Q. of Hearts* I. 242 A *two-stall stable. **1833** Loudon *Encycl. Archit.* §1829 A *two-stalled stable. **1854** M. S. Cummins *Lamplighter* iii. 13 A decent *two-storied house. **1874** W. Black *Princess of Thule* (ed. 2) I. i. 12 It was a square, two-storeyed substantial building of stone. **1878** Smiles *Robt. Dick* ii. 9 A two-storied..house. **1977** P. G. Winslow *Witch Hill Murder* II. xvi. 212 The lovely, two-storeyed drawing-room. **1796** *Aurora* (Philadelphia) 15 Apr., That certain one-story Frame shop in front, and *Two Story Frame messuage. **1866** A. D. Richardson *Secret Service* ii. 38 We took a two-story car of the Baronne street railway. **1880** J. Dunbar *Pract. Papermaker* 9 A two-storey building. **1977** *Times* 9 Sept. 2/3 Spacious late-nineteenth-century two-storey terrace houses. **1982** W. Boyd *Ice-Cream War* (1983) II. ii. 120 He passed the..two-storey building. **1851** H. Melville *Moby Dick* I. ix. 65 Shipmates, it is a *two-stranded lesson. **1976** P. Collard *Development Microbiol.* v. 64 Synthetic two-stranded RNA polyinosinic acid-polycytidylic acid. **1776** Burney *Hist. Mus.* I. 206 This dichord, or *two-stringed instrument. **1918** *Jrnl. R. Naval Med. Service* IV. 317 A '*two-stripe doctor'. **1860** W. Whitman in *N.Y. Times* 27 June 2/1 The Princes of Asia, swart-cheek'd princes, First comers, guests, *two-sworded princes. **1891** S. Mostyn *Curatica* 47 Peace be to his *manes*—this, dear ladies, is a *two-syllable word. **1933** A. N. Whitehead *Adventures of Ideas* xv. 230 Also we may well ask whether there are not subtle variations of meaning stretching far beyond the competence of the *two-term vocabulary—Judgment, Proposition. **1964** R. H. Robins *Gen. Linguistics* i. 26 A two-term relation between the word and the referent. **1968** Fox & Mayers *Computing Methods for Scientists & Engineers* i. 4 A better approach is to observe that, with a single integration by parts, we can find the two-term recurrence relation. **1981** *Times* 6 Aug. 8/7 A programme which can be implemented only by a two-term Government. **1933** *Mind* LXII. 45 If we consider *Russia is happy, England fears France, Germany prefers England to France, Italy believes that Germany prefers England to France*, we see that these facts form a series in that the first is one-termed, the second *two-termed, the third three-termed and the fourth four-termed. **1964** E. Bach *Introd. Transformational Gram.* vii. 157 Prepositional phrase in English is usually a two-termed relation. **1932** *Times* 26 Nov. 12/3 If their system were a *two-tier system, the element of uncertainty was reduced to a minimum. **1933** [see stack *sb.* 1 d]. **1937** *Burlington Mag.* Oct. 194/1 Ionic impost capitals,..two-tier capitals. **1969** *Punch* 1 Jan. 26/3 It is now working a good deal harder and will work even harder still when the reforms with their two-tier system of voting and non-voting but speaking Peers come into force. **1975** J. P. Morgan *House of Lords & Labour Govt.* ii. 75 The House can be persistent when an issue catches its imagination—favourites of the 1966–70 Parliament were decimal currency, the two-tier postal service, and the anti-Stansted campaign. **1969** *Listener* 23 Jan. 103/2 The debate is *two-tiered: the violence of Chicago..and the violence of the TV shows. **1979** *Arizona Daily Star* 5 Aug. D2/2 The Natural Gas Policy Act of 1978..wiped out the two-tiered pricing structure. **1601** Holland *Pliny* XVIII. vi. I. 557 If it be stonie, it would be digged with a mattocke or *two tined forkes. **1781** Pennant *Hist. Quad.* II. 496 *Two-toed S[loth] with a round head. **1872** Coues *N. Amer. Birds* 49 The two-toed birds. **1910** *Motor Man.* (ed. 12) iii. 75 The layshaft is driven by a chain instead of the usual *two-to-one gear wheels. **1975** *New Yorker* 17 Nov. 117/1 The Court of Appeals for the District of Columbia Circuit, in a two-to-one vote, upheld the claim. **1742** W. Ellis *Mod. Husbandman* Sept. xxvi. 124 These are the right profitable sort for Fatting, and not the *two-toothed sheep. **1802** R. Hall *Elem. Bot.* 192 Two-toothed, *bidentatus*. **1828** Stark *Elem. Nat. Hist.* II. 57 Shell fusiform,..aperture two-toothed. **1616** Chapman *Homer's Hymne to Apollo* 47 Their farr-stretcht valleys, and their *two-topt Hill. **1636** T. Heywood in *Ann. Dubrensia* (1877) 69 Two-top't Pernassus. **1902** J. Torrance *Story Marātha Missions* vii. 62 The two-topped hill of Sitabaldi. **1811** *Boston Patriot* 23 Jan. 3/2 A *two top-sail sch[ooner] was at H Hole on Saturday. **1944** J. Masefield *New Chum* 137 There used to be that kind of schooner. She was called a 'two-topsail schooner' or a 'maintopsail schooner'. **1934** *New Statesman* 27 Oct. 602/2 It is useless approaching these circles with *two-track class-war propaganda. **1961** G. A. Briggs *A to Z in Audio* 200 Regular supplies of high quality $7\frac{1}{2}$"/sec pre-recorded stereo tapes will be available, giving twice the playing time of previous two-track issues. **1977** *N.Y. Rev. Bks.* 13 Oct. 18/1 Had President Kennedy been pursuing a 'two-track' policy of offering Castro friendship while plotting his murder? **1649** Milton *Eikon.* xxvii, To whip us with his *two-twisted Scorpions, both temporal and spiritual Tyranny. **1676** Hobbes *Iliad* 375 A high *two-valved door. **1771** *Phil. Trans.* LXI. 232 Two valved shells. **1889** *Science-Gossip* XXV. 219 Fruit,..two-valved, dehiscing longitudinally. **1925** I. A. Richards *Princ. Lit. Criticism* 1 In a pamphlet or in a *two-volume work. **1978** *Early Music* Oct. 544/1 Silvestro Ganassi's two-volume treatise on the viol..is perhaps the most interesting and significant instrumental tutor to have survived from the 16th century. **1744** W. Ellis *Mod. Husbandman* Jan. i. 16 He plowed up the Surface..with a *two-wheel pecked Share-Plough. **1800** *Hull Advertiser* 19 July 2/4 A new two-wheel cart barrow. **1663** Butler *Hud.* I. II. 328 A *two-wheel'd Chariot. **1733** Tull *Horse-Hoeing Husb.* xxi. 300 A common Two-Wheel'd-Plow. **1886** C. E. Pascoe *Lond. of To-day* xliii. (ed. 3) 376 Two-wheeled cabs. **1861** *Eng. Wom. Dom. Mag.* III. 44 What they call a 'gig' in those parts—a tall *two-wheeler. **1753** Chambers *Cycl. Supp., Ox-fly*,..a species of *two-winged fly. **1918** D. H. Lawrence *New Poems* 41 Who then sees the two-winged Boat down there? **1949** E. Pound *Pisan Cantos* lxxvi. 45 Benecomata dea Under the two-winged cloud. **1974** *Encycl. Brit. Macropædia* V. 819/1 Diptera, the two-winged, or 'true', flies. **1930** *Engineering* 28 Feb. 278/3 Power distribution is at 230 volts in the *two-wire system. **1961** W. F. Leopold in Saporta & Bastian *Psycholinguistics* (1961) 357/1 *Two-word verbs of the type 'wake up'. **1977** N. Sahgal *Situation in New Delhi* xi. 115 They had labelled him with destructive little one and two-word flourishes that could smear an image for millions of readers.

2. Special Combinations: **two-address** *a.* *Computers*, having two addresses (see quot. 1953); **two and eight** *Rhyming slang*, a state (of agitation); **two-backed beast** = *the beast with two backs* s.v. beast *sb.* 4 b; **two-bagger** *N. Amer. Baseball*, a hit that enables the batter to reach second base safely; **two-bill**, = twibill; **two-bit** *a. U.S.* [bit *sb.*² 8 b], (*a*) of the value of a quarter of a dollar; (*b*) *fig.*, cheap, petty, worthless (*slang*); †**two-blade(s** = twayblade; **two-blocks** *adv.* = *block and block* (block *sb.* 5 b), *chock-a-block* (chock *adv.* c); **two-body** *a. Physics*, involving or pertaining to two objects or particles; **two-bottle** *a.*, applied to one who can drink two bottles of wine at a sitting; **two-by-four** orig. *U.S.*, a post or batten measuring 2 inches by 4 in cross-section; also (*U.S.*) *fig.* in *attrib.* use: small, insignificant; **two-cent** *a. U.S.*, (*a*) of the value of two cents; (*b*) *fig.* = *two-bit* (*b*) above (*slang*); **two cheers**, catch phr. expressing qualified enthusiasm *for* something, as opposed to the traditional three cheers (see three *a.* 1 g); **two-China(s)** *a. U.S. Pol.*, designating a proposal or policy for admitting to the United Nations representatives of both Communist China and Taiwan; **two-clang**, *Acoustics* [CLANG *sb.* 3], a compound tone consisting of two simple tones; **two-coat** *a.*, requiring two coats, as work in plastering and painting; **two cultures**: see CULTURE *sb.* 5c; **two-cycle** *a.*, completing a series of operations in two cycles or strokes, as a gas-engine; **two-eared** *a.*, having two ears; two-handled; **two-egg** *a.* = DIZYGOTIC *a.*; **two-ended** *a.*, having two ends (*spec.* with different properties, as a magnet); hence **two-endedness**; **two-eyed** *a.*, having two eyes; involving or adapted for the use of both eyes; **two-eyed stance** *Cricket* (see quot. 1924); **two-eyes** (*U.S. local*) = *twinberry* (see TWIN C.), from the two calyx-marks on the fruit (*Cent. Dict.* 1891); **two-field** *a.*, denoting a system of agriculture in which two fields are cropped and fallowed alternately; **two-finger**, one of a tribe in Surinam with deficient hands and feet (see quot.); **two fingers**, two fingers made into a V-sign as a coarse gesture of contempt; **two-fisted** *a.*, (*a*) (*dial.* or *colloq.*), awkward with the hands, clumsy; (*b*) *U.S. colloq.*, tough, aggressive; vigorous; (*c*) *Tennis*, of a backhand stroke: played with both hands on the racket; **two-for-his-heels**, used jocularly for 'knave' (in allusion to the expression for the dealer's score on turning up a knave at cribbage: see HEEL *sb.*[1] 1d); **two-forty**, *U.S. colloq.*, an expression for a high speed (properly, at the rate of a mile in 2 min. 40 sec., formerly a 'record' pace for trotting); **two-four** (usually $\frac{2}{4}$), *Mus.*, denoting a 'time' or rhythm with two crotchets in a bar; **two-furrow** *a.*, adapted for ploughing two furrows at once; **two-group**, a group of two, *e.g.* of two sound-units, as syllables forming an iamb or trochee; so **two-grouping**; **two-hearted** *a.*, double-hearted, deceitful; **two-heeled** *a.*, having two heels; in quot., two-edged (cf. HEEL *sb.*[1] 7b); **two-high** *a.*, having two rolls one over another, as a rolling-mill (cf. *three-high* s.v. THREE B. III. 2); **two-holer** *N. Amer.*, a privy or lavatory accommodating two people; **two-horse** *a.*, (*a*) drawn or worked by, or used with, two horses; (*b*) (of a race or other contest) in which only two of the contestants are likely winners; **two-knot** *a.*, running two knots (see KNOT *sb.*[1] 3); **two-line**, **two-lined** *adjs.*, (*a*) in *Printing*, extending through two lines, as a large capital letter; (*b*) occupying two lines, being two lines long; (*c*) underlined twice; *spec.* applied to a notice of forthcoming parliamentary business in which the attendance of members is requested with two underlines, indicating less urgency than a three-line whip (now the strongest one); **two-lipped** (-lɪpt) *a.*, having two lips; *esp.* in *Bot.* of a corolla, calyx, etc.; bilabiate; **2LO** (tuːel'əʊ) [*Lo*(*ndon*)], the call-sign of a radio station established in London in 1922 and taken over the same year by the newly-formed British Broadcasting Company, which used it as call-sign until 1924 and as a name of a programme service until 1930; the station itself; **two-lofted** (*Sc.* twa-) *a.*, two-storied; **two-meal** *a.*, (*a*) of cheese: see quots. (cf. MEAL *sb.*[2] 3a); (*b*) of or involving two meals a day; **two(-)minute(s') silence** = SILENCE *sb.* 2e; **two-monthly** *a.*, occurring every two months; see also quot. 1867; **two nation(s)**, used, chiefly *attrib.*, with reference to two irreconcilable groups or factions within a nation; **two-oar**, a two-oared boat; **two-one**, a place in the upper division of the second class in a degree class-list; (a graduate having) an upper-second-class degree; also represented as 2(1), etc.; **two-pair** *a.* (in full, *two-pair-of-stairs*), situated above two 'pairs' or flights of stairs, i.e. on the second floor; also *ellipt.* as *sb.* (*scil.* room); **two-piece** *a.* and *sb.*, (a suit) consisting of two garments (as a jacket and trousers, or coat and dress) matching or meant to be worn together; (a swimming costume) consisting now of a brassière and briefs, a bikini; also (*U.S.*) **two-piecer**; **two-place** *a.*, applied to an aeroplane with seats for two people; so **two-placer**; †**two-plait** (*two plette*), a double plait; **two-power standard** (see quot. 1910); **two-revolution** *a. Printing*, applied to a cylinder press in which the impression cylinder rotates continuously, alternately printing and delivering sheets as the forme moves to and fro; abbrev. **two-rev** (also *absol.*); **two-rhythm**, duple rhythm; **twos and threes**, a children's chasing game for six or more players; †**two-sea'd** *a.*, situated between two seas (tr. L. *bimaris*); **two-seater**, something (as a vehicle or settee) that has two seats; freq. *attrib.*; †**two-shafted** *a.*, of cloth, woven with two web-shafts (see SHAFT *sb.*[2] 9, and cf. THREE-*shafted*); **two-shear**, *a.* of a sheep, that has been shorn twice; *sb.* a two-shear sheep; also, the time or age of the second shearing; **Two-shoes**, nickname of the girl heroine of the History of Little Goody Two-shoes; hence, a quasi-proper name for a child; **two-shot**, a cinema or television shot of two people together; **two-spot** *U.S.*, (*a*) a playing card with two pips, a deuce; (*b*) a two-dollar banknote; (*c*) *transf.*, an insignificant or worthless person; a two-year prison sentence; **two-star** *a.*, (*a*) given two stars in a grading system in which more stars indicate higher quality (cf. STAR *sb.*[1] 10c); (*b*) having or being a military rank that has two stars on the shoulder-piece of the uniform, e.g. major-general or rear-admiral in the U.S. (cf. STAR *sb.*[1] 6c); **two-state** *a.*, capable of existing in either of two states or conditions; **two-step**, (*a*) a round dance characterized by sliding steps in duple rhythm; also, the music for such a dance; also *attrib.*; also as *v. intr.*, to dance a two-step; (*b*) *a.*, having or consisting of two successive actions; two-stage; **two-sticker** *colloq.*, a two-masted boat; **two-suiter**, (*a*) *Bridge* (see quot. 1923); (*b*) orig. *U.S.*, a suitcase large enough to hold two suits and accessories; **two-tailed** *a.*, (*a*) having two tails; (*b*) *Statistics*, applied to a test that tests for deviation from the null hypothesis in both directions; cf. *one-tailed* adj. s.v. ONE *numeral a.*, *pron.*, etc. B. 33; **two-teeth**, **-tooth**, *a.*, applied to sheep of from one to two years old: having two full-grown permanent teeth, double-toothed; also as *sb.*; **two-throw** *a.*, having two throws, as a crank (see THROW *sb.*[2] 2); **two-tone** *a.*, (*a*) in two colours or two shades of the same colour; (*b*) being or producing two notes, usu. alternately at intervals; also *fig.*; so **two-toned** *a.*, in the same sense; **two-tongued** *a.*, having two tongues; *fig.* double-tongued, deceitful; **two-two**, (*a*) (usu. represented as .22), used *attrib.* and *absol.* to designate (ammunition for) a gun with a calibre of 0.22 inch; (*b*) (also represented as 2(2), etc.), a place in the lower division of the second class in a degree class-list; see also sense II. 2g; **two-water** *a.*, *Naut.*, diluted with twice its bulk of water; **two-week** *dial.*, a fortnight; **two-year** *a.*, (*a*) = TWO-YEAR-OLD; (*b*) lasting or valid for two years; also *transf.*; **two-yearer**, (*a*) a voyage lasting two years; (*b*) a pupil who has been at (Harrow) school two years; †**two-yearing** *a.*, of a beast, two years old; **two-yearling**, a beast of two years old; also *attrib.*

1948 *Two-address [see *three-address* adj. s.v. THREE *a.* and *sb.* III. 2]. **1953** *Computers & Automation* Dec. 22 *Two-address*, in programming, a system of instructions whereby each complete instruction includes an operation and specifies the location of two registers, usually one containing an operand and the other the result of the operation. **1961** [see SEQUENCING *vbl. sb.*]. **1982** G. LEE *Hardware to Software* xx. 339 With 3-address instructions (as for 2-address), it is not necessary to have an accumulator. **1938** 'J. CURTIS' *They drive by Night* ix. 103 Give us a hand out, will you? I'm in a right *two and eight. **1960** M. CECIL *Something in Common* 129 Poor old Clinker! Bet she's in a proper two-and-eight! *a* **1693** *Two-backed beast [see BEAST *sb.* 4b]. **1925** G. GREENE *Babbling April* 5 The two-backed beast went trotting in my head. **1939** DYLAN THOMAS *Map of Love* 63 Here dwell, said Sam Rib, the two-backed beasts. He pointed to his map of Love. **1973** L. SNELLING *Heresy* II. i. 60 Hubby gor on to us. Came within an ace of catching us making the two-backed beast in his car. **1880** *Globe* (San Francisco) 16 May 1/4 Willigrod, Smith and J. Whitney led at the bat, the two former getting in each a *two-bagger. **1946** *N.Y. Herald Tribune* 24 Mar. VIII. 19/1, I hit a two-bagger with the bases full. **1619** S. ATKINSON *Gold Mynes Scotl.* (Bann. Cl.) 1 To digg the next ground under that sodd ..with a mattocke, picke, or *towbill. **1714** *Lond. Gaz.* No. 5228/4 Henry Bray..did give..Edward Hurly..a mortal Wound on the Head with a Two-Bill. **1807** VANCOUVER *Agric. Devon* (1813) 127 The grubbing of roots is generally performed with the two-bill, or double-bitted mattock. **1888** ELWORTHY *W. Somerset Word-bk.*, *Two-bill*, a double-ended mattock. Sometimes both ends are alike. **1802** J. DRAYTON *View South-Carolina* 215 Hence the origin of this society; which, from the contributions, being a sum of money called *two bitts*, became known by the appellation of the **two bitt* club. **1873** *Harper's Mag.* May 799 Thompson's Two-bit House, Front St. **1928** S. LEWIS *Man who knew Coolidge* I. 51 There's a man..always got a good story and a two-bit cigar for you. **1932** E. CALDWELL *Tobacco Road* xvii. 208 Tom said she used to be a two-bit slut. **1978** T. WILLIS *Buckingham Palace Connection* viii. 155 Some other two-bit General will try shooting us up. **1605** TIMME *Quersit.* III. 177 Take of the rootes of angelica,..of bifolium or *two-blades. **1728** BRADLEY *Dict. Bot.*, *Ophris*, sive *Bifolium*,..Twy-blade and Twablade. **1828** *Craven Gloss.*, *Twa-blade*, a plant with two leaves. *Ophrys ovata.* **1841** DANA *Seaman's Man.* 99 *Chock-a-block.* When the lower block of a tackle is run close up to the upper one, so that you can hoist no higher... Also called hoisting up **two-blocks.* **1956** *Nature* 11 Feb. 268/2 A principal aim of the theory is to show that, using only such *two-body forces, one can achieve nuclear separation. **1978** PASACHOFF & KUTNER *University Astron.* xxvi. 648 The effects that the planets have on each other are much less than the effect that the sun has on each, and the mutual interactions of the planets are treated as small deviations..from the situation that would be present if only the sun-planet two-body problem had to be solved. **1855** THACKERAY *Newcomes* lix, This *two-bottle Mentor. **1874** L. STEPHEN *Hours in Library* (1876) II. 163 The two-bottle men who lingered till our day were..relics of the type which then gave the tone to society. **1884** E. W. NYE *Baled Hay* 23 The managing editor of the mill lays out the log in his mind, and works it into dimension stuff, shingle bolts, slabs, edgings, *two by fours. **1897** 'O. THANET' *Missionary Sheriff* 13 'That how she makes a living?' 'Yes—little two-by-four bakery.' **1916** 'B. M. BOWER' *Phantom Herd* v. 77 Houses..bald behind as board fences save where two-by-fours braced them from falling. **1939** J. B. PRIESTLEY *Let People Sing* i. 3 A little two-by-four provincial agency..giving itself airs now! **1978** *Maledicta* II. 7 You hit him over his ossified skull with a two-by-four. **1979** J. VAN DE WETERING *Maine Massacre* xix. 226 De Gier saw a tableau made out of barn boards, framed neatly by weathered two-by-fours. **1859** L. A. WILMER *Our Press Gang* 42 The Express was a *two-cent cash paper. **1899** 'J. FLYNT' *Tramping* I. v. 119 The next higher type of the town tramp is the 'two-cent dosser'—the man who lives in stale-beer shops. **1902** ELIZ. L. BANKS *Newspaper Girl* xiv, Dinah got a letter through the American mail. She had fivepence to pay on it, because only a common two-cent stamp had been stuck on it. **1908** Two-cent [see GUNK 3]. **1951** E. M. FORSTER (*title*) *Two cheers for democracy. **1977** *Times* 5 Sept. 6/7 Two cheers for..the National Theatre's debut in community drama. **1962** E. SNOW *Other Side of River* (1963) xx. 149 Mao and other Chinese continued to respect Chiang Kai-shek for one thing, however: he had declined to support the '*two-Chinas' plan aimed at removing Taiwan from the sovereignty of China. **1979** H. KISSINGER *White House Yrs.* xviii. 719 This was close to the two-China solution always vehemently rejected by both Taipei and Peking. **1894** CREIGHTON & TITCHENER tr. *Wundt's Hum. & Anim. Psychol.* v. §2. 69 Similar simple periods are found to recur in the other harmonious *two-clangs [Ger. *Zweiklängen*]. **1833** LOUDON *Encycl. Archit.* §936 All the ceilings..are to be finished with fine *two-coat plasterwork. **1847** SMEATON *Builder's Man.* 127 Lath, laid and set,..in plastering, signifying two-coat work. **1903** *Motor. Ann.* 273 He suggests the *two-cycle engine without valves as the most economical motor. **1520** *MS. Acc. St. John's Hosp., Canterb.*, A *ij ered basket. **1685** *Lond. Gaz.* No. 2068/4 One Tea Pot, one Silver Tankard wrought, one two Ear'd Pot. **1704** *Ibid.* No. 3984/4 A..Two-ear'd Cup. **1959** *Listener* 29 Oct. 728/2 *Two-egg twins..are derived from the separate eggs fertilized by two different sperms. **1971** Two-egg [see *multiple birth* s.v. MULTIPLE *a.* 4c]. **1863** TYNDALL *Heat* xv. §755. (1870) 522 The polarity of a magnet consists in its *two-endedness. **1864** *Reader* 19 Nov. 642/1 'A *Two-eyed Steak',..a Yarmouth bloater. **1876** STEWART & TAIT *Unseen Univ.* 21 Another class who regard a two-eyed man as a monster. **1892** GREENER *Breech-Loader* 92 The sportsman may..dispense with shooting correctors, two-eyed sights, *et id genus omne.* **1924** A. C. MACLAREN *Cricket Old & New* viii. 73 What is called 'the *two-eyed stance' or the turn of the head to enable the batsman to see the ball with as full a face as possible but without taking the left shoulder off the line of the ball. **1977** *Sunday Times* 3 July 28/2 Hughie Trumble..condemned the two-eyed batting stance. **1907** M. C. F. MORRIS *Nunburnholme* 250 The *two-field or three-field shift system. **1796** STEDMAN *Surinam* II. xxvi. 255 The Accorees, or *Two-fingers, live amongst the Seramaca negroes. **1971** G. EWART *Gavin Ewart Show* III. 50 Meanwhile on the roof of the Playboy Club..one Bunny Flag. Two ears, like sensual man's *two-fingers-up to Culture. **1977** *Zigzag* June 24/1 There's nothing more the kids want to see than The Pistols at the top of the chart, two fingers pointed at the TV, radio, printing firms and council officials who've tried to stifle them. **1774** P. V. FITHIAN *Jrnl.* (1900) 223 He was Director, and appointed a sturdy *two-fisted Gentleman to open the Ball with Mrs. Tayloe. **1859** GEO. ELIOT *A. Bede* vi, As poor a two-fisted thing as ever I saw, you know you was. **1878** MRS. STOWE *Poganuc P.* vi, A stout, two-fisted farmer. **1908** [see CLEAN *v.* 4c]. **1925** E. E. CUMMINGS *Let.* 3 Sept. (1969) 108 [I] was not made to match wits with twofisted go-getters. **1960** *Times* 16 June 18/6 The two-fisted back-hand of Australia's Howe. *Ibid.* 16 Sept. 52 Hamdinger..being, as the menu says, 'for two-fisted appetites'. **1978** *Times* 4 July 19/4 Miss Kruger, a steady and tenacious competitor with a two-fisted backhand. **1979** *Tucson Mag.* Mar. 18/3 Bonanno..is going to have a two-fisted fight on his hands. The U.S. Criminal Justice system is also bearing down on Bonanno. **1837** DICKENS *Pickw.* xxvii, I am ashamed o' you, old *two-for-his-heels. **1889** FARMER *Americanisms*, *Two-forty.* To go at *two forty, or at two forty pace, is to proceed at a high rate of speed. The allusion is to the record pace at trotting matches, at one time a mile in two minutes forty seconds being considered very good. **1896** G. HUNTINGTON in *Chicago Advance* 26 Mar. 450/3 Now, get a two forty move on you, nags! **1848** RIMBAULT *First Bk. Piano.* 95 Where does the Accent fall in *Two-four Time? **1805** R. W. DICKSON *Pract. Agric.* I. 8 The double or *two-furrow plough. **1901** C. R. SQUIRE in *Amer. Jrnl. Psychol.* July–Oct. 535 The *two-group is psychologically simpler than the three-group. *Ibid.* 536 The natural tendency to a *two-grouping. **1654** A. GRAY *Serm.* (1755) 80 Many of us would be found *two-hearted men. *a* **1610** HEALEY *Theophrastus* (1636) 88 His *two-heel'd sword. **1875** KNIGHT *Dict. Mech.* s.v. *Rolling-mill Train*, *Two-high grooved rolls. **1971** *Islander* (Victoria, B.C.) 3 Jan. 12/2 Gone were the woodshed and the *two-holer discreetly removed from the house. **1974** S. ALSOP *Stay of Execution* II. 224 The house.. is a shooting lodge, built in 1929... There is one bathroom for the ladies, and one for the men, each with a two-holer. *c* **1780** 'J. H. St. J. DE CRÈVECŒUR' *Sk. 18th-Cent. Amer.* (1925) 138 You have often admired our *two-horse waggons. **1798** R. DOUGLAS *Agric. Surv. Roxb.* 50 The plough is drawn by a strong stretcher, commonly called a two-horse-tree. **1799** J. ROBERTSON *Agric. Perth* 525 Two-horse ploughs. **1812** SIR J. SINCLAIR *Syst. Husb. Scot.* I. 58 A two-horse cart. **1900** KROPOTKIN *Mem. Revolutionist* (1906) I. i. 4 Two-horse sledges. **1976** *Newmarket Jrnl.* 16

Dec., [Darts] With White Lion beating Wellington 7-2 it seems to be a two-horse race at the top. **1977** *Evening Gaz.* (Middlesbrough) 11 Jan. 14/1 [Association football] The two-horse race in Division B looks like continuing. **1984** *Times* 22 Feb. 1/5 If, as is expected, he comes second in New Hampshire, it could turn into a two-horse race. **1889** WESTGARTH *Austral. Progr.* 124 A *two-knot northerly current inshore. **1771** LUCKOMBE *Hist. Print.* 30 He used *two-line letters of a Gothic kind. **1892** A. OLDFIELD *Man. Typogr.* iv, Chapter Headings are usually set in a two-line titling. **1901** G. B. SHAW *Admirable Bashville* in *Cashel Byron's Profession* (rev. ed.) Pref. 288, I like the melodious sing-song, the clear simple one-line and two-line sayings, and the occasional rhymed tags. **1958** WILDING & LAUNDY *Encycl. Parl.* 603 Sir Wilfrid Lawson explained pithily that a one-line whip meant 'you ought to attend'; a two-line whip 'you should attend'; a three-line whip 'you must attend'. **1962** W. NOWOTTNY *Lang. Poets Use* v. 110 One usually expects of couplets that the sense of the passage will fall into two-line chunks. **1976** H. WILSON *Governance of Britain* iii. 46 The chief whip then indicates the kind of whip he will issue for each day—one-line, two-line or three. **1978** W. WHITE in W. Whitman *Daybks. & Notebks.* I. 121 'Roaming in Thought' is a two-line poem, published in the 1881 *Leaves of Grass*. **1683** MOXON *Mech. Exerc., Printing* xxii. ¶5 He begins his Chapter..with a *Two-lin'd Letter. **1787** *Fam. Plants* I. 4 Nectary..*two-lip'd. **1808** *Med. Jrnl.* XIX. 75 *G[enista] tinctoria*... Cal[yx] two-lipped. **1853** MISS PRATT *Wild Flowers* II. 18 They have..square stems, opposite leaves and two-lipped blossoms. **1923** *Radio Times* 28 Sept. 3/1 (*heading*) A recent talk broadcast from *2LO. **1924** A. R. BURROWS *Story of Broadcasting* viii. 59 A station known as 2LO, a 100-watt set contained in a small teak cabinet, and housed in the cinema theatre on the top floor of Marconi House, London. **1961** E. WILLIAMS *George* xxvi. 415, I would sit for an hour while the faint dream-sounds of 2LO echoed in my head. **1969** *Listener* 17 Apr. 514/3, 30 years after the introduction of broadcasting from 2LO, radio was the dominant or only means of electronic communication. **1981** S. BRIGGS *Those Radio Times* 9/2 The pre-Savoy Hill 2LO studio at Marconi House. **1818** SCOTT *Br. Lamm.* xxiv, Folk are far frae respecting me as they wad do if I lived in a *twa-lofted sclated house. **1741** W. ELLIS *Mod. Husbandman* May vii. 112 It is generally made with half skim, and half new; or what is more properly called *Two-meal Cheese. **1784** TWAMLEY *Dairying* 57 What is generally known by the name of Two-meal Cheese,..being made from one meal New Milk and one of old, or skimmed Milk. **1805** R. W. DICKSON *Pract. Agric.* II. 1011 Where two milkings are blended, or two-meal cheese made. **1901** *Daily Chron.* 3 Sept. 7/4 The generality of the two-meal system in hot countries. **1919**, etc. *Two(-)minute(s') [see SILENCE *sb.* 2 e]. **1811** *Regul. & Ord. Army* 95 The Monthly Settlement in the Infantry and the *Two-Monthly Settlement in the Cavalry..have been duly made by the Captains. **1867** SMYTH *Sailor's Word-bk.*, *Two-monthly book*, a book kept by the captain's clerk, to be forwarded every two months, when possible. [**1711** ADDISON in *Spectator* 24 July, There cannot a greater Judgment befall a Country than such a dreadful Spirit of Division as rends a Government into two distinct People, and makes them greater Strangers and more averse to one another, than if they were actually two different Nations.] **1845** DISRAELI *Sybil* I. II. v. 149 *Two nations; between whom there is no intercourse and no sympathy; who are as ignorant of each other's habits, thoughts, and feelings, as if they were.. inhabitants of different planets... The rich and the poor. **1913** *Times* 8 May 10/3 Rightly or wrongly, the Protestants of Ulster hold to the 'two nations' theory. **1958** O. CAROE *Pathans* xxvi. 434 Only when the British Government's move to bring British authority to an end acquired a momentum so unmistakable that even the unbelieving were compelled to read the signs..was the two-nation theory translated into practical politics. **1976** *Equals* Oct./Nov. 1/5 In contemporary Britain the Two Nations are not so obviously the rich and the poor or the blacks and the whites or the townspeople and the country people, as the urban deprived and the rest of us. **1857** MRQ. DALHOUSIE in *Life* (1895) 208 Lots of eighteen-penny *two-oars. **1937** 'M. INNES' *Hamlet, Revenge!* I. ii. 34 Gott with his tutor's instinct was placing this young lady's mind provisionally among the good *Two-ones. **1963** *Times* 10 May 6/4 The survey showed that 10 per cent of the firsts and 25 per cent of the 2.i (upper second) were earning less than £1,250 a year. **1964** *Guardian* 23 Oct. 14/2 It is argued..that examiners who can award 'two ones' are less ready to give firsts. **1969** M. KELLY *Write on Both Sides of Paper* 17 He was..a two-one graduate. **1976** *Times* 6 Sept. 10/5 For quite a number of years, New Hall got more firsts and 2/1s combined than any other college. **1984** *Oxf. Univ. Gaz.: Suppl.* 16 Feb. 506/1 It [*sc.* division of the second class] will ..greatly help the II(1) in competition with officially recognized II(1)s from other universities. **1749** FIELDING *Tom Jones* XIV. iv, Nightingale should procure him either the ground-floor, or the *two pair of stairs. **1755** KIDGELL *Card* II. 179 The very two-pair-of-stairs Apartment. **1836** DICKENS *Sk. Boz, Our Parish* i, I rents a two-pair back, gentlemen. **1840** THACKERAY *Shabby-genteel Story* vii, There was a light in the garret, and another in the two-pair front. **1841** —— *Gt. Hoggarty Diamond* ii, We occupied a very genteel two-pair. *c* **1880** in *Amer. Mail Order Fashions* (1961) 11 A very neat little *two-piece suit of calico. **1895** *Montgomery Ward Catal.* Spring & Summer 501/2 Bathing Suits... Two-piece suits. Consisting of quarter sleeve shirts and knee pants. **1933** AUDEN *Dance of Death* 8 Revealing handsome two-piece bathing suits. **1956** *Times* 28 May 13/3 The two-piece, which has now become the generic term for a dress with a matching jacket, has to a great extent replaced the suit for special occasions. **1978** L. DEIGHTON *SS-GB* iii. 29 She was dressed in a tailored two-piece of pink wool. **1963** *New Yorker* 1 June 110 Soak up the sun in our beautifully brief, terry *two-piecer. **1978** *Detroit Free Press* 5 Mar. (Spring Fashion Suppl.) 17 (Advt.), The Pierrot collared two-piecer has a gently shirred skirt, with side pockets. **1916** HALL & NILES *One Man's War* (1929) 160 He was flying a *two-place fighter. **1971** *Flying* Apr. 35/2 The jet works the same as a two-place trainer. **1916** HALL & NILES *One Man's War* (1929) 190 It wasn't long until Luf spied a *two-placer. **1641** BEST *Farm. Bks.* (Surtees) 148 Bandes..made of the smallest haver-strawe,..first well twined, and after that twined togeather againe, after the manner of a *two plette. **1901** *To-Day* 26 Sept. 280 In men and ships..the British Navy is distinctly above the '*two-Power standard'. **1910** *Encycl. Brit.* IV. 613/2 It has..been accepted as a fundamental axiom of defence that the British navy should exceed in strength any reasonable combination of foreign navies which could be brought against it, the accepted formula being the 'two-power standard', *i.e.* a 10% margin over the joint strength of the next two powers. **1914** G. B. SHAW *Fanny's First Play* III. 223 Your honest and sensible statesmen demand for England a two-power standard. **1980** *Two-rev [see *stop cylinder* s.v. STOP *sb.*[2] 29]. **1902** *Encycl. Brit.* XXXII. 5/2 The *two-revolution cylinder.. makes two revolutions to each impression and can be made to produce 1500 or more impressions on a large sheet in one hour. **1967** *Elsevier's Dict. Printing* 328/2 The cylinder on a two-revolution press constantly rotates, printing a sheet on its first revolution and delivering the sheet on its second. **1901** C. R. SQUIRE in *Amer. Jrnl. Psychol.* July–Oct. 536 Others explain this preference for the *two-rhythm as due to its accordance with the bodily rhythms, the expiration and inspiration of respiration, the diastole and systole of the heart [etc.]. **1896** E. TURNER *Little Larrikin* xxiii. 279 The frantic rushes of the game of '*twos and threes'. **1935** N. MITCHISON *We have been Warned* III. 236 After dinner there were games with the crew... They had fox-and-geese and twos-and-threes. **1983** G. MITCHELL *Greenstone Griffins* ii. 14 Some traditional party games were played... A game of Twos and Threes was in progress. **1621** G. SANDYS *Ovid's Met.* VI. (1626) 118 With all that *two-sead Isthmos Streights include. **1891** H. C. BUNNER *Zadoc Pine* 172, I climbed into his '*two-seater', and sat behind talking to Mrs. Tom. **1906** Two-seater car [see SEATER 2]. **1918** T. E. LAWRENCE *Lett.* (1938) 248 Our Bristol Fighter the same day brought down a German two-seater in flames. **1931** *Daily Express* 31 Jan. 7/4 The two-seater airplane which crashed in Bushy Park. **1973** R. LUDLUM *Matlock Paper* xviii. 150 He sat in the Early American two-seater in the outer office. **1977** P. HILL *Fanatics* 145 The helicopter ..was a two-seater. **1979** R. JAFFE *Class Reunion* (1980) III. i. 305 Emily..drove to her analyst..in the little two-seater Mercedes. *c* **1440** *Promp. Parv.* 497/2 *Toschappyd clothe (*S.* tooschaptyd cloth), *bilix*. **1788** W. MARSHALL *Yorks.* II. 260 The wedders will fat at *two-sheer (that is, two to three years old) to thirty pounds a quarter. *c* **1830** *Glouc. Farm Rep.* 16 in *Libr. Usef. Knowl., Husb.* III, The two-shear, or four-teeth ewes. **1898** *Speaker* 5 Feb. 181 [The lamb] attained to the dignity of a two-shear. **1766** *Hist. Goody Two-Shoes* I. iii, The Pleasure she took in her two Shoes.. by that Means [she] obtained the Name of Goody *Two-Shoes. **1858** GEO. ELIOT *Scenes Clerical Life* I. 166 Little Bessie Parrot, a flaxen-headed 'two-shoes', very white and fat as to her neck. **1870** EMERSON *Soc. & Solit., Dom. Life* Wks. (Bohn) III. 43 What a holiday is the first snow in which Twoshoes can be trusted abroad. **1949** N. STREATFEILD *Painted Garden* xxi. 228 Movies are made with a long shot, a *two-shot and a close-up of each person, each taken separately. **1978** *Broadcast* 27 Mar. 8/3 Two grey-suited figures, held in two-shot, recapped results interminably. **1885** *Narragansett Hist. Reg.* III. 213 We were shown a play-card, the *two-spot of clubs. **1896** ADE *Artie* vi. 50 You're nothin' but a two-spot. **1901** 'J. FLYNT' *World of Graft* 184 They convicted me at last and I got a two-spot. **1909** 'O. HENRY' *Roads of Destiny* xviii. 305 We get the heelers out with the crackly two-spots. **1936** H. HAGEDORN *Brookings* v. 73 He knew..when to be discreet and when to bluff on a two-spot. **1951** *Observer* 27 May 4/5 He cannot do better than buy the Michelin Guide to France and tour the *two- or even three-star restaurants. **1960** *John o' London's* 7 Apr. 403/1 The unknown two-star general.. accumulated power for himself in the name of France. **1976** *Daily Mail* (Hull) 30 Sept. 11/3 The Galant..will do over 35 miles to the gallon on two-star petrol. **1982** 'E. LATHEN' *Green grow Dollars* ii. 16 Two-star generals are less accustomed to being balked than most men. **1959** G. TROUP *Masers* iii. 35 The *two-state molecules under consideration. **1971** J. H. SMITH *Digital Logic* i. 1 Although most digital devices are 'two state', the essential requirement of a digital device is that it should change from one discrete state to another and not settle into any intermediate state or position. **1900** in *Westm. Gaz.* 12 Apr. 2/3 The best dancer is the best man. She falls in love with him to the tune of a sighing waltz. She marries him to the tune of a *two-step. **1909** *Daily Chron.* 27 Jan. 7/4 The most popular steps are the two-step, waltz, schottische, three-step, and glide waltz. **1910** *Punch* 30 Mar. 223/2 But when the maid my signal sees She '*two-steps' by like winking. **1929** S. LEWIS *Dodsworth* i. 9 The aristocracy of Zenith were dancing... They two-stepped on the wide porch. **1940** *Chambers's Techn. Dict.* 874/1 *Two-step relay. **1948** A. C. CLARKE *Across Sea of Stars* (1959) 13 The A. 20 was a two-step rocket. **1978** *Bull. Amer. Acad. Arts & Sci.* Feb. 13 The two-step mechanism of translocation of estradiol finds a precise counterpart in the action of other steroid hormones. **1884** *Leisure Hour* Aug. 505/2 Of modern racing schooners ..the fastest *two-sticker ever designed. **1895** Two-sticker [see JACK *sb.*[1] 25]. **1931** *Canad. Geogr. Jrnl.* II. 391/1 Our 'two-sticker with a kicker' lies in Sandy Bay harbour, Nova Scotia. **1923** M. C. WORK *Auction Bridge of 1924* vi. 60 A hand containing two suits both strong enough to bid is called a '*two-suiter'. **1958** *Which?* Winter 25/1 The boot accommodated one two-suiter and one week end case, or three week-end cases. **1979** *Arizona Daily Star* 5 Aug. I. 12/1 North had to have a monstrously powerful major two-suiter for his repeated cue-bids, and they invariably took a preference to six spades. **1981** L. DEIGHTON *XPD* xxvii. 223 Stuart lifted a Samsonite two-suiter onto the bed. **1904** *Oxford Mag.* 16 Mar. 275/2 When imported Labour Yellow should eliminate the Fellow, And the Head of every College be a *two-tailed Mandarin! **1922** JOYCE *Ulysses* 491 His twotailed black braces dangling at heels. **1931** *Times Lit. Suppl.* 1 Oct. 747/2 They [*sc.* Norman clerks] used a two-tailed capital F. **1945** *Biometrics Bull.* I. 70 If querist has other alternatives to be considered, he may be interested in the two-tailed test discussed in following answers. **1976** *Lancet* 30 Oct. 922/1 Data were analysed by Student's two-tailed *t* test. **1875** KNIGHT *Dict. Mech.*, **Two-throw Crank*. **1906** GOODCHILD & TWENEY *Technol. & Sci. Dict.* 800/2 **Two tone*,..a term applied to lace composed of cotton of the natural colour (ecru) interspersed with objects of white. **1940** R. CHANDLER *Farewell, My Lovely* xviii. 115 A couple of very nice two-tone Buicks. **1963** *Listener* 21 Feb. 349/2 There are signs, in the two-tone sketchiness of some of the scenes..that the book was written at speed. **1965** G. MCINNES *Road to Gundagai* x. 167 The sad two-tone cadence of the mopoke or Australian owl. **1966** *Statutory Instruments 1966* III. 3501 'Two-tone horn' means an instrument or apparatus which, when operated, automatically produces a sound which alternates at regular intervals between two fixed notes. **1977** *Harpers & Queen* Sept. 51/2 The usual luxury touches like electric windows, two-tone horns. **1981** *Country Life* 22 Jan. 226/3 Deep burgundy *bouclé* jacket.. two-tone belt. **1897** *Sears, Roebuck Catal.* 238/1 Striped Undershirts... Neat *two toned shades, silver gray predominating. **1951** T. STERLING *House without Door* v. 47 A two-toned gong rang... He opened the door. **1982** R. LUDLUM *Parsifal Mosaic* xviii. 271 He climbed out of the two-toned coupé. **1393** LANGL. *P. Pl.* C. XXIII. 162 Here syre was a sysour þat neuere swor treuthe, On tomme *two-tounged. **1636** G. SANDYS *Paraphr. Ps.* xxvi. 35, I hate the two-tongu'd Hypocrite. **1815** MALCOLM *Sk. Persia* (1828) II. 156 'The fiery steed of the two-tongued pen' [a split reed] is allowed to run wild. **1776** *Carlisle Mag.* 13 July 22 It [the goggles] generally..attacks the younger sheep, more particularly the *two tooths. **1778** *Lett. & Pap. Agric. to Soc. at Bath* I. 42 The sheep most subject to it [the disease goggles] are two teeth. *c* **1830** *Glouc. Farm Rep.* 16 in *Libr. Usef. Knowl., Husb.* III, The young or two-teeth ewes. **1945** N. MARSH *Died in Wool* viii. 180 A couple more dirty two-tooths for the herd to shear. **1962** *Coast to Coast 1961–62* 26 Kangaroos, goannas and two-tooth ewes constitute the characteristic fauna of Coorabin. **1972** P. NEWTON *Sheep Thief* iii. 26 As two-tooths they all go out to Cow Creek with the ewes. **1980** D. HART-DAVIS *Heights of Rimring* xviii. 212 'What the hell's a two-tooth ewe?' 'A hogget—a second-year ewe. The best mutton there is.' **1895** *Army & Navy Co-op. Soc. Price List* 921 The Remington single shot rifle. Shooting the *·22 rim fire American Cartridge. **1944** 'N. SHUTE' *Pastoral* i. 11 A little gun, his own. Two-two. **1973** 'M. HEBDEN' *Dark Side of Island* xvi. 134 'What sort was it? Shotgun?' 'No. Two-two.' **1976** J. H. SPENCER *Surgenor Campaign* i. 11 His own Tripos degree class in history, a Two-Two in place of the expected First, had been a disappointment. **1981** LD. HAREWOOD *Tongs & Bones* v. 90, I..at least got a II:ii..; in those days the only respectable thing was either a First or a Third. **1905** *Two-water..grog [see *three-water* s.v. THREE B. III. 2]. **1900** H. SUTCLIFFE *Shameless Wayne* 119 It's a *two-week come yesterday sin' they fought i' th' kirk-yard. **1596–7** *Durham Wills* (Surtees) II. 268, iiij *two-yere cattell. **1927** A. H. MCNEILE *Introd. Study N.T.* v. 141 St. Paul returned [to Ephesus] for his two-year visit. **1962** E. SNOW *Other Side of River* (1963) i. 19 There were six of them..on their way to serve two-year contracts as technical advisers in China. **1975** *Whitaker's Almanack 1976* 802 Institutions of higher education include universities, colleges, professional schools, and two-year colleges. **1894** DOYLE *Mem. S. Holmes* 81 I'm just off a *two-yearer in an eight-knot tramp. **1899** *Tit-Bits* 1 July 276/3 A 'three-yearer' may..be recognised by his stand-up collar and his tie-pin,..which an unfavored 'two-yearer' may look and long for. **1600** in W. F. Shaw *Mem. Eastry* (1876) 226 Item vij kine iij *towyearing beasts and four twelve monthings. **1577** B. GOOGE *Heresbach's Husb.* I. (1586) 43b, My young breede, Yeerelinges, and *Twoyeerelinges. **1884** *W. Sussex Gaz.* 25 Sept., 10 good two-yearling wellbred Steers.

twoche, obs. form of TOUCH.

'two-,decker. [f. TWO + DECK *sb.*[1] + -ER[1]: see DECKER[2].]

1. A two-decked ship or boat; formerly *spec.* a line-of-battle ship carrying guns on two decks.

1790 BEATSON *Nav. & Mil. Mem.* II. 140 We could perceive the ships to be French, the largest being a two-decker. **1833** MARRYAT *P. Simple* xiii, I was in the dock-yard, looking at a two-decker in the basin.

2. *transf.* and *fig.* Something consisting of two ranges or divisions, as a tram-car with seats on the roof and an additional roof over them; in quot. 1902, a play in two acts. Also *attrib.*

1884 Two Decker Oven [see DECKER[2] 1]. **1902** *Westm. Gaz.* 20 Aug. 3/1 Unfortunately, it is a theory of managers that one poor three-act play is better than two good two-deckers. **1904** *Daily Chron.* 18 July 3/1 L.C.C. Two-deckers ..on the..tramways south of the Thames. **1905** *Outlook* 23 Dec. 903/2 The two-decker bed with its red and yellow curtains.

two-di'mensional (also 'tuː-), *a.* **1.** Having or appearing to have length and breadth but no depth.

1883 [see DIMENSIONAL *a.* 2]. **1898** SIR W. CROOKES in *Daily News* 8 Sept. 6/3, I was like some two-dimensional being who might stand at the singular point of a Riemann's surface, and thus find himself in..inexplicable contact with a plane of existence not his own. **1954** M. RICKERT *Painting in Britain: Middle Ages* viii. 201 Two-dimensional compositions for glass panels. **1967** E. SHORT *Embroidery & Fabric Collage* i. 8 Without realising what effect they will have when translated into a two-dimensional design.

2. *fig.* Lacking depth or substance; shallow, superficial.

1934 C. LAMBERT *Music Ho!* v. 310 It is possible to detach Stravinsky's methods from their contents and apply Stravinsky scoring to any piece of music. Like everything else in his music, it is two-dimensional. **1959** *Times Lit. Suppl.* 9 Oct. 573/4 By comparison *Heart to Heart* seems both shallow and hollow, a two-dimensional manufactured thing for an obvious mass market. **1977** *Broadcast* 7 Nov. 13/1 'Hard Times'..is less a novel than..a strip cartoon with two-dimensional characters.

Hence **two-dimensionality**, the property of being two-dimensional; **two-dimensionally** *adv.*, in, or in terms of, two dimensions; **two-dimensionalness** (*rare*).

1926 H. READ *Eng. Stained Glass* i. 11/1 Two-dimensionality. No attempt is made to put the scene in strict spatial perspective. **1956** *Essays in Criticism* VI. 219 The two-dimensionality of the canvases. **1958** S. SPENDER *Engaged in Writing* 116 Her general two-dimensionalness permitted her to appear different on each side. **1961** WEBSTER, Two-dimensionally. **1968** *Jrnl. Physical Soc. Japan* XXV. 934/1 The computations were made two-dimensionally. **1975** I. STEWART *Concepts Mod. Math.* ii. 22 It is a consequence of the two-dimensionality of the plane that any rigid motion is uniquely specified by what it does to a (non-degenerate) triangle. **1978** *Spectator* (New Canaan High School, Connecticut) 65 The world has become two-dimensionally black and white. **1979** *Jrnl. R. Soc. Arts* July 509/1 The criticisms..that Ruskin saw architecture only two-dimensionally, and that he never seems to have looked at a building structurally, are refuted with ample quotations.

two-edged (-ɛdʒd, *poet.* -ɛdʒɪd), *a.* Having two edges; esp. of a sword, axe, etc., having two cutting edges, one on each side of the blade.

In quot. 1712–14 applied humorously to a pair of scissors.

1526 TINDALE *Heb.* iv. 12 The worde off god is..sharper then eny two edged swearde. **1546** *Lanc. Wills* (Chetham Soc.) II. 27 My greit twoo edged sword and my lesse tow edged sword. **1578** LYTE *Dodoens* IV. xxxi. 489 Turner calleth it..Axeworte, bycause Dioscorides saith the seede is lyke a two edged Axe. **1648** HEXHAM II, *Een twee-snijdigh swaert*, a two-edged sword. **1712–14** POPE *Rape Lock* III. 128 Clarissa drew..A two-edg'd weapon from her shining case. **1776** J. LEE *Introd. Bot.* Explan. Terms, *Anceps*, two-edged, flattened with two opposite sides sharp. **1850** W. IRVING *Mahomet* etc. xxxviii. II. 344 Alashtar..wielded a two-edged sword. **1875** BENNETT & DYER *Sach's Bot.* 410 The..apical cell..of *Isoëtes lacustris* is, according to Hofmeister, two-edged when the stem has two furrows.

b. *fig.* or in figurative allusion.

a **1625** FLETCHER *Hum. Lieutenant* III. iv, She has two-edged eyes; they kill o' both sides. **1661** BOYLE *Style of Script.* (1675) 126, I find all these Topicks..such two-edg'd Weapons, that they are as well applicable to the service of Falshood, as of Truth. **1878** BOSW. SMITH *Carthage* 82 Elephants were found to be a two-edged weapon which might be fatal to the hand which wielded it.

twoer (ˈtuːə(r)). *colloq.* [f. TWO + -ER[1].] Something consisting of or counted as two; in quot. 1889, a hit at cricket for which two runs are or may be obtained.

1887 W. S. CHURCHILL *Let.* 3 May in R. S. Churchill *Winston S. Churchill* (1967) I. Compan. I. iv. 131 We had a game of Cricket this afternoon, I hit a *twoer*, as the expression goes, my first runs this year. **1889** *Boys' Own Paper* 23 Mar. 400/1 If he hits the ball far enough away for a twoer, he must run it. **1899** *N. & Q.* 9th Ser. III. 185/2 The value of the buttons..varied. There was the average unit, then 'twoers', as well as others of increased value. **1899** C. ROOK *Hooligan Nights* iv. 64, I..went froo the till. It wasn't much of a 'aul... I don't fink there was more'n free twoers worf to be nicked. **1970** G. F. NEWMAN *Sir, you Bastard* iii. 98 Sneed flipped the notes without undoing the band. 'A twoer there,' Doleman said.

ˈtwo-faced (-feɪst), *a.*

1. Having two faces: = DOUBLE-FACED 1.

1659 T. PECKE *Parnassi Puerp.* 160 Janus..The Two-fac'd God. **1793** MARTYN *Lang. Bot.* s.v., Two-faced leaves. **1861** J. G. SHEPPARD *Fall of Rome* i. 13 January presents itself under the influence of the 'Two-faced Janus'.

2. *fig.* Deceitful, insincere: = DOUBLE-FACED 2.

a **1619** FLETCHER, etc. *Q. Corinth* III. ii, Who can trust The gentle looks and words of two-faced man? **1720** WELTON *Suffer. Son of God* II. xiv. 364 People, who, in Private..approve of the principles of Religion, but act the Libertine in the Face of the World... These loose and Two-fac'd Christians. **1864** in J. H. Newman *Apol.* v. 429 Two-faced persons, who did not go simply and straightforwardly to work.

Hence **two-facedness**.

1882 in *Jamieson's Sc. Dict.* IV. 647. **1889** TALMAGE *Serm.* in *Voice* (N.Y.) 10 Oct., What subterfuge, what double-dealing, what two-facedness.

twofer (ˈtuːfə(r)). *U.S. colloq.* Also too-, -fah, -for, -fur. [f. TWO + (representation of) FOR *prep.*]

1. A cigar sold at two for a quarter; hence, any cheap cigar.

a **1911** D. G. PHILLIPS *Susan Lenox* (1917) I. xx. 351 He smoked five-cent cigars instead of 'two-furs'. **1922** S. LEWIS *Babbitt* v. 63 'I do like decent cigars—not these Flor de Cabagos you're smoking——' 'That's all right now! That's a good two-for.' **1923** WODEHOUSE *Inimitable Jeeves* xiii. 143, I found him..lying on the bed with his feet on the rail, smoking a toofah. **1943** *Sun* (Baltimore) 3 Feb. 24/6 The latest items on the list of wartime shortages are the 'toofer', the 'nickel cigar' and the '10-center'.

2. a. A coupon that entitles a person to buy two tickets for a specified theatre show for the price of one.

1948 *N.Y. Herald Tribune* 9 Aug. 8/1 Twofers, as they are called in the slang of the trade, entitle the holder to two seats for a given show for the price of one. **1959** P. BULL *I know Face* iii. 56 It was a constant embarrassment to me to watch a nice customer..buy two expensive stalls for 27*s.*, only to be followed by a 'twofer' lady who got the same thing for 13*s.* 6*d.* **1971** *It* 2–16 June 11/3 Me and the missus got twofers for the show. **1982** *Eastern Province* (S. Afr.) *Herald* 5 Aug. 17/2 Twofers are usually available only for near-to-flop shows or those looking tatty after a long run.

b. *transf.*; also *spec.* a Black woman appointed to a post, the appointment being seen as evidence of both racial and sexual equality of opportunity.

1969 *Britannica Bk. of Year* (U.S.) 801/1 *Twofer, specif.*, a blazer with matching trousers. **1977** *Time* 3 Jan. 36/1 By appointing her, Carter got a kind of 'twofer': as a black and as a woman, she is proof that the President-elect is trying to open his Cabinet to both groups. **1978** *N.Y. Times* 29 Mar. A11/2 (Advt.), Another terrific two-for. This sun dress..becomes city-smart when you float the boxy jacket over it. **1979** *Daily Tel.* 2 June 10 Personnel departments [in the United States] are told always to try and hire a 'twofer'. **1982** *Record Business* 11 Jan. 2/1 Ian Miles..had best-sellers with..a Wout Steenhuis twofer and a Harry Secombe-Moira Anderson album of duets.

twofold (ˈtuːfəʊld), *a.*, (*sb.*), *adv.* Forms: α. 2, 5– *Sc.*, twafald, 5 *Sc.* twa faulde, 9 *Sc.* twafauld, (twa-fall). β. 3 twouold; 4 two-folde, 6 two folde, twofoulde, 7 twofolde; 5–6 two fold, 7–9 two-fold, 7– twofold. [app. orig. a refashioning of TWIFOLD, after TWO; in later use perh. independently f. TWO + -FOLD.]

A. *adj.*

†**1.** Double (in *fig.* sense); double-minded, wavering. *Obs.*

c **1175** *Lamb Hom.* 151 Anfald oðer twafald is ech mon... þe twafalde Mon is unstaþelfest on alle his weies.

2. a. Consisting of two folds or layers.

a **1225** *Ancr. R.* 50 þe cloð in ham beo twouold.

b. Folded or bent double. (Cf. B. 1.) *Sc.*

1821 *Blackw. Mag.* Jan. 402/1 My auld auntie, wha's twafauld with the rheumatics.

3. Consisting of two combined; composed of two parts or elements; existing in two relations or manners; of two kinds; double, dual.

a. in abstract or general sense.

1559 W. CUNNINGHAM *Cosmogr. Glasse* 17, I finde a twofoulde difference betwixt a sphere, and a circle. **1610** HOLLAND *Camden's Brit.* (1637) 102 A twofold victorie. **1691** NORRIS *Pract. Disc.* 321 The object of the Divine Will..is Twofold, either the object of his Will Decreeing, or..of his Will Commanding. **1774** GOLDSM. *Nat. Hist.* (1776) I. 399 The earth..seen with its twofold motion; producing, by the one, the change of seasons; and, by the other, the..vicissitudes of day and night. **1875** HELPS *Ess.*, *Self-Discipl.* 19 Man, a creature of twofold nature, body and soul.

b. in concrete sense, of material objects.

1605 SHAKS. *Macb.* IV. i. 121 Some..That two-fold Balles, and trebble Scepters carry. *a* **1721** PRIOR *2nd Hymn of Callimachus* 64 Ewes, that erst brought forth but single Lambs, Now drop'd their Two-fold Burdens. **1794** NELSON in Nicolas *Disp.* (1845) I. 379 Two three-fold blocks, and two two-fold blocks. **1888** *Lady* 25 Oct. 374/3 The two-fold [photograph] screens with..space for panel portraits.

4. Double in amount; twice as great.

1812 CRABBE *Tales* xii. 176 More charming grew the Fair, And seem'd to watch him with a two-fold care. **1873** B. STEWART *Conserv. Force* iii. 49 The double system will now attract the single system with twofold force.

5. Of yarn: Consisting of two strands twisted into one.

1880 *Daily News* 7 Dec. 2/8 Two-fold yarns are rather more in request. **1883** *Ibid.* 22 Oct. 7/1 Two-fold yarns..command improved rates more readily than single wefts. **1894** *Ibid.* 20 Mar. 7/3 The trade in twofold yarns shows some improvement.

b. as *sb.* Also *attrib.*

1884 W. S. B. MCLAREN *Spinning* (ed. 2) 239 Twisting two or more threads together that have already been each made into two-fold. **1888** *Daily News* 25 Sept. 2/5 Transactions in twofolds and singles are still somewhat restricted. **1895** *Ibid.* 3 Feb. 2/5 Twofold spinners are getting more work. **1910** *Encycl. Brit.* VII. 277/1 (*Cotton*), 40*s* mule, water twists and twofolds.

B. *adv.*

1. In two folds; so as to be folded or doubled. Chiefly *Sc.* of persons.

c **1394** *P. Pl. Crede* 516 þe glose is so greit in gladding tales, þat turneþ vp two-folde vnteyned opon trewþe. *c* **1425** WYNTOUN *Cron.* VIII. xxxii. 5595 A stane..has hym ourtane, And twa faulde [*v.r.* twafald] downe can him bere. **1523** FITZHERB. *Husb.* §62 Bynde a clothe two or thre folde vpon his foreheed. **1721** RAMSAY *Ode to Ph——* ix, Before auld age..lay ye twafald o'er a rung. *a* **1802** *Johnie of Breadislee* xviii. in Scott *Min.*, He's laid him twa-fald ower his steed. **1894** 'IAN MACLAREN' *Bonnie Brier Bush, Highl. Mystic* i, He wes bent twa fad; a' doot it's a titch o' rheumatism, or maybe lumbago.

2. To twice the amount, twice as much, doubly.

1526 TINDALE *Matt.* xxiii. 15 Ye make hym two folde more the chylde off hell then ye youre selves are. **1637** GILLESPIE *Eng. Pop Cerem.* II. i. 6 It twofolde more scandalizeth such a one.

Hence **ˈtwofoldly** (also 2 **twafaldeliche**) *adv.*, in a twofold manner, doubly; **ˈtwofoldness**, the quality of being twofold, doubleness, duality. So **twoˈfolded** *ppl. a.* [f. TWO *sb.* + FOLDED], folded in two, folded double.

1887 MORRIS *Odyss.* XII. 361 Wrapping it round *two-folded. *c* **1175** *Lamb. Hom.* 5 Nu ic eou habbe þet godspel iseid anfaldeliche, nu scule ȝe understonden *twafaldeliche þet hit bi-tacnet. **1648** HEXHAM II, *Tweevoudighlick*, Two-foldly or Double. **1827** COLERIDGE in *Lit. Rem.* (1839) IV. 310 The *twofoldness of the Christian Church. **1861** W. BARNES in *Macm. Mag.* June 128 That we should have two legs, or two hands,..this twofoldness of life-forms.

two-foot (ˈtuːfʊt), *a.*

1. †**a.** Having two feet, two-footed (*obs.*). **b.** Performed or executed with both feet (*rare*).

1620 ROWLANDS *Night Raven* 3, I haunt not barnes, for either Mouse or Rat, As doth the searching two-foote flying Cat. **1902** *Munsey's Mag.* XXVI. 477/1 The two foot spin is one of the most sensational movements in figure skating.

2. Measuring two feet; two feet long, wide, or thick. ***two-foot rule***, a measuring rule two feet long. So **two-foot-wide** *a.*

1664 BUTLER *Hud.* II. III. 13 A two-foot Trout. **1679** MOXON *Mech. Exerc.* vii. 129 If there be odd Inches, they measure them with the Two-foot Rule. **1855** J. PHILLIPS *Man. Geol.* 193 Two-foot coal. **1891** C. JAMES *Rom. Rigmarole* 127 Squeezed in between the two-foot-wide pavement and the centre of the roadway..was a row of canvas booths. **1903** *Heart of Heretic* xx. 152 We measure Him [God] by our little two-foot rule.

two-footed (ˈtuːˌfʊtɪd), *a.*

1. a. Having two feet; biped; two-legged; standing on two feet.

c **1374** CHAUCER *Boeth.* v. pr. iv. 128 (Camb. MS.) Man is a reasonable two foted beest. **1495** *Trevisa's Barth. De P.R.* v. liv. (W. de W.) 171 The fete of fowles and of two foted beestes. **1601** HOLLAND *Pliny* I. 305 The Mice and Rats of Ægypt..walke like as if they were two-footed. **1607** [see BIPEDAL *a.* 2]. *a* **1661** HOLYDAY *Juvenal* ix. 170 He neglects me, and now seeks some other Two-footed sturdy asse. **1802** SHAW *Gen. Zool.* III. 311 Two-footed cylindric Lizard. **1839** CARLYLE *Chartism* iv. 125 There is not a horse willing to work but can get food..; a thing this two-footed worker has to seek for. **1864** TENNYSON *Aylmer's F.* 127 He [the dog] rose Twofooted at the limit of his chain.

b. *transf.* Performed by the two feet.

1898 R. F. HORTON *Commandm. Jesus* i. 7 The third step in the two-footed progress.

2. Of a footballer: able to kick equally well with either foot.

1948 *Sporting Mirror* 19 Nov. 6/2 He's a fine two-footed defender, very speedy in recovery and cool under pressure. **1969** *Listener* 3 Apr. 473/3 Arsenal's Jimmy Robertson, naturally two-footed. **1978** *Sunday Express* 19 Mar. 29/5 Robson drafted the inexperienced but talented, two-footed Russell Osman into his depleted defence.

twofor, var. TWOFER.

two-forked (ˈtuːfɔːkt), *a.* Having two divisions or branches like the prongs of a fork; bifurcate; dichotomous. Also *fig.*

1579 FULKE *Heskins' Parl.* 107 This two forked reason. **1617** MORYSON *Itin.* I. 95 Towards the West-side of the City is a large market place twoforked. **1638** FEATLY *Strict. Lyndom.* II. 46 A dilemma or two-forked argument. *c* **1789** *Encycl. Brit.* (ed. 3) III. 440/2 *Caulis dichotomus*, a dichotomous or two-forked stem. **1793** MARTYN *Lang. Bot.* s.v., Two-forked, see *Dichotomous*. [Hence in Webster (1828), and in later Dicts.] **1923** D. H. LAWRENCE *Birds, Beasts & Flowers* 113 He..flickered his two-forked tongue from his lips.

twofur, var. TWOFER.

ˈtwo-hand, *a.* Also 5 two-handes.

1. Requiring both hands to wield or manage: = next, 1.

c **1410** *Master of Game* (MS. Digby 182) xi, Makary had a gret twohande staffe. *a* **1440** *Sir Degrev.* 1643 Two-honde swerde. *c* **1500** *Melusine* xxii. 145 He held a two handes ax. **1630** *R. Johnson's Kingd. & Commw.* 312 Men of large stature..[who] serve onely with the Pike or two-hand-sword. **1807** HOGG *Gilmanscleuch* lvii, His twa-hand sword hang round his neck.

2. Done, or worked, by two persons: = next, 2. †***two-hand battle***, a single combat, a duel (*obs.*).

c **1500** *Arnolde's Chron.* Index (1811) 2 That noo citezen doo twoo hand batayle. **1538** *MS. Acc. St. John's Hosp., Canterb.*, Payd for haftyng off the ij hand saw. **1614** *Ibid.*, Payd for the baryng of a too hand sawe xij d.

†**3.** Leading in two directions (right-hand and left-hand). *Obs. rare*$^{-1}$.

1607 HIERON *Defence* I. 38 At some crosse or two hand way.

ˈtwo-ˈhanded (stress var.), *a.*

1. Wielded with both hands, as a sword, etc. (= prec. 1); involving the use of both hands.

1432–50 tr. *Higden* (Rolls) VII. 243 Tailefer..toke a too-honded swerde, and..did slee oon of Ynglishe men. **1588** *Reg. Privy Council Scot.* IV. 277 With hagbute, bow, speir, or twa-handit swerd. **1637** MILTON *Lycidas* 130 That two-handed engine..Stands ready to smite. **1667** —— *P.L.* VI. 251 With huge two-handed sway Brandisht aloft the horrid edge came down. **1814** SCOTT *Diary* 22 Aug., in *Lockhart*, The effigy of a warrior completely armed..with his hand on his two-handed broadsword. **1837** *Penny Cycl.* VIII. 283/1 This was probably the finger-alphabet from which our present two-handed one was derived. **1874** SWINBURNE *Bothwell* IV. ii, The sword Which was my grandsire's, whose two-handed stroke Did such-like service.

2. Wielded or worked by the hands of two persons, as a saw; engaged in or played by two persons, as a card-game, etc.: = prec. 2.

1657 R. LIGON *Barbadoes* (1673) 41 Cutting it with two-handed Saws. **1680** COTTON *Compl. Gamester* x. 83 Some play at two handed, or three handed whist. **1827** J. WILSON *Noct. Ambr.* Wks. 1855 I. 274 I'm real happy..to think that we're to hae a twa-handed crack. **1853** SIR H. DOUGLAS *Milit. Bridges* vi. (ed. 3) 303 A plank..upon which..two men may stand to..work, conjointly, a heavy two-handed beetle. **1898** *To-Day* 5 Nov. 19/2 The Captain sat down to play two-handed poker with Chris.

3. *colloq.* Big, bulky, strapping. ? *Obs.*

1687 T. BROWN *Saints in Uproar* Wks. 1730 I. 73 A huge two-handed lubber, St. Christopher I think they call him. **1692** tr. *C'tess D'Aunoy's Trav.* iii. (1706) 44 The Hair..being..kept behind their Ears with a great Twohanded [mistranslating Fr. *doublé* 'lined'] Hat. *a* **1700** B. E. *Dict. Cant. Crew*, *Strapping-Lass*, a swinging two-handed Woman. **1749** FIELDING *Tom Jones* IX. iii, This Susan was as two-handed a wench (according to the phrase) as any in the country. **1830** LAMB *Let. to Wordsworth* 22 Jan., [Vulcan] the two-handed skinker.

4. Having two hands.

1847 CARPENTER *Zool.* 132 *Bimana*, or two-handed Mammals. *Ibid.* 137 Man alone is two-handed.

5. Using both hands equally well, ambidextrous; dexterous, handy, efficient.

1861 WHYTE MELVILLE *Good for Nothing* xxvii, A man soon learns to be two-handed in the bush.

6. *U.S. colloq.* Generous, open-handed.

1929 D. RUNYON in *Cosmopolitan* July 57/1 Miss Missouri Martin..puts the blast on her plenty for chasing a two-handed spender..out of the joint. **1933** G. ADE *Let.* 12 Sept. (1973) 173 He was..a two-handed drinker who could not carry his rum because he was too frail and intellectual.

Hence **two-handedly** *adv.*, with or in both hands; **two-handedness**; **two-hander,** (*a*) a two-handed sword; (*b*) *Theatr.*, a play with a cast of two; †**two-handy** *a.* = sense 1.

1927 KIPLING *Verse 1885–1926* 730 *Two-handedly tossing me jewels. **1981** M. KENYON *Zigzag* xxi. 143 Peckover, pickaxe two-handedly poised..stepped towards him. **1891** *Home Missionary* (N.Y.) Jan. 389 A holy *two-handedness. **1888** *Archæologia* LI. 512 The sword..is an exceedingly handsome example of the *two-hander of the sixteenth century. **1976** *Listener* 20 May 648/3 The play was ..a two-hander, finely acted by Maurice Denham and Colette O'Neil. **1981** H. BALDRY *Case for Arts* 9 The ever-diminishing casts of the plays which our theatre directors can afford to present... This is the time of the three-hander and the two-hander. **1648** HEXHAM II, *Een Slach-swaerdt*, a *two-handie Sword.

two-headed (ˈtuːˌhɛdɪd), *a.*

1. Having, or represented with, two heads.

two-headed snake or *worm*, the amphisbæna (AMPHISBÆNA 2), formerly supposed to have two heads, one at each end of the body.

1596 SPENSER *F.Q.* v. x. 10 His two-headed dogge that Orthrus hight. **1596** SHAKS. *Merch. V.* I. i. 50 By two-headed Ianus. **1708** SEWEL II, *Tweehoofdig*, two-headed. **1752** J. HILL *Hist. Anim.* 102 The Amphisbæna..has obtained, among the English, the name of the two-headed worm. **1796** MORSE *Amer. Geog.* I. 221 The two-headed snake. **1867** LATHAM *Black & White* 62 A two-headed iron bolt. **1899** T. NICOLL *Rec. Archæol. & Bible* vi. 193 The two-headed eagle of the Hittites..survives..as the symbol of imperial power in Austria and Russia to-day.

2. *fig.* Having or governed by two chiefs or rulers.

1885 W. WILSON *Congress. Govt.* iv. 220 Doubts as to the ..advantage of a two-headed legislature. **1888** T. W. HIGGINSON *Women & Men* 93 If two business partners can work successfully on the two-headed plan, why [can] not two married persons do it?

two-leaf, *a.* = next, a.

1634 in *Archæologia* XXXV. 199 One two-leaf wyndowe. **1890** *Sale-Catal. Suffield House near Derby*, Deal table.. Two-leaf ditto.

two-leaved (ˈtuːliːvd), *a.* Also 7 -leaf(e)d. Having or consisting of two leaves. **a.** Having two hinged or folding parts, as a door, table, etc. Also *fig.*

1610 GUILLIM *Heraldry* II. i. (1660) 50 The two leaved silver gates. **1611** MIDDLETON & DEKKER *Roaring Girl* II. ii, The two-leav'd tongues of slander or of truth. **1611** COTGR., *Valve*, a foulding, or two-leafed doore, or window. **1626** tr. *Featly's Parallel.* A ij, A two leafed Tablet. *a* **1644** QUARLES *Sol. Recant.* ch. xii, Then shall the Castles two-leafd gates be barr'd. **1847** C. BRONTË *J. Eyre* xii, The great dining-room, whose two-leaved door stood open.

b. Having two foliage-leaves, or two petals or sepals; having leaves growing in pairs.

1688 R. HOLME *Armoury* II. 115/2 Bifoile, or two leafed flower. **1793** MARTYN *Lang. Bot.*, Two-leaved calyx. **1894** J. MUIR *Mount. California* viii. 201 The Two-leaved Pine [*Pinus contorta*], more than any other, is subject to destruction by fire.

c. Of a book: Consisting of two leaves.

1726 AYLIFFE *Parergon* 191 Her Register..was a two-leav'd Book of Record.

two-legged (ˈtuːlɛgd, -ˌlɛgɪd), *a.* Having two legs: usually as an epithet suggestive of a human being having the qualities of the animal named. Also *fig.*

1561 B. GOOGE *Palingenius' Zodiac Life* I. A vj b, What a sort ther be of twolegd Asses clothed In gold and silke and purple. **1575** *Gamm. Gurton* v. ii, Thy neighbours hens yᵘ takest, and playes the two legged fox. **1693** DRYDEN *Juvenal* x. 388 Next to the Raven's Age, the Pylian King Was longest liv'd of any two-legg'd thing. **1719** DE FOE *Crusoe* (1840) I. xix. 348 A kind of two-legged wolves. **1815** SCOTT *Guy Mann.* xlviii, The mate of the two-legged Cerberus. **1858** CARLYLE *Fredk. Gt.* v. v. (1872) II. 97 Countries..infested with a new species of predatory two-legged animals: Prussian recruiters. **1930** W. K. HANCOCK *Australia* i. 28 In the very best wheat country the farmer will keep a flock of sheep, not only to make his economy 'two-legged', but also because sheep are an essential agricultural implement. **1976** *Milton Keynes Express* 16 July 39 Whereas last season the winners and runners-up of each section met in the semi finals, the winner and runner-up of the one league will meet in a two-legged final.

twolf, obs. form of TWELVE.

twoling (ˈtuːlɪŋ). *rare*⁻⁰. [f. TWO + -LING[1] 2.] A twin crystal (*Cent. Dict.*, 1891).

twoll, twolue, obs. ff. TWELVE.

twolthe, obs. f. TWELFTH.

twon, twone, obs. pa. pples. of TWINE *v.*[1]

two natures, *sb. pl. Theol.* The divine and human natures united in the person of Christ. Also (hyphened) *attrib.*

1600, 1651 [see HYPOSTASIS 5]. **1797** *Encycl. Brit.* VII. 43/1 He [*sc.* Eutyches] appeared to allow of two natures, even before the union. **1874** J. H. BLUNT *Dict. Sects, Heresies* 332/2 The Monophysites held that the two Natures were so united, that although the 'One Christ' was partly Human and partly Divine, His two Natures became by their union only one Nature. **1946** E. L. MASCALL *Christ, Christian & Church* iii. 49 In no case is the divine nature seen acting in separation from the human. The two natures are distinct and their union is unimaginably intimate. **1977** D. CUPITT in J. Hick *Myth of God Incarnate* vii. 136 Liddon ..did not see in the full two-natures doctrine any threat to the unity of Christ's person. **1982** *Church Times* 24 Dec. 8/3 The doctrine of the 'two natures' in the one person of Christ ..does not mean that Jesus was in any sense schizophrenic, acting at one moment as man and the next as God.

twoness (ˈtuːnɪs). [f. TWO + -NESS.] The fact or condition of being two; duality, doubleness.

1648 HEXHAM II, *Tweeheydt*, Twonesse, or Dualitie. **1829** JAS. MILL *Hum. Mind* (1869) II. 92 Abstract terms..in place of which, the words oneness, twoness, threeness, might be substituted. **1892** SWEET *N. Eng. Gram.* 49 The singular expresses 'oneness'..The dual expresses 'twoness'. **1908** C. BIGG *Orig. Chr.* xxxii. (1909) 407 The original unity ..is now perceived to be a twoness.

†**twoops.** *Obs.* (*colloq.* or *slang.*) Twopenny ale.

1729 *Dulcinead* 5 Her Health he drinks when o'er his Cups, Which are brimful of Fitzy's Twoops.

'two-part, *a.* Containing, consisting of, having, or involving two parts; composed in two parts, as a piece of music, or for two actors, as a play.

1854 *Cherubini's Counterpoint* 20 It is prohibited in three-part-counterpoint, as in two-part-counterpoint, to make concealed fifths. **1894** S. FISKE *Holiday Stories* (1900) 207 Two-part comediettas.

So **two-parted** *a.*, divided into two parts, bipartite.

1793 MARTYN *Lang. Bot.*, *Two-parted leaf, perianth*,.. divided in two down to the base. **1830** LINDLEY *Nat. Syst. Bot.* 57 Calyx..tubular, with a two-parted limb.

twopence (ˈtʌpəns). Forms: see TWO and PENNY A. 2; also 6–7 **tuppens,** 7–9 **tuppence,** 8–9 *Sc.* **tippence;** and 20 (with reference to decimal coinage) **two pence,** *attrib.* **two-pence.**

Since the introduction of decimal coinage in Britain in 1971 also pronounced (tuː ˈpɛns) when a sum of money is meant (as in senses 1, 2, and 6).

1. A sum of money equal to two pennies.

†*penny of twopence* = sense 2: see PENNY 3.

1477 *Rolls of Parlt.* VI. 183/1 The Grotes, Pens of two Pens, and Pens, of this Reame. **1514** in *Eng. Gilds* (1870) 144 To the beddell of the seid Gilde Tuppens. **1641** *Sc. Acts Chas. I* (1817) V. 510/1 They might sell at tuppens a groatt & Sexpens..They micht sell..the deirest for a tippens. **1772–84** COOK *Voy.* (1790) I. 299 They were accosted by several Indians..and one of them undertook to carry them over..at two-pence per head. **1785** BURNS *Holy Fair* viii, A greedy glowr Black Bonnet throws, An' we maun draw our tippence. **1812** H. & J. SMITH *Rej. Addr., Theatre* 61 Boys who long linger at the gallery-door, With pence twice five —they want but twopence more. **1857** HUGHES *Tom Brown* I. ii, What can you expect for tuppence? **1872** RUSKIN *Fors Clav.* (1896) I. xix. 376 Work that will pay no dividend on their twopences.

2. a. An English silver coin of the value of two pennies: = HALF-GROAT (since 1662 coined only as Maundy money). **b.** A copper coin of this value issued in the reign of George III.

c **1450** *Mankind* 457 in *Macro Plays* 17 He louyth no grotis, nor pens or to-pens. **1597** SHAKS. *2 Hen. IV*, IV. iii. 55 Like gilt two-pences. **1653** WALTON *Angler* xii. 231 A piece of reed..as big about as the compass of a two pence. **1684** E. CHAMBERLAYNE *St. Gt. Brit.* I. (ed. 15) 217 To scatter new-coyned two-pences in the..places where the King passes. **1712** *Mus. Thoresby.* (1713) 361 A very fair Canterbury Twopence [*temp.* Hen. VIII]. **1818** SCOTT *Br. Lamm.* xxxv, A when silver tippences to the poor folk. **1820** —— *Let. to J. Ballantyne* 28 Mar., in *Lockhart*, I care not a bent twopence about their quarrels.

3. a. As type of a very small amount: now esp. in phr. (*not*) *to care twopence.* Also *for twopence*, very easily, with the smallest encouragement.

1691 BAXTER *Repl. Beverley* 2 All our righteousness is not worth two-pence. *a* **1744** BRAMSTON *Art Politicks* 193 He cares not two-pence for the land-tax bill. **1752** FOOTE *Taste* I. (1781) 18 It does not signify Two Pence. **1894** G. W. APPLETON *Co-Respondent* I. 65 He asked me if you really cared twopence for Kate. **1934** R. H. MOTTRAM *Bumphrey's* i. 37 I'm all heavy with that stuff. I could go to sleep for tuppence! *a* **1960** E. M. FORSTER *Maurice* (1973) xxvi. 132 I'd jump out of the window for twopence.

b. *fig.* Applied to a person of very little worth.

1866 SARTORIS *Week in French Country Ho.* (1902) 213 She was a wretched twopence of a woman.

c. *twopence coloured* adj. phr.: orig. with reference to prints of characters for toy theatres that were sold in the early nineteenth century at one penny (1d) for black and white ones and two pennies (2d) for coloured ones; hence, excessively theatrical; cheap and gaudy.

1859, etc. [see *penny plain* adj. s.v. PENNY 12 c]. **1879** R. L. STEVENSON *Trav. with Donkey* 82 If landscapes were sold, like the sheets of characters of my boyhood, one penny plain and twopence coloured, I should go to the length of twopence every day. **1887** *Art Jrnl.* Apr. 105/1 Picturesque melodrama..has given place to every-day drama.. unsusceptible of twopence coloured treatment. **1908** E. TERRY *Story of my Life* x. 243, I never cared much for Henry [Irving]'s Mephistopheles—a two-pence coloured part, any way. **1911** G. K. CHESTERTON *Innocence of Father Brown* xi. 304 It was a twopence coloured sort of incident. **1926** W. DE LA MARE *Connoisseur* 311 My American adventure..is of the 'twopence coloured' variety, rather than the 'penny plain'. **1932** *N. & Q.* 27 Feb. 151/2, I have two very unusual specimens of the twopence coloured. They..have very little brush-work, being decorated in every possible part with foil of different colours. **1948** *Eng. Stud.* I. 95 The Rape of Heraclide is a magnificent specimen of the 'twopence coloured' style. **1966** A. L. COBURN *Autobiogr.* iv. 48 The toy theatre of Stevenson's childhood and mine. A penny plain and twopence coloured. **1968** *Economist* 9 Nov. p. v/1 Almost too much painful detail, which is of no intrinsic interest except by double proof of the horror of the whole; and perhaps slightly twopence-coloured; but brilliantly readable. **1978** *Guardian Weekly* 24 Sept. 20/3 A penny-dreadful dramatisation..that has been bumped up into a tuppence-coloured theatrical event by sheer production values.

4. twopence halfpenny: a sum of money equal to two pennies and a halfpenny. Also *attrib.*

In attrib. use *twopenny-halfpenny* was more usual (see after next word), but in Sc. *twopence-halfpenny* was regular when the precise sum was intended, as in *a twopence-halfpenny stamp.*

16.. *Black Bk. Admiralty* (Rolls) I. 13 Each sea boy shall have twopence halfpenny per diem. **1849** THACKERAY *Pendennis* xl, Twopence-halfpenny for your thoughts. **1890** LE GALLIENNE *Meredith* 155 He does not weave two-pence-halfpenny mysteries.

5. *herb twopence*: name given by Turner to the plant *Lysimachia Nummularia*, also called *two-penny grass* (see next, 3) or MONEYWORT, from its pairs of rounded leaves.

1548 TURNER *Names of Herbes* H ij, Centimorbia otherwise called Nummularia..may be called in englishe Herbe .ij. pence or two penigrasse because it hath two and two leaues standyng together of ech syde of the stalke lyke pence. **1597** GERARDE *Herbal* II. clxxxix. 505 Nummularia.. herbe Two pence, and Two pennie grasse. **1756** WATSON in *Phil. Trans.* XLIX. 815 The Nummularia, Moneywort, or Herb Twopence. **1861** MISS PRATT *Flower. Pl.* IV. 238 Creeping Loosestrife, Moneywort, or Herb-Twopence.

6. *attrib.* (= next, 1, 2) and *Comb.* Cf. TWOPENNY *a.* 1 a.)

1762 STERNE *Tr. Shandy* V. xxxix, 'Tis not two-pence matter. **1827** SCOTT *Two Drovers* ii, Robin..proceeded to light his pipe, and call for a pint of twopenny. 'We have no twopence ale', answered..the landlord. **1889** STEVENSON *Let. to S. Colvin* 2 Dec., If we only had twopenceworth of wind. **1972** J. WILSON *Hide & Seek* ii. 28 Alice found she had a two-pence piece in the pocket of her jeans. **1976** DEAKIN & WILLIS *Johnny go Home* ii. 50 Annie called him from a coin box..using a two-pence piece that had been given her. **1979** M. PAGE *Pilate Plot* vi. 94 Dick Goddard pushed a two-pence coin into the slot.

two-penneth, -pennorth, -penn'orth, colloq. contractions of TWO PENNYWORTH.

twopenny (ˈtʌpənɪ), *a.* and *sb.* Forms: see TWO and PENNY; also 9 **tuppeny;** *Sc.* 8 **tippony, tippanny,** 8–9 **tippenny, tippeny,** 9 **tip'ny.**

A. *adj.* **1. a.** Of the value of, amounting to, or costing twopence.

twopenny faith, the name by which Archbishop Hamilton's tract, *Ane Godlie Exhortatioun*, etc., published in 1559, was popularly known in Scotland.

1532 *Acc. Ld. High Treas. Scot.* VI. 156 Item, for vj scoir tuapenny breid..xxs. **1558–9** KNOX *Hist. Ref.* I. Wks. (1846) I. 291 The Bischoppis..sett furth somewhat in print, which of the People was called 'The Twa-penny Fayth'. **1589** NASHE *Anat. Absurditie* 17 The sum of their diuinitie consists in twopennie Catichismes. **1603** H. CROSSE *Vertues Commw.* (1878) 116 For a two-penny almes he may be throughly taught and made a perfect good scholler. **1625** MASSINGER *New Way* III. ii, Even starv'd for want of two-penny chops. **1705** *Lond. Gaz.* No. 4107/4 A Sable Tippet, with a black Two-peny Ribbon. **1825** JEFFERSON *Autobiog.* Wks. 1859 I. 106 A two-penny duty on tea. **1852** THACKERAY *Esmond* I. ii, His nephew slunk by..to his twopenny ordinary. **1873** RUSKIN *Fors Clav.* (1896) II. xxxviii. 295 People will eat twopenny herrings..when they wouldn't touch half-penny ones.

(*b*) *twopenny piece*, any coin of the value of twopence (cf. TWOPENCE 2); in mod. use (freq. pronounced (ˈtuːˌpɛnɪ)), a bronze coin first issued in Britain with the introduction of decimal currency in 1971.

1607 E. TOPSELL *Foure-Footed Beasts* 358 A round peece of leather, as broad as a two penny peece. **1907** *Westm. Gaz.* 11 Nov. 8/2 The same firm was authorised by George III to manufacture penny and twopenny pieces. **1972** A. ROSS *London Assignment* 65 The old witch outside began to rap on the glass door [of the telephone kiosk] with her tuppenny pieces. **1974** [see PHONE *v.* a]. **1976** *Daily Tel.* 5 Nov. 13/6 There were plastic bags of tuppenny pieces from current juniors who had held raffles in 'break'. **1979** J. SCOTT *Clutch of Vipers* viii. 141 The chunk as the Twopenny piece fell.

b. Involving an outlay of twopence; for the use of or admission to which there is a charge of twopence.

twopenny tube, a popular name for the Central London Railway (see TUBE *sb.* 7 b), on which the fare was originally twopence for any distance.

1599 *Contract building Globe Theatre* in *Henslowe Papers* (1907) 6 The gentlemens roomes and Twoepennie roomes. **1601** B. JONSON *Poetaster* v. i, In taverns, two-penny rooms, tyring houses. **1765** *Chron.* in *Ann. Reg.* 70/1 Letting out two-penny lodgings. **1768** TUCKER *Lt. Nat.* (1834) I. 41 He ..sits among his fellow topers at the two-penny club. **1814** J. BOSWELL in *Songs Justiciary Opera* (1816) 9 Mine's a tippeny eatin house. **1831** D. E. WILLIAMS *Life & Corr. Sir T. Lawrence* II. 23 Sources of petty gains—mere two-penny shows. **1900** [see TUBE *sb.* 7 b]. **1903** MCNEILL *Egregious English* 199 They saw Peter Robinson's and the tuppenny tube.

c. *twopenny ale* (or *beer*), a quality of ale originally sold at twopence per quart; in Scotland, at twopence a Scotch pint (= 3 imperial pints).

1710 *Lond. Gaz.* No. 4668/1 Every Barrel of Twopenny Ale. **1798** W. HUTTON *Autobiog.* 6 My father treated us with a quart of twopenny beer. **1819** SCOTT *Leg. Montrose* iv, A huge barrel of twopenny ale.

d. ***twopenny post***: the London post (1801–1839) for conveyance of letters, etc. at an ordinary charge of twopence each. Also *attrib.*, as ***twopenny postman***, etc.

1797–8 JANE AUSTEN *Sense & Sens.* xxvi, Marianne.. requested the footman..to get that letter conveyed..to the two-penny post. **1838** DICKENS *O. Twist* xxix, To make an appointment by the twopenny post. **1887** T. A. TROLLOPE *What I remember* I. ii. 44 The twopenny post was considered an immense boon to Londoners.

1812 L. HUNT in *Examiner* 25 May 321/1 The two-penny postmen should ride about upon elephants. **1813** MOORE (*title*) Intercepted Letters; or, The Twopenny Post-Bag. **1830** *Parl. Papers* XIII. 46 The twopenny-post riders convey greater weights than the general-post riders.

e. Of iron: Costing twopence per pound.

1858 GREENER *Gunnery* 239 Making Double and Single Guns, with 'Twopenny' or 'Wedgebury Skelp Iron'.

†**f.** ***twopenny rope***: a cheap lodging-house (see quot. 1836). *Obs.*

1836 [see ROPE *sb.*[1] 2 f]. **1850** [see *lie-down* s.v. LIE *sb.*[2] 6].

g. ***twopenny library*** (*Hist.*): a lending library, usu. operated from a shop, from which a book could be borrowed for twopence a week.

1935 W. G. TAYLOR in J. Hampden *Bk. World* 85 That the 'reading public' is growing rapidly seems evident from the growth of the 'twopenny library'. **1942** J. B. PRIESTLEY *Black-Out in Gretley* iii. 23 Twopenny libraries bright with book jackets. **1963** 'R. FINDLATER' *What are Writers Worth?* 7 The 'twopenny libraries' which spread rapidly throughout the country before the war, and have vanished nearly as quickly in the past decade. **1978** S. HODGES *Gollancz* v. 115 The twopenny libraries..had come into their own..in the mid-thirties.

2. *fig.* as a disparaging epithet: Of very little value; paltry, trumpery, trifling, worthless; esp. in phr. ***(not) to care*** (or ***give***) ***a twopenny damn*** (or ***hang***); also *ellipt.*

1560 JEWEL *Corr. Cole* I iv, To make the people thinke that we reade nothyng els but ij. penny doctoures, as ye cal them. **1643** S. MARSHALL *Lett.* 5 Even in a two-peny matter. **1739** CIBBER *Apol.* (1756) I. 243 Twopenny criticks must live as well as eighteenpenny authors. **1848** THACKERAY *Van. Fair* lxi, This woman, with her twopenny gentility. **1897** W. S. MAUGHAM *Liza of Lambeth* xi. 215, I don't care a twopenny 'ang for all them blokes. **1898** R. FRY *Let.* 5 Sept. (1972) I. 172 The date for Bissolo's death, for which I don't care just now a tuppenny damn. **1924** LAWRENCE & SKINNER *Boy in Bush* 58, I don't believe she cares a tuppenny for 'em. **1980** D. K. CAMERON *Willie Gavin* ix. 86 It was rich in its lairds, men who..gave not a tuppeny damn ..for anybody.

b. ***twopenny upright***, a prostitute. *slang.*

1958 L. DURRELL *Balthazar* ii. 41 A little old tart, button-eyed and razor-nosed—a tart of the Waterloo Bridge epoch, a veritable Tuppeny Upright. **1978** *Maledicta* II. 258 At the turn of the century, an Iowa woman was awarded $200 for being called a 'whore', while in England, at about the same time, a woman was denied any award for being called a 'two-penny upright'.

†**3.** ***twopenny grass***, Herb twopence (see prec. 5).

1548, 1597 [see TWOPENCE 5]. **1578** LYTE *Dodoens* I. liv. 78 This herbe is now called..in English..two penny grasse.

†**4.** Applied to a ward in a prison. (The allusion is obscure.) *Obs. rare*[−1].

1605 CHAPMAN, etc. *Eastward Hoe* v. i. G iv b, I never knew..Prisoners..more deuout. They will sit you vp all night singing of Psalmes,..onely, Securitie sings a note too high, sometimes, because hee lyes i' the Two-penny ward, farre off, and cannot take his tune.

B. *sb.* (ellipt. use of the adj.)

1. a. Short for *twopenny ale*: see 1 c above.

1711 RAMSAY *On Maggy Johnstoun* i, To braw tippony bid adieu. **1729** *Dulcinead* 5 *note*, The Old Swan in the Butcher-Row, noted for good Twopenny. **1762** BP. FORBES *Jrnl.* (1886) 181 To drink Tippanny and Whiskie. **1815** SCOTT *Guy M.* vi, The gossip over the good twopenny in every alehouse. **1858** M. PORTEOUS *Souter Johnny* 13 To appease their 'lowin' drouth' either with the Smith's 'tippeny' or the Landlord's 'strong drink'.

b. Short for *twopenny post* or *letter*: see 1 d above.

1818 KEATS *Let.* Oct. (1931) I. 263 Haslam..has taken all the Letters except this sheet, which I shall send him by the Twopenny. **1832** DICKENS *Let.* ? Aug. (1965) I. 9 The place has no other name, but a twopenny directed as above will no doubt find us.

2. A twopenny piece (= TWOPENCE 2), or the sum of twopence.

1736 DRAKE *Eboracum* I. vi. 189 Pennyes or two pennyes, halfpennyes or farthings.

3. A jocular name for a child.

1844 MARY HOWITT *My Own Story* viii, 'Well, little Twopenny'... I..did not like to be called 'little Twopenny'.

4. *slang.* The head. [See quot. 1931.]

1859 in HOTTEN *Dict. Slang.* **1889** W. S. GILBERT *Gondoliers* II. 34 A Lord High Archbishop might tell a Lord High Chancellor to tuck in his tuppenny, but certainly not a cook. **1906** GALSWORTHY *Man of Property* III. iv. 321 Fast after him walked George. If the fellow meant to put his 'twopenny' under a bus, he would stop it if he could! **1928** C. E. MONTAGUE *Action* 150 'Into it, Jemmy', I yelled. 'Into the sewer and tuck in your tuppenny.' **1931** 'G. ORWELL' *Coll. Essays* (1968) I. 71 The hop-pickers..also used the abbreviated rhyming slang, e.g. 'Use your twopenny' for 'Use your head'. This is arrived at like this: head, loaf of bread, loaf, twopenny loaf, twopenny.

So **twopenny-halfpenny** (ˌtʌpənɪˈheɪpənɪ) *a.*, of the value of twopence-halfpenny; usually *fig.* as an epithet of disparagement (cf. A. 2 above).

1809 SOUTHEY in Robberds *Mem. W. Taylor* (1843) II. 268 Some little dirty twopenny-halfpenny piece of roguery. **1827** LYTTON *Pelham* II. xii, He..filched a twopenny-halfpenny gilt-chain out of..the pawnbroker's window. **1872** H. KINGSLEY *Hornby Mills* I. 30 They had lost a law-suit, a twopenny-halfpenny squabble about a trespass. *Mod.* A twopenny-halfpenny stamp.

two pennyworth (ˌtuːˈpɛnɪwəθ), contr. **twopenneth, -penn'orth, -pennorth** (-ˈpɛnəθ). As much as is worth or costs twopence. Freq. *fig.*, a small or contemptible amount. See PENNYWORTH.

1851 H. MAYHEW *London Labour* I. 75/2 Two penn'orth for a whet. **1865** 'L. CARROLL' *Alice's Adv. Wonderland* x. 160 Who would not give all else for two p [rhyme with 'soup'] ennyworth only of beautiful Soup? **1870** *Punch* 5 Nov. 194/1, I walked down the street with just two-penn'orth of swagger on. **1896** G. B. SHAW *Let.* 5 Dec. in *Ellen Terry & Shaw* (1931) 134 You thought two pennorth of flattery all that the occasion demanded. **1924** WODEHOUSE *Leave it to Psmith* vi. 90 Within reason—and if undetected —I see no objection to two-pennorth of crime. **1965** G. MELLY *Owning Up* ix. 105 After it [*sc.* the band] broke up I used to go along every other Tuesday to 'The Three Brewers'..and put in what Mick would call 'my two penn'orth'. **1979** *SLR Camera* Mar. 16/1 No meter, only years of experience and twopenneth of glass.

two-pile (ˈtuːpaɪl), *a.* Applied to velvet in which the loops of the pile-warp are formed by two threads, producing a pile of double thickness: see PILE *sb.*[5] 2, and cf. THREE-PILE. Also **two-piled** *a.* (in quot. *fig.*: cf. THREE-PILED 2).

1611 COTGR. s.v. *Poil*, *Velours à deux poils*, two-pile Veluet. **1678** DRYDEN *Limberham* I. i, Then she's a two-pil'd Punk, a Punk of two Descents.

two-ˈpipe, *a.* **a.** Applied to a system of hot-water heating in which a flow pipe supplies the radiators and a separate return pipe receives water from them.

1897 F. DYE *Hood's Pract. Treat. Warming Buildings* (ed. 3) xviii. 328 The arrangement of pipes is on the ordinary two-pipe principle. A flow and return is carried in different directions almost from a central point. **1970** [see ONE-PIPE *a.* a].

b. Applied to a system of plumbing in which separate waste-pipes and soil-pipes are employed.

1946 E. MOLLOY *Plumbing & Gas-Fitting* x. 203 The 'dual' or 'two-pipe' system, in which the removal of excretal matters..is effected by a pipe connected direct to the drain, and the removal of waste water..effected by a second pipe ..discharging..over or into a properly trapped gully. **1972** T. A. TOMPSON *Guide Sanitary Engin. Services* vii. 226 The two-pipe system of sanitation is rarely used today and has been largely replaced by a more economic design.

twos (tuːz), *v. U.S. colloq.* [f. TWO sb.] *intr.* To keep company with a person of the opposite sex. Hence **ˈtwosing** *vbl. sb.*

1920 S. LEWIS *Main Street* 2 She played tennis,..went 'twosing', and joined half a dozen societies for the practice of the arts. **1924** *Dialect Notes* V. 291 *Twosing*,..going in couples. **1940** W. FAULKNER *Hamlet* II. ii. 119 They chose one another monotonously in the twosing games.

two-sided (ˈtuːˈsaɪdɪd: stress var.), *a.* Having two sides, bilateral; *fig.* having two parts or aspects. Hence **two-ˈsidedness**.

1863 TYNDALL *Heat* xv. §755 (1870) 522 A kind of two-sidedness. **1869** —— *Notes Lect. Light* iii. (1873) 116 The two-sidedness of that [polarized] light, in contrast to the all-sidedness of ordinary light. **1884** BOWER & SCOTT *De Bary's Phaner.* 409 To the second type belong..flat horizontal leaves... The chlorophyll-parenchyma..is severed into two different layers, each of which corresponds to one surface of the leaf. It may accordingly be termed the two-sided, the bifacial type. **1896** MRS. CAFFYN *Quaker Grandmother* 192 It's..in this case a two-sided custom.

twosome (ˈtuːsəm), *sb.* and *a.* Orig. *Sc.* (4–6 twasum, 9 twasome). [f. TWO + -SOME. Cf. WFris. *twaresom, -sum.*]

A. *sb.* **1.** Two persons together; two in company; a pair of lovers.

c **1375** *Sc. Leg. Saints* l. (*Katerine*) 691 Full Ioyfull þane þire twasum war. **1489** *Barbour's Bruce* x. 19 Twasum samyn mycht nocht rid. *a* **1578** LINDESAY (Pitscottie) *Chron. Scot.* (S.T.S.) I. 276 Thair was nane left onslaine bot himselff his brother and twasum with thame. *a* **1802** *Auld Maitland* liii. in Scott *Minstr. Scott. Bord.* (1869) 157 The twa-some they hae slayne the ane. **1816** SCOTT *Bl. Dwarf* viii, The rest disperse by twasome and threesome. *c* **1870** *Jethart Worthies* (ed. 3) 58 The twosome kept the secret for a season or two. **1893** CROCKETT *Stickit Minister* x. 120 When the twasome had been haein' denner thegither. **1926** [see FOURSOME B. *sb.* 2]. **1945** L. SHELLY *Jive Talk Dict.* 19/2 *Twosome*,..lovers. **1959** *Manch. Guardian* 12 Aug. 6/2 For the leaders of the nations..the rule is two by two. What is one to think of these twosomes? **1972** *Guardian* 4 Dec. 12/1 Government in Australia and New Zealand has become a socialist twosome. **1973** L. SNELLING *Heresy* I. i. 8 Shockley and..Rosamund became a definite twosome in Rome. **1978** J. IRVING *World according to Garp* xii. 232 Along came another Land Rover, as if they were a separated twosome from a column of an army on the move. **1982** H. ENGEL *Ransom Game* xvii. 101 Eddie Milano..used to spend a lot on her. They didn't keep house..—there's a Mrs. Milano out in Fort Erie, I think—but they were known as a twosome in the joints.

2. A game, dance, etc. for two persons.

1911 in *Conc. Oxf. Dict.* **1977** *Washington Post* 3 Sept. D7/4 Irwin and Weiskopf..had to roll in 25-foot birdie putts at the 18th in the last twosome of the day. **1983** *Ibid.* 6 Nov. C2/1 The [golf] competition..also includes two some matches.

B. *adj.* Performed by two together.

1825 JAMIESON, *Twasum* is still used to denote a dance, in which two persons are engaged; *a twasome dance*, i.e., a strathspey. **1830** GALT *Lawrie T.* VI. i, Whisking round and round the room to a two-some reel.

ˈtwo-stroke, *a.* (and *sb.*) [STROKE *sb.*[1] 12 c.] Working mechanically by means of a succession of reciprocal movements, in and out or up and down; applied *esp.* to (vehicles having) internal-combustion engines in which the power cycle is completed in one upward and one downward stroke of a piston. Also as *sb.*, a two-stroke engine or vehicle.

1855 BAIN *Senses & Int.* I. ii. §21. (1864) 59 The two-stroke movement of the lungs. **1900** *Engineering Mag.* XIX. 788/1 Two-Stroke Oil Engines. **1902** P. N. HASLUCK *Automobile* vi. 113 Motors of the four-stroke cycle consume less fuel than motors of the two-stroke cycle. **1936** *Economist* 2 May 234/1 In a two-stroke engine, each cylinder gives an impulse at every revolution of the crankshaft. **1963** L. DEIGHTON *Horse under Water* xiv. 59 Fernie propped his two-stroke against the baker's shop. **1972** J. MCCLURE *Caterpillar Cop* ii. 19 The lights pulsed to the quick beat of the two-stroke. **1975** D. MALOUF *Johnno* x. 109 All one scorching summer I blazed from suburb to suburb on a Fanny Barnet two-stroke. **1982** *Sunday Tel.* 1 Aug. 6/1 It [*sc.* a free-wheel device] was..also used by Saab, mainly on its two-stroke models.

twot: see TWAT.

ˈtwo-time, *a. slang* (orig. *U.S.*). **1.** [f. *two times* adv. phr. s.v. TWO B. 1 d.] Characterized by something that has happened or been done twice; ***two-time loser***: see LOSER 4.

1897 R. M. JOHNSTON *Middle Georgia* 113 Is a widder, even a two-time widder, got nothin' else to do but..go about grievin' for them that's gone? **1960** *Guardian* 14 July 9/1 A threat to unseat one man..for his two-time allegiance to Eisenhower. **1972** *Publisher's Weekly* 3 Jan. 9 This book by a two-time ABC Master Tournament winner. **1979** A. V. BADGLEY *Rembrandt Decisions* (1980) xv. 212 Maybe they won't go [*sc.* be stolen] any more... Maybe it was just a two-time snatch.

2. [f. the vb.] Double-crossing, two-timing.

1937 E. S. GARDNER *Case of Dangerous Dowager* xii. 231 You think I'm a two-time, chiseling crook.

ˈtwo-time, *v. slang* (orig. *U.S.*). *trans.* To deceive (esp. a person to whom one owes loyalty); to be unfaithful to (a spouse or lover); to double-cross. Also *absol.* or *intr.*

1924 J. EDWARDS in P. Oliver *Screening Blues* (1968) ii. 64 She'll two-time you like she double-crossed me. **1926** E. HEMINGWAY *Sun also Rises* I. vii. 66 The drummer shouted: 'You can't two time ——'. **1937** WODEHOUSE *Summer Moonshine* (1938) xxiv. 287, I can tell you it pretty near broke me up when I found you were two-timing me that way. Letting another guy send you jewellery. **1959** 'M. M. KAYE' *House of Shade* v. 63 You can't go two-timing the police and skipping out of the country on a stolen passport. **1959** M. RENAULT *Charioteer* vi. 117 In return you've done nothing but two-time me. **1975** *Time Out* 10 Jan. 65/2 Do all attractive slim girls think it clever to lie and two-time? **1981** *Sunday Times* 8 Mar. 8/2 Judith Exner..two-timed the late President John Kennedy with a leader of organised crime.

Hence **two-timing** *vbl. sb.* and *ppl. a.*; also **two-timer**, one who double-crosses or is unfaithful.

1927 K. NICHOLSON *Barker* I. ii. 53 You dirty two-timer, you can't get away with that. **1927** 'C. WOOLRICH' *Children of Ritz* viii. 149 Two-timing was what they called that, when a wife went out in other company. **1927** *Columbia Record Catal.* 205/2 My two-timing papa. **1935** *Discovery* Nov. 346/2 His criticism of the hypocritical quakers and 'two-timing' politicians..is too strong. **1942** *Daily Mirror* (N.Y.) 7 Aug. 5/4 The girl had a gun..and told McNaughton: 'You're a two-timer and no good... I'm going to kill you.' **1959** N. MARSH *False Scent* (1960) i. 36 You little, two-timing, double-crossing, dirty rat. **1974** G. JENKINS *Bridge of Magpies* xii. 182 I'd written him off as a two-timer who'd run away to save his own skin. **1982** N. PAINTING *Reluctant Archer* iii. 36 Goneril's two-timing of her worthy but dull husband. **1984** *Listener* 26 Jan. 31/3 Rogers plays a chorus girl out to make a show business reputation by confessing to the murder of her two-timing lover.

twound, pa. t. and pple. of TWIND *v. Obs.*

ˈtwo-up, *sb.* and *adv.* (*a.*) [UP *adv.*[2]] **A.** *sb.*

1. *Austral.* and *N.Z.* A gambling game played by tossing two coins, bets being laid on the showing of two heads or two tails.

1898 *Bulletin* (Sydney) 3 Sept. 32 At 'loo he'd lately scooped the pool; He'd simply smashed the two-up school. **1898** [see KIP *sb.*[6]]. **1911** L. STONE *Jonah* vi. 213 He marked pak-a-pu tickets, took the kip at two-up, and staked his last shilling more readily than the first. **1916** G. THORNTON *Wowser* viii. 108 Forty young men..were..playing that favourite but not intellectual game of chance, 'two-up'. **1936** 'R. HYDE' *Passport to Hell* viii. 137 Two dozen mounted police charged the two-up schools, involving a heavy loss of stakes as the men scattered. **1948** V. PALMER *Golconda* iv. 27 A fellow of some power, a fellow who had been used to handling the rough crowds of two-up rings. **1952** J. CLEARY *Sundowners* 229 Who's for a game of two-up? Got just the place out the back? **1960** P. WILSON in C. K. Stead *N.Z. Short Stories* (1966) 129 Some had a two-up school going on in the corner. **1965** B. WANNAN *Fair Go, Spinner* IV. 192 The landlord of the pub, who ran the two-up school, roared out to them, 'Stay where you are, around the ring, but put your dough outa sight!' **1980** *Courier-Mail* (Brisbane) 19 June 3/4 Two-up is banned in Queensland.

1982 G. Greer in *Observer* 8 Aug. 21/3 Two-up is Australia's very own way of parting a fool and his money.

2. two-up (and) two-down, a house with two reception rooms downstairs and two bedrooms upstairs. Also *attrib.* or as *adj. phr.* So ***two-up-and-two-downer***.

1958 *Listener* 7 Aug. 212/1 The microphone popped in and out of the two-up-and-two-downers. **1962** *Radio Times* 2 Aug. 37/2 Recalling such local institutions [in Liverpool] as 'the two-up, two-downs'. **1970** J. Sangster *Touchfeather, Too* v. 125 A smart little two up and two down somewhere in the suburbs. **1973** *Times* 18 May 4/5 Long, straight terraces of miners' cottages, typically two up, two down. **1978** *Times* 18 May 18/4, I am a poor cotton town boy who grew up in a two-up two-down. **1978** M. Kenyon *Deep Pocket* vi. 71 The two-up, two-down brick and dinginess of Ensign Terrace.

B. *adv.* Two at a time, two together.

1926 [see double-bank *v.* 2]. **1967** Cox & Grose *Organization & Handling Bibl. Rec. by Computer* II. 25 Master output for photo-litho reproduction 'two-up'.

two-'valued, *a.* Chiefly *Logic.* Able to take one or other of only two values; characterized by the usual two truth-values, i.e. truth and falsity.

1918 C. I. Lewis *Survey Symbolic Logic* iv. 222 The first procedure..interprets the elements of this system as propositions, and adds to it a postulate which holds for propositions but not for logical classes. The result is what has been called the 'Two-valued Algebra'. **1933** *Mind* XLII. 269, I attempt to show that there are fourteen different meanings of implication in a two-valued logic. **1946** *Nature* 14 Sept. 357/1 Ordinary symbolic logic.. represents two-valued logic. **1965** N. Chomsky *Aspects Theory Syntax* 232 We can regard..number [in German grammar] as a two-valued dimension. **1970** O. Dopping *Computers & Data Processing* i. 26 All logical connections between two-valued variables can be expressed by means of the three functions not, and, and or.

two-way, *a.* and *sb.*

Hexham (1648) renders Du. *twee-wegh* by 'a Two-way, or a double way'.

A. *adj.* **1. a.** Having, or connected with, two ways, roads, or channels; situated where two ways meet.

two-way cock, one with two outlets, which may act together or alternatively.

1571 Golding *Calvin on Ps.* xxv. 12 We stand as it were in a twowayleete, in every of our dooings, we hang in doubt, and are at our wittes end. **1618** Bolton *Florus* I. ix. 36 Being situated in the middest betweene Latium and Tuscanie, as it were in a two-way-leet. **1844** Stephens *Bk. Farm* II. 209 The gauge-cock, of which there are usually two, but sometimes one, a two-way cock.

b. Of a plug or adaptor: able to accommodate two plugs at the same time.

1923 *T. Eaton & Co. Catal.* Spring & Summer 357 Two-way socket plug. **1977** *Times* 24 Sept. 22/2 You can use two or three-way adaptors..but do be careful not to overload your current supply.

c. Of a loudspeaker: having two separate drive units for different frequency ranges.

1950 *Audio Engin.* Aug. 15/2 Many loudspeakers are two-way: that is, the frequency range is divided and each portion is handled by separate radiating systems. **1960** [see three-way *a.* b]. **1978** *Detroit Free Press* 16 Apr. 18A/1 (Advt.), Two-way bass reflex speaker system. 8-in. woofer, 3-in. tweeter.

2. Extending in two directions or dimensions, or having two modes of variation. (In quot. 1894 coinciding with sense 1.) ***two-way stretch*** attrib. phr., designed to stretch in both length and width; also *ellipt.* such an elastic corset.

1891 *Cent. Dict.* s.v., A surface is a two-way spread. **1894** Cayley *Math. Papers* XIII. 507 The link may rotate in either direction..that is, *B* may move from B_1 along *b* in either of the two opposite senses, say B_1 is a 'two-way point'. **1932** [see girdle *sb.*[1] 1 d]. **1959** *News Chron.* 19 Aug. 3/8 A girdle of Ellen Terry's—'I mean a sash, not a two-way stretch.' **1964** *Observer* 22 Mar. 3/1 Mr Clutson invented the two-way stretch elastic. **1977** *Summit* (Austin Reed, Ltd.) Autumn 44 Men's two-way stretch riding breeches from £18.

3. *Electr.* Of a switch, wiring, etc.: that enables a light or other device to be switched on or off at either of two points.

1893 W. P. Maycock *Electric Lighting & Power Distribution* III. xv. 382 Fig. 240 shows a double-pole, 2-way switch, which would be connected in a parallel circuit in the manner illustrated. **1903** *Daily Rec. & Mail* 15 Dec. 4 As a burglar may be driven out of the house by judicious handling of a two-way switch. **1933** D. L. Sayers *Murder must Advertise* vii. 113 The hall-light..was fitted with two-way wiring. **1960** *Practical Wireless* XXXVI. 395/1 A two-way switch is provided so that C9 may be connected to either.

4. a. Involving or permitting movement or communication in each of two opposite directions; (of a radio) capable of both transmitting and receiving.

1922 *Encycl. Brit.* XXXII. 1027/2 A problem of practical importance is that of two-way radiotelephony enabling two communications to speak and hear simultaneously. **1927** *Glasgow Herald* 16 Apr. 7 The purpose..is to strengthen the direct connection between Great Britain and the Middle Western group of American States by increasing the two-way tonnage exchange clearing through the Virginian ports. **1938** *Radio Times* 1 July 6/3 A two-way broadcast arranged by the BBC and the Columbia Broadcasting System of America. **1957** L. F. R. Williams *State of Israel* viii. 144 There is a growing two-way traffic in literature between Israel and other countries. **1967** 'R. Stark' *Damsel* (1968) II. 47 Eight lanes of two-way traffic were flanked by broad swaths of green grass. **1971** A. Price *Alamut Ambush* x. 127 He was fixing up the two-way speaker in the porch..so that I could answer the door from here. **1976** L. Deighton *Twinkle, twinkle, Little Spy* xxi. 207 Has he got a two-way radio in the car? **1981** R. Hayman *K* xii. 156 A solitude which was unbroken by the two-way traffic in fantasies that went on in his correspondence.

b. Occurring or existing in two directions; reciprocal; ***two-way street*** (*fig.*), a situation of mutual action; something that works both ways.

1950 J. Jenks *From Ground Up* ii. 17 The agri-cultural relationship is, like all vital relationships, two-way. **1951** *Sun* (Baltimore) 14 Dec. 5/6 'An amendment..provided that if any company..gave so much as a cigar to a Government employé, the contract should be cancelled... Do you think that should be made stronger?'.. 'Yes, it is a two-way street.' **1959** *Times* 19 Sept. 6/3 In sharp contrast with other days this week the market was more 'two-way'—that is, there was more buying to offset the selling. **1968** H. Waugh *Con Game* xi. 101 'Our aim in this racket is to use you.' 'I prefer to think of it as a two-way street.' **1969** T. F. Torrance *Theol. Sci.* ii. 67 The relation between God and the creature is a two-way relation. **1975** *Language for Life* (Dept. Educ. & Sci.) xiv. 214 Some will have had very little sustained two-way conversation in the home. **1975** *Times Lit. Suppl.* 21 Nov. 1392/5 Tolerance..was a two-way street: if the Germans were to learn to live with the Jews, so too must the Jews learn to live with the Germans. **1982** *Times* 12 Jan. 12/3 The jobbers..encountered a fair amount of two-way business.

c. *two-way mirror*, a mirror which lets through enough light for an observer at the back to see through it, without being seen from the front.

1967 J. Gardner *Madrigal* i. 3 They directed total concentration through the sighting side of a two-way mirror. **1974** *Times* 23 Jan. 2/5 Everyone laughed at a show business party when looking through a two-way mirror at couples having sexual intercourse. **1982** R. Hill *Who guards a Prince* I. viii. 57 Locking doors was an empty gesture in these days of two-way mirrors.

B. *sb.* A two-way radio.

1963 'W. Haggard' *High Wire* v. 54 There's an operator with a two-way somewhere near the junction. I'm picking up his message. **1974** V. Brome *Day of Destruction* v. 51 We've just received a message over the two-way to say he's stuck..in the middle of a swamp.

'two-year-old, *a.* and *sb.*

A. *adj.* Of the age of two years. Chiefly of animals, *esp.* colts.

1601 in *T. Pont's Topogr. Acc. Cunningham* (Maitland Cl.) 180 Item, ane twa ȝeir auld bull. *c* **1686** *Depred. Clan Campbell* (1816) 31 [Three] tuo year old stots. **1805** R. W. Dickson *Pract. Agric.* II. 1176 Young horses, as two-year old colts. **1835** Jekyll *Corr.* (1894) 338 The two-year-old person on the throne of Spain. **1838** *Penny Cycl.* XII. 307/2 A three-year-old colt has his form and energies much more developed than a two-year-old one.

B. *sb.* **a.** An animal (*esp.* a colt) or child of two years of age. Also *attrib.*

1594-5 *Durham Wills* (Surtees) II. 254, iiij kyne and their calves, and fowre two-yere oldes. *a* **1600** in *T. Pont's Topogr. Acc. Cunningham* (Maitland Cl.) 178 Item, xiiij ȝoing beystis,..four twa ȝeir auldis and five ane ȝeir auld. *c* **1686** *Depred. Clan Campbell* (1816) 57 Nyne great coues, 2 tuo year olds. **1831** Youatt *Horse* viii. 141 Is it possible to give this mouth to an early two-year-old? **1856** H. H. Dixon *Post & Paddock* iii. 56 Two-year-old racing lays the seeds of infirmity. *Ibid.* iii. 79 Very few two-year-olds were then trained. **1895** P. Hemingway *Out of Egypt* i. iv. 46 The two-year-old [child] regarded him wonderingly.

b. As the type of a youthful and energetic person.

1912 *Punch* 19 June 470/1 Feeling as he did like a two-year-old, he was convinced that an immeasurable advantage to the country would be gained by placing the ballot in the hands of babies. **1928** Galsworthy *Swan Song* III. xvi. 342 Mr. Forsyte was a proper wonder—went at it like a two-year old. **1936** [see stinker 6 c].

twrn(e, twrss, obs. Sc. ff. turn, truss.

twussle, Sc. var. twistle.

†**twy**, *v.* *Obs. rare.* (Meaning uncertain.)

A ME. survival of OE. *twīȝan*, northern var. of *twēoȝan*, *twēon*, to doubt, hesitate, would suit the first passage, but not the second, unless a negative has been omitted. The sense of 'turn' would be appropriate in both passages.

c **1400** *Destr. Troy* 6360 The xij vnthwyuond, þat twyet not in fight Was..mightfull Henex. *Ibid.* 6378 With xxij vnthwyuond twyet to filde Dyomede, the derfe kyng.

twy, obs. f. tway, two; var. twie *Obs.*, twice.

twy-: see twi-.

twyblade, obs. f. twayblade.

twych, obs. Sc. f. touch.

twych, -e, etc., obs. ff. twitch.

twychell, obs. f. twitchel[1].

twychen: see note to twitchel[1].

twye, var. twie *Obs.*, twice.

†**'twyeling.** *Obs. rare.* (Meaning uncertain.)

(Perh. an error for *wyeling*, var. of *wiȝeling*, *-ung*, OE. *wiȝelung* sorcery, witchcraft.)

c **1275** *Duty of Christians* i. in *O.E. Misc.* 141 Crist..yeue vs þat we moten fleo euer suneȝynge And þene feond and al his gleo and al his twyelinge.

twyer, -ere, var. tuyere.

twyes, obs. form of twice.

†**twyfyl.** *Obs. rare.* (Meaning uncertain.)

c **1460** *Towneley Myst.* xxx. 324 And nell with hir nyfyls of crisp and of sylke, Tent welle youre twyfyls, youre nek abowte as mylke.

twyght, twyȝt, -e, obs. pa. t. and pple. of twitch *v.*[1]

twyis, -iss, obs. ff. twice.

twyk, obs. f. twick.

twyle, twyll, etc.: see twill, etc.

twylt, var. twilt (obs. and dial. form of quilt *sb.*[1], etc.).

twyn, obs. f. 'tween, twin.

twynch, -e, twyncle, obs. ff. twinge, twinkle.

twyne, twynn(e, obs. ff. twin.

†**twynrys.** *Obs. rare*$^{-1}$. (Form and meaning doubtful.)

1513 Douglas *Æneid* xii. vii. 55 (1553) Wyth his twynrys [*ed. Small* wynris] and grippand turkas sle, To thrist the hede and draw furth pressis he.

†**twynt.** *Obs. rare.* Also **twynte.** [a. MDu. *twint* in similar use.] In negative expressions: a jot, a particle.

1399 Langl. *Rich. Redeles* iii. 81 Thus lafte þey þe leder þat hem wrong ladde, And tymed no twynte, but tolled her cornes. **14..** *Beryn* 433 So he þat payd for all in feer, [ne] hadde nat a twynt.

twynt(t)er, obs. ff. twinter.

twyrle, obs. f. twirl.

twys, twyse, twyss, obs. ff. twice.

Twysday, obs. f. Tuesday.

twysker, twysle, var. tuskar, twisel *v.* *Obs.*

twyte, var. thwite, to cut; obs. f. twit; obs. pa. t. and pple. of twitch *v.*[1]

twyter, obs. f. twitter *v.*[1]

twyvel, obs. f. twibill.

†**twyvete.** *Obs. rare.* Also **twyfet.** App. variant of twibit (cf. *twyvel*, var. twibill).

c **1500** *Debate Carpenter's Tools* 145 in Hazl. *E.P.P.* I. 84 ȝe, ȝe, sayd the twyvete, Thryft I trow be fro your fette. *Ibid.* 157 Then be-spake the polyff,..How, ser twyfet, me thinke ȝou grevyd.

twyys, obs. f. twice.

ty, obs. form of tie.

-ty, *suffix*[1], denoting quality or condition, representing ME. *-tie*, *-tee*, *-te* (early ME. *-teð*), from OF. *-te* (mod.F. *-té*), earlier *-tet* (*-ted*):—L. *-itātem*, nom. *-itās*. Such Latin types as *bonitātem*, *feritātem*, were in OF. normally reduced to two syllables (*bontet*, *fertet*) by elision of the *-i-* between the two stresses, so that *-tet*, later *-te*, became the regular form of the suffix. The final dental still appears in some early adoptions in ME., as *plenteð*, *plenteth* plenty (*c* 1250, in use till *c* 1600), and is characteristic of the Scottish forms *bountith*, *daintith*, and *poortith* (q.v.). The reduced form *-te*, however, is found in words recorded from shortly before or after 1200, such as *bonte* bounty, *cruelte* cruelty, *deboneret* debonairness, *deinte* dainty (sb.), *plente* plenty, *poverte* poverty, *purte* purity, and *vilte* vileness. Among others which appear somewhat later are *certeynte* certainty, *Cristente* Christenty, *freelte* frailty, *novelte* novelty, and *sotelte* subtlety. Varying forms of the stem are found in the words now or formerly represented by *beauty*, *fealty*, *lealty*, †*lewty*, *loyalty*, †*realty*, †*rialty*, and *royalty*. From the types *lealte*, *realte*, the ending *-alte* (mod.F. *-auté*) was in OF. extended to formations from different stems, and many words of this form (ultimately written with *-alty*) established themselves in English, as *admiralty*, *casualty*, *commonalty*, †*generalty*, *mayoralty*, †*principalty*, †*regalty*, *severalty*, *specialty*, *spiritualty*, *temporalty*. Most of these date from the 14th or early 15th century; *penalty* appears to be of later introduction (1512). An obsolete type of formation is exhibited by *curiouste*, *hid(e)ouste*, and *joyouste*. In OF. certain analogies led to the frequent substitution of *-ete* for *-te*, but this form of the suffix is only occasionally adopted in English, as in the obsolete *noblete*, *purete*, and *simplete*; the early *sauvete* is now represented by *safety*. Under Latin influence many words in

OF. also appear with *-ite* (mod.F. *-ité*) in place of *-(e)te*; hence English forms in -ITY, which in many cases (as in F.) have supplanted those in *-ty*.

Although occurring in a large number of words the suffix has shown little productive power in English; *evelte*, *everlastingte*, and *overte* occur in the 14–15th cent., and *shrievalty*, *sheriffalty*, have had currency from the beginning of the 16th cent., but such formations are very rare.

Such words as *faculty*, *difficulty*, *honesty*, *modesty*, *puberty*, represent Latin formations in which the suffix *-tās* is directly added to a consonantal stem. The number of these in English, as in French, is very small.

The early form of the suffix (*-te*, or *-tee*) remained in use down to the 16th cent., but from the 15th was gradually supplanted by *-tie*, *-tye*, and the surviving *-ty*.

-ty, *suffix*², denoting 'ten', forming the second element of the decade numerals from 20 to 90 (in OE. to 120), as *twenty*, *thirty* (OE. *twentiȝ*, *þritiȝ*), etc. The OE. *-tiȝ* (gen. sing. *-tiȝes*, gen. pl. *-tiȝa*, *-tiȝra*, dat. pl. *-tiȝum*) corresponds to OFris. *-tich*, *-tech* (pl. *-tiga*, *-tega*), MDu. *-tigh* (Du. *-tig*), OS. *-tig* (*-thig*), *-teg*, *-tich*, *-tech* (MLG. and LG. *-tig*), OHG. *-zug*, *-zuc*, *-zoch* (MHG. *-zec*, *-zic*, G. *-zig*), and is the same as ON. *tigr*, *tegr*, *tøgr*, *tugr* (pl. *tigir*, etc.) and Goth. *tigus* (pl. *tigjus*), which are not suffixed but remain independent words, as ON. *tveir tigir*, Goth. *twai tigjus*, twenty. For examples of the OE. forms and syntactical usage, see the various numerals.

†**tyage** ('taɪɪdʒ). *Obs. rare.* [f. TIE *v.* + -AGE.] The action of tying or mooring a vessel.

1504 *Sel. Cases Crt. Star Chamb.* (Selden) 212 Euery of the kynges liege people..at their pleasure takyth there ancre holde & tyage in the seid streme & Reuer. *Ibid.* 223 He hath ..payd yerely for his Trow..xxd. for his haling tyage and hoking att the seide brugge.

tyal, tyall, variants of TIAL, *Obs.*

tyar, obs. f. TEAR *sb.*¹, TIAR, TIRE *v.*¹

tyara, obs. f. TIARA.

tyare, obs. f. TIAR.

tyauve, tyave, Sc. var. TAVE *v.*

Tyburn ('taɪbən). Forms: 4 **Tybourne**, 4–7 **Tyborne**, 5–6 **Tiborne**, 5–7 **Tyburne**, 6 **Tibourne**, **-burne**, 6–7 **Tiburn**, 7 **Tiborn**, 8 **Tybourn**, 7– **Tyburn**. The place of public execution for Middlesex until 1783, situated at the junction of the present Oxford Street, Bayswater Road, and Edgware Road. Hence in allusive use.

[*a* **1200** RALPH DE DICETO *Chron.* (Rolls) II. 143 (Hanging of Will. FitzOsbert in 1196) Per mediam civitatem trahitur ad furcas prope Tyburnam. Suspensus est.]

1377 LANGL. *P. Pl.* B. XII. 190 *Dominus pars hereditatis mee* is a meri verset, þat has take fro tybourne twenti stronge þeues. **1393** *Ibid.* C. VII. 368 þe hangeman of tyborne. *c* **1450** *Brut* 443 To be drawe fro þe Toure of London thorugh þe Citee to Tiborne, & þere hangede & quartrede. *c* **1520** SKELTON *Magnyf.* 423 At the laste I brynge hym ryght to Tyburne, where they hange on hyght. **1580** CAMPION in *Hanmer's Answ.* (1581) 24 We haue a league, all the Iesuits in the worlde..neuer to dispayre your recouerye whiles we haue a man left to enioy your tyburne or to be racked wyth your torments [etc.]. **1603** H. CROSSE *Vertues Commw.* (1878) 138 Many idle persons..fall into offence of lawe, and are many times eaten vp by Tyborne. **1705** HICKERINGILL *Priest-cr.* II. iii. 30, I pity the Fate of Malefactors (as they go up Holborn towards Tybourn) though they deserve to be hang'd. **1783** *New Annual Reg.* II. 48 (Sept. 20) The malefactors..convicted last week at the Old Bailey..were executed at Tyburn.

fig. **1598** E. GILPIN *Skial.* (1878) 32 It is the scourge, the Tamberlaine of vice, The three square Tyborne of impieties.

transf. **1736** DRAKE *Eboracum* I. v. 171 August 23 [1649] were executed at Tyburn near York, Colonel John Morrice and Lieutenant Blackburn. **1904** DOM BEDE CAMM *Tyburn & Eng. Mart.* Introd. 12 The blessed Edmund Campion himself inaugurated this pilgrimage, just as the venerable Margaret Clitheroe began that to the York Tyburn.

b. *attrib.* and *Comb.*, as ***Tyburn check, coach, collop, face, jig, piccadill, saint, stretch, string, tie, tiffany, tribe, wright***; **Tyburn blossom**: see quot. 1796; **Tyburn ticket**, a certificate formerly granted to one who secured the conviction of a felon, exempting the holder from all parochial duties in the parish where the offence was committed; **Tyburn tippet**: see TIPPET *sb.* 2; **Tyburn top**: see quot.; hence **Tyburn-topped** *a.*; **Tyburn tree**, the gallows.

1796 *Grose's Dict. Vulg. T.*, *Tyburn *Blossom*, a young thief or pickpocket, who in time will ripen into fruit borne by the deadly never-green. **1827** LYTTON *Pelham* lxxxi, As pretty a Tyburn blossom as ever was brought up to ride a horse foaled by an acorn. *c* **1520** SKELTON *Magnyf.* 911 A *Tyborne checke Shall breke his necke. **1829** CARLYLE *Misc.* (1857) II. 27 At the tenth mile this *Tyburn-coach breaks down! *c* **1420** ? LYDG. *Assembly of Gods* 697 *Tyburne coloppys, and pursekytters. *c* **1515** *Cocke Lorells B.* 11 Tyburne collopes and peny pryckers. **1695** CONGREVE *Love for L.* II. vii, He has a damn'd *Tyburn-Face, without the Benefit o' the Clergy. **1698** FARQUHAR *Love & Bottle* II. ii, Which is best, Mr. Nimblewrist, an easy Minuet, or a *Tyburn Jigg? **1620** J. TAYLOR (Water P.) *Hempseed* Preamble 38 Till they put on a *Tyburne Pickadill. **1785** WOLCOTT (P. Pindar) *Odes to R. Acad.* v. 16 Your *Tyburn Saints will not your fame increase. **1573** TUSSER *Husb.* (1878) 214 To beg in age, Or else to fetch a *Tibourne stretch. **1882** J. WALKER *Jaunt to Auld Reekie* 4 He should dangle in a *Tyburn string. **1796** COLQUHOUN *Police of Metropolis* 203 For apprehending, and prosecuting to conviction, any person charged with horse-stealing, a *Tyburn ticket. **1813** *Examiner* 12 Apr. 232/1 Mr. Burton was also robbed,..for which a man suffered death, on whose conviction the worthy old man received a Tyburn Ticket. **1816** *Rep. Committee on Police of Metropolis* 4 Is it not customary to give what is called 'a Tyburn Ticket' on some occasions? **1828** *Lights & Shades* II. 186 His brother was about to endure..the '*Tyburn-tie'. **1612** ROWLANDS *Knave of Harts* 4 Neuer regarding Hang-mans feare, Till *Tyburne-tiffany he weare. **1549** *Tyburn tippet [see TIPPET *sb.* 2]. **1647** TRAPP *Comm. 1 Cor.* xiii. 3 And how many of our Popish Martyrs..have worne the Tiburn-tippet, as Father Latimer phraseth it? **1830** MRS. BRAY *Fitz of F.* xxiv, Your glories aspire to a Tyburn tippet, and that will be the end of them. **1796** *Grose's Dict. Vulg. T.*, **Tyburn Top*, or *Foretop*, a wig with the foretop combed over the eyes in a knowing style. **1774** FOOTE *Cozeners* I. Wks. 1799 II. 153 See him on the turf, at Newmarket, in his *Tyburn-topp'd wig, tight boots, and round hat. **1727** GAY *Begg. Op.* III. xiii, I wonder we han't better Company, Upon *Tyburn Tree! **1851** BORROW *Lavengro* xxxix, Tyburn tree had long since been cut down. **1717** ROWE *Cruel Gift* Epil. 29 That *Tyburn-tribe of speech-making Non-jurors. **1589** [? LYLY] *Pappe w. Hatchet* B iij b, We neither feare Martin,.. nor of what occupation hee be, be a ship-wright, cart-wright, or *tiburn-wright.

c. ***to preach at Tyburn cross***, to be hanged; in reference to the speeches permitted to those about to be executed.

1576 GASCOIGNE *Steele Gl.* (Arb.) 55 That Soldiours sterue, or prech at Tiborne crosse.

Tyburnia (taɪ'bɜːnɪə). [mod.L., f. TYBURN + -IA¹.] A former literary name for the residential district built in the nineteenth century and extending along the Bayswater Road from Marble Arch to Lancaster Gate and north-wards.

1848, *a* **1852** [see BELGRAVIA]. **1878** A. J. C. HARE *Walks in London* II. 104 Tyburn still gives a name to the white streets and squares of *Tyburnia*, which are wholly devoid of interest or beauty. **1902** G. W. E. RUSSELL *For Better? For Worse?* iv. 58 The most gorgeous mansion in Cromwell Road or Tyburnia could never for a moment be quoted as supplying the place of the Hall or the Manor. **1973** *Country Life* 15 Nov. 1528/1 By the mid-1830s in Tyburnia stucco was replacing brick-facing.

Hence **Ty'burnian** *a.*

1850 THACKERAY *Pendennis* II. xi. 104 The great lawyers are giving grand dinner parties at their houses in the Belgravian or Tyburnian districts. **1860** *Once a Week* 28 July 124/2 The gallows, called 'Tyburn Tree'..had been for years a standing fixture on..the Edgware Road,..but this was..the second Tyburnian location of the gallows. **1973** *Country Life* 15 Nov. 1528/1 The circular turrets.. contemporary with the earliest Tyburnian example.. appear in Victoria Square.

tyce, variant of TICE *v.*

tychism ('taɪkɪz(ə)m). [f. Gr. τύχη chance + -ISM.] The doctrine that objective account must be taken of the element of chance in (philosophical, cosmological, etc.) reasoning.

1892 C. S. PEIRCE in *Monist* II. 533, I endeavored to show what ideas ought to form the warp of a system of philosophy, and particularly emphasised that of absolute chance..which it will be convenient to christen *tychism* (from τυχη, chance). **1926** J. LAIRD *Study in Moral Theory* viii. 173 The theory that every event..is necessary (or *must* occur precisely as it does occur) I shall call *determinism*... The opposite theory I shall call *tychism*, such tychism being either general or restricted. **1978** *Sci. Amer.* July 18/1 At a time when determinism dominated physics Peirce's doctrine of 'tychism' maintained that pure chance—events undetermined by prior causes—are basic to the universe.

tychite ('taɪkaɪt). *Min.* [f. Gr. τύχη fortune, chance + -ITE¹, in reference to its accidental discovery.] A rare mineral consisting of carbonate and sulphate of magnesium and sodium, crystallizing in colourless octahedrons.

1909 in *Cent. Dict. Suppl.*

tycho- (taɪkəʊ), combining form repr. Gr. τύχη fortune, chance, used in a few recent scientific terms. **ˌtychoˌparthenoˈgenesis**, exceptional or occasional parthenogenesis. **tycho'potamic** *a.* [Gr. ποταμός river], of occasional occurrence in or near rivers.

1900 B. D. JACKSON *Gloss. Bot. Terms*, *Tychopotamic*.. *Plankton*, the floating organisms of pools and river overflows (Zimmer). **1909** *Cent. Dict. Suppl.*, Tychoparthenogenesis.

Tychonian (taɪ'kəʊnɪən), *a.* and *sb.* [f. mod.L. *Tychon-*, stem of *Tycho*, Latinized form of the Danish personal name *Tyge* + -IAN.] **a.** *adj.* = TYCHONIC. **b.** *sb.* A disciple or adherent of Tycho Brahe or of his system of astronomy. *rare.*

1647 BOYLE *Let.* 8 Apr., in Birch *Life* B.'s Wks. 1772 I. p. xxxix, The dissenting opinions of the Ptolemeans, the Tychonians [etc.]. **1710** J. HARRIS *Lex. Techn.* II, *Tychonian System* or *Hypothesis*, is so called from having been advanced to solve the Phænomena of Astronomy by the Noble Tycho Brahe. **1901** *Nature* 7 Nov. 7/1 In..the Prague Town Hall an exhibition was held of several Tychonian relics.

Tychonic (taɪ'kɒnɪk), *a.* [f. as prec. + -IC.] Of or pertaining to the Danish astronomer Tycho Brahe (died 1601), or to his system of astronomy.

1670 FLAMSTEED in Rigaud *Corr. Sci. Men* (1841) II. 97, I had first notice of this star's varying from the Tychonic canon. **1678** CUDWORTH *Intell. Syst.* Pref. 3 The other (vulgarly so called) systems of the world..the Ptolemaick, Tychonick, and Copernican. **1715** tr. *Gregory's Astron.* (1726) I. 187 The same Forces that are required in the Semi-Tychonic System, are required also in the Tychonic, since the same Motion of the Sun and Planets are supposed in both. **1870** R. A. PROCTOR in *Eng. Mech.* 4 Mar. 598/3 His ellipses were..as available for the Tychonic system as for the Copernican.

tycht, Sc. pa. pple. of TIGHT *v.*¹ *Obs.*

tyck, tyckett, tyckle, obs. ff. TICK, etc.

tycoon (taɪ'kuːn). Also **taikun**. [ad. Jap. *taikun* great lord or prince, f. Chinese *ta* great + *kiun* prince.]

1. The title by which the shogun of Japan was described to foreigners.

1857 T. HARRIS *Diary* 28 Oct. (1930) 406 Today, I am told *Ziogoon* is not the proper appellation of their ruler, but that it is *Tykoon*. *Ziogoon* is literally 'Generalissimo' while *Tykoon* means 'Great Ruler'. **1858** *Times* 9 Nov. 7/1 This treaty, in the first place, engages that there shall be perpetual peace and friendship between Her British Majesty and the Tycoon of Japan. **1863** ALCOCK (*title*) The Capital of the Tycoon: A narrative of a three years' residence in Japan. *Ibid.* II. 491 The name by which this officer is commonly known is 'the Tycoon of Japan'. **1875** W. E. GRIFFIS in *N. Amer. Rev.* CXX. 287 There never was but one emperor in Japan, the Shogun was military usurper, and the bombastic title 'Tycoon' a diplomatic fraud. **1881** SIR R. ALCOCK in *Encycl. Brit.* XIII. 584/2 The title of *taikun* (often misspelt *tycoon*) was then for the first time used; it..was employed for the occasion by the Tokugawa officials to convey the impression that their chief was in reality the lord paramount. **1887** L. OLIPHANT *Episodes* (1888) 186 Soldiers of the Tycoon, or Temporal Emperor [of Japan], as he was then [1861] called.

2. An important or dominant person, esp. in business or politics; a magnate. Also *attrib.* orig. *U.S.* (as a nickname of Abraham Lincoln).

1861 J. HAY *Diary* 25 Apr. in *Lincoln & Civil War* (1939) 12 Gen. Butler has sent an imploring request to the President to be allowed to bag the whole nest of traitorous Maryland Legislators. This the Tycoon..forbade. **1886** *Outing* (U.S.) IX. 164/1 The tycoon of the baggage car objected to handling the boat. **1926** *Time* 14 June 32/3 *Married.* Fred W. Fitch, 56, rich hair-tonic tycoon. **1947** AUDEN *Age of Anxiety* (1948) 36 With diamonds to offer, A cleaned tycoon in a cooled office, I smiled at a siren. **1952** *Manch. Guardian Weekly* 3 July 7/3 Warren has..been the preferred choice of..oil and aviation tycoons with delusions of grandeur. **1958** [see TYCOONISH *a.*]. **1960** R. W. MARKS *Dymaxion World of B. Fuller* 62/1 Pictures of his latest projects appear regularly on the front cover of the magazines which symbolize the tycoon press. **1982** M. RUSSELL *Rainblast* iii. 21 She has a thing going with Marcus Hicks, the stores tycoon.

Hence **ty'coonate**, the office or dignity of a tycoon or the tycoons; **ty'coonery** [-ERY], the behaviour or status of a tycoon or tycoons; a group of businessmen; **tycoo'ness**, a female tycoon (sense 2); **ty'coonish** *a.*, characteristic of a tycoon (sense 2); **ty'coonism**, the system of temporal government by the tycoon; **ty'coonship**, the status or position of a tycoon (sense 2); the fact of being a tycoon.

1863 ALCOCK *Capital Tycoon* I. v. 135 The '*Tycoonat*', created by the strong arm and determined will of *Taikosama*. **1876** E. W. CLARK *Life Japan* 128 Shidz-u-o-ka..became the St. Helena of Tycoonism. **1956** *Time* 24 Dec. 47/2 Instead of making a budget, Falk decided to indulge in a bit of extracurricular tycoonery. **1958** *Times* 3 Dec. 6/4 Tycoons are not quite as tycoonish as they were before. **1959** *Ibid.* 19 Nov. 15/5 This immensely long.. novel gives us a new Tom Sawyer and takes him up to tycoonery. **1960** *Guardian* 28 Oct. 8/4 A high-powered tycooness must have sharp claws within the velvet paw. **1962** *Punch* 26 Sept. 443/3 The *Express* group stands alone among the major press tycooneries. **1964** R. WARD *Penguin Bk. Austral. Ballads* 15 Rugged individualists separately thrusting their ways..to an industrial tycoon-ship. **1965** 'R. ERSKINE' *Passion Flowers in Business* iv. 48, I..thought it tycoonish in an exciting way. **1970** 'D. HALLIDAY' *Dolly & Cookie Bird* viii. 119 Janey's father..had..several irritating habits of tycoonery. **1976** 'M. INNES' *Gay Phoenix* iii. 43 Business affairs... A high degree of continuity in their direction was..a *sine qua non* of successful tycoonship. **1983** *Listener* 27 Oct. 34/3 He was busy trying to set up a rival consortium to buy the Sunday Times, competing with (and losing to) Murdoch in tycoonery.

tyd, obs. f. TIDE *sb.* and *v.*, TITE *adv.*; var. TID *a. Obs.*

tydance, -and(e, -annes, -ant, obs. ff. TIDING, TIDINGS.

tyddie, obs. f. TIDY.

tyde, obs. f. TIDY; obs. pa. t. of TIE *v.*

tydely: see TIDELY *adv.*

tyden, obs. f. TIDE *v.*[1]

tyder, obs. f. THITHER.

† **tydie.** *Obs. rare*—[1]. The name of some small bird; ? = TIDIFE.
1612 DRAYTON *Poly-olb.* xiii. 79 And of these chaunting fowls, the goldfinch not behind, That hath so many sorts descending from her kind. The tydie for her notes as delicate as they.

tydie, obs. f. TIDY.

tydond, tydynde, obs. ff. TIDING, TIDINGS.

tye, tie (taɪ), *sb.*[1] *Obs.* exc. *dial.* and *local.* Forms: α. 1 téaȝ, tæȝ, téȝ, 5 tee; β. 1 tíȝ, 5 tigh, ty, 4- tye, 5-6, 9 tie. [OE. *téaȝ, téah,* which agrees in forms with TIE *sb.* and TYE *sb.*[2], and is treated by Bosw.-Toller and Sweet as the same word. The sense-history is unknown; the connexion of the senses here included is also uncertain.]

†**1.** A small box or case for jewels and other valuables; a casket. *Obs.*
α. c725 *Corpus Gloss.* (O.E.T.) 1300 *Mantega,* taeȝ. *Ibid.* 2010 *Tehis* [for *techis, thecis*], teȝum, fodrum. c1000 ÆLFRIC *Saints' Lives* xxiii. 764 þa feng se port-ȝerefa to þære teȝe and..hi uninsæȝlode. 1027-34 *Laws of Cnut* II. c. 76 §1 Hyre hordern and hyre cyste and hyre teȝe [*MS. B.* tæȝan]. 1477 *Inventory* in *Lanc. Wills* (1884) 4 A Tee wth other coofers.
β. c1050 *Gloss* in Wr.-Wülcker 443/8 *Mantega,* tiȝ. 1390 GOWER *Conf.* II. 246 Tho tok sche forth a riche Tye Mad al of gold and of Perrie, Out of the which sche nam a Ring. c1400 *Laud Troy Bk.* 5870 Thei robbed clene al that thei founde..Off gold, siluer, & riche druri, That thei fond in coffres and ty. *Ibid.* 9983 ȝoure brochis brode & al ȝoure byes That now ligges In ȝoure tyes. c1425 *Seven Sag.* (P.) 2951 Scho..broght the rynge anoon That lay loken in hir tie [*rime* eie]. 1460 *Will of Spenser* (Somerset Ho.), Cum duabus cistis..altera vocata spruce tigh. 1535 in Weaver *Wells Wills* (1890) 116 A croke, a tye, and v silver spones.

2. *Mining* (*Cornwall*). A deep trough or box used for collecting the dross and refuse in washing ore.
1531-2 *Act 23 Hen. VIII,* c. 8 §1 Onelesse the saide diggar owner or wassher shall make..sufficient hatches and tyes in the end of thir buddels and cordes and therin putt..all the sande stones gravell and robell digged about the inserching fynding and washing of the said Tynne there to be holly and suerlie kepte by the said hatches and ties oute and frome the said fresshe rivers. 1839 DE LA BECHE *Rep. Geol. Cornw.,* etc. xv. 578 The tye is a long, narrow, inclined furrow, through which passes a stream of water, three or four times larger than that used in buddling. 1839 URE *Dict. Arts* 1245 The latter is sometimes thrown away, and at others is subjected to the operation called the tie, viz., a washing upon the sloping bottom of a long trough.

3. A pit or trench from which turf or peat is dug. *local* (*Devonsh.*).
1836 A. E. BRAY *Descr. Tamar & Tavy* I. xx. 348 A turf tye, that is, a pit from which they dig turfs for fuel. 1873 *Q. Rev.* July 159 Dartmoor turf-cutters..labouring in the solitary 'ties', as the turf-trenches are called.

4. The stuffed case forming a mattress or pillow: = TICK *sb.*[2] Also *bed-tye, pillow-tye.* (Cf. TAY, TEY.) Now *dial.*
1615 CROOKE *Body of Man* 143 This Membrane..is rowled in plentifull fat, & so serueth the Kidneyes instead of a couering, of a tye, and of a soft pillow or bolster. 1847-78 [see PILLOW *sb.* 6]. 1893 BARING-GOULD *Cheap Jack Z.* I. vii. 110 We'll lift you on to a feather tye. 1898 MRS. C. P. PENBERTHY *Warp & Woof Cornish Life* ii. 13 The bed-tie and pillows..was..in a pawn shop... There was the very tie, I knawed un in a minute.

5. *attrib.* and *Comb.* (in sense 2): **tye-lift** (see LIFT *sb.*[2] 12); **tye-pit**, a pit for collecting the refuse in washing ore.
1602 CAREW *Cornwall* 154b, They have a tye-pit, not so much satisfying use, as relieving necessitie. 1778 W. PRYCE *Min. Cornub.* 16 To take up the superficial streams, by..grooves cut in the walls..of the Lode, to convey them either into the adit or tye lift of pumps. 1905 *Eng. Dial. Dict.* s.v. *Tye* (*Devon.*), 'Be careful now and don't go near the tie-pit.'

tye, tie (taɪ), *sb.*[2] *local.* Forms: 1 téaȝ, 5- tye (also 7 tie). [OE. *téaȝ,* by Bosw.-Toller and Sweet held to be the same word as TIE *sb.* and TYE *sb.*[1]; but the connexion of sense is unexplained. Bosw.-Toller also compares ON. *teigr* a strip of field or meadow-land, a close or paddock, which occurs freq. in names of meadows; but OE. *téaȝ* and ON. *teigr* are not phonetically related.] An enclosed piece of land, enclosure, close; also, an extensive common pasture; a large common.
832 *Test. of Werhard* in Birch *Cart. Sax.* I. 559 Mansionem..et clausulam quod Angli dicunt *teaȝe,* quæ pertinet ad prædictam mansionem. 853 *Charter of Ætheluulf* ibid. II. 61 Circumcincta est..a meritie Bromteaȝ. 1407 in *Essex Rev.* XIII. 204 [A freehold called] Tye-lond. 1488 *Maldon, Essex, Liber B.* lf. 39 (MS.) All that lane till they came dovne to Lymborn-broke on to the tye & comon ayenst Brodehedis. 1670 BLOUNT *Law Dict., Tigh* or *Teage*..a Close or Enclosure, a Croft... The word *Tigh* is still used in Kent in the same sense. c1700 *Churchw. Acc. St. Dunstan's, Canterb.,* Woolvysty 3 acres of land lying within a cross. 1708 *Lond. Gaz.* No. 4453/4 Lost.., from the Tye in the Parish of Blackthorne.., a black Gelding. a1825 FORBY *Voc. E. Anglia, Tye,* an extensive common pasture. There are several tyes a few miles South of the central part of Suffolk; but in no other part of East Anglia. There are also some on the Northern border of Essex. 1884 *Daily News* 23 Sept. 6/6 In almost every parish was a 'heath', tie, common, or green, where the poor of the parish had certain rights. 1887 PARISH & SHAW *Dict. Kentish Dial., Tye, Tie,* an extensive common pasture. Such as Waldershare Tie.

tye, tie, *v. Mining.* (*local.*) [f. TYE *sb.*[1] 2.] *trans.* To separate (the ore) from the dross or refuse by means of a 'tye'. Hence **'tying** *vbl. sb.*
1757 in J. Lloyd *Old S. Wales Iron Works* (1906) 23 Pipes for carrying Air or Water underground through their lands, or Tying of Wase or Wases. 1839 DE LA BECHE *Rep. Geol. Cornw.,* etc. xv. 578 Some kinds of ore..required other operations after roasting, generally either tying by itself, or tying and jigging. 1881 RAYMOND *Mining Gloss., Strake* (*Corn.*), an inclined launder for separating or tying ground ore in water.

tye, obs. form or var. of TIE.

‖**tyee, tyhee** ('taiiː). [Chinook jargon.]
1. A chief; a person of distinction. *N. Amer. slang.*
1792 in E. HEALEY *Hist. Alert Bay* (1958) 15 The Ty-ee, or chief, of the village paid us an early visit. 1866 J. K. LORD *Naturalist in Brit. Columbia* I. 161, I was presented to the chiefs as a Hyas tyee (great chief), one of 'King George's' men. 1877 *Puget Sound* (Washington) *Argus* 23 Nov., With the coming of the military among us came a big church 'tyhee', who told us that the soldiers were come to protect us. 1880 D. M. GORDON *Mountain & Prairie* 117 We were surprised to find, at the head of Stewart Lake, a well-stocked farm, owned and worked by the Indian 'tyhee'. 1909 in *Cent. Dict. Supp.* 1911 *Chambers' Jrnl.* July 439 Thither when a tyhee [*i.e.* a wealthy Chinaman] dies, wends a noisy procession. 1927 [see HIGH-MUCK-A-MUCK]. 1963 *Brit. Columbia Digest* Oct. 54/2 A British officer..may have told the Chief that he was now the great Tyee of the country. The Indian took the words literally and elevated himself to top position. 1966 H. MARRIOTT *Cariboo Cowboy* v. 54 The agricultural tyees in both Canada and the United States have taken a wise view.

2. The king-salmon or quinnat (*Oncorhynchus chouicha* or *quinnat*). Also *attrib.*
1902 JORDAN & EVERMANN *Amer. Food & Game Fishes* 151 Chinook Salmon... Other names by which this fish is known are quinnat salmon,..tyee, tchaviche, and tschawytscha. 1903 *Blackw. Mag.* Mar. 373/1 The quinnat, chinook, or ty-hee (chief) commonly known as the Spring Salmon. 1909 *Morn. Leader* 6 Feb. 4/4 He caught four and Mr. Bonnell two 'Tyee' salmon;..only three other 'Tyees' were taken.

tyen, obs. var. T'IEN.

tyer, obs. f. TEAR *sb.*[1], TIRE *sb.*[1] and *v.*[3], TYRE *sb.*[1]; var. TIER *sb.*[2], TIRE *v.*[2], TYRE *sb.*[4]

tyerce, tyercell(e, obs. ff. TIERCE, TERCEL.

tyere, obs. f. TIRE *v.*[1] and [3]; var. TYRE *sb.*[1] *Obs.*

tyers(e, obs. ff. TIERCE.

Tyesday, Sc. f. TUESDAY.

tyf(e, tyff(e, obs. ff. TIFF *v.*[1]

† **tyft**, app. an obs. variant of TUFT *sb.* 3.
c1450 *Godstow Reg.* 458, iij. acris of arable lond..with the mansion, tyftis of roddis, thorptis or croftis, and medis, at wyke. *Ibid.,* All the forsaid lond with the mansion, tyftis of twyggis, thorptis, medis,..and all other thyngis longyng to the said lond [cf. 139 toft of roddys; 679 tofte of Roddys].

tyg, tig (tɪg). [Origin unknown.] A name said to have been formerly given in the Staffordshire potteries to a porringer; now applied by antiquaries and collectors to a drinking-cup with two or more handles, attributed to the 17th and 18th c.
1838 BOSWORTH *Anglo-Sax. Dict.* s.v. *Tigel,* To this day porringers are called tigs by the working potters. 1855 H. DE LA BECHE & T. REEKS *Catal. Specimens Brit. Pottery,* etc., *Mus. Pract. Geol.* 116 Three handled tyg, a drinking cup of the time, so handled that three different persons, drinking out of it, and each using a separate handle, bring their mouths to different parts of the rim. 1865 ELIZA METEYARD *Life J. Wedgwood* I. 76 The tyg or cup with two or more handles, was a favourite drinking vessel in the sixteenth and seventeenth centuries. 1880 C. H. POOLE *Gloss. Stafford, Tyg,* a two-handled cup. 1892 RAINE *Handbk. to York Museum* 169 Cruses and tygs of black and brown ware.

tyger, obs. f. TIGER.

tyȝe, obs. f. TIE *v.*

tyȝl, tyȝt, obs. ff. TILE, TITE.

tyght(e, obs. f. THEAT, TIGHT; var. TITE *adv.*

tyhee, obs. f. TEE-HEE *int.*; var. TYEE.

tyik, obs. Sc. f. TICK *sb.*[2], case for bed.

tying ('taɪɪŋ), *vbl. sb.*[1] [f. TIE *v.* + -ING[1].]
1. The action of the verb TIE in various senses; fastening with a cord or string; connexion, binding, etc. Also *attrib.*
1480 *Wardr. Acc. Edw. IV* (1830) 123 For vj teyng haltres, price the pece xvj d. 1505 *Sel. Cases Crt. Star Chamb.* (Selden) 219 The kinges leege people..att ther pleasur take ther tying in the seide streme and on ther land adioyning. 1651 *Fuller's Abel Rediv., Melancthon* (1867) I. 279 It was a tying void of sense and reason, to yield a subscription unto ..things which..he did neither know nor understand. 1760-72 H. BROOKE *Fool of Qual.* (1809) III. 89, I was still sore from the tyings and the bruises which I had received. 1809 *Med. Jrnl.* XXI. 424 When..ulceration takes place after the tying of an artery. 1833 LOUDON *Encycl. Archit.* §16 Cow-house, with a tying-post and trough for food. 1906 *Macm. Mag.* Apr. 447 A March brown [angling fly]..of the popular local tying.

2. *concr.* Something used for tying; something that ties, binds, or connects; a tie. ? *Obs.*
1548 UDALL *Erasm. Par. Luke* i. 27 By and by..was the tying of his tounge looced. 1608 TOPSELL *Serpents* (1658) 652 A short stalk or tying, by which the Comb [in a wasps' nest]..is fastened..to the earth, or some tree. 1844 N. PATERSON *Manse Gard.* 119 The paper may be kept in its place by pins, or a tying of twine.

tying, *vbl. sb.*[2]; see TYE *v.*

'tying, *ppl. a.* [f. TIE *v.* + -ING[2].] That ties: see the verb.
In some of the quots. this may be the vbl. sb. used *attrib.*
1552 HULOET, Tiynge bonde, *ligamentum.* 1688 R. HOLME *Armoury* III. 261/2 *Tying course,* [the bricks] as cover the top of the Arch. 1781 P. BECKFORD *Hunting* xx. 68 Old tyeing hounds..are..contrary to the true spirit of fox-hunting.. continually bringing the pack back again. 1826 *Sporting Mag.* XVII. 233 Like unto the tying beagle which dwells upon the stale scent. 1827 SYD. SMITH in *Edin. Rev.* XLV. 429 A tying-up..action. 1901 *J. Black's Illustr. Carp. & Build., Home Handicr.* 61 Mortised through the tying rails.

tyir, obs. Sc. f. TIRE *v.*[1]

tyisce, tyist(e, obs. Sc. ff. TICE *v.*

Tyisday, obs. Sc. f. TUESDAY.

tyke (taɪk). Chiefly *Sc.* and *north. dial.* Also 6 tyk, 6-9 tike. [a. ON. *tík* female dog, bitch (Norw. *tik,* also she-fox, vixen, Sw. dial. *tik,* older Da. *tig*); also MLG. *tike* bitch.]
1. A dog; usually in depreciation or contempt, a low-bred or coarse dog, a cur, a mongrel.
c1400 *Melayne* 1325 Says Charls: 'þou false hethyn hownde,..aythire of thies dayes Ilyke Hase þou stollen a waye lyke a tyke'. 1500-20 DUNBAR *Of James Dog* 14 Poems (S.T.S.) He barkis lyk ane midding tyk. 1570 LEVINS *Manip.* 122/25 A Tyke, dogge, *canis.* 1575 CHURCHYARD *Chippes* (1817) 182 At great dogs the lttle tikes doe snarre. 1634 HEYWOOD *Lanc. Witches* II. Wks. 1874 IV. 199 Are Mr. Robinsons dogges turn'd tykes with a wanion? 1786 BURNS *Twa Dogs* 29 He was a gash an' faithfu' tyke, As ever lap a sheugh or dike. 1815 SCOTT *Guy M.* lv, The mad randy gipsy, that had..been hounded like a stray tike from parish to parish. 1844 STEPHENS *Bk. Farm* II. 89 A drover of sheep should always be provided with a dog,..a knowing cautious tyke. 1861 J. BROWN *Horæ Subs.* II. 138 Toby was the most utterly shabby, vulgar, mean-looking cur I ever beheld—in one word, a tyke.

2. *transf.* Applied opprobriously to a man (rarely with similar force to a woman): A low-bred, lazy, mean, surly, or ill-mannered fellow; a boor. (Cf. DOG *sb.*[1] 3a, HOUND *sb.*[1] 4a.) Also said in playful reproof to a child; hence (unreprovingly), a child, esp. a small boy; occas., a young animal (*U.S.*).
?a1400 *Morte Arth.* 3642 Hewe downe hertly ȝone heythene tykes! ?a1500 *Chester Pl.* vii. 275 Lyther tyke,.. thy deedes are done. 1567 *Satir. Poems Reform.* xiv. 42 For me that Nobill of Renoun With ane Tyke, Tratour Hammiltoun, Was schot. 1599 SHAKS. *Hen. V,* II. i. 31 Base Tyke, cal'st thou mee Hoste? 1625 B. JONSON *Staple of N.* v. iv. 57 Yo'are a dissembling Tyke. 1681 COLVIL *Whigs Supplic.* (1751) 87 Yet many utterly mislikes, That butcher Presbyterian tykes Should flee upon their throats and faces. 1806 JAMIESON *Gude Wallace* in *Ball. & Songs* (1806) II. 174 Tyke, by the rude thou 'scapes nat sae. 1825 BROCKETT *N.C. Words, Tike* or *Tyke,* a person of bad character, a blunt or vulgar fellow. 1868 [see *tykishness* below]. 1894 *Daily News* 4 Oct. 7/2 Mr. R——..exclaimed, 'You dirty little tyke'. 1902 *Dialect Notes* II. 248 *Tyke, n.,* a child. 1930 W. FAULKNER *As I lay Dying* 30 'That poor boy,' Cora says. 'The poor little tyke.' 1942 H. K. SMITH *Last Train from Berlin* v. 174 If you think the present Gestapo is brutal, just wait until these little tykes..grow up and become the rulers of Victorious Germany. 1979 *Tucson* (Arizona) *Citizen* 20 Sept. 1E/4 The stripes are nature's way of protecting the tapir tyke until it's old enough to fend for itself. 1981 *Verbatim* VII. III. 23/2 What hours of chair-side fun await the tyke supplied with 'three 6-oz. cans of modeling compound'!

3. A nickname for a Yorkshireman: in full ***Yorkshire tyke.***
(Perhaps originally opprobrious; but now accepted and owned. It may have arisen from the fact that in Yorkshire *tyke* is in common use for *dog.*)
a1700 B. E. *Dict. Cant. Crew., Yorkshire-Tike,* a Yorkshire manner of Man. a1714 PRIOR *Wandering Pilgrim* vii, Could Yorkshire-Tyke but do the same, Then He like Them might thrive. 1761 *British Mag.* II. 464 I'se a poor Yorkshire tyke. 1820 SYD. SMITH in *Life* x. (1884) 249 Give a tyke a bridle and he'll soon have a horse. 1856 [H. H. DIXON] *Post & Paddock* vi. 92 The tykes, who were very jealous of the honour of their jocks, did not relish their defeat. 1901 HARPER *Great North Road* I. 268 By common consent, whatever its origin may have been, 'tyke', applied to a Yorkshireman, is taken in the complimentary sense.

4. [Assimilated or altered f. TEAGUE.] A Roman Catholic. *Austral.* and *N.Z. slang.*
1941 BAKER *Dict. Austral. Slang* 76 *Tike, tyke,* a Roman Catholic. 1948 R. PARK *Harp in South* xxi. 268 I'll do what I like when I like without the interference of any bone-headed tike. 1961 P. WHITE *Riders in Chariot* viii. 232, I would never ever of suspected you Rosetrees of being tykes. Only the civil servants are Roman Catholics here, and the politicians, if they are anything at all. 1977 D. AITKIN *Second Chair* xviii. 172 Baxter's a tyke (you wouldn't think it from his name..) and he goes to mass each Sunday. 1981

M. Gee *Meg* xvii. 189 Once it fell to me to.. explain to a pair of Jehovah's Witnesses that we were all good Catholics in this house... 'At least the tikes have got some style... Shall I nail a crucifix on the door?'

5. *attrib.* and *Comb.*, as *tyke dog, -man, -sticker.*

a **1585** Polwart *Flyting w. Montgomerie* 787 Tyk stickar, poysond viccar, pot lickar! **1826** *Sporting Mag.* XVII. 283 A provincial touch.. between Bob Luckman, a tyke-man, and John Bouck, a rat-trap. **1895** Crockett *Men of Moss-Hags* xxxiv, A great debate concerning this tyke dog.

Hence (*nonce-wds.*) **'tykedom**, the realm or community of tykes; humorously, Yorkshire (see 3); **'tykish** *a.*, characteristic of a tyke; **'tykishness**, the character of a tyke.

1868 E. H. Yates *Wrecked in Port* iii, As the 'tyke' grew up she dropped all outward signs of tykeishness. **1888** G. M. Hopkins *Let.* 20 May (1956) 392 There is an old Adam of barbarism, boyishness, wildness, rawness, rankness, the disreputable, the unrefined in the refined and educated. It is that I meant by tykishness (a tyke is a stray sly unowned dog)... Ancient Pistol is the typical tyke,.. and the tykish element undergoing dilution in Falstaff and Prince Hall [*sic*] appears to vanish.. in Henry V as king. **1905** *Westm. Gaz.* 18 Dec. 3/1 At Bradford or Sheffield or some other murky stronghold of Tykedom.

tyke: see TIKE[1]; obs. f. TICK *sb.*[1] and [2].

tykele, -ell, obs. ff. TICKLE.

‖**tykhana** (taɪ'kɑːnə). *E. Ind.* [ad. Urdū (Pers.) *tahkhāna* nether house.] In India, an underground chamber to which to retire during the heat of the day.

1859 Lang *Wand. India* 196 These walls are those of the ty-khana—a vault beneath the dwelling from which the light is excluded. **1862** Beveridge *Hist. India* III. ix. iv. 629 Their families found good shelter in the tykhanas, or underground rooms. **1913** *Blackw. Mag.* May 687/2 Almost under our feet are the tykhanas.

tykkatt, tykke, tykle, -yl(l, obs. ff. TICKET, TICK *sb.*[2], TICKLE.

tyl, obs. form of TILL *prep.* and *conj.*

tyld, tylde, var. TELD, TILD, *Obs.*

tyle: see TILD, TILE, TILL *v.*[1] and [3].

tyle, in *tyle seed*: see TILLY *sb.*[1]

tyle-berry. The coral-plant, *Jatropha multifida.*

1866 *Treas. Bot.* 1185.

tylectomy ('taɪlɛktəmɪ). *Surg.* [f. TYLO- + -ECTOMY.] The excision of a lump or swelling, esp. a cancerous one.

1972 H. Atkins et al. *Brit. Med. Jrnl.* 20 May 423/2 We are indebted to Dr. W. J. Mann, who has proposed the term 'tylectomy'.. for excision of a lump and we use the term 'extended tylectomy' instead of 'wide excision' throughout the paper. **1978** *Jrnl. R. Soc. Med.* LXXI. 341 Stage I cases treated by tylectomy and HVT in the Guy's Hospital trial.. had local recurrence rates of 15% at three years and 20% at five years.

tyler, obs. f. or var. TILER.

Tylerism ('taɪlərɪz(ə)m). [f. proper name *Tyler* (see defs.) + -ISM.]

1. *U.S. Politics.* The practice or methods of President Tyler (see below).

1844 *Hallowell* (Maine) *Liberty Standard* 4 Apr., They would vote for Harrison.. and have fallen under Tylerism.

2. The theological system of Dr. Bennet Tyler of Connecticut (1783–1858), which reaffirmed the doctrines of the older Calvinism as against Taylorism.

1891 in *Cent. Dict.*

So **'Tylerize** *v., intr.* to abandon the party to which one owes one's position or office, as President Tyler (1841–5) did; also *trans.* in causal sense.

1865 *Nation* (N.Y.) 24 Aug. 227 The Democratic party.. had two ways of returning.. to office... They might either .. unseat the Administration, or else persuade the Executive to Tylerize. **1866** Pres. Johnson in *Morn. Star* 16 Mar. 5/3 It has been said.. that here is a President who was elected by a party, and who on coming into power abandoned that party; that he has 'Tylerised' his Administration.

tylet, var. TILLET[2] *Obs.*, lime-tree.

tylhexactine: see TYLO-.

tylie, obs. f. TILL *v.*[1]

tyll, obs. f. THILL[1], TILL; var. TILD *Obs.*

tylle, obs. f. TILL, TWILL *sb.*[1]

†**tyllole.** *Obs. rare*[−1]. [a. OF. *tillole* (also *tignole*) in the same sense.] A device for bending a cross-bow.

1489 Caxton *Faytes of A.* ii. xxv. I v b, Tournes al newe for to bende crosbowes with all.. othre tylloles for to bende crosbowes.

†**tyllshite,** app. obs. for *twill-sheet*, TWILL *sb.*[1] c.

1586 *Shuttleworths' Acc.* (Chetham Soc.) 34 Tyntie yardes of grete canves for to be a grete tyllshite, vij[s].

tylo- (taɪləʊ), before a vowel or *h* **tyl-** (tɪl), combining form repr. Gr. τύλος knob, or τύλη callus, cushion, used in a few terms of zoology. **tylhe'xactine** [see *hexactine* under HEXA-], a six-rayed sponge-spicule having a knob at the end of each ray. **'tyloclad** [Gr. κλάδος shoot, branch], a sponge-spicule knobbed at one end and branched at the other. **'tylopod** [Gr. πούς, ποδ- foot], *a.* having pads on the digits instead of hoofs; belonging to the *Tylopoda*, a group of ruminants comprising the camels and llamas (synonymous with *Camelidæ*); *sb.* a member of the *Tylopoda*; so **ty'lopodous** *a.* **'tylostyle** [Gr. στῦλος pillar] (also in L. form **tylo'stylus**), a sponge-spicule of the form of a rod with a knob at one end (the other end being pointed); also *attrib.* or as *adj.*; so **tylo'stylar, tylo'stylote,** *adjs.*, pertaining to, or of the form of, a tylostyle.

1909 *Cent. Dict. Suppl.*, *Tylhexactine. **1888** Sollas in *Challenger Rep.* XXV. p. lv, **Tyloclad.* The esactine is tylote and the ecactine cladose. [**1878** Bell *Gegenbaur's Comp. Anat.* 483 In the Tylopoda and Solidungula this end of the ulna has quite disappeared.] **1891** *Cent. Dict.*, *Tylopod, *Tylopodous. **1902** *Cassell's Encycl. Dict., Suppl.*, *Tylostylar. **1886** R. von Lendenfeld in *Proc. Zool. Soc.* 21 Dec. 574 The supporting skeleton, composed of bundles of monaxonid not *tylostyle spicules, is strengthened by spongin. *Ibid.*, Spicules tetraxon, monaxon (tylostylus), or absent. **1887** Sollas in *Encycl. Brit.* XXII. 423/1 (*Sponges*) *Polymastidae.*—Skeleton consisting of styles radiately arranged and cortical tylostyles. **1886** R. von Lendenfeld in *Proc. Zool. Soc.* 21 Dec. 590 Spicules polyact, tetract, lithistid, *tylostylote, or stylote, never cemented with spongin.

tylose ('taɪləʊs). *Bot.* Also **thylose.** [a. F. *tylose* (Van Heurck), f. G. *thyllen* (1845), *tüllen* sb. pl., of doubtful origin.] An intrusive growth of the wall of a cell into the cavity of a vessel in woody tissue.

1872 Thiselton-Dyer in *Geol. Mag.* June 242 The most curious feature about this wood is.. the cellular mass (Tylose) with which the interior of the ducts is filled up. *Ibid.* 243 Many instances of Tylose are now known. **1884** Bower & Scott *De Bary's Phaner.* 170 The formation of fresh thyloses may continue for a long time in a portion of a vessel.

tylosin ('taɪləʊsɪn). *Vet. Sci.* [Etym. unkn.; see -IN[1].] A macrolide antibiotic, $C_{46}H_{77}NO_{17}$, produced by *Streptomyces fradiæ* and used esp. to treat respiratory infections in animals.

1961 J. M. McGuire et al. in *Antibiotics & Chemotherapy* (N.Y.) XI. 326 Tylosin, a new antibiotic substance, has been obtained from soil isolates tentatively identified as strains of *Streptomyces fradiae* (Waksman and Curtis) Waksman and Henrici. **1968** [see MACROLIDE]. **1981** *Antimicrobial Agents & Chemotherapy* XX. 214/1 Tylosin is a complex macrolide antibiotic which is produced commercially by a strain of *Streptomyces fradiae*.., it is also produced by strains of *Streptomyces rimosus*.. and *Streptomyces hygroscopicus.*

‖**tylosis** (taɪ'ləʊsɪs). [mod.L., in sense 1 ad. Gr. τύλωσις formation of a callus (Galen), f. τύλος or τύλη: see TYLO- and -OSIS.]

1. *Path.* **a.** An inflammatory disease of the eyelids, characterized by thickening and hardening of their edges. **b.** An affection of the mucous membrane of the lips and mouth, characterized by whitish spots; leucoplacia. **c.** Callosity.

1890 in Billings *Med. Dict.* **1899** *Syd. Soc. Lex.*, *T[ylosis] palmæ*.. callosity of the palm. *T. plantæ*.., a callosity occurring in the foot. **1899** *Allbutt's Syst. Med.* VIII. 689 Tylosis is usually painless.

¶**2.** *Bot.* = TYLOSE.

Perh. an erron. use arising from the pl. *tyloses* being taken as Latin.

1876 J. H. Balfour in *Encycl. Brit.* IV. 87/1 These portions appear as cells filling the interior of the vessel, and are described under the name of *tylosis*. **1899** in *Syd. Soc. Lex.* **1900** B. D. Jackson *Gloss. Bot. Terms, Tylose, Tylosis* .., a cell intruding into a duct.

tylostyle, etc.: see TYLO-.

tylote ('taɪləʊt), *sb.* (*a.*) *Zool.* Also in L. form **tylotus** (taɪ'ləʊtəs). [ad. Gr. τυλωτός knobbed, vbl. adj. f. τυλοῦν to make knobby, f. τύλος knob.] A sponge-spicule of the form of a cylindrical rod with a knob at each end; also *attrib.* or *adj.* Hence **'tylotate** *a.* [-ATE[2]], shaped like a tylote, knobbed; ‖**tylo'toxea** [OXEA], a spicule resembling a tylote but pointed at one end (whence **tylo'toxeate** *a.*, shaped like a tylotoxea).

1887 Sollas in *Encycl. Brit.* XXII. 416/2 (*Sponges*) The spicular rays often become cylindrical;.. they are.. frequently rounded off (*strongylate*), or thickened into knobs (**tylotate*), or branched (*cladose*). *Ibid.* 417/2 The distal ends.. becoming slightly tylotate. *Ibid.* 417/1 The rhabdus .. if knobbed at both ends [is known] as a **tylote.* **1888** —— in *Challenger Rep.* XXV. p. lviii, *Tylostyle.* A style which is tylote at the origin. **1887** —— in *Encycl. Brit.* XXII. 417/1 The tylote if pointed at one end is a **tylotoxea.* **1891** *Cent. Dict.* (citing Sollas) *Tylotoxeate. **1886** R. von Lendenfeld in *Proc. Zool. Soc.* 21 Dec. 561 *Tylotus. A cylindrical rod with a knob at each end.

tylotic (taɪ'lɒtɪk), *a.* *Path.* [f. TYLOSIS: see -OTIC.] Of, pertaining to, or affected with tylosis.

1883 *Quain's Dict. Med.* 1645 The tylotic coating [of the tongue] presents a silvery or snow-white appearance. **1899** *Syd. Soc. Lex., Tylotic*, pertaining to, or affected with, a callosity.

tylsent, early perverted form of TINSEL *sb.*[3]

†**tylye,** obs. form of TAILYE.

1666 *Caldwell Papers* (Maitl. Cl.) I. 135, I heirby bind me, my aires of tylye and provisione, to pay [etc.].

tylye, obs. form of TILL *v.*[1]

†**tylyester.** *Obs.rare.* Also **tylyystere.** [f. OE. *tili-an* (cf. TELING *vbl. sb.*) + *-estre* -STER.] An enchantress, sorceress.

14.. *Voc.* in Wr.-Wülcker 582/4 *Facimia*, a forspeker or a tylyystere. *Ibid.* 582/22 *Fascennina, i. femina que novit incantare*, a tylyester.

†**tymar,** var. TIMAR *Obs.*, a Turkish military fief.

c **1618** Moryson *Itin.* iv. (1903) 17 For reuenues of Land, the Tymars giuen in farme only for life,.. pay tythes and other duties to the Emperor.

Tymba, var. TEMBU.

tymbal, var.TIMBAL.

tymbal, var. TIMBAL

tymber, -ir, -re, -ur, -yr, obs. ff. TIMBER, TIMBRE.

tymble, obs. f. THIMBLE.

tymbrel, -ell(e, -ill, obs. ff. TIMBREL.

†**tymburnar.** *Obs. rare*[−0]. [Cf. TABORNER and TIMBRER.] A player on a timbrel.

14.. *Nom.* in Wr.-Wülcker 693/13 *Hec timpanizatrix*, a tymburnar.

tyme, obs. f. TEAM *sb.*, THYME, TIME; var. TEME *v. Obs.*

†**tymer,** *v. Obs. rare*[−0]. [Of obscure origin.] *intr.* To work idly.

c **1440** *Promp. Parv.* 494/1 Tymeryn, *idem quod* tyffyn *supra.* [= TIFF *v.*[1] 3.]

tymer, tymeral, tymerous, obs. ff. TIMBER *sb.*[1], TIMBREL *sb.*[2], TIMOROUS.

tymir, -ire, obs. ff. TIMBER.

tymlie, obs. Sc. f. TIMELY *adv.*

tymmer, -ir, -yr, obs. ff. TIMBER, TIMBRE.

†**tymor, -our.** *Obs. rare*[−1]. The name of some bird (if the reading is correct).

? *a* **1400** in Horstm. *Altengl. Leg.* (1881) 370/152 The pyly-cane & þe popyne-Jay The tymour & [*v.rr.* tymor and, tenure of] þe turtell trewe.

tymorous, obs. f. TIMOROUS.

tymous, obs. f. TIMEOUS.

tymp (tɪmp). Also 7 **timpe, timp.** [app. an abbreviation of TYMPAN. So F. *tympe, timpe.*]

1. The mouth of the hearth of a blast-furnace, through which the molten metal descends; formed by an arch of masonry (*tymp-arch*), or a block of stone or iron (*tymp-stone, tymp-plate*), or by two of these together.

1645–50 Boate *Irel. Nat. Hist.* (1860) 113 The [melted] Iron.. descendeth to the lowest part of the furnace, called the Hearth; the which being filled.. they unstop the Hearth and open the Mouth thereof (or the Timp as the Arts-men call it). **1686** Plot *Staffordsh.* 162 Which four walls have the following names; that next the bellows, the tuarn or tuiron wall; that against it, the wind-wall or spirit-plate; that where the Metall comes out, the Timp or fire plate; that over against it, the back-wall. **1859** R. Hunt *Guide Mus. Pract. Geol.* (ed. 2) 195 A strong blast of air is.. injected through *tuyeres*.., which are fixed in holes just above the level of the *tymp*, or block of sandstone which is adjusted at the base of the furnace.

b. *attrib.*, as ***tymp arch, plate, stone, stopping.***

1665 D. Dudley *Metallum Martis* (1855) 32 The Founder['s] terms,.. as the Timpe stones, the Wind-wall stones,.. the Boshes. **1825** J. Nicholson *Operat. Mechanic* 331 Tymp-stone.. Tymp-plate [*both mispr.* Lymp-]. **1839** Ure *Dict. Arts* 691 [Iron blast furnace] Fig. 584 represents the hearth and boshes.. *a* is the tymp stone, and *b* the tymp plate for confining the liquid metal in the hearth... The space under the tymp plate.. is rammed full, for every cast, with strong loamy earth, or even fine clay; a process called the tymp stopping. **1876** Routledge *Discov.* 29 The glassy looking slags.. continually flowing over the tympstone. **1881** Raymond *Mining Gloss., Tymp*, a hollow iron casting, cooled interiorly by a current of water, and placed to protect the tymp-arch, or arch over the dam, in a blast furnace having a fore-hearth.

2. *Coal Mining.* A horizontal piece of timber for supporting the roof; also called *bar, cap,* or *lid.*

1883 in Gresley *Gloss. Terms Coal Mining.*

tympan (ˈtɪmpən). Also 1 **timpana**, 3–7 **timpane**, **timpan** (also 9 in sense 1 b), 4–8 **tympane**, (6 **tymphan**, **timphan**). [ad. L. *tympanum*, TYMPANUM, or a. OF. *tympan*, *timpan* (12th c. in Hatz.-Darm.; mod.F. *tympan*, = Pg. *tympano*, Sp. and It. *timpano*, in various senses). Cf. OHG. *timpana*, OIcel. *timpan*. In OE. and early ME. only in renderings of Biblical passages.]

1. A drum or similar instrument, as a timbrel or tambourine. *arch.*

c825 *Vesp. Psalter* lxvii. 26 In midle iungra plæȝiendra timpanan. **c897** K. ÆLFRED *Gregory's Past. C.* xlvi. 346 Lofiað God mid tympanan, ond on choro. **c1000** ÆLFRIC *Gen.* xxxi. 27 Mid lofsangum, & mid timpanum, & mid hearpum. **a1300** *E.E. Psalter* cxlix. 3 In timpan and sautre to him singe þai. *Ibid.* cl. 4 Loves him in crouth and timpane. **1303** R. BRUNNE *Handl. Synne* 7128 As þe bras, And as þe tympan, þat bete was. **c1400** *Lanfranc's Cirurg.* 283 þese ben þe propre signes of tympanites: his wombe & þe regioun of his stomac schulen oonly be to-swolle, & alle his oþere lymes..wolen bicome smal, & if þou smitist him vpon his wombe, it wole soune as it were a tympan. **1413** *Pilgr. Sowle* (Caxton 1483) v. viii. 99 Dauyd ordeyned.. instrumentes..organs and harpes, Symbals and sawtryes, Kroudes and tympans, Trompettes and tabours. **1503** *Acc. Ld. High Treas. Scot.* II. 392 Item..ane pair of tympanes to the King xxiiij s. **1606** G. W[OODCOCKE] *Hist. Ivstine* XLI. 128 They vse not to sound a trumpet, but a Timpane. **a1682** SIR T. BROWNE *Tracts* vi. (1684) 122 Bacchus gave the signal of Battel..not with Trumpets but with Tympans and Cymbals.

b. [Ir. *tiompan*.] An ancient Irish stringed instrument played with a bow.

1432–50 tr. *Higden* (Rolls) I. 355 Men of Irlonde be experte specially in ij. kyndes of musike,..an harpe, and a tympan [L. *tympano*] stryngede and armede with cordes of brasse. **1862** O'CURRY *Anc. Irish* xxxvi. (1873) III. 362 The poem affords another proof that the Timpan was a stringed instrument; and..shows that it was..played on with a wand and hair, words that plainly enough describe a fiddle-bow. **1891** W. B. YEATS *C'tess Cathleen* Poems (1908) 10, I thought I heard far off tympans and harps.

†**2. a.** = TYMPANITES, TYMPANY 1. *Obs. rare.*

1530 PALSGR. 281/2 Tympan a dysease in the bely, *enfleure.*

†**b.** *transf.* (See quot.) *Obs.*

1555 EDEN *Decades* 142 The smaulest [pearls] differ from the byggest in a certayne swellynge or impostumation whiche the Spaniardes caule a tympane.

†**3.** = TYMPANUM 2. *Obs.*

1549 COVERDALE, etc. *Erasm. Par. Jas.* 28 The worde of the Gospell..knocketh in vayne at the tympane of the ears; vnles it light depe in to the inwarde partes of the hearte. **1639** J. S. *Clidamas* 24 If what I speake may befit the tender tympane of a Ladyes eare. **1688** BURNET *Lett. Pres. St. Italy* 181 The violent noise..weakened the Tympan of his Ear. **1706** PHILLIPS (ed. Kersey), *Tympan*,..the Drum of the Ear.

4. An appliance in a printing-press, interposed between the platen or impression-cylinder and the sheet to be printed, in order to soften and equalize the pressure; in a hand press consisting of two frames (***outer*** and ***inner tympan***) with sheets of parchment or strong linen stretched upon them, and inclosing a packing either of blanket, rubber, or other soft substance, or sheets of paper, cardboard, cloth, or other harder material, according to the nature of the work to be printed.

1580 HOLLYBAND *Treas. Fr. Tong, Le Chassis*, the tympane of a Printers presse. **1594** R. ASHLEY tr. *Loys le Roy* 22 Placing the leafe that is to be printed, on a double tympan or parchmin. **1683** MOXON *Mech. Exerc., Printing* x. ¶10 The Tympan is a square Frame. **1728** CHAMBERS *Cycl.* s.v. *Printing*, On the Front of the Coffin are three Frames.., *viz.* the two Tympans and Frisket. **1824** J. JOHNSON *Typogr.* II. xv. 529 The tympans are covered with vellum, forrels, or parchment. **1869** W. B. in *Eng. Mech.* 24 Dec. 362/1 Make a tympan of thick cardboard. **1880** *Printing Times* 15 Mar. 63/1 Too much packing in a tympan is a great and common fault. **1885** C. G. W. LOCK *Workshop Receipts* Ser. IV. 404/1 A sheet of smooth card..should be laid over the picture before the leather tympan is closed down upon it.

5. *Arch.* = TYMPANUM 3.

1704 J. HARRIS *Lex. Techn.* I, *Tympan of an Arch*, is a triangular Table placed in its Corners. *Ibid.*, *Tympan*, is also attributed to the Pannels of Doors..and to the Dye or Square of Pedestals. **1767** DUCAREL *Anglo-Norman Antiq.* 88 Within the Tympan or panel of the pediment is a basso relievo. **1825** JAMIESON, *Timpan, tympany*, the middle part of the front of a house, raised above the level of the rest of the wall, resembling a gable... This is also called a *Tympany gavel.* **1893** E. H. BARKER *Wand. Southern Waters* 89 The composition, which fills the tympan of the scarcely-pointed arch, represents Christ surrounded by the twelve Apostles.

6. = TYMPANUM 4 b.

1858 LARDNER *Hand-bk. Nat. Phil., Hydrost.* etc. 123 *The tympan.*—A form of wheel, which has received this name, is also used in France for irrigation.

7. A tense membrane or thin plate in any mechanical apparatus, e.g. in a phonograph.

1883 GREER *Dict. Electr.* 170 This [carbon] lozenge is pressed gently by a tympan. **1900** *Daily News* 17 Nov. 6/3 The vibrating plate or tympan had not force enough to imprint the feeble sounds on the wax of the cylinder, and form a good record. *Ibid.*, This varying current in passing through the telephone..makes the iron plate or tympan vibrate and give out..a fairly correct imitation of the speaker's voice.

8. *attrib.* (in sense 4), as ***tympan-cloth***, ***-frame***; **tympan-sheet**, a sheet of paper, etc. laid on or fixed in the tympan, originally as a guide for placing the sheets to be printed.

1683 MOXON *Mech. Exerc., Printing* xxiv. ¶7 He takes a Sheet of Paper..for a Tympan-sheet. *Ibid.* ¶19 This Tympan-cloath is a Fine and even Linnen Cloath. **1771** LUCKOMBE *Hist. Print.* 345 The Tympan sheet..is only as a standing mark to lay all the other sheets exactly even upon. **1841** T. C. HANSARD *Print. & Type-founding* 109 They now choose their points, which are thin iron arms, having a short point projecting from the end, and made to screw on to the tympan-frame. **1911** WEBSTER s.v., In hand presses the tympan is double and consists of two sheets, usually of parchment, stretched on the tympan frame.

Hence †**ˈtympaned** *a.* (*obs. nonce-wd.*), affected as with a 'tympan' (sense 2); inflated, puffed up; **ˈtympaning** (tɪm-) *vbl. sb.* (*nonce-wd.*), the playing of a tympan (sense 1 b).

a1640 DAY *Peregr. Schol.* (1881) 56 Philosophos..swolne and timpaned with presumption. **1862** O'CURRY *Anc. Irish* xxxvi. (1873) III. 363 The harper has exclusive harping... The Timpanist has exclusive timpaning (or Timpan playing).

tympanal (ˈtɪmpənəl), *a.* (*sb.*) *Anat.* and *Zool.* [f. TYMPAN-UM + -AL[1]. So F. and Pg. *tympanal.*] = TYMPANIC 1.

1822–9 GOOD *Study Med.* (ed. 3) IV. 273 An impeded motion of the air in the tympanal cavity. **1875** SIR W. TURNER in *Encycl. Brit.* I. 806/2 Alexander Achillini of Bologna..the first who described the two tympanal bones, termed *malleus* and *incus*. **1887** *Amer. Naturalist* XXI. 579 The only organs [in insects] which might be interpreted as answering functionally to an ear are the so-called tympanal organs of Orthoptera.

B. *sb.* A tympanal or tympanic bone.

1875 C. C. BLAKE *Zool.* 202 The upper jaw is represented by the vomer, the palatines, and the tympanals. **1883** *Science* I. 506/2 The tympanal is a horseshoe-like bone.

tympanectomy: see TYMPANO-.

tympani, var. TIMPANI.

tympanic (tɪmˈpænɪk), *a.* (*sb.*) [f. as TYMPANAL + -IC; cf. Gr. τυμπανικός suffering from tympanites. So F. *tympanique*, Pg. *tymp-*, Sp. *timpanico.*]

1. *Anat.* and *Zool.* Of, pertaining to, or connected with the tympanum, or drum of the ear (as ***tympanic artery***, ***bulla***, ***cavity***, ***membrane***, ***muscle***, ***nerve***, ***ossicle***, etc.); of the nature of a tympanum.

tympanic bone, in mammals, a bone of annular to tubular form supporting the tympanic membrane and surrounding the external auditory meatus (in the adult forming part of the temporal bone); in lower vertebrates, one of several bones variously supposed to be homologous with this, esp. the quadrate bone, which supports the lower jaw. ***tympanic pedicle***, the slender bone or series of bones by which the lower jaw is suspended in fishes. ***tympanic plate***, ***ring***, the tympanic bone of mammals.

1808 *Med. Jrnl.* XIX. 410 Other branches of the same nerve which supply the tympanic muscles. **1840** E. WILSON *Anat. Vade M.* (1842) 277 The Tympanic branch [of the glossopharyngeal nerve] is small. **1849** LYELL *2nd Visit U.S.* (1850) II. 75 The convoluted tympanic bones.. characteristic of cetaceans. **1851** RICHARDSON *Geol.* viii. (1855) 308 The lower jaw is articulated to a tympanic bone as in reptiles. **1851** CARPENTER *Princ. Physiol.* §825 The purpose of this Tympanic apparatus is..to receive the sonorous vibrations from the air, and to transmit them to the membranous wall of the labyrinth. **1860** TYNDALL *Glac.* 225 These aërial waves enter the external ear, meet..the so-called tympanic membrane. **1860** MAYNE *Expos. Lex.*, *Tympanic Pedicle*,..the large and long pedicle which supports the mandible in fishes,..subdivided into sometimes two or three, and commonly into four pieces. **1876** *Nature* 20 July 253/2 Sawing out the temporal bone,.. and exposing the tympanic bulla. **1893** NEWTON *Dict. Birds* 180 The quadrate bone..in Mammals..is reduced and modified into the comparatively insignificant tympanic ring.

b. as *sb.* Short for *tympanic bone*.

1851 RICHARDSON *Geol.* (1855) 287 The lower jaw..is articulated to the upper jaw by a distinct bone (the tympanic). **1881** MIVART *Cat* 65 Between the anterior end of the tympanic and the post-glenoid process is a narrow chink..which transmits the chorda tympani nerve.

2. Pertaining to or resembling a drum; in *Path.* tympanitic.

1891 *Cent. Dict.* s.v., *Tympanic resonance*, typanitic resonance.

3. *Arch.* Pertaining to a tympanum.

1909 *Spectator* 6 Nov. Suppl. 713/1 The 'Doom' often vividly depicted on the tympanic background, and the Saviour upon the cross in connexion with it.

†**tymˈpanical**, *a.* *Obs. rare.* [f. as prec. + -ICAL.] = TYMPANITIC.

1623 COCKERAM, *Tympanicall*, of or belonging to the tympanie. **1647** LILLY *Chr. Astrol.* xliv. 262 The Dropsie or Tympanicall humours.

tympanichord (ˈtɪmpənɪ-, tɪmˈpænɪkɔːd). *Anat.* [f. TYMPANUM + Gr. χορδή CHORD *sb.*[1]] The *chorda tympani*, a branch of the facial nerve which traverses the mucous membrane of the tympanum. Hence **tympaniˈchordal** *a.*, pertaining to the tympanichord.

1887 COUES (cited in *Cent. Dict.*).

tympanicity (tɪmpəˈnɪsɪtɪ). [f. TYMPANIC + -ITY.] The condition of being tympanic, or affected with tympanites.

1899 in *Syd. Soc. Lex.* **1903** *Lancet* 11 July 98/1 The area of gastric tympanicity was only slightly enlarged.

tympanie, obs. form of TYMPANY.

tympaniform (ˈtɪmpənɪ-, tɪmˈpænɪfɔːm), *a.* *Nat. Hist.* [ad. F. *tympaniforme* (Cuvier), f. TYMPANUM + *-forme*, -FORM.] Having the form of a drum, or (usually) of a drum-head; stretched like a drum-head: *spec.* applied to certain membranes in the bronchi of birds.

1854 BUSHNAN in *Circ. Sc.* (c 1865) I. 291/1 It is to this usually large portion of the wall of each bronchus that Cuvier gives the name, tympaniform membrane. **1893** NEWTON *Dict. Birds* 58 In almost all birds..the bronchi are strengthened by cartilaginous semirings; the ends of these.. are closed by the inner tympaniform membrane. *Ibid.* 940 *Syrinx trachealis*... Both inner and outer tympaniform membranes exist in the Bronchi. **1900** in B. D. JACKSON *Gloss. Bot. Terms.*

†**tymˈpanious**, *a.* *Obs.* *rare*$^{-1}$. [f. TYMPANY + -OUS.] Pertaining to or of the nature of a tympany.

1704 D'URFEY *Heir Adopted* cx, The dangerous secret of his life Shall never swell again a wife With a tympanious matter.

tympanism (ˈtɪmpənɪz(ə)m). *rare*$^{-0}$. [cf. Gr. τυμπανισμός a beating of drums, ἀποτυμπανισμός a cudgelling: see TYMPANIZE and -ISM. So F. *tympanisme*, in sense 2.]

†**1.** (See quot., and cf. TYMPANIZE *v.* 3.) *Obs.*

1661 BLOUNT *Glossogr.* (ed. 2), *Tympanism*..a kind of torturing, used by the Jews, by beating one to death with Cudgels or Drum-sticks, *Heb.* 11. 35. *2 Mac.* 6. 19.

2. *Path.* (See quot., and cf. TYMPANITES.)

1890 BILLINGS *Med. Dict.*, *Tympanism*, state of being distended with gas.

tympanist (ˈtɪmpənɪst). Also 9 **tim-**. [ad. F. *tympaniste*, It. *timpanista*, L. *tympanista*, G. τυμπανιστής, f. τυμπανίζειν TYMPANIZE, or f. *timpan* TYMPAN + -IST.] One who beats or plays upon a drum, a drummer. In quot. 1862, one who plays a tympan (TYMPAN 1 b). Now *spec.*, one who plays upon a kettledrum.

1611 COTGR., *Tympaniste*, a Timpanist; a player on a Timpan, &c. **1656** BLOUNT *Glossogr.*, *Tympanist*, a Drumster or Taberer. **1862** in O'Curry *Anc. Irish* xxxi. (1873) III. 236 'Why is the *Timpan* called *Timpan Naimh* (or saint's Timpan), and yet no saint ever took a Timpan into his hands?' 'I do not know', said the timpanist. **1906** *Daily Chron.* 22 Sept. 1/3 Solo for Six Timpani and Orchestra... Timpanist—Mr. G. G. Cleather. **1930** *Melody Maker* Jan. 72/3 All that need trouble the tympanist in regard to the minor chords is [etc.]. **1955** L. FEATHER *Encycl. Jazz* 195/1 He studied with Saul Goodman, tympanist with the N.Y. Philharmonic.

So †**tympanister** [ad. L. *tympanistria*, a. Gr. τυμπανίστρια], a female player on a drum or tambourine.

1382 WYCLIF *Ps.* lxvii. 26 The princis camen befor ioyned with the singeris; in the myddel of the ȝunge wymmen tympanystris.

‖**tympanites** (tɪmpəˈnaɪtiːz). *Path.* [Late L. *tympanītēs*, a. Gr. τυμπανίτης (Galen), f. τύμπανον drum: cf. ASCITES. So Pg. *tympanites*, F. *tympanite* (OF. *timpanides*), It. *timpanite.*] Distension of the abdomen by gas or air in the intestine, the peritoneal cavity, or the uterus.

1398 TREVISA *Barth. De P.R.* VII. lii. (Bodl. MS.) lf. 64 b/1 þe ferþe [kind of dropsy] hatte Tympanytes..for if þe wombe is ysmete it sowneþ as a taboure oþer a tymber. **c1400** *Lanfranc's Cirurg.* 282 þe .iij. [maner dropesie] is engendrid of greet wynd resolued of coold mater, & fallip into þe holownes of þe wombe, & is clepid tympanites. *Ibid.* 283 [see TYMPAN 1]. **1651** BAXTER *Inf. Bapt.* 260 If a Physitian ask, How many Tympanites have you known cured? **1694** SALMON *Bate's Dispens.* (1713) 7/1 Water of black Cherries compound..is a most powerful Remedy in the Cure of a Tympanites. **1767** GOOCH *Treat. Wounds* I. 411 The Abdomen was..distended, as if the patient had been afflicted with an Ascites or Tympanites. **1872** T. G. THOMAS *Dis. Women* (ed. 3) 261 Abdominal enlargement from tympanites. **1899** [see TYPHOID *a.* 2 b].

tympanitic (tɪmpəˈnɪtɪk), *a.* [ad. L. *tympanīticus*, f. *tympanītēs*: see prec. and -IC. So Pg. *tymp-*, Sp. and It. *timpanitico.*] Pertaining to, characteristic of, or affected with tympanites. ***tympanitic note***, ***resonance***, or ***sound***, a sound somewhat like that of a drum produced by percussion over the abdomen or other part when distended with gas or air.

1834 J. FORBES *Laennec's Dis. Chest* (ed. 4) 481 Some.. were of opinion that the..tympanitic resonance, on percussion, is of itself sufficient to point out pneumothorax. **1843** R. J. GRAVES *Syst. Clin. Med.* xiii. 142 His tongue was black and parched, his belly tympanitic. **1853** MARKHAM *Skoda's Auscult.*, etc. 255 The percussion-sound of the abdomen..being at one time distinctly tympanitic and clear, at another indistinct. **1860** TANNER *Pregnancy* ii. 67 Tympanitic distension of the intestines. **1899** *Allbutt's Syst. Med.* VII. 644 A tympanitic note on skull-percussion is suggestive that the abscess is situated in the cerebellum.

b. Giving a tympanitic sound.

1900 *Jrnl. Exp. Med.* 25 Oct. 140 The skin and subcutaneous tissues of the face, neck and chest were markedly swollen, and tympanitic on percussion.

So †**tympaˈnitical** *a.* *Obs.* (in quot. 1772 *fig.*; cf. TYMPANY 2).

1656 BLOUNT *Glossogr.*, *Tympanitical*, that hath a Tympany or dropsy. **1772** NUGENT tr. *Hist. Friar Gerund*

II. 202 Filling it with airy conceits, tympanitical thoughts, ..and fantastical dissertations.

‖**tympanitis** (tɪmpəˈnaɪtɪs). *Path.* [In sense 1, an alteration of TYMPANITES; so Pg. *tymp-*, Sp. *timpanitis*, It. *timpanitide*. In sense 2, f. TYMPAN-UM + -ITIS.]

1. = TYMPANITES.

1797 M. BAILLIE *Morb. Anat.* (ed. 2) 205 When air is accumulated in very large quantity,..it forms a..disease called tympanitis... The belly is extremely swelled, with a very tense feeling. **1876** *Trans. Clinical Soc.* IX. 103 Bowels still unrelieved... The tympanitis has increased.

2. Inflammation of the lining membrane of the tympanum.

1857 DUNGLISON *Med. Lex.* **1890** BILLINGS *Med. Dict.*

†ˈ**tympanize,** *v. Obs.* Also 6–7 **tim-**. [ad. Gr. τυμπανίζειν to beat a drum, f. τύμπανον TYMPANUM; or late L. *tympanizāre* (in med.L. in sense 1 b below); cf. F. *tympaniser* (16th c.), to proclaim or decry loudly, Pg. *tympanisar* (med.).]

1. *trans.* To affect with a tympany (*lit.* or *fig.*); to distend (the abdomen, etc.) with gas; to inflate, puff up (with pride, etc.).

1593 NASHE *Christ's T.* (1613) 118 The therd sonne of Pride is Atheisme, which is when a man is so timpaniz'd with prosperity,..that he forgets he had a Maker. **1623** COCKERAM II, Swolne with watrish humors, *tympaniz'd*. **1647** C. HARVEY *Schola Cordis* XII. vi, My windy thoughts with pride are tympaniz'd. **1679** J. GOODMAN *Penit. Pard.* I. iv. (1713) 114 To have that element [water] forced down a man's throat till all the vessels of his body are stretched and tympanized.

b. *intr.* To be affected with a tympany; to swell (*lit.* and *fig.*).

1607 R. C[AREW] tr. *Estienne's World of Wonders* 157 Our Ladies..haue so many *prophylactica* to keepe their bellies from tympanizing. **1635** HEYWOOD *Hierarch.* VI. 352 Pride in their hearts doth swell and tympanise.

2. *intr.* To beat or play on a drum. *rare*⁻⁰.

1623 COCKERAM II, To beate a Drum, *tympanize*. **1656** BLOUNT *Glossogr.*, *Tympanize*, to play on a Drum, Taber or Tymbrel.

3. *trans.* To stretch on the rack.

A former interpretation of τυμπανίζειν in Heb. xi. 35 (prob. rather = to beat with a drum-stick: cf. TYMPANISM 1).

1647 TRAPP *Comm. Heb.* xi. 35 Ἐτυμπανίσθησαν.. They were tympanized, distended, stretched upon the rack as a sheeps-pelt is upon a drum-head. **1652** OLEY *Life G. Herbert* in *Rem.* A xj b, To be sawn asunder as Esay, stoned as Jeremy, made a Drum, or Tympanised, as other Saints of God were.

Hence †ˈ**tympanizing** *ppl. a.*

1607 WALKINGTON *Opt. Glass* i. 7 Swolne with timpanizing pride.

tympano- (tɪmpənəʊ), before a vowel sometimes **tympan-**, combining form repr. Gr. τύμπανον or L. TYMPANUM, in recent terms of anatomy, etc. **tympaˈnectomy** [Gr. ἐκτομή excision], excision of the tympanic membrane. ˌ**tympano-ˈcervical** *a.* [CERVICAL], affecting the tympanum and the neck. ˌ**tympano-Euˈstachian** (-juːˈsteɪkɪən) *a.*, constituted by the tympanum and the Eustachian tube. ˈ**tympanogram**, a graphical record of pressure changes obtained in tympanometry; so **tympaˈnography.** ˌ**tympanoˈhyal** *a.*, pertaining to the tympanum and the hyoid arch; epithet of a small bone or cartilage at the base of the styloid process, which in early life becomes fused with the temporal bone; *sb.* = t. bone or cartilage. ˌ**tympanoˈmalleal** *a.*, pertaining to the tympanic bone and the malleus; applied to a bone in the skull of batrachians and fishes. ˌ**tympanomanˈdibular** *a.*, pertaining to the tympanum, or the tympanic bone, and the mandible or lower jaw-bone. ˌ**tympanoˈmastoid** *a.*, pertaining to the tympanum and the mastoid cells. **tympaˈnometry**, the measurement, for diagnostic purposes, of changes in the compliance of the tympanic membrane as the air pressure is altered in the passage of the external ear; hence ˌ**tympanoˈmetric** *a.* ˌ**tympano-ocˈcipital** *a.* and *sb.*, applied to a small bone or ossification connected with the ear and the exoccipital bone in birds, and held to be homologous with the tympanic bone in mammals (*Cent. Dict.* 1891). ˌ**tympano-periˈotic** *a.*, consisting of the tympanic bone and periotic bones united; *sb.*, a tympanoperiotic bone, as the ear-bone of a cetacean. **tympaˈnophony** [Gr. φωνή voice], a sensation of ringing in the ears (cf. TYMPANUM 2). ˈ**tympanoˌplasty** *Surg.* [-PLASTY], an operation to repair the middle ear; hence ˌ**tympanoˈplastic** *a.* ˌ**tympanoscleˈrosis** *Med.* [SCLEROSIS], thickening of the tympanic membrane, and of the connective tissue in the tympanic cavity; hence ˌ**tympanoscleˈrotic** *a.* ˌ**tympanosquaˈmosal** *a.*, pertaining to the tympanic and the squamosal bones. ˌ**tympanostaˈpedial** *a.*, 'pertaining to the tympanum and the stapes' (Dorland *Med. Dict.* 1900–13). ˌ**tympanoˈtemporal** *a.*, 'pertaining to the tympanum and the region over the temporal bone' (*ibid.*). **tympaˈnotomy** [Gr. τομή cutting], incision through the tympanic membrane.

1900–13 DORLAND *Med. Dict.*, *Tympanectomy. *Ibid.* s.v. *Abscess*, **Tympanocervical a[bscess]*, an abscess arising in the tympanum and extending to the neck. **1890** BILLINGS *Med. Dict.*, **Tympano-Eustachian passage*, the tympanum and Eustachian tube considered together as a branchial cleft. **1969** *Arch. Otolaryngol.* LXXXIX. 217/2 The *tympanogram has a normal configuration. **1979** J. J. KNIGHT in H. A. Beagley *Auditory Investigation* viii. 158 A flat tympanogram with a negative middle ear pressure is suggestive of serous otitis media. **1977** *Proc. R. Soc. Med.* LXX. 824/1 Surgery should not be undertaken until after *tympanography has been done and tomograms taken to exclude abnormalities of cochlear anatomy. **1984** *Lancet* 19 May 1112/2 A sound case can be made for including tympanography in the routine screening tests at school entry. **1872** MIVART *Elem. Anat.* 81 The styloid process.. is at birth separate from a little cylindrical piece of bone which afterwards forms its root, and which is called the *tympano-hyal. **1881** —— *Cat* 78 At the end of the stylo-hyal is a cylindrical cartilage, the tympano-hyal. **1891** *Cent. Dict.*, *Tympanomalleal. **1900–13** in DORLAND *Med. Dict.* *a* **1909** STARKS *Synon. Fish Skeleton* 513 (Cent. D. Supp.). **1891** *Cent. Dict.*, *Tympanomandibular. *c* **1900** *Buck's Handbk. Med. Sci.* III. 697 (Cent. D. Supp.) *Tympano-mastoid. **1970** *Arch. Otolaryngol.* XCII. 255/2 *Tympanometric characteristics provide information in analysis of the conductive pathological abnormality. **1984** *Jrnl. Speech & Hearing Res.* XXVII. 257 The influence that repeated tympanometric trials have on the aural-acoustic admittance characteristics of the middle-ear transmission system was studied in 24 young adults. **1956** H. ANDERSON et al. in *Acta Oto-Laryngol.* XLVI. 384 This method—for which we propose the name *tympanometry—may..yield very important additional information for the diagnosis of hearing impairments. **1980** *Ibid.* LXXXIX. 480/1 The patients were regularly checked with audiometry and tympanometry. **1870** ROLLESTON *Anim. Life* 8 A lamina of bone, which..serves..to keep the *tympano-periotic..in place. **1871** HUXLEY *Anat. Vert. Anim.* viii. 405 When the tympano-periotic bone and all the facial bones are removed. **1899** *Syd. Soc. Lex.*, **Tympanophony*, abnormal sounds in the ear, as echoes, &c. **1955** *Jrnl. Laryngol.* LXIX. 654 Of 110 *tympanoplastic cases..60 per cent. have retained or regained 'social' hearing. **1977** *Lancet* 16 July 119/2 Tympanoplastic surgery is a logical development of the modified radical techniques and aims to avoid their main disadvantages—deafness and an open cavity in the mastoid—by creating a functioning middle ear in a healthy closed system. **1955** *Acta Oto-Laryngol.* XLV. 457 It seems advisable in some cases..to operate in two stages: first a conservative radical operation..and, secondly, *tympanoplasty. **1960** J. GRANT *Come again, Nurse* xvi. 97 Now a tympanoplasty is different again. That is a plastic repair to the middle ear with a skin graft, to help the sound waves. **1977** *Lancet* 16 July 119/1 Grafting the drum constitutes the simplest and most successful form of tympanoplasty. **1961** *Brit. Med. Dict.* 1491/1 *Tympanosclerosis. **1965** I. B. THORBURN in W. G. Scott-Brown et al. *Dis. Ear, Nose & Throat* (ed. 2) II. xx. 454 Tympanosclerosis. Zöllner (1955) drew fresh attention to this condition which was first described as 'Paukensclerose' by von Tröltsch in 1873. **1978** *Jrnl. R. Soc. Med.* LXXI. 354 Scars and tympanosclerosis were only present in the ears with grommets. **1965** I. B. THORBURN in W. G. Scott-Brown et al. *Dis. Ear, Nose & Throat* (ed. 2) II. xx. 454 On otomicroscopic examination a keratinizing appearance distinguishes cholesteatoma, whereas the white *tympanosclerotic focus is covered by an intact healthy mucous membrane. **1981** *Brit. Med. Jrnl.* 14 Feb. 501/1 Tympanosclerotic plaques are commonly seen in the drum after the use of grommets. **1891** *Cent. Dict.*, *Tympanosquamosal. *c* **1900** *Buck's Handbk. Med. Sci.* III. 672 (Cent. D. Supp.) *Tympanotomy.

tympanoid (ˈtɪmpənɔɪd), *a. Nat. Hist.* [ad. Gr. τυμπανοειδής, f. τύμπανον drum: see -OID.] Resembling a drum, or a drum-head.

1863 BERKELEY *Brit. Mosses* Gloss. 313 *Tympanoid*, resembling the head of a drum.

†ˈ**tympanous,** *a. Obs.* [f. TYMPAN-UM or TYMPAN-Y + -OUS.] Swollen as with a tympany; usually *fig.* inflated, puffed up; turgid, bombastic; hollow, empty, vain.

1624 MIDDLETON *Game at Chess* II. i, His proud tympanous master, swell'd with state-wind. **1635** HEYWOOD *Hierarch.* IV. 208 A Puny shall assume the name of Poet; And in a Tympanous and Thrasonicke stile [etc.]. **1648** SYMMONS *Vind. Chas. I* p. ii, Those new hopes being likely to prove tympanous. **1660** WATERHOUSE *Arms & Arm.* 26 That tympanous humour that swells up..light minds. **1669** COKAINE *Poems* 164 Her tympanous belly.

‖**tympanum** (ˈtɪmpənəm). Pl. **tympana.** [L. *tympanum* drum, wheel for raising weights, face of pediment, etc., a. Gr. τύμπανον drum, f. root of τύπτειν to strike, beat.]

1. A drum or similar instrument, as a tambourine or timbrel (esp. ancient); also, the stretched membrane of a drum, a drum-head.

1675 COVEL in *Early Voy. Levant* (Hakl. Soc.) 203, 6 Drumes, 4 trumpets, 2 kettle-drumes, and 4 tamburs (or tympanums) like sives cover'd with parchment at bottome. **1830** *Hobart Town Almanack* 92 The little tympanums which the Chinese hawk about the streets to amuse children. **1847** LEITCH tr. *C. O. Müller's Anc. Art* §395 (1850) 520 She [Cybele] is recognised by the crown of flowers, the tympanum as a symbol of her enthusiastic worship, and the car yoked with lions. **1908** SIR H. JOHNSTON *Grenfell & Congo* I. xvi. 394 The slipping of his fingers down the cane set up a vibration of the tympanum of the drum.

2. *Anat.* The drum of the ear (med.L. *tympanum auris*, Albertus Magnus *c* 1255); the middle ear, consisting of a cavity in the temporal bone, filled with air, separated from the outer auditory canal by the tympanic membrane (*membrana tympani*) and from the inner ear by the membranes of the *fenestra ovalis* and *fenestra rotunda*, and containing the chain of small bones (auditory ossicles), or in lower vertebrates the single bone (*columella*), by which sound-vibrations are conveyed to the inner ear. Also often applied to the tympanic membrane simply.

In insects, a similar membrane with connected parts, in some cases supposed to constitute an organ of hearing (cf. quot. 1887 s.v. TYMPANAL *a.*).

1619 PURCHAS *Microcosmus* ix. 99 The passage auditorie being anfractuous, lest the *Tympanum* should by directer incursions be endangered. **1691** RAY *Creation* II. (1692) 38 At the end of this hole is a Membrane..stretched like the head of a Drum, and therefore by Anatomists called also *Tympanum.* **1709** STEELE *Tatler* No. 47 ¶3, I recited some Heroick Lines..which operated so strongly on the Tympanum of his Ear [etc.]. **1726** MONRO *Anat. Bones* (ed. 3) 97 The Cavity of the Ear, called *Tympanum.* **1840** G. V. ELLIS *Anat.* 282 The tympanum or middle ear is a circular space, situated in the base of the petrous portion of the temporal bone..; a chain of small bones crosses the cavity, to convey the undulations of sound to the labyrinth that is internal to it. **1856** TODD & BOWMAN *Phys. Anat.* II. 63 The tympanum..communicates..with the cavity of the throat through..the Eustachian tube, whereby air has a free access into the tympanum. **1868** DUNCAN *Figuier's Insect W.* Introd. 6 The membrane..represents a trace of the tympanum which exists among the higher animals. **1871** ROSSETTI *Poems, Dante at Verona* xlvi, A Jester,..a ribald mouth to shout In Folly's horny tympanum Such things as make the wise man dumb. **1880** GÜNTHER *Fishes* 116 A tympanum, tympanic cavity [etc.] are..absent in..fishes.

b. *Ornith.* (*a*) Each of the two inflatable air-sacs at the sides of the neck in certain birds, as grouse. (*b*) Applied to the bony labyrinth at the base of the trachea in certain species of duck, having resonant membranes in its walls.

1873 COUES *Birds N.W.* (1874) 416 An illy-defined white area on each side of the neck, over the tympanum. **1896** NEWTON *Dict. Birds* 984 [In] the males of many..*Anseres*, some 6 or 8 of the lowest rings [of the trachea are] fused together..forming..the *bulba ossea* or labyrinth... This.. becomes very complicated in the group of 'Diving Ducks', forming in many cases a *tympanum*, whose bony walls are fenestrated and the spaces filled with a resonant membrane.

3. *Arch.* **a.** The die or cubical portion of a pedestal. **b.** The vertical recessed face of a pediment, often adorned with sculpture.

The sense 'panel of a door', given in the Glossary to Gwilt's *Encycl. Archit.*, and thence in mod. Dicts., is app. only Latin (Vitruvius).

1658 tr. *Porta's Nat. Magic* XIX. v. 393 And in the upper surface of the Tympanum, bore the basis quite through with a little pipe, which enters into the hollow of the Tympanum. **1680** EVELYN *Diary* 18 Apr., The tympanum or gabal at the front [of Cashiobury] is a bass-relievo of Diana hunting. **1723** CHAMBERS tr. *Le Clerc's Treat. Archit.* I. 111 The Tympanum is either Triangular or Circular. **1841** W. SPALDING *Italy & It. Isl.* I. 161 The statues..which filled the tympana, or triangular spaces of the pediments at both ends of the temple. *a* **1878** SIR G. G. SCOTT *Lect. Archit.* (1879) I. 166 In the tympanum are sculptured scenes from Scripture history.

4. *Mech.* †**a.** The barrel of a capstan or similar apparatus for raising weights (? only Latin). *Obs.* **b.** A kind of wheel (originally drum-shaped) with curved radial partitions, used for raising water. **c.** A hollow wheel turned by two or more persons walking inside it, and communicating motion to a machine (*Cent. Dict.* 1891).

1704 J. HARRIS *Lex. Techn.* I, *Tympanum*, in Mechanicks, is a Cylinder, but larger and shorter than the common Axis or Cylinder,..and..usually placed upon that Axis, and is much the same with the *Peritrochium*, which is a kind of Wheel..in whose Circumference are Staves or Levers to turn the Axis easily about, in order to raise the Weight required. **1875** KNIGHT *Dict. Mech.*, *Tympanum*, 1. An ancient form of wheel for elevating water... The Roman form of the *tympanum* is described by Vitruvius,..and was derived from Egypt... The *tympanum*, under the name of the *scoop-wheel*, is much used in the drainage of the fens in the East of England.

5. *Bot.* A membrane stretching across the mouth of the spore-case in some urn-mosses.

1832 LINDLEY *Introd. Bot.* 201 Sometimes one membrane only remains,..stretching across the orifice of the theca, which is closed up by it; this is sometimes named the *tympanum.*

tympany (ˈtɪmpənɪ). Also 6 **tympanye,** 6–7 **tym-, timpanie, timpany.** [ad. med.L. *tympanias*, a. Gr. τυμπανίας, f. τύμπανον TYMPANUM.]

1. a. = TYMPANITES; also sometimes used vaguely for a morbid swelling or tumour of any kind. Common from 16th to 18th c. (with *a*, *the*, or without article).

(*a*) **1528** PAYNEL *Salerne's Regim.* C iij b, A tympany..is ingendred..by coldenes of the stomake, and lyuer, not sufferyng mans drynke or meate to be conuerted in to good humours, but tourneth them in to ventosities. **1547** BOORDE *Brev. Health* cccxlv. 111 b, A tympany..doth make ones bely to swel lyke a taber. **1577–87** HOLINSHED *Chron.* III. 1131/1 Some..affirmed that she was deceiued by a timpanie ..to thinke hirselfe with child. **1611** COTGR., *Mole*, a

Timpanie, or Moone-calfe; a shapelesse lump of flesh, or hard swelling, in the wombe. **1635** N. R. *Camden's Hist. Eliz.* Introd., Q. Mary..left her life..of a sixe months Fever and a Tympany. **1706–7** FARQUHAR *Beaux' Strat.* I. i, She cured her of Three Tympanies, but the Fourth carried her off. **1754–64** SMELLIE *Midwif.* II. 82 She was grown very big; a circumstance she imputed to a dropsy or rather a tympany. **1860** EMERSON *Cond. Life, Culture* Wks. (Bohn) II. 363 Nature has no mercy,..makes a dropsy or a tympany of him.

(*b*) **1542** BOORDE *Dyetary* xxviii. (1870) 299 Yet the lyuer is drye, whether it be alchytes, Iposarca, Leucoflegmancia, or the tympany. **1612** WOODALL *Surg. Mate* Wks. (1653) 68 Cummin seed..is good against the chollick and tympany. **1661** LOVELL *Hist. Anim. & Min.* 178 It helps..the collick, tympany, and nephritick passion. **1747** WESLEY *Prim. Physic* (1762) 109 The Tympany or Windy Dropsy. **1844** BABINGTON tr. *Hecker's Epid. Middle Ages* 88 This practice of swathing was resorted to on account of the tympany which followed these spasmodic ravings.

(*c*) **1731** *Gentl. Mag.* I. Index, The Diseases and Casualties this year... Tympany, 3. **1796** E. DARWIN *Zoon.* (1802) III. 208 Tympany consists in an elastic tumor of the abdomen, which sounds on being struck. **1881** *Trans. Obstet. Soc.* XXII. 135 The movements of a coil of distended intestine as in some forms of tympany. **1901** W. OSLER *Princ. & Pract. Med.* i. 26 Obliteration of the liver flatness in the nipple line may be caused by excessive tympany. **1923** G. H. WOOLDRIDGE *Encycl. Vet. Med., Surg. & Obstetr.* II. 1023/2 Tympany is..a common accompaniment of rumenitis. **1970** W. H. PARKER *Health & Dis. in Farm Animals* xiv. 186 The swelling in cases of tympany is primarily on the left.

†**b.** *transf.* or *allusively*, esp. in reference to pregnancy. *Obs.*

1580 LYLY *Euphues* (Arb.) 238 My pursse now swelling with a timpany, I thought to serch al countries for a remedy. **1590** [TARLTON] *News Purgat.* (1844) 78 The maid fell sicke, and her disease was thought to be a timpany with two heeles. **1613** PURCHAS *Pilgrimage* IX. vii. 865 Sometimes the neighbour hils..tumble downe..in the plaine, thereby so amazing the fearefull Riuers, that they runne quite out of their Channels..or else stand still..and..fall into an vncouth tympanie, their bellies swelling into spacious..lakes. **1649** DAVENANT *Love & Hon.* IV. ii, Midwives believe that it foretells A hopefull timpany to come. **1663** DRYDEN *Wild Gallant* v. ii, A mere tympany..raised by a cushion. **1707** MRS. CENTLIVRE *Platonick Lady* II. i, If she has not twice slipt aside for a natural Tympany. **1711** ADDISON *Spect.* No. 127 ¶10 To Unhoop the Fair Sex, and cure this fashionable Tympany that is got among them.

2. *fig.* A swelling, as of pride, arrogance, self-conceit, etc., figured as a disease; a condition of being inflated or puffed up; an excess *of* something figured as a swelling; something big or pretentious, but empty or vain; inflated style, turgidity, bombast. Now *rare* or *Obs.*

1581 J. BELL *Haddon's Answ. Osor.* 389 Why could your holy mother Church suffer so horrible a Tympany, and Imposthume within her owne bowels. **1602** WARNER *Alb. Eng.* Epit. (1612) 387 To this the Dukes Tympanie, the Commons..became Midl-wiues,..vntill..they had brought him a bed of a Kingdome. **1610** DONNE *Pseudo-martyr* 365 This Timpany, or false conception, by which spirituall power is blowne vp, and swelled with temporall. **1616** B. JONSON *Epigr.* xxviii, H' has tympanies of businesse, in his face. **1621** BURTON *Anat. Mel.* I. ii. III. xiv. (1651) 122 Puffed up with this Timpany of self conceit. **1639** FULLER *Holy War* v. xvii. 258 Some would cut off the flesh of the Churches necessary maintenance, under pretense to cure her of a tympanie of superfluities. **1676** E. BURY *Medit.* 214 Wealth many times swells men into a tympany, not easily cured. **1680** EARL ROSCOM. *Horace's Art Poetry* Poems (1780) 105 Others, that affect A lofty style, swell to a tympany. *a* **1703** BURKITT *On N.T.* Luke xiv. 11 He that before their eyes had cured a man of a bodily dropsy, attempts to cure [them] of the tympany of pride. **1723** DK. WHARTON *True Briton* No. 27 I. 233 What..was observ'd of Sejanus holds true of many later Tympanies of Grandeur. **1828** *Blackw. Mag.* XXIV. 906 Dr. Johnson..he charges..with a plethoric and tautologic tympany of sentence. **1829** SOUTHEY *Sir T. More* (1831) II. 288 He was afflicted with a tympany of mind produced by metaphysics. **1842** *Blackw. Mag.* LI. 15 It was the conceit..which turned out to be the sober truth; and our modesty..it was which turned out a windy tympany.

3. = TYMPAN 1, TYMPANUM 1. *rare. Obs.* or *arch.*

1535 *Goodly Primer, Matins* Ps. cl. 4 Praise him with tympany and tabret. **1557** *Sarum Primer* B ij, Let them sing unto him with timpanie and harpe. **1875** BROWNING *Aristoph. Apol., Herakles* 950 By the tympanies and the thyrsos hoist Of the Bromian revel-rout.

4. *Arch.* = TYMPAN 5, TYMPANUM 3 b. *Sc.*

1825 [see TYMPAN 5].

5. *attrib.* and *Comb.*, as ***tympany gavel*** (GABLE *sb.*^{1}), ***window*** (sense 4); ***tympany-like*** adj.

1658 BROMHALL *Treat. Specters* I. 98 Out of a tympany-like ostentation. **1825** Tympany gavel [see TYMPAN 5]. **1849** *Glasgow Past & Present* (1884) I. 106 An old house with tympany windows.

Hence †**tympanied** *ppl. a.* (*obs. nonce-wd.*), inflated as with a tympany, puffed up.

1637 HEYWOOD *Dial., Pelop, & Alope* Argt., Wks. 1874 VI. 297 More simple truth in their chaste loves, Than greater Ladies, tympany'de With much more honour, state, and pride.

tymper, obs. f. TEMPER *sb.*

†**tymyame**, var. *thymyame*, THYMIAMA *Obs.*

1382 WYCLIF *Ezek.* xvi. 18 Myn oyle and my tymyame, [*gloss*] or encense.

tymyr, -yre, obs. ff. TIMBER.

tymze, obs. form of TEMSE, sieve.

tyn, obs. f. TIN, TINE *v.*^{2}; var. TINE *a. Obs.*

tynacle, -akle, obs. ff. TUNICLE.

tynage, -axe, variants of TINAJA, *Obs.* a jar.

tyncke, obs. f. TINK *v.*^{1}

†**tynclare**, obs. form of TINKLER^{1}.

1560 *Abst. Protocols Town Cl. Glasgow* (1896) II. 79.

†**tyncte.** *Obs.* app. = TAINT *sb.* 3.

1456–7 *Paston Lett.* I. 406, I had lever paye xx. marke,..with myn enemyndz good love, than to yelde me to preson ayens here entent, and sewe forth the tyncte. And no trost ..that he wele bere owt the cost of the tyncte.

tynd(e, var. TIND *v. Obs.* to kindle; obs. f. TINE *sb.*^{1}, *v.*^{1}; obs. pa. pple. of TINE *v.*^{2}

Tyndall (ˈtɪndəl). The name of John *Tyndall*, an English physicist (1820–1893), used *attrib.* with reference to the scattering of a beam of light by small particles and the blue colour that the scattered light often has (described by Tyndall in 1869).

1910 H. H. HODGSON tr. *Pöschl's Introd. Chem. of Colloids* ii. 12 The Tyndall effect is the basis of ultra-microscopy. **1915** M. H. FISCHER et al. tr. *Ostwald's Handbk. Colloid-Chem.* 8 Liquids which show no definite Tyndall light-cone ..are molecular-disperse solutions. **1925** G. BARGER tr. *Freundlich's Elem. Colloidal Chem.* 125 All colloidal solutions with colourless particles show a blue Tyndall light. **1939** H. B. WEISER *Colloid Chem.* xii. 160 There is no pigment in blue eyes; the color is a Tyndall blue which is more intense the finer the particles that give rise to the blue color. **1964** *Oceanogr. & Marine Biol.* II. 366 With the searchlights [of the bathyscaph] on, it is possible to discern very minute particles..by the Tyndall effect. **1966** *McGraw-Hill Encycl. Sci. & Technol.* XIV. 169/1 In aqueous gold sols..strong Tyndall cones are observed. **1971** *Nature* 19 Feb. 573/1 Drops smaller than 1 μm form a 'blue haze' due to selective Tyndall scattering of shorter light wavelengths.

Hence **ˈTyndallmeter** (also as two words), **Tyndaˈllometer**, an instrument that makes use of the Tyndall effect for measuring aerosols and suspensions.

1919 TOLMAN & VLIET in *Jrnl. Amer. Chem. Soc.* XLI. 297 (*heading*) A Tyndallmeter for the examination of disperse systems. **1937** *Nature* 25 Sept. 553/1 The hygienic importance of the reduction of dust lends interest to means for its measurement, and the Tyndallometer shown by E. Leitz (London) provides a new and rapid means of its measurement. **1957** H. C. VAN DE HULST *Light Scattering by Small Particles* xix. 405 This problem, of obvious importance in the testing of gas masks, was studied by Gucker and by O'Konski. A Tyndall meter is insufficient for the concentrations of 10^{-9}g/liter and lower that have to be investigated.

tyndallization (ˌtɪndəlaɪˈzeɪʃən). [f. the name of John Tyndall (see prec.); cf. PASTEURIZATION.] A method of sterilization in which time is allowed between repeated heatings for bacteria to develop; fractional or intermittent sterilization. So **ˈtyndallize** *v. trans.* to sterilize by this process (Webster, 1911).

c **1900** *Buck's Handbk. Med. Sci.* I. 686 (Cent. D. Supp.) Tyndallization. **1900–13** in DORLAND *Med. Dict.*

tynder, obs. form of TINDER.

†**tyndesawe.** *Obs. rare*$^{-1}$. [app. f. *saw* SOW *sb.*^{3}, with obscure first element.] A designation of a Lenten sowing.

c **1300** *Battle Abbey Custumals* (1889) 150 Ad semen Quadragesimale quod vocatur Tyndesawe.

†**tyne**, app. an error for *cyue*, var. *cyuey*, *cyvey* (see CIVET *sb.*^{3}) occurring in the same passages.

c **1430** *Two Cookery-bks.* 49 Take flowre, Almaunde milke, & Safroune, & make þer-of .iiij. tynez, & frye þi tynez in Oyle. *Ibid.* 50 Ley on þin cyvey a-bouyn þin Fyssche,..and caste a-bouyn Sugre of Alysaundre, & þer-vppe-on þine tyne.

tyne, obs. f. THYINE, TIN, TIND, TINE.

†**tynel, tynnell.** *Obs. rare.* [a. OF. *tinel* (= It. *tinello*) tub, vat, dim. of *tine* TINE *sb.*^{3}] A vessel for holding liquids.

1336–7 *Acc. Exch. K.R.* 19/31 m. 5 (P.R.O.) In ij. naugers emptis ad eandem..viij. d. Et in xxiiij tynels emptis de Rogero Hirdelere ad dictam nauem purificandam .ij. s. **1540** in V. Green *Hist. Worcester* (1796) II. App. 5 Inprimis, a holy water tynnell of selver and gylte.

Tyneside (ˈtaɪnsaɪd). [SIDE *sb.*^{1} 7 a.] The area adjacent to the banks of the river Tyne in England, *spec.* the city of Newcastle-on-Tyne, used *attrib.* to designate things, esp. speech, characteristic of this area.

1824 R. GILCHRIST *Coll. Original Songs* 9 Hail, Tyneside lads! in collier fleets. **1844** R. NICHOLS in M. A. Richardson *Local Historian's Table Bk.* II. 370 (*heading*) The Tyneside angler. **1872** T. & G. ALLAN (*title*) Tyneside songs. **1896** R. O. HESLOP *Bibliogr. List Wks. Illustr. Dialect Northumberland* 6 Two tales of sixty years sin seyne, as related by the late Thomas Bewick, of Newcastle, in the Tyneside dialect. **1923** A. HERBERT *Northumberland* viii. 127 In the Hancock Museum of National History may be seen the matchless collection of birds set up by the Tyneside naturalist, John Hancock. **1949** H. L. HONEYMAN *Northumberland* II. ii. 219 If there is anything that can be called a Tyneside type it is perhaps the rather small, wiry kind of man. **1955** P. STREVENS *Papers in Lang. & Lang. Teaching* (1965) ix. 114 A uvular fricative *r*, similar to that used in Tyneside pronunciation of English or in Parisian French. **1978** *Early Music Gaz.* Oct. 3/3 The senior minstrel, aged about 12, gave his mates a good Tyne-side dressing-down for being late and playing wrong notes the night before!

Tynesider (ˈtaɪnsaɪdə(r)). [f. prec. + -ER^{1}.] A native or inhabitant of Tyneside. Cf. CLYDESIDER, MERSEYSIDER.

1895 *Tyneside* May 146/1 The Life of Sir Charles Palmer has been frequently written and is familiar enough to every Tynesider. **1923** A. HERBERT *Northumberland* v. 69 The word 'keel' on Tyneside..was the name for an entire boat. .. It is the word for which all Tynesiders have most regard. **1950** S. MIDDLEBROOK *Newcastle upon Tyne* xviii. 222 In the 'forties the practice began of holding an annual skiff race.. either between two local champions, or between a Tynesider and some challenger from the Thames. **1978** M. STOPPARD in D. Abse *My Medical School* 173 Tynesiders were proud of their College.

tynie, obs. f. TINY.

tynke, obs. f. TINK *v.*

tynnacle, -akel, -akil, etc., obs. ff. TUNICLE.

tynne, obs. f. TIN, TIND.

tynsel, -il, -yll (-in, -yn), obs. ff. TINSEL *sb.*^{3}

tynt, obs. f. TENT *sb.*^{4}, *v.*^{1}; obs. pa. t. and pple. of TINE *v.*^{2}

tyntare, obs. f. *tine-tare*: see TINE *sb.*^{4} b.

†**tynte.** *Obs. rare.* [Of obscure origin: cf. ON. *tinta* fem., a small bottle, Norw. dial. *tint* a small vessel or measure; these are probably not native Scand. words.] (See quots.)

c **1440** *Promp. Parv.* 494/2 Tynte, mesure, *satum. Ibid.* 222/2 Half a buschel, or eytendele (..*H., P.* or tynt), *satum.* **1552** HULOET, Tynte or halfe parte of a bushell, *semimodius.*

Tynwald (ˈtɪnwəld, ˈtaɪn-). Also 7 Tynwold, 7–8 Tinewald, 7, 9 Tinwald. [ad. early ON. **þingwall-*, stem of ON. *þingvǫllr* (gen. *-vallar*), f. *þing* THING *sb.*^{2} + *vǫllr* field, level ground. The initial *t* for *th* is due to Manx phonetics. Of the same origin are the place-names *Tinwald* in Dumfriesshire, *Dingwall* in Ross-shire, and *Tingwall* in Shetland.] (Also ***Tynwald Court.***) In the Isle of Man, an annual convention attended by the governor (representing the sovereign), a council acting as the upper house, and the House of Keys, at which the laws which have been enacted are proclaimed to the people. Also *attrib.*, as ***Tynwald chapel, day, hill, mount.***

The MS. source of the earliest quots. dates from the beginning of the 17th century.

1422 *Acts Sir John Stanley* (Manx Soc., vol. III) 71 This is..how you shalle be governed upon your Tynwald dayes. *Ibid.* 92 That the Tynwold be houldene two tymes in the yeare at the leaste. **1610** in *Mills' Statute Laws Isle of Man* (1821) 81 It is agreed..that after Midsomer Day next noe Tinwald shall be holden in this Isle upon the Lord's day. **1656** J. CHALONER *Descr. I. of Man* iv. in D. King *Vale Royall* IV. 16 The said Governour and Officers do usually call the 24 Keyes of the Island, especially once every year, *viz.* upon Midsummer day, at St. John's Chappel, to the Tinewald Court there, where upon a Hill near unto the said Chappel, all the Inhabitants of the Island, standing round about a fair Plain, they may hear the Laws and Ordinances agreed upon before in the Chappel aforesaid, published and declar'd unto them. *Ibid.* 17 If any Orders be agreed upon by the Officers, and 24 Keys, they are..at the next Tynwald, after, proclaimed for absolute Laws. **1701** in *Cowell's Interpr.* s.v. *Tinewald.* **1739** [see KEYS]. **1798** FELTHAM *Tour Isle of Man* xii. 144 The annual mode of promulgating the laws, is at the Tynwald hill. **1836** *Encycl. Brit.* (ed. 7) XIV. 211/2 [A law of the House of Keys] must be promulgated by the lieutenant-governor..on the top of an ancient tumulus called the Tynwald Mount. **1860** *All Year Round* No. 68. 420, I believe..though the language is still employed in some official formulæ of the Tynwald (or ancient court).. the ancient idiom of Mona is very near extinction. **1871** W. HARRISON (*title*) Records of the Tynwald and Saint John's Chapels in the Isle of Man. **1894** HALL CAINE *Little Man Isl.* 15 The open-air Parliament..meets once a year at St. John's, in the centre of the island, on the mount known as Tynwald Hill.

typ, obs. form of TIP.

typacanthid, typarchical: see TYPO-.

typal (ˈtaɪpəl), *a.* [f. TYPE *sb.*^{1} + -AL^{1}.]

1. Of the nature of, serving as, or answering to a type, pattern, or specimen; representative; typical.

1853 BRIMLEY *Ess., My Novel* 277 True typal varieties of English life. **1861** BERESF. HOPE *Eng. Cathedr. 19th C.* i. 18 The 'literate' may become the typal incumbent of England, and..the English clergyman—gentleman and scholar as well as Christian—become a thing of the past. **1882** DORLING in *Sunday Mag.* 196 A charming glimpse of a typal Welsh preacher.

2. Pertaining or relating to a type or symbol; symbolic; emblematic.

1893 E. DINGLE (*title*) The typal use of the 22 letters of the Hebrew alphabet in the Psalms &c.

3. Of or pertaining to printing type; typographical.

1882 J. Parker *Apost. Life* I. 62 There are palpitations which cannot be reported, and tones which have no typal representation.

type (taɪp), *sb.*[1] Also 6–7 **tipe.** [ad. F. *type* (16th c. in Littré) or L. *typus*, a. Gr. τύπος impression, figure, type, f. the root of τύπτειν to beat, strike.]

1. a. That by which something is symbolized or figured; anything having a symbolical signification; a symbol, emblem; *spec.* in *Theol.* a person, object, or event of Old Testament history, prefiguring some person or thing revealed in the new dispensation; correl. to *antitype*. ***in (the) type***, in symbolic representation.

c **1470** Henryson *Mor. Fab.* (S.T.S.) 579 Suppose this be ane Fabill, And ouerheillit with typis figurall. **1590** 'Hobynoll' *To Learned Sheph.* v. in *Spenser's F.Q.* (Pref. Verses), That fare Ilands right, Which thou dost vayle in Type of Faery land, Elizas blessed field, that Albion hight. **1607** Hieron *Wks.* I. 104 The people of Israel were a tipe of Gods people: Canaan a tipe of heauen. **1654** Jer. Taylor *Real Pres.* v. 103 He offered wine not water in the type..of his bloud. **1706** Prior *Ode to Queen* xxxiv, The British Rose, Type of sweet Rule, and gentle Majesty. **1781** Fletcher *Lett.* Wks. 1795 VII. 236 [Marriage] the most perfect type of our Lords union with his church. **1829** *The Bengallee* 182 The Hookah's monstrous snake... That type of eastern Luxury's excess. **1851** Kingsley in *Life* (1878) I. 255 It is only in proportion as we appreciate and understand the types that we can understand the anti-types. **1863** Mary Howitt *F. Bremer's Greece* II. xii. 29 A river is always the type of human life. **1875** Manning *Mission H. Ghost* i. 15 Ceremonial actions, and washings, and purifications, which were the types and shadows of things to come.

b. An imperfect symbol or anticipation *of* something. *nonce-use.*

1754 Foote *Knights* I. Wks. 1799 I. 62 The very abstract of penury! Sir John Cutler, with his transmigrated stockings, was but a type of him.

†2. a. A figure or picture of something; a representation; an image or imitation. *Obs. rare.*

1559 W. Cunningham *Cosmogr. Glasse* 10 This Type do represent the world. *Ibid.* 156 Wherfore behold the tipe before placed. **1572** Gascoigne *Herbs*, *Voy. into Holland* 7, I must endite..A tipe of heauen, a liuely hew of hell. **1774** J. Bryant *Mythol.* II. 445 Lunar amulets, or types of the Ark in the form of a crescent.

b. *Numism.* The figure on either side of a coin or medal.

1785 Holcroft tr. *Mme. de Genlis' Tales Castle* (ed. 2) I. Notes 292 On the two sides..of a medal..are distinguished the type, and the inscription or legend. The type, or device, is the figure represented. **1853** Humphreys *Coin-Coll. Man.* vi. 61 The crab, being perhaps at an early period made sacred to the river deity, became the principal type of the money of this city [Agrigentum]. **1904** W. M. Ramsay *Lett. Seven Churches* xix. 262 Homer is one of the most frequent types on coins of the city.

3. A distinguishing mark or sign; a stamp. *rare.*

1593 Shaks. *3 Hen. VI*, I. iv. 121 Thy Father beares the type of King of Naples. **1613** —— *Hen. VIII*, I. iii. 31 Tennis and tall Stockings, Short blistred Breeches, and those types of Trauell. **1692** Prior *Ode Imit. Horace* viii. 28 Heav'n as plainly pointed out the King, As when he at the Altar stood, In all his Types and Robes of Powr. **1862** Burton *Bk. Hunter* (1863) 11 The types of a really hospitable country house were an anker of whisky always on the spigot, a caldron ever on the bubble with boiling water. *Ibid.* 44 All these things were the types of an intellectual vitality.

4. *Path.* The characteristic form of a fever; *esp.* the character of an intermittent fever as determined by its period. Cf. *type-fever* in 10. [So L. *typus*.] *Obs.* or merged in 5.

1601 Holland *Pliny* xxii. xiv. II. 122 The fever also, Of what type or kind it is. *Ibid.* xxvi. xi. 260 Some are wont to give of Cinque foile three leaves in a Tertian, and foure in a Quartane, and so rise to more according to the period or type of the rest. **1776** W. Cullen *First Lines Pract. Physic* §30 With respect to the form, or Type, of fevers. **1818–20** J. Thompson *Cullen's Nosol. Method.* (ed. 3) 187 [Fever] with intermission, varying (*a*) in type or period. **1858** Copland *Dict. Pract. Med.* I. 937 The type of masked ague is generally quotidian.

5. a. The general form, structure, or character distinguishing a particular kind, group, or class of beings or objects; hence *transf.* a pattern or model after which something is made.

1843 Mill *Logic* iv. ii. §3 (1856) II. 192 When we..see a creature resembling an animal, we compare it with our general conception of an animal; and if it agrees with that general conception, we include it in the class. The conception becomes the type of comparison. **1857** Maurice *Ep. St. John* i. 3 The type upon which the whole was constructed. **1860** Motley *Netherl.* (1868) I. i. 15 His face had lost all resemblance to the type of his heroic family. **1864** *Soc. Science Rev.* 3 Diseases are founded on types like animals, plants, systems of worlds [etc.]. **1874** Blackie *Self-Cult.* 4 The fundamental unity of type which the Divine reason has imposed on all things. **1874** Parker *Goth. Archit.* i. i. 1 The original type of all Christian churches is universally acknowledged to have been the Roman Basilica. **1877** Roberts *Handbk. Med.* (ed. 3) I. 12 A few diseases exhibit well-marked types. **1880** *Mem. J. Legge* vi. 76 Every creature has a type, a peculiar character of its own.

b. *Ch. Hist.* [Gr. τύπος τῆς πίστεως type of the faith.] An edict of the Emperor Constans II, promulgated A.D. 648, prohibiting further discussion of the Monothelite controversy.

1727–41 Chambers *Cycl.*, *Type*, τυπος,..a name given to an edict of the Emperor Constans II... It had the name type, as being a kind of formulary of faith. **1854** Milman *Lat. Chr.* iv. vi. (1864) II. 322 The Ecthesis of Heraclius was replaced by the Type of Constans. The Type..aspired to silence by authority this interminable dispute. **1902** J. K. Mann *Hist. Popes* I. i. 381 Paul caused the Emperor Constans to issue the 'Type'... The 'Type' ordered the Ecthesis to be taken down, and forbade anyone in future to speak of either one or two wills or operations in Our Lord.

6. a. A kind, class, or order as distinguished by a particular character.

1854 Brewster *More Worlds* iv. 73 On a planet more magnificent than ours, may there not be a type of reason of which the intellect of Newton is the lowest degree? **1855** Macaulay *Hist. Eng.* xx. IV. 531 The Queen was sinking under small pox of the most malignant type. **1879** M. Arnold *Ess.*, *Porro unum est necess.* 152 The instruction in both is of the same type. **1888** Bryce *Amer. Commw.* II. xlviii. 220 Three types of rural local government are discernible in America. **1897** D. W. Forrest *Christ of Hist. & Exp.* i. 31 It is a different type of moral character: another order of humanity. **1898** *Jrnl. Sch. Geog.* (U.S.) Oct. 306 The dominant weather type was clear, with light southerly winds and temperatures between 50° and 55°. This type was interrupted by two spells of cloudy weather, with northerly winds.

b. Preceding a sb. with ellipsis of *of*, = type of. Cf. -TYPE 2. *U.S. colloq.*

1966 *Word Study* Dec. 2/2 He could not pick out things like a bridge from 'this type distance'. **1979** *Nature* 22 Nov. p. xvii/1 The 110C systems may be used with virtually any type projector.

7. *transf.* **a.** A person or thing that exhibits the characteristic qualities of a class; a representative specimen; a typical example or instance.

1842 Prichard *Nat. Hist. Man* (ed. 2) 333 The Tahitians are considered by Lesson as the type of the whole Polynesian race. *a* **1854** Reed *Lect. Brit. Poets* v. (1857) 172 Shakspeare may be contemplated as the type of modern intellect and the representative of the European mind. **1865** Dickens *Mut. Fr.* iii. viii, It is a type of many. **1873** Ruskin *Fors Clav.* xxxiv. (1896) II. 236 Sir Roger de Coverley is a character, as well as a type.

b. *spec.* A person or thing that exemplifies the ideal qualities or characteristics *of* a kind or order; a perfect example or specimen *of* something; a model, pattern, exemplar.

1847 Emerson *Repr. Men, Goethe* Wks. (Bohn) I. 392 He is the type of culture. *a* **1853** Robertson *Lect., Wordsw.* 228 Arnold of Rugby is the type of English action; Wordsworth is the type of English thought. **1858** J. H. Newman *Hist. Sk.* (1873) III. ii. i. 221 Plato is the very type of soaring philosophy.

c. A person of a certain (specified or implicit) character; ***one's type***, the sort of person to whom one is attracted (usu. in neg. or interrog. contexts). Also simply, a person; as a gallicism, also with pronunc. (‖tip), derogatory. *colloq.*

1922 [see ABANDON *sb.*[3]]. **1930** Kipling *Limits & Renewals* (1932) 327, I played piquet with our schoolmaster... *That* was a type upon whom our War had done bad work. **1931** K. Boyle *Plagued by Nightingale* xv. 123 Luc could fish with Nicholas... It's exactly what the poor *type* would prefer anyway! **1933** 'G. Orwell' *Down & Out in Paris & London* xxix. 216 'Low types,' said the old Etonian, 'very low types.' **1934** F. B. Cuthrell *Innocent Bystander* vii. 130 Richardson did not interest her, he was not her 'type'. **1942** T. Rattigan *Flare Path* ii. i. 127 You're the actor type, aren't you? **1948** 'N. Shute' *No Highway* ii. 41 It didn't do Fisher any good with the R.A.F. types. **1951** J. G. Fennessy *Sonnet in Bottle* i. v. 28 'Oh, by the way, do you know these types?' and he introduced the two men with him. **1956** 'A. Bridge' *Lighthearted Quest* 199, I went to look for Colin in that red-haired type's house. **1962** A. Lurie *Love & Friendship* xiii. 250 You wouldn't like him... He's not your type. He's a little fat man. **1965** R. & D. Morris *Men & Snakes* i. 16 Although an intrepid explorer type, he made a hasty exit. **1968** M. Jones *Survivor* iii. 51 'I'm asking you if you think she's at all his type.' Stuart shrugged. 'I shouldn't care to say what Martin's type is. Come to think of it, I'd say he has no type.' **1971** D. E. Westlake *I gave at Office* 136, I was not alone in the room. Three army types were there.. tall, fat, khaki-uniformed. **1974** J. Aiken *Midnight is Place* iv. 142 That *type*... He is a brigand! **1979** R. Jaffe *Class Reunion* ii. ii. 145 I've always thought you were very beautiful, Annabel. You always were just my type. **1979** A. Fraser *King Charles II* vii. 102 These were scarcely the types to risk life and limb. **1981** 'M. Hebden' *Pel is Puzzled* xi. 113 'Type over here... He recognises it.' The 'type over here' was a man about thirty-five with long blond hair.

8. Technical uses from senses 5–7.

a. *Nat. Hist.*, etc. A certain general plan of structure characterizing a group of animals, plants, etc.; hence *transf.* a group or division of animals, etc., having a common form or structure.

1850 McCosh *Div. Govt.* ii. ii. (ed. 2) 162 In the organic kingdoms, there is an all-pervading system of types: there is a type for every particular species of plant and animal; a type for every leaf and every limb. **1850** Tennyson *In Mem.* lv, So careful of the type she seems, So careless of the single life. **1867** Dk. Argyll *Reign Law* iv. 215 The adaptability of the one Vertebrate Type to the..variety of Life to which it serves as..a home. **1872** Oliver *Elem. Bot.* ii. 122 You must try to refer to its type every flowering plant you meet with. **1877** Huxley *Anat. Inv. Anim.* i. 49 Such types or common plans as those of the *Arthropoda*, the *Annelida*, the *Mollusca* [etc.]. **1878** Gurney *Crystallogr.* 30 By the type of symmetry of a crystal we mean the number and arrangement of its symmetral planes. **1892** Westcott *Gospel of Life* 10 The product of any particular seed is fixed within the limits of a type.

b. *Nat. Hist.* A species or genus which most perfectly exhibits the essential characters of its family or group, and from which the family or group is (usually) named; an individual embodying all the distinctive characteristics of a species, etc., *esp.* the specimen on which the first published description of a species is based.

1840 Whewell *Philos. Induct. Sci.* viii. ii. I. 476 A Type is an example of any class, for instance, a species of a genus, which is considered as eminently possessing the characters of the class. **1851** Woodward *Mollusca* i. 61 The type of each genus should be that species in which the characters of its group are best exhibited, and most evenly balanced. **1858** Mayne *Expos. Lex.*, *Salicornieus*,..a tribe of the *Chenopodeæ* established by C. A. Meyer, having the *Salicornia* for their type. **1893** O. Thomas in *Proc. Zool. Soc.* 242 The following are..the definitions now suggested for the different terms: A Type is a single specimen either unaccompanied by others at the time of description, or else deliberately selected as such by the author out of a series. **1951** G. H. M. Lawrence *Taxonomy of Vascular Plants* ix. 205 The term type, used alone and unqualified, generally refers to the holotype. **1964** *Internat. Code Zool. Nomencl.* xiii. 59 The 'type' affords the standard of reference that determines the application of a scientific name. **1970** *Watsonia* VIII. 156 A herbarium sheet stated..to be the 'type'..is, however, quite different.

c. *Chem.* A simple compound taken as representing the structure of more complex compounds.

1852 Watts tr. *Gmelin's Handbk. Chem.* VII. 15 Dumas' Theory of Substitution and of Types. **1857** Miller *Elem. Chem.* (1862) III. 48 Water, hydrochloric, and hydrosulphuric acid are, therefore, the patterns or types upon which these several bodies are formed. **1868** Watts *Dict. Chem.* V. 926 Bodies analogous in constitution, and exhibiting analogous reactions, are said to belong to the same type... In a wider sense, the formula HCl may be taken as the type of chlorides, bromides, iodides, fluorides, and cyanides.

d. *Math.* (See quots.)

1891 *Cent. Dict.*, *Type* 12. In *math.*, a succession of symbols susceptible of + and − signs. **1911** Webster, *Type* ..6, the simplest of the forms equivalent with respect to a group.

e. *Semiotics*, etc. A sign representing a category or set of instances, as opposed to the individual tokens by which the category is instantiated. Cf. TOKEN *sb.* 1 f.

1908 [see TOKEN *sb.* 1 f]. **1966** *Publ. Amer. Dial. Soc.* xlvi. 13 The incidence of tokens is..equal to the sum of all forms. .. The incidence of types..is equal to the number of different forms. **1976** *Biometrika* LXIII. 435 Shakespeare's known works comprise 884 647 total words, of which 14 376 are types appearing just one time, 4343 are types appearing twice, etc.

9. a. A small rectangular block, usually of metal or wood, having on its upper end a raised letter, figure, or other character, for use in printing. ***in types***, in type (see b). Also *fig.*

1713 J. Watson *Hist. Art Printing* 54 Christopher Plantin ..printed..that fine Bible..whose Types were casten and made at Paris. **1727–41** Chambers *Cycl.* s.v. *Printing*, The printing letters, characters, or types, as they are sometimes called. **1751** Berkeley *Let. to Prior* 30 Mar., Wks. 1871 IV. 327 They are going to print..two editions..of Plato's works, in most magnificent types. **1799** *Monthly Rev.* XXX. 290 A method of printing maps and charts of any size by means of moveable types. **1829** Macaulay *Westm. Reviewer's Def. Mill* (*ad fin.*), The preceding article was written, and was actually in types, when [etc.]. **1849** Ruskin *Sev. Lamps* v. §3 The types which once had the die of thought struck fresh upon them. **1880** Vern. Lee *Stud. Italy* iii. ii. 102 Musical types had..been invented by an Italian.

b. *sing.* Types collectively; letter. ***in type***, set up ready for printing.

1778 V. Knox *Ess.* xxxviii. 305 To trace the art in its gradual progress from the wooden and immoveable letter to the moveable and metal type. **1784** J. Belknap in *B. Papers* (1877) II. 179, I believe some brethren of the type are offended at it. **1837** Sir F. Palgrave *Merch. & Friar* Ded. (1844) 4 The work..had been kept in type for nearly a twelve-month. **1852** Dickens *Lett.* (1880) I. 291 This story goes straightway into type. **1869** Tyndall *Notes Lect. Light* §71 Compositors arrange their type in this backward fashion, the type being reversed by the process of printing. **1882** J. Southward *Pract. Print.* (1884) 9 A bill of type is a table showing the number of each of the several sorts in a fount. **1904** R. J. Farrer *Garden Asia* 63 Not China, but Korea, was the inventor of movable type, and the true parent of printing.

c. *transf.* A printed character or characters, or an imitation of these.

1784 Cowper *Task* v. 419 To read engraven on the mouldy walls [of the Bastille] In stagg'ring types, his predecessor's tale. **1831** Brewster *Optics* xxxviii. §183. 320 To see small objects distinctly..such as..a small type. **1841** J. T. Hewlett *Parish Clerk* I. 125 It was directed in the well-known type of Davy Diggs. **1872** Ruskin *Fors Clav.* (1896) I. xvi. 321 Here it is in full type, for it is worth careful reading.

10. *attrib.* and *Comb.*, as ***type-animal***, ***category***, ***-character***, ***description***, ***-figure***, ***-fossil***, ***index***, ***-man***, ***-name***, ***-number***, ***-phase***, ***-phenomenon***, ***-sample***, ***-series***, ***-set***, ***-ship***, ***-symptom***, ***-theme***, ***-tragedy***; in sense 9, as ***type-arrangement***, ***-body*** (BODY *sb.* 13), ***-case***, ***-composition***, ***-foundry***, ***-mould***, ***-punch***, ***-size***; objective, instrumental, etc., as ***type-founder***; ***type-composing***, ***-creating***, ***-distributing***, ***-founding***, ***-making***, sbs. and adjs.; ***type-blackened***, ***-marked*** adjs.; **type approval** (see quot. 1979); **type area**, (*a*) the part of a page covered by print; (*b*) the location of a type-specimen or an area taken as typical of a particular group; *Geol.* = *type site* below; **type-ball**, a spherical ball on certain kinds of electric typewriter on which all the type is mounted; = *golf ball* (*b*) s.v. GOLF *sb.* b; **type-bar**, (*a*) a line of type cast in a solid bar, as by the linotype; (*b*) in a typewriter, each of the bars carrying the letters or characters; **type basket**, the assembly of type-bars in a typewriter; **type-block**, a block having raised characters on its face, used to impress words or figures, as in gilding (Knight *Dict. Mech.* 1875); **type-blow**, the impact of the type on the paper in a typewriter; **type-carriage**, in a printing-machine, a frame carrying the form; **type-chart**, a chart or outline of a typical object or structure; **type-copy** *sb.* (*arch.*), a typewritten copy; so **type-copy** *v. trans.* (*arch.*); **type-cutter**, one who engraves the dies or punches from which types are cast; a punch-cutter; so **type-cutting**; **type-cylinder**, the cylinder on which the types or plates are fastened in a rotary press; **type-desk**, a desk or table at which typewriting is done; **type-dressing**, the scraping, polishing, etc., of newly cast type: in quot. *attrib.*; **type face**, a set of printing type of a particular design; cf. FACE *sb.* 22, FOUNT[2]; **type facsimile**, a copy of a piece of printing which is either a page-for-page copy using type as close as possible to the original or an exact photographic reproduction; **type-fallacy** *Logic*, the fallacy or mistake of including amongst the members of a type or category something belonging to another type or category (see quot. 1908); †**type-fever**, an intermittent fever, an ague; **type-form**, (*a*) = FORM *sb.* 20; (*b*) a typical or representative form; **type-gauge**, (*a*) a gauge used by type-founders to test the size of type-bodies; (*b*) a type-measure (*Cassell's Encycl. Dict.*, 1888); **type-genus**, the genus which most perfectly exemplifies the essential characters of the family to which it belongs; *esp.* the genus from which the name of the family is taken; **type height** = HEIGHT *sb.* 1 c; **type-high**, *a.* of the standard height of type (i.e. in Great Britain formerly ·9175 in., now and in *U.S.* ·918 in.); *adv.* as high as, so as to correspond in height with, type; **type-holder**, an instrument for holding types, used for stamping or lettering books (*Cent. Dict.* 1891); **type-larval**, *a.* of or pertaining to a *type larva*, i.e. one which exhibits features characteristic of the group to which it belongs, which do not appear in the adult form; **type-letter**, each of the types or letters of a typewriter; **type-lever**, a lever by which a type or character is impressed, as in a linotype; **type locality** = *type-area* (*b*), above, *type site* below; **type-matter**, printed matter, letterpress; **type-measure, -measurer** (Knight *Dict. Mech.*), a rule showing the depth of the various kinds of type, used in calculating the number of lines or ems in composed type; **type-metal**, an alloy of lead and antimony, sometimes with tin or bismuth, of which printing types are cast; **type-music**, music printed from types; **type-page**, the page of type or letterpress as distinct from the paper-page on which it is printed; **type-paper**, paper suitable for typewriting; **type-printed** *a.*, printed from types; also, type-written; so **type-printing**; **type-psychology**, psychological study or theory based on the classification of people or phenomena by type; **type-rule** (*Funk's Stand. Dict.*, 1895); **type-scale** = *type-measure* (*Cent. Dict.* 1891); **typescript** [cf. *typoscript* TYPO-], *sb.* type-written matter or copy; *a.* typewritten; hence **typescript** *v. trans.*, to record in typescript; **typescripted** *ppl. a.*; **typescripting** *vbl. sb.*; **typesetter**, a compositor; also, a composing-machine; so **typesetting**, *sb.* and *a.*, **typeset** *a.*; **type site** *Archæol.*, *Geol.*, etc., a site the features of which are used to define, or are paradigmatic of, a culture, stratigraphic level, etc.; **type-slug** = *type-bar* a (*Funk's Stand. Dict.*, 1895); **type-species**, *Nat. Hist.* a species which most perfectly exemplifies its genus; *esp.* the species on which the genus is based; **type-specimen**, (*a*) *Nat. Hist.* a specimen or individual on which the species is based, and from which the specific name is taken; also *fig.*; (*b*) a printed sheet or booklet showing the variety of type-faces a printer or founder has available; **type-sticker**, a compositor (*slang*); **type-system**, a system of teaching by types or representative specimens; **type test** *sb.* (esp. *Aeronaut.*), a test conducted to determine whether a new piece of equipment meets its specifications; also *attrib.*; hence **type-test** *v. trans.*; **type-theory**, *Chem.* the theory of the derivation of compounds from types (sense 8 c) by substitution; **type-token** *attrib.*, in *Semiotics*, etc., pertaining to types and tokens, involving the relationship of type to tokens (see TOKEN *sb.* 1 f, sense 8 e above); **type-transliteration**, transliteration into modern type or letterpress; **type-value**, value as a type or standard of comparison; **type-wash**, a washing medium for type or plates (Webster, 1911); **type-wheel**, a wheel with raised characters on its periphery, as in the printing telegraph and in some typewriters; **type-work**, letterpress; also type-setting, composing. Also TYPEWRITER, etc.

1850 *Jrnl. Asiatic Soc. Bengal* Jan. 35 This rare and beautiful creature [the giraffe], *type-animal of their land. *Ibid.* 36 The elephant is evidently with these people, the type-animal. **1967** *Economist* 15 Apr. 270/1 The Europeans are used to the '*type approval' on which most Continental governments insist before [motor] models can be sold. **1979** *Gloss. Terms Quality Assurance* (*B.S.I.*) 11/2 *Type approval*, the status given to a design that has been shown by type tests to meet all the requirements of the product specification and which is suitable for a specific application. **1916** W. H. HAZELL et al. *Estimating for Printers* 19 Before an estimate.. can be worked out, the following points must be decided: Number of words in bookwork..; size of type,..and *type area of page. **1937** *Burlington Mag.* June 309/2 Consideration of primitive work as craftsmanship..is no more essential for an æsthetic evaluation than the geographical location of type-areas. **1969** *Proc. Geol. Soc.* Aug. 146 Customary stratigraphical usage should be maintained by placing the marker-points as near to the stratigraphical correspondence with traditional boundaries as possible, although not necessarily in the traditional type-area. **1973** S. JENNETT *Making of Books* (ed. 5) xvi. 338 There is a theory that the type area should be about 50 per cent of the page area. **1975** Type area [see *type site* below]. **1877** W. BOYD *Descr. Model Newspaper*, A sheet..regarding *type-arrangement, Excellent. **1971** *Computers & Humanities* VI. 43 The character set..is limited to the Selectric *type-balls specified by the scanning service. **1977** *Daily Tel.* 3 Aug. 3/5 There has been a real search for a type ball from one of the IBM electric typewriters that were in the office. **1886** *Science* 17 Sept. 252/2 As the *type-bar of a type-writer is connected with its key. **1891** in *Cent. Dict.* **1931** M. CROOKS *Bk. of Underwood Typewriter* ii. 10 Above and behind the keyboard, occupying practically the centre of the framework, is the type—this part of the machine is known as the *Type-Basket. **1968** *Typing* ('Know the Craft' Series) 4/1 Every machine has a type basket and a carriage. **1900** KIPLING in *Daily Express* 26 June 4/6 Allen wagged a *type-blackened forefinger across the table. **1901** *Phonetic Jrnl.* 15 June 371/1 In..an electrical typewriter..the *type-blow, or the hammer-blow, will be automatic. **1895** *Funk's Standard Dict.* s.v. *Point system*, Under this system the old names of *type-bodies, as *nonpareil* (now 6-point), *bourgeois* (now 9-point), etc., are in disuse. **1825** J. NICHOLSON *Operat. Mechanic* 307 By the farther motion of the *type carriage, the ink-table is caused to pass under four small elastic rollers. **1891** *Cent. Dict.*, *Type-case. **1909** H. HART in *Periodical* Feb. 294 A double-windowed room..was fitted up with compositors' frames and type-cases. **1947** *Amer. Jrnl. Sociol.* LII. 293 Kinship, its relationships and institutions, are the *type categories of experience and the familial group is the unit of action. **1931** *Times Lit. Suppl.* 5 Nov. 865/3 Mr. Strauss hits off the foibles of his *type-characters with wit and acumen. **1887** J. G. WOOD in *19th Cent.* Mar. 386 There are *type-charts of each organ. **1878** JEVONS *Prim. Pol. Econ.* 71 Some compositors still object to work in offices where *type-composing machines are introduced. **1890** H. JAMES *Let.* 10 Nov. (1981) III. 307 A shorter story..which I am just sending off to be *typecopied. **1893** *Ibid.* 2 July 416, I have determined to dispatch by the same post as this note, in another cover, a fresh *type-copy of the said first act. **1854** GEO. ELIOT tr. *Feuerbach's Essence Christianity* vii. 75 Mind presenting itself as at once *type-creating, emotional, and sensuous, is the imagination. **1881** *Instr. Census Clerks* (1886) 51 *Type cutter, founder. **1890** *Athenæum* 1 Mar. 281/3 He was a die-sinker and type-cutter. **1839** T. C. HANSARD *Print. & Type founding* (1841) 156 An inking apparatus was applied to the *type-cylinder, and the paper was to be impressed by passing between the two. **1905** *Type-description [see PROTOLOGUE]. **1962** J. A. FORD *Quantitative Method for deriving Cultural Chronol.* iii. 16 Other workers have sought to achieve greater precision by dealing not with types but with various elements, attributes, or 'modes'..that are usually hidden away in the type description. **1967** J. DEETZ *Invitation to Archaeol.* 51 An artifact type description is..a statement of a set of somewhat variable attributes which can be observed to occur together in the majority of cases. **1901** F. HARRISON in *19th Cent.* June 918 Every girl at a *type-desk or a telegraph office may live to reside in Fifth Avenue. **1875** KNIGHT *Dict. Mech.* 2676/1 *Type-distributing machines have frequently been invented as companion machines to those for composing. *Ibid.*, **Type-dressing machine*..passes the type set up in rows between a pair of knife-blades set in exact parallelism. **1887** T. B. REED *Hist. Old Eng. Letter Foundries* i. 40 It now remains to trace briefly the origin and development of the leading *type-faces used in English Typography. **1923** S. MORISON *On Type Faces* p. v, The choice of type face is always a matter of immediate and insistent importance. **1980** B. CRUTCHLEY *To be a Printer* v. 65 Bodoni..produced in his lifetime over four hundred type faces. **1900** (*title*) *Type Facsimile Society. Publications of the Society for the year 1900. **1966** *Eng. Studies* XLVII. 298 It [*sc.* old spelling] does no harm, provided the reader is not misled into using the book as a type-facsimile. [**1908** B. RUSSELL *Logic & Knowl.* (1956) 75 The division of objects into types is necessitated by the reflexive fallacies which otherwise arise. These fallacies.. are to be avoided by what may be called the 'vicious-circle principle'; i.e., 'no totality can contain members defined in terms of itself'.] **1935** *Mind* XLIV. 150 Now, of course, the word 'about' is very ambiguous; but, in one sense of it, to say that a proposition is about itself is to commit the simplest of *type-fallacies. **1952** *Mind* LXI. 130 The type-fallacy that only moral goodness itself is good. **1967** *Philos.* XLII. 3 A transition from one to the other would then become tantamount to a category-mistake or type-fallacy. **1819** SIR A. BOSWELL in *Poet. Wks. & Mem.* Introd. 33 Being infected with the *type-fever the fits have periodically returned. **1897** *Westm. Gaz.* 16 Mar. 2/1 Mr. Meredith.. has himself drawn the great *type-figure of modern fiction ..'The Egoist'. **1839** URE *Dict. Arts* 1035 To adapt this method of inking to a flat *type-form machine. **1875** *Ibid.* III. 660 Mr. Applegarth..decided on abandoning the reciprocating motion of the type-form. **1900** F. H. STODDARD *Evol. Eng. Novel* 218 Mankind demands that it shall show conformity to a certain type-form. **1901** *Nature* 19 Dec. 168/1 The author divides the species into the type-form and four varieties. **1854** MURCHISON *Siluria* iii. 52 The *type-fossils..have not yet been detected. **1797** M. L. WEEMS *Let.* 13 July in *Works & Ways* (1929) II. 84 A letter was written..containing an order on Mr. Baine the *Type Founder for some money. **1801** *Tilloch's Philos. Mag.* X. 270 A new art, that of the type-founder. **1888** BURGON *Lives 12 Gd. Men* I. iii. 349 A heavy assortment of great and small pica, newly arrived from the type-founder. **1839** T. C. HANSARD *Print. & Type-founding* (1841) 222 The invention of the art of *type-founding was a very early consequence of the discovery of the rude art of taking impressions from laboriously excised letters of wood and metal. **1875** W. BLADES in *Bks. in Chains* (1892) Introd. 24 The first positive notice we have of type-founding in England is the fount of Saxon cut by John Day for Archbishop Parker and used in 1567. **1809** T. JEFFERSON *Let.* 28 June in *Writings* (1904) XII. 295 The foundation of printing..is the *type-foundry. **1843** *Penny Cycl.* XXV. 454/1 The first and most important operation of a type-foundry is the formation of the punches. **1840** WHEWELL *Philos. Induct. Sci.* VIII. ii. I. 477 The type-species of every genus, the *type-genus of every family, is, then, one which possesses all the characters and properties of the genus in a marked and prominent manner. **1896** H. WOODWARD *Guide Fossil Reptiles Brit. Mus.* 65 Dr. Filhol records the type-genus from the Upper Eocene Phosphorites of France. **1905** C. T. JACOBI *Printers' Handbk.* (ed. 3) 22 There is some uncertainty as to what is *type-height, and therefore all those engaged in supplying blocks..to the printer should remember that type-height is ·9175 inch. **1931** R. R. KARCH *Printing & Allied Trades* iii. 9 Type heights differ in foreign countries. In England the height is ·917; France, Germany and Spain ·928. **1973** S. JENNETT *Making of Books* (ed. 5) ii. 40 Type height, or height to paper, is not the same thing as height of face. **1896** T. L. DE VINNE *Moxon's Mech. Exerc.*, *Printing* 406 Brass Rule..cut in strips *type-high. **1890** W. J. GORDON *Foundry* 213 The copper electro is mounted type-high, and becomes the block from which the printing is made. **1943** *Mind* LII. 271 In *Principia* the need to avoid a small number of objectionable trains of argument is made the occasion for wholesale elaboration of symbolism (the introduction of *type-indices). **1972, 1973** Type index [see *motif-index* s.v. MOTIF 4]. **1884** HYATT in *Proc. Boston Soc. Nat. Hist.* 5 Mar. 122 Their embryonic history has no stage which exhibits.. a distinct *type-larval stage. **1876** *Nature* 18 May 43/2 Two keys struck at the same time must consequently cause two *type-letters to clash in their attempt to reach the same spot, the centre of the circle. **1908** *Daily Chron.* 26 Aug. 5/2 The typist has at his disposal all kinds of type on type wheels which are fixed at the end of *type levers. **1934** WEBSTER, *Type-locality. **1937** *Brit. Birds* XXXI. 10 Dr. Ticehurst has given as type-locality Lincolnshire. **1940** *Chambers's Techn. Dict.* 874/2 *Type locality*, the locality from which a rock, formation, etc., has been named and described, usually because of its characteristic occurrence there. **1962** GORDON & LAVOIPIERRE *Entomol. for Students of Med.* liii. 325 The locality from which the holotype was collected is known as the 'type locality'. **1969** *Proc. Geol. Soc.* Aug. 159 Donovan ..stated Watchet to be the type-locality of the index species of the zone, but gave no type-locality for the zone itself. **1872** T. L. CUYLER *Heart Life* 25 He is the *type-man for thorough-going fidelity. **1906** DK. ARGYLL *Autobiog. & Mem.* I. ii. 32 The type-man was Wolfe Tone, the unscrupulous Villain. **1866** G. M. HOPKINS *Jrnl.* 16 May (1959) 137 Hawthorn especially when thrown up with may is very clearly *type-marked. **1892** *Advt.* in *Photogr. Ann.* II. p. clxiv, Phototype Prints are the best for reproducing Portraits [etc.]..*Type Matter requires a second printing. **1800** tr. *Lagrange's Chem.* I. 445 Antimony and lead form a most valuable mixture; it is that used for printing-types, and is called *Type-Metal. **1818** TODD, *To stereotype*, to make type-metal plates to print from at the letter-press. **1850** ANSTED *Elem. Geol.*, *Min.* etc. §475 [Antimony] is used in the manufacture of type metal, of which it forms from one fourth to a twelfth part, the rest being lead, with a little tin, bismuth, and copper. **1882** J. SOUTHWARD *Pract. Print.* (1884) 15 Type metal is of two kinds, ordinary and hard. **1843** *Penny Cycl.* XXV. 454/1 A *type-mould [illustrated]. **1882** J. SOUTHWARD *Pract. Print.* (1884) 342 This system undoubtedly brings *type-music into disrepute. **1928** L. P. SMITH *Words & Idioms* 40 Some of these *type-names give evidence of the impression made on foreigners by the travelling Englishmen of rank. **1974** *Encycl. Brit. Micropædia* X. 219/2 *Type names*,..those names given by the dramatist to characters in his play so that their personalities may be instantly ascertained. **1871** KINGSLEY *At Last* xiii, The nut ought to have..not one ovule, but three, the *type-number in palms. **1910** *Athenæum* 19 Mar. 348/1 The relation of *type-page to paper-page is..still open, within certain limits, to individual taste. **1906** *Daily Chron.* 27 Jan. 6/4 They make the better-class papers known as 'banks', '*type' papers, 'drawing' papers, and high-class writing papers. **1911** *Edin. Rev.* July 103 Isolated..caprices rather than *type-phases of animal literature. **1892** *Daily News* 26 Feb. 7/3, I searched Sampson before leaving..and found..two *type-printed statements relating to the charge. **1839** T. C. HANSARD *Print. & Type-founding* (1841) 59 There does not appear to be any vestige of an art in any degree similar (such as block-printing) having been practised prior to the introduction of *type-printing. **1876** *Nature* 18 May 43/1 The sewing-machine or the more novel type-printing apparatus. **1932** *Brit. Jrnl. Psychol.* July 77 The considerable growth of '*type' psychologies has been a leading characteristic of recent psychological and clinical study and speculation. **1952** H. Read *Philos. Mod. Art* iv. 83 The science of typology—or type-psychology as it is more often called—is comparatively modern. **1888** *Arts & Crafts Catal.* 94 The current hand-writing may be elegant enough to be.. used as a model for the *type-punch engraver. **1894** *Daily News* 12 Sept. 7/1 *Type-samples of unmanufactured tobacco sent for trade purposes. **1893** A. Estoclet in *Nation* (N.Y.) 6 July 10/3 Writing.. concerning a typewritten document.., I half apologetically used the word '*type-script'. **1906** N. W. Thomas *Kin. Org. & Group Marr. Austral.* Pref., He has read twice over my typescript MS, and my proofs. **1907** H. Wyndham *Flare of Footlights* xxix, Adrian recognized it as the typescript of his one-act play. **1976** *Amer. Speech 1974* XLIX. 19 H. Rex Wilson.. was probably the first linguistic geographer to propose *typescripting entire interviews. **1979** *Amer. N. & Q.* Mar. 106/1 Nor did Fisher ever mention to Crane or to me his *Plowshare* publications of Greenberg, which included 'The Charming Maiden' (June 1918) 'Serenade in Grey', 'Regret At Parting', and 'Where Sweepest Thou' (January 1920), all later typescripted by Hart Crane. **1980** *Amer. Speech 1976* LI. 204 A *typescripted record represents several weeks of tedious work. **1981** *Ibid.* LVI. 258 The *typescripting or computer-taping and indexing of LAGS field records are now considered supplemental descriptive components of the atlas. **1887** J. G. Wood in *19th Cent.* Mar. 395, I would have a *type-series of the vertebrates, so that in going through the galleries the visitors would recognise the creatures they had seen grouped. **1903** *Westm. Gaz.* 17 Nov. 2/1 A *type set of the collections representing the massive rocks of the island. **1867** Brande & Cox *Dict. Sc.*, etc. s.v. *Telegraph*, The *type-set message. *Ibid.*, Ten *type-setters under Bonelli's system can compose at least 300 despatches per hour. **1888** *Cassell's Encycl. Dict.*, *Type-setter*, 2, a type-setting or composing machine. **1899** *Daily News* 24 June 4/4 When women first began as type-setters in Boston, the male type-setters struck. **1911** *T.P.'s Weekly* 29 Dec. 844/1 Young's Patent Composing Machine.. was the name of the first practical type-setter, seventy years ago. **1846** S. F. Smith *Theatrical Apprenticeship* ii. 30 She.. would then dismiss us to our *type-setting. **1848** *De Bow's Rev.* VI. 52 But the printer is too important.. to have his usefulness set aside by the multiplication of type-setting and press-working machines. **1867** Brande & Cox *Dict. Sc.* etc. s.v. *Telegraph*, Converting the telegraph stations.. into so many type-setting work-shops. **1875** Knight *Dict. Mech.*, *Type-setting machine*, a composing-machine for type. **1886** *Science* 17 Sept. 254/1 Justification will be as easily accomplished as in ordinary type-setting. **1901** *Feilden's Mag.* IV. 421/1 The *type-ship, which has been tried on the measured mile. **1935** *Proc. Prehistoric Soc.* I. 6 The Late Bronze Age assemblage to which the *type site offers no significant parallel. **1959** J. D. Clark *Prehist. Southern Africa* vi. 159 Bambata is the type site for the Stillbay Culture in Rhodesia. **1969** *Proc. Geol. Soc.* Aug. 157 Table 1.. gives the sequence of stages so far defined for the Quaternary of the British Isles. The stage names are based either on type-sites or type-areas. **1975** J. G. Evans *Environment Early Man Brit. Isles* i. 8 Each interglacial is named after a type site or area where deposits of that stage occur. **1981** P. Salway *Roman Britain* 7 A 'type-site' is, in archaeological jargon, the site after which a culture is named, often the site at which it was first discovered or recognized as distinct. **1922** D. B. Updike *Printing Types* I. ii. 32 It [*sc.* the point system] placed *type sizes upon a basis comprehensible to the meanest intelligence. **1978** *Early Music* Oct. 597/3 The physical presentation of *Clementi* is also gratifying. Type sizes are unusually ample. **1840** Whewell *Philos. Induct. Sci.* viii. ii. I. 476 All the species which have a greater affinity with this *type-species than with any others, form the genus. **1875** W. Blades *Some Early Type Specimen Bks.* 3 When printers were their own type-founders their works were their own *type-specimen. **1891** *Cent. Dict.*, Type specimen. **1894** *Geol. Mag.* Oct. 435 J. Sowerby's type-specimens of *Ammonites Brocchii* are much more inflated than the present species. **1904** G. L. Kittredge *Eng. & Scot. Pop. Ball.* p. xxvi, 'The Hangman's Tree' is a survival of an archaic type-specimen. **1922** D. B. Updike *Printing Types* I. xi. 133 A few 'type specimens' were issued by founders, and some by printers. **1842** H. Greeley *Corr. R. W. Griswold* (1898) 104 Which you will keep out of the dirty hands of all *type-stickers. **1899** *Allbutt's Syst. Med.* VII. 591 All the *type symptoms of cerebellar abscess were present. **1901** *Nature* 26 Sept. 526/1 Prosecuting a more detailed study of individual forms, as with the now universal *type-system. **1922** *Flight* XIV. 267/1 The Bristol 'Lucifer' engine.. has successfully passed its *type-tests in accordance with British Air Ministry Type-Test Schedule of May, 1920. **1978** *Proc. Internat. Conf. Noise Control Engin., San Francisco* 743 Because of the complexity and cost of conducting certification type tests, a study was undertaken to determine the feasibility of using an alternative scheme to obtain approach and takeoff noise levels. **1979** *Gloss. Terms Quality Assurance (B.S.I.)* 11/2 *Type test*, a test or series of tests directed towards approval of a design, conducted to determine whether an item is capable of meeting the requirements of the product specification. **1946** *Sun* (Baltimore) 17 May 6 (Advt.), For sale: Stinson cabin monoplanes... Have been *type-tested and declared eligible for certification by CAA. **1901** *Daily Chron.* 14 June 3/4 In 'Rosmersholm' Ibsen has seized upon one of the great *type-themes of modern life. **1868** Watts *Dict. Chem.* V. 927 The law of substitution is the expression of facts, which the *type-theory was intended to explain. **1960** G. Herdan (*title*) *Type-token mathematics: a textbook of mathematical linguistics. **1971** *Computers & Humanities* V. 133 A type/token ratio is computed for each text, where type is the number of different words occurring in the text and token is the total number of occurrences of all words in the text. **1979** *Sci. Amer.* Feb. 61/2 The type-token ratio, a parameter that reflects the size of the vocabulary employed by the author, was determined for each text. **1931** S. Beckett *Proust* 7 The tragedy of the Marcel-Albertine liaison is the *type-tragedy of the human relationship whose failure is preordained. **1896** *Periodical* No. 1. 4 The unique MS... has been reproduced.. in photo-facsimile and *type-transliteration. **1909** Marett *Threshold Relig.* Introd. (1914) 25 When.. a set of useful contrasts is obtained by means of such bundles, each bundle.. is said to have '*type-value'. **1849** Noad *Electricity* viii. (ed. 3) 381 The rotatory motion given to the *type wheel.. until the required letter arrives opposite the paper. **1886** *Science* 17 Sept. 252/2 Fitted in vertical grooves in the periphery of the type-wheel are a number of steel types. **1910** H. C. G. Moule in *Fundamentals* II. vi. 107 The compositor 'justifies' a piece of *typework, when he corrects, brings into perfect order, as to spaces between words and letters, and so on, the types which he has set up.

Hence (*nonce-wds.*) ˈ**typeful** *a.*, having the quality of a type; typical; symbolic; **typefy** (ˈtaɪpɪfaɪ), *v. trans.* to put into type, to print; ˈ**typeless** *a.*, untyped, unprinted.

1889 Lucia E. F. Kimball in *Chicago Advance* 16 May, How *typeful this lovely blossom of the rare, sweet souls who strive.. to make the bare, ugly places brighter and better. **1856** Strang *Glasgow & Clubs* 25 The blatant blusterings of every charlatan.. must be pencilled and *typefied, before the lapse of a few hours. **1845** Ford *Handbk. Spain* ii. 708/1 Many authors.. content to remain .. in *typeless obscurity.

type, *sb.*²: see tipe *sb.*¹

†**type**, *sb.*³ Obs. var. of tipe *sb.*², trap.

1799 *Hull Advertiser* 2 Feb. 3/3 [A] labourer.. charged with entering the warren.. and breaking open the lock of a type, and killing a rabbit therein.

type (taɪp), *v.* [f. type *sb.*¹; cf. F. *typé* adj. (Littré), *typer* (ibid. *Suppl.*).]

1. *trans.* **a.** *Theol.* To prefigure or foreshadow as a type; to represent in prophetic similitude. Also ***type forth, out***.

1596 H. Clapham *Briefe Bible* i. 58 That specially typed out Our spotles Priest Iesus. **1606** J. Carpenter *Solomon's Solace* xxvii. 111 Wee see how he typeth the holy Messiah. **1633** Bp. Hall *Hard Texts, N.T.* 268 Which same thing is also typed forth unto us by Sinai and Jerusalem. **1690** C. Nesse *O. & N. Test.* I. 66 Adam.. offer'd sacrifice which typed out Christ. **1827** Pollok *Course T.* v. 894 A time Typed by the Sabbath-day.. When all had rest and peace.

b. To be the type or symbol of; to represent by a type or symbol; to symbolize: = typify 1.

1836 E. Howard *R. Reefer* xxxii, The old man's look.. was so wretched,.. yet so fond—and was typed to my fancy so strongly by his little boat [etc.]. **1837** Campbell *Lines on Poland* 130 The Rainbow types Heaven's promise to my sight. **1839** Bailey *Festus* xi. (1848) 32/2 All nature typeth Thee and Thine. **1875** Tennyson *Q. Mary* iii. iv, The cataract typed the headlong plunge and fall Of heresy to the pit.

2. a. To be an example or specimen of; to exemplify: = typify 2. *rare.*

1627 W. Sclater *Exp. 2 Thess.* (1629) 263 Pauls maine intention in typing or lineing out in his owne practise, what he prescribed to others. **1866** Blackie *Homer & Iliad* I. 25 The peculiar character.. of Scottish piety, as it has been typed in Scotland now for more than three hundred years.

b. To be or furnish the pattern or model for.

1836 Lytton *Athens* (1837) II. 55 On the Shield He bears his haughty ensign—typed by stars Gleaming athwart the sky.

3. To reproduce by means of type; to print. *rare.*

1736 [see typing *vbl. sb.*]. **1841** Miall in *Nonconf.* I. 13 A host of abstractions typed off with capital letters.

4. a. To write or copy by means of a typewriter; also with *out*, *up*. **b.** *intr.* To practise typewriting; to typewrite.

1888 *Scott. Leader* 28 Aug. 3 The operator.. types at the rate of from fifty to sixty words a minute. **1888** *Pall Mall G.* 6 Oct. 15/1 Shorthand Evidence 'typed' from Dictation. **1897** G. Allen *Type-writer Girl* xvi, I went back to my machine and began typing mechanically. **1900** E. Wallace *Writ in Barracks* 114 ''Tis the dainty hand that types it. **1948** A. Keith *Three came Home* xv. 255 The news that came over the radio was typed out. **1961** 'E. Lathen' *Banking on Death* xvii. 135, I want you to.. type up a copy of the Hoffman contract. **1981** C. Dexter *Dead of Jericho* xxxvi. 202 We've got to.. get it down in writing, then typed up, and signed.

5. a. *trans.* To assign to a particular type; to classify; esp. in *Biol.* and *Med.*, to determine the type to which (blood, tissue, etc.) belongs.

1900, etc. [see typing *vbl. sb.* 1]. **1929** L. H. Snyder *Blood Grouping in Relation to Clin. & Legal Med.* iii. 13 They called attention to the fact that the methods used for typing an unknown blood are based upon the assumption that there are only four iso-agglutination groups and that the blood of every person belongs to one of the four. **1939** *Jrnl. Bacteriol.* XXXVII. 136 Sixty-seven of the double-zone strains have been serologically 'typed' by Lancefield or Plummer. **1946** Gerth & Mills *From Max Weber* (1947) iii. 56 Less 'rational' actions are typed by Weber in terms of the pursuit of 'absolute ends', as flowing from affectual sentiments, or as 'traditional'. **1959** *Times Lit. Suppl.* 3 Apr. 194/4 The simple character, long ago 'typed' and pigeon-holed, often turns out to be much more complex in the light of his correspondence. **1964** *McCall's Sewing* iii. 41/1 Zippers are typed according to their purpose. **1967** A. S. Byatt *Game* xi. 154 Her clothes.. typed her: grey pleated skirt, cable-stitch sweater, brogue shoes. **1968**, etc. [see *tissue-type* vb. s.v. tissue *sb.* 9b]. **1969** *New Yorker* 12 Apr. 85/1 The exobiologists have insisted that.. the astronauts' microflora .. have all been typed and catalogued for comparison later. **1977** *Time* 7 Mar. 43/2 The kidney was.. then 'typed' so that doctors could choose a patient whose body tissue matched it. **1977** *Jrnl. R. Soc. Arts* CXXV. 87/1 We like to label periods in our history as we like to 'type' people.

b. = type-cast *v.*

1933 *Sat. Even. Post* 17 June 14/3 The danger of being 'typed' by the producers, which, in turn, fixes you irrevocably in the public eye, is one of those haunting fears that an actor must meet and conquer. **1939** J. Gielgud *Early Stages* ix. 151 Refusing to be typed in 'silly society' parts, she [*sc.* Edith Evans].. achieved her greatest triumph as Millamant. **1959** *Times Lit. Suppl.* 27 Feb. 118/1 There is an inevitable tendency in novels about soldiers and sailors for characters to be typed; but though some of Mr. Armstrong's ship's company conform, others are distinct individuals. **1959** *Listener* 9 July 72/1 This was good documentary in that the characters were not in the least typed. **1960** *Guardian* 20 Oct. 8/7 They were in revolt against the whole Broadway system of typing actors and thus limiting their development.

Hence ˈ**typing** *ppl. a.*

1897 *Daily News* 21 Sept. 7/2 To transform.. the secretaries into shorthand and typing clerks.

-type (taɪp), *suffix.*

1. Repr. F. *-type*, L. *-typus*, Gr. -τυπος, f. root of τύπτειν to beat, strike: cf. type *sb.*¹ The termination -τυπος was used in Greek to form adjs., in sense 'struck, driven, moulded', as ἀντίτυπος repelled, reflected (also in active sense 'repelling'), ἀρχέτυπος first-moulded, πρωτότυπος original, primitive (also used *absol.* as sbs.). These have been anglicized as sbs., *antitype*, *archetype*, *prototype*; and many technical words connected with printing and other modern processes of copying have been formed on the model of them, with the sense 'type, block, or plate for printing from', as in *electrotype*, *logotype*, *phonotype*, *stereotype*; 'impression or picture', also 'process of reproduction', as in *autotype*, *calotype*, *chrysotype*, *collotype*, *cyanotype*, *ferrotype*, *phototype*, *platinotype*, etc.; also in hybrid formations on Eng. words, as *colourtype*.

2. [type *sb.*¹] Appended to adjs. and sbs. or sb. phrs. forming adjs. with the sense 'of the specified type; typical or characteristic of (..), reminiscent or imitative of (..)'. Cf. type *sb.*¹ 6.

1887 New-type [see new *a.* 10b]. **1907** *Yesterday's Shopping* (1969) 97/2 *Australian*... Claret type.. Burgundy type. **1922**, etc. [see *shell-type* adj. s.v. shell *sb.* 40]. **1924** *Sat. Even. Post* 13 Sept. 80 (Advt.), Has the car you have in mind a European type, high compression motor? **1936** *Discovery* Aug. 237/2 Eight astronomical-type stainless steel mirrors. **1939** W. S. Churchill in *War Illustr.* 29 Dec. 522/2 The submarine had not long been in her patrol area before she sighted a big-type U-boat. **1940** *Illustr. London News* 28 Dec. 821 The outbreak of the war found the Fleet Air Arm using for the most part adapted land-type machines. **1949** *Here & Now* (N.Z.) Oct. 23/3 Following the old Spanish custom still prevalent at California-type barbecues, the meat can be served with some version of hot, tangy tomato sauce. **1959** *Chambers's Encycl.* IV. 693/2 The indulines and nigrosines are important azine type dyes. **1960** *Farmer & Stockbreeder* 8 Mar. 77/1 He showed slides of some of his farm-made, 'home-grown' Dutch-barn-type buildings which he believed in putting up. **1970** *Daily Tel.* 18 Aug. 11 Ocean Spirit is the biggest-type glass fibre boat ever made in this country. **1973** *New Statesman* 19 Oct. 557/3 Fifties-type social realist films. **1976** *Derbyshire Times* (Peak ed.) 3 Sept. 15/1 (Advt.), A very spacious older type house.

type-cast (ˈtaɪpkɑːst, -æ-), *a.* Also as one word. [f. type *sb.*¹ + cast *ppl. a.*]

1. Formed into type for printing.

1876 *Nature* 18 May 43/2 This hammer.. carries at its extremity a type-cast letter.

2. Of an actor, etc.: that has been type-cast (see type-cast *v.*); identified with a particular kind of part. Also *transf.* and in extended use.

1946 S. H. Adams *Alexander Woollcott* 314 He is type-cast if ever a man was. **1952** *Time* 2 June 92/2 Hollywood noticed Jules in 1938, changed his name to John Garfield, and launched him on a type-cast screen career of playing himself —the narrow-eyed, rock-hard underdog. **1964** L. Deighton *Funeral in Berlin* xxiv. 135 'So I am type-cast as the loser?' 'It's a one-horse race,' said Samantha. **1965** *Spectator* 29 Jan. 137/2 He is in danger of becoming typecast. **1971** *Daily Tel.* 9 June 13/5 David Shepherd is type-cast as the man who paints elephants and this bothers him. He wants to be known as 'a painter'. **1976** M. Gilbert *Night of Twelfth* xvi. 149 Naval Officers are deceptive people. They're usually type-cast as bluff simple extroverts. .. Actually, their training, and the lives they have to lead, are calculated to produce the most complex introverts. **1982** M. Babson *Death beside Seaside* v. 41 One gets the feeling she's typecast in her show. **1984** *Listener* 19 Jan. 37/2 It is only in New York, in my experience, that truly typecast events occur.

type-cast (ˈtaɪpkɑːst, -æ-), *v.* Also as one word. [Back-formation from type-casting *vbl. sb.* 2.] *trans.* To cast (an actor) in a role or roles for which he appears to be physically or temperamentally suited or of a kind in which he has been successful; to allocate continually to the same type of part. Also *transf.* and *fig.*, and in extended use, to represent or regard as a stereotype.

1946, etc. [implied in type-cast *a.* 2]. **1952** Granville *Dict. Theatr. Terms* 192 *Type cast*, to assign parts to artistes who approximate the type drawn in the play. **1958** R. Hoggart in N. Mackenzie *Conviction* 136 We.. will no longer type-cast regional accents by class or comedy. **1958** *Wall St. Jrnl.* 6 Nov. 6/2 Right-to-work has been type-cast as a villain in the public mind. **1959** *Times* 9 Nov. 6/4 Sir Thomas Beecham's gifts tend to typecast him as an interpreter of even-numbered Beethoven. **1971** *Country Life* 20 May 1252/1 But it is by using plants in this category as ornamentals in their own right instead of type-casting them purely as herbs for the herb garden that they become most useful in the garden. **1981** *N. & Q.* Oct. 448/2 Hardy's contemporaries, having type-cast him as a novelist, were dubious if not contemptuous of his poetry. **1982** *Daily Tel.* 16 July 15/4 People are not as likely to be typecast by their accents as they once were.

type-casting ('taɪpkɑːstɪŋ, -æ-), *vbl. sb.* Also as one word. [f. TYPE *sb.*¹ + CASTING *vbl. sb.*]

1. The forming of metal, wood, etc., into type for printing. Also *attrib.* So **type-caster**.

1847 in *Inquiry Yorksh. Deaf & Dumb* (1870) 19 As a type-caster..we consider him a good hand. **1864** T. L. NICHOLS *Forty Years Amer. Life* I. 381 By the use of type-casting machines a workman can cast ninety brevier types a minute. **1875** KNIGHT *Dict. Mech.*, Type-casting,..Type casting and setting machine. **1897** *Daily News* 2 Feb. 2/1 The Wicks Rotary Type-Casting Machine can cast..from 40,000 to 60,000 letters per hour. **1967** V. STRAUSS *Printing Industry* ii. 66/1 Hot-metal machines are type-casting equipment.

2. The casting of an actor in a role or roles for which he appears to be physically or temperamentally suited or of a kind in which he has been successful; the fact of being so cast. Also *transf.* and in extended use, representation as a stereotype or stereotypes.

1927 *Observer* 25 Sept. 13/4 Please do not conclude that I believe in 'type-casting'; an actor should in his time play many sorts of part. **1947** A. MENEN *Prevalence of Witches* xi. 190 He says..why pick on *him* to work a miracle? He says it's his beard..; he says its just type-casting, like they do in pictures. **1960** *Twentieth Cent.* Dec. 588 These Dickensian names suggest the general feeling of type-casting. **1977** 'E. CRISPIN' *Glimpses of Moon* iii. 38 Film-music composers are just as liable to type-casting as actors and actresses. **1979** D. ARKELL *Looking for Laforgue* iii. 78 Laforgue was invariably given the part of Colline, the philosopher... It would appear to have been excellent type-casting.

typed (taɪpt, *poet.* 'taɪpɪd), *ppl. a.* [f. TYPE *v.* or *sb.*¹ + -ED.]

1. Of or pertaining to a (specified) type; having a (certain) type or general character.

1839 BAILEY *Festus* xv. (1852) 170 Sun, planet, satellite, all typéd spheres..it is mine To search and pass through. **1881** *Builder* XLI. 442 Medieval Church architecture..is characteristic and strongly typed.

2. In combination: That is printed in or with type of a specified kind.

1831 J. BROWN *Lett.* (1907) 7 A larger typed Testament which I think will suit your eyes.

3. That is printed or reproduced by means of a typewriter; typewritten. Also with *out*, *up*.

1890 *Daily News* 24 Feb. 5/6 'Typing' from copy,.. dictation from 'typed matter'. **1895** A. W. TUER in *Athenæum* 15 June 773/1 Some typed sample chapters. **1971** D. E. WESTLAKE *I gave at Office* 200 They had this typed-out paper, and it would be everything you said... So you'd read it and sign it. **1977** A. HUNTER *Gently Instrumental* viii. 116 Gently found Leyston glooming over the policewoman's typed-up notes.

†**typed**, *a.* *Obs. rare.* [f. TYPE *sb.*³ + -ED².] Furnished with tipes or traps.

1799 A. YOUNG *Agric. Lincoln.* 385 A warren..carefully typed to catch all extra bucks.

typembryo (taɪ'pembrɪəʊ). *Biol.* [f. TYPE *sb.*¹ + EMBRYO.] The stage in the development of an embryo when the characteristic structure of its phylum or subkingdom begins to appear.

1887 HYATT in *Proc. Boston Nat. Hist. Soc.* 16 Nov. 398 Naming the embryo in these last stages the Typembryo. *Ibid.* 399 Typembryos serve to connect the earlier stages of the Neoembryos with the true larval stages which succeed the former.

typer ('taɪpə(r)). [f. TYPE *v.* + -ER¹.] A typewriting machine: = TYPEWRITER 1.

1892 in *Boston* (Mass.) *Jrnl.* 27 May 4/7 For 'typewriter' (the machine) say 'typer'. **1915** *Morn. Post* 5 Feb. 2/1 It is ..typewritten, for..'we have bagged another German typer'.

typewrite ('taɪpraɪt), *v.* [Back-formation from TYPEWRITER.] *trans.* To print by means of a typewriter; to type; also *intr.* to use a typewriter, to practise typewriting.

1887 in *Athenæum* 31 Dec. 878/1 Authors' MSS...type-written at 1d. per folio. **1894** *Westm. Gaz.* 20 June 3/2 Eighteen machines,..the simplest of which type-writes a message by means of a single wire. **1897** G. ALLEN *Type-writer Girl* x, With my maimed fingers, it would be impossible for me to type-write for three days at least. **1898** *Westm. Gaz.* 5 Feb. 2/1 His..hero—a literary character—had fallen madly in love with the young lady who came to typewrite his novel.

So **'typewriting** *vbl. sb.* and *ppl. a.*, **'type-written** *ppl. a.*

1867 *Sci. Amer.* 6 July 3/1 The subject of type writing is one of the interesting aspects of the near future. **1881** *X-Y-Z Guide* (N.Y.) Oct. 161 For sale..a type writing machine. **1885** *Pall Mall G.* 5 May 6/1 That new convenience of civilization a type writing office... Constant employment is now afforded to eight ladies in type-writing. **1888** *Ibid.* 6 Oct. 15/1 Typewritten documents cost no more than Law Engrossing. **1894** *Athenæum* 21 July 90/2 She forges type-written letters. **1897** G. ALLEN *Type-writer Girl* ii, Type-writing as an accomplishment is as diffused as the piano. **1912** *Times* 19 Dec. 13/2 A type-written copy of all the memoranda.

typewriter ('taɪp,raɪtə(r)). [f. TYPE *sb.*¹ + WRITER.]

1. A writing-machine having types for the letters of the alphabet, figures, and punctuation-marks, so arranged on separate rods (or on the periphery of a wheel) that as each key of the machine is depressed the corresponding character is imprinted in line on a moving sheet.

1868 C. L. SHOLES et al. *U.S. Patent* 79,265 23 June 4 Thus made, the type-writer is the simplest, most perfectly adapted to its work. **1875** KNIGHT *Dict. Mech.* s.v., The Sholes type-writer..is about the size of the sewing-machine, and is worked with keys arranged in four banks or rows. **1881** *X-Y-Z Guide* (N.Y.) Oct. p. iv, Manufacturers of the best Type Writer in the market. **1897** G. ALLEN *Type-writer Girl* iii, My type-writer continued to go click, click, click. **1899** *Allbutt's Syst. Med.* VIII. 25 One typewriter.. is worked by means of a handle which is grasped.

2. One who does typewriting, esp. as a regular occupation; = TYPIST 2.

1884 *N. York Herald* 27 Oct. 7/2 Situation wanted—by lady, rapid stenographer and typewriter. **1887** *St. James's Gaz.* 22 Dec., Women..beat them [men] altogether as type-writers and 'dry-goods clerks'. **1895** *How to get Married* 86 The marriage of the type-writer and her employer is so frequent that it has passed into a joke.

3. A machine-gun or sub-machine-gun. *slang.*

1915 A. D. GILLESPIE *Let.* 3 Mar. in *Lett. from Flanders* (1916) 31 The only typewriter here is the machine-gun—the men's nickname for it. **1930** *Sun* (Baltimore) 25 Oct. 10/3 When the 'typewriters', as machine guns are called, rattle, it is natural for the police to suspect these 'independents' even of shooting each other. **1959** 'J. CHRISTOPHER' *Scent of White Poppies* vii. 101 'You associate typewriters with more than one guy.'.. 'Typewriters?' Bella asked. 'Submachine gun. Browning, maybe..firing automatic.' **1973** P. EVANS *Bodyguard Man* iii. 25 Al Capone['s]..torpedoes..were mean with a Thompson 'type-writer'.

4. *attrib.* and *Comb.* as ***typewriter cover***, ***ribbon***, etc.

1889 *Pall Mall G.* 22 Oct. 2/1 The typewriter industry.. is a thing to itself. **1897** G. ALLEN *Type-writer Girl* xi, Ten thousand type-writer girls crowd London to-day. **1900** DOYLE *Green Flag* 13 The typewriter-like clicking of the hopper. **1902** ELIZ. L. BANKS *Newspaper Girl* 4 My fingers ..flew over the typewriter keys. *Ibid.* 155, I took my typewriter brush out, as though to wash it in the kitchen sink. **1903** *Christendom* 13 June 393 Please furnish..12 typewriter ribbons. **1934** WEBSTER, Typewriter cover. **1966** D. FRANCIS *Flying Finish* i. 8 Maggie's..typewriter cover askew. **1975** 'D. JORDAN' *Black Account* xiv. 74 She was busy..with her typewriter ribbon.

typey ('taɪpɪ), *a.* Also **typy**. [f. TYPE *sb.*¹ + -Y¹.] Of a domestic animal: exhibiting the distinctive characteristics of the breed; being a perfect specimen of the breed.

1931 *19th Century* Feb. 210 It is not registered bulls that are needed, nor 'typey' bulls, but proved bulls, whether registered or not. **1951** *Sun* (Baltimore) 9 Oct. (B ed.) 11/3 One bull might be as 'typy' (Angus argot for conforming to perfect physical standards) as another bull. **1976** *Horse & Hound* 10 Dec. 67/4 (Advt.), Pure Arabian filly... Very typey with large eyes and one of the best movers we have ever seen. **1980** *Hunting Ann. 1981* 107 (Advt.), Typey pups sired by our top studs and from matings within our own pack.

typh (taɪf). [Deduced from TYPHUS, TYPHOID.] **typh fever** (also simply **typh**): see quots.; **typh poison**, poison causing typh fever.

1861 T. K. CHAMBERS *Lect.* (1864) vi. 70 You saw a case of continued low fever (or as I shall call it for shortness Typh-fever) admitted four days ago. *Ibid.* 75, I have been led to believe that the exciting cause of typh-fever enters usually by the digestive canal. **1890** BILLINGS *Med. Dict.*, *Typh fever*, a name proposed by Dr. Thomas King Chambers to include both typhus and enteric fevers. **1891** *Cent. Dict.*, Typh-poison. **1900–13** DORLAND *Med. Dict.*, *Typh, typh-fever*, typhus and typhoid viewed together.

†**typh**, obs. form of TIPHE.

1600 SURFLET *Country Farm* v. xvii. 688 Typh wheate is very like to our rye, and doth make a very blacke bread.

‖**Typha** ('taɪfə). *Bot.* [mod.L., f. Gr. τύφη cat's-tail.] A genus of aquatic herbs (type of the N.O. *Typhaceæ*), containing the common cat's-tail or reed-mace (*T. latifolia*).

1548 TURNER *Names of Herbes* (E.D.S.) 79 Typha groweth in fennes and water sydes among the reedes... It is called in englishe cattes tayle, or a Reedmace. **1796** H. HUNTER tr. *St.-Pierre's Stud. Nat.* (1799) II. 143 The water-lentil of our marshes, as well as the typha of our rivers, has the middle of it's leaf swelled. **1838** MARY HOWITT *Birds & Fl., Lit. Streams* 23 Typha strong, and green bur-reed. **1861** BENTLEY *Man. Bot.* 688 The pollen of some species of *Typha* is edible.

typhaceous (taɪ'feɪʃəs), *a.* *Bot.* [f. mod.L. *Typhācē-æ*, f. *Typha*: see prec. and -ACEOUS.] Belonging to the Natural Order *Typhaceæ*.

1909 in *Cent. Dict. Suppl.*

typhe, obs. form of TIPHE.

typhic ('tɪfɪk), *a.* *Path.* [f. TYPH-US + -IC; cf. F. *typhique*.] = TYPHOUS.

1860 MAYNE *Expos. Lex.*, *Typhosepsis*, term for typhic or typhous putrefaction. **1890** BILLINGS *Med. Dict.*, *Typhic*, typhoid.

typhine ('taɪfɪn). [f. TYPH-US + -INE⁵.] The hypothetical infectious principle of typhus.

1864 FARR in *Rep. Regr. General* 34 Any zymotic matter such as varioline, scarlatinine, or typhine.

typhization (taɪ-, tɪfɪ'zeɪʃən). *Path.* [f. TYPH-US + -IZE + -ATION.] Production of a morbid state by exposure to the infection of typhus.

1895 in *Funk's Stand. Dict.* **1900–13** in DORLAND *Med. Dict.*

‖**typhlitis** (tɪ'flaɪtɪs). *Path.* [mod.L., f. Gr. τυφλόν the cæcum or blind gut (neut. of τυφλός blind) + -ITIS.] Inflammation of the cæcum, cæcitis (often including that of the *appendix vermiformis*, now distinctively called *appendicitis*).

1857 in DUNGLISON *Med. Lex.* **1866** A. FLINT *Princ. Med.* (1880) 427 Inflammation of the caecum..constitutes an affection called *typhlitis, tuphlo-enteritis,* or *caecitis*. *Ibid.* 429 The term typhlitis is applied to inflammation of the vermiform appendix as well as to caecitis. **1891** *Pall Mall G.* 13 May 6/3 She died, after a short illness, of typhlitis.

Hence **typhlitic** (tɪ'flɪtɪk) *a.*, pertaining to, of the nature of, or affected with typhlitis.

1891 in *Cent. Dict.*

typhlo- (tɪfləʊ), before a vowel regularly **typhl-**, ad. Gr. τυφλο-, combining form of τυφλός blind: occurring in a few recent scientific and technical words, chiefly pathological and surgical terms relating to the cæcum (Gr. τυφλόν: see prec.). **typhlatony** (-'ætənɪ), atony of the cæcum. **ty'phlectomy** [Gr. ἐκτομή excision], excision of the cæcum. **typhlente'ritis**, more regular form of *typhlo-enteritis*. **typhlodicliditis** (-dɪklɪ'daɪtɪs) [Gr. δικλίς, δικλιδ- folding door], inflammation of the ileo-cæcal valve. **typhlo-enteritis** (also **tuphlo-**) [Gr. ἔντερον intestine] = TYPHLITIS. **'typhlograph** (-grɑːf, -æ-) [-GRAPH: cf. F. *typhlographe* (Littré)], an apparatus for assisting the blind to write evenly; also = NYCTOGRAPH. **,typhloli'thiasis** [LITHIASIS], formation of calculi or hard concretions in the cæcum. **ty'phlology** [-LOGY], the scientific knowledge relating to blindness. **'typhlopexy** [Gr. πῆξις fixation], the operation of fixing the cæcum to the wall of the abdomen. **,typhloste'nosis** [Gr. στένωσις straitening, contraction], constriction of the cæcum. **ty'phlotomy** [Gr. τομή cutting], incision into the cæcum.

1900–13 DORLAND *Med. Dict.*, **Typhlatony*, inefficiency of the motor activity of the cæcum. *Ibid.*, *Typhlectomy... *Typhlenteritis... *Typhlodicliditis. **1857** DUNGLISON *Med. Lex.*, *Tuphlo-enteritis. *Ibid.*, Typhlo-enteritis. **1866** [see TYPHLITIS]. **1891** *Typhlograph [see NYCTOGRAPH]. **1896** *Westm. Gaz.* 2 May 2/3 Messrs. Jarrold send us a sample of what they..term 'The Typhlo-graph'. It consists of a neat slope of hard wood with grooves on the surface, and it is designed to enable the blind to produce ordinary hand-writing in a straight line. **1898** *Internat. Cycl.* (N.Y.) II. 641 Mr. Gall's typhlograph is a much more perfect instrument. **1890** BILLINGS *Med. Dict.*, **Typhlolithiasis*. **1872** W. H. LEVY (*title*) Blindness and the Blind: or, a Treatise on the Science of *Typhlology. **1900–13** DORLAND *Med. Dict.*, Typhlopexia, *typhlopexy. **1890** BILLINGS *Med. Dict.*, *Typhlostenosis. **1903** *Lancet* 30 May 1511/1 Other operations may be required to relieve the patient, such as *typhlotomy, colotomy.

typhlope ('tɪfləʊp). *Zool.* *rare*⁻⁰. [ad. mod.L. *Typhlop-*, *-ops*, ad. Gr. τυφλώψ, f. τυφλός blind + ὤψ eye, face.] A snake of the genus *Typhlops* or family *Typhlopidæ*; a blindworm.

1891 in *Cent. Dict.*

typhlophthalmic (tɪflɒf'θælmɪk), *a.* *Zool.* *rare*⁻⁰. [f. mod.L. *Typhlophthalmi* (f. Gr. τυφλός blind + ὀφθαλμός eye) + -IC.] Belonging to the *Typhlophthalmi*, a superfamily of pleurodont lizards in Cope's classification.

1891 in *Cent. Dict.*

typhlosole ('tɪfləʊsəʊl). *Zool.* Also **-solis**. [irreg. f. Gr. τυφλός blind + σωλήν channel, pipe.] A ridge or fold extending along the inner wall of the intestine and partly dividing the cavity of it, in various animals, as lampreys and certain ascidians, molluscs, and worms.

1859 *Todd's Cycl. Anat.* V. 297/2 In the Earth-worm, there is a singular apparatus, the typhlosole. **1877** HUXLEY *Anat. Inv. Anim.* x. 604 In many Ascidians, a strong fold of the endoderm of the intestine projects into its interior, as in Lamellibranchs and in the Earthworm, where such a fold constitutes the so-called typhlosole. **1881** DARWIN *Veg. Mould* 19 The intestine [of the earth-worm] presents a remarkable structure, the typhlosolis. **1888** ROLLESTON & JACKSON *Anim. Life* 435 The mid-gut..in the Lampreys contains a projecting fold or typhlosole.

Hence **typhlo'solar** *a.*, pertaining to or of the nature of a typhlosole.

1887 BENHAM in *Q. Jrnl. Microsc. Sci.* Mar. 566 The dorsal trunk divides into two. A subneural vessel is present and a typhlosolar vessel.

typho- (taɪfəʊ), ad. Gr. τῦφο-, combining form of τῦφος (see TYPHUS): used as combining form of TYPHUS or TYPHOID, in recent terms of pathology, etc. **typho-ady'namic** *a.* [ADYNAMIC], characterized by prostration as in typhus or typhoid fever. **typhogenic** (-'dʒenɪk) *a.* [see -GEN and -IC], producing typhus or typhoid fever. **typholysin** (taɪ'fɒlɪsɪn), a lysin which destroys the bacilli of typhoid fever. **typhomalarial** (-mə'lɛərɪəl) *a.*, applied to a fever exhibiting both typhoid and malarial symptoms, or to typhoid fever with malarial complications or of supposed malarial origin.

ˌ**typhopneu'monia**, pneumonia complicated with typhoid fever, or exhibiting typhoid symptoms. **typho'toxin** [see TOXIN], a poisonous ptomaine obtained from cultures of the bacillus of typhoid fever.

1898 P. MANSON *Trop. Diseases* ii. 66 The fever may assume the *typho-adynamic type. **1900–13** DORLAND *Med. Dict.*, *Typhogenic. **1902** *Brit. Med. Jrnl.* 12 Apr. 920 *Typholysin, the lysin of cholera [etc.]. **1863** J. J. WOODWARD *Outl. Chief Camp Diseases U.S. Armies* iii. 87 In all the cases of *typho-malarial fever,.. three several trains of phenomena are to be noted: the malarial, the typhoid, and the scorbutic. **1884** *Lisbon* (Dakota) *Star* 29 Aug., A severe attack of typho-malarial fever. **1898** P. MANSON *Trop. Diseases* vi. 109 These cases are typho-malarial,.. typhoid with a malarial complication. **1878** A. HAMILTON *Nerv. Dis.* 62 Typhoid, in some of its forms, or *typho-pneumonia, may resemble tubercular meningitis. **1890** BILLINGS *Med. Dict.*, *Typhotoxine, $C_7H_{17}NO_2$. **1901** W. OSLER *Princ. & Pract. Med.* i. (ed. 4) 8 Brieger isolated from cultures [of typhoid bacilli] a poison belonging to the group of ptomaines—typhotoxin.

† **ty'phodial**, *a. Obs. rare*$^{-1}$. [f. Gr. *τυφώδης* (f. *τῦφος*, TYPHUS + *εἶδος* form) + -IAL.] Resembling typhus: = TYPHOID *a.* 1.

1869 E. A. PARKES *Pract. Hygiene* (ed. 3) 72 Eight persons were affected with more or less typhodial symptoms.

Typhœan (taɪ'fiːən), *a.* [Properly *Typhoëan*, f. *Typhōeus*, Gr. *Τυφωεύς*, name of a giant of Greek mythology. (Cf. TYPHON[1].)] Belonging to or characteristic of Typhoeus.

1667 MILTON *P.L.* II. 539 Others with vast Typhœan rage ..Rend up both Rocks and Hills, And ride the Air in whirlwind.

typhoid ('taɪfɔɪd), *a.* (*sb.*) *Path.* [f. TYPHUS + -OID; cf. Gr. *τυφώδης*, F. *typhoïde*, Pg. *typhoideo*, Sp., It. *tifoideo*.]

A. *adj.* **1.** Resembling or characteristic of typhus; applied to a class of febrile diseases exhibiting symptoms similar to those of typhus, or to such symptoms themselves, esp. to a state of delirious stupor occurring in certain fevers.

1800 *Med. Jrnl.* III. 95 In its first stage, this fever did not appear to be contagious; but it was evidently so after the eleventh or fourteenth day, when the typhoid state was induced. **1813** J. THOMSON *Lect. Inflam.* 175 In low typhous fever, and in typhoid inflammatory affections. **1846** G. E. DAY tr. *Simon's Anim. Chem.* II. 245 The state of the urine in typhoid fevers. **1897** *Allbutt's Syst. Med.* II. 38 Acute general tuberculosis or acute typhoid tuberculosis as it is sometimes called. **1905** H. D. ROLLESTON *Dis. Liver* 316 A 'typhoid' or comatose condition ushers in death.

2. a. ***typhoid fever***: a specific eruptive fever (formerly supposed to be a variety of typhus), characterized by intestinal inflammation and ulceration: more distinctively, and now more usually, called *enteric fever*.

1845 BUDD *Dis. Liver* 70, I have never seen abscess of the liver noticed in conjunction with ulcerated intestine in typhoid fever. **1877** ROBERTS *Handbk. Med.* (ed. 3) I. 119 Typhoid fever originates from a specific poison, which is quite distinct from that causing typhus. **1890** *Lancet* 22 Nov. 1133/1 As to typhoid fever, the principal factor in its propagation was.. drinking-water.

b. Of or pertaining to, characteristic of, or affected with typhoid fever.

1871 TYNDALL *Fragm. Sc.* (1879) I. v. 178 So surely does the typhoid virus increase and multiply into typhoid fever. **1890** BILLINGS *Med. Dict.*, *Typhoid.. tongue*, the black, dry tongue seen in enteric and typhus fevers. **1899** *Allbutt's Syst. Med.* VII. 483 The typhoid patient has some tympanites as a rule. *Ibid.* 600 A typhoid rash came out. **1904** *Brit. Med. Jrnl.* 10 Sept. 596 Infection with the typhoid bacillus.

3. ***Typhoid Mary***, nickname of Mary Mallon (d. 1938), Irish-born cook who transmitted typhoid fever in the U.S.A. Also *fig.*, a transmitter of undesirable opinions, sentiments, etc.

1909 *N.Y. Times* 17 July 3/5 Mary Mallon, known to fame as 'Typhoid Mary',.. must remain at Riverside Hospital. **1961** S. P. HAYES in *Webster* s.v., Authoritarianism.. is carried by Typhoid Marys, unwitting sources of infection. **1971** 'L. EGAN' *Malicious Mischief* (1972) vii. 118, I went to the library.. and asked. And of course they looked at me as if I was—was Typhoid Mary. **1976** *Ann. Rev. Microbiol.* XXX. 438 During the next 15 years Typhoid Mary infected well over 200 persons. **1979** R. JAFFE *Class Reunion* II. vi. 180 Alexander's own misery was the most important thing in Alexander's life, and whatever he gave of it to others was unimportant to him; he was simply unaware. Alexander was the Typhoid Mary of angst.

B. *sb.* **a.** Short for *typhoid fever*: see 2 above. ***pig typhoid***, a name for swine fever.

1861 TANNER *Pract. Med.* II. i. (ed. 4) 153 The fatal cases in typhus and typhoid are one in between five and six. **1887** *Times* 1 Feb. 9/6 Swine fever.. being known in different parts of Great Britain by the names of pig typhoid, pig distemper. **1893** *Syd. Soc. Lex.*, *Pig typhoid*, swine plague. **1898** *Daily News* 13 Dec. 3/4 Jenner's great contribution to medical knowledge was the differentiation of typhus and typhoid. **1902** R. BAGOT *Donna Diana* xxi, In typhoid there are often relapses.

b. A case of typhoid; a patient suffering from typhoid. *colloq.*

1890 *Pall Mall G.* 8 Sept. 2/3, I have heard of nurses who started out of their sleep and got out of bed under the impression they had still, as they put it, their 'two-hour typhoids to feed'. **1900** *Westm. Gaz.* 27 June 1/2 There were 316 patients, of whom half were typhoids.

c. *Comb.* as ***typhoid-bacillus***, ***-carrier***, ***-infection***; ***typhoid-contaminated***, ***-like***, ***-poisoned*** adjs.

1897 *Allbutt's Syst. Med.* IV. 154 Pansini.. obtained typhoid-like bacilli in three dysenteric abscesses. **1899** CAGNEY tr. *Jaksch's Clin. Diagn.* vi. (ed. 4) 246 The typhoid-bacillus.. infests the discharges of this disease. **1902** *Daily Chron.* 18 Dec. 5/1 Typhoid-contaminated sewage. **1903** *Daily Mail* 10 Sept. 3/4 Typhoid-poisoned oysters. **1908** *Daily Chron.* 8 Sept. 4/4 Typhoid-infection on a large scale. *Ibid.*, 'Typhoid carriers', persons.. long cured.. of the active disease, yet act as culture-merchants of its germs.

typhoidal (taɪ'fɔɪdəl), *a.* [f. prec. + -AL[1].] Pertaining to or characteristic of typhoid fever; resembling or having the character of typhoid fever.

1882 *St. James's Gaz.* 15 Nov. 6 The milk-pail reeks with fever germs, The pump with seeds typhoidal. **1890** in *N.Y. Voice* 17 Apr., Miasmatic and typhoidal conditions. **1899** *Allbutt's Syst. Med.* VIII. 467 The fever.. may be.. ephemeral, remittent,.. continuous, typhoidal, according to the circumstances.

typholysin, typhomalarial: see TYPHO-.

‖ **typhomania** (taɪfəʊ'meɪnɪə). *Path.* [mod.L., ad. Gr. *τυφωμανία* (Hippocrates, Galen), f. *τῦφος* (see TYPHUS) + *μανία* madness, MANIA; by modern writers taken as f. TYPHUS (in the mod. sense) + MANIA.] Delirium accompanied with stupor, occurring in typhus and other fevers.

1693 tr. *Blancard's Phys. Dict.* (ed. 2), *Typhomania*, a Delirium with a Phrensy, and a Lethargy. **1783** W. CULLEN *First Lines Pract. Phys.* §293 In the Nosology, I added the Typhomania to the character of Phrenitis. **1822–9** GOOD *Study Med.* (ed. 3) IV. 622 Imperfect lethargy,.. the Typhomania of the Greek writers; the Coma Vigil of many later pathologists. **1857** DUNGLISON *Med. Lex.*, *Typhomania*, the kind of delirium common in typhus. **1876** BRISTOWE *The. & Pract. Med.* (1878) 185 Occasionally the delirium [in typhus] is violent and maniacal,.. but much more commonly it is of the low muttering kind, known by the name of 'typhomania'.

Typhon[1] ('taɪfɒn). [a. L. *Tȳphōn*, a. Gr. *Τῡφῶν*, name of a giant (see below); also, a tempestuous wind (see next); also applied to a comet or meteor.] The name of a giant or monster of ancient Greek mythology (according to Hesiod, the son of Typhoeus (see TYPHŒAN), and father of the Winds; later identified with Typhoeus), fabled to have been buried under Mount Etna, and represented as having a hundred heads and breathing out flames; also used as a name for the Egyptian evil divinity Set. Hence *allusively*.

1592 KYD *Sol. & Pers.* I. iii, *Bas.* What, wouldst thou haue me a Typhon, To beare vp Peleon or Ossa? *Pist.* Typhon me no Typhons. **1610** GUILLIM *Heraldry* I. i. (1660) 7 Ulysses bare a Dolphin and a Typhon breathing out flames of fire. **1611** SPEED *Hist. Gt. Brit.* IX. xx. §14 This aery Typhon [Lambert Symnell], which grasped at the embracement of the two Kingdomes of England and Ireland. *a* **1649** DRUMM. OF HAWTH. *Poems* Wks. (1711) 40 Those brazen Typhons, which disgorge.. metal, flame, and smoak. **1820** T. MITCHELL *Aristoph.* I. 202 He marches all elate 'Gainst that Typhon of the state, Storm and hurricane and tempest combining. *a* **1864** T. ARCHER in Macfarlane *Mem.* vii. (1867) 190 Boring away at Berosus and Sanchoniatho.. at Demi-gods and Typhons.

Comb. **1598** SYLVESTER *Du Bartas* II. i. II. *Imposture* 637 Wo to the vain bravados Of Typhon-like invincible Armados. **1859** J. C. FAIRBAIRN *Hymns & Poems* 92 That brindled monster, typhon-born.

'**typhon**[2]. ? *Obs.* [ad. Gr. *τῡφῶν*: see prec. In later use partly suggested by TYPHOON. Cf. F. *typhon*, Sp. *tifon*, It. *tifone*.] A whirlwind, cyclone, tornado; a violent storm of wind, a hurricane.

1555 EDEN *Decades* 21 These tempestes of the ayer (which the Grecians caule *Tiphones* that is whyrle wyndes) they caule, *Furacanes*. **1585** T. WASHINGTON tr. *Nicholay's Voy.* I. xi. 13 A wind called by the Gretians Typhon, of Plinie Vertex or Vortex. **1601** HOLLAND *Pliny* II. xlvii. I. 24 If the clift or breach bee not great, so that the wind be constrained to turn round, to rol and whirle in his discent,.. it makes a whirlepuffe or ghust called Typhon. **1627** MAY *Lucan* VII. 177 Cloud breaking Typhons did arise. **1686** PLOT *Staffordsh.* 27 There happen'd a Typhon or Tornado-wind, ..not above forty yards broad. **1699** Typhones [see TYPHOON β]. **1727–46** THOMSON *Summer* 984 The circling Typhon, whirl'd from point to point, Exhausting all the rage of all the sky. **1761** *Chron.* in *Ann. Reg.* 126/1 On the 4th of May, a most violent whirlwind of that kind commonly known by the name of Typhons, passed down Ashley river [S. Carolina]. **1820** T. S. HUGHES *Trav. Sicily* I. iv. 121 A violent sirocco blew from the S.E... As long as this Typhon prevails, the streets are generally deserted. **1826** HOOD *She is far fr. the Land* 21 All the sea-dangers,.. Tornadoes and typhons, And horrible syphons.

† **b.** Applied erroneously to a waterspout. (Cf. quot. 1625 s.v. TYPHOON α) *Obs. rare*$^{-1}$.

1774 GOLDSM. *Nat. Hist.* I. xxi. 394, I am at a loss whether we ought to reckon these spouts called typhons; which are sometimes seen at land, of the same kind with those so often described by mariners, at sea.

† **c.** *spec.* = TYPHOON b. *Obs.*

1783 JUSTAMOND tr. *Raynal's Hist. Indies* III. 186 The storms they call typhons, which are peculiar to the seas of China.

Typhonian (taɪ'fəʊnɪən), *a. Mythol.* [f. TYPHON[1] + -IAN; cf. Gr. *Τῡφώνιος*, L. *Tȳphōneus*.] Pertaining to or connected with Typhon or Set.

1837 *Fraser's Mag.* XVI. 409 The greater bear appears under the typhonian figure of a pig standing on his hind-legs. **1863** G. TREVOR *Anc. Egypt* ix. 200 Some of the paintings represent the spirits of the dead in Tartarus, armed with lances, fighting with the Typhonian animals, the hippopotamus, serpent, tortoise, and ass. **1877** S. LANE POOLE in *Encycl. Brit.* VII. 783/1 A gallery supported by Typhonian columns.

typhonic (taɪ'fɒnɪk), *a.* [ad. Gr. *Τῡφωνικός*, f. *Τῡφῶν*: see TYPHON[1] and -IC.]

1. Having the character of a whirlwind or tornado; tempestuous. (In quots. in allusion to Gr. *τυφωνικός* in Acts xxvii. 14.)

[**1382** WYCLIF *Acts* xxvii. 14 The wynd Tiffonyk [**1388** Tifonyk: Vulg. *ventus typhonicus*], that is clepid north eest, or wynd of tempest.] **1865** *Pall Mall G.* 25 Aug. 11/1 Captain Spratt.. was for some time in the Fair Havens, and ..was caught by a real Euroclydon,.. the gale having acquired a truly typhonic character by rushing down from the high land. **1895** W. M. RAMSAY *St. Paul the Trav.* xiv. §4. 326 There struck down from the island a typhonic wind.

2. = TYPHONIAN.

1874 BIRCH *1st & 2nd Egypt. Rooms Brit. Mus.* 19 Wooden head of a hippopotamus.. sacred to Typhon, Thoueris and other Typhonic deities. **1894** *Western Daily News* 19 Sept., The history of Saturn is Typhonic or Satanic ..; he is said to devour his children.

typhoon (taɪ'fuːn). Forms: α. 6 **touffon**, 7 **tuffon, -one, -in, tufon, -faon, tufan**, 8 **typhawn**, 9 **tuphan, toofan, touffan, tūfān**. β. 7–9 **tuffoon**, 8–9 **tiffoon**. γ. 8 **tay-fun**, 9 **ty-foong, tifoon, tyfoon, typhoon**. [Two different Oriental words are included here: (1) the α-forms (like Pg. *tufão*, †*tufõe*) are a. Urdū (Persian and Arabic) *ṭūfān* a violent storm of wind and rain, a tempest, hurricane, tornado, commonly referred to Arab. *ṭāfa*, to turn round (nouns of action *ṭauf*, *ṭawafān*), but possibly an adoption of Gr. *τῡφῶν* TYPHON[2]; (2) the β- and γ- forms represent Chinese *tai fung*, common dialect forms (as in Cantonese) of *ta* big, and *fêng* wind (hence also G. *teifun*). The spelling of the β-forms has apparently been influenced by that of the earlier-known Indian word, while that now current is due to association with TYPHON[2].]

a. A violent storm or tempest occurring in India (†occas. with reference to other localities); **b.** A violent cyclonic storm or hurricane occurring in the China seas and adjacent regions, chiefly during the period from July to October.

α. **1588** T. HICKOCK tr. *Frederick's Voy.* 34 b, I went a boord of the Shippe of Bengala, at which time it was the yeere of Touffon. *Ibid.* 35 This Touffon or cruell storme endured three dayes and three nightes. **1614** PURCHAS *Pilgrimage* IV. xix. 448 The winde, which they call Tufan is so violent, that it driueth ships on the land, ouerthroweth men and houses. **1616** R. COCKS *Diary* (Hakl. Soc.) I. 163 Over-cast wether, with a stiff gale wynd.. towardes night proved a tuffon. **1625** PURCHAS *Pilgrims* I. I. vi. 20 Tempests, Huricanos, Tufons, Water-spouts. **1665** SIR T. HERBERT *Trav.* (1677) 11 It may also be remembred, that during this late tuffon, lightning was seen to fall and hang like fire. **1674** J. JOSSELYN *Two Voyages to N.-E.* 54 In the West-Indies in August and September the forcible North-wind, which though some call Tuffins or Hurricanes we must distinguish. **1793** W. HODGES *Trav. India* 132 The country people call them aundees, and typhawns. **1811** MRS. SHERWOOD in *Life* xxiii. (1847) 382 During a most tremendous touffan. **1826** HOCKLEY *Pandurang Hari* I. iv. 48, I.. inquired how this *toofan* or storm had arisen. **1850** FANNY PARKS *Wand. Pilgr.* xliii. II. 53 The whirling clouds of the tūfān. **1885** LEWIN *Fly on Wheel* ii. 61 We ought to make ready for the coming 'tuphan' or tempest.

β. **1699** DAMPIER *Voy.* (1729) II. I. 35 The violent Storms called Tuffoons (Typhones). **1727** A. HAMILTON *New Acc. E. Ind.* II. xxxix. 89 September, they reacht the Coast of China, where meeting with a Tuffoon, or a North-east Storm, that often blows violently about that Season, they were forced to bear away. **1745** P. THOMAS *Voy. S. Seas* 274 Those dreadful Gusts of Wind called here [near Canton] by the Name of Tuffoons, of which the Chinese relate very amazing and incredible Effects. **1773** *Chron.* in *Ann. Reg.* 202/1 We had another tiffoon in August, when all the European ships at Wampoo drove with three anchors a-head. **1802** CAPT. ELMORE in *Naval Chron.* VIII. 381 In the event of a tuffoon coming on. **1831** TRELAWNY *Adv. Younger Son* I. 281, I should as soon have thought of anchoring on the sand-heads in a tiffoon.

γ. **1771** J. R. FORSTER tr. *Osbeck's Voy.* I. 169 Exceeding great storms (called Tay-fun by the Chinese). **1806** *Naval Chron.* XV. 465 A Danish.. ship.. encountered a Ty-foong. **1819** SHELLEY *Prometh. Unb.* II. iv. 170 My coursers.. outstrip the Typhoon [*rime* moon]. **1832** LYELL *Princ. Geol.* II. 98 Captain W. H. Smyth informs me, that when cruizing.. amidst the Philippine Islands, he has.. seen, after those dreadful hurricanes called typhoons, floating islands of wood, with trees growing upon them. **1848** S. W. WILLIAMS *Middle Kingd.* I. ii. 49 The increased temperature on the southern coast during.. June and July operates.. to produce violent storms along the seaboard, called tyfoons, from the Chinese *ta-fung*, or 'great wind'. **1900** *Jrnl. Sch. Geog.* (U.S.) June 224 The typhoon of the western Pacific Ocean is in many respects the counterpart of the West Indian hurricane.

fig. **1851** J. MILNE *Poems* 295 Thoughts have their Typhoons. **1898** *Allbutt's Syst. Med.* V. 807 Its [the heart's] workings.. lie.. in the track of emotional gales and typhoons.

c. *attrib.* and *Comb.*

1880 Miss Bird *Japan* II. 124 It was what they call a 'typhoon rain', without the typhoon. **1901** Hall & Osborne *Sunshine & Surf* ii. 17 Our track was well out of the typhoon district. **1907** *Manila Cablenews* 21 Aug. 8/5 The building is of concrete, earthquake- and typhoon-proof.

Hence **typhoon** *v. trans.* (*nonce-word*), to batter with the force of a typhoon; **ty'phoonish** *a.*, resembling or portending a typhoon.

1880 Clark Russell *Sailor's Sweetheart* vi, That was a bright flash! Gad! That looked typhoonish! **1893** K. T. Webber in *Columbus* (Ohio) *Dispatch* 22 Nov., The weather ..had been very 'typhoonish'. **1953** Dylan Thomas *Under Milk Wood* (1954) 50 But with blue hazy eyes the fishermen gaze at that milkmaid whispering water with no ruck or ripple as though it blew great guns and serpents and typhooned the town.

typhopneumonia, -toxin: see typho-.

typhous ('taɪfəs), *a. Path.* [f. typh-us + -ous.] Pertaining to or having the character of typhus.

1805 *Med. Jrnl.* XIV. 341 The district..has been..more free from typhous fever, than the more distant parts of the metropolis. **1822-9** Good *Study Med.* (ed. 3) II. 91 Prisoners confined in jails with typhous miasm around them. **1844** Babington tr. *Hecker's Epidemics Mid. Ages* 237 Such opposite states are usual in all typhous fevers. **1857** Dunglison *Med. Lex.*, *Typhous Deposit*, a peculiar substance of new formation found in the areolar membrane ..of the patches of Peyer in typhoid fever. **1897** *Allbutt's Syst. Med.* II. 364 The renal secretion..is..dark-coloured from typhous dissolution of the blood.

typhus ('taɪfəs). [Late L. *tȳphus* in sense 1, and mod.L. (De Sauvages, 1759) in sense 2, ad. Gr. τῦφος smoke, vapour, conceit, vanity, stupor, f. τύφειν to smoke, smoulder. So (in sense 2) F. *typhus*, Sp. *tifus*, Pg. *typho*, Sp. and It. *tifo*.]

†**1. a.** Pride, haughtiness, conceit. *Obs.*

1643 Tuckney *Balme of G.* 31 To bring down our loftinesse and pride,..to take down the Typhus of a *Britannia triumphans*, as some few yeares since we vainly boasted. [**1681** *Ess. Peace & Truth Ch.* 18 Proud and haughty Prelates (full of that *Typhus Secularis*—The old bane of the Church).]

2. *Path.* **a.** An acute infectious fever, characterized by great prostration and a petechial eruption; chiefly occurring in crowded tenements, etc.

1785 D. Campbell *Observ. Typhus* 7 We shall therefore, in speaking of this fever, either employ the technical term *Typhus*; or call it a low contagious fever. **1822-9** Good *Study Med.* (ed. 3) II. 239 The heavier, severer, or putrid typhus chiefly differs from the mild in the violence and rapidity of its march. **1866** A. Flint *Princ. Med.* (1880) 967 The fever called typhus, known from the earliest antiquity, has received a great variety of names. The name typhus, introduced by Sauvages in 1759,..derived from τυφος, denoting stupor,..relates to a feature..usually more or less prominent in this disease. **1875** B. W. Richardson *Dis. Mod. Life* ii. 14 The black death is still represented in malignant typhus. **1897** *Allbutt's Syst. Med.* II. 354 Previous to the time of de Sauvages typhus was known as 'Pestilential' or 'Putrid Fever', or by some name suggested by the eruption or expressive of the locality in which it appeared, as 'Camp', 'Jail', 'Hospital' or 'Ship Fever'.

b. Also *typhus fever*.

1789 G. Buchanan (*title*) Treatise on the Typhus Fever. **1818** Scott *Let. to Laidlaw* Mar., in *Lockhart*, Many of the better ranks are ill of the typhus fever. **1877** Roberts *Handbk. Med.* (ed. 3) I. 110 Typhus fever is generated by a specific poison, and is highly contagious.

c. *attrib.*, as *typhus case, contagion, epidemic, eruption, patient*; **typhus-louse**, a louse of the kind responsible for transmitting typhus.

1799 J. Franks (*title*) On the Non-Existence of Typhus Contagion. **1843** R. J. Graves *Syst. Clin. Med.* iv. 41 The chief causes of typhus epidemics. **1876** Bristowe *The. & Pract. Med.* (1878) 189 It is important that typhus patients should be treated in large, airy, well-ventilated chambers. **1885-8** Fagge & Pye-Smith *Princ. Med.* (ed. 2) I. 146 He had headache and fever, and the typhus eruption followed in due course. **1939** Auden & Isherwood *Journey to War* 136 Their upholstery often contained typhus-lice.

typic ('tɪpɪk), *a.* [a. F. *typique* (1582 in Hatz.-Darm.), ad. L. *typicus*, a. Gr. τυπικός typical, figurative, f. τύπος type; see -ic. So Pg. *typico*, Sp. and It. *tipico*.]

1. = typical *a.* 1.

1610 Donne *Pseudo-martyr* 5 Those Typique times, and Sacrifices of the old law. **1692** J. Salter *Triumphs Jesus* 7 Of various colour'd Plumes their wings are made The Rainbows to 'em are but Typick shade. **1839** Bailey *Festus* x. (1848) 110 This air-filled bowl is typic of the world. **1856** Mrs. Browning *Aur. Leigh* ix. 134 Already swearing at my feet That I'm the typic She. **1886** Swinburne *Stud. Prose & Poetry* (1894) 181 With what passionate magnificence of rapture the poet would have sung the fall of the typic prison.

2. Of a fever: Conforming to a particular type (see type *sb.*[1] 4); recurring at regular intervals; intermittent; periodic. ? *Obs.*

1601 Holland *Pliny* xxviii. xvi. II. 335 As touching feavers,..if it bee any of these Typicke and Periodicall agues, which be intermittent and returne by fits. **1857** Dunglison *Med. Lex.*, *Typic, typical*,..characterized by periodicity, as a 'typical fever'; or one which observes a particular type.

typical ('tɪpɪkəl), *a.* [ad. med.L. *typicālis* figurative, symbolic (Thomas Aquinas, *c* 1150), f. L. *typicus* typic: see -ical.]

1. Of the nature of, or serving as, a type or emblem; pertaining or relating to a type or types; symbolical, emblematic.

1612 T. Taylor *Comm. Titus* i. 6 (1619) 99 Were they not all typicall representations of that spirituall holines, wherin even we ought to resemble them? **1616** Bullokar *Eng. Expos.*, *Typicall*, mysticall, or that which serueth as a shadow and figure of an other thing. **1631** Gouge *God's Arrows* iii. §72. 319 Both the Psalmes are typicall, and prophesie of Christ, and his joyfull comming. *a* **1661** Fuller *Worthies, York* (1662) ii. 230 He renewed the custome of expounding Scripture in a typicall way. **1711** Hickes *Two Treat. Chr. Priesth.* (1847) II. 188 The typical Melchisedec, the sacerdotal king of Salem. **1784** Cowper *Task* iv. 218 Ensanguin'd hearts, clubs typical of strife, And spades, the emblem of untimely graves. **1860** Pusey *Min. Proph.* 601 In the daily sacrifice..the lamb..was typical of the precious blood-shedding of the Lamb without spot upon the Cross. **1865** R. W. Dale *Jew. Temp.* xiv. (1877) 159 The typical character of Old Testament ritualism, and of Old Testament history. **1898** C. Bell tr. *Huysman's Cathedral* xi. 223 Samuel, in many ways typical of Christ.

2. Having the qualities of a type or specimen; serving as a representative specimen of a class or kind.

1860 Tyndall *Glac.* ii. App. 434 The facts which I have brought before you are typical facts. **1861** Bentley *Man. Bot.* 359 A perfectly normal and typical flower should possess a calyx, corolla, stamens, and carpels. **1874** Parker *Goth. Archit.* i. v. 162 Exeter Cathedral is..the best typical example of the early part of this style. **1875** Fortnum *Maiolica* ix. 81 Their style would be..typical of the Valencian pottery. **1881** Froude *Short Stud.* (1883) IV. ii. vi. 249 Horace is a typical Roman of the intellectual sort.

b. *Nat. Hist.* That is the type of the genus, family, etc.

1847 Webster, *Typical*,..2. In *natural history*, pertaining to or constituting a type. **1861** *Rep. Smithsonian Instit.* 1860, 192 The typical genus, *Pleurotoma*.

c. *Path.* Of a fever: = typic 2.

1857 [see typic 2]. **1875** tr. *von Ziemssen's Cycl. Med.* II. 599 Masked intermittents usually show themselves as typical neuralgia.

3. Of or pertaining to a type or representative specimen; distinctive, characteristic.

1850 McCosh *Div. Govt.* ii. i. (1874) 123 The normal or typical number of toes is ten,..corresponding to the typical number of the digits. **1862** Burton *Bk. Hunter* (1863) 290 Hitting off the deeper and typical characteristics of Scottish life. **1891** Swinburne *Stud. Prose & Poetry* (1894) 18 The typical English vices of egotism, hypocrisy, and envy.

4. Of or pertaining to printers' type; typographical. Now *rare* or *Obs.*

1770 G. Faulkner in *Abp. Boulter's Lett.* I. p. vii, I have ..corrected some typical errors that are in the London Edition. **1822** *Blackw. Mag.* XI. 7 Should you ever descend from your correctorship of typical errata. **1837** Lockhart *Scott* xliv. (1839) VI. 87 Numerous typical errors which sprang of necessity from the author's inability to correct any proof-sheets.

Hence **typi'cality** = typicalness.

1863 H. James *Substance & Shadow* 222 Such men..have spurned the empty typicality of the church. **1890** W. Whitman in *Pall Mall G.* 26 Aug. 7/2 If America is only for the rule and fashion and small typicality of other lands (the rule of the *état-major*) it is not the land I take it for. **1900** *Speaker* 22 Dec. 317/2 The propriety, justice and typicality of the picture.

typically ('tɪpɪkəlɪ), *adv.* [f. typical + -ly[2].] In a typical manner.

1. By way of or by means of a type or types; figuratively; symbolically; emblematically.

1605 Willet *Hexapla Gen.* 455 It typically also setteth the practises of the scribes. **1617** Collins *Def. Bp. Ely* ii. x. 506 How could the Priesthood of our Sauiour Christ be typically shaddowed and prefigured by two? **1692** Bentley *Boyle Lect.* ix. 334 The things they typically represented were come to pass. **1786** A. Maclean *Christ's Commission* i. 15 The nations of this world are neither typically nor spiritually related to God as His Church and Kingdom. **1836** J. Gilbert *Chr. Atonem.* Notes (1852) 335 What is true typically of the legal sacrifices, is true really of Christ's sacrifice. **1873** Symonds *Grk. Poets* iv. 193 We find the fundamental moral law of Nemesis as a part of the Divine government of the world expressed typically..in the Oresteia.

2. So as to constitute a type; in conformity with the type; representatively; characteristically.

1868 Carpenter in *Sci. Opinion* 6 Jan. (1869) 174/2 Numerous specimens of the typically triradiate. **1872** Yeats *Growth Comm.* 10 The Phoenicians were typically a nation of traders. **1910** Seligmann *Melanesians Brit. N. Guinea* Introd. 2 The character of its [the nose's] bridge varies, typically the nostrils are broad.

typicalness ('tɪpɪkəlnɪs). [f. as prec. + -ness.] The character or quality of being typical; *esp.* symbolic character.

1633 Ames *Agst. Cerem.* i. 24 All Interpreters terme the types of the ould law ceremonies; for that spiritual disposition they have, and typicalnes which the Lord set upon them. **1649** Roberts *Clavis Bibl.* 560 His Typicalnesse herein remarkable; for Ionas was a singular type of Iesus Christ. **1865** *Lit. Churchman* 21 Oct. 443 Typicalness is a matter of the interior nature. **1903** A. B. Davidson *O. Test. Proph.* xiv. 238 The Divine design is no part of their typicalness.

typification (ˌtɪpɪfɪ'keɪʃən). [Noun of action f. typify *v.*: see -fication.] The action of typifying; representation by a type or symbol; also, that which typifies, or serves as a type, symbol, or specimen of something: an exemplification.

1811-31 Bentham *Lang.* Wks. 1843 VIII. 334 A distant and fanciful analogy which there is between the event typified and the real event made use of for typification. **1845** *Blackw. Mag.* LVII. 731 The four-paned rattling window of that clumsy typefication of slowness, misnamed a diligence. **1850** A. Baker *Plea for Romanizers* 26 The typification, the earnest and the pledge by outward miracle, of the reality of the sacramental grace. **1893** E. L. Wakeman in *Columbus* (Ohio) *Dispatch* 19 Dec., A perfect typification of Norwegian childhood.

typify ('tɪpɪfaɪ), *v.* [f. L. *typus* type *sb.*[1]: see -fy; cf. F. *typifié* (Littré).]

1. *trans.* To represent or express by a type or symbol; to serve as a type, figure, or emblem of; to symbolize; to prefigure.

1634 Wither *Emblemes* 5 Glorie by the wreath is typifide. **1646** Sir T. Browne *Pseud. Ep.* v. viii. 246 We cannot well conceive the wood a burthen for a boy, but such a one unto Isaac, as that which it typified was unto Christ. **1673** Penn *The Chr. a Quaker* xvi. 570 How can Christ be said to be typified out? **1730** Waterland *Script. Vind.* Pref. 8 That Fact expresses, prefigures, or typifies, another Fact of a higher and more important Nature. **1833** Ht. Martineau *Loom & Lugger* ii. v. 103 A double death was to be typified by its fate. **1858** J. H. Newman *Hist. Sk.* (1873) III. ii. ii. 233 The Euxine! that strange mysterious sea, which typifies the abyss of outer darkness. **1864** Bowen *Logic* viii. (1870) 248 A Syllogism, which is a union of three Judgments, is appropriately typified by a triangle, a union of three lines.

2. To serve as the typical specimen or characteristic example of (a class, family, etc.); to exhibit the essential characters of; to exemplify.

1854 Murchison *Siluria* i. (1867) 7 Fossils which might typify such supposed older sediments. **1868** Owen *Anat. Vertebr. Anim.* III. 374 The second deciduous molar.. typifies the form of the upper sectorial, which is retained in the permanent dentition of several Viverrine and Musteline species.

Hence **'typified** *ppl. a.*, **'typifying** *vbl. sb.* and *ppl. a.* Also **'typifier**, one who typifies (*rare*).

1653 Baxter *Worc. Petit. Def.* 13 The typifying use may cease. **1685** —— *Paraphr. N.T.* Matt. v. 17 The Ceremonial part..was but a Typifying prediction of me. **1745** Warburton *Remarks Occas. Refl.* ii. xviii. 95 A modern Typifier, who deals only in Similitudes and Correspondences. **1851** Wardlaw *Zech.* v. (1869) 98 As the typical Zerubbabel finished the typical temple, so surely shall the typified finish His.

typing ('taɪpɪŋ), *vbl. sb.* [f. type *v.* + -ing[1].]

1. The action of type *v.* in various senses. Also *attrib.*

a **1638** Mede *Wks.* (1672) 43 The Seven Arch-angels,.. and the typing of them by the Seven Eyes and Horns of the Lamb. **1736** Byrom *Jrnl. & Lit. Rem.* (1856) II. i. 82 Dr. Mainwaring brought me a piece of Torlock's typing. **1876** Mrs. Whitney *Sights & Ins.* vi, Somebody near, not going very deep, yet observing faintly a typing in it. **1900** W. Myers tr. *Ehrlich & Lazarus' Histol. of Blood* 32 The simple 'typing' of several hundred cells. **1927** H. W. Jones in *Osler's Mod. Med.* (ed. 3) V. 191 The institution of blood typing has made the operation of blood transfusion reasonably safe. **1928**, etc. [see *blood-typing* vbl. sb. s.v. blood *sb.* 21]. **1960** *Guardian* 3 Nov. 8/4 The rigid typing of her as a dumb blonde... Hollywood has destroyed..talent by typing. **1962** *Brit. Med. Bull.* XVIII. 64/1 (*heading*) The genetic basis of bacteriophage typing. **1965**, etc. [see *tissue typing* s.v. tissue *sb.* 9 b]. **1971** *Nature* 9 July 141/2 Each centre coordinates the typing and distribution of cadaveric kidneys to and from a group of collaborating hospitals.

2. *attrib.* and *Comb.*, as *typing agency, bureau, course, error, paper, pool* (see pool *sb.*[3] 5 c), *purposes, school, speed*.

1973 W. M. Duncan *Big Timer* xi. 75, I should like..a list of the typing agencies within say, roughly, a half-mile. **1935** D. L. Sayers *Gaudy Night* v. 97 [She] ran what was ostensibly a Typing Bureau. **1974** R. Rendell *Face of Trespass* i. 17 My friend Molly that I used to have my typing bureau with. **1952** Leslie & Pepe *Methods Teaching Typing Simplified* (1954) 85 A slightly condensed verbatim report of an actual teaching period within the first week of the typing course. **1981** C. Storr *Vicky* xviii. 128 She'd taken a typing course and she had a job. **1936** A. Dvorak et al. *Typewriting Behavior* xiii. 395 Typing errors are signs of interference, due partly to drills on isolated letter strokes. **1979** M. Page *Pilate Plot* i. 21 He looked at it three times to make sure it was not a typing error. **1944** Mrs. Belloc Lowndes *Let.* 4 June (1971) 249, I got a packet of *pre-war* typing paper—finest quality! **1889** *Pall Mall G.* 21 Jan. 6/1 The application of the Tainter graphophone..to typing purposes. **1966** 'G. Black' *You want to die, Johnny?* xii. 223 There are certainly duller jobs waiting for a graduate of typing school than being the secretary to a Regent. **1936** A. Dvorak et al. *Typewriting Behavior* xi. 286 Typing speed grows, but fast motions must also be present from the start. **1976** 'A. York' *Dark Passage* xiv. 182 Her typing speeds and general ability as a secretary were excellent.

typism ('taɪpɪz(ə)m). *rare*[−1]. [f. type *sb.*[1] + -ism.] The character or quality of being typical or symbolic; symbolism.

1850 J. Brown *Disc. & Sayings our Lord* (1852) I. ii. 65 The economy, whose great characters were externality and typism, is about to close.

typist ('taɪpɪst). [f. type *sb.*[1] + -ist.]

1. One who uses type; a printer, a compositor. In quot. *attrib. rare*[−1].

1843 J. W. Croker in *C. Papers* 5 Dec. (1884) III. 13 Some of them are probably typist errors.

2. One who does typewriting; = TYPE-WRITER 2.

1885 FREWEN in *Pall Mall G.* 5 May 6/2 The feelings with which a 'typist' contemplates the clumsy goose quill. *Ibid.* 9 May 2 If they are quick writers, the typists earn more than the sum mentioned. **1890** *Daily News* 24 Feb. 5/6 The Society of Typists announces a meeting at Exeter Hall on March 17 for the examination of 'type writer operators'. **1902** ELIZ. L. BANKS *Newspaper Girl* ii, I was a sort of private secretary and confidential typist to the proprietor of the *Daily Hustler*.

typiste (taɪˈpiːst). [Alteration of TYPIST, with Fr. termination as in *modiste*, misinterpreted as fem.] A female typist.

1923 *Daily Mail* 26 Feb. 8 An actress who played the part of a typiste. **1969** *West Australian* 5 July 65/1 (Advt.), Shorthand typiste.

typo (ˈtaɪpəʊ), *sb.* (*a.*) *slang.* [Short for *typographer* or *typographic(al)*.] **a.** A typographer, a printer; *spec.* a compositor. **b.** A typographical error. **c.** *attrib.* or as *adj.* = TYPOGRAPHIC.

1816 *Massachusetts Spy* 7 Aug. (Thornton), [Printers] will confer a favour on a brother typo [etc.]. **1858** *Printer* Dec. (Bartlett), A manuscript written in 1714–1716, by two ambitious typos. **1880** *Stationer* XXXV. 3 From the humble typo to the grand publisher in his chair. **1891** *Anthony's Photogr. Bull.* IV. 110 Good pressmen for color work, for litho. and typo. presses... What does a typo pressman know about lithographic inks, damping, [etc.]? **1892** I. ZANGWILL *Childr. Ghetto* III. II. iii. 24 My men..don't like to pass anything till it's free from typos. **1893** LELAND *Mem.* I. 286 The typos, reporters, and subs [on a newspaper staff]. **1945** E. B. WHITE *Let.* 10 July (1976) 266 As for the 'her'—'hen' typo, I guessed that it was a typo and that it would be caught. **1963** C. D. SIMAK *They walked like Men* vi. 36, I went through the story again and caught a couple of typos and fixed up another place or two to make language better. **1978** *Times Lit. Suppl.* 15 Sept. 1031/5 Since few proof-readers are perfect, a typo here and there is easily forgiven.

typo- (ˈtaɪpəʊ, ˈtɪpəʊ), before a vowel **typ-**, combining form repr. Gr. τύπος TYPE *sb.*[1], used chiefly in forming scientific and technical terms, and some nonce-words. **typacanthid** (taɪp-, tɪpəˈkænθɪd), *a.* [Gr. ἄκανθα spine], having the typical arrangement of spines, as a star-fish. **tyˈparchical** *a. nonce-wd.* [Gr. ἀρχή rule: cf. ARCHICAL], of or pertaining to the control of the printing-press. **ˈtypocrat** [after DEMOCRAT], one who rules by means of the press; so **typoˈcratic** *a.* (*nonce-wds.*). **typo-etching**: see quot. **ˈtypogravure**, a method of printing pictures from half-tone blocks prepared by photo-engraving, and set up for printing with type-matter; also, a picture produced by this process. † **typolite** (ˈtɪpəlaɪt), *Geol.* (also *typolith*) [-LITE]: see quot. 1828. **typoliˈthography**, a process in which impressions from printers' type are reproduced by lithography (Webster, 1911); hence † **typoliˈthography** *v. trans.* to reproduce by this process; **typolithoˈgraphic** *a.* pertaining to or produced by typolithography (Webster 1911). **typoˈmania** (*nonce-wd.*), (*a*) a craze for seeing one's writings or name in print; (*b*) a craze for typology or symbolism. **tyˈpometer**, an instrument for measuring type-bodies. **typonym** (ˈtaɪpənɪm), *Nat. Hist.* [after *eponym*, etc.], a name based on a type or specimen; hence **typonymal** (-ˈɒnɪməl), **typonymic** (-əˈnɪmɪk), *adjs.* **ˈtypophil(e** [-PHIL, -PHILE], one who has a fondness for or interest in typography. **typoradiˈography**, a method of making copies of a writing, etc. on sensitized sheets or films by radiography. **typoˈrama** [Gr. ὅραμα view, spectacle], a model or representation in facsimile. **ˈtyposcribe**, a typist. **ˈtyposcript**, typewriting, type-script. **typo-ˈtelegraph**, a telegraph instrument which automatically prints the messages it receives; so **typo-teˈlegraphy**. **typotheter** (-ˈɒθɪtə(r)) [Gr. θετήρ, f. τιθέναι to set, place], a type-setting machine.

1881 F. J. BELL in *Proc. Zool. Soc.* 3 May 502 When the spines retain the simpler disposition..seen in..most of the better known forms, we may speak of the arrangement as being *typacanthid. **1835** SOUTHEY *Doctor* cii. (1848) 233/2 Old Mr. Strahan the printer (the founder of his *typarchical dynasty). **1858** BAILEY *Age* 15 The *Typo-crat now rules from coast to coast. **1854** E. MICHELSEN *England* 186 The English Constitution..is *typocratic, and written every day. **1888** J. SOUTHWARD in *Encycl. Brit.* XXIII. 704/1 In ..*typo-etching, the drawing is made with ordinary lithographic ink on stone, or on paper and transferred to stone. It is then re-transferred to a plate of polished zinc by the ordinary lithographic process. **1885** *Academy* 20 June 445/2 A new process—'*typogravure'. **1890** WOODBURY *Encycl. Photogr.* 535 The Typogravure process is a method of obtaining half-tone pictures from copper relief plates. **1828** WEBSTER, **Typolite*, in natural history, a stone or fossil which has on it impressions or figures of plants and animals. *Cyc.* **1860** MAYNE *Expos. Lex.*, *Typolithus*,..a typolith. **1825** HONE *Every-day Bk.* I. 1038 A new musical work *typolithographied. **1882** O. W. HOLMES in *Atlantic Monthly* LI. 66 The slender intellectual endowments.. which are so very frequently observed in association with *typomania. **1890** P. H. HUNTER *After Exile* II. iii. 57 The Jewish-Christian, misled by the prevailing typomania of his age. **1884** COUES in *Auk* Oct. 321 **Typonym*, a name based upon indication of a type species, or of a type specimen. **1889** *Pall Mall G.* 16 Feb. 1/2 Two publications which will receive and deserve the attention of all *typophils. **1958** *Times Lit. Suppl.* 3 Jan. 12/3 It is only sad that the Typophile Chap Books are not more widely available. **1975** *Dalhousie Rev.* Summer 206 Berenson..was the recognized leader of an energetic group which included..Bertram Goodhue, architect, book-designer and typophile. **1982** *Amer. N. & Q.* Jan./Feb. 89/2 It is good reading, at least for typophiles. **1899** *Sci. Amer.* 28 Jan. 51/1 Dr. Kolle now declares..that the process of *typo-radiography is..a self-evident and systematic method of procedure. *a* **1891** *First Year Silken Reign* 214 (Cent.) The *typorama, a plaster of Paris model of the Undercliff, Isle of Wight. **1893** N. H. DOLE in *Nation* (N.Y.) 13 July 27/2 For upwards of ten years ..I have..spoken and written of work thus composed as *typoscript. **1910** *Times* 26 Sept. 8/1, 40,000 articles..in the form of corrected typoscripts. **1888** *Encycl. Brit.* XXIII. 120/1 The automatic *typo-telegraph of Bonelli. **1903** *Electr. World & Engin.* 3 Oct. 377 (Cent. D. Supp.) *Typo-telegraphy. **1888** *Pall Mall G.* 10 Sept. 11/1 The *typotheter is a machine used for..setting type,..and requires no change in the type, material, or appliances now in use.

† **typocosmy.** *Obs. rare* [ad. mod.L. *typocosmia*, a. Gr. type *τυποκοσμία, f. τύπος type + κοσμεῖν to set in order.] A method or system, intended as an aid to learning, in which words or terms are grouped according to types or classes.

Blount's definition appears to be erroneous.

1605 BACON *Adv. Learn.* II. xvii. §14 Such was the trauaile of Raymundus Lullius, in making that Art, which beares his name; not vnlike to some Bookes of Typocosmy, which haue beene made since, beeing nothing but a Masse of words of all Arts. **1605** CAMDEN *Rem.* (1636) 112 To reduce surnames to a Methode, is matter for a Ramist, who should haply finde it to be a Typocosmie. **1656** BLOUNT *Glossogr.*, *Tipocosmy* or *Typocosmy* (*typocosmia*), a type or figure of the world.

typograph (ˈtaɪp-, ˈtɪpəgrɑːf, -græf). [a. F. *typographe* (1554 in Hatz.-Darm.), ad. med.L. *typographus*, f. Gr. τύπος (see TYPO-) + -γραφος (see -GRAPH). So Pg. *typographo*, Sp. and It. *tipografo*.]

1. A typographer or typographist.

1737 OZELL *Rabelais* III. 281 A Fault of Mr Typograph's. **1833** MOORE *Mem.* (1854) VI. 329, I recollect having a little struggle with Simmons, my valuable Typograph, on this very point. **1880** (*title*) The Enemies of Books. By William Blades, Typograph.

2. A writing-machine for the blind in which pressure upon raised types causes the corresponding characters to be printed.

1820 *Gentl. Mag.* May 446/1 A Duplex Typograph.. enables the blind to receive and communicate ideas by means of letters, upon a principle adapted to the sense of feeling. **1851** *Rep. Jurors, Exhibition of 1851* 311 Hughes.. has exhibited a portable typograph or writing machine for the blind.

3. (See quot.)

1886 *Science* 17 Sept. 252/1 There is now being perfected ..a machine intended to dispense with type and type-setters in certain kinds of printing. The 'standard typograph' is the name selected for it... The typograph is in reality a kind of type-writer, but, instead of printing upon paper, it produces indented or depressed characters upon a sheet of soft metal, from which an electrotype may be made.

typographer (taɪp-, tɪˈpɒgrəfə(r)). [f. med.L. *typographus* (see prec.) + -ER[1].]

1. One who is skilled in typography; a printer.

1643 SIR T. BROWNE *Relig. Med.* I. §24 To maintain the trade and mystery of Typographers. **1683** MOXON *Mech. Exerc.*, *Printing* i, By a Typographer, I do not mean a Printer... But by a Typographer, I mean such a one, who.. can either perform, or direct others to perform..all the Handy-works and Physical Operations relating to Typographie. **1715** M. DAVIES *Athen. Brit.* I. Pref. 9 The Vatican Typographers.., in Printing several Treatises. **1778** WARTON *Hist. Eng. Poetry* II. Addit. kj, A very antient edition..without date, place, or typographer. **1837** LOCKHART *Scott* II. i. 17 Whenever the poet hesitated about taking the hints of the zealous typographer.

†**2.** = TYPEWRITER I. *Obs. rare.*

1829 *Mechanics' Mag.* XII. 128 A curious machine.. called a typographer. *Ibid.*, The time is near when a man.. will instantly resort to his typographer, instead of his pen and ink.

3. A beetle, *Bostrychus* (or *Tomicus*) *typographicus*, which makes print-like markings in the bark of trees. Also called ***typographic beetle***. Also ***typographer*** (***bark-***) ***beetle***.

1840 LOUDON tr. *Köllar's Treat. Insects* 357 The Typographer Bark-beetle. *Ibid.* 358 The larvæ..gnaw tortuous passages,..which, on account of their resemblance to letters, have obtained for the beetle the name of typographer. **1847** CARPENTER *Zool.* §656 The Typographer beetle..devours, both in the larva and perfect states, the soft wood beneath the bark,..and thus causes the death of the tree.

typographic (taɪp-, tɪpəˈgræfɪk), *a.* [ad. med.L. *typographic-us* (1540 in *Corpus Reform.* (1843) XI. 818), f. *typographus* TYPOGRAPH: see -IC. So F. *typographique* (1710 in Hatz.-Darm.), Pg. *typographico*, Sp. and It. *tipografico*.] Of or pertaining to printing, typographical.

1778 WARTON *Hist. Eng. Poetry* (1840) II. xxviii. 403 It was printed..in the infancy of the typographic art. **1794** MATTHIAS *Purs. Lit.* (1798) 337 My only objection is to the typographick pomp and expence of a book on such a subject. **1840** DE QUINCEY *Style* Wks. 1859 XI. 283 This typographic mystery..awoke and went back to sleep many times over from mere defect of materials. **1898** *Blackw. Mag.* Aug. 266/1 Typographic nudges and leers conveyed to the reader by capital letters, italics, dashes and asterisks.

typographica (taɪpəˈgræfɪkə), *sb. pl.* [see TYPOGRAPHIC *a.*] Examples of fine printing; in quot. 1949 used as the title of a journal dealing with typography.

[**1858** S. L. SOTHEBY (*title*) Principia typographica.] **1931** *Times Lit. Suppl.* 25 June (Salon Int. du Livre d'Art Suppl.) p. i/3 The former [publishing] house has issued a series of *feuillets d'imprimerie* which..are coveted by collectors of typographica. **1949** *Typographica* I. 3 The first purpose of Typographica will be to present serious analyses of various aspects..of contemporary typography. **1959** *Times Lit. Suppl.* 15 May 289/4 Your account of the George A. Poole collection of typographica..contains one inaccuracy.

typographical (taɪp-, tɪpəˈgræfɪkəl), *a.* [f. as TYPOGRAPHIC *a.* + -AL[1]: see -ICAL.]

1. Of or pertaining to typography or printing; connected or dealing with printing.

1593 J. UDALL *Key Holy Tongue* Printer's Note, The Typographical faultes, which perhaps haue scaped vs. **1611** in *Coryat's Crudities* Pref. Verses d vij, To Topographicall Typographicall Thomas. **1677** W. HUBBARD *Narrative* Pref., Faults..such as are meerly Typographical. **1757** BLACKSTONE *Let. to Dr. Randolph* 21 May 11 Mr. Mussendine's typographical character was entirely forgot in the university. **1790** V. KNOX *Winter Even.* (ed. 2) II. xxxiii. 229 That providential discovery, the typographical art. **1837** HALLAM *Hist. Lit.* I. iii. §141 Some cities..had acquired a typographical reputation somewhat disproportioned to the local demand for books. **1847** L. HUNT *Men, Women, & B.* II. xi. 267 There were no stars, or other typographical symbols, indicating the passages omitted. **1874** ANDERSON *Missions Amer. Bd.* IV. xxxviii. 345 One of the most beautiful books, in its typographical execution, in the Arabic language.

b. Produced or expressed by typography or in print; printed.

1803 SYD. SMITH *Wks.* (1859) I. 50/2 Not..a picture presenting us with an interesting epitome of the whole; but a typographical plan, detailing, with minute and fatiguing precision, every trifling circumstance, and every subordinate feature. **1806** in R. S. Fisher *Amer.* II. (1854) 323 That typographical thunder..has been muffled on this side of the Atlantic. **1868** *Pall Mall G.* 23 July 3 Typographical emphasis was given to the following advantages.

†**2.** (See quot.) *Obs. rare*$^{-0}$.

1755 JOHNSON, *Typographical*, 1, emblematical; figurative. [Hence in later dicts.]

typoˈgraphically, *adv.* [f. prec. + -LY[2].]

1. In a typographical way; in relation to or with respect to typography.

1755 JOHNSON, *Typographically adv.*..2, after the manner of printers. **1802** WOODHOUSE in *Phil. Trans.* XCII. 88 Typographically considered, these expressions are more commodious than [etc.]. **1845** MISS MITFORD in L'Estrange *Life* (1870) III. xi. 197 Selling, for five shillings, books typographically worth about eightpence—poetically, good for nothing. **1893** J. L. SMITH in *World's Congr. Instr. Deaf* 254 An important requirement of the ideal institution newspaper is a high standard of excellence typographically.

†**2.** (See quot.) *Obs. rare*$^{-0}$.

1755 JOHNSON, *Typographically*, 1, emblematically; figuratively. [Hence in later dicts.]

typographist (taɪp-, tɪˈpɒgrəfɪst). *rare.* [f. as TYPOGRAPH-ER + -IST.] One versed in the history or art of printing; a student of typography.

1851 *Tait's Edin. Mag.* Oct. 636/1 The public had a thousand or so of quarto pages for which they paid a folio price, nearly three-fourths of which price was a clear gain to the colluding typographists. **1890** *Athenæum* 27 Sept. 412/1 [The origin of printing] seems still to excite strange passion in the minds of German and Dutch typographists... The grouping of [printing] types and the investigation of their evolution and relationship is the *ultima ratio* of the typographist.

So **tyˈpographize** *v.* (*nonce-wd.*), *trans.* to treat typographically, to describe in print.

1811 BYRON *Bards & Rev.* liii. (ed. 5) *note*, He topographised and typographised King Priam's dominions.

typography (taɪp-, tɪˈpɒgrəfɪ). Also 7 tipo-. [a. F. *typographie* (1577 in Hatz.-Darm.), ad. mod.L. *typographia* (B. Veronensis, 1493), f. Gr. τύπος type + -γραφία writing: see TYPO- and -GRAPHY. So Pg. *typographia*, Sp. and It. *tipografia*.]

1. The art or practice of printing.

1641 EVELYN *Diary* 28 Aug., The happy Monke whom they report to have been the first inventor of Typography. **1646** SIR T. BROWNE *Pseud. Ep.* I. viii. 34 Those diminutive, and pamphlet Treaties.., pieces maintaining rather Typography then verity. **1679** C. NESSE *Antichrist* 94 Typography or publick printing, a rare engine for communicating the knowledge of the truth. **1759** JOHNSON *Idler* No. 69. ¶3 Caxton taught us typography about the year 1474. **1831** CARLYLE *Sart. Res.* I. vi, I consider those printed Paper Aprons, worn by the Parisian Cooks, as a new vent, though a slight one, for Typography. **1875** SCRIVENER *Lect. Text N.T.* 3 The first fruit of typography, the beautiful Latin Bible known as Cardinal Mazarin's.

†**b.** A printing establishment, a press. *Obs.*

1660 in Blackstone *Let. to Dr. Randolph* 21 May 1757, 20 The overplus of the money..to be imployed in setting up and maintaining a learned typographie.

2. The action or process of printing; *esp.* the setting and arrangement of types and printing from them; typographical execution; hence, the arrangement and appearance of printed matter.

1697 G. Keith *Sec. Narr. Proc. Turn.-Hall* 39 A Literal Fault in the Typography, as for *read* it was printed *real*. **1793** Boswell *Johnson* (ed. 2) Advert., The typography of both editions does honour to the press. **1817** Cobbett *Wks.* XXXII. 8 My name is placed in large characters,..here, merely in the typography of the thing, is a proof that [etc.]. **1853** Humphreys *Coin-Coll. Man.* xxvi. (1876) 405 Whose book is a fine monument of the typography of the period. **1900** *Jrnl. Sch. Geog.* (U.S.) Apr. 160 The typography is clear.

b. *transf.* Printed matter; letterpress. *rare.*

1644 Milton *Areop.* (Arb.) 53 To catalogue all those Printers who are found frequently offending, and forbidd the importation of their whole suspected typography.

†**3.** (See quot.) *Obs. rare*$^{-0}$.

1755 Johnson, *Typography*, 1, emblematical, figurative, or hieroglyphical representation.

typologic (taɪp-, tɪpə'lɒdʒɪk), *a. rare.* [f. as next + -ic.] = next; in quot., relating to the study or subject of organic types (type *sb.*[1] 8 a).

1890 *Smithsonian Rep.* July 514 It is only very seldom.. that we can follow the typologic development.

typological (taɪp-, tɪpə'lɒdʒɪkəl), *a.* [f. typology + -ical.]

1. Of or pertaining to typology; relating to the study or interpretation of symbols.

1845 P. Fairbairn *Typology Script.* (1857) I. i. 32 The typological System of the Cocceian School. **1868** J. A. Wylie *Road to Rome* iii. 30 The close of the typological dispensation. **1905** *Edin. Rev.* Oct. 333 No typological connexion was to be assumed between the subjects of the nave and the arch.

2. Pertaining to the art of printing, typographical.

1882 *Trübner's Record* 127/2 Future writers on the Invention of Printing should..treat the question from a purely historical and typological point of view.

3. Pertaining to the study of numismatic types.

1891 *Athenæum* 24 Oct. 554/1 From the evidence of recent finds and the author's typological studies it would further be shown that the whole chronological arrangement of the Syracusan coin-types..required radical revision.

4. Pertaining to typology 3.

1913 E. T. Leeds *Anglo-Saxon Settlements* 28 A large amount of information can be obtained from the purely typological method. **1929** V. G. Childe *Danube in Prehist.* 246 By correlating the several stages in the evolution of celts, daggers,..&c...it is possible to divide the Bronze Age up into several typological phases. **1930** *Psyche* X. iii. 80 (*heading*) Typological methods in experimental psychology. **1942** *Antiquity* XVI. 61 What typological evidence there is ..confirms the standard view of the invasion in its secondary stages. **1964** R. H. Robins *General Linguistics* viii. 325 It is..possible to compare languages..simply by reference to any significant general features of form or structural organization that they share at any level of analysis... Comparison of languages on this basis is usually distinguished..by the title of *typological comparison.* **1968** *Internat. Encycl. Soc. Sci.* XVI. 178/1 Typological classification, as a subdivision of taxonomy, has characterized a considerable part of the culture of the social sciences. **1971** J. Z. Young *Introd. Study Man* xxvii. 386 We are bound therefore to use arbitrary typological groupings, that is to say to put together those we think seem most alike in appearance or some other character. **1972** *Jrnl. Social Psychol.* LXXXVI. 55 The first definition refers to..the characteristics rather than the persons being used for typological identification. **1980** *Nature* 27 Mar. 341/1 Isaac has stated that it is likely that Olorgesailie may date to before 400 kyr BP and it is suggested on typological grounds that Namib IV is of similar antiquity.

Hence **typo'logically** *adv.*, by means of, in terms of, or according to typology.

1895 in *Funk's Standard Dict.* **1921** M. C. Burkitt *Prehistory* vii. 94 If a series be made out they are found to grade on the one hand into what typologically are Mousterian points, and on the other into a sort of pseudo-Solutrean. **1943** C. L. Wrenn *Word & Symbol* (1967) 134 Collingwood typologically demonstrates on historical artistic grounds that the inscription belongs to the close of the eighth century. **1964** R. H. Robins *General Linguistics* viii. 326 Languages are typologically classified according to the similarities of form they exhibit with other languages at any level or levels. **1976** G. W. H. Lampe in M. F. Wiles et al. *Christian Believing* (C. of E. Doctrine Cmn.) 55 The Church continued to read it [*sc.* the Old Testament] in its supposed 'spiritual' sense, or typologically. **1980** *Nature* 27 Mar. 340/2 Typologically..Namib IV may closely be paralleled by East African industries from Olorgesailie, Kilombe and Olduvai IV.

typologist (taɪ'pɒlədʒɪst). [f. typology + -ist.] A student of typology.

1841 W. L. Alexander *Connect. O. & N. Test.* viii. (1853) 314 If typologists had but kept fast hold of the principle, that nothing is typical which is not also symbolical [etc.]. **1898** J. H. Wilkinson in *Expositor* July 50 Justin..proceeded further to apply the ὕδωρ πιστόν to the wine of the Sacrament —no great liberty in a typologist.

typologize (taɪ'pɒlədʒaɪz), *v.* [f. typology + -ize.] *trans.* and *intr.* To interpret or classify typologically. Hence **ty'pologizing** *vbl. sb.*

1895 *Funk's Stand. Dict.* II. 1955/2 *Typologize,*..To interpret by types; treat typologically... To deal in or with types or figures. **1959** A. Farrer in *Proc. Oxf. Soc. Hist. Theol.* 8 Questions, which..theologians and exegetes are not going to let alone, whether they typologise or not:—for example, why St Mark put several paragraphs in the order in which he placed them. *Ibid.* 9 Here..is an example of the prefiguration scheme which the greatest enemy of typologising can scarcely deny. **1964** *Harvard Educ. Rev.* XXXIV. ii. 356 Then in a sort of neo-Jespersenian typologizing, we find that there are three sorts of monemes. **1969** P. Worsley in Ionescu & Gellner *Populism* 218 When actors see themselves as part of a shared tradition or organized movement..we are plainly dealing with a quite different kind of typologizing, based upon self-identification. **1976** *Times Lit. Suppl.* 12 Mar. 288/2 One might even say they [*sc.* the anthropologists Benedict and Radcliffe-Brown] shared the impulse to typologize. **1978** *Ibid.* 17 Feb. 217/1 It is possible to typologize military regimes.

typology (taɪ'pɒlədʒɪ). [f. Gr. τύπος: see typo- and -logy.]

1. The study of symbolic representation, *esp.* of the origin and meaning of Scripture types; also *transf.* symbolic significance, representation, or treatment; symbolism.

1845 P. Fairbairn *Typology Script.* (1857) I. i. 1 The Typology of Scripture has been one of the most neglected departments of theological science. **1850** W. M. Hetherington in *Chr. Sabbath* (1852) X. 277 The true character of the Sabbath and the misapplication to it of the principle of typology. **1856** *Tait's Mag.* XXIII. 241 There is typology as well as a teleology in nature. **1862** Neale *Hymns East. Ch.* (1866) 82 S. Stephen the Sabaite is not deficient in richness of typology. **1867** H. Macmillan *Bible Teach.* vii. (1870) 139 He who understands the typology of plants, finds an eloquent tongue in every leaf. **1882** Farrar *Early Chr.* I. 105 Contrast the numerous errors and monstrously crude typology of the former [the Epistle of Barnabas] with the splendid spiritualism of the latter [the Epistle to the Hebrews].

2. The study of or a discourse on printing types or printing.

1882 [implied in typological *a.* 2].

3. The study of classes with common characteristics; classification, esp. of human products, behaviour, characteristics, etc., according to type; the comparative analysis of structural or other characteristics; a classification or analysis of this kind.

1886 *Academy* 8 May 332/1 In his former publications the learned writer gave too high a place to typology. **1929** V. G. Childe *Danube in Prehist.* p. vii, Where stratigraphical or geological evidence is lacking, we must have recourse to typology. This depends on the assumption that types evolved (or degenerated) regularly. **1930** S. Casson *Archæol.* 43 Even after Schliemann archæologists are to be found who will still prefer a typology which is established by *a priori* methods. **1930** *Psyche* X. iii. 82 Scheler..tries to construct a typology on a purely philosophical and phenomenological basis. **1937** J. R. Firth *Tongues of Men* i. 17 Language is the typology of the common elements in your speech and mine, yesterday, to-day, and to-morrow. **1950** T. W. Adorno *Authoritarian Personality* xix. 744 Hardly any concept in contemporary American psychology has been so thoroughly criticized as that of typology. **1953** C. E. Bazell *Linguistic Form* 80 There will therefore be different typologies of language according to the system which is taken as starting-point. **1959** J. J. Michaels in S. Arieti *Amer. Handbk. Psychiatry* I. xix. 358/1 The absence of a psychoanalytic typology may also be explained by the absence of a complete theory of character structure. **1962** [see a-historical *a.*]. **1964** M. Argyle *Psychol. & Social Probl.* i. 17 One typology in common use is that of mental disorders, largely derived from a classification due to Kraepelin. **1971** *New Scientist* 27 May 534/3 A sort of 'typology' of unsafe drivers, dividing them into groups. **1974** P. H. Matthews *Morphology* 17 In some [languages], grammarians speak of a 'word' without internal grammatical structure: according to the first typologies these were 'isolating' languages... This typology has..been criticised and elaborated. **1977** H. C. Triandis *Interpersonal Behav.* i. 21 The..most important function of the model is to guide investigations of typologies of behaviors, settings and people. **1977** *Dædalus* Summer 89 One direction in which the comparative analogical approach can lead is toward what might be called a typology of cultures and of process.

typothetae (taɪ'pɒθɪtiː, ˌtaɪpə'θiːtiː), *sb. pl.* [mod.L., f. Gr. τύπος typo- + θετός, f. τίθεναι to set, place.] Master printers collectively; *spec.* the members of a N. Amer. association of master printers.

1825 T. C. Hansard *Typographia* i. ii. 43, I cannot find that Gutenberg was encouraged in his labours by the smiles of royal influence. This is the more remarkable, as the then reigning sovereign of Germany, Frederic III, was a monarch 'deeply versed in the learning of the times'... The ..emperor..permitted printers to wear gold and silver, and granted coat-armour to the *Typothetae* and *Typographi*, to perpetuate the honour of the discovery. This armorial bearing is still claimed by the professors of the art of Germany. **1865** *N.Y. Times* 22 Mar. 5/2 (*heading*) Inauguration of the Typothetæ. *Ibid.*, At a recent general meeting of master printers of this city, it was decided to organize a permanent association for the general benefit of the trade and the improvement of the typographic art. A constitution was adopted and the name of 'Typothetæ' was given to the new association. **1888** (*title*) Banquet given by the Typothetae of New York to the delegates of the United Typothetae of America, September 20, 1888. **1915** E. G. Gress in *Fifty Years Typothetae City of N.Y.* 6 The reign of Frederick III., who recognized the German Typothetae, was from 1440 to 1493. **1921** *Daily Colonist* (Victoria, B.C.) 30 Mar. 1/4 The Boston typothetae today announced a reduction of $4 a week in the pay of journeymen printers, and $3 a week in the pay of journeywomen printers.

typto, -ton, etc.: see tiptoe.

typtology (tɪp'tɒlədʒɪ). *rare*$^{-0}$. [irreg. f. Gr. τύπτειν to strike + -ology.] The theory or subject of spirit-rapping. So **typto'logical** *a.*, pertaining to typtology; **typ'tologist**, a producer of, or believer in, spirit-rappings.

In recent Dicts.

typy, var. typey *a.*

tyr, obs. f. tire *sb.*[1] and *v.*[1]

†**tyr,** *int. Obs. rare.* A call used to drive or direct sheep.

c **1460** *Towneley Myst.* xii. 113 *Secundus pastor.* I say, tyr! *Primus pastor.* I say, tyr, now agane!.. *Secundus pastor.* Wold thou neuer so fane, Tup, I say, whyr!

tyramine ('taɪərəmiːn). *Biochem.* Also **tyramin.** [f. tyr(osine + amine.] A crystalline sympathomimetic amine derived from tyrosine and occurring naturally in cheese and other foods, which can cause dangerously high blood pressure in people taking a monoamine oxidase inhibitor; 2-(*p*-hydroxyphenyl)ethylamine, $HO{\cdot}C_6H_4{\cdot}\ CH_2{\cdot}CH_2{\cdot}NH_2$.

1910 *Biochem. Jrnl.* V. 236 Tyramine,..an organic base which can be produced from tyrosine by action of certain bacteria. **1939** Tyramine [see hypertensin]. **1974** Passmore & Robson *Compan. Med. Stud.* III. lxii. 22/2 Cheese, red wine, yeast extracts and pickled herrings may contain large amounts of tyramine, and this is normally metabolized by monoamine oxidase... In patients receiving MAO [*sc.* monoamine oxidase] inhibitors, tyramine is absorbed intact and releases the large amounts of stored noradrenaline causing a hypertensive crisis.

tyran, -and, etc., obs. ff. tyrant.

†**tyrandise.** *Obs.* Forms: 4–5 tir-, **tyraundise, -ys, -andise, -yse, tyrauntyse, tyrannyse.** [a. OF. *tirandise* (14th c. in Godef.), var. of *tirannise*, f. *tiran* tyrant + *-ise*:—L. *itia*: see -ise[2].]

1. The sway of a tyrant; absolute or despotic rule: = tyranny 1. *rare.*

1387 Trevisa *Higden* (Rolls) III. 269 þat tyme þe firste Denys usede tiraundise [*v.r.* tyraundys] in Sicilia.

2. Oppressive or despotic government, action, or treatment: = tyranny 3.

1382 Wyclif *Wisd.* xvi. 4 It bihouede to them, hauntende tiraundise, deth to comen on with oute excusacioun. **1387** Trevisa *Higden* (Rolls) III. 283 Socrates was wel nygh alway in batayle, oþer in tyrauntise [**1480** Caxton, tyrannyse], oþer in fredom, hardiere þan bataille oþer tiraundise. **1390** Gower *Conf.* III. 382 He schal..Governe and lede in such a wise, So that ther be no tirandise. *c* **1450** *Cursor M.* 253 (Laud) To hem speke I alle-ther-most.. That spendyþ her lyf in tyrandyse [*v.r.* truandis].

†**'tyranful,** *a. Obs. rare*$^{-1}$. [f. *tyran*, tyrant + -ful.] Tyrannical, tyrannous.

1533 Bellenden *Livy* iii. xii. (S.T.S.) I. 299 Traisting ay the mair distant and ferrare thay war fra the cumpany of þir ten tyranfull men, to be the ferrare fra every trubil approcheing.

tyranlie, variant of tyrantly.

tyranness ('taɪərənɪs). [f. L. *tyrann-us* tyrant + -ess; cf. med.L. *tyrannissa* (1372 in Du Cange).] A female tyrant. Chiefly *fig.*

1590 Spenser *F.Q.* i. v. 46 They were by law of that proud Tyrannesse [Dame Pride],..Condemned to that Dongeon mercilesse. **1607** Topsell *Four-f. Beasts* 462 Semiramis the Babilonian tyrannesse. **1614** Raleigh *Hist. World* ii. xxi. §2 The house of David..was..rooted up, and the Crown of Juda in..possession of a cruel Tyrannesse. **1643** Milton *Divorce* i. xiii, Not to canonize Marriage either as a tyranness or a goddess over the enfranchised life and soul of man. **1706** Watts *Horæ Lyr.* ii. xvi. (1743) 171 Custom, that Tyranness of Fools. **1754** Richardson *Grandison* (1781) III. xi. 84 She was..indeed a tyranness, to all beneath her. **1814** Scott *Let. to J. B. S. Morritt* 11 Nov., in *Lockhart*, My Muse is a Tyranness, and not a Christian Queen. **1824** Heber *Narr. Journ. India* xix. (1828) II. 278 She [the Begum Sumroo] is, however, a sad tyranness. **1844** *Blackw. Mag.* LVI. 84 The lovely marble-souled tyranness has..turned back..a hundred, all worthily born.

†**tyrannesse.** *Obs. rare.* [f. as prec. + -ess[2].] = tyrandise 2.

1432–50 tr. *Higden* (Rolls) III. 283 Socrates was alle moste contynually other in tyrannesse other in liberte moore cruelle and grevous then batayle.

†**ty'rannial,** *a. Obs.* [f. L. *tyrann-us* tyrant + -ial.] = tyrannic.

1651 W. Jane Εικων Ακλαστος 216 Mahometts..Tyraniall vsurpation. **1788** Priestley *Lect. Hist.* v. xl. 291 The very names which have been used to express these tyrannial governments have grown..odious.

tyrannic (tɪ-, taɪ'rænɪk), *a.* Also 7 tir-. [ad. L. *tyrannicus*, a. Gr. τυραννικός, f. τύραννος tyrant; cf. F. *tyrannique* (14th c. in Hatz.-Darm.), Pg. *tyrannico*, Sp. *tiranico*, It. *tirannico.*] = next.

1491 Caxton *Vitas Patr.* (W. de W. 1495) ii. 272/2 We wyll dyscerne thabstynence dyuyne & holsome fro that whiche is tyrannyke & dyabolyke. *c* **1636** Denham *Passion of Dido* 115 Ah cruel Love!.. Again she feels the smart Of a fresh wound from his tyrannic dart. **1695** Blackmore *Pr. Arth.* i. 52 The Pow'r of Hell and Sin's Tyrannick Yoke. **1704** Pope *Windsor For.* 74 The oppressor ruled tyrannick where he durst. **1768** H. Walpole *Hist. Doubts* 63 Henry was a tyrannic husband. **1793** Burke *Cond. Minority* Wks. VII. 267 Unprovoked rebellion and tyrannick usurpation. **1829** Hood *Dream of Eugene A.* xxvii, One stern tyrannic thought, that made All other thoughts its slave. **1868** M. E.

G. Duff *Pol. Surv.* 85 The Anglo-Saxon, amongst weaker races, is apt to join the tyrannic School.

tyrannical (tɪ-, taɪˈrænɪkəl), *a.* Also 6–7 tir-. [f. as prec. + -AL[1].]

1. Of, pertaining to, or befitting an absolute ruler or his government; arbitrary; despotic.

1560 Daus tr. *Sleidane's Comm.* 410 Certain places of thempire wer brought into his tirannical power. **1601** R. Johnson *Kingd. & Commw.* (1603) 193 His gouernment is rather tyrannicall then kinglike: for he is absolute Lord of all the demeanes of the kingdome. **1603** Daniel *Def. Rhime* Wks. (1717) 14 Nor is this certain Limit observed in Sonnets, any tyrannical Bounding of the Conceit, but rather a reducing it in *girum*. **1638** Baker tr. *Balzac's Lett.* (vol. II) 3 So Tyrannicall an usurpation upon the liberty of mens spirits. **1706** Phillips (ed. Kersey), *Tyrannical*, or *Tyrannous*, belonging to Tyranny, imperious. **1838** Thirlwall *Greece* II. xii. 104 Miletus, after the overthrow of a tyrannical dynasty, was split into two factions.

2. a. Of the nature or character of a tyrant; acting or operating in an oppressive, cruel, or unjustly severe manner.

1538 Starkey *England* I. iv. 115 We must schake of al such tyrannycal custumys and vnresonabyl bandys. *a* **1548** Hall *Chron., Hen. VI*, 167 A tyrannicall gouernor. **1606** Warner *Alb. Eng.* xiv. lxxxv. (1612) 351 A wretch so vitious, insolent, tyrannicall and prowd. **1618** D. Dyke *Two Treat., Sch. Afflict.* 328 Those tygerly and tyrannicall persecutours. **1685** Baxter *Paraphr. N.T.* 1 Cor. vii. 12 Such will be tyrannical and malicious Adversaries. **1791** Mrs. Radcliffe *Rom. Forest* v, If you must be tyrannical, Madam, indulge your humour in private. **1836** Marryat *Midsh. Easy* xii, Like all those who are seldom in command, the master was proportionally tyrannical and abusive. **1872** Morley *Voltaire* i. (1886) 12 A dark and tyrannical superstition.

b. Of, pertaining to, or befitting a tyrant; severely oppressive; despotically harsh or cruel.

1579 E. K. *Gloss. Spenser's Sheph. Cal.* July 173 *In purple*, spoken of the Popes and Cardinalles, which vse such tyrannical colours and pompous paynting. **1592** tr. *Junius On Rev.* ix. 13 The first execution done upon the world by the tyrannical powers thereof. **1641** *More's Rich. III* Ded., The troublesome and tyrannicall government of usurping Richard the third. **1653** H. Cogan tr. *Pinto's Trav.* lxi. 248 They shall be chastised by the hand of the Most High God for the crimes of their tyrannicall lives. **1796** Morse *Amer. Geog.* II. 290 As to the king of Prussia, his conduct in Poland was the most tyrannical and oppressive that can be conceived. **1812** Scott *Let. to Southey* 4 June, in *Lockhart*, I am always prepared to expect the most tyrannical proceedings from professed demagogues. **1884** Pae *Eustace* 23 To his inferiors, his behaviour was most tyrannical.

ty'rannically, *adv.* [f. prec. + -LY[2].]

1. In a tyrannical manner; oppressively; despotically.

1560 Daus tr. *Sleidane's Comm.* 216 Luther was in dede condemned.. violently and tyrannically. **1653** H. Cogan tr. *Pinto's Trav.* lxi. 248 God hath made you Kings to use clemency towards men,.. not to kill them tyrannically. **1699** Dampier *Voy.* II. i. iv. 78 These poor Prisoners.. are tyranically insulted over by their rigid Creditors, till the debt is satisfied. **1756** C. Smart tr. *Horace, Sat.* ii. ii. (1826) II. 101 Such a man will not.. be tyrannically cruel. **1839** James *Louis XIV*, III. 145 Colbert.. pursuing not only eagerly, but somewhat tyrannically, his schemes. **1874** Spurgeon *Treas. Dav.* Ps. xcix. 4 His power never exerts itself tyrannically.

†**2.** As an intensive: Exceedingly; violently; vehemently. *Obs. colloq.*

1602 Marston *Antonio's Rev.* v. iii, I am most tyrannically hungry. **1602** Shaks. *Ham.* ii. ii. 356 That crye out on the top of question; and are most tyrannically clap't for't. **1607** *Puritan* i. iv. 73, I warrant, my Kinsman's talking of me, for my left eare burnes most tyrannically.

So **ty'rannicalness**, tyrannical character. *rare.*

1649 Roberts *Clavis Bibl.* 588 Which Chaldeans are described.. By their.. Tyrannicalnesse. **1727** in Bailey vol. II.

tyrannicidal (tɪ-, taɪˌrænɪˈsaɪdəl), *a.* [f. next + -AL[1].] Pertaining or relating to tyrannicide; disposed or inclined to tyrannicide.

1801 W. Dupré *Lexicographia-Neologica Gallica* 282 Projet *tyrannicide*—A *tyrannicidal* scheme. **1814** W. Taylor in *Monthly Rev.* LXXIII. 456 The seditious and tyrannicidal spirit. **1837** Hallam *Hist. Lit.* I. i. iv. §46. 290 He has introduced a limitation of his tyrannicidal doctrine. **1853** Grote *Greece* ii. lxxxv. XI. 197 Such affection had to be overcome before he [Timoleon] accompanied his tyrannicidal friends to the acropolis. **1892** *Illustr. Lond. News* 8 Oct. 450/3 Dynamitical and tyrannicidal schemes.

tyrannicide[1] (tɪ-, taɪˈrænɪsaɪd). [a. F. *tyrannicide* (1583 in Hatz.-Darm.), ad. L. *tyrannicīda*, f. *tyrannus* TYRANT: see -CIDE 1. So It. *tirannicida*.] One who kills a tyrant.

1657 W. Blois *Mod. Policies*, etc. (ed. 7) C vij, An honest Scot, who complains, that there are not some glorious rewards appointed for Tyrannicides. **1692** Washington tr. *Milton's Def. Pop.* v. M.'s Wks. (1847) 380/1 They.. erect statues in their temples to the honour of tyrannicides. **1700** Toland *Harrington's Oceana* Pref. 9 Cremutius Cordus, who was condemn'd by that Monster Tiberius for speaking honorably of the immortal Tyrannicides Brutus and Cassius. **1809** *Edin. Rev.* Apr. 227 [Debry] proposed the formation of a corps of Tyrannicides. **1832** Carlyle *Misc., Boswell's Johnson* (1840) IV. 77 The English Nation had rebelled against a Tyrant; and, by the hands of religious tyrannicides, exacted stern vengeance of him. **1874** Symonds *Sk. Italy & Gr.* (1898) I. xv. 344 Memories of.. Brutus, and other exalted tyrannicides, exalted his imagination. **1904** *Sat. Rev.* 30 July 144 The exact amount of blood-money received by each of the 'patriots', who posed as tyrannicides.

ty'rannicide[2]. [a. F. *tyrannicide* (16th c. in Hatz.-Darm.), ad. L. *tyrannicīdium*: see prec. and -CIDE 2. So Pg. *tyrannicidio*.] The killing or assassination of a tyrant.

1650 Hobbes *De Corp. Pol.* 165 Tyrannicide, that is, the killing of a Tyrant, not onely Lawful, but also Laudable. **1751** Hume *Princ. Mor.* ii. iii. 29 Tyrannicide or the Assassination of Usurpers and oppressive Princes was highly prais'd in antient Times. **1790** Burke *Fr. Rev.* 93 It was in the most patient period of Roman servitude that themes of tyrannicide made the ordinary exercise of boys at school. **1809–10** Coleridge *Friend* i. xv. (1865) 212 It is difficult to conceive a case in which a good man would attempt tyrannicide. **1852** Miss Yonge *Cameos* (1877) II. xxiv. 263 Julian the Apostate is the first instance of tyrannicide that is adduced. **1873** Symonds *Grk. Poets* iii. 87 Theognis in one place actually advises tyrannicide.

†**ty'rannicly**, *adv. Obs. rare*[−1]. In 6 -ykly. [f. TYRANNIC + -LY[2].] = TYRANNICALLY.

1539 Cromwell in Merriman *Life & Lett.* (1902) II. 188 The Duke of Holtz usurpatour of the kingdom of Denmerke by whose meanes his brother in lawe king christierne is kept tyrannykly in prison.

tyrannine (ˈtɪrənaɪn), *a. Ornith.* [f. mod.L. *Tyranninæ* (see def.), f. L. *tyrannus* TYRANT: see -INE[1].] Of or pertaining to the *Tyranninæ*, the typical subfamily of the tyrant-birds.

1888 P. L. Sclater *Argentine Ornith.* I 148 The Bienteveo is in its habits the most interesting member of the Tyrannine family.

†**ty'rannious**, *a. Obs. rare.* [f. L. *tyrannus* TYRANT + -IOUS.] = TYRANNOUS. Hence †**ty'ranniously** *adv. Obs.* = TYRANNOUSLY.

c **1561** T. Preston *Cambyses* D iv, The King is a tirant tirannious. **1584** Hudson *Du Bartas' Judith* iv. 224 Manasses then his wife would not controule Tyranniously. **1624** Bedell *Lett.* vii. 115 Doth hee tyranniously inforce his Colleagues to obedience also?

tyrannis (tɪˈrænɪs). *Gr. Hist.* [L., a. Gr. τυραννίς rule of a despot.] = TYRANNY *sb.* 1. Also *transf.*

1878 T. D. Woolsey *Political Science* I. ix. 406 His [*sc.* Plato's] forms of polity.. are.. aristocracy, timocracy, oligarchy, democracy, and the *tyrannis*. Oligarchy arises from overgrown wealth, tyrannis from overgrown liberty. **1910** *Encycl. Brit.* XII. 446/2 Between the Roman principate and the Greek *tyrannis* there are two essential differences. **1920** *Glasgow Herald* 6 Apr. 6 D'Annunzio.. proceeded to establish a tyrannis quite on the classical model.

†**'tyrannish**, *a. Obs. rare.* In 4 tirannyssh. [f. as prec. + -ISH[1].] = TYRANNICAL.

1390 Gower *Conf.* III. 246 The proude tirannyssh Romein Tarquinus. *Ibid.* 256 And thus this tirannysshe knyht Was soupled.

†**tyrannism**. *Obs. rare*[−1]. [f. as prec. + -ISM.] The action or rule of a tyrant; absolute government; despotism.

1591 Greene *Disc. Coosnage* (1859) 4 None could decipher Tyranisme better then Arestippus, not that his nature was cruell, but that he was nourtured with Dionisius.

†**ty'rannity**. *Sc. Obs. rare*[−1]. [ad. OF. *tirannité*, or med.L. *tyrannitās* (Du Cange), f. *tyrannus*: see TYRANT and -ITY.] Tyranny.

1535 Stewart *Cron. Scot.* (Rolls) I. 91 Fra mansuetude and greit humanitie To tigirnes and greit tirannitie.

tyrannize (ˈtɪrənaɪz), *v.* Also 6–7 tir-. [a. F. *tyranniser* (14th c. in Hatz.-Darm.), f. *tyran* TYRANT; cf. late L. *tyrannizāre* to act the tyrant, Gr. τυραννίζειν to side with a tyrant; also Pg. *tyrannizar*, Sp. *tiranizar*, It. *tirannizare*.]

1. a. *intr.* To be a despot or absolute ruler; to exercise absolute rule. Const. *over*.

1590 Spenser *F.Q.* ii. x. 57 Then gan Carausius tirannize anew, And gainst the Romanes bent their proper powre. **1628** Hobbes *Thucyd.* (1822) 9 Polycrates, who.. tyrannized in Samos. **1737** Whiston *Josephus, Antiq.* i. vi. §2 Nimrod.. stayed and tyrannized at Babylon. **1889** Jacobs *Æsop* 33 Here [at Athens] he 'tyrannised' in an easy-going way for ten years.

†**b.** *trans.* To have absolute sovereignty in or over; to rule over or dominate with absolute power. (Cf. 4.) Also *fig. Obs.*

1583 Stocker *Civ. Warres Lowe C.* i. 6 The 12. articles.. inuented and practised by the Spanish Inquisition, to the end they might inuade, get, and tyrannize the Belgique prouinces. **1651** *Nicholas Papers* (Camden) 270 That whisperinge calumniator who hath of late tyrannized their eares. **1670** Milton *Hist. Eng.* i. Wks. 1851 V. 5 Giants, who tyranniz'd the Ile, till Brutus came. **1795** Wraxall *Hist. France* III. 175 His hopes of retaining the duchy of Brittany which he had tyrannized during a number of years.

2. *intr.* To reign tyrannically; to rule despotically or oppressively. Const. *over* (†*on, upon*).

1494 Fabyan *Chron.* vi. cl. 138 Sigebertus was thus depryuyd.. when he.. had reygned or tyrannysyd two yeres. **1588** *Marprel. Epist.* (Arb.) 21 Oppressing and tyrannizing ouer her Maiesties subiects. *a* **1604** Hanmer *Chron. Irel.* (1809) 136 Athelfrid the Saxon King of Northumbers, so tyrannized over the Britaines, that they were faine to take Ireland for their refuge. *a* **1641** Bp. Mountagu *Acts & Mon.* i. (1642) 20 The King of Egypt after Iosephs death.. did tyrannize upon them with all extremity. **1741** Pulteney in *Johnson's Debates* 16 Apr. (1787) I. 388 That power by which.. the administration has tyrannized without controul. **1807** G. Chalmers *Caledonia* I. ii. vi. 309 The kings.. had strengths, wherein they lived; and whence they tyrannized. **1814** Scott *Let. to J. S. B. Morritt* 30 Apr., in *Lockhart*, A glorious and stable peace with the country over which he tyrannized, and its lawful ruler.

b. *trans.* To spend (time) in tyrannizing. *rare.*

1649 Milton *Eikon.* xxvii, Idlely raigning.. he either tyranniz'd or trifl'd away those seventeen yeares of peace.

3. *intr.* To act tyrannically, play the tyrant; to exercise power or control oppressively or cruelly. Const. as in 2.

1529 Frith *Antithesis* (1829) 314 Think you they would not let you know the cause and judgment, if they did justice & not tyrannize. **1590** Marlowe *Edw. II*, i. ii, What! will they tyrannize upon the Church? **1621** Burton *Anat. Mel.* i. ii. i. i. (1651) 38 A sacrilegious Frenchman.. became frantick.. tyrannizing over his own flesh. **1639** Fuller *Holy War* iii. xxvii. (1840) 167 They within the city, being themselves safe on shore, tyrannized on their poor brethren in ship-wreck. **1690** C. Nesse *O. & N. Test.* I. 59 Popish prelates.. tyrannizing also over the bones of the dead. **1749** Fielding *Tom Jones* i. vi, It is the nature of such persons.. to insult and tyrannise over little people. **1817** Shelley *Rev. Islam* Ded. iv, The selfish and the strong still tyrannize Without reproach or check. **1846** S. Sharpe *Hist. Egypt* xi. 364 The great were not allowed to tyrannize over the poor.

b. *fig.* of things.

1588 Shaks. *Tit. A.* iii. ii. 8 This poore right hand of mine, Is left to tirranize vppon my breast. **1615** W. Lawson *Country Housew. Gard.* (1626) 39 A long, proud, and disorderly Cyon,.. bearing no fruit, till it haue tyrannized ouer the whole tree. **1670** Dryden *1st Pt. Conq. Granada* v. i, Affairs of State.. should not tyrannize on Love, but wait. **1805** Foster *Ess.* iv. vii. 217 The influences which tyrannise over human passions and opinions. **1833** J. H. Newman *Arians* i. ii. (1876) 25 [The Arian heresy] made its way into the highest dignities of the Church.. and tyrannized over the majority of her members who were orthodox believers. **1838–9** Fr. A. Kemble *Resid. in Georgia* (1863) 19 The cold.. tyrannizing over your region.

4. *trans.* To rule or govern tyrannically; to treat tyrannically, play the tyrant to or over. (Cf. 1 b.) Now *rare.*

a **1533** Ld. Berners *Gold. Bk. M. Aurel.* (1546) H hij, That one with tyranny shuld tyrannise dyuers other. **1594** Daniel *Cleopatra* ii. i, But that he must.. tyrannize Th' afflicted Body of a woefull Woman. **1596** Danett tr. *Comines* (1614) 183 Their subiects, whom they tyrannize and oppresse.. without any compassion. **1649** Milton *Eikon.* iv, Had.. rather sit still, and let his Country be tyrannized, than that the people.. should.. demand their rights. **1675** G. R. tr. *Le Grand's Man without Passion* 34 The Proud Mistresses of Beauty, that Tyrannize the Spirits of indiscreet men. **1761** Murphy *Old Maid* ii. i, Do not tyrannize me thus with alternate doubts and fears. **1783** Justamond tr. *Raynal's Hist. Indies* V. 268 They are tyrannized, mutilated, burnt, and put to death. **1896** *Daily News* 20 Feb. 6/1 A poor, weak ruler he was. The tyrant was tyrannised by the set about him.

b. *fig.* of things.

1588 W. Byrd *Psalmes*, etc. xxviii. 2 Pleasure.. doth tirannize the ship. **1621** Burton *Anat. Mel.* i. ii. iv. vi. (1628) 147 Poverty, which doth so tyrannize, crucifie, and generally depresse vs. **1741** Mrs. Montagu *Lett.* (1813) I. 271 Happier are they who are governed by another's will than such as are tyrannized by their own. **1887** G. Meredith *Solon* iv, But shall the Present tyrannize us?

†**5.** To render tyrannical; to make oppressive. *Obs. rare*[−1].

1643 Milton *Divorce* ii. xx, The canon law.., whose boisterous edicts tyrannizing the blessed ordinance of marriage into the quality of a most unnatural.. yoke [etc.].

Hence **'tyrannized** *ppl. a.*, **'tyrannizing** *vbl. sb.* and *ppl. a.*; whence **'tyrannizingly** *adv.*

1589 *Hay any Work* 41 For their tyrannizing ouer him. **1611** Speed *Hist. Gt. Brit.* vii. xviii. §5. 290 His Christian heart pitying at such heathenish tyrannizings. **1642** Milton *Apol. Smect.* Wks. 1851 III. 320 A slavish obedience without law; which is the known definition of a tyrant, and a tyranniz'd people. **1650** A. B. *Mutat. Polemo* 9 A self willed and wildly-Tyrannizing Monarch. *c* **1680** *Roxb. Ball.* (1887) VI. 290 Cupid, leave thy Tyrannizing! **1756** *World* No. 206 ¶7 In.. a few months, from being a restless, tyrannized, tormented wretch, I found myself a husband, a cuckold, and a happy man. *a* **1774** Tucker *Lt. Nat.* (1834) II. 80 The crown, the church, and the barons, struggling which should have the tyrannizing over the people. **1790** Han. More *Relig. Fash. World* (1791) 89 Those tyrannizing inclinations, which have so natural a tendency to enslave the human heart. **1832** H. Melvile in *Preacher* III. 221/1 That infidelity which shall rule tyrannizingly over Christendom. **1881** *Athenæum* 27 Aug. 268/1 Intolerant of mean compliances and tyrannizing superiors. **1905** *Daily Chron.* 16 Feb. 5/2 The Church of the Concordat will be succeeded either by a free Church or by a tyrannised Church.

tyrannizer (ˈtɪrənaɪzə(r)). [f. prec. + -ER[1].] One who or that which tyrannizes; a tyrant.

1577 Patericke tr. *Gentillet* Pref. A iv b, Small potentates and tyrannizers. **1629** Sir W. Mure *True Crucifix* 2960 Maisters.. May learne.. To rule aright, not Tyrannizers proue. **1689** *Def. Liberty agst. Tyrants* 124 The Tyrannizer of Tyrants, Fear. **1882** P. Hood *O. Cromwell* xvii. 226 When the will of the king became the tyrannizer of the country.

tyranno- (tɪ-, taɪˈrænəʊ), before a vowel **tyrann-**, repr. Gr. τυραννο-, combining form of τύραννος TYRANT, occurs in a few nonce-formations, as **tyrannoctonic** (-ɒkˈtɒnɪk) *a.* [Gr. τυραννοκτόνος killer of a tyrant], tyrant-slaying; **tyranno'phobia** [-PHOBIA], dread of tyrants.

1651 Hobbes *Leviath.* ii. xxix. 171 A certain *Tyranno-phobia*, or feare of being strongly governed. **1789** Parr *Let. to Burney* Wks. 1828 VII. 411 What say you to this tyranno[c]tonic rigour which has overtaken Joseph and Gustavus?

tyrannoid ('tɪrənɔɪd), *a. Ornith.* [f. L. *tyrannus* TYRANT + -OID.] Resembling or related to the tyrant-birds.

1891 in *Cent. Dict.*

tyrannosaurus (tɪˌrænəʊ'sɔːrəs). Also **ty'rannosaur.** [mod.L. (H. F. Osborn 1905, in *Bull. Amer. Mus. Nat. Hist.* XXI. 259), f. TYRANNO- + Gr. σαῦρος lizard.] A large bipedal dinosaur of the genus of the same name, known from fossil remains found in North America. Also *fig.*

1906 H. F. OSBORN in *Bull. Amer. Mus. Nat. Hist.* XXII. 281 *(heading)* Tyrannosaurus, Upper Cretaceous carnivorous dinosaur. **1927** HALDANE & HUXLEY *Animal Biol.* xi. 240 The Tyrannosaur [was adapted] for preying on large animals. *Ibid.* xiii. 314 The Tyrannosaurus.. stood over twenty feet high. **1934** [see ANKYLOSAURUS]. **1957** L. EISELEY *Immense Journey* 64 Tyrannosaurs, enormous bipedal caricatures of men, would stalk mindlessly across the sites of future cities. **1984** J. WAIN in *Listener* 23 Aug. 37/1 Peter Ustinov and Alec McCowen play two 19th-century American railroad barons—Cornelius Vanderbilt and Jay Gould... The two tyrannosaurs fought to a standstill.

2. ***Tyrannosaurus rex***, the only species of the genus *Tyrannosaurus*; also *fig.*

1906 *Bull. Amer. Mus. Nat. Hist.* XXII. 284 Tyrannosaurus rex... The complete skeleton of this animal is restored. **1972** D. BLOODWORTH *Any Number can Play* viii. 56 A stupid, feudal autocrat.. who believes in the divine right of all Kings, starting with tyrannosaurus rex. **1976** 'J. Ross' *I know what it's like to Die* xxiv. 150 A crane, fancifully recognisable to him as an orange-painted *Tyrannosaurus Rex*, towered above a metal-crushing plant.

tyrannous ('tɪrənəs), *a.* Also 6–7 tir-. [f. L. *tyrann-us* TYRANT + -OUS.]

1. Characterized by or inclined to tyranny; ruling or acting tyrannically; despotic.

1491 *Act 7 Hen. VII*, c. 18 Richard the iij^{de}.. of his cruell and tyrannous disposicion.. caused [etc.]. **1531** TINDALE *Expos. 1 John* Prol. (1538) 3 b, When God visiteth vs with sycknes, pouerte, or what so euer aduersite it be, he doth it not of a tyrannous mynde to satisfye hys luste. **1577** tr. *Bullinger's Decades* (1592) 114 The tyrannous handes of any earthly Pharao. *c* **1600** SHAKS. *Sonn.* cxxxi, Thou art as tiranous.. As those whose beauties proudly make them cruell. **1641** *Vind. Smectymnuus* 8 Those Bishops were Popish Tyrannous Bishops. **1760–72** H. BROOKE *Fool of Qual.* (1809) III. 34 Gave up the innocent many for a prey to the tyrannous few. **1876** GEO. ELIOT *Dan. Der.* III. xxv, To speak freely of a tyrannous patron behind his back.

b. *fig.* Exercising absolute dominion in some way; overpowering, irresistible; relentless; inexorable; severe.

1549 BIBLE *Ps.* xxv. 18 They beare a tyrannous hate agaynst me. **1592** SHAKS. *Rom. & Jul.* I. i. 176 Alas that loue so gentle in his view, Should be so tyrannous and rough in proofe. **1604** —— *Oth.* III. iii. 447 Yeeld vp (O Loue) thy Crowne.. To tyrannous Hate. **1644** MILTON *Educ.* Wks. (1847) 99/1 Flattery and court-shifts and tyrannous Aphorisms appear to them the highest points of wisdom. **1665** BOYLE *Occas. Refl.* IV. xvii, That Tyrannous thing, which we misname Civility. **1797–8** COLERIDGE *Anc. Mar.* I. xi, The Storm-blast.. was tyrannous and strong. **1841–4** EMERSON *Ess.* Ser. II. i. (1876) 36 We have yet had no genius in America, with tyrannous eye, which knew the value of our incomparable materials. **1873** B. STEWART *Conserv. Force* v. 139 [Nature] is only tyrannous on the surface. **1876** GEO. ELIOT *Dan. Der.* IV. xxxii, To have spoken once is a tyrannous reason for speaking again. **1890** *Century Mag.* Feb. 574/1 The tyrannous moral Sense.

2. *transf.* Of the nature of or involving tyranny; oppressive, unjustly severe or cruel.

1556 OLDE *Antichrist* 51 b, The tyrannous power that they hade long wished for. **1585** T. WASHINGTON tr. *Nicholay's Voy.* IV. xxxi. 153 b, Princes should not vsurpe vpon tyrannous force. **1602** SHAKS. *Ham.* II. ii. 482 The parching streets That lend a tyrannous and damned light. **1637** EARL MONM. tr. *Malvezzi's Romulus & Tarquin* 146, I hold a good Principalitie as free, as a bad Common-wealth tyranous. **1709** STRYPE *Ann. Ref.* I. lvii. 583 That the election of ministers and bishops at this day was tyrannous. **1845** J. H. NEWMAN *Ess. Developm.* 167 As soon as the Empire relaxed its tyrannous oppression of the Church. **1870** J. R. SEELEY in *Macm. Mag.* Sept. 354/2 The Press.. would have an exceptional and almost tyrannous power.

3. Comb., as ***tyrannous-minded***.

1590 HARINGTON *Apol. Poetrie* in *Orl. Fur.* ¶vj, For Tragedies.., that.. of Richard the 3. would moue (I thinke) Phalaris the tyraunt, and terrifie all tyrannous minded men.

tyrannously ('tɪrənəslɪ), *adv.* [f. prec. + -LY^2. Cf. OF. *tiranneusement.*] In a tyrannous manner; with tyrannical oppression or cruelty; despotically. Also *fig.*

1545 BRINKLOW *Compl.* xxii. (1874) 53 Let the kyngs grace consyder how tyrannosly.. thei vsed part of his progenytors, kynges of Ingland. **1559** *Mirr. Mag., Rich. Plantagenet* iv, Waye how vsurpers tyrannously warke. **1596** SPENSER *F.Q.* v. ii. 13 They each at other tyrannously flew. **1612–16** *Liber Depositionum Archid. Colcestr.* lf. 70 b (MS.) Margaret Adams did vse her husband extreamly cruelly and tiranously. **1670** MILTON *Hist. Eng.* II. Wks. 1851 V. 46 Julius.. tyrannously had made himself Emperor of the Roman Common-wealth. **1844** *Fraser's Mag.* XXX. 460/2 Monarchies more tyrannously monarchical. **1859** GEO. ELIOT *A. Bede* xxviii, His deed.. was already governing him tyrannously. **1865** KINGSLEY *Herew.* Prelude, Right tyrannously.. he lords it over her.

So **'tyrannousness**, tyrannous character or quality.

1870 M. ARNOLD *St. Paul & Protestantism* 17 This proves well what the narrowness and tyrannousness of Puritanism dominant had really been. **1870** J. H. NEWMAN in *Life* (1912) II. xxix. 289, I cannot bear to think of the tyrannousness and cruelty of its advocates.

tyranny ('tɪrənɪ), *sb.* Forms: 4–6 tir-, **tyrannye, -ie,** (5 **thir-, thyrannye, tirandye, tyreny, terannye),** 6 **tiranni, tyranye** (*Sc.* -y), **tyrranie,** 6–7 **tiranny** (**tirr-**), **tyrannie,** (7 **tirany**), 5– **tyranny.** [a. F. *tyrannie* (13th c. in Hatz.-Darm.), = Prov. *tirannia*, Sp. *tirania*, It. *tirannia*, a. med.L. *tyrannia*, f. L. *tyrannus*, Gr. τύραννος TYRANT; cf. Gr. τυραννία (rare).]

1. The government of a tyrant or absolute ruler; the position or rule of a tyrant (in sense 1).

c **1374** CHAUCER *Anel. & Arc.* 66 And whan that old Creon [king of Thebes] gan espie How that the blode riall was brought edoun, He heled that Cite by his Thyrannye. **1579–80** NORTH *Plutarch* (1595) 94 They say that he aunswered his friendes, that principalitie and tirannie was indeede a goodly place. *Ibid.* 106 Solon liued long time after Pisistratus had vsurped the tyranny. **1614** RALEIGH *Hist. World* IV. vi. §6 The Athenians.. were fallen.. vnder the tyranny of Lachares. **1671** MILTON *Samson* Pref., Of that honour Dionysius the elder was no less ambitious, then before of his attaining to the Tyranny. *a* **1727** NEWTON *Chronol. Amended* i. (1728) 124 Pisistratus began to affect the Tyranny of that city [Athens]. **1835** *Penny Cycl.* III. 15/1 Pisistratus and his son held the tyranny of Athens for thirty-six years. **1887** *Encycl. Brit.* XXII. 19/1 The tyranny of Dionysios fell, as usual, in the second generation.

b. In general sense: Absolute sovereignty.

1651 HOBBES *Leviath.* IV. xlvi, From Aristotle's civil philosophy, they have learned, to call all manner of common-wealths but the popular.. tyranny. **1668** H. MORE *Div. Dial.* IV. vii. (1713) 300 Is it not absolute and unlimited Sovereignty,.. which we from the Greeks call Tyranny? **1681** NEVILE *Plato Rediv.* 38 Aristotle.. calls Tyranny the Corruption of Monarchy.

c. With *a* and *pl.* A state ruled by a tyrant or absolute prince; an absolute or despotic government.

1605 BACON *Adv. Learn.* I. viii. §3 Honour in free Monarchies and Common wealths, had a sweetness more, than in Tyrannies. **1628** HOBBES *Thucyd.* (1822) 8 In most of the cities there were erected Tyrannies. **1672** TEMPLE *Ess. Govts.* Wks. 1731 I. 97 Some of the smaller States, but especially those of the Cities, fell often under Tyrannies, which spring naturally out of Popular Governments. **1712** SWIFT *Let. Eng. Tongue* ¶5 The change of their [*i.e.* the Roman] government to a tyranny, which ruined the study of eloquence. **1838** ARNOLD *Hist. Rome* (1846) I. xxi. 454 All the ancient writers.. call the Government of Dionysius a tyranny. **1881** JOWETT *Thucyd.* I. 10 The revenues of her [Hellas'] cities increased, and in most of them tyrannies were established; they had hitherto been ruled by hereditary kings, having fixed prerogatives.

2. The action or government of a tyrannical ruler; oppressive or unjustly severe government.

c **1385** CHAUCER *L.G.W.* Prol. 375 Tyrauntis of lumbardye That vsyn wilfulhed & tyrannye [*v.r.* tirandye]. **1390** GOWER *Conf.* III. 201 Of crualte the felonie Engendred is of tirannie. *c* **1430** LYDG. *Min. Poems* (Percy Soc.) 82 Roote of discorde is froward tyrannye. **1494** FABYAN *Chron.* I. vii. 12 Of this [Madan] is lytell or no memory made.., except y^t some wryte of hym y^t he vsed great Tyranny amonge his Brytons. **1495** *Trevisa's Barth. De P.R.* VI. xviii. (W. de W.) niij/1 Ryghtful lordshyp ouersettith not his subgettes by tyranny, but he defendyth theym. **1555** EDEN *Decades* 258 The patriarch of Constantinople was oppressed by the Tiranni of the Turkes. **1586** T. B. *La Primaud. Fr. Acad.* I. (1594) 601 We may call that a tyrannie, when the prince accounteth all his will as a just law, and hath no care eithre of pietie, justice, or faith. **1594** SHAKS. *Rich. III*, v. iii. 168 The last was I that felt thy Tyranny. **1596** DALRYMPLE tr. *Leslie's Hist. Scot.* II. (S.T.S.) I. 137 The fyfte quha helde the gouernement.. for his gret tirannie.. he is slane. **1636** E. DACRES tr. *Machiavel's Disc. Livy* I. 172 That part of the nobility, that hath not a share in the Tyrannie, is alwayes enemy to the Tyrant. **1667** MILTON *P.L.* XII. 95 Tyrannie must be, Though to the Tyrant thereby no excuse. **1724** DE FOE *Mem. Cavalier* II. 167 Parliament Tyranny began to succeed Church Tyranny. **1792** *Anecd. W. Pitt* III. xl. 87 The House, in committing the City Magistrates to prison, without hearing their defence upon the point of privilege, had been guilty of a gross and palpable act of tyranny. **1835** THIRLWALL *Greece* I. x. 396 A monarchy, in which selfish aims predominate, becomes a tyranny. **1836** HOR. SMITH *Tin Trump.* (1876) 203 Sir Thos. More transported himself from the tyranny of Henry VIII into Utopia. **1863** FROUDE *Hist. Eng.* VII. i. 9 The accession of Mary had found the new opinions equally dishonoured by tyranny. **1883** —— *Short Stud.* IV. iii. 263 In political catastrophes revolution is nearest when tyranny is at its worst.

3. Arbitrary or oppressive exercise of power; unjustly severe use of one's authority; despotic treatment or influence; harsh, severe, or unmerciful action; with *a* and *pl.*, an instance of this, a tyrannical act or proceeding.

c **1368** CHAUCER *Compl. Pite* 6 The cruelte and Tyrannye [*v.rr.* tirannye, thirannye] Of loue. **1390** GOWER *Conf.* III. 207 The tirannies whiche he wroght. *c* **1402** LYDG. *Compl. Bl. Knt.* 665 Jelousye.. That hath so longe.. Werreyed Trouthe with his tirannye. *a* **1533** LD. BERNERS *Gold. Bk. M. Aurel.* (1546) O j, He that hath muche, doeth tyranny to hym that hath but littell. **1560** DAUS tr. *Sleidane's Comm.* 449 It is a starke tyranny that maried priestes should be put from the holy ministery. **1568** JEWEL *Let. to Abp. Parker* 7 May, I am afraid of printers. Their tyranny is terrible. **1613** PURCHAS *Pilgrimage* (1614) 546 He delights to see men.. torn with Elephants. Of these tyrannies he reckons many particulars which he saw. **1642** FULLER *Holy & Prof. St.* IV. x. 285 'Tis tyranny to trample on him that prostrates himself. **1664** H. MORE *Myst. Iniq.* xvii. 62 All the Frauds and Tyrannies of this Unchristian, though over-much Anointed, Priesthood. **1709** STRYPE *Ann. Ref.* I. liii. 537 Among other his tyrannies,.. the boy was gotten into Boner's house, and there whipped with rods in a most lamentable manner. **1747** BUTLER *Serm.* Wks. 1874 II. 302 The tyranny of our own lawless passions is the.. most dangerous of all tyrannies. **1843** PRESCOTT *Mexico* I. iii. (1864) 27 The worst kind of tyranny—that of a blind fanaticism. **1853** KANE *Grinnell Exp.* xl. (1856) 364, I commenced the anti-scorbutic tyranny at once. **1856** KINGSLEY *Lett.* (1878) I. 474 Lifting up your voice to expose the tyranny of 'Union' strikes. **1886** SHELDON tr. *Flaubert's Salammbô* 24 The tyrannies of discipline.

b. Violent or lawless action; violence, outrage, villany. *Obs.* or *arch.*

1475 *Rolls of Parlt.* VI. 138/2 For fere of which Robberies and Tyrany, doon by the said Henry Bodrugan. **1547** *Reg. Privy Council Scot.* I. 75 The greit preparationis and tyrany divisit and ordanit be our saidis auld ynemeis. **1568** GRAFTON *Chron.* II. 250 When the Scottishe king had finished this hys tiranny vpon the Towne. **1570** *Sat. Poems Reform.* xx. 102 Be tyrannie, To sla our rycht Regent. **1603** KNOLLES *Hist. Turks* (1621) 142 Which crueltie he used, because they a little before had used the like tyrannie against his Turks.

Hence †**'tyranny** *v., intr.* = TYRANNIZE *v.* 3. *Obs. rare*$^{-1}$.

1650 GENTILIS *Considerations* 45 Our sense doth with ease tyranny over us.

tyrannykly, var. TYRANNICLY *adv. Obs.*

tyrant ('taɪərənt), *sb.* Forms: *α.* 4 **tyraun,** 4–7 **tyran, -anne,** 5–7 **tyrane,** 6 **tiran, -anne,** 7 **tyrann,** *Sc.* 4 **terane,** 5–6 **tirrane,** 6 **tirane, tyran(ne;** *β.* 3–5 (6 *Sc.*) **tir-, tyrand,** 4–5 **-ande, tir-, tyraund, terand** (also 6 *Sc.*), 5, 6 *Sc.* **tirr-, tyrrand,** (7 **tyrannd**); *γ.* 3 *pl.* **tyraunz,** 3–7 **tirant,** 4–5 **terant, -aunt,** 4–6 **tir-, tyraunt, -e,** (4 **tir-,** 5 **terawnte,** 6 *Sc.* **tirrant),** 6 **tyrante,** 5– **tyrant.** [a. OF. *tyrant* (12th c.), *tiran* (13th c.), F. *tyran* (14th c.) = Prov. *tiran*, Cat. *tira*, Sp. *tirano*, Pg. *tyranno*, It. *tiranno*, a. L. *tyrannus*, Gr. τύραννος.

The spelling with final *t* arose in OF. from association of the ending with that of present participles; cf. *suffragant* as variant of *suffragan.*]

1. One who seizes upon the sovereign power in a state without legal right; an absolute ruler; a usurper. (Chiefly in reference to ancient rulers, and in early use with suggestion of sense 3.)

a **1300** *Cursor M.* 21001 (Cott.) Vnder a tirant hight egeas Bonden on a rod he was. *c* **1330** R. BRUNNE *Chron.* (1810) 51 A bastard no kyngdom suld hald Bot if þat he it wan.. Of tirant or of Sarazin. *c* **1374** CHAUCER *Boeth.* III. pr. v. 59 (Camb. MS.) A tyraunt þat was kyng of sysile. *c* **1470** HARDING *Chron.* XXXI. ii, Eche Tyraunt was a Conqueroure. **1513** DOUGLAS *Æneis* VI. ix. 197 Sum.. Sald and betrasit thar natiue realm and land And tharin brocht a michty tirrand strang. **1542** UDALL *Erasm. Apoph.* 39 The thirtie tyrannes had invaded & usurped the governance. **1593** SHAKS. *3 Hen. VI*, III. iii. 71 To proue him Tyrant, this reason may suffice, That Henry liueth still. **1622** BACON *Hen. VII*, 1 Richard the third of that name, King in fact onely, but Tyrant both in Title and Regiment. **1653** GATAKER *Vind. Annot. Jer.* 47 He.. landed his forces, surprised Syracusa, and drave out the Tyranne. **1763** J. BROWN *Poetry & Mus.* vii. 151 This Event happened.. thro' the Authority of the thirty Tyrants. **1821** BYRON *Juan* III. lxxxvi, The tyrant of the Chersonese Was freedom's best and bravest friend; *That* tyrant was Miltiades! **1882** *Gd. Words* 181/1 In the fifth century before Christ, the tyrant Gelon extended its limits to embrace Acradina.

†**2.** A ruler, governor, prince. *Obs.*

a **1340** HAMPOLE *Psalter* xxxii. 10 Princes, þat is,.. tirauntis of þis warld. **1382** WYCLIF *Dan.* i. 3 The sonys of Yrael, and of the kyngus bloode, and the children of tyrauntis. *c* **1430** LYDG. *Min. Poems* (Percy Soc.) 118 The hors.. Withe his bellis and boosis brode of gold, Estate of tirauntis the poraile dothe expresse. *c* **1477** CAXTON *Jason* 38 b, Dyomedes.. brought with him xxx. of his tyrants. **1555** W. WATREMAN *Fardle Facions* I. vi. 90 The Troglodites .. haue their heade ouer them, whome they call Tiraunte. **1609** BIBLE (Douay) *Dan.* iii. 2 The king sent to cal together the nobles, the magistrates, and judges, dukes, and tyrants, and rulers. **1737** WHISTON *Josephus, Hist.* I. xii. §2 Cassius .. set tyrants over all Syria.

3. A king or ruler who exercises his power in an oppressive, unjust, or cruel manner; a despot.

1297 R. GLOUC. (Rolls) 7689 To hom þat wolde is wille do debonere he was & milde & to hom þat wiþsede strong tirant [*v.r.* tyraund]. *c* **1375** *Sc. Leg. Saints* ii. (*Paulus*) 647 Nero, þat tyran kene. *Ibid.* 796 þe tyrand tuk on hand For to byrne þe gret cite Of rome. **1390** GOWER *Conf.* III. 201 Evere yit it hath so stonde, That god a tirant overladde. **1422** tr. *Secreta Secret., Priv. Priv.* 181 Yf y [Cæsar] were a tyraunte, thow sholdyst Say no more so. *c* **1471** FORTESCUE *Wks.* (1869) 453 Whan a Kyng rulith his Realme onely to his own profytt, and not to the good of his Subgetts, he ys a Tyraunte. **1542** UDALL *Erasm. Apoph.* 262 b, Sylla.. afterwarde weaxed a cruell tyranne. **1587** GOLDING *De Mornay* xii. (1592) 172 Tyrannes.. be but Gods scourges which he will cast into the fire when he hath done with them. **1601** SHAKS. *Jul. C.* v. iv. 5 A Foe to Tyrants, and my Countries Friend. **1617** BP. HALL *Quo Vadis* §18 Their late Patron.. was, after his death, in their Pulpits proclaimed *Tyran*, and worse. **1727** GAY *Fables* I. xlix. 5 Do not tyrants .. Think men were born for slaves to kings? **1831** SIR J. SINCLAIR *Corr.* II. 145 When Bonaparte put the Duke d'Enghien to death, all Paris felt so much horror.. that the throne of the tyrant trembled under him. **1875** STUBBS *Const. Hist.* II. xvi. 350 The king had never been a tyrant. **1888** BRYCE *Amer. Commw.* I. iv. 42 The weak points which had enabled George III to play the tyrant.

4. Any one who exercises power or authority oppressively, despotically, or cruelly; one who treats those under his control tyrannically.

c **1290** *Beket* 750 in *S. Eng. Leg.* I. 128 Ore louerd helpe nouþe seint thomas.. A-mong so manie tyraunz for-to come þat weren alle is fon. *Ibid.* 753 In þe castel sat þe motinge of þis tyraunz ech-on. *a* **1340** HAMPOLE *Psalter* ii. 9 þou sall noght be tyraunt til þaim. **1387** TREVISA *Higden* (Rolls) VI. 209 þe abbotes..for grete richesse beeþ proude, and bycomeþ tyrauntz. **1610** SHAKS. *Temp.* II. ii. 166 A plague vpon the Tyrant that I serue. **1750** GRAY *Elegy* 58 Some village Hampden, that..The little Tyrant of his fields withstood. **1792** in *Gentl. Mag.* Dec. 1199/1 A man of republican levelling principles, who was the greatest of *tyrants* to his wife and family. **1817** MISS MITFORD in L'Estrange *Life* (1870) II. i. 2 A sad tyrant, as my friends the Democrats sometimes are. **1848** THACKERAY *Van. Fair* lxvii, It was William who defended him against a tyrant at the school where they were. **1908** R. BAGOT *A. Cuthbert* iv, The marriage had not proved a happy one... He had been a domestic tyrant.

†**b.** By extension: Any one who acts in a cruel, violent, or wicked manner; a ruffian, desperado; a villain. Hence as a term of reproach. *Obs.*

c **1375** *Sc. Leg. Saints* i. (*Petrus*) 289 He folawit.. Agan þat Terane [Simon Magus] for to stryfe. *Ibid.* xix. (*Cristofere*) 528 His tyranis furth can ryn, & did as he þaim bad in haste. **1377** LANGL. *P. Pl.* B. I. 199 Attache þo tyrauntz [**1393**, tyrauns].. And fettereth fast falsenesse.. And gurdeth of gyles hed. *c* **1430** *Chev. Assigne* 84 Tytlye tyrauntes tweyne ..by þe byddynge of matabryne a-non þey her hente. *c* **1440** *York Myst.* xxxii. 227 Fals tiraunte [Judas], for þi tratoury þu art worþi to be hanged. **1457** HARDING *Chron.* in *Eng. Hist. Rev.* Oct. (1912) 745 Your Iustyse of pese darr nought reply Suche tyrauntes that perteyne to any lorde. **1526** TINDALE *1 Tim.* i. 13, I was a blasphemar, and a persecuter, and a tyraunt. **1561** S. WYTHERS tr. *Calvin's Treat. Relics* H vij b, The tirauntes that stoned him [Stephen]. *a* **1578** LINDESAY (Pitscottie) *Chron. Scot.* (S.T.S.) I. xix. 86 He suburnit sum blody tyrantis to ly in ane quyit place.. awaitand for the slaughter.

c. *fig.* Anything of which the action is likened to that of a tyrannical ruler.

1508 DUNBAR *Lament Makaris* 25 That strang vnmercifull tyrand [i.e. Death]. **1528** PAYNEL *Salerne's Regim.* Oj, A pike (called the tyranne of fishes). **1579** SPENSER *Sheph. Cal.* Oct. 98 Lordly loue is such a Tyranne fell. **1611** SHAKS. *Cymb.* I. i. 84 O dissembling Curtesie! How fine this Tyrant Can tickle where she wounds? **1757** GRAY *Bard* 130 Horrour, Tyrant of the throbbing breast. **1796** ELIZA HAMILTON *Lett. Hindoo Rajah* (1811) I. 11 When the tyrant pain had a little loosened the fetters of her power. **1847** HELPS *Friends in C.* I. viii. 132 Public opinion, the greatest tyrant of these times.

5. *Ornith.* Any bird of the family *Tyrannidæ*; *esp.* any of several species of the genus *Tyrannus* (as *T. carolinensis*, the KING-BIRD or bee-martin), noted for attacking and driving off any other bird approaching its nesting place. Also called *tyrant-bird*, *tyrant-flycatcher*.

1730 MORTIMER in *Phil. Trans.* XXXVI. 433 *Muscicapa coronâ rubrâ*, the Tyrant... He puts to Flight all Birds, both great and small, that come near his Station. **1731** M. CATESBY *Nat. Hist. Carolina* I. 55 The Tyrant... The courage of this little Bird is singular. *a* **1841** SWAINSON in *Penny Cycl.* XXI. 415/2 The lesser tyrants (*Tyrannulæ*) are spread over the whole of America, where they represent the true flycatcher... The tyrants are bold and quarrelsome birds, particularly during the season of incubation. **1869** GILLMORE tr. *Figuier's Rept. & Birds* (1870) 538 The Tyrants (*Tyrannus*) owe their name to their courageous, audacious, and quarrelsome character. **1895** NEWTON *Dict. Birds*, *Tyrant* or *Tyrant-bird*, Catesby applied it solely to.. the King-bird.., but apparently as much in reference to its bright crown..as to its tyrannical behaviour to other birds.

6. *attrib.* or as *adj.* That is a tyrant, tyrannical, tyrannous; also, characteristic of a tyrant.

1297 R. GLOUC. (Rolls) 8005 Milce nas þer mid him [King William] non..Ac as a tirant [*v.r.* terant] tormentor in speche & ek in dede. *c* **1375** *Sc. Leg. Saints* xvii. (*Martha*) 290 A tyrand man in vord & vark. **1390** GOWER *Conf.* II. 316 That tirant raviner [Tereus], Whan that sche was in his pouer..Foryat he was a wedded man. *Ibid.* III. 148 Cirus the king tirant sche tok. **1456** SIR G. HAYE *Law Arms* (S.T.S.) 32 Wikkit tyrane Emperouris and princis. **1572** *Reg. Privy Council Scot.* II. 140 Thair inordinat proceidingis, tirrant and tressonable attemptattis. **1585** T. WASHINGTON tr. *Nicholay's Voy.* III. iii. 74b, Sundry emperors tirants. **1600** SHAKS. *A.Y.L.* I. ii. 300 Thus must I from the smoake into the smother, From tyrant Duke, vnto a tyrant Brother. **1624** QUARLES *Job Militant* xv. 26 Hidden roots, wherewith they might appease Their Tyran'-stomakes. **1691** SWIFT *Athenian Soc.* x. Wks. 1755 IV. I. 236 The deluding muse..changes all to beauty, and the praise Of that proud tyrant sex of hers. **1730–46** THOMSON *Autumn* 222 When tyrant custom had not shackled man. **1775** ABIGAIL ADAMS *Fam. Lett.* (1876) 124 A reconciliation between our no longer parent state, but tyrant state, and these colonies. **1810** CRABBE *Borough* xxiv. 287 The tyrant-boy, whose sway All hearts acknowledge. **1835** LYTTON *Rienzi* I. i, The excuse for these tyrant hypocrites to lift up their hands. **1839** BAILEY *Festus* xxxi. (1852) 514 Those basest few who thought to win The tyrant monster's favour.

†**b.** as *adj.* in predicate. *Obs. rare.*

1297 R. GLOUC. (Rolls) 8615 So cruel ne so tirant ich wene no mon ne say. **1422** tr. *Secreta Secret., Priv. Priv.* 212 A man his..Tyraunt & Slow as a bere. *c* **1440** *Jacob's Well* 86 He is pruddere, þe more teraunt, þe more ouerledere, þe more cursyd lyvere, for his good. **1529** RASTELL *Pastyme* (1811) 19 He was most tirant and cruell of all emperours.

7. *attrib.* and *Comb.*, as ***tyrant-air***, ***-craft***, ***-killing***, ***-kind***, ***-murder***, ***period***; ***tyrant-hater***, ***-killer***, ***-queller***, ***-slayer***, ***-tamer***; ***tyrant-hating***, ***-quelling***, ***-ridden***, ***-scourging*** adjs.; ***tyrant-like*** adj. and adv.; **tyrant-bird**: see sense 5; **tyrant-chat** (see quot.); **tyrant-fish**, a West Indian cutlass-fish, *Evoxymetopon tæniatus* (*Cent. Dict. Supp.*, 1909); **tyrant-flycatcher**, **tyrant-shrike**, species of *Tyrannus*, resembling, and formerly confused with, the *Muscicapidæ* and *Laniidæ*; **tyrant-wren**: see quot. for *tyrant-chat*.

1746 LOCKMAN *To 1st Promoter of Cambrick & Tea Bills* 29 [He] Lords it, with *tyrant-airs, o'er beast and man. **1888** *Cassell's Encycl. Dict.*, *Tyrant-bird. **1892** W. H. HUDSON *Natur. La Plata* 35 Puma..following and harassing it [the jaguar] as a tyrant-bird harasses an eagle or hawk. **1885** *Stand Nat. Hist.* IV. 468 We may now style various birds *tyrant-chats, tyrant-wrens, tyrant-flycatchers, etc., according to the more or less obvious resemblance they may have to the true (oscinine) chats, wrens, or flycatchers. **1812** CRABBE *Tales* xiv. 349 With *tyrant-craft, he then was still and calm. **1783** LATHAM *Synopsis Birds* III. 357 *Tyrant Fl[ycatcher]. Size of the Red-backed Shrike, or a trifle bigger... Inhabits Cayenne. **1839** DARWIN *Voy. Nat.* xi. (1873) 237 Occasionally the plaintive note of a white-tufted tyrant-fly catcher..may be heard. **1879** E. P. WRIGHT *Anim. Life* 243 The Tyrant Fly-catcher (*Tyrannus intrepidus*) is one of the migratory visitors of the United States, and often bears the name of 'King', as well as 'Tyrant'. **1819** BYRON *Juan* Ded. x, He [Milton] closed the *tyrant-hater he begun. **1866** M. C. TYLER *Glimpses Eng.* (1898) 146 Two centuries of *tyrant-hating Russells. *a* **1586** SIDNEY *Arcadia* II. (1622) 128 Killing many guiltlesse persons, either for affinitie to the tyrant, or enmitie to the *tyrant-killers. **1649** CANNE *Gold. Rule* 36 Those monuments of tyrant-killers by antiquity were so honored. **1648** MILTON *Tenure Kings* (1650) 20 Among the Jews this practice of *tyrant-killing was not unusual. **1726** POPE *Odyss.* XVIII. 97 Echetus..A tyrant, fiercest of the *tyrant-kind. **1532** BECON *Pomander of Prayer* (1578) 38 Forgeuing them, & praying for them whiche most *tyrauntlike handled thee. **1571** GOLDING *Calvin on Ps.* xlv. 7 Salomon reigneth not tyrantlike, as many Kynges do. **1629** H. BURTON *Truth's Triumph* 21 The Prince of darkenesse, who tyrant-like ruleth in the children of disobedience. **1894** tr. *Pastor's Hist. Popes* IV. II. v. 290 This crime was a *tyrant-murder of the ancient type. **1898** *Q. Rev.* July 106 Certain of the Mycenaean types..outlived the *Tyrant period. **1542** UDALL *Erasm. Apoph.* I. 115b, Harmodius & Aristogiton had been *tyrannequellers. **1819** SHELLEY *Prometh. Unb.* IV. i. 272 Golden spears With *tyrant-quelling myrtle overtwined. **1848** MRS. JAMESON *Sacr. & Leg. Art* (1850) 6 The *tyrant-ridden serf. **1591** SYLVESTER *Ivry* 385 Those King-correcting, *Tyrant-scourging Braves. **1809** SHAW *Gen. Zool.* VII. 304 *Tyrant Shrike..usually measuring about eight inches in length. **1826** STEPHENS *ibid.* XIII. II. 133 Tyrant-Shrike..these inhabit the American continent: they..are said to defend their young against the attacks of Eagles. **1692** WASHINGTON tr. *Milton's Def. Pop.* ii. M.'s Wks. (1847) 354/1 The same emperour honoured the memory of Thraseas, and Helvidius [etc.], who all were *tyrant-slayers. **1910** P. GARDNER in *Encycl. Brit.* XII. 480/1 The tyrant-slayers, Harmodius and Aristogiton. **1605** SYLVESTER *Du Bartas* II. iii. IV. 704 Thy gracious God, the glorious *Tyrant-tamer. **1613** HEYWOOD *Silver Age* III. i, Nor will we cease till we haue pruchas'd vs The name of Tyrant-tamer through the world.

Hence **'tyrant** *v. intr.*, to play the tyrant, to tyrannize (also with *it*); whence **'tyranting** (†**tyranning**) *vbl. sb.*; **'tyrantess**, a female tyrant, a tyranness.

1596 SPENSER *F.Q.* IV. vii. 1 Great God of love,..What glorie, or what guerdon hast thou found In feeble Ladies tyranning so sore? **1622** in Foster *Eng. Factories Ind.* (1908) II. 177 Hee persisted in his tyraninge. *a* **1661** FULLER *Worthies, Bucks.* (1662) I. 134 This encouraged the Irish Grandees (their *O's* and *Mac's*) to Rant and Tyrant it in their respective seignieuries. **1890** E. L. ARNOLD *Phra* iv, I was sorry for the tyrantess.

†**'tyrantly**, *adv.* *Obs. rare.* Also **tyranlie**. [f. TYRANT + -LY[2].] Tyrannically.

c **1470** HARDING *Chron.* XX. iv. (MS. Arch. Seld. B. 10) lf. 19 He..His commons alle with taxes did distreyne So tirantly he lefte þeim noght to spende. **1501** DOUGLAS *Pal. Hon.* III. xxxii, I saw..How tyranlie he Jowrie all opprest. **1560** BECON *Flower Godly Prayers* Wks. II. 171 A multitude of enemies..haue all ready most tyrantelye spoyled me of my garmentes.

†**'tyrantry**. *Obs.* Also 4 **tyrauntyre**, 4–5 **tir-**, **tyra(u)ntry**, **-ie**, **-ye**, **-e(e**, 5 **tyraunterie**, **terawntrye**; 4–5 **ter(r)andry**, 5 **tyrandry**, **-ie**; **tyranry**, **-ie**. [f. TYRANT + -RY. Cf. OF. *tirannerie*.] = TYRANNY (in various senses).

13.. *E.E. Allit. P.* (Morris) B. 187 Traysoun, & trichcherye, & tyrauntyre boþe. **1340** HAMPOLE *Pr. Consc.* 1601 Now es luff turned tyll lychery, And ryghtwisnes tyll tyrauntry. **1382** WYCLIF *Prol. Bible* iii. 4 The persecucioun and tirauntrie of Farao. *a* **1387** in *Archæologia* XVI. 83 His extorciones & his mayntenances and his tirranttrie of þat he hath take falsly ageyne þe Kynges lawes. *a* **1400–50** *Alexander* 4251 þi [Alexander's] tent is all on terrandry & tourment of armys. **1435** MISYN *Fire of Love* I. xxxi. 68 Slike forsoth,..be power of þer tyrantry þe smale oppres. *c* **1449** PECOCK *Repr.* III. iv. (Rolls) 302 Into the avail of the vndirlingis; and not..by tyranrie into the avail oonli of the ouerers. *c* **1470** HENRY *Wallace* IX. 206 In tyranry thus haiff we rongyn lang. **1483** *Cath. Angl.* 389/1 Tyrandry, *tirannides*. **1496** *Dives & Paup.* (W. de W.) I. lix. 100/2 Neyther they myght ne durste made suche solempnyte for tyrauntrye of the hethen people.

tyrantship ('taɪərəntʃɪp). *rare.* [f. TYRANT + -SHIP.] The condition or state of a tyrant, tyranny; also (with possessive), the personality of a tyrant.

c **1470** ASHBY *Active Policy Prince* 332 Rightwisnesse withoute pite is tiranship. *a* **1643** CARTWRIGHT *Siedge* II. iv, Saving your Tyrantship, you are a Fool. **1885** *Pall Mall G.* 19 Nov. 3/1 Tyrantship, not necessarily tyranny, was in those days a recognized profession.

†**tyranture.** *Obs. rare*$^{-0}$. = TYRANTRY.

c **1460** *Promp. Parv.* (E.E.T.S.) 476 Tyranture, *tirannis*.

tyraund, **-aunt**, **-aundise**, etc.: see TYRANT, TYRANDISE.

†**tyre**, **tire**, *sb.*[1] *Obs.* Forms: 5–6 **tire**, **tyre**, 6 **tyer(e**. [app. named from Tyre in Syria. Cf. OF. *tire*, *tyre*, silk cloth from Tyre.

'*Tire*, if not of Syrian growth, was probably a Calabrian or Sicilian wine, manufactured from the species of grape called [in Italian] *tirio*' (Furnivall in Note to quot. *c* 1460).]

A strong sweet wine imported in the 15th and 16th centuries. Also *attrib.*

1429 *Rolls of Parlt.* IV. 361/1 Tires and Romeneys at iiii marc'. *c* **1440** *Promp. Parv.* (E.E.T.S.) 483 Tyre wyne, or wyne tyre. *c* **1460** J. RUSSELL *Bk. Nurture* 119 The namys of swete wynes..Rompney of modon, Bastard, Tyre, Ozey. **1519** *Interl. Four Elem.* (Percy Soc.) 22 Ye shall have Spayneshe wyne and Gascoyn..Tyre, capryck, and malvesyne. **1526** *Pilgr. Perf.* (1531) 53b, There groweth the myghty swete wynes, as malueseys, tyeres & muscadels. **1556** WITHALS *Dict.* (1566) Hj/2 Tyre, *Vinum Tyrense, ex Tyro insula.* **1587** HARRISON *England* II. vi. in Holinshed *Chron.* I. 167/2 Whereof..Bastard, Tire, Oseie..are not least of all accompted of, bicause of their strength and valure.

†**tyre**, *sb.*[2] *Obs.* [ad. med.L. *tirus* (Du Cange), *tyrus*, of uncertain origin. So OF. *tir*, *tyr*, *thire*.] The name of an alleged venomous snake of Syria and Arabia.

1471 RIPLEY *Comp. Alch.* III. ix. in Ashm. *Theatr. Chem. Brit.* (1652) 141 Thys Water ys lyke to the venemous Tyre, Wherewyth the myghty Tryacle ys wrought. **1608** TOPSELL *Serpents* (1658) 792 Of the Tyre. There be some which have confounded this Serpent with the Viper, and taken them both to be but one kinde or at least the Tyre to be a kinde of Viper, because the Arabians call a Viper *Thiron*. *Ibid.*, This Tyre is called in Latine *Tyrus* and *Tyria*, and also among the Arabians..*Eosmari*, and *Alpfahex*.

†**tyre**, *sb.*[3] *Obs. rare*$^{-1}$. [ad. med.L. *tyria*, *tiria*, ? fem. of *Tyrius* TYRIAN.] Name of a kind of leprosy: see quot.

1547 BOORDE *Brev. Health* cccxlix. (1557) 112b, One of the kyndes of Leprousnes named Tiria. Tiria is the Latin worde. In Englyshe it is named the tyre or the propertie of an adder which is full of skales, so is this kynde of leprousnes full of skales and scabbes, corodyng the fleshe.

‖**tyre**, **tyer** (taɪə(r)), *sb.*[4] *E. Ind.* Forms: 7 **tayer**, 7–8 **tair**, 7–9 **tire**, 8 **tayar**, 8–9 **tyer**, 9 **tyre**. [ad. Tamil *tayir*.] Name in India for curdled milk and cream beginning to sour.

1613 PURCHAS *Pilgrimage* v. xi. 428 Some held..that there were seuen Seas; one of salt-water, the second of fresh, the third of honey, the fourth of milke, the fift of Tair (which is creame beginning to sowre). **1699** DAMPIER *Voy.* II. I. 139 Tire is sold about the Streets there: 'tis thick sower milk. **1776** N. B. HALHED *Code Gentoo Laws* Pref. 41 Flesh, or Milk, or *Tyer* (Sour Cream) or *Ghee*, or bitter Oil. **1822** BABINGTON tr. *Beschi's Gooroo Paramartan* v. 80 A repast, in which there was no lack of ghee, or milk, or tyer. **1844** SOUTHEY *Life A. Bell* I. 192 He had been greatly displeased to see the bad milk and bad tire with which they were frequently supplied.

tyre (taɪə(r)), *sb.*[5] [A variant spelling of TIRE *sb.*[2], both being used indifferently in 15th and 16th c. In 17th c. *tire* became the settled spelling, and has so continued in U.S.; but in Gt. Britain *tyre* has been revived for the pneumatic tires of bicycles, carriages, and motor-cars, and is also sometimes used for iron or steel tires.]

1. The iron or steel rim of a wheel, *esp.* the steel rim of the driving wheel of a locomotive: = TIRE *sb.*[2] 2a.

1796 W. FELTON *Carriages* Gloss., *Tyre*, the iron which rims the wheels. **1801** *Ibid.* II. 13 Extras to Wheels. Hooped tyre. Patent ditto. **1825** J. NICHOLSON *Operat. Mechanic* 647 The advantage of hooping cast iron wheels with malleable iron tyres or trods. **1838** BOURNE & BARTLEY *Patent Specif.* No. 7795, 6 Sept. 3 The felloe turned..to receive an ordinary outside hoop or tyre. **1862** SMILES *Engineers* III. 365 There are limits to the strength of iron,..and there is a point at which both rails and tyres must break. **1865** *Athenæum* 30 Sept. 442/1 Prior to the invention of weldless tyres. **1889** G. FINDLAY *Eng. Railway* 130 A steel tyre, spun from a solid block of Bessemer steel, without a weld.

2. a. A rubber cushion around the wheel of a bicycle, motor-car, etc.: = TIRE *sb.*[2] 2b.

1875 *Encycl. Brit.* III. 665/1 India-rubber tyres..were brought into requisition to relieve jolting. **1890** *Patent Specif.* No. 4206 Large rubber tyres..known commercially as (1) Pneumatic tyres, (2) Cushion tyres. **1891–1898** [see PNEUMATIC 1b]. **1902** *Encycl. Brit.* XXVII. 325/1 In 1846 Mr. William Thompson had taken out a patent for a pneumatic tyre for carriages.

b. ***spare tyre***: see SPARE *a.* and *adv.* 1a(a).

3. *attrib.* and *Comb.*, as ***tyre-bar***, ***-burst***, ***-carrier***, ***cast***, ***-cover***, ***-fitter***, ***-hoop***, ***-inflator***, ***lever***, ***-maker***, ***mark***, ***pressure***, ***-pump***, ***-rim***, ***track***, ***tread***, ***-wheel***. **tyre chain**, a chain fastened to a tyre to prevent wheel-skid, esp. in snow. (See also TIRE *sb.*[2] 3.)

1862 *Catal. Internat. Exhib., Brit.* II. No. 6264 Specimens of iron and steel, and Stocker's patent combined metal *tyre-bars. **1935** 'R. WEST' *Harsh Voice* ii. 91 A *tyreburst made him turn towards the road. **1909** *Westm. Gaz.* 17 Nov. 5/2 The general fittings consist of two head-lights, wind-screen, clock, speedometer, two horns, and *tyre-carrier. **1971** J. WAINWRIGHT *Dig Grave* 67 We're busy taking *tyre-casts... Taking plaster of Paris casts of tyre-marks. **1958** L. DURRELL *Mount-olive* iii. 80 His ears had caught the slither and scrape of *tyre-chains on the frosty drive outside. **1903**

Motor. Ann. 294 Brakes which act directly on the *tyre-cover cause it to deteriorate at an expensive rate. **1909** *Westm. Gaz.* 11 May 7/2 Carriage-builders, wheelwrights, carpenters, *tyre-fitters. **1865** *Athenæum* 30 Sept. 442/1 *Tyre-hoops for railway wheels. **1901** *Daily Chron.* 23 Sept. 8/5 Most of the *tyre inflators now made are provided with handles which telescope over the barrel. **1927** *Cycling Man.* (ed. 7) (Advt.), *Tyre levers. The famous 'Jiffy' has no rival. **1959** I. JEFFERIES *Thirteen Days* vii. 92 Once he found a receptive bitch he wouldn't leave her.. until he was prized off with tyre-levers. **1936** 'N. BLAKE' *Thou Shell of Death* xiv. 258 They had stopped at a fork. Blount was out, scanning the road surface for *tyre marks. **1971** Tyre mark [see *tyre cast* above]. **1931** *Man. Morris Minor Car* (Morris Motors, Ltd.) 50 Gauges for testing balloon *tyre pressures can be bought from all reputable motor dealers. **1959** *Motor Manual* (ed. 36) v. 130 A word or two should be said on the subject of tyre pressures. The basic fact to be remembered is that it is the air that carries the load. **1906** *Daily Chron.* 8 Sept. 3/7 Most *tyre pumps have a gauge on them to show the correct pressure. **1896** *Westm. Gaz.* 2 May 6/7 The Beeston Pneumatic Tyre Company.. being unable to fulfil its orders for *tyre rims [etc.]. **1931** D. L. SAYERS *Five Red Herrings* iii. 38 A fresh set of *tyre-tracks in the dust showing where the car had been taken out. **1971** M. KELLY *Twenty-Fifth Hour* i. 23 There were tyre tracks, wide ones, in the shingle reef at each edge of the road. **1925** *Motor* 29 Dec. 1091/3 (*heading*) Oil grooves and *tyre-tread grooves compared. **1978** R. WESTALL *Devil on Road* xi. 73 There were hoofprints in the dried-up mud... Wheeltracks too, but no tyre-treads. **1801** W. FELTON *Carriages* II. 38 A neat town Coach has.. hooped *tyre wheels with moulded fellies.

Hence **tyre** *v., trans.* to furnish with a tyre or tyres (= TIRE *v.*^{4}); **tyred** *ppl. a.*, furnished with a tyre or tyres: chiefly in compounds (= TIRED *ppl. a.*^{2}); **'tyreless** *a.*, having no tyres.

1909 MISS G. GUINNESS *Peru* xxi. 222 Sufficient rubber to *tyre 300,000 motor-cars. **1884** G. L. HILLER in *Longm. Mag.* III. 491 Using his *tyred but tireless steed [a bicycle]. **1886** Rubber-tyred [see RUBBER *sb.*^{1} 13 c]. **1896** Pneumatic-tyred [see PNEUMATIC *a.* 5]. **1906** C. MANSFIELD *Girl & Gods* xv, The discordant hoot of the motor horn, the rumble of *tyreless vehicles.

†**tyre**, Sc. aphetic f. *en-*, *intyre*, INTER *v.*

a **1500** *Wyntoun's Cron.* IX. 1096 (Cott. MS.) To Scoyne his men hym bare And honorably hym tyrit [*v.rr.* entyrit, enteryd] þar.

tyre, obs. form of TIER *sb.*^{1}, TIRE.

tyrefull, var. *tereful* obs., tedious: see TERE *a.*

tyrein ('taɪəriːɪn). *Chem. rare*$^{-0}$. [f. Gr. τυρός cheese, after *casein*.] A synonym of CASEIN.

1860 MAYNE *Expos. Lex.*, *Tyreina*, the same as *Casein*: tyrein. **1890** in BILLINGS *Med. Dict.*

tyreling, var. TIRELING *Obs.*

†**tyr(e)ment**, Sc. aphetic f. INTERMENT.

1504 *Acc. Ld. High Treas. Scot.* II. 257 Quhen he passit to Sanct Androis to the Beschopes tyrement. **1513** DOUGLAS *Æneis* XI. ii. *heading*, 3ong Pallas corps is till Evander sent, With all honour accordyng hys tyrment. **1541** *Acc. Ld. High Treas. Scot.* VIII. 39 To cum to the quenis tyrement.

‖**tyremesis** (taɪ'rɛmɪsɪs). *Path.* [mod.L., f. Gr. τυρός cheese + ἔμεσις vomiting.] (See quot.)

1857 DUNGLISON *Med. Lex.*, *Tyremesis*, vomiting of curdy matter, in infants especially.

tyreny, obs. form of TYRANNY.

†**tyret, tyrette**, obs. ff. TERRET.

1575 TURBERV. *Falconrie* Verses Commend. Hawking, To shape hir Jesse, hir Tyrets and hir line.

Tyrian ('tɪrɪən), *a.* and *sb.* [f. L. *Tyri-us* (f. *Tyrus* Tyre) + -AN.] **A.** *adj.* **a.** Of or belonging to, native of, or made in Tyre, an ancient Phœnician city on the Mediterranean, the centre of an extensive commerce.

In quot. 1634 alluding to the use of the pole-star (CYNOSURE 1) as a guide in navigation by the merchants of Tyre.

1513 DOUGLAS *Æneis* IV. iv. 67 The Tyrian men3e skalis wydequhair. **1582** STANYHURST *Æneis* I. (Arb.) 28 Of Tyrian virgins too weare thus a quiuer is vsed. **1596** SHAKS. *Tam. Shr.* II. i. 351 My hangings all of tirian tapestry. **1634** MILTON *Comus* 342 Thou shalt be our star of Arcady, Or Tyrian Cynosure. **1746** FRANCIS tr. *Horace, Sat.* II. iv. 102 What! sweep with dirty broom a floor inlaid, Or on foul couches Tyrian carpets spread? **1893** M. G. EASTON *Illustr. Bible Dict.* (1894) 677/1 Tyrian merchants were the first who ventured to navigate the Mediterranean waters.

b. *spec.* In reference or allusion to the purple or crimson dye anciently made at Tyre from certain molluscs: see PURPLE B. 1 a.

1616 DRUMM. OF HAWTH. *Poems* I. D iij, Nor Temples spread with Flackes of Virgine Snow, Nor Snow of Cheekes with Tyrian Graine enroll'd. **1693** DRYDEN *Persius* ii. 117 Another finds the way to dye in Grain, And make Calabrian Wool receive the Tyrian Stain. **1700** —— *Secular Masque* 56 The sprightly green has drunk the Tyrian dye [*i.e.* blood]. **1738** *Gentl. Mag.* VIII. 211/1 'Tis true, my form no Tyrian purples grace. **1877** G. F. MACLEAR *St. Mark* vii. (1879) 85 The dyes of the celebrated Tyrian purple. **1890** BILLINGS *Med. Dict.*, *Tyrian blue*, aniline dye, of violet color; a nuclear stain for alcoholic preparations.

B. *sb.* A native or inhabitant of Tyre.

1513 DOUGLAS *Æneis* I. viii. 141 Betuix ane Troiane and ane Tiriane Na difference. *Ibid.* xi. 82 3ow, my awin Tirianis. *c* **1614** SIR W. MURE *Dido & Æneas* I. 511 Even so the Tyrians, some a stately stage On arches rais'd for comedyes ereck. **1770** J. Z. HOLWELL *Orig. Princ. Anc. Bramins* viii. §125 (1770) 165 The histories of the ancient Phenicians, Tyrians, and Carthaginians. **1893** M. G. EASTON *Illustr. Bible Dict.* (1894) 677/1 In the time of David, a friendly alliance was entered into between the Hebrews and the Tyrians.

C. *Comb.*, as ***Tyrian-dyed, -hued*** adjs.

1847 C. BRONTË *Jane Eyre* I. xi. 194 A wide arch.. hung ..with a Tyrian-dyed curtain. **1903** AGNES M. CLERKE *Probl. Astrophysics* 259 To put off its crocus-veil and shine Tyrian-hued. **1910** *Sat. Westm. Gaz.* 19 Feb. 6/1 The Tyrian-dyed curtain.

'tyring, *vbl. sb.* [f. *tyre* vb. s.v. TYRE *sb.*^{5} + -ING^{1}.] The action of furnishing with a tyre or tyres (= TIRING *vbl. sb.*^{4}). Freq. *attrib.*

1923 G. STURT *Wheelwright's Shop* xxiii. 117 A great business was this tyring—if possible deferred.. until a number of tyres could be put on in a batch, being 'hotted up' in one fire. *Ibid.* xxiv. 125 Armed with tyring dogs, the three of us watched, expectant. **1936** *Automobile & Carriage Jrnl.* Dec. 153/2 The exhibits will include the tyring platform and tyre-bending machine. **1945** *Daily Herald* 31 Aug. 4/2 (Advt.), Much of the work had lain in its adaptation to the tyring of tank bogie wheels. **1968** J. ARNOLD *Shell Bk. Country Crafts* 159 The construction of a wheel, before the tyring stage was reached, required long experience.

tyrite ('taɪəraɪt). *Min.* [f. Norw. *Tyr*, ON. *Týr*, the god of war (cf. TUESDAY) + -ITE^{1}.] A variety of, or mineral allied to, FERGUSONITE.

1855 FORBES in *Edin. New Philos. Jrnl.* I. 67 Tyrite.. was found.. by Mr. Dahl, at a place called Hampemijr, and was crystallized in prisms, having a quadratic section. **1857** —— in *Philos. Mag.* Feb. 96 Tyrite and Fergusonite are closely allied, and may possibly be even identical. **1868** DANA *Min.* (ed. 5) 524 Tyrite.. occurs in square pyramidal crystals like those of fergusonite. *Ibid.* 525 Tyrite is associated with euxenite at Hampemyr.. and Helle.

†**tyrl**, obs. f. THIRL *v.*^{1}, to perforate.

1519 HORMAN *Vulg.* 108 Boxen pypes be lyghtlyer tyrld through, or made holowe, than yuery pypis.

tyrleis, obs. Sc. var. TRELLIS.

tyrment: see TYREMENT.

tyro, tyrocinium, etc.: see TIRO, etc.

tyrocidine (taɪrəʊ'saɪdɪn, -diːn). *Pharm.* Also **tyrocidin.** [f. mod.L. *Tyro-thrix* (see TYROTHRICIN) + -CID(E + -IN^{1}, -INE^{5}, after GRAMICIDIN.] (Any of) a group of crystalline monocyclic decapeptide antibiotics which along with the gramicidins are the active components of tyrothricin, as ***tyrocidine A*** $(C_{66}H_{87}O_{13}N_{13})$, ***tyrocidine B*** $(C_{68}H_{88}O_{13}N_{14})$, ***tyrocidine C*** $(C_{70}H_{88}O_{13}N_{15})$.

1940 HOTCHKISS & DUBOS in *Jrnl. Biol. Chem.* CXXXVI. 803 This substance was described earlier under the name *graminic acid* before its low chlorine content was recognized; it will be referred to hereafter as *tyrocidine hydrochloride*. **1952** BATTERSBY & CRAIG in *Jrnl. Amer. Chem. Soc.* LXXIV. 4021/2 Crystalline tyrocidine hydrochloride is in fact a family of polypeptides... The major peptides have been called tyrocidine A, tyrocidine B, tyrocidine C according to their partition ratios in the solvent system. **1969** Tyrocidin [see GRAMICIDIN]. **1977** J. S. GLASBY *Encycl. Antibiotics* 350/1 Most of the bacteriological examination has been carried out on the mixture of tyrocidins.

Tyrode ('taɪrəʊd). *Med.* Also **tyrode.** The name of Maurice Vejux *Tyrode* (1878–1930), American pharmacologist, used *attrib.*, in the possessive, and *ellipt.* as ***Tyrode's***, to designate a type of physiological saline solution used to irrigate tissue and in laboratory work.

1923 *Jrnl. Pharmacol. & Exper. Therapeutics* XXI. 218 Lowering of pH values of the blood did not occur regularly after injection of.. Tyrode's solution. **1962** HARRIS & GRUBER in A. Pirie *Lens Metabolism Rel. Cataract* 374 The cation transport can be measured reasonably well in a fairly simple medium. Originally, we used Tyrode's solution. **1964** W. G. SMITH *Allergy & Tissue Metabolism* iii. 36 These experiments.. consisted simply of replacing the oxygenated tyrode solution in which the tissue was bathed with tyrode solution containing either 48/80, stibamidine protamine sulphate or toluidine blue. **1975** *Nature* 31 Jan. 353/1 The sperm were recovered from the albumin by centrifugation at 2,500*g* and washed once in Tyrode's.

tyrogenous (taɪ'rɒdʒɪnəs), *a. rare*$^{-0}$. [f. Gr. τυρός cheese + -GEN + -OUS.] 'Originating in cheese' (Dorland *Med. Dict.* 1900–13).

tyroglyphid (taɪ'rɒglɪfɪd), *sb.* and *a. Zool.* [f. mod.L. *Tyroglyphid-æ*, pl., f. *Tyroglyphus*, name of the typical genus, f. Gr. τυρός cheese + γλύφειν to carve.] **a.** *sb.* An acarid of the family *Tyroglyphidæ*, including the cheese-mites. **b.** *adj.* Belonging to this family.

1909 in *Cent. Dict. Supp.* **1914** *Brit. Mus. Return* 180.

tyroid ('taɪərɔɪd), *a. rare*$^{-0}$. [f. Gr. τυρός cheese: see -OID.] Resembling cheese; cheesy.

1900–13 in DORLAND *Med. Dict.*

Tyrolean (tɪrəʊ'liːən, tɪ'rəʊliːən), *a.* and *sb.* Also **-ian.** [f. *Tyrol* (see def.) + -EAN. Cf. F. *tyrolien.*]

a. *adj.* Belonging to Tyrol (often called 'the Tyrol'), a former crown land of Austria-Hungary, embracing the present Austrian province of Tyrol and parts of northern Italy. ***Tyrolean hat***, a soft felt hat with a brim turned up at the sides and usu. a feather cockade. **b.** *sb.* A native or inhabitant of Tyrol. Also = *Tyrolean hat* above. So **Tyroler** ('tɪrələ(r)) [G. *Tyroler*, *Tiroler*: see -ER] (*a*) *sb.*, = *Tyrolean* b; also, the dialect of German spoken in the Tyrol; (*b*) *adj.*, = *Tyrolean* a; **Tyrolese** (-'iːz) *a.* and *sb.* = *Tyrolean*; ‖**tyrolienne** (tɪrəʊlɪ'ɛn) [F., fem. of *tyrolien* Tyrolean], a dance or song of the Tyrolese peasants, or in the style of this.

1805 *Times* 7 Nov. 2/3 The greatest part of those prisoners taken.. belong to.. the *Tyrolian Chasseurs. **1809** *Repos. of Arts* II. 388/1 The attachment of the Tyroleans.. to their emperors was always firm. **1859** *Habits Gd. Soc.* vi. (new ed.) 232 Except for the occasional playing of Tyrolean minstrels, [the zither is] unknown in this country. **1906** *Temple Bar Mag.* Jan. 33 Green Tyrolean hats with feathers. **1909** *Cent. Dict. Supp.*, Tyrolian. **1957** M. B. PICKEN *Fashion Dict.* 361/2 *Tyrolean hat*, soft brimmed felt hat. **1973** T. PYNCHON *Gravity's Rainbow* III. 495 Von Göll tips an invisible Tyrolean to old ladies in black who've come out in pairs to get some sun. **1887** M. HOWITT *Let.* 21 June in *Autobiogr.* (1889) II. ix. 345 Father Paul.. has been ill.., but being able to say Mass this morning, he, a *Tyroler Benedictine, remembered our Queen's Jubilee, and made it his intention. **1891** *Cent. Dict.*, Tyroler. **1899** *Daily News* 20 Dec. 6/6 They got guides familiar with the ground, and.. outflanked the Tyrolers. **1923** E. HEMINGWAY *Three Stories & Ten Poems* 18 Part of the time he talked in D'Ampezzo dialect and sometimes in Tyroler German dialect... Peduzzi decided to talk altogether in Tyroler. **1963** I. FLEMING *On H.M. Secret Service* (U.S. ed.) xxvii. 295 A dark-grey Tyroler outfit with the traditional dark-green trimmings and stag's-horn buttons. **1809** *Repos. of Arts* II. 388 Portrait of the *Tyrolese Deputies. *Ibid.* 389 He stipulated that the privileges of the Tyrolese.. should remain entire. **1844** A. P. DE LISLE in E. Purcell *Life* (1900) I. vii. 131 Columns of white Tyrolese marble. **1872** RUSKIN *Fors Clav.* (1896) I. xix. 373 The Tyrolese mountains. **1898** *Review of Rev.* Feb. 181/2 The Tyrolese.. a sterling, sober-minded people. **1889** W. B. SQUIRE in Grove *Dict. Mus.* IV. 198 The best-known example of an artificial '*Tyrolienne' is the well-known 'Chœur Tyrolien' in Act iii of Rossini's 'Guillaume Tell'.

tyroleucin (taɪərəʊ'l(j)uːsɪn). *Chem.* Also **-ine.** [f. Gr. τυρός cheese + LEUCIN.] A white crystalline substance $(C_7H_{11}NO_2)$ produced by the decomposition of proteins.

1878 KINGZETT *Anim. Chem.* 366 Among the new products recently described by Schützenberger is a substance termed by him tyroleucin. **1881** WATTS *Dict. Chem.* VIII. 1682 Tyroleucine is a white crystalline deposit of chalky aspect, nearly tasteless.

tyroline ('tɪrəlaɪn). [? f. TYR-IAN *a.* + -OL + -INE^{5}.] A variety of aniline-violet.

1867 *Ure's Dict. Arts* (ed. 6) I. 170.

tyrolite ('tɪrəlaɪt). *Min.* [ad. G. *tirolit* (Haidinger, 1845), f. *Tyrol*, where found: see -ITE^{1}.] 'Hydrous arsenate of copper, found usually in reniform masses of pale green colour' (Chester).

1854 DANA *Min.* (1868) 570.

‖**tyroma** (taɪ'rəʊmə). *Path.* [mod.L., ad. Gr. τύρωμα, f. τυροῦν to make into cheese, curdle, f. τυρός cheese.] A morbid formation or tumour of a cheesy consistence. Hence **ty'romatous** *a.*, of the nature of a tyroma.

1848 CRAIGIE *Elem. Anat.* I. xi. 222 *Tyroma glandularum.* Tyromatous deposition. *Ibid.*, I think that the term *Tyroma* (*Τυρος*, caseus) is most suited to express its nature. *Ibid.*, This tyromatous substance. **1880** W. AITKEN *Sc. & Pract. Med.* (ed. 7) II. 476 Strumous tumors, as tubercles of the brain, or tyroma.

†**'tyro,mancy.** *Obs.* Also **tiro-.** [ad. F. *tyromantie* (Rabelais), f. Gr. τυρός cheese: see -MANCY.] Divination by means of cheese.

1652 GAULE *Magastrom.* xix. 166 *Tyromancy* [mispr. *Typomancy*], [divining] by the coagulation of cheese. **1656** BLOUNT *Glossogr.*, *Tiromantie.* *a* **1693** *Urquhart's Rabelais* III. xxv, To have the truth.. more fully.. disclosed.. by Tyromancy, whereof we make some Proof in a great Brehemont Cheese.

tyronic, -ism, -ist, -ize: see TIRONIC.

tyrosin: see TYROSINE.

tyrosinæmia (taɪrəsɪ'niːmɪə). *Med.* Also (chiefly *U.S.*) **-emia.** [f. prec. + Gr. αἷμα blood + -IA^{1}.] Any of several conditions marked by the presence in blood and urine of abnormally high amounts of tyrosine.

1965 J. GENTZ et al. in *Jrnl. Pediatrics* LXVI. 670/1 Tyrosinemia as defined in the present report is a disorder characterized biochemically by a continuous high urinary excretion of tyrosine and tyrosyl compounds and a high plasma tyrosine level, while the concentrations of other amino acids are normal or rather low. **1982** T. I. DIAMONDSTONE in T. M. Devlin *Textbk. Biochem.* xii. 589 Transient tyrosinemia of the newborn appears to be due to delayed development of tyrosine transaminase and/or *p*-hydroxyphenylpyruvate oxidase... Persistent tyrosinemia without liver or kidney disease has been reported in six patients, all of whom are retarded. **1983** *Oxf. Textbk. Med.* I. IX. 94/1 A single metabolic lesion to explain all the findings has not yet been identified, and it has been argued that Type I tyrosinaemia is not in fact primarily a disorder of tyrosine metabolism.

tyrosinase ('taɪərəs-, taɪ'rɒsɪneɪz). *Biochem.* [a. F. *tyrosinase* (G. Bertrand 1896, in *Compt. Rend.* CXXII. 1216): see TYROSINE and -ASE.] A copper-containing oxygenase found in many plants and animals which catalyses the formation of quinones from phenols and polyphenols (e.g. melanin from tyrosine) by the addition and then the oxidation of hydroxyl groups.

1896 *Jrnl. R. Microsc. Soc.* 430 In the root of the dahlia and beet, as well as in several fungi.. M. G. Bertrand finds a hitherto undescribed diastase, to which he gives the name *tyrosinase*, from its connection with tyrosin. **1904** *Proc. R. Soc.* LXXIV. 313 An extract can be made from the skins of certain pigmented animals.., which will act upon tyrosin and produce a pigmented substance. This action suggests the presence of a tyrosinase. **1931** [see PHENOLASE]. **1974** [see *polyphenol oxidase* s.v. POLY- 2]. **1982** T. I. DIAMONDSTONE in T. M. Devlin *Textbk. Biochem.* xii. 614/2 Melanin is formed from tyrosine via L-dopa as intermediate; however, the enzyme that catalyzes the formation of L-dopa in this pathway is not tyrosine hydroxylase, but a copper-containing oxygenase known as tyrosinase.

tyrosine (ˈtaɪərəʊsiːn). *Chem.* Also † -in. [irreg. f. Gr. τῡρός cheese + -IN[1].] An amino-acid that is the precursor of several hormones, including adrenalin; 3-(*p*-hydroxyphenyl)alanine. Also *attrib.*

1857 MILLER *Elem. Chem.* III. 627 Tyrosine..was obtained by Liebig from the products of the fusion of well-dried cheese, fibrin, or albumen, with hydrate of potash. *Ibid.* 628 Tyrosine forms long fibrous crystals, which are very sparingly soluble in cold water. **1873** RALFE *Phys. Chem.* 72 Tyrosin... Associated with leucin it has been obtained from all the glandular organs and secretions of the body. *Ibid.*, On cooling, crystals of tyrosin will be deposited. **1897** *Allbutt's Syst. Med.* IV. 100 Tyrosin crystals were found in the urine. **1926** [see DEAMINATION]. **1955** *Sci. Amer.* July 75/2 The six virus strains were analyzed for their content of three amino acids: tyrosine, tryptophan and phenylalanine. **1965** LEE & KNOWLES *Animal Hormones* v. 91 Basically, thyroid hormone consists of iodine conjugated with tyrosine. **1982** [see TYROSINASE].

tyrosinosis (taɪrəʊsɪˈnəʊsɪs). *Med.* [f. TYROSINE + -OSIS.] A rare condition of unknown ætiology in which there is increased excretion of the early metabolites of tyrosine but no liver or kidney damage; also (now *rare*) = TYROSINÆMIA.

1932 G. MEDES in *Biochem. Jrnl.* XXVI. 938 The essential feature in our patient..consists in a complete stoppage of the oxidation of tyrosine at the stage of *p*-hydroxyphenylpyruvic acid... Thus results an excretion not only of *p*-hydroxyphenylpyruvic acid and..*l*-*p*-hydroxyphenyllactic acid, but also of tyrosine and ..*l*-3:4-dihydroxyphenylalanine. For this condition, the name tyrosinosis is proposed. **1942** [see L-DOPA]. **1969** [see *homocystinuria* s.v. HOMOCYSTINE]. **1974** PASSMORE & ROBSON *Compan. Med. Stud.* III. xlvii. 8/1 Formerly hypertyrosinaemia or tyrosinosis was considered to be a single, exceedingly rare abnormality. **1982** T. I. DIAMONDSTONE in T. M. Devlin *Textbk. Biochem.* xii. 589/1 Tyrosinosis and the tyrosinemias have certain biochemical features in common.

‖**tyrosis** (taɪˈrəʊsɪs). *Path.*, etc. [mod.L., ad. Gr. type *τῡ́ρωσις, f. τῡροῦν: see TYROMA and -OSIS.] **a.** Curdling of milk, esp. in the stomach: = CASEATION a. **b.** = TYREMESIS. **c.** Cheesy degeneration: = CASEATION b.

1693 tr. *Blancard's Phys. Dict.* (ed. 2). **1857** DUNGLISON *Med. Lex.*, *Tyrosis*, Tyremesis. Also, the curdling of milk in the stomach. **1896** *Allbutt's Syst. Med.* I. 175 Caseation or Tyrosis is a mode of termination of necrosis.

tyrothricin (taɪrəʊˈθraɪsɪn, -ˈθrɪsɪn). *Pharm.* [f. *Tyrothrix* (see quot. 1940), f. Gr. τυρό-ς cheese + θρίξ, τριχ- hair: see -IN[1].] A preparation of gramicidin and tyrocidine which has antibiotic properties, esp. against Gram-positive bacteria, and has been used externally to treat local infections.

1940 HOTCHKISS & DUBOS in *Jrnl. Biol. Chem.* CXXXVI. 804 Gramicidin will continue to be used as the name of the crystalline neutral substance described before. It is proposed here to apply the name tyrothricin to the bactericidal agent prepared as an alcohol-soluble, water-insoluble material and containing both gramicidin and tyrocidine. This name is derived from the word *Tyrothrix*, a generic name first used by Duclaux to designate sporulating aerobic bacterial species, several of which have since been found to exhibit antagonistic activity toward other microorganisms. **1959** *Sunday Graphic* 25 Jan. 4 (Advt.), Antibiotic throat lozenges contain the highly effective antibiotic tyrothricin. **1974** M. C. GERALD *Pharmacol.* xxvi. 453 Tyrothricin proved too toxic for systemic use in animals.

‖**tyrotoxicon** (taɪərəʊˈtɒksɪkɒn). *Chem.* [mod.L., f. Gr. τῡρός cheese + τοξικόν poison.] A poisonous ptomaine (diazobenzene hydroxide, $C_6H_5N.N.OH$), produced by a microbe in stale cheese and milk; cheese-poison.

1886 *Sci. Amer.* 21 Aug. 112/3 About a year ago, Dr. Victor C. Vaughan, of the University of Michigan, succeeded in isolating from some samples of cheese..a highly poisonous ptomaine, which he named tyrotoxicon (cheese poison)... Further investigations have led to the discovery that tyrotoxicon may be developed in milk.

So **tyro'toxin** [TOXIN] = *tyrotoxicon*; **tyro'toxism**, cheese-poisoning.

1899 CAGNEY tr. *Jaksch's Clin. Diagn.* v. (ed. 4) 189 Vaughan obtained one of these bodies (tyrotoxin) from rotten cheese and bad milk. **1900–13** DORLAND *Med. Dict.*, *Tyrotoxism*, cheese-poisoning.

tyrran, -and, -anie, etc. obs. ff. TYRANT, TYRANNY.

tyrret, obs. form of TERRET.

Tyrrhene (ˈtɪriːn, tɪˈriːn), *a.* and *sb.* Forms: 4–5 Tyren, 5 Tyrene, 6 Tirrene, 6–7 Tyrrhen, 6– Tyrrhene. [ad. L. *Tyrrhēnus* of or pertaining to the *Tyrrhēnī* (Gr. Τυρρηνοί) or Etruscans.] = next.

1387 TREVISA *Higden* (Rolls) II. 445 He passede.. Hercules his pilers, and com in to þe see Tyren. **1432–50** tr. *Higden* (Rolls) VI. 369 From the occean of Briteyne unto the see Tyrene. **1513** DOUGLAS *Æneis* VII. xii. 54 In Itale strandis at the cost Tyrrhene. *Ibid.* VIII. viii. 164 Wyth brag of weyr and Tirrene trumpis sovn. **1634** MILTON *Comus* 49 Coasting the Tyrrhene shore. **1697** DRYDEN *Æneid* VIII. 729 The Trojan band, Who wait their leader to the Tyrrhene land. **1736** AINSWORTH *Lat. Dict.*, *Mezentius*,..a prince of the Tyrrhenes. **1882** 'OUIDA' *Maremma* I. 147 One of the forgotten kings of the Tyrrhene people.

Tyrrhenian (tɪˈriːnɪən), *a.* and *sb.* [f. L. *Tyrrhēn-us* (see prec.) or *Tyrrhēnia* Etruria.] **a.** *adj.* Of or pertaining to the Tyrrheni or their country; Etruscan, Etrurian. **b.** *sb.* One of the Tyrrheni; an Etruscan.

Tyrrhenian Sea, the sea lying between the mainland of Italy and the islands of Corsica, Sardinia, and Sicily.

1660 STANLEY *Hist. Philos.* IX. *Pythagoras* i. (1687) 492/1 Suidas saith, That Pythagoras was..by birth a Tyrrhenian. **1711** J. CLARKE tr. *Grotius' Chr. Relig.* II. xii. 112 *note*, [See] Diodorus, Book v, concerning the Tyrrhenians. **1788** LEMPRIÈRE *Class. Dict.*, *Mezentius*, a king of the Tyrrhenians when Æneas came into Italy. **1797** *Encycl. Brit.* (ed. 3) XVI. 327 Æneas..steered his course for Italy across the Tyrrhenian sea. **1857** BIRCH *Anc. Pottery* (1858) II. 77 The amphora called Tyrrhenian differs only in its general proportion from the two preceding kinds.

tyrse. *rare.* ? *Obs.* Also **thirsé**. [Properly *tirsé* (Forskål, 1775), *tyrsé* (G. Saint-Hilaire and Cuvier), ad. Arab. *tirsa^h*, f. *turs* shield.] The Egyptian soft-billed turtle, *Testudo triunguis*.

1807 HUNTER tr. *Sonnini's Trav. in Egypt* I. 301 The advantage with which this *thirsé* of the Egyptians and Nubians wages war with the crocodile. **1834** MCMURTRIE *Cuvier's Anim. Kingd.* 171 *T. Ægyptiacus*... The Tyrse. **1839** *Encycl. Brit.* (ed. 7) XIX. 132/2 The Egyptian species or tyrse, the soft turtle of the Nile.

Tyrtæan (təˈtiːən), *a.* [f. proper name *Tyrtæus*, Gr. Τυρταῖος (see def.) + -AN.] Pertaining to or in the style of Tyrtæus, a Greek poet of the 7th century B.C., who composed martial songs for the Spartans; martial, warlike.

1879 SWINBURNE *Stud. Shaks.* (1880) 114 There was nothing of the dry Tyrtæan twang, the dull mechanic resonance. **1898** G. W. E. RUSSELL *Collect. & Recollect.* 380 Twenty years ago..the music-halls rang with the 'Great MacDermott's' Tyrtæan strain:—We don't want to fight; but, by Jingo, if we do [etc.].

tyrtle, -tyll, obs. forms of TURTLE *sb.*[1]

tysan, -ane, -ant, obs. ff. PTISAN.

tysche, Tysday, obs. Sc. ff. TISSUE, TUESDAY.

tyse, var. TICE *v.*, to entice.

Tysonian (taɪˈsəʊnɪən), *a.* *Anat.* [f. proper name *Tyson* (see def.) + -IAN.] Pertaining to or discovered by Edward Tyson, an English anatomist (1649–1708); applied to the sebaceous glands of the prepuce, also called *Tyson's glands*.

1891 in *Cent. Dict.* **1900–13** in DORLAND *Med. Dict.*

tysonite (ˈtaɪsənaɪt). *Min.* [f. the name of S. T. *Tyson*, from whom it was received + -ITE[1].] A rare native fluoride of the cerium metals.

1880 ALLEN & COMSTOCK in *Amer. Jrnl. Sc. & Arts* XIX. 390 The formula (Ce, La, Di)$_2$ Fl$_6$ appears.. to express the composition of the mineral... It should be regarded as a new species. We propose for it the name *Tysonite*.

tyss, obs. Sc. f. TICE *v.*, to entice.

tyssew, tysshewe, etc., obs. ff. TISSUE.

† **tyssyke, tysyke**, obs. forms of PHTHISIC.

c **1450** *Nom.* in Wr.-Wülcker 708/5 *Hec tisis*, the tyssyke. *c* **1520** SKELTON *Magnyf.* 555 Can you a remedy for a tysyke?

tyst, var. TICE *v.*, to entice.

tyster, -yre, obs. Sc. ff. TESTER, canopy.

tystie (ˈtaɪstɪ, ˈtiːstɪ). *local.* Also 8 **taisté**, 9 **tysté, -ty, -tie, -tey, teisty, teistie, testie, tiestie**. [Of Norse origin: cf. Norw. *teist(e*, OIcel. *þeist*, *þeisti*.] The Black Guillemot.

1774 LOW *Fauna Orcad.* (1813) 106 The taisté build in holes of the earth: lay but one egg. **1837** R. DUNN *Ornith. Orkney & Shetl.* 102 Uria Grylle...Tystie. Black Guillemot. Greenland Dove. **1847** *Zoologist* V. 1909 The black guillemot..or the testie. **1876** D. GORRIE *Summers & Wint. Orkneys* v. 153 Bevies of teisties were disporting themselves in front and rear. **1892** G. STEWART *Shetland Fireside T.* iv. (ed. 2) 27 He turned as fat as a tiestie. **1893** COZENS-HARDY *Broad Norfolk* 50 Sometimes there is quite a family of similar names..of the same origin. Thus the Black Guillemot is..the *tyste, taiste, toyst*, and *tysty*. **1952** U. VENABLES *Tempestuous Eden* iii. 50 This was an ideal nesting-ground for black guillemots or tysties. **1964** A. L. THOMSON *New Dict. Birds* 69/1 The Tystie (or Black Guillemot)..and its congeners constitute the tribe Cepphini. **1980** *Birds* Summer 51/2 There is a small brackish loch near the shore where tysties display in spring.

tyt, obs. f. TIT, TITE.

tytandis, obs. f. TIDINGS.

tyte, tytely, obs. ff. TITE, TITELY.

† **tytelet**, ? obs. f. TITLED *ppl. a.*

13.. *Gaw. & Gr. Knt.* 1515 F[or] to telle of þis teuelyng of þis trwe kny3tez, Hit is þe tytelet token, & tyxt of her werkkez.

† **tyte tust, tytetuste.** *Obs. rare*⁻¹. [app. related to *titty*, TUTTY *sb.*[2], in same sense; cf. TISTY-TOSTY, TUZZY-MUZZY.] A nosegay, posy.

c **1440** *Promp. Parv.* 494/2 Tyte tust, or tusmose of flowrys or othyr herbys [*S.* tytetuste or tussemose], *olfactorium*.

tythance, -and(es), -aundes, obs. ff. TIDING(S.

tythe, var. TITHE.

tythimal(l, var. TITHYMAL *Obs.*

tything, obs. f. TIDING; var. TITHING.

tythondys, obs. f. TIDINGS.

tytill, tytle, obs. ff. TITLE, TITTLE.

tytt(e obs. ff. TEAT, TITE.

† **ˈtytyfer.** *Obs.* Also 6 **tedyffre**. [Origin obscure: perh. akin to TIDIFE.] The name of some small bird.

c **1500** *Parl. Byrdes* 193 in Hazl. *E.P.P.* III. 177 The Tytyffer. I say, sayd the Tytyfer, we kentysshe men [*Lansdowne MS.*, Syth, quod the Tedyffre with the Norfolk men], We may not geue the Crow a penne.

tytyl, -yll, obs. ff. TITLE, TITTLE.

tytynge, obs. f. TIDING.

tytyuell, -villus: see TITIVIL.

tyuyamunite (tjuːjəˈmuːnaɪt). *Min.* [ad. Russ. *tyuyamunit'* (K. A. Nenadkevicha 1913, in *Izvestiya imper. Akad. Nauk"* VI. 945), f. *Tyuya Muyun*, name of a village near Osh, Kirgiziya, U.S.S.R.: see -ITE[1].] A hydrous uranyl vanadate of calcium, $Ca(UO_2)_2(VO_4)_2.5-8H_2O$, occurring as soft, yellowish orthorhombic crystals and mined for its uranium content.

1913 *Amer. Jrnl. Sci.* CLXXXV. 440 The calcium carnotite experimented with is probably identical with the tuyamunite of Nenadkevich. **1957** *Financial Times Ann. Rev. Brit. Industry* 39/3 Important secondary ore mineral[s] ..are the calcium-uranium vanadate tyuyamunite,..and tobernite. **1979** *Mineral. Abstr.* XXX. 362/1 The San Rafael mining area is situated along the east flank of the San Rafael Swell in east-central Utah... Coffinite is the most abundant primary ore mineral, and tyuyamunite is the most abundant secondary ore mineral.

Tyvys-, Tywes-, Tywysday, obs. ff. TUESDAY.

tywele, variant of TWILLY *sb.*[1] *Obs.*

tywell, tywlle, obs. forms of TWILL *sb.*[1]

† **tyxhyl**, obs. f. THIXEL (*dial.*).

c **1475** *Pict. Voc.* in Wr.-Wülcker 807/19 *Hec acia*. a tyxhyl.

tyxste: see TEE *v.*[2]

tyxt, tyxte, obs. ff. TEXT.

tyyn, obs. f. THYINE.

tzaddik, -iq, varr. TSADDIK.

Tzakonian, var. TSAKONIAN *sb.* and *a.*

tzantza, var. TSANTSA.

tzar, etc.: see TSAR.

‖**tzedaka(h)** (tsɛˈdɔka). [Heb. *ṣĕdāqāh* righteousness.] Charity, the obligation to help one's fellow Jews.

1959 D. D. RUNES *Conc. Dict. Judaism* 225/2 *Tzedakah*, righteousness; charity. **1962** *New Jewish Encycl.* 87/1 The Jewish concept of 'charity' has..been refined to mean more than the mere giving of alms; it has been considered as 'Tzedakah', an act of justice and righteousness. **1968** L. ROSTEN *Joys of Yiddish* 417 Maimonides set down variously rated forms of *tzedaka*. **1973** *Synagogue Light* Sept. 30/1 To all who have helped our brothers overseas in the year 5733, let me say that there can be no finer act of Tzedakah. **1978** *Jewish Chron.* 6 Oct. 23/3 Acceptance of the mitzvot, the ritual acts of prayer, *tzedaka* and so on.

tzeiran, var. DZEREN.

[**1662** J. DAVIES tr. *Olearius' Voy. Ambass.* 226 A kind of Deer, which the Turks call *Tzeiran*, and the Persians, *Ahn*.] **1862** *Chambers' Encycl.* IV. 692/1 The bear of Tibet, the musk-deer, the tzeiran.., the Mongolian goat [etc.].

Tzeltal (tsɛlˈtɑːl, ˈtsɛltɑːl; s-), *sb.* (and *a.*) Also Tzendal, Tzental. Pl. -al, -ales (-ˈɑːlɪs), -als. [a. Sp., earlier also *Tzendal*, *Sendal*, name of one of the three regions of Chiapas as divided by the

Spaniards; ulterior origin uncertain.] (A member of) an Indian people inhabiting parts of southern Mexico; the Mayan language of this people. Also *attrib.* or as *adj.*

1868 C. H. BERENDT in *Ann. Rep. Board of Regents Smithsonian Inst. 1867* 426, I visited the ruins of Palenque, and..was enabled..to collect vocabularies of the Putum and Tzental languages, both spoken in Chiapas. **1871** L. H. MORGAN *Systems of Consanguinity* II. vi. 263 The Chontal language is allied to the Maya of Yucatan. It also affiliates with the Chol and Tzental of Chiapa. **1875** H. H. BANCROFT *Native Races Pacific States N. Amer.* I. vi. 645 South of them [*sc.* the Chontales] in Chiapas are the *Choles, Tzendales, Zotziles,* [etc.]. *Ibid.* III. x. 760 Most..are related to..the Maya, of which a dialect called the Tzendal is said to be the oldest language spoken in any of these countries. **1927** O. LA FARGE in *Tribes & Temples* II. xv. 326 The language itself has been variously named Cendal, Tzendal, Cendales, Tzental, and Tzeltal. I have taken the latter form, as it most nearly represents the Indians' own form, *ts'eltal*, varied in careless speech to *tceltal*. *Ibid.* 325 They speak the Tzeltal language, belonging to that branch of the great Mayance stock more closely related to Maya. **1939** REDFIELD & VILLA in *Contrib. Amer. Anthropol. & Hist.* V. XXVIII. 107 Mr. Villa..does not speak Tzeltal. *Ibid.* 110 Most Tzeltal communities are without beehives. **1949** [see INTRANSITIVIZE *v.*]. **1964** E. A. NIDA *Toward Sci. Transl.* x. 239 Among the Tzeltals in Southern Mexico the coming of missionaries..resulted in the conversion of many hundreds of persons, who responded, in their eagerness to describe their spiritual experiences, by creating many new phrases. *Ibid.*, At the same time, the Tzeltal people were undergoing certain adjustments of experience to new elements of language. **1979** L. CAMPBELL in Campbell & Mithun *Lang. Native Amer.* 902 Examination of numerals shows every other one to be Tzeltal alternating with Tojolabal.

tzetse, tzetze, var. TSETSE.

‖**tzigane** (tsɪ'gɑːn), *sb.* and *a.* Also **tsigan(e, tzigan,** † **zigan.** [a. F. *tzigane*, = Russian *tsÿgan*, Ruthenian *tsÿhan*, Slovenian *cigan*, Romanian *ţigan*, Lithuanian *cigonas*, Bulgarian *tsiganin*, Croatian *ciganin*; all from Magyar *cigány*, ('tsigaːŋ). The spelling with *tz-* originated in German; a better Eng. spelling would be *tsigan*: cf. *Tsar*.]

A. *sb.* A Hungarian gipsy.

1851 BORROW *Lavengro* xc. (1893) 352 Like the forge and tent of a wandering Zigan. **1887** *Pall Mall G.* 3 Mar. 5/2 The fiery Magyar, the melancholy Roumanian, the stolid Saxon, the merry, thieving Tzigane. **1898** *Tit-Bits* 7 May 114/1 The finest-looking people of Europe are the Tsiganes, or gipsies of Hungary. **1906** *Reader* 24 Nov. 124/1 The humblest peasant, even the nomad Tzigan, greasy, wild, and unkempt in appearance.

B. *adj.* That is a tzigane; pertaining to or consisting of tziganes.

1885 MABEL COLLINS *Prettiest Woman* vi. The Tzigane musicians were playing most exquisite music. **1888** E. GERARD *Land beyond Forest* II. xxvii. 13 Stripping a young Tzigane girl quite naked. **1912** *Daily News* 12 Apr. 6 The ..inevitable tzigane bands, valses, cake-walks.

Hence **tziganologist** (tsɪgə'nɒlədʒɪst), **tzi'ganologue** (also **ts-**), one who studies or treats of the tziganes.

1909 *Cent. Dict. Suppl.*, *Tsiganologist*, same as *Zinganologist*. **1911** *19th Cent.* Sept. 550 We owe our knowledge of it [Shelta] to Charles Godfrey Leland, a keen tsiganologue.

tzimmes ('tsɪməs). Also **tsimmes, -is; tzimmas, -is, -us; (t)zimes.** Pl. same. [a. Yiddish *tsimes* of obscure origin.] A stew or casserole of sweetened vegetables or vegetables and fruit, sometimes with meat. Also *fig.*, a fuss, a confused affair.

1892 I. ZANGWILL *Childr. Ghetto* I. v. 136 Esther sometimes compounded *Tzimmus*, a dainty blend of carrots, pudding, and potatoes. **1893** *Pall Mall Mag.* Oct. 870 It was a good and simple meal of fish, fowl, and fruits, no 'borsch', no 'tabeches', no 'tzimmas'. **1903** *Jewish Encycl.* IV. 256/1 *Zimes*, or compote, consists generally of cooked fruits..or of vegetables, well spiced. **1923** A. YEZIERSKA *Children of Loneliness* 142 *Tzimmes—blintzes*—a golden-roasted goose swimming in its own fat ravished the senses. **1925** S. RAPHAELSON *Jazz Singer* 125 Brother Levy, I am the chairman of the Executive Committee. Make yourself a *tsimmes* from it... All right—*all* right. **1925** A. YEZIERSKA *Bread Givers* vi. 102 You ought to taste her *gefülte* fish! Her *tzimes*! **1946** D. RUNYON *Short Takes* 199 Why is he making a big tsimmis out of a grunt? **1958** J. GROSSINGER *Jewish Cookery* p. xi, Rosh Hashonah..one of the many different styles of *tzimmes* is a regular part of the holiday's menu. **1968** L. ROSTEN *Joys of Yiddish* 411 Since making *tsimmes* took time and various mixings, the word came to mean:..A prolonged procedure; an involved business; a mix-up. **1970** S. ELLIN *Bind* xxxviii. 186 I'll be owing money before this *tzimmis* is over. **1970** [see KISHKE]. **1974** R. L. SIMON *Wild Turkey* (1976) vii. 39 Why are you making such a *tsimmis*? Hecht is dead. **1975** G. MEIR *My Life* iii. 37 The Sabbath meal—chicken soup, *gefilte* fish, and meat braised with potatoes and onions, with a carrot-and-prune *tzimmes* on the side. **1978** *Times* 29 July 9/2 On a recent visit, latkes were greasy and tzimmis boring.

tzirid, obs. f. JERID, wooden javelin.

tzitzit(h), varr. TSITSITH.

tzolkin ('tsɔːlkɪn, s-). [Mayan.] The cycle of two hundred and sixty days constituting the sacred calendar of the Maya.

1931 GANN & THOMPSON *Hist. Maya* viii. 208 After giving the position of a day in their sacred calendar or Tzolkin, as it was probably called, they proceeded to give the position in their 365-day year. **1948** A. L. KROEBER *Anthropol.* (rev. ed.) 549 The 260-day tzolkin..had heavy religious and astrological import. **1977** G. CLARK *World Prehistory* (ed. 3) viii. 374 The Maya maintained two distinct counts. For religious purposes they used a sacred year (*tzolkin*) made up of thirteen twenty-day units.

tzores, var. TSORES.

Tzotzil ('tsəʊtsɪl, tsəʊt'sɪl; s-), *sb.* (and *a.*) Also **Zotzil.** Pl. **-il, -iles** (-'iːlɪs), **-ils.** [a. Sp., ad. Tzotzil *sočil* bat people.] (A member of) an Indian people inhabiting parts of southern Mexico; the Mayan language of this people. Also *attrib.* or as *adj.*

1875 [see TZELTAL]. **1927** O. LA FARGE in *Tribes & Temples* II. xv. 326 Their [the Bachajons'] immediate neighbors of the Highlands are the Zotzil. [They] speak a language differentiated from Tzeltal only by a shift of *a, e,* and *b* to Zotzil *o, i,* and *m*. **1939** REDFIELD & VILLA in *Contrib. Amer. Anthropol. & Hist.* V. XXVII. 110 Wheat is.. grown in the Tzotzil towns of Chamula and Huistán. **1940** F. JOHNSON in *Maya & their Neighbors* vi. 108 The Chañabal, and Tzotzil Languages. **1964** E. A. NIDA *Toward Sci. Transl.* ix. 218 The same period may be spoken of in very different ways in diverse languages; e.g. the Biblical 'tenth hour' (or 4 P.M.) is called..'the sun is astride the mountain' (Tzotzil) and 'time for untying the oxen' (Bolivian Quechua). **1977** *Language* LIII. 464 Tzotzil is a Mayan language with more than 120,000 speakers, all living in the State of Chiapas, Mexico.

Tz'u Chou (tsuː dʒuː). Also **Cizhou.** [Chinese *Tz'u Chou* (Wade-Giles), *Cizhou* (Pinyin), place-name in northern China.] Pottery made at Tz'u Chou, or in similar styles elsewhere, from the Sui dynasty onwards.

1910 S. W. BUSHELL *Chinese Art* II. 22 The Ting-chou and Tz'u-chou porcelains. **1915** R. L. HOBSON *Chinese Pott. & Porc.* I. viii. 103 By far the largest group of the Tz'ŭ Chou family consists of the painted wares. Like the rest of the Tz'ŭ Chou pottery..these have a greyish buff body of porcellanous stoneware..covered with a transparent glaze. .. On this glaze..the painters executed rapid, bold.. designs in shades of brown, varying from black to a soft sepia colour. **1934** *Burlington Mag.* May 214/2 The most characteristic Tz'ŭ Chou product is a buff or grey stoneware dressed with white slip. **1972** *Guardian* 15 Nov. 7/1 A firm of New York dealers..yesterday paid £50,000 for a vase of Tz'ŭ Chou stoneware of the Sung dynasty at Sotheby's. **1980** *Sotheby's Preview Calendar of Sales* Apr.–May p. xxiii (*caption*) A Cizhou (Tz'u Chou) pillow... Jin (Chin) dynasty.

tzuica, var. TSUICA.

tzuris, var. TSORES.

U

U (juː), the 21st letter of the modern English, and the 20th of the ancient Roman alphabet, was in the latter identical in form and origin with V (q.v.), the same symbol being employed both as a vowel and a consonant. In Latin MSS. written in capitals the form V is retained; but in uncial MSS., of which the earliest specimens belong to the third or fourth century, the modified form U appears, and is continued in the later half-uncial (from *c* 500) and minuscule MSS. (from the eighth century) as u. In Anglo-Saxon MSS. the latter form (u) was regularly employed as a minuscule to denote the vowel *u*, the corresponding form in capitals being either V or U. In early MSS. *u* and *uu* are also employed with the value of *w*, and very rarely *u* in place of *b* (later *f*) to denote intervocalic *v*; in late MSS. the substitution of *u* for *f* (= v) becomes fairly common, usually between vowels but sometimes also initially. In ME., after continental usage, the two symbols *u* and *v* were employed, but without clear distinction in value, each of them being used to denote either the vowel *u* or the consonant *v*. The practice with regard to the employment of the two forms varied considerably, but the general tendency was to write *v* initially and *u* in other positions, regardless of phonetic considerations, e.g. *vnder, vpon, vse* but *cure, full, huge*, and *vain, vice, vile* but *saue, euer, giuen*. For the sake of clearness, however, *v* was frequently preferred to *u*, especially in conjunction with *n* and *m*, as in *tvne, rovnd, mvse*. (In Scottish MSS. intervocalic *u* with the value of *v* is much rarer than in English, its place being largely taken by *f, ff, v* or *w*.) The early printers followed the common usage with regard to *u* and *v* in small letters; in capitals they employed only one symbol, viz. 𝖀 in black letter, and V in Roman. During the sixteenth century, however, continental printers began to distinguish between *u* and *v*, using the former as a vowel and the latter as a consonant. The distinction is found in Italian printing as early as 1524, but its general introduction dates from 1559–60, when it was employed in the *Grammatica* of Ramus; apparently the innovation was due to the printer rather than to the author. In English there were several attempts to introduce the distinction before 1600; after 1600 it rapidly became more common, and had come to be general by 1630. In capitals, however, V for some time continued to serve in the old double function, although U had been introduced in the work of Ramus. This was subsequently adopted and remained the usual form for the capital vowel until the close of the 17th century, after which it rapidly gave way to U, a form which is employed, though at first sparingly, from at least 1625. (In italic type the vowel was *V*, the consonant *V*.) From about 1700 the regular forms have been U u for the vowel, and V v for the consonant.

One result of the long-continued confusion of *u* and *v* was that in dictionaries, indexes, etc., words beginning with the vowel and with the consonant were combined in one list, *va-* being followed by *vb-* (i.e. *ub-*), *ve-* by *vf-*, etc. This practice was very commonly continued even after the two letters had been distinguished, and in English dictionaries remained as late as Todd's edition of Johnson (1818) and Richardson's dictionary (1837). When the two letters were separated, *v-* was sometimes placed before *u-*; a late example of this occurs in Jodrell's dictionary (1820). The modern arrangement, by which *u-* precedes *v-*, is found from at least the early part of the 18th cent., and has been usual in English dictionaries from that of Webster (1828) onwards.

In OE. the vowel-sounds denoted by *u* were those of Latin *u*, short and long, in the former case corresponding to that of mod.E. *pull, bush*, in the latter to that of *rude, brute*. In ME. the short *u* in native words partly retained its own sound, and was partly altered by lengthening or other phonetic changes; in some words the sound remained while the spelling was altered, as in *wolf* (OE. *wulf*), *woll* (OE. *wull*). The long *u* also retained its sound (unless when shortened before certain consonants), but was denoted by the new symbol *ou* derived from French spelling. Short and long *u* also freely occurred in words of French and Latin origin, but differed in quality from those of the native words, having the value of *ü, ǖ*; in the case of *ū* the difference continued to be marked, and the resultant sounds are now quite distinct. Under the influence of these forms southern ME. scribes substituted *u* for OE. *y, ý* (which had expressed the sounds *ü, ǖ*), writing *cun, cuðen*, etc., for OE. *cyn, cýðan*, which in midland and northern dialects became *kin, kithe*.

In mod.E. the short *u* of OE. (apart from changes due to lengthening, etc.) has normally become (ʌ) (written *u* or *o*), as *dumb, sun, thus* = OE. *dumb, sunne, þus*, or *some, love* = OE. *sum, lufu*. This change apparently had not proceeded far enough to be clearly noticeable until the middle of the 17th century, and was probably not generally completed until the beginning of the 18th. Over all the north of England, however, and a large part of the midlands, the original sound of *u* remains in words of this class, and even in standard English it is preserved in a few instances after labial consonants, as in *bull, full, pull, bush, put*. Short *u* also has this sound in some common words not of native origin (mostly with labial initials), as *bushel, butcher, pudding, pulpit, push, sugar*. The OE. *ū* (ME. *ou*) has normally become the diphthong (aʊ), written *ou* or *ow*, as in *thou, town* = OE. *þú, tún*, but in a few instances has been shortened, as in *plum, thumb*. The ME. *ū* from French or Latin, on the other hand, has become the diphthong (juː, jʊə), written *u, ue*, or *u-e*, as in *huge, mute, future, cure*, with reduction to (uː, ʊə) after *s* (= ʃ, ʒ), *j*, and *r*, as in *sure, jury, brute, rule*, optionally after *l*, as in *lute, lure*, and more widely in American usage. This mode of spelling has also been extended to some native words which originally had a diphthong, and would normally be written with *ew*, as *hue, rue, true, truth* (compared with *new, grew, strew*). The same sounds (juː, uː) are also represented by *ui* in a few words, as *nuisance, bruise, fruit*.

In combination with other vowels *u* is employed in the groups *au* (ɔː), *eu* (juː), *ou* (with varying value, as in *foul, soul, four, young, route*), *ue* and *ui* (see above). It is silent after *g* in many words, as *guard, guide, plague*, and in final *-que*, as masque, grotesque. It has the value of *w* after *q* in other positions, and in various words after *g* and *s*, as *queen, quick, inquest; guano, iguana, anguish; suave, persuade*, etc.

The name of the letter down to the 16th century was *u*, pronounced like the long *u* of French or Latin origin, and consequently undergoing the same change to (juː) which took place in ordinary words. The completion of the change is indicated by the use of the letter (*u* or *v*) to represent the personal pronoun *you* in such passages as Shaks. *L.L.L.* v. i. 60 and Dekker and Webster *Westward Hoe* II. i. (Cf. IOU.) In Scotland the name (u) was locally in use as late as the 19th century.

I. 1. a. Illustrations of the use of the letter or of its name.

a. *c* **1000** ÆLFRIC *Gram.* ii. (Z.) 6, *h* and *k* ȝeendiað on *a* æfter rihte, *q* ȝeendað on *u*. *Ibid.* xxxi. (Z.) 197 *Mortuus sum* on twam uum, swaswa nan oðer. **1530** PALSGR. 7 *U*, in the frenche tong, where so ever he is a vowel by hym-selfe, shall be sownded like as we sownde *ew*. **1588** SHAKS. *L.L.L.* v. i. 60 *Peda.* I will repeat them: a e i. *Pag.* The Sheepe, the other two concludes it o u. **1668** O. PRICE *Eng. Orthogr.* 29 The u is two fold. 1. Short, as in but, must, burst. 2. Long, as in lute, muse, refuse, as if it were the compound of iw. **1727** SWIFT *Misc. in Verse* Wks. 1841 I. 783/1 And Q maintain'd 'twas but his due Still to keep company with U. **1768** BOSWELL *Corsica* Pref. p. xviii, Leaving out..u in the last syllable of words which used to end in our. **1843** *Penny Cycl.* XXV. 484/1 U is at one extremity of the series of vowel sounds, lying next to the vowel *o*. **1867** A. J. ELLIS *E.E. Pronunc.* I. iii. 136 Many words now spelled with *u* were written with *ew* in the XVIth century. **1888** JACOBI *Printers' Vocab.*, U is the nineteenth signature of the printer's alphabet.

β. **1526** *Pilgr. Perf.* (W. de W. 1531) 291 He reciteth an example of one Masseus a frere,..the whiche in suche ioye or iubile coude speke nothyng but .v.v.v. *c* **1532** DU WES *Introd. Fr.* in Palsgr. 899 Ye shal pronounce..*v* after the Skottes, as in this worde *gud*. **1611** COTGR. *Brief Direct.* I *V*, is sounded as if you would whistle it out, as in the word, a Lute. **1616** BULLOKAR, *Orthographie*, the art of writing words truely; as sonne of man, with an O: sunne that shineth, with the vowell v. **1710** SHAFTESB. *Charac.* I. III. III. i. 288 The vowel *O* was form'd by an orbicular Disposition of the Mouth;..The Vowel *V* by a parallel Protrusion of the Lips.

b. = YOU *pron.*, esp. in U.S. commercial and Black use. ***U-Haul*** (U.S. proprietary name for) a small rented truck or a trailer. See also IOU.

1840 SIR N. C. TINDAL in Manning and Granger *Reports* I. 48 There was no one but the plaintiff to whom the 'U' in the document [an IOU] could be applied. **1862** HARDY *Let.* 3 Nov. (1978) I. 2, I wish you wd tell me how u.r. when u. write. **1923** *Dialect Notes* V. 231 Call Tel-U-Where for our nearest distributor... Fits-U Eyeglasses. U All Kno After Dinner Mints. Uneeda Biscuit. **1924**, etc. [see PUT-YOU-UP]. **1929** *Amer. Speech* V. 24 U-Bet-U It's Good Candy. *Ibid.*, U Drive It (cars for hire),..Shine While U Wait, Hats Cleaned While U Wait,..Motor Boats to Rent—U Drive,.. Did U Eat? (card in window of restaurant). **1951** *Washington Yellow Pages Classified Telephone Directory* (Chesapeake & Potomac Telephone Co.) Nov. 846/3 Rent a 'U-Haul Co.' trailer. You can rent here and leave in other major cities. **1963** *Official Gaz.* (U.S. Patent Office) 26 Feb. TM 154/2 Arcoa Inc., Portland, Oreg... *U-Haul*. For Rental of Trucks and Automobile Freight Trailers. First use Oct. 15, 1945. **1970** S. SANCHEZ in S. Henderson *Understanding New Black Poetry* (1973) 275 U blew away our passsst. **1971** *Black World* June 48 That scag Reefers Wine That send u spinnen into witeness. **1972** *Guardian* 11 July 10/6 The.. catalogue essay..is a masterpiece of myth-making, art history while-u-wait. **1974** R. M. PIRSIG *Zen & Art of Motorcycle Maintenance* I. iv. 48 It would probably be normal about this time to wonder what sort of U-Haul trailer all this is in. **1976** *Billings* (Montana) *Gaz.* 27 June 2-D/6 Roberts lost his gas station and is residing in a U-Haul propped on cinder blocks. **1980** 'D. SHANNON' *Felony File* viii. 193, I had the hell of a time getting hold of a U-Haul truck. **1981** M. C. SMITH *Gorky Park* III. iv. 356 Painted everywhere were signs: NO TRESPASSING THIS MEANS U and BEWARE OF DOGS.

c. *attrib.*, as ***u-sound***, ***-vowel***.

1852 *Proc. Philol. Soc.* V. 198 The long vowel expressed by the diphthong *ou* is weakened, but not to the extinction of the *u* sound. **1886** *Encycl. Brit.* XXI. 272/1 Original root-syllables contained no simple *i-* and *u-*vowels, except as the second element of..diphthongs. **1888** *Ibid.* XXIII. 715/2 At the same time begins the corruption of *u* to the (so-called) *ŭ* sound in 'but,' 'shut', &c.; this is not a *u* sound at all.

2. a. Used with reference to the shape of the (capital) letter, esp. *attrib.* or *Comb.*, as ***U-like*** adj., ***U-shape***. ***U-shaped*** adj.: *spec.* designating or pertaining to a valley having such a cross-section, esp. as a result of glacial erosion.

1822–7 GOOD *Study Med.* (1829) I. 493 A minute semi-lunar bone, which, from its resemblance to the Greek letter *υ* or u-psilon, is called the hyoid or u-like bone. **1842** PARNELL *Chem. Anal.* (1845) 457 The water in the bottle is withdrawn, air entering through the U-shaped tube at the same time. **1857** W. K. LOFTUS *Trav. & Res. Chaldæa & Susiana* xxi. 270 Three mud bricks were laid down in the form of the capital letter U. **1872** COUES *N. Amer. Birds* 234 Below, the spots fewer, brown, U-shaped. **1875** BENNETT & DYER tr. *Sachs's Bot.* 88 The mother-cells are so developed that from the young..epidermis-cell, a small piece is cut out on one side by a wall bent in a U-shape. **1894** *Jrnl. Geol.* II. 350 Glacial cañons are..U shaped rather than V shaped in cross-profile. **1909** *Bull. Geol. Soc. Amer.* XX. 409 (*heading*) Striations and U-shaped valleys produced by other than glacial action. **1970** R. J. SMALL *Study of Landforms* xi. 367 Virtually all U-shaped valleys in glaciated areas have been produced by the glacial modification of pre-existing river valleys.

b. *attrib.*, in the sense 'shaped like the letter U', as ***U-bend***, ***bolt***, ***cross profile***, ***-frame***, ***-magnet***, ***piece***, ***plate***, ***-rail***, ***-section*** (hence ***-sectioned*** adj.), ***-tube***, ***-turn*** (also *fig.* and as *v. intr.* and *trans.*), ***-valley*** (see prec. sense).

1797 J. CURR *Coal Viewer* 63 The strength of the U plates must be the same as the spear plates. **1819** M. EDGEWORTH *Let.* 4 Mar. (1971) 177 Excellent lecture room well lighted with *gas* spouting from U tubes at the bottom of the gallery. **1850** *Athenæum* 31 Aug. 922/2 By Arrangements of Coloured Liquids in a U Tube. **1868** *Rep. to Govt. U.S. Munitions War* 273 Iron rolled in the fashion of the ordinary U-rail for railroads. **1878** ABNEY *Photogr.* 289 A mirror..is suspended on two axes, xx, working a U-piece, ss. **1884** KNIGHT *Dict. Mech.* Suppl. 911/1 *U bolt*, a clevis for the attachment of axles, rods, etc., in machinery and vehicles. **1884** W. J. MCGEE in *Proc. Amer. Assoc. Adv. Sci.* XXXII. 238 The effect of temporary occupancy of a typical water-cut cañon by glacier ice will be to..change the original V to a U cross profile. **1888** *Scribner's Mag.* Aug. 177/2 Immediately below the bend of the U-magnet are the commutator segments. **1909** WEBSTER, *U section*, or *U-section*. **1928** BLUNDEN *Undertones of War* viii. 80 A support line was being made, and very nice and proper it looked.. with its clean U-frames..and symmetrical wire anchorages. **1937** *Sun* (Baltimore) 27 July 6/3 He will enforce new ordinances barring U turns in the public square and regulating parking. **1947** AUDEN *Age of Anxiety* (1948) iii.

62 Let down From U-valleys like yarn, Waterfalls.. Quietly encourage me on. **1950** 'S. RANSOME' *Deadly Miss Ashley* xi. 145 The driver U-turned into the wake of the police car. **1954** 'N. BLAKE' *Whisper in Gloom* xvi. 232 The armoured car..made a sudden sweeping u-turn. **1958** R. STOUT *Champagne for One* vii. 82, I do the driving, and I wanted one [*sc.* a car] I could U-turn when the occasion arose. **1959** *Sunday Express* 17 May 6/1 His wife offered him a cup of tea. .. He U-turned again. **1959** *Times* 30 Sept. 13/6 (Advt.), We don't care *what* you call us so long as you *do* call us when you are in need of cold drawn precision tubes... Not to mention..'U' bends. **1961** WEBSTER, *U-turn*.., something held to resemble a U-turn (as a reversal of policy) < stated that the Administration is making an economic *U-turn*—T. R. Ybarra >. **1963** A. ROSS *Australia 63* ii. 49 At weekends motor boats churn up the water and skiers make U-turns past the koala farm. **1969** E. H. PINTO *Treen* 26 Early folding umbrellas were heavy and clumsy... The most important patents were that of Henry Holland..and that of Samuel Fox & Co. of Stockbridge, Sheffield, for the lighter U-section steel rib in 1852. **1969** *Jane's Freight Containers 1968–69* 578/1 The Conjack is a U-frame container lifter and transporter. **1972** A. ROTH *Heath & Heathmen* i. 16 One of the things which surprised even close observers was the ease with which Heath made a complete U-turn between his first rightwing, or Mark I phase of 1970–1, and his second, leftwing or Mark II phase of 1971–2. **1974** 'A. GARVE' *File on Lester* xx. 93 His wife had once lost a ring down a wash basin waste pipe and it had stuck in a U-bend. **1974** H. MACINNES *Climb to Lost World* ix. 132 Don was carrying up more climbing gear, pitons and bongs—large U-sectioned pieces of alloy or steel..which, when hammered into cracks as climbing aids, emit a resounding 'bong-bong'. **1975** J. G. EVANS *Environment Early Man Brit. Isles* iii. 69 We cannot see..the U-valleys of Lakeland with their sheer rock walls ..without feeling the drama and immediacy of the Pleistocene ice. **1977** *Western Morning News* 30 Aug. 2/3 Reg. Cann, F.S.V.A., will sell by Auction,..steel U-sections. **1981** R. LEWIS *Seek for Justice* iii. 81 The car ahead slowed, then turned in a wide U-turn.

c. Something shaped like the letter U.

1873 J. H. BEADLE *Undevel. West* xxv. 521 Four miles from Wingate the valley makes a great U to the north-ward. **1897** *Allbutt's Syst. Med.* III. 814 The apex of the V or the bend of the U may become adherent to the mesentery.

d. = *U-turn*, sense 2 b above.

1971 'G. BLACK' *Time for Pirates* iv. 80, I was gambling on the lane doing a U and coming down again beyond the building. **1973** J. GORES *Final Notice* xv. 95 Ballard went by, U-ed, came back into the parking area.

3. Used to denote serial order.

Also employed as a symbol for purposes of calculation in quaternions, hydrodynamics, the theory of heat, etc.

1900 *Dundee Advertiser* 14 Mar. 5 U Battery, which occupied a position to the north of the Boer centre, shelled the ridge thoroughly.

4. Symbolic uses: *U* is a coefficient representing the rate at which heat is lost through a structure, in B.Th.U. per hour per square foot per degree difference in temperature between the two sides (or the metric equivalent). Also *U factor*, *value*.

1928 *Jrnl. Amer. Soc. Heating & Ventilating Engineers* XXXIV. 63 Let U = coefficient of heat transmission. **1958** *Times Rev. Industry* Sept. 24/1 To specify the standard the Ministry [of Power] has approved the U value of thermal transmittance coefficient. **1975** R. H. WARING *All about Home Heating* v. 40 For the same actual *thickness* of brick, an 11 inch cavity wall has a U factor of about 0·33, compared with a value of 0·43 for a solid brick wall. **1982** *New Scientist* 10 June 692/3 All the external walls are insulated... This should cut the 'U' value from 1·7 to 0·5.

II. 5. a. Abbreviations. (All abbreviations given here with a full stop are frequently used without it; those without can also be used with.) ***u*** (Physics) [f. G. *ungerade* odd], used to designate functions, esp. wave functions, which change sign on inversion through the origin (cf. ODD *a.* 5), and atomic states, etc., represented by such functions; U, universal, designating (a certificate given to) films suitable for exhibition to audiences of all age-groups; also *ellipt.* and *fig.*; ***u*** (Physics), up, a quark flavour; U, uranium; also with following or preceding numeral indicating the mass number of the isotope symbolized; **U.A.B.**, Unemployment Assistance Board; **U.A.E.**, United Arab Emirates; **U.A.P.**, United Australia Party; **U.A.R.**, United Arab Republic; **U.A.W.(A.)** (*U.S.*), United Automobile Workers (of America); **UB40** [*UB* = unemployment benefit; the name was changed from UI40 (= unemployment insurance) in the early 1970s], (the index number of) a card issued to a claimant for unemployment benefit in the UK; also *transf.*, an unemployed person; **U.C.**, upcast shaft; **UCCA** (ˈʌkə), Universities Central Council on Admissions; **U.C.D.**, University College, Dublin; **U.C.L.**, University College London; **U.C.L.A.**, University of California at Los Angeles., **U.D.A.**, Ulster Defence Association; **U.D.C.**, universal decimal classification; **U.D.C.**, Urban District Council; **U.D.I.**, unilateral declaration of independence (orig. of Rhodesia from the U.K.); **UDM**, Union of Democratic Mineworkers; **UDN** (*Vet. Sci.*), ulcerative dermal necrosis, a disease of fish; **U.D.R.**, Ulster Defence Regiment; **U.D.S.R.** [F. *Union Démocratique et Socialiste de la Résistance*], Democratic and Socialist Union of the Resistance, a left-wing French party under the Fourth Republic; **UEFA** (juːˈeɪfə), Union of European Football Associations; **U.F.**, United Free (Church, of Scotland); also, a member of this; **U.F.F.**, Ulster Freedom Fighters; **U.G.C.**, University Grants Committee; **UHF, uhf**, ultra-high frequency; **UHT**, ultra heat treated; ultra-high temperature; **U.I.L.**, United Irish League; **UJ**, universal joint; **U.K.**, United Kingdom; **U.K.A.E.A.**, United Kingdom Atomic Energy Authority; **ULCC**, ultra-large crude carrier; **ULMS**, underwater long-range missile system; **UMNO, Umno** (ˈʌmnəʊ), United Malay(s) (*later* Malaysia) National Organization; **U.N.**, United Nations; **UNCTAD, Unctad** (ˈʌŋktæd), United Nations Conference on Trade and Development; **UNDP**, United Nations Development Programme; **U.N.E.F.**, United Nations Emergency Force; **UNEP**, United Nations Environment Programme; **UNESCO, Unesco** (juːˈnɛskəʊ), United Nations Educational, Scientific, and Cultural Organization; **UNHCR**, United Nations High Commissioner for Refugees; **U.N.I.A.** (*U.S.*), Universal Negro Improvement Association; **UNICEF, Unicef** (ˈjuːnɪsɛf), United Nations International Children's Emergency Fund (now officially the United Nations Children's Fund); **UNIDO**, United Nations Industrial Development Organization; **UNIDROIT, Unidroit** [F. *Institut international pour l'unification du droit privé*], International Institute for the Unification of Private Law; **UNIP, Unip** (ˈjuːnɪp), United National Independence Party (of Zambia); **UNITA, Unita** (juːˈniːtə) [Pg. *União Nacional por Independência Total de Angola*], National Union for the Total Independence of Angola; **UNO, Uno** (ˈjuːnəʊ), United Nations Organization; **U.N.P.**, United National Party (of Sri Lanka (Ceylon)); **UNREF, Unref** (ˈʌnrɛf), United Nations Refugee Emergency Fund; **UNRRA, Unrra** (ˈʌnrə), United Nations Relief and Rehabilitation Administration; **UNRWA (PRNE)**, United Nations Relief and Works Agency (*orig.* for Palestine Refugees in the Near East); **U.P.**, United Party (*spec.* of South Africa); **U.P.**, United Presbyterian; **U.P.**, United Press; **U.P.**, United Provinces (of Agra and Oudh, India), now, Uttar Pradesh; **U.P.C.**, Uganda People's Congress; **UPC**, universal product code; **U.P.I.**, United Press International; **U.P.N.I.**, Unionist Party of Northern Ireland; **U.S.**, **U.S.A.**, United States (of America); **u/s, U/S, U.S., u.s.**, unserviceable; **U.S.A.A.F.**, United States Army Air Forces; **U.S.A.F.**, United States Air Force; **U.S.C.**, Ulster Special Constabulary; **U.S.I.A.**, United States Information Agency; **USM**, unlisted securities market; **U.S.N.**, United States Navy; **U.S.O.** (*U.S.*), United Service Organization; **U.S. of A.** (*colloq.*), United States of America; **U.S.P.**, United States Pharmacopœia; **U.S.S.**, United States Ship; **U.S.S.R.**, Union of Soviet Socialist Republics (Russ. *Soyuz sovetskikh sotsialisticheskikh respublik*); **U.T.**, Universal Time; **U.U.U.C.**, United Ulster Unionist Council; **U.V.**, ultraviolet; **U.V.F.**, Ulster Volunteer Force; **U.W.C.** Ulster Workers' Council; **UXB**, unexploded bomb. See also UFO.

1930, **1962** **u* (= *ungerade*) [see g s.v. G III. f]. **1965** J. N. MURRELL et al. *Valence Theory* x. 143 Only if there is an odd number of electrons in *u* orbitals can a state of *u* symmetry (e.g. $He_2{}^+$) exist. **1922** *Times* 11 Mar. 8/2 An attempt may be made to secure a rather broader interpretation of the division of films into '*U' and 'A' classes. The former are passed for universal exhibition... The 'U' certificate is very difficult to obtain. **1929** M. ALLINGHAM *Mystery Mile* xxiv. 224 They collected the evidence: Datchett collected the blackmail. Not a certificate 'U' production. **1935** [see A, adult s.v. A III]. **1958** *Spectator* 15 Aug. 221/3 *A Cry from the Streets* (..'U' certificate) is about children. **1968** *Guardian* 26 Sept. 15/2 About the only British medium-budget U showing in London's West End is 'Yellow Submarine'. **1972** D. BLOODWORTH *Any Number can Play* xviii. 182 This particular prophecy was to whom it may concern. U-certificate. Kitay, Americans, British, it didn't matter. **1977** *Punch* 21 Jan. 80 'Hell!' cried the priest. 'What kind of penitent *are* you? Did you at least make love to your wife, see a U film, buy *Reader's Digest?*' 'No,' said the confessant, 'none of those.' **1964**, etc. **u* (Particle Physics) [see S 15]. **1975** *Sci. Amer.* Oct. 43/1 Just two of the quarks, the *u* and the *d*, suffice to explain the structure of all the hadrons encountered in ordinary matter. **1982** *McGraw-Hill Yearbk. Sci. & Technol.* 386/1 Neutron decay corresponds to a transition $d \rightarrow u$ and Λ° decay to a transition $s \rightarrow u$. **1844** FOWNES *Man. Chem.* 290 The equivalent of uranium is 60·. Its symbol is *U. **1938** R. W. LAWSON tr. *Hevesy & Paneth's Man. Radioactivity* (ed. 2) xxiii. 221 Uranium is a mixture of three isotopes, uranium I (^{238}U), uranium II (^{234}U), and ^{235}U. **1940** *Manch. Guardian Weekly* 10 May 367 The discovery of a natural substance whose chief characteristic is the release of great energy is announced... It is known as U-235. **1968** *Listener* 22 Aug. 230/3 But an analysis of the radioactive fallout associated with the bombs showed that they were made from U235 and not plutonium as had generally been expected. **1979** A. G. MADDOCK in Harbottle & Maddock *Chem. Effects Nucl. Transformations in Inorg. Systems* xxi. 388 In uranyl sulphate solution most of the ^{239}U appears as uranyl ion. **1937** 'G. ORWELL' *Road to Wigan Pier* v. 77 When a man's stamps are exhausted..he receives twenty-six weeks' 'transitional benefit' from the *U.A.B. (Unemployment Assistance Board). **1972** *Whitaker's Almanack 1973* 958/1 The United Arab Emirates (formerly the Trucial States) is composed of seven Emirates... The approximate area of the *U.A.E. is 32,000 square miles. **1979** *Financial Times* 12 Jan. 3/4 The Iranian community based on the UAE, which, in the northern Emirate of Dubai, runs into thousands. **1936** *Age* (Melbourne) 4 May 8/5 The attitude likely to be adopted by the full-blooded protectionist members of the *U.A.P. towards the Government's proposal for abolition of duty on cement from Great Britain. **1964** J. JUPP *Austral. Party Politics* vi. 130 The U.A.P. leader, R. G. Menzies, called a conference at Canberra in October 1944. **1958** *Spectator* 20 June 793/1 There is no more reason to think that they [*sc.* the Lebanese] want to join the *UAR in the immediate future than there is that the UAR wants them to join it. **1966** M. WOODHOUSE *Tree Frog* xxv. 190 The U.A.R. were supposed to be developing a delta-wing of their own. **1981** *Economist* 24 Jan. 43/1 In 1963, when a second attempt was made at a UAR, this time a tripartite one, the Syrians and Iraqis spent weeks in Cairo arguing against Nasser's federal ideas. **1946** W. WEINSTONE *Case against David Dubinsky* iv. 35 They now have in Walter P. Reuther and the presidency of the *U.A.W. a strong base from which to operate more effectively. **1970** *Toronto Daily Star* 24 Sept. 35/1 There is some possibility that the UAW strike at General Motors will reduce the number of UAW delegates. **1936** *Business Week* 5 Dec. 16/2 The *U.A.W.A. has a remarkable story to tell of its growth. **1983** *Time Out* 8 Sept. 75/4 Half price tickets to *UB40s and OAPs on Wednesdays. **1983** *Responsibilities of Claimants while Unemployed* (Dept. Employment Leaflet UBL18) 3 When you start work or a training course complete and return your attendance card (UB40) and your P45 will be sent to you. **1986** *Capital Gay* 8 Aug. 9/3 Eight introductions will cost £95, although there is a reduction for students and holders of UB40s. **1883** GRESLEY *Gloss. Coal-M.* 266 *U.C., upcast shaft. **1963** F. D. FAWCETT *Cycl. Initials & Abbrev.* 149/1 **UCCA*, Universities Central Council for Admissions. **1971** *Where* Dec. 357/3 The particular sections on the UCCA form which need careful filling in. **1976** *Times Higher Educ. Suppl.* 6 Aug. 8/2 A Nigerian universities joint matriculation scheme, which includes a combined school leaving and university entrance examination, and a form of UCCA selection. **1955** R. J. SCHWARTZ *Compl. Dict. Abbrev.* 179/2 **UCD*, University College, Dublin. **1962** B. INGLIS *West Briton* vii. 123 The 'National', as U.C.D. was known in Trinity. **1979** U.C.D. [see *T.C.D.* s.v. T 6 a]. *a* **1912** W. T. ROGERS *Dict. Abbrev.* (1913) 192/2 **U.C.L.*,..University College, London. **1979** W. H. CANAWAY *Solid Gold Buddha* xiv. 101 Das had a first class degree in law..and had studied full-time for it at UCL. **1941** B. SCHULBERG *What makes Sammy Run?* viii. 185 We drove past Westwood Village, the home of *UCLA..Hollywood's version of campus life. **1977** H. FAST *Immigrants* iv. 290 He asked how far it was to the U.C.L.A. campus at Melrose and Vermont. **1972** *Times* 15 May 2/6 One *UDA man said today [etc.]. **1978** D. MURPHY *Place Apart* vii. 134 The main loyalist paramilitary force, the UDA, is not illegal. **1935** *ASLIB Information* Dec. 4/2 (*heading*) English edition of the *U.D.C. **1965** *Rev. Internat. Documentation* XXXII. 19/1 For many years the problems of indexing and retrieving information have involved the use of tree-structured classification schemes such as the UDC system. **1905** F. H. COLLINS *Author & Printer* 383/1 **U.D.C.*, Urban District Council. *a* **1974** R. CROSSMAN *Diaries* (1977) III. 576 There were the C.C.A., the A.M.C., the London boroughs, the G.L.C., the U.D.C.s and R.D.C.s. **1965** *Economist* 8 May 634/1 They shrug off..the threat of Britain imposing sanctions if Mr Ian Smith's government made a unilateral declaration of independence ('*UDI'). **1966** *Listener* 17 Feb. 251/3 The British often 'lean over backwards' in their determination to do justice to George Washington and the other U.D.I. heroes. **1972** A. PRICE *Col. Butler's Wolf* ix. 99 He lived in Rhodesia...left shortly after UDI. **1980** *Times* 30 July 13/2 Both he and his wife Avis are from Yorkshire —not quite the kind that think Yorkshire should declare UDI. **1985** *Times* 3 Aug. 34/6 The leaders of the Fledgling *UDM are confident that the coal board..will extend recognition to other coalfields. **1986** *Financial Times* 12 Dec. I. 14 The offer, which would apply to pits where the UDM is the majority union, would increase basic grade rates. **1968** CARBERY & STRICKLAND in *Irish Veterinary Jrnl.* XXII. 171/2 This paper describes the symptoms, gross and microscopic lesions, epizootiology and bacteriology of *UDN. **1972** *Trout & Salmon* Feb. 9/1 The effects on spawning stocks of UDN..are dangers just as significant. **1969** *Times* 20 Nov. 5/5 The Bill provided the necessary legal framework for the establishment of the *U.D.R. **1978** D. MURPHY *Place Apart* iii. 53 No UDR, no British army patrols, nothing to flaw the impression of a traditional rural community. **1945** *Times* 25 Oct. 3/3 Joint Socialist and *U.D.S.R. (*Union Democratique et Socialiste de la Résistance*) lists, 961, 704. **1965** F. R. WILLIS *France, Germany, & New Europe* vi. 138 The Pleven cabinet, a coalition of the four most 'European' parties in the Assembly (Socialists, MRP, Radicals and UDSR), hoped in this way to avoid a national German army and advance European integration at the same time. **1963** I. WILKES *British Initials & Abbrev.* 102/2 **UEFA*, Union of European Football Associations, P.O. Box 16, Berne, 15, Switzerland. **1972** *Rothman's Football Yearbk. 1972–73* 808 Last season, the U.E.F.A. took over the running of this colourful competition, re-named it the U.E.F.A. Cup and clearly stated that only clubs which finished high in their respective domestic leagues will be accepted. **1982** *Daily Tel.* 23 Dec. 16/1 UEFA have joined FIFA in their condemnation of the referee clampdown. **1913** *Northern Whig* 3 Dec. 8/5 The Rev. John C. Ingles, minister of the North *U.F. Church, Crieff. **1922** 'R. WEST' *Judge* I. i. 17 The snatching of the Church funds from the U.F.'s by the

Wee Frees. **1973** *Times* 13 Nov. 2/6 The *U.F.F...have claimed responsibility for at least 10 murders. **1947** *Universities Q.* Aug. 326 There is..another field of major importance which the *UGC is not touching; the whole issue of the aims and methods of university teaching. **1979** *Jrnl. R. Soc. Arts* Oct. 707/2 In 1964..the U.G.C. lost its distinctive rôle of a body advising the Treasury directly. **1937** *RCA Rev.* II. 30 For low-power *u-h-f transmitters and receivers, special tubes having low internal capacities.. are available. **1939** *Amat. Radio Handbk.* 161/1 The devices of Fig. 16 are satisfactory for matching U.H.F. aerials to open wire lines. **1955** *Times* 27 July 9/6 Its task is confused by the haphazard growth of early v.h.f. (very high frequency) stations and the consequent need to resort to the u.h.f. (ultra-high frequency) band for many of the new licences. **1978** *Jrnl. R. Soc. Arts* CXXVI. 437/1 Chief Officer Rowe..remained with the lifeboats and maintained communication with the rescue vessels using portable UHF radio. **1968** *Sunday Truth* (Brisbane) 27 Oct. 32/3 Local sale of *UHT milk. **1981** *Economist* 24 Jan. 49/3 The UHT process—sterilisation by heating to 132 degrees centigrade —produces milk that keeps for months without refrigeration, but tastes peculiar. **1983** *Times* 7 Feb. 10/2 A repellent whitish fluid..known as ultra heat treated (UHT) milk. [**1963** J. F. Hogerton *Atomic Energy Handbk.* 569/1 (*heading*) Ultra high-temperature reactor experiment (UHTREX).] **1968** E. Pugh *Dict. Acronyms & Abbrev.* 174 **UHT*, ultra high temperature. **1901** *Notes from Ireland* 1 Dec. Suppl., A *U.I.L. meeting in Longhrea. **1976** J. V. O'Brien *William O'Brien* viii. 194 UIL circles in America. **1970** K. Ball *Fiat 600, 600D Autobook* 165/2 *UJ Universal joint. A coupling between shafts which permits angular movement. **1892** *Daily News* 27 Oct. 7/4 The supplies at sea for *U.K. have decreased 32,000 quarters on the week... Supplies at sea for U.K. have further slightly decreased. **1959** *Times Rev. Industry* Aug. 17/1 *U.K.A.E.A. research section. **1983** *Listener* 24 Nov. 5/2 In 1955 a new quango, the UKAEA, was created from various research and production units of the Ministry of Supply. **1973** *Sunday Post-Herald* (Hong Kong) 20 May (Business sect.) 5/3 The European yards..worry that their..share of new orders for VLCCs and *ULCCs will remain small. **1981** E. Corlett *Revolution Merchant Shipping* 26/1 The world was about to be presented with new initials, VLCC and ULCC—the very large and the ultra large crude carriers were at hand. **1970** B. Wedertz *Dict. Naval Abbrev.* 234/1 **ULMS*, Underwater Long-range Missile System. **1973** *New Scientist* 30 Aug. 483 The ULMS will have a greater range than either Polaris or Poseidon. **1946** *Malay Mail* 14 May 4/5 Delegates from the newly formed United Malays National Organization will..attend. A two-day conference..has just ended at which delegates from all over Malaya and Singapore passed and ratified a charter incorporating the *U.M.N.O., as the new organization will in future be known. **1979** *Straits Times* 27 Nov. I. 12/8 Umno Youth leader Haji Suhaimi bin Datuk Haji Kamaruddin. **1946** *N.Y. Times* 11 Apr. 1/6 If the *U.N. remained at Hunter or went to Lake Success, it would have to erect an auditorium. **1946** J. S. Huxley *Unesco* I. iii. 14 Other U.N. agencies such as the F.A.O. and the World Health Organisation. **1978** L. Heren *Growing up on The Times* iii. 84 The assassination of the UN mediator had frightened most Israelis. The UN had been the indispensable midwife at the birth of their country. **1964** *Newsweek* 6 Apr. 31 *UNCTAD..might very well lead to a major realignment of global power, with the world's poor nations in solid opposition to the rich. **1967** *Economist* 19 Aug. 670/1 Unctad, the United Nations body which tries to help the less developed countries. **1977** *Arab Times* 14 Dec. 6/6 A five-day session of an UNCTAD committee. **1966** *U.N. Monthly Chron.* Feb. 21/1 (*heading*) New Projects Approved by *UNDP Governing Council. **1956** *N.Y. Times* 29 Nov. 12/6 The United Nations Emergency Force has been in Egypt..two weeks... It may be..the *UNEF, in terms of potential effectiveness.., must be rated as equivalent to a substantially larger military body. **1964** *Ann. Reg. 1963* 141 Owing to the continued failure of a number of Member States to pay their assessed contributions to the costs of the U.N. Emergency Force in the Middle East (U.N.E.F.)..the financial situation remained serious. **1974** P. Gore-Booth *With Great Truth & Respect* 364 The Israelis had not helped their case by refusing to allow the UNEF to operate on their side of the frontier. **1973** *U.N. Monthly Chron.* Aug.-Sept. 84/1 The Council adopted..a resolution noting the report of the Governing Council of *UNEP on its first session. **1980** *Africa* Jan. 43/2 UNEP's plans for the Red Sea. **1946** J. S. Huxley (*title*) *UNESCO: its purpose and its philosophy. **1946** A. Huxley *Let.* 27 Oct. (1969) 551, I was delighted.. to learn that all goes well with you and the infant Unesco. **1948** *Hansard Commons* 11 Mar. 1504 Someone was being brought from U.N.E.S.C.O. in order to help formulate an education policy. **1955** *Times* 17 June 5/2 The Universal Copyright Convention, which has been promoted by Unesco, will at last come into force on September 16. **1983** *Whitaker's Almanack 1984* 964 (*heading*) United Nations Educational, Scientific and Cultural Organization (UNESCO). *Ibid.*, In most Member States National Commissions serve as a link with Unesco. **1953** *U.N. Yearbk. 1952* 492/2 The report of the United Nations High Commissioner for Refugees (*UNHCR)..dealt with the activities of the High Commissioner's Office. **1984** *Listener* 8 Mar. 12/2 The UNHCR includes Laotian and Kampuchean exiles in its total of 891,967 resettled up to the end of 1983. **1921** *Nation* (N.Y.) 28 Dec. 750/1 Any phenomenon among the colored population, like the *U.N.I.A., white persons at first..regard as a huge joke. **1977** *Western Political Q.* XXX. 171 Thus we arrive at an understanding of the enhanced emotionality/reduced intellectuality characteristic of groups like the UNIA. **1948** *U.N. Bull.* 1 Mar. 184/2 The word *UNICEF, pronounced 'Uni-sef', is now known far and wide in Europe. **1958** *Listener* 5 June 952/3 Danny Kaye's touching film..about the part played by Unicef in conquering disease among children all over the world. **1982** *Whitaker's Almanack 1983* 962/1 United Nations Children's Fund (UNICEF). **1967** *Ann. Rep. Sec. Gen.* [*U.N.*] *16 June 1966–15 June 1967* xi. 145/1 The General Assembly decided that the United Nations Industrial Development Organization (*UNIDO) should function as an autonomous organization. **1980** *Jrnl. R. Soc. Arts* June 440/2 At this moment, UNIDO III—the third conference of the UN International Development Organization—is in its final hours in Delhi. **1959** *Uniform Law Cases* (*UNIDROIT) p. iii, One of the activities collateral to the unification of law, which the International Institute for the Unification of Private Law (UNIDROIT) has taken over, has been the study of the most appropriate measures to ensure uniformity in the interpretation of texts of uniform law. **1974** A. Watson *Legal Transplants* xv. 91 The work of the legal committees of the Council of Europe and of Unidroit is regarded as important as an indication of European trends. **1959** *Central African Post* 26 Oct. 1 (*heading*) Chona's Congress merges with *U.N.I.P. **1961** *Times* 2 Nov. 9/2 Youth branches of Unip in the Western Province. **1977** *Times of Zambia* 7 Sept. 6/5, I see UNIP everywhere and I see it as one of the best organised parties in the world. **1967** *N.Y. Times* 17 Sept. I. 17/3 Two Angolan nationalist organizations, the Popular Movement for the Liberation of Angola and the *Unita, have been sending small guerrilla bands into eastern Angola from Zambia. **1972** J. Biggs-Davison *Africa—Hope Deferred* i. 9 U.N.I.T.A. of Angola and C.O.R.E.M.O. of Mozambique. **1978** *Guardian Weekly* 2 July 6 Secretary of State Cyrus Vance..defeated a move by President Carter's national security advisor, Zbigniew Brzezinski, proposing the covert sending of arms to UNITA guerrillas fighting in Angola against the Marxist Government of President Agostinho Neto. **1945** *Tuscaloosa* (Alabama) *News* 15 Nov. 4/4 The ideas range like this..let the United Nations Organization (*UNO) handle it [etc.]. **1946** H. H. Henson *Let.* 14 May (1950) 181 The degraded haggling of the international market to which the cosmic idealism of U.N.O. has now degenerated. **1953** P. Scott *Alien Sky* I. iii. 32 An official observer from Uno or one of those dreary organisations. *a* **1974** R. Crossman *Diaries* (1976) II. 353 The arrival of the U.N.O. troops who are there to police the peace settlement between the Greeks and Turks. **1946** *Ceylon Daily News* 9 Sept. 4/2 The speech of Mr. D. S. Senanayaka, the leader of the State Council, at a meeting of the Executive Committee of the United National Party..is..remarkable for its fairness and vigour... The leader delivered his speech under the auspices of the *U.N.P. **1979** *Round Table* Jan. 49 No defeat in the annals of Sri Lanka's volatile parliamentary history is quite as comprehensive as that suffered by the rivals of the United National Party (UNP) in July 1977. **1954** *U.N. Yearbk. 1953* 845/2 **UNREF*, United Nations Refugee Emergency Fund. **1959** *Economist* 17 Jan. 229/2 In Austria, where the UN has a much freer hand than in Germany, the Unref building schemes are progressing much faster than government projects. **1943** *Times* (Weekly ed.) 24 Nov. 4 *U.N.R.R.A. has already reached an agreement to share the cost by a levy of one per cent. on the national incomes of the contributing countries. **1943** *Times* 15 Dec. 5/6 The great success achieved by the United Nations Relief and Rehabilitation Administration (Unrra) conference. **1944** J. S. Huxley *On Living in Revolution* xiii. 139 UNRRA, the United Nations Relief and Rehabilitation Agency,..is preparing the vast stores we shall need to rush into Europe as soon as the 'cease fire' sounds—food and medical supplies, feeding-stuffs for the surviving livestock, seed and new breeding-stock. **1975** J. Cleary *Safe House* i. 23 The UNRRA parcels had began arriving from overseas. **1951** *U.N. Yearbk. 1950* 1014/3 **UNRWAPRNE*, United Nations Relief and Works Agency for Palestine Refugees in the Near East. **1955** *Times* 24 May 8/3 Some U.N.R.W.A. experts admit that the completion of the High Dam is necessary for the full realization of their scheme. **1943** *Cape Times* 29 July 4/7 The first election result to arrive at this office last evening was Major Piet van der Byl's at Bredasdorp—a smashing *U.P. victory. **1959** *Ann. Reg. 1958* 101 On 10 November, the detention of 43 members of the U.P. was ordered after government allegations of a plot to assassinate Dr. Kwame Nkrumah, Prime Minister. **1971** *Progress* (Cape Town) May 1/2 Cutting the U.P. majority in North Rand by 1688 votes..Progressive candidate John Wilding has shown a considerable swing to the Progressive Party. **1865** *Slang Dict.* 265 *U.P., United Presbyterian. Scotch clerical Slang. **1878** *Chambers's Encycl.* IX. 647/1 Protracted negotiations for union between the U.P. and Free Churches have been without result. **1915** *Oregon Daily Jrnl.* 13 Apr. 1/2 London, April 13.—(*U.P.)—French aviators dropped bombs upon Hamburg..yesterday. **1943** C. Hollingworth *German just behind Me* v. 84 The Ministry of Propaganda issued a statement from the Ministry of Foreign Affairs which denied the U.P. story entirely. **1960** R. St. John *Foreign Correspondent* x. 222 We were forty-eight hours ahead of UP. **1908** *Resolution on Administration Famine Relief in United Provinces of Agra & Oudh 1907 & 1908* ii. 18 (*table*) Statement showing percentage outturn of the autumn harvest in terms of normal yield on normal area... Total, *U.P. of Agra and Oudh. 39 31. **1919** *Indian Ann. Reg.* IV. 148 U.P. Provincial Conference. Special Session—11 Aug. 1918. **1947** G. Cunningham *Diary* in N. Mitchell *Sir George Cunningham* (1968) vii. 146 He has been in Kashmir (Uri front) for three-and-a-half-months with 200 of his 'fanatics' (mostly U.P. Muslims). **1963** *Listener* 21 Mar. 520/2 One would pass them [*sc.* Gurkhas] in the U.P. foothills. **1975** *Ibid.* 30 Oct. 558/3 Mrs Naidu, the famous poetess..was..Governor of the UP. **1961** *Times* 22 Mar. 10/6 The *U.P.C. has committed itself more emphatically to an East African Federation. **1980** *Economist* 9 Aug. 31/2 There are old grievances against the UPC. **1974** *McGraw-Hill Yearbk. Sci. & Technol.* 357/2 The Universal Product Code (*UPC) is coming to the general merchandise store, too. **1982** *Sci. Amer.* Sept. 119/1 UPC bars are the set of thick and thin lines now printed on essentially all prepared-food items. **1958** *N.Y. Times* 25 May 1/4 The United Press Associations and the International News Service announced yesterday they had merged into a new agency called United Press International... The new *U.P.I. agency announced that it would take over key I.N.S. employees. **1972** J. Belfrage in G. W. Turner *Good Austral. Eng.* vi. 103 You will find very likely that..the UPI stories, and various others taken from agency sources are written with less colour..than local stories written by Australians for Australians. **1975** *Times* 22 Apr. 2/8 The leaders of the three power-sharing parties, Alliance, SDLP and *UPNI. **1975** *Irish Times* 9 May 1/1 The standing orders committee—seven Loyalists, three S.D.L.P members, and one member from each from the Alliance and U.P.N.I. **1834** McCulloch *Dict. Commerce* (ed. 2) 843 American Tonnage. Entered into the *U.S... Departed from U.S. **1867** *Chambers's Encycl.* IX. 649/2 The U.S. are rich in mineral productions. **1901** *Daily Chron.* 12 Aug. 5/2 On Saturday we asked what language is U.S., which is announced as 'spoken' in the window of a City office. **1942** *Tee Emm* (Air Ministry) II. 84 If your helmet is *u/s, then your wireless mechanics have wasted their time. **1948** 'N. Shute' *No Highway* xii. 305 'What was the Machmeter showing?' 'I never look at that,' he said. 'It's no bloody good, that thing. Half the time it's U/S.' **1966** D. Francis *Flying Finish* v. 65 The de-icers were U.S. last week... It's O.K., I've checked them..since they were repaired. **1971** O. Norton *Corpse-Bird Cries* ii. 35 His brakes were u.s., I daresay. The usual story. **1978** M. Duffy *Housespy* v. 110 The device seems to have gone U.S. They're dodgy things because they're so small. **1943** *Times* 22 Dec. 4/5 The bombers, all of which returned safely, were escorted by *U.S.A.A.F., R.A.F. and Dominion fighters. **1973** M. Calvert *Slim* 55/1 (*caption*) Brigadier-General Old (USAAF). **1947** *Air Force Times* 23 Sept. 1/2 The *USAF is a reality! This first issue of Air Force Times.. coincides with the birth of the independent Air Force. **1955** *Times* 24 Aug. 6/4 It makes the project the exclusive property of the United States Air Force. Regular progress reports are being made to the U.S.A.F.'s air research and development command headquarters at Baltimore. **1977** *R.A.F. News* 11–24 May 3/5 The Deputy Chief of Staff Personnel USAF, paid an official visit. **1963** I. Wilkes *Brit. Initials & Abbrev.* 106/2 **USC*, Ulster Special Constabulary. **1973** J. Callaghan *House Divided* vii. 91 They said that the USC had been the victim of a propaganda campaign. **1982** M. Wallace *Brit. Govt. Northern Ireland* ii. 28 The disbanding of the U.S.C. **1953** *U.S. Congr. House Hearings Comm. Govt. Operations Reorganization Plans 7 & 8* 43 *USIA, which is United States Information Agency, will go through here [indicating the box marked 'State']. **1975** *New Yorker* 26 May 27/3 The Stanton panel, after working on the problem for over ten months and taking testimony from over a hundred witnesses, recommended that the cultural activities of the U.S.I.A...be combined with the cultural activities of the State Department. **1979**, etc. *USM [see unlisted *ppl. a.* 2 a]. **1863** *Rebellion Rec.* V. II. 177 All our fleet,..under Commodore Davis, *U.S.N.,.. was under way. *a* **1968** R. S. Churchill *Winston S. Churchill* (1969) II. Compan. I. 635 Rear Admiral Charles Davis, USN. **1974** L. Deighton *Spy Story* xviii. 189 We changed into U.S.N. khakis. **1941** *Christian Century* 30 Apr. 597/1 When on June 3 solicitation begins for $10,765,000 for the *U.S.O. the public will..know that another organization is in the field. The letters stand for 'United Service Organization'. **1966** *Sunday Times* (Colour Suppl.) 4 Dec. 73/4 GI Jargon *USO*, United Services Organisation, nearest equivalent of ENSA. **1973** *Black World* Apr. 90 A Moslem man..marries an Afro-American Catholic woman while on an extended visit to the *u.s. of a. **1982** A. Melville-Ross *Trigger* xxiv. 284 You'll be told..that won't be until you're back in the US of A under tight security wraps. **1909** *Cent. Dict.* Suppl. 1408/3, *U.S.P. **1946** F. Schneider *Qualitative Organic Microanalysis* vi. 171 This technique is based upon the original U.S.P. directions in that the concentrations of the solutions are the same. **1961** R. D. Baker *Essent. Path.* viii. 129 The absorption of some of the substances by the ventral area [of a rat] denuded of skin is sufficient to cause death; specifically, alcohol (95 per cent) causes acute alcoholism and solution of hydrogen peroxide (U.S.P. half strength) causes gaseous cardiac embolism. *a* **1912** W. T. Rogers *Dict. Abbrev.* (1913) 194/2 **U.S.S.*,..United States ship. **1957** 'N. Shute' *On Beach* i. 9 I'm posting you as liaison officer in the U.S.S. *Scorpion*. **1981** G. Markstein *Ultimate Issue* 17 The *USS Sharkfin* wasn't due to surface for another nine weeks. **1927** *19th Cent.* Nov. 653 The..execution of two Italian anarchists in America stirred up the human soul far more than the mass executions, mass tortures, mass deportations, that have been taking place almost daily in the *U.S.S.R. for ten painful years. **1959** E. H. Carr *Socialism in One Country* II. xx. 231 The year 1924 saw the constitution of the USSR in full operation on lines which were to remain substantially unchanged till 1936. **1982** *Whitaker's Almanack 1983* 961/2 There are five *permanent members* (China, France, U.K., U.S.A., U.S.S.R.). **1929** *Trans. Internat. Astron. Union* III. 224 The terms Greenwich Civil Time (G.C.T.), Weltzeit (W.Z.) and Universal Time (*U.T.) denote time measured from Greenwich Mean Midnight, and are not ambiguous. **1974** *Nature* 1 Nov. 25/1 The balloon was launched at 0830 UT and it reached a ceiling height of 3.8 mbar. **1974** *Times* 22 June 1/3 Members of the Democratic Unionist Party, one of the three Protestant groups in the *UUUC. **1982** M. Wallace *Brit. Govt. in Northern Ireland* vi. 125 The overall UUUC vote rose from 366,703 to 407,778. [**1925** E. H. & W. K. Russell *Ultra-Violet Radiation & Actinotherapy* 261/2 (Index), Veterinary uses of U.V.R.] **1928** *Moderna Språk* XXII. 188 Popularly one also hears *U.V.-treatment, light treatment, light bath. **1940** A. L. M. Sowerby *Wall's Dict. Photogr.* (ed. 15) 431 Ultra-violet light is only present in sufficient amounts to be harmful on very clear days at sea-level, or at high altitudes... In such circumstances it should be excluded by a U.V. filter if it is desired to obtain photographs not showing the characteristics associated with the use of the ordinary yellow filter. **1979** *Nature* 29 Mar. 484/1 The ultraviolet region of the solar spectrum, which has somewhat arbitrarily been divided into three sections —UV-C (wavelength 200–290 nm), UV-B (290–320 nm) and UV-A (320–400 nm). **1913** *Northern Whig* 27 Nov. 8/5 They knew that the letters '*U.V.F.' stood for Ulster Volunteer Force. **1983** *Listener* 11 Aug. 3/1 The two supergrasses have helped to convict over 50 people they once worked with: Black in the IRA, Bennett in the UVF. **1974** *Times* 9 Sept. 2/2 Mr Murray resigned from the *UWC but was later reappointed. **1975** *Irish Times* 30 May 4/6 The Ulster Loyalist Central Co-ordinating Committee (made up of the para-military groups, the U.W.C., and political representatives). **1955** R. J. Schwartz *Compl. Dict. Abbrev.* 184/3 **UXB*, unexploded bomb. **1979** P. Way *Sunrise* vii. 72 Once a UXB was in position—then, until this Unexploded Bomb had been dealt with, it was necessary to cordon off an entire block.

b. U, upper class, esp. with reference to linguistic usage; as *sb.*, U persons or characteristics collectively, U language. Hence *U-ness*. Cf. non-U *a.* and *sb.*

1954, etc. [see non-U *a.* and *sb.*]. **1956** *Times* 1 Mar. 11/5 He is what, in old-fashioned 'U' was called a 'rattle' and, in 'Non-U', a 'scream'. **1956** Auden *Making, Knowing & Judging* 15 Poets and scholars have one thing in common. They are not gentlemen. The U is that which both, being non-U, with passion worship. **1956** A. S. C. Ross in N.

Mitford *Noblesse Oblige* 26 *Fault, also, Balkans*,..are pronounced by the U as if spelt *fawlt, awlso, bawlkans*. **1957** E. HYAMS *Speaking Garden* vi. 68 *Spinacia oleracea* of Linnaeus... I must say, at the risk of being accused of gastronomic U-ness..is the only one I care to eat. **1958** *Oxf. Mag.* 15 May 432/2 He..dropped the final 'g's' of his present participles in a manner then 'U'. **1959** *New Statesman* 17 Oct. 499/1 My own personal participation.. was to go and speak for Fenner Brockway at Eton and Slough. For me, he is a nostalgic figure of the old Labour Party into which I was born, and therefore more sympathetic than the later U intake. **1962** A. LURIE *Love & Friendship* ix. 166 'I don't think he's really U, though, do you?' 'Oh no. Shabby genteel, maybe.' **1968** *New Society* 22 Aug. 266/1 In London, Mayfair, once so very U, is still so in some sort, but few U people live there as it is so expensive. **1970** *Daily Tel.* (Colour Suppl.) 27 Nov. 12 The point is not so much that U-speech and U-behaviour are, by some absolute standard, superior but that they are indicators. If you want to be unobtrusive, or effective, in a U context, you must adopt U manners. **1977** D. BENNETT *Jigsaw Man* xii. 225 He had spoken with a distinct English accent. Very U, indeed.

6. *slang* or *colloq.* **U.P.**, the spelling pronunciation of UP *adv.*, = over, finished, beyond remedy.

1838 DICKENS *O. Twist* xxiv, It's all U.P. there,..if she lasts a couple of hours, I shall be surprised. **1854** MISS BAKER *Northampt. Gloss.* 370 'It's all U.P. with him'; i.e. all up either with his health, or circumstances. **1861** WHYTE MELVILLE *Good for Nothing* xxvii. II. 18 It's a long lane that has no turning, but I did think for five minutes afore I saw your fire that it was about U.P.

U^{2} (uː, juː). [Burmese.] A Burmese honorific, used as the Burmese equivalent of Mr.

1930 *Outlook* 17 Dec. 607/2 Noting that the Burmese delegates were becoming restive, U Ba Pe, their chief, forced the issue. **1953** STEVENSON & EVELETH *Judson's Burmese-English Dict.* p. vii, In 1893 Mr. Robert C. Stevenson, aided by U Si, U Thiri of Danubyu, U Pho U, and U San Ngyeing of Monywa, prepared an enlarged edition. **1971** *Whitaker's Almanack 1972* 813/2 *Secretary-General* (1966–71), U Thant (*Burma*).

u, obs. var. YEW; var. *yu*, dial. f. YULE.

ua-, frequent ME. spelling for VA-.

uakari (wəˈkɑːrɪ). Also **ouakari, wakari.** [a. Tupi.] A short-tailed monkey of the genus *Cacajao*, found in the upper Amazon basin, esp. *C. rubicundus*, which has a red face and shaggy reddish-brown fur.

1863 H. W. BATES *Naturalist on Amazons* II. v. 306 These red-faced apes belonged to a species called by the Indians Uakari. **1894** H. O. FORBES *Hand-bk. Primates* I. 174 The Uakari monkeys..are at once recognised by their short tail. *Ibid.* 175 The Uakaris are arboreal monkeys, very gentle and timid. **1966** R. & D. MORRIS *Men & Apes* iii. 67 The curious uakari monkeys with their shaggy coats, abbreviated tails and sad, naked, almost human faces. **1975** *New Yorker* 12 May 46/2 He slew a wallaby and a lemur and a trio of ouakaris.

-ual *suffix* of adjs., repr. late L., med.L. *-uālis*, *-uāle*, as in *conceptual* (med.L. *conceptuālis*), *sensual* (late L. *sensuālis*); in adjs. formed from sb. stems in *-u-*, as *accentual* (L. *accentus*), *eventual* (L. *eventus*); and in adjs. derived from L. adjs. in *-uus*, as *individual* (med.L. *individuālis*, f. L. *individuus*), *perpetual* (L. *perpetuālis*, f. L. *perpetuus*). (Further information is given at -AL *suffix*.)

uald, uas, obs. Sc. ff. *would, was*.

‖**U-bahn** (ˈ(j)uːbɑːn). [Ger., f. *U*, abbrev. of *untergrund* underground, + *bahn* railway.] The underground railway in any of several of the major cities of Germany and Austria.

1938 G. CONKLIN *All about Subways* x. 193 After the construction of the Paris subway came the *Untergrundbahn*, Berlin's thirty-nine-mile subway, which Berliners always refer to as the *U-Bahn*. **1957** S. CLARK *All Best in Germany & Austria* ix. 117 Only in trips to East Berlin would I recommend the U-Bahn or S-Bahn, where you can lose yourself in crowds and feel at ease. **1964** L. DEIGHTON *Funeral in Berlin* xl. 238 The U-bahn station across the road. **1974** P. HIGHSMITH *Ripley's Game* v. 58 He gets off the U-bahn at the Steinstrasse station every day around six-fifteen. **1983** *Railway Mag.* Jan. 15/3 When I was in Vienna in April 1982, the prototype of the city's U-Bahn e.m.us was being *completely* rebuilt.

Ubaid (ʊˈbaɪd). *Archæol.* [f. the name of the tell Al *ʿUbaid* near Ur in the Euphrates valley.] Used *attrib.* of the culture thought to have flourished throughout Mesopotamia in the fifth millennium B.C., and of the artefacts associated with it.

[**1927** HALL & WOOLEY *Ur Excavations* I. viii. 165 Two types of kiln were employed by the al-ʿUbaid potter. *Ibid.* ix. 217 All of the al-ʿUbaid skulls have assumed..a reddish grey colour. **1936** S. LLOYD *Mesopotamia* ii. 40 The familiar greenish-painted pottery..known as Al'Ubaid ware.] **1952** V. G. CHILDE *New Light on Most Anc. East* i. 13 Still older and purely prehistoric are villages of the Ubaid culture. **1961** G. CLARK *World Prehist.* iv. 92 On the Ubaid foundation Sumerian civilization developed comparatively rapidly in the south. **1976** *Times* 3 Sept. (Qatar Suppl.) p. iv/6 Recently Ubaid pottery has been found farther down the Gulf in Saudi Arabia.

u-batch, var. *yu batch*: see YULE.

ubble, ubbly(e, obs. ff. OBLEY.

ub(b)ubboo, variant of HUBBUBOO.

1702 FARQUHAR *Twin-Rivals* v. iii, Ububboo, a Witch, a Witch. **1851** BORROW *Lavengro* xi, Cut-throat kens, where thirty ruffians..would spring up with brandished sticks and an 'ubbubboo, like the blowing up of a powder-magazine'.

‖**über alles** (ˌyːbər ˈaləs), *phr.* [Ger.] Above all else.

In quots. 1967 and 1983 prob. influenced by a misunderstanding of the opening words of the German national anthem, 'Deutschland über alles', as 'Germany supreme'.

1967 *Listener* 21 Sept. 365/3 Advertising..is now advertising *über Alles*: it has become very big business indeed. **1979** *Guardian* 18 June 9/7 Monetarism, in the sense of giving precedence uber alles to restraining the growth of money supply. **1983** *Times* 22 Feb. 10/3 An exhibition..presented..by the British-Soviet Friendship Society...astronauts, Red Square, Lenin *über alles*.

†**ˈuberant,** *a. Obs. rare.* [ad. L. *ūberant-*, *ūberans*, pres. pple. of *ūberāre*, f. *ūber* rich, plentiful.] Abundant, copious.

1622 G. FITZ-GEFFRY *Elisha* 14 Where the fountaine is vberant, needs must the streames bee fluent. **1624** *Gag for Pope* 56 Like vberant springs to send forth flowing streams of truth into the world. **1624** T. SCOTT *Belg. Souldier* 38 Whose vertue proued like an Vberant spring.

†**uberate,** *v.*^{1} *Obs.*$^{-0}$ Also **hub-**. [f. ppl. stem of L. *ūberāre*: cf. prec.] (See quots.)

1623 COCKERAM, *Huberate*, to make plentifull. **1656** BLOUNT *Glossogr.*, *Uberate*, to make plenteous and fruitfull.

†**uberate,** *v.*^{2} *Obs.*$^{-0}$ [f. L. *ūber* udder.] (See quot.)

1623 COCKERAM, *Vberate*, to give suck, to fatten with the brest. [Hence in Blount.]

‖**Überfremdung** (yːbərˈfrɛmdʊŋ). [Ger., f. *überfremden* to give foreign character to, f. *über* over + *fremd* foreign + *-ung* -ING^{1}.] The admission or presence of too many foreigners.

1965 *Economist* 27 Feb. 910/1 The vulgar prejudice against *Überfremdung* of which Dr Abs has recently chosen to become the spokesman. **1969** *Britannica Bk. of Year* 709 The issue of Überfremdung ('over-alienation'; i.e., the high percentage of foreign workers in Switzerland) continued to make news. **1970** *Time* 8 June 39 Nowhere in Europe have relations between guest and host become more acrimonious than in Switzerland. Uberfremdung (over-foreignization) has been a battle cry of the far right for the past five years.

‖**überhaupt** (yːbərˈhaʊpt), *adv.* [Ger.] In general, (taken) as a whole; as such; par excellence.

1875 W. JAMES *Let.* 14 Nov. in R. B. Perry *Thought & Character W. James* (1935) I. 361 This element, which I suppose lawyers and men of society and business *überhaupt*, must necessarily lose. **1909** —— *Pluralistic Universe* 381 But what made them at all? What propels experience *überhaupt* into being? **1927** C. R. S. HARRIS *Duns Scotus* II. i. 50 It is only by supposing that universals have some reality which is quite independent of our thinking that the objectivity of thought *überhaupt* can be maintained. **1954** *Ethics* LXIV. 277/2 We seek..the form of particular truths *überhaupt*. **1976** *Times Lit. Suppl.* 3 Dec. 1507/1 Psychology was regarded by Dewey as the philosophic science *überhaupt*, in the Hegelian sense.

‖**Übermensch** (ˈyːbərmɛnʃ). Also **Ueber-**. Pl. **-menschen.** [Ger.: see SUPERMAN.] = SUPERMAN. Also in extended and weakened senses. Similarly **übermenschlich** (ˈyːbərmɛnʃlıç) *a.*, superior; like a superman, superhuman; **Übermenschlichkeit** (ˈyːbərˌmɛnʃlıçkaıt), the quality of a superman, superhumanity.

1902 *Pall Mall* XXVI. 405/1 Where Bismarck exerted the full..strength of the *Uebermensch*, Bülow always remains the polite orator. **1907** G. B. SHAW *Major Barbara* Pref. 152 It is assumed, on the strength of the single word Superman (Übermensch) borrowed by me from Nietzsche, that I look for the salvation of society to the despotism of a single Napoleonic Superman. **1911** J. WARD *Realm of Ends* xx. 451 The struggle for existence and the survival of the fittest.. will lead, he teaches, to a yet higher being, the *Uebermensch* or Over-man. **1920** D. H. LAWRENCE *Women in Love* xxix. 439 One really does feel übermenschlich—more than human. **1922** JOYCE *Ulysses* 417 Mead of our fathers for the *Übermensch*. **1931** W. STEVENS *Harmonium* 131 If it were lost in Übermenschlichkeit Perhaps our wretched state would soon come right. **1939** L. MACNEICE *Autumn Jrnl.* vii. 32 Take one's paltry measures against the coming Of the unknown Uebermensch. **1950** BLESH & JANIS *They All played Ragtime* v. 85 A subtle but devastating caricature of the white *Übermensch*, employing the blackface like an African ceremonial mask. **1963** *Economist* 13 July 103/1 Doctor and detective *übermenschen*. **1977** *Times* 2 Sept. 11/4, I should like to know whether the Irish would be reckoned by him among the Übermenschen or the Untermenschen.

uberous (ˈjuːbərəs), *a.* Now *rare*. [f. L. *ūber* rich, full, fruitful, abundant, etc. + -OUS, or ad. med.L. *ūberōsus*. Cf. mod.F. *ubéreux*.

Bailey (1727, vol. II) gives *uberose*, and (1721) *uberosity*.]

1. Supplying milk or nourishment in abundance. Said (*a*) of animals, etc., or (*b*) of the breasts.

In this sense prob. associated with L. *über* udder.

(*a*) **1624** QUARLES *Sion's Elegies* IV. vii, Milke, from the vberous Cow, Was ne're so pure in substance. **1632** —— *Div. Fancies* I. xxxvii, How do our Pastures flourish, and refresh Our uberous Kine, so fair, so full of flesh! *a* **1635** NAUNTON *Fragm. Reg.* (Arb.) 51 My Lord..drew in too fast, like a childe sucking on an over-uberous Nurse. **1644** QUARLES *Sheph. Orac.* i, Our uberous ewes were evermore supplyed With twins, attending upon either side.

(*b*) **1634** SIR T. HERBERT *Trav.* 17 The women giue their Infants sucke as they hang at their backes, the vberous dugge stretched ouer her shoulder. **1635** QUARLES *Embl.* I. xii. 2 The ub'rous breasts, when fairly drawn, repast The thriving infant with their milkie flood. **1869** BROWNING *Ring & Bk.* IX. 53 Each feminine delight of florid lip,.. Marmoreal neck and bosom uberous.

b. Rich in fertilizing moisture. *rare*$^{-1}$.

a **1706** EVELYN *Sylva* II. viii. (1776) 426 This [water from ponds] approaches nearest to that of rain dropping from the uberous cloud, and is certainly the most natural and nursing.

†**2.** Of places: Richly productive; fertile. *Obs.*

a **1626** MIDDLETON *Mayor of Queenborough* II. iii, About the fruitful flanks of uberous Kent. **1634** SIR T. HERBERT *Trav.* 20 Cotton they [the Malagasy] haue store of, but most vberous in Fruits. **1651** HOWELL *Venice* 26 She [Padua] is situated in a most delightfull and uberous plain.

3. Abundant, copious, full.

1633 T. ADAMS *Exp. 2 Peter* iii. 18 If the young and tender grace of thankfulness do not fall into the hands of uberous and fruitful obedience, it will languish and pine away. **1747** *Gentl. Mag.* 242 Her uberous store, To these, parturient Earth unmidwif'd yields. **1839** *New Monthly Mag.* LVII. 408 Addressing himself to a lady of most uberous presence.

Hence **ˈuberousness**, plentifulness, fertileness.

1727 BAILEY (vol. II).

‖**uberrima fides** (juːˈbɛrɪmə ˈfaɪdiːz), *sb. phr. Law.* Also gen. **uberrimae fidei.** [L.] The utmost good faith.

1850 MACNAGHTEN & GORDON *Rep. Cases High Court of Chancery* (1851) II. 243 The application for a special injunction is very much governed by the same principles which govern insurances, matters which are said to require the utmost degree of good faith, 'uberrima fides'. **1880** *Law Rep. Appeal Cases* 954 In policies of insurance, whether marine insurance or life insurance, there is an understanding that the contract is *uberrima fides*. **1899** *Law Rep. Queen's Bench Div.* I. 792 There are some contracts in which our Courts of law and equity require what is called 'uberrima fides' to be shewn by the person obtaining them. **1946** *Rep. Patent, Design, & Trade Mark Cases* LXIV. 6 The Petitioner must provide complete disclosure of all the circumstances and furnish all relevant accounts..; the matter is one *uberrimae fidei*. **1959** JOWITT *Dict. Eng. Law* II. 1797/1 Contracts of suretyship and partnership, though not strictly contracts *uberrimae fidei*, are..such as to require full disclosure and the utmost good faith. **1979** H. S. KENT *In on Act* iii. 37 He said that there was a very good relationship, based upon *uberrima fides*, the utmost good faith.

uberty (ˈjuːbətɪ). Now *rare*. Also 5 **vberte, uberte(e**; 7 **ubertie.** [a. OF. *uberté* (= It. *ubertà*, Pg. *uberdade*), or ad. L. *ūbertās*, f. *ūber*: cf. UBEROUS *a.* and -TY.] Rich growth, fruitfulness, fertility; copiousness, abundance.

? *a* **1412** LYDG. *Two Merchants* 613 Greyne oppressith to moche vberte. *c* **1440** *Pallad. on Husb.* III. 104 A vine abundaunt ek thow take hem fro, And not hem take that ber a grape or too, But hem that kneleth doun for vberte. *Ibid.* VIII. 88 Of pasturyng they must haue vberte, Fro breris fer. **1491** CAXTON *Vitas Patr.* (W. de W. 1495) I. vii. 11 b/1 An ydolle, whyche somtyme was by prestes & other peple born in processyon for to obteyne uberte & habundaunce of rayne. **1603** FLORIO *Montaigne* I. xxx. (1632) 104 They yet enjoy that naturall ubertie and fruitfulnesse, which..doth in such plenteous aboundance furnish them with all necessary things. **1623** COCKERAM, *Vbertie*, fertility, abundance. [Hence in Blount, Phillips, etc.] **1900** *Westm. Gaz.* 6 Apr. 7/3 So these happy volatile fellows talk on, with a uberty of optimism.

‖**ˈubi.** *Obs.* [L. *ubi* where. So Sp. *ubi* place, room.]

1. Place, position; location. (In common use *c* 1640–1740.)

1614 T. ADAMS *Physicke fr. Heaven* in *Diuells Banket*, etc. 321 Euery spirtuall Phisitian must keepe his right *vbi*. **1644** DIGBY *Nat. Bodies* i. (1645) 8 It is but assigning an Ubi to such a spirit and he is presently riveted to what place you please; and by multiplying the Ubies [etc.]. **1661** GLANVILL *Van. Dogm.* 101 Nor are we solicitous for the *Ubi* of Vertue, or any other Immaterial accident. **1704** NORRIS *Ideal World* II. iii. 223 Spirit cannot resist body, as being capable of coexisting in the same *ubi* with it. **1740** CHEYNE *Regimen* 215 That Bodies..must have an *Ubi*, a local permanent Situation at last, is certain.

2. Present place or location; whereabouts.

1778 H. WALPOLE *Let. to W. Mason* 15 May, The *ubi* of the Toulon squadron is not ascertained.

†**ubiˈation.** *Obs.*$^{-1}$ [Cf. prec. and next.] The action of occupying a (new) place.

1624 F. WHITE *Repl. Fisher* 422 No substantiall thing is produced, but one substance succeedeth in the roome of another, by that which they stile vbiation.

ubication (juːbɪˈkeɪʃən). [ad. mod.L. **ubicātio* (cf. Sp. *ubicacion*, Pg. *ubicação*), f. **ubicāre* (Sp. *ubicarse* to be in a determinate place), f. L. *ubi* UBI.] The condition or fact of being in, or occupying, a certain place or position; location.

1644 DIGBY *Nat. Soule* v. §9. 400 We conceiue these modifications of the thing, like substances; and..we call them by substantiue names, Whitenesse, Action, Vbication, Duration, &c. **1661** GLANVILL *Van. Dogm.* 101 Relations, Ubications, Duration, the vulgar Philosophy admits into the list of something. **1699** BURNET *39 Art*, xxviii. (1700) 324 They are accustomed to think that Ubication, or the being in a Place, is but an Accident to a Substance. **1837** WHEWELL *Hist. Induct. Sci.* II. vi. ii. §5. 45 Arriaga, who wrote in 1639, ..suggests that the board affects the upper weight, which it does not touch, by its ubication, or whereness. **1866** T. N. Harper *Peace through Truth* Ser. I. 212 The *terminus ad quem* is already existing, and merely receives a new ubication. **1892** *Standard* 5 Aug., The constant identity of the ubication and direction of the lines [in Mars] proved their connection with the soil.

ubicity (juːˈbɪsɪtɪ). *rare.* [f. L. *ubi* UBI: see -ICITY.] Whereabouts.

1922 Joyce *Ulysses* 388 No man knows the ubicity of his tumulus. **1938** E. Pound *Let.* 9 Jan. (1971) 305 If letter via *Criterion* don't reach him, I will indaginare his ubicity.

ubiety (juːˈbaɪɪtɪ). [ad. mod.L. **ubietās*, f. L. *ubi* UBI.] Condition in respect of place or location; local relationship; whereness.

1674 N. Fairfax *Bulk & Selv.* 77 Being no wayes beclam'd with body as to ubiety or whereness. **1686** H. More *Real Pres.* 25 To make a body in this sense independent of Place or Ubiety, is as unconceivable as to make it independent of Time. **1733** Watts *Scheme Ontol.* xii, Of time, and place, and ubiety. **1834** Southey *Doctor* cxcii. (1848) 509 O Soul of Sir John Cheke, thou wouldst have led me out of my way, if that had been possible,—if my ubiety did not so nearly resemble ubiquity. **1855** Bailey *Mystic*, etc. 81 Vervain and magic haschisch, which endows Thought with ubiety. **1866** R. Hobson *Chas. Waterton* iv. 92 Notwithstanding her uncertain tenure of ubiety,..she [the coot] patiently yielded to her lot.

ubiquarian (juːbɪˈkwɛərɪən), *sb.* and *a.* Also 8 **ubiquerian**. [f. L. *ubīque* wherever, anywhere, everywhere.]

A. *sb.* † **1.** *pl.* A society or club existing in the 18th cent. Also *attrib. Obs.*

1737 (*title*), A modest vindication of the illustrious order of Ubiquarians. *Ibid.* 23 The Ubiquarian Senate do not yet admit of this Difference. **1755** J. Witsell in *Connoisseur* 27 Nov. 581 Laws, Rules, Regulations, or Orders, shall be formed for the Anti-Gallicans, Ubiquarians, Gregorians, or any private clubs and societies. **1761** *Ann. Reg., Charac.* II. 51/1 He was a respectable member of the Killers of Care, The Silenians,..Ubiquarians, &c.

2. A person who goes everywhere. *rare.*

1767 *Ann. Reg., Charac.* 62/2 The English being by their nature Ubiquarians, and seldom in one place long, must have painted canvas as quick as their ideas. **1812** *Sporting Mag.* XL. 281 That sporting ubiquarian, Colonel Thornton.

B. *adj.* **1.** Being or existing, present or found, everywhere; ubiquitous, ubiquitary.

1762 *Gentl. Mag.* Sept. 440/1 Happiness our friend shall be, Ubiquerian deity! **1784** Cowper *Tiroc.* 266 Have ye, ye sage intendants of the whole, An ubiquarian presence and controul. **1819** MacCulloch *West. Isl. Scot.* II. 321 Fingal ..the ubiquarian king and warrior is said to have occupied them. **1848** Hampden *Bampt. Lect.* (ed. 3) 147 The Universal Governor, overshadowing all things with the ubiquarian tutelage of his Providence. **1891** C. Dixon *Idle Hours w. Nat.* 108 The ubiquarian House Sparrow has his home amongst the girders of the roof.

2. Met with or experienced everywhere.

1825 *Monthly Rev.* CVI. 490 It will facilitate, also, to men of note, who have occasion to travel, an ubiquarian reception.

ubiquinone (juːˈbɪkwɪnəʊn, juːbɪˈkwɪnəʊn, -kwɪˈnəʊn). *Biochem.* [Blend of UBIQUITOUS *a.* and QUINONE.] Any of a class of dimethoxy-, methyl-, and polyisoprenyl-substituted quinones, (the number of isoprene units depending upon the biological source) which act as electron-transfer agents in cell respiration.

1958 R. A. Morton et al. in *Biochem. Jrnl.* LXVIII. 16P/2 Because of its widespread distribution..and properties, the name *ubiquinone* is proposed. **1979** *Biochimica & Biophysica Acta* DLXXXII. 400 The ubiquinones in malaria parasites ..differ from those in mammalian cells. **1982** M. S. Olson in T. M. Devlin *Textbk. Biochem.* vi. 310 The final component of the mitochondrial respiratory chain, which is neither a nucleotide species nor a protein, is a lipophilic electron carrier called coenzyme Q or ubiquinone.

† **u'biquious**, *a. Obs. rare.* [f. as UBIQUARIAN *sb.* and *a.* + -IOUS.] Ubiquitous.

1782 W. Stevenson *Hymn to Deity* 31 Thro' stretch ubiquious, measureless expanse,..Abroad he moves in majesty of state. **1835** *Tait's Mag.* II. 93 The ubiquious Princess had arrived suddenly at Ostend.

'ubiquism. *rare*$^{-1}$. [Cf. next and -ISM. So Sp. *ubiquismo*.] = UBIQUITISM.

1891 *Athenæum* 28 March 403/3 In Switzerland he [Montaigne] questions Felix Plater..in regard to heretical doctrines such as Ubiquism.

'ubiquist. *rare.* [a. F. *ubiquiste* (= Sp., Pg. *ubiquista*), f. L. *ubīque* everywhere: see -IST.]

† **1.** (See quots.) *Obs.*

[**1706** Phillips (ed. Kersey), *Ubiquiste*, a Divinity-Doctor that belongs to no particular College in the University of Paris.] **1721** Bailey, *Ubiquist* [from prec.]. **1728** Chambers *Cycl.* s.v., In the University of Paris,..the Ubiquists are called simply Doctors in Theology.

2. = UBIQUITARIAN *sb.* 2.

1728 Chambers *Cycl.* s.v., All the Ubiquists, however, are not agreed: Some of 'em, and among the rest the Swedes, hold that Jesus Christ, even during his Mortal Life, was every where. **1842** Brande *Dict. Sci.*, etc. *Ubiquists*, or *Ubiquitarians*, in Ecclesiastical History, a school of Lutheran divines; so called from their tenet that the body of Christ was present in the Eucharist in virtue of his divine omnipresence.

† **ubiquit**, *v. Obs.*$^{-1}$ [Back-formation from UBIQUITOUS or -ITY.] *trans.* To make ubiquitous.

1676 Marvell *Mr. Smirke* 33 This being done, then the Exposer ubiquits himself, peeping at the Key-holes, or picking the Locks of the Bed-chambers of all the Great Ministers.

† **u'biquitair**, *a. Obs.*$^{-1}$ [a. F. *ubiquitaire*.] = UBIQUITARY *a.* 2.

c **1645** Howell *Lett.* VI. xiii. (1650) I. 198 Of Him, whom Earth nor Air, Nor the vast mould Of Heaven can hould, Cause he's Vbiquitair.

† **u'biquitant.** *Obs.*$^{-1}$ [Cf. prec. and -ANT.] = UBIQUITARY *sb.* 1.

1654 Vilvain *Theol. Treat.* i. 9 They cannot be ubiquitants every wher or elsewher at once.

ubiquitarian (juːˌbɪkwɪˈtɛərɪən), *sb.* and *a.* [See UBIQUITARY and -IAN.]

A. *sb.* † **1.** = UBIQUITARY *sb.* 1. *Obs.*

1644 *Thomasson Tracts* (Brit. Mus.) CLXIII. No. 12 A 4, He cannot heare..that Prince Rupert is approaching anything neare Yorke, yet they..prepare for him least that ubiquitarian steale on them unawares. **1663** R. Head *Hic et Ubique* 40 Why that Ubiquitarian, and his antick comrade Phantastick have lately borrowed monies of me. **1670** Clarke *Nat. Hist. Nitre* 19 It [nitre] is an Ubiquitarian, though no place wil scarce hold it. *a* **1734** North *Lives* (1826) III. 136 And I, that was no housekeeper, became an ubiquitarian till his lordship's death.

2. One of those Lutherans who maintained the doctrine that Christ's body was everywhere present at all times. Chiefly in *pl.*

1651 *Fuller's Abel Rediv., Sohnius* 384 Confuting the Ubiquitarians..so boldly, that he chose rather to hazard banishment then to connive at errors. **1660** Hacket *Serm. at Whitehall* 22 Mar. 20 The unrelenting Ubiquitarians among the rigid Lutherans. **1676** Glanvill *Ess.* v. 25 The Ubiquitarians defend their Errors, by denying the judgement of Reason. **1704** Norris *Ideal World* II. xii. 511 Nay, perhaps, the Ubiquitarians may of the two have the better plea. **1798** Hey *Lect. Divinity* IV. IV. xxviii. § 10. 325 *note*, Luther is said to have given up this ubiquity as a proof of Christ's corporal presence in the Eucharist; but rigid Lutherans were still Ubiquitarians. **1874** J. H. Blunt *Dict. Sects*, etc. (1886) 603 The Ubiquitarians are strong opponents of the Calvinistic and Zwinglian theories of the Holy Eucharist.

B. *adj.* **1.** Of or pertaining to, holding or maintaining, the doctrine of the Ubiquitarians.

1640 Bp. Hall *Chr. Moder.* II. x. 79 The Calvinists brand Schlusselburgius for an Ubiquitarian hereticke. **1673** Hickman *Quinquart. Hist.* Ep. a b, The late Ubiquitarian Lutherans make a difference where they [Zwinglius and Luther] found none. *Ibid.* II. 366 Frederick the Prince was from his youth trained up and instructed in the Ubiquitarian Doctrine. **1882** Farrar *Early Chr.* I. 350 *note*, The old Ubiquitarian controversy as to whether 'the right hand of God is everywhere'.

2. = UBIQUITARY *a.* 2. *rare.*

1641 Ld. Brooke *Disc. Nat. Episc.* II. ii. 71 No one man living could..Over-see it; except he could get the Pope to Transubstantiate him also, and so get a Ubiquitarian Body. **1828** *Examiner* 25/1 No ubiquitarian order should exist, with duties and interests paramount to those of national allegiance.

Hence **ubiqui'tarianism** = UBIQUITISM.

1885 Schaff *Christ & Christianity* 75 The absolute ubiquitarianism of the Swabian school, and..the relative or hypothetical ubiquitarianism of the Saxon school.

† **u'biquitariness.** *Obs. rare.* [f. next + -NESS.] The quality of being ubiquitary.

1655 Fuller *Ch. Hist.* x. i. §26 The Prelaticall party complained..of the ubiquitarinesse of some hands, the same being alwayes present at all Petitions. *a* **1661** —— *Worthies, Lanc.* II. (1662) 119 He..was very obstreperous in arguing the case for Transubstantiation, and the Ubiquitariness of Christs body.

ubiquitary (juːˈbɪkwɪtərɪ), *sb.* and *a.* [ad. mod.L. *ubīquitārius*, f. L. *ubīque* everywhere. Hence also F. *ubiquitaire*, Sp. and Pg. *ubiquitario*.]

A. *sb.* **1.** One who, or that which, is or can be everywhere at once. Now *rare.*

1587 Holinshed *Chron.* III. 579/2 There must needs be an errour..vnlesse we will grant the king and queene..to haue beene *Hic ibi simul*, which priuilege is granted to none but Ubiquitaries. **1599** B. Jonson *Cynthia's Rev.* II. iv, A Nymph..all motion, an ubiquitarie, Shee is euery where. **1615** P. Small in Farr *S.P. Jas. I* (1848) 332 Time is of the Ubiquitaries' race,—Time's here, Time's there, Time is in every place. **1638** Bp. Mountague *Art. Enq. Norwich* D2, The Bishop is no Ubiquitary, that hee can discover every thing done. **1657** R. Ligon *Barbadoes* (1673) 63 Tables, cupbords, beds, stools, all are covered with them [*sc.* ants], so that they are a kind of Ubiquitaries. **1826** *Sporting Mag.* XVII. 262 Could it have been possible to have been an ubiquitary, I should have been with the Warwickshire, as well as with the Duke's hounds.

† **b.** *spec.* (See quot.) *Obs.*$^{-1}$

1615 J. Stephens *Ess. & Charac.* xiv. 189 A Vbiquitarie Is a Iourney-man of all Trades, but no sauer because no setter vp.

† **c.** A clergyman having no settled benefice but taking duty anywhere. *Obs.*

1646 T. Edwards *Gangrena* I. 72 In a word, our Sectaries are become Pluralists, Nonresidents, and some of them Ubiquitaries, and are well paid for it. **1654** Gayton *Pleas. Notes* III. viii. 117 The Priest being himself unbenefic'd, and an Ubiquitary, made bold..to pay the Non-Residentiaries ..for not stopping his mouth with a Living. **1663** Bp. Nicholson *Expos. Catech.* Ep. Ded. A 3 These are not Ubiquitaries, and consequently are forced to be Non-residents.

† **2.** = UBIQUITARIAN *sb.* 2. *Obs.*

1585–7 T. Rogers *39 Art.* (1625) 19 We altogether dissent ..from the Germaine Vbiquitaries..saying that Christ as man, is not onely in heauen, but in earth too at this instant. **1595** in Ellis *Orig. Lett.* Ser. III. IV. 116 A condemnacion of other reformed Churches, that did not agree with the Ubiquitaryes. **1614** Bp. Hall *No Peace with Rome* §181 Either Aquinas is false, or the papists vbiquitaries. **1654** Jer. Taylor *Real Pres.* 156 To this the Answer is the same in effect which is given by the Roman Doctors, and by the Ubiquitaries, whom they call Hereticks. **1681** R. L'Estrange *Apol. Protestants* IV. i. 98 There is no collecting from their Writings whether they were Consubstantiators or Ubiquitaries. **1709** Strype *Ann. Ref.* XXV. 252 Martyr in his lifetime dedicated to him his dialogue..against the Ubiquitaries.

B. *adj.* † **1.** = UBIQUITARIAN *a.* 1. *Obs.*

1599 Sandys *Europæ Spec.* (1632) 213 Besides the absurdity of their Ubiquitarie Chimera. *a* **1603** T. Cartwright *Confut. Rhem. N.T.* (1618) 721 The Iesuites deride the ubiquitarie Protestants, for that they could not finde how Christ should be present in all places by his Humanity, unlesse his Humanity were in every place where his Godhead is.

2. = UBIQUITOUS *a.* **a.** Of single persons, or the Deity. Now *rare* or *Obs.*

1609 *Ev. Woman in Hum.* IV. i. in Bullen *O. Pl.* IV, Nay looke up, beholde yon Christall pallace. There sits an ubiquitarie Judge. **1631** Massinger *Emperor East* I. ii, She can conjure, And I am her ubiquitary spirit. **1647** Ward *Simple Cobler* 57, I can as well admit an ubiquitary King as another. **1673** Dryden *Marr. à la Mode* I. i, Besides the Court, she's the most eternal Visiter of the Town: And yet manages her time so well, that she seems ubiquitary. **1707** J. Stevens tr. *Quevedo's Com. Wks.* (1709) 393 Then Jove said [to Olympus], Thou Vbiquitary God, shoot thy self into the World, and in a trice drag Fortune hither by the Ears. **1710** Steele *Tatler* No. 244 ¶6, I remember at a full Table in the City, one of these ubiquitary Wits was entertaining the Company with a Soliloquy.

b. Of individual things, qualities, etc.

1625 Jackson *Creed* V. xxvii. §2 The fruition of His presence..cannot make saints or angels so capable of this ubiquitary knowledge as personal union with Him..might make Christ's body of ubiquitary local presence. **1640** Howell *Dodona's Gr.* 43 For wealth and an ubiquitary commerce none can exceed her. **1645** —— *Twelve Treat.* (1661) 338 Their faculties have a kind of ubiquitary freedom, though the body be never so under restraint, as the Authors is. **1713** Steele *Englishman* No. 22. 146 The ubiquitary Assistance of the Deity is celebrated by..the Psalmist. **1738** *Phil. Trans.* XL. Suppl. 41 Whether God himself be not the immediate, acting, ubiquitary Cause of centripetal power. **1823** Palmerston *Opin. & Policy* (1852) 28 The surest though it may be the slow resource of Spain, is the desultory but ubiquitary resistance of her population.

c. Of a kind or class of persons or things.

1610 Donne *Pseudo-martyr* §35. 141 These vbiquitary Monks haue the aduantage of all others. **1642** Fuller *Holy & Prof. St.* III. xxiv. 220 It was in vain to erect any structure therein to restrain and keep his Ubiquitary beams. **1669** Baxter *Power Mag. & Ch. Past.* I. (1671) 6 The Clergy are so numerous, subtile, ubiquitary and potent. **1709** Mrs. Manley *Secret Mem.* (1720) II. 150 The God of Love finds little more Difficulty in Subduing the Grave than the Gay; the Desires he gives are alike Ubiquitary. **1853** G. Johnston *Nat. Hist. E. Bord.* I. 121 A few, such as the Dandelion and the Daisy, may be said to be almost ubiquitary. *a* **1865** J. Young *Life J. Welsh* v. i. (1866) 280 Scotsmen, in all ages roving and ubiquitary, were, at that time, settled in unprecedented numbers in..France. **1888** *Co-operative News* 4 Aug. 784 As I passed on I met two more of the ubiquitary fraternity.

3. Extending to all quarters; extremely wide or extensive. *rare.*

1652 Urquhart *Jewel* Wks. (1834) 194 [English] by its promiscuous and ubiquitary borrowing consisteth almost of all languages. *a* **1661** Fuller *Worthies, Barkshire* I. (1662) 92 It is impossible for any Author of a Voluminous Book consisting of several persons and circumstances..to have such Ubiquitary intelligence, as to apply the same infallibly to every particular. **1803** *Ann. Rev.* I. 257 The research displayed is ubiquitary, the materials are judiciously proportioned.

† **u'biquiter.** *Sc. Obs. rare.* [Cf. prec. and -ER^1.] = UBIQUITARIAN *sb.* 2.

1589 R. Bruce *Serm. Sacram.* iii. (1590) M vj b, Will ȝe speare at the Vbiqviter, gif the trew bodie of Christ be present? *a* **1599** Rollock *Lect. Passion*, etc. xxxix. (1616) 381 If one goe to Germanie, he wil be an Vbiquiter, and in Rome a Papist, in Scotland a Christian.

ubiquitism (juːˈbɪkwɪtɪz(ə)m). [f. UBIQUIT-ARY + -ISM.] The doctrine of the omnipresence of Christ's body.

1617 Collins *Def. Bp. Ely* II. x. 413 Vnles you wil be so wood now, as to adde brutish Ubiquitisme to your barbarous Cyclopisme. **1630** Donne *Serm., Easter-day* (1640) 253 *For he is risen*; And if this be a good reason, there is no Transubstantiation, no Ubiquitisme, for then Christ might have been there, though he were risen. **1728** Chambers *Cycl.* s.v. *Ubiquists*, G. Hornius will only allow Brentius to be the first Propagator of Ubiquitism. **1857** Pusey *Real Presence* i. (1869) 122 The 'Formula Concordiæ' admitted very little of the Ubiquitism of Breur; but it retained the original Ubiquitism of Luther.

† **u'biquitist.** *Obs.*$^{-1}$ [Cf. prec. and UBIQUIST 2.] = UBIQUITARIAN *sb.* 2.

1687 *Good Advice* 40 At this time there were Papists, Protestants, Evangelists, Præcisians, Ubiquitists, Familists or Enthusiasts and Anabaptists in England.

u'biquitory, *sb.* and *a. rare.* [-ORY.]

A. *sb.* = UBIQUITARY *sb.* 1.

1645 *Sacred Decretal* 4 Hee's such an Ubiquitory, wee know not how to deale with him.

B. *adj.* = UBIQUITARY *a.* 2b.

1643 R. O. *Man's Mort.* v. 33 His humanitie not being vbiquitorie, that is, everie where at once, he must be in the creation, and in some certaine place of the creation. **1841** *Blackw. Mag.* L. 585 The arts have claimed .. an ubiquitory citizenship everywhere.

ubiquitous (ju:ˈbɪkwɪtəs), *a.* [f. as UBIQUITARY + -OUS.] Present or appearing everywhere; omnipresent: **a.** Of single persons or things.

Of persons freq. with humorous exaggeration = 'turning up everywhere'.

1837 MISS SEDGWICK *Live & let Live* (1876) 60 Mrs. Broadson, who had an ubiquitous pair of ears. **1852** THACKERAY *Esmond* III. i, Here, as he lay nursing himself, ubiquitous Mr. Holt reappeared. **1860** PUSEY *Min. Proph.* 428 Heathendom was as a beleaguered city, mastered by an ubiquitous Presence, which they knew not how to meet. **1879** S. C. BARTLETT *Egypt to Pal.* i. 14 On crossing to the Continent, the marks of this ancient and ubiquitous force grew more continuous.

b. Of a kind or class of persons or things.

1840 E. NEWMAN *Brit. Ferns* (1844) 210 This fern appears to be ubiquitous in the moist woods and marshes. **1847** GROTE *Greece* II. xvii. III. 306 Informing himself, moreover, of passing events by means of ubiquitous spies and officials. **1878** BOSW. SMITH *Carthage* 4 Wherever a ship could penetrate, .. there we find these ubiquitous, these irrepressible Phœnicians. **1887** *Pall Mall G.* 17 Dec. 2/2 The ubiquitous and unabashed British tourist.

Hence **u'biquitously** *adv.*, **u'biquitousness**.

1864 *Daily Tel.* 16 Aug., In spirit Mr. Dicey remains *ubiquitously impartial. **1882** *Standard* 25 Dec. 5/1 The modern spirit is ubiquitously triumphant. **1874** *Contemp. Rev.* XXV. 135, I have a spirit of which *ubiquitousness is an attribute. **1887** *Pall Mall G.* 8 Feb. 2/2 The coolness and courage he infused into his young troops by his ubiquitousness on the battlefield.

ubiquity (ju:ˈbɪkwɪtɪ). [ad. mod.L. *ubīquitas* (cf. F. *ubiquité* (17th c.), Sp. *ubicuidad*, Pg. *ubiquidade*), f. L. *ubīque* everywhere: see -ITY.]

1. *Theol.* The omnipresence of Christ or of his body, as maintained by the Ubiquitarians.

1579 FULKE *Heskins' Parl.* 173 If we found as good authoritie for the vbiquitie, or pluralitie of placing of his body as we finde for the feeding vs thereby into eternall life. **1597** HOOKER *Eccl. Pol.* v. lxvii. §10 Out of which vbiquitie of his body they gather the presence thereof with that sanctified bread and wine. *a* **1617** BAYNE *On Eph.* (1618) 388 We see Vbiquity and all real Presence .. ouer-throwne. **1624** BEDELL *Lett.* ii. 48 One side fetches arguments against vbiquitie from these places, and thereupon saith, the question is about these Articles. **1674** HICKMAN *Quinquart. Hist.* (ed. 2) 131 It seems, if men be never so violent for Ubiquity, .. if they be but against Predestination, they shall pass for .. Melancthonians. **1798** HEY *Lect. Div.* IV. IV. xxviii. §10. 325 Luther .. supported it [*sc.* consubstantiation], by what was called Ubiquity; by affirming, that the Son of God was every where, *ubique*. **1839** HALLAM *Hist. Lit.* II. ii. §23 After the death of Melanchthon, a controversy, relating to the ubiquity, as it was called, of Christ's body, proceeded with much heat. **1882-3** SCHAFF *Encycl. Relig. Knowl.* III. 2414 Ubiquity is the doctrine .. of the omnipresence of the humanity, and more especially of the body, of Christ.

2. The capacity of being everywhere or in all places at the same time: **a.** In general use.

1597 HOOKER *Eccl. Pol.* v. liii. §4 In the one there is attributed to God .. death, whereof diuine nature is not capable; in the other vbiquitie vnto Man, which humane nature admitteth not. **1604** R. CAWDREY *Table Alph.*, *Vbiquitie*, presence of a person in all places. **1625** EARL CARLISLE in *Fortescue Papers* (Camden) 214, I could wishe .. that you would borrow so muche of ubiquity as that your persone could be in the several places where your sufficiensy is so necessary. **1655** CLEVELAND *Gen. Poems*, etc. (1677) 142 Knowing that no place in the Nation is so remote, as not to share in the Ubiquity of your Care. **1713** CLARKE *Several Letters* (1716) 16 The Reason why you do not apprehend Ubiquity to be necessarily connected with Self-Existence. *a* **1721** PRIOR *On Coronation* i, Giving Poets to partake (Like those Deities they make) Of infinite Ubiquity. **1796** COLERIDGE *Destiny of Nations* 45 One all-conscious Spirit, which informs With absolute ubiquity of thought .. All his involved Monads. **1823** SCOTT *Quentin D.* xvi, The attention and activity which Quentin bestowed .. had in it something that gave him the appearance of ubiquity. **1838** PRESCOTT *Ferd. & Is.* (1846) I. x. 427 Their vigilant adversary, who seemed now in their eyes to possess the powers of ubiquity. **1864** BOWEN *Logic* xiii. 422 It is admitted that this doctrine of the ubiquity of the mind to the body is incomprehensible.

b. As an attribute of God.

Variously taken as synonymous with, or as distinct from, *omnipresence*.

1607 J. DAVIES *Summa Totalis* E 2, For, so they must by his Immensitie, Which is the cause of his Vbiquity. **1664** H. MORE *Myst. Iniq.* ii. 36 It is an acknowledgement of one of the incommunicable Excellencies of God, viz. his Ubiquity. **1704** SWIFT *T. Tub* viii, This God, though endued with Ubiquity, was yet supposed to possess one peculiar Habitation. **1748** HARTLEY *Observ. Man* II. i. 34 By God's Omnipresence, or Ubiquity, we must be understood to mean that his Power and Knowlege extend to all Places. **1855** MILMAN *Lat. Chr.* VII. vi. (1864) IV. 167 The impartial ubiquity of God, the equable omnipresence of the Redeemer and the Holy Spirit throughout the whole universe. **1885** LYMAN ABBOTT in *Chr. World Pulpit* XXVIII. 179 Most Christians do not believe in the omnipresence of God; they only believe in His ubiquity.

c. *Law.* (See quots.)

1765 BLACKSTONE *Comm.* I. vii. 260 A consequence of this prerogative is the legal *ubiquity* of the king. His majesty, in the eye of the law, is always present in all his courts, though he cannot personally distribute justice... From this ubiquity it follows, that the king can never be nonsuit. **1841** in Peters *Rep. Supr. Crt. U.S.* XV. 6 The United States, in their sovereign capacity, have no particular place of domicile but possess, in contemplation of law, an ubiquity throughout the Union.

†**3.** Locality, region. *Obs.*$^{-1}$

1633 B. JONSON *Love's Welcome* Wks. (1640) 275 A solemne Wight As you should meet In any street, In that Ubiquitie.

‖**ubi sunt** (ˌʊbɪ ˈsʊnt). *Literary Criticism.* [L., lit. 'where are'.] An interrogatory phrase taken from the opening words or the refrain of certain mediæval Latin works, used chiefly *attrib.* to designate a mood or theme in literature of lament for the mutability of things.

1914 B. C. WILLIAMS *Gnomic Poetry in Anglo-Saxon* 45 The *ubi sunt* motivation is an old one, perhaps of equal age with riddle, charm, and spell. **1957** N. FRYE *Anat. Crit.* 160 Themes of .. the wheel of fortune in social affairs, of the *ubi sunt* elegy. **1965** *English Studies* XLVI. 307 Cresseid's *ubi sunt* lament underscores the narrator's sympathy. **1969** DUNNING & BLISS *Wanderer* 97 The adaptation of the *Ubi sunt* commonplace from a Latin *milieu* to an Anglo-Saxon one takes place in the sermon in much the same fashion as in *The Wanderer*. **1977** *Times Lit. Suppl.* 25 Feb. 224/4 The *ubi sunt* motif ('where are Caesar and Alexander [now]?'). **1977** M. McC. GATCH *Preaching & Theology in Anglo-Saxon England* 229/1 Characteristically, the device is employed in discussions of the brevity of life ('Brevis est hujus mundi felicitas, modica est hujus saeculi gloria, caduca est et fragilis temporalis potentia. Dic ubi sunt reges? ubi principes? ubi imperatores?..'—Isidore of Seville, *Synonyma* II. 91... Ælfric's use of the rhetorical tag *ubi sunt?*, however, is quite different here... I know of no strict *ubi sunt?* passage in Ælfric.

'**ubity.** *rare.* [f. L. *ubi* UBI + -TY.] Place, locality.

1624 F. WHITE *Repl. Fisher* 451 An Angell being a finite creature, is at one instant difinitiuely in one vbitie onely. *Ibid.* 452 That which mooueth and passeth from one vbitie to another, is not in both the places at once. **1964** AUDEN in *Listener* 1 Oct. 525 Your influence is welcome at any hour in my ubity.

uble, ubli, ubly, obs. forms of OBLEY.

u-block, variant of *yu-block*: see YULE.

U-boat. [ad. G. *U-boot*, abbrev. of *Unterseeboot* 'under-sea-boat'.] A (German) submarine. Also *attrib.*

'In recent use (1913-).' *N.E.D.*

1916 *Times* 11 July 6/4 The U boat is stated to be unarmed. **1918** *Glasgow Herald* 27 Aug. 4/6 The Maura Cabinet will stand firm in its attitude towards Germany on the question of the U-boat sinkings. **1928** C. MACKENZIE *Extremes Meet* 115 I'm frightened of what the Germans will do presently with their U-boats. **1943** J. B. PRIESTLEY *Daylight on Saturday* xxxi. 249 Sinking all the U-boats, putting out all the incendiaries, bombing the Ruhr. **1975** tr. *Melchior's Sleeper Agent* (1976) vii. 161 Two reporters .. had walked boldly up and down Times Square clad in full Nazi U-boat commander uniforms. **1979** A. PRICE *Tomorrow's Ghost* ii. 22 The Atlantic is very big and a U-boat is very small.

Ubykh (ˈu:bɪx). [Native name.] An almost extinct language of the North-West Caucasian group, now spoken only in Turkey.

1951 W. K. MATTHEWS *Languages U.S.S.R.* v. 87 A third type of North-West Caucasian is usually listed, viz. Ubykh, which is now almost extinct along the north-east coast of the Black Sea and survives chiefly in Asia Minor. **1965** W. S. ALLEN *Vox Latina* 9 The number of consonants .. varies from 8 in Hawaiian .. to 80 in Caucasian Ubykh. **1977** *Language* LIII. 450 Ironically, the language which has been the most extensively documented, Ubykh, is the most seriously moribund.

†**uch(e, vch(e,** obs. Sc. and north. ff. OUCH *sb.*

c **1375** [see OUCH *sb.* 1 β]. **1464** *Registr. Aberdon.* (Maitland) II. 163 Betuix þe tua vchis ij. litil garnatis; beneth þe secunde vche .ij. litil garnatis. **1488** *Acc. Ld. High Treas. Scot.* I. 81 In a litill paper within the said box, ane vche with a diamant. **1549** *Registr. Aberdon.* (Maitland) II. 196 In þe heid of þe samyn [monstrance] ane propir vch of gold. **1552** *N. Country Wills* (Surtees, 1908) 221 My best jewell which is an uche of golde after the fac[i]on of a bucle.

uch(e, obs. forms of EACH *a.*

Uchee: see YUCHI.

‖**uchiwa** (ˈu:tʃiwa). [Jap. f. *utsu* to strike, shake + *ha* feather.] A flat Japanese fan (FAN *sb.*[1] 3) that does not fold.

1877 W. E. GRIFFIS *Mikado's Empire* II. xv. 518 Fukiu has a few shops where *ogi* (folding fans) and *uchiwa* (flat fans) are made. **1898** A. DIÓSY *New Far East* v. 268 The Japanese *uchi-wa*, or non-folding fan .. is often decorated with a highly coloured print. **1970** J. KIRKUP *Japan behind Fan* 164 One should .. carry in one's left hand an *uchiwa*, that broad, flat paper fan printed with cool summer subjects.

uckers (ˈʌkəz). Also **ukkers.** [Origin unknown.] A board game resembling ludo, played in the Navy.

1946 J. IRVING *Royal Navalese* 180 Uckers. A game very similar to Ludo, and played on a large board by teams of three or four men. **1976** C. CAUSLEY in *Cornish Short Stories* 63 The rest of the members of the mess—arguing, scuffling, singing, writing, playing uckers. **1978** *Navy News* Aug. 2/5 A 50-hour uckers match .. raised £277 for the Spina Bifida Association. **1979** *Daily Tel.* 3 Dec. 20 That nautical form of ludo known as 'ukkers', and tombola, too, have given way in the patrol craft HMS Vigilant to war-games.

ucky (ˈʌkɪ), *a. colloq.* Also **ukky.** [Cf. YUCKY *a.*] Sticky and dirty; disgusting.

1963 J. T. STORY *Something for Nothing* i. 7 It's ucky. That's what it is. It's ucky. **1969** *Sydney Morning Herald* 7 June 2/1 According to the organiser, Mrs Kemp, it will do away with 'ukky little pastel colours, fairy tales and endless nursery rhyme jingle stuff', replacing them with modern paintings, bright orange curtains and hi-fi sets playing classical music and jazz. **1974** 'D. FLETCHER' *Lovable Man* I. 61, I guess it would be awfully ucky... You know, sticky, muddy.

ud, var. OUD.

Ud, minced form of GOD. (Cf. AD, OD, UDS.)

1759 D. MALLET *Prol. to The Brothers* Wks. I. 41, I wish he would appear .. Ud! I would give it him.

'ud, abbrev. form of *would* WILL *v.*

udad, var. AOUDAD.

udal (ˈju:dəl). Forms: α. 6 **outhale,** 6-7 **outhell, owthell,** 7 **owthall;** 6 **uthall, -ail,** 6-7 **-ale,** 7 **-el.** β. 6-7 **owdaill,** 6- **udal,** 7 **udail, udell, uddal, utal.** [Orkney and Shetland form of Norw. *odal, odel*, ON. *óðal* ODAL.]

1. *attrib.* **a.** *udal land* or *lands*, land(s) in Orkney or Shetland held by the old native form of freehold tenure.

α. ? **1502** in Peterkin *Rentals Orkney* (1820) I. 6 Tankarnes xij d terre uthall land. **1576** in *Reg. Mag. Sig. Scot.* (1890) 479/2 The said James outhale landis of Gartht, lyand within the parochin of Stronnes, Menland of Orknay. **1592** *Ibid.* (1892) 118/1 The haill skatt of the uthail land within the said yle baith butter and wadmell. **1609** *Ibid.* 129/1 Et omnium lie owthall-landis in dicto rentali content.

β. **1576** *Reg. Privy Council Scot.* II. 488 Being heretour of the udall land of the Yle of Gairsay in Orknay. **1633** *Reg. Mag. Sig. Scot.* 757/1, 1½ den. ex antiquo lie kingisland et ½ den. lie utalandis nuncupat. *Ibid.* 757/2, 24 den. kingisland et udailland in dicta villa. **1649** *Ibid.* 769/2 Towmale of uddalland vocat. Skegebuster. **1664** in Gifford *Descr. Zetland* (1886) 65 The lands called Udell-lands lying within the said earldom. **1707** *Ibid.* 68 Sundry isles, .. udell-lands, and other lands. **1795** *Statist. Acc. Scot.* XV. 393 Some of the udal lands pay a small proportion of yearly rent to the King, and to the kirk. **1805** G. BARRY *Hist. Orkney Isl.* II. v. 219 These udal or allodial lands are directly opposed to fees or feus. **1884** *Scotsman* 26 July 3/1 Two Merks and One-Half Merk Udal Land.

†**b.** Placed after the sb. (sometimes in contrast to 'royal'). *Obs.*

1584 *Reg. Mag. Sig. Scot.* 264/1 Cum .. scattis terrarum regalium et outhell de Southerbie .. et owthell de Noltland. *Ibid.*, Cum scattis .. terrarum regalium et owdaill de Sandweik. **1602** in A. Peterkin *Notes Orkney & Zetl.* (1822) App. 40 The richt and tytil of 6 mark land uthel, lyand in the town of Gruting. **1627** in Peterkin *Rentals Orkney* (1820) III. 45 Lynais is ane d. land outhell.

c. With other sbs., as *men, right, tenure*, etc.

c **1500** in A. Peterkin *Orkney & Zetl.* (1822) 88 The uthale men. **1587** in *Edinb. Antiq. Mag.* (1849) 60 He hes Reft and spulzeit diuerss of the uthallmen and heretors .. of Orknay and Zetland of yair proper heritaige. **1669** in Peterkin *Orkney & Zetl.* (1822) 190 That their udal right may be sustained valid in all tyme coming. *a* **1688** J. WALLACE *Descr. Orkney* (1693) 94 *Udall-lands*, such as are possessed by the Udall-right, a possession the natives have successively without either Charter or Seasin. **1750** in Hibbert *Descr. Shetl. Isl.* (1822) 192 The udalmen were likewise called Rothmen or Roythmen; that is, self-holders. **1765-8** ERSKINE *Inst. Law Scot.* II. iii. §18 The udal right of the stewartry of Orkney and Zetland is of the same nature. **1793** *Statist. Acc. Scot.* VII. 239 There are three kinds of tenure of lands in Scotland... Thirdly, the Udal, being a right compleat without writing. **1805** G. BARRY *Hist. Orkney Isl.* II. v. 219 The laws by which this udal property was inherited, sold, redeemed, or transmitted from one person to another. **1814** SCOTT *Diary* 4 August in *Lockhart*, The Udal proprietors have ceased to exist, yet proper feudal tenures seem ill understood. **1821** —— *Pirate* xix, The wide Udal possessions of their father .. were divided betwixt the brothers. **1909** J. GUNN *Orkney Bk.* 110 In Scotland land was held according to the feudal system, in Orkney according to the udal system.

2. The form of freehold tenure characteristic of Orkney and Shetland; land held in this way.

1588 *Reg. Mag. Sig. Scot.* 547/1 To be haldin .. off our soverane lord .. in fie, heretage, frie uthall and blensche for evir. **1750** in Hibbert *Descr. Shetl. Isl.* (1822) 192 Their udals, at this day, are not transmitted like other lands, but with the .. compleat propriety and demesne of the subject.

udaller (ˈju:dələ(r)). Also 8 **udiller, udelar,** 9 **udeler, uddaler.** [f. prec. + -ER. Cf. ODALLER.] A tenant of land by udal right. Also *attrib.*

1669 in Peterkin *Orkney & Zetl.* (1822) 190 [An act] for the udallers of Orknay and Zetland. **1671** *Shetland Doct.* in *Proc. Soc. Antiq. Scot.* (1892) XXVI. 194 He .. shall not suffer the same [lands] to be incrotched upon be the ffewaries, udallers and uythers. *Ibid.*, The ffewares, udallers, tennendes, occupiers of the landis [etc.]. **1733** GIFFORD *Descr. Zetland* (1886) 9 The head courts .. where all the Udillers were obliged to convene. **1798** *Statist. Acc. Scot.* XX. 269 There are six udelars in Deerness. **1805** G. BARRY *Hist. Orkney Isl.* I. ii. 28 Men here called Udallers, who are little proprietors of land, that has never been held by the feudal tenure, nor subjected to either service or payment to any superior. **1821** SCOTT *Pirate* xvii, The stout-hearted and experienced general, for so the Udaller might be termed. **1884** *Gd. Words* Nov. 747/2 The last remains of the old udallers are to be found amongst the 'peerie (small) lairds' of Fladdabister.

'**udally,** *adv.* [f. as prec. + -LY².] By udal right or tenure; under the udal system.

1909 J. GUNN *Orkney Bk.* 111 It must not be supposed that all the land in Orkney was held udally, or that all the inhabitants were udallers.

‖**udarnik** (u'darnɪk). Pl. -i. [Russ.] A shock-worker (SHOCK *sb.*³ 4 c).
1931 S. N. HARPER *Making Bolsheviks* vii. 162 *Udarnik* is the member of a 'shock brigade'. **1939** G. B. SHAW *Geneva* I. 25 In her youth she was a udarnik, what you call a shock worker. **1966** *Economist* 29 Oct. 464/1 Various forms of 'socialist competition' were gradually introduced, first with the aid of shock workers or *udarniki*, and then by the encouragement of Stakhanovites.

udder ('ʌdə(r)). Forms: α. 1 udr-, 4 vddre, 5 vddyr (6 *Sc.* vdyr), 5–7 vdder (6 vtter, odder), 6– udder; 5–6 uther (9 *Sc.*), 6 other. β. 5 iddyr, 6 ydder. [OE. *úder* (once), = OS. *ûdar*, *ûder-*, MLG. (LG.) *ûder*, MDu. *ūder*, *uyder* (Du. *uier*, *uijer*, WFlem. *eur*; cf. WFris. *ûr* teat), OHG. *ûtar* (and *ûtiro*), MHG. *ûter* and *iuter* (G. *euter*):—OTeut. **ūdr-*, = Gr. οὖθαρ, Skr. *ūdhar*, *-as* (also *ūdhan*), L. *ūber*. By unexplained consonant change the corresponding ON. form is *júgr* EWER³, YURE. It is doubtful whether an OTeut. variant, or an entirely different stem, is represented by OFris. *iader* (EFris. *jader*, *jæder*, NFris. *jidder*, etc., WFris. *jaer*), older Du. *jadder* (dial. *jaar*), OS. *geder*, MLG. *geder*, *jeder* (LG. *jidder*, *judder*). In English the original long vowel has been regularly shortened before the consonant-group *-der*.]

1. a. The pendulous baggy organ, provided with two or more teats or nipples, by which the milk is secreted in certain female animals.
a **1000** *Kentish Gl.* 203 *Uberibus*, of udrum. **1398** TREVISA *Barth. De P.R.* XVIII. xviii. (Bodl. MS.), Þe Camel haþ foure tettes and tweyne vddres as þe cowe haþ. *a* **1425** tr. *Arderne's Treat. Fistula*, etc. 12 Wolle þat groweth atuix þe leggez of ane ewe about þe vdder. *c* **1440** *Promp. Parv.* 258/2 Iddyr, or vddyr of a beeste, *Uber.* **1515** BARCLAY *Egloges* iv. (1570) C iij b/2 Your cowes others of milke replete and full. *Ibid.* C iiij/1 Leane be my lambes,.. And yet their dammes they dayly sucke so dry, That from the uthers no licoure can we wring. *c* **1518** SKELTON *Magnyf.* 1814, I saw a fox sucke on a kowes ydder; And with a lyme rodde I toke them bothe togyder. *c* **1534** in *Suss. Star Chamber Proc.* (1913) 21 The ..Kyn were in suche payn for lake of mylkyng that the mylke rane oute of there odderens and so lyke to be all perishte. **1577** B. GOOGE *Heresbach's Husb.* III. (1586) 139 b, The Lambe.. must be sette on foote, and put to the dammes vdder. **1613** PURCHAS *Pilgrimage* IV. xi. 349 Next to the doore on the womens side.. there is an Image with a Cowes Vdder for the women,.. on the other side another with a Mares Vdder for the men. **1665** BOYLE *Occas. Refl.* IV. iii. 16, I.. approach'd the place where the fair Milk-maid was solliciting the Udder of a fresh Cow. **1684** *Lond. Gaz.* No. 1910/4 A Red Cow of about 5 or 6 years old, with a White Udder. *c* **1720** W. GIBSON *Farrier's Guide* I. ii. (1738) 19 The Udder is another part peculiar to a Mare. **1773** JOHNSON in *Boswell* (1831) III. 47 Milk pressed from the swelling udder by the gentle hand of the beauteous milk-maid. **1799** *Med. Jrnl.* I. 314 A spurious cow-pox.. arising from pustules on the nipples or udder of the cow. **1847** W. C. L. MARTIN *Ox* 41/1 A twin heifer.. which.. was very handsome, with a well-formed udder, and was a good milker. **1867** BAKER *Nile Trib.* v. (1872) 75 The distended udders of thousands of camels were an assurance of plenty.

b. This part of an animal as an article of food.
1474 in *Househ. Ord.* (1790) *32 The purveyors of beeves and muttons.. hath to theire fees the oxe heads, muttons heades, the rumpes of every beefe, and the intrayles of every beaste excepte the oxe feete, and the uthers. **1598** *Epulario* J iiij, Fifteene Egs, with a Cowes Udder wel sodden. **1660** PEPYS *Diary* 11 Oct., Mr. Creed and I to the Leg in King Street, where he and I, and my Will had a good udder to dinner. **1675** HANNAH WOOLLEY *Gentlew. Comp.* 158/1 Neats tongue and Udder roasted. **1721** *Queen's Closet* 99 To Roast a Cows Udder. **1842** A. COMBE *Physiol. Digestion* (ed. 4) 35 Four pounds of cow's udder and ten pounds of raw beef.

2. *poet.* (in *pl.*) A dug or teat. *rare.*
1582 STANYHURST *Æneis* II. (Arb.) 55 Theyre whelps neere starued ar eager And expect vdders with dry iaws. **1600** SHAKS. *A.Y.L.* IV. iii. 115 Vnder which bushes shade A Lyonesse, with vdders all drawne drie, Lay cowching head on ground. **1887** BOWEN *Virg. Ecl.* III. 30 Twice each day she is milked; though still at her udders we leave Two young calves.

3. The breast of a woman. *rare.*
a **1704** T. BROWN *Pleas Lett. to Gent.* Wks. 1709 III. II. 16 Their Udders swagging down to their Navils. **1933** DYLAN THOMAS *Let.* Nov. (1966) 53 Farmers' boys pressed amorously upon the udders of their dairymaids.

4. *attrib.* and *Comb.*, as ***udder-cattle***, ***-flank***, ***part***; **udder-clap**, inflammation in the udder; **udder-ill** (see quot. 1847); **udder-lock** *sb.* (see quot. *a* 1808); *v. trans.*, to pull away the wool from the udders of (sheep).
a **1722** LISLE *Husb.* (1757) 214 The oak-buds killed five of the udder-cattle. *Ibid.* 345 It was the udder-flank, or throat, that they usually bit the sheep in. **1798** R. DOUGLAS *Agric. Roxb.* 156 *note*, All sheep are *udder-locked*, as it is here called, that being thought refreshing and salutary. **1806** A. HUNTER *Culina* (ed. 3) 256 Under the udder part of a leg of veal, there is a large piece of meat. *a* **1808** *Essays Highl. Soc.* III. 250 (Jam.) Udderlocks are the wool plucked from the udder. **1825** JAMIESON, *Udder-clap*, a sort of schirrous tumour affecting the udder of ewes, by an unexpected return of milk after being sometime *eild*. Teviotd. **1844** H. STEPHENS *Bk. Farm* II. 620 After recovery from lambing, the only complaint the ewe is subject to is inflammation in the udder, or *udder-clap*, or *garget*. **1847** W. C. L. MARTIN *Ox* 172/2 Loss of milk, or milk of a disgusting taste and odour, and consequently unfit for use, results from derangement of the digestive organs, and especially from morbid affections of the fourth stomach, and the animal is said to labour under 'udder-ill'.

Hence '**udderful** *a.*, having a full udder; *sb.*, as much (milk) as an udder will hold. '**udderless** *a.*, unsuckled, motherless.
1818 KEATS *Endym.* I. 210 All ye gentle girls who foster up Udderless lambs. **1879** MEREDITH *Egoist* Prelude, Listen.. to an unleavened society: a low as of the udderful cow past milking hour! **1922** JOYCE *Ulysses* 416 Drink, man, an udderful!

udder, -ir, dial. and obs. Sc. forms of OTHER.

'**uddered**, *a.* [f. UDDER + -ED.]
†**1.** Suckled. *Obs.*⁻¹
1582 STANYHURST *Æneis* IV. (Arb.) 108 Amydst rocks, Caucasus haggish Bred the, with a tigers soure milck vnseasoned, vdderd.

2. Having an udder or udders; provided with a teat or teats.
1652 BENLOWES *Theoph.* XII. cxv, See where the udderd Cattle finde us food. **1714** GAY *Sheph. Week* II. 11 Marian, that soft could stroke the udder'd cow. **1725** POPE *Odyss.* IX. 282 Big-udder'd ewes, and goats of female kind. **1826** *Blackw. Mag.* XX. 782 A mother-matron, with a baboon visage, and uddered like a cow. **1870** MORRIS *Earthly Par.* III. 278 Deep-uddered kine Went lowing towards the pails at eventide. **1875** —— *Æneid* VIII. 45 There lieth she All white along, and piglings white around her uddered sides.

3. Contained in the udder.
a **1814** A. BECKET *Genii* i. in *New Brit. Theatre* I. 518 Nor let the heifers of the vale In udder'd treasure ever fail.

†'**uddery**, *a.* *Obs.*⁻¹ [f. UDDER + -Y.] Soft as the flesh of an udder.
1398 TREVISA *Barth. De P.R.* v. xlviii. (Bodl. MS.), Constantine seiþ þat these stones þe substaunce of ham is ymade of vddry and cruddy flessch.

‖**uddiyana** (u'di:jana). [ad. Skt. *uddīyana* rising up.] One of the physical exercises in Yoga (see quots.).
1949 S. KUVALAYÂNANDA *Popular Yoga* I. iii. 51 Uḍḍiyâna means *rising up* and Bandha means *contraction of particular anatomical parts.* This exercise is called Uḍḍiyâna-Bandha because the muscular contractions.. enable the spiritual force to rise up. Anatomically this Bandha may be called Uḍḍiyâna because it raises the diaphragm. **1960** J. HEWITT *Yoga* II. 42 *Uddiyana* can be counted as one of the physical exercises. **1960** KOESTLER *Lotus & Robot* iii. 117 Udiyama [*sic*]— drawing in the abdominal muscles, while forcing the viscerae and diaphragm upwards.

ude, var. of *yode* went: see GO *v.* A 3.

udelar, -er, obs. forms of UDALLER.

udell, obs. form of UDAL.

udell, variant of ALUDEL.
1894 ROSCOE & SCHORLEMMER *Treat. Chem.* (new ed.) I. 201 Each cover is fitted with a leaden pipe, and this is connected with a series of glass or earthenware condensers, termed udells, fitting one into the other.

uder, obs. Sc. form of OTHER.

†**Udfoot**, variant of *Ud's foot*: see UDS.
1620 I. C. *Two Merry Milk-maids* I. iii. C 4, *Fer.* Vdfoot, what will the young Duke doe trow? *Ibid.*, *Iul.* Vdfoot, we shalbe whipt anon for this Abuse.

†**udge**, var. JUDGE *v.* (attributed to Welsh speakers).
1598 SHAKS. *Merry W.* I. i. 191 So got-udge me, that is a vertuous minde. **1603** DEKKER *Patient Grissill* 588 By Cods vdge me, is all true.

udged, *a.* *Mining.* (see quot.)
1883 GRESLEY *Gloss. Coal-M.* 266 *Udged*, loose, weak, liable to fall, sounding hollow, or unsound. A roof or a piece of side is said to *knock udged* when it produces a dead, hollow, unsafe sound, upon being knocked upon with a hammer, &c.

Udi ('u:di:). [Native name.] An almost extinct north-east Caucasian language of Daghestan. Also *attrib.*
1948 [see ALBANIAN *sb.*³ 2]. **1951** W. K. MATTHEWS *Languages U.S.S.R.* v. 86 Udi, which is the language of two villages, in South-East Daghestan. **1974** *Encycl. Brit. Macropædia* III. 1013/2 One village of Udi speakers is located in Georgia. *Ibid.*, The Udi language is supposed to be one of the languages of ancient Caucasian Albania.

udiller, obs. form of UDALLER.

udimia, obs. f. ŒDEMA.

udir, obs. Sc. f. OTHER.

udometer (ju:'dɒmɪtə(r)). [ad. F. *udomètre*, f. L. *ūdus* wet, damp: see -METER.] A rain-gauge.
1825 *Reg. Arts & Sci.* III. 142 An improved Udometer, to shew the quantity of Rain fallen. **1873** *Routledge's Young Gentl. Mag.* Feb. 162/1 His thermometers,.. hygrometers, and udometers.

Hence **udo'metric** *a.* [F. *udométrique.*]
1891 *Cent. Dict.*

‖**udon** ('u:dɒn). [Jap.] A kind of noodle made from wheat flour.
1920 *Japan Advertiser* 22 Aug. 5/2 Udon is an alternative for soba.. but is made of wheat flour instead of buckwheat and is cut in thicker strings. **1959** *Encounter* Jan. 26/1 Bowls of *udon*, a kind of noodle-soup. **1978** *Chicago* June 236/2 There's also terrific chicken teriyaki, and reliable sukiyaki and udons ($1.75–2.25).

†**Uds.** *Obs.* Also 7 ud's, udds, udz. [Minced form of *God's*, possessive of GOD *sb.*, or of *God s'* = God save. Cf. ADS and OD¹.] A form of the name of God common in expletive oaths in the 17th century.

1. In possessive phrases (cf. GOD *sb.* 14), frequently written as one word, as ***Ud's blood***, ***bluff***, ***bobblekens***, ***-bows***, ***-bud***, ***-buddikins***, etc.
1607 DEKKER & WEBSTER *Northw. Hoe* II. i, *Vds bloud ile laie him crosse vpon his coxcomb next daie. **1664** H. BOLD *Poems* 162 They swore Udz niggs, we swore *Udz bluffe. **1681** T. FLATMAN *Heraclitus Ridens* No. 42 (1713) II. 21 *Udds Bobblekens, quoth he, I were wet to the skin. **1684** D'URFEY *Sev. New Songs* 9 *Udsbows, cries my Country-man John, Was ever the like before seen? **1681** OTWAY *Soldier's Fort.* II. i, Ah! *udds-bud, they'd.. have stript for t'other Bottle. **1689** SHADWELL *Bury F.* II. 19 A very good jest! Udsbud, there's a pair of Gloves of the same mettle, to stop your pretty Mouth. **1740** tr. *De Mouhy's Fort. Country Maid* (1741) I. 59 *Udsbuddikins, were I in Colin's Place, I know what I would do. **1607** DEKKER & WEBSTER *Westw. Hoe* v. iii, *Vds Daggers? cannot sinne be set a shore once in a raigne vpon your Country quarters, but it must haue fidling? **1821** SCOTT *Kenilw.* iii, Uds daggers! I tell thee, man, mine own stock of assurance was too small to trade upon. **1607** DEKKER & WEBSTER *Westw. Hoe* IV. ii, *Vds death speake, or ile kil thee. **1702** VANBRUGH *False Friend* II. i, Keep a woman honest? Udsdeath! I'd as soon undertake to keep Portocarero honest! **1854** H. AINSWORTH *Flitch of Bacon* I. v. 43 'Uds-death! I wish he hadn't arrested him here,' the landlord said. **1698** MOTTEUX *Quix.* (1733) I. 269 *Uds-diggers, quoth Sancho, I know her full well. *a* **1586** SIDNEY *Pansies Penshurst & Wilton* vi, Doth she call the faith of man In question? nay, *'uds foot, she loves thee than. **1608** DAY *Hum. out of Br.* IV. iii, Vdsfoot, your iaylor, my lord. **1623** WEBSTER *Devil's Law-Case* IV. ii, Vd's foot, we are spoyled. **1630** DEKKER *2nd Pt. Honest Wh.* IV. i, Vds foot, Giue me some meate. **1676** D'URFEY *Madam Fickle* III. i, *Udshash! I'd like to have spoil'd all, I took him for a Morrice-Dancer. **1614** J. COOKE *Greene's Tu Quoque* E 1 b, *Vdslid, I'le not be out-brau'd. *Ibid.*, Vdslid, I am gleek't this time. *Ibid.* H 3 b, *Vds'life, this is excellent: now she talkes. **1706** VANBRUGH *Mistake* I. 92 Udslife! Sir! attack her with a fiddle! **1611** MIDDLETON & DEKKER *Roaring Girl* II. ii, *Vds light the tide's against me. **1618** N. FIELD *Amends for Ladies* I. (1639) B 2 b, Vd'slight whats the matter, wring him by the nose. **1632** MASSINGER & FIELD *Fatal Dowry* II. ii, Vd's-light, enioy your wishes. **1680** DRYDEN *Limberham* IV. i, *Saint.* *Uds Niggers, but I will... *Wood.* Uds Niggers, I confess, is a very dreadful Oath. **1664** *Uds nigs [see *Uds bluff* above]. **1719** D'URFEY *Pills* IV. 96 Uds nigs, quoth I, what a Kirk beth' here. **1614** J. COOKE *Greene's Tu Quoque* B 2 b, *Vds pitty! unbutton man, thou'lt stifle her else. **1613** BEAUM. & FL. *Honest Man's Fort.* II. iv, *Udsprecious, we have lost a brother. **1821** SCOTT *Kenilw.* iv, Uds precious! madam, what make you here out of bounds? **1611** MIDDLETON & DEKKER *Roaring Girl* IV. ii. K ij, *Vds so Mol, where's that Trapdore? **1659** *Lady Alimony* II. i. B iij b, Uds so, will their dainty fingers tug in Alume work? **1695** CONGREVE *Love for L.* I. vi, Udso that's true, Mr. Valentine, I love Mirth, but Business must be done. **1697** VANBRUGH *Relapse* v. v, *Udsookers! they set my old blood a-fire! **1777** SHERIDAN *Trip Scarb.* v. ii, Udzookers! Now six words more, and I'll forgive them directly. **1611** MIDDLETON & DEKKER *Roaring Girl* IV. ii. I iij, *Vd' soule do but name that rascall. **1697** VANBRUGH *Relapse* III. v, *Udswoons! I'll give my wench a wedding-dinner. **1698** —— *Æsop* II. 457 '*Udzwooks!' quoth he, 'With all your meat, I will maintain a dish of pease.. Is much a better treat'. **1721** AMHERST *Terræ Fil.* No. 44 (1726) 236 Udzooks, I believe 'tis the hugest varsity alive.

2. In *Uds me*, *uds my life*: see GOD *sb.* 8 b.
1635 [GLAPTHORNE] *Lady Mother* IV. i. in Bullen *O. Pl.* (1883) II. 169 Udsme, my lady! **1668** DRYDEN *Maiden Queen* v. i, Uds my life! here's the queen's music just going to us. **1702** FARQUHAR *Inconstant* II. ii, Uds my life—here's one.

Uebermensch, var. ÜBERMENSCH.

uein, ueir, uell, southern ME. varr. FAIN *adv.*, FAIR *a.*, FELL *v.*

uell, obs. Sc. f. WEAL *sb.*

uerry, southern ME. var. *ferre* FAR *v.*; obs. Sc. f. VERY *adv.*

uewe, obs. f. VIEW *sb.*

U-ey ('ju:i:). *Austral. slang.* Also youee. [f. U + -Y⁶.] A U-turn.
1976 *Bulletin* (Sydney) 28 Feb. 27 Ted Heath, like Fraser, began as a professed opponent of big government but was soon 'doing a youee' (U-turn) all over the place. **1983** *Truckin' Life* Aug. 70/1 The turning circle is 15.2 m (49.8 ft). Not natural U-ey material but adequate for a six tonner.

ufel, obs. f. EVIL.

ufemest, var. OVEMEST *a. Obs.*

ufenan, -en, varr. OVENON, -AN *Obs.*

ufer ('ju:fə(r)). Also 9 upher. [Variant spelling of JUFFER. See also EUPHROE.] (See quot. 1842.)
1754 T. GARDNER *Hist. Dunwich* 257 The Master found an Expedient to make a Stage with Ufers (he had on board), and Planks, to bear the Carriages. **1795** *Act 35 Geo. III*, c. 20 Sch. A, Ufers, imported from any Part of Europe, five Inches square and under eight Inches square, or if twenty-four Feet in Length or upwards. **1812** J. SMYTH *Pract. of Customs* (1821) 426 Ufers, being 5 inches square or upwards, are subject and liable to the Duties payable on Fir Timber. **1833** *Rep. Sel. Comm. on Munic. Corporations* 320 Water-

bailiffs dues, payable to Corporation of Hull... Ufers, double..—, single. **1842** Gwilt *Archit.* 1049 *Uphers*, fir poles, from four to seven inches in diameter, and from twenty to forty feet in length.

ufere, uferr-mar, obs. ff. over *a.*, over-more *adv.*

uff (ʌf), *int.* An exclamation as of someone panting with exertion or difficulty.
1922 Joyce *Ulysses* 244 O, my corns!.. Come upstairs for goodness' sake till I sit down somewhere. Uff! Ooo! **1958** O. Caroe *Pathans* xxiv. 394 One day the fisherman caught—uff!—an enormous fish.

uffish (ˈʌfɪʃ), *a.* [f. h)uffish *a.*] = huffish *a.*
1871 'L. Carroll' *Through Looking-Glass* i. 22 And as in uffish thought he stood. **1926** C. Mackenzie *Fairy Gold* xviii. 200 I'm sorry if I was uffish. **1942** Berrey & Van den Bark *Amer. Thes. Slang* §301/6 *Arrogant, haughty*,.. uffish. **1960** *Guardian* 5 Oct. 9/5 Watson looks a trifle uffish. **1977** *Times* 24 June 14/5 The infant Levin sat for a while in uffish thought.

UFO (ˈjuːfəʊ, juːɛfˈəʊ). orig. *U.S.* Also **U.F.O.**, Ufo, ufo. [Acronym.] An unidentified flying object; a 'flying saucer'.
1953 D. E. Keyhoe in *Air Line Pilot* Oct. 9/3 The UFO was estimated to be between 12,000 and 20,000 feet above the jets. **1956** E. J. Ruppelt *Rep. Unidentified Flying Objects* 13 UFO is the official term that I created to replace the words 'flying saucers'. **1957** *Flying Saucer Rev.* III. vi. 9/2 Andrew Vaccari, of London Road, Neath, saw a crescent-shaped U.F.O. travelling at a terrific speed from the direction of Wern Mountain, Port Talbot, towards Mumbles. **1959** 'Wyndham' & Parkes *Outward Urge* ii. 86 Radar Watch here, sir.. Two ufos observed approaching south-east by south. **1966** *New Statesman* 8 July 58/2 Flying saucers or Ufos.. continue. They are now seen in all parts of the world and in increasing numbers. **1977** *New Yorker* 27 June 51/2 She talked to people who had seen strange sights —UFOs or sea monsters. **1983** *Out of Town* July 14/2 A relative of the marquess, celebrated for her obsession with flying saucers, scans the skies and.. UFOs obligingly hover overhead.
Hence **ˈUFOish** *a.*, having characteristics of a UFO.
1973 G. S. Hawkins *Beyond Stonehenge* vii. 117 We found no extraterrestrial artifacts. Nothing the least bit UFO-ish. **1978** J. Updike *Coup* (1979) iv. 130 Steely, spherical UFOish IBM type elements.

ufology (juːˈfɒlədʒɪ). [f. prec. + -logy.] The study of UFOs. Hence **ufoˈlogical** *a.*, of or pertaining to ufology; **uˈfologist**, one who makes such a study.
1959 *Times Lit. Suppl.* 23 Jan. 44/4 The articles, reports, and bureaucratic studies which have been written about this perplexing visitant constitute 'ufology'. **1963** *New Scientist* 19 Sept. 613/2 Long before the frustrated ufologist has realised that even the finest binoculars do not help in finding ufos, he will have discovered that there are other sports and pastimes than ufology. **1966** *New Yorker* 9 Apr. 32 The ufological definition of a flap is a concentration of sightings in a small area within a short period. **1973** *Nature* 31 Aug. 582/1 He was not writing..another addition to the burgeoning literature of Ufology. **1981** *Guardian* 29 Aug. 1/3 Cley Hill is the Loch Ness of the Ufologist. Flying saucers, it is claimed, cannot keep away from its flat top. **1984** *Spectator* 21 July 30/1 George Adamski..wrote, in collaboration with Desmond Leslie,..the first ufological best-seller, *Flying Saucers Have Landed*.

uforbium, obs. form of euphorbium.

ufreet, variant of afreet, efreet.
1847 L. Hunt *Jar Honey* i. (1848) 3 The vapour reached its height, and condensed,..and became an Ufreet (evil spirit), his head in the clouds, and his foot on the soil.

ug, *sb. Obs.* exc. *dial.* [a. ON. *ugg-r*: cf. next. In mod. dial. use perh. from the vb.] Fear, dread.
a **1240** *Lofsong* in *O.E. Hom.* I. 209 For-ȝif me mine sunnen;..louerd, ich i-seo ham wið muchel ugge of þin eie.

ug (ʌg), *v. Obs.* exc. *dial.* Forms: 3 *subj.* **uggi**, 4–6 **ugge** (**vgge**, 5 **vggyn**, **-one**), 5–6, 9 **ugg** (*Sc.* 5 **owgg**, 6 **vgg**, **wgg**), 5–6, 8–9 **ug** (5–6 **vg**, 6 *Sc.* **wg**); 5 **ughe**, **uge**. [a. ON. *ugga* to fear, dread, apprehend: cf. prec. and hugge *v.*]
1. *trans.* To inspire or affect with dread, loathing, or disgust.
a **1225** *Ancr. R.* 92 Ȝe schulen biholden sumetime touward te pine of helle, þet ou agrüse aȝean ham [*Titus MS.* þet ow uggi wið ham]. **1434** Misyn *Mending Life* 122 If my handis schyne as clennes,..ȝit sall þou toche me with fylth,..& my clothes sall vg me. *c* **1440** *Alph. Tales* 157 He spewid oute a grete froske... And when Nero lukid þervppon, hym vggid þerwith. *c* **1450** *St. Cuthbert* (Surtees) 7069 What he suld do he na wyste With þe sacrement..; him vgged to vse it and to ete. **1560** Rolland *Seven Sages* 124 My flesche it vggis quhen yᵗ I tuitche his hyde. **1894** Heslop *Northumbld. Gloss.* 754 He was ugged wi' eatin the stuff.
2. *intr.* To feel dread or apprehension, disgust or loathing. Usu. const. *at*, *of*, or *with*.
a **1340** Hampole *Psalter* xxxiv. 7 Wha is þat vggis not with a way þat is bath myrke & sliþer. *c* **1340** —— *Pr. Consc.* 6419 For þa paynes er swa fel and hard,.. þat ilk man may ugge, batheyhunge and alde, þat heres þam be reherced and talde. *c* **1380** Wyclif *Sel. Wks.* III. 117 Ne ugge þou not wiþ seknesse of þyn evyn Cristyn. *c* **1400** *Sc. Trojan War* II. 1097 Nought at the deth sche wggis there. **14..** *Tundale's Vis.* 317 Of hit was Tundale fulle yrke. When he hit sawe, he ugged sore. **1434** Misyn *Mending of Life* 122 My flesch makis me vg of my-self. *c* **1440** *Alph. Tales* 209 He vgged so with þe fend þat he cryed hugelie, & said he wold nott go with hym. *c* **1590** J. Stewart *Poems* (S.T.S.) II. 228 Glottonnie he vas so filthie fy, I vggit vith the discheis quhilk he buir. **1865** Janet Hamilton *Poems* (1885) 100 It's no the wife that curls her nose At cogs o' sowens or cadger's brose, An' uggs at lang-kail.
†**b.** Const. *to* with inf. *Obs.*
a **1395** Hylton *Scala Perf.* II. xv (W. de W. 1494), It is made..soo dredfull to her thynkynge that they uggen & lothen for to thinke vpon it. **1435** Misyn *Fire of Love* 43 þa vg..to be borne to þer lust. *c* **1440** *Alph. Tales* 478 Becauce þou vggid to sla so mych innocent blude. *c* **1560** A. Scott *Poems* xxxiv. 119, I vg, for villanie, ȝour vycis to reherss. **1562** Winȝet *Vincent. Lirin.* xi. Wks. (S.T.S.) II. 31 Quhat materis I pray ȝow? I wg to tell.
c. *Sc.* (See quot.)
1824 Mactaggart *Gallovid. Encycl.*, Ugg, to vomit.
3. *trans.* To abhor, loathe, detest.
a **1340** Hampole *Ps.* xli. 13 He þis felid of þe swetnes of heuen, and vggid þe perils of þe warld. *c* **1400** *Apol. Loll.* 109 Wylful begging of stalworþ men..of Salomon..is vggid, and many fold reprouid of holy doctoris. **1435** Misyn *Fire of Love* 64 A trew sawle..lufys meyknes; vaynglory it vggis, for myrth euer-lastyng onely desyrand. *a* **1568** '*My Mistres*' 26 in *Bannatyne Poems* (1881) vii. 1081, I hate and vgg hir greedie dispositioune. **1721** Ramsay *To Earl Dalhousie* 47 What his kind frighted mother ugs, Is music to the soger's lugs. **1793** T. Scott *Poems* 367 Thus ane aye seekin' what another ugs. **1825** Brockett *N.C. Gloss.*, *Ug*, to feel abhorrence at.
Hence †**ugged** *ppl. a.*, horrid, loathsome. *Obs.*⁻⁰ **ˈugging** *ppl. a.*, causing loathing or disgust. *Sc.*
1570 Levins *Manip.* 49/20 Vgged, *fædus*. **1832–53** A. MacLaggan in *Whistle-binkie* Ser. II. 118 I'm neither sae auld, auld, Nor am I sae gruesome or uggin.

‖**ugali** (uːˈgɑːliː). [Swahili.] A type of maize porridge eaten in east and central Africa. Also *attrib.*
1970 *Kenya Farmer* Feb. 24/4 A maizemeal consumer in Kaloleni said that although the taste of the 'ugali' prepared from the new cereal was similar to that of 'ugali' prepared from ordinary granulated maizemeal, the new cereal was coarser and darker. **1974** *Sunday News* (Tanzania) 29 Sept. 4/7 We would get out early in the morning—work for a few hours before stopping at about ten thirty for an ugali break —then everyone would disperse and resume their normal jobs.

Uganda (juːˈgændə). The name of a central African State used *attrib.*, as **Uganda kob**, a large brown waterbuck, *Adenota kob thomasi*, found in parts of Uganda.
1915 Roosevelt & Heller *Life-Histories Afr. Game Animals* II. xvi. 511 The Uganda kob differs from the typical race by its larger size and darker coloration. **1964** C. Willock *Enormous Zoo* ii. 30 Uganda kob stare from the tall grass.

Ugandan (juːˈgændən), *a.* and *sb.* [f. prec. + -an.] **A.** *adj.* **1.** Of or pertaining to Uganda or its people.
1962 *Times Index* Nov.–Dec. 79/1 Ugandan and Tanganyikan Prime Ministers to appeal to Mr. Macmillan. **1969** *Times* 15 Sept. (Uganda Suppl.) p. i/3 One of the most delicate feats of balance facing the Ugandan Government. **1972** *Listener* 7 Sept. 291/2 A poll in the *Daily Express*.. showed that only six out of every 100 people wanted to see the Ugandan Asians allowed in immediately. **1982** *Daily Tel.* 4 Dec. 6/7 Anyone convicted of giving away examination papers to candidates will be liable to two years in jail..under a Bill approved by the Ugandan Parliament yesterday.
2. A euphemism for 'sexual' adopted by the British satirical magazine *Private Eye*.
[**1975** *Private Eye* 21 Mar. 5/3 After dinner..the party became more informal and discussions of African affairs began to take place while a film featuring Linda Lovelace and an Alsatian dog was shown.] *Ibid.* 11 July 6/3 Margaret, Duchess of Argyll..depicts this charming old gentleman, who often kisses young girls outside Annabel's, as a narrow-minded, boring Ugandan expert. *Ibid.* 25 July 5/3 There is even talk of his writing the Duke's life story, a saga of wine, gambling and Ugandan Affairs. **1983** *Times* 7 Sept. 11/2 Amin's most spectacular accusation was that [Princess] Elizabeth [of Toro] had made love to a Frenchman at Orly Airport. It was a strange charge..but one that nevertheless received worldwide publicity and gave rise to the phrase 'Ugandan practices'. **1983** C. Adam *Let.* in *Ibid.* 13 Sept. 13/7 The phrase 'Ugandan practices'..was coined by *The Sunday Times* theatre critic some 11 years ago at a party in my house when I suggested to Mr James Fenton that he should go into a room where an interesting exile was 'talking about Uganda'. He was doing no such thing; and *Private Eye* soon picked up the phrase as one of their house jokes. **1985** *Computing* 9 May 88/3 Despite not being rational creatures..they can at least enjoy activities of a Ugandan nature.
B. *sb.* A native or inhabitant of Uganda.
1963 *Punch* 3 July 4/2 A tall Ugandan in his ankle-length white robe. **1977** *Whitaker's Almanack 1978* 588/1 President Amin declared that neither he nor any other Ugandans would attend the Commonwealth Conference in London.

Uˌgandaniˈzation. [f. prec. + -ization.] In Uganda, the replacement of settlers and Asians by Ugandan Africans in government posts, the civil service, and other occupations.
1962 *Economist* 13 Oct. 132/1 The government's recent adoption of the term 'Ugandanisation' in place of 'Africanisation'. **1969** *Times* 15 Sept. (Uganda Suppl.) p. i/4 In filling new jobs, the Government has had to choose between Ugandanization, which allows Asian citizens to qualify, and Africanization, which looks at colour rather than citizenship. **1970** [see Kenyanization].

Ugaritic (uːgəˈrɪtɪk), *sb.* and *a.* [f. *Ugarit*, the name of an ancient city in northern Syria + -ic.] **A.** *sb.* A pre-Phoenician Semitic language examples of which were first discovered at the site of Ugarit by Claude Schaeffer in 1929. **B.** *adj.* Of or pertaining to this language.
1936 H. L. Ginsberg in *Orientalia* V. 179 There is excellent reason for believing that Phoenician was almost identical with Ugaritic. **1938** A. Goetze in *Jrnl. Amer. Orient. Soc.* LVIII. 266 The student who approaches the Ugaritic epics.. is startled by the fact that the long narrative passages..are for the most part in the 'imperfect' (ygtl). **1951** A. M. Honeyman in H. H. Rowley *Old Testament & Mod. Study* 279 The precise linguistic affiliation of the Ugaritic tongue was for some time the subject of keen debate, Bauer and Goetze holding that..Ugaritic cannot be classed as a Canaanite dialect. **1955** *Proc. Prehistoric Soc.* XXI. 177 There is a curious knife from Galilee which has a cuneiform inscription on the blade in the Ugaritic of the second half of the second millennium. **1963** *Listener* 31 Jan. 213/2 In northern Syria the thirty-letter Ugaritic cuneiform alphabet was already a precise instrument for recording phonetically several quite distinct tongues. **1973** A. R. Millard in D. J. Wiseman *Peoples of Old Testament Times* ii. 47 The tremendous impetus given to Hebrew studies by the recovery of the Ugaritic texts. **1981** *Word 1980* XXXI. 222 We have here an important isogloss for the chronological division of the Semitic languages into languages with *š* (Akkadian, Ugaritic, Eblaite,..), languages with *h* [etc.].

uge, ME. variant of huge *a.*

†**ugertful**, *a. Sc. Obs.* Also ogert-. [f. ogart.] Proud; nice, squeamish.
1755 Forbes *Jrnl. fr. London* 29 Ye ken well enough that I was never vera ogertfu'. *c* **1770** Beattie *To Alex. Ross* 63 Our fine newfangle sparks, I grant ye,.. They're grown sae ugertfu' and vaunty. **1808** Jamieson.

ˈugging, *vbl. sb.* [f. ug *v.* + -ing¹.] Dread, fear, horror, loathing.
c **1250** *Gen. & Ex.* 950 Ðo cam on him vgging [L. *horror*] and friȝt. *Ibid.* 2826 Vgging and dred me haueð numen. *a* **1340** Hampole *Psalter, Song Moses* ii. 13 He fand him in land deserte: in stede of vggynge [L. *in loco horroris*], and in waste wildirnes. *Ibid.*, In þe wrechidnes of þis life, in þe qwilke is vggynge for drede of wa. **1650–1** R. Baillie *Lett. & Jrnls.* (1842) III. 126 The ugging of sundrie good people to see numbers of grievous bloodshedders ready to come in.

†**ˈuggle**, *a. Obs.*⁻⁰ [f. the stem of ug *sb.* and *v.* Cf. ougle *a.*, and mod.Norw. *uggall* (Ross).] = ugly *a.* 1.
1499 *Promp. Parv.* (Pynson), Vggyll, *horridus, horribilis*. Pynson has also the verb *ugglyn* for *uggyn*, *uggone* (see ug *v.*) of the manuscripts.]

ugglesome (ˈʌg(ə)lsʌm), *a.* Now *rare.* Also 6–7 **vgle-**; 9 **ogglesome**. *β.* 6–7 **ouglesome**. [app. f. prec. + -some.] Fearful, horrible, gruesome.
α. **1561** T. Hoby tr. *Castiglione's Courtyer* iii. (1577) Q viij, Some are compelled by their fathers to take olde men ful of diseases vglesome and wayward. *Ibid.* iv. X iij b, A face darke, vglesome, vnpleasaunt, and to be shunned for yll. **1576** Foxe *A. & M.* (ed. 3) 1904/2 When I beholde the amiable countenance of Christ..yᵉ vglesome [1563 vgsome] face of death doth not greatly trouble me. **1583** Stubbes *Anat. Abus.* i. (1877) 188 They shal be punished in fire and brimstone amongest the terrible Company of vgglesome Deuills. **1591** —— *Christal Glasse* C ij b, As though she saw some filthie vgglesome, and displeasant thing. **1617** J. Moore *Mappe Mans Mort.* i. viii. 58 It shewed..our vglesome shape, most monstrous to beholde.
1855 *Chambers' Jrnl.* 7 July 13 This 'ugglesome beast' seldom troubles me, for his dwelling is in some secluded cleft of the stone. **1864** Sala in *Daily Tel.* 14 Nov., That weird and ogglesome beast the Wangdoodlum.
β. **1575** Vautrollier *Luther on Ep. Gal.* 260 In the wilde wildernes, which being burnt vp with the heat of the Sunne, yeldeth an ouglesome habitation to the Monkes. **1608** Dod & Cleaver *Expos. Prov.* xi–xii. 69 In the froward he seeth the work of the diuell, whereby they are deprauued and made most vile & ouglesome. **1622** S. Ward *Life of Faith in Death* (1627) 26 When I behold the ouglesome face of death, I am afrayd, but when I consider Christs amiable Countenance, I take heart againe. [Cf. quot. 1576 above.]

uggliness, uggly, obs. varr. ugliness, ugly.

ugh (ʊh, ʌh, ɜːh, ʊx, etc.), *int.* and *sb.* [Imitative.]
1. A representation of an inarticulate sound of the nature of a hollow cough; a sound or utterance of this nature.
1765 Foote *Commissary* i. (1782) 12 Ugh, ugh, ugh— [coughs]. **1822** Scott *Nigel* xxiii, The usurer..concluded his speech with a dry 'ugh, ugh'. **1859** Thackeray *Virgin.* li, The next moment,..with an *ugh*, the Indian fell over my chest dead. **1887** L. Oliphant *Episodes* (1888) 70 My address was frequently interrupted by what Fenimore Cooper calls 'expressive ughs'.
2. An interjection expressive of disgust.
1837 Howitt *Rur. Life* ii. v. (1862) 140 The overhanging banks of the most transparent streams—ugh! they are now the very lurking-places of danger! **1855** Browning *Childe Roland* xxi, It may have been a water-rat I speared, But, ugh! it sounded like a baby's shriek. **1878** Dale *Lect. Preach.* viii. 242 Physic..all the year round;..ugh!—it is intolerable.

ugh(e, obs. forms of yew.

ughin, var. of dial. *agin* again *prep.*
1767 S. Paterson *Another Trav.* I. 368 Six to four ughin your lordship, and I say done first.

†**ˈughten.** *Obs.* Forms: 1 **uhtan**, 3 **uhhtenn**, 4 **vȝten**, **vghtene**. See also oughten. [Common Teutonic: OE. *úhtan*, obl. form of **úhte* wk.

fem. = OS. *ûhta* (MLG. *uchten*, LG. *ucht*; MDu. *uchten*, *ochten*, Du. *ucht-*, *ochtend*), OHG. *ûhtâ*, *uohtâ* (MHG. *uohte*, *uhte*), Goth. *ūhtwō*, ON. and Icel. *ótta* (Norw. and Sw. *otta*) in the same sense: relationship to forms outside of Germanic is uncertain. In ME., as in MLG. and MDu., the oblique case in which the word commonly occurred was adopted in place of the original nominative.]

1. The part of the night immediately before daybreak; early morning.

Beowulf 126 Ða wæs on uhtan mid ærdæge Grendles guðcræft gumum undyrne. **971** *Blickling Hom.* 47 Syxtan siþe on niht ær he ræste, seofoþan siþe on uhtan. *c* **1000** *Saxon Leechd.* III. 20 Læt standan þreo niht; syle drincan ær uhton lytelne scænc fulne. *c* **1200** ORMIN 2484 Godess enngell comm himm to Onn uhhtenn þær he sleppte. *a* **1300** *K. Horn* 1474 (Camb. MS.), Hi sloȝen & fuȝten, þe niȝt & þe vȝten. **13..** *E.E. Allit. P.* B. 893 Ruddon of þe day-rawe ros vpon vȝten, When merk of þe mydnyȝt moȝt no more last. **13..** *St. Erkenwolde* 118 in Horstm. *Altengl. Leg.* (1881) 268 Ser Erkenwolde was vp in þe vghtene ere þene.

2. *attrib.* in **ughten-tide**; also **ughten-song**, = UHTSONG.

c **900** tr. *Bæda's Eccl. Hist.* IV. xii. 300 Neowe steorra.. in uhttide [*Ca.* uhtantide] wæs upeornende. *c* **950** *Lindisf. Gosp.* Mk. xiii. 35 On uhte tid [*Rushw.* uhtu-tid] *vel* on honcroed. *c* **1200** ORMIN 5832 Hu Crist ras upp off dæþe Onn uhhtenntid te þridde daȝȝ. *Ibid.* 6360 Wiþþ daȝȝsang & wiþþ uhhtennsang, Wiþþ messess & wiþþ beness. **13..** [see next].

Hence **'ughtening** (also *dial.* oachenin), in the same sense.

a **1300** *E.E. Psalter* lxxii. 14, I was swongen al þe dai, And in vghteninges [*Harl. MS.* uhtentide] mi þhraying ai. *Ibid.* c. 9 In vghteninge I slogh with hand Alle þe sinful of þe land. *c* **1900** *Eng. Dial. Dict.* (Caithness dial.), *Oachenin*, the early dawn.

uȝten, variant of UGHTEN *Obs.*

uglesome, variant of UGGLESOME *a.*

Ugli ('ʌglɪ). Also ugli(fruit). [Alteration of UGLY *a.*] The proprietary name of a hybrid citrus fruit, first produced in Jamaica by crossing the Seville orange *Citrus aurantium*, the grapefruit *C. paradisi*, and the tangerine, *C. reticulata*. Cf. TANGELO.

1934 *Daily Gleaner* (Kingston, Jamaica) 26 Feb. 19 Should the name of 'ugli' fruit be changed to a more beautiful name? **1938** *Trade Marks Jrnl.* 7 Dec. 1498 *Ugli*, ..fresh citrus fruits...2nd August, 1938. **1943** WEBBER & BATCHELOR *Citrus Industry* I. 650 The Ugli is a very interesting fruit, probably a hybrid, that first came to the writer's attention..in February, 1934. **1951** *Amer. Speech* XXVI. 35 *Ugli*...The mother tree..was discovered near Brown's Town, Jamaica, about 1914. **1958** *Spectator* 13 June 770/2 Passion fruit, mangoes, uglifruit, and pomegranates. **1975** *Austral. Post* 31 July 27/1 Prince Charles loves an ugli, so said the Queen when she opened London's new Covent Garden market recently.

uglification (ʌglɪfɪ'keɪʃən). [f. next: see -FICATION.]

1. The action or process of making ugly.

1820 SHELLEY *Œd. Tyr.* I. 409 Where, for more glory, let the ceremony Take place of the uglification of the Queen. **1863** *N. & Q.* 3rd Ser. IV. 521 A more thorough uglification of our written or spoken language could hardly have been devised. **1890** *Longm. Mag.* Mar. 506 Their experiments in the science of comparative uglification.

2. That which renders ugly.

1893 *Westm. Gaz.* 8 Apr. 1/3 London..has no street architecture. It has no decorations, though it has many uglifications.

uglify ('ʌglɪfaɪ), *v.* [f. UGLY *a.* + -FY.] *trans.* To make ugly or repulsive in appearance; to disfigure.

1576 NEWTON *Lemnie's Complex.* II. iii. 117 It defourmeth and vglyfyeth the skinne wyth dry, skuruye, skalie, mangie, and fylthye eruptions. **1650** B. *Discolliminium* 46 These derne, dreery, direfull dayes condunghill'd and uglified me into a darke dense lumpe. **1792** MME. D'ARBLAY *Diary* V. VII. 313 She is..completely a beauty... She uglifies everything near her. **1834** *Tait's Mag.* I. 613/1 When Mr. Luke marvelled at his daughter, disguised and uglified. **1857** HAWTHORNE *Eng. Note-bks.* (1870) II. 317, I remember little or nothing of this edifice, except that the Covenanters had uglified it with pews and a gallery, and whitewash. **1898** J. A. HOBSON *Ruskin* 304 The power exercised by irresponsible wealth..to uglify the outward aspects of life.

Hence **'uglifying** *ppl. a.*

1886 *New Princetown Rev.* I. 107 A protest against that uglifying process by which women are coaxed into resignation to old age and death.

uglily ('ʌglɪlɪ), *adv.* Also 4 vgglili, 6–7 ouglily. [f. UGLY *a.* + -LY².] In an ugly manner, in senses of the adj.

a **1300** *Cursor M.* 29297 þe man..þat kirkes brinnes or vgglili þar inwit sinnes,..he es cursd. *a* **1586** SIDNEY *Arcadia* III. (1912) 388 Fowler deaths had ouglily displayed their trayling guttes. **1615** G. SANDYS *Trav.* 134 Charon grim Ferri-man these streames doth guard, Vglily nastie. **1668** H. MORE *Div. Dial.* III. xv. (1713) 208 His Head uglily starting out from the midst of his Breast. **1685** —— *Paralip. Prophet.* Pref. p. xxiii, Two statuary Poppets..must needs bear out Aaron's Breast-plate, very uglily and ill-favour'dly while they are there. **1755** JOHNSON, *Uglily*, filthily; with deformity; in such a manner as to raise dislike. **1834** SOUTHEY *Doctor* lxxxvii. (1848) 191 In those representations man indeed was not more uglily than fearfully made. **1869** D. W. FRESHFIELD *Central Caucasus & Bashan* ii. 19 The town is..uglily picturesque, if one may use such a phrase.

ugliness ('ʌglɪnɪs). Forms: 4, 6– ugli- (4, 6–7 vgli-), 4, 7–8 ugly- (5 vgly-); 5 vgg(e)ly-, 7 uggli-; 6 ougly-, 6–7 ougli-, 9 *dial.* oogli-; also 4–5 -nes, 5–7 -nesse. [f. UGLY *a.* + -NESS.]

†**1.** Horror, dread, loathing. *Obs.*

c **1325** *Metr. Hom.* 21 For folc sal duin for din of se, And for baret that than sal be, Ouer al this werd bes rednes, Wandreth, and uglines. **1340** HAMPOLE *Pr. Consc.* 6832 'þar nan ordre wonand es,' says he, 'Bot uglynes [L. *horror*] þat ever mare sal be'. *a* **1395** HYLTON *Scala Perf.* I. xxxvii. (W. de W. 1494), Some men he tempteth also and namely solitary men & wymmen by dredes and vglynes, and quakynges and shakynges. *a* **1400** *Relig. Pieces fr. Thornton MS.* 43 Whare we sulde hafe vgglynes als vn-till oure body, for to ete flesche, and drynke blude of man, oure Lorde Ihesu Criste turnede his flesche and his blude in liknes of brede and of wyne. *a* **1425** tr. *Arderne's Treat. Fistula*, etc. 8 þof-al I suffre no-þing, vgglynes [L. *horror*] of suffryng holdeth me.

†**b.** A cause of horror or loathing. *Obs.*

1587 GOLDING *De Mornay* xvi. 294 What an ouglynesse then ought it to be vnto vs, when wee see how men..doe euery howre kill..and roote out one another?

2. The state of being ugly to look at; repulsiveness or marked inelegance of appearance: **a.** As an abstract quality.

Stronger in earlier than in later use.

c **1340** HAMPOLE *Pr. Consc.* 917 Aftir man,..vermyn es, And aftir vermyn stynkand uglynes. *c* **1440** *Promp. Parv.* 509/2 Vggelynesse, *horribilitas*. **1596** SPENSER *F.Q.* VI. vi. 10 But all her hinder parts did plaine expresse A monstrous Dragon, full of fearefull vglinesse. **1623** MIDDLETON *More Dissemblers* V. ii. 102 A thing whose face, through ugliness, frights children. **1642** MILTON *Apol. Smect.* Wks. 1851 III. 316 Which to dresse up and garnish with a devis'd bravery ..addes nothing but a deform'd uglinesse. **1703** ROWE *Fair Penit.* II. 22 You blast the Fair with Lies because they scorn you, Hate you like Age, like Ugliness and Impotence. **1756** BURKE *Subl. & B.* III. xxi, Though ugliness be the opposite to beauty it is not the opposite to proportion and fitness. **1798** S. & HT. LEE *Canterb. T.* II. 25 Her features had every disadvantage of ugliness, but that of being remarkable. **1820** KEATS *Lamia* I. 164 Of all these bereft, Nothing but pain and ugliness were left. **1844** KINGLAKE *Eothen* xvii, The awful haggardness that gave something of character to the faces of the men was sheer ugliness in the poor women. **1885–94** R. BRIDGES *Eros & Psyche* March v, She was as far From pictured beauty as is ugliness.

b. As a quality of particular things or persons.

c **1340** HAMPOLE *Pr. Consc.* 2364 Sen þe devel þus has tane his uglines Of þe filth of syn, þat swa filand es. *c* **1400** *Cursor M.* 27638 (Cott. Galba), When he wex proud..out of heuyn he fell to hell, And al his vglines he toke Of sin of pride. **1608** WILLET *Hexapla Exod.* 97 The Egyptians..were.. punished..with the number and vglines of them [frogs]. *a* **1618** SYLVESTER *Mem. Mortalitie* iii, Death's ougliness is but imagined; Under foule Vizard a faire Face shee wears. **1658** T. WALL *Charact. Enemies Ch.* 31 The ugliness of its [the leopard's] shape would more affright then the sweetness of its scent allure. **1756** MRS. CALDERWOOD in *Coltness Collect.* (Maitl. Cl.) 193 And what adds to the uglyness of the town is the dirty smoaky look it has. **1826** F. REYNOLDS *Life & Times* I. 19, I was perfectly startled at his ugliness. **1849** MACAULAY *Hist. Eng.* vi. II. 69 Charles, though he liked her conversation, laughed at her ugliness. **1861** M. PATTISON *Ess.* (1889) I. 45 High above, the Imperial double eagle figured in all its ugliness, like a scarecrow nailed to a barn door.

c. An instance of this quality; an ugly thing or feature.

1856 HAWTHORNE *Eng. Note-bks.* (1879) I. 313 All full of monstrosities and horrible uglinesses.

3. Moral repulsiveness or offensiveness; disgusting wickedness.

1601 BARLOW *Serm. Paules Crosse* B vij b, We, being commanded by authority,..did describe the nature and vglinesse of the rebellion. **1646** HAMMOND *Death-bed Repent.* 66 A consideration of the..detestable uglynesse of sinne. **1684** *Contempl. St. Man* I. ix. (1699) 95 The ugliness likewise of Human Nature shall be discovered. **1844** KINGLAKE *Eothen* v, A shock of this kind disclosing the *ugliness* of a cheat, is more..convincing than any mere proofs. **1858** HAWTHORNE *Fr. & It. Note-bks.* (1871) II. 3, I should like to know what it was..that made him insist upon having his actual likeness perpetrated, with all the ugliness of its animal and moral character. **1869** MᶜLAREN *Serm.* Ser. II. vii. 113 The Bible tells the shameful history in all its naked ugliness.

4. *dial.* Bad temper; disagreeableness.

1889 MABEL PEACOCK *Tales* 76, I knaw what he is, when he's full o' his ugliness.

†**'uglisome**, *a. Obs. rare.* Also 6 oug(g)lisom(e. [f. next + -SOME. Cf. UGGLESOME *a.*] Horrible, horrid; ugly.

1530 PALSGR. 328/1 Uglysome, *horryble, execrable*. **1583** STUBBES *Anat. Abus.* II. (1882) 51 Barbers are verie necessarie, for otherwise men should grow verie ougglisom and deformed.

ugly ('ʌglɪ), *a.*, *adv.*, and *sb.* Forms: *α.* 3 uglike (iglic), 4–5 vg-, ugli, 4- ugly (4–7 vgly, 5 igly, *Sc.* wgly, 5, 7 vgely), 6 vg-, uglye, 6–7 vg-, uglie (6 *Sc.* wg-); 4 uggeli, 5–6 vggely(e, vggly(e, 5–7 vggly; 4 ogli, 6 oglie, oggly. *β.* 5 oughlye, 7 oughly; 5–6 owgly, 6 ouglye, 6–7 ougly, -lie, 9 *dial.* oogly. *γ.* 4 hoggyliche, hogely, 6 hogly; 4–6 hugly, 5 hughely, 5–6 houghly, 6 hougly. [ad. ON. *ugglig-r* to be feared or dreaded, f. *ugga* UG *v.*: see -LY¹.

The forms *iglic* in *Gen. & Ex.* 2918 and *igly* in the Harl. MS. of Chaucer *Clerk's T.* 673 are difficult to account for.]

A. *adj.* **1.** Having an appearance or aspect which causes dread or horror; frightful or horrible, esp. through deformity or squalor. (Now merged in sense 3.)

α. c **1250** *Gen. & Ex.* 2805 [Moses] it warp vt of hise hond, And wurð sone an uglike snake. *Ibid.* 2918 Moyseses migtful wond..wurð bi-foren pharaon An Iglic snake sone on-on. *a* **1300** *Cursor M.* 11606 þar þai þam thoght to rest and slepe, þar did þai mari for to light, Bot son þai sagh an vgli sight. *c* **1340** HAMPOLE *Pr. Consc.* 860 Nathyng es swa ugly, Als here es a mans dede body. *Ibid.* 6683 Swylk filthe and stynk es in þat ugly hole. **1423** JAS. I *Kingis Q.* clxii, And vnderneth the quhele sawe I there Ane vgly pit, was depe as ony helle. *c* **1470** HENRY *Wallace* II. 247 Thai chargyt the geyler..to..bryng him wp out of that vgly sell. **1500–20** DUNBAR *Poems* xi. 20 Ȝit may thow be, within ane ȝeir, Ane vgsum, vglye tramort. *a* **1547** SURREY *Æneid* IV. 626 Agamemnons son:..That sitting found within the temples porche The vglie furies his slaughter to revenge. **1594** KYD *Cornelia* II. 13 Fayne would I die, but darksome vgly Death With-holds his darte, and in disdaine doth flye me. **1613** PURCHAS *Pilgrimage* VIII. vi. 639 The faces of their Priests are painted as vgly as they can deuise. **1643** A. ROSSE *Mel Helic.* 77 His snakie hairs doe shew how uggly he [*sc.* Cerberus] is in the sight of good men. **1667** MILTON *P.L.* XI. 464 O sight Of terrour, foul and ugly to behold, Horrid to think, how horrible to feel! **1680** OTWAY *Orphan* II. i, I struck The ugly brindled Monster to the heart. **1789** T. RUSSELL *Sonn.* xi, Uglier far than have been feign'd or fear'd, Ten thousand Phantoms to my sight appear'd.

β. **1426** LYDG. *De Guil. Pilgr.* 11036 Somwhyle, off dyrknesse And off the owgly ffoul thyknesse,..Thow shalt lese the syht off me. *c* **1430** LYDG. *Min. Poems* (Percy Soc.) 145 Yif he hadde..Seyn that owgly careyn lamentable. **1550** CRAWLEY *Epigr.* 376 A greate mastyfe dogge and a foule ouglye beare. **1587** HOLINSHED *Chron.* III. 835/1 Suddenlie came out..eight wildmen,..with ouglie weapons & terrible visages. **1595** *Locrine* III. i. 7 Those ougly diuels of black Erebus, That might torment the damned traitors soule! **1601** HOLLAND *Pliny* XXVI. i. II. 240 These new-come diseases verely were..so foule and filthie, so loathsome and ougly, that a man would have chosen rather to die..than to bee so disfigured. **1633** P. FLETCHER *Purple Isl.* I. xl, Darknesse headlong fell, Frighted with suddain beams,.. And plung'd her ougly head in deepest hell. **1640** GLAPTHORN *Ladies Privilege* III, But know the shape of Death Is not ougly to me.

γ. **13..** *Adultery* 85 in Herrig's *Archiv* LXXIX. 420 He ledd hym to an hogely hylle; þe erthe openyd & in þei ȝede. *c* **1375** *Sc. Leg. Saints* ii. (*Paul*) 1151 þan come a schadow full hugly, blak & blay, & stud hyme by. *c* **1470** HARDING *Chron.* CVII. vi. (1543) 107 b, Echeon their nose and ouer lippe ful right Cut of anone which was an hougly [*v.r.* hogly] sight. **1555** W. WATREMAN *Fardle Facions* I. iv. C ij, There be in it [Ethiopia] dyuers peoples of sondry phisonomy and shape, monstruous and of hugly shewe. **1565** STAPLETON tr. *Bede's Hist. Ch. Eng.* 95 These foure fyres encreasing by litle and litle so farr at the length extended, that ioyning altogether they grew to a great and houghly flame.

†**2. a.** Of events, times, etc.: Dreadful, terrible.

a **1300** *Cursor M.* 22519 Uggeli sal be þe fift dai, Mare þan ani tung can sai. *a* **1340** HAMPOLE *Psalter* ix. 37 Vgly is it to fall in þere hend, for þou bihaldis þe trauaile and þe sorow þat he has doen till haly men. **13..** *E.E. Allit. P.* B. 892 Bot þay wern wakned..Of on þe vglokest vnhap þat euer on erd suffred. *c* **1460** *Towneley Myst.* xvi. 142 Sich panys hard neuer man tell, For vgly and for fell. *a* **1586** SIDNEY *Ps.* (1823) VI. iii, Turn thee, sweete Lord, and from this ougly fall, My deere God, stay me. **1597** J. PAYNE *Royal Exch.* 41 This wylie feynd geves not his onsett after his vglie and terrible maner.

b. Of sounds. (Passing into sense 6.)

c **1400** *Destr. Troy* 3701 With an ugli noise, noye for to here, Hit sundrit þere sailes & þere sad ropis. *c* **1400** MAUNDEV. (Roxb.) xxxi. 138 In þis vale er oft tymes herd.. voices vggly and hidous. *c* **1440** *York Myst.* xxxvii. 101 What! heris þou noȝt þis vggely noyse. **1513** DOUGLAS *Æneid* III. iv. 31 The Harpyes..voce also was wglie for to heir. **1550** LYNDESAY *Sq. Meldrum* 738 Than rais the reik with vglie crakkis. *a* **1585** MONTGOMERIE *Flyting* 503 The cry was sa ouglie, of elfes, aips, and owles. **1603** G. OWEN *Pembrokeshire* (1892) 249 At certaine tymes there is vgglye and terrible noyses and soundes hard to proceede from the same pitte. **1725** DE FOE *Voy. round World* (1840) 87 Great numbers came down to the shore, staring at us, and making confused ugly noises.

3. Offensive or repulsive to the eye; unpleasing in appearance; of disagreeable or unsightly aspect: **a.** Of persons.

α. c **1375** *Sc. Leg. Saints* ii. (*Paul*) 778 þan sperit he [*sc.* Nero] rycht besyly, gyf þat he wes sa wgly Quhen he wes borne. *c* **1386** CHAUCER *Clerk's T.* 673 This vgly sergeant.. Hath hent hire sone þat ful was of beautee. *c* **1400** MAUNDEV. (Roxb.) xvii. 77 þir wymmen er riȝt blak and vggly to behold. *c* **1480** HENRYSON *Test. Cres.* 372 He luikit on hir vglye Lipper face, The quhilk befor was quhite as Lillie flour. **1509** BARCLAY *Ship of Folys* (1570) 198 The uggly Maurians are also of this sect. *a* **1548** HALL *Chron.*, *Hen. VIII*, 130 b, If the Frenche Quene, whiche was lame and ugly were dedde,..then waies might bee founde. **1580** H. GIFFORD *Gilloflowers, Dream* xv, An oggly creature, all in blacke. **1606** SHAKS. *Ant. & Cl.* II. v. 96 Had'st thou Narcissus in thy face to me, Thou would'st appeere most vgly. **1634** SIR T. HERBERT *Trav.* 49 They are the most vgly and impudent Whoores, in all Persia. *a* **1687** VILLIERS (Dk. Buckhm.) *Speeches* (1775) 237 Like ugly foolish children, whom, because of their deformity and want of wit, the parents are ashamed of. **1717** PRIOR *Alma* II. 350 Dames, who Native Beauty want, Still uglier look, the more They paint. **1742** BERKELEY *Lett.* Wks. 1871 IV. 286 You would be less zealous were the Queen old and ugly. **1794** S. WILLIAMS *Vermont* 195 They have all the same sallow complexion, deformed features, ugly appearance. **1815** SCOTT *Guy M.* liii, The fairy bride of Sir Gawaine..was more decrepit probably, and what is commonly called more ugly, than Meg Merrilies. **1858** HAWTHORNE *Fr. & It. Note-bks.* (1871) I. 98 A very ugly old man indeed—wrinkled, puckered, shrunken. **1879** FARRAR *St. Paul* (1883) 390 The ugly Greek who was the noblest of all Greeks.

absol. **1766** GOLDSM. *Vicar* xxxi, After having tried in vain [to find a wife], even amongst the pert and the ugly.

β. c 1400 *Rom. Rose* 3038 He was so hidous and so oughlye, I mene this that Trespasse hight. c 1407 Lydg. *Reson & Sens.* 1934 This lady, Dame hatrede, To-rent and owgly in her wede. 1548 Udall *Erasm. Par. Mark* i. 16 Hence with this ougly and abhominable creature. 1598 R. Haydocke tr. *Lomazzo* II. 133 Though a woman be faire, merry, and healthy and yet be dishonest, shee must needes seeme most ougly to an ingenuous and honest minde. 1610 Shaks. *Temp.* IV. i. 192 And, as with age, his body ouglier growes, So his minde cankers.

γ. 1562 Bullein *Bulwarke, Sicke Men* 13 Keepe the mouth, teeth, and tongue cleane,..whych els shalbe corrupted, defiled, and so anoyed, that it shalbe..hugely and noysome to the beholders.

b. Of animals.

c 1375 *Sc. Leg. Saints* ii. (*Paul*) 780 þat vgly padok þan gert he ta. 1444 *Pol. Poems* (Rolls) II. 218 The owgly bakke wyl gladly fleen be nyght Dirk cressetys and laumpys that been lyght. 1508 Dunbar *Flyting* 185 Thow pure-hippit, vgly averill, With hurkland banis, holkand throw thy hyd. 1587 Turberv. *Trag. T.* (1837) 31 Two monstrous mastyves eke he sawe that ran Close by her side, two ugly curres they were. 1614 Sylvester *Bethulia's Rescue* II. 175 Millions of millions of foule Frogs hee makes To cover Memphis with their ougly Frie. 1643 Sir T. Browne *Relig. Med.* I. 102 16, I cannot tell by what Logick we call a Toad, a Beare, or an Elephant, ugly. 1699 Dampier *Voy.* II. II. ii. 59 The Monkies that are in these Parts are the ugliest I ever saw. 1774 Goldsm. *Nat. Hist.* (1776) V. 355 In quadrupedes, the smallest animals are noxious, ugly and loathsome.

c. In miscellaneous uses.

α. 13.. *Seuyn Sages* (W.) 2782 With lang noses and mowthes wide, And vgly eres on ether syde. ? a 1400 *Morte Arth.* 1086 Erne had he fulle huge, and vgly to schewe, Wiþ eghne fulle horreble. c 1440 *York Myst.* xi. 265 Full vgly and full ill is it, þat was ful faire and fresshe before. 1561 T. Norton *Calvin's Inst.* I. 52 Although we graunt that the Image of God was not altogether defaced and blotted out in him, yet was it so corrupted, that all that remaineth, is but vggly deformitie. 1577 in Hakluyt *Voy.* (1589) 626 For her ougly hewe and deformitie, we let her goe. 1604 E. G[rimstone] *D'Acosta's Hist. Indies* v. xii. 360 They entred backward to their idol, and so went bending their bodies and head, after an vglie manner. 1680 C. Nesse *Church-Hist.* 122 An ugly image, half a fish and half a man. 1687 A. Lovell tr. *Thevenot's Trav.* I. 26 The streets of Constantinople are very ugly, being for the most part narrow, crooked, up-hill and down-hill. 1763 J. Brown *Poetry & Music* xiii. 227 *note*, May not the Voice and Figure of a distressed or joyous Object be so..ridiculous or ugly, as..to destroy the Sympathy of those who hear and see it? 1803 Mar. Edgeworth *Manufacturers* i, She made him pronounce an absurd eulogium on the ugliest thing in the room. 1865 Trollope *Belton Est.* i. 5 The house itself was an ugly residence..built in the time of George II. 1875 J. P. Hopps *Princ. Relig.* i. (1878) 6 Even poor savages who have never been taught any better, cling to an ugly idol,..rather than be without a god at all.

β. 1547 Baldwin *Mor. Philos.* (Palfr.) 124 Wherewith..the figure of man is as it were by enchantment transformed into an ougly and loathsome image. 1581 A. Hall *Iliad* x. 181 This Dolon was of ougly shape. 1600 Fairfax *Tasso* VII. cxvi, Heau'ns glorious lampe wrapt in an ouglie vaile Of shadowes darke. 1607 Norden *Surv. Dial.* 222 Without the aid and industrie of a skilfull husband, fairest grounds will become ougly.

d. In figurative contexts.

c 1440 *Jacob's Well* 246 Thynke of goddys presence, and be raysed to heuen be holy thouȝt. þanne se þe world foul & vggly, voyde of al goodnes. 1576 Fleming *Panopl. Epist.* 339 An infinite number, whose malice is infected with many a foule and ougly disease. a 1586 Sidney *Arcadia* v. (1605) 445 While each conceite an ougly figure beares. 1601 Yarington *Two Lament. Trag.* II. i. in Bullen *O. Pl.* IV, Where shall we hide this trumpet of your shame, This timelesse ougly map of crueltie? 1615 J. Castle in *Crt. & Times Jas. I* (1848) I. 378 Those holy men..had made him see this fearful error, and the ugly face of his sin. 1663 Davenant *2nd Pt. Siege of Rhodes* IV. i, Amazement is the uggli'st shape of fear. 1884 *Congregationalist* Jan. 14 The honest man must allow that there are ugly truths and lies with beautiful faces.

e. ***ugly duckling***, a young person who shows no promise of the beauty, success, etc., that will come with maturity (in allusion to the story by Hans Andersen first translated into English in 1846). Also *transf.*

[1871 Geo. Eliot *Middlem.* (1872) I. p. vii, Here and there a cygnet is reared uneasily among the ducklings. 1877 M. W. Chapman in H. Martineau *Autobiogr.* III. 151 Those early days..when she seems to have been like the 'ugly duckling' of Hans Christian Andersen.] 1885 A. Edwardes *Girton Girl* I. xiv. 258 As a girl she never went through that chrysalis or ugly-duckling stage. 1927 M. Sadleir *Trollope* 138 He [*sc.* Trollope] rose in the hierarchy of the Post Office. .. His ugly-duckling days were done. 1934 G. B. Shaw *Too True to be Good* Pref. 10 When one of their ugly ducklings becomes a revolutionist it is not because countryhouse life is idle, but because its activities are uncongenial. 1940 V. W. Brooks *New England: Indian Summer* xxi. 440 He had grown up in a Boston family, a strange, alien, lonely child, a duckling, far from ugly, in whom perceptive eyes foresaw the swan. 1963 B. Friedan *Feminine Mystique* xiv. 356 The feminine mystique..often forced the unhappy ones, the ugly ducklings, to find themselves while the girls who fitted the image became adjusted 'happy' housewives. 1977 D. Ramsay *You can't call it Murder* I. 49 A big, gawky ugly duckling like me. 1978 *Nature* 26 Jan. 303/3 Mass spectrometers have been something of an ugly duckling in magnetospheric research. Initially too heavy, magnetically dirty and ill suited for hot plasma measurements, they have come of age and are now invited to all the best satellite projects. 1982 M. Hinxman *Telephone never Tells* xviii. 134 The ugly duckling gawkiness of her youth had matured and mellowed.

4. a. Morally offensive or repulsive; base, degraded, loathsome, vile. In later use also in weaker sense: Offending against propriety; highly objectionable.

α. a 1300 *Cursor M.* 1106 þai thoght þat kynd him mond for-bede To haf don suilk an ogli dede. *Ibid.* 27612 þai þat sua vgli athes suers, wonder es hou þis erth þam bers. c 1340 Hampole *Prose Tr.* 33 A full forsakynge of..syne and of unclenes, with a gastely syghte of it how foule how vggly and how paynfull þat it es. c 1440 *Alph. Tales* 142 On a tyme þer was a scoler at Parissh, þat had done many vglie syn. 1583 Babington *Commandm.* (1590) 54 Sight of vglie sinne lodging still in mee..will make mee praise His name. 1608 Willet *Hexapla Exod.* 393 The most vile monstrous and vgely sinnes. 1650 Bulwer *Anthropomet.* 199 Tokens that God was grievously offended with such ugly deeds. a 1658 Cleveland *Rustick Ramp.* (1687) 431 An abominable Ceremony, which had made their Impiety more ugly. 1732 Berkeley *Alciphr.* III. §11 Is it not..an ugly system in which you can suppose no law and prove no duty? 1816 J. Wilson *City of Plague* II. v. 110 But cutting throats in a churchyard Is something new, and 'tis an ugly practice. 1879 Geo. Eliot *Theo. Such* 128, I cannot consider such courses any the less ugly because they are ascribed to temper. 1894 Simpkinson *Life & Times Laud* vi. 118 Gentlemen..who were sentenced to..do public penance in their own parish church for ugly acts of immorality.

β. 1584 Constable *Diana* III. ii, Like catife wretch by time and travell taught, His ougly ills in others good to hide. 1594 T. B. *La Primaud. Fr. Acad.* II. To Rdr., Surely of all Sathans delusions wrought by him in the hearts of vnbeleeuers, this monstrous error of atheisme is most ougly. 1602 Warner *Alb. Eng.* XIII. lxxvii. (1612) 320 Wherein were acted ouglier things than to be found mong'st beasts. 1611 Cotgr., *Landie deschiquetée*, an ouglie nickname for an ouerridden Hackney (or Harlot).

b. ***Ugly*** (or ***ugly***) ***American*** (in allusion to the title of the book: see quot. 1958), an American who behaves offensively abroad.

1958 Lederer & Burdick (*title*) The ugly American. 1965 *Atlantic Monthly* May 152 A host of odd and funny foreigners: bogus Russian counts, semi-aristocratic Slavic ladies, German officers, and an early type of the ugly American abroad. 1968 *Sat. Rev.* (U.S.) 9 Mar. 76 I don't think we were Ugly Americans; perhaps just unaware, or Unlettered. 1980 D. Williams *Murder for Treasure* x. 100 That awful man..thinks you're swinging the deal and he needs Edgar to blow it by acting the Ugly American.

5. Offensive or unpleasant to the smell or taste; noisome, nasty.

c 1400 *Destr. Troy* 8732 How the korse might be keppit..likyng to se; And not orible, ne vgly of odir to fele. 1668 Culpepper & Cole *Barthol. Anat.* I. xxviii. 70 Stinking things have filthy and ugly Vapors. 1693 Evelyn *De la Quint. Compl. Gard.* II. 148 Those kinds of rotten Dung are accompanied with an unpleasing smell that infects the Plants raised upon such Beds, and gives them an ugly Taste. 1707 Mortimer *Husb.* (1721) II. 43 It yields an ugly stench in burning. 1712 W. Rogers *Voy.* (1718) 149 The wind always blowing fresh over the land, brought any ugly noisome smell aboard from the Seals ashore. 1876 Geo. Eliot *Dan. Der.* x, Archery has no ugly smell of brimstone.

6. a. Offensive to refined taste or good feelings; objectionable, disagreeable, unpleasant, not nice.

1621 Burton *Anat. Mel.* I. iv. III. i. 272 In the midst of these squalid, vgly, and such irksome dayes, they seek at last..to be eased of all by death. 1671 Clarendon *Hist. Reb.* XI. §243 When a Man might reasonably believe that less than a universal Defection of three Nations, could not have reduced a great King to so ugly a fate. 1697 tr. *C'tess D'Aunoy's Trav.* (1706) 126, I thought it very ugly, that an Old Woman such as that was which I saw there, should come and spurt Water out of her Mouth, in my Face. 1720 *Lett. Lond. Jrnl.* (1721) 48 It would be very pleasant, if it were not for the Abuse and ugly Language you meet with. 1722 De Foe *Plague* (1754) 204 They call'd me..to an ugly and dangerous Office. 1754 W. Goodall *Exam. Lett. Mary Q. Scots* I. i. 33 To affirm that it was to be found there, when it is not, has an extreme ugly aspect. 1806 Surr *Winter in Lond.* III. 128 The idea of having a daughter of sufficient age to be presented carries with it..an ugly memento of the age of her mother. 1874 'Max Adeler' *Out of Hurly-burly* xiv. (Rtldg.) 176 With an ugly word upon his lips, he sprang from his seat. 1888 Burgon *Lives 12 Gd. Men* II. v. 18 The one person who comes out of that strife with an ugly stain upon his shield..was the Prime Minister.

b. Causing disquiet or discomfort; of a very troublesome or awkward nature.

1645 in *Verney Memoirs* (1904) I. 328 Sir Ralph replies at great length about 'this ugly business'. 1660 Marvell *Corr.* Wks. (Grosart) II. 40 The last of December here was an ugly false report got abroad, that his Majesty was stabb'd. 1672 —— *Reh. Transp.* I. 105 After things have been laid with all the depth of humane Policy, there happens lightly some ugly little contrary Accident. 1687 A. Lovell tr. *Thevenot's Trav.* II. 11 Fearing that the Galleys..might serve him some ugly trick, he caused the Entry of it to be stopt up. 1711 Swift *Jrnl. To Stella* 4 Jan., I had an ugly giddy fit last night in my chamber. 1751 *Affect. Narr. of Wager* 17 For the more expeditiously retrieving this ugly Accident, the Commodore ordered several Carpenters on board her. 1792 Burke *Let. to Sir H. Langrishe* Wks. 1842 I. 550 It is putting things into the position of an ugly alternative, into which I hope in God they never will be put. 1826 Disraeli *Viv. Grey* II. xi, A horse which he was endeavouring to cure of some ugly tricks. 1852 Thackeray *Esmond* I. xiii, My Lord Mohun (of whose exploits and fame some of the gentlemen of the University had brought down but ugly reports). 1890 *Spectator* 19 Apr., The Under-Secretary for Foreign Affairs..admitted some ugly facts.

7. a. Somewhat hazardous or perilous.

1654 *Nicholas Papers* (Camden) II. 45, I know it is an ugly time to mention goeing into England. 1711 Swift *Jrnl. to Stella* 21 Jan., It is very ugly walking; a baker's boy broke his thigh yesterday. 1889 in *Eng. Dial. Dict.*

b. Suggestive of trouble or danger.

1660 *Trial Regic.* 161, I was in the hall when that ugly Proclamation was proclaimed. 1719 De Foe *Crusoe* II. (Globe) 352 They..let fall some dangerous ugly Words. 1780 Cowper *Lett.* Mar., A long preface such as mine is an ugly symptom and always forebodes great sterility in the following pages. 1801 S. & Ht. Lee *Canterb. T.* IV. 376, I had an ugly presentiment of what was to be the subject of our conversation. 1853 Kane *Grinnell Exp.* xxix. (1856) 244 Poor Sir John Franklin! this night-drift is an ugly omen. 1888 E. Money *Dutch Maiden* 133 You think this looks ugly, but..a stern chase is a long chase.

c. Of the weather, sea, etc.: Unpleasantly or dangerously rough, stormy, or boisterous.

1744 *Lond. Mag.* 143 But little Wind, and an ugly Swell. 1781 Archer in *Naval Chron.* (1804) XI. 289 Hold fast! that was an ugly sea... Another ugly sea: sent a Midshipman to bring news from the pumps. 1840 R. H. Dana *Bef. Mast* xxxv, It is blowing harder, and an ugly head sea is running. 1844 Kinglake *Eothen* xvii, With an ugly black sky above, and an angry sea beneath. 1847 Alb. Smith *Chr. Tadpole* xxiii. (1879) 207 The flashes of lightning..shewed that it was going to be an ugly night. 1900 J. H. Harris *Our Cove* ii. 14 You know the weather is going to be 'ugly', which means anything from tricky to downright bad.

d. In phr. ***ugly customer***, a person who is likely to cause trouble, or be difficult to deal with.

1811 *Sporting Mag.* XXXVIII. 56 He is a very ugly customer. 1819 *Metropolis* I. 241 Coachee, you've picked up an ugly customer there. 1844 Dickens *Mart. Chuz.* xliii, In any such a cause you will find me, my young sir, an Ugly Customer! 1884 E. Yates *Recoll.* II. 207 The tone of the letter was exceedingly offensive and dictatorial, and it was evident that he was a very ugly customer.

e. ***the ugly man***, the actual perpetrator of an act of garroting, as distinguished from his two accomplices. (Cf. nasty *a.* 6.)

1888 *Cassell's Encycl. Dict.*

8. a. Cross, angry, ill-tempered.

1687 Alice Hatton in *H. Corr.* (Camden) II. 65, I am sorry my ugly letter gave you any disturbance. 1848 Dickens *Dombey* liv, He turned upon her with his ugliest look. 1855 Haliburton *Nat. & Hum. Nat.* I. ix. 286 Don't rile me, for I have an ugly pen, an ugly tongue, and an ugly temper. 1894 H. Gardener *Unoff. Patriot* 163 I've had to buck up to some pretty ugly talk first and last.

b. In predicative use, esp. ***to feel*** or ***look ugly***.

1796 R. Bage *Hermsprong* xxv, Lord Grondale looked ugly; the doctor did not know how to look. 1836 Haliburton *Clockmaker* Pref., I don't know as ever I felt so ugly afore since I was raised. *Ibid.* I. xii, Don't say that are any more.., for it makes me feel ugly. 1864 *Louie's Last Term* 122 You make me ten times worse every time I see you, you make me so ugly I don't know myself. 1896 *Daily News* 25 Feb. 3 It is amusing to see the clever promptitude with which they manage the brutes who look at all ugly.

9. *Comb.*, as ***ugly-clouded, conditioned, faced, -headed, -tempered, visaged*** adjs.; also ***ugly-looking*** adj.

(*a*) 1593 Marlowe & Chapman *Hero & Leander* IV. 331 So most vgly clowded was the light, That day was hid in day. 1602 Carew *Cornwall* I. 34 b, The Seale..is..not vnlike a Pigge, vgly faced, and footed like a Moldwarp. 1634 Milton *Comus* 695 What grim aspects are these, These oughly-headed Monsters? 1655 in *Verney Mem.* (1904) II. 25 The Example of very many..might somewhat excuse my signing that ugly conditioned Bond. 1849 Cupples *Green Hand* xi. (1856) 113 Ye're too tarnation ugly-faced for it, let alone colour. 1885 J. G. Waller in *Archaeologia* XLIX. 205 On the opposite side is another ugly visaged figure. 1897 *Outing* XXIX. 590/2 A good-sized, well-fed, ugly-tempered creature, with a pair of magnificent tusks.

(*b*) 1771 Smollett *Humph. Cl.* 31 May, A parcel of ugly-looking fellows came running into the water, and laid hold on our boat with great violence. 1820 Belzoni *Egypt & Nubia* III. 425 A sort of short ugly-looking fellow, turned up nose, long teeth out of his mouth, and uncommon thick lips. 1839 Sir C. Napier in Bruce *Life* iv. (1885) 132 A hundred fellows may get ugly-looking gashes.

B. *adv.* Horribly; terribly; uglily.

c 1375 *Sc. Leg. Saints* xxxiv. (*Pelagia*) 232 þe feynde þarfor hye can cry, þat mony herde, ful vgly. c 1420 *Chron. Vilod.* 3988 An horribulle, foulle grome..hoggyliche lokede vpone herre w^t horrible chere. c 1440 *Alph. Tales* 51 Yone yong man..stynkis more vglie in þe sight of God..þan done all þe carion of þis werld. c 1440 *Promp. Parv.* 509/2 Vggely, or vggely wyse, *horribiliter*. 1678 Bunyan *Pilgr.* (ed. 2) I. 187 But they desired him to let them go; with that he looked ugly upon them. 1876 [see plug-ugly]. 1897 E. Phillpotts *Lying Prophets* III. xi. 344 I'm punished ugly enough.

C. *sb.* **1.** An ugly person, animal, etc.

1755 H. Walpole *Lett.* (1846) III. 100 There were all the beauties, and all the diamonds, and not a few of the uglies of London. 1790 Mrs. Wheeler *Westmld. Dial.* (1821) 16 Monny a lump ea brass he hes teaan frae his poor barns an me, to carry to thor uglys. 1889 *Pall Mall G.* 27 June 6/1 Artists and actors,..peers and judges, beauties and uglies—they were all in the highest spirits. 1895 J. G. Millais *Breath fr. Veldt* (1899) 161 There lay old Ugly *in extremis* with his..fine tusks directed towards us.

2. a. A kind of hood or shade attached to the front of a lady's bonnet or hat as a protection to the eyes. (In use c 1850.)

1850 Thackeray *Kickleburys on Rhine* (1851) 25 'Those hoods!' she said; 'we call those hoods Uglies!' 1856 H. Mayhew *The Rhine* 107 The broad eaves project so far over that they remind you almost of a lady's 'ugly'. 1891 *Eng. Illustr. Mag.* Dec. 197 Most hideous folding shades of silk drawn on wires were affixed to the front of these bonnets, and deservedly called 'uglies'.

b. A knitted face-protector formerly worn in Canada.

1895 *Funk's Standard Dict.*

3. ***the uglies*** (slang), depression, bad temper; (see also quots. 1903 and 1974).

1846 *Swell's Night Guide* 77, I know as how I've got the uglies. 1903 Farmer & Henley *Slang* VII. 251/1 *Ugly*,.. In *pl.* = delirium tremens; the horrors. 1939 N. Last *Diary* 18 Oct. in *N. Last's War* (1983) 20 A gloom seems over us all. I've shaken off my fit of the uglies, but I felt I'd just like to crawl into a hole. 1974 *Petroleum Rev.* XXVIII. 672/1 Nitrogen narcosis, popularly called 'raptures of the deep' but perhaps more accurately described as 'the uglies', is the malady caused by nitrogen under pressure, interfering with the normal function of the nervous system.

Hence **'ugly** *v. trans.*, to make ugly; to uglify; also with *up*.

1740 RICHARDSON *Pamela* (1824) I. 97 It is impossible I should love him; for his vices all ugly him over, as I may say. **1770** C. JENNER *Placid Man* v. iv, The idea of a ticket-porter stuck to every part of him, and uglied him all over. **1946** *Sun* (Baltimore) 5 Feb. 8/7 Hands uglied by winter weather? **1965** *New Statesman* 26 Nov. 850/2 He uglies up the very places where one expects an opposite treatment. **1979** *Listener* 23 Aug. 248/2 Ever since *Grease* uglied up the Fifties.. the nostalgia industry has taken a curiously tough turn.

ugly'ography. [f. UGLY *a.* + -OGRAPHY. Used only by Southey.] Bad handwriting; uncouth spelling. Hence **ugly'ographize** *v. trans.*, to spell uncouthly.

1804 SOUTHEY *Lett.* (1856) I. 285, I do beseech you mend your uglyography. **1805** —— *Madoc* (1807) II. Notes 200 Quetzalcohuatl, for such is the *uglyography* of his name. **1834** —— *Doctor* ccxxiii. (1848) 604 How it would have been ..*uglyographised* by Elphinstone.. I know not.

Ugrian ('u:grɪən, 'ju:g-), *a.* and *sb.* [f. *Ugri*, the name given by early Russian writers to an Asiatic race dwelling east of the Ural Mountains.]

A. *adj.* Belonging to, of or pertaining to, a division of Ural-Altaic peoples, which includes the Finns and Magyars.

1838 *Jrnl. R. Geogr. Soc.* VIII. 390 He will investigate in that region the primitive as well as the present abodes of the nations belonging to the Ugrian race. **1841** PRICHARD *Phys. Hist. Mankind* III. 277 The fourth branch are the Ugorian races, the Ougres or Ugrian tribes. *Ibid.* 322 The proper Ostiaks of Ugrian origin. **1861** HULME tr. *Moquin-Tandon* I. v. 32 Taurainans... Divisions: 1, the Mongolian stock;..4, the Ugrian stock; 5, the Peninsular stock. **1889** S. BRYANT *Celtic Ireland* 5 The early Finnish or Ugrian type, that wandered westwards from the north-east.

B. *sb.* **1.** A member of the Ugrian stock.

1841 PRICHARD *Phys. Hist. Mankind* III. 274 In Asia various Tartar or Turkish tribes have encroached on the southern borders of the Tschudes and Ugrians. **1862** LATHAM *Elem. Compar. Philol.* 127 The Ugrians lead not only from Asia to Europe, but to America as well. **1889** S. BRYANT *Celtic Ireland* 5 Later immigrations.. may have included.. mixtures of the Ugrian with the Celt.

2. The language of the Ugrians. Also *attrib.*

1862 LATHAM *Elem. Compar. Philol.* 150 The Votiak is the Ugrian of the Government of Viatka. **1877** *Encycl. Brit.* VII. 183/1 The following is the order of the groups, some of the more important languages.. standing alone:—..Celtic, Lithuanic, Slavonic, Ugrian, Turkish.

Ugric ('u:grɪk, 'ju:g-), *a.* (*sb.*) [f. as UGRI-AN + -IC. Cf. *Finno-Ugric* (1879) s.v. UGRO-.] = UGRIAN *a.* Also as *sb.* = UGRIAN *sb.* 2.

1854 MAX MÜLLER in C. Bunsen *Christianity & Mankind* III. 445 If we compare the Ugric and Tamulic Numerals. *Ibid.* 453 In Mandshu.. we find juan for 10, the same root we met before in Ugric. **1884** *Imp. Dict.*, *Ugric* a., same as Ugrian. **1886** M. A. MORRISON in *Jrnl. R. Asiatic Soc.* XVIII. II. 178 Finn. This group is almost altogether confined to Europe. Its four sub-branches are the Ugric, Finn proper, Volga-Finn, and Perm-Finn. *Ibid.*, The Magyar, on of the languages of the Ugric sub-branch. **1964** J. ATKINSON tr. *Vuorela's Finno-Ugric Peoples* 2 Ugric comprising Vogul, Ostyak and Hungarian.

†**ugriness.** *Sc. Obs.*⁻¹ [Cf. UG *v.*] Horror.

c **1375** *Sc. Leg. Saints* vii. (*James Min.*) 716 In harte þai had sike wgrines, þat þai had no word for to say.

ugrio-, variant of UGRO-.

1889 S. BRYANT *Celtic Ireland* 5 Later immigrations.. may have included mixtures of a Ugrio-Iberian.. stock.

Ugro- ('u:grəʊ, 'ju:g-), combining form of UGRIAN *a.*, used in a few terms, as ***Ugro-Altaic***, ***-Finn***, ***-Finnic***, ***-Finnish***, ***-Samoyede***, ***-Slavonic***, ***-Tartarian***.

1848 J. C. PRICHARD in *Rep. Brit. Assoc. 1847* 241 The Turanian, or as I shall term them, Ugro-Tartarian languages, or the languages of High-Asia and other regions ...Ugro-Tartarian nations. **1852** *Todd's Cycl. Anat.* IV. II. 1347 The Turanian, or Ugro-Tartarian [languages]..; spoken by the (Mongolian) people of High Asia and of certain parts of Northern Europe. **1862** *Temple Bar* Nov. 549 The Ugro-Finns, whom they have driven northwards. **1879** *Encycl. Brit.* IX. 210/1 The term Finns.. being, with its adjective Finnic or Finno-Ugric or Ugro-Finnic, the collective name of the westernmost branch of the great Uralo-Altaic family. **1880** A. H. SAYCE *Introd. Sci. of Lang.* II. viii. 190 It is more than doubtful whether we can class the Mongols physically with the Turkish-Tartars or the Ugro-Finns. **1883** MORFILL *Slavonic Lit.* ii. 31 In 681 the Slavonic settlers fell under the power of a tribe of Bulgarians, a Ugro-Finnish race. **1886** M. A. MORRISON in *Jrnl. R. Asiatic Soc.* XVIII. II. 177 Broadly speaking,..the Ugro-Altaic languages are spoken over a region extending through more than 100 degrees of longitude. **1887** *Encycl. Brit.* XXII. 11/2 The Yeniseians were followed by the Ugro-Samoyedes. **1896** KEANE *Ethnology* ix. 201 [The] Bulgarians [are] Ugro-Slavonic.

ugsome ('ʌgsəm), *a.* Chiefly *north.* and Sc. Forms: 5 vg-, ugsom, 6 vgsoom; 5-6 vgsome (5 hwg-), 6 ougsome, 6- ugsome; *Sc.* 5-6 vg-, wgsum, 6-8 ugsum (6 -sume). [f. UG *v.* + -SOME.] Horrible, horrid, loathsome.

In older use common down to the latter part of the 16th cent. Literary currency in the 19th cent. is prob. due to the influence of Scott.

c **1400** *Destr. Troy* 877 He.. was ware sone Of þe orible oxin, vgsome to see. *Ibid.* 12497 A thoner and a thicke rayne .. With an ugsom noise. *c* **1425** WYNTOUN *Cron.* II. xi. 1011 Off þat incest fel murthir keyn, And ane vgsum maniory Off wlatsum corssis and vgly. *c* **1440** *Alph. Tales* 470 þer he saw many vgsom turment and many dyvers kyndes of paynys. **1475** *Cath. Angl.* 191/2 Hwgsome, *abhominabilis.* **1509** FISHER 7 *Penit. Ps.* xxxviii. Wks. (1876) 49 Lyke as þe mornynge is a meane bytwene þe grete clerenes of þe sonne & þe vgsome derkenes of the nyght. **1549** LATIMER *7th Serm. bef. Edw. VI* (Arb.) 186 Such an euyl fauoured face, such an vgsome countenaunce, such an horrible vysage. **1566** J. STUDLEY *Seneca's Medea* (1581) 134 O ougsome bugges, O gobblins grym of hell, I you intreat. **1583** MELBANCKE *Philotimus* C ij, And Morpheus [shall] present the with vgsome sights.

1724 RAMSAY *Vision* x, Infernal be thair hyre, Quha.. flang us Into this ugsum myre! **1790** A. WILSON *3rd Epist. to W. Mitchell* Poet. Wks. (1846) 180 The carle.. Aye puffin', or stuffin' Wi' ugsome chews his cheek. **1816** SCOTT *Antiq.* xxi, Like an auld dog that trails its useless ugsome carcass into some bush or bracken. **1832** LYTTON *Eugene A.* II. viii, ''Tis an ugsome bit of road,' said the corporal. **1875** BROWNING *Aristoph. Apol.* 1360 Attestation of the Muse That low-and-ugsome is not signed and sealed Incontrovertibly man's portion here.

Hence **'ugsomely** *adv. rare.*

c **1440** *Alph. Tales* 181 Sodanlie as he lay, he began to cry vgsomlie. *a* **1578** LINDESAY (Pitscottie) *Chron. Scot.* (S.T.S.) I. 67 Thir same wordis war more wgsumlie crayit nor befoir. **1876** *Whitby Gloss.* 204 'It leuk'd at us varry ugsomely', savagely.

ugsomeness ('ʌgsəmnɪs). Also 5-6 vgsomnes (6 ug-), 5 hugsomenes, 6 *Sc.* wgsumnes. [f. prec. + -NESS.] †**a.** Loathing. *Obs.* **b.** The quality of being ugsome; loathsomeness; ugliness.

c **1440** *Alph. Tales* 117 He had lepre folk in so grete vgsomnes þat he myght not suffer to se þaim. **1483** *Cath. Angl.* 401/2 An Vgsomnes, *abhominacio.* **1509** FISHER 7 *Penit. Ps.* xxxviii. Wks. (1876) 81 Suche as be ouercomen by temptacyons are very blynde not perceyuynge þe vgsomnes of synne. **1549** LATIMER *7th Serm. bef. Edw. VI* (Arb.) 185 The horrour and vgsomnes of death is sorer then death it selfe. *a* **1672** J. LIVINGSTONE in Tweedie *Sel. Biogr.* (Wodrow Soc.) I. 273 When sinlesse nature did sinlesly scunder at the infinite ugsomenes of the cup of wrath. **1834** WILSON in *Blackw. Mag.* XXXVI. 564 Some hideous witch-hag, to look on whose ugsomeness would be to die.

uguisu (u:'gwi:zu:). [Jap.] A bush warbler of delicate olive-green plumage, *Cettia diphone*, native to Japan.

1871 A. B. MITFORD *Tales of Old Japan* I. 37 The *uguisu*, by some enthusiasts called the Japanese nightingale. **1941** N. TAKATUKASA *Jap. Birds* 40 Pride of place among the native songbirds is therefore given to the *uguisu*. **1974** K. REXROTH *New Poems* 33 Maple leaves, an uguisu Sings as if in spring.

uh (ʌh, ʌ), *int.* [Imitative: cf. UGH.]

a. A representation of an inarticulate sound, such as that produced in coughing.

1605 B. JONSON *Volpone* I. iii, I feele mee going, (vh, vh, vh, vh.) I am sayling to my port, (vh, vh, vh, vh?) **1678** OTWAY *Friendship in F.* II. i, Uh gud murther, I had rather you had offer'd me a Toad. **1818** SCOTT *Br. Lamm.* xiii, Nae ill come ower them, I trust? Uh? **1818** —— *Rob Roy* xxxi, Uh! uh! &c. &c. I am very happy to have this joyful opportunity.

b. *U.S.* Expressing hesitation: = ER.

1962 J. D. MACDONALD *Only Girl in Game* vi. 85 'Are you cashing cheques?'.. The man hesitated. 'Uh... Yes, we are.' **1973** *National Observer* (U.S.) 3 Feb., He wanted most awfully to see the one in the advertisement about being, uh, well, you know. **1977** *N.Y. Rev. Bks.* 4 Aug. 32/4 'Perhaps we should, uh, wait,' I said.

c. = EH *int.* 3.

1977 'E. TREVOR' *Theta Syndrome* ii. 28 'Was it okay, Doc?' 'Uh?' 'The tube.' 'Oh, sure.' **1978** G. GREENE *Human Factor* v. iii. 272 'Weren't those my very words?' 'Uh,' Mr Barker said.

uh (ʌ), repr. the indefinite article in the speech of U.S. Blacks.

1893 H. A. SHANDS *Some Peculiarities of Speech in Mississippi* 65 *Uh*, the common negro form for the indefinite article *a*. This is generally written *er* by dialect writers, but no sound of *r* is ever apparent in the negro pronunciation. **1933** *Publ. Texas Folklore Soc.* XI. 105 Dey's jes' ez good uh fish in de creek ez evah been caught. **1973** *Black World* Oct. 74 Locking up folks lives For stealing less than uh hundred dollars.

uh-huh ('ʌhʌ; see quot. 1982), *adv. colloq.* (orig. *U.S.*). [Imitative.] A spoken affirmative or non-committal response to a question or remark; 'yes', 'oh yes?'

1924 *Dialect Notes* V. 278 *Uh-húh*, yes. **1925** *Ladies' Home Jrnl.* May 22/3 The policeman behind the desk said to Buckbarrow: 'Here's something! A runaway kid.'.. 'Uh-huh,' commented Buckbarrow. **1941** E. CARR *Klee Wyck* 111 'Uh huh,' he nodded. **1947** 'N. BLAKE' *Minute for Murder* v. 111 'You ought to go on the films, Blount.' 'Uh-huh?' **1969** D. DALBY in A. Dundes *Mother-Wit* (1973) 139/1 African usage can also explain the frequent use by Americans of the interjections uh-huh, for 'yes', and uh-uh for 'no'. Similar forms, especially for 'yes', occur in scattered parts of the world, but nowhere as frequently and as regularly as in Africa. **1978** J. A. MICHENER *Chesapeake* iii. 123 'You're to.. mind your manners. This is your last chance.' 'Uh-huh,' Timothy grunted, staring with contempt at the wretched spot to which he was being taken. **1982** J. C. WELLS *Accents of English* III. vi. 556 There are also the grunts sometimes spelt *uh-huh* and *uh-uh* respectively. The first, 'yes', is phonetically [ˈə̃hə̃, ˈʌ̃hʌ̃, ˈm̩m̩], hence nasal or nasalized; it usually has a rising tone pattern... The second, 'no', is [ˈʔəˀʔə, ˈʔʌ̃ˀʔʌ, ˈʔm̩ˀm̩]..; it is not necessarily nasal, and has an accented final syllable, with an obligatory falling tone pattern.

‖**uhlan** ('u:lən, 'ju:lən). Also 8-9 ulan; 8 houlan, 9 hulan. [a. F. *uhlan, hulan, houlan*, G. *uhlan, ulan* (Da. and Sw. *ulan*, It. *ulano*), a. Polish *ułan*, *hułan* (Czech *ulan, hulan*, Serb. *ulan*, Russ. *ulan*), ad. Turk. *oghlān* (pop. *ōlān*), son, youth, servant.] A special type of cavalryman or lancer in various European armies (originally in Slavonic countries, esp. Poland; subsequently spec. in the German Empire).

α. **1753** *Scots. Mag.* Jan. 3/2 The surplus.. consisted of Tartars and Ulans, whom he chose to keep in his pay. **1799** W. TOOKE *View Russian Emp.* I. 418 In their clothes they resembled the Poles, or rather the polish Ulans. **1802** JAMES *Milit. Dict.* s.v., The Ulans generally engage the enemy in small platoons or squads.

β. **1768** *Ann. Reg., Chron.* 126 They write from Warsaw, that an officer of Houlans.. has been grievously insulted by a Russian officer. **1809** R. K. PORTER *Trav. Sk. Russia & Sweden* (1813) I. 171 One of the most superb regiments in the Russian service is that of the Hulans, commanded by the Archduke Constantine. **1837** CARLYLE *Fr. Rev.* III. I. i, Flying hulans and hussars have been seen on the Châlons road. **1851** GALLENGA *Italy* 131 Three squadrons of *hulans* and four companies of Croatians.

γ. **1771** *Gentl. Mag.* XLI. 478 The King [of Poland] was not escorted as usual by his guard of twelve Uhlans. **1809** *Lond. Chron.* 6 July 18/2 Three regiments of infantry, one of uhlans, and a battalion of the Bohemian Landwehr. **1889** BADEN-POWELL *Pigsticking* xi. 71 In that campaign, Hans Breitmann, serving as a uhlan, observed the number of sows that were about in the Ardennes.

attrib. **1812** *Examiner* 7 Dec. 781/1 Three Uhlan regiments of Guards. **1887** SIR W. W. HUNTER in Skrine *Life* xviii. (1901) 367 The horses go well, and my Uhlan groom is careful and intelligent.

transf. **1886** *Pall Mall G.* 6 March 5/2 Those uhlans of commerce who have lately been so urgently calling for the establishment of railway communication with China through Burmah.

Hence **'uhlaner.**

1886 W. J. TUCKER *E. Europe* 265 The cavalry officer, be he of the huszárs, the uhlaners, or of any other mounted body of men, represents in most cases blood and fortune.

uht-song (u:xt-). *Eccl.* Now *Hist.* [OE. *úhtsang, -song*, f. *úhte* UGHTEN. Cf. OHG. *uhtisang*, ON. and Icel. *óttusǫngr* (MSw. *otto-, otta-, ottesang*, Sw. *ottesång*).] The ecclesiastical office celebrated just before daybreak; nocturns or matins.

a **900** *O.E. Martyrol.* 23 June 102 From uhtsanges tide heo a wunode.. on hire ȝebede oð dæȝ. *c* **900** tr. *Bæda's Eccl. Hist.* IV. xxv. 348 Hu neah þære tide wære, þætte þa broðor arisan scolden.. & heora uhtsong singan. *c* **960** *Rule St. Benet* ix. (Schröer) 33 On wintres timan is se uhtsang þus to beȝinnenne. *a* **1225** *Ancr. R.* 18 þer efter anonriht vre Leafdi vhtsong siggeð oþisse wise. *Ibid.* 22 Biuoren Uht-song & efter Prime.

1720 JOHNSON *Canons Ch. Engl., Elfric's Can.* xix, Let them sing.. the Uht-song, the Prime-song, the Undern-song [etc.]. **1844** LINGARD *Anglo-Sax. Ch.* (1858) I. vii. 272 *note*, The night-song.. was frequently joined with the *uht-song*. **1853** ROCK *Ch. of Fathers* III. II. 11 The 'invitatory' at the beginning of uht-song or matins.

uh-uh (ʌ'ʌ; see quot. 1982 at UH-HUH), *adv. colloq.* (chiefly *U.S.*). [Imitative.] A spoken negative response to a question or remark; 'no'.

1924 *Dialect Notes* V. 278 *Uh-uh*, negation. **1930** D. HAMMETT *Maltese Falcon* xvi. 194 'Do you know who he is?' .. 'Uh-uh,' he said, 'but I'd guess he was Captain Jacobi.' **1970** H. WAUGH *Finish me Off* (1971) 133 She shook her head. 'Uh-uh. He's my daddy.' **1977** *Sounds* 9 July 19/1 Uh-*uh*. I thought not.

Uhuru (ʊ'hu:ru:). Also uhuru. [a. Swahili, = freedom.] National independence of an African country, *spec.* Kenya.

1961 *Times* 4 Aug. 11/5 The British base in Kenya will be liquidated, all British troops evacuated, and the police totally Africanized. These are the basic conditions of *uhuru*. **1976** *Drum* (E. Afr. ed.) June 4/2 Kenya became independent in 1963. Much has been done to defend and demonstrate the hard-won uhuru. **1980** *Oxford Diocesan Mag.* Jan. 18/1 Any Christian struggle for *uhuru* in South Africa must involve the church as well as the state. **1982** D. BAGLEY *Windfall* xx. 192 The coming of Uhuru [to Kenya] must have been painful for the [club] membership who had to adapt to a determinedly multiracial society. **1984** *Listener* 24 May 11/1 An entire continent has seemed hell-bent on self-destruction, despite uhuru, despite the bright hopes of the many thousands who died seeking it.

‖**Uighur** ('wi:gʊə(r)), *sb.* and *a.* Also 8 Uigure, 9 Uigur, Ouigour. [ad. East Turkish *uighur*, f. *ui* to follow, fit, agree + *-gur* adj. suffix.]

A. *sb.* **1.** A member of the eastern branch of the Turkish race, which was prominent in Central Asia from the 8th to the 12th century.

1785 *Archaeol.* VII. 227 Perhaps it was the Uigures or Igureans, from whom the great founder of the Mongol monarchy first received letters and the art of writing. **1844** PRICHARD *Phys. Hist. Mankind* IV. 311 The celebrated Turkish race of the Ouigours. **1874** F. E. BURNETT tr. *Vambéry's Cent. Asia* 132 The Uigurs have played a very remarkable part in the history of the civilisation of Central Asia. **1888** *Encycl. Brit.* XXIII. 658/2 When we speak of Uigurs and Tatars, we mean tribes who style themselves

Turks and really are such. **1966** D. WILSON *Quarter of Mankind* vii. 89 Unlike the Tibetans, Mongols and Uighurs, these are relatively primitive people. **1969** *Listener* 3 July 6/2 There are millions of people living in the border areas, who speak neither Russian nor Chinese. They're Khazaks, Uzbeks, Uighurs, Tartars, many of them still leading nomadic lives, herdsmen born to the saddle. **1977** *Times* 4 July 5/4 The eight to ten million inhabitants of Sinkiang, the majority of whom are Uighurs and Kazakhs.

2. The language spoken by the Uigurs.

1843 *Penny Cycl.* XXV. 406/1 The Uighur was originally written with fourteen, and afterwards with sixteen letters, which..there is reason to believe..have been invented by the Uighurs themselves. **1862** LATHAM *Compar. Philol.* 102 Theoretically, the main differences between the Tshagatai and Uighur are considerable.

B. *adj.* Of or pertaining to, used by, the Uigurs.

1747 *Astley's Gen. Coll. Voy.* IV. II. iv. 457/2 He says, they are the same with the Wigûr, Oygûr, or Jugur Characters. **1844** PRICHARD *Phys. Hist. Mankind* IV. 312 The Ouigour dialect..preserves the true characteristics and analogies of an oriental Tartarian idiom. *Ibid.* 313 He was the founder of the Ouigour empire. **1862** LATHAM *Compar. Philol.* 100 The Uighur Turks were the first of their stock to use an alphabet. *Ibid.* 102 A Uighur alphabet makes a Uighur work. **1870** HOWORTH in *Jrnl. Ethnol. Soc.* (N.S.) II. 87 The remains of the Ouigour literature.

Hence **Ui'gurean, Ui'gurian, Ui'guric** *adjs.*

1773 *Archaeol.* II. 228 The Oigurian or Uigurean alphabet of 14 characters. **1844** PRICHARD *Phys. Hist. Mankind* IV. 316 As the Ouigourian and Mongolian alphabets have the same origin and form. **1874** F. E. BURNETT tr. *Vambéry's Cent. Asia* 131 The Uigurian race of the Turks. **1888** *Encycl. Brit.* XXIII. 662/1 But the oldest Turkish alphabet, the Uigurian, is a direct transformation of the Syriac. *Ibid.* XXIV. 2 The unassimilated Uiguric *kilur-im* answers to the Osmanli *kilur-um.*

uile, obs. form of OIL *sb.*[1]

uillean pipes ('ɪljɪn), *sb. pl.* Also **-ann.** [See UNION PIPES *sb. pl.*] = UNION PIPES *sb. pl. Rarely* in *sing.*

The etymological relationship between the two terms is uncertain. This name is now the usual one.

[**1876**: see WOOLLEN *a.* 1 ¶.] **1906** *Grove's Dict. Mus.* (ed. 2) II. 509/1 The later bagpipe, the Uillean or Union pipe, blown with a bellows, became popular in Ireland. **1962** *Times* 16 Nov. 16/1 Ceilidh bands of the venerable Uilleann pipes. **1974** *Irish Democrat* Nov. 2/4 Irish concert in.. Acton Town Hall... Tommy McCarthy (Uillean pipes and concertina). **1980** *Observer* 10 Feb. 14/8 The ensemble consists of two fiddles, flute, harp, a single-headed drum called the bodhran and the uillean pipes. **1984** *Listener* 3 May 28/1 Making extensive use of the most beautiful sound on earth, that of uilleann pipes in skilled hands, it was first and foremost a portrait of a contented man.

uintaite (juː'ɪntəaɪt). *Geol.* Also **uintahite.** [f. the name of the *Uinta* Mountains, Utah + -ITE[1].] = GILSONITE.

1888 [see GILSONITE]. **1904** G. P. MERRILL *Non-Metallic Minerals* xiii. 373 The principal use of uintaite thus far has been in the manufacture of varnishes for ironwork and baking japans. **1951** E. N. TIRATSOO *Petroleum Geol.* xi. 291 The following are the principal bitumens found:—(a) Uintaite.., also called Gilsonite. **1974** *Encycl. Brit. Micropædia* IV. 546/2 *Gilsonite*, also called uintaite, lustrous, jet-black, natural bitumen.., an asphaltite.

‖**Uitlander** ('ɔɪt-, 'eɪtlændə(r), ‖'œʏtlandər). [(Cape) Du., f. *uit* out + *land* land. Cf. G. *ausländer.*] = OUTLANDER b.

1892 [see OUTLANDER b]. **1893** *Natal Times* 30 Sept., The *uitlanders'* petitions for redress had been received with silence. **1901** *Contemp. Rev.* March 313 One of the most grievous blunders committed by the military authorities, has been in connection with the Uitlanders.

attrib. **1894** *Daily News* 31 May 2/6 The uitlander opinion, even in the Transvaal, was strongly alive to the advantages of the union. **1895** *Westm. Gaz.* 12 Dec. 7/1 He aims at the Presidency and counts on large uitlander support.

transf. **1902** *Fortn. Rev.* March 376 Disputes will not be avoided as the uitlanders [in Korea] become more numerous and powerful.

‖**ujamaa** (udʒa'maː). [Swahili, = consanguinity, brotherhood, f. *jamaa* family, a. Arab. *jamāʿa* group (of people), community.] The name given by President Nyerere of Tanzania to a kind of socialism he introduced in that country in the 1960s, in which village co-operatives were established based on equality of opportunity and self-help; so ***ujamaa village.***

1962 J. K. NYERERE *Ujamaa: Basis of African Socialism* in *Ujamaa: Ess. Socialism* (1968) 12 'Ujamaa', then, or 'Familyhood', describes our socialism. **1962** *Economist* 8 Sept. 892/2 Mr Nyerere's thesis that Ujamaa (familyhood) is the basis of African socialism. **1969** *Reporter* (Nairobi) 13 June 21/1 *Ujamaa* villages will be encouraged, to spread more wealth across the rural areas. **1970** *Drum* (E. Afr. ed.) Feb. 19/2 Tanzania is now well under way with its second Five-Year Development Plan, a £400 million investment programme tailor-made for the strengthening of ujamaa throughout the land. **1971** *Standard* (Dar es Salaam) 7 Apr. 1/8 A sum of 15,422/20 is to be spent by the government on drilling ten bore-holes in various villages of Hanang district, including two ujamaa villages. **1979** *New African* Mar. 57/2 Out of Tanzania's total 16 m. population, more than 13 m. are living in about 8,000 *ujamaa* villages. **1983** *N.Y. Times* 15 Aug. C14/6 Most of the cast participate in the theater arts and black studies programs of Ujamaa.

‖**uji** ('udʒi). [Jap.] In feudal Japan, a name indicating which ancestral noble family the bearer belonged to; a patriarchal lineage group comprising all those with the same *uji.*

1876 W. E. GRIFFIS *Mikado's Empire* (1877) I. xii. 117 The family name (*uji*) precedes the personal..name. **1896** F. BRINKLEY *Japanese-Eng. Dict.* 1555/1 Although the offshoots from these noble families took various names.., yet these were not, strictly speaking, the family names or *uji* in the now-accepted sense. **1931** G. B. SANSOM *Japan* I. ii. 36 The society consisted of patriarchal units called *uji*, which were communities formed of a number of households of the same ancestry. **1970** J. W. HALL *Japan* iv. 29 Being of the upper class the *uji* possessed surnames and bore titles of respect. **1974** *Encycl. Brit. Micropædia* X. 238/1 The *uji* members..were supported by the labour of common workers, who were organized into subunits of the *uji*... Imperial rule over the various autonomous *uji* remained weak until the adoption of centralized government in the early 8th century.

‖**ujigami** (udʒi'gaːmi). [Jap., f. *uji* UJI + *kami* god.] In feudal Japan, the ancestral deity of an *uji*; later, the tutelary deity of a particular village or area.

1897 L. HEARN *Gleanings in Buddha-Fields* i. 18 The peasants were going to celebrate their harvest by a dance in the court of the *ujigami*. **1931** G. B. SANSOM *Japan* I. ii. 36 The members of a clan all worshipped a guardian god, the *uji-gami*, or clan god. **1970** J. W. HALL *Japan* iv. 32 The *uji-gami* venerated by members of certain *uji* were human or totemistic progenitors.

‖**ukase** (juː'keɪs). Also 8 **oukauze, ukause,** 9 **(o)ukaz.** [ad. Russ. *ukaz*, f. *ukazatʹ* to show, direct, order, decree. Hence also F. *ukase, oukase*, Pg. *ukase*, Sp. *ucase*, G., Da., Sw. *ukas.*]

1. A decree or edict, having the force of law, issued by the Russian emperor or government.

α. **1729** CONSETT *Pres. State Russia* Pref. p. lxiv, A true Oukauze or Edict sign'd with her Imperial Majesty's own hand. **1797** W. TOOKE *Cath. II* (1798) III. 204 A gracious *ukause*..put an end to every process of more than ten years standing. **1833** R. PINKERTON *Russia* 62 The ukaz, which expelled them from the empire,..was dated March 13, 1820. **1877** D. M. WALLACE *Russia* i. 12 Fifteen years ago the domestic serfs were emancipated by Imperial Ukaz. **1894** *Times* 11 Dec. 8/3 In execution of the Imperial Oukaz to the Minister of Finance.

β. **1775** *Ann. Reg., Chron.* 120 The Empress of Russia issued an ukase, whereby various taxes are abolished. **1810** E. D. CLARKE *Trav. Russia* (1839) 28/1 A ukase had appeared, which forbade the importation of any kind of foreign literature. **1889** GUNTER *That Frenchman* xv. 193 The ukase of September has been issued—proclaiming, in time of peace, military law.

2. *transf.* Any proclamation or decree; an order or regulation of a final or arbitrary nature.

1818 LADY MORGAN *Fl. Macarthy* II. ii. (1819) 106 (Stanf.), He was even half inclined to send out an ukase to Jemmy Bryan, and his myrmidons, to hold themselves in readiness. **1859** KINGSLEY *Misc., Plays & Purit.* II. 136 That New England ukase of Cotton Mather's, who punished the woman who should kiss her infant on the Sabbath day. **1880** MRS. WHITNEY *Odd or Even?* xxx, Whatever the Autocrat of the Breakfast Table may have found true, or have recorded by his ukase, twenty years ago.

ukata, var. YUKATA.

uke[1] (juːk), colloq. abbrev. of UKULELE.

[**1915** *N.Y. World* 18 July 2M/4 Those who pretend to know say that the euk did more than anything else to put the lulu in Honolulu.] **1921** *Quill* July 21 The music store of Gino Polluce on Blocker Street was raided by Inspector Bullem but no ukes were captured. **1949** L. FEATHER *Inside Be-Bop* i. 7, I fooled around with the uke. **1960** N. HILLIARD *Maori Girl* 133 A big grey hair. It looks just like a uke-string, it's that big. **1976** W. GOLDMAN *Magic* III. xiv. 227, I won't sing no more 'Cause I ain't got my uke.

‖**uke**[2] ('uːke). [Jap., f. *ukeru* to receive, be passive, defend.] In Judo, the passive partner, the one who is acted upon.

1956 [see REAP *v.*[1] 2 e]. **1961** *New Statesman* 22 Sept. 402/2 The thrower's body is turned facing the same way as the Uke's... He gets both feet inside the Uke's. **1972** *Judo Illustrated* Sept. 48/2 Tori and uke should be friends and know each other's attitudes well. **1984** *Coaching Award Scheme* (Brit. Judo Assoc.) 6/2 If nage-no-Kata is mastered it vastly widens tori's repertoire, but just as vital, it will eliminate uke's fears of falling—right or left side.

ukeke (uː'keɪkeɪ). [a. Hawaiian *ʿūkēkē.*] A Hawaiian stringed instrument consisting of a strip of wood with two or three strings that are played with the fingers and mouth.

1891 W. D. ALEXANDER *Brief Hist. Hawaiian People* xiv. 91 The *ukeke* was a strip of flexible wood or bamboo, mounted with two or three strings of *olona* or of cocoanut fiber. **1970** *Western Folklore* XXIX. 239 The guitar was introduced [into Polynesia]..in 1879 by Portuguese immigrants, the only native stringed instrument being the two- or three-stringed *ukeke*, which was never played with a slider. **1980** *New Grove Dict. Mus.* XIX. 323/2 There is no string instrument native to Hawaii other than the *ukeke*, a musical bow.

ukelele, var. UKULELE.

‖**ukemi** ('uːkemi). [Jap., f. *uke* UKE[2] + *mi* body.] In Judo, the art of falling safely.

[**1942** C. YERKOW *Mod. Judo* ii. 26 *Ukemi* is the Japanese word and means 'to fall away'. The aim is to break the fall *before* the body reaches the mat or ground, so that no jar or shock is felt. Thus the equivalent for 'ukemi' might be *break*-falling.] **1956** K. TOMIKI *Judo* iii. 54 It is essential to learn the art of falling. This is called *ukemi* (breakfall). **1969** G. R. GLEESON *Anatomy of Judo* iv. 66 In spite of the much vaunted effectiveness of traditional ukemi..very few indeed considered they were capable of taking the falls in the last two sets of nage-no-kata. **1984** *Coaching Award Scheme* (Brit. Judo Assoc.) 29/2 No ukemi is asked as such, but in the first section, the candidate is required to act as Uke and Tori.

‖**ukiyo-e** (ukijo'jeː). Also **ukiyo-we, -ye,** and without hyphen. [Jap., f. *ukiyo* fleeting world (f. *uku* to float, go by fleetingly + *yo* world) + *e* picture.] A Japanese art-form consisting of wood-block prints or paintings of scenes from everyday life simply treated; a picture belonging to this art-form. Usu. *attrib.*

1879 *Trans. Asiatic Soc. Japan* VII. 358 Its founder is still celebrated as the author of the *Ukiyo-we* or popular style. **1898** L. HEARN *Gleanings in Buddha-Fields* v. 115 The Ukiyo-yé artist drew actualities, but not repellent or meaningless actualities... He looked for dominant laws.. for the order of the beautiful as it was and is. **1915** *Dial* LIX. 375/1 In the forty years or thereabout since the color prints by the Ukiyoe masters first came to the attention of art lovers ..the circle of their ardent admirers has steadily widened. **1955** *N.Y. Times* 24 Apr. 11-1. 9/1 Japanese tend to see things flatly. This is..most noticeable in the ukiyoe prints. **1957** *Encycl. Brit.* XII. 966/2 Ukiyo-e grew to be almost exclusively the art of the populace of Edo. **1971** *Times Lit. Suppl.* 20 Aug. 997/3 The 'Pictures of the Passing World', the *ukiyo-e*, which from the late seventeenth century constituted the latest and most inventive phase of the Popular School. **1983** *Sunday Tel.* (Colour Suppl.) 26 June 31/2 The tradition of the *Ukiyo-E* print, which had been bought by a Japanese public uninfluenced by Western work, was effectively dead by the 1880s.

ukkers, ukky, varr. UCKERS, UCKY.

†**Uk'rainer.** *Obs. rare.* [f. as next + -ER.] = UKRAINIAN *sb.* a.

a **1815** *Gentl. Mag.* LXXXV. II. 114 That by the Malo-russians and Ukrainers is meant the same people, none are ignorant. **1815** *Ibid.* 602.

Ukrainian (juː'kreɪnɪən), *a.* and *sb.* [f. *Ukraine*, an extensive district in the south of Russia, ad. Polish *Ukraina* or Russ. *Ukraĭna*, specific use of *ukraĭna* border, frontier, marches, f. *u-* at, beside + *kraĭ* edge, brink, etc.] **A.** *adj.* Of or pertaining to the Ukraine. **B.** *sb.* **a.** A native or inhabitant of the Ukraine. **b.** The Slavonic language spoken in the Ukraine; formerly also called Malo-Russian, Ruthenian.

1804 M. WILMOT *Jrnl.* 12 Aug. in Londonderry & Hyde *Russian Jrnls.* (1934) I. 124 His dress a jacket lin'd with Ukrainian sheeps' skin. **1816** *Gentl. Mag.* March 212 The so much vaunted liberty of the Ukrainian Kozaks. **1823** [ROBERTSON & BYERLEY] *Percy Anecd.* XIII. II. 79 Ukrainian Singers. *Ibid.*, The sweetness and unlimited combination and range of the voice of the Ukrainians. **1886** *Encycl. Brit.* XXI. 80/2 In western Russia, printing in Ukrainian is prohibited, and 'Russification' is being carried on among Ukrainians by the same means as those employed in Poland.

ukulele (juːkə'leɪliː). Also **ukelele.** [a. Hawaiian *ʿukulele*, f. *ʿuku* flea + *lele* jumping: see quot. 1957.] A small four-stringed Hawaiian guitar that is a development of a Portuguese instrument introduced to the island *c* 1879.

1896 *Hawaiian* Feb.–Mar. 789 Then comes the twang of the *ukelele*, the soft, melodious cadence of the hula song. **1900** *Century Mag.* June 164/2 Kolomono..holds the ukulele, a stringed instrument which may or may not be indigenous to the island. **1913** R. BROOKE *Coll. Poems* (1918) 28 Somewhere an eukaleli thrills and cries. **1919** WODEHOUSE *Damsel in Distress* vi. 93 You see the handsome sophomore from Yale sitting beside her on the porch playing the ukalele. **1932** D. L. SAYERS *Have his Carcase* xii. 146 Campers..brought gramophones or concertinas or ukeleles. **1950** 'D. DIVINE' *King of Fassarai* xviii. 144 Queer the notions you get about South Sea islands,..all..hula-hula skirts..and ukeleles. **1957** *Amer. Speech* XXXII. 309 The machete was heard one day by the vice-chamberlain of King Kalakaua's court, who..asked to be taught to play it... This vice-chamberlain was a British army officer named Edward Purvis; but the Hawaiians..called him *ukulele* because his lively playing and antics and his small build suggested a leaping flea. The new instrument became a great success,.. and someone started calling them *ukeleles*. **1978** L. THOMAS *Ormerod's Landing* iv. 67 The simple boy produced a dramatic strumming chord on the ukelele.

ulalu, var. ULULU

ulama, ulan, variants of ULEMA, UHLAN.

-ular, *suffix*, representing L. *ulāris* (whence also F. *ulaire*, Sp. and Pg. *-ular*, It. *-ulare, -olare*), formed by the addition of *-āris* -AR[1] to the diminutive suffix *-ul-*, and employed in adjs. derived from nouns ending in *-ulus, -ula, -ulum*, as *populāris, rēgulāris, sēculāris*, f. *populus, rēgula, sēculum.* A considerable number of these are recorded from classical or post-classical Latin, as *angulāris, annulāris, caniculāris, circulāris, fistulāris*, etc., and many of these have at various dates been adopted in English in the forms *angular, annular*, etc. Many others are derived either from mediæval or modern Latin formations, or have been directly formed on Latin sbs., as *auricular, capsular, cellular, corpuscular, funicular, globular, jugular*, etc., the use of the suffix having steadily become more frequent (especially in scientific use) since the 17th century. When the primitive noun as well as the diminutive exists in English, and is in common use, the adj. in *-ular* is usually associated with it; thus *glandular* and *globular* commonly correspond to *gland*, *globe*, rather than to *glandule*, *globule*. This, however, has not given rise to much independent use of the suffix, which is normally confined to the above types.

ulcer (ˈʌlsə(r)), *sb.* Also 5–7 vlcer, 5–6 vlcere, 6 ulcere. [ad. L. *ulcer-*, *ulcus* neut. (related to Gr. ἕλκος), whence also It. *ulcera* fem., *ulcero* masc., Sp. and Pg. *ulcera* fem., F. *ulcère* masc. (†and fem.), OF. *ulcere* (1314).]

1. *Path.* An erosive solution of continuity in any external or internal surface of the body, forming an open sore attended with a secretion of pus or other morbid matter.

c **1400** *Lanfranc's Cirurg.* 215 Þe cure of vlcers þat ben olde. *a* **1425** tr. *Arderne's Treat. Fistula*, etc. 35 Þe clensyng of þe vlcer of flessh mortified by þe forseid poudre. *Ibid.* 89 Sanguis veneris heleþ wele..depe woundez..and holow vlcerez. **1541** R. Copland *Galyen's Terap.* 2 F iv, Yf the lyppes of the vlcere appere harde and stony, they must be cutte. **1589** Nashe *Almond for Parrat* 10 The disease of disobedience proceeds from the swelling of pride, as madness from some vntollerable vlcer. **1615** H. Crooke *Body of Man* 56 Why if a bone be caued or hollowed by an vlcer..the flesh can neuer be generated ouer it? **1637** Nabbes *Microcosm.* v, Conscience stain'd Is like a fretting ulcer. **1694** Ray in *Lett. Lit. Men* (Camden) 201 The ulcers upon my leg..are..broken out again. *c* **1720** W. Gibson *Farrier's Guide* II. lv. (1738) 210 A small ulcer is more easily managed than one that is large. **1772** W. Buchan *Dom. Med.* I. 712 Ulcers may be the consequence of wounds, bruises, or imposthumes improperly treated. **1797** M. Baillie *Morb. Anat.* (1807) 154, I have reason to believe that ulcers of the stomach are often slow in their progress. **1846** Brittan tr. *Malgaigne's Oper. Surg.* 270 These foreign bodies introduced by the wound finished by transforming it into an ulcer. **1877** F. T. Roberts *Handbk. Med.* (ed. 3) I. 48 When inflammation destroys the tissues on a surface, an ulcer is formed.

transf. **1606** Shaks. *Tr. & Cr.* I. i. 52 Thou..Powr'st in the open Vlcer of my heart, Her Eyes, her Haire [etc.].

b. Used in sing. as a generic term.

1623 Lodge *Poor Mans Talent* 13 For the Cancer, vlcer, and Noli me tangere. **1667** Milton *P.L.* XI. 484 Intestin Stone and Ulcer, Colic pangs. **1749** Hartley *Observ. Man* I. 126 The subsequent Pain is to be referred to the Heads of Inflammation and Ulcer. **1820** Good *Nosology* 274 For so closely is ulcer connected with gangrene, that it can-not exist without it. *c* **1837** in A. Combe *Physiol. Digestion* (1842) ix. 250 Scurvy, typhoid fever, dysentery, and ulcer, which up to the period of the change had produced great havoc. **1884** Bryant *Pract. Surg.* (ed. 4) I. 83 *marg.*, Local causes of ulcer. *Ibid.*, Constitutional causes of ulcer.

c. *attrib.* and *Comb.*

1611 Cotgr., *Vlceratif*,..vlcer-breeding. **1843** R. J. Graves *Syst. Clin. Med.* xxvi. 336 Enlargements of the tonsils, without any ulcer-like cavities, were not unfrequently observed. **1897** *Allbutt's Syst. Med.* II. 765 The mucous membrane overhanging the ulcer cavity is œdematous.

2. *fig.* Any corroding or corrupting influence; a morally diseased or unsound element; a plague-spot.

1592 tr. *Junius on Rev.* xvi. 2 It doeth signifie a spirituall ulcer. **1613–8** Daniel *Coll. Hist. Eng.* Wks. (Grosart) IV. 211 Hee would not wrest any thing by an Imperiall power from the Kingdome (which might breed vlcers of dangerous nature). **1643** Baker *Chron.*, *Q. Eliz.* 105 This was the right way to finde, whether the ulcer of his minde were throughly cured or no. **1873–4** Dixon *Two Queens* XXI. iii. IV. 138 His enmity to some of the Reformers..was the ulcer of his fame.

b. Applied to persons. *rare.*

1602 Marston *Antonio's Rev.* I. iv, Yon putred ulcer of my roiall bloode. **1615** Brathwait *Strappado* (1878) 34 This wicked vlcer that corrupts the state, Nere thinkes of death, till that it be too late.

ulcer (ˈʌlsə(r)), *v.* Now *rare.* [f. prec. In first quot. after F. *ulcérer.*] a. *absol.* To cause an ulcer or ulcers. b. *trans.* To ulcerate. Also *fig.*

1590 C'tess Pembroke *Antonie* 284 And his [*sc.* Love's] sweet shafts, with whose shot none are kill'd, Which ulcer not. **1642** Fuller *Holy & Prof. St.* v. vi. 379 This by degrees abates the reverence of religion, and ulcers mens hearts with profaneness. **1694** *Acc. Sev. Late Voy.* Introd. p. xxii, The cold had prodigious effects on our men in Greenland,..as blistering, and ulcering their flesh. **1829** Lytton *Disowned* xiv, Thought, feeling, the faculties and impulses of man, all ulcered into one great canker—Gain.

ˈulcerable, *a.* *rare*⁻⁰. [Cf. prec. and -ABLE.] 'That may become ulcerated.'

1846 Worcester (citing *Quart. Rev.*).

†**ˈulcerate**, *ppl. a.* *Obs.* [ad. L. *ulcerātus*, pa. pple. of *ulcerāre*: see next. So It. *ulcerato*, Sp. and Pg. *ulcerado*, F. *ulcéré.*] Ulcerated. Also *fig.*

a **1425** tr. *Arderne's Treat. Fistula*, etc. 2 Bothe his buttokis was so vlcerat and putrefied with-in. **1541** R. Copland *Galyen's Terap.* 2 A iv, For the mystemperaunce of yᵉ flesshe vlcerate, or for the gatheryng of humours. **1609** [Bp. W. Barlow] *Answ. Nameless Cath.* 104 Vlcerate Apostemes must be launced. **1654** Earl Monm. tr. *Bentivoglio's Wars Flanders* 367 So the ulcerate part of Flanders makes the body of your whole Empire daily languish. **1720** W. Gibson *Diet. Horses* i. (1726) 17 When the Cornet is large, it denotes an over-great Relaxation and Moisture in that Part, which is apt to turn ulcerate.

ulcerate (ˈʌlsəreɪt), *v.* [f. ppl. stem of L. *ulcerāre* (whence It. *ulcerare*, Sp. and Pg. *ulcerar*, F. *ulcérer*), f. *ulcer-*, *ulcus* ULCER *sb.*: see -ATE.]

1. *intr.* To form an ulcer; to break out into ulcers or purulent sores; to fester.

a **1425** tr. *Arderne's Treat. Fistula*, etc. 37 Þis sikenes lurkeþ wiþ in þe lure in þe bigynnyng, but after processe of tyme it vlcerate, & fretyng þe lure goþe out. **1623** Cockeram, *Vlcerate*, to blister, to breake out into sores. **1753** N. Torriano *Gangr. Sore Throat* 45 The Tonsils, says he, are often exposed to ulcerate. **1813** J. Thomson *Lect. Inflam.* 387 A part never ulcerates till it has become inflamed. **1826** S. Cooper *First Lines Surg.* (ed. 5) 190 Inflaming the whole swelling, and causing it to ulcerate and slough. **1898** *Hutchinson's Arch. Surg.* IX. 313 The patches do not ulcerate or inflame.

fig. **1833** I. Taylor *Fanat.* ii. 49 When an affection, more sensitive than any other, is left to bleed and ulcerate in open air. **1850** Blackie *Æschylus* I. 154 More than a house may bear, whose wounds yet bleed, And ulcerate from the fangs of fate.

2. *trans.* To cause ulcers in or on.

c **1550** H. Lloyd *Treas. Health* 5 Sinapismus is an emplaster made of mustard to vlcerate the skynne & make the same red. **1604** R. Cawdrey *Table Alph.*, *Vlcerate*, to make full of sores, to blister. **1684** tr. *Bonet's Merc. Compit.* VII. 249 When signs of a Gangrene begin to appear..we must ulcerate the parts..with deep scarifications. **1753** *Phil. Trans.* XLVIII. 149 If either the stalks or leaves of this valuable plant are applied to the skin, they heat and ulcerate it. **1788** *Med. Commun.* II. 208 The discharge..excoriates or ulcerates the membrane. **1843** Youatt *Horse* (ed. 2) i. 14 The fetlock would be chafed and ulcerated, if the horse was ridden over ploughed grounds.

3. *fig.* To affect after the manner of an ulcer; to irritate; to wound or poison.

1647 N. Bacon *Disc. Govt. Eng.* I. lxiv. 214 Wherein the King dealt with a tender hand, as if he feared to ulcerate any part, and especially the Clergy. **1768–74** Tucker *Lt. Nat.* (1834) II. 656 By knowing the true place of the wound, we shall prevent its ulcerating the mind herself. **1792** Burke *Let. to Sir H. Langrishe* Wks. VI. 362 The only reason which can be assigned for this disfranchisement, has a tendency more deeply to ulcerate their minds than the act of exclusion itself. **1849** Macaulay *Hist. Eng.* vi. II. 46 A small knot of Roman Catholics whose hearts had been ulcerated by old injuries. *Ibid.* vii. II. 255 When her heart had been ulcerated by disasters and mortifications. **1879** Farrar *St. Paul* viii, To brand consciences, already ulcerated by a sense of guilt.

ˈulcerated, *ppl. a.* [f. prec. + -ED.]

1. Converted into an ulcer; afflicted with ulcers; eroded with purulent sores.

1547 Boorde *Brev. Health* § 377 Some be playne woundes .., some be festered, some be vlcerated and some hath fyssures. **1580** Hester tr. *Fioravanti's Disc. Chirurg.* 25 b, The cure of an Vlcerated legge. **1651** Baxter *Inf. Bapt.* 274 It is only the ulcerated parts that honey doth bite and purge. **1695** J. Edwards *Perfect. Script.* 273 The falling out of his ulcerated bowels. **1721** R. Keith tr. *T. à Kempis, Vall. Lillies* 56 The poor and ulcerated Lazarus, who after Death was joyfully received into Abraham's Bosom. **1787** *Med. Commun.* II. 384 The ulcerated sore-throat. **1797** M. Baillie *Morb. Anat.* (1807) 383 In advanced stages of the ulcerated uterus. **1799** *Med. Jrnl.* II. 89 The prevailing method of treating ulcerated legs. **1843** R. J. Graves *Syst. Clin. Med.* xxiii. 280 The lungs were extensively solidified, black, and ulcerated. **1872** Cohen *Dis. Throat* 89 Ulcerated sore throat is indicated by its name.

transf. **1842** Loudon *Suburban Hort.* 649 Manure.. causes the roots to branch and their rind to become ulcerated.

b. *fig.* (Cf. ULCERATE *v.* 3.)

1634 Ford *Perk. Warbeck* v. ii, Scorne weares onely Such fashion, as commends to gazers eyes Sad vlcerated Novelty. **1700** T. Brown *Amusem. Ser. & Com.* ix. (1709) 99 They.. say that his conscience is Ulcerated. **1759** Dilworth *Life of Pope* 28 Wrangling Dennis..with others of a like ulcerated understanding plied all the severity of censure they could, against it. **1875** Jowett *Plato, Gorgias* (ed. 2) II. 399 The ulcerated and swollen condition of the State.

†2. Of matter: Rendered purulent. *Obs. rare.*

1580 Hester tr. *Fioravanti's Disc. Chirurg.* 21 b, It is a grosse and vlcerated matter. **1660** R. Coke *Power & Subj.* 170 The wound is to be inquired into by good counsel; then the ulcerated matter, which does inwardly putrifie, is to be let out, that is, he purge himself through confession.

3. Of diseases: Characterized by the formation of ulcers in the affected part.

1706 Phillips (ed. Kersey), s.v. *Cancer*, It is call'd an Occult, Latent, or Blind Cancer, but when bigger and open'd, it bears the Name of an Ulcerated Cancer. **1762** R. Guy *Pract. Obs. Cancers* 46 An ulcerated Cancer in the Breast. **1826** S. Cooper *First Lines Surg.* (ed. 5) 201 Another event, still more rare, is the actual cicatrization of an ulcerated cancer. **1878** Habershon *Dis. Abdomen* (ed. 3) 21 Ulcerated Stomatitis is especially seen in young children of 4 to 10 years of age.

ˈulcerating, *ppl. a.* [f. as prec. + -ING².]

1. Giving rise to ulcers. *rare*⁻⁰.

1611 Cotgr., *Vlceratif*, vlceratiue, vlcerating, vlcer-breeding.

2. Developing into an ulcer or ulcers.

1843 R. J. Graves *Syst. Clin. Med.* xxix. 390 A few ulcerating points on the surface, were touched with nitrate of silver. **1890** *Retrospect Med.* CII. 384 An ulcerating malignant growth of the anterior vaginal wall.

ulceration (ʌlsəˈreɪʃən). *Path.* Also 5 vlceracio(u)n, 6 -cyon, -tion. [ad. L. *ulcerātiōn-*, *ulcerātio*, noun of action f. *ulcerāre*: see ULCERATE *v.* Hence also F. *ulcération* (1314), Sp. *ulceracion*, Pg. *-ação*, It. *-azione.*]

1. The action, process, or state of forming ulcers or of becoming ulcerated.

c **1400** *Lanfranc's Cirurg.* 214 Þis wole not suffre þat þe matere schal make noon vlceracioun ne no fretyng. *a* **1425** tr. *Arderne's Treat. Fistula*, etc. 37 Signes, forsoþe, of his vlceracion bene þise. *c* **1530** *Judic. Urines* III. vii. 51 b *marg.*, Vlceracyon of the bladder. Vlceracyon of yᵉ reines. Vlceracyon of yᵉ liuer. **1541** R. Copland *Guydon's Form.* R iij b, Before the vlceracyon fyrste ought to be mynystred medycyns that be colde. **1611** Cotgr., *Vlceration*, an ulceration; a making or growing vlcerous, a drawing to an vlcer. **1676** Wiseman *Chirurg. Treat.* II. ii. 169 Where the Part hath been long affected with Vlceration, it..is very difficult to cicatrize. **1804** Abernethy *Surg. Obs.* 160 Some of these sores spread by ulceration, and some by sloughing. **1847** E. J. Seymour *Severe Dis.* I. 16 Adhesion of the gall-bladder to the bowels and subsequent ulceration. **1876** Bristowe *Th. & Pract. Med.* (1878) 44 In ulceration the destruction of parts is molecular, or by small fragments, and progessive.

2. An ulcerous formation; an ulcer or group of ulcers.

1580 T. Newton *Approved Medicines* 57 b, Pryuet.. healeth vlcerations of the Mouthe that often happe in Children. **1599** A. M. tr. *Gabelhouer's Bk. Physicke* 178/2 A little bagge, as bigge that it may cover the vlceration. **1718** Quincy *Compl. Disp.* 120 All Medicines of this Intention are suppos'd..to..fill up with new Flesh, all Ulcerations, and Foulnesses. **1725** *Fam. Dict.* s.v. *Lucatellus Balsam*, Such Coughs as give Suspicion of Tubercles and Ulcerations in the Lungs. **1804** Abernethy *Surg. Obs.* 124 He had an ulceration which spread over the palate. **1829** Cooper *Good's Study Med.* (ed. 3) III. 513 The disease generally commences on the alæ of the nose, with small tubercules, which gradually change into ulcerations.

ulcerative (ˈʌlsəreɪtɪv, -ətɪv), *a.* [ad. med.L. *ulcerātīv-us*: see ULCERATE *v.* and -IVE. So F. *ulcératif*, *-ive* (1495), Sp., Pg., It. *ulcerativo.*]

1. Causing ulceration.

1575 J. Banister *Treat. Chyrurg.* 138 The properties of vlceratiue medicins, is to breake & blister the skinne, in what places they are laide. **1601** Holland *Pliny* II. 158 The dregs of vinegre, must of necessitie be much more sharpe, biting, and ulcerative, than wine lees. **1813** J. Thomson *Lect. Inflam.* 379 One, two, or three parts..were more susceptible of the ulcerative stimulus than the others.

2. Of the nature of ulceration.

1800 *Med. Jrnl.* IV. 489 Extensive erysipelas..followed in most [instances] by an immediate ulcerative process. **1835–6** *Todd's Cycl. Anat.* I. 444/2 The process of ulcerative absorption in any structure is scarcely understood. **1872** Cohen *Dis. Throat* 116 The ulcerative process may involve its cartilages as well as its mucous membrane. **1878** T. Bryant *Pract. Surg.* I. 44 Opium is an admirable drug when the ulcerative action is present.

3. Accompanied or characterized by the formation of ulcers.

1813 J. Thomson *Lect. Inflam.* 223 Mr. Hunter has divided inflammation..into adhesive, suppurative, and ulcerative. **1850** F. Churchill *Dis. Children* II. vi. (1858) 471 Ulcerated sore mouth. Ulcerative stomatitis. **1879** *St. George's Hosp. Rep.* IX. 411 Ulcerative endocarditis of the heart-wall.

4. Due to, produced by, ulceration.

1876 Bristowe *Th. & Pract. Med.* (1878) 45 The chief removal of ulcerative detritus.

ˈulceratory, *a.* [Cf. prec. and -ORY.] Ulcerative. (1891 *Cent. Dict.*)

ˈulcered, *ppl. a.* [f. ULCER *sb.* or *v.* + -ED.]

1. = ULCERATED *ppl. a.* 1.

1575 J. Banister *Treat. Chyrurg.* 81 What meates are to be vsed as touching diet in vlcered bodies. **1576** G. Baker tr. *Gesner's Jewell of Health* 58 b, This water..cureth the Bladder ulcered. **1610** Healey *St. Aug. Citie of God* I. xi. (1620) 19 One farre more sumptuous did the ministring Angell prepare for the poore vlcered begger in the sight of God. **1654** Whitlock *Zootomia* 386 Comparing his own sound Arme, with the Ulcer'd one of the Diseased. **1708** *Phil. Trans.* XXVI. 229 A Youth of Ten Years old, had his Gums much swelled and ulcered. **1807** Southey *Espriella's Lett.* II. 311 Colonel Despard..had been confined there.. without fire, till his feet were ulcered with the frost. **1844** H. G. Robinson *Odes of Horace* I. xxv, When that lust, and hot desire,..Shall round your ulcer'd liver reign.

b. *fig.* = ULCERATED *ppl. a.* 1 b.

1602 Marston *Antonio's Rev.* v. i, Now gin the leprous cores of ulcered sins Wheale to a heade. **1616** R. C. *Times Whistle* (1871) 88 Lop of these vlcerd members of our land. **1699** R. L'Estrange *Erasm. Colloq.* (1725) 162 Your Soul is yet fouler, than your Body, more putrid and ulcer'd, and yet more dangerously wounded. **1747** Francis tr. *Horace, Epist.* I. xvi. 32 For Fools alone their ulcer'd Ills conceal.

†2. = ULCERATED *ppl. a.* 3. *Obs.*⁻¹

1622 R. Banister *113 Diseases Eyes* O 10 b, Of vlcered Cancers, those onely are cut and seared, which are in the vppermost part of the body.

ulcerogenic (ʌlsərəʊˈdʒɛnɪk), *a.* *Med.* [f. ULCER + -O- + -GENIC.] = ULCERATIVE *a.* 1.

1959 *Amer. Jrnl. Digestive Dis.* IV. 903 (*heading*) Ulcerogenic drugs. **1971** *Nature* 15 Oct. 498/1 These results strengthen the hypothesis that nicotine sensitizes the duodenum to the ulcerogenic property of acid flowing from the stomach.

ulcerous (ˈʌlsərəs), *a.* [ad. L. *ulcerōs-us*, f. *ulcer-*, *ulcus* ULCER *sb.* Hence also It., Sp., Pg. *ulceroso*, F. *ulcéreux*, *-euse* (1554), Da. *ulcerøs.*]

1. Of the nature of an ulcer or ulcers; forming a purulent sore.

1577 B. Googe *Heresbach's Husb.* III. (1586) 144 The vlcerous places must be nointed with Vinegar. **1592** Greene *Groat's W. Wit* (1617) 43 For my gluttony, I suffer hunger: ..for my adulterie, vlcerous sores. **1603** Holland *Plutarch's Mor.* 97 Honie..being applied to a sore or ulcerous place, at the first doth smart and sting. **1607** Shaks.

Timon IV. iii. 39 Shee, whom the Spittle-house, and vlcerous sores, Would cast the gorge at. **1744** BERKELEY *Siris* §21 In obstructions and ulcerous erosions of the inward parts. **1752** —— *Th. Tar-water* Wks. 1871 III. 499 Good against ulcerous eruptions. **1789** A. DUNCAN *Mariner's Chron.* (1805) IV. 42 Their lips began to break out in watery and ulcerous blisters. **1834** J. FORBES *Laennec's Dis. Chest* (ed. 4) 279 The disease is curable..after the softening of the tubercles and the formation of an ulcerous excavation. **1897** *Allbutt's Syst. Med.* III. 886 In some instances the foreign bodies had escaped from the appendix through the ulcerous openings they had made in its walls.

fig. **1601** [? MARSTON] *Pasquil & Kath.* v. 20 Why, now the vlcerous swelling of my hate Is broken forth. **1602** MARSTON *Antonio's Rev.* IV. iii, The polluting filth Of ulcerous sinne.

2. Afflicted with an ulcer or ulcers; exhibiting ulceration.

1599 B. JONSON *Ev. Man out of Hum.*, *The Stage* 73 Euery seruile imitating spirit..striues to fling His vlc'rous body in the Thespian spring, And streight leaps forth a Poet. **1600** R. CAWDREY *Treasurie* 266 Scuruie, Scabbie, and vlcerous persons. **1605** SHAKS. *Macb.* IV. iii. 151 Strangely visited people All swolne and Vlcerous..he cures. **1662** HIBBERT *Body Divinity* I. 313 They observed..whether the bowels were of an unnatural colour, or ulcerous. **1899** *Allbutt's Syst. Med.* VI. 105 Cavities resulting from their destruction present irregular, anfractuous, ragged and ulcerous walls.

absol. **1889** H. M. STANLEY in *Stanley & Africa* xvii. (1890) 392 Assiduously dressing and trimming up the ulcerous ready for the march to Zanzibar.

b. *fig.* (Cf. ULCERATED *ppl. a.* 1 b.)

1611 SPEED *Hist. Gt. Brit.* IX. xvi. §20 A weauer (the Bailiffe of the Towne) was the vlcerous head, to which that corruption gathered. **1643** MILTON *Divorce* II. iii. Wks. 1851 IV. 65 Did God for this come down..to patch up an ulcerous and rott'n commonwealth with strict and stern injunctions? **1660** T. M. *C. Walker's Hist. Independ.* IV. 22 Belching forth the scandalous language of their ulcerous tongues to incense the People. **1879** H. GEORGE *Progr. & Pov.* X. v. (1881) 494 A just man would crush with his foot such an ulcerous ant-hill!

3. Developed in, proceeding from, ulcers.

1660 O. SEDGWICK in Spurgeon *Treas. David* Ps. xix. 12 Methinks sin is..like evil and ulcerous humours. **1718** QUINCY *Compl. Disp.* 121 Ulcerous Exudations, which by their loose situations are easily carried along with the Medicine. **1844** G. S. FABER *Eight Dissert.* (1845) II. 311 By reason of some colouring ulcerous matter, the skin of the sufferer would pass through the different successive shades of dark red and lead colour and complete black.

4. Characteristic of, appropriate to, ulcers.

1641 in Rushw. *Hist. Coll.* (1692) III. I. 218, I cannot but admire how this..Body of Judicature should swell up into such a vast and ulcerous dimension. *c* **1720** W. GIBSON *Farrier's Dispens.* III. xiv. (1721) 268/2 To dry up watry Corruptions, which create an ulcerous Disposition in the Legs. **1842** TENNYSON *St. Sim. Styl.* 13 Thrice ten years, Thrice multiplied by superhuman pangs,..In coughs,..ulcerous throes and cramps. **1896** *Allbutt's Syst. Med.* I. 127 The development of ulcerous conditions when the process affects free surfaces.

5. = ULCERATED *ppl. a.* 3.

1751 FOTHERGILL (*title*), Account of the Ulcerous Sore Throat. **1761** *Phil. Trans.* LII. 264 His disorder has been a malignant or ulcerous sore throat. **1859** SEMPLE *Diphtheria* 84 Severe and obstinate ulcerous inflammations of the skin and mucous tissue. **1889** DUNCAN *Clin. Lect. Dis. Women* (ed. 4) xxii. 189 A disease exactly resembling the acute ulcerous stomatitis of children.

Hence **'ulcerously** *adv.*; **'ulcerousness.**

1727 BAILEY (vol. II), *Ulcerousness*, ulcerous State, Condition, or Quality. **1847** WEBSTER, *Ulcerously*.

'ulcery, *a. rare*$^{-1}$. [f. ULCER *sb.*] Of the nature of an ulcer.

1611 COTGR., *Mammelons*, be certaine little, red, hard, vlcerie, and teat-like swellings, which break out of the skin of the head.

ulche, ME. variant of EACH *a.*

'ulcuscle. *rare*$^{-1}$. [ad. L. *ulcusculum*, dim. of *ulcus* ULCER *sb.*] A small ulcer.

1794 E. DARWIN *Zoon.* I. 400 The specific medicines..act only by increasing the absorption of the matter in the ulcuscles of those diseases.

So **ul'cuscule.** (Webster, 1847.)

ulde, -ere, -est, ME. ff. ELD, -ER, -EST.

†**uldron,** variant of *oldron* OLERON *Obs.*

1550 *Admir. Crt. Exemplifications* 3, No. 167, Serten packes of canvas namyd uldrons of Methernek.

ule, obs. var. OIL *sb.*[1]; obs. f. OWL *sb.*, YULE.

ule, var. HULE.

-ule, *suffix*, representing the Latin diminutive ending *-ulus, -ula, -ulum* (whence also F. *-ule*, Sp. and Pg. *-ulo, -ula*, It. *-ulo, -ula, -olo, -ola*), as in *globulus* globule, *glandula* glandule, *grānulum* granule. Among words now current with this ending a certain number correspond to actual Latin forms, as *capsule, cellule, ferule, macule, nodule, pustule, spherule, valvule*; others are of modern formation, as *anguillule*. Only a few of these were in use before the 17th century. Some examples, as *angule, circule, scrupule*, failed to establish themselves against the earlier forms of French origin in *-le*; others, as *formule*, have given way to the purely Latin form. In some cases both forms exist in scientific use, as *ligule* and *ligula, macule* and *macula, valvule* and *valvula*; in some the Latin form is commonly or exclusively employed, as *lingula, tabula*.

‖**ulema** (uːlə'mɑː, 'uːləmə, uː-, juː'liːmə). Also 7 **ulemi,** 9 **oulema, uhlema, oolama, ulama.** [a. Arab. (also Turk. and Pers.) *ʿulemā*, pl. of *ʿālim* knowing, learned, f. *ʿalama* to know. Hence also Sp. *Ulema*, Pg. *Ulemas*, F. *Uléma*.]

1. *pl.* or *collect.* Those who have had special training in the knowledge of Muslim religion and law, and are regarded by Muslims as the authorities on these matters; *spec.* the body of Muslim doctors under the headship of the Sheik-ul-islam, which exercised great political influence in the Turkish empire.

1688 *Lond. Gaz.* No. 2313/2 The next day was a great Consultation held with the Ulemi or Interpreters of their Law. **1768** SIR J. PORTER *Observ. Turks* Pref. (1771) 30 They have the Ulema..composed of all the members of the church or law; a body of men..who stand as an intermediate order between the prince and people. **1803** *Edin. Rev.* II. 292 Russia, and imperial Rome, had its prætorian guards. Turkey has its *uhlema*. **1848** LAYARD *Nineveh* (1849) I. Introd. p. xxiv, The ulema having at length pronounced that these figures were the idols of the infidels, the Mohammedans..destroyed them. **1892** TENNYSON *Akbar's Dream* 45 But our Ulama..Are like wild brutes new-caged.

attrib. **1847** MRS. A. KERR tr. *Ranke's Hist. Servia* v. 89 The establishment of the influence of some great Ulema families which had become almost hereditary. **1888** *Encycl. Brit.* XXIII. 654/2 The juridical and spiritual precepts of the Koran and its *'ulemá* interpreters.

2. A Muslim doctor or divine.

a **1843** in Southey *Comm.-pl. Bk.* Ser. II. (1849) 350 A great part of the oulemas and of the people in office delayed not to partake of this luxury. **1848** W. H. KELLY tr. *L. Blanc's Hist. Ten Y.* I. 260 The divan was rescued from the mystic domination of the ulemas. **1882** *Macm. Mag.* XLVI. 474 The army was accompanied by a number of moullas and ulemas.

‖**ulendo** (ʊ'lɛndəʊ). [Nyanja.] In central Africa: a trek, a safari.

1921 *United Free Church Miss. Rec.* June 189/1 The settlements near the missions may not be so interesting to visit as those one sees on ulendo or trek in the more backward districts. **1927** *Other Lands* Oct. 14/2 Two months on ulendo through Nyasaland would be an ideal holiday. **1971** *Countryman* Autumn 88 A month-long *ulendo* on foot into the western side of the Luangwa Valley in the wet season was one of the moments of my life. **1979** C. ALLEN *Tales from Dark Continent* vi. 79 Touring through the district, a process..known as a safari in East Africa, as *ulendo* in Central Africa and as 'going to bush' or 'going on trek' in West Africa.

-ulent, *suffix*, ad. L. *-ulentus* employed to form adjs., usually with the force of 'abounding in', 'full of' (some thing or quality), as *fraudulentus* fraudulent, *opulentus* opulent, *truculentus* truculent, etc. (Variant forms of the suffix are *-olentus*, as in *vinolentus* vinolent, *violentus* violent, and *-ilentus* as in *gracilentus* slender, *pestilentus* pestilent.) A considerable number of the formations occurring in Latin have been adopted in English, and a few have been added either from mediæval or modern Latin, or by direct formation on Latin stems, as *cinerulent, flatulent, herbulent, nidorulent, torpulent*.

‖**ulex** ('juːlɛks). *Bot.* [mod.L. (Linnæus, 1737), a. L. *ulex* (Pliny) a shrub resembling rosemary.] A genus of thorny papilionaceous shrubs belonging to the order *Leguminosæ*; a plant belonging to this genus, esp. *Ulex Europæus* the common furze, gorse, or whin.

1753 *Chambers' Cycl.* Suppl. s.v. **1755** *Dict. Arts & Sci.*, *Ulex*, in botany, a genus..of plants, with a papilionaceous flower; and an oblong turgid pod for its fruit. **1859** DARWIN *Orig. Spec.* xiii. (1860) 439 The embryonic leaves of the ulex or furze..are pinnate or divided like the ordinary leaves of the leguminosæ.

ulexine ('juːlɛksaɪn). *Med.* [f. prec. + -INE.] An alkaloid prepared from the seeds of gorse.

1887 *Brit. Med. Jrnl.* 21 May 1144/2 The value..of kavaine and ulexine as local anæsthetics. **1888** F. H. LESCHER *Recent Mat. Medica* (ed. 3) 88 Ulexine;..discovered by A. W. Gerrard. A powerful organic base, soluble in water, insoluble in ether.

ulexite ('juːlɛksaɪt). *Chem.* [See quot. 1867.] (See quots. and BOROCALCITE.)

1867 BRANDE & COX *Dict. Sci.*, etc. III. 892/2 *Ulexite*, a name given to native borate of lime (Hayesine), after Ulex, by whom it was analysed. **1875** *Ure's Dict. Arts* (ed. 7) III. 1050 *Ulexite*, a native borate of lime and soda, known also as Boronatrocalcite. It occurs at Iquique, in Peru; and in the Province of Tarapaca.

uley, obs. Sc. variant of OIL *sb.*

†**ulȝeat.** *Sc. Obs.*$^{-1}$ [var. *olyet* OILLET.] A stud for armour.

1507 *Acc. Ld. High Treas. Scot.* III. 254 For I stuthes with ruffis callit ulȝeatis for the King is panses and mailȝeis, weyand v unce j quartar, iijli, xixs. ijd.

ulican, variant of ULLAGONE.

ulicon, var. EULACHON.

ulie, obs. Sc. variant of OIL *sb.*

u'liginal, *a. Bot.* [f. L. *ūlīgin-* (see next) + -AL[1].] Growing in moist or wet ground.

1863 J. G. BAKER *N. Yorksh. Stud. Bot.*, etc. 181 Aboriginal species characteristically paludal, uliginal, ericetal, and sylvestral.

uligi'nose, *a. rare.* [ad. L. *ūlīginōs-us* full of moisture, f. *ūlīgin-*, *ūlīgo* moisture, marshiness. Cf. It., Sp., Pg. *uliginoso*, F. *uligineux*.]

1. = ULIGINOUS *a.* 2 b. *rare*$^{-1}$.

c **1440** *Pallad. on Husb.* x. 29 This moone in lond vliginose or lene,..In thicked lond also, is to demene, When day and nyght yliche longe is holde.

2. *Bot.* = ULIGINAL *a.*

1866 *Treas. Bot.*, *Uliginose*, growing in swampy places. **1967** V. NABOKOV *Speak, Memory* vi. 138 Pretty Cordigera, a gemlike moth, buzzed all over its uliginose food plant.

uliginous (juː'lɪdʒɪnəs), *a.* [f. as prec., or directly f. L. *ūlīgin-* + -OUS. Cf. F. *uligineux* (of soil or plants).]

1. Of a watery, slimy, or oozy nature.

1576 NEWTON *Lemnie's Complex.* II. iii. 109 b, For it is a certayne vliginous moystishnes and superfluous excrement, which ought rather to be sent out and purged. **1610** W. FOLKINGHAM *Art of Survey* I. x. 24 It reuiues the radicall and vliginous humour. *a* **1656** USSHER *Ann.* VI. (1658) 240 One Proxenus..found a spring of a fatty, and uliginous, or oily liquor. **1669** *Phil. Trans.* IV. 1132 The Birch and Alder feed more kindly on a thin uliginous moisture. *a* **1728** WOODWARD *Fossils* (1729) I. 118 The uliginous lacteous Matter,..in the Coral Fishings upon the Coast of Italy, was only a Collection of the Corallin Particles thus sustained in the Sea Water.

2. Of places: Soaked with water or moisture; water-logged, plashy, swampy.

1610 W. FOLKINGHAM *Art of Survey* I. x. 33 Their vliginous and soaked Mosses doe recompence their meane ayre with vnctious Turffes. **1620** VENNER *Via Recta* i. 20 Contrary to this is that which is of a laxe and open substance, such as is commonly growen in low and vliginous places. **1664** EVELYN *Sylva* xv. 32 The water-galls, and uliginous parts of Forests that hardly bear any grass, do many times spontaneously produce it in abundance. **1699** —— *Acetaria* (1729) 155 Those who live in marshes and uliginous Places like the Hundreds of Essex. **1867** SMYTH *Sailor's Word-bk.* 705 *Uliginous channels*, those connecting the branches of rivers, by cuts through the soil.

b. Similarly of soil.

1650 CHARLETON tr. *Van Helmont's Paradoxes* 15 If..they are..buried in a muddy uliginous earth; when they begin to putrifie, they then operate upon..the Patient. **1802** R. HALL *Bot.* 192 *Uliginous Soil*,..spongy, filled with putrid water.

†**3.** Of air: Damp, moist. *Obs. rare.*

1661 EVELYN *Fumifugium* Misc. Writ. (1805) I. 217 The impure and uliginous [air], as that which proceeds from stagnated places, is..the most vile and pestilent. **1697** R. PEIRCE *Bath Mem.* 85 He liv'd near the Fenns, to which Uliginous Air, was ascrib'd the beginning of his Illness.

†**ulipy.** *Sc. Obs.* Also **vly-.** [Prob. ad. older Du. or Flem. **oliepij(e*, f. *olie* oil + *pij(e* PEE *sb.*[1] Cf. the equivalent WFlem. *oliebaai*.] ? An oilskin coat or jacket.

1529 *Acc. Ld. High Treas. Scot.* V. 369 For ane coit of ulipy in all uncostis. *a* **1568** in *Bannatyne MS.* fol. 158 b, His clais is oft in wanting and sic is his gyis, He thrawis and he puttis fast at his vly pyis.

ulk, ME. var. ILK *adjs.*; obs. Sc. f. WEEK.

ulken, obs. var. EULACHON.

ulklie, obs. Sc. f. WEEKLY.

'ull, dial. f. WILL *v.*

ullage ('ʌlɪdʒ), *sb.* Forms: 5 **oylage, vlage,** 6 *Sc.* **vlege,** 8– **ullage.** [ad. AF. *ulliage*, OF. *ouillage*, *eullage* (*heulliage*), *œillage* (also Anglo-L. *oliagium, oyll-, ull-, ulagium*), Pr. *ulhage*, *oulhage*, f. OF. *ouiller, eullier, oiller, œiller* (Anglo-L. *oillare*), Pr. *ulha, oulha*, to fill up (a barrel).

Forms with initial *a-* are also given by Godefroy, viz. *aouillage* and *aouillier, aoillier, aeullier*, etc. (1295–).]

1. The amount of wine or other liquor by which a cask or bottle falls short of being quite full (originally the quantity required to make good the loss by leakage or absorption).

[**1297** *Chanc. Misc.* (P.R.O.) Bd. 2 No. 15 (5), Tradidi etiam eidem vnam pipam pro oliagio predictorum doleorum. **1329** *Exchequer Rolls Scotl.* (1878) I. 224 De ij doliis et j pipa vini... Et in vllagio..j et dimidium. *a* **1377** *Rolls of Parlt.* II. 384 Item par Adam le Ken pur ulliage es Vins mesme l'an 1 ton' 1 pip'.]

1444 *Compota Domest.* (Abbotsf. Cl. 1836) 26 In vlage et lecage per tempus predictum, [84] lagene [bere]. **1481–90** *Howard Househ. Bks.* (Roxb.) 288 Paid for iiij. galons wyne, iij. qrtes. for oylage for the ton wyne, iij. s. ij. d. **1565** *Burgh Rec. Edinb.* (1875) III. 211 The twn of wyne at this present ..xvj crownis of the sone;..item, of fraucht xvj crownis sone; item, for vlege vj li. **1706** PHILLIPS (ed. Kersey), *Ullage* of a Cask, is what such a Vessel wants of being full. **1749** W. YEO *Ullaging & Inching* 3 As often as these Lines are used for determining the Ullages of Casks. **1755** *Dict. Arts & Sci.* s.v., The ullage of a vessel, whose axis is parallel to the horizon, may be found thus. **1833** LOUDON *Encycl. Archit.* §1324 It is usually tunned into hogsheads of a hundred gallons each, leaving a few gallons ullage. **1835** MARRYAT *Olla Podr.* III. 297 (*Moonshine*), I held the bottle up to the candle to ascertain the ullage. **1885** W. ECOCKES in

Civilian 3 Jan. 141/2 A work..comprising tables of ullages of casks, whose bung diameters range from 15 to 40 inches.

b. *on ullage*, (in a vessel) not completely full.
1863 T. G. SHAW *Wine, Vine & Cellar* xi. 302 It is injurious to Rhenish wine to be left on ullage. **1880** *Act 43 & 44 Vic.* c. 24 §43 The casks in which spirits are removed may be either full or..on ullage. **1883** *Times* 17 Nov. 10 The wines should not remain long on ullage.

2. a. (See quots.)
1832 S. ROOSE *Ullaging* 5 By knowing the vacuity, and subtracting it from the whole content, leaves the Ullage or the quantity of liquor then in the cask. **1867** SMYTH *Sailor's Word-bk.* 705 *Ullage*, the remainder in a cask or package which has leaked or been partially used. **1883** *Encycl. Brit.* XVI. 28/2 The quantity of liquor contained in a cask partially filled and the capacity of the portion which is empty are termed respectively the wet and dry ullage.

b. *slang.* (See quots.)
1874 *Slang Dict.* 332 *Ullages*, the wine of all sorts left in the bottoms of glasses at a public dinner. **1889** *Pall Mall G.* 21 Aug. 2/1 'Pray what is "ullage"?' 'The washings out of casks, sir,' replied my friend.

3. *transf.* **a.** Liquid that has oozed through a substance.
1824 T. HOGG *Carnation* 50 Upon this stratum or bed of dung..the ullage occasioned from time to time by the rains will all be received.

b. The waste of metal in engraving.
1860 *Cornh. Mag.* I. 272 In graving deep, tiny spirals of gold and silver curl away from the trenchant tool, and there is precious ullage in chasing and burnishing—spirals and ullage worth money in the market.

c. *Naut.* (See quots.)
1901 *Daily Chron.* 23 May 5/1 The mass of her crew will all too probably be 'ullage'—to use the naval term for a preponderance of undesirables. **1904** KIPLING *Traffics & Discov.* 113 'You're a disgrace to the Service, and your boat's offal.' 'Awful?' I said. 'No—offal—tripes—swipes—ullage.'

4. *attrib.*, as ***ullage bottle, cask, contents.***
1743 BULKELEY & CUMMINS *Voy. S. Seas* 46 This Morning found the Store Tent robbed of Brandy; filled up all the ullage Casks. **1784** J. BOYDELL (*title*), The Ullage Cask Gauger; comprised in a series of Tables..whereby the Ullage Contents of any Cask..is at one view known. **1812** J. SMYTH *Pract. of Customs* (1821) 363 The ullage cask..must be re-gauged, as must all casks entered for exportation. *Ibid.* 409 Landing Ullage Contents. **1864** *Daily Tel.* 4 June, There is scarcely a ship..in which the examining officer's attention is not called to ullage casks. **1889** *Pall Mall G.* 19 Jan. 7 It might have been made by putting two ullage bottles into one.

ˈullage, *v.* [f. prec.]
1. *trans.* To calculate the amount of ullage in (a cask).
1749 W. YEO (*title*), The Method of Ullaging and Inching all sorts of Casks and other Utensils used by Common Brewers, Victuallers, Distillers, &c. **1832** S. ROOSE *Ullaging* 11 To Ullage a Cask in the form of the frustum of a Cone.

2. a. To draw or tap to a slight extent. **b.** To fill up again (an ullaged cask, etc.).
1881 *Standard* 3 Oct. 2/1 There..a cask of some rare vintage was 'ullaged,' with a biscuit and cheese accompaniment. **1888** *Wine, Sp. & Beer* 8 Mar. 186/1 To stir in some pure olive oil..and then flood the oil out by ullaging.

Hence **ˈullaging** *vbl. sb.*
1749 W. YEO *Ullaging & Inching* p. iii, That part of it [*sc.* gauging] which relates to the Ullaging of Casks. **1832** S. ROOSE *Ullaging* 5 The Ullaging of a Cask is to find how much liquor there is in it, when it is not full.

ˈullaged, *ppl. a.* [f. prec. or the sb. + -ED. Cf. *unullaged* (1646).]
1. Of a cask or bottle: Short of contents.
1549 in R. G. Marsden *Sel. Pleas Crt. Admir.* (Selden Soc.) II. 59 One hundreth and fyftie tonnes of wyne full and ullagid. **1867** SMYTH *Sailor's Word-bk.* 705 *Ullaged* is used for damaged, short of contents. **1908** ATTON & HOLLAND *King's Customs* 195 A demijohn or two in the captain's locker, and an ullaged anker in the forecastle.

2. Of wine: Affected in quality by the presence of ullage.
1907 *Sat. Rev.* 29 June 815/1 Without..the clash of personalities the story is like a bottle of ullaged wine.

3. *transf.* Of inferior quality; refuse.
1892 *Spectator* 9 Jan. 41/1 If you have to feed ten men on twopence, you must buy ullaged flour.

ˈullager. [f. ULLAGE *v.*] One who ascertains the amount of ullage.
1885 W. ECOCKES (*title*), The Ullager's Pocket Gem, comprising tables for finding the ullages of casks.

‖**ullagone,** *sb.* and *int.* *Anglo-Irish.* Also **ullagoane, ullaghone, ul(l)agon, hullagone, ullagawn, ulican, yoolughan.** [ad. Ir. Gael. *olagón, ologón, olagán*, of imitative origin.] A cry of lamentation, a wail; *spec.* a funeral lament. Also as *int.*
1819 [RENNIE] *St. Patrick* II. 118 I'll gar her set up her yoolughans there, the limmer, an I had ance an arrow. **1828** T. C. CROKER *Fairy Leg. & Tradit. S. Irel.* II. 191, I heard the dismallest ullagoane in the world, enough to break any one's heart. *Ibid.* 236 Oh ullagone, ullagone! this is a wide world. **1845** MRS. S. C. HALL *Whiteboy* v, A scream—loud and long—as of a woman in bitter trouble; it was, in fact, a 'keen', a regular 'ullagawn'. **1901** W. BARRY *Wizard's Knot* 219 (E.D.D.), It was a dirge, an ulagón, over Cathal, and his ruined walls.

Hence ‖**ullagone** *v. intr.*, to wail or lament loudly.
1828 T. C. CROKER *Fairy Leg. & Tradit. S. Irel.* II. 76 Then the poor woman began to cry and ullagoane so finely that it would do any one good to hear her.

ulle, obs. Sc. var. OIL *sb.*

ulli, var. HULE.

ullmannite (ˈʌlmənaɪt). *Min.* [From the name of Prof. J. C. *Ullmann* + -ITE[1]; in sense b named by J. Fröbel in 1850.] (See quots.)
†**a. 1839** *Penny Cycl.* XIV. 382/1 Phosphate of Manganese and Iron: Ullmannite... Occurs at Limoges in France.
b. 1868 WATTS *Dict. Chem.* V. 936 *Ullmanite*, antimonial or antimonio-arsenical nickel-glance. **1875** *Ure's Dict. Arts* (ed. 7) III. 1050 *Ullmannite*, an antimonio-sulphide of nickel, occasionally containing arsenic. It occurs at Freusberg, in Nassau.

ˈullo (ʌˈləʊ), *int.* Also **ullo.** Colloq. or joc. pronunc. of HULLO *int.*
1895 A. W. PINERO *Second Mrs. Tanqueray* III. 112 'Ullo, 'ullo! Whisky and potass! **1955** M. ALLINGHAM *Beckoning Lady* ii. 31 'Ullo, now what? **1968** P. DICKINSON *Skin Deep* iii. 36 Ullo, ullo! The other fellah caught in the nest, eh? **1980** *Daily Mail* 17 Jan. 4/1 [*Cartoon: policeman speaking*] 'Ullo, 'ullo, 'ullo..and where do you think *you're* going?

ully, obs. Sc. variant of OIL *sb.*

ulˈmaceous, *a.* *Bot.* [f. mod.L. *Ulmace-æ*, an order of plants including the elm, f. L. *ulm-us* ULME.] (See quot.)
1849 CRAIG, *Ulmaceous*, pertaining to the elm; belonging to the order Ulmaceæ.

ulmate (ˈʌlmət). *Chem.* [f. ULM-IC *a.*: see -ATE[4]. So F. *ulmate*, Pg. *ulmato.*] A salt produced by the action of ulmic acid.
1836 BRANDE *Man. Chem.* 924 A brown liquid is obtained (ulmate of potassa), from which acids throw down ulmin. **1843** *Penny Cycl.* XXV. 491/1 When cold, the product, which contains ulmate of potash, is dissolved in water.

ulme. *Obs.* or *dial.* [ad. L. *ulm-us* elm. Cf. G. *ulme*, Du. *olm.*] An elm-tree. (Cf. ULM-TREE.)
The forms *olm, holm, ulm*, are recorded as surviving in northern English and southern Scottish dialects in the latter part of the 19th cent.
1567 DRANT *Horace, Epist.* I. vii. D vj, Our cittizen is now a Corridon. He trimmes his ulmes. **1698** J. FRYER *Acc. E. India & P.* 295 A Catalogue of Plants growing at Spahaun. .. Sycamore. Ivy... Poplar. Ulmes. Willows.

ulmic (ˈʌlmɪk), *a.* *Chem.* [f. L. *ulm-us* elm, after ULMIN. Cf. F. *ulmique*, Pg. *ulmico.*] ***ulmic acid***:
a. = ULMIN 1.
A distinction between ulmic acid and ulmin or ulmine has been made by various chemists, but without agreement in the precise application of the terms.
1831 T. THOMSON *Chem. Inorg. Bodies* II. 105 Ulmic acid appears to be a vegetable substance of very great importance ..obtained from the exudation of the elm by dissolving the exudation in water and precipitating the ulmic acid. **1836** BRANDE *Man. Chem.* 923 As it [*sc.* ulmin] combines with bases, Boullay terms it *ulmic acid*... He represents ulmin, or ulmic acid, as a compound [etc.]. **1868** WATTS *Dict. Chem.* V. 936 The name 'ulmic acid', or 'ulmin', was given by Klaproth to a gummy substance contained in the black alkaline excrescences on the stems of unhealthy trees, especially of elms.
b. = ULMIN 2.
1843 *Penny Cycl.* XXV. 491/1 Ulmic acid plays an important part in manures and soils, and what is called moss-water owes its peculiar properties to its presence. **1868** WATTS *Dict. Chem.* V. 936 The ammoniacal solution.. deposits brown or black gelatinous flocks of ulmic acid.

ulmin (ˈʌlmɪn). *Chem.* Also **ulmine.** [f. L. *ulm-us* elm + -IN: named by Thomson. Cf. F. *ulmine*, Pg. *ulmina.*]
1. A substance which exudes spontaneously from the inner bark of the elm and some other trees; *spec.* the final stage of this as a distinct chemical principle.
α. **1813** T. THOMSON *Syst. Chem.* (1817) IV. 48 Ulmin.. was first noticed in 1804, by Klaproth, who found it in a spontaneous exudation from the elm. **1819** BRANDE *Chem.* 366 Ulmin is of a dark brown colour, with scarcely any taste or smell... The exudation from the elm is generally combined with carbonate of potassa, and is therefore readily soluble in water. **1842** *Penny Cycl.* XXII. 26/1 Simaruba is the bark of the root of the Simaruba amara... Its chief constituents are..ulmin, mucilage, and some salts.
β. **1838** TUPPER *Proverb. Philos.* Notes 219 With reference to the elm, I would remark, that no use has yet been discovered in the principle called 'ulmine'. **1853** ROYLE *Mat. Med.* (ed. 2) 632 It [the bark of Elm] contains Tannin ..and a peculiar mucilaginous or gummy principle, called Ulmine.
2. A dark-brown or black product resulting from the decay of wood or vegetable matter, or artificially obtained by the action of powerful chemical agents on sugar and some other substances.
α. **1843** *Penny Cycl.* XXV. 491/1 Ulmin, or ulmic acid, may be artificially obtained..by the following process. **1857** MILLER *Elem. Chem., Org.* 54 If the solution [of sugar] be kept boiling for some hours,..a certain quantity of formic acid, and of a brown sparingly soluble substance termed *ulmin*, are produced. **1868** WATTS *Dict. Chem.* V. 936 Ulmin is also the name of a brown pigment, produced by the action of strong acids or alkalis on various organic bodies.
β. **1848** FOWNES *Chem.* (ed. 2) 371 *note*, This [substance] is generally called ulmic or humic acid, and its origin ascribed to the reaction of the alkali on the ulmine or humus of the soil. **1861** GESNER *Coal, Petrol.*, etc. (1865) 128 The decay of wood is produced by oxidation, and ulmine is the result.

ˈulmous, *a.* *Chem.* [f. as prec. + -OUS.] Partaking of the character of ulmin.
1868 WATTS *Dict. Chem.* V. 936 Ulmous or Humous Substances.

†**ulm-tree.** *Obs. rare.* [f. L. *ulm-us* elm + TREE *sb.* Cf. ULME and MHG. *ulmboum*, Du. *olmboom.*] An elm-tree.
c **1000** ÆLFRIC *Gloss.* in Wr.-Wülcker 138 *Ulmus*, ulmtreow. **1382** WYCLIF *Isaiah* xli. 19, I shal sette in desert fyrr tree, and vlm tree, and box togidere.

‖**ulna** (ˈʌlnə). *Anat.* [L. *ulna* (hence also It., Pg. *ulna*), related to Gr. ὠλένη and OE. *eln* ELL[1] (cf. ELBOW *sb.*).]
1. The large inner bone of the fore-arm, extending from the elbow to the wrist.
1541 R. COPLAND *Guydon's Quest. Chirurg.* G j b, The arme..is deuyded in thre great partyes. One is called vlna, the other lytel arme. *Ibid.* G ij, Howe many bones are in yᵉ fyrste parte of the great hande that is named vlna or adiutor? **1646** SIR T. BROWNE *Pseud. Ep.* IV. iv. 184 The other or lower division of the artery descendeth by the ulna. **1693** tr. *Blancard's Phys. Dict.* (ed. 2), *Ulna*,..the greater Bone, betwixt the Arm and the Wrist, which is jointed upward with the Shoulder. **1726** MONRO *Anat. Bones* (1741) 252 At the superior Extremity of the Ulna are two Processes. **1728** CHAMBERS *Cycl.* s.v., The Ulna lies on the inside of the Fore-Arm, reaching from the Elbow to the Wrist. **1803** *Med. Jrnl.* X. 558 The head of this bone was separated from the surrounding parts, as well as its union with the ulna. **1825** T. HOOK *Sayings* Ser. II. *Doubts and F.* i, Who conceived that some desperate injury had been done to her Ladyship's radius or ulna. **1881** *Med. Temp. Jrnl.* XLVI. 86 There was discharge from incisions both at the back and front of the hand and over the lower part of the ulna.
2. The corresponding bone of the foreleg in quadrupeds, and of the wing in birds.
1831 YOUATT *Horse* xiii. 236 The long and front bone, called the *radius*, is nearly straight... The short and hinder bone is called the *ulna*. **1839** *Penny Cycl.* XIV. 69/1 In the ruminants generally the ulna is scarcely more than an appendage to the radius. **1879** E. P. WRIGHT *Anim. Life* 57 The fore-arm [in bats] consists of a rudimentary ulna, and a long, curved radius. **1884** COUES *N. Amer. Birds* 107 The enlarged proximal extremity of the ulna is called the olecranon, or 'head of the elbow'.
3. *Palæont.* and *Ichthyol.* (See quots.)
(*a*) **1839** G. ROBERTS *Dict. Geol.*, *Ulna*.., the bone or plate which, together with the radius, forms the first row, after the humerus, in the *front* paddles of an ichthyosaurus and plesiosaurus.
(*b*) *a* **1843** *Encycl. Metrop.* (1845) VII. 303/1 Between the lower edge of the spoke-bone and the upper edge of the ulna or cubit. **1854** OWEN *Orr's Circ. Sci.*, *Org. Nat.* I. 175 Of the two flat bones connecting the fin with the coracoid, the upper one is the 'ulna'.

ˈulnad, *adv.* [f. prec. + -AD.] Toward the ulnar aspect of the forearm.
1803 BARCLAY *New Anat. Nomencl.* 166 Ulnad will signify towards the ulnar aspect. **1808** —— *Muscular Motions* 384 When it is rolled radiad or ulnad, the power of the one will be necessarily increased proportionally as that of the other is diminished.

ulnage (ˈʌlnɪdʒ). *Obs.* exc. *Hist.* [ad. med.L. *ulnagium* (14th c.), f. L. *ulna* after OF. *aulnage* ALNAGE.]
1. = ALNAGE 1.
1447 *Ord. exchequer* 35. c. 62 (6) A v b, For euerye foreyn accompte of sheryffes and vlnage. **1454** *Rolls of Parlt.* V. 247 The Fermours of the Ulnage in the Counte of Somers[et] yerely. **1495** *Act 11 Hen. VII*, c. 62 §1 The fermour of Ulnage in the Citie of Coventre.
2. = ALNAGE 2.
1450 in *Archaeol.* (1770) I. 92 The issues and profits coming of the ulnage and subsidue of wollen clothes. **1450** *Rolls of Parlt.* V. 186/1 To be taken of the Subsidie and ulnage of Clothes. **1545** *Lanc. Wills* (Chetham Soc.) II. 61 My lease wyche I have of the ulnage and subsidie within the countie palatyne of Lancast[er].

ulnager (ˈʌlnɪdʒə(r)). *Hist.* [f. prec. + -ER[1].] = ALNAGER.
1750 in *10th Rep. Hist. MSS. Comm.* (1885) App. I. 304 [Prosecuting his suit for the recovery of the patent office of] Ulnager [in Dublin]. **1832** *Rolls Parlt.* VII. 953/1 Office of Ulnager of Worsteds. **1867** BRANDE & COX *Dict. Sci.*, etc. III. 893/2 These officers were called *alnagers* or *ulnagers*, and the accounts rendered by them to the exchequer are still preserved.

ulnar (ˈʌlnə(r)), *a.* and *sb.* *Anat.* [f. ULN-A + -AR. So F. *ulnaire*, Pg. *ulnar*, Sp. *ulnario.*]
1. Pertaining to the ulna, in various senses:
a. In ***ulnar artery, nerve, vein***, etc.
1741 MONRO *Anat. Nerves* (ed. 3) 70 The ulnar Nerve is in the Palm of the Hand. **1800** *Phil. Trans.* XC. 103 The median proceeding along the arm, with the large blood-vessels, and giving off two branches of communication with the ulnar nerve. **1813** J. THOMSON *Lect. Inflam.* 267 As the brachial [artery] is sometimes observed to be divided..into radial and ulnar arteries. **1840** E. WILSON *Anat. Vade Mecum* vi. 318 The posterior ulnar vein. **1870** ROLLESTON *Anim. Life* 9 The ulnar sesamoid bone, or 'os pisiforme', is not reckoned as a carpal bone. **1885** *Buck's Handbk. Med. Sci.* I. 313/2 The ulnar nerve is placed to the inner side of the artery in the wrist.
b. With other sbs.
1803 [see ULNAD *adv.*]. **1808** BARCLAY *Muscular Motions* p. xx, An aspect..towards the side on which the ulna is situated [is] *ulnar*. **1846** BRITTAN tr. *Malgaigne's Man. Oper. Surg.* 6 During the operation the ulnar border of the left hand should be pressed on the skin behind the right. **1854** OWEN in *Orr's Circ. Sci.*, *Org. Nat.* I. 190 The ulnar portion

of the bone developes a short..olecranon. **1872** HUMPHRY *Myology* 185 Towards the ulnar side of the hand these tendons are usually absent.

2. *absol.* as *sb.* The ulnar nerve.

1899 *Allbutt's Syst. Med.* VIII. 9 The physician then examines the nerve-trunks of both limbs simultaneously by means of gentle pressure on the ulnars behind the olecranons.

ulno- (ˈʌlnəʊ), combining form (on Greek types) of ULNA, occurring in a few technical terms, as ***ulnocarpal, -metacarpal, -radial***.

a **1843** *Encycl. Metrop.* (1845) VII. 327/2 In the Penguins, the Ulno-carpal bone..is largely developed.

ulo'dendroid, *a. rare*⁻¹. [f. mod.L. *Ulodendron* (see def.), f. Gr. οὖλος crisp, curly + δένδρον tree.] Of or connected with *Ulodendron*, a genus of extinct fossil plants.

1900 *Nature* 15 Nov. 53/2 The nature of the large scars on the well-known Ulodendroid branches.

uloid (ˈjuːlɔɪd), *a.* and *sb. Path.* [f. Gr. οὐλή scar + -OID.] **a.** *adj.* Having the appearance of a scar or cicatrix. **b.** *sb.* A scar-like spot or mark on the skin.

1901 DORLAND *Med. Dict.* (ed. 2).

-ulose, *suffix*[1]. A compound adjectival suffix representing L. *-ulōsus*, formed by the addition of *-ōsus* (see -OSE) to stems in *-ul-us, -a, -um*, as *angulōsus* from *angulus, fābulōsus* from *fābula, perīculōsus* from *perīculum*. Such formations are rare in earlier Latin, but a considerable number are employed by post-Augustan writers, as Pliny, Columella, etc. Among the English examples which have their source in classical or post-classical forms are *angulose, calculose, fabulose, fistulose, glandulose, nebulose, pustulose, ramulose, sabulose, vermiculose*. On the analogy of these, various others have been introduced, as *flosculose, globulose, granulose, scrofulose, siliculose, tubulose, tumulose*. These forms are parallel to a certain number of those in -ULOUS, being as a rule either obsolete variants of these, or introduced later in order to convey the distinction commonly observed between the endings -OSE and -OUS.

-ulose (-jʊləʊz), *suffix*[2]. *Biochem.* [f. LÆV)ULOSE.] Used (in place of -OSE[2]) to form the systematic names of ketoses from the names of the corresponding aldoses, esp. ketoses having the carbonyl group at the second carbon atom; as *hexulose*, RIBULOSE, SEDOHEPTULOSE.

ulotrichan (juːˈlɒtrɪkən). [Cf. next.] A person belonging to the 'crisp-haired' division of mankind (see next).

1888 *Cassell's Encycl. Dict.*

ulotrichous (juːˈlɒtrɪkəs), *a.* Also oulo-. [f. mod.L. *Ulotrichi* (see def.), f. Gr. οὖλος crisp, curly + -τριχος -haired, f. τριχ-, θρίξ hair. Cf. F. *ulotrique*, Pg. *ulotrico*.] Of or belonging to the *Ulotrichi*, the division of mankind (in Bory de St. Vincent's classification) defined as having crisp or woolly hair. Hence **u'lotrichy**, woolly-hairedness.

1857 MAYNE *Expos. Lex.* 847/2 Oulotrichous. **1884** *Imp. Dict.* **1909** A. C. HADDON *Races of Man* 3 These three varieties [of hair, *i.e.* straight, wavy, and woolly] are now termed leiotrichous, cymotrichous, and ulotrichous. **1924** A. C. HADDON *Races of Man* (ed. 2) i. 5 *Ulotrichy*, or woolly hair. **1936** [see CYMOTRICHY].

-ulous, a compound adjectival suffix representing the two Latin endings *-ulōsus* and *-ulus*. In the former case there are frequently variants in *-ulose*, which in modern use are as a rule more specific in meaning. To this class belong *angulous, calculous, fabulous, fistulous*, etc. (see -ULOSE); also *crapulous, meticulous, populous, scrupulous*, etc. The number of purely modern formations is not large. To the group which corresponds to Latin forms in *-ulus* belong *bibulous, credulous, emulous, garrulous, pendulous, sedulous, stridulous, tremulous*. In a very few instances both forms occur in Latin, as *querulus*, rarely *querulōsus*, querulous; *rīdiculus*, rarely *rīdiculōsus*, ridiculous.

‖**ulpan** (ul'pan). Pl. **ulpanim** (-'im). [mod. Heb. *ulpān*.] An intensive course in the Hebrew language, orig. for immigrants to the modern state of Israel; a centre providing such a course; also in extended use.

1950 *Israel Govt. Yearbk.* 119/1 The intensive Hebrew language courses (Ulpanim) are attended by lawyers, engineers, teachers, newspapermen..and senior officials. **1973** *Jewish Chron.* 19 Jan. 7/1 The erection of temporary classrooms and religious ulpanim. **1975** *Times* 27 May 2/3 The courses, run by the extramural department of the University of Wales, are a development of the Ulpan method of language teaching. **1977** *New Yorker* 9 May 42/3 You should go downtown..where they got regular language factories... They even got an *ulpan*, like in Israel.

†**ulpic.** *Obs. rare.* In 5 vlpike. [ad. L. *ulpicum*.] A kind of leek.

c **1440** *Pallad. on Husb.* II. 224 Al the route Of rucul serue hit like this, cool also, Garlec, vlpike ek sowe hem now bo too. *Ibid.* IV. 166, XII. 71.

Ulster (ˈʌlstə(r)). [The name of the most northerly of the four provinces of Ireland.

The name occurs in ME. (14–15th cent.) as *Ulster* (also *Hulster*) and in the fuller form *Ulvester* (in Sc. also as *Ullister, Ulsister*, and *Ulcister*), = AF. (*a* 1225) *Ulvestre* (*Hulv-*), Anglo-L. (*c* 1200) *Ulvestera, -tira, -tria*, corresponding to ON. *Ulfastir*, a variant of the more usual *Ulaztir, Ulaðstir* (also *Ulaþscir*), the first element of which is the Irish *Ulaidh* (gen. *Uladh*), men of Ulster. The origin of the suffix, which also appears in Leinster and Munster (Ir. Gael. *Laighean, Mumha*), is not clear, but it may represent Ir. *tír* land.]

1. *pl.* Ulstermen (forming a regiment). *rare.*

1649 CROMWELL *Let.* 19 Dec. (Carlyle), Being informed that..Lieutenant-general Ferral with his Ulsters was to march out of Waterford,..I ordered Colonel Zanchy..to march..to the relief of our friends. *Ibid.*, The Ulsters.. made indeed for the time a good resistance.

2. The king-of-arms for Ireland.

1552 EDWARD VI *Jrnl.* in *Lit. Rem.* (Roxburghe Cl.) II. 395, [February] 2. Ther was a king of armes made for Irland, whose name was Ulster, and his province was al Irland. **1627** CHAS. I in *State Papers, Ireland* (1900) 223 You shall also see Ulster (who is the Chief Herald) countenanced in a herald's commission of visitation of various places in Ireland. **1712** *Lond. Gaz.* No. 4970/2 Coat of his Arms carried by Ulster King of Arms. **1857** *Lit. Rem. Edw. VI* (Roxb. Cl.) II. 395 *n.*, The arms given to the office of Ulster were, Argent, St. George's cross, and on a chief gules a lion between a harp and portcullis, all or. **1880** *Encycl. Brit.* XI. 688/1 In Ireland also there is but one king-at-arms, Ulster.

3. A long, loose overcoat of frieze or other rough cloth, frequently with a waist-belt.

The 'Ulster Overcoat' was introduced by J. G. M'Gee & Co. of Belfast in 1867; the abbreviated name has been in common use from 1879.

1876 L. TROUBRIDGE *Jrnl.* 31 Dec. in J. Hope-Nicholson *Life amongst Troubridges* (1966) 149 [I] came swaggering into Dulcie's bedroom..in an ulster, revealing the immortal check trousers. **1877** TROLLOPE *Amer. Senator* I. xx. 209 She once offered to lay an Ulster to a sealskin jacket. **1878** H. S. LEIGH *Town Garland* 87 When the Ulster descends from its home on the hook, And the warmth-giving wrappers return from the wash. **1879** MISS BRADDON *Cloven Foot* xii. 110 Celia running home..with all her wedding finery smothered under a waterproof Ulster. **1888** RIDER HAGGARD *Col. Quaritch* III. xi. 169 He put on a pair of shooting-boots, an old coat, and an ulster.

attrib. **1878** *Era Almanack* 35 The ulster epidemic was raging even at this time. **1879** E. O'DONOVAN *Merv Oasis* xvi. (1883) 174 Over my shoulders was a drenched leopard skin, beneath which could be seen my travel-stained, much-worn ulster overcoat. **1880** *Cassell's Family Mag.* 122 The ulster muff is of a rectangular shape.

4. *attrib.* **a.** Used to designate the custom prevalent in Ulster by which a tenant has certain rights of occupancy, disposal, or compensation, in regard to land held by him; usually ***Ulster tenant-right***.

1870 *Act 33–34 Victoria* c. 46 §1 The usages prevalent in the province of Ulster, which are known as, and in this Act intended to be included under, the denomination of the Ulster tenant-right custom, are hereby declared to be legal. **1878** [see TENANT-RIGHT]. **1879** H. GEORGE *Progr. & Pov.* VI. i. (1881) 291 If what is known as the Ulster tenant right were extended to the whole of Great Britain, it would be but to carve out of the estate of the landlord, an estate for the tenant. **1882** M. ARNOLD *Irish Ess.*, etc. 28 It has been suggested..by the Ulster custom of compensating them [*sc.* tenants] for their improvements, and letting them sell the value which by their improvements they had added to the property.

b. ***Ulsterman, Ulsterwoman***, a native or inhabitant of Ulster.

Cf. ULTONIAN.

1845 CARLYLE *Cromwell* I. 497 'Lieutenant-General Ferral with his Ulsters;' *note*, Ulster-men. **1868** (*title*), Modern Ireland: its Vital Questions, Secret Societies, and Government: by an Ulsterman. **1971** *Guardian* 18 Sept. 9/6 A lady assures us that she is proud to be an Ulsterwoman. **1981** A. T. Q. STEWART *Edward Carson* v. 87 An Ulsterwoman who was the wife of a high official.

c. ***Ulster fry*** (see quots.).

1941 J. D. CARR *Case of Constant Suicides* 43 That stuff that looks like slices of boloney is called Ulster Fry. **1978** J. GALWAY *Autobiogr.* (1979) v. 57, I remember eating liver and sausages, roast beef for dinner on Sunday and, of course, an Ulster fry for breakfast—bacon, eggs, potato and soda bread. **1979** *Guardian* 22 June 19/5 The notorious 'Ulster fry'—most things you can think of cooked in a pan.

Hence **'Ulsterite** *temporary*, a native or inhabitant of Ulster; also **Ulsteri'zation**, the policy of replacing British security forces in Northern Ireland by Northern Irish ones; also in extended use; (from sense 3) **'ulstered** *a.*, wearing an ulster; **ulste'rette**, a small or light ulster; **'ulstering**, material suitable for ulsters.

1880 MISS BROUGHTON *Second Thoughts* I. v. 62 A few *ulstered, comforted men, stamping up and down, waiting for the night mail. **1889** SKRINE *Mem. Thring* 201 The group of flannelled and ulstered players. **1881** J. W. BUEL *Border Outlaws* 187 Each wearing a long linen *ulsterette over a heavy fall coat. **1887** J. ASHBY STERRY *Lazy Minstrel* (1892) 171 My smart ulsterette, e'en a poet might sing, 'Tis white corduroy, with a rose-coloured lining! **1888** *Cambridge* (Mass.) *Tribune* 24 Nov., These 'Inverness' overcoats are close-fitting, and when worn without the cape have the appearance of an ulsterette. **1888** *Myra's Jrnl.* 1 Nov. 656/1 Patterns of Cloths, Homespuns, and *Ulsterings for ladies' and children's jackets and ulsters. **1890** *Textile News* 20 June (List Manufacturers), Fancy meltons, ulsterings, costumes, coatings, &c. **1920** *Glasgow Herald* 11 Nov. 9 The amendment was criticised by a number of members in addition to the *Ulsterites. **1921** LLOYD GEORGE *Let.* 24 Nov. (1973) viii. 195 The Irish negotiations have taken a turn for the worse... This time it is the Sinn Feiners. Last week it was the Ulsterites. **1925** J. O'CONNOR *Hist. Ireland 1798–1924* II. xx. 260 Southerners hope and think, and the Ulsterites fear and affect to think that the four counties could not stand by themselves. **1977** *Belfast Tel.* 28 Feb. 1/6 Attempts by the Government to move towards an '*Ulsterisation'..of the security forces. **1979** *An Phoblacht* 29 Sept. 1/3 Given Britain's Ulsterisation policy, then that increased repression is likely to be led by the RUC. **1980** *Times* 15 Sept. 12/3 One could be speaking about the ultimate 'Ulsterization' of the West Bank and Gaza.

ult., abbrev. of ULTIMO.

1750 DUNCOMBE in *Lett. Eminent Persons* (1772) II. 170, I have read yours of the 30th ult. with great pleasure. **1767** J. GARDEN *Elegant Epist.* (1790) 730/1, I am..favoured with your's of the 25th ult. **1798** *York Courant* 1 Oct. 2/5 On Saturday the first ult a new peal of six bells..was opened. **1815** *Sporting Mag.* XLV. 354 On the 3d ult. they fell in with a fox. **1935, 1962** [see PROX.].

†**Ultagh, -ogh.** *Anglo-Irish. Obs.* Also **Ultock**. [a. Ir. Gael. *Ultach*, f. *Ult-*, stem of OIr. *Ulaid* (d. pl. *Ultaib*, a. pl. *Ultu*) men of Ulster.] An Ulsterman.

1649 in *Contemp. Hist. Irel.* (Ir. Archæol. Soc.) II. 335 Those under the command of George Monro, part whereof were formerly his own, and part were of Owen ONeals Ultoghs. **1652–3** *Ibid.* III. 370 Created Earle of Tyrone, by the Ultaghes. **1690** J. MACKENZIE *Siege London-Derry* 48/1 Great numbers of Women and Boys (which the Ultoghs always carry along with them, when they expect spoil).

attrib. **1688** in Somers *Tracts* (1814) XI. 451 How often do we now hear the Ultock Irish boast of their merit.

ulterior (ʌlˈtɪərɪə(r)), *a.* and *sb.* [a. L. *ulterior* further, more distant, comp. of **ulter* (cf. *ultrā, ultrō* advs.) that is beyond. Hence also It. *ulteriore*, Sp. and Pg. *ulterior*, F. *ultérieur* (16th c.).]

A. *adj.* **1.** Lying beyond that which is immediate or present; coming at a subsequent point or stage; further, future.

1646 SIR T. BROWNE *Pseud. Ep.* II. i. 49 If the prescription of time, and numerositie of assertors, were a sufficient demonstration, we might sit downe herein, as an unquestionable truth; nor should there need *vlterior* disquisition. **1661** BOYLE *Style of Script.* 211 The Ulterior Accomplishment of that Part of it [*sc.* Scripture], which once Promis'd God's People, that Kings should be its Nursing Fathers. **1816** A. KNOX *Rem.* (1834) I. 54 These changes were meant by Providence to subserve ulterior movements. **1827** JARMAN *Powell's Devises* II. 75 The principle which confers upon him the ulterior interest in the lands directed to be sold would seem to exclude him in the converse case. **1856** FROUDE *Hist. Eng.* (1858) I. iv. 336 The request was only preparatory to ulterior measures. **1884** *Manch. Exam.* 10 May 5/4 The attitude and disposition of those Powers, as bearing upon their ulterior action, necessarily enter into the question.

b. *spec.* Lying beyond what is openly stated, avowed, or evident; intentionally kept in the background or concealed.

1735 BOLINGBROKE *Study Hist.* viii. (1752) II. 98 By reserving still a right of making ulterior demands, they reduced the Carthaginians at last to the necessity of abandoning their city, or of continuing the war. **1825** T. HOOK *Sayings* Ser. II. *Man of Many Fr.* (Colburn) 86 Without any knowledge of her uncle's ulterior intentions on the subject. **1856** *N. Brit. Rev.* XXVI. 197 There is no reason for suspecting him of ulterior designs of a deeper and more treacherous dye. **1877** FROUDE *Short Stud.* (1883) IV. I. iii. 30 He was..the most unlikely..to have adopted a course so marked without some ulterior purpose.

2. Lying on the further side of a point or boundary; more remote in position.

1721 BAILEY, *Ulterior*, on the farther Side. **1798** *Phil. Trans.* LXXXVIII. 167 This scale..containing three parallel lines engraven thereon, on the exterior and ulterior of which are three divisions. **1817** CHALMERS *Astron Disc.* iii. (1852) 68 To shoot afar into those ulterior regions which are beyond the limits of our astronomy. **1864** BAILEY *Festus* (ed. 7) 120 The thunderous bars Of Heaven's ulterior orb.

B. *sb.* A further aim or end.

1843 CHALMERS in Hanna *Mem.* (1852) IV. xviii. 351 This will open..a bright and beautiful ulterior, to which every eye should be directed.

Hence **ulteri'ority**, an ulterior thing or matter.

1814 PARR *Let. to S. Butler* 1 Apr., Wks. 1828 VII. 363, I shall say something about the ulteriorities, and you must sympathise and co-operate with me.

ul'teriorly, *adv.* [f. ULTERIOR *a.* + -LY².] At (or to) a further stage or point; subsequently; afterwards.

1818 BENTHAM *Ch. Eng.*, *Catech. Exam.* 209 The future probable Bell-taught and ulteriorly teachable Parish School-boy. **1833** CARLYLE *Misc. Ess.*, *Diderot* (1888) 32 Nor do the generality, on either side, yet see whither ulteriorly it is tending. **1854** J. S. C. ABBOTT *Napoleon* (1855) II. xxxv. 663 Beneath its lofty dome, where the massive tomb of Napoleon was ulteriorly to be erected, a magnificent cenotaph was reared.

ultima (ˈʌltɪmə). [L. *ultima* (sc. *syllaba*), fem. of *ultimus* last.] The last syllable of a word.

1913 [see AFFECTION *sb.* I b]. **1964** *Language* XL. 24 PItW [*sc.* Proto-Italo-Western] posttonic syllables survived into

Rhaeto-Romance (1) in paroxytones if the ultima was /a/. **1977** *Amer. Speech 1975* L. 46 It also occurs in unstressed position, for example, in the ultima of *always* and the penult of *annihilated*.

ultimacy ('ʌltɪməsɪ). [f. ULTIM-ATE *a.*: see -ACY.] The quality or state of being ultimate.

1842 SIR W. HAMILTON *Diss.* in *Reid's Wks.* II. 760 The simplicity, ultimacy, and incomprehensibility of our original apprehensions. *a* **1848** W. A. BUTLER *Hist. Anc. Philos.* (1856) I. 161 The ultimacy of the laws of motion has been lately made the subject of disquisition. **1893** FAIRBAIRN *Christ in Mod. Theol.* II. II. iii. 430 As to the ultimacy of the will Calvin is explicit.

‖**ultima ratio** ('ʌltɪmə 'reɪʃɪəʊ). [L.] Final sanction.

1848 MILL *Polit. Econ.* I. II. ix. 375 The Irish cottier.. protects himself by the *ultima ratio* of a defensive civil war. *a* **1902** S. BUTLER *Way of All Flesh* (1903) lxv. 292 There can be no doubt about faith and not reason being the *ultima ratio*. **1910** G. K. CHESTERTON *George Bernard Shaw* 26 The very logic of the Irishman makes him regard war or revolution as extra-logical, an *ultima ratio* which is beyond reason. **1933** *Times Lit. Suppl.* 29 June 436/4 The rod is still the *ultima ratio* of so many teachers. **1969** P. ANDERSON in Cockburn & Blackburn *Student Power* 226 The cultural limitations of bourgeois reason in England were thus politically rational: the *ultima ratio* of the economy founded both.

ultimata, pl. of ULTIMATUM *sb.*

ultimate ('ʌltɪmət), *a.* and *sb.* [ad. late L. *ultimāt-us*, pa. pple. of *ultimāre* to be at the end, f. *ultimus* last, final: see ULTIME *a.*]

A. *adj.* **1.** Of ends, designs, etc.: Lying beyond all others; forming the final aim or object.

1654 JER. TAYLOR *Real Pres.* i. 10 The faithful and pious communicants receive the ultimate end of his presence, that is, spiritual blessings. **1664** POWER *Exp. Philos.* I. 67 In the obtainment of which he hath come to the ultimate design of his endeavours. **1675** BAXTER *Cath. Theol.* I. I. 61 God is this ultimate End of man,.. to which all are means. *a* **1721** PRIOR *Dial. Dead* iii. Wks. 1907 II. 258 The beginning, Progress, and Ultimate end of Thought. **1758** JOHNSON *Idler* No. 1 ¶3 To be idle is the ultimate purpose of the busy. **1782** PRIESTLEY *Corrupt. Chr.* I. Pref. p. xiii, If my proper and ultimate object be considered. **1847** G. HARRIS *Life Ld. Hardwicke* I. iv. 354 A far higher and nobler reward is their ultimate aim. *a* **1871** GROTE *Eth. Fragm.* iv. (1876) 72 They would.. esteem different agents in proportion as they tended to assist these same ultimate purposes. **1892** H. LANE *Differ. Rheum. Dis.* (ed. 2) vi. 119 The ultimate goal of all our investigations and observations.

2. a. Coming at the end of a process, course of action, etc., or as the last in a succession or series; arrived at as a final result or in the last resort.

1660 R. COKE *Justice Vind.* 8, I am content with Aristotle's definition of the will,.. That it is the ultimate resolution, end, or determination of counsel. **1671** MILTON *P.R.* III. 210 My harbour and my ultimate repose, The end I would attain, my final good. **1755** YOUNG *Centaur* ii. Wks. 1757 IV. 159 All agree, that several goods being proposed for our ultimate enjoyment, it is impossible in our nature not to chuse the best. **1785** PALEY *Mor. Philos.* VI. xii. (1818) II. 426 Containing that which in peace and war is equally unjustifiable—ultimate and gratuitous mischief. **1827** FARADAY *Chem. Manip.* ii. (1842) 30 The oscillations.. will be found to be quick and the beam will soon take its ultimate state of rest. **1841** MIALL in *Nonconf.* I. 2 Ultimate success will require union, patience, persevering energy. **1860** RUSKIN *Unto this Last* (1862) 8 No man ever knew, or can know, what will be the ultimate result to himself, or to others, of any given line of conduct. **1890** H. LANE *Differ. Rheum. Dis.* 5 Not to exhaust the subject, nor even to lead the way to the ultimate hope of eradicating the source and the origin of the evil.

b. Of resolves, etc.: Final, determinate, absolute.

1687 MIÉGE *Gt. Fr. Dict.* II. s.v., This is the ultimate Resolution. **1779** J. MOORE *View Soc. France* (1789) I. i. 4, I have now formed an ultimate resolution against gaming. **1786** JEFFERSON *Writ.* (1859) I. 570 An ultimate opinion should not be formed till we see Mr. Randall. **1803** in Gurw. *Wellington's Desp.* (1837) II. 138 *note*, I consented to wait till then for their ultimate decision.

c. Putting an end to further continuance, development, or action; final, decisive.

1755 JOHNSON, *End*,.. ultimate state; final doom. **1781** COWPER *Hope* 640 Nature opposes.. This riving stroke, this ultimate divorce. **1803** MALTHUS *Popul.* (1817) I. 17 The ultimate check to population appears then to be a want of food. **1827** POLLOK *Course T.* VI. 365 Some disaster great and ultimate. **1838** PRESCOTT *Ferd. & Is.* Introd. ii. I. 79 To protect the subject from the oppressions of the crown and its officers, over all which cases it possessed original and ultimate jurisdiction. **1870** MOZLEY *Univ. Serm.* iii. (1877) 60 The natural philosopher is practically assured from the concurrence of data before him, of a result, before the ultimate test is got.

d. Forming a final stage, point, or limit; beyond which there is no advance or progress.

1794 G. ADAMS *Nat. & Exp. Philos.* I. v. 204, I informed them that the creatures [larvæ] before us were not in their ultimate state, but were the produce of the bee-fly. **1815** J. SMITH *Panorama Sci. & Art* II. 34 This salt.. causes the hair to contract itself, until it has attained the ultimate limit of its contraction. **1869** RANKINE *Mach. & Millwork* 497 The ultimate shearing strength, or modulus of resistance to shearing. **1878** B. TAYLOR *Deukalion* III. v. 127 Why should I conceal The ultimate barrier where I needs must pause?

e. Applied to the values of a mechanical property corresponding to fracture or breakage of the object concerned.

1858 W. J. M. RANKINE *Man. Appl. Mech.* II. iii. 273 The Ultimate Strength of a solid is the stress required to produce fracture in some specified way. **1869** —— *Man. Machinery & Millwork* 485 The column headed 'Ultimate Extension' gives the ratio of the elongation of the piece, at the instant of breaking, to its original length. **1876** [see STRESS *sb.* 5 c]. **1922** GLAZEBROOK *Dict. Appl. Physics* I. 156/2 The ultimate stress was in some cases greater when the extension was fast than when it was slow. **1962** READ & WATSON *Introd. Geol.* viii. 446 The properties which control the reactions of rocks are ..the values of the elastic limit and the ultimate strength.

f. ***ultimate Frisbee*** U.S., a form of the game of Frisbee (see FRISBEE, FRISBEE).

1972 in *Amer. Speech 1974* (1976) XLIX. 301 In *ultimate Frisbee*, two seven-man teams play on a field 60 yards by 40 yards each game lasting 48 minutes. **1980** *Boston Globe* 7 Mar. 32 The game of Ultimate Frisbee now is included on the list of activities accepted for academic credit at prestigious Worcester Polytechnic Institute, one of the nation's top five suppliers of engineers. **1984** *New Yorker* 9 Apr. 36/1 Ultimate Frisbee.. bears only a slight resemblance to the mellow.. Frisbee played on beaches.

3. a. Beyond which no advance can be made by investigation or analysis; forming a limit or final stage in respect of nature or quality; fundamental or elemental.

1659 PEARSON *Creed* ii. 147 We must acknowledge that the actuall giving of salvation to us, is the ultimate and conclusive ground of the title *Saviour*. **1681** *Ess. Peace & Truth Ch.* 9 Man therefore is justly defined to be a Rational Religious Creature, therein consisting the formal ultimate difference from a Brute. **1739** HUME *Hum. Nat.* Introd. (1874) I. 308 Any hypothesis, that pretends to discover the ultimate original qualities of human nature. **1749** HARTLEY *Observ. Man* II. 32 Since God is the ultimate Author of all Motion, we must suppose him to be immaterial. **1792** N. CHIPMAN *Rep.* (1871) 53 The King was, in view of the law, the ultimate owner of all lands within his dominions. **1808** JEBB in *Knox & Jebb's Corr.* (1834) I. 453 There are ultimate truths, far above human ken. **1836** J. GILBERT *Chr. Atonem.* iv. (1852) 113 The ultimate law of moral agents must be the will of God. **1850** MCCOSH *Div. Govt.* III. i. (1874) 295 In the inquiry into virtue and vice, we come back to ultimate principles, on which all morality rests. **1880** SAYCE *Introd. Sci. Lang.* (1890) I. 113 The sentence, in short, is.. the ultimate starting-point of all our linguistic inquiries.

b. Of material things, *esp.* of the component particles of matter.

1808 BARCLAY *Muscular Motions* 273 These fibres, composed of the fibres that are called *ultimate*, are seldom seen extending from the one extremity of a muscle to the other. **1815** J. SMITH *Panorama Sci. & Art* II. 303 All that can be affirmed of the state in which the ultimate particles of matter exist, is only the result of conjecture. **1836–41** BRANDE *Chem.* (ed. 5) 1053 Although the ultimate principles of vegetable substances are few in number. **1857** MILLER *Elem. Chem., Org.* 11 To determine the relative proportion in which each of the ultimate elements exists. **1871** TYNDALL *Fragm. Sci.* (1879) II. vi. 81 This formative power,.. ready to.. build the ultimate particles of matter into definite shapes.

transf. **1831** T. P. JONES *New Convers. Chem.* xxviii. 282 When we decompose them [*sc.* proximate principles], to ascertain how much they contain of each of the simple bodies, the operation is called *ultimate analysis*. **1857** MILLER *Elem. Chem., Org.* 6 The determination of the proportions.. furnishes an illustration of what is meant by *ultimate* organic analysis.

c. *Math.* ***ultimate ratio***, the final limiting ratio between two variable quantities which simultaneously approach definite fixed values or limits. (Correl. to ***prime ratio***: see PRIME *a.* 9 d.)

1729 A. MOTTE tr. *Newton's Principia* I. 46 The ultimate ratio of the arc, chord, and tangent, any one to any other, is the ratio of equality. **1749** HARTLEY *Observ. Man* II. 32 According to the mathematical Doctrine of ultimate Ratios, not even an infinite Series.. could remove it. **1818** VINCE *Fluxions* (ed. 5) 16 The ingenious.. Author of the *Analyst*.. went upon the term *ultimate* ratio, assuming equality where it was never intended. **1842** BRANDE *Dict. Sci.*, etc. 974/2 They are called prime ratios, or ultimate ratios, according as the ratios of the variables are considered as receding from, or approaching to, the ratios of the limits.

4. Not followed by another; last. *rare*$^{-1}$.

1728 MORGAN *Algiers* II. iv. 292 Returning home, he bad farewel to the fluid Element; this being his ultimate Expedition.

5. Forming a result or conclusion of a character different from the starting-point or present state; eventual, resultant.

1777 PRIESTLEY *Disc. Philos. Necess.* Ded. p. ix, All seeming discord is real harmony, and all apparent evil, ultimate good. **1795** BURKE *Th. Scarcity* Wks. 1842 II. 253 The quiet of the town is purchased by the ruin of the country, and the ultimate wretchedness of both. **1832** HT. MARTINEAU *Homes Abroad* ix. 127 One yields temporary benefit to a few at the expense of ultimate injury to the many. **1874** GREEN *Short Hist.* iv. §1. 161 Neither trick nor conquest could shake the firm faith of the Celt in the ultimate victory of his race.

6. Final, last; occurring in, or falling on, the last syllable of a word.

1837 G. PHILLIPS *Syriac Gram.* 28 If the ultimate syllable be perfect without the terminating consonant. **1862** MARSH *Lect. Eng. Lang.* 380 The great frequency of ultimate and penultimate accentuation.

7. Most remote in space or position. *rare*$^{-1}$.

1848 JOHNSTON in *Proc. Berw. Nat. Club* II. 297 The ultimate [joint] armed with a long curved.. claw.

B. *sb.* **1.** The final point or result; the end or conclusion; the last step. ***the ultimate*** (const. *in*), the best that can be achieved or imagined; the 'last word'.

1681 RYCAUT tr. *Gracian's Critick* 113 Ordinary Toyes, applauded by a Castilian, for but being his own, with praises as might befit the ultimate of all Perfection. **1718** J. FOX *Wanderer* 72, I.. once hoped I might attain to the very Ultimate of what you propos'd by Sunday last. **1728** ELIZA HEYWOOD tr. *Mme. de Gomez's Belle A.* (1732) II. 2 Thelamont,.. having now obtain'd the ultimate of his Desires, appear'd more bright and gay than ever. **1794** HUTTON *Philos. Light*, etc. 211 A proper fulminating composition, which seems to be the ultimate to which we may proceed. **1820** SHELLEY *Ess. & Lett.* (1852) II. 225, I shall write to you the ultimates of my Commission in my next letter. **1852** BAILEY *Festus* (ed. 5) 534 Ends and beginnings mingle at the last; All ultimates are foreordained. **1890** BOOTH *Darkest Eng.* II. iv. 230 They carried their principles of freedom and license to the logical ultimate. **1958** S. J. PERELMAN *Most of S. J. Perelman* 343 The Central Hotel,.. advertised as the ultimate in gaiety and chic. **1971** *Hi-Fi Sound* Feb. 67/1 In the medium-cost category our ideal is a system in which the most attractive 'top' features are recognisable while the ultimate in power handling or 'monitoring' capability has been lost. **1981** P. DAVIES *Edge of Infinity* viii. 168 The ultimate in elaborate organization is the human body and mind. **1981** *Monitor* (McAllen, Texas) 8 July III. 1/1 Shop for your man on the first floor and yourself on the second. They have *the ultimate* in fashions.

2. The point at which investigation or analysis stops; a final or fundamental fact or principle.

1709 MRS. MANLEY *Secret Mem.* (1720) IV. 101 It was not her Fault that she became not Mistress of the great Secret, the Ultimate of Chymistry. **1774** J. BRYANT *Mythol.* I. p. xii, The Deluge.. was esteemed.. the ultimate of Gentile history. *Ibid.* II. 267 The ancient Poet.. spoke of him as the father of mankind. In short he was the ultimate, to which Grecian history referred. **1841** *Blackw. Mag.* XLIX. 152 Mind seems as it were to be getting loose upon space. It reposes upon no religious ultimates. **1862** H. SPENCER *First Princ.* II. iii. §50 (1875) 169 We come down then finally to Force, as the ultimate of ultimates. **1866** E. P. WHIPPLE *Character & Characteristic Men* 268 If he calls his notion Law and makes law an ultimate, beyond which the human reason cannot go.

ultimate ('ʌltɪmeɪt), *v.*[1] [f. prec. or L. *ultimāt-*, ppl. stem of *ultimāre* (cf. It. *ultimare*, Sp. and Pg. *ultimar* to finish).]

1. *trans.* To carry to an end; to complete.

1849 E. H. SEARS *Regeneration* III. i. (1859) 131 Works are filled and vitalized by that angelic benevolence which is not complete until clothed and ultimated in action. **1866** BESSIE R. PARKES *Vignettes* 399 My parents had seen my education ultimated in practical life. **1881** E. S. HOLDEN *Sir W. Herschel* 53 His researches on the construction of the heavens would have been made; those were in his brain, and must have been ultimated.

refl. **1860** EMERSON *Cond. Life* viii. 169 It is the soundness of the bones that ultimates itself in a peach-bloom complexion. **1880** HOWELLS *Undisc. Country* iii. 50 A ferment of the kind he speaks of in the world of spirits would be more apt to ultimate itself here in the mind than in the stomach. **1885** L. OLIPHANT *Sympneumata* 14 The moral forces which ultimate themselves dynamically in the actions of men.

2. *intr.* To result finally; to end (*in* something).

c **1834** A. H. STEPHENS in Johnston & Browne *Life* (1878) 95 How the thing will ultimate I cannot tell. **1868** L. OLIPHANT *Let.* in *Life* (1891) viii. II. 41 We have no place here for those who like to meditate, unless the meditation ultimates in useful work. **1887** *Pop. Sci. Monthly* Aug. 564/2 Believing that they.. must ultimate.. in an increase of egoism.

'**ultimate**, *v.*[2] *rare.* [Back-formation from ULTIMATUM *sb.*] *trans.* = ULTIMATUM *v.*

1892 *Black & White* 30 Jan. 135/2 President Harrison has at last 'ultimated' Chili, as the Americans will probably soon be saying. **1898** *Pall Mall G.* 28 Sept. 2 At last the four Powers are going to ultimate the Sultan about the Turkish troops in Crete.

ultimately ('ʌltɪmətlɪ), *adv.* [f. ULTIMATE *a.* + -LY[2].]

1. In the last resort; when carried to the natural or logical conclusion; fundamentally.

1660 R. COKE *Justice Vind.* Pref. 13 If I could not ultimately resolve the Dictates of my Reason as a Christian, into plain places of Scripture. **1690** LOCKE *Hum. Und.* II. i. §2 In one word, From Experience: in that, all our Knowledge is founded; and from that it ultimately derives it self. ? **1743** in *10th Rep. Hist. MSS. Comm.* App. I. 279 To which nevertheless their Immunities must ultimately resort. **1775** JOHNSON *Tax. no Tyr.* 23 All government is ultimately and essentially absolute. **1776** GIBBON *Decl. & F.* vi. (1782) I. 185 The young emperor, on whose personal qualities the happiness or misery of the Roman world must ultimately depend. **1835** NEWMAN *Par. Serm.* (1837) I. iv. 64 What will it ultimately profit a man to profess without understanding? **1866** CRUMP *Banking* v. 131 Credit given to the holder of a bill by the person ultimately liable is considered equivalent to payment. **1869** MOZLEY *Univ. Serm.* i. (1877) 18 Every kingdom ultimately depends on moral influence and not on physical force.

2. In the end; at the last: **a.** As the conclusion or final stage of a process, course of action, etc.

1755 JOHNSON, *Finally*, 1. Ultimately; lastly; in conclusion. [Quoting Milton *Samson A.* 1296.] **1794** MATTHIAS *Purs. Lit.* (1798) 306 All passions submit ultimately.. to the inability of gratifying them. **1796** MME. D'ARBLAY *Camilla* IX. iii, The heart-breaking event to which it had ultimately led. **1818** MRS. SHELLEY *Frankenst.* iii, I doubted not that I should ultimately succeed. **1839** JAMES *Louis XIV*, III. 235 It became daily apparent to all parties that war must ultimately be the result. **1860** HOLLAND *Miss Gilbert* ii. 19 It was supposed by the gossips of the village that Dr. Gilbert would ultimately marry Aunt Catharine. **1878** LECKY *Eng. in 18th C.* I. iii. 452 It is of the nature of a constitution so formed as ours.. ultimately to work well.

b. As a point in a series, or in time.

1818 CRUISE *Digest* (ed. 2) II. 430 A feoffment was made to the use of the feoffor for his life.. and ultimately to the use of himself and his heirs for ever. **1827** FARADAY *Chem.*

Manip. ii. (1842) 37 It economises time to have the smaller weights arranged in order..and ultimately the large weights. **1880** TROLLOPE *Duke's Children* I. iii. 35 Frank's mother..would sometimes surmise..that the entire property must ultimately come to him. **1884** THOMPSON *Tumours of Bladder* 33 He..suffered much for a long time; ultimately there was some improvement.

3. In a final or conclusive manner; definitely.

1785 JEFFERSON *Corr.* Wks. 1859 I. 342 These questions, however, cannot be decided, ultimately, at this day. **1793** —— *Writ.* (1830) IV. 479 It had no right to dismember or alienate any portion of territory once ultimately consolidated with us. **1798** S. & HT. LEE *Canterb. T.* II. 206 Yet nothing but a favourable judgment from the civilians in England could ultimately relieve [his] mind.

'ultimateness. [f. as prec. + -NESS.] The quality of being ultimate; finality.

1884 *Century Mag.* XXVIII. 636 To have in it a certain completeness, ultimateness, and sacredness.

ultima Thule: see THULE.

ultimation (ʌltɪ'meɪʃən). [f. L. *ultimāt-*, *ultimāre*: see ULTIMATE *v.*[1] Cf. It. *ultimazione.*] The action or process of bringing to an ultimate result; final issue or development.

1791 H. WALPOLE *Let. to Miss Berry* 23 June, As this must take its passage..early to-morrow morning,..I shall perhaps not know the ultimation, but you probably will before you receive this. **1805** EUGENIA DI ACTON *Nuns of Desert* I. 117 The ultimation of their meditated kindness, was only to bestow upon her an indisputable right to the title of a penitent. **1858** SEARS *Athan.* III. ii. 258 The words *heaven* and *hell*, as they are used in popular speech, describe the complete ultimations of good and evil. **1883** L. OLIPHANT *Altiora Peto* II. 65 When a sufficient number have..attained a sufficient development for the ultimation of new results.

So **ˌultimati'zation.** *rare.*

1885 L. OLIPHANT *Sympneumata* 117 Because of this abnormal ultimatisation of organisms in this subsurface world.

'ultimative, *adj. rare*[−1]. [f. as prec.] That tends to produce some final result.

1885 L. OLIPHANT *Sympneumata* 239 The ultimative or operative region of earthly manhood.

ultimatory (ʌltɪ'meɪtərɪ), *a.* [f. ULTIMATE *a.* + -ORY[2].] Having the character of an ultimatum.

1928 E. BLUNDEN *Undertones of War* xi. 127 The company ..was..exhausted, and its commander appealed..for relief in ultimatory terms.

ultimatum (ʌltɪ'meɪtəm), *sb.* Pl. **-ata** (-'eɪtə). [ad. late L. *ultimātum*, neut. sing. of *ultimātus*, pa. pple. of *ultimāre*: see ULTIMATE *v.*[1] So in F., It., Pg., G., Du., etc.]

1. In diplomacy, the final terms presented by one power (or group of powers) to another, the rejection of which may lead to the severing of diplomatic relations, and eventually to a declaration of war.

sing. **1731** *Gentl. Mag.* Jan. 39/1 There are privately handed about here Copies of the *Ultimatum* (or last Proposals) of the Allies of Sevile, as transmitted hither from Paris. **1759** SMOLLETT *Hist. Eng.* VIII. (ed. 3) IX. 143 He delivered to the mediator an ultimatum, importing, That he adhered to the treaties of Westphalia and Nimeguen. **1784–5** *Ann. Reg., Hist. Europe* 107/1 A new statement of the emperor's claims and demands, described as his *ultimatum*, was presented to the Dutch ministers. **1832** tr. *Sismondi's Ital. Rep.* xiii. 287 Charles still insisted on disgraceful conditions, which his secretary read as his ultimatum. **1876** BANCROFT *Hist. U.S.* VI. lviii. 482 Fitzherbert.. reflected that peace with the United States would be the best means of forcing France and Spain to declare their ultimatum.

pl. **1773** *Ann. Reg., Hist. Europe* 40/2 The delegates were also appointed..to receive the ultimata of the three powers. **1796** HAMILTON *Wks.* (1886) VII. 121 In general, where more had been obtained by a treaty than the *ultimata* prescribed to the negotiator, it would be inexpedient to publish those *ultimata*. **1859** L. OLIPHANT *China & Japan* I. 98 Mr. Wade..proceeded..to Canton, and delivered the *ultimata* of the French and English plenipotentiaries. **1883** *Harper's Mag.* April 676/1 *note*, Different ultimata had been adopted with respect to the boundaries.

b. *transf.* A final condition or stipulation; one's last word on a matter.

1733 SWIFT *Let. to Pope* 31 Mar., But, there must be some stipulations for my riding, with other necessary postulatums, and ultimatums. **1787** M. CUTLER in *Life*, etc. (1888) I. 299 We therefore begged leave to state to the Board of terms on which we were ready to close the contract, and that those terms must be our *Ultimatum*. **1813** *Examiner* 11 Jan. 23/1 His Lordship would require, as the ultimatum,.. that a competent portion of the natives shall perform duty under British Officers. **1848** DICKENS *Dombey* xl, I have state my *ultimatum*, Madam. **1869** TROLLOPE *He knew*, etc. xxxvii. (1878) 207 The official shrugged his shoulders and signified that his ultimatum had been pronounced.

2. The final point, extreme limit; an ultimate end or aim.

1748 RICHARDSON *Clarissa* (1768) III. 53 That single pressure..delighted me more than ever I was delighted with the *Ultimatum* with any other woman. **1793** R. WILLETT in *Archaeologia* XI. 196 The size of our ships seems now to have reached nearly its ultimatum. **1804** JEBB *Corr.* (1834) I. 153 And now I will tell you an ultimatum, which I would far prefer,..the librarianship of Armagh. **1804** EUGENIA DE ACTON *Tale without Title* II. 26 Their ultimatum was obtained, and they were considered as persons of consequence.

b. Const. *of.*

1770 *Monthly Rev.* 502 This surely is the *ultimatum* of astronomical precision. **1790** *Bystander* 308 The ultimatum of earthly enjoyment was to give him invitations to their houses. **1802** MRS. E. PARSONS *Myst. Visit* I. 132 To be married was still the ultimatum of her wishes. **1812** SHELLEY *Proposals* Pr. Wks. 1888 I. 280 The attainment of the good which I propose as the ultimatum of philanthropic exertion. **1856** KANE *Arct. Expl.* I. x. 114 At last we came to the Esquimaux ultimatum of simplicity,—raw meat and a fur bag. **1888** J. ELLIS *New Chr.* ii. 51 If..all chemical and mechanical changes, or effects, are but the ultimatum of spiritual causes.

c. Final lot or destiny. *rare*[−1].

1861 G. MOORE *Lost Tribes* iv. 84 To trace the meaning of God's handwriting concerning the origin and ultimatum of our race.

†**3.** *slang.* The hinder parts; the buttocks. *Obs.*

1823 C. WESTMACOTT *Points of Misery* iii. 31 Old Brummagem and the fat lady being thrown head downwards, formed an excellent step-ladder with their *ultimatums* for the purpose. **1824** in *Spirit Pub. Jrnls.* (1825) 38 He..at the same time felt his spinal extremities and his ultimatum covered by a shower of slimy material of a very offensive odour. **1825** C. WESTMACOTT *Eng. Spy* I. 165 As for the inexpressibles they hung round his *ultimatum* like petticoat trousers.

4. A primary element, beyond which analysis becomes impossible; something fundamental.

1858 O. W. HOLMES *Aut. Breakf.-t.* i. (1859) 10 No men can have satisfactory relations with each other until they have agreed on certain *ultimata* of belief not to be disturbed in ordinary conversation. **1867** H. MACMILLAN *Bible Teach.* i. 22 The truth is, that all our scientific investigations will never conduct us to the ultimatum—the commencement of matter. **1868** BAIN *Ment. & Mor. Sci., Ethics* II. 498 Sensible Perception,..whereby we perceive that the triangle before us is a geometrical ultimatum.

5. Furthest destination; most distant point (to be) reached.

1862 CARLYLE *Fredk. Gt.* XI. ii. III. 44 Almost to the coast of the Baltic; their ultimatum there a place called Köslin.

Hence **ulti'matum** *v. trans.*, to present with an ultimatum. (Cf. ULTIMATE *v.*[2])

1897 *Pall Mall G.* 23 Sept. 2 General Woodford never ultimatumed the fiery untamed Duke of Tetuan.

†**ultime,** *a. Obs.* Also ultim. [ad. L. *ultim-us*, superl. of **ulter*: cf. ULTERIOR. So It., Sp., Pg. *ultimo*, OF. *ultime.*] Ultimate, final.

1626 BACON *Nat. Hist.* §99 Whereby the true and Ultime Operations of Heat are not attained. **1654** H. L'ESTRANGE *Chas. I* (1655) 105 Nothing was wanting now to the perfecting of this League, but the ultime and compleating act, the solemn confirmation by Oath. **1659** —— *Alliance Div. Off.* 295 The perficient and ultim act of marriage.

ultimity (ʌl'tɪmɪtɪ). Now *rare.* [f. as prec. + -ITY. Cf. med.L. *ultimitas.*]

1. The final point or ultimate development of an action or thing; the last stage.

1613 BACON *Let. to Jas. I*, Wks. 1868 XI. x. 369 That those tragical arguments and (as the schoolmen call them) ultimities of persuasions which were used last Parliament should for ever be abolished. **1626** —— *Sylva* §838 The Degrees of Alteration, of one Body into another, from Crudity to Perfect Concoction; which is the ultimity of that Action, or Processe. *a* **1706** EVELYN *Hist. Relig.* (1850) I. 77 [The Almighty] knows all that does not actually exist, even the ultimities of what can or may be.

2. An ultimate principle or fact.

1898 *Expositor* June 453 In everything appertaining to origins and causes, to ultimities and universalities.

†**ultimo,** *sb. Obs.*[−1] [? a. It., Sp., or Pg. *ultimo*: see ULTIME *a.*] = ULTIMUM.

1622 in Foster *Eng. Factories Ind.* (1908) II. 11 Which is as farr as the Nabobs perwanna importes, and is the ultimo of there and our owne expectacions.

‖**ultimo** ('ʌltɪməʊ), *a.* and *adv.* [L. *ultimō* (sc. *diē* or *mense*), abl. sing. masc. of *ultimus* last. So in G., Du., Sw., etc.]

†**1.** On the last day (of a specified month). *Obs.*

1582 ALLEN *Martyrd. Fr. E. Campion* (1908) 17 In the xxij yere of the raigne of our soveraine Lady the Queene, Maij vltimo. **1682** SCARLETT *Exchanges* 102 If it be dated *ultimo* February, then its not due till the *ultimo* March. *Ibid.*, If for the 30th of June he write *ultimo*, it will not be due till *ultimo* July.

2. Of last month. (Abbreviated ULT. and ULTO.)

1616 R. COCKS *Diary* (Hakl. Soc.) I. 125, I receved a letter from Mr. Wickham, dated..the 22th ultimo. **1683** W. HEDGES *Diary* (Hakl. Soc.) I. 63 Letters from Cassumbazar advised Thomas Bromly dyed y[e] 29 Ultimo. **1754** WASHINGTON *Let.* Writ. 1889 I. 70 The 25th ultimo,..I received ye news of your Honour's arrival. **1792** *Ibid.* (1891) XII. 242, I was very glad to receive your letter of the 31st ultimo. **1823** COL. HAWKER *Diary* (1893) I. 261 The morning of the 31st ultimo. **1841** HAWTHORNE in J. Hawthorne *N. Hawthorne & Wife* (1885) I. 227, I took up my abode here on the 12th ultimo.

ˌultimo'branchial, *a. Anat.* [f. L. *ultim-us* last + -O + BRANCHIAL *a.*; so called because the gland develops from the most caudal pharyngeal pouches.] Applied to a gland in the neck which in many lower vertebrates regulates the calcium level in the body but in man and several higher vertebrates is absorbed into the thyroid during embryonic life.

1913 *Gray's Anat.* (ed. 18) 123 A pair of diverticula arise from the fifth branchial pouch and form what are termed the ultimobranchial bodies..: these fuse with the thyreoid gland, but probably contribute no true thyreoid tissue. **1968** *New Scientist* 15 Feb. 375/2 The ultimobranchial glands are small and situated in the neck region in birds and reptiles, but are generally absent in mammals. **1976** *Path. Ann.* XI. 222 Parafollicular C cells are not restricted to the thyroid, but can also be found in other structures embryologically connected with the ultimobranchial body, ie, parathyroid IV and thymus IV.

ultimo'geniture. [f. L. *ultim-us* last; after PRIMOGENITURE.] The mode of succession by which the right of inheritance pertains to the youngest of a family, as in borough-english.

1882 C. ELTON *Orig. Eng. Hist.* 185 'Ultimogeniture,' the awkward term proposed by the Real Property Commissioners of the last generation. **1883** GOMME in *Athenæum* 29 Dec. 865/3 The divergent lines of succession known as ultimogeniture and primogeniture.

†**'ultimum.** *Obs.*[−1] [L., neut. sing. of *ultim-us* last.] The final point or limit.

1649 G. DANIEL *Trinarch., Rich. II*, liv, Something has euer bin The Vltimum; and there is yet one step Beyond a Possibilitie to heap.

†**'ultion.** *Obs. rare* Also 6 *Sc.* vltioun. [ad. L. *ultiōn-*, *ultio*, noun of action f. the stem of *ulcisci* to avenge. So OF. *ultion*, *ulcion*, It. *ulzione.*] Vengeance, revenge, avengement.

c **1550** ROLLAND *Crt. Venus* III. 582 Quhairfoir the greit vltioun First come on him and his pepill Ilkone. **1623** COCKERAM, *Vltion*, reuenge. **1657** TOMLINSON *Renou's Disp.* 132 A medicament..should leave in the mouth the ultion of the fault therein committed. **1682** SIR T. BROWNE *Chr. Mor.* III. §12 To do good for evil [is] a soft and melting ultion, a method taught from Heaven to keep all smooth on Earth. **1901** G. B. SHAW *Admirable Bashville* III. 323 My mission here Is to wreak ultion for the broken law.

Ultisol ('ʌltɪsɒl). *Soil Sci.* [f. ULTI(MATE *a.* + -SOL.] A type of highly weathered, leached, red-yellow or red acid soil marked by a clay-rich B horizon and found in warm, humid climates.

1960 *Soil Classification: 7th Approximation* (U.S. Dept. Agric.) xv. 226/1 The Ultisols include most soils that have been called Red-Yellow Podzolic soils, Reddish-Brown Lateritic soils, and Rubrozems in the United States. **1972** J. G. CRUICKSHANK *Soil Geogr.* iv. 132 In their geographical distribution, the Ultisols—otherwise known as red-yellow podsolics or ferruginous soils—merge into grassland soils on their arid margins and into Alfisols and Inceptisols (brown earths) on their cool humid margins (eg, in North America).

ulto., abbrev. of ULTIMO *adv.* 2.

1796 BP. G. HAY in *Ushaw Mag.* Dec. (1913) 284, I had left Edinr. on the 29 Ulto. **1847** *Theatr. Times* 7 Aug. 247 This house opened for a week's season on the 24th ulto.

Ultonian (ʌl'təʊnɪən), *a.* and *sb.* [f. med.L. *Ultonia* Ulster, f. OIr. *Ult-*, *Ulaid*: see ULTAGH.]

A. *adj.* Of or belonging to Ulster.

1766 O'CONOR *Dissert. Hist. Irel.* 50 The Ultonian Heberlans followed the Example. *Ibid.* 158 The Establishment of the Ultonian Oeconomy by Kimbaoth. **1865** S. FERGUSON *Lays Western Gael, Tain-Quest* 23 In the ransom-races..to run 'Gainst the fleet Ultonian horses. **1880** *Encycl. Brit.* XIII. 245/2 The origin of the clan of Degaid is obscure; one story makes it Ultonian, and the other Erimonian.

B. *sb.* An inhabitant or native of Ulster.

1781 C. VALLANCEY *Lit. Irish in Heathen Times* 9 He..was banished by the Ultonians the year following. **1837** W. F. SKENE *Highlanders* I. viii. 210 The Ultonians, or inhabitants of the north of Ireland, were Cruithne. **1880** *Encycl. Brit.* XIII. 246/1 If the Scots failed to subdue the south thoroughly, they succeeded in crushing the Ultonians.

ultra ('ʌltrə), *a.* and *sb.* [Independent use of ULTRA-, orig. as an abbreviation of F. *ultra-royaliste*, and app. mainly due to Lady Morgan. Cf. F. *ultra* sb. (in senses B. 1 and 2).]

A. *adj.* **1.** Ultra-royalist.

1817 LADY MORGAN *France* II. (1818) I. 225 The gradual alteration in tone and manner of the *ultra* circles, during my residence at Paris, was extremely obvious. **1818** —— *Autobiog.* (1859) 236 The ministry, it is thought, will be ultra. **1819** HELEN M. WILLIAMS *Lett. France* 195 No sooner did the tidings..reach Nismes, than the *Ultra*-party seized a pretext for new disturbances. **1828** LYTTON *Pelham* xv, Monsieur d'A——, a man of much conversational talent and some celebrity as an ultra writer.

2. Of persons or parties: Holding extreme views in politics or other matters of opinion.

1820 H. MATTHEWS *Diary of Invalid* (ed. 2) 492 Shifting its support as it may find danger from the encroachment of either of the ultra parties of the state. **1837** LOCKHART *Scott* (1839) IX. 119 The lofty impartiality with which Scott treats the personal character of Buonaparte was of course sure to make all ultra-politicians at home and abroad condemn his representation. **1864** J. H. NEWMAN *Apol.* 401 The said authority may be supported by a violent ultra-party.

3. Going beyond what is usual or ordinary; excessive, extreme, immoderate.

attrib. **1818** in *Lady Morgan's Autobiog.* (1859) 213 It will afford me equal pleasure if Lady Morgan should turn into ridicule, and excite to ultra rage, those who are envious of her. **1824** W. IRVING *T. Trav.* II. 147 A little wearied by this story, and by the ultra zeal of his countrymen. **1834** SIR W. HAMILTON *Discuss.* (1853) 502 Bishop Marsh,..whom no one assuredly will suspect of aught but ultra reverence to the Church of England.

pred. **1819** *Metropolis* III. 122 The term over-dressed does not mean over-clad, but applies to their being ultra in the caricature of fashion. **1864** LOWELL *Lincoln* Prose Wks. 1890 V. 187 All that he did was sure to be virulently attacked as ultra by one side. **1884** JEFFERIES *Life of Fields* 246 It is so great and ponderous, and ultra in size.

4. Expressive of extreme views.

1827 SCOTT *Let. to Lockhart* 26 Apr., I own I thin Ultra-writing only disgusts people, unless it is in the way of a downright invective.

B. *sb.* **1.** An ultra-royalist (in France).

1817 LADY MORGAN *France* II. (1818) I. 237 The royalists abuse the *ultras*; the *ultras* abuse the government; the constitutionalist laugh at both. **1821** MOORE *Mem.* (1853) III. 253 Went with Villamil to dine with General Fuller at Versailles; a party of ultras. **1831** in Gen. P. Thompson *Exerc.* (1842) I. 475, I remember a deputy, a good ultra too, once saying..that Charles X was losing the confidence and affection of his people. **1864** *Month* I. 357 She [Madame Récamier] equally welcomed ultras and liberals.

2. One who holds extreme opinions, particularly in religion or politics.

1823 H. MORE *Let.* in R. B. Johnson *Lett. Hannah More* (1925) 201 My friend F. is an ultra of the first magnitude. The poor must not only read English, but ancient history, and even the sciences are to be laid open to them. **1826** SCOTT *Diary* 20 Jan., Making mutual concessions and balancing the constitution against the ultras of both parties. **1829** *Blackw. Mag.* XXV. 273 It must therefore stigmatize every man who..acts upon principle as an Ultra and a person of extreme opinions. **1860** FROUDE *Hist. Eng.* V. 391 To the last he was considered by the ultras as timid and intellectually weak. **1884** *American* IX. 69 The ultras of their own party denounce the Ministry as having betrayed their friends.

3. One who goes to the extreme of fashion.

1819 F. MACDONOGH *Hermit in Lond.* I. 55 Bad horsemen and pedestrian women, ultras in conceit and in dress. **1825** T. HOOK *Sayings* Ser. II. *Passion & Princ.* v, Even the parson dined at five, and he was the village *ultra* in points of fashion and etiquette. **1828** P. CUNNINGHAM *N.S. Wales* (ed. 3) II. 112 Cards are ceremoniously left, and rules of precedence..punctiliously insisted on by some of our *ultras*.

‖**ˈultra**, *prep.* [L. *ultrā* beyond. Cf. F., Pg. *ultra*, It. *oltre*.]

1. In the phr. ***ultra vires*** (ˈvaɪəriːz), beyond the powers or legal authority (*of* a person, etc.; also used with ellipse of *for*).

1793 [EARL DUNDONALD] *Descr. Estate Culross* 59 This has proved, and must always prove, *ultra vires* or any one individual. **1806** G. HUTCHESON *Treat. Justice of Peace*, etc. II. 564 *note*, This judgment has been appealed from, as *ultra vires*, as far as regards the directions for building the cruive dike. **1884** *Law Times* LXXVIII. 116/1 It was not *ultra vires* the directors to advance money on such security.

2. Lying beyond. (Cf. ULTRA- 1 c.)

1876 *Law Times Rep.* XXXIV. 697/2 Here she was asked to do something which was no part of her service..it being something *ultra* her service to go to the kitchen. **1883** *Ch. Times* XXI. 939/2 As the human eye is sensible only of impressions of light ranging from red to violet, it follows that we cannot be conscious of any hue ultra either of these.

3. In the L. phr. ***ultra crepidam*** (ˈkrɛpɪdæm) [see ULTRA-CREPIDARIAN *a.* and *sb.*], on matters beyond one's knowledge.

1883 G. M. HOPKINS *Let.* 7 Nov. (1956) 332 Pope was the great master of metre of his day,..but..he was nothing *ultra crepidam*. **1895** *Econ. Jrnl.* V. 589 Meeker than the ancient master, he has refrained from breaking out against the criticisms which have been *ultra crepidam*.

ultra- (ˈʌltrə), *prefix*, representing L. *ultrā* beyond, employed as a prefix in the post-classical *ultrāmundānus* ultramundane, and the later *ultrāmarīnus* ultramarine, and *ultrāmontānus* ultramontane. On these models are formed the types illustrated in senses 1 and 2. The further development represented by sense 3 apparently originated in French with the terms *ultra-révolutionnaire* and *ultra-royaliste*, and has become very prolific in English use, as well as in the Romanic languages and in German, Swedish, and Danish.

1. Signifying 'lying spatially beyond or on the other side of': **a.** With sbs., as ***ultraequinoctials*** (pl.), those who live beyond the equinox.

1551 ROBINSON tr. *More's Utopia* I. (1895) 112 For (as there Cronicles testifie) before our arriuall ther they neuer harde any thinge of vs, whome they call the ultraequinoctialles.

b. With adjs., as ***ultra-Gangetic, -Martian, -median, -stellar, -terrene, -terrestrial, -zodiacal.***

Also *ultra-galactic, -tropical.* (In Dicts.).

1833 *Edin. Rev.* Oct. 197 The..hypothesis of Olbers respecting the formation of the four ultra-zodiacal planets. **1836** J. F. DAVIS *Chinese* I. iii. 81 The usual cautious and exclusive spirit of the ultra-gangetic nations. **1858** GLADSTONE *Homer* III. 288 Homer had conceived the existence of what we may call ultra-terrene parts, both westwards and eastwards. **1860** OLMSTEAD *Mech. Heavens* 271 The Asteroids, or Ultra-Zodiacal Planets. **1902** *Proc. Zool. Soc. Lond.* 115 On the hind wing the ultramedian blue band is replaced by a narrow line. **1905** *Athenæum* 11 Mar. 312/3 [A rotation] longer than that of any of the great ultra-Martian planets. **1906** Ultra-stellar [see *night-web* s.v. NIGHT *sb.* 13 a].

c. ***ultra-red***, A former name for INFRA-RED *a.* and *sb.* (So F. *ultra-rouge*; cf. ULTRAVIOLET *a.* and *sb.*)

1870 TYNDALL *Heat* (ed. 4) xiii. §612. 439 The failure.. proved the invisible rays to be exclusively ultra-red. **1875** tr. *Vogel's Chem. Light* vii. 60 We name the invisible tones of colour above violet ultra-violet, and those beyond red ultra-red.

2. a. With adjs., signifying 'going beyond, surpassing, or transcending the limits of' (the specified concept), as ***ultra-human, -natural, -pecuniary***, etc.

Also *ultra-atomic, -gaseous, -material.* (In Dicts.)

1818 COLERIDGE in *Lit. Rem.* (1836) I. 185 All other super or *ultra-human beings. **1856** R. A. VAUGHAN *Mystics* (1860) I. 99 The intellectual refinements of an ultra-human spiritualism. **1883** JEFFERIES *Story of my Heart* 63 All things being ultra-human and without design. **1850** GROTE *Greece* II. lxvii. (1862) VI. 29 The *ulta-natural sublimity of the legendary characters disappears. **1802–12** BENTHAM *Ration. Judic. Evid.* (1827) V. 138 Suppose the punishment *ultra-pecuniary: suppose man's life at stake. **1850** GROTE *Greece* II. lxvii. (1862) VI. 70 The word Existence, as they understood it, did not mean phænomenal, but *ultra-phænomenal existence. **1865** —— *Plato* I. ii. 97 The real, absolute, ontological, ultra-phenomenal, or Noumenal world. **1883** J. PARKER *Tyne Chylde* 152 Is it possible..to return to the meridian of absolute neutrality as regards *ultraphysical questions? **1894** B. KIDD *Soc. Evolution* vii. 184 That *ultra-rational system of ethics upon which our civilisation is founded. **1895** *Educational Rev.* Sept. 117 Science itself not unfrequently derives motive power from an *ultra-scientific source. **1851** MANSEL *Proleg. Log.* (1860) 18 It would not be difficult to shew that the *ultra-sensational philosophy is that which could most easily dispense with the necessity of introducing language at all. **1882** TYNDALL in *Longm. Mag.* I. 35 There is..boldness.. in the attempt to make these *ultra-sensible actions generally intelligible. **1833** CARLYLE *Extr. Jrnl.* 28 Oct., in Froude *First Forty Y.* (1882) II. xvi. 372 The *ultra-sensual surrounds the sensual and gives it meaning.

b. In the sense of 'exceeding in respect of quantity or number', as ***ultra-centenarianism*** (of human life), ***-dimidiate, -total.***

1847 HAMILTON *Let. to De Morgan* 43 If the one extreme coincide with the middle, to the extent of a half (dimidiate quantification); and the other, to the extent of aught more than a half, (ultradimidiate quantification). *Ibid.* 41 In regard to the ultratotal quantification of the middle term. **1864** BOWEN *Logic* viii. 251 This notation can represent equally total and ultratotal distribution. **1879** W. J. THOMS *Longevity* p. xxvi, A very large number of cases of alleged ultra-Centenarianism.

c. With sbs. in this sense, as ULTRA-FILTRATION, -MICROSCOPE, etc.

3. a. Signifying an excessive or extreme degree of the quality or condition expressed by the adjective forming the second element of the compound, as ***ultra-affected, -Anglican, -Arctic, -believing, -beloved, -bourgeois, -Catholic, -cautious, -civilized, -clean, -clear, -clerical, -critical, -fashionable, -fast, -feminine, -generous, -German, -intellectual, -left, -leftist, -militant, -miniature, -miniaturized, -nationalist, -nationalistic, -patriotic, -professional, -pure, -rapid, -rationalist, -respectable, -revolutionary, -rightist, -romantic, -sentimental, -smart, -tropical, -violent,*** etc.

First in *ultra-fashionable, -revolutionary*, but in very common, and steadily-increasing, use from about 1830. Only a few of the earlier or more important examples are given here. The distinction from sense 2 is not always quite clear.

1819 *Metropolis* I. 234 The *ultra-affected D-s-y gave us a drop in for a few minutes. **1834** SIR W. HAMILTON *Discuss.* (1853) 533 [Bishop Marsh] peculiarly affects an *ultra-Anglican orthodoxy. **1866** *Ch. Times* 27 Jan., The narrow and intolerant spirit of the ultra-Anglican School. **1856** KANE *Arct. Expl.* I. xx. 205 The ability of Europeans or Americans to inure themselves to an *ultra-Arctic climate. **1829** SOUTHEY *Sir T. More* I. 259 The unbelieving clergy are better than the *ultra-believing in this respect. **1923** D. H. LAWRENCE *Birds, Beasts & Flowers* 183 Everybody so dear, and yourself so *ultra-beloved. **1836** J. GILBERT *Chr. Atonem.* vii. (1852) 190 The patrons of this theory are *ultra-benevolent towards the transgressors of law. **1934** G. B. SHAW *On Rocks* Pref. 161 Even Lenin and his colleagues, all *ultra-bourgeois (otherwise they would never have so absurdly overestimated the intellectual resources of the proletariat [etc.]). **1830** J. S. MILL *Let.* 20 Aug. in *Victorian Stud.* (1957) I. 143 Three were printers of an *ultra-Catholic and royalist journal. **1930** G. B. SHAW *John Bull's Other Island* Pref., in *Works* XI. 71 The ubiquitous sodalities of that new ultra-Catholic Church called Socialism. **1946** *Mind* LV. 141 To suppose that no improvement can be effected by so doing is an *ultracautious and conservative position. **1842** E. A. POE in *Graham's Mag.* Feb. 125/2 Hugh has grown to a stalwart man—the type of man *the animal*, as his father is of man the *ultra-civilized. **1931** E. BLUNDEN *Votive Tablets* 170 Byron ..with his ultra-civilised fraternisation with the gentlemen. **1970** *Ultraclean [see *sonication* s.v. SONICATE *sb.* and *v.*]. **1907** W. JAMES in *Jrnl. Philos., Psychol. & Sci. Methods* IV. 295 Your letter is so *ultraclear. **1938** *New Statesman* 23 July 162/1 Maria-Cristina's *ultra-clerical court. **1816–30** BENTHAM *Offic. Apt. Maximized, Extr. Const. Code* (1830) 11 Repugnant to these same principles is all *ultra-concomitant remuneration. **1868** BOYD *Lessons Mid. Age* 106 Excellent men, *ultra-conservative in all things. **1870** DISRAELI *Lothair* I. viii. 69 Theodora is..*ultra-cosmopolitan and has invented a new religion. **1907** W. JAMES *Pragmatism* v. 192 Common science or corpuscular philosophy, *ultra-critical science..or idealistic philosophy, all seem insufficiently true. **1838** LOWELL *Lett.* (1894) I. 33 I am fast becoming *ultra-democratic. **1861** G. MUSGRAVE *By-Roads* 323 Owing to ultra-democratic feeling and low radicalism. **1841** F. E. PAGET *Tales Village* Ser. II. x. 197 There is more than one society, which..has already assumed (if I may coin such a word) *ultra-episcopal functions. **1831** *Eclectic Rev.* Apr. 307 A fearless and uncompromising asserter of..*ultra-evangelical doctrines. **1802** in *Spirit Pub. Jrnls.* VI. 91 No female, in the dress of the *ultra-fashionable, can be seen in the streets with the smallest regard to decency. **1841** THACKERAY *Ess., Lett., Sk.*, etc., *Men & Coats* Wks. 1900 XIII. 369 A person who sports an ultra-fashionable costume. **1939** *Sun* (Baltimore) 28 Jan. 2/6 *Ultrafast American two-engined light bombers, capable of being used for combat after they have dropped their bomb loads. **1977** J. HEDGECOE *Photographer's Handbk.* 41 Ultra-fast films are most useful for working in dim existing-light conditions. **1964** *Ultra-feminine [see SLIMLINE, SLIM-LINE *a.* a]. **1976** *Time* 27 Sept. 94/2 Melba Till Allen owes much of her success at the polls to her charming, ultrafeminine manner. **1859** *All Year Round* No. 33. 150 Its combination of the *ultra-feudal with the ultra-modern. **1842** DE QUINCEY *Mod. Greece* Wks. 1890 VII. 351 The Italian, in many features of Gallic insensibility, will be found *ultra-Gallican. **1903** W. JAMES *Let.* 8 Apr. in R. B. Perry *Thought & Char. W. James* (1935) II. 375 Your review..was as usual *ultra-generous, and I thank you for it. **1837** E. A. POE in *Amer. Monthly Mag.* June 566 Young men..alive with an exaggerated sense of honour. They abound in the most *ultra German opinions respecting the *duello*. **1843** MILL *Logic* I. iii. §7 The ultra-German and ontological character of his philosophy. **1848** MRS. JAMESON *Sacr. & Leg. Art* (1850) 107 What may be called the ultra German style. **1866** MRS. H. WOOD *St. Martin's Eve* xxii. (1874) 259 He was given to be *ultra honourable, and to maintain silence in such a case. **1927** T. S. ELIOT in *Seneca's Tenne Tragedies* p. xliii, It is assumed..that Shakespeare had acquired some extra- or *ultra-intellectual knowledge superior to a philosophy. **1954** KOESTLER *Invisible Writing* xv. 186 He had discovered both its weaknesses as a play, and its *ultra-Left tendency. **1977** P. JOHNSON *Enemies of Society* xviii. 240 Ulrika Meinhof..became the ideological leader of the German Baader-Meinhof gang of ultra-Left terrorists. **1947** *Partisan Rev.* XIV. 398 Gorky's became an 'opposition school' for '*ultra-leftist' Bolsheviks. **1824** SCOTT *Redgauntlet* ch. xvii, The most frank-hearted and *ultra-liberal lass that had ever lived. **1856** GEO. ELIOT *Ess.* (1884) 117 Börne..was a remarkable political writer of the ultra-Liberal party in Germany. **1881** *Times* 3 Jan. 9/4 One of the most notorious consequences of this *ultra-logical mode of conducting affairs is the instability of French Ministries. **1861** MAY *Const. Hist.* (1863) I. iii. 144 A joint address was agreed upon by both Houses,—*ultra-loyal, according to the fashion of the time. **1848** THACKERAY *Van. Fair* xxvi, Who does not know how *ultra-maternal grandmothers are? **1970** *Times* 11 Mar. 6 A new, *ultra-militant shopkeepers' organization, known as the 'Tour du Pin Movement'. **1968** *Sci. News* 7 Dec. 573 An *ultra-miniature vacuum pump..will be worn directly under the astronaut's chin. **1968** *World Book Sci. Ann. 1968* 215 Using a multitude of ICs, *ultraminiaturized, working in parallel, together with functional circuits, he may build electronic devices tomorrow that seem like impossible dreams even today. **1840** EARL ABERDEEN in Charteris *Life Jas. Robertson* v. (1863) 112 It will only be approved of by the old *ultra-moderate party. **1843** *Penny Cycl.* XXV. 296/2 The followers of the *ultra-modern school. **1830** *Fraser's Mag.* II. 598 His *ultramulish obstinacy in persisting. *a* **1832** BENTHAM *Deontol.* xii. (1834) I. 171 They spread into divers circles, domestic,..national, *ultra-national, universal. **1877** GEIKIE *Christ* lvi. (1879) 676 He would embitter Himself with the ultra-national party. **1927** H. DOBBS in *Lett. Gertrude Bell* II. 555 It had indeed alarmed the *ultra-nationalist party to find a section of the British press averse from the extension of the alliance. **1977** *Time* 27 June 22/3 Some are concerned about Israeli intransigence and afraid that the new ultranationalist Premier-designate, Menachem Begin..may make a settlement all the harder to achieve. **1974** *Daily Colonist* (Victoria, B.C.) 1 Oct. 5/1 The Chinese call the Amur the Black Dragon River, and the Japanese named one of their most *ultranationalistic societies after it in the days when they were itching to go to war with Russia. **1876** C. M. DAVIES *Unorth. Lond.* 60 He will see nothing but an *ultra-ornate service of the most decorous kind. **1830** PUSEY *Hist. Enq.* II. 327 It is not clear from this extract whether he is immediately speaking of *ultra-orthodox or fanatic opponents. **1801** W. DUPRÉ *Lexicographia-Neologica Gallica* 283 Some *ultra-patriotic writers and journalists have likened Bonaparte to the conquerors who plundered Greece. **1926** J. S. HUXLEY *Ess. Pop. Sci.* 159 Proud and ultra-patriotic Gods. **1844** *Civil Eng. & Arch. Jrnl.* Oct. 376/1 The *ultra-Pecksniffian taste displayed in the portico. **1842** BORROW *Bible in Spain* xxxviii, Several of the *ultra-popish bishops, then resident in Madrid, had denounced the Bible. **1928** E. O'NEILL *Strange Interlude* IV. 147 In his *ultra-professional manner—like an automation of a doctor. **1841** A. P. DE LISLE in E. Purcell *Life* (1900) I. vi. 108 The *Ultra Protestant Parsons are quite beside themselves, they rave like maniacs. **1846** HOOK *Ch. Dict.* (ed. 5) 853 Some ultra-protestant sects..have irreverently used sitting as the posture of receiving the Lord's Supper. **1847** L. HUNT *Men, Women, & B.* (1876) 343 Lady Mary herself had an *ultra-prudent sympathy with her husband. **1961** *Ultra-pure [see CONDUCTIVITY 2]. **1973** *Nature* 13 Apr. 482/3 The preparation, handling containment and analysis of ultrapure materials. **1820** SHELLEY *Œd. Tyr.* I. 200 Prating there of commerce, public faith, Economy,..And other topics, *ultra-radical. **1845** LD. CAMPBELL *Chancellors* xxxviii. (1857) II. 151 There were a few ultra-radical members still not satisfied. **1921** *Sci. Amer.* 9 Apr. 288 Diagram of the multiple prism ring used for the *ultra-rapid camera. **1969** *Jane's Freight Containers 1968–69* 445/1 The Boeing has three baggage/cargo compartments. Two, fully containerised for ultra-rapid ground handling. **1907** W. JAMES *Pragmatism* iii. 123 A mere mess of anarchy and confusion..will pragmatism often seem to *ultra-rationalist minds in philosophy. **1925** T. DREISER *Amer. Trag.* (1926) II. i. 152 Older and more conservative families who constituted the *ultra-respectable element of the city. **1958** *People* 4 May 2/3 The workers have captured even the ultra-respectable Royal Academy this year. **1826** SOUTHEY *Vind. Eccl. Angl.* 198 Music and poetry were as much in request.. in those days as they are now among the most *ultra-refined circles. **1890** 'R. BOLDREWOOD' *Col. Reformer* (1891) 369 An ultra-refined aristocrat. **1831** CARLYLE in Froude *First Forty Years* (1882) II. viii. 177 They were all prophetical, Toryish, *ultra-religious. **1850** GROTE *Greece* II. lix. (1862) V. 248 His decorous private life and ultra-religious habits. **1793** HELEN M. WILLIAMS *Lett. France* (1795) II. 13 He had sufficient address to lead them to make some extravagant proposition, which he denominated *ultra-revolutionary, and for which he sent them to the scaffold. **1845** *Encycl. Metrop.* XIII. 370/2 Robespierre..accordingly..took an early occasion to associate the ultra-revolutionary party with the foreign enemies of the republic. **1974** tr. *Wertheim's Evolution & Revolution* i. 47 The ultra-revolutionary Red Guards in turbulent China,..the dissatisfied students in France or the rebellious young Negroes in the United States—all of them are..rebelling against the *status quo.* **1974** *Ann. Reg. 1973* 313 Whereas previously most criticism had accused him of being ultra-leftist, the media now argued that most of his faults were in fact *ultra-rightist. **1846** E. A. Poe in *Godey's Mag. & Lady's Bk.* Mar. 135/1 As a drama, we find 'Elfrida' faulty in the extreme. Its situations are *ultra-romantic, or improbable. **1931** *Times Lit. Suppl.* 14 May 385/1 Young Browning in his period of ultra-romantic chaos. **1819** Helen M. Williams *Lett. France* 61 A party, too well known by the denomination of *ultra-royalist. **1821** *Edin. Rev.* XXXVI. 139 This ultra-royalist spirit, diffused by the priests and emigrants. **1836** H. Coleridge *North. Worthies* (1852) I. 38 Their intolerant and ultra-royalist principles. **1926** E. O'Neill *Great God Brown* Prologue 11 The sound of the school quartet rendering 'Sweet Adeline' with many *ultra-sentimental barber-shop quavers. **1823** Bentham *Mem. & Corr.* Wks. 1843 X. 536 Then came the servile poet and novelist, Sir Walter Scott: and then the *ultra-servile sack guzzler, Southey. **1904** *N.Y. World Mag.* 1 May 6/1 She is likewise one of the prettiest girls in society, and *ultra-smart. **1939** O. Lancaster *Homes Sweet Homes* 74 Ultra-smart householders who reacted instantaneously to every change of fashion. **1832** Coleridge *Table-t.* 16 Aug., The discipline at Christ's Hospital in my time was *ultra-Spartan. **1853** Miss Yonge *Heir of Redclyffe* vii, Really it is so *ultra-splendid as to deserve notice! **1885** *Spectator* 18 July 945/2 He does not emulate the *ultra-strict veracity of the Quaker. **1829** Moore *Mem.* (1854) VI. 41 Murray full of *ultra-Tory predictions about Peel; that he is a ruined man [etc.]. **1843** Syd. Smith *Wks.* (1850) 683 Let me beg of my dear Ultras not to imagine..that they could form an Ultra-tory Administration. **1848** E. A. Poe *Eureka* 83 On the Melville islands..we find traces of **ultra-tropical* vegetation. **1851** G. F. Richardson *Geol.* (1855) 438 Groves and forests of the luxuriant vegetation of an *ultra-tropical climate were swept away by floods and inundations. **1972** *Daily Colonist* (Victoria, B.C.) 3 Mar. 5/3 Another standard argument for the *ultraviolent film is that in real life, violence is not the gunshot flash and quick dissolve, [etc.].

b. In some special terms, as ***ultra-brachy-cephalic, -dolichocephalic, -elliptic.***

1886 J. G. Garson in *Jrnl. Anthropol. Inst.* XVI. 14 The ..third group on either side is called ultradolichocephalic and *ultrabrachycephalic respectively. **1900** Deniker *Races of Man* ii. 58 *note*, Cephalic index of the skull:..from 90 and upwards, ultra-brachycephalic. **1877** Cayley *Math. Papers* X. 162 Göpel and Rosenhain each connect the theory with that of the *ultra-elliptic functions involving the radical $\sqrt{x}$ [etc.].

c. Similarly with advs.

1871 Miss Mulock *Fair France* i. 9 And what possible harm can it do a man to greet his neighbour civilly, even ultra-politely, rather than grumpily? **1883** Meredith *Poems & Lyrics* 139 All in honour still; Oh, all in honour ultra-honourably!

4. With sbs. in the same sense: **a.** Denoting persons as ***ultra-Catholic, -feminist, -leftist, -modernist, -nationalist -patriot, -rationalist, -rightist, -royalist,*** etc.; also with adj. used as collective sb., as ***ultra-feminine, -left, -right.***

Many of these are adjs. used substantively.

1817 Mar. Edgeworth *On Bores* Wks. 1833 XVIII. 318 Well-bred persons, abhorring the pedantry of the blues, are usually *anti-blues*, or **ultra-antis.* **1850** Marsden *Early Purit.* (1853) 338 Whitgift..was, in modern language, an *Ultra-Calvinist. **1837** J. S. Mill in *Westm. Rev.* XXVIII. 71 The *ultra-Catholics with their bigotry and pretensions to priestly domination. **1907** *Cambr. Mod. Hist.* X. xvi. 530 Belgium..was divided.., as it is still, into two irreconcilable parties, the ultra-Catholics or Clericals, and the Liberals. **1868** G. Duff *Pol. Surv.* 12 The struggles between *ultra-centralizers and ultra-federalists. **1836** Gen. P. Thompson *Let.* in *Exerc.* (1842) IV. 124 Among the names..are many, like Hermes, Nereus,..which modern *ultra-christians would have thought formidably heathenish. **1821** H. More in Roberts *Mem.* (1835) IV. 179 The *ultra-educationist would despise these limits. **1834** Mar. Edgeworth *Helen* xxxv. III. 66 One born and bred such an *ultra exclusive as Louisa Castlefort. **1829** T. Hook *Bank to Barnes* 146 The forthcoming novel has long kept the *ultra fashionables on the tiptoe of expectation. **1868** *Ultra-federalist [see *ultra-centralizer*]. **1926** W. de la Mare *Connoisseur, & Other Stories* 184 Mr. Thripp indeed was no lover of the *ultra-feminine. **1979** *Maledicta* III. 17 Even though many *ultra-feminists have attacked you.., you still insist that women are superior to men. **1866** G. Talbot in E. Purcell *Life A. P. de Lisle* (1900) I. xv. 408 The [architectural] designs excited the admiration even of the *Ultra-Goths present. **1818** Byron *Juan* Ded. xvii, Is it not so, my Tory, *ultra-Julian? **1971** *New Scientist* 30 Sept. 740/2 The *ultra-left found its voice by protesting against the new Tokyo international airport. **1971** *Time* 11 Oct. 13 As an *ultra-leftist, of course, Wu would hardly expect a warm welcome from as revisionist a country as the Soviet Union. **1824** Miss Mitford *Village* Ser. i. (1863) 208 He is an *ultra-liberal, quotes Cobbett, and goes rather too far. **1860** W. G. Clark in *Vac. Tour* (1864) 6 The ultra-liberals are blind to facts and consequences. **1857** Pusey *Real Presence* i. (1869) 112 The error of the Sacramentaries was opposed by the error of the *Ultra-Lutherans. **1816** Southey *Ess.* (1832) I. 281 The *amateurs outrés* of horse-racing, or *ultra-men of the turf. **1926** H. W. Fowler *Mod. Eng. Usage* 709/1 Let us not be *ultra-modernists & assume that *whence* & *whither*..are dead & buried. **1936** G. B. Shaw *Millionairess* Pref. 121 Only the stupidest or craziest *ultra-Nationalists believe that people corralled within the same political frontier are all exactly alike. **1852** S. R. Maitland *Eight Ess.* 158 'Just so,' replies the *ultra-papist; 'I believe you'. **1938** *Ultra-patriot [see *samurai-minded* adj. s.v. samurai 2]. **1976** *Times Lit. Suppl.* 21 May 602/4 De Mille and the ultra-patriots who had been smearing the guild's president..for opposing the introduction of a compulsory loyalty oath. **1827** G. Higgins *Celtic Druids* 136 The *ultra pietists make a terrible outcry.

1818 Bentham *Ch. Eng., Catech. Exam.* 334 If the number of livings be greater than two,..he may be termed an *Ultra-Pluralist. **1818** *Q. Rev.* XVIII. 504 In the opinion of the *ultra-presbyterians. **1835** Hook *Ch. Dict.* (1842) 501 The use of the ring in marriage used to be regarded as a remnant of Popery by *ultra-protestants. **1841** A. P. de Lisle in E. Purcell *Life* (1900) I. xi. 208 That still more monstrous idea held by ultra-Protestants that the Catholick Church consists of all sects of nominal Christians. **1850** Marsden *Early Purit.* (1853) 49 The *ultra-puritans regarded them as semi-papists. **1834** Greville *Mem.* (1874) III. 54 Lord Wharncliffe..says that the constituency of the great towns is composed of *ultra-Radicals. **1871** M. Collins *Marq. & Merch.* II. iii. 58 You're an ultra-Radical. **1909** W. James *Pluralistic Universe* 352 Mr. Bradley, for instance, is an *ultra-rationalist. **1858** Froude *Hist. Eng.* IV. 114 At home, the virulence of the *ultra-reactionaries.. recommenced. **1867** Latham *Black & White* Pref. p. vi, They are the successful men, who have made money, and are not disposed to be *ultra-Republicans in future. **1845** *Encycl. Metrop.* XIII. 370/2 The progress of Hebert and the *ultra-revolutionists was still more distasteful to him [Danton] than to Robespierre. **1977** *Time* 21 Nov. 39/3 She's willingly making herself a stalking horse for the *ultra-right. **1976** *New Yorker* 8 Mar. 28/1 In 1973, he [*sc.* Lin Piao] became an '*ultra-rightist'. **1848** Blackie in *Class. Mus.* V. 72 Dante..said many things in his divine poem.. offensive to the *ultra-Romanists. **1817** *Ann. Reg. 1816* 109/2 The latter were accordingly eminently monarchical in their principles, and were invidiously branded with the title of **ultra-royalists.* **1818** Lady Morgan *Autobiog.* (1859) 276, I dread the machinations of the ultra royalists and the Bourbon princes. **1845** Ld. Campbell *Chancellors* xcv. (1857) IV. 302 It was thought fit to balance them by some determined ultra-royalists. **1816** Southey *Ess.* (1832) I. 356 Such was the system of government established in France by the Perfect Emperor of the *Ultra-Whigs and Extra-Reformers.

b. Denoting actions, qualities as ***ultra-leftism, -liberalism, -marathon, -nationalism, -Protestantism, -radicalism, -rationalism, -speed, -supernaturalism, violence,*** etc.

1858 H. Martineau *Hist. Peru* 169 The government was declared to have gone over to *ultra-abolitionism. **1845** Ford *Handbk. Spain* ii. 656 Napier, in his *ultra advocacy of Soult, says [etc.]. **1831** *Edin. Rev.* LIV. 387 He parades an *ultra-Byronism. **1841** Miall in *Nonconf.* I. 73 In connection with Laudism and *ultra-churchism. **1850** L. Hunt *Autobiog.* I. ii. 70, I found myself..cultivating a perplexed *ultra-conscientiousness with my mother. **1828** P. Cunningham *N.S. Wales* (ed. 3) II. 16 His *ultra-dandyism of speech, dress, and manner, made his presence a sort of *sine qua non* in every merry meeting. **1863** A. Blomfield *Mem. Bp. Blomfield* I. iv. 106 Reports of his *ultra-discipline..may have reached you. **1949** *Horizon* May 315 'Trotskyism' (i.e., *ultra-leftism). **1835** J. E. Alexander *Sk. Portugal* viii. 192 The priest..seized a musket by the barrel and hit him a crack with the butt over the head to show his *ultra-liberalism, (priests being generally suspected of being anti-constitutional). **1856** R. A. Vaughan *Mystics* (1860) I. 279 It is sickening to hear the unctuous talk with which now-a-days ultra-liberalism will sometimes stretch out a hand to spiritual tyranny. **1857** Pusey *Real Presence* i. (1869) 122 Amid the conflict of parties, the 'Formula Concordiæ' moderated the extremes of *Ultra-Lutheranism. **1847** L. Hunt *Men, Women, & B.* II. v. 70 The account is singular and interesting, as a specimen of the highest *ultra-manners of those times. **1977** J. F. Fixx *Compl. Bk. Running* xxiv. 268 Corbitt knows as much about long races—*ultramarathons, runners call them—as anyone alive. **1949** *Horizon* June 398 Men who have grown old in the ways of self-interest and *ultranationalism. **1877** C. Geikie *Christ* lvi. (1879) 676 With craft, the *ultra-orthodoxy of the Pharisaic party allied itself with the loyalist faction. **1818** Bentham *Ch. Eng.* 336 In these cases of *Ultra-Pluralism, whereabouts are the eyes of the Archbishop? **1839** J. S. Mill *Let.* 27 Dec. in *Wks.* (1963) XIII. 415 The principal peculiarity of this school is hostility to what they call *ultra-Protestantism. **1842** Pusey *Crisis Eng. Ch.* 30 Cases in which persons who were going over from Ultra-Protestantism, have been thankful to be stayed, and found their rest in the true doctrines of our Church. **1858** Sears *Athan.* iii. ii. 267 It is only our ultra Protestantism that involves us in these difficulties and absurdities. **1825** Hazlitt *Spirit of Age* 147 They are a relief to the mind..heated with *ultra-radicalism. **1949** I. Deutscher *Stalin* 405 The Comintern was now indeed engaged in a mock fight. Its ultra-radicalism was so unreal. **1899** W. S. Churchill *Let.* 19 Jan. in R. S. Churchill *Winston S. Churchill* (1969) II. Compan. i. p. xxvii, Who should draw the line where the maximum of human pain and doubt may be allayed and the minimum of *ultra-rationalism be incurred? **1946** *Mind* LV. 109 This ultra-rationalism, as I may call it, put forward by Leibniz. **1847** W. C. L. Martin *Ox* 63/1 There is, perhaps, something of *ultra-refinement in this view of the matter. **1816–30** Bentham *Offic. Apt. Maximized, Extr. Const. Code* (1830) 12 Completely needless, and thence unjustifiable, is all such *ultra-remuneration. **1865** *Ch. Times* 28 Oct. 341 The Puritan outcry about the '*ultra-ritualism' at St. Michael's Church. **1815** *Ann. Reg. Gen. Hist.* 94 A preponderance of what is called *ultra-royalism, which opposes the moderation of the court. **1963** C. R. Cowell et al. *Inlays, Crowns, & Bridges* ix. 103 Some operators..then undertake most of the rest of the preparation at *ultra-speed. **1871** Lowell *Pope* Prose Wks. 1890 IV. 18 The *ultra-spiritualism of the Puritans. **1950** R. A. Knox *Enthusiasm* i. 2 If I could have been certain of the reader's goodwill, I would have called my tendency '*ultrasupernaturalism'. For that is the real character of the enthusiast; he expects more evident results from the grace of God than we others. **1829** Moore *Mem.* (1854) VI. 44 Some of the Handelian part of the selections might be called the *ultra-Toryism of music. **1972** *Times* 6 May 9/2 It will serve as a textbook study of how to photograph acts of *ultraviolence without giving offence. **1977** *Time* 24 Jan. 14/2 It was like an orgy of 'ultra-violence' from Stanley Kubrick's *A Clockwork Orange*... About 200 masked youths rioted last week in the industrial town of Mestre near Venice.

†**ultra-, ultrequidance,** variants of outrecuidance *Obs.*

1541 *St. Papers Hen. VIII*, VIII. 545 He made.. protestation, that the same..passed him..only uppon wilfulness and ultraquidance, which he confessed had been in him.

ultrabasic (ʌltrəˈbeɪsɪk), *a.* (*sb.*) *Petrol.* [f. ultra- 3 + basic *a.*] Of an igneous rock: having a silica content that is lower than that of the basic rocks (cf. basic *a.* 2 b), *spec.* less than 45 per cent by weight. Also as *sb.*

1881 J. W. Judd *Volcanoes* (ed. 2) 317 There are some rarer materials..that present a most wonderful resemblance to the stony portions of meteorites. These materials we may call 'ultra-basic rocks'. **1885** —— in *Q. Jrnl. Geol. Soc.* XLI. 354 Those rocks which contain an excessive proportion of the bases, especially magnesia and ferrous oxide, and are therefore composed largely of unisilicates, may be conveniently classed as ultra-basic rocks. **1893** Geikie *Text-bk. Geol.* (ed. 3) vi. i. 681 Crystalline rocks, which range from amorphous masses..to basic or even what are called 'ultra-basic' compounds. **1898** *Nature* 3 Feb. 315/2 He.. had arrived at certain very definite views concerning the constant association of the crystalline form of carbon with the ultrabasic rocks. **1938** R. W. Lawson tr. *Hevesy & Paneth's Man. Radioactivity* (ed. 2) xxv. 274 Stone meteorites are still more strongly basic than the ultrabasic terrestrial rocks. **1964** *Economic Geol.* LIX. 804 In the low-lying regions the ultrabasics are largely masked by soil. **1970** *Nature* 28 Mar. 1227/2 Most of the volcanics were basic, but during the upper Cretaceous ultrabasics..were intruded. **1977** *Sci. Amer.* Mar. 96/3 In a typical greenstone belt early volcanic activity has produced ultrabasic and basic lavas.

ultracentrifuge (ʌltrəˈsɛntrɪfjuːdʒ), *sb.* [f. ultra- 2 c + centrifuge *sb.*] A very high-speed centrifuge, now usu. generating over 100,000*g*, used to separate small particles and large molecules in a liquid and to determine their sedimentation rate (and hence their size).

1924 Svedberg & Rinde in *Jrnl. Amer. Chem. Soc.* XLVI. 2678 In analogy with the naming of the ultra-microscope and ultra-filtration apparatus we propose the name *ultra-centrifuge* for this apparatus. **1939** *Ann. Reg. 1938* 374 The ultracentrifuge showed the presence in plant juices of carbohydrates of well-defined molecular weight. **1948** *New Biol.* V. 33 Tiny air-driven turbine ultra-centrifuges which rotate at speeds up to 5,000 revolutions per second, giving forces equal to half a million times that of gravity, will stratify many of the finest cell inclusions. **1968** *New Scientist* 3 Oct. 6/3 A pilot plant for enriching uranium by the ultracentrifuge method. **1978** H. McLeave *Borderline Case* (1979) xiii. 132 The laboratory..had everything, including ..several ultracentrifuges.

Hence ˌ**ultracentrifugal** (stress variable) *a.*, involving or employing an ultracentrifuge; ˌ**ultracentrifugally** (stress variable) *adv.*, by means of an ultracentrifuge; with respect to the ultracentrifuge.

1930 *Jrnl. Amer. Chem. Soc.* LII. 2904 The ultracentrifugal study of gelatin solutions has been fruitful in revealing the heterogeneous nature of the sols. **1943** *Jrnl. Exper. Med.* LXXVII. 460 Gratia and Paillot had reported polyhedral bodies and ultracentrifugally purified material from jaundiced blood to be serologically unrelated to ultracentrifugally purified material from the blood of normal silkworms. **1953** *Jrnl. Amer. Chem. Soc.* LXXV. 67/2 Recently they succeeded in preparing an electrophoretically and ultracentrifugally homogeneous mucoprotein. **1962** M. Rabaey in A. Pirie *Lens Metabolism Rel. Cataract* 310 Ultracentrifugal analysis permitted us to classify this protein as a member of the so-called group of β-crystallins. **1977** *Lancet* 8 Oct. 742/1 A typical ultra-centrifugal scan and the distribution of IgE in the corresponding fractions is shown.

ultraˈcentrifuge, *v.* [f. prec. sb.: cf. centrifuge *v.*] *trans.* To spin in an ultracentrifuge. Chiefly as **ultraˈcentrifuged** *ppl. a.*, **ultraˈcentrifuging** *vbl. sb.* Also ˌ**ultracentrifuˈgation**, the action or process of ultracentrifuging.

1934 *Proc. Soc. Exper. Biol. & Med.* XXXI. 707 (*heading*) Effect of ultracentrifuging on Paramecium. **1936** *Trans. Faraday Soc.* XXXII. 301 In this case again, analogous to those of viscometry and ultracentrifugation, the dilutest solutions yield the clearest result. **1946** *Nature* 5 Oct. 488/2 Virus can be separated by differential ultracentrifuging into fractions with widely different properties. **1947** *Ann. Rev. Microbiol.* I. 364 Ultracentrifuged concentrates of virus. **1971** *Nature* 18 June 447/1 The extract was spun at 25,000*g* for 20 min to remove large particles before being subjected to ultracentrifugation at 105,000*g* for 90 min to sediment out the microsomes and membrane fractions. **1974** *Ibid.* 13 Dec. 605/2 The injection of adult mice with ultracentrifuged heterologous γ globulin induces immunological unresponsiveness to a subsequent injection of the globulin. **1977** *Lancet* 8 Oct. 742/1 The distribution of radioactivity in a radiolabelled (^{125}I) myeloma IgE preparation ultracentrifuged under identical conditions.

ˌ**ultraˈcold,** *sb.* and *a.* [f. ultra- 3 + cold *a.*, *sb.*] **A.** *sb.* Extreme coldness.

1967 *Britannica Bk. of Year* (U.S.) 804/3 *Ultracold*, excessive coldness especially near absolute zero. **1977** A. Hallam *Planet Earth* 15/1 The Moon's atmosphere.. provides little protection from the direct heat of the Sun, and little insulation from the ultracold of space.

B. *adj. Nucl. Physics.* Of a neutron: having an energy of the order of 10^{-7} eV or less.

1969 *JETP Lett.* IX. 26 Ultracold neutrons are produced and propagate in accordance with the theoretical expectations. **1978** *Nature* 9 Mar. 127/1 Ultracold neutrons are slow neutrons with velocities of less than 7 m s^{-1}. **1979**

Sci. Amer. June 106/1 A striking property of ultracold neutrons is their total reflection from solid surfaces.

ultra-crepi'darian, *a.* and *sb.* [f. the Latin phrase *ultrā crepidam* 'beyond the sole' in allusion to the reply of Apelles to the cobbler.
The form in which the reply is given by Pliny (*Nat. Hist.* xxxv. x. §36) is *ne supra crepidam judicaret.* Valerius Maximus (VIII. xii. 3) expresses it by *supra plantam ascendere vetuit.*]

A. *adj.* Going beyond one's proper province; giving opinions on matters beyond one's knowledge.

1819 HAZLITT *Letter to W. Gifford* Wks. 1902 I. 368 You have been well called an Ultra-Crepidarian critic. **1822** —— *Table-T.* II. vi. 143 The last sort I shall mention are verbal critics—mere word-catchers. [*Note*] The title of Ultra-Crepidarian critics has been given to a variety of this species. **1832** *Examiner* 662/1 He takes a fancy to teach that 'Ultra-crepidarian Critic' his own theory. **1872** F. HALL *Rec. Exemplif. False Philol.* 112 His assumption of judicial assessorship, as a critic of English, is, therefore, to borrow a word from Hazlitt, altogether ultra-crepidarian.

B. *sb.* One who ventures beyond his scope; an ignorant or presumptuous critic.

1825 BEDDOES *Let.* in *Poems* (1851) p. xxxviii, The 'Fatal Dowry' has been cobbled, I see, by some purblind ultra-crepidarian. **1831** *Q. Rev.* XLIV. 77 Two of these ultra-crepidarians are included in Mr. Southey's present chapter of chronicles.

Hence **ultracrepi'darianism**. †**ultra-'crepidast**, = B. above. *Obs. rare*$^{-1}$. **ultra-'crepidate** *v. intr.*, to venture beyond one's scope. **ultracrepi'dation, -'crepidizing**, the action or fact of criticizing ignorantly.

1640 HENSHAW *Horæ Succ.* II. Ep. Ded. 1, I cannot but condemne those *ultra-crepitasts* [*sic*] that, with Festus, will teach Saint Paul divinity. **1800** COLERIDGE in *Sir H. Davy's Rem.* (1858) 78, I was a well-meaning *sutor* who had ultra-crepidated with more zeal than wisdom. *Ibid.* 83 All this is ultra crepidation. **1837** S. R. MAITLAND *6 Lett. Fox's A. & M.* p. ix, There is among the infinity of anonymous writing, compiling, concocting, .. so much pretence (if I may make a word.., so much ultracrepidizing) that [etc.]. *a* **1876** M. COLLINS *Pen Sketches by Vanished Hand* (1879) I. 242 A brochure on *The Laws of Verse*, which is curious as exemplifying what a great wit called 'ultracrepidarianism'. **1882** FARRAR in *Contemp. Rev.* Mar. 374 It is always dangerous, as Coleridge phrased it, to ultra-crepidate.

,ultracyto'chemistry. *Biol.* [f. ULTRA (*structural* adj. s.v. ULTRASTRUCTURE + *cyto-chemistry* s.v. CYTO-.] Ultrastructural cytochemistry. So **,ultracyto'chemical** *a.*; **,ultra-cyto'chemically** *adv.*

1963 *Proc. Amer. Assoc. Cancer Res.* IV. 16/1 Ultracytochemical studies of the thymus of birds with myeloblastosis .. revealed adenosinetriphosphatase activity. **1965** *Virology* XXV. 162/1 The technique for ultracytochemistry .. was proved to be an effective method for investigating intracellularly developing viruses. **1981** *Physiol. Plant Path.* XVIII. 339 (*heading*) Phenolic ultracytochemistry of tobacco cells undergoing the hypersensitive reaction to *Pseudomonas solanacearum*. *Ibid.*, The objective of this study was to ultracytochemically determine if any phenolic deposition and PPO [*sc.* polyphenoloxidase] might be detected. *Ibid.* 343 With the ultracytochemical method, particulate as well as soluble activity can be demonstrated.

ultradian (ʌl'treɪdɪən), *a.* [f. ULTRA- + L. *di-ēs* day + -AN.] Designating cycles of physiological activity which recur with a period shorter than one day but longer than one hour. Cf. CIRCADIAN *a.*

1961 F. HALBERG in *39th Rep. Ross Conf. Pediatric Res.* 15 Observations have been made on frequencies higher than circadian, yet lower than the respiratory or cardiac cycles (ultradian), and frequencies lower than circadian, but higher than the menstrual cycle (infradian). **1978** *Nature* 3 Aug. 490/1 In humans, REM sleep .. occurs every 90–110 min and is presumed to be under the control of an underlying ultradian oscillatory mechanism.

ultrafiche ('ʌltrəfiːʃ). [f. ULTRA- 2 c + FICHE.] A microfiche in which the linear reduction of the image size is of the order of 100 or more; documentary material of this kind.

1971 *Collier's 1971 Year Book* 322/1 (*caption*) On one card, over 3,000 pages are reduced to microscopic proportions... The cards, called ultrafiches or microfiches, are magnified in the reader. **1972** *Physics Bull.* Sept. 522/1 Flat sheets of film, known as ultrafiche and measuring 6 in × 4 in can contain more than 3000 pages of normal text. **1972** *Times* 1 Dec. (Suppl.) p. ii/6 Ultrafiches of the photochronic micro image process store up to 4,000 pages on a 4 in by 6 in film. **1975** *New Yorker* 22 Dec. 30/1 They brought out the Bible on an ultrafiche... The whole book on a piece of film two inches square. **1976** P. HARCOURT *Dance for Diplomats* xii. 135 The really vital thing is a bit of ultrafiche—that's some form of microfilm. **1981** JACOBSTEIN & MERSKY *Fund. Legal Res.* (ed. 2) 447 In some instances up to 1700 pages can be placed on a single sheet of ultrafiche.

ultra'fidian, *a.* [f. the L. phrase *ultrā fidem* 'beyond faith'.] Going beyond mere faith; blindly credulous. Also **ultra'fidianism**.

1825 COLERIDGE *Aids Refl.* viii, Sir Thomas Brown.. could answer all the objections of the Devil and Reason 'with the old resolution he had learnt of Tertullian: Certum est quia impossibile est!' .. Now this I call Ultra-fidianism. *a* **1849** H. COLERIDGE *Ess.* (1851) II. 96 The great moralist, who balanced an ultrafidian credulity in the supernatural with an extraordinary degree of scepticism in things natural and human. **1865** *Reader* 14 Jan. 43/2 It must be, however, a strangely incurious and ultrafidian mind that can consent to rest there .. simply at another's bidding.

ultra'filtrate. *Biol.* [f. next, after *filtration, filtrate.*] Liquid that has passed through an ultrafilter.

1928 *Biochem. Jrnl.* XXII. 633 There was slightly less inorganic phosphorus in the ultrafiltrate than in either the original or the residual plasma. **1957** G. E. HUTCHINSON *Treat. Limnol.* I. xv. 811 Two determinations of the copper content of ultra filtrates indicate that about 80 per cent of the so-called organic copper is associated with colloidal material. **1977** *Lancet* 18 June 1294/1 Ultrafiltrates of pepsin digests of the mucosa.

,ultrafil'tration. *Biol.* [f. ULTRA- 2 c + FILTRATION.] The action or process of filtration through a medium sufficiently fine to retain colloidal particles, certain viruses, or large molecules.

1908 *Chem. Abstr.* II. 1155 Ultrafiltration... Filtration of this type is accomplished by forcing under pressure the solutions through colloid membranes such as collodium, glacial acetic acid-collodium and hardened gelatin. **1946** *Nature* 9 Nov. 665/2 The blood pressure reduction cannot have augmented the osmotic pressure by more than .. about 3·2/1000 of the total osmotic pressure. This change is so small that ultra-filtration cannot play any considerable part in the formation of aqueous humor. **1959** *New Scientist* 15 Jan. 135/3 Most marine animals possess some type of ampullary excretory organ... It is probable .. that these organs produce an excretory fluid by a process of ultrafiltration. **1964** [see GRADOCOL]. **1978** *Sci. Amer.* July 88/2 The pores of an ultrafiltration membrane are on the scale of 10^{-9} meter, or one nanometer; average pore diameters range from less than a nanometer to about 10 nanometers.

So **'ultrafilter** *sb.*, a medium or membrane used for ultrafiltration; also as *v. trans.*, to subject to ultrafiltration; **ultra'filterable** *a.*, capable of passing through an ultrafilter.

1908 *Chem. Abstr.* II. 3183 (*heading*) Porosity of ultra filters. **1911** *Ibid.* V. 2 Ultrafiltration... A discussion of the merits of the Bechhold and Burian ultrafilters and of the author's modifications. **1920** *Biochem. Jrnl.* XIV. 539 The oxygenase remains on the ultrafilter. **1928** *Ibid.* XXII. 633 A large proportion of the inorganic phosphate of the plasma is ultrafilterable through cellophane. **1946** *Physiol. Rev.* XXVI. 586 The first indication that the adrenotrophic factor could be ultrafiltered was presented .. in 1934. **1961** *Lancet* 5 Aug. 284/2 The plasma was ultrafiltered. **1974** *Nature* 8 Nov. 176/1 The haemagglutinating activity in galactose .. was found in the retentate and could be concentrated quantitatively and washed free of monosaccharide by ultrafiltration over an XM-50 ultrafilter (Amicon) which nominally retains proteins of molecular weight greater than 50,000. **1976** *Ibid.* 8 Apr. 487/1 The rise in brain tryptophan .. correlates .. with the fraction of tryptophan which is not protein bound (free or ultrafilterable). **1978** *Ibid.* 2 Mar. 65/2 The supernatant was ultrafiltered twice .. to separate the proteins into three fractions with molecular weights .. above 50,000, between 10,000 and 50,000 and below 10,000.

ultrage, obs. form of OUTRAGE.

ul'trageous, *a. rare.* [f. ULTRA *a.* or *sb.*, after *outrageous.*] Violently extreme.

1823 G. CANNING *Let.* in *Q. Rev.* July (1897) 129 The French Government .. suffered themselves to be driven on .. by the Ultrageous party of their followers. *Ibid.*, Another of an opposite sort may spring up, in an Ultrageous fashion.

ultra-high (ʌltrə'haɪ), *a.* [f. ULTRA- 3 + HIGH *a.*] **1.** *Radio.* Of a radio-frequency: in the range 300 to 3,000 megahertz. Abbrev. UHF s.v. U 4 a.

1932 *Proc. IRE* XX. 95 Among the significant and comparatively recent developments in electrical engineering is the efficient and dependable production of ultra-high-frequency oscillating circuits. **1935** *Discovery* Sept. 278/2 Special valves are being developed suitable for direct signal amplification at the ultra-high frequencies. **1940** *Jrnl. R. Aeronaut. Soc.* XLIV. 216 Another application of ultra-high frequencies is to provide a system of instrument landing. **1951** *Electronic Engin.* XXIII. 452 The use of ultra high frequencies for communication purposes is a relatively new and rapidly developing branch of radio. **1978** *Dædalus* Spring 212 There is already a good deal of listening in the ultrahigh frequency radio bands.

2. *gen.* Exceedingly high; freq. in attrib. phr. in comb. with following sb.

1936 *Discovery* Mar. 88/1 The G.W.R. and the L.N.E.R. have been even more enterprising in introducing some ultra-high-speed expresses. **1962** F. I. ORDWAY et al. *Basic Astronautics* vii. 327 Ultrahigh-risk equipment. **1966** D. G. BRANDON *Mod. Techniques Metallogr.* iv. 184 Methods for obtaining ultra-high vacua (UHV) are now highly developed. **1972** D. HALBERSTAM *Best & Brightest* 558 At West Point he again had ultrahigh visibility and he impressed everyone. **1977** P. JOHNSON *Enemies of Society* i. 4 The extended family also dissociated procreation from the responsibility to maintain offspring, and so produced ultra-high birthrates. **1981** *Economist* 24 Jan. 49/3 How long can Britain go on protecting its farmers from competition from imported UHT (Ultra-High Temperature, or long-life) milk?

ultraism ('ʌltrəɪz(ə)m). [f. ULTRA *a.* + -ISM. So Sw. *ultraism*, G. *ultraismus*. Cf. F. *ultracisme.*] The principles or tenets of one who holds extreme opinions on any question; the fact of holding such opinions.

1821 H. MORE in Roberts *Mem.* (1835) IV. 178, I think there is ultraism on both sides of the question. **1842** G. S. FABER *Prov. Lett.* (1844) II. 116 The Ultraism of those, who .. would fain establish a bundle of Unscripturalities as the catholic doctrine of the primitive Church. **1880** O. JOHNSON *W. L. Garrison* 32 How foolish to throw away all chances of doing any good by such ultraism!

b. An instance of this.

1824 MEDWIN *Convers. Byron* II. 5 To the great horror of the former, she soon sported her Ultraisms. **1857** O. BROWNSON *Convert* Wks. 1882–7 V. 46 My alleged Ultraisms and tendency to run to extremes. **1865** J. H. NEWMAN in Ward *Life* (1912) xxiii. II. 102, I abominate the fierce tyranny which .. calls to account everyone who ventures to keep clear of ultra-isms.

ultraist ('ʌltrəɪst). [f. as prec. + -IST. So Sw. *ultraist.*] One who holds extreme opinions; an extremist.

1842 G. S. FABER *Prim. Doctr. Election* (ed. 2) I. i. 5 *note*, Those high-vaulting Ultraists, who professedly treat with contempt the harmonious voice of Aboriginal Antiquity. **1875** O. W. HOLMES *Old Vol. Life, Crime and Automatism* (1891) 357 Obviously these reformers are not fanatics; they are not ultraists or Utopians.

Hence **ultra'istic** *a.*, tending to extremes in opinion or practice.

1840 G. S. FABER *Christ's Disc. Capernaum* Ded. p. xx, Our ultraistic friend, .. in his own insulated strength confident against the world in arms. **1877** SPARROW *Serm.* ix. 115 This unmeasured, exaggerated and ultraistic mode of drawing inferences.

ultralight, *a.* and *sb.* [f. ULTRA- 3 + LIGHT *a.*[1]] **A.** *adj.* (Stress variable.) Extremely light-weight; *spec.* applied to a small, low-speed, inexpensive, usually one-seater aircraft that has a small engine but can also soar and whose fuselage is an open framework without an enclosed cockpit. **B.** *sb.* (Stressed '*ultralight.*) An ultralight aircraft.

1974 *Soaring* Jan. 44/1 (Advt. heading), Ultralights. **1974** *Flying* Mar. 30/1 Hang gliders have been in the news... Sometimes called 'ultralight gliders', they represent the minimum machine capable of controllable sustained flight. **1974** *Nat. Geographic* Dec. 771/2 His ultralight 30-foot canoe was a perfectly balanced sailing machine. **1982** *Sci. Amer.* July 60/1 Only within the past few years has the conjunction of the hang glider and the small engine (Go-Kart or snowmobile) brought the long-sought objective into being as the ultralight airplane. **1982** *N.Y. Times* 22 Aug. I. 1/4 Swarms of these new craft—known to enthusiasts as ultralights—are filling the air. **1983** *Economist* 27 Aug. 47 First on the runway is likely to be Eipper Aircraft of California, the biggest maker of ultralights (almost the same as microlights in Europe).

ultramafic (ʌltrə'mæfɪk), *a.* (and *sb.*) *Petrol.* [f. ULTRA- 3 + MAFIC *a.*] Of an igneous rock: composed chiefly of mafic minerals. Also as *sb.*

1933 R. A. DALY *Igneous Rocks & Depths of the Earth* ii. 31 The more important groups [of igneous rocks] are the granite clan .., the ultramafic clans, and the 'feldspathoidal' clans. *Ibid.* xxii. 565 Each of the ultramafic and ultrabasic species .. treated in this chapter has its own unsolved problems. **1948** *Bull. Oregon State Dept. Geol. & Mineral.* XXXIX. 8 The ultramafics include bodies of dunite, pyroxenite, and gabbro which have been extensively altered to hornblendite and serpentine. **1965** G. J. WILLIAMS *Econ. Geol. N.Z.* x. 143/1 The useful non-metallic minerals are more abundant in those ultramafics which have been subjected either to metamorphic or metasomatic changes. **1967** P. J. WYLLIE *Ultramafic & Related Rocks* 1/1 Ultramafic monomineralic rocks composed of the following mafic minerals would certainly be ultrabasic .. forsterite .. fayalite .. hornblende .. biotite. **1971** I. G. GASS et al. *Understanding Earth* i. 23/1 Only in the ultramafic rocks .. does Al_2O_3 fall to significantly lower values than those quoted.

ultramarine (ʌltrəmə'riːn), *a.* and *sb.* [ad. med.L. *ultrāmarīn-us*, f. L. *ultrā* beyond + *mare* sea: see ULTRA-. Cf. Sp. and Pg. *ultramarino*, It. *oltramarino*, OF. *ultremarin*, *oltre-* (obs. F. *outremarin*); also as sb. (sense B. 1) Sp. *ultramarino*, G., Sw., Da. *ultramarin*, Du. *-marijn*; Sp., Pg. *ultramar*, F. *outremer.*]

A. *adj.* **1.** Situated beyond the sea. Now *rare.*

1652 FRENCH *Yorksh. Spa* vii. 65 In a moorish, boggie ground, ariseth a Spring of a Vitrioline tast.., resembling much those ultramarine Spaws. **1681** H. NEVILE *Plato Rediv.* 47 In the several Countries of Padua, Brescia, Vicenza, Verona, .. as also in the Ultramarine Provinces. **1769** BURKE *Obs. Pres. St. Nat.* Wks. 1842 I. 80 He tells them that the loss of her ultramarine dominions lessens her expences. **1828** SIR W. NAPIER *Penins. War* I. ii. I. 15 The ultramarine dominions of the exiled family to be equally divided between the contracting parties. **1852** GROTE *Greece* II. lxxix. X. 419 The project of stretching across the Ægean for ultramarine dependencies.

2. (See defs.)

1656 BLOUNT *Glossogr.*, *Ultramarine*, coming from beyond Sea. **1802** JAMES *Milit. Dict.*, *Ultramarine*, from beyond the sea—foreign.

3. ***ultramarine blue*** (or *colour*): **a.** A pigment or colouring matter of various shades of blue, originally obtained from the mineral lapis lazuli and named with reference to the foreign origin of this. (†Also with *green.*)

So Sp. and Pg. *azul ultramarino*, It. *azzurro oltremarino.*

1686 AGLIONBY *Painting Illustr.* I. 23 In imploying of fine Colours, as fine lacks Ultra Marine Green, &c. **1698** FRYER *Acc. E. India & P.* 332 From this Stone [*sc.* Lapis Lazuli] is made that Colour they name Ultra-marine Blue. *a* **1775** J. HILL (Jod.), To it the painters are indebted for their beautiful ultramarine colour, which is by a calcination of lapis lazuli. **1816** P. CLEAVELAND *Min.* 258 Its chief use is to furnish the ultramarine blue, a pigment remarkable for the durability of its color. **1879** *Cassell's Techn. Educ.* IV. 222/1

If the body is to be blue, mix ultramarine blue with one half raw oil and turpentine.

b. A blue colour like that of this pigment.

1781 [see next]. **1845** *Florist's Jrnl.* 229 It differs materially in the colour, the flowers of the present species being a bright ultra-marine blue. **1882** *Garden* 22 Apr. 283/3 The glowing ultramarine blue of the flowers is strikingly brilliant.

4. Of a special deep-blue colour. (Cf. sense 3 above.)

1781 LATHAM *Gen. Synop. Birds* I. 413 Ultramarine R[oller]... The whole plumage of a rich glossy ultramarine blue. **1783** *Ibid.* III. 301 Ultramarine F[inch]. The plumage wholly of a fine deep blue. **1867** MISS BRADDON *Rupert Godwin* I. i. 5 The deep crimson of the brick-work,.. sharply defined against an ultramarine sky.

B. *sb.* **1.** = A. 3.

1598 HAYDOCKE tr. *Lomazzo's Artes* III. v. 101 Of Blewes, ..the greater part of Azures, specially the vltramarine. *c* **1650** NORGATE *Miniatura* (1919) 49 The rest of the skie.. is made with Ultramarine and White. **1677** GREW *Disc. Colours Plants* iii. §28 The Flower of Lathyrus or Parseverlasting.. is changed from a Peach, to as pure a Blew, as the best Vltramarine. **1683** TRYON *Way to Health* 229 Take Indigo, Vltramarine, or any Blew, and mix it with White, and it makes a Skie to what degree you please. **1731** *Gentl. Mag.* I. 449 Capt. Goslin presented some blue Colour, with a Specimen which shew'd it to exceed the common Ultramarine. **1762–71** H. WALPOLE *Vertue's Anecd. Paint.* (1786) II. 234 It would be a very long time before the worth of 20*ol.* in ultramarine could be employed in miniatures. **1816** P. CLEAVELAND *Min.* 258 The particles of the ultramarine, being thus rendered smooth and slippery, escape. **1859** R. HUNT *Guide Mus. Pract. Geol.* (ed. 2) 256 An artificial ultramarine is prepared by mixing clay, carbonate of soda, and sulphur. **1880** J. DUNBAR *Pract. Paper-maker* 60 The above tests are.. a safeguard to any paper-maker in buying ultramarines.

attrib. **1839** URE *Dict. Arts* 1262 The remainder of the mass.. yields an inferior pigment, called ultramarine ashes. **1868** WATTS *Dict. Chem.* V. 937 A pale-blue powder called ultramarine ash. **1881** *Instr. Census Clerks* (1885) 58 Ultramarine Maker. Verditer Maker. **1888** *Encycl. Brit.* XXIII. 721/2 There are very few ultramarine works in other countries, and none, as far as we know, in Great Britain.

b. With distinguishing terms (see quots.).

1728 CHAMBERS *Cycl.* s.v., There is another Kind, call'd Common or Dutch Ultramarine. **1867** *Chambers' Encycl.* IX. 625 The term *Yellow Ultramarine* is sometimes given commercially to chromate of baryta, a yellow insoluble powder used as a pigment. **1868** WATTS *Dict. Chem.* V. 937 The green ultramarine thus obtained is ground in a mill, and then roasted, with addition of sulphur, to convert it into blue ultramarine. **1879** *Cassell's Techn. Educ.* I. 221/2 The best imitation, or German ultramarine. *Ibid.* III. 20/1 The blue colour of artificial ultramarine. **1888** *Encycl. Brit.* XXIII. 722/1 Silica ultramarine is soda-ash ultramarine in whose preparation a quantity of finely divided silica.. has been added. *Ibid.*, Since 1873 the Nuremberg works have been producing four varieties of magnificently violet ultramarine.

2. = A. 3 b.

1695 DRYDEN tr. *Dufresnoy's Art Paint.* §354 Red Oker is one of the most heavy Colours... Ultramarine, or azure, is very light and a very sweet Colour. **1696** PATRICK *Comm. Exod.* xxv. (1697) 479 Mainonides expresses it the Colour of the Firmament; and Kimchi calls it ultramarine. **1860** TYNDALL *Glac.* I. iv. 34 The lake at some distance was of a deep ultramarine. **1868** W. S. O. tr. *Figuier's Ocean World* i. (1872) 13 The ocean, seen by reflection, presents a fine azure blue or ultramarine.

So †**ultrama'rinish** *a.*, = prec. A. 3. *Obs.*

1667 DENHAM *Direct. Paint.* I. iv, Use nothing but Ultra-Marinish Blue.

ultramicro- (ʌltrəˈmaɪkrəʊ), *prefix* and quasi-*adj. Chem.* [f. ULTRA- 2 + MICRO- 2 a, 8 b.] Formative element denoting chemical analysis or research which involves very minute quantities (of the order of a few microgrammes or less), as in ***ultramicroanalysis***, ***-analytical*** adj., ***-chemistry***, ***-chemical*** adj. Also used without a hyphen as an independent word.

1937 *Ann. Rev. Biochem.* VI. 90 The methods of capillary colorimetry are necessarily more difficult than the other ultramicro methods which have been discussed. **1940** *Ibid.* IX. 599 Drop analysis.—Ultramicrochemical methods have been advanced.. in regard to the number of constituents determinable. **1946** *Chem. Abstr.* XL. 6017 (*heading*) Ultramicroanalysis. III. A method for enriching copper by selective adsorption and for destroying organic matter in the determination of copper. **1946** *Chem. & Engin. News* XXIV. 1195/2 The field which embraces the chemical study of material on this minute scale of operation has been given the name 'ultramicrochemistry' by P. L. Kirk, a pioneer investigator in the field of quantitative chemistry on the microgram scale. **1946** *Nature* 31 Aug. 313/1 (*heading*) Ultra-micro methods in nuclear chemistry. **1962** H. HEATH in A. Pirie *Lens Metabolism Rel. Cataract* 365 Ultra-microanalytical methods have to be used to detect the last traces of ascorbic acid. **1971** *Analytical Biochem.* XLIV. 503 (*heading*) Quantitative ultramicroanalysis of amino acids in the form of their DNS-derivatives. **1973** *Biol. Abstr.* LVI. 1717/1 (*heading*) Ultramicrochemical methods for the analysis of tissues and cells of the inner ear. **1979** MA & RITTNER *Mod. Organic Elemental Analysis* xi. 366 Since it is now possible to carry out organic synthesis at the microgram level, the applications of ultramicro analytical methods become apparent.

ultra'microfiche. [ULTRA- 3.] = ULTRAFICHE.

1967 in WEBSTER Add. **1974** *Encycl. Brit. Macropædia* IX. 569/1 Film has not been used widely as a medium of primary distribution. One example is the Library of American Civilization, a retrospective collection on ultra-microfiche of the full original text of about 20,000 titles.

ultra'microscope. [f. ULTRA- 2 c + MICROSCOPE *sb.*, or a back-formation from next.] An optical microscope used to detect particles smaller than a wavelength of light by illuminating them at an angle, so that the light scattered by the particles (Tyndall scattering) can be observed against a dark background.

1906 *Jrnl. R. Microsc. Soc.* 366 The ultramicroscope is adapted to the determination of the identity and purity of oils. **1927** [see *polydispersity* s.v. POLYDISPERSE *a.*]. **1936** *Discovery* Nov. 347/2 The ultramicroscope, which by specially illuminating fine particles so that they themselves shine with reflected light, makes them perceptible through an ordinary microscope when they would not otherwise be so. **1974** *Sci. Amer.* May 88/2 We examined samples of oil in an ultramicroscope.

Hence **ultrami'croscopy**, the art or practice of using an ultramicroscope.

1906 *Jrnl. R. Microsc. Soc.* 366 (*heading*) Ultramicroscopy of oleosole. **1910** [see TYNDALL]. **1961** R. D. BAKER *Essential Path.* i. 7 Advances in histochemistry and ultramicroscopy are increasing the scope of pathologic anatomy as an investigative science.

ˌultramicro'scopic, *a.* Formerly also with hyphen. [f. ULTRA- 2 + MICROSCOPIC *a.*] Of such minute size as to be invisible or indeterminate under the ordinary light microscope; of or pertaining to the use of the ultramicroscope.

1870 TYNDALL *Heat* (ed. 4) xv. §754. 521 To make our precipitated particles grow from an infinitesimal and altogether ultra-microscopic size. **1905** *Daily News* 18 May 8 An optical appliance for making visible ultramicroscopic particles in fluids. **1932** *Nature* 2 Jan. 21/1 Optical ultra-microscopic examination of.. films. **1946** F. SCHNEIDER *Qualitative Organic Microanalysis* iv. 103 An instrument for estimating the refractive index of particles of ultramicroscopic size. **1958** *Times Lit. Suppl.* 17 Jan. 33/2 A description of this extraordinary population of all shapes and sizes from rabbits to ultramicroscopic organisms. **1978** *Nature* 22 June 610/1 Proteolytic enzymes.. are emitted through ultra-microscopic pores in the eggshell.

Hence **ˌultramicro'scopical** *a.*, in the same sense; **ˌultramicro'scopically** *adv.*

1904 *Jrnl. R. Microsc. Soc.* 711 There is a very disturbing adsorption effect of the glass planes on the ultra-microscopical particles. **1906** *Ibid.* 366 Fats and ethereal oils were treated with chlorides of the metals, and the products of reaction ultramicroscopically studied. **1929** A. S. C. LAWRENCE *Soap Films* v. 88 Microscopically, we see the actual particles; ultramicroscopically, we only see the light diffracted by particles themselves invisible. **1976** *Jrnl. Compar. Path.* LXXXVI. 516 Light and ultra-microscopical features of spontaneous glomerular lipoidosis are described. **1981** *Jrnl. Protozool.* XXVIII. 308 Thin sections of treated cells, examined ultramicroscopically, exhibited vacuolations.. and severe mitochondrial damage.

ultra'microtome. [f. ULTRA- 2 c + MICROTOME.] A microtome for cutting sections thin enough for electron microscopy (typically about 300 nanometres thick).

1953 *Jrnl. Electron Microsc.* I. 44 (*heading*) A simplified thermal expansion type ultramicrotome. **1966** D. G. BRANDON *Mod. Techniques Metallogr.* 92 A plate glass or diamond knife ultramicrotome has proved to be the most successful method available for producing thin sections of biological specimens for electron microscope examination, and serious attempts have been made to adapt the technique to metallurgical specimens. **1980** *Amer. Jrnl. Tropical Med. & Hygiene* XXIX. 775/1 Ultra-thin sections.. were cut with either glass knives or diamond knives on an ultramicrotome.

Hence **ultra'microtomed** *ppl. a.*, sectioned with an ultramicrotome; **ultrami'crotomy**, the practice or technique of using the ultra-microtome.

1949 *Science* 15 July 66/2 A promising new development in ultramicrotomy is presented. **1976** *Nature* 8 Apr. 513/1 Detailed examinations of a Georgia kaolinite using high resolution electron microscopy of ultramicrotomed section of the kaolinite mineral revealed not only the expected 7 Å (001) spacing, but also occasional 10 and 14 Å spacings. **1978** *Ibid.* 30 Mar. 433/1 Ultramicrotomy and ion beam thinning of films.. have provided greater information on film morphology and composition. **1982** *Electrochimica Acta* XXVII. 245 Electron microscopy.. of stripped anodic films and ultramicrotomed sections of the aluminium substrate and the anodic film have been used to examine directly the general film growth over the macroscopic metal surface.

ultramontane (ʌltrəˈmɒnteɪn), *sb.* and *a.* Also 7 **-an, -aine;** 7 **oltra-**. [ad. med.L. *ultrāmontān-us*, f. L. *ultrā* beyond + *mont-*, *mons* mountain (sc. the Alps). So F. *ultramontain* (1323; also OF. *outremontain, -an*), Sp. and Pg. *ultramontano*, It. *oltramontano*; G. *ultramontan*, Du. *-montaan*. Cf. TRAMONTANE *a.* and *sb.*]

A. *sb.* **1.** *Eccl. Hist.* **a.** A representative of the Roman Catholic Church north of the Alps as opposed to the ecclesiastics in Italy. Now *rare.*

1592 BACON *Obs. Libel* in *Resuscitatio* (1657) 147 Those that know any Thing of the Respects of Conclaves, know, that he is not Papable: First, because he is an Vltramontane, of which sort, there hath been none, these Fifty years. **1620** BRENT tr. *Sarpi's Hist. Council of Trent* v. 463 The Cardinals saw no other meanes to oppose these attemp[t]s, but by sending a great number of Italian Prelats, who, being vnited together, will overcome all the Vltramontans. **1651** *Life Father Sarpi* 157 The Oltramontanes.. did greedily reade and receive whatsoever came abroade. **1769** ROBERTSON *Chas. V*, III. ¶46 Perhaps the cardinals durst not venture to provoke the people of Rome.. by placing another *ultra-montane* on the papal throne. **1855** MILMAN *Lat. Chr.* VI. 10 He [Pope Urban VI] openly avowed his design to make so large a nomination [of cardinals] that the Italians should resume their ascendancy over the Ultramontanes.

b. A strong adherent or supporter of the Papal authority; an ultramontanist. (Cf. B. 1 b.)

In this connexion the point of view is that of France or other countries north of the Alps.

1829 *Dublin Even. Post* 3 Oct. 3/1 Supposed that the Catholic Clergy in Ireland were *Ultramontanes* of the same class. **1845** J. H. NEWMAN *Ess. Devel. Christian Doctrine* ii. 129 An unbeliever, as Gibbon, assumes one hypothesis, and an Ultra-montane, as Baronius, adopts another. **1865** E. B. PUSEY *Eirenicon* 326 The present Ultramontanes have apparently changed the old Ultramontane doctrine of the inerrancy of the Pope. **1873** SPENCER *Stud. Sociol.* xii. (1874) 299 To the Ultra-montane, holding that the temporal welfare no less than the eternal salvation of men depends on submission to the Church, it is incredible that Church-authority has but a transitory value. **1876** GLADSTONE in *Contemp. Rev.* June 4 The most violent Ultramontane, the most determined Agnostic, may alike make excellent Erastians. ? **1882** TENNYSON *In Mem. W. G. Ward* 4 My friend, the most unworldly of mankind, Most generous of all Ultramontanes, Ward.

2. An inhabitant or native of a country north of the Alps.

c **1618** MORYSON *Itin.* IV. (1903) 429 In Bologna.. the Vltramontans and Citramontans are each governed by their owne Statutes. **1626** C. POTTER tr. *Sarpi's Hist. Quarrels* 331 The Venetians.. resolued.. to make ready all their Troupes, Italians and Albans, with some others of the Vltramontans. **1696** PHILLIPS (ed. 5) s.v., The Italians call all on this side the Alpes, Ultra-montanes, or People living beyond the Alpes. **1730** A. GORDON *Maffei's Amphith.* 195 The Original was bought by some Ultramontane or another, and so published we know not by whom. **1851** GALLENGA *Italy* II. iii. 74 Schiller was, of course, the best understood and appreciated of all the ultramontanes.

3. (See quot.)

1875 *Dublin Mag.* Sept. 317 A group of troubadours in the most northerly districts of Provence, who were called 'Ultramontanes' by the poets of the plains south of the Garonne and the Cevennes.

B. *adj.* **1. a.** Of or belonging to, connected with, derived from, the countries or peoples lying to the north of the Alps.

c **1618** MORYSON *Itin.* IV. (1903) 427 The Rector Vltramontane (that is of the nations beyond the Alps) must be chosen by the former yeares Rectour and by the newe Counselors. **1687** *Lond. Gaz.* No. 2209/2 An Officer in the service of the Duke of Savoy, has agreed with the Senate to raise 600 Ultra-montaine Horse. **1829** SCOTT *Anne of G.* xxx, Your speech smacks of the northern, or Norman-French... But you are a minstrel, perhaps, from these ultramontane parts. **1832** tr. *Sismondi's Ital. Rep.* v. 128 Henry VII. departed from Pisa, commanding 2500 ultramontane and 1500 Italian cavalry. **1855** MILMAN *Lat. Chr.* VI. 12 The Ultramontane Cardinals would not tamely abandon a power which had given them.. the spiritual supremacy of the world for seventy years. *Ibid.* 19 The Pope's courtiers of ultramontane birth or opinions.

b. Of, belonging to, or characteristic of, the Italian party in the Church of Rome; holding or implying extreme views in favour of the papal authority. (Cf. A. 1 b.)

1728 CHAMBERS *Cycl.* s.v. *Tramontan*, The French Lawyers give the same Title of.. Ultramontane Doctors to the Italian Canonists.. who go upon Rules and Maxims, too favourable to the Court of Rome. **1819** HELEN M. WILLIAMS *Lett. France* 100 Nations are tired of those ultra-montane mysteries. **1846** G. OLIVER *Monast. Dioec. Exon.* 424 *note*, A papal bull settled the question respecting the capacity of the mendicant orders to purchase in a manner eminently ultramontane. **1873–4** DIXON *Two Queens* XIII. v. III. 27 The ultra-montane school of canonists asserted, that a pope had power to publish such an act.

transf. **1899** T. G. SELBY *Unheeding God* xi. 201 Some of his [Darwin's] most fervent disciples no longer adopt that ultramontane attitude.

2. In general sense: Situated beyond, belonging to the other side of, the mountains.

1786 JEFFERSON *Writ.* (1859) I. 587 How may the ultra-montane territory be disposed of so as to produce the greatest.. benefit to the inhabitants of the maritime States of the Union? **1809** A. HENRY *Trav.* 325 They were in possession of several ultramontane prisoners, two of whom we purchased.

ultramontanism (ʌltrəˈmɒntənɪz(ə)m). [ad. F. *ultramontanisme* (18th c.), = Sp., Pg. *ultramontanismo*: see prec. and -ISM.] The principles and practice of the ultramontane party in the Church of Rome; the doctrine of absolute papal supremacy.

1827 *Westm. Rev.* Jan. 80 That what he calls ultramontanism may be maintained.. to be an orthodox tenet of the Catholic church. **1854** LD. HOUGHTON in T. W. Reid *Life* (1891) I. xi. 498 Cullen's ultramontaism is doing good in denationalising the priesthood. **1878** DOWDEN *Stud. Lit.* 323 Ultramontanism in its strictest form was the creed of Lamennais.

ultra'montanist. [Cf. prec. and -IST.]

1. An adherent of ultramontane principles and doctrines; a supporter of the absolute supremacy of the Pope.

1826 SOUTHEY *Vind. Eccl. Angl.* 3 The English Romanists will proudly acknowledge you for their advocate (whatever may be thought by the Ultra-Montanists), as one in whose hands their cause will lose nothing in strength. **1839** HALLAM *Hist. Lit.* III. ii. §12 This opposition to the extreme line of the ultra-montanists might be well compatible with a tendency towards much that the reformers had denounced. **1885** W. W. ROBERTS *Pontif. Decrees* Introd. 12 How can the

Ultramontanist meet the mistake that Rome made in condemning heliocentricism?
attrib. **1839** *Fraser's Mag.* XIX. 274 This paper..is an ultra-montanist paper. **1884** *Encycl. Brit.* XVII. 754/2 This bold proclamation of Ultramontanist doctrine.

2. = ULTRAMONTANE *sb.* 1 a. *rare*$^{-1}$.
1855 MILMAN *Lat. Chr.* VI. 13 As Ultramontanists it was their interest, their inclination, to espouse the Ultramontane cause.

ultra'montanizing, *vbl. sb.* [Cf. prec. and -IZE.] The process of making ultramontane in character.
1893 *Dublin Rev.* Apr. 250 The Romanising or Ultramontanising of English worship, as it would be called in our days.

ultramundane (ʌltrə'mʌndeɪn), *sb.* and *a.* [ad. late L. *ultrāmundānus*, f. *ultrā* beyond + *mundus* the world. Cf. F. *ultramondain*, Sp. *ultra-*, It. *oltramundano*.]

†**A.** *sb. pl.* Matters lying outside the physical world; metaphysics. *Obs.*$^{-1}$
1549 CHALONER *Erasm. on Folly* M ij, He had spent whole xxxvi yeeres togethers in studiyng the Phisicals and Vltramundans of Duns and Aristotle.

B. *adj.* Lying beyond or outside of the world; of or belonging to things beyond the limits of the solar system.
1656 BLOUNT *Glossogr.*, *Ultramundane*,..supercelestial, beyond or above the sky. Dr. Charl. **1665** BOYLE *Occas. Refl.*, *Occas. Medit.* 35 A Faculty.. by whose help the restless mind..roves about in the ultra-mundane spaces, and considers how farr they reach. **1697** J. SERGEANT *Solid Philos.* 180 They will needs conceit there is some Ultramundane kind of Thing existent out of the world. **1807** *Edin. Rev.* X. 147 The particles by which this effect is brought about, are called by Le Sage..the ultramundane atoms. **1845** J. H. NEWMAN in Ward *Life* (1912) iii. I. 80 He dies a Pantheist denying that there is an Ultramundane God. **1876** P. G. TAIT *Rec. Adv. Phys. Sci.* (1885) 368 The very ingenious idea of the ultra-mundane corpuscles, the outcome of the lifework of Le Sage.

ultra-'short, *a.* Also **ultrashort.** [ULTRA- 3.]

a. *Radio.* Applied to radio waves significantly shorter than the usual 'short waves': in mod. use, shorter than 10 metres, corresponding to a frequency greater than 30 MHz (i.e. in the VHF range).
1926 E. V. APPLETON in *Proc. Cambridge Philos. Soc.* XXIII. 155 (*heading*) On the diurnal variation of ultra-short wave wireless transmission. [*Note*] The term 'ultra-short' is here applied to wave-lengths less than the critical band indicated by the magneto-ionic theory (i.e. about 200 meters). It seems desirable, for historical reasons, to retain the term 'short waves' for the broadcasting wave-lengths 200–600 metres. **1935** *Discovery* Sept. 278/1 A difficulty is.. the limited range of these ultra-short wave-lengths, as we are dependent upon the direct waves propagated more or less parallel to the earth's surface. **1947** *Nature* 4 Jan. 16/1 The electrical interference from motor-car ignition systems ..is a serious factor in the reception of ultra-short waves. **1974** *Radio Engin. & Electronic Physics* Dec. 20 (*heading*) Multiple diffractor amplification of ultrashort waves.

b. *gen.* Extremely short (in length or duration).
1962 R. H. SMYTHE *Anat. Dog Breeding* 29 An ultra-short loin. **1975** *Bio Systems* VII. 45 Accordingly, we may introduce an ultrashort time scale. **1977** *Jrnl. R. Soc. Arts* CXXV. 766/1 The same lasers can be used to generate ultrashort light pulses.

ultrasonic (ʌltrə'sɒnɪk), *a.* [f. ULTRA- 2 + SONIC *a.*] **1. a.** The more usual synonym of SUPERSONIC *a.* 1.
1923 *Proc. & Trans. R. Soc. Canada* XVII. III. 145 The wave-lengths of ultra-sonic waves are very convenient for experiment. **1926** *Encycl. Brit.* III. 592/1 The utilisation of ultrasonic waves by Professor Langevin..in connection with deep-sea sounding. **1928** *Observer* 30 Dec. 3/6 This was the first occasion in this country on which the 'ultrasonic' waves have been shown to an audience. **1938, 1948** [see HYPERSONIC *a.* 1]. **1957** *New Scientist* 9 May 26/3 Owing to the restricted frequency response of the human ear, those organisms which produce ultra-sonic sounds, as do many insects and bats, for example, have in particular been thought of as 'dumb'. **1976** R. DAWKINS *Selfish Gene* iv. 67 The..song of the humpback whale, with..its frequencies spanning the whole of human hearing from subsonic rumblings to ultrasonic squeaks. **1985** *Sunday Times* 27 Jan. 80/8 An ultrasonic beam passed through liquid generates bubbles which act as a cleansing agent.

b. Employing or operated by sound waves or vibrations having a frequency above the range of human hearing (i.e greater than 15–20 kHz); used esp. with reference to devices and techniques which make use of the reflected echo of an ultrasound pulse.
1923 *Proc. & Trans. R. Soc. Canada* XVII. III. 142 Two ultra-sonic generators..were placed facing one another, 60 cms. apart, in a large tank of water. **1935** [see REFLECTOMETER]. **1949** A. R. WEYL *Guided Missiles* 25 Photo-electric, magnetic, acoustic (ultra-sonic) and other methods have been successfully used for proximity fuses. **1961** *Lancet* 30 Sept. 750/1 Ultrasonic methods have been described for the detection of intra-abdominal masses, breast tumours, [etc.]. **1976** *Offshore Platforms & Pipelining* 174/1 Ultrasonic inspection followed the completion of the welds.

2. Designating speeds above that of sound; supersonic. *rare*$^{-1}$.
1942 [see INFRASONIC *a.* 2].

Hence **ultra'sonically** *adv.*, by means of ultrasound.
1955 *Sci. News Let.* 26 Mar. 206/3 Ultrasonically treated honey..showed no signs of crystallizing. **1968** *Amer. Mineralogist* LIII. 1558 Samples of the ash were cleaned ultrasonically. **1974** *Nature* 2 Aug. 410/2 Electrodeposition in an ultrasonically agitated solution.

ultrasonication (ˌʌltrəsɒnɪ'keɪʃən). [f. ULTRA- 2 c + SONICATION.] = *sonication* s.v. SONICATE *sb.* and *v.*
1965 *Dissertation Abstr.* XXV. 4366/1 Ultrasonication causes the complete shedding of the embryonic periderm leaving a residual layer of originally basal cells. **1979** *Chem. & Physics of Lipids* XXIV. 257 The solubility of the three steroid hormones..was measured after shaking and ultrasonication.

So **ultra'sonicate** *v. trans.* = SONICATE *v.*; **ultra'sonicated** *ppl. a.*
1969 *Bot. Mag.* (Tokyo) LXXXII. 162 (*heading*) Electron microscopy of replicas from ultrasonicated *Chara* oosporangial walls. **1974** P. PULIDO in K. Elliott et al. *Trypanosomiasis & Leishmaniasis* (Ciba Symp. No. 20) 280 Lyophilized *T. cruzi* was resuspended in buffer and ultrasonicated. **1980** *Exper. Parasitol.* L. 360/1 Two milliliters of the suspension was ultrasonicated on ice.

ultrasonics (ʌltrə'sɒnɪks), *sb. pl.* [f. ULTRASONIC *a.*: see -IC 2.] **a.** Ultrasonic waves; ultrasound.
1924 *Ann. Rep. Canadian Nat. Research Council* 23 Ultra Sonics are sound vibrations of a pitch higher than those which are audible. **1931** *Nature* 21 Feb. 284/2 Prof. F. L. Hopwood discussed ultra-sonics or inaudible sounds. **1957** A. C. CLARKE *Deep Range* i. 10 Sub 5 was still close enough to the mother ship for radio to work, but before long he'd have to switch to the ultrasonics. **1960** *New Biol.* XXXI. 32 The bacteria which have been treated by ultrasonics.. cannot multiply any more. **1972** R. E. ORNSTEIN *Psychol. of Consciousness* (1975) ii. 19 We normally consider that our senses are the 'windows' to the world... But such a view.. is not entirely true, for a primary function of sensory systems taken as a whole is to discard 'irrelevant' information, such as X-rays, infrared radiation, or ultrasonics.

b. The branch of science and technology concerned with the study and use of ultrasonic waves. Const. as *sing.*
1940 [see ASDIC]. **1959** *Sunday Times* 21 June 3/2 Ultrasonics has..been established for a number of years in submarine detection, underwater signalling, echo-sounding, fish location, flaw detection in metals and in many fields of industrial measurement and control. **1977** *Time* 28 Nov. 56/2 Since the original development of the technique for cardiology in the 1950s, ultrasonics has been used to explore other areas of the body, notably, the developing fetus in the mother's uterus.

ultrasonography (ʌltrəsəʊ'nɒgrəfɪ). *Med.* [f. ULTRA- (in *ultrasound*) + SONO- + -GRAPHY.] A technique which makes use of echoes of ultrasound pulses to delineate objects or areas of different density within the body, esp. for diagnostic purposes.
1960 *Arch. Ophthalmol.* LXIV. 180/1 Ultrasonography is an invaluable aid in the diagnosis and management of orbital disease because it can visualize and localize the position of orbital lesions when all other tests are negative. **1967** *New Scientist* 26 Jan. 195/2 Ultrasonography..is capable of detecting pregnancy even before a woman's urine test becomes positive. **1980** *Brit. Med. Jrnl.* 29 Mar. 940/2 Serum luteinising hormone concentrations and serial ovarian ultrasonography are helpful screening procedures.

So **ultra'sonogram**, an image obtained by ultrasonography; **ultra'sonograph**, an apparatus for producing ultrasonograms. Also **ultraso'nographer**, one who specializes in ultrasonography.
1958 *Arch. Ophthalmol.* LX. 266/2 The ultrasonogram represents a horizontal section, or planigram, through a level of the eye. **1975** *Proc. 2nd European Congr. Ultrasonics in Medicine* 129 Ultrasonographs employed to visualize internal eye structures use focusing systems which concentrate the ultrasonic beam into a small area. **1975** *Daily Tel.* (Colour Suppl.) 7 Feb. 21/1 Now the second generation of ultra-sonographs—some capable of using a computer to 'freeze' the movement of a single heartbeat—are extending the boundaries of medical knowledge. **1979** *Brit. Med. Jrnl.* 13 Oct. 934/2 They are not in conflict with the ultrasonographers' longitudinal data. **1981** *Daily Tel.* 24 Apr. 3/3 Hydrocephalus occurs in about two of every 1,000 babies. With the use of ultra-sonograms..doctors can usually detect the condition while the foetus is developing.

ultrasound ('ʌltrəsaʊnd). [f. ULTRA- 2 c + SOUND *sb.*[3]] Sound waves or vibrations with frequencies greater than those audible to the human ear, or greater than 20,000 Hz; also, ultrasonic techniques.
1923 *Proc. & Trans. R. Soc. Canada* XVII. III. 143 When the electrical exciting sources were alternating in potential, the tonic trains of ultra-sound so produced—120 pulses per second—could be heard in the stethoscope. **1936** *Jrnl. R. Aeronaut. Soc.* XL. 25 Ultra-sound waves are generated by a quartz oscillator arc propagated through a surrounding liquid medium. **1953** J. Y. COUSTEAU *Silent World* 104 Are porpoises equipped with sonic or ultra-sound apparatus by which their squeaks give them the feel of unseen bottom topography? **1958** *Oxford Mail* 30 June 4/4 Some firms now use ultrasound to detect flaws in metal. **1968** *New Scientist* 16 May 347/1 The moth's sensitivity to ultrasound may have other uses. **1984** *Times* 16 Nov. 12/4 Any woman who is worried about malformations would be subject to a detailed ultrasound scan.

ultrastable (ʌltrə'steɪb(ə)l), *a.* [f. ULTRA- 3 + STABLE *a.*] Stable against all subsequent disturbances, even those not taken into account in the design of the system. Hence **ultrasta'bility**.
1952 W. R. ASHBY *Design for Brain* viii. 91 This process is most clearly shown in what I shall call an ultra-stable system: one that is absolute and contains step-functions in a sufficiently large number for us to be able to ignore the finiteness of the number. *Ibid.*, The principle of ultrastability will be stated formally: an ultra-stable system acts selectively towards the fields of the main variables, rejecting those that lead the representative point to a critical state but retaining those that do not. **1967** R. WHITEHEAD in Wills & Yearsley *Handbk. Management Technol.* 66 Cybernetics seeks to produce an ultra-stable solution between an organism and its environment. *Ibid.*, If self-regulation and ultra-stability are desirable things..then we must be prepared to learn from the systems that exhibit them. **1970** G. ORDISH tr. *R. Chauvin's World of Ants* 203 What do we mean here by the word 'adaptation'? It should mean a series of successive changes of tactics which only stop, as Ashby says, when the system reaches an 'ultrastable' state within the limits set by the physiology of the individuals in question. **1976** *Listener* 24 June 821/4 Such thought..would itself become an historical system—in the modern jargon, an 'ultra-stable' system, one which could take its own corrective action when things went wrong.

'ultraˌstructure. [f. ULTRA- 2 + STRUCTURE *sb.*] Structure of biological material that is visible only under greater magnification than can be obtained with optical microscopy.
1939 F. O. SCHMITT in *Physiol. Rev.* XIX. 270 The term ultrastructure as used in this review denotes the submicroscopic organization of cellular and tissue components. **1948** *New Biol.* V. 34 Experiments with the centrifuge and micromanipulator show..that organised development can be interfered with by breaking up this ultrastructure, but as we have seen, it often reforms itself after such a breakdown. **1970** *Jrnl. Neurosurg.* XXXII. 142/2 The ultrastructure of the capillaries in human malignant brain tumors has been studied. **1977** J. L. HARPER *Population Biol. Plants* v. 131 A seed that is going to germinate may begin to show marked changes in the ultrastructure of its cells within 30 min of welting.

Hence **ultra'structural** *a.*, of or pertaining to ultrastructure; **ultra'structurally** *adv.*, with regard to ultrastructure.
1939 *Physiol. Rev.* XIX. 270 To learn the details of the ultrastructural organization of such systems it is necessary to know the chemical composition and the physical and chemical properties of the molecules which compose the system. **1971** *Nature* 2 Apr. 334/2 Ultrastructurally, as well as by light microscopy, the human parafollicular cells were similar to those of other mammals. **1975** *Ibid.* 7 Aug. 459/3 Ultrastructurally, the size (diameter 600 ± 150 Å), but not the number, of nuclear pores is remarkably constant in all eukaryotic cells. **1977** *Proc. R. Soc. Med.* LXX. 670/2 The anatomical, histological, ultrastructural and physiological aspects of normal peripheral nerves.

Ultrasuede ('ʌltrəsweɪd). *U.S.* Also **ultrasuede.** [f. ULTRA- + SUEDE.] A proprietary name for a synthetic non-woven fabric resembling suede. Also as *sb.*, a garment made of this.
1973 *Official Gaz.* (U.S. Patent Office) 13 Mar. TM 96/2 Spring Mills, Inc., Fort Mill, S.C... *Ultrasuede.* For non-woven suede-like fabrics... First use Nov. 24, 1971. **1974** [see MAN-MADE *a.*]. **1976** *National Observer* (U.S.) 2 Oct. 16/1 Rich chocolate-brown carpet, white ultrasuede couch, and..two pink ultrasuede armchairs. **1977** *Detroit Free Press* 11 Dec. 22-A/2 She dressed in Von Furstenberg shirtwaists and Halston ultrasuedes. **1981** A. CROSS *Death in Faculty* i. 8 Her suit, ultra-suede, was worn over a turtleneck knit.

ultra'thin, *a.* Also **ultra-thin.** [f. ULTRA- 3 + THIN *a.*] Extremely thin; *spec.* in *Biol.*, applied to a section cut with an ultramicrotome.
1949 *Science* 15 July 68/2 The new technique provides an inexpensive, practical method for producing ultrathin sections of tissue in almost a routine fashion. **1961** *Technology* Feb. 52/4 Fabrics treated with an ultrathin coating of a polyamide..are said to retain the soft texture of wool, and yet may be washed repeatedly without shrinking. **1962** *Sci. Survey* III. 164 These ultra-thin sections are today about 250 times thinner than the conventional sections used in light microscopy. **1969** *New Scientist* 16 Oct. 131/2 The new ultrathin transistor is particularly important for uhf applications. **1976** *Ann. Rev. Microbiol.* XXX. 116 (*caption*) Ultrathin section of cell from a diseased mushroom.

ultraviolation (ˌʌltrəvaɪə'leɪʃən). *slang.* [Humorous blend of ULTRAVIOLET *a.* and *sb.* and VIOLATION.] Irradiation with ultraviolet light. So **ultra'violate** *v. trans.*
1978 *Oxf. Univ. Gaz.* 23 Oct. Suppl. I. 167 (*heading*) Why does yeast die from ultra-violation? **1979** *Amer. Speech* LIV. 119 Ultraviolation. William J. Payne tells us that, when cells are subjected to ultraviolet radiation (for mutagenesis), they are said to have been ultraviolated. Editors..strike the term from papers submitted for publication, but scientists frequently use it in conversation. **1984** *New Scientist* 3 May 46/1 At Stanford University..medical scientists no longer expose cells to UV light... They prefer to ultraviolate them.

ultra'violet, *a.* and *sb.* Also with hyphen. [f. ULTRA- 1 c + VIOLET *sb.*[1]] **A.** *adj.* **1.** Lying beyond the violet end of the visible spectrum: the epithet of electromagnetic radiation (and of the part of the spectrum containing it) which has a wavelength shorter than that of violet light (about 420 nm.) and (in modern use) no shorter than that of the longest X-rays (of the order of 4 to 40 nm.).

1840 [see LAVENDER *a.* 2]. **1870** J. TYNDALL *Nine Lect. Light* 36 As regards the ultra-violet rays; when they are permitted to fall upon certain substances.. they render the substance luminous. **1875** tr. *Vogel's Chem. Light* vii. 60 We name the invisible tones of colour above violet ultra-violet, and those beyond red ultra-red. **1887** *Encycl. Brit.* XXII. 375/2 The remarkable series of ultra-violet lines.. in the spectra of some stars. **1904** *Sci. Siftings* 12 Mar. 320/2 These ultra-violet rays.. are most effective in the treatment of such diseases as tuberculosis of the skin, *i.e.*, lupus. **1928** GALSWORTHY *Swan Song* I. xi. 84 They talk about these ultra-violet rays. Plain sunshine used to be good enough. **1935** *Discovery* Aug. 225/1 Those physical agents which have been found of service in the treatment of various diseases—such agents as ultra-violet and infra-red radiation. **1947** *Sci. News* IV. 43 Ultra-violet light is a strong bleacher. **1955** *Times* 2 July 7/7 Ultra-violet radiation is useful, both to the naked eye and by photography, to determine whether varnish has perished. **1979** T. B. AKRILL et al. *Physics* xviii. 248/1 The mercury vapour spectrum also includes a considerable amount of ultra-violet radiation.

2. a. Involving, producing, or pertaining to ultraviolet radiation or its use; ***ultraviolet catastrophe***, an indefinite increase that the Rayleigh-Jeans law predicts should occur in the radiation emitted by a black body at successively shorter wavelengths (where the law in fact becomes invalid).

1922 [see LAVENDER *a.* 2]. **1934** *Discovery* May 138/1 In the detection of forgery, the deciphering of illegible or faded documents, over-writing and the like.. ultra-violet photography is the most useful process to employ. **1935** J. DOUGALL tr. *Born's Atomic Physics* vii. 189 We have here what is called the 'ultra-violet catastrophe'. **1958** *New Biol.* XXVII. 12 The conclusion reached on a chemical basis regarding the presence of lignin has been confirmed using the ultra-violet microscope for spectro-micrographic purposes. **1966** M. JAMMER *Conceptual Devel. Quantum Mech.* i. 17 A situation which was later, following Ehrenfest, referred to as the 'ultraviolet catastrophe'. [*Note*] P. Ehrenfest,.. *Annalen der Physik* 36, 91–118 (1911). The fourth chapter of this paper is entitled 'Die Vermeidung der Rayleigh-Jeans-Katastrophe im Ultravioletten', where the term 'ultraviolet catastrophe' appeared for the first time. **1974** *Daily Tel.* 17 Jan. 17/6 An ultra-violet photograph taken from an Aerobee rocket.. has revealed the development of a huge ball of hydrogen. **1976** *Progress in Sci. Culture* (E. Majorana Centre) Spring 20 The paradox is the ultra-violet catastrophe of the theory of black-body radiation, which was predicted on the basis of classical statistical mechanics and Maxwell's theory of radiation.

b. Sensitive to ultraviolet radiation.

1940 *Chambers's Techn. Dict.* 875/2 Ultra-violet cell. **1969** *Rev. Sci. Instruments* XL. 311 (*heading*) A secondary standard vacuum ultraviolet detector. **1975** J. TAYLOR *Superminds* iii. 52 At this point the primitive ultra-violet detector was used.

B. *ellipt.* as *sb.* The ultraviolet part of the spectrum; ***near, far ultraviolet***, the part close to, or far from, the visible spectrum.

1887 *Encycl. Brit.* XXII. 375/2 A number of lines in the ultra-violet. **1931** *Discovery* Mar. 86/2 The possibility is discussed of extending the study of the spectrum of stars into the regions of the ultra-violet. **1954** *Jrnl. Amer. Chem. Soc.* LXXVI. 3847/1 Samples of barium and calcium titanates were sealed in quartz tubes containing phosphorus pentoxide for 72 hours and then exposed to ultraviolet. **1962** L. S. SASIENI *Optical Dispensing* xiii. 326 In snow glare protection is required against the ultra-violet. **1974** *Nature* 4 Jan. 44/1 At the molecular level, the effects of far-ultraviolet (<300nm) and near-ultraviolet (300 to 420nm) on biological systems are quite different.

†ultrice. *Obs.*$^{-1}$ [a. OF. *ultrice*, ad. L. *ultrīcem*, *ultrix*, fem. of *ultor* avenger.] A female avenger.

1490 CAXTON *Eneydos* xxvii. 99 O cruelle vltryces, wycked vengeresses, Furyes infernalle & Iusticers of helle.

ultro-mo'tivity. *rare*$^{-1}$. [f. L. *ultrō* (see next) + MOTIVITY.] Capability of spontaneous movement.

1854 HICKOK *Sci. Mind* 278 Pure spontaneity has.. merely a simple ultro-motivity to its object.

ultroneous (ʌl'trəʊnɪəs), *a.* [f. L. *ultrōne-us*, f. *ultrō* of one's own accord, voluntarily. Cf. Sp., Pg., It. *ultroneo*.] Made, offered, etc., of one's own accord; spontaneous, voluntary.

1637 GILLESPIE *Eng. Pop. Cerem.* II. ix. 43 This Argument of Scandall, the Pastor can make good against the Fornicator, out of his owne ultroneous and unrequired concession of the indifferency of Fornication. **1657** J. WATTS *Vind. Ch. Eng.* 144 A superiour may do an ultroneous honour, if he will, to his inferior. **1817** J. FERGUSSON *Rep. Consist. Crt. Scotl.* 257 *note*, Testimony given by a witness not cited is liable to objection, as ultroneous. **1852** SIR W. HAMILTON *Discuss.* (1853) App. iii. 811 The exercise of the student in the University classes, should be partly exigible, partly ultroneous. **1894** BRETT in *19th Cent.* June 914 That worthy body of doctrinaires were responsible for the ultroneous rule of Palmerston.

b. *Sc. Law.* Of witnesses: (see quots.).

1824 G. TAIT *On Evidence* 379 Witnesses.. if they come into Court.. without being cited.. are called ultroneous witnesses. **1838** W. BELL *Dict. Law. Scot.* 371 Ultroneous witnesses, *i.e.* witnesses who offer their testimony without being regularly cited, were formerly inadmissable; but this objection seems now only to affect their credibility.

ul'troneously, *adv.* [f. prec. + -LY[2].] Of one's own accord; spontaneously, voluntarily.

1627 W. SCLATER *Exp. 2 Thess.* (1629) 75 Is it warrantable vltroneously to offer our selues to Martyrdome? **1657** REEVE *God's Plea* 28 He [God] doth love himselfe necessarily, but all other things ultroneously. **1847** SIR W. HAMILTON *Let. to De Morgan* 30 In the second, (what you omit to mention,) copies were through your friend Dr. —— ultroneously proffered. **1883** *Saturday Review* 21 July 65 Mr. Gladstone and his colleagues wantonly, ultroneously,.. have themselves interpreted and settled a.. complicated point.

ul'troneousness. *rare.* [f. as prec. + -NESS.] Voluntary action; spontaneity.

1623 W. SCLATER *Tythes* f 2 b, Law is not here opposed to no Law, or iniunction to vltroneousnesse of Tything. **1858–61** J. BROWN *Horae Subs.* (1863) 222 The law of personality, of ultroneousness, of free will, that which in a great measure makes us what we are.

‖**ulu**[1] ('u:lu:). Also oo(d)loo. [Eskimo.] An Eskimo woman's knife having a crescent-shaped blade.

1864 C. F. HALL *Life with Esquimaux* I. 291 One of the Innuit women slit them down with her oodloo till they did fit. **1940** *Beaver* (Winnipeg) Mar. 24 The women then take their semicircular knives or 'ooloos', and flench the hide from the blubber. **1958** W. WILLETTS *Chinese Art* I. ii. 77 They [*sc.* knives] are especially common in the North-western Eskimo area, where they occur as the 'woman's knife' or *ulu*, mounted in wood or ivory handles. **1964** *Nat. Geogr. Mag.* May 718/2 Some Eskimo women want their favourite ulu to be buried with them. **1972** S. BURNFORD *One Woman's Arctic* (1973) ii. 35 Tabitha.. hacked off some bannock with her round, razor-sharp ooloo.

‖**ulu**[2] ('u:lu:). Also Ulu. [Malay (*h*)*ulu* head, upper part.] The upstream, interior part of Malaya; the Malayan jungle.

1878 F. MCNAIR *Perak & Malays* xxxv. 424 Futreu surveys will confirm this description of the Ulu—interior, or up-stream. **1936** R. H. BRUCE LOCKHART *Return to Malaya* II. iii. 108 In my time every healthy young man preferred the 'ulu' to the town, not merely because he found the life more attractive in itself, but also because it offered greater chances for promotion. **1963** J. KIRKUP *Tropic Temper* 106 In the ulu or deep jungle country, no Chinese would ever dare to look at a Malay girl. **1977** *Borneo Bull.* 7 May 4/3 The ulu people may now be less willing to flock into a town which can cope only primitively with big numbers of visitors.

†ululable, *a. Obs.*$^{-0}$ [ad. L. (post-classical) *ululābilis*.] 'Howling, yelling' (Bailey, 1721).

ululance ('ʌljʊləns). *rare*$^{-1}$. [f. as ULULANT *a.*: see -ANCE.] Ululation.

1951 W. FAULKNER *Requiem for Nun* III. 244 At last, the last of silence too: the county's hollow inverted air one resonant boom and ululance of radio.

ululant ('ʌljʊlənt, 'ju:l-), *a.* [a. L. *ululant-*, *ululans*, pres. pple. of *ululāre*: see next.]

1. Having the character of ululation.

1868 G. MACDONALD *R. Falconer* xxx, He burst out laughing, after a doubtful and ululant fashion. **1901** EDITH RICKERT in *Academy* 16 Mar. 236/2 An ululant tumult, that bounds and rebounds.

2. Ululating, howling.

1896 A. LANG *Walton's Angler* Introd. p. xli, They were better than Quakers, naked and ululant.

ululate ('ʌljʊleɪt, 'ju:l-), *v.* [f. L. *ululāt-*, ppl. stem of *ululāre* (hence It. *ululare*, Sp., Pg., Pr. *ulular*, Fr. *ululer*), of imitative origin: cf. *ulula* screech-owl.] *intr.* To howl or wail; to lament loudly.

1623 COCKERAM, *Vlulate*, to howle like a dog or wolfe. **1638** SIR T. HERBERT *Trav.* (ed. 2) 124 Troopes of Jackalls .. all the while ululating and in offensive noises barking and ecchoing out their sacriledge. **1826** *Lancet* 59 Poor Sir Peter ululates plaintively as an Irish Benshee over the fate of his College. **1832** GEN. P. THOMPSON *Exerc.* (1842) II. 321 Men must have been sadly beaten, when they ululate in this sort. **1893** 'Q' (QUILLER COUCH) *Delect. Duchy* 171 The widow so often interrupted the service to ululate that the town clock had struck four when I hurried back.

Hence **'ululating** *ppl. a.*

1894 N. BROOKS *Tales Maine Coast* 8 Nance Pegg knew the times and seasons of the ululating and melancholy loon.

ululation (ʌljʊ'leɪʃən, 'ju:l-). [ad. L. *ululātiōn-*, *ululātio*, noun of action f. *ululāre*: see prec. So obs. F. *ululation*, *-acion*.]

1. A howl or wail; a cry of lamentation.

1599 R. LINCHE *Fount. Anc. Fiction* O j b, Scilla,.. with her vncouth and lowd barking and howling, make[s] the waters thereabout resound with an incredible report and eccho of such her strange vlulations. **1606** DEKKER *Newes fr. Hell* Wks. (Grosart) II. 130 What tongue is able to relate the grones and vlulations of a wretch so distressed? **1654** R. CODRINGTON tr. *Iustine* XII. 191 They did by instinct break forth into the sacred ululations of the God. **1689** R. COX *Hibernia Angl.* I. *Appar.* 12, They bury their Dead with great Ululations or *Allelews*. **1812** COLMAN *Poet. Vagaries, Lady of Wreck* xxxi, Again the horns were fill'd by all, And ululations shook the Hall. **1827–39** DE QUINCEY *Murder* Postscr., Wks. 1854 IV. 100 The ululation of vengeance which ascended instantaneously from the individual street. **1856** F. E. PAGET *Owlet of Owlst.* 169 Master Maximilian checked his ululations. **1881** *Blackw. Mag.* Sept. 341 The women.. burst forth in a shrill scream, with a quaver or ululation resembling the note of the screech-owl.

2. The action of howling or wailing.

?**1799** COLERIDGE *Mahomet* 11 The people with mad shouts Thundering now, and now with saddest ululation Flew. **1848** LOWELL *Biglow P.* Ser. I. ix. Introd., The laborers.. are heard to shout from behind the scenes in a singular tone resembling ululation. **1886** SWINBURNE *Misc.* 98 Who uttered in public or in private such high-pitched notes of ululation and imprecation.

†'ululative, *a. Obs.*$^{-1}$ [See ULULATE *v.* and -ATIVE.] Wailing, lamenting.

1490 CAXTON *Eneydos* xxvii. 99 Lady & mastresse of alle artes & scyences magyques, ryght often called wyth voyces vlulatyue,.. in tyme of nyght obscure.

ululatory (ʌlju:'leɪtərɪ, 'ju:l-), *a.* [Cf. prec. and -ATORY.] = ULULANT *ppl. a.*

1831 *Fraser's Mag.* IV. 931 The matutinal ululatory summons of the dairy-maid. **1890** *Sat. Rev.* 13 Sept. 326/1 The overworked and ululatory brains ['that called out so loudly for rest'].

ulu'lu. Also u-lu-lu, ulalu, ul-ul-loo, ululalu. [Imitative. Cf. dial. *whillilew*, *whillaloo*, Ir. Gael. *uileliúgh*.] A wailing cry; a wail of lamentation.

1834 *Knickerbocker* IV. 15 Well may they raise the ul-ul-loo. **1854** THOREAU *Walden, Sounds* (1884) 135 When other birds are still the screech owls take up the strain, like mourning women their ancient u-lu-lu. *a* **1873** MRS. SPOFFORD in *Casquet of Lit.* (1873) IV. 13/2, I raised such a ululu that presently mother took me in hand again severely. **1889** W. B. YEATS *Wanderings of Oisin* 80, I must away by wood and sea And lift an ulalu forlorn And fling my laughter to the sun. *a* **1955** W. STEVENS *Opus Posthumous* (1957) 26 'Olu' the eunuchs cried. 'Ululalu.'

‖**ulus** ('u:lu:s). Also †Oolooss. [Turk.] In Afghanistan, a tribe.

1815 M. ELPHINSTONE *Caubul* II. ii. 159 The name of Oolooss is applied either to a whole tribe, or to one of these independent branches. The word seems to mean a clanish commonwealth. **1902** *East India (N.-W. Frontier) Mahsud-Waziri Operations* 125 in *Parl. Papers* (Cd. 1177) LXXI. 649 In return for the allowances, both Maliks and Levies are expected to serve Government, to control the body of the clansmen, the 'ulus', and to arrange that individual offenders are surrendered for trial. **1953** O. CAROE *Soviet Empire* iii. 35 The Mongol *ulus* or hordes.

‖**Ulva** ('ʌlvə). *Bot.* [L. *ulva* sedge.] An alga forming the typical genus of the order *Ulvaceæ*; the laver or sea-lettuce.

1706 PHILLIPS (ed. Kersey), *Ulva*, Reet, or Weed of the Sea, Sea-grass; also Weeds growing in Pools, or standing Waters. **1753** *Chambers' Cycl.* Suppl. s.v., Bauhine makes the Ulva a purple sea-moss allied to the alga. **1850** MISS PRATT *Comm. Things of Sea-side* ii. 160 The Ulvæ, or Lavers, are flat green leaves, very transparent, and easily torn, and when laid on paper are scarcely thicker than gold-beater's skin. **1857** J. G. WOOD *Comm. Objects Sea-shore* 44, I found that the ulva had risen in the water, and was hanging in most elegant festoons from the surface. **1871** KINGSLEY *At Last* i, Here and there floated large fronds of a lettuce-like weed, seemingly an ulva.

ul'vaceous, *a. Bot.* [f. mod.L. *Ulvace-æ*: see prec.] Resembling or belonging to the *Ulvaceæ*.

1891 *Cent. Dict.*

†ul'vose, *a. Obs.*$^{-0}$ [See ULVA and -OSE.] 'Full of reeds or weeds' (Bailey, vol. II. 1727).

ulvöspinel (,ʌlvəʊspɪ'nɛl). *Min.* Also ulvo-. [ad. Sw. *ulvöspinell* (F. Mogensen 1943, in *Blad för Bergshandt. Vänner* XXVI. 135), f. the name of the *Ulvö* islands, Sweden: see SPINEL.]

A mineral of the spinel group, Fe_2TiO_4, frequently found as lamellæ in magnetite.

1947 *Mineral. Abstr.* X. 6 X-ray examination shows two spinel phases with cell edges 8·40 and 8·47Å., close to the values for magnetite (8·37) and ferrous orthotitanate Fe_2TiO_4 or titanspinel (8·50). It is assumed that the ore contains a large amount (100,000 tons) of the latter which is named Ulvöspinel. **1963** D. W. & E. E. HUMPHRIES tr. *Termier's Erosion & Sedimentation* i. 6 The Curie point is 575°C. for pure magnetite and 675°C. for magnetite; it alters in the solid solutions of magnetite (Fe_3O_4) and ulvo-spinel. **1970** *Sci. Jrnl.* May 32/3 If the lava lake was sufficiently enriched in titanium dioxide, its base would tend to collect concentrations of ilmenite, ulvospinel and pseudobrookite. **1971** *Nature* 3 Dec. 264/1 The rock contains relatively small amounts of the phases that we have found in other Apollo basalts (nickleliferous iron, troilite ulvöspinel, ilmenite, [etc.]).

uly(e, obs. Sc. variants of OIL *sb.*, OILY *a.*

ulyie, obs. Sc. form of OIL *sb.*[1]

ulys ('ju:lɪs). *nonce-wd.* [Coined by W. de la Mare.] An imaginary mountain flower.

1912 W. DE LA MARE *Listeners* 58 The icy hills far off from me With frosty ulys overgrown.

Ulyssean (ju:'lɪsi:ən), *a.* [f. L. *Ulysses* (also *Ulixes*), ad. Gr. *'Οδυσσεύς* Odysseus, king of Ithaca and hero of the Odyssey.] Of, belonging to, or connected with Ulysses; *spec.* characteristic of, or resembling, Ulysses in craft or deceit, or in extensive wanderings.

In quots. 1700, 1746 the metre shows the stressing to be *Uly'ssean*.

1639 T. BANCROFT *Epigr. & Epit.* B 3 b, This Vlyssean course of yours Vs of your worthier qualities assures. **1676** BP. N. FRENCH *Vnkinde Desertor* xvi. Wks. 1846 II. 151 His subuerting our union with Vlyssean practizes. **1700** DRYDEN *Ovid's Met.* XIII. 100 That this is not a Fable forg'd by me, Like one of his, an Ulyssean Lie. **1746** FRANCIS tr. *Horace, Epist.* I. vi. 95 Then let us.. like th' abandon'd Ulyssean Crew, Our Ithaca forgot, forbidden Joys pursue. *a* **1850** MARG. FULLER *Life Without & Within* (1862) 55 It is said.. that the modern Greeks are Ulyssean in this respect, never telling straightforward truth, when deceit will answer the purpose. **1875** W. D. GEDDES in *Contemp. Rev.* July 256 The pathos culminates in the Ulyssean part of the 'Iliad', the humour in the 'Odyssey' itself. **1889** *Scottish Leader* 13 April 6 Sir Samuel Baker..is one of the best living specimens of the Ulyssean Englishman.

Ulysses (juː'lɪsiːz, 'juːlɪsiːz). [See ULYSSEAN *a.*] Used as the type of a traveller or adventurer; occas. also, of a crafty and clever schemer.

1611 CORYAT *Crudities* 160 Famous Sir Iohn Mandeuil our English Vlysses. **1876** GEO. ELIOT *Dan. Der.* II. III. xxii. 68 Klesmer was as versatile and fascinating as a young Ulysses. **1915** J. BUCHAN *Salute to Adventurers* iv. 68, I had been dreaming of foreign parts..and here on a Glasgow stairhead I had found Ulysses himself. **1959** T. H. WHITE *Godstone & Blackymor* 172 That Ulysses, that circumnavigator, that..cheated husband. **1981** P. VANSITTART *Death of Robin Hood* II. vii. 84 Richard [Lionheart]..was invisibly present, a resentful Ulysses marking his victims.

ulzie, obs. Sc. form of OIL *sb.*[1]

um, 'um, var. of 'EM, HEM *pron.*

Common in 17th c. writers; now only *dial.*

1606 CHAPMAN *Gentlem. Usher* II. i. 82 Come strew this roome afresh; spread here this carpet... Come sir Giles Goosecap, I must do all my selfe, lay me vm thus. *c* **1610** BEAUM. & FL. *Philaster* I. i, But ever when he turned His tender eyes upon 'um, he would weep. **1664** DRYDEN & HOWARD *Ind. Queen* v. i, How can the Gods delight in humane blood? Think 'um not cruel; if you think 'um good. **1689** *Pol. Ballads* (1860) II. 12 May they all repent 'um And to Holland be sent home, On condition we lose all the money we lent 'um. **1859** J. RICHARDSON *Song. Sol.* v. 3 I've weish't my feet; hoo s'all I soil um? **1887** JEFFERIES *Amaryllis* iii. 19 Th' pigeons have been at um, they be 'mazing fond of um, so be the larks.

um ((ə)m), *int.* [Imitative. Cf. HUM *int.*]

1. Used to indicate hesitating or inarticulate utterance on the part of a speaker.

1672 VANBRUGH *Mistake* IV. i, Certain Immotions, which —um—cause, as one may suppose, a sort of convulsive—yes —Hurricanious—um—Like in short; a Woman, is like the Devil. **1748** RICHARDSON *Clarissa* VI. 101 'Madam—I cannot excuse myself'—um, um, um, um, um, um—'I must own to you, Madam, that [etc.]'. **1933** P. MACDONALD *Mystery of Dead Police* viii. 63 'I don't think,' she said, 'that you two know each other..Mr. Revel—Captain Um-ha'. **1974** C. HAMPTON *Savages* v. 39, I publish, I mean I have had published, a few what we used to call slim volumes of verse, um, poetry, you know.

2. Used to indicate hesitation or doubt in replying to another.

1777 SHERIDAN *Trip Scarb.* III. ii, *Love[less]*. (Kissing her.) In matters of love, a woman's oath is no more to be minded than a man's. *Ber.* Um! **1818** SCOTT *Rob Roy* x, 'Was this selection of studies Rashleigh's choice, or your own, Miss Vernon?' I asked. 'Um!' said she, as if hesitating to answer my question. **1844** ALB. SMITH *Adv. Mr. Ledbury* (1856) I. xiii. 99 Um! I don't see the..necessity. **1898** 'MERRIMAN' *Roden's Corner* ii. 19 'Is it..the Victoria Cross?' she asked. 'Um—yes,' admitted White.

3. Used to indicate assent.

1913 J. VAIZEY *College Girl* vii. 98 'Shall I tell you?'.. 'Um!' 'Very well, then.' **1964** L. DEIGHTON *Funeral in Berlin* xlii. 271 'You knew I was working for the Israeli Intelligence.' 'Is that who you work for?' I said... 'Um,' she said. **1974** N. FREELING *Dressing of Diamond* 49 'Um,' said Vera vaguely... The 'um' was only a symbol.

Hence as *v. intr.*, to make an utterance indicative of hesitation; also as *sb.*

1913 KIPLING *Songs from Books* 74 Sometimes in a smoking-room, through clouds of 'Ers' and 'Ums'. **1962** P. PURSER *Peregrination 22* vii. 35, I ummed in agreement. **1980** J. O'FAOLAIN *No Country for Young Men* iii. 67, I drink to doubt..and stutters and ums and ahs. Beware of the smooth-speaker.

†**um-**, *prefix*, a reduced form of UMB-, perh. directly ad. ON. *um-* (Icel. and Norw. *um-*. MSw. *um-*, *om-*, Sw. and Da. *om-*); a similar reduction has taken place in OFris. *um-* (Fris. *om-*, *âm-*), MDu. *um-*, *om-* (Du. *om-*), MLG. and MHG. (also G.) *um-*, and in the occasional OE. *ym-*, *em-* for *ymb-*, *emb-*. The more important words with this form of the prefix are UMBRACE *v.*, UMBRAID *v.*, UMGANG *sb.*, etc.; the following rarer verbs are chiefly found in northern texts of the 14th century:—**umbehold** to look about; **umcast** (see quot.); **umclap**, to surround, invest; **umclead**, to clothe about; **umclip**, to surround; **umclose**, to close in, invest; **umfold**, to enclose, surround, **umgripe**, to embrace, enfold; **umheed**, to look about; **umhill**, to cover; **umsee** (*refl.*), to take heed; **umseek**, to search for; **umshade, -shadow**, to shade about, to protect; **umshine**, to shine about; **umstand**, to stand round, to guard; **umtiff**, to deck out, adorn; **umwrithe**, to wind round, entwine.

The majority of these have corresponding forms in UMBE-, and a certain number also appear with UMB-. In the cognate languages the following parallel forms with similar significations occur:—umclead, MDu. *omcleeden* (p.p. *omghecleet*), Norw. *umklædd* p.p.; umfold, Da. *omfolde*, G. *umfalten* (MHG. *umbefalten*), Du. *omvouwen*; umgripe, MDu. *omme-*, *omgripen* (Du. *omgrijpen*), MLG. *ummegripen* (MHG. *umbegrîfen*), NFris. *âmgrip*, MSw. *umgripa*, older Da. *omgribe*; umsee, WFris. *omsjen*, NFris. *âmse*, MDu. *omme-*, *om-*, *umsien* (Du. *omzien*), MSw. *umsea*, older Da. *omse* (also OFris. *umbesia*, MDu. *ombesien*, OHG. *umbisehan*, *umbesehen*, OE. *ymbséon*); umseek, MDu. *omme-*, *omsoeken*, MSw. *omsökia*, older Da. *omsøge*; umshade, MLG. *ummescheden*, NFris. *âmskadi*; umshadow, MDu. *ommescaduwen* (Du. *omschaduwen*), MHG. *umbeschatewen*, *-schetewen*; umshine, MDu. *omme-*, Du. *omschijnen*, MHG. *umbeschînen*, MSw. *omskina*, OE. *ymbscínan*; umstand, MDu. *omme-*, *omstaen* (Du. *omstaan*), G. *umstehen*, older Da. *omstande*; umwrithe, Da. *omvride*, Sw. *omvrida*.

a **1400-50** *Alexander* 731 (Ashm. MS.), *Vn-behalde þe wele on ilk halfe & haue a gud eȝe. **1887** *Jamieson's Sc. Dict.* Suppl. 250/1 'To **umcast* a splice,' to fasten it by a wrapping of cord. *a* **1400-50** *Alexander* 2473 (Ashm. MS.), With þat þe kyng & his kniȝtis *vm-clappis þe cite. *a* **1340** HAMPOLE *Psalter* xliv. 15 þe doghtirs of þe kynge..in hemmyngis of gold, *vmcled in sernesis. *a* **1300** *E.E. Psalter* xlvii. 11 Vmgiues Syon, and *vmklippes it; Telles in his toures yhit. *c* **1400** *Destr. Troy* 4255 [A place] *Vmclosit with a course of the colde ythes, With a serkle of the se þat soght þere aboute. *Ibid.* 9027 The Duke of Athens..& derf Menelaus.. Vmcloset the kyng and his knightes als. **1515** *Scottish Field* 268 in *Chetham Misc.* (1856) II, He umclosed that castell, clene round aboute. *a* **1400-50** *Alexander* 4717 Now gase he ..& a fild entris, *Vmfaldin with a faire wod. *a* **1300** *E.E. Psalter* lxxviii. 8 Ne mine of our alde wickenesses, for-þi; Tite *vmgripe vs þi merci. *a* **1400-50** *Alexander* 731 (Dubl. MS.), *Vmhede þe wele on ilke halfe & haue a god Eȝe. *a* **1340** HAMPOLE *Psalter* xliii. 21 þe shadow of ded *vmhild vs. *Ibid.* liv. 5 Dred and qwakynge com on me, and myrknes vmhild me. *a* **1400-50** *Alexander* 3728 For-þi..*vmse þe be tyme, Quat tene & torfare may tide, & tent to þine ende. *a* **1300** *Cursor M.* 15846 Quar-for haf yee taken me, And als a theif *vm-soght? *c* **1460** *Towneley Myst.* x. 128 The holy gost shall light in the,..he shall *vmshade and fulfyll That thi madynhede shall neuer spyll. *a* **1300** *E.E. Psalter* xc. 4 With his sculdres sal he *vmschadow þe al. *a* **1340** HAMPOLE *Psalter* cxxxix. 8 þou vmshadoud abouen my heuyd in day of bataile. *Ibid.* xc. 4 He sall gif þe vmshadowynge. *a* **1400** *New Test.* (Paues) Acts. xxvi. 13 A lyghte þat *vmschone me and hem þat wore wiþ me. *a* **1300** *E.E. Psalter* cxl. 3 Set, lauerd, to mi mouth yheming, And to mi lippes doer of *vmstanding [L. *ostium circumstantiæ*]. *Ibid.* cxliii. 14 Doghtres of þam samen-dight, *Vmtiffed als licknes of kirke bright. *a* **1340** HAMPOLE *Psalter* cxviii. 61 Cordis of synful has *vmwrithyn me.

Uma, var. HUMA.

umage, obs. f. HOMAGE.

'uman, Sc. f. WOMAN.

umangite ('juːməŋgaɪt). *Min.* [ad. G. *umangit* (F. Klockmann 1891, in *Zeitschr. f. Krist. und Min.* XIX. 265), f. the name of Sierra de *Umango* in Argentina: see -ITE[1].] A copper selenide, Cu_3Se_2, found as dark red, violet, or black tetragonal crystals.

1891 *Jrnl. Chem. Soc.* LX. 1435 The author has found three rare minerals of great interest... 2. Umangite.—Associated with eukairite, there occurs a mineral..which proved on analysis to be a variety of copper selenide... The new mineral occurs in finely granular masses. **1978** *Mineral. Abstr.* XXIX. 198/2 Umangite (Cu_3Se_2), berzelianite ($Cu_{2-x}Se$), and athabascaite ($Cu_{5.1}Se_4$) are found in fracture fillings in a carbonatized mafic intrusive rock from Christopher Island, Baker Lake, North West Territories.

umast, variant UMEST *a. Sc. Obs.*

Umayyad (ʊ'maːjæd), *sb.* and *a.* Also *α.* **Umeiyad**; *β.* **Om(m)ay(y)ad, Omeyyad, Ommiyan**, etc. [f. the name of *Umayya*, ancestor of Muhammad.] **A.** *sb.* A member of a Muslim dynasty which ruled the Empire of the Caliphate from 660 (or 661) to 750 and founded an emirate in Spain in 756. **B.** *adj.* Of or pertaining to this dynasty.

1758 tr. *de Marigny's Hist. Arabians* II. 331 The descendants of Abbas had always refused to acknowledge the Ommiyans as lawful Caliphs. *Ibid.* III. 5 Abdollah.. vented his rage on the tombs of the Ommiyan Caliphs. **1788**, **1872** [see ABBASID, -IDE *a.* and *sb.*]. **1907** D. S. MARGOLIOUTH tr. *Zaydân's Umayyads & 'Abbâsids* ii. 63 The pivot on which the policy of the Umayyads turned.. was the recovery of the sovereignty which they had enjoyed in pagan days. *Ibid.*, The Umayyad desire for exclusive sovereignty..led them to commit many acts which blacken their memories. **1924** W. MUIR *Caliphate* (ed. 2) lx. 432 In passing from the Umeiyad to the 'Abbâsid Caliphate, we reach..a fresh departure... The first new feature is, that while the Umeiyad Caliphate..was co-ordinate with the limits of Islâm, this is no longer true of the 'Abbâsid. *Ibid.* 433 Of the Umeiyads, the Syrians remained the last support. **1927** D. HOGARTH in *Lett. Gertrude Bell* I. xiii. 353 Her journey was a pioneer venture which..cast much new light on the history of the Syrian desert frontiers under Roman, Palmyrene, and Ummayad domination. **1950** B. LEWIS *Arabs in Hist.* iv. 68 Umayyad society was based on the domination of the Arabs. *Ibid.* 78 The last of the Umayyads, Marwān II.., was a clever and capable ruler, but he had come too late to save the dynasty. **1975** F. HEER *Charlemagne & his World* viii. 106 In 750 the Ommayyad dynasty was overthrown by the Abbassids, descendants of Mohammed's uncle... One Ommayyad..escaped the massacre of his dynasty in Baghdad..and made his way to Spain, where he became emir. **1981** *Economist* 24 Jan. 43/1 It is taken for granted that present day Damascus and Baghdad automatically oppose each other because of the hostility between the Ummayad and Abbasid dynasties 1,200 years ago.

umb, variant of UMBE *prep. Obs.*

†**umb-**, *prefix*, app. ad. ON. *umb-* (earlier form of *um-* UM-), corresponding to MLG. and MHG. *umb-*, OE. *ymb-*, *emb-* (see UMBE-). In ME. this form of the prefix is much rarer than the reduced UM- or the extended UMBE-, and occurs only in the following verbs:—**umbcast**, to surround; **umbclose**, to enclose; **umbfold**, to embrace; **umblay**, to wrap round; **umblook**, to look round; **umbset, -stead**, to surround; **umbthink**, to bethink (oneself *of* something).

The OE. *ymb-* was extensively employed in compound verbs, as *ymbclippan*, *-lócian*, *-settan*, *-sniðan*, *-standan*, *-þencan*, etc., and although not the phonetic antecedent of ME. *umb-* may have had some influence on its use.

c **1400** *Destr. Troy* 10420 Achilles..meuyt to his Mirmydons in maner before, þe kyng to *vmbcast, & close hym with-in. *c* **1330** R. BRUNNE *Chron. Wace* (Rolls) 4080 Lud..*vmb-closed it [*sc.* London] wyþ a walle. *c* **1400** *Destr. Troy* 8496 Sho braid with the barne to þe bare erthe, *Vmbfoldyt his fete, felle vnto swone. *a* **1300** *Cursor M.* 22069 (Edinb.), And als it in ur leuedi liȝte, þe hali gaste þurȝ godis miȝte, Ane *umblaide hir wiþ his leme To brede þate blisful barneteme. *c* **1375** *Ibid.* 26406 (Fairf), þer-of saltow þe *vmbloke, of cases iiij, I finde in boke. *c* **1400** *Destr. Troy* 10433 þe Mirmydons to Menon myghtily þronge, *Vmbset hym on yche side, sesit hym onon. *c* **1450** *Mirk's Festial* 64 Techyng his good chyldryn, forto haue yn mynde how hard he ys *vmbstad wyth deth on yche syde. *a* **1300** *Cursor M.* 21667 (Edin.), Qua wil *umbþink him in his mode Mai finde fele takins of þe rode. *c* **1375** *Ibid.* 19891 (Fairf.), Quiles saint peter him vmbþoȝt of þis siȝt quat hit takin muȝt.

†**umbe**, *prep.* and *adv. Obs.* Forms: 1-2 ymbe (imbe), 1-5 umbe (3 ummbe), 3-4 umben; 5 umb. [Partly (1) OE. *ymbe* (with equivalent forms in the other Germanic languages; see below), whence southern ME. *ümbe* (see also EMBE *prep.*); partly (2) an adoption of ON. *umb* (earlier form of *um*; cf. UM- and UMB-), whence the midland and northern forms. The form *ummbe* in the Ormulum is disyllabic (cf. *inne*, *onne*, *offe*, etc.), and so presumably are the ME. examples of the adv.

The Germanic forms corresponding to OE. *ymbe (embe)*, *ymb*, are OFris. *umbe*, *umme*, *um*, *ombe*, *omme*, *om* (WFris. *om*), MDu. *omme*, *om* (Du. *om*), OS. *umbi*, *um* (MLG. *umbe*, *umb*, *umme*), OHG. *umbi (umpi)*, *umbe* (MHG. *umbe*, *umme*, *umb*, *umm*, *um*; also *ümbe*, etc.; G. *um*), ON. *umb*, *um* (Icel. and Norw. *um*, Sw. and Da. *om*). The stem is represented in other Indo-European languages by Gr. ἀμφί (ἀμφίς), ἀμφι-, L. *ambi-*, Gaulish *ambi-*, Irish *imb-*, *im(m)-*.]

A. *prep.* **1.** Around, about.

Beowulf 2883 Werȝendra to lyt þrong ymbe þeoden. *Ibid.* 3170 þa ymbe hlæw riodan hildedeore. **971** *Blickling Hom.* 141 Ealle þa þe ymbe me standaþ. *c* **1000** *Sax. Leechd.* I. 218 Wið þæt reng-wyrmas ymbe þone nafolan deriȝen. *a* **1310** in Wright *Lyric P.* ix. 35 Hire gurdel of bete gold is al, Umben hire middel smal. **13..** *E.E. Allit. P.* B. 879 þus þay þrobled & þrong & þrwe vmbe his erez. **13..** *Gaw. & Gr. Knt.* 1830 Ho laȝt a lace lyȝtly, þat leke vmbe hir sydez. *a* **1400-50** *Alexander* 2209 (Dubl. MS.), Alexander als belyfe all vmbe þe cyte Mase iiij Mille to fonde. *c* **1400** *Destr. Troy* 335 Vmbe the sercle of the Citie was sothely a playne. *Ibid.* 8745 A tabernacle triet & tristyly wroght;..Hit was atiryt vmb the top all with triet stones.

2. About, concerning, of.

Beowulf 2070 Ic sceal forð sprecan ȝen ymbe Grendel. *c* **900** tr. *Baeda's Hist.* v. xii. (1890) 422 Se arwyrða bisscop ..feorr & wide Godes work ymbe Cristes ȝeleafan bodade & lærde. *c* **1000** *Ags. Psalter* (Thorpe) xxxvii. 18 Forþæm ic andette Gode min unriht, and ic þence ymbe mine synna. ? *a* **1100** *O.E. Chron.* an. 1070, þa þa hi þyder comon & umbe oþer þing ȝesprecon hæfdon umbe þæt hi sprecan woldon. *c* **1175** *Lamb. Hom.* 95 He dude þet heo weren..bodiende umbe godes riche. *Ibid.* 147 þreo roden beoð þa ich umbe speche. *c* **1200** ORMIN 304 þatt tiss Elysabæþ, þatt we nu mælenn ummbe, Wass þuss off Aaroness kinn.

b. Busied with, aiming at, seeking after.

c **1000** ÆLFRIC *Hom.* I. 12 Ac hi æfre beoð ymbe þæt an, hu hi maȝon Gode hyrsumian. *a* **1200** *St. Marher.* 6 Helle hundes..haueð al biset me, ah þu, hehe healent, beo umbe me to helpen. *a* **1225** *Ancr. R.* 218 He..makeð hire ueire cheres, & is vmbe eueriches weis þet heo him luuie inwardliche in hire heorte. *c* **1225** in *Rel. Ant.* II. 5 For-þi he is eaver umben to reare sum laððe.

3. After (in time).

c **1000** ÆLFRIC *Gen.* xvii. 21 Min wedd soðlice ic sette to Isaace, þone þe Sarra þe acenð on þisre tide nu ymbe twelfmonð. *a* **1122** *O.E. Chron.* Pref. (Laud MS.), And þa ȝelamp hit imbe ȝeara rina, þæt Scotta sum-dæl ȝewat of Ybernian on Brittene. *c* **1205** *Lay.* 2632 Vmben ane stunde, þa scipen ȝaru weoren. *Ibid.* 6617 Hit wes vmbe fif winter, seoððe he heonne ferde. *a* **1225** *Leg. Kath.* 518 þes sondesmon, umbe long, þa he hefde al þet lond ourgan & þurhsoht, com [etc.].

4. *umbe throwe.* = UMBEWHILE *adv.* 2.

a **1310** in Wright *Lyric P.* iv. 25 We shule aryse ur fader byfore, thah fon us fallen umbe throwe.

B. *adv.* About, round.

Beowulf 2597 Nealles him on heape hand-ȝesteallan, æðelinga bearn, ymbe ȝestodon. **13..** *E.E. Allit. P.* C. 309 þe grete flem of þy flod folded me vmbe. *a* **1400-50** *Alexander* 2762 (Dubl. MS.), The ledes oute of Landace & all þe Landes vmbe. *c* **1400** *Destr. Troy* 1455 Grete Troy was vp tild with mony toures vmbe. *c* **1440** *Pallad. on Husb.* VII. 106 Do donge vppon and vmbe on euery side, And bynde hit to.

†**umbe-**, *prefix* (also 3 ummbe-, 4-5 vmbe-, 5 vnbe-, unbe-, 6 *Sc.* wmbe-, ombe-; 4 vnbi-, 4-5 vmbi-, 5 vmby-, unby-, 6 *Sc.* onby-), partly (in southern ME. texts) representing OE. *ymbe-* (see prec.), but chiefly either an extended form of UMB- (cf. prec.) or a combination of UM- with BE-. Forms with the double prefix (*ommebe-* or *ombe-*) are very common in Middle Dutch, not infrequent in older Danish (*ombe-*), and occur occasionally in MLG.; it is possible that their prevalence in MDu. may have contributed to

the extensive use of such forms in ME. Originally the *um-* was probably added to verbs which already had the prefix *be-* (as *beclip*, *belap*, etc.), and in most cases the two forms (with *be-* and *umbe-*) coexist with the same signification. In addition to those treated as main words (viz. UMBECAST, -CLIP, -GO, -LAP, -LAY, -SET, -THINK) the following examples occur in ME. texts chiefly of the 14th and 15th centuries :—**umbebraid**, to turn round; **umbecarve**, to circumcise; **umbeclap**, to embrace, to enclose; **umbeclead**, to clothe, wrap up; **umbeclose**, to enclose, enwrap; **umbedelve**, to dig round; **umbedraw**, to withdraw; **umbefold**, to surround, to embrace; **umbegang**, to go round, to surround; **umbegild**, to gild about; **umbegive**, to surround; **umbegrip**, to grasp; **umbegrow**, to grow round, overgrow; **umbelie**, to surround; **umbelook**, to look about; **umbelouk**, to include, comprehend; **umbepitch**, **umbereach**, to surround; **umberow**, to row about; **umberun**, to surround; **umbeshadow**, to shade about; **umbeshear**, to circumcise; **umbeshine**, to shine about; **umbesiege**, to besiege, environ; **umbespread**, to spread about; **umbestand**, to stand round, surround; **umbeswey**, to encircle; **umbethonre**, to encompass, surround; **umbetigh**, to encircle, surround; **umbeviron**, to environ; **umbewalt**, to surround; **umbeweave**, to enwrap; **umbewend**, to imbed, enclose; **umbewet**, to wet about.

Of these the following have parallels with the compound prefix (*um-be-*) in the cognate languages:—umbeclead, MDu. *ommebecleden* (p.p. *-cleet*); umbegrip, older Da. *ombegribe* (cf. MDu. *ombegrijp* sb.); umbelie, MLG. *ummebeliggen*; umbelook, NFris. *ombiluke*; umbelouk, MDu. *omme-*, *ombeluken* (p.p. *-beloken*); umbeshine, MDu. *ombeschijnen*; umbestand, NFris. *ombistunn*, MDu. *omme-*, *ombestaen* (p.p.); umbetigh, NFris. *ombitiin*. Several of these, and many of the others, also correspond in sense to OE. formations with *ymb-* (less commonly *ymbe-*) or to equivalent forms in the other languages, e.g. umbecarve, OE. *ymbceorfan*; umbedelve, (OE. *ymbȝedelf* sb.), MDu. and Du. *omdelven*; umbegang, OE. *ymbgangan*, OFris. *ummegunga*, OHG. *umbigangan*, etc.: cf. the examples given under UM-.

13.. *E.E. Allit. P.* B. 1622 When he com bifore þe kyng & clanly had halsed, Baltazar *vmbe-brayde hym & 'leue sir', he sayde. *a* **1240** *Lofsong* in *O.E. Hom.* I. 207 Ich bide þe..bi his blodi rune þat ron,..In *umbekeoruunge, in his blod swetunge. ? *a* **1400** *Morte Arth.* 1779 Thane syr Cador of Cornewayle *Umbeclappes the cors, and kyssez hyme ofte. *a* **1400–50** *Alexander* 4171 þan vmbyclappis þaim a cloude & couirs all ouire. *c* **1400** *Anturs of Arth.* x. (Thornton MS.), Alle glowede als gledis the gaste whare scho glydis, *Vmbyclede in a clowde. *c* **1400** *Ibid.* ix. (Ireland MS.), Alle bare was the body, and blak by the bone, *Vmbeclosut in a cloude, in clething evyl clad. *c* **1440** *Pallad. on Husb.* III. 533 Ek now is to repare Rosayres olde & drynesse of to pare. Now *vmbedelue hem. *Ibid.* IV. 324 In heruest & in ver hem vmbidelue. **1456** SIR G. HAYE *Law Arms* (S.T.S.) 53 Thai war fayn..to *unbedraw thame agayne to thair pavilliones. **1513** DOUGLAS *Æneid* XII. Prol. 6 Mars onbydrew, for all his grundin glave. **13..** *Gaw. & Gr. Knt.* 181 Fayre fannand fax *vmbe-foldes his schulderes. **14..** *Siege Jerus.* (E.E.T.S.) 12/219 To seint Peter þe pope 30 platte to þe grounde, Vmbe-felde his fete, & to þe freke saide. *c* **1200** *Trin. Coll. Hom.* 191 Alse þe apostle seið..Ðurch onde com deað in to þe worelde al *umbegonge. *c* **1440** tr. *Palladius on Husb.* IV. 437 With seefroth other haue hem vmbiyonge [L. *circumdederunt*]. *a* **1400–50** *Alexander* 4899 ȝit was a mynstir on þe mounte of metall as þe nobill, *Vmbegildid with a garden of golden vynes. *a* **1400** in *Hampole's Psalter* (1884) p. xviii, For *vmbegyuen me hathe euels of þe whiche noumber is noght. ? *a* **1400** *Morte Arth.* 3758 Bot sir Gawayne..*Vmbegrippys a spere, and to a gome rynnys. *Ibid.* 3944 Sir Gawayne.. Vmbegrippede the girse, and one grouffe fallene. **13..** *E.E. Allit. P.* B. 488 A bronch of olyue, Gracyously *vmbegrouen al with grene leuez. *Ibid.* B. 836 þe borȝ was al vp; ..To *vmbe-lyȝe lothez hous þe ledez to take. *a* **1300** *Cursor M.* 8468 O prouerbes es þat toper boke, þat lers man him *vm-biloke Agains þis werld wikcedhede. *Ibid.* 23705 Yee cristen men, yow vmbilok,..O yur lijf þat yee her lede. *a* **1400** *Pistill of Susan* 291 Vmbiloke ȝou, lordes, such lawes ben leiþ. **1357** *Lay Folks Catech.* (T.) 259 This ten Comandementz that I haue nowe rekend Er *umbilouked in twa of the godspell. **13..** *E.E. Allit. P.* A. 1052 þe hyȝe trone þer moȝt ȝe hede With alle þe apparaylmente *vmbepyȝte. **1513** DOUGLAS *Æneid* II. x. 155 The fader of goddis and king of men With thunderis blast me smate.. And with his fyry lewyne me *wmberauch. *Ibid.* VI. i. 134 Thocht..hard fortoun has wmberaucht The Troianis, and persewit vnfreindfully. *c* **1205** LAY. 114 Eneas þe duc, mid his driht folcke,..moni lond *umbe-rowen. *c* **1440** *Pallad. on Husb.* I. 324 Wyth orchard, or with gardyn, or with mede, Se that thyn hous with hem be *vmbironne. **14..** *With an O and an I* in *Anglia* XXVII. 286 þe haly gast ..*Vmbeschadow þe sall wiþouten ony syn. *c* **1450** *Mirk's Festial* 106 þe Holy Gost wythouten any werke of man, þat schall vmbeschadow þe wythout. *c* **1200** ORMIN 4132 þatt cnif wass..Forr *tummbesherenn shapp þærwiþþ Off þeȝȝre cnapechilldre. *Ibid.* 4080 To wurrþenn ummbeshorenn, swa To clennsenn hemm off sinne. **13..** *E.E. Allit. P.* C. 455 þe schyre sunne hit *vmbe-schon. **1422** YONGE tr. *Secreta Secret.* 182 The grete lordis of laynyster, seynge har Prynce i-putte to myschefe, and in euery Partie *vmbesegid wyth enemys. **1513** DOUGLAS *Æneid* X. ii. 85 The Troiane adulterar Ombesegyt the cite of Spartha. *c* **1400** *Laud Troy Bk.* 10563 Alle that feld was *vmbesprade Off dede knyȝtes. *c* **1300** *Havelok* 1875 Huwe rauen..saw how þe laddes wode Hauelok his louerd *umbistode, And beten on him. **13..** *E.E. Allit. P.* B. 1380 þe bourȝ [Babylon] was so brod & so bigge alce,..*Vmbe-sweyed on vch a syde with seuen grete wateres. *a* **1400–50** *Alexander* 3857 þan come he streke on a staunke..*Umby-thonred with a thike wod thre mile a-boute. *Ibid.* 4806 þai ware vmbe-thonrid in þat thede with slike a thike cloude, þat þai miȝt fele it with þaire fiste. **13..** *Gaw. & Gr. Knt.* 770 A castel..Pyched on a prayere, a park al aboute, With a pyked palays, pyned ful þik, þat *vmbe-teȝe mony tre mo þen two myle. **1375** BARBOUR *Bruce* XI. 640 (Edin. MS.), I will me speid To help hym, for he has ned; All *umbeweround with hys fayis is he. **13..** *E.E. Allit. P.* B. 1181 þe gentylest of Iudee in Ierusalem [he] biseged, *Vmbe-walt alle þe walles wyth wyȝes ful stronge. **13..** *Gaw. & Gr. Knt.* 581 þe brawden bryne of bryȝt stel ryngez, *Vmbe-weued þat wyȝ, vpon wlonk stuffe. **1338** R. BRUNNE *Chron.* (1725) I. 117 A hede þat was of smyten,..þis squier..sette it on a spere, in an orfreis vnbiweued. *c* **1440** *Pallad. on Husb.* XII. 221 The rootis wel in dongynge *vmbiwende. In faat lond moyst thei ioyfulliche ascende. *Ibid.* III. 675 The rootes ek ycutte & *vmbiwette With donge is good her spryngyng forto glade.

b. In the advs. **umbetrin**, **-turn**, round about.

c **1200** ORMIN 17563 Onn heffness whel all ummbetrin, þurrh Godd tatt swillc itt wrohhte. **13..** *Gaw. & Gr. Knt.* 184 A much berd as a busk ouer his brest henges, þat wyth his hiȝlich here, þat of his hed reches, Was euesed al vmbetorne, a-bof his elbowes.

†**umbecast**, *v.* *Obs.* Forms: 4 vmbecast (5 *p.t.* -caste), 4 (5 *p.t.*) vmbekest; 4 *p.t.* vmbikest, 5 vmbycast(e. [f. UMBE- + CAST *v.* (or UM- + BECAST *v.*). Cf. *umbcast* s.v. UMB-, and *umcast* s.v. UM-.]

1. *trans.* To surround, encircle.

c **1350** *Will. Palerne* 2319 þei herd an huge route of horse þat hel al a-boute, & herd þat quarrere vmbe-cast & al þe cuntre wide. *Ibid.* 4693 Whan al þe cuntre was umbe-cast with clene men of armes. *c* **1400** *Laud Troy Bk.* 5505 The Gregeis vmbikest his cart With many a knyȝt hardi and smart. *c* **1410** *Master of Game* (MS. Digby 182) xxv, þen ought þe lymmer..vmbycaste with his lymer þe whart þat þe deere is into.

b. To make the circuit of; to go round.

13.. *E.E. Allit. P.* B. 478 When ho fyndez no folde her fote on to pyche, Ho vmbe-kestez þe coste & þe kyst sechez. *c* **1475** *Rauf Coilȝear* 410 He vmbekest the countrie outwith the toun. He saw na thing on steir, Nouther fer nor neir.

2. To enclose, confine.

c **1440** *York Myst.* xxxiii. 467, *i Mil.* All in cordis his coorse vmbycast. *ii Mil.* Late vs bynde hym in bandis all bare.

3. To consider, meditate (*that*, etc.).

1375 BARBOUR *Bruce* V. 552 He vmbethocht him at the last, And in his hert can vmbecast, That the king had in custum ay [etc.]. *c* **1425** WYNTOUN *Cron.* VII. viii. 2029 (Wemyss MS.), All þarby Off þat thing thocht gret ferly, And vmbekest in þare entent.

4. *intr.* Of a hunting dog: = CAST *v.* 60.

1470–85 MALORY *Arthur* XVIII. xxi. 764 Whan the hynde came to the welle..the dogges came after and vmbecaste aboute, for she had lost the veray parfyte feaute of the hynde.

umbeclap, -clead: see UMBE-.

†**umbeclip**, *v.*[1] *Obs.*[−1] In 3 ummbeclippenn. [f. UMBE- + CLIP *v.*[2]] *trans.* To circumcise.

c **1200** ORMIN 15009 Forr he let hise kinness menn Hiss shapp himm ummbeclippenn.

†**umbeclip**, *v.*[2] *Obs.* In 4–5 vmbeclyppe, -clippe, 5 vmbiclyppe. [See UMBE- and BECLIP *v.*[1] OE. *ymbclyppan* occurs in the same sense.] *trans.* To surround, encircle.

13.. *Gaw. & Gr. Knt.* 616 þe cercle was more o prys. þat vmbe-clypped hys croun. *a* **1395** HYLTON *Scala Perf.* (W. de W. 1494) II. xxxvii, Sothfastnes shall vmbiclyppe [ed. 1533 becleppe] the wyth a sheelde. *c* **1400** *Anturs of Arth.* x. (Douce MS.), Al glowed as a glede þe goste þere ho glides, Vmbeclipped him with a cloude, of cle[th]yng vnclere. *c* **1450** *Mirk's Festial* 64 The sykyngys of deth hauen vmbeclypped me.

umbeclose, -delve, -draw, etc.: see UMBE-.

†**umbego**, *v.* *Obs.* Also 4 vnbigo, 5 vmbego, vmbigo, vmbygo. [f. UMBE- + GO *v.* Cf. MDu. *ommebegaen*, and UMGO *v.*] *trans.* To go around, to encircle; to surround *with* something.

c **1300** *Havelok* 1842 þe laddes were kaske and teyte, And vn-bi-yeden him ilkon, Sum smot with tre, and sum wit ston. **13..** *E.E. Allit. P.* A. 210 Her lere leke al hyr vmbegon. *c* **1400** *Laud Troy Bk.* 9468 Rofe and wal and euery a gable,..Courbel, beme, and euery a ston, With riche gold was vmbygon. **1430–40** in *MS. Bodl. 423* fol. 186 b, A weddynge cote,..the whiche shulde be a maydens cote, vmbigoon with diuersitees of vertues. *c* **1440** *Pallad. on Husb.* II. 197 In herbis letuce vmbigoon wol growe.

umbegrip, -grow, -hold: see UMBE-, UM-.

umbel (ˈʌmb(ə)l). Also 6–9 umbell, 6–8 umble, 8 umbil. [ad. L. *umbella* sun-shade, parasol, dim. of *umbra* shadow. So Sp. *umbela*, Pg. and It. *umbella*, F. *ombelle*, †*umbelle* (16th c.), Sw. *umbell*. Cf. It. *ombrella*.]

1. *Bot.* A mass of inflorescence borne upon pedicels of nearly equal length springing from a common centre. Cf. UMBELLA 1.

1597 GERARDE *Herbal* I. xvi. 19 His stalke is long, big and square,..and on his top a chaffie vmbel or tuft like vnto the true Cyperus. *Ibid.* II. ccccxiv. 904 The flowers stande at the tops of the stalkes in small spokie vmbles. **1634** T. JOHNSON *Parey's Chirurg. Wks.* XXVII. xii. 1103 Almost all hearbes that carry their flowres and seeds in an umbell, have seeds of a hot, subtle, and aiery substanc. **1652** CULPEPPER *Eng. Physic.* 48 The middle part being hollow and low, and the outer stalks rising high, maketh the whole Umbel to shew like a Birds nest. **1682** *Nat. Hist. Coffee*, etc. 28 On the top of the Branches [of the elder]..there spring sweet and crisped umbels, swelling with white odoriferous Flowers. **1731** P. MILLER *Gard. Dict.* s.v. *Umbella*, That Umbel which consists of Pedicles only, is call'd a Simple Umbel; that which is compos'd both of Rays and Pedicles, is call'd a Compound Umbel. **1785** MARTYN *Lett. Bot.* v. (1794) 54 At first sight you would say, here is an umbellate plant. In looking at it, you would find a large or universal umbel, a small or partial umbel [etc.]. **1832** *Veg. Subst. Food* 192 The water-parsnip bears its flowers in umbels close upon the fruits of the stem. **1859** GEO. ELIOT *A. Bede* ii, The gently-curving stems of the feathered grass..and the white umbels of the hemlocks lining the bushy hedgerows. **1882** *Garden* 11 Feb. 93/1 Nearly the whole of the flowers composing the umbel were succeeded by capsules.

attrib. and *Comb.* **1683** J. REID *Scots Gard'ner* (1907) 98 The wild service,..when spread over with their umbel-fashion'd bright red fruit. **1712** PETIVER in *Phil. Trans.* XXVII. 420 The Flowers pale,..in an umbel-like tuft. **1725** *Fam. Dict.* s.v. *Guaiacum*, The Flowers appear umbel-wise and are of a pale yellow. **1802** R. HALL *Elem. Bot.* 192 *Umbelliferous*,..umbel-bearing. **1829** LOUDON *Encycl. Pl.* (1836) 268 Umbel-flowered. **1858** R. HOGG *Veg. Kingd.* 370 Umbelliferæ.—Umbelflowers. **1861** S. THOMSON *Wild Fl.* II. (ed. 4) 121 The fruit of the composites, like that of the umbel-bearers, looks like a seed. **1870** HOOKER *Stud. Flora* 166 *Silaus pratensis*... Umbel-rays 1–2 in., few or many, incurved.

†**b.** An umbelliferous plant. *Obs. rare.*

1702 FLOYER in *Phil. Trans.* XXIII. 1167, I refer the Umbells to the Grasses, because of their Sweetness and Joynted Stalks. **1713** PETIVER *Ibid.* XXVIII. 189 The Peculiarity of this Umbell, is to have its Root Leaves deeply cut.

2. *Zool.* An umbelliform arrangement of parts.

1870 H. A. NICHOLSON *Man. Zool.* I. 311 *Umbellate*,.. forming an umbel; i.e. a number of nearly equal *radii* all proceeding from one point. **1891** *Cent. Dict.*, *Umbellularia*, ..a genus of deep-sea alcyonarian polyps, having the polypites clustered in an umbel on top of the polypidom.

†**umbelap**, *v.* *Obs.* Forms: 5 um-, vmbelappe (6 vn-); 4–5 um-, vmbilappe, vmbylap(p. [See UMBE- and BELAP *v.*, and cf. UMLAP *v.*] *trans.* To encompass, surround.

a **1350** *St. Andrew* 243 in Horstm. *Altengl. Leg.* (1881) 7 þar come a light in Doun fro þe heuyn..And vmbilappid his bodi about. ? *a* **1400** *Morte Arth.* 1819 The kynge of Lebe has laughte a stede þat hym lykede, And comes in lordely.., Umbelappez þe lumpe, and lattes in sondre. *c* **1400** MAUNDEV. (Roxb.) xxviii. 128 A thikke mirkness.. vmbelapped þe emperour and all his oste. *c* **1440** *Alph. Tales* 423 When I dyed devuls vmbelappid me. *c* **1440** *Gesta Rom.* xcv. 426 (Add. MS.), Thou mayste aske, why this man disserued contricion, that wes vmbelapped with so many synnes. **1502** ATKYNSON tr. *De Imitatione* III. lxii. (1893) 254 If it touch the, yet let it nat throwe þe downe, ne longe vnbelappe the.

†**umbelay**, *v.* *Obs.* Also 4 vmbelai, vmbilay; vmbe-, vmbi-, vmbyley. [See UMBE- and BELAY *v.* (and cf. *umblay* s.v. UMB-, and UMLAY *v.*). So MDu. *omme-*, *ombeleggen*.] *trans.* To beset, surround, encompass.

a **1300** *Cursor M.* 1336 þis tre, þat i of for-wit said, A neddur hit hade al vmbilaid. **13..** *Ibid.* 22069 (Gött.), Als it in vr leuedi light,—þe hali-gast wid goddes might,—And vmbilaid hir wid his leme To brede þat blisful barnteme. *c* **1330** R. BRUNNE *Chron. Wace* (Rolls) 8278 Totenesse was vmbyleyd Wyþ schipes. **1338** —— *Chron.* (1810) 297 þat was his folie, so long in his bed gan ligge, Untille þe Waleis partie had vmbilaid þe brigge.

umbelic(k, -ique, obs. forms of UMBILIC *sb.*

umbelical, obs. form of UMBILICAL *a.*

umbelie: see UMBE-.

‖**umbella** (ʌmˈbɛlə). [L.: see UMBEL.]

1. *Bot.* An umbel.

[**1693** tr. *Blancard's Phys. Dict.* (ed. 2), *Umbellæ*, the Tops of Plants that are like a Bird's Nest.] **1699** EVELYN *Acetaria* 25 Fennel..expels Wind, sharpens the Sight, and recreates the Brain; especially the tender *Umbella* and Seed-Pods. **1725** *Fam. Dict.* s.v. *Moly*, Bearing a great Umbella of starlike purple Flowers, that continue long before they decay. **1832** LINDLEY *Introd. Bot.* 111 Unless they applied the same term to the umbella, the spica, and all other forms of inflorescence. **1856** HENSLOW *Dict. Bot. Terms* 206 *Umbelliferns*, bearing umbels. Assuming the form as an umbella.

2. *Zool.* A more or less convex disk supporting the tentacula in Medusæ.

1834 MᶜMURTRIE *Cuvier's Anim. Kingd.* 480 The tentacula, whether situated on the margin of the umbella or round the mouth, vary, not only according to the species, but to the age of the animal.

umbellal, *a.* *Bot.* [Cf. prec. and -AL[1].] Consisting of plants with umbellate flowers.

1836 LINDLEY *Nat. Syst. Bot.* (ed. 2) 21 A plant of the Umbellal alliance. **1846** —— *Veg. Kingd.* 773 Umbellal Exogens, with didymous fruit, and a double epigynous disk.

ˈ**umbellar**, *a.* *Bot.* [f. as prec. + -AR.] 'Pertaining to an umbel; having the form of an umbel' (Webster, 1828–32).

umbellate ('ʌmbɛlət), *a.* [ad. mod.L. *umbellāt-us*, f. L. *umbella* parasol, UMBELLA: see -ATE². So Sw. *umbellat*, F. *ombellé*.]

1. *Bot.* **a.** Of flowers: Forming, arranged in, an umbel or umbels.

1760 J. LEE *Introd. Bot.* I. xix. (1765) 50 An *Umbellate* Flower is an aggregate one, consisting of many Florets placed on a Receptacle, on fastigiate Peduncles that are all produced from the same point. **1793** [see UMBELLED *a.*]. **1807** J. E. SMITH *Phys. Bot.* 239 Its ultimate terminations are sometimes obscurely umbellate, especially while in blossom. **1826** SAMOUELLE *Direct. Collect. Insects & Crust.* 28 Alighting on the blossoms of trees and shrubs, and particularly on flowers of the umbellate kind. **1872** OLIVER *Elem. Bot.* II. 184 Common Ivy... A climbing evergreen shrub, with..inconspicuous umbellate flowers.

b. Of plants: Having flowers in umbels.

1785 MARTYN *Lett. Bot.* v. (1794) 53 This then is the proper character of the umbellate tribe. **1822-7** GOOD *Study Med.* (1829) I. 174 The umbellate order affords also a rich variety of carminatives.

2. *Zool.* Provided with, or forming, an umbel; umbelliferous; umbelliform.

1870 [see UMBEL 2].

Hence **'umbellately** *adv.*, in umbels.

1887 GARNSEY & BALFOUR tr. *De Bary's Fungi* v. 153 A creeping endophytic mycelium and straight erect simple sporophores ending in umbellately arranged heads of basidia.

'umbellated, *a. Bot.* [f. as prec. + -ED.] = UMBELLATE *a.* 1: **a.** Of flowers, etc.

1676 GREW *Anat. Flowers* II. App. §15 [Flowers] stand.. either without Stalks..or with Stalks, that is, Umbellated as Fenil, &c. **1756** P. BROWNE *Jamaica* 183 The flowers are disposed in umbellated groups. **1797** HOLCROFT tr. *Stolberg's Trav.* III. xc, A plant which bears an umbellated flower, or tuft.

b. Of plants.

1731 P. MILLER *Gard. Dict.* s.v. *Jacobæa*, Shrubby African Ragwort, with hoary Leaves like the umbellated Wormwood. **1812** *New Bot. Garden* I. 97 Umbellated Butomus, or Flowering Rush. **1871** GARROD *Mat. Med.* (ed. 3) 413 Chimaphila, or umbellated winter green.

'umbelled, *a. Bot.* [f. UMBEL + -ED².] = prec.

1793 MARTYN *Lang. Bot.* s.v. *Umbella*, Flowers growing in this manner are called *Umbellati*, Umbellate or Umbelled flowers. **1812** *New. Bot. Garden* I. 7 The peduncles from the summit of the stem, umbelled, villose. **1830** LINDLEY *Nat. Syst. Bot.* 29 Inflorescence panicled or umbelled. **1869** RUSKIN *Q. or Air* §77 In the celery and radish, you have the two great groups of umbelled and cruciferous plants.

'umbellet. *Bot. rare.* [f. UMBEL + -LET.] = UMBELLULE.

1793 MARTYN *Lang. Bot.*, *Umbellula*, an Umbellule or Umbellet. **1806** GALPINE *Brit. Bot.* 127 Umbels trifid, naked: umbellets 3-seeded. **1857** A. GRAY *First Less. Bot.* xi. 81 Here the whole is termed a *compound umbel*; and the smaller or partial umbels take the name in English of *umbellets*.

um'bellicle. *Bot. rare*⁻⁰. [f. UMBEL or UMBELLA.] An umbellule.

1828-32 WEBSTER, *Umbellicle*, a little or partial umbel.

umbellifer (ʌm'bɛlɪfə(r)). *Bot.* [mod.L.: see UMBELLIFEROUS *a.*] A plant belonging to the natural order *Umbelliferæ*, having umbellate flowers.

1718 OZELL tr. *Tournefort's Voy.* II. vi. 214 It is an Umbellifer, to speak like a Botanist, the Root whereof goes a foot and a half down. **1727** BAILEY (vol. II), *Umbellifer*, signifies a Plant that bears many Flowers, dispos'd somewhat like an Umbrella, growing upon many Foot-stalks proceeding from the same Center. **1846** LINDLEY *Veg. Kingd.* 773 If Botanists form their ideas of an Umbellifer from the ordinary appearance of such plants in Europe. **1861** S. THOMSON *Wild Fl.* II. (ed. 4) 120 The blossoms of umbellifers vary. **1872** OLIVER *Elem. Bot.* II. 183, So many species are dangerous, that Umbellifers generally are regarded as suspicious.

umbelliferone (ʌmbɛ'lɪfərəʊn). *Chem.* Also -on. [f. prec. + -ONE.] A colourless, tasteless, crystalline substance obtained from the bark of mezereon, and, by distillation, from various umbellifers.

1868 WATTS *Dict. Chem.* V. 938 Umbelliferone forms colourless rhombic prisms, having a faint silky lustre. **1876** HARLEY *Royle's Mat. Med.* (ed. 6) 598 The resin yields oils of a green or purple tint, and about ¼ per cent. of umbelliferone, $C_9H_6C_3$, which is isomeric with quinone.

umbelliferous (ʌmbɛ'lɪfərəs), *a.* [f. mod.L. *umbellifer*, f. L. *umbella* UMBELLA + *-fer* bearing: see -FEROUS. Cf. It. *umbellifero* (*ombrellifero*), Sp. *umbelifero*, F. *ombellifère*, †*umbellifère* (1698).]

1. *Bot.* Bearing flowers arranged in umbels; of or belonging to the order of *Umbelliferæ*.

1662 RAY *Rem.* (1760) 260, I observed, creeping upon the Ground, a small umbelliferous Plant. **1668** WILKINS *Real Char.* II. iv. §4. 88 Umbelliferous herbs whose leaves are more broad and less finely cut. **1731** MILLER *Gard. Dict.* s.v. *Foeniculum*, Fennel..is an Umbelliferous Plant, whose Leaves are divided into Capillaceous Jags. **1776** WITHERING *Brit. Plants* Introd. p. xxxv, Carrot,..an example of the Umbelliferous or Rundle-bearing plants. **1785** MARTYN *Lett. Bot.* v. (1794) 55 The umbelliferous tribe is numerous. **1842** LOUDON *Suburban Hort.* 651 The parsnep..is an umbelliferous biennial. **1862** H. W. BELLEW *Pol. Mission Afghanistan* 471 A great variety of labiate and umbelliferous herbs. **1887** BENTLEY *Man. Bot.* (ed. 5) 576 The poisonous or non-poisonous properties of some other species of Umbelliferous plants.

2. Produced by or grown on umbelliferous plants.

1753 *Chambers' Cycl.* Suppl., *Apium*,..a genus of plants... The flower is of the umbelliferous kind, and is rosaceous. **1847** in Royle *Mat. Med.* 420, I have examined another kind of Umbelliferous fruit in the collection of Dr. Royle. **1876** HARLEY *Royle's Mat. Med.* (ed. 6) 581 Cumin is carminative like the other umbelliferous fruits.

3. Umbelliform.

1896 *Westm. Gaz.* 10 Sept. 3/2 That gored and umbelliferous skirt, that monster hat.

'umbelli,florous, *a. Bot.* [Cf. prec.] Having an umbellate inflorescence.

1895 *Funk's Stand. Dict.*

um'belliform, *a. rare*⁻¹. [f. L. *umbella* (cf. above) + -(I)FORM. Cf. F. *ombelliforme*.] Having the form of an umbel.

1891 *Cent. Dict.*, *Umbellate*,..umbelliferous,.. umbelliform. **1898** H. C. PORTER tr. *Strasburger's Bot.* 544 The designation of the whole order as *Umbellifloræ* has reference to the umbelliform manner of branching displayed in the floral region.

umbellule (ʌm'bɛljuːl). *Bot.* [ad. mod.L. *umbellula*, f. UMBELLA: see -ULE. Cf. F. *ombellule*.] A partial or secondary umbel; an umbellet.

Also (in recent Dicts.) *umbellulate*, *-ated* adjs.

1793 MARTYN *Lang. Bot.*, *Umbellula*, an Umbellule or Umbellet. **1796** WITHERING *Brit. Plants* (ed. 3) I. 204 Leafits acute, as long as the umbellule. **1812** *New Bot. Garden* I. 8 The flowers in umbels, umbellules..in pairs. **1843** *Penny Cycl.* XXV. 498/1 If the primary pedicels have other smaller pedicels, which form of themselves a smaller umbel,..the umbel is said to be compound, and the smaller umbels are called umbellules. **1861** BENTLEY *Man. Bot.* 190 Another [involucre] at the base of each of the partial umbels or umbellules.

umbelook, -louke, -pitch: see UMBE-.

umber, *sb.*¹ Now *dial.* Forms: 4-7 vmbre, umbre, 4-7 vmber (7 vmbier), 5- umber; 5 owmbre, ovmbre, ovmbere; *dial.* 7 oumar, 7-9 oumer, 9 oumber, oomer, etc. [a. OF. *umbre* (*ombre*) or ad. L. *umbra* shade, shadow. Cf. F. *ombre*, Pr. *umbra*, *ombra*, It. *ombra*, It. and Sp. *ombria*, Sp. and Pg. *umbria*.]

1. Shade, shadow.

a **1300** *Cursor M.* 8017 Qua mai rest him in þer vmber, Es nathing þat mai him cumber. *Ibid.* 8451 Vnder þe vmber o þat tre, þe kind o thinges lerd he. **13..** *E.E. Allit. P.* B. 524 Sesounez schal yow neuer sese of sede ne of heruest, Ne hete, ne no harde forst, vmbre ne droȝþe. **1382** WYCLIF *Ps.* cvi. 10 The sitteris in dercnessis, and in the vmbre of deth. *c* **1407** LYDG. *Reson & Sens.* 1242 Pallas..Fleyng had about her hede Of Cynetys ful grete novmbre, Makyng in maner of an ovmbre. *c* **1440** *Pallad. on Husb.* XI. 329 Or flouris swete of vyne or other tre, In vmbre dried, may reserued be. **1470-85** MALORY *Arthur* VIII. i. 274 Thenne the gentylwoman leyd her vnder an vmbre of a grete tree. **1549** *Compl. Scot.* vi. 56 The mune is maid obscure..be rason that the vmbre and schaddou of the eird empeschis hyr to resaue lycht fra the soune. **1572** BOSSEWELL *Armorie* II. 25 Of whatsoever colour the fielde is of, the vmbre or shadowe of the token or signe borne in the fielde is traced of a contrarie color. **1673** *Yorkshire Dial.* 32 (E.D.S.), Put th' Whyes a-mel yon Stirks an' Steers, I' th' Oumar, an' sneck the lear-deers. **1677** NICOLSON *Cumbld. Gloss.* in *Trans. Roy. Soc. Lit.* (1870) IX. 317 *Oumer*, shade. [Hence in Ray, etc.] **1781-** in northern dial. glossaries (*Eng. Dial. Dict.* s.v. *Oumer*).

†**b.** The shadow of the pointer on a sundial or quadrant. *Obs.*

1382 WYCLIF *2 Kings* xx. 11 The prophete..brouȝt aȝeyn the vmbre by the lynys..in the orloge of Achaz. *a* **1400** in Halliwell *Rara Mathem.* (1841) 58 Byholde vpon what place of þe quadrant þe perpendicle falles, for ouþer it wille falle on þe vmbre toward or on þe vmbre froward.

†**c.** Reflection. (Cf. SHADOW *sb.* 5.) *Obs.*

c **1407** LYDG. *Reson & Sens.* 3846 Love him shal so dysfigure, To doon hys besy myght and peyn Hys ovne vmbre to restreyn.

†**2.** In various figurative uses. *Obs.*

c **1380** WYCLIF *Sel. Wks.* I. 355 þe vertue of God makiþ umbre, whanne in a lowe place it lettiþ heete of synne. *c* **1425** *St. Mary of Oignies* II. x. 30 in *Anglia* VIII. 176 After þat she hadde sitten..vndir þe vmbre of hym þat she desyred. **1430-40** LYDG. *Bochas* I. xii. (1544) 23 In euery cost his renoun did shyne. The fame therof was clipsed wᵗ none vmbre. *c* **1450** —— *Secrees* 402 Your studye ay stood, and your dilligence bryght as Apollo, with oute shadwe or Owmbre. **1481** CAXTON *Botoner's Tulle on Old Age* Pref., Whiche lytil volume I haue emprysed tenpryntе vnder the vmbre and shadowe of the noble protection of our moost dradde souerayn. **1573** in *Cath. Tractates* (S.T.S.) 26 In the synagoge, quhilk wes bot ane schaddou and vmbre of the trew kirk. **1581** *Ibid.* 137.

†**3.** *under* (*the*) *umber of* (or *for*), under the cloak or colour of; on pretence of. *Obs.*

1423 JAS. I *Kingis Q.* cxxxiv, Suich feynit treuth is all bot trechorye, Vnder the vmbre of hid ypocrisye. **1430** *Rolls of Parlt.* IV. 501/1 To considre..how under ye umbre of such Vidimus, all an hole Navy of Adversaries myght..daily vetaill, stuffe and refreshe yair partie. **1475** *Bk. Noblesse* (Roxb.) 3 Tho roughe subtile wirkingis conspired and wroughte be the Frenshe partie undre the umbre and coloure of trewis. **1518** H. WATSON *Hist. Oliver of Castile* (Roxb.) P 4 How Arthur vnder the vmbre for to goo to Saynt James, departed for to fynde his felowe Olyuer.

†**4.** The visor of a helmet. Cf. UMBRERE. *Obs.*

14.. *Guy Warw.* (C.) 8346 He opyned vmber that tyde, And keeled hym on euery syde. **1555** *Lydgate's Chron. Troy* III. xxii. P j/2 His swerde so mightely gan race Through the vmber [*MSS.* vmbrere, vmbrel] into Troylus face, That he hym gaue a large mortall wounde. *Ibid.* P ij/2 Cedeus wᵗ his swerde such a stroke him sette, That through yᵉ vmber out his eye he smette. **1603** STOW *Surv.* 385 The Esquier tooke his axe, and smote many blowes on the knight, and made him let fall his axe, and brake vp his vmber three times. **1616** J. LANE *Contn. Sqr.'s T.* XI. 261 The next that entred was a mightie knight..Whose bever and his vmbier closd vp weare.

umber ('ʌmbə(r)), *sb.*² Forms: 5 vmbre, 6- umber (6-7 vmber), 7, 9 humber, 7-8 omber; 7 omer, 9 *dial.* oumer. [a. OF. *umbre*, *ombre* (also *humble*; mod.F. *umble*, *omble*; Sp. *umbla*, *ombla*, Pg. *umbla*), or ad. L. *umbra* UMBRA².] = GRAYLING.

1496 *Fysshynge w. Angle* (1883) 23 The grayllynge by a nother name callyd vmbre is a delycyous fysshe to mannys mouthe. *a* **1550** LELAND *Itin.* (1769) V. 68 In the Lake be Umbers, yn Walsche *Cangans*, and great Store of Pykes, wherof many cum into Wy River. **1615** MARKHAM *Pleas. Princes* iv. (1635) 23 The Humber haunts the clayie Rivers of hie Countries. *Ibid.* vi. 32 The Barbell, or Grayling, which some call the Vmber, are very crafty Fishes. **1662** R. VENABLES *Exper. Angler* v. 55 The Umber is generally taken with the same baits as the Trout. *a* **1672** WILLUGHBY *Hist. Pisc.* (1686) Tab. N. 8 *Thymus et Thymalus* Salv[ian], a Greyling or Omer. *Eboracensibus.* **1740** R. BROOKES *Art of Angling* I. ix. 33 The Grayling or Umber..is in proportion neither so broad nor so thick as a Trout. **1758** *Descr. Thames* 178 Next to the Trout I place the Graylin or Umber, which are thought by some to differ. **1817-22** *Encycl. Metrop.* (1845) XIV. 585/1 The Grayling, or Umber, spawns in May, and is in the best condition in November. **1853** J. JACKSON (*title*), The Practical Fly-Fisher, more particularly for Grayling or Umber.

'umber, *sb.*³ Also 6-9 umbre, 6-7 vmber. [ad. F. *ombre* (also *terre d'ombre*) or It. *ombra* (also *terra di ombra*), either meaning 'shadow' (see UMBER *sb.*¹) or from L. *Umbra*, fem. of *Umber*, belonging to the province Umbria (cf. *Umbrica crēta*, Pliny). Hence also G. *umbra*, *umber-erde*, Da. and Sw. *umber*, *umbra*, Du. *omber*, but Sp. and Pg. *sombra* (= shadow) and *tierra* (Pg. *terra*) *de sombra*.]

1. A brown earth used as a pigment; also, the colour of this.

1568 [see *umber-colour*, sense 3]. **1599** B. JONSON *Cynthia's Revels* v. ii, The gloves are right, sir: you shall bury them.. seven years, and they shall still retain their first scent, true Spanish. There's ambre in the umbre. **1600** SHAKS. *A.Y.L.* I. iii. 114 Ile put my selfe in poore and meane attire, And with a kinde of vmber smirch my face. **1612** PEACHAM *Gentl. Exerc.* 80 Vmber is a more sad colour. *c* **1650** in Norgate *Miniatura* (1919) 97 For the Black Cercle of the eye take Umber, Coale black, and a little whyte. **1753** *Chambers' Cycl.* Suppl. *App.*, *Umber*. This earth when burnt makes a good shade for gold. **1755** *Gentl. Mag.* XXV. 447/2 Sea sand, that in colour resembles unburnt umber, but is lighter and more yellow. **1815** J. SMITH *Panorama Sci. & Art* II. 744 Dark back-grounds may be composed of bistre, umber, or Cologne earth. **1842** LOUDON *Suburban Hort.* 167 Certain colours, having a greater affinity for water than for oil (such as blacks, umbers, and ochres), are liable to be affected by damp. **1899** *Pall Mall Mag.* Jan. 90 The scheme of colour is composed of the yellows, umbers, and reds which Rembrandt loved so intensely.

b. ***burnt umber***, a special preparation of the pigment rendering it redder in colour. Also *attrib.*

c **1650** NORGATE *Miniatura* (1919) 40 The deepning being made with Lake and burnt Umber, the heigthning of pure Gold. **1660** *Albert Durer Revived* 12 Shadow it with the water of Burnt Umber. **1787** W. WILLIAMS *Mechanic Oil Colours* 42 Burnt umber, a very quick drier. **1843** WINSOR & NEWTON *Hand-bk. Water Col.* 27 Burnt Umber, a quiet brown colour, affording clear and warm shadows. **1843** THACKERAY *Jerome Paturot* Wks. 1900 XIII. 388 The Jew-boy.., the burnt-umber Malay who sweeps crossings, save money. **1886** RUSKIN *Præterita* I. 396 To crumble burnt umber with a dry brush for foliage and foreground.

2. One or other of various moths.

1832 J. RENNIE *Consp. Butterfl. & M.* 103 The Scarce Umbre (*L. prosapiaria*) appears in October or November. *Ibid.*, The Umbre (*C. defoliaria*) appears the end of October, in woods and copses. **1887** *Nicholson's Illustr. Dict. Gardening* IV. 122 *Hybernia defoliaria*, or the Mottled Umber.., and *H. aurantiaria*, or the Scarce Umber.

3. *attrib.* and *Comb.*, as ***umber-colour***; ***umber-black***, ***-brown***, ***-coloured***, ***-rufous***, ***-tinted*** adjs.; †***umber-owe***, a kind of madder.

1845 *Encycl. Metrop.* XXV. 882/2 A tufted *umber-black plant. **1832** T. BROWN *Bk. Butterflies & M.* (1834) I. 171 The pupa is of a burnt *umber-brown colour. **1859** B. CLEMENS *Tineina N. Amer.* (1872) 25 The head is umbre-brown. **1887** W. PHILLIPS *Brit. Discomycetes* 59 The hymenium is dark umber brown, externally a little lighter. *c* **1568** in Swayne *Sarum Churchw. Acc.* (1896) 116 Yᵉ paynter for *vmber coller. **1816** W. SMITH *Strata Ident.* 3 The soil is of a mellow brown or umber colour. **1817** STEPHENS in *Shaw's Gen. Zool.* X. II. 335 The upper parts of the body *umber-coloured. **1832** T. BROWN *Bk. Butterflies & M.* (1834) I. 217 With..three umber-coloured spots towards the lower edge of the under wings. **1881** *Instr. Census Clerks* (1885) 85 *Umber Mine Agent. *Ibid.*, *Umber Miner. *a* **1661** FULLER *Worthies, Kent* II. (1662) 57 There are three kinds thereof. 1. Crop-Madder. 2. *Umber-owe. 3. Pipe or Fat-Madder. **1836** BERKELEY *Fungi* in *Smith's Eng. Flora* V. II. 17 Pileus dry squamulose *umber-rufous. **1895** *Daily News* 20 Dec. 5/2 Delicately arched nostrils, sensuously-moulded lips, and *umber-tinted hair.

b. Attrib. in the sense of 'umber-coloured'.

1802 SHAW *Gen. Zool.* III. I. 226 Umbre Lizard. **1803** *Ibid.* IV. II. 384 Umbre Acanthurus. **1832** J. RENNIE *Consp. Butterfl. & M.* 103 The Umbre Link (*Hibernia connectaria*) appears in November and December. **1866** MISS MULOCK *Noble Life* x, The black woods—black, or with a faint umber shadow running through them. **1870** DISRAELI *Lothair* xxxviii, The golden and umber vapours fell into forms that ..depicted the objects of his frequent meditation. **1881** ELEANOR A. ORMEROD *Injur. Insects* (1890) 337 The caterpillar of the Mottled Umber Moth is a 'looper'.

umber *sb.*^{4}, aphetic f. NUMBER *sb.*

The form *imber* (sb. and v.) is found in modern East Anglian dialect. (Cf. UMBER *v.*^{2})

c **1400** *Laud Troy Bk.* 4319 He sclow that tyme withouten vmbre Mo Troyens that I can numbre. **1746** *Exmoor Vocab.* in *Gentl. Mag.* July 408 *Umber*, number.

umber, variant of UMBRE (the bird).

'umber, *v.*^{1} Chiefly *dial.* In 5 **oumbre, owmbre,** 7 **vmbre,** 9 *dial.* **oumer, owmer, oomer,** etc. [ad. OF. *umbrer*, *ombrer* (mod.F. *ombrer* to shade in painting), ad. L. *umbrāre* (whence also It. *ombrare*), f. *umbra* UMBER *sb.*^{1}] *trans.* To shade, to protect.

c **1400** MAUNDEV. (Roxb.) xvii. 78 It will couer and oumbre all his body for þe sonne. *Ibid.* xxii. 100 It will couer all þe body and owmbre it fra þe sonne. **1611** COTGR., *Ombré*, vmbred, or shadowed; (a tearme in Blason). **1790** GROSE *Prov. Gloss.*, *Oumert*, shaded with trees or buildings. **1828** *Craven Gloss.* (ed. 2), *Oumer*, to shadow. *Ibid.*, That birk oumers 't gait. *a* **1867** in Harland & Wilkinson *Lanc. Folk-Lore* 60 T' leaves on t' trees, they owm'ered t' land, And fadin' was the summer light.

Hence **'umbering** *ppl. a.*

1872 DIXON *Milkin' Time* (E.D.D.), The branches of the owmering yew. **1880** A. B. TODD *August* Poet. Wks. (1906) 209 When winds grew hush'd, and umbering trees were still.

† **'umber**, *v.*^{2} *Obs.*$^{-1}$ In 5 **vmbre.** [Aphetic f. NUMBER *v.* Cf. UMBER *sb.*^{4}] *trans.* To number.

c **1400** *Laud Troy Bk.* 370 He sclow champions withouten nombre, So manye that no man myȝt hem vmbre.

'umber, *v.*^{3} Also 7 **vmbre,** 7–8 **umbre.** [f. UMBER *sb.*^{3}] *trans.* To stain or paint with umber; to make of a dark brown colour.

1610 B. JONSON *Alch.* v. v, You..told her, you had tane the paines To dye your beard, and vmbre o'er your face. **1615** MARKHAM *Pleas. Princes* ii. (1635) 7 He which is a master in this Art will Vmber, and darken the Rod. **1623** MIDDLETON & ROWLEY *Sp. Gipsy* II. i, No red-ochre rascals umbered with soot and bacon as the English gipsies are. **1735** *Dict. Polygraph.* I. Q5 After the faces have been umbred, shadow the hair. **1813** HOGG *Queen's Wake* I. *Young Kennedy* i, When the gusts of October had rifled the thorn, Had dappled the woodland, and umbered the plain.

umbereach: see UMBE-.

'umbered, *ppl. a.* Also 9 **umbred.** [f. UMBER *sb.*^{3} or *v.*^{3} + -ED.] Stained or painted with umber; made of a dark brown colour; embrowned, darkened.

In some quots. the sense 'shadowed, darkened by shade' (cf. UMBER *v.*^{1}) is possible.

1599 SHAKS. *Hen. V*, IV. Prologue 9 Fire answers fire, and through their paly flames Each Battaile sees the others vmber'd face. **1624** HEYWOOD *Captives* II. ii. in Bullen *O. Pl.* IV, Fayre flesh and cleane they bothe appeare And not like gypsies umber'd. **1716** POPE *Iliad* VIII. 706 Full fifty guards each flaming pile attend, Whose umber'd arms, by fits, thick flashes send. **1805–6** CARY *Dante, Inf.* III. 110 Thus go they over through the umber'd wave. **1813** SCOTT *Trierm.* I. x, Amid whose yawning gulfs the sun Cast umber'd radiance red and dun. **1860** O. W. HOLMES *Elsie V.* xi. (1891) 154 The bistred or umbered beauties of mingled blood among whom he had been living. **1877** MALLOCK *New Republic* v. i. II. 232 A circular domed temple of umbred marble.

umberere, variant of UMBRERE *Obs.*

† **umberment.** *Obs.* [Cf. UMBER *sb.*^{4} and *v.*^{2}] Number, multitude.

Modern Kentish dial. *umblement* 'number, complement', is prob. a survival of this.

1550–3 *Decaye Eng.* in *Supplic.* (1871) 96 Where tillage was wont to be, nowe is it stored wyth greate vmberment of shepe, & they that haue great vmberment of shepe, must nedes haue greate store of woll.

umberow: see UMBE-.

umbershoot ('ʌmbəʃuːt), *nonce-wd.* [Perh. fanciful formation f. UMBRELLA and SHOOT *sb.* Cf. UMBER *sb.*^{1}] (A word of obscure meaning.)

1922 JOYCE *Ulysses* 189 Crosslegged under an umbrel umbershoot he thrones an Aztec logos.

† **umberst**, *a.* *Obs.*$^{-1}$ [? superl. of **umberous* NUMBEROUS *a.* Cf. UMBER *sb.*^{4}] ? Most numerous.

1599 *Warn. Faire Wom.* II. 198 Methought you..went into a garden, and there was the vmberst sorte of flowers that euer I see.

† **umberty.** *Obs. rare.* In 6 **omberty, vmbertie.** [App. an alteration of UBERTY, after UMBER *sb.*^{4}] Abundance.

1575 LANEHAM *Lett.* (1871) 30 In Philosophy..I think he be az naturally ouerseen: beside poetrie and Astronomie, and oother hid sciencez, as I may gesse by the omberty of hiz books. **1589** *Marprel. Epit.* E iij b, What bommination vmbertie of reasons here be,..and yet euerye one fause.

umberun: see UMBE-.

'umbery, *a.* [f. UMBER *sb.*^{3} + -Y.] Of the colour of umber; dark brown.

1834 H. MILLER *Scenes & Leg.* vi. (1857) 76 They admitted..a sort of umbery twilight. **1862** THORNBURY *Turner* I. 55 Turner..sketching the river and boats with the conventional Indian ink and umbery sails. **1902** *Academy* 28 June 22/2 The flesh is not white, but umbery gold.

† **umbeschew**, *v.* *Sc. Obs.* Also 5 **umbechew,** 6 **vm-, wmschew, vmchev-, vmchow.** [f. UMB- + ESCHEW *v.* The reason for the prefix is not clear.] *trans.* To avoid, shun. Hence † **umschewing** *vbl. sb.*

a. **1456** SIR G. HAY *Gov. Princes* Wks. (S.T.S.) II. 120 Off sik thing men suld have counsale of medicineris as maladyes that men may nocht gudely umbechew. *a* **1500** in *Ratis Raving*, etc. 90 Thir ar the thewis..Quilkis fullis oys comonly; Quhay lovis honor suld thaim vmbeschew. **1514** *Extr. Aberd. Rec.* (1844) I. 90 It is thoucht expedient,..to vmbeschew the said seknes, that thar be bot thre portis haldin oppin for cuming of strangearis.

β. **1530** *Extr. Aberd. Rec.* (1844) I. 448 To ewaid and vmchow trubill of thair innymeis. **1547** *Rec. Elgin* (1903) I. 91 The vmcheving of the apperand schayth and damagh of the haill commond veill.

† **umbeset**, *v.* *Obs.* In later use *Sc.* Forms: *α.* 4– **umbeset,** 4–5 **vmbesette,** 5–6 **-set(t, wmbeset,** 6 **-sett,** 6 **ombeset(t;** 4 **umbisett(e,** 4 **vmbi-,** 5 **vmbysett.** *β.* 5 **vnbesette,** 6–7 **-set,** 6 **unbeset, wnbesett.** [See UMBE- and BESET *v.*, and cf. *umbset* s.v. UMB- and UMSET *v.* So MDu. *omme-, ombeset* p.p., MDa. *ombesat* p.p.] *trans.* To surround, encompass, beset.

α. *a* **1300** *Cursor M.* 7179 Þai vmbisett þat tun a-bute. *Ibid.* 19775 Petre..to þis licam com þat lai, Wit pouer widus vm-bi-sett. **1375** BARBOUR *Bruce* VI. 535 The kyng wes in gret iuperdy, That wes on athir syde vmbeset With fayis. *Ibid.* IX. 706 He till the hous went hastely, And vmbeset it all about. *c* **1400** *Apol. Loll.* 48 Þe auter is vmbeset wiþ stonis. *c* **1470** HENRY *Wallace* v. 168 At syndry furdis the gait thai vmbeset. **1513** DOUGLAS *Æneid* XI. xiv. 22 Quhou huge dolfnes, and schamful cowardice, Hes ombeset ȝour myndis apon sik wys. *c* **1550** ROLLAND *Crt. Venus* I. 113 With Iacinth fine, and Topazion sa fair,..Was vmbeset his body ouir all quhair. **1587** *Reg. Privy Counc. Scot.* IV. 162 Thai ..umbesettis thair hie wayes in thair ganging and cuming fra thair parroche kirk.

β. *c* **1440** *Gesta Rom.* lxv. 281 (Add. MS.), Whan the Steward was thus vnbesette with thise iij. bestes, he was right sory. *a* **1575** *Diurn. Occurr.* (Bann. Cl.) 168 Certane personis..quha was werry bent to haue vnbesett him in the waij betuix Edinburgh and Berwick. **1582–8** *Hist. James VI* (1804) 112 Thairfoir Lord Claud Hamiltoun unbeset the way with sum chosen men. **1624** in *Abbotsford Club Misc.* 144 Thomas Logie..meitting ane number of cattis..quhilk vnbesett him, the said Thomas saw ȝour face vpoun ane of [the] cattis.

Hence † **umbe'setting** *vbl. sb.* *Obs.*

1543 *Acc. Ld. High Treas. Scot.* VIII. 244 To underly the law for thair tressonable umbesetting of the gait. **1551** *Ibid.* X. 35 To have underlyne the lawis for unbesetting of the said Alexander Cummyng of Alteir gait. **1624** in *Abbotsford Club Misc.* 144 Anent the vnbesetting of the cattis.

umbeshadow, -shear, -shine, -siege, -spread, -stand: see UMBE-.

† **umbestound**, *adv.* *Obs.* Forms: 3 **vmbe stunde, umbestunde,** 4 **vmbesto(u)nde,** 5 *Sc.* **vmbestount.** [OE. *ymbe* (*embe*) *stunde*: see UMBE *prep.* and STOUND *sb.*^{1}] **a.** At times; sometimes. **b.** After a (short) time.

[**993** *Battle of Maldon* 271 Æfre embe stunde he sealde sume wunde.] *c* **1205** LAY. 11969 Þa vmbe stunde ne sæȝe heo noht of londe. *a* **1225** *Ancr. R.* 344 Ich am of-dred leste I go driuinde oðerhwules to swuðe uorðward upe fole þouhtes, and fule umbestunde. *a* **1300** *Havelok* 2297 He is birkabeynes sone, Þe king þat was vmbe stonde wone For to yeme [us] and wel were. **13..** *E.E. Allit. P.* C. 122 O Folez in folk felez oþer whyle, & vnderstondes vmbestounde,.. Hope ȝe þat he heres not þat eres alle made? **1375** BARBOUR *Bruce* VII. 398 The kyng..Wes in Carrik, quhar vmbestount He vald vend vith his men till hount.

So † **umbestounds** *adv.* *Obs.*

13.. *E.E. Allit. P.* C. 7 Þen is better to abyde þe bur vmbe-stoundes, Þen ay þrow forth my þro, þaȝ me þynk ylle.

umbeswey: see UMBE-.

umbe'think, un-, *v.* *Obs.* exc. *dial.* Forms: *α.* 3 **ummbeþennkenn,** 5 **umbethenke;** 4 **vmbethynk(e,** 4–6 **vmbe-, umbethink** (5–6 *Sc.* **wmbe-**); 4 **vmby-,** 4–5 **vmbithynk(e.** *β.* 4–7 **vnbethink** (4 **vnbi-;** 6 **-thynk**), 7, 8–9 *dial.*, **unbethink** (9 *dial.* **on-**). [See UMBE- and BETHINK *v.*^{1} and cf. UMTHINK *v.*]

† **1.** *trans.* (with objective clause). To think about, to consider; to remember (*how*, *that*, etc.). *Obs.*

c **1200** ORMIN 2953 Ʒiff þatt icc..mikell ummbeþennke, Whillc gate icc muȝhe cwemenn Godd. *c* **1340** HAMPOLE *Psalter* lxxxvi. 13 Londe of forgettinge is in þas þat vnbethinks not þat þai salbe demed rightwisly. *c* **1380** WYCLIF in *MS. Bodl. 288* fol. 250/1 Makiþ knowen in þe folk þe fyndingis of him: vmbiþinkiþ for his name is hiȝ. **1483** *Cath. Angl.* 403/1 To Vnbethynke, *recogitare*. **1501** DOUGLAS *Pal. Hon.* I. lxx, I vmbethocht how Joue and auld Saturne, Intill ane wolf thay did Lycaon turne.

2. *refl.* To bethink (oneself); to call to mind: **a.** With obj. clause or inf.

α. *a* **1300** *Cursor M.* 2999 For I me vm-bithoght Yee war men þat godd duted noght. *c* **1340** HAMPOLE *Prose Tr.* 10 Vmbethynke the þat thou halowe þi halydaye. **1375** BARBOUR *Bruce* v. 613 'A! schir, vmbethinkis ȝow,' said he, 'How neir to ȝou that I suld be'. *c* **1400** *Ywaine & Gaw.* 1583 Sir Ywaine umbithought him than He had forgeten his leman. *c* **1425** WYNTOUN *Cron.* IV. ii. 130 He.. wmbethoucht [*v.r.* (*c* 1520) vnbethocht] hym inkyrly Withe qwhat turmentis men mycht be Punyst for þar iniquite. *c* **1460** *Towneley Myst.* i. 123 Therfor, felow, hold thi peasse, and vmbithynke the what thou saysse.

β. *c* **1520** [see 2 *a*]. **1685** COTTON *Montaigne* (1711) I. xii. 60 The Lacedæmonian Foot..unbethought themselves to disperse and retire. *Ibid.* II. xii. 365 Nicetas of Syracusa unbethought him to maintain, that it was the Earth that mov'd. **1703** A. DE LA PRYME *Short View Hist. Winterton* in *Archaeol.* XL. 234 William the Conqueror haveing the whole Nation at Command begun to unbethink himself, how he might gratify his Favourites. **1863** MRS. GASKELL *Sylvia's L.* vii, They'll prize what I leave 'em if I could only onbethink me what they would like.

b. Const. *of* or *on*. Also *intr.*

α. *c* **1375** *Cursor M.* 1325 (Fairf.), Of steppis he vmbe-þoȝt him þan þat falowed for syn of man. **1375** BARBOUR *Bruce* III. 352 The king umbethocht him off a thing. **1422** tr. *Secreta Secret., Priv. Priv.* 150 Vmbethynke vs of the moste noble lordis as to worthely lorshuppe that afor this tymes weryn. **1456** SIR G. HAYE *Govt. Princes* (S.T.S.) 164 Will thou umbethink the wele of all that I have said. **1513** DOUGLAS *Æneid* I. x. 32 Quharfore I vmbethink me of ane trane, This quene first for to caucht in luvis lace. **1560** ROLLAND *Seven Sages* 87 He vmbethocht him self of ane consait.

β. ? *a* **1500** *Chester Pl.* xxiv. 430 How durst you euer doe amysse, when you vnbethoughte you of this? ? *a* **1600** *Sir Lionel* 35 in *Percy Folio, Ball. & Rom.* (1867) I. 76 He.. vnbethought him of a while [= wile], how he might that wilde bore beguile. **1630** W. FREAKE *Doctrines Jesuites* II. 59 The Iesuites vnbethought themselues further of this Stratagem. **1686** G. STUART *Joco-Ser. Disc.* 4 When I unbethink me of thae frights and fears This poor auld grey beard hangs dreeping with tears. *c* **1746** J. COLLIER (Tim Bobbin) *View Lanc. Dial.* Wks. (1862) 11 On then I unbethowt meh o me Sawt. **1788** W. H. MARSHALL *Rur. Econ. Yorks.* II. s.v., I unbethought myself on't. **1892** SARAH HEWETT *Peas. Sp. Devon* 139 Well, I'm baggered ef I ant ajist unbethowted o' 't.

c. Without const.

α. *a* **1300** *Cursor M.* 3622 A wyel sco hir vmbithogt. **1375** BARBOUR *Bruce* XVII. 40 Quhen the marschall the letteris saw, He vmbethoucht him than a thraw. *c* **1440** *Alph. Tales* 17 Sho satt still & vmbethoght hur, & knew his falssett well enogh. *Ibid.* 237 Als oft sithes as I se a tade, I vmbethynk me, & thankis God þat gaf me so fayr a form. *a* **1500** in *Ratis Raving*, etc. 13 Quhen I wmbethocht me, and turnyt my mynd in my self, thinkand of al my warldly werkis.

β. **1535** COVERDALE *2 Sam.* xiv. 14 And God will not take awaye the lyfe, but vnbethynketh himselfe. **1603** *Philotus* lxxvi, Quhen I haue vnbethocht me thryse, I can na better way deuyse. *a* **1666** C. HOOLE *School-Colloquies* (1688) 190 Let me unbethink myself a little. *c* **1800** PEGGE *Anecd. Eng. Lang.* (1814) 250 Similar to this word *un*beknown is an expression used in some parts of England, where people say, 'I un-bethought myself': i.e. I recollected. **1857** WAUGH *Lanc. Life* 207 He's the very mon for yo! Aw've just unbethought mo! **1879** MISS JACKSON *Shropsh. Wordbk.* 460, I should a done that wrung, if I 'adna jest unbethought me in time.

3. In *pa. pple.* After reflection.

1422 tr. *Secreta Secret., Priv. Priv.* 138 If hit happe a kynge to do any thynge vnawyssely, he owyth hit repel vmbethoght avysely, and wyth reyson know his defaute.

Hence **umbe'thinking** *vbl. sb.*; **umbe'thought** *ppl. a.*

1422 tr. *Secreta Secret., Priv. Priv.* 155 The more ryche man be and manaunt, the more hym be-howyth that he be vmbethoght. *Ibid.* 157 Whoso wyse is and vmbethoght, he wille not begyle, ne begilid he nel not be. *c* **1440** *Alph. Tales* 293 To restrene hur wepyng sho lefte thynkyng of þe manhede of Criste & toke hur to vmbethynkyng of His godded. **1548** UDALL *Erasm. Par., Luke* xii. 115 To take folie and unbethinking to be of his counsayle.

umbethonre, -tigh, -trin, -turn, -viron, -wall, -weave, -wend, -wet: see UMBE-.

† **umbe'while**, *adv.* *Obs.* Also 3 **umbe hwile,** 4 **vmbywhile** (4 **unbe-,** 5 **vnbi-**). [OE. *ymb(e) hwíle*: see UMBE *prep.* and WHILE *sb.* Cf. UMWHILE.]

1. After a time.

971 *Blickling Hom.* 217 Þa wæs ymb hwile, ða ʒefelde he þæt se deada man his leomu ealle astyrede. *a* **1225** *Leg. Kath.* 12 Weox umbe hwile [*Royal MS.* umbe hwiles] wreððe ham bitweonen.

2. At times; sometimes.

c **1230** *Hali Meid.* 27 Nawt ane on ende; ah eauer umbehwile. *a* **1310** in Wright *Lyric P.* xv. 49 Sleuthe ant slep mi bedyner, that weneth me unbe-while. Umbe-while y am to whene, when y shal murthes meten. **1393** LANGL. *P. Pl.* C. VII. 396 (MS. Laud 656), [They] setyn til euesang range & songe vmbywhile.

umbfold: see UMB-.

umbier, variant of UMBER *sb.*^{1}

† **umbil.** *Obs.*$^{-0}$ [ad. L. *umbil-īcus*: see next. F. *nombril* is used in the same sense.] (See quot.)

1688 R. HOLME *Armoury* II. 85/1 The umbil is the navel, or daulk in any fruit, just against the stalk; it is also taken for the crown, top, or head of an apple, where the blossom is.

umbilic (ʌm'bɪlɪk), *sb.* Forms: *α.* 7 **vmbilike, -icke, umbilick, umbelic(k,** 7, 9 **umbilic.** *β.* 7 **vmbilique, umbelique.** [ad. L. *umbilīc-us* UMBILICUS, related to Gr. *ὀμφαλός*, and ultimately to NAVEL *sb.* Hence also F. *ombilic*, †*umbilic* (1556), It. *um-*, *ombilico*, *ombellico*, Sp. *ombligo*, Pg. *umbigo*. In sense 1 prob. stressed *umbi'lic*.]

†**1.** The centre; the middle point or part. *Obs.*
α. **1607** BP. J. KING *Serm. 5 Nov.* 23 For the perpetration of it they went downe into the bowells of the earth, but for the inuention to the very vmbilicke, and centre of the earth. **1608** —— *Serm. 24 Mar.* 19 The verie middle and vmbilicke of natures prefined time. **1638** SIR T. HERBERT *Trav.* (ed. 2) 113 Ormus is as it were the umbelick of the gulph. *Ibid.* 265 Hell is in the Umbelic or navell of the world.
β. **1612** PEACHAM *Gentl. Exerc.* III. 143 It was round, and equall from the vmbelique or middle point, to euery side. **1615** SIR E. HOBY *Curry-combe* vi. 248 Not only in Wales and Scotland, but euen in the vmbilique of the Saxons Dominion. **1638** SIR T. HERBERT *Trav.* (ed. 2) 214 In the umbelique or mid-part of this spatious Court is a quadrangular Tanck or Pond.
2. *Geom.* (See quots. 1875–6.)
1843 MACCULLAGH in *Proc. R. Irish Acad.* (1846) II. 458 The focal hyperbola of the ellipsoid and the focal ellipse of the hyperboloid of two sheets, are umbilicar focals, and pass through the umbilics of these surfaces. **1875** P. FROST *Solid Geom.* (ed. 2) I. 166 The point-circles in which the variable circle terminates are called *umbilics*. **1876** *Handbk. Sci. App. S. Kens.* 46 At special points, called umbilics, the greatest and least curvatures (and therefore all the curvatures) are equal to one another. The sphere has the peculiarity that every point on it is an umbilic.

†**umˈbilic**, *a. Obs.* Also 6 vm-, 7 umbilique, 8 umbilick. [ad. L. *umbilīc-us* (see prec.), the ending being taken as adjectival.]
1. ***umbilic point***, a central point.
a. *Her.* **1586** FERNE *Blaz. Gentrie* 105 Counterchanging of them by the fesse or vmbilique point of the sheeld. *Ibid.* 184 This scutcheon..was of old named fessey target bycause that the fesse or vmbilique point of the coate armor is occupied with a targe or sheeld.
b. *Math.* **1700** MOXON *Math. Dict.*, *Umbilique Points*, or the 2 Focus or Centre-Points in an Elipsis.
2. (See quot.)
1681 tr. *Willis' Rem. Med. Wks.* Vocab., *Umbilic*, belonging to the navel, or of the likeness or shape of the navel.

umbilical (ʌmˈbɪlɪkəl, ʌmbɪˈlaɪkəl), *a.* and *sb.* Also 6 **vmbelycall**, 8 **umbelical**, 7 **vm-**, **umbilicall**, 8 **umbillical**. [ad. med.L. *umbilīcāl-is*, f. *umbilīcus* UMBILIC *sb.* Cf. It. *umbilicale*, *ombelicale*, Sp. and Pg. *umbilical*, F. *ombilical* (1541), †*umbilical* (Cotgr.).]
A. *adj.* **1.** *Anat.* **a.** Of or pertaining to the umbilicus or navel.
1541 R. COPLAND *Guydon's Quest. Chirurg.* Hij, The party vmbelycall synual is fro yͤ nauyll downwarde. **1704** J. HARRIS *Lex. Techn.* I, *Umbilical Region*, is that part of the Abdomen lying round about the Navel. **1728** CHAMBERS *Cycl.* s.v. *Liver*, One [fissure] thro' which the Umbilical Ligament passes. **1808** BARCLAY *Muscular Motions* 348 A tendon, which..divides in the region called *umbilical* into two strata. **1846** BRITTAN tr. *Malgaigne's Man. Oper. Surg.* 434 The umbilical ring..is but slightly resistant and very dilatable for some time after birth. **1859** BULLOCK *Cazeaux' Midwif.* 128 The umbilical depression, which in the two first months seems deeper, disappears gradually as gestation progresses. **1881** MIVART *Cat* 185 On this account the ventral part of the groove is called the umbilical fissure.
b. In ***umbilical artery***, ***vein***, ***vessel***.
1615 CROOKE *Body of Man* 710 The Infant..draweth the nourishment into the Liuer through the vmbilicall veine by a naturall instinct. **1656** BLOUNT *Glossogr.*, *Umbilical Arteries*, are two Arteries marching from the Navil, through *Peritonæum* to the sides of the Bladder. **1667** *Phil. Trans.* II. 512 The Embrio doth breath, but not feed, through the Umbilical vessels. **1725** *Fam. Dict.* s.v. *Liver*, These two Lobes [of the Liver] are separated by a Scissure or Cleft, through which the Umbelical Vein enters. **1774** GOLDSMITH *Nat. Hist.* (1862) I. ii. 158 The bloodvessels that go to the placenta..are plainly seen issuing from the navel (being therefore called the umbilical vessels). **1831** R. KNOX *Cloquet's Anat.* 715 The umbilical artery always furnishes three or four, which ramify in the walls of the bladder. **1841** T. R. JONES *Anim. Kingd.* 629 The arteries..represent the umbilical arteries of the human fetus.
c. *Path.* and *Med.* Affecting, proceeding from, or applied to, the navel.
1797 *Encycl. Brit.* (ed. 3) XVIII. 155 In umbilical hernia the parts protruded pass out at the umbilicus, and are commonly the intestines, or omentum, or both. **1862** HABERSHON *Dis. Abdomen* (ed. 2) 570 Strumous Peritonitis. Fæcal Abscess. Umbilical Discharge. **1875** KNIGHT *Dict. Mech.* 2678/1 *Umbilical bandage*,..a broad band of fabric which is buckled around the umbilical region of the body to serve as an abdominal supporter and for palliating umbilical hernia. *Ibid.*, An umbilical truss, designed for the same purpose.
d. Connected on the female side.
1888 *N. & Q.* 7th Ser. V. 493/2 The direct lineal ancestress in the female line, or what is sometimes termed umbilical or uterine ancestress.
2. ***umbilical cord***: **a.** The flexible string which attaches the fœtus to the placenta; the navel-string.
1753 *Chambers' Cycl.* Suppl. s.v. *Navel*, The umbilical cord or navel-string of the new-born infant. **1803** *Med. Jrnl.* IX. 74 He combats the opinion..that the death of the child necessarily follows from the neglect of tying the umbilical cord after delivery. **1847** W. C. L. MARTIN *Ox* 167/2 Some farmers after the birth of the calf attach a small weight to the umbilical cord, in order to facilitate the separation and expulsion of the placenta. **1888** *Buck's Handbk. Med. Sci.* VI. 22/2 The umbilical cord normally presents torsions.
fig. **1847** EMERSON *Repr. Men, Swedenborg* Wks. (Bohn) I. 334 With a force of many men, he could never break the umbilical cord which held him to nature. **1859** I. TAYLOR *Logic in Theol.* 217 That intercourse which..is linking England with India—that umbilical cord through which the circulation, to and fro, is going on.

b. *Bot.* The small peduncle which attaches a seed to the placenta. Similarly ***umbilical bundle***, ***vessel***.
1731 P. MILLER *Gard. Dict.* s.v. *Vegetation*, This fermented Liquor is convey'd by the Umbilical Vessel to the Trunk of the little Plant. **1819** LINDLEY tr. *Richard's Obs. Fruits & Seeds* 6 Every visible process of the trophosperm which bears a single seed is known by the name of umbilical chord. **1830** —— *Nat. Syst. Bot.* 150 Seeds attached by umbilical cords to placentæ. **1875** BENNETT & DYER tr. *Sachs's Bot.* 252 From it [an umbilicus] a denser bundle of threads runs downwards to the peridium, the umbilical bundle.
c. *transf.* (*a*) *Astronaut.* A cable or other linking device supplying essential liquid or electrical services; *spec.* the connection between a guided missile and its launching equipment, or that joining a space-walking astronaut to his craft. Similarly ***umbilical connection***, ***pipe***, ***tower***, etc.
1948 *Gloss. Guided Missile Terms* (U.S. Research & Development Board) 69 *Umbilical cord*, a cable fitted with a quick disconnect plug at the missile end, through which missile equipment is controlled and tested while missile is still attached to launching equipment or parent plane. **1958** *Times* 1 Mar. 6/3 The 'umbilical pipes' through which liquid oxygen was being pumped to top up its [*sc.* the missile's] fuel tanks. **1959** *Manch. Guardian* 3 Jan. 5 The 'umbilical cord' is a widely detachable cable through which the missile is powered and controlled while still on its 'ivory tower'. **1962** J. GLENN in *Into Orbit* 188 A special countdown started for dropping the umbilical cord which had been providing external power and cooling for the capsule until now. **1963** *Times* 31 May 19/4 The Apollo spacecraft and the three-stage Saturn MK.5 launch vehicle will be erected in the vertical position, together with the umbilical tower on a fabricated base. **1966** *Daily Tel.* 12 Oct. 21/5 The value of the umbilical tether employed on all space walks so far is being questioned. **1967** *Economist* 23 Dec. 1237/2 (*caption*) That grip of gold: umbilical cord linking astronaut to his space ship. **1970** N. ARMSTRONG et al. *First on Moon* vii. 147 We can see the LM umbilical connection quite well.
(*b*) A cable or pipe providing a deep-sea diver with essential electrical and similar supplies. Similarly ***umbilical cable***, ***link***, ***pipe***, etc.
1968 *New Scientist* 17 Oct. 127/2 Helium-distorted speech, picked up through the microphone, is transmitted by shielded cables in the umbilical pipe. **1969** *Ibid.* 2 Oct. 11/2 Life support requirements have been provided by way of an umbilical link to a surface station. **1970** R. BARTON *Oceanology Today* v. 123 It submerges and then travels along the seabed on four large hydraulically driven wheels. .. Power is provided through an umbilical cable. **1975** *Offshore* Sept. 115/2 Moreover, the Globule has..an emergency life support of 96 hours and batteries which can be recharged when in operation through the umbilical cable and the induction cable. **1979** *Daily Tel.* 11 Aug. 2/5 The divers asked for their chamber to be lowered to the sea-bed by means of their life-support umbilical cord. **1981** *Times* 23 May 3/3 He found the umbilical lifeline to the [diving] bell ..in tatters.
(*c*) In other misc. uses.
1962 *New Scientist* 9 Aug. 285/1 Steering was done from another car travelling behind and a little to one side of the crash car by an attachment which is referred to by the research workers as an umbilical cord. **1968** *Listener* 15 Aug. 200/1 Tiny portable cameras carried by stalwart chaps loaded with power packs and aerials and umbilical cords like a spaceman operating outside his spaceship. **1977** *Rolling Stone* 30 June 117/3 Their giant electrostatic Model One.. was the first electrostatic speaker system I know of that got rid of that cumbersome 'umbilical cord' (the line cord you had to connect to a wall outlet to power its high-voltage polarizing supply).
3. *Conchol.* Provided or connected with, of the nature of, an umbilicus.
1755 *Gentl. Mag.* XXV. 128 The particular species of the *Nautilus*, as shells, are the papiraceous, the eared, and the umbilical. **1822** J. PARKINSON *Outl. Oryctol.* 147 In some instances the umbilical termination [of a shell] is filled, as if by an exudation of callus. **1894** *Geol. Mag.* Oct. 438 The Australian form is distinguished by the greater prominence of its short umbilical ribs.
4. *Geom.* Forming, or pertaining to, an umbilicus.
1728 CHAMBERS *Cycl.*, *Umbilical Points*, in Mathematicks, the same with *Foci*. **1841** J. R. YOUNG *Math. Dissert.* ii. 34 Dupin..clearly saw that Mouge had misinterpreted this symbol in his investigation of umbilical points. **1851** SYLVESTER in *Lond.* etc. *Phil. Mag.* Feb. 136 *note*, As the two surfaces jut one close into the other at this point, it would perhaps be not improper to designate the contact at such point as umbilical. **1863** FROST & WOLSTENHOLME *Solid Geom.* 144 The fixed point is called an umbilical focus, the intersection of the planes a directrix, and the constant ratio the umbilical modulus.
5. Occupying a central point or position.
1742 *De Foe's Tour Gt. Brit.* (ed. 3) II. 293 The Chapter-house is large, supported, as to its arched Roof, by one umbilical pillar. **1760** STERNE *Tr. Shandy* I. xxiii, His soul might as well, unless for mere ceremony, or the trifling advantage which the umbilical point gave her,..play the fool out o' doors as in her own house. **1774** J. BRYANT *Mythol.* I. 243 The Ætolians were stiled umbilical; and looked upon themselves as the central people in Greece.
B. *sb. pl.* **1.** The umbilical vessels.
1774 COOPER in *Phil. Trans.* LXV. 316 It is plain also, that the blood passed..through the hypogastrics and umbilicals to the placenta.
2. *transf.* and *fig.* (also in sing.).
1936 W. FAULKNER *Absalom, Absalom!* 259 That River which runs not only through the physical land of which it is the geologic umbilical. **1960** *Times* 18 Oct. 13/6 The umbilicals are..expendable power lines which nurture the bird (missile) while it is on the ground and vanish when it takes flight. **1966** J. A. CHAMIER *Cannonball* iv. 34 He picked up a microphone with its spring-spiral umbilical from its recess. **1974** *Petroleum Rev.* XXVIII. 674/3 Underwater vehicles may be..tethered (powered by an umbilical from a surface vehicle) or untethered (free swimming). **1977** *Times* 17 Oct. 14/7 On the humid roof sat batteries of television crews... Wires and umbilicals led..to a generator outside. **1982** D. HART-DAVIS *Level Five* i. 9 Newman held the end of the hot-water umbilical... The steady flow began, cold at first, then warm, then hot... He..felt the warm jets course through the [diving] suit.

†**umbiliˈcality.** *Obs.* [f. prec. + -ITY.]
1. A close or intimate connexion.
1646 SIR T. BROWNE *Pseud. Ep.* v. v. 240 In his immortall and diviner part hee seemed to hold a nearer coherence, and an umbilicality even with God himselfe.
2. An umbilical cord.
1658 J. ROBINSON *Endoxa* vii. 44, I know, after two or three days incubation, that there is a Sanguine-like string;.. but that that should be the Umbilicality of the Chicken, is not by sight demonstrable.

umˈbilically, *adv.* [f. as prec. + -LY².] By means of an umbilicus or umbilical cord; in the region of the navel. Also *transf.* and *fig.*
1821 W. P. C. BARTON *Flora N. Amer.* I. 97 Seeds numerous, attached umbilically to a central receptacle. **1936** D. GASCOYNE *Man's Life is this Meat* 19 Umbilically detached, of sorrowful mien and at the same time tricked out in cobwebs,—these vanquished ones, whose breathings propagate violence and fear. **1951** M. MCLUHAN *Mech. Bride* (1967) 51/1 The self-consciousness and uneasiness of those still umbilically attached to such guides. **1963** *Adv. Space Sci. & Technol.* V. 241 Mass transfer (gas, liquid, solid cargo, and personnel) can be done umbilically or by docking. **1979** G. MACDONALD *Camera* xiii. 187/2 After being linked umbilically to the visual arts for half of the last century, the cultural influence of the contemporary photograph is now slight.

umbiliˈcanimism. *rare.* [f. L. *umbilīc-us* UMBILICUS + *anima* soul, after late Gr. ὀμφαλόψυχος.] The practice of looking steadfastly at the navel, followed by the Hesychasts, in expectation of an outward exhibition of the light supposed to dwell within the soul of man.
1874 J. H. BLUNT *Dict. Sects* 192/1 The Light theory and Umbilicanimism of the Hesychasts.

umˈbilicar, *a. Geom.* [f. UMBILIC-US + -AR. Cf. late L. *umbilīcāris* (Tertullian).] Of or belonging to the umbilicus.
1843 MACCULLAGH in *Proc. R. Irish Acad.* (1846) II. 458 A focal which is not modular may be called *umbilicar*, because it intersects the surface in the umbilics. *Ibid.* 469 A focal point which is at once modular and umbilicar. **1870** CAYLEY *Math. Papers* VIII. 326 The contacts arise, as will appear, from the umbilici of the ellipsoid, and may be termed 'umbilicar centres', or 'omphaloi'.

†**umˈbilicary**, *a. Obs.*⁻¹ [f. obs. F. *umbilicar* (Rabelais), ad. late L. *umbilīcāris*: see prec.] Lying in the region of the navel.
a **1693** *Urquhart's Rabelais* III. xxxiv. 290, I will..grope her Pulse, and see the Disposition of her Hypogaster, together with her Umbilicary Parts [F. *parties umbilicares*].

umbilicate (ʌmˈbɪlɪkət), *a.* [ad. L. *umbilīcāt-us*, f. *umbilīcus* UMBILICUS. Cf. It. *umbilicato*, *ombelicato*, F. *ombiliqué*.] Resembling a navel; having a depression like the navel.
1698 W. KING tr. *Sorbière's Journ. Lond.* 15 He has several other Curiosities; among the rest was a Roman Glass, whose very bottom was smoth and very little umbilicate. **1785** MARTYN *Lett. Bot.* xxxii. (1794) 499 Umbilicate [section], or hollowed like the navel, and sooty, or appearing black, or as if burnt. **1826** KIRBY & SP. *Entomol.* IV. 270 *Umbilicate*,.. when a variole, tubercle granule, &c. has a depression in its centre. **1842** JOHNSTON in *Proc. Berw. Nat. Club* II. 30 There is no spire, nor is the apex umbilicate. **1897** W. E. STEELE *Field Bot.* 81 Cal[yx] with 30 furrows, conical, umbilicate at base.

umˈbilicate, *v.* [Cf. prec. and UMBILICATION.] *intr.* To become umbilicate.
c **1900** *Buck's Handbk. Med. Sci.* VII. 250 (Cent. Suppl.).

umˈbilicated, *a.* [f. as prec. + -ED.] Having a depression like the navel; umbilicate. (Chiefly in special applications: see quots.)
a. **1698** W. KING tr. *Sorbière's Journ. Lond.* 15 He show'd me, likewise, a great Rummer of two Quarts..: I found that the foot of the latter was more Vmbilicated than the former.
b. *Bot.* **1693** *Phil. Trans.* XVII. 928 The Fourth Section contains such Trees and Shrubs as have an Umbilicated Fruit. **1725** SLOANE *Jamaica* II. 76 To that follows many crown'd or umbilicated berries. **1756** P. BROWNE *Jamaica* 203 The larger Colts-foot, with umbilicated leaves. **1771** DUCHESS PORTLAND *Let.* in Mrs. Delany *Life & Corr.* Ser. II. (1862) I. 359, I fancy I left the umbilicated lichen at Ilam. **1845** *Florist's Jrnl.* (1846) VI. 196 The plant..is at first rotund, in age becoming more oblong, umbilicated at the top.
c. *Conch.* **1776** DA COSTA *Elem. Conchol.* x. 202 The umbilicated whitish thin Snail. **1822** J. PARKINSON *Outl. Oryctol.* 155 The columella umbilicated and slightly grooved at its base. **1851** S. P. WOODWARD *Mollusca* I. 100 The axis of the shell, around which the whorls are coiled, is sometimes open or hollow; in which case, the shell is said to be perforated, or umbilicated. **1880** *Linn. Soc. Jrnl.* XV. 95 Shell high, conical, tectiform, carinated, umbilicated, with a flattish depressedly conical base.
d. *Ent.* **1819** SAMOUELLE *Entomol. Compend.* 190 Black, shining, impressed-punctate, cicatriculose; the punctures umbilicated, the umbilici perforate. **1826** KIRBY & SPENCE

Entomol. III. 509 In *Fulgora Diadema* they [stemmata] are also umbilicated, but the *umbilicus* is circular.

e. *Path.* and *Anat.* **1834** *Cycl. Pract. Med.* III. 738/2 This central depression, or *umbilicated* form of vesicle (as it is sometimes called), is very characteristic of small-pox. **1877** COUES *Fur Anim.* i. 13 At each side of this fossa.. is found an umbilicated papilla. **1897** *Allbutt's Syst. Med.* II. 519 A pustular rash,.. but without umbilicated pustules.

umbilication (ʌmbɪlɪˈkeɪʃən). *Path.* [f. L. *umbilīc-us* UMBILICUS + -ATION.] A central depression on the upper part of a pock or other vesicle on the skin; also, the condition of being so depressed.

1873 F. T. ROBERTS *Handbk. Med.* 182 After a while the umbilication disappears, the pock becoming either rounded or pointed at the top. **1880** A. FLINT *Princ. Med.* 618 The umbilication, which can sometimes be felt on the cancerous nodules, may be of assistance in the diagnosis. **1899** *Allbutt's Syst. Med.* VIII. 876 As the tumour increases in size, one or more depressions, or umbilications, are observed on the surface.

umbiˈliciform, *a. rare.* [f. L. *umbilīc-us* + -(I)FORM.] Having the form of an umbilicus; navel-like.

1867 [see AFTER-SHAFT]. **1893** GADOW in Newton *Dict. Birds* 239 The umbiliciform pit,.. which marks the point of junction with the rhachis and hyporhachis.

umbiˈlicular, *a. rare*⁻¹. [f. L. *umbilīc-us* (see next) + -ULAR.] Directed towards the navel.

1883 BOODLE in *Pop. Sci. Monthly* Feb. 513 The writers who have drawn attention off mere umbilicular contemplation.

‖**umbilicus** (ʌmbɪˈlaɪkəs, ʌmˈbɪlɪkəs). Pl. -ici (-ˈaɪsaɪ, -ɪsaɪ). [L. *umbilīcus*: see UMBILIC *sb.*]

1. *Anat.* The central depression in the abdomen, marking the point of attachment of the umbilical cord; the navel.

[**1615** CROOKE *Body of Man* (1631) 81 They are called *Vasa Vmbilicalia*, because they passe through the Nauell which is called *Vmbilicus.* **1693** tr. *Blancard's Phys. Dict.* (ed. 2), *Umbilicus*, the Navel, or Boss in the middle of the Abdomen, to which the Navel-string in a Fœtus is joined. **1728** CHAMBERS *Cycl.* s.v. *Abdomen*, The middle part of the Umbilical [region], is called the *Umbilicus*, or Navel.] **1799** *Med. Jrnl.* I. 422 Immediately over the left rectus muscle, at its half intersection below the umbilicus. **1834** J. FORBES *Laennec's Dis. Chest.* (ed. 4) 345 This tumour increased and extended towards the umbilicus. **1876** BRISTOWE *Th. & Pract. Med.* (1878) 650 In which case the general symmetry of the belly is maintained, but the umbilicus is usually deeply sunk.

b. *Bot.* The part of a seed by which it is attached to the placenta.

1837 P. KEITH *Bot. Lex.* 89 They are then nourished by means of an *umbilicus*, which we cannot but regard as an external root. **1857** M. J. BERKELEY *Cryptog. Bot.* §108. 135 *Acetabularia* bears a whorl of threads,.. seated on a delicate peduncle, with a few free-branched threads springing from the umbilicus. **1866** *Treas. Bot.* 1190/1 *Umbilicus*, the hilum of a seed; the scar formed by its separation from the placenta.

c. *transf.* The central point.

1897–8 G. T. STOKES *Worthies Irish Ch.* i. 5 Killare in the county of Westmeath, formerly regarded as the umbilicus of Ireland.

†**2.** (See quot.) *Obs.*

1688 R. HOLME *Armoury* II. 363/1 An Umbilicus or Navel shell.. is a kind of writhen cockle or shell fish wrinkled and turned in on the top like a Navel.

3. *Geom.* †**a.** A focus. *Obs.*

1704 J. HARRIS *Lex. Techn.* I, *Umbelicus* in an Ellipsis, &c. is that Focus about which the Motion of any Revolving Body is made, and which it respects as its Centre. So that either Focus may be called by this Name. **1728** CHAMBERS *Cycl.* s.v. *Moon*, These smaller [planets] must move in Ellipses having their Umbilici in the Centres of the larger.

b. A point in a surface through which all its lines of curvature pass.

1841 J. R. YOUNG *Math. Dissert.* ii. 36 The perplexities and mistakes in the theory of umbilici. **1863** P. FROST & WOLSTENHOLME *Solid Geom.* 418 To determine the conditions for an umbilicus. *Ibid.* 420 To determine the number of umbilici on a surface of the nth degree.

4. A small depression or hollow suggestive of a navel. (Chiefly in special applications.)

a. *Bot.* **1809** BROWN in *Trans. Linnean Soc.* (1811) X. 36 It is not accompanied by the usual position or even uniformity in the situation of the external umbilicus. **1812** *New. Bot. Garden* I. 42 The berries are round with a depressed umbilicus. **1845** *Florist's Jrnl.* (1846) VI. 196 In the umbilicus alone, whence the flowers appear, there are a few small brown rigid setæ rather than spines.

b. *Ent.* **1819**, **1826** [see UMBILICATED *a.* d]. **1828** STARK *Elem. Nat. Hist.* II. 380 An indistinct style inclosed in an umbilicus at its extremity.

c. *Zool.* **1822** J. PARKINSON *Outl. Oryctol.* 147 The substance round which the turns are formed, is on the left side of the shell, and terminates at its base; sometimes in a point, and sometimes in a hollow, which is termed an umbilicus. **1851** WOODWARD *Mollusca* I. 84 The umbilicus is small or obsolete in the typical nautili. **1890** *Science-Gossip* XXVI. 242/2 A variety of *Helix hortensis*.. having.. traces of white between the bands,.. and white continuous over the umbilicus.

d. *Ornith.* **1878** DUNMAN *Gloss. Biol. Terms* (1889) 152 *Umbilicus*,.. the name given to two apertures (*superior* and *inferior*) in the calamus of a bird's feather.

e. *Path.* *a* **1883** FAGGE *Princ. & Pract. Med.* (1886) II. 612 The cavity is 'pocketed' and shows a central depression or *umbilicus.*

umbisett(e, umbith: see UMBESET, UMBOTH.

umblay: see UMB-.

umble, var. HUMBLE *a.*, HUMMEL.

umblement, *dial.*: see UMBERMENT.

umbles (ˈʌmb(ə)lz). Also 5 **owmlys**, 6 **umblys**, **vmblis**, 7–9 (in comb.) **umble-**. [var. of NUMBLES: see also HUMBLE *sb.*]

1. The edible inward parts of an animal, usually of a deer.

14.. *Voc.* in Wr.-Wülcker 616 *Tispatum*, umbles. **14..** *Nom.* Ibid. 678 *Hoc burburium*, owmlys. *a* **1500** *For to serve a Lord* in *Babees Bk.* (1868) 377 Brawne with mustard, umblys of a dere or of a sepe. **1523** SKELTON *Garl. Laurel* 1240 The vmblis of venyson.. To fayre maistres Anne that shuld haue be sent. **1558** PHAER *Æneid* v. M 2 On umbles fat they feede, and broche, and broyle. **1587** HARRISON *England* II. xix. (1877) I. 305 The ordinarie fee, and parts of the deere giuen vnto the keeper by a custome, who.. hath the skin, head, vmbles, chine, and shoulders. **1616** SURFL. & MARKH. *Country Farme* 585 Fine, daintie, and tender bodies, as.. Umbles, Chickens, Calves feete, or any other good thing. **1662** J. DAVIES tr. *Mandelslo's Trav.* 208 They sell the flesh of them to the Chineses,.. eating themselves onely the Umbles and Paunch. **1665** PEPYS *Diary* 13 Sept., He did give us the meanest dinner, (of beef, shoulder and umbles of venison). **1725** *Fam. Dict.*, *Black Puddings*;.. the best Method to make them.. is, to boil the Umbles of a Hog tender. **1741** *Compl. Fam. Piece* I. ii. 175 Take the Umbles of a Deer, parboil them, clear off all the Fat from them. **1826** SCOTT *Woodst.* iii, Where.. monarchs.. amused themselves with broiling the umbles, or dowsets, of the deer, upon the glowing embers.

b. *transf.* and *fig.* (of persons).

1536 in W. H. Turner *Select. Rec. Oxford* (1880) 137, I trust shortly to wash my hands in yᵉ umbles of yᵉ.. knaves. **1611** MIDDLETON & DEKKER *Roaring Girl* III. i, A good well-set fellow, if his spirit Be answerable to his umbles. **1826** SCOTT *Woodst* xviii, I'll give them leave to give mine umbles to the kites and ravens if they find me conferring my confidence where it is not safe.

2. *attrib.* in ***umble-pie***. (Cf. HUMBLE PIE, and *numble-pie* s.v. NUMBLES β.)

1663 PEPYS *Diary* 8 July, Mrs. Turner.. did bring us an umble pie hot out of her oven. **1683** *Accomplisht Lady's Delight*, 17 A dish of fruits. 18 An umble pye. **1728** E. SMITH *Compl. Housew.* A viij, First Course.. Westphalia-Ham and Chickens.. Venison Pasty.. Umble-Pies. **1736** BAILEY *Household Dict.* s.v., [To make] An Umble Pye. Boil the umbles of a deer till they are very tender [etc.]. **1864** LOWELL *McClellan or Lincoln?* Prose Wks. 1890 V. 158 Disguise it as you will, flavor it as you will, call it what you will, umble-pie is umble-pie, and nothing else.

†**umblete**, var. HUMBLETE (humility). *Obs.*

1377 LANGL. *P. Pl.* B. v. 629 (MS. Rawl. Poet. 38) fol. 24 þere aren seven ȝiftes, þat seruen treuthe euere;.. þat on hatte abstinence, and vmblete an other.

†**umbliˈcometry**. *Obs.*⁻¹ (Meaning doubtful.)

Perhaps intended for *umbilicometry*, as the passage deals with methods of judging character from physical peculiarities.

1653 R. SANDERS *Physiogn.* 145 These Greeks know also *Umblicometry*, and divers others; but as for Physiognomie they place it according to this Figure.

umblook: see UMB-.

umbly, obs. form of HUMBLY *adv.*

‖**umbo** (ˈʌmbəʊ). Pl. **umbones** (ʌmˈbəʊniːz), **umbos.** [L. *umbo, umbōnis* shield-boss, knob, projection, etc. Cf. F. *ombon* (in sense 1).]

1. The boss of a shield, usually in or near the centre, and sometimes having a sharp point.

1721 SWIFT *Poems, George-nim-Dan-Dean's Answ. to Sheridan* 33 Like the umbo of the Romans Which fiercest foes could break by no means. **1753** *Chambers' Cycl.* Suppl., *Umbo*, in antiquity, the round protuberant part of a shield. **1851** D. WILSON *Preh. Ann.* II. iv. 268 Many of the shields of the same period were made chiefly of wood and leather, with the central umbo of bronze. **1899** R. MUNRO *Prehist. Scot.* vii. 240 Similar relics.. were associated with the iron umbo of a shield.

2. A projection of a round or conical form; a knob.

1753 *Chambers' Cycl.* Suppl., *Umbunculus*.. was afterwards used to express the inequalities on the surfaces of flints and agates, which frequently are roundish and obtuse and represent a kind of umbones. **1832** GELL *Pompeiana* I. vi. 116 The hot-water bath.. consists in a vase or tazza of white marble... In the centre is a projection, or umbo, rising from the bottom.

3. a. *Conch.* The point at which a univalve shell, or each valve of a bivalve shell, is most protuberant.

sing. **1822** J. PARKINSON *Outl. Oryctol.* 228 *Terebratula semiglobosa*:.. tumid, very smooth; umbo raised, margin entirely without plicæ. **1877** SIR C. W. THOMSON *Voy. Challenger* II. i. 5 The carina is a handsome plate, very uniformly arched, with the umbo placed at the apex.

pl. **1824** *Q. Jrnl. Sci.* XVII. 16 The umbones, which are unusually small, have scarcely any convexity. **1849** DANA *Geol.* (1850) App. i. 699 A byssiferous canal passing out of the umbos at the margin of the shell. **1870** ROLLESTON *Anim. Life* 54 The bivalve shell of the fresh-water mussel,.. with its ligament and its umbones.

b. *Ent.* (See quot.)

1826 KIRBY & SP. *Entomol.* III. 368 *Umbones* (the Bosses), two moveable bosses surmounted by a spine, with which the Prothorax of the Coleopterous genus *Macropus* is armed.

c. *Bot.* The knob or prominence in the centre of the pileus of a fungus.

1836 BERKELEY *Fungi* in *Smith's Eng. Flora* V. II. 28 *Agaricus rufus*... Pileus 3 inches broad, plano-convex, slightly or strongly umbonate with a depression round the umbo as the plant advances. **1871** M. C. COOKE *Handbk. Brit. Fungi* 186 Pileus 1–2 in. broad, purple brown,.. umbonate, the umbo generally subumbilicate.

d. *Zool.* One of the perforated ambulacral plates of echinoderms.

1877 *Encycl. Brit.* VII. 630/1 The ambulacra.. have near their outer edge small shield-like spaces, *umbones*,.. perforated by pairs of small orifices or pores for the protrusion of the feet.

4. *Path.* A central patch in an efflorescence or other affection of the skin.

1822–7 GOOD *Study Med.* (1829) V. 559 Efflorescence in blushing patches;.. often alternately fading and reviving; sometimes with a colourless umbo. *Ibid.* 625 Even the area partakes of the vesication and becomes an umbo.

5. *Anat.* (See first quot.)

1877 BURNETT *Ear* 51 The lower end of the manubrium draws the *membrana tympani* inward very markedly, and forms that depressed spot in the centre called the umbo. **1902** HUGHES & KEITH *Man. Pract. Anat.* III. 281 The membrane is concave externally, the umbo forming the deepest point of the concavity.

umbo, umbois, variants of UMBOTH *Sc. Obs.*

umbonal (ˈʌmbəʊnəl), *a.* [f. L. *umbōn-, umbo* UMBO + -AL¹.] Of, belonging to, situated near, the umbo; of the nature of an umbo.

1854 S. P. WOODWARD *Mollusca* II. 316 Shell smooth, oblong;.. umbonal rib extending across the interior of the valve. **1866** R. TATE *Brit. Mollusks* ii. 12 In the interior of the shell, the following.. are to be distinguished: The umbonal cavity corresponding to the umbo [etc.]. **1888** ROLLESTON & JACKSON *Anim. Life* 124 A line.. drawn to the ventral margin from the centre of the umbonal region.

umbonate (ˈʌmbəʊnət), *a.* [f. as prec. + -ATE.]

1. Furnished with, rising up in, an umbo or boss. Chiefly *Bot.*

1829 LOUDON *Encycl. Plants* (1836) 987 *Agaricus asper*... Cap somewhat umbonate rough with acute warts. **1857** BERKELEY *Cryptog. Bot.* §532 In the other genus [Cryptangium].., the operculum is acuminate instead of umbonate. **1887** W. PHILLIPS *Brit. Discomycetes* 393 Spermogonia.. punctiform, black, acutely umbonate.

2. Formed into an umbo or knob.

1891 *Cent. Dict.*

So **ˈumbonated** *a. rare*⁻¹.

1752 HILL *Hist. Anim.* 127 The fine, roundish, umbonated Cochlea. **1847** WEBSTER, *Umbonated*, in botany, having a boss or elevated point in the middle.

umboˈnation. *rare*⁻¹. [Cf. prec. and -ATION.] A formation of the nature of an umbo.

1872 H. C. WOOD *Fresh-Water Algæ* (1874) 101 Tubercles, obtuse or sharp simple or forked spines, hair-like processes, umbonations, &c.

ˈumbone. Now *rare* or *Obs.* [ad. L. *umbōn-*, stem of *umbo* UMBO.]

†**1.** *Bot.* A style or pistil. *Obs.*

1633 *Gerarde's Herbal* I. xcii. 166 Each of these floures hath six leaues,.. with so many white chiues or threds, and a little blewish umbone in the midst. **1708** KERSEY, *Umbone or Horn*,.. any pointed Style or Head in the middle of a Flower. **1725** *Fam. Dict.* s.v. *Virginia Climber*, The Leaves are of a whitish Colour,.. but the strongest Part is the Umbone, which rises in the middle. **1728** CHAMBERS *Cycl.* s.v., There is also an Umbone call'd doubly-pointed, or by-parted, as in the Peony; and sometimes the Umbone has four sharp Points.

2. *Conch.* = UMBO 3 a.

1867 MURCHISON *Siluria* (ed. 4) ix. 195 Beneath the beak or umbone a small area pierced by a round foramen.

umbones, pl. of UMBO.

umˈbonial, *a. rare*⁻¹. [Cf. UMBONAL *a.*] Of or belonging to the umbo of a shell.

1824 *Q. Jrnl. Sci.* XVII. 16 Four series of short oblique grooves, or of indented wrinkles, three of which are arranged in a direction with the umbonial slope.

So **umˈbonic** *a.*

1877 HUXLEY *Anat. Inv. Anim.* viii. 473 Sometimes the umbonic cone is prolonged and bent inwards.

umˈbonically, *adv. rare*⁻¹. [f. L. *umbōn-, umbo* UMBO: cf. prec. and -AL¹, -LY.] In the manner of an umbo or shield-boss.

1654 GAYTON *Pleas. Notes* IV. viii. 218 The Trunke hose, and Codpiece umbonically prominent, and significant as a Digitus Mercurialis.

umˈbonulate, *a. Bot.* [ad. mod.L. *umbonulāt-us*, f. L. *umbōn-* UMBO: see -ULE and -ATE.]

1866 *Treas. Bot.* 1190/1 *Umbonulate*, terminated by a very small boss or nipple.

†**umboth.** *Ork.* and *Shetl. Obs.* Also 6 **umbuth**, **umbo**, **umbuss**, **-bois**, 9 **umbith.** [a. ON. *umboð* (Norw. *umbod*, Sw. and Da. *ombud*) agency, office, f. *um-* UM- + *boð* command, etc.]

1. Agency, procuratory, part (in affairs).

1509 *Earldom of Orkney* (S.H.S.) 84 Schir Nycol Haucru,.. persone of Orphare, in his said fadaris umbuth. **1510** in *Scottish Jrnl. Topog.* etc. II. 88 Sir Vilȝem Sinclar.. sueand for Justice Rychert Sinclar, in ye umbuss of Jhone Adesone one ye tayne part, and Vilȝam flet in h[i]s awyne umbuss on ye tother part.

2. (See quots. *a* 1688 and 1733.) Also ***umboth duty, tithe.***

1577 *Reg. Privy Council Scot.* II. 648 To pay the Bischoppis dewitie callit the bischoppis umbois in Zeitland, quhilk he hes in tak and assedatioun. *a* **1688** J. WALLACE *Descr. Orkney* (1693) 94 *Umboth*, the great Tiend of either half of the Parish: so called because every other year it was changed with the Minister for his half: for the word *Umboth* signifieth time about. **1733** T. GIFFORD *Descr. Zetland Islands* (1886) 56 That rent called Umboth duty, that is the bishop's rents of Zetland, for which..the bishop has the equivalent rent in Orkney. *Ibid.* The Umboth tythes are for the most part a rental tythe. *a* **1800** *MS. Acc. Lands Unst* 2 (Jam.), In the Parish of Unst, the teind of which being umboth, or free parsonage teind, is..payable to Lord Dundas,..who has right to the Bishop's reserved teinds. **1809** EDMONDSTON *Zetl. Isl.* I. iv. 163 The corn teind is divided between the minister and the proprietor of the crown rents, and the share of the latter is denominated *umbith* or *umboth* duty. **1866** EDMONSTON *Shetland Gloss.* 135.

†**umbothman.** *Obs.* Also 5 vmbythisman. [a. ON. *umboðsmann* (nom. *-maðr*; = Norw. *umbodsmann*, Sw. and Da. *ombudsman*), f. *umboð*: see prec.] An agent or procurator.

1482–3 in *Rec. Earldom of Orkney* (S.H.S.) 194 Andro Quhitquiysson and Jonat Mawnus..witht consent of our vmbythisman..have sauld a half penny land lyand in Wasbuster. **1557** *Ibid.* 108 Thome.. maid Villiam Corgell yongest his procuratour and umbothman, and gave him his full power to defend his landis, housis, and heritage.

‖**umbra**¹ ('ʌmbrə). Pl. umbræ ('ʌmbriː). [L. *umbra* shade, shadow, UMBER *sb.*¹ Cf. It. *ombra*, *ombria*, F. *ombre*.]

1. The shade of a deceased person; a phantom or ghost. Also *fig.*

1599 B. JONSON *Cynthia's Rev.* Induct., The *umbræ* or ghosts of some three or four playes, departed a dozen yeeres since. **1654** GAYTON *Pleas. Notes* III. iii. 78 Such kind of Tones as these the *Umbræ* use, when they call upon Charon for a Boat. **1654** tr. *Scudery's Curia Pol.* Pref., I have not troubled their famous umbra's, whom an innocent kind of Magick hath so often summoned from their Royal Tombs. **1878** BESANT & RICE *Celia's Arb.* xi, The faint and dimly-seen ghost of a possible repentance,..a special umbra pointing heavenward. **1883** *Sat. Rev.* 21 Apr. 486/1 Had Lord Beaconsfield ever indulged in such rashness, his *umbra* might point out..the disaster and the disgrace which have followed on their neglect of the warning.

b. (See quot.)

a **1652** J. SMITH *Sel. Disc.* v. 176 The spiritual vehicle of the soul,..a kind of umbra or aërial mantle in which the soul wraps herself.

2. A mere shadow of something. In quot. *fig.*

1634 RAINBOW *Labour* (1635) 33 The pride of those..who are their owne umbra's, the servants and shadowes of their owne reflected shadowes.

b. An uninvited guest accompanying one who is invited.

1696 S. SEWALL *Diary* 7 May, And let my dear Wife and all my children partake in this priviledge, and that not as Umbras, but on their own account. **1724** MOFFET *Hesperineso-gr.* (1755) 9 Most of the guests their umbra's brought And sauce that money never bought. *c* **1800** R. CUMBERLAND *John De Lancaster* (1809) II. 71 Mr. David Owen and his umbra in the bottle green were missing. **1834** LYTTON *Pompeii* I. iii, The sixth banqueter, who was the umbra of Clodius,..muttered also 'Ædepol'.

3. Shade; shadow.

1638 SIR T. HERBERT *Trav.* (ed. 2) 5 To all in the temperate Zone, in the Sunnes Meridian their shadowes cast North, having past the Zenith, the shade or umbra becomes contrary. **1856** RUSKIN *Mod. Paint.* IV. v. v. §11 If any of these wayward umbræ are faithfully remembered and set down by the painter, they nearly always have an unaccountable look.

4. *Astr.* **a.** The shadow cast by the earth or moon as visible in an eclipse; now *spec.* that portion in which the shadow is complete, as contrasted with the *penumbra*.

1679 MOXON *Math. Dict.*, *Umbra*, a shadow, a word oft used in the obscuration [*sic*] of Eclipses. **1812** WOODHOUSE *Astron.* xxxv. 344 The cones of the umbra and penumbra.. formed by lines drawn from the Sun and touching the Earth's surface. **1833** HERSCHEL *Astron.* vi. 225 Owing to the great size of the earth, the cone of its umbra always projects far beyond the moon. **1868** LOCKYER *Elem. Astron.* §237 If the Sun were a point of light merely, the shadow would be all umbra.

b. In sun-spots: (see quots.).

The earlier *nucleus* and *umbra* correspond respectively to the modern *umbra* and *penumbra*.

1788 *Encycl. Brit.* (ed. 3) II. 434/2 The increase of a spot is gradual, the breadth of the nucleus and umbra dilating at the same time. *Ibid.*, Small umbræ are often seen without nuclei. **1860** OLMSTED *Mech. Heavens* x. 103 A solar spot usually consists of two parts, the nucleus and the umbra... The umbra is a wide margin, of lighter shade, and is often of greater extent than the nucleus. **1868** LOCKYER *Guillemin's Heavens* (ed. 3) 32 The spots consist almost invariably of one or several dark portions called umbræ, which seem black when compared with the luminous parts of the disk. **1878** NEWCOMB *Pop. Astron.* III. ii. 245 The shaded penumbra seems to form the sides of the cavity, while the umbra is the invisible bottom.

5. *Algebra.* A symbol which requires to be paired with another in order to denote a quantity.

1851 SYLVESTER in *Lond.* etc. *Phil. Mag.* Apr. 296 Each quantity is now represented by two letters; the letters themselves, taken separately, being symbols neither of quantity nor of operation, but mere umbræ or ideal elements of quantitative symbols. **1855** RANKINE *Misc. Sci. Papers* (1881) 139 The tasinomic coefficients for oblique axes may be regarded as compounded of umbræ.

‖'**umbra**². *rare.* [L. *umbra*, perh. the same word as prec.]

1. The grayling; = UMBER *sb.*²

1610 HOLLAND *Camden's Brit.* 627 Both these rivers are full of salmons and trouts, but Wy of the twaine is the better, affording the best kind of them which they call Vmbras. **1708** KERSEY, *Umbra*,..the Vmber, a sort of Fish. **1769** PENNANT *Brit. Zool.* III. 262 It is a very swift swimmer and disappears like the transient passage of a shadow, from whence we believe is derived the name of Umbra.

2. A sciænoid fish of the genus *Umbrina*, esp. the Mediterranean species *U. cirrosa*.

1753 *Chambers' Cycl.* Suppl. s.v. **1755** *Dict. Arts & Sci.*, *Sciæna*,..this genus comprehends the umbra and the umbrino. **1854** BADHAM *Halieut.* 43 A sandy bottom, though not absolutely bad for flat fish, suits the pelagians.. best; such as, e.g. auratas, the dentex, and Punic and indigenous umbras.

umbra, obs. form of OMRAH.

†**umbrace**, *v.* *Obs. rare.* [Alteration of EMBRACE *v.*, by substitution of UM-.] *trans.* To surround; to obtain.

c **1350** *St. Agatha* 101 in Horstm. *Altengl. Leg.* (1881) 46 And with fire if þou [? me] vmbraste With dew of heuin it sal be waste. **13..** *Adultery 46 Ibid.* 369 With schryft of mouth & penans smerte They wene þer blys forto vnbrace [*v.rr.* vmbrace, vmbras].

um'bracious, *a.* *rare.* [Irreg. f. L. *umbra* UMBRA¹.] Shady, umbrageous.

1839 STONEHOUSE *Axholme* 226 Planted with elms, sycamores, and chesnuts.., which have already become very umbracious. **1983** P. LEVI *Flutes of Autumn* i. 12 That scruffy umbracious margin where the town was just beginning to dissolve the countryside in its dark acid.

um'braciousness. *rare*⁻¹. [Cf. prec.] The quality of giving shade.

1661 MORGAN *Sph. Gentry* I. viii. 109 The umbraciousnesse of the Tree he compaires to the dark life of Man, through which the Sun is not able to pierce.

†**umbracle.** *Obs.* Also 6 *Sc.* vmbrakill, -kle. [ad. L. *umbrăcul-um* shady place, etc., dim. of *umbra* UMBRA¹. Cf. obs. F. *ombracle*, It. *ombraculo*, *-colo*, F. (bot.) *umbracule*.] Shade or shadow; a shady place.

c **1500** KENNEDY *Passion of Christ* 14 Haill, beyme to skaill of ded þe dirk vmbrakill! *Ibid.* 1312, 1395. **1500–20** DUNBAR *Poems* lxxxv. 20 Quhilk king ws bring vnto his ryng, Fro dethis dirk vmbrakle. **1609** J. DAVIES (Heref.) *Holy Roode* Wks. (Grosart) I. 15/1 That Tree (that Soulerefreshing Vmbracle Together with our Sinne) His shoulders teares. **1653** R. MASON in Bulwer *Anthropomet. Let. to Author*, Here were the Alleys and umbracles of his ordinary recesses.

um'braculate, *a.* *Ent.* [ad. mod.L. *umbrăculāt-us*, f. L. *umbrăcul-um*: see prec.] (See quot.)

1826 KIRBY & SP. *Entomol.* xlvi. IV. 307 *Umbraculate*.., when there is upon the head an umbrella-shaped process.

umbraculi-, the stem of L. *umbrăcul-um* sunshade (see UMBRACLE), employed in the botanical adjs. **umbracu'liferous**, **um'braculiform** [F. (bot.) *umbraculiforme*]: (see quots.).

1847 WEBSTER, *Umbraculiform*, having the form of an umbraculum or arbor. **1857** A. GRAY *First Less. Bot.* 235 *Umbraculiform*, umbrella-shaped, like a Mushroom, or the top of the style of Sarracenia. **1862** MAYNE *Med. Voc.* 422 *Umbraculiferus*,..*Bot.*, formed like a parasol: umbraculiferous.

umbrage ('ʌmbrɪdʒ), *sb.* Also 7–9 ombrage. [a. OF. *umbrage*, *ombrage* (F. *ombrage*), = Pr. *umbratge*:—L. *umbrāticum*, *-icus*, f. *umbra* shadow.]

†**1.** Shade, shadow. *Obs.*

1426 LYDG. *De Guil. Pilgr.* 22310 The party off my vysage Whiche is clowded with vmbrage, Off cleernesse scholde haue no reporte. **1513** DOUGLAS *Æneid* XIII. Prol. 40 All the bewtie of the fructuus feyld Was wyth the erthis vmbrage clene ourheild. **1544** BETHAM *Precepts War* I. cci. I vij b, The lyghte, and also..the false vmbrage whych the Moone doth shewe fourthe. **1616** DRUMM. OF HAWTH. *Poems* II. (S.T.S.) I. 65 Deare amber Lockes gaue Vmbrage to her Face. **1654** tr. *Scudery's Curia Pol.* 129 If we be worsted in our nocturnall and more secret attempts, the darknesse will give an umbrage, and obscure our shame. **1655** F. G. tr. *Mlle. De Scudery's Artamenes* IV. II. 83 The Sun setting that Evening without any cloudy umbrage, it might almost be said that the Sun-beams did guild the whole Countrey. **1687** NORRIS *Coll. Misc.*, *Ode to Darkness* v, The Blest above do thy sweet umbrage prize. When Cloy'd with light, they veil their eyes.

b. *transf.* and *fig.* (Very common in the 17th c.)

a. *c* **1642** *Observ. his Majesty's late Answ. & Expresses* 18 To look into termes a little more narrower, and dispell umbrages. **1663** *Aron-bimnucha* 30 Those Clouds and Umbrages that did eclipse and darken the glory of the Gospel. **1684** HOWE *Redeemer's Tears* Wks. 1862 II. 269 A mind led..to transmit through a dark umbrage some glimmerings only of that excellent majesty which his Sonship..entitled him to. **1711** SHAFTESB. *Charac.* (1737) III. 322 Great Mysterys,..so wrap'd in Clouds, or hid in Umbrages,..that they may seem to have been left as Trials of our Industry. **1727** A. HAMILTON *New Acc. E. Ind.* I. xxiii. 279 [To] live..under the Badge and Umbrage of Ignominy and Shame. *a* **1763** SHENSTONE *Progr. Taste* II. 102 And o'er her charms with caution shown, Be still a graceful umbrage thrown.

β. **1660** MILTON *Free Commw.* 448 Kingship, though looking big, yet indeed most pusillanimous,..startl'd at every Ombrage. **1669** TEMPLE *Lett.* (1701) II. 65 To suspect that it was Artificial, and only intended to give an Ombrage or false Light to the Court of Sueden.

2. *spec.* Shade or shadow cast by trees or the like.

a. **1540–1** ELYOT *Image Gov.* xxi. (1544) 38 b, The sayd trees gaue a commodyous and plesant vmbrage. *Ibid.* xxii. 42 Which trees did cast ouer the walles a pleasant vmbrage or shadowe. **1664** EVELYN *Sylva* vi. 24 [Ash-trees are] not to be planted for Umbrage, or Ornament; especially neer the Garden. **1665** SIR T. HERBERT *Trav.* (1677) 115 The boughs ..so circle the bole or trunk that it resembles an arch'd circumference affording umbrage and refreshment to some hundred men. **1675** EVELYN *Terra* (1676) 94 All shade is not unpropitious, where the Soil and Climate are benign, as well as that which casts the umbrage. **1757** DYER *Fleece* I. 399 Accustom'd to the barriers of the rick, Or some warm umbrage. **1849** C. BRONTE *Shirley* xiii, Often..she would spend a sunny afternoon in lying stirless on the turf, at the foot of some tree of friendly umbrage. **1865** A. RALEIGH in *Rec. Life* xi. (1881) 138 We had crept up slowly through the leafy woods, and all at once we emerged from the umbrage and stood upon the hill-top. **1888** R. BUCHANAN *City of Dream* VIII. 171 The steed sprang on across the golden glade and plunged into the umbrage suddenly.

β. **1604** R. CAWDREY *Table Alph.*, *Ombrage*, shade, harbor, or bower to rest vnder. **1866** J. B. ROSE tr. *Ovid's Met.* I. 447 On sounding pinions Cupid sped his flight To the deep ombrage of Parnassus' height.

b. Const. *of*, or with possessives.

1596 R. L[INCHE] *Diella* (1877) 22 Where vnder vmbrage of some aged Tree, With lute in hand I sit. **1667** MILTON *P.L.* IX. 1087 In some glade Obscur'd, where highest Woods impenetrable To Starr or Sun-light, spread thir umbrage broad. **1677** PLOT *Oxfordsh.* 159 Under the umbrage of which Tree..no less than 324 horses, or 4374 men, may sufficiently be shelter'd. **1708** J. PHILIPS *Cyder* I. 141 They run To Grots, and Caves, and the cool Umbrage seek Of woven Arborets. **1772** S. WHYTE *Poems* (1795) 186 In the brown umbrage of the wood. If lonely you retire. **1793** *Minstrel* II. 109 The heat increasing, the deep umbrage of the forest invited her into its closest paths. **1830** J. G. STRUTT *Sylva Brit.* 118 Branches..spreading their umbrage to the circumference of two hundred and seven feet. **1875** MISS BRADDON *Strange World* i, Two figures are seated.. beneath the umbrage of an ancient thorn.

c. The foliage of trees, etc., affording shade.

1657 TOMLINSON *Renou's Disp.* Pref. b ij, Here you may view..the pleasant Umbrages sporting with Zephyrus-Nectar-Blooms. **1659** HAMMOND *On Ps.* cxxviii. 3 Olive-plants..were usually planted (as in arbours) to shade the table, entertainments being made without doors, in gardens, under that umbrage. **1727–46** THOMSON *Summer* 626 Beside the dewy border let me sit,..There in that hollow'd rock, grotesque and wild,..and over head By flowering umbrage shaded. **1767** JAGO *Edge-hill* I. 357 Beneath their waving Umbrage Flora spreads Her spotted Couch. **1789** E. DARWIN *Bot. Gard.* I. (1791) 207 Delighted Thames through Tropic umbrage glides, And flowers antarctic, bending o'er his tides. **1811** SHELLEY *St. Irvyne* xi, The tall ash and oak, in mingled umbrage, sighed far above their heads. **1833** LYTTON *Godolphin* xv, Then abruptly they rose, over-spread with thick and tangled umbrage, several feet above the level of the river. **1885** BUCHANAN *Annan Water* ix, In one corner was an arbour almost buried in umbrage.

transf. **1739** R. BULL tr. *Dedekindus' Grobianus* 222 Mustachio's, far beyond the vulgar Size; O'er all thy Mouth their hairy Umbrage spread. **1828** WORDSW. *Triad* 188 Her brow hath opened on me—see it there, Brightening the umbrage of her hair.

fig. **1822** DE QUINCEY *Confess.* II. 81 The calamities of my noviciate in London..shot up and flourished afresh, and grew into a noxious umbrage that has overshadowed and darkened my latter years. **1871** TYNDALL *Fragm. Sci.* (1879) I. xviii. 462 The light of law was for a time obscured by the thick umbrage of novel facts.

3. A shadowy appearance or indication, a semblance, outline, or faint representation, a glimmering or trace, *of* something. Now *rare.* (Common in 17th c.)

a. **1604** SHAKS. *Ham.* v. ii. 125 (Q. 2), His semblable is his mirrour, & who els would trace him, his vmbrage, nothing more. **1644** BULWER *Chirol.* 143 The arme shadowes out the second Person in the Trinity... The fingers give an umbrage of the Holy Spirit. **1686** PLOT *Staffordsh.* 417 There yet remains some umbrage of a Dean and Prebends here to this very day. **1756** in *Palatine Note-book* (1881) I. 118/2 His whole Life..may be look'd upon as an Umbrage of Troubles and Perplexities among vexatious Neighbours. **1856** FABER *Creator & Creature* II. i. (1886) 110 Joys angelical..are all but a manifold umbrage of the one joy of God.

β. **1640** HOWELL *Dodona's Grove* 30 It will breed scruples and ombrages of doubts in her confederats. **1652** —— *Giraffi's Rev. Naples* II. 57 The people had shrewd ombrages of fear that he came to no good purpose.

†**b.** Without const.: An appearance or semblance. *Obs.*

1639 FULLER *Holy War* v. xxv. 272 Some of them [*sc.* essays] being umbrages and State-representations rather than realities. **1649** JER. TAYLOR *Gt. Exemp.* II. viii. 78 A penitent is not taken with umbrages and appearances, nor quits a reall good for an imaginary. **1678** MARVELL *Growth Popery* Wks. 1875 IV. 395 It looks and gives an umbrage as if what he was to do was by your leave. **1680** DE BRITAINE *Hum. Prud.* ii. 5 But Wise-men cannot be content to be abused with Umbrages, nor is the World any longer to be entertained with Dark Lanthorns.

†**c.** In emphatic or intensive use, with *all*, *any*, *even*, *the least*, etc. *Obs.*

a. **1649** FULLER *Just Man's Funeral* 10 The very umbrage of Religion hath a soveraign virtue in it. **1668** EARL ORRERY in *St. Lett.* (1743) II. 340 To avoid even the umbrages of suspicion. **1675** V. ALSOP *Anti-Sozzo* 556 Our Author,.. without any umbrage of a pretence from the Text,..has laid them in saltire. **1703** BP. T. WILSON in Keble *Life* v. (1863) 192 That so all umbrage of arbitrary government may be removed. *a* **1734** NORTH *Examen* II. v. §139 (1740) 402 Let any one see in that extended Sum of the Evidence..if there be the least Umbrage of a Reflection upon this Accident. **1737** [S. BERINGTON] *Mem. G. de Lucca* (1738) 35 To take off all Umbrage of Jealousy, I give you leave to sell him to some honourable Person for a Slave.

β. *c* **1645** HOWELL *Lett.* (1650) I. 75 They parted for that time without the least ombrage of discontent. **1650** —— *Giraffi's Rev. Naples* I. 17 Hereupon the Vice-Roy went unto them to take off all ombrages of distrust. **1692** BEVERLEY *Conciliatory Disc.* 19 Thus are the Secrets of all Hearts, judged according to the Apostles Gospel... Some Ombrage of which Heathens have.

†**d.** A figure or type. *Obs.*

1657 W. MORICE *Coena quasi Κοινὴ* xvi. 297 Sometime they think hereticks set forth under the umbrage of Tares.

†**4.** A feeling of suspicion or doubt. *Obs.*

α. **1624** BACON *Consid. War with Spain* (1629) 8 I say iust feare,..not out of vmbrages, light iealousnesse, apprehensions a farre off, but out of cleare foresight of imminent danger. **1639** FULLER *Holy War* I. ix. (1840) 15 Though umbrages and light jealousies..be too narrow to build a fair quarrel on. **1656** HEYLIN *Extraneus Vapulans* 63 He took some time to consider of it,..for removing of all such umbrages and misapprehensions, as otherwise that interparlance might have occasioned.

β. **1604** BACON *Apol.* 27 And therefore good my Lord carie it so, as you take away by all meanes all ombrages and distasts from the Queene. *c* **1645** HOWELL *Lett.* VI. i. (1650) 180 Ther were som ombrages, and not only so, but open and actuall differences.

†**b.** A suspicion, hint, inkling, or slight idea, *of* a matter. *Obs.*

1654–66 EARL ORRERY *Parthen.* (1676) 800 They neuer had the least umbrage of the Truth. **1697** DAMPIER *Voy.* (1729) I. 310 We..found no Canoas, or People, that might give us any umbrage of a City, or place of Trade near at hand. *a* **1734** NORTH *Examen* I. iii. §59 (1740) 160 Nor is it less remarkable that such Preparations of Fleets, Transports, Armies,..were to be dispatched..and no Neighbour Nation jealous, nor England (so near) haue any Intelligence or Umbrage of it.

†**c.** A reason or ground for suspicion, or for some opinion. *Obs.*

1664 JER. TAYLOR *Dissuas. Popery* I. x. 70 S. Peter did not carry himself so as to give the least overture or umbrage to make any one suspect he had any such preheminence. **1673** *Lady's Call.* II. ii. §3 Therefore they must be nicely careful to give their husbands no color, no least umbrage for it [*sc.* jealousy]. **1704** *Lond. Gaz.* No. 4054/1 Every Man..did his Duty, without the least Umbrage for Censure or Reflection. **1737** L. CLARKE *Hist. Bible* (1740) II. 288 But there is not the least umbrage for such a conjecture to be found in the scripture. **1760–72** tr. *Juan & Ulloa's Voy.* (1807) I. 6 All umbrage would be thus removed from persons who might not be sufficiently acquainted with the nature of their design.

†**5.** Shelter, protection, screen. *Obs.*

1607 DAY *Trav. Eng. Bro.* Ded. (1881) 3 Wee our selues should haue a safe harbor and vmbrage for our well willing yet weake labours. **1658** R. FRANCK *North. Mem.* Ded. (1694) p. iv, In this Dilemma I left the University to seek Umbrage in the City of London. **1698** J. FRYER *Acc. E. India & P.* 98 Humble Suiters for the Umbrage of any of Quality, to skreen them from this Violence. **1730** T. GENT *Hist. York* Pref. p. iii, So that it flies to the Umbrage of the courteous Reader, to be favourable in its Reception. **1740** S. RICHARDSON in *Corr.* (1804) I. p. lxxvi, I therefore..struck a bold stroke,..having the umbrage of the Editor's character to screen myself behind.

†**b.** In the phr. ***under the umbrage of.*** *Obs.*

The material sense in quot. 1741 is unusual.

1677 W. HUBBARD *Narrative* Pref., The Historicall discourse ensuing might pass into publick view under the umbrage of your Protection. **1683** W. ROGERS *Scourge for G. Whitehead* 10 Whitehead, now sinking in his Reputation, ..seems to shelter himself under the Umbrage of W.P. **1709** MRS. MANLEY *Secret Mem.* (1720) III. 207 A Prince..is still answerable for all the Evil he suffers others to commit under the sacred Umbrage of his Name. **1741** A. HILL in *Richardson's Corr.* (1804) I. 71 Little Harry Campbell..had been listening all this while upon the floor, under the umbrage of a pair of out-strutting hoops. **1776** P. OLIVER in *T. Hutchinson's Diary*, etc. (1886) II. 109, I entered the House of Lords under the umbrage of Lord Polworth.

†**6.** A pretext or pretence; a colour or false show. *Obs.*

1634 BP. HALL *Contempl. N.T.*, *Christ before Pilate*, It is al the care of hypocrites to seek umbrages, and pretences for their hatefull purposes. **1662** HICKERINGILL *Apol. Distressed Innoc.* Wks. 1716 I. 272 Veiling the Murder with the Umbrage of Devotion and Justice. *a* **1693** LD. DELAMER *Wks.* (1694) 107 Truth will appear from under all the false glosses and umbrages that men may draw over it. **1706** *Phil. Trans.* XXV. 2416 So convincing an Experiment as this, which..leaves no manner of umbrage for any other Hypothesis to take place in it.

†**b.** In the phr. ***under the umbrage of.*** *Obs.*

Slight differences of usage are represented in the different groups of quotations.

(*a*) **1674** *Case of Bankers & Creditors* Pref. 3 This grievance of ours hath been represented to his Majesty under the pretence and umbrages of Royal Prerogative. **1681** HICKERINGILL *Sin Man-Catching* Wks. 1716 I. 174 [Villains] that commit the greatest Rapacities..under the umbrage, pretence and colour of Law and Justice. **1696** C. LESLIE *Snake in Grass* (1697) 90 Otherwise, they may commit Theft, Sacrilege, and all other Immoralities under this Umbrage. **1727** A. HAMILTON *New Acc. E. Ind.* II. xlvii. 176 To make him accuse rich Men,..that he might seize their Estates under the Umbrage of Justice and Law. **1735** BOLINGBROKE *On Parties* (ed. 2) viii. 87 To form a Party, and maintain a Struggle for personal Power, under the Pretence and Umbrage of Principle.

(*b*) **1679** J. SMITH *Narr. Popish Plot* 30 Under the Umbrage of Repairing a College, they were providing for the Ruine of a Kingdom.

(*c*) **1709** SACHEVERELL *Serm.* 5 Nov. 9 Should we cover such a False Apostle under the Sacred Umbrage of a True Church-Man? **1720** GORDON & TRENCHARD *Independ. Whig* (1728) 284 Under the Colour and Umbrage of Significant and decent Ceremonies, the most ridiculous and immodest Usages have been introduced. **1723** DK. WHARTON *True Briton* I. 234 Under the Umbrage of Adorers, [they] make themselves Masters.

†**7.** *to be*, or *to stand, in* (..) ***umbrage***, to be in disfavour. *Obs.*

a **1635** NAUNTON *Fragm. Reg.* (Arb.) 31 On the fall of the Duke he stood some yeers in umbrage, and without imployment. **1647** CLARENDON *Hist. Reb.* II. §102 Being suspected at least a Favourer of the Papists,..by which he was in great umbrage with the People. *a* **1649** DRUMM. OF HAWTH. *Hist. Jas. V*, Wks. (1711) 110 He knew Sir James stood in some umbrage with the King.

8. Displeasure, annoyance, offence, resentment: **a.** In the phr. *to give* (..) ***umbrage*** (*to* a person or persons).

1620 BRENT tr. *Sarpi's Hist. Council Trent* I. 28 He.. therefore besought them to take away all those words that might give him any Vmbrage. **1668** DRYDEN *Evening's Love* IV, It will not be convenient to give him any umbrage, by seeing me with another person. *a* **1700** EVELYN *Diary* 5 May 1686, Which dispensation..gave umbrage (as well it might) to every good Protestant. **1740** SOMERVILLE *Hobbinol* I. 242 Be thou, my Muse! No leaky Blab, nor painful Umbrage give To wealthy Squire. **1771** J. FLETCHER *Checks* Wks. 1795 II. 8 How often do men sneakingly forsake their friends, for fear of giving umbrage to a superior party or interest. **1796** WASHINGTON *Let.* Writ. 1892 XIII. 263 Unless my pacific disposition was displeasing, nothing else could have given umbrage by the most rigid construction of the letter. **1842** H. ROGERS *Ess.* (1874) I. i. 5 The sermon, when printed, gave great umbrage to the parliamentary party. **1869** RAWLINSON *Anc. Hist.* 314 Both Antiochus and Seleucus..abstained from any proceedings that could give umbrage to their new subjects.

b. In the phr. *to take* (..) ***umbrage*** (*at*; also without const. or with clause).

(*a*) **1680** FOUNTAINHALL *Chronol. Notes* (1822) 5 The Bishop..took umbrage at his freedom of speech in the pulpit anent the government. **1683** TEMPLE *Mem.* Wks. 1720 I. 439 The Allies had taken great Umbrage at my Journey to the Hague. **1725** DE FOE *Voy. round World* (1840) 300 If any opposition should be offered them in the country, or any umbrage taken at their design. **1759** ROBERTSON *Hist. Scot.* VIII. Wks. 1813 II. 49 James himself, though he prudently concealed it, took great umbrage at her behaviour. **1796** MME. D'ARBLAY *Camilla* x. xiv, However, as to his having called me a blockhead, it's not what I take umbrage at. **1827** HALLAM *Const. Hist.* v. (1876) I. 284 We find no mention of any umbrage being taken at certain strains of prerogatives. **1862** KINGSLEY *A. Locke* Pref. p. v, Many of them..have taken umbrage at certain scenes of Cambridge life drawn in this book. **1883** SIR T. MARTIN *Ld. Lyndhurst* ix. 231 A less kindly-tempered man..would have taken umbrage at the tone of this letter.

(*b*) **1723** *Present State of Russia* I. 197 The subjects of the Can of Schirvan began to take Umbrage. **1748** SMOLLETT *R. Random* xi, Fearing the captain and his lady would take umbrage, and leave his carriage. **1813** SCOTT *Rokeby* III. xxi, Our stout Knight..Took umbrage that a friend so near Refused to share his chase and cheer. **1841** D'ISRAELI *Amen. Lit.* (1867) 594 Many close at hand took umbrage lest they themselves were being supplanted.

c. In other constructions.

1724 R. WODROW *Corr.* (1843) III. 140 They all have your case very much at heart, and all the umbrage is over. **1768** H. WALPOLE *Hist. Doubts* 23 Whether the steps taken by the queen gave them new cause of umbrage. **1856** LEVER *Martins of Cro' M.* xx, A very good-natured laugh from the others showed how little umbrage the frank avowal excited.

umbrage (ˈʌmbrɪdʒ), *v.* Also 7 ombrage. [f. prec., or ad. F. *ombrager*, *-ier*, †*umbrager*, *-ier*, f. *ombrage*: see prec. Cf. also It. *ombreggiare*.]

1. *trans.* To shade or shadow; also *fig.*, to overshadow, put in the shade.

α. **1647** HEXHAM I, To Vmbrage or shadow, *beschaduwen.* **1658** JAS. WEBB tr. *Calprenède's Cleopatra* VIII. 93 A man.. whose valour umbraged theirs, and whose words they had found so true to their confusion. **1738** [G. SMITH] *Cur. Relat.* I. iv. 465 They were separated from one another with Rails, and umbraged with a Sort of Canopy. **1804** ANNA SEWARD *Mem. Darwin* 123 Rude gives an idea of barrenness, and Matlock is luxuriantly umbraged. **1888** *Harper's Mag.* April 733/2 A ridge or hillock heavily umbraged with the rounded foliage of evergreen oaks.

β. **1648** HEXHAM II, *Omschaduwen*,..to Shaddowe About, or to Ombrage. **1652** F. KIRKMAN *Clerio & Lozia* 16 His Hat was ombraged with a plume of black Herons Feathers.

†**2.** To colour over, disguise. *Obs.*⁻¹

1675 R. BURTHOGGE *Causa Dei* 312 If she mentioned others, it was by way of caution, only to secure her self, and Umbrage what she said that it might down the better.

†**b.** To give a pretext or ground for. *Obs.*⁻¹

1689 HICKERINGILL *Modest Inquiries* 35 Like that young Gallant, studying what he should see in her [*sc.* an old woman] to Vmbrage the fondness of his Embraces.

3. To offend, displease. *rare.*

a **1894** STEVENSON *St. Ives* xxiv, May I help myself to wine without umbraging you.

Hence **ˈumbraged, ˈumbraging** *ppl. adjs.*

1663 SIR G. MACKENZIE *Religious Stoic* i. 12 Intimating thereby that umbrag'd silence was an excellent Shryn for sincere devotions. **1683** PETTUS *Fleta Min.* I. Ded., They are divulged either by umbraging Sophistications, or concealed under the Name of Philosophical Secrets. **1890** *Lippincott's Mag.* May 667 A park, a wood, an umbraged lane.

umbrageous (ʌmˈbreɪdʒəs), *a.* Also 6–8 umbragious, 7, 9 ombrageous (7 -ious). [ad. F. *ombrageux* (OF. also *-eus*), f. *ombrage* (see UMBRAGE *sb.*); or directly f. UMBRAGE *sb.* + -OUS.]

1. a. Forming or affording shade; shady.

1587 A. DAY *Daphnis & Chloe* (1890) 69 First ranne hee to the foot of a hie and umbragious rocke. **1614** GORGES *Lucan* II. 63 Where these vmbragious mountaines stand. **1675** EVELYN *Terra* (1676) 93 Lastly, by shade Ground is render'd barren, and by the dripping of umbragious trees. **1725** POPE *Odyss.* VI. 149 Where the grove with leaves umbrageous bends, With forceful strength a branch the Heroe rends. **1790** *Phil. Trans.* LXXX. 351 Their tops are so very thick and umbrageous as to prevent even a very heavy rain from reaching the ground underneath. **1826** SCOTT *Woodst.* x, The towers of Woodstock arose high above the umbrageous shroud which the forest spread around the..mansion. **1846** J. BAXTER *Libr. Pract. Agric.* (ed. 4) I. 99 A handsome umbrageous tree, with a smooth bark, and shining leaves. **1873** SYMONDS *Grk. Poets* x. 310 Oaks with their umbrageous foliage..belong to the forests of the North.

b. Abounding in shade; shaded by trees or the like; overshadowed.

1612 DRAYTON *Poly-olb.* xxii. 1619 Those past times.. When as that woody kind, in our umbrageous wild,.. In this their world of waste, the sovereign empire sway'd. **1632** LITHGOW *Trav.* iii. 81 A secure place of repose in a vmbragious Caue. **1666** HARVEY *Morb. Angl.* 215 Walk daily in a pleasant, airy, and umbragious Garden. **1742** GRAY *Propertius* III. 3 Fast by th' umbrageous vale lull'd to repose, Where Aganippe warbles as it flows. **1774** R. CUMBERLAND in *Westm. Mag.* II. 148 No cooling Grottoes, no umbrageous Groves, To win the Graces, and allure the Loves. **1811** SHELLEY *St. Irvyne* xi, The umbrageous loveliness of the surrounding country. **1846** HAWTHORNE *Mosses* I. I. 13 It makes us shiver to think of these deep umbrageous recesses. **1891** FARRAR *Darkn. & Dawn* lvi, Everyone should wander at will about the green copses, and the umbrageous retreats.

c. Caused by thick foliage.

1830 J. G. STRUTT *Sylva Brit.* 54 The religious Mahometans chose to pray under old trees,..piously believing that the holy men of former times had prayed and meditated under their umbrageous shade. *a* **1854** J. WILSON in *Casquet of Lit.* (1896) V. 178/2 Dew and dreams dropping through their umbrageous twilight at eve or morn.

2. Of persons: Suspicious; jealous; apt or disposed to take offence.

α. **1601** R. JOHNSON *Kingd. & Commw.* 169 The inhabitants,..partly by their forme of gouernment, whereby they are made vile, base and vmbragious, haue little valour or manhood left them. **1652** J. WRIGHT tr. *Camus' Nat. Paradox* III. Argt. 48 The King made jealous of the Queen, shee no less umbragious of him, and both for Iphigenes. **1758** WARBURTON *Div. Legat.* Pref., Of which, doubtless, the Romans were very jealous,..though not so extravagantly umbragious as our Critic's hypothesis obliges him to suppose. **1768** HURD in Warburton *Lett.* (1809) 425 Both susceptible of high passions in love and friendship; but, of the two, the Italian more constant, and less umbrageous. **1846** GROTE *Greece* II. vi. II. 503 The rural costume..which the Helot commonly wore, and the change of which exposed him to suspicion, if not to punishment, from his umbrageous masters. **1874** SYMONDS *Sk. Italy & Greece* (1898) I. vi. 107 The people are idle, haughty, umbrageous, fiery, quarrelsome [etc.].

β. **1630** DONNE *Serm.* lv. (1640) 557 At the beginning some men were a little ombrageous, and startling at the name of the Fathers. **1803** [? SIR L. HANSON] *Hist. Acc. Orders Knighth.* II. 306 Most punctilious with respect to forms and Ceremonies: and excessively ombrageous, with regard to the Non-observance of trivial points.

b. Of disposition or nature.

c **1639** WOTTON *Let. Sir. E. Bacon* in *Reliq.* (1672) 430 But lest you should mistake, as some others have been apt to do here, in the present constitution of the court (which is very ombragious). **1652** J. WRIGHT tr. *Camus' Nat. Paradox* XII. 321 Let your rigour execute mee..all that your umbragious or Cholerick humour can suggest. **1667** G. DIGBY *Elvira* I. i, What power meer appearances have had..to destroy, With an umbragious nature, all that Love Was ever able.. To found and to establish.

†**3.** Obscure; dubious. *Obs.*

1635 J. REYNOLDS *God's Revenge* III. xiii. 256 That there was none other present but himselfe when his Master De Merson was murthered, it is umbragious, and leaves a.. sting of suspition in their heads. *a* **1649** DRUMM. OF HAWTH. *Hist. Jas. II*, Wks. (1711) 24 By umbragious Ways he nourished Discontentments in all Parts of the Country. **1651** H. L'ESTRANGE *Answ. Mrq. Worcester* 61 We blesse God for the light they had, though umbrageous and clouded, yet was it such as discovered the nakednesse and shame of the Church of Rome.

Hence **umˈbrageously** *adv.*; **umˈbrageousness.**

1639 DRUMM. OF HAWTH. *Mag. Mirror* Wks. (1711) 175 He had Intention to bring Novations into our Religion; tending *umbrageously, and under a Mask, to the Introduction of Popery. **1834** AINSWORTH *Rookwood* I. i, One tree..out-flings..its arms umbrageously. **1614** RALEIGH *Hist. World* I. iv. §3. 69 The exceeding *umbrageousnesse of this tree he compareth to the darke and shadowed life of man. **1755** JOHNSON, *Shadiness*,.. umbrageousness. **1823** *Examiner* 106/2 Trees..spreading sideways with Asiatic grace and umbrageousness. **1837** *Blackw. Mag.* XLI. 512 A face incapable of a blush, partly from the umbrageousness of the whiskers. **1871** *Daily News* 28 July, The familiar umbrageousness of Croydon.

†**umbraid**, *sb. Obs.* Forms: 4 vmbreyd, 4–5 vmbreide, 5 vm-, vnbreid; 5 vmbrayd(e, vnbraide. [var. of UPBRAID *sb.*: cf. next.] Upbraiding, reproach.

c **1330** R. BRUNNE *Chron. Wace* (Rolls) 3485 Wiþ suche vm reides þey hem missayde. *Ibid.* 7999 When wraþe bygynneþ, þen comeþ vmbreyd. *a* **1400–50** *Alexander* 1800 (Dubl. MS.), Lett neuer it be broght on brade for vmbrayd of shame, Ye dout for þe dityng of darius pistell. *a* **1425** *Cursor M.* 5673 (Trin.), Moises for þis vmbreide Was dredinge in his herte. *a* **1470** HARDING *Chron.* CLIV. iv, He.. letters sent hym, defyals and vmbrayde, Of hys suraunce and othe that he had erred.

†**umbraid**, *v. Obs.* Forms: 4 vmbreyde, -breide, 5 vmbreid; 4–5 vmbraide, 5–6 vmbrayde (6 um-), 5 vmbrayed, 6 vmbrayd, -braid, -brade; 5

vnbrayd(e, -braide. [Alteration of UPBRAID *v.*, under the influence of verbs in UM-.] *trans.* To upbraid, reproach.

c **1330** R. BRUNNE *Chron. Wace* (Rolls) 8004 3yf þou me vmbreyde, þe schame ys þyn. **1390** GOWER *Conf.* II. 296 If so be that he him umbreide Of oght that hath be speke or do. *a* **1400** *Sir Beues* (S.) 2417 Thow shalt neuer vmbraide me. When þou comest hoom to my contre. **1432-50** tr. *Higden* (Rolls) III. 81 Then the suster of that Oracius.. vmbraydede here brother for the sleenge of here howsebonde. *c* **1450** *Mirk's Festial* 132 þes þat.. be vsed to swere horrybull oþys by Godys sydys and his blod, and vmbrayden God of his passyon. *c* **1489** CAXTON *Sonnes of Aymon* xvi. 377 Many tyme he hath vnbrayd vs therof. **1530** PALSGR. 766/1 What though he have done a mysse, it was nat thy parte to umbrayde hym. **1557** EDGEWORTH *Serm.* Repert., Fastinge.. in the rogation weke is vmbrayded and mocked of noughty lyuers. **1597** J. PAYNE *Royal Exch.* 24 Manie a good Christian have bene no less vmbraded and reproched.

Hence †**um'braiding** *vbl. sb. Obs.*

1597 J. PAYNE *Royal Exch.* 15 Men love better gentle admonitions then bytter vmbradings.

umbral ('ʌmbrəl), *a.* [f. UMBRA[1] + -AL[1].]

1. *Algebra.* Based on the use of umbræ in notation; consisting of umbræ.

1851 SYLVESTER in *Lond.* etc. *Phil. Mag.* Apr. 297 My system of umbral or biliteral notation. **1852** —— in *Cambr. & Dubl. Math. Jrnl.* VII. 78 *note*, The umbral method of denoting such a function. **1893** CAYLEY *Math. Papers* (1897) XIII. 306 It does not appear that there is any monomial umbral expression for the last-mentioned form.

2. *Astr.* Pertaining to the umbra of sun-spots or eclipses.

1867-77 G. F. CHAMBERS *Astron.* 7 *note*, The umbral structure [of a sun-spot] is quite complete, and made up of sunken banks of filaments. **1879** NEWCOMB & HOLDEN *Astron.* 286 The observations consisted in measuring the relative amounts of umbral, penumbral, and photospheric radiation. **1885** AGNES M. CLERKE *Pop. Hist. Astron.* 201 Vapours which are dispersed over the unbroken solar surface are accumulated in the umbral cavity.

3. *Geol.* The special designation of a series of rocks occurring in Pennsylvania.

1858 H. D. ROGERS *Geol. Pennsylv.* I. 144 The Umbral Series contains, in Pennsylvania, but one formation—the Umbral Red Shale... Its prevailing character, which is that of a dark-brownish red shale and red sandstone, it steadily maintains throughout its range.

Hence **'umbrally** *adv.*

1852 SYLVESTER in *Cambr. & Dubl. Math. Jrnl.* VII. 87 Express *H* umbrally under the form [etc.]. **1853** —— in *Phil. Trans.* CXLIII. 429 The determinants thus umbrally represented.

†**um'brana, -'brano,** app. ad. It. *umbrina*: see UMBRINA.

1607 BEAUM. & FL. *Woman-Hater* I. i, Is the Umbranoes head as we commanded, sent to the sad Gondarino, our General? *Ibid.* I. ii, For the Dukes owne Table, the head of an Umbrana.

†**umbrary.** *Obs.*[−1] [Cf. UMBRERE, and obs. F. *ombraire* umbrella (Cotgr.).] Visor.

c **1442** *Chron. London* (ed. Nicholas, 1827) 130 In brekynge of his gauntelette and reysyng of his umbrary [*MS. Cleop. C. iv.* umbray].

†**umbrate,** *a. Obs.* [ad. L. *umbrāt-us*, pa. pple. of *umbrāre*: see next.]

1. Shady; umbrageous.

1501 DOUGLAS *Pal. Hon.* I. Prol. 40 The vmbrate treis that Tytan about wappit War portrait.. Be goldin bemis.

2. *Her.* = UMBRATED *a.*

1572 BOSSEWELL *Armorie* II. 25 b, But yet in my iudgement, they myghte alwayes (with conuenient differences) haue borne the same whole, and not vmbrate.

†**umbrate,** *v. Obs.* [f. ppl. stem of L. *umbrāre* (whence It. *ombrare*, F. *ombrer*), f. *umbra* UMBRA[1]. Cf. the earlier *adumbrate*, *obumbrate*.]

1. *trans.* To shadow. Also *fig.*

1623 COCKERAM, *Vmbrate*, to shadow. *c* **1630** RISDON *Surv. Devon* §42 (1810) 48 Instead of *lux fiat*, it may be verified that they are umbrated thereby.

2. To adumbrate, indicate.

1675 J. SMITH *Chr. Relig. Appeal* II. viii. 84 The Gospel .. exhibits to us the Substance of the Law's Types; wherein the things pertaining to the Person, Office, and Kingdom, of the Messias, were umbrated.

'umbrated, *a. Her.* Also 7 umbreted. [See prec. and -ED[1]. So F. *ombré*.] Indicated or drawn in a faint or shadowy manner.

1486 [see UMBRATION I]. **1562** LEGH *Armory* 79 He beareth On a Lion Saliaunte vmbrated. This is as muche to saye, as the shadowe of a Lion;.. he is but traced with a pencell. vpon the fielde. So that the fyelde sheweth throwghe him. **1572** BOSSEWELL *Armorie* II. 25 This crosse so vmbrated is thus to be blazed. A. beareth Or, a crosse Moloyne Vmbre. **1610** GUILLIM *Heraldry* II. iii. 42 The portraicting out of any thing umbrated, is nothing else but a sleight and single draught or purfle traced out with a pensile, expressing to the view a vacant forme of a thing deprived of all substance. **1688** HOLME *Armoury* IV. viii. (Roxb.) 354/1 Morholt de Irland. A. Barry vmbreted ouer all a Lion rampant G. *c* **1828** BERRY *Encycl. Her.* I. Gloss. s.v., A sun umbrated does not show the face as it is usually represented.

umbratic (ʌm'brætɪk), *a. rare.* [ad. L. *umbrātic-us* staying in the shade, f. *umbra* UMBRA[1]. So Sp. and Pg. *umbratico*, It. *ombratico*, F. *ombratique*, †*umbratique*.]

1. Shadowy, foreshadowing.

a **1677** BARROW *Serm.* (1683) II. xxvii. 386 By virtue wherof those.. umbratick representations.. did obtain their substance, validity and effect.

2. Confined to the shade or to retirement; retired, secluded.

1839 DE QUINCEY in *Tait's Mag.* VI. 364 The torpid dreams of what the Romans called an umbratic experience.

†**um'bratical,** *a. Obs.* [f. as prec. + -AL[1].]

1. Remaining in retirement or seclusion.

1636 B. JONSON *Discov.* Wks. (1641) 94 So I can see whole volumes dispatch'd by the umbraticall Doctors on all sides. **1656** COLLOP *Poesis Rediv.* 18 On the Umbraticall Doctors on the Romish party.

2. Serving as a shadow or imperfect representation of something.

1633 AMES *Agst. Cerem.* II. 219 If all umbraticall rites be Iudaicall, and therefore unlawfull, then all religious significant Ceremonies are Iewish and unlawfull. **1633** BP. HALL *Hard Texts, N.T.* 333 Whose service was altogether umbraticall and typical, shadowing and representing heavenly things. **1683** *Case of Inf.-Baptism* 24 The purging and cleansing Virtue in their Blood.. was also but a faint and umbratical resemblance of the more noble and efficacious cleansing Virtue of his Blood.

3. Serving as a disguise or cloak.

1662 HIBBERT *Body Div.* II. 122 Ye have learned.. not to be guided by the ostentation or umbratical shews of any plausible tongue.

Hence †**um'bratically** *adv. Obs.*

1683 *Case of Inf.-Baptism* 25 It never did Umbratically initiate Believers, or Umbratically, and in shew and Similitude only, confirm the Covenant.

umbratile ('ʌmbrətaɪl, -ɪl), *a.* and *sb.* [ad. L. *umbrātil-is* keeping in the shade, private, retired, etc., f. *umbra* UMBRA[1]. So It. *umbratile*, *ombratile*, Pg. *umbratil*, F. *ombratile*, †*umbratile*.]

A. *adj.* **1.** †**a.** Spent within doors. *Obs.*[−1]

1592 BACON *Confer. Pleasure* (1870) 24 A health.. that hath not ben softened by an vmbratill life still vnder the rooffe.

b. Carried on in retirement or seclusion; not public or practical.

1640 BP. REYNOLDS *Passions* xxxix. 511 The same speech may be excellent in an umbratile Exercitation, which would be too pedanticall, and smelling of the Lampe in a matter of serious and weighty debate. **1840** *British Critic* XXVIII. 370 Christianity.. was not once that umbratile thing, that feeble exotic, shut up in churches, parsonages and parlours. **1845** M. PATTISON *Ess.* (1889) 3 A time of peace and security tends to foster an umbratile and academic science.

c. Staying or living in the shade or within-doors; recluse, retiring.

1850 *Tait's Mag.* XVII. 431/2 Umbratile spectators may inquire what ought to be done. **1888** DOUGHTY *Arabia Deserta* II. 29 The third brother.. was an umbratile young man, and very fanatical. **1898** L. JOHNSON in *Post Liminium* (1911) 207 Octavius the 'umbratile', quiet man was content with a miniature immortality.

2. Of, belonging to, or resembling a shadow or shadows.

1632 B. JONSON *Magn. Lady* III. iii, Shadows have their figure, motion, And their umbratil action, from the real Posture and motion of the body's act.

b. Of a shadowy nature; unsubstantial; unreal. Now *rare* or *Obs.* (Common in 17th c.)

1647 H. MORE *Song of Soul* Notes 337 But this life that we live disjoyned from God is but a shadow, and umbratil imitation of that. *Ibid.* 433 A kind of an umbratil vitalitie that the soul imparts to the body in the enlivening of it. **1656** JEANES *Fuln. Christ* 131 Body is opposed unto shadowes; and so a bodily inhabitation unto an umbratile. **1678** CUDWORTH *Intell. Syst.* 854 As themselves are juniors,.. so are their effects.. but slight, ludicrous and umbratil. *a* **1706** EVELYN *Hist. Relig.* (1850) I. p. xxvii, All we have of precious and worthy our solicitude in this umbratile and transitory passage. **1806** KNOX *Corr.* (1834) I. 290 As far as thought could proceed, without feeling,.. the umbratile, without the real apprehension,—few men could outdo him.

†**c.** Serving as a token or type. *Obs.*[−1]

1663 J. SPENCER *Prodigies* (1665) 199 The honor of being received at least as the umbratile Sign and Coming of the Son of Man.

3. Giving shade; shady.

1659 GAYTON *Art Longevity* 79 Under a Sycamore Which with umbratile leaves will let no Sun Hurt your Silk-gown. **1866** BLACKMORE *Cradock Nowell* lxiii. (1883) 439 His hat was umbratile, as of the Pilgrim Fathers.

†**4.** Of colour: Shaded, dark. *Obs.*[−1]

1678 *Phil. Trans.* XII. 949 Appearing sometimes of a more flourishing colour tending to Carnation; and sometimes more umbratile.

B. *sb.* One who spends his time in the shade.

1888 DOUGHTY *Arabia Deserta* I. 248 Many thus are umbratiles in the Arabian boothies, and give themselves almost to a perpetual slumber.

†**um'bratilous,** *a. Obs.* [f. as prec. + -OUS.] Shadowy, unreal; faint.

1637 IRONSIDE *Seven Quest. Sabbath* To Rdr. B iij b, Least thou shouldst perhaps think I affected a Sciomachy or Umbratilous skirmish. **1640** G. WATTS tr. *Bacon's Adv. Learn.* III. iv. 165 The handling of Finall Causes in the Physiques.. hath given men occasion to rest satisfied in such specious, and umbratilous Causes. **1669** W. SIMPSON *Hydrol. Chym.* 273 An humane embryo.. without sexual discrimination, onely an umbratilous figuration of the microcosme.

†**um'bration.** *Obs. rare.* [ad. L. type **umbrātio*, f. *umbrāre*: see UMBRATE *v.* So It. *ombrazione*.]

1. *Her.* A faintly outlined figure; = ADUMBRATION 4.

1486 *Bk. St. Albans, Her.* c viij, Another sampull is sene of the vmbracion of a certayn cros, and thys cros is calde a cros floree vmbratid;.. bot truly spekyng and propurli it is no cros, bott a shadow of such a cros.

2. A shadowy indication or faint representation (*of* something).

a **1706** EVELYN *Hist. Relig.* (1850) I. 192 Which, though resembling, are yet but faint shadows and umbrations of that sublime nature. *Ibid.* 241 Nor all this by transient and superficial knowledge, figures, and umbrations, but immediate and intuitive notices.

†**um'bratious,** *a. Obs.*[−1] [Irreg. f. UMBRACE *sb.*] Suspicious.

a **1639** WOTTON *Parall. Essex & Buckhm.* in *Reliq.* (1651) 11 He was to wrastle with a Queens declyning, or rather with her very setting Age,.. which.. is commonly even of it selfe the more umbratious and apprehensive.

umbrave, -brawe, -braye, obs. ff. OMRAH.

umbre ('ʌmbə(r)). Also **umber.** [ad. L. *umbra* or F. *ombre* shade, shadow, after mod.L. *umbretta*, F. *ombrette*, Brisson's name for the bird.] An African bird (*Scopus umbretta*) with deep-brown plumage; the hammerhead or African crow. (Cf. UMBRETTE.)

1773 PENNANT *Gen. Birds* 44 Umbre. Bill, strong, thick, strait, compressed, the upper mandible composed of several pieces. **1785** LATHAM *Gen. Synop. Birds* III. I. 30 Tufted Umbre... Size of a Crow... The bill is three inches and a half in length. **1819** STEPHENS *Shaw's Gen. Zool.* XI. II. 636 Crested Umbre, with the whole body fuscous. **1848** *Maunder's Treas. Nat. Hist.* 716/1 The Crested Umbre (*Scopus umbretta*).. is.. of an umber colour, and the male is crested. **1890** *Sat. Rev.* 1 Feb. 139/2 The umbre.. feeds upon fish and frogs, worms, snails, and insects.

umbre, obs. variant of OMBRE, UMBER *sb.*

†**umbrel**[1]. *Obs.* Also 6 **-ell.** [ad. OF. *ombrel* shade: cf. UMBRERE.] The visor of a helmet.

[**1437** in Meyrick *Ant. Armour* (1824) II. 127 Arma in primis v galee cum v umbrell[s] et iiii ventells.] *c* **1470** *Lydgate's Chron. Troy.* III. 1636 (MS. Digby 230), With his swerde so my3tely [Ulysses] gan race Thoru3 þe vmbrel in to Troylus face. **1530** PALSGR. 285/1 Umbrell of an heed pece, *uisiere.*

†**umbrel**[2]. *Obs.* [Anglicized f. UMBRELLA; in first quot. ad. F. *ombrelle*.]

1. = UMBRELLA 1.

1603 FLORIO *Montaigne* III. ix. 583 These Vmbrels or riding canapies, which since the ancient Romanes, the Italians vse, doe more weary the armes, then ease the head. **1617** MORYSON *Itin.* III. 21 In hot regions, to avoid the heat of the sun in some places (as in Italy) they carry Umbrels, or things like a little canopy over their heads. **1694** D'URFEY *Don Quixote* I. 9 Thou shouldst walk in the Streets with thy Train held up, and two Embroidered Laqueys holding an Umbrel over thee.

2. (See quot.)

1688 HOLME *Armoury* III. 271/1 Antiquity did ever set forth the Virgin Mary after this form with her Umbrel or Shady Hat.

um'brell, umberell, dial. forms UMBRELLA 2.

1816 U. BROWN *Jrnl.* 18 Aug. in *Maryland Hist. Mag.* (1916) XI. 151 Never was as wet in my Clothing, through Great Coat umbrell & all. **1857** WAUGH *Lanc. Life* 31 Aw've no moor use for a book nor a duck has for a umbrell. **1883** *Harper's Mag.* May 845/1 Better take this umbrell, hadn't ye? **1910** G. B. MCCUTCHEON *Rose in Ring* I. i. 5 The drizzling rain.. blew softly into the faces of the few who enjoyed the luxury of 'umberells'.

umbrella (ʌm'brɛlə). Also 7 **umbrellia, umbrilla.** *β.* 7-9 **umbrello** (7 vn-), 7 **vmbrillo,** 8 **umbrellow.** *γ.* 7-8 **ombrella.** [ad. It. *ombrella* and *ombrello*, f. *ombra*:—L. *umbra* shade, UMBRA[1]. Cf. F. *ombrelle*, Sp. *umbrela* (zool.).]

1. a. A light portable screen or shade, usually circular in form and supported on a central stick or staff, used in hot countries as a protection for the head or person against the sun.

α. **1611** CORYAT *Crudities* 111 Many of them doe carry other fine things.. which they commonly call in the Italian tongue 'umbrellaes'... These are made of leather something answerable to the forme of a little caunopy and hooped in the inside with divers little wooden hoopes that extend the umbrella in a pretty large compasse. **1668** DAVENANT *Man's the Master* II. i, A very desperate man.. coming near so bright a Sun as you are without a Parasol, Umbrellia, or a Bondgrace. **1695** MOTTEUX *St. Olon's Morocco* 148 An Umbrella was carry'd over me, which in some manner defended me from the Heat of the Sun's Rays. **1716** GAY *Trivia* I. 213 Let Persian dames th' umbrella's ribs display, To guard their beauties from the sunny ray. *a* **1739** JARVIS *Don Quix.* I. I. iv, They carried umbrellas, and were attended by four servants on horseback. **1797** HOLCROFT tr. *Stolberg's Trav.* (ed. 2) III. lxxxix. 479 The heat began so early in the day that, at six o'clock, we were obliged to use our umbrellas. **1832** G. DOWNES *Lett. Cont. Countries* I. 341 The costume is very picturesque in this part of Tuscany, always excepting the monstrous yellow umbrella, which is part and parcel of it. **1860** EMERSON *Cond. Life, Culture* Wks. (Bohn) II. 373 In the city of Palermo, the street was in a blaze with scarlet umbrellas. **1875** JOWETT *Plato* (ed. 2) III. 103 He sees the rich man under an umbrella puffing and panting.

β. **1610** W. STRACHEY in Purchas *Pilgrims* (1625) IV. 1739 So broad are the leaves [of palms] as an Italian *Vmbrello*. **1611** COTGR., *Ombrelle*, an Vmbrello; a (fashion of) round and broad fanne, wherwith the Indians (and from them our great ones) preserue themselues from the heat of a scorching Sunne. **1662** J. DAVIES tr. *Mandelslo's Trav.* II. 138 Of the leaves they make sayles;..they make of them likewise Umbrelloes, Fans, Tents, Mats and Hats. **1697** DAMPIER *Voy.* (1699) 407 The Chinese..when they walk abroad..carry a small Umbrello in their Hands, wherewith they fence their Head from the Sun or the Rain. **1697** *Lady's Trav. Spain* (1706) 249 He commanded them to bring Umbrellos to defend us from the Sun. **1753** HANWAY *Trav.* II. xlii. I. 286, I observed that the Persians are not cautious ..of the sun in any degree equal to the Portugueze; for the last seldom travel without a cloak and umbrello. **1755** SMOLLETT *Quix.* I. I. iv. I. 21 Six merchants of Toledo..who travelled with umbrelloes.

γ. *c* **1620** MORYSON *Itin.* IV. v. i. (1903) 442 Then followes the Duke in his Robes,..a Scudiero carying his ombrella betweene him and the sunne. **1710** C. SHADWELL *Fair Quaker Deal* IV. 40 Your Baubles of China, your Indian Ombrella, your Hair-Ring, and your own Picture.

b. In some Oriental and African countries used as a symbol of rank or state.

a. **1682** *Lond. Gaz.* No. 1721/4 In the Evening he visited his Highness Prince Rupert, to whom he presented the two great Umbrella's. **1718** *Entertainer* No. 16. 109 To score out a Pattern of Umbrella's for the King of Bantam. **1727** A. HAMILTON *New Acc. E. Ind.* II. xxxvi. 45 King of the White Elephant, and of the twenty four Somereroes or Umbrellaes. **1745** P. THOMAS *Jrnl. Anson's Voy.* 201 Mandarines..accompanied with all the Officers of their Tribunal, who surround them with Umbrella's and other Marks of their Dignity. **1849** LAYARD *Nineveh* I. x. 337 He is attended by two eunuchs, one holding the umbrella, the other his quiver and mace. **1888** *Times* 30 Oct. 6/1 The Shereefian Umbrella does not pass necessarily from father to son.

β. **1653** H. COGAN tr. *Pinto's Trav.* xxxiv. 135 Then next to them marches twelve men on horsback, called *Peretandas*, each of them carrying an Umbrello of carnation Sattin. **1678** J. PHILLIPS *Tavernier's Trav.* II. II. viii. 123 Upon each side of the Throne are plac'd two Parasols, or Umbrellos, the handles whereof are about eight foot high. **1688** HOLME *Armory* IV. xi. (Roxb.) 431/2 Then 24 Vnbrello's richly adorned and them as carry them 2 and 2 together. **1719** J. T. PHILLIPS tr. *Thirty-four Confer.* 331 Women..attended him with Umbrello's,..and all the other Court Employments within Doors were all done by Women. **1745** ELIZA HEYWOOD *Female Spect.* No. 18 (1748) III. 301 Twelve stout Indians carried a canopy of yellow and green silk, under which all the royal family walked:—the rest had umbrelloes, supported by their own particular slaves.

2. A portable protection against bad weather, made of silk or similar material fastened on slender ribs, which are attached radially to a stick and can be readily raised so as to form a circular arched canopy.

a. **1634** SIR T. HERBERT *Trav.* 149 A Shagg or Yopangee which riding serues [in Persia] as an Vmbrella against raine. **1716** GAY *Trivia* I. 211 Good houswives..underneath th' umbrella's oily shed, Safe thro' the wet on clinking pattens tread. **1765** H. WALPOLE *Let. to J. Chute* 3 Oct., Servants.. walk about the streets in the rain with umbrellas to avoid putting on their hats. **1787** *Phil. Trans.* LXXVII. 291 If the weather be rainy, an insulated umbrella may be carried in one hand. **1833** COL. HAWKER *Diary* (1893) II. 52 It poured with rain, and my umbrella broke all to pieces. **1856** EMERSON *Eng. Traits, Manners* ¶6 An Englishman walks in a pouring rain, swinging his closed umbrella like a walking-stick. **1882** MISS BRADDON *Mt. Royal* I. i. 34 She always carried her stout little umbrella, winter or summer.

β. **1697** [see 1 β]. **1704** SWIFT *T. Tub* xi, A large Skin of Parchment..served him for a Night-cap when he went to Bed, and for an Umbrello in rainy Weather. **1709** W. KING *Art of Love* 99, I might have made you such a fellow, As should have carry'd my Umbrello, Or bore a flambeau by my chair. **1731** *Phil. Trans.* XXXVII. 32 An Umbrello, suspended by a Packthread tied to the Handle of it, became strongly Electrical. **1732** *Inventory Sir R. Sutton's Goods* 7 Four Umbrellows.

3. Used in comparisons or similes, esp. with reference to shape.

a. **1616** B. JONSON *Devil an Ass* IV. iv, I saw i' the Court of Spaine once, A Lady fall i' the Kings sight, along. And there shee lay, flat spred, as an Vmbrella. **1630** DRAYTON *Muses Elizium* (1892) 15 Doues..Which..shall..like Vmbrellas with their feathers Sheeld you in all sorts of weathers. *a* **1680** BUTLER *Rem.* (1759) II. 99 Hats..With broad Brims sometimes like Umbrellas, And sometimes narrow as Punchinello's. **1726** SHELVOCKE *Voy. round World* (1757) 66 On this bank, or shoal, we saw great numbers of Clubbers appearing, like the tops of umbrellas. **1726** J. HOBSON *Diary* 8 Oct., in *Yorks. Diaries* (Surtees) 258 Out of all..came pyramidicall streams of light,..forming such a figure as a ladies' umbrella. **1796** WITHERING *Brit. Plants* (ed. 3) III. 646 The florets diverging from the centre, spreading outwards and downwards like an umbrella.

β. **1710** STEELE *Tatler* No. 116 ¶1 An engine of several legs, that could contract or open itself like the top of an umbrello. **1740** L. WHYTE *Dissert. Fashions* 66 Erst have I seen a little fellow, With Hat as large as Vmbrellow; It was the Mode for young and old.

†**4.** *fig.* **a.** A means of shelter or protection.

a. **1609** DONNE *Lett.* (1651) 63 We have an earthly cave, our bodies, to go into by consideration, and cool our selves; and..we have within us a torch, a soul, lighter and warmer than any without: we are therefore our own umbrella's and our own suns. **1624** FLETCHER *Rule a Wife* III. i, Is your heart at rest, Now you have got a shadow, an umbrella To keep the scorching worlds opinion From your fair credit. **1648** J. RAYMOND *Il Merc. Ital.* Pref. 1 A weather beaten Traveller needs no such Umbrilla as a Patron to shroud under. *a* **1734** NORTH *Examen* I. ii. (1740) 89, I have been, perhaps, too long in exposing the Author for holding up an Umbrella to keep his Earl in a Shade.

β. **1652** H. L'ESTRANGE *Amer. no Jewes* To Rdr., No other dedicatory Umbrello do I seek..to defend this work from the scorch of censure. **1670** PHILIPOT *Antiq. Hierol. & Gent.* Ded., This Treatise implores your Patronage as an Umbrello to over-shadow it. **1690** *Secr. Hist. Chas. II & Jas. II*, 112 The popular gentlemen were only made use of as Umbrello's to shade the conspirators from the scorching heat of the people's discontent.

†**b.** A screen or disguise. *Obs.*

1623 T. SCOTT *Tongue-Combat* 80 Yorke, Patton, and Symple, with many others, who may haue Dispensations for their Oathes, and Vmbrilloes for their humours. **1653** JER. TAYLOR *Serm. for Year* I. vi. 77 We shall dishonour the sufferings of our blessed Saviour, if we make them to be a Umbrello to shelter our impious and ungodly living. **1658** OSBORNE *Mem. Jas. I*, 45 These brainsick fooles as..made Religion an Umbrella to impiety.

5. a. Anything serving as a protection or shelter from the sun, rain, etc.

1654 WHITLOCK *Zootomia* 403 How do they lessen the stately wonders of the Eye, into Cottages (I may say Snaile-like Umbrellos) meer shades, and Dormitorys. **1674** C. F. *Wit at a Venture* 38 Shroud the Sun, and let each tree To her a kind umbrella be. **1701** WOLLEY *Jrnl. New York* (1860) 25 Nature kindly..shelters it with the umbrella's of all sorts of Trees from pernicious Lakes. **1718** OZELL tr. *Tournefort's Voy.* I. 66 To skreen themselues from the sun, they haue no other way but to make a sort of Umbrella of their Handkerchief. **1838** BARHAM *Ingol. Leg.* Ser. 1, *Witches' Frolic* (1905) 99 The straggling yew, His leafy umbrella, was wet through and through; Rob was half dead with cold. **1907** *Westm. Gaz.* 9 Feb. 2/2 Here and there a stone-pine with its great umbrella of dark foliage cast a more impenetrable shade.

†**b.** A sun-blind. *Obs.*

1687 MIÉGE *Gt. Fr. Dict.* II. s.v., To have an Umbrello before his Window to keep off the Sun [Fr. *un Paillasson*]. **1706** PHILLIPS (ed. Kersey), *Umbrello*,..a Wooden Frame cover'd with Cloth or Stuff, to keep off the Sun from a Window. **1709** MRS. MANLEY *Secret Mem.* I. 33 The Weather violently Hot, the Umbrelloes were let down from behind the Windows, the Sashes open.

c. A screen of fighter aircraft or a curtain of fire put up as protection against enemy aircraft.

1941 [see *air umbrella* s.v. AIR *sb.*[1] III. 2]. **1942** *Hutchinson's Pict. Hist. War* 18 Mar.–9 June 102 The task of a fleet working in confined waters is a most difficult one. It is eased if long-range fighters or aircraft-carriers..are available to provide a protective umbrella. **1945** *Sun* (Baltimore) 17 Mar. 2-0/5 The giant bombers of the United States 15th Air Force, continuing their methodical pounding of Germany's vital fuel sources, were escorted by an umbrella of fast American fighters. **1946** *Ibid.* 26 June 8/3 Gun crews pumped deadly umbrellas of anti-aircraft fire above the harbor. **1967** *Electronics* 6 Mar. 73 (Advt.), The Army's new Missile Mentors..now provide major U.S. cities with air defense umbrellas.

6. a. A structure resembling in shape an outspread umbrella, or serving for protection against something.

1680–4 DINGLEY *Hist. from Marble* (Camden Soc.) p. xxxix, The Umbrello in yᵉ Bath was erected and leaded by Mr. Coo. **1719** D'URFEY *Pills* II. 125 Tho' at Cales they scap'ed our Guns, By strong wall'd umbrello. **1742** B. LANGLEY *Anc. Archit. Restored* Plate xxxi, The work contains several designs for Umbrellos, by which term the author indicates a roofed structure with open sides to be placed at the termination of a walk in a garden. **1844** H. H. WILSON *Brit. India* III. 51 A spire surmounted by a Tee or umbrella of open iron-work. **1883** GRESLEY *Gloss. Coal-m.* 266 *Umbrella* [= *Bonnet*, the overhead cover of a cage or swinging bont]. **1904** *Daily Chron.* 26 Oct. 4/5 It requires a pretty good umbrella of a trench to protect men from this death-shower.

b. Anything which temporarily or permanently has the form of an umbrella.

c **1770** *Art of Angling* 48 in Ruddiman *Coll.* (1773) 277 But mine is not the glory to unfurl The net's umbrello, with Herculean whirl. **1846** J. BAXTER *Libr. Pract. Agric.* (ed. 4) I. 106 The feathery-like points of the down..uniting together form a kind of inverted umbrella. **1866** E. C. RYE *Brit. Beetles* 225 The larvæ in this family have an ingenious but unpleasant habit of forming their excrement into an umbrella, as in *Crioceris*. **1885** *Pall Mall G.* 11 Mar. 11/1 The araucaria forests..fringing the tops of the hills..with delicate, long stilted umbrellas.

c. A broad-brimmed hat.

a **1803** C. L. LEWES in *Mem.* (1805) I. 25 A large slouched beaver umbrella, that wanted only a crape hatband to sanctify it for a funeral.

d. *U.S. Mil. slang.* A parachute.

1933 C. K. STEWART *Speech Amer. Airman* 99 *Umbrella*, parachute. **1980** J. DITTON *Copley's Hunch* II. i. 117 It takes ages to come down on an umbrella... Then you have to get rid of the chute.

7. a. *Bot.* A part of a plant resembling an outspread umbrella.

1658 SIR T. BROWNE *Gard. Cyrus* iii. 47 Elegant clusters of Dragons.. with an *umbrella* or skreening Leaf about them. **1712** tr. *Pomet's Hist. Drugs* I. 6 The Flowers grow in Umbrellos on the Tops of the thick Branches. **1809** *Naval Chron.* XXII. 493 The cap of a mushroom, which M. P... names umbrella.

b. *Zool.* The gelatinous disk or bell-shaped structure of a jelly-fish.

1834 GRIFFITH tr. *Cuvier* XII. 482 *Medusa* have a disk more or less convex above, similar to the head of a mushroom, and to which the name of *umbrella* has been given. **1861** J. R. GREENE *Man. Anim. Kingd., Cœlent.* 38 In the umbrella of the *Lucernaridæ*, both vesicles and pigment-spots seem to become united into a single organ. **1881** E. R. LANKESTER in *Jrnl. Microsc. Sci.* Jan. 122 The manubrium of Limnocodium is a somewhat quadrangular tube, which depends during life below the margin of the umbrella.

c. *Conch.* A limpet-like gastropod of the genus *Umbrella*; also the part of the shell resembling an open umbrella.

1841 *Penny Cycl.* XXI. 217/2 Umbrella with a flattened shell; the disk of the lower surface not radiated. **1861** P. P. CARPENTER in *Rep. Smithsonian Instit. 1860*, 230 The shell ..entirely covers the animal; which..can move its long neck freely under its large umbrella. *Ibid.* 234 The Umbrellas are very large creatures, wearing a flat limpet on the middle of the back.

†**8.** ***white umbrella***, the elder-tree. *Obs.*$^{-1}$

1658 SIR T. BROWNE *Gard. Cyrus* iii. 47 The white umbrella or medicall bush of Elder, is an Epitome of this order.

9. Authority, protection, means of defence; controlling or unifying agency. Freq. in phr. ***under the umbrella*** and varr.

1948 *Hansard Commons* 22 Jan. 388 Giving the smaller Powers a chance to evolve, under the umbrella of the Four Powers. **1949** *Ibid.* 24 May 1213, I am not taking away from the occupants of these flats the umbrella which the law intends to give them. **1952** *Sun* (Baltimore) 15 Feb. (B. ed.) 2/6 The big broad budgetary umbrella under which all manner of wasteful sin is committed. **1958** *Economist* 25 Oct. 297/2 The political division of Germany may become once more a looming *casus belli*, to be contested by the conventional forces that can regain their freedom of action under the atomic umbrella. **1962** H. E. BEECHENO *Introd. Business Stud.* xi. 93 What they have done is to bring all the operations, or most of them, under the umbrella of one firm and cut out various 'middlemen' as separate concerns. **1965** *Listener* 1 July 7/2 Europe seems unenthusiastic to exchange the American nuclear umbrella for a French one. **1973** E. BULLINS *Theme is Blackness* 7 Theater workers and institutions that presently work from under the Black umbrella. **1976** *Howard Jrnl.* XV. I. 55 Many of the former approved schools continue in their former practices, albeit under a new umbrella. **1983** *Listener* 12 May 5/3 The harsh truth is that Sweden is not under the NATO umbrella.

10. *attrib.* and *Comb.* **a.** ***umbrella-case, -cover, covering, frame, -silk, -stand, -stick, -trade; umbrella-bearer, -maker, -mender; umbrella-shaped, -topped*** adjs.; ***umbrella-wise*** adv.; (sense 5 c) ***umbrella barrage***; (sense 9) ***umbrella basis, policy***.

1852 BONOMI *Nineveh & Palaces* (1853) 176 The king.. is accompanied by his charioteer and *umbrella-bearer. **1891** KINNS *Graven in Rock* xvi. 599 In the left hand of the umbrella-bearer is an object like a fan or fly-trap. **1850** THACKERAY *Pendennis* lvii, His despatch-boxes and *umbrella-cases, his guide-books, passports, maps, and other elaborate necessaries of the English traveller. **1944** T. H. WISDOM *Triumph over Tunisia* 134 There was..an intense *umbrella barrage over the two Tunisian ports. **1961** *Wall St. Jrnl.* 30 Nov. 19/3 Companies with assembly plants, warehouses and other properties in 15 countries, for example, are realizing it is to their advantage to write insurance on an '*umbrella' basis. **1888** *Encycl. Brit.* XXIII. 723/1 In 1848 William Sangster patented the use of alpaca as an *umbrella covering material. **1837** HEBERT *Engin. & Mech. Encycl.* II. 829 *Umbrella frames of the usual construction. **1793–4** *Matthews's Bristol Directory*, Ashbury, William, *Umbrella-maker, Hope Square, Hotwells. **1813** *Examiner* 31 May 350/2 She has given 'mirth' to nobody except it be the ducks and the umbrella-makers. **1884** *Harper's Mag.* Feb. 375/1 An umbrella-maker had established his open-air shop. **1848** DICKENS *Dombey* iii, The summer sun..came with the water-carts and the old clothes-men,..and the *umbrella-mender. **1963** *Daily Tel.* 23 Sept. 21/6 Miss Hawkes said that CND's '*umbrella policy' of accepting any group simply because it had pacifist aims, was not acceptable to her. **1796** WITHERING *Brit. Plants* (ed. 3) I. 387 Capsule cylindrical, sitting on a hollow nearly globular or *umbrella-shaped receptacle. **1837** P. KEITH *Bot. Lex.* 298 The pileus or cap is the conical or umbrella-shaped organ that surmounts the stipe of the Agarics. **1862** ANSTED *Channel Isl.* II. ix. (ed. 2) 239 The umbrella-shaped body of this animal. **1888** *Encycl. Brit.* XXIII. 723/1 *Umbrella silk is principally made at Lyons and Crefeld. **1837** DICKENS *Pickw.* xxxiv. 378 A mahogany *umbrella stand. **1862** *Catal. Internat. Exhib., Brit.* II. No. 6061, Fenders, fire-irons, hat and umbrella stands. **1879** MEREDITH *Egoist* xxv, He stepped to the umbrella-stand. There was then a general question whether Clara had taken her umbrella. **1875** KNIGHT *Dict. Mech.* 2679/1 In preparing an ordinary *umbrella-stick, it passes through 19 separate processes or movements. **1850** R. G. CUMMING *Hunter's Life S. Afr.* (1902) 61/1 Some friendly grove of *umbrella-topped mimosas. **1835** *Penny Cycl.* IV. 446/1 The *umbrella trade arose from the demand for the brass furniture of these useful contrivances. **1725** *Fam. Dict.* s.v. *Elder-Tree*, Its Flowers grow somewhat like Roses at the Tops of the Branches *Umbrella or Parasole-wise.

b. In names of plants or trees, denoting 'shaped like, resembling, an umbrella', as ***umbrella acacia, bush, fern, -fir, grass, leaf, palm, -pine, -plant, -wort***.

1882 *Garden* 11 March 166/3 The *Umbrella Acacia.. forms a dense globular head, which is certainly very conspicuous. **1889** MAIDEN *Useful Pl.* 363 *Acacia Oswaldi*, ..often called *Umbrella Bush, as it is a capital shade-tree. **1882** T. H. POTTS *Out in Open* 53 There Cunningham's *Gleichenia* grows marvellously robust, its stiff many-branched fronds rise, tier above tier, in curved fan-like form —which habit, doubtless, induced settlers to call this species the '*umbrella fern'. **1959** A. MCLINTOCK *Descr. Atlas N.Z.* 30 Where the forest has been cleared and burnt, the resulting cover is all too often low scrub, rushes, and umbrella fern. **1884** MILLER *Plant-n.* 247/2 *Sciadopitys*, *Umbrella-, or Parasol-, Pine or Fir. *Ibid.* 58/1 *Umbrella Grass. *Fuirena squarrosa* and *Panicum decompositum*. **1898** MORRIS *Austral Eng.* 487/1 It is called Umbrella-grass, from the shape of the branches at the top of the stem representing the ribs of an open umbrella. **1866** *Treas. Bot.* 412/1 The only species, *Diphylleia cymosa*, a native of Japan, and of the southern United States, is there called the *Umbrella Leaf. **1798** NEMNICH *Allg. Polyglotten-Lex.* II. 928 *Umbrella palm. *Corypha umbraculifera*. **1884** MILLER *Plant-n.* 210/1 *Kentia Canterburyana*, Umbrella Palm. **1873** HEMSLEY *Handbk. Trees & Shrubs* 435 *Sciadopitys verticillata*, *Umbrella-Pine. A large evergreen tree from 50 to 150 feet high. **1893** G. ALLEN *Scallywag* I. 141 Among the rosemary bushes and the scanty umbrella-pines. **1874** *Treas. Bot.* Suppl. 1350/1 *Umbrella-plant, *Saxifraga peltata*. **1829**

LOUDON *Encycl. Plants* (1836) 36 *Calymenia.* *Umbrella-Wort. **1852** JOHNSON *Cottage Gard. Dict.* 671/2 *Oxybaphus,* Umbrella-wort.

c. In names of birds, etc., as ***umbrella-ant, -bird, chatterer, shell, snake.***

1883 W. FARREN *White Ants* vi. 61 In some ant colonies more than two distinct forms of workers are found. I may instance the Sauba, or *Umbrella ant of Brazil. **1891** *Cent. Dict., Umbrella-ant,* a parasol-ant or leaf-carrying ant. **1850** A. R. WALLACE in *Ann. & Mag. Nat. Hist.* (1851) Ser. II. VIII. 429 The *Umbrella Bird is about the size of a crow. **1863** BATES *Nat. Amazon* II. iv. 283 The rare and curious Umbrella bird (*Cephalopterus ornatus*);..decorated with a crest of long, curved, hairy feathers having long bare quills, which, when raised, spread themselves out in the form of a fringed sun-shade over the head. *Ibid.* II. vi. 387 Birds and monkeys, in this glorious forest, were very abundant,..the *Umbrella Chatterer and curl-crested Toucans amongst the most beautiful of the birds. **1861** P. P. CARPENTER in *Rep. Smithsonian Instit. 1860.* 234 Family *Umbrellidæ.* (Chinese *Umbrella Shells.) **1881** *Cassell's Nat. Hist.* V. 226 The 'Chinese Umbrella-shell' has a small depressed Limpet-like shell, marked by concentric lines of growth. **1904** *Westm. Gaz.* 23 April 2/3 The natives call it Mtaba, or the *umbrella snake.

11. Special Combs., as **umbrella bridge**, a temporary raised traffic lane with ramp approaches, in use while building work is conducted below; **umbrella defence**, in Amer. football, an alignment of the backs resembling the shape of an open umbrella; **umbrella field** *Cricket*, an arrangement of close fieldsmen (esp. in the slips) spread in a cordon about the batsman; **umbrella gingham**, gingham employed for covering umbrellas; **umbrella hat**, a hat similar in size or shape to an umbrella; **umbrella man**, (*a*) one who mends or sells umbrellas; (*b*) a street-vendor who displays his wares in an inverted open umbrella; **umbrella organization**, an organization which represents and protects separate member bodies; **umbrella print-seller**, = *umbrella man* (*b*); **umbrella roof**, an arched roof resembling an umbrella; **umbrella sail**, a sail constructed partly on the principle of an umbrella; **umbrella tent**, a tent made on the umbrella principle; **umbrella type**, used (freq., with hyphen, *attrib.*) to denote any structure which resembles (part of) an umbrella in shape; **umbrella warping** *Naut.* (see quot.).

1962 *Daily Tel.* 14 Sept. 15/7 Supports will be sunk to take a steel '*umbrella' road bridge while the Oxford Circus underground station is rebuilt. **1973** *Times* 24 Mar. 2/8 A temporary 'umbrella' bridge is to be erected in the Charring Cross railway station forecourt. **1950** *Sun* (Baltimore) 23 Oct. 17/3 An *umbrella backfield defense..had no special name. It was..a formation to provide width and depth for pass defence. It has the general shape of an umbrella. **1972** J. MOSEDALE *Football* x. 145 Owen installed what was called 'the umbrella defense', so-called because the alignment of the defensive backfield resembled an open umbrella. **1954** MILLER & WHITINGTON *Gods or Flannelled Fools?* vi. 225 Hassett had been loath to set the..'*Umbrella' field..with eight men stationed in an inner arc behind the batsman from backward point to square-leg. **1963** *Courier-Mail* (Brisbane) 21 Nov. 17/1 The conversation..consisted of snippets like ..'in an umbrella field'. **1834** *Tait's Mag.* I. 72/2 *Umbrella ginghams have remained steady for some time. **1817** COLERIDGE *Biog. Lit.* (1907) II. 150 Dutch women with large *umbrella hats shooting out half a yard before them. **1851** MAYHEW *Lond. Labour* I. 303 I learned from one '*umbrella man' that, six or seven years previously, he used to sell more portraits of 'Mr. Edmund Kean, as Richard III.', than of anything else. **1889** *Belgravia* Sept. 333 The umbrella-man..stopped beside a stile and put down his bundle of umbrellas. **1950** *Times* 8 May 2/7 The domestic poultry-keepers could also win independence, and it is doubtful whether either group needs an '*umbrella' organization set up at the Ministry of Agriculture. **1983** *Out of Town* Dec. 17/1 They [*sc.* naturalist rectors] showed an equally native disposition to flourish best as part of an amiable, protective institution. Today the BBC has replaced the Church as the umbrella organisation. **1851** MAYHEW *Lond. Labour* I. 303 Sometimes, too, an '*umbrella print-seller' will have a few 'pictures in frames', on a sort of stand alongside the umbrella. **1847** LEITCH tr. *C.O. Müller's Anc. Art* §106 (1850) 74 The Odeion also, a smaller theatre with an *umbrella roof, received its form at Athens. **1900** *Pearson's Mag.* Aug. 143 The *umbrella sail can be set or furled in a minute; it does not close up as does an umbrella, but each side shuts up like a fan. **1895** *Army & Navy Co-op. Soc. Price List* 15 Sept. Index p. lxxv, *Umbrella Tents. *Ibid.* 449 The Umbrella Garden Tent with Sloping Walls. **1913** *Wireless World* June 210/1 M. V...asks..whether the '*umbrella type' of aerial would be most suitable, or whether the use of another mast, 10 feet high,..would improve matters. **1940** *Chambers's Techn. Dict.* 876/1 *Umbrella-type alternator*.., a vertical-shaft alternator,..in which the field system is overhung and revolves around the stationary armature. **1962** *Daily Tel.* 4 Dec. 15/3 An open market..has been replaced by a modern covered market. It has an attractive umbrella-type roof. **1963** *Guardian* 27 Feb. 5/2 Why on a semisports car should the handbrake be of the 'umbrella' type? **1971** *Jamaican Weekly Gleaner* 17 Nov. 9/1 The promenade..would contain umbrella type shops and stalls to accommodate the present proliferation of peddlers. **1867** SMYTH *Sailor's Word-bk.* 705 **Umbrella-warping*, a contrivance similar to an umbrella, by which ships in a calm can be warped ahead.

12. *attrib.* passing into *adj.* Of words, names, etc.: covering a number of meanings or associated terms; general, catch-all.

1949 G. RYLE *Concept of Mind* vi. 198 The range of higher order acts and attitudes, which are apt to be inadequately covered by the umbrella-title 'self-consciousness'. **1957** *Listener* 8 Aug. 201/1 Cancer is one of the umbrella words. It covers a number of disease conditions. **1974** *Country Life* 5 Dec. 1723/1 The numerous [Ilex] hybrids which are gathered beneath the umbrella name of *I.* × *altaclarensis.* **1977** *Times Lit. Suppl.* 29 Apr. 530/3 Any one of half a dozen umbrella titles would equally well match the variety of the contents of this military miscellany, *War and Society.*

um'brellaed, *ppl. a.* [f. prec. + -ED[1].]

1. Protected or covered as by an umbrella. Also *fig.*

c **1800** SOUTHEY *Inscriptions* xvi. *Under An Oak* (1854) 100 This ancient oak Will parasol thee if the sun ride high, Or, should the sudden shower be falling fast, Here mayst thou rest umbrella'd. **1858** H. W. BEECHER *Life Thoughts* 142 Many..believe that they must come to Him [*sc.* God] under the covert of some apology, or beneath some umbrellaed excuse. **1885** W. P. BREED *Aboard & Abroad* 127 The landscape lovingly umbrellaed by smiling clouds that took turns in the task of keeping the direct sunbeams from our faces.

2. *Ornith.* (See quot. and cf. UMBRELLA 9 c.)

a **1807** SHAW *Nat. Misc.* XXI. pl. 897 The Umbrella'd Ampelis... Black Ampelis, with the vertical crest and pendent breast-feathers glossed with violet. The Umbrella'd Chatterer. *Cephalopterus ornatus.*

3. Provided with an umbrella or umbrellas.

1834 *Tait's Mag.* I. 42/1 Who in their senses might hope to escape the drench?..umbrellaed or umbrellaless they must have it. **1863** *Morn. Star* 21 May, When the umbrellaed multitude swarmed down the centre of the course, the effect was most extraordinary. **1887** M. B. EDWARDS *Next of Kin Wanted* I. x. 135 Groups of mackintoshed, umbrella'd, behooded travellers.

um'brellaless, *a.* [f. as prec. + -LESS.] Unprovided with an umbrella.

1834 [see prec. 3]. **1864** MISS YONGE *Trial* II. 224 Pacing on, umbrellaless, was a figure which made her hurry to overtake him. **1898** *Daily Tel.* 14 Dec. 10/2 The umbrellaless man who in a shower of rain, sought to run between the drops.

um'brella-like, *a.* [f. as prec. + -LIKE.] Resembling an umbrella.

1796 WITHERING *Brit. Plants* (ed. 3) IV. 340 Pileus umbrella-like, gold coloured. **1857** DUFFERIN *Lett. High Lat.* xi. 290 A dark mantle of tempestuous clouds, that stretched down in umbrella-like points towards the horizon. **1895** CLIVE HOLLAND *Jap. Wife* ix, A wonderful umbrella-like hat of huge diameter.

um'brella-tree. [f. as prec. + TREE *sb.*]

1. One of various American magnolias, especially *Magnolia tripetala*, having the leaves arranged umbrella-wise at the ends of the branches.

1738 *Phil. Trans.* XL. 350 *Magnolia, amplissimoflore albo, fructu coccineo.* The Umbrella-tree. **1796** W. H. MARSHALL *Planting* II. 210 The wood of the Umbrella Tree..is more spongy than any of the other species of Magnolia. **1814** PURSH *Flora Amer. Septentr.* II. 381 *Magnolia tripetala*..is generally known by the name of Umbrella-tree. **1832** *Planting* 94 (L.U.K.), Magnolia tripetala, umbrella-tree, is found in soils deep and fertile in the northern parts of New York. **1884** *Cassell's Fam. Mag.* Mar. 239/1 Here the umbrella-trees shaded the streets.

2. One of a variety of trees whose leaves or habit of growth resemble an umbrella.

c **1790** *Encycl. Brit.* (ed. 3) V. 482/1 *Corypha,* Mountain Palm, or Umbrella Tree. **1834** CAUNTER *Orient. Ann.* v. 53 The chatta, or umbrella-tree, begins here to be plentiful. **1866** *Treas. Bot.* 1190/1 Umbrella-tree,..*Thespesia populnea* and *Pandanus odoratissimus.* *Ibid.*, Guinea Umbrella-Tree, *Paritium guineense.* **1883** *Sunday Mag.* Aug. 511/2 We saw a good many specimens of the 'umbrella-tree', as it is called, a sort of acacia. **1889** MAIDEN *Useful Pl.* 387 *Brassaia actinophylla*,..Umbrella Tree, the large leaves being set, like umbrella-ribs, at the top of numerous stems.

†**um'brellian,** *a. Obs.*[−1] [f. as next + -IAN.] Serving the purpose of an umbrella.

1721 RAMSAY *Tartana* 101 On each motion wait th' umbrellian Plaids, Repelling dust when winds disturb the air.

um'brelliform, *a. Zool.* [f. UMBRELL-A + -(I)FORM.] Having the shape of an umbrella.

1857 GOSSE *Omphalos* xi. 304 The pulmonigrade umbrelliform stage.

umbrello(w, obs. variants of UMBRELLA.

†**'umbrere.** *Obs.* Also 5 oumbrer, owmbrer(e, vmberere, 6–7 vmbriere, 7 umbrier. [app. a. AF. **umbrere*, f. *umbre* shade, shadow; cf. obs. F. *ombriere* umbrella (Cotgr.).] The visor of a helmet.

a **1400** *Sir Perc.* 678 For to see hyme with syghte, He putt his umbrere on highte. ? *a* **1400** *Morte Arth.* 943 To þe creste of þe clyffe he clymbez one lofte; Keste upe hys vmbrere, and kenly he lukes. **1448–9** J. METHAM *Wks.* (1916) 37 At þe fyrst metyng Amoryus þis odyr gan smyght Vp-on hys vmbrere. **1470–85** MALORY *Arthur* VIII. xli. 338 Thenne sire Lamorak knelyd adoune, and vnlaced fyrst his vmberere, and thenne his owne. **1590** SPENSER *F.Q.* III. i. 42 But the braue Mayd would not disarmed bee, But onely vented vp her vmbriere. **1596** *Ibid.* IV. iv. 44 He..therewith smote him on his vmbriere. **1655** tr. *Sorel's Com. Hist. Francion* VII. 4 It was cloven in the middle, as if it were the Umbrier of some Troopers old Head-piece.

†**umbretary,** misprint for VULNERARY *a.*

1601 HOLLAND *Pliny* II. 111 Being applied as a cataplasme with oyle rosat and milke, it is a vmbretarie medicine.

umbreted, obs. variant of UMBRATED *a.*

um'brette. [ad. mod.L. *umbretta* or F. *ombrette.*] = UMBRE.

1884 *Athenæum* 29 Nov. 698/3 Communications and papers were read..by Mr. F. E. Beddard, on the anatomy of the umbrette (*Scopus umbretta*). **1890** *Daily News* 9 Jan. 3/8 Occasionally the umbrette relaxes the severity of its demeanour and executes a fantastic dance with outspread wings.

Umbrian ('ʌmbrɪən), *sb.* and *a.* [f. L. *Umbr-*, *Umber* (a. and sb.) or *Umbria* (see def.) + -(I)AN.]

A. *sb.* **1.** An inhabitant or native of Umbria, a province of central Italy; *esp.* a member of the Italic race anciently inhabiting this district.

1601 HOLLAND *Pliny* I. 36 The Babylonians count for day all the time betweene two sunne risings... The Vmbrians from noone to noone. **1693** DRYDEN *Persius* III. 140 The Greaz'd Advocate, that Grinds the Poor, Fat Fees from the defended Umbrian draws. **1843** MACAULAY *Horatius* xxii, The terror of the Umbrian, The terror of the Gaul. **1867** *Chambers' Encycl.* IX. 630/1 The Umbrians were considered in ancient times to be the oldest people of Italy. **1890** *Contemp. Rev.* Aug. 266 The pile dwelling in the Lake of Fimòn, near Vicenza,..must have been founded very soon after the Umbrians first reached Italy.

2. The language anciently spoken in Umbria.

1854 C. C. J. BUNSEN *Christianity & Mankind* III. 91 In Umbrian, the *D* between two vowels passes into a specific *R*, expressed in the national alphabet by a peculiar letter, in Latin by *RS.* **1858** G. ROBERTSON *Earliest Inhabitants Italy* 9 The differences between the Oscan and the Umbrian with its kindred dialects. **1864** F. W. NEWMAN *Iguvine Inscriptions* p. xiv, The vowel-declensions of Umbrian. **1882** C. S. HALSEY *Etym. Latin & Greek* I. i. 2 This [division] includes..2. The Latin, akin to which were the Oscan and the Umbrian of central Italy.

B. *adj.* **1.** Of or belonging to ancient Umbria, its inhabitants or langauge.

1601 HOLLAND *Pliny* II. Index s.v., Vmbrian earth or chalke, for what it is good. **1697** DRYDEN *Æneid* XII. 1088 The persecuted creature..Turns here and there, to escape his Umbrian foe. **1845** *Encycl. Metrop.* XXV. 1345/1 The Umbrian, Oscan, and Samnite characters, are, with a few trifling exceptions, nearly identical with the Etruscan. **1864** F. W. NEWMAN *Iguvine Inscriptions* p. iii, The Umbrian tendency to assimilate *n* even in the middle of words. **1890** *Contemp. Rev.* Aug. 264 We now come to the third Italian race, which may be called the Umbrian or Latin race.

2. Of or pertaining to mediæval or modern Umbria. ***Umbrian School***, the Italian school of painting developed in Umbria in the 15th century.

1836 *Dublin Rev.* July 443 The continuous efforts of the Umbrian School, even after..the death of Perugino. **1841** W. SPALDING *Italy & It. Isl.* II. 252 The Umbrian painters appear to have at first studied both the older Florentines and the decaying school of Siena. **1845** MRS. JAMESON *Early Italian Painters* I. 204 In the sentiment of their works they resembled the Umbrian school, but the manner of execution is different. **1883** W. SHARP in E. A. Sharp *Life* (1910) 88 Watching the sunset over the far-stretching Umbrian country.

umbridawes: see EMBER[2] 2.

um'briferous, *a.* [f. L. *umbrifer* (f. *umbra* shade) + -OUS. Cf. It. *ombrifero.*] Affording or giving shade; umbrageous.

1616 W. FORDE *Serm.* Ep. Ded., She had, to shadow her from the sunnes scorching beames, a beautifull and umbriferous tree. **1665** SIR T. HERBERT *Trav.* (1677) 382 Several other sorts of Trees there are... One I took special notice of was above five yards about and of a reasonable height, but umbriferous it was not. **1819** H. BUSK *Vestriad* I. 576 Nor cypress, plane, and cedar interlace Their arms umbrif'rous.

Hence **um'briferously** *adv.*; **um'briferousness.**

1727 BAILEY (vol. II), *Umbriferousness*, Shadow-bringing Quality. **1884** *Imp. Dict.* (citing Tyndall), *Umbriferously*, so as to make or cast a shade.

†**umbril**[1]. *Obs. rare.* [ad. It. *umbrella* UMBRELLA. Cf. UMBREL[2].] A sun-shade, parasol, umbrella.

1610 R. TOFTE *Hon. Acad.* II. 10 Her amorous eye-browes, somewhat blacke, serving as an Umbrill for her diamond-like-eyes. **1612** SHELTON *Quix.* I. I. viii. 54 Two monkes..wore masks with Spectacles in them, to keepe away the dust from their faces, and each of them besides bore their Vmbrilles.

†**umbril**[2]. *Obs. rare.* [ad. F. *nombril* navel.] A centre. Also *attrib.*

1630 WESTCOTE *View Devonsh.* (1845) 135 The great conduit which stands in the umbril point of the city. *Ibid.* 139 The umbril of the city where standeth a great water conduit.

umbril[3]. *Hist.* [var. UMBREL[1].] **a.** A part of a helmet projecting above the eyes. **b.** A visor.

1824 MEYRICK *Ant. Armour* II. 221 The helmet of the king is the casquetel, having no covering for the face, but merely an umbril. **1864** WEBSTER, *Umbrere*,..an umbril; a visor. **1892** H. PYLE *Men of Iron* xxxii. 306 The Constable advanced to his side, and formally raising the umbril of the helmet, looked him in the face.

‖**um'brina.** *Zool.* [mod.L. (Cuvier), a. Sp. and It. *umbrina* (It. also *ombrina*, F. *ombrine*,

†*umbrine*), f. *umbra* UMBER *sb.*^{2}] A fish of the genus *Umbrina*, chiefly found in warm seas.

1834 McMURTRIE *Cuvier's Anim. Kingd.* 197 Some of the species, such as the King-fisher (an *Umbrina*), inhabit the American seas. **1840** tr. *Cuvier's Anim. Kingd.* 296 Some of them are silvery, and attain the size of an Umbrina. **1884** *Longman's Mag.* March 530 The Umbrinas of European seas are well known for the drumming sound they make.

†um'briphilous, *a. Obs.*$^{-1}$ [f. L. *umbra* shade: see -PHIL and -OUS.] Shade-loving; growing in the shade.

1592 R. D. *Hypnerotomachia* 32 Heleborous [*sic*] Niger, or Melampodi, Trayfles, and such other Vmbriphilous hearbes.

Umbro- ('ʌmbrəʊ), comb. form, on Gr. models, of L. *Umbr-*, *Umber* (see UMBRIAN), occurring in a few terms, as ***Umbro-Etruscan***, ***-Latin***, ***-Oscan***, ***-Roman***, ***-Sabellian***, ***-Samnite***. Also, with reference to the Umbrian school of painting, ***Umbro-Florentine***, ***-Siennese*** (1866).

1853 *Jrnl. Ethnol. Soc.* (1856) IV. 67 This inscription differs from those which are found in the Umbro-Etruscan or Rasenic districts. **1858** G. ROBERTSON *Earliest Inhabitants Italy* 46 The migration of the Umbro-Sabellian races. **1858** *Bibliotheca Sacra* XV. 99 The Latin stands related to all this Umbro-Samnite class of special dialects, as, in Greek, the Ionic to the Doric dialect. **1862** T. CLARK *Handbk. Compar. Grammar* 24 The Latin language has..some such relation to the Umbro-Samnite, as the Ionic has to the Doric. **1880** *Encycl. Brit* XIII. 496/1 The features common to Umbro-Roman and the Neapolitan dialects. **1890** *Contemp. Rev.* Aug. 265 This Umbro-Latin Aryan race must have entered Italy considerably more than two thousand years before the commencement of our era.

umbrose (ʌm'brəʊs), *a. rare.* [ad. L. *umbrōs-us*, f. *umbra* shade. Cf. Sp. and Pg. *umbroso*, It. *ombroso*, OF. *ombros*.]

1. Shady; giving shade.

a **1425** tr. *Arderne's Treat. Fistula*, etc. 75 Hyng it in ane vmbrose place vnto þat þer be had nede þer-of. **1721** BAILEY, *Umbrose*, shady, casting a great Shade. **1871** MACDONALD *Wks. Fancy & Imag.*, *Roadside Poems* III. 187 Still as a pool in its own place, Unsunned within an umbrose wood.

2. *Ornith.* Dusky.

1783 LATHAM *Gen. Synop. Birds* IV. 437 Umbrose W[arbler];..upper parts greyish brown: on the back obscurely marked with black.

†um'brosity. *Obs. rare.* [ad. L. *umbrōsitas*, f. *umbrōsus*: see prec. and -ITY. Cf. It. *ombrosità*, obs. F. *ombrosité*, *umbrosité*.] The state or condition of being shady.

1646 SIR T. BROWNE *Pseud. Ep.* II. i. 55 Oyled paper.. becommeth more transparent, and admits the visible rayes with lesse umbrosity. **1650** BULWER *Anthropomet.* v. (1653) 100 Kypler would not have this notion neglected, that the Haires of the Eye-lids do chiefly conduce to their umbrosity.

†um'brosous, *a. Obs.*$^{-0}$ [f. L. *umbrōs-us*.] 'Full of shadow' (Cockeram, 1623).

umbrous ('ʌmbrəs), *a.* Also 5 **vmbreuse.** [ad. F. *ombreux*, †*umbreux*, or L. *umbrōs-us*: cf. UMBROSE *a.*]

1. Lying in the shade; shady, shadowed.

1480 CAXTON *Myrr.* III. i. 130 The Sonne..maketh the day to growe byfore hym, and on that other parte the erthe is vmbreuse & derke by hynde hym. **1480** —— *Ovid's Met.* x. i, The Kynge and the quene comanded that Erudice shold be called forth, which was in the umbrous valeye. **1657** TOMLINSON *Renou's Disp.* 334 It grows..in margins of fields, that are not umbrous. **1821** T. G. WAINEWRIGHT *Ess. & Crit.* (1880) 227 A meadow..umbrous with orange and cedar trees.

†**2.** *fig.* (See quot.) *Obs.*$^{-1}$

1483 CAXTON *Gold. Leg.* 108 b/1 He was umbrouse or shadewous, that is to saye he was colde and refrigerat fro all concupyscence of the flesshe.

umbset, -stead, -think: see UMB-.

umbuss, umbuth: see UMBOTH.

†umbwhile, *adv. Obs.* = UMBEWHILE *adv.* 2.

1393 LANGL. *P. Pl.* C. VII. 396 Bargeynes and beuereges by-gunne to aryse, And setyn so til euesong rang and songe vmbwhyle [*v.r.* vmbwyle, vmbwhile].

umbyll, obs. f. HUMBLE *a.*

umchew, var. UMBESCHEW *v. Obs.*

umclap, -clead, -clip, -close: see UM-.

umeer, variant of AMEER.

umellete, obs. f. HUMILITY.

'umest, *a. Sc.* Now *rare.* Also 5 **humest,** 6 **vmest, wmest,** 8–9 **umist,** 9 **eemest;** 5 **humast,** 5–6 **um-, vmast,** 9 **eemost, yimost.** [OE. *ufemest*: see OVEMEST *a.*]

†**1.** Of clothes: Uppermost, outermost; *spec.* applied to the coverlet of a bed, claimed by the priest as a perquisite on the death of a parishioner.

c **1400** *Sc. Trojan War* II. 1932 Pallamydes..tuke of baith hois & schone, And syne his vmast clath. *c* **1470** HENRY *Wallace* IX. 707 Wallace gert tak in haist thar humest weid. **1535** LYNDESAY *Satyre* 3900 From this day furth, thay salbe cleane denudit Baith of cors-present, cow, and vmest claith. **1567** *Gude & Godlie B.* (S.T.S.) 196 Preistis, tak na kyis, The vmest claith ȝe sall quyte clame. *a* **1578** LINDESAY (Pitscottie) *Chron. Scot.* (S.T.S.) I. 349 Thow gaif againe to the parochinaris the kow and the wmest cloth.

2. Of things or places: Lying uppermost or highest.

c **1425** WYNTOUN *Cron.* VIII. xxvii. 4652 Endlange þe wode war wayis twa: þe erl in þe vmast lay of þa. **1456** SIR G. HAY *Gov. Princes* Wks. (S.T.S.) II. 123 The ground of the stomak is..mare forcy of degestioun na the humast part of the stomak. **1513** DOUGLAS *Æneid* XII. vi. 172 Turnus..evin betwix the helm can him arras And vmast roll or hem of his curas. **1537** *Reg. Privy Seal Scot.* II. 352/2 The umest hous and duelling place of the land callit the Abbay ȝet. **1566** in Ramsay *Bamff Charters* (1915) 103 Quhill it cum to the entres of the umest forkis of the burn. **1710** RUDDIMAN *Gloss. Douglas' Æneis, Umist*, S. upmost, uppermost. *c* **1800–** in glossaries and texts (Kinc., Aberdeen, Moray, Caithness, etc.: *Eng. Dial. Dict.* s.v. *Eemost*).

3. Most important or prominent. ? *Obs.*

1513 DOUGLAS *Æneid* I. vi. 66 Lang war the iniuris, the dowtis lang to be tawld; Bot I the vmest of the mater sall hauld. *a* **1578** LINDESAY (Pitscottie) *Chron. Scot.* (S.T.S.) I. 284 The Earle of Angus become werie prude and insolent.., thinkand quho ewer had right to the autorietie he sould be vmest.

umfaan ('ʊmfa:n). *S. Afr.* Also **†oomfaan, umfane.** [Afrikaans, ad. Zulu *umFana* small boy.] A young African boy, esp. one employed in domestic service.

1852 C. BARTER *Dorp & Veld* xiv. 213 The Kaffir *umfane* (boy) when he becomes an *indola* (man), shaves his head, and *sews* into the scalp a circular coronet of reeds. **1878** H. A. ROCHE *On Trek in Transvaal* iii. 39 Your wife..if she be so lucky as to have floors at all, will make..that provoking '*Oomfan*' clean them for her. **1907** P. FITZPATRICK *Jock of Bushveld* 194 Jim had fought at 'Sandhlwana, and could tell of an umfaan sent out to herd some cattle within sight of the British camp to draw the troops out raiding. **1932** F. W. FITZSIMONS *Snakes* xiv. 173 No! Snakes do not suck milk from cows; but Kafir umfaans and pigs do. **1964** S. MILNE *False Witness* xv. 167 'You have a servant on the premises?' 'Yes, an *umfaan*. He is sixteen years old.' **1977** J. McCLURE *Sunday Hangman* ii. 13 He'd strung himself up on a thorn tree... Some umfaans made a report.

umff, var. UMPH.

umfold: see UM-.

umfundisi (ʊm'fʊndɪsɪ, ʊmfʊn'di:zɪ). *S. Afr.* Also 9 **fundis, umfundis(e; mfundisi.** [a. Nguni *umFundisi*, *Mfundisi* teacher.] A teacher, a minister, a missionary; also used as a respectful form of address.

1825 W. SHAW *Diary* in C. Sadler *Never Young Man* (1967) 64 The Caffres knew me to be a 'Fundis' (teacher). **1833** S. KAY *Trav. Caffraria* iii. 73 Never have we been safe; but the *Umfundis* shall be our bush. *Ibid.* xii. 317 But if we neglect her, the *Umfundis* (Missionary) will be angry. **1837** F. OWEN *Diary* 12 Oct. (1926) 44 We don't know what we have learned this morning, for the Umfundis (teacher) sent us away so soon. **1863** J. S. DOBIE *S. Afr. Jrnl.* (1945) 78 Called at a kraal and got enlightened on road to the umfundisi (missionary). **1905** G. CALLOWAY *Sk. Kafir Life* 9 Oh! Mfundisi; I am weak, I cannot work to-day. **1923** *Other Lands* Oct. 19/1 Their dear old *Umfundise* was the Moderator-elect. **1948** A. PATON *Cry, Beloved Country* I. ii. 14, I bring a letter, umfundisi. *Ibid.* iii. 21 They saw his clerical collar, and moved up to make room for the umfundisi. **1973** *Eastern Province Herald* 6 Aug. 6/7 Job's comforters are..the unfundisi and a cheerful scavenger from the municipal rubbish dump.

†umgang. *Obs.* In 4–5 **vm-,** 6 *Sc.* **wn-;** 4 **vmgong.** [ME. *umgang* (see UM- and GANG *sb.*^{1}), = ON. *umgangr* (Norw. *um-*, MSw. *um-*, *omgang*, Sw. *omgång*, Da. *omgang*), WFris. *omgong*, NFris. *omgang*, *âmgung*, MDu. *omme-*, *omganc* (Du. *omgang*), MLG. *umb(e)-*, *ummegank*, OHG. *umbiganc* (MHG. *umbe-*, *umbganc*, G. *umgang*), OE. *ymb(e)gang*.]

1. The act of going round; the distance covered in this way; circuit, circumference.

a **1300** *E.E. Psalter* xvii. 13 And he set mirkenes his lurking lang, His telde to be in his vmgange, Mirke watres þat war of hewe. *a* **1300** *Cursor M.* 9192 In his [Josiah's] time was Fordon þe tune of niniue, þat was of vmgang thre iorne. *a* **1340** HAMPOLE *Psalter* xi. 9 Vs þou kepis, bot wickid men gas in vmgange. *c* **1400** MAUNDEV. (Roxb.) xxi. 97 It es a grete ile and a faire; and þe vmgang þeroff es nere a thowsand myle. **1456** SIR G. HAYE *Law Arms* (S.T.S.) 56 [Carthage] had sexty thousand pass about the vmgang [*printed* vin-] of the toune. **1505** *Charters Crosraguel Abbey* (1886) I. 63 Becaus the said hous, smedy, orchard, and yarde ar within the yettis and umgang and wallis of the said abbay.

2. A turn or spell of work. *rare*$^{-1}$.

1538 *Aberdeen Reg.* XVI. (Jam.), For the parting of the said maisteris fysche thre tymmez on ane wngang, quhar thai suld be twa tymmez partit on ane haill day.

So **†um'ganging** *vbl. sb.*, going round. *Obs.*

a **1340** HAMPOLE *Psalter* cxii. 3 By þe vmgangynge of þe sone..he signyfyes þe warld.

‖**Umgangssprache** ('ʊmgaŋsʃpra:xə). [Ger., = colloquial speech.] The vernacular language between standard and dialect speech customarily used as a means of communication within a linguistic community.

1934 PRIEBSCH & COLLINSON *German Lang.* viii. 350 The schools..are playing a considerable part in removing the *Umgangssprache*..from local influences by basing the language of instruction more strictly upon the literary language. **1961** R. E. KELLER *German Dialects* i. 8 Wherever the ideal of the standard has led to the abandonment of the native dialect a third form arises between the two: the *Umgangssprache*. **1976** *Amer. Speech 1973* XLVIII. 215 We assume that the Swiss immigrants on their arrival in Wisconsin used Swiss German as their 'Umgangssprache' and had at least some knowledge of standard German.

†umgive, *v. Obs.* [f. UM- + GIVE *v.* Cf. WFris. *omjowн* (p.p.), NFris. *âmjiw*, Du. *omgeven* (p.p.), OHG. *umbigeban* (MHG. *umbe-*, *umbgeben*, G. *umgeben*), Sw. *omgifva*, Da. *omgive*.] *trans.* To enclose, surround, environ.

a **1300** *E.E. Psalter* iii. 6 Noght sal i drede a thousand Of folk, ar me vmgyuand. *Ibid.* vii. 7 Rise, lauerd, in bode þou sent to be, And kirke of folke sal vmgif þe. *a* **1340** HAMPOLE *Psalter* iii. 6 All vices, þe whilk vmgifs men to dissaif þaim. *Ibid.* xxxix. 16 For vmgifen me has illes of þe whilke noumbire is noght. *a* **1400** *New Test.* (Paues) Acts xxviii. 20 Forwhi for þo hope of Israel I am vmgyuen (or, bounden) with þis cheyne.

†umgo, *v. Obs.* [f. UM- + GO *v.* Cf. WFris. *omgean*, MDu. *omme-*, *omgaen* (Du. *omgaan*), MSw. *um-*, *omga* (Sw. *omgås* refl.), Da. *omgaa*, OE. *ymbgán*, MLG. *umb-*, *umm(e)gân*, OHG. *umbi-*, *umbegân* (G. *umgehen*). See also UMBEGO *v.*] *trans.* To go around; to encompass.

a **1300** *E.E. Psalter* xxvi. 11, I vmyhode, and offred in telde hisse Offrand of berand steuen þat isse. *Ibid.* lviii. 7 þai be torned at euen, and hunger thole þa Als hundes, and cite þai sal vmga. *a* **1340** HAMPOLE *Psalter* xxvi. 11, I vmȝed & i offird in his tabernakile þe hoste of heghynge of voice.

umgripe: see UM-.

†umh, um'h, obs. varr. of UM or UMPH.

1614 J. COOKE *Greene's Tu Quoque* B 4, *Bub.* Vmh, vmh, vmh. **1616** S. S. *Honest Lawyer* IV. G 1, Vm'h, my doubts Wrappe me in further maze. **1668** DRYDEN *Evening's Love* IV, Umh! thou awaken'st a most villainous apprehension in me! **1702** FARQUHAR *Inconstant* II. i, Umh.—before that any young..Rakelly Fellow shou'd play such Tricks with me, I wou'd wear my Teeth to the stumps. **1740** CIBBER *Apol.* (1756) II. 31 With a slow hesitation..he reply'd—Umh! the best—umh!—I have tasted a great while.

umheed, -hill: see UM-.

umiak ('u:mɪæk). Also **umiack, umyak, oomia(c)k.** [Eskimo.] A large Eskimo boat, consisting of a wooden frame with skins drawn over it, and propelled by paddles.

1769 FALCONER *Dict. Marine* (1789) L b, The canoe is called *kaiak*, or man's boat, to distinguish it from *umiak*, the woman's boat. **1819** SIR J. ROSS *Voy. Disc.* I. iv. 55 The boat was called an umiack. **1845** *Life T. Simpson* xiii. 258, I procured an oomiak or family canoe. **1863** A. YOUNG *Naut. Dict.* (ed. 2) 431 In Greenland, the umyak is the boat worked exclusively by the women, as the kayak is by the men. **1884** *Good Words* Feb. 96/1 We quitted the whale-boat..and took a small umiak, on account of weight. **1894** *Outing* (U.S.) XXIII. 390/1 Huge, lumbering oomiacks, loaded to the rail with a mixed cargo of men, women, children, and dogs, all howling, is an entertaining..sight. **1900** *Scribner's Mag.* Sept. 294/2 Well-made models of kayaks and umiaks.

Umklapp ('ʊmklæp). *Physics.* Also **umklapp.** [tr. G. *umklappprozess* (R. Peierls 1919, in *Ann. d. Physik* III. 1073), f. *umklappen* to turn down or over.] Used *attrib.* to designate interactions in a crystal lattice in which their total momentum is not conserved, and the momentum of the initial excitations is reversed. Abbrev. ***U-*** or ***u-process***.

[**1937** *Physical Rev.* LII. 690/1 These authors neglect transitions due to the '*Umklappprozesse*' of Peierls.] **1951** *Proc. R. Soc.* A. CCVIII. 90 Further measurements made on a corundum crystal confirm the importance of the 'Umklapp' processes, postulated by Peierls, in causing thermal resistance. **1960** J. M. ZIMAN *Electrons & Phonons* iii. 133 We shall refer to *U*-processes, and, where wave vector is conserved,..*N*-processes. **1974** H. E. HALL *Solid State Physics* viii. 207 An Umklapp process can be thought of as one in which a phonon is Bragg reflected simultaneously with absorbing or emitting another phonon. **1975** H. M. ROSENBERG *Solid State* vi. 99 In a continuous medium u-processes cannot occur. **1976** F. CAP tr. *Busch & Schade's Lect. Solid State Physics* 67 At low temperatures the umklapp processes are essential for the establishment of thermal equilibrium in the crystal.

†umlap, *v. Obs.* [f. UM- + LAP *v.*^{2} Cf. UMBELAP *v.*] *trans.* To encompass, surround.

a **1300** *Cursor M.* 2778 þaa foles feluns þat war fuus, All vmlapped loth huse. *c* **1340** HAMPOLE *Pr. Consc.* 6937 þai salle umlapp þam alle oboute, And gnaw on ilka lym and souke. *c* **1375** *Sc. Leg. Saints* ii. (Paul) 537 Fra hewine schane don a mekil lycht, And vmlappyt hym son all. *c* **1400** tr. *Secreta Secret.*, *Gov. Lordsh.* 109 þe nombre of ten ys þe perfeccion of hem þat enbracen ffourhede, & vmlappys it yn nombres. *c* **1440** *Alph. Tales* 367 Sodanlie he was vmlappid with a grete flok of myce. *Ibid.* 521 þe se-flude vmlappid bothe hym & þe cow & þe calfe.

umlaut ('ʊmlaʊt). *Philol.* [G., f. *um-* about + *laut* sound.]

a. A change in the sound of a vowel produced by partial assimilation to an adjacent sound (usually that of a vowel or semivowel in the following syllable); = MUTATION 4 b.

[**1844** T. H. KEY *Alphabet* 169 The Influence of Assimilation. *Footnote*, Sometimes called by Germans 'umlaut']. **1852** *Trans. Philol. Soc.* 25 June V. 200 The cognate languages clearly exhibit the fact, that the umlaut in these words has been produced by the weak vowel of a lost suffix. **1873** EARLE *Philol. Eng. Tongue* (ed. 2) §127 The

Umlaut of the Indo-European languages is a phenomenon of a different order. Here the vowel of the after-member of the word influences that which has gone before.
attrib. **1873** Earle *Philol. Eng. Tongue* (ed. 2) §128 Nowhere is any structural signification attached now to an Umlaut form, except [etc.]. **1879** *Ibid.* (ed. 3) §381 The modern s being imposed upon the old umlaut plural. **1879** *Encycl. Brit.* X. 519/2 In most [German] Midland manuscripts no special signs for the Umlaut vowels are used, except *e*.

b. The diacritical sign (¨) placed over a vowel to indicate that such a change has taken place.
1938 H. Faulk *Common-Sense German Course* 3 The so-called modified vowels are distinguished by the modification mark or umlaut(¨) on the vowel. **1952** M. Pei *Story of Lang.* I. ix. 93 English makes use of no subsidiary characters, save for the apostrophe. Many other languages use accent-marks, umlauts, cedillas. **1970** [see computer 2 b].

Hence as *v. trans.*, to make such a change; **'umlauted** *a.*, modified by umlaut; containing a vowel or vowels modified in this way; **'umlauting** *vbl. sb.* and *ppl. a.*
1852 *Trans. Philol. Soc.* 25 June V. 200 In particular the umlaut-ed plurals appear not to have yet found a fitting explanation in English grammars. **1879** Earle *Philol. Eng. Tongue* (ed. 3) §381 It should be observed that there is no natural connection between Umlauted forms and Plurality. **1938** W. F. Twaddell in *Monatschr. f. Deutschen Unterricht* XXX. 177 The *i*, *ī*, or *j* which 'caused' the umlauting was no longer present in MHG. **1943** E. A. Nida *Handbk. Descriptive Linguistics* II. v. 84 What changes the stems so materially is the umlauting produced by the *e* vowel of -*et*. **1976** *Language* LII. 154 Moulton..assumes that all instances of [a] were umlauted simultaneously to [ä]. **1977** *Ibid.* LIII. 18 As a result of this second rule, back vowels are created on the surface which, unlike all the other back vowels, fail to umlaut in umlauting environments. **1983** *Word* XXXIV. 120 The color of prothetic vowels, unless and until umlauted by the next syllable, was that of the laryngeal which was vocalized.

†**umlay**, *v. Obs.* [f. um- + lay *v.*[1] Cf. MDu. *omme-*, *omleggen* (Du. *omleggen*), Da. *omlægge*; OS. *umbileggian* (MLG. *ummeleggen*), MHG. *umbe-*, *umblegen* (G. *umlegen*). See also umbelay *v.*] *trans.* To surround.
a **1300** *Cursor M.* 1010 Paradis is..euer vmlaid wit lem and light. *Ibid.* 22069 In vr leuedi light þe hali-gast.., And vmlaid hir wit his lem.

Umlimo, var. Mlimo.

†**umlouk**, *v. Obs.* Also -luke, -lok(e. [f. um- + louk *v.*[2] Cf. MDu. *omme-*, *omluken* (Du. *omluiken*), and see *umbelouk* under umbe-.] *trans.* To surround, enclose.
a **1300** *Cursor M.* 22705 The see þat vmlukes þe land, And watres all that rinnes in strand, Al sal turn again to noght. *a* **1300** *E.E. Psalter* lxxvii. 68 He vmlouked in swerd his folke to be. *a* **1340** Hampole *Psalter* cxliv. 3 He is incomprehensibil, for na stede, na thoght, may vmlouke him. *a* **1400–50** *Alexander* 4672 With soft serkis of silke ȝoure sidis [ȝe] vm-loke.

‖**umma** ('uma). Also Umma, ummah. [Arab. *'umma* people, community, nation.] **1.** The Islamic community, founded by Muhammad at Medina, comprising individuals bound to one another by religious ties on a tribal model.
1885 T. P. Hughes *Dict. Islam* 654/2 *Ummah*,..a people, a nation, a sect. The word occurs about forty times in the Qur'an. *Ummatu Ibrāhīm*, the people of Abraham .. *Ummatu Muhammad*, the people of Muhammad. **1919** H. U. W. Stanton *Teaching of Qur'an* vi. 71 The..term ..*ummah*, i.e. religious community. Of this it is said that mankind were originally one *ummah*, and that Allāh, had He pleased, could have kept them so. **1934** *Encycl. Islam* IV. 1015/2 Muhammad frequently discusses the question why mankind consists of a plurality of ummas and has not remained a unit. **1974** B. Lewis in Schacht & Bosworth *Legacy of Islam* (ed. 2) iv. 157 From the start, the Islamic *umma* had a dual character. On the one hand it was a political society..; on the other it was a religious community, founded by a prophet and ruled by his deputy. **1976** *Jrnl. R. Soc. Arts* CXXIV. 613/1 The flexibility of government in Islam goes back—doesn't it?—to the concept of 'Umma' in Islam, the idea that Islam came actually to build up an Umma, a community, rather than impose a doctrine. **1979** *Economist* 5 May 82/2 The governance of the Moslem community, the *umma*.
2. (With capital initial.) The name of a nationalist political party founded in the Sudan in 1945.
1946 *Economist* 9 Mar. 369/1 The western Sudanese.. speak through the Umma or nationalist party, which wants 'a union in which the two partners enjoy internal and external autonomy'. **1946** *Times* 30 Sept. 4/5 The Umma Party of Sudan. **1958** *Listener* 21 Aug. 256/2 Both these ministers are members of the Umma, the Mahdist party. **1965** K. D. D. Henderson *Sudan Republic* vii. 89 There emerges in March 1945 a new political party calling itself the *Umma*, the Community Party with the slogan of 'the Sudan for the Sudanese'. **1979** M. Deeb *Party Politics in Egypt* ii. 40 The defunct Umma Party. **1981** *Economist* 24 Jan. 43/2 There are parochial or communal parties which do not favour or are fearful of, absorption into larger units: these include the Christian Phalange in Lebanon, the Umma in Sudan, the Neo-Destour in Tunisia.

umman, dial. form of woman.

umohoite (juːməʊ'həʊaɪt). *Min.* [See quot. 1953.] A hydrous uranyl molybdate, $UO_2MoO_4.4H_2O$, found as monoclinic and orthorhombic, usu. dark-coloured, crystals.
1953 P. F. Kerr in *Rocks & Minerals* XXVIII. 480/1 The name 'umohoite' is given to the mineral by combining the chemical symbols U, Mo, H, and O with the mineral suffix 'ite'. **1980** *Mineral. Abstr.* XXXI. 82/2 Umohoite from Shinkolobwe, Shaba, Zaïre.., is regarded as a magnesian variety: dark green to black, 0·65% Mg, ortho-rhombic... Two other varieties are described.

umor, umour, obs. ff. humour.

ump (ʌmp), *slang* (chiefly *U.S.*). Abbrev. of umpire *sb.*, *spec.* in baseball. Also **umps** (cf. -s[2]).
1915 'High Jinks, Jr.' *Choice Slang* v. 74 Every time that Umps starts talking his tongue gets twisted around his eye tooth and he can't see what he's saying. **1942** *Sun* (Baltimore) 30 June 12/4 (*heading*) Durocher fined..for quarrel with umps. **1952** B. Malamud *Natural* 46 I'd've thrown him out too if I was the ump. **1975** *New Yorker* 17 Feb. 25/3 That's why Nick Colosi, National League ump, was a featured attraction at the Auto Show last week. **1979** *Arizona Daily Star* 8 Apr. c1/6 A few bad calls by the rookie umps will no doubt be cause for more outcries from the baseball world.

umpah, var. oompah.

umph ((ə)mh), *int.* Also 6 vmff. [Imitative: cf. humph and umh.] An inarticulate sound, expressive of hesitation, doubt, or dissatisfaction.
a **1568** in *Bannatyne MS.* (Hunter. Club) 461/21 Vmff, quod the Helandman, and swere be yon kirk [etc.].
1782 Miss Burney *Cecilia* iv. vi, He only looked at her, and said 'umph?' *Ibid.* vii. ix, I really believe the gentleman's deaf! he won't so much as say *umph* and *hay*, now. **1800** Mrs. Hervey *Mourtray Fam.* II. 119 'Umph!' thought Emma, 'is he abusing the Turk now by way of a blind?' **1822** Scott *Nigel* v, 'Umph!' repeated Master George,..'what does *umph* mean?' **1826** —— *Woodst.* iii, Commands—umph —I think the damsel might have tarried. **1894** A. Gordon *Northward Ho* 87 An occasional 'Oich! Oich!' from John, and a sympathetic 'Umph! Umph!' from Eppie.
Hence **umph** *v. intr.*, to ejaculate 'umph'.
1894 Hall Caine *Manxman* i. x. 48 Cæsar *umpht* and grunted. **1900** *Daily News* 30 June 4/1 'Umph,' replied Mr. Rhodes, in his grim, gruff way, 'Umph!' and he went away umphing.

umph, var. oomph.

umpirage ('ʌmpaɪrɪdʒ). Forms: α. 5 owmpreght, 7 umpridge, umpiridge, umperage, umpeerage. β. 6– umpirage (7 umpireage). [f. next + -age.] The act of umpiring; the office or power of an umpire; the decision of an umpire, arbitration.
α. *c* **1490** *Plumpton Corr.* (Camden) 84 Wher it is so, uncle, at the matter betwyxt my servant and John Forest is put to iiij men, and the owmpreght of you. **1609** *N. Riding Rec.* (1884) I. 173 The arbitrament..of Tho. Warcupp and Anth. Byarley, gent., with the umpridge of Mr. Parson Lascells. **1649** Bp. Hall *Cases Consc.* 301 The Prophet Malachi..hath so fully decided the cause, as if it had been expresly referred to his umperage. **1661** *Andronicus* iii. i. D 4 b, Here's Cleobulus, We will refer it to his Umpeerage. **1679** W. Penn *Addr. Prot.* ii. 180 The Scriptures are made more doubtful than they are by such as would fain preserve to themselves the Umpiridge and Judgship of their Meaning.
β. **1519** *Plumpton Corr.* (Camden) 223 *n.*, The parties to abide the umpirage of Thomas Lord Cardinal..if given before the feast of All Saints. **1633** Bp. Morton *Discharge Five Imput.* 144 S. Augustine his Vmpirage and full Determination of this whole question, concerning the exposition of Christ his speech. **1643** Nethersole *Proj. for Peace* (1648) 21 The finall Umpirage of such..matters, as cannot be resolved without the admission of forein arbitrement. **1675** J. Smith *Chr. Relig. App.* i. 18 Augustus ..referring the choice of an Heir, where he had so bad choice, to the umpirage of the Divine Wisdom. *a* **1715** Burnet *Own Time* (1766) I. 48 They hoped the umpirage of the war would fall into their hands. **1768** Blackstone *Comm.* III. i. 17 Enacting..that their submission of the suit to arbitration or umpirage shall be made a rule of any of the king's courts of record. **1805** *East's Reports* V. 189 The time for making the umpirage was further extended. **1846** Sumner *Scholar, Jurist*, etc. 62 When, in our age, two nations..appeal to war.., they voluntarily adopt this unchristian umpirage of right. **1890** *Law Times* LXXXVIII. 358/1 We do not think it would be fair to cast upon the County Court judges the responsibilities of umpirage.

umpire ('ʌmpaɪə(r)), *sb.* Forms: α. 5 owmpere, ovmper, ompar. β. 5–6 umpere (6 vn-), 6 vmppere, 6–7 umpeer(e. γ. 5–7 umper (5 unpar). δ. 6–7 umpyer, -pier (6 impier). ε. 6– umpire (7 umpyre). [Later form of noumpere, by transference of the *n*- to the indefinite article, as in *adder*, *apron*.]
1. One who decides between disputants or contending parties and whose decision is usually accepted as final; an arbitrator.
α. ?*c* **1400** Lydg. *Æsop's Fab.* vi. 43 Among these owmperis was werre none, ne stryf. *c* **1440** *Promp. Parv.* 360/1 Nowmpere, or owmpere, *arbiter, sequester*. **1483** *Cath. Angl.* 263/2 An Ovmper (A. Ompar), *impar*.
β. *c* **1430** *Wyclif's Prol. Rom.* (MS. Rawl. C. 257 fol. 90 b/2), þe apostle putte him bitwene as a meene, distriynge alle her questiouns, as a good vmpere. **1450** *Paston Lett.* I. 120 Take ȝe one, and he another; and if they may not accorde, ȝe and I to be umpere, for we stande bothe in like cas. **1552–3** in E. B. Jupp *Carpenters' Co.* (1887) 376 John abbott Richard tylton George Kyng John revell..for days men and master Russell for vmppere. **1567** Jewel *Def. Apol.* ii. 312 He is no indifferente umpeere, that firste diuideth Offices equally bitweene twoo, and afterwarde alloteth bothe offices to One alone. **1576** A. Hall *Acc. Quarrell* (1815) 25 The just and consionable dome of so grave umpeers. **1601** R. Johnson *Kingd. & Commw.* (1603) 255 They constitute him their arbitraitour and chiefe Vmpeere. **1649** Ball *Power of Kings* 6 These things they may doe as Judges Allegate, or Umpeeres for the People. **1688** R. Holme *Armoury* ii. 394/2 Being desired to be Umpeer between Apollo and Pan,..Midas passed his verdict against Apollo.
γ. **1464**, **1556** [see 2]. **1580** Lyly *Euphues* (Arb.) 421 The Ladie Flauia..commaunded them both to silence, willing Euphues as vmper in these matters, briefly to speake his minde. **1606** Bp. W. Barlow *Serm.* E j b, The best course.. will bee..to make him the vmper, whom they make our Accuser. **1611** Grimeston *Hist. France* 969 Cardinall Medicis..was, as it were, an Vmper of all difficulties in this good and holy reconciliation.
δ. **1551** Robinson tr. *More's Utopia* Ded. (1895) 3 Some as an vmpier or a judge with my sentence finallye to discusse. **1577** *F. de L'isle's Legendarie* A vij b, The controuersie was referred vnto the arbitrement of three vmpiers. **1581** J. Bell *Haddon's Answ. Osor.* 168 If this Aunswere..shall seeme but of small credite with you, I will bryng you Augustine for an umpyer betwixt us. **1609** Holland *Amm. Marcell.* 23, I rest waiting upon you as umpiers to know what ye advise. **1641** Prynne *Antip.* 274 The Lords in Parliament tooke an Oath to be indifferent umpiers betweene the Bishop and Duke.
ε. **1599** *Broughton's Let.* vii. 25 He, whom you..made vmpire of that..controuersie. **1606** J. Carpenter *Solomon's Solace* xxviii. 115 If a man sinne against God, who shall bee his Umpire, or Dayes-man? **1640** Quarles *Enchirid.* (1641) 13 When the Frog and the Mouse could not take up the Quarrell, the Kite was umpyre. **1681** H. Nevile *Plato Rediv.* 152 A great person was to be chosen every Parliament, who should be as it were an Umpire between the King and his People. **1717** J. Keill *Anim. Œcon.* (1738) 54 How could I wish for a more impartial Judge, or how could I choose a more proper Umpire? **1751** Smollett *R. Random* xvii, The constable..pleaded our cause so effectually, that she condescended to make him umpire. **1815** *Zeluca* III. 268, I must become umpire between you and Mrs. Wolsey. **1835** Lytton *Rienzi* x. iii, We might call in an umpire—a foreigner who had no interest in either faction. **1875** Jowett *Plato* (ed. 2) I. 152 To choose an umpire of discourse would be unseemly.
b. *transf.* Something which serves to decide or settle a matter.
1583 W. M. in Foxe *A. & M.* (ed. 4) II. 2139 Let Gods word be vnpere, To try our true religion, From this euill fauoured geere. **1600** Rowland *Lett. Humours Blood* v. 73 Make Steele and Iron vmpiers to the Fray. **1647** N. Bacon *Disc. Govt. Eng.* i. xvi. 48 As if the Law were the sole umpire between King and people. **1662** Stillingfl. *Orig. Sacræ* iii. i. §9 It is a sign there is little of reason left, where sense is made the only Umpire of all kinds of Beings. **1696** Dogget *Country-Wake* iii. ii. 30 Your Conscience must be Umper in this Case. **1718** Rowe tr. *Lucan* i. 205 The Sword is now the Umpire to decide. **1784** Cowper *Tiroc.* 29 The judgment, umpire in the strife That grace and nature have to wage through life. **1805–6** Cary *Dante, Inf.* xxii. 140 In the boiling lake both fell. The heat Was umpire soon between them. **1878** Browning *La Saisiaz* 55 Take thou, soul, thy solitary stand, Umpire to the champions Fancy, Reason.
†**c.** Something which stands between others either by way of connexion or separation. *Obs.*
1598 Sylvester *Du Bartas* ii. i. *Eden* 392 For spirits ..'Twixt God and man retein a middle kinde; And (Umpires) mortall th' immortall joine. **1610** Holland *Camden's Brit.* i. 745 Those mountaines, which..interpose themselves as Umpiers and Bounders between diverse shires.
2. *Law.* A third person appointed or called upon to decide a matter submitted to arbitrators who cannot agree. Cf. referee *sb.* 2.
1464 *Cov. Leet Bk.* 329 If in the mean tyme the seid iiij arbitrours can not accorde that then the seid Mair to be unpar. *Ibid.*, That..as the a-fore named iiij arbitrours.. cowde not accorde, that then the seid mair to be vmper. **1552** Huloet, Impier or umpier, a iudge or mediatoure taken besydes arbitors to deme a matter debated, wher the arbitrors can not agree, *sequestor*. **1556** in W. H. Turner *Select. Rec. Oxford* (1880) 257 To abyde the arbytrament of ..arbytrators,..and that Mr. Pollard shalbe umper. **1706** Phillips (ed. Kersey), *Umpire*, a third Person chosen to put a final End to a Controversy left to the Determination of two Arbitrators. **1768** Blackstone *Comm.* III. 16 If they [*sc.* the arbitrators] do not agree, it is usual to add, that another person be called in as umpire (*imperator*), to whose sole judgment it is then referred. **1838** W. Bell *Dict. Law Scot.* 692 An oversman is an umpire appointed by a submission to decide where two arbiters have differed in opinion, or he is named by the arbiters themselves. **1843** *Penny Cycl.* XXV. 501/2 The word umpire..in its legal sense..means a person named in the Submission, or under its authority, by the arbitrators to decide the matters referred, which the arbitrators either cannot or will not decide.
3. In games or contests: One to whose decision all doubtful points are referred, and who sees that the rules of the game or sport are not broken. Cf. referee *sb.* 3 b.
1714 in Parkyns *Inn-Play* (ed. 2) 63 [Wrestling], And in case they can't Decide such Differences, then they shall be referr'd solely to the Decision of the said Sir Thomas Parkyns as Umpire. **1778** C. Jones *Hoyle's Games Impr.* 201 The Umpires are the sole Judges of fair and unfair Play, and have a Power to determine all Disputes. **1837** Dickens *Pickw.* vii, The umpires were stationed behind the wickets. **1857** Hughes *Tom Brown* ii. viii, Their leading men and umpire inspected the ground, criticising it rather unmercifully. **1884** *Times* 15 Sept. 7/3 [Football], Mr. Walker officiated as referee, and Messrs. Davies and Bryan as umpires.
attrib. **1889** *Infantry Drill* 406 Umpire Regulations. *Ibid.* 407 Orders from the Umpire Staff are to be considered as emanating directly from the Umpire-in-Chief.

'umpire, *v.* Also 7 vmpeere, vmper. [f. prec.]

†**1.** *trans.* To adjudge, appoint (a person to an office), in virtue of being umpire. *Obs.*⁻¹

1592 BACON *Observ. Libel* in *Resuscitatio* (1657) 123 That no King of Spain, nor Bishop of Rome, shall umpire, or promote, any beneficiary, or feodatory, King, as they designed to do.

†**2.** To decide between (persons) as umpire; to act as umpire to. *Obs. rare.*

1611 T. JAMES *Corrupt. Scripture* IV. 19 Who shall reconcile or vmpire them, decide doubts, determine questions, and take vp all controuersies? *a* **1657** R. LOVEDAY *Lett.* (1663) 19 He is now the great Cardinal that umpires almost all Christendom.

3. To settle or decide (a matter in dispute) as umpire or after the manner of an umpire.

1611 SPEED *Hist. Gt. Brit.* IX. viii. 24 The Pope..therfore vndertooke to vmpeere the debates betwixt those two great Enemies. **1622** MABBE tr. *Aleman's Guzman d'Alf.* I. 101 The Clergy-men interposed themselues; they were to vmpire the businesse betweene vs. **1637** CARTWRIGHT *Royal Slave* IV. iv, I have Two or three servants within call here, they Shall umpire this your variance. **1675** R. BURTHOGGE *Causa Dei* 379 It was the Office of the Druids..to decide and umpire Controversies. **1710** R. WARD *Life H. More* 121, I have heard him pleasantly speaking, How he was fain to umpire the matter between his Mirth and his Sadder Tempers.

b. *transf.* Of things.

1609 [BP. W. BARLOW] *Answ. Nameless Cath.* 322 The question also then in hand beeing to bee vmper'd onely by the holy Scripture. **1629** N. CARPENTER *Achitophel* II. (1640) 115 Queasi stomacks had rather appetite should umpire their desires, then judgement. **1674** T. FLATMAN *Desperate Lover* 2/8 A turfe of grass or Monument of Stone Umpires the petty competition.

4. *spec.* To supervise (games or contests) in the capacity of umpire.

1861 *Times* 12 July, The regatta yesterday was exceedingly well managed, and the races umpired by gentlemen of the Universities. **1884** *Harper's Mag.* Oct. 726/1 It is not an unusual sight to see a game among the officers 'umpired' by some..non-commissioned officer. **1887** *Field* 13 Aug. 283/3 The various competitions were umpired from the bows of a launch.

b. To give (a player) *out*, as umpire.

1894 *Daily News* 20 June 5/2 Conceivably, he 'umpired out' the other side whenever he had an opportunity.

5. *intr.* To act as umpire. Also const. *between, betwixt.*

1613 PURCHAS *Pilgrimage* (1614) 328 We list not to vmpire betwixt Geographers. *a* **1638** MEDE *Wks.* (1672) 746 Even Cæsar at first umpired between her and her brother, in matters of difference between them. *a* **1688** CUDWORTH *Freewill* (1838) 42 In this contest there is no necessary understanding interposing and coming in to umpire between, that does unavoidably and irresistibly determine one way or other. **1716** M. DAVIES *Athen. Brit.* II. 243, I am sure nothing can be justly pleaded in Bar to their undoubted Prerogative..to Umpire in this Contest about Primitive Christianity. **1881** W. THOMSON *Bacon & Shakespeare* 29 None will be readier than he to umpire justly. **1901** *Weekly Register* 22 Nov. 649/2 The famous cricketer, who often used to umpire at boys' matches.

b. With *it.*

1620 BRATHWAIT *Five Senses* in *Archaica* (1815) II. 51 Nobly interposing himself..to umpire it, that it may be more evenly carried, and more equally composed. **1627** W. SCLATER *Exp. 2 Thess.* (1629) 299 While Thomas..must vmpire it in Religion. **1695** J. SAGE *Article* Wks. 1844 I. 268 She umpired it between the Queen of Scotland and those who appeared for her son.

Hence †**'umpirer**, an umpire. *Obs. rare.*

1650 FULLER *Pisgah* I. x. 32 If the extent of their dominions be surveyed, and our eye in the Map made umpirer therein, the case is clear. **1675** J. SMITH *Chr. Relig. Appeal* IV. 97 The Umpirers of Difference among the Nations of the World.

'umpireship. Also 6 umpeere-, 6–7 umpier-. [f. UMPIRE *sb.*] The office of umpire, or the discharge of this; umpirage.

1565 HARDING *Confut. Apol.* I. ix. 31 We refuse not tharbitrement and vmpireship of the holy ghost. **1567** JEWEL *Def. Apol.* 65 Ye saie, ye refuse not the Umpeereship, and iudgemente of the Holy Ghoste. **1613** JACKSON *Creed* II. xxvii. §4. 431 Tyrannicall claime of soueraigntie, and imperiall vmpiership over all other Churches. **1819** MOORE *Mem.* (1853) II. 264, I..was proceeding to talk to him about our joint umpireship on Byron's poem. **1869** *Daily News* 26 May, He withdrew from the umpireship of a dog show because he objected to the admission of mutilated dogs.

'umpiress. Also 7 ump(e)resse, 8 umpress. [f. UMPIRE *sb.* + -ESS.] A female umpire.

1602 MARSTON *Ant. & Mel.* v. Wks. 1856 I. 58 Give mee the golden harpe: faith with your favour, ile be umperesse. **1651** HOWELL *Venice* 4 She [Venice] hath allwayes bin more inclined to peace than war, and chosen rather to be a Spectatrix or Umpresse, than a Gamestresse. **1715** tr. *C'tess D'Aunoy's Wks.* 18, I became an Umpress among the Wits, and Judge of their Works. **1889** *Pall Mall G.* 4 Mar. 1/2 Umpires, or rather umpiresses, for the women folk of the village had been invited to give judgment.

'umpiring, *vbl. sb.* [f. UMPIRE *v.* + -ING¹.] The action of acting as an umpire, esp. of deciding doubtful points in games.

1851 W. CLARK in W. Bolland *Cricket Notes* vii. 149 Umpiring is a very arduous and often unthankful office. **1884** *Pall Mall G.* 15 July 5/1 Construction of asphalte courts; treatises on umpiring, the same on handicapping. **1894** *Westm. Gaz.* 30 July 3/2 Most of these faults would be checked by good umpiring.

attrib. **1884** *Marshall's Tennis Cuts* 102 Our suggestion of a band on these occasions was scouted with scorn by the eminent in the umpiring line. **1896** KNOWLES & MORTON *Baseball* 56 The whole season was a very trying one for the gentlemen who occupied the umpiring positions.

'umpirism. *rare*⁻¹. [f. UMPIRE *sb.*] Umpirage.

1792 ANNA SEWARD *Lett.* (1811) III. 150 If the umpireism of dispassionate examination is to be rejected, and the ardours of zeal confided in implicitly.

†**umple.** *Obs.* Also 5 umpull. [a. OF. *omple* 'étoffe unie' (15th c. in Godefroy).] A fine kind of linen stuff.

1457 *Inv. Ornaments in Lady Chapel Cirencester Abbey Ch.*, A new Kerchon of umpull. **1463** *Rolls Parlt.* V. 505 Kerchiefs..of..Lawne, Nyfels, Umple. *a* **1500** *Assemb. Ladies* 471 Bicause the wallis shone so bright, With fyne umple they were al over-sprad, To that intent, folk shuld nat hurte hir sight. ? *a* **1500** *London Lickpenny* (MS. Harl. 542) x, One bad me come nere, and by fine cloth of lawne, paris thred, Coton, and vmple.

umpra, obs. form of OMRAH.

umpteen ('ʌm(p)tiːn, ʌm(p)'tiːn), *a.* and *sb. colloq.* Also **umteen.** [f. UMP(TY + TEEN *sb.*² after *thirteen*, etc.]

A. *adj.* An indefinite number, used in the sense 'many, several', etc. **B.** *sb.* Such a number in the abstract.

1918 *Blackw. Mag.* Mar. 290/1 Men from five continents and umpteen colonies. **1919** *Athenæum* 1 Aug. 695/1 As 'umpty' means 'dash', it is fairly evident that..'umpteen' (or 'umteen'), which means 'any number of times', comes from this source. **1922** *Public Opinion* 11 Jan. 48/2, I entered into it and prepared to drop umteen floors. **1923** [see UMPTY *sb.*] **1930** J. B. PRIESTLEY *Angel Pavement* ii. 82 I've got umpteen things for him to sign. **1973** K. GILES *File on Death* ii. 39, I leave business to the Estate managers, six of 'em with umpteen clerks and typists. **1976** A. PRICE *War Game* I. viii. 141 A potential offender against section umpteen of the Road Traffic Act.

Hence **umpteenth** (stress variable) *a.* Phr. ***the umpteenth time***, used of something repeated unbearably or irritatingly often.

1918 E. A. MACKINTOSH *War, the Liberator* 99 That's the umpteenth Bosche that I've killed today. **1921** *Blackw. Mag.* Apr. 475/1 It was our umteenth breakdown. **1952** M. LASKI *Village* v. 89 'I always did say I'd go back if..she needed me,' she said for the umpteenth time. **1980** P. HARCOURT *Tomorrow's Treason* 19 For the umpteenth time I'm telling you. I haven't done anything.

umpty ('ʌmptɪ), *sb.* and *a.* [A fanciful verbal repr. of the dash (—) in Morse code. Cf. IDDY-UMPTY.] **A.** *sb.* An indefinite number, usu. fairly large. (Often used on an analogy with *twenty*, etc.) *Mil. slang.*

1905 *Outing* July 389/2 The undergraduates..whisper to their guests, who stroked the crew in umpty-seven, the year we won by twenty lengths. **1919** W. LANG *Sea Lawyer's Log* 70 Umpteen or 'umpty', it should be explained, is to the Navy what x is to Euclid—the symbol of an unknown or unmentionable quantity. **1923** *Daily Mail* 3 Sept. 1 (Advt.), Umpteen to umpty Fahrenheit, Wolsey keeps you comfy, quite. **1924** KIPLING in *Hearst's Internat.* July 16/2 The bettin' was even on my drawin' a V.C. or getting Number Umpty Rest-Camp.

B. *adj.* **1.** An indefinite number of this kind, in adjectival use.

1917 P. MACGILL *Gt. Push* xii. 250 When I go back to blighty I'll go to bed and I'll not get up for umpty-eleven months. **1939** J. D. CARR *Black Spectacles* xx. 289 Again, once more, and for the umpty-umph time, we had been hocussed by still *another* of Chesney's ingenious tricks. **1959** W. FAULKNER *Mansion* xv. 354 'I never got to Heidelberg,' Charles said. 'All I had was Harvard and Stalag umpty-nine.' **1974** R. L. SIMON *Peking Duck* xi. 84 A drill press of umpty-ump kilotons' capacity.

2. *fig.* Of a person, place, or circumstance: unpleasant.

[**1925** FRASER & GIBBONS *Soldier & Sailor Words & Phrases* 294 *Umpty iddy, to feel,* so so. Not very well. All upside down.] **1948** M. ALLINGHAM *More Work for Undertaker* xiii. 158 Things a bit umpty at home, I rather suspect. **1970** A. DRAPER *Swansong for Rare Bird* vii. 54, I was worried in case the guvnor was umpty about the night before. The last thing I wanted was a slanging match. **1974** N. MARSH *Black as he's Painted* iii. 76 Very umpty little dump. **1980** C. FREMLIN *With no Crying* xix. 117 This rather umpty friend of his.

Hence **'umptieth** *a.*

1917 'CONTACT' *Airman's Outings* 216 The umptieth squadron then had the only machines of this type in France. **1984** *Business Rev. Weekly* 25 Feb.–2 Mar. 92/2 Two hours later, after being wiped out for the umptieth time, frustration rears its ugly head.

umquhile, umwhile ('ʌmhwaɪl), *adv.* and *a.* Now only *arch.* Forms: α. 2 um-wile, 4–5, 7–9 **umwhile** (4 homwill), 4, 6 **umwhyle.** β. *north.* 4–5 **umquile** (**umquil**, 4 **umquille**), **vmqwhyle**; *Sc.* 5 **umqwhile** (9 **umquwhile**), 5– **umquhile** (5–6 **wmquhile**), 5–7 **umquhyle** (5 **wmquhyle, vm-, wmqwhyle**); 5 **umquhil**, 5–7 **umquhill** (**wm-**; 7 **wmquill**). [Representing OE. *ymb hwīle* (see UMBEWHILE *adv.*), with substitution of UM- for *ymb-*. In later use specifically Scottish, whence the usual spelling with *-quh-*.]

A. *adv.* †**1.** At times; sometimes. *Obs.*

α. **1154** *O.E. Chron.* (Laud MS.) an. 1137, Hi læiden gæildes on the tunes æure um wile & clepeden it tenserie. **1303** R. BRUNNE *Handl. Synne* 2780 Fallace ys, as who seye, 'gyle', As many one sweryn vmwhyle. *c* **1330** —— *Chron. Wace* (Rolls) 1415 Vmwhile west, vmwhile est, þer schipes driuen in many tempest. *a* **1340** HAMPOLE *Psalter* cxli. 6, I fled noght fra tribulacioun in saule, thof i fled vmwhile in body. **1377** LANGL. *P. Pl.* B. v. 345 þere was laughyng and louryng..And seten so til euensonge and songen vmwhile. *a* **1529** SKELTON *Agst. Garnesche* ii. 11 Ye countyr vmwhyle to capcyously, and ar ye be dysiryd.

β. *a* **1300** *Cursor M.* 4319 Sua þou mai þe driue to ded, To ded vmquil, and to langur. *Ibid.* 10323 þof godd vmquil be funden still. **1375** BARBOUR *Bruce* III. 262 To stand agayne thar fayis mycht, Wmquhile with strenth, & quhile with slycht. *c* **1400** MAUNDEV. (Roxb.) vi. 20 Ay when him list, he gase to visit þam, and vmqwhyle ledes þam aboute with him. *a* **1500** *Ratis Raving* I. 1448 And eild..Wmquhill is twrnyt with inwy, And wmquhill led with lichory. **1535** STEWART *Cron. Scot.* (Rolls) III. 525 That all this warld hes bene full of variance; Vmquhill in plesure and prosperitie, Vmquhill in pane and greit penuritie. *a* **1568** in *Bannatyne MS.* (Hunterian Cl.) 633 Vmquhile I syche and vmquhile I sing. .. Vmquhill I lawche and quhill I weip and wring.

2. At one time; at some previous time; formerly. *Obs.* exc. *arch.*

c **1375** *Sc. Leg. Saints* iii. (*Andrew*) 863 Ane bischope vmquhile, I herd say..Sancte Andrew in affecione Had ay. *a* **1400–50** *Alexander* 23 Oute in þe erth of Egipt enhabet vmquile þe wysest wees of the werd. *Ibid.* 3079 (Dubl. MS.), Nowe am I kest vnder, þat had of the Orient all ouer homage vmwhile. **1456** SIR G. HAYE *Law Arms* (S.T.S.) 2 Chaumerlayn umquhyle to..king Charles of Fraunce. *c* **1470** HENRY *Wallace* II. 207 O der Wallace, wmquhill was stark and stur, Thow most o neide in presoune till endur. **1508** DUNBAR *Poems* vii. *heading*, Lord Barnard Stewart,.. Conquereur of Naplis and vmquhile constable general of the same. *c* **1550** LYNDESAY *Tragedy* Prol. 40 I am Dauid, that cairfull Cardinall,..That vmquhyle had so gret preeminens. **1567** *Satir. Poems Reform.* iv. 1 I, Henrie Stewart, vmquhile of Scotland King. **1832** F. TROLLOPE *Dom. Manners Amer.* I. vii. 93 A drawing..representing Hebe and the bird, umquhile sacred to Jupiter. [**1890** SERVICE *Notandums* 88 Her white cheek, umquhile red.]

†**3.** At some later time; by-and-by. *Obs.*

1375 BARBOUR *Bruce* III. 256 For nane wate, in how litill space That god wmquhile will send his grace. **1513** DOUGLAS *Æneid* II. x. 209 And I wmquhill quhilk sal be clepit thi spous, Quham to sall we be left in this waist hous?

B. *adj.* Former, late: **a.** Of persons; *esp.* = now deceased.

In the first quot. perhaps still adverbial.

1431 *Munim. de Melros* (Bann. Cl.) 521 Patrike off Dunbarr,..brothir vmquhile of a hee & mychti lorde Sir George of Dunbarr. **1477** *Exch. Rolls Scotl.* VIII. 403 *note*, Landis..the quhilkis umquhile Cuthbert Colvile had of ws of before. **1490–1** *Acc. Ld. High Treas. Scot.* I. 197 A compositioun maid with vmquhile the Master of Craufurd. **1535** STEWART *Cron. Scot.* (Rolls) III. 519 James Stewart, Sone and Air..to vmquhill King Robert Stewart. **1583** in *Montgomerie's Poems* (S.T.S. 1910) 300 The testament.. pertening to vmquhile ane richt honorabill Ladie Margaret Fraser.., relict of vmquhile Iohne Montgummerie. **1633** *Sc. Acts, Chas. I* (1870) V. 26/1 The fruites of benefice givin by his Majestie his said vmquhyle dearest father. *a* **1670** SPALDING *Troub. Chas. I* (1829) 9 Lachlan M'Intosh,.. brother to the umquhile laird of M'Intosh, William M'Intosh,..son to umquhile Lachlan Angus-son. **1714** RAMSAY *Elegy J. Cowper* xiii, Of umquhile John to lie or bann, Shaws but ill will. **1784** in *Nairne Peerage Evidence* (1874) 72 The goods and gear which pertained and belonged to umq^le miss Brabazone Nairne. **1814** SCOTT *Wav.* x, The estate which devolved on this unhappy woman by a settlement of her umwhile husband. **1816** —— *Old Mort.* iii, His uncle, as well as his umquhile father, is a roundhead, I presume. **1874** HISLOP *Bk. Sc. Anecdote* 725/1 The 'leader of the psalmody', as umquhile 'precentors' are now termed. **1886** RUSKIN *Præterita* I. 408 Her father visited his umquwhile clientage at the coal-wharves. **1934** J. BUCHAN *Free Fishers* ii. 40 What do you think of your umquhile pupil, Professor? **1976** *Times Lit. Suppl.* 21 May 606/3 The reference to the *ci-devant* Lord Stansgate is notoriously getting shorter and shorter;..with further reduction en by en the umquhile peer will disappear completely.

b. Of things. *rare.*

1548 *Compl. Scotl.* i. 21 Quhat sal be said of athenes, the vmquhile fontane of sapiens. **1842** F. TROLLOPE *Vis. to Italy* I. x. 161, I went to see Europe's umwhile wonder and delight. **1854** H. MILLER *Sch. & Schm.* (1858) 356 When I last passed along the Coal-hill, I saw my umquhile house existing as a bit of dingy wall.

umra, var. OMRAH.

umschew, var. UMBESCHEW *v. Obs.*

umsee, -seek: see UM-.

†**umset,** *v. Obs.* Also 6 vnsett. [f. UM- + SET *v.*¹ Cf. MDu. *omme-, omsetten* (Du. *omzetten*), MSw. *omsätia*, Da. *omsætte*; OHG. *umbi-, umpisezzan* (MHG. *umbesezzen, -setzen*, G. *umsetzen*), OE. *ymbsettan.*] *trans.* To surround, invest.

a **1300** *Cursor M.* 195 How Iuus iesu oft vmsette And for his sermon thrali thrette. *Ibid.* 15012 Wit harp and pipe, and horn and trump, þe strette þai him vmsette. *c* **1340** HAMPOLE *Pr. Consc.* 1250 For-why here we er on many wyse Alle umset with sere enmys. *a* **1352** MINOT in *Pol. Poems* (Rolls) I. 77 With him come mani a kumly knight And all umset the bare obout. *c* **1400** *Destr. Troy* 6964 Cassibilan kynd brether þen þe kyng segh,..Vmset hym full sone in a sop hole. *a* **1600** *Flodden Field* lxxi. in Child *Ball.* III. 358/1 Sir Rice..Came with a feirce menye; He bent his bowes on the bent to abyde, And cleane vnsett the gallow-tree.

umshade, -shadow, -shine: see UM-.

†**umsiege,** *v. Obs.* [f. UM- + SIEGE *v.* Cf. *umbesiege* under UMBE-.] *trans.* To besiege.

a **1325** *Prose Psalter* xxi. 16 þe counseil of wicked vmseged me. *a* **1340** HAMPOLE *Psalter* xxi. 11 Fat bulles me has vmseged. *c* **1440** *Alph. Tales* 220 When Titus had vmsegid Jerusalem ij yere. *Ibid.* 226 What cetie at þai vmsegid, þai trustid to gett & wyn itt.

umstand: see UM-.

†**um'stound,** *adv. Obs.* Also 4 **vmbstont, vmstount, -stunt,** 5 **vmstonte;** 4 **vmstond.** [ad. ON. *um stund* for a time. Cf. UMBESTOUND *adv.*] Sometimes.

a **1300** *Cursor M.* 4451 Ioseph sagh þam ai vmstunt To comforth þam wel was he wont. *Ibid.* 14033 A man quilum was wont Penis for to lene vm-stunt [*Gött.* vmstount]. *Ibid.* 28330 Ben i haue vmstond quare barne Wit-vten cristening was for-farne. *a* **1340** HAMPOLE *Psalter* Prol. 4 Vmstunt he spekis of crist in his godhed, vmstunt in his manhed. *c* **1450** *St. Cuthbert* (Surtees) 3323 His brethir come to him vmstonte, To visit him, as þai were wonte.

um'strid, *adv. north. dial.* Also 9 (h)umpstridden. [Pa. pple. next.] Astride, strideways.

1674 RAY *N.C. Words, Umstrid,* astride, astridlands. [Hence in Bailey and Grose.] **1828**- in dial. glossaries (Yks., Lancs.).

†**um'stride,** *v. Obs. rare.* [f. UM- + STRIDE *v.*] *trans.* To bestride.

a **1352** MINOT in *Pol. Poems* (Rolls) I. 68 The King of Beme had cares colde, That was ful hardy and bolde A stede to umstride. *c* **1400** *Ywaine & Gaw.* 1302 When he was dight in seker wede, Than he umstrade a nobil stede.

†**umstroke.** *Obs. rare.* [f. UM- + STROKE *sb.*[1]] Edge, circumference.

1650 FULLER *Pisgah* I. xiv. 46 Such Towns as stand (as one may say) on tiptoes, on the very umstroke, or on any part of the utmost line of any Map. *Ibid.* v. xx. 182 Places situate on the Um-stroke (such the location of Aleppo in our Map) are not in their exact position.

†**umthink,** *v. Obs.* Also 4 **vmthinc(k,** 5 *Sc.* **wmthink;** 4-6 **vmthynk(e,** 6 **vnþ-.** [f. UM- + THINK *v.*[2] Cf. WFris. *omtinke*, MSw. *omtänkia*, older Da. *omtænke*, obs. Icel. *umþenkja*, MLG. *ummedenken*, OE. *ymbþencan*. See also UMBETHINK *v.*]

1. *intr.* To bethink, consider, reflect. Also const. *of*, or with inf.

a **1300** *Cursor M.* 717 Sathan.. vmthoght o þat thing to stint þat godd til ending god had mint. *Ibid.* 23709 (Edinb.), Quasum graiþeli wil vmþink, þis werd es fals and ful of swink. *a* **1340** HAMPOLE *Psalter* xxi. 28 þe kirke of all þe warld sall vmthynke of God, for þai had forgetyn him: & swa vmthynkand, þai sall be turnyd till him.

b. In *pa. pple.* Having taken thought.

c **1340** HAMPOLE *Psalter, Cant. Mariæ* 9 He receyfyd israel his barne, vmthouȝt [L. *recordatus*] of his mercy.

2. *refl.* To bethink (oneself). Also const. *of*, or with obj. clause or inf.

a **1300** *Cursor M.* 529 If þow wil þe vm-think, þow may þam find with litul suink. *Ibid.* 5722 He vmthoght him in his hert Of his hiht lang siþen es gan. *c* **1325** *Metr. Hom.* (1862) 79 He umthoght him what was best, How he might this ilk nonne fange. *c* **1340** HAMPOLE *Psalter* ix. 12 Sekand þe blode of þaim he has vmthoght him. *Ibid.* He has vmthoght him to glorifie his seruantes. *a* **1400** *New Test.* (Paues) Acts xi. 16 Forsoþe I vmþoghte me of þo wordes of oure Lorde. *c* **1440** *Alph. Tales* 31 'Son, vmthynk þe if þou hafe dissayvid any man be þis stane.' And at þis wurde he vmthoght hym & said [etc.]. *Ibid.* 351 þat evur when he lukid þer-vppon, he sulde vmthynk hym of his dead. **15..** *Chester Pl.* xxiv. 430 (MS. Bodley 175), How durst you euer doo amisse When you vnþought you of þis?

umtiff: see UM-.

‖**umu** ('ʊmʊ). *N.Z.* [Maori.] = HANGI; also, the food prepared in this oven.

Also used in other Polynesian areas in the Pacific.

1845 E. J. WAKEFIELD *Adventure in N.Z.* I. iv. 75 The tangi had terminated; the *umu* or 'cooking holes' were smoking away for the feast. **1889** S. P. SMITH in *Trans. N.Z. Inst.* XXII. 98 An oven of stones, exactly like a Maori *umu* or *hangi*. **1950** *Landfall* IV. 85 The passage describes in detail the well-remembered lighting of the *umu* fires. **1972** M. SHADBOLT *Strangers & Journeys* xxii. 474 Mother, grandmother, and children scattered around in vague blue smoke for their *umu*, or earth oven. **1974** T. HEYERDAHL *Fatu-Hiva* i. 46 No banquet.. can better regale guests than such a juicy, fresh.. Polynesian *umu* served without cost.. in the open air of a tropical night.

umutsha, var. MOOCHA.

‖**Umwelt** ('ʊmvɛlt). Pl. **Umwelten.** [Ger., = environment.] The outer world, or reality, as it affects the organisms inhabiting it.

1964 M. KING *Heidegger's Philos.* II. ii. 96 One suggestion which Heidegger undoubtedly intends to convey with *Umwelt* is of a world that is closest and most familiar to man. .. We shall paraphrase *Umwelt* by 'the first and nearest world'. **1966** J. S. BRUNER *Beyond Information Given* (1974) xviii. 318 Modern ethnological conceptions are centrally concerned with representation in such mechanisms as releasers and imprinting, much of it deriving from the originating idea of the *Umwelt* first proposed by von Uexküll. **1971** E. O. WILSON *Insect Societies* (1972) xi. 209/2 The various species of ants are generally similar to the honeybee in their *Umwelten*. **1977** A. SHERIDAN tr. *J. Lacan's Écrits* i. 4 To break out of the circle of the *Innenwelt* into the *Umwelt* generates the inexhaustible quadrature of the ego's verifications.

umwhile: see UMQUHILE.

umwrithe: see UM-.

umyak, var. UMIAK.

umzimbeet (ʊmzɪm'biːt). *S. Afr.* Also **umzimbit(i).** [a. Xhosa *umSimbithi* ironwood.] A South African tree, *Millettia grandis* or *M. caffra* (family Leguminosæ), which bears clusters of pink or purple flowers, may be evergreen or deciduous, and has very heavy, hard wood; the wood itself.

[**1851** R. GRAY *Jrnl. Bishop's Visitation Tour Cape Colony* II. 99 There are several kinds of valuable wood unknown in the colony. Two of the hardest and most useful are called by the natives 'Unizimbeti' and 'Umnebelala'.] **1870** C. HAMILTON *Life & Sport S.-E. Afr.* 6 The wheels are made of the famous Natal wood called 'umsimbiti' or ironwood, from its strength and durability. **1902** G. S. BOULGER *Wood* II. 335 Umzimbit.. Known also as 'White Ironwood'. **1907** T. R. SIM *Forests & Forest Flora Cape of Good Hope* 203 Umzimbeet is a light-demanding tree. **1950** [see *flat-crown* s.v. FLAT *a.* 15]. **1955** W. GADDIS *Recognitions* II. i. 293 Bird-of-paradise flowers.. among the native white pear.. and umzimbiti. **1972** PALMER & PITMAN *Trees S. Afr.* II. 923 The umzimbeet is a medium to large tree of the coastal forests. *Ibid.* 925 The wood of the umzimbeet is extremely heavy, hard, and strong.

un, *sb.* An instance of the negative prefix UN-[1].

1650 B. *Discolliminium* 7 It was a thousand pities those two *Un's* were put in.

un, 'un[1], later dial. f. HIN(E *pers. pron.* 'him'. (*Eng. Dial. Dict.* s.v. *En*).

1633 B. JONSON *Tale Tub* I. iv, *Pup.* He is high Constable, And who should reade above un, or avore 'hun? **1749** FIELDING *Tom Jones* VI. ii, Allworthy is a queer dog, and money has no effect o' un. **1785** [see HIN(E]. **1821** SCOTT *Kenilw.* xi, 'And what if I did see un, Master Crane?' replied Jack Hostler. **1919** G. B. SHAW *Heartbreak House* III. 109 Right in the gravel pit: I seen it. Serve un right! **1932** D. L. SAYERS *Have his Carcase* xi. 134 Soon as I come in zight of 'un, I zee un. **1977** P. HILL *Liars* x. 140 The ladies liked 'un.

un, 'un[2], dial. f. ONE *pron.* (senses 22 and 24).

c **1810** W. HICKEY *Mem.* (1960) iv. 64 The young 'un there wanted to be off. **1821** SCOTT *Kenilw.* xii, Here's a gentleman.. has given Sir Hugh a draught that is worth twenty of yon un. **1859** GEO. ELIOT *A. Bede* xx, 'It [a rose] smells very sweet,' he said; 'those striped uns have no smell'.

un, obs. form of ON *prep.*, dial. f. AND *conj.*

un-, *prefix*[1], expressing negation, representing OE. *un-*, = OFris. *un-*, *on-*, *oen-* (WFris. *ûn-*, *on-*, EFris. *ûn-*, NFris. *ün-*), MDu. (and Du.) *on-*, OS. (MLG., LG.), OHG. (MLG., G.), and Goth. *un-*, ON. *ú-*, *ó-* (Icel. *ó-*, Sw. *o-*, Norw. and Da. *u-*), corresponding to OIr. *in-*, *an-*, L. *in-* (*im-*, *il-*, *ir-*, *i-*), Gr. ἀν-, ἀ-, Arm. *an-*, Skr. *an-*, *a-*, Indo-Eur. *ṇ, an ablaut-variant of *ne* not: see NE *adv.* The prefix has been very extensively employed in English, as in the other Germanic languages, and is now the one which can be used with the greatest freedom in new formations.

2. In OE. the number of recorded forms in *un-* is very large, the prefix being freely applied with a purely negative force to several parts of speech, which may be classified as follows: (*a*) simple adjectives, as *unbeald*, *unbliðe*, *unbrád*, *unclǽne*, *uncúþ*, *undéop*, etc., derivative adjs., as *unbealoful*, *unblódiȝ*, *ungyltiȝ*, *unmeahtiȝ*, *unclǽnlic*, *uncúðlic*, *uncynlic*, etc., and composite forms, as *uncampróf*, *undéopþancol*, *unfæstrǽd*, etc.; (*b*) simple adverbs, as *unéaðe*, *unefne*, *unfæȝere*, *unfeorr*, etc., and derivative forms, as *unclǽnlíce*, *uncúðlíce*, *unéaðelíce*, *unfæstlíce*, etc.; (*c*) past participles of strong and weak verbs, as *unbeden*, *unbegunnen*, *unboren*, *undrifen*, *unȝeboden*, *unȝecnáwen*, etc., *unbyrȝed*, *undǽled*, *unȝedered*, *unclǽnsod*, *unȝeendod*, *unȝehálȝod*, *unboht*, etc.; (*d*) present participles, as *unberende*, *unbirnende*, *uncwaciende*, *uncweðende*, *unfélende*, etc.; (*e*) simple nouns, as *unár*, *unbealu*, *uncyst*, *unfriþ*, *unlaȝu*, *unþanc*, etc., and derivative forms, as *unclǽnness*, *unfæȝerness*, *uncáfscipe*, *unwísdóm*, etc. A prominent feature of the OE. examples is the prevalence of long derivative or compound formations, usually based upon, or corresponding to, Latin formations with *in-*, *im-*, *il-*, as *unaberendlic* intolerable, *unaberendlíce* intolerably, *unbegrípendlic* incomprehensible, *unbescéawodlíce* inconsiderately, *unforhæfedness* incontinence. The greater number of such forms were no doubt artificial, and had little or no currency in ordinary language. In a small number of nouns *un-* appears with a pejorative in place of a negative sense, as *unǽt* excessive eating, *uncoðu* an evil disease, *uncræft* an evil art, and similarly *undǽd*, *undóm*, *unlaȝu*, *unrǽd*, *unsíþ*, *untíma*, *unweder*. Altogether the number of *un-* words recorded in OE. is about 1250, of which barely an eighth part survived beyond the OE. period.

3. The disappearance of so many of the OE. formations left early ME. with a very limited supply of *un-* words, even when new (or apparently new) examples are added to those inherited from the older language. A fair proportion even of this reduced stock proved unable to survive for more than half a century, and had passed out of use by 1250. A few of these, especially such as obviously had some general currency, are entered in their alphabetical places, but the greater number are given here (together with a few of somewhat later date) as properly belonging to the older period and having no direct influence upon the later development of the prefix. Most of these are composed of purely native elements, but a few show the beginnings of Scandinavian and French influence, as *ungrith*, *unhaȝerliȝ*, *unskatheful*; *unbispused*, *uncoverlich*.

In ME. transcripts of OE. homilies a few additional words are found, as *unafillendlich*, *unasecgliche*, *uniredliche*, *unisewenlich*, *untodele(n)dlich*, *unȝearu*.

una'gin *a.* [cf. AGIN *v.*], without beginning; **una'nemned** *ppl. a.* [OE. *ánemnan* to declare], unnamed, indescribable; **un'awned** *ppl. a.* [f. AWN *v.*[2]], unmanifested, undeclared; **una'ȝeten** *ppl. a.* [f. ANGET *v.*], unperceived; **un'baleful** *a.* [OE. *unbealoful*], harmless; **un'barmed** *ppl. a.* [f. BARM *v.*], unleavened; **unbi'buried** *ppl. a.* [OE. *unbebyriȝed*], unburied; **unbi'heve** *sb.* [cf. next] = *unbihoof*; **unbi'heve** *a.* [OE. *unbehéfe*], disadvantageous, unprofitable; **unbi'hoof, -'hofthe** [BEHOOF, BIHOFTHE], disadvantage, detriment; **unbi'se(h)iness** [f. pa. pple. of BESEE *v.*], inattention, carelessness; **unbi'sorȝeliche** *adv.* [OE. *unbesorh* not cared for], roughly; **unbi'spused** *ppl. a.* [after OE. *unbeweddod*], unmarried; **unbi'wene** *a.* [cf. OE. *unwéne*], unexpected; **un'boned** *ppl. a.* [f. BOON *v.*], unentreated; **un'botelich** *a.* [f. BOOT *sb.*[1]], irremediable; **un'coverlich** *a.* [f. COVER *v.*[2] 2], irrecoverable; **un'cunne** [cf. OE. *uncynn* a.], improper conduct; **un'cunneliche** *v.* [f. OE. *cynn* KIN[1]], to denaturalize; **un'cunness** [f. OE. *cunnan* to know], ignorance; **un'cuððe** [OE. *uncyððu*], a strange land; **un'deaðlich** *a.* [OE. *undéaþlic*], immortal; **un'deaðlichness** [OE. *undéaþlicnes*], immortality; **undeaþ'shildiȝness** [f. OE. *déaþscyldiȝ*], exemption from death; **un'derf,** *a.* [f. DERF *a.*], irresolute, weak; **un'dreint** *p.p.* [f. DRENCH *v.*], undrowned; **un'drinkled** *p.p.* [f. DRENKLE *v.*], = *undreint*; **un'endliche** *adv.* [cf. ON. *úendiliga*], infinitely; **un'faken** *a.* [OE. *unfácne*], guileless, innocent; **un'few** *a.* [ON. *úfár*], many; **unfor'golden** *p.p.* [OE. *unforgolden*], unrequited; **unfor'gult** *ppl. a.* [f. FORGUILT *v.*], not affected with guilt; **un'frame** [cf. ON. *úframi* backwardness], disadvantage, loss; **un'freme** [OE. *unfremu*], = *unframe*; **un'frith** [OE. *unfriþ*, ON. *úfriðr*], dissension, strife; **un'fulhtned** [f. FULHTNE *v.*], unbaptized; **unfull'making** [cf. *fullmake* v., and OE. *unfulfremming*], imperfection; **unȝe'rim** *a.* [OE. *unȝerím* sb.], numberless; **un'ghere** *adv.* [OE. *unȝéara*], soon, quickly; **un'grete** [cf. OE. *grýto*], want of size, smallness; **un'grith** [f. GRITH *sb.*], insecurity, hurt; **un'haȝherliȝ** *adv.* [see HAGHER *a.*, and cf. ON. *úhagliga*], unskilfully, awkwardly; **un'hersumness** [OE. *unhiersumnes*], disobedience; **un'huhtlic** *a.* [f. OE. *hyhtlic* HIGHTLY *a.*], unpleasant; **uni'cunde** *a.* [OE. *unȝecynde*], not native, foreign; **uni'feie** *a.* [OE. *unȝeféȝe*], = next; **uni'foh, -i'voh,** *a.* [OE. *unȝefóȝ*], immense; *adv.* extremely; **uni'hoded** *ppl. a.* [OE. *unȝehádod*], not ordained; **uni'limp** [OE. *unȝelimp*], misfortune, mishap; **uni'loȝe** *p.p.* [f. ME. *iloȝe*, p.p. of LIE *v.*[2]], without falsehood; **uni'make** [OE. *unȝemaca*], a non-equal, a superior; **uni'meað** *adv.*, = *unmeðe* (see below); **uni'queme** *a.* [OE. *unȝecwéme*], unpleasant, inconvenient; **uni'riht** [f. OE. *ȝeriht*], injustice, wrong; **uni'rimed** *ppl. a.* [OE. *unȝerímed*], unnumbered; **uni'rude** *a.* [OE. *unȝerýde*], = UNRIDE *a.*; **uni'saht** *ppl. a.* [see SAUGHT *v.*], unreconciled; **uni'sele** *sb.* [cf. SELE *sb.*], unhappiness, misery; **uni'sele** *a.* [f. ISELE *a.*], = next; **uni'seli** *a.* [OE. *unȝesǽliȝ*: cf. ISELI *a.*], unhappy, wretched; **uni'seliche** *adv.* [OE. *unȝesǽlíce*], unhappily, wretchedly; **uni'selth** [OE. *unȝesǽlþ*: cf. ISELTH], unhappiness, misfortune; **uni'sibbe** [cf. OE. *unsib* and *ȝesib* a.], dissension, strife; **uni'some** *a.* [OE. *unȝesóm*: cf. ISOM(E *a.*], at variance; **uni'sunde** [cf. ISUNDE], unsoundness, injury; **uni'tharf** [cf. THARF *sb.*], evil, mischief; **uni'vele** *a.*, = UNFELE *a.*; **uni'weald** [OE. *unȝeweald*: cf. IWALD *sb.*], lack of control; **uni'welde** *a.* [OE.

unᵹewielde], unwieldy; **uni'widere** [OE. *unᵹewidere*], bad weather; **uni'will** [cf. IWILL], unwillingness; **uni'wine**, = UNWINE (an enemy); **uni'wrast** *a.*, = UNWRAST *a.*; **uni'wrench**, = UNWRENCH *sb.*; **un'laȝeliche, -like** *adv.* [f. LAWLY *adv.*], unlawfully; **un'lef** *a.* [OE. *unᵹeléaf*], unbelieving; **un'leflich** *a.* [OE. *unᵹeléaflic*], incredible; **un'lepped** *ppl. a.* [f. *lep* LAP *v.*], uncovered; **un'lif** *a.*, unleavened; **un'limp**, = *unilimp*; **un'liȝel** *a.* [f. LIE *v.*²], truthful; **un'lothness** [cf. LOATHNESS 1], harmlessness, innocence; **un'lude** [f. LUDE¹], an unpleasant noise; **un'luved** *ppl. a.* [OE. *unlýfed*, *-líefed*], unallowed, illicit; **un'meaðeliche** *adv.* [OE. *unmǽðlíce*], immoderately; **un'meðe** *adv.*, = *unmeaðeliche*; **un'meðlich** *a.* [OE. *unmǽðlic*], immoderate, excessive; **un'meðship** [cf. prec.], impatience; **un'miðe** [f. MITHE *v.*], open speech; **un'mundlunge** *adv.* [OE. *unmyndlinga*], unexpectedly; **un'ned, -'net** *p.p.* [OE. *unᵹeníedd*], unconstrained; **un'neod** [f. NEED *sb.*], disadvantage, loss; **un'neomelich** *a.* [f. NIM *v.*], untakable; **un'recheleas** *a.* [see 5 a], reckless, careless; **un'roless** *a.* [see 5 a], restless; **un'seȝendlic** *a.* [cf. OE. *unásecgendlic*], unspeakable; **un'seȝendlike** *adv.* [cf. OE. *unásecgendlice*], unspeakably; **un'seȝenlic, -'sehelich** *a.* [OE. *unᵹeseᵹenlic*], invisible; **un'seȝenlike** *adv.* [cf. OE. *unᵹesewenlíce*], invisibly; **un'shathiȝ** *a.* [OE. *unsceaþþiᵹ*], harmless, innocent; **un'shathiȝness** [OE. *unsceaþþiᵹnes*], innocence; **un'shrivel** *a.* [f. SHRIVE *v.*], neglectful of confession; **un'sibbe**, = *unisibbe*; **un'sithe** [OE. *unsíþ*], mishap, misfortune; **un'skatheful** *a.* [cf. OE. *unsceaþful*], harmless; **un'smethe** *a.* [OE. *unsméðe*], unsmooth; **un'stathelfest** *a.* [OE. *unstaðolfæst*], unsteadfast; **un'streoned** *p.p.* [f. STRENE *v.*], unbegot; **un'talelich** *a.* [f. TALE *sb.*], indescribable; **un'theode** [f. THEDE], strangers; **un'tholelich** *a.* [f. THOLE *v.*], unendurable; **un'throwlich** *a.* [cf. OE. *unþrówiᵹendlic*], incapable of suffering; **un'thuldeliche** *adv.* [cf. OE. *unþyldlicnes*], with lack of endurance; **un'timing** [f. TIMING *vbl. sb.* 1], mishap, ill fortune; **unto'britned** *ppl. a.* [f. TO-BRITTEN *v.*], undivided; **unto'deled** *ppl. a.* [OE. *untódǽled*], = *untobritned*; **unto'delinde** *ppl. a.* [cf. prec.], indivisible; **un'trowness** [cf. OE. *untréow*, *-tréowþ*], unfaithfulness, breach of trust; **un'tuderi** *a.* [cf. OE. *untydrende*], barren; **un'tuhtle** [see TUHTLE], a bad habit or custom; **un'twemed** *ppl. a.* [f. TWEME *v.*], undivided; **un'vonded** *ppl. a.* [cf. OE. *unᵹefandod*], untried; **un'waker** *a.* [f. WAKER *a.*], unwatchful; **un'waldes** *adv.* [OE. *unᵹewealdes*], unintentionally; **un'weawed** *ppl. a.*, ?uncovered; **un'wend** *p.p.* [f. WEND *v.*], unturned; **un'weote** [OE. *unwita*], an ignorant person; **un'weoteness**, = *unwiteness*; **un'wharfed** *p.p.* [f. WHARF *v.*], unturned, unaltered; **un'whate** [f. WHATE *sb.*], misfortune; **un'wille** *a.* [cf. UNWILL *sb.*], unwilling; **un'wisdomness** [f. UNWISDOM], folly; **un'witeness** [cf. *unweote* above], ignorance; **un'witless** *a.* [see 5 a], senseless, insensible; **un'witship** [cf. WITSHIP], folly; **un'zyginde** *ppl. a.* [cf. OE. *unásecgende*], indescribable.

a **1225** *Juliana* 3 (Bodl. MS.), An godd *unagin, euch godes ful. *c* **1175** *Lamb. Hom.* 43 Innan þan ilke sea weren *unaneomned deor. *c* **1200** Ormin 2003 Forr þatt itt shollde *unnawwnedd ben & all unncuþ & dærne. *Ibid.* 7227, 7381. *c* **1205** Lay 25797 Ȝif þu hine ifindest..and þu al *un-aȝeten [*c* **1275** on-aȝete] aȝein miht iwende. *c* **1200** *Trin. Coll. Hom.* 49 Duue ne harmeð none fuȝele..and ðus kið þat hie is admod & *unbaleful. *c* **1200** Ormin 1591 Forr þerrflinng bræd iss clene bræd, Forr þatt itt iss *unnberrmedd. *a* **1225** *Leg. Kath.* 2243 He het..bihefden ham..& leauen hare bodies *unbiburiet alle, fode to wilde deor. *c* **1200** *Trin. Coll. Hom.* 121 Ure drihten..seh þat alle hie turnden fro him hem seluen to *unbihefe. *Ibid.* 7 Do þat ure sowle & ure lichame be biheue, & forlaten al þat hem beð *unbiheue. *a* **1240** *Sawles Warde* in *O.E. Hom.* I. 265 Nes na lessere mi tale þen wes murhðes sondes ne unbihefre to ow. *c* **1205** Lay. 8576 Forð ferde þe king..to his muchelen *vnbihoue [*c* **1275** unbiofþe]. *a* **1225** *Ancr. R.* 344 [The sin] of keorfunge, oðer of hurtunge, þuruh *unbiseinesse [*v.r.* -sehenesse]. *c* **1175** *Lamb. Hom.* 43 Herefter iseh paul hwer .iii. deoflen ledden an meiden swiðe *unbisorȝeliche. *c* **1200** *Trin. Coll. Hom.* 13 Þat man þe spuse haueð,..& þo þe beð *unbispused. *c* **1250** *Gen. & Ex.* 3777 Alle he sunken ðe erðe wið-in,..Swilc endesið *vn-bi-wen hauen. *c* **1200** Ormin 17081 Forrþi toc Crist forrþrihht anan Unnbedenn & *unnbonedd Allræresst towarrd Nicodem. *c* **1230** *Hali Meid.* 17 Flih alle thinges, & forhuh ȝeorne þat tus *unbotelich lure of mahe arisen. *Ibid.* 27 Wið swuch *uncouerlich lure as meidenhades menske is. *c* **1200** *Trin. Coll. Hom.* 11 After clepenge, & ascinge, & *uncunne, & warienge,..& fele swilche deueles craftes. *c* **1230** *Hali Meid.* 35 Þis is sunne, & ec *uncunnelicheð þe. *c* **1250** *Hymn* in *Trin. Coll. Hom.* App. 258 Vre neode wel þu wost, & ure *unkunnesse in þine hond is michte mest; louerd þu vs blesce. **1357** *Lay Folks Catech.* (L.) 390 For non schuld excuse hym of vnkunnys for to cun hem. *a* **1225** *Ancr. R.* 140 Uor heo is her in *uncuðoe, iput in one prisune. *c* **1200** *Trin. Coll. Hom.* 133 Adam..was *undeaðlich forte he sinede. *a* **1225** *Leg. Kath.* 2292 Þet þing þet schal arisen ..of deað to lif undeðlich. *c* **1200** *Trin. Coll. Hom.* 33 Ðe [deflen] bireueden him alle his riche weden þat waren unerned giue, & *undeðlicnesse, & loðlesnesse. *c* **1200** Ormin 17571 Sawle iss ec wurrþlike shridd..Wiþþ *unndæþshildiȝnesse. *a* **1225** *Leg. Kath.* 1174 Ah al þe weane..wente upon þe unstrencðe of þet *underue flesch, þet he neodeles nom. *c* **1175** *Lamb. Hom.* 141 Þe see.. adreinte pharao and al his ferede mid him, swa þet nes þere nefre an bileued *un-dreint. *c* **1250** *Gen. & Ex.* 3280 Of hem alle bi-leaf non fot *Vn-drincled in ðat salte spot. *a* **1225** *Ancr. R.* 398 Ne schal neuer heorte þenchen swuch seluhðe, þet ich nulle ȝiuen more uor þine luue, vnimeteliche and *vnendliche more. *c* **1200** Ormin 4149 Forr Crist iss strang & stedefasst & findiȝ & *unnfakenn. *Ibid.* 13327. *Ibid.* 159 Oþre *unnfæwe shulenn ec Full glade & bliþe wurrþenn. *Ibid.* 792 Oþre menn unnfæwe. *c* **1175** *Lamb. Hom.* 41 Ne scule ȝe neure god don *unforgolden. *a* **1200** *Moral Ode* 59 (Lamb. MS.), Ne scal nan ufel bon unbocht ne nan god unforȝolden [*v.rr.* -ȝolde, -gulde]. *a* **1225** *Leg. Kath.* 231 Þes heouenliche lauerd luueð treowe bileaue & nowðer blod ne ban of *unforgult ahte. *c* **1230** *Hali Meid.* 43 And te oðre þat halden ham vnforgult & cleane, beon ase sikere. *c* **1250** *Gen. & Ex.* 1566 Riȝt is his name hoten iacob, to min *un-frame. *Ibid.* 3037 Knowen sal ben, ðe to un-frame, In euerilc lond min miȝte name. *a* **1200** *Moral Ode* 226 (Lambeth MS.), Ich ..wille..Warni hom wið hore *unfrome [*v.r.* unfreme] ȝif ho me wulleð lusten. *c* **1200** *Trin. Coll. Hom.* 195 Ðe man noteð wel his ȝiepshipe þe birgeð him seluen wið his aȝene soule unfreme, & erneð after his soule freme. *c* **1205** Lay. 2557 Membriz hefde inomen þat grið, ah sone he makede *unfrið. *Ibid.* 19404 Octa heold muche vnfrið, & Lot faht him ofte wið. *c* **1200** Ormin 16895 Þatt lede þatt primmseȝȝnedd iss & iss ȝet all *unnfullhtnedd. *a* **1300** *E.E. Psalter* cxxxviii. 15 Þine eghen segh *unfulmaking mine. *c* **1200** Ormin 18993 Forr mikell follc & *unnȝerim Iss ȝet to daȝȝ onn erþe. *c* **1250** *Gen. & Ex.* 3047 O morgen, ..ðhunder, and hail, and leuenes fir, Cam wel *vnghere. *a* **1250** *Owl & Night.* 752 (Jesus Coll. MS.), Hwy atwitestu me myne vnstrengþe & myne *vngrete & myn vnlengþe? *c* **1200** Ormin 16280 Forr hefiȝ & forr sware *unngriþþ Þatt hæþenn follc þær wrohhte. *Ibid.* 425 Forr swa we don *unnhaȝherrliȝ Whattse we don to gode. *Ibid.* 4277 Þatt dæþess wunde, Þatt Adam haffde ȝifenn uss Þurrh hiss *unnherrsummnesse. *Ibid.* 13425. *c* **1205** Lay. 5101 Nis hit noht *un-huhtlic incker moder inc hateð. *Ibid.* 18429 Swa we scullen of londe driuen *vnicunde [*c* **1275** onicunde]. *Ibid.* 5573 Ferde he hauede inoh muchel and *vnifeie. *Ibid.* 8674 Of þon folke he sloh muchel & *unifoh [*c* **1275** onifoh]. *Ibid.* 23518. *Ibid.* 17883 Þe leome þe toward France droh, he wes briht *vnifoh. *a* **1250** *Owl & Night.* 1178 (Jesus Coll. MS.), Ertu ihoded oþer þu cursest *vnihoded? *c* **1200** *Trin. Coll. Hom.* 177 Ðe water stremes on-heueden up here undes, þat is þat folc þe sore bimurneð, & swiðe bimeneð swich *unilimp. *a* **1250** *Prov. Ælfred* 148 in *O.E. Misc.* 110 Strong..hit is to swynke a-yeyn vnylimpe. *c* **1380** *Sir Ferumb.* 511 Ȝunder at my sadel boȝe hongeþ o botel, Ful of baume *oun-y-loȝe ys he euery del. *c* **1205** Lay. 17961 Biuoren þa steorre wes þæ drake elcches wurmes *vnimake [*c* 1275 onimake]. *Ibid.* 19125. *a* **1225** *Juliana* 5 (Bodl. MS.), Wið *unimeað muchel hird & wið heh duheðe. *a* **1250** *Prov. Ælfred* 444 in *O.E. Misc.* 128 Þanne deþ hit sone þat þe biþ *vnyqueme. *c* **1205** Lay. 10281 In his herede he makede grið, & lette awæi þat *vniriht. *Ibid.* 433 Þa lette he riden *vnirimed folc. *a* **1240** *Sawles Warde* in *O.E. Hom.* I. 253 [To] þolien & a-beoren hare *unirude duntes. *c* **1175** *Lamb. Hom.* 39 Þu scalt sahtnien þa þe beoð *unisahte mid alle þine mahte. *c* **1205** Lay. 21788 Þa Scottes weoren to-deled mid muclen *vniselen ȝeond þa monie munten. *Ibid.* 26446 Þe cniht was *unisele. *c* **1250** *Moral Ode* 101 in *E.E.P.* (1862) 28 Niere no man elles dieð ne sic, ne non vn-ysele [*v.r.* vnsele]. *c* **1175** *Lamb. Hom.* 31 He his *uniseli ȝif him is lað to donne þis. *c* **1205** Lay. 4014 Þe uniselie moder mid sexe hine to-snæde. *a* **1225** *Ancr. R.* 68 Sum uniseli..haueð ischriuen hire al to wundre. *c* **1205** Lay. 7022 Seoððen wes his sune king þe *vniseliche [*c* **1275** onselliche] luuede. *a* **1200** *Moral Ode* 198 Þurh him deð com in þis middenerd and oðer *uniselðe [*v.r.* unisalðe, vnyselyhþe]. *c* **1205** Lay. 2545 Bi-tweonen heom aræs..sleȝht & muchel seorwa, al for heora uniselðe. *Ibid.* 9845 Betere weore sæhte Þene swulc *vnisibbe [*c* **1275** onsibbe]. *a* **1250** *Owl & Night.* 1522 (Cott. MS.), For hit itit ofte & ilome, þat wif & were beoþ *unisome. *c* **1205** Lay. 18452 Heo droȝen heore þermes mid muchele *vnisunde. *c* **1200** *Trin. Coll. Hom.* 65 *Pes cucurrit ad malum*, fot ȝide to *uniðor[f]. *c* **1205** Lay. 21744 Þat is a seolcuð mere..mid fiscen & mid feoȝelen, mid *uniuele þingen. *c* **1200** *Trin. Coll. Hom.* 63 Þat we hauen agilt..oðer þurh nuteluste, oðer þurh *uniweald,..oðer recheluste. *c* **1205** Lay. 5901 Fifti hundred cnihtes, mid alle heore wepnen, þe weoren *vniwælde; Þa oðere weoren swifte, heore wepnen weoren lihte. *c* **1175** *Lamb. Hom.* 115 Þene bið his erd ihened,..ȝe on hungre, ȝe on cwalme, ȝe on *uniwidere. *Ibid.* 69 Halde we us from *uniwil, & habben feir lete & ec skil. *c* **1205** Lay. 14466 Ȝif þu wult þe awraken ..& don þine *vniwinen [*c* **1275** onwines] wa. *Ibid.* 29609 Heom sceomeden wel sære þat þat *vniwraste moncun heom iscend hafden. *c* **1250** *Death* 94 in *O.E. Misc.* 174 For þine fule sunnen & for þin *uniwrenche [*v.r.* vny-]. *c* **1175** *Lamb. Hom.* 115 Wa þere þeode..þer þa aldormen etað on erne marȝen *u[n]laȝeliche. *c* **1200** Ormin 15867 All alls he draf ..Ut off hiss Faderr temmple Þatt follc þatt he þærinne sahh Unnlaȝhelike himm ledenn. *c* **1200** *Trin. Coll. Hom.* 125 For þu art *unlef mine worde, þu shalt beo dumb forte þat child beo boren. *Ibid.*, And for þese þre þing [he] let hit *unleflich, & ne lefde hit noht, þat þe engel him seide. *a* **1225** *Leg. Kath.* 345 Þet alle ower leasunges beoð unlefliche. *a* **1225** *Unlepped [see *unweawed* below]. *c* **1250** *Gen. & Ex.* 3153 Heued and fet, and in-rew meten, lesen fro ðe bones and eten, Wið wriðel and *vn-lif bread. *c* **1200** *Trin. Coll. Hom.* 61 Oðer þurh roberie, oðer þurh unrihte dom,..oðer þurh oðer *unlimp. *Ibid.* 195. *a* **1225** *Ancr. R.* 274 Al þis unlimp is icumen þuruh þe ȝetewardes slepe. *c* **1200** *Trin. Coll. Hom.* 131 *Un-liȝel man selde liȝeð, & soð-saȝel man seið ofte soð. *c* **1175** *Lamb. Hom.* 97 Heo deð þere monnan heortan..þet heo beoð liðe þurh un-cladnesse [*read* *un-laðnesse]. *a* **1225** *Ancr. R.* 340 Edmodnesse, & abstinence, kulure unloðnesse, & oðer swuch uertuz. *a* **1275** *Prov. Ælfred* 689 in *O.E. Misc.* 138 He wole maken fule luden; he wole grennen, cocken, & chiden, & hewere [= ever] faren mid *vnluden. *c* **1200** *Trin. Coll. Hom.* 71 Ȝif hit was don on untime, oðer on *unluuede stede, oðer mid unluued lete, oðer on unluued wise. *a* **1200** *St. Marher.* 15 Lutle ich mei makien to muchelin *unmeaðeliche, ȝef me hut ant heleð hit. *a* **1225** *Juliana* 4 (Royal MS.), Wið *unmeð muchel hird & unduhti duheðe. *a* **1225** *Ancr. R.* 238 And so hit *unmeðluker is, wrinnen aȝean þe uestluker. *Ibid.* 122 Auh nu is muche wunder of ure muchele *unmeðschipe. Understondeð þis word. *c* **1250** *Gen. & Ex.* 3973 Quuað ðis asse ðus wið *vn-miðe, 'Qui betes ðu me ðis ðridde siðe?' *a* **1225** *Ancr. R.* 280 Mid þen ilke turn he mei hine *unmunlunge aworpen. *a* **1240** *Sawles Warde* in *O.E. Hom.* I. 249 Hire wune is to cumen bi stale ferliche & unmundlunge hwen me least weneð. *c* **1200** Ormin 11457 To don summ hæfedd sinne, All hise þannkess, all *unnnedd. *a* **1225** *Ancr. R.* 340 Vor þe eorðe al unnet.. bringeð forð misliche flures. *c* **1205** Lay. 308 Þe fader heo bi-eode to his aȝre *unneode [*c* **1275** on-neode]. *Ibid.* 8741 To þes kinges unneoden. *a* **1225** *Leg. Kath.* 1180 Ne mahte me nowðer godd,..ne halden ne neomen ȝet, for godd is *unneomelich. *a* **1225** *Ancr. R.* 388 Heo underueng al ase on *unrecheleas þing. *c* **1230** *Hali Meid.* 35 Þat *unroles uuel, þat pine upo pine, þat wondrende ȝeomerunge. *c* **1200** Ormin 2823 Þin seollþe iss all *unnseȝȝenndlic. *Ibid.* 11177 O Godess name, þatt iss an Unnseȝȝenndliȝ Þrimmnesse. *Ibid.* 1760 *Unnseȝȝenndlike mare inoh Þann aniȝ wihht maȝȝ þennkenn. *Ibid.* 17296 Forr gast iss all *unn-seȝhennlic Biforenn flæshlic eȝhe. *Ibid.* 19465. *a* **1225** *Leg. Kath.* 254 Alre þinge schuppent, þet is godd unsehelich. *Ibid.* 904. *c* **1200** Ormin 17241 Þær iss þa þatt illke mann *Unnseȝhennlike wharrfedd Fra flæsh till gast. *Ibid.* 19720. *Ibid.* 2889, I þatt tatt he ne wollde nohht *Unnshaþiȝ wimmann wreȝhenn. *Ibid.* 15946 Þatt shep iss all unnshaþiȝ der. *Ibid.* 1171 Ȝiff þatt tu follȝhesst soþ meocleȝȝc & soþ *unnshaþiȝnesse. *Ibid.* 14473. **1340** *Ayenb.* 32 Huanne he is sleuuol,..*onssriuel, uoryetinde, slak, and fallinde. *a* **1250** *Owl & Night.* 1164 (Cott. MS.), Þu ne singst neuer one siþe Þat hit nis for sum *unsiþe. *c* **1200** Ormin 1176 Forr shep iss all *unnskaþefull & stille der & liþe. *Ibid.* 7915. *Ibid.* 9209 Whærse iss all *unnsmeþe get Þurrh bannkess & þurrh græfess. *c* **1175** *Lamb. Hom.* 151 Þe twafalde Mon is *un-staþelfest on alle his weies. *a* **1225** *Ancr. R.* 208 Vnstaðeluest bileaue aȝean holi lore, nis hit of prude? *c* **1205** Lay. 18882 For ȝet he beoð *unstreoned þa sturieð al þa þeoden. *a* **1225** *Ancr. R.* 144 Þe *untaleliche pinen þet no tunge ne mei tellen. *Ibid.* 410 Þeo blisse..is untalelich to alle world-liche tungen. *a* **1240** *Sawles Warde* in *O.E. Hom.* I. 251 Hell is.. ful of sorhe untalelich, for ne mei na muð..rikenin hit ne tellen. *a* **1225** *Ancr. R.* 312 *Unðeode ledden uorð þis child in his warde. *a* **1240** *Sawles Warde* in *O.E. Hom.* I. 251 Helle is..ful of stench *unþolelich. *a* **1225** *Leg. Kath.* 1155 Godd, þe is *unþrowlich, þrowede, oðer þolede pine oðer passiun, o þe deore rode. *Ibid.* 161 Heo..ifont ter swiðe feole ..þeotinde *unþuldeliche wið reowfule reames. *c* **1250** *Gen. & Ex.* 1180 On dreme him cam tiding for-quat He ðrowede and ðolede *un-timing ðat. *c* **1200** Ormin 11179 Faderr, & Sune, & Haliȝ Gast, An Godd all *unntobrittnedd. *Ibid.* 11518 An Godd all *unntodæledd. *Ibid.* 18512, I Godess herrte..All hal & unntodæledd. **1340** *Ayenb.* 266 Ich yzeȝ þe ilke onspekynde an *on-todelinde mageste of þe holy trinyte be-gynnynge ne ende ne heþ. *a* **1200** *Moral Ode* 265 Þer inne boð..þa þe *untrownesse duden þon þe ho sculden bon holde. *c* **1250** *Gen. & Ex.* 964 Siðen bi-fel ðat sarrai, for ȝhe was longe *untuderi, Ȝhe bitagte abre maiden agar. *c* **1205** Lay. 24655 Elche *untuhtle heo talden vnwurðe. *a* **1225** *Juliana* 54 (Royal MS.), Nawt þreo godes, ah is an euer ihwer *untwemet [*Bodl. MS.* untweamet]. *a* **1225** *Ancr. R.* 232 Hwat wot, he seið, Salomon, þe þet is *unuonded? *Ibid.* 272 Hwon Recabes sunen..ivindeð so *unwaker & so nesche ȝeteward. *c* **1175** *Lamb. Hom.* 23 Hit nis nan wunder þah mon sunegie oðer hwile *unwaldes. *a* **1225** *Ancr. R.* 424 No mon ne i-seo ham *unweawed [*v.r.* unlepped] ne open heaued. *c* **1200** *Trin. Coll. Hom.* 163 Ac seðen hie henen wenden, atlai þat lond *unwend, & bicam waste. *a* **1225** *Ancr. R.* 8 Ȝif eni *unweote acseð ou of hwat ordre ȝe beon. *a* **1225** *Leg. Kath.* 1054 Unweoten, þe weneð þet hit beo swa as hit on ehe bereð ham. *a* **1240** *Sawles Warde* in *O.E. Hom.* I. 255 Þurh *unweotenesse ne mei ha nawt sunegin. *c* **1200** Ormin 18794, I Godess herrte,..Þat aȝȝ iss all *unn-wharrfedd. *Ibid.* 18822. *a* **1250** *Owl & Night.* 1148 (Cott. MS.), Al þat þu singst raþe oþer late Hit is euer of manne *unwate [*v.r.* vnhwate]. *Ibid.* 1267. *a* **1225** *Ancr. R.* 238 Þeo uihteð treouliche þet..wiðsiggeð þe graunt þerof mid *unwille heorte. *c* **1200** *Trin. Coll. Hom.* 39 Ðe unwreste herde sit on *unwisdomnesse, for he ne can is orf ȝemen. *a* **1225** *Ancr. R.* 278 Sunne & ignorance, þet is, unwisdom & *unwitenesse. *a* **1225** *Leg. Kath.* 245 He ȝelt þe wurðmunt to witlese [*R.* *unwitlese, *B.* unwitelese] þing. *a* **1240** *Wohunge* in *O.E. Hom.* I. 275 For sunne & *unwitschipe, ne hafdes tu nowðer. **1340** *Ayenb.* 268 Hy byeþ glede of god *onzyginde, hy byeþ glede of zuo moche of hare oȝene holynesse.

4. a. When the words included in the previous section are eliminated, the early ME. instances of the prefix resolve themselves into the following classes: (*a*) survivals of OE. forms, chiefly adjectives, as *unclene*, *uncouth*, *unfele*, *unfere*, *unhole*, *unmilde*, *unorne*, *unsely*, and nouns, as *unhele*, *unlaȝe*, *unmiȝt*, *unrede*, *unriȝt*, *unsele*, *unthank*, *unclenenes*, *unwisdom*, and a few past participles, as *unbegun*, *unborn*, *unboȝt*, *unheled*, *unwemmed*, *unwounded*; (*b*) new formations from native elements, as *unbuȝsom*, *uncomely*, *unhende*, *unsiker*, *untidy* adjs., *unhope*, *unstrength*, *unwinne* sbs., *unbeten*, *undone*, *unshriven*, *undemed*, *unsouȝt* pa. pples.; (*c*) adoptions of Scandinavian forms, or new formations on Scandinavian bases, as *unmeek*, *unnait*, *unsauȝt*, *unsleȝe* adjs.; *unhap*, *unsauȝt*, *unskill* sbs., *unbigged* pa. pple.; (*d*) new formations on French bases, as *ungracious*, *unsavoury*, *untrussed*.

Down to 1300 these additions were comparatively few, and barely compensated for the disuse of obsolescent forms. About that date a southern writer like Robert of Gloucester uses only a small number of *un-* words, and most of these belong to the traditional stock. On the other hand, the northern *Cursor Mundi* has a rich variety of both old and new forms, and indicates clearly the beginning of a fresh period of development. The features which are most notable in this are: (*a*) the increased proportion of past pples. in comparison with adjs. and nouns; (*b*) the reappearance of pres. pples. (as *undeiand*, *unfeland*, *unseand*), which are wanting in earlier ME. texts; (*c*) the increase in the French element, as *uncertain*, *undevote*, *undispensed*, *unfelun*, *unfruitand*, *unlele*, *unleute*, *unmesure*, *unpais*, *unponist*, *unpurvaid*, *unquit*, *unresun*, *unresunable*, *unvised*, *unwily*. With this revival of the past and pres. pples., and the introduction of *-able*, the way was opened for some of the commonest uses of *un-* in the later language. The tendency thus indicated is clearly marked before the middle of the 14th century; Dan Michel uses pres. pples., as *onconnynde*, *onspekynde*, *onwytynde*, while Hampole has *unconable*, *uncurable*, *unsufferable*, and even *unfillable*, *unstirrable*. Before 1400 the period of free employment of the prefix had fully begun, as shown by the number of new formations appearing in the works of Chaucer, Wyclif, Trevisa, and others.

b. As in OE., the usual force of *un-* in ME. is purely negative. The pejorative sense however survived in a few words, as *unrede*, *unsithe*, *unthew*, *unwether*, *unwine*, *unwrench*, and appears also in *unlede*, *unlude*, *unthede*, *unwiȝt*; in *unbeast* it is employed with a French base.

c. The usual form of the prefix in ME. is *un-*, but *on-* appears in some English texts (as the later version of Layamon, the *Ayenbite*, and the *Promp. Parv.*), and is common in older Scottish, esp. in the 16th century; this form is still current in midland and south-western dialects and in Scotland. In *Sir Ferumbras* (*c* 1380) the form *oun-* is employed, and a pronunciation corresponding to this (uːn-) is still heard in Aberdeenshire. In detached use (see 5 d) the form (oːn), sometimes written *ohn*, is also employed in the same locality.

5. Some peculiarities in the use of *un-*, arising in the ME. period but surviving beyond it, require special notice.

a. It is sometimes redundantly prefixed to adjs. ending in *-less*. Early instances are *unrecheleas* reckless, *unroless* restless, *unwitles* insensible (see 3 above), and *ungiltles* guiltless (*Sir Tristr.* 2144). The type, however, chiefly belongs to the later 16th and the 17th cent.; among the instances from that period are *unboundless*, *uncomfortless*, *undauntless*, *uneffectless*, *unfathomless*, *unhelpless*, *unmatchless*, *unmerciless*, *unnumberless*, *unrecomptless*, *unremorseless*, *unrespectless*, *unshameless*, *unshapeless*, *untimeless*; as late as 1786 *unquestionless* is found, and *unrestless* exists in modern dialect.

b. From the 14th century onwards there was considerable variation, when the base was of Latin origin, between the Latin *in-*, *im-*, etc., and the native *un-*. Early examples of forms with *un-*, which either then or a little later have variants with *in-*, *im-*, are *unability*, *uncorrigible*, *uncorrupt*, *uncurable*, *undign*, *undiscreet*, *unmeasurable*, *unmovable*, *unnumerable*, *unperfect*, *unperfection*, *unportable*, *unpossible*. Similar formations continued to multiply during the following centuries, so that a large proportion of the words beginning with *il-*, *im-*, *in-*, *ir-* had corresponding forms in *un-*, as *unadequate*, *unadvertence*, *unarticulate*, *unartificial*, *unattentive*, *unaudible*, *unauspicious*, *uncapable*, etc. The culminating period of the double forms lies in the 17th century; since that time the tendency has been to differentiate, and to discard one or other of the doublets, the forms with *in-*, etc., being very commonly preferred when the whole word has a distinctively Latin character, as *inadequate*, *inadvertence*, *inarticulate*, etc. Even with such forms there is no absolute rule, and doublets are still numerous, as *in-* or *un-advisable*, *in-* or *un-alienable*, etc. (See IN-².)

By inadvertence, or simple errors in printing, *un-* or *vn-* sometimes appears in works of the 16–17th cent. for *im-*, *in-*, or *em-*, *en-*, as *vncoraged* encouraged, *unlarge* enlarge, *unployed* employed, *unpoysonynge* empoisoning, *unflam'd* inflamed, *unpostumed* imposthumed.

c. When two or more negative terms occurred in the same clause and were coupled by *and* or *or*, the prefix was sometimes employed only with the first. The following are examples of this practice, which is especially common in Scottish of the 16th century.

c **1380** WYCLIF *Wks.* (1880) 129 To kepe hym self vnblekkid or defoulid fro þis world. *c* **1460** J. RUSSELL *Bk. Nurture* 944 Lett neuer wollyn cloth.. passe a seuenyght to be vn-brosshen & shakyn. *a* **1500** in *Ratis Raving* 3 The synis that he has done wnconfessyt of or rapentyt. **1506** in *Charters, &c., Edinb.* (1871) 189 Throw selling of clayth.. vnsene or customit be yow. **1565** *Rec. Earld. Orkney* 274 Uncoackit, compellit, or seducit be ony way. **1603** KNOLLES *Hist. Turks* (1621) 83 The insolent souldiers.. nothing dedicated to the seruice of God, left vnpolluted and defaced. *Ibid.* 91 Which companies.. came neere vnto the towne vnseene or discouered. **1707** MORTIMER *Husb.* 608 Eggs, unbroken or crack'd.

d. When *un-* is prefixed to present or past participles, these are rarely employed in a true participial function, but become adjectival in character. Examples of the present participle, however, occasionally occur with a following object, or with a prepositional construction; and in Scottish use, from at least the 15th century, *un-* in such cases has acquired the sense of 'without'. More rarely, in the older language, it has the same sense with passive participles. Both constructions are still retained in north-eastern Scottish dialect, with the prefix in the form *on* or *ohn*, frequently written separate from the participle. (The spelling *ohn* is due to, or has led to, a false association with G. *ohne* without.) Examples of these uses are:—

(*a*) **1456** SIR G. HAYE *Law Arms* (S.T.S.) 155 All that I may gett apon him, unslaand him. *Ibid.* 163 How may than a man do till othir sik dissait, ungrevand God? **1573** *Reg. Privy Council Scot.* II. 215 [To] gif to thame.. gude entreatment.. unrasand the present pryces in ony thing. *a* **1578** LINDESAY (Pitscottie) *Chron. Scot.* (S.T.S.) II. 122 Sa mony as the bot wald hauld on drowning thame sellffis. **1588** *Reg. Privy Council Scot.* IV. 279 Thay depairtit furth agane.., undoing ony violent deid. **1621** LADY M. WROTH *Urania* 103 Vnknowne, and vndiscouering your selfe to any, you come among vs. **1632** LITHGOW *Trav.* I. 7 The harmlesse innocent, vnexpecting euill, may suddenly bee surprised. **1786** BURNS *Ep. Young Friend* viii, Resolutely keep its laws, Uncaring consequences. **1796** MRS. M. ROBINSON *Angelina* I. 176, I could perceive him.. leaning pensively on his hand, and for whole hours unvarying his attitude. **1816** BYRON *Ch. Har.* III. xlvii, As stands a lofty mind, Worn, but unstooping to the baser crowd. **1845** BAILEY *Festus* (ed. 2) 375 Earth.. basks in her own free light Unfed, unaided, unrequiring aught. **1885** A. O. LEGGE *Unpop. King* II. 295 To mount a ladder.. untouching the rounds with their feet.

(*b*) **1456** SIR G. HAYE *Law Arms* (S.T.S.) 185 Be quhat resoune than suld he consent.. till his awin scathe.., unmaid sekir to be amendit? **1597** *Trials for Witchcraft* in *Spalding Club Misc.* (1841) I. 91 To ryss airlie befoir the sone, on betechit hir self to God, and on spokin. **1871** W. ALEXANDER *Johnny Gibb* xlii, I'm nae responsible to gae afore Sir Simon onhed my papers upo' me. **1879** G. MACDONALD *Sir Gibbie* xxii, Wad ye hae a fellow-cratur live to a' eternity ohn been ashamed o' sic a thing's that?

6. a. During the 15th, 16th, and 17th centuries the use of *un-* steadily increased, a large number of words being thus formed which have permanently established themselves in the language, besides many more which occur only incidentally or rarely. The freedom with which the prefix could be used in new formations appears clearly in the dictionaries of Florio and Cotgrave, who constantly employ it in rendering Italian and French negative terms in *in-*, etc. As the use of *un-* or *in-* (see 5 b) was still largely a matter of choice, and many of the older formations were still current, the vocabulary of the 17th century exhibits many types in common use which are now rare or obsolete, and in general is extremely rich in words beginning with *un-*. During the 18th century many of the older forms disappeared, and new formations became more limited in number and variety, but the sense of freedom in the use of the prefix when desired is clearly shown by a large number of the examples given by Ash in his dictionary in 1775. These were obviously manufactured for the purpose, and when added to the genuine words which he has included, make up a total of about 5,000 entries. In this way Ash frequently anticipates the actual introduction of new formations. In the 19th century the use of the prefix became still more common, it being freely applied to almost any adjectival or participial form, until its employment has become almost unrestricted, within certain limits indicated below. On this account it is impossible to make a complete enumeration even of forms which have actually been used, still less of those which may be created at any time.

b. The form of the prefix indicates that it was originally unstressed (although in OE. poetry it may have stress and carry the alliterative letter), and normally it still bears this relationship to the main part of the word. There is, however, considerable tendency to give stress to it in rare or casual formations, and whenever the negation or contrast which it implies is at all emphatic. In such cases the compound may either have two equal stresses, or the prefix may have the stronger stress; the latter degree of emphasis is usually indicated by underlining or italicizing, and the use of the hyphen; e.g. 'he is distinctly *un*-literary'.

c. The following sections illustrate the usual types of current formations, with illustrations drawn from unimportant modern examples, which might be indefinitely increased. All older examples in actual use, and all words important either in themselves or on account of their source, are given in their alphabetical place in the main series. As a large number of these are purely negative and self-explanatory, the place of a definition is supplied by a reference to the section of this article under which the precise type of formation is explained and illustrated.

The entries in Ash (see above) have been regarded as worthy of note only when they anticipate the appearance of a word in actual use. In these cases a reference to Ash is given within parentheses.

A purely artificial formation (suggested by Euphuistic diction) is *un-to-be-imitated* (Scott *Monast.* xx).

7. a. *Un-* is freely prefixed to adjectives of all kinds, except where a Latin form in *in-*, etc., has definitely established itself in common use. Both forms, however, may co-exist, and in some cases a new formation with *un-* has been introduced when that with *in-* has acquired a connotation which it is desirable to avoid. The form with *un-* is then purely negative, while the other may have almost a positive sense, e.g. *unmoral* in contrast with *immoral*. (When the form with *un-* has similarly acquired a positive implication, the simple negative or neutral sense is expressed by the use of NON- or NOT-.) There is also considerable restriction in the use of *un-* with short simple adjectives of native origin, the negative of these being naturally supplied by another simple word of an opposite signification. There is thus little or no tendency now to employ such forms as *unbroad*, *undeep*, *unwide*, *unbold*, *unglad*, *ungood*, *unstrong*, *unwhole*, *unfew*, etc., which freely occur in the older language. On the other hand, derivative forms in *-al*, *-ant*, *-ar*, *-ary*, *-ent*, *-ful*, *-ic*, *-ical*, *-ile*, *-ish*, *-ive*, *-ly*, *-ory*, *-ous*, *-y*, etc., are too numerous to be completely recorded. The general character of the less usual or permanent of these and other adjectival forms is illustrated by the following examples, which are a severly restricted selection, and could be indefinitely increased by the addition of less noteworthy material.

In dictionaries of various dates many formations are given of which no real instance has been found. Levins (1570) has *unhateful*, *unprecious*. Florio (1598 and 1611) renders equivalent Italian words in *in-* by such forms as *unavailful*, *unbrittle*, *uncontinuall*, *uncoy*, *unempty*, *unfrail*, *unnice*, *unoffensible*, *unopen*, *unplenteous*, *unshrill*, *unvalorous*. Ash (1775) gives *unalphabetical*, *unattendant*, *uncohesive*, *uncompatible*, *uncompressible*, *uncompulsive*, etc. (about 80 in all). Later dictionaries (Webster, Worcester, etc.), with or without indication of source, have the entries *unabundant*, *unbiographical*, *uncogent*, *uncollectible*, *undeceptive*, *undeliberative*, etc.

Recent formations include: ***unadult***, ***un-African***, ***unairworthy***, ***unambivalent***, ***unarcadian***, ***unarchæological***, ***un-Australian***, ***unbitchy***, ***unblameworthy***, ***unblasé***, ***unbureaucratic***, ***un-Byronic***, ***uncerebral***, ***uncharismatic***, ***unchic*** (also *absol.*), ***un-Chinese***, ***unchipper***, ***unchoosy***, ***un-Christmassy***, ***uncomfy***, ***uncomposite***, ***uncomradely***, ***unconscient***, ***uncool*** [esp. COOL *a.* 4 e] (also *absol.*), ***uncooperative***, ***uncosy***, ***uncranky***, ***uncreditworthy***, ***uncuddlesome***, ***uncuddly***, ***un-Darwinian***, ***undeducible***, ***un-Dickensian***, ***undimensional***, ***undisastrous***, ***undoctrinaire***, ***undynamic***, ***unecological***, ***uneconomic***, ***unecstatic***, ***unecumenical***, ***unegoistic***, ***unegotistic***, ***unegotistical***, ***unerotic***, ***unetymological***, ***unexotic***, ***unfaery*** (poet.), ***unfeline***, ***unfeminist***, ***unflamboyant***, ***unflashy***, ***unfond***, ***unfresh***, ***unfurtive***, ***un-Gaelic***, ***ungay***, ***ungimmicky***, ***unglamorous***, ***ungroovy***, ***unhep*** (also *absol.*), ***unhip*** (also *absol.*), ***unhors(e)y***, ***unideological***, ***unintrospective***, ***unirksome***, ***unironic***, ***unironical***, ***un-Islamic***, ***un-Italian***, ***un-Jamesian***, ***un-Japanese***, ***unjingoistic***, ***unkeen*** (also *absol.*), ***unkosher***, ***unlegendary***, ***unlocal***, ***unmarital***, ***un-Marxist***, ***unmawkish***, ***unmeritocratic***, ***unneurotic***, ***unodoriferous***, ***unopen***, ***unpacifist***, ***unphonemic***, ***unphon(e)y*** (also *absol.*), ***unphotogenic***, ***unplatonic***, ***unpolemical***, ***unpolicemanly***, ***unpositive***, ***unprestigious***, ***unpriggish***, ***unprivate***, ***un-Proustian***, ***unpugnacious***, ***unradiogenic***, ***unresilient***, ***unrevolutionary***, ***unrisky***, ***unroadworthy***, ***un-Russian***, ***unscenic***, ***unseductive***, ***unselective***, ***unsemantic***, ***unsexy***, ***un-Shelleyan***, ***unsnobbish***, ***unsorry***, ***un-Spanish***, ***unspecial***, ***unspectacular***, ***unstarchy***, ***unsterile***, ***unstiff***, ***unstuffy***, ***unsycophantic***, ***unsymmetric***, ***untendentious***, ***untense***, ***untherapeutic***, ***unthistly***, ***unticklish***, ***untogether***, ***untouristy*** (also *absol.*), ***untraditional***, ***untrendy***, ***unurgent***, ***unutilitarian***, ***unviable***, ***un-Victorian***, ***unviolent***, ***unvisual***, ***un-Western***, ***un-with-it***, ***unworthwhile***, ***unyoung***.

1888 *Pall Mall G.* 6 Oct. 6/1 That *unacoustic chamber in the Town Hall. **1944** A. L. ROWSE *Eng. Spirit* xxxiii. 229 There was something curiously *unadult, ungrown-up about him. 1976 R. B. Parker Promised Land xxiv. 152 She's not a fool, but she's misled, maybe unadult. 1883 Contemp. Rev. June 815 The Scotch are..the most *unæsthetical. 1923 D. H. Lawrence Birds, Beasts & Flowers 31 An ultimate desperateness, *un-African. 1979 Guardian 6 Sept. 11/7 Parliament [in Kenya] has just thrown out as 'un-African' a Marriage Bill which would have outlawed wife-beating. 1907 Cornh. Mag. May 617 For such a motion the machine would be longitudinally unstable, and, shall we say, '*unairworthy'—to coin an analogue for the word 'unseaworthy', as applied to ships. 1979 Daily Tel. 8 Nov. 3/5 A fine..has been imposed on Braniff International Airways for conducting hundreds of flights with aircraft that were allegedly in an 'unairworthy condition'. 1842 De Morgan Diff. & Int. Calculus 3, I should not care if anyone thought this Treatise *unalgebraical. 1977 Lancet 2 July 36/2 We felt that obstetricians and midwives should remain *unambivalent in their efforts to advise smoking mothers to give up the tobacco habit during pregnancy. 1981 London Rev. Bks. 5–18 Feb. 9/1 No such vision is likely to be utterly unambivalent, regret being as intrinsic to the human condition as is hope. 1862 Carlyle Fredk. Gt. xiii. i. (1872) V. 6 *Unanarchic, disciplined at all points. 1962 Auden Dyer's Hand (1963) 350 If the landscape of New England is *unarcadian, so is its social life. 1927 Observer 11 Dec. 16/5 The workmanship and designs of ancient Peruvian pottery ..seemed, to my *unarchaeological eye, so like the Etruscan as to be almost identical. 1965 J. A. Michener Source (1966) 890 Swinging his pick with un-archaeological vigor he felt its point bite through a thin layer of semi-rock and then leap forward into nothingness. 1867 Macm. Mag. Feb. 355/1 These found it consistent with their *unarduous duties to hold livings at a distance. 1880 Warren Book-plates viii. 95 The only *unarmorial book-plates. 1877 'H. A. Page' De Quincey I. viii. 151 Certain solitary *unassimilative elements in Wordsworth's character. 1881 Athenæum 2 Apr. 461/3 The *un-Attic character of the diction of the tragic poets. 1841 Bosanquet Rights Poor Vind. 298 The sweeping and cleansing of the Augean Church, from motives the..most wholly *unaugean. 1965 G. McInnes Road to Gundagai v. 82 The larder was notable for two very *un-Australian.. gadgets. 1846 Mrs. Gore Eng. Char. (1852) 132 Certain fools cavil at Lady Consol's box at the Opera as *unbankerish and prodigal. 1804 Coleridge in Mem. Coleorton (1887) I. 56 The effect of my own *unbellerophontic countenance. 1861 W. Barnes in Macm. Mag. June 128 Where..a man's..arms are so short or *unbendsome. 1963 S. Farrar Death in Wrong Bed x. 148 You're the *unbitchiest woman I know. 1973 Country Life 18 Oct. 1210/3 This most readable and unbitchy of biographies. 1883 Q. Rev. Jan. 188 His picturesque, naïve, and *unbitter narrative. 1966 S. Smith Frog Prince 78 Touch, where the feeling is most vulnerable, *Unblameworthy. 1860 Queen Victoria Let. 6 June in R. Fulford Dearest Child (1964) 258, I like them extremely, so nice, natural, sensible, quiet and so *un-blasé. 1977 C. Wood James Bond, Spy who loved Me vii. 58 Only the most skilful and unblasé eye would be able to detect an unfamiliar outline. 1833 Fraser's Mag. VIII. 433 She is a very nice, *unbluestockingish, well-dressed..young lady. 1833 Moore Mem. (1854) VI. 343 Considering all the *un-Brahminical things he has done. 1825 Jamieson, *Onbraw,..Ugly, not handsome;..Unbecoming. 1970 Daily Tel. (Colour Suppl.) 16 Oct. 68/1 The first stages.. were remarkably easy, *unbureaucratic, and free from the famous red tape. 1936 F. R. Leavis Revaluation vii. 270 The aesthete who achieved so *un-Byronic and so un-Shelleyan a note in the contemplation of human suffering. 1959 Times Lit. Suppl. 23 Jan. 45/4 Even his forged confessions have an unbyronic slime about them. 1846 Mrs. Gore Eng. Char. (1852) 91 He should look well-fed and *uncareworn. 1934 F. Scott Fitzgerald Tender is Night ii. i. 153 His criterion of *uncerebral phrase-making was that it was American. 1971 P. Ziegler King William IV ii. 29 The Hanoverians had brought their own style of home-spun and singularly *uncharismatic monarchy to England. 1960 Guardian 6 May 10/6 Anything thicker is totally *unchic. 1975 51 Newsmagazine 12 Sept. 2/2 You'll read about New York's politics, events, labor, the chic and unchic. 1934 Webster, *Un-Chinese. 1974 Dawa Norbu Red Star over Tibet xi. 176 Norzin-la occasionally uttered the words 'San fan, shuang jian' in her un-Chinese accent before the uneducated masses. 1969 J. Fowles French Lieutenant's Woman lvii. 403 The evening that saw him so *unchipper in his place of refreshment. 1948 M. Allingham More Work for Undertaker xiv. 177 The Fuller gang..made quite a name for themselves as being remarkably *unchoosy. 1927 D. H. Lawrence Let. 12 Dec. (1962) II. 1026 The post is so tiresome here, and altogether one feels so *unchristmassy. 1982 Daily Tel. 24 Dec. 1/6 The Leader of the Opposition ..was in a most unChristmassy temper. 1826 J. Gilchrist Lecture 43 Too theoretic..for plain, *uncollegian understandings. 1888 Kipling Wee Willie Winkie (1889) 51 I'm so *uncomfy! Come and tuck me up. 1925 A. Huxley Those Barren Leaves iii. vi. 222 Such an uncomfy house! 1981 'A. Hall' Pekin Target xvii. 181 Put it under my head ..no need to be uncomfy. 1920 W. B. Yeats Michael Robartes & Dancer 3 It follows from this Latin text..that all beautiful women may Live in *uncomposite blessedness. 1968 Listener 23 May 654/3 The foreign editor charges his chief with suppressing news vital to Party comrades: his chief has rebuked him to the extent of three columns for 'the anarchy of emotions and passions that give rise to *uncomradely and irresponsible actions'. 1883 Sir H. Oakeley Bible Psalter Pref. p. v, That the extensive compass of many of them renders their melodies *uncongregational. 1929 R. Bridges Testament of Beauty iv. 184 Like as in *unconscient things where conscience came, ther is also thru'out conscient life. a1831 Bentham Univ. Gram. Wks. 1843 VIII. 357/2 Interjections may be termed the *unconstructural parts of speech. 1863 Life in South II. 196 The British Consul..was deeper than ever in the pressure of *unconsular business. 1866 N. & Q. 22 Sept. 221 A slim middle-aged man, in quaint *uncontemporary habiliments. 1851 H. D. Wolff Madrilenia (1853) 51 That timid and *uncontemptuous smile so much their characteristic. 1835–6 Todd's Cycl. Anat. I. 253/2 An *uncontractile ligamentous capsule. 1887 D. C. Murray Old Blazer's Hero x, With an eminently *unconversational aspect. 1953 W. Burroughs Junkie (1972) vi. 61 'It's better to meet alone like this.' His smile was ambiguously sexual. 'Nick is a very *un-cool guy.' Ibid. xiv. 145, I learned the new hipster vocabulary..'cool', an all-purpose word indicating anything you like or any situation that is not hot with the law. Conversely, anything you don't like is 'uncool'. 1958 G. Lea Somewhere there's Music xx. 175 Like, buy my forthcoming book on what's uncool in American education. 1960 [see daddy-o]. 1961 R. Russell Sound v. 101, I dunno, old man, to the average colored person, the average gray acts like he's in a sweat most of the time. Hungup. Uncool. 1966 Punch 30 Nov. 824 The uncool in the audience clapped heartily. The hip young watched in stony contempt. 1968 It 1–14 Nov. 16/1 The whole place [sc. Turkey]..is very very uncool. The Turks seem to be ready to turn with a malicious vengeance on young Europeans for the least (often no) provocation. 1979 Guardian 5 July 9/3 Those men who keep their cool are dragged, willy nilly, into violence not of their making and are then tarred with the same brush as their uncool brethren. 1934 Webster, *Uncooperative. 1944 J. S. Huxley On Living in Revolution xi. 114 The neighbours had at first been wholly unco-operative. 1970 Morning Star 11 May 4/4 The kindergarten teacher told me that she deals in the same way with unco-operative children. 1893 M. Beerbohm Let. 3 Dec. (1964) 82, I thought the streets would be rather *un-cosy. 1976 Times Lit. Suppl. 26 Mar. 344/2 Paris, where they knew nobody, and where their collègues de carrière were, at the outset at least, singularly uncosy. 1935 E. Bowen House in Paris ii. vii. 159 Mrs. Michaelis joined two more *un-cranky committees. 1941 Scrutiny IX. 376 Yet, if it is his weakness to seem unaware of the amount of *uncreditworthy coinage he puts into circulation, at least he knows the problems which must beset anyone who writes poetry to-day. 1960 Times 29 Feb. 14/7 Cases which the banks would consider uncredit-worthy. 1881 Blackw. Mag. Mar. 369 A ripe scholar of old-fashioned and *uncrotchety beliefs. 1817 H. T. Colebrooke Algebra, etc. 12 The first [digit] is a cube's place; and the two next *uncubic. 1946 M. Dickens Happy Prisoner vii. 122 Elizabeth..began to give Heather more help with the children, which she did on modern hospital lines, *un-cuddlesome, but extremely efficient. 1963 Punch 13 Nov. 693/1 Huge animals all around; gross, *uncuddly. 1800 Coleridge Unpubl. Lett. to Estlin (1884) 78 How I did think of your Sunday suppers, their light *uncumbrous simplicity. 1899 A. H. Japp Cuckoo iii. 162, I regard this phrase as in itself very unhappy—and, in fact, *un-Darwinian. 1955 H. Hodgkinson Doubletalk 43 'The modern theory of mutations' is regarded as un-Darwinian. 1977 D. Cory Bennett iv. 121 If he..had evolved from a mere something..to a sentient personality, then Bennett in a most un-Darwinian way gave an opposite impression. 1812 W. Tennant Anster F. iv. lxxiv, No man *undeaf could stockishly refrain. 1813 Examiner 12 Apr. 228/2 Questions..of that innoxious and *undeceptious cast. 1802–12 Bentham Ration. Judic. Evid. (1827) II. 643 Evidence being subservient to justice no otherwise than in so far as it is *undeceptitious. 1854 Geo. Eliot tr. Feuerbach's Essence Christianity viii. 84 The differentia specifica..is always in the ordinary sense inexplicable, *undeducible. 1952 Mind LXI. 267 What is unexpectable —or unpredictable or undeducible. 1862 T. W. Higginson Army Life (1870) 34, I am equable and *undepressible. 1870 Sat. Rev. 5 Feb. 194/2 The *undestructive revolution which his theory..was certain to bring about. 1879 S. C. Bartlett Egypt to Pal. xvii. 367 Various indications,.. some of which are too general, or too *undeterminal, to aid in solving the question. 1948 F. R. Leavis Great Tradition iii. 133 The *un-Dickensian subtlety—the penetrating analysis. 1982 Times 30 June 8/5 Damn un-Dickensian sentimentality. 1847 H. Bushnell Chr. Nurt. iii. (1861) 283 This unetherial and *undiffusive kind of bliss. 1940 W. Faulkner Hamlet iii. i. 173 She owns no dimension against the lambent and *undimensional grass. 1931 V. Sackville-West All Passion Spent iii. 218 He managed to be an *undisastrous Prime Minister of England during five.. difficult years. 1963 Economist 28 Dec. 1317/2 Moving.. towards undisastrous answers. 1962 Times 4 Apr. 6/5 Her sensibility inclines her to an *undoctrinaire approach. 1976 Daily Tel. 2 Dec. 18 He was sensible, un-doctrinaire, moderate—a consensus man. 1844 B. Jowett in Life Dean Lake (1901) 166 The old Bishop, like Lee, is very *undonnish. 1872 Howells Wedding Journ. (1892) 101, I speak of the *un-dressful sex alone. 1960 C. Day Lewis Burial Day vii. 140 E., despairing..of so *un-dynamic a lover..married a don. a1974 R. Crossman Diaries (1975) I. 33 Their proposals..struck me as extremely undynamic and dull. 1976 N. Postman Crazy Talk 7 What is wrong with Orwell's advice is that it is *unecological. It places language outside of any context in which it is used. 1909 Webster, *Uneconomic. 1953 Maori Affairs Act (N.Z.) 71 For the purposes of this Part of the Act, the expression 'uneconomic interest' means a beneficial freehold interest the value of which..does not exceed the sum of twenty-five pounds. 1971 'G. Black' Time for Pirates ii. 40 Vicious, totally uneconomic price cutting. 1858 Queen Victoria Let. 28 July in R. Fulford Dearest Child (1964) 125 With your.. poetical, romantic mind how can you be so *unecstatic? 1953 Essays in Criticism III. 95 A universe..forever beyond ..tomorrow's unecstatic nights at home. 1970 Irish Jurist V. 97, I have given these individuals the benefit of the doubt (if the phrase is not *unecumenical). 1845 Mrs. Carlyle in Froude Lett. & Mem. (1883) I. 338, 'I find your toast *unegoist,' said he. 1934 Webster, *Unegoistic. 1942 E. Bowen Bowen's Court x. 270 Henry was unegoistic. 1939 D. Cecil Young Melbourne i. 25 She cared for few people; but these she loved with a strong, *unegotistic affection. 1977 Gramophone Aug. 309/3, I should stress that this is a completely unegotistic performance, devoid of any mannerisms or interpretative point-making. 1932 E. Wharton in Scribner's Mag. Feb. 113/1 Like many perfectly *unegotistical women Catherine Glenn had no subject of conversation except her own affairs. 1858 Wilkinson in Rawlinson Herodotus ii. cxi. II. 182 note, The story about the women is equally *un-Egyptian. 1878 J. Payn By Proxy x, His system of morality..is singularly deficient and *unelemental. 1856 Olmsted Slave States 120 In the words of a certain *un-eminent Southern divine. 1814 Ann. Reg., Chron. 284 He had demanded the place of marshal of the admiralty, not an *unemolumentary place. c1813 Epitaph Gen. Fitzpatrick (Jod.), Through life he walk'd *unemulous of Fame. 1885 Stevenson Prince Otto iii. iv, I had no merit but a love, slavish and *unerect. 1930 V. Sackville-West Edwardians vi. 275 Morning is bleak and *unerotic. 1962 Auden Dyer's Hand (1963) 374 The personal relation was completely unerotic. 1876 Fortn. Rev. 1 Apr. 568 What is now called the etymological or historical spelling of words, is, in many cases, utterly *unetymological and un-historical. 1960 P. H. Reaney Orig. Eng. Place-Names i. 13 A similar unetymological -ham- appears in the early forms of Alphamstone, Alfelmestune 1086, Alfhampston 1318, 'Ælfhelm's farm'. 1828 E. Irving Last Days 102 The word in our text is 'not eucharistical or *uneucharistical'. 1818 Bentham Ch. Eng. Introd. 18 The one short and *unexcludible prayer excepted. 1827 Moore Hist. Irel. I. i. 5 The yet *unexcursive Greeks. 1934 Webster, *Unexotic. 1951 'J. Wyndham' Day of Triffids vi. 116 Her pleasant though unexotic countenance. 1983 Out of Town Dec. 16/3 For a haunt of Jungle Jims the BBC at Bristol is distinctly unexotic. 1802–12 Bentham Ration. Judic. Evid. (1827) IV. 599 The limited and *unextensible quantity of time allowed. 1885 W. B. Yeats in Dublin Univ. Rev. May 83/1 Peace, peace, the earth's a-quake. I hear Some barbarous, *un-faery thing draw near. 1869 'Mark Twain' Innocents Abroad ix. 87 Their *unfeline conduct in eating up all the Tetouan cats aroused a hatred toward them in the breasts of the Moors. 1930 Times Lit. Suppl. 4 Sept. 698/3 Rachel, sweet and serene, destined to be the loyal and unfeline friend. 1862 Bagehot Lit. Stud. (1879) I. 236 The whole tide of abstract discussion is quite *unfemale. 1924 Blackw. Mag. Jan. 73/2 It is only my retrograde feminine mind that will jump to these *unfeminist conclusions. 1980 M. Drabble Middle Ground 2 'I know my limitations,' said Kate. 'That's a very unfeminist remark,' said Hugo provocatively. 1873 Mrs. H. Wood Master of Greylands i, Enough to give an *unfinancial man the night-mare. 1934 Webster, *Unflamboyant. 1962 Times 12 Nov. 4/1 Camberabero..had a neat and unflamboyant partner in Laforgue. 1981 J. Johnston Christmas Tree 6 The older ladies would wear hats, neat, unflamboyant hats. 1967 Punch 29 Nov. p. x/2, *Unflashy surroundings designed to relax diners... Very good French cooking. 1979 Guardian 9 Oct. 19/8 King is a quiet, unflashy man. 1804 D. O'Connell Let. 20 Aug. (1972) I. 115, I know you are *unfond of that expedition—But if I do go I solemnly pledge myself to you that I will not put my foot in other than Capt. O'Sullivan's own boat. 1964 Punch 11 Nov. 732/2 A medley of mutually unfond nationalities. 1980 Country Life 3 July 69/4 She was not un-fond of her children, but they stood in the way of..a full working life. 1816 Coleridge Lay Serm. (Bohn) 329 The *unfoodful trees in the shadowy world of Maro. 1889 Skrine Mem. Thring 251 The subtle, tender, yielding, *un-forceful growth of tree and herb. 1871 Palgrave Lyr. Poems 78 Sigh not, if the smiling band Their *unforethoughtful brightness keep. 1840 Carlyle Heroes vi. (1904) 209 The King coming to them in the rugged *unformulistic state shall be no King. 1870 Standard 14 Dec., Till there is not a battered and *unfoul place left. 1854 C. M. Yonge Heartsease II. iii. iv. 164 In spite of clinging *unfresh muslin and shrinking figure, with the unmistakable air of high breeding. 1976 J. Colville Footprints in Time xi. 63 The unfresh air of the Central War Room. 1879 F. W. Robinson Bridge of Glass i. i, When the victim is reticent and *un-fretful. 1881 A. Knox New Playgr. xiii. 315 These *un-frisky matrons were certainly safe. 1875 Blake Zool. 26 Two principal toes, with two *unfunctional and rudimentary ones. 1967 J. Porter Chinks in Curtain vii. 68, I spun round and assumed as *unfurtive an air as possible. 1949 St. J. Ervine Craigavon ii. lix. 278 His singularly *un-Gaelic name. 1977 A. T. Q. Stewart Narrow Ground i. i. 28 The markedly un-Gaelic physical characteristics of the people now living in the Irish-speaking areas of the south and west. 1936 M. Franklin All that Swagger xxxv. 273 Laura and Humphrey, both big and *ungay, would make a fine buggy pair. 1977 Logophile iv. 9/2, I have known some very, very un-gay homosexuals, and many gay heterosexuals. 1856 Gosse Tenby v. 49 To be easily procured by the most *ungeological virtuosi. 1963 Punch 22 May 753/3 An *ungimmicky, original writer. 1977 Times 15 Feb. 8/6 It is the goblet that captures me. I love the ungimmicky, familiar and simple lines. 1934 Webster, *Unglamorous. 1960 Times 15 Jan. 16/4 Mr. David Tindle's unglamorous but sympathetically conceived 'Girl dressing'. 1810 S. Green Reformist I. 206 The *ungothic, and more modern, ménage of their master's sons. 1866 Howells Venet. Life v. 67 A certain gliding, *ungradual locomotion, altogether spectral. 1856 J. A. Symonds Let. in Life (1895) I. iii. 81, I pick up a good many words and phrases in an easy and *ungrammary way. 1856 Kane Arct. Expl. II. i. 23 A manner so *un-grandisonian that I leave a special description..to my note-book. 1967 P. Welles Babyhip (1968) viii. 73 They're so *ungroovy but we have to do it this way. 1944 C. Calloway Hepsters Dict., *Unhep, not wise to the jive, said of an icky, a Jeff, a square. 1961 L. Hughes Ask your Mama xii. 84 (heading) Liner notes for the poetically unhep. 1844 Tupper Heart ii. 15 Notwithstanding all these *unheroinals, no one..could look upon Maria without pleasure. 1864 Grosart Lambs all Safe (1865) 96 My answer here is again *unhesitant and direct. 1940 Music Makers May 37/3 *Unhip, not wise to the jive, an icky..a square. 1959 C. MacInnes Absolute Beginners 131, I climbed in the rear seat, with a fine view of their..un-hip Jermyn street hair-dos. 1968 Esquire Apr. 88/2 There is nothing more detrimental to anything hip than to have it fall into the square hands of the hopelessly unhip. 1974 H. L. Foster Ribbin', jivin', & playin' Dozens v. 180 Because the teacher may be unhip and square middle class, he has no idea that the game is being run. 1840 C. O. Müller's Hist. Lit. Greece vi. §4. 68 Yet the fundamental ideas of the Cypria are so *un-Homeric. 1931 Ld. Wodehouse in 'Marco' Introd. Polo p. v, Living in the '*unhorsey' atmosphere of ships. 1955 H. Smith Horseman through Six Reigns xvi. 163 A very un-horsy and rather ungainly lady. 1849 Herschel Ess. (1857) 626 Some *unhygrometric, non-metallic substance. 1935 N. Mitchison We have been Warned iii. 298 Tom refused to admit that there is anything *unideological about cafés. 1981 Daily Tel. 28 Nov. 12/5 To live as an ordinary, totally un-ideological private person. 1886 H. Sweet in Academy 6 Feb. 94 In spite of the *unimpartial and personal tone of his remarks. 1810 Bentham Packing (1821) 265 Its only cognoscible, determinate and *unimpostrous state. 1887 Athenæum 8 Jan. 57/2 A series of accurate, but singularly *unincisive lectures. 1839 [Mrs. Maitland] Lett. fr. Madras (1843) 275 The tracts which come from England are altogether *un-Indian, and unfit to translate. 1831 Edin. Rev. LIII. 390 Not allowed to slumber in the quiescence of an *uninfringible monopoly. 1883 Mrs. Oliphant Sheridan v. 170 Genial, not *uninnocent amusement. 1879 Expositor IX. 116 Modern editors have..treated the poem as *unintensive. **1913** Webster, *Unintrospective. **1931** *Times Lit. Suppl.* 26 Mar. 241/2 Such a straightforward lie was possible to so unintrospective an artist as Milton, but not to Donne. **1929** W. Faulkner *Sartoris* III. viii. 259 And so there was another bond between them, but *unirksome. **1938** G. Greene in *Spectator* 4 Nov. 782/2 Miss Richardson's *unironic and undetached method. **1979** L. Lerner *Love & Marriage* i. 18 Poetry like this is essentially unironic. **1934** Webster, *Unironical. **1942** *Scrutiny* X. 345 Shakespeare's power to present acceptably and movingly the unironical vision (for us given in Miranda and Ferdinand) goes with his power to contemplate the irony at the same time. **1958** O. Caroe *Pathans* i. 13 The *un-Islamic flavour of the names of the two sons of Sarbanr.. will not escape notice. **1984** *Times* 31 Mar. 4/8 Artifical methods of birth control are un-islamic. **1934** Webster, *Un-Italian. **1939** *Burlington Mag.* May. 227/2 Both of them have an un-Italian flavour. **1973** P. Evans *Bodyguard Man* iv. 36 The mainlanders.. think of the people from the islands as being un-Italian. **1931** T. H. Pear *Voice & Personality* iv. 35 The workings of the mind are.. designated in single stark letters. Their messages are *un-Jamesian and un-Proustian, but concise. **1979** F. Kermode *Genesis of Secrecy* iv. 81 This model,.. a useful way of thinking about the relation of character to narrative structure.. is a very un-Jamesian way. **1934** Webster, *Un-Japanese. **1974** *Country Life* 28 Mar. 716/1 The more convincing the make-up, the more disconcerting are un-Japanese physiques. **1962** *Economist* 15 Sept. 990/2 A majority of the *unjingoistic people in the country. **1978** Cadogan & Craig *Women & Children First* viii. 185 An honest picture of the practical, unjingoistic attitudes which characterized most RAF personnel. **1894** *Law Notes* XIII. 227/1 These remarks are uncalled for and very '*unjudgely'. **1966** A. E. Lindop *I start Counting* iv. 67 Grandad was on edge until he'd settled his mice... Aunt Lucy had been a bit *un-keen to have them. **1971** *Daily Express* 7 Dec. 1/5 Mrs. Indira Gandhi and Mrs. Golda Meir do make one feel tremendously unkeen on Women's Lib. **1983** Barr & York *Official Sloane Ranger Diary* 4/2 The Keen have to put up with the Unkeen. **1924** G. B. Stern *Tents of Israel* i. 20 For nearly fourteen years she must have been.. cooking for them *unkosher food. **1965** *Guardian* 4 Aug. 6/4 The Israeli Embassy.. had almost been faced with an Israeli parliamentary inquiry into its allegedly sinful un-kosher way of life. **1762** H. Walpole *Let. to Lady Hervey* 1 Oct., You are one of those *un-Lacedæmonian mothers. **1939** S. Spender *Still Centre* 97 In you The Caesars tamed by dying, fired again Their lives in the *unlegendary sky. **1854** Geo. Eliot tr. *Feuerbach's Essence Christianity* xxii. 215 God sees.. all locality in an *unlocal manner. **1977** Unlocal [see un-central *a.*]. **1855** Pusey *Doctr. Real Presence* i. (1869) 101 An *un-Lutheran tone of teaching. **1880** S. Lanier *Poems* (1884) 110 Bring large Lucretius, with *unmaniac mind. **1876** Trollope *Prime Minister* III. iv. 65 That coarse *un-marital and yet marital roughness. **1956** M. McCarthy *Sights & Spectacles* p. xii, The notion that abstract reasoning can crush a fact.., a wholly *un-Marxist notion, was nonetheless the principle on which most of our criticism was practiced. **1966** *Punch* 13 Apr. 524/2 His exquisite black-and-white short *Shorts*.., with its touching yet *unmawkish dwelling upon the hemline. **1802–12** Bentham *Ration. Judic. Evid.* (1827) I. 159 That self-criminative consciousness.. which distinguishes it from *unmendacious falsehood. **1852** *Meanderings Mem.* I. 15 A thing *unmental, mannerless and crude. **1966** *Guardian* 10 Oct. 16/8 The present pattern is in many ways strikingly *unmeritocratic. **1849** E. W. Benson in *Life* (1899) I. iv. 80 The *unmilitant part of the Church. **1839** J. Sterling *Ess.*, etc. (1848) I. 310 Compare.. a missionary Swartz with an *un-missionary Lord Clive or Hyder Ali. **1847** Ld. Cockburn *Jrnl.* (1874) II. 172 A mendicant peer is very *unmonarchical. **1874** Hazlitt *Mary & C. Lamb* 15 The sentence seemed *un-motto-ish. *a* **1851** Moir *Poems* (1852) II. 130 Before her stood the household wheel *unmurmurous, and the thread Still in her fingers lay. **1861** [Mrs. Penny] *Romance Dull Life* xl. 295 An *unnervous nature, blessed with social effrontery. **1938** D. Jones *Let.* 15 Feb. in R. Hague *Dai Greatcoat* (1980) ii. 85 The *only* time of day when I feel more or less *un-neurotic.. is after dinner. **1980** S. Brett *Dead Side of Mike* x. 113 A very balanced and unneurotic personality. **1818** J. Brown *Psyche* 137 In honesty, the *unnew notion Of giving Psyche loco-motion, Is traceable to merry Prior. **1880** Freeman in *Contemp. Rev.* June 971 The present *unnormal state of Thessaly, and.. the causes which made it unnormal. **1887** Saintsbury *Hist. Elizab. Lit.* (1894) 366 His stepmother appears to have been most *unnovercal. **1850** S. Dobell *Roman* vii, The *unoblivious sun hath paused not once; Our time is far spent. *a* **1861** Clough *Poems*, etc. (1869) I. 333 Have we anything that will.. be as bright and *un-obsolete a hundred and fifty years hence? **1856** Bagehot in *National Rev.* Oct. 365 If Miss Westbrook had married.. a gentleman, suppose, in the tallow line.. her society would have been a gentle relief from *unodoriferous pursuits. **1862** Mrs. H. Wood *Mrs. Hallib.* (1864) III. xxiv. 461 Hovey Fair used to be an unsightly and unodoriferous place. **1823** R. H. Froude *Let.* 12 Aug. in G. Battiscombe *John Keble* (1963) iv. 75 Keble.. is neither positive on this subject nor *un-open to conviction on any. **1981** 'A. Cross' *Death in Faculty* v. 47 The few older men.. were so stuffy, so unopen to any views but their own. **1885** *Pall Mall G.* 30 June 5/2 The popular, terse, and *unornate style. **1916** J. Buchan *Greenmantle* iii. 30 He got a brussels-sprout in the eye, at which.. he swore in a very *unpacifist style. **1976** S. Hynes *Auden Generation* vii. 195 The book is pacificist propaganda.., but the position he takes is an oddly belligerent and un-pacifist one. **1826** G. S. Faber *Diffic. Romanism* (1853) p. lxii, An *unpaginal reference to a pamphlet which he had published. **1860** Poynting *Glimpses Heaven* Introd. p. xxi, The conception of God here presented is intensely *unpantheistic. **1844** J. T. Hewlett *Parsons & W.* xix, Added to all these *unpapaverous influences. **1854** Ferrier *Inst. Metaph.* 444 A clear, detached,.. genuine, or *un-parasitical Being. **1868** Dickens *Lett.* 23 Jan., A clever, *unparsonic, and straightforward man. **1876** Bernstein *Five Senses* 282 Noise is produced by irregular, *un-periodical movements of those bodies which convey sound. **1871** Earle *Philol. Eng. Tongue* 385 It would be *un-philological to let them be absorbed into any class of words whatever. **1965** W. S. Allen *Vox Latina* i. 15 Such a complication.. is '*unphonemic'. **1974** D. G. Scragg *Hist. Eng. Spelling* iv. 61 Mulcaster.. was frequently forced to compromise his endeavour to be guided by sound because what he calls custom favoured a flagrantly unphonemic spelling. **1959** *News Chron.* 19 Aug. 4/3 'I'm no intellectual,' he says with *unphoney modesty. **1973** *Publishers' Weekly* 26 Mar. 61/3 Individually these British lads (and lass) are enjoyably unphony. **1982** *Listener* 11 Feb. 27/3 Let our final words honour the exceptionally unphoney—the first performance of Edward Cowie's.. Concerto for orchestra. **1934** C. Lambert *Music Ho!* iv. 244 The present vogue for mechanical realism.. is bound to disappear.. as the Turneresque steam engine gives way to the *unphotogenic electric train. **1977** R. Lacey *Majesty* 14 She is actually quite small.. and.. really rather unphotogenic. **1749** J. Cleland *Mem. Woman Pleasure* II. 219 Our acquaintance.. innocent, at first.. changed nature, and ran into *unplatonic lengths. **1866** J. S. Mill in *Edin. Rev.* CXXIII. 340 The answer of the Xenophontic Sokrates to the question of Hippias is very un-Platonic. **1875** Jowett *Plato* (ed. 2) I. p. xxi, Respecting the un-Platonic character of the Laws. **1882** Morris in Mackail *Life* (1899) II. 74 The surroundings of life are so stern and *unplayful. **1934** Webster, *Unpolemical. **1936** *Mind* XLV. 397 Philosophy, according to Jaspers, is 'un-polemical'. **1965** *Times Lit. Suppl.* 25 Nov. 1079/2 There is evidence of good, unpolemical work being done. **1936** 'M. Innes' *Death at President's Lodging* ix. 164 Appleby had brought out his notebook—not without a certain diffidence over the remains of the Dean's elegant and *un-policemanly luncheon. **1980** P. G. Winslow *Counsellor Heart* xi. 148 Manning.. sitting quietly at his desk, might have been an accountant. For once his unpolicemanly appearance did not amuse Capricorn. **1865** Mill *Comte* 80 Political economy.. he deems unscientific, *unpositive, and a mere branch of metaphysics. **1868** H. Bushnell *Serm. Living Subj.* 17 She is a person too unpositive.. to be affirmatively capable of anything. **1968** 'D. Halliday' *Photogenic Soprano* xiv. 160 All the sordid and *un-prestigious details of your warm friendship with Kenneth. **1980** *Word* 1979 XXX. 197 Speakers of unprestigious urban dialects were sharply disadvantaged in education and employment. **1933** H. Walpole *Vanessa* III. 484 She learnt now to be patient, tolerant and *unpriggish. **1969** J. Clarke *Foxon's Hole* xxii. 133 Roger really was feeling rebellious, and Gawaine.. found it much easier to tell this new, unpriggish Roger.. about Mick. **1871** *Sat. Rev.* 4 Feb. 137/1 Prim English matrons, and Yankee girls of a very *unprim type indeed. **1974** P. Gzowski *Bk. about this Country* 190 I'd.. have to become what I call an *unprivate person in relation to social issues. **1882** *Athenæum* 11 Nov. 631/3 A family hitherto remarkable for its *unproliferous nature. **1931** *Un-Proustian [see *un-Jamesian* above]. **1981** *Times* 2 Mar. 6/2 Scott Moncrieff's unProustian style. **1934** Webster, *Unpugnacious. **1962** Auden *Dyer's Hand* (1963) 305 As creatures go, he [*sc.* the ant-eater] is unpugnacious. **1981** *Daily Tel.* 18 July 28/3 He fought an uncomplicated, unpugnacious and honest campaign. **1968** *Earth & Planetary Sci. Lett.* V. 220/1 Hamilton invoked the melting of Lewisian rocks to account for the *unradiogenic leads in the Skye acid rocks. **1858** H. Bushnell *Nat. & Supernatural* iii. (1864) 66 The immense array of mythologic and formally *unrational religions. **1864** Grosart *Lambs all Safe* (1865) 83 Wishing to be as brief, and.. *unrepetitive as possible. **1949** St. J. Ervine *Craigavon* II. lxvi. 296 Whose *unresilient and unimaginative mind. **1963** *Times* 17 May 7/2 (Advt.), They took an ordinary piece of hard, unresilient plastic and 'let the air in'. **1976** *Gramophone* Mar. 1499/1 The music is steam-rollered into a kind of impersonal uniformity, its lines unphrased, its rhythms unresilient, and the subtle interaction of words and notes quite lost. **1881** H. James *Portr. Lady* lv, Whose footfall, on the *unresonant turf,.. she had not heard. **1858** H. Bushnell *New Life* (1860) 229 The respectable sin.. shades into the *unrespectable. **1888** Bryce *Amer. Commw.* II. II. xliii. 121 The criticisms of a very *unreticent press. *Ibid.* III. IV. lxxx. 55 Religion apart, they are an *unreverential people. I do not mean irreverent. **1974** Moore & Parry *Twentieth-Cent. Russ. Lit.* ii. 22 His *unrevolutionary deed in surrendering to despair and killing himself. **1909** 'Mark Twain' *Is Shakes. Dead?* 13 When an *unrisky opportunity offered.. and he was feeling good, I showed it to him. **1934** Webster, *Unroadworthy. **1955** *Times* 20 Aug. 5/1 The cars hired by correspondents to take them to the frontier were unroadworthy. **1978** N. Freeling *Night Lords* xxxii. 147 Being suddenly told your home is unhygienic and your car unroadworthy. **1864** Spencer *Illustr. Progr.* 437 Out amid the fields, a formal house.. strikes us as *unrural. **1919** tr. *Turgenev's Smoke* x. 73 A dandified air utterly *un-Russian. **1976** W. Greatorex *Crossover* 159 She took in the flared tartan trousers... He looked so un-Russian she laughed. **1879** C. Geikie *Eng. Reform.* xxiv. 428 [The Prayer Book] was made more thoroughly *unsacramentarian than it has ever been since. **1886** *Athenæum* 23 Oct. 528/2 The *unsacrificial nature of Buddhist worship. **1835** *Chamb. Jrnl.* 25 July 205 Now how little chance is there of all these being effected *un-sanguineously. **1926** G. Frankau *My Unsentimental Journey* xiii. 178 And so away from Denver by this route which seems not so *unscenic. **1978** J. Updike *Coup* (1979) vi. 219 His trip down from the Massif, by the unscenic highway. **1842** G. S. Faber *Prov. Lett.* (1844) II. 119 The cheap penalty of his *unschismatical independence. **1883** *Athenæum* 27 Jan. 128/2 Some of his sculptures are very effective, but *unsculptural. **1791** E. Inchbald *Simple Story* I. ii. 12 Nor upon that event did he think it necessary.. to fly the roof of two such *unseductive innocent females as Mrs. Horton and her niece. **1937** M. Borden *Black Virgin* ii. 26 He looked at.. her neat unseductive clothes and thanked God she was like that. **1934** Webster, *Unselective. **1956** *Nature* 10 Mar. 489/1 Government shooters co-operated in recording results of unselective shooting [of red deer] to make these data available. **1968** *Punch* 24 Jan. 105/2 Flat-rate, unselective welfare was possible when the vast majority of people were earning poor wages and when taxation was relatively light. **1933** L. Bloomfield *Language* x. 158 The situations of the several speakers contain some common features, and.. the differences between these situations are irrelevant (*unsemantic). **1968** *N.Y. Times* 21 Feb. 56/1 His barrage of blithely unsemantic bombast sweeps you up in such phraseology as 'the political hue that blightens the eye' and the oracular 'protocol takes precedence over procedure'. **1837** Carlyle *Fr. Rev.* III. III. iii, Marat.. is heard to articulate these most *un-senatorial ejaculations. **1886** H. Tennyson *Jack & Bean Stalk* 11 Oh! what a cramp'd-up, small, *unsesquipedalian object! **1959** *News Chron.* 25 Aug. 6/6 He thought the most *unsexy things a woman could wear were trousers, boat necklines, and high-heeled shoes. **1973** M. Amis *Rachel Papers* 193, I would get.. a kind of hollow pressure at the back of my throat (.. not unsexy) which nevertheless I had to lose, and the only way to lose it was to go on coughing. **1936** *Un-Shelleyan [see *un-Byronic* above]. **1865** *Cornh. Mag.* Mar. 299 His kindly, unpretentious, but not *unshrewd, talk. **1865** D. W. Thompson *Odds & Ends* iii. 26 In our ordinary *unsilentious services. **1880** A. Raleigh *Way to the City* 266 To be unworldly is to be unsordid, *unslippery, unselfish. **1887** E. Johnson *Antiqua Mater* 251 Your *unslothful love unto the glory of God. **1797** *Monthly Mag.* III. 516 The cause.. of unwearied power, and of *unsluggish energy. **1896** 'M. Rutherford' *Clara Hopgood* iv. 41 His *unsnobbish, deferential behaviour.. showed that he understood who they were and that the little house made no difference to him. **1959** G. D. Painter *Proust* I. vii. 100 She was unmusical, non-political, and in the social sense unsnobbish. **1821** *Monthly Mag.* LI. 12 The Romans appear to have had a strange propensity to the harsh and *unsonorous letters j and s. **1871** Morris in Mackail *Life* (1899) I. 237 Things pushing up through the clean *unsooty soil. **1934** Webster, *Unsorry. **1963** J. Fowles *Collector* II. 195 I'm not really sorry. But I'm not absolutely unsorry. **1973** 'G. Butler' *Coffin for Pandora* viii. 163 Alice had departed.., not unsorry, I thought, to get away. **1862** T. W. Higginson *Army Life* (1870) 9 Something so *un-Southern, the camp of a regiment of black slaves. **1846** R. Ford *Gatherings from Spain* xxiii. 330 Some muscular.. performer.. screams forth his couplets.. to the imminent danger of his own trachea, and of all *un-Spanish acoustic organs. **1959** H. Thomas *Establishment* 15 Spain, where for four hundred years any idea.. which had not existed in the golden sixteenth century has been automatically frowned upon as 'Un-Spanish'. **1970** T. Hilton *Pre-Raphaelites* v. 151 Here is a dull day, *unspecial, cold and leaden, and yet a momentous day for those people who are leaving home. **1983** *Woman's Weekly* 8 Jan. 18/1 Anna, feeling very un-special indeed, agreed.. that there was no point in looking back. **1808** Wilford *Sacr. Isles* in *Asiat. Res.* VIII. 247 The first impression, originating from no *un-specious reasons. **1926** *Public Opinion* 30 Apr. 433/3 An *unspectacular honesty and a certain literary sobriety.. mark this novel. **1977** M. V. Brian *Ants* 11 Most of the species have wide temperate Eurasian distributions and, though unspectacular compared with some tropical types, play an important part in terrestrial ecosystems. **1674** N. Fairfax *Bulk & Selv.* 129 So the seeds.. when sown become barren or *unsproutful. **1968** R. Marett *Through Back Door* iv. 37 The bluff, nautical and *unstarchy Chief Press Censor. **1934** Webster, *Unsterile. **1953** R. Lehmann *Echoing Grove* 29 But still the stones seemed rocked, the unsterile mounds, reimpregnated, exhaled dust's fever; a breath, impure, of earthbound anguish. **1977** *Lancet* 26 Mar. 688/1 Unsterile cystoscopes have been in use for years. *c* **1873** V. Montagu *Let.* in G. Battiscombe *Queen Alexandra* (1969) ix. 127 It is very jolly here indeed,.. very *unstiff and only a certain amount of etiquette. **1958** J. Pope-Hennessy in *Lonely Business* (1981) III. 248 They said above all she.. was 'such a *darling*'—such fun—so unstiff. **1881** Dowden in *Academy* 8 Jan. 21 An *unstrenuous mood of lingering delight. **1929** D. H. Lawrence *Pansies* 117 Space, of course, is alive. That's why it moves about; and that's what makes it eternally spacious and *unstuffy. **1974** K. Clark *Another Part of Wood* vi. 220 To be one of Lady Cunard's regular guests was to have reached somewhere very near the top of unstuffy, new world society. *a* **1861** D. Gray *Poet. Wks.* (1874) 48 The *unsubvertive temple of the soul! **1865** Carlyle *Fredk. Gt.* XVIII. v, Next evening.. Prince of Prussia strikes his tents again; rolls-off in very *unsuccinct condition. **1830** Disraeli in Monypenny *Life* (1910) I. ix. 161 The dry, round, *unsugary fig is a great whetter. **1873** Miss Broughton *Nancy* III. 11 He shall see how patient I am! how *unsulky! **1933** H. Walpole *Vanessa* II. 414 Will's love for [his master] Adam had been.. protective, selfless, and also gay, simple, *unsycophantic, man to man. **1964** *Punch* 23 Sept. p. xv, Cockney writers.. are refreshingly unsycophantic. **1878** H. G. Guinness *Approaching End of Age* (1881) 129 The Apocalypse.. translated into *unsymbolic language. **1909** Webster, *Unsymmetric. **1957** L. Fox *Numerical Solution Two-Point Boundary Probl.* iv. 103 In this case we would have to use some unsymmetric formula involving only internal points. **1809** *Med. Jrnl.* XXI. 207 Judgment weaker; memory *untenacious. **1935** J. Laird *Enquiry into Moral Notions* 10 In my view the times are propitious for attempting an *untendentious comparison of ethical ideas.. with equity and.. patience. **1962** *Times* 5 Dec. 17/6 (*heading*) Untendentious story of the Berlin Wall. **1934** Webster, *Untense. **1959** *Punch* 25 Feb. 277/2 To become untense you must relax. **1974** *Times Lit. Suppl.* 8 Nov. 1248/4 A melodrama in a curiously untense key. **1880** Goldw. Smith in *Atlantic Monthly* No. 268. 210 *Untheistic science can take cognizance of nothing but facts. **1961** *Lancet* 2 Sept. 549/1, I.. support your editorial.. questioning the value of euthanasia... Justification for such *untherapeutic therapy can rest only on a total lack of understanding of the nature.. of Man. **1978** *Sci. Amer.* Feb. 50/2 Untherapeutic though many nursing homes are, living conditions in most of them are at least tolerable. **1906** Kipling *Puck of Pook's Hill* 6 They sat down in the *unthistly centre of the Ring. **1953** Auden in R. Humphries *New Poems by Amer. Poets* 7 The water-scorpion finds it quite *unticklish. **1858** E. W. L. Davies *Algiers* i. 5 The *untidal character of the sea. **1674** N. Fairfax *Bulk & Selv.* 40 'Tis hoped we may have leave to settle Gods whole Everlastingness, as *untimesom. **1969** Fabian & Byrne *Groupie* xxix. 206 As a group they are something else, but off-stage they're pretty *untogether, and they need someone like me to get them to the top. **1976** Untogether [see staggeringly *adv.*]. **1962** *Harper's Bazaar* Aug. 57/3 Basutoland is for the sophisticated traveller seeking the *untouristy. **1979** *Homes & Gardens* June 23/2 Today more visitors bring their cars and instead of making an automatic beeline for London they venture into the most remote and 'untouristy' localities. **1934** Webster, *Untraditional. **1958** *Times* 16 Dec. 11/1 We await the rest of the season with untraditional excitement. **1971** 'E. Ferrars' *Stranger & Afraid* xii. 187 The understanding that the university should be one of the new ones and as untraditional as possible. **1815** Mar. Edgeworth *Patronage* xxviii, The language of fine feeling is absolutely untranslateable, *untransfusible. **1968** *Guardian* 26 Sept. 8/5 A BBC man, worried that Priestley might be too *un-trendy for the 'Wednesday Play'. **1978** *Times* 4 Sept. 13/2 My untrendy and doubtless outdated opinions about the high seriousness of political debate. **1867** H. BUSHNELL *Mor. Uses Dark Th.* 202 This most *untropical institution we call home. **1811** SPENCER *Poems* 65 Love's yet *untruant pinions. **1934** WEBSTER, *Unurgent. **1939** C. DAY LEWIS *Child of Misfortune* II. iv. 212 There was something intimate yet unurgent in the touch. **1949** *New Yorker* 18 June 24/2 The mist incorporates the pulse, rapid but unurgent, of a motorboat. **1907** H. RASHDALL *Theory of Good & Evil* I. vi. 158 Such an obviously *unutilitarian precept as that which condemns cannibalism. **1955** S. SPENDER *Making of Poem* i. 16 Architecture.. expresses the tension of the aesthetic against the useful. At the other extreme, music is completely unutilitarian. **1824** in *Spirit Pub. Jrnls.* (1825) 303 Milton, ..in a very *un-uxorious spirit, calls a wife—'A thorn intestine,.. A cleaving mischief'. **1858** G. H. LEWES *Sea-Side Stud.* 223 He is, with all his learning, quite as *unveridical as Giulia Grisi. **1859** HAMLEY in Shand *Life* (1895) I. vi. 127 At present I am a kind of clean and *unverminous lazzarone. **1931** *Times Lit. Suppl.* 7 May 360/3 Courses which are ultimately impolitic though not formally '*unviable'. **1964** G. WHEELER *Mod. Hist. Soviet Central Asia* 234 The steady proliferation of independent although economically unviable states. **1982** M. WALLACE *Brit. Govt. Northern Ireland* i. 18 The Irish negotiators.. had clearly felt that a commission would so reduce the area of Northern Ireland that it would become unviable. **1916** L. STRACHEY *Let.* 25 Feb. in *Virginia Woolf & Lytton Strachey* (1956) 56 Oh, it's very, very *unvictorian! **1981** F. INGLIS *Promise of Happiness* v. 144 Ideal parents.. so un-Victorian but also so excellently authoritative. **1866** BLACKMORE *Cradock Nowell* xxiv, To tell the plain, *unvinous truth. **1934** WEBSTER, *Unviolent. **1963** *Listener* 3 Oct. 522/3 Even his rhetorical phrases.. came out with a lack of ferocity which has great charm for people enamoured of unviolent politicians. **1980** U. CURTISS *Poisoned Orchard* x. 100 That tranquil, unviolent setting. **1931** V. WOOLF *Waves* 168, I may find something *unvisual beneath [the mind's eye]. **1943** H. READ *Education through Art* 147 This leaves two of our categories un-accounted for, the expressionist and the decorative, but a little consideration will show that one of these is *a priori* excluded from Bullough's apperceptive types, because it is essentially un-visual. **1869** RUSKIN *Q. of Air* (1874) 168 The swallow, in that noisy, but modestly upside-down Babel of hers under the eaves, with its *unvolcanic slime of mortar. **1668** WILKINS *Real Char.* III. vii. 341 A person insolutive.. is a Bankrupt; *Vnwalkative, is a Cripple. **1889** STEVENSON *Master Ballantrae* ix, About the top of it ran considerable bulwarks, which made the ship *unweatherly. **1903** *Lippincott's Monthly Mag.* Aug. 230 To tell the truth, Barrett's calm philosophy irritated her not a little. It was painfully *un-Western. **1981** G. MACBETH *Kind of Treason* xii. 116 The Japanese were traditionally un-Western in their attitude to declarations of war. **1965** K. AMIS *James Bond Dossier* ix. 88 These days there are few things more *un-with-it than feeling.. the slightest anti-American sentiment. **1977** *Grimsby Even. Tel.* 5 May 8/3 There is only one word for them, a word so passé, fuddy-duddy and un-with-it that one blushes to use it. **1882** *Macm. Mag.* XLVI. 213/1 His method of describing its inhabitants is.. *un-Wordsworthian. **1959** *Economist* 23 May 716/2 The importation or maintenance of party ardours.. must seem singularly *un-worthwhile. **1974** *Nature* 19 Apr. 715/3 Contributions so speculative as to make such an effort unworthwhile. **1925** 'H. H. RICHARDSON' *Way Home* III. v. 281 Emmy with the hard and *unyoung look her face assumed when she spoke of her stepmother. **1972** *National Observer* (U.S.) 27 May 12/1 An unyoung 'youth' leader travels about the country urging audiences to 'kill your parents'.

b. The use of *un-* with adjs. in *-able*, beginning in the 14th cent. (see 4 above), soon became common, and gave rise to a large number of formations in the 16th and subsequent centuries. In the modern period the examples become too numerous for illustration; in addition to those entered as main words, those given below will serve as specimens of the freedom with which new formations are created. These are sometimes due to an antithesis of the form 'not only.. but', as 'not only unpainted but unpaintable'. The unusual types *uncome-at-able* (1694–), *unget-at-able* (1862–) are later in date than the corresponding positive terms; for illustrations of similar forms see (*b*).

Cotgrave (1611) has *unaboardable, unaccompanable, unaccostable, uncorruptable, undisplayable, unendable, unexceedable, unexpressable, unexterminable*, etc. Florio (1611) has *unaccommodable, uncolourable, uncompassionable, unsuccourable, untrafficable, unwadable*, and Hexham (1648) *unbesteadable, unbindable, unlabourable*. Ash (1775) introduces about twenty-five new forms, as *unadmittable, unappropriable, uncreditable, unexhalable, unexterminable*. An extreme instance is *un-in-one-breath-utterable* (B. Jonson *Ev. Man in Hum.* I. v.).

Recent formations include: (*a*) ***unactionable, unarrangeable, unbackable, unbilletable, unbiodegradable, unblinkable, unbroadcastable, unbudgeable, unbuggable, unbuildable, uncapturable, uncashable, unclaimable, unclearable, uncollectable, uncondonable, unconfessable, unconfusable, unconsortable, uncontactable, uncopyrightable, uncounterfeitable, uncrackable, undeflectable, undevelopable, undeviable*** [DEVIABLE *a.*], ***undiagnosable, undisseverable, undownable, undreamable*** (also *absol.*), ***unexorcizable, unexperienceable, unexploitable, unfak***(e)***able, unfalsifiable, unfaultable, unfilmable*** (also *absol.*), ***unfulfillable, unidentifiable, unignorable, uninterruptable, unjammable, unkinkable, unkissable*** (also *absol.*), ***unmanœuvrable, unmeltable, unoccupiable, unpatentable, unplaceable, unplumbable, unpoliceable*** (also *absol.*), ***unquantifiable*** (also *absol.*), ***unrecapturable, unregenerable, unrejectable, unreviewable, unruffl***(e)***able, unsayable*** (also *absol.*), ***unshar***(e)***able, unshockable, unskiable, unsmoothable, unsplinterable, unsplittable, unsquashable, unstageable, unstat***(e)***able, unstressable, unswallowable, untappable, untestable, untippable, untransmittable, unverbalizable, unvintageable, unweighable, unwettable, unwipeable, unwithstandable***; (*b*) ***unputdownable, unswitchoffable, unwearoutable***.

(*a*) **1952** *Federal Suppl.* (U.S.) CVI. 1019/1 All this might still be *unactionable but for the fact that [etc.]. **1980** *Times* 16 Nov. 3/1 The case was dismissed by the High Court in London in preliminary proceedings as 'un-actionable in English law'. **1821** *Blackw. Mag.* X. 525 An *unarrangeable mass of contraries and shades of difference. **1982** *Book Collector* Winter 457 Vivaldi was virtually un-arrangeable. **1928** *Daily Express* 2 Aug. 13/1 Zahrat.. walked away from three moderate rivals in the Alexandra Handicap. She was ..*unbackable, odds of nine to two having to be laid on. **1973** *Nation Rev.* (Melbourne) 24–30 Aug. 1418/3 Who's Who was literally unbackable on form and treble figure odds ought to have been obtainable. **1831** *Blackw. Mag.* XXX. 105 His picture swam in lustre *unbedimmable by the mist of years. **1940** *Daily Mirror* 17 Dec. 2/2 My wife was asked to give temporary lodging to some young girls who were described by the authorities as *unbilletable. **1977** *Water SA* (S. Afr.) Jan. 18/1 The influent TKN [*sc.* Total Kjeldahl Nitrogen] is split into three fractions (i) an *unbiodegradable fraction [etc.]. **1978** D. BLOODWORTH *Crosstalk* xxxi. 239 An imitation crocodile handbag in some unbiodegradable plastic. **1936** *Times Lit. Suppl.* 31 Oct. 884/4 A stark *unblinkable picture of life as it is being lived somewhere to-day. **1966** *Guardian* 28 Dec. 7/2 There is, finally, the unblinkable fact that the [U.S.] Cabinet is weary. **1834** *Tait's Mag.* I. 439/2 The mighty treasures laid up unbonded and *un-bondable within the teeming womb of Nature. **1975** *Listener* 6 Feb. 163/1 The interview was quite *unbroadcastable, due.. to the Venerable brother's imperfect English. **1936** L. C. DOUGLAS *White Banners* iv. 73 'Now that's where you're wrong, Marcia.' Paul was kind, but *unbudgeable. **1981** *Time* 7 Dec. 74/2 It is an almost unbudgeable popular belief.. that cats and dogs have an instinctive rivalry. **1979** R. CASSILIS *Arrow of God* II. vi. 33 The Service's beautiful new, and allegedly *unbuggable headquarters. **1956** R. A. HEINLEIN *Door into Summer* v. 82 Take the great Leonardo da Vinci, so far out of his time that his most brilliant concepts were utterly *un-buildable. **1887** *Pall Mall G.* 15 Oct. 4/1 Land in London is almost *unbuyable. **1851** H. MELVILLE *Moby Dick* II. xxxix. 274 The only spout in sight was that of a Fin-Back, belonging to the species of *uncapturable whales, because of its incredible power of swimming. **1925** *Glasgow Herald* 7 Feb. 4 In the translation something elusive and.. un-capturable has vanished. **1832** CHALMERS *Pol. Econ.* vi. 206 Food, speaking generally, is far more bulky and *uncarriageable than workmanship. **1906** 'MARK TWAIN' *Autobiogr.* (1924) II. 288, I don't know what Dick got, but it was probably only *un-cashable promises. **1978** *Daily Tel.* 28 Oct. 1/4 The £100,000 cheque handed to Korchnoi as defeated finalist in the World Chess Championship is uncashable until he signs a declaration that he has lost the title. **1884** *Sat. Rev.* 29 Nov. 16 They [groups of boroughs] are almost *uncaucusable. **1866** RUSKIN *Crown Wild Olive* (1873) 60 They are as the *uncharmable serpent. **1881** R. G. WHITE *England* 363 A dismal, cheerless, *uncheerable dankness. **1817** W. KITCHENER *Apicius Rediv.* (1822) 77 Till they are trapped to buy some *unchewable old poultry. **1884** W. JAMES in *unitarian Rev.* XXII. 205 Whether the world be the better or the worse for having either chances or gifts in it will depend altogether on *what* these uncertain and *unclaimable things turn out to be. **1955** *Bull. Atomic Sci.* Apr. 146/3 Most unfortunate is the cleared scientist who marries into an *unclearable family. **1984** *Sunday Express Mag.* 26 Feb. 28/1 The RE major.. has abandoned whole fields and beaches as 'unclearable'. **1884** *Punch* 30 Aug. 101/1 He is such an obstinately *uncoaxable man. **1927** *Glasgow Herald* 18 July 10 They had huge outstanding accounts up country, which were *uncollectable. **1981** *Sunday Tel.* 26 July 19/6 Some £12 million that is now officially designated as 'almost uncollectable'. **1861** VAN EVRIE *Negroes* 100 The negress.. with her short, stiff, *uncombable fleece of seeming wool. **1802–12** BENTHAM *Ration. Judic. Evid.* (1827) III. 564 An uncompleted and perhaps *uncompletable sentence. *Ibid.* V. 290 A suit.. carried on upon unpremeditatable, *unconcertable, cross-examined evidence. **1935** W. DE LA MARE *Early One Morning* 136 Hatred of elderly and yet not wholly *uncondonable cant. **1919** C. B. JORDAN tr. *Ibañez's Four Horsemen of Apoc.* I. v. 143 The infallible remedy for the most *unconfessable of diseases. **1967** P. WHITE in *Coast to Coast 1965–6* 232 He lied smiling, ashamed.. of his.. unconfessable experience. **1840** ALISON *Hist. Eur.* (1859) VIII. 670 *Unconfrontable excitement among the people. **1934** WEBSTER, *unconfusable. **1935** W. DE LA MARE *Early One Morning* 533 Each is in accord with its writer's after-work and unconfusable with the work of any other poet. **1873** *Contemp. Rev.* XXII. 835 The desperate determination to conserve the *unconservable. **1907** JOYCE *Chamber Music* xxi, He who hath glory lost, nor hath Found any soul to follow his... That high *unconsortable one. **1976** *Daily Tel.* 26 Oct. 1/6 The 3,500-ton Swiftsure class hunter-killer vessel is said to be '*uncontactable' beneath the Arctic ice-pack at the North Pole. **1865** D. W. THOMPSON *Odds & Ends* iii. 5 We are *uncontentable hangerels. **1845** STOCQUELER *Handbk. Brit. India* (1854) 114 The grounding of the adventurer in this description of *unconveyable knowledge. **1884** *Pop. Sci. Monthly* Apr. 774 These volatile oils, when heated,.. are *uncookable. **1926** WHITEMAN & MCBRIDE *Jazz* viii. 178 The earliest jazz was found *uncopyrightable by certain judges. **1982** *Amer. Speech* LVII. 308 It seems possible that other dictionary makers may well have adopted this simple method of protecting their essentially uncopyrightable labors. **1912** E. POUND in *Poetry Rev.* Feb. 73 A man's rhythm must be interpretative, it will be, therefore, in the end, his own, uncounterfeiting, *uncounterfeitable. **1932** *Blue Book Mag.* Sept. 12/1 He owned that uncounterfeitable trait which goes with what we call good birth. **1959** 'B. MATHER' *Achilles Affair* I. ii. 21 The code we were using was as near to *uncrackable as any code can be. **1875** HELPS *Soc. Pressure* ii. 24 It is almost *undealable with. **1954** W. FAULKNER *Fable* 263 The forsaken.. betrothed pursuing, ..*undeflectable. *a* **1866** J. GROTE *Moral Ideals* (1876) xv. 371 The other kind of knowledge lies at the base.., insoluble and *undevelopable. **1878** ABNEY *Photogr.* xxxiv. 274 The image becomes undevelopable. **1929** S. LESLIE *Anglo-Catholic* xiv. 199 This continuity stretching back beyond modern history, undeviating and *un-deviable. **1951** W. FAULKNER *Requiem for Nun* II. 210 Who am I.. to set the puny appanage of my office in the balance against that simple undeviable aim? **1926** *Jrnl. Amer. Med. Assoc.* 20 Nov. 1721/2 Some intangible,.. *undiagnosable sinus disease. **1978** R. BANNISTER *Brain's Clinical Neurol.* (ed. 5) p. iii, Disorders either undiagnosable or untreatable or both. **1811** MISS L. M. HAWKINS *C'tess & Gertr.* 364 By the natural and *undiscardable stratagem of her nature. **1834** *Blackw. Mag.* XXXV. 419 Sheer, downright,.. and *undislodgeable obstinacy. **1897** H. JAMES *Spoils of Poynton* xiii. 152 Mona was *undisseverable from her prey. **1884** GOLDW. SMITH in *Contemp. Rev.* Apr. 527 The ruler is an *undomicilable alien. **1957** *Sci. Amer.* Apr. 50/2 The *undownable question remained: Why were tau and theta [particles] exactly alike in every respect except this one? **1978** J. UPDIKE *Coup* (1979) vi. 224 His motionlessness a mask for his suffocating struggle with the resurging, undownable fact of Sheba's absence. **1864** F. W. ROBINSON *Mattie* I. 141 The driest, hardest, and most *undrawable of cigars. **1906** W. DE LA MARE *Poems* 81 In its future loomed the *undreamable. **1957** L. MACNEICE *Visitations* 53 When the undreamable Dream comes clearer. **1884** E. ABBOTT *Flatland* 86 Remaining henceforth thy docile pupil, thy *unemancipable slave. **1876** M. COLLINS *From Midn. to Midn.* II. ii. 250, I have had.. the most labyrinthine and *unentangleable nightmares. **1922** *Blackw. Mag.* June 800/2 Because of those *unexorcisable.. Oriental ancestors of his, nothing will ever bring him to regard the game [*sc.* golf].. with the laconic reverence that a Scotsman.. expects. **1879** H. W. WARREN *Recr. Astron.* xii. 261 But nature sustained by *unexpendable forces must abide. **1909** W. JAMES *Meaning of Truth* p. xii, Things of an *unexperienceable nature may exist ad libitum, but they form no part of the material for philosophic debate. **1976** *Word 1971* XXVII. 130 If grammar is 'autonomous and independent of meaning', then it is unexperienceable in the surface structure of sentences—therefore unlearnable, and therefore innate. **1923** *Blackw. Mag.* Sept. 398/1 A rich spring of natural oil, as yet unexploited, and perhaps, on account of the climate and neighbours, forever *unexploitable. **1978** A. GILCHRIST *Cod Wars* vi. 42 Such resources were largely hidden or disregarded or unexploitable until modern techniques could be applied. **1831** J. WILSON *Unimore* I. 85 Th' *uneyeable sun flames up the heavens. **1955** P. LARKIN *Less Deceived* 41 You cannot always keep That *unfakable young surface. **1977** H. OSBORNE *White Poppy* xxii. 160 That loud wah-wah voice that.. was the unfakeable mark of an English gentleman. **1934** WEBSTER, *Unfalsifiable. **1963** *Guardian* 25 Jan. 7/6 Any.. existential statement which is unrestricted in scope and therefore unfalsifiable. **1977** P. JOHNSON *Enemies of Society* xi. 153 The proposition was left sufficiently vague to allow for it to be updated.. in the light of scientific advances; it is thus a classic example of an unverifiable, or unfalsifiable, statement, and as such scientifically useless. **1668** WILKINS *Real Char.* III. vii. 341 A person insolutive,.. Unwalkative, .. Non-surrective,.. *Unfattable. **1965** *Punch* 21 Apr. 572/3 They plump for a return to this hotel, reminding each other of its *unfaultable charms. **1928** *Sunday Express* 29 Apr. 4 'Piccadilly', Arnold Bennett's original story.., is said to be not wholly disconnected with his novel 'The Pretty Lady', the great unfilmed (and *un-filmable). **1958** *Times Lit. Suppl.* 15 Aug. p. xxviii/4 Film studio executives sat up and took notice of the work of writers whom they had previously dismissed as un-filmable. **1963** E. HUMPHREYS *Gift* II. iv. 238 It didn't matter how unfilmable the book might be, other producers were after it. **1983** *Listener* 6 Jan. 28/1 Le Carré is on record as saying that it is unfilmable. **1884** J. PAYN *Lit. Recol.* 14 Vivian had reached the rather *unfloggable age of seventeen. **1934** WEBSTER, *Unfulfillable. **1968** *Punch* 4 Sept. 337/1, I ended up spending the night with my friend.., after signing numerous, apparently unfulfillable bonds and promises for the Customs officer. **1982** H. KISSINGER *Years of Upheaval* vi. 197 A demand as seemingly reasonable as it was unfulfillable. *a* **1860** J. YOUNGER *Autobiog.* (1881) 206 This became an *ungratifiable passion. **1835** T. B. THORPE in Griswold *Prose Writers Amer.* (1851) 549/2 That bar [= bear] was an *unhuntable bar, and died when his time come. **1909** WEBSTER, *Unidentifiable. **1923** M. SADLEIR *Desolate Splendour* ix. 142 The small girl, in charge of her young uncle and the unidentifiable Margery, gambolled.. across an uneven field. **1971** S. HILL *Strange Meeting* iii. 179 The hammering noise went on, only slightly muffled and then another, unidentifiable sound, though the voices had ceased. **1955** P. LARKIN *Less Deceived* 26 A tense, musty, *unignorable silence. **1981** *London Rev. Bks.* 18 June–1 July 7 The speed, wit and range of the book make it unignorable and exhilarating. **1875** POSTE *Gaius* (ed. 2) I. Introd. 14 That is involuntary (*unimputable) which is caused by external compulsion or by ignorance. **1880** R. G. WHITE *Every-Day Eng.* 143 The peculiar indescribable and *unindicable French sound. **1843** LANE *Select. fr. Kúran* Introd. 13 A vast desert to all but Arabs *unindwellable. **1977** *Sociology* XI. 99 We would observe the syntactical momentum employed for an *uninterruptable delivery. **1959** *Economist* 11 Apr. 140/2 The [Soviet] government fears that this information has already become *unjammable. **1963** *Daily Tel.* 4 Mar. 1/7 Typhon is designed to knock down aircraft and winged missiles by homing on them with its 'unjammable' radar. **1813** LADY LYTTELTON *Corr.* (1912) vii. 174 Men and women always in two distant and *unjoinable squadrons at the end of the room. **1802–12** BENTHAM *Ration. Judic. Evid.* (1827) II. 176 The testimony of expatriate and *unjusticiable witnesses. **1935** *N. & Q.* 4 May 314/1 **Unkinkable.* A new cable-trade term, applied to a fresh and useful flexible electric cord, which is guaranteed not to ravel or ruck up when in use. **1977** *Offshore Engineer* May 16/2 (Advt.), The right rope for the job... H and T Multiplait is:.. unkinkable. **1936** G. B. SHAW *Simpleton* II. 63 His poor little secret vice of cigaret smoking?.. Faugh! The *unkissable... The air poisoner. **1847** BURTON *Ld. Lovat* iii. 72 That *unlearnable self-estimate which insensibly exacts obedience. **1831** *Blackw. Mag.* XXX. 507 The Reformers owe us an *unliquidateable debt of gratitude. **1962** M. DRABBLE *Summer Bird-Cage* vi. 99, I was standing stock still and quite *unmanoeuvrable. **1940** W. FAULKNER *Hamlet* II. ii. 141 He brought a gross with him in the suitcase, specially made up for him outen asbestos, with *unmeltable snaps. **1810** BENTHAM *Packing* (1821) 137 To persevere in defeating the express words as well as *unmisconceivable intention, of a law. **1831** —— *Corr.* Wks. 1843 XI. 70 My advice to jurymen is plain and *unmisunderstandable. **1885** R. BRIDGES *Nero* I. IV. iii. 1933 Out of thy cold *unmotionable ashes. **1829** S. MARTIN in J. Duns *Mem.* iii. 36 He complains of being..*unmouldable.. and difficult to impress. **1922** JOYCE *Ulysses* 697 A thatched .. 2 storey dwellinghouse..with agreeable prospect..over unoccupied and *unoccupyable interjacent pastures. **1854** *U.S. Reports* (U.S. Supreme Court) LVI. 132 If the inventor of printing had..claimed his art as something distinct from his machinery, the doctrine now advanced, would have declared it *unpatentable to its full extent as an art. **1980** *TWA Ambassador* Oct. 21/3 Left unpatentable are elements of nature—a newly discovered wildflower, for instance—and laws of nature such as philosophical theories and mathematical principles. **1805** SAUNDERS *Min. Waters* 493 A dry *unperspirable state of the skin. **1935** *Sun* (Baltimore) 10 Jan. 22/4 The increase in the number of *unplaceable children taken under care. **1940** DYLAN THOMAS *Portrait of Artist as Young Dog* 117 We stood in the scooped, windy room of the arch, listening to the noises from the muffled town,..unplaceable sounds,..an engine coughing like a sheep on a hill. **1972** *Human World* Feb. 21 The absence of unplaceable graduates in Britain and the U.S.A. was one of the chief causes of the relative immunity of these countries to Marxism. **1984** *New Yorker* 9 Apr. 39/2 The music was unplaceable. It must have been a Russian idea of American pop. **1921** H. WILLIAMSON *Beautiful Years* 118 The man certainly was queer: he no longer thought as he had at first, that there was anything deep in his nature. Either that, or it was so deep as to be *unplumbable. **1929** S. LESLIE *Anglo-Catholic* x. 122 The pitiless unplumbable spaces filled him with terrors. **1980** D. MORAES *Mrs Gandhi* viii. 116 While she usually answers complex and difficult questions fluently, perfectly innocuous queries seem to drive her back into unplumbable depths of silence. **1971** *Nature* 3 Sept. 2/2 This device let the Vienna agency escape from the invidious position of policing the *unpoliceable into which it has been jockeyed. **1981** *Times* 25 July 5/1 Protests in other centres would render the rest of New Zealand unpoliceable. **1888** LANE-POOLE *Stratford de Redcliffe* I. 365 Some described him as 'the most *unpumpable of men'. **1838** TUPPER *Proverb. Philos.* (1852) 415 Life is a constant force, spirit an unquietable impetus. **1890** A. C. FRASER *Locke* 147 The idea of the **unquantifiable* is 'suggested' by the positive ideas of spaces and times which we have had in our sense experience. *Ibid.*, We are *as* remote from the unquantifiable infinite..as we were at the beginning of the process. **1979** *Financial Times* 2 Apr. 27/4 Job security is more generally regarded as unquantifiable. **1870** MISS BROUGHTON *Red as a Rose* (1878) 127 Most energetic, most *unrebuffable. **1925** T. DREISER *Amer. Tragedy* I. II. xxii. 307 So wild and *unrecapturable is the fever of youth. **1964** W. MCCORD in I. L. Horowitz *New Sociology* 428 We must eschew..the romanticism which longs for the virtues of an unrecapturable past. **1883** *Harper's Mag.* Feb. 347/2 [There are] such a variety of.. legends that they are quite *unrecountable. **1930** *Times Lit. Suppl.* 30 Oct. 884/3 The *unregenerate and unregenerable realm of life. **1982** *Observer* 17 Jan. 31/9 It is typical of my unregenerable soul that I can only see this as a marvellous theme for a novel. **1851** W. H. GOOLD in *Owen's Wks.* IX. 461 *note*, The *unreiterable sacraments, to which ordination ..belongs. **1934** WEBSTER, *Unrejectable. **1963** M. DRABBLE *Summer Bird-Cage* viii. 127, I felt rather guilty.., as if I had been reading a diary instead of simply receiving unrejectable impressions. **1884** *Century Mag.* XXIX. 81 An *un-restrictable commercial access to the markets and workshops of Europe. **1934** WEBSTER, *Unreviewable. **1955** *Bull. Atomic Sci.* Apr. 129/3 With so much unreviewable power in the executive there is bound to be doubt whether the company is getting the information which it really needs. **1968** *Guardian* 15 Nov. 6/7, I find Mary McCarthy's account of her visit to North Vietnam almost unreviewable. **1884** *Church Bells* 21 June 682/2 The bells of this church have been *unringable for some time. **1862** *Jrnl. Roy. Dubl. Soc.* 347 Rough vascular tissue, which is probably *unrollable spiral fibres. **1960** E. W. SWANTON *West Indies Revisited* 226 Worrell, however, is *unruffleable. **1981** F. INGLIS *Promise of Happiness* ii. 65, I read them for..the unrufflable, wholly impossible calm of big boys. **1870** W. KNIGHT *Colloquia Peripatetica* p. xii, The thought might penetrate into that shadowy region where language almost breaks down in the effort, as he put it, 'to say the *unsayable'. **1905** E. F. BENSON *Image in Sand* vii. 99 The only things worth saying are just those which are unsayable. **1954** R. JARRELL *Pictures from Institution* IV. 150 Her name was not Rosenbaum on the [gramophone] records but her own real unsayable Russian name. **1979** 'J. LE CARRÉ' *Smiley's People* (1980) iv. 49 Strickland incanted the unsayable: 'No coat-trailing..No émigrés. No bugger all.' **1861** THOREAU *Lett.* (1865) 205 Excuse these pencil marks, but my inkstand is *unscrewable. **1902** W. JAMES *Varieties Relig. Experience* xx. 499 That *unshareable feeling which each one of us has of the pinch of his individual destiny. **1976** *Daily Tel.* 19 Oct. 2/1 He said the doctor's belief in independence was fostered by the ultimately unshareable responsibility he accepted for his patient. **1928** C. BELL *Civilization* vi. 173 At this time of day a civilized person, male or female, should be *unshockable. **1980** FIRST & SCOTT *Olive Schreiner* iv. 132 The tenor of the history..was ..cool and unshockable. **1950** *Times* 15 Feb. 7/5, I should like to ask Lord Montgomery what he does when the 'soft' snow is practically *unskiable. **1978** *Detroit Free Press* 2 Apr. 17D/3 Help came in the form of the snow drought during the 1976–77 ski season that left Western and New England slopes unskiable. **1851** H. MELVILLE *Moby Dick* III. xxvii. 176 'Canst thou smooth this seam?'..'Aye, man, it is *unsmoothable.' **1925** 'R. CROMPTON' *Still—William* xi. 207 William watched him, smoothing back his unsmoothable hair. **1924** *Motor* 21 Oct. 623/3 An M.E. rear screen with Triplex *unsplinterable glass. **1962** L. S. SASIENI *Optical Dispensing* xiii. 329 Unsplinterable lenses are provided as protection. **1926–7** *Army & Navy Stores Catal.* 101/3 Shaving brushes..with *unsplittable handles. **1945** R. KNOX *God & Atom* i. 13 It might be possible..to resolve the molecule into its component parts, but beyond that lay something smaller yet, completely indivisible; it was christened accordingly 'the atom'—the unsplittable thing. **1978** M. MIDGLEY *Beast & Man* (1979) x. 214 Language.. seems an unmistakable, unsplittable single thing. **1956** M. STEWART *Wildfire at Midnight* ii. 26 He's little and round and quite, quite sorbo..*Unsquashable. **1975** *Daily Tel.* 7 Apr. 9/1 Ghastly statistics about the vast number of totally *unstageable scripts that come pouring through the post on to the desks of successful theatre people. **1981** *Times Lit. Suppl.* 13 Feb. 161/5 The work [*sc.* a Russian play] is unstageable today. **1881** *Nature* XXIII. 585 To show the hypothesis to be *unstateable. **1955** P. HERON *Changing Forms of Art* p. xiv, Indeed, as with all good art, the whole truth is unstatable. **1963** *Times Lit. Suppl.* 24 May 376/4 This appeal to unstateable personal and inter-personal experience. **1972** *Language* XLVIII. 83 Of course, one can state rules in global grammar that are unstatable as transformations. **1883** *Pall Mall G.* Suppl. 2 June, Unsinkable boats,..*unstaveable life-boats. *a* **1843** SOUTHEY *Comm.-pl. Bk.* (1851) IV. 429 Toads..so tough as to be almost *unstoneable. **1950** D. JONES *Phoneme* 150 Semi-vowels, such as j and w, would appear to be essentially *unstressable. **1886** EARL LYTTON *Lett.* (1906) II. xxi. 307 Churchill's 'Tory Democracy' they find still more *unswallowable. **1968** *Economist* 14 Dec. 21/1 Shifting to the side of their cheeks some unswallowable differences, they agreed to put up common candidates in 1969's general election. **1910** *Chambers's Jrnl.* 10 Sept. 644/1 The secrecy provided by the use of cryptic combinations of meaningless consonants can be equally assured by the various methods used for rendering the electric waves '*untappable'. **1979** C. MCCARRY *Better Angels* II. ii. 115 'I found that a computer out there..knew some things that only our computer was supposed to know.'.. 'But I thought our equipment was untappable.' **1909** WEBSTER, *Un-testable. **1964** F. BOWERS *Bibliogr. & Textual Criticism* III. vii. 93 Generalized opinions that are not only untested..but are also (usually) untestable. **1850** H. BUSHNELL *God in Christ* 311 We must bring this astounding *untheorizable fact into theory. **1950** O. NASH *Family Reunion* (1951) 102 Where hotels and restaurants and service stations are operated by *untippable unoffendable machinery. **1968** *Listener* 27 June 851/1 Even in Europe—where tipping started—there are such things as untippable taxis, though one has perhaps to go to Helsinki to find them. **1877** E. G. SQUIER *Peru* (1878) 348 Some of these [causeways] are now so ruined as to be *untransitable. **1978** *Broadcast* 28 Aug. 19/2 This commercial..took place in almost undecipherably muddy twilight. They can't really mean that, I thought.. it looks *un-transmittable. **1833** *Blackw. Mag.* XXXIII. 125 The *untroubleable regions of the skies. **1834** *Tait's Mag.* I. 39/2 Those..vehicles, that once rolled in slow and *unupsettable solemnity along. **1953** J. S. WILKIE *Sci. Mind & Brain* iv. 41 Some things are virtually *unverbalizable: is it at all credible that one could verbalize the face of a friend? **1978** *Language* LIV. 268 A variant of this position holds that experience, to be authentic, must be unverbalizable ('the idea, once expressed, is a lie'). **1877** O. WILDE in *Irish Monthly* Dec. 746, I stood by the *unvintageable sea. **1915** Unvintageable [see POLYPHLOISBIC *a.*]. **1879** *Cassell's Techn. Educ.* IV. 46/1 These slabs must be *unwarpable. **1886** *American* XII. 164 Railroad property..spread over an unmanageable and *unwatchable area. **1845** O. BROWNSON *Wks.* 188. V. 358 A firm, unwavering and *unwaverable conviction. **1909** WEBSTER, *Unweighable. **1938** R. W. LAWSON tr. *Hevesy & Paneth's Man. Radioactivity* (ed. 2) xi. 132 A parent substance present in unweighable quantities. **1971** *Nature* 23 July 260/2 By trapping the effluent from gas chromatographic columns we have obtained unweighable samples (< 50μg) of the natural pheromone. **1955** *New Biol.* XVIII. 112 Flowers, if floating, must be more or less cup-shaped, and even if lifted above the water surface must, like the leaves, be *unwettable. **1977** J. L. HARPER *Population Biol. Plants* ii. 46 When light unwettable seed lands on water, it tends to become concentrated at the edges of the water. **1845** STOCQUELER *Handbk. Brit. India* (1854) 103 Thus they become..worn..into such *unwhetstonable bluntness. **1912** G. B. SHAW *Let.* 10 Dec. in *B. Shaw & Mrs. Campbell* (1952) 68 There would be some terrible breach of etiquette some *unwipable-out insult, if she gave me a card for you. **1971** *Daily Tel.* (Colour Suppl.) 4 June 39/1 This little hole (felt-lined usually, and utterly unwipeable)..which they actually call a glove-box. **1981** *Times* 4 July 10/1 Tape costing a quarter of the price of these unwipeable tapes. **1931** *Times Lit. Suppl.* 12 Mar. 196/2 The episodes of Susan's life..and her ruthless imposition of herself upon..her third husband, and upon his Poor Christians as a kind of *unwithstandable Deborah—are told with admirable spirit. **1970** R. PRICE *Gt. Roob Revolution* 5 The classic rube withstood the unwithstandable winter at Valley Forge.

(*b*) *c* **1850** 'DOW JR.' in Jerdan *Yankee Hum.* (1853) 89 Ovid, whose veracity is *uncomoverable, and can't be disputed. **1844** J. T. HEWLETT *Parsons & W.* xi, *Un-do-without-able, which I think is a much more applicable word than indispensable. **1888** G. GROSSMITH *Society Clown* iv, A ..bottle of 'undryupable ink'. **1873** MISS BRADDON *Str. & Pilgr.* I. ix, Miss Disney is really the most *un-get-on-able-with girl. **1840** J. T. HEWLETT *P. Priggins* i, Weather hot —blow-flies *un-keep-off-able. **1947** R. CHANDLER *Let.* 5 Jan. in *R. Chandler Speaking* (1966) 66, I found it absolutely ..*unputdownable. **1982** *Brit. Med. Jrnl.* 15 May 1466/2 The novel is highly readable and quite unputdownable. **1840** DE QUINCEY *Style* Wks. 1859 XI. 244 Alcibiades..was too unsteady and..'unrelyable'; or, perhaps, in more correct English, too '*unrelyuponable'. **1974** *Guardian* 21 Mar. 10/4 The immediacy which makes TV sometimes.. absolutely *un-switch offable. **1984** *Listener* 10 May 38/1 Alfred Brendel's recording of Beethoven's Five Piano Concertos, with the Chicago Symphony Orchestra conducted by James Levine..is unswitchoffable. **1862** H. MARRYAT *Year in Sweden* I. 407 In the earlier period of Scandinavian history, serpents and dragons were looked upon as *untalkaboutable subjects. **1968** *Economist* 25 May 89/2 The engine..is a neat—and presumably *unwearoutable—air-cooled flat-four unit in the back of the car. **1979** *Field* 3 Oct. 942/1 (Advt.), Almost un-wearoutable socks. *a* **1864** HAWTHORNE *Dr. Grimshawe* xxii. (1891) 301 The record..of a foot stamped down there in guilt and agony, and oozing out with *unwipeupable blood.

c. The use of *un-* with adjectives in *-like* is found from at least the close of the 16th cent., when *ungentlemanlike* appears. Others occur in the following century, as *unbodylike, ungodlike, unwarlike.* The free use of such forms, however, is characteristic of the 19th cent., and especially of the latter part of it. The following are examples of casual formations.

Recent formations include: ***unbridegroomlike, unbutlerlike, uncatlike, unpolicemanlike.***

1886 *Pall Mall G.* 1 Nov. 13 So contemptible, detestable, and *un-actor-like a proceeding. **1674** N. FAIRFAX *Bulk & Selv.* 88 Their *unbodylike way of being somewhere. **1830** M. O'BRIEN *Jrnl.* 15 May (1968) xii. 114 Mary and Fanny exclaimed at this most *unbridegroomlike proceeding. **1845** FITZBALL *Maritana* II. i. 18 Your costume is somewhat unbridegroom-like. **1847** L. HUNT *Men, Women, & B.* I. 74 The hand [of the monkey]..mortifies one: it looks so very *unbrute-like. **1854** GRACE GREENWOOD *Haps & Mishaps* 14 He met my advances in a most gracious and *un-Bumble-like manner. **1841** J. T. HEWLETT *Parish Clerk* II. 37 He.. killed it afterwards in a most *unbutcherlike way. **1924** J. SUTHERLAND *Circle of Stars* iii. 24 His manner was unimpeachable, his tone superlatively correct, but somewhere in his eyes was a most *unbutler-like gleam. **1955** AUDEN *Shield of Achilles* i. 22 For an *uncatlike Creature who has gone wrong, Five minutes on even the nicest mountain Is awfully long. **1865** VISCT. MILTON & W. B. CHEADLE *N.-W. Passage by Land* viii. (1867) 112 Feeling very dismal and *un-Christmaslike. **1850** MARG. FULLER *Wom. 19th C.* (1862) 190 Gazing up at the clouds in a most *uncitizen-like fashion. **1838** JAS. GRANT *Sk. Lond.* 160 Whose manner..is the most *undeliberative-like that the human mind could fancy. **1856** LEVER *Martins of Cro' M.* 249 Suffering a 'sea change'..as *unearthlike as well may be imagined. **1807** in *Spirit Pub. Jrnls.* XI. 352 Your scandalous and *un-Englishmanlike behaviour. **1823** *Blackw. Mag.* XIV. 563 An excessive dread of being caught in the *unfreeman-like sin of blushing. **1826** MISS MITFORD *Village* Ser. II. (1863) 451 Her manners were quite as *ungipsy-like as her apparel. **1823** in *Spirit Pub. Jrnls.* 151 The professor thought this conduct extremely rude and *ungoldsmithlike. **1868** LANIER *Jacquerie* I. 24 The pack.. took revenge as bloody as a man's, *Unhoundlike, sudden. **1884** *Century Mag.* XXVII. 678 The rows of unhomelike and even *unhouse-like dwelling-places. **1851** MAYNE REID *Scalp Hunt.* xxi, This was said in well-accentuated and most *un-Indian-like English. **1822** MRS. SHELLEY in *Mem.* (1859) 215 Pardon me that I still write in this incoherent and *unletterlike manner. **1841** THACKERAY *Men & Coats* Wks. 1900 XIII. 610 An affair of brocade that has always struck me as absurd and *un-Macbethlike. **1860** TRISTRAM *Gt. Sahara* vi. 93 The strange and most *unmoslem-like ceremony of sacrificing a goat. **1803** *Edin. Rev.* II. 427 And it would have been highly *unneighbour-like to have neglected them. **1978** D. WILLIAMS *Treasure up in Smoke* xx. 186 There was a most *un-policeman-like implication in the Chief Inspector's tone. **1879** DOWDEN *Southey* v. 117 Southey had a most *unprophet-like craving for the creature comforts of beef and bread. **1851** G. H. KINGSLEY *Sp. & Trav.* (1900) 452 In a most *unsalmon-like manner. **1846** MRS GORE *Eng. Char.* (1852) 155 Thrusting his paraphernalia into a drawer, with a most *unsecretary-like blush. **1802** MRS. E. PARSONS *Myst. Visit* II. 257 The *unsex-like wickedness of Mrs. Hood. **1805** *Edin. Rev.* V. 399 The..*unsquire-like employment of writing, printing and publishing. **1878** A. H. MARKHAM *Gt. Frozen Sea* xvi. 229 Conducting itself in a very erratic and *unstarlike manner. **1880** *Cassell's Mag.* June 440 Another *unsummer-like fashion is asserting itself this year. **1885** GLADSTONE in Morley *Life* (1905) II. VIII. x. 426 It is so *unsundaylike and unrestful. **1825** J. WILSON *Noct. Ambr.* Wks. 1855 I. 2 So bright wavering and *unsurelike was the haill living world. **1828** *Lancet* 19 Jan. 592 I The unfeeling, *unsurgeon-like conduct of Mr. Heyderman. **1877** S. COX *Salv. Mundi* Preface p. x, It is surely an undignified and *unteacherlike procedure. *a* **1849** POE *Poems* (1859) 66 *Unthought-like thoughts that are the souls of thought. **1869** H. BUSHNELL *Wom. S.* i. 13 What could be more *un-university-like? **1855** SMEDLEY *Occult Sciences* 150 Its water..extinguished torches.., but it possessed also the most *unwaterlike power of relighting them. **1797** MRS. M. ROBINSON *Walsingham* III. 41 The *un-zephyrlike hand of the angry Lady Fusby forcibly held me.

8. The prefixing of *un-* to past participles, common in OE. and revived in ME., was subsequently extended until it became the commonest of all uses of the prefix. The following varieties may be distinguished in the usual formations:

a. Simple past pples. in *-ed.* These form an inexhaustible class, largely represented among the main words, and including many more similar to those in the following list.

A few casual forms are employed by Florio (1611), as *uncomparted, unnotted,* and various others by Hexham (1648), as *unbalsamed, unbedabbled, unblued, uncalumniated, unchested,* etc. Ash (1775) carries this type of formation to great lengths, and enters about 800 words which are either not recorded, or are of rare occurrence, in actual use, as *unabetted, unaccited, unacquitted, unadjudged, unallured, unamplified, unappraised,* etc.

As subdivisions of this type, forms in *-ated* and *-ized* may be specially noted on account of their frequency. These are also largely represented in Ash's dictionary, which contains about 150 unused or rare forms in *-ated,* as *unaccumulated, uncamphorated, uncircumstantiated,* etc., and a score or so in *-ized,* as *unapostrophized, unaromatized, uncantonized,* etc.

On the double meaning of forms like *undressed, unhoused, unsheathed,* etc., see UN-[2] 8.

Recent formations include: (*a*) ***unacclaimed, unaddled, unaffrayed*** (arch.), ***unassessed, unattributed, unbeglamoured, unbobbed*** [BOBBED *a.* b], ***unbombed, unbothered, unbuffered, unbugged, unbypassed, uncaked, uncatalysed, uncloned, uncluttered, uncobbled, uncoded, uncopyrighted, uncouponed, undeafened, undepicted, undiffused, undisbursed, undistanced, unearmarked, unenhanced, unenthused, uneroded, unexploded, unfaked, unfattened, unfazed, unfilmed, unflustered, unfocus(s)ed, unformatted, unfussed, ungrazed, ungritted, unhipped*** [HIP *v.*[5]], ***unhousetrained, uniced, uninjected, unkeepered, unladdered*** [LADDER *v.* 2], ***unlaundered, unlenited, unmonitored, unneutered, unoriented, unpackaged, unpadded, unphotographed, unplanned, unposed, unpowered, unprogrammed, unprovenanced, unrationed, unrattled, unseeded, unshingled*** [SHINGLED *ppl. a.*[1] 3], ***unsignposted, unslanted, unsliced, unslipped*** [SLIPPED *ppl. a.*[3]], ***unsourced,*** *unspayed, unsponsored, unstaffed, unstreamed* [STREAMED *a.* 2], *unstructured, unsupercharged, unsurfaced, untagged, untelevised, untenured, unupholstered, unvetted*; (*b*) *unacculturated, unactivated, unagglutinated, unallocated, uncalibrated, unchlorinated, undemarcated, unencapsulated, unexhilarated, unfractionated, unintegrated, unmotivated* (also *absol.*), *unmyelinated, unpatinated, unrefrigerated, unreplicated, unsegregated, unsublimated, unsyncopated, unvegetated*; (*c*) *unactualized, un-Americanized, unanæsthetized, unanatomized, un-Anglicized, unbowdlerized, uncolonized* (cf. UNCOLONIZE *v.*), *undiphthongized, un-Hellenized, unindustrialized, unlemmatized, unnationalized, unnormalized, unparasitized, unpasteurized, unplasticized, unpoliticized, unpolymerized, unpressurized, unpublicized, unsclerotized, unsocialized, unstabilized, unstandardized* (also *absol.*), *unsterilized, ununionized, unvandalized, unverbalized.*

(*a*) *general.* **1921** W. DE LA MARE *Mem. Midget* xlvi. 314 That other less professional *début* which poor Mr. Crimble . . had left *unacclaimed. **1899** *Leeds Mercury Weekly Suppl.* 5 Aug. (E.D.D.), We should call money that had been acquired without effort, '*unaddled brass'. **1935** W. DE LA MARE *Early One Morning* xiv. 179 Flattery of the young is so usual that it is remarkable that a child with a 'fine head' manages to keep the brains in it un-addled. **1935** T. S. ELIOT *Murder in Cathedral* i. 20 Archbishop, secure and assured of your fate, *unaffrayed among the shades. **1922** *Times* 15 Nov. 13/6 That *un-assessed quantity, the man in the street. **1970** *Jrnl. General Psychol.* LXXXII. 146 Ebbinghaus was faced with a similar problem of unassessed previous experience in learning phenomena. **1972** N. FREELING *Long Silence* II. 233 He had been to look at a picture... The price was high, and might have been a great deal higher but that it was, as he pointed out, quite *unattributed. **1846** WORCESTER (citing Haslam), **Unbandaged.* **1901** G. B. SHAW *Three Plays for Puritans* Pref. p. xxix, A thing compared to which Falstaff's *unbeglamored drinking and drabbing is respectable. **1884** *Pall Mall G.* 15 Jan. 6/2 Who seldom see even an *unbesmutted blade of grass. **1827** POLLOK *Course T.* VIII. 91 No king, no subject was; unsutcheoned all, . . uncoroneted, *unbestarred. **1846** WORCESTER (citing Scott), **Unboasted.* **1927** *Blackw. Mag.* Nov. 601/1 By her own account the only *unbobbed head in Hampstead. **1931** W. FAULKNER in *Harper's Mag.* Sept. 394/2 The fine, soft cloud of her unbobbed hair gleamed like the chestnut's flank. **1928** M. BEERBOHM *Variety of Things* 128 One likes to think of him there among the *unbombed Lakes. **1980** A. PRICE *Hour of Donkey* iv. 63 One un-bombed veteran to another obviously much-bombed one. **1912** W. DEEPING *Sincerity* xxviii. 216 Wolfe . . seemed to brush Turrell's arms aside as though they were mere sticks. His crisp, sinewy punches landed serenely. He looked unmarked, *unbothered. **1965** J. A. MICHENER *Source* (1966) 794 Bagdadi, apparently unbothered by history, pressed on. **1936** *Nature* 7 Nov. 800/1 The native hæmoglobin of the horse, in *unbuffered dilute salt solutions at the isoelectric point. **1966** *Punch* 2 Feb. 169/2 If any Tom, Dick or Harry can meet in a collapsible plastic balloon and chatter away *unbugged, there is no knowing what they will say. We shall be back to the old, bad days of secret diplomacy. **1883** *Athenæum* 11 Aug. 182/3 It is a question . . what power of resistance a solid '*unburrowed' soil might have offered. **1962** SIMPSON & RICHARDS *Physical Princ. Junction Transistors* xi. 255 A better solution is to leave a portion of the emitter bias resistor *un-by-passed, thereby introducing negative-current feedback. **1954** T. GUNN *Fighting Terms* 44, I . . felt my body sweet, *Un-caked blood in all its channels flowing. **1939** *Jrnl. Organic Chem.* IV. 434 No *uncatalyzed addition has yet been observed. **1976** *Nature* 24 June 659/1 After the establishment of the kinetic orders of the catalysed and uncatalysed reactions a mechanism consistent with all the results was deduced. **1971** *Ibid.* 2 Apr. 276/1 If single-cell clones of cultured cells are derived from women heterozygous for *X*-linked genes determining enzyme variants, each clone shows the activity of only one of the two possible genes, whereas *uncloned cultures derived from many cells show both. **1980** *Jrnl. Immunol. Methods* XXXIV. 153 Uncloned and cloned populations. **1925** *Glasgow Herald* 6 Nov. 8 The adjective *uncluttered is an American term of strong commendation when used to describe a wall, a mantelpiece or even a whole room. **1960** J. STROUD *Shorn Lamb* xxii. 239 New modern houses . . with their plate-glass and uncluttered lines. **1980** *Times* 29 Feb. 26 (Advt.), Spring-time in Greece. Uncluttered beaches, [etc.]. **1922** JOYCE *Ulysses* 422 An *uncobbled tramsiding set with skeleton tracks. **1918** J. W. GERARD *Face to Face with Kaiserism* xx. 230 The bags were secretly opened and our *uncoded despatches and letters read. **1971** B. PATTEN *Irrelevant Song* 24 A bleak and uncoded message whispers Down all the nerves. **1852** MRS. STOWE *Let.* 27 Sept. in N. Spain *Mrs Beeton* (1948) I. iv. 51, I do not conceive that I have any *claim* on an English publisher for any of the profits of an *uncopyrighted work. **1950** A. LOMAX *Mister Jelly Roll* 292 He established *The Tempo-Music Publishing Company* to protect, publish, and push Morton's uncopyrighted and unpublished works. **1846** WORCESTER (citing West. Rev.), **Uncountervailed.* **1935** *Economist* 9 Nov. 930/1 They had actually harvested rather more than that quantity, but the balance, being *uncouponed stock, had been carried forward to the current season's account. **1967** *Punch* 13 Sept. 388/1 Unfortunately the police caught him with several bales of uncouponed suit material. **1935** W. B. YEATS *Dramatis Personae* vii. 25 Only at pictures did he look *undeafened and unblinded. **1979** *New Scientist* 17 May 537/2 It also sings normally next season, and goes through the usual subsong and plastic song again in the same way as undeafened birds. *c* **1884** E. DICKINSON in *Poems* (1955) III. 1120 Bugles call the least of us To *un-depicted Realms. **1940** W. FAULKNER *Hamlet* III. ii. 212 That perfect marriage of will and ability with a single *undiffused object. **1964** *Economist* 7 Mar. 917/3 Loans still undisbursed. **1893** G. ALLEN *Scallywag* I. 206 Quite *undiscomposed by this . . most startling announcement. **1951** W. FAULKNER *Requiem for Nun* III. 262 There is the clear *undistanced voice as though out of the delicate antenna-skeins of radio. *a* **1868** *Unearmarked [see EARMARK *v.* 3]. **1971** *Oxf. Univ. Gaz.* 25 Feb. 709/2 That the Curators of the University Chest be authorized to expend from the unearmarked money in the Higher Studies Fund a sum of £10,000. **1878** ABNEY *Photogr.* 117 The *unemulsified collodion for the wet process. **1883** *Encycl. Brit.* XVI. 653/2 Others . . discharge their eggs *unenclosed in capsules freely into the sea-water. **1934** WEBSTER, *Unenhanced. **1942** R. FROST *Witness Tree* 41 We gave ourselves outright . . to the land vaguely realizing westward, but still unstoried, artless, unenhanced. **1963** *Punch* 9 Oct. 516/2 It [*sc.* industry] is markedly *unenthused about the Tories. **1977** M. KENYON *Rapist* ix. 109 Keane, unenthused, watched from the door. **1924** *Brit. Weekly* 13 Nov. 147/3, There is no 'basalt and bronze' for a Prime Minister like a still *uneroded majority of 210. **1978** J. UPDIKE *Coup* (1979) ii. 48 Its façade is topped with eight marble statues of an unreal whiteness, uneroded in this climate. **1889** *Cent. Dict.*, *Unexploded. **1924** A. D. SEDGWICK *Little French Girl* II. i 100 Their mutual secret . . that Giles visualized as an unexploded bomb . . liable at a touch to . . scatter the family happiness to fragments. **1952** A. COHEN *Phonemes of English* 28 We find that . . in *nipped* [the [p] is] unexploded. **1981** B. LANGLEY *Autumn Tiger* ii. 21 *Berlin, February 1945* . . . a sign in red paint which warned 'Danger! Unexploded Bomb.' **1865** EARLE *Sax. Chron.* Introd. p. iv, Their *unfagged memory was richly stored with the events of their own day. **1902** KIPLING *Let.* 30 Nov. in C. Carrington *Rudyard Kipling* (1955) xv. 369 A grey stone lichened house . . with old oak staircase, and all untouched and *unfaked. **1968** A. DIMENT *Bang Bang Birds* vi. 102 One of the Birds, gazing at them with apparently unfaked adoration. **1895** HARDY *Jude* I. viii. 58 Three young *unfattened pigs had escaped from their sty. **1951** T. CAPOTE *Grass Harp* ii. 50 'Of course they are nearer God,' he said, *unfazed by the disapproving, sober faces around him. **1977** P. ROTH *Professor of Desire* 55 They were all screaming at one another, but he just walked along, unfazed. **1872** W. R. GREG *Enigmas of Life* vii. 260 Naked truth, *unfilmed eyes, will do all that the most righteous vengeance could desire. **1928** Unfilmed [see *unfilmable*, sense 7 b above]. **1887** *Encycl. Brit.* XXII. 386 The 'jerk' or *unflated aspirate. **1887** *Pall Mall G.* 8 Aug. 12/1 They wanted the line between the *unflogged class . . and the flogged masses to remain. **1913** H. WALPOLE *Fortitude* II. ii. 165 Beaming, calm, and *unflustered as though he had just come from the next street. **1967** T. STOPPARD *Rosencrantz & Guildenstern are Dead* II. 58 (*He turns away.* GUIL *grabs him and spins him back violently.*) (*Unflustered.*) Now if you're going to be subtle, we'll miss each other in the dark. **1886** HARDY *Mayor of Casterbridge* II. xii. 307 His eyes lighting on them with an *unfocused gaze. **1939** H. NICOLSON *Diary* 4 Feb. (1966) 390 V. and I go round to the Beales where there is a Television Set... Compared with a film, it is a bleary, flickering, . . unfocused, interruptible thing. **1979** G. MACDONALD *Camera* xii. 165/1 The greatest portraitist of Victorian England was the unfocussed Julia Margaret Cameron. **1967** E. R. LANNON in Cox & Grose *Organiz. & Handling Bibliogr. Rec. by Computer* IV. 82 The second type of data, sometimes called *unformatted, takes on special meaning due to its surrounding elements. **1982** *Which Computer?* June 30/3 The M20 has . . an on-line unformatted data storage capacity of 320 KB. **1873** H. A. WISE *Seven Decades Union* 282 As large a solid piece of it as was left *unfrasseled by the concussions. **1871** NOYES *Hymns Mod. Man* 39 Perfection *unfreckled by flaws. **1907** T. HODGKIN *Let.* 27 Oct. in L. Creighton *Life & Lett. T. Hodgkin* (1917) xii. 282 When Christ . . said that he would have us *unfussed' he meant almost what we mean by '*unfussed'. **1981** N. FREELING *One Damn Thing after Another* xxxii. 236 She phoned home. To hear Arthur's voice, unfussed and matter-of-fact. **1903** KIPLING *Five Nations* 155 For the *ungrazed upland, the untilled lea Cry, and the fields forlorn. **1972** J. L. HARPER *Population Biol. Plants* 450 Within this zone of taller, ungrazed herbage the balance of competitive interactions is changed. **1977** *Belfast Tel.* 19 Jan. 1/2 Environment Department officials were caught napping today by the heavy overnight frost, which left a network of icy Ulster roads *ungritted. **1938** *Amer. Speech* XIII. 314/2 *Jump salty*, implies an un-expected change in a person's . . knowledge... An *un-hipped person may become hipped. **1944** D. BURLEY *Orig. Handbk. Harlem Jive* 90, I hunch the pinball layout, Jack, and it's an unhipped tilt. **1883** GRESLEY *Gloss. Coal-m.* 268 **Unholed*, boardgates or other headings which are not driven through or thirled into the adjoining roadway. **1870** E. PEACOCK *Ralf Skirl.* I. 106 Because some . . kitchen-girl has left the cow *unhoppled. **1955** AUDEN *Shield of Achilles* iii. 66 Where should we be but for them? Feral skill, *un-housetrained. **1967** A. WILSON *No Laughing Matter* III. 232 He's doing PPE. Whatever that may be. It sounds very un-housetrained. **1864** GEO. ELIOT *Let.* 8 Mar. (1956) IV. 138 Iced water is what I always long for . . while water **un*-iced is detestable to me. **1971** 'J. BELL' *Hole in Ground* iv. 53 A plate of scones and an uniced cake. **1881** ROMANES in *Nature* XXIV. 185 Sources of intermediate or *uninferred knowledge. **1934** WEBSTER, *Uninjected. **1946** *Nature* 31 Aug. 311/2 There are two natural folds of skin in cattle at . . the root of the tail, and the uninjected fold serves as a control. **1977** P. DICKINSON *Walking Dead* I. i. 20 He only injected three pairs of rats in a batch . . . Nor could he run uninjected rats. **1938** J. W. DAY *Dog in Sport* xi. 143 There were partridges, naturally bred, more or less *un-keepered. **1977** H. DOUGLAS-HOME *Birdman* vi. 71 Keepering established a balance which could not have existed in the earlier predator dominated times. Anyone who doubts this need only take a train from Edinburgh to Glasgow, unkeepered country today. **1956** 'C. BLACKSTOCK' *Dewey Death* v. 102 She was . . her well-groomed self, with . . *unladdered stockings. **1978** J. GOODMAN *Last Sentence* i. 28 She and Cecil were entered . . at the Streatham Locarno . . and she *had* to have unladdered hose for that. **1844** A. MALLALIEU *Buenos Ayres*, etc. 62 The untamed *unlassoed steed. **1895** *Montgomery Ward Catal.* Spring & Summer 36/3 Soft or *Unlaundered Waists. **1965** T. CAPOTE *In Cold Blood* ii. 125 Some bits of unlaundered laundry. **1978** 'R. CASSILIS' *Winding Sheet* III. 199 Politicians . . should never be allowed to hear unlaundered secrets. It made them uncomfortable. **1953** K. JACKSON *Lang. & Hist. in Early Britain* 554 Original *unlenited Brit. *b*. **1977** *Word 1972* XXVIII. 99 Three of the 7 semi-speakers showed switching between lenited and un-lenited forms of *daor* 'expensive'. **1883** *Pall Mall G.* 28 Dec. 5/1 Dr. Schliemann recognized . . in the objects of gold the *unlooted 'treasure of Priam'. **1844** *Ayrshire Wreath* 190 Egbert *unlured by vow or gift Gaid furth withouten fear. **1966** R. H. RIMMER *Harrad Experiment* (1967) 92 Locating my leopard coat under a heap of fur coats in the *unmonitored cloak room. **1976** *Guardian* 23 July 15/6 Now at last it seems that a researcher from Stirling University may begin work, and both staff and inmates see this as a positive development, while regretting that the first years have slipped past largely unmonitored. **1844** FRIEDLÄNDER tr. *F. Bremer's Neighbours* II. 201, I was half fearful after this of expressing my yet *unmooted fears in reference to himself. **1884** *Pall Mall G.* 29 Aug. 2/1 Not only did they receive their rations in full, but also their pay *unmulcted. **1962** G. BUTLER *Coffin in Oxford* ii. 38 The undying burning hate of one *un-neutered tom for another. **1971** *Nat. Geographic* May 735/2 The Seigneur [of Sark] . . exercises the right to keep the Island's only 'unneutered' bitch. **1931** V. WOOLF *Waves* 205 Here am I marching up and down the terrace alone, *unoriented. **1947** [see ORIENTED *ppl. a.* 2]. **1962** U. WEINREICH in Householder & Saporta *Probl. Lexicogr.* 30 Features of a geographic area can be studied even from an unoriented map. **1969** W. R. R. PARK *Plastics Film Technol.* ii. 33 Unoriented film is very brittle at below zero temperatures. **1875** ROLLESTON *Addr. Dept. Anthrop. Brit. Assoc.* 7 The possession of an *unoverwhelmed numerical representation. **1948** A. N. KEITH *Three came Home* xi. 199, 100 cigarettes, *unpackaged and unlabelled. **1984** *Times Lit. Suppl.* 10 Feb. 148/1 Here is a manual for the unpackaged, mildly enterprising and tolerably well-heeled holidaymakers. **1923** A. HUXLEY *Antic Hay* x. 152 The wearing exhaustion to which long-protracted sitting on *unpadded seats subjects them. **1979** A. BUCK *Dress in 18th-C. Eng.* ii. 31 The coat was losing its stiffness, and the pleats of its skirts, now unpadded, were set further back. **1884** BOURKE *Snake Dance Moquis* vii. 68 The stones were uncut or *unpecked. **1886** *Pall Mall G.* 9 Dec. 3/2 The unregenerate and, as yet, *unpermeated Tory. **1914** G. BELL *Let.* 21 Jan. (1927) I. xiii. 327 And we came at two o'clock to the last of the castles, Baîr, as yet unplanned and *unphotographed. **1929** 'E. QUEEN' *Roman Hat Mystery* v. 86 You are by no means an unphotographed young lady—I saw your picture in the paper to-day. **1981** J. WAINWRIGHT *All on Summer's Day* 80 An inspection which (literally) left no square inch unsearched or un-photographed. **1909** WEBSTER, *Unplanned. **1914** [see *unphotographed* above]. **1942** J. S. HUXLEY in *Harper's Mag.* Sept. 346/1 The need for entering upon our revolution consciously . ., deliberately guiding its course instead of allowing its blind forces to push and buffet our un-planned lives. **1959** *Listener* 4 June 981/1 These people are spontaneous in almost all they do. Children are 'un-planned'. **1961** 'J. LE CARRÉ' *Call for Dead* xvii. 186 The obviously unplanned and unproductive selection of files. **1973** *Times* 19 Apr. 19/2 Nearly half of *all* pregnancies are unplanned. **1981** N. TUCKER *Child & Book* i. 45 A shoe . . may . . house a large and almost certainly unplanned family. **1934** WEBSTER, *Unposed. **1960** *Guardian* 13 July 7/2 The best pictures of people are unposed and are taken while they are intent on what they are doing. **1968** E. HYAMS *Mischief Makers* i. 12 This unselfconscious, unposed animation was not what I was used to. **1963** *Times* 26 Feb. 9/4 After being boosted to orbital speed, the 45ft. long Dyna-Soar will be capable of manoeuvering freely during reentry into the earth's atmosphere, and then making a horizontal landing. As it will be *unpowered at that stage this will call for particular skill and judgment by the pilot. **1975** S. JOHNSON *Urbane Guerilla* III. 108 The canal . . plunging . . through a half-mile tunnel forbidden to unpowered craft. **1887** *Q. Rev.* Oct. 537 *Unprenticed and ingenuous new voters. **1941** W. C. HANDY *Father of Blues* (1957) xiv. 194 Other New York composer-conductors were introduced here and there and asked to play *unprogrammed numbers. **1953** *Sun* (Baltimore) 12 Mar. 2/1 The 'unprogrammed' funds referred to come to the Army from several sources. **1959** *New Biol.* XXVIII. 113 In order to keep such a process going in its most elementary form, some prearrangement, in the form of strings of unprogrammed material to be used, has been found necessary. **1974** *Sci. Amer.* May 61/2 When the machine is off or unprogrammed, the knob moves freely in all directions. **1976** H. WILSON *Governance of Britain* iv. 85 Apart from pre-arranged ministerial meetings with documents circulated and written and sometimes oral briefing, each day sees a number of often unprogrammed meetings with ministers. **1967** *Antiquaries Jrnl.* XLVII. 209 Another animal . . is the springing canine with collar on an *unprovenanced ?flagon handle also in the British Museum. **1882** *Garden* 14 Jan. 24/2 The chief danger with *unputtied glass is found when fierce wind-storms prevail. **1919** A. P. HERBERT in *Punch* 22 Jan. 62/1 The free *unrationed blotting-pad. **1940** C. E. MILBURN *Diary* 10 Mar. (1979) 26 To church . . then home for the last unrationed meat dinner. **1982** T. FITZGIBBON *With Love* I. v. 31 We would have friends to dinner, and with food rationing becoming stringent, stuff and braise un-rationed sheeps' hearts. **1934** WEBSTER, *Unrattled. **1953** *Manch. Guardian Weekly* 20 Aug. 7 He was quite unrattled, in good physical shape. **1976** J. COLVILLE *Footprints in Time* xxvii. 144 His second-in-command at the Embassy . . was unrattled by the crescendo of disaster to the allied cause. **1864** *Realm* 18 May 5 Formless clothes whose folds, *unretrenched by artifice, follow nature's laws. **1838** *Penny Cycl.* X. 378/1 The sides of their ditches being *unreveted. **1884** *Gentl. Mag.* Feb. 125 He fell at the head of his own *unrevolted regiment. **1879** LANIER *Poems, To B. Taylor* 23 Not [to] drudge *unriched. **1881** R. G. WHITE *Eng.* 371 Sheridan . . leaves this trait of speech *unridiculed. **1952** *N.Y. Times* 8 Sept. 27/5 The third-seeded player, Irene Rawcliffe of Nutley High, was eliminated by *unseeded Lynn Anderson of Mount St. Mary's Academy 6–1, 6–1. **1977** *Washington Post* 9 Mar. D4, I think anybody, including the unseeded squads, has a chance to make the final. **1928** *Daily Express* 23 May 8/4 Among the fifty horsewomen only five have *un-shingled hair. **1933** A. G. MACDONELL *England, their England* xiv. 246 A network of narrow lanes, *unsignposted. **1981** M. E. ATKINS *Palimpsest* ii. 12 Breakdowns *always* occurred in foul weather on unsignposted roads. **1885** WARREN & CLEVERLY *Wand. Beetle* 52 The Gunner saw no fun in leaving stunning things *unsketched. **1964** F. BOWERS *Bibliogr. & Textual Criticism* VI. i. 165 With selected though *unslanted evidence, a point should be reached at which our common-sense view of probability rebels at being asked to accept any more coincidence as the result of mere chance. **1974** J. IRVING *158-Pound Marriage* vi. 131 It was an old-fashioned, unslanted, glass windshield. **1889** *Cent. Dict.*, *Unsliced. **1968** D. E. ALLEN *Brit. Tastes* iii. 77 Bread, being . . made more by small local bakers, tends to be unwrapped (and . . unsliced) more frequently than elsewhere. **1978** *Times* 15 Apr. 3/6 There will be bloomers, cobs, . . sliced and unsliced, white and brown loaves on the shelves. **1940** R. E. Smith in *Maya & Their Neighbors* xvi. 243 *Unslipped jars with flaring necks. **1977** *Sci. Amer.* Mar. 130/2 The pots range from rough, unslipped pieces—'earthenware' in modern terminology—to thinner-walled pieces with smooth and glossy surfaces. *c* **1890** *Fred Wilson's Fate* 80 His record out of office [was] not by any means *unsmudged. **1851** H. Melville *Moby Dick* III. xviii. 128 This ante-mosaic, *unsourced existence of the un-speakable terrors of the whale. **1977** *Kuwait Times* 1 Nov. 6/3 In an unsourced report from Bucharest, the Egyptian agency also said that a decision whether to reconvene the Geneva conference would be made within the next two weeks. **1939** J. R. Kinney *How to raise a Dog* vi. 144 During their periods the *unspayed bitch is sometimes an aesthetic problem because of the discharge. **1979** 'J. Ross' *Rattling of Old Bones* ix. 83 The woman . . [had] the sexual hunger of an unspayed cat in her eyes. **1930** E. Rice *Voyage to Purilia* i. 7 We wanted to travel quietly and unobtrusively. . . This could be done only if our voyage was *unsponsored and unheralded. **1979** *Tuscon* (Arizona) *Citizen* 20 Sept. 2D/1 The Patio Pools team amassed 4,882 pins . . against Diamond Life and unsponsored Team No. 4 in the first round of action. **1884** *Spectator* 4 Oct. 1326/1 She has left some wood *un-stacked at home. **1934** Webster, *Unstaffed. **1957** [see remotely *adv.* 2 b]. **1979** V. L. Pandit *Scope of Happiness* xxxvii. 288 The Embassy remained closed and unstaffed. **1876** Brickwood *Boat-Racing* 63 Rowing with *unstraightened arms, or slackened muscles. **1962** *Guardian* 30 Mar. 10/4 A large **unstreamed* school in which these distinctions have no place. **1981** *Indexer* XII. 152/2 Six unstreamed classes in a local comprehensive school. **1936** F. & G. M. Heider tr. *Lewin's Princ. Topological Psychol.* xii. 134 If one puts a rat into the maze without food, he gets a chance to 'orient' himself, which means that what is first an *unstructured field becomes structured. **1948** M. Sherif *Outl. Soc. Psychol.* vii. 181 Psychological principles which are . . applicable in the case of the individual facing an unstructured situation. **1965** *Times Lit. Suppl.* 25 Nov. 1049/3 This was . . an anarchically 'unstructured' society. **1973** *Computers & Humanities* VII. 171 The current trend in elementary education is in the direction of open, unstructured classrooms. **1977** *Lancashire Life* Mar. 106/2 Spring coats are lean and unstructured, with their line emphasised with braid or other fabric trimming in contrast colour. **1984** *Guardian* 5 Mar. 11/4 Jackets are loose and unstructured. **1888** Doughty *Arabia Deserta* I. 31 The unwilling contribution of the few *unsubmitted Idumean villages. **1863** Dicey *Federal St.* I. 27 Wherever there is a free and *unsubventioned press, you may be sure [etc.]. **1830** Mackintosh *Progr. Eth. Philos.* Wks. 1846 I. 128 That Dr. Adam Smith's ethical speculations are not so *unsuggested as they are beautiful. **1929** V. W. Pagé *Mod. Aviation Engines* I. xii. 343 A supercharged plane requires a somewhat larger propeller than an *unsupercharged one. **1974** *Encycl. Brit. Macropædia* VII. 936/1 The loss in power suffered by unsupercharged engines at high altitudes can be largely restored [by supercharging]. **1880** McCarthy *Own Times* III. 208 So long as the Bill of 1832 remained *unsupplemented. **1953** W. Moore *Bring Jubilee* (1955) ii. 13 It was impossible to maintain *unsurfaced highways in good condition. **1971** D. Potter *Brit. Eliz. Stamps* vi. 68 A few copies of the 10d on un-surfaced paper . . were found in 1970. **1788** T. Munro, etc. *Olla Podrida* 25 Of difficulties *unsurmounted. **1909** Webster, *Untagged. **1957** D. L. Bolinger in *Publ. Amer. Dial. Soc.* xxviii. 112 The evolution of the secondary towards tag-ness has not reached the point of admitting an untagged secondary on the second A of the most conducive intonation. **1967** *Oceanogr. & Marine Biol.* XVI. 440 The basis for this is an assumption that tagged and untagged fish are caught in the same proportions. **1876** Stone in *Jrnl. R. Geog. Soc.* XLVI. 58 The bodies of the men are often *untattooed. **1868** Visct. Strangford *Select.* (1869) II. 104 They would not have let the triumph pass untold and *untelegraphed. **1962** *Punch* 11 Apr. 555/2 Shakespeare, *untelevised and unrecorded, was never asked to take it all back and substitute some more ethical appeal. **1971** *Guardian* 25 Aug. 8/5 'Polaris—The Secret World' (Yorkshire) was wholly untelevised territory. **1969** *Federal Suppl.* (U.S.) 11 Dec. 1053/1 Person, even though *untenured, may not be denied public employment for unconstitutional reason. **1981** 'A. Cross' *Death in Faculty* v. 49 An untenured professor in search of 'contacts'. **1883** *Athenæum* 8 Sept. 300/2 Untrodden districts— . . *untoured, unspoiled. **1887** *Spectator* 20 Aug. 1111 What is the Channel, so long as it remains *untunnelled. **1919** G. B. Shaw *Heartbreak House* I. 1 A row of books under the window provides an *unupholstered window-seat. **1938** S. Beckett *Murphy* v. 63 Two massive upright unupholstered armchairs. **1843** Tizard *Brewing* 444 New or *unvatted porter. **1871** *Athenæum* 3 June 679 Let them be *unvaunted and unpublished. **1962** *Guardian* 15 Feb. 6/6 Unscripted, *unvetted discussion programmes. **1979** T. Wiseman *Game of Secrets* viii. 100 The company . . in certain cases actually prohibited un-sanctioned intercourse with unvetted outsiders. **1867** *Routledge's Ev. Boy's Ann.* Aug. 471 In the *unvivified condition it absolutely becomes a poison instead of a vivifier.

(*b*) ending in *-ated*. **1969** *Nature* 26 July 419/1 European children, during their first year at school, were like *unacculturated African tribal adults in that many failed to interpret the perspective features of a picture as representing depth. **1956** A. Huxley *Adonis & Alphabet* 156 The problem of what we may politely call '*unactivated sludge'. **1950** Race & Sanger *Blood Groups in Man* iii. 34 Such points as . . the shaking free of *unagglutinated cells enmeshed in agglutinates are skilfully dealt with. **1979** *Jrnl. R. Soc. Med.* LXXII. 450 An unagglutinated suspension of the recipient's blood. **1869** *Bradshaw's Railway Man.* XXI. 183 Deducting all proper expenses and interest on the *unallocated debt. *a* **1974** R. Crossman *Diaries* (1977) III. 953 It looks to me as if he might find himself unallocated and put back into the pool. **1965** *Canad. Jrnl. Linguistics* Fall 45 The whole process is wasteful, much as if one were to work with a number of highly sensitive but quite *uncalibrated scientific instruments. **1974** *Jrnl. Water Pollution Control* XLVI. 2153 (*heading*) Bacteriology of chlorinated and *unchlorinated wastewater effluents. **1884** *American* VIII. 236 The oddest theory . . with which *unconjugated individuals ever comforted themselves. **1886** C. Scott *Sheep-Farming* 208 Cotton cake, *undecorticated. **1902** G. F. Stout in H. Sturt *Personal Idealism* I. 42 All demarcated figure presupposes what we may call *undemarcated figure. **1967** M. Ayub Khan *Friends not Masters* x. 161 A similar situation could arise on our own undemarcated borders in the Sinkiang and Baltistan areas. **1886** B. Harte *Snow-bound* 18 The remaining and *undenominated passenger turned to Hale. **1884** *Spectator* No. 2914. 587/1 Mr. Besant's bowdlerised presentment cannot but tempt to the perusal of the *undepurated loot. **1882** *Pall Mall G.* 8 Apr. 3 The universal *undigitated stocking need not fear its rival. **1846** Worcester (citing Fleming), **Undisintegrated*. **1965** *Amer. Jrnl. Clin. Path.* XLIII. 112/2 The tumor was . . usually *unencapsulated and often diffusely infiltrated the adjacent muscle. **1851** H. Melville *Moby Dick* I. xxxiii. 235 He swings himself to the deck and in an even, *unexhilarated voice, saying 'Dinner, Mr Starbuck,' disappears into the cabin. **1887** *Pall Mall G.* 5 Nov. 7/1 With *unexpropriated landlords . . some sort of arrangement will be come to. **1881** *Standard* 7 Apr. 7/4 There are numerous dead and wounded still *unextricated from the ruins. **1956** *Nature* 18 Feb. 326/2 The *unfractionated polymer . . gives crystals which are smaller and more opaque to electrons. **1885** *Athenæum* 12 Dec. 772/3 The medium . . is *ungranulated ether. **1889** Geddes & Thomson *Evol. Sex* 78 The liberation of *unindividuated sex elements. **1889** *Cent. Dict.*, *Unintegrated. **1920** R. R. Marett *Psychology & Folk-Lore* vi. 121 An un-integrated or imperfectly rational type. *a* **1974** R. Crossman *Diaries* (1977) III. 484 An absolutely self-perpetuating oligarchy of R.H.B.s completely unintegrated with the community services of the local authorities. **1881** *Nation* (N.Y.) XXXII. 426 A manuscript *unmanipulated by them would be of priceless value. **1922** J. Riviere tr. *Freud's Introd. Lect. Psycho-Anal.* iv. 48 They [*sc.* acts] also appear to be *unmotivated, insignificant and unimportant. **1947** *Mind* LVI. 353 Witness the familiar sort of situation where someone has met with misfortune from a natural, apparently unmotivated, cause. **1953** E. Simon *Past Masters* I. 18 The house . . bleak despite a mass of unmotivated Victorian architectural curlicues. **1964** M. Argyle *Psychol. & Social Probl.* v. 70 A man with an unmotivated tendency to attack perambulators and handbags. **1973** *Sci. Amer.* July 22/3 A fairly simple change yielded a considerable response from a group of patients who had previously been characterized . . as 'unmotivated' to seek postpartum checkups. **1977** P. Strevens *New Orientations Teaching of English* i. 10 They are unmotivated towards learning English and sometimes even hostile towards doing so. **1978** H. R. F. Keating *Long Walk to Wimbledon* II. 18 His world was at the mercy of the unmotivated. **1915** *Brain* XXXVIII. 384 The *unmyelinated fibres of spinal nerves are distributed chiefly to the skin. **1980** *Jrnl. R. Soc. Med.* LXXIII. 268 Using the electronmicroscope, Frank . . described unmyelinated nerve fibres in the inner third of fully formed human coronal dentine. **1926** *S. Afr. Jrnl. Sci.* XXIII. 785 The Earlier Stone Age implements are heavily patinated, the later are *unpatinated or only slightly so. **1946** F. E. Zeuner *Dating Past* vi. 193 The gravel has yielded . . in a fresh, unabraded and unpatinated condition: a middle Levalloisian comparable with that found by Burchell. **1934** Webster, *Unrefrigerated. **1964** *Supermarket & Self-Service* (Johannesburg) Feb. 5/2 On the left is a 12 ft. long cabinet with three unrefrigerated shelves. **1968** D. E. Allen *Brit. Tastes* 234 Milk was scarce and the sealed, sterilised variety would stay fresh, though unrefrigerated, for seven days. **1971** *Nature* 25 June 491/3 This fact enabled Hill and Hillova to separate . . the newly replicated double helices . . from *unreplicated DNA. **1976** *Billings* (Montana) *Gaz.* 20 June 12-A/1 It would be 'almost criminal to look upon this unreplicated study as representative'. **1881** Le Conte *Light* 172 Now a rectangular cross-image, if *unrotated, would project as the crosses in the corners. **1905** *Rep. Evolution Committee R. Soc.* II. 110 Some gametes are bearing r.p. [*sc.* the characters of both 'rose comb' and 'pea comb' together (in poultry)] *unsegregated. **1954** *Harper's Mag.* Sept. 47/2 On the first day of the fall term, Amy Miller . . was so apprehensive about entering an unsegregated school that she persuaded her father, a truck driver, to accompany her. **1977** *Listener* 17 Feb. 215/3 One of the motives . . was to bring an unsegregated band to perform before an unsegregated audience. **1923** J. S. Huxley *Ess. Biologist* vii. 271 We may perhaps best say that a sublimated instinct has more and higher values attached to its satisfaction than one *unsublimated. **1952** Gerth & Martindale tr. *Weber's Anc. Judaism* v. 126 Acculturation is generally productive of entirely new . . phenomena given the . . compelling need of absorbing a series of as yet unsublimated ideas. **1967** N. Marsh *Death at Dolphin* iv. 94 An actor . . was embarrassed rather than released by unsublimated chunks of raw association. **1887** Cook *Sievers' O.E. Gram.* 168 The middle vowel has again forced an entrance from the *unsyncopated forms. **1922** W. J. Locke *Tale of Triona* ix. 97 A company of women groping . . after ideals in unsyncopated time. **1950** Blesh & Janis *They all played Ragtime* (1958) ii. 44 The second and third themes, printed unsyncopated, cry out for syncopation when one plays them. **1953** K. Jackson *Lang. & Hist. in Early Britain* 689 The AS. *Cerdic* seems to have been borrowed . . from a syncopated Pr. W. **Car'dig* . . side by side with unsyncopated *Ceredig*. **1939** *Geogr. Jrnl.* XCIV. 221 A high pyramid of *unvegetated sand was a prominent landmark. **1970** *Nature* 2 May 429/2 The unvegetated mudflats of Sanderson's Gulf.

(*c*) ending in *-ized*. **1938** A. Farrer in T. E. Jessup et al. *Christian Understanding of Man* 211 Christianity asserts . . that there is a true nature of man . . actual in the Divine mind and never wholly *unactualized in men. **1875** A. J. C. Hare *Days near Rome* I. 1 The real, true, un-Anglicized, *un-Americanized country. **1931** *Times Lit. Suppl.* 18 June 481/4 An un-Americanised . . honest English England. **1950** O. Nash *Family Reunion* (1951) 134 He undergoes the lecturing Like *unanesthetized vivisecturing. **1934** Blunden *Mind's Eye* IV. 256 A world as yet *unanatomized by scientific accuracy. **1875** *Un-Anglicized [see *un-Americanized* above]. **1964** B. Trnka in D. Abercrombie et al. *Daniel Jones* 186 The French nasals in the occasionally un-Anglicized pronunciation of Modern French words. **1873** J. Davies *Hesiod, & Theognis* II. i. 130 The shape in which the poetry of Theognis has come down to us is as unlike the original form and drift as a handbook of maxims from Shakespeare is unlike an undoctored and *un-Bowdlerised play. **1957** *Times Lit. Suppl.* 6 Dec. 738/2 A quarter of a century ago the complete, unbowdlerized edition of 1951 might have made a stir. **1886** *Pall Mall G.* 1 Oct. 4/1 A father of limited means and *uncapitalized income. **1885** Seth *Scott. Philos.* iv. 136 To this *uncategorised perception . . Kant allows a wide range. **1852** *Meanderings of Mem.* I. 76 Hope, *un-celestialized by heathen hand. **1862** J. S. Mill in *Westm. Rev.* XXII. 510 The vast *uncolonized region of Arkansas, and Texas. **1979** *Jrnl. Brit. Interplanetary Soc.* XXXII. 222/1 The relative availability of uncolonized stars will be rapidly and dramatically restricted. **1921** E. Sapir *Language* 176 The long *un-diphthongized *u* is still preserved in Lowland Scotch. **1951** W. K. Matthews *Languages U.S.S.R.* iii. 35 Undiphthongised long *e* and *o*. **1860** W. C. Lake in *Life* (1901) 199 Liddell, whom I found quite different and *un-donicised (by the side of Whewell at least). **1907** G. Murray *Rise Greek Epic* ii. 55 It was a hard task for an island in that position to keep itself *un-Hellenized. **1934** A. Toynbee *Study of Hist.* II. 79 This region remained unhellenized much longer than many places that were far more distant from the Aegean. **1960** C. S. Lewis *Studies in Words* ii. 24 In defiance of chronology, we begin with some account of the Latin and English words in their un-hellenised condition. **1855** Milman *Lat. Chr.* xiv. vi. (1864) IX. 218 Toulouse owns only her own *unidealised unromanticised Counts. **1934** Webster, *Unindustrialized. **1962** *Rep. Constitution Commission, Pakistan 1961* iv. 40 The unindustrialized portion of Bengal. **1978** R. Mitchison *Life in Scotland* viii. 154 The Scottish pattern of tall tenements . . is to be found in older unindustrialized burghs. **1885** *Athenæum* 20 June 788/1 The author's liberal use of *unitalicized . . French words. **1971** *Un-lemmatized [see *key-word-in-context* s.v. key *sb.*[1] 18]. **1968** O. Wynd *Sumatra Seven Zero* ii. 16 She'll have a handsome income for as long as the place stays *un-nationalized. **1957** L. Fox *Numerical Solution Two-Point Boundary Probl.* vii. 170 This constant is the reciprocal of the corresponding current estimate of λ, obtained as the ratio of successive *unnormalized first components. **1889** *Cent. Dict.*, *Unparasitized. **1949** *Proc. Soc. Exper. Biol. & Med.* LXX. 580/2 To make such values really comparable with those obtained for unparasitized blood it is necessary to know both the parasite count, and the proportions present of parasites of different sizes. **1909** Webster, *Unpasteurized. **1955** J. G. Davis *Dict. Dairying* (ed. 2) 789 Special fluting arrangements to prevent any unpasteurised milk seepages from reaching the outlet connection. **1975** *Listener* 14 Aug. 205/2 The beer here is unpasteurised, unassisted into the glass by CO_2. **1946** *Electronic Engin.* Feb. 54/3 *Unplasticised polyvinyl chloride. **1982** Sears & Darby *Technol. of Plasticizers* v. 301 Rigid, unplasticized PVC . . essentially obeys Hooke's Law for quite some distance. **1976** D. Davin *Woman-Work* (1978) ii. 57 Communist experience in the towns had been limited to clandestine work in which contact with the mass of *unpoliticized women was very difficult. **1879** *Jrnl. Chem. Soc.* XXXV. 758 They [*sc.* terpenes] are ultimately rendered optically inactive, a considerable proportion remaining *unpolymerised. **1976** *Jrnl. Molecular Biol.* CV. 527 Is there an appreciable amount of unpolymerized protein free within the cytoplasm, as there probably is for microtubules? **1958** A. Toynbee *East to West* 37 Even this *unpressurized plane would fly high enough to make certain of that [*sc.* flying blind]. **1963** *Economist* 2 Feb. 413/2 Some of the best thinking had been done under pressure . . far from . . optimum conditions. . . Its case for an unpressurised future might have seemed stronger. **1974** P. Gore-Booth *With Great Truth & Respect* 57 But I did, between Chicago and Minneapolis, take my first aeroplane flight; nobody warned me what an unpressurized flight does to your ears. **1978** S. Radley *Death & Maiden* xiii. 123 The real, unpressurised Adnams Suffolk ale. **1978** *Detroit Free Press* 16 Apr. E2/4 (Advt.), Package of 3 Nassau brand unpressurized tennis balls. **1959** *Times* 28 May 16/6 Equally important is a constant, *unpublicized two-way exchange. **1977** M. Edelman *Polit. Lang.* vii. 123 Both the publicized and the un-publicized aspects of policymaking processes have functions to serve. **1967** *Ann. Entomol. Soc. Amer.* LX. 1134/1 The second type of integument is found in the softer *unsclerotized regions of the body. **1976** D. J. Horn *Biol. Insects* v. 212 Greater freedom of movement between sclerotized parts is afforded by thin, unsclerotized membranes at joints of moveable body parts. **1934** Webster, *Unsocialized. **1948** H. V. Hodson *Twentieth-Cent. Empire* x. 112 The still unstabilized and unsocialized citizens. **1964** P. Meadows in I. L. Horowitz *New Sociology* 451 Locating the sources of human hostility in . . unsocialized, primitive impulse, Freudian social theory provided the same kind of conservative blast at political and economic radicalism. *a* **1861** Cunningham *Hist. Theol.* (1864) II. xxiv. 325 The sounder or *unsocinianized Arminians. **1830** Lamb *Let.* 24 May, I . . know no more of stave and crochet Than did the *Un-Spaniardised Peruvians. **1864** *Sat. Rev.* 3 Dec., A mere *unspurgeonized profane grocer. **1948** *Unstabilized [see *un-socialized* above]. **1960** *Times* 23 Feb. 12/2 The other [class of satellite] was a smaller unstabilized instrumentation package of 50 lb. **1975** *Petroleum Rev.* XXIX. 89/3 Unstabilised raw crude oil consisting of crude oil and natural gas liquids will be pumped at increasing rates of throughput to Teesside. **1909** Webster, *Unstandardized. **1920** S. Alexander *Space, Time, & Deity* II. 262 Error is real only as possessed by the unstandardised believer. **1930** E. Weekley *Adjectives & Other Words* 154, I need hardly say that he was one of the elderly and unstandardized—the sort of man . . who says *onct* for *once*. **1909** Webster, *Unsterilized. **1945** *Mind* LIV. 327 Pasteur found that putrescible liquids exposed to unsterilised air . . developed infusoria. **1979** *United States 1980/81* (Penguin Travel Guides) 333 The atmosphere in this 19th-century structure is distinctly unmodern . . and un-sterilized. **1885** *Pall Mall G.* 23 Jan. 5/1 *Unsubventionized English steamers. **1858** *Brownson's Q. Rev.* Apr. 198 Salvation lies in the supernatural order, and is not secured in the *unsupernaturalized by the simple negative merit of not sinning. **1844** Draper in *Philos. Mag.* July 2 The *untithonized chlorine shows no disposition to unite with its hydrogen. **1973** *Guardian* 23 Feb. 17/2 The American unions seemed to accept a situation in which some 68 million workers . . remained *ununionized. **1984** *Listener* 1 Mar. 15/2 There is . . an inability to see what this feels like from the point of view of people who may be unskilled workers who are still predominantly ununionised. **1968** P. Dickinson *Skin Deep* iii. 42 There was still a telephone kiosk . . momentarily *unvandalised too. **1844** Noad *Electricity* (ed. 2) 267 If even the smallest quantity of liquid remains in the capsule, *unvaporized. **1909** W. James *Pluralistic Universe* 348 Its purity is only a relative term, meaning the proportional amount of *unverbalized sensation which it [*sc.* experience] still embodies. **1977** P. STREVENS *New Orientations Teaching Eng.* xii. 149 The internalized, unverbalized rules according to which sentences are created.

b. Past pples. with other endings, from strong or weak verbs. These form a much smaller class, but include a considerable number in common use, as *unbegun*, *unblown*, *unborn*, *unbought*, etc. A few are found with *-ate* for *-ated*, as *unevaporate*, *-exaggerate*, but these and others not permanently established in the language are of rare occurrence.

Examples in Ash are *unbeset*, *uncast*, *uninterwoven*, *unshotten*, *unshown*, *unslung*, etc.

c. Participial formations with *un-* frequently have a suffixed adverb or preposition (usually with a hyphen when the formation is used attributively). An early example of this is *unborne-away* (Caxton, 1483); others make their appearance in the 16th and 17th centuries, as *uncalled-for*, *uncared-for*, *unheard-of*, *unlooked-for*, *unthought-of*, etc. A number of these have become permanent and are in general use; the following are examples of more casual formations.

1884 H. SPENCER in *Contemp. Mag.* 613 Exceptional communities unaggressive and from special causes *unaggressed upon. **1858** FROUDE *Hist. Eng.* IV. 496 Unvouched for, *unalluded to by any contemporary authority as yet discovered. **1887** *Daily News* 3 Nov. 2/5 You have..allowed your conduct to remain unexplained and *unapologised for. **1855** BROWNING *Bp. Blougram's Apol.* 894 Not simply unbutted at, *unbickered with. **1847** MEDWIN *Shelley* I. 105 This startling and *unborne-out proposition. **1970** D. FRANCIS *Rat Race* ix. 116 The Derrydowns Six had been hired by an *un-clued-up trainer. **1982** *Times* 20 Apr. 1/5 Cardinal Hume..said..'I am terribly unclued up on what constitutes a war.' **1873** WATERFORD in Hare *Two Noble Lives* (1893) III. 325 [For my dance] I expect so many very young and pretty girls—the *un-come-out Durhams and Tankervilles. **1860** E. VENABLES *Isle of Wight* 332 Many a lovely nook ..*unencroached upon as yet by gentility. **1836** R. M. M'CHEYNE in *Mem.* (1872) 296 It had left some footpath *unglared across. **1832** TENNYSON *Sonn., Alexander* 12 High things were spoken there, *unhanded down. **1863** GROSART *Small Sins* (ed. 2) 79, I do not say that his prayer will go unheard, much less *unhearkened to. **1839** BURGON *Life & Times Gresham* I. ii. 57 His administration..was very nearly *uninterfered with. **1830** J. G. STRUTT *Sylva Brit.* 11 The extent to which the oak will throw its broad arms..when *unintruded upon. **1648** HEXHAM II, *Een Onbeslapen dochter*, a maide *Vnlien with, or a Virgine. **1828** *Craven Gloss.*, **Unmelled-on*, not meddled with. **1849** MILL *Ess.* (1859) II. 335 Justice..demand[s] that these unmerited attacks should not remain *unprotested against. **1871** MACDUFF *Mem. Patmos* vii. 90 As they sob their tale of *unresponded-to anguish. **1849** M. ARNOLD *Fragm.* '*Antigone*' i. [He] makes his own welfare his *unswerv'd-from law. *a* **1674** CLARENDON *Hist. Reb.* XVI. §17 After he had lived some years in Paris *untaken notice of, indeed unknown.

d. A type of formation which is not very frequent is that in which the participle is preceded by a noun, usually with instrumental sense, as in the following examples.

1595 *Polimanteia* (1881) 36 For not..aged censoring Cato might challenge greater priuiledge of trueth, then your free toongd and *vn-aw-bound skill. **1765** [E. THOMPSON] *Meretriciad* 26 She never vended goods *unduty paid. **1829** BENTHAM *Justice & Cod. Petit.* 104 Because by the judges, *unfee-fed as they would be, nothing would be to be got by it. **1895** L. A. TOLLEMACHE *B. Jowett* 135 The barren laurels of an *un-heaven-rewarded martyrdom. **1659** FULLER *App. Inj. Innoc.* II. 68 That single and signal instance of that *Unparliament-impowred Convocation. **1598** BARRET *Theor. Warres* 5 The *vnsouldier-learned, to the vnlettered souldier may be paralleld as the Phisition Theorike to the grosse practitioner. **1605** SYLVESTER *Du Bartas* II. iii. IV. *Captains* 1022 Where, Learned men, *un-soule-clog'd (as it were) With servile gyves of Kings imperious Fear, Fly even to Heav'n. **1879** RUTLEY *Study Rocks* xiv. 300 Consisting partly of angular and comparatively *unwater-worn.. materials.

9. a. Adjectival forms in *-ed*, from substantives, of the type *unbearded*, *unbodied*, *unfeathered*, etc. These are anticipated in OE. by such rare formations as *unȝefeþered*, *unȝewintred*, *unwǣded*, but otherwise belong to the 16th and subsequent centuries. The usual sense is 'not provided or furnished with', but sometimes 'not affected by', 'not treated with', etc.; in the latter case the use is not clearly distinguishable from the purely participial.

Ash gives such instances as *unaproned*, *unbrooched*, *unbuskined*, *unchevroned*, *uncliented*, *uncodded*, etc.

Recent formations include: ***unautumned***, ***unaveraged***, ***unbanked*** (also *absol.*), ***unbra-ed***, ***unbrassièred***, ***undentisted***, ***ungated***, ***ungoggled***, ***unillusioned***, ***unjacketed***, ***unmooned***, ***unpupilled***, ***unrectored***, ***unscripted***, ***unspeeched***.

1881 J. M. BROWN *Student Life* 13 The *unancestored genius. **1920** J. MASEFIELD *Enslaved* 6 The old *unautumned beauty that never goes away. **1905** WEBSTER, *Un-averaged. **1924** G. B. SHAW *St. Joan* p. xli, The unaveraged individual, representing life..never at its merely mathematical average. **1965** *Economist* 19 June p. vii, One way of jerking the clearing banks into providing better facilities for the great *unbanked public. **1980** *Daily Tel.* 9 Dec. 15 The banks are well aware that they can best pay their own wages bills by drumming up more business from the great unbanked. **1873** *Daily News* 22 Aug., The barbarous exposure of them, *unblanketed in piquet line. **1962** J. P. CARSTAIRS *Pardon my Gun* i. 20 The large cusp-like *un-bra-ed bosom..stood, prow-like. **1965** G. MCINNES *Road to Gundagai* ix. 148 He touched his hat to local Mums with shapeless *unbrassiered bosoms. **1981** M. GEE *Dying, in Other Words* 74 She had pressed her unbrassièred breasts on his shoulders and said he was gorgeous. **1846** WORCESTER (citing *Ed. Rev.*), **Unbuoyed*.., not buoyed. **1892** STEVENSON *Across the Plains* 13 A butler perhaps rides as high over the *unbutlered. **1882** *Encycl. Brit.* XIV. 862/2 The *uncathedralled paganisms of American scenery and life. **1864** SALA in *Daily Tel.* 25 Feb., I wonder whether the *unchattelled farmer will keep his oath. **1885** *Jrnl. Science* July 389 The sewage of an *unclosetted town. **1877** BLACKMORE *Cripps* (1887) 240 His simple, unpractised, and *un-cored heart. **1886** *Pall Mall G.* 3 Aug. 6/2 A supplementary *uncostumed choir.. supported the singing. **1873** 'SUSAN COOLIDGE' *What Katy did at Sch.* xi. 183 As she looked up at the *uncottoned space at the top of the window. *a* **1916** H. JAMES *Sense of Past* (1917) 290 His perfect and soignées teeth..which that *undentisted age can't have known the like of. **1860** *All Year Round* No. 47. 493 With paint washed off and *undiamonded hair. **1887** D. A. LOW *Machine Drawing* Pref. p. iii, An *undimensioned scale drawing. **1883** *19th Cent.* May 858 *Unfountained from above, the higher moral virtues would decay for lack of a meaning. **1954** *Norfolk Mag.* June 57/2 Immediately beyond the farmhouse is the now *ungated entrance to the grounds. **1978** C. TOMLINSON *Shaft* 21 Did Eden Greet us ungated? **1914** M. BEERBOHM in *Eng. Rev.* Dec. 18 From time to time (for I too was *ungoggled) I looked round to nod and smile. **1940** G. FRANKAU *Self-Portrait* lxii. 385, I drove like a fool, the car open and my eyes ungoggled. **1864** ELIZ. MURRAY *Ella Norman* II. 270 That on the left was a treeless, *ungrassed elevation. **1887** RIDER HAGGARD *Jess* xiv, You must either knock under..or trek on into the *unhostelled wilderness. **1934** WEBSTER, *Unillusioned. **1940** W. FAULKNER *Hamlet* II. ii. 130 The father, the lean pleasant shrewd unillusioned man..had been betrayed at the last. **1982** *London Rev. Bks.* IV. XXIV. 23/2 We competitors are unillusioned about the lipservice of the walls of leaning bodies and megaphone hands that we sprint between. **1860** *All Year Round* No. 41. 344 A draught of pure *unincensed air from the open window. **1878** B. TAYLOR *Deukalion* II. v. 90 Druid oaks *Univied, stretch their stubborn arms abroad. **1925** *Times* 17 Aug. 6/2 A single *unjacketed saucepan of a capacity equal to twice the amount of water to be put into it. **1970** D. DODGE *Hatchetman* iii. 52 They used lead bullets, unjacketed; illegal, under the Hague Convention. **1980** N. MARSH *Photo-Finish* iv. 86 He..came upon a book... It was unjacketed and the spine was rubbed. **1880** MISS BIRD *Japan* I. p. xxii, An *unmatted floor. **1926** S. LESLIE *Cantab* (ed. 2) x. 115 The *unmooned sky inked out the Universe. **1940** W. FAULKNER *Hamlet* II. ii. 127 The long return through night-time roads across the mooned or unmooned sleeping land. **1821** *Examiner* 5 Aug. 482/1 The unbeneficed and *unparked. **1844** POE *Mesmeric Rev.* Wks. 1864 I. 113 Until we arrive at a matter *unparticled—without particles. **1888** RUTLEY *Rock-Forming Min.* 142 A band of unstriated or *unpegged crystal. **1874** J. ADDIS *Eliz. Echoes* (1879) 110 Defiant Chestnuts prick the air, *Unpennon'd battle-spears arraying. **1914** R. BROOKE *Let.* Mar. (1968) 568 They come to you by night,..& their eyes—*unpupiled balls of white —fall out too, & they stink & shine. **1955** W. GADDIS *Recognitions* I. vii. 231 He did not move, nor did his unpupiled eyes betray any surprise. **1861** *Times* 25 Feb. 8/5 The banks of our river *unquayed. **1863** *Not an Angel* II. 260 The *unrailwayed inhabitants of that neighbourhood. **1836** F. MAHONY *Rel. Father Prout* (1859) 394 As for your critic,..We *unrancoured hope to see him. **1944** AUDEN *For Time Being* 31 She cannot conceivably tolerate in her presence..the rival..who does not rule but defiantly is the *unrectored chaos. *a* **1871** DE MORGAN *Budget Parad.* (1872) 75 The following, of which I have an *unreferenced note. **1887** MEREDITH *Poet. Wks.* (1912) 332 Idly the flax wheel spun *unridered. **1877** BLACKMORE *Erema* xi, The riders struck the savage, *unrowelled spur into them. **1822** WILKINS *Body & Soul* I. 123 The picturesque appearance of the *unsabled mourners. **1953** *Ann. Reg. 1952* 449 Previously an *unscripted defamatory broadcast was treated as slander. **1966** G. N. LEECH *Eng. in Advertising* ix. 89 So far my remarks about the spoken language have applied mainly to unrehearsed and un-scripted speech. **1852** *Meanderings of Mem.* I. 5 Worn As weary nakedness, *unshooned, unshorn. **1854** HOOKER *Himal. Jrnls.* I. xi. 252 The ridge was *unsnowed a little way down the east flank. **1880** 'MARK TWAIN' *Tramp Abroad* I. 144 The only 'distinguished dead' who went down to the grave *unsonnetted. **1831** SCOTT *Jrnl.* 26 Nov., I got home about mid-night; but remain unpoetised and *unspeeched. **1922** JOYCE *Ulysses* 49 His mouth moulded issuing breath, unspeeched. **1648** HEXHAM II, *Ongespitst*, Vnpointed, or *Vnspired. **1866** in *Cassell's Techn. Educ.* (1879) IV. 108/2 The fold-yards are also kept *unspouted. **1823** E. MOOR *Suffolk Words* 23 Where words occur, not readily understood by the *Unsuffolked reader, he is to take them as Suffolcisms. **1872** G. B. CHEEVER *Lect. Pilgr. Progr.* xiv. 345 What we know of the..state of *untabernacled souls is but little. **1890** 'R. BOLDREWOOD' *Col. Reformer* (1891) 244 The serene *untempested heavens of the isles of the blest. **1860** O. W. HOLMES *Elsie V.* xiv, There are states of mind.. which remain not only unworded, but *unthoughted. **1867** H. CONYBEARE in *Fortn. Rev.* Nov. 514 There is a breadth of effect in the..*untraceried windows. **1888** YEATS *Wand. Oisin* Poems (1908) 259 His vast foot that lay Half in the *unvesselled sea. **1866** CRICHTON *Rambles Orcades* 34 Over country 'unrailway-ed' and '*unvilla-ed'.

b. Instances in which the noun is preceded by a qualifying word are not numerous, and such formations are usually individual or casual.

[**1650** TRAPP *Comm. Lev.* xxi. 18 Lest his Ministerie bee sleighted for..unheavenlie mindedness.] **1870** *Routledge's Ev. Boy's Ann.* May, Suppl. 3/1 Plain white unwatermarked paper. **1872** RUSKIN *Fors Clav.* xix. 6 My notion of..charity is, by no means..the giving to unable-bodied paupers. **1964** *Economist* 19 Dec. 1356/1 A straightforward, unfootnoted historical narrative.

10. The use of *un-* with present participles, revived about 1300 (see 4 above), subsequently became common, and has given rise to a large number of permanent words, such as *unbecoming*, *unbending*, *unchanging*, *undoubting*, etc. (On the participial use of such forms see 5 d.) Examples of casual formations are given below.

Others occurring in Ash's dictionary are *unbeguiling*, *unbiasing*, *unblinding*, *unbuilding*, *unenticing*, *unflowing*, etc.

Recent formations include: ***unalloying***, ***unarresting***, ***uncompelling***, ***unconflicting***, ***unendearing***, ***unenticing***, ***unexhilarating***, ***unexpanding***, ***unfascinating***, ***unflowering***, ***unforfending***, ***unforthcoming***, ***unmatching***, ***unminding*** (cf. UNMINDING *vbl. sb.*), ***unmourning***, ***unselfpitying***, ***unselfregarding***, ***unselfseeking***, ***unswinging*** [SWINGING *ppl. a.* 3 b, c], ***unthreatening***.

1812 SHELLEY *Retrospect* in *Compl. Poet. Wks.* (1904) 970/2 When mountain, meadow, wood and stream With *unalloying glory gleam. **1883** R. BRIDGES *Prometh.* 79 Hope..to cheer with visions fair Their *unamending pains. **1844** WARDLAW *Prov.* xxxix. (1869) II. 44 Doctrines of this easy *unannoying description. **1873** RUSKIN *Fors Clav.* xxx. 2 He showed his wisdom in pleasant and *unappalling ways. **1845** R. W. HAMILTON *Pop. Educ.* iii. (ed. 2) 40 Agriculture, ..in the ordinary processes of its labour,..has been simple and *un-arousing. **1906** G. HIGGINS in A. Smith *Life of St. Agnes* p. viii, It may be objected..that a book treating of times and persons and occurrences of so ancient a date must be dull and *unarresting. **1958** *Times* 25 Nov. 14/4 It was disconcerting to hear..so musically unarresting an account from her of so genial a work. **1876** MRS. WHITNEY *Sights & Ins.* II. xxxviii. 673 There had been two wonderful tides, that which carried them forth, all uncertain, *unbelonging, separate. **1870** G. T. DODDS in Bonar *Life* ii. (1884) 70 Our study will be comparatively useless and *unbenefiting. **1885** *Pall Mall G.* 6 Feb. 6/1 A safe and *unblundering guide through the mazes. **1862** FURNIVALL *Handlyng Synne* Pref. p. ix, Ready to turn to account, though in an *unboring way, every opportunity. **1873** C. E. NORTON *Lett.* (1913) I. viii. 471 Carlyle seemed a little weary, perhaps weakened by the mild *unbracing weather. **1837** WHITTOCK *Bk. Trades* (1842) 358 None of these ends can be accomplished..unless this be done in a neat '*unbungling' manner. **1886** *Academy* 14 Aug. 109/1 The Gaelic tribes of Ireland—that 'heap of *uncementing sand'. **1884** *Harper's Mag.* Apr. 659/2 Da Porta's..*uncommenting way of telling the story. **1857** LD. GRANVILLE in *Life* (1905) I. x. 260, I encourage the correspondence by commonplace *uncommitting acknowledgements. **1920** W. J. LOCKE *House of Baltazar* xi. 130 We sought for possible imperative objectives, and one so apparently *un-compelling as China never occurred to us. **1977** *Gramophone* Jan. 1139/3 How best to write about a set which is noteworthy but ultimately uncompelling? **1784** R. BAGE *Barham Downs* I. 101 *Unconcatenating blockhead! **1899** 'J. OXENHAM' *Rising Fortunes* xxvii. 182 His was a character of sharp contrasts—of perfect consistency, from his own point of view—of *unconflicting opposites. **1938** F. SCOTT FITZGERALD *Let.* 18 Apr. (1964) 29 We are unconflicting on 90% of things. **1858** FABER *Spir. Confer.* 136 Of all saving things, fear..is..the most *undeluding. **1823** D. M[c]NICOLL *Wks.* (1837) 118 *Undemurring confidence. **1856** RUSKIN *Mod. Paint.* IV. v. 20 To burn *undisdaining upon the reeds of the river. **1865** GROSART *Mem. H. Palmer* 38 His was the omnipotence of the light,.. silent *undisplaying might. **1805** *Med. Jrnl.* XIV. 495 A simple *unembarrassing method of stopping the screw from being relaxed. **1926** W. DE LA MARE *Connoisseur* 49 The eyes ..were now peering vacantly..over a trim but *unendearing moustache at the crumbs on his empty plate. **1981** F. INGLIS *Promise of Happiness* viii. 202 That is a lapse into avuncularity... In the novel..it is not un-endearing. **1915** W. J. LOCKE *Jaffery* v. 63 Mountains..were made for goats and cascades and lunatics..; and the more jagged and *unenticing they are, the greater is their specious air of stupendousness. **1948** D. WELCH *Brave & Cruel* 95, I wondered that Mr. Mellon could show such fondness for Phyllis; she seemed so very unenticing to me. **1978** *Observer* 16 Apr. 38/1 The furniture was unenticing, but some American dealer would take a 40-foot container of assorted items. **1811** JANE AUSTEN *Sense & Sensibility* II. xiii. 253 The nature of her commendation..was..very *unexhilarating to Edward. **1909** W. J. LOCKE *Septimus* x. 114 He walked to the window and looked out into the unexhilarating street. **1968** *Punch* 3 Jan. 32/2 With such an unexhilarating cast-list you'd expect a muted, subfusc drama. But there are surprises in store. **1905** *Spectator* 11 Mar. 363 Countries which exclude coloured labour,.. though possessing a larger area and..advantages of soil and climate, continue to suffer from..*unexpanding revenue, heavy taxation, and a stationary population. **1957** 'O. EDWARDS' *Talking of Books* 231 The time came, alas—as it always must in the case of expanding collections of books and unexpanding homes—when something had to go. **1866** GEO. ELIOT *Felix Holt* III. xliii. 149 The love of this not *unfascinating man. **1883** *Athenæum* 15 Dec. 774/3 The stories are as unfascinating as they can be made. **1887** J. HUTCHISON *Lect. Phil.* xvii. 187 The *unfaultfinding complacency with which he contemplated one of his later works. **1942** T. S. ELIOT *Little Gidding* iii. 12 Being between two lives—*unflowering, between The live and the dead nettle. **1891** HARDY *Tess* III. lvii. 255 Their every idea was temporary and *un-forefending, like the plans of two children. **1920** 'O. DOUGLAS' *Penny Plain* xiv. 141 He might be so shy and *unforthcoming that he would put people off. **1934** R. A. KNOX *Still Dead* xii. 152 He was certainly a very repressed, unforthcoming sort of boy. **1966** I. JEFFERIES *House-Surgeon* i. 13 Smiling uncomfortably and looking round for unforthcoming support from Grant. **1981** 'E. LATHEN' *Going for Gold* xvi. 183 They were guarding a secret... It tells us why Miss Deladier..was so unforthcoming when we spoke to her. **1865** MRS. CARLYLE *Lett.* (1883) III. 263 She is so kind and *unfussing. *c* **1860** FABER *Hymn, Sacr. Heart* iii, In that *ungrowing vision nothing deepens, nothing brightens. **1876** MEREDITH *Beauch. Career* II. iv. 64 The *unlettering elusive moon. **1887** MORRIS *Odyss.* XII. 325 But *unlulling blew the south-wind. **1881** R. G. WHITE *Eng.* 74 This *unmarring modesty of outward show. **1939** D. WALLACE *E. Anglia* ii. 35 This unique church with its two *unmatching towers. **1969** C. ARMSTRONG *Seven Seats to Moon* xiii. 119 A bottle and two unmatching glasses. **1945** DYLAN THOMAS in *Life & Lett.* July 28 Under the *unminding skies. **1945** —— in *New Republic* 14 May 675/2 By the *unmourning water Of the riding Thames. **1867** J. Thomson *Vane's Story*, etc. (1881) 113 Their eyes..flashed..like swift swords That leapt *unparrying to each other's heart. **1873** Miss Broughton *Nancy* II. 216, I pass and re-pass the cold River Gods of the *unplaying fountain. **1862** Mrs. Crosland *Mrs. Blake* II. 131 Men..profess..a certain horror of an '*unpraying' woman. **1822–7** Good *Study Med.* (1829) III. 18 In a pure and healthy, or *unpredisposing atmosphere. **1866** J. G. Murphy *Comm., Exodus* xxi. 14 The milder sentence of the *unpremeditating manslayer. **1866** S. B. James *Duty & Doctr.* (1871) 290 Eternity hastens on, and so many are unprepared, are *unpreparing, to meet it. **1864** *Realm* 24 Feb. 2 *Unpresaging of the complaints which will ere long issue from the offices. **1867** H. Bushnell *Mor. Uses Dark Things* 195 Tropical consciences, which are out-door, self-indulgent, *unpronouncing consciences. **1862** R. H. Patterson *Ess. Hist. & Art* 403 Secluded in position and *unproselytising in spirit. **1885** *Athenæum* 24 Oct. 533 His life was an *unprotesting protest against convention. **1821** Cobbett *Rur. Rides* (1885) I. 38 It is no very *unprovoking reflection. *c* **1800** Macneill *To Eliza* 43 Plaguing her plain, *unpuffing spouse, About his former oaths and vows. **1882** H. S. Holland *Logic & Life* (1885) 24 These impulses cannot be altogether blind and *unpurposing. **1881** Ruskin *Bible Amiens* iv. §10 On the *unquaking and fruitful earth. *a* **1859** De Quincey *Posth. Wks.* (1891) I. 220 To explain the true character of note-writing—how compressed and *unrambling and direct it ought to be. **1878** S. Cox *Salv. Mundi* vii. (ed. 3) 145 Doomed to an endless and *un-redeeming torment. **1880** S. Lanier *Sunrise* Poems (1884) 8 The wave-serrate sea-rim sinks unjarring, *un-reeling. **1874** L. Tollemache in *Fortn. Rev.* Feb. 229 We are..led to describe the poet..as an *unreforming optimist. **1869** Mrs. H. Wood *Roland Yorke* III. 173 To submit to it in *unrefuting tameness. **1854** Faber *Growth in Holiness* xiii. 223 Go walk by the shore of that *unresounding sea. **1858** J. Robertson *Poems* 78 As light is mixed in the *unretreating air. **1864** A. de Vere in *Reader* 30 Apr. 545/1 We part..With *unreverting faces, not ingrate. **1868** Pusey *Serm. Pharisaism* 11 Monuments..scarce held in being by our *unsacrificing gifts. **1845** *Florist's Jrnl.* (1846) VI. 177 An upright *unscrambling habit, and very blunt leaflets. **1932** W. Faulkner *Light in August* xi. 221 The hard, untearful and *unselfpitying..yielding of that surrender. **1983** *N. & Q.* Dec. 576/1 The voice that emerges..is that of a writer who is..generous in spirit, self-aware and unself-pitying. *a* **1945** E. R. Eddison *Mezentian Gate* (1958) ii. 21 An ambiency of beauty that lived in her whole frame and posture, an easefulness and reposefulness of *un-selfregarding grace. **1982** W. J. Walsh *R. K. Narayan* i. 27 An oblique and as unself-regarding a treatment as anything like an autobiography could possibly be. **1931** W. S. Churchill *World Crises* VI. iii. 53 Fop, dandy, la-di-da; amiable, polite and curiously *un-selfseeking. **1963** *Times* 7 June 7/3 Edward Grey, 'the most completely unselfconscious and unselfseeking politician I have ever known'. **1888** Meredith *Poems* (1898) II. 143, I saw, *unsighting: her heart I saw. **1880** A. Raleigh *Way to City* (1881) 282 His goodness is a full and *unslacking stream. **1674** N. Fairfax *Bulk & Selv.* 47 All tastless, nothing relishing; all *unsmelling, nothing scented. **1873** Pater *Stud. Hist. Renaiss.* 74 This last passion would be the most *unsoftening..of all. **1848** Buckley *Iliad* 193 Both heard an *unsoothing reply. **1883** R. Bridges *Prometh.* 395 To sow thy seed Year after year in this *un-sprouting soil. **1815** Chalmers *Let.* in *Life* (1851) II. 25 The more *unstaggering your faith is..the more is God well pleased with it. **1834** De Quincey *Autob. Sk.* Wks. 1853 I. 211 We were detained a few days in those *unsteaming times by foul winds. **1863** W. Lancaster *Præterita* 43, I lean on this *unstumbling oracle, And nourish hope. **1958** K. Goodwin in P. Gammond *Decca Bk. Jazz* xiii. 153 Rumsey—himself a rather dull, plodding, completely *unswinging bassist. **1967** *Punch* 23 Aug. 275/2 It only takes you a day or two in this utterly unswinging country to realise what a frightful crushing bore the legendary London Scene has become. **1969** *Daily Tel.* 29 May 22/7 An unswinging Anglo-Irishman who stands for the common decencies now so acutely unfashionable. **1972** *Jazz & Blues* Feb. 22/1 Marshall is a little unswinging in places but Weston is suitably solid. **1844** G. S. Faber *Eight Dissert.* (1845) II. 127 An *unsystematising perusal of the prophecy itself. **1885** *Irish Monthly* Nov. 598 The white monotony of *unthawing snow. **1903** E. Wharton *Sanctuary* I. i. 11 The very lifting of the cloud—remote, *unthreatening as it had been. **1858** H. Bushnell *Serm. New Life* 100 More ambitious and more *untransforming to the people. **1865** *Pall Mall G.* 29 Sept. 10/1 Novel sensations wherewith to enliven the *untravelling reader. **1888** A. S. Wilson *Lyric Hopeless Love* 162 Nor vow..nor sacred rite The *ununiting can unite. **1880** W. Watson *Prince's Quest*, etc. (1892) 94 So forward piloted.., she held her way *Unveering. **1878** Jessie Fothergill *First Violin* vi. iv, To finger, or blow into, or beat the dumb, *unvibrating things. **1878** B. Taylor *Deukalion* I. iv. 34 Gray sedges wave *Unwhispering ever, o'er the slimy flats. **1887** Morris *Odyss.* x. 282 Whither away..dost thou wander,..*Unwotting of the country?"

11. a. In OE. adverbial formations in *-lice* formed a large portion of the words in *un-*. Very few of these survived in ME., but additions were gradually made which maintained the existence of the type (ending in *-liche* in southern dialects and *-ly* in the northern). Subsequently the use of *un-* with *-ly* again became common, independent of the form of the central element, which may be an adjective, present or past pple., etc. There are however two ways in which such formations may arise. Either the suffix *-ly* is added to a form already beginning with *un-*, or *un-* is prefixed to an adverb already formed with *-ly*. In most cases the difference in sense is slight or immaterial, but at times the distinction becomes important. If *unprofessionally* is formed from *unprofessional* it means 'at variance with, contrary to, professional rules or etiquette', if from *professionally* it means 'not in a professional manner or capacity'.

The following are miscellaneous examples of recent formations: ***unarguably, unassessably, unboringly, unbridgeably, unconsciently, unhungrily, unidentifiably, unignorably, unprotestingly, unselectively, unurgently.***

A few others occur in early dictionaries, as *unaccessively, unbewailably, unfalsely, unrecoverably.*

1887 H. S. Holland *Creed & Char.* 126 So He pityingly, *unangrily pronounced. **1929** *Daily Express* 3 Jan. 8/6 'You know Mr. Umph, don't you?' with an intonation implying that not to know Mr. Umph leaves one *unarguably in the certifiable class. **1978** *Nature* 20 Apr. 666/3 By excluding a sizable class of environmental variables, high within group heritability, unarguably does raise the probability of the remaining classes of possible explanations. **1937** J. R. R. Tolkien *Hobbit* xii. 231 Surely, O Smaug the *unassessably wealthy, you must realize that your success has made you some bitter enemies? **1921** F. G. Ellerton *Let.* 6 Sept. in *John Bailey* (1935) 214 You do his life most frightfully well and *unboringly and your observes on *Paradise Lost* and *Paradise Regained* are most excellent. **1932** *Times Lit. Suppl.* 21 Jan. 33/3 The unique, the *unbridgably different. **1979** *Church Times* 30 Nov. (Christmas Bk. Suppl.) p. xi/1, Christ and God are presented as living in a world unbridgeably remote. **1842** *Murray's Hand-bk. N. Italy* 21/2 The Cardinal..had most *uncardinally directed the painter [etc.]. **1869** W. G. Ward *Ess.* (1884) II. 243 These *uncatholicly educated Catholics who are the Church's most dangerous enemies. **1824** J. Gilchrist *Etym. Interpr.* 150 Many verbs..are employed both causatively and *un-causatively. **1816** Bentham *Chrestom.* Wks. 1843 VIII. 38 The short time necessary..would not be *unchrestomathically employed. **1929** R. Bridges *Testament of Beauty* ii. 51 So, tho' slowly and *unconsciently, he remembereth. **1871** Tyndall *Fragm. Sci.* (1879) II. viii. 130 If you wish to speak to me, plainly, honestly, and *un-disputatiously. **1830** W. Taylor *Hist. Surv. Germ. Poetry* II. 369 The very words, which twice before They said by heart so *unerroneously. **1887** *Pall Mall G.* 18 Oct. 1/1 That her eyes are set not *ungreedily upon Morocco is notorious to every one. **1838** *Tait's Mag.* V. 279 She told her weeping tale..so mildly, and so *unhatingly towards the prisoners. **1783** *Satanical Remembrancer* 16 Our Irish Native *Van Sighè*, vulgarly and *unhibernically called *Banshee*. **1842** Pusey *Crisis Eng. Ch.* 9 It may be, that we may all together learn humility, and none..think *un-humbly of them. **1922** Joyce *Ulysses* 172 His eyes *un-hungrily saw shelves of tins, sardines, gaudy lobsters' claws. **1965** 'R. Macdonald' *Far Side of Dollar* xxiii. 204 Susanna broiled me a steak, and chewed unhungrily on a piece of it. **1885** Stevenson in *Contemp. Rev.* Apr. 555 The groups which..break up the verse for utterance, fall *uniambically. **1934** F. M. Ford *Let.* 27 Sept. (1965) 235, I never guyed you either identifiably or *unidentifiably. **1982** A. Price *Old Vengeful* ii. 42 The new voice..was..unidentifiably classless. **1960** E. Bowen *Time in Rome* ii. 41 No tribute to an assassinated uncle can have been ever more *unignorably placed. **1884** W. M. Baker in *Harper's Mag.* Mar. 561/2 No woman could have done more, and so naturally and *unintrusively. **1884** A. C. Bickley *Geo. Fox* vii. 96 Lambert defended himself not altogether *unjesuitically. **1737** *Gentl. Mag.* VII. 13/2 *Unliterally and ungrammatically. **1833–40** J. H. Newman *Ch. of Fathers* 264 Olybrius, our virgin's father, who..was *unmaturely carried off. **1873** B. Gregory *Holy Catholic Ch.* xv. 162 What boots it that the chain of bishops has become..inextricably entangled and *unmendably snapped? **1838** R. Bagot *Let.* in Liddon *Life Pusey* (1893) II. xxi. 57 Feeling sure that you will not think that I ever..acted *unopenly towards you. **1887** J. A. Wylie *Hist. Scott. Nation* II. xxii. 279 Heads so *unorthodoxically shorn. **1862** S. Lucas *Secularia* 327 He received an ostensible letter of recall, and with it a private letter apprising him that '*unostensibly his proceedings were approved of'. **1824** *Westm. Rev.*. Jan. 143 Who had unprofessionally and *unpecuniarily burthened his memory with the dull details. **1953** R. Lehmann *Echoing Grove* 80 'I didn't realize she was so completely your kept woman.' 'She wasn't,' he said *unprotestingly. **1972** P. Cave *Judas Freaks* xv. 104 She followed unprotestingly. **1875** Howells *Foregone Concl.* xv. 259 Some..harmless thing that she had *unpurposely bruised. **1889** Saltus *Truth about T. Varick* 165 The..most *unrebuffably good-natured scoundrel that he had ever encountered. **1882** W. R. Greg *Misc. Ess.* ii. 31 As briefly and *unrhetorically as possible. **1859** Boyd *Recreat. Country Parson* (1862) 36 The massive foolscap..over which the pen so pleasantly and *unscratchingly glides. **1929** A. N. Whitehead *Process & Reality* 161 The pattern refers *unselectively to any eternal objects. **1977** *Nature* 3 Nov. 15/2 Quantitative measurements..show hydroxyl radicals ..to interact unselectively with most biological molecules at rates which are practically diffusion controlled. **1834** *New Monthly Mag.* XLII. 53 *Unsilenceably resounded in his ears the mandate. *a* **1864** Hawthorne *Amer. Note-bks.* (1883) 352 Last night was the most uncomfortably and *unsleepably sultry that we have experienced. **1980** V. Cunningham *Spanish Civil War Verse* 45 Jack Lindsay's Declamation now seems *un-urgently lengthy and even turgid. **1855** Lynch *Rivulet* lxxvii. ii, *Unvauntingly, yet with defiance, One man the world may meet. **1852** Smedley *L. Arundel* xliii. 331 His..tail, which was crumpled up *un-wag-ably in the corner.

b. *Un-* is seldom prefixed to simple adverbs. Even in OE. such formations are rare, though a few do occur, as *unéaðe, unefne, unfæȝere, unfeorr, unseldan, unsófte*. ME. retained most of these, but the number has at no time been greatly added to, and the later tendency is to discard such forms altogether.

12. a. The OE. use of *un-* with substantives (see 2 e above) survived very fully in ME., not only by the retention of old forms but by the introduction of many new, which continue to multiply in the later periods of the language. From the beginning the nouns have been almost entirely restricted to those of an abstract nature, so that forms with suffixes are numerous. In OE. and ME. the commonest of these is *-ness* (occasionally *-dom* and *-ship*); subsequently *-ation*, *-ity*, and *-ment* are frequent, as in the following selection of miscellaneous examples.

Florio (1611) has a certain number of casual formations, as *unacknowledgement, unartness, unbrittleness, undwellingness, uneloquence, unfrailness*, etc. Ash gives *unadequateness, uncommensurability, -ableness, unfrugalness, unliableness, unorganicalness*, and various others.

Recent formations include: ***unaccentuation, unamaze, unamazement, unbook, unclarity, uncomfiness, uncountry, uncrackability, uncreditworthiness, undeath, undeathliness, undecrease, undeviation, uneducation, unenlightenment, unfreshness, unfulfilment, unglamorousness, unimportancy, unintelligentsia, uninterruptability, uninvolvement, unlight, unmeritocracy, unpriggishness, unrepose, unsurprise, unwettability.***

1883 A. Stewart *Nether Lochaber* l. 316 The *unabidingness..of all sublunary things. **1879** G. M. Hopkins *Let.* 27 Feb. in Hopkins & Dixon *Corr.* (1955) 22 Wherever there is an accent or stress, there there is also so much *unaccentuation, so to speak, or slack. **1887** *Athenæum* 6 Aug. 177/2 Some decidedly clever.. observations upon the *unactuality of old art. **1853** Miss E. S. Sheppard *Ch. Auchester* II. 211 Here I suddenly arrested myself, for my *unaddress stared me in the face. **1884** *N. & Q.* 6 Sept. 189 The Church only crossed the Jordan, and that on dry land and in the purest *unalarm. **1936** W. Faulkner *Absalom, Absalom!* i. 8 Then in the long *unamaze Quentin seemed to watch them. **1954** —— *Fable* 369 Thinking in a sort of quiet *unamazement, Yes, I probably knew from the moment he sent for me what door I should have to emerge from. *a* **1866** J. Grote *Exam. Utilit. Philos.* (1870) 324 The *unassociativeness of different races of man. **1864** Lowell *Fireside Trav.* 263 The picturesque vivacity and ever-renewing *unassuetude of the whole scene. **1884** *Athenæum* 23 Aug. 238 The onesidedness and *unbalancement of our best efforts. **1965** *Probl. Communism* July/Aug. 56 (*heading*) Another *un-book. **1982** *Underground Grammarian* Nov. 5/1 Reading experts always need tricky new gimmicks to put in their unbooks. **1868** Ruskin *Time & Tide* (1872) 31, I must get back to the evil light, and *uncalm, of the places I was taking you through. **1844** Kinglake *Eothen* (1845) 324 *Unchangefulness in the midst of change. **1934** Webster, *Unclarity. **1936** *Mind* XLV. 503 Prof. Reichenbach's discussion of material, formal, and tautologous implication ..suffers from the same unclarity. **1980** 'J. le Carré' *Smiley's People* v. 54 'Vladimir telephoned the Circus at lunch-time today, sir,' Mostyn began, leaving some unclarity as to which 'sir' he was addressing. **1914** L. S. Woolf *Wise Virgins* ii. 39 'I hate being uncomfortable. But then I don't think I often am, except when I..cut my nails.' 'Oh, that sort of *uncomfyness!' said Gwen. **1862** F. Hall *Hindu Philos. Syst.* 143 Atheism, injury to others, *uncompassion, falsehood, and so forth. **1873** Mrs. Whitney *Other Girls* xxx, *Unconsent to the divine impulse comes of incongruity. **1862** Spencer *First Princ.* (1870) 281 That increase of internal motion involves a progressing *unconsolidation. **1964** W. Golding *Spire* ix. 178 In this *un-country there was blue sky and light, consent and so sin. **1923** *Daily Mail* 10 Jan. 9 (Advt.), The Vitreosil Globe, because of its '*uncrackability', lies close to the mantle. **1966** *Economist* 22 Oct. 413/2 Even the unlucky companies mentioned above are..credit worthy enough: the depths of *uncreditworthiness below remain murky indeed. **1882** *Ch. Times* XX. 938 All that the State can aim at is *un-crime, whereas the work of the Church is to inculcate virtue. **1865** W. Kay *Crisis Hupfeldiana* 23 The *à priori* criticism, the *uncriticism, which is..chiefly intent on proving 'two main conclusions'. **1933** L. Riding *Poet* v. 125 The sum of the first and second sign Shall be *undeath of the moon. **1974** *Globe & Mail* (Toronto) 24 July 13/4 There is, every now and then, a film that escapes this sort of un-death. **1922** Joyce *Ulysses* 379 She prayed to God the Allruthful to have his dear soul in his *undeathliness. **1898** Hardy *Wessex Poems* 5 Knowing that, though Love cease, Love's race shows *undecrease. **1858** Sir C. Napier in *Times* 24 Nov. 9/5 This country must not be left in a state of *undefence. **1893** Goldw. Smith in *Contemp. Rev.* Dec. 800 There is also *undesign,..there is waste, there is failure. **1932** W. Faulkner *Light in August* xix. 435 He was going fast too,.. with..the implacable *undeviation of Juggernaut or Fate. **1853** Herschel *Fam. Lect. Sci.* vi. §42 (1873) 258 The three primary colours,.. each in its highest degree of purity and *undilution. **1886** *Pall Mall G.* 12 July 10/1 Full of calmness, and courage, and quiet *undismay. *a* **1936** G. K. Chesterton *Common Man* (1950) vii. 39 It is not their *uneducation but their education that I scoff at. **1866** Carlyle *Remin.* (1881) II. 21 My feeling with him was that of *unembarrassment. **1882** *Century Mag.* XXIV. 44, I had no power to return to my original *unembodiment. **1950** T. S. Eliot *Cocktail Party* ii. 110 While still in a state of *unenlightenment, *You* could always say: 'he could not love any woman.' **1967** T. Keneally *Bring Larks & Heroes* xxii. 178 A creature of dish-eyed unenlightenment. **1868** Dilke *Greater Brit.* I. i. vi. 70 A fog of *unenterprise hung over the land. **1877** M. Collins *Sweet & Twenty* i. xi, The *unfragrance of money adheres to him. **1889** *Pall Mall G.* 25 Mar. 2/3 The palpable *unfrankness of the addendum. **1897** St. L. Strachey *From Grave to Gay* 288 We can keep the *unfreshness of our eggs to ourselves, but not so the unfreshness of our jokes. **1969** J. Cheever *Bullet Park* vi. 79 She..exhaled the faint unfreshness of humanity at the end of the day. **1851** H. Melville *Moby Dick* (U.S. ed.) lxxxi. 397 Oh! that *unfulfilments should follow the prophets. **1881** 'L. Malet' *Counsel of Perfection* xiv. 323 There is a wonderful compensation in the un-fulfilment of prophecy. **1978** F. King *Action* ii. 12 The pathos of his unfulfilment. **1958** *Economist* 26 July 277 He has probably had to contend ..also with the poor pay offered and the *unglamorousness of the whole proceeding. **1886** *Encycl. Brit.* XX. 610/1 A more curious instance of *ungreediness for pelf than earlier cases which we have cited. *a* **1960** E. M. Forster *Maurice* (1971) xlvi. 226 Excuse me if I work at *unimportancies for a bit now. **1852** De Morgan in Graves *Life Sir W.R. Hamilton* (1889) III. 418 A unanimous *uninfallibility would be just as drowsy a dormitory as an infallible Church. **1930** G. B. Shaw *Philanderer* Pref., in *Works* VII. 68 That far more numerous body which may be called the *Unintelligentsia was as unconscious of Ibsen as of any other political influence. **1964** R. H. Robins *Gen. Linguistics* v. 211 The unitary behaviour of such forms in sentences and their *uninterruptability..are the grounds for ascribing single word status to them. **1966** *Punch* 2 Nov. 682/2 He remains an aloof catalyst. Yet his very *uninvolvement has a value of its own. **1796** W. H. MARSHALL *W. England* II. 16 The roads, their *unlevelness apart, are among the best in the kingdom. *a* **1973** J. R. R. TOLKIEN *Silmarillion* (1977) viii. 74 A cloak of darkness she wove about them..an *Unlight, in which things seemed to be no more, and which eyes could not pierce, for it was void. **1843** *Civil Eng. & Arch. Jrnl.* VI. 40/1 A property almost peculiar to wrought iron, namely its all but *unmeltableness. **1970** *New Scientist* 31 Dec. 586/2 Large families are not the prerogative of the feckless poor whether in the Third World or in the urban ghettoes of the *unmeritocracy. **1847** H. BUSHNELL *Chr. Nurt.* iii. (1861) 65 The ostrich is nature's type of all *unmotherhood. **1879** G. MACDONALD *Sir Gibbie* xii, The earthly hitherto—the final obstacle of *unobstancy. **1862** MRS. H. WOOD *Mrs. Hallib.* II. xv. 225 Cyril was looking on. .. His *unoccupation caught the Quaker's eye. **1884** *Harper's Mag.* June 73/2 The most..commendable feature of the charity is its privacy and *unostentation. **1877** BLACKMORE *Cripps* II. ii. 23 Every single fall or rise of nature's work..led her into various veins of inductive *unphilosophy. **1955** S. SPENDER *Making of Poem* 75 There are standards of sensibility or of '*unpriggishness' which are a development of what Samuel Butler approvingly called 'being a nice person'. **1866** *Pall Mall G.* 12 May 12 Gaze down into the future upon the hateful Land of *Unpromise. **1802–12** BENTHAM *Ration. Judic. Evid.* (1827) II. 140 The publicity or *unpublicity of the process. **1883** E. CLODD in *Knowl.* 15 June 352/2 The *unrelation between religion and formulated theology. **1873** MRS. WHITNEY *Other Girls* xxviii, The old story of worry, discontent, *unreliance, disruption. **1868** J. H. NEWMAN *Verses on Various Occasions* 312 The prison where they roam in hopeless *unrepose. **1954** W. FAULKNER *Fable* 343 Thicker and denser than the stars in its concentration of anguish and unrepose. **1868** *Edin. Rev.* Apr. 435 Making due allowance..for a considerable amount of *unrepresentation on the part of our manufacturers. **1853** FABER *All for Jesus* 163 Anything like *unrespectability has been so completely avoided. **1825** HOGG *Queen Hynde* 104 To veil *unsanctitude within. **1865** W. G. PALGRAVE *Arabia* II. 230 An event followed by much confusion, shouting, and awkward *unseamanship. *c* **1843** CARLYLE *Hist. Sk. Jas. I & Chas. I* (1898) 269 The English noses in their shapes and *unshapes. **1872** H. BUSHNELL *Serm. Living Subj.* 335 What kind of *unsociety we suffer when we have about us only persons very unequal. **1881** G. S. HALL *German Cult.* 230 The very possibility of *unspaciality or punctuality. **1878** J. W. REYNOLDS *Supernat. in Nat.* (1883) 109 Making stuff pass from a no sort of *unstickingness into some sort of holding-togetherness. **1872** HOWELLS *Wedding Journ.* (1892) 296 The young girls..had the true touch of provincial *unstylishness. **1802–12** BENTHAM *Ration. Judic. Evid.* (1827) I. 293 Suggestedness and *unsuggestedness. **1932** W. FAULKNER *Light in August* xvii. 371 He seemed to stand aloof,..thinking with a kind of grim *unsurprise: 'Byron Bunch borning a baby.' **1955** W. GADDIS *Recognitions* II. iii. 393 A, M, D, G, sequence of unsurprise (Lao-tse's 84-year gestation), right Nicodemus? **1846** G. S. FABER *Lett. Tractar. Secess.* 271 To flounder in all the comfortless *untenacity of an ever-shifting quicksand. **1886** W. J. AMHERST *Hist. Cath. Emanc.* I. 271 Ireland's *ununanimity —if I may coin an expression—is England's opportunity. **1864** RUSKIN in *Daily Tel.* 28 Oct., Intrinsic value or goodness in some things, and..intrinsic *unvalue or badness in other things. **1937** *Nature* 26 June 1107/2 The *unwettability of natural cotton is generally ascribed to the existence of a film of wax or oil covering its outer surface.

b. The prefixing of *un-* to nouns used attributively is rare and usually not intended seriously.

1673 PENN *The Chr. a Quaker* i. Wks. (1726) 523 The Unchange-Gospel-Rule to Believers. **1771** LADY MARY COKE *Jrnl.* 13 Aug., The reason of the discontent of the unquality Ladys is that they were laugh'd at by the great Ladys. **1823** BYRON *Age of Bronze* xiv, Alas, the country! how shall tongue or pen Bewail her now *un*country gentlemen? **1852** S. R. MAITLAND *Eight Ess.* 236 It was a whim of the artist to sketch his subject in that occasional, uncompany costume. **1880** *Spectator* 3 Jan. 9/2 Single women, widows, and unbusiness men, are those on whom the blow chiefly fell.

Other examples are *uncurrency-style* (1852), *undining-room* (1845), *unhousehold-name* (1894), *unsociety-people* (1898).

13. In OE. there are a few instances of *un-* with verbal substantives in *-ung*, as *unbletsung*, *-brosnung*, *unmeltung*, etc. None of these survive in ME., and new forms in *-ing* are rare; *untiming* occurs *c* 1250, *uncunning* *c* 1300, *unknowing*, *unpunishing* *c* 1340. In the later language the usage also remains rare, and in nearly all verbal sbs. the prefix *un-* is UN-²; a few exceptions are recorded here.

1538 ELYOT, *Insolentia*,..vnhauntinge of a place. **1598** FLORIO, *Insepoltura*, the vnburying of one. *Ibid.*, *Ingenerabilita*, vnbegetting, ingenerabilitie. **1611** FLORIO, *Inconniuenza*, an vnmoouing or not twinkling of the eies. **1853** R. S. SURTEES *Sponge's Sp. Tour* iii, His sellings and his returning, his lettings and his unlettings. **1886** LINSKILL *Haven under Hill* lxii, The great beauty which had been to Ermengarde Salvain as a hurt and an unblessing. **1887** *Daily Tel.* 20 Dec. (Cassell's), Why was this unowning of the plays necessary? **1930** AUDEN *Poems* 8 Unforgetting is not today's forgetting For yesterday.

14. In OE. the use of *un-* with verbs is limited to formations from negative adjectives, as *unclǽnsian*, *unrótsian*, *untrumian* from *unclǽne*, *unrót*, *untrum*. (More commonly *ȝe-* is prefixed, as in *ȝeunclǽnsian*, *ȝeunrétan*, etc.) This type barely survived in ME., but *un-* began to be sparingly prefixed to ordinary verbs, as *untrowen* (*a* 1200) to disbelieve, *untrusten* (*a* 1225) to distrust, *unbetide* not to happen, *unbe* not to be, and similar formations are fairly common in the 16–17th c., as *unbecome*, *unbefit*, *unbelieve*, *unbeseem*, *uncomprehend*, *unconcern*, etc. Many of these are obviously suggested by the participial adjectives (*unbecoming*, etc.), which are quite regular in formation (see 10 above). The type is now rare, but occasional examples occur.

Recent formations include: (nonce-wds.) ***unbloom***, ***undie***, ***unfulfil***, ***untouch***, ***unvision***.

a **1175** *Twelfth Cent. Hom.* 118 Swa mucele swiðor him biteriæð & unswetiæþ alle þas eorðlice þing. *c* **1205** LAY. 11547 Vnhæle & ælde hæueð þene king vnbalded [*c* **1275** onbalded]. *Ibid.* 15037 þa þat folc was icumen, þa was þe king swiðe untrumed [*c* **1275** ontromed]. *a* **1300** *Maximian* 65 (MS. Digby 86), Forþi min herte keldeþ And mi bodi ounbeldeþ.

1898 HARDY *Wessex Poems* 8 And why unblooms the best hope ever sown? **1952** DYLAN THOMAS *Coll. Poems* p. x, These seathumbed leaves That will fly and fall Like leaves of trees and as soon Crumble and undie. **1922** HARDY *Late Lyrics & Earlier* 37 Though duties due that press to do This whole long day I unfulfil. **1843** E. JONES *Poems, Sens. & Event* 71 But the world unrecognized his visions of goodness. **1884** LORD R. CHURCHILL in *Pall Mall G.* 11 Aug. 10/1 This measure..which, instead of improving the representation of the people, would only fatally unrepresent the people. **1922** HARDY *Late Lyrics & Earlier* 34 And time untouched me with a trace Of soul-smart or despair. **1917** —— *Moments of Vision* 207 I'll not unvision A shape which, somehow, there may be. **1902** *St. James's Gaz.* 31 Dec. 12/2 On the ground that the state of trade absolutely unwarrants it.

15. By confusion of thought, *un-* is sometimes used redundantly, especially in the 16th and 17th centuries, where a positive term is really intended. For examples see *undated* (1637), *undifference* (1654), *undifferency* (1583).

16. In telegrams *un-* is sometimes used in nonce formations with any part of speech to avoid a separate negative.

1936 E. WAUGH *Waugh in Abyssinia* 161 Cables were soon arriving... '*Require earliest name life story photograph American nurse upblown* [*sc.* bombed] *Adowa.*' We replied '*Nurse unupblown*,' and after a few days she disappeared from the news. **1967** *Observer* 8 Oct. 2/5 Regret expelled by Syrians after twenty-four hours unreason given. **1968** *Punch* 3 Apr. 485/3 All those compound words like 'unproceed'.. in press cables.

un-, *prefix*², expressing reversal or deprivation, representing OE. *un-*, *on-*, = OFris. *und-*, *unt-*, *un-*, *ond-*, *ont-*, *on-*, MDu. and Du. *ont-*, OS. *ant-*, OHG. *ant-*, *int-* (MHG. and G. *ent-*), Goth. *and-*, originally identical with AND- *prefix*.

2. a. From OE. more than a score of reversive verbs formed with *un-* (or its variant *on-*) are recorded, as *unbindan*, *uncnyttan*, *undón*, *unfealdan*, *ungyrdan*, *unhelian*, *unlúcan*, etc. Some of these were in common use; others occur rarely or in single instances. About half of the number (including all those mentioned above) survived in ME., and various new formations appear in texts from the first half of the 13th century, as *unbenden*, *undytten*, *unfast(n)en*, *unhaspen*, *unhillen*, *unlimen*, *unmensken*, *unsteken*; even at that date the prefix is used with verbs which are not of native origin. Similar formations from later ME. are *unbuckle*, *uncatch*, *unclench*, *uncover*, *unfetter*, *unkevel*, *unsew*, *unshut*, *unwrap*, *unyoke*. The following are examples of obsolete ME. forms :—**un'hadien** [OE. *unhádian*], to deprive of ecclesiastical orders; **un'mensken** [f. MENSK *v.*], to dishonour; **un'rone** [f. RONE *v.*], to make desolate; hence ***un'roningness***; **un'teon** [f. *teon* TEE *v.*¹ 6 b], to fall apart.

c **1205** LAY. 13169 Buten he him plihte þæt he wolden vorð rihtes *vnhadien [*v.r.* onhodi] Costanz. *Ibid.* 13174 þar he vnhadede his broðer. *a* **1200** *St. Marher.* 14 Heanlunges makeð ham wið heouenlich hirð ant *unmenskeð hamseolf bimong eorðlich men. *a* **1300** *E.E. Psalter* lxxviii. 7 For þai ete Jacob ilka lim, And *vnroned þe stede of him. *Ibid.* lxxii. 19 Hou ere þai made in vnronyngnesse! *a* **1310** in Wright *Lyric P.* 101 The fleyhs shal rotie from the bon, The senewes *untuen everuchon.

b. In the 16th century new formations with *un-* become very numerous and varied, and in the 17th the prefix is used with much greater freedom than is now possible. The lexicographers Florio and Cotgrave constantly employ it in rendering Italian words in *dis-* and *s-* and French words in *de-*, *des-*. By this time the prefix had developed several variations of sense which are still current, and are illustrated by modern examples in the following sections.

3. In OE. most of the forms with *un-* have for their second part a simple verb, either strong (as *unbindan*, *unfealdan*, *unlúcan*, etc.) or weak (as *uncnyttan*, *undón*, *ungierwan*, *ungyrdan*, etc.). In either case the prefix denotes a simple reversal of the action of the verb. Many of the new formations in ME. are of the same type, as *unbend*, *unclench*, *uncover*, *unfasten*, *unhasp*, *unhide*, *unshut*, etc., and additions to this class continue to be freely made at all subsequent periods. In addition to the numerous examples entered as main words, many others have been casually employed, similar to those here illustrated.

Florio and Cotgrave make extensive use of this type, e.g. *unastony*, *unbrand*, *uncancel*, *unclumse*, *unclutter*, *uncompass*, *uncurd*, *unfester*, *unflow*, etc. Ash gives *unbaste*, *unmoble*, *unsolder*, *unsort*, etc.

Recent formations include: ***unbake***, ***unban***, ***unbatten***, ***unbore***, ***unclutter***, ***undip*** [DIP *v.* 6 d], ***unendear***, ***uninvent***, ***unjumble***, ***untape***, ***untease***.

1865 *Sat. Rev.* 9 Sept. 330/2 A boisterous English captain ..annexed them for a few weeks, and then had to *unannex them. **1864** G. M. HOPKINS *Poems* (1967) 15 Wasteful wide huge-girthèd Nile *Unbakes my pores, and streams, and makes all fresh. **1968** *Guardian* 5 Sept. 9/2 Book censorship has eased since the Dail passed a law which *un-bans a book after 12 years in purdah. **1983** *Bookseller* 4 June 2072/3 *Lady Chatterley's Lover*: unbanned in South Africa in 1980, it has been selling through Leserskring at a steady 1,000 a quarter. **1788** W. BLIGH in R. M. Bowker *Mutiny* (1978) iii. 90 *Unbattened all the Hatchways. **1927** R. A. FREEMAN *Certain Dr. Thorndyke* iv. 62 Osmond..unbattened the doors, and, opening them, slid the wriggling captive down the ladder on to the cabin floor. **1838** [MRS. MAITLAND] *Lett. fr. Madras* (1843) 223 You had betrayed his intention. .. You tried to **un-betray* it afterwards,..but in vain. **1922** M. A. VON ARNIM *Enchanted April* xiii. 213 Rose felt right down at her very roots that if you have once thoroughly bored somebody it is next to impossible to *unbore him. **1862** DE MORGAN in Graves *Life Sir W.R. Hamilton* (1889) III. 576 My belief is, that if you call *h* and *k* differentials, the community..will *uncall them. ? **1774** *Monody Death Goldsmith* 13 G.'s Wks. (1816) p. li, Thus some magician ..*Uncears the pond'rous tombs. **1886** *Pall Mall G.* 22 Dec. 2/2 When he has changed his mind no power on earth can induce him to *unchange it. **1888** J. C. AMBROSE in *Union Signal* (Chicago) 19 Apr., The first hard work..on butter is to *unchurn it. **1891** M. COLE *Cy Ross* 12 Pull up for the night, *uncinch the packs. **1859** SEMPLE *Diphtheria* 316 Is this leading circumstance..sufficient to make us *unclassify this disease? **1930** *Times* 29 Nov. 13/6 Sadler's Wells..appears to go farthest in *uncluttering the conditions for witnessing the performance. **1977** A. SCHOLEFIELD *Venom* III. 90 He liked to clear everything away, to unclutter the stage. **1851** W. R. GREG *Creed of Christendom* xvi. 268 That everything done is done irrevocably—that even the Omnipotence of God cannot *uncommit a deed. **1860** TROLLOPE *Framley P.* xvii, Do no such thing, or you may too probably have to *uncongratulate me again. **1775** ASH, **Uncrook*.., to reduce from crookedness. **1868** E. YATES *Rocks Ahead* III. vii, I could hardly uncrook your fingers. **1966** T. WISDOM *High-Performance Driving* x. 104 Drivers..use their headlights badly. They do not *undip them fast enough after meeting other traffic. **1885** S. TROMHOLT *Aurora Borealis* II. 20 She looked as if she had never *undonned her funny garb since I saw her last. **1865** G. M. HOPKINS *Poems* (1967) 21 Still thou bind'st me to fresh fealty..for nothing here Nor elsewhere can thy sweetness *unendear. **1825** COLERIDGE *Aids Refl.* (1848) I. 288 To break this sensual charm, to *unfascinate these bedazzled brethren. **1818** COBBETT *Pol. Reg.* XXXIII. 527 To unthink their present thoughts and *unfeel their present feelings! **1862** [W. COOPER] *Yacht Sailor* xi. 142 The only perfect self acting fid I ever saw ..'fids' and '*unfids' itself. **1873** MISS BROUGHTON *Nancy* II. 241, I have my flax hair..curled, plaited, frizzed, and again *unfrizzed. **1891** ZANGWILL *Bachelor's Club* 35 His brow began to *un-furrow itself. **1883** *Century Mag.* Oct. 946/2 We could see them all busy *ungriping their lee boat. **1896** E. BERDOE *Browning & Chr. Faith* 180 It is not in him to *unhate his hates. **1889** *Blackw. Mag.* Oct. 456 It was unprecedented that..a weak hysterical subject should, after being *unhypnotised, remain so long in prostrate exhaustion. **1844** NOAD *Electricity* (ed. 2) 69 *Uninsulating the ball, insulating it, and then observing what change it had acquired. **1888** JACOBI *Printers' Vocab.*, **Uninterleave*, to withdraw the sheets which have been placed between printed work to prevent set-off. **1962** *Guardian* 4 Oct. 6/5 It may not be possible to *un-invent the motor-car. **1982** *Church Times* 22 Oct. 5/1 Nuclear weapons cannot be uninvented. **1839** J. STERLING *Ess. & T.* (1848) I. 327 Self is thus..dis-individualized, *unisolated, rather universalized and idealized. **1775** ASH, **Unjamb*,..to free from a pressure between two bodies. **1900** *Daily News* 7 Mar. 8/7 The gun..jammed less than any other machine gun, and could be easily unjammed. **1966** J. DERRICK *Teaching English to Immigrants* v. 206 Pupils can also be asked to *unjumble and write out in correct order a series of sentences that should obviously follow a certain sequence (such as the description of a picture story or of a series of actions). **1979** J. GARDNER *Nostradamus Traitor* xliii. 204 He's the bloody expert on Nostradamus. He's even.. unjumbled the prophecies. **1888** LEES & CLUTTERBUCK *B.C.* xxviii. (1892) 314 Presently..the monster had *unkilled himself..and swam happily away. **1611** FLORIO, *Dismentire*, to *vnlie. **1882** *Ch. Times* 10 Feb. 83 It is hardly necessary to 'unlie' the insinuation, as the French would say. **1845** *P. Parley's Ann.* VI. 361 How long it took to *unmat their hair. **1887** *Pall Mall G.* 19 Oct. 2/1 To *un-mesmerize all those Christians whom the devil has mesmerized. **1809** *Ann. Reg.*, *Chron.* 339/2 For heaven's sake, do not be *unmodelling my accounts again. **1817** PETTIGREW *Mem. Lettsom* II. 230 Let any person..*unprejudice his mind. **1844** WHEWELL in *Life* (1881) 308 Having puzzled and *unpuzzled myself. **1889** SAINTSBURY *Ess. Eng. Lit.* (1891) 31 You could play on Crabbe that odd trick..and *unrhyme him. **1812** J. H. VAUX *Flash Dict.*, **Unslour*, to unlock, unfasten, or unbutton. **1860** NARES *Seamanship* 112 *Unsnatch and shift the mast rope. **1887** in Prothero *Life of Bradshaw* (1888) 78 Some one '*unsported' him with a dinner-knife. **1833** *Fraser's Mag.* VIII. 309 It *unsquatted the incubus which so long oppressed me. **1856** J. STRANG *Glasgow & Clubs* 395 To *unswing a golden fleece was a common trick. **1968** 'R. MACDONALD' *Instant Enemy* xxxiv. 217 He *untaped my wrists and ankles. **1981** E. WARD *Baltic Emerald* xxi. 175 Henry untaped the envelope and photographs from my back. **1932** AUDEN in *Rev. Eng. Stud.* (1978) Aug. 287 A piece of paper, neatly Folded in a hexagon shape Which Sampson took and *unteased and read. **1869** ABBOT *Shaks. Gram.* Pref., So far from training we are *untraining our understanding. **1896** *Globe* 19 Dec. 1/4 It would have been as easy to take the stripes as to *unwhip those boys.

4. a. A small number of OE. verbs in *un-* imply removal or deprivation; these end in *-ian*, as *unhádian* to deprive of orders, *unhlidian* to remove the lid from, *uninseȝlian* to unseal, *unscóȝian* to unshoe. In ME. the type remains rare, but occurs in *unclead*, *unclothe*, *unhair*. At a later date it becomes more frequent, and is common in modern use.

Florio is especially lavish in new formations which have not obtained subsequent currency, as *unblossom*, *unbrain*, *unbridge*, *uncheek*, *uncheese*, *uncorn*, *uncorner*, *unflank*, *unfringe*, *ungarland*, etc.

Recent formations include: ***unblouse***, ***undogcollar*** (nonce), ***unpearl*** (nonce).

1882 R. G. INGERSOLL, etc. *Chr. Relig.* 44 Cradles would be robbed, and women's breasts *unbabed. **1922** JOYCE *Ulysses* 254 Miss bronze *unbloused her neck. **1798** FERRIAR *Illustr. Sterne* i. 8 In like manner, *unbolster Falstaff and his wit will affect us less. **1836** T. HOOK *G. Gurney* II. 260, I found the task of '*unbooting' one of much greater difficulty than I had anticipated. **1886** *Pall Mall G.* 2 Dec. 6 A native *unbraceleting or ungartering himself. **1611** COTGR., *Desbrodequiner*, to *vnbuskin; to plucke, or draw, off buskins. **1831** *Soc. Life Eng. & France* 198 Some subsequent attempts to unbuskin tragedy. **1611** COTGR., *Escremé*, *vncreamed. **1886** *Pall Mall G.* 28 Sept. 11/2 Adulterated or uncreamed..milk. **1826** BEDDOES *Let. to B. Procter* Poems (1851) 170 To rob him,—to *uncypress him in the light—To unmask all his secrets. **1874** S. LANIER *Poems, Corn* 190 Discrowned, *undaughtered, and alone. **1846** LANDOR *Imag. Conv.* Wks. I. 144/2 The chalice of poison,..by which their own hands were..*undirked, and paralysed. **1953** DYLAN THOMAS *Under Milk Wood* (1954) 74 Esau,..*undogcollared because of his little weakness, was scythed to the bone one harvest by mistake. **1855** BAILEY *Mystic*, etc. 127 He, to his fate divine, *uneyes himself in vain. **1878** J. W. REYNOLDS *Supernat. in Nat.* (1880) 4 To *unfaith men takes from them everything which can preserve from evil and lead to good. **1859** SALA *Gas-light & D.* v. 62 He would..run down the doomed legislator.., and..*unfrank him on the spot. **1829** GEN. P. THOMPSON *Exerc.* (1842) I. 84 That the man..who goes to bed a freeholder, does not wake *un-freeholded on the morrow. **1791** LADY HAMILTON in Gamlin *Romney* (1894) 223 The little picture with the black hat. I wish you would *unfrill it. **1897** F. THOMPSON *Sel. Poems* 125 She..Her hand *ungauntlets in mild amity. **1861** *Temple Bar Mag.* III. 197 A hand of light *Unjewelleth the robe of night. **1821** *Sporting Mag.* IX. 51 Both were *unmettled by fast work. **1936** A. E. HOUSMAN *More Poems* 18 For these of old the trader *Unpearled the Indian seas. **1804** LARWOOD *No Gun Boats* 10 Let England *unpoignard her Dwarf Assassins. **1852** R. REDGRAVE in *Life* iv. (1891) 83 Here we were disrobed and *unsashed. **1888** 'B. CANE' *Haunted Tower* 307 He had *unspiled the water-cask. **1865** WILBERFORCE in *Life* (1882) III. 189 If he did not *unsurplice his choir and degrade his service to their Dissenting level. **1839** HOOD *Lines to Friend at Cobham* iii, Of hen and cock you'll have a stock, And death will oft *unthrob 'em. **1808** E. S. BARRETT *Miss-led General* 69 We must either embowel them, or they will *untripe us. **1889** TALMAGE *Serm.* 28 Apr., God is not dead. The chariots are *unwheeled.

b. A modification of this sense is that of freeing or releasing from something. This appears in ME. in *unfetter*, *unkevel*, *unyoke*, although in origin these may be simply reversive. In the later period the type has also become common, and is very largely represented from the close of the 16th century.

Florio and Cotgrave afford numerous examples, as *unbarb*, *unbit*, *unbunch*, *unchaff*, *uncrupper*, *ungravel*, *unhunger*, etc.

1899 T. S. MOORE *Vinedresser* 74 His sword fell noisy to the ground While he *unbrooched his cloak. **1888** F. H. STODDARD in *Andover Rev.* Oct., [Matthew] Arnold has *un-Coleridged criticism. **1839** in Marindin *Lett. Ld. Blachford* (1896) 57, I can't fancy any more magnificent practice for a fidgety person who wanted to be *unfidgeted. **1839** BAILEY *Festus* 118 When heaven's light Pours itself on the page,..*unglooming all its mighty meanings. **1868** EARL CLARENDON in *Life & Lett.* (1913) II. xxiii. 355, I wish he were *unhandcuffed from the party with which he can have no sympathy. **1881** *Cheq. Career* 335 *Unhobble the spare horses. **1888** JACOBI *Printers' Vocab.*, **Unlead*, to take out the leads from leaded matter. **1814** SCOTT *Wav.* lvi, *Unplaid yourself on the first opportunity. **1840** R. H. HORNE *Gregory VII*, IV. v. 74 It is his change That hath *unscarfed mine eyes. **1800** *Naval Chron.* IV. 523 The labourers..*unshored the St. Joseph..in the great dock. **1878** A. H. MARKHAM *Gt. Frozen Sea* xviii. 257 'Woolwich' was also '*unsnowed'. **1832** *Regul. & Instr. Cavalry* II. 43 The men..strap and *unswivel their carbines. *a* **1722** LISLE *Husb.* (1757) 387 If it is impracticable to accomplish both, the oats should be left *unthistled rather than the barley. **1897** MARY KINGSLEY *W. Africa* 280 To devote the rest of his evening..to *unthorning himself. **1845** T. W. COIT *Puritanism* 237 *Untrammeling human opinion and human will. **1815** T. SHUFFLETON *Amat. Wks.* 116 *Unzone the veil! produce the prize Which long has charm'd my roving eyes! **1907** JOYCE *Chamber Music* xi, Begin thou softly to unzone Thy girlish bosom into him.

5. a. The use of *un-* to denote the removal or extraction (forcibly or otherwise) of a person or thing from a place or receptacle occurs in the 14th cent. in *unhouse*, and later in *unbody*, *unearth*, but does not become prominent till the beginning of the 17th, when Florio and Cotgrave afford many examples. In a few instances the sense passes into that of releasing or setting free from confinement, as in *uncage*, or of revealing to others, as in *unbosom*.

Among the instances occurring in Florio and Cotgrave are *unaerie*, *unbench*, *unborough*, *unbrake*, *unbranch*, *unchamber*, *unchest*, *unfurnace*, etc.

1865 E. BURRITT *Walk to Land's End* 375 Then he *unbasketed our dinner. **1897** *Outing* XXIX. 491/1 The request that a number of soldiers be sent back to *unbog the wagon. **1822** W. TENNANT *Thane of Fife* VI. xxiii, He..had *uncav'd his jars to heave their spirits up. **1883** H. DRUMMOND *Nat. Law in Spir. W.* i. (1884) 30 To do that, and rest in the contemplation, it has first to *uncentury itself. **1859** SALA *Tw. round Clock* (1861) 228, I fear the awful committee that ..can *unclub a man for a few idle words inadvertently spoken. **1929** W. FAULKNER *Sound & Fury* 235, I went on to the back, where old Job was *uncrating them [*sc.* cultivators]. **1963** *Ann. Reg. 1962* 520 In addition, jet bombers, capable of carrying nuclear weapons, are now being uncrated and assembled on Cuba. **1870** T. W. HIGGINSON *Army Life* 195 She shouted with delight at being suddenly *un-cribbed and thrust into her little scarlet cloak. **1851** G. W. CURTIS *Nile Notes* xxv. 112 The cavalcade was magically *undonkeyed, the savages..tumbled off, while their beasts were yet in full motion. **1888** *Public Opinion* 29 June 811 Hearing that a mammoth had been unearthed, or rather *uniced, near the mouth of the Lena. **1883** *Daily News* 18 Sept. 3/3 Until the furniture and other articles.. stored hastily..have been *unstored and examined. **1846** LANDOR *Imag. Conv.* Wks. II. 45/1 All her wars for six hundred years have not done this; and the first trumpet will *untrance her. **1884** *Law Rep. 12 Chanc. Div.* 631 No offence was committed until the pigs were *untrucked, and the appellants had..no part in untrucking them.

b. In some formations belonging to this type *un-* is prefixed to a word either denoting the thing removed or the action of removal; in the latter case the sense of the prefix passes into that of *out*. Examples of these uses are:—

1598 FLORIO, *Sbacciellare*,..to vngraine, or take out of the cods. **1611** COTGR., *Escerner*, to vnkernell; to take or cut a thing cleane out of the round place wherein it was. **1877** TALMAGE *Serm.* 316 He it is who undirks the lightning from the storm cloud.

6. In OE. the fact or process of depriving a person or thing of a certain quality or property was not expressed by the reversive *un-*, but by verbal formations based on adjectives already having the negative prefix (see UN-[1] 14). *Unable*, appearing towards the end of the 14th cent., may still belong to this type, but from the middle of the 16th century forms become frequent in which the prefix is clearly the reversive *un-* , employed both with adjs. and sbs. Both types are largely represented in Florio, and to a less extent in Cotgrave. **a.** When the formation has an adjectival base, the adjective may be used in its simple form, or with the suffix *-en*.

Examples from Florio and Cotgr. of the simple adj. form are *unbald*, *unbig*, *uncorrect*, *undizzy*, *ungiddy*, *unhoar*, etc.; and of forms in *-en*, *unfatten*, *ungreaten*, *unmoisten*, *unsharpen*, *unthicken*, *unweaken*.

1888 RUSKIN in *Pall Mall G.* 27 Oct. 5/2 Rosalind is extremely glad to get her face *unbrowned again. **1893** *Columbus* (Ohio) *Dispatch* 10 Sept., They found..the shops ill-regulated and the Frenchmen *un-Frenched. **1827** HARE *Guesses* (1859) 488 You may abuse and misuse: you cannot *ungood. **1747** E. POSTON *Pratler* I. 223 Thy Brother.. almost had the Name undone, And almost did *ungrand it. **1825** SOUTHEY *Let. to Mrs. S.* 7 July, Freshmen are called *greens*, and a ceremony was (and perhaps is) used in *ungreening them. **1827** O'CONNELL *Let.* in *Daily News* 17 Dec. (1888) 3/6, I will *un-Orange Ireland. **1887** BROWNING *Parleyings, F. Furini* i, Straight your bag *Unplumped itself. **1826** SCOTT 19 Mar. in *Croker Papers*, If you *unscotch us you will find us damned mischievous Englishmen.

b. Substantives are similarly employed without ending.

Florio has a number of examples, as *unbride*, *uncitizen*, *uncoward*, *undoctor*, *undwarf*, etc. Casual formations are frequently employed by Fuller, as *uncardinal*, *unchaplain*, *uncity*, *unmartyr*, etc.

1867 SIR J. Y. SIMPSON in Duns *Mem.* xiv. (1873) 482 Often I wish I could *unbaronet myself. **1839** J. D. COLERIDGE in *Life Ld. Coleridge* (1904) I. 71 Herman Merivale *unbeared himself for five minutes. **1800** MACKINTOSH in *R. Hall's Wks.* (1832) VI. 129 They ought not to *uncitizen Tom Paine. **1797** MRS. A. M. BENNETT *Beggar Girl* (1813) V. 94 Recollections, unsupported by proofs, could neither *uncountess her nor rob her of the adoration her beauty excited. **1876** *Unfather [see UNCHILD *v.*]. **1857** HEAVYSEGE *Saul* (1869) 145 It me *unfiends to see and listen to him. **1860** READE *8th Commandm.* 24 It would be 'nefas' to *ungenius our geniuses. **1889** TALMAGE *Serm.* in *Voice* (N.Y.) 31 Oct., Every day there are Samsons *ungianted. **1870** C. W. COLLINS *Anc. Classics for Eng. Readers, Virg.* 182 An occasional burst of tears on Æneas's part would not have *unheroed him in our estimation one whit. **1839** J. ROGERS *Antipopopr.* i. §7. 87 They unavoidably fancy all other kirks to be no real or right kirks at all, *unkirking them. **1860** MILMAN in *Archaeol.* XXXVIII. 22 The remedy applicable to the condition of the Marches of Mercia and Wales was..to reduce and, so far, **unmarch* them. **1865** J. GROTE *Explor. Philos.* I. 229 This.. is described first as seeing nature in masquerade, and then as *unmasquerading her. **1877** E. FITZGERALD *Lett.* (1889) I. 408 Thence I lately took down Mr. Lowell's (I have proposed to **un-mister* him too), Lowell's Essays. **1870** C. READE *Put yourself in his Place* I. v. 68 The hair, not in ropes —yet not so as to cord the mass, and *unsatin it quite. **1890** *Chamb. Jrnl.* 21 June 387/2 To break her spirit, and *unshrew her into somebody's very humble servant. **1674** N. FAIRFAX *Bulk & Selv.* 75 Our Watch would without more ado be utterly *unwatcht.

c. From sbs. (rarely from adjs.) there are numerous formations in *-(i)fy*, and from both sbs. and adjs. in *-ize*. Other endings, as *-ate*, are less usual.

(*a*) **1857** DUFFERIN *Lett. High Lat.* viii. 201 The idea of fog and ice in the month of June seemed so completely to *uncockneyfy us. **1834** SOUTHEY *Doctor* vi. (1848) 107 Unipsefying and *unegofying the *Ipsissimus Ego*. **1837** DARWIN in *Life* (1887) I. 282, I think my silicified wood has *unflintified Mr. Brown's heart. **1882** SALA *Amer. Revis.* (1883) 241 A city on a scale of vastness which Sesostris, could he '*unmummify' himself, might admire. **1866** RUSKIN *Eth. Dust* 36 What will you gain by *unpersonifying it? **1858** FABER *Foot of Cross* (1872) 231 Why should she stay her devotion, or *unsimplify her worship?

(*b*) **1883** *American* VII. 117 Foreign interests and alien population tend to *un-Americanize the place. **1895** *Spectator* 23 Nov. 731 The author scarcely deserves to be *unanonymised. **1860** READE *8th Commandm.* 335 A noble international measure that..would have done much to *unbohemianize writers. **1891** W. S. LILLY *Shibboleths* 186 A certain number of the clergy..wished to *unclericalize themselves. **1876** *N. Amer. Rev.* Oct. 255 Its consequence was to *undemocratize the Democratic party. **1871** PROCTOR *Light Science* 338 To pluralize some of the objects,..to *undualize others. **1870** *Standard* 24 Nov., If the *unequalising process is to be carried any further. **1882** *St. James' Gaz.* 29 Mar. 3/1 We are invited to view..the Fenians *unfenianized. **1830** PUSEY *Hist. Enq.* II. 392 The great body, which their excellent predecessors had endeavoured to *unformularize. **1898** BODLEY *France* I. I. i. 67 German intermarriages have *un-gallicised the Swedish dynasty. **1852** BRISTED *Five Yrs. Eng. Univ.* (ed. 2) 343 Unmanning and *un-gentlemanizing themselves to any extent. **1898** BODLEY *France* I. I. iv. 222 As for the Alsacians, France took little pains to *un-germanize them. **1853** *Blackw. Mag.* LXXIV. 101 A hero, with out-staring eyes,..is sadly *unheroised. *a* **1876** HT. MARTINEAU *Autobiog.* (1877) II. 287 Let us *un-individualize ourselves. **1875** SHALDERS tr. *Godet's Comm. Luke* I. 386 Jesus desired..to reclaim the people, and prevent their being still more *unjudaized. **1862** DE MORGAN in Graves *Life Sir W.R. Hamilton* (1889) III. 571 He had..to back out of infinitesimals, in order to *unleibnitize his system. **1874** H. BUSHNELL *Forgiveness & Law* iv. 222 To *unlocalize, universalize, and make victorious the great salvation. **1838** G. S. FABER *Inquiry* 48 The paradoxical vineyard of *unmanicheanised Manicheism. **1884** STOUGHTON *Relig. in Eng.* I. 337 How could it, without *un-methodising Methodism? **1833** R. H. FROUDE *Rem.* (1838) I. 332 To..un-Protestantise, *un-Miltonise them. **1885** MASSON *Carlyle* ii. 71 Mystics he could make nothing of except by *unmysticising them. **1833** *Blackw. Mag.* XXXIV. 540 Such a taste is there to vulgarize, to *unpoetize nature. **1852** SMEDLEY *L. Arundel* xxix. 218 It will take me longer to *unpuppyise myself than I was aware of. **1889** *Times* 23 Feb. 7/1 His great anxiety was to *unradicalize himself. **1842** *Blackw. Mag.* LI. 163 The effect produced,..was, if the expression may be allowed, to *unrevelationize revelation. **1852** C. WORDSWORTH *Occas. Serm.* IV. 14 England romanized Ireland: and England ought to *un-romanize it. **1885** *Cornh. Mag.* Mar. 271 Some of the chaunting was rather fine, but the orchestral accompaniment was decidedly *unsolemnising. **1899** R. WALLACE *Geo. Buchanan* iv. 70 Had he been all his detractors call him, that would not have *unstoicized him. **1854** FABER *Growth in Holiness* x. (1872) 163 Human respect *unsupernaturalizes actions which are good in substance. **1852** LEWIS *Meth. Observ. & Reas. in Pol.* I. 96 There are numerous influences at work to *untechnicalize it. **1873** J. SKINNER *Let.* in *Life* xvi. (1884) 318 Those mad attempts to *untheologize (if I may coin a word) the language of theology.

7. With rare exceptions, the OE. verbs in *un-* are transitive, and this has always remained the prevailing use. In ME., however, intransitive uses of some common words are found, as *unbend*, *unclose*, *unlouk*, and in casual formations as *unbody*. In the later language the usage increases to some extent (as in *unfold*, etc.), but is chiefly confined to words having some currency.

Florio employs *unday*, *undebt*, *undroop*, *unsicken*, *unswell*. The following are rare modern instances.

1816 COLMAN *Br. Grins, Champernoune* ii, His courtiers swore..They'd broil a pope to keep a place, So all unpapalized apace. **1831** TRELAWNY *Adv. Younger Son* II. 113 Look at him, he is unturbaning! **1862** HELPS *Org. Daily Life* 108 The organization grinds on,..and it is very difficult to make the thing ungrind. **1922** JOYCE *Ulysses* 461 The Timepiece (*Unportalling.*) Cuckoo. Cuckoo. Cuckoo.

8. Verbal substantives, participial adjectives, and agent-nouns are naturally formed from verbs in *un-* as from simple verbs. These forms begin to appear in the 14th century, and become common in the later language.

Many of the past pples. and ppl. adjs., as *unbent*, *unbound*, *undressed*, *unfastened*, etc., coincide with formations in which the prefix is UN-[1], and the distinction in meaning is not always sufficiently clear to admit of an absolute separation between the forms. Either prefix is normally unstressed in all participial formations used predicatively, but commonly receives the main stress when employed attributively, as *an 'unbent bow, an 'unbound book*.

9. The redundant use of *un-* is rare, but occurs in OE. *unlíesan*, and ME. *unloose*, which has succeeded in maintaining itself. Later instances are *unbare*, *unsolve*, *unstrip* (16–17th cent.), and the modern dialect forms *unempt(y)*, *unrid*, *unthaw* (also locally *uneave*). Another redundant or extended use (= 'peel off') exists in UNPEEL *v.*

For occasional misuses of *un-* see *unloaden*, *unranked*.

Una ('juːnə). [From the name of the first boat of the kind brought from America to England in 1853.] A catboat. Also *attrib.*

1878 D. KEMP *Man. Yacht Sailing* xvi. 171 In less than a year there was a whole fleet of Unas at Cowes. *Ibid.* 174 The Cowes Una boat of the present time. **1880** G. C. DAVIES *Pract. Boat Sailing* 42 The mast is more inboard than the real Unas. **1889** E. F. KNIGHT *Sailing* 36 The Cat or Una rig is generally preferred by the Americans.

una'bandoned, *ppl. a.* (UN-[1] 8.)
1745 YOUNG *Refl. Public Sit. Kingd.* 107 Which honest counsels never fail to fix In favour of an unabandon'd land.

†**una'based,** *ppl. a.*[1] *Obs.* Forms: 5 unabaiste, *Sc.* -abasit, -yt, 6 *Sc.* onabasit, unabaset. [Northern and Sc. var. UNABASHED *a.*] Undaunted.
?*a* **1400** *Morte Arth.* 1378 Sir Boys vn-abaiste alle he buskes hyme a-gaynes. *c* **1470** HENRY *Wallace* II. 48 He vnabasyt, and nocht gretlie agast, Vpon the hed ane with the steing hitt he. **1513** DOUGLAS *Æneid* VI. iv. 54 Eneas vnabasit..Followis his gyde. *Ibid.* XI. xvi. 12 Opis..onabasit did behald the ficht. **1596** DALRYMPLE tr. *Leslie's Hist. Scot.* II. 437 At the altar he stude vnabaset without al feir.

una'based, *ppl. a.*[2] (UN-[1] 8.)
1659 GAUDEN *Tears Ch.* III. iv. 274 They easily preserved the doctrine of Christian Religion uncorrupted,..the reverence of Religion unabased.

†**una'basedly,** *adv. Sc. Obs.* Forms: 4-5 un-, onabasytly, 5 wn-, unabasitly (6 -lie), wnabayssitly, 6 unabaisitly (-lie). [f. UNABASED *ppl. a.*[1] + -LY[2].] Dauntlessly, boldly.
1375 BARBOUR *Bruce* VI. 20 Var he nocht outrageous hardy, He had nocht swa vnabasitly Sa smertly seyn his avantage. *c* **1425** WYNTOUN *Cron.* V. xi. 3032 He Wnabasitly maid entre..Wndere erd to þe dragoune. **1501** DOUGLAS *Pal. Hon.* III. xxviii, Vnabasitlie this campioun saw I gang In a deip cisterne, and thair a lyoun sleuch. **1573** *Satir. Poems Reform.* xxxix. 359 He..stoutlie tuik on hand Richt vnabasitlie all that gait to gang.

una'bashable, *a.* (UN-[1] 7 b.)
1848 LANDOR *Exam. Shaks.* Wks. II. 290 It must be an unabashable man that ever shook his sides in their company. **1872** LEVER *Ld. Kilgobbin* xiv, He is the most unabashable villain in Europe.

unabashed (ʌnə'bæʃt), *ppl. a.* [UN-[1] 8.] Not abashed; bold, undaunted; not disconcerted or put out.
1571 GOLDING *Calvin on Ps.* xxvii. 1 If wee dare not with unabashed minde set him ageinste all oure enemies. **1592** WARNER *Alb. Eng.* VIII. xl. 177 Shee vnabashed, mounting now the Skaffold, theare attends The fatall Stroke. **1728** POPE *Dunc.* II. 147 Earless on high, stood unabash'd De Foe. **1772** PRIESTLEY *Inst. Relig.* (1782) II. 104, I..shall show an unabashed..countenance. **1851** MRS. BROWNING *Casa Guidi Wind.* II. 749 Fix thy brave blue English eyes on mine ..With unabashed and unabated gaze. **1891** FARRAR *Darkn. & Dawn* xxxii, Detected in their theft, the priests were still unabashed.
Hence **una'bashedly** *adv.*
1890 TALMAGE in *Voice* (N.Y.) 13 Feb., We go easily and unabashedly into sin.

una'batable, *a.* (UN-[1] 7 b.)
1788 T. PAINE *Amer. Crisis* (1817) 170 The enmity is perpetual, unalterable, and unabateable. **1837** CARLYLE *Fr. Rev.* I. III. iv, The wise man..sees..all the symptoms he has ever met with in history,—unabateable by soothing Edicts.

una'bated, *ppl. a.* (UN-[1] 8.)
?*a* **1611** BEAUM. & FL. *Four Plays in One* Wks. 1912 X. 296 Behold a princess..playing here the slave, To keep her husbands greatness unabated. **1676** HOBBES *Iliad* XIX. 295, I think yet Another time for Feast had better been;..whilst yet unabated is my Spleen. **1781** GIBBON *Decl. & F.* xxxi. (1787) III. 194 The king of the Goths..still advanced with unabated vigour. **1796** MME. D'ARBLAY *Camilla* III. 393 Mrs. Arlbery felt provoked to find his power thus unabated. **1840** R. H. DANA *Bef. Mast* xxv, For three days and three nights the gale continued with unabated fury. **1857** BUCKLE *Civiliz.* I. vii. 456 For nearly fifty years the movement has continued with unabated speed.
Hence **una'batedly** *adv.*
1828 CARLYLE *Misc.* (1857) I. 132 They chaunting unabatedly her extreme deficiency in personal charms. **1898** *Westm. Gaz.* 27 July 5/1 The war would be carried on unabatedly until something more tangible in the way of terms was proposed.

una'bating, *ppl. a.* (UN-[1] 10.)
1768-74 TUCKER *Lt. Nat.* (1834) II. 103 That unabating activity, that serenity..which are characteristics of a perfect disciple. **1779** HERVEY *Nav. Hist.* II. 165 The fleet remained ignorant of what had happened, and the fight was continued with unabating warmth. **1831** D. E. WILLIAMS *Life & Corr. Sir T. Lawrence* II. 264 The whole of which time he appeared in unabating spirits, and with not the slightest appearance of weakness. **1894** *Daily News* 5 Sept. 5/6 His unabating zeal for the Irish cause.
Hence **una'batingly** *adv.*
1793 *Minstrel* I. 174 The storm continued unabatingly.

una'bbreviated, *ppl. a.* (UN-[1] 8.)
[**1775** ASH.] **1805** TOOKE *Purley* II. viii. 498 Without taking..into our language the same unabbreviated verb. **1886** *Athenæum* 27 Nov. 714/1 Many of the 'points' in the narrative have been selected for printing without their context, but unabbreviated.

una'bhorred, *ppl. a.* (UN-[1] 8.)
1608 SYLVESTER tr. *Mathieu, Mem. Mortality* I. lxxx, Th' art loth to leave the Courts Delights, Devices Where None lives long vnbrav'd, or vnabhorred.

una'biding, *ppl. a.* (UN-[1] 10.)
c **1430** *Life St. Kath.* (1884) 49 To see what medes and rewardes þay be þat crist ȝeueth to hyse seruauntys for þese vnabydyng thynges. **1849** FROUDE *Nemesis of Faith* 226 Markham's new faith fabric had been reared upon the clouds of sudden violent feeling, and no air castle was ever of more unabiding growth.

una'bidingly *adv.* (UN-[1] 11). **una'bidingness** (UN-[1] 12).
1847 WEBSTER.

†**una'bility.** *Obs.* Also 5-6 unabilite, 6 -itie, -itye; 6-7 unhabilitie, 6 -habylytee, *Sc.* wnhabilietie. [UN-[1] 12, after OF. *inhabilité* (14th c.) or med.L. *inhabilitas* INABILITY.] The quality of being unable; inability. Freq. const. *for, of, to,* etc.
c **1400** *Apol. Loll.* 28 þer ontrowþ, and vndisposicoun, and vnabilite to reseyue. **1509** FISHER *Serm.* Wks. (1876) 268, I knowe well myne vnworthynes & vnhabylytees to this so grete a mater. **1565** STAPLETON *Fortr. Faith* 122 b, S. Basill excuseth him selfe of vnabilite to extoll sufficiently the vocation of couent Monkes. **1617** R. WILKINSON *Barwick Bridge* 31 The highest stile of praise is to professe our unability of expressing. **1644** QUARLES *Barnabas & B.* (1651) 223 Thy unability for the work prophesies the impossibility of the reward. **1711** in *10th Rep. Hist. MSS. Comm.* App. V. 152 They alleadge for their justification an unability in stopping the foe. **1769** in *Cath. Rec. Soc. Publ.* (1914) XIV. 149 Not admitting any Solace but when constrain'd by an absolute Unability.

un'abject, *a.* (UN-[1] 7.)
1850 LEIGH HUNT *Autobiog.* xxv. III. 269 Such humble, yet un-abject, and truly religious souls, as cannot accept unintelligible and unworthy ties of conscience.

unab'jured, *ppl. a.* (UN-[1] 8.)
1549 LATIMER *7th Serm. bef. Edw. VI* (Arb.) 189, I wyl aduyse you fyrst..to abiure al your fryendes, all your frindeshipe, leaue not one vnabiured.

unable (ʌn'eɪb(ə)l), *a.* Forms: α. 4-7 unhable, (6 *Sc.* wnhable, unhabil). β. 4- unable, 5 unabille, -abyll(e, -abull, 5-6 unabil(l; 5 onable, 6 -abil. [UN-[1] 7 + ABLE *a.*, after OF. *inhabile* or L. *inhabilis* INHABILE *a.* Cf. MDu. *onabel.*]
1. Not able, not having ability or power, *to* do or perform (undergo or experience) something specified. (Chiefly of persons.)
α. *c* **1380** WYCLIF *Wks.* (1880) 422 Al þes þat han chirchis aproprid faylen of þis trewe seruyss herfore, & þus þei ben vnhable to preye, but preyen aȝen þer oune hed. **1552** LATIMER *Serm. Gosp.* vi. 190 The person of the Church is ignoraunt and unhable to teach the word of God. **1590** SPENSER *F.Q.* I. iv. 23 Vnfit he was for any worldly thing And eke vnhable once to stirre or go. **1596** *Ibid.* VI. i. 16 Me first he tooke, vnhable to withstond.
β. **1382** WYCLIF *Isaiah* xl. 20 The stronge tree, and the vnable to roten ches the wise craftes man. *c* **1420** LYDG. *Ballad Commend. Our Lady* 15 Alas! unworthy I am and unable To love suche oon. *c* **1470** HENRY *Wallace* VII. 119 My witt vnabill is To runsik sic, for dreid I say off myss. **1526** *Pilgr. Perf.* (W. de W. 1531) 98 Thou shalte make thy selfe vnable to ryse and growe in goostlynesse. **1598** YONG *Diana* 57 To tell you now the life, that I led in his absence, ..my toong is far vnable. **1651** HOBBES *Leviath.* II. xxx. 181 Many men..become unable to maintain themselves by their labour. **1700** PRIOR *Carm. Sec.* xxiii, Lost in trackless Fields of shining Day, Unable to discern the Way. **1774** GOLDSM. *Nat. Hist.* (1776) III. 402 As they are unable to escape by flight, the hunters..easily overpower them. **1836** THIRLWALL *Greece* III. xvii. 3 The Persian governor, unable to hold out, and disdaining to surrender, set fire to the town. **1891** FARRAR *Darkn. & Dawn* xx, Panting with wrath, he was unable even to return the greeting of Nero.
b. Const. *for* or *to* (with sbs.).
(*a*) **1456** SIR G. HAYE *Law Arms* (S.T.S.) 109 Gif he be ane unworthy persone, and unhable tharto,..he degradis him. *a* **1470** H. PARKER *Dives & Pauper* (W. de W. 1496) v. xviii. 220/1 Though his woodnes passe yet he is yrreguler & unable to goddes aulter. **1513** *Life Henry V* (1911) 83 The Kinge his father, who at that time was lymited, was vnable to the charge of the realme.
(*b*) **1568** GRAFTON *Chron.* II. 382 He was maymed with the stroke of an horse in his youth, and so made unhable for the governaunce of the Realme. **1598** GRENEWEY *Tacitus, Ann.* I. i. (1622) 2 Agrippa they accounted..yoong, and raw in state matters; vnable for so great a charge. **1668** WILKINS *Real Char.* II. i. §4. 41 Either by restoring what is due, or by being rendred unable for it. **1841** CHAMBERS *Pop. Rhymes Scotl.* (1870) 76 She could not spin at all, and found herself quite unable for it.
†**c.** Used attributively with *to* following the noun. *Obs. rare.*
1560 PILKINGTON *Expos. Aggeus* (1562) 59 An unable priest to teach, is good to nothinge in that kynde of lyfe or ministerye. *a* **1586** SIDNEY *Arcadia* I. xii. (1912) 80 Those troblesome effects..be not the faults of love, but of him that loves; as an unable vessel to beare such a licour. *c* **1640** J. SMYTH *Lives Berkeleys* (1883) II. 141, I stand an unable man to determine of either opinion.
d. Not knowing, ignorant. *rare*[−1].
a **1721** EUSDEN in *Addison's Cato* A.'s Misc. Wks. 1721 I. 267 Silent we stand, unable where to praise.
2. Of persons: Lacking ability in some implied respect; incompetent, inefficient.
1395 PURVEY *Remonstr.* (1851) 112 It is gouernid by symonient bisshopis and vnable curatis. **1407** WILLIAM OF THORPE in Foxe *A. & M.* (1570) I. 648/2 These vnable priestes haue bene, and yet are, and shalbe, chiefe cause of pestilence of men. *a* **1513** FABYAN *Chron.* (1811) 548 Weale I wote, and knowlege, and deme myselfe to be and haue ben vnsuffycyent and vnable and also vnprofytable. **1544** BETHAM *Precepts War* I. cxcviii. I vj b, To sende forth thyne vnable souldyours.. to be as a bayte..to thyne enemyes. **1612** BRINSLEY *Lud. Lit.* p iv, This indeuor..thus vndertaken by me the vnablest of many thousands. **1668** R. STEELE *Husbandman's Calling* v. (1672) 139 What if I leave a shiftless wife, and unable children behind me? **1710** SHAFTESB. *Charac., Adv. Author* (1737) I. 224 The greatest actions lose their force, and perish in the custody of unable and mean writers. *a* **1774** GOLDSM. *Hist. Greece* II. 167 No hopes of succour from such unable protectors. **1856** EMERSON *Eng. Traits, Manners* ¶8, I hesitated to read and threw out for its impertinence many a disparaging phrase.. about poor, thin, unable mortals. **1877** OWEN *Wellesley's Desp.* p. xxvii, What would become of the system in *unable* hands?
b. Of faculties, actions, etc.: Characterized by want of ability; inefficient, ineffectual.
1387-8 T. USK *Test. Love* III. i. (Skeat) l. 171 If any thing be insufficient or els mislyking, wyte that the leudnesse of myne unable conning. *c* **1400** MAUNDEV. (1839) xxxi. 315, I ..have ben..at many a faire Dede of Armes (alle be it that I dide none my self, for myn unable insuffisance). **1584** CONSTABLE *Diana* VII. vi, A dombe restraint Breakes forth in teares from mine unable mind. **1633** COWLEY *Constantia & Philetus* To Rdr. ii, As shee my vnabler quill did guide, Her briny teares did on the paper fall. *a* **1699** J. BEAUMONT *Psyche* XXI. lxxv, I..see thee more By this unable and denying Sight, Than they [etc.]. **1795** BURKE *Abridgm. Eng. Hist.* Wks. 1842 II. 523 Vortigern..opposed a mixture of timid war and unable negociation.
†**3. a.** Of persons: Incapable of, not qualified for, some position. *Obs.*
c **1380** WYCLIF *Wks.* (1880) 465 þat pope þat fayliþ heere oþer for kunnyng or for wille is vnhable to take to pope & lede his floc. **1390** GOWER *Conf.* III. 202 His nase of and his lippes bothe He kutte, for he wolde him lothe Unto the poeple and make unable. **1426** LYDG. *De Guil Pilgr.* 5108 But I sawh ther in presence, Somme pressen to the table That wer vnworthy & vnhable.
†**b.** Of things: Unfit or unsuitable for some purpose. *Obs.*
1390 GOWER *Conf.* III. 104 Which of the poeple be forlete As lond desert that is unable, For it mai noght ben habitable. *c* **1440** *Pallad. on Husb.* I. 222 Diuide hit thus: that fatte & bering, able, Let plowe hit vp, & leef the lene, vnable, Couert in woode. **1444** *Maldon* (Essex) *Rec.* Liber 'A.' fol. 32 b, Item, that no bocher sle, ne selle, none vnhable flessh.
†**4. a.** Not able to be (done); impossible. *Obs.*
c **1400** *Destr. Troy* Prol. 46 How goddes foght in the filde, folke as þai were, And other errours vnable þat after were knowen, That poyetis of prise have preuyt vntrew. **1548** GESTE *Pr. Masse* 78 The wyche, as it is an attempte too unreasonable and unable, so passynge wycked, presumptuouse and detestable. **1567** *Reg. Privy Council Scot.* I. 512 How unabill it salbe to the nobilitie..alwayis to abyde and continew at Court.
†**b.** Awkward; unlucky. *Obs.*[−1]
1572 *Satir. Poems Reform.* xxxi. 94 Sen Fortoun, with a Reill, Hes wrocht thame ane vnabill charr.
5. Lacking in physical ability or strength; incapable of much bodily exertion; weak, feeble. In later use *Sc.*
1577 B. GOOGE *Heresbach's Husb.* III. (1586) 144 b, Hee waxeth feeble, and vnable, before he bee sixe yeeres olde. **1591** SHAKS. *1 Hen. VI*, IV. v. 4 When saplesse Age, and weake vnable limbes Should bring thy Father to his drooping Chaire. **1621** BURTON *Anat. Mel.* III. iii. I. ii, I haue an old grimme sire to my husband as bald as a gourde, as little and as vnable as a child. **1685** BAXTER *Paraphr. N.T.* Matt. xxv. 46 This doth not extend to condemn Infants or poor unable persons for not doing what they could not. **1764** GOLDSM. *Hist. Eng. in Lett.* (1772) I. 168 Though unable by disease, yet they recompensed the defect by valour. **1818** SCOTT *Br. Lamm.* xv, Those unarmed and unable Mephibosheths, that are sure to be a burden to every one that takes them up. **1858-61** J. BROWN *Horæ Subs.* (1863) 163 No one could have suffered from..the misery of an unable body. **1896** CROCKETT *Grey Man* iv, He..was ever thereafter unable of his legs.
transf. **1601** YARINGTON *Two Lament. Trag.* i. ii. in Bullen *O. Pl.* IV, We do assure us of your love And care to guide his weake unhable youth In pathes of knowledge. **1607** HEYWOOD *Wom. Killed w. Kindn.* (1617) C 2 b, Sir I accept it, and remaine indebted Euen to the best of my vnable power.

†**un'able,** *v. Obs.* Also 5 unabyl, 6 -abill; 5-6 unhable. [UN-[2] 6 a, or f. UNABLE *a.*]
1. *trans.* To render unable, to unfit or incapacitate, *to* do something. Sometimes *spec.* in *Law*: To make legally incapable.
c **1380** WYCLIF *Sel. Wks.* I. 147 Myche more shulde worldely lordship unable men now to take þis Goost. *c* **1400** *Destr. Troy* 9423 He woundit hym wickedly in his wale face, And vnablit after with angur to fight. *a* **1470** HARDING *Chron.* CLVII. iii, This Edmond thelder soonne of Kyng Henry, Broke backed and bowbacked bore, Was vnabled to haue the monarche. **1567-9** JEWEL *Def. Apol.* (1611) 195 Then doth it [the vow] not of necessitie and fine force vnable a man to contract Matrimonie. **1613** SHERLEY *Trav. Persia* 32 The eldest son of the King remained at the Court of his father, administring all that, which his fathers defect of light vnabled him to doe. **1640** HABINGTON *Edw. IV*, 67 They.. had been unabled to pay their usuall tribute to the King. *a* **1774** GOLDSM. *Hist. Greece* I. 207 Until both were utterly unabled to withstand the smallest efforts of foreign invasion.
refl. *c* **1380** WYCLIF *Wks.* (1880) 191 þei vnablen hem self to do þe office of prestis. *c* **1380** —— *Serm.* Sel. Wks. II. 36 þre ordris in Cristis tyme unabliden hem to be of þis rewme.
b. Const. *to* (or *of*) an action, office, etc.
a **1395** HYLTON *Scala Perf.* II. xv. (W. de W. 1494), How louers of this worlde unable hem in dyuers maners to the refourmyng of her owne soule. *a* **1470** H. PARKER *Dives & Pauper* (W. de W. 1496) I. xxxviii. 79/1 He sholde be pryued of his benefyce yf that he hadde ony. Yf he had no benefyce he sholde be unabled and dysposed therto. **1560** KNOX *Bk. Common Order* (1901) 20 The crimes and vices that might unable them of the Ministry.
2. Without const.: To unfit or incapacitate, to deprive of ability or power, in some respect; to disable physically.
c **1380** WYCLIF *Sel. Wks.* I. 105 Siþ he..wiþdrawiþ never his grace, but ȝif man unable him selfe. *Ibid.* 219 As distempour of þe eir shal sle men and unable þe erþe. *c* **1450** in Aungier *Syon* (1840) 281 Whom eurychone and eche

trespasyng in the premysses, we unable for euermore in the selfdede doyng. **1503** *Rolls of Parlt.* VI. 547/1 To the use, profitte or behove of any persone or persones by this Acte not attaynted nor unabled. **1582** Stanyhurst *Æneis* iii. (Arb.) 80, I through pangs vncoth vnhabled, With stutting stamering at leingth thus fumbled an aunswer. *a* **1641** Bp. Mountagu *Acts & Mon.* (1642) 285 That old Leacher, worne out and unabled, though he dyed his haire black that he might seeme to be young. **1654** Gayton *Pleas. Notes* iii. v. 100 That is to say, with three hard words, un-mule, un-leg, and un-able, Alanso Lopez. **1775** Johnson *Let.* in *Boswell* (1831) III. 255 Poor Lucy Porter has her hand in a bag, so unabled by the gout that she cannot dress herself.

b. To annul or cancel. *rare*[-1].

1611 Speed *Hist. Gt. Brit.* ix. xxi. §134 Hee prepared himselfe to make his Wil, wherein howsoeuer titles had been vnhabled in Parliaments, he ordained his three children to succeede each after others.

Hence †**un'abling** *vbl. sb. Obs.*

1475 *Rolls of Parlt.* VI. 147/2 As if the said Acte of atteyndre or unablyng never had been made. **1503** *Ibid.* 548.

†**un'abled,** *ppl. a. Obs. rare.* [un-[1] 8.]

1. Unqualified.

1497–8 in *Archæol. Jrnl.* XLIII. 168 It[e]m for a fyne lost by Will[ia]m Birchwold for settyng to werke a child vnabled & vnbound [= unapprenticed], x[d]. **1653** Gauden *Hierasp.* 226 Compleating those sad effects, which disorderly, unordeined, unsent, and unabled Teachers..have already begun.

2. Not endowed with strength or vigour.

1597 Middleton *Wisd. Solomon* ii. 11 Wee are the cedars, they the mushromes bee, Vnabled shrubs, vnto an abled tree.

†**un'ableness.** *Obs.* [f. unable *a.*] The condition of being unable; inability, incapacity; disability. (Very common *c* 1500–1660.)

c **1380** Wyclif *Wks.* (1880) 245 Siche men as desiren benefices schulden not haue hem, but men þat fleen hem for drede of vnabilnesse of hemself & grete charge, as dide moyses. *c* **1425** *Found. St. Bartholomew's* (E.E.T.S.) 4 Promysynge that he wolde be ware of alle passid vnhabilnesse, and yeue affectualy his diligence and laboure to that he hathe promysyd. **1501** in *Lett. Rich. III & Hen. VII* (Rolls) II. 100 The..commissary hath full power to dispense with that irregularity and to take away all infamy and unableness. **1560** Pilkington *Expos. Aggeus* (1562) 172 He biddeth us when we feele oure weakness & unablenes to fulfil his law, to come unto hym. **1638** Junius *Paint. Ancients* 37 There is in us a certaine unablenesse of imitating such things as doe not very well agree with our naturall disposition. **1648** Boyle *Seraph. Love* xiii. (1700) 71 To convince the World of their unableness to emerge and recover out of that deep Abyss, wherein the load of Sin.. had precipitated Fall'n Man. **1727** Bailey (vol. II) s.v. *Inability*.

†**un'ablety.** *Obs.* In 4–5 vnablete, -abilte. [f. unable *a.* + -ty, prob. after OF. *inhabileté*.] = unability.

c **1380** Wyclif *Wks.* (1880) 67 God wole not and may not brynge vnable men in-to benefices of þe chirche for his riȝt-wysnesse & vnablete of hem self. *c* **1400** tr. *Secreta Secret., Gov. Lordsh.* 67 He may falle yn-to syknes, ffebylnes, and ynto oþer vnabiltez. **1425** *Rolls of Parlt.* IV. 267/2 Ye grete unabilte and unsuffisante, that the same Wauter felte in hymself, to touche thing yat was so chier.

un'ably, *adv.* Now *rare* or *Obs.* [un-[1] 11.] In an unable or incapable manner.

a **1400–50** *Alexander* 2308 Quat, & has þou ossed to Alexander þis ayndain wirdes, And me þus ill? vn-ably þine abet þou weris. *c* **1658** in *Lovelace's Poems* (1904) 212 Thy but unably-comprehending clay, To what could not be circumscrib'd gave way. **1710** Shaftesb. *Charac.* (1711) I. 346 Facts unably related, tho with the greatest Sincerity and good Faith, may prove the worst sort of Deceit.

una'bolishable, *a.* (un-[1] 7 b.)

1643 Milton *Divorce* Wks. 1851 IV. 57 That Law [has been] proved to be morall, and unabolishable. **1645** —— *Tetrach.* Ibid. IV. 215 By that unabolishable equity which it convaies to us. **1682** H. More *Annot. Glanvill's Lux O.* 257 There may be many other..habitudes of Terms..every jot as unabolishable as this.

una'bolished, *ppl. a.* (un-[1] 8.)

1577 Holinshed *Chron.* I. 4/1 They [*sc.* Bards], of all the other sectes before specified, were suffred only to continue vnabolished in all ages. **1594** Hooker *Eccl. Pol.* iv. xiv. §1 The number of needlesse lawes vnabolisht, doth weaken the force of them that are necessarie. **1667** *Phil. Trans.* II. 579 With art and care those channels may be preserved un-abolisht. **1837** Carlyle *Fr. Rev.* ii. vi. i, Your unabolished Staff of the Guard..is in these very moments privily deliberating at the General's.

una'braded, *ppl. a.* (un-[1] 8.)

1827 Faraday *Chem. Manip.* iii. (1842) 72 The learner should practise first on a piece of waste glass tube, commencing both from an unabraded surface and from a cross line. **1886** *Athenæum* 18 Dec. 830/1 In an area of about forty feet square were found nearly six hundred unabraded worked flints.

una'bridg(e)able, *a.* (un-[1] 7 b.)

1802–12 Bentham *Ration. Judic. Evid.* (1827) IV. 154 The establishment of long and unabridgable intervals between these times.

una'bridged, *ppl. a.* [un-[1] 8.] Not abridged, reduced, or shortened. In mod. use spec. of literary works.

1599 Sandys *Europæ Spec.* (1632) 111 In those places where their power remaineth yet unabridged. **1772** Mason *Eng. Gard.* i. 20 To the lawn [to] restore Its ample space, and bid it feast the sight With verdure pure, unbroken, unabridg'd. **1840** Ainsworth *Tower of Lond.* (1864) 234 By which means your authority would be unabridged. **1864** Pusey *Lect. Dan.* i. (1876) 49 Daniel and Ezra use unabridged, and so, older forms. **1894** A. E. Waite *Paracelsus' Writ.* Title-p., Paracelsus the Great, now for the first time translated faithfully and unabridged into English.

b. *absol.* A copy of the 'unabridged edition' of Webster's Dictionary.

1860 O. W. Holmes *Prof. Breakf.-T.* ii. 36 You small boy there, hurry up that 'Webster's Unabridged'! **1894** H. Gardener *Unoff. Patriot* 302 I'm not sure that I've spelled some of these words right, but my unabridged is not handy.

un'abrogated, *ppl. a.* Also 6 *Sc.* vnabrogat. (un-[1] 8 and 8 b.)

1535 Stewart *Cron. Scot.* (Rolls) I. 101 To caus thair lawis keip the strenth..that tha had maid vnabrogat at lenth. **1577** tr. *Bullinger's Decades* (1592) 410 The law, so far as it is the rule howe to liue well and happely,..doth remaine vnabrogated. **1818** G. S. Faber *Horæ Mosaicæ* II. 29 These priests must obviously have been priests according to the still unabrogated patriarchal dispensation. **1849** Ruskin *Seven Lamps* i. §6. 14 Let us not now lose sight of this broad and unabrogated principle.

una'brupt, *a.* (un-[1] 7.)

1865 Meteyard *Life Wedgwood* I. 168 The highest effects are obtained from subdued tones, and unabrupt contrasts of colour, light and shade.

†**unab'soiled,** *ppl. a. Obs.*[-1] [un-[1] 8: cf. assoil *v.* 6.] Unsettled.

1521 Wolsey in *St. Papers Hen. VIII* (1830) I. 67 Soo that doubte remaynethe yet unabsoiled, as it did byfore my writyng.

†**un'absolute,** *a. Obs.* (un-[1] 7.)

1697 Collier *Ess. Mor. Subj.* i. (1709) 174 Where Goodness is mutable, and Reason unabsolute, there must be Rigour to..check the Abuse of Liberty.

unab'solvable, *a.* (un-[1] 7 b.)

1635 J. Hayward tr. *Biondi's Banish'd Virg.* 17 The Gods are not so firmely bound by the unabsolveable oathes they vow by the infernall Lake.

unab'solved, *ppl. a.* [un-[1] 8. Cf. G. *unabsolviert*.]

1. Not absolved. Also const. *of*.

1611 Florio, *Innassolto*, vnabsolued. **1681** Baxter *Acc. Sherlocke* iv. 186 Who shall Absolve the Patriarchs, Primates,..&c.? Must they be Unabsolved till a General Council do it? **1765** Sterne *Tr. Shandy* vii. xxiv, If we are ravished and die unabsolved of them. **1819** Scott *Ivanhoe* xliii, Slay him not,..unshriven and unabsolved. **1844** Lady G. Fullerton *Ellen Middleton* III. xxi. 68 [I] always let him draw near to the altar alone; for, unforgiven, unabsolved, unreconciled, I dared not approach it.

†**2.** Unsettled, undecided. *Obs.*

An alteration of unabsoiled *ppl. a.*

1721 Strype *Eccl. Mem.* I. 33 So that doubt remaineth not [*sic*] unabsolved.

unab'sorbable, *a.* (un-[1] 7 b.)

1846 Worcester (citing Davy). **1899** *Westm. Gaz.* 6 Dec. 10/1 The carbon in the 'fog mixture' being of an unabsorbable nature.

unab'sorbed, *ppl. a.* (un-[1] 8.)

1766 *Phil. Trans.* LVII. 99, I think we may fairly conclude that this unabsorbed part was intirely common air. **1791** *Ibid.* LXXXI. 370 Being then taken out, and the unabsorbed water hastily wiped from their surface, they were again weighed. **1863** Tyndall *Heat* ix. (1870) 305 Where the waves pursue their way unabsorbed no motion of heat is imparted. **1885** *Pall Mall G.* 28 July 5/2 Within ten years the list of unabsorbed country banks will probably be a short one.

un'abstract, *a.* (un-[1] 7.)

1840 Herschell *Ess.* (1857) 73 A theory..rude and unabstract in the form of its statement.

unab'surd, *a.* (un-[1] 7.)

1742 Young *Nt. Th.* vii. 514 What less than infinite, makes un-absurd Passions, which all on earth but more inflames? *c* **1815** Jane Austen *Persuas.* viii, Doing it with so much sympathy and natural graces as showed the kindest considerations for all that was real and unabsurd in the parent's feelings.

†**una'builyeit,** *ppl. a. Sc. Obs.*[-1] [un-[1] 8.] Unarrayed.

c **1530** W. Stewart *To the King* 8 (Bann. MS.), Of alkin clething nakit and denud, Bair, vnabulyeit [*Maitl. MS.* onabilȝeit], as scho borne was.

una'bused, *ppl. a.* (un-[1] 8.)

1661 Glanvill *Van. Dogm.* 100 More sober heads have a set of misconceits, which are as absurd to an unpassionated reason, as those to our unabused senses. **1678** Cudworth *Intell. Syst.* 69 The Opinion, that such Spirits were Incorporeal and Immaterial, could never enter into the minds of men by Nature, Unabused by Doctrine. **1864** Pusey *Lect. Daniel* i. (1876) 19 Human greatness is, when unabused, a majestic sight.

una'busing, *ppl. a.* (un-[1] 10.)

a **1628** F. Grevil *Let. Hon. Lady* (1633) C iv, To giue all, and take nothing, proceeds of an uncaused goodnesse, and so necessarily of an vnabusing.

unaca'demic, *a.* (un-[1] 7. Cf. G. *unacademisch*.)

1844 H. Rogers *Ess.* (1874) I. ii. 45 Having absented himself from certain 'exercises', and otherwise been guilty of sundry unacademic irregularities. **1897** Flandrau *Harvard Episodes* 78 Probably the most..unacademic person that ever answered to an official name.

unaca'demical, *a.* (un-[1] 7.)

1840 Mozley *Lett.* (1885) 98 Therefore his conduct is so much the more unacademical.

unac'celerated, *ppl. a.* (un-[1] 8.)

a **1774** Goldsm. *Surv. Exp. Philos.* (1776) I. 135 The product will be the space described by the unaccelerated motion continued after the fall. **1893** *Brit. Jrnl. Photogr.* XL. 751 A simple unaccelerated drop-shutter.

unac'cented, *ppl. a.* [un-[1] 8.] Not accented or stressed; unemphasized.

Hence (in recent use) ***unaccentedness***.

1598 Florio, *Disaccentato*, vnaccented, without an accent or due sound. **1728** Chambers *Cycl.* s.v. *Accent*, Every Bar or Measure is divided into accented and unaccented Parts. **1768** *Phil. Trans.* LVIII. 256 As neither the Samnites nor the Etruscans had in their alphabet O, they used the simple unaccented V for that element. **1808** L. Murray *Eng. Gram.* I. 332 Unaccented syllables are generally short. **1873** H. C. Banister *Music* 12 In all measures, certain beats are accented, and the others unaccented. **1893** *Nation* (N.Y.) 12 Jan. 33/3 His outline drawings..are round and unaccented, and show little sense of structure.

unac'centuated, *ppl. a.* (un-[1] 8. Cf. G. *unaccentuirt*, Sw. *oaccentuerad*.)

1716 M. Davies *Athen. Brit.* II. 373 Of the same 12th Century were Folmar, Abaillard, Arnaldus Brixiensis [etc.], ..all whose unaccentuated and recanted Arianism perish'd together. **1887** Cook *Sievers' O.E. Gram.* 114 This change occurs most frequently in an unaccentuated syllable.

unac'cept, *v. rare*[-1]. [un-[2] 3.] *trans.* To cancel the acceptance of (a bill).

1665 Marius *Adv. Conc. Bills Exchange* 24 The Acceptor would (if he could) unaccept the Bill, or make voyde his Acceptance thereof.

unaccepta'bility. (un-[1] 12.)

[**1775** Ash.] **1852** Ld. Cockburn *Jeffrey* I. 387 The people maintained..that popular unacceptability was of itself a ground on which the courts were entitled to reject. **1863** H. Spencer *Ess.* III. 325 We shall find that its unacceptability becomes still more conspicuous when the analysis is pursued to the end.

unacceptable, *a.* [un-[1] 7 b and 5 b. For pronunciation see note to acceptable *a.*] Not acceptable.

Catch.-phr. ***the unacceptable face of***——: see quot. 1973.

1483 *Cath. Angl.* 2/2 Vn Acceptabylle, *ingratus,..non acceptabilis.* **1540** Wyatt in Flügel *Neuengl. Lesebuch* I. 349, I can not ellis se what shold move this rigour..onles I peraventure be vnacceptable vnto hym. **1594** Hooker *Eccl. Pol.* ii. iv. §5 To the author and God of our nature, how shal any operation proceeding in naturall sort, be in that respect vnacceptable? **1634** Canne *Necess. Separ.* 27 A vaine worship: and therefore vnacceptable altogether to the Lord. **1697** Bentley *Phal.* (1699) 83 It will not be unacceptable to the Reader, to see some of it here corrected. **1710** Prideaux *Orig. Tithes* v. 241 The new Laws of King Henry being very unacceptable to the English. **1753** Warburton in Harris *Hardwicke* (1847) II. 481 No favours from such a hand could be unacceptable. **1855** Macaulay *Hist. Eng.* xxi. IV. 551 He still called himself a Whig, and was not unacceptable to many of the Whigs. **1880** Meredith *Tragic Com.* (1881) 165 An honourable son-in-law could not be unacceptable to him. **1973** E. Heath in *Hansard Commons* 15 May 1243 It is the unpleasant and unacceptable face of capitalism, but one should not suggest that the whole of British industry consists of practices of this kind. **1973** *Times* 5 June 1/6 He called the actions of the *News of the World* 'the unacceptable face of journalism'. **1975** A. Beevor *Violent Brink* vii. 210 Let us look at the unacceptable face of Communism. **1982** *Guardian* 8 Jan. 18/1 The unacceptable face of modern men's tennis was seen again during the Barratt world doubles championship..yesterday when Hank Pfister.. swore at the match umpire and then accused him of cheating.

Hence **unacceptableness; unacceptably** *adv.*

1648 Hexham ii, *On-aengenaemheydt*, *Un-acceptableness. **1660** Ingelo *Bentiv. & Ur.* i. (1682) 72 To correct the un-acceptableness of his story. **1697** Collier *Ess. Mor. Subj.* i. (1709) 2, I hope this Alteration does not arise from any natural Antipathy I have to Sense; but from the unacceptableness of the Subject I am upon. **1873** Mrs. Whitney *Other Girls* xxi, A tone timid with an apprehension of some possible unacceptableness. **1648** Hexham ii, *On-aenge-naemlick*, *Vn-acceptably. **1828–** in various Dicts.

unac'ceptance. [un-[1] 12.] Lack of acceptance.

1865 M. Arnold *Ess. Crit.* iv. (1875) 148 Saint Theresa endured twenty years of unacceptance and of repulse in her prayers. **1898** Saintsbury *Short. Hist. Eng. Lit.* xi. iii. (1900) 772 Mr. Ruskin's ideas, when their first stage of unacceptance and their second of acceptance were over, came to be cavilled at.

unac'ceptant, *a.* (un-[1] 7.)

1865 Ruskin *Eth. Dust* v. (1883) 85 Whatever dead substance, unacceptant of this energy, comes in their way, is ..rejected.

unac'cepted, *ppl. a.* [un-[1] 8.] Not accepted; rejected.

1612 T. Taylor *Comm. Titus* i. 8 Such cups of cold water shall not be vnaccepted nor unrewarded of him. **1718** Prior *Solomon* ii. 212 Restless I follow'd this obdurate Maid.., Offer'd again the unaccepted Wreath. **1809** R. Langford *Introd. Trade* 35 Unaccepted bills must be protested..on the very day when they become due. **1857** Miss Winkworth tr. *Tauler's Serm.* xviii. 322 Therefore, His gifts, which He offers without ceasing to every man, remain unaccepted. **1899** Miss B. Harraden *Fowler* 234 Davy always kept up the rôle of being an unaccepted sweetheart.

†**unac'cessible**, *a.* *Obs.* Also 6–7 -able. [UN-[1] 5 b.] = INACCESSIBLE *a.*
α. **1596** RALEIGH *Discov. Guiana* 97 Whosoeuer shall first possesse it, it shall bee founde vnaccessable for anie Enemie. **1611** COTGR., *Vn lieu condemné*, an vncouth, or vnaccessable place. **1645** SLINGSBY *Diary* (1836) 167 By y[e] wayes we took thro' y[e] almost unaccessable mountains of Wales.
β. **1600** E. BLOUNT tr. *Conestaggio* 263 Hauing viewed the Iland fortified on all parts where he might descend, and by nature vnaccessible. *a* **1641** BP. MOUNTAGU *Acts & Mon.* (1642) 536 The place was.. unaccessible; none did or could come there but the High Priest, once every yeere. **1704** RAY *Creation* (ed. 4) I. 200 Things.. too remote and unaccessible for us to penetrate or discover. **1768–74** TUCKER *Lt. Nat.* (1834) I. 527 The Creator dwells in unaccessible light, whereto we cannot draw near.
Hence †**unac'cessibleness**; †**unac'cessibly** *adv.* *Obs.*
1615 G. SANDYS *Trav.* 183 Mountains; whereof some are cut (or naturally so) in degrees like allies, which would be else vnaccessably fruitlesse. *a* **1676** HALE *Prim. Orig. Man.* II. iv. (1677) 155 We cannot attain to any clear sensible discovery of them.. by reason of their remoteness, distance, and unaccessibleness.

unac'cessional, *a.* (UN-[1] 7 and 5 b.)
1655 EARL ORRERY *Parthen.* I. II. 95 The Princess.. has all the guifts of Nature in so unaccessionall a Degree, that nothing can excel the perfectnesse of her body but that of her Minde.

unac'cessory, *a.* (UN-[1] 7.)
1660 INGELO *Bentiv. & Ur.* II. (1682) 155 Altogether unaccessory to their Calamities. **1753** W. MELMOTH tr. *Cicero's Lett.* II. 145 Nor were you entirely unaccessory to my error.

unacci'dented, *a.* (UN-[1] 9.)
c **1740** J. BROWN in R. Mackenzie *Life* (1918) iii. 23 Reason told me that at least our unaccidented tongue could not much change names from what they were in the Greek.

una'cclimated, *ppl. a.* (UN-[1] 8.)
1846 WORCESTER (citing Patterson). **1852** T. ROSS tr. *Humboldt's Trav.* I. xi. 379 Their death often alarmed the unacclimated Europeans. **1883** *Cent. Mag.* July 425/2 The fatality of the epidemics was principally among the unacclimated.

unaccli'mation. (UN-[1] 12.)
1866 A. FLINT *Princ. Med.* (1880) 1023 Unacclimation is a condition pertaining to individual susceptibility.

una'cclimatized, *ppl. a.* (UN-[1] 8. Cf. G. *unacclimatisirt.*)
1863 *Waitz' Introd. Anthropol.* I. 125 Negroes of the third and fourth generation, who, after being acclimatized in North America had returned to Africa,.. became subject to the same climatic diseases as other unacclimatized individuals. **1891** KIPLING *City Dreadf. Nt.* 80 The air.. brings about, to the unacclimatised, a singing in the ears.

†**una'ccommodate**, *ppl. a.* *Obs.* [UN-[1] 8 b and 5 b.] Unsuited; unaccommodated.
a **1676** HALE *Prim. Orig. Man.* III. vi. (1677) 282 Yet in the first state of Humane Production all these Suppositions must be laid aside, as unaccommodate to that state. **1736** T. PRINCE *New Eng. Chronol.* II. i. 103 Infected with the Scurvy & other Diseases, which their long Voyage and unaccommodate [**1621** inacomodate] Condition brought upon them.

una'ccommodated, *ppl. a.* [UN-[1] 8.] Not accommodated; not possessed *of*, unprovided *with*.
1605 SHAKS. *Lear* III. iv. 109 Vnaccommodated man, is no more but such a poore, bare, forked Animall as thou art. **1627** DONNE *Serm.* 41 Not angry so as that he left Moses unsatisfied or unaccommodated for the maine businesse. **1680** MOXON *Mech. Exerc.* 226 Being at that time.. unaccommodated of a Lathe of my own, I intended to put them out to be Turned. **1726** WELSTED *Dissemb. Wanton* I. i, The resource of stale virgins, and unaccommodated prudes. **1818** LADY MORGAN *Autobiog.* (1859) 7, I hear that travelling in Italy is beyond everything desolate and unaccommodated. **1842** F. E. PAGET *Milf. Malv.* 161 So soon as he perceived a body of strangers unaccommodated with seats of any kind, he immediately opened his pew door, and beckoned them in.

una'ccommodating, *ppl. a.* (UN-[1] 10.)
1790 BEATSON *Nav. & Mil. Mem.* I. 94 His manners and temper were unaccommodating. **1854** DICKENS *Hard T.* I. i, His very neckcloth, trained to take him by the throat with an unaccommodating grasp,.. helped the emphasis. **1897** HINDE *Fall Congo Arabs* 106 We had taken prisoner the unaccommodating chief.

una'ccompanied, *ppl. a.* [UN-[1] 8.]
1. Not accompanied or attended. Also const. *by*, or *with*.
1545 RAYNALDE *Byrth Mankynde* 21 b, God.. neuer createth no speciall pleasure vnaccompanyed with some sorowe. *a* **1600** HOOKER *Eccl. Pol.* VII. xxiv. §18 The travels and crosses wherewith prelacy is never unaccompanied. **1605** SHAKS. *Macb.* I. iv. 40 Our eldest, Malcolme, whom we name hereafter, The Prince of Cumberland: which Honor must Not vnaccompanied, inuest him onely. **1709** *Tatler* No. 120 ¶3 As I was single and unaccompanied, I was not permitted to enter the temple. **1763** J. BROWN *Poetry & Music* v. 47 The Melody of Instruments, unaccompany'd by Dance or Song. **1800** *Asiat. Ann. Reg., Misc. Tr.* 84/2 Persic odes, unaccompanied with translations. **1827** POLLOK *Course T.* x. 351 Thou goest.. Not unaccompanied; all these, my saints, Go with Thee. **1891** FARRAR *Darkn. & Dawn* liii, Unaccompanied by Philetus, the actor went to the meeting.
2. Lacking instrumental accompaniment.
1818 BUSBY *Gram. Mus.* 475 In Unaccompanied Recitative, the modulation has little or no dependence. **1876** STAINER & BARRETT *Dict. Mus. Terms* s.v. *Anthem*, Those choirs in which an unaccompanied service is sometimes performed.

una'ccomplishable, *a.* (UN-[1] 7 b.)
1675 *Art Contentm.* I. §12. 179 It must be exceedingly bitter, to be thus condemned to endless unaccomplishable desires. **1812** CARY *Dante, Parad.* XXVI. 126 Or ever Nimrod's race Their unaccomplishable work began. **1868** RUSKIN *Sesame* (1871) 161 At these visions of theirs we have mocked, and held them for idle and vain, unreal and unaccomplishable.

una'ccomplished, *ppl. a.* [UN-[1] 8.]
1. Not accomplished or achieved; uncompleted.
1525 LD. BERNERS *Froiss.* II. cxiv. 329 Your wysshes and enterprises are more lyke to be vnacomplysshed than atchyued. **1590** SWINBURNE *Testaments* 133 The same is neither accompted for accomplished,.. neither yet for vnaccomplished or deficient. **1667** MILTON *P.L.* III. 455 All th' unaccomplisht works of Natures hand, Abortive, monstrous, or unkindly mixt. **1736** THOMSON *Liberty* IV. 161 Yet dark beneath The suffering feature sullen vengeance lowrs Shame, indignation, unaccomplish'd rage. **1821** SHELLEY *Hellas* Prol. 51 Assemble, sons of God, To speed or to prevent or to suspend.. The unaccomplished destiny. **1850** TENNYSON *In Mem.* xci, The hope of unaccomplish'd years Be large and lucid round thy brow.
2. Of persons: Not socially or intellectually accomplished.
a **1729** CONGREVE tr. *Ovid's Art Love* III, Still unaccomplish'd may the maid be thought, Who gracefully to dance was never taught. **1796** MME. D'ARBLAY *Camilla* II. 357 How many are there, amongst the untaught and unaccomplished, who would think [etc.]. **1826** MISS MITFORD *Our Village* Ser. II. (1863) 274 Unaccomplished they were of course, but they could never have been thought ignorant. **1874** MISS MULOCK *My Mother & I*, xiv, Not that she is ill-educated, or unaccomplished.

una'ccomplishment. (UN-[1] 12.)
1643 MILTON *Divorce* Introd., Wks. 1851 IV. 4 Custom being but a meer face,.. rests not in her unaccomplishment, untill by secret inclination she accorporat her self with error. *Ibid.* 24 Where the mind and person pleases aptly, there some unaccomplishment of the bodies delight may be better born with.

†**una'ccomptably**, *adv.* *Obs.* (UN-[1] 11.)
a **1677** BARROW *Serm.* Wks. 1686 III. 260 The which are alledged, not with intent to imply that God ever acteth unaccomptably, or without highest reason.

†**unaccompted**, *ppl. a.* *Obs.* (UN-[1] 8.)
a **1483** *Liber Niger* in *Househ. Ord.* (1790) 65 In case the accomptes passe, for lack of appearance of one of them [*sc.* the steward or treasurer], three dayes unaccompted.

†**una'ccomptible**, *a.* *Obs.* (UN-[1] 7.)
1678 B. R. *Let. Pop. Friends* 4 What Protestant Scammony is strong enough to make a.. Catholick Disgorge Infallibility, or the Popes unaccomptible Power?

†**una'ccomptibly**, *adv.* *Obs.* (UN-[1] 11.)
1678 CUDWORTH *Intell. Syst.* I. iii. Contents §10. 102 These Materialists.. assigned no cause of Motion, but introduced it into the world unaccomptibly.

una'ccordable, *a.* (UN-[1] 7 b.)
1456 SIR G. HAYE *Law Arms* (S.T.S.) 30 Thai ar.. unacordable with wysare than thame self. **1611** FLORIO, *Inaccordabile*, vnaccordable, not to bee agreed vpon.

†**una'ccordance.** *Obs.*$^{-1}$ [UN-[1] 12 and 5 b.] Disagreement.
c **1449** PECOCK *Repr.* 263 These preiers, whiche mowen be seid as mad to the cros, mowen be saued fro inconuenience and vnaccordaunce.

una'ccordant, *a.* (UN-[1] 7 and 5 b.)
a **1470** HARDING *Chron.* CV. xiii, Athelbold.. His stepdame wed, menne saied it was not faire,.. Again the lawe and christen conscience, Vnaccordant with his magnificence. **1798** *Geraldina* II. 268 The present disposition of my spirits is not unaccordant to the sentiments of affection. **1879** FARRAR *St. Paul* I. 384 The rhythmic conclusion is not unaccordant with the style of his most elevated moods.

una'ccorded, *ppl. a.* [UN-[1] 8.] Not agreed upon; not granted or bestowed.
1645 BP. HALL *Peace-Maker* v. 43 The Divines.. professed their agreement in all the maine and important points; leaving those parcels unaccorded, which are meet to be sent, and confined to the Schooles. **1883** R. BRIDGES *Prometheus* 1215 O Right's toil unrewarded! O Love's prize unaccorded.

†**una'ccording**, *ppl. a.* *Obs.* [UN-[1] 10.] Inaccordant.
1398 TREVISA *Barth. De P.R.* IX. xv. (Bodl MS.). Þe Caniculer daies bygynneþ,.. alle hoote passions encreseth, and þat tyme is moste disconuenient and vnacording to medicyne. *c* **1400** tr. *Secreta Secret., Gov. Lordsh.* 60 By þe wyndes comes corrupcions of þe eyr and norschight dedly venyms, and many oþer vnacordand þinges comes þerof. *a* **1470** HARDING *Chron* XXX. iv, Drunken he was echedaye expresse, Vnaccordynge to a prince of worthynesse. **1530** R. WHYTFORD *Werke for Househ.* H 3 Ferre vnacordynge ben thy for housbandes and ware housholders. **1756** PITT in Walpole *George II* (1822) II. 34 From such an unaccording assemblage of separate.. powers with no system, a nullity results.
Hence †**una'ccordingly** *adv.* *Obs.*
c **1449** PECOCK *Repr.* 207 Ellis it wolde folewe that ther yn thei diden vnaccordingli and vnsemeli. **1519** HORMAN *Vulg.* 77 Many be occupyed vncomly, and vnaccordynglye about childrens matters. **1533** tr. *Erasmus' Com. Crede* 63 Yf ony man dyd tourne a temple made of stone.. into a showemakers shope wolde not all men crye out that it were shamefully and vnaccordyngly don?

unaccounta'bility. (UN-[1] 12. See next.)
1704 SWIFT *Let. to Tisdall* 20 Apr., There is more unaccountability in your letter's little finger than in mine's whole body. **1794** ANNA SEWARD *Lett.* (1811) IV. 31 With all his good taste in literature and ladies, he has some unaccountabilities—I was going to have said eccentricities. **1851** SIR F. PALGRAVE *Norm. & Eng.* I. 68 Moreover, many anomalies and unaccountabilities accompanied the growth. **1871** TYLOR *Prim. Cult.* I. 17 The notions of arbitrary impulses, causeless freaks, chance and nonsense and indefinite unaccountability.

una'ccountable, *a.* and *sb.* [UN-[1] 7 b, 5 b.]
A. *adj.* **1. a.** That cannot be accounted for or explained; inexplicable. Also *absol.*
1643 MILTON *Divorce* II. xxi. Wks. 1851 IV. 120 The unaccountable and secret reasons of disaffection between man and wife. **1689** [see UNACCOUNTED 2]. **1709** ADDISON *Tatler* No. 123 ¶7 Those unaccountable Antipathies which some Persons are born with. **1776** DALRYMPLE *Ann. Scot.* I. 9 To this hardy atchievement, an unaccountable inactivity succeeded. **1834** LYTTON *Pompeii* I. v. 25 A sudden and unaccountable gloom came over each as they thus gazed. **1871** TYLOR *Prim. Cult.* I. 4 Where events look unaccountable,.. to wait and watch in hope that the key to the problem may some day be found. **1895** MRS. WILSON 5 *Years India* 281 The Hindu accounts for the unaccountable by calling it divine.
b. Of persons: Difficult to account for or make out; of a strange or puzzling disposition.
1711 ADDISON *Spect.* No. 1 ¶4, I.. left the University, with the Character of an odd unaccountable Fellow, that had a great deal of Learning, if I would but show it. **1748** RICHARDSON *Clarissa* (1811) III. 329 Indeed, Mr. Lovelace, you are a very unaccountable man. **1774** FOOTE *Cozeners* II. Wks. 1799 II. 161 The family above.. are a strange unaccountable tribe: Pray, who the deuce are they? **1801** MAR. EDGEWORTH *Moral T.*, *Angelina* i, A self-willed, unaccountable romantic girl. **1873** 'OUIDA' *Pascarel* II. 240 We Italians are an unaccountable people.
2. Not liable to be called to account; irresponsible: **a.** Of power, etc.
1649 MILTON *Eikon.* xi. Wks. 1851 III. 420 Hee met at first with Doctrines of unaccountable Prerogative; in them hee rested, because they pleas'd him. **1695** J. SAGE *Cyprianic Age* 67 The Acknowledgment of his Supream and Unaccountable Power within his own District. **1724** R. FIDDES *Morality* Pref. p. lxxxiii, If man had an unaccountable power.. a single tyrant.. might lawfully destroy all the rest. **1736** *Gentl. Mag.* VI. 303/2 They have never since made any Demand for the Deficiencies; not that We are to suppose that it is supply'd by the Revenue's being unaccountable. **1861** LD. BROUGHAM *Brit. Const.* viii. 105 Each estate should have powers independent of all the others, and in the exercise of which it is unaccountable and supreme.
b. Of persons, etc.
1677 *Spottiswood's Hist. Ch. Scot.* App. 31 The King is an absolute and unaccountable Monarch. **1683** *Brit. Spec.* 173 Governed by one Supreme, Absolute, Independent, Undeposable, and Unaccountable Head. **1713** BERKELEY *Guard.* No. 3 ¶1 The Pleasures for which their Doctrines leave them [*sc.* abandoned young men] unaccountable. **1827** POLLOK *Course T.* II. 38 All else was.. unaccountable, by instinct led. But man He made of angel-form erect.
†**3.** Incalculable; uncountable. *Obs.*
169. TEMPLE *Pop. Discontents* ii. ¶6 It is unaccountable what Treasures it would save this Nation, by preventing so many Wars.. abroad. **1722** WOLLASTON *Relig. Nat.* v. §14 To shew him.. still more and more of these fixt lights, and to beget in him an apprehension of their unaccountable numbers.
B. *sb.* **1.** An unaccountable person.
1748 RICHARDSON *Clarissa* (1811) V. 314, I never heard of or saw such a dear unaccountable. **1825** BROCKETT *N.C. Gloss.* s.v. **1854** MISS BAKER *Northampt. Gloss.* s.v., He's quite an unaccountable.
2. An unaccountable thing or event. *rare.*
1789 M. CUTLER in *Life*, etc. (1888) I. 448 It was an event, however, I could not fail of recording in my book of unaccountables. **1799** MRS. J. WEST *Tale of Times* II. 250 It.. must be set down in the catalogue of my unaccountables. **1833** R. DYER *Nine Yrs. Actor's Life* 66 His non-engagement in London is amongst the unaccountables of metropolitan management. **1961** 'J. LE CARRÉ' *Call for Dead* viii. 83 Of all the unaccountables in the case, that worried him most.

una'ccountableness. (UN-[1] 12.)
1676 W. ALLEN *Address Nonconf.* 156 The unsafeness or unaccountableness of the way in which you conduct the people. **1696** C. LESLIE *Snake in Grass* (1697) 254 What is an Universal Liberty, but Independancy and Unaccountableness in Practice and Conversation? **1713** BERKELEY *Guard.* No. 70 The Unaccountableness of some Step of Providence or Point of Doctrine to his narrow Faculties. **1748** RICHARDSON *Clarissa* (1811) V. 106 Jealousy of itself, to female minds, accounts for a thousand unaccountablenesses. **1814** JANE AUSTEN *Mansf. Park* xxxii, As her unaccountableness was confirmed, his displeasure increased. **1874** PUSEY *Lent. Serm.* 6 God has placed no limit to the wonderfulness, the unaccountableness of His mercies.

una'ccountably, *adv.* [UN-[1] 11.]
†**1.** Without being liable to be called to account; irresponsibly. *Obs.*
1679 OATES *Narr. Popish Plot* Ded. a 2 b, More to trust and rely upon Your Two Houses of Parliament.. than to any.. Ministers whatsoever, unaccountably, who may pretend to more Loyalty.
2. Inexplicably.
1694 F. BRAGGE *Disc. Parables* xiii. 427 So unaccountably stupid and thoughtless are men for the generality. **1733** CHEYNE *Eng. Malady* II. ix. §7 (1734) 214 Which

Symptoms, as they will come on unaccountably, .. will go off as unaccountably. **1794** Mrs. Radcliffe *Myst. Udolpho* lv, He had felt suddenly and unaccountably reassured of her innocence. **1847** Meeson & Welsby *Rep.* XVI. 645 *note*, The season had proved unaccountably injurious to meat. **1885** *Manch. Exam.* 13 Jan. 5/4 The indifference of the clergy themselves to a defect which their flocks have so unaccountably condoned.

una'ccounted, *ppl. a.* [un-[1] 8, 8 c.]

1. a. Not taken account *of*. *rare*[−1].

1587 Golding *De Mornay* xxi. 328 A people being conquered, caried away, .. vnaccounted of, .. as the Iewes were.

b. Not accounted *for*.

1799 J. Robertson *Agric. Perth* 392 Allowing the average of this increase to the fourteen unaccounted for. **1834** *Tait's Mag.* I. 697/1 Sir Robert Walpole .. had left a million and a half of the public money unaccounted for. **1884** *Manch. Exam.* 22 Nov. 4/7 The voting papers were scrutinised with the exception of 547 remaining unaccounted for.

2. Of which no account is given.

1689 *Apol. Fail. Walker's Acc.* 19 Those unaccounted (but not unaccountable) baffles giv'n to the reliefs sent to Derry. **1812** *Examiner* 5 Oct. 633/1 Which suffers an Irish Defaulter of unaccounted millions, to remain unaudited. **1827** Hallam *Const. Hist.* II. 56 *note*, They reported unaccounted balances of 1,509,161*l.*, besides much that was questionable in the payments.

una'ccoutred, *ppl. a.* (un-[1] 8.)

1749 Mrs. R. Goadby *Carew* ii. (1750) 24 He exchanged his Habit .. for only an old Blanket... Being thus accoutred, or rather unaccoutred, he was now no other than poor Mad Tom.

una'ccreditated, *ppl. a.* (un-[1] 8.)

1806 R. Cumberland *Mem.* (1807) II. 53 He was driven to allude to these unaccreditated propositions.

una'ccredited, *ppl. a.* (un-[1] 8.)

1828–32 Webster s.v., The consul remained unaccredited. **1850** Kingsley *A. Locke* x, They're the unknown great—the unaccredited heroes, as Master Thomas Carlyle would say. **1882** Farrar *Early Chr.* I. 83 It is singular how very little is narrated of the rest [of the apostles], and how entirely that little depends upon loose and unaccredited tradition.

†**un'accuracy**. *Obs.*[−1] [un-[1] 12 and 5 b.] = inaccuracy.

1702 S. Parker tr. *Cicero's De Finibus* ii. 73 We'll not fall out with him for the Confusedness of his Method, because he professes and vindicates Unaccuracy and Negligence.

†**un'accurate**, *a. Obs.* [un-[1] 7 and 5 b. Cf. G. *unaccurat.*] = inaccurate *a.*

1660 Boyle *New Exp. Phys. Mech.* xxxvi. 288 Some learned men have attempted it by wayes so unaccurate that they seeme to have much mistaken it. *a* **1680** Glanvill *Sadducismus* i. (1682) 1 The unaccurate product of a little leisure. **1723** Waterland *2nd Vind. Christ's Div.* 188 The latter has indeed, in an unaccurate Work, or perhaps corrupted, mentioned the Distinction.

†**un'accurately**, *adv. Obs.* [un-[1] 11 and 5 b.] = inaccurately *adv.*

1674 Boyle *Excell. Theol.* 159 A Mathematician, when he probably conjectures at the compass of the Terrestrial Globe, .. divides, .. unaccurately, its Surface, first, into proportions of Sea and Land. **1710** *Managers' Pro & Con* M j b, The Parliament expressed themselves unaccurately. **1719** Waterland *Vind. Christ's Div.* 186 If ποιητὴς signified more than δημιουργὸς, Origen spoke very unaccurately.

†**un'accurateness**. *Obs.* [un-[1] 12 and 5 b.] Inaccuracy.

?**1648** Boyle *Seraphic Love* To Rdr. (1660) A 3 b, They will passe by such unaccuratenesses as are wont to be incident to Composures of this Later Nature. **1665** Hooke *Microgr.* 247 The great unaccurateness of artificial works. **1705** Hearne *Collect* 29 Aug. (O.H.S.) I. 38 The unaccurateness of divers particulars.

una'ccursed, una'ccurst, *ppl. a.* (un-[1] 8.)

a **1674** T. Traherne *Poems Felicity* (1910) 16 All that in Visibles is Good, Or Pure, or Fair, or Unaccurst. **1727** Thomson *Britannia* 113 Pure is thy reign; when, unaccurs'd by blood, Nought, save the sweetness of indulgent showers, Trickling distils into the vernant glebe. **1828** Campbell *Emigrants for N.S. Wales* 70 With laws from Gothic bondage burst, And creeds by chartered priesthoods unaccurst.

una'ccusable, *a.* (un-[1] 7 b. Cf. late L. *inaccūsābilis*, F. *inaccusable.*)

1582 *Reg. Privy Council Scot.* III. 538 The saidis nobill men .. salbe untroublid and unaccusabill for that caus in tyme cuming. **1589** *Ibid.* IV. 406 To be free and unaccusable for thair ressett and furnissing grantit to the saidis Erllis. **1651** Stanley *Poems*, etc. 256 Persons exact and unaccusable in every part. **1853** Ruskin *Stones Ven.* II. vi. 160 They thus receive the results of the labour of inferior minds; and out of fragments full of imperfection, .. indulgently raise up a stately and unaccusable whole. **1886** —— *Præterita* (1899) I. iv. 117 As much trigonometry as made my mountain work .. unaccusable.

Hence **una'ccusably** *adv.*

1859 Ruskin *Arrows of Chace* (1880) I. 199 Every man .. unaccusably accomplished .. for his place and function. **1870** —— *Lect. Art* vi. 161 The slightest attempts to copy them will show you that the terminal lines are .. unaccusably true.

una'ccused, *ppl. a.* (un-[1] 8.)

1508 *Reg. Privy Seal Scotl.* I. 250/1 We .. respittis thame to be .. unaccusit, unpersewit, unfolowit in the law or by the law. **1520** *Caxton's Chron. Eng.* iv. 36 b/2 Also that no man vnaccused in a cryme shold be put frome his dygnyte or degree tyll he were conuycted. **1580** Lupton *Sivquila* 93 Many should be unaccused, that now are falsely accused. **1624** Heywood *Gunaik.* iv. 178 This was three times prooved, and he still came off unaccused. **1784** Cowper *Task* v. 398 There dwell the most forlorn of human kind; Immur'd though unaccus'd, condemn'd untried. **1796** Mme. D'Arblay *Camilla* III. 31 He felt .. some consolation to find that Edgar .. was untainted by deceit, unaccused of any evil. **1897** *Daily News* 15 Mar. 5/4 Ismail Pacha has also amused himself during the past week in making many arrests in the town of unaccused persons.

una'ccusing, *ppl. a.* (un-[1] 10.)

1827 Pollok *Course T.* vii. 569 To censure, unaccusing minds .. Opposing.

una'ccustom, *v.* (un-[2] 3).

1580 Hollyband *Treas. Fr. Tong*, *Desaccoustumer*, to vnaccustome, to disuse. **1591** Percivall *Sp. Dict.*, *Desabituar*, to vnaccustome. *Ibid.*, *Desabituacion*, vnaccustoming.

†**una'ccustomable**, *adv. Obs.* [un-[1] 7 b.] Unusual. Hence †**una'ccustomably** *adv. Obs.*

1584 Lodge *Hist. Forbonius & Prisc.* (Shaks. Soc.) 94 Let it not seeme straunge unto thee, to beholde thine aged father's unaccustomable accesse, since he is now perplexed with unacquainted feares. **1651** Biggs *New Disp.* ¶ 230 The veins being now unnaturally and unaccustomably emptied.

†**una'ccustomarily**, *adv. Obs.* [un-[1] 11.] Unusually, abnormally.

1634 T. Johnson *Parey's Chirurg.* xviii. vii. Wks. (1678) 417 These .. are now suddenly and unaccustomarily suppresт. **1655** Culpepper, etc. *Riverius* xiii. iii. 364 If the Belly be unaccustomarily bound, or loose.

una'ccustomed, *ppl. a.* [un-[1] 8.]

1. Not customary; unfamiliar, unusual, strange.

1526 *Pilgr. Perf.* (Pynson) 92 By the reason of their glorious presence and excellent lyght, unaccustomed to the sayd persons. **1560** Daus tr. *Sleidane's Comm.* 452 Such unaccustomed vices, and not everywhere used. **1621** in Foster *Eng. Factories Ind.* (1906) I. 260 Such unaccustomed raynes .. hath drowned the greatest parte of new indicoe in the countryes. **1656** Earl Monm. tr. *Boccalini's Advts. fr. Parnass.* i. xii. (1674) 15 [He] was met with unaccustomed demonstrations of honour. **1742** Gray *Propertius* ii. i. 27 Nor I with unaccustomed vigour trace Back to its source divine the Julian race. **1840** Dickens *Old C. Shop* xvii, At sight of the strange room and its unaccustomed objects she started up in alarm. **1871** Morley *Crit. Misc.* Ser. i. 283 Firmer souls were not only exhilarated, but intoxicated by the potent and unaccustomed air.

†**b.** Const. *to* with inf. *Obs.*[−1]

1607 Topsell *Four-f. Beasts* 64 They were wont also to sacrifice a bul to Neptune... But vnto Iupiter it was vnaccustomed to be offered.

2. Not accustomed or habituated. Const. *to*.

1611 Bible *Jer.* xxxi. 18, I was chastised, as a bullocke vnaccustomed to the yoke. *a* **1680** Glanvill *Serm.* i. (1681) 90 The first steps are roughest to those feet that have been unaccustomed to it. **1728** Eliza Heywood tr. *Mme. de Gomez's Belle A.* (1732) II. 82 Your Heart, unaccustom'd to feel any very tender Impressions, felt some Concern for those you have inspir'd me with. **1797** S. & Ht. Lee *Canterb. T.* (1799) I. 352 Lothaire was unaccustomed to fear. **1846** Mrs. A. Marsh *Father Darcy* II. ii. 67 The abhorrence of bloodshed is common to all who are unaccustomed to it. **1891** Farrar *Darkn. & Dawn* lvii, Familiar with crime, he was unaccustomed to be charged with it.

b. Used (attrib. or absol.) without const.

1653 W. Ramesey *Astrol. Restored* 170 Phlebotomy is not any wise dangerous to those that are accustomed therewith, but it may prove dangerous to the unaccustomed. **1794** Mrs. Radcliffe *Myst. Udolpho* xxxv, Circumstances that united to elevate the unaccustomed mind of Blanche to enthusiasm. **1859** Mansel *Lett., Lect.*, etc. (1873) 192 Quaint as the nomenclature may sound to unaccustomed ears. **1875** Whyte Melville *Katerfelto* xix, An unaccustomed horse would have stuck fast up to its girths before it had gone fifty yards.

†**3.** = uncustomed *ppl. a. Obs.*

1701 *Lond. Gaz.* No. 3737/4 Liable to be .. seized in like manner as Prohibited and Unaccustomed Goods. **1715** *Ibid.* No. 5298/3 Prosecutions .. concerning unaccustomed and Prohibited Goods.

Hence **una'ccustomedness**; **una'ccustomedly**.

1611 Cotgr., *Desaccoustumance*, a disuse, vnwontednesse, vnaccustomednesse. **1659** *Gentl. Calling* 435 The main cause of that disgust men have to this spiritual entercourse, is their unaccustomedness to it. **1866** *Lond. Rev.* 8 Dec. 623 It is permissible when it leads the worshipper to God, and does not, by its unaccustomedness, splendour, or intricacy, interpose itself as a veil between God and him. **1881** Mrs. Oliphant in *Macm. Mag.* Apr. 493/1 He was seated, not in any familiar corner, but with the forlornest unaccustomedness, in the middle of it. **1659** Torriano, Unaccustomedly. **1963** *Economist* 2 Nov. 472/1 Unaccustomedly emotional language. **1980** H. Curtiss *Poisoned Orchard* iii. 22 She had put her car away, unaccustomedly, because of the sub-zero temperature forecast.

una'chievable, *a.* (un-[1] 7 b.)

1657 Farindon *Serm.* 484 If .. it should be unatchievable, not to be attained to by some. **1845** Carlyle *Cromwell* (1871) IV. 238 Projects unachievable, even the preface of them. **1899** *Westm. Gaz.* 15 Feb. 2/1 A reader of less nimble wits who has not caught the trick of suppressing the verbs and leaping to a meaning unachievable by syntax.

una'chieved, *ppl. a.* (un-[1] 8.)

1603 Holland *Plutarch's Mor.* 794 The combat remained unatchived and unperfect, neither had it a certaine and doubtlesse conclusion. **1831** Scott *Ct. Rob.* x, So it is, the spell remains unachieved.

un'aching, *ppl. a.* (un-[1] 10.)

1607 Shaks. *Cor.* ii. ii. 155 To brag vnto them, thus I did, and thus Shew them th' vnaking Skarres, which I should hide. **1721** Cibber *Love in Riddle* i. i, The winter of unaching Age. **1757** Dyer *Fleece* i. 642 Pleasing weariness Soon our unaching heads to sleep inclines. **1822–7** Good *Study Med.* (1829) I. 532 Compressible Polypus, .. unaching, chiefly pale-red. **1828** Landor *Imag. Conv.* III. 312 Days of happiness like this I could recall and look back upon with unaching brow.

†**un'achteled**, *ppl. a. Obs.*[−1] [un-[1] 8 + *achtel*, *aghtle* ettle *v.*] Unestimated.

c **1250** *Gen. & Ex.* 796 God gaf him ðor siluer and gold, .. Vn-achteled welðe he ðor bi-gat.

una'cidulated, *ppl. a.* (un-[1] 8.)

[**1775** Ash.] **1860** Grove *Corr. Phys. Forces*, etc. (1874) 416 With distilled water unacidulated I could observe no effect of electrolysis.

unack'nowledged, *ppl. a.* (un-[1] 8.)

1583 Golding *Calvin on Deut.* iii. 17/1 See (I say) how God is vnacknowledged of vs in his benefites. **1647** Clarendon *Hist. Reb.* i. §160 The fear .. of what was to come .. from an unknown, at least an unacknowledg'd Successor, to the Crown. **1687** Rycaut *Hist. Turks* II. 228 The Ambassadour remained aboard unsaluted and unacknowledged by the publick Ministers of the City. **1751** Earl Orrery *Remarks Swift* (1752) 76 From the same causes, Stella remained an unacknowledged wife. **1796** Mme. D'Arblay *Camilla* x. xiii, A reciprocal confidence that left .. not an action unrelated, not even a thought unacknowledged. **1835** T. Mitchell *Acharn. of Aristoph.* 230 *note*, The consequent dread that prevailed lest any of those gifts should appear to pass unacknowledged. **1871** Tylor *Prim. Cult.* i. 2 Nor .. in investigating the lower functions even of man, are these leading ideas unacknowledged.

unack'nowledging, *ppl. a.* (un-[1] 10.)

1611 Cotgr., *Mescognoissant*, vnacknowledging, ignorant, vngratefull. **1656** Earl Monm. tr. *Boccalini's Advts. fr. Parnass.* i. xxxiii. 38 He .. desired, that as an unacknowledging and ungrateful man, he might receive condign punishment. **1697** Collier *Ess. Mor. Subj.* ii. (1709) 35 Who could have imagined People so strangely stupid and unacknowledging? **1752** Mrs. Lennox *Fem. Quixote* iii. viii. 208 Your Condition shall be never the worse for Miss Glanville's unacknowledging Temper... You are almost as unacknowledging as your Sister.

una corda (ˈuːnə ˈkɔːdə). *Mus.* [It., = one string.] As a direction in music for the piano, etc.: use the soft pedal (which on grand pianos softens the tone by shifting the hammers so as to strike only one or two strings instead of two or three for each note). Also *attrib.*, designating such a pedal mechanism. Cf. soft pedal *sb.*

1849 *Hamilton's Celebrated Dict.* s.v., *Una corda* (Italian). Implies that a passage is to be played upon only one string. **1876** Stainer & Barrett *Dict. Mus. Terms* 444/1 *Un, Una, Uno* (It.), one; as *Una corda*, one string. **1909** *Cent. Dict.* Suppl. s.v. *pedal* n., The direction *una corda* signifies simply the use of this [shifting] pedal. **1931** D. F. Tovey *Beethoven Sonatas for Pianoforte* xxix. 140 Beethoven's double shift from *tre corda* through *due corda* to *una corda*. **1961** [see escapement 3]. **1979** *Sci. Amer.* Jan. 99/2 To prevent this the piano is equipped with the una corda pedal, whose mechanical function is to shift the entire keyboard so that a hammer strikes only two strings of a unison triplet.

una'cquaint, *a.* Chiefly *Sc.* [un-[1] 7.] = unacquainted *ppl. a.* (Usu. const. *with.*)

1587 T. Hughes *Misfort. Arthur* Induct., Good ladies, unacquaint with cunning reach. **1587** W. Fowler *Wks.* (S.T.S.) I. 26 The habit proude, vnsene, vnvsd, all new and vnacquent, I thair beheld. **1611** Sir W. Mure *Misc. Poems* ii. 47 Scho, spying me ȝit wnacquaint in loue, Hir new got dairts throught my puir hert did roue. **1628** —— *Doomesday* 643 Satietie, which vnacquent With loathing, doth arise. *a* **1699** Kirkton *Hist. Ch. Scotl.* (1817) 280 Maxwell, .. because he was unacquaint in the town, .. came running into Nicol Moffat, stabler, his house in Horse-Wynd. **1716** Wodrow *Corr.* (1843) II. 216 Your Reverend colleague, to whom, though unacquaint, I give my dearest respects. *a* **1758** Ramsay *Some of the Contents* v, Thair forbeirs were unacquaint with feir. **1822** Galt *Provost* xxvi, We were unacquaint with the character of the man. **1840** Lowell *Irene* 23 And, though herself not unacquaint with care, Hath in her heart wide room for all that be.

†**una'cquaint**, *v. Obs. rare.* [un-[2] 6 a.] *trans.* To deprive of acquaintance.

1557 N.T. (Genev.) Epist. *iiii, What thing can ther be then that might vnacquaynte vs and dryue vs backe from this Gospel? **1697** J. Sergeant *Solid. Philos.* 360 Nor can the contrary be sustaind any other way, but by unacquainting us with our selves and our own kind.

una'cquaintance. (un-[1] 12 and 5 b.)

1598 Florio, *Inesperientia*, inexperience, vnskilfulnes, vnacquaintance. **1627** Bp. Hall *Gt. Impostor* 507 Of this vnacquaintance, secondly, arises a dangerous mesprison of a mans selfe. **1659** T. Pecke *Parnassi Puerp.* 49 Therefore how many, and how Qualifi'd; By unacquaintance, could not be descry'd. **1786** A. Gib *Sacr. Contempl.* 381 There will be no unacquaintance among the individuals of the redeemed in heaven. **1882** Ld. Acton in *Life & Lett. Bp. Creighton* (1904) I. 229, I shall be very glad if I may consider the stage of unacquaintance as gone by.

b. Freq. const. *with*.

1646 R. Baillie *Anabaptism* (1647) 49 Through unacquaintance with the minde of the most. **1676** Glanvill *Ess.* vi. 28, I scorn the ordinary Tales of Prodigies, which proceed from superstitious Fears, and unacquaintance with Nature. **1716–20** *Lett. fr. Mist's Jrnl.* (1722) I. 300 Our as yet utter Unacquaintance with the real Folly and Vanity there is in every thing. **1777** Robertson *Hist. Amer.* vii.

(1778) II. 319 The Peruvians, from their unacquaintance with the use of arches,.. could not construct bridges either of stone or timber. **1814** SCOTT *Wav.* xxxi, Your.. unacquaintance with the manners of the Highlands. **1895** HUNTER *Old Missionary* iv. 106 Their unacquaintance with English made it difficult for them to master the.. new Penal .. Codes.

una'cquainted, *ppl. a.* [UN-[1] 8.]

†**1.** Of persons: Not personally known (to one). *Obs.* (Cf. 4.)

1529 MORE *Suppl. Souls* Wks. 288/1 Your humble & vnacquaynted, and half forgotten supplyantes. **1586** J. HOOKER *Hist. Irel.* in *Holinshed* II. 155/2 He was more like a father than a freend, and more like a freend than an vnacquainted countriman. **1607** DEKKER & WEBSTER *Northw. Hoe* I. i, Being a Londoner though altogether vnacquainted, I haue requested his company at supper.

†**2.** Of things: Unknown, unfamiliar, strange, unusual. *Obs.* (Common *c* 1560–1640.)

1551 T. WILSON *Logike* Ep. to King A iv, I haue.. enterprised to ioyne an acquaintaunce betwiene Logique, and my countrymen, from the whiche they haue bene hetherto barred, by tongues vnacquaynted. **1565** JEWEL *Reply Harding* (1611) 53 Certainly this phrase was so farre vnacquainted and vnknowen in that World, that the very Originals of these Decrees haue it not. **1577** tr. *Bullinger's Decades* (1592) 467 The name of merites is an vnacquainted terme, not vsed in the scriptures. **1632** LITHGOW *Trav.* x. 458, I was confident to dye a fearefull and vnacquainted death. **1672** MARVELL *Reh. Transp.* I. 126 Although the other punishments are more severe, yet this being more new and unacquainted, I cannot pass it by.

†**b.** Const. *to. Obs. rare.*

1572 BUCHANAN *Detection Marie Q. of Scottes* H ij b, The kinde of disease, strange, vnknawin to the pepill, vnacquainted to phisitiones. **1598** YONG *Diana* 452 Marcelius, Diana, and Ismenia, were lodged in two chambers in the Palace,.. lodgings vnacquainted to simple Shepherds.

3. Of persons (rarely of things): Having no acquaintance *with* (= knowledge of) something.

(*a*) **1563** GOLDING *Cæsar* III. (1565) 70b, Conueying thyther by water wold be very combersome, bycause the Romanes were vnacquainted wyth those countryes. **1647** CLARENDON *Hist. Reb.* I. §143 Sir Dudley Carleton.. was unacquainted with the Government, Laws, and Customs of his own Country. **1736** BUTLER *Anal.* I. ii. Wks. 1874 I. 36 There may be some impossibilities in the nature of things, which we are unacquainted with. **1771** *Junius Lett.* lviii. (1788) 312, I profess to be unacquainted with his private character. **1815** SCOTT *Guy M.* liv, Hazlewood, unacquainted with their plan of assault, was a moment later. **1860** TYNDALL *Glac.* II. ix. 269 To those unacquainted with the fact of their motion,.. the assertion that a glacier moves must appear.. startling and incredible.

(*b*) **1605** VERSTEGAN *Dec. Intell.* i. (1628) 1 The Irish language.. is.. vtterly vnacquainted with the names of England and of Englishmen. **1615** SANDYS *Trav.* IV. 254 A bay.. vnacquainted with tempests. **1646** P. BULKELEY *Gospel Covt.* IV. 303 Faith being.. yet unacquainted with the Lords dealing with his people. **1860** ADLER *Prov. Poet.* 351 This poetry was unacquainted with the dramatic form.

†**b.** Const. *in, of,* or *to. Obs.*

a **1586** SIDNEY *Arcadia* (1622) 360 So that poor Apollo was faine to leade a very miserable life, vnacquainted to worke, and never vsed to begge. **1704** SWIFT *T. Tub* Ded., Being very unacquainted in the style and form of dedications. **1787** CHARLOTTE SMITH *Romance Real Life* I. 290 A species of torture, but of the nature of which we are happily unacquainted in this country. **1805** tr. *Lafontaine's Hermann & E.* IV. 181 She is unacquainted of this circumstance, and she must remain in ignorance of it.

c. Without const.: Inexperienced; ignorant. Also with *that* and clause.

In quot. 1791 = in ignorance.

1581 ALLEN *Apol.* 121 Death and dungeons be not so terrible things to Christes souldiars, as they seeme to the vnacquainted. **1581** STUDLEY *Medea* A v, Not any guilt thou shalt with unacquainted hand assay. **1632** LITHGOW *Trav.* x. 426, I thinke it best to show the vnacquainted Reader, a reasonable satisfaction for [etc.]. **1663** BOYLE *Usef. Exp. Nat. Philos.* I. i. 3 The surprizing spectacle of so many and various Objects, as presented themselves to her unacquainted Sight. **1791** J. LEARMONT *Poems* 15 Tho' unacquaintit she has wooet Wi' ane that is his fae. **1796** MME. D'ARBLAY *Camilla* IV. v, Is she unacquainted that a little knowledge of books and languages is what alone I have been taught?

4. Of persons: Not having acquaintance, not being on terms of personal knowledge, *with* another. Also without const.: Not mutually acquainted.

1633 MASSINGER *Guardian* v. iv, You know the proscribed Severino,—he not unacquainted, but familiar, with The most of you. **1657** REEVE *God's Plea* 263 The Omniscient God is not unacquainted with them that are most dear to him, his Elect. **1766** GOLDSM. *Vicar* xxviii, Sir,.. you are unacquainted with the man that oppresses us. **1818** SCOTT *Br. Lamm.* xx, Were my mother to see you.. I am sure she would approve; but you are unacquainted personally. **1892** H. LANE *Differ. Rheum. Dis.* (ed. 2) Pref., The exceeding kindness.. with which friends, as well as critics, with whom I was personally unacquainted, received my first literary venture.

una'cquaintedness. [UN-[1] 12.] The state or fact of not being acquainted: **a.** Const. *with.*

1617 HIERON *Wks.* (1620) II. 380 Doe not cherish thy selfe in thy vnaccquaintednesse with this broken heart. **1682** FLAVEL *Fear* 115 We may be excused for our fears, by reason of our own unacquaintedness with sufferings. **1764** T. HUTCHINSON *Hist. Mass.* i. (1765) 5 From unacquaintedness with the geography of the country. **1825–9** MRS. SHERWOOD *Lady of Manor* II. xiv. 257, I have no doubt that I uttered many shocking avowals of my entire unacquaintedness with these things. **1851** I. TAYLOR *Wesley* 250 With our.. unacquaintedness with the manners and habits of the lower classes.

b. With *in, of,* or without const.

1667 *Inconveniences of Toleration* 6 It is nothing but unacquaintedness which makes them lyable to be so scared with all those terrible and groundless Stories. **1669** EARL ORRERY *Parthen.* III. v. 44 By their unacquaintedness in using of an Oar [they were] unable to Row. **1729** 'PHILALETHES' *Enq. Price Coals* 35 What proceeded from an Unacquaintedness in some Part of this Affair. **1748** RICHARDSON *Clarissa* (1811) II. xxxvii. 272 To what might not my youth, my sex, and unacquaintedness of the ways of that great, wicked town expose me?

una'cquirable, *a.* (UN-[1] 7 b.)

1640 BP. REYNOLDS *Passions* xiii. 121 Sinners, conceiving happinesse as unacquirable by them, do grow to the Hating of it. **1882** G. MACDONALD *Weighed & Wanting* II. vi. 53 An unacquirable gift, not necessarily associated with anything noble.

una'cquirableness. (UN-[1] 12.)

1768–74 TUCKER *Lt. Nat.* (1834) I. 217 As to the unacquirableness of virtue, this somewhat resembles Whitfield's day of grace, which being not yet come or being once past, no man can attain to righteousness.

una'cquired, *ppl. a.* [UN-[1] 8.]

1. Not acquired; unattained.

1653 JER. TAYLOR *Serm. for Year* I. xii. 154 The work of God is left imperfect, and our persons ungracious, and our ends unacquired. **1656** W. MONTAGUE *Accompl. Wom.* Ep. Ded., So that this cannot enform your understanding in any new unacquired grace or vertue.

2. Not obtained from without; innate.

1793 HOLCROFT tr. *Lavater's Physiog.* xxix. 136 Can we call this feeling, internal unacquired sensation? **1870** LOWELL *Among my Bks.* Ser. I. 164 We recognize his truth to Nature by an innate and unacquired sympathy.

†**unacquit,** *ppl. a. Obs.*[−1] [UN-[1] 7.] Unrequited.

1390 GOWER *Conf.* I. 271 For it was nevere knowe yit That charite goth unacquit.

unac'quitted, *ppl. a.* (UN-[1] 8.)

1770 HAILES *Anc. Sc. Poems* 327 *Unquyt*, unacquitted, unpaid.

†**unacquitting,** *vbl. sb.* [UN-[1] 13.] Failure in acquitting or clearing.

1648 W. BROWNE *Polexander* II. IV. ¶¶¶¶j, He.. besought his pardon for the long unacquitting himselfe of what he owed him.

†**unact,** *v. Obs. rare.* [UN-[2] 3.] *trans.* To reverse in act; to undo.

1594 W. PERCY *Cœlia* (1877) 5 My doome is past, nor can be now vnactit. **1628** FELTHAM *Resolves* II. lxxxix. 257 The Act remaines adultery still:.. nor can a Man vnact it againe.

un'actable, *a.* [UN-[1] 7 b.] That cannot be acted (on the stage); unsuitable for dramatic representation. Hence (in recent use) **unacta'bility.**

1810 BYRON *Let. to Hodgson* 3 Oct., Before the fire was out, he writes.. to inquire whether this farce was not converted into fuel, with about two thousand other unactable manuscripts. **1830** MISS MITFORD in L'Estrange *Life* (1870) II. xiii. 298 Goldoni is the most insipid writer I ever read; Alfieri is a very fine one but unactable. **1871** *Public Opinion* 16 Dec. 778 Mr. Browning has written brief unactable dramas.

un'acted, *a.* [UN-[1] 8.]

1. Not acted or carried out in action; unperformed.

1593 SHAKS. *Lucr.* 527 The fault vnknowne, is as a thought vnacted. **1613** SHERLEY *Trav. Persia* 52 To leaue no meanes vnacted which might both assure them more, and him selfe with them. *a* **1688** JORDAN *Muses Melody, To his disdainful Mistress* 17 Must I For some offence unacted, or unknown, Be tortur'd thus? **1706** [? PRIOR] *Ep. after Battle of Ramillies* 290 My sons lament, in distant dungeons thrown, Unacted crimes, and follies not their own. **1789** W. BLAKE *Marr. Heaven & Hell, Proverbs*, Sooner murder an infant in its cradle than nurse unacted desires. **1825** SCOTT *Talism.* xvii, I would buy with every jewel I have, that our fatal jest had remained unacted.

b. Const. *on, upon.*

1794 G. ADAMS *Nat. & Exp. Philos.* III. xxiv. 21 A mass of [units] lying together, unacted upon by a mechanical material agency. **1825** T. HOOK *Sayings* Ser. II. *Passion & Princ.* iv, I wish you to peruse it alone, and unacted upon by any extraneous influence. **1857** MILLER *Elem. Chem., Org.* 67 The second portion remains unacted on in the liquid.

2. Not acted upon; unformed. *rare*[−1].

1700 W. SHIPPEN in Rowe *Amb. Step-Moth.* III. ii, When Matter yet unacted lay.

3. Not performed on the stage. Also *absol.* as *sb.*, those whose plays are not acted.

In recent use.

un'acting, *ppl. a.* (UN-[1] 10.)

1736 HERVEY *Mem.* I. 82 The state of his mind.. seemed still to be an entire apathy, unacting and unmoved. **1745** *Phil. Trans.* XLIV. 156 It is the white unacting Globules that do thus.

†**un'action.** *Obs.*[−1] [UN-[1] 12, 5 b.] Inaction.

1698 tr. *Fénelon's Maxims of Saints* 98 'Tis better to remain in an absolute Unaction.

†**un'active,** *a. Obs.* [UN-[1] 7 and 5 b.]

1. Habitually or naturally inactive; indisposed or unable to act; hence, sluggish, slothful: **a.** Of persons (or animals).

1591 G. FLETCHER *Russe Commw.* (Hakl. Soc.) 146 For the most part, they are unwieldy and unactive withall. **1657** AUSTEN *Fruit Trees* II. 177 It is an intolerable shame to some professors especially, to see them so lukewarme and unactive in the waies of God. **1696** STANHOPE *Chr. Pattern* (1711) 126 When advancement to Heaven.. is offered, they are slothful and unactive. **1726** GIBSON *Dieting Horses* 14 Flanders Horses.. are thereby render'd the more heavy and unactive. **1741** *Compl. Fam.-Piece* II. ii. 346 Chub.. are a strong unactive Fish.

absol. **1708** *Diss. Drunkenness* 12 It charms the Unactive, the Desperate and Crafty of either Sex.

b. Of material things.

1638 QUARLES *Hieroglyph.* ii. (1669) 27 Nor hath unactive matter pow'r to soil Her pure and active form, as Jars corrupt their Oyl. **1694** SALMON *Bate's Dispens.* (1713) 528/2 The Points of the Acid of the Tartar.. are too unactive, gross or blunt to insinuate themselves into the Pores of this Salt. **1704** NORRIS *Ideal World* II. iii. 253 What a dead unactive thing matter is. **1729** BUTLER *Serm. Hum. Nat.* i. Wks. 1874 II. 387 The mere material body.., without the mind being a dead unactive thing.

c. Of mind or disposition.

1647 CLARENDON *Hist. Reb.* v. §340 The drowsy and unactive Genius of the Kingdom. *Ibid.* VI. §182 The faculties and understandings of the lay councillors [grew] more dull, lazy, and unactive. **1704** J. TRAPP *Abra-Mulé* II. i. 544 Melancholy Blood retards the Springs Of his unactive Soul. **1724** R. FIDDES *Morality* Pref. p. xxxviii, Disquisitions of this kind are an argument of an unactive wit. **1746** *Brit. Mag.* 98 The Ignorance, or unactive inexperimenting Spirit of our Manufacturers.

d. Of immaterial things.

1649 JER. TAYLOR *Gt. Exemp.* Ep. Ded. 1 The calentures of men breathe out in problemes and unactive discourses. **1686** W. DE BRITAINE *Hum. Prudence* xvi. 74 He.. may escape many dangers by his wary Conduct, but will fail of as many Successes by his unactive Fearfulness. *c* **1705** BP. BERKELEY in Fraser *Life* (1871) 445 Uneasiness, &c. are ideas, therefore unactive, therefore can do nothing. **1761** HUME *Hist. Eng.* III. xlviii. 45 His unactive virtue, the more it was extolled, the greater disregard was it exposed to.

2. Not active at a particular time; remaining quiescent or idle.

1599 DANIEL *Musoph.* (1602) c iij b, That these more curious times, they might diuorce From the opinion.. Of our disable and vnactiue force. **1643** WITHER *Campo Musæ* 2 When I shall be dead, And lie unactive in a loanly roome. **1670** COTTON *Espernon* I. III. 107 Neither was he in his retirement.. either unactive in himself, or in a Scene improper for his Majesties Service. **1715** POPE *Iliad* IV. 425 Can'st thou, remote, the mingling Hosts descry, With Hands unactive, and a careless Eye? **1756** JOHNSON *Misc. Lives, K. of Prussia* Wks. 1787 IV. 557 All the vegetative powers are kept unactive by a long continuance of drought. **1757** BURKE *Abridgm. Eng. Hist.* Wks. 1842 II. 516 The legates in Britain.. remained unactive till it could be determined for what master they were to conquer.

3. Marked or characterized by inaction.

1621 G. SANDYS *Ovid's Met.* II. (1626) 41 To Enuie's caue her course shee bent,.. Repleat with sadnesse, and vnactiue cold. **1652** EVELYN *St. France* Misc. Writ. (1805) 81 The Gentry.. are universally given to solitary and unactive lives in the country. **1711** ADDISON *Spect.* No. 93 ¶14 For the Employment of our dead unactive Hours. **1736** BUTLER *Anal.* v. 89 Nothing which we at present see, would lead us to the Thought of a solitary unactive State hereafter. **1777** JOHNSON *Let. to Mrs. Thrale* 27 Aug., I am here in unactive obscurity.

†**un'active,** *v. Obs.* [UN-[2] 6 a.] *trans.* To unfit for action.

1639 FULLER *Holy War* 52 Though bookishnesse may unactive, yet learning doth accomplish a Prince. **1655** —— *Ch. Hist.* VIII. ii. 19 A man so buried in the speculations of School-Divinity, that it unactiv'd him to be practical in persecution.

†**un'actively,** *adv. Obs.* [UN-[1] 11 and 5 b.] = INACTIVELY *adv.*

1611 SPEED *Hist. Gt. Brit.* VII. viii. 236 That his time was so peaceably and vnactiuely spent, that it ministred not matter whereof to indite. **1661** FELTHAM *Resolves* II. xlix. 281 He.. that is illiterate, and unactively lives hamletted in some untravail'd village. **1693** LOCKE *Educ.* §125 Mark how he spends his Time, whether he unactively loiters it away.

†**un'activeness.** *Obs.* [UN-[1] 12.] = next.

1647 JENKYN *Serm. bef. Peeres 27 Jan.* Pref. Cast off the spirit of sleep in respect of unactivenesse. **1683** TEMPLE *Mem.* Wks. 1720 I. 406 To make amends for the Unactiveness of this Campaign in Flanders, the Confederates by Concert on all sides fell upon an Enterprize of great *Eclat.*

†**unac'tivity.** *Obs.* [UN-[1] 12 and 5 b.] = INACTIVITY.

1654 FULLER *Two Serm.* 5 By their easinesse and unactivitie [they] betray themselves to that condition. *a* **1676** HALE *Prim. Orig. Man.* (1677) 98 To suppose them in an eternal rest and unactivity,.. were to suppose them eternally kept in a useless, needless, imperfect state. **1740** CHEYNE *Regimen* iv. 174 The human Soul.. now confin'd to Darkness, Silence, and Unactivity.

un'actual, *a.* (UN-[1] 7.)

1871 FRASER *Berkeley* x. 377 Our now unactual past or future sense experience.

un'actuated, *ppl. a.* (UN-[1] 8.)

1661 GLANVILL *Van. Dogm.* xvi. 153 The Peripatetick matter is a pure unactuated Power: and this conceited Vacuum a meer Receptibility. **1774** *Trinket* 50 The sprightly friend, unactuated by any softer passion. **1802** tr. *Ducray-Duminil's Victor* I. 171 What reliance was to be placed upon the faith of a banditti, unactuated by any sentiment of honour or delicacy? **1827** SCOTT *Let.* in *Lockhart* (1839) IX. 148 Unactuated by any feeling excepting the wish to do justice to all parties.

una'cute, *a.* (UN-[1] 7.)
1775 J. HARRIS *Philosoph. Arrangem.* (1841) 349 Acute sentiments often escape the comprehension of unacute hearers.

una'cuted, *ppl. a.* (UN-[1] 8.)
1804 MITFORD *Inquiry* 268 Though..Latin..can have a long penultimate following an acuted antepenultimate,..yet ..long vowels unacuted are numerous.

unadapta'bility. (UN-[1] 12 and 5 b.)
1829 BENTHAM *Justice & Cod. Petit.* Suppl. 11 So they be —either by unadaptability, or by their narrowness—.. obstructive of all..change.

una'daptable, *a.* (UN-[1] 7 b and 5 b.)
1882 A. GRAY in *Electic Mag.* XXXV. 738 Natural Selection continually took away the unadaptable, to give room and opportunity to the better-adapted. **1886** *Athenæum* 17 Apr. 530/2 'Tom Jones' is, in fact, unadaptable [as a play].

una'dapted, *ppl. a.* (UN-[1] 8.)
[**1775** ASH.] **1805** J. FOSTER *Ess.* II. ii. (1806) I. 148 They may form a strong character, in spite of the counteraction of an unadapted constitution. **1879** H. SPENCER *Data of Ethics* xiii. §84. 223 The material aids to happiness which each received would be more or less unadapted to his requirements.

una'daptedness. (UN-[1] 12.)
1846 WORCESTER (citing Foster). **1871** in Napheys *Prev. & Cure Dis.* II. iv. 557 The choicest articles of food are injurious to some persons by an obscure and inexplicable unadaptedness.

una'daptive, *a.* (UN-[1] 7 and 5 b.)
1841 MYERS *Cath. Th.* III. §27. 99 The words which Jesus ..spoke in answer to the instincts of the unadaptive Baptist.

un'added, *pa. pple.* (UN-[1] 8.)
1610 HEALEY *St. Aug. Citie of God* IX. xi. (1620) 332 Romulus..instituted the *Lemuralia* to be kept the third day of May, at such time as February was vnadded to the yeare.

una'ddicted, *ppl. a.* (UN-[1] 8.)
1583 GOLDING *Calvin on Deut.* xciv. 1203 It behoued them to forget both father and mother, and to be vnaddicted to their fleshly affections. *a* **1670** HACKET *Abp. Williams* I. (1692) 9 To be unaddicted to belly-pampering, sleep, and carnal wantonness. **1670** G. H. *Hist. Cardinals* II. I. 119 A Pope..unaddicted to the advancement of his private Family. **1844** KINGLAKE *Eothen* xvii, Marlen..is.. unaddicted to the practice of magical arts. **1859** SALA *Tw. round Clock* (1861) 317 The serious world is not at all unaddicted to good living.

†**una'dditionable**, *a. Obs.*—[1] [UN-[1] 7 b.] Not worth counting in or adding.
1716 M. DAVIES *Athen. Brit.* II. To Rdr. p. xiii, Some few Despicable Unadditionable Units or Unitarians.

†**una'dditioned**, *a. Obs.*—[1] [UN-[1] 8.] Not provided with a title.
a **1661** FULLER *Worthies, Hereford* II. (1662) 46 He was a Knight, howsoever it cometh to passe he is here unadditioned.

†**un'addle**, *a. Obs.*—[1] [UN-[1] 7.] Not addled.
1611 *Panegyr. Verses* in Coryat *Crudities* d vij, In Odcombe parish yet famous with his cradle, A chicke he hatcht was of an egge vnaddle.

una'ddressed, *ppl. a.* (UN-[1] 8. Cf. G. *unaddressirt.*)
[**1775** ASH.] **1885** *Athenæum* 5 Dec. 732/3 A letter from Mrs. Byron..perhaps to Mr. Becker is unaddressed, and not dated further than 'Thursday 13th'.

una'dept, *sb.* and *a.* [UN-[1] 12, 7, and 5 b.]
a. *sb.* One who is not an adept. **b.** *adj.* Not adept or proficient. Also *absol.*
1742 YOUNG *Nt. Th.* IX. 649 I'll point out to thee Its various lessons; some that may surprise An un-adept in mysteries of Night. **1817** KEATINGE *Trav.* I. 42 The un-adept in the valuable science of botany. **1818** MRS. SHELLEY *Frankenst.* ii, Thus for a time I was occupied by exploded systems, mingling, like an unadept, a thousand contradictory theories. **1830** BENTHAM *Offic. Apt. Maximized, Public Account Keeping* 10 To an unadept mind, what other idea than this is it in the nature of this appellation to suggest?

†**un'adequate**, *a. Obs.* [UN-[1] 5 b.] = INADEQUATE *a.*
1644 MILTON *Bucer on Div.* Wks. 1851 IV. 303 Be not bound about..by the scanty and unadequat and inconsistent Principles of such as condemn others for adhering to Traditions. **1651** BIGGS *New Disp.* ¶35 The preposterous ignorance of the Constitution of man in generall..hath..been a meanes to usher in that incongruous form of unadæquat remedies. **1709** HEARNE *Collect.* (O.H.S.) II. 234 Those who are unadequate Judges.

unad'herence. *rare*[−1]. [UN-[1] 12. Cf. next.] Non-adherence.
1728–31 *Lett. fr. Fog's Jrnl.* (1732) I. 17 In such a Government, Unadherence to the Rights and Privileges..of the Court, manifest a glorious Fortitude of Mind.

unad'herent, *a.* (UN-[1] 7 and 5 b.)
1836–9 *Todd's Cycl. Anat.* II. 598/1 The inner surface [of the pericardium], like that of all the other serous membranes, is unadherent, smooth, and shining.

unad'hesive, *a.* (UN-[1] 7 and 5 b.)
1815 KIRBY & SP. *Entomol.* xiii. (1816) I. 419 The unadhesive radii and exterior threads remain unsoiled. **1840** MARRYAT *Olla Podr.* III. 246 Her imperishable beauty and unadhesive cleanliness of person.

un'adjectived, *ppl. a.* (UN-[1] 9.)
1805 TOOKE *Purley* II. vii. II. 469 As the Noun Adjective always signifies all that the unadjectived Noun signifies,..so must the Verb Adjective signify all that the unadjectived Verb signifies, and no more. **1815** RICHARDSON *Eng. Philol.* 28 We have also borrowed..adjectived signs from other languages, without always borrowing the unadjectived signs of the same ideas.

una'djourned, *ppl. a.* (UN-[1] 8.)
1648 HEXHAM II, *Ongedaeght*, Vncited, or Vn-adjourned. **1865** DICKENS *Mut. Fr.* IV. xi, Mrs. Sprodgkin was left still unadjourned in the hall.

una'djust, *v.* (UN-[2] 3.)
1785 *Phil. Trans.* LXXV. 475 *note*, I have myself repeatedly adjusted the wires eight or ten times running, allowing another person to read off and unadjust each time.

una'djusted, *ppl. a.* (UN-[1] 8.)
1775 JOHNSON *Tax. no Tyr.* 17 In countries where life was yet unadjusted and policy unformed. **1812** *Ann. Reg., Gen. Hist.* 2 Important differences between this country and the United States of America remained unadjusted. **1899** *Allbutt's Syst. Med.* VIII. 274 That his conduct is unadjusted to his circumstances is manifest.

unad'ministered, *ppl. a.* [UN-[1] 8.] Not administered (esp. in law).
1590 SWINBURNE *Testaments* 171 He maie commit the administration of the goods of the deceased vnadministred by thee. **1684** *Secr. Serv. Money Chas. & Jas.* (Camden) 97 Of the goods and chattels of John Eaton unadministred. *a* **1814** *Forgery* II. v. in *New Brit. Theatre* I. 455 Inquiry would perhaps but probe the wound, Leaving the cure still unadminister'd. **1884** *Law Times Rep.* 12 Apr. 205/2 The latter died on the 12th Dec. 1879, leaving the estate of the testatrix partly unadministered.

un'admirable, *a.* (UN-[1] 7 b.)
1853 RUSKIN *Stones Ven.* III. ii. §3. 34 That the antagonistic Renaissance is, in the main, unworthy and unadmirable,..it was my principal purpose to show. **1866** CARLYLE *Remin.* I. 218 Very sumptuous, very cockneyish, strange and unadmirable to me.

unad'mired, *ppl. a.* (UN-[1] 8.)
1707 MRS. BEHN in *Muses Mercury* Oct. 237 Then all your Glories unadmir'd will lie. **1781** V. KNOX *Lib. Educ.* xxi. 186 The story was entertaining, but the diction and the sentiment passed unadmired. **1827** POLLOK *Course T.* IX. 480 Nor 'mong the fairest unadmired..Distinguished stood the bard. **1865** TREVELYAN *Cawnpore* 6 The furniture..is scattered about in most unadmired disorder.

unad'miring, *ppl. a.* (UN-[1] 10 and 5 d.)
1858 CARLYLE *Fredk. Gt.* II. xii. (1872) I. 119 Unadmiring posterity has confirmed the nickname. **1881** *Times* 20 Aug. 9/2 Before an impatient and unadmiring audience.
b. Used with ppl. construction.
1876 MISS BROUGHTON *Joan* xxi, Joan looks away again, utterly unadmiring herself.
Hence **unad'miringly** *adv.*
1862 'SHIRLEY' *Nugæ Crit.* iii. 150 One, whose massive brow and chiselled eyelids you..have noted not unadmiringly.

unad'mitted, *ppl. a.* [UN-[1] 8.]
1. Not allowed to enter.
1616 in *Harl. Misc.* (Malh.) III. 327 It was not lawful for a Christian to enter unadmitted. **1801** SOUTHEY *Thalaba* IX. xxvi, On the sympathizing wax, The unadmitted flames play powerlessly.
2. Unacknowledged, unconfessed.
1895 *Thinker* VIII. 440 Science has almost out-dogmatized the dogmatists, by teaching a practical though unadmitted atheism.

unad'monished, *ppl. a.* (UN-[1] 8.)
a **1591** H. SMITH *Serm. Punishm. Jonah* i. Wks. 1867 II. 224 Let us take heed that a wicked one be not found amongst us unadmonished. **1645** MILTON *Tetrach.* Introd., Wks. 1851 IV. 136 Who..hath not forborn to scandalize him, unconferr'd with, unadmonisht, undealt with by any Pastorly or brotherly convincement. **1667** —— *P.L.* v. 245. **1751** WARBURTON in *Pope's Works* IV. 138 *note*, He would not bear to see a friend..live in the miserable abuse of one of Nature's best gifts unadmonished of his folly. **1781** COWPER in *Priv. Corresp.* (1824) I. 106, I am sure you would not suffer me unadmonished to add myself to the multitude of insipid rhimers. **1862** T. A. TROLLOPE *Marietta* i, The pony, unadmonished save by a word, started off at a brisk trot.

una'doptable, *a.* (UN-[1] 7 b.)
1843 CARLYLE *Past & P.* II. xvii, The good [prayers] were found adoptable by men;..the bad, found inappropriate, unadoptable, were gradually forgotten.

una'dopted, *ppl. a.* (UN-[1] 8.)
1659 MILTON *Civ. Power* Wks. 1851 V. 328 Hence it planely appeers, that if we be not free we are not sons, but still servants unadopted. **1765** LANGHORNE *Observ. Collins' Ode to Evening*, Blank verse.., though it has been generally received in the latter [kind of poetry], it is yet unadopted in the former. **1902** *Westm. Gaz.* 27 Oct. 4/2 Put aside, too, and unadopted by the Jewish writers are the statements of the extreme critical..school. **1938** [see ADOPTED *ppl. a.* 1 b]. **1963** *Times* 18 May 10/7 It is virtually undistinguished except for the number of roughly surfaced streets compelling a glance at signs proclaiming that they are unadopted. **1970** J. BURKE *Four Stars for Danger* ii. 21 That road up to Bryncroeso Hall is unadopted. If the people at the Hall don't want to do anything about it, nobody's going to make them.

una'dored, *ppl. a.* (UN-[1] 8.)
1621 G. SANDYS *Ovid's Met.* VIII. (1626) 157 Nor vnreueng'd, said she, Though vn-adored, shalt they vant we be. **1667** MILTON *P.L.* I. 738 Nor was his name unheard or unador'd In ancient Greece. **1742** YOUNG *Nt. Th.* IV. 383 By Thee, Oh most adorable! most unador'd! **1816** WORDSW. *Ode General Thanksgiving* 32 Thou..for thy bounty wert not unadored.

una'doring, *ppl. a.* (UN-[1] 10.)
1748 RICHARDSON *Clarissa* (1811) IV. 137 The complaisant gallant is so often preferred to the cold, the unadoring husband. **1845** MOZLEY *Ess.* (1878) II. 119 In proportion to the extent to which such a view obtains, worship must become necessarily unimpassionate and unadoring.

una'dorned, *ppl. a.* (UN-[1] 8.)
1634 MILTON *Comus* 23 All the Sea-girt Iles That like to rich and various gemms inlay The unadorned bosom of the Deep. **1667** —— *P.L.* IV. 305 Shee as a vail down to the slender waste Her unadorned golden tresses wore. **1730** THOMSON *Autumn* 213 For loveliness Needs not the foreign aid of ornament, But is when unadorn'd adorn'd the most. **1777** SHERIDAN *Sch. Scand., Portrait* 231 She, adorning fashion, unadorned by dress. **1813** BYRON *Br. Abydos* II. ix, That dagger..No longer glitter'd at his waist, Where pistols unadorn'd were braced. **1865** W. G. PALGRAVE *Arabia* I. 80 It is a very simple and unadorned construction. **1871** DARWIN *Desc. Man* II. xiii. (1890) 391 Eight or nine specimens..retained their unadorned winter plumage.. throughout the year.
b. In transf. or fig. applications.
1647 CLARENDON *Hist. Reb.* I. §142 A man..unadorned with parts of vigour and quickness. **1692** ATTERBURY *Serm., Ps. l. 14* (1726) I. 31 Majestick Plainness and Simplicity of Thought..Unadorn'd by Words, Unenliven'd by Figures. **1744** AKENSIDE *Pleas. Imag.* I. 550 Where Virtue..doth forsake The unadorned condition of her birth. **1796** MME. D'ARBLAY *Camilla* VII. viii, The artlessness of unadorned truth. **1837** HALLAM *Hist. Lit.* I. iv. §22 The speeches in this tragedy are sometimes too long, the style unadorned.
Hence **una'dornedly** *adv.*, **una'dornedness.**
1727 BAILEY (vol. II), *Plainness*,..Unadornedness. **1820** *Monthly Rev.* XCI. 278 The merit of having recorded faithfully, and unadornedly, the observations made by him. **1847** H. MILLER *First Impr. Eng.* vii. (1857) 105 It was placed there, in its naked unadornedness.

una'droit, *a.* (UN-[1] 7.)
1841 S. WARREN *Ten Thousand a Year* iii. I. 101 Various faint but unadroit hints and feelers of his had been thrown away.

una'droitly, *adv.* (UN-[1] 11.)
1839 THACKERAY *Major Gahagan* iv, The..scimitar, fiercely but unadroitly drawn.

una'dulterate, *ppl. a.* [UN-[1] 8 b and 5 b.] Not adulterated or corrupted. Also *absol.*
1664 H. MORE *Myst. Iniq.* 206 It cannot be judged pure and unadulterate Christianity. **1697** TUTCHIN *Search Honesty* iii, The Unadulterate Priesthood never knew The Glory, Strength, nor Lewdness of the New. **1716** GAY *Journ. to Exeter* 99 On unadulterate wine we here regale. **1798** CHARLOTTE SMITH *Yng. Philos.* IV. 71 You would have ..a beautiful piece of unadulterate clay, which you might mould as you would. **1841** I. TAYLOR *Spir. Chr.* 79 This doctrine when unadulterate..animates orthodoxy. **1879** MEREDITH *Egoist* xxxvii, The unadulterate is to be had only by faith in it or by waiting for it.
So **una'dulterately** *adv.*
1638 W. GILBERTE in *Ussher's Lett.* (1686) 494 By Inductions, fresh and unadulteratly drawn from those Observations [of the Heavens].

una'dulterated, *ppl. a.* (UN-[1] 8.)
a **1719** ADDISON *Evid. Chr. Relig.* v. (1733) 41, I have only discovered one of those channels by which the history of our Saviour might be conveyed pure and unadulterated, through those several ages. **1765** BLACKSTONE *Comm.* I. 64 That these customs..continued down..to the present time, unchanged and unadulterated. **1823** J. BADCOCK *Dom. Amusem.* 30 Flour which is pure and unadulterated. **1881** WESTCOTT & HORT *Grk. N.T.* Introd. §38 An unadulterated transcript of the original text.
Hence **una'dulteratedly** *adv.*
1891 KIPLING *City Dreadf. Nt., Railway Folk* i, Jamalpur is unadulteratedly 'Railway'.

una'dulterously, *adv.* (UN-[1] 11.)
1643 MILTON *Divorce* 10 Many beasts in voluntary and chosen couples live together as unadulterously, and are as truly maried in that respect.

unad'vanced, *ppl. a.* Also 4–5 -avanced, 5 -avaunced. [UN-[1] 8.] Not advanced or promoted; not pushed forward.
1390 GOWER *Conf.* II. 205 If it is along on me Of that ye unavanced be,..The sothe schal be proved nou. **1411–2** HOCCLEVE *De Reg. Princ.* 5274 So manny a worthi clerk famouse, In Oxinford, and in Cambrigge also, Stonde vnavanced. **1491** *Act 7 Hen. VII*, c. 12 *Preamble*, His Highnes..entendith to provyde..his children unavaunced to be preferred. **1603** KNOLLES *Hist. Turks* (1621) 832 In the meane time..matters stood stil altogether vnaduanced. **1741** T. ROBINSON *Gavelkind* App. Qq iv b, The youngest Son..was the Child, if any, left unadvanced at the Death of his Father. **1856** OLMSTED *Slave States* 367 Young men.. unadvanced beyond the lowest knowledge of the elements of primary school learning. **1892** *Pall Mall G.* 26 Sept. 3/3 Both advanced and unadvanced members of unincorporated societies.

unad'vancing, *ppl. a.* (UN-[1] 10.)
1819 *Metropolis* III. 209 Her habit, her unadvancing air of modest timidity,..all conspired to render her irresistible. **1850** L. HUNT *Autobiog.* III. xxv. 267 Let the imagination of him who thinks otherwise sit for ever with his unadvancing legs in the ditches of his ancestors.

†**unad'vantageable,** *a. Obs.*$^{-1}$ [UN-[1] 7 b.] Not advantageous or profitable.

1603 CHETTLE *Engl. Mourn.-Garm.* B 4 b, So potent, that the Deputie had many dangerous and vnadvantageable skirmishes against him.

unad'vantaged, *ppl. a.* (UN-[1] 8.)

a **1661** FULLER *Worthies, Stafford.* (1840) 145, I have not met with a more noble family, measuring on the level of flat and unadvantaged antiquity. **1755** AMORY *Mem.* (1769) I. 149 Divine faith shines forth in breasts unadvantaged with human requirements.

unad'ventured, *ppl. a.* (UN-[1] 8.)

1548 HALL *Chron.* 261 For whose defence,.. if necessitie require, my persone shall not be vnaduentured.

unad'venturing, *ppl. a.* (UN-[1] 10.)

1824 GODWIN *Hist. Commw.* I. 4 Men of a more cautious and unadventuring character.

unad'venturous, *a.* [UN-[1] 7 and 5 b.]

Hence, in recent use, ***unadventurously, -ness.***

1671 MILTON *P.R.* III. 243 The wisest, unexperienc't, will be ever.. Irresolute, unhardy, unadventrous. **1861** CRAIK *Hist. Eng. Lit.* I. 35 His attempts are of the slightest character, and unadventurous as they are, nobody can undertake to say.. whether they are well or ill done. **1890** 'R. BOLDREWOOD' *Col. Reformer* (1891) 312 The shorthorns and unadventurous beeves of more.. succulent pastures.

†**unad'vertance.** *Obs.*$^{-1}$ [ad. OF. *inadvertance.*] Inadvertence.

1483 CAXTON *Cato* F vj, To the ende that thou be not ouertaken by unaduertaunce or unwyttyngly.

†**unad'vertedly,** *adv. Obs.*$^{-1}$ [UN-[1] 11.] Without being noticed.

1660 tr. *Amyraldus' Treat. conc. Relig.* III. iii. 343 As Sugar blended with his poisonous doctrines to make them be swallow'd more pleasingly and unadvertedly.

†**unad'vertency.** *Obs.* [UN-[1] 12 and 5 b.] = INADVERTENCY.

1653 R. BAILLIE *Dissuas. Vind.* (1655) 62 In this unadvertency M. Marshall.. has the good luck to be set at my side. **1656** EARL MONM. tr. *Boccalini's Advts. fr. Parnass.* 385 It was neither unadvertency, nor bestiality which made me do that to my Master Apuleius.

un'advertised, *ppl. a.* [UN-[1] 8 and 8 c.]

†**1.** Not advertised or warned; uninformed (*of* something). *Obs.*

1450 *Paston Lett.* I. 176 My Lord York, unadvertised of the trouth, sent a lettre to my Lord Oxford. **1535** STEWART *Cron. Scot.* (Rolls) III. 362 All this.. wes done In that intent to turne agane richt sone, Quhen that his fais sould wnaduerteist be. *a* **1548** HALL *Chron., Hen. VI,* 174 The kyng was not ignorant of this assemble, nor yet vnaduertised of the dukes intent. **1627** *Lisander & Cal.* VIII. 157 Thus Lisander, unadvertized, could not come to the court within the time hee was expected. **1652** LOVEDAY tr. *Calprenede's Cassandra* III. 212 That it was impossible for Roxina to be long unadvertis'd of his love.

2. Not announced or made known.

1864 *Daily Telegraph* 6 Aug., Strange storms, unadvertised by Admiral Fitzroy,.. go eddying round us. **1874** A. WHITNEY *We Girls* xi. 229 The little unadvertised resources of New York.

un'advertising, *ppl. a.* (UN-[1] 10.)

1548 *Reg. Cupar Abbey* II. 55 Give ony of thame.. permittis ony vtheris to.. tak away ony of the samyn [wood] vnaduertissand or stoppand at thair powar. **1834** *Tait's Mag.* 735/2 Lazarus with the dogs (the unadvertising dogs) licking his sores!

unad'visable, *a.* [UN-[1] 7 b and 5 b.]

1. Of persons: That cannot or will not be advised; not open to advice.

1673 O. WALKER *Educ.* 77 Of angry persons some are.. sullen, intractable, unadvisable (a disposition mixed up of pride and melancholy). **1692** WOOD *Life* (O.H.S.) IV. 27, I hope his lordship will admit me to his favour, and not think I am unadviseable. **1762** WESLEY *Jrnl.* 3 July, There were none of them headstrong or unadvisable, none that were wiser than their teachers. **1802** H. MARTIN *Helen of Glenross* III. 216 Till now I have ever considered you, though too unadvisable, to be a man possessed of a considerable share of talents and understanding. **1865** CARLYLE *Fredk. Gt.* XIX. viii. (1873) VIII. 265, I am Astolpho warning Roger.. not to trust himself to the Enchantress Alcina; but Roger was unadvisable.

2. Of things: Inexpedient, imprudent.

1758 LOWTH *Life Wm. of Wykeham* v. 155 Extreme rigour would have been unadviseable in the beginning of a new reign. **1837** CARLYLE *Fr. Rev.* I. v. i, Nay were resistance unadvisable, even dangerous, yet surely pause is very natural. **1897** *Allbutt's Syst. Med.* IV. 619 Alcohol in the form of diluted brandy or whisky is unadvisable.

Hence **unad'visably** *adv.*

1702 *Lond. Gaz.* No. 3822/2 A Soldier.. firing unadvisably upon a Centinel. **1877** RUSKIN *Fors Clav.* lxxxi. 257 It was unadvisably allowed by me to remain in small print.

unad'visableness. [f. prec. + -NESS.] The quality of being unadvisable: **a.** Of persons.

1771 WESLEY *Wks.* (1872) V. 476 As he grows in pride, so he must grow in unadvisableness and in stubbornness also.

b. Of things.

In recent use (1891–) also ***unadvisability*** (for earlier *inadvisability*).

1833 GEN. P. THOMPSON *Exerc.* II. 374 In proof of the unadviseableness of permitting the extension of manufacturing industry. **1841** CRAIK in *Pict. Hist. Eng.* IX. vii. IV. 853/1 The impossibility or unadvisableness of carrying it [the Licensing Act] rigorously into execution. **1877** M. ARNOLD *Last Ess. on Church* 217 The unadvisableness of using the occasion of burial for passing sentence of condemnation.. against the particular person dead.

unad'vised, *a.* and *adv.* Forms: α. 4 **onauysed,** 5 **-yd, onavised;** 4–5 **unauysed** (4, 6 **-id**), 5–7 **unauised** (5 **-yd**); 4–5 **unavised** (5 **-ede, -id**), 4–6 **unavysed** (4 **-id,** 5 **-et**). β. 5–6 **unaduysed,** 6–7 **unaduised** (6 *Sc.* **-it**), **-uized,** 6– **unadvised.** [UN-[1] 8. Cf. MDu. *ongeavijst.*]

1. Of acts, words, etc.: Done or spoken without due consideration; rash, inconsiderate.

α. **13..** *E.E. Allit. P.* A. 292 Þre wordez has þou spoken at ene, Vn-avysed, for soþe, wern alle þre. *c* **1380** WYCLIF *Wks.* (1880) 389 So herode schuld have broke his oþe,.. and sore a-repentid hym for his vnavysid swerynge. *a* **1450** *Knt. de la Tour* (1868) 126 Ofte tymes by vnauised speche of right is made the wronge. **1537** CROMWELL in Merriman *Life & Lett.* (1902) II. 86 They haue him in the lesse estimatyon for his vayn tytle and vnauised procedinges to the same.

β. **1526** *Pilgr. Perf.* (W. de W. 1531) 158 For.. suche cogitacions vnaduysed, eyther be lytell synne or none. **1579** NORTHBROOKE *Dicing* (1843) 168 By dauncing commeth filthie talke and communications, vnaduised promises. **1612** WOODALL *Surg. Mate* Wks. (1653) 334 Fearfull dangers ensue often by unadvised bleeding.. in contagious times. **1677** W. HUBBARD *Narrative* 83 Provoked by the rash, unadvised, cruel act of some of the English. **1753** RICHARDSON *Grandison* (1781) III. xxix. 338 Lady Sforza.. hinted, that the last interview between the young lady and me was an unadvised permission. **1769** BLACKSTONE *Comm.* IV. 123 Contempts against the king's title.. are the denial of his right to the crown in common and unadvised discourse. **1833** I. TAYLOR *Fanat.* Pref. p. iv, An unskilful or unadvised treatment. **1876** BANCROFT *Hist. U.S.* I. vi. 155 Complaining.. of his unadvised and dangerous dealings with the Indians.

2. Of persons: Imprudent, indiscreet, thoughtless. Also *transf.* of things.

α. **1382** WYCLIF *Prov.* xiii. 3 Who forsothe is vnauysid to speken, shal felen euelis. **1390** GOWER *Conf.* II. 43 Thou miht so per cas Ben ydel, as somtime was A kinges dowhter unavised. **1412–20** LYDG. *Chron. Troy* IV. 4617 Hem list no þing to be so rekkeles, Nor vn-avysed what hem ouȝt to do. *a* **1475** G. ASHBY *Dicta Philos.* 385 Unauised men, foles bene repute. **1530** PALSGR. 328/1 Unavysed, *maladuisé.*

β. **1535** COVERDALE *Prov.* xxi. 5 He y[t] is vnaduysed, commeth vnto pouerte. **1566** PAINTER *Pal. Pleas.* II. 175 Here they may see the damage and hurt that unadvised youth incurreth. **1640** BP. HALL *Episc.* III. 223 Some bold unwarranted suggestion from an unadvised adversary. **1656** EARL MONM. tr. *Boccalini's Advts. fr. Parnass.* I. i. (1674) 3 Flies.. which some unadvised men endeavouring to chase away.. with a Dagger, have.. cut their own Noses. **1726** LEONI *Alberti's Archit.* II. 99 Faults which the negligent and unadvised easily fall into. **1819** LAMB *St. Crispin to Mr. Gifford* 1 All unadvised, and in an evil hour,.. you daft The lowly labours of the Gentle Craft. **1831** SCOTT *Ct. Rob.* xv, The thoughtless insult which the Count had been unadvised enough to put upon the Emperor the preceding day.

transf. **1600** S. NICHOLSON *Acolastus* (1876) 10 O vnaduised, Treason-working eyes, You are the cause my ife in passion dyes. **1621** QUARLES *Argalus & P.* I. Wks. (Grosart) III. 250/2 Her unadvised sickle shall not thrust Into her hopefull Harvest, ere needs must.

b. Similarly of conduct, disposition, etc.

1390 GOWER *Conf.* III. 274 Ther is yit more forto sein Of love which is unavised. *c* **1412** HOCCLEVE *De Reg. Princ.* 3104 A Prince mot.. his angir refreyne, & ire, Lest þat vnavisid commocioun.. sette his hert on fire. **1440** J. SHIRLEY *Dethe K. James* (1818) 25 O ye.. mercilesse Scottisshe folke,.. full replet of unavisid folie. **1553** *Act 1 Mary* Sess. II. c. I. §2 Taking his foundation partly vpon his owne vnaduised judgment of the Scripture. **1590** SPENSER *F.Q.* I. iv. 34 His ruffin raiment.. Which he had spilt.. Through vnaduized rashnesse woxen wood. **1610** HOLLAND *Camden's Brit.* (1637) 454 Preserving.. the Realme from that confusion which it after fell into by King John's unadvised carriage. **1638** QUARLES *Hieroglyph.* I. iii. 6 His knowledge climbs.. and sometimes slips Through unadvised hast. **1726** LEONI *Alberti's Archit.* I. 21 b, Nero's unadvised fondness for building.

†**c.** Quasi-*adv.* Without consideration or reflection; unwarily, heedlessly. *Obs.*

α. **1420–2** LYDG. *Thebes* III. 4651 Wherfor ech man be war Vnavysed a werre to bygynne. *c* **1440** *Gesta Rom.* lxv. 289 (Add. MS.), He, as he rode vnavised, fille into one, and myght not come out, for the pitte was depe. **1483** *Vulgaria abs Terentio* 6 b, It forseth nott whedyr a woman do all thynges auysed or vnauysed.

β. **1535** COVERDALE *Prov.* xiii. 3 Who so speaketh vnaduysed, fyndeth harme. **1606** G. WOODCOCK *Lives Emperors* in *Hist. Ivstine* K k 5 The matter being vnaduised done, hee lost many of his men. **1627** MAY *Lucan* I. 543 The madd people all With hasty steppes so vnaduised runne, As if no way at all were left to shunne Their imminent, and feard distruction.

d. Not having consulted *with* another; not having been consulted *with.*

1579 FENTON *Guicciard.* (1618) 4 So Ludouyke Sforce,.. unadvised with others, had given counsell that the Embassadors.. should all enter Rome in one day. **1649** MILTON *Eikon* xii. Wks. 1851 III. 431 What should move the King.. to hold such frequent and close meetings with a Committy of Irish Papists.. while the Parlament of England sate unadvis'd with. **1836** BROWNING & FOSTER *Life Strafford* (1892) 160 The Catholics.. unadvised with each other, and utterly unprepared.

3. Not advised or warned. *rare*$^{-1}$.

c **1374** CHAUCER *Troylus* I. 378 Thus argumented he yn his gynnynge, Ful vnauysed of his wo comynge.

†**4.** Not announced or foreshadowed. *Obs.*

c **1386** CHAUCER *Pars. T.* ¶449 Whan they sourden by freletee vnauysed and sodeynly withdrawen ayeyn. *a* **1395** HYLTON *Scala Perf.* II. xliii. (1507) Z viij b, The ghostly presence of Ihesu.. bryngeth to his mynde.. the wordes.. of holy wrytte vnsoughte and vnauysed one after a nother.

†**b.** As *adv.* Without warning; unexpectedly.

1390 GOWER *Conf.* I. 133 The Camelion, Which.. moste newe His colour, and thus unavised Fulofte time he stant desguised. *c* **1450** tr. *De Imitatione* I. xxiii. 31 Many men dien sodenly & unavised. **1483** CAXTON *Gold Leg.* 377/2 To thende that sodaynly he shold falle up on this kyng unaduysed.

5. Not supplied with advice.

1851 TENNYSON *Q. Mary* II. ii, We.. set no foot theretoward unadvised Of all our Privy Council. **1864** in Ld. Fitzmaurice *Life Granville* (1905) I. 469 How fearful it is to be suspected—uncheered—unguided and unadvised! **1876** J. C. BROWN *Reboisement in France* IV. v. §10. 294 From the forbidding nature of the precipice, few would be bold enough to make the essay unadvised.

unad'visedly, *adv.* Forms: as prec. + -lie, -ly(e (also 4 **unauyssedly,** 6 *Sc.* **onavisitly**). [f. prec. + -LY[2].]

1. Without consideration or reflection; imprudently, injudiciously; thoughtlessly, rashly, inadvisedly.

α. *c* **1340** HAMPOLE *Prose Tr.* 11 Þat þay say to þam na wordes of myssawe.. ne of displesance vnauyssedly. *a* **1513** FABYAN *Chron.* VII. (1811) 666 Robert Byfelde, one of the shyreffs, vnauysidly knelyd downe nygh vnto the sayd mayer, wherof the mayer after reasonyd hym and layd it to his charge. **1513** DOUGLAS *Æneid* X. vii. 151 Quhill Alesus onavisitly Cled with hys scheyld Imaonus, hym by,.. Hys breist stud nakyt.

β. **1474** CAXTON *Chesse* III. iv. G 4 b, It cometh of nature often tymes to women to geue counceyl shortly and unaduysedly to thynges that ben in doubte or perilous. **1581** MULCASTER *Positions* xxxvi. (1887) 138 By appointment, either vnaduisedly made, or aduisedly marred. **1620** VENNER *Via Recta* viii. 189 If it be immoderately, vntimely, and vnaduisedly vsed, it is no lesse hurtfull then Intemperance. **1657** TRAPP *Comm. Job* xlii. 4 He would speak no more so rashly, and unadvisedly as he had done, to God's dishonour. **1709** *Tatler* No. 147 ¶8, I shall decide nothing unadvisedly in Matters of this Nature. **1765** BLACKSTONE *Comm.* I. 187 Charles the first.. having unadvisedly passed an act to continue the parliament then in being. **1808** SCOTT *Let. to Gifford* Oct. in *Lockhart,* If a weak brother will unadvisedly put forth his hand to support even the ark of the constitution, I would expose his arguments. **1866** GEO. ELIOT *F. Holt* v, There are ranks and degrees —and those who can serve in the higher must not unadvisedly change what seems to be a providential appointment.

†**2.** Without warning; unexpectedly. *Obs.*

c **1535** in Strype *Eccl. Mem.* (1721) I. App. xlv. 125 Antichrist shal sodenly and unadvisedly come, and.. destroy al mankind through his error. **1577** HANMER *Anc. Eccl. Hist.* (1663) 175 Petrus, who.. suddenly and unadvisedly by the commandment of Maximinus was beheaded. **1699** N. MARSH in *Lett. Lit. Men* (Camden) 296 The pretended Mathematician has quite mistaken his measures, and, soaring too high, hath unadvisedly dropt into the pit.

unad'visedness. [f. as prec. + -NESS.] The quality of being unadvised; want of consideration or reflection; imprudence, rashness; an instance of this.

c **1449** PECOCK *Repr.* 357 It is to be bileeued that Girald was bigilid (as manie othere writers bi liȝtnes and unavisidnes han be). **1542** UDALL *Erasm. Apoph.* 256 b, There was nothyng more unconvenable for a perfecte good Capitaine, then over muche hastyng & unavisednesse. **1583** GOLDING *Calvin on Deut.* cxlii. 875 How many faults do we commit through vnaduisednesse, when we thinke not on them? **1611** SPEED *Hist. Gt. Brit.* IX. xxiv. (1632) 1229 By his owne vnaduisednesse.. hee clouded his honour. **1681** KETTLEWELL *Chr. Obedience* (1715) 564 All his unwill'd ignorances, and innocent unadvisednesses, upon his prayers for pardon shall be abated. **1780** BENTHAM *Princ. Legisl.* IX. §16 In the case of *un*-advisedness with respect to any of the circumstances. *Ibid.* §17 Un-advisedness coupled with heedlessness, and mis-advisedness coupled with rashness. **1853** JAS. HAMILTON *Life Bp. J. Hall* 167 The circumstance which implicated him was, at the worst, an act of unadvisedness.

†**unad'visely,** *adv. Obs.* Also 4 **vnauisely,** 4–5 **-auysely,** 5 **-awyssely.** [f. UN-[1] 11 + *avisé* ADVISY *a.* + -LY[2]. Cf. UNAVISY *a.*] = UNADVISEDLY *adv.*

c **1380** WYCLIF *Wks.* (1880) 383 Þis symony & heresi so vnauysely brouȝte in-to þe chirche. **1422** tr. *Secreta Secret., Priv. Priv.* 138 If hit happe a kynge to do any thynge vnawyssely. *a* **1455** *Lett. Marg. Anjou & Bp. Beckington* (Camden) 99 Summe of your officers.. unadvisely toke fro day to day the horses of our said tenants.

†**unad'visement.** *Obs. rare.* In 6 **vnaduyse-,** *Sc.* **vnadwysment.** [UN-[1] 12.] Want of consideration or judgement.

1526 *Pilgr. Perf.* (W. de W. 1531) 90 b, Inconstancy or vnstablenes, heddynes or vnaduysement, inordinate loue that man or woman hath to them selfe. *a* **1600** MONTGOMERIE *Devot. Poems* v. 2 Since vnadwysment wraks or thou be war, To call for grace betyms at God begin.

†**unad'vising,** *ppl. a. Obs.*$^{-1}$ [UN-[1] 10.] Imprudent.

1721 SOUTHERNE *Spartan Dame* II. i, The repented rashness of my youth, Whose unadvising folly gave me to Your sister's bed, now surfeited, and loath'd.

un'aerated, *ppl. a.* (UN-[1] 8.)

1796 KIRWAN *Elem. Min.* (ed. 2) I. 170 Here [it] is remarkable.. that magnesia and calx should be unaerated. **1835–6** *Todd's Cycl. Anat.* I. 143/2 In this instance.. the aerated and unaerated blood require to be.. prevented from commingling. **1887** MOLONEY *Forestry W. Afr.* 152 The cloth is dipped into the extract unaerated, then freely exposed to the air.

unæs'thetic, *a.* (UN-1 7. Cf. INÆSTHETIC *a.*, and G. *unæstetisch.*)
1832 [S. AUSTIN] tr. *Tour Germ. Prince* III. xii. 332 This morning I went to church, with a full intention of being pious; but it did not succeed. Everything was too cold, dry, and unæsthetic. **1846** MILMAN *Ess., Newman* (1870) 352 Our unpoetic and unæsthetic (may we venture the word?) spirituality.

una'feard, -ed, *a.* Now arch or *dial.* Also 6 **vnaffear'd,** *Sc.* **onaffeired.** [UN-1 8.] Unafraid.
15.. *Christ's Kirk* in *Bannatyne MS.* (Hunt. Club) 287 Than followit feymen rycht on-affeird. **1595** DANIEL *Civ. Wars* III. lxxviii, The king..plies his hands vndaunted, vnaffear'd, And with good hart, and life for life he stird. **1812** TENNANT *Anster F.* VI. xli, I was not unafeared. **1868** MORRIS *Earthly Par.* (1870) I. I. 400 The weasel peered From out the wheat stalks on her unafear'd. **1898** N. MUNRO *J. Splendid* viii, Down at the shore, unafeared of man, would be solitary hinds.

un'affable, *a.* (UN-1 7.)
1603 DANIEL *To Sir T. Egerton* xvii, When surly Law, sterne and vnaffable, Cares onely but itselfe to satisfie. **1633** T. ADAMS *Exp. 2 Peter* ii. 19 Nabal's servant was wearie of so unaffable, uncharitable, unreasonable a Master. **1736** NEAL *Hist. Purit.* III. 542 He [Charles I] was unaffable and difficult of address. **1770** ARMSTRONG *Imitations of Shaks.* 119 Of walking statues, ghosts unaffable. **1834** DE QUINCEY *Autobiog. Sk.* Wks. 1854 II. 189 Southey disliked in Wordsworth the air of dogmatism, and the unaffable haughtiness of his manner.

una'ffected, *ppl. a.* [UN-1 8. Cf. G. *unaffectirt.*]
I. 1. Not adopted or assumed: **a.** Of qualities, feelings, etc.: Not simulated or pretended; real, genuine, sincere.
1592 DANIEL *Compl. Rosamund* lxxviii. A happy Country mayde, Whose vnaffected innocencie thinks No guilefull fraude. **1622** PEACHAM *Compl. Gent.* x. (1634) 90 Hee.. cannot with Virgill containe himselfe within that sweet, humble, and unaffected moderation. *a* **1656** BP. HALL *Serm. on Eccl. iii. 4* Wks. 1808 V. 571 Not in a hypocritical way of ostentation,..but in a wise, sober, seemly, unaffected deportment. **1710** STEELE *Tatler* No. 198 ⁋2 There appeared in the Face of Cælia a Chearfulness, the constant Companion of unaffected Virtue. **1796** MME. D'ARBLAY *Camilla* III. 184 Sir Sedley received them with the most unaffected pleasure. **1825** SCOTT *Talism.* xvii, A hurried glance of undisguised and unaffected terror. **1884** *Manch. Exam.* 22 May 5/2 A war which the great majority of the nation regard with unaffected dislike.
b. Of style or discourse: Free from affected words or phrases; simple, natural.
1598 HAKLUYT *Voy.* Pref. ⁋8 The harsh and vnaffected stile of his substantiall verses and the olde dialect of his wordes. **1619** T. MORE in A. Newman *Pleas. Vis.* A iij b, Like to thy modest selfe, thy happy veine Is vnaffected. **1659** RUSHW. *Hist. Coll.* I. Pref., I have esteemed the most unaffected and familiar Stile the best. **1711** STEELE *Spect.* No. 2 ⁋3 Sir Andrew having a natural unaffected Eloquence. *a* **1721** SHEFFIELD (Dk. Buckhm.) *Wks.* (1723) I. 180 Here sweet Eloquence does always smile, In such a choice, yet unaffected Style, As must both Knowledge and Delight impart. **1818** SCOTT *Let.* in *Lockhart* (1837) IV. iv. 137 The letters you have published are, I think, his very best—lively, entertaining, and unaffected.
c. Of conduct, bearing, etc.: Free from affectation or artificiality.
1712 STEELE *Spect.* No. 284 ⁋1 An unaffected Behaviour is without question a very great Charm. **1791** MRS. RADCLIFFE *Rom. Forest* v, His Manners were unaffected and graceful rather than dignified. **1848** THACKERAY *Van. Fair* li, She said the wickedest things with the most simple unaffected air. **1876** MISS BRADDON *J. Haggard's Dau.* I. 67 Oswald was impressed by the simple pathos, the unaffected power, of the speaker.
†**2.** Not desired or aimed at. *Obs. rare.*
1611 SPEED *Hist. Gt. Brit.* VII. xliv. §3. 358 A cloud appearing of bloud and fire, immediately after his vnaffected Coronation.
3. Of persons: Not affected, unartificial or unpretentious, in manners.
1677 MIEGE *Fr. Dict.* II, Unaffected, *qui n'est pas affecté.* *a* **1721** SHEFFIELD (Dk. Buckhm.) *Wks.* (1723) II. 266 Montagu, methinks, represents Adam in his innocence..; naked, but not ashamed, because unblemished and unaffected. **1729** T. COOKE *Tales*, etc. 88 Hence, says the Bird of Venus, Boaster fly..Me Men, and Gods, with Admiration view, Plain, unaffected, with my glossy Hue. **1818** LADY MORGAN *Autobiog.* (1859) 21 He seems eminently intellectual, unaffected, and kind. **1889** LANG *Prince Prigio* ii. 13 What nice, unaffected princes they are!
b. Sincere, honest (in some respect).
1796 MME. D'ARBLAY *Camilla* V. 221 An unaffected admirer of all she had heard of [her] good qualities.
II. 4. Not affected or influenced in mind or feeling; untouched, unmoved. Also const. *by*, †*to*, †*with.*
c **1586** C'TESS PEMBROKE *Ps.* LVIII. ii, The aspick..On whom the charmer all in vaine applies His skillful'st spells .., self-deaf, and unaffected lies. *c* **1616** FLETCHER *Thierry & Theod.* II. i, A poor, cold, unspirited, unmanner'd, Unhonest, unaffected, undone, fool. **1729** LAW *Serious C.* iv. 67 The mock ceremony, instead of blessing our victuals, does but accustom us to trifle with devotion, and give us a habit of being unaffected with our prayers. **1741** RICHARDSON *Pamela* I. 177 How unaffected People were to the Distresses of others. **1803** *Censor* 1 Sept. 100 There is something..so moving in the narrative, that I think it is impossible any reader, however stoical, can remain unaffected. *c* **1820** MRS. SHERWOOD *Orange Grove* 17 The old man was quite unaffected, and looked quite stupid.
†**b.** Not inclined to a side or party. *Obs.*$^{-1}$
1619 SIR E. HERBERT in *Eng. & Germ.* (Camden Soc.) 85, I hope his Majestie will find this state so unaffected and neutrall, that..their irresolution will keep them indifferent.
5. Not attacked by disease or illness.
1797 M. BAILLIE *Morb. Anat.* (1807) 408 Scirrhous tumours occasionally arise in the vagina itself..when the uterus is unaffected. **1873** T. H. GREEN *Introd. Pathol.* (ed. 2) 281 In this stage [of nephritis] the tubes and their epithelium are unaffected.
6. Not acted upon or altered *by* some agent or influence.
1830 MACKINTOSH *Eth. Philos.* Wks. 1846 I. 24 That happiness consisted in virtuous pleasure, chiefly dependent on the state of mind, but not unaffected by outward agents, was the doctrine of both. **1875** JOWETT *Plato* (ed. 2) III. 615 Free from old age and unaffected by disease.
b. Similarly without const.
1833-4 J. PHILLIPS *Geol.* in *Encycl. Metrop.* (1845) VI. 656 A tremour which might shiver elastic flint,..but leave the chalk unaffected. **1890** *Retrospect Med.* CII. 182 Out of six cases treated..two were cured (?), three slightly relieved, and one unaffected.

una'ffectedly, *adv.* [f. prec.] In an unaffected manner; without affectation.
1677 MIEGE *Fr. Dict.* II, Unaffectedly, *sans affectation.* **1693** CONGREVE *Old Batchelor* v. i, Yet, she was unaffectedly concern'd, he says; and often blush'd with Anger and Surprize. **1782** V. KNOX *Ess.* xxiii. (1819) I. 131 The purpose of history is truth, and truth requires no more than to be fairly, openly, and unaffectedly exhibited. **1794** R. J. SULIVAN *View Nat.* I. Pref. 7 He has unaffectedly to solicit the indulgence of the reader. **1808** L. MURRAY *Eng. Gram.* I. 232 A girl unaffectedly modest. *Ibid.* 270 He spoke unaffectedly and forcibly. **1896** T. F. TOUT *Edw. I*, iv. 68 Edward was deeply and unaffectedly religious.

una'ffectedness. [f. as prec.] The quality of being unaffected.
†**1.** Impassiveness, indifference. *Obs.*
1670 *Devout Commun.* (1688) 203 Charge not upon me.. my unpreparedness, unaffectedness. **1681** KETTLEWELL *Chr. Obedience* (1715) 528 The coldness and unaffectedness, the unsettledness and distractions, which they find in themselves when they are at prayers. **1694** —— *Comp. Penitent* 55, I am grieved..for all my neglects of thy service, and for my insincerity and unaffectedness in performing it.
2. Freedom from affectation; naturalness.
1685 H. MORE *Paralip. Prophet.* vi. 38 Which Letter, as I said, is written with..unaffectedness and punctualness withal. **1752** *Narr. Journ. through Eng.* (1869) 32 She seemed to have all that delicacy and unaffectedness requisite to persons of the first rank. **1783** BLAIR *Lect.* xix. I. 398 The simplicity or unaffectedness of his manner, is the crowning ornament. **1861** THACKERAY *Four Georges* iv. (1862) 192 Not ill liked by the nation, which pardons youthful irregularities readily enough for the sake of pluck, unaffectedness and good-humour. **1882** J. A. ALLEN *Love Story Col. & Mrs. Hutchinson* 39 What dignity of bearing! yet withal What simple, winning unaffectedness!

†**una'ffectible,** *a.* *Obs.*$^{-1}$ [UN-1 7.] That cannot be affected.
1678 CUDWORTH *Intell. Syst.* I. iv. §36. 561 To what purpose any Devotional Addresses should be made by us to such an Unaffectible, Inflexible,..and Adamantine Being.

una'ffecting, *ppl. a.* [UN-1 10.]
†**1.** Free from affectation. *Obs.*
1602 *Ld. Cromwell* III. iii. 13 A most learned, yet vnaffecting spirit. **1713** STEELE *Spect.* No. 423 ⁋2 He carries on an unaffecting Exactness in his Dress and Manner. **1814** WORDSW. *Excurs.* VI. 578 Though a vulgar face..And unaffecting manners might at once Be recognised by all.
2. Not affecting or touching; having no effect upon the feelings.
1647 N. WARD *Simple Cobler* 87 Affected termes are unaffecting things to solid hearers. **1719** WATERLAND *Vind. Christ's Div.* 277 Abstract Reasons of Esteem, Honour, and Regard are unaffecting, without a mixture of something relative to Us. **1763** J. BROWN *Poetry & Music* xiii. 233 The Ode must be written in the Style of Passion; not with the Parade of unaffecting Imagery, or tedious Allegory. **1812** CRABBE *Tales* viii. 354 In her tall mirror then she shows a face, Still coldly fair with unaffecting grace. **1823** J. WILSON *Trials Marg. Lyndsay* i. 3 The narrative of whose fortunes may perhaps not be unaffecting to those who [etc.].

una'ffectionate, *a.* [UN-1 7 and 5 b.]
†**1.** Unbiassed; impartial. *Obs.*$^{-1}$
1588 A. KING tr. *Canisius' Catech.* G vij b, I think it sall be acceptable to the vnaffectionat redar, giff..I sall pen ye occasion [etc.].
†**2.** Not endowed with feeling. *Obs.*$^{-1}$
1645 MILTON *Tetrach.* Wks. 1851 IV. 236 A helplesse, unaffectionate, and sullen masse whose very company represents the visible and exactest figure of lonelines it selfe.
†**3.** Not well affected. *Obs.*$^{-1}$
1787 JEFFERSON *Writ.* (1859) II. 108 His devotion to the principles of pure despotism, renders him unaffectionate to our governments.
4. Not affectionate; devoid of affection.
1815 MRS. PILKINGTON *Celebrity* III. 13 Sir Ferdinand,.. returning to her hand the unaffectionate production, said [etc.]. **1830** H. N. COLERIDGE *Grk. Poets* (1834) 304 His demeanour towards his mother..is generally unaffectionate. **1875** RUSKIN *Fors Clav.* liv. 167 Not..that I grew up selfish and unaffectionate.
Hence **una'ffectionately** *adv.*
1847 H. BUSHNELL *Chr. Nurt.* II. i. (1861) 241 If the child is..simply laid aside unaffectionately, in no warmth of motherly gentleness.

una'ffectioned, *ppl. a.* (UN-1 8.)
1788 D. GILSON *Serm.* xv. 434 When..the sayings of Jesus are lost upon unaffectioned spirits. **1911** K. HARE *Green Fields* 5 His tuneable unaffectioned voice that loved the matter Has in the grey room conjured up the sunshine.

una'ffective, *a.* *Obs.*$^{-1}$ (UN-1 7.)
1689 *Myst. Iniq.* 22 A superficial and unaffective Glance.

una'ffianced, *ppl. a.* (UN-1 8.)
1750 CARTE *Hist. Eng.* II. 612 The duke of Bourgogne, or the count of Hainault,..had no daughters unmarried or unaffianced. **1829** B. W. PROCTER in *Gem* 284 Did they not say this girl Was unaffianced? Ay, unwoo'd, unsought. **1898** TALMAGE in *Chr. Herald* (N.Y.) 19 Jan. 44/1 That at least that number of women shall be unaffianced for life.

una'ffied, *ppl. a.* [UN-1 8.] = prec.
1527 in Grose *Antiq. Rep.* (1809) IV. 670 The saide Andrewe then to be vnmarryed, vnaffied and vncontracted. *c* **1625** in *Verney Mem.* (1904) I. 72 That the ward unmarried, unaffyed, and uncontracted should..be sent to Lady Denham. **1857** EMERSON *Poems, Woodnotes* II. 231 Not unrelated, unaffied, But to each thought and thing allied.

†**una'ffiled,** *ppl. a.* *Obs.*$^{-1}$ [UN-1 8.] Unpolished, rude.
1390 GOWER *Conf.* I. 119 No strengthe of love bowe mihte His herte, which is unaffiled.

una'ffiliated, *ppl. a.* (UN-1 8.)
1849-50 ALISON *Hist. Eur.* II. vii. §23. 134 No precautions [were] adopted..against the admission of unaffiliated members. **1859** *Sat. Rev.* 17 Dec. 728/2 Not to trust upright and able servants unaffiliated to the Society of Loyola.

una'ffirmed, *ppl. a.* (UN-1 8.)
1620 DONNE *26 Serm.* (1660) 48 That Council [of Trent] will not say, that..we leave any truth unaffirmed, which the Primitive Church affirm'd to be necessary to salvation.

una'ffixed, *ppl. a.* (UN-1 8). Also as *adj.* [UN-9 a].
1602 WILLIS *Stenographie* D ij b, Vnaffixed Particles, as: furlong, despise. **1964** R. H. ROBINS *Gen. Linguistics* vi. 260 In Japanese the formation of words..referring to more than one entity..leaves the resultant words syntactically equivalent to unaffixed forms.

una'fflicted, *ppl. a.* (UN-1 8.)
1599 DANIEL *Musophilus* 13 The whiles my vnafflicted minde doth feed On no vnholy thoughts for benefit. **1647** BP. HALL *Satan's Fiery Darts* II. iv. 163 Tell mee if thou canst, which of those Saints that are now shining bright in their heaven, hath got thither un-afflicted? **1665** BP. N. FRENCH *Hist. Wks.* (1846) I. 135 If such an one may not pass his days unafflicted. **1742** YOUNG *Nt. Th.* v. 333 Truth, radiant goddess!..shews the real estimate of things; Which no man, unafflicted, ever saw. **1872** RUSKIN *Fors Clav.* xvi. 13 [Wine] mellowed by pure chalk rock and unafflicted sunshine.

una'fflicting, *a.* (UN-1 10.)
a **1771** KEN *Hymns Evang.* Poet. Wks. 1721 I. 174 And on the Stone an angel they behold, His Face like unafflicting Lightning bright. —— *Christophel* Ibid. I. 420 As Moses.. once saw God's trayling Beams with unafflicting Aw.

una'fflictingly, *adv.* (UN-1 11.)
a **1711** KEN *Hymns Evang.* Poet. Wks. 1721 I. 94 Forth from the bosom of the fontal Sire Came the Eternal Word to wear our Clay And Godhead unafflictingly display.

una'ffordable, *a.* (UN-1 7 b.)
1825 BENTHAM *Offic. Apt. Maximized, Indic.* (1830) 77 The space and research necessary for such distinctions [is] altogether unaffordable.

una'ffranchized, *ppl. a.* (UN-1 8.)
1611 COTGR. s.v. *Morte-main*, Illegitimated bastards, vnnaturalized strangers, and vnaffranchized villaines.

una'ffrighted, *ppl. a.* (UN-1 8.)
1586 MARLOWE *1st Pt. Tamburl.* IV. i, As Crocodiles that vnaffrighted rest While thundring Cannons rattle on their Skins. *c* **1620** FLETCHER & MASS. *Little Fr. Lawyer* I. i, He that through all these dreadfull passages Pursued and overtook them, unaffrighted, Deserves reward. **1641** T. HAYNE *M. Luther* 21 Multitius..with sharp wordes and threates so daunted the man, till now a clamorous, unaffrighted, bold face, terrible to all. **1718** *Entertainer* No. 13. 84 Henderson.., whom they traduced as timorous.., they found..unaffrighted with Threats, Reproaches, and Dangers. **1742** RICHARDSON *Pamela* III. 211, I was not guilty of any Freedoms, that her Modesty, unaffrighted, could reproach itself with having suffered. **1852** M. ARNOLD *Self-Depend.* v, Unaffrighted by the silence round them, Undistracted by the sights they see. **1886** A. WEIR *Hist. Basis Mod. Europe* (1889) 554 A generation grew up..which was unaffrighted by visions of fanaticism.
Hence **una'ffrightedly** *adv.*
1891 H. HERMAN *His Angel* 121 When they could unaffrightedly bask in the sunshine of their mutual happiness.

una'ffronted, *ppl. a.* [UN-1 8.]
1. Not affronted or insulted.
1753 RICHARDSON *Grandison* (1781) III. xxx. 355 You went away unhurt and unaffronted. **1820** KEATS *Lamia* I. 101 And by my power is her beauty veil'd To keep it unaffronted, unassail'd By the love-glances of unlovely eyes.
2. Not confronted or faced.
1840 BROWNING *Sordello* I. 547 Rife With grandeurs, unaffronted to the last, Equal to being all! **1856** F. E. PAGET *Owlet of Owlst.* 57 But unaffronted, (we invent a very expressive word for the occasion,) he is impregnable.

†**una'ffrontive,** *a.* *Obs.*$^{-1}$ [UN-1 7.] Unresisting.
1720 WELTON *Suffer. Son of God* II. xxxi. 801 Such an unaffrontive Patience, and Resigned Disposition, is ever acceptable to God.

unaflow, var. UNIFLOW *a.*

una'fraid, *a.* [UN-1 7.] Not afraid; undaunted, undismayed. Also const. *of*.

1423 JAS. I. *Kingis Q.* xxxv, Therewith vnaffraid,.. From beugh to beugh thay hippit and thai plaid. **1535** STEWART *Cron. Scot.* (Rolls) I. 247 King Caratac, with curage vnaffrayit, Upoun ane plane the battell hes arrayit. **1584** HUDSON *Du Bartas' Judith* IV. (1608) 64 This while, the worthie widdow with her maid Past towards th' enmies camp not vnafraide. **1635** QUARLES *Embl.* IV. xiv. (1818) 251 Hath thy all-glorious Deity ne'er a shade.. Where I might sit refreshed and unafraid? **1672** DRYDEN *Def. Epilogue* Ess. (ed. Ker) I. 169 By *unfeared* he [B. Jonson *Catiline* IV. i. 32] means *unafraid*: words of quite a contrary signification. **1725** RAMSAY *Gentl. Sheph.* III. i, He,.. unafraid of fate, Contented spends his time. **1748** THOMSON *Cast. Indol.* II. xxviii, Where free, and unafraid, Amid the flowering brakes each coyer creature stray'd. **1856** MRS. BROWNING *Aur. Leigh* III. 169 Serene and unafraid of solitude I worked the short days out. **1895** CLIVE HOLLAND *Jap. Wife* iii, I never felt so unafraid of Lou.. in all my life.

† **unagain'sayably**, *adv. Obs. rare.* [UN-1 11.] Undeniably.

c **1449** PECOCK *Repr.* I. xx. 130 This firste parte of this present book and The iust apprising of Holi Scripture.. schewen vndoutabli and vnaȝenseiabily, that [etc.]. *Ibid.* III. xvi. 380. *c* **1456** —— *Bk. of Faith* (1909) 222 If this be trewe, as it is unaȝenseiabili trewe.

† **unagain'standably**, *adv. Obs.*-1 [UN-1 11.] Irresistibly.

c **1449** PECOCK *Repr.* V. ix. 533 If a manys riȝt iȝe sclaundre him (that is to seie, violentli and ferseli and as it were vnaȝenstondeabli bringith him into synne).

† **un'aged**, *a. Obs.*-1 [UN-1 9.] Not of age.

1486 *Bk. St. Albans, Her.* A vi b, Whan an unaged prynce is made Knyght or be crowned King.

un'ageing, *ppl. a.* (UN-1 10.)

1860 PUSEY *Min. Proph.* 414 He who admitteth faith and love to dwell in his heart hath as a requital, un-aging life. **1887** MORRIS *Odyss.* VII. 257 She.. meant to make me be A deathless man for ever, and unageing all my days.

un'aggravated, *ppl. a.* (UN-1 8.)

1746 WESLEY *Princ. Methodist* 12 This is the real unaggravated charge. **1777** POTTER *Æschylus, Agamemnon* 284, I tremble now Hearing th' unaggravated truth. **1816** J. SCOTT *Vis. Paris* (ed. 5) 130 It is a sign that the virtue of a nation is spurious and debased, not that its vice is scanty and unaggravated.

un'aggregated, *ppl. a.* (UN-1 8.)

1871 FRASER *Berkeley* x. 390 Things I say, not mere unaggregated phenomena.

una'ggressive, *a.* (UN-1 7 and 5 b.)

1862 *Edin. Rev.* CXVI. 223 In the unaggressive position which England assumes these interests are identical. **1867** LEWES *Hist. Philos.* II. 207 There was something in the noble calmness and unagressive fearlessness of his attitude which acted like a mental tonic.

una'ggressively, *adv.* (UN-1 11.)

1899 MISS B. HARRADEN *Fowler* 8 Carrying everything before them, but carrying it gallantly and unaggressively.

una'ggressiveness. (UN-1 12.)

1870 *Pall Mall G.* 16 Dec. 3 It would be absurd to give credit for national unaggressiveness to a country parcelled out among a lot of squabbling princelings.

† **una'ghast**, *a. Sc. Obs.* [UN-1 7.] Not aghast; unafraid.

a **1510** DOUGLAS *K. Hart* I. 184 Sone thai can thame dres, Full glaid thai glyde as gromes vnagaist. **1535** STEWART *Cron. Scot.* (Rolls) III. 249 To quhome agane richt sone in to that place He ansuer maid, rycht scharplie wnagast. *a* **1600** MONTGOMERIE *Misc. Poems* xiv. 32, I pas the tym but pain, And vnagast.

un'agitated, *ppl. a.* [UN-1 8.]

1. Not physically moved or disturbed.

1638 SIR T. HERBERT *Trav.* (ed. 2) 128 Commonly the clouds here at Larr are undigested.. and unagitated by the wind. **1747** *Gentl. Mag.* 523 The air stable, and the water unagitated.

2. Not mentally disturbed; not stirred or excited by emotion or unrest.

1772 *Test Filial Duty* II. 88 Unagitated by alternate hope and fear, the heart is quiet. **1844** *Mem. Babylonian Princess* II. 257 The steady and unagitated tread of some sea-man. **1857** RUSKIN *Pol. Econ. Art* i. 34 What we mainly want, therefore, is a means of sufficient and unagitated employment.

Hence **un'agitatedly** *adv.*

1894 MRS. DYER *Man's Keeping* (1899) 64 There was a perceptible pause before he spoke again, during which Urquhart unagitatedly waited.

† **un'aglet**, *v.* (UN-2 4.)

1530 PALSGR. 766/1, I unaglet a poynte, or lace, *je defferre.* .. I pray you, unaglet this poynt.

una'greeable, *a.* Now *rare.* [UN-1 7 b.]

1. Not agreeable or pleasing; not to one's liking or taste; disagreeable, uncongenial. Also const. *to, unto.*

c **1374** CHAUCER *Boeth.* I. met. i. (1868) 4 But now.. myn vnpitouse lijf draweþ a-long vnagreable dwellynges in me. **1491** CAXTON *Vitas Patr.* (W. de. W. 1495) I. clxiv. 173/1 In all maner of her dedes she was unagreable to god. **1547** SIR W. PAGET in Strype *Eccl. Mem.* (1721) II. vii. 57 Then shall it be well don.. to send an express man, not unagreeable to any of both the parts. **1671** CLARENDON *Hist. Reb.* IX. §1 We are now entering upon a time, the representation.. whereof must be the most unpleasant.. to the reader.. and as unagreeable and difficult to the writer. **1683** J. L. in J. Pordage *Mystic Div.* To Rdr. 5 His Soul, which then groaned to be set loose from so unagreeable a Bodie. **1725** *Fam. Dict.* s.v. *Box*, The Excellency of its Wood makes amends for its unagreeable Smell. **1808** JANE AUSTEN *Lett.* (1884) I. 361 Mr. M. was not unagreeable, though nothing seemed to go right with him. **1866** *Lond. Rev.* 5 May 499/2 There is another class of persons who.. are what one might call (if there were such a word in the English language) 'unagreeable' people.

† **2.** Unconformable or unsuitable *to*, inconsistent or incongruous *with*. *Obs.*

1550 BALE *Apol.* 57 Here, how inconstaunt, unagreable, and contraryouse he is also to hymselfe. **1566** PAINTER *Pal. Pleas.* (1569) 86 b, Thinkinge it better.. to haue a wife unagreable to his estate, then to suffer him to die for her sake. **1580** E. KNIGHT *Trial Truth* 12 The millers hackney vnagreeable with the true rules and accident of armes. **1624** HEYWOOD *Gunaik.* III. 151 Least any abject thing or unworthie may be objected against us unagreable with our blood and qualitie. **1667** MILTON *P.L.* x. 256 Let us try Adventrous work, yet to thy power and mine Not unagreeable. **1684** H. MORE *Answer* 42 Also it is unagreeable with the making the Christian Emperours the seventh Head. **1702** H. DODWELL *Apol.* §14 in S. Parker *Cicero's De Finibus* b 4 b, This was thought to be the case of the *Biothanatoi*.. which made it unagreeable to the Principles of Philosophy for any to imitate it.

Hence **una'greeableness.**

1658 *Whole Duty Man* xii. §8 That unagreeableness that was betwixt their practice, and their law. **1667** *Decay Chr. Piety* xvi. ¶2 A doctrine, whose unagreeableness to the gospel-œconomy rendred it suspicious.

una'greeably, *adv.* [UN-1 11.]

† **1.** Inconsistently. *Obs.*-1

1546 BALE *Eng. Votaries* I. (1550) 4 b, Which thynge hath bene hytherto in all Englysh Chronicles, doubtfullie, vnagreablye, yea and vntruly treated.

2. Unpleasantly, disagreeably.

[**1775** ASH.] **1850** L. HUNT *Autobiog.* I. vii. 291 They.. were not unagreeably sprinkled with quotation.

una'greed, *ppl. a.* [UN-1 8.]

1. Not agreed or in accord (*with*).

1525 LD. BERNERS *Froiss.* II. clxxxiv. 556 Thoughe the lordes departed euery daye vnagreed, yet they departed asonder right amiably. **1557-75** *Diurn. Occurr.* (Bann. Cl.) 188 Thaj depairtit agane unaggreit with the said regent. **1667** *Decay Chr. Piety* xi. §8 If he find them unagreed upon the way, one disputing for this, and another for that,.. he would sure retract his confidence.

† **2.** With *of*: Not agreed upon. *Obs.*-1

1661 BOYLE *Style of Script.* (1675) 172 Which [part] is not onely less considerable, but is changeable and unagreed of.

una'greeing, *ppl. a.* (UN-1 10.)

1611 COTGR., *Incongruë*, incongruous, vnagreeing; absurd. **1654** COKAINE *Dianea* I. 9 The knight.. conceived it unagreeing to his generous spirit to be cruell to a Carkass.

un'aidable, *a.* (UN-1 7 b and 5 b.)

1664 (SHAKS.) *All's Well* II. i. 122 (3rd Fol.) That labouring art can never ransome nature From her unaydible [1623 inaydible] estate. [**1755** JOHNSON.] **1866** CARLYLE *Remin.* (1881) II. 265 What a look,.. unaidable, and like to break one's heart. **1871** —— in *Lett. Mrs. Carlyle* (1883) III. 179 Such a deluge of.. indescribable, unaidable pain, as I had never seen or dreamt of.

† **un'aidant**, *a. Obs.*-1 [UN-1 7.] Not helpful.

1667 WATERHOUSE *Fire Lond.* 170 Incontributive to the publique Charge, as well as unaydant to their own Expences.

un'aided, *ppl. a.* [UN-1 8.] Not aided; unassisted: **a.** In predicative use; also const. *by*.

1667 MILTON *P.L.* VI. 141 Who,.. with solitarie hand Reaching beyond all limit, at one blow Unaided could have finisht thee. **1791** COWPER *Iliad* XVI. 652 Thy allies, who, for thy sake,.. Perish, unaided and unmiss'd by thee. **1796** MME. D'ARBLAY *Camilla* V. 376, I cannot support it unaided. **1860** TYNDALL *Glac.* I. i. 5 Mere reasoning, unaided by experiment, was incompetent to answer. **1888** BARRIE *When a Man's Single* (1900) 71/1 Angus is longing to pull us up the river unaided.

b. Attrib.; in later use esp. of the eye.

1676 GLANVILL *Ess.* iii. 24 The distance of the Heavens is so vast, that our unaided Senses can give us but extreamly imperfect Informations of that Upper World. **1712** BLACKMORE *Creation* II. 77 Counting those the unaided eye Can see, or by invented tubes descry. **1773** *Observ. State Poor* 63 The terrors of unaided poverty would happily operate to the advantage of those, who.. prodigally waste those earnings. **1827** SCOTT *Chron. Canongate* Introd., I had therefore the task of avowing myself.. as the sole and unaided author of these Novels of Waverley. **1855** BAIN *Senses & Int.* III. iii. §2 The multiplication of unaided eyes could never equal the vision of one person with a telescope.

Hence **un'aidedly** *adv.*

1859 G. WILSON *Mem. E. Forbes* ii. (1861) 42 Forbes.. had.. unaidedly discovered the true scope of his intellect.

un'aiding, *ppl. a.* (UN-1 10.)

1716 POPE *Iliad* VIII. 581 From fields forbidden we submiss refrain, With arms unaiding see our Argives slain.

un'ailing, *ppl. a.* (UN-1 10.)

1846 WORCESTER (citing Chatham), *Unailing*, a., free from disease; healthy.

† **un'aimable**, *a. Obs.*-1 In 4 uneymable. [UN-1 7 b.] Unreckonable.

1382 WYCLIF *Job* xxxvi. 26 Lo! God gret, ouercomende oute kunnyng; the noumbre of the ȝeris of hym uneymable [L. *inestimabilis*].

un'aimed, *ppl. a.* [UN-1 8.] **a.** Not aimed or pointed at a mark. **b.** With *at*: Not taken as a mark.

1648 HEXHAM II, *Ongemickt*, Vn-aimed, Vnleveled. **1669** COKAINE *Poems, Let. to Earl Huntingdon* 86 So you (my Lord) for sweet conditions known, Parallels to your high birth, stand alone, Unaim'd and unarriv'd at. **1805** WORDSW. *Prelude* IV. 315 With din of instruments and shuffling feet,.. And unaimed prattle flying up and down. **1835** BROWNING *Paracelsus* V. 629 The tumult of unproved desire, the unaimed, Uncertain yearnings, aspirations blind. **1888** *Daily News* 6 Sept. 6/5 Swept by artillery fire and unaimed rifle fire at long ranges.

un'aiming, *ppl. a.* (UN-1 10.)

1691 DRYDEN *K. Arthur* I. i, Your Charming Daughter, who like Love, Born Blind, Un-aiming hits, with surest Archery, And Innocently kills. *a* **1735** GRANVILLE *Poems* (1790) 86 The noisy Culverin, o'er-charg'd, lets fly, And burst unaiming in the rended sky.

un'airable, *a. Obs.*-1 [UN-1 7 b. Cf. AIRABLE *a.*] † Not capable of forming good music.

a **1619** CAMPION *Counterpoint* Wks. (1909) 217 If this be the right Base,.. what a strange vnaireable change must the key then make from *F.* with the first third sharp to *G.* with *B.* flat.

un'aired, *ppl. a.* [UN-1 8.]

† **1.** Untravelled. *Obs.*-1 (Cf. AIRED *ppl. a.* 2.)

? *a* **1616** BEAUM. & FL. *Q. Corinth* II. iv, Be not so improvident To forget your travelling pace, 'tis a main posture, And to all unayr'd Gentlemen will betray you.

2. Not exposed to the air or to heat so as to remove stagnant air or damp. (Cf. AIR *v.* 1, 2.)

1682 OTWAY *Venice Preserved* III. ii, What feminine Tale hast thou been listening to, Of unayr'd shirts; Catharrs and Tooth Ach got By thin-sol'd shoos. **1740** MRS. DELANY in *Life & Corr.* (1861) II. 122 We are, I think, too much invalids to go into an unaired house. **1763** *Brit. Mag.* IV. 405 The ladies were under terrible apprehensions about damp sheets and unaired beds. **1826** SCOTT *Woodst.* iii, The state-rooms are unaired, and in indifferent order. **1865** TROLLOPE *Belton Est.* ix. 95 She had been wrong to go into such a place as the cold, unaired Court House.

unait, variant of UNNAIT. *a. Obs.*

† **unaker.** *Obs.* (See quots.)

1744 in *Dict. Nat. Biogr.* (1889) XX. 300/1 The material [for making china-ware] is an earth, the produce of the Cherokee nation in America, called by the natives *unaker.* **1885** *Encycl. Brit.* XIX. 641/1 The clay, which was called 'unaker,' was brought from America, and was probably an impure kind of kaolin.

una'kin, *a.* (UN-1 7.)

1864 F. W. ROBINSON *Mattie, a Stray* III. 175 Twice had the answer been deferred, for reasons unakin to each other. **1878** MISS FOTHERGILL *First Violin* VI. i, In former days there had been in his face something not unakin to this stormy, free night.

unal ('juːnəl), *a.* [f. L. *ūn-us* one + -AL1.] Single; that is one only; based on unity.

1883 MOMERIE *Personality* Introd. (ed. 2) 12 It [metaphysics] seeks a unal basis for the phenomena of nature and of human nature. **1892** 'UNITAS' *Unalism* Pref., The neglected Unal principle has its source in the Divine Oneness.

una'larm, *v.* (UN-2 3.)

1722 DE FOE *Plague* (1754) 21 The Distemper intermitted often at first; so they were as it were, alarm'd, and unalarm'd again.

una'larmed, *ppl. a.* (UN-1 8.)

1756 MRS. DELANY in *Life & Corr.* (1861) III. 419, I am still unalarmed about the invasion, but don't find people are so apprehensive as at first. **1769** G. WHITE *Selborne* xxvi, A tame snake, which was.. as sweet as any animal while in good humour and unalarmed. **1820** W. JAY *Prayers* 89 Unalarmed by fears, undistressed by pain. **1897** ANNE PAGE *Afternoon Ride* 61 A large iguana, waddling with serious mien and unalarmed leisure towards the drift.

una'larming, *a.* (UN-1 10.)

1760-72 H. BROOKE *Fool of Qual.* (1792) III. 9 The seasonable precaution of breaking the matter to our father by unalarming degrees. **1803** *Ann. Rev.* I. 364 A disposition to make.. slight unalarming reforms. **1868** MISS BRADDON *Dead Sea Fr.* III. iv. 61 Her illness was of a very slight and unalarming character.

† **un'alchemy**, *v. Obs.*-1 [UN-2 3.] *trans.* To decompose chemically.

1661 FELTHAM *Resolves* II. viii. 194 Like the only true Philosophers stone, he can unalchimy the Allay of life.

un'alcoholized, *ppl. a.* (UN-1 8.)

[**1775** ASH.] **1881** *Daily News* 21 June 6/8 During those two years.. they were experimenting in the production of Unalcoholized Sherry. **1884** *Ch. Bells* 2 Feb. 214/1 *Vino Sacro*, the pure unalcoholised Sacramental wine.

una'lert, *a.* (UN-1 7.)

1811 SOUTHEY *Inscript.*, *Affair Arroyo Molinos* 17 He.. deem'd the British soldiers all too slow, To seize occasion, unalert in war. **1892** 'M. FIELD' *Sight & Song* 92 The offender callous, unalert.

un'alienable, *a.* [UN-1 7 b and 5 b.] = INALIENABLE *a.*

1611 COTGR., *Inalienable*, vnalienable; which cannot be sold, or passed away. **1641** EARL MONM. tr. *Biondi's Civil Warres* v. 125 Those countries.. which for safety and reputation ought to be unallienable from the Crowne of England. **1688** *Answ. Talon's Plea* 27 This Monsieur Talon maintains to be an unalienable right of the Crown of France. **1743** J. MORRIS *Serm.* vii. 197 God.. gives all men their being, and has an unalienable claim to their obedience. **1771** GOLDSM. *Hist. Eng.* II. 307 Giving these petty tyrants a power of selling their estates, which before his time were unalienable. **1841** STEPHEN *Comm. Laws Eng.* (1874) II. 13 Personal chattels cannot in any instance be rendered unalienable beyond the period prescribed. **1855** MACAULAY *Hist. Eng.* xvii. IV. 115 That all men were endowed by the Creator with an unalienable right to liberty.

un'alienably, *adv.* [UN-[1] 11 and 5b.] = INALIENABLY *adv.*
1702 *Toleration* 3 It is..evident..that no Man may arrogate what is unalienably appropriated unto God. **1765** WILKES *Corr.* (1805) II. 193, I hope my friends..think of me..for my life unalienably attentive to my country. **1809** E. CHRISTIAN in *Blackstone's Comm.* I. 329 The parliament had the wisdom..to vest unalienably in commissioners the sum of 1,000,000 *l.* annually. **1881** EMMA WORBOISE *Sissie* xxv, The pittance that remained was hers—hers unalienably.

un'alienated, *ppl. a.* [UN-[1] 8.]
1. Not estranged in feeling.
1798 S. & HT. LEE *Canterb. T.* II. 513 Even if his heart should stand the test, and remain wholly uncorrupted, and unalienated. **1859** FARRAR *J. Home* 414 An effort was made by his few remaining and unalienated friends to provide for him the means of emigration.
2. Not alienated or transferred in respect of ownership.
1851 SIR F. PALGRAVE *Norm. & Eng.* I. 5 His resources.. arose only from the very few royal domains as yet unalienated from the crown. **1887** MOLONEY *Forestry W. Africa* 6 The absence of compiled information of extent of lands sold and unalienated.

†**un'aliened**, *ppl. a.* [UN-[1] 8.] Unalienated.
1596 BACON *Use Com. Law* (1635) 28 Some action must bee brought against the heire whilest the land or other inheritance resteth in him unaliened away. **1674** STAVELEY *Rom. Horseleech* 131 Her example was not followed by any of the Nobility, or others, who had incorporated any of the Abby Lands into their estates, but the Queen restored only what remained in the Crown un-aliened from the same.

una'ligned, *ppl. a.* [UN-[1] 8.] **1.** Not physically aligned.
1936 F. M. FORD *Let.* 2 July (1965) 254 This damned new machine—unaligned a's and all which means that it will have to go back to the shop. **1962** CORSON & LORRAIN *Introd. Electromagn. Fields* iii. 107 An unaligned dipole therefore has greater energy than an aligned one.
2. = NON-ALIGNED *a.* Also *absol.* as *sb.*
1961 *Guardian* 28 Jan. 2/3 India and the 'unaligned nations'. **1962** C. B. MARSHALL in L. W. Martin *Neutralism & Nonalignment* ii. 13 (*heading*) On understanding the unaligned. **1965** *Listener* 10 June 851/1 Africans feel the need to be wholly African, unaligned, even in their form of government.

una'like, *adv.* [UN-[1] 11b.] Differently.
1616 GATAKER *Lots* 337 Which stickes if they light and lye both alike on the flat side, they account it a good signe; if unalike, an evill signe.

una'like, *a.* [UN-[1] 7.] Different; not alike.
1934 'L. G. GIBBON' *Grey Granite* 210 If Ewan had been as that other Ewan..and she paused... Was he so unalike? **1944** *Penguin New Writing* XX. 61 Arthur continued to wonder..how these two unalike girls had come to set up together. **1961** B. VAWTER *Conscience of Israel* v. 127 If they are two prophets in agreement on fundamentals, they are also severely unalike in numerous ways. **1978** D. MURPHY *Place Apart* xii. 250 Cycling is by far the best way to travel around the North where regions only twenty miles apart can be so very unalike.

unali'mentary, *a.* (UN-[1] 7.)
1822 GOOD *Study Med.* I. 182 Unalimentary substances swallowed through bravado or by mistake, as knives, metallic money, or pieces of glass.

'unalism. [f. UNAL *a.* + -ISM.] (See quot.)
1892 'UNITAS' *Unalism* i. 2 Unalism..has nothing whatever to do with Unitarianism. It means a system of thought and action which is in accordance with the Unal Rule.

unalist ('juːnəlɪst). [f. UNAL *a.* + IST; cf. *pluralist.*] **a.** A holder of only one benefice. **b.** A believer in unalism.
1743 R. NEWTON *Pluralities Indefensible* 198, I do deny, that, in the general, Pluralists have Greater Merit than Unalists. **1892** 'UNITAS' *Unalism* i. 2 Christian nations and Churches generally..are Double Deists, or Ditheists, instead of being Unalists, as they ought to be.

una'live, *a.* [UN-[1] 7.] **a.** Not fully susceptible or awake *to* something.
1828 L. HUNT *Byron & Contemp.* (ed. 2) I. 377 Dry, mechanical theorists, unalive to sentiment and fancy. **1855** BAGEHOT *Lit. Stud.* (1879) I. 16 An experienced and erudite Frenchman, not unalive to artistic effect. **1893** G. ALLEN *Scallywag* III. 9 He was not unalive to the advantages of keeping up his dormant connection.
b. Lacking in vitality; not living. Also *fig.*
1905 M. DODS *Let.* 14 Apr. (1911) 176 How you can think yourself empty and unalive I don't know. **1931** H. S. WALPOLE *Judith Paris* II. v. 338 All the members of the Herries family, with whom she had so lately been, seemed unreal and unalive. **1935** E. BOWEN *House in Paris* II. x. 209 The street reflected the blind windows and a strip of unalive wet sky. **1954** R. SPEAIGHT *George Eliot* iv. 51 The true criticism of Stephen is not that he is unattractive but that he is unalive.

una'llayable, *a.* (UN-[1] 7b.)
1801 SOUTHEY *Thalaba* VII. xvi, Belike he shall exchange ..its cups of joy For the unallayable bitterness of Zaccoum's fruit accurst.

una'llayed, *ppl. a.* [UN-[1] 8.] Not allayed or mixed; unmixed, unqualified.
1519 HORMAN *Vulg.* 165b, He drynketh wyne vnalayed. **1648** BOYLE *Seraph. Love* i. (1700) 2 Unallay'd satisfactions are joys too Heavenly to fall to many men's shares on Earth. **1682** NORRIS *Hierocles* 90 Yet by the conjunction of good, he ..at last enjoys pure and unallai'd pleasure with his vertue. **1796** CHARLOTTE SMITH *Marchmont* I. 46 Althea received this news with unallayed transport. **1817** COLERIDGE *Biogr. Lit.* xx. II. 114, I can bring to my recollection three persons ..who had read the poems..with more and more unallayed pleasure. **1887** BOWEN *Æneid* v. 608 Deep her mighty designs, and her ancient wrath unallayed.
b. Const. *with* or *by*.
a **1676** HALE *Prim. Orig. Man.* IV. viii. (1677) 375 By this means their enjoyments are sincere, unallayed with fears or suspitions. **1751** SMOLLETT *Per. Pic.* civ, The most elevated transports of joy, unallayed with the least mixture of grief. **1762** FALCONER *Shipwr.* II. 379 Where perils unallay'd by hope appear. **1791** ANNA SEWARD *Lett.* (1811) III. 199 A source of lasting happiness..unallayed by private or public calamity.

una'lleged, *ppl. a.* (UN-[1] 8.)
1587 GOLDING *De Mornay* xiv. (1592) 224 If I haue left any thing vnalledged which might make to this purpose,.. he which feeleth himself conuicted in himself, needeth no more diligent proofe than hath been made already.

unalle'gorical, *a.* (UN-[1] 7. Cf. G. *unallegorisch.*)
1776 MICKLE tr. *Camoens' Lusiad* Introd. 138 *note*, The unallegorical opposition or concert of Christian and Pagan ideas.

una'lleviable, *a.* (UN-[1] 7b.)
1816 SOUTHEY *Ess.* (1832) I. 241 It was vehement grief,.. unalleviated..and..unalleviable. **1887** H. DRUMMOND in G. A. Smith *Life* (1899) xi. 274 The thing that crushes is to look on silently at the unalleviable pain of those we love.

una'lleviated, *ppl. a.* (UN-[1] 8.)
1750 SECKER *Serm. 11 Mar.* (1771) 194 All Mischief of all Kinds befall us,..through the whole Course of Life, unalleviated by a Prospect of Recompense after Death. **1816** [see prec.]. **1866** J. C. COLQUHOUN *Wilberforce* 408 It is no wonder that he felt, and showed in his looks, the unalleviated strain. **1882** FARRAR *Early Chr.* I. 107 The world was settling into the sadness of unalleviated despair.

una'lliable, *a.* (UN-[1] 7b.)
1740 CHEYNE *Regimen* 37 They are not incompatible and unallyable,..but they are contrary. **1792** BURKE *Corr.* (1844) III. 394 They had long shown themselves wholly adverse to, and unalliable with, the party. **1792** —— *Let. to Langrishe* Wks. VI. 355 We look upon you..as perpetual and unalliable aliens.

una'llied, *ppl. a.* [UN-[1] 8.]
1. Not allied or related.
1663 BOYLE *Usef. Exp. Nat. Philos.* II. v. 290 The greater their experience,..the greater indisposition it would give them to credit so unallied a truth. **1697** COLLIER *Ess. Mor. Subj.* II. (1703) 85 Extension and cogitation are unallied in their ideas. **1852** M. ARNOLD *Empedocles* II. 359 Still Thought and Mind Will hurry us..Over the unallied unopening Earth. **1862** SPENCER *First Princ.* II. xiv. §113 (1875) 323 Year by year are established certain connexions among orders of phenomena that appear unallied.
b. Const. *to.*
1697 COLLIER *Ess. Mor. Subj.* I. (1709) 143 'Tis a Principle ..absolutely unallied to Reason and Good-nature. **1789** COWPER *Annus Mem.* 59 The eyes that never saw thee, shine With joy not unallied to thine. **1818** SCOTT *Br. Lamm.* xviii, She seemed to be an angel..unallied to the coarser mortals among whom she deigned to dwell for a season. **1864** CARLYLE *Fredk. Gt.* XVI. iii. IV. 280 He..regards with sublime pity, not unallied to contempt, all other diplomatic beings.
2. Having no ally or allies.
a **1797** H. WALPOLE *Geo. II* (1847) II. iv. 127 Unallied we could make no diversion to France. **1898** *Westm. Gaz.* 15 Apr. 5/3 Spain..enters upon the conflict unallied.

una'llotted, *ppl. a.* (UN-[1] 8.)
[**1775** ASH.] **1869** *Sat. Rev.* 9 Jan. 44/2 This shows how wise it is to have a spare hour or two unallotted in the scheme of days. **1883** *Law Rep. 24 Chanc. Div.* 375 As there were so many shares remaining unallotted, it shews that there were no other persons ready to take them.

una'llowable, *a.* [UN-[1] 7b.] Not allowable; inadmissible, impermissible.
1560 DAUS *Sleidane's Comm.* ij b, He neyther bringeth Scripture for hym, nor any thinge out of the auncient Doctours, but certein dreames of his owne, receiued of scoolemen by an vnallowable euill custome. **1577** tr. *Bullinger's Decades* (1592) 134 If we shall goe about to performe those..vnallowable othes, then shal we..incurre the heauie wrath of the reuenging Lorde. **1645** MILTON *Tetrach.* To Parlt. A2b, It can be no immoderate, or unallowable course of seeking so.. needfull reparations. *a* **1678** H. SCOUGAL *Disc. Imp. Subj.* (1735) 268 An unallowable patience in hearing his master dishonoured. **1726** BUTLER *Serm.* Pref., It is very unallowable for a work of imagination or entertainment not to be of easy comprehension. **1799** *Monthly Rev.* XXVIII. 526 The inferences deduced from them would still be unallowable. **1842** DE MORGAN *Diff. & Int. Calc.* 384 An infinite number of unallowable points. **1867** MACFARREN *Harmony* ii. 40 Whatever is unallowable for all the notes is, of course, forbidden for each particular one.

una'llowed, *ppl. a.* (UN-[1] 8 and 8c.)
1632 SHERWOOD, Unalowed, *desavoüé.* **1686** HORNECK *Crucif. Jesus* xiv. 322 No unallowed of miscarriages, I mean miscarriages against the settled bent and resolutions of our souls, can be said to null this covenant. **1785** *Liberal Amer.* II. 257, I saw two virtuous hearts struggling with an unallowed passion. **1842** PUSEY *Crisis Eng. Ch.* 26 There must be risk that persons will seek unity in unallowed ways of their own. **1874** —— *Lent. Serm.* 84 To use unallowed what is another's is to steal.

una'lloyed, *ppl. a.* (UN-[1] 8.)
fig. *a* **1672** STERRY *Freed. Will* (1675) 9 Being it self in its absoluteness,..unalloyed by any differences of mixtures. **1737** WEST *Let.* in *Gray's Poems* (1775) 27 Four-and-twenty hours of pure unalloy'd health together. **1796** MME. D'ARBLAY *Camilla* V. 183 A pity..unalloyed with any blame. **1860** MOTLEY *Netherl.* vi. (1868) I. 358 There is hardly a character in history upon which the imagination can dwell with more unalloyed delight. **1869** TOZER *Highl. Turkey* I. 131 The purest religious influences, unalloyed by superstition.
lit. **1760–72** H. BROOKE *Fool of Qual.* (1792) V. 216 A coffin of unalloyed and beaten silver. **1812** SIR H. DAVY *Chem. Philos.* 385 Iron..is capable of acquiring magnetism, though in its unalloyed state it retains it only a very short time.

una'llurable, *a.* (UN-[1] 7b.)
1812 *Monthly Rev.* LXVII. 296 Uniformity in religious opinion was the unallurable phœnix, for which reformation professed to spread her nets.

una'lluring, *ppl. a.* (UN-[1] 10.)
[**1775** ASH.] **1805** M. A. SHEE *Rhymes on Art* (1806) 106 *note*, Our national mode of worship;..there is a coldness about it, an unalluring formality. *c* **1855** LYTTON in *Life* (1883) I. iii. 26 Those Muses which had seemed so unalluring to her childhood took a softer aspect. **1863** —— *Caxtoniana* II. 201 They maintained the continuance after death of an unsatisfactory, unalluring state of being.

un'almsed, *a.* (UN-[1] 9.)
1827 POLLOK *Course T.* III 279 He..with a look Which hell might be ashamed of, drove the poor Away unalmsed.

un'alphabeted, *a.* [UN-[1] 9.] Not acquainted with the alphabet. Also *fig.*
1799 COLERIDGE *Lett.* (1895) 305 The inhabitants..are bigots, unalphabeted in the first feelings of liberality. **1832** —— *Ibid.* 764 An almost unalphabeted but very sensible woman.

unalpha'betic, *a.* (UN-[1] 7.)
1883 BURTON & CAMERON *Gold Coast* I. v. 127 In fact, the Guanches of Tenerife were unalphabetic.

un'altarlike, *a.* (UN-[1] 7c.)
1640 SIR E. DERING *Carmelite* (1641) 34 You may guesse how un-altar-like these Tables were.

unaltera'bility. (UN-[1] 12 and 5b.)
1847 SMEATON *Builders' Man.* 143 It is used for housepainting, less..in regard to its unalterability, than to its solubility. **1885** *Law Times* LXXVIII. 315/2 Not that there was any sanctity or unalterability inherent in the memorandum.

un'alterable, *a.* [UN-[1] 7b and 5b.] That cannot be altered or changed: **a.** In general use.
1611 FLORIO, *Inpermutabile*, vnalterable. **1656** BRAMHALL *Replication* 5 The essences of things are unalterable. **1694** F. BRAGGE *Disc. Parables* xii. 397 Whatever alteration is made in the state..of the soul..shall be from henceforth for ever unalterable. **1729** POPE *Let. to Swift* 9 Oct., The doctor is unalterable, both in friendship and quadrille. **1794** HUTTON *Philos. Light*, etc. 286 Space, which is unalterable, and in which bodies are conceived to move. **1815** J. SMITH *Panorama Sci. & Art* II. 451 Alone, it [*sc.* silex] is unalterable by the strongest heat. **1864** BOWEN *Logic* xii. 400 What is called physical necessity is nothing but a conviction that the relation of an Efficient Cause to its effect is unalterable.
b. Of resolves, decisions, laws, etc.
1631 GOUGE *God's Arrows* I. §67. 112 Vow with an unalterable resolution to performe what you vow. **1699** BURNET *39 Art.* xxxiv. 370 No rule made in such matters is to be held unalterable, but may be changed upon occasion. **1779** *Mirror* No. 67, Her resolution was taken; and she repeatedly assured me, that her motives made it unalterable. **1781** COWPER *Conversat.* 467 'Tis an unalterable fix'd decree, That none could frame or ratify but she. **1815** J. CORMACK *Abol. Fem. Infanticide Guzerat* x. 195 Not less unalterable did the Jahrejahs of Guzerat pronounce the horrid practice of infanticide. **1890** 'R. BOLDREWOOD' *Col. Reformer* (1891) 199, I do not see why it should be an unalterable law.
c. Of feelings. (Common in 18th cent.)
1716 POPE *Let. to Lady Montagu* 18 Aug., With all unalterable esteem and sincerity. **1776** MICKLE tr. *Camoens' Lusiad* Dissert. 160/1 Perceiving the unalterable hatred which the League bore to his religion. **1841** BREWSTER *Mart. Sci.* II. iii. (1856) 133 Tycho received..an assurance of his Majesty's unalterable attachment.

un'alterableness. [f. prec.: see UN-[1] 12.] The quality of being unalterable.
1620 BP. HALL *Hon. Marr. Clergy* I. xxii. 123 When he finds an vnalterablenesse in the determination of these degrees. **1649** F. ROBERTS *Clavis Bibl.* 372 The unalterablenesse of Gods work. **1699** BURNET *39 Art.* xxxiv. 372 The Second Branch of this Article is against the Unalterableness of Laws made in matters indifferent. *a* **1728** WOODWARD *Fossils* I. 186 The Unalterableness of the Corpuscles. **1817** HAZLITT *Char. Shaks.* (1838) 287 The unalterableness of his resolutions. **1850** L. HUNT *Autobiog.* III. xxv. 283 A bull declaring the unalterableness of every papal dogma. **1866** GEO. ELIOT *F. Holt* xxxiv. III. 6 Our minds get tricks and attitudes as our bodies do—and age stiffens them into unalterableness.

un'alterably, *adv.* (UN-[1] 11.)
1643 LIGHTFOOT *Glean. Ex.* (1648) 22 That must be of a Lambe or kid unalterably. **1697** COLLIER *Ess. Mor. Subj.* I. (1703) 90 It is the part of true magnanimity to adhere unalterably to a wise choice. **1725** BOLINGBROKE *Let. to Swift* 24 July, To pass an act, which fixing my fortune unalterably to this country, fixes my person here also. **1796** MME. D'ARBLAY *Camilla* I. 9 His temper was unalterably

sweet. **1830** HERSCHEL *Study Nat. Phil.* I. iii. 39 These primary qualities originally and unalterably impressed on matter. **1894** H. GARDENER *Unoff. Patriot* 56 Upon that point his mind was clearly and unalterably made up.

†**un'alterate**, *ppl. a. Sc. Obs.*$^{-1}$ [UN-^{1} 8 b.] Unaltered.

153. BELLENDEN *Benner of Pietie* 35 (Bann. MS.), Thy word eterne but end is permanent, Vnalterat but mvtabilitie.

unalte'ration. (UN-^{1} 12.)

a **1676** HALES *Prim. Orig. Man.* I. iii. (1677) 86 The supposition..of any corruptible or alterable Being, in a state of incorruption or unalteration.

un'altered, *ppl. a.* [UN-^{1} 8.] Unchanged. Of an animal: not castrated.

1551 RECORDE *Pathw. Knowl.* I. v, Then do I set one foote of the compas vnaltered in D, and stretch the other in the circular line. **1597** HOOKER *Eccl. Pol.* v. liv. §5 Neyther are ..the state and qualitie of our substance so vnaltered, but that there are in it many glorious effects proceeding from so neere copulation with deitie. **1615** CHAPMAN *Odyss.* v. 148 Affirming that th' unaltered Destinies..have decreed he shall not die. **1653** W. RAMESEY *Astrol. Restored* 226 The Government or Rule then setled shall continue firm and unaltered 57 years. **1763** SIR W. JONES *Caissa* Poems, etc. (1777) 131 In one unalter'd line they tempt the fight. **1796** MME. D'ARBLAY *Camilla* IV. 302, I should have assured you of my unaltered regard. **1855** MACAULAY *Hist. Eng.* xix. IV. 315 The valuation made in 1692 has remained unaltered down to our own time. **1882** MINCHIN *Unipl. Kinemat.* 27 The distance between them being altered or unaltered. **1946** H. A. SMITH *Rhubarb* ii. 28 An unaltered cat is by nature inclined to wildness. **1967** A. LEWIN *Unaltered Cat* II. iv. 117 Have you ever tried keeping an unaltered cat in an apartment?

un'altering, *ppl. a.* (UN-^{1} 10.)

1813 SHELLEY *Q. Mab* VII. 6 Tempered disdain in his unaltering eye, Mixed with a quiet smile, shone calmly forth. **1877** 'H. A. PAGE' *De Quincey* II. xix. 166 Unaltering friendship for him remains as his record in this particular.

un'alumed, *ppl. a.* (UN-^{1} 9.)

1811 *Self-Instructor* 536 A scabrous matter, such as unallumed cloth is.

una'malgamable, *a.* (UN-^{1} 7 b.)

1828 SOUTHEY *Lett.* (1856) IV. 86 Coarse materials predominate in the unamalgamable composition. **1865** C. J. VAUGHAN *Plain Words* vi. (1866) 106 That remote and unamalgamable thing we have always fancied to be religion.

una'malgamated, *ppl. a* (UN-^{1} 8. Cf. G. *unamalgamirt*.)

1825 *Monthly Rev.* CVI. 19 His three unamalgamated provinces. **1844** NOAD *Electricity* (ed. 2) 184 Gas from the unamalgamated part of the copper. **1855** I. TAYLOR *Restor. Belief* (1856) 42 The mass combines the two unamalgamated and adverse elements.

una'malgamating, *ppl. a.* (UN-^{1} 10.)

1820 T. L. PEACOCK *Misc.* Wks. 1875 III. 335 A heterogeneous congeries of unamalgamating manners. **1865** W. G. PALGRAVE *Arabia* II. 271 An influence hardly to be understood by our own unamalgamating Anglo-Saxon.

una'massed, *ppl. a.* (UN-^{1} 8.)

1700 S. PARKER *Six Philos. Ess.* 4 Why might it not be as well a drift or shower of Atoms yet unamass'd, disorderly dancing one amongst another, and at various distances?

una'mazed, *ppl. a.* (UN-^{1} 8.)

1598 FLORIO, *Interrito*, without feare, vnamazed. **1624** QUARLES *Job* xvii. 50 Who comprehends the Lightning, or the Thunder? Who sees, who heares them, vnamaz'd with wonder? **1667** MILTON *P.L.* IX. 552 Into the Heart of Eve his words made way, Though at the voice much marveling; at length Not unamaz'd, she thus in answer spake. **1899** *Westm. Gaz.* 28 Sept. 3/3 It is possible to be unamazed at the modesty of the man who Englished it.

unambi'guity. (UN-^{1} 12.)

1842 G. S. FABER *Prov. Lett.* (1844) II. 203 Its unambiguity is the more fully established, because the language is not that of a single individual.

unam'biguous, *a.* (UN-^{1} 7.)

1751 CHESTERF. *Lett.* xlv. (1774) II. 189 Every paragraph should be so clear, and unambiguous, that the dullest fellow in the world may not be able to mistake it. **1785** REID *Intell. Powers* II. viii. 273 Malebranche is perfectly clear and unambiguous in this matter. **1804** *Phil. Trans.* XCIV. 219 The concise and unambiguous expression of the conditions of a problem in algebraic language. **1883** in *Law Times Rep.* (1884) 26 Apr. 273/2 If..that had been intended, the Legislature would have so enacted in express and unambiguous terms.

Hence **unam'biguously** *adv.*

1790 G. WALKER *Serm.* II. xxiii. 164 The promises of the Gospel..do clearly and unambiguously confirm the hope. **1802** *Phil. Trans.* XCII. 111 The law of the series is truly and unambiguously represented. **1866** J. MARTINEAU *Ess.* I. 162 All the physical indications point unambiguously the same way.

unam'bition. [UN-^{1} 12.] Lack of ambition.

1781 EARL MALMESBURY *Diaries & Corr.* I. 487 The idea of the moderation and unambition of the French Ministry is ..solidly established. **1850** F. W. NEWMAN *Phases of Faith* 31 Now indeed they are weak: now they profess unworldliness and unambition.

unam'bitious, *a.* [UN-^{1} 7 and 5 b] Not ambitious or aspiring; devoid of ambition. **a.** Of thoughts, occupations, productions, etc.

16.. *Nobody & Someb.* in Simpson *Sch. Shaks.* (1878) I. 332 My unambitious thoughts have bin long tird With this great charge. **1656** COWLEY *Praise Pindar* iv, Whilst, alas, my tim'erous Muse Unambitious tracks pursues. **1713** *Guard.* No. 167 ¶3 Train them up in the humble unambitious Pursuits of Knowledge. **1768** BOSWELL *Corsica* Dedication p. v, Predicting greatness to those who afterwards pass their days in unambitious indolence. **1814** WORDSW. *Excurs.* v. 111 The calm delights Of unambitious piety he chose. **1862** LATHAM *Channel Isl.* III. xviii. (ed. 2) 430 The bottom of this unambitious window..is but four feet from the ground. **1887** *Spectator* 25 Mar. 421/2 He can produce an unambitious though not unsatisfying tiny cabinet picture.

b. Of persons, the mind, etc.

1621 G. SANDYS *Ovid's Met.* I. (1626) 3 Then, vnambitious Mortals knew no more, But their owne Countrie's Nature-bounded shore. **1728** YOUNG *Love Fame* II. 291 Is thy ambition sweating for a rhyme; Thou unambitious fool, at this late time? **1784** COWPER *Task* IV. 798 An unambitious mind, content In the low vale of life. **1816** BYRON *Ch. Har.* III. lxiv, Stainless victories, Won by the unambitious heart and hand Of a proud, brotherly, and civic band. **1893** LIDDON *Life Pusey* I. App. 455 That unenterprising and unambitious but useful class of the English gentry.

Hence **unam'bitiously** *adv.*, **-ness.**

1746 HERVEY *Medit.* (1818) 120 While others, free from all aspiring views, creep unambitiously on the ground, and look like the commonalty of the kind. *a* **1755** CONYBEARE (Mason), Others through unambitiousness of temper are gradually sinking. **1791** COLERIDGE *Math. Problem* iii. 10 Unambitiously join'd in equality's band. **1814** WORDSW. *Excurs.* VII. 473 That monumental stone..unambitiously relates How long..The sad privation was by him endured. **1847** LYTTON *Lucretia* 19 He felt a lively satisfaction at the thought of leaving his friend honourably, if unambitiously, provided for.

unam'brosial, *a.* (UN-^{1} 7.)

1839 J. STERLING *Ess.*, etc. (1848) I. 316 Jove, whose shake of his un-ambrosial wig once ruled the world.

un'ambush, *v.* (UN-^{2} 3.)

1650 FULLER *Pisgah* II. xii. 254 Such ambushes are now adays unambushed, by the general suspicion all have of them.

una'menability. (UN-^{1} 12.)

1865 *Cornh. Mag.* May 591 One set of features characteristic of pestilence is the suddenness of its onset; its unamenability to the resources of the healing art.

una'menable, *a.* (UN-^{1} 7 b.)

1771 E. LONG *Trial of Dog 'Porter'* in Hone *Every-day Bk.* II. 209 Laws to which he was unamenable. **1802–12** BENTHAM *Ration. Judic. Evid.* (1827) II. 599 Superior and unamenable power. **1868** VISCT. STRANGFORD *Select.* (1869) II. 251 Tibet, Afghanistan, and all Indian frontier countries are classed in the same category as unamenable to civilised laws. **1877** SIR H. TAYLOR *Autobiog.* (1885) I. 139 The good easy Chancellor of the Exchequer was overruled by the stout and unamenable Secretary.

una'mendable, *a.* (UN-^{1} 7 b.)

c **1450** HOLLAND *Howlat* 928 'My first making,' quoth scho, 'was vnamendable'. *c* **1550** CHEKE *Let.* in *Athenæum* 28 Aug. (1909) 237/2 If you think yourself unamendable. **1561** DAUS tr. *Bullinger on Apoc.* (1573) 112 His vnamendable wickednes and continuall blasphemy. **1583** GOLDING *Calvin on Deut.* i. 6 Let vs aduise our selues to make our profit therof and let vs not be vnamendable. **1646** BAILLIE *Lett. & Jrnls.* (1841) II. 378 The Independents miserable unamendable designe to keep all things from any conclusion. **1653** tr. *Carmeni's Nissena* 10 Struck with admiration to behold those..unamendable beauties. **1729** POPE *Let. to Swift* 9 Oct., [Gay] is the same man. So is every one here that you know: mankind is unamendable. **1817** BENTHAM *Parl. Reform* Introd. 174 A pure and ever unamendable despotism. **1853** WHEWELL *Grotius* II. 277 When a man who is unamendable is removed from life, that he may not commit more or greater crimes.

una'mended, *ppl. a.* (UN-^{1} 8.)

1382 WYCLIF *2 Chron.* Prol., Bot to the blame of wrijters it is to wijten, while of the vnamendid thei wrijten vnamendide thingis. **1525** LD. BERNERS *Froiss.* II. ccxxxv. [ccxxxi.] 729 This can nat longe endure vnamended. **1549** COVERDALE, etc. *Erasm. Par. 2 Cor.* 63 So wryte I..also to all such, as are offenders, yf I fynde them vnamended. **1583** GOLDING *Calvin on Deut.* iii. 681 Forasmuch as God hath called you and you continue vnamended. **1648** HEXHAM II, *Ongebetert*, Vnbettered, or Vn-amended. **1726** THEOBALD (*title*), Shakespeare restored: or, a Specimen of the Many Errors, as well Committed, as Unamended, by Mr. Pope in his Late Edition of this Poet. **1779** JOHNSON *L.P.*, *Pope* Wks. IV. 105 He never passed a fault unamended by indifference. **1853** LD. J. RUSSELL in Walpole *Life* (1889) II. 187 We surely cannot again present to him the same note unamended. **1884** *Law Times* 24 May 59/2 The present clause of the Bill, if unamended, would change that law; hence his proposal.

una'merced, *ppl. a.* (UN-^{1} 8.)

[**1775** ASH.] **1872** BROWNING *Fifine* xxxiii, Such tribute body pays to time: but, unamerced, The soul..boasts old treasure multiplied.

un-A'merican, *a.* [UN-^{1} 7.] Not in consonance with American characteristics; contrary to the ideals and interests of the United States of America.

Hence **un-Americanism.**

1818 M. BIRKBECK *Notes Amer.* 28 Ninety marble capitals have been imported at vast cost from Italy,..and shew how *un*-American is the whole plan. **1893** H. B. FULLER *Cliff-Dwellers* xviii. 242 Does it seem unreasonable that the State [*sc.* Illinois]..which has done most..to check alien excesses and un-American ideas, should also be the State to give the country the final blend of the American character and its ultimate metropolis? **1894** *Daily News* 30 Apr. 5/3 However it came about, it is un-American and should be repudiated by the people. **1902** ELIZ. BANKS *Newspaper Girl* 55 She refused on the ground that it was both unbecoming and un-American. **1917** T. ROOSEVELT *Let.* 10 Jan. in *Proc. Congr. Constructive Patriotism* 172 Everything is un-American that tends either to government by a plutocracy or government by a mob. **1921** *N.E.D.*, Un-Americanism, un-American-looking. **1936** F. R. MARVIN (*title*) Fools gold: an exposé of un-American activities and political action in the United States. **1938** *N.Y. Times* 27 May 2/2 The House ..today passed a resolution providing for the appointment of a seven-man committee to investigate un-American propaganda in the United States. **1955** C. L. SEWREY in *Comprehensive Dissert. Index* (1973) XXVIII. 116/3 The alleged 'un-Americanism' of the Church. **1958** E. H. CLEMENTS *Uncommon Cold* iii. 97 Visas aren't handed out by Americans to anyone. They are averse to Communists, criminals, all un-American activities. **1960** *Guardian* 26 Aug. 5/1 To question either now seems tantamount to un-Americanism. **1978** *Amer. Speech 1975* L. 315 The sin is neither as recent a matter of concern nor as diagnostic of un-Americanism as Dwight Bolinger implies. **1980** in S. Terkel *Amer. Dreams* 363 The Red scare was on, the witch hunt. The House Un-American Activities Committee came to town.

unamia'bility. [UN-^{1} 12.] Unamiableness.

1829 BEDDOES *Let.* in *Poems* (1851) p. lxxxvi, The ruling unamiability of the principal characters. **1866** SEELEY *Ecce Homo* 154 There is an extreme degree of unamiability which quenches this love in us. **1880** 'OUIDA' *Moths* II. iii. 55 It would be impossible to suspect the Princess of unamiability.

un'amiable, *a.* [UN-^{1} 7 b and 5 b.] Not amiable, in senses of that adj.: **a.** Of things (chiefly abstract) or acts.

c **1480** HENRYSON *Fables, Trial of Fox* xx, My mycht is.. Angrie, austerne, and als vnamiable To all that standis fray to myne estait. **1565** COOPER *Thesaurus, Inamabilis*,.. vnamiable: without grace or pleasantnesse woorthie fauour. **1603** HOLLAND *Plutarch's Mor.* 1140 If love be away,..the act thereof remaineth altogether not expetible, dishonourable, without grace and unamiable. **1708** J. PHILIPS *Cyder* I. 563 Nor are the Hills unamiable, whose Tops To Heav'n aspire. **1796** MME. D'ARBLAY *Camilla* V. 83 Extremes, nearly as pernicious, though not so unamiable as the vices. **1849** MACAULAY *Hist. Eng.* iv. I. 500 Three poor labouring men, deeply imbued with this unamiable divinity, were arrested. **1884** *St. James's Gaz.* 9 Sept. 6/1 The Greenore steamer..surmounted the unamiable waves of the Channel.

b. Of persons.

1711 ADDISON *Spect.* No. 261 ¶4 True Love has ten thousand Griefs..that render a Man unamiable in the Eyes of the Person whose Affection he sollicits. **1778** MISS BURNEY *Evelina* xl, The distaste I already felt for these unamiable sisters. **1832** LYTTON *Eugene A.* i. 4 What in the world makes a man of just pride appear so unamiable as the sense of dependence? **1884** *Spectator* 4 Oct. 1325/1 There is no more unamiable character in the whole of history than Frederick William I.

c. Of conduct, disposition, etc.

1774 MRS. DELANY in *Life & Corr.* (1862) II. 65 His conduct had been unamiable and careless. **1779** *Mirror* No. 33, A tolerable person, and I think not an unamiable temper. **1818** SCOTT *Hrt. Midl.* xlv, This unamiable..disposition of mind broke forth in sundry unfounded criticisms. **1849** MACAULAY *Hist. Eng.* iv. I. 450 His countenance and his voice must always have been unamiable. **1890** BAKER *Wild Beasts* I. 306 The difficulty was increased by the cheetah making unamiable faces as the man approached.

Hence **un'amiableness, un'amiably** *adv.*

1611 FLORIO, *Inamabilità*, *vnamiablenesse, vnlouingnesse. **1668** WILKINS *Real Char.* III. vii. §6. 341 Passive, to be done, *Unamiableness*. *a* **1797** H. WALPOLE *Mem. Geo. II* (1847) III. vi. 162 The unamiableness of the characters he blamed imprinted those dislikes. **1840** L. HUNT *Leg. Florence* I. i, He does her the honour of making her..Grateful return for his unamiableness, Love without bounds, in short, for his self-love. **1874** RUSKIN *Val D'Arno* cxxxi. (1886) 63 Pacific Florence, in her pride of victory, was beginning to show unamiableness of temper. **1849** MACAULAY *Hist. Eng.* ix. II. 423 Their national antipathies were, indeed, in that age, unreasonably and *unamiably strong.

un'amicable, *a.* (UN-^{1} 7 b and 5 b.)

1732 BERKELEY *Serm. to S.P.G.* Wks. 1871 III. 245 That narrowness of spirit which formerly kept them at such an unamicable distance from us.

un'amorous, *a.* (UN-^{1} 7.)

1668 WILKINS *Real Char.* 341 Adjective,..Active, to do, *Unamourous*. **1877** SIR H. TAYLOR *Autobiog.* (1885) I. 52 My admiration was wholly unamorous, but it was very ardent.

†**una'moved**, *ppl. a. Sc. Obs.*$^{-1}$ [UN-^{1} 8.] Unmoved.

1513 DOUGLAS *Æneid* IX. iii. 113 The hie curage and forcy hardyment Baid onamovit in Turnus stout entent.

una'musable, *a.* (UN-^{1} 7 b.)

1812 *Monthly Rev.* LXVII. 143 With the revenues of a nation at his fingers-ends, he was still unamusable. **1841** *Tait's Mag.* VIII. 620 An unamusable and capricious fashionable audience. **1865** MISS BRADDON *Sir Jasper* v, Ambitious Madame de Maintenon found it a hard thing to amuse the unamusable.

una'mused, *ppl. a.* (UN-^{1} 8.)

1742 YOUNG *Nt. Th.* II. 246 O ye Lorenzos of our age! who deem One moment unamus'd a misery Not made for feeble man! **1795** V. KNOX *Chr. Philos.* lv. 405 They fly to various scenes of public resort, in the midst of amusements, unamused. **1809** SYD. SMITH in Lady Holland *Mem.* (1855) II. 55 Instead of being unamused by trifles, I am..amused by them a great deal too much. **1890** 'R. BOLDREWOOD' *Col. Reformer* (1891) 264 He played..well enough..to enliven their somewhat unamused evenings.

una'musing, *ppl. a.* (UN-^{1} 10.)

1794 F. BURNEY *Jrnl.* 2 Mar. (1973) III. 43 He found it very unamusing to have a Walk without any *but*. **1799** *Mirror* No. 10, To a stranger it would have been not unamusing. **1812** *Q. Rev.* VII. 384 It cannot be unamusing to speculate on what Warburton would have achieved. **1893** SWINBURNE *Stud. Prose & Poetry* (1894) 74 'Wit at Several Weapons,' a violent farce, outrageous but not unamusing.

Hence **una'musingly** *adv.*

1889 SWINBURNE *Study B. Jonson* I. 76 It is neither coarse nor tedious, and takes up but very little space; and that not unamusingly.

una'musive, *a.* (UN-[1] 7.)

1755 SHENSTONE *Lett.* lxxxiii. Wks. 1777 III. 254, I have passed a very dull and unamusive winter.

unanacre'ontic, *a.* (UN-[1] 7.)

1809 MALKIN *Gil Blas* VIII. ix. ¶13, An ode of Anacreon, translated into most un-anacreontic Spanish verse.

†**una'nalied**, *ppl. a. Sc. Obs.*[−1] [UN-[1] 8.] Unalienated.

1508 *Reg. Privy Seal Scotl.* I. 253/1 For keping of his heretage..unsparpalit and unanalyt in favouris of his sone.

unana'logical, *a.* (UN-[1] 7.)

1755 JOHNSON, *Shine*, n.s.,..is a word, though not unanalogical, yet ungraceful, and little used.

una'nalogous, *a.* (UN-[1] 7.)

1782 ELIZ. BLOWER *Geo. Bateman* III. 83 For reasons totally unanalogous to real humanity. **1816** BENTHAM *Chrestom.* Wks. 1843 VIII. 181 An objection not unanalogous to that which is above applied to the word power. **1837** LYTTON *Athens* II. 326 A conflict between the negroes and the planters in modern times, may not be unanalogous to that of the helots and the Spartans.

un'ana,lysable, *a.* (UN-[1] 7b.) Hence **un,analysa'bility**.

1829 JAS. MILL *Hum. Mind* (1869) II. 146 We have an indivisible, unanalysable, mode of consciousness, distinct from all modes of passive sensation. **1882** SEELEY *Nat. Relig.* 47 Witness the instinctive, as we say, and unanalysable skill sometimes possessed by savages. **1941** *Mind* I. 335 The sort of unanalysability which the P[ure] E[go] theory attributes to class (1) 'someone' sentences. **1973** E. JONG *Fear of Flying* i. 3 There were 117 psychoanalysts on the Pan Am flight to Vienna and I'd been treated by at least six of them... God knows it was a tribute either to the shrinks' ineptitude or my own glorious unanalyzability that I was now..more scared of flying than when I began my analytic adventures some thirteen years earlier.

un'analysed, *ppl. a.* (UN-[1] 8.)

1668 BOYLE *Phys.-Chym. Ess., Salt-Petre* §5 Some large Crystals of refin'd and unanalyz'd Nitre..appear'd to have each of them six flat sides. **1754** WARBURTON *Bolingbroke's Philos.* ii. 164 There he would stop: and leave the other side of the eternal reason, unanalyzed. **1794** HUTTON *Philos. Light*, etc. 326 To attempt to philosophise with those vulgar notions, or unanalysed ideas, leads only to the confusion of our knowledge. **1820** HAZLITT *Table-T.* Ser. II. ii. (1869) 37 This sort of unmeaning, unanalysed reputation. **1865** MRS. WHITNEY *Gayworthys* II. 116 There was a joy of claim and confidence, unanalysed, between them in that instant. **1871** R. H. HUTTON *Ess.* (1876) I. 9 Moral freedom..may be superseded..by the single unanalysed predominance of another's wish.

unana'lytic, *a.* (UN-[1] 7.)

1865 *North Brit. Rev.* XLIII. 27 Reflective Realism is only a change in the unanalytic manner of thinking about objects. **1884** BROWNING *Ferishtah, Cherries* 93 My father took The..gold, Nor cared to count what sparkled here and there, Sagely unanalytic.

unana'lytical, *a.* (UN-[1] 7.)

1840 MILL *Diss. & Disc.* (1859) I. 450 It would be difficult to find,..in the works of analytical minds, anything more entirely unanalytical. **1884** J. TAIT *Mind in Matter* IV. 128 In unanalytical ages, the knowledge of God was moral rather than intellectual.

una'natomizable, *a.* (UN-[1] 7b.)

1861 T. L. PEACOCK *Gryll Gr.* xiii, What can be more pitiable than the right-hand man..with the dish twisted round.., digging..for a joint which he cannot find, and wishing the unanatomisable *volaille* behind a Russian screen with the footmen?

un'ancestried, *a.* (UN-[1] 9b.)

1864 LOWELL *Study Wind.* (1870) 163 As God made Adam, out of the very earth, unancestried, unprivileged, unknown.

un'anchor, *v.* [UN-[2] 4b. Cf. Du. *ontankeren.*] *trans.* To loose from anchor.

1648 HEXHAM II, *Ontanckert*, un-anckred, or, the Ancker wound up. **1649** G. DANIEL *Trinarch.* To Rdr. 193 Whose Cable Pietie vn-Anchored, Yet fixt her vessell steddie, in the Bed Of many waters meeting. **1847** DE QUINCEY *Span. Mil. Nun* Wks. 1854 III. 10 Now, then, through three-fourths of an hour Kate will have free elbow-room for unanchoring her boat.

refl. and *absol.* **1878** DALLINGER in *Proc. Roy. Soc. Lond.* XXVII. 337 [It attaches] itself to one of the springing forms, which at once unanchors itself, and both together swim freely and vigorously about. [**1878** *Pop. Sci. Monthly* Aug. 511/2 It soon comes in contact with a colony of the organism in the perfectly flagellate condition, attaches itself to one of them, which soon unanchors, and both swim away.]

un'anchored, *ppl. a.* (UN-[1] 8.)

1651 DAVENANT *Gondibert* II. VII. xxxix, She dreams Her-self into possession of desires, And trusts unanchored hope in fleeting streams. **1652** BENLOWES *Theoph.* IV. xxxv, All Hope's unanchor'd but in that. **1725** POPE *Odyss.* IX. 158 A port there is, inclos'd on either side, Where ships may rest, unanchor'd and unty'd. **1876** MRS. WHITNEY *Sights & Ins.* II. xxxvii. 663, I had lived such a wandering, unanchored life. **1880** L. WALLACE *Ben-Hur* 457 Over all the clouds floated like sailed ships unanchored.

un'anchylosed, *ppl. a.* (UN-[1] 8.)

1839–47 OWEN in *Todd's Cycl. Anat.* III. 269/2 In the skull of the mature Wombat..the ex-occipitals were still unanchylosed. **1854** —— in *Orr's Circ. Sc., Org. Nat.* I. 217 Their pleurapophyses are unanchylosed.

una'neled, *ppl. a.* Forms: 7 vnnaneld, 8 unanell'd, 9 -el'd, -eled; 8 unanneald, 8–9 -ealed, 9 -eal'd, unaneal'd, -ealed. [UN-[1] 8.] Not having received extreme unction. Also *fig.*

1602 SHAKS. *Ham.* I. v. 77 Cut off euen in the Blossomes of my Sinne, Vnhouzzled, disappointed, vnnaneld. ? **1740** W. THOMPSON *Hymn to May* xxix, O may the man that shall his image scorn,.. Die unanell'd and dead, by dogs and kites be torn. **1759** STERNE *Tr. Shandy* II. x, Obadiah had led him in as he was, unwiped, unappointed, unannealed. **1816** BYRON *Siege Cor.* xxvii, Unanel'd he pass'd away,..To the last a Renegade. *a* **1851** MOIR *De Quincey's Rev.* II. viii, How awful it is for the soul of man Unanneal'd to pass away! **1897** ABP. BENSON *Cyprian* 98 The divine acceptance of the unaneled penitent.

un-'angel, *v.* (UN-[2] 6b.)

1641 'SMECTYMNUUS' *Vind. Answ.* §13. 140 Rather then you will not prove the Angell of Thyatira to be an individuall Bishop, you will *un-Angell* him.

unan'gelic, *a.* (UN-[1] 7.)

1890 S. J. DUNCAN *Soc. Depart.* 236 We,..to persuade ourselves that we had not really died and gone to heaven, took a most unangelic tiffin. **1893** W. H. HUDSON *Idle Days in Patagonia* 230 We are hardly in a position just yet to dispense with the unangelic qualities, even in this exceedingly complex state.

unan'gelical, *a.* (UN-[1] 7.)

a **1711** KEN *Edmund* Poet. Wks. 1721 II. 96 Angel he seems, but yet methinks his speech Strives something unangelical to teach.

un'angered, *ppl. a.* (UN-[1] 8.)

1813 T. BUSBY *Lucretius* II. VI. 465 Strike with consuming flame the Good, the Wise, And bring destruction from un-angered skies. **1909** *Westm. Gaz.* 31 July 13/1 Unhorrified, unangered, suave and grand [he] Looked on the Cid.

un'anglican, *a.* (UN-[1] 7.)

1842 G. S. FABER *Prov. Lett.* (1844) II. 15 Episcopal admonitions and censures..directed against their own unscriptural and unanglican speculations.

un'angry, *a.* (UN-[1] 7.)

1876 MORRIS *Sigurd* II. 159 Look down with unangry eyes on us to-day alive.

un'angular, *a.* (UN-[1] 7.)

1756 BURKE *Subl. & B.* III. xxiv, His state of mind, on feeling soft, smooth, variegated, un-angular bodies.

Unani, var. YUNANI.

unanimad'verted, *ppl. a.* (UN-[1] 8c.)

1816 KEATINGE *Trav.* I. 125 The state of..refinement of a people is to be judged of by what they applaud on a theatre, where the emotion may be gratified unanimadverted on.

un'animalized, *ppl. a.* (UN-[1] 8.)

a **1778** C. DARWIN *Acc. Retrograde Motions* (1780) 47 A great quantity of pale unanimalized urine is discharged.

†**un'animate**, *a. Obs.*[−1] [f. L. *ūnanim-is, -us* + -ATE[2].] Of one mind.

1633 COWLEY *Pyramus & Thisbe* 32 Age had cracked the wall which did them part, This the vnanimate couple soone did spye.

unanimate (juː'nænɪmeɪt), *v.* [f. as prec. + -ATE[3].] *trans.* To make of one mind; to cause to be unanimous.

1702 C. MATHER *Magn. Chr.* IV. vi. 190/1 Even such was the Friendship, that Vnanimated our Oakes and our Shepard. **1886** *Sat. Rev.* 20 Nov. 683 It has become.. necessary for the great Liberal party..to unite and unanimate itself still further by a League of its own.

†**un'animate**, *ppl. a. Obs.* [UN-[1] 8b and 5b.] = UNANIMATED *ppl. a.* 1.

1614 TOMKIS *Albumazar* II. v. (1615) Eij, I'le rather change fiue, then apparrell one: For men haue liuing soules, cloathes are vnanimate. **1652** EARL MONM. tr. *Bentivoglio's Hist. Relat.* 13 The..Mariners, who are the animated Instruments of Navigation,..yield not in number to the other unanimate necessaries.

un'animated, *ppl. a.* [UN-[1] 8. Cf. prec.]

1. Not animated or endowed with life.

1697 DRYDEN *Æneis* Ded., Ess. (ed. Ker) II. 231 Part of them kindled into life, and part a lump of unformed unanimated mud. **1799** CORRY *Sat. Lond.* (1803) 60 How infinitely superior are those animated originals of feminine perfection,..when compared with the unanimated beauties of even the Venus de Medici. **1834** W. GODWIN *Lives Necromancers* 144 The ghost of the dead man stood erect before her, trembling at the view of his own unanimated limbs.

2. Dull, inanimate; not enlivened.

1734 *Prompter* 19 Nov. 2/1 The empty, unanimated Briskness of a Fop, a Fool, or a Courtier. **1779** JOHNSON *L.P., Thomson* Wks. IV. 172 Of a dull countenance, and a gross, unanimated, uninviting appearance. **1815** SCOTT *Paul's Lett.* (1839) 193 The total absence of cattle from the fields, gives a dull and unanimated air to a French land-scape. **1816** —— *Old Mort.* xviii, A square face, and a set of stupid and unanimated features.

3. Not inspired or actuated *by* something.

1856 R. A. VAUGHAN *Mystics* (1860) I. III. iii. 70 The understanding had been over-tasked—set to work unanimated and unaided by the conscience and the heart.

†**u'nanimately**, *adv. Obs. rare.* [f. UNANIMATE *a.*] = UNANIMOUSLY *adv.*

1599 NASHE *Lenten Stuffe* 49 To the water foules vnanimately they recourse, and besought Ducke, and Drake,..of their oary assistance. **1610** MARCELLINE *Triumphs Jas. I*, 49 So that all vnanimately or with one consent, were in duty compelled to respect him.

u'nanimating, *ppl. a.* (UN-[1] 10.)

[**1775** ASH.] **1785** REID *Intell. Powers* IV. iv. 388 Whose imagination..grovels in a field of mean, unanimating, and uninteresting objects. **1790** BURKE *Fr. Rev.* Wks. V. 131 The still unanimating repose of publick prosperity.

†**unanime**, *a. Obs.* Also **unanim.** [ad. L. *ūnanim-is, -us*, f. *ūn-us* one + *animus* mind. So F., Sp., Pg., It. *unanime.*] = UNANIMOUS *a.*

Common 1610–1650, esp. with *consent.*

1610 DONNE *Pseudo-martyr* 213 For your first title.. you haue the intire and vnanime consent and concurrence of the whole Christian Church. **1635** PAGITT *Christianogr.* App. 20 First, they make a generall Confession, which they follow the Priest in: and assent in an Unanim Amen. **1656** A. WRIGHT *Five Serm.* 157 The frame and context of the place hath drawn that unanime Exposition from all.

Hence †**u'nanimely** *adv. Obs.*

1625 DONNE *Serm.* 3 Apr. 15 Those Fundamentall things, which are unanimely professed by both. **1626** —— *Serm., John xiv.* 2 (1640) 740 Where all the Fathers are unanimely and diametrally against them.

unanimism (juː'nænɪmɪz(ə)m). Also ‖**unanimisme** (ynanimism). [ad. F. *unanimisme*, f. *unanime* unanimous + *-isme* -ISM.] A French poetic movement of the early twentieth century which emphasized the submersion of the poet in the group consciousness and which was characterized by simple diction, absence of rhyme, and strongly accented rhythms.

1931 [see POPULISM b]. **1936** *Times Lit. Suppl.* 7 Mar. 197/3 But Mr. Buchanan is not indulging in the fallacies of *unanimisme*. **1959** *Oxf. Compan. French Lit.* 724/1 *Unanimisme*, a 20th-century poetic movement which owes much to the Whitmanesque doctrine of universal brotherhood as well as to more modern psycho-philosophical theories of group emotion. **1964** *Listener* 27 Aug. 315/2 This man [*sc.* Apollinaire]..under the banner of Unanimism..had loudly and proudly identified himself with everything quick and living. **1971** J. WILLETT in A. Bullock *Twentieth Century* x. 235/2 Jules Romains, whose faith in the anonymous mass..inspired his short-lived doctrine of Unanimism.

¶ **una'nism**, ‖**unanisme.**

1919 W. B. YEATS *If I were Four-&-Twenty* (1940) ii. 4 There has been a development in various forms of literature —in French 'unanisme' for instance—towards the expression..of an emotional agreement with some historical or local group. **1958** *Times Lit. Suppl.* 4 July 383/1 A study ..of unanism in the plays of Jules Romains.

unanimist (juː'nænɪmɪst), *sb.* (and *a.*) Also ‖**unanimiste** (ynanimist). [ad. F. *unanimiste*: see prec., -IST.] An adherent of unanimism. Also *attrib.* or as *adj.*

1915 A. HUXLEY *Let.* Dec. (1969) 88 This good man [*sc.* D. H. Lawrence].. proposes..to go to the deserts of Florida there..to found a sort of unanimist colony. **1918** [see SURREALIST *a.* and *sb.*]. **1929** V. PAYEN-PAYNE in M. S. McLaren *Douze Sonnets de Varlet* 9 Varlet..has been classed among the Unanimists because of his friendship with Jules Romains and Georges Duhamel. **1938** *Times Lit. Suppl.* 10 Sept. p. iii/1 From such an incident does the writer, with something like the *unanimiste* technique of Jules Romains..develop a theme of nation-wide, or even world-wide, import. **1959** *Oxf. Compan. French Lit.* 724/2 The *unanimistes* had their own, fairly recognizable, technique of versification. **1974** *Encycl. Brit. Micropædia* X. 253/1 The Unanimiste theories of prosody..resembled those of the American poet Walt Whitman.

unanimity (juːnə'nɪmɪtɪ). Also 5 -te, 6 -tee, 6–7 -tie. [ad. OF. *unanimite* (14th c.; F. *unanimité*, = It. *unanimità*, Sp. *-idad*, Pg. *-idade*), ad. L. *ūnanimitās* (rare), f. *ūnanimis, -us*: see UNANIME *a.*] The state of being unanimous or of one mind; agreement in opinion.

1436 *Libel Eng. Policy* in *Pol. Poems* (Rolls) II. 201 Set many wittes wythoutene variaunce To one accorde and unanimite. **1579** FULKE *Heskins' Parl.* 478 Our Lords sacrifices doe declare the Christian vnanimitie, which is knitted vnto him with an insuperable vnitie. **1581** LAMBARDE *Eiren.* I. ii. (1588) 8 To reduce the people to an uniuersall unanimitie (or agreement of minds). **1603** B. JONSON *K. Jas.'s Entertainm.* Wks. (1616) 847 Her selfe personating the vnanimity, or consent of soule, in all inhabitants of the city to his seruice. **1680** C. NESSE *Church-Hist.* 425 Christian Princes..might have by their unanimity and united armies given a stop to..this severe scourge. **1762** in *10th Rep. Hist. MSS. Comm.* App. I. 345 May it produce Peace abroad, and cheerful unanimity at home. **1781** JOHNSON *Let. to Mrs. Thrale* 14 Nov., I..love them because they love each other. Of this consanguineous unanimity I have had never much experience. **1822** BYRON *Juan* VII. li, A general council, in which unanimity, That stranger to most councils, here prevail'd. **1859** MILL *Liberty* ii. (1865) 28/1 Persons..who form an exception to the apparent unanimity of the world on any subject. **1897** GLADSTONE *E. Crisis* 16 Parliament, upon that question, would speak with unanimity.

b. Const. *of.*

1712 STEELE *Spect.* No. 280 ¶2 A certain Unanimity of Taste and Judgment. **1815** *Ann. Reg., Gen. Hist.* 65 The acceptance of the new act by nearly a unanimity of votes. **1839** JAMES *Louis XIV*, II. 291 This unanimity of object seems to me to have given ultimate predominance to the royal party. **1869** FARRAR *Fam. Speech* iii. (1873) 106 Animated by a sublime unanimity of purpose.

unanimous (juːˈnænɪməs), *a.* [f. L. *ūnanim-is, -us*: see UNANIME *a.*]

1. Of persons: Of one mind or opinion; agreed. **1624** DONNE *Serm.* Wks. 1839 IV. 585 Be the fathers as clear, and as unanimous as they will in it. **1637** R. HUMFREY tr. *St. Ambrose* I. 70 Let not thine unanimous friend nor thy brother know what thou dost. **1697** ADDISON *Ess. Georgics* ¶1 All are Unanimous in giving him the Precedence to Hesiod in his Georgics. **1744** HARRIS *Three Treat.* Wks. (1841) 43 You cannot forget (for we were both unanimous) the contempt in which we held those superficial censurers. **1783** W. THOMSON *Watson's Philip III*, VI. 475 The council was unanimous that he ought immediately to be recalled. **1849** MACAULAY *Hist. Eng.* vi. II. 146 The English Roman Catholics..were almost unanimous in favour of the Act of Settlement. **1873** HAMERTON *Intell. Life* x. v. 388 Physicians are unanimous in their preference of early to late work.

2. Of beliefs, statements, actions, etc.: Exhibiting general agreement or consent. **1675** tr. *Camden's Hist. Eliz.* III. 402 The universall and unanimous Belief of all men carried it for certain Truth, that a most invincible Armada was rigged and prepared in Spain against England. **1691** WOOD *Ath. Oxon* II. 685 Dr. Atkins was nominated by the unanimous Votes of the said Presbytery. *a* **1727** NEWTON *Chronol. Amended* vi. (1728) 352 By the unanimous consent of all Chronologers. **1772** BURKE *Corr.* (1844) I. 363 Without their own vigorous and unanimous efforts in their own cause, our endeavours will be of no service. **1856** FROUDE *Hist. Eng.* (1858) II. vii. 22 The nation seemed to unite in an unanimous declaration of freedom. **1875** JOWETT *Plato* (ed. 2) V. 3 The genuineness of the Laws is sufficiently proved..by the unanimous voice of later antiquity.

uˈnanimously, *adv.* [f. prec. + -LY².] In a unanimous manner.

†**1.** In unanimity or harmony. *Obs.* *a* **1619** FOTHERBY *Atheom.* I. v. §2 (1622) 31 'Religion [is] the foundation of euery Citie,' both gathering men, and holding them vnanimously together. **1633** BP. HALL *Hard Texts, Ps.* cxxii. 3 Jerusalem is stately built,..And is strongly, and unanimously compacted together. **1648** STANLEY *Aurora* 44 Pausanias and Aurora living and loving so unanimously that every day seemed the first of their marriage.

2. With unanimity; with agreement in aim, opinion, or action. **1611** SPEED *Hist. Gt. Brit.* IX. viii. §5. 485/1 Him they had all..vnanimiously [*sic*] Elected. **1631** *Star Chamb. Cases* (Camden) 64 It was unanimously declared by the whole Court that his Majestie proceeded herein legally and rightfully for the benefit of his crowne and people. **1737** WATERLAND *Eucharist* 2 It is of great Moment..to observe what they unanimously agreed in. **1794** R. J. SULIVAN *View Nat.* xliv. II. 272 The collecting of the Sacred Writings is unanimously ascribed by both Jews and Christians to Ezra. **1826** F. REYNOLDS *Life & Times* II. 165 Being unanimously elected, I immediately assumed..the uniform of the club. **1855** MACAULAY *Hist. Eng.* xi. III. 40 An address was unanimously voted requesting the King to take effectual steps for the suppression of the rebellion. **1884** A. R. PENNINGTON *Wiclif* ix. 289 They had unanimously resolved that they [*sc.* books] should be committed to the flames.

†**3.** In combination; conjointly. *Obs.* **1655** MRQ. WORCESTER *Cent. Inv.* §16 A Sea-castle or Fortification..to divide it self into three Ships... And even whilest it is a Fort or Castle they shall be unanimously steered. *Ibid.* §98.

uˈnanimousness. [f. as prec. + -NESS.] The quality or fact of being unanimous. [**1775** ASH.] **1828–32** WEBSTER s.v., The unanimousness of a vote.

†**uˈnanimy**, *v.* *Obs.*⁻¹ [f. L. *ūnanim-is*: see UNANIME *a.*] *trans.* To combine harmoniously. **1602** WARNER *Alb. Eng.* XI. lxvii. 285 With Marriage, that preferreth vs, and stayes vs in content, Vnanimieth weale or woe, as either vs is sent.

unaˈnnealed, *a.* [UN-¹ 8.] Untempered. **1745** *Phil. Trans.* XLIII. 505 Some Experiments lately made..upon the Fragility of unannealed glass Vessels. **1753** *Chambers' Cycl.* Suppl. s.v., Unannealed Bottles, or Bologna Bottles. *a* **1853** PEREIRA *Polarized Light* (1854) 149 The dissected unannealed glasses, sold in the opticians' shops. **1869** SIR E. REED *Shipbuild.* xvi. 312 We find that the drilled unannealed plates gave an average of 41·075 tons per square inch. *fig.* **1855** BREWSTER *Newton* II. xvii. 134 The stability of a mind unannealed by the world.

unannealed, variant of UNANELED *ppl. a.*

unaˈnnexed, *ppl. a.* (UN-¹ 8.) [**1775** ASH.] **1867** BURTON *Hist. Scot.* i. I. 44 The unannexed districts of the British Isles. **1884** *Pall Mall G.* 11 Oct. 1/1 The internationalization of all the unannexed lands of the world.

unaˈnnihilable, *a.* (UN-¹ 7 b.) **1678** CUDWORTH *Intell. Syst.* I. iv. §36.559 They were not only Eternal Emanations..but also necessary, and therefore are they both also absolutely undestroyable, and unannihilable.

unaˈnnihilate, *ppl. a.* (UN-¹ 8 b.) **1804** BLAKE *Milton* Poet. Wks. (1913) 372 Lest the Last Judgement come and find me unannihilate.

unaˈnnihilated, *ppl. a.* (UN-¹ 8.) [**1775** ASH.] **1797** *Monthly Rev.* XXIII. 569 A portion even of the interest of the unannihilated debt is now discharged in specie.

unˈannotated, *ppl. a.* (UN-¹ 8.) **1859** G. WILSON *Mem. E. Forbes* v. (1861) 153 It is partly a Commonplace Book for unannotated extracts, partly a record of original observations. **1884** *Athenæum* 8 Mar. 310/3 An unannotated edition of the 'Poetical Works of Keats'.

unaˈnnounced, *ppl. a.* (UN-¹ 8.) [**1775** ASH.] **1825** SCOTT *Talism.* xviii, Behind him glided as a spectre, unannounced, yet unopposed, the savage form of the hermit of Engaddi. **1891** HARDY *Tess* liii, Her letter made him ask himself if it would be wise to confront her unannounced in the presence of her parents.

unaˈnnoyed, *ppl. a.* (UN-¹ 8.) *a* **1470** HARDING *Chron.* CIV. vii, To the sea they went agayne vnanoyed. **1791** COWPER *Iliad* XIV. 487 The double guard preserv'd him unannoy'd. **1865** W. G. PALGRAVE *Arabia* II. 224 Next morning we took a small boat, and unannoyed this time by the custom-house officers..we crossed over to Moharrek.

unaˈnnulled, *ppl. a.* (UN-¹ 8.) **1579** *Reg. Privy Council Scot.* III. 239 In respect of the said marriage standing unannullit. **1832** SOUTHEY *Hist. Penins. War* III. 63 For sanctioned it was by being allowed to appear in the Regency's Gazette unannulled and uncensured.

unaˈnointed, *ppl. a.* (UN-¹ 8.) **1649** LOVELACE *Lucasta* Poems (1904) 82 Sweeter and sweeter whisleth He To un-anointed Axel-tree. **1726** BAILEY (ed. 3), *Unannealed*, unanointed, *i.e.* without extreme Unction. **1846** R. FORD *Gatherings fr. Spain* (1906) 304 In order to ensure success, no step in the official ladder must be left unanointed. **1885** *Harper's Mag.* Dec. 90/1 The wind..waltzing about with screaming and creaking an unanointed weather-cock.

unˌansweraˈbility. (UN-¹ 12.) *a* **1849** POE *Marginalia* cii, The beauty of these *exposés* must lie in the precision and unanswerability with which they are given.

unˈanswerable, *a.* [UN-¹ 7 b.]

†**1.** Wanting in correspondence or agreement; discrepant, dissimilar. *Obs.* **1611** FLORIO, *Inrispondéuole*, vnanswerable. **1665** SIR T. HERBERT *Trav.* (1677) 86 His good will was much, but the success unanswerable. **1674** N. FAIRFAX *Bulk & Selv.* 133 Another man..may make over the beginnings of manliness.., with a liveliness no ways unanswerable.

†**b.** Const. *to.* Also quasi-*adv.* *Obs.* (*a*) **1614** W. B. *Philosopher's Banquet* (ed. 2) 244 A man of so large a stature and bodie,..a woman so small and vnanswereable therevnto. **1616** J. HAYWARD *Sanct. Troub. Soul* I. xv. (1620) 325, I yeeld thee praises (O Lord) although base and bare, and farre vnanswerable to thy deserts. **1660** *Seas. Exhort.* 13 Our barrenness and unanswerable walking to the Gospel of Christ. (*b*) **1657** AUSTEN *Fruit Trees* II. 93 When the enemies of God see professours..behave themselves unanswerable to their profession, these things reflect even upon God. **1670** *Devout Commun.* (1688) 175, I have walked..unanswerable to those multiplied obligations laid upon me.

2. That cannot be answered; not admitting of an answer. **1613** PURCHAS *Pilgrimage* IX. xv. 747 A Bishop in America hath written a large and vnanswerable Treatise of the..vnchristian Antichristian proceedings in the new World. **1690** C. NESSE *O. & N. Test.* I. 29 The unanswerable argument of [*i.e.* for] his knowledge and wisdom. **1709** BERKELEY *Th. Vision* §1 A new and unanswerable proof of the Existence and immediate Operation of God. **1796** MME. D'ARBLAY *Camilla* VIII. x. IV. 379 Edgar sighed, but acknowledged this question to be unanswerable. **1814** BYRON *Corsair* II. xv, Oh! too convincing—dangerously dear —In woman's eye the unanswerable tear! **1852** MRS. STOWE *Uncle Tom's C.* xxviii, A solving of all moral problems by an unanswerable wisdom! **1894** MRS. DYAN *Man's Keeping* (1899) 271 She never plied him with embarrassing, unanswerable questions.

3. Unable to answer; irresponsible. **1884** *Manch. Exam.* 21 July 4 He committed the offence..whilst suffering from a fit, and unanswerable for his acts.

unˈanswerableness. [UN-¹ 12.]

†**1.** The character of not answering or being responsive. Also const. *to.* *Obs.* **1625** BP. HALL *Serm. Thanksgiving* (1626) 21 How can we but hate this vnkind, and vnjust, vnanswerablenesse. *a* **1656** —— *Rem. Wks.* (1660) 26 Being conscious..of my unanswerableness to so great expectation. **1677** GILPIN *Demonol.* (1867) 315 The greatness of the disappointment under special service, the unworthy neglect and unanswerableness to special favours, are extraordinary provocations.

2. The condition of not admitting of an answer. **1627** PERROT *Tithes* Ep. Ded. A ij b, That great opinion that most men have of the unanswerablenes of Mr. Seldens History of Tithes. *a* **1631** DONNE *Serm., Ps. lxxxix. 47* (1640) 267 We shall first, for our generall humiliation, consider the unanswerablenesse of this question, There is no man that lives, and shall not see death. **1817** SHELLEY *Rev. Islam* Preface *note*, A commentary illustrative of the unanswerableness of 'Political Justice'. **1879** MINTO *Defoe* 33 He proved with provoking unanswerableness that all honest Dissenters were noways concerned in the Bill.

unˈanswerably, *adv.* [UN-¹ 11.]

1. In a manner not capable of being answered or refuted; irrefutably. **1584** FENNER *Def. Ministers* (1587) 107 But vnto this we haue answered unanswerably. **1624** GATAKER *Transubst.* 68 So plainely and unanswerably doe they teach the literal understanding of our Saviours words. **1679** MARG. MASON *Tickler Tickled* 6 This was certainly and unanswerably a knowledge sufficient of the persons. **1710** STEELE *Tatler* No. 195 ¶6, I have unanswerably proved, that Jointures and Settlements are the Bane of Happiness. **1782** MME. D'ARBLAY *Let.* May, All you say about the annuity and the money appears to me unanswerably right. **1802** SYD. SMITH *Wks.* (1859) I. 14/2 Errors that have been so frequently, and so unanswerably exposed. **1884** LD. COLERIDGE in *Law Times Rep.* 2 Aug. 694/2 The judgment..interprets the statute quite rightly and unanswerably.

2. Unconformably, unsuitably. **1656** BAXTER *Reformed Pastor* (1862) 209[To] deliver the message of God so..unanswerably to its dignity, and the need of men's souls.

unˈanswered, *ppl. a.* (UN-¹ 8.) **1390** GOWER *Conf.* I. 250 Bot for nothing that evere he can He mihte as thanne noght ben herd, So that his cleym is unansuerd. **1464** *Cov. Leet Bk.* 323 That hit were doughtfull sich suggestion to remayn vnanswered. **1532** MORE *Confut. Tindale* III. 281 Tyndale wolde haue sayed I hadde dissymyled, and lefte vnanswered his chyefe reason of all. **1585** T. WASHINGTON tr. *Nicholay's Voy.* I. xix. 22 [They began] to shoote at the castle with great furie, which was not leaft vnanswered. **1611** SHAKS. *Wint. T.* v. i. 229 Your Petition Is yet vn-answer'd. **1653** W. RAMESEY *Astrol. Restored* 37 The Art remains still unshaken, and it [= a book] unanswered. **1738** WESLEY *Ps.* VI. iv, Weary of my unanswered Groans, Yet still with never-ceasing Moans I languish for Relief. **1796** MME. D'ARBLAY *Camilla* II. xi, His unanswered observations contributed but little to enliven the walk. **1843** MRS. CARLYLE *Lett.* (1883) I. 276 She has left my last letter unanswered. **1901** *Spectator* 20 July 92/2 The arguments so ably re-stated..are not only unanswered but unanswerable.

unˈanswering, *ppl. a.* (UN-¹ 10.) **1624** SANDERSON *Serm.* I. 226 Many of the creatures being now rebellious and noysom unto man, and unanswering his commands and expectations. **1861** SIR T. MARTIN *Catullus, To Calvus* 4 When..friendship weeps, and clasps the unanswering urn.

unantagoˈnistic, *a.* (UN-¹ 7.) **1858** STOPFORD BROOKE in Jacks *Life & Lett.* (1917) I. 110 They are on the whole such lifeless, unantagonistic creatures.

unanˈtagonized, *ppl. a.* (UN-¹ 8.) **1862** SPENCER *First Princ.* (1870) 246 An unantagonized force in one direction. **1899** *Allbutt's Syst. Med.* VII. 376 The occurrence of rigidity..is due to the 'unantagonised' or 'unrestrained' influence exerted by the cerebellum.

unanˈticipated, *ppl. a.* (UN-¹ 8.) *a* **1779** WARBURTON *Div. Legat.* v. App., Wks. 1788 III. 183 This possibly might have recurred to his Lordship, while he was boasting of his new and unanticipated objection. **1827** FARADAY *Chem. Manip.* xxiii. 565 Those who have suddenly had occasion to collect gas from natural or unanticipated sources. **1891** MEREDITH *One of our Conq.* xxv, They left hurriedly; I think it was unanticipated by Nesta.

unanˈticipatingly, *adv.* (UN-¹ 11.) **1891** MEREDITH *One of our Conq.* xxvii, She had come unanticipatingly, without design, except perhaps to get a superior being to..restrain a gambler's hand.

unanˈticipative, *a.* (UN-¹ 7.) **1847** H. MILLER *First Impr. Eng.* xvii. (1857) 309 They perished ignorant of the past, and unanticipative of the future. **1891** V. C. COTES *2 Girls on Barge* 6 He stood with unanticipative resignation, this old carpenter.

unˈantiquated, *ppl. a.* (UN-¹ 8.) **1859** RUSKIN in *R. & Rossetti* (1899) 230, I plead with you for entire clearness of modern and unantiquated expression.

unˈanxious, *a.* (UN-¹ 7.) **1742** YOUNG *Nt. Th.* I. 414 When young, indeed, In full content, we sometimes nobly rest, Unanxious for ourselves. *a* **1774** TUCKER *Lt. Nat.* (1834) II. 642 To keep the mind..unanxious for success in her eagerest pursuits. **1844** THACKERAY *B. Lyndon* vi, I am not unanxious to experience on myself the effect of the war passion. **1870** W. R. GREG *Polit. Problems* 161 The career of these classes, instead of being easier and more unanxious than it was,..has become ..a ceaseless struggle.

Hence **unˈanxiously** *adv.* **1762** *J. Philips' Poems, Life* 10 This gentleman..sat as unanxiously easy as he did, even in a much humbler fortune. **1861** WISEMAN *Lenten Past.* in *Times* 12 Feb. 5/6 We can safely and unanxiously commit to..our devoted clergy the task [etc.]. **1885** FINLAYSON *Biol. Relig.* 52 He ought to do all these things unanxiously.

unaˈpocryphal, *a.* (UN-¹ 7.) **1644** MILTON *Areop.* (Arb.) 43 Yet God in that unapocryphall vision, said..Rise Peter, kill and eat.

unapoloˈgetic, *a.* (UN-¹ 7. Cf. G. *unapologetisch.*) **1834** LYTTON *Pompeii* II. iv, With that sort of quiet and unapologetic air, which seemed to consider the right as a thing of course. **1868** W. R. GREG *Lit. & Soc. Judgm.* 203 The unapologetic and as it were physiological coolness of his analysis. **1892** SWINBURNE *Stud. Prose & Poetry* (1894) 236 The humorous little word of unapologetic apology.

unaˈpostatized, *ppl. a.* (UN-¹ 8.) **1684** H. MORE *Answer* 77 The Vision..prefigures the purity and unapostatized state of the primitive Church. *Ibid.* 367 Characterizing the true Church and unapostatized Evangelical Christians.

unaˈpostatizedness. (UN-¹ 12.) **1684** H. MORE *Answer* 411 The Purity and Unapostatizedness of the Primitive Church.

unapoˈstolic, *a.* (UN-¹ 7. Cf. G. *unapostolisch.*) **1675** [BP. CROFT] *Naked Truth* 25, I know full well this unapostolick way of Preaching was used by some of the Ancient Fathers. **1850** F. W. NEWMAN *Phases of Faith* 14

My repugnance to Infant Baptism was really intense, and my conviction that it is unapostolic as strong then as now. **1876** RUSKIN *Fors Clav.* lxv. 160, I can't think whom the unapostolic William was named after.

unapo'stolical, *a.* (UN-^{1} 7.)
1837 SYD. SMITH *Let. to Singleton* Wks. 1859 II. 158/2 An opulence which my clever friend the Examiner would pronounce to be unapostolical.

unapo'stolically, *adv.* (UN-^{1} 11.)
1868 J. A. WYLIE *Road to Rome* xi. 142 They died, and were succeeded by others unapostolically ordained. **1884** W. S. LILLY *Anc. Relig. & Mod. Th.* 64 [Evangelicalism] had ended unapostolically in the preaching of foolishness.

†**una'ppair,** *v. Obs.*$^{-1}$ [UN-^{1} 15.] *intr.* To become impaired, to fade.
1426 LYDG. *De Guil. Pilgr.* 19210 Lyche a ffloure that dothe vnapayre Whanne it is plukkyd and leyde lowe.

†**una'ppairable,** *a. Obs.*$^{-1}$ [UN-^{1} 7b.] Incapable of being impaired; unfading.
1574 tr. *Marlorat's Apocalips* 300 It signifieth y^t the blissed sort are crowned with an vnappairable & flaming crowne of euerlasting life.

†**una'ppaired,** *ppl. a. Obs.* [UN-^{1} 8.] Unimpaired.
1561 T. NORTON *Calvin's Inst.* IV. 161 Y^t euery man may kepe his own safe & vnappeired. **1571** GOLDING *Calvin on Ps.* ii. 4 His power..contineweth sauf and unappayred, whatsoever men doo practise against it. **1587** —— *De Mornay* xiv. 199 Ye shall see a man forgoe all his sences.. and yet haue both life and reason vnappayred.

una'ppalled, *ppl. a.* (UN-^{1} 8.)
1578 BANISTER *Hist. Man* VII. 89 Others, with senses vnappalled,..haue plowed a path directly over the mountaine. **1586** T. B. *La Primaud. Fr. Acad.* (1589) 282 Sustaining also with a great and unappalled hart, most cruel torments. **1611** SPEED *Hist. Gt. Brit.* IX. vii. §68 Applying vnto him certaine verses of Lucan, in commendation of his vnapalled constancy. **1671** MILTON *P.R.* IV. 425 Some bent at thee thir fiery darts, while thou Sat'st unappall'd in calm and sinless peace. **1713** YOUNG *Last Day* III. 168 The sons of light scarce unappal'd look down. *a* **1774** TUCKER *Lt. Nat.* (1834) II. 229 Unhurt by toils and labours, unappalled by dangers. **1821** SCOTT *Pirate* xxxvii, The unappalled, dignified, and commanding manner of Minna Troil overawed him. **1851** LONGF. *Gold. Leg.* I. *Castle of Vautsberg,* Unappalled By fear of death, or priestly word.

†**una'pparel,** *v. Obs.* [UN-^{2} 4.] *trans.* To disrobe, undress. Also *fig.*
1577 HANMER *Anc. Eccl. Hist.* (1663) 65 The fiery pile being prepared, he unapparelled himself. **1586** J. MUSH *Life Margt. Clitherow* (1849) 194 She requested them that the women might unapparel her. **1602** MIDDLETON *Blurt Master Constable* II. ii. D ij, Ladies vnapparell your deare beauties. **1614** DONNE *Obsequies Ld. Harrington* 12 That I can studie thee, And, by these meditations refin'd, Can unapparell and enlarge my minde.

una'pparelled, *ppl. a.* (UN-^{1} 8.)
1622 BACON *Holy War* (1629) 103 In Peru, though they were unapparelled People, according to the Clime [etc.]. **1624** QUARLES *Job* Sect. xv. M j b, If e're (alone) my lips did taste my bread,..Or bent my hand to doe the Orphane wrong, Or saw him naked, vnapparell'd long. **1656** HEYLIN *Surv. France* 118 Most immodestly unapparelled. **1872** CALVERLEY *Fly Leaves* (1903) 93 All unapparell'd, barefoot all, She ran to that old ruin'd wall.

una'pparent, *a.* (UN-^{1} 7.)
1554 KNOX *Faythfull Admon.* F8b, To..obeye that whych God commaundeth be it neuer so harde, so vnapparent or contrarie to their affeccions. **1614** LATHAM *Falconry* (1633) 102 For the liuer or the disease thereof, is so secret and vnapparant, that..it is neuer mistrusted nor thought of. **1645** MILTON *Tetrach.* Wks. 1851 IV. 193 Bitter actions of despight too suttle and too unapparent for Law to deal with. **1667** —— *P.L.* VII. 103 He heares..the rising Birth Of Nature from the unapparent Deep. **1725** POPE *Odyss.* II. 152 On foreign shores Ulysses treads, Or glides a ghost with unapparent shades. **1755** YOUNG *Centaur* i. Wks. 1757 IV. 129 A fire elemental is diffused through all nature, though..unapparent in most parts of our globe. **1816** SHELLEY *Dæmon* I. 42 The dark blue orbs that burn below With unapparent fire. **1890** HOSMER *Anglo-Sax. Freedom* 129 Nowhere, probably, was the popular moot utterly unapparent.
absol. **1821** SHELLEY *Adonais* xlv, The inheritors of unfulfilled renown Rose from their thrones, built beyond mortal thought, Far in the Unapparent.
Hence **una'pparently** *adv.*
1599 SANDYS *Europæ Spec.* (1632) 94 To avoid the contagion of the disease or seducement by the dangerously and unapparently diseased.

†**una'ppassionate,** *a.* (UN-^{1} 7), **-ately** *adv.* (UN-^{1} 11.)
1598 YONG *Diana* 53 If Paris had iudged like a prudent and vnappassionate iudge. *Ibid.* 148 But thinking of the matter vnappassionately, it was now better for me.

una'ppealable, *a.* [UN-^{1} 7b.] That cannot be appealed against (or *from*).
1635 J. HAYWARD tr. *Biondi's Banish'd Virg.* 30 An unappealable sentence of death. **1642** *Vind. King* 15 The sole unappealable Judge of all things. **1678** CUDWORTH *Intell. Syst.* I. v. 898 There being no ultimate judgment unappealable from, there could never be any final determination of controversies. **1747** CARTE *Hist. Eng.* I. 259 The Bishops..maintaining their just and unappealable authority. **1786** SEWARD *Lett.* (1811) I. 229 A man of ability, with an air of unappealable decision, perpetually pronouncing in modern poets that to be obscure, which is clear as day-light. **1860** LD. LYTTON *Lucile* II. iv. §1. 11 Muse or Spirit, that inspirest..the deep drama of man!.. First and last unappealable arbitress, thou! **1874** GLADSTONE *Rome* etc., *Vatican Decrees* 38 The judgments of this Pope..are unappealable and irreversible.
Hence **una'ppealableness, -ably** *adv.*
1651 DURHAM *Maran-atha* (1652) 23 The unappealablenesse from this judgement. **1840** DE QUINCEY *Mod. Superstit.* Wks. 1854 III. 314 The *victa causa*..stood, as regarded heavenly verdicts, unappealably condemned.

una'ppealing, *ppl. a.* (UN-^{1} 10.)
1846 WORCESTER (citing South). **1856** RUSKIN *Mod. Paint.* IV. v. xviii. §9 Without some correlative understanding in the spectator, Titian's work..must be utterly dead and unappealing to him. **1865** C. STANFORD *Symb. Christ* vii. (1878) 190 Hidden meanings sparkle out from lines in his Bible that before seemed blank and unappealing.

†**una'ppearing,** *ppl. a. Obs.* [UN-^{1} 10.] Unapparent.
1554 KNOX *Faythf. Admon.* H7b, God hath a thousand meanes (very unapperyng to mannes iudgement) wherby he wyll delyuer..his afflicted churche. **1638** MAYNE *Lucian* (1664) 388, I plainly see the Images of all things, you unappearing; my self elsewhere. **1640** FULLER *Joseph's Coat* I. (1867) 108 Their knowledge..[being] increased insensibly and by unappearing degrees.

una'ppeasable, *a.* [UN-^{1} 7b.] That cannot be appeased or placated; implacable, insatiable:
a. Of feelings, activities, etc.
1561 T. NORTON *Calvin's Inst.* II. vii. (1634) 158 They presse us, I say, and doe pursue us with an unappeasable rigour. **1571** GOLDING *Calvin on Ps.* xxxiv. 1 He..burned against him with unappeasable hatred. **1581** J. BELL *Haddon's Answ. Osor.* 407 Such unappeasable contention and brawlyng about the mainteynaunce of Purgatory. **1602** WARNER *Alb. Eng.* Epit. 360 They pursued such vnapeasable and tyrannous warre that [etc.]. **1671** MILTON *Samson* 963 Thy anger, unappeasable, still rages, Eternal tempest never to be calm'd. **1779** JOHNSON *L.P., Addison* ¶37 The author..wandered..behind the scenes with restless and unappeasable solicitude. **1822** LAMB *Elia* I. *Artif. Comedy,* The eternal tormenting unappeasable vigilance..of present fashionable tragedy. **1845** HAMILTON *Pop. Educ.* ix. (ed. 2) 256 The ambition of the Papal See is unappeasable. **1870** LOWELL *Among my Bks.* Ser. I. (1873) 292 The unappeasable apprehension of a German for his biographer.
b. Of persons (or other agents).
1577 tr. *Bullinger's Decades* (1592) 574 There is no faith in a hard, stubborne, and vnappeasable man. **1578** *Chr. Prayers* in *Priv. Prayers* (1851) 543 Set thyself in our defence against this our unappeasable adversary. **1611** SPEED *Hist. Gt. Brit.* IX. xx. 31 The turbulent, and vnappeaceable Dutchesse of Burgundy. **1632** LITHGOW *Trav.* I. 26 [They are] so vnappeasable in anger, that they cowardly murther their enemies. *a* **1711** KEN *Hymns Festiv.* Poet. Wks. 1721 I. 234 With envious Rage I saw them swell, All unappeasable as Hell. **1839** DICKENS *Nickleby* xliii, A real live furious and most unappeasable Saracen. **1872** M. COLLINS *Two Plunges for Pearl* I. ix. 183 One makes it a vast machine, moving blindly in an unalterable groove, driven by an unappeasable fate.
Hence **una'ppeasableness, -ably** *adv.*
1611 FLORIO, *Implacabilita,* vnappeasablenesse. [Also in Bailey and Ash.] **1647** HEXHAM I, Vnappeasably, *onversoenelicken.* **1837** LYTTON *Athens* II. 310 Those twin rocks..between which the sea..roars unappeasably through its mists of foam. **1865** CARLYLE *Fredk. Gt.* XXI. v. (1872) X. 63 He grieves unappeasably to have lost Friedrich. **1871** LOWELL *Stud. Wind.* (1886) 129 He is pertinaciously and unappeasably dull.

una'ppeased, *ppl. a.* (UN-^{1} 8.)
1588 SHAKS. *Tit. A.* I. i. 100 Giue vs the proudest prisoner of the Gothes, That we may..sacrifice his flesh:..That so the shadowes be not vnappeas'd. **1597** HOOKER *Eccl. Pol.* v. xlviii. §9 Gods heauie indignation and wrath towards mankinde as yet vnappeased. *a* **1637** B. JONSON *Horace's Art Poet.* 172 If againe Honour'd Achilles' chance by thee be seiz'd, Keepe him still active, angry, un-appeas'd. **1718** POPE *Iliad* XIV. 567 Not unappeased he enters Pluto's gate, Who leaves a brother to revenge his fate. **1828** LYTTON *Pelham* III. xiii, He was too lost in his still unappeased rage to heed me. **1864** R. F. BURTON *Mission to Gelele* I. 9 The unappeased elements gathered strength for a fresh outburst.

†**una'ppellable,** *a. Obs.*$^{-1}$ [UN-^{1} 7b: cf. APPELLATE *ppl. a.*] = UNAPPEALABLE *a.*
1661 FELTHAM *Resolves* (ed. 8) II. lxxxiii. 370 Who shall be Judg, whether..I shall take upon me to be supreme and unappellable?

una'ppendaged, *a.* (UN-^{1} 9.)
1827 POLLOK *Course T.* VIII. 107 It was a congregation vast of men: Of unappendaged and unvarnished men.

†**unapperceived,** *ppl. a. Obs. rare.* [UN-^{1} 8.] Unperceived.
1390 GOWER *Conf.* II. 337 Wher that Diane hirselve stod, Sche thoghte come unaperceived. *Ibid.* 367 His pourpos aboute he broghte, And wente awey unaparceived.

unapper'taining, *ppl. a.* (UN-^{1} 10.)
1645 SYMONDS *Diary* (Camden) 274 Tire others easier eares with these Unapperteyning storyes. **1800** W. TAYLOR in Robberds *Mem.* (1843) I. 344, I steadily disadvise spoiling your new edition of Chatterton by tacking to it any unappertaining stuff of mine.

un'appetizing, *ppl. a.* (UN-^{1} 10.)
1884 *Graphic* 18 Oct. 399/2 The food is too often frequently coarsely-prepared, pretentious and unappetising. **1890** *Times* 15 Mar. 11/2 Within the unappetizing husk which surrounds the question there is a kernel of interest.

una'pplauded, *ppl. a.* (UN-^{1} 8.)
1739 R. BULL tr. *Dedekindus' Grobianus* 153 You'll something find to act, as well as they, Nor unapplauded be for what you say. *a* **1774** GOLDSM. tr. *Scarron's Com. Romance* (1775) I. 9 His merit did not pass unobserved or unapplauded. **1855** [J. R. LEIFCHILD] *Cornwall* 293, I should envy the man that faith of assurance which could support him in such an extremity..unwitnessed, unapplauded. **1863** KINGLAKE *Crimea* II. 112 The patient unapplauded toil by which he prepared the end.

una'pplausive, *a.* (UN-^{1} 7.)
1837 CARLYLE *Fr. Rev.* II. v. x, At which Festival the Public again assists, *un-applausive.* **1872** GEO. ELIOT *Middlem.* xx, The cold, shadowy, unapplausive audience of his life.

†**una'ppliable,** *a. Obs.* [UN-^{1} 7b.] Inapplicable.
1588 J. HARVEY *Disc. Probl.* 96 Shall you not find the said esteemed number of that yeere vnapliable to any such purposes, or intents? **1644** MILTON *Areop.* (Arb.) 44 Best books to a naughty mind are not unappliable to occasions of evill. *a* **1661** FULLER *Worthies, Cambridge.* I. (1662) 150 All unappliable in any peculiar manner to the people of this County. **1675** R. BURTHOGGE *Causa Dei* 116 Who seeth not how unapplyable to either Proposition in the mention'd Argument this Answer is?

una'pplianced, *a.* (UN-^{1} 9.)
1844 TALFOURD *Athenian Captive* IV. ii, The sun-like face Of unapplianced virtue.

†**un'applicable,** *a. Obs.* [UN-^{1} 7b.] = INAPPLICABLE *a.*
1647 CLARENDON *Hist. Reb.* v. §11 His Majesty..saw all those..either totally aliened from his service,..or, like men in a trance, unapplicable to it. **1690** LOCKE *Hum. Und.* IV. xii. §7 The Ideas that demonstratively shew the equality or inequality of unapplicable Quantities. **1741** C. MIDDLETON *Cicero* I. vi. 406 A consecration, legally performed, made the thing consecrated unapplicable ever after to any private use. **1765** BLACKSTONE *Comm.* I. 12 The Roman pandects will furnish us with a piece of history not unapplicable to our present purpose.

una'pplied, *ppl. a.* [UN-^{1} 8.] Not applied, in various senses.
1540 HYRDE tr. *Vives' Instr. Chr. Wom.* I. i. 1 Quintilian in his boke, where he doth instruct and teache an oratour, wylleth his begynnyng and entrance to be taken from the cradel, and no tyme to be slacked vnaplied towarde thende and purpose of the facultee entended. **1605** BACON *Adv. Learn* II. xxi. §5 Because they were men dedicated to a private, free, unapplied course of life. **1681** FLAVEL *Meth. Grace* i. 2 Never was any wound healed by a prepared, but unapplied plaister. **1751** WARBURTON *Pope's Wks.* IV. 28 *note,* While a character is unapplied, all the various parts of it will be considered together. **1785** J. PHILLIPS *Treat. Inland Nav.* 39 The money would lie useless and unapplied a great part of the time. **1832** BABBAGE *Econ. Manuf.* xxxv. (ed. 3) 388 We may remark that the sea itself offers a perennial source of power hitherto almost unapplied. **1889** S. WALPOLE *Ld. J. Russell* I. 272 The remedies which Lord John had desired to provide were still unapplied.

una'ppoint, *v.* [UN-^{2} 3.] *trans.* To cancel.
1682 MRS. BEHN *City Heiress* IV. i, 'Twas an appointment only, hum, which I shall now make bold to unappoint, render null, void, and of none effect.

una'ppointable, *a.* (UN-^{1} 7b.)
1664 H. MORE *Myst. Iniq.* 95 This Infallible Judge being not appointed by God, and being unappointable by man. **1836** CARLYLE *Corr. w. Emerson* (1883) I. 103, I suppose there is no more unpromotable, unappointable man now living in England than I.

una'ppointed, *ppl. a.* [UN-^{1} 8.]
1. Not appointed, in various senses.
1560 PILKINGTON *Expos. Aggeus* I iij, Nay how shall they come together, except place and time be appoynted? How shal they know when and whither to resort, vnappoynted? *a* **1586** SIDNEY *Arcadia* III. v. (1912) 377 Else the very griefe & feare would prove her unappointed executioners. **1782** V. KNOX *Ess.* vi. (1819) I. 34 The operations of this engine of oppression, in the hands of an interested plebeian, unappointed, unauthorised. **1800** *Law Rep.* 29 *Ch. Div.* 521 So much thereof as should remain unappointed or undisposed of.
2. Not fitted out with requisites; unequipped.
1579 GOSSON *Sch. Abuse* (Arb.) 64 Finding them selues vnappointed for the fielde, [they] keepe a farre off. **1759** [see UNANELED *ppl. a.*]. **1837** CARLYLE *Fr. Rev.* II. v. xi, Troops badly commanded, shall we say? Or troops intrinsically bad? Unappointed, undisciplined, mutinous.

una'pportioned, *ppl. a.* (UN-^{1} 8.)
[**1775** ASH.] **1792** A. HAMILTON *Wks.* (1886) VII. 53 This second process leaves a residue of eight out of the 120 members unapportioned.

un'appositely, *adv.* (UN-^{1} 11.)
1680 H. MORE *Apocal. Apoc.* Epil. 292 To the fourth and last [argument] he answers not unappositely.

una'ppreciable, *a.* [UN-^{1} 7b and 5b.] Inappreciable.
1801 F. BURNEY *Let.* 29 Oct. (1975) V. 21 My dear Charlottina, whom I regard as an unappreciable consolation & delight to you. **1822** *Blackw. Mag.* XII. 53 After reading the above unappreciable epistle..we forthwith sweetened our fragrant lymph with two supernumerary lumps. **1849** F. W. NEWMAN *Soul* iv. §2 Where that holy spirit of Intercession lives, the whole man must be wonderfully perfect, nor would this be an unappreciable fact. **1864** *Times* 24 Dec., It was never worth while for the sake of a sum which would be unappreciable as a national debt to create an unpopular..system of national taxation.

una'ppreciated, *ppl. a.* [UN-[1] 8.] **a.** Not duly appreciated or valued. **b.** Not properly estimated.

1828–32 WEBSTER. **1835** *Court Mag.* VI. 132 Though her powers in parts of passion, energy and pathos, are not unappreciated. **1868** MISS BRADDON *Run to Earth* III. i. 5 She loves him, although she knows that her affection is unreturned, unappreciated. **1893** LIDDON, etc. *Life Pusey* I. xi. 271 The yet unappreciated power of Romanism.

una'ppreciating, *ppl. a.* (UN-[1] 10.)

1833 S. AUSTIN *Charac. Goethe* I. 304 The unworthy and unappreciating mention of such names as Wordsworth, Southey, and Coleridge. **1871** TYLOR *Prim. Cult.* I. 20 The unappreciating hatred and ridicule that is lavished by narrow hostile zeal on Brahmanism, Buddhism, Zoroastrism.

unappreci'ation. (UN-[1] 12 and 5 b.)

1886 *Pall Mall G.* 29 Jan. 8/2 A singular unappreciation of the condition of things.

una'ppreciative, *a.* (UN-[1] 7 and 5 b.)

1840 J. S. MILL *Let.* 23 Dec. in *Wks.* (1963) XIII. 453 A man of Molesworth's sort of limitation has a natural tendency to be intolerant, because unappreciative of ideas & persons unlike him & his ideas. **1857** C. E. NORTON *Lett.* (1913) I. iv. 172 The reviews are cold and unappreciative. **1868** VISCT. STRANGFORD *Selection* (1869) I. 202 It is full time to enter into a special examination of his Eastern policy, contrasting it, when necessary, with his own curiously unappreciative exposition of the same.

unappre'hended, *ppl. a.* [UN-[1] 8.]

1. Not apprehended by the mind.

1597 HOOKER *Eccl. Pol.* v. ii. §1 They of whom God is altogether vnapprehended, are but few in number. **1668** CLARENDON *Vind.* Tracts (1727) 48 Bringing heinous crimes to light..by means unapprehended by the guilty. **1896** A. MORRISON *Child of the Jago* xxi. 205 He had a shapeless, unapprehended notion that Canary was the sole creature alive that could understand and feel with him.

2. Not arrested.

1611 COTGR., *Descalengé*, vnarrested, vnapprehended. **1764** BURN *Poor Laws* 207 The clause..whereby a rogue and vagabond..was to be sent to the place where he last passed unapprehended. **1977** *Daily Tel.* 5 Mar. 3/1 It included 341 multi-offenders and concluded with 60 unapprehended men wanted in Dallas this year.

unappre'hending, *ppl. a.* [UN-[1] 10.] Lacking in apprehension.

1794 GODWIN *Caleb Williams* 112 How much had he to struggle with in this respect in the unapprehending obstinacy of some of his Macedonians? **1891** HARDY *Tess* xxxv, You are an unapprehending peasant woman.

† **unappre'hensible,** *a. Obs.* [UN-[1] 7, 5 b.]

1. That cannot be apprehended.

1613 SIR W. ALEXANDER in Sidney *Arcadia* (1622) 333 O how the soule, apt for all impressions transcending reason, can comprehend unapprehensible things! *a* **1715** SOUTH *Serm.* (1744) VII. 94 Which assertions..leave it unapprehensible what place can reasonably be left for addressing exhortations to the will. *a* **1761** LAW *Behmen's Myst. Magnum* xx. (1772) 85 It stood hidden in God, and was unapprehensible.

2. Incapable of apprehending.

1613 HEYWOOD *Bras. Age* II. ii, How harshly doth your wisedome sound in th'eares Of these Barbarians, dull, vnapprehensible.

unappre'hensive, *a.* [UN-[1] 7 and 5 b.]

1. Not apprehensive or quick to understand; stupid, unintelligent.

1624 DONNE *Devot.* Med. xiv. (ed. 2) 321 When they [*sc.* honours and pleasures] come in an vnapprehensive Age, they come..as a Pardon, when the head is off. **1670** MILTON *Hist. Eng.* III. Wks. 1851 V. 130 Unapprehensive, yet impudent; suttle Prowlers, Pastors in Name, but indeed Wolves. **1770** GRAY in *Corr. w. Nicholls* (1843) 104 Pray let the next you send me be halt and blind, dull, unapprehensive, and wrong headed. **1786** *Francis the Philanthropist* I. 66 The wine was sour, the sheets wet,..and the servants unapprehensive and impertinent. **1825** SCOTT *Betrothed* v, Frame not thyself more unapprehensive than nature hath formed thee. **1840** J. H. NEWMAN *Par. Serm.* (1842) V. iii. 41 They look at them as infants gaze at the objects which meet their eyes, in a vague unapprehensive way.

2. Not anticipative or fearful *of* danger, etc.

1666 W. BOGHURST *Loimographia* (1894) 28 The patient being unapprehensive of his danger. **1672** WILKINS *Nat. Relig.* 267 That stupor and benummedness of spirit, whereby men are made unapprehensive of their afflictions. **1728** ELIZA HEYWOOD tr. *Mme. de Gomez's Belle A.* (1732) II. 227 Unapprehensive of the Destiny which attended him. **1805** WORDSW. *Prelude* II. 455 And for this cause to thee I speak, unapprehensive of contempt. **1854** J. S. C. ABBOTT *Napoleon* (1885) I. xxvi. 409 For there were thousands of travelers on the Continent, unapprehensive of danger.

b. With clause, or without const.

a **1705** J. HOWE *Living Temple* I. ii. §8, I am not unapprehensive that I might..have proceeded in another method. **1742** BLAIR *Grave* 477 In gamesome Mood To frolick on Eternity's dread Brink, Unapprehensive. **1753** RICHARDSON *Grandison* (1781) I. xxxix. 283 My heart is a little lighter: Yet not unapprehensive. **1829** SCOTT *Anne of G.* ix, In the hour of unaffected and unapprehensive ease and simplicity. **1853** KANE *Grinnell Exp.* xxxvii. (1856) 340 *note*, The animals were entirely unapprehensive.

unappre'hensively, *adv.* [UN-[1] 11 b.] † Undiscoverably, imperceptibly.

a **1659** OSBORNE *Observ. Turks* Wks. (1673) 317 Till a reverence..be real, or unapprehensively feigned, it is folly to expect performance of Oaths in the Members.

unappre'hensiveness. [UN-[1] 12.] Lack of apprehension.

1661 BAXTER *Mor. Prognost.* (1680) I. §4 If..a Natural Unapprehensiveness Blocks up the Way, even Time and Labour will never..bring any, to any great Eminency of Understanding. **1671** WOODHEAD *St. Teresa* II. xix. 127 By reason of the Unapprehensiveness which God puts into us. **1748** RICHARDSON *Clarissa* (1811) III. ii. 6 Unthinking creatures have some comfort in the shortness of their views; in their unapprehensiveness. *c* **1833** MRS. SHERWOOD *Life* xxxi. (1854) 567 That unaccountable unapprehensiveness which so often foreruns any severe affliction.

una'pprenticed, *ppl. a.* (UN-[1] 8.)

[**1775** ASH.] **1809** *Crit. Rev.* XVI. 500 How many await, unapprenticed, for the interference of some overseer in their behalf?

una'pprised, *ppl. a.* [UN-[1] 8.] Not apprised or informed: **a.** Const. *of*.

1728 R. MORRIS *Ess. Anc. Archit.* p. xxii, Those who are unappriz'd of the minuter Proportions. **1798** S. & HT. LEE *Canterb. T.* II. 58 But he, unapprised of the anxious expectation he excited, loitered by the way. **1835** I. TAYLOR *Spir. Despot.* iv. 144 The author must not be supposed.. unapprised of the vast controversy of which it has been the subject. **1852** MUNDY *Antipodes* (1857) 211 Aware that Darlington had been a Probation Station, and unapprised of its abandonment.

b. With dependent clause, or without const.

1742 YOUNG *Nt. Th.* v. 539 Some mischievously weep, not unappris'd, Tears, sometimes, aid the conquest of an eye. **1746** WESLEY *Princ. Methodist* 49, I suppose, you are not unapprized, That during this Period..they were continually relieved by the Prayers of the Faithful. **1783** POTT *Chirurg. Wks.* II. 65, I also am not unapprized what influence a successful operation has had. **1816** P. HERVÉ *Beauties of Paris* I. 238 Truly mortifying is it to the unapprized visitor to one of the first theatres in Europe, to find [etc.] **1847** GROTE *Greece* II. xxxii. (1862) IV. 268 They doubtless were not unapprised that the Spartans had actually equipped an army for the support of Crœsus.

unapproacha'bility. (UN-[1] 12 and 5 b.)

1846 MRS. GORE *Eng. Char.* Introd., My Lord Duke, no longer arrayed in his star, garter, and unapproachability, can be trafficked with. **1902** S. E. WHITE *Blazed Trail* xxx, The lumber-jack demands in his boss a certain fundamental unapproachability.

una'pproachable, *a.* (and *sb.*). [UN-[1] 7 b and 5 b.]

1. Of things or places: That cannot be approached; inaccessible.

1581 A. GILBY *Test. 12 Patriarchs* 28 We went to a strong walled, and vnapprochable Citie..whiche threatened to kill vs. **1583** GOLDING *Calvin on Deut.* xxii. 130 To the ende that wee shoulde learne to be humble and to know that hee dwelleth in vnapprochable light. **1625** K. LONG tr. *Barclay's Argenis* III. vii. 175 The Hill is unapproachable toward the Sea-side. **1685** BOYLE *High Veneration* §6. 5 God..is said to inhabite an unapproachable Light, which humane Speculations cannot penetrate. **1742** YOUNG *Nt. Th.* IX. 850 He resides above them all, In glory's unapproachable recess. **1816** SCOTT *Old Mort.* xliii, All alone, and in a place of almost unapproachable seclusion. **1891** FARRAR *Darkn. & Dawn* l, There were districts in which the heat was so intense that they were unapproachable.

fig. **1686** tr. *Chardin's Trav. Persia* 51 Which sort of Policy, having neither Art nor Principles, was as it were unapproachable.

2. That cannot be approached in confidence or intimacy.

1848 DICKENS *Dombey* liii, Mr. Dombey is unapproachable by any one, and his state of mind is haughty, rash, unreasonable, and ungovernable, now. **1865** —— *Mut. Fr.* III. viii, All such things she would hear discussed, as we..in our unapproachable magnificence never hear them. **1904** MRS. M. CREIGHTON *Life Bp. Creighton* vi. I. 158 The fisherfolk..had..the most imagination, and the hinds were the most unapproachable.

3. Beyond the reach of rivalry; matchless.

1831 CARLYLE *Sart. Res.* III. xi, The epithet *schneidermässig* (tailor-like) betokens an otherwise unapproachable degree of pusillanimity. **1856** FROUDE *Hist. Eng.* (1858) I. i. 68 Out of the illuminations arose those paintings which remain unapproached and unapproachable in their excellence. **1871** E. F. BURR *Ad Fidem* xiv. 280 A sermon of unapproachable eloquence, and pathos.

4. *absol.* as *sb.* One who, or that which, cannot be approached or equalled.

1800 COLERIDGE *Piccolom.* III. i, We shall view The Unapproachable glide out in splendour. **1821** SHELLEY *Sonn. Byron* 6 A worm whose life may share A portion of the unapproachable. **1886** *Academy* 22 May 357/3 One or two [translations] from Heine come as near to the unapproachable as can fairly be expected.

Hence **una'pproachableness, -ably** *adv.*

1727 BAILEY (vol. II), *Inaccessibleness*, *unapproachableness. **1825** *Eng. Life* II. 82 He became resolutely silent and did not attempt to overcome his unapproachableness. **1874** LISLE CARR *J. Gwynne* I. iii. 94 The unapproachableness of the disdainful governess. **1846** WORCESTER, **Unapproachably*, so as not to be approached. Dr. Allen. **1863** LD. LYTTON *Ring Amasis* I. 36 The habitual consciousness of an unapproachably high social position. **1890** 'R. BOLDREWOOD' *Miner's Right* (1899) 177/2 The illustrious Jake Challerson, unapproachably apparelled, redolent of fabulous wealth.

una'pproached, *ppl. a.* [UN-[1] 8.] Not approached; not reached by advance (in space or attainment).

1667 MILTON *P.L.* III. 4 Since God is light, And never but in unapproached light Dwelt from Eternitie. **1725** POPE *Odyss.* XIX. 53 Celestials, mantl'd in excess of light, Can visit unapproach'd by mortal sight. **1817** WORDSW. *Lament Mary Q. Scots* 19 Me, unapproached by any friend, Save those who to my sorrows lend Tears due unto their own. **1856** [see UNAPPROACHABLE *a.* 3]. **1864** *Realm* 22 June 8 To form..a national style such as is yet unapproached by native composers.

absol. *c* **1854** FABER *Hymn, 'Harsh Judgements'* x, Thou art the Unapproached, whose height Enables Thee to stoop.

una'ppropriate, *ppl. a.* [UN-[1] 8 b, 5 b.]

1. Not appropriated or assigned.

1767 WARBURTON *Serm.* Wks. 1788 V. 513 Goods, which God, at first, created un-appropriate; and Nature threw in common to all her children. **1832** C. M. GOODRIDGE *Voy. South Seas* Title-p., A Statistical View of Van Diemen's Land, Giving its..Roads and Public Works, Unappropriate Land [etc.].

2. = INAPPROPRIATE *a.*

1818 BENTHAM *Ch. Eng., Catech. Exam.* 153 With the exception of the Scriptural, and surely not unappropriate, part of the subject. **1822** T. TAYLOR *Apuleius* 234 He assigned unappropriate causes. **1898** *Daily News* 12 May 7/5 He would not say that the treatment..would be unappropriate for pelvic inflammation.

Hence **una'ppropriateness.**

1838 [MRS. MAITLAND] *Lett. fr. Madras* (1843) 208 They had contrived with great ingenuity every possible unappropriateness that could be devised.

una'ppropriated, *ppl. a.* [UN-[1] 8.]

1. Not allocated or assigned to a special person, thing, or purpose.

1756 J. WARTON *Ess. Pope* I. iii. 147 Ovid could not restrain the luxuriancy of his genius..from wandering with an endless variety of flowery and unappropriated similitudes. **1791** BOSWELL *Johnson* II. 365 He has not owned to whom he was obliged; so that the acknowledgement is unappropriated to his Grace. **1806** SURR *Winter in Lond.* I. 21 There remained thirty thousand pounds unappropriated, and the whole was at her own disposal. **1872** HOWELLS *Wedding Journ.* (1892) 310 She had found..certain odd corners in her trunks still unappropriated.

2. Not taken in possession by any one.

1776 BURNEY *Hist. Mus.* I. 1 The land of conjecture, however, is so extensive and unappropriated, that every new cultivator has a right to break up fresh ground. **1796** MATHIAS *Purs. Lit.* II. (1797) 24 This character..shall ever remain unappropriated by me. **1814** JANE AUSTEN *Mansf. Park* viii, The envied seat, the post of honour, was unappropriated. **1884** *Law Times Rep.* 19 Apr. 230/2 A common supply of unappropriated water in deep water-bearing strata.

una'ppropriating, *vbl. sb.* (UN-[2] 3.)

1641 MILTON *Reform.* II. 85 The unappropriating, and unmonopolizing the rewards of learning and industry, from the greasie clutch of ignorance, and high feeding.

una'pprovable, *a.* (UN-[1] 7 b.)

1647 TRAPP *Comm., 2 Cor.* xiii. 6 We are no reprobates, counterfeits, or unapprovable, opposed to approved. **1685** H. MORE *Reflect. Baxter* 1 Seven unapprovable Particulars noted in the said Advertisement.

una'pproved, *ppl. a.* [UN-[1] 8.]

† **1.** Not proved to be skilled. *Obs.*[−1]

1421 *Rolls of Parlt.* IV. 158/1 Many unconnyng an[d] unapproved in the forsayd science practiseth.

† **2.** Not demonstrated; unproved. *Obs.*

1597 SHAKS. *Lover's Compl.* 53 O false blood thou register of lies, What vnapproued witnes doost thou beare! **1597** HOOKER *Eccl. Pol.* v. lxii. §16 The nullity of baptism in regard of the like defect is only a few men's new, ungrounded, and as yet unapproved imagination. **1598** FLORIO *Dict.* Ep. Ded., Rashnes in assuming so much for it that yet is vnapprooued.

3. Not approved or sanctioned.

1667 MILTON *P.L.* v. 118 Evil into the mind of God or Man May come and go, so unapprov'd, and leave No spot or blame behind. **1812** CRABBE *Tales* ix. 77 A Doctor Campbell ..Declared his passion, and proclaim'd his worth; Not unapproved. **1827** POLLOK *Course T.* VIII. 193 Unprofitable seemed, and unapproved That day, the sullen, self-vindictive life Of the recluse. **1902** *Westm. Gaz.* 20 May 3 He recognised forces unapproved by the Royal College of Surgeons.

una'pproven, *ppl. a. Sc.* [UN-[1] 8 b.] = prec. 1.

1619 A. SIMSON in *Sel. Biog.* (Wodrow Soc.) I. 105 Our unapproven hand may loss them and tyne our travells.

una'pproving, *ppl. a.* (UN-[1] 10.)

Also in recent use, with adv. ***unapprovingly***.

1787 HAWKINS *Life Johnson* 225 He looked upon the restraints on a life of pleasure with an unapproving eye.

unapropos (ʌnæprə'pəʊ, ʌn'æprəpəʊ), *a.* and *adv.* [UN-[1] 7, 11 b.] Not apropos; irrelevant(ly); inappropriate(ly).

1840 H. MOZLEY *Let.* 13 Oct. in D. Mozley *Newman Family Lett.* (1962) III. 92, I have none of the un-a-propos propensities that would stand in the way of engagement with some ladies. **1940** J. POPE-HENNESSY *Let.* in J. Lees-Milne *Ancestral Voices* (1975) 267 Christianity..seems a clear and tranquil stream running parallel to but utterly detached from the turgid river of the war, and..too unapropos for words. **1956** R. ROBINSON *Landscape with Dead Dons* xxi. 194, I was chatting to Christelow when it occurred to me quite unapropos that one of the things they had in common was *The Book*.

un'apt, *a.* [UN-[1] 7 and 5 b.]

† **1.** Of persons or things: Unfitted or unfit *to* do something. *Obs.*

c **1374** CHAUCER *Troylus* I. 971 Was neuere man ne woman yet bygete, That was vnapt to suffren loues hete Celestial. **1504** ATKYNSON tr. *De Imitatione* II. viii. 186 Whan grace deperteth fro the soule it is faynt & frayle, vnapte to do or to suffre that vertue commaundith. **1597** HOOKER *Eccl. Pol.* v. lxi. §1 *note*, Those which were baptized in their beds were thereby made vnapt to haue any place amongst the clergie. **1610** J. Dove *Advt. Seminaries* 52, I might happily have persuaded them,..had they not been as a plot of ground unapt to receive good seed. **1654** Gayton *Pleas. Notes* iv. v. 199, I had some guests that were very unapt to sleep anywhere but in their own houses. **1682** Norris *Hierocles* 19 Those which constantly contemplate God, and are unapt to converse on earth. **1726** De Foe *Hist. Devil* (1840) 106 The wood unapt to burn by the moisture which fell, scarce received the fire I brought to kindle it. **1736** Butler *Anal.* ii. vi. 225 In Proportion to Defects in the Understanding, Men are unapt to see lower Degrees of Evidence.

2. Unfit or unsuited *for* some use or purpose: **a.** Of persons.

a **1513** Fabyan *Chron.* vii. 408 A great nombre of olde men and women, and children, vnapt for ye warre. **1595** Daniel *Civ. Wars* iv. xxix, The Earle being..Vnapt for issue, it must needes descend on those of his being next of Clarence race. *a* **1648** Ld. Herbert *Hen. VIII* (1683) 33 Courtiers have those [arts] by which they govern their Princes, when through any indisposition they grow unapt for affairs. **1654** H. L'Estrange *Chas. I* (1655) 1 He was exceeding feeble in his lower parts,..whereby he was unapt for exercises of activity. **1791** Cowper *Odyss.* xxi. 159, I shall prove of little force Hereafter, and for manly feats unapt. **1850** Ht. Martineau *Hist. Eng.* II. 224 Unapt for combination..as his colleagues were, his..indifference went to increase the evil.

b. Of things.

1579 Fulke *Heskins' Parl.* 20 A minde vnapte for the contemplation of this doctrine. **1608** Willet *Hexapla Exod.* 836 Such beasts..being vncleane, and vnapt for food. **1633** Bp. Hall *Occas. Medit.* 108 Is there any thing more heavy, and unapt for motion then Iron, or steele? **1736** Butler *Anal.* i. vi. 116 Whoever will consider, how unapt for Speculation, rude and uncultivated Minds are. **1765** Sterne *Tr. Shandy* vii. xxx, I..have a brain so entirely unapt for every thing of that kind. **1826** Kirby & Sp. *Introd. Entomol.* III. xxxiv. 429 In the Lamellicorn beetles..they [*sc.* mandibles] are soft, membranous, and unapt for mastication. **1873** M. Arnold *Lit. & Dogma* (1876) 9 There are heads unapt for this sort of work.

†**3.** Unsuited or unadapted *to* some end. *Obs.*

1539 N.T. (Cranmer) *Tit.* i. 16 They are..vnapte vnto euery good worcke. **1579** Gosson *Sch. Abuse* (Arb.) 72 We must neither be laboured too muche..nor loyter too long, for making ourselues vnapt to any thing. **1620** Venner *Via Recta* viii. 179 Men after a full meale are..very vnapt vnto any labour.., either of minde or body. **1647** Jer. Taylor *Lib. Proph.* ii. 47 That..every clause in the Creed should be clear, and..inopportune and vnapt to variety of interpretation.

4. Without const. Unfitted, unsuited, unadapted: †**a.** Of persons. *Obs.*

a **1513** Fabyan *Chron.* vii. (1811) 422 An vnredy and dispurueyed hoost for the warre, as..spyrytuell men of the churche, with husbonde men and other vnapte people. **1577** tr. *Bullinger's Decades* (1592) 269 He must be no litherbacke, vnapt, or slothfull fellow. *a* **1621** Bacon *Disc. Saville* in *Resuscitatio* (1657) 230 The contrary Advantage (in Natures very dull, and unapt) of working Alacrity, by framing an Exercise with some Delight, or affection. *a* **1656** Hales *Gold. Rem.* (1688) 277 The longer we defer, the more unapt still we grow. *a* **1680** Butler *Rem.* (1759) I. 402 Such Men are commonly the most unapt in Things, that require Judgment and Reason.

b. Of things.

1588 Lambarde *Eiren.* iv. Epil., I may neyther altogether condemne it as unapt, nor reiect it as unserviceable. **1598** Greene *Jas. IV*, ii. ii, When the mould is barraine and vnapt, They toyle, they plow, and make the fallow fatte. **1638** Penkethman *Artach.* K4 The whole Earth..is growne more unapt and backwards in bearing. **1650** Jer. Taylor *Holy Living* ii. §6. 132 There are many worse [diseases] then to dye with an atrophy or Consumption, or unapt and courser nourishment. **1818** Cruise *Digest* (ed. 2) IV. 261 Such a union was very unapt and improper. **1842** H. Rogers *Introd. Burke's Wks.* I. 56 Thus disorders become incurable..by the unapt and violent nature of the remedies.

5. Of language, etc.: Unsuitable, inappropriate.

1553 Wilson *Art Rhet.* 88 *marg.*, Vnapte vsyng of apt wordes. **1588** E. Yorke in *Antiq. Rep.* (1807) I. 261 Of which worde of Calibre, came first this unapt terme wee use to call a Harquebuze a Calliver. **1634** W. Tirwhyt tr. *Balzac's Lett.* A2 Those, who with unapt complements imagine they have composed a good letter. **1783** Colman *Prose Sev. Occas., Ep. Pisos* (1787) III. 13 Chaunting no odes between the acts, that seem unapt, or foreign to the general theme. **1796** Mrs. M. Robinson *Angelina* I. 228 Seldom she speaks: if question'd, she returns The answer incoherent and unapt. **1821** Scott *Pirate* xxv, No unapt representation of the sea in the Vision of Mirza. **1866** Geo. Eliot *F. Holt* xvi, Your comparison is not unapt, sir.

6. Of things: Not readily tending or likely *to* do something.

1587 Turberv. *Trag. T.* (1837) 64 But commonly when men in fancie burne, Then womens hartes are most unapt to turne. **1597** Hooker *Eccl. Pol.* v. iii. §1 Feare..is of all affections (anger excepted) the vnaptest to admit any conference with reason. *a* **1628** F. Grevil *Cælica* liv, Rage, feare, griefe, Powers as unapt to take, as give reliefe. **1665** Hooke *Microgr.* 13 The parts of the body of some are so loose from one another, and so unapt to cohere,..that [etc.]. **1819** Scott *Ivanhoe* xl, A mind which was unapt to apprehend danger. **1856** Bryant *Yellow Violet* v, Unapt the passing view to meet, When loftier flowers are flaunting nigh.

b. Of persons: Not apt or prone, not readily disposed, *to* do something.

1640 Wilkins *New Planet* ii. 32 Men being naturally unapt to beleeve any thing that seemes contrary to their senses. **1665** Hooke *Microgr.* 242, I am not unapt to think, that the Vale may have Vegetables analogous to our Grass, Shrubs, and Trees. **1785** T. Balguy *Disc.* 5 Unaccustomed to suffer harm, we are unapt to suspect it. **1828** Scott *F.M. Perth* viii, You may have thought me unapt to be moved by light complaints. **1874** Micklethwaite *Mod. Par. Churches* 241 Men of little creative power, but not unapt to take up ideas suggested to them.

c. Without const.: Unready, backward.

1849 Mill *Ess.* (1859) II. 401 Lord Brougham has condescended to bestow upon these unapt scholars his view of some of the essential requisites of a popular Constitution.

†**un'apt**, *v. Obs.* [f. prec., or un-[2] 6a + apt *a.*] *trans.* To render unapt.

1593 Nashe *Christ's T.* (1613) 156 Our full platters.. vnapt vs to any exercise of Christianitie. **1628** R. Hobart *Edw. II*, cccxvii, Let not..false surmises Unapt their meanes, and crosse their owne devises. **1641** *Exam. Abstr. Answ. agst. Votes Bps. in Parl.* 77 It puts them out of their Calling, unapts them for the proper worke of it.

†**un'aptitude.** *Obs.*[−1] [un-[1] 12 and 5b.] Inaptitude. (Const. *of* = for.)

1545 Raynald *Byrth Mankynde* 144 Most communely the vnaptitude of conception (in women hauynge ther helth) springeth of the superfluyte of cold & moyst humours.

un'aptly, *adv.* [un-[1] 11 and 5b.] Inaptly.

1548 Udall, etc. *Erasm. Par. Luke* Pref., Why than should the ghospell seme to be vnapteley sent vnto those which are handlers and louers of the ghospell? **1579** W. Wilkinson *Confut. Fam. Love* 20 Yet are these places by him very vnskilfully cited and vnaptly to the purpose. *c* **1643** Ld. Herbert *Autobiog.* (1824) 56 It may be not unaptly called the paying our debts with another Man's money. **1659** *Gentl. Calling* 57 In this respect therefore I may not unaptly apply that Exhortation which the Apostle makes in another. **1748** Smollett *R. Random* xxxiii, This composition was, by the sailors, not unaptly stiled *Necessity*. **1798** S. & Ht. Lee *Canterb. T.* II. 101 Dennis, my silver-headed foster-father, may not unaptly personate my real one. **1852** Mrs. Stowe *Uncle Tom's C.* xi, Mr. Wilson's mind was one of those that may not unaptly be represented by a bale of cotton. **1866** Felton *Anc. & Mod. Gr.* I. 168 A soft, yet spicy vivacity, in which it has been not unaptly compared to the Castillian.

un'aptness. [un-[1] 12 and 5b.] Inaptitude.

1557 *Act 4 & 5 Phil. & Mary* c. 3 §1 The same Disability and Unaptness notwithstanding, the same unable and unmeet Persons..have been also released. **1595** Daniel *Civ. Wars* iv. xviii, And languishing luxuriousnes had spred Feeble vnaptnes ouer all the land. **1605** Verstegan *Dec. Intell.* ix. 291 The trees grow but low..by reason of the vnaptnesse of the soyle. **1652** W. Hartley *Inf. Bapt.* 12 The prohibition hath peculiar relation to the unaptness of the sacrificers. **1676** *Phil. Trans.* II. 739 That seminal root.. hindred by the unaptness of the place. **1710** Norris *Chr. Prud.* ii. 98 He often fails as to his Means, as well as to his End, I don't mean as to their unaptness.

b. Const. *for, to* (with sb. or inf.).

1548 Elyot, *Prosedanium*, a disease which happeneth to ..beastes, which is vnaptenesse to generacion through to muche labour. **1600** W. Watson *Decacordon* (1602) 165 M. Blackwels simplicitie and vnaptnesse to gouerne. **1654** *Nicholas Papers* (Camden) II. 55 The naturall unaptness hee has for that exercise. **1670** Clarendon *Contempl. Ps.* Tracts (1727) 729 An unaptness to be confident of what they see and feel. *a* **1688** W. Clagett *17 Serm.* (1699) 216 There will be laziness and slothfulness, and unaptness for instruction. **1860** Rawlinson *Herodotus* ix. lxx. IV. 442 *note*, A general unaptness for the mechanical arts?

unaraced: see unraced *ppl. a. Obs.*

un'arbitrariness. (un-[1] 12.)

1825 Coleridge in *Lit. Rem.* (1836) II. 359 The coincidences would bring the truth, the unarbitrariness, of the preceding exposition as near to demonstration as can rationally be required.

un'arbitrary, *a.* (un-[1] 7.)

1793 Holcroft tr. *Lavater's Physiog.* iv. 35 If unarbitrary Nature patched up countenances like arbitrary Art.

un'arbitrated, *ppl. a.* (un-[1] 8.)

1821 Shelley *Let. to T. L. Peacock* 10 Aug., All these [animals]..walk about the house, which every now and then resounds with their unarbitrated quarrels.

unarch (ʌn'ɑːtʃ), *v.* [un-[2] 3.] *trans.* and *intr.* To uncurve; to straighten.

1598 Florio, *Disarcare*, to vnbend, to vnarche. **1885** Jefferies *Open Air* (1890) 234 His flexible back bends and undulates, arches and unarches, rises and falls as a wave rises and rolls on.

unarch'deacon, *v.* (un-[2] 6b.)

1555 Philpot *Exam.* 100 In dede M[aster] D[octor] ye haue among you vnarchediaconed me as nowe.

un'arched, *a.* [un-[1] 9.]

1. Not covered over with an arch.

1658 Osborne *Adv. Son* (1896) 132 [A] tomb also hinders the variety of such contingent Resurrections as unarched Bodies enjoy.

2. Not provided with arches.

1832 Froude in *Rem.* (1838) I. 299 The awkwardness of mixing up arched and unarched architecture is thus entirely avoided.

unarchi'tectural, *a.* [un-[1] 7.]

1. Not in accordance with the principles of architecture.

1849 Ruskin *Sev. Lamps* ii. §18. 47 It is lawful to paint either pictures or patterns... But it is not less true, that such practices are essentially unarchitectural. **1862** E. Falkener *Ephesus* i. iv. 49 The old style of building, which, from its irregularity and unarchitectural character, resembled that still used in Eastern climates. **1873** Mrs. Whitney *Other Girls* xxxi, An odd rambling wing,..slanting off at a wholly unarchitectural angle from the main house.

2. Not skilled in architecture.

1884 *Pall Mall G.* 18 July 11/1 It is difficult from the mere text of this report for the unarchitectural reader to get a clear notion of what is proposed.

un'arguable, *a.* (un-[1] 7b and 5b.)

1881 *Times* 11 May 6/5 The President said that point was wholly unarguable. **1885** *Law Times* LXXIX. 244/1 The case for the first mortgagee would have been absolutely unarguable.

un'argued, *ppl. a.* (un-[1] 8.)

1616 B. Jonson *Epigr.* i. cx, He wrote with the same spirit that he fought; Not that his work lived in the hands of foes, Unargued then. **1628** Bp. Hall *Old Relig.* Ep. Ded. ¶vj, No corner of truth hath lyen vnsearcht, no plea vnargued. **1667** Milton *P.L.* iv. 636 To whom thus Eve..: My Author and Disposer, what thou bidst Unargu'd I obey; so God ordains. **1777** Howard *Prisons Eng.* (1780) 152 The orders given by the commissary of the marines encharged with the care of prisoners are to be strictly complied with unargued and undisputed.

unargu'mentative, *a.* (un-[1] 7.)

1722 *Lett. fr. Mist's Jrnl.* I. Pref. p. ii, The most.. impudent and unargumentative weekly Paper the Town was ever infested with. **1837** G. S. Faber *Prim. Doctr. Justif.* v. 235 The doctrine would not have been a whit the worse, had the..unargumentative curses been omitted. **1870** J. H. Newman *Gram. Assent* i. v. 119 The inward voice of that solemn Monitor, personal, peremptory, unargumentative.

Hence **unargu'mentatively** *adv.*

1840 G. S. Faber *Prim. Doctr. Regen.* 66 Just as if the writers unargumentatively thought, that no one..could ever doubt its propriety.

una'risen, *ppl. a.* (un-[1] 8b.)

1865 Swinburne *Hesperia* 74 Now that the white skies thrill with a moon unarisen. **1894** *Woman's Signal* 5 Apr. 224/2 A working principle..as yet unarisen in the public mind.

unaristo'cratic, *a.* (un-[1] 7.)

1841 in Monypenny *Disraeli* (1912) II. 123 We do not know the latest appointments; but up to the latest, except Gladstone, there is not one single untitled or unaristocratic individual. **1863** *Sat. Rev.* 7 Feb. 183/2 Stung at times into unaristocratic ebullitions of rather helpless spleen.

unarith'metic, *a.* (un-[1] 7.)

1789 H. Walpole *Let. to Mrs. H. More* 4 Nov., My head is as un-mechanic as it is un-arithmetic, un-geometric, un-metaphysic, un-commercial. **1953** *Trans. Amer. Inst. Electr. Engineers* LXXII. 597/2 The unarithmetic representation for zero is standard in the 2-out-of-5 code.

unarith'metical, *a.* (un-[1] 7.)

1671 Crowne *Juliana* 1, Five times ten hundred crowns! most monstrous, prodigious, gigantique, pedantique, unarithmetical sum. **1858** Miss Mulock *Th. about Wom.* vi. 156 Unarithmetical ladies, who have always reckoned their accounts by sixpences.

un'ark, *v.* (un-[2] 5.)

1611 J. Davies *Sco. Folly* cclxxxv, Till thou be left vpon Th' Armenian mount of safety, ioy and rest; Where when thou art thou maist thyselfe vn-arke.

un'arm, *v.* Also 4–5 onarm (4 oun-), 4–7 unarme (5 *Sc.* wnarm). [un-[2] 4.]

1. *trans.* To relieve (a person) of armour; to assist in putting off armour.

13.. *Sir Beues* (A.) 1081 King Ermin..clepede is douȝter & saide: 'Iosian, þe faire maide, Vn-arme Beues, he wer at mete. *c* **1386** Chaucer *Sqr.'s T.* 173 This knyght is to his chambre lad anoon, And is vnarmed, and vn to mete yset. **1470–85** Malory *Arthur* vii. xviii. 241 The mayden Lynet ..vnarmed hym and serched his woundes. *c* **1489** Caxton *Sonnes of Aymon* xv. 357 He made hym to be vn-armed, and made his wounde to be wrapped. **1568** Grafton *Chron.* II. 252 Assoone as the King was vnarmed, he..went vp to the Castell to salute the Countesse of Sarisbury. **1573** in Feuillerat *Revels Q. Eliz.* (1908) 202 [To] Roger Tyndall.. for his seruauntes Attendaunces to arme & vn-arme the children in the play. **1606** Shaks. *Tr. & Cr.* iii. i. 163 Sweet Hellen, I must woe you, To helpe vnarme our Hector..You shall..disarme great Hector. **1720** Mrs. Manley *Power of Love* (1741) 337 [He] commanded the Conqueror should be unarm'd and set before his Face, to receive the Reward due to his Valour.

absol. **1606** Shaks. *Ant. & Cl.* iv. xiv. 35 Vnarme Eros, the long dayes taske is done, And we must sleepe.

b. *refl.* To free or strip (oneself) of armour. (Also with *head* as obj.)

13.. *Guy Warw.* (A.) 5506 Otus to his pauiloun he ȝede, & vnarmed him of his wede. *c* **1400** *Laud Troy Bk.* 10241 Vn-Arme the at my prayere. *c* **1430** *Pilgr. Lyf. Manhode* i. cxxxiv. (1869) 70 Allas, whi woldest thou euere vnarme thee? *c* **1477** Caxton *Jason* 7b, The Iousters vnarmed them, And put hem in fayr araye. *a* **1533** Ld. Berners *Huon* lix. 206 They vnarmyd them, and went to dyner. **1581** A. Hall *Iliad* iv. 66 He soft vnarmes him, and his scarfe, and Curet off doth take. **1609** Heywood *Brit. Troy* xiii. lxxxv, King Priam by Antenors mouth desires To vnarme him streight and to the Courte returne. **1624** —— *Gunaik.* v. 246 When with the slaughter of his enemies tyred He doff'd his cushes, and unarm'd his head. **1719** D'Urfey *Pills* I. 175 The Great Mars of the Battle unarms him and plays.. **1823** Scott *Quentin D.* xxxvi, Go, tell no man to unarm himself; and let them shoot, in case of necessity.

absol. *c* **1450** *Merlin* xxvii. 555 Elizer was besy to serue sir Gawein..and helped him to vn-arme. **1606** Shaks. *Tr. & Cr.* i. i. 1 Call here my Varlet, I vnarme againe. *Ibid.* v. iii. 3 Vnarme, vnarme, and doe not fight to day. *a* **1625** Fletcher *Hum. Lieut.* iii. vi, Will ye unarm, and yield your selves his prisoners?

†**2.** To deprive of arms or armour; to disarm.

1560 Daus tr. *Sleidane's Comm.* 101 To send their ayde agaynst the Turke..were to unarme them selves and to cut their owne senewes. **1569** J. Sanford tr. *Agrippa's Van. Artes* 125b, To kill them, to take them, to unarme them, to spoile them. *a* **1618** RALEIGH *Maxims St.* in *Rem.* (1661) 43 To unarm his people of weapons, money, and all means, whereby they may resist his power. **1635** PAGITT *Christianogr.* I. ii. (1636) 48 The Turke usually in his Conquests unarmeth the Christians. **1654** EARL MONM. tr. *Bentivoglio's Wars Flanders* 106 A Brigade of the Spanish foot forthwith entered the Town, and unarmed every one therein.

†**b.** *transf.* and *fig. Obs.*

1568 GRAFTON *Chron.* II. 757 If deuision and dissencion of their friendes had not vnarmed them, and left them destitute. **1646** SIR T. BROWNE *Pseud. Ep.* 385 Galen.. would not leave unto the world too subtile a Theory of Poisons; unarming thereby the malice of venemous spirits. *a* **1668** DAVENANT *Epithal.* Wks. (1673) 312 So an excessive purity of Love Unarmes you to invite offence.

†**3.** To empty or strip of arms. *Obs.*

1560 DAUS tr. *Sleidane's Comm.* 405 By unarmyng the armaries, and openyng the waye to confiscation. **1636** G. SANDYS *Paraphr., Ps.* xlvi, He breaks their Bowes, unarmes their Quivers, The bloody Speare in pieces shivers. **1665** MANLEY *Grotius' Low C. Wars* 209 The Queen.. Commands by her Letter, the Lord Admirall Howard.. that he should unarm and discharge the best of her Ships.

†**4.** To disarm, render harmless. *Obs.*[-1]

1700 DRYDEN *Ovid's Met.* VIII. *Meleager* 120 No blood he drew; Dian unarm'd the Javelin as it flew.

un'armed, *ppl. a.* Also 3 uniarmed, 5 *Sc.* unermyt, onarmed. [UN-[1] 8.]

1. Not armed; having no armour or weapons.

1297 R. GLOUC. (Rolls) 11274 Vn iarmed out he wende to þe barons wel stille. *c* **1330** *Arth. & Merl.* 6947 (Kölbing), Vnarmed were þe paiens alle, Our folk hem gun to talle. **1387** TREVISA *Higden* (Rolls) I. 353 þey fiȝteþ vnarmed, naked in body. **1412–20** LYDG. *Chron. Troy* III. 1719 Cruelly þei had his hede of smet, For he vnarmyd al at meschef stood. **1456** SIR G. HAYE *Law Arms* (S.T.S.) 113 A man that is outhir unarmyt, or evill armyt may nocht hald felde in bataill place. *a* **1533** LD. BERNERS *Huon* lxvii. 230 All his company were vnarmed, & all the other .xl. were clene armed. **1579** W. WILKINSON *Confut. Fam. Love* Ep. Ded. *iij, Neither are able many of them being vnarmed to withstand the enemy. **1632** W. LITHGOW *Trav.* III. 89, I neuer could see a Greeke come forth of his house vnarmed. **1671** MILTON *P.R.* IV. 626 He all unarm'd Shall chase thee with the terror of his voice. **1748** *Anson's Voy.* II. vi. 200 He came down unarmed to a centinel of ours. **1794** S. WILLIAMS *Vermont* 170 An unarmed defenceless stranger. **1839** THIRLWALL *Greece* VI. 223 The Thracians were keeping very negligent guard, and, in imagined security, were mostly unarmed. **1882** DE WINDT *Equator* 69 The remainder of the tribe were unarmed, as it is made a strict rule in Sarawak that ..all arms..shall be left behind.

absol. **1590** BARWICK *Disc. Weapons* 10 b, The musket.. will kill the armed of proofe at ten skore yardes,..and the vnarmed at thirty skore.

transf. **1634** MILTON *Comus* 582 Th' unarmed weakness of one Virgin Alone, and helpless! **1827** POLLOK *Course T.* IX. 965 Sin's dark tactics, such as boyish man, Unarmed by strength divine, could ill withstand.

b. Phr. ***unarmed combat.***

1947 'N. SHUTE' *Chequer Board* ix. 262 'You went on to a course in unarmed combat. What did they teach you to do there?' 'We was taught how to attack an armed man just with our hands and feet.' **1957** J. BRAINE *Room at Top* xxx. 252 A hand on my shoulder..started the Unarmed Combat reflexes working. **1973** J. R. L. ANDERSON *Death on Rocks* ii. 39 If I could get my hands on him—well, I'd been quite good at what the Army calls unarmed combat.

2. Of animals, etc.: Not fitted for attack; not furnished with horns, teeth, or the like.

1398 TREVISA *Barth. De P.R.* XVIII. lxxx. (Bodl. MS.), The schepe..is a nesche beeste and bereþ wolle & is vnarmed & plesinge in herte. **1649** LOVELACE *Lucasta* Poems (1904) 95 A Falcon.. Unarm'd of Wings and Scaly Oare. **1804** SHAW *Gen. Zool.* V. I. 14 Unarmed Silure, *Silurus Inermis.* **1834** MCMURTRIE *Cuvier's Anim. Kingd.* 495 *Furcularia*... The body is unarmed. **1855** *Orr's Circ. Sci., Inorg. Nat.* 108 Reptiles..whose two tusks, in an otherwise unarmed jaw, strikingly distinguish them from any of their contemporaries. **1869** TANNER *Clin. Med.* (ed. 2) 309 The unarmed or beef tape-worm,..as its name implies, is unfurnished with hooks around its head.

3. Of plants: Destitute of prickles, spines, or thorns.

1676 GREW *Anat. Flowers* II. App. §11 The Top is Thorny, as in Furz; or Vnarmed. Vnarmed, either produced, that is, poynted, or at least, Roundish. **1793** MARTYN *Lang. Bot., Inerme folium*, an unarmed leaf. **1845** STEELE *Field Bot.* 218 Bracts of invol. linear-lanceolate, almost unarmed. **1855** MISS PRATT *Flower. Pl.* II. 298 Unarmed Hornwort. Fruit without either spines or tubercles. **1870** HOOKER *Stud. Flora* 107 *Prunus communis*, ..Sub-sp. *domestica*;..branches straight unarmed.

4. Of things: Not provided with anything that assists or strengthens.

1693 DRYDEN *Juvenal* x. 319 The same foulness does to Age belong, The self same Palsie,..And Gums unarm'd to mumble Meat in vain. *a* **1721** PRIOR *Journ. to Copt-Hall* 12, I mount, and great as Hudibrass, With unarm'd kick urge on my horse. **1860** TYNDALL *Glac.* I. xxvii. 200 Pattens..sank less deeply than the unarmed feet. **1860** EMERSON *Cond. Life* v. 156 In Siberia, a late traveller found men who could see the satellites of Jupiter with their unarmed eye.

†**5.** Of a magnet: Not provided with an armature. *Obs.*

1662 J. BARGRAVE *Pope Alex. VII* (1867) 120 Two large loadstones, one armed with steel... The other..is unarmed. **1730** *Phil. Trans.* XXXVI. 325, I placed the Pole of the upper Armour about 4 or 5 Inches from the Top of the unarmed Bar. **1777** *Ibid.* LXVII. 135 A fine, smooth, unarmed load-stone.

Hence **un'armedness.**

1684 H. MORE *Answer* 208 This Lamblike condition of it is chiefly represented in this present Vision, its seeming harmlesness and unarmedness.

un'armoured, *a.* [UN-[1] 9.]

1. Of vessels: Not armour-clad.

1869 SIR E. REED *Our Iron-Clad Ships* iv. 73 When we pass from unarmoured to armoured ships, the contrast is still more striking. **1879** *Cassell's Techn. Educ.* IV. 61/1 In the unarmoured iron ships recently built for the navy tie-plates have been entirely dispensed with.

2. Of persons: Not protected by armour.

1873 MORRIS *Love is Enough* 18 Barehanded, unarmoured, he handled the spear-shaft. **1892** TENNYSON *Foresters* IV, And walkest [thou] here Unarmour'd? all these walks are Robin Hood's And sometimes perilous.

una'roused, *ppl. a.* (UN-[1] 8.)

1855 SINGLETON *Virgil* II. 207 Burns Unaroused and moveless hitherto Ausonia.

una'rraignable, *a.* (UN-[1] 7 b.)

1886 SWINBURNE *Misc.* 52 Work unarraignable alike by fair means or foul.

una'rraigned, *ppl. a.* (UN-[1] 8.)

1595 DANIEL *Civ. Wars* III. xxii, Neuer shall this poore breath of mine consent That he..Should here be iudgd vnheard, and vnaraignd. **1858** MERIVALE *Hist. Rom. Emp.* lii. (1865) VI. 286 He did not venture to command his execution, unarraigned and unconvicted.

una'rranged, *ppl. a.* (UN-[1] 8.)

[**1775** ASH.] **1791** BOSWELL *Johnson* an. 1737, The *disjecta membra* scattered throughout, and as yet unarranged. **1840** CARLYLE *Heroes* v. (1904) 160 How many powerful forces are seen working in a wasteful, chaotic, altogether unarranged manner. **1897** PULLEN BURRY *Blotted Out* 51 Death is an unsurveyed land, an unarranged science.

†**una'rray**, *v. Obs.* [UN-[2] 4.] *trans.* To deprive of array; *esp.* to undress, disrobe.

14.. *Chaucer's Sqr.'s T.* 173 (Camb. MS.), This knyght.. is on-arayed [*other MSS.* vnarmed] & to mete i-set. *a* **1483** *Liber Niger* in S. Pegge *Cur. Misc.* (1782) 79 Two [Esquires of the Body] to be attendant on the King's person to array and unarray him. **1483** *Cath. Angl.* 12/1 To vn Aray, *exornare, & cetera*; *vbi* to dysaray. **1590** STOCKWOOD *Eng. Accidence* 65 This verbe *exuo*, of araying, or rather indeed of vnaraying, hath two accusative cases. **1601** LAMBARDE *Dict. Angl. Topogr.* (1730) 69 She forth-with unarrayed her selfe, untrussed her Heare.

una'rrayed, *ppl. a.* [UN-[1] 8.]

1. Not arrayed or put in order.

c **1340** HAMPOLE *Prose Tr.* 28 If þou..latis þame spill for defaute of kepynge—unarayede, unkepide,..thou pleses Hym noghte. **1390** GOWER *Conf.* III. 175, I sih also The noble peple of Irahel Dispers as schep upon an hell, Withoute a kepere unarraied. *c* **1400** *Brut* 13 Whan Humbar saw hem come, he was sore adrad, forasmyche as his men wist it not, & also þey were vnarrayed. **1727** BAILEY (vol. II), *Unarrayed*, not ranged in Order of Battle.

2. Not dressed; unclothed; unarmed.

c **1380** *Sir Ferumb.* 821 Duke Roland þan was sore amayed, So wern þe doþþepers,..for þay wern oun-araid. *c* **1440** *York Myst.* xxiv. 6 We will bere witnesse..How we hir raysed all vnarayed,..Wher sche was with hir leman laide. *a* **1450** *Knt. de la Tour* (1906) 153 There shall now be sheued you of the good ladyes that were vnaraied, duellynge in Rome. **1611** COTGR., *Desabillé*, vncloathed, vndressed, vnarrayed. **1665** DRYDEN *Ind. Emp.* I. i, As if this Infant World, yet unarray'd, Naked and bare, in Nature's Lap were laid. **1685** —— *Thren. August.* 54 Half unarray'd he ran to his Relief, So hasty and so artless was his Grief. **1839** BAILEY *Festus* 187 Thou art as the cloudless moon, Undimmed and unarrayed; No robe hast thou.

una'rrestable, *a.* (UN-[1] 7 b), **-ably**, *adv.* (UN-[1] 11).

1855 PRINCE ALBERT *Sp. in B'ham* 22 Nov., The former is an unarrestable movement towards the fountain of truth. **1884** E. ABBOTT *Flatland* 75, I could feel him slowly and unarrestably slipping from my contact.

una'rrested, *ppl. a.* [UN-[1] 8. Cf. MDu. *ongearresteert.*]

1. Not arrested or apprehended.

c **1400** *Beryn* 2188, I woll..assay, yf I may, in eny maner wise, Ascapen vnarestid more in suche maner wise. **1498**, **1531** [see UNATTACHED *ppl. a.* 1]. **1533** MORE *Apol.* 259 b, By thys pacyfyers good deuyse, heretykes maye go unarrested. **1611** COTGR., *Descalengé*, vnarrested, vnapprehended. **1891** E. KINGLAKE *Australian at Home* 77 The wife of a certain unarrested absconder was observed to have command of plenty of money.

2. Not stopped or checked.

1733 TULL *Horse-Hoeing Husb.* xiv. 199 The under Stratum must be the richer for receiving what the upper Stratum lets pass Unarrested. **1859** TENNENT *Ceylon* II. VII. v. 197 The temples of Kandy..are dilapidated edifices, apparently perishing from unarrested decay. **1869** G. LAWSON *Dis. Eye* (1874) 79 If the disease be unarrested by treatment, the whole pupillary margin becomes sealed to the lens capsule.

una'rrived, *ppl. a.* [UN-[1] 8.]

1. Not yet arrived (at a place, or in time).

1626 in Foster *Eng. Factories India* (1909) III. 155 The shipps expected and unarrived. **1742** YOUNG *Nt. Th.* IX. 294 These, as two monarchs, on their borders meet, (Monarchs of all elaps'd, or unarriv'd!)

b. That has not yet attained success.

1902 *Academy* 25 Jan. 76/2 Liverpool offers great possibilities to the unarrived novelist.

2. Not yet arrived *at*; unattained.

1669 [see UNAIMED *ppl. a.*].

un'arrogant, *a.* (UN-[1] 7.)

1831 D. E. WILLIAMS *Sir T. Lawrence* I. 12 He had an unarrogant self-possession which few men enjoy.

un'arrogating, *ppl. a.* (UN-[1] 10.)

1742 MELMOTH *Fitzosborne Lett.* (1763) 349 Whoever pursues his speculations with this humble unarrogating temper of mind [etc.]. **1864** E. SARGENT *Peculiar* I. 152 The quiet unarrogating air of one whose nobility is a part of his nature.

†**un'arted**, *a. Obs.* [UN-[1] 9.]

1. Ignorant of the arts; unskilled.

1603 FLORIO *Montaigne* I. li. 166 They are..rude, simple, and unarted in the combate of talking. **1606** WARNER *Alb. Engl.* XIV. To Rdr., Shunne Eares vnarted, rude, precise. **1699** CIBBER *Xerxes* II, I am unarted, Sir, in any grace of speech To stir the soul! My words are plain and honest.

2. Unartificial; plain.

1628 FELTHAM *Resolves* II. xcix. 291 Wise Innocence, friends like, and good Vnarted-meat, kind neighbourhood.

un'artful, *a.* [UN-[1] 7.]

1. Not artificial or contrived; artless.

1669 DRYDEN & DAVENANT *Tempest* III. (1670) 32 I'm sure unartful truth lies open In her mind, as Crystal streams their sandy bottom shew. **1693** CONGREVE in *Dryden's Juvenal* XI. (1697) 291 A chearful Sweetness in his Looks he has, And Innocence unartful in his Face. **1713** *Guard.* No. 127 *Crt. Venus* 70 Unartful Tears, and hectick Looks, that show With silent Eloquence the Lover's Woe. **1763** FALCONER *Fond Lover* 14 Since all her thoughts by sense refined, Unartful truth express. **1820** W. TOOKE tr. *Lucian* I. 147 Much less can it be affirmed, that it [*sc.* spunging] is an unartful art. **1899** VERRAL in A. C. Brown *Life E. W. Benson* (1900) I. 219 The same delightful and unartful arts were displayed.

b. Free from artifice or cunning.

1703 ROWE *Fair Penit.* II. ii. 596 This Son, if Fame mistakes not, is more hot, More open, and unartful.

2. Displaying no technical skill; inartistic.

1675 COCKER *Morals* 49 Rashness draws crooked and unartful Lines. **1703** SAVAGE *Lett. Antients* ix. 52 Beneath this humble Roof he stood, and this plain unartful Floor supported him. **1712** BLACKMORE *Creation* III. 179 So full of faults is all the unartful frame. **1759** GOLDSM. *Bee* No. 5. 90 To have almost every personage on the scene almost of the same character..was unartful in the poet to the last degree. **1883** *Pall Mall G.* 24 Nov. 4/2 Prose which borrows in a manner pleasant enough in result, and by no means unartful, the more obvious and seductive attractions of verse.

b. Of persons: Unskilful, maladroit. *rare.*

1683 MRS. BEHN *Yng. King* II. iii, I am a man, whose martial disposition Renders unartful in my language. **1709** MRS. MANLEY *Secret Mem.* (1720) IV. 88 A swift and sure Contempt succeeds upon what-ever the unartful Husband shall happen to do after.

Hence **un'artfully** *adv.*

1724 SWIFT *Drapier's Lett.* iii. Wks. 1841 II. 17/2 The report, which, although it be not unartfully drawn,..yet there was no great skill required to detect the many mistakes ..in it. **1726** —— *Gulliver* IV. ii, Matts of straw, not unartfully made. **1793** *Minstrel* III. 137, I discovered a door, not unartfully concealed by some rude chizeling in the rock. **1840** THACKERAY *Pict. Rhapsody* 116 This plan has been not unartfully contrived.

unar'ticulate, *a.* [UN-[1] 7 and 5 b.]

†**1.** = INARTICULATE *a.* 2. *Obs.*

1603 J. DAVIES (Heref.) *Microcosmos* Wks. (Grosart) I. 12/2 No Beast..But in his voice (though vnarticulate) Salutes these times. **1611** COTGR., *Sphinge*, the..Sphinx..; his vnarticulate voice like that of a hastie speaker.

2. = INARTICULATE *a.* 1.

1855 PUSEY *Doctr. Real Presence* Note 440 The one..is upright, articulate,..but the other..is round, unarticulate, inanimate.

unar'ticulated, *ppl. a.* [UN-[1] 8. Cf. G. *unarticulirt*, Sw. *oarticulerad.*]

1. Not articulated or distinct.

a **1700** KEN *Hymnarium* Poet. Wks. 1721 II. 25 God from the Moment we draw breath,..Our words, when unarticulated, hears. **1823** LAMB *Let. Old Gentl.* Misc. Wks. (1871) 451 That unarticulated language, which was before the written tongue. **1840** WILLIS *Loiterings* II. 139 The touching attitudes and utter abandonment of all around to their unarticulated devotions.

2. Not jointed; not fitted together.

1861 HULME tr. *Moquin-Tandon* II. VII. xiii. 399 The egg encloses a short unarticulated embryo. *a* **1894** C. H. PEARSON in Stebbing *Life* (1900) 77 A cupboard full of unarticulated human bones.

unarti'ficial, *a.* [UN-[1] 7 and 5 b.]

1. Not displaying special art or skill; unskilful, inartistic, clumsy. Now *rare* or *Obs.*

1591 HARINGTON *Orl. Fur.* Pref., If I shold confesse..that my verse is vnartificiall, the stile rude, the phrase barbarous. **1597** MORLEY *Introd. Mus.* 80 It is an vnartificiall kinde of descanting in the middle of a lesson, to let the plainsong sing alone. **1602** CAMPION *Art Eng. Poesie* Ded., The vulgar and vnarteficiall custome of riming. **1702** S. PARKER tr. *Cicero's De Finibus* III. 154 The Common-Places and suggestions of your Advocates for Pleasure are, at best, but very Shallow and Unartificial. **1790** BURKE *Fr. Rev.* 275 They have levelled and crushed together all the orders which they found, even under the coarse unartificial arrangement of the monarchy. **1825** BENTHAM *Ration. Reward* 204 Art and science, on the one hand, and unartificial practice and unscientific knowledge, on the other.

2. Not artificial; simple, natural.

1603 FLORIO *Montaigne* III. xii. 628 It representeth in an vn-artificiall boldnesse, and infantine securitie, the pure impression and first ignorance of nature. **1656** EARL MONM. tr. *Boccalini's Advts. fr. Parnass.* I. lxxvii. (1674) 100 Men who live in sincerity.., with an undisguised and unartificial goodness. **1799** *Monthly Rev.* XXX. 345 Example arising from a natural unartificial developement of incidents. **1982** *N. & Q.* Aug. 361/2 He demonstrates that Wordsworth considered a good epitaph to be an expression in unartificial language of the deep feelings of the bereaved for the dead.

unarti'ficially, *adv.* [f. prec.] † Inartistically, unskilfully.

1591 HARINGTON *Orl. Fur.* Pref., And yet for Ariostos tales that many thinke vnartificially brought in, Homer him selfe hath the like. **1598** HAKLUYT *Voy.* I. 484 The barrel is rudely and vnartificially made. **1622** PEACHAM *Compl. Gent.* x. (1634) 89 Hee goeth unartificially to worke even in the very beginning. **1670** MILTON *Hist. Eng.* III. Wks. 1851 V. 102 The material being only Turf, and by the rude multitude unartificially built up.., avail'd them little. **1706** STEVENS *Span. Dict.* I, *Inhabilmente*, unhandily, unartificially, unskilfully, ignorantly.

unar'tistic, *a.* (UN-[1] 7 and 5 b.)

1854 GRACE GREENWOOD *Haps & Mishaps* 68 It certainly strikes the unartistic as a most unsuitable alliance. **1865** *Athenæum* No. 1955. 520/3 A vague unartistic tale.

un'artistlike, *a.* and *adv.* (UN-[1] 7 c and 11 b.)

1654 GAYTON *Pleas. Notes* III. iii. 81 It was very improper, and unartist-like done in Sancho, to permit him to sleep. **1757** GROSE *Voy. E. Indies* 173 Their naval, like their other architecture, has always something clumsy, unfinished, and unartist-like in it. **1837** LYTTON *Athens* II. 115 The elaborate description of this work [a bridge] given by Herodotus proves it to have been no clumsy or unartistlike performance.

† **'unary**, *sb. Obs.*[-1] [f. L. *ūn-us* one.] A unit.

1576 FLEMING tr. *Caius' Dogs* (1880) 36 This countrey was cleerely discharged of rauenyng wolfes, & none at all left, no, not to the least number, or the beginnyng of a number, which is an Vnari.

unary ('juːnərɪ), *a.* [f. L. *ūn-us* one + -ARY[1], after BINARY, TERNARY *adjs.*] **1.** *Chem.* Of a chemical system: consisting of a single component.

1923 A. C. D. RIVETT *Phase Rule* i. 25 For systems of one, two, three, four, five (and so on) components, one uses the terms unary, binary, ternary, quaternary, quinary (and so on), respectively. **1980** *Mineral. Abstr.* XXXI. 311/1 Sixteen possible configurations of phase diagrams have been deduced for unary four-phase multi-systems.

2. *Math., Logic,* and *Linguistics.* Of an operator, operation, or transformation: involving or operating on a single element.

1931 *Bull. Amer. Math. Soc.* XXXVII. 487 Let *p* be the result of an undefined unary operation on a *K*-element *p*, and *p* + *q* the result of an undefined binary operation on the *K*-elements *p, q.* **1940** [see SINGULARY *a.*]. **1961** *Jrnl. Assoc. Computing Machinery* VIII. 579 The five binary arithmetic operators (↑, ×, /, +, −), the two unary arithmetic operators (+, −). **1965** *Language* XLI. 270 Robert Stockwell has described rules that indicate the colorless patterns for kernel sentences and unary transformations. **1968** J. J. C. SMART *Betw. Sci. & Philos.* ii. 24 'Not' can be thought of as a unary sentence connective. **1973** C. W. GEAR *Introd. Computer Sci.* iii. 104 The unary arithmetic operators take precedence over all of the binary operators and must be performed first. **1976** J. S. GRUBER *Lexical Structures in Syntax & Semantics* II. i. 266 If the treatment is through a unary transformation that alters structure, the dependency of the transformation on apparently semantic factors becomes a matter of graver theoretical consequences.

3. Composed of a single item or element.

1968 P. M. POSTAL *Aspects Phonol. Theory* i. 13 Natural languages have structures which are such that the markers on every level can be looked upon as sets (sometimes unary sets) of strings of elements. **1968** *Amer. Documentation* Jan. 73/1 Items are either unary or multiple, depending upon whether they are composed of a single piece of information (which may itself be composed of any number of characters or words) or of two or more separate pieces of information.

una'scendable, *a.* (UN-[1] 7 b.)

1615 G. SANDYS *Trav.* 171 He..confined the Royall progeny within high and vnascendable mountaines. **1628** FELTHAM *Resolves* II. [I.] xxix. 90 A Hill almost vnascendable. **1801** SOUTHEY *Thalaba* XII. xvi, The depth was unascendable.

una'scended, *ppl. a.* (UN-[1] 8.)

1820 SHELLEY *Prometh. Unb.* III. iv. 203 The loftiest star of unascended heaven. **1821** —— *Adonais* xlvi, It was for thee yon kingless sphere has long Swung blind in unascended majesty. **1861** F. W. JACOMB in *Peaks, Passes & Glaciers* Ser. II. I. 315 Removing a mountain from the unascended list.

una'scendible, *a.* (UN-[1] 7.)

1801 SOUTHEY *Thalaba* VII. iv, The heights precipitous, Impending crags, rocks unascendible.

unascer'tainable, *a.* (UN-[1] 7 b.)

1802–12 BENTHAM *Ration. Judic. Evid.* (1827) V. 237 It is only..to an amount altogether precarious and unascertainable, that it does away the mischief. **1876** A. S. MURRAY *Mythol.* 14 By keeping constantly before the mind a sense of the unascertainable and infinite powers of nature.

unascer'tained, *ppl. a.* [UN-[1] 8.] †**a.** Not certified or apprised. *Obs.* **b.** Not ascertained or known.

1628 in Foster *Eng. Factories India* (1909) III. 193 What is become of Beale, whether living or dead, we are yett unascertained. **1751** HARRIS *Hermes* II. i. (1765) 217 The Article (A) leaves the Individual itself unascertained, whereas the Article (The) ascertains the Individual also. **1784** COOK *Third Voy.* VI. iv. III. 269 The only part of the Russian empire that now remains unascertained. **1815** J. SMITH *Panorama Sci. & Art* II. 319 The standard temperatures desired, remained unascertained till the time of Newton. **1879** *St. George's Hosp. Rep.* IX. 127 An unascertained quantity of oxalic acid and white precipitate.

† **una'scried**, *ppl. a. Obs.*[-1] [UN-[1] 8.] Undescried, unobserved.

a **1548** HALL *Chron., Hen. VIII*, 32 So that alwaies it was forsene that..the Frenchemen shoulde not come on them sodainly vnaskryed.

una'shamed, *ppl. a.* (UN-[1] 8.)

Hence **una'shamedly** *adv.*; **una'shamedness** (1921 *N.E.D.*).

1600 FAIRFAX *Tasso* V. lxxi, This foolish crew of louers, vnashamed,..Ran forward still, in this disordred sort. **1619** H. HUTTON *Follie's Anat.* (Percy Soc.) 24 See this incarnate monster of her sex Play the virago, unashamde, perplext. **1827** POLLOK *Course T.* VIII. 782 Lust of wealth and power Inordinate, and lewdness unashamed. **1855** BROWNING *Two in Campagna* vii, Let us, O my dove, Let us be unashamed of soul. **1887** LOWELL *Democracy*, etc. 100 Coleridge's words have the unashamed nakedness of Scripture. **1905** W. J. LOCKE *Morals of Marcus Ordeyne* iv. 50 She was wearing a deep red silk peignoir,..unashamedly Parisian, which clung to every salient curve of her figure. **1928** *Manch. Guardian Weekly* 10 Aug. 115/2 They break out.. into dance measures of an unashamedly negroid vigour. **1983** M. GILBERT *Black Seraphim* iii. 35 Amanda..was listening unashamedly.

un'asinous, *a.* [f. L. *ūn-us* one + *asinus* ass, after *unanimous.*] Agreeing in stupidity.

1656 HOBBES *Six Lessons* vi. ad fin., Go your wayes you uncivil Ecclesiasticks... De-doctors of Morality, unasinous collegues [etc.].

un'ask, *v.* (UN-[2] 3.)

1843 GEO. ELIOT in Cross *Life* (1885) I. 120, I cannot desire that you should unask violin and Flute, unless a postponement would be..as agreeable to you and them.

un'askable, *a.* (UN-[1] 7 b.)

1854 FERRIER *Inst. Metaph.* IX. xxxv. 498 The truths which it has reached renders that question absurd. It is unanswerable, because it is unaskable.

un'asked, *ppl. a.* Also 6, 9 *dial*, unaxed. [UN-[1] 8, 8 c.]

1. Without being asked; not requested or intreated; uninvited.

a **1255** *Ancr. R.* 338 þe hwule þet tu const siggen out [in shrift], seie al unasked. **1456** SIR. G. HAYE *Law Arms* (S.T.S.) 139 Gyf a knycht..had gevyn a coursour to the Provost of Paris unaskit. **1582** STANYHURST *Æneis* II. (Arb.) 55 In gentil manner thus he soone discoursed, vnasked. **1618** J. TAYLOR (Water P.) *Penniless Pilgr.* Wks. (1630) 123/1 Master Taylor, at the Sarazen's head, Vnask'd (vnpaid for) me both lodg'd and fed. **1697** DRYDEN *Virg. Past.* III. 100 Fair Amyntas comes unasked to me, And offers love. **1710** PRIOR *Examiner, To Earl Godolphin* 10 Unask'd you offer, and unseen you give. **1746** FRANCIS tr. *Hor., Sat.* I. iii. 3 Sing they can never at a friend's request, Yet chant it forth, unask'd, from morn till night. **1810** CRABBE *Borough* xviii. 56 He shows the shipping;..He makes (unask'd) their ports and business known. **1879** MEREDITH *Egoist* xxiv, She went to the music rack and gave the song unasked.

†**b.** Left uninvited. *Sc. Obs.*

c **1730** BURT *Lett. N. Scot.* (1754) II. 204, I have several times been unasked to eat.

2. Not asked for; not made the subject of a request.

1456 SIR G. HAYE *Law Arms* (S.T.S.) 96 Quhat thingis.. has sauf condyt be privilege unaskit at the princis. **1529** S. FISH *Supplic. Beggars* (1871) 8 There was giuen theim ynough vnaxed. **1592** SHAKS. *Ven. & Ad.* 102 Yet hath he.. begg'd for that which thou unask'd shalt have. **1618** J. TAYLOR (Water P.) *Penniless Pilgr.* Wks. (1630) 123/2, I thought it no good manners to refuse, But thank'd him for his kinde vnasked gift. **1658** OSBORNE *Jas. I*, 53 The Scots, by whom nothing was unasked, and to whom nothing was denied. **1712** ADDISON *Spect.* No. 357 ¶10 Adam.. expostulates with his Creator for having given him an unasked Existence. **1751** WARBURTON *Pope's Wks.* IX. 247 *note*, To the issue of that unasked and unsought compliment these words allude. **1819** SCOTT *Leg. Montrose* x, He delivered his unasked opinion as follows. **1870** MORRIS *Earthly Par.* II. III. 426 Indeed I thought That news of ill unasked would soon be brought.

b. Similarly with *for.*

1714 MANDEVILLE *Fab. Bees* (1733) II. 117 The unask'd-for bounty and downright generosity of this benefactor. **1861** LADY LYTTELTON *Let.* 15 Dec., The Queen..sent me an account on the 10th (unasked for..) through Lady Augusta Bruce. **1876** T. HARDY *Ethelberta* xxxvi, An unasked-for concession to their cause.

un'asking, *ppl. a.* (UN-[1] 10.)

1722 WOLLASTON *Relig. Nat.* v. 116 That he..should have many things granted him, which are not given to the careless, obdurate, unasking part of mankind. **1799** in *Spirit Pub. Jrnls.* III. 271 Laid under contribution to the unasking necessities of the pupil of Mercury. **1876** LANIER *Clover* 97 This cool, unasking Ox Comes browsing o'er my hills and vales of Time.

b. In ppl. use: Without asking for. (UN-[1] 5 d.)

1754 SHEBBEARE *Matrimony* (1766) I. 225 Unasking more, he implored only the Continuation of Health to himself and Family.

† **una'spected**, *ppl. a. Obs.*[-1] [UN-[1] 8: cf. ASPECT *v.* 1.] Unsuspected, unexpected.

1578 FLORIO *1st Fruites* 86 The forreyne knyfe doothe disbarke it [*sc.* a tree], the bee of unaspected causes dooth consume it.

† **una'spective**, *a. Obs.*[-1] [UN-[1] 7 + ASPECT *v.*] Unregardful.

1661 FELTHAM *Resolves* II. lxxiv. 348 In which the Holy Ghost is not wholly unaspective to the custome that was used among men.

† **una'spied**, *ppl. a. Obs.* = UNESPIED *ppl. a.*

c **1400** *Destr. Troy* 1428 Of a sparke unaspied, spred vnder askys, May feston vp fyre to mony freike sorow. **1508** DUNBAR *Tua Mariit Wemen* 427 That I may spy, vnaspyit, a space me beside.

un'aspirated, *ppl. a.* (UN-[1] 8. Cf. G. *unaspirirt.*)

[**1775** ASH.] **1793** PARR *Combe's Horace* Wks. 1828 III. 33 Lambin gives ὀρημι for the Æolic verb unaspirated. **1887** *Pall Mall G.* 26 Aug. 3/1 Mr. and Mrs. Williamson's unaspirated piety might have been spared with advantage.

una'spiring, *ppl. a.* (UN-[1] 10.)

a **1729** J. ROGERS *Serm.* (1736) 173 An easy unaspiring Temper which rests satisfy'd with its present Share of the Bounties of Providence. **1806** R. MANT *Poems, To Bp. Durham* I. 2 She loves..To cheer with unaspiring lay The dear domestic shade. **1852** LD. COCKBURN *Jeffrey* I. 103 The unaspiring life, I believe, has the least positive wretchedness.

Hence **una'spiringness.**

1681 *Whole Duty Nations* 64 The Humility, Modesty, and unaspiringness of Christianity. **1861** MILL *Repr. Govt.* iii. 64 Inactivity, unaspiringness, absence of desire, are a more fatal hindrance to improvement than any misdirection of energy.

un'ass, *v.* (UN-[2] 5.)

1654 GAYTON *Pleas. Notes* IV. iii. 184 Gines Passamont.. With Sancho's Asse unto a Fare was packing; The quick-eyed Bore had spied him, and unass'd him.

unassailability. (UN-[1] 12.)

a **1921** *N.E.D.* s.v. *Unassailable* a. **1952** *Mind* LXI. 504 Its unassailability has been bought at the price of making no claim about the world. **1957** J. S. HUXLEY *Relig. without Revelation* i. 27 The unassailability of private property.

una'ssailable, *a.* [UN-[1] 7 b.]

1. Not assailable; not open to assault or attack. Also *fig.*

1596 SPENSER *F.Q.* V. ix. 5 Thereto both his owne wylie wit (she sayd), And eke the fastnesse of his dwelling place, Both vnassaylable, gaue him great ayde. **1601** SHAKS. *Jul. C.* III. i. 69, I do know but One That vnassayleable holds on his Ranke, Vnshak'd of Motion. **1825** J. NEAL *Bro. Jonathan* III. 121 He was always the same,..alike unassailable—inscrutable. **1841** ELPHINSTONE *Hist. Ind.* I. 543 The chief had occupied an unassailable position, but was drawn out by a pretended flight. **1871** MACDUFF *Mem. Patmos* xii. 167 They have a..heritage of tribulation: but their spiritual safety is unassailable.

2. Not open to adverse criticism.

1830 MACKINTOSH *Progr. Eth. Philos.* Wks. 1846 I. 120 In both cases he occupies the unassailable ground of an appeal to consciousness. **1884** *Manch. Exam.* 17 Sept. 4/6 The President's address..does not actually lead us to any unassailable conclusions.

Hence **una'ssailableness; -ably** *adv.*

1854 GEO. ELIOT tr. *Feuerbach's Essence Christianity* xiv. 136 The truth and unassailableness of their subjective feelings. **1870** *Pall Mall G.* 20 Oct. 3 America possesses over us the advantages of distance and unassailableness. **1876** BANCROFT *Hist. U.S.* VI. xxxvii. 184 The two oceans, between which the republic has unassailably intrenched itself.

una'ssailed, *ppl. a.* (UN-[1] 8.)

a **1586** SIDNEY *Arcadia* III. vii. (1912) 385 The quietnesse of his unassailed senses. **1593** SHAKS. *2 Hen. VI*, VI. ii. 18 It greeues my soule to leaue thee vnassail'd. **1634** MILTON *Comus* 220 The Supreme good..Would send a glistring Guardian if need were To keep my life and honour unassail'd. **1735** THOMSON *Liberty* III. 456 Unarm'd he stray'd, unguarded, unassail'd. **1819** SCOTT *Ivanhoe* xliv, If unassailed, we depart assailing no one. **1887** MOLONEY *Forestry W. Africa* 194 Nevertheless the trade in jute holds its own unassailed.

una'ssassinated, *ppl. a.* (UN-[1] 8.)

1842 POE *Marie Roget* Wks. 1865 I. 227 If starting from the living Marie, we find her, yet find her unassassinated.

una'ssaultable, *a.* (UN-[1] 7 b.)

1571 GOLDING *Calvin on Ps.* xlviii. 11 A Citie very wel fortified and unassaultable. **1582** BENTLEY *Mon. Matrones* 334 When I bethinke me what a tower of strength..and unassaultable habitation thou hast euer beene. **1611** SPEED *Hist. Gt. Brit.* IX. xxiii. 114 A breach made in the wall, not farre from the Water-gate, but yet vnassaultable, the English within so maintained the defence. **1653** A. WILSON *Jas. I*, 216 It is a great disadvantage for living Bodies to fight against dead Walls, being so high, and unassaultable. *a* **1711** KEN *Christophil* Poet. Wks. 1721 I. 516 O Realm of undisturb'd repose, Thrones unassaultable by Woes!

una'ssaulted, *ppl. a.* (UN-[1] 8.)

1611 SPEED *Hist. Gt. Brit.* V. vi. §17. 37 The German Saxons..neuer left their attempts vnassaulted till they set the glorious diademe thereof vpon their owne heads. **1655** MOUFET & BENNET *Health's Improv.* (1746) 207 He..left no fair Woman unassaulted. *a* **1711** KEN *Psyche* Poet. Wks. 1721 IV. 209 That I secure may grow, When unassaulted by my Foe. **1758** JOHNSON *Idler* No. 20 ¶11 The commanders ..durst not leave the place unassaulted.

una'ssayed, *ppl. a.* (UN-[1] 8.)

c **1374** CHAUCER *Boeth.* II. pr. iv. (1868) 42 Alwey to euery man þere is..somwhat þat vnassaied he ne wot not, or ellys he drediþ þat he haþ assaied. *c* **1403** LYDG. *Temple Glas* 1249 For vn-assaied men may no troupe preue. **1513** DOUGLAS *Æneid* VIII. iv. 58 Na maner of wickitnes nor dissait Mycht be, that he ne durst nocht tak on hand, Ne onassait leif. **1560** DAUS tr. *Sleidane's Comm.* 195 b, Who leaveth no waye unassayed to accomplyshe his ambition. **1617** MORYSON *Itin.* I. 275 These good fellowes leave nothing unassaied, in the wished discovery of these fraudes. **1649** MILTON *Eikon.* xi. Wks. 1851 III. 427 To be ridd of these mortifying Propositions he leaves no tyrannical evasion unassaid. **1708** PHILIPS *Cyder* I. 362 They sedulously think To meliorate thy Stock; no Way, or Rule Be unassay'd. **1784** COWPER

Task III. 451 To raise the prickly and green-coated gourd,.. is an art..at this moment unassay'd in song. **1912** LADY BURGHCLERE *Life Dk. Ormonde* I. x. 317 He could not afford to leave unassayed any issue that promised escape.

una'ssenting, *ppl. a.* (UN-1 10.)
1836 SIR H. TAYLOR *Statesman* xiii. 88 Otherwise the hand, if an unassenting one, will carry an advantage over the head. **1883** MISS BETHAM-EDWARDS *Disarmed* xx, Arthura smiled, a sad, unassenting smile.

una'sserted, *ppl. a.* (UN-1 8.)
[**1775** ASH]. **1856** LEVER *Martins of Cro'M.* lxv, He is now back here once more; come to insist upon his long unasserted rights.

una'ssertive, *a.* (UN-1 7.)
1861 DICKENS *Gt. Expect.* lvii, He would sit and talk to me ..in the old unassertive protecting way. **1882** *Ch. Q. Rev.* Apr. 140 Unanxious and unassertive, where certainty fails it.

†**una'sserved,** *ppl. a. Obs. rare.* [UN-1 8.]
a. Unserved. **b.** Undeserved.
c **1400** *Beryn* 56 'Graunt mercy, gentil Sir!' quod she, 'þat yee been vnaservid'. *c* **1400** *R. Gloucester's Chron.* 1256 (MS. Digby 205), I haue holde him on his londe and my mede þer of is That he me wolde dryue awey and unasserued j wis.

una'ssiduous, *a.* (UN-1 7.)
1776 BENTHAM *On. Govt.* Wks. 1843 I. 295 All these leading points,..with as many points of detail subservient to each as a meditation not unassiduous has suggested.

una'ssignable, *a.* (UN-1 7 b.)
Hence, in recent use, ***unassignability.***
1674 N. FAIRFAX *Bulk & Selv.* 62, I see this roomthiness in the whole, must as well have unassignable parts or such as cannot be laid out. **1780** T. TWINING in R. Twining *Recreat. & Stud.* (1882) 76 In gracing, he does the most beautiful, most unassignable..things I ever heard. **1780** BENTHAM *Princ. Legisl.* xii. §15 Such party may be either an assignable individual..or else a multitude of unassignable individuals. **1883** SIR. E. E. KAY in *Weekly Notes* 15 Dec. 212/1 A vested reversionary interest subject to a life interest in leasehold property..[is] not an unassignable possibility.

una'ssigned, *ppl. a.* (UN-1 8.)
1495 *Cov. Leet Bk.* 565 Yf..eny persone vnassigned take vppon hym to ruyde contrarie to þis ordenaunce, they to lese at euery defalt x s. **1812** WOODHOUSE *Astron.* xvii. 181 Effects with unassigned causes. **1870** SWINBURNE *Ess. & Stud.* (1875) 341 Many sketches by hands unknown... Also unassigned, is a vigorous drawing of a monk's head.

una'ssimilable, *a.* (UN-1 7 b and 5 b.)
1873 E. H. CLARKE *Sex in Educ.* 23 Our girls revel in those unassimilable abominations. **1882** *Athenæum* 4 Mar. 286/1 America is being invaded by Socialist Germans..and unassimilable Chinese.

una'ssimilatable, *a.* (UN-1 7 b.)
1858 J. H. BENNET *Nutrition* iv. 89 The kidneys ..[remove] from the circulating fluid effete unassimilatable nutritive elements.

una'ssimilated, *ppl. a.* (UN-1 8. Cf. G. *unassimilirt.*)
1748 HARTLEY *Observ. Man* I. iii. §6. 393 It circulates with the Fluids in an unassimilated State. **1811** ABERNETHY *Surg. Wks.* (1827) II. 201 Much unassimilated matter being conveyed into the blood with the chyle. **1866** WHIPPLE *Char. & Charac. Men* 11 Unassimilated knowledge—knowledge that does not form part of the mind, but is attached to it.

una'ssimilating, *ppl. a.* (UN-1 10.)
1796 MME. D'ARBLAY *Camilla* I. i, [Fortune's] most rapid vicissitudes, her most unassimilating eccentricities, are.. distanced by the wilder wonders of the Heart of man.

una'ssistant, *a.* (UN-1 7.)
1796 *Plain Sense* (ed. 2) III. 203 To suffer..her most strenuous protector, thus to depart unassistant to her wants, ..pressed..heavily on her mind.

una'ssisted, *ppl. a.* (UN-1 8.)
Hence, in recent use, ***unassistedly*** adv.
1614 GORGES *Lucan* v. 179 Cæsar..As vnassisted now he stands: And almost left to his owne sword. **1705** CLARKE *Disc. Attributes* II. xiii, Many of them not discoverable by bare Reason unassisted with Revelation. **1751** EARL ORRERY *Remarks Swift* (1752) 120 The pure instincts of brutes, unassisted by any knowledge of letters. **1820** SCOTT *Monast.* ii, In case of assault, the proprietor would have to rely upon his own unassisted strength. **1849** RUSKIN *Sev. Lamps* ii. §7. 33 The pillars would be, if unassisted, too slight for the weight.
b. *spec.* Of the eye or sight: Unaided, naked.
1661 BOYLE *Certain Physiol. Ess.* (1669) 196 Notwithstanding the unassisted Eye can discern no such matter. **1707** *Curios. in Husb. & Gard.* 27 A naked and unassisted Eye. **1781** COWPER *Retirem.* 56 Contrivance intricate, express'd with ease, Where unassisted sight no beauty sees. **1794** G. ADAMS *Nat. & Exp. Philos.* I. i. 28 Microscopical observations that discover animals, thousands of which could scarce form a particle perceptible to the unassisted sense. **1865** MRS. L. L. CLARKE *Common Seaweeds* ii. 42 How could we with the unassisted eye see aught that is lovely in those dark purple or olive-brown tufts?

una'ssisting, *ppl. a.* (UN-1 10.)
1694 DRYDEN *Love Triumph.* IV. i, They stretch their unassisting Hands in vain, But none will plunge into the raging Main, To save the sinking Passenger from Death. **1716** POPE *Iliad* v. 395 Nor Sthenelus, with unassisting hands, Remain'd unheedful of his lord's commands.

una'ssized, *ppl. a.* [UN-1 8.] †Not brought up to the proper assize; under weight.
1616 *Southampton Court Leet Rec.* (1907) III. 512 We have ..from each of them..taken some smale quantities of there howesholde vnassized bread.

una'ssociable, *a.* (UN-1 7 b.)
1816 J. GILCHRIST *Philos. Etym.* 215 Not to mention the unassociable, repellent natures of their tastes and styles. **1829** JAS. MILL *Hum. Mind* (1869) I. 98 There is therefore a further condition required to render two ideas unassociable.

una'ssociably, *adv.* (UN-1 11.)
1892 PATER *Marius* II. 72 The immemorial waterfall, plunging down so unassociably among those human habitations.

†**una'ssociate,** *ppl. a. Obs.* [UN-1 8 b.] = next. (Const. *of* = with.)
1545 RAYNALD *Byrth Mankynde* 17 Nether is there any notable vaine vnassotiat of an artyre. *Ibid.* 33 None of this vaynes run to the matrice or otherwhere, vnassosiat of an Artyre.

una'ssociated, *ppl. a.* (UN-1 8.)
1709 SHAFTESB. *Charac.* (1711) II. 313 Even on the supposal, that there was ever such a Condition or State of Men, when as yet they were unassociated, unacquainted. **1790** HAMILTON *Wks.* (1886) VII. 48 The accommodation ..of unassociated persons and families who may emigrate thither. **1839** DE LA BECHE *Rep. Geol. Cornwall*, etc. x. 286 The manganese ores of North Devon are, however, unassociated with trappean rocks. **1897** *Westm. Gaz.* 17 Mar. 2/2 In this case the unassociated schools were better off than the associated.

una'ssoiled, *a.* [UN-1 8.]
1. Not assoiled; not absolved from sin.
c **1440** *Alph. Tales* 16 He was wrothe þat þis monke died vnasoylid. *a* **1513** FABYAN *Chron.* VII. 335 This Frederyke dyed vnassoylyd. **1844** MRS. BROWNING *Lost Bower* xxxiv, Unassoiled by Ave Marys Which the passing pilgrim prays. **1888** LOWELL *Heartsease & Rue* 71 The unclean bird Hooting to unassoiled shapes as they pass.
†**2.** Not settled; undecided. *Obs. rare.*
1387 TREVISA *Higden* (Rolls) VII. 451 þe pope..now.. leveþ þe stryf al unassoilled [L. *indeterminatum*]. *a* **1513** FABYAN *Chron.* VII. ccxxviii. 257 The pope gaue suche a defuse sentence in this mater y^t he lefte ye stryfe vndetermyned & vnassoyled.

una'ssorted, *ppl. a.* (UN-1 8. Cf. G. *unassortirt.*)
[**1775** ASH.] **1865** GLADSTONE *Farew. Addr. Edin. Univ.* 24 They were no longer a chaotic assemblage of unassorted or even conflicting units. **1877** RAYMOND *Statist. Mines & Mining* 253 Assays, unassorted, from $200 to $300.

una'ssuageable, *a.* (UN-1 7 b.)
1611 FLORIO, *Inplacabile*, vnasswageable. **1802–12** BENTHAM *Ration. Judic. Evid.* Wks. 1843 VII. 436 No mischief is so unassuageable as that which employs for its instrument a mass of corrupted language. **1817** SHELLEY *Address* Pr. Wks. 1888 I. 374 A calamity..such as the English nation ought to mourn with an unassuageable grief. **1884** G. MACDONALD *Unspoken Serm.* Ser. II. 39 The unassuageable rest of repulsion with which he regards such conditions.

una'ssuaged, *ppl. a.* (UN-1 8.)
1654 R. BAKER tr. *Balzac's Lett.* (vol. II) I. 119 There is no ..pain unasswaged by his words before it be expelled by his wit. **1784** COWPER *Task* VI. 463 The pangs Of hunger unassuag'd. **1799** CAMPBELL *Pleas. Hope* II. 434 That spark ..shall beam on Joy's interminable years, Unveiled by darkness, unassuaged by tears. **1815** WORDSW. *Artigal & Elidure* 35 Till she, in jealous fury unassuaged, Had slain his paramour. **1892** *Pall Mall G.* 11 Oct. 2/3 The unassuaged agony of the animal.

una'ssumed, *ppl. a.* (UN-1 8.)
[**1775** ASH.] **1818** HAZLITT *Table T.* xviii, The true, unassumed equality of greatness.

una'ssuming, *ppl. a.* [UN-1 10.] Free from assumption; unpretentious: **a.** Of persons.
1726 THOMSON *Winter* 772 See now the cause, Why unassuming worth in secret liv'd, And dy'd, neglected. **1780** *Mirror* No. 90, In his manners simple and unassuming. **1839** DICKENS *Nickleby* xviii, A very unassuming young woman. **1862** CALVERLEY *Verses & Transl.* (ed. 2) 49 Once, an unassuming Freshman Through these wilds I wandered on.
b. Of character or manners.
1796 MME. D'ARBLAY *Camilla* IV. 401 His character [was] unassuming. **1797** S. & HT. LEE *Canterb. T.* (1799) I. 369 The unassuming and simple dignity of Lothaire. **1805** SOUTHEY in *Ann. Rev.* III. 570 A gentleman of unassuming talents. **1875** JOWETT *Plato* (ed. 2) II. 392 He walks about on the sea shore in an unassuming way.
c. Of things.
1805 WORDSW. *Prelude* XIII. 46 The unassuming things that hold A silent station in this beauteous world. **1838** LYTTON *Alice* I. v, The expensive, yet unassuming *robe de soie*. **1896** MRS. CAFFYN *Quaker Grandmother* 146 Stopping to hit at the blackened unassuming remains of a dock.
Hence **una'ssumingness.**
Also, in recent use, ***unassumingly*** adv.
1768 *Woman of Honor* I. 48 An unassumingness, which was the result of most perfect modesty. **1799** SOUTHEY in Robberds *Mem. W. Taylor* (1843) I. 303 Davy is a surprising young man, and one who, by his unassumingness,..soon conciliates our affections. **1830** JAMES *Darnley* xxi, A sort of unassumingness, which seemed to hold his own high qualities as light, silenced much envy. **1876** MRS. WHITNEY *Sights & Insights* xii. 124 That unassumingness which is conscious of nothing to assume.

†**una'ssure,** *a. Obs.*–1 [Cf. UNASSURED and SURE *a.*] Unreliable.
1531 in Ellis *Orig. Lett.* Ser. III. II. 216, I..wyll prove myselff, though the powrest,..yet not the vnassurest or vntrustiest of your frends.

†**una'ssure,** *v. Obs.*–1 [UN-2 3.] *trans.* To cancel the assurance of.
1643 CARYL *Sacr. Covt.* 20 When at any time ye can..be resolved that these are insufficient grounds of making a Covenant,..ye may goe, and un-assure the Covenant which ye make this day.

una'ssured, *ppl. a.* [UN-1 8.]
1. Not assured or safe; insecure.
c **1430** LYDG. *Min. Poems* (Percy Soc.) 76 Riche with wysshis, pore of possessioune; Stable unassured, assured eke unstable. **1596** SPENSER *Hymn of Love* 263 The doubts, the daungers, the delayes,..The fayned friends, the unassured foes. **1611** COTGR., *Desassurer*, to disassure;..to make vnsetled, vnassured. **1647** N. BACON *Disc. Govt. Eng.* I. xlv. 117 In the middest of his strong and conquering army he held himselfe unassured. **1896** *Daily News* 29 Oct. 6/5 The confusion..superinduced by unassured peace.
2. Not certain or sure (*of* something).
a **1529** SKELTON *Replyc.* 93 Your selfe thus ye discured As clerkes vnassured, With ignorance obscured. **1577** tr. *Bullinger's Decades* (1592) 504 The sentence definitive is suspended or else it is otherwise ghessed at by humane and vnassured suspition. **1646** SIR T. BROWNE *Pseud. Ep.* 194 To invent or assign a cause, when we remain unsatisfied or unassured of the effect. **1651** HOBBES *Leviath.* II. xxvii. 156 When men are by any accident unassured they have slept, [dreams] seem to be reall Visions. **1736** THOMSON *Liberty* v. 718 As thick to view these varied Wonders rose, Shook all my soul with transport, unassur'd, The Vision broke. **1776** M. MORGANN *Ess. Dram. Char. Falstaff* (1777) 12 Their ill-gotten..gold feels loose in their unassured grasp.
3. Not self-possessed or confident; not sure of oneself or of one's safety.
1627 *Lisander & Cal.* v. 81 A troubled countenance and an unassured voice. **1697** COLLIER *Ess. Mor. Subj.* II. (1709) 153 He that is Embarrassed in his Liberty, is apt to be unassur'd in his Actions. **1713** *Guard.* No. 32 ¶8 He moved towards her with an easie but unassured air. **1760–72** H. BROOKE *Fool of Qual.* (1809) IV. 73 [They] stood yet awhile, pale, astonished, and unassured. **1821–2** WORDSW. *Eccl. Sonn.* III. xxxvii. 8 Had we, like them, endured Sore stress of apprehension,..From month to month trembling and unassured. **1825** SCOTT *Betrothed* xxvii, Lady Eveline approached his bedside with unassured steps, fearing she knew not what.
4. Not insured against loss or damage.
1828–32 WEBSTER s.v.
Hence **una'ssuredly** *adv.*, **una'ssuredness.**
1648 HEXHAM II, *Ongewisselick*, Vncertainly, or Vnassuredly. **1660** INGELO *Bentiv. & Ur.* I. (1682) 130 Incredulous Philosophers, of whose vitious lives I cannot but think their unassuredness in this matter to have been a great cause.

una'stonished, *ppl. a.* (UN-1 8.)
1533 BELLENDEN *Livy* v. xxi. (S.T.S.) II. 220 Fabius.. past sturdelie throw all þe statiouns and watche of Inemyis vn-astonist be ony of þare wourdis or terrouris. *c* **1605** ROWLEY *Birth Merl.* IV. i, Mother speak freely and unastonished; That which you dared to act, dread not to name. **1621** SANDYS *Ovid's Met.* VIII. 267 She..vnlocks a posterne doore; Then past the foe (bold by her merit made), Vnto the King not vn-astonisht, said. **1828** CARLYLE *Misc.* (1857) I. 224 Cool, unastonished, holding his equal rank from Nature herself. **1891** CONST. MACEWEN *3 Women in 1 Boat* 117 Xenia rose slowly, indifferently, and quite unastonished from her lounge.

†**una'strained,** *ppl. a. Obs.*–1 In 5 *Sc.* **vnastrenȝet.** [UN-1 8.] Unconstrained.
c **1375** *Sc. Leg. Saints* iii. (*Andrew*) 341 He tholit þar one for to hynge, vnastrenȝet, bot of fre will.

unastro'nomical, *a.* (UN-1 7.)
a **1849** POE *Eureka* Wks. 1865 II. 127 The difficulty, if not impossibility, of presenting..to the unastronomical, a picture at all comprehensible. **1887** RUSKIN *Præterita* II. 391 This—unastronomical readers will please to note—being one of the leaden influences on me of the planet Saturn.

unat, variant of UNNAIT *a. Obs.*

unate (juː'neɪt), *a. Math.* [f. L. *ūn-us* one + -ATE2.] Of a logical function: containing no variable in both negated and unnegated forms. Hence **u'nateness.**
1960 *Proc. IRE* XLVIII. 1336/1 The first of these, Theorem 1, gives one of the most easily recognized properties of a setting function, unateness... A unate function is defined as one from which one of each pair of complementary literals..can be eliminated. **1978** S. C. LEE *Mod. Switching Theory* iv. 118 Any threshold function is unate.

unath'letic, *a.* (UN-1 7.)
1759 H. WALPOLE *Let. to Mann* 13 Sept., With your unathletic constitution I think you will have a greater weight of glory to represent than you can bear. **1888** *Daily News* 25 Aug. 5/2 The absence of nerves in the unathletic Chinaman.

unatmo'spheric, *a.* [UN-1 7.] That conveys no suggestion of tone or mood; that fails to evoke associations. Hence **unatmo'spherically** *adv.*
1913 E. F. BENSON *Thorley Weir* iii. 68 Arthur..found this peremptory young savage slightly alarming. For himself he demanded that social intercourse should be conducted in a serene atmosphere of politeness, of manners. .. He thought he had seldom seen anybody so unatmospheric. *Ibid.* 69 Frank looked at him quite unatmospherically. **1938** *Scrutiny* VII. 179 His [*sc.*

Roussel's] instrumentation is unatmospheric. **1963** *Listener* 28 Feb. 393/2 A couple of very stagy and unatmospheric outdoor sets. **1976** *Gramophone* Oct. 584/2 The 'Royal Hunt and Storm' begins unatmospherically, with the strings at once forceful and casual, carrying none of the sense of light slowly dawning on a classical landscape.

una'tonable, *a.* Also **-eable.** [UN-[1] 7 b.]
†**1.** Unaccordable. *Obs.*[-1]
1645 MILTON *Tetrach.* Wks. 1851 IV. 267 He who sees not this argument how plainly it serves to divorce any untunable, or unattonable matrimony, sees little.
2. Irreconcilable.
1683 HOWE *Union among Prot.* Wks. 1724 II. 243 If such men were capable of being reason'd with..I would ask them, 'What, are you altogether unatoneable? Will nothing divert you from this pursuit?' **1830** W. TAYLOR *Hist. Surv. Germ. Poetry* I. 213 How the waves rush, the thunders roar, and the voice of winds tells of this unatonable vengeance. **1853** RUSKIN *Stones Ven.* II. viii. §45. 312 The great unatoneable division between the disciple and the adversary.
3. That cannot be atoned for or expiated.
1689 *Apol. Fail. Walker's Acc.* 19 The unattoneable Guilt of retarding the Conveyance of those Arms and Ammunition. **1881** W. COLLINS *Black Robe* I. x, I have committed the one unatonable and unpardonable sin.

una'toned, *ppl. a.* [UN-[1] 8, 8 c.]
1. Not atoned for or expiated. Also with *for*.
(*a*) **1727** THOMSON *Britannia* 60 And his guilty stores, Won by the ravage of a butcher'd world, Yet unatton'd, sunk in the swallowing deep. **1771** MRS. GRIFFITH *Hist. Lady Barton* III. 220 There is a hope beyond the grave, and nought but vice, unatoned by penitence and piety, need ever urge despair! **1811** SCOTT *Don Roderick* II. xlix, Nor unatoned, where freedom's foes prevail, Remain'd their savage waste. **1837** LYTTON *Athens* II. 7 Time past on, the injury was unatoned, the remembrance remained.
(*b*) **1753** RICHARDSON *Grandison* (1781) V. x. 50, I acquainted her with his former fault, unatoned for as it was. **1856** LEVER *Martins of Cro' M.* 279 The great fact remained unatoned for—his family, his own connexions, 'had done nothing for him'. **1876** BANCROFT *Hist. U.S.* III. i. 316 They cherished a deep sense of the wrongs unatoned for and unavenged.
†**2.** Unreconciled. *Obs.*[-1]
1730 T. BOSTON *View Covt. Grace* (1734) 167 That Spirit they could not have from an unattoned God.

una'toning, *ppl. a.* (UN-[1] 10.)
1838 LYTTON *Alice* XI. iv, What hand could dare to send a criminal..so black with crime, unatoning, unrepentant, and unprepared, before the judgment seat of the All-Just?

una'ttach, *v.* [UN-[2] 4 b.] *trans.* To free from attachment.
1671 F. PHILIPPS *Reg. Necess.* 246 When it is and hath been not unusual for the Judges..to free or unattach goods attached in the City of Lond.

una'ttachable, *a.* (UN-[1] 7 b.)
1843 in *Life A. Fonblanque* (1874) 257 There is no temple, and there is to be no temple, and the unattached and unattachable gates are mere lumber.

una'ttached, *ppl. a.* Also 5–6 *Sc.* **-attechit.** [UN-[1] 8.]
†**1.** Not arrested or seized. *Obs.*
1498 *Reg. Privy Seal Scotl.* I. 34/2 All his men..to be unesumond, une-attechit, une-arrestit, in his or thairis persoun or gudis. **1531** *Ibid.* II. 134/2 The saidis personis..to be unattechit, unarrestit,..and untrublit. **1639** R. JUNIUS *Sin Stigm.* 368 He that is pursued, will cry, Stop Theife, that by this meanes he may escape unattached.
2. Not attached or united (*to* something).
In the first set of quots. used with reference to physical attachment or connexion.
(*a*) **1822** J. PARKINSON *Outl. Oryctol.* 96 Mr. Mantell.. ascertained it to have been an unattached animal, and without a column. **1861** H. MACMILLAN *Footn. fr. Page Nat.* 46 It [the bog-moss] has no roots whatever, but floats unattached in an upright position in the water. **1878** ABNEY *Photogr.* 100 Bromide of silver with unattached atoms of metallic silver, is formed.
(*b*) *a* **1821** V. KNOX *Spir. Despotism* §34 True patriotism and true philosophy, unattached to names of particular men, or even to parties. **1844** DISRAELI *Coningsby* VIII. vi, Her eye soon glanced over the page, unattached by its contents. **1885** 'MRS. ALEXANDER' *At Bay* iii, 'Pray do not trouble yourself,' returned Deering hastily, 'I can exist for half an hour in an unattached condition'.
3. Of persons: Not attached to, or definitely associated with, a particular body, institution, sphere of work, etc.: **a.** Of military officers: Not attached to a particular regiment or company.
1796 *List Officers Army* 13 Thomas Nesbitt,..Capt. of Foot, unattached. **1806** *Ibid.* 17 Late Unattached Officers. **1826** *Gentl. Mag.* I. 638 Promotions..J. Haverfield, from unattached full pay. **1835** MARRYAT *Olla Podr.* vii, He was put on full pay unattached. **1852** BURN *Naval & Milit. Dict.* s.v. *Disponibilité*, To place on the unattached list. **1859** J. LANG *Wand. India* 363 As a General of Division, he had been unattached, and had never done a single day's duty. **1876** VOYLE & STEVENSON *Milit. Dict.* 445/1 *Unattached list*, in the British army, officers not attached to regiments.
b. Of clergy: Not attached to a particular diocese or church.
1865 PUSEY *Truth Eng. Ch.* 285 *note*, Lord Westbury has ..declared him in fact an unattached Bishop. **1902** R. BAGOT *Donna Diana* v. 43 One of the unattached priests to be met with by hundreds in the streets of Rome.
c. Of students: Not attached to any college; non-collegiate. Also *transf.* and as *sb.*
1870–1 *Ann. Rep. Deleg. Stud. not attached* 16 A Grocers' Company's Exhibitioner and Unattached Student in the University of Oxford. *Ibid.* 4 The amount of intellectual life and industry developed by the Unattached system. **1897** ESCOTT *Soc. Transform. Vict. Age* xiv. 184 The Davis scholarship in Chinese was for the fifth time won a few years ago by an unattached.
d. In miscellaneous uses.
1888 'R. BOLDREWOOD' *Robbery under Arms* xl, We must get you in the police force..or make you an inspector, unattached. **1893** JOYCE *Short Hist. Irel.* 70 The oldest.. passed out of the organization altogether, and became an ordinary unattached member of the tribe. **1899** *Daily News* 26 June 8/4 Reporters attached to no particular journal have dashed up with news.., though the importance of the unattached men has waned.
4. a. Not engaged or married. Also *absol.*
1874 LISLE CARR *J. Gwynne* II. vii. 184 You lovers have such a provoking way of showing your immense superiority to us unattached creatures. **1897** *Westm. Gaz.* 9 Dec. 10/1 We are absolutely out of single young ladies just now, and.. they specially invited some charming 'unattached' from Johannesburg.
b. Not belonging to any family, owner, etc.
1888 *Pall Mall G.* 11 Oct. 11/2 That would bring to decent places the unattached children. **1898** *Tit-Bits* 26 Feb. 420/2, 40000 cats,..of which half are 'unattached', and live largely on refuse.
c. Not assigned to any special group.
1899 *Allbutt's Syst. Med.* VIII. 855 The Microsporon Audouini is as yet 'unattached'.
Hence **una'ttachedness.**
1936 WIRTH & SHILS tr. *Mannheim's Ideology & Utopia* III. iv. 140 The 'unattachedness' of the intellectuals. **1981** M. WARNER *Joan of Arc* iv. 86 The..unattachedness of the displaced and the poor.

una'ttackable, *a.* [UN-[1] 7 b.]
1. Not liable or open to assault.
1805 LD. GRENVILLE in Dk. Buckingham *Mem. Geo. III*, (1855) III. 457, I am confident that Toulon is absolutely unattackable with such a force as you speak of. **1862** CARLYLE *Fredk. Gt.* XIII. xii. (1872) V. 122 Height which he judged unattackable, and on the side of which he pitches his camp accordingly.
2. Not susceptible to the effects of detrimental or dissolvent agencies.
1881 *Nature* XXIV. 249/1 The oxides formed on the surface may preserve it by their very presence, furnishing a sort of unattackable varnish. **1882** *U.S. Rep. Prec. Met.* 649 To make some of the particles of gold wholly unattackable by mercury.
Hence **una'ttackably** *adv.*
1865 CARLYLE *Fredk. Gt.* XVIII. xiii. (1872) VIII. 56 So unattackably strong was this position at Klein Kamin.

una'ttacked, *ppl. a.* (UN-[1] 8.)
1663 COWLEY *Cutter Coleman-St.* Pref. ad fin., There are others..who think it a sign of weakness or stupidity to let anything pass by them unattaqued. **1693** *Mem. Ct. Teckely* II. 145 It having not been imagin'd that the Turks would leave behind them Comorra and Raab unattack'd. **1772** BURKE *Sp. Acts Uniformity* Wks. 1812 V. 325 However, as none of them wholly abandon that post, it will not be safe to leave it behind me unattacked. **1828** LYTTON *Pelham* III. iii, I am undisturbed and unattacked in the enjoyments best suited to my taste. **1878** ABNEY *Photogr.* 28 Treat all these residues with nitric acid, and they will all be found to remain unattacked by it.

unattaina'bility. (UN-[1] 12 and next.)
1850 CARLYLE *Latter Day Pamphlets, Jesuitism* 29 Moral evil is unattainability of Pig's-wash; moral good, attainability of ditto.

una'ttainable, *a.* and *sb.* [UN-[1] 7 b and 12.]
A. *adj.* That cannot be attained or reached.
1662 BP. HOPKINS *Serm., Funeral* (1685) 52 Those thirty or forty years, which were judged by thee in thy childhood an unattainable age. **1690** LOCKE *Hum. Und.* II. xxi. §40 The will..cannot, at any time, be moved towards what is judged, at that time, unattainable. **1736** POPE *Let. to Swift* 25 Mar., A View of the useful and therefore attainable, and of the un-useful and therefore un-attainable, Arts. **1771** *Junius' Lett.* lxiii. (1788) 334 This, though a wicked purpose, is neither absurd nor unattainable. **1809** *Edin. Rev.* XIV. 283 The great body of the people never yet engaged eagerly in the pursuit of an unattainable object. **1860** RUSKIN *Unto this Last* (1862) 80 Though absolute justice be unattainable, as much justice as we need for all practical use is attainable.
B. *sb.* **1.** An unattainable thing. *rare.*
1661 GLANVILL *Van. Dogm.* 112 *Temperamentum ad pondus*, may well be reckon'd among the three Philosophical unattainables. **1786** COWPER *Let. to Lady Hesketh* 10 Apr., Range and jack [in a kitchen] are not unattainables; they may be easily supplied.
2. With *the*: That which is not attainable.
1857 MAURICE *Ep. St. John* xx. 340 In one sense I can admit that man is always striving after the unattainable. **1882** MISS BRADDON *Mt. Royal* I. iii. 101 All women sigh for the unattainable.
Hence **una'ttainableness; -ably** *adv.*
1690 LOCKE *Hum. Und.* II. xx. §11 Despair is the thought of the unattainableness of any Good. **1863** HAWTHORNE *Our Old Home* (1879) 371 A strange repulsion and unattainableness in the very spell that made her beautiful. **1894** HALL CAINE *Manxman* III. xxv, She would be with him always;..the more reproachfully and unattainably, because she would be the wife of another man.

una'ttained, *a.* and *sb.* [UN-[1] 8.]
†**1.** Untouched, unaffected. *Obs.*[-1]
1613 SIR A. SHERLEY *Trav. Persia* 136 Any of those bring extrinsicke danger, or intrinsicke errours, from both which you must liue free and vnattained.
2. Not attained or reached.
1671 CLARENDON *Dial.* Tracts (1727) 326 The art of Logick..is rarely unattained there by any who spend their time there with any application. **1774** GOLDSMITH *Nat. Hist.* (1776) II. 92 When the mind reflects with regret upon some good unattained or lost. **1794** MRS. RADCLIFFE *Myst. Udolpho* xxvi, Unless the crime..was instigated merely by resentment,..its object must be unattained till the niece was also dead. **1868** MORRIS *Earthly Par.* (1870) I. II. 585 Days once bright, With foolish hopes of unattained delight.
b. *sb.* With *the*: That which is not attained.
1854 LONGF. *Epimetheus* xii, Thou makest each mystery clearer, And the unattained seems nearer. **1870** WHITTIER *My Triumph* vii, I better know than all How little I have gained, How vast the unattained.

una'ttaining, *a.* (UN-[1] 10.)
1831 CARLYLE *Sart. Res.* II. iv, No mortal's endeavour or attainment will..content the as yet unendeavouring, unattaining young gentleman.

una'ttaint, *a.* [UN-[1] 7: cf. next.]
1. = UNATTAINTED *ppl. a.* 2.
1649 G. DANIEL *Trinarch., Rich. II*, cclxxv, These, by a Publicke Act, stand vnattaint. *Ibid., Hen. IV*, xxii, The rest who fell Confederates with them, are vn-attaint.
2. = UNATTAINTED *ppl. a.* 1.
1850 S. DOBELL *Roman* ii, Unattaint, Perchance the Arethusan blood of Rome Hath coursed the conduits of a tyrant's veins. **1856** E. FITZGERALD *Salaman* (1909) 59 From Darkness came to Light a Child, Of Carnal Composition unattaint.

una'ttainted, *ppl. a.* [UN-[1] 8.]
1. Unstained, unspotted; free from blemish.
1592 SHAKS. *Rom. & Jul.* I. ii. 90 With vnattainted eye, Compare her face with some that I shall show. **1600** W. WATSON *Decacordon* (1602) 274 [The catholics] liue in sorrow, heauiness, and suspition had of their vnattainted loyalties in generall, for some priuate offences in speciall. **1641** MILTON *Reformation* II. Wks. 1851 III. 54 To..ingage the unattainted Honour of English Knighthood..for so unworthy a purpose. **1716** SWIFT *Misc. Poems, To Earl of Oxford* 8 Virtue repuls't, yet knows not to repine; But shall with unattainted Honour shine. **1845** HIRST *Com. Mommoth*, etc. 44 That bears on high in knightly fight An unattainted crest.
2. Not attainted in law.
1794 W. HUTCHINSON *Hist. Cumbld.* I. 378 Whereupon it was adjudged that the title remained unattainted. **1821** BYRON *Two Foscari* I. i, Wouldst thou have His state descend to his children, as it must, If he die unattainted?

una'ttempered, *ppl. a.* (UN-[1] 8.)
[**1775** ASH.] **1884** WYLIE *Hist. Protestantism* VIII. i. I. 411/1 Nor have their souls remained unattempered by the grandeurs amid which they daily move.

una'ttemptable, *a.* (UN-[1] 7 b.)
1656 CROMWELL *Let.* 28 April (Carlyle), Whether Cadiz itself be unattemptable. **1865** CARLYLE *Fredk. Gt.* XX. v. (1872) IX. 94 Hopes there were of getting back Dresden itself; but that, on closer view, proved unattemptable.

una'ttempted, *ppl. a.* [UN-[1] 8.]
1. Not attempted or tried.
a **1548** HALL *Chron., Hen. VI*, 105 b, Thei..assauted the walles, and left no thyng vnattempted, whiche might bee to them, any aduantage. *a* **1586** SIDNEY *Arcadia* II. xv. (1912) 250 Leaving no meanes unattempted of destroying his son. **1655** *Nicholas Papers* (Camden) II. 191 Yet no meanes shall bee vnattempted to discharge my duty. **1667** MILTON *P.L.* I. 16 Things unattempted yet in Prose or Rhime. **1734** *Col. Rec. Pennsylv.* III. 561 That we might leave no means unattempted for the Relief of these..Men. **1744** AKENSIDE *Pleas. Imag.* I. 696 To adorn This unattempted theme. **1816** BENTHAM *Chrestom.* 239 The imperfection, so long as the work has any use, will not afford any sufficient reason for leaving it unattempted. **1846** MRS. A. MARSH *Father Darcy* II. xiii. 230 Whatever the work left unattempted at home [etc.].
2. Upon, or against, which no attempt has been made.
1595 SHAKS. *John* II. i. 591 My hand, as vnattempted yet, Like a poore begger, raileth on the rich. **1687** SHADWELL *Juvenal* 372 While flourishing Troy Yet unattempted, did full peace enjoy. *a* **1704** T. BROWN *Walks round London, Westm.-Abby* (1709) 48 The Thief stole the Head and left the Trunk unattempted.

una'ttempting, *ppl. a.* [UN-[1] 5 d and 10.]
†**a.** Not attempting. *Sc. Obs.* **b.** Unenterprising.
1585 *Reg. Privy Council Scot.* III. 759 That thay contene thameselffis, in peceable and quiet maner at this tyme, unattempting ony..revenge aganis ony Englishman. **1730** WATERLAND *Script. Vind.* Pref. 23 Many have been too forward and enterprizing in that way..; and many also have been too cautious and unattempting.

una'ttendance. [UN-[1] 12.] †Inattention.
c **1449** PECOCK *Repr.* IV. ix. 470 Al tho lay persoonys..y biseche for to attende into these thingis,..whos vnattendaunce hath causid ful myche yuel.

una'ttended, *ppl. a.* [UN-[1] 8.]
1. Not attended or waited upon; unaccompanied.
1603 DRAYTON *Bar. Wars* V. xxiv, Car'd for of none, nor look'd on, vnattended, Sadly returning, with a heauie Heart. **1667** MILTON *P.L.* VIII. 60 Forth she went; Nor unattended, for on her as Queen A pomp of winning Graces waited still. **1708** POPE *Lett.* (1735) I. 66 What a Number have here drop'd off, and left the poor surviving seven unattended! *a* **1795** PHILIDOR *Studies of Chess* (1817) 36 The unattended king should advance to intercept the pawn. **1846** MRS. GORE *Eng. Char.* (1852) 60 It suited him to ride thither unattended. **1895** SWETTENHAM *Malay Sk.* 119 The Shabandar, unarmed and unattended, accompanied him.
b. Of horses, etc.: With no one in attendance.
1796 COLERIDGE *Destiny of Nations* 197 In the first entrance of the level road An unattended team! **1897** *Daily News* 5 Oct. 6/3 When vehicles were left unattended the wheels should be chained.

2. Not attended or accompanied *by* or *with* some thing, circumstance, etc.

(*a*) **1687** DRYDEN *Hind & P.* III. 607 Night came, but unattended with repose. **1768–74** TUCKER *Lt. Nat.* (1834) II. 678 Every benefit..procured for any individual,..if unattended with bad consequences, is a profit made to the whole. **1787** W. TICKELL *Acc. New Chym. Med.* (title-page), Its specific virtue in..all coughs unattended with inflammation. **1837** LYTTON *Athens* II. 4 It seldom happens that their renown in life was unattended with reverses equally signal. **1885** *Manch. Exam.* 6 Jan. 5/2 The collision was unattended with grave consequences.

(*b*) **1726** POPE *Odyss.* XIX. 601 Unattended by sincere repose, The night assists my ever-wakeful woes. **1749** FIELDING *Tom Jones* VIII. xi, I could have gladly embraced Death,..if it had offered itself to my Choice unattended by Shame. **1847** W. C. L. MARTIN *Ox* 11/1 Nor is the chase unattended by danger, for a wounded bison often turns on his assailant. **1884** *Manch. Exam.* 12 Sept. 5/3 The accident to the Fenella..was fortunately unattended by worse consequences.

3. Not attended *to*. (Also without prep.)

1729 BOYER *Dict. Royal* 11, Unattended to, (disregarded) ..*negligé.* **1791** COWPER *Retired Cat* 66 The sun descended, And puss remain'd still unattended. **1803** *Edwin* III. ix. 150 No circumstance, however trivial, should be unattended to, from whence aid to our purpose may be derived. **1874** RUSKIN *Fors Clav.* IV. xxxvii. 4, I don't suppose any man with a tongue in his head and zeal to use it was ever left so entirely unattended to.

una'ttending, *ppl. a.* [UN-1 10.] Inattentive.

1634 MILTON *Comus* 272 Nay gentle Shepherd ill is lost that praise That is addresst to unattending Ears.

una'ttention. *Obs.*$^{-1}$ (UN-1 12 and 5 b.)

1691 NORRIS *Pract. Disc.* 290 Our Unattention is the Shield that repels thy Darts.

†**una'ttentive,** *a. Obs.* [UN-1 5 b.] = INATTENTIVE *a.*

1591 HARINGTON *Orl. Fur.* Pref., A loose vnattentiue reader will hardly carrie away any part of the storie. **1665** BOYLE *Occas. Refl.* IV. Advt., A Reader that is not Unattentive, may easily collect..That they were written several years ago. **1710** STEELE *Tatler* No. 167 ¶3 Young Men, who are too unattentive to receive Lectures. **1768–74** TUCKER *Lt. Nat.* (1834) II. 547 There is a virtue in keeping one's self unconcerned at abuse or slander, unattentive to noise and impertinence.

Hence †**una'ttentively** *adv.*, **-ness.** *Obs.*

1611 COTGR., *Sourdement*, deafely; also vnattentiuely. *a* **1649** DRUMM. OF HAWTH. *Hist. Jas. III*, Wks. (1711) 44 By the ambition and unattentiveness of his friends, his worth was made the scaffold of his ruine. **1682** NORRIS *Heirocles* 133 Their unattentiveness to the Instructions of others.

una'ttenuated, *ppl. a.* (UN-1 8.)

1727 *Vin. Britan.* 42 The gross and unattenuated Parts of the Liquor. **1826** *Art of Brewing* (ed. 2) 31 Keeping a quantity of this fermentable matter unattenuated. *c* **1900** *Buck's Handbk. Med. Sci.* VI. 833 (Cent. Suppl.), Rabbits inoculated with unattenuated rabies virus.

una'ttested, *ppl. a.* (UN-1 8.)

1665 J. SPENCER *Vulg. Proph.* 83 All these unattested Prophets generally fail in all their Prophecies. *a* **1677** BARROW *On the Creed* (1697) 27 Thus..God has not left himself unattested, doing good. **1818** CRUISE *Digest* (ed. 2) VI. 84 A charge by an unattested codicil will not be good. **1853** GROTE *Greece* II. lxxxviii. XI. 454 *note*, This is the best opinion which I can form on matters lamentably unattested and uncertain. **1858** LD. ST. LEONARDS *Handy-bk. Prop. Law* xviii. 143 If there are any interlineations in your will unattested, it will be presumed that they were made after the execution of your will.

una'ttire, *v.* (UN-2 7.)

1791 MME. D'ARBLAY *Diary* (1842) V. 209 We both left Mrs. Schwellenberg to unattire.

una'ttired, *ppl. a.* [UN-1 8.] Unclothed.

c **1400** *Laud Troy Bk.* 8300 Sithen I se the, I haue desired to se the, Ector, vn-atired. **1624** BOLTON *Nero* 247 Coignes represent that lady in this vnattired dresse, and posture. **1781** COWPER *Table T.* 722 Unattir'd in that becoming vest Religion weaves for her, and half undress'd. **1813** *J. N. Brewer's Beauties Eng. & Wales* XII. II. 449 Mrs. Lucy Waters, with an unattired infant.

una'ttractable, *a.* (UN-1 7 b.)

1802 *Phil. Trans.* XCII. 188, I separated the particles attractable by a magnet; and digested the unattractable portion with nitric acid.

una'ttracted, *ppl. a.* (UN-1 8.)

1727 THOMSON *To Mem. Newton* 55 The tide revertive, unattracted, leaves A yellow waste of idle sands behind. **1909** *Pall Mall G.* 12 Apr. 6/2 Those who are unattracted by the South Pole.

una'ttracting, *ppl. a.* (UN-1 10.)

1776 S. J. PRATT *Pupil of Pleas.* (1777) I. 219 A woman whom even the depredations of four lingering months, passed in the languors of sickness, have not rendered unattracting.

una'ttractive, *a.* (UN-1 7.) Also *Comb.*

[**1775** ASH.] **1813** SHELLEY *Q. Mab* v. 29 Compelled, by its deformity, to screen..Its unattractive lineaments. **1880** MCCARTHY *Own Times* IV. 56 It was evident..that the proposed measure was only..a compromise of the most unattractive kind. **1897** *Outing* (U.S.) XXX. 242/1 A very unattractive-looking dog that put us into precipitate flight.

Hence **una'ttractively** *adv.*, **-ness.**

1836 JAS. GRANT *Random Recoll. Ho. Lords* xvi. 379 The unattractiveness of his manner. **1862** [ELIZ. JOHNSTON] *Gifts & Graces* xvi. 159 The..condition of lady-like unattractiveness so indispensable in a governess. **1863** A. GILCHRIST *Life Blake* (1880) I. 426 They are very small and very unattractively engraved.

una'ttributable, *a.* (UN-1 7 b).

1812 [LEIGH HUNT] in *Examiner* 11 May 289/2 Whatever may be the..cause of the misfortune, and however unattributable to the people. **1967** *Listener* 9 Nov. 594/2 The 'unattributable' story, which is valid information to be published as long as the source is not identified. **1972** T. LILLEY *K Section* xli. 229 The information is unattributable and for your ears only.

una'ttuned, *ppl. a.* (UN-1 8.)

[**1775** ASH.] **1792** *Elvina* II. 23 Spirits..so unattuned as mine. **1806** SURR *Winter in Lond.* III. 185 Wild and unattuned to the social duties. **1887** SWINBURNE *Stud. Prose & Poetry* (1894) 135 A poor creature whose ear was yet unattuned to the cadence of 'chants democratic'.

‖**unau** ('juːnɔː). *Zool.* [Brazilian of the Island of Maranhão.] The South American two-toed sloth, *Cholopus didactylus.*

Adopted by Buffon from C. d'Abbeville *Mission des Pères Capucins*, etc. (1614) 252. Of the two kinds there mentioned by the names of *Unaü* and *Unaü ouassou* the former is Buffon's *Aï*, the latter his *Unau.*

1774 GOLDSM. *Nat. Hist.* IV. xxii. 343 Of the sloth there are two different kinds,..the one, which in its native country is called the unan [*sic*], having only two claws upon each foot. **1834** MCMURTRIE *Cuvier's Anim. Kingd.* 93 Only one species [of *Bradypus*] is known, the Unau.., less uniform in its organisation than the Aï. **1872** HUMPHRY *Myology* 21 A recess and dimple in the astragalus of Unau and of Aï.

†**un'audible,** *a. Obs.* [UN-1 7 and 5 b.] = INAUDIBLE *a.*

1611 FLORIO, *Inaudibile*, vnaudible, not to be heard. **1650** R. STAPYLTON *Strada's Low C. Wars* VII. 68 The man read it in French, and Low Dutch, but with such a hoarse vnaudible Voyce, that very few understood him. **1667** *Decay Chr. Piety* ii. ¶18 Shall the superaddition of our Religion damp ours into a whisper, a soft unaudible sound. **1784** R. BAGE *Barham Downs* II. 106 Only heaven has blessed him with the gift of unaudible sighing.

un'audienced, *ppl. a.* (UN-1 8.)

1748 RICHARDSON *Clarissa* (1811) V. 183 To send back to town, un-audienced, unseen, a man of his business and importance!

un'audited, *ppl. a.* (UN-1 8.)

1812 *Examiner* 5 Oct. 633/1 Which suffers an Irish Defaulter of unaccounted millions, to remain unaudited.. after his dismissal. **1869** J. MARTINEAU *Ess.* II. 57 Honorable men do not wish their accounts to pass unaudited.

unaug'mentable, *a.* (UN-1 7 b.)

1868 W. R. GREG *Lit. & Soc. Judgm.* 372 If, indeed, there were only a certain fixed and unaugmentable quantity of work to be done.

unaug'mented, *ppl. a.* [UN-1 8.] Not augmented or increased; in later use *spec.* of Greek verbs (see AUGMENT *sb.* 2).

1555 EDEN *Decades* (Arb.) 296 The residue of the nyght that receaueth no light by the sayde..twilightes, is accomplysshed by the lyght of the moone, so that the nyghtes are seldome vnaugmented. **1648** HEXHAM II, *Ongegrooted*, vnaugmented. **1776** RICHARDSON *Arabic Grammar* 28 Chiefly from the simple or unaugmented three-letter words and their feminines. **1848** VEITCH *Irreg. Grk. Verbs* (1856) s.v. *Ἀναλίσκω*, Thuc. and the Trag. seem to have preferred the unaugmented, Plato and the Orators the augmented forms.

†**un'augurate,** *a. Obs.*$^{-1}$ [UN-1 8 b: cf. AUGURATE *v.*] Unconsecrated by augury.

1600 HOLLAND *Livy*, *Topogr. Rome* vii. 1365 In it the Senat sate in counsell, because they might not assemble in any place unaugurate or unhallowed.

†**unau'spicious,** *a. Obs.* [UN-1 7 and 5 b.] = INAUSPICIOUS *a.*

1601 SHAKS. *Twel. N.* v. i. 116 To whose ingrate, and vnauspicious Altars My soule the faithfull'st offrings haue breath'd out. **1656** EARL MONM. tr. *Boccalini's Advts. fr. Parnass.* II. I. (1674) 200 Some unauspicious Aspects of the Heavens. **1708** ROWE *Royal Convert* IV, Seo. Haste, and break off your unauspicious Rites: The instant Dangers summon you away. **1768** *Woman of Honor* II. 232 To consummate so unauspicious a sacrifice as that must be.

Hence †**unau'spiciously** *adv. Obs.*

a **1797** H. WALPOLE *Mem. Geo. II* (1847) III. x. 276 A Minister so unauspiciously seconded by fortune.

unau'stere, *a.* (UN-1 7.)

1740 in Richardson *Pamela* (1741) I. p. xix, A gradual moral Sunshine of un-austere and compassionate Virtue shall break upon the World.

unau'thentic, *a.* (UN-1 7 and 5 b.)

1631 BRATHWAIT *Whimzies, Zealous Brother* 119 He vents such unauthenticke stuffe, as it proves pregnantly from what spirit it comes. **1660** GAUDEN *God's Gt. Demonstr.* 51 Thy humane traditions, and unauthentick because uncatholick observations, instead of Christ's institutions. **1778** WARTON *Dissert.* in *Hist. Eng. Poetry* (1781) p. xx, Shakespeare is thought to have formed his play [*Anthony and Cleopatra*] on this story from North's translation of Amyot's unauthentic French Plutarch. **1831–3** E. BURTON *Eccl. Hist.* xxii. (1845) 474 The evidence is equally unauthentic, which speaks of Zoticus, an Armenian Bishop, being put to death at this same period. **1851** I. TAYLOR *Wesley* (1852) 132 But the Methodists took orders in another manner, less direct and explicit indeed, but yet..not unauthentic or unimportant.

unau'thentical, *a.* (UN-1 7.)

1549 COVERDALE, etc. *Rev.* xxii. 40 Nor it is not lawfull to confirme and mainteyne any maner of doctrine, concerninge our faithe and relygion by the auctoritie of any suche vnauenticall bookes.

unau'thentically, *adv.* (UN-1 11.)

1600 W. WATSON *Decacordon* IX. x. (1602) 332 A maxime in the lawes, either vnauthentically defined, or remaining litigious. **1975** *Daily Tel.* 17 Mar. 10/2 John Constable's amusingly, if probably unauthentically, informal continuo-comments.

unau'thenticated, *ppl. a.* (UN-1 8.)

1787 WHITAKER *Mary Q. Scots Vind.* I. 62 They thus condemn the Queen..upon letters unauthenticated by the producers. **1823** LINGARD *Hist. Eng.* VI. 316 The contradictory and unauthenticated statements of her friends and enemies. **1882** FARRAR *Early Chr.* II. 533 No Apostolic Church would have paid attention to an unauthenticated epistle.

unauthen'ticity. (UN-1 12.)

1776 MICKLE *Camoens' Lusiad* Introduction 130 Though Voltaire still retains this sentence, its unauthenticity has been detected by several critics. **1862** LATHAM *Channel Isl.* II. xiii. (ed. 2) 325 The general unauthenticity of all the earliest monastic grants and charters. **1890** GLADSTONE *Impregnable Rock* v. 187 The question is not so much what particulars can be convicted of unauthenticity.

unau'thenticness. (UN-1 12.)

1657 J. SERGEANT *Schism Dispach't* 533 The perfect weaknes of his corroboratory proof, and utter unauthenticknes of the Welsh Pueriles.

un'authorish, *a.* (UN-1 7.)

1798 COLERIDGE *Let.* in *Biogr. Epist.* (1911) I. 161 May God love you and me, who am, with most unauthorish feelings, your true friend.

unau'thoritative, *a.* (UN-1 7 and 5 b.)

1644 HUNTON *Vind. Treat. Monarchy* v. 39 Is that.. Authoritative; or merely Consiliarie and unauthoritative? **1780** BENTHAM *Princ. Legisl.* xix. §22 A Book of expository Jurisprudence is either authoritative or unauthoritative. **1851** H. W. TORRENS *Jrnl. Asiat. Soc. Bengal* 14 The vague and unauthoritative character of this learned writer's deductions. **1884** DOWELL *Taxation* IV. iii. I. 67 An abstract, imperfect and unauthoritative, of the Regent's Act of confirmation.

Hence **unau'thoritatively** *adv.*; **-ness.**

1644 HUNTON *Vind. Treat. Monarchy* iv. 27 It brings an illegality and unauthoritativenesse on acts exceeding. *a* **1827** in Bentham *Ration. Judic. Evid.* V. 595 *note*, To speak of the unauthoritatively..described act as evidence of the authoritatively..expressed one.

unau'thoritied, *ppl. a.* [UN-1 8.] Unauthorized.

1641 MILTON *Animadv.* Wks. 1851 III. 185 Nor to do thus are we unautoritied either from the morall precept of Salomon..nor from the example of Christ.

un'authorize, *v.* Also 6 -ysh. [UN-2 3.] *trans.* †To reject or annul the authority of.

1554 BALE *Declar. Bonner's Art.* xix. 68 He hathe vnauthoryshed his owne naturall king Edwarde the syxte, notynge hym an vsurper. **1611** COTGR., *Exauthorer*, to exauthorize, or vnauthorize; to dispossesse of, or degrade from, authoritie.

un'authorized, *ppl. a.* (UN-1 8.)

1596 WARNER *Alb. Eng.* XII. lxxii. (1612) 300 To armor vnauthorised should subiects neuer ronne. **1597** HOOKER *Eccl. Pol.* v. lxii. §16 The exercise of vnauthorized iurisdiction. *a* **1637** B. JONSON *Underw., Vis. Muses M. Drayton* 46 A wild and an unauthoris'd wickedness! **1684** T. GODDARD *Plato's Demon* 14 Any private person, who unauthoriz'd by our lawful Government, shall publish..any arguments or discourse [etc.]. ? **1760–1** GRAY *Metrum* Wks. 1884 I. 325 [To] insert words and syllables, unauthorized by the oldest manuscripts. **1858** FROUDE *Hist. Eng.* IV. 290 Henry so far listened..as to forbid the sale of unauthorized editions. **1885** J. MARTINEAU *Types Eth. Th.* II. II. iii. i. §1 He was threatened with penalties still unrepealed for unauthorised theological teaching.

Hence **un'authorizedly** *adv.*

1854 GROSART *Spenser's Wks.* III. 29/2 The spelling and grammatical forms, etc., of the later date are made to supplant..the earlier—unauthorisedly.

una'vail, *v.* [UN-1 14, after *unavailing*.] *trans.* and *intr.* To be of no avail (to); to fail.

1866 J. B. ROSE tr. *Ovid's Met.* 23 Aye, all my knowledge unavails its lord. *Ibid.* 186 And lest medicaments should unavail [Medea] Chanted another magic silent spell.

unavailability. (UN-1 12.)

1855 D. G. ROSSETTI *Let.* 29 July (1965) I. 265 If Mr. Oakes should..be no longer in the above capacity,..let me know at once of Mr. O.'s unavailability. **1967** *Listener* 13 July 61/2 In England the young composer is sadly hampered by the unavailability of one possible salvation—electronic equipment. **1980** J. KRANTZ *Princess Daisy* xvi. 267 *That's* what drives him crazy..your essential *unavailability.*

una'vailable, *a.* [UN-1 7 b and 5 b.]

1. Unavailing; inefficacious; ineffectual.

1549 COVERDALE, etc. *Erasm. Par. Jas.* 31 b, Of like sorte doubtles shall the profession of faith, whiche consisteth only in worde and worketh nothynge in dede, bee vnauayleable, but lyeth slugging like as it were deade. *a* **1600** HOOKER *Eccl. Pol.* VII. xi. §2 Their proofs are unavailable to shew, that Scripture affordeth no evidence for the inequality of Pastors. **1616** J. HAYWARD *Sanct. Troub. Soul* I. v. (1620) 86 Where shall I hide?.. To go forward it will bee intolerable, ..to turne aside vnauailable. **1673** DRYDEN *Marr. à la Mode* IV. i, Your pity, madam, Is generous, but 'tis unavailable. **1746** HERVEY *Medit.* 81 What can they do in this Day of Visitation?.. To fly, will be impossible; to justify themselves, impracticable; and now, to make any Supplications, unavailable. **1777** POTTER *Æschylus, Prom. Chained* 12 To complain, or not complain, alike Is unavailable. **1808** *Mem. Female Philos.* II. 91 They displayed..the greatest valour and patriotism, but they were, alas, wholly unavailable in opposition to a superior force. **1850** MERIVALE *Rom. Emp.* xiii. (1865) II. 120 He unburdened his feelings to Atticus in unavailable lamentations.

2. Not available; incapable of being used.

1855 *Orr's Circ. Sci., Inorg. Nat.* 202 Storage in reservoirs ..if the river supply is for any reason unavailable. **1888** BRYCE *Amer. Commw.* III. lxx. II. 558 In the event of the man they chiefly favour proving 'unavailable'.

una'vailableness. (UN-^{1} 12.)

1548 GESTE *Pr. Masse* E j b, Whych dyde [= deed] as it is a grounded proufe of falshode so of y^e vnauaileablenes of y^e masse. **1599** SANDYS *Europæ Spec.* (1605) L 3 b, Doubting else the vnavaileablenesse of those former inconveniences. **1611** W. SCLATER *Key* (1629) 130 Vncertaintie,.. vnprofitablenesse, and vnauaileablenesse eyther to decline wrath, or procure saluation. **1638** —— *Serm. Experimentall* 63 The unavailablenesse of all outward benefits, to stead us in the day of Gods wrath. **1829** E. BATHER *Serm.* II. 564 The utter unavailableness of man's presumed merits. **1870** RUSKIN *Lect. Art* v. 123 The impossibility of using it [oil-colour] with safety..and its unavailableness for note-book sketches and memoranda.

una'vailably, *adv.* (UN-^{1} 11.)

1860 RUSKIN *Mod. Paint.* V. VI. viii. §5, I know that nearly all in such matters must be said or shown, unavailably.

una'vailing, *ppl. a.* (UN-^{1} 10.)

1670 DRYDEN *Conq. Granada* III. i, I..would your unavailing Valour call, From aiding those whom Heav'n has doom'd to fall. **1728** ELIZA HEYWOOD tr. *Mme. de Gomez's Belle A.* (1732) II. 286 In hope that..I might bring him to a just Sense of his Folly, and cure a Passion so unavailing. **1788** GIBBON *Decl. & F.* l. V. 216 Their mummies were embalmed..to preserve the ancient mansion of the soul, during a period of three thousand years. But the attempt is partial and unavailing. **1843** BETHUNE *Sc. Fireside Stor.* 117 The heavy sea which was then running, rendered their efforts unavailing. **1891** FARRAR *Darkn. & Dawn* lv, The inventiveness of cruelty which Tigellinus and Nero studied ..amid the faint, unavailing remonstrances of Poppæa.

Hence **una'vailingly** *adv.*

1748 RICHARDSON *Clarissa* IV. 170 Must..those arms.. be used to repel brutal force; all their strength, unavailingly perhaps, exerted to repel it? **1810** LEE *Odes Pindar* vii. 83 Approaching age serene I view, Nor unavailingly deplore The time, when I shall be no more. **1885** *Law Rep.* 10 *P.D.* 99 Every effort was unavailingly made to avoid the collision.

†**una'valuable,** *a. Obs.*$^{-1}$ [UN-^{1} 7 b + obs. F. *avaluer* (Cotgr. *avalluer*) to value.] Inestimable.

1638 KNYVETT in Ellis *Orig. Lett.* Ser. III. IV. 211 For not only the estate went to wrack, but neglected my education and breeding, a loss to me unavalleuable.

unava(u)nced, obs. ff. UNADVANCED.

una'vengeable, *a.* (UN-^{1} 7 b.)

1814 WORDSW. *Excurs.* III. 375 Wrongs unredressed, or insults unavenged And unavengeable.

una'venged, *ppl. a.* Also 6 **vnad-.** (UN-^{1} 8.)

1481 CAXTON *Reynard* ii. (Arb.) 6 That shal I neuer hyde ne suffre it vnauengyd. **1548** UDALL, etc. *Erasm. Par. Rev.* xxii. 40 God wyll not suffer any suche thing to be vnpunysshed nor vnaduenged. **1670** MILTON *Hist. Eng.* IV. 169 They were by him and his Heathen Neighbours cruelly butchered; yet not unaveng'd. **1790** [see UNAVOWED *ppl. a.*]. **1816** SCOTT *Old Mort.* xxvii, The sword of liberty..is in my hand, and I will neither fall meanly nor unavenged. **1859** TENNYSON *Marriage of Geraint* 1544 Tyrants in their day of power, With life-long injuries burning unavenged. **1876** [see UNATONED *ppl. a.* 1].

una'venging, *ppl. a.* (UN-^{1} 10.)

1827 CAMPBELL *Lines St. Greece* vi, To see her unavenging ships Ride fast by Greece's funeral pile.

un'avenued, *a.* (UN-^{1} 9.)

1827 POLLOK *Course T.* IX. 1173 The gulf Of an unavenued,..Interminable, dark Futurity.

una'verred, *ppl. a.* (UN-^{1} 8.)

[**1775** ASH.] **1850** MRS. BROWNING *Sonn. fr. Portug.* xxxi, With souls that tremble through Their happy eyelids from an unaverred Yet prodigal inward joy.

una'vertable, -ible, *a.* (UN-^{1} 7 b and 5 b.)

1829 SOUTHEY in *For. Rev. & Cont. Misc.* III. 3 The Moorish historian considers it as an unavertable fatality. **1882** *U.S. Rep. Prec. Met.* 540 The theory of an unavertable decline of the Australian gold fields. **1897** J. L. ALLEN *Choir Invisible* vi. 78 Their own inescapable tombs, their own unavertible ruins. **1929** *Daily Tel.* 15 Jan. 11/7 The public is seldom concerned with the future until it has become an unavertible disaster.

una'verted, *ppl. a.* (UN-^{1} 8.)

1753 RICHARDSON *Grandison* (1781) VI. xlii. 264 He stole gently my handkerchief from my half-hid face; with it he dried my unaverted cheek. **1820** SHELLEY *Œd. Tyr.* I. 374 Let not man or beast Behold their face with unaverted eyes! **1836** J. H. NEWMAN in *Lyra Apost.* (1849) 3 Upon Death's unaverted day As I speed upward.

unavertible, var. of UNAVERTABLE *a.*

un'avian, *a.* (UN-^{1} 7.)

1890 W. H. HUDSON *Natur. La Plata* ii. (1892) 27 Its [the rhea's] figure and carriage have a quaint majestic grace, somewhat unavian in character.

unavised, -ly, obs. varr. UNADVISED, -LY.

†**unavisy,** *a. Obs. rare.* [f. UN-^{1} 7 + *avisy* ADVISY *a.*] Not well-advised.

c **1420** *Prose Life Alex.* 13 Þe vnavesy lightenesse of ȝonge men. *c* **1425** *St. Mary Oignies* in *Anglia* VIII. 138 Soo þat hee, vnavisy man,..leeryd with schame by experiens what hee schulde doo.

‖**una voce** ('ju:neɪ 'vəʊsi:). [L. *ūnā* abl. sing. fem. of *ūnus* one + *vōce*, abl. sing. of *vox* voice.] With one voice; unanimously.

1567 HARMAN *Caveat* vi. 14 And, *vna voce* all sayde that no such man dwelte in their streate. **1619** BACON *Lett. & Rem.* (1734) 100 Unto which..all the Lords and the rest *unâ voce* assented. *a* **1708** T. WARD *Eng. Reform.* I. (1710) 113 The Congregation hearing this, Cry'd, *Vnâ voce*, So it is. **1758** J. S. *Le Dran's Observ. Surg.* (1771) 194 We concluded, *una Voce*, to leave all Things in the same Condition. **1834** DICKENS *Sk. Boz, Mrs. J. Porter*, 'It's sure to do.' 'Sure! sure!' cried all the performers *unâ voce*.

unavoidability. (UN-^{1} 12.)

1858 D. G. ROSSETTI *Lett.* (1965) I. 336 Three evenings a week at least are..used up away from work by unavoidabilities. **1938** *Mind* XLVII. 47 Arguments which seek to prove unavoidability by reference to determinism are to be dismissed as ridiculous.

una'voidable, *a.* [UN-^{1} 7 b and 5 b.]

1. Not avoidable; that cannot be avoided or escaped; inevitable.

1577 tr. *Bullinger's Decades* (1592) 511 If..meere and vnauoidable violence is offered to a godlie man. **1600** E. BLOUNT tr. *Conestaggio* 241 Beeing an vnauoydable passage for the ships that come from the Indies. *a* **1688** CUDWORTH *Immut. Mor.* (1731) 11 The necessary and unavoidable Consequences of this Opinion. **1718** LADY M. W. MONTAGU *Let. to C'tess Mar* 10 Mar., Surprise at her beauty and manner..is unavoidable at the first sight. **1782** MISS BURNEY *Cecilia* v. xiii, The change of habitation that now seemed unavoidable. **1826** F. REYNOLDS *Life & Times* II. 406 Within, and without, the walls of his theatre, he has a host of unavoidable enemies. **1885** 'MRS. ALEXANDER' *At Bay* i, You may be sure the delay was unavoidable or I should not have kept you waiting.

2. *Law.* Not liable to be voided.

1628 COKE *On Litt.* 2 b, But if the man of non sane memory recouer his memory, and agree vnto it, it is vnauoydable.

Hence **una'voidableness.**

1599 SANDYS *Europæ Spec.* (1632) 115 The unavoidablenesse of those former inconveniences. **1653** GATAKER *Vind. Annot. Jer.* 103 The unavoidablenes of the Evils by these signs portended. *a* **1688** W. CLAGETT 17 *Serm.* (1699) 206 The unavoidableness of heresies in the church. **1894** *Current Hist.* (Buffalo, N.Y.) IV. 900 Francis Joseph, convinced of the unavoidableness of the proposed reforms, supported his ministers steadfastly.

una'voidably, *adv.* (UN-^{1} 11 and 5 b.)

1608 H. CLAPHAM *Errour Left Hand* 86 Then it vnauoidably followeth, that [etc.]. **1695** LD. PRESTON *Boeth.* II. 66 They whom they have left must unavoidably submit to Poverty. **1744** BERKELEY *Siris* §256 Natural evils will sometimes unavoidably ensue. **1798** COXE *Walpole* I. 727 The time unavoidably to be taken up in drawing orders at the exchequer. **1827** JARMAN *Powell's Devises* II. 177 Different minds will almost unavoidably form different opinions. **1861** MILL *Repr. Govt.* (1865) 4/1 There have been states of society in which even a monarchy.. unavoidably broke up into petty principalities.

una'voided, *ppl. a.* [UN-^{1} 8.]

1. Not avoided or escaped.

1565 GOLDING *Ovid's Met.* II. 24 b, Phebus..by and by with deadly stripe of unauoyded blow strake through the breast. **1596** DRAYTON *Legends* iv. 670 O powerfull Doome of unavoyded Fate. **1616** B. JONSON *Epigr.* I. xciv, Yet, Satires, since the most of mankind bee Their vn-auoided subiect, fewest see. **1642** H. MORE *Song Soul* IV. xix, The silent Preachers thoughts..will..Find each man out, and in a moment hit With unavoyded force. **1842** IS. WILLIAMS *Baptistery* I. ix. (1874) 109 Every night He sends his image, wraps us in his cove Of unavoided sleep.

†**2. a.** Unavoidable; inevitable. *Obs.*

1591 SHAKS. 1 *Hen. VI*, IV. v. 8 A terrible and vnauoyded danger. **1594** —— *Rich. III*, IV. iv. 218 All vnauoyded is the doome of Destiny.

†**b.** Unexceptionable; irrefutable. *Obs.*$^{-1}$

1617 MIDDLETON *Fair Quarrel* v. i, Mine accusation shall haue firme euidence. I will produce an unauoided witnes.

una'vouchable, *a.* (UN-^{1} 7.)

1650 FULLER *Pisgah* III. xii. 403 What ever politick palliations may be pleaded for the contrary, such sacrilidge was unavouchable in it self. *Ibid.* v. iii. 149 An opinion.. unavouchable by any strong arguments.

una'vouched, *ppl. a.* (UN-^{1} 8.)

1628 GAULE *Pract. The.* (1629) 182 They lash out the largest pennyworths, whose Ware is either vnknowne, or vnauouched.

una'vowable, *a.* (UN-^{1} 7 b.)

[**1775** ASH.] **1802** BENTHAM *Panopt. Corr.* Wks. 1843 XI. 140 Any such clandestine and dishonourable, and unavowable and unavowed assurance. **1892** *Times* 26 Apr. 9/3 Gladstonian adhesion to crazy and unavowable schemes.

una'vowed, *ppl. a.* (UN-^{1} 8.)

[**1775** ASH.] **1790** BURKE *Fr. Rev.* 124 If the French king ..has in his own person..really deserved these unavowed, but unavenged, murderous attempts. **1850** L. HUNT *Autobiog.* xii. II. 94 Coleridge..lamented that an endeavour unavowed had been made to catch his tone. **1876** GLADSTONE in *Contemp. Rev.* June 5 Votaries who are scattered and isolated; or whose creed is unavowed.

Hence **una'vowedly** *adv.*

1861 MAINE *Anc. Law* ii. (1866) 31 The moment the judgment has been rendered and reported, we slide unconsciously or unavowedly into..a new train of thought.

†**unawait,** error for *in* (or *on*) *await*: see AWAIT *sb.* 1 b.

1452 *Paston Lett.* I. 238 Item, iij. of the seid felechep lay unawayte upon Emond Brome,..and toke hym presoner.

una'wakable, *a.* (UN-^{1} 7 b.)

1691 E. TAYLOR *Behmen's Theos. Philos.* 348 In the Eternal Nature lyeth the Turba, though unawakable.

una'waked, *ppl. a.* [UN-^{1} 8.] = next.

1647 HEXHAM I, Vnawaked, *ongeweckt*. **1721** YOUNG *Revenge* IV. i, How soft the breast, on which I laid my peace For years to slumber, unawak'd by care! **1742** —— *Nt. Th.* II. 618 Strange! the theme..shou'd sleep unsung! And yet it sleeps, by genius unawak'd.

una'wakened, *ppl. a.* (UN-^{1} 8.)

1705 ATTERBURY *Serm. Luke xvi. 31* (1726) II. 57 Every day the Impression loses somewhat of its Force,..till at length it comes..to operate..faintly upon careless unawaken'd Minds. **1762** WESLEY *Jrnl.* 29 July (1827) III. 103 A harmless, unawakened..woman came to one of the meetings for prayer. **1819** SHELLEY *Ode West Wind* 68 Be through my lips to unawakened earth The trumpet of a prophecy! **1860** W. L. COLLINS *Luck of Ladysmede* (1862) I. 275 The eyes..in whose soft depths a mighty unawakened love had seemed always sleeping. **1899** *Educ. Rev.* Dec. 472 The dull and unawakened have their rights.

Hence **una'wakenedness.**

1879 MEREDITH *Egoist* x, Chewing the cud in the happy pastures of unawakenedness.

una'wakening, *ppl. a.* (UN-^{1} 10.)

1846 WORCESTER (citing Foster). **1866** M. ARNOLD *Thyrsis* xvii, There thine earth-forgetting eyelids keep The morningless and unawakening sleep.

una'waking, *ppl. a.* (UN-^{1} 10.)

1863 [H. W. WHEELWRIGHT] *Spring Lapl.* 131, I should.. gradually pass off into an unawaking slumber.

una'warded, *ppl. a.* (UN-^{1} 8.)

[**1775** ASH.] **1897** *Outing* XXX. 346/1 The cup offered.. to the member who should ride upon the road the greatest number of days..is unawarded after a whole year having elapsed.

unaware (ʌnə'wɛə(r)), *adv.* and *a.* [UN-^{1} 11 b and 7: cf. UNIWARE and UNWARE.]

A. *adv.* **1.** = UNAWARES *adv.* 1 a.

1592 SHAKS. *Ven. & Ad.* 823 As one that unaware Hath dropp'd a precious jewel in the flood. **1667** MILTON *P.L.* II. 156 Will he, so wise, let loose at once his ire, Belike through impotence, or unaware. **1700** DRYDEN *Pal. & Arc.* II. 18 To his Keeper this [beverage] he brought, Who swallow'd unaware the sleepy Draught. *a* **1800** COWPER *Odyss.* (ed. 2) XIX. 634 She pours her echoing voice,..Deploring Itylus, whom she destroy'd (Her son by royal Zethus) unaware. **1862** MRS. BROWNING *False Step* ii, Thou only hast stepped unaware,—Malice, not one can impute.

2. = UNAWARES *adv.* 2.

1667 MILTON *P.L.* III. 547 Some high-climbing Hill, Which to his eye discovers unaware The goodly prospect. **1700** DRYDEN *Pal. & Arc.* I. 258 A Glance of some new Goddess gave the Wound, Whom, like Acteon, unaware I found. **1818** KEATS *Endym.* IV. 879 Long have I sought for rest, and, unaware, Behold I find it! **1885–94** R. BRIDGES *Eros & Psyche* Apr. xxviii, A Zephyr..gathering round her unaware Fill'd with his breath her vesture and her veil.

3. In phr. *at unaware*: cf. UNAWARES *adv.* 4.

1598 R. BERNARD tr. *Terence, Heautont.* IV. i, Thou doest all things at unaware and unadvisedly. **1644** T. CASE *Serm., Quarrel of the Covenant* 6 Floods of wrath and vengeance might break in upon them at unaware. **1700** DRYDEN *Pal. & Arc.* I. 492 A Serpent shoots his Sting at unaware. **1855** BROWNING *An Epistle* 296 So we met In this old sleepy town at unaware, The man and I. **1866** CHR. ROSETTI *Prince's Progr.*, etc. 20 At unaware They met eye to eye.

B. *adj.* **1.** Not aware; not cognizant; ignorant. Const. *of*, or with clause.

1704 SWIFT *T. Tub* i, I am not unaware how the Productions of the Grub-street Brotherhood have..fallen under many Prejudices. **1809–10** COLERIDGE *Friend* (1865) 121 Of this important fact Rousseau was by no means unaware. **1866** G. MACDONALD *Ann. Q. Neighb.* iii. (1878) 34 He spoke in the most matter-of-fact tone, unaware of anything poetic in what he said.

2. Reckless; lacking caution; unwary.

1817 SHELLEY *Rev. Islam* VI. xv, I lost all sense or care, And like the rest I grew desperate and unaware.

Hence †**una'wared** *a.*; **una'waredly** *adv.*; **una'wareness.**

1652 SPARKE *Prim. Devot.* (1663) 114 A barbarous surprise of unawared sufferers, affording them neither opportunity of defence or preparation. **1847** L. HUNT *Men, Women & B.* I. ix. 145 He stood holding the door open,.. in the blandest tones of unawareness saying—'Ah, dear me —I'm very—I beg pardon'. **1895** W. SHARP in *Life* xv. (1910) 244 It is unawaredly that she whispers to me.

unawares (ʌnə'wɛəz), *adv.* Also 6 **unawarres,** 7 **unawars.** [f. as prec. + -s^1. Cf. UNIWARES, UNWARES *advs.*]

1. a. Without being aware; unconsciously; inadvertently; unintentionally. Cf. UNAWARE *adv.* 1.

1535 COVERDALE *Josh.* xx. 5 They shall not delyuer the deedslayer in to his handes, for so moch as he hath slayne his neghboure vnawarres. **1585** T. WASHINGTON tr. *Nicholay's Voy.* II. vi. 35 b, If any drinke of it vnawares. **1641** J. JACKSON *True Evang. T.* I. 70 Lactantius was slipt unawares into this opinion, and S. Ierome doth..animadvert him for it. **1699** R. L'ESTRANGE *Erasm. Colloq.* (1725) 276 Money might lie upon the Ground, and they tread upon it unawares. **1726** BERKELEY *Let.* Wks. 1871 IV. 139, I have unawares run into this long account. **1787** BENTHAM *Def. Usury* xiii. 184 So great a master having fallen unawares into an error. **1832** HT. MARTINEAU *Weal & Woe* ix. 133, I might have spoken unawares, with authority. 1865 Kingsley *Heroes* II. ii, I will tell you, lest you rush upon your ruin unawares.

b. Without being noticed; unobserved.

1667 Dryden & Davenant *Tempest* III. ii, I fear'd the pleasing form of this young man Might unawares possess your tender breast. 1690 Locke *Hum. Und.* III. i. §5 By which we may give some kind of guess,.. how Nature, even in the naming of Things, unawares suggested to Men the Originals and Principles of all their Knowledg. 1718 Prior *Solomon* Pref. ¶8 Age steals upon Us unawares. 1796 Mme. D'Arblay *Camilla* V. 531 [In] confidence unlimited.. hours might have passed, unnumbered and unawares.

2. Without intimation or warning (given or received); unexpectedly, suddenly.

1535 Coverdale *Ps.* xxxiv. 8 Let a sodane destruccion come vpon him vnawarres. 1584 R. Scot *Discov. Witchcr.* II. ii. (1886) 16 Witches must be examined as suddenlie, and as unawares as is possible. 1657 Trapp *Comm. Job.* i. 19 No guest cometh unawares to him who keeps a constant table. 1667 Milton *P.L.* II. 932 He.. meets A vast vacuitie: all unawares Fluttring his pennons vain plumb down he drops. 1712 Steele *Spect.* No. 504 ¶1 Commend me also to those who.. do not give up their Pretensions to Mirth. These can slap you on the Back unawares. 1796 Mme. D'Arblay *Camilla* II. 353 He had just surprised her in tears, by coming upon her unawares. 1812 Byron *Ch. Har.* II. lxxi, He that unawares had there ygazed With gaping wonderment had stared aghast. 1869 Freeman *Norm. Conq.* vii. (1877) II. 63 The King, accompanied by the three great Earls, came unawares upon the Lady.

b. In the phr. *to take* (or *catch*).. *unawares*.

1593 Shaks. *3 Hen. VI*, IV. viii. 63 Away betimes, before his forces ioyne, And take the great-growne Traytor vnawares. 1791 Burns *Tam O'Shanter* 86 Glowring round wi' prudent cares, Lest bogles catch him unawares. 1849 Lytton *Caxtons* I. iii, He seemed incapable of acting for himself; he,.. if taken unawares, was pretty sure to be the dupe. 1865 Kingsley *Herew.* ii, The famous soubriquet of 'Wake'; the Watcher, whom no man ever took unawares.

3. In quasi-adj. use: †**a.** Ignorant, not aware, *of* something. *Obs.*$^{-1}$ (Cf. unaware *a.* 1.)

1548 Coverdale, etc. *Erasm. Par. Acts* 36 b, But thou, in persecucion of my disciples,.. doest persecute me also, vnawares thereof. 1567 Maplet *Gr. Forest* 86 b, He, as they are vnawares of him, sodainely snatcheth vp with his Pawes certaine of them.

b. Unknown, unperceived, unrealized. Const. *to* or †*of* (oneself or another).

1548 Udall, etc. *Erasm. Par. John* 94 b, Neyther is it vnawares to me that ye shall not fully vnderstande these thynges whiche I nowe speake. 1584 *Leycesters Commonw.* (1641) 36 They sent on day (unawares to her) for Doctor Bayly, and desired him to perswade her to take some little potion at his hands. 1635 J. Hayward tr. *Biondi's Banish'd Virg.* 140, I submissively kneeling down, and kissing his [hand] unawares of him. 1643 E. Symmons *Loyal Subjects Belief* 75 It is not wisdome for any man.. to trust himself in a suspicious path, lest unawares to himselfe and them, he be on the sudden *in mediis malis*. 1748 Richardson *Clarissa* (1811) VI. 70 Unawares to myself, I had moved onward. 1857 Kingsley *Two Y. Ago* I. 144 She found.. that she watched, almost unawares to herself, for his passing. 1874 S. Wilberforce *Ess.* II. 15 The very features of men.. assume, unawares to themselves, something of unnatural severity.

4. In phr. ***at unawares***: **a.** = sense 2.

1564 Haward *Eutropius* III. 31 Anniball assaultinge Eneus Fulvius at unawares beinge then in Italye slue him. 1593 Shaks. *3 Hen. VI*, IV. iv. 9 He is taken prisoner, Either betrayd by falshood of his Guard, Or by his Foe surpriz'd at vnawares. 1622 R. Hawkins *Voy. S. Sea* (1847) 90 We used all our best endevours to take them at unawares, yet comming within fortie paces, we were discovered. *a* 1667 Cowley *Ess. in Verse & Pr.*, *Avarice*, He.. Must run the danger.. of the rapid stream it self which may At unawares bear him perhaps away. 1737 Whiston *Josephus, Antiq.* II. x. §2 Serpents.. some of which.. fly in the air, and so come upon men at unawares. *a* 1774 Goldsm. *Hist. Greece* II. 225 Darius fearing he should be attacked at unawares,.. obliged his soldiers to coutinue the whole night under arms. 1822 Scott *Halidon Hill* I. ii. 167 You might slay him At unawares before he saw your blade drawn. 1868 Nettleship *Ess. Browning* i. 40 It is like coming to the edge of a precipice at unawares.

b. = sense 1 a and 1 b.

1595 Danett tr. *Comines* (1614) 129 The King feared especially.. least some word should escape him at vnawares. 1613 Purchas *Pilgrimage* (1614) 570 A Roman, at vnawares hauing killed a Cat, could not.. be detained from their butcherly furie. 1679 C. Nesse *Antichrist* 213 It stole into the world.. unsensibly and at unawares. 1853 Miss Yonge *Heir of Redclyffe* xv, All this was told at unawares, drawn forth by different questions and remarks, till Guy inquired how much 'it would take to give them a start?' 1870 Chr. Rossetti *Poems* (1904) 65 When friend shall no more envy friend Nor vex his friend at unawares.

†**una'warnist**, *ppl. a. Sc. Obs.* [un-^{1} 8: cf. unwarnist.]

Unannounced. So †**una'warnistly** *adv.*, without warning. *Obs.*

1533 Bellenden *Livy* II. x. (S.T.S.) I. 165 Brokin of þare purpois be vnawarnist cummyng of romane legiouns. *Ibid.* IV. xii. II. 89 This l. posthvmeus.. Invadit þe Inemyis vnawarnistlie.

un'awed, *ppl. a.* [un-^{1} 8.] Not awed or awestruck. Also const. *by*.

1693 Dryden *Ovid's Met.* I. 116 Unforc'd by Punishment, un-aw'd by fear, His words were simple, and his Soul sincere. 1728 Pope *Dunciad* III. 223 Persist, by all divine in Man unaw'd. 1768–74 Tucker *Lt. Nat.* (1834) I. 669, I have proceeded all along with an unawed freedom, doing my utmost to cast all prejudices aside. 1807 Byron *Episode of Nisus* 95 With anxious tremors, yet unawed by fear, The faithful pair before the throne appear. 1867 H. Macmillan *Bible Teach.* 73 The pine.. standing lonely and unawed.. in the midst of fearful horizons of snow-mountain and glacier.

un'awful, *a.* [un-^{1} 7.]

†**1.** Not inspired or tinged with awe. *Obs.*

1627 Wren *Serm. bef. King* 17 Feb. 33 All negligent and perfunctorie performance of our Religion, all slight and unawful Expressions in it, as in Gods presence, are the foulest Scorn and Abasement that may be. 1656 Jeanes *Fuln. Christ* 70 Men come with as unprepared, unreverent, unawfull, and undevout thoughts and affections to a sermon, as to a play.

2. Not inspiring or causing awe.

1799 H. T. Colebrooke in *Life* (1873) 422 In the valleys the gloomy confined view is not unawful. 1826 Milman *Anne Boleyn* iii. 50, I go.. where wild men howl around Their blood stain'd altars—to uplift th' unknown, Unawful Crucifix.

†**un'awned**, *ppl. a. Obs.* (See un-^{1} 3.)

un'awned, *a.* [un-^{1} 9.] Awnless.

1821 W. P. C. Barton *Flora N. Amer.* I. 105 Anthers linear, unawned.

un'azotized, *ppl. a.* [un-^{1} 8.] Not deprived of oxygen.

1828 *Lancet* 29 Mar. 940/1 Unazotised food increased the symptoms. 1861 Bentley *Man. Bot.* 726 The various azotized and unazotized compounds which are concerned in the development of new tissues.

un-'backboarded, *a.* (un-^{1} 9.)

1858 Mrs. Gore *Heckington* xvi, God be praised! there is still one good, natural, honest, un-backboarded girl left in the world.

un'backed, *a.* [un-^{1} 8.]

1. Of horses: Unmounted; untrained.

1592 Shaks. *Ven. & Ad.* 320 The vnbackt breeder full of fears, Iealous of catching, swiftly doth forsake him. 1613 W. Browne *Brit. Past.* I. v. 98 A stubborne Nagge of Galloway; Or vnback'd Iennet, or a Flanders Mare. 1656 Stanley *Hist. Philos.* IV. (1687) 136/2 Being demanded how the Learned differ from the unlearned, he answered, as Horses unback'd from such as are well manag'd. 1753 Hogarth *Anal. Beauty* xvii. 223 A fine Arabian war-horse, unbacked, and at liberty, and in a wanton trot. 1787 *Generous Attachment* II. 66 My Louisa's long unbacked mare.. frisked like a fawn across the neighbouring meadow.

2. Not backed or supported; not endorsed.

1609 Daniel *Civ. Wars* III. lxxix, He.. will not avouch thy fact, But let the weight of thine owne infamie Fall on thee, vnsupported, and vnbackt. 1642 H. More *Song of Soul* To Rdr., Nor is reason unback'd with better principles mathematically satisfiable in matters of this kind. 1658 Earl Monm. tr. *Paruta's Wars Cyprus* 34 Most.. were new men, and unexperienced, especially being unback'd by Horse. 1846 Mrs. Gore *Eng. Char.* (1852) 115 A sucking politician unbacked by parliamentary interest. 1854 H. Miller *Sch. & Schm.* (1858) 548 They were in danger of being put down, unbacked by the popular support which in such a cause they deserved. 1892 *Daily News* 25 May 2/3 An arrangement which gives only an unbacked promise of half interest.

b. Not backed by betting.

1883 *Times* 22 Oct. 10/2 This year he took part in the race for the Great Yarmouth Handicap,.. but he was unbacked and unplaced.

3. Not furnished with a back or backing.

1861 *Daily Tel.* 19 Aug., The target fired at was an unbacked slab of wrought iron. 1895 *Funk's Stand. Dict.*, *Unbacked*, having no back, as a stool.

†**unbad**, obs. variant of unbid *ppl. a.*

1642 H. More *Song of Soul* II. ii, Men ybrought Into some spacious room, which when they've had A turn or two, go out, although unbad.

un'badged, *ppl. a.* (un-^{1} 8.)

1875 Browning *Aristoph. Apol.* 195 No unbadged buffoon is licensed here To shame us all.

un'baffleable, *a.* (un-^{1} 7.)

1827 *Examiner* 642 Extraordinary penetration and unbaffleable acuteness.

un'baffled, *ppl. a.* (un-^{1} 8.)

1795 Southey *Joan of Arc* I. 251 'Maiden, thou hast done Thy mission here,' the unbaffled fiend replied. 1829 Lytton *Disowned* ii, The first glow and life of youth,.. unbaffled in a single hope. 1855 Browning *Old Pict. Florence* xxxvi, That morning the scaffold Is broken away, and the long-pent fire.. unbaffled Springs from its sleep.

un'bag, *v.* [un-^{2} 5.] *trans.* To take or let out of a bag.

1611 Florio, *Dissaccare*, to emptie out of a sacke, to vnbag. 1854 De Quincey *War* Wks. 1862 IV. 279 To carry the knaves like foxes in a bag to the English border and there unbag them. 1860 Geo. Eliot *Mill on Floss* III. iii, Mrs. Tulliver, with a confused impression that it was a great occasion, like a funeral, unbagged the bell-rope tassels, and unpinned the curtains. 1884 *Pall Mall G.* 5 Mar. 3/2 A crowd of spectators assembled to see the fox unbagged.

un'bailable, *a.* [un-^{1} 7 b.] **a.** Not entitled to be released on bail. **b.** Not admitting of bail.

1627 in Birch *Crt. & Times Chas. I* (1848) I. 295 If the cause be unexpressed, he shall be unbailable. *a* 1718 Penn *Life* Wks. 1726 I. 228 We are.. then thrown into a noisom Gaol, and there we must lie unbailable. 1861 W. S. Perry *Hist. Ch. Eng.* I. iv. 185 The unbailable imprisonment which lighted upon those who declined it. 1884 *Imp. Dict.* s.v., The offence is unbailable.

un'bain, *a.* Now only *dial.* Also 4–5 vnbayn(e, -bein, 5 -beyne, 9 *dial.* unbane. [f. un-^{1} 7 + bain *a.*, or ad. ON. *úbeinn* not straight, crooked (Norw. *ubein* crooked, awkward).]

†**1.** Not ready or willing; disobedient. *Obs.*

a 1300 *Cursor M.* 17735 He sal find mani bern vnbain, For mani sal him sai again. *c* 1400 *Rule St. Benet* (Verse) 1639 If ony be so vnbayne In word or werk to groch ogayn,.. With penance sal scho be chastid. *c* 1460 *Towneley Myst.* xxiv. 356 Thou shall forthynk it, in fayth; Fy, what thou art fre! vnbychid, vnbayn! ? *a* 1500 *Chester Pl.* II. 338 Thus shalt thou lyve,.. for thou hast bene to me vnbeyne.

†**b.** Unfriendly, disagreeable. *Obs.*

a 1300 *Prov. Hending* in *Anglia* IV. 186 Drawe þine honde sone aȝein, ȝef man doth þe ouht unbein, þar þine herte is ilende.

†**2.** Slow, inactive. *Obs.*$^{-1}$

a 1470 Harding *Chron.* LXIII. xii, So was he kyng of Brytain then again, And sone then after, he fell in age vnbain.

3. *dial.* Inconvenient, awkward.

1828 *Craven Gloss.*, *Unbane*, inconvenient, distant. 1863 Mrs. Toogood *Spec. Yorksh. Dial.* (MS.), I ought to have a fork; the spade is very unbane for the work. 1899 *Leeds Merc. Suppl.* 5 Aug. (E.D.D.), T' doors is as unbane as can be.

un'bait, *v.* (un-^{2} 4.)

1598 Florio, *Disinuescare*, to vnsnare, to vnbaite. 1844 *P. Parley's Ann.* V. 231 As to cheese, I'll unbait all the mousetraps for you; but you shall not eat dry bread.

un'baited, *ppl. a.* [un-^{1} 8.]

1. Not baited or worried by dogs.

15.. J. Balnavis '*O Gallandis all*' 86 (Bann. MS.), Ouer oft to hound in vnkowth ground, Thow ma tak vp vnbaittit. 1672 in Picton *L'pool Munic. Rec.* (1883) I. 341 A bull unbaited.

2. Not furnished with bait.

1880 Carnegie *Pract. Trapping* 61 A sure way of catching this destructive little animal.. is to cut a groove in some of the posts or gate posts, in which set an unbaited steel trap. 1905 *Macm. Mag.* Dec. 90 Two rods dangled an unbaited hook and a bedraggled fly in the water.

un'baized *a.* (un-^{1} 9.)

1853 C. Bronte *Villette* xxviii, It slid down the polished slope of the varnished and unbaized desk.

un'baked (ʌnˈbeɪkt), *ppl. a.* Also 6 unbackte. [un-^{1} 8. Cf. Sw. *obakad*, Da. *ubagt*.]

1. Of tiles, brick, etc.: Not baked in a kiln; not exposed to heat.

1563 Hyll *Art Garden.* (1574) 32 Ye water, in which the vnbaked Tile hath bene soked, poured vpon their holes, doth destroy them. 1579 Langham *Gard. Health* (1633) 191 The stones burned in an vnbaked pot.. and the ashes burnt wil serue for Spodium. 1598 Florio, *Mattoni crudi*, vnbaked brickes, white bricks. 1787 *Phil. Trans.* LXXVII. 291 This handle consists of turned unbaked mahogany. 1853 J. Lang *Wetherbys* 171 Badly-built walls, which had been made of unbaked bricks to save expense! 1869 Tozer *Highl. Turkey* I. 375 Miserable hovels of unbaked brick.

2. Of bread, etc.: Not prepared by baking.

1577 tr. *Bullinger's Decades* (1592) 370 There was offered .. cleane meale vnbaked. 1578 Lyte *Dodoens* II. cxvi. 310 Maynardus.. putteth it into the midle of an vnbackte loafe, so letting it bake vntil the bread be wel backte. 1611 Florio, *Incotto*, vnsodden, vnbaked, vnrosted, vnboyled. 1727 Bailey (vol. II), *Dough*,.. the Mass of Bread unbaked. 1769 Cook *Voy. round World* I. xvii. (1773) 202 A quart of the pounded bread-fruit, which is as substantial as the thickest unbaked custard.

3. *fig.* Left in an unfinished or immature state.

1601 Shaks. *All's Well* IV. v. 3 All the vnbak'd and dowy youth of a nation. *a* 1625 Fletcher *Elder Brother* II. ii, A little unbak'd Poetry, such as the Dablers of our time contrive. 1635 Pagitt *Christianogr.* II. vi. (1636) 40 Their Masse was then unmoulded, Transubstantiation unbaked.

†**un'baken**, *ppl. a. Obs.*$^{-1}$ [un-^{1} 8 b. Cf. MDu. *ongebacken* (Du. *-bakken*), OHG. *ungipachan* (MHG. *ungebachen*, G. *-backen*).] = prec. 1.

1549 *Compl. Scot.* vi. 46 Ane of the tabilis vas of baikyn stane, and the tothir tabil of onbaykyn stane.

un'balance, *sb.* (un-^{1} 12.)

1887 *Alienist & Neurol.* Oct. 524 The paralyzing influence.. arising from congenital deficiency and unbalance. 1895 *Strand Mag.* Oct. 383/1 His mind was still in a terrible state of unbalance.

un'balance, *v.* [un-^{2} 3.]

†**1.** *trans.* = unballast *v.* 1. *Obs.*$^{-1}$ (Cf. balance *v.* 17.)

1586 B. Young *Guazzo's Civ. Conv.* IV. 193 b, He.. without anie more wordes unballanced [It. *votò*] the ship.

2. To throw (a person or thing) off the balance.

1856 Ruskin *Mod. Paint.* III. IV. xii. §10 His ways are stedfast; it is not this or that new sight which will at once unbalance him. 1892 *Pall Mall G.* 21 Jan. 3/2 Alcohol.. disturbs and unbalances the nervous system.

Hence **un'balancing** *vbl. sb.*

1889 *Pop. Sci. Monthly* July 368 A further unbalancing of the relations between the railroad companies and the public.

un'balanceably, *adv.* (un-^{1} 11.)

1661 Feltham *Resolves*, etc. 392 Albeit his loss without Gods mercy was unbalanceably irrecoverable.

un'balanced, *ppl. a.* [un-^{1} 8.]

1. Not balanced or equably poised: **a.** Of the mind, judgement, etc., or persons in respect of these.

1650 Bp. Hall *Cases Consc.* (ed. 2) 388 Wherein yet I cannot much blame an unballanced judgement, whiles I find the Septuagint contrary to themselves. 1737 Pope *Hor. Epist.* I. vi. 25 Thus good or bad, to one extreme betray Th' unbalanc'd Mind, and snatch the Man away. **1882** J. PARKER *Apost. Life* I. 62 We know what he has been up to this time, ardent, impulsive, unbalanced, enthusiastic, cowardly. **1886** A. WEIR *Hist. Basis Mod. Europe* (1889) 111 Interference with the old order was so far-reaching, that the minds of all were quite unbalanced.

b. Of material things.

1732 POPE *Ess. Man* I. 251 Let Earth unbalanc'd from her orbit fly. **1784** COWPER *Task* v. 40 No needless care, Lest storms should overset the leaning pile Deciduous, or its own unbalanc'd weight. **1835** *Court Mag.* VI. 192/1, I was several times unbalanced, and on the very point of being hurled backward into the gulf. **1901** *Feilden's Mag.* IV. 442/2 A running test of 16 hrs. with an average unbalanced load of 3,000 lbs.

c. *fig.* or *transf.* in various senses.

1712 BLACKMORE *Creation* III. 487 Then would unbalanc'd heat licentious reign. **1818** BYRON *Ch. Har.* IV. cxxxii, Thou, who never yet of human wrong Left the unbalanced scale. **1855** BAIN *Senses & Int.* II. ii. §9 The variegated aspects of the fields and gardens..have more beauty than the unbalanced verdure of the leaf. **1879** R. K. DOUGLAS *Confucianism* iii. 91 He hated those who possess valour unbalanced by the observance of propriety. **1899** *Allbutt's Syst. Med.* VIII. 333 Deviation takes place in the opposite direction through the unbalanced action of the healthy muscles on the unparalysed side.

2. Of an account: (see BALANCE *v.* 14).

1828–32 WEBSTER, *Unbalanced*,..not brought to an equality of debt and credit. **1902** *Daily Chron.* 25 Nov. 6/2 Complicated, confused, and unbalanced accounts.

un'bale, *v.* [UN-[2] 5.] *trans.* To undo (goods) from a bale or bales. Hence **un'baled** *ppl. a.*

1752 *Phil. Trans.* XLVII. 516 There should be found very honest men..who will take the trouble of seeing all the good unbaled, and every particular parcel exposed to the air. **1879** T. H. S. ESCOTT *England* I. 221 The unbaled cotton..passes through a series of machines.

un'balked, *ppl. a.* (UN-[1] 8.)

1888 TALMAGE in *Voice* (N.Y.) 10 May, That passion of jealousy, livid, hungry, unbalked, rages on.

un'ball, *v.* [UN-[2] 5: cf. UNBALE *v.*] *trans.* To unpack.

a **1694** SIR A. BALFOUR *Lett.* (1700) 96 You must..then cause unball them at the Custom-house, and set your Mark upon them.

†**un'ballassed**, *ppl. a. Obs.* Also 7 **vnballac't, -aced.** [UN-[1] 8.] = UNBALLASTED.

1606 BP. HALL *Heaven upon Earth* §25. 185 A light, vnballaced vessell, that rises and falls with euery wave. **1621** G. SANDYS *Ovid's Met.* II. (1626) 25 As vnballac't ships are rockt and tost With tumbling Waues. **1694** ADDISON *Ovid's Met.* II. Wks. 1721 I. 157 As at sea th' unballassed vessel rides Cast to and fro.

†**un'ballast**, *ppl. a. Obs.* [var. of prec. Cf. Du. *ongeballast.*] = UNBALLASTED.

1622 T. SCOTT *Belg. Pismire* Pref., I have..saved much I might have lost, had I ventured any thing in so light, weake, and vnbalast a bottom. **1655** GURNALL *Chr. in Arm.* I. 275 The opinion of others, whose breath of applause possibly was a means to over-set thy unballast spirit. **1659** W. CHAMBERLAYNE *Pharonnida* II. 103 The vexed prince,..to entertain Them now with strength unballast, calls in haste His late neglected Council.

un'ballast, *v.* [UN-[2] 4. Cf. Du. *ontballasten.*]

1. *Naut.* To clear (a ship) of ballast. Also **un'ballasting** *vbl. sb.*

a **1684** LEIGHTON *Com. Pet.* v. 6 (1849) II. 460 It is necessary time and pains that is given to the unballasting of a ship. **1769** FALCONER *Dict. Marine* (1780), *To unbalast*, to discharge the ballast of a ship. [Hence in later dicts.] *Ibid.* (French Terms), [The] *Maître de quai*..is besides to appoint the proper places for ballasting and unballasting vessels.

2. *fig.* To render unsteady.

1836 *Blackw. Mag.* XXXIX. 466 This pleasure..more completely unballasts the mind than any other.

un'ballasted, *ppl. a.* [UN-[1] 8.]

1. Of vessels: Not ballasted or rendered steady by ballast.

1657 F. COCKIN *Div. Blossomes* 22 And such a heart, like an unballast'd Ship, Is turned o'r with e'ry breath of wind. **1678** CUDWORTH *Intell. Syst.* I. iv. §31. 472 These have cut off the most excellent Fulcrum of the Soul,..by means whereof, like unballasted ships, they are tossed up and down perpetually. **1829** I. TAYLOR *Enthus.* ii. 41 Yesterday the unballasted vessel was seen hanging out all the gaiety of its colours. **1897** *Outing* (U.S.) XXX. 334/1 No better demonstration of the superiority of the light-draught and unballasted sailboat over the deep, heavy one has been given.

b. *fig.* Not steadied or kept in order by serious or solid qualities.

1644 MILTON *Educ.* 2 To be tost and turmoild with their unballasted wits in fathomles and unquiet deeps of controversie. **1670** C. GATAKER in *Gataker's Antid. Errour* Ep. Ded. A iij, The shame and misery will light heavie at last upon these unballasted mindes. **1697** COLLIER *Ess. Mor. Subj.* I. (1703) 182 An unexperienced unballasted Divine must be an improper missionary. **1701** —— *M. Aurel., Life* p. xxiv, Lucius Verus had none of these good Qualities; his Inclinations were eager, unballasted, and lewd. **1796** CHARLOTTE SMITH *Marchmont* III. 144 The unballasted head of Linda..was quite overset. **1809** SOUTHEY *Lett.* (1856) II. 151 Both these men are such unballasted politicians, that the public mind could not be worse guided. **1870** LOWELL *Study Wind.* 179 Percival..offers an example ..of the poetic temperament unballasted with those less obvious qualities, which make the poetic faculty.

2. Of a railway line: Not filled in with ballast.

1887 M. ROBERTS *Western Avernus* 204, I could not step in between, for the line was unballasted. **1891** *Cycling* 21 Feb. 75 Riding over the 'sleepers' on an unballasted railroad would be preferable.

un'bandage, *v.* [UN-[2] 4.] *trans.* To remove the bandage from. Also *absol.*

1840 MARRYAT *Poor Jack* xliii, The hospital mates unbandaged Spicer's leg. **1857** R. TOMES *Amer. in Japan* viii. 181 Dr. Parker prevailed upon a girl of thirteen, who was a patient in the hospital, to unbandage in the presence of her mother. **1899** *Westm. Gaz.* 8 Sept. 3/2 Mr. L. (the oculist..) unbandaged the weak eye for a few moments.

un'banded, *ppl. a.* [UN-[1] 8.] Not furnished with a band or bands. Also *fig.*

1570 *Wills & Inv. N. Co.* (Surtees, 1835) 329 It[e]m I do gyue and bequiethe vnto my doughtor margreatt dychbourne a brass pan vnbanded. **1600** SHAKS. *A. Y. L.* III. ii. 397 Your hose should be vngarter'd, your bonnet vnbanded, your sleeue vnbutton'd. **1608** *Merry Devil Edmonton* v. i. 85 Did not this good knight..Confesse with you,..To deale with him about th' unbanded marriage Betwixt him and that faire young Millisent?

†**un'bandoned**, *ppl. a. Sc. Obs.*[−1] [UN-[1] 8.] Not kept under control; loose.

1375 BARBOUR *Bruce* x. 382 (Camb. MS.), Richt as thai ky and oxin weir, That war vnbawndonit left therout.

un'banished, *ppl. a.* (UN-[1] 8.)

1533 BELLENDEN *Livy* v. xv. (S.T.S.) II. 197 Quhen Camyllus..was on þis wise exilit, quhilk remanand still.. vnbanist, Rome micht never haue bene tane. **1597** WARNER *Alb. Eng.* v. xxvii. 137 Make-shifts, and Bawdes did thriue, Nor was an ancient English Peere vnbanisht or aliue. **1648** HEXHAM II, *Ongebannen*, Vnbanished, or Vn-exiled. **1821** BENTHAM *Lib. Press* 17 Under whom it has hitherto been my good hap to live unhanged, unsabred, unimprisoned, unbanished, and unruined.

un'bank, *v.*[1] [UN-[2] 4.]

1. *trans.* To free from a bank or barrier. In quot. *fig.*

1842 SIR H. TAYLOR *Edwin the Fair* I. v. 36 Unbank the hours To that soft overflow which bids the heart Yield increase of delight.

2. To clear (a fire) from banked-up matter.

1890 *Sci. Amer.* 17 May 315/3 The first duty of an engineer..is to ascertain how many gauges of water there are in his boilers. Never unbank or replenish the fires until this is done.

un'bank, *v.*[2] (UN-[2] 4: cf. BANK *sb.*[3] 7.)

1834 CALHOUN *Wks.* (1874) II. 363 We must..use a bank to unbank the banks, to the extent that may be necessary.

un'bankable, *a.* (UN-[1] 7 b.)

1864 *Weekly Times* (N.Y.) 9 Apr., The loss the treasury may sustain from unbankable notes. **1890** GILDERSLEEVE *Ess. & Stud.* 55 A poor exchange for the treasure of German idealism, unbankable as it is.

un'banked, *ppl. a.* (UN-[1] 8.)

[**1775** ASH.] **1898** *Cycling* 82 [The cycle-tracks] were unbanked, and in some cases the corners were very sharp.

un'bannered, *ppl. a.* (UN-[1] 8.)

1827 POLLOK *Course T.* VII. 421 Innumerable armies rose, unbannered all.

unbap'tize, *v.* [UN-[2] 3.] *trans.* To divest (a person) of the effect of baptism. Also *absol.*

1611 FLORIO, *Sbattezzare*, to vnchristen, to vnbaptize. **1641** MILTON *Ch. Govt.* II. ii. 55 Ye have bin bold,.. baptizing the Christian infant with a solemne sprinkle, and unbaptizing for your own part with a profane and impious forefinger. **1709** J. JOHNSON *Clergym. Vade M.* II. p. lxxi, The Priest can baptize, but he can't un-baptize. *a* **1714** M. HENRY *Treat. Baptism* Wks. 1853 I. 549/1 To unchurch, unchristianize, unbaptize, all those who are not in every thing of our length, is..destructive to the catholic church. **1841** A. R. C. DALLAS *Past. Superintend.* 147 Therefore, a person who acts thus would become a heathen if he could unbaptize himself. **1858** *Edin. Rev.* July 220 In the Roman Catholic Church..a man can no more be unmarried than he can be unbaptized.

unbap'tized, *ppl. a.* (UN-[1] 8.)

c **1375** *Sc. Leg. Saints* xxxiii. (*George*) 789 Quhat..sal be of me gyf I de in sic degre vnbaptyst ȝet? **14..** *With an O and an I* in *Anglia* XXVII. 288 He þat will lende Vnbaptist, he bese feffed wiþ þe fende. **14..** *Siege Jerus.* (E.E.T.S.) 155 ȝit vnbaptized wer boþe Barnabe & Poule. **1534** MORE *Treat. Passion* Wks. 1287/2 As for infantes dyeng vnbaptised.., many men wil peraduenture thynk otherwyse. **1586** WARNER *Alb. Eng.* IV. xxi. (1592) 90 He putteth all to Sword and Seas that vnbaptized wair. **1651** BAXTER *Inf. Bapt.* 71 It is true that many unbaptized are in the Kingdom of Christ. **1689** SHERLOCK *Death* iii. §7 They are in the state of unbaptized Jews. **1708** J. PHILIPS *Cyder* II. 652 Th' unbaptiz'd Turk Dreads War from utmost Thule. **1796** COLERIDGE *To a Friend* 11 And with those recreant unbaptized heels Thou'rt flying from thy bounden ministeries. **1826** SCOTT *Woodst.* ii, Unbaptized dog, speak civil of the Martyr in my presence. **1867** PEARSON *Hist. Eng.* I. 153 He bethought himself of asking what fate his unbaptized ancestors were undergoing.

unbap'tizing, *ppl. a.* (UN-[1] 10.)

1846 WORCESTER (citing Coleridge), *Unbaptizing*, *a.*, not baptizing.

unbar, *v.* [UN-[2] 3 and 7.] **a.** *trans.* To remove the bar from (a door or gate, etc.); to unfasten, undo. Also *absol.*

13.. *Gaw. & Gr. Knt.* 2070 The brygge was brayde doun, & þe brode gatez Vnbarred, & born open. **1433** LYDG. *St. Edmund* III. 1201 A-nother [thief] besy..To vnpyke lokys, a-nother to vnbarre. *c* **1450** *Mirk's Festial* 42 Thomas ȝede to þe dyr, and vnbarret þe dyrre. *c* **1530** LD. BERNERS *Arth. Lyt. Bryt.* (1814) 81 He vnbarred helmes, and claue asounder sheldes. **1590** SPENSER *F.Q.* II. xi. 17 He behight Those gates to be vnbar'd, and forth he went. **1603** KNOLLES *Hist. Turks* (1621) 995 The Turkes..vncouered and vnbarred their artillerie against the assailants. *c* **1620** FLETCHER & MASSINGER *Trag. Barnavelt* v. iii, Who Unbard the Havens that the floating Merchant Might clap his lynnen wings up to the windes. **1700** DRYDEN *Ovid's Met., Ajax* XIII. 573 Sure I may..Enter the Town, I then unbarr'd the Gates, When I remov'd their tutelary Fates. **1752** JOHNSON *Rambler* No. 190 ¶7 The servant immediately confessed that he unbarred the door. **1815** SCOTT *Guy M.* xlv, The house-door was next unbarred, unlocked, and unchained. **1859** DICKENS *Haunted House* iv, With soothing words the sister bade her wait, Until she brought the key to unbar the gate.

b. In fig. context.

1601 WEEVER *Mirr. Mart.* C iij b, Looke when the sun.. doth rise, Soone as the morne vnbarres her christall gate. **1611** SHAKS. *Cymb.* v. iv. 8 Th' sure Physitian, Death, who is the key T' vnbarre these Lockes. **1667** MILTON *P.L.* VI. 4 Till Morn..with rosie hand Unbarr'd the gates of Light. **1725** POPE *Odyss.* IV. 412 The morn..Unbarr'd the portal of the roseate East. **1746** HERVEY *Medit.* (1818) 87 The returning hours have unbarred the gates of light. **1855** BREWSTER *Newton* II. xvii. 133 That intellectual strength which had unbarred the strongholds of the universe. **1867** RUSKIN *Time & Tide* iv. §17 You practical English!—will you ever unbar the shutters of your brains? **1878** SEELEY *Stein* III. 565 There is nothing he likes better than unbarring restrictions, throwing open closed doors.

c. *intr.* To undergo unbarring.

1748 RICHARDSON *Clarissa* (1811) IV. 396, I heard her lady's door, with hasty violence unbar, unbolt, unlock, and open.

Hence **un'barring** *vbl. sb.* and *ppl. a.*

1611 FLORIO, *Sbaraglio*, rout, vnbarring, scattring. **1829** SCOTT *Anne of G.* xix, They heard the noise of the unbolting and unbarring of the gates of the inn. **1834** MARRYAT *P. Simple* xix, The unbarring of the prison doors. **1857** DICKENS *Dorrit* I. xvi, The possibility of her father's release from prison by the unbarring hand of death.

un'barbarize, *v.* [UN-[2] 6 c.] *trans.* To render less barbarous; to civilize. Hence (or f. UN-[1] 8) **un'barbarized** *ppl. a.*, civilized.

1648 J. BEAUMONT *Psyche* VIII. ccxxv, Mothers Who in their arms their tender Burdens brought, A sight which might all Beasts unbarbarize. **1719** OZELL tr. *Misson's Mem.* 150 Of these original Irish, most of the Persons of Quality understand English, and lead a Life totally unbarbarized. **1752** CHESTERF. *Lett.* cclxxviii (1792) III. 275 The courts of Manheim and Bonn I take to be a little more unbarbarised than some others. **1812** SOUTHEY *Let. to Landor* 16 April, Peru may be unbarbarized— made worse than it was under the Incas by the victory of the Indians. **1893** G. TYRRELL in M. D. Petre *Life* (1912) II. ii. 57 If Newman were studied and assimilated it would tend to unbarbarise us.

†**un'barbed**, *ppl. a.*[1] *Obs.* [UN-[1] 8. See BARB *v.* 1 and 2.]

1. Of cloth: Not barbed or clipped.

1535 *Act 27 Hen. VIII*, c. 13 §1 No wollen cloth..shuld be conveyed ouer the See unrowed, unbarbed and unshorne. **1541–2** *Act 33 Hen. VIII*, c. 19 Any coloured Clothe above the value of thre poundes, unrowed, unbarbed or unshorne. **1643** *Docq. Lett. Pat. at Oxf.* (1837) 363 To transporte all wollen clothes vnrowed, vnbarbd, vnshorne, and not fully drest.

2. *poet.* Unmown, uncut.

1612 DRAYTON *Poly-olb.* xiii. 112 When with his hounds The laboring Hunter tufts the thicke unbarbed grounds Where harbor'd is the Hart. **1652** BENLOWES *Theoph.* XII. lvii, The Virgin-meads, whose gaies Unbarb'd perk up to prank the curled stream.

un'barbed, *ppl. a.*[2] [UN-[1] 8 + BARBED *ppl. a.*[2]] Unarmed; not caparisoned; unbarded.

1565 COOPER *Thesaurus*, *Equus patens vulneri*, a horse vnbarbed, and in daunger to be wounded. **1607** SHAKS. *Cor.* III. ii. 99 Must I goe shew them my vnbarb'd Sconce?

un'barbed, *ppl. a.*[3] [UN-[1] 8 + BARBED *ppl. a.*[1]] Not furnished with a barb or barbs. Also *fig.*

1844 J. TOMLIN *Mission. Jrnls.* 84 The point sharp as the finest needle, but unbarbed. **1880** DAWSON *Fossil Men* v. (1882) 135 In the north barbed bone spears were used, and also little unbarbed bones with two elastic pieces of wood at the sides.

b. Const. *by.* (Cf. BARB *v.* 4.)

1863 MISS BRADDON *Aurora Floyd* i, The busy tongues.. were not unbarbed by malice.

un'barbered, *ppl. a.* (UN-[1] 8.)

1845 THACKERAY *Journ. fr. Cornhill to Cairo* ix, We'd a hundred Jews to larboard, Unwashed, uncombed, unbarbered. **1891** *Century Mag.* Dec. 236 Their long black locks unbarbered.

un'barded, *ppl. a.* [UN-[1] 8.] = UNBARRED *ppl. a.*[2]

1598 BARRET *Theor. Warres* v. ii. 142 Well mounted vpon a strong horse vnbarded. **1846** H. W. TORRENS *Rem. Milit. Hist.* 95 The real Grecian cavalry..used un-barded horses.

†**un'bare**, *a. Obs.*[−1] [UN-[2] 9.] = UNBARED *ppl. a.*

1624 HEYWOOD *Gunaik.* VIII. 391 The people stare To see my garments torne, and brests unbare.

un'bare, *v.* Now *rare.* [UN-[2] 9.] *trans.* To lay bare, to expose to view. (Cf. BARE *v.*)

1530 PALSGR. 766/1, I unbare a thyng, *je desnue. Ibid.*, Sythe I se the vysage, it is ynough, I wyll unbare nothing else. **1598** TOFTE *Alba* (1880) 108 Because thou seest myselfe with Love I cloathe, Another shall despoyle me and vnbare. **1615** SYLVESTER *Job Triumphant* II. 204

Destruction's Sword shall hunt him every hower, Consume his Sinews, and un-bare his Skin. **1630** LORD *Banians* Ep. Ded. A 2 b, Not unbaring the roote of their guilt and criminalitie. **1650** H. MORE *Observ.* in *Enthus. Tri.*, etc. (1656) 108 He has not done that which is impossible to doe, unbare to us the very substance of the Form. **1858** FARRAR *Eric* II. ii, The least boys seemed the greatest proficients in unbaring, without a blush, its hideous ugliness.

Hence **un'bared** *ppl. a.*, **un'baring** *vbl. sb.*

1585 Q. ELIZ. in Motley *Netherl.* (1868) I. vi. 340 This is no small succour, and no little unbaring of this realm of mine. *a* **1665** J. GOODWIN *Filled w. the Spirit* (1867) 203 When there is an unbared arm of God, then the work is said to be done from heaven. **1879** FARRAR *St. Paul* (1883) 418 The unbared palpitations of his inmost being.

un'bargained, *ppl. a.* (UN-[1] 8.)

1839 *Times* 1 Apr., An unbought, unbargained support to the Conservative government. **1874** H. SIDGWICK *Meth. Ethics* IV. iii. 409 Some-times such unbargained requital is even legally obligatory.

un'bark, *v.*[1] [UN-[2] 4 + BARK *sb.*[1]] *trans.* To deprive or strip of bark. (Cf. BARK *v.*[2] 3.)

c **1557** ABP. PARKER *Ps.* lxxviii. 224 He dyd unbarke of vyne the trees. **1589** FLEMING *Virg. Georg.* II. 30 Smooth canes and poles of byrch Peeld or vnbarkt. **1626** BACON *Sylva* §654 A Branch of a Tree being Un-barked some space at the Bottome. **1654** GAYTON *Pleas. Notes* IV. 209 Spoyling the stick and unbarking that body, which is vitiated.. by the approach of outward air. **1677** PLOT *Oxfordsh.* 165 The Tree being within as hollow as a Drum, and its out-most surface, where unbark'd, dead and dry beside. **1719** LONDON & WISE *Compl. Gard.* 103 In speaking of good and bad Roots, it may be thought, that the meaning of these is only such as are broken, or unbarked.

un'bark, *v.*[2] Now *dial.* or *Obs.* [UN-[2] 5 + BARK *sb.*[2]] To disembark.

1555 EDEN *Decades* (Arb.) 194 The gouernour had vnbarked .xvi. horses which were also at the battayle. **1560** DAUS tr. *Sleidane's Comm.* 83 The Emperoure unbarked hym selfe in spayne & arryved at Genes. **1599** HAKLUYT *Voy.* II. I. 214 Where they.. doe vnbarke themselues and vnlade their goods. *c* **1850** in *Eng. Dial. Dict.* (Devonshire dial.).

un'barked, *ppl. a.* [UN-[1] 8 + BARK *v.*[2]]

†**1.** Not treated with bark; untanned. *Obs.*[−1]

So Sw. *obarkad*, Da. *ubarket.*

1569 *Richmond. Wills* (Surtees) 218, ij barked horse skyns, and one vnbarked.

2. Not stripped of bark.

1839 MARRYAT *Diary Amer.* Ser. I. I. 237 The other had an unbarked hiccory stick. **1890** 'R. BOLDREWOOD' *Col. Reformer* (1891) 185 The unbarked pine-posts of the rude verandah.

un'barking, *ppl. a.* (UN-[1] 10.)

1833 MRS. BROWNING *Prometh. Bound* Poems 1850 I. 177 The griffins, those unbarking dogs of Zeus.

unbarmed: see UN-[1] 4.

un'barrable, *a.* (See UN-[1] 7 b and next.)

1818 CRUISE *Digest* (ed. 2) V. 525 An entail.. had lasted three hundred and sixty years... Its having been so long unbarred, gives a presumption, that the owners knew it was unbarrable.

un'barred, *ppl. a.* [UN-[1] 8.]

1. Of harbours: Not obstructed by a bar.

a **1550** LELAND *Itin.* III. (1907) 192 Ther cam to this place ons, the haven beyng onbarrid and syns chokid with tynne workes, good talle shippes. **1796** MORSE *Amer. Geog.* II. 177 These are.. the principal unbarred havens.

2. Not secured or blocked with a bar or bars.

1603 HOLLAND *Plutarch's Mor.* 165 Making no resistance to his appetites and demaunds, but letting all ly unfortified, unbard, and unlockt. **1708** J. PHILIPS *Cyder* I. 656 Weymouth,.. whose hospitable Gate, Unbarr'd to All, invites a numerous Train Of daily Guests. **1811** LD. DUDLEY *Lett. to 'Ivy'* (1905) 147 The doors are all left unbarred, and yet I never heard of anything being stolen. **1871** *Daily News* 18 Sept., Gallopers explored the railway line right and left to find sound bridges or unbarred level crossings.

3. *Law.* Not excluded or blocked. (BAR *v.* 5 b.)

1818 [see UNBARRABLE *a.*]. **1877** BLACKMORE *Erema* li, As to the property,.. the greater part would descend to me under unbarred settlement.

4. Not marked with a bar or minus sign.

1878 GURNEY *Crystallogr.* 16 All of these numbers are unbarred.

5. Of music: Not divided into bars.

1879 *Grove's Dict. Mus.* I. 137/2 In this kind of unbarred music the relative value of the notes must be.. preserved. **1901** *Westm. Gaz.* 5 Feb. 1/3 Old madrigals from the separate and unbarred part books for the Musical Antiquarian Society.

un'barrel, *v.* (UN-[2] 5.)

1611 FLORIO, *Sbarillare*, to vnbarrell. [**1775** ASH.] **1889** J. L. HILL in *Minutes Congreg. Council* 295 How can we, upon the spot, unbarrel the salt?

un'barrelable, *a.* (UN-[1] 7.)

1838 EMERSON *Addr., Lit. Ethics*, Truth is.. so.. unbarrelable a commodity, that it is as bad to catch as light.

un'barrelled, *ppl. a.* (UN-[1] 8.)

1482 in *Charters*, etc. *Edinb.* (1871) 168 Salmound and sic lyke fish vnbaralit.

un'barrenness. (UN-[1] 12.)

1656 JEANES *Fuln. Christ* 161 From all which he concludeth the perpetuity, indeficiency, and unbarrennesse of the Church.

un'barricade, *v.* [UN-[2] 4.] *trans.* To free from a barricade or barrier.

1623 WEBSTER *Duchess Malfi* v. v, You shall not unbarracade the doore To let in rescew. **1768** STERNE *Sent. Journ., Passport*, The Bastile is not an evil to be despised —but.. unbarricade the door—.. the evil vanishes.

unbarri'cadoed, *ppl. a.* (UN-[1] 8.)

[**1775** ASH.] **1795** BURKE *Let. to W. Elliott* Wks. VII. 351 What he could find in the glutted markets, the unbarricadoed streets.

†**un'barrowed**, *ppl. a. Obs.* [UN-[1] 8: cf. BAROWE *v.* and UNBERRIED.] Unthreshed.

1569 *Richmond. Wills* (Surtees) 218 Haver barrowid and unbarrowed bye estimacion xv quertars..; l. stroke queat unbarrowed.

un'base, *a.* (UN-[1] 7.)

1601–3 DANIEL *Cert. Epist.* 42 Wks. (Grosart) I. 218 How should we know thy soule had beene secur'd In honest counsels and in way vnbase!

un'based, *a.* (UN-[1] 8.)

1860 PUSEY *Min. Proph.* 82 From that unsolid, unbased, inflated greatness it vanisheth in air. **1884** H. SPENCER in *Contemp. Rev.* July 25 The theory commonly accepted is ill-based or unbased.

†**un'bashed**, *ppl. a. Obs.*[−1] [UN-[1] 8.] = UNABASHED *ppl. a.*

1536 *Stories & Proph. Script.* H viij, Geue vs a bolde and an onbashed harte to resiste all temptacions.

un'bashful, *a.* (UN-[1] 7.)

1563 MAN *Musculus' Commonpl.* 13 b, The benefite of clere conscience, and the unbashfull [L. *intrepidæ*] familiaritie with God. **1600** SHAKS. *A. Y. L.* II. iii. 50 In my youth I.. did not with vnbashfull forehead woe The meanes of weaknesse and debilitie. **1611** FLORIO, *Inuerecondo*, vnbashfull, impudent. **1834** WORDSW. *Even. Voluntaries* vi. 17 Meek eve shuts up the whole usurping host (Unbashful dwarfs each glittering at his post). **1858** MASSON *Milton* I. 280 Throughout all Milton's works there may be discerned a vein of noble egotism, of unbashful self-assertion. **1887** SWINBURNE *Stud. Prose & Poetry* (1894) 140 The laurels of Gotham, with which the critical sages.. have bedecked his unbashful brows.

Hence **un'bashfully** *adv.*, **un'bashfulness**.

1795 *Monthly Rev.* XVIII. 129 Probably Mr. Pye cared not unbashfully to contest the authority of Aristotle. **1611** FLORIO, *Inuerecondia*, vnbashfulnes, impudency.

un'bastardized, *ppl. a.* (UN-[1] 8.)

1769 H. WALPOLE *Let. to Mr. Cole* 12 Aug., Abp. Wareham's tomb at Canterbury being.. the last example of unbastardized Gothic. **1794** W. ROBERTS *Looker-on* No. 90 III. 448 A line of honest yeomanry, untainted by spurious grandeur,.. unbastardized by kings and nobles.

unbastilled, *a.* (UN-[1] 9.)

1817 BENTHAM *Parl. Reform* (1818) 77 So long, in a word, as it shall be my lot to remain alive, unkilled, and unbastiled.

un'bated, *ppl. a.* [UN-[1] 8.]

1. = UNABATED *ppl. a.*

1596 SHAKS. *Merch. V.* II. vi. 11 Where is the horse that doth vntread againe His tedious measures with the vnbated fire, That he did pace them first? **1611** B. JONSON *Cataline* III. iv, My guards Are you, great Powers, and the unbated strengths Of a firm conscience. **1670** COTTON *Espernon* I. II. 80 His brave, and unbated Courage. **1680** OTWAY *Orphan* IV. vi, I still love him with unbated Passion. **1810** SCOTT *Lady of L.* I. vii, Alone, but with unbated zeal, That horseman plied the scourge and steel. **1892** 'M. FIELD' *Sight & Song* 95 Yet round the place whence flows Thy blood Thy conscious palm with fervour of unbated will doth cling.

2. Not bated or blunted.

1602 SHAKS. *Ham.* IV. vii. 139 You may choose A Sword vnbaited, and in a passe of practice, Requit him for your Father. **1815** W. H. IRELAND *Scribbleomania* v, At ye I point the lance unbated by the poison of envy. [**1826** SCOTT *Woodst.* xxxii, I would have struck him through.. with an unbated weapon, as Will says.] **1979** A. WILLIAMSON *Funeral March* xv. 81 'Do you know how Andersson died?' .. 'Well—I suppose it was the unbated spear?'

un'bathed, *ppl. a.* (UN-[1] 8.)

1570 FOXE *A. & M.* (ed. 2) I. 57 He leaped out of the bathe vnbathed, because he feared the bathe shoulde haue fallen. *a* **1625** FLETCHER, etc. *Love's Pilgr.* III. ii, Let her but shew me A ruin'd cheek like mine, that holds his colour;.. An unbathed body. **1697** DRYDEN *Æneis* VII. 1103 Her flying feet unbathed on billows hung. **1700** —— *Cymon & Iph.* 599 The Blade return'd unbath'd, and to the Handle bent. **1791** COWPER *Odyss.* XIX. 409 For how, my honour'd inmate! shalt thou learn.. if unbathed, unoil'd, Ill-clad, thou sojourn here? **1803** VISCT. STRANGFORD *Poems of Camoens, Sonn.* xx. (1810) 106 Not unbath'd by Memory's warmest tear! **1888** *Pall Mall G.* 12 Sept. 2/2 During the three days that we spent under his roof I remained unbathed.

un'bating, *ppl. a.* (UN-[1] 10.)

1744 AKENSIDE *Pleas. Imag.* III. 373 The virgin's radiant eye, Superior to disease,.. Shines with unbating lustre.

un'batterable, *a.* (UN-[1] 7 b.)

1576 FLEMING *Panopl. Epist.* 266 Not taking strong towers, huge castles, and unbatterable walls for their fortifications.

un'battered, *ppl. a.* (UN-[1] 8.)

1603 KNOLLES *Hist. Turks* (1621) 324 If these wals stood still firme, and vnbattered. **1605** SHAKS. *Macb.* v. vii. 19 Else my Sword with an vnbattered edge I sheath againe vndeeded. **1607** DEKKER *Knt.'s Conjur.* iv. F ij, Captains, some in guilt armour (vnbattred), some in buffe Ierkens. **1837** CARLYLE *Fr. Rev.* III. I. vii, Brunswick may recross the dell,.. not unbattered by the way.

unbawndonit: see UNBANDONED *ppl. a.*

unbay, error for *im-*, EMBAY *v.*[1] 1.

1625 J. GLANVILLE *Voy. to Cadiz* (1883) 111 It was dangerous, in tyme of Winter, to unbay our selves soe deepelie as wee must doe by touching att Bayon.

†**unbay**, *v. Obs.*[−1] [UN-[2] 4 b + BAY *sb.*[5]] *trans.* To free from barrier or restraint.

1687 NORRIS *Coll. Misc.* 326, I ought now to let loose the reins of my affections, to unbay the current of my Passion.

†**un'bazled**, *ppl. a. Sc. Obs.* [UN-[2] 4: cf. Sc. dial. (Roxb.) *bizzel* 'a hoop or ring round the end of any tube' (Jam.).] ? Having the ring(s) started or loose.

1719 in W. R. Mackintosh *Glimpses of Kirkwall* (1887) 81 The guns belonging to the Brugh have been long unwrought for whereby they or some of them may be unbazled.

un'be, *v.*[1] *rare.* [UN-[1] 14.] *intr.* To lack being; to be non-existent.

1434 MISYN *Mending Life* 122 As qwo say: syn in vs may vnrene [= not reign], bot it may not vnbe. *a* **1795** *Bonnie James Campbell* iv. in Child *Ballads* IV. (1890) 143/2 My house is unbigged, my barn's unbeen. **1885** R. F. BURTON *Arab. Nts.* IV. 248 This ecstasy would see my being unbe. **1898** T. HARDY *Wessex Poems* 182 But for the charge that blessed things I'd liefer have unbe.

un'be, *v.*[2] [UN-[2] 4.] To deprive of being; to make non-existent.

1624 *Trag. Nero* III. iii. in Bullen *O. Pl.* (1882) I. 51 How oft, with danger of the field beset Or with home mutineys, would he unbee Himselfe. **1646** S. BOLTON *Arraignm. Err.* 13 God.. could as easily destroy them, as subdue them, unbee them as conquer them. **1759** R. SHIRRA in *Rem.* (1850) 118 He would not only dethrone, but un-be God, un-God him.

un'beaconed, *ppl. a.* (UN-[1] 8.)

1828 CAMPBELL *Departure of Emigrants* 72 Where shipless seas now wash unbeaconed crags. **1850** *Illustr. London News* 25 May 372/1 Her starboard bow suddenly struck upon the dangerous and unbeaconed rocks in question.

un'beamed, *ppl. a.* (UN-[2] 8.)

a **1843** SOUTHEY *Comm.-Pl. Bk.* (1851) IV. 198 The barber... Without his wig he is Jove without his thunder. Venus uncestused, Phœbus unbeamed.

un'bear, *v.* [UN-[2] 4 b.] *trans.* To free (a horse) from the bearing-rein.

1853 DICKENS *Bleak Ho.* lvi, Unbear him half a moment to freshen him up.

un'bearable, *a.* [UN-[1] 7 b.] Unendurable, intolerable.

c **1449** PECOCK *Repr.* v. v. 507 This man hath a bodili sijknes.. bi which he schal lyue in huge vnberable peine or be deed. **1601** SIR W. BROWN in A. Collins *Lett. & Mem. State* (1746) II. 228 The hurt Men.. make such a noysom Smell in the Towne, that is allmost vnberable. **1690** C. NESSE *O. & N. Test.* I. 175 The first covenant.. hath impossible as well as unbearable conditions. **1791–3** in *Spirit Public Jrnls.* (1799) I. 159 The consumption of provisions in such an army as this, may be objected to as unbearable. **1812** J. HENRY *Camp. agst. Quebec* 212 He was almost unbearable to many men. **1875** C. L. KENNEY *Mem. M. W. Balfe* 60 This state of mind was heightened to an almost unbearable strain of suspense.

Hence **un'bearableness**, **un'bearably** *adv.*

1730 BAILEY (fol.), *Insupportableness*, *unbearableness. **1867** MISS BROUGHTON *Cometh up like a Flower* vi, This bearableness or unbearableness of the various burdens laid on the shoulders of poor humanity. **1873** *Daily News* 26 Aug., An ordinary mortal would have found the beach in the middle of the day hot to unbearableness. **1809** MALKIN *Gil Blas* VII. i. ¶11 You are become so *unbearably hateful to her. **1862** C. H. AÏDÉ *Carr of Carlyon* II. 255 Since her dog's death she had been more unbearably silly.. than ever.

un'beard, *v.* (UN-[2] 4.)

1598 FLORIO, *Sbarbare*,.. to vnbeard, to cut off ones beard. **1786** tr. *Dulaure's Pogonologia* 127 One of their lay brethren.. unbearded all of them whilst they were asleep.

un'bearded, *a.* [UN-[1] 9. Cf. NFris. *ünbiarded*, Du. *ongebaard* (Kilian *onghebaerdt*), G. (botan.) *ungebartet*.]

1. Of persons: Not having a beard.

1560 BECON *Jewel of Joy* Pref., What a swarme of popyshe shauelyngs brought he forth,.. some bearded, some vnbearded. **1567** DRANT *Horace, Ep.* A v, Unbearded youth, at last rid from the Tutors barring charge. **1586** J. DAVIS in Hakluyt *Voy.* (1600) III. 104 The people are of good stature ..; the most part vnbearded,.. and close toothed. *a* **1637** B. JONSON *Horace, Art Poet.* 230 Th' unbearded youth, his guardian once being gone, Loves dogs and horses. *a* **1653** G. DANIEL *Idyll.* iii. 162 Truth shall find A Narrow Roome to tread in, and the few Vn-bearded Criticks, Cloth her out a new. **1855** SINGLETON *Virgil* II. 186 O'er it stand amazed The inexperienced and unbearded groups. **1891** KINNS *Graven in Rock* xvi. 599 Behind the king stands an unbearded officer.

2. Of plants, etc.: Not furnished with bristles or hairy tufts; awnless.

1688 DRYDEN *Brit. Rediv.* 260 As when a sudden Storm of Hail and Rain Beats to the ground the yet unbearded Grain. **1882** *Garden* 28 Jan. 66/3 The throat of the flower is unbearded.

un'bearing, *ppl. a.* [UN-[1] 10. Cf. OHG. *unberenti*, *-perendi*, Goth. *unbairands*.] Unfertile, unproductive, barren.

c **825** *Vesp. Psalter* cxii. 9 Se eardian doeð unbeorende [L. *sterilem*] in huse modur bearna. *c* **950** *Lindisf. Gosp.* John xv. 2 *marg.*, þæt unberende treo he ȝenimes. *c* **1000** ÆLFRIC

Deut. vii. 13 Ne bið mid eow nan þing unberendes ne on mannum ne on nytenum. *c* **1200** *Trin. Coll. Hom.* 125 Þe holi man.. was of michel elde, & his woreldes make was.. unberinde. **1685** DRYDEN *Horace, Ep.* ii. 21 [He] Does.. with his pruneing hook disjoyn Unbearing Branches from their Head. **1863** J. G. MURPHY *Comm., Gen.* xi. 6 Unwittingly provide a store for the unbearing period of the year. **1874** C. R. SMITH *Rural Life Shaks.* 4 Fruit-trees must be continually lacerated to decrease the growth of unbearing wood.

† **un'beast**, *sb. north.* and *Sc. Obs.* Also 4–5 vnbest(e, 6 wn-, vnbeast, 6 vn-, 9 unbeist, 8 *Sc.* onbeast. [UN-[1] 12. Cf. MDu. and Du. *ondier*, MHG. and G. *untier*, Da. and Norw. *udyr*, Sw. *odjur*.] A wild beast; a monster; a ravenous or vile animal. Also *transf.*

a **1300** *Cursor M.* 19859 Quen petre þais vnbestes sagh, O þaim þan thoght him mikel agh. *c* **1375** *Sc. Leg. Saints* xvi. (*Magdalene*) 502 Pytuisly þe prince can pray, þat þai hyr kest nocht in þe se, met til vnbestis to be. *c* **1400** *Destr. Troy.* 7766 He auntrid on this Vnbest angardly fast. *a* **1585** MONTGOMERIE *Flyting* 258 (Tullibardine MS.), Bot this bargane, vnbeist, deir sall þou by it. **1629** Z. BOYD *Last Battell* i. 47 Fye upon barnes, a nest for myce and rattons. Would yee desire to liue for to enjoye the leauinges of vnbeastes? **1768** ROSS *Helenore* I. 8 Has the onbeast your lambie taen awa'? *Ibid.* I. 18. **1808** JAMIESON s.v. *Onbeast, Unbeist*,.. a noxious member of human society; Ang[us].

un'beast, *v.* (UN-[2] 6 b.)

1611 FLORIO, *Disbestiare*, to vnbeast, to vnrude. **1621** G. SANDYS *Ovid's Met.* II. (1626) 35 Let him vnbeast the beast .. and her wanton shape restore.

† **unbeat**, obs. variant of UNBEATEN *ppl. a.*

1533 BELLENDEN *Livy* II. v. (S.T.S.) I. 145 Nocht was left þareof vnbet doun bot ane small parte. **1635** BRATHWAIT *Arc. Princ.* Ded., You shall here meet with an Author walking in an unbeat path.

un'beatable, *a.* (UN-[1] 7.)

1897 *Outing* (U.S.) XXIX. 483/2 The dogs.. were, however, very pretty and almost unbeatable on the show-bench.

un'beaten, *ppl. a.* [UN-[1] 8 b.]

1. Not beaten or struck.

a **1275** *Prov. Ælfred* 448 in *O.E. Misc.* 129 Betere is child vnboren þenne vnbeten. *a* **1635** CORBET *Iter Bor.* Poems (1647) 12 His Mare went truer then his Chronicle; And even for Conscience sake unspurr'd, unbeaten, Brought us sixe miles, and turn'd taile to New-Eaton.

b. Not pounded; not broken up or softened by pounding.

1607 TOPSELL *Four-f. Beasts* 515 Yoong mice being beaten into small bits or peeces... The same being vnbeaten and roasted. **1655** MOUFET & BENNET *Health's Improvement* 169 Stockfish whilst it is unbeaten is called Buckhorne, because it is so tough; when it is beaten upon the stock, it is termed stockfish. **1903** *Westm. Gaz.* 3 June 5/3 The daily labour required is the picking of 2 lb. of unbeaten or 4 lb. of beaten oakum.

2. Not beaten or trodden down. Also *fig.*

1617 MORYSON *Itin.* I. 294 The unbeaten waies make them [miles] seeme longer. **1634** W. WOOD *New Engl. Prosp.* I. ii, To hit home through the unbeaten Woods, was strange. **1690** T. BURNET *Theory Earth* II. 142 Natural reason can determine neither of these, sees no tract to follow in these unbeaten paths. **1716** SWIFT *Horace* III. ii. 12 Some new unbeaten passage to the sky. **1796** MORSE *Amer. Geog.* I. Pref. p. iii, He does not pretend that this design is completed;..he has trodden, comparatively, an unbeaten path. **1807** T. THOMSON *Chem.* (ed. 3) II. 144 One of the first excursions made by that illustrious philosopher into the then unbeaten tracts of pneumatic chemistry. **1880** MISS BIRD (*title*), Unbeaten Tracks in Japan.

3. Not conquered or defeated.

1757 *Pol. Ballads* (1860) II. 338 What joy it must be to a nation like Britain, To see such a Fleet return safe and unbeaten! **1884** ST. L. HERBERT in *Fortn. Rev.* Feb. 243 The Basutos, unbeaten, are thrown back upon the Imperial Government.

4. Not scoured for game.

1882 *N.Y. Tribune* 12 July, With these companions the sportsman is taken over unbeaten ground.

un'beauteous, *a.* (UN-[1] 7.)

a **1660** HAMMOND *Serm. Luke xviii. 11* Wks. 1684 IV. 610 The sanctifying spirit that beautifies the soul, is an humbling spirit also, to make it unbeauteous in its own eyes. **1839** LADY LYTTON *Cheveley* i, They.. turned away from every inn within that most dirty and unbeauteous town. **1876** MARY M. GRANT *Sun-Maid* i, The long tracts through which the railroad passes.. are very dreary and unbeauteous.

un'beauteousness. (UN-[1] 12.)

1886 MISS BRADDON *One Thing Needful* x, She had felt keenly the sting of her own unbeauteousness.

un'beautified, *ppl. a.* (UN-[1] 8.)

1625 QUARLES *Sion's Sonn.* xii. 4 Thy Necke (vnbeautifyde with borrow'd grace) Is whiter then the Lillies of thy face. **1680** C. NESSE *Church-Hist.* 137 Nature had spent all her strength in beautifying their bodies,.. but she had left their souls altogether unbeautified. **1871** SMILES *Charac.* xi. 314 Fine features unbeautified by sentiment or good-nature.

un'beautiful, *a.* (UN-[1] 7.)

1495 *Trevisa's Barth. De P.R.* XIX. viii. (W. de W.) hh vij b/2 Euery mannes face is moste made bewtefull or vnbewtefull with colour. **1580** LUPTON *Sivquila* 60 Both fayre and foule, beautiful and unbeautiful, go so al alike, that none can know the fair from the foule. **1647** CLARENDON *Contempl. Ps.* Tracts (1727) 503 If we.. by.. adorning it [*sc.* guilt] with specious Excuses.. render it less unbeautiful and unpleasant to our View. *a* **1680** CHARNOCK *Attrib. God* (1834) II. 223 To.. deny him this, is to frame him as an unbeautiful monster, a deformed power. **1692** SOUTH *Serm.* (1727) III. xi. 434, I cannot persuade myself, that God ever designed his Church for a rude, naked, unbeautiful Lump. **1828** TENNYSON *Lover's Tale* I. 342 Nothing in nature is unbeautiful. **1870** SWINBURNE *Ess. & Stud.* (1875) 379 No good art is unbeautiful; but much able and effective work may be, and is.

absol. **1887** HISSEY *Holiday on Road* 299 Once the unbeautiful puts her foot in anywhere, there.. she remains.

Hence **un'beautifully** *adv.*; **un'beautifulness** (1727 Bailey).

1847 WEBSTER, Unbeautifully. **1879** GEO. ELIOT *Let.* 5 Mar. (1956) VII. 111 The margin seems perilously and unbeautifully narrow. **1922** *Daily Mail* 23 Nov. 8 A Frenchwoman would as soon be seen in shabby shoes as with wisps of hair escaping unbeautifully from her coiffure. **1984** A. PRICE *Sion Crossing* xi. 222 His lip twisted unbeautifully.

un'beautify, *v.* [UN-[2] 6 c.] *trans.* To render unbeautiful.

1570 LEVINS *Manip.* 98 To vnbeautifie, *dedecorare.* **1611** FLORIO, *Disabellire*,.. to vnbeautyfie. *a* **1680** CHARNOCK *Attrib. God* (1834) I. 753 Sin unbeautifies man, and ravisheth his excellency. **1729** W. REEVE *Serm.* 20 They depreciate and unbeautify the whole work of Redemption. **1798** LAMB *The Witch* in Lucas *Lamb & Lloyds* (1898) 94 Heaven's music, which is order, seems unstrung, And this brave world.. unbeautify'd, Disorder'd, marr'd. **1876** W. ALEXANDER *Witness Ps. to Christ* (1877) 181 It is characteristic that the same hand should have unbeautified the Psalms for a shallow generation.

† **un'beauty**, *v. Obs. rare.* [UN-[2] 4.] = prec.

1495 *Trevisa's Barth. De P.R.* XVII. lxxv. (W. de W.) U iv b/2 The floure.. defoyleth nother vnbewtieth the rodde: but makyth it.. perfyte & fayr. **1611** FLORIO, *Disbellettare*, to vnpaint, or vnbeautie.

un'beavered, *a.*[1] (UN-[1] 9 or UN-[2] 4 + BEAVER *sb.*[1])

1720 GAY *The Espousal* 81 Brethren unbeaver'd then shall bow their head.

un'beavered, *a.*[2] (UN-[1] 9 or UN-[2] 4 + BEAVER *sb.*[2])

a **1851** MOIR *Sir Eliduc* xvi, From the echoing streets of Exeter March'd a thousand men and more, With banners, and unbeaver'd all.

unbe'clogged, *ppl. a.* (UN-[1] 8.)

1674 N. FAIRFAX *Bulk & Selv.* 40 'Tis hoped we may have leave to settle Gods whole Everlastingness, as untimesom, and altogether unbeclogg'd with onwardness.

unbe'clouded, *ppl. a.* (UN-[1] 8.)

1709 WATTS *Hymn*, '*There is a land*' v, Oh! could we.. see the Canaan that we love With unbeclouded eyes! **1857** SUSANNA WINKWORTH tr. *Life Tauler* 251 The beams of the eternal and divine sun.. shining with unbeclouded force. **1884** J. PARKER *Apost. Life* III. 68 On another day, unbeclouded and infinite in light, thou wilt show the answer to the riddle.

unbe'come, *v.*[1] [UN-[2] 4.] *trans.* To deprive (*of* something).

1624 HEYWOOD *Captives* I. i, Shall I, bycause hee perisht in the sea,.. Despoyle my shipps, and unbecom the deepes Of theire fayre Sayles and tackles?

unbe'come, *v.*[2] [UN-[1] 14: cf. UNBECOMING *ppl. a.*] *trans.* To fail to become or suit; to be unbecoming to.

1628 ABP. WILLIAMS *Serm.* 8 It doth not vnbecome fortunate men to swell a little. **1653** SHIRLEY *Court Secret* II. i, It will not unbecome your royal justice To let me know his crime. **1679** PENN *Addr. Prot.* II. vi. (1692) 221 They draw to Strife,.. Hatred and Persecutions, which unbecome the Man of God. **1716** M. DAVIES *Athen. Brit.* III. Ded. A j b, I thought it did not unbecome me.. to pay and raise such Tribute of Loyalty and Gratitude as lay in my Power. **1893** YEATS *Celtic Twilight* p. x, I.. shall be well content if it do not unbecome me.

† **unbe'comed**, *ppl. a. Obs.*[−1] [UN-[1] 8 c: the sense of *become* is unusual.] Unadorned *with* something.

1646 J. GREGORY *Notes & Obs.* 113 The Earth was without Forme and voide, i.e... unbecomed with that glorious furniture which now it hath.

† **unbe'comely**, *a. Obs.* Forms: 3 unbicomelich, -cumeliche, 4 onebycomeleche. [UN-[1] 11.] Unbecoming; unsuitable.

c **1200** *Trin. Coll. Hom.* 97 Hwu come þu [h]ider in mid unbicumeliche weden? *a* **1300** *K. Horn* 1145 He makede him vn-bicomelich, Hes [= as] he nas neuremore ilich. *c* **1315** SHOREHAM *Poems* VII. 589 One-by-comeleche þyng hyt were, ȝef eny loȝ þer leþy were.

unbe'coming, *vbl. sb.* (UN-[2] 8.)

1883 MAUDSLEY *Body & Will* III. vii. 317 Are we to look forward to a continued becoming or to an ultimate unbecoming of things? Will evolution on earth go on for ever?

unbe'coming, *ppl. a.* [UN-[1] 10 and 5 d.] Not becoming or befitting; unsuitable; improper.

a. Without const.

1598 FLORIO, *Inconueneuole*,.. vnbeseeming, vnbecomming. **1605** SHAKS. *Macb.* III. i. 14 If he had beene forgotten, It had bene as a gap in our great Feast, And all-thing vnbecomming. **1659** W. CHAMBERLAYNE *Pharonnida* III. 187 Some this bold Act of her's Term un-becoming Passion. **1688** in Ellis *Orig. Lett.* Ser. II. IV. 155 One of his own officers.. had provoked Mr. Howard to give him some unbecoming language. **1727** SWIFT *To Young Lady* Wks. 1755 II. II. 49 Those of our sex, who presume to take unbecoming liberty before you. **1775** SHERIDAN *St. Patrick's Day* I. ii, It is very unbecoming in you to want to have the last word with your Mamma. **1816** J. WILSON *City of Plague* II. i. 209 With frantic outcry and with violent steps Most unbecoming mid the hush of death. **1855** MACAULAY *Hist. Eng.* xxi. IV. 541 They pointed out.. with a grave irony which is not unbecoming, the absurdities.. of the statute. **1885** SIR J. HANNEN in *Law Rep. 15 Q.B.D.* 143 It would be highly unbecoming if the justices were present when the medical man made his examination.

b. Governing a sb. (Cf. BECOME *v.* 8 b.)

1658 *Whole Duty Man* x. §23 This savageness.. is so unbecoming the nature of a man, that [etc.]. **1670** COTTON *Espernon* I. I. 12 An assiduity and diligence unbecoming his Spirit, and Blood. **1749** FIELDING *Tom Jones* v. viii, Behaviour, so unbecoming a Christian. *a* **1774** GOLDSM. *Hist. Greece* I. 21 They.. had a power of arresting.. their kings, if they acted unbecoming their station. **1830** SCOTT *Pirate* vii. *note*, The woman's dwelling and appearance were not unbecoming her pretensions. **1842** TENNYSON *Ulysses* 53 Some work of noble note may yet be done, Not unbecoming men that strove with Gods. **1882** *Daily News* 22 Aug. 6/4 Temper unbecoming of all places the Judgment seat.

c. Const. *of.*

1741 CHESTERF. *Lett.* May, What was not unbecoming of a child would be disgraceful to a youth. *c* **1800** R. CUMBERLAND *John De Lancaster* (1809) II. 254 You must not do what is unbecoming of your situation. **1803** *Censor* 1 Nov. 124 He never offered any thing unbecoming of a man who has serious intentions of wedding a woman. **1862** J. F. STEPHEN *Def. Rowl. Williams* 180 It would be unbecoming, I think, of the character of any man [etc.].

d. Const. *to.*

1893 WILDE *Lady Windermere's Fan* III. 90 There is nothing in the whole world so unbecoming to a woman as a Nonconformist conscience. **1901** G. B. SHAW *Capt. Brassbound's Conversion* II. 245 Brandyfaced Jack: I name you for conduct and language unbecoming to a gentleman. **1980** *Washington Post* 1 June A17 But to set out to fix blame is.. unbecoming to America. **1982** *Financial Times* 21 Aug. 4 Rumours flew about in a manner most unbecoming to the month.

e. *ellipt.* after a sb. in ***conduct unbecoming*** (*sc.* of a military officer); also *transf.*

1971 B. ENGLAND (*title*) Conduct unbecoming. **1976** *Time* 5 July 46/3 The Merchant Marine Academy, which classifies copulation in the barracks as conduct unbecoming and worthy of dismissal. **1976** *Times Lit. Suppl.* 6 Aug. 988/4 Conduct unbecoming in a man of letters must be reprimanded.

unbe'comingly, *adv.* (UN-[1] 11.)

1653 H. MORE *Conject. Cabbal.* (1713) 203 He has unbecomingly and indiscreetly ventured out of his own Sphere. **1742** RICHARDSON *Pamela* IV. 231 A Gentleman would not attempt to penetrate unbecomingly, thro' the Disguises that a Lady thinks proper to assume. **1749** CHESTERF. *Lett.* 7 Feb. (1774) I. 393 What Cicero, very absurdly and unbecomingly for a Philosopher, says with regard to Plato. **1843** BETHUNE *Sc. Fireside Stor.* 99 For one so near her grave,.. I must confess I have acted unbecomingly. **1876** T. HARDY *Ethelberta* xlviii, Why did you come so mysteriously, and, I must say, unbecomingly?

unbe'comingness. (UN-[1] 12.)

1652 J. HALL *Height of Eloquence* p. ix, All these extream unbecomingnesses have defaced Eloquence. **1693** LOCKE *Educ.* §75 If Words are sometimes to be used, they ought to be grave, kind and sober, representing the ill, or unbecomingness of the Fault. **1810** BENTHAM *Packing* (1821) 98 Flippancy... Deviation from decency... Unbecomingness. **1872** GEO. ELIOT *Middlem.* xxxiv, She felt the unbecomingness of saying anything that might convey a notion of it to others.

un'bed, *v.* [UN-[2] 5.] *trans.* To remove from a bed; to disembed. Also *refl.*

1611 FLORIO, *Dislettare*, to vnbed, to vncouch. **1653** WALTON *Angler* v. 129 That learned man has made me to believe that Eeles unbed themselves, and stir at the noise of the thunder. **1821** CLARE *Vill. Minstr.* II. 122 The plough unbeds the worms. **1883** R. BRIDGES *Prometheus* 102 In the ruined dwellings and old tombs He dug, un-bedding from the wormed ooze Vessels and tools.

un'bedded, *ppl. a.* [UN-[1] 8.]

1. *Geol.* Not arranged in beds.

1842 SEDGWICK in *Hudson's Guide Lakes* (1843) 198 Great masses of granite and other kinds of crystalline unbedded rock. **1890** *Q. Jrnl. Geol. Soc.* Aug. 393 There are two crags,.. of which one is slate, striking directly at the other which is unbedded grit.

2. Not put to bed. (In quot. *spec.*)

1877 SIR H. TAYLOR *Edwin the Fair* III. viii. Wks. II. 121 We deem'd it best that this unbedded bride Should visit Chester, there to live recluse.

unbe'dewed, *ppl. a.* (UN-[1] 8.)

[**1775** ASH.] **1860** PUSEY *Min. Proph.* 14 The soul of the sinner.. is unbedewed by God's grace, unwatered by the Fountain of living waters.

unbe'dimmed, *ppl. a.* (UN-[1] 8.)

[**1775** ASH.] **1840** WORDSW. *Misc. Sonn.* III. xxxii, 'Tis a fruitless task to paint for me, Who.. By the habitual light of memory see Eyes unbedimmed. **1857** SUSANNA WINKWORTH tr. *Life Tauler* 333 There reigns perpetual light, clear and unbedimmed.

unbe'dinned, *ppl. a.* (UN-[1] 8.)

1816 L. HUNT *Rimini* I. 131 A princely music unbedinned with drums.

† **un'beened**, *ppl. a. Obs.*[−1] [UN-[2] 8: cf. UNBE *v.*[2]] Deprived of existence.

1642 H. MORE *Song of Soul* II. I. I. xv, The hidden might And root of motion unliv'd, unbeen'd they leave In their vain thoughts.

unbe'fit, *v.* [UN-[1] 14.] *trans.* To be unfitting or unbecoming for.

1621 QUARLES *Hadassa* Med. 10 Wks. (Grosart) II. 57/2 Kings by their Royall priuiledge may doe, What vnbefits a mind to search into. **1624** —— *Job* xvi. 104 It vnbefits our wills, to stint his pleasure.

unbe'fitting, *ppl. a.* [UN-[1] 10 and 5 d.] Not befitting or suitable: **a.** Without const.

1588 SHAKS. *L.L.L.* v. ii. 770 Loue is full of vnbefitting straines. **1659** MILTON *Civ. Power* 48 Then was the state of rigor, childhood, bondage and works, to all which force was not unbefitting. **1836** J. GILBERT *Chr. Atonem.* ix. (1852) 275 To imagine that,..were of all extravagances the most wild and unbefitting. **1864** PUSEY *Lect. Daniel* viii. 472 It would be unbefitting to speak of the Creator as the 'throne' of the creature. **1891** MEREDITH *One of our Conq.* xxx, Mrs. Blathenoy resented her unbefitting queenly style.

b. Governing a sb. (Cf. BEFIT *v.* 1.)

a **1643** J. SHUTE *Judgem. & Mercy* ix. (1645) 198 Moses.. loved not to..provoke him [Pharaoh] and use him unbefitting a Magistrate. **1667** MILTON *P.L.* IV. 759 Farr be it, that I should..think thee unbefitting holiest place. **1815** L. HUNT *Feast Poets* 70 The stanza..has always an air of direct imitation, which is unbefitting the dignity of an original seriousness. **1880** MISS BRADDON *Just as I am* vii, She never wore a garment unbefitting her years. **1890** 'R. BOLDREWOOD' *Col. Reformer* (1891) 115 A species of rest.. not unbefitting the day.

Hence **unbe'fittingly** *adv.*, **unbe'fittingness**.

1871 MACDUFF *Mem. Patmos* iv. 49 The form which these seven letters or addresses assume is unique; or, as it has not unbefittingly been called, 'artistic'. **1865** PUSEY *Truth Eng. Ch.* 194 The longing for the vision of God, from which the unbefittingness, yet cleaving to her, still excludes her.

unbe'fool, *v.* (UN-[2] 3.)

a **1684** LEIGHTON *Serm. Ps. cvii. 43* Wks. (1859) 512/2 The strange woman..calls the fools to befool them:..but wisdom calls them, to unbefool them. *a* **1716** SOUTH *Serm.* (1744) VII. viii. 175 He that recovers a fool must first unbefool him to that degree, as to perswade him of his folly.

unbe'friend, *v.* (UN-[1] 14.)

1884 *American* XXIX. 104 And will not unbefriend the enterprising any more than the timid.

unbe'friended, *ppl. a.* (UN-[1] 8.)

1628 WITHER *Brit. Rememb.* VIII. 1212 All those reeds on which thou hast depended, Will faile thy trust, and leave thee unbefriended. *a* **1661** FULLER *Worthies, Berkshire* I. (1662) 94 God and himself raised him to the eminency he attained unto, unbefriended with any extraction. **1767** *Woman of Fashion* I. 134, I am..convinced of your Readiness to afford an Asylum to hopeless and unbefriended Innocence. **1800** CAMPBELL *Scene in Bavaria* viii, Forsaken scene, how like to thee The fate of unbefriended Worth! **1842** MIALL in *Nonconf.* II. 1 Alone and unbefriended,..it set out on its course. **1877** 'H. A. PAGE' *De Quincey* I. iv. 72 Whilst he had every hardship to face that is most painful in unbefriended poverty.

absol. **1717** KILLINGBECK *Serm.* xiii. 287 The Patronage of the Poor and Unbefriended.

unbe'get, *v.* [UN-[2] 3.] *trans.* To annul or undo the begetting of.

a **1625** FLETCHER *Hum. Lieut.* IV. ii, I'le raise 'em to a Regiment, and then command 'em, When they turn disobedient, unbeget 'em. **1676** DRYDEN *Aurengzebe* I. i, He .., Repining that he must preserve his Crown, Wishes..he could unbeget Those Rebel-Sons, who dare t' usurp his Seat. *a* **1721** SHEFFIELD (Dk. Buckhm.) *Wks.* (1753) II. 200 There would be yet a greater pleasure in unbegetting such a Son, if possible. *c* **1825** BEDDOES *Poems, Torrismond* I. iv, Unwrap me of my years, And hunt me..Into my mother's womb! there unbeget me!

†**unbegete** (also -ȝet), obs. var. UNBEGOTTEN.

a **1300** *XV Signa* 31 in *E.E.P.* (1862) 8 We wold louerd þat we ner in world icome forto bene and vnbeȝet of ure fader wer. *c* **1450** *Cov. Myst.* (Shaks. Soc.) 274 Bettyr it hadde hym for to a be Bothe unborn and unbegete.

un'beggared, *ppl. a.* (UN-[2] 8.)

1538 LATIMER *Let. to Cromwell* 6 Oct., Rem. (Parker Soc.) 403 Popishness changed into holiness, beggars unbeggared to avoid beggary.

un'begged, *ppl. a.* [UN-[1] 8.] **a.** Not begged or entreated. **b.** Not obtained by begging.

1579 *Sc. Acts Jas. VI* (1814) III. 141/1 To see quhat they may be maid content..to accept daylie to leif on vn-beggit. **1634** MASSINGER *Very Woman* Epil., If you are pleased, unbegged you will bestow A gentle censure. **1648** HEXHAM II, *Ongebedelt broodt*, Vnbegged bread. **1683** E. HOOKER *Pref. Pordage's Mystic Div.* 91 His (unexpected, undeserved, tho' I trust not undesired and unbegged) Mercie. *c* **1828** PRAED *Poems, Parting* ix, When between us lay Long tracks of sand and sea, The carrier pigeon went his way Unbegged, unbought, by me.

unbe'gilt, *ppl. a.* (UN-[1] 8 b.)

1850 S. DOBELL *Roman* viii. Poet. Wks. 1875 I. 151 That uncrown'd presence, unbegilt, unfeather'd, Naked and full of God. **1850** SIR H. TAYLOR *Virgin Widow* v. v. 178 Sire, the sense Of loyal service done is, unbegilt, Worth..the ransom of a King.

unbe'ginning, *ppl. a.* [UN-[1] 10.] Having no beginning.

1591 SYLVESTER *Du Bartas* I. i. 343 [The world is] nought but all, in't selfe including All; An un-beginning, midlesse, endlesse Ball. **1756** LAW *Lett. Important Subj.* 118 The unbeginning, never-ending, never-changing trinity of love. *a* **1761** —— *Behmen's Myst. Magnum* iv. (1772) 18 Threefold in its eternal unbeginning Birth. **1842** MRS. BROWNING *Grk. Chr. Poets* IV. ad fin., That unbeginning light of Thine. **1887** E. JOHNSON *Antiq. Mater* 217 The doctrine of the unbeginning and unknowable God.

Hence **unbe'ginningly** *adv.*, **-ness**.

1674 N. FAIRFAX *Bulk & Selv.* 165 You can no wayes halve them, and say, This half is unbeginningly, and that unendingly. **1862** F. HALL *Hindu Philos. Syst.* 35 By the unbeginningness of transmigration.

unbe'girt, *ppl. a.* (UN-[1] 8 b.)

1603 DEEBLE in J. Davies (Heref.) *Microcosmos* P p, That curious Hand Which could the Pen most perfectly commaund Had not a Finger unbegirt with Gold.

unbe'got, *ppl. a.* [UN-[1] 8 b.] = next.

1593 SHAKS. *Rich. II*, III. iii. 88 They shall strike Your Children yet vnborne, and vnbegot. **1604** *Primer Blessed Virgin, Hymns* 20 Vnto the father unbegot, And to his sole begotten sonne. **1667** MILTON *P.L.* x. 988 In thy power It lies, yet ere Conception to prevent The Race unblest, to being yet unbegot. **1936** A. E. HOUSMAN *More Poems* 14 This is for all ill-treated fellows Unborn and unbegot.

unbe'gotten, *ppl. a.* [UN-[1] 8 b.] Ungenerated.

1532 SIR T. MORE *Confut. Tindale* IV. Wks. 580/2 Wherein the sonnes will that is yet vnbegotten, can nothyng make nor marre. **1561** T. NORTON *Calvin's Inst.* I. 40 By the Scriptures we teach..that the essence as well of the Sonn as of the Holy ghost is vnbegotten. **1587** GOLDING *De Mornay* (1592) 133 The world euerlasting and unbegotten. **1613-31** *Primer our Lady* (1669) 367 Glorie to th' unbegotten Father, And to the sole begotten Son. **1678** CUDWORTH *Intell. Syst.* I. iv. §36. 587 The First Divine Hypostasis is altogether Unbegotten from any other. **1884** ADDIS & ARNOLD *Cath. Dict.* (1897) 895/2 The Father is unbegotten, the Son begotten.

Hence **unbe'gottenly** *adv.*, **unbe'gottenness**.

1631 I. R. *Pair Spectacles* ix. 340 Consubstantiality of the sonne, Diuinity of the Holy Ghost, and euen vnbegottenesse of the Father. **1736** CHANDLER *Hist. Persec.* 49 The son co-exists with God unbegottenly.

†**unbe'grave**, *ppl. a. Obs.* [UN-[1] 8 b + BEGRAVE *v.* 1. Cf. MDu. and Du. *onbegraven*, MHG. and G. *unbegraben*, Da. *ubegraven*, etc.] Unburied.

1513 DOUGLAS *Æneid* XI. i. 54 Lat ws to erd haue The corpsis of our fallowis onbegraue.

unbe'guile, *v.* [UN-[2] 3.] *trans.* To undeceive.

1601 DANIEL *Let. fr. Octavia* li, Break from these snares —thy judgment unbeguile. **1654** H. L'ESTRANGE *Chas. I* (1655) 182 The Archbishop..resolved to speak out, and unbeguile them both. *a* **1711** KEN *Preparat.* Poet. Wks. 1721 IV. 58 Our God in that great King design'd To unbeguile each Worldly mind.

unbe'guiled, *ppl. a.* (UN-[1] 8.)

a **1533** LD. BERNERS *Gold. Bk. M. Aurel.* xlii. (1535) 76 b, And to the entent thou lyue vnbegiled I will tell the a secrete. *a* **1729** CONGREVE *Homer's Hymn to Venus* 14 Blue-ey'd Minerva free preserves her heart, A virgin un-beguil'd by Cupid's art. **1820** SHELLEY *Hymn Merc.* xxvi, The Goddess, his fair mother, unbeguiled, Knew all that he had done being abroad. **1833** TENNYSON *Lady Clara Vere De V.* 5 At me you smiled, but unbeguiled I saw the snare.

unbe'guileful, *a.* (UN-[1] 7.)

1604 R. CAWDREY *Table Alph.* (1613), *Infallible*, undeceiueable, vnbeguilefull.

unbe'guilefulness. (UN-[1] 12.)

c **1456** PECOCK *Bk. of Faith* (1909) 156 He knewe bi experience the treuthe and the sadnes and the unbigilefulnes of hise felowis.

unbe'gun, *ppl. a.* Forms: 1 unbegunnen, 3 unnbigunnenn, 4 unbegunne (7 vn-), 6 vnbegon(ne, vnbegun, 7- unbegun. [UN-[1] 8 b. Cf. Du. *onbegonnen*, OHG. *unbegunnen*.]

1. That had no beginning; ever existent.

c **1000** ÆLFRIC *Saints' Lives* I. 16 An ælmihtiȝ god æfre unbegunnen and unȝeændod. *c* **1200** ORMIN 18574 Forr eȝȝþerr iss wiþþutenn ord, & æfre all unnbigunnenn. **1390** GOWER *Conf.* III. 275 The myhti god, which unbegunne Stant of himself. **1610** J. HEALEY *St. Aug. Citie of God* XII. xvii. 458 Hee needed none of these creatures,..hauing continued..blessed without them, from all vn-begunne eternity. *a* **1680** CHARNOCK *Attrib. God* (1834) I. 375 We were nothing from an unbegun eternity. **1872** LIDDON *Elem. Relig.* ii. 79 That unbegun, unending, self-existent Life; that boundless Intelligence,..what is He, our God, to us?

2. Not yet begun; not commenced.

1562 W. WIGHTMAN Ep. Ded., in Phaer *Æneid* (ed. 2) 1 He..promised to vse all hys possible diligence for the finishing of the other three bookes then vtterly vnbegonne. *a* **1568** ASCHAM *Scholem.* II. (Arb.) 159 The other part of the head beyng hidden, the bodie and the rest of the members vnbegon. **1597** HOOKER *Eccl. Pol.* v. lvi. §5 A worke vn-begun is in the Artificer which afterward bringeth it into effect. **1706** WATTS *Horæ Lyr.* III. 266 Nations unborn, and ages unbegun. **1738** *Gentl. Mag.* VIII. 485/2 Therefore, tho' more than half my days are done, My days of life are un-begun. **1812** *Monthly Mag.* XXXIV. 14 We prevent what is unbegun, we hinder what is unfinished. **1868** MRS. WHITNEY *P. Strong* xvi, The smoothness of that which is unbegun.

unbe'headed, *ppl. a.* (UN-[1] 8.)

a **1578** LINDESAY (Pitscottie) *Chron. Scot.* (S.T.S.) II. 49 *marg.*, The erle of angus eschaippit onbeheiddit be meanis of the lard of blanerne.

unbe'held, *ppl. a.* (UN-[1] 8 b.)

1667 MILTON *P.L.* IV. 674 These then, though unbeheld in deep of night, Shine not in vain. **1796** ANNA SEWARD *Lett.* (1811) IV. 172 In my best days, however I might admire and revere unbeheld excellence,..yet [etc.]. **1819** SHELLEY *Cenci* II. i. 192 Constellations quenched in murkiest cloud, In which I walk secure and unbeheld Towards my purpose. **1867** G. MACDONALD *Poems* 3 The good, the heavenly land, Though unbeheld, quite near them lay.

unbe'holdable, *a.* (UN-[1] 7 b.)

1855 PUSEY *Doct. Real Presence* Note 2. 173 Afterwards his face is changed by brightness unbeholdable. **1862** R. H. PATTERSON *Ess. Hist. & Art* 392 The mystery of whose unbeholdable splendours not unaptly symbolised the presence of Him.

unbe'holden, *ppl. a.* [UN-[1] 8 b.]

1. Not under an obligation (*to* a person); independent. *rare.*

1674 N. FAIRFAX *Bulk & Selv.* 18 Both unmade by God, and unbeholden to, or independent on God. *c* **1848** J. KEEGAN *Leg. & Poems* (1907) 489 Dandy Delaney and his family grew rich all at once. People..wondered how the mischief he grew so 'unbeholden' in a moment.

2. Unbeheld, unseen.

1820 SHELLEY *Skylark* 48 Like a glow-worm golden.. Scattering unbeholden Its aëreal hue. **1867** JEAN INGELOW *Poems, Tired* v, And were it good to go, And unbeholden in the vessel's wake Look on the man thou lovedst, and forgive. **1876** SWINBURNE *Erechtheus* 813 At a shrine unbeloved of a God unbeholden a gift shall be given for the land.

Hence **unbe'holdenness.** *rare*[−1].

1674 N. FAIRFAX *Bulk & Selv.* 63 They who hold this wild emptiness, hold also..its independency on, or unbeholdenness to, God himself.

†**unbe'holding**, *ppl. a. Obs.* [UN-[1] 10.] = UNBEHOLDEN 1.

1615 G. SANDYS *Trav.* 182 Where we saw..a fountaine not vnbeholding to Art. **1654-66** EARL ORRERY *Parthen.* (1676) 164 Perhaps I have not been unbeholding to her.

†**unbe'hovable**, *a. Obs. rare.* Also 5 vnbehuvable. [UN-[1] 7 b.]

Unsuitable; unprofitable.

c **1440** *Alph. Tales* 63 þan Joseph thoght þat & sho hatid euer-ilk a man, sho sulde not be vnbehuvable vnto hym. **1550** CHEKE in *Harington's Nugæ Ant.* (1804) I. 42 Heareby all sortes of students..be..enabled to attaine to a greater and perfecter trade of learning, not unbehovable for the commonwelthe.

†**unbe'hoveful**, *a. Obs.* [UN-[1] 7.] Not profitable or useful; unnecessary.

1429 *Rolls of Parlt.* V. 417/2 [Fortresses and places] suche as shall be thoght..unbehovefull. *c* **1520** BARCLAY *Jugurtha* 4 b, Neuertheles so to do it is vnbehouefull & vnexpedyent. **1619** W. SCLATER *Exp. 1 Thess.* (1630) 554 Things lawfull in themselues may be vnseemely for our state and calling; vnbehouefull also to benefit of others. **1624** BP. MOUNTAGU *New Gagg* 205 We hold it needlesse,..as unbehoovefull, and to no purpose. **1648** HEXHAM II, *Onbehoeflick*, Vnbehovefull.

†**unbe'hovely**, *a. Obs. rare.* [UN-[1] 7.] = prec.

1390 GOWER *Conf.* III. 123 Scorpio..of his kinde is moiste and cold And unbehovely manyfold. *Ibid.* 372, I am unbehovely Your Court fro this day forth to serve. **14..** *Voc.* in Wr.-Wülcker 588 *Illicitus*, vnbehouely *vel* unleffул.

unbe'hoving. (UN-[1] 12.)

1844 MRS. BROWNING *Woman's Shortcoming* v, Unless you can dream that his faith is fast, Through behoving and unbehoving.

un'being, *vbl. sb.* [UN-[1] 13.] Absence or lack of being; non-existence.

1435 MISYN *Fire of Love* 84 To deed hastand & to vnbeingis to mevingis of fleschly affeccions. **1587** GOLDING *De Mornay* ii. (1592) 22 A tending to the vtter vnbeing or not being of the whole. *Ibid.* 23 Which matter they termed the verie vnbeing, that is to saye, in verie troth no being at all. **1935** G. BARKER *Janus* 16 The lighter bird of being, obstructing my line of sight, entirely conceals the form of the bird of unbeing. **1936** T. S. ELIOT *Coll. Poems 1909–35* 191 Love is itself unmoving... Caught in the form of limitation Between un-being and being. **1944** L. MACNEICE *Springboard* 17 From the lubber depths of my unbeing.

†**un'being**, *ppl. a. Obs.* [UN-[1] 10.] Non-existent.

1607 J. DAVIES (Heref.) *Summa Totalis* Wks. (Grosart) I. 23/1 Those Things haue euer an vnbeing Beeing Which in his Vnderstanding onely Bee. *a* **1631** DONNE *Ess. Divinity* (1651) 130 All [those] now eminent and in actions, and all yet undiscovered, and unbeing. **1682** SIR T. BROWNE *Chr. Mor.* 119 He must answer, who asks it; who understands entities of preordination, and beings yet unbeing.

unbe'kend, -kent, *ppl. a. Sc.* and *north.* [UN-[1] 8, 8 b. Cf. WFris. *on-*, *ûnbikend*, Du. and Flem. *onbekend*, †*onbekendt*, G. *unbekannt*, Sw. *obekant*, Da. *ubekendt*.] Unknown.

1513 DOUGLAS *Æneid* VIII. ii. 15 And thou, O haly fader Tiberyne,..Ressaue Eneas to ȝou onbekend [*v.r.* vn-]. *Ibid.* IX. vii. 61 Quham the dissaitfull onbekend [*v.r.* vm-] dern way..Betrasit had. **1808** JAMIESON, *Unbekent.* **1894** HESLOP *Northumbld. Gloss.* 754.

unbe'known, *ppl. a.* Also *dial.* onbeknown, unbeknawn, etc. [UN-[1] 8 b.]

1. In absolute or adverbial const. in the phrase *unbeknown to*, without the knowledge of.

1636 T. GOODWIN *Return of Prayers* iv. 75 To sympathize with another in praying for such a thing unbeknowne one to another. **1836-7** DICKENS *Sk. Boz, Seven Dials*, If my 'usband had treated her with a drain..unbeknown to me, I'd tear her precious eyes out. **1837** —— *Pickw.* xxxiv, 'I was there,' resumed Mrs. Cluppins, 'unbeknown to Mrs. Bardell'. **1885** *Law Times* 28 Feb. 321/2 The chalk had been opened..unbeknown to the tenant. **1947** *Sun* (Baltimore) 31 Oct. 10/3 That this number is insufficient is being quietly demonstrated at the present time, unbeknown to the general public. **1952** J. L. WATEN *Alien Son* 121 Unbeknown to our parents we sneaked away from the street one summer day.

ellipt. **1866** READE *G. Gaunt* xvi, I shall send you some stock from the castle, and you can cook his vegetables in good strong gravy, unbeknown. **1896** HOUSMAN *Shropshire*

Lad xxi, My love rose up so early And stole out unbeknown. **1901** J. Barlow *From Land of Shamrock* 215 Openin' it at the breakfast-table, unbeknown, to set people passin' remarks, and risin' a laugh on him.

2. Unknown; lying outside of one's knowledge or acquaintance. Also *absol.*

1824 *Monthly Mag.* LVII. 408 They agreed to be both at the tourney, But unbeknown and clad in common armure. **1861** Clough *Poems*, etc. (1869) I. 262 Gentlemen unbeknown to ladies give their arms to ladies aforesaid, to conduct them into dinner. **1888** *Pall Mall G.* 7 May 2/2 He..is loath to prophesy as to what is possible or is not possible in that 'land of the unbeknown'. **1976** *Jrnl. Lakeland Dial. Soc.* No. 38. 39 Ah nivver really spock t' dialect proper, but Ah hev a gey lot ev dialect sayings Ah offen let slip oot, unbeknawen like!

unbe'knownst, *a.* or *adv.* Orig. *colloq.* and *dial.* Also **unbeknowns**, etc. [f. prec. The analogy on which the *-s* or *-st* has been added is not clear: cf. the earlier UNKNOWNST.] = UNBEKNOWN 2. Also, = UNBEKNOWN *ppl. a.* 1.

Now of much wider currency than in the 19th. cent.

1848 Mrs. Gaskell *Let.* 11 Nov. (1966) 61 You don't see me, but I often am sitting in the rocking-chair unbeknownst to you. **1854** Huxley in L. Huxley *Life & Lett.* (1910) I. 111, I hate doing anything of the kind 'unbeknownst' to people. **1854** *Poultry Chron.* I. 331/1 It was found that she was sitting on a nest of eggs,—unbeknownst. **1887** Kipling *Plain Tales fr. Hills* (1888) 147 Perhaps they were afraid that their wives had come from Homo unbeknownst. **1907** J. M. Synge *Playboy of Western World* III. 70 Burying your poor father unbeknownst when..we could have given him a decent burial. **1932** W. Faulkner *Light in August* i. 16 Interfering with his work unbeknownst to him. **1952** A. Christie *They do it with Mirrors* xiii. 122 One of those smart lads may have got out of the College buildings unbeknownst. **1979** *Dædalus* Summer 99 Here, illusion, unbeknownst to those who believed they had overcome it, made its most triumphant reentry. **1982** *London Rev. Bks.* 20 May–2 June 3 A whole other wife and children all unbeknownst to Ackerley until after his father's death.

unbe'lawyered, *a.* (UN-[1] 9.)

1830 *Westm. Rev.* Oct. 445 Not to speak of unsold justice, unbelawyered justice.

un'belched, *ppl. a.* (UN-[1] 8.)

1854 S. Dobell *Balder* xxiv. 169 Like an embowelled earthquake yet unbelched.

unbeld, obs. variant of UNBOLD *a.*

unbeleue, obs. f. UNBELIEF, -LIEVE *v.*[1]

unbe'lied, *ppl. a.* (UN-[1] 8.)

[**1775** Ash.] **1834** Wordsw. '*Soft as a Cloud*' 24 If yet To-morrow, unbelied, may say, I come to open out [etc.].

unbe'lief. Forms: α. 2 unbelefe, 4 vnbylefe; 3 unbileue, -leaue, 4 vnbi-, vnbyleue, 4, 6 unbeleue (4 -leeue, 6 -leve). β. 6 vnbelefe, 6–7 -leefe, -liefe, 6– unbelief (6–7 -liefe). [UN-[1] 12.] Absence or lack of belief; disbelief, incredulity.

a. In matters of religion.

α. *c* **1160** *Hatton Gosp.* Mark xvi. 14 Heom atewede se hælend & here unbelefen & heora heorten ʒe-tremede. *c* **1200** *Trin. Coll. Hom.* 81 He..blamede here un-bileue & here unwreste liflode. *a* **1225** *Leg. Kath.* 259 Wið neauer an ne keccheð he creftiluker cang men, ne leadeð to unbileaue. **1382** Wyclif *Matt.* xiii. 58 He dide nat there manye vertues, for the vnbyleue of hem. *a* **1400** *New Test.* (Paues) Heb. iii. 12 Loke ʒe, wheþer þer be in any of ʒou an efel herte of vnbylefe. **1526** Tindale *Rom.* xi. 20 Be cause of vnbeleve they are broken of. **1567** *Gude & Godlie B.* (S.T.S.) 13 Saif vs..from dispair, From unbeleue, and Lollardis lair.

β. **1531** Tindale *Exp. 1 John* ii. (1538) 39 The doctrine of them..that say, vnbelefe to be the mother of al vyce. **1597** Hooker *Eccl. Pol.* v. xxii. §4 Their vnbeleefe in that case we may not impute vnto any weakness..in the meanes. **1634** Milton *Comus* 519 Such there be, but unbelief is blind. **1680** Flavel *Meth. Grace* xxxii, Positive Unbelief, is the Sin of Men and Women under the Gospel. **1705** Atterbury *Serm.* (1726) II. 51 For the Mind doth, by every degree of affected Unbelief, contract more and more of a general Indisposition towards Believing. **1809–10** Coleridge *Friend* (1865) 57 As much as I love my fellow-men, so much and no more will I be intolerant of their heresies and unbelief. **1858** J. Martineau *Stud. Chr.* 27 The second of these books would be condemned for heresy, and the first for unbelief. **1897** Liddon, etc. *Life Pusey* IV. iii. 73 Those forms of German unbelief with which..he had become painfully familiar at Göttingen.

b. In general use.

1649 J. Taylor (Water P.) *Western Voy.* 15 It is a hazard of the losse of a traveller's liberty by either their unbeliefe or misprision. *a* **1800** Cowper *Odyssey* (ed. 2) xiv. 177 Since, hopeless of thy lord's return, Thou art thus resolute in unbelief. **1855** *Poultry Chron.* II. 566/1 The tables were turned on me by the man, who had I suppose observed my previous gesture of unbelief. **1900** *Longm. Mag.* Mar. 465, I had received the news with contemptuous unbelief.

c. Personified.

1744 Akenside *Pleas. Imag.* III. 122 Where watchful Unbelief Darts through the thin pretence her squinting eye. **1781** Cowper *Truth* 445 Thus often unbelief, grown sick of life, Flies to the tempting pool, or felon knife.

† **unbe'liefful**, *a. Obs.* Forms: α. 4–5 unbileveful, vnbileueful. β. 4–5 vnbelefful, vnbileefful(l, vnbyleefful. [UN-[1] 7, or f. prec. + -FUL.]

1. Unbelieving; wanting in belief. Also *absol.*

α. *c* **1380** Wyclif *Sel. Wks.* II. 149 He þat is unbileveful to þe sone, shal not se þe blis of hevene. **1388** —— *Deut.* i. 26 ʒe weren vnbileueful to the word of oure Lord God.

β. *c* **1380** Wyclif *Wks.* (1880) 45 Who euere of freris bi inspiracioun of god wilen goon among sarasyns & oþere vnbelefful. **1382** —— *Acts* xxvi. 19, I was not vnbileefful to heuenly visioun. *c* **1430–40** *R. Gloucester's Chron.* (Rolls) 4920 + 20 To byleue [= remain] þere Among mys bylyuede [MS. ε vnbeleffful] men.

2. Incredible. *rare*[−1].

1388 Wyclif *Judg.* xx. 5 Thei bitraueliden my wijf with vnbileueful woodnesse of letcherie.

Hence † **unbe'lieffulness.** *Obs.*[−1]

1382 Wyclif *Mark* ix. 23 Lord, I bileue; help thou myn vnbileuefulnesse.

unbelieva'bility. (UN-[1] 12: see next.)

Also, in recent use, *unbelievableness.*

1851 Carlyle *Sterling* I. xv, Boiling mud-oceans of Hypocrisy and Unbelievability.

unbe'lievable, *a.* Also 6 vnbeleu(e)able, 6–7 vnbeleeu(e)able; 7 unbeleavable; 6 unbelieuable. [UN-[1] 7 b.] That cannot be believed; incredible.

1548 Geste *Pr. Masse* A viij b, Which graunt [= admission] as it is erronyouse and vnbeleueable so vngodly and exchuable. **1549** Coverdale, etc. *Erasm. Par. Acts* vii. 36 Though it semed to be a thynge vnbeleuable that was promysed,..Abraham beleued. **1580** *Apol. Prince of Orange* liv, Some..will thinke it vnbeleeueable, that euer there could be founde, such great inconstancie in them. **1624** Heywood *Gunaik.* VII. 346 Hugotio..began to recite many unbeleavable things concerning his appetite in his youth. **1633** J. Done tr. *Aristeas' Hist. Septuagint* 63 This is a thing yet more admirable, and almost vnbeleeuable. **1797** Mrs. Radcliffe *Italian* xxii, However unbelievable it may seem, you may depend upon it, it is all true. **1833** Carlyle *Misc. Ess., Diderot* (1888) V. 52 He believes that pleasure is pleasant: that a lie is unbelievable. **1895** Saintsbury *Corrected Impressions* xv. 144 Almost unbelievable faults of taste.

Hence **unbe'lievably** *adv.*

1839 Bailey *Festus* 359 Made pure, and unbelievably uplift Above their present state. **1893** *Chamb. Jrnl.* 19 Aug. 514/1 It seemed almost unbelievably sweet.

unbe'lieve, *v.*[1] Also 6 vnbeleue, 7 -leeue. [UN-[1] 14.] To disbelieve: **a.** *trans.*

1547 Baldwin *Mor. Philos.* (1550) G v b, Aristotle..beeyng asked what vauntage a man might get by lying, he answered: to be vnbeleued whan he telleth truth. **1615** Daniel *Hymen's Triumph* II. ii, A counterfeited shew Of passion, which you may..Make him as easily to vnbeleeue, As what he neuer saw. **1646** Sir T. Browne *Pseud. Ep.* I. viii. (1686) 24 Such as amass all relations, must erre in some, and may without offence be unbelieved in many. **1672** Eachard *Lett.* 70, I must desire you to unbelieve all that you have said. **1711** *Medley* No. 42 He seems to think he may..make us unbelieve what we have seen. **1813** J. Adams *Wks.* (1856) X. 57 What does Priestley mean by an unbeliever, when he applies it to you? How much did he unbelieve himself? **1872** Lever *Ld. Kilgobbin* lxxix, Fellows who are realistic,..who have little to speculate on and less to unbelieve.

b. *intr.* or *absol.*

1687 *Reason. Toleration* 2 Let neither Her nor Him that unbelieves depart, if pleased to stay. *a* **1718** Penn *Tracts* Wks. 1726 I. 451 Where Men believe, not because it is True, but because they are required to do so, there they will unbelieve. **1855** Browning *Bp. Blougram's Apol.* 263 And so you live to sleep as I to wake, To unbelieve as I to still believe?

unbe'lieve, *v.*[2] [UN-[2] 4.] *trans.* To give up belief in; to discard or abandon (belief).

1605 Daniel *Queen's Arcadia* v. iv. (1606) K iij, How were I cleer'd of griefe, Had I the power to vnbeleeue beliefe. **1795** Paine *Age of Reason* II. 8 To believe therefore the Bible to be true, we must unbelieve all our belief in the moral justice of God. **1837** Ht. Martineau *Soc. Amer.* II. 38 *note*, You know nothing of those people. They will believe everything, and unbelieve nothing.

unbe'lieved, *ppl. a.* Forms: 3 unbilefde, -bileued; 4 vnbylefed, 5 vnbeleued, etc.; 7– unbelieved. [UN-[1] 8.]

†1. Unbelieving. *Obs.*

c **1200** *Trin. Coll. Hom.* 81 Þe grimliche wordes þe ure helende..gaf to andswere þe unbilefde iudeuisshe men. *a* **1225** *Ancr. R.* 260 Unbileued he is þet luueð to muchel & ʒisceð worldes weole & wunne. *a* **1400** *New Test.* (Paues) Titus i. 16 Þei beþ abhomynabel, & vnbylefed, & reprefabel to eferich good werk. *c* **1450** *Mirk's Festial* I. 139 Phylyp was send..forto prech Godis worde to þe vnbeleued pepull.

†2. Unbelievable, incredible. *Obs.*

c **1425** in *Anglia* X. 342 Turmentede with vnbylevede sorowe. **1581** Sidney *Apol. Poetrie* (Arb.) 19 Nay, to so vnbeleeued a poynt hee proceeded, as that no earthly thing bred such wonder to a Prince, as to be a good horseman. **1611** Beaum. & Fl. *King & No King* II. ii, I made his valour stoop, and brought that name soar'd to so unbeliev'd a height, to fall beneath mine.

3. Not believed; disbelieved.

1603 Shaks. *Meas. for M.* v. i. 119 Heauen shield your Grace from woe As I thus wrong'd, hence vnbeleeued goe. *a* **1619** Fotherby *Atheom.* Pref. (1622) B ij b, But yet specially, in the first point, of beleeuing that there is a God, that is of all the rest the most vnbeleeued. **1655** J. Jane in *Nicholas Papers* (Camden) II. 223 It cannot be long vnbeleeved, being soe farr advanced especially in the French leauge. **1819** Wordsw. *Haunted Tree* 27 Nor is it unbelieved, By ruder fancy, that a troubled ghost Haunts the old trunk. **1844** Kinglake *Eothen* viii, The unbelieved Cassandra was right after all. **1877** Ruskin *Fors Clav.* lxxxi. 250 All which teachings have..passed from deed and truth into mere monotony of unbelieved phrase.

unbe'liever. [UN-[1] 12.] One who does not believe; *spec.* one who does not accept a particular religious belief, an infidel.

1526 Tindale *2 Cor.* vi. 14 Beare nott the yooke wyth the vnbelevers. **1597** Hooker *Eccl. Pol.* v. lxxx. §2 The name of Pagans, which properly signifieth country people, came to be used in common speech for the same that infidels and vnbeleeuers were. **1618** J. Taylor (Water P.) *Pennyles Pilgr.* F ij, This sounds like a lie to an vnbeleeuer; but I..knowe that I speake within the compasse of truth. **1653** W. Ramesey *Astrol. Restored* 32 In the dark corners of the Gentiles, who were then unbelievers. **1709** Addison *Tatler* No. 111 ¶4 To become conspicuous, [he] declares that he is an Unbeliever. **1777** Priestley *Matt. & Spir.* I. Pref. (1782) p. viii, The cry against me as an unbeliever..was..general and loud. **1825** Scott *Talism.* iii, The miseries imposed by the unbelievers upon the Latin Christians in the Holy Land. **1837** W. A. Butler *Serm. Doctr. & Pract.* Ser. II. xx. (1856) 202 The unbeliever may chafe at the mysteries of faith.

unbe'lieving, *vbl. sb.* [UN-[1] 13.] The action of not believing; disbelief; an instance of this.

a **1400** *New Test.* (Paues) Heb. iii. 19 Þei ne myʒte not entren in-to his reste for hure vnbylefynge. **1611** Cotgr., *Incredulité*,..vnbeleeuing, lacke of beliefe. **1627** R. Ashley *Almansor* 60 God permitteth vnbeleeuing in this world. **1883** J. M. Wilson *Theory Inspiration* ii. 30 It is as wrong to count a man a fool for believing as for unbelieving.

unbe'lieving, *ppl. a.* [UN-[1] 10.] Not giving or having belief (esp. in religious matters); incredulous; infidel.

a **1400** *New Test.* (Paues) Heb. iii. 18 To whom swor he þat þei schulden noʒt entren in-to his reste, bote to þilke þat weren vnbylefynge? **1526** Tindale *1 Cor.* vii. 14 For the vnbelevynge husbande is sanctifyed by the wyfe: and the vnbelevynge wyfe ys sanctifyed by the husbande. **1567** Jewel *Def. Apol.* II. vi. Div. 3. 141 As often as he shutteth vp the Gate of the Kingdome of Heauen against vnbeleeuing, and stubborne persons. **1613–6** W. Browne *Brit. Past.* II. iv, Which vnbeleeuing man, that is not mov'd To credit aught, if not by reason prov'd,..Held as most fabulous. *a* **1656** Hales *Gold. Rem.* I. (1673) 95 'Tis true indeed, in spight of unbeleiving miscreants, it hath pleased God..to save those that are his. **1725** Pope *Odyss.* XIV. 431 And why, oh swain of unbelieving mind!..Doubt you my oath? **1728** Eliza Heywood tr. *Mme. de Gomez' Belle A.* (1732) II. 270 There is nothing I would not endeavour to suffer, or perform, to keep you mine, indifferent and unbelieving as you are. **1825** Scott *Talism.* iii, A barefooted friar would have been a better associate than the gay but unbelieving Paynim. **1864** Pusey *Lect. Daniel* (1876) 110 It is no uncommon resource of unbelieving criticism. **1875** Jowett *Plato* (ed. 2) III. 41 The age of miracles has ceased, and the world is an unbelieving world.

absol. **1526** Tindale *Rev.* xxi. 8 The fearfull and vnbelevynge, and the abhominable, and murdres. **1594** Drayton *Sonn.* Minor Poems (1907) 7 See myracles, ye vnbeleeuing; see A dumbe-born Muse made to expresse the mind.

Hence **unbe'lievingly** *adv.*; **-be'lievingness.**

1685 Baxter *Paraphr. N.T.* 1 Pet. ii. 7 Even they that *unbelievingly reject..the Gospel, and disobey it. *a* **1708** Beveridge *Thes. Theol.* (1711) I. 340 He is angry with them [*sc.* the wicked]..For all Actions; as done 1) From wrong Principle. 2)..Inobedientially. 3. Unbelievingly. **1850** Lynch *Theoph. Trinal* vii. 134 Many true things we unbelievingly say. **1561** T. Norton *Calvin's Inst.* I. 34 It is therfore no maruell if Christ alleged his miracles to confound the *vnbeleuingnesse of the Jewes. **1581** J. Bell *Haddon's Answ. Osor.* 231 The fault hereof is their own unbeleevingnes, not the will of God.

unbe'loved, *ppl. a.* (UN-[1] 8.)

1597 Warner *Alb. Eng.* IX. xlvi. 217 Eccho, an amiable Nymph, long amorous of him, But louing, vnbeloued. **1647** Clarendon *Hist. Reb.* II. §101 If it had not concerned a person notoriously unbeloved, and so the more unpitied. **1697** Dryden *Æneid* I. 536 Whoe'er you are..not unbeloved by Heaven..—Have courage. **1706** Watts *Horæ Lyr.* I. 118 Wild and wand'ring all alone, Unbeloved and unknown. **1815** Shelley *Summer Evening* 5 Silence and Twilight, unbeloved of men. **1890** Baker *Wild Beasts* I. 230 A tiger or some unbeloved animal was before them.

absol. **1820** Lamb (*title*), The Unbeloved.

† **un'belt**, *ppl. a. Obs.* [UN-[1] 8 b.] Unbelted.

1662 Hibbert *Body Divinity* I. 130 Truely here (as one saith well) if ever *unbelt unblest*; he is a loose man that wants this girdle of sincerity.

un'belt, *v.* [UN-[2] 4 and 5.]

1. *trans.* To ungird.

1483 *Cath. Angl.* 27/2 To vn Belte, *discingere, incingere.*

2. To detach or remove (a sword, etc.) by unfastening the belt.

1814 Scott *Lord of Isles* III. xxiii, But why waste time in idle words? Sit to your cheer—unbelt your swords. **1825** —— *Talism.* xxvii, As if thy knight, who hath not yet buckled on his armour, were unbelting it in triumph. **1879** J. D. Long *Æneid* IX. 389 From off His shoulder he unbelts the golden sword.

un'belted, *a.* (UN-[1] 9.) Also *absol.* as *sb.*

1814 Byron *Lara* I. xii, They..snatch'd in startled haste unbelted brands. **1870** Bryant *Iliad* XVI. 135 Sarpedon as he saw his friends The unbelted Lycians. **1880** L. Wallace *Ben-Hur* 32 He wears..a loose gown, sleeveless, unbelted, and dropping from the neck to the knee. **1970** *Guardian* 24 Aug. 7/4 An unbelted driver can die (and has died) at speeds as low as 13 miles an hour. **1973** [see NON-TRIVIAL *a.*]. **1977** *Times* 5 July 15/5 A higher proportion of belted than unbelted drivers remain in control of their vehicles.

unbe'moaned, *ppl. a.* (UN-[1] 8.)

1623 tr. *Favine's Theat. Hon.* v. i. 41 By his vnbemoaned death, Henry his Brother..came to enioy the Crowne of England. *a* **1711** Ken *Hymns Evang.* Poet. Wks. 1721 I. 375 When he..Had no known Sin left unbemoan'd, And with fresh Tears had God aton'd. **1827** Pollok *Course T.* II. 773 God..lets them ever try..To walk alone, unguided, unbemoaned, Where Evil dwells.

un'bend, *v.* [UN-[2] 3 and 7.]

I. *trans.* **1.** To release or relax (a bow) from tension; to unstring.

c **1250** *Gen. & Ex.* 483 Lamech wið wreðe is knape nam, Vn-bente is boȝe, and bet, and sloȝ. *c* **1290** *St. John* 331 in *S. Eng. Leg.* I. 412 Þare-aftur sone he nam is bouwe, and unbende it ase he couþe. *c* **1375** *Sc. Leg. Saints* v. (*John*) 481 Þar-for he his bow vnbent. Þane sad sancte Iohne: 'tel þi entent, quhy þu vnbent þi bow sa sone'. **1390** GOWER *Conf.* I. 108 Thanne was I furthest ate laste, And as a foll my bowe unbende. **1413** *26 Pol. Poems* 53 Pray we god his bowe of wraþþe vnbende. *c* **1440** *Alph. Tales* 274 Þe apostell askid hym whi it was vnbendid. **1503-4** *Act 19 Hen. VII*, c. 4 Yf ..servauntes..shote with their Crosebowe otherwyse than ..to unbend the same. **1530** PALSGR. 766/1 Unbende your bowes, syrs, nowe you come in to the towne. **1614** PURCHAS *Pilgrimage* VI. v. (ed. 2) 590 Others 3. times vnbent their bows, & thrice again bent them whiles their horses ran. **1627** DRAYTON *Agincourt* 61 Their bloody swords they quietly had sheath'd, And their strong bowes already were unbent. **1825** SCOTT *Talism.* xii, Unbend thy arblast, and come into the moonlight.

†**b.** To uncock (a fire-arm). *Obs.*$^{-1}$

1632 LITHGOW *Trav.* VIII. 351 Holding vp my hand, and imploring for our liues.., they vnbend their fire-locks, and ..did me homage.

†**2.** To slacken or weaken. *Obs.*

1605 SHAKS. *Macb.* II. ii. 45 You doe vnbend your Noble strength, to thinke So braine-sickly of things. **1611** —— *Cymb.* III. iv. 111 Why hast thou gone so farre To be vnbent? **1831** JAMES *Phil. Augustus* vi, My curse upon time! for he..saps our castles, and unbends our sinews.

3. *fig.* To relax, to give relaxation to (one's mind, etc.); to free from serious occupations.

1594 SOUTHWELL *M. Magd. Funeral Teares* (1823) 139 Unlesse thou wilt unbend her thoughts, that her eyes may fully see thee. **1604** MARSTON *Malcontent* III. ii. E j b, Thou that..Vnbendst the feebled vaines of sweatie labour. **1656** COWLEY *Pindar. Odes, To Dr. Scarborough* vi, Unbend sometimes thy restless care. **1725** POPE *Odyss.* I. 335 Social mirth unbent his serious soul. **1753** HANWAY *Trav.* VII. xcviii. (1762) I. 459 In this palace..the king most unbends his mind. **1839** HALLAM *Hist. Lit.* III. vi. §5 The extemporaneous comedy had always been the amusement.. of all who wished to unbend their minds. **1856** *N. Brit. Rev.* XXVI. 217 The mind of the reader is unbent, he puts aside for a time his own cares.

refl. **1672** WYCHERLEY *Love in Wood* v. ii, Men in office too, that adjourn their cares and businesses, to come and unbend themselves at night here. **1711** ADDISON *Spect.* No. 93 ¶10 The Mind never unbends itself so agreeably as in the Conversation of a well chosen Friend. **1791** BOSWELL *Johnson* Ded., Dr. Clarke..was unbending himself with a few friends in the most playful and frolicksome manner. **1891** L. FALCONER *Mlle. Ixe* ii. 38 A very different person from the Mademoiselle Ixe who unbent herself with Evelyn.

4. *Naut.* To unfasten, untie, undo (a cable, line, or sail).

1627 CAPT. SMITH *Seaman's Gram.* vii. 30 [To] vnbend the Cable, is..to take it away, which we vsually doe when we are at Sea. **1720** DE FOE *Capt. Singleton* (1906) 220 We immediately unbent all our sails,..and set up seven or eight tents with them. **1745** P. THOMAS *Jrnl. Anson's Voy.* 27 We split the Foresail and unbent it, and bent another. **1793** SMEATON *Edystone L.* §158 We found it equally difficult to get the bridle chain unbent from the swivel. **1840** R. H. DANA *Bef. Mast* xxvi, We unbent the mainsail, and formed an awning with it. **1875** *Board of Trade Instr. Saving Life by Rocket*, Unbend the Rocket Line from the Warp. **1882** NARES *Seamanship* (ed. 6) 124 What ropes are bent and unbent from the sail?

5. To allow or cause (the brow) to relax from a serious, severe, or frowning aspect.

1718 PRIOR *Henry & Emma* 6 Wilt thou awhile unbend thy serious Brow? *Ibid.* 138 A softer Look unbends his op'ning Brow. **1811** LAMB *Hogarth* Wks. 1909 I. 110 The ..joke which has unbent his care-worn hard-working visage. **1816** BYRON *Parisina* xx, But never..smile his brow unbended.

6. To straighten from a bent or curved position; to unfold. Also *refl.*

1663 BP. PATRICK *Parab. Pilgr.* xxx, They are the Souls whose Prayers God hears, who employ their hands as soon as they have unbent their knees. **1817** KIRBY & SPENCE *Entomol.* xxiii. II. 315 These [spines] are of great use in pushing them off when the legs are unbended. **1834-6** P. BARLOW in *Encycl. Metrop.* (1845) VIII. 99/2 A spring, which, in order that it may exert any force or give motion to a Machine, must first unbend itself. **1886** *N. Zealand Herald* 8 Nov. 6/5 Three nets were unbent and a number of opening games played.

absol. **1816** KIRBY & SP. *Entomol.* xxiii. (1817) II. 315 They bend their legs like the grasshoppers, and then unbending kick them out with violence.

II. *intr.* or *absol.* †**7.** To abandon an effort or attempt. *Obs. rare.*

a **1400-50** *Alexander* 1744 (Dubl. MS.) For-þi is better vnbende & of þi brathe leue. *Ibid.* 1974 For-þi it wer better vnbenden or þou bale suffre.

8. a. To free oneself from constraint or ceremony; to act in an unconstrained or genial manner; to relax one's seriousness or severity.

1746 FRANCIS tr. *Horace, Epist.* I. xviii. 106 Yet oft at home you can unbend, And even to trifling Sports descend. **1784** COWPER *Tiroc.* 608 Ev'n in his pastimes he requires a friend, To warn, and teach him safely to unbend. **1831** D. E. WILLIAMS *Life & Corr. Sir T. Lawrence* II. 351 *note*, He seemed to unbend, and give way to his humour. **1869** FREEMAN *Norm. Conq.* vii. (1877) II. 28 In private company though he never forgot his rank, he could unbend.

b. Of the features: To lose severity; to relax.

1818 SCOTT *Rob Roy* xviii, His hard features gradually unbent. **1897** A. DOBSON *Poems, Tale of Polypheme* xviii, Soon the Child Filled the lone shore with louder merriment, And e'en the Cyclops' heavy brow unbent.

c. To relax in purpose.

1877 C. GEIKIE *Christ* xxxv. (1879) 413 His soul never unbent from its grand enthusiasm.

9. To alter from a bend or curve; to become straight or less curved.

1815 J. SMITH *Panorama Sci. & Art* II. 35 The spring, by unbending at the same time, loses a part of its power. **1861** GEO. ELIOT *Silas M.* xii, But the complete torpor came at last: the fingers lost their tension, the arms unbent. **1867** AUGUSTA WILSON *Vashti* xxx, The brow wore its heavy cloud, and the arch of the lip had not unbent.

un'bendable, *a.* (UN-[1] 7 b.)

[**1775** ASH.] **1884** G. MACDONALD tr. *Lett. fr. Hell* (1885) 62 In such things her will was unbendable. **1889** BADEN-POWELL *Pigsticking* 94 The neck connecting the socket to the blade should be strong and unbendable.

un'bended, *ppl. a.*[1] [f. UNBEND *v.*] Relaxed.

1693 *Humours Town* A 6 b, If it does but Contribute to your Diversion, at your more unbended Hours. **1745** ELIZA HEYWOOD *Female Spect.* No. 10 (1748) II. 192 The constantly cheerful and entertaining companion of his more unbended moments. **1751** SMOLLETT *Per. Pick.* ii, His features were a little unbended. **1751** JOHNSON *Rambler* No. 89 ¶12 A wise and good man is never so amiable as in his unbended and familiar intervals.

un'bended, *ppl. a.*[2] [UN-[1] 8.] Not bent.

1648 HEXHAM II, *Onbesweken*, Vnbowed, or Vnbended. **1726** POPE *Odyss.* XXI. 62 She..To the proud Suitors bears in pensive state Th' unbended bow, and arrows wing'd with Fate.

un'bender. *rare*$^{-1}$. [f. UNBEND *v.*] That which unbends or relaxes.

1637 QUARLES *Elegie* i, Away, those Ioyes:..The late vnbenders of my thoughtfull minde.

un'bending, *vbl. sb.* [f. UNBEND *v.*] The action of the verb, esp. in senses 3 and 8.

1552 HULOET, Vnbendinge, *remissio.* **1611** COTGR., *Destenture*, an vnbending, vnstretching, slackening, loossing. **1648** HEXHAM, *Ontspanninge*, a Loosening, an Vnbending, or an Vnspanning. **1693** DRYDEN *Juvenal's Sat.* Ded. (1697) p. xxix, Recreation, for the unbending of our Minds. **1709** MRS. MANLEY *Secret Mem.* (1720) IV. 105 He found his Understanding return with double Force after such Unbendings. **1756** *Monitor* No. 53 II. 12 The rest of the evening was spent in table talk, and the easy unbendings of these little nocturnal assemblies. **1840** DICKENS *Old. C. Shop* xxxvi, With such unbendings did Richard..relieve the tedium of his confinement. **1859** G. A. SALA *Tw. round Clock* 218 He was of a disposition, save in casual moments of unbending, quite surprising for its saturnine taciturnity.

b. *attrib.* (or *ppl. a.*).

1701 ROWE *Amb. Step-Moth.* Ded., I hope it may indifferently Entertain your Lordship at an unbending hour. **1740** CIBBER *Apol.* I. Ded. (1756) p. viii, Where like the fam'd orator of old, when publick cares permit, you pass so many rational unbending hours.

un'bending, *ppl. a.* [UN-[1] 10.]

1. Not giving way or departing from a position or principle; unyielding, inflexible, steady: **a.** Of feelings, dispositions, etc.

a **1688** CUDWORTH *Immut. Mor.* (1731) 270 Truth is the most Unbending and Uncompliable..Thing in the World. **1800** MRS. HERVEY *Mourtray Fam.* IV. 115 Recollect, that Mr. Silbourne is rather of an unbending temper. **1848** LYTTON *Harold* VIII. iv, His unbending hate of all that was Norman. **1861** MAY *Const. Hist.* (1863) I. i. 82 A kind but most unbending answer was returned to Mr. Pitt.

b. Of persons.

1796 MATHIAS *Purs. Lit.* (1798) 128 Firm, constant, and unbending, he has the principles of a man, who knows and feels what is demanded of him by his country. **1831** SCOTT *Ct. Rob.* xxxiii, The veteran and unbending conspirator, Harpax, thus strengthened..the failing spirits of Stephanos. **1871** C. GIBBON *Lack of Gold* viii, Annie knew how doggedly unbending her father was.

2. Not bending or curving; rigid; *esp.* of persons, remaining erect, not stooping.

1709 POPE *Ess. Crit.* 373 Swift Camilla..Flies o'er th' unbending corn. **1726-45** THOMSON *Winter* 1064 Ye noble few! who here unbending stand Beneath life's pressure, yet bear up a while. **1802** PALEY *Nat. Theol.* xvi, The short unbending neck of the elephant is compensated by the length and flexibility of his proboscis. **1884** F. M. CRAWFORD *Rom. Singer* I. 25 The tall old foreigner stood erect and unbending.

Hence **un'bendingly** *adv.*, **un'bendingness.**

1847 WEBSTER, *Unbendingly. **1894** C. N. ROBINSON *Brit. Fleet* 439 The usage of the time was unbendingly severe. **1824** LANDOR *Imag. Conv.* I. 96 *note*, *Unbendingness, in the moral as in the vegetable world, is an indication as frequently of unsoundness as of strength. **1855** I. TAYLOR *Restor. Belief* (1856) 59 The spread of Christianity, ..[considering] its unbendingness, and the furious hostility it encountered,..is proof of its reality. **1891** MEREDITH *One of our Conq.* xxxviii, She met them with the slender unbendingness that was her own.

†**unbene**, *a. Obs.*$^{-1}$ [UN-[1] 7: see BEIN *a.*] Ungenial, wild and rugged.

13.. *Gaw. & Gr. Knt.* 710 Þe kny3t tok gates straunge, In mony a bonk vnbene.

un'beneficed, *ppl. a.* (UN-[1] 8.)

1623 MARSTON *Duchess of Malfi* III. ii, No question but many an unbenefic'd scholar Shall pray for you for this deed. **1697** COLLIER *Ess. Mor. Subj.* I. (1709) 50 There would be a strange Improvement in the unbeneficed Clergy, if they had a better Salary. **1749** FIELDING *Tom Jones* XIV. viii, The brother..married the daughter of an unbeneficed clergyman. **1828** *Q. Rev.* XXXVII. 39 Some hoary, unbeneficed Oxonian unburthening his heart in a garret. **1884** *Gentl. Mag.* Feb. 106 Me the unbeneficed and insignificant, with my wretched pittance of £80 per annum.

unbe'neficent, *a.* (UN-[1] 7.)

1822 'P. BEAUCHAMP' (Geo. Grote) *Anal. Infl. Nat. Relig.* (1875) 21 If..he is depicted as unbeneficent—as having personal affections seldom co-incident with human happiness. **1864** *Sat. Rev.* XVIII. 398/2 Mr. Sturm..had a face..fit to belong to some wood-god (not unbeneficent) of heathen fable.

unbene'ficial, *a.* (UN-[1] 7.)

1626 BP. H. KING *Serm. Deliverance* 63 Salubrity or Aire is His Gift; shift of Places, smells to prepossesse the Senses, but for Him had been vnbeneficiall. **1687** NORRIS *Coll. Misc.* (1699) 125 That it becomes unbeneficial to him [*sc.* God].. is purely by accident. **1718** *Entertainer* No. 24. 162 If duly apply'd, it may be, not unbeneficial. **1828** P. CUNNINGHAM *N.S. Wales* (ed. 3) II. 70 It would admit an exchange among ourselves beneficially, instead of an unbeneficial exchange with distant parts. **1839** PALMERSTON in G. H. Francis *Opin. & Pol.* (1852) 418 We shall be doing that which will not be unbeneficial or unacceptable to some of those persons.

un'benefitable, *a. rare.* (UN-[1] 7 b.)

1688 NORRIS *Love* I. v. 59 This is plain in God, who..is the most self-sufficient and unbenefitable..Being.

un'benefited, *ppl. a.* (UN-[1] 8.)

1735 POPE *Let. to Swift* Wks. 1751 IX. 195 A friend and benefactor even to your un-friended and un-benefited Nation. **1753** RICHARDSON *Grandison* (1781) V. xxvii. 166 Religion..will not, I hope, leave me unbenefited by its all-chearing influence. *a* **1821** V. KNOX *Liberal Educ.* App. Wks. 1824 IV. 263 Men who have acquired their excellence ..uninstructed by the tuition, unbenefited by the foundations, and undignified by the graduation of Oxford and Cambridge. **1879** *St. George's Hosp. Rep.* IX. 57 Unbenefited by treatment.

unbe'nevolence. *rare.* (UN-[1] 12.)

1688 COLLIER *Several Disc.* (1725) 352 To imagine God has ordered this World for the Advantage of..Pride, of Sordidness, and Unbenevolence,..seems inconsistent with his Attributes. **1720** —— *Further Def. Restor. Prayer-bk.* 79 I'm sorry to see such Marks of Unbenevolence.

unbe'nevolent, *a.* (UN-[1] 7.)

1697 COLLIER *Ess. Mor. Subj.* I. (1703) 106 To be fond of anything,..because the generality of mankind wants it,.. arises from an unbenevolent and ungenerous temper. **1701** —— *M. Anton.* (1726) 205 If not, they [the gods] must either be mistaken in their measures, or unbenevolent in their design. **1775** S. J. PRATT *Liberal Opin.* iv. (1783) I. 83 To prevent an action, which I thought, on all hands, unlawful and unbenevolent. *a* **1832** BENTHAM *Deontol.* i. (1834) II. 65 The meekness of a man whose meekness is pernicious to others, and useless to himself, is unbenevolent, and the contrary of virtuous. **1853** G. J. CAYLEY *Las Alforjas* II. 291 Another interstice of apathy, followed by a frown of unbenevolent impatience.

unbe'night, *v.* [UN-[2] 4 b.] *trans.* To free from night or obscurity.

1621 QUARLES *Argalus & P.* I, Wks. (Grosart) III. 252/2 When sad Athleia's dreame had unbenighted Her slumbering eyes, her busie thoughts were frighted. **1638** —— *Hieroglyph.* i. 20 Ibid. 187/1 Thou great Originall of Light, Whose errour-chacing beams do unbenight The very soul of darkness. **1674** N. FAIRFAX *Bulk. & Selv.* 40 Having thus far unbenighted our selvs, and clear'd our way.

unbe'nighted, *ppl. a.* (UN-[1] 8.)

1667 MILTON *P.L.* x. 682 To them Day Had unbenighted shon.

unbe'nign, *a.* (UN-[1] 7.)

1651 CROMWELL *Let. to Greenwood* 4 Feb. (Carlyle), I should wrong it..if, either by pretended modesty or in any unbenign way, I should dispute the acceptance of it. **1667** MILTON *P.L.* x. 661 When to joyne In Synod unbenigne. **1698** *Christ Exalted* cix. 88, I proceed to convince..my Dear Kratiste of his unbenign Temper. **1809-14** WORDSW. *Excurs.* IV. 1014 As if the act removed..all traces from the good Man's heart Of unbenign aversion.

Hence **unbe'nignly** *adv.*

a **1892** TENNYSON *Hendecasyllabics* 21 As some..half coquette-like Maiden, not to be greeted unbenignly.

unbe'nignant, *a.* (UN-[1] 7.)

1856 HAWTHORNE *Eng. Note-bks.* (1879) II. 76 A thoughtful..and not unbenignant face. **1860** GEO. ELIOT in Cross *Life* (1885) II. 202 A really grand woman of fifty, with firm mouth and knitted brow, yet not unbenignant.

unbe'nignity. (UN-[1] 12.)

1867 H. BUSHNELL *Mor. Uses Dark Th.* 188 We have, in our winter, a whole season of the year that bears a look of unbenignity.

un'bent, *ppl. a.* [UN-[1] 8 b; also (in sense 1) f. UNBEND *v.*]

1. Not bowed or curved; also, freed from bending, straightened.

1483 *Cath. Angl.* 28/1 Vn Bent, *laxus, relaxus.* **1611** COTGR., *Desbandé*, disbanded; vnbent; vnbound. **1813** BYRON *Giaour* 27 His queen, the garden queen, his Rose, Unbent by winds, unchill'd by snows. **1860** GOSSE *Rom. Nat. Hist.* 61 These venerable giants of the forest, that have stood unbent beneath the weight of a thousand years.

b. Of a bow: Not bent; released from a bent state.

1513 DOUGLAS *Æneid* XI. xvii. 18 [They] on thar wery schuldris wyth greit schame Thar byg bowys onbent has tursit hame. **1601** DONNE *Progr. Soul* 390 Like an unbent bow, carelesly His sinewy Proboscis did remisly lie. **1663** BP. PATRICK *Parab. Pilgr.* xxii, Do not think you shall be in danger to lose the Victory over them, if you suffer your Bow sometimes to be unbent. **1728** ELIZA HEYWOOD tr. *Mme. de Gomez's Belle A.* (1732) II. 41 She had a Quiver at her Back, and an unbent Bow in her Hand. **1830-4** WHITTIER *Mogg Megone* 386, I only meant To draw up again the bow unbent.

2. Not wrinkled or knit.

1593 SHAKS. *Lucr.* 1509 An humble gate, calme looks, eyes wayling still, A brow vnbent that seem'd to welcome wo.

3. *fig.* Not subdued or made subservient.

1697 DRYDEN *Æneis* VI. 143 Thou, secure of soul, unbent with woes. *a* **1718** PRIOR *Solomon* II. 554 She looks with Majesty, and moves with State: Unbent her Soul, and in Misfortune great, She scorns the World. **1825** SCOTT *Betrothed* xxix, The high-spirited entreaties of Eveline, unbent by adversity and want, gradually lost effect on the defenders of the castle. **1845** [see UNBETTERED *ppl. a.*].

unbe'numb, *v.* [UN-^{2} 3.] *trans.* To free from numbness. Hence **unbe'numbing** *vbl. sb.*

1598 SYLVESTER *Du Bartas* II. i. IV. *Handy-cr.* 237 The fire Dries his dank Cloathes,.. And un-benums his sinnews and his flesh. **1603** FLORIO *Montaigne* III. iii. 492 Most wittes haue neede of extravagant stuffe, to vn-benumme and exercise themselues. **1611** COTGR., *Desdormissement*,.. a quickening, or vnbenumming. **1624** QUARLES *Job* xvi. 25 The vertue of his breath, can vnbenumme The frozen lips, and strike the speaker dumme. **1706** STEVENS I, *Desentorpecer*, to unbenum.

unbe'numbed, *ppl. a.* (UN-^{1} 8.)

1861 GEO. ELIOT *Silas M.* xii, She knew this well; and yet, in the moments of wretched unbenumbed consciousness [etc.].

unbe'pissed, *ppl. a.* (UN-^{1} 8.)

a **1550** *Image Hypocr.* III. 172 in *Skelton's Wks.* (1843) II. 435/1 He is sutch a scolde, That no play may hym holde For anger vnbepyst.

unbe'pranked, *ppl. a.* (UN-^{1} 8.)

1594 CAREW *Tasso* (1881) 31 And of her wooers vnbepranct and sole, Both from the land, and from the lookes she stole.

unbe'queathed, *ppl. a.* Also 5 **unbequethyn, -queithen,** 6 **-queith.** [UN-^{1} 8 and 8b.] Not bequeathed.

α. **1483** in *Somerset Med. Wills* (1901) 243 My money and plate that remayneth unbequethyn to be kept by my seid executours. **1494** [see UNBESET]. **1521** in *Test. Ebor.* (Surtees) VI. 4 The residew of.. my goodes unbequeith I freely gif unto Jenett my wif. **1553** *Wills & Inv. N.C.* (Surtees, 1835) 141 The Resydew off all my goods vnbequeith I gyue to my brother.

β. *c* **1525** *Lanc. Wills* (Chetham Soc.) I. 3, I will and beqweth.. all the residew of my goodes unbeqwethed unto the mariage of my son. **1544** *Knaresb. Wills* (Surtees) I. 42, I gyffe all my goodes unbequythed to the usse of Richard my sonne. *a* **1613** OVERBURY *Characters* (1615) Hj b, He croakes like a raven against the death of rich men, and so gets a Legacy vnbequeath'd. **1618** in *Buccleuch MSS.* (Hist. MSS. Comm.) I. 253 He hath.. given him the residue of his goods unbequeathed. **1655** FULLER *Hist. Cambr.* (1840) 214 She left.. five thousand pounds, besides her goods unbequeathed, for the erection of a College. **1829** S. H. CASSAN *Lives Bps. Bath & Wells* 224 The residue, unbequeathed, was applied to the Vicars' Close at Wells. **1846** GROTE *Greece* II. vi. (1862) II. 475 Conflicting claims at law for the hand of an unbequeathed orphan heiress.

fig. **1622** MAY *Heir* II. D j, Her Ladies heart doe yet stand free And vnbequeath'd to any.

†**unbe'quest(ed,** *ppl. a. Obs.* [UN-^{1} 8, 8b.] = prec.

1506 *Test. Ebor.* (Surtees) IV. 255 All my oder goods unbequest I gyf them to Kateryn my wife. **1527** *Lanc. Wills* (Chetham Soc.) I. 18, I will that all my goodis moveable and unmoveable unbequest be sold. **1540** *Test. Ebor.* (Surtees) VI. 108 Residue of my goodes unbequested I put unto the full disposicion of my sones. **1564** *Richmond. Wills* (Surtees) 175 All my goods unbequested I give and bequeth to Cecile Swale my wiff.

†**unbe'quothen,** obs. var. of UNBEQUEATHED.

1482 MARG. PASTON in *P. Lett.* III. 288 The residewe of the stuffe of myn houshold unbiquothen.

unbe'reaved, *ppl. a.* (UN-^{1} 8.)

1889 *Sat. Rev.* 23 Mar. 359/2 That iron philosopher.. had, in his unbereaved moments, a keen eye for the main chance.

unbe'reaven, *ppl. a.* (UN-^{1} 8b.)

1849 MRS. BROWNING *Child's Grave* xxiv, Arms, empty of her child, she lifts, With spirit unbereaven.

unbe'reft, *ppl. a.* (UN-^{1} 8b.)

1621 G. SANDYS *Æneis* I. 411 Lost Phrygia I with twenty ships forsooke;.. seauen, unbereft By seas, and cruell stormes, alone are left. **1648** HEXHAM II, *Onberooft*, Vnbereft, or Vnspoiled. **1820** WORDSW. *River Duddon, Faery Chasm* 3 A sky-blue stone, within this sunless cleft, Is of the very footmarks unbereft Which tiny Elves impressed. **1839** WHITTIER *Relic* 24 Flower of a perished garland left, Of life and beauty unbereft!

†**unbe'risped,** *ppl. a. Obs.*$^{-1}$ [ad. Du. and Flem. *onberispt*, f. *berispen* BERISP *v.*] Uncensured, unreproved.

1481 CAXTON *Reynard* xvi. (Arb.) 36 Tho commanded the kynge openly that eche of them shold be stylle, and suffre the foxe to saye vnberisped what that he wolde.

unbe'rouged, *ppl. a.* (UN-^{1} 8.)

1778 *The Auction* 3 Half-dress'd and unberoug'd, she hastes away.

un'berried, *ppl. a.* [UN-^{1} 8: see BERRY *v.*^{1}, and cf. UNBARROWED *ppl. a.* So Norw. dial. *ubard*, *obart*.] Unthreshed.

1570 *Wills & Inv. N.C.* (Surtees, 1835) 341 In vnberied whete xiiij thraves;.. in pease vnberied iij quarters. **1582-3** *Durham Wills* II. 77 In corne berryed and vnberyed.

un'berthed, *ppl. a.* [UN-^{1} 8: see BERTH *v.*^{2}] Unboarded.

1589 in *N. & Q.* 9th Ser. X. 373/2 The church stool which is appointed for women to sit in, is very insufficient, being unbirthed and kept very fowle. **1640** *Ibid.* VII. 505/2 That many of the pews.. are old, ruinous, unbirthed.

‖**unberufen** (ʊnbəˈruːfən), *int.* [Ger., unauthorized, gratuitous.] 'Touch wood!' (TOUCH *v.* 29b).

1858 QUEEN VICTORIA *Let.* 10 Apr. in R. Fulford *Dearest Child* (1964) 88 Poor Leopold.. bruises as much as ever but unberufen 1000 times—is free from any at present. **1911** BEERBOHM *Zuleika D.* xv. 225, 'I will choose.. whatever moment within my brief span of life shall seem aptest to me. *Unberufen*,' he added, lightly tapping Mr. Druce's counter. **1960** N. MITFORD *Don't tell Alfred* xvi. 180 'My point is that going to Eton will have minimized the danger of such extreme phases in the case of Charlie and Fabrice.' 'Unberufen,' said Alfred.

unbe'seem, *v.* [UN-^{1} 14.]

1. *trans.* To be unseemly or unbecoming for (a person); to suit (one) badly.

a **1657** R. LOVEDAY *Lett.* (1663) 30, I.. write his Letters, and [do] whatever else that unbeseems not his command or my obedience. **1678** GALE *Crt. Gentiles* IV. III. Pref. A ij, Passionate emotions, personal reflexions, or whatever may unbeseem one that lies under essential obligation [etc.]. **1846** H. G. ROBINSON *Odes of Horace* II. xii, Whom it ne'er unbeseem'd to bear foot in the dance.

2. To fail in, fall short of.

1812 BYRON *Ch. Har.*, *To Ianthe* ii, Ah! may'st thou ever be what now thou art, Nor unbeseem the promise of thy spring. **1870** CREASY *Hist. Eng.* II. 336 But he soon unbeseemed that promise.

unbe'seeming, *a.* [UN-^{1} 10 and 5d.]

1. With object: Not beseeming or befitting (a person, etc.); unbecoming or inappropriate to. (Very common in 17th c.)

1583 GOLDING *Calvin on Deut.* lxv. 394 Nowe it were vnbeseeming his power that hee coulde not execute the thing that he had determined with himselfe. **1586** T. B. *La Primaud. Fr. Acad.* I. 191 They judged the verie remembrance thereof to be unwoorthie & unbeseeming men of honor. **1631** GOUGE *God's Arrows* I. §27 You shall find them all to be very toyes, much unbeseeming Gods excellent Majesty. **1651** WITTIE tr. *Primrose's Pop. Err.* I. ii. 40 But some thinke it a thing unbeseeming the dignitie of a physician, to prepare his Medicines. **1676** HALE *Contempl.* I. 493 An unnecessary breaking of the rest of this day, and unbeseeming the solemnity of it. **1721** in *Cath. Rec. Soc. Publ.* VIII. 301 As being a thing Unbeseeming a Religious house. *a* **1721** SHEFFIELD (Dk. of Buckhm.) *Wks.* (1753) II. 153 The truth of it is, a criminal there had put me into a passion, a little unbeseeming a Judge. **1880** SWINBURNE *Study Shaks.* (1895) 60 An office.. no more unbeseeming the pupil hand of the future master, than [etc.].

†**b.** In quasi-adverbial use. *Obs.*

1645 TOMBES *Anthropol.* 9 Ye doe unbeseeming your priviledge. **1655** GURNALL *Chr. in Arm.* II. xviii. §2. 190 He dare not think or speak unbeseeming the glory or goodnesse of God.

2. Unbecoming; offending against propriety or good taste. (Very common in 17th c.)

1594 HOOKER *Eccl. Pol.* I. viii. §9 All those things which men by the light of their naturall vnderstanding euidently know.. to be beseeming or vnbeseeming. **1621** BURTON *Anat. Mel.* I. ii. III. xiii, They.. break many times into violent passions, oaths, imprecations and unbeseeming speeches. **1664** PEPYS *Diary* 23 Sept., Minnes took occasion, in the most childish and unbeseeming manner, to reproach us all. **1671** H. M. tr. *Erasm. Colloq.* 433 What is more unbeseeming, than that an ignoble merchant should have store of money. **1716** M. DAVIES *Athen. Brit.* I. 296 Larding their unbeseeming and inconsistent Prophecies, with.. incongruous Latin. **1825** LAMB *Elia* II. *The Wedding*, The unbeseeming artifices, by which some wives push on the matrimonial projects of their daughters. *a* **1843** SOUTHEY *Doctor* ccxxii, Nor has it any unbeseeming levity, like this which is among Browne's poems. **1860** GEO. ELIOT in Cross *Life* (1885) II. 244 The Almighty above is as unbeseeming as painted Almighties usually are.

Hence **unbe'seemingly** *adv.*, **-'seemingness.**

1617 COLLINS *Def. Bp. Ely* II. x. 497 They dare not for horrour say that our Sauiour did vnwisely, or any way *vnbeseemingly. **1660** STANLEY *Hist. Philos.* IX. (1687) 521/2 They, under the pretence of his Doctrine, do many strange things, inveigling the young men unbeseemingly. *a* **1677** BARROW *Serm. Phil. iv. 11* Wks. 1686 III. 63 All reason dictateth.. that in being discontented we behave our selves very unbeseemingly and unworthily. **1623** BP. HALL *Contempl., O.T.* XVIII. iv, Against the disguise she had pleaded the *unbeseemingnesse for her person and state. **1674** N. FAIRFAX *Bulk & Selv.* 191 That would be an unbeseemingness. **1723** DK. WHARTON *True Briton* No. 48 II. 422 He is to learn from the Unbeseemingness and Intemperances of others Passions, the better how to govern his own.

unbe'seemly, *a. rare.* [UN-^{1} 11.] Unseemly.

1648 HEXHAM II, *Onbehoorlick*, Vnbeseemly. **1801** ELIZ. HELME *St. Mag.'s Cave* xi. (1819) I. 121 It is unbeseemly for youth to press thus before age to the grave.

†**unbe'seen,** *a. Obs.*$^{-1}$ [UN-^{1} 8b.] Unprovided, destitute, devoid.

1390 GOWER *Conf.* III. 280 Love, which is unbesein Of alle reson, as men sein.

†**unbe'seenness.** *Obs.*$^{-1}$ [Cf. prec.] Heedlessness; want of care.

a **1225** *Ancr. R.* 344 Of alle kudde & kuðe sunnen, ase.. of keorfunge, oðer of hurtunge, þuruh unbiseinesse [*MS. T.* unbisehenesse].

unbeset, var. UMBESET *v. Obs.*

†**unbe'set,** *ppl. a. Obs.* [UN-^{1} 8b + BESET *v.* 8.] Not bestowed or apportioned.

1494 *Will Maude Parterich* 23 Feb. (Somerset Ho.), As long as my goodis vnbyset and vnbequeithen will strecche to.

unbe'sieged, *ppl. a.* (UN-^{1} 8.)

1610 HEALEY *St. Aug. Citie of God* 148 But Sulmo.. being unbesieged.. was.. appointed for a direct spoile. **1644** PRYNNE & WALKER *Fiennes' Trial* 89 Unlesse they leave the Castles unbesieged.

unbe'sot, *v. rare.* [UN-^{2} 3.] *trans.* To free from dulness or stupidity.

1603 FLORIO *Montaigne* III. v. 532 He that could recouer or vn-besot man, from so.. verball a superstition, should not much prejudice the world. **1611** COTGR., *Dessoter*, to vnbesot; to quicken, refine, or cleere a dull vnderstanding.

unbe'sotted, *ppl. a.* (UN-^{1} 8.)

1875 RUSKIN *Fors Clav.* liii. 126 The meaning of the parable, heard with ears unbesotted, is this.

unbe'sought, *ppl. a.* (UN-^{1} 8b.)

1667 MILTON *P.L.* x. 1058 Least Cold Or Heat should injure us, his timely care Hath unbesaught provided. **1739** 'R. BULL' tr. *Dedekindus Grobianus* 173 In case they come, which sure no Mortal ought, Unlook'd for, unexpected, unbesought, Receive 'em not. **1827** POLLOK *Course T.* VII. 20 Thus the bard, Not unbesought, again resumed his song. **1874** HOLLAND *Mistr. Manse* iv. 30 Poor precious gift, that goes for nought From willing heart and ready hand, And wins no favor unbesought.

†**unbe'sound,** *ppl. a. Obs.*$^{-1}$ [UN-^{1} 8b.] Not sounded.

c **1532** DU WES *Introd. Fr.* in *Palsgr.* 898 What letters shall be lefte unbesounde.

†**unbe'speak,** *v. Obs.* [UN-^{2} 3.] *trans.* To countermand; to cancel an order or request for.

1661 PEPYS *Diary* 30 Oct., Pretending that the corps stinks, they will bury it to-night privately, and so will unbespeak all their guests. **1693** —— *Let.* in *Academy* 9 Aug. (1890) 109/3 You will force me elce to.. unbespeake ye continuance of a Kindenesse I cannot repay. **1740** GARRICK *Lying Valet* 1, I can immediately run back and unbespeak what I have order'd. **1743** MRS. DELANY in *Life & Corr.* (1861) II. 207 He says he has not strength to perform the journey. The lodgings are unbespoke, the coach forbid.

unbe'spoken, *ppl. a.* Also 8 **unbespoke.** [UN-^{1} 8b.] Not bespoken; not ordered, engaged, or arranged for.

1681 DRYDEN *Abs. & Achit.* I. 242 Swift, unbespoken Pomps, thy steps proclaim. **1796** *Campaigns 1793-4* I. I. ix. 85 Oh, spare me a Muse (if there's one unbespoke). **1843** GEO. ELIOT in Cross *Life* (1885) I. 124 We need not be idle in imparting all that is pure and lovely to children whose minds are unbespoken. **1860** EMERSON *Cond. Life* vi. (1861) 118 The horses come up with the family carriage unbespoken to the door.

unbe'sprinkled, *ppl. a.* (UN-^{1} 8.)

1653 URQUHART *Rabelais* II. xxii. 153 These villainous dogs.. left none of her attire unbesprinkled with their staling.

unbe'stowed, *ppl. a.* (UN-^{1} 8.)

1534 MORE *Comf. agst. Trib.* III. xiii. P vj, He woulde not haue lefte them vnbestowed, if he had foreknowen the chaunce. **1581** MULCASTER *Positions* xxxvi. (1887) 137 Is not that most dangerous.. as the vnbestowed scoller by profession is? **1622** BACON *Hen. VII*, 216 Hee had now but one Sonne, and one Daughter vnbestowed. **1794** WORDSW. *Guilt & Sorrow* lix, Comfort by prouder mansions unbestowed Their wearied frames, she hoped, would soon regale.

†**un'bet,** *ppl. a. Obs.* [UN-^{1} 8b + BEET *v.* Cf. OE. *ungebétt*, ON. *úbǿttr*.] Unamended.

c **1200** *Trin. Coll. Hom.* 173 He bit here unbette sennes.. cumen biforen hem. *a* **1300** *Cursor M.* 26649 A sin or tua Vnbette þai drau ai toward maa. *Ibid.* 28371 My suernes me has don for-gette And many sinnes left vn-bett.

un'bet, *v. rare*$^{-1}$. [UN-^{2} 3.] *trans.* To free from a bet.

1668 DRYDEN *Even. Love* v. i, I'll be unbetted again if you please, Sir, and leave you all the Honour of it.

†**unbe'teaming,** *ppl. a. Obs.*$^{-1}$ [UN-^{1} 10 + BETEEM *v.*] Unconsenting.

1642 D. ROGERS *Naaman* 274 Cease thine enmity, thine hard thoughts, thine unbeteaming heart.

unbe'teared, *ppl. a.* (UN-^{1} 8.)

1635 J. HAYWARD tr. *Biondi's Banish'd Virg.* 30 With unbeteared eyes to see him at parting. *Ibid.* 217 There was not an unbeteared eye among all the spectators.

unbethink, variant of UMBETHINK *v.*

unbe'thought, *ppl. a.* [UN-^{1} 8b. Cf. MDu. *onbedocht*, *-dacht* (Du. *-dacht*), G. *unbedacht* thoughtless.]

1. Unpremeditated; also as *adv.*, without premeditation, unintentionally, unexpectedly. Now *dial.*

1558 PHAER *Æneid* II. D 4 b, As one that unbethought hath hapt some snake among the briers To tread. **1823** E. MOOR *Suffolk Words* 458 *Unbethowt*, unpremeditated, unintentionally. ''Twas wholly unbethowt o' me.' **1854** MISS BAKER *Northampt. Gloss.* 368.

2. Unthought of, unrealized.

1855 Bailey *Mystic*, etc. 135 When, i' th' end, Unnumbered times, duration unbethought, Have passed.

†unbe'tide, *v. Obs. rare.* [UN-^{1} 14.] *intr.* To fail to happen.

c **1374** Chaucer *Boeth.* v. pr. iv. (1868) 161 þilke þinges þat þe prescience woot byforn ne mowen nat vnbitide, þat is to seyn þat þei moten bitide. *Ibid.* pr. vi. 175 þat þilke þinge þat god seeþ to bytide it ne may nat vnbytide.

unbe'token, *v.* (UN-^{1} 14.)

1844 Ld. Houghton *Mem. Many Scenes* 151 Like a glorious maiden dreaming music in the drowsy heat, Lies the City, unbetokening where its myriad pulses beat.

unbe'trayed, *ppl. a.* (UN-^{1} 8.)

1595 Daniel *Civ. Wars* iii. xli. 52 For many being priuy to the fact How hard it is to keepe it vnbetray'd? **1805** Wordsw. *Sonn. fr. Michael Angelo* i. 2 Yes! hope may with my strong desire keep pace, And I be undeluded, unbetrayed. **1821** Shelley *Epipsych., Fragm.* 42 Start not—the thing you are is unbetrayed.

unbe'traying, *ppl. a.* (UN-^{1} 10.)

1788 Anna Seward *Lett.* (1811) II. 8 It is either genuine, or assumed with guarded and unbetraying art. **1893** K. Graham *Pagan Papers* 64 Only we three, the wide world over, she and I, and the unbetraying gate.

unbe'trothed, *ppl. a.* (UN-^{1} 8.)

1577 tr. *Bullinger's Decades* ii. x. (1592) 231 Some..are of opinion that they are not culpable of adultery, if they haue the company of an vnbetrothed maiden. **1660** R. Coke *Power & Subj.* 153 If a man corrupt a virgin unbetrothed,.. let him be fined. **1904** Howitt *Native Tribes S.E. Australia* v. 178 Some other woman..who has an unbetrothed daughter.

un'betterable, *a.* [UN-^{1} 7 b.] Incapable of being improved.

1806 *Ann. Rev.* IV. 82 The country is not only bad but unbetterable. **1874** Ruskin *Fors Clav.* xl. IV. 76 A lovely, classic, unbetterable sentence of Marmontel's, perfect in wisdom and modesty.

un'bettered, *ppl. a.* [UN-^{1} 8. Cf. Du. *ongebeterd*, MHG. *ungebezzert* (G. *-bessert*), MSw. *obätrad*.] Not made better; unimproved.

1628 Wither *Brit. Rememb.* iv. 941 All they that goe Unbetter'd from such objects, worse doe grow. **1648** Sparke *Pref. to J. Shute's Sarah & Hagar* b j, He..so tempered the wine and oil together, that none (but through his own default) might go away unbettered. **1813** Shelley *Q. Mab.* iv. 81 From kings, and priests, and statesmen, war arose, Whose safety is man's deep unbettered woe. **1845** Bailey *Festus* (ed. 2) 310 Even these..Unbent, unbettered will again rush forth In all the might of madness and despair.

†un'betty, *v. Cant.* [UN-^{2} 3.] (See quot.)

1812 J. H. Vaux *Flash Dict.* s.v. *Betty*, To *unbetty*, or *betty* a lock, is to open or relock it, by means of the betty [= a picklock].

un'bevelled, *ppl. a.* (UN-^{1} 8.)

1592 Kyd *Sp. Trag.* iii. xi. 23 A sonne, The more he growes.., The more vnsquard, unbeuelled he appeares. **1621** Quarles *Div. Poems, Esther* Med. 19 The Law of God ..doth iustly paize The ballances of his [*sc.* man's] vnbeuelled wayes. **1851** Ruskin *Stones Ven.* I. xvi. §5 The bevelled wall cannot conveniently carry an unbevelled arch. **1875** *Carpentry & Join.* 47 A chisel is inclined to draw into the work on the plain or unbevelled side.

unbe'wailed, *ppl. a.* (UN-^{1} 8.)

1586 W. Warner *Alb. Eng.* iv. xxi. (1592) 88 He wandred vnbewailed long, as man whom men exempt From house, and helpe. **1606** Shaks. *Ant. & Cl.* iii. vi. 85 But let determin'd things to destinie Hold vnbewayl'd their way. **1661** Hickeringill *Jamaica* 99 Not unbewail'd was his Catastrophe. **1676** Hobbes *Iliad* 338 Why should this come now into my head, When unbewail'd Patroclus lieth still? **1837-8** Southey *Poems, To Hymen* iii, Tho' doomed perchance to die Alone and unbewailed.

unbe'wailing, *ppl. a.* (UN-^{1} 10.)

1820 Shelley *Prometh. Unb.* ii. iv. 16 The radiant looks of unbewailing flowers. *Ibid.* ii. v. 71.

†unbe'ware, *adv. Obs.* [Alteration of unware *adv.*, after beware *v.*] = unaware *adv.*

1489 Caxton *Faytes of A.* i. x. 28 To com by thees wayes vpon theyre enemyes vnbeware. *c* **1489** —— *Blanchardyn* xxx. 113 A grete sorowe toke hym at his herte of that he was so taken vnbeware. **1565** Golding *Ovid's Met.* i. (1593) 7 He meant..To steale upon me in the night and kill me unbeware.

†unbe'wares, *adv. Obs.* [Cf. prec.] = unawares *adv.*

1483 *Vulgaria abs Terentio* 23 b, He com vnbywarse. **1508** Fisher *7 Penit. Ps.* cii. Wks. (1876) 192 Leest perauenture sodeynly vnbewares it fall in decaye. **1550** Bale *Apol.* 25 Fulfyll not that thou hast vowed vnbewares. *a* **1557** Abp. Parker *Ps.* F ij, And thus I offend unbewares, thoughe afterwards I perceiue it.

unbe'wilder, *v.* (UN-^{2} 3.)

1668 H. More *Div. Dial.* v. xvii. (1713) 464 For it can be no unbecoming office to unbewilder some over-serious Souls, that may be too much captivated with such kind of Writers.

unbe'wildered, *ppl. a.* (UN-^{1} 8.)

[**1775** Ash.] **1805** Wordsw. *Prelude* vi. 41 What keen research, Unbiassed, unbewildered, and unawed. **1855** Milman *Lat. Chr.* xiv. iii. VI. 461 Yet he himself seems to walk unbewildered in his own labyrinth.

unbe'witch, *v.* [UN-^{2} 3.] *trans.* To deliver from witchcraft; to disenchant.

1584 R. Scot *Discov. Witchcr.* xii. xviii. (1886) 219 There be masses of purpose for this matter, to unbewitch the bewitched. **1646** Gaule *Cases Consc.* 4 Their bewitched body or goods has served to unbewitch them. **1679** Oates *Serm. at St. Michaels* Pref. A 4 b, That God..would unbewitch this Roman Catholick Synagogue, who believe none to be Christians but themselves. **1751** Lavington *Enthus. Meth. & Papists* iii. (1754) 194 Barbara Dorea.. confessed that she had unbewitched several whom she herself had bewitched.

unbe'witched, *ppl. a.* (UN-^{1} 8.)

1648 Bp. Hall *Select Th.* §12 A Christian can hold his eyes and yet behold beauty, unbewitched. **1827** Pollok *Course T.* ix. 242 By fashion's revelry uncharmed, By honour unbewitched—he left the chase Of vanity.

unbe'witching, *ppl. a.* (UN-^{1} 10.)

1859 G. Meredith *R. Feverel* xxi, A similar unbewitching fear.

unbe'wrayed, *ppl. a.* (UN-^{1} 10.)

1605 Daniel *Philotas* iii. i, And that the keeping of it [i.e. an offence] vnbewraid, Was that I held the rumor vaine to be.

unbe'written, *ppl. a.* (UN-^{1} 8.)

1820 in Mrs. Wyndham *Corr. Lady Lyttleton* (1912) 228 This perfectly fresh and unbewritten sort of subject.

un'bias, *v.* [UN-^{2} 3.] *trans.* To free from bias.

1708 Swift *Sent. Ch. Eng. Man* Wks. 1755 II. i. 54 The truest service a private man may hope to do his country is, by unbiassing his mind as much as possible.

un'biassable, *a.* (UN-^{1} 7 b.)

1714 G. Lockhart *Mem. Affairs Scot.* (ed. 3) 214 His being esteem'd by People of all Parties, on Account of his eminently unbyassable Honesty and Integrity.

unbias(s)ed (ʌn'baɪəst), *a.* Forms: 7-8 unbyassed, 7- unbiassed, 8- unbiased; 7- 8 unbyass'd (7 -byas'd), unbiass'd (7, 9 -bias'd), 8 unbyast. [UN-^{1} 8.]

1. Of bowls, etc.: Having no bias.

1607 G. Wilkins *Miseries Enforced Marr.* iv, These men ..headlong run, like an unbias'd bowl. **1825** J. Nicholson *Operat. Mechanic* 173 The piston, therefore, being in an unbiassed state, as regards the pressure, will again be raised to its original situation by the counterpoise weights.

2. *fig.* Not unduly or improperly influenced or inclined; unprejudiced, impartial:

a. Of persons.

1647 Clarendon *Hist. Reb.* ii. §77 They were as sure, that so many so unbiass'd men, would never be elected again. **1686** W. Hopkins tr. *Ratramnus* Dissert. v. (1688) 100 Which are the Sentiments of Ratramnus, as will evidently appear to any unbyass'd Reader. **1710** *Tatler* No. 235 ¶2 My Lady..is wholly unbiassed in dispensing her Favours among them. **1775** Wesley *Calm Address* 12, I am unbiassed: I have nothing to hope or fear from either side. **1823** Keble *Serm.* iii. (1848) 72 A considerate unbiassed man, acting steadily by this rule. **1861** Brougham *Brit. Const.* xvii. 265 Its [the House of Lords'] veto upon all the measures that pass the Commons,..its more calm deliberation on all questions, unbiassed by mob clamour.

absol. *c* **1721** Mrq. Tullibardine in *10th Rep. Hist. MSS. Comm.* App. I. 126 The unbiass'd are strangely disjoynted through the busie artifice of those who find their account in unexpressable confusion.

b. Of the judgement, mind, feeling, standards of action, etc.

1654 Whitlock *Zootomia* 209 In humane Learning I appeale to every Mans own impartiall Breast, whether he can boast an unbiassed Judgement? **1673** Dryden *Amboyna* Ded. A iij, You have serv'd him with unbyass'd Honor, and with unshaken resolution. **1724** Swift *Drapier's Lett.* Wks. 1755 V. ii. 104 The minds of a jury, which ought to be wholly free and unbyassed. **1776** Gibbon *Decl. & F.* x. I. 252 He submitted the choice of the censor to the unbiassed voice of the senate. **1808** Helen St. Victor *Ruins of Rigonda* II. 6 A heart, unbiassed to any particular individual. **1846** Mrs. Gore *Eng. Char.* I. 117 The Linkman sees with unbiassed eyes, and declaims with unblushing enunciation. **1873** C. M. Davies *Unorthod. Lond.* (1876) 104 And probably in no section of religious development is this unbiassed judgement more essentially necessary.

c. Of particular actions, opinions, etc.

1668 Temple *Let. to Bridgman* Wks. 1720 II. 63 The general Opinion conceived here, of your Lordship's.. unbiass'd Pursuit of the true Interest of the Kingdom. **1690** Locke *Hum. Und.* i. iv. §25 Without any other design, than an unbiass'd enquiry after Truth. **1742** Richardson *Pamela* III. 248 He will judge us according to the unforced and unbyassed Use we make of that Light. **1791** Burke *Corr.* (1844) III. 193 All..which a man without authority can give,—his unbiassed opinion, his honest advice, and his best reasons. **1812** Sir H. Davy *Chem. Philos.* 25 Every field of enquiry was open for the free and unbiassed exercise of the powers of genius. **1843** Bethune *Sc. Fireside Stor.* 72 Upon these concurring circumstances—supported as they were by the unbiassed testimony of Dr. G——, he was set at liberty. **1862** H. Spencer *First Princ.* i. i. §6 (1875) 20 An unbiassed consideration of its general aspects.

3. As *adv.* = next. *rare*$^{-1}$.

1796 Mme. D'Arblay *Camilla* vii. iv, If impartially and unbiassed, the Major is refused.

Hence **un'biassedly** *adv.*, **un'biassedness**.

1676 *Doctrine of Devils* 159 As is plain, if any man do but *unbyassedly consider the several places, where the word is used, as I have intimated afore. **1699** Locke in Fox Bourne *Life* (1876) II. xv. 472 With a free mind that unbiassedly pursues truth it cannot be other wise. **1718** Hickes & Nelson *J. Kettlewell* iii. ciii. 443 Who..shall Faithfully and Unbyasedly Persue the Blessed Work of Christian Union. **1886** *Cyclist* 25 Aug. 1165/1 The same printer very unbiassedly turned out both bills. **1660** *Bp. Hall's Remains* Pref. b ij b, He claims the liberty of reserving his own Judgement, and more especially to pag. 387, where in the close of the Tract his *unbyassedness is clearly professed. **1692** Locke *Toleration* Wks. 1714 III. 462 'Tis Want of Attention and Unbyassedness in you, that puts your Religion past doubt with you.

un'biblical, *a.* (UN-^{1} 7. Cf. Du. *onbijbelsch*, G. *unbiblisch*, Sw. *obiblisk*.)

1828 Pusey *Hist. Eng.* i. 92 Even unbiblical terminology, except what was admitted by the universal church, was excluded. **1875** E. White *Life in Christ* v. xxviii, The custom..of representing Faith and Reason as opposites, is unbiblical and pernicious.

un'bibulous, *a.* (UN-^{1} 7.)

1864 J. Ormsby *Autumn Rambles N. Africa* 44 Bushes of an unbibulous kind of brushwood that seemed to have taken a pledge of total abstinence early in life.

†un'biched, *a. Obs.*$^{-1}$. App. = bicched *a.*

c **1460** *Towneley Myst.* xxiv. 356 Thou shall forthynk it, in faythe; Fy, what thou art fre! vnbychid, vnbayn!

un'bickered, *ppl. a.* (UN-^{1} 8 c.)

1855 Browning *Bp. Blougram* 894 You are not I—Who needs must make earth mine and feed my fill Not simply unbutted at, unbickered with, But [etc.].

un'bid, *ppl. a.* Also 5 vnbedde. [UN-^{1} 8 b.]

1. = unbidden *ppl. a.*

14.. *Gosp. Nicodemus* (A.) 174 þis messagere to ihesu kneled;..þes baners sone gan helde And bowed to ihesu vnbedde. **1593** Shaks. *3 Hen. VI*, v. i. 18 Oh vnbid spight, is sportfull Edward come? **1623** J. Taylor (Water P.) *Discov. by Sea* A vij, The waues amaine (vnbid) oft boorded vs. **1661** Pepys *Diary* 3 Feb., So to Mr. Fox's, unbidd; where I had a good dinner and special company. **1700** Dryden *Iliad* i. 784 He said no more but crown'd a Bowl, unbid: The laughing Nectar overlook'd the Lid. **1715** Pope *Iliad* ii. 485 And Menelaus came, unbid, the last. **1725** —— *Odyss.* vii. 269 As yet, unbid they never grac'd our feast. **1827** Pollok *Course T.* viii. 16 The ministers Of God's unsparing vengeance waited, still Unbid. **1876** [see unboden *ppl. a.* 1].

†2. Unprayed for. *Obs.*

1590 Spenser *F.Q.* i. ix. 54 He chose an halter from among the rest, And with it hung himselfe, vnbid vnblest.

un'bid, *v.* [UN-^{2} 3.] *absol.* To cancel a command or invitation.

1597 J. King *On Jonas* (1618) 450 A man may impute it to unconstancy, to bid, and vnbid. **1598** Florio, *Disinuitare*, to vnuie at any game, to vnbid, to disinuite.

un'biddable, *a.* (UN-^{1} 7 b.)

1825 Jamieson. **1831** Cobbett *Eng. Spelling-Bk.* 91 He was not in general what is called an unbidable child. **1899** Crockett *Black Douglas* xxi, A great ram-stam, unbiddable, unhallowed deevil he is.

un'bidden, *ppl. a.* Forms: 1, 4-5 unbeden (3 *Orm.* unnbedenn); 4 vnbiden, 5 -bidyn, -byden; 4, 6-7 vn-, 6- unbidden. [UN-^{1} 8 b. Cf. NFris. *ünbeden*, MDu. and Du. *ongebeden*, MHG. and G. *ungebeten*, ON. *úbeðinn*, Icel. *óbeðinn* (Norw. *ubeden*).] Not asked or invited; not commanded or directed.

pred. *c* **1010** Ælfric *Past. Ep.* xlix. in Thorpe *Anc. Laws* (1840) II. 386 Sume preostas..unbedene gaderiað hi to ðam lice. *c* **1200** Ormin 17081 Forrþi toc Crist forrþrihht anan Unnbedenn & unnbonedd..To mælenn & to spellenn. *a* **1300** *Cursor M.* 14912 He wil him all vnbiden [*v.r.* vnbidden] bede. *c* **1380** Wyclif *Serm.* Sel. Wks. II. 120 And siþ alle þes failen to men, how shulden þei fiȝ te unbeden of God? *c* **1400** *Destr. Troy* 9943 Breisaid the burd, vnbidyn of hir fader, Full duly to Dyamede dressit to wend. **1427** *Wills & Inv. N.C.* (Surtees) I. 74 þai þat come thidir þat tyme vnbyden be fewe. **1583** in Strype *Ann. Ref.* (1709) III. xvi. 183 The painful pastors and ministers of the Word..are condemned,..Some for leaving the Holidays unbidden. **1608** Dod & Cleaver *Expos. Prov.* xi-xii. 122 That we goe not unsent, nor come unbidden. **1685** Baxter *Paraphr. N.T.* Matt. xiv. 28 Yet none must tempt God, nor go unbidden into danger. **1726** Pope *Odyss.* xvii. 365 Adown his cheek a tear unbidden stole. **1796** Mme. D'Arblay *Camilla* x. x, Thou art come, uncalled, unbidden, thy task unfulfilled, thy peace unearned. **1842** Manning *Serm.* ii. (1848) I. 30 Thoughts..thrust themselves unbidden now into the abode where they were wont to be welcomed before. **1859** Tennyson *Merlin & V.* 426 And beasts themselves would worship; camels knelt Unbidden. **1873** Black *Pr. Thule* iv. 47 Tears had sprung to her eyes unbidden.

attrib. *a* **1425** *Cursor M.* 14243 (Trin.), þere were fele hem to rewe And also mony vnbeden iewe þider coom. **1548** Udall, etc. *Erasm. Par. Luke* vii. 74 She did not onely ieoperde as an vnbidden geaste boldely to entre into the house of a Pharisee, but [etc.]. **1573** G. Harvey *Letter-bk.* (Camden) 42 He lookith like..an unbidden geste that knowes not where to sitt him downe. **1620** Brinsley *Virgil* 58/3, I do not sing vnbidden (vncommanded) things. **1697** Dryden *Virg. Georg.* i. 227 Burrs and Brambles, an unbidden Crew Of graceless guests, th' unhappy Field subdue. **1718** Pope *Iliad* xiv. 396 Glad earth..from her bosom pours Unbidden herbs, and voluntary flowers. **1805** Scott *Last Minstrel* iv. xxv, Gush'd to her eye the unbidden tear. **1850** F. W. Newman *Phases Faith* 163 Judaism also unlearnt polygamy, and made an unbidden improvement upon Moses.

unbide, variant of onbide.

un'bigged, *ppl. a.* Also *Sc.* 5-6 vnbiggit. [UN-^{1} 8. Cf. ON. and Icel. *ú-*, *óbygðr* (Norw. *ubygd*, older Da. *ubygget*, *ubygt*, Sw. *obyggd*).]

a. Uninhabited. **b.** Unbuilt. **c.** Not built upon.

c **1200** Ormin 3199 He..flæh himm inntill wesste land þær itt wass all unnbiggedd. **1496** *Acc. Ld. High Treas. Scot.* I. 270 For tymmir and diuers odir expens maid apone the bigging of the harnes mill, quhilk ȝit is vnbiggit. **1555** *Sc. Acts, Mary* (1814) II. 490/1 Gif the awnaris lattis the ground to be vnbiggit. **1597** Skene *De Verb. Sign.* s.v. *Annuell*, Quhen the ground and propertie of onie land bigged or vnbigged, is disponed and annalied. a **1795** *Bonnie James Campbell* iv. in Child *Ballads* IV. (1890) 143/2 My house is unbigged,..My corn's unshorn.

un'bigoted, *a.* (un-¹ 9.)

1711 Addison *Spect.* No. 213 ¶15 Erasmus, who was an unbigotted Roman Catholick. **1784** R. Bage *Barham Downs* II. 311 Sir George has free notions; the Professor is an unbigotted Catholic. **1841** F. E. Paget *Tales of Village* (1852) 317 He is..so unbigotted, has such a liberal mind,.. that it was quite impossible not to admire him. **1894** Blackmore *Perlycross* xliv, A Protestant not quite unbigoted.

† **unbiheve**, *sb.* and *a.*: see un-¹ 3.

un'bilified, *ppl. a.* (un-¹ 8.)

1823 Lockhart *Reg. Dalton* II. vii, A firm, sound, unseasoned, and unbilified stomach.

un'billed, *ppl. a.* [un-¹ 8.] Not enrolled.

1587 Harrison *England* II. xvi. (1877) I. 280 A third part of this like multitude [of soldiers] was left vnbilled and vncalled.

un'billeting, *vbl. sb.* (un-¹ 13.)

1654 H. L'Estrange *Chas. I* (1655) 78 Personal liberty being thus setled, next they fall upon..the unbilleting of Souldiers and nulling of Martiall Law in times of peace.

un'bind, *v.* Forms: (see un-² and bind *v.*). [OE. *unbindan* (f. un-² 3 + bind *v.*), *onbindan*, = Du. *ontbinden*, G. *entbinden*.]

1. *trans.* To free from a band, bond, or tie; to make loose or free by undoing a band, etc. Also *absol.*

c **950** *Lindisf. Gosp.* Matt. xxi. 2 ðe infindes asal ȝebunden & fola mið hia, unbindas & to-lædas me. *Ibid.* Luke xiii. 15 An eȝhuelc iuer on symbel-doeȝ ne unbindeð *vel* woxo his *vel* assald of bósih. c **1175** *Lamb. Hom.* 5 Ure drihten sende his .ii. apostles..þet heo unbunden þat assa. c **1250** *Gen. & Ex.* 2223 Quan men ðo seckes ðor un-bond, And in ðe coren ðo aȝtes fond. **1382** Wyclif *Luke* xix. 31 And if ony man schal axe, whi ȝe vnbynden [*sc.* the ass], thus ȝe schulen seye to him. **1426** Lydg. *De Guil. Pilgr.* 3038 Pereyl off deth..ys a cause evydent That thow mayst wel..The swerd ydrawe, ..And the keyes vnbynde also. c **1450** Lovelich *Grail* xlix. 213 Thanne let this Sarrazin Iosephe vnbynde his hondis that bownden weren behinde. **1484** Caxton *Fables of Alfonce* ix, Whanne the nyght was come, the labourer vnbonde his oxen. **1596** Shaks. *Tam. Shr.* I. i. 4 For these other goods, Vnbinde my hands, Ile pull them off my selfe. **1669** Sturmy *Mariner's Mag.* I. ii. 17 Get the Sail into the Ship, and unbind all things clear of it. **1683** J. Reid *Scots Gard'ner* (1907) 71 Set the graff on the west-side... Unbind when you find their bands harme them. **1707** Mortimer *Husb.* (1721) II. 262 When you unbind them you may discern which are good and have taken, and which not. **1791** Mrs. Radcliffe *Rom. Forest* ix, The ruffians unbound me from my horse. **1821** Scott *Kenilw.* xxxix, He unbound his horse from the tree.

fig. c **1000** Ælfric *Hom.* I. 352 þæs fæder tungan his nama unband. c **1400** *Rom. Rose* 2226 To vilayne speche in no degre Late never thi lippe vnbounden be. **1859** Tennyson *Guinevere* 164 O maiden,..Sing, and unbind my heart that I may weep.

b. *transf.* To loosen, open up or out, set free, detach, etc.

1577 Grange *Golden Aphrod.*, etc. S j b, So doth the morne (me thinkes) vnclose and eke vnbinde, Each thing whiche in the night, are closed in their kynde. **1633** Fletcher *Purple Isl.* I. xxxvi, Vain men, too fondly wise, who plough the seas,..The earths vast limits dayly more unbinde! **1697** Dryden *Virg. Georg.* I. 64 While Earth unbinds Her frozen Bosom to the Western Winds. **1735** A. Hill *Zara* v. 60 His absence shall unbind his sister's tongue. **1743** Francis tr. *Hor., Odes* I. xxii. 18 Place me where never Summer Breeze Unbinds the Glebe, or warms the Trees. **1781** Cowper *Tiroc.* 439 The most disint'rested and virtuous minds, In early years connected, time unbinds. **1817** Shelley *Rev. Islam* VII. xl, Like wind Which..can wake the still cloud, and unbind The strength of tempest.

c. To take the bandage off (a limb or wound).

1639 T. de Gray *Expert Farrier* 30 Binde upon it a linnen cloth,..then..unbinde the foot. **1699** Dampier *Voy.* II. II. 91 The next Morning the Cloath being rubb'd off, I unbound it, and found the Worm broken off, and the Hole quite healed up. **1821** Byron *Sardanap.* III. i, I will unbind your wound and tend it.

2. *fig.* **a.** In renderings of Matt. xvi. 19, etc. Cf. loose *v.* 1 c.

c **950** *Lindisf. Gosp.* Matt. xvi. 19 Suæ huæt ðu unbindes ofer eorðu bið unbunden in heofnum. c **1000** Ælfric *Hom.* I. 542 Swa hwæt swa hi unbindað ofer eorðan, þæt bið unbunden on heofonum. c **1200** *Trin. Coll. Hom.* 65 Al þat prest bindeð soðliche buð ibunden & al þat he unbindeð beð unbunden. **1382** Wyclif *Matt.* xviii. 18 What euere thingis ȝee shulen vnbynde vpon erthe, tho shulen be vnbounden and in heuenes. c **1400** Love *Bonavent. Mirr.* (1908) 123 What that ȝe vnbynde in erthe schal be vnbounden in heuene.

absol. **1820** Wordsw. *Processions* 67 That licentious craving in the mind To act the God among external things, To bind, on apt suggestion, or unbind. **1822** —— *Eccl. Sonn.* I. xxxix, Through earth and heaven to bind and to unbind!

† **b.** To free from sin or its consequences; to absolve. *Obs.*

c **950** *Lindisf. Gosp.* Luke, Contents lxxvi, Ðone aldormono unbaund [L. *absoluit*] seðe cuom hal ȝedoe þætte losade. c **1000** Ælfric *Hom.* I. 234 Forði sceolon ða lareowas ða unbindan fram heora synnum þa ðe Crist ȝeliffæst þurh onbryrdnysse. a **1200** *Vices & Virtues* 53 Hwa se..is mid heued-senne ibunden, þe naure ne mai ben unbunden bute ðurh priestes muðe oðer ðurh biscopes. c **1275** *Passion Our Lord* 630 in *O.E. Misc.* 55 þeo þat ye aleseþ here of heore sunnes bende, Hi schulle beon vnbunden euer buten ende. **1303** R. Brunne *Handl. Synne* 1014 Certys we ouȝt þan with ful mynde To preye god vs of synne vnbynde. c **1400** *Rom. Rose* 6416, I am unbounde;..For he that myght hath in his honde, Of alle my synnes me unbonde. a **1450** *Knt. de la Tour* (1906) 53 The deuell holdithe hem bounde in his seruice till thei be vnbounde by confession.

absol. a **1300** *Cursor M.* 28742 Sin crist is buxum to vnbind, Qui sal man preist ouer hard find. **1340** *Ayenb.* 172 He ssel zeche zuych ane confessour, þet conne bynde and onbynde. **1396–7** in *Eng. Hist. Rev.* (1907) XXII. 301 þei seyn þat..þei mown cursyn and blissin, byndin and unbyndin at here owne wil. c **1440** *Jacob's Well* 63 Here it semyth þat acursyng byndyth, & absolucyoun vnbyndyth.

† **c.** To set free, deliver, cure (from sickness or trouble). *Obs.*

c **950** *Lindisf. Gosp.* Luke xiii. 16 Ðios..dohter abrahames ..ne were..reht to unbindanne *vel* to undoanne of bend ðissum dæȝe symbles? c **1000** *Saxon Leechd.* I. 98 ðyf hwa on þære untrumnysse sy þæt he sy cis, þonne meaht ðu hine unbindan. c **1385** Chaucer *L.G.W.* 1339 *Dido*, O cloth, whil Jubiter hyt leste, Take now my soule, vnbynd me of thys vnreste. c **1430** *Hymns Virgin* (1867) 97 How myȝt god me of care vnbinde Siþen god loueþ trouþe so verrili? c **1440** *Jacob's Well* 63 3ysterday, whan þe absolucyoun was red ouyr my graue, I was vnboundyn of my peyne.

† **d.** To make free, to release, from some legal restraint or obligation. Also *absol.* *Obs.*

1297 R. Glouc. (Rolls) 3370 In oþer halue he founde Ioye in is herte, uor þe contasse of spoushod was vnbunde. *Ibid.* 649 þo was he al clene louerd, to binde & unbinde. **1340** *Ayenb.* 97 Laȝe is yzed þeruore þet hy hare-zelue ne byn ake þe oþre byndeþ and þis onbynt. **1382** Wyclif *Rom.* vii. 6 Now forsothe we ben vnbounden fro the lawe of deeth. c **1386** Chaucer *Merch. Prol.* 14 Were I vnbounden al so moot I thee I wolde neuere eft comen in the snare [of marriage]. a **1470** H. Parker *Dives & Pauper* (W. de W. 1496) IV. vi. 166/2 By his relygyon he is unbounden from this commaundement. **1491** Caxton *Vitas Patr.* (W. de W. 1495) v. xiv. 344/2, I praye the that it please the to doo to me that grace..to unbynde me of the sentence of excomynycacyon in whiche I am bounden. **1581** Marbeck *Bk. of Notes* 978 New things, that is, the sweete tidings of yᵉ Gospell to vnbinde us.

† **e.** *absol.* To give up an enterprise. *Obs. rare.*

a **1400–50** *Alexander* 1744 (Ashm. MS.), Forthi is bettir vnbynd & of þe brathe leue. *Ibid.* 1974 For-þi ware bettir vnbynde or þou bale suffire.

3. a. To set (a person) free from bonds; to restore to personal liberty in this way. Also in fig. context.

c **950** *Rit. Eccl. Dunelm.* (Surtees) 7 From synna bendum unbundeno..vsig..ȝihald. c **1000** Ælfric *Hom.* I. 466 Æfter his behate ic ðe unbinde, þæt þu fare to westene. a **1023** Wulfstan *Hom.* (1883) 83 Æfter þusend ȝearum bið Satanas unbunden. c **1200** Ormin 3682 Forr þatt he wollde unnbindenn uss Off hellepiness bandess. c **1300** *Havelok* 601 [They] Vnkeueleden him, and swiþe unbounden. c **1350** *Will. Palerne* 1227 þan þei him vnbond bliue & brouȝt him his stede. **1382** Wyclif *Acts* xxii. 30 Forsoth in the day suynge he..vnbound him. a **1425** *Cursor M.* 14912 (Trin.) þat wiþ þe fend dwellynge ware He wolde hem vnbynde in dede. **1483** Caxton *Gold. Leg.* 180/1 Thenne came an aungel that unbonde them. a **1533** Ld. Berners *Huon* l. 168, I requyre the vnbynd me & brynge me out of this dolouros payne. **1588** Shaks. *Tit. A.* III. i. 24 Vnbinde my sonnes, reuerse the doome of death. **1635** *Life Long Meg of Westm.* (1871) 27 Help to unbind me, for I am undone, and almost killed. **1799** *Hull Advertiser* 3 Aug. 4/1 A..girl..tied up by both arms to a tree... I implored that she might be immediately unbound. **1817** Shelley *Rev. Islam* III. xiii. 2 They bore me to a cavern in the hill Beneath that column, and unbound me there. **1839** Whittier *World's Convention* 228 Methinks I see my country rise:..Her captives from their chains unbound. **1851** —— *Pris. Naples* 13 Whom man hath bound let Thy right hand unbind.

fig. **1390** Gower *Conf.* III. 369 Sche which mai the hertes bynde In loves cause and ek unbinde. **1400–10** Clanvowe *Cuckow & Night.* ii, The god of love..can binden and unbinden eke What he wol have bounden or unbounde.

† **b.** To deliver (a woman). *Obs.*⁻¹

c **1325** *Lai le Freine* 85 Sone therafter bifel a cas, That hirself with child was. When God wild sche was unbounde, And deliuerd.

† **c.** To clear of phlegm. *Obs.*⁻⁰

1552 Huloet, Vnbynde the breaste, *expectoro*.

4. To unfasten, untie, undo (a bond, cord, etc.).

c **950** *Lindisf. Gosp.* Luke iii. 16 Ðæs ne am ic wyrðe to unbindanne ðuongas sceoea his. c **1200** Ormin 10412 þa shollde an oþerr cumenn forþ..& shollde unnbindenn þin shoþ wang. c **1205** Lay. 5926 Heo unbunde þa locun, drowen ut þa baiȝes. **1382** Wyclif *Acts* xvi. 26 And a-noon alle the doris ben openyd, and the bondis of alle ben vnbounden. **1426** Lydg. *De Guil. Pilgr.* 22028 For the osyers nygh echon Were broke ffyrste.., Wherffore the hoopys were vnbounde. **1596** Spenser *F.Q.* VI. xi. 8 But she resolu'd no remedy to fynde,..Till Fortune would her captiue bonds vnbynde. **1697** Dryden *Æneis* VII. 563 Unbind your fillets, loose your flowing hair. **1757** W. Wilkie *Epigon.* VI. 170 They..the helmet loos'd, the buckled mail unbound. **1791** Cowper *Odyss.* V. 419 Unbind the zone, Which thou shalt cast far distant from the shore Into the deep. **1812** Byron *Ch. Har.* III. civ, 'Twas the ground Where early Love his Psyche's zone unbound. **1820** Shelley *Vis. Sea* 56 The sharks and the dogfish their grave-clothes unbound.

b. In fig. context.

c **950** *Lindisf. Gosp.* Mark vii. 35 Sona untyndo woeron earo his & un-bunden wæs ȝebend tungæs his. a **1200** *Moral Ode* 188 in *O.E. Hom.* I. 171 Vre bendes he vnbond & bohte us mid his blode. **1388** Wyclif *Isaiah* lviii. 6 Vnbynde thou the byndingis togidere of vnpitee. a **1500** *Ratis Raving* I. 1067 Gyf thai twa frendis can nocht find That scho may syk a band [*sc.* as that of marriage] wnbynd, I pray thee, reul the as thai red. **1559** *Mirr. Mag., Dk. Clarence* xi, Loves strongest bandes vnkindnes doth vnbinde. **1728** Pope *Dunc.* I. 24 Whether thou..magnify Mankind, Or thy griev'd Country's copper chains unbind. **1744** Berkeley *Siris* §302 Theology and philosophy gently unbind the ligaments that chain the soul down to the earth. **1810** Scott *Lady of L.* v. xxviii, Those cords of love I should unbind, Which knit my country and my kind. **1843** Whittier *Knight of St. John* 70 Then let the Paynim work his will, And death unbind my chain.

c. *fig.* To dissolve, undo, destroy.

c **1200** Ormin 15590 Ure Laferrd..seȝȝde: Unnbindeþþ all þiss temmple, & icc Itt i þre daȝhess reȝȝse. c **1374** Chaucer *Troylus* IV. 675 Al þe world ne koude here loue vnbynde, Ne Troylus out of here herte caste. c **1386** —— *Pars. T.* ¶511 Thanne cometh discord that vnbyndeth alle manere of freendshipe. c **1430** *Pilgr. Lyf Manhode* IV. l. (1869) 200 þis byndinge, quod she, is cleped silence; Benedicite, þis is þilke þat oonliche vnbynt it. **1490** Caxton *How to Die* (1491) 19 Thou vnbondest the synne of all the worlde. **1529** More *Suppl. Soulys* 28 b, By thys place ye se ..that cryste at hys resurreccyon dyd lose and vnbynd paynys in hell. **1643** Baker *Chron., Hen. VIII*, 19 Both Kings had given authority..to the Cardinall to affirme and confirme, to bind or unbind, whatsoever should be in difference betweene them. **1697** Dryden *Æneis* IV. 704 Her charms unbind The chains of love, or fix them on the mind. *Ibid.* XII. 304 No force, no fortune, shall my vows unbind, Or shake the steadfast tenor of my mind.

† **5. a.** *absol.* To aid the natural flux of the bowels. **b.** *trans.* To detach, clear away. *Obs.*

1398 Trevisa *Barth. De P.R.* VII. lxix. (Bodl. MS.) fol. 73 b/2 With laxatyue medicens we laxeþ & vnbindeþ as with scamony. **1541** *Bk. Properties Herbs* E ij, Thys herbe..wyll vnbinde wormes in a mannes stomake.

6. *intr.* † **a.** To dissolve. *Obs.*⁻¹

c **1450** *M.E. Med. Bk.* (Heinrich) 220 Tak gomme of chyrytrees, or of plumtrees,..& put hyt in old wyn forto onbynde.

b. To become loosened.

1827 Keble *Chr. Year* St. Peter xvi, Touch'd he upstarts —his chains unbind.

Hence **un'binder**, one who unbinds.

1837 Lytton *Athens* II. 17 Bacchus,..the God of the Vineyard and the 'Unbinder of galling cares'.

un'binding, *vbl. sb.* [f. prec. + -ing¹.] The action of the verb in various senses.

1382 Wyclif *Prol. Bible* ii. 3 In the tyme of Antecrist, and of vnbyndyng of Sathanas. **1382** —— *1 Cor.* vii. 27 Thou art boundyn to a wyf, nyle thou seke vnbyndyng. c **1400** tr. *Secreta Secret., Gov. Lordsh.* 101 But it nedys be doon with consideracion..yn byndynge, & vnbyndynge. **1598** Florio, *Stralciamenti*, vntanglings, vnbindings, vntyings. **1641** Milton *Animadv.* 52 There comes another strange Gardener that..challenges as his right the binding or unbinding of every flower. **1875** Poste *Gaius* III. (ed. 2) 443 Nothing more natural than the likeness of the means of binding and of unbinding.

un'binding, *ppl. a.*¹ [un-¹ 10.] Not binding; *esp.* having no binding force, invalid.

1652 *Persuasive to Compliance* 14 Rules..unbinding to the Parliament. **1803** in *Spirit Publ. Jrnls.* VII. 189 Assurances of the most satisfactory and yet unbinding nature. **1846** M'Gee *Gallery Irish Writers* 121 He published a treatise against the proceedings of the nuncio as uncanonical and unbinding. **1853** Kane *Grinnell Exp.* xxx. (1856) 263 It is drawn on like the shirt, and, except at the neck, is perfectly loose and unbinding.

un'binding, *ppl. a.*² [f. unbind *v.*] Loosening, dissolving.

1791 Cowper *Yardley Oak* 78 a (MS.), All-binding frost and all unbinding thaw.

unbio'logical, *a.* [un-¹ 7 a.] **a.** Not in accord with the findings of biology. **b.** Not such as occurs in the course of nature, as studied in biology.

1934 *Mind* XLIII. 519 Positivism and Kantianism were pre-evolutionary and unbiological. **1950** [see stereotyped *ppl. a.* c]. **1977** P. Johnson *Enemies of Society* xv. 197 Many of the central ideas of psychoanalysis are profoundly unbiological.

un'birdlimed, *ppl. a.* (un-¹ 8 and un-² 8.)

1800 Coleridge in Campbell *Life* (1894) vi. 112 If God grant me health, I shall have my wings wholly unbirdlimed.

un'birdly, *a.* [un-¹ 7.] Unlike a bird; not maintaining the character of a bird.

a **1667** Cowley *Verses & Ess., Ode upon Liberty* iii, None so degenerous and unbirdly prove,..None but a few unhappy Houshold Foul. [**1834** K. H. Digby *Mores Cath.* v. vi. 185 If we would not degenerate below our species, and even unbirdly prove, we should rise to salute the dawn.]

un'birsed, *ppl. a.* *north.* and *Sc.* [un-¹ 8.] Unbruised.

1435 Misyn *Fire of Love* II. vi. 82 Goddis holy lufar in cristis name onbyrsyd & als [it] wer without stryfe gladynde. **15..** *Christ's Kirk* xv. (Bann. MS.), He come hame with vnbirsd banis, Quhair fechtaris wer mischevit.

un'birthday. (un-¹ 12 b.)

1871 'L. Carroll' *Through Looking-Glass* vi, 'What *is* an un-birthday present?' 'A present given when it isn't your birthday, of course.' **1930** W. de la Mare *On the Edge* 272 'Have you one really simple, lovely..trinket suitable for a lady?..An un-birthday present?' **1977** *Lancet* 2 July 31/2 A friend who has come to the front door, unexpectedly bearing a small unbirthday present.

un'bishop, *v.* [un-² 6 b and 4.]

1. *trans.* To deprive of the office of bishop.

1598 Florio, *Smetriare*, to vnmytre, to vnbishop, to degrade from a mytre. **1628** in *Cosin's Corr.* (Surtees) I. 153 You in the north, I in the south, are the object of toungs and penns, and I must be unbishop't a-geyne. **1657** TRAPP *Comm. Job* xxxi. 30 The one died ere he came home, and the other was unbishoped. **1691** GRASCOMBE *Reply Vind. Disc. Unreasonableness New Separation* 11/2 It was in their power to take away our Orders, and Unpriest and Unbishop us. *refl.* **1641** MILTON *Reform.* I. Wks. 1851 III. 11 When he steps up into the Chayre of Pontificall Pride,..then he degrades, then he un-Bishops himselfe. **1680** *Spirit of Popery* 15 By which he did really unbishop himself.

2. To deprive (a place) of a bishop. *rare*$^{-1}$.

a **1661** FULLER *Worthies, Glouc.* I. (1662) 368 Some questioned its Charter, and would have had it Un-Citied, because Un-Bishoped in our Civil Wars.

Hence **un'bishop(p)ing** *vbl. sb.*

1636 PRYNNE (*title*), The Vnbishoping of Timothy and Titvs. **1641** *Lords Spiritual* 7 That this un-bishoping intends onely the losse of his Barony and place in Parliament. **1711-2** M. HENRY *Life P. Henry* vii. Wks. 1853 II. 691/2 Much was said, *pro* and *con*, touching..the bishoping and unbishoping of Timothy and Titus [etc.].

un'bishoply, *a.* (UN-^{1} 7.)

1865 RUSKIN *Sesame* i. §22 The most unbishoply character a man can have is therefore to be Blind. **1876** FREEMAN *Norm. Conq.* V. xxv. 576 After the days of the unbishoply Ulf had passed away.

un'bishop(p)ed, *ppl. a.*^{1} Also 5 *Sc.* wnbyschoppyt. [UN-^{1} 8.]

1. Not blessed or confirmed by a bishop.

a **970** *Canons Edgar* c. 15 And we lærað..þæt ænig man to lange unbiscopod ne wurðe. *a* **1023** WULFSTAN *Hom.* (1883) 120 We lærað, þæt man ænigne ne læte unbiscpod [*v.r.* unbiscopod] to lange. *a* **1225** *Ancr. R.* 208 Al so as..longe beon unbishoped, & falsliche igon to schrifte. *c* **1470** HENRY *Wallace* VII. 549 Wnbyschoppyt ȝeit, for suth I trow ye be; Your selff sall fyrst his blyssyng tak for me. [**1844** LINGARD *Anglo-Sax. Ch.* (1858) I. vii. 298 *note*, That no man remain unbishoped too long.]

2. Not consecrated as a bishop.

1601 F. GODWIN *Bps. of Eng.* 373 Much against his will he died vnbishopped twelue daies after his nomination.

un'bishop(p)ed, *ppl. a.*^{2} [UN-^{2} 8, or f. UNBISHOP *v.*] Deprived of the status of a bishop.

1563 FOXE *A. & M.* 1353/1 Shaxton byshop of Salisburye resigned also with him his bishoprick. And so these two remained a great space vnbishopped. **1607** HARINGTON *Nugæ Ant.* (1804) II. 32 Once I thought to have sayd somwhat of Bonner, because I may remember him living in the late Queens tyme unbishopped. **1666** SOUTH *Dolben Consecr. Serm.* 2, I must profess that I cannot look upon Titus as so far Vnbishopt yet but that he still exhibits to us all the Essentials of that Jurisdiction.

un'bit, *ppl. a.* (UN-^{1} 8 b.)

1742 YOUNG *Nt. Th.* IV. 108 Some avocation deeming it—to die; Unbit by rage canine of dying rich.

un'bit, *v.* [UN-^{2} 4 b.] *trans.* To free (a horse) from the bit. Also *absol.*

1565-6 BLUNDEVIL *Horsemanship* IV. lxx. (1580) 29 b, Then vnbitte him, and if it bee in Winter, offer him a hande full of Wheaten strawe. **1639** T. DE GRAY *Expert Farrier* 116 Let him stand upon his trench foure or five houres,..then unbit him, and give him sweet hay. **1662** J. DAVIES tr. *Olearius' Voy. Ambass.* 228 We were told the Herb of it is..venemous,..upon which accompt it was, that we durst not unbit that day. **1775** S. J. PRATT *Liberal Opin.* cxi. (1783) IV. 51 Jack Bookwit..unbitted his horse.

un'bitt, *v.* [UN-^{2} 3.] *trans.* To uncoil or unfasten (a cable) from the bitts. Also *absol.*

1769 FALCONER *Dict. Marine* (1780), *Unbitting*, the operation of removing the turns of a cable from off the bits. *Ibid.*, *Débitter le cable*, to unbit the cable. *a* **1860** H. STUART *Seaman's Catech.* 54 It is used for stoppering the cable, when bitting or unbitting. **1883** *Man. Seamanship for Boys* 189 A..Blake's stopper..is used for stoppering the cable to bitt or unbitt it.

Hence **un'bitted** *ppl. a.*^{1}

1864 *Daily Tel.* 25 Feb., In what particular the public money is running through Admiralty hawse-pipes like an unbitted cable.

un'bitted, *ppl. a.*^{2} [UN-^{1} 8.] Not furnished with a bit; unbridled, unrestrained. Also *fig.*

a **1586** SIDNEY *Astr. & Stella* Sonn. xxxviii, This night while..vnbitted thought Doth fall to stray. **1604** SHAKS. *Oth.* I. iii. 335 We haue Reason to coole our raging Motions, our carnall Stings, or vnbitted Lusts. **1628** FELTHAM *Resolves* II. xciii. 270 A limitlesse tongue is a strange vnbitted Beast, to worry one with. **1826** MRS. SHELLEY *Last Man* II. 248 Like a troop of unbitted steeds. **1882** STEVENSON *Mem. & Portr.* xii. (1887) 211 The same fatal conflicts of unbitted nature with too rigid custom.

un'bitten, *ppl. a.* (UN-^{1} 8 b.)

1796 W. H. MARSHALL *Rur. Econ. W. England* II. 204 Instance of unbitten aftergrass.

un'blacked, *ppl. a.* (UN-^{1} 8.)

1836 *Hood's Comic Ann.* 80 So like Othello, with his face unblack'd. **1887** T. HARDY *Woodlanders* II. viii. 143 He..had sometimes been..seen on Sundays with unblacked boots.

un'blackened, *ppl. a.* (UN-^{1} 8.)

1864 *Lond. Rev.* 28 May 563 A fair spring day, with the young green of the trees still unscorched by sun and unblackened by smoke. **1867** M. ARNOLD *Epil. to Lessing's Laocoon*, The grass had still the green of May, And still the unblacken'd elms were gay.

un'blade, *v.* [UN-^{2} 6 b.] *trans.* To divest of the character of a blade or ruffian.

1633 SHIRLEY *Gamester* v. i, I shall take it as a favour too If, for the same price that you made him valiant, You will unblade him.

un'blameable, un'blamable, *a.* [UN-^{1} 7 b.] Blameless, irreproachable.

1531 TINDALE *Exp. 1 John* (1537) 100 A man of maruaylous integrete and vnblameable. **1579** W. WILKINSON *Confut. Fam. Love* Ep. Ded. *iij b, [They] would fayne in lyfe seeme innocent and vnblameable. **1612** T. TAYLOR *Comm. Titus* i. 6 (1619) 93 *margin*, The most commendable conformitie is to ioyne to vncorrupt doctrine an vnblameable life. **1693** *Apol. Clergy Scot.* 15, I know not a more unblamable Company of men upon Earth than the Episcopal Clergy of Scotland. **1738** WARBURTON *Div. Legat.* I. v. I. 72 His Followers, whom their very Enemies acknowledged to be unblameable in their actions. **1781** COWPER *Hope* 622 If, unblameable in word and thought, A *man* arise. **1840** CARLYLE *Heroes* iv. 230 That Scotland would forgive him [Knox] for having been worth to it any million 'unblamable' Scotchmen that need no forgiveness!

Hence **un'blam(e)ableness.**

1638 BP. REYNOLDS *Serm. 12 July* 42 Piety and unblameablenesse of living. *a* **1661** FULLER *Worthies, Lanc.* II. (1662) 107 Elizabeths unblameableness,..the Canaanitish Womans faith, Mary Magdalens charity. **1698** KILLINGBECK *Serm.* (1717) 23 The Integrity of his Heart, and the Unblamableness of his Life.

un'blameably, un'blamably, *adv.* [UN-^{1} 11.] Blamelessly, irreproachably.

1539 BIBLE (Great) *1 Thess.* ii. 10 Ye are witnesses..how holyly and iustly and vnblameably we behaued ourselues. **1612** T. TAYLOR *Comm. Titus* ii. 7 It is possible for a man by grace to liue vnblameably. **1650** JER. TAYLOR *Holy Living* I. iii. 33 It is a great..ingagement to do unblameably, when we act before that Judge, who is infallible in his sentence. **1712** ADDISON *Spect.* No. 343 ¶4 From that time forth I lived so very unblameably, that I was made President of a College of Brachmans. **1883** F. D. HUNTINGTON in J. G. Butler *Bible-Work* (1887) II. 266 Even in these self-seeking earthly streets the Christian is to walk unselfishly and unblamably.

un'blamed, *ppl. a.* [UN-^{1} 8. Cf. MDu. *ongeblaemt.*] Not found fault with; uncensured.

14.. *Love-Longing* in *Rel. Ant.* I. 71 Wo worth hope unblamyd! **1570** LEVINS *Manip.* 50 Vnblamed, *inculpatus.* **1596** SPENSER *F.Q.* VI. ii. 43 Ioying together in vnblam'd delight. **1603** B. JONSON *Sejanus* II. iv, They that durst to strike At so exampless, and unblamed a life. **1651** STANLEY *Poems, Moschus* 42 Before unblam'd Europa's feet he stood. **1700** DRYDEN *Flower & Leaf* 513 And all her Train with leavy Chaplets crown'd Were for unblam'd Virginity renown'd. **1725** POPE *Odyss.* I. 207 Unblam'd abundance crown'd the royal board. **1767** SIR W. JONES *Seven Fountains* Poems (1777) 38 Say, gentle damsel, may I ask unblam'd, How this gay isle, and splendid seats are nam'd? **1840** CARLYLE *Heroes* vi. 359 Now he was, there as he stood recognised unblamed, the virtual King of England. **1876** GEO. ELIOT *Dan. Der.* lxii, The bright, unblamed young fellow.

† **un'blameful**, *a. Obs.*$^{-1}$ [UN-^{1} 7.] Blameless. So † **un'blamefully** *adv.*

c **1400** *Apol. Loll.* 17 Þe kirk may not do it iustli, ne vnblamfully. **1570** LEVINS *Manip.* 186 Vnblameful, *inculpabilis.*

un'blanched, *ppl. a.* [UN-^{1} 8.] Not bleached.

a **1420** *Liber Cocorum* (1862) 11 Take almondes unblanchyd, wasshe hom and grynd. **1598** *Epulario* D j, Take a pound and a half of Almonds vnblanched. **1658** A. FOX *Würtz' Surg., Children's Bk.* 342 Course unblanched linnen. **1725** *Fam. Dict.* s.v. *Sallet*, With unblanch'd Endive, Succory and Purslane. **1842** LOUDON *Suburban Hort.* 677 The points of the unblanched leaves are used to flavour soups.

† **un'blanked**, *ppl. a. Obs.*$^{-1}$ [UN-^{1} 8 + BLANK *v.* 2.] Not disconcerted or silenced.

1570 FOXE *A. & M.* (ed. 2) I. 753/1 Yet was ther none of al those that interrupted him which scaped vnblanckt, but he brought them all to confusion.

un'blasted, *ppl. a.* (UN-^{1} 8.)

1589 WARNER *Alb. Eng.* v. xxiii. (1592) 102 We here a blisfull Vintage gayne, That..euermore vnblasted may remaine. **1612** PEACHAM *Minerva Brit.* 209 Th' vnblasted bay, to conquests due. **1742** YOUNG *Nt. Th.* III. 79 Those Few our noxious Fate unblasted leaves In this inclement Clime of human Life. **1819** BYRON *Proph. Dante* I. 16 Midst whom..Beatrice..led the mortal guest, Unblasted by the glory, though he trod From star to star.

un'blazoned, *ppl. a.* (UN-^{1} 8.)

[**1775** ASH.] **1830** W. COBBETT *Rur. Rides* (1853) 578 The memory of the virtuous Catharine is unblazoned. **1859** TENNYSON *Elaine* 378 When Lavaine Returning brought the yet-unblazon'd shield.

un'bleached, *ppl. a.* [UN-^{1} 8. Cf. MDu. and Du. *ongebleekt*, G. *ungebleicht*, Sw. *oblekt*, Da. *ubleget*, *-blegt.*] Not bleached. Also *ellipt.*

1531-2 *Durham Househ. Bk.* (Surtees) 68 Et in 15½ ulnis unbleched emptis. **1570** *Wills & Inv. N.C.* (Surtees, 1835) 337 Thre peces of vnbleched lynne xxx^{s}. **1648** HEXHAM II, *Ongebleyckt lijnwaedt*, Vnbleached linen. **1756** F. HOME *Exper. Bleaching* 182 Into this mixture the same quantity of the same unbleached cloth was put. **1842** MRS. CARLYLE *Lett.* (1883) I. 175 Mr. Byng..was dressed from head to foot in unbleached linen. **1880** *Plain Hints Needlework* 79 In the North,..unbleached diaper can be procured.

transf. and *fig.* **1815** JANE AUSTEN *Emma* lv, The stain of illegitimacy, unbleached by nobility or wealth, would have been a stain indeed. **1865** *Slang Dict.* 264 *Unbleached American*, the new Yankee term for coloured natives of the United States.

un'bleaching, *ppl. a.* (UN-^{1} 10.)

1812 BYRON *Ch. Har.* I. lxxxviii, Let their bleach'd bones, and blood's unbleaching stain, Long mark the battle-field with hideous awe.

† **un'blecked**, *ppl. a. Obs.* [UN-^{1} 8.] Unstained.

c **1380** WYCLIF *Wks.* (1880) 129 Þis is clene religion..to kepe hym self vnblekkid and defoulid fro þis world. *Ibid.* 211 Ypocritis of feyned religion..kepe not hem self vnbleckid fro þis world. **1535** STEWART *Cron. Scot.* (Rolls) III. 130 Syne efter that this ladie he did wed.., Quhilk..Martha.. In all hir tyme wnblekkit wes with blame.

un'bled, *ppl. a.* (UN-^{1} 8 b.)

1835 SANGRADO (*title*), The Great Unbled. An Allegorical Tale.

un'bleeding, *ppl. a.* (UN-^{1} 10.)

a **1619** DANIEL *To Sir T. Egerton* v. in *Panegyrike*, etc. (1623) 50 Making as deepe, although unbleeding wounds. **1812** BYRON *Ch. Har.* I. xci, To..mix unbleeding with the boasted slain.

un'blemishable, *a.* (UN-^{1} 7 b.)

1607 DEKKER *Knt.'s Conjur.* (1842) 69 It went away chaste and vnblemishable. **1625** *Modell Wit* 67 Her inhærent vnblemishable vertue and honor. **1651** W. JANE *Image Unbroken* 229 A sobrietie vnblemishable by a Traytours malice. **1720** WELTON *Suffer. Son of God* II. xiv. 369 So Pure and Unblemishable was His conversation, that He defied His Enemies to convince Him of any sin. **1875** MYERS *Poems* 98 Her sweet unblemishable soul.

un'blemished, *ppl. a.* Forms: (see BLEMISH *v.*). [UN-^{1} 8.]

1. Free from moral blemish or stain: **a.** Of persons. Also *absol.*

13.. *E.E. Allit. P.* A. 782 Vnblemyst I am wyth-outen blot. **1626** QUARLES *Feast for Worms* 1594 His Spouse is chaste, vnblemisht with a spot. **1646** CRASHAW *Sospetto d'Herode* xxiv, The unblemisht Lambe, blessed for ever, Should take the marke of sin, and paine of sence. **1711** POPE *Temp. Fame* 523 Unblemish'd let me live, or die unknown! **1784** COWPER *Task* III. 83 'Twas..an wholesome rigour in the main, And taught th' unblemish'd to preserve with care That purity, whose loss was loss of all. **1800** *Misc. Tr.* in *Asiat. Ann. Reg.* 58/2 Fines are enacted for abandoning an unblemished girl, and forgiving a blemished damsel. **1870** BRYANT *Iliad* VI. I. 194 Priam's sons in law And their unblemished consorts.

b. Of honour, name, character, etc.

1432 *Paston Lett.* I. 35 The said Erle..desired, and ever shal, to kepe his trouthe and worship unblemysshed. *a* **1475** ASHBY *Dicta Philos.* 1155 Thus ye shul..come to grete glory and noble fame Thurgh your goode liffe & vnblemyshed name. **1634** MILTON *Comus* 215 O welcom pure-ey'd Faith, ..And thou unblemish't form of Chastity. **1670** PETTUS *Fodinæ Reg.* 45 They must be Men of upright and unblemisht Lives and Conversations. **1738** WARBURTON *Div. Legat.* II. iv. I. 139 He should be of an unblemished and virtuous Character. **1779** *Mirror* No. 33, I am now in affluent circumstances, and I have reason to think that I am so with an unblemished character. **1823** SCOTT *Quentin D.* xviii, For the unblemished faith and unfaded honour of Scotland. **1855** MACAULAY *Hist. Eng.* xix. IV. 387 All the authority which belongs to unblemished integrity.

2. Not substantially or materially blemished or impaired.

c **1450** *St. Cuthbert* (Surtees) 6802 Þe text of wangels fell in þe water... Þe text was foun vnblemyst þare. *c* **1460** FORTESCUE *Abs. & Lim. Mon.* vii. (1885) 125 For be this meane þe kynges estate shall alwey be kept vnblemyshed. *a* **1500** in *Arnolde's Chron.* (1811) 19 So that all the forsayd citezens of London..haue alle the frauncheses of the wareyn and forest vnblemyssyd. **1596** SPENSER *F.Q.* v. xi. 62 What foule disgrace is this,..To blot your beautie that vnblemisht is? **1598** HAKLUYT *Voy.* I. 618 The religious houses only being spared, and left vnblemished. **1625** QUARLES *Sion's Sonn.* xvii. 3 His eyes are..Vnblemisht, vndistayned with a spot. **1883** SCHAFF *Encycl. Relig. Knowl.* 2365 The tenth one [of cattle, etc.] being set apart, no matter whether it were bad or good, blemished or unblemished.

Hence **un'blemishedness.**

1656 JEANES *Fuln. Christ* 239 The unblemishednesse required in all the Priests, that ministered in the sanctuary. **1680** H. MORE *Apocal. Apoc.* 58 After a due search into their Pedigree, and the unblemishedness of their body. **1681-6** J. SCOTT *Chr. Life* (1747) III. 148 The Necessity of a moral Cleanness and Unblemishedness.

un'blemishing, *ppl. a.* (UN-^{1} 10.)

1661 FELTHAM *Serm. Luke xiv. 20* in *Resolves*, etc. (ed. 8) 392 If at most they leave a Mote behind, it is but dead, and with the next fair wind unblemishing blowes away.

un'blenched, *ppl. a.* [UN-^{1} 8.]

1. Not blenched or turned aside; undismayed, unflinching.

1634 MILTON *Comus* 430 Yea there, where very desolation dwels,..She may pass on with unblench't majesty. **1839** HALLAM *Hist. Lit.* (1855) IV. 101 His eye roams unblenched in the light, before which that of Pascal had been veiled in awe. **1863** IS. WILLIAMS *Baptistery* II. xxiv. (1874) 90 He who seem'd an unblench'd eye to bear. **1876** BANCROFT *Hist. U.S.* IV. xxiv. 494 Wesley's mental constitution was not robust enough to gaze on the future with unblenched calm.

2. Unstained, untarnished.

Perh. vaguely associated with BLENCH *v.*^{2}

1813 COLERIDGE *Night-Scene* 66, I swore to her, that were she red with guilt, I would exchange my unblenched state with hers. **1815** — *Zapolya, Prelude* i. 286 Let the Queen Dowager, with unblench'd honours, Resume her state.

un'blenching, *ppl. a.* (UN-^{1} 10.)

[**1828** WEBSTER.] **1837** R. NICOLL *Poems* (1842) 132 The Poor and Honest Man can stand, With an unblenching brow, Before Earth's highest. **1843** PRESCOTT *Mexico* v. iii. (1864) 293 He looked with an unblenching eye on his past reverses. **1898** WATTS-DUNTON *Aylwin* II. iv, So different from the unblenching child who loved to stand hatless!

un'blenchingly, *adv.* (UN-^{1} 11.)

1864 E. SARGENT *Peculiar* I. 27 Mrs. Charlton..looked him unblenchingly in the face. **1885** *Athenæum* 3 Jan. 8/3 He takes his death as the English hero should take death, unblenchingly.

un'blendable, *a.* (UN-1 7 b.)

1716 M. DAVIES *Athen. Brit.* III. 67 The Romists value themselves to an unblendable Obstinancy, upon such pretended Superiority of Parts and Performances.

un'blended, *ppl. a.* (UN-1 8.)

c **1340** HAMPOLE *Prose Tr.* 8 Thay hafe othyr vertus vnblendide with þe fylthe of syne and vnclene luste. **1611** FLORIO, *Immescolato*, vnmingled, vnblended. **1624** QUARLES *Job* vi. 31 The Hiue No hony yeelds, vnblended with the Wax. **1661** GLANVILL *Van. Dogm.* vii. 65 It dwels no where in unblended proportions on this side the Empyreum. **1795** ANNA SEWARD *Lett.* (1811) IV. 108 Her lilies and roses are exchanged for the unblended flush of sun-burnt health. **1820** SHELLEY *Arethusa* iii, Behind her descended Her billows, unblended With the brackish Dorian stream. **1887** MORRIS *Odyss.* IX. 204 The drink of the Gods, unblended sweet wine, for me did he pour Into twelve fulfilled pitchers.

un'blent, *ppl. a.* (UN-1 8 b.)

1835 *Court Mag.* VI. 229/1 Nothing could exceed the distortion of those naturally large and unblent lineaments. **1882** *Good Literature* 8 Apr., Born of the old Puritan stock, unblent with other strains.

un'bless, *v.* [UN-2 3.] *trans.* To deprive of a blessing or of happiness.

1600 SHAKS. *Sonn.* iii. 4 That face should forme an other, Whose fresh repaire if now thou not renewest, Thou doo'st beguile the world, vnblesse some mother. **1631** QUARLES *Samson* Wks. (Grosart) II. 149/1 Too great excesse Makes Ioy a Madnesse, and does quite unblesse So sweet a gift. **1641** M. FRANK *Serm., Annunc.* (1672) 319 Because they bless her too much, these unbless her quite.

un'blessed, un'blest, *ppl. a.* Forms: (see BLESS *v.*). [UN-1 8.]

1. Not formally blessed or consecrated.

c **1310** in Horstm. *Altengl. Leg.* (1881) 231 Þer ich finde a wiif þat liȝter is of barn, .. ȝif it be vnblisced, y croke it fot or arm. **1340** *Ayenb.* 41 Huanne me stelþ .. be kueade skele out of holy stede yblissede þinges oþer onblissede, huet þet hit by. *c* **1530** MORE *Answ. Frith* Wks. 842/2 Whether the blessed sacrament be consecrate or vnconsecrate,.. [he] biddeth care not but take it for all that vnblessed as it is. **1546** *Wyclif's Wycket* A viij, Ye gyve vs after the breade wyne and water, and sometymes clene water vnblessed rather coniured.

b. Deprived of, excluded from, left without, a blessing or benediction.

1590 SPENSER *F.Q.* I. ix. 54 He chose an halter from among the rest, And with it hung himselfe, vnbid vnblest. **1633** BP. HALL *Contempl., N.T.* IV. xii, 'Ungirt, unblessed,' was the old word; as not ready till they were girded. **1687** DRYDEN *Hind & P.* III. 637 He breath'd his last, exposed to open air, And there his corps, unbless'd, is hanging still. **1757** GRAY *Bard* 102 Stay, oh stay! nor thus forlorn Leave me unbless'd, unpitied, here to mourn. **1783** CRABBE *Village* I. 346 The crowd retire distress'd, To think a poor man's bones should lie unbless'd. **1818** BYRON *Ch. Har.* IV. lxviii, Pass not unblest the Genius of the place! **1847** H. BUSHNELL *Chr. Nurt.* II. ii, This always unblessed, tedious look of sanctimony.

2. Not blessed in fortune or lot; unfortunate, wretched, miserable.

1340–70 *Alex. & Dind.* 1124 ȝe ben vn-blessed of lif, for .. þat ȝe holden so her holsome dedes Gret wante is of wo & wikkede paine. *c* **1375** *Cursor M.* 13108 (Fairf.), Þat man salle vn-blessed be þe quilk trawes noȝt in me. *c* **1400** *Laud Troy Bk.* 5883 That day the Troyens were glad... But Ector was that day vnblessed, Off grace certes that day he myssed. *c* **1450** *Myrr. our Ladye* 220 O moste blyssed of women, socoure vs vnblyssed synners. **1592** WARNER *Alb. Eng.* VII. xxxvii. 166 What might remaine but death for me that liued so vnblest? **1604** SHAKS. *Oth.* V. i. 34 Minion, your deere lyes dead, And your vnblest Fate highes. **1649** MILTON *Eikon.* ix. 79 That unblest expedition to the Jle of Rhee. **1675** HOBBES *Odyssey* (1677) 25 Unblest Ulysses, who at Ilium Together with you fought. *a* **1721** PRIOR *Fortune-Teller* 27 What matters, if unblest in love, How long or short my life will prove? **1798** *Monthly Mag.* IV. 48 Unchang'd, eternal be your misery. I rule you, and am only more unblest. **1848** BAILEY *Festus* (ed. 3) 169 Which is more unblest Whose love is shunned or sought let time attest! **1865** DICKENS *Mut. Fr.* III. i, Gaslights flared in the shops with a haggard and unblest air.

absol. **1814** WORDSW. *Excurs.* II. 596 That poor Man taken hence to-day .. must be deemed, I fear, Of the unblest.

3. Unhallowed, unholy; wicked, evil, malignant.

1388 WYCLIF *Ecclus.* xxvii. 24 To schewe opynli the pryuytees of a frend, is dispeir of a soule vnblessid. **1426** AUDELAY *Poems* (Percy Soc.) 15 We were put in paradise to have wele withoutyn woo Hent we had unblest brokyn the commaundmentis of our Kyng. *c* **1450** *Mirk's Festial* 219 Then sayde Laurens: 'Vnblessyd, þes tormentys I haue ȝore desyred'. *c* **1520** SKELTON *Magnyf.* 134 If Lyberte sholde lepe and renne where he lyst, It were no vertue, it were a thynge vnblyst. **1591** SPENSER *M. Hubberd* 915 For none but such as this bold Ape vnblest Can euer thriue in that vnluckie quest. **1610** BP. CARLETON *Jurisd.* 71 This vnblessed deuise of forgerie, being attempted in a number of decretall Epistles. **1667** MILTON *P.L.* I. 238 Such resting found the sole Of unblest feet. **1697** DRYDEN *Virg. Georg.* I. 229 Oats unblest, and Darnel domineers, And shoots its head above the shining Ears. **1761** GRAY *Odin* 35 Who is he, with voice unblest, That calls me from the bed of rest? **1793** HOLCROFT *Lavater's Physiog.* i. 11 Wilt thou teach man the unblessed art of judging his brother by the ambiguous expressions of his countenance? **1800** COLERIDGE *Christabel* II. 529, I had vowed with music loud To clear yon wood from thing unblest. **1837** CARLYLE *Fr. Rev.* II. v. v, Why were not [they] .. in their beds, that unblessed Varennes Night! **1840** —— *Heroes* v. 304 The world .. can either have it as blessed continuous summer-sunshine, or as unblessed black thunder and tornado.

4. Not favoured or made happy *by* or *with* something.

1743 FRANCIS tr. *Hor., Odes* I. xx. 15 My meagre Cup's unblest With the rich Formian, or Falernian Vine. **1795** CAMPBELL *Elegy* 13 The cloudy heavens unblest by summer's smile. **1844** H. G. ROBINSON *Odes of Horace* I. xxxi, Nor let me an old age prolong, Unhonour'd or unblest by song. **1848** W. H. KELLY tr. *L. Blanc's Hist. Ten Y.* II. 269 Lyons was plunged into a silence, unblessed with repose.

Hence **un'blessedness**.

1549 COVERDALE, etc. *Erasm. Par. Rev.* xix. 32 An euerlasting supper of al bitternes & vnblessednes wherof they maye eate and be partakers altogether. **1836** T. HOOK *G. Gurney* I. 141 Without having changed her state of single-unblessedness. **1881** BRUCE *Chief End Rev.* vi. 302 The grace of God is represented as finding men in a state of serious moral corruption and consequent unblessedness.

un'blessing, *ppl. a.* (UN-1 10.)

1760–72 H. BROOKE *Fool of Qual.* (1809) IV. 11 All the .. fond relations .. must ever have remained, unblessing and as dead. **1842** GEO. ELIOT in Cross *Life* (1885) I. 116, I .. have thought .. my life the shallowest, muddiest, most unblessing stream.

† **un'blestful**, *a. Obs.*−1 [UN-1 7.] = UNBLESSED *ppl. a.* 2.

1608 SYLVESTER *Du Bartas* III. II. iv. *Schisme* 417 Th' unsavory breath of Serpents crawling o're The Lybians pest-full and un-blest-full shore.

un'blighted, *ppl. a.* (UN-1 8.)

1784 COWPER *Task* IV. 334 In such a world; so thorny, and where none Finds happiness unblighted. **1792** CHARLOTTE SMITH *Desmond* II. 217 That world which has, at your age, and with your unblighted prospects, so many charms. **1827** LYTTON *Falkland* 233 She went to that last home with a blest and unblighted name. **1861** H. MACMILLAN *Footnotes Page Nat.* 34 Though subjected to the scorching rays of the summer's sun, they [*sc.* mosses] continue green and unblighted.

Hence **un'blightedly** *adv.*

[**1847** WEBSTER.] **1871** B. TAYLOR *Faust* V. vi. 373 Roses .. Branching unblightedly, Budding delightedly.

un'blind, *a.* (UN-1 7.)

1818 KEATS *Visit Burns's Country* 48 That he may .. keep his vision clear from speck, his inward sight unblind.

un'blind, *v.* [UN-2 3. Cf. Du. *ontblinden.*]

1. *trans.* To free from blindness.

In some instances implying sense 2.

1598 MARLOWE & CHAPMAN *Hero & Leander* III. 365 We know not how to vow, till loue vnblinde vs. **1605** SYLVESTER *Miracle of Peace* xxiv, Unblinde thy blinde soule, ope thine inward sight. **1681** RYCAUT tr. *Gracian's Critick* 202 How well is my innocency .. rewarded, wherewith I desire to unblind the World.

2. = UNBLINDFOLD *v.*

1590 R. W[ILSON] *Three Lords & Ladies Lond.* I. I iij b, Wel one day he wil pay for all. Vnblind Simplicity. **1608** ARMIN *Nest Ninn.* (1842) 20 They all shout aloud and cry rarely well done, and on unblindes him, while another puts the glove on the speare. **1632** BROME *Crt. Beggar* III. i, Here set him downe: unbind him and unblind him. **1655** tr. *Sorel's Com. Hist. Francion* IX. 16 Having unblinded him, they demanded of him, who did put him there?

un'blinded, *ppl. a.* [UN-1 8.]

1. Not blinded or deprived of sight.

1611 FLORIO, *Inorbato*,.. vnblinded. **1833** TENNYSON *Pal. Art* 42 Who shall gaze upon My palace with unblinded eyes?

2. *fig.* Not deluded or deceived.

1755 *Man* No. 20. 8 A man unblinded by prejudice, is not far from being a Christian. **1797** COLERIDGE *Let. to Cottle* 8 June, I speak with heartfelt sincerity and, I think, unblinded judgment. **1802–12** BENTHAM *Ration. Judic. Evid.* (1827) I. 287 A judgment unblinded by prejudice. **1871** RUSKIN *Fors Clav.* vii. 24 Learn .. how to obey good Men, who are living, breathing unblinded law.

un'blinded, *a.* [UN-1 9.] Not furnished with, or covered by, a window-blind.

1862 MRS. NORTON *Lady of La Garaye* IV. 113 The cold fine star That glitters through the unblinded window-pane. **1876** T. HARDY *Ethelberta* xlv, An unblinded window revealed inside it a room bright and warm.

un'blindfold, *v.* Also 5 vnblyndfelle, 6 vnblindefilde. [UN-2 4.] *trans.* To unbandage (the eyes); to free (a person or animal) from a bandage over the eyes. Also *fig.*

c **1430** *Pilgr. Lyf Manhode* IV. xix. (1869) 186 Þat þei vnblyndfelle so here eyen þat þei mown biholde to þe heuene. **1580** HOLLYBAND *Treas. Fr. Tong, Dessiller*, to vnwrappe his eies,.. to vnblindefilde. **1596** SPENSER *F.Q.* VI. vii. 33 He bad his eyes to be vnblindfold both, That he might see his men. **1607** MARKHAM *Cavel.* VIII. (1617) 28 You may blindfolde the horse and .. after vnblindfolde him. **1643** PRYNNE *Sov. Power Parl.* II. 79 Which I hope will fully unblindfold the hood-winkt world.

unblinking, *a.* (UN-1 10.)

1909 in WEBSTER. **1923** *Chambers's Jrnl.* 10 Nov. 791/1 John .. could see only the unblinking stars. **1965** G. MCINNES *Road to Gundagai* xvi. 283 The unblinking stare of the lizard on the sun-baked rock.

un'blinkingly, *adv.* (UN-1 11.)

1867 AUGUSTA WILSON *Vashti* v, Her large, brilliant eyes followed the sinking sun as steadily—as unblinkingly—as an eagle's. **1888** *Daily News* 7 Dec. 3/2 Until now he had looked none in the face. Now, however, he did it unblinkingly.

un'bliss. [UN-1 12. So OE. *unbliss.*] Lack of bliss; unhappiness.

a **1628** F. GREVIL *Poems, Inquisition upon Fame and Hon.* II. xix, So as between perfection, and unblisse, Man, out of man, will make himself a frame.

un'blissful, *a.* [UN-1 7.] Unhappy; destitute of bliss. Hence **un'blissfully** *adv.*

1340–70 *Alex. & Dind.* 543 To ȝoure souorain of sinne [ye] sacrifice maken Wiþ þat vnblisful blod þat þei bled hauen. **1382** WYCLIF *Prov.* xix. 26 Who tormentith the fader, and fleeth the modir, shenful shal be, and vnblisful [L. *infelix*]. **1833** TENNYSON *Dream Fair Wom.* xxi, From within me a clear under-tone Thrill'd thro' mine ears in that unblissful clime. **1849** C. BRONTË *Shirley* III. iv. 107 His whole nature seemed serenely alight: he stood .. musing not unblissfully. **1868** MORRIS *Earthly Par.* (1870) I. I. 149 Ah! soothly, well remembered Was that unblissful wretched home.

† **un'blithe**, *a. Obs.* Forms: (see UN-1 and BLITHE *a.*), = MDu. *onblide* (Kilian *-blijde*), OHG. *unblîdi*, *-plîdi* (MHG. *unblîde*), ON. and Icel. *ú-*, *óblíðr* (Sw. *oblid*, Da. *ublid*).] [OE. *unbliðe* (f. *un-* UN-1 7 + *bliðe* a.).]

1. Unhappy; sad, sorrowful; not delighted.

Beowulf 131 Mære þeoden .. unbliðe sæt, þolode ðryðswyð, þegnsorge dreah. *c* **897** K. ÆLFRED *Gregory's Past C.* xxvii. 187 Moniȝe beoð ðeah bliðe & eac unbliðe .. for ðæs blodes styringe. *c* **1000** ÆLFRIC *Saints' Lives* xxxiii. 348 Þa se abbod þis gehyrde þa wearð he swyðe unbliðe. *a* **1250** *Owl & Night.* 1585 Þe lauerd into þare þeode Fareþ ut .., An[d] is þat gode wif unbliþe For hire lauerdes houdsiþe. *a* **1300** *Cursor M.* 14867 Þai went þam ham, all þat sith, Bath wrath, waful, and vn-blith. **13..** *Gaw. & Gr. Knt.* 746 With mony bryddez vnblyþe vpon bare twyges, Þat pitosly þer piped for pyne of þe colde. *c* **1400** *Destr. Troy* 8029 For Bresaide the bright vnblithe was his chere. **1535** STEWART *Cron. Scot.* (Rolls) II. 272 So Columba tuik on him greit cuir And bissines, quhopis he wes wnblyth.

2. Of things: Unpleasant, disagreeable.

In OE. also of persons = showing displeasure.

c **1320** *Sir Tristr.* 240 As god wil, it schal be, Vnbliþe. **13..** *E.E. Allit. P.* B. 1017 Þer faure citees wern set, nov is a see called,.. Blo, blubrande, & blak, vnblyþe to neȝe. *a* **1400–50** *Alexander* 48 Þan was him bodword vnblyth broȝt to þe sale.

Hence † **un'blithely** *adv. Obs.*

1415 *Pol. Poems* (Rolls) II. 127 Many of hem her hertblode Unblythly bledden upon that bent.

un'block, *v.* [UN-2 3.]

1. *trans.* To free from an obstruction; to open up, to clear. Also *fig.*

1611 COTGR., *Desblouquer*, to vnblocke, or open the (blockt-vp) passages of. **1656** BAXTER *Reformed Pastor* 193 Our credit may do much to remove prejudice, and to unblock the entrance into mens minds. **1969** H. PERKIN *Key Profession* v. 186 Even that .. did not unblock the channels of advance. **1974** J. MANN *Sticking Place* ii. 30 She did not want to un-block drains or carry the dustbins.

2. *Cards.* To give free scope to (a partner's suit) by playing an unnecessarily high card. Also *absol.*

1885 'CAVENDISH' *Whist Developments* Pref. p. x, The cases where the leader's partner, when he does not head the trick, should play to unblock by retaining his lowest card (playing a higher one). **1899** MELROSE *Solo Whist* 12 This principle is known in whist as 'unblocking' partner's suit.

Hence **un'blocking** *vbl. sb.*

1885 'CAVENDISH' *Whist Developments* Pref. p. x, Hitherto it has been left to the ingenuity of individuals .. to decide when and how the unblocking should be done.

un'blocked, *ppl. a.* (UN-1 8 c.)

1662 GURNALL *Chr. in Arm.* III. 83 This River is unblockt up which makes glad the City of God.

un'blooded, *ppl. a.* [UN-1 8.]

1. = next 1.

[**1775** ASH.] **1784** COWPER *Task* V. 215 The shrew'd Contriver who first .. forced the blunt and yet unblooded [**1800** unbloodied] steel To a keen edge. **1818** MILMAN *Samor* 78 To Hela's realm, Unblooded, woundless, must the maid descend. **1831** SCOTT *Ct. Rob.* vii, As a man who dies in peace, and with unblooded hand.

2. Of an animal: 'Not marked or distinguished with improved blood'.

1860 WORCESTER (citing J. N. Brown).

un'bloodied, *ppl. a.* [UN-1 8.]

1. Not smeared or stained with blood.

1593 SHAKS. *2 Hen. VI*, III. ii. 193 Who finds the Partridge in the Puttocks Nest, But may imagine how the Bird was dead, Although the Kyte soare with vnbloudied Beake? **1791** HUDDESFORD *Salmag., Monody Death of Dick* 138 Within the tender velvet of his paw Tho' yet unbloodied lurks each virgin claw. **1825** SCOTT *Betrothed* xv, The spirit of the murdered person,.. if favourable,.. appears with a smiling aspect, and crosses them with her unbloodied hand. **1881** SWINBURNE *Mary Stuart* I. i. 29, I am sick with shame to hear men's jangling tongues Outnoise their swords unbloodied.

† **2.** = UNBLOODY *a.* 2 b. *Obs.*−1

1644 SIR E. DERING *Prop. Sacr.* 39 Your Sacrifice is ἀναίμακτος, *unbloudyed*.

un'bloodily, *adv.* Also 6 vnbloudely, 7 unbloudily. [UN-1 11.] In a bloodless manner; without shedding of blood. (Chiefly *Theol.*)

1548 GESTE *Pr. Masse* C vi b, Ye ones offering of christ neuer to be reuyued eyther .. bloudely or vnbloudely to purge our synnes withal. **1565** HARDING *Answ. M. Ivelles Chalenge* 145 The lambe of God being layed and sacrificed of priestes vnbloudely. **1624** GATAKER *Transubst.* 46 He saith, that Christs blood is offered in the Eucharist, unbloodily, or not as blood. **1670** C. GATAKER *Harmony Truth* 67 To beleive that the blood of Christ is really shed in the Sacrament unbloodily. **1749** WESLEY *Wks.* (1872) X. 120 In the sacrifice of the mass, the same Christ is contained, and unbloodily offered.

un'bloody, *a.* [UN-^{1} 7. So OE. *unblódiȝ* (once), = Du. *onbloedig*, G. *unblutig*, ON. *úblóðigr*, Da. *ublodig*, Sw. *oblodig*.]

1. Not attended with (much or any) bloodshed.

1544 BETHAM *Precepts War* I. cxciv. I v, Nothynge is more profytable,.. then by vnbloudye battayle to wynne the mastrye. **1553** BRENDE *Q. Curtius* IV. 47 b, There were slaine of the Percians and Arabies ten thousand, and the victorye was not vnblodye vnto the Macedones. **1607** TOPSELL *Four-f. Beasts* 88 The Spartanes.. esteemed more of an vnbloudy then a bloudy victory. **1654** R. CODRINGTON tr. *Iustine* v. 82 They fell not in a sluggish or an unbloody war, but fought to the last man. **1670** MILTON *Hist. Eng.* II. Wks. 1851 V. 64 Petilius Cerealis.. had to doe with the populous Brigantes in many Battails, and som of those, not unbloodie. **1870** BRYANT *Iliad* XVII. II. 177 The strife was not unbloody, though of Greeks There perished fewer.

2. Not involving the shedding of blood; not characterized by bloodshed.

1548 [see b]. **1577** HANMER *Anc. Eccl. Hist.* (1663) 201 The unbloody and spiritual Sacrifices of prayers. **1590** SWINBURNE *Testaments* 67 Verie likelie it is to bee vrged with more violent arguments.. then by the vnbloodie blowes of bare words. **1606** SYLVESTER *Du Bartas* II. iv. *Magnif.* 868 Here, many a Mars un-bloudy Combats fights. **1649** MILTON *Eikon.* ix. Wks. 1851 III. 402 Those many.. corporal inflictions wherwith his raign also before this Warr was not unbloodie. **1702** ECHARD *Eccl. Hist.* (1710) 26 Prohibiting the use of wine, and using only inanimate and unbloody sacrifices. *a* **1797** H. WALPOLE *Mem. Geo. II* (1822) I. 324 By the character of the age that disposition is systematized into little mischiefs and unbloody treacheries. **1858** FROUDE *Hist. Eng.* III. 154/2 *note,* The cause of the unbloody termination of the crisis was more creditable to the rebel leaders. **1899** CAPT. A. T. MAHAN *Lessons of War with Spain*, etc. (1900) iii. 106 Blockade.. is but one form of the unbloody pressure brought to bear upon an enemy by interruption of his commerce.

b. *Theol.* Used with reference to the eucharist, esp. in the phrase ***unbloody sacrifice.***

1548 GESTE *Pr. Masse* C vi b, Theyr auouching.. our synnes clerely to be clensed wyth theyr vnsufferable & vnbloudye sacryfyce of christ. **1599** BP. SCOTT in Strype *Ann. Ref.* (1709) I. App. x. 30 Manyfestly affirmynge Christe to be offered daylye after an unbloody manner. **1581** J. BELL *Haddon's Answ. Osor.* 432 That unbloudy Sacrifice of the body and bloud of Christ, which is dayly exequuted by so many handes of sacrificing shavelinges. **1620** BP. HALL *Hon. Marr. Clergy* Conclusion, I leave my refuter.. to the acting of his vnbloudie executions of the Sonne of God. **1651** C. CARTWRIGHT *Cert. Relig.* I. 71 S. Clem. Apost. calleth it a reasonable, unbloudy, and Mysticall Sacrament. **1712** P. METCALFE *Life St. Winefride* (1917) 23 Saint Beuno was preparing to offer the Unbloody Sacrifice of our Redemption. **1753** CHALLONER *Cath. Chr. Instr.* 81 In the Sacrifice of the Altar he [Christ] only dies mystically, and therefore this is an unbloody Sacrifice. **1833** J. WATERWORTH tr. *Veron's Rule Cath. Faith* 127 In this divine sacrifice.. the same Christ is present and offered in an unbloody manner, who.. offered himself in a bloody manner. **1860** PUSEY *Min. Proph.* 595 To Malachi alone it was reserved to prophesy of the unbloody Sacrifice.

3. Not covered or smeared with blood. ***unbloody grave,*** that of one who has not died by bloodshed.

a **1590** *1st Pt. Contention* E 3, Although the kyte soare with unbloodie beake. *a* **1699** J. BEAUMONT *Psyche* XVI. xciv, Prayers and Persuasions her Engins be, Prepared pure unbloody Bays to gain. **1733** [see UNBRIBED]. **1819** SCOTT *Leg. Montrose* xiv, You might yet lay your head on an unbloody pillow to-night. **1829** —— *Anne of G.* xx, As thou desirest to sleep in an unbloody grave, let me warn thee, that the secrets of this night shall remain with thee.

†**4.** Having no blood; bloodless. *Obs.*$^{-1}$

1615 CROOKE *Body of Man* 258 All these kinds of generation are maimed and imperfect, and therfore the creatures so procreated, are called.. vnbloodye and insectile creatures.

5. Not bloodthirsty; averse to bloodshed.

c **1665** MRS. HUTCHINSON *Mem. Col. Hutchinson* (1846) 339 His unbloody nature desiring to spare the rest of the delinquents. **1824** LANDOR *Imag. Conv.* I. 324 Such is the characteristic expression of this brave unbloody people.

Hence **un'bloodiness.**

1851 W. ANDERSON *The Mass* iv. 48 The unbloodiness of the Mass.

un'bloomed, *ppl. a.* (UN-^{1} 8.)

1501 DOUGLAS *Pal. Hon.* I. iii, Muscane treis.., Combust, barrant, vnblomit and vnleifit. **1528** LYNDESAY *Dreme* 76 Because vnblomit was baith bank and braye. **1892** *Daily News* 20 Dec. 3/8 Unbloomed pieces of Odontoglossum.

un'blossomed, *ppl. a.* (UN-^{2} 8, UN-^{1} 9.)

1611 FLORIO, *Sfioreggiato*, vnblossomed, disflowred. **1861** W. BILLINGTON *Sheen & Shade* 23 Like dainty fruit on the unblossomed boughs.

un'blossoming, *ppl. a.* (UN-^{1} 10.)

1699 EVELYN *Kal. Hort.* (ed. 9) May 60 You may now give a third Pruning to Peach-trees, taking away and pinching off unblossoming Branches.

un'blotted, *ppl. a.* (UN-^{1} 8.)

a **1548** HALL *Chron., Hen. VI*, 172 Few or none of this company were unblotted, or undestroied by this dolorous drink of dissimulacion. **1612** BRINSLEY *Lud. Lit.* 39 That the schollars.. keep their copies and books fair, vnblotted and vnscrauled. **1615** SYLVESTER *Job Triumph.* I. 69 A man.. Of Life unblotted, and unspotted Fame. **1809** [see UNBLURRED]. **1841** D'ISRAELI *Amen. Lit.* (1867) 475 He seems to have been satisfied with his first unblotted thoughts. **1862** T. A. TROLLOPE *Marietta* vii, You would by such an alliance blot the hitherto unblotted scutcheon, which [etc.].

†**un'blowed,** *ppl. a.* *Obs.*$^{-1}$ [UN-^{1} 8.] = UNBLOWN *ppl. a.*^{2}

1623 (SHAKS.) *Rich. III*, IV. iv. 10 Ah my poore Princes! ah my tender Babes: My vnblowed [*Quartos* vnblowne] Flowres, new appearing sweets.

un'blown, *ppl. a.*^{1} [UN-^{1} 8 b, 8 c + BLOWN *ppl. a.*^{1}]

1. Not driven, tossed, or fanned by the wind.

1638 G. SANDYS *Paraphr. Job* XX. 27 Thick darknesse shall infold, a fire unblowne Devoure his Race. **1648** B. DUPPA *Soules Solil.* 17 He.. might the next year at his return find the same Letters un-blowne away. **1835** CAMPBELL *Fragm. Oratorio Bk. Job* 29 By the fire of his conscience he perisheth In an unblown flame. **1878** B. TAYLOR *Deukalion* III. v. 125 Groping first on fields of unblown mist.

2. With *-out*: Not extinguished.

1642 H. MORE *Song of Soul* I. II. cxviii, When others eyes plainly can nothing see, Then thy prodigious lamps by night unwet And unblown-out, can read right readily.

3. Not sounded.

1815 BYRON *Hebrew Mel., Destr. Sennacherib* v, The tents were all silent, the banners alone, The lances unlifted, the trumpet unblown.

un'blown, *ppl. a.*^{2} [UN-^{1} 8 b + BLOWN *ppl. a.*^{2}] Of flowers: Unopened; still in the bud.

1587 GOLDING *De Mornay* xiii. 213 The little flowers, which wee see vnblowen in the morning and withered at night. **1775** T. PERCIVAL *Ess.* (1776) III. 203 A purple flower, unblown, was suspended in the vessel with the lilas. *a* **1822** [see UNBORN *ppl. a.* 1 b]. **1845** BALLARD & GARROD *Mat. Med.* 226 *Rosa Gallica.* The dried petals of the shops are the unblown flower-buds. **1850** *Jrnl. Asiatic Soc. Bengal* XIX. 18 *note,* The formation shaped like the unblown water-lily.

fig. **1594** SHAKS. *Rich. III* (1597) IV. iv. 10 Ah my young princes, ah my tender babes! My vnblowne flowers. *a* **1625** FLETCHER *Hum. Lieut.* II. iv, How yet unripe we were, unblown, unharden'd. *a* **1625** —— *Love's Pilgrimage* III. ii, I hold my beauty.. As right and rich as hers,.. My youth as much unblown. **1784** COWPER *Tiroc.* 446 Boys are at best but pretty buds unblown. **1821** SHELLEY *Epipsych.* 265 As hair grown gray O'er a young brow, they hid its unblown prime With ruins of unseasonable time. **1893** B. CARMAN *Lyrics, Why* i, A name unknown, Whose fame unblown Sleeps in the hills.

un'blunder, *v.* (UN-^{2} 4 b.)

1665 J. SERGEANT *Sure Footing* 214 In the mean time let him consider what Logick tells us, that The Conclusion is in the Premises, which reflexion will much unblunder his Thoughts.

un'blunted, *ppl. a.* (UN-^{1} 8.)

1656 COWLEY *Davideis* III. 12 A Sword whose weight without a blow might slay, Able unblunted to cut Hosts away. **1775** S. J. PRATT *Liberal Opin.* lvi. (1783) II. 168 My feelings were, as yet, unblunted by habitual trespasses. **1779** *Mirror* No. 67, While the warm feelings of benevolence remain unblunted by those artificial manners. **1818** BYRON *Juan* XVI. cix, Anacreon only had the soul to tie an Unwithering myrtle round the unblunted dart Of Eros. **1867** MRS. WHITNEY *L. Goldthwaite* viii. (1873) 127 The full white light of such unblunted day. *a* **1894** STEVENSON *South Seas* II. ii, [I] woke again with an unblunted sense of my surroundings.

un'blurred, *ppl. a.* (UN-^{1} 8.)

1809 W. BLAKE *Descr. Catal.* 51 Mr. B. left it [a picture] unblotted and unblurred. **1880** BARING-GOULD *Mehalah* iii. (1884) 43 The sky was absolutely unblurred, and thick besprint with stars.

un'blush, *v.* [UN-^{2} 7.] *fig.* To cease to be ashamed.

1620 tr. *St. Augustine's Confessions* VIII. ii. 350 Esteeming himselfe guilty.. if he should be ashamed,.. he did vnblush, and shew a bold face against errour.

†**un'blushed,** *ppl. a.*^{1} *Obs.*$^{-1}$ [Prob. ad. Du. or Flem. *ongebluscht*: see BLESCHE *v.*] Unslaked.

c **1550** *Vertuous Scholehous* B ij b, Nowe arte thou lyke vnto vnblusshed lymestone, whiche, whan colde water is poured vpon it,.. smoketh and burneth vnnaturally.

un'blushed, *ppl. a.*^{2} (UN-^{1} 8.)

1854 S. DOBELL *Balder* i. 4 Who to me Is as your airy fragrance and mere hues To your unblushed substantial.

un'blushing, *vbl. sb.* [UN-^{1} 13 or UN-^{2} 8.] The fact of not blushing or of recovering from a blush.

1596 WARNER *Alb. Eng.* XI. lxvi. (1597) 280 Her blusshing, and vnblushing, made that Stafford doubted whether It pleased, or displeased.

un'blushing, *ppl. a.* [UN-^{1} 10.]

1. Not blushing or reddening.

1595 DANIEL *Civ. Wars* II. lvi, People vntrue To God and man,.. And with vnblushing faces formost thrust. *a* **1711** KEN *Hymnotheo* IX, That [Beauty] modest, pure, this full of Stain, Unblushing, vain. *a* **1757** T. EDWARDS *Sonn.* xiv. 3 That bold bad man.. pretending still With hard unblushing front the public good. **1773** GOLDSM. *Stoops to Conq.* Epil., Th' unblushing Barmaid at a country inn. **1815** W. H. IRELAND *Scribbleomania* 124 Bold and unblushing comes Theodore Hooke, For ever enroll'd in rank plagiary's book. **1865** ELLEN C. CLAYTON *Cruel Fort.* I. 207 The very next day, perhaps, she would utter a falsehood with the most unblushing face.

2. Immodest, shameless, unabashed.

1736 THOMSON *Liberty* v. 180 The buzz Of masquerade unblushing. **1776** MICKLE *Camoens' Lusiad* Introd. 128 This last unblushing falsity, that Gama prays to Christ. **1849** MACAULAY *Hist. Eng.* ix. II. 415 He tried to show.. that strenuous and unblushing servility, even when least successful, was a sure title to his favour. **1875** JOWETT *Plato* (ed. 2) V. 14 In several passages the Athenian praises himself in the most unblushing manner.

Hence **un'blushingly** *adv.*, **un'blushingness.**

1752 RICHARDSON *Let.* 18 Apr. (1964) 207 For the word *Love* has enabled some People to talk of a Passion fearlessly, *unblushingly. **1782** V. KNOX *Ess.* viii. I. 38 They.. end with bankruptcy as naturally, as unreluctantly, and as unblushingly, as if it had been the object of their pursuit. **1812** 'LUCIUS' in *Examiner* 5 Oct. 633/1 Though undenied, and even unblushingly acknowledged. **1894** SIR E. SULLIVAN *Woman* 26 They so unblushingly affect virtues that they have not got. **1891** MEREDITH *One of our Conq.* xxxviii, The appalling theme.. was taken for a proof of the girl's *unblushingness.

un'boarded, *ppl. a.* (UN-^{1} 8.)

1825 J. NICHOLSON *Operat. Mechanic* 451 It is at last brought to a part that is left unboarded and it falls through into troughs placed to receive it. **1892** G. HAKE *Mem. 80 Y.* lxvi. 281 The floor is, in one place, ostentatiously unboarded, to show the foundation to be rock.

un'boastful, *a.* (UN-^{1} 7.)

1727-46 THOMSON *Summer* 684 Oft in humble station dwells Unboastful worth, above fastidious pomp. **1747** COLLINS *Ode Simplicity* ii, O chaste, unboastful Nymph, to thee I call! **1868** MILMAN *St. Paul's* xix. 494 Unlike most great men, the more he is revealed to posterity, [Wellington] shows more substantial, unboastful, unquestionable greatness. **1890** LD. COLERIDGE in J. E. Butler *Recoll. G. Butler* (1893) 483 An athlete quite unboastful, a sportsman silent about his exploits.

un'boasting, *ppl. a.* (UN-^{1} 10.)

1802 MRS. J. WEST *Infidel Father* III. 346 The same manly virtue.. and unboasting goodness. **1854** CDL. WISEMAN *Fabiola* (1855) 174 So frank, so generous, so brave, yet so unboasting.

un'boated, *ppl. a.* [UN-^{2} 8.] Disembarked; landed from a boat.

1688 R. HOLME *Armoury* III. xv. (Roxb.) 26/2 The Oare by beating the water forceth the boate forward to the place desired: the hooks holds it close to the shoare till all be vnboated.

un'boden, *ppl. a.* *Obs.* exc. *dial.* [UN-^{1} 8 b. Cf. OE. *unȝeboden*, = MDu. and Du. *ongeboden*, MHG. and G. *ungeboten*, ON. and Icel. *ú-*, *óboðinn* (Norw. *uboden*, Da. *ubuden*, Sw. *objuden*).]

1. Uninvited; unbidden.

a **1300** *Cursor M.* 14243 þar was fele boden, als i tru, And mani als-sua vnboden Iuu þider com. **1876** ROBINSON *Whitby Gloss.* 204 *Unbid*,.. or *Unbodden*, uninvited.

†**2.** *Sc.* Not provided with arms. *Obs.*$^{-1}$

1456 *Sc. Acts, Jas. II* (1814) II. 45/2 And at na pure man, na vnbodyn, be chargyt to cum to ony raidis in Inglande.

un'bodied, *a.* and *ppl. a.* [UN-^{1} 9 and UN-^{2} 8.]

1. Of souls or spirits: Having no body; not invested with a body; also, removed from the body, disembodied.

The two senses are not clearly distinguishable.

attrib. **1532** MORE *Confut. Tindale* Wks. 387/1 By his power mai the bodily water as wel be a working instrument upon ye vnbodied & vnbodily soule. **1589** WARNER *Alb. Eng.* VI. xxxii. (1592) 143 He wonne his Subiects loue,.. But, as must ours, so lastly his vn-bodied Soule departs. **1643** DIGBY *Observ. Sir T. Browne's Relig. Med.* 10 A Separated and unbodyed Soule. **1696** STANHOPE *Chr. Pattern* (1711) 177 To indulge those longings and pleasures, which refined and unbodied spirits feel. **1711** POPE *Temple Fame* 101 These.. call'd th' unbody'd shades To midnight banquets in the glimm'ring glades. **1721** TICKELL *Epist. Death of Addison* 48 In what new region to the just assign'd, What new employments please the unbodied mind? **1791** COWPER *Iliad* IX. 510 No force arrests Or may constrain th' unbodied spirit back. **1810** CRABBE *Borough* xxii. 327 There were they, hard by me in the tide, The three unbodied forms. **1827** KEBLE *Chr. Year* 2 Lent v, Then may th' unbodied soul in safety fleet Through the dark curtains of the world above.

pred. **1513** DOUGLAS *Æneid* III. v. 42 Oft wald sche cleip and call, and oneith stint, Apone the saulis that wnbodeit war, Besyde Hectouris void tomb standand thair. **1665** J. SPENCER *Vulg. Proph.* 71 The Souls of men become half unbodyed, while they hang upon the lips of these extraordinary persons. **1678** *Lively Oracles* III. §23 (1684) 270 We must be unbodied our selves before we can perfectly conceive what he is. **1726** POPE *Odyssey* XXIV. 19 The spectres.. rest at last, where souls unbodied dwell. *c* **1750** COLLINS *Ode Superst. Highl.* 60 When, o'er the wat'ry strath, or quaggy moss, They see the gliding ghosts unbodied troop. **1818** BYRON *Ch. Har.* IV. ix, My spirit shall resume it—if we may Unbodied choose a sanctuary.

2. Of abstract or immaterial things: Not having a corporeal form.

1606 SHAKS. *Tr. & Cr.* I. iii. 16 That vnbodied figure of the thought That gaue't surmised shape. **1678** CUDWORTH *Intell. Syst.* I. iii. §37. 157 As Knowledge and Understanding only, which is Art naked, abstract and unbodied. *c* **1800** H. K. WHITE *On Survey Heavens* v, Say, foolish one—can that unbodied fame.. Give a new zest to bliss? **1820** SHELLEY *Skylark* 15 Thou dost float and run; Like an unbodied joy whose race is just begun. *a* **1851** MOIR *Poems, Night-Hawk* xiii, Most lonely voice! most wild unbodied scream!

3. Of substances or material things: Not having a definite form.

1630 DAVENANT *Just Italian* Wks. (1673) 457 Wilt thou not bleed? not yet? I skirmish with unbodied air. **1651** FRENCH *Distill.* v. 163 Salts unbodied are farre more acid then when they have assumed a body. **1652** —— *Yorksh. Spa* vii. 67 Those spirits,.. becoming to be unbodied (for before they were incorporated with the water),.. penetrate even the glass it self. **1845** BAILEY *Festus* (ed. 2) 215 Command of mind alone, and of the world Unbodied and all-lovely.

un'bodily, *a.* Now *rare.* [UN-¹ 7.] Incorporeal.
1398 TREVISA *Barth. De P.R.* III. iii. (Tollem. MS.), A soule is an unbodili..substance. **1435** MISYN *Fire of Love* 76 þe lufar..byrnand into vnbodily halsynge. *c* **1491** *Chast. Goddes Chyld.* 47 Whanne the insighte of the sowle..is cleerly fastnyd in unbodely substaunce. **1532** MORE *Confut. Tindale* Wks. 387/1 That yᵉ bodely water can not worke vpon the vnbodyly soule. **1587** GOLDING *De Mornay* xiv. (1592) 203 Herevpon inseweth another controuersie, whether this substance bee a bodily or an vnbodily substance. **1610** HEALEY *St. Aug. Citie of God* XI. xxi. 424 His intention runnes not from thought to thought, all thinges hee knowes are in his vnbodily presence. **1686** PARR *Life of Ussher* App. 14 The real presence of a Body, and yet unbodily; I suppose those that speak thus, understand as little as I do. **1876** EMERSON *Lett. & Soc. Aims, Immort.* Wks. (Bohn) III. 288 Thinking the soul as unbodily among bodies,..the wise man casts off all grief.
Hence **un'bodiliness**.
1611 FLORIO, *Incorporeita*, vnbodilinesse.

un'boding, *ppl. a.* [UN-¹ 10 and 5 d.]
1. *Sc.* 'Unpropitious, unpromising' (Jam., 1825).
2. Not anticipating.
1842 TENNYSON *Will Waterproof* vi, I grow in worth, and wit, and sense, Unboding critic-pen.

un'bodkined, *a.* (UN-¹ 9.)
1844 MRS. BROWNING *Duchess May* lxii, Calm she stood; unbodkined through, fell her dark hair to her shoe.

un'body, *v.* [UN-² 7 and 3.]
†**1.** *intr.* To leave or quit the body. *Obs.*
c **1374** CHAUCER *Troylus* v. 1550 The fate wold his soule sholde vnbodye, And shapen hadde a mene it out to dryue. **1387–8** T. USK *Test. Love* I. i. (Skeat) l. 88 These diseses mowen wel, by duresse of sorowe, make my lyfe to unbodye, and so for to dye.
2. *trans.* To remove from the body; to disembody.
a **1548** HALL *Chron., Hen. VI*, 83 Death..vnbodiyng the solle of this godly prince,..appalled the hertes..of the Englishe nacion. **1577** HOLINSHED *Chron.* I. *Hist. Scot.* 138/1 Herevpon followed a feuer..that after xiiij. monethes space vnbodied his ghost. **1602** WARNER *Alb. Eng.* Epit. (1612) 394 Prince Edward,..also formerly vnbodied by that Tyrant Gloucester. **1650** T. VAUGHAN *Anthroposophia* 53, I am unbodi'd by thy Books, and Thee, And in thy Papers finde my Extasie. **1753** A. MURPHY *Gray's-Inn Jrnl.* No. 60 II. 46 As soon as the Spirit shall be unbodied, it will instantly smile at our wisest Employments in this World. **1787** *Generous Attachment* I. 174 Would to heaven it was in my power to unbody myself, and like a celestial being, to come to you on a sun beam!
fig. **1678** CUDWORTH *Intell. Syst.* I. ii. 51 Plato and Aristotle..took..the Theology and Doctrine of Incorporeals, but Unbodied, and Devested of its most Proper and convenient Vehicle, the Atomical Physiology.
†**b.** *Chem.* To render amorphous. *Obs.*⁻¹
1651 FRENCH *Distill.* v. 163 We must..consider which way we may unbody Nitre (because it is scarse possible to get it before it hath received its body).

unbodylike, *a.*: see UN-¹ 7 c.

un'boggy, *a.* (UN-¹ 7.)
1887 RUSKIN *Præterita* II. 358 One of the best bits of unboggy ground by the Tummel.

un'boiled, *ppl. a.* (UN-¹ 8.)
1611 FLORIO, *Incotto*, vnsodden, vnbaked, vnrosted, vnboyled. **1622** MALYNES *Anc. Law-Merch.* 233 Strong wort new runne, or vnboyled wort also luke warme. **1698** *Phil. Trans.* XX. 439 When as the same Water un-boyl'd rose ⅞. **1756** F. HOME *Exper. Bleaching* 273 Six grains of the effete lime required 26 drops..to saturate it; 6 gr. of the unboiled, 41 drops. **1794** G. ADAMS *Nat. & Exp. Philos.* II. xx. 378 Where this transparent blue colour of the unboiled lobster is thinner. **1847** W. C. L. MARTIN *Ox* 149/1 This disease generally occurs in stalled cattle fed upon unboiled potatoes. **1875** HUXLEY & MARTIN *Elem. Biol.* (1877) 29 In a day or two abundant Bacteria will be found in the unboiled flask.

un'boisterous, *a.* (UN-¹ 7.)
1768–74 TUCKER *Lt. Nat.* (1834) II. 404 Christians of all denominations..will find themselves actuated by the same spirit of a steady, unboisterous zeal.

unbokel, variant of UNBUCKLE *v.*

un'bold, *a.* ? *Obs.* Forms: α. 1 unbeald, 3 onbald, 1, 3–6 un-, vnbald (4 -baald, -balde), 6, 9 *Sc.* unbauld; 4–5 un-, vnbolde, 4, 6 onbolde, 6–7 vnbould. β. 4–5 un-, vnbelde. [UN-¹ 7. Cf. OHG. *unbald.*] Lacking in boldness; deficient in self-confidence or energy; timid, bashful; backward, slow.
α. *c* **897** K. ÆLFRED *Gregory's Past. C.* xl. 289 He for his monnðwærnesse aslawað, & wierð to unbeald. *a* **900** CYNEWULF *Juliana* 427 Wende ic, þæt þu þy wærra weorþan sceolde..& þy unbealdra. *c* **1205** LAY. 16306 Þer fore maȝen Bruttes beon muchele þe vnbaldur [*c* **1275** onbaldere]. *Ibid.* 28159 Þa weoren Bruttisce men swiðe vnbalde uorþæn. *a* **1310** in Wright *Lyric P.* xxxvi. 100 When we shule suen thy wounde blede, to speke thenne we bueth unbolde. **13..** *Minor Poems of Vernon MS.* xxxvii. 172 As a lord schalt þou be cald, þer oþure schul stonde behynde vnbald. *c* **1460** *Lament. Virg.* in *Chester Pl.* (Shaks. Soc.) II. 206/2 But whan he lyste they were on slepe, For to wakyn they were unbolde. *c* **1480** HENRYSON *Thre Deid Pollis* 8 (Bann. MS.), Off thy self, man, thow may be richt vnbald. **1530** PALSGR. 632, I make unbolde or shamfull. *Ibid.*, Twenty honest women can nat make her onbolde agayne. **1611** FLORIO, *Inaudace*, vndaring, cowardly, fearefull, vnbould. **1825** JAMIESON, *Unbauld*, humble, self-abased, *Clydes*[*dale*].
β. **13..** *Sir Beues* (A.) 47 Man, whan he falleþ in to elde, Feble a wexeþ and vnbelde þourȝ riȝt resoun. **13..** *Metr. Hom.* (Vernon MS.) in Herrig's *Archiv.* LVII. 277 Whon þis Monk com to feir elde To worchen ouht he was vnbelde. *a* **1470** HARDING *Chron.* CCIX. iii, The which the duke of Burgoyn wold haue weld, Because to hym they were so vnbelde, Theim to haue slayn.

un'boldened, *ppl. a.* (UN-¹ 8.)
1591 DANIEL *To C'tess Pembroke* Wks. (Grosart) I. 33 My vnboldned Muse is forced to appeare so rawly in publique.

un'boldness. (UN-¹ 12.)
c **1520** BARCLAY *Jugurth* 81 b, For a great part therof is wasted and spent..by the vnbol[d]nesse and cowardyse of their captayns. **1611** FLORIO, *Sbaldanza*, vnboldnesse, vnhardinesse.

†**un'bolne**, *v. Obs. rare.* [UN-² 7.] *intr.* Of a swelling: To go down; to subside.
a **1425** tr. *Arderne's Treat. Fistula*, etc. 93 It makeþ þe place for to vnbolne, and it remeueþ þe rede colour.

un'bolt, *v.* [UN-² 7 and 3.]
1. *intr.* Of a door: To have the bolt withdrawn.
1470–85 MALORY *Arthur* XI. i. 571 And when he came to the chamber..the dores of yron vnlocked and vnbolted. **1680** OTWAY *Orphan* III. *Stage Direct.*, The door unbolts. **1711** MRS. CENTLIVRE *Marplot* I, Ha! the door unbolts; which way shall I get rid of this puppy? **1748** [see UNBAR *v.* c].
2. *trans.* To draw back the bolt of, to unfasten (a door, etc.).
1598 FLORIO, *Discadenacciare*, to vnboult a doore, to vnbar. **1606** SHAKS. *Tr. & Cr.* IV. ii. 3 Ile call mine Vnckle down; He shall vnbolt the Gates. **1650** ALSOP *Serm.* in A. B. Grosart *Small Sins* (1863) 75 *note*, They bring little boys along with them,..who..unbolt the doors, and let in the whole company of thieves. **1760–72** H. BROOKE *Fool of Qual.* (1809) IV. 124 He..unbolted a door that opened into a garden. **1767** *Phil. Trans.* LVIII. 7, I tried the experiment of unbolting my windows. **1819** SCOTT *Ivanhoe* xx, The hermit speedily unbolted his portal. **1835** DICKENS *Pickwick* xxvii, Putting his arm over the half-door of the bar, coolly unbolting it, and leisurely walking in. **1887** BOWEN *Æneid* II. 266 [They] unbolt Troy's gates, to the hosts of the fleet Entrance give.
b. In fig. contexts.
1601 DENT *Pathw. Heaven* 258 To betray vs into the hands of Satan: ye to vnbolt the doore, and let him in to cut our throats. **1648** BP. HALL *Breathings Devout Soul* (1851) 194 To enable me with strength to turn the key, and to unbolt this unwieldy bar of my soul. **1828** T. BROWN *Serm.* 116 We cannot unbolt or break open the gate of the temple of Knowledge.
†**c.** *absol.* To unfold, explain. *Obs.*
1607 SHAKS. *Timon* I. i. 51 *Painter.* How shall I vnderstand you? *Poet.* I will vnbolt to you.
3. To withdraw, draw back (a bolt).
1655 MRQ. WORCESTER *Cent. Inv.* §69 To bolt and unbolt ..an hundred Bolts through fifty Staples, two in each.
4. To detach by the removal of bolts.
1793 *Trans. Soc. Enc. Arts*, etc. (ed. 2) V. 207 By unbolting and taking off the side pipe.
Hence **un'bolting** *vbl. sb.*
[**1775** ASH.] **1829** SCOTT *Anne of G.* xix, The noise of the unbolting and unbarring of the gates.

un'bolted, *ppl. a.*¹ [UN-¹ 8 and UN-² 8.]
1. Not fastened with a bolt; released by withdrawal of a bolt.
c **1580** *Bugbears* I. ii. 132 A window which I left unbolted. **1711** MRS. CENTLIVRE *Marplot* I, Let me see, is my trap-door unbolted? **1779** JOHNSON *L.P., Milton* (1868) 45 To sleep with doors unbolted. **1874** SWINBURNE *Bothwell* II. xviii, The strait garden-plot..Whereto the door that opens from beneath Shall stand unbolted. **1891** C. ROBERTS *Adrift Amer.* 57 Most are content to hunt for an unbolted end door.
2. Not fastened together with a bolt or bolts.
1793 SMEATON *Edystone L.* §262 The bolt and shackle.. had got its forelock broken or beat out, and then..it could not be long before the shackle became unbolted.

un'bolted, *ppl. a.*² Also 6 vnbulted, 6–7 unboulted. [UN-¹ 8.] Not bolted or sifted.
1598 FLORIO, *Semolato*, a kind of course vnboulted bread, full of branne. **1611** COTGR., *Pain de fenestre*,..bread made of vnboulted corne. **1616** SURFL. & MARKH. *Country Farme* v. xx. 577 It is made of meale vnboulted, the brannè and the meale being all knodden together. **1857** R. TOMES *Amer. in Japan* ix. 200 The flour, however, remains unbolted, but makes a good and sweet bread. **1871** NAPHEYS *Prev. & Cure Dis.* II. i. 406 Take a tablespoonful of unbolted flour.
fig. **1570** FOXE *A. & M.* (ed. 2) III. 2033/2 Leauyng the very truth of the matter vnboulted out by the word of God. **1605** SHAKS. *Lear* II. ii. 70, I will tread this vnboulted villaine into morter, and daube the wall of a Iakes with him.

†**un'bombast**, *v. Obs.*⁻¹ [UN-² 3.] *trans.* To take the stuffing out of.
1596 NASHE *Saffron-Walden* Wks. (Grosart) III. 49, I came to vnrip and vnbumbast this Gargantuan bag-pudding, and found nothing in it but dogs-tripes..and sheepes gutts.

unbonairty: see UNDEBONAIRTY *Obs.*

un'bonded, *ppl. a.* (UN-¹ 8.)
1878 ABNEY *Photogr.* 102 The unbonded atom of silver in the subsalt. **1880** F. G. LEE *Ch. under Q. Eliz.* I. p. xlii, Without it the others are unbonded together.

un'bone, *v.* (UN-² 4.)
1570 LEVINS *Manip.* 168 To Vnbone, *exossare.* **1598** FLORIO, *Dissosare*, to vnbone, to pull out the bones. **1611** COTGR., *Desossé*, vnboned; whose bones are taken out. **1642** MILTON *Apol. Smect.* Wks. 1851 III. 267 So many of the young Divines..have bin seene so oft upon the Stage writhing and unboning their Clergie limmes.

un'boned, *ppl. a.* [UN-¹ 8.]
1. Not finished with a bone; boneless.
a **1650** MAY *Satir. Puppy* (1657) 32 Her Chastitie being starv'd..and her Fort vanquisht by an unboned Member (the Tongue).
2. Not manured with bones.
1849 JOHNSTON *Exp. Agric.* 57 On the old boned field, the crop was four times as bulky as on the unboned field.
3. Of meat: Not having the bone(s) removed.

un'bonnet, *v.* [UN-² 7 and 4.]
1. *intr.* To remove the bonnet.
1810 SCOTT *Lady of L.* v. xvii, With that he.. Unbonneted, and by the wave Sate down his brow and hands to lave. **1850** MRS. GASKELL *Let.* in *Life of C. Bronte* (1857) II. vii. 171, I went up to unbonnet, &c.; came down to tea.
b. *esp.* To do this as a mark of respect; to uncover. Also *refl.*
1821 SCOTT *Kenilw.* vii, They hurried to bespeak favour by hastily unbonneting. **1829** —— *Anne of G.* xxxii, Do nothing but rise, unbonnet yourself, and be silent. **1879** DIXON *Windsor* I. ii. 14 His pride disdained to unbonnet in the presence of a King of Scots.
2. *trans.* To remove the bonnet from.
1828 MISS MITFORD *Village* II. 62 She sat down on her dear sofa, and was forthwith unclogged..and unbonneted. **1868** F. E. PAGET *Lucretia* 183 When people attempt to exert a power which they do not possess,—be they judges unbonneting quakers, or bishops exasperated at 'ribbons'. **1896** *Daily News* 4 Apr. 2/3 Even a foreigner may only disregard the pious custom..at the imminent risk of being rudely 'unbonneted' by any devout Russian whom he may happen to encounter.
Hence **un'bonneting** *vbl. sb.*
c **1844** MRS. BROWNING *Lett. R. H. Horne* xliii. (1877) II. 24, I excuse the unbonneting. You are Orion, and I can estimate you.

un'bonneted, *ppl. a.* [UN-¹ 8.]
1. Not wearing a bonnet; having the head uncovered, *spec.* as a mark of respect. Also *fig.*
1604 SHAKS. *Oth.* I. ii. 23 My demerites May speake (vnbonneted) to as proud a Fortune As this that I haue reach'd. **1605** —— *Lear* III. i. 14 (Qo. 1), This night.. vnbonneted he runnes, And bids what will take all. **1818** LAMB *Sonn.* x, Wet and chilly on thy deck I stood Unbonnetted and gazed upon the flood. **1823** SCOTT *Quentin D.* xxvi, 'No,' replied the gray-headed seneschal, who attended upon him unbonneted. **1863** THORNBURY *True as Steel* I. 208 Standing unbonneted before his good master.
2. Of the head: Not covered by a bonnet.
1820 SCOTT *Monast.* xi, Halbert, his head unbonneted,.. sped up..the little valley of Glendearg. **1876** MARIA M. GRANT *Sun-Maid* ix, A broad parasol shielded her unbonneted head.

un'bonny, *a. dial.* (UN-¹ 7.)
1830 J. WILSON *Noctes Ambr.* (1856) III. 71 *North.* She sat and smiled to see her long dishevelled tresses reflected in the Fairy's Pool. *Shepherd.* That's no unbonny. **1894** CROCKETT *Lilac Sunbonnet* 34 'Deed I'm nane sae unbonny yet.

un'booked, *ppl. a.* [UN-¹ 8. Cf. Du. *ongeboekt*, G. *ungebucht.*] **a.** Not entered, registered, or recorded in a book. **b.** Not booklearned.
Also, in recent use, 'not pre-engaged by booking'.
1586 HOOKER *Hist. Irel.* in *Holinshed* II. 140/1 If any of them were found vnbooked and not registered, that he should be used as a fellon where so euer he was taken. **1859** MASSON *Brit. Novelists* iv. 220 There are rich fields of yet unbooked English life both in northern and in southern England. **1870** LOWELL *Study Wind.* 139 From the unbooked freshness of the Scottish peasant to the most far-sought phrase of literary curiosity.

un'bookish, *a.* [UN-¹ 7.]
1. Not bookish or studious; unlearned.
1604 SHAKS. *Oth.* IV. i. 102 His vnbookish Ielousie must construe Poore Cassio's smiles, gestures, and light behauiours Quite in the wrong. **1644** MILTON *Areop.* (Arb.) 36 It is to be wonder'd how museless and unbookish they were. **1792** G. WAKEFIELD *Mem.* (1804) II. 135 Alexander, like the unbookish bigots who are molesting me, would take offence at the speculations of his preceptor. **1863** *N. & Q.* 3rd Ser. III. 349 We would submit the following explanation of the unbookish housekeeper's little bill. **1882** *Century Mag.* XXIII. 951 Even the most unbookish reader will kindle into a momentary sympathy.
2. Free from bookishness.
1887 *Spect.* 19 Mar. 382 Luther, the most unbookish of men.

un'booklearned, *ppl. a.* (UN-¹ 8 d.)
1633 D. R[OGERS] *Treatise of Sacr.* ii. 67 Meane folkes who ..being unbook-learned cannot comprehend such depths as these. *a* **1661** FULLER *Worthies, Northampton* (1662) II. 291 The History of the Bible..hath done as much good to un-book-learn'd people, as any of that kind.

un'boot, *v.* [UN-² 4 and 7.]
1. *trans.* To take the boots off (a person).
1598 FLORIO, *Distiuallare*, to vnboote, to pull off boots. **1611** COTGR., *Dehousé*,..vnbooted, or whose boots are pulled off. **1865** J. M. LUDLOW *Epics Mid. Ages* II. 219 Has he no servant nor squire to unboot him? **1893** *Voice* (N.Y.) 21 Sept., 'I will never unboot the son of a slave,' was the lady's gracious response, referring to a marriage ceremony of the time.
2. *absol.* To take off one's own boots.

1812 BYRON *Waltz* To Publ., I unbooted, and went to a ball. 1873 LELAND *Egypt. Sketch-Bk.* 97 They were very particular at the door in making us unboot and put on canoes of the native pattern.

un'booted, *ppl. a.* (UN-[1] 8 or UN-[2] 8.)
1727 BAILEY (vol. II). 1881 *Cheq. Career* 39 Their comely unbooted feet in the stirrup-irons.

†**un'bore**, *ppl. a. Obs.* [UN-[1] 8 b.] = UNBORN *ppl. a.*
*a*1250 *Prov. Alfred* 449 in *O.E. Misc.* 128 Betere is child vnbore þane vnbuhsum. *c*1290 *S. Eng. Leg.* I. 19/2 Miracle ore louerd dude for him þe ȝuyt he was un-bore. 1390 GOWER *Conf.* I. 149 Sche wissheth forto ben unbore. *c*1400 *Beryn* 1210 It wer better he were vnbore, For he doith nat ellis, save atte hazard pley. 1605 SYLVESTER *Du Bartas* II. iii. II. *Fathers* 133 But (O!) more millions of Babes yet un-bore, Then there be sands upon the Libyan shore.

un'bored, *ppl. a.* Also 7 unboared. (UN-[1] 8. Cf. Du. *ongeboord*, G. *ungebohrt*.)
1598 FLORIO, *Disforato*, without holes, vnbored. 1626 B. JONSON *Staple of N.* II. iv, We ha the dullest, Most unboar'd Eares for verse amongst our females. 1799 G. SMITH *Laboratory* I. 16 It is best to give the turner an unbored rocket. 1829 *Nat. Philos.* I. *Heat* ii. 4 (L.U.K.), He took an unbored cannon, with the large projecting piece..which is usually cast with cannon to ensure solidity. 1861 *Rep. Smithsonian Instit. 1860* 215 A flat, spiral shell exactly like an unbored *Haliotis*. 1868 G. STEPHENS *Runic Mon.* II. 576 The unbored and therefore current Roman Coins.

un'born, *ppl. a.* [OE. *unboren* (UN-[1] 8 b), = OFris. *un-, oen-, onbern* (WFris. *on-, ûnberne*), MDu. and Du. *ongeboren*, OHG. *ungi-, ungaporan* (MHG. *ungeborn*, G. *-boren*), ON. and Icel. *ú-, óborinn* (MSw. *oborin, -burin*, Norw. *uboren*, Da. *ubaaren*).]
1. Not yet born; still to be born. (Freq. with preceding *yet*.) Also in fig. context.
*c*897 K. ÆLFRED *Gregory's Past. C.* xlviii. 367 Mid ðy ðe hie ofsniðen mid ðy seaxe hefiȝlices ȝedwolan ða unborenan bearn, ðe..beoð mid wordum ȝeeacnode on ȝeleaffullra mode. *c*1000 ÆLFRIC *Lives Saints* xxiii. 429 Ure hælend se þe unborenum cildum lif sylð on heora modra innoðe. *c*1200 ORMIN 17327 Forr þatt Nicodem wass ȝet Unnborenn i þatt time Off Haliȝ Gast. *c*1375 *Cursor M.* 12232 (Fair.), I wende my make ware vnborne [*Cott.* noght born]. *c*1386 CHAUCER *Melib.* ¶2231 Ther is ful many a child vnborn of his mooder that shal sterue yong by cause of that ilke werre. *c*1465 *Chevy Chase* 9 The chylde may rue that ys vn-born, it wos the mor pitte. 1535 COVERDALE *Eccl.* iv. 2 Wherfore I iudged..him that is yet vnborne to be better at ease then they both. 1560 DAUS tr. *Sleidane's Comm.* 118b, Young chyldren, as well borne as unborne. 1624 ELIZ. JOCELIN (*title*), The Mothers Legacie, To her vnborne Childe. 1695 PRIOR *Ode after Queen's Death* iii, Ages to come, and Men unborn Shall bless her Name. 1717 POPE *Iliad* x. 61 Yet such his acts, as Greeks unborn shall tell. 1779 WARNER in Jesse *Selwyn & Contemp.* (1844) IV. 294 They had just discovered, by what means I know no more than the child unborn, that [etc.]. 1818 CRUISE *Digest* (ed. 2) VI. 190 The devise would have been void, being to an unborn person for life. 1840 THIRLWALL *Greece* VII. lvi. 169 The throne was to be shared between an idiot and an infant yet unborn. 1887 *Spectator* 22 Oct. 1406 The total abolition of settlements upon unborn lives.
b. *transf.* or *fig.* Of time, etc.
1596 SHAKS. *1 Hen. IV*, v. i. 21 A Portent Of broached Mischeefe, to the vnborne Times. 1667 MILTON *P.L.* VII. 220 Nor staid [He], but..in Paternal Glorie rode Farr into Chaos, and the World unborn. 1712 *Spect.* No. 316 ¶5 The present Time alone is ours, the future is yet unborn. 1757 GRAY *Bard* 108 Ye unborn Ages, crowd not on my soul! 1776 GIBBON *Decl. & F.* i. (1782) I. 26 Venice was yet unborn; but the territories of that state..were inhabited by the Venetians. 1822 SHELLEY *Unfinished Drama* 203 A nook of unblown violets And lilies-of-the-valley yet unborn. —— *To Jane, Invit.* 7 The brightest hour of unborn Spring. 1884 *Chr. Treasury* Feb. 92/2 It is not a function of human intellect to read the secrets of unborn ages.
2. Not born; deprived of birth. Also *fig.*
*a*1275 *Prov. Ælfred* 447 in *O.E. Misc.* 129 For betere is child vnboren þenne vnbeten. *a*1300 *Cursor M.* 15372 To mare blis it had him ben Vnborn if þat he ware. *c*1386 CHAUCER *Shipman's T.* 1372 Yet were me leuere that I were vnborn Than me were doon a sclaundre or vileynye. 14.. *Lat. & Eng. Prov.* (MS. Douce 52) fol. 27 Better is a chylde vnborne þen vnlerned. *c*1450 *Mirk's Festial* 87 Yf God had don vengeans, anon the world had ben endyd mony a day agoo, and so mony had be vnborne, þat now ben holy sayntys yn Heuen. 1546 J. HEYWOOD *Prov.* (1867) 20 Better vnborne than vntought, I haue heard saie. 1595 DANIEL *Civ. Wars* II. xcvii, This mighty burthen wherewithall they goe Dies vndeliuered, perishes vnborne. 1618 BP. HALL *Contempl. N.T.* I. i, Many a father repents him of his fruitfulnesse, and hath such sons as he wishes unborne. *c*1645 HEYWOOD & ROWLEY *Fortune by Land & Sea* III, These mischiefs make me wish my self unborn. *a*1661 [see UNBRED *ppl. a.* 2].
transf. 1390 GOWER *Conf.* II. 109 Withdrawgh the Banere of thin Armes, And let thi lyhtes ben unborn.
3. Existing without having been born.
1821 SHELLEY *Hellas* 769 Look on that which cannot change—the One, The unborn and the undying.

un'borne, *ppl. a.* [UN-[1] 8b.] Not borne or carried *away* or *out*.
1483 CAXTON *Gold. Leg.* 89/1 On a tyme whan the Jewe was oute theuys cam and robbed alle his goodes and lefte unborn away only thymage. 1847 MEDWIN *Shelley* I. 105 This startling and unborne-out proposition.

un'borrowed, *ppl. a.* [UN-[1] 8. Cf. obs. Da. *uborget*.] Not borrowed or taken on loan; esp. *fig.*, not adopted from another, native, inherent, original. (Common from *c* 1700.)
1638 G. DANIEL *Eclog* i. 256 Oh doe not thinke but She may be as faire In nature's bounties, with vnborrwed haire. 1697 DRYDEN *Virg. Past.* IV. 52 The luxurious father of the fold, With native purple and unborrowed gold, Beneath his pompous fleece shall proudly sweat. 1704 *Moderat. Displ.* ix, Bathillo, in his own unborrow'd Strains, Young Sacharissa's Angel Form profanes. 1742 RICHARDSON *Pamela* III. 325 For your Arguments are always new and unborrow'd. 1793 W. ROBERTS *Looker-on* No. 43 (1794) II. 144 His taste was unborrowed, as well as the principles on which he supported it. 1828 LD. GRENVILLE *Sinking Fund* 55 Every portion of unborrowed wealth which this fund has ever received. 1871 FRASER *Life Berkeley* ix. 351 His unborrowed, evidently self-elaborated thought.

un'borrowing, *ppl. a.* (UN-[1] 10.)
1776 MICKLE tr. *Camoens' Lusiad* Introd. 134 In this unborrowing sameness, he artfully interweaves the history of Portugal.

unbosom, *v.* [UN-[2] 5. Cf. Du. *ontboezemen*.]
1. a. *trans.* To bring out from the breast or heart; to give vent to; *esp.* to disclose, reveal.
1588 SHAKS. *L.L.L.* v. ii. 141 Their seuerall counsels they vnbosome shall. 1645 QUARLES *Sol. Recant.* v. 31 Here may thy Griefs unbosome all their grones. *a*1652 J. SMITH *Sel. Disc.* ix. (1821) 412 But God..is pleased to unbosom his secrets, and most clearly to manifest the way into the holiest of all. 1715 DE FOE *Fam. Instruct.* I. i. (1841) II. 9, I have longed a great while to unbosom my sorrows to somebody. 1749 FIELDING *Tom Jones* XVI. viii, He then unbosomed the violence of his passion to Lady Bellaston. 1844 THIRLWALL *Greece* VIII. 149 It was difficult to find a friend to whom he could safely unbosom his views or wishes. 1854 J. S. C. ABBOTT *Napoleon* (1855) II. xxv. 468 He was freely unbosoming his perplexities and his anguish to General Coletta.
b. *refl.* To disclose or reveal one's thoughts, secrets, etc.
1628 T. BALL *Life Preston* (1885) 171 To him he, therefore, now unbosomed himselfe. 1673 *True Worship God* 44 When men unbosome themselves to their Ministers. 1712 STEELE *Spect.* No. 528 ¶1, [I] have now taken Pen, Ink, and Paper, and am resolv'd to unbosom my self to you. 1749 FIELDING *Tom Jones* XIV. ix, Mr. Nightingale, taking the old gentleman with him up stairs,..unbosomed himself as follows. 1803 *Censor* 1 Oct. 110 Having been lately in great distress of mind,..I was led..to unbosom myself to several friends. 1848 THACKERAY *Van. Fair* vi, The fat fellow could not be brought to unbosom himself of his great secret.
c. *absol.* = prec.
1733 P. SHAW tr. *Bacon's De Sap. Vet.* B.'s Phil. Wks. I. 593 Princes usually treat such Persons familiarly; and..think they may with safety unbosom to them. 1772 FOOTE *Nabob* I. Wks. 1799 II. 295 Similarity of sentiments..may have induced him to unbosom to you. 1804 H. K. WHITE *Lett. to B. Maddock* Sept., I am long before I can unbosom to a friend. 1879 MEREDITH *Egoist* xxix, She was really the last person to whom he could unbosom.
2. To lay open or disclose to the eye.
1610 G. FLETCHER *Christ's Vict. & Tri.* II. xi, Rose-buds bright, Unbosoming their brests against the light. 1728–46 THOMSON *Spring* 526 Along these blushing borders, bright with dew,..Fair-handed Spring unbosoms every grace. 1845 BAILEY *Festus* (ed. 2) 258 The world in vain unbosometh her beauty, We have no list to live.
3. To empty or exhaust (the bosom). *rare*$^{-1}$.
1610 G. FLETCHER *Christ's Vict. & Tri.* I. xiii, Greefes companie..That lankes the cheekes, and pales the freshest sight, Unbosoming the cheerefull brest of all delight.
Hence **un'bosomer**; **un'bosoming** *vbl. sb.*
1850 THACKERAY *Pendennis* xxiv, That great unbosomer of secrets, a cigar. 1895 PURCELL *Life Cdl. Manning* I. xxii. 475 Not as a teacher, but as an unbosomer of his own burdens. 1910 *Blackw. Mag.* Jan. 57 And with a voice of growing strength renewed His vague unbosomings. 1935 DYLAN THOMAS *Poems* (1971) 46 Summer to him Is the unbosoming of the sun.

unbo'tanical, *a.* (UN-[1] 7.)
[1775 ASH.] 1883 G. ALLEN in *Longm. Mag.* July 306 The two plants really differ sufficiently to attract the attention of an unbotanical eye.

un'bottle, *v.* [UN-[2] 5.] *trans.* To extract from, or let out of, a bottle. Also *fig.*
1821 *Q. Rev.* XXIV. 497 As good an insight..as Don Cleophas, by the help of the unbottled Asmodeus, obtained into the intrigues of Madrid. 1862 CARLYLE *Fredk. Gt.* XII. iii. (1872) IV. 149 The general population..turned out, with emotion again like to unbottle itself. 1895 *Advance* (Chicago) 18 Apr. 1038/2 Without warning he [a blue-jay] unbottled his shrillest whistle.

un'bottom, *v.* [UN-[2] 4 and 7.]
1. *trans.* To divest of a bottom or foundation; †*fig.*, to deprive of support or stay; to unsettle or make unstable.
1598 FLORIO, *Diffondare*, to vnbottom. 1642 D. ROGERS *Naaman* 156, I am willing to be informed,..yea, to unbottome my selfe of my old rotten mixtures. 1655 GURNALL *Chr. in Arm.* I. 252 This one consideration might be of excellent use to unbottom a sinner, and abase him so as never to have high thought of himself. 1693 G. FIRMIN *Rev. Davis's Vind.* i. 6 Commonly when we speak of unbottoming a Man from himself, we mean [from] his own goodness.
2. *intr.* To make oneself bare-breeched.
1651 CLEVELAND *Poems, News fr. Newcastle* 45 Then you'll unbottom, though December blow, And sweat i' th' midst of Isicles and Snow.

un'bottomed, *ppl. a.*[1] [UN-[1] 8.]
1. Having no bottom; bottomless. Also *fig.*
1615 SYLVESTER *Tobacco Battered* 192 Tobacco's smoakie Mists Which..No small addition of Adustion fit Bring to the smoak of the Unbottom'd Pit. 1630 J. TAYLOR (Water P.) *World's Eighth Wonder* Wks. II. 67/1 The nine and forty wenches, water filling, In tubs vnbottom'd, which was euer spilling. 1667 MILTON *P.L.* II. 405 Who shall tempt with wandring feet The dark unbottom'd infinite Abyss? 1704 *Moderat. Displ.* x, From Faction's dark unbottom'd Cell I come. 1778 *Conciliation* 7 Mir'd and flound'ring in th' unbottom'd Pit. 1802 LEYDEN *Mermaid* 44 If, from the unbottom'd deep,..The sea-snake heave his snowy mane.
b. *fig.* Unfathomable.
1760–72 H. BROOKE *Fool of Qual.* (1809) I. 150, I will no longer..make my ignorance a sounding-line for his [God's] unbottomed wisdom.
2. Having no proper foundation; unsupported; not founded *on* or *in* something.
1640 GAUDEN *Love of Truth* (1641) 21 For errour is so feeble and unbottomed, that it must have some butresses and seeming basis of truth to support it. 1650 ASHMOLE *Chym. Collect.* Prol. 3 Others there are, who out of Ignorance or Mistake, have delivered blinde and unbottomed Fictions. 1675 H. MORE in R. Ward *Life* (1710) 272 The Question,..whether there be no Love unbottomed on Self-love? 1742 YOUNG *Nt. Th.* VIII. 801 Can joy, unbottom'd in reflection, stand? And, in a tempest, can reflection live?

un'bottomed, *ppl. a.*[2] [UN-[2] 8.] Deprived of a bottom or foundation; unsettled.
1674 PENN *Christian Quaker* I. xxv. 126 Thus is this Man Unravel'd, Unreligion'd, Unbottom'd as to his former State. *a*1684 LEIGHTON *Comm. 1 Pet.* iii. (1849) 263 You are your own deceivers in it,..and are not careful to have your souls really unbottomed from themselves, and built upon Christ.

unbought (ʌnˈbɔːt), *ppl. a.* Forms: (see BUY *v.*). [UN-[1] 8 b.]
1. Not bought; unpurchased.
*c*950 *Lindisf. Gosp.* Matt. x. 8 Unboht *vel* unceaped [L. *gratis*] ȝie onfengon, unboht sellas. *a*1300 *Prov. Hendyng* in *Rel. Ant.* I. 114 Of un-boht hude men kerveth brod thong. *a*1300 *Cursor M.* 5410 In all egypti lefte he na land Vn-boght in-til þe king hand. 1535 STEWART *Cron. Scot.* (Rolls) II. 451 Thus tha strave about ane wnbocht gait. *a*1593 MARLOWE *Ovid's Elegies* I. x. 43 Thankes worthely are due for things vnbought. *c*1600 CHALKHILL *Thealma & Cl.* (1683) 24 On unbought Delicates their Hunger fed. 1637 COWLEY *Sylva, A Vote* xi, In this true delight, These unbought sports, and happy state, I would not feare, nor wish my fate. *c*1720 PRIOR *Pontius & Pontia* 23 Some hair I have, I'm sure, unbought, Pray bring your brother-wits to see't. 1790 BURKE *Fr. Rev.* 113 The unbought grace of life ..is gone! 1845 *Kitto's Cycl. Bibl. Lit.* (1847) I. 604/1 Wandering shepherds..depending solely upon the unbought gifts of nature. 1895 CORNISH *Wild England* 310 The unbought beauty of the county is still its main and most potent charm.
†**2.** Unpunished. *Obs.*$^{-1}$
*a*1200 *Moral Ode* 59 (Lamb. MS.), Ne scal nan ufel bon unboht, ne nan god unforȝolden.

un'bound, *ppl. a.*[1] Forms: (see BIND *v.*). [UN-[1] 8 b. Cf. MDu. and Du. *ongebonden*, MHG. and G. *ungebunden*, NFris. *ünbünjen*, ON. and Icel. *ú-, óbundinn* (Da. *unbunden*, Sw. *obunden*).]
1. a. Not bound or tied up; unfastened. Also with *up*.
α. *a*900 *Laws of Ælfred* c. 35 Ȝif he hine to preoste bescire unbundenne, mid xxx scill. ȝebete. *a*1000 *Ags. Riddles* xxiii. [xxiv.] 15 Nelle ic unbunden æniȝum hyran, nymðe searosælod. *c*1375 *Sc. Leg. Saints* xlvii. (*Euphemia*) 49 Vnbundine [he] gert hir cum þare Ymang þame þat bundyn var sar. 1523 FITZHERB. *Husb.* §28 So the barley lyeth vnbounden .iii. or .iiii. dayes.., and than to bynde it.
β. *c*1440 *Alph. Tales* 357 With þe ta syde of hur heade vnbun vpp sho ran to feght agayn þaim of Babilon. 1570 LEVINS *Manip.* 221 Vnbound, *liber*. 1600 FAIRFAX *Tasso* XVI. xviii, Her lockes vnbound, wau'd in the wanton winde. 1667 MILTON *P.L.* III. 603 Though..they binde Volatil Hermes, and call up unbound In various shapes old Proteus from the Sea. 1757 W. WILKIE *Epigon.* II. 47 Now, tam'd by age, his coursers stood unbound. 1808 SCOTT *Marm.* IV. iv, Some damsel flying fast, With hair unbound, and looks aghast. 1892 GUNTER *Miss Dividends* (1893) 248 The moonlight shining through the car window gets into her unbound hair.
b. *fig.* Unconfined, unconstrained; not bound by any engagement, vow, etc.
1390 GOWER *Conf.* II. 393 It helpeth more..than forto crave Of othre men and make him bounde, Wher elles he mai stonde unbounde. *c*1470 *Gol. & Gaw.* 1040 Bot ilk berne has bene vnbundin with blame. 1532 MORE *Confut. Tindale* Wks. 684/1 God..hauing his power absolute, fre, and vnbounden vnto any maner of hys ordinary course. 1603 J. DAVIES (Heref.) *Microcosmos* Wks. (Grosart) I. 66/1 To court bright beauty match'd, as t'were vnbound. 1790 COWPER *Mother's Pict.* 87, I should ill requite thee to constrain Thy unbound spirit into bonds again. 1859 TENNYSON *Elaine* 1377 Yet thee She fail'd to bind, tho' being, as I think, Unbound as yet.
c. Not bound as apprentice. *rare.*
1497–8 in *Archæol. Jrnl.* XLIII. 168 A fyne lost by R. Bancrofte for..settyng to werk a child vnbound & vnablid.
2. Not secured with a band or border of some strong material.
1531 *Rec. St. Mary at Hill* 38, viij kettelles bound and vnbond. 1547 in Feuillerat *Revels Edw. VI* (1914) 17 One Black chest bounde with Irone & ij other Chestes vnbounde.
3. Of books: Not provided with a binding or cover. Also with *up*.
1541 *Acts Privy Council* 25 Apr., Anthony Marler..might sell the bibles of the Gret volume unbounde for x. s sterl[ing]. 1549 (Mar.) *Bk. Com. Prayer* Colophon, That no maner of person do sell this present booke unbounde, aboue the price of ii. Shyllynges the piece. 1690 LOCKE *Hum. Und.* III. x. §27 A Book-seller, who had in his Ware-house Volumes that lay there unbound, and without Titles. 1720 HEARNE *Collect.* (O.H.S.) VII. 161 The Textus..will be

sent unbound as desired. **1831** CARLYLE *Sart. Res.* I. xi, One other leaf of that mighty volume..left to fly abroad, unprinted, unpublished, unbound up. **1896** T. L. DE VINNE *Moxon's Mech. Exerc., Printing* 401 The complete book on printing, unbound, then cost 14s. 4d.

fig. **1592** SHAKS. *Rom. & Jul.* I. iii. 87 This precious Booke of Loue, this vnbound Louer, To Beautifie him, onely lacks a Couer.

4. Of substances: In a loose or free state. Also of a particle: = FREE *a.* 14 b.

1697 DRYDEN *Virg. Georg.* I. 98 While the Turf lies open, and unbound, Succeeding Suns may bake the Mellow Ground. **1902** *Brit. Med. Jrnl.* 14 June 146 Their methods ..would only extract and precipitate the unbound purin. **1971** *Sci. Amer.* June 25/1 Once a few unbound electrons are produced on the surface of the solid hydrogen isotope, these free electrons rapidly pick up energy from the incident oscillating electric field.

un'bound, *ppl. a.*^{2} *rare*$^{-1}$. [UN-^{1} 8 + BOUND *ppl. a.*^{1}] Unprovided, destitute.

a **1300** *Cursor M.* 24034, I stakerd sua i moght not stand, Bot als þai me up-held wit hand Vn-bun was i o bote.

†**un'bound,** *ppl. a.*^{3} *Obs.* [UN-^{1} + BOUND *v.*] Unbounded; boundless.

1593 Q. ELIZ. *Boeth.* II. pr. vii. 53 The lasting of any longest tyme, if it be matcht with vnbounde eternitie, not small but none shall seeme. *a* **1619** FOTHERBY *Atheom.* II. ii. §1 (1622) 198 The vnlimited and vnbound extension of the Appetites of Man. *c* **1658** *Elegy on Cleveland* 16 C.'s Wks. (1687) 284 Such was the Fate of my weak Streams, that ran To drown themselves in th' unbound Ocean. *c* **1725** RAMSAY *Some of Contents* ii, Dunbar does with unbound ingyne, In satyre, joke, and in the serious schyne.

un'bound, *v. rare.* [UN-^{2} 3.] *trans.* To deprive of bounds or limits.

1598 SYLVESTER *Du Bartas* III. ii. *Colonies* 178 The thirst of Vengeance, and that puffing breath Of elvish Honour.. Un-bound all Countries. **1612** DRAYTON *Poly-olb.* v. 104 Gowr, whose promontory (plac'd to check the ocean's pow'r) Kept in Severne yet herself, till being growne too great Shee with extended armes unbounds her ancient seat.

unbound, pa. pple. of UNBIND *v.*

un'boundable, *a.* (UN-^{1} 7 b.)

1622 R. HARRIS *Gods Goodnes* 17 Mercy in the first sense, is Negatiuely endlesse, that is, vncapable of end, because vnboundable for being. **1837** EMERSON *Misc.* (1855) 91 Who shall set a barrier on any one side to this unbounded, unboundable empire?

un'boundably, *adv.* (UN-^{1} 11.)

1607 DEKKER *Westw. Hoe* Wks. 1873 II. 289, I am so infinitly, so vnboundably beholding to you.

un'bounded, *ppl. a.* [UN-^{1} 8.]

1. Not bounded or limited in extent. Also *fig.*, of the Deity.

1598 FLORIO, *Interminato*, vnbounded, boundles, vnlimited. **1667** MILTON *P.L.* x. 471 With what paine [I have] Voyag'd th' unreal, vast, unbounded deep Of horrible confusion. *a* **1711** KEN *Hymns Festiv.* Poet. Wks. 1721 I. 270 God's Presence is himself; for none Unbounded is but God alone. **1730** THOMSON *Autumn* 902 Mean-time, light-shadowing all, a sober calm Fleeces unbounded ether. **1808** SCOTT *Marm.* IV. Introd. 160 The wild unbounded hills we ranged. **1821** BYRON *Heav. & Earth* I. iii, Earth shall be ocean! And no breath, Save of the winds, be on the unbounded wave! **1870–2** LIDDON *Elem. Relig.* iv. §1 The Unbounded, All-powerful Being is alone the good.

b. Unlimited in amount.

1646 CRASHAW *Steps to Temple, Miracle of Multiplyed Loaves* 3 See here an easie Feast,..A subtle Harvest of unbounded bread. **1695** PRIOR *Ode Queen's Death* xxiii, As Waters from her Sluces, flow'd Unbounded Sorrow from her Eyes. **1709** HEARNE in *R. Glouc. Chron.* (1724) II. 603 Ador'd and flatter'd upon account of their Dignity and unbounded Wealth. **1763** WILKES *Corr.* (1805) I. 89 Testimonies of an unbounded confidence in your veracity and good faith. **1849** MACAULAY *Hist. Eng.* vii. II. 257 The writers generally expressed unbounded reverence and affection for William. **1867** DICKENS *Lett.* (1880) II. 272 The enthusiasm has been unbounded. **1897** MARY KINGSLEY *W. Africa* 474 Owing entirely to..her own unbounded courage and energy.

2. Not restrained or kept within limits; unchecked, uncontrolled.

Not always clearly distinguishable from prec. sense.

1608 CHAPMAN *Byron's Consp.* II. i. 47 In such air breathe his unbounded spirits, Which therefore well will fit such conjurations. **1647** N. WARD *Simple Cobler* 49 They are a good People, that undoe not their Prince, by any one of their unbounded Liberties. **1736** BUTLER *Anal.* I. v. Wks. 1874 I. 108 Prosperity itself..begets extravagant and unbounded thoughts. **1794** R. J. SULIVAN *View Nat.* I. iii. 14 Their unbounded claims..to temporal..dominion. **1823** SCOTT *Quentin D.* i, A tone of romantic and chivalrous gallantry (which, however, was often disgraced by unbounded license). **1830** HERSCHEL *Study Nat. Phil.* 7 Cherishing as a vital principle an unbounded spirit of enquiry. **1854** BANCROFT *Hist. U.S.* I. ii. 34 Leaving his wife to govern the island, he and his company, full of unbounded expectations, embarked for Florida.

3. Of persons (and animals): Unchecked or uncontrolled in action.

1612 *Two Noble K.* I. ii. 70 A most unbounded Tyrant. **1656** COWLEY *Davideis* IV. 241 Let his power loose, and you shall quickly see How mild a thing unbounded Man will be. **1681** DRYDEN *Abs. & Achit.* I. 762 Then they are left Defenceless, to the Sword Of each unbounded, Arbitrary Lord. **1725** DE FOE *Voy. round World* (1840) 312 The fellows were so rude, so ungovernable and so unbounded in their hunting after gold. **1728** SAVAGE *Bastard* 19 Nature's unbounded son, he stands alone, His heart unbiass'd, and his mind his own. **1818** SCOTT *Hrt. Midl.* xxxvi, Numberless flocks and herds, which seemed to wander unrestrained and unbounded through the rich pastures.

b. Profusely generous or liberal.

a **1704** T. BROWN *Praise Drunken.* Wks. 1730 I. 35 Their darling humour, avarice, is lost, and their hearts become unbounded, and free as the God by whom they are possess'd. **1825** SCOTT *Talism.* xxiii, It is well known that the high esteem of the European knowledge and courage made the Soldan unbounded in his gifts to those who..had been induced to take the turban.

un'boundedly, *adv.* [f. prec.] Without limitation; beyond all bounds.

1611 COTGR., *Librement*, freely, frankly, vnboundedly. **1619** HIERON *Wks.* II. 431 Nor to bee so vnboundedly subiect vnto kings, as not to regard what is owing from us vnto God. **1674** *Govt. Tongue* ix. §1. 150 So unboundedly mischievous is that petulant member, that heaven and earth are not wide enough for its range. **1781** H. DOWNMAN tr. *Voltaire's Dram. Wks.* I. 248 My heart relies upon thy faith, Unboundedly relies. **1845** BAILEY *Festus* (ed. 2) 227, I was born To gratify myself unboundedly, So that I wronged none else. **1881** MRS. H. HUNT *Child. Jerus.* 122 She was unboundedly fond of babies.

un'boundedness. [f. as prec.] Unlimitedness, boundlessness.

1640 BP. REYNOLDS *Passions* xviii. 192 This unboundednesse of Desires we are to take heed of. **1678** CUDWORTH *Intell. Syst.* 389 The unlimitedness and unboundedness of its power, declareth it to be infinite. **1715** CHEYNE *Philos. Princ. Nat. Relig.* II. ii. 58 Infinitude [imports] the unboundedness of these Degrees of Affections, or Properties. **1839** BAILEY *Festus* 240 When thus to one poor spirit He gives His hand, He seems to impart His own unboundedness Of bliss. **1860** PUSEY *Min. Proph.* 321 With increased knowledge of Him, come higher perceptions of the unboundedness of God's love to us.

unbounden, obs. var. UNBOUND *ppl. a.*, and obs. pa. pple. of UNBIND *v.*

†**un'boundless,** *a. Obs.*$^{-1}$ [UN-^{1} 5 a.] Unbounded, boundless.

1624 in Capt. J. Smith *Virginia* III. ii. 45 Thus God vnboundlesse by his power, Made them thus kind.

un'bounteous, *a.* (UN-^{1} 7.)

1645 MILTON *Tetrach.* Wks. 1851 IV. 156 Nay such an unbounteous giver we should make him, as in the fables Jupiter was to Ixion.

un'bountifulness. (UN-^{1} 12.)

1660 INGELO *Bentiv. & Ur.* I. (1682) 144 Want..is not from God's unbountifulness, but men's folly and wickedness. **1730** BAILEY (fol.), *Illiberality*,.. unbountifulness.

†**un'bow,** *v. Obs.* [UN-^{2} 3.] *trans.* To unbend, to straighten.

1538 ELYOT, *Decircino*,..to vnbowe, or to bringe out of compasse, or roundenesse. **1621** QUARLES *Hadassa* ii. Wks. (Grosart) II. 57/2 Her lowly bended body she vnbow'd. **1653** H. MORE *Antid. Ath.* II. i. §6 As in little pieces of Wood naturally bow'd like a Man's Elbow, the Carver doth not unbow it but..shapes it into the Compleat Figure of a Man's Arm.

fig. **1639** FULLER *Holy War* III. vi. (1840) 124 Because looking back would unbow his resolution.

†**un'bowable,** *a. Obs.* [UN-^{1} 7 b.] Unbendable, inflexible.

1537 BIBLE (Matthew) *Ps.* ii. 9 *note*, A rodde of yron for a sure and unbowable domynyon. **1583** STUBBES *Anat. Abus.* I. (1879) 76 So long as a sprigge, twist, or braunche, is yong, it is flexible and bowable.., but if we tarie till it be a great tree, it is inflexible and unbowable. **1611** COTGR., *Imployable*, inflexible, vnbowable.

un'bowdlerized. *ppl. a.* (UN-^{1} 8.)

1894 WILKINS & VIVIAN *Green Bay Tree* II. 50 A private and unbowdlerized version of 'Helen of Troy'. **1896** MRS. CAFFYN *Quaker Grandmother* 54 An entirely unbowdlerised library.

un'bowed, *ppl. a.* [UN-^{1} 8.] Not bowed or bent. Freq. *fig.*

c **1374** CHAUCER *Boeth.* IV. met. vii. (1868) 148 þe laste of his labours was þat he sustenede þe heuene vpon his nekke vnbowed. **1593** SHAKS. *2 Hen. VI*, III. i. 16 He..passeth by with stiffe vnbowed Knee. **1610** —— *Temp.* I. ii. 116 Confederates..To giue him Annuall tribute..and bend The Dukedom yet vnbow'd..To most ignoble stooping. **1648** HEXHAM II, *Ongekromt*, Vncrooked, or Vnbowed. **1816** BYRON *Ch. Har.* III. xxxix, He stood unbow'd beneath the ills upon him piled. **1865** W. G. PALGRAVE *Arabia* I. 205 His tall stature, absolutely unbowed by years. **1879** M. PATTISON *Milton* 131 In Andrew Marvel Milton found one congenial spirit, incorruptible amid poverty, unbowed by defeat.

un'bowed, *a.* [UN-^{1} + BOW *sb.*^{1}] Of pigs: Not furnished with a bow-shaped piece of wood to impede their movements.

1624 in H. Maclean *Watermillock Reg.* (1908) 157 That none..shall keep their swine unbowed..sub poena for every swine so unbowed iiij d. **1794** W. HUTCHINSON *Hist. Cumbld.* I. 163 *note*, The tenants are subject to pains..for swine going unbowed in the time of harvest.

†**un'bowel,** *v. Obs.* [UN-^{2} 4.]

1. *trans.* To disembowel (a person or animal); to eviscerate, exenterate.

1552 HULOET, Vnbowell, *exentero*. **1591** R. W[ILMOT] *Tancred & Gism.* Argt., Afterward..he commanded the Earle to be attached, imprisoned, strangled, vnbowelled. **1606** S. GARDINER *Bk. Angling* 123 The hand of this cunning worke-man vnbowelleth him. **1651** HOWELL *Venice* 84 After the Duke is dead, he is unbowell'd, his body embalm'd. *a* **1691** BOYLE *Hist. Air* (1692) 182 This prepared, they first unbowelled the corps.

fig. **1592** NASHE *Four Lett. Confut.* Wks. (Grosart) II. 198 Before I vnbowell the leane Carcase of thy book any further. **1654** COKAINE *Dianea* IV. 336 All Vices are Vices; but Cruelty holds the preheminence. It spoiles, unbowels, unsoules the World. **1713** C'TESS WINCHELSEA *Misc. Poems* 389 Wou'd you then have me live, when thus unbowell'd, Without the Charms of my Aristor's presence?

b. *refl.* (*a*) To exhaust oneself; to expend one's strength or means; (*b*) to unbosom oneself.

(*a*) **1647** A. ROSS *Mystag. Poet.* i. (1675) 30 Covetous men are like spiders, they unbowel, that is they consume and spend themselves with care and toyl to catch a fly. **1650** HOWELL *Giraffi's Rev. Naples* I. 27 With such cries..they did unbowell themselves to provide furniture for the War.

(*b*) **1650** H. BROOKE *Conserv. Health* 205 Thus..did this famous Deviner unbowel himself and thereby..made some amends for his former impostures. **1655** SANDERSON *Serm.* (1681) II. Pref., Since I had thus adventured to unbowel my self.

2. *fig.* To empty of contents; to open up; to make hollow. Also in fig. context.

1597 J. KING *On Jonas* (1618) 78 They ransack all the corners of the shippe, vnbowell her inmost cells, throwe out commodities. **1610** *Histrio-m.* III. 62 Then stooping suiters ..May groaning come, unbowelling the bagges Of their rich burthens in your wide-mouth'd deskes. **1646** GATAKER *Mistake Removed* To Rdr. 2 Partly to unbowel and lay open some part of that unsound stuff that lies closely couched in this covert vault. *a* **1785** GLOVER *Athenaid* XXVII, A native arch..Expands before an excavation deep, Unbowelling the hill.

b. To open up or disclose by investigation or exposition. (Common in 17th c.)

1606 J. KING *Serm.* Sept. 15 The whole book of God must be vnbowelled, and all the wit of man ransackt, to finde out a stile honorable enough for their new erected presbytery. **1659** E. HOPTON *Encomium* in T. Barker *Art of Angling* (ed. 2), Thou hast unbowell'd Dame Natures part In a *Vade mecum*. **1693** NORRIS *Pract. Disc.* (1698) IV. 178 When this Great Thought comes to be open'd and unbowell'd, to be unravell'd and laid bare.

c. To display or reveal.

1650 BAXTER *Saints' R.* I. vii. 91 When we shall feed at Josephs own house,..when he shall fully unbowel his love unto us, and take us to dwell in Goshen by him.

Hence †**un'bowelling** *vbl. sb. Obs.*

a **1639** SPOTTISWOODE *Hist. Ch. Scot.* (1655) VI. xiii. 306 Whether they perceived any sign of poyson at his unbowelling. *a* **1653** BINNING *Serm.* (1845) 340 The not unbowelling of our hidden affections. **1694** WESTMACOTT *Script. Herb.* 41 The embalmer..then salted, without any Incision or unbowelling, the whole body with Sal Nitri.

†**un'bowelled,** *ppl. a. Obs.* [f. prec.] Disembowelled. Also *fig.*

1592 KYD *Sp. Trag.* I. ii. 61 There legs and armes lye bleeding on the grasse, Mingled with weapons, and vnboweld steedes. **1637** N. WHITING *Albino & Bellama* 32 Th' hollow belly of th' un-boweld earth. **1655** VAUGHAN *Silex Scint.* I. (1858) 27 Unbowel'd nature, shew'd thee her recruits And change of suits.

un'bowelled, *a.* [UN-^{1} 9.] Having no bowels; *fig.* unaffectionate, pitiless.

1592 R. D. *Hypnerotomachia* 17, I issued foorth of the unbowelled monster. **1656** EARL MONM. tr. *Boccalini's Advts. fr. Parnass.*, etc. 241 The unbowel'd love which they bear unto them, is more prejudicial to them, then is their enemies implacable hatred. *Ibid.*, *Pol. Touchstone* 403 That unbowel'd beyond sea Renegado. **1815** MILMAN *Fazio* (1821) 81 As deaf and hollow as the unbowell'd winds.

un'bowing, *ppl. a.* [UN-^{1} 10.] Unbending, unyielding. Hence **un'bowingness**.

a **1300** *Cursor M.* 27243 Wandring in quere, Vn-boandnes a-bote þe autere. *Ibid.* 27796 O suernes cums..Hardnes of hert and vnboand [*v.rr.* vnbowand, vnboghande]. **1382** WYCLIF *Heb.* x. 23 We..holde the confessioun of oure hope vnbowynge, or that may not be foldyn.

un'bowsome, *a. Obs.* exc. *dial.* [UN-^{1} 7. Cf. NFris. *ünbügsom*, MDu. *onboochsam*, Du. *onbuigzaam*, G. *unbeugsam*.]

1. = UNBUXOM *a.* 1.

c **1290** *S. Eng. Leg.* I. 266/185 Ake þat ich onbouȝsum ne beo i-seie..I-chulle bidde for þe, mi leoue fader. **1340** *Ayenb.* 21 þou hest y-by onboȝsam to þine uader and to þine moder. *c* **1340** HAMPOLE *Pr. Consc.* 8596 Grysely devels salle gang and com On þe synfulle þat tylle God war unbowsom. **1818** HOGG *Brownie of B.* i, Ye hae a dour, stiff, unbowsom kind o' nature in ye.

2. *dial.* Unbending, stiff.

1818 HOGG *Wool-gatherer* Tales (1866) 80/2 It makes.. but an unbowsome overleather. **1894** HESLOP *Northumbld. Gloss.* 755 He's..ungainly an' unbowsome.

Hence **un'bowsomeness**.

1340 *Ayenb.* 33 þe uerste [point] is onboȝsamnesse, huanne þe man nele do þet me him zayþ ine penonce. *c* **1400** *Cursor M.* 27616 (Cott. Galba), Of pride cumes als vnbowsumnes. *c* **1450** *St. Cuthbert* (Surtees) 3377 þai wer glad and somwhat shamed,..þaim shamed of þair vnbowsomnes.

un'box, *v.* [UN-^{2} 5.] *trans.* To take out of a box.

1611 COTGR., *Desboëter*, to vnbox, or take out of a box. **1817** KEATS *Let.* Wks. 1889 III. 51, I went and unbox'd a Shakespeare. **1864** P. M. IRVING *Life W. Irving* IV. 31 He brought home also a picture... After tea he took mallet and chisel, and proceeded to unbox it. **1883** *Standard* 10 Aug. 2/1 Minehead reached, horses were quickly unboxed.

un'boy, *v.* [UN-^{2} 7 and 6 b.] **a.** *intr.* To grow out of boyhood. **b.** *trans.* To divest of boyishness; to make a man of.

1611 FLORIO, *Sgarzonare*, to become from a boy to a man, to vnboy, to vnlackie. **1647** CLARENDON *Hist. Reb.* VIII. §179 He began to say..that it was now time to unboy him, by putting him into some action and acquaintance with business.

un'boyish, *a.* (UN-^{1} 7.)

1838 S. G. GOODRICH *Fireside Educ.* 107 Charles, the eldest boy, with a patience most *unboyish*, was holding a skein of yarn for grandmamma to wind. **1864** MISS YONGE *Trial* I. 277 The steady low voice, and unboyish language. **1881** MARY C. HAY *Missing*, etc. II. 43 It might have grown into an idle and unboyish habit.

un'brace, *v.* [UN-^{2} 3.]

1. *refl.* or *trans.* To free (oneself or another) from bands or braces forming part of clothing or armour. Also *absol.*

c **1400** *Laud Troy Bk.* 7007 Ector affter euere chases, At eche a lepe his stede vnbrasis. **1420–2** LYDGATE *Thebes* 4284 He alighte doun, And brotherly, with a pitous face, To saue his lyf gan hym to vnbrace. **1598** FLORIO, *Sbracciarsi*, to vnbrace ones selfe. **1633** ROWLEY *Match at Midn.* IV, *Widow.* You will not be so uncivil to unbrace you here?.. *Alex.* I will off with my doublet to my very shirt. **1637** HEYWOOD *Pleas. Dial.* xviii. 147 *Par.* Have them all stript naked... *Merc.* Vnbrace your selues, put off, and nothing hide.

b. *fig.* To lay open; to disclose, reveal.

1607 TOURNEUR *Rev. Trag.* IV, Now y'are both present, I will unbrace such a close private villain Unto your vengeful swords.

2. *trans.* To undo, to loosen or untie, to relax (a band, grasp, etc.).

c **1475** *Rauf Coilȝear* 629 The ȝaip ȝeman to the ȝet is gane; Enbraissit [*read* vn-] the bandis beliue. *c* **1475** *Lament. Mary Magd.* xxxi, Than gan I there min armes to vnbrace Up lifting my handes ful mourningly. **1590** SPENSER *F.Q.* II. iv. 9 The knight..Knit all his forces, and gan soone vnbrace His grasping hold. **1598** YONG *Diana* 189 A faire and daintie hand he did vnbrace. **1718** POPE *Iliad* XIV. 245 The queen of love..from her fragrant breast the zone unbraced. **1762–9** FALCONER *Shipwr.* II. 521 Arion..The cordage of the leeward guns unbraced.

b. To loosen, detach, or set free by the undoing or removal of braces or bonds.

1593 NASHE *Christ's T.* Wks. (Grosart) IV. 71 The resplendent eye-out-brauing buildings of your Temple, (like a Drum) shal be vngirt & vnbraced. **1627** DRAYTON *Agincourt* ccix, Now with mayne blowes their Armours are vnbras'd. **1654** WHITELOCKE *Jrnl. Swed. Emb.* (1772) II. 365 The gunner was so amazed with the daunger, that he forgott to unbrace the gunnes, and shott away the maine sheate. **1714** 'NESTOR IRONSIDE' *Orig. Canto Spenser* xli, So gan they soon her Armoury unbrace. **1813** SCOTT *Trierm.* II. xxiv, Gay shields were cleft, and crests defaced, And steel coats riven, and helms unbraced. **1828** LANDOR *Imag. Conv.* III. 133 Unbrace his armour—loose the helmet first.

c. To relax the tension of (a drum).

1593 [see 2 b]. **1636** MASSINGER *Bashf. Lover* IV. i, Had you been Employed to mediate your father's cause, My drum had been unbraced, my trumpet hung up. **1691** DRYDEN *K. Arthur* III. i, Furl up our Colours, and Unbrace our Drums.

†**3.** To carve (a mallard or duck). *Obs.*

The two earlier instances are repeated in many later copies of the list of 'proper terms'.

c **1470** *Hors, Shepe, & G.* (Roxb.) 33 A malard unbrased; a cony unlaced. **1508** W. DE WORDE *Bk. Keruynge* in *Babees Bk.* (1868) 265 Vnbrace that malarde. **1687** J. SHIRLEY *Rich Closet of Rarities* 52 In unbracing a Mallard, Observe that you raise up the pinion and leg, not taking them off. **1688** R. HOLME *Armoury* III. 78 Unbrace that Duck or Mallard. **1771** MRS. HAYWOOD *New Present for Maid* 269 To unbrace a Duck. *Ibid.* 270 To unbrace a Mallard. **1804** FARLEY *Lond. Art Cookery* (ed. 10) 293 To unbrace a mallard or duck, first raise the pinions and legs.

4. *fig.* †**a.** To allow or make (the heart) to relax in feeling; to free (oneself) from restraint.

c **1485** SKELTON *Death Edw. IV*, 93 O ye curtes commyns, your hertis vnbrace Benyngly now to pray for me also. ? *a* **1500** *Chester Pl., Ador. Sheph.* 448 Nowe pray we to hym with good intent, And sing I will, and me unbrace. ? **1511** SIR T. PHELYPPIS in *Early XVI Cent. Lyrics* lxvii. 24 The rose I suppose thyn hart vnbrace.

b. To render lax or slack; *esp.* to deprive of firmness or strength in this way; to enfeeble, weaken.

1711 ADDISON *Spect.* No. 249 ¶5 Laughter, while it lasts, slackens and unbraces the Mind, weakens the Faculties. **1715** POPE *Iliad* IV. 365 But wasting years, that wither human race, Exhaust thy spirits, and thy arms unbrace. **1758** JOHNSON *Idler* No. 9 ¶2 What rules has he proposed totally to unbrace the slackened nerve? **1799** *Phil. Trans.* XC. 2 The muscles of the malleus having been deemed sufficient for bracing and unbracing it. **1865** LOWELL *Wks.* (1890) V. 293 The war..which invigorated bolder men, unbraced him. **1884** *Fortn. Rev.* Jan. 37 Everything has been done that could be done..to unbrace the sinew of national resistance.

c. *absol.* To become lax; to lose firmness.

1693 DRYDEN *Juvenal* VI. 210 Let her Eyes lessen, and her Skin unbrace. **1699** GARTH *Dispens.* 37 At thy Approach the Springs of Nature start, The Nerves unbrace. *a* **1718** PARNELL *Gift of Poetry* 455 When spirits stop their course, when nerves unbrace, And outward action and perception cease.

un'braced, *ppl. a.* [UN-^{1} 8 or UN-^{2} 8.]

1. With dress or part of dress unfastened or loosened.

c **1510** BARCLAY *Mirr. Gd. Manners* (1570) E v, Their false heare inuolued, in nettes intricate, Their brestes vnbraced, their smerking paynted chin. *a* **1529** SKELTON *E. Rummyng* 134 Some wenches come vnlased, Some huswyues come vnbrased. **1601** HOLLAND *Pliny* II. 308 Women,..with their haire hanging loose about their eares, vngirt, vnlaced, and vnbraced. **1602** SHAKS. *Ham.* II. i. 78 Lord Hamlet with his doublet all vnbrac'd, No hat vpon his head. **1622** FLETCHER *Sea-Voy.* II. i, Methought a sweet young man..Stole slylie to my Cabin all unbrac'd. **1821** SCOTT *Kenilw.* xiv, He found Lord Sussex dressed, but unbraced and lying on his couch. **1875** WHYTE MELVILLE *Katerfelto* xiii. 120 Presently steals in a slipshod drawer, unbraced, uncombed, unwashed.

2. Of a drum: Not made tight or tense; released from tension.

1625 B. JONSON *Staple of N.* Induct., He doth sit like an vnbrac'd Drum with one of his heads beaten out. **1669** DRYDEN *Tyrannic Love* I. i, Like the hoarse murmurs of a trumpet's sound, And drums unbraced. **1703** PRIOR *Advice to Painter* 43 Near this, erected on a Drum unbrac'd, Let Heaven's and James's Enemy be plac'd. **1713** MRS. CENTLIVRE *Wonder* II. i, Poor Gentleman, he is as melancholy as an unbraced drum.

3. Loosened, relaxed. Also *fig.*

1621 QUARLES *Argalus & P.* (1678) 55 The little winged god with arm unbrac'd, And Bow unbent. **1760** *Cautions & Adv. Officers of Army* 98 Little Good can be expected from him whose..unbraced Nerves..denote him fitter for his Grave..than for his Duty. **1776** PAINE *Com. Sense* (1791) 73 The property of no man is secure in the present unbraced system of things.

4. Not braced or strengthened (*by* something).

1809–10 COLERIDGE *Friend* (1865) 216 Their sensibilities unbraced by the co-operation of fixed principles. **1883** H. DRUMMOND *Nat. Law in Spir. W.* (1884) 354 His character untouched, his will unbraced.

un'braceleted, *a.* (UN-^{1} 9.)

1855 PATMORE *Angel in Ho.* II. iii. 2 With arm and wrist All warmth and light, unbraceleted.

†**un'brack**, *v. Obs.* (UN-^{2} 5: cf. BRACK *sb.*^{5})

1611 FLORIO, *Scassare vn pezzo*, to vnstocke, to vnbracke or dismount a piece.

un'bragging, *ppl. a.* (UN-^{1} 10.)

1570 LEVINS *Manip.* 137 Vnbragging, *inglorius.*

un'braid, *v.* (UN-^{2} 3.)

1828–32 WEBSTER, *Unbraid*, to separate the strands of a braid. **1880** J. COOK *Monday Lect.* Ser. I. 6, I shall unbraid the reasoning and show its strands.

un'braided, *ppl. a.* [UN-^{1} 8.]

†**1.** Untarnished, undamaged. *Obs.*$^{-1}$

1611 SHAKS. *Wint. T.* IV. iv. 204 Thou talkest of an admirable conceited fellow, has he any vnbraided Wares?

2. Not braided or plaited.

1821 SCOTT *Kenilw.* vii, Her unbraided hair escaping from under her midnight coif. **1879** H. W. WARREN *Recr. Astron.* ii. 30 Just above the color vibrations of the unbraided sunbeam.

un'brailed, *ppl. a.* [UN-^{1} 8.] Not confined by a brail or thong.

1618 LATHAM *Falconry* (1633) 97 Beware you giue no traines vnbrayld of both wings, vntill the Hawke be well blouded.

†**un'brained**, *ppl. a. Obs.*$^{-1}$ [UN-^{1} 8.] Not deprived of brains.

c **1614** FLETCHER *Wit at Sev. Weapons* IV. i, Hast thou ever hope To come i' the same roome where lovers are; And scape unbrain'd with one of their velvet slippers?

un'bran, *v.* [UN-^{2} 4.] *trans.* To divest of bran. Hence **un'branning** *vbl. sb.*

1848 *Rep. Comm. Patents 1847* (U.S.) 373 In addition to the *unbraning* of the berry, the wheat undergoes an operation [etc.]. **1863** WYNTER *Subtle Brains* 383 The invaluable process of unbranning wheat. **1884** KNIGHT *Dict. Mech.* Suppl. 911/1 *Unbranning machine*, a machine for removing the bran or cuticle of the wheat grain.

un'branched, *a.* [UN-^{1} 9.]

1. Of trees or plants, their stems, etc.: Not furnished with branches.

1665 REA *Flora* 96 The Lily Asphodells flower in the end of May;..the unbranched kind is the first and the branched the last. **1731** MILLER *Gard. Dict.* s.v. *Palma*, The Palm-Tree..hath a single unbranch'd Stalk. **1753** *Chambers' Cycl.* Suppl. s.v. *Filix*, The unbranched, dentated fern. **1855** MISS PRATT *Flower. Pl.* (1861) V. 314 Unbranched Upright Bur-reed. **1897** MARY KINGSLEY *W. Africa* 464 A great hard wood forest tree, which has a tall unbranched stem, terminating in a crown of branches.

2. Not divided into branches; having no ramifications. Chiefly *Bot.* and *Zool.*

1796 WITHERING *Brit. Plants* (ed. 3) III. 755 Leaves generally unbranched. **1847** W. E. STEELE *Field Bot.* 171 Leaves with unbranched mostly parallel ribs. **1857** T. MOORE *Handbk. Brit. Ferns* (ed. 3) 58 The veins, which are alternate, mostly unbranched, and extending to the margin. **1875** HUXLEY & MARTIN *Elem. Biol.* (1877) 37 A bud-like process is thrown out, which, usually, grows only into a very short unbranched hypha.

un'branched, *ppl. a.* [UN-^{1} 8.] Not deprived of branches.

1572 MASCALL *Plant. & Graff.* (1592) 37 The other sorts of Trees may well passe vnbranched, if they haue not too great or large branches.

un'branching, *ppl. a.* (UN-^{1} 10.)

1774 GOLDSM. *Nat. Hist.* III. iii. 80 The other has black unbranching hollow horns that never fall. **1826** KIRBY & SP. *Entomol.* III. xxviii. 12 He has made the first deviation from the beaten track of an unbroken and unbranching series.

un'branded, *ppl. a.* (UN-^{1} 8.)

1641 MILTON *Animadv.* Wks. 1851 III. 230 Lest his conversation unprohibited, or unbranded, might breath a pestilentiall murrein into the other sheepe. **1886** *Daily News* 4 June 6/3 Butter:..price of unbranded, 78*s*, 71*s*, 66*s*. **1890** 'R. BOLDREWOOD' *Col. Reformer* (1891) 232 Cows, unbranded calves, and pen-branded bullocks. **1892** *Academy* 23 Jan. 81/3 What is false and heartless is not allowed to pass unbranded under its screen of art.

un'brandied, *a.* (UN-^{1} 9.)

1862 T. A. TROLLOPE *Marietta* I. x. 195 Unbrandied juice of the grape.

†**un'brangled**, *ppl. a. Sc. Obs. rare.* [UN-^{1} 8.] Not shaken or made uncertain.

1671 R. MACWARD *True Nonconf.* 368 The more serious Presbyterians..remain stedfast and unbrangled with these delusions. *c* **1730** T. BOSTON *Life* ix. (1908) 182 God's calling me to the place remained clear, plain, and unbrangled.

unbranning: see UNBRAN *v.*

†**un'branslable**, *a. Obs.*$^{-1}$ [UN-^{1} 7 b: cf. BRANLE *v.*] Unshakable.

1633 LD. WARRISTON *Diary* (S.H.S.) I. 170 On the quhilk tuo my saule doeth bottom itself as one ane unbranslable rok.

†**un'brashed**, *ppl. a. Obs.*$^{-1}$ [UN-^{1} 8.] Unattacked, unassailed.

1596 DALRYMPLE tr. *Leslie's Hist. Scot.* (S.T.S.) I. 104 Quhen the armie is in sicht, the space of thrie dayes thay byd nocht vnbrachte with vs.

un'brave, *a.* (UN-^{1} 7.)

a **1681** T. RAYMOND *Autobiog.* (Camden) 35 Soe I had in this brave place [the Hague] a very unbrave life. **1896** *Godey's Mag.* Feb. 172/1 She saw before her his old self—strong, not unbrave, not disloyal. **1981** *London Mag.* Oct. 18 The sensible thing, as many unbrave realised at the time, would have been to opt for ground duties with the RAF.

un'braved, *ppl. a.* (UN-^{1} 8.)

1608 SYLVESTER tr. *Mathieu, Mem. Mortality* I. lxxx, Th' art loth to leave the Courts Delights, Devices, Where None lives long vnbrav'd, or vnabhorred.

un'braze, *v.* (UN-^{2} 4.)

[**1775** ASH, *Unbraze*.., to unsolder brass.] **1898** *Cycling* 19 A useful bar is made by unbrazing the central lap-joint.

un'breachable, *a.* (UN-^{1} 7 b.)

1866 M. ARNOLD *Thyrsis* 156 Unbreachable the fort Of the long-batter'd world uplifts its wall.

un'breached, *ppl. a.* (UN-^{1} 8.)

1876 SWINBURNE *Erechtheus* 1451 Unbreached of warring waters Athens like a sea rock stands.

un'breakable, *a.* (UN-^{1} 7 b.)

c **1480** HENRYSON *Orpheus & Eurydice* 405 Hard is þi law, þi bandis vnbrekable. **1611** COTGR., *Irrefragable*,.. vnbreakable. **1845** BAILEY *Festus* (ed. 2) 130 He made earth, ..Lined it with fire, and round its heart-fire bowed Rock-ribs unbreakable. **1890** *Spectator* 20 Sept. 374/2 This Moloch that devours young girls' lives is an idol that appears unbreakable. **1929** T. M. JOHNSON *Our Secret War* iv. 180 Is there an unbreakable code? **1944** H. MCCLOY *Panic* 73 There's no such thing as an unbreakable cipher! **1963** R. V. JONES in Brown & Foote *Early Eng. & Norse Studies* 223 An unbreakable W/T code.

un'breakfasted, *a.* (UN-^{1} 9.)

1646 J. HALL *Poems* 43 Three such as you Unbreakfasted might sterve Seraglio. **1826** DISRAELI *V. Grey* v. ii, I see you smile at my supposing a horseman unbreakfasted. **1847** L. HUNT *Men, Women & B.* I. ix. 159 This personage.. persisted in giving poor unbreakfasted Jack in charge. **1865** TREVELYAN *Cawnpore* 115 Half-clad, unbreakfasted,..our countrymen huddled..into the precincts of the fatal earthwork.

un'breaking, *ppl. a.* (UN-^{1} 10.)

1869 MORRIS *Earthly Par.* II. III. 183 And ever as the shadows fell, More formless grew the unbreaking swell Far out to sea. **1876** GEO. ELIOT *Dan. Der.* xl, Part of my Jewish heritage is an unbreaking patience.

un'breast, *v.* [UN-^{2} 5.] *trans.* To take or force out from the breast; to unbosom. Chiefly *fig.*

1559 *Mirr. Mag.* (1563) C vii, My fault wherein because mine vncle tolde..I found the meanes his bowels to vnbrest. **1603** FLORIO *Montaigne* I. xvii. 28 Feare then vnbreasts all wit, That in my minde did sit. **1631** P. FLETCHER *Pisc. Eclogs* IV. xxiv, Could'st thou unmask their pomp, unbreast their heart, How would'st thou laugh at this rich beggerie! **1633** —— *Purple Isl.* XII. lxiii, Out from his mouth a two-edg'd sword he darts;..And with his keenest point unbreasts the naked hearts.

Hence **un'breasted** *ppl. a.*

1610 G. FLETCHER *Christ's Tri.* II. xl, To whose open eye The hearts of wicked men unbrested lie.

un'breathable, *a.* (UN-^{1} 7 b.)

1846 WORCESTER (citing F. Butler). **1862** *Cornh. Mag.* VI. 485 No one pretends that the worst air in a closed railway carriage is unbreathable. *c* **1882** CHR. ROSSETTI *Resurgam* Poems (1891) 378 He stumbles on the darkened mountain-head, Left breathless in the unbreathable thin air.

un'breathe, *v.* [UN-^{2} 7.] *intr.* To cease to breathe; to expire, die.

1589 WARNER *Alb. Eng.* VI. xxxiii. 144 Now is the time and place (sweete Frends) and we the Persons be That must giue England breath, or els vnbreath for her must we.

un'breathed, (*ppl.*) *a.* [UN-¹ 8, 8c, 9. For pronunc. see BREATHED *ppl. a.*]

†**1.** Unexercised; unpractised. *Obs.*

1590 COKAINE *Treat. Hunting* C 4 Who so hunteth vnbreathed hounds at the Bucke first in hot weather. **1590** SHAKS. *Mid. N.* V. i. 73 Hard handed men,..Which neuer labour'd in their mindes till now; And now haue toyled their vnbreathed memories With this same play. **1620** QUARLES *Jonah* 99 A Muse vnbreath'd, vnlikely to obtaine An easie honour, by so stout a Traine. **1644** MILTON *Areop.* (Arb.) 45, I cannot praise a fugitive and cloister'd vertue, unexercis'd and unbreath'd.

2. a. Not having recovered breath.

1692 PRIOR *Ode Imit. Hor.* v, Yon' Hero, crown'd with blooming Victory,..And yet unbreath'd from Battles gain'd.

b. Not out of breath or exhausted.

1901 KIPLING *Kim* 369 Kim's messenger dropped from the steep pasture as unbreathed as when she had set out.

3. Not breathed (*upon*); not respired.

1817 MOORE *Lalla Rookh*; *Veiled Prophet* II. 186 When from those lips, unbreath'd upon for years, I shall again kiss off the soul-felt tears. **1831** WORDSW. *Yarrow Revisited* VI. 9 Rocks, rivers, and smooth lakes more clear than glass Untouched, unbreathed upon. **1884** *Imp. Dict.* s.v., Air unbreathed.

4. Not uttered or whispered.

a **1827** J. HISLOP *Cameronian's Dream* 30 The vengeance that darkened their brow was unbreathed.

un'breathing, *ppl. a.* [UN-¹ 10.]

1. Not breathing or respiring; *esp.* holding the breath; breathless.

1709 *Rowe's Shaksp., Rich. III*, III. vii. 25 Like dumb statues or unbreathing stones. **1736** A. HILL *Zara* V. i, Th' unbreathing World is hush'd, as if it heard, And listen'd to, your Sorrows. **1789** E. DARWIN *Bot. Gard.* II. (1791) 53 Silent with upturned eyes unbreathing crowds Pursue the floating wonder to the clouds. **1814** WORDSW. *Excurs.* IV. 1281 Hushed As the unbreathing air, when not a leaf Stirs in the mighty woods. **1824** GALT *Rothelan* III. 237 The audience sat in silent admiration and unbreathing astonishment. *a* **1867** WILLIS *Lazarus & Mary* 68 A fearful and unbreathing hush, Stiller than night's last hour.

2. Not taking breath; continuous.

1893 *Scribner's Mag.* June 821/1 It is neither recital, analysis, nor exposition; but soaring, sweeping, unbreathing rhapsody.

un'bred, *ppl. a.* [UN-¹ 8b.]

†**1.** Unborn. *Obs.*⁻¹

c **1600** SHAKS. *Sonn.* civ, For feare of which, heare this thou age vnbred, Ere you were borne was beauties summer dead.

2. Not properly bred or brought up; not imbued with good manners; unmannerly, ill-bred.

1622 in Foster *Eng. Factories Ind.* (1908) II. 146 Borish unbred upstartts, whoe abound in all pryde and insolenceey. *a* **1661** FULLER *Worthies* I. (1662) 34 Seeing much of Truth is contained in our English Proverb, It is as good to be unborn as unbred. **1700** CONGREVE *Way of World* III. xvii, My nephew's a little unbred, you'll pardon him, madam. **1712** STEELE *Spect.* No. 492 ¶2 A little Country Girl..that makes her use of being young and unbred. **1760-2** GOLDSM. *Cit. W.* xxxix, Would he not be reckoned more fantastically savage than even his unbred footman?

b. Not trained *in*, not brought up *to*, some occupation.

a **1683** OLDHAM *Wks.* (1686) 68 Dull Northern Brains, in these deep Arts unbred, Know nought but to cut Throats. **1697** DRYDEN *Æneis* VII. 1096 A warrior dame; Unbred to spinning, in the loom unskilled. **1878** *N. Amer. Rev.* CXXVI. 304 With no education,..often unbred to any handicraft.

†**un'brede,** *v. Obs.*⁻¹ (Meaning obscure.)

13.. *Satire* in *Pol. Songs* (Camden) 156 Heore boc ase unbredes. Heo wendeth bokes in-brad.

un'breech, *v.* [UN-² 4. Cf. Du. *ontbroeken.*]

†**1.** *trans.* To remove the breech or breeching from (a cannon, etc.).

a **1548** HALL *Chron., Hen. VIII*, 259 b, The portes [were] left open,..and the greate ordinaunce vnbreched, so that when the ship should turne, the water entered, and sodainly she sanke. **1598** FLORIO, *Scalcagnare*,..to vnbreech, to vnheele, to vnstock, or dismount any kinde of great ordinance or artillerie. *c* **1620** FLETCHER & MASS. *Double Marriage* II. i, *Gun.* Let the worst come, I can unbreech a Cannon, and without much help Turn her into the Keel. **1625** MARKHAM *Souldiers Accid.* 8 He shall..shew them how to scoure their Pieces, and..how to vnbreetch them.

2. To strip (a person) of breeches.

1598 FLORIO, *Scalciáre*, to vnhose, to unshoe,..to vnbreech. **1835** *Court Mag.* VI. 20, I was afraid of feeling for my snuff-box, lest I should unbreech half Naples. **1846** LANDOR *Imag. Conv.* Wks. I. 29 Kings have been stripped bare, and emperors unbreeched, by the popes. *a* **1896** MORRIS *Sundering Flood* (1897) 123 If I catch thee not and unbreech thee and whip thee as a grammar master his scholar, then [etc.]

Hence **un'breeching** *vbl. sb.*

1598 FLORIO, *Scalciatura*, an..vnhosing, vnbreeching.

un'breeched, *a.* [UN-¹ 9.] Not dressed in breeches.

1611 SHAKS. *Wint. T.* I. ii. 158 Me thoughts I did requoyle Twentie three yeeres, and saw my selfe vn-breech'd, In my greene Veluet Coat. **1800** WORDSW. *Two Thieves* 13 The One, yet unbreeched, is not three birthdays old. *c* **1837** HAWTHORNE *Twice-told T.* (1851) I. vi. 112 All at once, the devil of their fathers entered into the unbreeched fanatics. **1879** DOWDEN *Southey* i. 5 Southey, an unbreeched boy of three years, was borne away one morning..to be handed over to the tender mercies of a school-mistress.

unbrent, obs. f. UNBURNT.

unbresed, obs. f. UNBRUISED.

un'brewed, *ppl. a.* (UN-¹ 8.)

1725 *Fam. Dict.* s.v. *Straw*, In case you have not sweet Wine, take some thick or unbrew'd Wine of the Colour of Bulls Blood. **1742** YOUNG *Nt. Th.* VII. 288 They graze the turf untill'd; they drink the stream Unbrew'd, and ever full.

†**un'brewing.** *Obs.*⁻¹ A fanciful name for a 'company' (of carvers).

1486 *Bk. St. Albans* f vij, A vnbrewyng of kerueris.

un'bribable, *a.* (UN-¹ 7b.)

1661 FELTHAM *Resolves* (ed. 8) II. lxxxiii. 68 Though it be cry'd up for impartial and unbribeable, yet I do not see but in many 'tis erroneous, mutable, and uncertain. **1678** CUDWORTH *Intell. Syst.* I. iv. §16. 291 God is..the Head or Leader of all Good, Unbribable. **1849** THOREAU *Week Concord Riv.* Wedn. 304 The impartial and unbribable beneficence of Nature. **1862** THORNBURY *Turner* II. 169 My object is..to draw his real likeness with the unbribable fidelity of a photograph. **1893** SALTUS *Madam Sapphira* 166 Beyond that we won't go. The unbribable Comstock won't let us.

un'bribed, *ppl. a.* [UN-¹ 8.]

1. Not bribed; not corrupted by bribery.

1607 TOURNEUR *Rev. Trag.* I. ii, The justice Of that unbribed euerlasting law. **1646** G. DANIEL *Poems* Wks. (Grossart) I. 56 She commands Who ballanceth the world with unbrib'd hands. **1668** DRYDEN *Dram. Poesy* Ess. (ed. Ker) I. 44 That praise or censure is certainly the most sincere, which unbribed posterity shall give us. **1733** POPE *Ess. Man* III. 158 Unbrib'd, unbloody, stood the blameless priest. **1796** MME. D'ARBLAY *Camilla* V. 230 [He was] unbribed by the high praise of his son. **1802-12** BENTHAM *Ration. Judic. Evid.* (1827) II. 424 Two hundred unbribed witnesses agree in deposing that..he was seen by them at Prague. **1845** ELIZA COOK *Old Man's Marvel* xix, It [the heart] stands unbribed by an Eastern mine—For a ducat of dross 'tis bought and sold.

fig. **1608** BEAUM. & FL. *Four Pl. in One* Wks. 1912 X. 340 Have I not here enough to thank Heaven for?.. The water that I touch, unbrib'd with odours To make me sweet to others.

2. Not obtained or brought about by bribery.

1667 R. WILD *Poems* (1870) 75 Unbribed loyalty! his highest reach Was to be Master Calamy, and preach. **1735** THOMSON *Liberty* I. 79 The commonweal inspiring every tongue With fervent eloquence, unbrib'd, and bold. **1781** COWPER *Hope* 580 Paul's love of Christ, and steadiness unbrib'd. **1802-12** BENTHAM *Ration. Judic. Evid.* (1827) V. 93 Perjury, if unbribed, will be without a motive.

†**un'briche,** *a. Obs.* In 4 **vnbryche.** [OE. *unbrȳce*: see BRICHE *a.*] Useless, unserviceable.

1303 R. BRUNNE *Handl. Synne* 6786 God..deyneþ nat to nemne hys name,..But calleþ hym yn þe gospel, ryche, As vnkynde and vnbryche.

un'brick, *v.* [UN-² 4.] *trans.* To remove bricks from; to open up, set free, by the removal of bricks.

1598 FLORIO, *Smattonare*, to vnpaue, to vnbrick, to pull downe bricks. **1873** WHITNEY *Other Girls* xx, Couldn't the fire-place be unbricked? **1900** *Academy* 4 Aug. 90/2 A climber had stuck there [in a narrow chimney] and died before he could be unbricked.

fig. **1894** B. PAIN *Kindn. Celestial* 179 Three days after the engagement he had unbricked 'a bright and sunny temperament' in my father.

un'bricked, *ppl. a.* (UN-¹ 8.)

1814 *Monthly Mag.* July 594 No more than 130 yards of the tunnel..were unbricked on the 31st of May. **1894** *Daily News* 6 Sept. 1/3 He desired to be buried in an unbricked grave.

un'bridgeable, *a.* (UN-¹ 7b.)

1799 SOUTHEY in *Sir H. Davy's Rem.* (1858) 37 One channel,..unbridgeable from its depth, unpassable from its whirlpools. **1879** LEWES *Study Psychol.* 50 An unbridgeable gulf, which no dexterity of speculation can pass. **1881** *Standard* 30 Aug. 3/4 Between them there was an all but unbridgeable abyss.

un'bridged, *ppl. a.* (UN-¹ 8.)

1800 WORDSW. *Brothers* 254 Every water-course And unbridged stream..Was swoln into a noisy rivulet. **1852** MRS. STOWE *Uncle Tom's C.* xiv. 121 The gulf of separation was unbridged by even a friendly word or signal. **1884** *Spectator* 4 Oct. 1322/1 The traveller who left England with the intention of proceeding overland to Ceylon, with the exception of the three unbridged channels.

un'bridle, *v.* [UN-² 4b. Cf. Du. *ontbreidelen.*]

1. *trans.* To remove the bridle from (a horse). Also *absol.*

? *a* **1400** *Morte Arth.* 2509 Thare vnbrydilles theis bolde, and baytes þeire horses. *c* **1435** *Torr. Portugal* 1552 Down light this gentille knyght..And vnbrydelid his stede. *c* **1450** *Mirk's Festial* 56 He fell wod, and so vnbrydylt his hors þat bare hym into a maner of þe lordes. **1530** PALSGR. 766/2 Unbridell my horse and gyve hym otes. **1607** MARKHAM *Cavel.* III. (1617) 31 Then you shal come vnto him and vnbridle him. **1643** TRAPP *Comm. Gen.* xxiii. 2 They would neither unbridle their horses, nor untie their armor. **1809** MALKIN *Gil Blas* VI. ii. ¶1 We unbridled our horses, and turned them out to grass. **1890** L. C. D'OYLE *Notches* 134 He led the horses by their bridles down to the gate of the enclosure; here he unbridled them and let them go.

b. *transf.* and *fig.* To free from restraint.

a **1440** *Found. St. Bartholomew's* (E.E.T.S.) 57 The tonge was vnbridillid to blasfemy and rybawdy. **1567** *Trial Treas.* (Percy Soc.) 23, I doubte not but I shal be unbridled by Luste. **1576** GASCOIGNE *Philomene* li, Forth he floong the raines, Unbridling blinde desire. **1604** T. WRIGHT *Passions* I. iii. 14 Selfe-love..inticeth the citizens..to prosecute pleasures, unbridle their senses. **1648** J. BEAUMONT *Psyche* VIII. cclvii, Loe, There unbridle thy Extremitie, And give thee leave in free carreer to goe.

c. *absol.* (in fig. use). To stop or halt.

1653 URQUHART *Rabelais* I. xxii, Then did he sleep without unbrideling until eight a clock.

2. *Surg.* To free (a wound) from a bridle. (See BRIDLE *sb.* 5b.)

1758 J. S. *Le Dran's Observ. Surg.* (1771) 333, I had not sufficiently unbridled it, nor penetrated deep enough into the Body of the Muscles.

un'bridled, *ppl. a.* [UN-¹ 8. Cf. MDu. *ongebreidelt.*]

1. *fig.* Not restrained or held in check; absolutely uncontrolled or ungoverned: **a.** Of conduct, feeling, utterance, etc.

c **1374** CHAUCER *Troylus* III. 429 He..in hym self wiþ manhod gan restreyne, Eche rakel dede and eche vnbrydled chere. *c* **1412** HOCCLEVE *De Reg. Princ.* 2433 Vnbridlid wordes ofte man by-weepiþ. **1412-20** LYDG. *Chron. Troy* I. 2019 No cher vnbridled þat tyme hir asterte. *c* **1530** *Remedy of Love* Prol., Seeing the manifolde inconuenience Falling by vnbrideled prosperitie. **1561** T. NORTON *Calvin's Inst.* I. 4 We reade of none that euer did breake forth into more presumptuous and vnbridled despising of God, than Caius Caligula. **1590** SWINBURNE *Testaments* 200 By this meane to restraine the vnbrideled lusts of some. **1626** T. H[AWKINS] *Caussin's Holy Crt.* 120 After the concupiscences of the belly, commeth vnbridled irreuerence. **1642** MILTON *Apol. Smect.* Wks. 1851 III. 273, I go on to shew you the unbridl'd impudence of this loose rayler. **1711** STEELE *Spect.* No. 38 ¶5 When we give the Passion for Praise an unbridled Liberty. **1751** EARL ORRERY *Remarks Swift* (1752) 99 A wild unbridled indulgence of his own humour and disposition. **1821** SCOTT *Kenilw.* xxxi, His flights are too unbridled for any place but Parnassus. **1855** PALEY *Æschylus* Pref. (1861) p. xxiii, To keep in check the otherwise unbridled passions of a fickle multitude. **1888** BRYCE *Amer. Commw.* I. iii. 25 *note*, An alarming example of what the unbridled rule of the multitude may come to.

b. Of persons, the mind, tongue, etc.

a **1547** SURREY *Paraphr. Ps. lv.* 13 Rayne those vnbrydled tungs; breake that coniured league. *a* **1548** HALL *Chron., Hen. V*, 56 b, When he had once tamed and framed to his purpose this young unbrideled gentleman. **1581** A. HALL *Iliad* IV. 69 After our vnbrideled youth coms sage and wrinckled yeares. **1606** SHAKS. *Tr. & Cr.* III. ii. 130 My thoughts were like vnbrideled children grow[n] Too head-strong for their mother. **1644** MILTON *Areop.* (Arb.) 37 Nævius was quickly cast into prison for his unbridl'd pen. **1676** HOBBES *Iliad* I. 322 That they may be To Gods and Men, and to th' unbridled man My witnesses. **1840** ALISON *Hist. Eur.* VIII. liii. §39. 433 The usual..intemperance of the unbridled populace of great towns. **1876** BANCROFT *Hist. U.S.* I. xviii. 517 They were exposed, without defence, to the fury of an unbridled soldiery.

c. Of natural forces.

? **1814** WORDSW. *Brownie's Cell* 64 Towers rent, winds combating with woods, Lands deluged by unbridled floods.

2. Not furnished with a bridle.

1553 EDEN *Treat. New Ind.* (Arb.) 16 They are all vnbrideled, hauinge neither withe nor coller aboute theyr neckes. **1600** HAKLUYT *Voy.* III. 315 They fel on running like vnbridled horses, through the middest of the thickest woods. **1656** EARL MONM. tr. *Boccalini, Pol. Touchstone* (1674) 253 That unbridled Horse which the State bears for her Ensign. **1694** MOTTEUX *Rabelais* IV. xlviii. 188 An unbridled Mule, with green Trappings. **1798** *Hull Advertiser* 8 Sept. 1/4 Our picquets were attacked; this caused some bustle, as our horses were all unbridled. **1841** SPALDING *Italy & It. Isl.* II. 27 Pride, clothed in a lion's skin, rushes forward on an unbridled horse. **1872** HEAD *Sel. Grk. Coins Brit. Mus.* 16 The unbridled horse may be a symbol of Liberty.

Hence **un'bridledly** *adv.*; **un'bridledness.**

1561 T. NORTON *Calvin's Inst.* I. 37 Yet the boldnesse of Sophisters could not be restrained by them from babling *vnbrideledly. **1591** SYLVESTER *Du Bartas* I. vii. 211 Yet true it is, that humane things (seem) slide Unbridledly with so uncertain tide [etc.]. **1571** GOLDING *Calvin on Ps.* v. 5 With howe muche more *unbrydlednesse his enemies ronne royet. *a* **1639** W. WHATELEY *Prototypes* II. xxvi. (1640) 65 The unbridlednesse of your evill natures. *a* **1684** LEIGHTON *Comm. 1 Pet.* v. (1819) II. 322 The presumption and unbridledness of youth require the pressing and binding on of this rule.

un'briefed, *ppl. a.* (UN-¹ 8.)

1889 *Pall Mall G.* 18 Dec. 6/2 The Great Unbriefed—or *un*learned counsel as they are sometimes called.

un'bright, *a.* (UN-¹ 7; cf. OE. *unbeorhte* adv.)

1523 [COVERDALE] *Old God* (1534) B j, Beynge through dust & longe beynge unoccupied, unbright and defiled with ruste. **1570** LEVINS *Manip.* 119 Vnbright, *illucidus.*

un'brightened, *ppl. a.* (UN-¹ 8.)

1827 COLERIDGE *Work without Hope* 11 With lips unbrightened, wreathless brow, I stroll. **1873** MORLEY *Rousseau* II. 29 Saint Preux's egoism is unbrightened by a single ray of tender abnegation.

un'brined, *ppl. a.* (UN-¹ 8.)

1733 TULL *Horse-Hoeing Husb.* xii. 144 The Oldest Farmer believ'd Brining to be but a Fancy, and sow'd his Seed Unbrined.

un-'British, *a.* (UN-¹ 7.)

1746 YOUNG *Thoughts on Late Reb.* 191 By thoughts inglorious, and un-British deeds, Their cancell'd will is impiously profaned. **1754** H. WALPOLE *Mem. Geo. II* (1822) I. 328 As un-British an age as ever was. **1755** YOUNG *Centaur* vi, May they cease from this hour to sing or dance ..our British, unbritish youth, manhood, and age, out of their senses! **1894** *Daily News* 12 Nov. 6/4 This extraordinary and most un-British freedom from prejudice.

unbrizzed, Sc. form of UNBRUISED.

un'broached, *ppl. a.* (UN-^{1} 8.)
1689 *Gazophyl. Angl.*, *To Blink beer*, .. to keep it unbroached, till it grow sharp. **1742** YOUNG *Nt. Th.* III. 319 His luxuries have left him .. No maiden relishes, unbroacht delights. *Ibid.* VIII. 671 His full draught of pleasure, from a cask Unbroach'd by just authority. **1824** MISS FERRIER *Inher.* iii, Which she was reading unconsciously for the third time with unbroached delight. **1871** HAWTHORNE *Sept. Felton* (1879) 176 Septimius .. left the box unbroached.

†**un'broaded**, *ppl. a. Obs.*$^{-1}$ [UN-^{1} 8: see BROWD *v.*] Unbraided.
1590 C'TESS PEMBROKE *Antonie* 302 The Comets flaming through the scat'red clouds With fiery beames, most like vnbroaded haires.

†**un'broid**, *v. Obs.*$^{-1}$ [UN-^{2} 3.] *trans.* To unbraid, disentangle, make plain.
1586 STANYHURST *Descr. Irel.* Ep. Ded. in *Holinshed*, That I maie the sooner unbroid the pelfish trash that is wrapt within this treatise.

†**un'broided, -en**, *ppl. a. Obs.* [UN-^{1} 8, 8 b.] Unbraided, loose, dishevelled.
c **1374** CHAUCER *Troylus* IV. 817 The myghty tresses of here sonnyssh herys Vnbroyden hangen al aboute here eris. **1582** STANYHURST *Æneis* II. (Arb.) 56 Lo ye; the wood virgin, with locks vnbroyded is haled Cassandra.

un'broiled, *ppl. a.* (UN-^{1} 8.)
1623 FLETCHER & ROWLEY *Maid in Mill* IV. ii, Do not look to find .. so much flesh unbroil'd of all that mountain, As a worm might sup on.

un'broke, *ppl. a.* [var. of next.]
1. = UNBROKEN *ppl. a.* 1.
a **1325** *MS. Rawl. B.* 520 fol. 31 b, þulke þat we graunteden to holde .. in þe forme hol bi-forseide ant vnbroke. *c* **1460** *Oseney Reg.* 14 Ordeynyng þat all maner possessions .. to þem, and to þere successours sure and vnbroke abyde. *Ibid.* 161 þat sure and vnbroke hit abide. **1593** SHAKS. *Rich. II*, IV. i. 215 God keepe all Vowes vnbroke are made to thee. *a* **1637** B. JONSON *Underw.*, *to Browne*, See, that thou By off'ring not more sureties, than inow, Hold thyne owne worth unbroke.
2. = UNBROKEN *ppl. a.* 2. Also *fig.*
1632 LITHGOW *Trav.* V. 182 These Iarres are all .. interlarded with pitch to preserue the earthen vessels vnbroke a sunder. **1725** POPE *Odyss.* VIII. 149 How broad his shoulders spread! By age unbroke! **1762** WILKES *Corr.* (1805) III. 43, I .. return it with the seal unbroke, as the clearest demonstration that I never have read the contents of it. **1805** SCOTT *Last Minstrel* IV. xxi, Unbroke by age, erect his seat. **1845** LONGF. *Arrow* iii, Long, long afterward, in an oak I found the arrow, still unbroke.
3. = UNBROKEN *ppl. a.* 4.
a **1716** ADDISON tr. *Horace* III. iii, Wild from the desart and unbroke: In vain they foam'd. **1743** FRANCIS tr. *Hor.*, *Odes* II. v. 1 See, thy Heifer's yet unbroke To the Labours of the Yoke. **1810** SOUTHEY *Kehama* VIII. ii, His neck unbroke to mortal yoke, Like Nature free the Steed must be. **1842** BORROW *Bible in Spain* xix, He was a black Andalusian stallion, .. unbroke, savage, and furious. **1865** TOM TAYLOR *Ballads & Songs of Brittany* 172 An unbroke filly.
4. = UNBROKEN *ppl. a.* 5.
1793 WORDSW. *Evening Walk* 429 The scene is waken'd, yet its peace unbroke, By silver'd wreaths of quiet charcoal smoke. **1808** SCOTT *Marm.* III. vi, All gaz'd at length in silence drear, Unbroke, save when .. Some yeoman .. whisper'd forth his mind. **1816** BYRON *Siege Cor.* xi, That deep silence was unbroke, Save where the watch his signal spoke.

un'broken, *ppl. a.* [UN-^{1} 8 b. Cf. MDu. and Du. *ongebroken*, MHG. and G. *ungebrochen*.]
1. Of compacts, etc.: Not broken or infringed; unviolated, inviolate.
a **1300** *Cursor M.* 611 Bot for to hald it wel vnbroken, þe forbot þat was be-twix þam spoken. **1580** HOLLYBAND, *Inviolé*, inuiolated, sound, vnbroken. **1667** MILTON *P.L.* II. 691 That Traitor Angel, .. Who first broke peace in Heav'n and Faith, till then Unbrok'n. **1743** FRANCIS tr. *Hor.*, *Odes* I. xvii. 20 To sing frail Circe's guilty Fire, And chaste Penelope's unbroken Vow.
2. Of material things: Not broken or fractured; intact, whole.
1495 *Trevisa's Barth. De P.R.* XIX. cxxx. 939 Men in olde tyme callyd a thynge y^{t} was hoole and vnbroken, *Solidum et Totum*. **1585** T. WASHINGTON tr. *Nicholay's Voy.* I. xviii. 21 [There are] many towers and goodly buildings ruined .., amongst which, one which was vnbroken. **1613** TOURNEUR *Pr. Henry* 97, I wonder how Or he or anye other souldier now Can hold his sword unbroken. **1697** DRYDEN *Virg. Georg.* IV. 426 His bowels, bruised within, Betray no wound on his unbroken skin. **1707** MORTIMER *Husb.* (1721) II. 357 Put into the Hogshead ten new-laid Eggs, unbroken or cracked. **1790** J. BRUCE *Source Nile* II. 460 The seal [was] examined, and declared to be the patriarch's, and unbroken. **1864** MRS. CARLYLE *Lett.* (1883) III. 218 There is hardly a kitchen utensil left unbroken. **1889** J. C. JEAFFRESON *Q. of Naples & Nelson* I. iii. 93 Escaping .. with unbroken bones.
fig. *a* **1650** CRASHAW *Carmen*, *Answ. for Hope* 16 Nor will the virgin joyes we wed Come lesse unbroken to our bed. **1753** RICHARDSON *Grandison* (1781) II. xxxvi. 341 My fortune, which is unbroken, is the same sum that he gave my Brothers.
3. Not crushed, humbled, or subdued; not impaired or weakened.
1513 DOUGLAS *Æneid* XII. i. 4 Turnus .. saw thar curage faill, .. Quhilk war tofor onbrokin and stout of hart. **1549** COVERDALE, etc. *Erasm. Par. 1 John* ii. 47 A mynde that is vnbroken and vnconquered agaynst al wanton enticementes. **1609** B. JONSON *Masque of Queenes* Wks. (1660) 960 A Heroine of a most inuincible and vnbroken fortitude. **1612** *Two Noble K.* V. iv. 101 If thy heart, Thy worthie, manly heart, be yet unbroken. **1697** DRYDEN *Æneis* X. 1102 But, glancing thence, the yet unbroken force Took a new bent obliquely. **1796** MME. D'ARBLAY *Camilla* V. 288 Her, as yet, unbroken powers of encountering adversity. **1817** LADY MORGAN *France* II. (1818) I. 261 Courage unsubdued, spirits unbroken, indignation unrestrained. **1856** KANE *Arct. Expl.* I. xviii. 219 The journey was an arduous one to be undertaken, even by unbroken men. **1907** *Verney Mem.* II. 239 Her .. cheerful spirits, unbroken by poverty and dependence.
4. Of horses, etc.: Not tamed or rendered tractable; untrained.
1538 ELYOT, *Indomitus*, wylde, vnbroken. **1542** UDALL *Erasm. Apoph.* 230 To ride the vnbroken horse Bucephalus. **1593** NASHE *Christ's T.* Wks. (Grosart) IV. 170 We are the vnbroken-Colt .. which hee [*sc.* Our Lord] commaunded (with the Asse) to be brought vnto hym. **1705** STANHOPE *Paraphr.* I. 30 A Colt unbroken on which never Man had sat. **1806–7** J. BERESFORD *Miseries Hum. Life* (1826) II. xxvii, Driving an unbroken horse. **1864** BOYD *Ess.*, *Commonpl. Philos.* vii. 203 No man likes to think that he is being managed as Mr. Rarey might manage an unbroken colt. **1908** *Animal Managem.* 252 Traders carrying unbroken horses through the tropics.
transf. **1743** FRANCIS tr. *Hor.*, *Epodes* vii. 7 Britons yet unbroken to our War, In Chains should follow our triumphal Car. **1747** RICHARDSON *Clarissa* (1811) I. xvii. 119 You are young and unbroken.
5. Not interrupted or disturbed; continuous, uniform.
1561 T. NORTON *Calvin's Inst.* I. 5 b, There ought to haue ben one continual vnbroken course of obedience in their whole lyfe. *a* **1578** LINDESAY (Pitscottie) *Chron. Scot.* (S.T.S.) I. 23 Sick amitie and freindscheip .. that all men supponit the samyn for to indure for ever and euer onbrokin. **1722** WOLLASTON *Relig. Nat.* iii. 60 Truth is the offspring of silence, unbroken meditations, and thoughts often revised and corrected. **1736** BUTLER *Anal.* II. vii. 260 An unbroken Genealogy of Mankind for many Ages. **1783** BURKE *Rep. Aff. India* Wks. 1842 II. 11 It required an unbroken attention, .. to form a true judgment. **1825** WATERTON *Wand. S. Amer.* I. (1903) 2 An unbroken range of forest covers each bank of the river. **1852** ROBERTSON *Serm.* Ser. III. xii. (1882) 151 One unbroken series of cruelty and crime. **1887** BOWEN *Æneid* I. 495 While yet silent he stands in a long and unbroken gaze.
b. Const. *by*.
1743 FRANCIS tr. *Hor.*, *Odes* I. xiii. 19 In equal rapture, and sincere delights, Unbroken by complaints or strife. **1796** MME. D'ARBLAY *Camilla* III. 137 Miss Dennel grew .. weary with the length of the way, unbroken by any company. **1809** CAMPBELL *Gert. Wyom.* I. x, Many a halcyon day he lived to see Unbroken but by one misfortune dire. **1882** DE WINDT *Equator* 66 The landscape being unbroken by hill or habitation of any kind.
6. Of ground: Not broken by ploughing or digging. Also with *up*.
1579–80 NORTH *Plutarch* (1595) 26 They did take off the plougheshare, and draw the ploughe, with leauing a certain space of earthe vnbroken up. **1638** JUNIUS *Paint. Ancients* 245 An unbroken and untilled ground doth now and then bring forth goodly hearbs. **1646** EARL MONM. tr. *Biondi's Civil Wars* IX. 206 The ground is for the most part unbroken up. **1697** DRYDEN *Virg. Georg.* I. 75 E'er we stir the yet unbroken Ground. **1746** FRANCIS tr. *Horace*, *Epist.* I. xiv. 36 You complain, that with unceasing Toil, You break, alas! the long unbroken Soil. **1855** DELAMER *Kitchen Garden* (1861) 142 If you are making a new garden on unbroken ground.
7. Not broken in ranks; not thrown into disorder.
1721 DE FOE *Mem. Cavalier* (1840) 129 The imperialists, eager in the pursuit, left him unbroken. **1781** GIBBON *Decl. & F.* xxx. III. 153 He .. withdrew from the field of battle, with the greatest part of his cavalry entire and unbroken. **1855** MACAULAY *Hist. Eng.* xvii. IV. 93 The obscurity enabled Sarsfield, with a few squadrons which still remained unbroken, to cover the retreat. **1898** *Westm. Gaz.* 24 Sept. 2/1 As cavalry are not ordinarily required to charge large masses of unbroken infantry.
8. *Bot.* Not variegated. (Cf. BREAK *v.* 32 c.)
1829 LOUDON *Encycl. Plants* (1836) 267 Instead of saving the seed .. from the finest variegated tulips, they prefer unbroken flowers or breeders.
Hence **un'brokenly** *adv.*, **un'brokenness**.
1850 LYNCH *Theoph. Trinal* xii. 232 The years *unbrokenly march on. **1866** LIDDON *Bampt. Lect.* vi. (1875) 322 Like a ray of light from the parent fire with which it is unbrokenly joined. **1849** ROCK *Ch. of Fathers* I. iii. 246 The unbroken wholeness of this Altar-stone was a symbol of the *unbrokenness of the Church. **1889** ABP. BENSON in A. C. Benson *Life* (1900) II. 284 The whole crowded congregation sing in most perfect unbrokenness.

un'brookable, *a.* (UN-^{1} 7 b.)
1633 T. ADAMS *Exp. 2 Peter* ii. 8 How unbrookable is dulness in any work to a man of spirit! **1835** HOGG *Tales & Sk.* (1837) V. 357 A feeling of horror that was quite unbrookable.

un'brosten, *ppl. a.* [UN-^{1} 8 b. Cf. OHG. and MHG. *ungebrosten*, Du. *ongeborsten*.] Unburst.
13.. *E.E. Allit. P.* B. 365 Was no brymme þat abod vnbrosten bylyue. **1876** *Whitby Gloss.* 204/2 *Unbrussen*.

un'brother, *v.* [UN-^{2} 6 b.] *trans.* To deprive of brotherhood.
1634 BP. HALL *Contempl. N.T.* IV. xxxiii. 520 It is not in the power of the sins of our infirmities to unbrother us. **1657** M. LAWRENCE *Use & Pract. Faith* 211 Yet he beareth with them; he will not presently cast them off, and unbrother them. **1752** YOUNG *Brothers* III. i, Unson'd! unbrother'd! nay, unhumaniz'd! Far from affection, as thou'rt near in blood! **1804** *Ann. Rev.* II. 197/2 Brother Broomhall turned metaphysician .. As they could not confute *Mr.* Broomhall (for of course he was immediately unbrothered) they excommunicated him.

un'brothered, *ppl. a.* [UN-^{1} 8.] Not provided with a brother. Also *fig.*
1798 *Monthly Mag.* VI. 454 He from Thrugelmer descends, Aurgelmer's unbrother'd son. **1853** MISS E. S. SHEPPARD *Ch. Auchester* III. 194 The perfect form, the distinct conception of this unbrothered work.

un'brotherlike, *a.* [UN-^{1} 7 c.] = UNBROTHERLY *a.*
1594 WEST *2nd Pt. Symbol. Chancerie* §118 To thintent onely and thereby of set purpose, malice, and unbrotherlyke dealing to defraude .. your said Orator. **1667** *Decay Chr. Piety* xvii. ¶3, I mean Victor's unbrotherlike heat towards the Eastern churches in the controversie about Easter. **1877** TENNYSON *Harold* v. i, O brother, most unbrotherlike to me, Thou gavest thy voice against me in my life.

un'brotherliness. (f. next. See UN-^{1} 12.)
1647 N. WARD *Simple Cobler* 32 Nor would I declaime of the uncomlinesse, unbrotherlinesse, unseasonablenesse and unreasonablenesse of these direfull digladiations. **1885** C. J. LYALL *Anc. Arab. Poetry* 112 Ye took your stand far away from unbrotherliness.

un'brotherly, *a.* [UN-^{1} 7. Cf. Du. *onbroederlijk*, G. *unbrüderlich*.]
Not brotherly or characteristic of a brother.
1586 FERNE *Blaz. Gentrie* 113 The treacherous and vnbrotherly attempts of .. the Kinges brother. **1605** WILLET *Hexapla Gen.* 470 Dishonouring their holy profession with vnbrotherlie strife. **1680** MATHER *Irenicum* 3 Forbearing and avoiding unbrotherly and provoking terms and words. **1741** RICHARDSON *Pamela* IV. 36 How did all their hearts burn with sordid and unbrotherly Envy against their Father's favourite Son? **1796** *Monthly Mag.* I. 200 The people no longer view them with .. mistrust, or unbrotherly emotions. **1829** SCOTT *Anne of G.* v, Here is the scroll, coldly worded, but far less unkindly than his unbrotherly message. **1891** F. W. NEWMAN *J. H. Newman* 21, I shall be told that these revelations are unbrotherly.

†**un'brotherly**, *adv. Obs.* [UN-^{1} 11. Cf. ON. *úbróðurliga*.] In a manner or spirit unbefitting a brother.
1574 WHITGIFT *Def. Aunsw.* i. 74 As the name was first by the Papistes maliciously inuented, so is it of you verie vnbrotherly confirmed. **1605** CAMDEN *Rem.* 202 Brotherly to pardon his manifolde offences, that he had vnbrotherly committed against him. *a* **1635** SIBBES *Confer. Christ & Mary* (1656) 31 They had dealt most unbrotherly with him.

un'brought, *ppl. a.* [UN-^{1} 8 b, 8 c.] Not brought (*forth*, *in*, or *into*).
1525 TINDALE *N.T.* Prol. A serpent yet yonge, or yett unbrought forthe. **1595** DANIEL *Civ. Wars* III. xxii, Iudges incompetent To iudge their king unlawfully detaind, And vnbrought forth to plead his guiltles cause. **1600** FAIRFAX *Tasso* X. xviii, If in thy skilfull hart this lore be writ To tell th' euent of things to end vnbrought. **1817** KEATINGE *Trav.* II. 138 Not a foot of vertical superficies should remain unbrought into account.

un'bruised, *ppl. a.* [UN-^{1} 8.]
1. Not injured by bruising or crushing.
c **1440** *Pallad. on Husb.* III. 353 So sawe hit that the bark vnbresed be. **1526** *Pilgr. Perf.* (W. de W. 1531) 83 A floure, whan it is fresshe, .. vnbrused & hole, is moche delectable & swete. **1579** SPENSER *Sheph. Cal.* Oct. 42 Doubted Knights, whose .. helmes vnbruzed wexen dayly browne. **1606** SHAKS. *Tr. & Cr.* Prol. 14 On Dardan Plaines The fresh and yet vnbruised Greekes do pitch Their braue Pauillions. *a* **1652** BROME *City Wit* v. i, Unbruised bones, and smooth fore-heads to face both. **1801** SURR *Splendid Misery* I. 172 Foul imps of ignominy will squat their loathsome forms on my unbruised bones. **1816** SCOTT *Antiq.* viii, The callant had come off wi' unbrizzed banes. **1900** F. T. BULLEN *Men Merch. Service* xxxii, One man .. beat me until there was not a square inch of my small body unbruised.
fig. **1455** *Rolls of Parlt.* V. 280/2 Alwey kepyng oure trouthe to his said Highnesse unspotted and unbrused.
2. Not crushed small; unpounded.
1607 TOPSELL *Four-f. Beasts* 327 It should seeme that none of his meate should fall thereinto vnbruised. **1802** PALEY *Nat. Theol.* ix. §6. 1 The rough action of the unbruised spiculæ. **1844** H. STEPHENS *Bk. Farm* II. 191 The horses fed on unbruised raw and on boiled grain, gave results .. very nearly alike.

un'brushed, *ppl. a.* (UN-^{1} 8.)
1640 FULLER *Joseph's Coat* vi. (1867) 167 Men of a rugged, unbrushed nature, such as were never licked, hewn, or polished. **1888** BARRIE *When a Man's Single* iii, The coat had hung unbrushed on a nail for many years.

†**un'brushen**, *ppl. a. Obs.* (UN-^{1} 8 b.)
c **1460** J. RUSSELL *Bk. Nurture* 944 Lett neuer wollyn cloth ne furre passe a seuenyght to be vnbrosshen & shakyn.

un'brutalize, *v.* (UN-^{2} 6 a *c.*)
1852 MILL *Lett.* (1910) I. v. 165 All reading .. which must tend to .. give them some of the meaning of self-devotion and heroism, in short, to unbrutalise them. **1862** H. KINGSLEY *Ravenshoe* lii, I am afraid of their getting too much unbrutalized for another struggle like ours.

un'brute, *v.* (UN-^{2} 6 b.)
1670 PENN *Lib. Consc.* Wks. 1782 III. 21 That it does not unbrute us, but unman us. **1687** A. LOVELL tr. *Bergerac's Com. Hist.* 49 Not being able to unbrute my self so soon.

un'brutify, *v.* (UN-^{2} 6 c.)
1812 TENNANT *Anster F.* III. xiv, The very waving of her arm Had pow'r a brutish lout to unbrutify and charm.

un'brutized, *ppl. a.* (UN-^{1} 8.)
a **1711** KEN *Hymnotheo* Poet. Wks. 1721 III. 336, I certain am I must the Godhead fear, Since all Men unbrutis'd some God revere.

†**un'bubble**, *v. Obs.*$^{-1}$ [UN-^{2} 3.] *trans.* To explode, dispel.

a **1640** JACKSON *Wks.* (1844) VII. 416 So may every novice in arts unbubble all that some great..schoolmen have been twenty or thirty years in contriving.

un'bucked, *ppl. a.* (UN-^{1} 8 + BUCK *v.*^{2})

1638 MAYNE *Lucian* (1664) 337 'Tis not in a Lyons skinne, as I have heard, said Dinomachus, but in a Virgin Hindes skinne unbuckt.

un'buckle, *v.* [UN-^{2} 4 b.]

1. *trans.* To unfasten the buckle of (a shoe, belt, etc.); to undo or set free in this way.

c **1386** CHAUCER *Sqr.'s T.* 555 Ne neuere..Ne koude man ..Countrefete the Sophymes of his Art Ne were worthy vnbokelen his galoche. **1393** LANGL. *P. Pl.* C. xx. 68 He vnbokelede hus boteles, and boþe he a-tamede. *c* **1430** *Pilgr. Lyf Manhode* I. cxxxviii. (1869) 72 Thanne the bocle j vnboclede. **1470–85** MALORY *Arthur* x. lx. 516 Soo the varlet wente to vnbockel his helme. **1548** UDALL, etc. *Erasm. Par. Luke* iii. 32 b, I..am vnworthy to vnbuccle the latchet of his shooes. **1577** *Test. 12 Patriarchs* (1604) 90 The young man unbuckled Joseph's shoes at the gate. **1606** SHAKS. *Ant. & Cl.* IV. iv. 12 He that vnbuckles this, till we do please To daft for our Repose, shall heare a storme. **1755** YOUNG *Centaur* v. Wks. 1757 IV. 223 This is a militant state; nor must man unbuckle his armour, till he puts on his shroud. **1820** SCOTT *Monast.* vi, He is like a miser, who will not unbuckle his purse to bestow a farthing. **1860** FROUDE *Hist. Eng.* V. 389 Dropping his cloak he unbuckled his sword. **1886** C. E. PASCOE *London of To-day* i. (ed. 3) 23 The Major..fell to unbuckling the straps of his trunk.

b. In fig. context. (Cf. MAIL *sb.*^{3} 1 c.)

c **1386** CHAUCER *Miller's Prologue* 7 This gooth aright vnbokeled is the Male; Lat se now who shal telle another tale. *a* **1400** *Partonope* 7308 Of þi woo vnbocle þi male, And tell me all the verey troupe. *a* **1600** DELONEY *Gentle Craft* II. viii. Wks. (1912) 186 Neuer be afraid man to vnbuckle Your Budget of close counsell to me. **1805** *Ann. Rev.* III. 164 We much doubt whether any one, not educated in the catholic schools, could have detected where the collar may best be unbuckled.

c. *fig.* To free or separate *from*; to open up, display; to detach, break off.

a **1548** HALL *Chron., Hen. VI*, 177 b, This noble realme.. shall neuer be vnbuckeled from her quotidian feuer. **1638** BRATHWAIT *Barnabees Jrnl.* (1818) 191 Some comfort unbuckle, my sweet honeysuckle. **1736** [CHETWOOD] *Voy. Vaughan* (1760) I. 264 The congregation immediately unbuckled their Devotions, and were crouding out as fast as they cou'd.

2. *absol.* To undo the buckle or buckles of a belt, garment, etc.

1611 BEAUM. & FL. *King & No King* III, Why do you wear a Sword then? Come unbuckle... Unbuckle I say, and give it me. **1611** SHAKS. *Wint. T.* IV. iv. 659 Vnbuckle, vnbuckle. Fortunate Mistresse..you must retire your selfe Into some Couert. **1649** DAVENANT *Love & Hon.* I. i. 160 Unbuckle, Calladine, the day is hott. **1836** DICKENS *Sk. Boz, Gt. Winglebury Duel*, Up started the ostlers..unstrapping, and unchaining, and unbuckling.

b. *transf.* To become slack.

1648 J. BEAUMONT *Psyche* XIII. clxxxii, His Joints unbuckled; and his Eyes did start; His hair stood staring up.

c. *fig.* To unbend, become less stiff.

1886 STEVENSON *Kidnapped* viii, Even the captain..would sometimes unbuckle a bit, and tell me of the fine countries he had visited.

Hence **un'buckling** *vbl. sb.*

1598 FLORIO, *Sfibbiatura*, an vnbuckling, an vnlacing. *a* **1859** DE QUINCEY *Posth. Wks.* (1891) I. 272 Through the unbuckling of human nature under higher inspirations.

un'buckled, *ppl. a.* [UN-^{2} 8 and UN-^{1} 8.]

a. Having the buckle undone. **b.** Having the buckle not fastened.

In quot. *c* 1723 misused for 'not unbuckled' (in sense 2).

c **1489** CAXTON *Sonnes of Aymon* i. 42 There sholde ye haue seen..many..helmes vnbocled and sore beten. **1667** MILTON *P.L.* XI. 245 His starrie Helme unbuckl'd shew'd him prime In Manhood. *c* **1723** RAMSAY *The Nuptials* 145 That zone..lang unbuckled grows a hatefu' thing. **1809** *Med. Jrnl.* XXI. 389 The girths being unbuckled, the whole of the back may be exposed and dressed. **1825** SCOTT *Talism.* ii, The long and ponderous Gothic war-sword which was flung unbuckled on the same sod. **1875** BEDFORD *Sailor's Pocket Bk.* vii. 220 Whilst in the boats they are to keep them unbuckled.

un'buckramed, *a.* (UN-^{1} 9.)

1813 COLMAN *Broad Grins, Vagaries Vind.* li, Thence I appeal, for judgment on my pen, To moral but unbuckram'd gentlemen.

un'bud, *v.* (UN-^{2} 4.)

1669 WORLIDGE *Syst. Agric.* (1681) 220 In a little time they have almost totally unbudded the Plum-trees, Currant-trees, &c. of a whole Town.

un'budded, *ppl. a.* (UN-^{1} 8.)

1820 KEATS *Lamia* II. 54 Like the hid scent in an unbudded rose.

un'budget, *v.* (UN-^{2} 3.)

1611 FLORIO, *Sbolgettare*, to vnbudget. **1843** [JAMES] *Commissioner* 62 Mr. Longmore was infinitely relieved by unbudgetting his griefs. **1886** *Gd. Words* 332 He had made the most extraordinary unbudgettings about his pet bees, guinea-pigs [etc.].

un'buffeted, *ppl. a.* (UN-^{1} 8.)

[**1775** ASH.] **1855** LYNCH *Rivulet* LXXXVIII. vi, While unconfused by riot, Unbuffeted by storm.

un'build, *v.* [UN-^{2} 3.] *trans.* To pull down, destroy, demolish (a building or structure).

1607 SHAKS. *Cor.* III. i. 198 To vnbuild the Citie, and to lay all flat. **1642** T. GOODWIN *Zerub.*, etc. 25 Thou didst unbuild Hierusalem and my Temple. **1684** T. BURNET *Theory Earth* I. 91 God builds and unbuilds worlds: and who shall build up that arch that was broke down at the deluge? **1751** LABELYE *Westm. Bridge* 81 Whilst the Arches were unbuilding and taking down. **1820** SHELLEY *Cloud* 84, I arise and unbuild it again. **1829** CARLYLE *Misc.* (1857) II. 49 The Ephesian Temple..could be unbuilt by one madman, in a single hour. **1878** BROWNING *Poets Croisic* 13 Priestesses Unbuilt and then rebuilt it every May.

b. In fig. uses. Also *absol.*

1640 HABINGTON *Edw. IV*, 75 The Almightie..permitted perjurie now to unbuild the greatnesse of Lancaster. **1667** MILTON *P.L.* VIII. 81 When they come to model Heav'n,.. how they will weild The mightie frame, how build, unbuild. *Ibid.* XII. 526 What will they then..but unbuild His living Temples, built by Faith to stand? **1856** R. A. VAUGHAN *Mystics* (1860) I. v. i. 112 First of all exerting his extraordinary will to the utmost to unbuild his body. **1875** WHITNEY *Life Lang.* iv. 74 The component elements of speech are first unified, then unbuilt and destroyed.

Hence **un'building** *vbl. sb.*

1879 TRENCH *Poems* 155 Build it this time..A holy house, ..And we, though in the unbuilding there be pain, Will still affirm,—'tis well.

un'builded, *ppl. a.* [UN-^{1} 8.]

1. = UNBUILT *ppl. a.*

1519 in *Somerset. & Dorset. N. & Q.* (1893) III. 244 Every half yere that the said sidehouse shall be unbuylded or unreedefyed. **1535** COVERDALE *Isaiah* vi. 11 Till the londe be also desolate, and lye vnbuylded. **1560** PILKINGTON *Expos. Aggeus* (1562) 163 Chuse you whether ye will let my house lye unbuylded stil,..or ye will repare it diligently.

fig. **1594** HOOKER *Eccl. Pol.* II. vii. §5 When bare and vnbuilded conclusions are put into their mindes..they fall into anguish and perplexitie.

2. Not employed in building.

1867 HOWELLS *Ital. Journ.* iii. 21 Mixing their weary brick and mortar with the earth's unbuilded dust.

un'built, *ppl. a.* [UN-^{1} 8 b, 8 c: cf. prec.]

1. Not (yet) built or erected.

1455–6 *Cal. Anc. Rec. Dublin* (1889) 290 Yf yt be unbylyt aftyr the fyrst yere..than the Mayre..shold require hym to repeyre hit. **1582** STANYHURST *Æneis* III. (Arb.) 74 Theare picht he his kingdoom, for then Troy cittye was vnbuylt, And castels stood not. **1612** DRAYTON *Poly-olb.* iv. 375 Tuisco, Gomer's son, from unbuilt Babel brought His people to that place. **1697** COLLIER *Ess. Mor. Subj.* II. (ed. 2) 5 The Rhodian Colossus had been lost;..the Egyptian Pyramids unbuilt. **1861** BERESF. HOPE *Eng. Cathedr. 19th C.* iv. 112 As I have given some unbuilt designs of modern architects.

b. Made without building.

1882 J. PARKER *Apost. Life* I. 48 Elijah hid himself in an unbuilt chamber in the rock.

2. Of land: Not occupied with buildings; not built *on* or *upon*.

1631 WEEVER *Anc. Funeral Mon.* 607 All which he pulled downe,..leauing the ground vnbuilt for a Cemitery or Churchyard. **1819** in Picton *L'pool Munic Rec.* (1886) II. 378 Such part of their unbuilt land as will be sufficient for a Public Market. **1855** [J. R. LEIFCHILD] *Cornwall* 66 Scarcely in any other district so open and unbuilt on, would you find the agriculturist so completely subdued. **1893** A. CAWSTON *Street Improv. London* 124 In the as yet unbuilt parts grounds are to be reserved.

un'bulk, *v.* (UN-^{2} 3.)

Probably an error for UNBUCKLE *v.* 1 b.

1536 *Pilgr. T.* 272 in Thynne *Animadv.* (1875) 84 'But her,' he sayd, 'cowd I tell a tall'. 'now I pray the,' quod I, 'vnbulke thy malle, and tell forthe'.

un'bulky, *a.* (UN-^{1} 7.)

1678 CUDWORTH *Intell. Syst.* 780 Incorporeal..activities, ..though they act upon bulk and extension, yet are themselves unbulkie, and devoid of quantity and dimensions. **1848** MILL *Pol. Econ.* III. xix. §2 (1876) 369 This..must be occasioned by..the unbulky character of these commodities.

un'bumptious, *a.* (UN-^{1} 7.)

1865 TENNYSON in Ld. Tennyson *Mem.* (1897) II. 28 Me, who am physically the most unbumptious of men and authors.

un'bunched, *ppl. a.* (UN-^{1} 8.)

1615 *Marr. & Wiving* xi. in *Harl. Misc.* (1809) II. 173 This destiny shall preserve him, to wear his brow..as unbunched as the front of a bachelor.

un'bundle, *v.* [UN-^{2} 3.]

1. *trans.* To unpack, take out of a bundle. Also *fig.*

1606 S. GARDINER *Bk. Angling* 111 Who so is a wise merchant will not vnbundle his seuerall wares to such. **1611** FLORIO, *Disfagottare*, to vnfaggot, to vnbundle. *a* **1739** JARVIS *Quix.* (1749) II. III. vi. 220 Unbundle your griefs, madam, and let us into the particulars.

2. To introduce a system of separate charging for (items previously charged for collectively, esp. computer hardware and software).

1969 *Datamation* XV. 69 (*heading*) IBM 'unbundles' hardware/services charges... Will software be next? **1971** *New Scientist* 15 July 140/1 Programs, courses, computer maintenance and systems engineering would be priced separately (or 'unbundled') from the computers themselves. **1977** *Business Week* 18 Apr. 83/2 Banks may then be forced to unbundle costs and charge an additional 30¢ or so for each check processed. **1983** *Austral. Microcomputer Mag.* Dec. 40/3 The 8086 processor has been unbundled and is now an option.

Hence **un'bundling** *vbl. sb.*, (the introduction of) a policy of separate charging for related items.

1969 *Datamation* XV. 69/1 IBM 'expects to make changes in the way it charges for and supports its data processing equipment'. The word for it is 'unbundling'. **1971** E. F. SCHOETERS in B. de Ferranti *Living with Computer* viii. 72 These arguments are becoming academic in the light of separate pricing of hardware, software, support and staff training, commonly known by the unlovely name of 'unbundling'. **1981** *Economist* 11 July 65/2 Independent Japanese software houses, helped by separate pricing ('unbundling') of software and hardware by computer makers, are starting to write their own packaged programmes.

un'bung, *v.* [UN-^{2} 3.] *trans.* To take the bung out of (a barrel). Hence **un'bunging** *vbl. sb.*

1611 COTGR., *Detapper*, to vnbung, to open the bung-hole of. *a* **1693** *Urquhart's Rabelais* III. Prol. 6 There did he.. unbung it,..unstopple it. **1694** MOTTEUX *Rabelais* IV. li. 199 This Stuff has unbung'd the Orifice of my Mustard-Barrel. **1742** *Lond. & Country Brew.* II. (1743) 143 When Servants have the Bunging and Unbunging of such Casks of Malt-Liquors.

un'bunged, *ppl. a.* (UN-^{1} 8 or UN-^{2} 8.)

1731 MILLER *Gard. Dict.* s.v. *Wine*, Let it [the vessel] stand unbung'd 'till cool. **1817** W. SELWYN *Law Nisi Prius* (ed. 4) II. 1261 The act of the warehouseman in leaving them unbunged after filling them up. **1897** *Daily News* 23 July 3/1 Unbunged barrels were left at the mercy of the rising water, the contents being spoilt.

un'buoyant, *a.* (UN-^{1} 7.)

1866 J. B. ROSE tr. *Ovid's Met.* 1 Unfirm the earth, unbuoyant was the wave.

un'burden, un'burthen, *v.* [UN-^{2} 4 b. Cf. G. *entbürden*.]

1. *trans.* To unload; to free from a load or burden. Chiefly *fig.*, to relieve (a person, the mind, etc.) by the removal or disclosure of something. Freq. const. *of*.

α. **1538** ELYOT Addit., *Exonero, -rare*, to discharge or vnburdeyn. **1568** *Gismond of Salerne* I. ii. 34, I may perhappes devise some way to be unburdened of my life. **1622** S. WARD *Life of Faith in Death* (1627) 105 The inner man ages not,..but rather lifts vp the head,..and expects to be unburdened. **1634** SIR T. HAWKINS *Pol. Observ.* 11 Tiberius by him unburdened from the greater toyles of Empire,..would not so soone..precipitate him. **1797** MRS RADCLIFFE *Italian* xii, I would fain sing to unburden it of some of its joy. **1846** MRS. A. MARSH *Father Darcy* II. xi. 204 She felt that irresistible necessity to unburden her heart. **1858** SEARS *Athan.* II. iii. 194 They unburden their minds to each other.

β. *a* **1595** SOUTHWELL *Hundred Medit.* (1873) 231 Thou.. commandest us to love to unburthen us of the heavy weight and griefs that we suffer. **1597** A. M. tr. *Guillemeau's Fr. Chirurg.* 22 b/2 Ther ensueth an effluxion of bloode, because that parte may be therof released and vnburthened. **1641** CHAS. I *Commons Remonstr.* Wks. 1662 II. 68 We desire to unburthen the Consciences of men of needless and superstitious Ceremonies. **1671** H. M. tr. *Erasm. Colloq.* 406 If I had not unburthened my Boat, I had been cast away together with my Boat, passengers, and fraught. **1777** SHERIDAN *Sch. Scand.* IV. iii, There is a subject, my dear Friend, on which I wish to unburthen my Mind to you. **1796** MORSE *Amer. Geog.* II. 17 The glutton..unburthens his stomach by squeezing himself between two close-standing trees. **1820** SHELLEY *Liberty* xix, As summer clouds dissolve, unburthened of their rain. **1875** WHYTE MELVILLE *Katerfelto* iv. 31 He unburthened his mind while watching Waif's stealthy movements.

b. *refl.*

1589 GREENE *Menaphon* (Arb.) 67 Fame..vnburdened hir selfe of hir secrets in the presence of yong Pleusidippus. **1600** HAKLUYT *Voy.* III. 81 It is not possible that so great course of floods..can be digested here without vnburdening themselues into some open Sea beyond this place. **1634** SIR T. HERBERT *Trav.* 54 A violent storme of raine vnburthened it selfe. **1674** tr. *Scheffer's Lapland* xxxiv. 146 Several less rivers unburdening themselves at last into the Bothnick sea. **1859** J. LANG *Wand. India* 400 A trooper in the dragoons.. thus unburthened himself. **1862** TROLLOPE *Orley F.* xxxi, She thought to herself that she would..then unburthen herself of the whole story.

2. To cast off, get rid of, discharge, after the manner of a burden; to disclose, reveal.

a **1593** MARLOWE & NASHE *Dido* v. i, The Sunne from Egypt shall rich odors bring, Wherewith his burning beames..Shall here vnburden their exhaled sweetes. **1596** SHAKS. *Merch. V.* I. i. 133 From your loue I haue a warrantie To vnburthen all my plots and purposes. **1830** LYTTON *P. Clifford* iv, All that rage which it was necessary for her comfort that she should unburthen somewhere. **1876** E. MELLOR *Priesth.* viii. 372 There is, at times, a great relief in unburdening to a friend the sins and sorrows of one's life.

Hence **un'burdening** *vbl. sb.*; **un'burdenment**.

1550 THOMAS *Ital. Dict.*, *Scaricamento*, a dischardge or vnburdenyng. **1848** MRS. GASKELL *Mary Barton* ii, The unburdening of her fears and thoughts to her friend. **1892** MRS. H. WARD *David Grieve* II. vii, A moment of unburdenment, of intimacy. **1902** *Fortn. Rev.* June 1048 The unburdening of sins is generally a more irksome task.

un'burdened, *ppl. a.* (UN-^{1} 8 and UN-^{2} 8.)

1548 *Act 2 & 3 Edw. VI*, c. 21 §1 Beinge free and unburdened from the care and coste of fyndinge Wyef and Children. **1605** SHAKS. *Lear* I. i. 42 Conferring them on yonger strengths, while we Vnburthen'd crawle toward death. **1724** SWIFT *Poems, On Dreams* 8 When in bed we rest our weary limbs, The mind unburden'd sports in various whims. **1775** BURKE *Sp. Concil. Amer.* Wks. III. 116 The obedient colonies in this scheme are heavily taxed; the refractory remain unburthened. **1875** C. L. KENNEY *Mem. M. W. Balfe* 148 His exchequer would be unburdened with superfluous expenses. **1883** STEVENSON *Silverado Sq.* 122

Even for a man unburthened, the ascent was toilsome and precarious.

un'burdensome, *a.* (UN-[1] 7.)
1792 G. WAKEFIELD *Mem.* (1804) I. 363 Judiciall processes, speedy, decisive, and unburdensome. **1817** COLERIDGE *Biog. Lit.* xi. (1882) 111 The establishment presents a patronage at once..effective and unburthensome.

un'burdensomeness. (f. prec.: see UN-[1] 12.)
1795 BENTHAM *Supply without Burthen* 27 Thus stands the resource in point of unburthensomeness.

un'burgessed, *a.* (UN-[2] 8.)
1671 E. CHAMBERLAYNE *Pres. St. Eng.* II. 136 The petty decayed Burroughs [petitioned] that they might not be obliged to send Burgesses to Parlament, whereby it came to pass that divers were unburgessed.

un'buriable, *a.* (UN-[1] 7 b.)
1853 G. J. CAYLEY *Las Alforjas* I. 203 It would be an inconvenience to have an unpleasant, unburiable moral corpse of an unjustly supposed immoral ancester always lying at their door. **1872** TENNYSON *Gareth & Lynette* 79 A yet-warm corpse, and yet unburiable.

un'burial. [UN-[2] 8.] Disinterment.
1872 RUSKIN *Fors Clav.* xv. 15 The persons thus reverenced in their burial, or unburial, being all, by profession, soldiers.

un'buried, *ppl. a.* Forms: (see BURY *v.*). [UN-[1] 8.] Not buried; not interred.
a **900** *O.E. Martyrol.* 22 Jan. 28 Se casere þa bebead þæt hine man forlete unbyrȝedne. *a* **1225** *Ancr. R.* 352 þe dead nis [*v.r.* ne wis] nout of, þauh he ligge unburied & rotie buuen eorðe. **1297** R. GLOUC. (Rolls) 4486 Men bysyde of þe lond he let burye is fon, Vor he ne kepte uor reuþe þat þer were vnburied non. *c* **1386** CHAUCER *Frankl. T.* 713 His loue rather for to dyen chees Than for to suffre his body vnburyed be. *c* **1430** *Life St. Kath.* (1884) 59 He bad þat.. her hedes [should be] smyten of and her bodyes left vnburyed. **1460** CAPGRAVE *Chron.* (Rolls) 75, xxx. dayes lay his body onburied, til Seynt Petir..bad him bery it. **1513** DOUGLAS *Æneid* XI. vii. 191 So that we..Be nocht down strowit in the feildis ded, In cumpaneis vnberyit or bewalit. **1560** DAUS tr. *Sleidane's Comm.* 286 b, Wherof the one departed xi yeares past,..and remayned unburied hitherto. **1600** HAKLUYT *Voy.* III. 806 Euery Fort had in it one cast peece, which peeces were buryed in the ground, the cariages were standing in their place vnburied. **1697** DRYDEN *Æneis* XI. 4 The pious chief, whom double cares attend For his unbury'd soldiers and his friend. *a* **1745** SWIFT *Hen. II*, Wks. 1768 IV. 317 When he..found that..he must draw upon himself the scandal of keeping a father unburied. **1836** THIRLWALL *Greece* III. xxvi. 449 The sight of the unburied dead struck their surviving friends with pious grief. **1891** FARRAR *Darkn. & Dawn* lxv, The stench of an unburied corpse which lay by the roadside.

unbur'lesqued, *ppl. a.* (UN-[1] 8.)
1827 POLLOK *Course T.* VII. 586 Unfaded work of Deity, And unburlesqued by mortal's puny skill. **1876** MEREDITH *Beauch. Career* i, Politics..(enough, when unburlesqued, to blow the down off the gossamer-stump of fiction..) must be treated of.

†**un'burly,** *a.* and *adv.* *Obs.* In 5 unborely, vnburely. [UN-[1] 7 and 11.] Uncomely; not elegant(ly).
a **1400** *Sir Perc.* 525 Thofe he unborely were dyghte. *c* **1475** *Rauf Coilȝear* 522 Thocht thair brandis be blak and vnburely. *Ibid.* 807 His blonk was vnburely, braid and ouir hie.

un'burn, *v.* [UN-[2] 3.] *trans.* To restore from the effects of burning.
1815 J. SMITH *Panorama Sci. & Art* II. 485 To deprive them of oxygen is virtually to unburn them. **1869** *Q. Rev.* CXXVI. 263 The duty of the plant, on the other hand, is to unburn carbonic acid, to sunder the molecules of that compound back again to their elements of carbon and oxygen.
Hence **un'burning** *vbl. sb.*
1866 ODLING *Anim. Chem.* 72 The heat absorbed in the unburning, so to speak, of the hydrogen.

un'burnable, *a.* (UN-[1] 7 b.)
1881 *Harper's Weekly* XXV. 455 There is scarcely a town that does not contain his unburnable chests [= safes].

un'burning, *ppl. a.* (UN-[1] 10; cf. OE. *unbyrnende*.)
1644 DIGBY *Nat. Bodies* vii. (1658) 61 The unburning fire (which we call light) streaming from the flame of a candle. **1822** T. TAYLOR *Apuleius* 263 The purity of the vivific and unburning fire of the heavens. **1867** MORRIS *Jason* II. 666 Some happy summer isle Whereon the kind unburning sun doth smile For ever.

un'burnished, *ppl. a.* (UN-[1] 8.)
1691 *Lond. Gaz.* No. 2654/4, 7 Silver Tankards, one unburnished weighing about 32 Ounces. **1795** SOUTHEY *Joan of Arc* VII. 40 Their bucklers lay Unburnish'd and defiled. **1842** TENNYSON *Ulysses* 23 How dull it is to pause, to make an end, To rust unburnish'd, not to shine in use! **1894** *Daily News* 11 Nov. 5/2 An olive branch in old unburnished gold is..thrown across the oak branches.

un'burnt, un'burned, *ppl. a.* Forms: (see BURN *v.*). [UN-[1] 8 and 8 b. Cf. MDu. *ungebernt, -brant,* Du. *ongebrand,* G. *ungebrannt,* ON. and Icel. *úbrendr, óbrendr* (Sw. *obrand,* Da. *ubrændt*).]
1. Not burnt or consumed by fire.
α. *c* **1290** *S. Eng. Leg.* I. 29/97 His bones þat weren bi-left vn-barnd amidde þe se to caste. *c* **1440** *Alph. Tales* 162 þat was fon vnbyrnyd emang þe hate colis. **1563** FOXE *A. & M.* 1224/1, I will geue vi fagottes to burne the with all or thou shuldest be vnburned. **1607** SHAKS. *Cor.* v. i. 27 He said, 'twas folly, For one poore graine or two, to leaue vnburnt, And still to nose th' offence. **1623** BINGHAM *Xenophon* 57 They came..to the vnburnt villages, setting afire the villages, where they last quartered. **1676** GREW *Exper. Luctation* iii. § 11 Egg-shells..being burnt, are far stronger Medicines, than when unburnt. **1715** DESAGULIERS *Fires Impr.* 133 Put what Wood is left unburn'd over them. **1849** THOMS tr. *Worsaae's Primeval Antiq. Denmark* 94 The ancient cromlechs or giants' chambers, with unburnt bodies and objects of stone. **1884** *Health Exhib. Catal.* 71/2 Stoves ..constructed specially to bring all the air into the room.. pure and warm but unburnt.
β. *c* **1384** CHAUCER *H. Fame* I. 173 Anchises..Bare the goddesse of the londe Thilke that vnbrende were. **1412–20** LYDG. *Chron. Troy* IV. 6527 þei ne lefte with-inne þe cite No þing vnbrent. *c* **1450** *Mirk's Festial* 163 So [he] sauet his bokes vnbrent þrogh þe grace and þe mercy of God. **1509** BARCLAY *Shyp of Folys* (1570) 171 Because the lightning or thunder violent..suffreth thee and thy house to be vnbrent. **1568** GRAFTON *Chron.* II. 346 They..made a road into Scotland,..and left nothing vnbrent to Edenbourgh.
γ. *c* **1375** *Sc. Leg. Saints* xxvii. (*Machor*) 188 þe barne stil can ly, Ay kepand it sa godis grace þat in þe fyr vnbrynt it was. *c* **1480** HENRYSON *Annunciation* 40 The low of luf haldand þe hete Vnbrynt full blithlie birnis. **1555** *Sc. Acts, Mary* (1814) II. 490/1 Gif samekill restis vnbrint of the haill tenement. **1571–2** *Reg. Privy Council Scot.* II. 121 For sauftie of the houssis..being within the same unbrint and dimolissit.
fig. *a* **1584** MONTGOMERIE *Cherrie & Slae* (1597) 243 Bot now na bluid in me remaines, Vnbrunt and bruilȝeit throw my vaines, Be luiffis bellowes blawin.
2. Not subjected to the action of fire for a specific purpose. Esp. of bricks, clay, lime, etc.
1626 BACON *Sylva* § 898 We see also, that burnt wine is more hard and astringent, than wine unburnt. *c* **1650** NORGATE *Miniatura* (1919) 15 Cologne Earth unburnt..is a very good colour for deepe shadowes. **1815** ELPHINSTONE *Acc. Caubul* (1842) I. 305 The commonest house by far is built of unburned brick. **1877** RAYMOND *Statist. Mines & Mining* 382 When the pile is finished the outside crust of unburned pyrites is taken off and put onto the next pile.

un'burrow, *v.* [UN-[2] 7 and 5.] **a.** *intr.* To come out of a burrow. Also *fig.* **b.** *trans.* To bring or force out of a burrow.
1744 in *10th Rep. Hist. MSS. Comm.* App. I. 280 If Ma[rsha]l Saxe will not unburrow I have advised our sending strong partys of horse [etc.]. **1827** J. MONTGOMERY *Pelican Isl.* III. 158 Hence the young brood, that never knew a parent, Unburrowed and by instinct sought the sea. **1860** DICKENS *Uncomm. Trav.* x, He feigns that he can bring down sparrows, and unburrow rats.

un'burse, *v.* *Obs.*[−0] (UN-[2] 5.)
1570 LEVINS *Manip.* 191 To Dispurse, *expendere.* To Disburse, *idem*... To Vnburse and Vnpurse, *idem.*

un'burst, *ppl. a.* (UN-[1] 8 b; cf. UNBROSTEN.)
1782 F. DOUGLAS *E. Coast Scot.* 44 In one of them, called the Murray-gate,..several bombs, unburst, were lately found, deep sunk in the earth. **1855** T. R. JONES *Anim. Kingd.* (ed. 2) 333 Another membrane, which in the unburst egg is external to this and lines the interior of the shell.

un'burstable, *a.* (UN-[1] 7.)
1890 *Times* 25 Oct. 5/1 The power that will make guns unburstable and armour impenetrable.

unburthen, -ed, -some, varr. UNBURDEN, etc.

un'bury, *v.* [UN-[2] 3.] *trans.* To disinter; to take out of the ground again.
14.. *Voc.* in Wr.-Wülcker 581 *Exhumo,* to vnberye. **1481** CAXTON *Godfrey* cvi. 162 Whan the peple afoote knewe this, they ranne, And there vnburyed them, And toke them out of theyr sepultures and graues. **1530** PALSGR. 766/2 It shulde seme that he hath done some great offence, that they unbury hym nowe. **1567** JEWEL *Def. Apol.* 100 The same Pope Steuin vnburied his Predecessour Pope Formosus, and defaced, and mangled his naked carkesse. **1605** WILLET *Hexapla Gen.* 250 The Sichemites..would rather haue vnburied them. **1647** TRAPP *Comm. Rev.* xi. 9 They unburied and burned the bones of Hermannus Ferrariensis after they had sainted him. **1848** GALLENGA *Italy* I. 61 As long as there remain..inscriptions to decipher, or ruins to unbury. **1876** LOWELL *Among my Bks.* Ser. II. 132 The medicine by which vampires were cured was to unbury them, drive a stake through them [etc.].
b. *fig.* or in *fig.* context.
1620 SHELTON *Quix.* II. xlix. 321 Because they come not in a fit time to haue audience: straight they back-bite..him, gnaw his bones, and vnbury his ancestors. *a* **1739** JARVIS *Quix.* (1749) II. III. v. 217 Speaking ill of us, unburying our bones, and burying our reputations. **1839** LYTTON *Richelieu* I. i, Your breast holds both my secrets; Never Unbury either! **1862** H. AÏDÉ *Carr of Carrlyon* I. 309 The secret is ours. No one has a right to demand us to unbury our past. **1887** BROWNING *Parleyings, Fust & Friends,* Unbury that brow! Look up, that thy judge may read clear in thine eyes!
Hence **un'burying** *vbl. sb.*
1899 S. BUTLER *Shaks. Sonn.* 117 To suppose that he sanctioned the unburying, is to deny the commonest instinct of humanity.

un'busied, *ppl. a.* (UN-[1] 8. Cf. Du. *ongebezigd.*)
1570 T. WILSON tr. *Demosth. Orat.* vii. 101 Why wouldest thou not rather follow a quiet and vnbusied life? **1628** J. DOUGHTY *Serm. Church-schismes* 13 Rather then rest vnbusied, they will doe some vnnecessary mischiefe. **1658** ROWLAND tr. *Moufet's Theat. Ins.* 920 Yet..they are not unbusied neither; but they build houses for the Kings.

un'business, (UN-[1] 12 b.)
1901 *Westm. Gaz.* 19 Mar. 4/2 The unbusiness methods which mark the administration of the War Office.

un'business-like, *a.* (UN-[1] 7 c.)
1824 SCOTT *Redgauntlet* ch. ii, His own very unbusiness-like mistake of shuffling the Provost's letter..among some papers belonging to Peter Peebles's affairs. **1862** HELPS *Organiz. Daily Life* 21 Great efforts will be made in a scattered, uncomprehensive, and unbusiness-like way.

un'busk, *v.* [UN-[2] 4 and 7.] *trans.* and *intr.* To undress.
1596 NASHE *Saffron Walden* Wks. (Grosart) III. 178, I would we might know her, and see her vnbuskt and naked once. **1673** R. HEAD *Canting Acad.* 29 We had got Money enough to new cloath our selves, which we did, having first unbusk'd.

un'busked, *ppl. a.* (UN-[1] 8.)
1798 MACNEILL *Poems, Sc. Muse* xxxiv, 'Tween pastoral Tweed and wand'ring Ayr, Whar unbusked nature blooms sae fair.

unbustling, *ppl. a.* (UN-[1] 10.)
1826 SHERER *Notes & Refl. Ramble in Germany* 123 She.. then resumed her occupation with a plain unbustling air.

un'busy, *a.* (UN-[1] 7.)
1731 A. HILL *Adv. Poets* Ep. p. xiv, I am so devoted a Lover of a private, and unbusy Life. **1747** RICHARDSON *Clarissa* (1811) I. xviii. 132 [She] continued looking into a drawer among laces and linen in a way neither busy, nor unbusy. **1827** COLERIDGE *Work without Hope* 5 All Nature seems at work,..And I, the while, the sole unbusy thing. **1852** *Meanderings of Mem.* I. 196 If bigotted, or most unbusy herd, O'er stocked with time and talent, were preferred.

un'busy, *v.* (UN-[2] 6 a.)
a **1657** R. LOVEDAY *Lett.* (1663) 120 Error has humbled my Reason, and unbusied my reaches at futurity to a quiet resignation to the great Disposer.

un'butchered, *ppl. a.* (UN-[1] 8.)
1835 LYTTON *Rienzi* IX. iv, To live unbutchered by the Barons, and untaxed by their governors.

un'butted, *ppl. a.* (UN-[1] 8 c.)
1855 [see UNBICKERED].

un'buttered, *ppl. a.* [UN-[1] 8. Cf. Du. *ongeboterd.*] Not spread (or cooked) with butter.
1584 COGAN *Haven Health* 29 The greene beanes they vse to butter, & the other they eate with salt vnbuttered. **1655** MOUFET & BENNET *Health's Improv.* 40 If it be too lean and dry..it is far worse, and nourisheth the body no more then a piece of unbuttered stockfish. **1869** MRS. WHITNEY *Hitherto* I. vii. 145 The going in to eat beans or porridge and unbuttered bread.

un'button, *v.* [UN-[2] 3.]
1. a. *trans.* To unfasten (buttons); to undo the buttons of (a garment).
c **1325** *Gloss. W. de Bibbesw.* in Wright *Voc.* 149 Unbotone [*glossing* Tachet]. *c* **1530** REDFORDE *Play Wit & Sci.* (Shaks. Soc.) 29 Unbuttun thy cote, foole; canst thow do nothyng? **1653** H. COGAN tr. *Pinto's Trav.* xxix. 113 Hereupon she unbottoned one of the sleeves of a red Satin Gown she had on. **1688** R. HOLME *Armoury* IV. xi. (Roxb.) 447/1 The oyntment being thus prepared, the Kings buttons are to be vnbuttoned. **1727** SWIFT *Circumcision E. Curll* Wks. 1755 III. I. 166 Six Jews..laid hands upon him, and unbuttoning his breeches threw him upon the table. **1829** LYTTON *Disowned* 28 The stranger slowly unbuttoned his gaiters. **1891** C. ROBERTS *Adrift Amer.* 118 Unbuttoning my coat I pulled my six-shooter round handy over my right hip.
fig. **1593** G. HARVEY *Pierce's Super.* Wks. (Grosart) II. 124 Vnbutton thy vanity, and Vnlase thy folly. **1652** J. WRIGHT tr. *Camus' Nat. Paradox* v. 107 Wee shall never have done contesting..unless I quite unbutton my breast to you. **1830** GALT *Lawrie T.* II. vii. (1849) 64 Unbuttoning my bosom and showing him all the profitable secrets I had learnt in business. **1892** STEVENSON *Across the Plains* 25, I.. unbuttoned my wrath under the similitude of ironical submission.
b. With personal object. Also *refl.*
1596 SHAKS. *1 Hen. IV,* I. ii. 3 Thou art so fat-witted with drinking of olde Sacke, and vnbuttoning thee after Supper. **1619** R. JONES *Serm. Resurr.* (1659) 64 Help them, good Women! unbutton the Souldiers, ye need not fear their Halberts. **1650** GREAVES *Seraglio* 5 He puts off his uppermost Coat,..then turns up his sleeves, and unbuttoneth himself. **1696** VANBRUGH *Relapse* II. i, Call a surgeon there.—Unbutton him quickly. **1784** COWPER *Tiroc.* 304 The little ones, unbutton'd, glowing hot, Playing our games.
absol. **1725** *Fam. Dict.* s.v. *Swoon,* The most common way of relieving the Patient, is to throw Water in his Face; to make him lie on his Back, to unbutton or unlace.
c. *absol.* To undo one's own buttons; also (quot. 1605), to become unbuttoned. Also *fig.*
1605 SHAKS. *Lear* III. iv. 112 Off, off you Lendings: Come, vnbutton heere. **1664** [J. SCUDAMORE] *Homer à la Mode* 54 Till th' were so cramd with beef and mutton, That every one was faine t' unbutton. *a* **1697** AUBREY *Lives* (1898) I. 110 A man that is buttond or laced too hard, must unbutton before he can be at his ease. **1760–72** H. BROOKE *Fool of Qual.* (1809) III. 142 Gluttony stuffs till it pants, and unbuttons and stuffs again. **1817–8** COBBETT *Resid. U.S.* (1822) 201 You are here disgusted with none of those eaters by reputation that are found..in England: fellows that unbutton at it. **1956** N. STREATFEILD *Judith* III. 235 She definitely unbuttoned about her letters. **1978** O. WHITE *Silent Reach* ix. 97 If I cleared you, he'd probably unbutton.
2. *transf.* To open up or unfold (a bud).
1663 BP. PATRICK *Parab. Pilgr.* xxxvii, It swells into small knobs or buttons... Suppose you should unbutton it as soon as it swells,..would you not endanger the spoiling of its beauties?
Hence **un'buttoning** *vbl. sb.*
1591 PERCIVALL, *Desabotonadura,* vnbuttoning. **1892** *Photogr. Ann.* II. p. xxxi, With the unbuttoning of a strap.. three legs unfold and give us a most rigid Tripod.

un'buttoned, *ppl. a.* [UN-[1] 8.]
1. Not furnished with a button or buttons.

1583 *Rates of Custome Ho.* F iv, Caps vnbuttoned English the dosen xvi s. viij d. **1902** *Daily Chron.* 8 Dec. 3/6 Woe to the man who has to encounter an enemy like M. Merignac with a duelling sword or an unbuttoned foil.

2. Not fastened with buttons; having the buttons unfastened. Also *fig.*

In some instances possibly f. UNBUTTON *v.*

1592 GREENE *Courtier* D iv b, A thredbare blacke coate vnbuttond before vpon the brest. **1600** SHAKS. *A.Y.L.* III. ii. 398 Your hose should be vngarter'd, your bonnet vnbanded, your sleeue vnbutton'd. **1645** MILTON *Colast.* Wks. 1851 IV. 368 This is not for an unbutton'd fellow to discuss in the Garret, at his tressle. **1711** ADDISON *Spect.* No. 129 ¶9 His new silk Waistcoat, which was unbutton'd in several Places to let us see that he had a clean Shirt on. **1790** J. C. SMYTH in *Med. Commun.* II. 477, I..found him ..sitting in a great chair with the collar of his shirt unbuttoned. **1832** LYTTON *Eugene A.* I. ii, The one short, dry, fragile, and betraying a love of ease in his unbuttoned vest. **1854** A. FONBLANQUE in *Life & Labours* vi. (1874) 513 If he had seen the same officer with an unbuttoned jacket, or any other disorder in his dress.

fig. **1885** G. MEREDITH *Diana of Crossways* I. i. 8 He was careless of social opinion, unbuttoned, and a laughter [*sic*]. **1898** *Westm. Gaz.* 27 Oct. 4/1 An example of the master in an unwontedly unbuttoned mood. **1918** 'K. MANSFIELD' *Let.* 6 Feb. (1928) I. 124 On my life, I'd almost rather, like that English lady, not know whether my husband went to the lavatory or not, than be so unbuttoned. *a* **1967** J. R. ACKERLEY *My Father & Myself* (1968) 23 An unbuttoned stage of mellowness and ease. **1983** *Maledicta 1982* VI. 90 They are not by any means considered polite or even acceptable, except in a mood of broad and unbuttoned humor among close friends.

un'buttressed, *ppl. a.* (UN-[1] 8.)

1849 FREEMAN *Archit.* 280 The analogy which its vast, unbroken, unbuttressed height bears to the campaniles of that country. **1893** *Archaeol.* LIII. 550 On account of its unbuttressed length.

†**un'buxom,** *a. Obs.* Forms: (see BUXOM *a.*). [UN-[1] 7. Cf. UNBOWSOME *a.*]

1. Not submissive or compliant; intractable, disobedient. Freq. const. *to.*

a **1250** *Prov. Ælfred* 450 in *O.E. Misc.* 128 Betere is child vnbore, þane vnbuhsum. *a* **1300** *Cursor M.* 28089 To crist ic haue vn-buxum bene. *c* **1330** R. BRUNNE *Chron. Wace* (Rolls) 15378 Monk ne clerk wolde þey non spare, For þey byforn unbuxom ware. **1380** *Lay Folks Catech.* 713 (Lamb. MS.), Rebel men..ben vnbuxum to cryst and his chyrche. *c* **1440** *Jacob's Well* 112 þis vyce makyth a mannys herte hard & vnbuxom to god. *a* **1470** H. PARKER *Dives & Pauper* (1496) IV. viii. 171/1 Childern unbuxum to fader & moder sholde be stoned to deth. **1559** AYLMER *Harborowe* Q 4 God punished that sinne with another by sending them vnbuxome hartes.

absol. **1389** in *Eng. Gilds* (1870) 5 ȝif eny be rebelle..þe forsaide bretherhede shul be helpyng aȝeins þe rebelle and vnboxhum.

2. Unready to bend; stiff.

c **1412** HOCCLEVE *De Reg. Princ.* 985 My bak unbuxum hath swich thyng forsworne, At instance of writing,..That stowpyng hath hym spilt with his labour.

Hence †**un'buxomly** *adv. Obs.*

1390 GOWER *Conf.* I. 88 Evere unbuxomly thei pleigne Upon fortune. *Ibid.* III. 212 The more unbuxomliche he cride. *a* **1400** *MS. Harl. 2260* fol. 3, I usedde wronge with my body, And serves the unbuxumly.

†**un'buxomhead.** *Obs.*[−1] [f. prec.]

a. Disobedience. **b.** Stiffness of body.

c **1250** *Gen. & Ex.* 345 Vn-buxumhed he hauen hem don, Vn-buxumhed is hem cumen on; Vn-welde woren..Here owen limes hem wið-in.

†**un'buxomness.** *Obs.* [f. as prec.]

Disobedience; obstinacy.

a **1300** *Cursor M.* 27616 O pride bicums vnbuxumnes, Strif, and strutt, and frawardnes. *c* **1315** SHOREHAM VII. 806 God wyste wel þat man schold erry, And þorȝ onboxamnesse uerry Fram alle healþe. **1390** GOWER *Conf.* I. 89 And in this wise I me confesse Of that ye clepe unbuxomnesse. **1426** AUDELAY *Poems* (Percy Soc.) 18 Aȝayns my gret goodnes Thai chewyn me unbuxumnes. *c* **1450** *Mirk's Festial* 22 When angeles seon þat hor Lorde was wroth wyth man for vnbuxamnes. *c* **1530** *Songs, Carols,* etc. (E.E.T.S.) 55 Marcy, God, & forgevenes For pride & for vnbuxvmnes!

unc, var. UNK *pron.*

unca, var. UNCO *Sc.*

un'cabined, *a.* (UN-[1] 9.)

1891 HARDY *Tess* ii, There was an uncribbed, uncabined aspect in his eyes and attire.

un'cabled, *a.* (UN-[1] 9.)

1791 COWPER *Odyss.* XIII. 117 Within it, ships (The port once gain'd) uncabled ride secure. **1872** J. S. JEANS *Western Worthies* 93 The uncabled oceans that separate the families of the earth.

unca'd, Sc. f. UNCALLED.

un'cadenced, *ppl. a.* (UN-[1] 8.)

c **1838** MRS. BROWNING *Pet-Name* i, I have a name, a little name, Uncadenced for the ear.

un'cage, *v.* [UN-[2] 5.] *trans.* To let or take out of a cage. Also *fig.*

1620 SHELTON *Quix.* II. xxxviii. 250 But pray vncage your griefes, and tell them us. **1659** TORRIANO, *Sgabbiare,* to uncage, to let loose. **1660** KATH. PHILIPS *Poems* (1664) 77 Thou wert all Soul, and through thy Eyes it shin'd: Asham'd and angry to be so confin'd, It long'd to be uncag'd. **1837** W. A. BUTLER *Serm.* Ser. II. xxii. (1856) 326 The aged saint,.. turning round, bade them uncage the lions. **1855** [J. R. LEIFCHILD] *Cornwall* 167 Let Imagination have her flight, uncage her, and sit down on the top of this smooth bank.

Hence **un'caged** *ppl. a.*[1]

1647 FANSHAWE *Poems, Virgil's Æneas* 296 This said, cut off her hayre, Heat left her, and th' uncaged Soule flew through the Ayre.

un'caged, *ppl. a.*[2] [UN-[1] 8.] Not shut up or confined in a cage.

a **1734** POPE *Epigr. Dennis* 7 Uncag'd then let the harmless monster rage. **1775** ASH, *Uncaged,*..not put into a cage. **1890** 'R. BOLDREWOOD' *Col. Reformer* (1891) 260 The capture of an uncaged bird. **1893** in J. H. Barrows *World's Parlt. Relig.* II. 820 The [Jewish] spirit..shows in this free land the elasticity of the uncaged eagle.

uncairdly, var. UNCAREDLY *adv. Obs.*

uncal'careous, *a.* (UN-[1] 7.)

1793 SMEATON *Edystone L.* §193 It may be accounted a pure limestone..as containing no uncalcareous matter.

un'calcified, *ppl. a.* (UN-[1] 8.)

1854 OWEN in *Orr's Circ. Sci., Org. Nat.* I. 295 Certain tracts of that soft and vascular substance were left uncalcified. **1880** HUXLEY *Crayfish* iv. 155 An uncalcified plate, bent into the form of a half cylinder.

un'calcined, *ppl. a.* (UN-[1] 8.)

1601 HOLLAND *Pliny* II. 588 The same are much used also crude and uncalcined..for the king's evill. **1676** GREW *Exper. Luctation* iii. §17 Millepedes likewise calcined, make a stronger Effervescence, than when uncalcined. **1796** KIRWAN *Elem. Min.* (ed. 2) I. 395 Limestones are frequently ejected from volcanos uncalcined. **1839** URE *Dict. Arts* 322 A small quantity of uncalcined matt must be introduced. **1861** SIR W. FAIRBAIRN *Iron* 76 The use of raw coal and uncalcined ore.

un'calculable, *a.* (UN-[1] 7b and 5b.)

1848 MILL *Pol. Economy* II. vii. §4. 337 The habit of foreign service, by opening to the children a career indefinite and uncalculable, sometimes calls forth a superabundant population.

un'calculableness. (UN-[1] 12 and 5b.)

1831 J. FOSTER *Lett.* in Ryland *Life* (1846) II. 192 There are few things more remarkable than the total uncalculableness, if I may make such a word, of the ultimate local destinations of a young family.

un'calculated, *ppl. a.* (UN-[1] 8.)

1828 *Life Planter Jamaica* 153 In addition to these uncalculated incidents, the wet weather retarded the forwarding of the work. **1856** KANE *Arct. Expl.* I. xxxii. 443 This uncalculated accession of numbers makes our little room too crowded. **1883** SIR N. LINDLEY in *Law Rep. 25 Chan. Div.* 355 If the Plaintiff were to sue the Defendant again for that uncalculated interest, his action would be considered frivolous.

un'calculating, *ppl. a.* (UN-[1] 10.)

a **1832** BENTHAM *Deontol.* ii. (1834) II. 84 That sacrifice is mere asceticism;..it is miscalculating or uncalculating blindness. **1861** GEO. ELIOT *Silas M.* iii, Trying to turn his gloom into uncalculating anger. **1873** W. CORY *Lett. & Jrnls.* (1897) 331 These uncalculating disinterested lovers of truth.

Hence **un'calculatingly** *adv.*

1852 HAWTHORNE *Blithedale Rom.* ix, She seemed ready to fling it away..uncalculatingly. *a* **1853** ROBERTSON *Lect.* ii. (1858) 192 It consecrated certain acts as right, uncalculatingly, and independently of consequences.

un'calendared, *ppl. a.* [UN-[2] 8 and UN-[1] 8.]

a. Removed from a calendar or roll. **b.** Not entered in a calendar.

1654 GAYTON *Pleas. Notes* III. vii. 113 He..is Uncalendred for ever, and his name expung'd the Ephemerides of King Arthurs Knights. **1850** BLACKIE *Æschylus* II. 39 The flower-strewn Spring, and the fruit-laden Summer, Uncalendared, unregistered, returned. **1898** *Westm. Gaz.* 7 Dec. 5/1 With certain other uncalendared manuscripts placed at his disposal by Lord Salisbury.

un'called, *ppl. a.* Also 8– *Sc.* unca'd. [UN-[1] 8, 8c. Cf. MSw. and Sw. *okallad,* Da. *ukaldet.*]

1. a. Not called or summoned; not invited.

a **1400–50** *Alexander* 832 And I to consaile vn-callid I can noȝt þar-on. *c* **1440** *Alph. Tales* 243 þis Hillarius come to þis cowncell vncallid. *a* **1500** in *Ratis Raving,* etc. 9 Be curtas ay in company: To consell cum þow nocht wncald. **1533** MORE *Debell. Salem* Wks. 973/1 The ordinary shal know who can tell more, and will also if they be called and sworen, and wyll not vncalled and vnsworen, tel no tale at all. **1587** HARRISON *England* II. xvi. (1877) 280 Yet were they not so narrowlie taken, but that a third part of this like multitude was left vnbilled and vncalled. **1667** MILTON *P.L.* IX. 523 Hee boulder now, uncall'd before her stood. **1697** DRYDEN *Virgil* Postscr., For who would give physic to the great, when he is uncalled? **1796** MME. D'ARBLAY *Camilla* x. iii, [He] would, uncalled, have given his whole attention. **1810** SHELLEY *Spectral Horseman* 20 The shade of a murdered man, Who has rushed uncalled to the throne of his God. **1856** MRS. BROWNING *Aur. Leigh* IV. 84 He came uncalled wherever grief had come. **1861** MRS. H. WOOD *East Lynne* III. xix, Uncalled, unprepared,..you hurried that unfortunate man into eternity.

b. *transf.* Of things.

a **1586** SIDNEY *Astr. & Stella* Sonn. lxi, Oft with true sighes, oft with uncalled teares,..I Stella's eyes assaid. **1751** JOHNSON *Rambler* No. 175 ¶2 The knowledge of crimes intrudes uncalled and undesired. *c* **1790** COWPER *Comm. Milton's P.L.* II. 220 Rhyme is apt to come uncalled, and to writers of blank verse is often extremely troublesome. *a* **1839** PRAED *Poems* (1865) II. 15 Sudden tears uncalled spring up. **1885** 'MRS. ALEXANDER' *Valerie's Fate* vi, Bestowing frequent sudden uncalled hugs and kisses on her friend.

2. *spec.* **a.** Not called or summoned by some power or influence to a special function or state.

1561 T. NORTON *Calvin's Inst.* IV. xviii. §9. 144 b, They must confesse y^t the honour is not of God, into which they haue with wicked rashnes broken in vncalled. **1619** HIERON Wks. I. 11 All preaching, all exercises of religion ayme at one of these two, either to conuert those that are vncalled, or to builde vp those which are conuerted. **1662** H. HIBBERT *Body Divinity* II. 155 We pray thee then, O Heavenly Father, to call the uncalled Jew and Gentile. **1690** C. NESSE *O. & N. Test.* I. 142 Such as continue in an uncall'd condition yield up themselves to Satan. *c* **1700** PRIOR *Sat. Poets* 128 Something beyond the uncall'd drudging Tribe, Beyond what Bayes can write, or I describe.

b. Not invited to a pastorate.

1854 H. MILLER *Sch. & Schm.* vii. (1860) 74/1 Better be a poor mason, better be anything honest, however humble, —than an un-called Minister.

3. With *for*: Not called for; not asked for or requested; unnecessary, intrusive.

Hence, in recent use, *uncalled-for-ness.*

pred. *a* **1610** HEALEY *Theophrastus* (1636) 90 When the people consult,..hee steppeth forth uncalled for. **1623** MASSINGER *Dk. Milan* I. iii, *Enter Francisco. Sforza.* Why, uncalled for? **1824** MISS L. M. HAWKINS *Annaline* II. 168 The thought comes uncalled for into my mind. **1846** J. BAXTER *Libr. Pract. Agric.* (ed. 4) I. p. xv, The course he had adopted was uncalled for. **1867** TROLLOPE *Chron. Barset* II. lxvii. 242 No one could now press uncalled-for into his study.

attrib. **1635–56** COWLEY *Davideis* III. ad fin., Uncall'd for sighs oft from her bosome flew. **1817** BENNET in *Parl. Deb.* 340 He would oppose..this arbitrary, impolitic, and uncalled-for measure. **1843** R. J. GRAVES *Syst. Clin. Med.* xxix. 393 The uncalled for administration of mercury. **1874** BURNAND *My Time* vi. 50 A satisfactory issue of an uncalled-for interference.

4. Of capital: Not called up.

1869 *Bradshaw's Railway Man.* XXI. 199 The financial statement to same date... Discount on shares, 1837—£400,000... Uncalled—£619,525. **1882** *Pall Mall G.* 26 July 6/1 The whole of the remaining uncalled capital would have to be called up in order to pay the creditors.

un'callow, *sb. local.* [f. next.] = CALLOW *sb.* 3.

1787 W. H. MARSHALL *Norfolk* (1795) I. 151 The depth of uncallow is generally very unequal. *Ibid.* II. Gloss., *Uncallow,* the earth which covers a jam of marl. **1841** *Civil Eng. & Arch. Jrnl.* IV. 341/2 To the above must be added the expenses for removing the uncallow. **1871** J. PHILLIPS *Geol. Oxf. & Vall. Thames* 471 Thick bed of 'Uncallow', consisting of gravel, brickearth, loam, and sand, in horizontal, curved, and aggregated masses.

un'callow, *v. local.* [UN-[2] 4 + CALLOW *sb.* 3.] *trans.* To clear (clay, marl, etc.) of the surface soil; to remove (soil) for this purpose. Also *intr.* Hence **un'callowing** *vbl. sb.*

1729 *Act 2 Geo. II,* 313 They are hereby obliged and required to uncallow and take off all the Soil, Mould, or other Compost, lying upon the said Earth. **1787** W. H. MARSHALL *Norfolk* (1795) I. 396 *note,* One individual gives 4d...and 6d...a load for casting; besides the uncallowing, which he pays for extra by the day. **1824** *Mechanics' Mag.* No. 33. 77 This is done by removing the vegetable mould from the surface, which is called uncallowing. **1842** *Civil Eng. & Arch. Jrnl.* V. 85/2 The uncallowing and resoiling together..must be taken at the lowest price of 3d. and 3½d.

un'calm, *sb.*: see UN-[1] 12.

un'calm, *v.* [UN-[2] 6 a.] *trans.* To deprive of calm; to agitate, disturb.

1655 VAUGHAN *Silex Scint., Storm* ii, Thus the enlarg'd, enraged air Uncalms these [waters] to a flood. **1665** DRYDEN *Ind. Emp.* II. iv, What strange disquiet has uncalmed your breast?

un'calm, *a.* (UN-[1] 7.)

1817 MOORE *Lalla Rookh, Veiled Prophet* I. 378 The momentary meteors sent Across th' uncalm, but beauteous firmament.

un'cambered, *ppl. a.* (UN-[1] 8.)

1881 COLQUHOUN *Let.* in *Times* 11 Apr. 10/5 If the boats were laid on a straight or uncambered keel.

un'camp, *v.* (UN-[2] 5.)

1670 MILTON *Hist. Brit.* Wks. 1851 V. 37 Freeing themselvs from the fear of like invasions heerafter,..if they could but now uncamp thir Enemies.

un'cancellable, *a.* (UN-[1] 7b.)

1606 *True & Perfect Relat.* H h 3 It is cleare that..onely by the character of regall unction uncancellable he was so far priviledged. **1646** EARL MONM. tr. *Biondi's Civil Wars* VIII. 136 To cancell the uncancellable memory of his cruelty. **1716** M. DAVIES *Athen. Brit.* II. 151 He would..have laid uncancellable obligations at home and abroad.

un'cancelled, *ppl. a.* (UN-[1] 8.)

1557 RECORDE *Whetst.* O j b, The whole nomber aboue that is vncancelled. **1594** CONSTABLE *Diana* VII. iv, When posteritie in time to come, shall finde th' uncanceld tenor of her vow. **1622** MALYNES *Anc. Law-Merch.* 226 The new bond being made, the old is void, and yet may be vncancelled. **1675** DRYDEN *Aurengz.* IV. (1676) 64, I onely mourn my yet uncancell'd score. **1772** *Phil. Trans.* LXII. 334 The first uncancelled number that appears in the series, after 3, is 5. **1836** KEBLE in *Lyra Apost.* (1849) 220 O trust his seal Baptismal, yet uncancelled on thy brow. **1875** JEVONS *Money* xviii. 218 Equal in amount to the aggregate of the uncancelled notes.

un'candid, *a.* [UN-[1] 7.] Not candid or open; disingenuous: **a.** Of opinions, utterances, etc.

1681 KETTLEWELL *Meas. Chr. Obed.* V. iii. 633 Peevish, or uncourteous, or uncandid, behaviour. **1694** —— *Compan. Penitent* 59, All the..evil and uncandid surmises..which I stand guilty of towards any. **1759** FRANKLIN *Ess.* Wks. 1840 III. 305 How grossly uncandid and clumsily crafty this rhapsody was, appears at the first glance. **1771** *Encycl. Brit.* I. 651/2 The experiment is incomplete, and the conclusion drawn from it uncandid and precipitate. **1825** COLERIDGE *Aids Refl.* (1848) I. 84 That Leighton attached a definite sense to the words above quoted, it would be uncandid to doubt. **1884** CHURCH *Bacon* i. 26 Bacon's reply..is not more one-sided and uncandid than the pamphlet which it answers.

b. Of persons.

1771 SMOLLETT *Humph. Cl.* 8 June, Will you be so uncandid as to exclaim against Italy for the practice of common assassination? **1784** COWPER *Task* III. 275 The proud, uncandid, insincere, Or negligent, inquirer. **1849** MACAULAY *Hist. Eng.* i. I. 27 The temper, not of judges, but of angry and uncandid advocates.

Hence **un'candidly** *adv.*; **un'candidness.**

1681 KETTLEWELL *Measures Chr. Obed.* v. iii. 633 Has any man..committed any action of..Uncandidness, Unmercifulness, Unpeaceableness, or the like? **1754** MISS TALBOT *Lett.* (1809) II. 160 The uncandidness of disliking and throwing aside such a book, on casually dipping into the midst of it. **1800** *Asiat. Ann. Reg., Proc. E. Ind. Ho.* 132/1 It had been most uncandidly, because untruly argued. **1852** READE *Peg Woff.* x. 195 She offered to come to him. He answered uncandidly.

un'candied, *ppl. a.* (UN-[2] 8. Cf. DISCANDY *v.*)

1612 *Two Noble K.* I. i. 115 O my petition was Set downe in yce, which by hot greefe uncandied Melts into drops.

un'candour. [UN-[1] 12.] Lack of candour.

1879 HOWELLS *L. Aroostook* (1884) II. 178 A generous uncandour like this. **1892** WHITNEY *Max Müller* 79 What I had more right to object to was the uncandour and misrepresentation.

un'cankered, *ppl. a.* (UN-[1] 8.)

1768-74 TUCKER *Lt. Nat.* (1834) II. 111 Provided he employ healthy stocks of the genuine kind, uncankered with prejudice or peculiarity..the fruits will be the same.

un'cannily, *adv.* [f. UNCANNY *a.*]

1. *dial.* (See quot.)

1825 BROCKETT *N.C. Gloss.*, *Uncannily*, unthinkingly, thoughtlessly.

2. In an uncomfortably strange manner; weirdly.

1822 A. CUNNINGHAM *Traditional Tales* II. 267 He skirls sae uncannilie. **1873** MURDOCH *Doric Lyre* 98 Slates an' tiles an' chimla cans Uncannily were fa'in'. **1888** R. BUCHANAN *Heir of Linne* xxv, He talks so uncannily. **1895** *Atlantic Monthly* Aug. 225 A gigantic eye which uncannily turns around.

un'canniness. [f. next.] The quality or state of being uncanny; unpleasant strangeness.

1860 GEO. ELIOT *Mill on Fl.* VI. iii, Now I see how it is you ..have learned so much since you left school; which always seemed to me witchcraft before—part of your general uncanniness. **1880** *Contemp. Rev.* Sept. 382 They gain a terrible reality from the uncanniness of their surroundings. **1893** LELAND *Mem.* I. 39 There was a quaint uncanniness, as of something unknown, in my nature.

un'canny, *a.* Orig. *Sc.* and *north.* Also 6-7 uncannie, 7 unkannie, 8 unkanny. [UN-[1] 7.]

†**1.** Mischievous, malicious. *Obs.*[−1]

1596 DALRYMPLE tr. *Leslie's Hist. Scotl.* II. 58 Sum now, vncannie sawers, sew sum causes of contentioun betuene the Chanceller and the Gouernour.

2. Careless, incautious.

1638 R. BAILLIE *Lett. & Jrnls.* (1841) I. 100, I [was].. made hopefull he would not suffer it to be spoiled by the imprudencie of mony uncannie hands which are about it. **1825** BROCKETT *N.C. Gloss.*, *Uncanny*, giddy, careless, imprudent.

†**3.** Unreliable, not to be trusted. *Obs.*

1639 R. BAILLIE *Lett. & Jrnls.* (1841) I. 211 It was thought meet..to make all, without dinn. march forward, leist his unkannie trewes-men should light on to call [= drive] them up in their rear. **17..** PENNECUIK *Coll.* (1787) 36 You're an hawk of an unkanny nest.

4. Of persons: Not quite safe to trust to, or have dealings with, as being associated with supernatural arts or powers.

1773 R. FERGUSSON *Poems* (1789) II. 8 For this some ca'd him an uncanny wight; The clash gaed round, 'he had the second sight'. **1815** SCOTT *Guy M.* liii, I wish she binna uncanny! her words dinna seem to come in God's name, or like other folk's. **1868** NETTLESHIP *Ess. Browning* II. 68 These gipsies were a queer uncanny folk. **1884** J. GILMOUR *Mongols* 241 The Mongols..were inclined to think him uncanny.

b. Partaking of a supernatural character; mysterious, weird, uncomfortably strange or unfamiliar. (Common from *c* 1850.)

1843 LYTTON *Last Bar.* I. vii, If men, gentlemen born, will read uncanny books,..why they must resolve to reap what they sow. **1856** EMERSON *Eng. Traits, Stonehenge*, We walked in and out, and took again and again a fresh look at the uncanny stones. **1882** MISS BRADDON *Mt. Royal* II. x. 229 A slate quarry under the cliff—a scene of uncanny grandeur.

c. In comb. *uncanny-looking* adj.

1861 MISS E. A. BEAUFORT *Egypt. Sepul. & Syr. Shr.* II. xx. 184 Between the hill of Ophel and the strange, uncanny-looking village of Siloam. **1886** CORBETT *Fall of Asgard* I. 38 Frightened at her uncanny-looking companion's strange talk.

5. Unpleasantly severe or hard.

1773 R. FERGUSSON *Poems* (1789) II. 69 Whinstanes.. May thole the prancing feet o' naigs, Nor ever fear uncanny hotches Frae clumsy carts or hackney-coaches. **1814** SCOTT *Wav.* lxvi, I rode whip and spur to fetch the Chevalier..; and an uncanny coup I gat for my pains.

6. Dangerous, unsafe.

1785 *Poems Buchan Dial.* 7 Thus wi' uncanny pranks he fights. **1837** LOCKHART *Scott* IV. vii. 217 He said it was *uncanny*, and would certainly have felt it very uncomfortable, not to welcome the new year in the midst of his family and a few old friends. *a* **1882** W. DICKINSON *Lit. Rem.* (1888) 193 (E.D.D.), Times was raderly uncanny than, An' laal better now.

unca'nonic, *a.* [UN-[1] 7.] = next.

a **1711** KEN *Dedicat.* Poet. Wks. 1721 I. 2 Forc'd from my Flock by uncanonick Heat, In singing Hymns, thus solace my Retreat. **1868** BROWNING *Ring & Bk.* x. 70 This act was uncanonic and a fault.

unca'nonical, *a.* [UN-[1] 7.]

1. Not in accordance with ecclesiastical canons.

1632 *Star Chamb. Cases* (Camden) 172 He sought for this place in an uncanonicall order. **1676** MARVELL *Gen. Councils* Wks. (Grosart) IV. 104 And God forbid too that any measure of wealth should render a clergyman uncanonical. **1693** LUTTRELL *Brief Rel.* (1857) III. 17 Yesterday lord bishop of Llandaff exhibited articles..against Dr. Jones.. for uncanonicall practices and misdemeanours committed by him. **1709** BINGHAM *Orig. Eccl.* II. 172 Among his other Irregularities he [*sc.* Novatian] was ordained at an uncanonical Hour. **1760** STERNE *Tr. Shandy* IV. xxvi, A single word and no more [was] uttered..—a word I am ashamed to write—yet must be written—must be read—illegal—uncanonical. **1845** LD. CAMPBELL *Chancellors* ix. (1857) I. 130 Uncanonical and forced elections..were made to vacant ecclesiastical dignities. **1872** FREEMAN *Hist. Ess.* (ed. 2) Pref., The marriage of his widow was uncanonical.

b. Of dress, pastimes, etc.: Unclerical; unbecoming to 'the cloth'.

1747 CARTE *Hist. Eng.* I. 676 Wearing long hair, and a dress in any respect uncanonical. **1809** MALKIN *Gil Blas* VII. vi. ¶1 In the archbishop's palace..all such profane shews were condemned as uncanonical. **1819** SCOTT *Ivanhoe* xvii, Are you not afraid he may pay you a visit during some of your uncanonical pastimes? **1829** —— *Anne of G.* xv, Begirt, not with a suitable sash such as clergymen wear, but with a most uncanonical buff-belt. **1867** FELTON *Anc. & Mod. Gr.* II. iii. 299 He [St. George] exhibited a most uncanonical greed for money.

2. Not belonging to the canon of Scripture.

1835 *Penny Cycl.* IV. 369/1 Lists of Biblical books were promulgated by the orthodox Greek church in order to prevent the use of Apocryphal or uncanonical books. **1884** CHURTON (*title*), The Uncanonical and Apocryphal Scriptures, being the additions to the Old Testament Canon.

Hence **unca'nonicalness.**

1655 FULLER *Ch. Hist.* III. 38 This made him connive at Jeffery Plantaginet his holding the Bishoprick of Lincoln, though uncanonicalness on uncanonicalness met in his person. **1684** BP. LLOYD *Ch. Govt. Brit.* vi. 130 Here was another Uncanonicalness,..that he intruded into a See, into which another had been Elected.

unca'nonically, *adv.* [f. prec.] Not canonically or in a canonical manner.

1713 E. CALAMY *Life Baxter* (ed. 2) I. 508 He admits that the deposed Bishop was unjustly depriv'd and the New one Uncanonically promoted. **1774** J. COLLYER *Hist. Eng.* II. 150 He had been uncanonically elected. **1842** WRIGHT *Biog. Brit.* 174 He had been consecrated uncanonically by British bishops. **1865** KINGSLEY *Herew.* i, Now, why were the two ecclesiastics so uncanonically kind to this wicked youth?

un'canonize, *v.* [UN-[2] 6 c.]

1. *trans.* To remove from the canon or calendar of saints.

1607 R. C[AREW] tr. *Estienne's World Wond.* 348 A Monke ..who was almost as soone vncanonized as canonized. **1651** JANE *Image Unbr.* 32 The Authors Pageantry playing with a picture is not the way to uncannonize a saint. **1751** LAVINGTON *Enthus. Meth. & Papists* III. (1754) 214 He [Boniface VIII] uncanonized St. Herman of France, and ordered his Bones to be dug up and burned.

2. To reject from the canon of Scripture, or of authoritative writings.

a **1706** EVELYN *Hist. Relig.* (1850) I. 409 And it is enough to read the two last verses of the second of Maccabees quite to uncanonize them. **1812** JEFFERSON *Writ.* (1830) IV. 179 The exclusion from the courts of the malign influence of all authorities after the *Georgium sidus* became ascendant, would uncanonize Blackstone.

un'canonized, *ppl. a.* [UN-[1] 8.]

1. Not admitted into the canon of Scripture.

1548 GESTE *Pr. Masse* 129 The last consayl..regestered ye bible bokes without any mencion made of the Machabees at al, which argueth that then the bokes of Machabees were unconanised. **1860** WESTCOTT in *Smith's Dict. Bible* I. 251/1 The uncanonical books were described simply as 'those without', or 'those uncanonized'.

2. Not formally recognized (as a saint).

a **1643** A. TOWNSHEND *Poems* (1912) 34 If he tooke the style before, And name uncanonized wore,..This Saint [etc.]. **1718** ATTERBURY *Serm. Acts xxvi. 26* (1734) III. 17 The Members of it boast very much of mighty Signs and Wonders wrought by some Canonized, and some Uncanonized Saints; their Legends, their Sermons are full of them. **1771** MRS. GRIFFITH *Hist. Lady Barton* III. 220, I passed six days with this uncanonized saint. **1862** MISS BRADDON *Lady Audley* xiv, The uncanonized saint and benefactress to the poor.

un'canopied, *ppl. a.* (UN-[1] 8.)

1613 W. BROWNE *Brit. Past.* I. iv. 74 Gladly I tooke the place the sheepe had giuen, Uncanopy'd of any thing but heauen. **1890** R. BRIDGES *Shorter Poems* III. xv. 61 Uncanopied sleep is flying from field and tree.

un'canvassed, *ppl. a.* [UN-[1] 8.] Not canvassed, in various senses of the verb.

[**1775** ASH.] *a* **1797** H. WALPOLE *Mem. Geo. II* (1847) II. i. 3 His brother..rose..to a distinguished situation entirely unsought, uncanvassed. **1822** T. MITCHELL *Com. Aristoph.* II. 246 Where the loud-voiced herald cries, 'Who's uncanvass'd?—let him rise!' **1884** *Law Times* 13 Dec. 120 There is not a large town in England except London in which such transactions would be allowed to pass uncanvassed.

un'cap, *v.* [UN-[2] 4.]

1. *trans.* To remove the cap from (the head or a person). Also *absol.*

1566 PAINTER *Pal. Pleas.* li. 219 All they that weare hornes, be pardoned to weare their capps... For they be so sweete and pleasaunt, as they vncappe no man. **1598** FLORIO, *Sberettare*, to vncap, to put off hat or cap. **1836** L. HUNT *Poems, Bodryddan* 98 The gard'ner..Uncapp'd his bent old silver hair. **1875** H. JAMES *Transatlantic Sk.* 247, I felt really like uncapping, with a kind of reverence.

2. To divest (a thing) of a cap or covering.

1688 R. HOLME *Armoury* III. xix. (Roxb.) 170/2 The Words of command for the pistolls. 1. Vncape your pistolls. 2. Draw forth your pistoll. **1711** *Milit. & Sea Dict.* (ed. 4), Uncap your Cartridges, Is to take off the Top of the Paper, which is folded down at the End, that so the Powder may fall loose to the Touch-hole. **1750** W. ELLIS *Mod. Husbandm.* VI. I. v. 28 Farmers are emboldened to let their wheat stand ..in the field without uncapping. **1859** JEPHSON & REEVE *Brittany* 88 Mr. Taylor was watching eagerly for a sign from me to uncap the lenses. **1859** F. A. GRIFFITHS *Artill. Man.* (1862) 112 No. 3 loads, assists to ram home, elevates, uncaps fuze when in bore.

†**uncapa'bility.** *Obs.*[−1] [Cf. next.] = INCAPABILITY.

c **1642** TWYNE in Wood *Life* (O.H.S.) I. 84 The Vice-chancellour's supposed uncapabilitie.

†**un'capable,** *a. Obs.* [UN-[1] 7 b and 5 b.]

1. = INCAPABLE *a.* 1.

1587 W. FOWLER *Wks.* (S.T.S.) I. 98 My daisled eyes, vncapable of suche a splendant light. **1634** ABP. WILLIAMS in *Laud's Wks.* (1857) VI. 405, I do endeavour, by my life and conversation, to make myself a vessel not altogether uncapable of that sacred oil. **1637** C. DOW *Answ. to H. Burton* 40 Men were uncapable of these doctrines. **1713** STEELE *Englishm.* No. 55. 356, I know some..uncapable of the deep Secrets which lie in their Bosoms.

2. = INCAPABLE *a.* 2.

1586 T. B. *La Primaud. Fr. Acad.* I. 191 The brutish part of the soule, depending of the feeding beast, and uncapeable of reason. **1597** HOOKER *Eccl. Pol.* v. xlix. §3 Such as should be vncapable of so great a blessing. **1626** PRYNNE *Perpet. Regen. Man's Est.* 55 These promises which I haue mentioned must needes be absolute.., because that most of them are vncapable of any condition. *a* **1677** HALE *Prim. Orig. Man.* I. v. 113 All which will produce multitudes uncapable of Infinitude, as much as the several individuals of Mankind. **1683** KENNET *Erasm. on Folly* (1709) 30 He would be..uncapable of any ease or satisfaction. **1737** WATERLAND *Eucharist* 111 Being utterly uncapable of any certain Proof, the Argument built thereupon, must of consequence fall to the Ground.

3. = INCAPABLE *a.* 3.

1611 TOURNEUR *Ath. Trag.* II. i, I am uncapable of comfort. **1651** HOBBES *Leviath.* I. xvi. 81 There are few things, that are uncapable of being represented by Fiction. **1717** J. KEILL *Anim. Œcon.* (1738) 263 Things that lessen Perspiration, by being uncapable of Reduction. **1758** REID tr. *Macquer's Chym.* I. 6 The Earth, which we look upon as uncapable of vitrification.

4. = INCAPABLE *a.* 4 and 4 b.

1596 SHAKS. *Merch. V.* IV. i. 5 Thou art come to answere A stonie aduersary, an inhumane wretch, Vncapable of pitty. **1619** NAUNTON in *Fortescue Papers* (Camden) 105 It would make him uncapable to do the service he pretends he can from Rome and other partes. **1642** *Complaint Ho. Comm.* 19 We shal be made uncapable of taking fruit by it. **1716** M. DAVIES *Athen. Brit.* II. 426 He is as uncapable to calculate Eclipses as he is unfit..to Judge of the three first Christian Centuries. **1745** P. THOMAS *Jrnl. Anson's Voy.* 154 Left us..to help ourselves, of which we were utterly uncapable. **1775** ADAIR *Amer. Ind.* 176 Which might.. render them uncapable of receiving the supposed divine inspiration. **1805-6** CARY *Dante, Inf.* XXXIII. 91 Them.. their tender years, thou modern Thebes, did make Uncapable of guilt.

5. = INCAPABLE *a.* 5. Also *absol.*

1627 HAKEWILL *Apol.* Preface c v, Nature hath not made vs more vncapable then our Auncestours. **1632** LITHGOW *Trav.* x. 437 Preachers..who make conscience of their calling, and liue as Lanthorns to vncapable ignorants. **1653** R. SANDERS *Physiogn.* A 3 b, The eyes of the uncapable and ignorant debase, rather than illustrate and adorn them. **1712** W. ROGERS *Voy.* (1718) 309 Who have put the care of the said ship under an uncapable command. **1719** in W. S. Perry *Hist. Coll. Amer. Col. Ch.* (1871) I. 221 Of which we are very uncapable Judges.

6. = INCAPABLE *a.* 6.

1589 *Act 31 Eliz.* c. 6 §2 Everie person, by whom..anye Monye..shalbe given or agreed to be payde,..shalbe uncapeable of that Place or Roome for that tyme or turne. **1602** *Hist. Eng.* in *Harl. Misc.* (1809) II. 439 A notorious offender, exempt from the ordinary protection of the laws, uncapable of any preferment. **1678** SIR G. MACKENZIE *Crim. Laws Scot.* I. xvii. §10 (1699) 93 For though the Law make them uncapable to succeed as Heirs, yet it does not make them uncapable to receive a Disposition. **1706** DE FOE *Jure Div.* VIII. 189 The League deposed Henry the IIId, and declar'd him a Tyrant, a Murtherer, and uncapable to Reign. **1726** SWIFT *Gulliver* I. vi, The disbelief of a divine Providence renders a man uncapable of holding any public station.

Hence †**un'capableness.** *Obs.*

1611 COTGR., *Incapacité*,..incapacitie, vncapablenesse. **1612** T. TAYLOR *Comm. Titus* iii. 6. 662 Oh let vs bewaile our owne vncapablenesse in the sence of our wants. **1657** J.

WATTS *Vind. Ch. Eng.* 106 By reason of your uncapableness of them, by your ignorance. **1727** BAILEY (vol. II), *Illacerableness*, wholeness, or uncapableness of being torn.

unca'pacious, *a.* (UN-[1] 7 and 5 b.)
1635 HEYWOOD *Hierarchy* II. 77 It is not fit..to enquire for that, which should we finde, Our limited and uncapacious minde Could not conceiue. *c* **1638** FELTHAM *Let. to Johnson* in *Resolves*, etc. (1661) 87 The poor and uncapacious Vulgar think him to be such as they see. **1854** JAMES *Ticonderoga* III. 81 The narrow-minded man, the man of an uncapacious soul. *a* **1859** DE QUINCEY *Posth. Wks.* (1891) I. 279 It is remarkable how mean, vulgar, and uncapacious has been the range of intellect in many first-rate Grecians.

†**unca'pacitate**, *v. Obs.* [UN-[2] 3.] *trans.* = INCAPACITATE *v.*
1668 H. MORE *Div. Dial.* iv. II. 17 Tell me the difference that uncapacitates the one from being the members of the Kingdom of God more then the other. **1693** *Mem. Ct. Teckely* I. 45 Separating from Count Strasoldo..instead of entring Bosnia with him after the defeat of the Basha: Which uncapacitated Scrasoldo [*sic*] to do anything.

†**unca'pacity.** *Obs.* (UN-[1] 12 and 5 b.)
1681 BAXTER *Answ. Dodwell* ii. 16 One who hath no Authority through uncapacity, or usurpation.

unca'parisoned, *ppl. a.* (UN-[1] 8.)
[**1775** ASH.] **1865** MRS. WHITNEY *Gayworthys* xv, The uncaparisoned steed.

†**un'cape**, *v. Obs.*[−1] (Of obscure meaning.)
The interpretations 'to unbag' or 'to uncouple' are not supported by any evidence.
1598 SHAKS. *Merry W.* III. iii. 173 Ile warrant wee'le vnkennell the Fox. Let me stop this way first: so, now vncape.

un'capped, *ppl. a.* (UN-[1] 8.)
1548–63 BECON *New Catech.* (1564) I. 330 b, A sorte of Popettes standing in euerye corner of the Church, some holdinge in theyr handes a Swoorde,..some capped, some vncapped. **1670** G. H. *Hist. Cardinals* II. III. 186 The Nuntio [was] uncapt for some time, and not one word to be heard of his promotion. **1850** L. HUNT *Autobiog.* xx. (1860) 347 The large wrinkled features of the old women, with their uncapped gray hair, strike you at first as singularly plain. **1902** FAIRBAIRN in *Expositor* Sept. 171 The great mountains raised..their uncapped heads crowned with perennial snow. **1955** *Times* 3 Aug. 4/6 (*caption*) The only uncapped player in the British Isles team to meet South Africa at Johannesburg on Saturday. **1977** *World of Cricket Monthly* June 92/2 The form of uncapped 24-year-old seamer Bill Bourne pierced the gloom like a ray of sunshine.

un'capper. [f. UNCAP *v.* 2.] A tool for removing an exploded cap from a gun.
1895 *Funk's Stand. Dict.*

un'capping, *vbl. sb.* [f. UNCAP *v.*] The action of removing a cap or cover. Also *attrib.*
1681 HICKERINGILL *Dial. Def. Fullwood's Leges Angl.* 6, I now find thy knack at capping of verses and uncapping of names. **1886** *Pall Mall G.* 23 Sept. 6/2, I claim that we are before them in the matter of uncapping machines [for honeycombs].

uncap'sizable, *a.* (UN-[1] 7 b.)
1883 *Fisheries Exhib. Catal.* 48 Life Boat Buoy, uncapsizable, carries provisions and water; also signal lights. **1883** *Harper's Mag.* Aug. 442/2 The rule produced a boat that was..uncapsizable.

un'captained, *ppl. a.* (UN-[1] 8.)
1895 MEREDITH *Amazing Marr.* xlvi, An uncaptained vessel in the winds on high seas.

un'captious, *a.* (UN-[1] 7.)
1661 FELTHAM *Resolves* II. xliii. (ed. 8) 267 Among uncaptious and candid Natures, plainness and freedom are the preserves of amity. **1860** *Times* 26 Oct. 5/1 Supporters of a fair and uncaptious interpretation of Government rights.

un'captivate, *v.* [UN-[2] 3.] *trans.* To free from captivity.
1611 COTGR., *Decaptiver*, to vncaptiuate; free from captiuite, set at libertie. **1681** RYCAUT tr. *Gracian's Critick* 134 To consult about a remedy which might uncaptivate his beloved Friend.

un'captivated, *ppl. a.* (UN-[1] 8.)
1678 CUDWORTH *Intell. Syst.* Pref. 12 Those of the most accomplished intellectuals and uncaptivated minds. **1700** *Paper to W. Penn* 21 And this may be a Conviction to any of them that are but uncaptivated to observe what they find usual, and will confess it.

un'captived, *ppl. a.* [UN-[1] 8: cf. prec.] Not made captive.
1601 DANIEL *Cleopatra* I. Wks. F v b, For come what will, this stands, I must die free, And die my selfe vncaptiu'd and vnwonne. **1629** H. BURTON *Truth's Triumph* 23 Innocent as Adam,..his will most free, vntainted, vncaptiued. **1669** *Address to Hopef. Yng. Gentry Eng.* 110 The first and wisest of men had not larger notices of the creation, than the uncaptiv'd spirit instantly enters upon.

un'captured, *ppl. a.* (UN-[1] 8.)
1885 *Pall Mall G.* 15 May 3/2 As long as Riel is uncaptured the Canadian Government is not out of the wood.

un'carded, *ppl. a.* (UN-[1] 8. Cf. Sw. *okardad.*)
[**1775** ASH.] *a* **1833** in Carlyle *Misc.* (1840) IV. 375 Uncombed, uncarded, like a mass of tarry wool.

un'cardinal, *v.* (UN-[2] 6 b.)
1642 FULLER *Holy & Prof. St.* v. vii. 383 Borgia's active spirit disliked the profession,..wherefore he quickly got a dispensation to uncardinall himself. **1654** GAYTON *Pleas. Notes* IV. ix. 230 Ungovern'd, Uncardinall'd, Unlorded, Outed of all his hopes, but not Unworded. **1746** YOUNG *Th. Late Rebellion* 87 On what then smote his heart, uncardinall'd, And sunk beneath the level of a man?

un'cared-for, *a.* [UN-[1] 8 c.] Not cared for or looked after; untended, neglected.
pred. **1597** HOOKER *Eccl. Pol.* v. i. §4 Their Kings..left their owne and their peoples ghostly condition vncared for. **1775** ASH, *Uncared*.., not regarded;..'It was uncared for'. **1818** SCOTT *Br. Lamm.* xxi, Circumstances which, in families of rank, are left uncared for, because it is supposed impossible they can be neglected. **1850** TENNYSON *In Mem.* ci, The brook shall.., Uncared for, gird the windy grove. **1894** *Persian Pict.* 40 Somewhat desolate and uncared for in appearance.
attrib. **1621** G. SANDYS *Ovid's Met.* II. (1626) 37 He fetcht a grone,..And now vncar'd-for odours powr'd vpon her. **1856** *N. Brit. Rev.* XXVI. 109 A slatternly wife and eight or ten uncared-for children. **1887** MOLONEY *Forestry W. Africa* 171, I have seen species of this plant in an uncultivated and uncared-for state in the interior districts of the Gold Coast.

†**un'caredly**, *adv. Sc. Obs.* [UN-[1] 11.] Without taking care; recklessly.
1590 BUREL *Pilg.* II. in Watson *Scots Poems* (1709) II. 45 Dispairdly, vncairdly, I hasert ouer the hill.

un'careful, *a.* [UN-[1] 7.]
1. Not exercising care; careless, not cautious or watchful.
c **1533** LATIMER in Foxe *A. & M.* (1563) 1317/1 We be secure & vncarefull, as though false Prophetes coulde not haue meddled with vs. **1592** BRETON *C'tess Pembrooke's Loue* Wks. (Grosart) I. 25/1 Vnhappy hart, that euer thee offended,..Vncarefull eare, that euer tale attended! **1604** T. WRIGHT *Passions* II. ii. 58 An vncarefull Magistrate neglecteth the good of the common-weale. **1647** BP. REYNOLDS *Passions* iii. 15 An eagernesse to take in, makes uncareful to retain. **1861** FLOR. NIGHTINGALE *Nursing* (ed. 2) 83 Careful nursing has done in a few weeks what uncareful medical observation has declared it impossible to do in less than two years. **1867** HOWELLS *Ital. Journ.* xi. (1883) I. 165, I had noticed (in an uncareful fashion enough, no doubt) the great changes which had taken place in Italy.
2. Not taking any care or consideration *of* or *for* (a thing or person).
1559–60 *MS. Cott. Caligula* B ix, Our eyes are opened, we espy how uncareful they have been of our weile at all tymes. **1572** H. MIDDELMORE in Ellis *Orig. Lett.* Ser. II. III. 7 So ame I not uncarefull of hir in any thinge that I maye knowe to be for hir preservation and good. **1662** J. CHANDLER *Van Helmont's Oriat.* 263 Such [Gods] as are uncareful of us, and despisers of small matters, and therefore also ignorant of us. **1664** CHAS. II *Sp. Both Ho. Parlt* 6 That Bill..passed in a Time very uncareful for the Dignity of the Crown, or the Security of the People. **1882** MRS. OLIPHANT *Lit. Hist. Eng.* I. 90 A delusion..which..he suddenly adopts and sanctions, uncareful of the misery which it might produce. **1897** *Ch. Times* 6 Aug. 135/2 The exclusiveness of official Anglicanism, un-careful of the masses, and caring only for the big purses.
3. Free from care; not anxious or troubled.
1643 QUARLES *Emblems* IV. xiii. 40 There shall thy soul possesse uncarefull treasure. **1646** —— *Judgem. & Mercy* Wks. (Grosart) I. 97/1 How hast thou liv'd O my uncarefull soule to see these prophesies fulfill'd? **1858** HAWTHORNE *Fr. & It. Note-bks.* II. 291 This journey from Rome has been one of the brightest and most uncareful interludes of my life. **1874** RUSKIN *Val D'Arno* (1886) 117 The uncareful happiness of men clothed without labour, and fed without fear.
Hence **un'carefully** *adv.*, **un'carefulness**.
1567 PAYNELL *Treas. Amadis of Gaule* 255 [We] shall soone breake them, being thus open, and it may be through uncarefulnesse and negligence chauncing unto them. **1654–66** EARL ORRERY *Parthen.* (1676) 548 He began so uncarefully to thrust at my Prince.

unca'ressed, *ppl. a.* (UN-[1] 8.)
1814 WORDSW. *Excurs.* IV. 577 He, whose hours Are by domestic pleasure uncaressed And unenlivened. **1825** LYTTON in *Life & Lett.* (1883) II. 23 Contempt for all encaged starlings, who have not the privilege of being as free and uncaressed as myself.

un'caricatured, *ppl. a.* (UN-[1] 8.)
1880 RUSKIN in *19th Cent.* June 948 That book is an earnest and uncaricatured record of states of criminal life.

un'caring, *ppl. a.* (UN-[1] 10 and 5 d.)
1786 BURNS *Ep. Young Friend* viii, Debar a' side-pretences, And resolutely keep its laws, Uncaring consequences. **1826** MISS MITFORD *Village* Ser. II. (1863) 275 She was so overflowing with health and spirits, so fearless and uncaring. **1844** KINGLAKE *Eothen* xxvii, A few Persian carpets,—thrown about near the divan,—give to the room an appearance of uncaring luxury. **1896** KIPLING *Seven Seas, Hymn bef. Action* ii, Deaf ear and soul uncaring, We seek Thy mercy now!
Hence **un'caringly** *adv.*; **un'caringness**.
1868 H. BUSHNELL *Serm. Living Subj.* 208 Put into language outspoken, it says, 'Plunge thyself uncaringly into evil'. **1930** A. HUXLEY *Brief Candles* 5 The superficial charm and good humour of the man seemed to overlie a fundamental hardness, an uncaringness, a hostility even. **1955** E. BOWEN *World of Love* iv. 78 Oh, how the vice of uncaringness had been hers; she had neither heart nor wish for a living creature.

†**un'carnate**, *a. Obs.*[−1] [UN-[1] 7, after INCARNATE.] Not incarnate.
1646 SIR T. BROWNE *Pseud. Ep.* VII. xvi. 372 Nor need we be afraid to ascribe that unto the incarnate Son, which sometimes is attributed unto the uncarnate Father.

†**un'carnating**, *vbl. sb. Obs.* [UN-[2] 8: cf. prec.] The action of rendering unincarnate.
1659 GAUDEN *Tears Ch.* II. xvi. 198 They set forth their pageantries of new-drest Divinity to be.. spirituall manifestations,..unheard-of emanations,..the uncarnating of a Christian [etc.].

uncar'nivorous, *a.* (UN-[1] 7.)
1822 T. L. PEACOCK *Maid Marian* xv, The fast-day dinner of an uncarnivorous friar.

un'carpeted, *a.* (UN-[1] 9.)
[**1775** ASH.] **1816** J. SCOTT *Vis. Paris* (ed. 5) 117 A small room or two, uncarpeted and bare, must be hired. **1860** MARIA L. CHARLESWORTH *Eng. Yeomen* xxx. (1861) 392 You scarcely heard a footfall, though the parlour boards were uncarpeted. **1894** DOYLE *S. Holmes* 63 Little rooms, uncarpeted and uncurtained.

un'carried, *ppl. a.* (UN-[1] 8.)
1584–5 *Act 27 Eliz.* c. 19 §3 In default therof, [to] pay.. for euerie such load [of gravel, etc.] due and uncaried, Two Shillings and Sixe Pence. [**1775** ASH.] **1890** *Pall Mall G.* 1 Sept. 5/1 Operations are..much hampered by the standing and uncarried crops.

un'cart, *v.* [UN-[2] 5.] *trans.* To take out of a cart; to unload from a cart.
1641 J. TAYLOR (Water P.) *Last Voy.* A 7 b, I being vncarted (with my boate) at a place called Stonehouse. **1857** GEO. ELIOT *Scenes Cler. Life, A. Barton* ii, He carted and uncarted the manure with a sort of flunkey grace. **1865** M. COLLINS *Who is the Heir?* xxxi, A noble deer was uncarted, and went straight away without a pause. **1890** BAKER *Wild Beasts* I. 300 We now uncarted a fresh cheetah.

un'cartable, *a.* [UN-[1] 7 b.] †On which carting is impossible.
1658 FRANCK *Northern Mem.* (1694) 195 What have we here? Cawses [= causeways] uncartable, and Pavements unpracticable, pointed with rocky stumpy Stones.

un'carved, *ppl. a.* [UN-[1] 8.]
1. Not carved or cut up for eating.
a **1592** GREENE *Jas. IV*, I. ii, I cannot abide..a fat capon vncaru'd.
2. Not carved or cut artistically or ornamentally.
1611 FLORIO, *Inscolpito*, vncarued, vngrauen. **1613–39** I. JONES in Leoni *Palladio's Archit.* (1742) II. 45 This Architrave is..uncarv'd. **1830** *Q. Rev.* XLIII. 21 It was a rude uncarved wooden log about six feet long. **1831** W. ELLIS *Polynesian Res.* (ed. 2) I. xiv. 354 A straight log of hard casuarina wood,..uncarved, but decorated with feathers.

uncase, *v.* [UN-[2] 4 and 5.]
1. *trans.* †**a.** To skin or flay (an animal or person). *Obs.*
1575 TURBERV. *Faulconrie* 12 As well the browne Eagles as the blacke are skynned and uncased as the Vultures be. **1591** SPENSER *M. Hubberd* 1380 The Foxe, first Author of that treacherie, He did vncase, and then away let flie. **1638** *Guillim's Heraldry* III. xiv. 176 You shall say a Foxe is Vncased. **1658–9** MORRICE in *Burton's Diary* (1828) IV. 191 Cambyses once uncased a corrupt judge, and made a cushion of his skin for his son to sit on. **1677** W. HUBBARD *Narrative* Postscr. 10 As men use to do with a slaughtered Beast before they uncase him.
absol. **1712** STEELE *Spect.* No. 473 ¶1 It can be proved upon him, that he cuts up, disjoints, and uncases with incomparable Dexterity.
b. To strip (a person); to undress.
1570–6 LAMBARDE *Peramb. Kent* (1826) 147 He was openly uncased, boxed about the eares, and sent to the next Iustice. **1599** NASHE *Lenten Stuffe* Wks. (Grosart) V. 261 He tare him from his throne, and vncased him of his habiliments. **1600** HOLLAND *Livy* XXIX. ix. 715 Whiles there was some time spent in turning them out of their apparrell and uncasing them. **1635** [GLAPTHORNE] *Lady Mother* I. i. in Bullen *O. Pl.* (1883) II. 107 If you uncase him, you will find his sattin dublett naught but fore sleaves and breast. **1699** FARQUHAR *Constant Couple* v. ii, I'll ha' you into the dungeon, and uncase you. **1823** MRS. SHERWOOD *Henry Milner* III. xxi, He..uncased him from a huge great coat.
refl. **1588** GREENE *Pandosto* (1843) 42 Dorastus..went to the grove where hee had his rich apparel, and there uncasing himself as secretly as might be [etc.]. **1596** SHAKS. *Tam. Shr.* I. i. 212 Tranio at once Vncase thee: take my Coulord hat and cloake. *a* **1634** CHAPMAN *Alphonsus* III. i. 227, I.. straight untruss'd my points, uncas'd myself. **1704** NORRIS *Ideal World* II. vii. 338 It seems impossible that bodies should thus intirely and simultaneously strip and uncase themselves of these their outer coats or membranes.
c. *absol.* To put off a garment or garments.
1588 SHAKS. *L.L.L.* v. ii. 707 Do you not see Pompey is vncasing for the combat? **1622** FLETCHER *Prophetess* IV. vi, I know that glory Is like Alcides's Shirt..: when we would uncase, It brings along with it both flesh and sinews. **1691** J. WILSON *Belphegor* III. v, The Sham won't pass on me—Come, come—uncase. **1733** FIELDING *Don Quix. in Eng.* II. vi, Sancho, uncase this instant, and handle that squire as he deserves. **1781** C. JOHNSTON *Hist. J. Juniper* I. 192 As soon as they arrived at the Jew's Kennel in Houndsditch, our hero directly uncased. **1837** BARHAM *Ingol. Leg.* Ser. I. *Leech of Folkestone*, Quick, Master Marsh! uncase, or you perish!
2. *fig.* To uncover, lay bare, expose to view or observation.
1587 HOLINSHED *Chron.* I. 77/1 He vncased the crooked conditions which he had couertlie concealed. *a* **1591** R. GREENHAM *Wks.* (1599) 56 Nakedly to vncase thy sins before God, is a hard thing to flesh and blood. **1627** HAKEWILL

Apol. (1630) 520 His hypocrisie shall be uncased and laid open to the view of the world. **1642** FULLER *Holy & Prof. St.* v. viii. 390 Thus God at last shall uncase the closest dissembler to the sight of men. **1677** GILPIN *Demonol.* (1867) 23 Those secret thinkings;..the very inside and outside of them are uncased, cut up and anatomised by his eye. **1710** PALMER *Proverbs* 167 A hypocrite shou'd be uncas'd and shewn to the world.

b. To strip or deprive *of* something.
1583 MELBANCKE *Philotimus* T ij b, Thy prickemedaintie Cornelius shallbee vncased of his vaine vizarde, and disburdened..of his hypocriticall apparitions. **1613** DAY *Dyall* xii. (1614) 326 What? to uncase themselves of al they had, and to give it to the Poore?

c. To take out of the body.
1629 QUARLES *Argalus & P.* I. Wks. (Grosart) III. 252/2 Death could ne'r uncase Thy soule. **1631** —— *Samson* Ibid. II. 160/1 Betwixt them both, his fury did uncase A thousand soules.

3. To free from a casing or covering.
1643 A. ROSSE *Mel Helic.* 41 O Lord, when thou dost call on me, Uncase my eyes, that I may see.

4. To draw or take out of a case or cover.
1589 GREENE *Tully's Love* Wks. (Grosart) VII. 126 As the foes of Perseus when hee vncased the head of Medusa. **1600–9** ROWLANDS *Knaue of Clubbes* (Hunterian Cl.) 8 A swaggering rogue breakes open dore, And's Rapier did vncase. **1688** R. HOLME *Armoury* III. xix. (Roxb.) 153/1 Take forth your Granade. Shut your pouch. Vncase your fuse. **1742** *Lond. & Country Brew.* I. (ed. 4) 19 Here they save the Charge of emptying or uncasing it out of the Bin. **1791** COWPER *Iliad* IV. 122 So Pallas spake, to whom infatuate he Listening, uncased at once his polish'd bow. **1802** JAMES *Milit. Dict.*, *To uncase*, in a military sense to display, to exhibit—As to uncase the colours. **1826** P. POUNDEN *France & Italy* 66 A crystal coffin in a small repository..being uncased to our view. **1893** *Daily News* 14 Dec. 2/2 The gun was here uncased by an officer and handed to the witness.

†**5.** To cast, throw off. *Obs.*$^{-1}$
1582 STANYHURST *Æneis* II. (Arb.) 58 The owtpeaking from weeds of poysoned adder,..His slougth vncasing.

Hence **un'cased** *ppl. a.*^{1}
1598 E. GUILPIN *Skial.* (1878) 42 Who for deluding vs, to plague their sinne, Are turnd to counterfaits, which their vncasde skin Quickly discouers. **1611** COTGR., *Salcoque*, an vncased Prawne. **1658** J. ROBINSON *Endoxa* i. 19 What an uncased or discovered Hypocrite is, I could never apprehend. **1760** *Impostors Detected* IV. viii. II. 232 D. Nunez was not a little surprised at seeing me at that time of night, and so uncased. **1791** COWPER *Odyss.* XI. 741 With uncas'd bow and arrow on the string. **1809** MALKIN *Gil Blas* I. ix. ¶4 Leaving the carriage and the uncased carcases by the road-side. **1818** SCOTT *Rob Roy* xxxi, He arose a forked, uncased, bald-pated, beggarly-looking scarecrow.

un'cased, *ppl. a.*^{2} [UN-^{1} 8.] Not cased.
1840 CLOUGH *Early Poems* i Come back again, my olden heart!—With incrustations of the years Uncased as yet.

un'casemated, *a.* (UN-^{1} 9.)
1611 COTGR., *Veues mortes*, close, or vncasemated windowes.

un'cashed, *ppl. a.* (UN-^{1} 8.)
1896 *Harper's Mag.* XCIII. 35/1 It happened..that I had two or three uncashed checks in my pocket.

un'casing, *vbl. sb.* [f. UNCASE *v.*] The action of taking out of a case, etc.
1589 NASHE *Almond for Parrat* 12, I am a shreud fellow at the vncasing of a fox. **1613** PURCHAS *Pilgrimage* (1614) 356 Goropius bestowes much paines in the vncasing of them. **1642** MILTON *Animadv.* Pref., In the serious uncasing of a grand imposture. **1693** EVELYN *Misc. Wks.* (1825) 719 Uncasing, for the taking them out of the case or vessel. *a* **1701** SEDLEY *Tyrant K. of Crete* II. iv, Sir, commit the uncasing Him to me!

un'cask, *v.* [UN-^{2} 5.] *trans.* To take or bring out of a cask; *fig.* to open up.
1594 NASHE *Unfort. Trav.* Wks. (Grosart) V. 69 Oratorie vncaske the bard hutch of thy complements, and with the triumphantest troupe in thy treasurie doe trewage vnto him. **1630** J. TAYLOR (Water P.) *Eighth Wond. World* Wks. II. 60/1 If thou in kindnesse wilt accept this taske, Hereafter I will better things vn-caske.

un'casque, *v.* (UN-^{2} 5.)
1818 MILMAN *Samor* 158 Through files of warriors, who uncasque their brows To fill their curious gaze, she hurries on. **1880** BARING-GOULD *Mehalah* xxi. 101 There she was wont to uncasque, and ruffle out her white cap.

†**un'cassable,** *a.*, **un'cassed,** *ppl. a. Obs.* (UN-^{1} 7 b, 8. See CASS *v.*)
1599 Q. ELIZ. in Moryson *Itin.* (1617) II. 56 You may keep the Captaines uncassed, but not give any warrant to them to supply their Companies with any more Irish. **1609** SKENE *Reg. Maj.* 12 In that case he affirmes the brieve to be valide, and vncassable.

un'cassock, *v.* (UN-^{2} 5.)
1645 *Sacred Decretal* 2 He hath so uncassock'd our misterious divinity.

un'cast, *ppl. a.* Also *Sc.* 5 vncastyne, 6 -castin. [UN-^{1} 8. Cf. Sw. *okastad.*]

1. Not cast or thrown.
c **1375** *Sc. Leg. Saints* vii. (*James*) 246 þat stane one stane in-to þat towne suld nocht be lefit vncastyne done. **1533** BELLENDEN *Livy* II. xx. (S.T.S.) I. 209 þe dartis war left vncastin on athir side. *a* **1547** SURREY *Æneid* II. (1557) Cj, But sone an other sort stept in theyr stede, No stone vnthrown, nor yet no dart vncast. **1662** R. VENABLES *Exper. Angler* x. 100 The flie were better uncast, because it frights the fish.

2. Not founded or moulded by casting.
1617 *Bk. Rates Marchandise* N j b, Leade..vncast the Fodder..xx.l...cast, the Fodder..xx.l.

3. Not reckoned (*up*) or calculated.
1598 SYLVESTER *Du Bartas* II. *Ded. Sonn.* ii, Our small Art's-stock..is even beggerd with th' uncast Expense. **1745** *De Foe's Eng. Tradesm.* xxxii. (1841) II. 58 Other accounts are left open and uncast up.

4. Not disfigured by a squint.
1629 GAULE *Holy Madn.* 328 He sees well, and his eyes were uncast.

un'cast, *v.* (UN-^{2} 3.)
1874 LD. COLERIDGE in *Life* (1904) II. 244 The die is cast: it cannot be uncast now.

†**un'castigate,** *ppl. a. Obs.*$^{-1}$ [UN-^{1} 8 b.] = next.
1539 TAVERNER *Bible* Ded., But now though many faultes perchaunce be yet left behind vncastigat,..I trust your maiestie..wyll pardon me.

un'castigated, *ppl. a.* (UN-^{1} 8.)
1657 TOMLINSON *Renou's Disp.* 582 Trochisks of Alhandal were safer then Coloquintida uncastigated. **1812** L. HUNT in *Examiner* 14 Sept. 589/1 Any uncastigated edition of such a writer. **1896** *Daily News* 7 Dec. 4/7 The editor alone walks the earth uncastigated.

un'castle, *v.* (UN-^{2} 5.)
1611 FLORIO, *Discastellare*, to vncastle. **1655** FULLER *Ch. Hist.* III. xii. 27 He uncastled Roger of Sarisbury, Alexander of Lincoln, and Nigellus of Ely. *a* **1661** —— *Worthies, Lond.* (1662) II. 197 The first of these [houses] is so uncastelled, the Glory of the second so obscured, that very few know.. where these houses were fixed. **1775** ASH, *Uncastle*.., to drive out of a castle.

un'castrated, *ppl. a.* [UN-^{1} 8.]

1. Not castrated; ungelded; entire.
1725 *Fam. Dict.*, *Ram*, the uncastrated Male of the Sheep-Kind. **1764** C. CHURCHILL *The Times* 29 Where is the Mother,..Who not permits, e'en for the sake of pray'r, A Priest, uncastrated, to enter there?

2. Not mutilated or expurgated.
1737 OLDYS *Librarian* 159 *note*, About the middle of the late King's Reign, an uncastrated Copy did arise. **1817** D'ISRAELI *Cur. Lit.* III. 196 *note*, It is a quarto tract,.. inserted in the uncastrated edition of Milton's prose works in 1738. **1822–56** DE QUINCEY *Confess.* (1862) 145 An uncastrated Decamerone or other dazzling κειμήλιον. **1886** *Athenæum* 16 Jan. 103/2 The genuine Giunta uncastrated edition [fetched] 81 *l.*

un'casual, *a.* (UN-^{1} 7.)
a **1618** SYLVESTER *Panaretus* 781 Besides th' off-cutting of All Passages,..Is even to conquer by uncasuall course.

†**un'casuistly,** *adv. Obs.* (UN-^{1} 11.)
1649 *Bounds Publ. Obed.* 3 With an acknowledgement of their authority and right, which is very uncasuistly and unconscienciously inserted here.

un'catalogued, *ppl. a.* (UN-^{1} 8.)
1837 J. H. NEWMAN *Proph. Office Ch.* 249 Unsorted and uncatalogued treasures. **1858** O. W. HOLMES *Aut. Breakf.-t.* iv. 81 Then we will go together into the solemn archives of Oblivion's Uncatalogued Library! **1870** J. H. NEWMAN *Gram. Assent* II. viii. 297 The combination of many uncatalogued experiences floating in my memory.

un'catchable, *a.* (UN-^{1} 7 b.)
1824 MISS MITFORD *Village* Ser. I. (1863) 152 She was a sad romp;..as uncertain as a butterfly, as uncatchable as a swallow! **1892** *Star* 13 May 1/7 Some Indian gentlemen with uncatchable names were much admired.

'uncate, *a. Bot.* [ad. L. *uncāt-us*, f. *unc-us* hook.] = UNCINATE *a.*
1865 *Treas. Bot.* 1191/1 *Uncate*,..hooked; curved suddenly back at the point.

uncatechized (ʌn'kætɪkaɪzd), *ppl. a.* [UN-^{1} 8.] Not formally instructed or examined in religion. Also *absol.*
1619 W. SCLATER *Exp. 1 Thess.* (1630) 28 The manner of ascending to assurance of Election,..wherein..these men are yet uncatechized. **1667** *Decay Chr. Piety* iii. §6. 218 But would God the uncatechiz'd were the only persons we had to complain of in this matter. **1685** J. SCOTT *Chr. Life* II. 137 The hair-brain'd and uncatechised youths of the Town. **1832** MACGILLIVRAY *Trav. Humboldt* xvii. 237 They found six houses inhabited by uncatechised Guahiboes. **1842** PUSEY in Liddon *Life* (1893) I. xi. 258 It will be thrust on minds unprepared, and on an uncatechised Church.

Hence **un'catechizedness.**
1659 GAUDEN *Tears Ch.* IV. xxiii. 619 What means the Uncatechisedness, the Sottishness, Profaneness, Impudence and Irreligion which are so much spreading and prevailing?

uncathedralled, *a.*: see UN-^{1} 9.

uncatholic (ʌn'kæθəlɪk), *a.* and *sb.* [UN-^{1} 7 and 12.]

A. *adj.* Not catholic or universal, in an ecclesiastical sense; also *spec.*, not Roman-Catholic.
1601 [? W. WATSON] *Imp. Consid. Sec. Priests* (1675) 61 This intolerable and very uncatholick course thus held by divers, to the great offence of many good Catholicks. **1660** GAUDEN *God's Gt. Demonstr.* 51 Thy humane traditions, and unauthentick because uncatholick observations, instead of Christ's institutions. **1678** T. JONES *Heart & its Sov.* 522 Our Romanists..are so restrain'd, and Vncatholick, and Jewish-like, in the bounds of their Church, which they so confine to Rome. **1685** J. SCOTT *Chr. Life* II. vii. §9 Now that Church which requires sinful or uncatholick Terms of Communion, doth hereby exclude..all Parts of the Catholick Church from its Communion. **1711** G. HICKES *Two Treat. Chr. Priesth.* (1847) I. 271 A new uncatholic mission of their own creating. **1845** J. H. NEWMAN *Ess. Developm.* 328 Such a doctrine is in no sense uncatholic. **1896** GORE *R.C. Claims* App. I. 210 We in the Church of England..are yet unfettered by any uncatholic dogma.
transf. **1624** MIDDLETON *Game at Chess* II. i, I'll tell thee what a most uncatholic jest He put upon me once.

B. *sb.* One who is not a Catholic.
1865 PUSEY *Truth Eng. Ch.* 133 The Bishop of Trèves doubted for a time on account of the un-Catholics, but decided that the decree would be advantageous.

unca'tholicalness. (See prec. and UN-^{1} 12.)
Also, in recent use, *uncatholicity*.
1695 J. SAGE *Fundamental Charter* (1697) 247 The impoliticalness, the uncatholicalness of most, if not all, of these Propositions.

unca'tholicize, *v.* (UN-^{2} 6 c.)
1806 G. S. FABER *Disc. Prophecies* (1814) II. 279 As I have no inclination to uncatholicise myself. **1842** PUSEY *Crisis Eng. Ch.* 126 Our Church has been in part un-Catholicized by those who helped in a degree to unsecularize her.

Hence **unca'tholicized** *ppl. a.*, **unca'thol-icizing** *vbl. sb.*
1822 C. BUTLER *Remin.* xv. 211 The uncatholicizing of the calendar. **1824** BENTHAM *Bk. Fallacies* Wks. 1843 II. 468/2 All the doctors..of the as yet uncatholicized university of Mexico. **1863** O'DWYER *Pius IX*, xxxi. 188 In reformed and uncatholicised England.

uncatholicly, *adv.*: see UN-^{1} 11.

un'cattle, *v.* (UN-^{2} 4.)
1643 *Merc. Brit.* No. 27. 213 Colonell Cromwell hath uncatteled them about Oxford, and..both drove away the Cattell & the Rebells into Oxford at the same time.

un'caught, *ppl. a.* (UN-^{1} 8 b.)
1340–70 *Alex. & Dind.* 38 þei þou fonde wiþ þi folk to fiȝhte wiþ us alle, We schulle us kepe on-cauȝt oure cauus wiþ inne. ? *a* **1500** *Chester Pl.* XVIII. 117 He scapeth not vncought. **1605** SHAKS. *Lear* II. i. 59 Let him fly farre: Not in this Land shall he remaine vncaught. **1619** HIERON *Wks.* I. 639 The state of men by nature, who bee as fishes ranging after their owne disposition, vncaught. **1711** GAY *Rural Sports* 145 His bosom glows with treasures yet uncaught. **1820** C. R. MATURIN *Melmoth* (1892) III. xxviii. 147 Whenever you have seen the tear, which your hand might have wiped away, fall uncaught. **1894** BARING-GOULD *Kitty Alone* II. 95, I live in fear of him as long as he is uncaught.

un'caulk, *v.* (UN-^{2} 3.)
1608 SYLVESTER *Du Bartas* II. iv. *Schisme* 949 The billows, beating round about the ship, Unchauk [*sic*] her keel, and all her seams unrip.

un'caulked, *ppl. a.* (UN-^{1} 8.)
1748 SMOLLETT *R. Random* xxiv. 164 Another observing my wounds, which remained exposed to the air, told me, my seams were uncaulked. **1841** LEVER *C. O'Malley* xxxi. 166 Where the uncaulked deck but filters every rain on your head.

†**un'cauponated,** *ppl. a. Obs.* [UN-^{1} 8.] Not sold, or tampered with, by hucksters.
a **1752** SMART *Hop Garden* I. 176 When great Eliza reign'd .., when our brave sires Drank valour from uncauponated beer.

un'caused, *ppl. a.* (UN-^{1} 8.)
Common from *c* 1730; hence (in recent use) *uncausedness*.
a **1628** F. GREVIL *Let. to Honorable Lady* (1633) C iv, To giue all, and take nothing, proceeds of an uncaused goodnesse, and so necessarily of an vnabusing. **1722** WOLLASTON *Relig. Nat.* v. 65 Where there is a subordination of causes and effects, there must necessarily be a cause in nature prior to the rest, uncaused. **1768–74** TUCKER *Lt. Nat.* (1834) I. 366 We know that He is almighty, self-existent, uncaused. **1796** BP. WATSON *Apol. Bible* 367 What think you of an uncaused cause of every thing? **1849** H. SPENCER in *Academy* 25 June (1904) 690/1 An uncaused deity is just as inconceivable as an uncaused universe. **1871** TYLOR *Prim. Cult.* I. 4 He has simply thrown out..the whole fabric of motiveless will and uncaused spontaneity.

†**un'cautelous,** *a. Obs.* [UN-^{1} 7 and 5 b.] Incautious, unwary.
1628 PRYNNE *Brief Survay* 2 They may the more insensibly Insinuate..themselues into the Hearts, and Intralls, of vncautelous, and ouer-credulous Christians. *a* **1656** HALES *Gold. Rem.* I. (1673) 284, I would you would advise him to beware of such uncautelous speeches. **1697** EVELYN *Numism.* ix. 316 Those of Savoy, Swisserland, and many parts of Germany, which abound in Foxes, etc., are the dullest, simplest, and most uncautelous of all their Neighbours.

Hence †**un'cautelousness.** *Obs.*
a **1656** HALES *Gold. Rem.* I. (1673) 256 He hath laid it down in such terms, that nothing but negligence and uncautelousness can hazard it.

†**un'cautioned,** *ppl. a. Obs.* = next.
1671 R. MACWARD *True Noncomf.* 383 Your blunt and uncautioned general, viz. that private persons may punish crimes in case of the supinness of the Magistrat.

†**un'cautious,** *a. Obs.* [UN-^{1} 7 and 5 b.] Incautious. Also *absol.*
1644 DIGBY *Nat. Bodies* xii. §6. 105 A man that was vncautious and sucked strongly that had his foreteeth beaten out by the blow of the bullett ascending. **1677** GILPIN *Demonol.* (1867) 31 There is no small cunning and working of Satan in them, insomuch that the uncautious and injudicious are deceived. **1710** PALMER *Proverbs* Pref. p. xiv, An uncautious wanton writer can possibly give the vice he

has too lusciously describ'd. 1741 RICHARDSON *Pamela* I. 205 O what has this uncautious man said?

Hence †**un'cautiously** *adv.*, †**un'cautiousness**.

1680 H. DODWELL *Two Lett.* (1691) 154 Arguments.. endangered by the very uncautiousness of the expression. 1721 WATERLAND *Case Arian-Subscr. Consid.* iv. 41 (Plea xiv. §4), It is very uncautiously and unaccurately said, that King Charles I. patronized the Subscribing the same Articles either in contradictory, or different Senses. 1759 GOLDSM. *Bee* No. 7. 128 Uncautiously suffering this jealousy to corrode in her breast.

†**unce.** *Obs.*[-1] [ad. L. *uncus.*] A claw.

1609 HEYWOOD *Brit. Troy* VII. lxxvi, The Riuer-waking-Serpent to make sleepe, Whose horride crest, blew scales, and vnces blacke, Threat euery one a death.

unce, obs. f. OUNCE *sb.*[1] and *sb.*[2]

†**un'ceasable**, *a. Obs.* [UN-[1] 7 b.] Incessant.

1604 DEKKER *Magnif. Entertainm. K. Jas.* Wks. 1873 I. 268 Zealous prayers, and unceasable wishes for his most speedy and longed-for arrivall. 1611 COTGR., *Incessible*, vnceasable, vnendable, vndeterminable.

un'ceased, *ppl. a.* (UN-[1] 8.)

1598 SYLVESTER *Du Bartas* II. ii. *Colonies* 244 Not that I send Sem, at one flight unceast, From Babylon unto the farthest East.

un'ceasing, *ppl. a.* Also 4–5 vnce(e)s(s)ynge, 5 vncecynge. [UN-[1] 10.] Never ceasing, incessant, continuous. (Common from *c* 1750.)

1382 WYCLIF *2 Pet.* ii. 14 Hauynge iȝen ful of auoutrie, and vncesynge trespasse, deceyuynge vnstedefast soules. 1410 *Prymer* in Maskell *Mon. Rit.* III. 16 To the cherubyn and seraphym crien with uncecynge vois. 1743 FRANCIS tr. *Hor., Odes* III. xxix. 9 Nor [do thou] with unceasing Joy survey Fair Æsula's declining Fields. 1774 GOLDSM. *Nat. Hist.* (1776) VIII. 157 Still millions more [of gnats] succeed, and produce unceasing torment. 1803 MALTHUS *Popul.* I. vi. 75 The efforts of the German nations to colonize or plunder were unceasing. 1842 MANNING *Serm.* i. (1848) I. 6 Carrying on unceasing, universal warfare against Heaven. 1873 LELAND *Egypt. Sketch-Bk.* 196 They are still singing, those unceasing children of Egypt, that quaint old refrain.

Hence **un'ceasingness**.

1727 BAILEY (vol. II), *Incessantness*, Continualness, Unceasingness. (Also in recent use.)

un'ceasingly, *adv.* Also 4 vncesendly, -cessandly, -seshandle; 5 vncessyngly, -sessyngly, unsessyngly. [f. prec. + -LY[2].] Without ceasing; incessantly.

c 1340 HAMPOLE *Prose Tr.* 3 Wharefore, what may do faile vn-to hym þat couaytes vn-cessandly for to lufe þe name of Ihesu? 1382 WYCLIF *Isaiah* Prol., For the present bacbityng by which me enemys vncesendely to-tern, he to me ȝelde meede in tyme to come. *c* 1425 *Found. St. Barth.* II. xxviii, All the benefetys.. that hath be don yn the portys of the see .. unsessyngly. 1435 MISYN *Fire of Love* 101 þat þai godis giftis knawand in al þer hart hym þa suld glorify & lufe vncessyngly. 1779 *Mirror* No. 37, To wear high feathers, and to wave them more unceasingly than any other ladies. 1809 PINKNEY *Trav. France* 147 They are temperate, unceasingly gay, and sufficiently clad. 1880 'OUIDA' *Moths* I. vii. 161 She was harassed by the sense of being unceasingly criticised.

un'ceiled, *ppl. a.* (UN-[1] 8.)

[1775 ASH.] 1819 CRABBE *T. of Hall* xii. 708 The roof, unceil'd in patches, gave the snow Entrance within. 1865 KINGSLEY *Herew.* iii, A low lean-to roof; the slates and rafters unceiled. 1891 T. HARDY *Tess* xxxviii, The room below being unceiled she could hear most of what went on there.

un'ceilinged, *a.* (UN-[1] 9.)

1849 LEVER *Con Cregan* v, In a large unceilinged room.. sat Betty in a straw chair.

uncele, var. UNSEEL *v. Obs.*

un'celebrated, *ppl. a.* [UN-[1] 8.]

1. Not observed with festivities or in some formal manner; not specially honoured or extolled.

1660 MILTON *Free Commw.* Wks. 1851 V. 425 Nor was.. our Victory.. unprais'd or uncelebrated in a written Monument. 1667 —— *P.L.* VII. 253 Thus was the first Day Eev'n and Morn: Nor past uncelebrated, nor unsung By the Celestial Quires. 1736 POPE *Let. to Swift* 30 Dec., I have seen a royal birth-day uncelebrated but by one vile Ode, and one hired bonfire. 1781 MRS. GRANT *Lett. fr. Mount.* (1813) II. xiv. 75 The freedom, ease, and gaiety, which.. has not passed uncelebrated or unsung. *a* 1843 SOUTHEY *Comm.-pl. Bk.* Ser. II. (1849) 138 Christmas *un*celebrated there.

2. Not famed or renowned.

1740 CIBBER *Apol.* (1756) II. 4 There came over from Dublin Theatre two uncelebrated actors to pick up a few pence among us. 1782 V. KNOX *Ess.* lxvi. I. 288 Such is that uncelebrated virtue, common and moral honesty. 1840 WILLIS *Loiterings Trav.* III. 38 This out-of-door's world, unvisited and uncelebrated.

unce'lestial, *a.* (UN-[1] 7.)

1661 FELTHAM *Resolves* (ed. 8) II. lvi. 301 It.. gives the lips a trembling; the eyes an uncelestial and declining look. 1742 YOUNG *Nt. Th.* IX. 713 'Tis nature's structure, broke by stubborn will, Breeds all that un-celestial discord there. 1860 TROLLOPE *Framley P.* xxiii, Any uncelestial envy or malice. 1897 BLACKMORE *Dariel* 193 And the last of these was Dariel, looking as if she had never dreamed of anything uncelestial.

un'cellar, *v.* (UN-[2] 5.)

1611 FLORIO, *Discantinare*, to vncellar. 1879 J. TODHUNTER *Alcestis* 78 Set the banqueting-hall in order; .. uncellar my choicest wines.

un'cellared, *ppl. a.* (UN-[1] 8.)

1564 *Reg. Privy Council Scot.* I. 299 That it remane within schip onsellarit to that effect for the space of four dayis.

unce'ment, *v.* (UN-[2] 3.)

a 1634 CHAPMAN & SHIRLEY *Chabot* IV. i. 56 They have frighted My fancy into my dreams with their close whispers How to uncement your affections.

unce'mented, *ppl. a.* (UN-[1] 8.)

1717 BERKELEY *Jrnl. Tour Italy* 28 May, Wks. 1871 IV. 552 Parched pasture, amidst wall of huge uncemented stones grown rough with age. 1841 W. SPALDING *Italy & It. Isl.* I. 312 Some huge fragments of uncemented blocks. 1851 RUSKIN *Stones Ven.* I. vi. §2 With all the joints, perhaps uncemented, or imperfectly filled up with cement, open to the sky.

b. *transf.* and *fig.*

1783 BEATTIE *Theory Lang.* II. iv. 480 This uncemented composition has of late become fashionable among the French and their imitators. 1792 CHARLOTTE SMITH *Desmond* II. 53 That, uncemented by blood, the noble and simply majestic temple of liberty will arise. 1856 MERIVALE *Rom. Emp.* XXXIX. (1865) IV. 379 The state itself has seemed .. to become a mere collection of uncemented atoms. 1864 PUSEY *Lect. Daniel* (1876) 412 Subdued, but warlike nations, uncemented into one with the conquering empire.

un'censored, *ppl. a.* (UN-[1] 8.)

1890 *Blackw. Mag.* Oct. 442 No foreign journalist may send uncensored telegrams to his editor.

uncen'sorious, *a.* (UN-[1] 7.)

a 1711 KEN *Edmund* Poet. Wks. 1721 II. 272 Her Speech was uncensorious and restrain'd. 1823 DE QUINCEY *Lett. to Yng. Man* Wks. 1860 XIV. 19 Leibnitz was always uncensorious, and yet patient of censure. 1881 L. A. TOLLEMACHE in *Jrnl. Educ.* Oct. 225 Straightway the dove was expelled for his uncensorious mildness.

un'censurable, *a.* (UN-[1] 7 b.)

1643 PRYNNE *Sov. Power Parl.* III. 121 Our Opposites must grant all Bishops, Priests, Ministers,.. as irresistible, uncensurable, undeprivable. 1678 CUDWORTH *Intell. Syst.* I. v. 897 These sovereign legislative powers may be said to be .. un-judicable or un-censurable by any humane court. 1810 BENTHAM *Packing* (1821) 58 An interest, than which.. nothing should be more innocent and uncensurable. *a* 1817 T. DWIGHT *Trav. New Eng.*, etc. (1821) II. 112, I have been informed.. that he was uncensurable in his life.

un'censured, *ppl. a.* (UN-[1] 8.)

1574 *Life 70th Abp. Canterb.* To Rdr. E 2 b, A masse of there intolerable supersticions deeds and sayinges vncensured. 1606 SYLVESTER *Du Bartas* II. iv. *Tropheis* 1055 But David's foule defect Was yet un-seen, un-censur'd, un-suspect. 1645 MILTON *Tetrach.* Introd., It was preacht before ye.. that there was a wicked Book abroad, and ye were taxt of sin that it was yet uncensur'd. 1693 DRYDEN *Persius* I. 219 Rather than so, uncensur'd let 'em be. 1728 R. MORRIS *Ess. Anc. Archit.* 65 From these considerations I pass not uncensur'd. 1767 WILKES *Corr.* (1805) III. 101 All these papers have passed uncensured.. by the two houses of parliament. 1849 MACAULAY *Hist. Eng.* vi. II. 11 This breach of the law for a time passed uncensured. 1879 FARRAR *St. Paul* (1883) 754 Children of God, uncensured in the midst of a crooked and distorted generation.

un'central, *a.* (UN-[1] 7.)

1782 PAINE *Let. Abbé Raynel* (1791) 54 The greater part of the Abbe's writings.. appear to me uncentral and burthened with variety. 1911 R. BROOKE *Let.* Mar. (1968) 292 One's whole personality was there—only, somehow without the point. One was curiously *uncentral*. 1977 D. JONES *My Friend Dylan Thomas* iv. 40 This unlocal, uncentral world where the pubs are bad and the people are sly.

un'centre, *v.* [UN-[2] 5.] *trans.* To remove from or as from a centre. Also *refl.*

1625 T. ADAMS *Serm.* Wks. (1629) 944 Let the heart be vncentred from Christ, it is dead. 1642 H. MORE *Song of Soul* III. 3 For then we fell,.. Uncentring our selves from our great stay. 1693 NORRIS *Pract. Disc.* III. 195 To find herself loosen'd and uncenter'd from the Creature, and not lodg'd upon God. 1788 WESLEY *Wks.* (1872) VI. 447 Whatever uncentres the mind from God does properly dissipate us.

Hence **un'centring** *vbl. sb.*

1669 *Address to hopef. yng. Gentry Eng.* Ep. Ded. A 2 b, His vanity to promise the uncentring of that vast body and unweildy.

un'centred, *ppl. a.* (UN-[1] 8.)

1652 BENLOWES *Theoph.* VII. xi, Jehovah's zone to this uncentred ball Ecliptick and meridionall. 1829 LYTTON *Disowned* xxxviii, Hers is the real and uncentred poetry of being, which pervades and surrounds her as with an air.

un'cereclothed, *a.* (UN-[1] 9.)

1862 GRATTAN *Beaten Paths* I. 142 The unsepulchred, uncoffined, and uncereclothed tailor.

un'ceremented, *ppl. a.* (UN-[1] 8.)

1880 T. HODGKIN *Italy & her Invaders* III. vii, The bodies were unwashed, unceremented.

uncere'monious, *a.* [UN-[1] 7.]

1. Of conduct, actions, etc.: Characterized by lack of ceremony or formality.

1598 CHAPMAN *Contn. Marlowe's Hero & Leander* III. 156 She vanisht, leauing pierst Leanders hart With sence of his vnceremonious part. 1727 BLACKWALL *Sacr. Class.* (ed. 2) I. 206 In the more plain and unceremonious times it [woman] was a title apply'd to ladies of the greatest quality and merit. 1779 J. MOORE *View Soc. France* II. lxxxv. 332 The unceremonious and easy manner, in which this great prince lives with his subjects. 1825 SCOTT *Talism.* viii, Expressing strongly the displeasure he felt at this unceremonious rebuke. 1891 FARRAR *Darkn. & Dawn* xxxix, Now the people laughed at the unceremonious way in which he shook one of them.

2. Of persons, etc.: Acting without ceremony.

1831 SCOTT *Ct. Rob.* xiii, If it happens that they actually need gold, they are sufficiently unceremonious in taking it. 1832 LYTTON *Eugene A.* I. v, Forgive me if I seem unceremonious—adieu.

Hence **uncere'moniously**, *adv.*, **uncere'moniousness**.

1755 JOHNSON, *Familiarly*, *unceremoniously; with freedom like that of long acquaintance. 1796 MME. D'ARBLAY *Camilla* VI. xv, Resentful of the liberty he had so unceremoniously taken. 1825 SCOTT *Betrothed* xvii, The message of the Archbishop, so unceremoniously delivered. 1878 CHURCH *Bacon* ix. (1884) 215 Setting down unceremoniously.. the real rules which he had felt to be true. 1815 JANE AUSTEN *Emma* xii, All the *unceremoniousness of perfect amity. 1866 GEO. ELIOT *F. Holt* v, 'Well, they're right enough there,' said Felix, with his usual unceremoniousness.

†**un'cert**, *a. Sc. Obs. rare.* [ad. L. *incert-us*: cf. UN-[1] 5 b.] Uncertain.

1543 *Sc. Acts, Mary* (1814) II. 440/2 Tharfor þe said decret of forfaltour is vncert, Inept, and generale, & following and promulgate vpoune ane vncert, Inept & generale libell.

un'certain, *a.* Forms: (see UN-[1] and CERTAIN *a.*). [UN-[1] 7; cf. F. *incertain* INCERTAIN *a.*, and L. *incertus*.]

1. a. Not determinate or fixed in point of time or occurrence; that may happen earlier or later.

a 1300 *Cursor M.* 23733 Es nathing certainur þan dede, Ne vncertainner þan es þe tide. *c* 1340 HAMPOLE *Pr. Consc.* 1952 What es mare uncertayn thyng, þan es þe tyme of the dede commyng. 1388 WYCLIF *Wisd.* x. 7 Trees hauynge fruytis in vncerteyn tyme. *c* 1480 HENRYSON *Thre Deid Pollis* 12 (Bann. MS.), The hour of deth and place Is vncertane. 1526 *Pilgr. Perf.* (W. de W. 1531) 240 Vncertayne is thy deth, remember thyne ende. 1549 *Compl. Scot.* 36 The terme of cristis cumming is schort, ande the day on-certane. 1560 DAUS tr. *Sleidane's Comm.* 462 b, To be differed to a tyme uncerten. *a* 1627 SIR J. BEAUMONT *Miserable St. Man* 39 Which fixe our minds on that vncertaine day When these shall faile, most certaine to decay. 1811 *Regul. & Ord. Army* 135 The Captain and Subaltern of the Day of each Regiment are to visit the Hospital at different and uncertain Hours.

b. Not determinate or fixed in amount, number, or extent.

1303 R. BRUNNE *Handl. Synne* 6688 Betwyxe oure ioye, and ȝoure peyne, ys endles tyme, and vncerteyne. 1382 WYCLIF *Job* xv. 20 The noumbre of ȝeris of his tiraundise is vncertein. *c* 1460 FORTESCUE *Abs. & Lim. Mon.* ix. (1885) 127 Sithyn the said extraordinarie charges bith so vncertayne þat thai be not estymable. 1725 *Fam. Dict.* s.v. *Yard-land*, This uncertain quantity in 28 of Edward IV. is call'd a Verge of Land. 1774 GOLDSM. *Nat. Hist.* I. 339 The activity of the winds, their continual change, and uncertain duration. 1775 JOHNSON *Tax. no Tyr.* 14 A duty of very uncertain extent. 1816 SHELLEY *Hymn Intell. Beauty* IV. 2 Love, Hope, and Self-esteem, like clouds depart And come, for some uncertain moments lent. 1839 STONEHOUSE *Axholme* 25 The warp along the shores of the Trent forms a bed of uncertain thickness.

c. Having no regular shape. *rare*[-1].

1742 LEONI *Palladio's Archit.* I. 81 It was pav'd with uncertain Stones, that is, such as had unequal sides and angles.

2. a. Not certain or determined in respect of occurrence; dependent on chance or accident.

1303 R. BRUNNE *Handl. Synne* 5995 Here mercy ys ful on-certeyn But þey ȝelde hem here gode aȝeyn. 1484 *Coventry Leet Bk.* 518 Because they shuld not come in þe market.. Howe-so-euer þe price of whete went higher or lower, which was thought vncerteyn. 1589 PUTTENHAM *Eng. Poesie* I. xix. 32 The things future, being also euents very vncertaine, and such as can not possibly be knowne because they be not yet. 1634 MILTON *Comus* 360 Peace brother, be not over-exquisite To cast the fashion of uncertain evils. 1818 CRUISE *Digest* (ed. 2) II. 269 Such remainder is contingent, because it is uncertain which of them will survive. 1853 ABP. THOMSON *Laws Th.* (ed. 3) §124. 332 Uncertain events are those wherein no cause or law appears, to determine the occurrence of one rather than of another. 1880 *Science-Gossip* XXV. 116/1 There are small ledges here and there formed.. by the uncertain deposit of material, or by the uncertain slip of shingle.

b. Devoid of, lacking in, certainty or settled character; liable to change or accident.

1477 *Rolls of Parlt.* VI. 168/1 The lyf of every creature is uncertayn. 1503–4 *Act 19 Hen. VII*, c. 25 *Preamble*, Lyfe [is] as uncertayne to suche as survyve as was to them now departed. 1526 TINDALE *1 Tim.* vi. 17 Charge them.. that they be not excedynge wyse, and that they trust not in the vncertayne riches, but in the livynge god. 1607 SHAKS. *Timon* V. i. 205 Their Aches, losses, Their pangs of Loue, with other incident throwes That Natures fragile Vessell doth sustaine In lifes vncertaine voyage. 1655 STANLEY *Hist. Philos.* III. (1687) 86/2 He ought not voluntarily to thrust himself into destruction..; that he should leave his Children in an uncertain mean estate. 1690 LOCKE *Hum. Und.* I. iii. §13 Truth and Certainty.. are not at all secured by them: But Men are in the same uncertain, floating estate with, as without them. 1743 FRANCIS tr. *Hor., Odes* III. xxix. 39 For the World's uncertain Fate Alarm'd. 1828 LYTTON *Pelham* III. x, My mother was much better, but still in a very uncertain and dangerous state of health. 1850 MCCOSH *Div. Govt.* II. ii. (1874) 163 There is nothing so uncertain as bodily health and human destiny. 1891 FARRAR *Darkn. & Dawn* xlv, His philosophic teacher.. persuaded him that a firm death was preferable to troubled and uncertain life.

3. a. About which one cannot be certain or assured; subject to doubt.

1338 R. BRUNNE *Chron.* (1810) 324 Who may now in Rome haf any sikernesse, þat þer is hiest dome, & ȝit vncerteyn es? *c* **1374** CHAUCER *Boeth.* v. pr. iii. (1868) 154 þan ne sholde þer ben no stedfast prescience of þinge to comen but raþer an vncerteyn oppinioun. **1382** WYCLIF *1 Cor.* ix. 26 Therfore I renne so, not as into an vncerteyn thing; thus I fiȝte, not as betynge the eyr. *c* **1400** *Destr. Troy* 9206 Hit semith me vnsertain, all serchyng of wayes. **1484** CAXTON *Fables of Auian* xvi, Men ought not to lete goo.. what they be sure of, hopynge to haue afterwards that.. whiche is vncertayne. **1555** EDEN *Decades* (Arb.) 126 Petrus Arias.. hath offered hym selfe to aduenture his lyfe.. vnder vncerteyne hope of gayne. **1596** SHAKS. *1 Hen. IV*, II. iii. 12 The purpose you vndertake is dangerous, the Friends you haue named vncertaine. **1634** SIR T. HERBERT *Trav.* 2 Vncertaine stories, which not only perplexe the hearers, but beget incredulitie, oftentimes amongst the credulous. **1669** STURMY *Mariner's Mag.* v. xii. 70 It is very difficult, and a thing uncertain also to arrive herein unto Exactness. **1718** PRIOR *Solomon* I. 740 Forc'd by reflective Reason I confess, That human Science is uncertain Guess. **1794** S. WILLIAMS *Vermont* (1809) I. vii. 221 If the facts had been true, the conclusions which have been drawn from them would have been wholly uncertain. **1798** WORDSW. *Tintern Abbey* 19 With some uncertain notice, as might seem Of vagrant dwellers in the houseless woods. **1827** FARADAY *Chem. Manip.* xxi. 548 New, important, and uncertain or unexpected results, are to be repeated once or twice.

absol. **1484** CAXTON *Fables of Auian* xvi, Men ought not to leue that thynge whiche is sure & certayne, for hope to haue the vncertayn. **1548** HALL *Chron. Hen. VI*, 129 It was not the poynt of a wiseman, to leave and let passe, the certain for the uncertain.

b. Of ways, etc.: Not clearly leading to a certain goal or destination.

c **1380** WYCLIF *Sel. Wks.* III. 363 Certis þat man were a fool þat wolde take þis uncerteine weie, and leeve þe certeyn witt and feyþ. **1565** COOPER *Thesaurus, Iter ambiguum*, vncertayne way. **1594** SHAKS. *Rich. III*, IV. ii. 64 Murther her Brothers, and then marry her, Vncertaine way of gaine. **1640** DENHAM *Cooper's H.* (1655) 295 He.. more Repents his courage, then his feare before; Finds that uncertaine waies unsafest are. **1653** J. TAYLOR (Water P.) *title*, The certain Travailes of an uncertain Journey. **1784** COWPER *Task* III. 3 One who, long in thickets and in brakes Entangled, winds now this way and now that His devious course uncertain, seeking home. **1805** WORDSW. *Prelude* VI. 696 Doubting not that.. by no uncertain path.. Led, as before, we should behold the scene. **1818** KEATS *Endym.* II. 48 For many days, Has he been wandering in uncertain ways: Through wilderness.

c. That cannot be relied on to produce a particular result.

1382 WYCLIF *Wisd.* ix. 14 The thoȝtis forsothe of deadli men [ben] dredful, and vncerteyn oure purueauncis. **1596** SPENSER *F.Q.* VI. iv. 25 So vp and downe he wandred many a mile, With wearie trauell and vncertaine toile. **1759** R. BROWN *Compl. Farmer* II. 119 Hops are a very uncertain crop. **1765** *Museum Rust.* IV. 314 He admits the spring-sowing to be uncertain. **1781** GIBBON *Decl. & F.* xxx. III. 175 These expensive and uncertain treaties. **1833** *Penny Cycl.* I. 186 In this arid region.. maize, barley, and caffre corn, afford the husbandman a miserable and uncertain crop.

4. a. Not known with certainty; not established or proved beyond doubt; doubtful, dubious.

a **1325** *Prose Psalter* l. 7 Þe vncerteyn þynges and pryue of þy wisdom þou made to me apert. **1338** R. BRUNNE *Chron.* (1810) 334 Roberte's men þei slowe, þe numbre vncerteyn. **1387** TREVISA *Higden* (Rolls) II. 63 Hit is vncerteyn who bulde first þis citee. **1538** STARKEY *England* (1878) 61 Fortune, or els what other name soeuer you wyl gyue to the blynd and vncertayne causys wych be not in mannys powar. **1561** T. NORTON *Calvin's Inst.* 22 Euen the wisest of them .. in theyr prayers do cal vpon vncertayne gods. *a* **1578** LINDESAY (Pitscottie) *Chron. Scot.* (S.T.S.) I. 68 The Earle of Saillisberrie quho was slaine be the schot of ane goun, wncertane hou or be quhat way. **1610** HOLLAND *Camden's Brit.* (1637) 288 Uncertaine it is, whether he made these buildings, or the buildings made him. **1639** LD. BALMERINO in *10th Rep. Hist. MSS. Comm.* App. I. 48 Occurrents heere are vncertain. **1732** BERKELEY *Alciphr.* VI. §5 What was uncertain in the primitive times cannot be undoubted in the subsequent. **1807** ROBINSON *Archæol. Græca* III. xiv. 260 It is uncertain who was the inventor of divination by sacrifices. .. By some it is ascribed to the Hetrurians. **1875** JOWETT *Plato* (ed. 2) IV. 121 The relation [of the Parmenides] to the other writings of Plato is.. uncertain.

b. Without clear signification; ambiguous. Phr. ***in no uncertain terms***, emphatically, very clearly indeed.

1382 WYCLIF *1 Cor.* xiv. 8 If the trumpe ȝyue vncerteyn vois [**1388** soune], who schal make him silf redy to bateil? **1611** BIBLE *1 Cor.* xiv. 8 If the trumpet giue an vncertaine sound. **1663** BP. PATRICK *Parab. Pilgr.* xvi, Metaphorical or borrowed words, which.. make an uncertain sound, and leave the mind in confusion. **1818** CRUISE *Digest* (ed. 2) IV. 298 *marg.*, Where a Deed is uncertain, it is void. **1905** G. THORNE *Lost Cause* x, When the most influential part of the Press began to speak with no uncertain voice. **1958** L. DURRELL *Balthazar* vi. 139 And what's more, I told Abdul so in no uncertain terms. 'Lay a finger on the girl.. and I'll get you run in.' **1976** J. SNOW *Cricket Rebel* 132 Here we were bowling them out so that they could take advantage of it [*sc.* a green wicket]. They did that in no uncertain terms. **1977** *Time Out* 28 Jan.–3 Feb. 7/1 Five months after the programme was axed, Edmonds was told in no uncertain terms why it didn't fit.

c. Not clearly identified, located, or determined. Phr. ***of uncertain age***.

1617 MORYSON *Itin.* I. 192 Which King Phillip Augustus began to build in.. 1257, the foundations being before laid by an uncertaine founder. **1631** WEEVER *Anc. Funeral Mon.* 518 The vncertaine buriall of Vortimer.. was in some part of this Citie. **1638** *Guillim's Heraldry* (ed. 3) I. vi. 41 According to that saying of an uncertaine Author. **1817** BYRON *Beppo* xxii, The years Which certain people call a 'certain age', Which yet the most uncertain age appears. **1821** SCOTT *Kenilw.* xxv, A large and massive Keep, which formed the citadel of the Castle, was of uncertain though great antiquity. **1877** F. H. BURNETT *Theo* v. 137 The blandishments of a single gentleman of uncertain age. **1900** A. S. MURRAY *Catal. Sculpt. Parthen. in Brit. Mus.* 77 No. 30 is a maiden holding an uncertain object, perhaps a footstool, on her left arm. **1930** A. CHRISTIE *Murder at Vicarage* iv. 33 There is no detective in England equal to a spinster lady of uncertain age with plenty of time on her hands. **1952** J. CANNAN *Body in Beck* vii. 152 The fair sex is very credulous, especially in the case of maiden ladies of uncertain age.

d. Not clearly defined or outlined.

1638 JUNIUS *Paint. Ancients* 89 The uncertaine shapes of clouds most commonly are likened unto anything our wandering minde conceiveth. **1833** TENNYSON *Palace of Art* 238 But in dark corners of her palace stood Uncertain shapes. **1853** KANE *Grinnell Exp.* xlvii. (1856) 444 Every thing, in short, grew blurred and uncertain.

5. a. Not certain to remain in one state or condition; unsteady, variable, fitful.

1591 SHAKS. *Two Gent.* I. iii. 85 How this spring of loue resembleth The vncertaine glory of an Aprill day. *c* **1600** —— *Sonn.* cxlvii, My loue is as a feauer,.. Feeding on that which doth preserue the ill, Th' vncertaine sicklie appetite to please. **1694** J. SMITH *Horolog. Disquisit.* 87 To make the more certain Guess at what Weather will after ensue, especially if the Glass be at Changeable and Uncertain. **1738** GRAY *Tasso* 48 As when athwart the dusky woods by night The uncertain crescent gleams a sickly light. **1743** FRANCIS tr. *Hor., Odes* I. xiii. 6 On my cheek th' uncertain color dies. **1753** MISS COLLIER *Art Torment.* I. i, When the weather is quite uncertain. **1794** MRS. RADCLIFFE *Myst. Udolpho* xxix, The moon gave a faint and uncertain light, for heavy vapours surrounded it. **1805** SCOTT *Last Minstrel* Introd. 85 Amid the strings his fingers stray'd, And an uncertain warbling made. **1828** SIR J. E. SMITH *Eng. Flora* II. 109 It may be observed that our uncertain summer is established by the time the Elder is in full flower. **1866** HOWELLS *Venetian Life* ii, I could see by that uncertain glimmer how fair was all, but not how sad and old.

b. Of persons: Variable, fickle, changeable, capricious.

? *a* **1611** BEAUM. & FL. *Four Plays, Tri. Death* ii, Uncertain as the Sea, Sir, Proud and deceitful as his sins Great Master. *a* **1625** FLETCHER *Double Marr.* I. i, Thou art constant; I an uncertain fool, a most blind fool. **1664** J. WILSON *A. Commenius* v. viii, The uncertain people, Constant to nothing but inconstancy. *a* **1721** PRIOR *Ess. Opinion* ¶13 If You trace this Man thro life.. You will find him always uncertain. **1808** SCOTT *Marm.* VI. xxx, O, Woman! in our hours of ease, Uncertain, coy, and hard to please.

6. a. Of persons: Not fully confident or assured *of* something.

c **1400** *Destr. Troy* 2050 Now Priam.. [was] Uncertain of his Sister for seyng hir euer. **1548** UDALL, etc. *Erasm. Par. Mark* xiii. 83 b, These seruauntes, because they be vncertayne of theyr Lordes returnyng home, do styl endeuoyre them selues to do theyr office & duety. **1596** SHAKS. *1 Hen. IV*, I. i. 61 He.. in the very heate And pride of their contention, did take horse, Vncertaine of the issue any way. **1631** WEEVER *Anc. Funeral Mon.* 579 He.. being infected with the plague,.. was landed about Portsmouth, and being vncertaine of any house, died vnder a hedge. **1670** MILTON *Hist. Eng.* III. 110 Thir [*sc.* the Saxons'] multitude wander'd yet uncertain of habitation. **1718** PRIOR *Solomon* III. 290 What is a King?.. To blind Events, and fickle Chance a Slave: Seeking to settle what for ever flies; Sure of the Toil, uncertain of the Prize.

b. Const. *how, what, whether*, etc.: Having no clear knowledge; in a state of doubt.

1526 *Pilgr. Perf.* (W. de W. 1531) 7 Whan he is vncerteyn whether he shall be iudged for euermore to ioye or to payne. **1560** DAUS tr. *Sleidane's Comm.* 444 b, And the people be lefte in this doubtfull state of thinges, to be uncertaine howe pacientlye all menne woulde take it. **1597** HOOKER *Eccl. Pol.* v. lxii. §18 St. Augustine was not himselfe vncertaine what to thinke. **1697** DRYDEN *Æneis* III. 9 Uncertain yet to find What place the gods for our repose assigned. **1794** MRS. RADCLIFFE *Myst. Udolpho* xxxiv, As she advanced, terrified and uncertain what to do. **1796** MME. D'ARBLAY *Camilla* VI. xiii, Camilla was still more agitated; for though uncertain if she were right or wrong in the appeal she meant to make [etc.]. **1851** THACKERAY *Eng. Hum.* vi. 302 He is always looking in my face, watching his effect, uncertain whether I think him an impostor or not. **1865** MRS. CARLYLE *Lett.* (1883) III. 253, I am uncertain how long he will be away.

c. Undecided; not directed to a definite end.

1382 WYCLIF *1 Sam.* xxiii. 13 Dauid.. and his men.. hidir and thider weren vagaunt vncerteyn [L. *incerti*]. **1607** SHAKS. *Cor.* v. vi. 17 The People will remaine vncertaine, whil'st 'Twixt you there's difference. **1697** DRYDEN *Æneis* VII. 692 Ascanius young, and eager of his Game, Soon bent his Bow, uncertain in his Aim. **1808** SCOTT *Marm.* III. xx, The King Lord Gifford's castle sought, Deep labouring with uncertain thought. **1821** —— *Kenilw.* xxv, That anxious and uncertain gaze, which indicated a doubt whether her brain was settled. **1855** *Poultry Chron.* III. 428/1 In their droning flight they move very irregularly, darting hither and thither, with an uncertain aim.

†**7.** ***into uncertain***, at random. *Obs.*

1382 WYCLIF *1 Kings* xxii. 34 A maner man bente a boowe, into vncerteyn [L. *in incertum*]. —— *2 Chron.* xviii. 33 Oon of the puple in to vncerteyn kast an arowe.

8. Quasi-*adv.* In an uncertain manner.

a **1718** PRIOR *Cloe Hunting* 4 She lost her Way, And thro' the Woods uncertain chanc'd to stray. **1784** COWPER *Task* I. 358 The constant flail, That seems to swing uncertain, and yet falls Full on the destin'd ear.

†**un'certain,** *v. Obs. rare.* [f. prec.] *trans.* To render uncertain.

1614 RALEIGH *Hist. World* I. i. §11. 14 It being manifest, that the diuersity of seasons, the Winters, and Sommers, more hot and cold, are not so vncertained by the Sunne and Moone alone. *a* **1619** FOTHERBY *Atheom.* I. xiii. §4 (1622) 145 It might greatly vncertaine the mindes of the people about it.

†**un'certained,** *ppl. a. Obs.*⁻¹ [UN-¹ 8.] = UNCERTAIN *a.* 6 b.

1470 *Reb. Linc.* (Camden) 16 The tewsday, in the mornyng, the King, uncerteined how they wolde demean theym upon the saide summons.., addressed hymself to the felde.

un'certainly, *adv.* [UN-¹ 11.]

1. In an uncertain or variable manner; at random, by chance or accident.

1387 TREVISA *Higden* (Rolls) III. 217 Þese trowed þat al þing was vncertenliche i-made. **1530** PALSGR. 160 They use these sixe.. uncertainly, somtyme of the masculyne gendre and somtyme of the feminyne. **1590** SIR J. SMYTH *Disc. Weapons* 12 With the swelling of the salt water.. they shall shoote verie vncertainlie. **1678** CUDWORTH *Intell. Syst.* Pref., That Motion of Sensless Atoms Declining Uncertainly from the Perpendicular. **1737** WHISTON *Josephus, Antiq.* v. vii. §7 The affairs of the Hebrews were managed uncertainly, and tended to disorder, and to the contempt of God.

b. At an indefinite time. *rare*⁻¹.

1683 E. HOOKER *Pref. Pordage's Mystic Div.* 25 When the inexorabl Messenger, whose Name is the First Death, shal com (as certenly, and yet, as uncertenly hee wil).

2. Without definite result, course, or aim.

1555 EDEN *Decades* (Arb.) 129 Whyle the matter was thus vncerteynly debated. **1567** JEWEL *Def. Apol.* 152 Therefore the Prieste iudginge that, yᵗ he cannot know, muste needes wander vncertainely, and be a very doubteful Iudge. **1603** HOLLAND *Plutarch's Mor.* 484 It were better for them to settle in any one certaine place whatsoever, than still to wander uncertainely upon the seas. **1662** PLAYFORD *Skill Mus.* III. (1674) 38 Doing that safely and resolutely which others attempt timorously and uncertainly. **1696** WHISTON *Th. Earth* III. (1722) 278 [They] floated in the Waters among one another uncertainly. **1883** *Century Mag.* XXVI. 44 The poor beast ran uncertainly in all directions.

3. Without clear or definite knowledge or statement; doubtfully, undecidedly.

1613 *William I* in *Harl. Misc.* (Malh.) III. 144 The slaughter of the English is uncertainly reported. **1664** PEPYS *Diary* 11 Nov., Some in Germany do derive them-selves from the patrician families of Rome, but that uncertainly. **1742** *Jura Ecclesiastica* II. 351 To that two great Objections were made, that this Custom is unreasonable in itself and uncertainly set forth. **1795** *Phil. Trans.* LXXXV. 154, I have perceived this phænomenon only eleven times with perfect certainty, and only a few other times uncertainly. **1860** PUSEY *Min. Proph.* 104 Joel fore-told, not as uncertainly, not as anticipation, or hope, or longing, but absolutely and distinctly, that [etc.]. **1878** LADY BRASSEY *Voy. Sunbeam* xv. 255 A group of low islets whose position is very uncertainly indicated in the charts.

un'certainness. *rare*⁻¹. [f. as prec.] = next.

1601 W. CORNWALLIS *Ess.* II. xxx. R iv b, All which.. carry man from his destinated mediocritie, & so leaues him to the pleasure of irresolution and vncertainenesse. **1677** MIEGE II. s.v., Uncertainness what to do.

un'certainty. [UN-¹ 12 and 5 b.]

1. a. The quality of being uncertain in respect of duration, continuance, occurrence, etc.; liability to chance or accident. Also, the quality of being indeterminate as to magnitude or value; the amount of variation in a numerical result that is consistent with observation.

For the phrase ***the glorious uncertainty of the law*** see GLORIOUS *a.* 5 b.

1382 WYCLIF *1 Tim.* vi. 17 Nethir for to hope in vncerteynte of richessis, but in quyk God. **1495** *Act 11 Hen. VII*, c. 36 *Preamble*, Greate uncertente and troble myght her-after growe bytwyne the seid Duches and the seid nowe Duke. **1526** *Pilgr. Perf.* (W. de W. 1531) 230 Bothe for the vncertaynty of the same [life], and also for the paynfulnes.. therof. *a* **1548** HALL *Chron., Hen. IV*, 20 Whose study was euer to procure malice, and to set al thynges in broile and vncertentie. *a* **1586** SIDNEY *Arcadia* II. xxvi. (1912) 318 The uncertainty of his estate made you take armes. **1617** MORYSON *Itin.* I. 278 By reason of the aforesaid uncertaintie in receiving money by billes of exchange. **1677** YARRANTON *Eng. Improv.* 19 Such hazards at Sea as attend Merchants, with the badness and uncertainty of Personal Security. **1755** EARL OF CORKE in J. Duncombe *Lett.* (1773) III. 29 The uncertainty of the weather was still more surprising than the cold: we have had all kinds of seasons in a day. **1794** R. J. SULIVAN *View Nature* I. 164 There is, besides this, great uncertainty of colour, according as the heat varies. **1810** SCOTT *Lady of L.* III. ii, Neither broken nor at rest; In bright uncertainty they lie. **1853** *Proc. R. Irish Acad.* V. 372 As to the sun and moon, it is more doubtful. In the transit they have larger probable errors than the stars. For the sun I obtained.. the first limb $\pm 0^{s}{\cdot}116$, the second $\pm 0^{s}{\cdot}087$;.. while stars.. had but $\pm 0^{s}{\cdot}097$. This greater uncertainty arises from the strong contrast between the bright and dark surfaces whose boundary we take. **1860** TYNDALL *Glac.* I. xi. 75 The uncertainty of the footing between the blocks of ice. **1861** G. B. AIRY *Theory Errors of Observations* I. 4 Strictly speaking, we ought.. to use the word 'uncertainty' instead of 'error'. For we cannot at any time assert positively that our estimate or measure, though fallible, is not perfectly correct; and therefore it may happen that there is no 'error', in the ordinary sense of the word. **1930** RUARK & UREY *Atoms, Molecules & Quanta* xviii. 619 If a coordinate q is measured with an error of the order Δq, the uncertainty, Δp, of the conjugate momentum introduced by our measurement is such that $\Delta q{\cdot}\Delta p \cong h$. **1943** M. W. WHITE et al. *Practical Physics* i. 12 As applied to the final result of a measurement, the accuracy is expressed by stating the uncertainty of the numerical result, that is, the estimated maximum amount by which the result may differ from the 'true' or accepted value. **1974** G. REECE tr. *Hund's Hist. Quantum Theory* xii. 161 We thus have the relationship $\Delta E\, \Delta t \approx h$ between the uncertainty in the determination of energy and the evaluation of a point in time. **1975** *Physics Bull.* Apr. 165/2 The PTB developed a new measuring apparatus capable of accurate measurements of diameter on pistons of 850 mm and cylinders up to 1200 mm in diameter. The uncertainty in *Q*, d*Q*/*Q*, was estimated to be 3 × 10⁻⁵.

b. With *a* and pl. Something of which the occurrence, result, etc., is uncertain.

1619 in Foster *Eng. Factories India* (1906) I. 174, I send him not uppon uncertayntyes but uppon sure grounds. **1653** J. HALL *Paradoxes* 37 We love to toyl for uncertainties, and in this are worse then children. **1691** *Andros Tracts* II. 251 Most of the Persons in our Government understand little or nothing of Trade, and so they leave it always at uncertainties. **1712** LADY M. W. MONTAGU *Let. to Mr. W. Montagu* 9 Dec., I would not advise you to neglect a certainty for an uncertainty. **1757** PITT in *10th Rep. Hist. MSS. Comm.* App. I. 214 Exposed to the most alarming Uncertainties. **1782** MISS BURNEY *Cecilia* III. ix, Mr. Arnott was wretched from a thousand uncertainties. **1846** MRS. A. MARSH *Father Darcy* II. viii. 141 Every thing seems so certain, so inevitable, a consequence of the enterprise—yet my mind is harassed by uncertainties. **1864** BOWEN *Logic* xiii. 443 The probability..of two independent uncertainties happening conjointly.

c. An uncertain gain or emolument.

1650 GREAVES *Seraglio* 168 He hath then but a thousand aspars a day, as the Cadeeleschers have..; howbeit their uncertainties amount alwayes to a far greater matter.

2. a. The state of not being definitely known or perfectly clear; doubtfulness or vagueness.

c **1380** WYCLIF *Sel. Wks.* II. 133 þat sum men graunten and sum men denyen, for uncerteynte of þe dede. **1395** PURVEY *Remonstr.* (1851) 47 The multitude and vncertaynte of siche lawis. **1565** COOPER *Thesaurus, Incertum*,.. doubtfulnesse: vncertaintie. **1599** HAKLUYT *Voy.* II. Pref. *4b, Besides the foresaid vncertaintie, into what dangers and difficulties they plunged themselues..I tremble to recount. *a* **1633** AUSTIN *Medit.* (1635) 95 This is the briefe of the uncertainty of the History. **1696** WHISTON *The. Earth* III. (1722) 285, I might..leave the following Conjectures to the same State of Uncertainty they have hitherto been in. **1765** *Museum Rust.* IV. 291 The uncertainty in which of the stages the delineation of the plant has been taken. **1802** T. THOMSON *Chem.* II. v. II. 189 He acknowledged..that there were two sources of uncertainty, which rendered his conclusions not altogether to be depended upon. **1869** FROUDE *Short Stud.* Ser. II. *Educ.* (1871) 322 So far as our special occupations go, there is no uncertainty. **1902** J. GAIRDNER *Eng. Ch. 16th Cent.* viii. 141 The name of the celebrant was kept a profound secret, and to this day it is a matter of uncertainty.

b. *Law.* In phr. ***bad,*** or ***void, for uncertainty.***

1818 CRUISE *Digest* (ed. 2) IV. 298 Where the words of a deed are so uncertain that the intention of the parties cannot be discovered, the deed will be void. Thus a gift..to one of the children of J. S., he having four children, is void for uncertainty. **1890** SIR A. CHARLES in *Law Times Rep.* LXIII. 767/1 There is some variation in the mode in which the custom is stated, but not enough to make it bad for uncertainty.

c. Something not definitely known or knowable; a doubtful point.

1387 TREVISA *Higden* (Rolls) II. 377 It is vncerteynte whiche Mercurius þis was. **1577** tr. *Bullinger's Decades* (1592) 24 What..is more euident than that which..no man doeth referre to darkenesse and vncertainties. **1590** SHAKS. *Com. Err.* II. ii. 187 Vntill I know this sure vncertaintie, Ile entertaine the free'd [*sic*] fallacie. **1653** W. RAMESEY *Astrol. Restored* 38 To what end..is it for a man to busie his head about such uncertainties. **1878** STANLEY *Addr. & Serm. U.S.* iii. (1883) 141 Many a one..has been perplexed by the uncertainties and contentions of history. **1889** *Renan's Bk. Job* p. xxxix, There is but one remedy for such uncertainties.

3. a. The state or character of being uncertain in mind; a state of doubt; want of assurance or confidence; hesitation, irresolution.

1548 ELYOT, *Suspensio*, a hangyng vp; also doubte or vncertayntee of the mynde. **1598** R. BERNARD tr. *Terence, Phormio* IV. iii, Let me vnderstande..if they will giue me her, that I may let this alone, least I stay in an vncertaintie. **1607** SHAKS. *Cor.* III. iii. 124, I banish you, And heere remaine with your vncertaintie. Let euery feeble Rumor shake your hearts. **1635** D. DICKSON *Expl. Hebr.* x. 242 Doeth not this Exhortation importe the Elects vnsetlednesse, and vncertayntie of perseverance? **1746** WESLEY *Princ. Methodist* 43 When I have been in great distress of soul, or in utter uncertainty how to act in an important case. **1794** MRS. RADCLIFFE *Myst. Udolpho* i, She was compelled to rest in uncertainty. **1851** HAWTHORNE *Ho. Sev. Gables* ix, Pacing the room..with the uncertainty that characterized all his movements. **1879** LUBBOCK *Addr. Pol. & Educ.* iii. 57 Uncertainty as to the educational value of Science.

pl. **1846** MRS. A. MARSH *Father Darcy* II. viii. 139, I marvel at..these hesitations and uncertainties in a man of your resolution. **1851** CARLYLE *Sterling* II. iii, I suppose, he was full of uncertainties.

†**b.** In phr. ***at uncertainty, upon uncertainties.***

1668 HOWE *Bless. Righteous* (1825) 267 Though he be upon great uncertainties as to his enjoyment of them. **1690** LOCKE *2nd Let. Toleration* Wks. 1714 II. 272 Whereby we are as much still at Uncertainty, as we were before, who those are who..are to be punished.

4. *Econ.* (The quality of) a business risk which cannot be measured and whose outcome cannot be predicted or insured against (see quots. 1921 and 1964). Cf. RISK *sb.* 2a.

1921 F. H. KNIGHT (*title*) Risk, uncertainty and profit. *Ibid.* i. 20 A *measurable* uncertainty, or 'risk' proper, as we shall use the term, is so far different from an *unmeasurable* one that it is not in effect an uncertainty at all. We shall accordingly restrict the term 'uncertainty' to cases of the non-quantitative type. It is this 'true' uncertainty..which forms the basis of a valid theory of profit. **1929** G. O'BRIEN *Notes on Theory of Profit* ii. 17 The assumption of uncertainty is therefore a disutility and must be rewarded. Is uncertainty bearing on this account, entitled to rank as a separate factor of production. **1964** GOULD & KOLB *Dict. Social Sci.* 606/1 In its broadest definition the term uncertainty is used by economists to refer to any situation in which a set of alternative outcomes is not fully predictable. **1969** D. C. HAGUE *Managerial Economics* vii. 137 To conform to established terminology we shall, from now on, use the word uncertainty to mean the same thing as non-insurable risk.

5. ***(Heisenberg's) uncertainty principle*** (Physics), a principle of quantum mechanics implying that certain pairs of observables (e.g. the momentum and position of a particle, the energy and lifetime of a quantum level) cannot both be precisely and simultaneously known, and that as one of any pair is more exactly defined, the other becomes more uncertain. Also *transf.* Cf. HEISENBERG, ***principle of indeterminacy*** s.v. INDETERMINACY b.

The principle is usually stated as an inequality such that the product of the uncertainties of the pair of observables cannot be less than a quantity of the order of Planck's constant.

[**1928** *Physical Rev.* XXXII. 570 The principle of uncertainty is particularly clear in this [*sc.* Weyl's] system.] **1929** CONDON & MORSE *Quantum Mech.* i. 21 (*heading*) The quantum uncertainty principle. **1931** *Times Lit. Suppl.* 5 Nov. 852/4 Perhaps the most remarkable discovery that has been made in connexion with atomic theory is the so-called Uncertainty Principle. **1955** W. HEISENBERG in W. Pauli *Niels Bohr* 15 It was now [*sc.* in 1927] assumed in quantum mechanics that real states can always be represented as vectors in Hilbert space (or as 'mixtures' of such vectors). The uncertainty principle was the simple expression for this assumption. **1977** *Time* 14 Mar. 74/1 Even in the age of the Uncertainty Principle and culture fracture, Warren has not lost his sense of life as a sustained drama. **1982** A. M. LESK *Introd. Physical Chem.* x. 309 What Heisenberg's uncertainty principle asserts is that for *no* state of *any* system can *all* dynamical variables be arbitrarily well-determined.

uncer'tificated, *ppl. a.* (UN-¹ 8.)

Frequent in recent use, esp. of teachers.

1836–7 DICKENS *Sk. Boz, Scenes* xiii, A disappointed eighth-rate actor, a retired smuggler, or an uncertificated bankrupt. **1868** M. PATTISON *Academ. Org.* iv. 88 Study not merely private and uncertificated, but evidenced by a regular appearance in the public schools for disputation.

un'certified, *ppl. a.* [UN-¹ 8.]

1. Not made certain; not assured.

1535 STEWART *Cron. Scot.* (Rolls) II. 170 Vncertifieit tha war into sic thing Into that cace quhome that tha wald mak king. **1801** SOUTHEY *Thalaba* VI. xviii, The astonish'd Thalaba..closed his eyes, And open'd them again; And yet uncertified, He prest them close.

2. Not attested as certain; not guaranteed by certification.

1681 *Calr. Treas. Bks.* 7 That he do not issue out process upon any uncertified bond. **1760–1** SMOLLETT *Launcelot Greaves* xx, The mercy of the legislature in favor of insolvent debtors, is never extended to uncertified bankrupts taken in execution. **1846** GROTE *Greece* I. xix. II. 47 Any chronological system which may be applied to it, must be essentially uncertified and illusory. **1876** MEREDITH *Beauch. Career* xxxiv, She touched the double chords within us which are..a divine discord if an uncertified harmony.

3. Not certified insane.

1889 G. B. SHAW *London Music in 1888–89* (1937) 101 Brinio..is a patriotic Batavian with two sisters, one of whom is mad and the other sane... Ada, the uncertified one, is beloved by Aquilius. **1938** S. BECKETT *Murphy* ix. 161 There were a few such fortunate cases, certified and uncertified, enjoying all the amenities of a mental hospital. **1969** M. PUGH *Last Place Left* xiv. 102 Some uncertified genius had hit upon a new virus mutation method.

un'certitude. [UN-¹ 12.] = INCERTITUDE.

1541 CRANMER in *St. Papers Hen. VIII*, I. 717 Wheropon myght growe most uncertitude of Your Graces succession, with..unquietnes..to this Realme. **1870** J. H. NEWMAN *Gram. Assent* II. vi. 194 That uncertitude on the subject is just the explanation..of the strange violence of language.

†**un'cessable,** *a. Obs.*⁻¹ = INCESSABLE *a.*

1596 Z. J. tr. *Lavardin's Hist. Scanderbeg* 212 Mahomet was noted aboue the rest to vse an vncessable kind of diligence.

†**un'cessant,** *a. Obs.* Also 6 vnceassa(u)nt, -cessaunt. [UN-¹ 7 and 5b.] = INCESSANT *a.* (Very common *c* 1550–1690.)

α. **1548** UDALL *Erasm. Par. Luke* xxiv. 178b, Hauyng within hymself a perpetuall vnceassaunt power to dooe whatsoeuer his wille is. **1592** KYD *Murther I. Brewen* Wks. (1901) 293 Bloud is an vnceassant crier in the eares of the Lord.

β. **1555** EDEN *Decades* (Arb.) 161 The vncessaunt mouynge and impulsion of the heauens. **1583** BABINGTON *Commandm.* (1590) 190 Parents, that take such intollerable and vncessant paines to leaue much vnto their children. *a* **1641** BP. MOUNTAGU *Acts & Mon.* (1642) 429 Wicked mens soules they thrust and imprison in a darksome roome below, where torments uncessant doe attend them. *a* **1661** HOLYDAY *Juvenal* (1673) 263 They..bid their sons with uncessant industry imploy their time. **1692** RAY *Creation* II. 47 The Heart..by its uncessant Motion distributing the Blood.

†**un'cessantly,** *adv. Obs.* Also 5 vncessantle, 6 vncessaunt(e)ly(e, 6–7 uncessantlie; 6 vnceassantly. [Cf. prec.] = INCESSANTLY *adv.* (Very common *c* 1550–1690.)

c **1460** *Towneley Myst.* iii. 147 It shall begyn full sone to rayn vncessantle. **1548** UDALL *Erasm. Par. Luke* xix. 147b, But the Iewes..kepyng sylence of the glorie of Christ.., the stones vnceasauntely crye it out. **1576** FLEMING *Panopl. Epist.* 282 Such a one searcheth the very heart and entrayles of the ground, for gold and siluer, unceassantly. **1600** HOLLAND *Livy* XXXII. xv. 817 The assault and batterie continuing uncessantly both night & day, overcame at length the..valour of the Macedonians. **1651** H. MORE *2nd Lash* in *Enthus. Tri.*, etc. (1656) 213 Putting the body..into a perpetuall motion, so that the parts fridge one against another uncessantly. **1691** NORRIS *Pract. Disc.* 329 They.. must needs..be carried out uncessantly and intirely toward the Supream Good.

†**un'cessantness.** *Obs.* [Cf. prec.] = INCESSANTNESS.

1627 H. SCUDDER *Chr. Daily Walk* xvi. §6 (1637) 639 Those [evil thoughts] which come onely from Satan, may usually bee knowne..by their suddennesse and uncessantnesse. **1677** GILPIN *Demonol.* III. 19 If they urge the uncessantness of the Devil's Attempts, Christ and others have felt the like.

un'cestused, *a.* (UN-² 8.)

a **1843** SOUTHEY *Comm.-Pl. Bk.* (1851) IV. 198 Without his wig he is Jove without his thunder. Venus uncestused, Phœbus unbeamed.

unch, obs. form of INCH *sb.*¹

†**unch,** reduced form of NUNCHEON.

Nunch is common in English dialect use.

1668 R. B. *Adagia Scot.* 7 An unch is a feast (of Bread and Cheese).

un'chafed, *ppl. a.* (UN-¹ 8.)

[**1775** ASH.] **1865** *Pall Mall G.* 19 June 4/2 One is glad.. to be dismissed in peace, unchafed and unwearied.

†**unchaghe.** *Obs.*⁻¹ [a. Ir. *óinseach.*] A foolish or wanton woman.

1534 *St. Papers Hen. VIII*, II. 215 That no Yryshe.. bardes, unchaghes, nor messangers, come to desire any goodes of any man dwellinge within the Inglyshrie.

un'chain, *v.* [UN-² 4b.]

1. *trans.* To set free, release, from a chain or chains; to remove the chain(s) from.

1582 N. LICHEFIELD tr. *Castanheda's Conq. E. Ind.* I. lxxiii. 150 Being in a readinesse to uncheine his Mastes, he was presently informed that the king of Calicut was reforming a new his Castles. **1591** SHAKS. *1 Hen. VI*, V. iii. 31 Vnchaine your spirits now with spelling Charmes, And try if they can gaine your liberty. **1664** DRYDEN & HOWARD *Ind. Queen* III. i, They may By force unchain, and crown him in a day. **1679** ALSOP *Melius Inq.* I. ii. 108 When the Righteous God saw it necessary to unchain the Devil, and let him loose upon the English Protestants. **1704** PRIOR *Prol. Her Majesty's Birth-day* 37 So was his Fame compleat, and Andromede unchain'd. **1831–7** PRAED *Bridal of Belmont* 113 The young Count clambered down the rock, Unfurled the sail, unchained the oar. **1868** DICKENS *Uncomm. Trav.* xxviii, He used his utmost influence to get the man unchained from the bedstead.

absol. **1836** DICKENS *Sk. Boz, Gt. Winglebury Duel*, Up started the ostlers..unstrapping, and unchaining, and unbuckling, and dragging willing horses out.

b. *transf.* and *fig.* To set free; to liberate.

1793 H. WALPOLE in Miss Berry *Jrnls. & Corr.* (1865) I. 425, I unchain my impatience, which has behaved like an angel. **1796** COLERIDGE *Destiny of Nations* 111 Yet the wizard her..Forces to unchain the foodful progeny Of the Ocean stream. **1811** H. G. KNIGHT *Phrosyne* 40 Stern Winter..Unleafs the forest, and unchains the wind. **1855** [J. D. BURN] *Autobiog. Beggar Boy* (1859) 13 You may form some little opinion of my position when my father unchained his lawless desires. **1890** 'R. BOLDREWOOD' *Col. Reformer* (1891) 175 The storm..swept over..as if a fresh blast had been unchained among the far south ice-fields.

2. To free from obstruction by the removal of a chain. Also *fig.*

1613–6 W. BROWNE *Brit. Past.* II. iii, Gaze on mine eyes, whose life-infusing beames Haue powre to melt the Icy Northern streames, And so inflame the Gods of those bound Seas They should vnchaine their virgin passages. **1663** DAVENANT *Siege of Rhodes* I. 31 Away! unchain the Streets, unearth the Ports!.. And bravely sally out from all the Forts!

Hence **un'chaining** *vbl. sb.*

[**1775** ASH.] *a* **1835** MRS. HEMANS *Carolan's Prophecy* 13 Many stood waiting around, in silent earnestness, Th' unchaining of his soul. **1871** W. B. JERROLD *At Home in Paris* II. vii. II. 147 It was a wicked, reckless unchaining of the hates long nursed, of the two foremost military nations of the world.

un'chainable, *a.* (UN-¹ 7b.)

c **1836** MANGAN *Poems* (1903) 9 Though he were even a pleasant salmon in the unchainable sea. **1899** F. T. BULLEN *Way Navy* 12 Like sentient monsters mad with unchainable energy.

un'chained, *ppl. a.* (UN-¹ 8.)

1660 INGELO *Bentiv. & Ur.* II. (1682) 184 The unchain'd Barges separated themselves from one another. **1704** PRIOR *Let. to M. Boileau Despreaux* 174 The Eagle,..Unchain'd and Free, directs her upward Flight. *a* **1721** —— *Female Phaeton* vi, Dearest Mamma, for once let me, Unchain'd, my Fortune try. **1742** YOUNG *Nt. Th.* IX. 614 Come, my Prometheus, from thy pointed rock Of false ambition if unchain'd, we'll mount. **1816** BYRON *Siege Cor.* viii, Given to none, Had young Francesca's hand remain'd Still by the church's bonds unchain'd. **1865** ESQUIROS *Cornwall* 156 One must have lived there to know what is the violence of the unchained winds.

un'chair, *v.* (UN-² 5.)

1645 TOMBES *Anthropol.* 10 What is this lesse then to unchaire Christ?

un'chalked, *ppl. a.*

[**1775** ASH.] **1786** *Phil. Trans.* LXXVII. 30 No other book would do the same, though the sides were scraped unchalked. **1938** J. STEINBECK *Long Valley* 113 The house was unscarred, uncarved, unchalked.

un'challengeable, *a.* (UN-¹ 7 b.)
1611 SPEED *Hist. Gt. Brit.* IX. xx. 731/1 Our vulgar Bookes extant can hardly passe with a Iury of ordinary Criticks and Censors for vnchallengeable euidence. **1824** SCOTT *St. Ronan's* xxxiii, His title and his paternal fortune, which he thought..might be rendered unchallengeable. **1847** LD. LINDSAY *Sk. Hist. Chr. Art* I. 61 The Byzantines.. maintained a pre-eminence, unchallenged and unchallengeable, in the three sister arts. **1880** MUIRHEAD *Gaius* II. §119 *note*, A man, whose position as heir under the civil law was unchallenged and unchallengeable.
Hence **un'challengeably** *adv.*
1827 SCOTT *Napoleon* c. VIII. 330 Annual expositions of national receipt and expenditure..which were, to outward appearance, unchallengeably accurate. **1866** F. G. STEPHENS *Eng. Children* (1867) 32 This is unchallengeably true.

un'challenged, *ppl. a.* (UN-¹ 8.)
a **1639** SPOTTISWOODE *Hist. Ch. Scot.* (1655) II. 97 He was ..much hated by the clergy... Notthelesse he went unchallenged and was not brought in question. **1805** SCOTT *Last Minstr.* v. xii, Unchallenged thus, the warder's post, The court, unchallenged, thus he cross'd. **1847, 1880** [see UNCHALLENGEABLE *a.*]. **1898** 'MERRIMAN' *Roden's Corner* xvii. 176 'Yes,' continued the unchallenged speaker, in..the typical voice of the tavern-talker.

un'chambered, *ppl. a.* (UN-¹ 8.)
1650 FULLER *Pisgah* 373 The east end where the Porch stood, was clear, and unchambered. **1870** E. T. STEVENS *Flint Chips* 392 *note*, Skulls from unchambered long barrows in South Wilts. **1895** *Chambers's Encycl.* VII. 409 This shell [of the nautilus] is unchambered, and peculiar to the females.

un'championed, *ppl. a.* (UN-¹ 8.)
1819 SCOTT *Ivanhoe* xxxix, Championed or unchampioned, thou diest by the stake and faggot. **1872** *Spectator* 5 Oct. 1261 Will he, isolated and unchampioned, have the courage solemnly to bring his matters of complaint before a committee of squires.

un'chance. *north.* and *Sc.* [UN-¹ 12. Cf. WANCHANCE.] Mischance, misfortune.
a **1400–50** *Alexander* 822* (Dublin MS.), [He] Comand kenely hys knyghtez to kepe to hys blonkez, þat no vnchaunce þaim achefe. **1535** STEWART *Cron. Scot.* (Rolls) III. 405 Quhen this wnchance wes to king Richart kend. **1823** GALT *Gilhaize* lxxvi, Those grevious unchances which darkened the latter days of so many of the pious.

un'chancellor, *v.* (UN-² 6 b.)
1676 ROW *Contn. Blair's Autobiog.* xii. (1848) 512 The King took from Hyde the great seals (so he was unchancellered).

un'chancy, *a.* Chiefly *Sc.* [UN-¹ 7. Cf. WANCHANCY *a.*]
1. Ill-omened, ill-fated, unfortunate.
1533 BELLENDEN *Livy* II. iv. (S.T.S.) I. 142 Sen his hous was vnchancy, & his son dede. **1536** —— *Cron. Scot.* (1821) II. 468 The lordis thocht that Johne was ane unchancy name to be ane king. **1589** WARNER *Alb. Eng.* VI. xxxii. 141 Lastly slaine By Edward, whilst he did vphold vnchancie Henries Raigne. **1768** ROSS *Helenore* II. 98, I..monie a weary foot synsyne hae gane, Born i' the yerd wi' that unchancy coat. **1863** *N. & Q.* 3rd Ser. IV. 264 Another of this difficult lady's unchancy wooers was a Scottish laird. **1893** STEVENSON *Catriona* xiii, The devil any other sight or sound in that unchancy place.
b. Inconvenient, ill-timed.
1860 TROLLOPE *Framley P.* xxix, Why had his Grace come at so unchancy a moment?
2. Dangerous; not safe to meddle with.
1786 BURNS *To J. Kennedy* i, Down the gate, in faith, they're worse, And mair unchancy. **1818** SCOTT *Rob Roy* xxiii, We gang-there-out Hieland bodies are an unchancy generation when you speak to us o' bondage. **1833** M. SCOTT *Tom Cringle* xii, A stalwart unchancy customer, who will not be gainsaid or contradicted. **1874** WOOD *Nat. Hist.* 281 The Brown Owl,..when roused to anger or urged by despair, is a remarkably unchancy antagonist.

unchangea'bility. [f. next.]
= UNCHANGEABLENESS.
c **1400** *Pilgr. Sowle* (Caxton, 1483) II. lii. 54 He myght not be refourmyd by cause of his vnchangeabylyte. **1813** T. BUSBY *Lucretius* I. I. Comm. p. xviii, Objections like these only serve to throw difficulties in the way of our faith in the unchangeability of the Divine Being. **1865** LIVINGSTONE *Zambesi* xxiv. 509 The African traditions which seem possessed of the same unchangeability as the arts to which they relate.

un'changeable, *a.* [UN-¹ 7 b and 5 b.] That cannot change or be changed; not liable to change; immutable, invariable.
Also, in recent use, 'not exchangeable'.
a **1340** HAMPOLE *Psalter* iv. 9 It is tendant in til lastandnes and vnchaungeabile ioy. *c* **1340** —— *Pr. Consc.* 8232 How God invysible es, And unchaungeable, and endles. **1382** WYCLIF *Job* xv. 15 Among his seintus noon is vnchaungable. *c* **1430** *Life St. Kath.* xiii. (1884) 28 For god is vnbodyly inuisible and vnchaungeable. **1434** MISYN *Mending Life* 106 Qwhat is turnyng fro god bot turnynge fro guyde vnchawngabyll to guyde chawngabyll. **1526** *Pilgr. Perf.* (W. de W. 1531) 271 b, Seynge in spiryt the immutable or vnchaungeable trewth of god. **1587** GOLDING *De Mornay* iv. (1592) 44 By this terme Vnchangeable we deny him to be lyke the immortall soules, which admit passions. *a* **1610** HEALEY *Cebes* (1636) 152 Shee giueth the true knowledge of profitable things a gift of unchangeable goodnesse and security. **1676** HALE *Contempl.* I. 191 An eternal state of unchangeable and perfect happiness shall succeed. **1732** BERKELEY *Alciphr.* VI. §31 Although the light of truth be unchangeable. **1774** GOLDSM. *Nat. Hist.* I. xx. 341 They.. talk of a friend or a mistress as fixed and unchangeable as the winds. **1817** J. SCOTT *Paris Revisit.* (ed. 4) 71 The latter method will inevitably produce..a more unchangeable fidelity. **1855** MACAULAY *Hist. Eng.* xiv. III. 450 The thousands of clergymen, who had so loudly boasted of the unchangeable loyalty of their order. **1867** H. MACMILLAN *Bible Teach.* xvi. 322 About the average age of forty, when the character becomes unchangeable.
absol. **1875** JOWETT *Plato* (ed. 2) III. 535 For the unchangeable is never older or younger.

un'changeableness. [f. prec. + -NESS.] Immutability.
1548 ELYOT, *Immutabilitas*,..vnchaungeablenesse, constancie. **1587** GOLDING *De Mornay* xvii. (1592) 279 Surely the vnchangeablenes of Spirits was created to depend vppon their linking in with their maker. **1607** HIERON *Wks.* I. 156 The stablenesse and vnchangeablenesse of that worke of saluation which is wrought by Christ Jesus. *a* **1653** GOUGE *Comm. Heb.* xii. (1655) 271 The Apostle giveth us to understand..the unchangeablenesse of the Gospel. **1736** CHANDLER *Hist. Persec.* 51 He expressly asserts the immutability and unchangeableness of the Son. **1777** PRIESTLEY *Matt. & Spir.* (1782) I. xvi. 190 The eternity and unchangeableness of the first cause stands upon the very same grounds. **1827** FARADAY *Chem. Manip.* ii. 28 This is fully compensated by the unchangeableness in weight. **1871** JOWETT *Plato* I. 427 The realm of purity, and eternity, and immortality, and unchangeableness.

un'changeably, *adv.* [f. as prec. + -LY.] Immutably.
a **1340** HAMPOLE *Psalter* lxxxviii. 35 Antyme, þat is, vnchaungabilly i sware in my haligh. **1608** WILLET *Hexapla Exod.* 790 God yet himselfe being vnchangeablie present. **1682** NORRIS *Hierocles* 17 Shining with him in a happy life, but not uniformly and unchangeably. **1743** J. MORRIS *Serm.* ii. 37 Him, who is so perfectly wise, so unchangeably happy. **1781** COWPER *Table-t.* 443 A dire effect, by one of nature's laws Unchangeably connected with its cause. **1829** SOUTHEY *All for Love* I. xxi, Therein to be for life and death Unchangeably array'd. **1875** J. P. HOPPS *Princ. Relig.* viii. 26 There is such a thing as the eternally right and the unchangeably good.

un'changed, *ppl. a.* [UN-¹ 8.] Unaltered.
1387 TREVISA *Higden* (Rolls) II. 431 [To] chaunge þe liknesse wiþ oute and leue þe kynde vnchaunged wiþ ynne. *c* **1420** LYDG. *Ballad Commend. our Lady* 95 Thu louyst hem unchaungid þat serue the. **1532** MORE *Confut. Tindale* 135 He shold rather haue kepte styll the worde *presbyteros* vnchaunged, bycause that worde is yt y^t^ sygnyfyeth authoryte wyth the grekes. *a* **1586** SIDNEY *Arcadia* I. v. (1912) 34 Malice sooner ceased, then her unchanged patience. **1633** P. FLETCHER *Purple Isl.* x. xli, The faces change prov'd th' hearts unchanged grace. **1667** MILTON *P.L.* VII. 24 More safe I Sing with mortal voice, unchang'd To hoarce or mute. **1718** PRIOR *Solomon* I. 64 Whilst the distinguish'd Yew is ever seen, Unchang'd his Branch, and permanent his Green. **1794** MRS. RADCLIFFE *Myst. Udolpho* xxxiv, Tell him my heart is unchanged. **1827** SCOTT *Highl. Widow* v, Noon found him in the same unchanged posture. **1894** SIR E. SULLIVAN *Woman* 23 Throughout Asia and Africa the relative position of women, legal and social, is unchanged.
Hence **un'changedness**.
1880 MRS. CRAIK *Poems, Immutable* 31 Yet still Our change yearns after Thine unchangedness.

un'changing, *ppl. a.* (UN-¹ 10.)
1593 SHAKS. *3 Hen. VI*, I. iv. 116 But that thy Face is Vizard-like, vnchanging,..I would assay..to make thee blush. *a* **1625** FLETCHER *Fair Maid Inn* III. i, The husband Of my remembrance and unchanging vowes. **1709** POPE *Ess. Crit.* 315 But true expression, like th' unchanging Sun, Clears and improves whate'er it shines upon. **1757** W. WILKIE *Epigon.* VII. 198 If fame's unchanging voice to all the earth, With truth, proclaims you author of my birth. **1792** BURNS *The Posie* 11 The hyacinth's for constancy wi' its unchanging blue. **1812** SIR H. DAVY *Chem. Philos.* 91 The summits [of the Andes] are covered with unchanging snows. **1856** KANE *Arct. Expl.* I. xxv. 326 The horizon showed an unchanging circle of ice. **1875** JOWETT *Plato* (ed. 2) I. 456 The soul..being in communion with the unchanging is unchanging.
Hence **un'changingness.**
1878 A. L. WALKER *Lady's Holm* II. viii. 163 No place.. has the same look of unchangingness.

un'changingly, *adv.* (UN-¹ 11.)
1435 MISYN *Fire of Love* 14 So þe generacion of þe sone with þe euerlastynge of þe godhede vnchaungyngly bydis. **1817** MOORE *Lalla Rookh, Nourmahal* 130 There's a beauty, for ever unchangingly bright. **1827** —— *Epicur.* xvii. (ed. 4) 271 God..proceeds..unchangingly to the great, final object of his providence. **1883** WHITELAW *Sophocles, Œd. Col.* 613 And the same spirit never of friend and friend, Or state with state, abides unchangingly.

un'channelled, (*ppl.*) *a.* (UN-¹ 8 and 9.)
1600 S. NICHOLSON *Acolastus* (1876) 65 Then brake th' vnchannel'd issue of mine eyes, My teares gaue vent vnto my tired soule. **1712** BLACKMORE *Creation* VII. 622 She next essay'd the embryo's rise to trace From an unfashion'd, rude, unchannell'd mass. [**1775** ASH.] **1872** *Daily News* 12 Oct., The lanes and byways unchannelled.

un'chanted, *ppl. a.* (UN-¹ 8.)
[**1775** ASH.] **1820** SHELLEY *Prometh. Unb.* I. 513 Leave Hell's secrets half unchanted To the maniac dreamer. **1840** MANGAN *Poems* (1903) 14 The Chief whom nothing daunted ..fell in distant Spain, unchronicled, unchanted!

un'chaperoned, *ppl. a.* (UN-¹ 8.)
1858 MISS MULOCK *Th. ab. Women* 33 Anxious mothers, who would not for worlds be guilty of the indecorum of sending their daughters unchaperoned to the theatre or a ball. **1886** MISS BRADDON *One Thing Needful* vii, She was willing..to allow her daughter to stroll across the fields unchaperoned.

un'chaplain, *v.* (UN-² 6 b.)
a **1661** FULLER *Worthies, Dorset* I. (1662) 280 Dr. Hackwel, for opposing the Spanish Match, was un-Chaplain'd and banished the Court.

un'chapleted, *ppl. a.* (UN-¹ 8.)
1864 SWINBURNE *Atalanta* (1865) 114 With unchapleted hair, With unfilleted cheek. **1870** MORRIS *Earthly Par.* III. IV. 51 Her golden head,..uncoifed, unchapleted.

un'character, *v.* (UN-² 6 b.)
1570 FOXE *A. & M.* (ed. 2) 193/1 Making of a priest a non priest, or a layman: vncharacteryng his owne order.

un'charactered, *ppl. a.* [UN-¹ 8.]
1. Having no distinctive sign.
1633 C. BUTLER *Eng. Gram.* To Rdr., If first wee reforme our Alphabet, by adding those uncharactered letters which are wanting, and giving fit names to those that want them.
2. Of persons: Destitute of moral character.
1841 GEN. P. THOMPSON *Exerc.* (1842) VI. 37 The profligate and the uncharactered of both sexes.

uncharacte'ristic, *a.* (UN-¹ 7.)
1753 RICHARDSON *Grandison* (1781) IV. xviii. 141 Wisdom itself..is sometimes thought to sit ungracefully, when it is uncharacteristick, not to the man, but to the times. **1807** OPIE in *Lect. Paint.* iv. (1848) 329 Important events disgraced by mean and uncharacteristic agents. **1853** RUSKIN *Stones Ven.* II. v. §26. 139 This cross, though graceful and rich,..is uncharacteristic in one respect. **1893** F. ADAMS *New Egypt* 41 Everything that is characteristic of the Egyptian is uncharacteristic of the Arabian.

uncharacte'ristically, *adv.* (UN-¹ 11.)
1753 RICHARDSON *Grandison* (1781) V. xxxi. 208 They won't let me write on,..or I should not have concluded so uncharacteristically. **1804** *Something Odd* II. 76 A quantity of fair hair floated gracefully (uncharacteristically I might also add) upon the shoulders. **1856** RUSKIN *Mod. Paint.* III. IV. xiii. §26 His ideas respecting all landscape being not uncharacteristically summed, finally, by Pallas herself. **1898** *Century Mag.* LV. 772 It ends, uncharacteristically enough, in rich simplicity.

un'characterized, *ppl. a.* (UN-¹ 8.)
1701 BEVERLEY *Apoc. Quest.* 13 Seeing the Time between the Weeks and the 1260 Days, would be otherways uncharacteriz'd, and the Space unknown. **1862** E. FALKENER *Ephesus*, etc. II. iv. 268 Vitruvius's definition of *hypæthros* is said to be uncharacterized by his usual precision.

un'charge, *v.* Now *rare.* [UN-² 3.]
1. a. *trans.* To free from a charge or burden.
1303 R. BRUNNE *Handl. Synne* 11942 But yn euery tyme þat þou shryuest þe, Of pyne shalt þou vncharged be. **1377** LANGL. *P. Pl.* B. xv. 338 For charite with-oute chalengynge vnchargeth þe soule. *c* **1430** *Pilgr. Lyf Manhode* II. xlvii. (1869) 94 So miche we dide, she and j, þat þe contracte was ouerthrowe from me, and j vncharged.
absol. **1340** *Ayenb.* 97 Þe oþere [law] chargeþ: and þis onchargeþ.
b. To acquit of guilt.
1602 SHAKS. *Ham.* IV. vii. 68 Euen his Mother shall vncharge the practice, And call it accident.
2. To unload; to discharge (a vessel).
13.. *Coer de L.* 2584 The drowmound..was drownyd in the flood, Ar halff unchargyd wer that good. **13..** *Propr. Sanct.* (Vernon MS.) in Herrig's *Archiv* LXXXI. 312/171 A beest þat charged is In plaas Mai not passe þorwh narwh paas Til he vncharged be þat tide. **1388** WYCLIF *Acts* xxi. 3 We..seiliden in to Sirie, and camen to Tire. For there the schip schulde be vnchargid. *c* **1425** *Eng. Conq. Ireland* 10 Thay vncharged hare shippes, & made ham loges on lond. *c* **1475** *Cath. Angl.* 59/1 To vn-charge: *vbi* to discharge.
transf. **1387** TREVISA *Higden* (Rolls) VII. 201 After mete þey wente into þe feeld by cause for to uncharge þaire stomakes.
3. To remove the charge from (a gun).
1687 MIÈGE *Gt. Fr. Dict.* I, *Decharger un Canon, en ôter la charge*, to uncharge a Gun. **1902** *Infantry Training* (War Office) I. 119 Charging and Uncharging Magazines in two ranks.

un'chargeable, *a.* (UN-¹ 7 b.)
1649 JER. TAYLOR *Gt. Exemp.* II. x. 136 Offer was made of private and unchargeable arbitrators. **1659** *Gentl. Calling* ix. §8 Will any man renounce a rich unchargeable reversion, when he is not only wooed, but bribed..not to disclaim it?

† un'chargeant, *a. Obs.*⁻¹ (UN-¹ 7.)
c **1380** WYCLIF *Sel. Wks.* III. 412 Siþ Crist ches to be unchargeaunte to þo puple, ne gif non occasioun of avarise to oþer, þei shulden fle þis doynge.

un'charged, *ppl. a.* [UN-¹ 8.]
1. †**a.** Not called upon; unsummoned. *Obs.*
1456 SIR G. HAYE *Law Arms* (S.T.S.) 91 Gyf a man gais to the weris unchargit, sall he tak wagis? **1539** *Reg. Privy Seal Scot.* II. 472/2 The said Johnne to be..unchargit to find souerte to the law.
b. Not burdened (*with* something).
c **1475** *Golagros & Gaw.* 435 Sen hail our doughty elderis has bene endurand, Thriuandly in this thede, vnchargit as thril. **1746** ELIZA HEYWOOD *Female Spect.* No. 24 (1748) IV. 317 When the Almighty, offended with our presumption, gives his fiat to our wishes, they seldom come uncharged with ills. **1896** *Westm. Gaz.* 23 Sept. 5/1 The national desire to be at any rate uncharged with responsibility.
c. Not formally accused.
1900 *Westm. Gaz.* 3 Apr. 3/2 His two native evangelists, who were arrested with him, are reported to be still in prison, untried and uncharged.
2. Unassailed, unattacked.
1607 SHAKS. *Timon* v. iv. 56 Then there's my Gloue Desend and open your vncharged Ports.
3. *Her.* Not furnished with a charge.

1610 GUILLIM *Heraldry* II. v. 49 The Bend containeth in breadth the fifth part of the Field, as it is vncharged. **1845** *Antiq. & Archit. Year Bk.* 312 Beneath each figure appears a shield, but uncharged.

4. a. Not loaded with powder and shot.

1719 DE FOE *Crusoe* I. (Globe) 307 Snapping an uncharg'd Pistol, close to the Powder, [I] set it on fire. **1745** MRS. ELIZ. MONTAGU *Corr.* (1906) I. 203 The first was my servant, valiantly armed with two uncharged pistols. *a* **1829** *Parcy Reed* xv. in Child *Ball.* III. 26/2 You have left me in a fair field standin, And in my hand an uncharged gun.

b. Not charged with electricity.

1815 J. SMITH *Panorama Sci. & Art* II. 263 A coating was then put on the uncharged glass. **1873** MAXWELL *Electr. & Magn.* I. 53 When they are gone, other uncharged particles [of air] take their place.

c. Not furnished with a load.

1796 T. TWINING *Trav. India*, etc. (1893) 157 The jolting of the uncharged machine became almost insupportable.

5. Not subjected to a financial charge.

1894 *Daily Tel.* 5 Dec. 5/7 A Four and a Half per Cent. Gold Loan, secured on the uncharged revenues of the Treaty ports.

un'chariot, *v.* (UN-[2] 5.)

c **1715** POPE *Lett.* (1735) I. 140 The poor distressed Roman Catholics, now unhors'd and uncharioted. **1877** TALMAGE *Serm.* 9, The Lord has unhorsed us, uncharioted us.

un'charitable, *a.* Also *Sc.* 5 **uncheritable.** [UN-[1] 7 b and 5 b.] Not charitable; lacking in charity: **a.** Of persons, etc.

1456 SIR G. HAYE *Law of Armes* (S.T.S.) 237 And rycht sa..gif thare war ane uncheritable prelate, quhilk war..a counsailour to mak were. **1548** UDALL, etc. *Erasm. Par. Mark* xi. 71 b, With his frownyng browes, with his stately loke, with his contencious or vncharitable mouthe. **1592** G. HARVEY *Four Lett.* iii. Wks. (Grosart) I. 195 His conclusion, That the worlde was vncharitable, and he ordained to be miserable. **1646** CRASHAW *Steps to Temple, Charity* 58 What can the poore hope from us, when we bee Uncharitable ev'n to Charitie? **1673** *Lady's Call.* I. i. §29 In this uncharitable age, things are apt to be denominated not from the greater but worser part. **1743** J. MORRIS *Serm.* ii. 49 If he remains uncharitable he is utterly unfit for heaven. **1828** LYTTON *Pelham* III. iv, Why be so uncharitable to this poor and persecuted principle? **1880** 'OUIDA' *Moths* III. 82 People are so horridly uncharitable.

absol. **1837** W. IRVING *Adv. Capt. Bonneville* II. 191 The uncharitable were apt to surmise that he had, in the interim, been well used up in a buffalo hunt.

b. Of actions, feelings, etc.

a **1631** DONNE *Serm., Ps. li.* 7 (1640) 640 An uncharitable condemning of other men. **1683** D. A. *Art Converse* 22 With most uncharitable exaggerations of their least, or fancied misdemeanours. **1764** BURN *Poor Laws* 137 It were an uncharitable action to relieve them in a course of idleness. **1814** WORDSW. *Excurs.* VII. 775 Her uncharitable acts, I trust, And harsh unkindnesses are all forgiven. **1833** H. COLERIDGE *Lives Northerns* 11 Marvell..never again uttered so uncharitable a surmise as that with regard to Morus.

un'charitableness. [f. prec. + -NESS.] The quality or character of being uncharitable.

1548–9 (Mar.) *Bk. Com. Prayer, Litany*, From enuy, hatred, and malice, and all uncharitablenes, Good lorde, deliuer us. **1581** SIDNEY *Apol. Poetrie* (Arb.) 35 The morrall common places of vncharitablenes, and humblenes. **1641** SMECTYMNUUS *Answ.* §18 (1653) 74 It is no unusuall thing with the Prelats..to charge such as protest..with uncharitablenes and Schisme. **1653** JER. TAYLOR *Serm. for Year, Winter* ii. 17 The uncharitablenesse of men towards his poor. **1719** WATERLAND *Christ's Div. Vind.* 418 There's no uncharitableness in believing, that He gives us at least his own true meaning. **1836** HOR. SMITH *Tin Trump.* (1876) 193 Those outpourings of envy or uncharitableness which inevitably harden the heart. **1867** AUGUSTA WILSON *Vashti* xxi, I never before heard you utter sentiments that trenched so closely upon harsh uncharitableness.

un'charitably, *adv.* [UN-[1] 11 b.] In an uncharitable manner; without charity.

c **1386** CHAUCER *Pars. T.* ⁋626 If he repreue hym vncharitably of synne..thanne apperteneth that to the reioysynge of the deuel. **1529** *Act 21 Hen. VIII*, c. 4 §1 The resydue of the same Executours uncharytably..have refused to intermedle..with the execucion of the said wyll. *a* **1548** HALL *Chron., Hen. IV*, 7 He uncharitably commaunded that no man..should once entreate him for the retourne of Henry nowe duke of Lancastre. **1624** GATAKER *Transubst.* 147 He very uncharitably passeth them by. **1656** COWLEY *Pindar. Odes, Life* iii, We..wish uncharitably for them, To be as long a Dying as Methusalem. **1728** ELIZA HEYWOOD tr. *Mme. de Gomez's Belle A.* (1732) II. 288, I know not..which of my Actions should make you judge so uncharitably of me. **1831** JAMES *Phil. Augustus* II. iv, You speak but uncharitably of the reverend canon of St. Berthe's. **1860** TRENCH *Serm. in Westm. Abb.* xi. 122 We pray that we may not speak uncharitably; but oh! let us pray that we may not think uncharitably.

un'charity. (UN-[1] 12 and 5 b.)

a **1548** HALL *Chron., Edw. IV*, 200 The mother of this pernicious commocion was uncharitie, or very impietie. **1598** E. GUILPIN *Skial.* A v, It is a strange seeld seene vncharitie, To make fooles of themselues to hinder thee. **1643** SIR T. BROWNE *Relig. Med.* I. §56 Thus we,..with as much uncharity as ignorance, doe erre..in points, not onely of our own, but on[e] anothers salvation. **1691** NORRIS *Pract. Disc.* 53, I might without any danger of Censoriousness or Uncharity, write Mystery upon the Triple crown. **1722** WODROW *Corr.* (1843) II. 655 Forgive the seeming uncharity in the supposition; I shall be glad it be groundless. **1837** JEFFREY in Ld. Cockburn *Life* (1852) II. 293 But I will have no uncharity. They too should have been richer. **1874** FARRAR *Christ* (ed. 2) II. xliv. 118 The frenzy which filled them when He set at naught their Sabbatarian uncharities.

un'charm, *v.* [UN-[2] 3.]

1. *trans.* To deprive of magical powers; to nullify the efficacy or virtue of (a charm).

1575 VAUTROLLIER *Luther on Ep. Gal.* (1577) 95 We labour both by preaching and wryting vnto you, to vncharme that sorcerie wherewith the false apostles haue bewitched you. **1612** J. DAVIES (Heref.) *Muse's Sacr.* Wks. (Grosart) II. 53/1 Vncharme the Charmes then, of these grieuous ioyes, that still allure my sense of them to taste. **1624** HEYWOOD *Gunaik.* VIII. 402 Amasis King of Egypt was by the like exorcisme bound..till those ligatorie spells were after uncharmed. **1860** J. WOLFF *Trav. & Adv.* I. 362 The Russians convinced them that they could uncharm a talisman.

2. To free from a spell or from enchantment; to deliver from the influence of a charm. Also *absol.*

1621 LADY M. WROTH *Urania* 554 He ran to take her vp, and try how to vncharme her, but he was instantly throwne out of the Caue in a trance. **1638** GODOLPHIN in G. Sandys *Paraphr. Divine Poems* Pref. Verses **j b, That Harp, whose Charms uncharm'd the brest Of troubled Saul. **1688** E. RAVENSCROFT *London Cuckolds* 71, I will go home to my Wife, and uncharm her Mouth, and set her Tongue at Liberty. **1779** MME. D'ARBLAY *Diary* 16 June, She charms and uncharms in a moment; she is a bane and an antidote at the same time. **1883** MEREDITH *Lett.* (1912) II. 341 Where to go this year I do not know; perhaps nowhere. My last year's experience uncharmed me.

b. To deprive or rob of charm or fascination.

1835 WILLIS *Pencillings* II. xli. 28 But one look at the terms that might describe it, written on paper, uncharms even the remembrance.

un'charmed, *ppl. a.* [UN-[2] 8.]

1. Not subject to a spell or charm; not invested with charm; not delighted or pleased.

1592 SHAKS. *Rom. & Jul.* I. i. 217 From loues weake childish Bow, she liues vncharm'd. **1757** H. WALPOLE *Let. to Mann* 20 Nov., Still uncharmed, he said it was too little! **1818** COLERIDGE *Let. to Mrs. Gillman* (1895) 691 We come to a wood, full of birds and not uncharmed by nightingales. **1857** TENNYSON *Merlin & Vivien* 549 That full heart of yours..may now assure you mine; So live uncharm'd.

2. *Particle Physics.* Not possessing the property known as charm.

1972 *Physics Lett.* XXXIX. B. 349 Hadrons containing the fourth type of quark may be as low as 700 MeV above their uncharmed counterparts. **1975** *Physics Bull.* Apr. 181/1 If SU(3) symmetry were perfect, one should clearly distinguish a neutral octet member..from a singlet.., even though they are both neutral, non-strange and of course uncharmed. **1977** *Sci. Amer.* Oct. 68 Charm..becomes manifest only in hadrons that include a charmed quark or antiquark in combination with uncharmed quarks. **1983** *Canad. Jrnl. Physics* LXI. 124/1 Uncharmed baryons.

un'charming, *ppl. a.* (UN-[1] 10.)

1687 DRYDEN *Hind & P.* III. 209 Conscience would not let him rest: I mean, not till..old, uncharming Catherine was remov'd. **1892** *Pall Mall G.* 15 Nov. 3/1 He earned no little distinction by keeping outside that uncharming circle.

un'charnel, *v.* [UN-[2] 5.] *trans.* To take out of a charnel. Hence **uncharnelled** *ppl. a.*

c **1805** H. K. WHITE *Poems* (1825) 366 They tell..of uncharnell'd spectres, seen to glide Along the lone wood's unfrequented path. **1817** BYRON *Manfred* II. iv. 82 *Nemesis.* Whom wouldst thou Uncharnel? *Man.* One without a tomb—call up Astarte. **1831** TRELAWNY *Adv. Younger Son* III. 232 More like corpses uncharnelled, than living men.

un'charred, *ppl. a.* Also 8 **-chared.** (UN-[1] 8.)

[**1775** ASH, *Uncharred.*] **1799** J. ROBERTSON *Agric. Perth* 30 It is also calculated for drying malt, to which the acid, the oily particles and phlegm of unchared coals would be detrimental. **1898** *Daily News* 23 Nov. 6/6 Charred wood was more active than uncharred.

un'charted, *ppl. a.* [UN-[1] 8.] Of which there is not a map or chart. (Common in recent use.)

[**1847** WEBSTER.] **1895** *Pop. Sci. Monthly* July 404 To establish the latitude and longitude of uncharted places. **1897** *Edin. Rev.* Oct. 322 In tracking the Siberian coast through the month of August, many uncharted islands were discovered.

†**un'charteral,** *a. Obs.*[−1] [UN-[1] 7.] Not in accordance with a charter.

a **1718** PENN *Tracts* Wks. 1726 I. 687 The most ignominious Death of our Country..was hardly satisfaction enough to the Kingdom, for their Uncharterall Proceeding.

un'chartered, *ppl. a.* [UN-[1] 8.]

1. *fig.* Not authorized as by the terms of a charter; irregular, lawless.

1805 WORDSW. *Ode to Duty* 37 Me this unchartered freedom tires. **1863** COWDEN CLARKE *Shaks. Char.* ix. 215 The unchartered wind that 'bloweth where it listeth'. **1885** *Athenæum* 25 July 105/1 Faust..has mistaken unchartered freedom and limitless desires for the true human ideal.

2. Not furnished with a charter; not formally privileged or constituted.

1812 *Weekly Reg.* II. 19/2 Those planters..who should place confidence in the paper of unchartered banks. **1818** HALLAM *Mid. Ages* (1872) III. 112 The representation of unchartered, or at least unincorporated boroughs. **1822** J. FLINT *Lett. Amer.* 283 At the time when this happened, the people had just become jealous of unchartered banks. **1901** *Harper's Mag.* CII. 700/1 The Squatters—or unchartered settlers—roamed, at first, rent free.

un'chary, *a.* (UN-[1] 7.)

1601 SHAKS. *Twel. N.* III. iv. 222, I haue said too much vnto a hart of stone, And laid mine honour too vnchary on't. **1818** KEATS *Endym.* II. 532 The unchariest muse To embracements warm as theirs makes coy excuse. **1856** MRS. BROWNING *Aur. Leigh* II. 622 To make a good man, which my brother was, Unchary of the duties of his house.

un'chased, *ppl. a.* (UN-[1] 8.)

a **1533** LD. BERNERS *Gold. Bk. M. Aurel.* (1535) 101 b, They leaue no cattayle vnslayne, no gardeyne vnrobbed, no wyld beest vnchased. **1533** BELLENDEN *Livy* I. xxi. (S.T.S.) I. 118 The vnchangeabil seit of god terminus (quhilk alanerlie..sal abide vnchasit away fra his mansioun). **1648** HEXHAM II, *Ongejaeght*, Vnhunted, or Vnchased.

un'chaste, *a.* [UN-[1] 7.] Not chaste; lacking chastity; impure, lascivious: **a.** Of persons, etc.

1382 WYCLIF *Rev.* xxii. 15 Forsothe with oute forth, houndes, and venym doers,..and vnchaast men, and manquellers. **1387** TREVISA *Higden* (Rolls) II. 173 Sardanapallus..was ful vnchast, and..þey þat beeþ swiþe vnchast beeþ i-cleped Sardanapally. *c* **1422** HOCCLEVE *Min. Poems* 216 This tale..is of a womman þat was vnchaast. **1526** *Pilgr. Perf.* (W. de W. 1531) 95 He is so incontynent & vnchaste y[t] his mynde is blynde. **1564** tr. *Martyr's Comm. Judges* xxi. 287 b, Sempronia a certayne lasciuious & vnchast woman. **1626** BACON *New Atl.* (1650) 23 Their usuall saying is, That whosoever is unchaste cannot reverence himselfe. **1671** MILTON *Samson* 321 To seek in marriage that fallacious Bride, Unclean, unchaste. **1780** COWPER *The Doves* 29 If, fickle and unchaste,..Thou couldst become unkind at last, And scorn thy present lot. **1856** MRS. BROWNING *Aur. Leigh* VII. 71 These unchaste girls are always impudent.

absol. **1390** GOWER *Conf.* III. 269 And thus thunchaste was chastised. **1712** STEELE *Spect.* No. 286 ⁋ 1 The Unchaste are provoked to see their Vice exposed. **1888** *Hooker's Wks.* III. 789/2 The unchaste, excluded from absolution by Tertullian.

b. Of life, habits, etc.

1541 *Act 33 Hen. VIII*, c. 21 §8 Withoute plaine declaracion before of her unchaste lief. **1546** BALE (*title*), The Actes of Englysh votaryes, comprehendynge their vnchast practyses and examples by all ages. **1605** SHAKS. *Lear* I. i. 231 It is..No vnchaste action or dishonoured step That hath depriu'd me of your Grace and fauour. **1663** BP. PATRICK *Parab. Pilgr.* xxiii. (1687) 237 What a loss they are at sometimes..to satisfie an unchaste desire? **1711** SHAFTESB. *Charac.* II. 109 Even the unchastest Love borrows largely from this Source. **1849** ROBERTSON *Serm.* Ser. I. ix. (1855) 145 You read of the victims of unchaste life hurried on the dark whirlwind for ever.

un'chastely, *adv.* [f. prec. + -LY[2].] In an unchaste manner; impurely.

c **1340** HAMPOLE *Prose Tr.* 6 A 3onge mane,..vn-chastely and delycyousely lyfande and full of many synnys. **1340–70** *Alisaunder* 36 Hue loued so lecherie & lustes of synne, þat her chylder hue chase unchastly to haue. **1548** UDALL, etc. *Erasm. Par. John* iv. 23 One that had naughtely & vnchastely misused her body with diuerse. *a* **1586** SIDNEY *Arcadia* II. xv. (1912) 245 She (unchastly attempting his wonted fancies) found..a bitter refusall. **1634** HABINGTON *Castara* I. (Arb.) 36 Who while he ey'd, Vnchastely, such a beauty, ..Turn'd marble. **1690** C. NESSE *O. & N. Test.* I. 316 Dinah,..whom..he had unjustly as well as unchastly possessed.

un'chastened, *ppl. a.* (UN-[1] 8.)

1641 MILTON *Ch. Govt.* II. Concl. 62 A sort of formal outside men..whose unchast'nd and unwrought minds [were] never yet..subdu'd under the true lore of religion. **1760–72** H. BROOKE *Fool of Qual.* (1809) III. 136 He..has left his own household unchastened and unguided. **1819** KEATS *Otho* I. ii, I blush to think of my unchasten'd tongue. **1846** RUSKIN *Mod. Paint.* II. III. x. §6 In language coarse, in thought undisciplined, in all unchastened. **1875** MAINE *Hist. Inst.* i. 6 A school [of thought] almost infamous for the unchastened license of its speculations on history and philology.

un'chasteness. [f. UNCHASTE *a.* + -NESS.] The quality or state of being unchaste; impurity.

1530 PALSGR. 285/1 Unchastnesse, *impudicité.* **1548** CRANMER *Catech.* 66 Wher yought doth both heare and see vnchastnes, there the infection of vncleannes spreadeth abrode. **1610** HEALEY *St. Aug. Citie of God* I. xviii. (1620) 27 It were no vnchastenesse in her to suffer the rape vnwillingly. **1653** BAXTER *Worcester Petit. Def.* 38 Would you permit any rogues that will, to have access to your wives, and solicit them to Unchasteness? **1828** E. IRVING *Last Days* 239 If I were to come to speak of unchasteness.

†**un'chastied,** *ppl. a. Obs.*[−1] [UN-[1] 8 + CHASTY *v.*] Unchastised.

c **1340** HAMPOLE *Pr. Consc.* 5544 Yhit sons and doghters þat unchastyd war Sal accuse þair fadirs and modirs þar.

uncha'stisable, *a.* Also 6 *Sc.* **vnchestiable.** (UN-[1] 7 b.)

1382 WYCLIF *Ezek.* ii. 4 The sones ben of hard face, and of herte vnchaastisable,..to whom I sende thee. *c* **1430** LYDG. *Min. Poems* (Percy Soc.) 57 A chield to thryve that is unchastisable,..It may wele ryme, but it accordith nought. [*c* **1580** *Maitland Folio MS.* (S.T.S.) lv. 36 A chyld to thryff quhilk is vnchestiable.] **1645** MILTON *Tetrach.* Wks. 1851 IV. 194 The hard hearts of others unchastisable in those judicial Courts, were so remitted there, as bound over to the higher Session of Conscience.

uncha'stised, *ppl. a.* (UN-[1] 8.)

c **1380** WYCLIF *Wks.* (1880) 272 A bischop þat consentiþ to oþer mennus synnes schulde raþere be clepid an vnchastised hound þan a bischop. **1388** —— *Ecclus.* xxx. 8 An hors vntemyd, ether vnchastisid, schal ascape hard, and a sone vnchastisid schal ascape heedi. *a* **1533** LD. BERNERS *Gold Bk. M. Aurel.* xlviii. (1535) 94, I neuer lefte ylnesse vnchastysed, nor goodnesse without rewarde. *a* **1547** SURREY *Paraphr. Eccles.* iv. 2 Wks. (1815) 73 When I bethought me well, under the restless Sun By folk of power what cruel works unchastised were done. **1688** SHADWELL *Sqr. Alsatia* III, Do you think you shall dishonour this family and debauch my sister, unchastiz'd? **1711** in *10th Rep. Hist. MSS. Comm.* App. V. 123 The rebells..must not goe unchastized. **1779** COWPER *Olney Hymns* xxxvii, Oh! hadst thou left me unchastiz'd, Thy precept I had still despis'd. *a* **1814** *Intrigues of a Day* III. i, in *New Brit. Theatre* I. 116, I think it my duty, as a member of society, not to let it pass unchastised.

un'chastity. [UN-^{1} 12 and 5 b.] Lack of chastity; sexual impurity; lasciviousness.

1382 WYCLIF *Rom.* xiii. 13 Not in couchis and vnchastitees, not in stryf and in enuye. *a* **1400** *Pauline Ep.* (Powell) 2 Cor. xii. 21 Penaunce of þeyre vnclennesse..and vnchastite þat þey han done. **1483** *Cath. Angl.* 60/1 Vn Chastite, *incontinencia*. **1550** BALE *Apol.* 141 b, They haue in confessions, made kinges wiues and daughters to make vowes of vnchastyte vnto them. **1599** NASHE *Lenten Stuffe* 42 That she might liue chaste vestall Priest to Venus the queene of vnchastitie. **1639** HABINGTON *Castara* II. (Arb.) 80 Against them who lay unchastity to the sex of Women. **1685** BAXTER *Paraphr. N.T.* 1 Tim. v. 1–2 Carefully shunning all that savoureth of Immodesty or Unchastity. *a* **1763** W. KING *Polit. & Lit. Anecd.* (1819) 49 It might perhaps be too severe a censure to charge a woman with unchastity, who had only transgressed with one man. **1846** WRIGHT *Ess. Mid. Ages* I. ii. 56 [In] the thirteenth century ..unchastity was certainly not regarded as one of the greatest of sins. **1871** B. TAYLOR *Faust* (1875) I. 297 Church-penance for unchastity was formerly common in England.

un'chaw, *v.* (UN-^{2} 3.)

1611 COTGR., *Desmacher*, to vnchaw. **1616** J. LANE *Contn. Sqr.'s T.* 95 *note*, Th' intestine motive wheareof tind his blood, and soone causd to vnchawe his late chawd cud.

un'chawed, *ppl. a.* [UN-^{1} 8.] = UNCHEWED.

1566 BLUNDEVIL *Horsemanship* IV. xl. (1580) 18 b, To let his meate fall out of his mouth, or at the least to keepe it in his mouth vnchawed. **1600** J. LANE *Tom Tel-troth* 609 Bits vnchaw'de in her bulke, as in a forge, Kindle the coales whereof foule lust is bred. **1693** DRYDEN *Persius* v. 8 Why wou'dst thou these mighty Morsels chuse, Of Words unchaw'd, and fit to choak the Muse?

So **un'chawn** *ppl. a.* (UN-^{1} 8 b.)

1648 HEXHAM II, *Ongeknauwt*, vnchawne.

un'cheat, *v.* (UN-^{2} 3.)

1650 H. MORE *Observ.* in *Enthus. Tri.*, etc. (1656) L 2 b, Nor could his lofty soul so low descend But to uncheat the World; a noble end. **1681** CROWNE *Hen. VI*, I, They are fools, and know not men, nor what they love; Uncheat 'em; but however save the King.

un'cheated, *ppl. a.* (UN-^{1} 8.)

1746–7 W. COLLINS *The Manners* 19 Youth of the quick uncheated sight, Thy walks, Observance, more invite! **1820** T. MITCHELL *Com. Aristoph.* I. 101 Uncheated he his stalls may spread, nor lose his time and labour.

†**un'check,** *v. Obs.*$^{-1}$ [UN-^{1} 14.] *trans.* To fail to check.

1607 SHAKS. *Timon* IV. iii. 447 The Lawes, your curbe and whip, in their rough power Ha's vncheck'd Theft.

un'checkable, *a.* (UN-^{1} 7 b.)

a **1734** NORTH *Lives* (1826) II. 217 His lordship used him in his most private and uncheckable trusts. **1836** T. HOOK *G. Gurney* (1850) III. 389 Wells,..whose volubility when once 'off' was uncheckable,..would not let me pause here. **1881** *Echo* 11 Apr. 3/6 Flying before the uncheckable onslaughts of the interviewers.

un'checked, *ppl. a.* [UN-^{1} 8.] Not checked or repressed; unrestrained. Also const. *by*.

1469 in *Househ. Ord.* (1790) 92 Clerkes at wages certein, unchekked, to have a yeoman and groome's parte. **1533** MORE *Apol.* xlvii. Wks. 921/1 Yet he they suffred boldely to talke vnchecked. **1577** G. WHETSTONE in Gascoigne *Steele Gl.*, etc. (Arb.) 18 Trueth is the garde, that keepeth men vnchect. **1667** MILTON *P.L.* VIII. 189 Apte the Mind or Fancie is to roave Uncheckt. **1683** BURNET tr. *More's Utopia* (1753) 114 If they were not strictly restrained from all unchecked Appetites. **1732** POPE *Ess. Man* II. 40 Man's superior part Uncheck'd may rise, and climb from art to art. **1783** BURKE *Rep. Aff. India* Wks. XI. 100 The effects of commercial servitude during its unchecked existence. **1813** SHELLEY *Q. Mab* IX. 84 The growing longings of its dawning love, Unchecked by dull and selfish chastity. **1844** H. H. WILSON *Brit. India* II. 170 The mountaineers..were committing unchecked ravages in retaliation for invaded rights. **1891** FARRAR *Darkn. & Dawn* lvi, Mankind was to see..unchecked power smitten with fatal impotence.

†**b.** Of a report: Uncontradicted. *Obs.*

1596 SHAKS. *Merch. V.* III. i. 2 It liues there vncheckt, that Anthonio hath a ship..wrackt on the narrow Seas. **1619** VISCT. DONCASTER *Let.* in *Eng. & Germ.* (Camden) 208 There is there an unchecqued report these three or foure dayes that the Count of Mansfelt [etc.].

un'cheered, *ppl. a.* (UN-^{1} 8.)

[**1775** ASH.] **1817** WORDSW. *Ode to Lycoris* 24 Yet cool the space within, and not uncheered..By stealthy influx of the timid day. **1849** M. ARNOLD *Resignation* 235 Who treads at ease life's uncheer'd ways. **1864** TREVELYAN *Compet. Wallah* (1866) 301 He must go through the dreary remainder of life uncheered by friendship.

un'cheerful, *a.* [UN-^{1} 7.]

1. Not enlivening or gladdening; cheerless.

c **1449** PECOCK *Repr.* II. xvi. 244 Forto cleue to a thing as to his Souereyn Lord..and ȝit for to haue noon homelynes with the same thing were an vncherful thing. **1586** BRIGHT *Melanch.* xvii. 103 The body thus possessed with the vnchearefull darknes of melancholie. **1593** SHAKS. *Lucr.* 1024 In vaine I raile at oportunitie, At time, at Tarqvin, and vncheareful night. **1648** MILTON *Ps.* lxxxviii. 11 My life at death's uncherful dore Unto the grave draws nigh. **1656** COWLEY *Davideis* IV. 536 'Twas the last Morning whose uncheerful Rise, Sad Jabes was to view with both their Eyes. **1798** JANE AUSTEN *Northang. Abb.* xxi, The furniture..was handsome and comfortable, and the air of the room altogether far from uncheerful. **1853** RUSKIN *Stones Ven.* II. iv. § 10. 63 The Cathedral square..laid out in rigid divisions of smooth grass and gravel walk, yet not uncheerful. **1856** HAWTHORNE *Eng. Note-bks.* (1879) I. 256 It is an uncheerful old hotel.

2. Not exhibiting, or partaking of, cheerfulness.

c **1550** *Dice Play* (Percy Soc.) 6 Stalking up and down.. with such heavy and uncheerful countenance, as if he had some hammers working in his head. **1596** SPENSER *F.Q.* V. vii. 18 But by the change of her vnchearefull looke, They might perceiue she was not well in plight. **1712** ADDISON *Spect.* No. 483 ¶1 People of gloomy uncheareful Imaginations. **1753** RICHARDSON *Grandison* (1781) I. v. 24, I cannot bear an uncheareful brow in a servant. **1882** C. E. NORTON *Lett.* (1913) II. x. 131 'Ah, Charles,' he answered, with a not uncheerful smile, 'there are no good days now'. **1892** G. HAKE *Mem. 80 Yrs.* lxviii. 293 A quiet, not uncheerful, but almost complaining way.

b. Not cheerfully performed.

a **1684** LEIGHTON *Comm. 1 Pet.* iii. 1 (1849) II. 4 Now, if it be such obedience as ought to arise from a special kind of love, then the wife would remember this, that it must not be constrained, uncheerful obedience. **1858** FABER *Spir. Confer.* 115 There is no vigour in uncheerful penance.

3. Of persons: Lacking in cheerfulness; melancholy, gloomy. Also *transf.*

1612 BP. HALL *Contempl., O.T.* IV. iv, Wheresoeuer meere Nature is, she is..niggardly in her grants, and vncheerfull. **1621** BURTON *Anat. Mel.* I. iii. I. i. 231 They be commonly leane, hirsute, vnchearefull in countenance. **1680–1** PENN in *Wks. I. Pennington* I. p. viii, When he did Speak, he was Serious, yet sweet and not uncheerful. **1740** CIBBER *Apol.* (1756) I. 17 Let them call me any fool but an uncheerful one. **1860** BUSHNELL *New Life* i. 7 There ought never to be a discouraged or uncheerful being in the world. **1862** LYTTON *Str. Story* xlviii, She said that Lilian was quiet, not uncheerful.

Hence **un'cheerfully** *adv.*

a **1628** PRESTON *New Covt.* (1634) 104 Who comes not more uncheerfully before God, because of it? **1753** RICHARDSON *Grandison* (1781) VII. xvii. 98 We had hopes.. she would be brought to give her hand, not uncheerfully, to the Count of Belvedere. **1890** 'R. BOLDREWOOD' *Col. Reformer* (1891) 299 Save for the inevitable death-scene of the morrow, the evening would have passed not uncheerfully.

un'cheerfulness. [f. prec. + -NESS.] The quality or state of being uncheerful.

1617 HIERON *Wks.* II. 342 It is a checke to our common lumpishnesse and vncheerefulnesse. **1647** CLARENDON *Hist. Reb.* VII. § 231 Those indispositions..grew into a perfect habit of uncheerfulness. **1712** ADDISON *Spect.* No. 494 ¶2 There are many Persons, who, by a natural Uncheerfulness of Heart,..love to indulge this uncomfortable way of Life. **1733** W. CRAWFORD *Infidelity* (1836) 211 Lumpish uncheerfulness may not be taken for gospel sorrow.

un'cheering, *ppl. a.* (UN-^{1} 10.)

1796 *Monthly Mag.* II. 451 The kiss of thy mistress shall be cold and uncheering. **1856** FROUDE *Hist. Eng.* I. 79 It is not uncheering to look back upon a time when the nation was in a normal condition of militancy against social injustice. **1871** B. TAYLOR *Faust* (1875) II. II. i. 87 The incomprehensible disappearing Of that great man to him is most uncheering.

†**un'cheerly,** *a. Obs.*$^{-1}$ (UN-^{1} 7.)

1627 J. CARTER *Plain Expos.* 109 A very narrow way or lane (which we know is often mirie, and many wayes vncheerly to travellers.)

un'cheery, *a.* (UN-^{1} 7.)

1760 STERNE *Serm.* (1760) I. ii. 31 The sad accidents of life, and the uncheary hours which perpetually overtake us. *Ibid.* IV. vii. 16 In some uncheary corner it nourishes its discontent. **1847** MARY HOWITT *Ballads* 58 The chill light from the window fades; The fire it burneth all uncheery. **1871** B. TAYLOR *Faust* (1875) II. III. 224 Bat-like to squeak and twitter In whispers uncheery and ghostly.

†**un'cheque,** *a. Obs.*$^{-1}$ [UN-^{1} 7: see CHECK *v.* 9.] Without check or stoppage.

1671 F. PHILIPPS *Reg. Necess.* 367 That such of them as have none Offices..to the value of two pence by the day, shall have the wages of six pence by the day uncheque.

un'chequered, *ppl. a.* (UN-^{1} 8.)

1796 MME. D'ARBLAY *Camilla* VII. ii, Ah! what in this lower sphere can be unchequered? **1825** JEFFERSON *Autobiog.* Wks. 1859 I. 51, I had lived the last ten years in unchequered happiness. **1840** ARNOLD *Hist. Rome* II. 243 Nor was even this latter period of the contest unchequered by some changes of fortune. **1877** R. H. HORNE in F. Collins *M. Collins' Lett. & Friendships* I. 37 My pleasant and unchequered memory of Mortimer Collins.

un'cherished, *ppl. a.* (UN-^{1} 8.)

13.. *E.E. Allit. P.* B. 1125 And if hit cheue þe chaunce vncheryst ho worþe. [**1775** ASH.] **1817** KIRBY & SP. *Entomol.* xix. II. 136 An infant..fed with unwholesome food, or uncherished by genial warmth. **1859** CORNWALLIS *Panorama New World* I. 186 The obscure light shed by the yet uncherished fires.

un'cherishing, *ppl. a.* (UN-^{1} 10.)

1876 GEO. ELIOT *Dan Der.* xxxiii, When the uncherishing years have thrust it far onward in the ever-new procession of youth and age.

unchestiable: see UNCHASTISABLE *a.*

un'chewed, *ppl. a.* [UN-^{1} 8. Cf. UNCHAWED *ppl. a.*, and MDu. *ongecouwet*, *-kauwet*, Du. *ongekaauwd*, G. *ungekaut*.] Not chewed.

1646 QUARLES *Sheph. Orac.* ix, Say, do you eat and grind it,..Or like an unchew'd Pill, but swallow't down? **1697** DRYDEN *Æneis* v. 1025 His mouth runs o're With unchew'd morsels. **1742** YOUNG *Nt. Th.* v. 973 All,..wide-expanding their voracious jaws, Morsel on morsel swallow down unchew'd. **1766** *Compl. Farmer* s.v. *Cubbitting* O 2/2, Horses addicted to this vice are but of small value; they drop a great part of their food unchewed. **1884** BROWNING *Ferishtah, Two Camels*, No sprig Of toothsome chervil must I leave unchewed!

fig. **1643–5** MILTON *Divorce* Introd., If she presume to bring forth ought, that sorts not with their unchew'd notions and suppositions. **1681** DRYDEN *Abs. & Achit.* I. 113 Not weigh'd or winnow'd by the Multitude, But swallow'd in the Mass, unchewed and crude.

un'chid, *ppl. a.* [UN-^{1} 8 b.] = next.

[**1846** WORCESTER.] **1860** *Macm. Mag.* Aug. 292 There, unchid, her tears may flow. **1893** *Westm. Gaz.* 22 Sept. 3/2 Meditating..on his own sins, and leaving the world to sin unchid.

un'chidden, *ppl. a.* (UN-^{1} 8 b.)

1472 *Paston Lett.* III. 50 We go not to bed unchedyn lyghtly, all that we do is ille doon. **1614** T. A. in Latham *Falconry* A iv, Pleasure it selfe hath still vnchidden stood. **1753** GLOVER *Boadicea* III. i, While massacre, unchidden, cloys his famine, And quaffs the blood of nations. **1826** MISS MITFORD *Village* Ser. II. (1863) 295 It was no time for scolding; so the whole chain of delinquents..escaped unchidden. **1870** MORRIS *Earthly Par.* II. III. 366 Still stronger grew that thought, Unheeded, and unchidden.

un'child, *v.* [UN-^{2} 4 and 6 b.]

1. To deprive of children; to make childless.

1605 EARL STIRLING *Alexandr. Trag.* IV. ii, First orphan'd, widow'd, and vnchilded last, A daughter, wife, and mother all accurst. **1607** SHAKS. *Cor.* v. vi. 153 Though in this City hee Hath widdowed and vnchilded many a one. **1791** COWPER *Iliad* XXII. 48 He hath unchilded me of many a son.

2. To deprive of the status of a child or of the qualities peculiar to childhood.

1615 BP. HALL *Contempl., O.T.* x. iii, Whosoever now dispose of themselves without their parents, they do wilfully unchild themselves. **1864** BROWNING *Mr. Sludge* Wks. 1888 VII. 230 In brief, she may unchild the child I am.

Hence **un'childing** *ppl. a.*

1876 G. M. HOPKINS *Wreck of Deutschland* xiii, in *Poems* (1967) 55 Wiry and white-fiery and whirlwind-swivelled snow Spins to the widow-making unchilding unfathering deeps.

un'childed, *ppl. a.* [f. prec. or UN-^{1} 8.] Destitute or deprived of children; childless.

1610 HEALEY *St. Aug. Citie of God* XV. xv. (1620) 521 Nor is it credible that their fathers liued all this while either immature or vnmarried or vnchilded. **1866** J. CONINGTON *Æneid* 58 With death in view, the unchilded sire Checked not the utterance of his ire. **1882** SWINBURNE *Tristr. of Lyonesse*, etc. 155 So bitter burned within the unchilded wife A virgin lust for vengeance.

un'childish, *a.* (UN-^{1} 7.)

1586 W. WEBBE *Eng. Poetrie* (Arb.) 45 Some..haue especially made choyse of such vnchildish stuffe, to reade vnto young Schollers. **1888** F. H. BURNETT *Sara Crewe* I. 22 She spoke in a strange, unchildish voice. **1925** V. WOOLF *Common Reader* 169 An astonishing and unchildish story, *Love and Friendship*.

un'childlike, *a.* (UN-^{1} 7 c.)

[**1775** ASH, *Unchildlike*.., unlike a child, unbecoming a child.] **1833** J. S. MILL in *Monthly Repos.* VII. 62 This most grown-up and unchildlike age. **1840** DICKENS *Barn. Rudge* xxv, Something infinitely worse, so ghastly and unchild-like in its cunning. **1879** MISS BIRD *Rocky Mts.* 53 The family consists of a grown-up son..and three hard, unchildlike younger children.

†**un'childly,** *a. Obs.*$^{-1}$ [UN-^{1} 7.] Unfilial, undutiful.

1597 BEARD *Theatre God's Judgem.* (1612) 222 He first remoued his lodging..to a base vnder roome, and after shewed him many other vnkind and vnchildlie parts.

un'chilled, *ppl. a.* (UN-^{1} 8.)

1794 MRS. RADCLIFFE *Myst. Udolpho* i, Yet, amidst the changing visions of life, his principles remained unshaken, his benevolence unchilled. **1813** BYRON *Giaour* 27 His Queen, the garden queen, his Rose, Unbent by winds, unchill'd by snows. **1856** KANE *Arct. Expl.* I. xxxi. 434 Even an Arctic temperature leaves the mind unchilled. **1890** 'R. BOLDREWOOD' *Col. Reformer* (1891) 130 The prompt and unchilled service atones fully for want of artistic merit.

un'chinked, *ppl. a.* (UN-^{1} 8.)

1819 *Niles' Reg.* XVII. 30/2 A year ago there were only 'five or six unchinked cabins' on the town plot. **1879** MISS BIRD *Rocky Mts.* 45 The roof was in holes, the logs were unchinked. **1883** *Harper's Mag.* Sept. 625 Her eyes wandered over..the unchinked, dirty cabin.

un'chipped, *ppl. a.* (UN-^{1} 8.)

1647 HERRICK *Noble Numb., Thanksgiving to God* 22 A little Byn, Which keeps my little loafe of Bread Unchipt, unflead. **1854** *Poultry Chron.* I. 296/2 Nine healthy living chicks and five unchipped eggs. **1865** LUBBOCK *Preh. Times* 251 One of these peculiar forms has one side left unchipped.

unchi'rotonize: see CHIROTONIZE *v.*

un'chiselled, *ppl. a.* (UN-^{1} 8.)

1772 J. IVES *H. Swinden's Gt. Yarmouth* Pref. 1 The unchizelled stone, or rudest hieroglyphic, accompanied the songs of the Bards, to perpetuate a whole nation. **1830** *Westm. Rev.* Jan. 46 Unchiselled stones, according to Pausanias, were the first images of the gods of the Greeks. **1854** GRACE GREENWOOD *Haps & Mishaps* 3 The pure and graceful Greek column makes no solid or defiant show of strength, like the unchiselled stone or the jagged rock.

un'chivalric, *a.* [UN-^{1} 7.] = next.

1851 *Westm. Rev.* April 12 With much self-gratulation on our own unchivalric aspect. **1868** W. R. GREG *Lit. & Soc. Judgm.* 217 A coarseness and a cruelty, as well as an unchivalric and ungenerous roughness.

un'chivalrous, *a.* (UN-[1] 7.)
1846 WORCESTER (citing Scott). **1853** C. BRONTE *Villette* xxxvii, Such a bad pupil, monsieur! so thankless, cold-hearted, unchivalrous, unforgiving. **1880** SWINBURNE *Stud. Shaks.* 274 A garb of transforming verse under a guise at once weak and wordy, coarse and unchivalrous.

Hence **un'chivalrously** *adv.*
[**1847** WEBSTER.] **1889** *Sat. Rev.* 26 Jan. 103 He somewhat unchivalrously refused her request..for a safe-conduct.

un'chivalry. (UN-[1] 12.)
1858 KINGSLEY *Misc., Winter-Gard.* I. 148 That world-famous ancestor of his, whose deeds of unchivalry were the delight..of knight and kaiser..in the Middle Age. **1865** —— *Herew.* xxvi, All the chivalry, and the unchivalry, of the Baltic shores.

un'choke, *v.* (UN-[2] 3.)
1588 LUCAR tr. *Tartaglia's Colloq. Shooting* 36 If the Artillery should be choked with nayles or otherwise, whether it be possible to devise a waie to unchoke quickly the same Artillery. **1888** *Times* (weekly ed.) 3 Feb. 3/3 She tried to unchoke it and took three parts of a pailful out.

un'choked, *ppl. a.* (UN-[1] 8.)
1833 POE *Tales, MS. in Bottle* (1902) 54 We found the pumps unchoked. **1860** H. GOUGER *Two Yrs. Imprisonment* xxiii. 255, I..again luxuriated in a well-cleansed exterior, and pores unchoked with grime.

un'choleric, *a.* (UN-[1] 7.)
1831 CARLYLE *Sart. Res.* II. iv, On some points, as his *Excellenz* was not uncholeric, I found it more pleasant to keep silence.

un'choosable, *a.* (UN-[1] 7 b.)
1858 CARLYLE *Fredk. Gt.* IV. iii. I. 407 A man.. unchoosable at hustings or in caucus.

un'choosing, *ppl. a.* (UN-[1] 10.)
a **1586** SIDNEY *Arcadia* I. (1598) 94 Like a Lambe, whose damme away is fet, (Stolne from her young by theeues vnchoosing-haste). **1660** JER. TAYLOR *Ductor* IV. i. rule i. §17 They are natural, or unavoidable, or the productions of fancy, or some other unchusing faculty.

un'chopped, *ppl. a.* (UN-[1] 8.)
1648 HEXHAM II, *Ongehackelt*, Vnhackt, or Vnchopt. **1891** C. ROBERTS *Adrift Amer.* 101 A large stack of unchopped firewood.

un'choral, *a.* (UN-[1] 7.)
1865 MISS YONGE *Clever Woman of Fam.* iii, Cathedral music had been too natural to him for the endurance of an unchoral service.

un'chorded, *ppl. a.* (UN-[1] 8.)
1859 LD. LYTTON *Wanderer* (ed. 2) 189 From the unchorded harp and vacant shell New notes reveal.

un'chosen, *ppl. a.* (UN-[1] 8 b.)
1529 MORE *Dyaloge* IV. Wks. 273/2 And that euery man is either chosen or vnchosen... And yf we bee of the vnchosen sorte, no good dede can auail vs. *c* **1592** MARLOWE *Jew of Malta* II, In spite of these swine-eating Christians, (Vnchosen Nation, neuer circumciz'd). **1644** MILTON *Areop.* (Arb.) 54 To be made the perpetuall reader of unchosen books and pamphlets. **1655** JER. TAYLOR *Unum Necess.* VI. i. §29 To be born, was a thing wholly involuntary and unchosen. **1712** BLACKMORE *Creation* V. 397 Can actions be denominated wise,..The means unchosen, and unknown the end? **1814** WORDSW. *Excurs.* VII. 309 [To] Beguile A solitude, unchosen, unprofessed. **1871** CARLYLE in *Mrs. Carlyle's Lett.* (1883) II. 249 [She] never did complain once of her unchosen sufferings..under the writing of that sad book.
absol. **1849** FROUDE *Nemesis of Faith* 127 The sucking children of the unchosen were not saved in Noah's flood.

un'chrisom, *a. rare*[-1]. [UN-[1] 7.] Unchristened.
1831 LAMB *Elia* II. *Shade of Elliston*, The schoolmen admitted a receptacle apart for Patriarchs and un-chrisom Babes.

†**un'christed,** *ppl. a. Obs.* [UN-[2] 6 b.] Deprived of the attributes or nature of Christ.
1646 EVANCE *Noble Ord.* 42 God blasphemed, Christ unchristed. **1654** T. WARREN *Unbeleevers* 145 Let some frenzy take them and bereave them of their reason..and they are un-Christed again. **1677** W. HUGHES *Man of Sin* II. iii. 45 Is She not..God Un godded, and Christ Unchristed; in saying, That at death there is none other Hope but She?

†**un'christen,** *a. Obs.* [OE. *uncristen* (see UN-[1] 7 and CHRISTEN *a.*), = ON. *úkristinn* (Da. *ukristen*, Sw. *okristen*), OHG. *unchristâni* (MHG. *unkristen*).] = UNCHRISTIAN *a.* Also *absol.*
c **1000** tr. *Baeda's Eccl. Hist.* IV. xvi. (MSS. O and Ca.) Ðeah ðe hi þa ʒyta uncristene wæron. **1362** LANGL. *P. Pl.* A. I. 91 Clerkes þat knowen hit scholde techen hit aboute, For Cristene and vn-cristene him cleymeþ vchone. *c* **1400** *Rowland & Otuel* 218 For-thi hathe he sent the worde by mee, þat þou schall vn-cristen bee. **1456** SIR G. HAYE *Law Arms* (S.T.S.) 86 And a cristyn man war in a bataill..agayn the uncristyn. *Ibid.* 298 Paganis that we call unCristyn men. **1509** BARCLAY *Shyp of Folys* (1570) 201 All the land about, Trembling for feare of the unchristen route, Of cursed Turkes and other infidels. **1553** *Respublica* I. i. 71 My veray trewe vnchristen Name ys Avarice.

Hence †**un'christenness.** *Obs.*[-1]
c **1548** in Strype *Cranmer* II. viii. (1694) 176 Making the same..a Den or Sink of all Unchristiness.

un'christen, *v.* [UN-[2] 3.]
1. *trans.* To reverse the christening of; to deprive of the name given at christening.
1598 FLORIO, *Sbattezzare*, to vnchristen, to forget ones proper name. **1831** *Q. Rev.* XLV. 416 The church of St. Geneviève was once more unchristened, and ana-paganized by its absurd name of the Pantheon. **1868** H. BUSHNELL *Serm. Living Subj.* 167 These desolating doubts..are present as powers of the air to unchristen the new born thoughts of religion as fast as they arrive. **1893** in J. H. Barrows *World's Parlt. Relig.* II. 1152 Before you can strip the discovery [of America] of its religious character, you must unchristen the admiral's flagship.

†**2.** = UNCHRISTIANIZE *v. Obs.*
1643–5 MILTON *Divorce* II. xxii, To constrain him furder were to unchristen him, to unman him. **1653** BAXTER *Chr. Concord* 50 They would unchristen all the Reformed Christians in all these Nations. **1670** —— *Cure Ch. Div.* 296 Therefore on one side let us take heed how we unchurch and unchristen any with whom we do not corporally join. **1718** CIBBER *Non-juror* Prol., There safe, he lets his thundring Censures fly, Unchristens, damns us, gives our Laws the Lie.

Hence **un'christening** *ppl. a.*
1659 BAXTER *Key Cath.* II. iii. 429 It would be a damning unchristening sin to deny the Headship of the Pope or General Council, if they were indeed the Head of the Church.

un'christened, *ppl. a.* [UN-[1] 8. Cf. MSw. *okristnadher*, and UNKIRSENED *ppl. a.*]
1. Not made Christian; not converted to Christianity, unbaptized.
c **1330** R. BRUNNE *Chron. Wace* (Rolls) 11974 Me þynkeþ hit were but tynt, þe stounde, To write þe names of so fele hounde þat were vncristned in þys mounde. *c* **1350** *Lybeaus Disc.* 1358 What wendest thou, fendes fere? Uncrystenede that were Tyll y saw the wyth syght. *c* **1400** *Apol. Loll.* 2 Corneli centurio, ʒet vncristund, is clensid wiþ þe Hooli Goost. *c* **1440** *Alph. Tales* 219 þai & all þer howsold become crestend, þat war haythen befor and vncristend. **1470–85** MALORY *Arthur* IX. xxvii. 381 Nay said syre Persydes, hit is syr Palomydes, that is yet vncrystened. *a* **1548** HALL *Chron., Hen. VII*, 23 b, The Moores or Mawritane nacion, beyng infideles and vnchristened people. **1570–6** LAMBARDE *Peramb. Kent* (1826) 211 A Pagan (or unchristened) King of Northumberland, had married a Christian woman. **1649** JER. TAYLOR *Gt. Exemp.* III. xvii. 74 The Holy-land is now in the dominion of unchristened Saracens. **1659** BAXTER *Key Cath.* II. iii. 429 Else most of the Christians of the world at this day are Apostates and unchristened. **1825** SCOTT *Talism.* xxv, Edith Plantagenet scorns the homage of an unchristened Pagan. **1868** J. H. NEWMAN *Verses Var. Occas.* 114 Why should we fear, the Son now lacks His place Where roams unchristened man? **1881** *Athenæum* 24 Sept. 393/2 A survival of the feasts of our unchristened forefathers.
transf. **1805** SCOTT *Last Minstrel* III. ix, Those iron clasps ..Would not yield to unchristen'd hand. **1899** R. BRIDGES *Poet. Wks.* (1912) 348 Thy soft unchristen'd smile, That shadows neither love nor guile.
b. *spec.* Of children. Also *transf.*
1725 RAMSAY *Gentle Sheph.* II. ii, At midnight hours o'er the kirkyard she raves, And howks unchristen'd weans out of their graves. **1777** BRAND *Pop. Antiq.* 74 *note*, Children dying unbaptized;..It is thought here very unlucky to go over their Graves. It is vulgarly called going over 'unchristened Ground'. **1791** BURNS *Tam o' Shanter* 132 Twa span-lang, wee, unchristen'd bairns. **1855** MACAULAY *Hist. Eng.* xiv. III. 462 Annihilation is the fate of the greater part of mankind, of heathens, of Mahometans, of unchristened babes.
2. Unnamed.
1832 MISS MITFORD *Village* Ser. v. (1863) 456, I do not mean, in this catalogue, to include the large proportion of bright, shallow trouting-streams, for the most part unchristened and unregistered. **1853** E. K. KANE *Grinnell Exp.* xxiv. (1856) 194 A large cape and several smaller headlands were seen,..all on the western side. They remain unchristened.

†**un'christenlike,** *a. Obs.*[-1] [UN-[1] 7 c.] = UNCHRISTIANLIKE *a.*
1570 DEE *Math. Pref.* A ij, Their particular deuises, fables,..and vnchristenlike slaunders.

†**un'christenly,** *adv. Obs.* [UN-[1] 11.] = UNCHRISTIANLY *adv.*
1535 SHAXTON in Strype *Eccl. Mem.* (1721) I. App. lxi. 152 Take al in good part... Construe nothing unchristenly: & become again my good Lord. *a* **1568** COVERDALE *Bk. Death* (1579) vii. 28 It is better to liue ill, then to dye well. Whiche wordes are very vnchristenly spoken.

un'christian, *a.* and *sb.* [UN-[1] 7 and 12. Cf. UNCHRISTEN *a.*]
1. Of persons: Not Christian; not professing, or converted to, Christianity; devoid of Christian principles or feeling.
1555 LATIMER in Foxe *A. & M.* (1563) 1373/1 That iurisdiction whiche the vnchristian Princes before by tyranny did resiste. **1594** HOOKER *Eccl. Pol.* II. v. §7 Whereupon grew a question, whether a Christian Souldier might herein doe as the vnchristian did. **1606** *Arraignem. & Execution Late Traitors* (1872) 5 They wanted nothing, that ..was thought fit, and, indeed, too good for so unchristian offenders. **1755** MAGENS *Insurances* II. 250 Any Turkish, Moorish, Barbarian or other unchristian Pirates. **1852** MRS. STOWE *Uncle Tom's C.* xiv, 'Well, I hate those old slaveholders!' said the boy, who felt as unchristian as became any modern reformer. **1864** MISS YONGE in *Mag. for Young* May 152 The allowing an untaught un-Christian population to grow up among them.
b. Imposed by non-Christians.
1816 BYRON *Siege Corinth* ix, Ere that faithless truce was broke Which freed her from the unchristian yoke.
c. *sb.* One who is not a Christian.
1827 CARLYLE *Germ. Rom.* III. 285 This morning the little Unchristian, my godson, was precisely the person least attended to.
2. Of actions, etc.: At variance with Christian principles; devoid of Christian spirit; unbefitting or unbecoming a Christian.
1581 ALDERSEY in Hakluyt *Voy.* (1599) II. 152 We are not indeede all good Christians, for there are in the ship some that hold very vnchristian opinions. **1585–7** T. ROGERS *39 Art.* iv. (1633) 18 Vtterly false then, and vnchristian is the opinion of those men. **1605** *London Prodigal* III. ii. 185 That were vnchristian, and an vnhumane part. **1651** HOBBES *Leviath.* III. xlii. 279 Disciples that obstinately continue in an unchristian life. **1679** SHARP *Serm. St. Margaret's 11 Apr.* 18, I mean the Unnatural, Un-Christian Feuds and Divisions that are amongst us. **1729** BERKELEY *Skel. Serm.* Wks. 1871 IV. 639 Their own unchristian life and neglect of instruction. **1755** YOUNG *Centaur* i. Wks. 1757 IV. 115 He was for making religion familiar and inoffensive. And so he did; and unchristian too. **1812** HENRY *Camp. agst. Quebec* 131 The unchristian wish, that he might be hanged. **1849** MACAULAY *Hist. Eng.* viii. II. 389 He..had repeatedly assailed them with unjust and unchristian asperity. **1876** BANCROFT *Hist. U.S.* I. v. 131 Some years later, John de Wycliffe asserted strongly the unchristian character of slavery.
b. Improper; unnatural; objectionable.
1630 *R. Johnson's Kingd. & Commw.* 475 The most Unchristian abuse is, that in every great towne he hath a Caback (or Tap-house) to sell Aqua-vite. **1633** FLETCHER & SHIRLEY *Night Walker* III, My Aunt has turn'd me out a doors, she has, At this unchristian hour. **1831** TRELAWNY *Adv. Younger Son* III. 89 This was the unchristianest, beastliest liquor I ever tasted.

†**un'christian,** *v. Obs.* [UN-[2] 6 a. Cf. Du. *ontchristenen* (Sewel).] = UNCHRISTIANIZE *v.*
1633 PRYNNE *Histrio-m.* 172 Is this a light..effeminacie, for men..thus..to vnman, vnchristian, vncreate themselues? **1658** BAXTER *Saving Faith* §8. 60 If I deny this, I must unchurch and unchristian almost all..of the Churches and Christians in the world. **1661** BEVERIDGE *Priv. Th.* II. (1730) 46 By this means, he renouncing his Baptism, blasphemes Christ, unchristians himself. **1712** BP. TALBOT *Charge* 16 How many Thousands does this Doctrine unchristian of those that were born..from..1648, to..1660?

un'christianed, *ppl. a.* (UN-[1] 8.)
1579 W. WILKINSON *Confut. Fam. Love* 53 b, Hee trembled and was affrayde..which was an vnchristianed Heathen man.

unchristi'anity. [UN-[1] 12.] Lack of Christianity.
1652 HEYLYN *Cosmogr.* 297 The customs have not more unchristianity in them, than this of those Scottish Christians. **1859** *Habits of Gd. Society* 46 It is not mere vulgarity, it is positive unchristianity, hopeless injustice. **1885** ABP. BENSON in A. C. Benson *Life* (1899) II. i. 60 Is Unchristianity and Antichristianity to invade us yet more?

un'christianize, *v.* [UN-[2] 6 c.] *trans.* To deprive of the character or status of being Christian; to render unchristian.
a **1714** M. HENRY *Treat. Baptism* v. Wks. 1853 I. 549/1 To unchurch, unchristianize, unbaptize, all those who are not in every thing of our length. **1746** *Brit. Mag.* 95 Debasing and unchristianizing the more polite and younger Part of the Nation. **1839** *Morn. Herald* 1 July, To enslave the people and un-Christianise the country. **1850** NEWMAN *Diffic. Anglic.* I. i. (1891) I. 24 Why, half the country is unbaptized. .. Shall the country unchristianize itself? *a* **1878** SIR G. SCOTT *Lect. Archit.* I. 13 Surely this does not unchristianise the already Christian architecture of the soldiers of the Cross.

Hence **un'christianized** *ppl. a.*[1], **-izing** *vbl. sb.*
1636 H. BURTON *Apology of Appeale* 20 The basenesse of Degenerate English Spirits, become so unchristianized, as [etc.]. **1853** BRIGHT *Sp., Admiss. Jews to Parlt.* (1868) 524 Whence this notion or feeling of unchristianising springs.

un'christianized, *ppl. a.*[2] (UN-[1] 8.)
1778 APTHORPE *Preval. Chr.* 43 These nations, as yet unchristianized, found no power in Italy more respectable than that of the bishops of Rome. **1849** KINGSLEY *Misc., N. Devon* (1860) II. 300 There before me great countries untilled, uncivilized, unchristianized. **1859** W. ANDERSON *Disc.* (1860) 88 That must be a lifeless heart which lies cold and inanimate within the bosom of every unchristianized man.

un'christianlike, *a.* (UN-[1] 7 c.)
1610 in *Harl. Misc.* (Malh.) III. 111 This vnchristian-like conspiracie. **1646** E. F[ISHER] *Marrow Mod. Divin.* (ed. 2) 3 Neither let us have such unchristianlike expressions amongst us. **1709** STEELE *Tatler* No. 38 ¶1 That Unchristian-like and Bloody Custom of Duelling. **1754** *Connoisseur* No. 13. 77 That unchristian-like instrument the Jews-Harp. **1824** MISS L. M. HAWKINS *Annaline* I. 188 Do not think that any observations I make are allied to so unchristianlike a spirit. **1866** *Routledge's Ev. Boy's Ann.* 197 It is one of the most ungentlemanly and blackguardly things .., not to say unchristianlike and despicable.

un'christianlike, *adv.* (UN-[1] 11 b.)
1700–1 R. GOUGH *Hist. Myddle* (1875) 184 Hee grievously complained that his nephew had soe unchristian-like used his owne father. **1784** P. WRIGHT *New Bk. Martyrs* 796/1, I thank God I have not led my life as unchristian-like as many have done.

†**un'christianly,** *a. Obs.* (UN-[1] 7.)
1643–5 MILTON *Divorce* II. xx, A most unnatural and unchristianly yoke. **1645** —— *Colast.* Wks. 1851 IV. 364 Whom to leave thus without remedy..I say is most unchristianly.

un'christianly, *adv.* (UN-[1] 11.)
1547 J. HARRISON *Exhort. Scottes* 209 The feldes lie ful of their bodies, whose deathes thei moste cruelly and vnchristianly haue procured. **1599** HAKLUYT *Voy.* II. 309 As they behaued themselues most vnchristianly toward their brethren, so and much more vngodly..did they towards God. **1654** GATAKER *Disc. Apol.* 71 A wicked and wretched censure, most uncharitable and unchristianlie passed upon persons of well-known piety. **1694** F. BRAGGE

Disc. Parables II. 50 Why must communicating with such ministers..be unchristianly abstained from? **1743** WESLEY *Jrnl.* (1749) 69, I look upon myself to be under no kind of obligation..to observe any thing contained in that scandalous paper, so unchristianly imposed upon me. **1879** MEREDITH *Egoist* xxxi, She feared he might be speaking unchristianly.

un'christianness. [f. UNCHRISTIAN *a.*] The character of being unchristian.

1648–9 *Eikon Bas.* xxiv. 207 The Unchristianness of those denials. **1667** *Decay Chr. Piety* xx. ⁋1 We have now seen the unhappy riddle of the unchristianness of Christians unfolded.

un'christlike, *a.* (UN-[1] 7 c.)

1869 W. P. MACKAY *Grace & Truth* (1875) 153 Un-Christlike divisions in the Church of the living God. **1884** *Oxf. & Cambr. Undergrad. Jrnl.* 14 Feb. 232/1 The most un-Christ-like outcome of a so-called science.

Hence **un'christlikeness.**

1882 'EDNA LYALL' *Donovan* xxxiv, The un-Christlikeness of Christians.

un'christly, *a.* (UN-[1] 7.)

1880 *World of Cant.* x. 73 Both your objects and your means are unchristly. **1901** *Pop. Sci. Monthly* LVIII. 435/1 Ages have..fought over..this subject until history points with scarlet finger to unchristly deeds and impotent creeds, all in His name.

Hence **un'christliness.**

1905 MRS. J. E. BUTLER *Autobiog.* (1909) 307 The manifest unchristliness of the teaching of many of the churches.

un'chronicled, *ppl. a.* (UN-[1] 8.)

1598 *Mucedorus* Epilogue 19 Studie to act deedes yet vnchronicled. **1833** L. RITCHIE *Wand. by Loire* 194 Events of the most stupendous magnitude passed unchronicled. **1840** [see UNCHANTED *ppl. a.*]. **1885** J. E. TAYLOR *Brit. Fossils* ii. 49 The heroes..of many an unchronicled feud and deed of daring.

unchrono'logical, *a.* [UN-[1] 7.]

1. Not chronological; not arranged in order of time; not in accordance with chronology.

1763 BURN *Eccl. Law* II. 320 This is unchronological and absurd. **1801** R. PATTON *Asiat. Mon.* 149 The history is called, 'A modern unchronological Account of Bengal'. **1841** L. HUNT *Seer* II. (1864) 18 But the truth of the painting makes amends, as in the unchronological pictures of old masters. **1882** FARRAR *Early Chr.* II. 348 *note*, The assertion ..is an unchronological guess.

2. Of persons: Not skilled in, not observing, chronology.

1817 BYRON *Let. to Murray* 26 Apr., What is necessary but a bust and..a date? the last for the unchronological, of whom I am one. **1827** G. S. FABER *Sacr. Calend. Prophecy* (1844) I. 29 All the matters, which unchronological prophets describe as taking place at the epoch of the Restoration of Judah.

Hence **unchrono'logically** *adv.*

1879 FARRAR *St. Paul* (1883) 7 Mentioned only so cursorily,..so unchronologically, that scarcely one of them can be dwelt upon.

un'church, *v.* [UN-[2] 4, 5, and 6 b.]

1. *trans.* To remove or exclude (individuals) from membership of a church; to shut out from church privileges; to excommunicate.

a **1620** J. DYKE *Sel. Serm.* (1640) 372 Hee will cast men out of the Temple, will unchurch them,..because men doe not buy in the Temple. **1655** FULLER *Ch. Hist.* IX. i. §52 These holy men..were loath to unchurch any, and drive them off from an Ecclesiastical communion for such petty differences. **1677** W. HUGHES *Man of Sin* II. xii. 217 Gregory 3d...lets fly against the Emperour Leo also, to Unchurch and Uncrown him together. *a* **1703** BURKITT *On N.T., 2 Cor.* i. 24 Our apostle doth not unchurch them.., but endeavours to reform their disorders. **1711** *Medley* No. 21. 243 All Candidates,..if they vote with Dissenters, are (however Orthodox themselves) *ipso facto* unchurch'd. **1876** FAIRBAIRN in *Contemp. Rev.* June 127 He did not mean to be unchurched, was thoroughly happy and at home in the Christian religion.

absol. *a* **1658** DURHAM *Comm. Revelation* ii. 6–7 (1660) 91 They might Excommunicate and un-Church for spiritual offences.

refl. **1813** BP. J. MILNER in Husenbeth *Life* (1862) 225 By his obstinacy in adhering to his schismatical errors, [he] does in fact unchurch himself.

2. To exclude (a number or class of persons) from participation in the Church (or some branch of it); to divest (a community) of the character of a church; to deprive of the possession of a church.

1633 SANDERSON *Serm.* (1681) II. 43 These our brethren ..of the separation are so violent and peremptory in unchurching all the world but themselves. **1657** J. WATTS *Vind. Ch. Eng.* 8 If they be able to unchurch England, they may unchurch also all the World. **1709** J. JOHNSON *Clergym. Vade M.* II. p. xcvi, We are told..that by this judgment and practice we unchurch all foreign protestants. **1752** CARTE *Hist. Eng.* III. 578 Unchurching all bodies of Christians who did not adopt this discipline of his predecessor Calvin's invention. **1773** J. ALLEN *Serm. at S. Mary's, Oxf.* 12 A contempt of morality would be a reason sufficient for unchurching any Communion. **1833** *Tracts for Times* No. 4. 5 Do you then unchurch all the Presbyterians, all Christians who have no Bishops? **1856** EMERSON *Eng. Traits, Relig.* Wks. (Bohn) II. 101 Of course, money will..steadily work to..unchurch the people to whom it was bequeathed. **1892** *Guardian* 28 Sept. 1447/1 It 'unchurches' whole communities of sincere Christians.

refl. **1679** C. NESSE *Antid. agst. Popery* 102 The Jews..did apostatize,..unchurching and uncovenanting themselves. *c* **1700** HOWE in H. Rogers *Life* x. (1863) 306 This church.. has not, by adding some much disputed things,..thereby unchurched itself.

b. With *church* as object. (Cf. *unkirk* UN-[2] 6 b.)

1636 PRYNNE *Unbish. Tim.* (1661) 80 They..Un-church most Protestant Churches in foreign parts, and Un-minister their Ministers. **1680** C. NESSE *Church Hist.* 404 He wrote those seven Epistles to the seven Churches which were not un-churched. **1711** G. HICKES *Two Treat. Chr. Priesth.* (1847) I. 270 Invidious clamor..for unchurching the reformed churches. **1830** CASSAN *Lives Bps. Bath & Wells* II. 36 His Lordship's argument thus practically unchurches the Church. **1889** GORE *R.C. Claims* x. 162 But undiscipline does not unchurch a church.

un'churched, *ppl. a.* [UN-[1] 8 and UN-[2] 8: cf. prec.] **a.** Excluded from, deprived of, (the status of) a church. **b.** Not provided or connected with a church. **c.** (See quot. 1727.)

1681 BAXTER *Answ. Dodwell* iii. 21 The Protestant Churches are in the same unchurched damnable case that have Bishops. **1727** BAILEY (vol. II), *Unchurched*, dissolved from being a Church, excommunicated; also not churched, as a Woman that has lain in. **1870** M. D. CONWAY *Earthw. Pilgr.* xxvi. 311 The great interests of our time gather about the unchurched world. **1889** J. H. WARD *Church in Modern Society* 224 There is more activity to-day in the churches, but there are also more unchurched people than ever before.

un'churching, *vbl. sb.* [f. UNCHURCH *v.*] The action of the verb, in various senses.

1655 BAXTER *Quaker's Catech.* Pref., The decrying of the Ministry, the unchurching of our Churches. *a* **1658** DURHAM *Comm. Revelation* ii. 6–7 (1660) 99 Un-Churching and Excommunication in such cases, is an Ordinance of Jesus Christ. *a* **1715** BURNET *Own Time* (1897) I. 247 King James..thought it went too far towards the unchurching of all those who had not bishops among them. **1852** H. NEWLAND *Lect. Tractar.* 61, I wish I had time to say a few words on..the unchurching of our neighbours.

un'churching, *ppl. a.* [f. as prec.] That unchurches.

1681 BAXTER *Search Schism.* ii. 26 Bishop Gunning and Mr. Dodwell hence draw dismal degrading and unchurching Consequences. **1721** A. CAMPBELL *Doctr. Mid. State* Pref., Those Men, who..valued themselves chiefly.. upon their own Unchurching Principles. **1846** G. B. CHEEVER *Lect. Pilgr. Progr.* vi. 79 He..was completely free from the unchurching spirit of his age.

un'churchlike, *a.* (UN-[1] 7 c.)

1642 MILTON *Apol. Smect.* Wks. 1851 III. 290 Shall not all the mischiefe which other men do, be layd to his charge, if they doe it by that unchurchlike power which he defends. **1711** *Medley* No. 21. 243 The Name Church-men..not only ..wipes off all former Blemishes how unchurch-like soever, but [etc.]. **1845** G. A. POOLE *Churches* i. 3 We have trim, parsimonious, unchurchlike preaching-houses, under the name of churches. **1881** *Lond. & Provinc. Music Trades Rev.* 15 Feb. 7/3 This anthem is..crude, amateurish, and unchurchlike.

un'churchly, *a.* (UN-[1] 7: cf. G. *unkirchlich.*)

1815 J. MAYNE *Jrnl.* 1 Jan. (1909) 237 For although the most wretched, spiritless animals had been purposely selected, yet the novelty of the scene and the shouts of the people would sometimes elicit an unchurchly amble. **1858** in *Lit. Churchman* 15 May 184/1 A sentence which, according to their own explanation, arose from the unchurchly tone of the lectures themselves. **1883** P. BROOKS *Serm. in Eng. Ch.* 280 Churchmen..bringing to the Church unchurchly hearts.

unchut, obs. variant of UNCOUTH *a.*

unci, pl. of UNCUS.

‖**uncia** ('ʌnʃɪə). Pl. **unciæ** ('ʌnʃiː). [L. *uncia* a twelfth part (spec. of a pound or foot): see INCH *sb.*[1] and OUNCE *sb.*[1]]

†**1.** *Math.* (See quot. 1704.) *Obs.*

1695 *Phil. Trans.* XIX. 60 That admirable Invention of Mr. Newton, whereby he determines the *Unciæ* or Numbers prefixt to the Members composing Powers. **1704** J. HARRIS *Lex. Techn.* I, *Unciæ*, in Algebra, signify those Numbers which are prefixed before the Letters of the Members of any Power produced from a Binomial, Residual, or Multinomial Root. **1763** W. EMERSON *Meth. Increments* 106 Where the numeral coefficients are the unciæ of the several powers of a binomial.

2. A Roman copper coin, equal in value to the twelfth part of the 'as'.

1834 *Penny Cycl.* II. 431/2 The *Uncia*,..or piece of one ounce, is marked by a single globule. **1853** HUMPHREYS *Coin-coll. Man.* I. 260 The uncia here engraved is of the same period as that of the 'as' of nine-and-a-half ounces.

uncial ('ʌnʃ(ɪ)əl), *a.* and *sb.* [ad. L. *unciāl-is* pertaining to a twelfth part, f. *uncia* UNCIA. In sense 2 after L. *unciales litteræ* (Jerome). Hence also It. *onciale*, Sp. *uncial*, Pg. *oncial*, F. *oncial* (*uncial*), G., Sw. *uncial.*]

A. *adj.* **1. a.** Pertaining to, connected with, etc., an inch or an ounce.

1650 J. WYBARD *Tactometria* 305 The solid measure of one ounce-troy will be (in unciall or inch-measure) 1·8947 inch; and of one ounce-avoirdupois, 1·72556 inch. **1656** BLOUNT *Glossogr.* [copying Cooper], *Uncial*, of or belonging to an ounce or inch. **1824** SCOTT *Redgauntlet* Concl., I am sorry I have not room (the frank being only uncial) for his farther observations.

b. Based on a duodecimal division; divided into twelve equal parts.

1842 *Smith's Dict. Grk. & Rom. Antiq.* s.v. *Uncia*, The uncial system was adopted by the Greeks of Sicily. **1853** HUMPHREYS *Coin-coll. Man.* II. 375 *note*, It seems probable that both the name of the weight, and the uncial coinage, may have been derived from Sicily. **1884** *Encycl. Brit.* XVII. 652/2 The denarius was struck at 80 to the pound, and the as became uncial.

2. Of letters or writing: Having the large rounded forms (not joined to each other) characteristic of early Greek and Latin manuscripts; also (in looser use), of large size, capital.

The term is also applied to letters having the form of the uncial, irrespective of size. When used in its strict sense, *uncial* is distinguished from *capital*, which denotes the more original, unrounded forms of the letters.

Jerome's *unciales litteræ* (Prol. Job) is commonly explained as meaning 'letters of an inch long'; his use of the word is accompanied by the phrase *ut vulgo aiunt*, and the literal sense was perhaps not seriously intended. The emendations *initiales* 'initial' and *uncinales* 'hooked, bent', have been suggested.

1712 HENLEY tr. *Montfaucon's Trav. Italy* ii. 19 The Book is writ in the Oblong uncial Character. *a* **1734** NORTH *Lives* (1826) I. 20 It is not well to write, as the fashion now is, uncial or semiuncial letters. **1784** ASTLE *Orig. & Progr. Writ.* 82 Uncial writing began to be adopted about the middle of the fifth century. **1844** S. R. MAITLAND *Dark Ages* 207 A copy of the Gospels,..written in uncial characters. **1869** J. J. RAVEN *Ch. Bells Cambr.* (1881) 12 Bells inscribed in the uncial mediæval lettering, commonly called Longobardic. **1881** T. WALROND in *Macm. Mag.* XLIV. 151 All those that have been mentioned are written in the great uncial or capital character.

Comb. **1885** *Encycl. Brit.* XVIII. 150/2 The minuscule character is maintained intact, without intrusion of larger or uncial-formed letters.

b. Written, cut, etc., in uncial characters.

1849 CURZON *Monast. Levant* xi. 134 The one [inscription] on the other side was either Coptic or uncial Greek. **1863** *Smith's Dict. Bible* III. 1201 *note*, An uncial MS., brought by Tischendorf from St. Catherine's Monastery. **1885** H. SWEET *Oldest Eng. Texts* 422 The latest uncial charter..is dated 736, and..it is Mercian.

c. Characterized by the use of large letters.

1876 GEO. ELIOT *Dan. Der.* II. xiv, The address was in a lady's handwriting (of the delicate kind which used to be esteemed feminine before the present uncial period).

B. *sb.* **1.** An uncial or capital letter.

1775 ASH, *Uncial*.., a letter of a larger size formerly used in inscriptions. **1784** ASTLE *Orig. & Progr. Writ.* 66 All writing may be divided into capitals, uncials, and small letters. **1860** I. TAYLOR *Ess.* iii. 203 His [Franklin's] name, until his later years, drew after it no cumbrous length of academic Uncials. **1875** SCRIVENER *Lect. Text N. Test.* 19 These uncials attract the eye for their minuteness.

b. An uncial style of writing.

So F. *onciale* fem., *oncial* masc.

1883 I. TAYLOR *Alphabet* viii. §6 II. 204 In the 7th century the Irish uncial..came into competition with the Roman uncial. **1885** *Encycl. Brit.* XVIII. 148/1 In this class of writing there is again the same dearth of dated MSS. as in the round uncial.

2. A manuscript written in uncial characters.

1881 WESTCOTT & HORT *Grk. N. Test.* Introd. §98 The Greek MSS. of the New Testament are divided into two classes,—Uncials and Cursives. **1883** SCHAFF *Hist. Chr. Church, Apost. Chr.* lxxxi. II. 642 *note*, It is omitted in several uncials and ancient versions.

'uncialize, *v.* [f. prec.] *trans.* To convert into uncial characters; to write in uncials. Hence **'uncialized** *ppl. a.*

1883 I. TAYLOR *Alphabet* viii. §6 II. 204 The Irish uncial, which was the old Roman cursive uncialized. *Ibid.*, The Glagolitic might prove to be merely an uncialized form of the Greek cursive.

'uncially, *adv.* [f. UNCIAL *a.*]

†**1.** In uncial measurement. *Obs.*

1650 J. WYBARD *Tactometria* 306 And so the solid measure of one pound-troy of water, wil be, Uncially, 22·7368; and of one pound-avoirdupois, wil be Uncially 27·609.

2. In uncial letters.

1885 H. SWEET *Oldest Eng. Texts* 422 As there is an entire absence of Northumbrian charters and of uncially written West-Saxon ones.

†**'unciary,** *a. Obs.*[−1] [ad. L. *unciāri-us*, f. *uncia* UNCIA. Hence also F. *onciaire.*] Amounting to a twelfth part. (Wrongly explained in quot.)

1586 T. B. *La Primaud. Fr. Acad.* I. 497 There was a lawe amongst the ancient Grecians and Romanes, which forbad all usurie surmounting one pennie for a hundred by the yeere, and they called it vnciarie vsurie.

un'cicatrized, *ppl. a.* (UN-[1] 8.)

[**1775** ASH.] **1841** T. R. JONES *Anim. Kingd.* 301 The wound remains uncicatrised until the next moult. **1854** DE QUINCEY *Autobiog. Sk.* Wks. II. 271 Nothing was new, nothing was raw and uncicatrized.

unciform ('ʌnsɪfɔːm), *a.* and *sb.* *Anat.* [ad. mod.L. *unciform-is*, f. L. *unc-us* hook. So F. and Sp. *unciforme.*] **A.** *adj.* Hook-shaped; esp. ***unciform bone, process.***

(*a*) **1733–4** G. DOUGLAS tr. *Winslow's Anat. Expos.* (1756) 84 In the fourth Bone..we are to consider the..hooked or Unciform Apophysis. **1831** R. KNOX *Cloquet's Anat.* 105 The inferior turbinated bone..which..seems suspended by its unciform process. **1855** HOLDEN *Hum. Osteol.* 74 The unciform process..is connected..with the inferior spongy bone and the superior maxillary bone.

(*b*) **1840** E. WILSON *Anat. Vade M.* 198 The *Flexor ossis metacarpi*..arises from the unciform bone and annular ligament. **1861** HULME tr. *Moquin-Tandon* I. ii. 4 The carpus has 8 bones arranged in two rows... In the second.. is the trapezium, the trapezoid, the os magnum, and the unciform bone. **1884** COUES *N. Amer. Birds* 107 A carpal bone, supposed to be *unciform*, later fusing with metacarpus.

B. *sb.* The unciform bone of the wrist.

Also used in the L. form *unciforme* (sc. *os*).
1840 G. V. ELLIS *Anat.* 439 One is placed on each side of the os magnum, uniting this bone to the trapezoides on the one hand, and to the unciform on the other.

un'ciliated, *ppl. a.* (UN-[1] 8.)
1851 G. F. RICHARDSON *Geol.* viii. 217 The Anthozoa have unciliated tentacula, no intestinal appendage to the stomach [etc.]. **1860** *Encycl. Brit.* (ed. 8) XXI. 1008/2 The majority of the species produce only unciliated gelatinous grains.

uncinate ('ʌnsɪnət), *a.* and *sb.* [ad. L. *uncīnātus*, f. *uncīn-us* hook. Hence also It. *uncinato*.]
A. *adj.* Hooked; furnished with hooks; unciform, uncinated: **a.** *Bot.*
1760 J. LEE *Introd. Bot.* I. xiv. (1765) 36 *Uncinate*, hooked. **1832** LINDLEY *Nat. Syst. Bot.* 58 Flowers in terminal and lateral racemes, covered with uncinate hairs. **1870** HOOKER *Stud. Flora* 375 Grasswrack;.. embryo large, ovoid, with a small uncinate subulate plumule.
b. *Anat.* and *Zool. spec.* in ***uncinate gyrus***, the hook-shaped anterior part of the hippocampus involved in the perception of olfactory stimuli.
1826 KIRBY & SP. *Entomol.* xlvi. IV. 322 Antennæ. Uncinate (*Uncinatæ*), when their apex is incurved so as to form a kind of hook. **1852** DANA *Crust.* I. 191 The moveable finger being very strongly uncinate. **1883** *Gray's Anat.* (ed. 10) 487 The uncinate gyrus extends from the posterior extremity of the hemisphere to the fissure of Sylvius. **1884** COUES *N. Amer. Birds* 142 These 'sacral ribs' are furthermore distinguished by being devoid of the epipleural or uncinate processes. **1980** *Gray's Anat.* (ed. 36) 999/1 The tail [of the uncinate gyrus] separates the rest of the inferior surface of the uncus into an anterior uncinate gyrus and a posterior intralimbic gyrus.
c. Involving or affecting the uncinate gyrus: applied to a type of epileptic fit in which hallucinatory sensations of taste and smell are experienced.
1899 J. H. JACKSON in *Lancet* 14 Jan. 79/2 There is very often the Dreamy State in cases of this group of epileptic fits —the Uncinate Group. **1948** A. BRODAL *Neurol. Anat.* x. 338 An uncinate attack may be followed by an ordinary epileptic fit, in which case the uncinate attack represents an aura. **1974** E. NIEDERMEYER *Compendium of Epilepsies* v. 109 In human epileptic conditions, Jackson's term of 'uncinate epilepsy' corresponds with amygdaloid insular seizure manifestations.
B. *sb.* An uncinate process.
1891 *Cent. Dict.* **1903** *Proc. Zool. Soc. Lond.* 17 Mar. 274 The third pair [of ribs] always bear uncinates. *Ibid.*, The uncinates are broad and strong.

'uncinated, *ppl. a.* [f. as prec. + -ED.] = UNCINATE *a.*
1752 J. HILL *Hist. Anim.* 579 The Capra, with erect, uncinated horns. The Rupicapra, or Chamoise. **1772** *Phil. Trans.* LXIII. 150 The whole skin tough, covered with five rows of uncinated scales. **1826** KIRBY & SP. *Entomol.* III. xxxv. 630 The uncinated, forked,.. and insulated nervures of Coleopterous insects. **1851** S. P. WOODWARD *Mollusca* I. (1856) 72 The uncinated calamaries are solitary animals, frequenting the open sea.

un'cinch, *v.* (UN-[2] 3 or 4 b.)
1891 M. COLE *Cy Ross* 12 Pull up for the night, uncinch the packs. **1900** VACHELL *J. Charity* xx. 272 He and Quijas had dismounted and had uncinched their horses.

un'cinct, *ppl. a.* (UN-[1] 8 b.)
1880 BROWNING *Pan & Luna* 28 She teemed Herself with whiteness,—virginal, uncinct By any halo.

un'cinctured, *ppl. a.* (UN-[1] 8.)
1775 H. DOWNMAN *Infancy* II. (1803) 97 Cloath'd be thy child;.. but in airy garb, Loose, and uncinctured. **1791** COWPER *Iliad* XVI. 510 When he saw Such havoc made of his uncinctured friends.

‖**uncinus** (ʌn'saɪnəs). *Zool.* Pl. uncini (-naɪ). [L. *uncīnus*, f. *uncus* hook.] A hook-shaped part or process; esp. one of the hook-like teeth of molluscs.
1851 S. P. WOODWARD *Mollusca* I. 113 Lingual dentition like murex erinaceus; teeth transverse, 3 crested; uncini small, simple. **1859** J. R. GREENE *Man. Anim. Kingd.* I. *Protozoa* 67 The 'setæ' or ciliary bristles of *Oxytricha*,.. the 'uncini' (hooks) and 'styles' of *Euplotes*. **1878** BELL tr. *Gegenbaur's Comp. Anat.* 360 The outermost uncini of the transverse rows may.. also be articulated.

†**un'cipher**, *v. Obs.* [UN-[2] 6 b.] *trans.* To decipher. (Common in 17th c.)
1598 FLORIO, *Disciferare*, to vncifer, to decifer. **1640** HOWELL *Dodona's Gr.* 170 The bookes of Kings are written in darke Characters which few can uncypher. **1644–5** in *Charles I's Wks.* (1662) 322 If You believe that I should be capable to shew them to any, onely to Lord Jer. to uncypher them. **1668** TEMPLE *Let. Ld. Arlington* Wks. 1720 II. 96 Your Lordship will have found that all I could uncipher in your last was already performed here. **1710** STEELE *Tatler* No. 195 ¶2, I wanted the true Key to uncipher your Mysteries. **1737** in *10th Rep. Hist. MSS. Comm.* App. I. 474 Send me his answer if you can Uncypher or guess the meaning of yᵉ Spanish Phisick Latin.

un'circular, *a.* (UN-[1] 7.)
1775 R. CHANDLER *Trav. Asia M.* (1825) I. 4 The other portion [of the sun] put on several uncircular forms.

un'circulated, *ppl. a.* (UN-[1] 8.) Also *absol.* as *sb.*
[**1775** ASH.] **1880** *Plain Hints Needlework* 39 We live in crowded rooms with gas-consumed and uncirculated air. **1938** J. COFFIN *Coin Collecting* viii. 100 It is highly doubtful just what price might be given for an 1804 silver dollar in uncirculated condition. **1962** L. BROWN *Coin Collecting* i. 17 Owing to modern methods of minting, where coins move along conveyor belts, slide down shutes and are packed into bags, it is almost impossible to obtain a modern coin.. in anything like FDC [perfect mint state] condition and so the term 'uncirculated' was introduced. **1978** J. L. HENSLEY *Killing in Gold* v. 61 I'll stay with crisp uncirculateds.. at least for type.

†**uncircumcided**, obs. var. UNCIRCUMCISED.
1382 WYCLIF *Josh.* v. 6 The puple that is bore in deseert bi fourti yeer.. were uncircumcidid to the tyme that thei weren wastid. **1382** —— *Jer.* vi. 10 Lo! vncircumcidid the eres of hem. **1535** COVERDALE *Gen.* xxxiv. 14 That can we not do, to geue oure sister to an vncircumcided man.

†**uncircumcis**, *ppl. a. Obs.*[−1] [Cf. CIRCUMCIS *pa. pple.*] = next.
c **1250** *Gen. & Ex.* 2841 Moyses and hise wif sephoram And hise childre wið him nam; And ðat on was vncircumcis.

un'circumcised, *ppl. a.* [UN-[1] 8 and 5 b.]
1. Not having undergone circumcision. Also *absol.*
1387 TREVISA *Higden* (Rolls) IV. 115 By ensample of hem meny of þe Iewes.. lefte hem uncircumsised, and cleped hem self Antiochenes. *c* **1400** *Apol. Loll.* 35 Ilk alien kynd & vncircumsisid in hert, and vncircumsisid in flesch, schal not go in to my sanctuari. **1526** TINDALE *Rom.* ii. 26 Yf the vncircumcised kepe the right thynges contayned in the lawe, shall nott his vncircumcision be counted for circumcision? **1565** ALLEN *Def. Purg.* xvii. 285 b, Iudas or any other in the lawe, offered for his friend, or any man elles being vncircumcised. **1608** BP. HALL *Epistles* v. iv, As a seale of the righteousnes of that faith, which he had when he was vncircumcised. **1668** DRYDEN *Evening's Love* III, We of the Uncircumcised, in a civil way, as Lovers, have somewhat the advantage of your Musullman. **1685** BAXTER *Paraphr. N.T.* Gal. v. 6 For in our State of Christianity.. a Man shall not be accepted and justified as circumcised, or as uncircumcised. **1825** SCOTT *Talism.* ix, I will not reason with one uncircumcised upon the virtue of the medicines. **1850** F. W. NEWMAN *Phases Faith* 180 In the conversion of Cornelius was the justification of Peter for admitting uncircumcised Gentiles.
transf. **1535** COVERDALE *Lev.* xix. 23 All maner trees wherof men eate..: thre yeares shal ye holde them for vncircumcysed. [Also in later versions.]
2. *fig.* Not spiritually chastened or purified; irreligious; heathen. Also *absol.*
a **1400** *New Test.* (Paues) Acts vii. 51 Harde-frownted ande vncircumsised hertes ande eares. *c* **1400** *Apol. Loll.* 34 Alien sonis vncircumsicid in hert. **1526** TINDALE *Acts* vii. 51 Ye stiffenecked and of vncircumcised hertes and eares: ye have allwayes resisted agaynste the holy goost. **1591** SYLVESTER *Du Bartas* I. ii. 1185 Uncircumcised! O hard hearts! At least Let's think that God those Waters doth digest In that steep place. **1642** MILTON *Apol. Smect.* Wks. 1851 III. 310 In the Hebrew text, which is so necessary to be understood, except it be some few of them, their lips are utterly uncircumcis'd. **1685** BAXTER *Paraphr. N.T.* Acts vii. 51 Ye are an unruly obstinate people, whose hearts are unreformed and uncircumcised. **1800** WEEMS *Washington* xi. (1877) 149 The pirates of Morocco laying their uncircumcised hands on our rich commerce in the Mediterranean. **1825** SCOTT *Betrothed* vii, Such an uncircumcised Philistine as thou or thy master.
Hence **uncircum'cisedness**.
1583 GOLDING *Calvin on Deut.* lxxii. 442 This people.. who therefore were oftentimes vpbrayded with the vncircumcisednes of their heartes. *a* **1639** WHATELEY *Prototypes* I. xvi. (1640) 158 We make use of the outward seale, thereby to be made to see and feel our uncircumcisednesse of heart.

uncircum'cision. (UN-[1] 12 and 5 b.)
1526 TINDALE *Rom.* ii. 25 But if thou breake the lawe thy circumcision is made vncircumcision. **1561** T. NORTON *Calvin's Inst.* II. 145 Now there is no respect of Greke or Jewe, circumcision or vncircumcision. **1643–5** MILTON *Divorce* II. vi, How vain then,.. to exact a circumcision of flesh from an infant,.. and to dispence an uncircumcision in the soul of a grown man. **1685** BAXTER *Paraphr. N.T.* Gal. vi. 16 Placing acceptable Religion in this, and not in Circumcision or Uncircumcision. **1816** SCOTT *Old Mort.* xxvii, Even while thou.. wert fighting in the ranks of uncircumcision. **1879** FARRAR *St. Paul* I. 163 The idle fancies that circumcision alone was enough to save them from God's wrath, and that uncircumcision was worse than crime.

uncircum'locutory, *a.* (UN-[1] 7.)
1808 BENTHAM *Sc. Reform* 104 Those instruments of distinct conception, as well as unambiguous and uncircumlocutory reference.

uncircum'scribable, *a.* (UN-[1] 7 b.)
1608 tr. *Gregory's Dial.* (1874) 216 He is uncircumscribable and invisible. **1698** NORRIS *Treat. Sev. Subj.* 395, I do not see how they can make it, or he can call it Uncircumscribable. *a* **1706** EVELYN *Hist. Relig.* (1850) I. 99 Now, that which was first has no parts or dimensions, and is therefore.. uncircumscribable, and immense. **1848** BAILEY *Festus* (ed. 3) 202 In so far as worded it is not The entire truth uncircumscribable.

un'circumscribed, *ppl. a.* (UN-[1] 8.)
1610 HEALEY *St. Aug. Citie of God* x. xiii. 379 Hee desired to behold that cleare vncircumscribed nature [of God]. **1642** CHAS. I. *Mess. both Houses* 28 Apr. 3 So arbitrary and uncircumscribed a Power. *a* **1672** STERRY *Freedom Will* (1675) 12 The uncircumscribed Amplitude and Majesty of God. **1713** *Guard.* No. 164 ¶3 The Pow'r of Pluto stretches all around, Uncircumscrib'd by Nature's utmost Bound. **1798** *Monthly Mag.* V. 280 They boast the proud recommendation of moral beauty, in the most extensive and uncircumscribed acceptation of the term. **1820** SHELLEY *Prometh. Unb.* III. iv. 194 The loathsome mask has fallen, the man remains Sceptreless, free, uncircumscribed. **1881** MRS. C. PRAED *Policy & P.* I. 264 Imagination presented an uncircumscribed field of action.
absol. **1635** A. STAFFORD *Fem. Glory* (1869) 184 Thou Circumscription (if I may so say) of the Uncircumscribed!
Hence **un'circumscribedness**.
1679 J. GOODMAN *Penitent Pardoned* I. ii. (1713) 27 The uncircumscribedness of the divine Goodness.

†**un'circumscript**, *ppl. a.* [UN-[1] 8 b.] = prec.
c **1374** CHAUCER *Troylus* v. 1865 Thow.. That regnest ay yn thre, and two, and oon, Vncircumscript [*v.r.* -scrit] and al mayst circumscryue. **1649** G. DANIEL *Trinarch., Hen. V*, xxix, The vnresisted Emanations Of a true Maiestie.. baffle Questions To their Activity vncircumscript.

uncircum'scriptible, *a.* (UN-[1] 7 and 5 b.)
1577 tr. *Bullinger's Decades* IV. iii. 606 His eternall.. power and vnspeakable maiestie are altogether vncircumscriptible.

uncircum'scription. (UN-[1] 12 and 5 b.)
1852 BP. FORBES *Nicene Cr.* 145 Immensity, and uncircumscription, and supralocal existence, are the qualities of the true God.

un'circumspect, *a.* [UN-[1] 7 and 5 b.]
1. Of persons: Not circumspect or cautious; imprudent, unwary.
1502 ATKYNSON tr. *De Imitatione* I. xxiii. 173 O thou vncircumspecte soule, of howe great perell & fere myghtest thou delyuer thy selfe of nowe. **1540** ELYOT *Image Gov.* 143 If there had been a senate uncircumspect,.. or an Emperour a tyranne. **1632** J. HAYWOOD tr. *Biondi's Eromena* 119 Yet was I not therein uncircumspect, for some of them I tooke .., others would I not take. **1669** CLARENDON *Ess.* Tracts (1727) 157 Such like trivial imaginations, which make us so unwary in all our actions, so uncircumspect throughout the course of our lives. **1886** A. WEIR *Hist. Basis Mod. Europe* (1889) 38 The evident connection between the causes of his failure and his uncircumspect philanthropic temperament.
2. Of actions, etc.: Not marked by circumspection; incautious.
1563 FOXE *A. & M.* 605/2 Dalaber goes on, '.. by this your vncircumspecte comminge vnto me, and speaking so before this yonge man, ye haue disclosed your selfe and vtterlye vndone me'. **1625** K. LONG tr. *Barclay's Argenis* IV. xi. 275 Of her owne will, with a rash and uncircumspect hastinesse, she looked upon the shoulder of the child. **1682** BUNYAN *Holy War* (1905) 220 Yet I cannot but (a little) chide you for your late uncircumspect action.

uncircum'spection. (UN-[1] 12 and 5 b.)
1598 GRENEWEY *Tacitus, Ann.* IV. viii. (1622) 101 The witlesse vncircumspection of such as thinke.. they can also extinguish the memory of future times. **1810** G. LAWSON *Serm.* ix. 314 Your spiritual ardour is greatly abated through your uncircumspection.

un'circumspectly, *adv.* (UN-[1] 11 and 5 b.)
1535 JOYE *Apol. Tindale* (Arb.) 30 Sithe he cannot iustifye his writing so vncircumspectly put forth. **1560** DAUS tr. *Sleidane's Comm.* 300 In case you wyll obstinatly perseuer in the opinion, whiche very vncircumspectly you haue ones embraced. **1611** SPEED *Hist. Gt. Brit.* VI. vi. §18. 63 They intercepted the scattered troopes of the Romanes that vncircumspectly wasted and spoiled the Country. **1669** EARL ORRERY *Parthen.* (1676) 746 He sounded his inclinations.. so uncircumspectly, that he discover'd his own.

un'circumstanced, *ppl. a.* [UN-[1] 8.] Not justified or supported by circumstances.
1678 RYMER *Trag. last Age* 113 Both the Kings behaviour and hers, uncircumstanc'd as we have them, are every way so harsh.. that [etc.]. **1766** *Museum Rust.* VI. 12 He should have considered, that no sensible man can pay any regard to so uncircumstanced an account as he gives. **1943** S. SASSOON in *Country Life* 25 June 1136/2 Cloud shadows.. Dwell and dissolve; uncircumstanced they pause and pass.

uncircum'stantial, *a.* (UN-[1] 7.)
1646 SIR T. BROWNE *Pseud. Ep.* VII. i. 340 The like particulars although they seem uncircumstantiall are oft set downe in holy Scripture. **1752** *Phil. Trans.* XLVIII. 18 Cleomedes, who perhaps saw the same treatise of Hipparchus, is as uncircumstantial as Theon. **1823** BENTHAM *Not Paul* 332 Note here two things—the narrator one of the party; the narrative so loose and uncircumstantial.

uncisor'd, obs. f. UNSCISSORED *ppl. a.*

un'cite, *v.* (UN-[2] 3.)
1721 AMHERST *Terræ Fil.* No. 24 (1726) 126 Whom he order'd to cite the two proctors of the university into the court; as soon as the proctor had done this, the vice-chancellor order'd him to uncite them.

un'cited, *ppl. a.* [UN-[1] 8.]
1. Not called or summoned.
1584 R. SCOT *Discov. Witchcr.* II. iii. (1886) 18 A witnesse uncited, and offering himselfe in this case is to be heard. **1622** in Rushw. *Hist. Coll.* (1659) I. 72 So principal a Person .. who uncited, unheard, and without all knowledge of the Cause hath been condemned. **1665** BOYLE *Occas. Refl.* v. v. 161 There being nothing more easie,.. than for Multitudes to pass uncited before Man's Tribunal, to receive their Condemnation at God's.
2. Not quoted or mentioned.
1581 J. BELL *Haddon's Answ. Osor.* 116 Here withall is also coupled that saying of Christ with like uncited place. 'They that' [etc.]. **1891** MEREDITH *One of our Conq.* xxxiv, She had her charges to bring against them for injustice: uncited, unstirred charges.

un'citied, *a.* (UN-[1] 9.)
1802 LANDOR *Crysaor* 80, I am Jove, Thou Neptune: happier in uncitied realms. **1844** LD. HOUGHTON *Mem. Many Scenes, Valentia* 202 For thou.. Wilt.. bid him dwell at peace with thee In thy uncitied modesty.

un'city, *v.* [UN-[2] 6 b.] *trans.* **a.** To deprive of the privileges of a city. **b.** To destroy as a city.
a **1661** FULLER *Worthies, Glouc.* I. (1662) 368 Seeing some questioned its Charter, and would have had it Un-Citied,

because Un-Bishoped in our Civil Wars. **1850** BLACKIE *Æschylus* I. 211 The ancient city of famous Priam thou Didst sheer uncity.

un'civic, *a.* (UN-^{1} 7.)
1791 MACKINTOSH *Vind. Gallicæ* Wks. 1846 III. 28 The spirit of resistance to uncivic commands broke forth at once in every part of the empire. **1828** *Lights & Shades* I. 129 So uncivic and anti-commercial an offence. **1892** J. W. HEADLAM in *Classical Rev.* 297/2 Anyone who incurred suspicion of uncivic conduct, either political or moral, would be summoned before the Council.
Hence **un'civically** *adv.*
1931 A. HUXLEY *Music at Night* II. 81 We do not admit.. that there should be citizens treated uncivically.

un'civil, *a.* [UN-^{1} 7 and 5 b.]
1. Not civilized; barbarous; unrefined: †**a.** Of persons. *Obs.*
1553 BRENDE *Q. Curtius* IV. 35 The Bactrians be the most hardiest people amongst these nations, uncivill men. **1590** SPENSER *F.Q.* II. vii. 3 He sitting found in secret shade, An vncouth, saluage, and vnciuile wight. **1630** *R. Johnson's Kingd. & Commw.* 336 Among all men that professe Christ, there is not a more uncivill creature than the Calabrian. **1644** [H. PARKER] *Jus Populi* 42 No creature is now so uncivill or untame as Man.
b. Of actions, places, times, etc.
1553 BRENDE *Q. Curtius* V. 86 This nacion for al their vncyuill and rude maner, could not escape to be subdued with the same force of fortune y^{t} others were. **1596** SPENSER *State Irel.* Wks. (Globe) 633/1, I thought this manner of lewd crying and howling not impertinent to be noted as uncivill and Scythian-like. **1650** BULWER *Anthropomet.* 113 They of Goa also eat their pottage with their hands, mocking at the use of spoons as if they were uncivil. **1663** DAVENANT *Siege of Rhodes* II. i, Their gladness is but an uncivil Noise. **1790** BURKE *Fr. Rev.* Wks. V. 88 Men cannot enjoy the rights of an uncivil and of a civil state together. **1890** *Charity Organis. Rev.* Jan. 5 So is their project of feeding a barbarous and uncivil method in civic administration.
†**2. a.** Undeveloped, rude, primitive. *Obs.*
1572 TWYNE *Dionysius' Surv. World* E vij b, These inhabite a very wilde, and vnciuile countrey, the mould beeing very sandy, and not meete for anye tillage. **1632** LITHGOW *Trav.* x. 433 Bad and unciuill Husbandry in Ireland.
†**b.** Irresponsive to culture. *Obs.*
1675 EVELYN *Terra* (1676) 69 That Soil may be so strangely alter'd.. as to render the harsh and most uncivil Clay obsequious to the Husbandman. **1733** TULL *Horse-hoeing Husb.* 50 *note*, I take harsh uncivil Clay to be the least Profitable of any to keep in Tillage.
3. Not civil or courteous, impolite; rough, rude, lacking in manners: **a.** Of actions, etc.
1591 SHAKS. *Two Gentl.* v. iv. 60 Ruffian: let goe that rude vnciuill touch, Thou friend of an ill fashion. **1596** *Edward III*, II. ii. 60 Now we thinke it an vnciuill thing, To trouble heauen with such harsh resounds. **1613** W. BROWNE *Brit. Past.* I. iv. 439 [They] Bad me begone; and then (in terms uncivil) Did call me counterfait, witch, hag, whore, divell. **1653** W. RAMESEY *Astrol. Restored* 25 The which rugged, preposterous and uncivil answer, caused me presently to believe him to be whom I found him at the last. **1685** BAXTER *Paraphr. N.T.* Acts xv. 12 The proud Magisterial Talkers.. stop and silence him by rude uncivil interruption, on pretence that he is too long. **1796** MME. D'ARBLAY *Camilla* VII. xi, I'm not going to offer any thing uncivil. **1824** SCOTT *St. Ronan's* xiii, Having found himself aggrieved by the uncivil behaviour of.. Francis Tyrrel. **1878** BROWNING *Poets Croisic* xciv, You've learnt your lesson.. By this uncivil answer of La Roque.
Comb. **1600** NASHE *Summers Last Will* iv, Presumptuous Ver, vnciuill-nurturde boy, Think'st I will be derided thus of thee?
b. Of persons.
1611 COTGR., *Mauduict*,.. ill brought vp, vnciuile, rude. **1619** BEAUM. & FL. *Knight of Malta* v. i, Hard-hearted, and uncivil Oriana. **1663** BP. PATRICK *Parab. Pilgr.* xxxv, He was forced to be more uncivil to her than otherwise he should have been. **1712** ARBUTHNOT *John Bull* I. viii, He was a very uncivil fellow to use such coarse language before People of Condition. **1758** JOHNSON *Idler* No. 16 ¶7 His riches neither made him uncivil nor negligent. **1845** JAMES *Arrah Neil* III. ii, We do not intend to be uncivil to you. **1882** MISS BRADDON *Mt. Royal* II. v. 87 He was not absolutely uncivil to his cousin.
4. Not decent or seemly; indecorous.
1586 T. B. *La Primaud. Fr. Acad.* I. 172 No effeminate or loose maners, no clownish or uncivill fashions are seene in him. **1611** SPEED *Theat. Gt. Brit.* xxvii. (1614) 53/1 Her faire haire.. so covered her nakednes, that no part of her body was uncivil to sight. **1682** BUNYAN *Holy War* (1905) 377 His two servants.. catcht them together in uncivil manner more than once. **1687** DRYDEN *Hind & P.* III. 1010 That he should.. vex th' Etherial Pow'rs With mid-night Mattins at uncivil Hours.
5. Not in accordance with civic unity; contrary to civil well-being.
1597 BEARD *Theatre God's Judgem.* (1612) 277 So that great trouble and vnciuill warres were growne vp.. in euerie corner of the realme. **1620** J. TAYLOR (Water P.) *Jack a Lent* B ij b, They run starke mad, assembling in routs and throngs numberlesse of ungouerned numbers, with vnciuill ciuill commotions. **1642–4** VICARS *God in Mount* (1844) 29 Our home-bred and inbred distractions and uncivill-civill warres. **1647** N. WARD *Simple Cobler* 2 Civill Commotions make roome for uncivill practises. **1871** R. ELLIS tr. *Catullus* lxvii. 13 Comes to the light some mischief, a deed uncivil arising.
†**6.** Not civilian. *Obs.*$^{-1}$
1590 SWINBURNE *Testaments* 67 To be decided and ruled by the dead stroke of vnciuill and martial cannons, rather then by anie rule of the ciuill or cannon lawe.

†**un'civil**, *v.* *Obs.*$^{-1}$ [UN-^{2} 6 a.] *trans.* To render uncivil.
1615 DANIEL *Hymen's Triumph* IV. iii, I trust your lonenesse hath not so Vnciuil'd you, to force a messenger To doe against good manners, and his will.

un'civilish, *a.* (UN-^{1} 7.)
1828 LANDOR *Imag. Conv.* III. 280 It is uncivilish to speak to a lady, with a leg of a turkey in limbo, between the gullet and grinder.

unci'vility. Now *rare.* [UN-^{1} 12 and 5 b.] Absence or lack of civilization or of civility.
1598 FLORIO, *Immodestia*, immodestie, intemperancie, vnciuilitie. **1612** PEACHAM *Gentl. Exerc.* II. ii. 121 His crabbed lookes signifie the sauage vnciuility of the people in those parts. **1648** GAGE *West Ind.* xiii. 73 Their uncivility and barbarous properties tell us that they are most like the Tartars of any. **1697** T. BROWN *Dispens.* II. Wks. 1709 III. III. 67 If thee woul't have no Excuse made for thy Uncivility, I have done. **1830** CUNNINGHAM *Brit. Paint.* II. 78 The uncivility of his opponents.

un'civilizable, *a.* (UN-^{1} 7 b.)
1879 M. PATTISON *Milton* 99 Though the savage Irish are barbarians, uncivilised and uncivilisable. **1880** MISS BIRD *Japan* II. 74 They are uncivilisable and altogether irreclaimable savages.

un,civili'zation. (UN-^{1} 12 and 5 b.)
[**1828–32** WEBSTER.] **1880** W. MORRIS *Hopes & Fears for Art* (1882) 107 The attainment of these very comforts is what makes the difference between civilisation and uncivilisation. **1884** *Blackw. Mag.* Mar. 307 They, in their uncivilisation, would have regarded me with contempt.

un'civilize, *v.* [UN-^{2} 6 c.] *trans.* To deprive of civil, civilized, or civic character; to decivilize. Also *absol.*
1603 J. DAVIES (Heref.) *Microcosmos* Wks. (Grosart) I. 18/1 When the civill Sword's vnciuilliz'd In mightiest Empires. **1633** ROWLEY *Match at Midn.* IV. H 2 b, I will uncivillize that injured civilitie which you so scurvily slander. **1690** T. BURNET *Theory Earth* II. 16 That is commonly the vanity of great empires, to uncivilize in a manner all the rest of the world. **1811** *Henry & Isabella* II. 207 If the principle of force is to be sanctioned, the tendency of it is to uncivilize. *Ibid.* 212 Nor do I mean to deny that.. it would not have the same effect of uncivilizing.

un'civilized, *ppl. a.* [UN-^{1} 8 and 5 b.] Not civilized; barbarous. Also *absol.*
1607 TOPSELL *Four-f. Beasts* 334 Vulgar, illiterate, and vnciuilized men, do participate in their conditions, the labors and enuye of brute beasts. **1647** COWLEY *Mistr.*, *Welcome* iii, What joy couldst take, or what repose In Countrys so unciviliz'd as those? **1711** ADDISON *Spect.* No. 119 ¶5 Several of our Men of the Town.. make use of the most coarse uncivilized Words in our Language. **1777** COOK *Voy. Pacific* I. viii. (1784) I. 159 They shew as much ingenuity, both in invention and execution, as any uncivilized nations under similar circumstances. **1825** T. HOOK *Sayings* Ser. II. *Man of Many Friends* I. 283 The young gentlemen.. with difficulty suppressed a most uncivilized laugh. **1869** DOWDEN *Stud. Lit.* (1890) 161 The first thing we are tempted to say of him.. is that he was emphatically an uncivilized man.
absol. **1900** tr. *J. Deniker's Races of Man* vii. 251 Among the uncivilised, it is not a question of absolute right, of absolute morality; everything is reduced to a very restricted altruism, not extending beyond kin and immediate neighbours.
Hence **un'civilizedness.**
1879 M. ARNOLD *Mixed Ess.*, *Equality* 86 We owe.. our uncivilisedness to inequality.

un'civilly, *adv.* [UN-^{1} 11.] In an uncivil manner; not in accordance with civility; roughly, rudely; †barbarously.
1577 tr. *Bullinger's Decades* II. v. (1592) 150 Al vertue.. is vtterly ouerthrown,.. virgins defiled, matrones vnciuilly dealt withall. **1581** PETTIE tr. *Guazzo's Civ. Conv.* I. (1586) 22, I must first aske if you know anie citizen which liueth unciuillie. **1600** HOLLAND *Livy* 897 He was loth to converse there uncivilly, at so unseasonable a time. **1646** SIR T. BROWNE *Pseud. Ep.* (ed. 2) I. i. 3 When he brake forth as desperately as before he had done uncivilly. **1676** SHADWELL *Libertine* III, Ha! 'tis uncivilly done to leave a man in a strange country. **1798** SOUTHEY *Lett.* (1856) I. 51 Some English soldiers storm the ale-house, and are proceeding to behave somewhat uncivilly to Joan and her sister. **1825** SCOTT *Betrothed* xvii, Turning sternly on the huntsman, as one who has been hastily and uncivilly roused from a reverie. **1888** FREEMAN *Four Oxford Lect.* ii. 99 Those Breton followers of Ralph of Wader whom Lanfranc so uncivilly called 'filth'.

uncizar'd, obs. f. UNSCISSORED *ppl. a.*

†**uncked**, *a.* *Obs.*$^{-1}$ [f. L. *unc-us* hook.] Hooked, uncate.
1621 QUARLES *Esther* Sect. vii, Enuie did ope her snake-deuouring Iawes, Foamd frothy blood, and bent her vnked [ed. 1717: uncked] Pawes.

†**unckle**, obs. var. INKLE *sb.*
c **1545** in *Fabric Rolls York Minster* (Surtees) 136 For ij peeces of buckerham, 12*s.* For ij do. of white unckle.., 7*d.*

unckle, obs. f. UNCLE.

un'clad, *ppl. a.* [UN-^{1} 8 b. Cf. MDu. *ongecleet* (Du. *ongekleed*), MHG. *ungekleidet*, *-kleit*, ON. and Icel. *ú-*, *óklæddr* (Norw. *uklædd*, MSw. and Sw. *oklädd*, Da. *uklædt*).] Not clad or clothed; undressed; naked.
c **1420** *Avow. Arth.* liv, Qwenne ho se him vnclad, Then the lady wex drede. **1500** *Ortus Vocab.* (W. de W.) S viij b, *Inuestitus*, vncladde. **1531** ELYOT *Gov.* II. xii, He was a shamed to approche nigh to it, beinge in so simple astate and unklad. **1647** HEXHAM I, Vnclothed or unclad, *ontkleedt.* **1761** GLOVER *Medea* I. i, Creon knows, thy altar Unclad with garlands still proclaims thy firmness Against his daughter's marriage. **1768** MURPHY *Desert Isl.* II, That I may sit, With unclad sides, upon some blasted heath. **1827** POLLOK *Course T.* IX. 1095 Decrepit, withered wretch, unhoused, unclad. **1855** MILMAN *Lat. Chr.* XIV. ix. VI. 601 Men, women, rose unclad from their tombs.

unclad, pa. t. and pple. of UNCLEAD *v.*

un'claimed, *ppl. a.* (UN-^{1} 8.)
1600 SHAKS. *A. Y. L.* II. vii. 87 If he be free, Why then my taxing like a wild-goose flies Vnclaim'd of any man. **1738** JOHNSON *London* 173 Has Heav'n reserv'd, in pity to the poor,.. No peaceful desert yet unclaim'd by Spain? **1783** CRABBE *Village* II. 26 Yet still, ye humbler friends, enjoy your hour, This is your portion, yet unclaim'd of power. **1826** SOUTHEY *Vind. Eccl. Angl.* 306 The quiet, unassuming, unclaimed influence of the one may appear to you less than it ought to be. **1867** SMYTH *Sailor's Word-bk.* 705 *Unclaimed*, as Derelict. Vessels found at sea.. are good prizes, if not claimed within 366 days.

unclainte, obs. pa. t. of UNCLENCH *v.*

un'clamorous, *a.* (UN-^{1} 7.)
1849 LYTTON *K. Arthur* v. xxvii, The Prophet mark'd the deep unclamorous vow Of the pent passion.

un'clamp, *v.* (UN-^{2} 3.)
1809 *Phil. Trans.* XCIX. 120 Unclamp the apparatus. **1849** HERSCHEL *Astron.* 106 Now unclamp the level, and.. turn round the circle on the axis. **1860** H. STUART *Seaman's Catech.* 46 The outside men will.. unclamp the booms.

†**unclap**, *v.* *Obs.* [UN-^{2} 3.] *trans.* To open up.
1621 T. WILLIAMSON tr. *Goulart's Wise Vieillard* A 4 b, My fingers did euen itch to set pen to paper, and to vnclappe so good a Worke.

un'clarified, *ppl. a.* (UN-^{1} 8.)
1591 PERCIVALL *Sp. Dict.*, *Agraz*, a sower grape, honie vnmade, oile vnclarified, Veriuice. **1599** A. M. tr. *Gabelhouer's Bk. Physicke* 45/2 Then take vnclarifyede rosin. **1620** VENNER *Via Recta* vi. 104 It is.. hurtfull to such as abound with winde, especially the crude and vnclarified honie. **1725** *Fam. Dict.* s.v. *Whey*, Its best they should take it unclarify'd. [**1755** JOHNSON (quoting Bacon), and in later Dicts.]

un'clashing, *ppl. a.* (UN-^{1} 10.)
1642 W. PRICE *Serm.* 24 Like the æviternall unclashing sway of the Orbs in the Heavens. **1825** R. WILSON *Sk. Hist. Hawick* 297 In this momentous matter [*sc.* religion] human interests are so *unclashing*,.. that [etc.]. **1854** CDL. WISEMAN *Fabiola* (1855) 312 Glorious Church of Christ! great in the unclashing combination of thy unity!

un'clasp, *v.* [UN-^{2} 3 and 7.]
1. *trans.* To unfasten the clasp(s) of.
1530 PALSGR. 766/2, I pray you, unclaspe my boke, for I am nat stronge ynough. **1592** *Soliman & Pers.* II. i. 85, I must vnclaspe me, or my heart will breake. **1611** COTGR., *Desagrafer*, to vnclaspe, vngraple, vnhaspe. *a* **1699** J. BEAUMONT *Psyche* XVI. xvii, Disrobe me of my Beauty..; Unclasp my Joints; unlace my nerves. **1798** EDGEWORTH *Pract. Educ.* (1811) I. 110 A little boy.. trying to clasp and unclasp a lady's bracelet. **1805** SCOTT *Last Minstrel* v. xxiv, His beaver did he not unclasp. **1859** TENNYSON *Elaine* 975 Then, when she heard his horse upon the stones, Unclasping flung the casement back. **1891** FARRAR *Darkn. & Dawn* xiv, He unclasped the armlet from his wrist.
b. In fig. context.
1592 DANIEL *Delia* i, Heere I vnclaspe the booke of my charg'd soule. **1607** DEKKER *Hist. Sir T. Wyatt* Wks. 1873 III. 100 When ere the blacke booke of my crime's vnclaspt. **1633** DRUMM. OF HAWTH. *Entertainm. Chas. I*, ii. 31 Heavens volume to unclaspe, wast pages spread, Mysterious golden cyphers cleere to reade. **1833–4** *Encycl. Metrop.* (1845) VI. 688/2 It will be prudent before thus entangling ourselves in fetters which it may be difficult to unclasp, to wait for a full investigation of the subject.
†**c.** *fig.* To open up, display. *Obs.*
1599 SHAKS. *Much Ado* I. i. 325, I will.. tell faire Hero I am Claudio, And in her bosome Ile unclaspe my heart. **1611** —— *Wint. T.* III. ii. 168 He.. to my Kingly Guest Vnclasp'd my practise. **1637** N. WHITING *Albino & Bellama* 5 All had their speakers which unclasp'd their graces.
2. To loosen the grasp or hold of; to open or force open (the clasped hand).
1627 MAY *Lucan* IV. G v, His fresh limmes vnclaspe the others hands. **1681** FLAVEL *Right Man's Ref.* 251 Neither of them.. can unclasp the arms of divine love. **1810** SCOTT *Lady of L.* II. xxxiv, Sullen and slowly they unclasp, As struck with shame, their desperate grasp. **1831** JAMES *Phil. Augustus* iv, Unclasping his arms from the slight, beautiful form round which they were thrown. **1898** 'MERRIMAN' *Roden's Corner* i, Von Holzen.. softly unclasped the dead man's hand, taking from it the crumpled notes.
b. *intr.* To relax a grip or grasp.
1608 SHAKS. *Per.* II. iii. 107 Vnclaspe, vnclaspe. Thankes Gentlemen to all. **1751** SMOLLETT *Per. Pic.* xxix, The cudgel flew from his unclasping hand. **1850** LYNCH *Theoph. Trinal* vi. 110 The jaws of their grave shall unclasp. **1851** LONGF. *Gold. Leg.* ii. *Village Church*, I feel my feeble hands unclasp, And sink discouraged into night!
3. *trans.* To release from a clasp or grip.
1885 'MRS. ALEXANDER' *At Bay* ix, He remained silent for a minute, his hands clasping and unclasping the arms of his chair.
Hence **un'clasping** *vbl. sb.*
1592 *Soliman & Pers.* II. i. 87 But inward cares are most pent in with greefe; Vnclasping, therefore, yeeldes me no releefe. **1599** B. JONSON *Ev. Man out of Hum.* II. ii, A whole volume of humour, and worthy the vnclasping.

un'clasped, *ppl. a.* [f. UNCLASP *v.* 1 or UN-[1] 8 + CLASPED *ppl. a.*] Having the clasp undone or not fastened. Also *fig.*

1609 J. DAVIES *Holy Roode* G, None other Booke but thy vnclasped Side (Wherein's contain'd all Skils Angelical). **1628** GAULE *Pract. The.* (1629) 24 In him Law and Gospell conspire together; the Law as a closed Gospell; the Gospell as an vnclasped Law. **1825** SCOTT *Talism.* viii, The hood which he wore,.. now unclasped and thrown back for heat. **1856** J. RICHARDSON *Recoll.* I. iii. 69 He was an incessant talker... When once unclasped, it was with difficulty he could again be closed. **1880** L. WALLACE *Ben-Hur* 474 Iras began, toying the while with one of her unclasped bracelets.

un'clasping, *ppl. a.*[1] (UN-[1] 10.)

1640 O. SEDGWICK *Christs Counsell* 174 The impotency.. of an unholding and unclasping memory.

un'clasping, *ppl. a.*[2] (See UNCLASP *v.* 2 b, quot. 1751.)

un'class, *v.* (UN-[2] 6 b.)

1873 MORLEY *Rousseau* I. 108 *note*, 'A bourgeois unclassed by an alliance with a tavern servant';.. but surely Rousseau had unclassed himself long before.

un'classable, *a.* (UN-[1] 7 b.)

1848 RICKMAN *Styles Archit. Eng.* 234 Roslyn chapel.. is certainly unclassable as a whole, being unlike any other building in Great Britain of its age. **1870** H. SPENCER *Psychology* (ed. 2) I. II. i. 148 Mind remains unclassable and therefore unknowable.

un'classed, *ppl. a.* (UN-[1] 8.)

1820 SHELLEY *Prometh. Unb.* III. iv. 195 The man remains.. Equal, unclassed, tribeless, and nationless. **1865** TYLOR *Early Hist. Man.* viii. 203 He would have to leave a large fraction of the whole in an unclassed heap.

un'classic, *a.* (UN-[1] 7.)

1728 POPE *Dunc.* III. 258 Angel of Dulness, sent to scatter round His magic charms o'er all unclassic ground. **1894** *Outing* (U.S.) XXIV. 46/2 It is now known as the unclassic and plebeian Bay de Vache.

un'classical, *a.* (UN-[1] 7.)

1725 BLACKWALL *Sacr. Class.* (1727) I. 76 That it [*sc.* the repetition] is not unclassical but pure, I shall shew by parallel forms of expression in the noblest classics. **1767** S. PATERSON *Another Trav.* I. 350 They are either too classical (You are unclassical) or too illiterate. *c* **1828** ARNOLD in Stanley *Life & Corr.* (1844) I. 50 If the sermons are read, I do not care one farthing if the readers think me the most unclassical writer in the English language. **1871** BLACKIE *Four Phases* i. 11 The Athenian philosopher made a jest of his unclassical nose.

Hence **un'classically** *adv.*

[**1775** ASH.] **1860** J. WHITESIDE *Italy* xvii. 168 As we reach the unclassically-named town of Poggibonsi.

un'classifiable, *a.* (UN-[1] 7 b.)

a **1849** POE *E. B. Browning* Wks. 1865 III. 401 Setting aside.. certain rare commentators..—creatures neither precisely men, women, nor Mary Wollstonecraft's—.. as unclassifiable. **1875** [see next].

un'classified, *ppl. a.* (UN-[1] 8.) Also *absol.* as *sb.*

1865 TYLOR *Early Hist. Man.* i. 12 Our accounts of the culture of the lower races, being mostly unclassified. **1875** WHITNEY *Life Lang.* v. 82 Neglecting the unclassified and perhaps in part unclassifiable residue. **1884** J. TAIT *Mind in Matter* 132 Like the flora and the fauna in nature, miracles are unclassified in the Bible. **1935** *City of Oxford Council Rep.* 1 Mar. 401 It is recommended that the following programme be submitted to the Ministry of Transport ..:—*Bridges... By-passes... Classified Roads... Unclassified Roads.* **1952** *Manch. Guardian Weekly* 14 Feb. 13 My work is unclassified, but the fund out of which I am paid comes from a government agency. **1958** M. KELLY *Christmas Egg* III. 129 The road was lonely, unclassified... He must walk back to A260. **1968** 'J. LE CARRÉ' *Small Town in Germany* v. 72 He's down here collecting the mail... Everything. Classified or Unclassified, it didn't make no difference. **1978** *Country Life* 8 June 1634/3 Of all the track-ways of these Lincolnshire Wolds the most romantic is the Bluestone Heath Road, now an unclassified lane. **1980** D. BLOODWORTH *Trapdoor* xxiii. 143 The file was not unclassified... It was marked Top Secret.

absol. **1972** O. SELA *Bearer Plot* iv. 28 He would swoop off the main roads onto undulating unclassifieds that sometimes were little more than dirt tracks.

un'clay, *v.* (UN-[2] 4 b.)

1655 JER. TAYLOR *Guide Devot.* 144 Oh, end the Strife, And part us, that in Peace I may Unclay My wearied Spirit. [**1706** STEVENS I, *Desembarrar*, to unclay, to undaub.] **1796** C. MARSHALL *Gardening* xx. (1813) 407 Graffs that have clearly taken, unclay and unbind.

un'clayed, *ppl. a.* (UN-[1] 8.)

1883 *Daily News* 26 Sept. 3/4, 600 bags unclayed Manilla [sugar].

uncle ('ʌŋk(ə)l), *sb.* Forms: α. 3-7 vncle (5 wncle), 4- uncle (5-6 oncle). β. 4, 6-8 unkle (vn-) 6-7 unckle (vn, 7 wn-). γ. 4 unkel, 5 vnkel, 6 unkell (vn-), 5-6 vn-, unkil(l, -kyll (5 hunckyl, oncyll, ownkyll, 6 onkill); 5 vn-, uncull, 6 unckall. See also NUNCLE. [a. AF. *uncle*, OF. *uncle*, *oncle* (mod.F. *oncle*, whence G., Da., Sw. *onkel*), = Pr. *oncle*, *avoncle*, Roum. *unchiu*:—L. *avunculus* mother's brother.]

1. a. A brother of one's father or mother; also, an aunt's husband (= uncle-in-law).

α. *c* **1290** *S. Eng. Leg.* I. 20/27 To his vncle he gan go, þe Erchebischop of caunterburi. **1297** R. GLOUC. (Rolls) 1937 þre vnclen is moder adde. *c* **1380** *Sir Ferumb.* 169 þe duk.. drow ys swerd anon, & wolde ys vncle þar-wiþ herte. **1387** TREVISA *Higden* (Rolls) III. 389 Alisaundre exiled dwelled awhile wiþ his uncle in Epirus. **1412-20** LYDG. *Chron. Troy* I. 3751 Iason.. gan his vncle in ful lowe maner First to þanke. **1475** *Bk. Noblesse* (Roxb.) 15 Henry the v[te].. made Thomas Beauford then erle Dorset hys oncle capteyn of yt. *c* **1500** *Melusine* xix. 97 For neuer I shall ete tyl that ye be hanged with your vncle. *c* **1520** BARCLAY *Jugurth* vi. (1557) 6 b, Se that ye worshipe and loue this Jugurth your worthy vncle. **1581** G. PETTIE tr. *Guazzo's Civ. Conv.* III. (1586) 120 b, In families there are the Uncle and the Nephew, the Father in law and the Sonne in law [etc.]. **1653** W. RAMESEY *Astrol. Restored* 109 [This] signifieth.. also the Uncle or Ant of the Querent by the fathers side. **1725** RAMSAY *Gentle Sheph.* v. iii, At last he spak and won, And hopes to be our honest uncle's son. **1756-7** tr. *Keysler's Trav.* (1760) IV. 214 Offering him the immediate payment of a debt due to his uncle. **1818** CRUISE *Digest* (ed. 2) III. 353 If the son, in this case, die without issue, and his uncle enter into the land. **1866** GEO. ELIOT *Felix Holt* i, Your uncle thought I ought to have you to myself in the first hour or two.

β. *c* **1380** WYCLIF *Sel. Wks.* III. 475 How may oure hyȝe prestis.. be grettur worldly lordis þen.. kyngus unklis ande kyngus sonys? **1565** COOPER *Thesaurus*, *Auunculus*, the vnkle on the mothers side. **1584** *Knaresb. Wills* (Surtees) I. 145 Ric. Roundell ther unckle. **1610** HOLLAND *Camden's Brit.* (1637) 696 King Edward the Fifth his Unkle by the mothers side. *a* **1699** LADY HALKETT *Autobiog.* (Camden) 32 Pretending his wife was dead,.. and that her unckle Sir Ralph S. had assured them both of itt. *a* **1727** NEWTON *Chronol. Amended* ii. (1728) 239 Orus, with his mother Isis, .. and unkle Typhon. **1779** JOHNSON *L.P.*, *Pope* Wks. IV. 15 She was obliged to converse only with those from whom her unkle had nothing to fear.

γ. **1387** TREVISA *Higden* (Rolls) IV. 235 Herodias, þat was afterwarde Phelip his wif, þat was Aristobolus his eme and unkel. **1415** SIR T. GREY in *43 Deputy Keeper Public Records* 585 þe Erle of Somerset zowr uncull. **1451** *Paston Lett.* I. 202 On of myn unkyll men.. told it myn unkill. **1472** *Ibid.* III. 41 Item, as for myn ownkyll William, I have spook with hym. **1539** *Cal. Anc. Rec. Dublin* (1889) 407 For as mych as my sayd unkyll ys well willyng. **1540** CROMWELL in Merriman *Life & Lett.* (1902) II. 255 A true copie of your unckall ys testament and last will. **1570** LEVINS *Manip.* 126 An Vnkil, *auunculus*.

b. *uncle-in-law*, the husband of one's aunt.

1561 *Child-Marriages* 3 All the premisses this deponent knowis to be true, bie cause he is Vncle-in-lawe to the said Homfrey. **1667** DUCHESS OF NEWCASTLE *Life Duke of N.* (1886) I. 2 These two brothers were partly bred with Gilbert, Earl of Shrewsbury, their uncle-in-law. **1779** *Mirror* No. 53 ¶8 Among the rest was my uncle-in-law's partner.

c. In allusive use.

In the first two quots. directly from French usage.

1578 H. WOTTON *Courtlie Controv.* 275 Wheras other men accustome to visite their vncle when they determine to take truce for a time with their amorous trauailes. **1611** COTGR. s.v. *Oncle*, He is my neerest friend that fills my bellie; or he is my kindest vncle who doth feed me. **1678** RAY *Prov.* 227 She is one of mine Aunts that made mine Uncle go a begging. **1785** GROSE *Dict. Vulgar T.* s.v., He is gone to visit his uncle, saying of one who leaves his wife soon after marriage.

d. *Welsh uncle* (see later quots.).

1747 T. CARTE *Hist. England* I. 210 Aeddon, who was welsh-uncle to Rydderch, made his escape to the Isle of Man. **1820** SOUTHEY *Wesley* II. 108 He was placed under the care of the husband of his father's first cousin; which remote relationship comes under the comprehensive term of a Welsh Uncle. **1868** FREEMAN *Norm. Conq.* II. App. 645 A 'Welsh uncle', that is the first cousin of a parent.

e. *Dutch uncle* (see quots.).

1838 J. C. NEAL *Charcoal Sk.* 201 If you keep a cutting didoes, I must talk to you both like a Dutch uncle. **1853** *N. & Q.* 1st Ser. VII. 65/2 In some parts of America, when a person has determined to give another a regular lecture, he will often be heard to say, 'I will talk to him like a Dutch uncle'; that is, he shall not escape this time. **1869** *East Anglian* III. 350 There were the squires on the bench, but I took heart, and talked to 'em like a Dutch uncle. **1873** HELPS *Anim. & Mast.* v. 131 Milverton.. began reasoning with the boys; talking to them like a Dutch uncle.. about their cruelty.

f. In B.B.C. Radio: formerly, a male announcer or story-teller for children's programmes. Cf. sense 2 b and AUNTIE b (b).

1923 *Wireless Weekly* 8 Aug. 183/3 The Director of Programmes received me into the actual studio, where he and the other Uncles have so much fun over the Children's Hour. **1981** S. BRIGGS *Those Radio Times* 12/1 Long before the Corporation was called 'Auntie'.. it had dozens of 'aunts' and 'uncles' on its staff. **1985** *Times Lit. Suppl.* 22 Mar. 330/3 Knight began to broadcast.. after the war, becoming extremely popular as Uncle Max on the children's programme *Nature Parliament*.

g. *universal uncle*: see UNIVERSAL *a.* 9 b.

h. A male friend or lover of a child's mother.

1962 *Listener* 31 May 935/2 His mother has never been married, has lived for some years at a time with a series of 'uncles' who have been the fathers of these siblings. **1968** *Ibid.* 1 Aug. 155/2 The play is a simple tale of a boy who, lacking a resident father, grows up under the influence of various temporary 'uncles'.

2. a. Used in addressing or designating one's uncle.

c **1374** CHAUCER *Troylus* II. 210 Nay blame haf I, my vncle, quod she þenne. **1547** EDWARD VI in Ellis *Orig. Lett.* Ser. I. II. 148 Derest Vncle,.. we have at good length vnderstanded.. the good success [etc.]. ? *c* **1570** *Bugbears* v. vii. 97 O good vncle Donatus, ther is cawse I shold love you. **1598** SHAKS. *Merry W.* III. iv. 49 Pray you Vncle, tel Mist. Anne the iest how my Father stole two Geese out of a Pen, good Vnckle. **1640** BROME *Antipodes* III. v, *Beg.* Sir excuse me... *Gal.* Yet good unkle. **1656** STANLEY *Hist. Philos.* Ded., The gratitude of, Dear Uncle, Your most affectionate Nephew. **1700** N. ROUS in *Jrnl. Friends' Hist. Soc.* (1912) IX. 184 With mine and Wifes.. kind respects to Unckle and Aunt Abrams,.. I rest [etc.]. **1793** MRS. INCHBOLD *Midn. Hour* II, Do not be alarmed, uncle; force is seldom used but to her that is willing. **1828** SCOTT *F.M. Perth* xxiii, Uncle, you are a good huntsman. **1850** TENNYSON *In Mem.* lxxxiv, When.. boys of thine Had babbled 'Uncle' on my knee.

b. Used as a form of address to non-relatives, esp. to elderly men (*local* and *U.S.*). Also in senses 1 f, h.

1793 *Gentl. Mag.* Dec. 1083/2 It is common in Cornwall to call all elderly persons Aunt or Uncle, prefixed to their names. **1830** S. P. HOLBROOK *Sketches by Traveller* 111 In many families.. the children are taught to address the older servant as *uncle* or *auntee*, and this is sometimes more than a figure of speech. **1835** J. H. INGRAHAM *South West* II. 241 Nor are planters indifferent to the comfort of their gray-headed slaves... They always address them in a mild and pleasant manner as 'Uncle' or 'Aunty'. **1853** LOWELL *Wks.* (1890) I. 16 Formerly, every New England town had its representative uncle. **1855** KINGSLEY *Westw. Ho!* xx, 'Put this coat on your back, uncle,' says some one. **1859** BARTLETT *Dict. Amer.* (ed. 2) 492 *Uncle*, used in the Middle and Southern States in accosting an elderly colored man. **1876** 'MARK TWAIN' *Tom Sawyer* xxviii. 216 He let's [*sic*] me, and so does his pap's nigger man, Uncle Jake. **1923** *Radio Times* 28 Sept. 11/2 Children's Stories—Uncle Donald and Auntie Betty. **1937** PARTRIDGE *Dict. Slang* 337/1 Her children call him 'Uncle'. **1945** T. RATTIGAN *Love in Idleness* I. 280 Oh, don't call him sir, Michael. Call him—I know—call him Uncle John. **1962** W. FAULKNER *Reivers* ii. 30 His wife.. was Delphine, Grandmother's cook. At that time he was 'Uncle' Ned only to Mother. I mean, she was the one who insisted that all us children.. call him Uncle Ned.

transf. **1847** EMERSON *Repr. Men, Plato* ad fin., Plain old uncle as he [Socrates] was,.. the rumour ran, that [etc.].

c. *Uncle Sam*, the government (or people) of the United States of America.

The history of the expression has been traced by A. Matthews in *Proc. Amer. Antiq. Soc.* XIX. 21-65; see also R. H. Thornton *Amer. Glossary* 916. The suggestion that it arose as a facetious interpretation of the letters U.S. is as old as the first recorded instances, and later statements connecting it with different government officials of the name of Samuel appear to be unfounded.

1813 *Troy Post* 7 Sept. (Matthews), Loss upon loss, and no ill luck stir[r]ing but what lights upon Uncle Sam's shoulders. **1839** N. HAWTHORNE in Longfellow *Life* (1891) I. 334 Uncle Sam is rather despotic as to the disposal of my time. **1850** N. HAWTHORNE *Scarlet L.* Introd. (1852) 3 The thirteen stripes turned vertically,.. thus indicating that a civil.. post of Uncle Sam's government is here established. **1884** *Harper's Mag.* June 48/1 To cheat Uncle Sam in revenue matters is regarded as a.. venial sin.

(*b*) *ellipt. spec.* (the members of) a federal agency.

1849 *Placer Times* (Sacramento, Calif.) 1 Sept., Two Express Lines have been established between our City and San Francisco. Our old Uncle will have to 'stir his stumps' else his 'regular' arrangements will become a *dead letter*. **1950** H. E. GOLDIN *Dict. Amer. Underworld Lingo* 231/1 *Uncle...* (Plural) G-men; agents of the Federal Bureau of Investigation. **1953** W. BURROUGHS *Junkie* x. 98 'He belongs to Uncle, now,' said the [police] captain to my wife as they left the house. **1966** T. PYNCHON *Crying of Lot 49* i. 17 The well-known portrait of Uncle that appears in front of all our post offices. **1971** G. V. HIGGINS *Friends of Eddie Coyle* ii. 14 That's not working for uncle, Eddie. You got to put your whole soul into it. **1978** 'P. MANN' *Steal Big* ii. 8 The nerve I had. Uncle had made me prove it time and again.

d. *Uncle George*, King George III.

1829 MARRYAT *F. Mildmay* iii, We make *uncle George* suffer for the stores.

e. *Uncle Tom Cobleigh* (or *Cobley*) *and all*: a name given to the last of a long list of persons (see quot. *c* 1800 for the ballad alluded to); a whole lot of people.

c **1800** *Widdicombe Fair* in G. Bantock *One Hundred Songs of Eng.* 72 Tom Pearce's old mare doth appear gashly white Wi' Bill Brewer, Jan Stewer, Peter Gurney, Peter Davy, Dan Whiddon, Harry Hawk, old Uncle Tom Cobleigh and all, Old Uncle Tom Cobleigh and all. **1933** E. A. ROBERTSON *Ordinary Families* xiii. 287 When Dru.. repeated to Margaret some gossip about an engagement, Margaret said casually, 'Oh, and to Uncle Tom Cobley an' all, I suppose!' **1941** J. D. CARR *Case of Constant Suicides* iv. 55 They're all here: the Fiscal, and the law-agent.. and Uncle Tom Cobleigh and all. **1963** L. KLEIN *Fabian Tract No. 349* i. 2 We.. are exhorted to pant along behind the industrious Germans, Japanese, Russians, Americans and Uncle Tom Cobley. **1966** *Guardian* 10 Sept. 14/8 It seems clear that a compromise, half-way solution had equally been ruled out by Government, Opposition, economists, press, TV, Uncle Tom Cobleigh and all. **1981** D. BOGGIS *Time to Betray* xxv. 130 Stupid little man, dragging in old Uncle Tom Cobley and all.

f. *Uncle Ned* (Rhyming slang), (*a*) bed (also ellipt. as *uncle*); (*b*) head.

1925 FRASER & GIBBONS *Soldier & Sailor Words* 294 *Uncle Ned*, bed. **1955** F. BROWN *Martians, go Home!* II. iii. 68 Hi *got* to speel or there's no weeping willow for my Uncle Ned. **1964** *Listener* 31 Dec. 1053/1, I have spent an hour fixing the big, loose curls on top of my Uncle Ned. **1974** J. GARDNER *Corner Men* xiv. 194 Get out of that Uncle Ned, slide into your threads, and come down the nick with us. **1982** J. SCOTT *Uprush of Mayhem* x. 105 'You did right, shoving him back in his uncle.'.. Uncle. Uncle Ned, Cockney rhyming slang for bed.

3. *slang.* A pawnbroker.

Usually preceded by a possessive pronoun.

1756 TOLDERVY *Hist. 2 Orphans* IV. 113 The next week carried the new cloaths, which they bought at Bath, to their uncle's (if Humphry's expression may be used). **1796** GROSE *The Olio* 230 A shirt and hose I'd at my uncle's lodg'd. **1807** E. S. BARRETT *Rising Sun* II. 131 The bed-furniture was carefully preserved by my uncle, and when.. I had gained a bed, and money enough to redeem the furniture, I put them up. **1855** THACKERAY *Newcomes* xii, 'Dine in your frock,.. if your dress-coat is in the country.' 'It is at present at an uncle's.' **1869** M. COLLINS *Ivory Gate* II. i. 19 You may want to take it to your uncle, you know, now that your secretaryship is about to be abolished.

4. *to cry* (*holler, say,* etc.) *uncle*, to acknowledge defeat, to cry for mercy. *N. Amer. colloq.*

1918 *Chicago Herald-Examiner* 1 Oct. 11 Sic him Jenny Jinx—make him say 'Uncle'. **1939** *Amer. Speech* XIV. 267 'He hollered "calf rope" or 'He hollered "uncle",' are publishments of his defeat. **1941** B. SCHULBERG *What makes Sammy Run?* vi. 139 Kit was the one who did him some good. 'Okay,' I said. 'I'll cry uncle.' **1962** W. STEGNER *Wolf Willow* III. iii. 237 With good hay land and good range [we can] make this God darned country holler uncle. **1972** D. DELMAN *Sudden Death* v. 122 'Stop it, darling, please.' 'Say uncle.' 'Uncle.' **1980** *Amer. Speech 1976* LI. 281 Most American schoolboys are..familiar with the expression *cry uncle* or *holler uncle*, meaning 'give up in a fight, ask for mercy'. *Uncle* in this expression is surely a folk etymology, and the Irish original of the word is *anacol* (*anacal, anacul*) 'act of protecting; deliverance; mercy, quarter, safety', a verbal noun from the Old Irish verb *aingid* 'protects'... My unscientific sampling of English speakers in Britain a few years ago indicated that *cry uncle* is not familiar in England or Scotland.

5. *appositive* and *Comb.*, as ***uncle devil, father, -figure, -guardian, -marquis; uncle-given*** adj.

1602 SHAKS. *Ham.* II. ii. 393 My Vnckle Father, and Aunt Mother are deceiu'd. **1638** FORD *Fancies* II. ii, Our great uncle-marquis, Disabled from his cradle. **1789** M. MADAN tr. *Persius* II. 292 *note*, The relish or savour of morose uncle-guardians. **1828** *Lights & Shades* I. 27 At the very first uncle-given dinner. **1897** MARY KINGSLEY *W. Africa* 93 Any leg or arm I saw that uncle devil pulling out to place within reach of the crocodiles; **1959** *Listener* 10 Sept. 375/1 To a majority of Americans, Adlai Stevenson is an uncle-figure—'good old Uncle Adlai'. **1975** *Times* 8 Mar. 7/4 Such an uncle-figure as Johnny Carson..on late night television.

Hence **'unclehood**; *rare*$^{-1}$; **'uncle-ish** *a.*

1846 B. BARTON *Select.* (1849) 100 Those five uncles of mine..grew not up to mature uncle-hood. **1928** A. HUXLEY *Point Counter Point* x. 160 An occasional chaste uncle-ish kiss on the forehead. **1981** P. DICKINSON *Seventh Raven* xii. 166 He'd get much more mileage out of seeming friendly and uncle-ish.

'uncle, *v.* [f. prec.]

1. *trans.* To address (one) as uncle.

1593 SHAKS. *Rich. II*, II. iii. 85 Grace me no Grace, nor Vncle me, I am no Traytors Vnckle. **1872** B. TAYLOR in *Life & Lett.* (1884) II. 592, I am 'uncled' from morning till night. **1884** J. T. TROWBRIDGE *Farnell's Folly* I. xix. 196 'Uncle! uncle!' chattered old Carolus,..'don't uncle me!'

†**2.** To cheat or swindle (*of* something). *Obs.*

Perhaps originally implying a pretence of being uncle to the person victimized; but the association with COZEN *v.* and *sb.*, which appears in the quots., makes it also possible that *uncle* is merely a punning variation of *cousin*.

*a***1592** GREENE *Selimus* (1594) H ij, This is some cousoning conicatching crosbiter, that would faine perswade me he knowes me, and so vnder a tence of familiaritie and acquaintance, vncle me of victuals. **1606** *Sir G. Goosecappe* v. i, And Neece tho you have cosind me in this, Ile uncle you yet in an other thing. **1608** DEKKER *Belman of London* Wks. (Grosart) III. 127 If the Cozen be such an Asse to goe into a tauerne, then he is sure to be vnckled.

†**b.** To deprive (an uncle) *of* life. *Obs.*$^{-1}$

1602 CHETTLE *Hoffman* I. (1631) C 3, Vncle, ile vncle thee of thy proud life.

-uncle, *suffix*, representing OF. *-uncle* (*-oncle*) and ultimately L. *-unculus, -uncula*, in a few words, in most of which it retains its diminutive force. The earliest of these is *carbuncle* from the 13–14th cent.; †*portiuncle* appears in the 15th, *caruncle, furuncle, homuncle* in the 17th, *peduncle* in the 18th, and *oratiuncle* in the 19th. New formations without Latin originals are rare, and the suffix has little independent existence though occasionally employed as in the following examples.

1825 BENTHAM *Offic. Apt. Maximized, Indic.* (1830) 71 Not a *reformatiuncle* of his (as Hartley would have called it) did Romilly ever bring forward, that he had not first brought to me. **1875** [see PSEUDONYMUNCLE].

un'clead, *v. Obs.* or *arch.* Also 4 vncleth(e; *pa. t.* 4 vnclede, 5 -cledde, 5–6 -cled; 4–5, 7, 9 unclad; *p.p.* 7 vncled, -clad. [UN-^{2} 4. Cf. MDu. *ontcleden* (*-cleiden*), Du. *ontkleeden*, G. *entkleiden*.]

1. *trans.* To unclothe, undress. Also *refl.*

*a***1300** *Cursor M.* 16339 Pilate..Of his clothes vn-clethes him. *c***1375** *Sc. Leg. Saints* xxx. (*Theodera*) 781 Þe abbot..vncled hyr, as custum was, þe ded body for to wesche. *c***1400** *Rule St. Benet* (Prose) 145 Þe Priores sal hafe hir befor þe auter & vncleth hir of hir seculer clething. **1483** CAXTON *Gold. Leg.* 85 b/1 He dyspoylled and unclad hym and gaf hys clothys unto the bochyers. *c***1520** M. NISBET *Matt.* xxvii. 31 Thai vncled him of the mantil. **1842** TENNYSON *Godiva* 48 Godiva..Unclad herself in haste.

2. *fig.* To divest oneself of; to put off.

1659 W. CHAMBERLAYNE *Pharonnida* I. 44 Argalia thus unclad Amazements dark disguise. *Ibid.* IV. 81 We there unclad All our deform'd misfortunes.

un'clean, *a.* Forms: (see CLEAN *a.*). [OE. *unclǽne*: see UN-^{1} 7 and CLEAN *a.*]

1. Morally impure or defiled; unchaste: **a.** Of persons.

*a***900** CYNEWULF *Crist* 1017 Woruldmonna seo unclæne ȝecynd. *a***1100** *Voc.* in Wr.-Wülcker 308 *Incestus*, unclæne. *c***1325** *Spec. Gy Warw.* 834 For ȝit wole he noht sinne fle: Iwis, vnclene he shal be. **1340–70** *Alex. & Dind.* 636 Þanne schulle ȝe for ȝour sinne soffre paine, For ȝe unclene bi cleped & cleuen in ȝour sinne. *c***1440** *Promp. Parv.* 364/2 Onclene, *immundus, inpurus.* **1490** in *Somerset Med. Wills* (1901) 292 After her deceese, other else that she mary, other leve unclene of her body ayenst the lawes of God. **1526** TINDALE *Eph.* v. 5 No whormonger, other vnclene person, or coveteous person. **1596** DALRYMPLE tr. *Leslie's Hist. Scot.* (S.T.S.) I. 240 Quhen he gathiret his vile, vnhonest, maist jmpure, and vncleine secte. **1667** MILTON *P.L.* IX. 1098 That this new commer, Shame, There sit not, and reproach us as unclean. **1680** *Charac. Town-miss* (Hindley, III) 8 She becomes a Loathsome thing, too unclean to enter into Heaven. **1738** WESLEY *Ps.* v. ii, In Souls unholy and unclean Thou never canst delight. **1755** —— *Jrnl.* (1761) III. 5 The fierce, unclean, brutish, blasphemous Antinomians.

absol. **1382** WYCLIF *Eccl.* ix. 2 Alle thingus euenli comen ..to the goode and to the euele, to the clene and to the vnclene. **1535** COVERDALE *Ibid.*, It goeth..with the good & cleane as with the vncleane. **1569** J. SANFORD tr. *Agrippa's Van. Artes* lviii. 83 b, Sinners with the faithfull,..the vncleane with yͤ cleane.

b. Of thoughts, conduct, etc.

*a***900** CYNEWULF *Crist* 1316 Þær we nu maȝon..ȝeseon on ussum sawlum..unclæne inȝeþoncas. **971** *Blickl. Hom.* 25 Moniȝe men syndon þe..beoþ besmitene mid þem unclænan firen-luste. **1297** R. GLOUC. (Rolls) 7208 Vor prustes mid vnclene honden & mid lechors mod Al isoyled sacrieþ godes fless & is blod. *a***1300** *Cursor M.* 28509, I haf þam wit delt..Wit handling vnhende, kissyng vnclene. **13..** *E.E. Allit. P.* B. 710 Now haf þay skyfted my skyl & scorned natwre, & henttez þem in heþyng an vsage vn-clene. *c***1400** *Prymer* 49 From vnclene þouȝtis, lord, deliuere us! *c***1480** HENRYSON *Test. Cres.* 285 Thus hir leuing vnclene and Lecherous Scho wald returne on me and my Mother. **1526** *Pilgr. Perf.* (W. de W. 1531) 84 b, With elacyon of mynde, or other vycyous and vnclene thoughtes. **1567** *Gude & Godlie B.* (S.T.S.) 1 Then sal thay..cause them to put away baudrie & vnclene sangis. **1605** BACON *Adv. Learn.* I. i. §3 It is mere imposture..to offer to the author of truth the unclean sacrifice of a lie. **1651** [see 2]. **1707** WATTS *Hymn*, '*Vain are the Hopes*' i, Their Hearts by Nature [are] all unclean. **1728** POPE *Dunciad* II. 99 Her servants..List'ning delighted to the jest unclean Of link-boys vile. **1781** COWPER *Tiroc.* 735 If thy table be indeed unclean, Foul with excess, and with discourse obscene. **1889** R. BUCHANAN in *Contemp. Rev.* Dec. 925 Unclean sexual pathology..now threatens the Drama.

2. *unclean spirit*, a wicked spirit; a demon. Also *transf.*

*c***950** *Lindisf. Gosp.* Mark i. 26 Se gast unclænæ..of-eode from him. *c***1000** ÆLFRIC *Gloss.* in Wr.-Wülcker 144 *Spiracula*, unclænra gasta wunungstow. *c***1200** ORMIN 4635 Forr deofell iss unnclene gast, & lufeþþ unnclænnesse. **1382** WYCLIF *Mark* i. 23 In the synagoge of hem was a man in an vnclene spirit. *a***1400** *New Test.* (Paues) Acts v. 16 Hem þat wore traueiled wiþ vnclene spirittes. [**1534** TINDALE *Luke* iv. 33 A man which had a sprete of an vncleane devell.] **1548** UDALL, etc. *Erasm. Par. Matt.* xii. 56 b, Whan the vnclene spirite is gone out of a man. **1651** HOBBES *Leviath.* I. viii. 38 The spirit of man, when it produceth unclean actions, is ordinarily called an unclean spirit. **1727** DE FOE *Syst. Magic.* I. ii. (1840) 53 A cage of devils, and as the text calls them, unclean spirits. **1861** PALEY *Æschylus* (ed. 2) *Supplices* 637 *note*, Hence μιάστωρ became a general term for an unclean spirit, or evil genius. **1870** DICKENS *E. Drood* i, He has to withdraw himself to a lean arm-chair..until he has got the better of this unclean spirit of imitation.

3. Of animals: Regarded as defiled or impure, and *esp.* as unfit to be eaten on that account. Hence also of food.

*c***900** tr. *Baeda's Hist.* I. xxvii. (1890) 80 Mid þy seo æ moniȝ þing bewereð to etanne swa swa unclæne. *a***1000** *Colloq. Ælfric* in Wr.-Wülcker 93 Hwæt ȝif hit unclæne beoþ fixas? Ic utwyrpe þa unclænan ut, & ȝenime me clæne to mete. *a***1300** *Cursor M.* 1960, I warn yow als-sua all be-deine Ete o na best o kind vn-clene. **1382** WYCLIF *Lev.* xi. 8 Ne towche ȝe the careyns, for thei ben vnclene to ȝow. *c***1400** *Destr. Troy* 11185 Let hir bones with baret abide in this aire, As a caren vncleane, for hir curst dedis. **1535** COVERDALE *Hosea* ix. 3 But Ephraim..eateth vncleane thinges amonge the Assirians. **1597** HOOKER *Eccl. Pol.* v. lxviii. §1 They are Dogges, swine, vncleane beasts. **1604** E. G[RIMSTONE] *D'Acosta's Hist. Indies* VII. ii. 497 They hunted..vncleane beasts, as snakes, lizards, locusts and wormes. **1671** MILTON *P.R.* II. 328 Nor mention I Meats by the Law unclean, or offer'd first To Idols. **1796** H. HUNTER tr. *St.-Pierre's Stud. Nat.* (1799) I. 347 Why are those animals pronounced unclean? **1841** LANE *Arab. Nts.* I. 18 The distinctions of clean and unclean meats. **1854** BADHAM *Halieut.* 61 The remarkable Divine interdict obliging the Jews to abstain from certain fish as unclean. **1864** PUSEY *Lect. Daniel* (1876) 322 Eating of unclean food.

b. In general use: Ceremonially impure.

*c***1200** ORMIN 1712 He wass unnclene þohh þatt daȝȝ anan till efenn. *c***1250** *Gen. & Ex.* 1867 Aȝte unclene ne wulde he beren, for he dredde him it sulde him deren. *a***1300** *Cursor M.* 19932 Nu wit sight i haf it sene þat o man-kind es nan vnclene. **1382** WYCLIF *Lev.* xii. 2 She shal be vnclene seuen dayes. *c***1450** *Mirk's Festial* 57 A woman þat was delyuerde of a man-chyld sculd be holden vnclene by þe lawe vii dayes aftyr hur burth. **1535** COVERDALE *Lev.* xi. 38 Whan there is water poured vpon the sede, and afterwarde eny soch deed carcase falleth theron, then shall it be vncleane vnto you. **1630** J. TAYLOR (Water P.) *Jack a Lent* Wks. 119/1, I hold it a conscience to abstaine from flesh-eating in Lent: not that I thinke it to bee vncleane to the cleane. **1643** CARYL *Expos. Job* I. 1326 The uncleanness of the giver renders his gift unclean. **1836** J. H. NEWMAN *Par. Serm.* (ed. 2) II. xxi. 335 The Gentiles were no longer common or unclean. **1855** PUSEY *Doctr. Real Presence* Note S. 429 But if he who is merely unclean..has so fearful a judgment, how much more will he, who is in sin,..draw upon himself a more dreadful punishment!

transf. **1880** MISS BRADDON *Just as I am* xxvii, Avonmore is one of the genteelest towns in England. There is positively nothing common or unclean in it.

4. Not physically clean; dirty, filthy, foul. Of the tongue: Coated with fur.

*a***1250** *Owl & Night.* 91 Þu art lodlich & vnclene Bi þine neste ich hit mene. **1297** R. GLOUC. (Rolls) 8969 Is þis wel ido þat þou þes vnclene limes handlest & kust so? **1390** GOWER *Conf.* I. 179 For who so wole his handes lime, Thei mosten be the more unclene. *a***1400** *Octavian* 885 Clement broght forthe schylde and spere, That were uncomely for to were, Alle sutty, blakk, and unclene. **1440** J. SHIRLEY *Dethe K. James* (1818) 17 The Kyng..cryed..that they shuld cume with shettes, and drawe hym up owt of that uncleyne place of the privay. **1552** HULOET, Vncleane,..Loke in filthy and fowle. **1600** SHAKS. *A.Y.L.* III. iii. 36 To cast away honestie vppon a foule slut, were to put good meate into an vncleane dish. **1609** DEKKER *Gull's Horn-bk.* iii. 14 To carry away all noisome filth that is swept out of vncleane corners. **1683** BURNET tr. *More's Utopia* 92 Nor do they suffer any thing that is foul or unclean to be brought within their Towns. **1800** *Med. Jrnl.* IV. 423 As soon as they see an unclean tongue, an emetic is pronounced unquestionably necessary. **1864** HAZLITT in *E.P.P.* III. 131 The moist and unclean thumbs of a wide circle of readers. **1898** *Westm. Gaz.* 12 May 5/2 A common way of introducing it to the system is by the use of an unclean instrument.

absol. **1382** WYCLIF *Ecclus.* xxxiv. 4 Of the vnclene what shal ben clensid?

†**b.** Of air or smells: Foul, impure. *Obs.*

*c***1400** *Destr. Troy* 1639 The clowdes hom clede in vnclene ayre. *c***1440** *Pallad. on Husb.* I. 35 Al this is preef of holsum aier and clene, And ther as is contrair is aier vnclene. *Ibid.* IV. 971 From bathes aliene, vnclene odure,..auyse Thee wel to been.

c. Of land: Foul with weeds, etc. *rare*$^{-1}$.

*c***1440** *Pallad. on Husb.* II. 74 The lond vnclene al doluen up mot be, Of rootis, fern, & weed, to mak hit fre.

d. Of fish: In an unhealthy or unwholesome condition.

1861 *Act 24–5 Vict.* c. 109 §14 No Person shall..wilfully take any unclean or unseasonable Salmon. **1883** *Standard* 13 Jan. 3/6 Summoned for being in the possession of five unclean salmon.

un'cleanable, *a.* (UN-^{1} 7 b.)

1724 SWIFT *Blunders & Misfort. Quilca* Wks. 1841 II. 78/2 The empty bottles all uncleanable.

un'cleaned, *ppl. a.* (UN-^{1} 8.)

1854 MRS. GASKELL *North & South* (1855) I. xiii. 157 The uncleaned corners of the room. **1859** R. F. BURTON *Centr. Afr.* in *Jrnl. Geog. Soc.* XXIX. 437 The Americans exported the gum uncleaned, because the operation is better performed at Salem. **1902** *Munsey's Mag.* XXVI. 492/1 Should father find the tables and counter and windows uncleaned, my back would suffer.

un'cleanliness. [f. next + -NESS. Cf. MDu. *onclein-, oncleenlijcheit.*]

1. Lack of moral cleanness; moral impurity.

1509 BARCLAY *Shyp of Folys* (1570) 238 The newe disguises hath..come to Englande, and eche vnclenlynes Doth leade vs wretches. **1540** HYRDE tr. *Vives' Instr. Chr. Wom.* Pref. A iv b, I wolde not fall in to any vnclenlynes, which were the grettest shame that can be, for hym that shulde be a maister of chastitie. **1603** SHAKS. *Meas. for M.* II. i. 82 My wife..might haue bin accus'd in fornication, adultery, and all vncleanlinesse there.

2. Want of physical cleanliness.

1542 UDALL *Erasm. Apoph.* 142 b, Beeyng chidden, for yͭ he was a goer into places full of..vnclenelynesse. **1598** FLORIO, *Immonditia*, vnclenlines, filthines. **1722** *Lond. Gaz.* No. 6057/1 The Poverty and Uncleanliness of the Parents. **1802** MRS. SHERWOOD *Susan Gray* 18 However poor you may be, there can be no necessity for uncleanliness. **1859** R. F. BURTON *Centr. Afr.* in *Jrnl. Geog. Soc.* XXIX. 417 The village..is not only healthier,..despite its uncleanliness, but is also more comfortable. **1899** *Allbutt's Syst. Med.* VIII. 747 Personal uncleanliness is a powerful general cause [of Acnitis].

un'cleanly, *a.* [OE. *unclǽnlic*: see UN-^{1} 7 and CLEANLY *a.* Cf. MDu. *oncleinlijc, oncleenlijc* foul, dirty.]

1. Morally or spiritually impure.

*c***950** *Rit. Eccl. Dunelm.* (Surtees) 110 *Contactus inlicitorum fugat*, cunnvnga þa vnclænlico ȝifliæ. **1340** *Ayenb.* 42 Ich clepie onclenlich: huanne þe seruises byeþ y-do uor onclenliche cause. **1526** TINDALE *2 Pet.* ii. 7 Lot vexed with the vnclenly conversacion off the wicked. **1548** UDALL, etc. *Erasm. Par. Acts* xii. 45 b, And princes on the other parte flatter the people, exhibitinge vnto them shewes to gase vpon, and vncleanly playes. **1598** TOFTE *Alba* Div. Poems (1880) 131 Soyled with beastly Thoughts vncleanly gore. **1604** SHAKS. *Oth.* III. iii. 139 Who ha's that breast so pure, Wherein vncleanly Apprehensions Keepe Leetes, and Law-dayes. **1710** ADDISON *Tatler* No. 224 ¶8, I cannot excuse my fellow-Labourers for admitting into their Papers several uncleanly Advertisements. **1788** V. KNOX *Winter Even.* li. (1790) II. 368 He pursues his subject so far, as frequently to lead his reader to uncleanly scenes. **1871** FARRAR *Witn. Hist.* iv. 138 Yet there was a needless and uncleanly abjectness in several of his precepts.

2. Lacking in physical cleanness; dirty, foul, filthy.

1398 TREVISA *Barth. De P.R.* XVII. xi. (1495) 609 Men that must nedes passe by stynkyng places other vnclenly rotyn places. **1502** ARNOLDE *Chron.* 108 Item that many of the priestis and clerkis often were foule and unclenly surplesis. **1548** ELYOT, *Incultus*, vncleanly apparaylyng, contrary to *Cultus*; negligence in apparaylyng. **1595** SHAKS. *John* IV. iii. 112 Th' vncleanly savours of a Slaughter-house. **1604** JAS. I. *Counterbl. to Tobacco* (Arb.) 100 The vncleanly and adust constitution of their bodies. **1670** CLARENDON *Ess.* Tracts (1727) 173 This uncomely and uncleanly wardrobe. **1756** C. LUCAS *Ess. Waters* III. 261 Who is there so uncleanly..as to wash his feet in the water used by another? **1805** *Med. Jrnl.* XIV. 340 The crouded and uncleanly parts of the town. **1849** ROCK *Ch. of Fathers* I. ii. 188 Long hair on a clergyman, besides being uncleanly, is quite against the canons of the Church. **1896** KIPLING *Seven Seas, The King* iii, By sleight of sword we may not win, But scuffle 'mid uncleanly smoke Of arquebus and culverin.

un'cleanly, *adv.* [OE. *unclǽnlíce*: see UN-[1] 11 and CLEANLY *adv.*] In an unclean manner; foully, filthily.

c **1000** ÆLFRIC *Hom.* I. 432 We wilniað mid urum hlaforde clænlice sweltan, swiðor ðonne unclænlice mid eow lybban. **1583** BABINGTON *Commandm.* (1590) 178 Wee walke and talke idlely, vainly, vncleanly, and vngodlily. **1584** COGAN *Haven Health* 262 Much people in small roume, liuing vncleanly and sluttishly. **1611** COTGR., *Impurement*, impurely, foulely, filthily, vncleanely. **1621** BURTON *Anat. Mel.* I. ii. II. v. (1651) 83 The inhabitants are slovens, and the streets uncleanly kept. **1727** BAILEY (vol. II), *Uncleanly*, filthily.

un'cleanness. [OE. *unclǽnnes*, f. *unclǽne* UNCLEAN *a.* Cf. CLEANNESS.]

1. The quality or state of being morally or spiritually unclean; moral impurity; an instance of this.

c **897** K. ÆLFRED *Gregory's Past. C.* xiii. 75 Se reccere sceal bion simle clæne on his ȝeðohte, ðætte nan unclænnes hine ne besmite. *c* **1000** *Ags. Gosp.* Matt. xxiii. 25 ðe synt innan fulle reaflaces and unclænnysse. *a* **1100** in Napier *O.E. Glosses* I. 4225 *Lascivæ obscenitatis*, wrænre unclænnysse. *c* **1200** ORMIN 2168 Swa summ þatt laþe maȝȝdenn iss þat sekeþþ unnclænnesse. **1297** R. GLOUC. (Rolls) 8949 Vor me ne miȝte hire neuere ise vnclannesse [*v.r.* vnclennysse] do ene. **1340** *Ayenb.* 203 Uoule wordes þet wendeþ to ribaudye and to onclennesse. **1382** WYCLIF *2 Pet.* ii. 20 Men forsakinge the defoulinges, or vnclennesses, of the world. **1411–2** HOCCLEVE *De Reg. Princ.* 3724 Natheles eschued he þe taast Of vnclennesse, and kepte his body chaast. *c* **1450** CAPGRAVE *Life St. Aug.* xxiv. 33 Sche defouled neuer hir lippis with no vnclennesse. **1526** *Pilgr. Perf.* (W. de W. 1531) 90 b, Scurrilite or spekynge of fylthy wordes, vnclenness, moche speche or many wordes. **1577** HOLINSHED *Chron.* II. 340/2 Diuers of those..myghte haply fall into moste horrible vncleannesse. **1611** BIBLE *Ezek.* xxxvi. 29, I wil also saue you from all your vncleannesses. **1643** MILTON *Divorce* 16 Let him not put her away for the meer surmise of Judaicall uncleannes. **1714** BERKELEY *Serm.* Wks. 1871 IV. 606 Their Sacred Rites were polluted with acts of uncleanness and debauchery. **1748** SMOLLETT *R. Random* vii, There being no scandal equal to that of uncleanness. **1865** C. J. VAUGHAN *Plain Words* iv. (1866) 70 Still is the living fountain open for all sin and all uncleanness.

2. Physical impurity; filthiness, foulness; squalor.

c **950** *Rit. Eccl. Dunelm.* (Surtees) 121 Svæ hvæd in hvsvm ..þas yð eft astræȝde beværle vnclænnisse [L. *careat immunditia*]. *a* **1100** in Napier *O.E. Glosses* I. 4455 *Olidos squalores*, fule unclænnessa. **1390** GOWER *Conf.* III. 100 The Splen doth him to lawhe and pleie, Whan al unclennesse is aweie. **1487** *Rolls of Parlt.* VI. 391/1 To great hurt and disease of the Kyngs Leige People..goyng..in the said Stretis and Suburbes, and also grete unclenness of the same. **1534** *Act 26 Hen. VIII*, c. 8 Vacant groundes..replenisshed with muche vncleanes & filth to the great annusance of the said inhabitantes. **1598** GRENEWEY *Tacitus, Ann.* XII. xi. (1622) 172 The horse-men..were put to flight..by reason of the difficulties and vncleannesse of the place. **1663** COWLEY *Ess. in Verse & Pr.* viii, Yet the very sight of Uncleanness is loathsome to the Cleanly.

un'cleansable, *a. rare*[-0]. (UN-[1] 7 b.)

1483 *Cath. Angl.* 66/1 Vn Clenceabylle, *jnexpiabilis, jnpurgabilis*.

un'cleanse, *v.* [UN-[2] 3; cf. OE. *unclǽnsian*.] *trans.* To make (or declare) unclean.

1585 T. WASHINGTON tr. *Nicholay's Voy.* IV. ii. 115 No drop of the bloud should fall into the water, least the same shuld therby be polluted and vncleansed. **1872** J. G. MURPHY *Comm., Lev.* xiv. 7 As the priest uncleanses, that is, pronounces unclean, the leper.

un'cleansed, *ppl. a.* [UN-[1] 8.] Not cleansed or made clean.

c **897** K. ÆLFRED *Gregory's Past. C.* vii. 51 Ðylæs ænig unclænsod dorste on swa micelne haliȝdom fon ðære clænan ðeȝnenga ðæs sacerdhades. *c* **1200** ORMIN 10617 þatt all follc wass unnclennsedd Off þatt missdede þatt wass don þurrh Adam & þurrh Eve. **1439** *Rolls Parlt.* V. 32/1 Eny such Espiceries ungarbeled and unclensyd. **1467** in *Eng. Gilds* (1870) 385 That no blode putte be vnclensyd ouer a day and a night. **1549** COVERDALE, etc. *Erasm. Par. 1 Cor.* xi. 32 b, He without reuerence, and with an vnclensed conscience presumed to come vnto so great a misterie. **1555** EDEN *Decades* (Arb.) 268 It is sould vnclensed or vnpurged. **1632** SHERWOOD, Uncleansed, *non nettoyé*. **1821** SCOTT *Kenilw.* xxxi, We forgive your audacity, and your uncleansed boots withal. **1886** *Encycl. Brit.* XXI. 712/1 The imperfectly cleansed sewage and the wholly uncleansed surplus.

Hence **un'cleansedness.**

1622 W. WHATELY *God's Husb.* II. 122 You would not suffer your selfe-loue to hinder you from taking notice of your vncleansednesse.

un'clear, *a.* [UN-[1] 7. Cf. W.Fris. *ûn-*, *onklear* (at variance), MDu. *onclaer* (*oncleer*), Du. *onklaar*, MLG. *unklâr*, G. *unklar*, ON. *úklárr* (Norw. *uklaar*, Da. *uklar*, Sw. *oklar*).]

1. Not clear or distinct; not easy to understand; obscure, dark.

13.. *E.E. Allit. P.* C. 307, I calde & þou knew myn vncler steuen. ?*a* **1500** *Chester Pl.* XVI. 279 But my might in this manere Will I not proue,..my cause unclear Were then, in good fay. *a* **1513** FABYAN *Chron.* 2 Ryght mysty storyes, doughtfull and vnclere. **1611** TOURNEUR *Ath. Trag.* IV. iii, The time, the place, All circumstances argue that uncleare. **1678** SIR G. MACKENZIE *Crim. Laws Scot.* II. xxix. §ii. (1699) 277 It were very hard upon testimonies, that have so unclear a *causa scientiæ*.., to take a way a mans life. **1798** *Monthly Mag.* VI. 99 The mythological allusions in the 10th, 11th and 12th verses are unclear. **1828** PUSEY *Hist. Eng.* I. p. xiv, To fix the stamp of misconception upon every thing else which is unclear in the work. **1884** LD. COLERIDGE in *Law Times Rep.* L. 297/2 That these otherwise clear and plain words are made doubtful and unclear by the 3rd clause of this section.

b. Not clear in understanding, perception, or statement; confused.

c **1430** LYDG. *Min. Poems* (Percy Soc.) 27 A philosophre.. Had a frend that somwhat was aged, In suche tymes as wyttes wex uncler. **1734** LD. HERVEY *Mem. Geo. II* (1848) I. 324 From having a most unclear head..he was absolutely useless to his brother. **1828** PUSEY *Hist. Enq.* I. 142 The unsystematic and unclear mind of his disciple. **1885** *Century Mag.* XXXI. 276 So unclear in their statements that we can make nothing of them.

c. Of persons: Uncertain, doubtful (about something).

1671 [R. MACWARD] *True Nonconf.* 172 If you be still unclear, answere this demand with your self in sobriety. **1715** WODROW *Corr.* (1843) II. 94 The whole brethren present seemed very unclear as to the abjuration. **1886** SIR J. PAGET *Let.* 7 Aug. in *Mem.* vi. 362, I am unclear as to their [*sc.* certain patients'] names.

2. Not clear *of*, not free from, fault or blame.

a **1400** *Pistill of Susan* 306 Nou schal þi concience be knowen, þat euer was vnclere. **1426** AUDELAY *Poems* 13 Thai are the lanternys of lyf..Bot thai be caȝt with covetyse with conscions unclere. **1607** TOURNEUR *Rev. Trag.* II. Divb, I haue great sins; I must haue daies..To lift 'em out, and not to die vncleere.

3. Not clear or bright; dark, thick.

c **1400** *Anturs of Arth.* x, Al glowed as a glede þe goste þere ho glides, Vmbeclipped him with a cloude, of cle[th]yng vnclere. **1527** ANDREW *Brunswyke's Distyll. Waters* Bij, Lyquor or sape, which ye wyl puryfye from all trowblous and unclere substaunces. **1535** COVERDALE *Esther* xi. 8 Ye same daye was full of darcknes & very vncleare, full of trouble & anguysh. **1594** CAREW *Tasso* (1881) 80 Sometimes the Sun shines through white cloud vncleere.

fig. *c* **1440** CAPGRAVE *Life St. Kath.* v. 1207 Fro al onclennesse Of lust and filthe, and fro that loue on-clere Whiche þei calle letcherie. **1639** G. DANIEL *Ecclus.* xvii. 80 Those Horrid Crimes of Mortalls Shall appeare Vgly and Monstrous, vile, deform'd, vncleare.

un'cleared, *ppl. a.* [UN-[1] 8.]

1. Not cleared off or settled; undischarged.

1637 RUTHERFORD *Lett.* (1664) 132 When he & I fall in reckoning, we are both behinde,..& so marches lie still unrid & counts uncleared betwixt us. **172.** RAMSAY *Evergreen* Gloss., *Unquit*, uncleared or unpaid.

2. Not cleared or freed from something which encumbers; *esp.* not cleared of trees.

1772 COOK *Voy.* I. v. (1773) 60 There was neither gnat nor musquito,..which perhaps is more than can be said of any other uncleared country. **1805** R. W. DICKSON *Pract. Agric.* I. 391 The water..is conveyed in a rut perpetually descending along the whole line of the uncleared moss. **1822** J. FLINT *Lett. Amer.* 239 In the uncleared woods, which are not suitable pastures for sheep. **1829** TYTLER *Hist. Scot.* (1864) I. 234 Savage animals abounded as much in Scotland as in the other uncleared and wooded regions of northern Europe. **1880** J. C. CRAWFORD *N. Zealand & Australia* 27 The whole distance traversed..was through dense and uncleared forest.

3. Not freed from the imputation of guilt.

1724 SAVAGE *Sir T. Overbury* IV. i. 35 To fly, wou'd be, to leave my Fame uncleár'd. **1903** *Westm. Gaz.* 26 Jan. 8/2 Were the Crown to..release the prisoner, he would for ever remain an 'uncleared' man.

4. Not cleared *up*; not removed or explained.

1802–12 BENTHAM *Ration. Judic. Evid.* (1827) II. 405 A repugnancy, which, for want of cross-examination, remains uncleared up. **1861** [F. W. ROBINSON] *Under the Spell* III. 237 That would necessitate another long night of suspense, with doubts 'uncleared'.

5. Not freed from impurities; not made clear or transparent.

1837 M. DONOVAN *Dom. Econ.* II. 343 It appears to me that uncleared coffee has a less agreeable taste than the same quality if transparent.

un'clearly, *adv.* (UN-[1] 11.)

1844 DARWIN in *Life & Lett.* (1887) II. 29 If I had seen how hypothetical [is] the little, which I have unclearly written, I would not [etc.]. **1875** WHITNEY *Life Lang.* xv. 317 The germs of all the most important modern doctrines, ..but unclearly apprehended.

un'clearness. [f. UNCLEAR *a.*] Lack of clearness; obscurity.

a **1658** DURHAM *Comm. Rev.* xvii. (1660) 665 From this unclearnesse it ariseth, that it is hotly disputed. *a* **1718** PENN *Tracts* Wks. 1726 I. 748 The Voluminousness of the Books is no small Token of the Unclearness of the Writers. **1811–31** BENTHAM *Logic* Wks. 1843 VIII. 242/2 Where unclearness (why not unclearness as well as uncleanness) has place in a discourse. **1842** PUSEY *Crisis Eng. Ch.* 51 It is no disrespect to speak of the unclearness or narrowness of a system. **1881** W. R. SMITH *Old Test. in the Jew. Ch.* v. 29 This unclearness of view rests upon an error.

un'cleavable, *a.* (UN-[1] 7 b.)

1839 URE *Dict. Arts*, etc. 744 Opal, or uncleavable quartz. **1855** *Orr's Circ. Sci., Geol.*, etc. 514 Uncleavable Staphyline Malachite.

un'cleave, *v.* [UN-[2] 7.] *intr.* To become unfastened or detached. So **un'cleaving** *vbl. sb.*

1596 THOMAS *Dict.* (1606), *Deglutinatio*, an vncleauing or vngluing. **1648** GAGE *West Ind.* xii. 45 Which did glew so strong, that it scarce ever uncleaved again.

un'cleaved, *ppl. a.* (UN-[1] 8.)

1882 GEIKIE *Text-bk. Geol.* IV. vi. 522 Fragments of cleaved rocks in an uncleaved conglomerate.

un'cleft, *ppl. a.* (UN-[1] 8 b. Cf. Du. *ongekliefd*.)

1611 COTGR., *Bois de brin*, round, or vncleft-small-wood. **1647** HEXHAM I, Vncleft, *ongedeylt*. [Also in later Dicts.]

†**un'clement**, *a. Obs.* [UN-[1] 7 and 5 b.] = INCLEMENT *a.*

1598 FLORIO, *Incleménte*,..mercilesse, sterne, fell, vnclement. **1611** COTGR., *Inclement*, vnclement; rigorous, austere. **1751** YOUNG *Nt. Th.* III. 80 Those few [buds which] our noxious fate unblasted leaves, In this unclement [**1742** inclement] clime of human life.

un'clench, *v.* [UN-[2] 3. Cf. UNCLINCH *v.*]

1. *trans.* To undo the clenching of (bars, etc.).

1340–70 *Alisaunder* 1172 Hee unclosed þe caue, unclainte þe barres. **1775** ASH, *Unclench*,..to raise the point of a bended nail. **1825** [see UNCLENCHING *vbl. sb.*].

2. To relax or open (the clenched hand, a grip or clutch, etc.).

[**1775** ASH.] **1816** *Monthly Mag.* XLI. 143 Nor dares unclench the hand of her relief. **1868** BROWNING *Ring & Bk.* x. 600 Revenge..would pluck pang forth, but unclench No gripe in the act, let fall no money-piece. **1888** 'J. S. WINTER' *Bootle's Childr.* vii, So he stood there clenching and unclenching his hands,..the very picture of misery.

fig. **1839** BAILEY *Festus, L'Envoi* 361 God was with him; and bade old Time, to the youth, Unclench his heart.

b. To cause to relax; to force open.

1793 *Minstrel* III. 70, I flew on the wretch who held him, unclenched his grasping hand from the throat of my darling. **1841** DICKENS *Barn. Rudge* lxxi, 'We have time for no more of this,' cried the man, unclenching her hands, and throwing her roughly off. **1888** G. E. POST in *Centen. Conf. Missions* I. 323 A grasp of iron which the crusaders could not unclench.

c. *refl.* and *absol.* Of the hand: To relax from a clenched state.

[**1755** JOHNSON.] **1900** *Daily News* 11 Oct. 3/1 The nervous hand, clenching and unclenching as his passions swayed him. **1901** MRS. E. L. VOYNICH *Jack Raymond* 87 He let his hand fall by his side, and unclench itself slowly.

3. *trans.* To loosen from a grasp or hold.

1860 FARRAR *Orig. Lang.* (1865) 2 Her lessons..have been unclenched by sheer labour from the granite hand of nature. **1871** R. ELLIS *Catullus* xxv. 9 Unglue the nails adroit to steal, unclench the spoil.

Hence **un'clenching** *vbl. sb.*

[**1775** ASH.] **1825** SCOTT *Betrothed* Concl., Hasten thy unclenching and undoing of rivets.

un'clergiable, *a.* (UN-[1] 7 b.)

1802–12 BENTHAM *Ration. Judic. Evid.* (1827) III. 556 In the penal branch, in cases of felony unclergyable and clergyable. **1819** MACDONALD in *Rep. fr. Comm., Crim. Laws* VIII. 49 The Black Act is full of unclergyable felonies.

un'clergy, *v. rare*[-1]. (UN-[2] 6 b.)

1695 HICKERINGILL *Lay-Clergy* Wks. 1716 I. 348 Till Holy Church was pleased to Depose, Disrobe, and unclergy the Traytor or Murderer.

un'clerical, *a.* [UN-[1] 7.] Not appropriate to, or characteristic of, the clergy or a clergyman.

1762 FOOTE *Orator* I. Wks. 1799 I. 201 Many individuals ..are obliged to have recourse to very unclerical professions for the support of themselves and families. **1788** V. KNOX *Winter Even.* (1790) II. xiii. 88, I have no doubt but that it is one reason why many clergymen are seen to take delight in unclerical occupations. **1848** THACKERAY *Van. Fair* xxxiv, I am a martyr to duty and to your odious unclerical habit of hunting. **1865** MRS. WHITNEY *Gayworthys* ii, A very unclerical gesture of—to say the least—impatience.

Hence **un'clerically** *adv.*

1883 *Harper's Mag.* June 5/2 The..canons unclerically.. fell upon him.

un'clerklike, *a.* (UN-[1] 7 c.)

1647 JER. TAYLOR *Lib. Proph.* vi. 118 Such an emendation as is a plain contradiction to the sense, and that so un-clerk-like.

un'clerkly, *a.* (UN-[1] 7.)

1875 BLACKMORE *Alice Lorraine* II. i. 4 This unclerkly clerk had a good supper. **1895** *Athenæum* 4 May 567/2 The manuscript..was a very unclerkly one.

un'clerkly, *adv.* (UN-[1] 11.)

1531 S. VAUGHAN in Ellis *Orig. Lett.* Ser. III. II. 208 You wrot that the answer whiche he made to the Chancellour was unclerkly done.

'uncleship. [f. UNCLE *sb.* + -SHIP.] The state or condition of being an uncle; the relationship of an uncle.

1742 RICHARDSON *Pamela* IV. 410 Must you, my Lord,.. add to my Plagues, if I have any? Is this your Uncleship? **1826** LAMB *Elia* II. *Wedding*, I feel a sort of cousinhood, or uncleship, for the season. **1827** SOUTHEY *Lett.* (1856) IV. 51 And how, Mr. Bedford, do you feel yourself under the honours of uncleship? **1881** *Athenæum* 24 Dec. 844/1 She was a niece of that unlucky General..whose uncleship bribed Southey into omitting a sentence in his 'Peninsular War'.

Uncle Tom. orig. *U.S.* [UNCLE *sb.* 2 b.] The name of the hero of *Uncle Tom's Cabin*, a novel (1851–2) by Harriet Beecher Stowe, used allusively for a Black man who is submissively loyal or servile to White men. Also *transf.* and in extended use.

1922 [see NEW NEGRO, NEW NEGRO]. **1942, 1960** [see *handkerchief-head* s.v. HANDKERCHIEF b]. **1971** *Guardian* 15 July 3/1 Arafat was always attacked by the Marxist-orientated militants as being a Palestinian 'Uncle Tom', neither sufficiently radical or violent. **1972** M. J. BOSSE *Incident at Naha* i. 37 Some people consider him an Uncle Tom because he doesn't study Afro-American culture. **1975** M. BRADBURY *History Man* v. 84 The girl I'm living with.. says I have a slave mentality... She says I'm an Uncle Tom. **1977** *New Yorker* 22 Aug. 66/3 Pryor goes through his part pop-eyed, playing Uncle Tom for Uncle Toms. **1978**

Church Times 24 Feb. 2/4 Many parishes do have a youngster on the PCC, but... It's only tokenism. The youngsters are 'Uncle Toms', in a way. **1981** *Bull. Amer. Acad. Arts & Sci.* May 41 Uncle Tom's virtues as a worker change when the vices of his condition have to go.

attrib. **1953** BERREY & VAN DEN BARK *Amer. Thes. Slang* (1954) §579/2 '*Straight jazz*',.. schmaltz,.. unadulterated corn, Uncle Tom music. **1959** 'F. NEWTON' *Jazz Scene* v. 88 The savage hostility to 'Uncle Tom' musicians, which for the first time split the community of jazz players. **1960** [see JIM CROW[1], JIM-CROW, JIM CROW 3]. **1971** *Black Scholar* Dec. 20 The harshest discrimination that I have encountered *in the political arena* is anti-feminism—from both males and brainwashed 'Uncle Tom' females. **1978** G. GREENE *Human Factor* III. iii. 127 Been to the African University in the Transvaal where Uncle Tom professors always produce dangerous students. **1979** *Guardian* 14 Apr. 8/8 You got an Uncle Tom figure there in your book?.. You know, kinda creepy black always trying to ingratiate himself with the white folks.

Hence **Uncle Tom** *v. intr.*, to act in a manner characteristic of an Uncle Tom; also with *it*; **Uncle Tom(m)ery, Uncle Tom(m)ing** *vbl. sb.*, **Uncle Tom(m)ish,** *a.*, **Uncle Tom(m)ism.**

1937 Uncle Tomism [see NIGGER *sb.* 1]. **1944** C. HIMES *Black on Black* (1973) 198 Here come a big Uncle Tomish lookin' cat in starched overalls. **1947** S. LEWIS *Kingsblood Royal* x. 52 Why, you gold-digging, uncle-tomming, old, black he-courtesan! **1950** PATTERSON & CONRAD *Scottsboro Boy* III. iv. 219 The prisoners clowned for the white folks—the guards, the prison heads, and their families. It looked like a lot of Uncle Tom-ing to me, and I didn't enjoy seeing whites laugh at the coloured guys' pranks. **1960** *New Left Rev.* Nov.-Dec. 49/1 Armstrong's clowning is just Depressing. It isn't that he 'uncle toms' but that the act is so automatic and lifeless. **1961** *Guardian* 1 Dec. 6/5 The Uncle-Tommish innocence of the.. Negro. **1967** *Listener* 23 Feb. 264/2 Not all Jews will like it, though. One of my acquaintance finds it patronizing and demeaning, the Jewish equivalent of Uncle Tommism. **1967** *Punch* 9 Aug. 210 An obligation.. applies constantly to all underdog groups, constantly tempted by rewards to uncle-tom, to pull the forelock. **1968** *New Yorker* 17 Aug. 21 The guests will be arriving any minute now. Please, Amanda, try to Uncle Tom it a little just for tonight. **1972** *Guardian* 21 Oct. 9/2 The young black studies' teacher.. was striking out against Uncle Tommery. **1976** *Gramophone* Feb. 1321/2 Now today it has almost the opposite effect from what was intended. Many blacks relate it to the era of Uncle Tom-ism. **1979** *N.Y. Times* 12 Feb. B13/1 To tell women that if they just behave nicer, if they shuffle and Uncle Tom a little more, that they will be more successful, is simply not accurate. **1981** *Cape Argus Mag.* 24 Oct. 2/2 With.. that substantial brush of Uncle Tommery with which his opponents have tarred him, Dr Cedric [Phatudi] is a walking.. paradox... He has none of the stridency of a Chief Buthelezi,.. or the bombast of a Matanzima.

un'clever, *a.* (UN-[1] 7.)

Also, in recent use, *uncleverly, uncleverness.*

[**1775** ASH.] **1870** *Daily News* 23 Dec., Those garments.. which her lazy or unclever fingers do not care to preserve tidy. **1890** SARA J. DUNCAN *Social Depart.* 112 We felt most clumsy and bungling and unclever.

un'clew, un'clue, *v.* [UN-[2] 3.]

1. *trans.* To unwind, undo; *fig.* to ruin.

1607 SHAKS. *Timon* I. i. 167 If I should pay you for't as 'tis extold, It would vnclew me quite. *c* **1645** HOWELL *Lett.* IV. Ded., They [*sc.* letters] can the Cabinets of Kings unscrue, And hardest intricacies of State unclue. **1654** E. JOHNSON *Wonder-wrkg. Provid.* 221 With watry tears unclued we will be, From creature-comforts. **1855** SINGLETON *Virgil* II. 72 Dædalus himself The cheats and windings of the dome unclewed.

refl. **1622** MABBE tr. *Aleman's Guzman d'Alf.* I. (To Vulgar), Who is he, that can be so happy, as to vnclue himselfe from this Labyrinth?

2. To let down the clews or lower ends of (a sail).

1855 SINGLETON *Virgil* I. 384 Take your seats upon the banks; Unclew the sails with speed. **1899** *Atlantic Monthly* Aug. 197 The sailboat.. lay alongside the wooden pier, with ballast stowed amidships and her mutton-ham unclewed.

'unclify, *v.* [f. UNCLE *sb.*] *trans.* To make an uncle of.

1799 LAMB *Let. to Southey* 21 Jan., Did Lord Falkland die before Worcester fight? In that case I must make bold to unclify some other nobleman.

un'climbable, *a.* (UN-[1] 7 b.)

In frequent use from *c* 1880.

1533 BELLENDEN *Livy* v. xv. (S.T.S.) II. 199 At þe fute of þe montanis, quhilkis stude sa hie agane his þat þai apperit vnclymabil. **1827** *Lincoln & Lincolnshire Cabinet* 9 The almost unclim[b]able street which, as before stated, runs directly up the hill. **1892** RIDER HAGGARD *Nada the Lily* 211 It was of no great height, and yet unclimbable, for.. the sides of it were sheer.

un'climbed, *ppl. a.* (UN-[1] 8.)

[**1775** ASH.] **1800** *Monthly Mag.* X. 426 When on mountains unclimb'd encamps tremendous a nigh storm. **1856** MASSON *Ess., Shaks. & Goethe* 24 Like a universal ivy, which has left no wall uncovered, no pinnacle unclimbed.

un'clinch, *v.* [UN-[2] 3.] *trans.* = UNCLENCH *v.* Hence **un'clinching** *vbl. sb.*

1598 FLORIO, *Sbrancare*,.. to rid or free from any pawes or clawes, to vnclinch. **1688** R. L'ESTRANGE *Brief Hist. Times* III. 158 When the Word was once pass'd, and the Charge Rivetted to Somerset-House, there was No Recalling, No Unclinching of it. **1699** GARTH *Dispens.* v. 66 The Hero thus his Enterprise recalls, His Fist unclinches, and the Weapon falls. **1720** *Humourist* 25 The Miser, when Love has once warm'd his Heart, unclinches both his Fists, and throws away his Money in Handfuls. **1752** YOUNG *Brothers* IV. i, Unclinch thy talons from thy prey. **1887** RIDER HAGGARD *Jess* ii, Clinching and unclinching his great hand.

un'clinched, *ppl. a.* (UN-[1] 8.)

1877 MORLEY *Crit. Misc.* Ser. II. 287 We may think the reasoning.. halt of foot; we may discern arguments unclinched.

un'cling, *v.* [UN-[2] 7 and 3.]

1. *intr.* To loosen hold.

1645 MILTON *Tetrach.* 11 A canonicall infection livergrown to their sides; which perhaps will never uncling, without the strong abstersive of som heroick magistrat. **1710** J. NORRIS *Chr. Prud.* viii. 358 When even this cleaving Folly.. shall uncling and drop from us.

2. *trans.* To unclasp; to loosen from clinging.

a **1711** KEN *Preparatives* Poet. Wks. 1721 IV. 34, I have got the Wing, You without Fear your Fingers may uncling. **1750** G. HUGHES *Barbados* 305 It is found to be a difficult task for a very able man to uncling one of them from the rocks.

unclip, *v. rare*[−1]. [UN-[2] 3.] *trans.* To unclasp.

1598 MARSTON *Sco. Villanie* I. (1599) 171 Daphne, vnclip thine armes from my sad brow.

un'clipped, -'clipt, *ppl. a.* [UN-[1] 8. Cf. Da. *uklippet*, Sw. *oklippt.*] Not clipped or cut: **a.** Of hair, wings, etc., or with reference to these.

1388 WYCLIF *2 Sam.* xix. 24 Myphibosech.. cam doun.. with berd vnclippid, in to the comyng of the kyng. **1483** *Cath. Angl.* 67 (Vn) Clippyd, *intonsus.* **1573** TUSSER *Husb.* (1878) 118 Let lambes go vnclipped, till June be halfe worne. **1586** FERNE *Blaz. Gentrie* 20 Hath your Eagle her wings vnclipped? **1658** *Melrose Regality Rec.* (S.H.S.) I. 193 He ought therefore to deliver the ewes with their lambs, unclipped. **1878** BROWNING *Poets Croisic* 101 Grant A fledgeling novice that with wing unclipt She soar her little circuit.

b. Of money.

1691 LOCKE *Consid. Money* Wks. 1714 II. 45 Clip'd and unclip'd money will always buy an equal quantity of any thing else. **1696** DE LA PRYME *Diary* (Surtees) 98, I have seen unclip'd half crowns that has weigh'd down fifteen shillings clipt. **1823** BYRON *Juan* XII. xii, Ingots, bags of dollars, coins (Not of old victors,.. But) of fine unclipt gold.

c. Not fastened with a clip.

1922 JOYCE *Ulysses* 23 Buck Mulligan stood on a stone,.. his unclipped tie rippling over his shoulder.

†**un'clipsed,** *ppl. a. Obs.*[−1] [UN-[1] 8.] Not eclipsed.

c **1485** *Digby Myst.* (1882) III. 1349 O, þe on-clypsyd sonne, tempyll of salamon!

un'clit, *v.* [UN-[2] 3: cf. CLITCH *v.*] *trans.* To unfasten.

1587 M. GROVE *Pelops & Hipp.* (1878) 91 My lady cals it follie plaine, With toong such hardned knot to knit, As all the teeth with helpe of braine, Shall ne be able to vnclit.

un'cloak, *v.* [UN-[2] 4.]

1. *trans.* To divest of, free from, a cloak. Chiefly *refl.* Also *absol.*

1598 FLORIO, *Smantellare*, to vnmantle, to vncloke. **1775** ASH, *Uncloak*.., to take off a cloak, to free from the incumberance of a cloak. **1816** SCOTT *Old Mort.* iii, The young plebian,.. as he took his stand, half-uncloaked his rustic countenance. **1826** —— *Woodst.* xxx, A bustle occurred in receiving the General, assisting him to uncloak himself. **1845** FORD *Handbk. Spain* I. 146 All men give the wall to her, many uncloak themselves. *Ibid.* 201 Spaniards always uncloak when.. the host or the king passes by.

2. *fig.* To expose, lay bare, reveal.

1659 *Gentl. Calling* (1696) 124 Will none have so much Charity, so much Zeal for publick Concern, as to uncloak this Impostor? *a* **1847** ELIZA COOK *Poems, He that is without Sin* ii, The herd, Whose dark and evil works are all uncloaked. **1877** MRS. OLIPHANT *Makers Flor.* xii. 302 The price of uncloaking the false pretensions of the.. priest.

Hence **un'cloaking** *vbl. sb.* Also *attrib.*

[**1775** ASH.] **1845** FORD *Handbk. Spain* xviii. 249 Uncloaking in Spain is.. a mark of respect, and is equivalent to our taking off the hat. **1877** MRS. FORRESTER *Mignon* II. 56 Kitty is awaiting her friend.. in the uncloaking room.

un'cloaked, *ppl. a.* [UN-[1] 8.] Not provided with, or covered by, a cloak. Also *fig.* and *absol.*

1540 MORYSINE *Vives' Introd. Wysd.* K iij, It is better, that all thinges be open, playne, uncloked, and symple. **1839** LEVER *Lorreq.* v. 34 It being now settled to my satisfaction, that Mr. Beamish and the great uncloaked were 'convertible terms'. **1862** J. SPENCE *Amer.* 164 It must stand out unshielded, uncloaked, in the light of open day.

un'clog, *v.*[1] [UN-[2] 4 b.] *trans.* To free from a clog, hindrance, or encumbrance.

1607 SHAKS. *Cor.* IV. ii. 47 Could I meete 'em But once a day, it would vnclogge my heart of what lyes heauy too't. **1678** G. G. in H. Scougal *Wks.* (1735) 304 Such ardent sighs, and groanings,.. as perhaps unclog'd his spirit, and made his soul take its flight, so soon. **1766** MRS. S. PENNINGTON *Lett.* III. 172 Soft magic welcome, welcome angel dream, Unclog me quick, and let me far expand. **1834** HT. MARTINEAU *Moral* III. 119 Which must.. unclog the system of manufactures and commerce. **1886** LESTER *Under Fig Trees* 161 You can't be stooping down for ever to unclog your machine.

un'clog, *v.*[2] [UN-[2] 4.] *trans.* To divest of clogs or pattens.

1828 [see UNBONNET *v.*[2]].

un'clogged, *ppl. a.* [UN-[1] 8.] Not clogged or hampered.

1563 FOXE *A. & M.* 1046/2 That we may liue and kepe our consciences vnclogged. **1654** WHITLOCK *Zootomia* 345 Ranging Licentiousnesse, which such Satyrists call Liberty, and unclogged Freedome. *a* **1721** SHEFFIELD (Dk. Buckhm.) *Wks.* (1753) I. 312 Our minds unclogg'd with farther care, Except to overcome or die. **1742** RICHARDSON *Pamela* III. 356 The Wheels of Nature being unclogg'd, new-oiled, as it were, and set right. **1839** DE LA BECHE *Rep. Geol. Cornwall*, etc. iv. 101 Thus leaving the subject unclogged by this kind of entanglement.

un'cloister, *v.* [UN-[2] 5.] *trans.* To turn out of, remove from, a cloister; to set free, liberate.

1611 FLORIO, *Dischiostrare*, to vncloister. **1687** NORRIS *Paraphr. 3rd Chap. Job* vi, Why did I not uncloister'd from the Womb Take my next lodging in a Tomb? **1795** tr. *Mercier's Fragm. Pol. & Hist.* II. 424 These.. burnt the archives, and uncloistered the monks and nuns. **1856** *N. Brit. Rev.* XXVI. 276 The monks and friars were uncloistered.

Hence **un'cloistered** *ppl. a.*[1]

1627 P. FLETCHER *Locusts* IV. x, Can that uncloist'red Frier with those light armes.. Wake all the sleeping world? **1853** CDL. WISEMAN *Ess.* iii. 97 He was brother to the patron and was.. an uncloistered friar.

un'cloistered, *ppl. a.*[2] [UN-[1] 8.] Not shut up in a cloister; not organized as a cloister.

1652 BENLOWES *Theoph.* XII. xxxiii, Uncloystred, we this course beyond Courts splendor love. **1859** SALA *Tw. round Clock* (1861) 115 These *preux chevalières* of womanhood, these uncloistered nuns. **1902** MRS. TOUT in *Owens Coll. Hist. Ess.* 51 This order arose in an uncloistered institute for the Christian education of young girls.

transf. **1874** RUSKIN *Val D'Arno* ii. §35 If you.. return to the uncloistered sunlight of the piazza.

un'closable, *a.* (UN-[1] 7 b.)

1820 L. HUNT *Indicator* No. 14, Another.. shall find his eyes as uncloseable as a statue's. **1866** NEALE *Sequences & Hymns* 139 Who are these that next the unclosable portals.. Gather in one.

un'close, *a.* Now *rare.* [UN-[1] 7.] **a.** Not closed; open. **b.** Unreserved. **c.** Not intimate; distant.

c **1400** *Destr. Troy* 4688 The Grekes.. Comyn to the castell, (vnclose were the yatis). **1605** SYLVESTER *Du Bartas* II. iii. *Captains* 1075 Known Designs are dangerous to act: And th' vnclose Chief did never noble fact. **1651** *Buchanan's Detection Mary Q. Scots* 59 A house.. not [only].. unclose, but [even] open to pass through. **1659** A. HAY *Diary* (S.H.S.) 227 Notwithstanding my unclose walking, yet the Lord had been very kind to me.

un'close, *v.* [UN-[2] 3 and 7.]

1. *trans.* To make open; to cause to open.

13.. *E.E. Allit. P.* B. 1438 He with keyes vn-closes kystes ful mony. *c* **1430** LYDG. *Min. Poems* (Percy Soc.) 23 Aurora, ageyne the morowe gray, Causith the daysy hir croune to unclose. **1530** PALSGR. 766/2 These letters shall nat be unclosed for me, I wot nat from whence they come. **1555** EDEN *Decades* (Arb.) 101 They vnclose and shake theyr handes. *c* **1586** C'TESS PEMBROKE *Ps.* (1823) LXXVIII. x, He unclos'd the garners of the skies. **1700** DRYDEN *Cymon & Iph.* 177 At length awaking, Iphigene the fair.. Unclos'd her eyes. **1761** GRAY *Descent Odin* 49 Unwilling I my lips unclose. **1794** MRS. RADCLIFFE *Myst. Udolpho* viii, She unclosed the casement to listen to the strains of the music. **1827** SCOTT *Surg. Dau.* ix, Surely the demons of Ambition and Avarice will unclose the talons which they have fixed upon this man. **1852** MRS. STOWE *Uncle Tom's C.* ix, The woman slowly unclosed her large dark eyes, and looked vacantly at her.

absol. **1426** LYDG. *De Guil. Pilgr.* 20333 Yiff they hadde commyssioun.. Bothe to shette and ek vnclose.

b. *fig.* To disclose, make known, reveal.

13.. *E.E. Allit. P.* B. 26 Me mynez on one amonge oþer, as maþew recordez, þat þus of clannesse vn-closez a ful cler speche. **1426** LYDG. *De Guil. Pilgr.* 2760 How sore aforn that they yt close, ye muste hem make yt to vnclose By trewe reuelacyon. **1446** —— *Two Nightingale P.* ii. 51 The briddes song I shal to the vnclose. **1877** MRS. OLIPHANT *Makers Flor.* viii. 212 He.. uncloses the treasures of that celestial wisdom which speaks to men.

†**c.** To detach, unharness. *Obs.*[−1]

1615 CHAPMAN *Odyss.* IV. 32 Inform your pleasure, if we shall unclose Their horse from coach.

2. *intr.* To become open.

c **1385** CHAUCER *L.G.W.* Prol. 65 Hire [the daisy's] chere is pleynly sprad in the brightnesse Of the sonne for ther yt wol vnclose. *c* **1400** *Destr. Troy* 807 In hor mouthe caste [it], And þai clappe shall full clene, & neuer vnclose aftur. *c* **1440** *Pallad. on Husb.* VI. 218 Take roses that bigynneth forto vnclose. **1725** POPE *Odyss.* XVIII. 235 Wak'd at their steps, her flowing eyes unclose. *a* **1785** GLOVER *Athenaid* XXVII, Now they reach The further mouth unclosing in a dale Abrupt. **1808** HELEN ST. VICTOR *Ruins of Rigonda* II. 94 She perceived her curtains unclose, and the form of her mother leaning over her. **1880** 'OUIDA' *Moths* I. 54 She heard the door underneath unclose.

†**3.** *trans.* To hatch. *Obs.* (Cf. DISCLOSE *v.* 3 b.)

1486 *Bk. St. Albans, Hawking* a ij, And when they [*sc.* hawks] bene unclosed and begynneth to feder any thyng of lengthe anoon be kynde they will draw somwatt out of the nest. **1581** MARBECK *Bk. of Notes* 325 Of Eagles it maie be taken, that their young ones doe sucke bloud anone after they be unclosed.

Hence **un'closing** *vbl. sb.*

1705 STEVENS II. s.v., An Unclosing of that which was shut, *abertura.* **1840** POE *W. Wilson* Wks. 1864 I. 428 The violent, although partial unclosing of the door. **1874** *Contemp. Rev.* Oct. 690 The unclosing of the potential parts of a plant in its development from a germ.

un'closed, *ppl. a.* [UN-[1] 8.]

1. Not enclosed or shut in; unenclosed.

c **1400** *Rom. Rose* 3921, I wole with siker walle Close bothe roses and roser. I have to longe.. Left hem unclosid wilfully. **1426** LYDG. *De Guil. Pilgr.* 3208 Thogh thow sest hem bothe two Ber swerd And keyes in ther hond Naked & vnclosyd. **1523** LD. BERNERS *Froiss.* I. cccexxx. 306 And a thre leages in yᵉ way there stode the towne of Mardyke, a great vyllage on the see syde vnclosed. **1543** *Act 35 Hen. VIII*, c. 17 §2 Every Month that the same Coppice..shall..be unclosed, not fenced, saved or preserved.

2. Not closed; open.

c **1450** *Merlin* xxix. 597 Than thei..be-helde towarde the see where thei saugh the cristin a litill vn-closed. *c* **1470** *Gol. & Gaw.* 60 The berne bovnit to the burgh with ane blith cheir, Fand the yettis vnclosit, and thrang in full thra. **1563** SHUTE *Archit.* C iij, The other side is lefte vnclosed. **1790** COLERIDGE *Inside the Coach* 2 'Tis hard on Bagshot Heath to try Unclosed to keep the weary eye. **1827** SCOTT *Highl. Widow* iv, Night by night..she removed from her unclosed door to throw herself on her restless pallet. **1888** HON. MORTEN *Sk. Hospital Life* 35 If a man..has the smallest unclosed wound on his body.

b. *transf.* Of an account. (See CLOSE *v.* 8.)

1723 STEELE *Consc. Lovers* IV. i. 63, I don't love to leave any part of the Account unclos'd.

3. Not joined so as to enclose a space. (Cf. CLOSE *v.* 11.)

1551 RECORDE *Pathw. Knowl.* I. Defin., To speake properlie, a figure is euer made by platte formes, and not of bare lines unclosed.

un'closing, *ppl. a.*[1] [UN-[1] 10.] Not coming close; keeping apart.

1643 MILTON *Divorce* 6 Where the minde and person pleases aptly, there some unaccomplishment of the bodies delight may be better born with, then when the minde hangs off in an unclosing disproportion.

un'closing, *ppl. a.*[2] [f. UNCLOSE *v.*] That unclose(s); opening.

1792 J. BARLOW *Conspir. Kings* 159 The hour is come, the world's unclosing eyes Discern with rapture where its wisdom lies. **1831** T. L. PEACOCK *Crotchet Castle* iv, The Captain anxiously watched the unclosing door for the form of his beloved. **1894** AUG. WEBSTER *Mother & Daughter* (1895) 28 The flower's unclosing growth.

un'clothe, *v.* [UN-[2] 4; cf. UNCLEAD *v.*]

1. *trans.* To divest (a person) of clothing; to undress; to strip.

c **1300** *Havelok* 659 Grim dede maken a ful fayr bed; Vncloþede him, and dede him þer-inne. **1382** WYCLIF *Matt.* xxvii. 28 And thei vnclothinge hym, diden aboute hym a rede mantel. **1485** in *Rutland Papers* (Camden) 16 Wher as the King shalbe vnraied and vnclothed by his Chamberlayn. **1556** *Aurelio & Isab.* (1608) P iv, They unclothede him of his garmentes. **1632** LITHGOW *Trav.* x. 476, I was..vnclothed to my skin. **1790** BURNS *Let.* in Cromek *Reliques* (1808) 101 Unclothing the naturalist [in a picture], and giving him a rather more resolute look.

transf. *c* **1440** *Pallad. on Husb.* IV. 449 In the wynter seson, Couert of stre their coldes most appeson. When somer comth, vnclothe hem.

b. *refl.* (†Also with double object.)

1382 WYCLIF *Ezek.* xliv. 19 Thei shuln vnclothe hem her clothingus. *c* **1489** CAXTON *Sonnes of Aymon* xxii. 491 He wente to his chambre, & vnclothed hymselfe from his goode raymentes. **1530** PALSGR. 766/2 Unclothe you at ones, for you shall be trymmed starke naked. **1585** T. WASHINGTON tr. *Nicholay's Voy.* II. xxi. 58 Seats..vppon the whiche they vncloth themselues. **1604** E. G[RIMSTONE] *D'Acosta's Hist. Indies* V. xxiv. 397 The ceremonies, dancing and sacrifice ended, they went to vnclothe themselves.

transf. **1661** MORGAN *Sph. Gentry* I. vi. 87 The Sheep doth uncloth it self to apparel man.

c. In various figurative uses.

1526 *Pilgr. Perf.* (W. de W. 1531) 82 To vnclothe our olde man and make hym all naked, that he may be renewed in god. **1586** T. B. *La Primaud. Fr. Acad.* I. 440 Let us learne to uncloath our harts of all envie and hatred. **1622** S. WARD *Life of Faith in Death* 104 Though they doe not Cynically reuile the body as a Clog, a prison,..yet are they willing, yea and sigh to be vncloathed. **1632** J. HAYWARD tr. *Biondi's Eromena* 23 You'l uncloath your owne shame, and thereby procure your selfe many losses and disgraces. **1671** FLAVEL *Fount. Life* v. 13 The Seleusians affirmed that He unclothed himself of His Humanity. **1849** STOVEL *Canne's Necess.* 55 The sombre but joyous magnanimity of Frith unclothed an element in human nature which human expedients can never overcome. **1870** NEWMAN *Gram. Assent* II. x, Why am I..unclothing my mind of that large outfit of existing thoughts,..desires, and hopes, which make me what I am?

2. To strip of leaves or vegetation.

In the first quot. perhaps *intr.*, 'to shed the leaves'.

a **1547** SURREY in *Tottel's Misc.* (Arb.) 16 When Boreas gan his raigne, And euery tree vnclothed fast, as nature taught them plaine. **1613** DENNIS *Secr. Angling* I. v, When ..blustring Boreas with his chilling cold, Vnclothed hath the Trees of Sommers greene. **1707** MORTIMER *Husb.* Ss 3 b, Nov[ember]..generally proves dry, and the Earth and Trees are wholly uncloathed.

3. To remove a cloth or cloths from.

In early quots. perh. strictly *uncloth*.

1607 MARKHAM *Cavel.* III. (1617) 21 First let your Groom vncloath him, then..dresse him in such sort as belongs to his place and office. **1623** —— *Eng. Housew.* v. 217 Couer it ouer with some thicke wollen clothes,..the warmth whereof will make it Come presently: which once perceiued, then forth-with vncloth it. **1825** J. NICHOLSON *Operat. Mechanic* 39 Many wind-mills are provided with flying-balls, which, by very ingenious mechanism, clothe and unclothe the sails just in proportion to the strength of the wind. **1893** *N. & Q.* 8th Ser. III. 75/2 When the force of the wind increased, the miller was obliged to bring each of the sails in succession to the ground, in order to 'unclothe' it.

Hence **un'clothing** *vbl. sb.*

1643 CARYL *Expos. Job* I. 104 Death is called an uncloathing,..because it pulleth all outward things off from a man. **1650** BAXTER *Saints' R.* v. §2. 54 If unclothing be the thing thou fearest; why, it is, that thou mayst have better clothing put on.

un'clothed, *ppl. a.* [UN-[1] 8.]

1. Not covered with clothes; bare, naked.

1440 J. SHIRLEY *Dethe K. James* (1818) 15 The Kyng.. stondyng in his night gowne, all unclothid save his shirt, his cape [etc.]. **1495** *Trevisa's Barth. De P.R.* XVIII. ix. 762 A serpent dredyth a nakyd man & dare not touche hym though he lepe on hym whan he is vnclothed. **1601** LD. MOUNTJOY *Let.* in Moryson *Itin.* II. (1617) 204 Then will the souldier be vnclothed, which rather then he will indure, he will runne away. **1616** SURFL. & MARKH. *Country Farme* I. xxviii. 128 Vpon his necke, and other outward parts which are vnclothed. **1816** BYRON *Siege Cor.* xxvi, Their leader's nervous arm is bare,..Unclothed to the shoulder it waves them on. **1862** SHARPE *Egypt. Antiq. Brit. Mus.* 13 The unclothed parts of their bodies are painted red. **1874** LISLE CARR *J. Gwynne* I. vii. 237 Prone to cravings after a savage ideal of untaught, unclothed freedom.

transf. **1581** HOWELL *Devises* (1906) 32, I sawe the naked Fields vnclothde on euery side. **1855** *Orr's Circ. Sci., Inorg. Nat.* 85 The unclothed jaws—covered with hard enamel instead of skin—are lined with a double row of teeth.

2. Not covered with a cloth or cloths.

1856 KANE *Arct. Expl.* II. ix. 93 [The table] still stands in its simple dignity, an unclothed platform of boards. **1891** E. KINGLAKE *Australian at Home* 94 A plainly furnished room with an unclothed deal table.

Hence **un'clothedly** *adv.*

a **1648** *Ess. on Death* in *Bacon's Remaines* (1648) 8 Forgetting how unclothedly they came hither, or with what naked ornaments they were arrayed. **1683** E. HOOKER *Pref. Pordage's Mystic Div.* 67 Where, unclothedly, uncoveredly, nakedly, uncompoundedly,..Hee stood.

un'clotted, *ppl. a.* (UN-[1] 8.)

1770 HEWSON *Blood* in *Phil. Trans.* LX. 380, I had the curiosity to compare..the clotted part with the unclotted.

un'cloud, *v.* [UN-[2] 4 b.]

1. *trans.* To clear or free from clouds.

1598 FLORIO, *Disnebbiare*, to vncloude, to cleere vp. *c* **1610** BEAUM. & FL. *Philaster* IV. i, 'Tis the King Will have it so, whose breath can still the winds, Uncloud the Sun. **1652** BENLOWES *Theoph.* v. lxxiii, This Monarch Star, Making his progresse through the Signes, unclouds the air.

2. *transf.* and *fig.* To free from obscurity or gloom; to clear, make clear.

1594 *Constable's Diana* Printer to Rdr., Obscur'd wonders ..visited me.., and I in regard of Aeneas honour, have vnclouded them vnto the worlde. **1607** EARL STIRLING *J. Cæsar* IV. i, When friend-ship one of them pretends, The other like-wise doth un-cloud the face. *a* **1711** KEN *Hymnotheo* Poet. Wks. 1721 III. 375 Down from high Heav'n rush'd a strong gracious Wind, Dispelling Mists, unclouding ev'ry Mind. **1789** T. TWINING *Aristotle's Treat. Poetry* (1812) I. 305 It is in the true spirit of a modern drinking song; recommending it to the servant to uncloud his brow. **1891** C. E. NORTON *Dante's Purgat.* xxviii. 179 The psalm..affords light which may uncloud your understanding.

refl. *a* **1672** P. S[TERRY] *Appear. God to Man* Wks. (1710) 328 Things seen in their Unseen and Divine Forms, unclouding themselves, shining out upon the Soul.

3. *absol.* To become clear.

1874 KINGSLEY *Lett.*, etc. (1877) II. 431, I am hopeful that as she gets weaker the brain will uncloud. **1879** G. MACDONALD *P. Faber* I. xv. 176 Every now and then she cast up a glance, and there were black suns unclouding over a white sea.

Hence **un'clouding** *vbl. sb.*

1704 NORRIS *Ideal World* II. iii. 162 It is for the unclouding of both, to observe a definitive strickness in the use of our words.

un'clouded, *ppl. a.* [UN-[1] 8.]

1. Not obscured or darkened by clouds.

1595 G. W. *On Spenser's Sonn.* 3 But when they see his glorious raies vnclowded, With steddy steps they keepe the perfect way. **1639** HABINGTON *Castara* II. (Arb.) 91 Th' unclouded Sun had never showne them day Till that bright minute. **1655** VAUGHAN *Silex Scint.* II. *Ascension-day* 46 All the Planets did unclouded pass. **1765** WILKES *Corr.* (1805) II. 160 A fine blue the arch of heaven is here,—pure, serene, and unclouded. **1796** H. HUNTER *St.-Pierre's Stud. Nat.* (1799) II. 36 The unclouded azure in the Heavens. **1858** LARDNER *Handbk. Nat. Phil.* 377 A clear unclouded sky in the absence of the sun radiates but little heat towards the earth. **1887** BOWEN *Æneid* III. 518 He beholds that the heavens are one unclouded expanse.

2. *transf.* and *fig.* Not darkened or obscured.

1641 MILTON *Ch. Govt.* II. ii, That more then angelick brightnes, the unclouded serenity of Christian Religion. *c* **1645** HOWELL *Lett.* (1650) I. 355 A clear unclouded countenance. *a* **1711** KEN *Sion* Poet. Wks. 1721 IV. 398 And where the Mind falls short, Love taking Flight, Obtains of God a more unclouded Sight. **1796** MME. D'ARBLAY *Camilla* V. 189 A brighter, though not unclouded scene, was exhibited at Cleves. **1821** SCOTT *Kenilw.* vi, The graceful ease and unclouded front of an accomplished courtier. **1847** C. BRONTË *J. Eyre* xxxviii, No fear of death will darken St. John's last hour: his mind will be unclouded. **1890** 'R. BOLDREWOOD' *Miner's Right* (1899) 160/2 My conscience was unclouded.

Hence **un'cloudedly** *adv.*; **un'cloudedness**.

1648 BOYLE *Seraph. Love* iii. (1700) 14 The Love..that makes nothing more conducive to it than the greatest uncloudedness of the Eye. **1804** EUGENIA DE ACTON *Tale without Title* I. 62 Why then, fond foolish heart, so sad! Think not to pass uncloudedly thy days.

un'cloudy, *a.* (UN-[1] 7.)

1675 GASCOIGNE in Rigaud *Corr. Sci. Men* (1841) I. 223 A clearer and more uncloudy sky than ordinarily England doth allow. **1711** GAY *Rural Sports* I. 108 Now..twinkling orbs bestrow th' uncloudy skies.

un'cloured, *ppl. a. Sc.* [UN-[1] 8.] Not injured with blows or hard knocks.

1719 RAMSAY *Ep. to Hamilton* 4 Aug. vii, Be thy Crown ay unclowr'd in Quarrel.

un'cloven, *ppl. a.* (UN-[1] 8 b. Cf. MDu. *ongecloven*, MSw. *oclyffvin*, Sw. *oklufven*.)

1620 FLETCHER *Chances* II. i, My skull's uncloven yet, let me but kill. **1725** *Fam. Dict.* s.v. *Animal*, There are those that are cloven-footed; as black Cattle; or uncloven, as Horses. **1842** BORROW *Bible in Spain* v, They will not partake of the beast of the uncloven foot. **1893** SWINBURNE *Stud. Prose & Poetry* (1894) 290 A sea uncloven by the share or by the prow of an adventurer in verse.

un'cloy, *v.* [UN-[2] 3.] *trans.* (See quots., and cf. CLOY *v.*[1] 1 and 4. In this sense *Obs.*)

1611 COTGR., *Descloüer*, to vnnayle, or vncloy; to loose, pull off, draw out, a nayle. **1627** CAPT. SMITH *Seaman's Gram.* xiv. 68 To uncloy her [*sc.* a gun], is to put..oile.. about the naile to make it glib, and by a traine giue fire to her by her mouth, and so blow it out.

un'cloyed, *ppl. a.* [UN-[1] 8.]

†**1.** Unhurt, uninjured. *Obs.*

1562 PHAER *Æneid* x. Dd ij b, Yet..let me Ascanius keepe vncloyed: Let me my nephew small withdraw from Mars.

2. Not cloyed or surfeited.

1627 SANDERSON *Serm.* I. 268 Depending upon the ministry thereof with unsatisfied ears and unwearied attention, and feeding thereon with uncloyed appetites. *a* **1703** POMFRET *Ode Gen. Conflagration* xiii, Where undisturb'd uncloyed they will possess Divine substantial happiness. **1797** GODWIN *Enquirer* I. xv. 139 The man of genius..feeds with an uncloyed appetite. **1827** KEBLE *Chr. Y., 4th Sun. Advent* viii, These eyes..In fearless love and hope uncloy'd For ever on that ocean bright Empower'd to gaze. **1866** LIDDON *Bampt. Lect.* v. (1875) 230 All His infinite powers and faculties turn ever inward with uncloyed delight.

un'cloying, *ppl. a.* (UN-[1] 10.)

1768–74 TUCKER *Lt. Nat.* (1834) II. 263 Thou endest not but in endless, uncloying fruition. **1819** SHELLEY *Cyclops* 364 The Cyclops vermilion, With slaughter uncloying, Now feasts on the dead. **1856** GRINDON *Life* xx. (1875) 253 The pure and uncloying charms of virtue and nature.

un'clubbable, *a.* (UN-[1] 7 b.)

Hence in recent use, ***unclubbability***.

? **1764** JOHNSON in Mme. D'Arblay *Diary* (1842) I. 66 Sir John was a most unclubable man! **1859** SALA *Tw. round Clock* (1861) 215 Moreover, they are a people who drink *standing*,..a most unclubable characteristic. **1867** E. YATES *Forlorn Hope* x, Kilsyth is not popular at Barnes's, being decidedly an unclubbable man.

unclue, var. UNCLEW *v.*

un'clung, *ppl. a.* (UN-[1] 8 b. Cf. CLUNG *ppl. a.* 2.)

1587 GOLDING *De Mornay* xv. 233 Or els the earth yet yoong..the seede thereof vncloong Reteined still in fruitfull wombe.

un'clutch, *v.* (UN-[2] 3.)

1667 *Decay Chr. Piety* iv. ¶3, If the terrors of the Lord could not have force enough..to unclutch his griping hand, or disseize him of his prey. **1816** SCOTT *Bl. Dwarf* viii, It unclutched the burden, and let it drop..upon the ground. **1864** E. SARGENT *Peculiar* III. 56, I should not feel much compunction in compelling such a man to unclutch his riches.

unco ('ʌŋkə), *a.*, *adv.*, and *sb. Sc.* and *north. dial.* Also 5 **vnkow**, 6 **vncow**, 7, 9 **uncow**, 8–9 **unko**, 9 **unco'**, **unca.** [Shortening of UNCOUTH *a.*]

A. *adj.* **1.** Unknown, strange; unusual.

c **1410** *Chaucer's Troylus* III. 1797 (Campsall MS.), And ouer al þis so wel koude he deuyse Of sentement and in so vnkow wyse, Al his aray, þat [etc.]. **1500–20** DUNBAR *Poems* xxxi. 13 He that..schuttis syne at an vncow schell,..He wirkis sorrow to him sell. **1596** DALRYMPLE tr. *Leslie's Hist. Scot.* (S.T.S.) II. 132 At this tyme an vncow and sair seiknes ..invadet hail Scotland. **1683** LAW *Mem.* (1818) 246 Taken with an uncow disease, like unto convulsion fits. **1725** RAMSAY *Gentl. Sheph.* III. ii, They're here that ken, and here that disna ken The wimpled meaning of your unko tale. **1785** BURNS *Halloween* xxviii, Wi' merry sangs, an' friendly cracks,..And unco tales, an' funnie jokes. **1816** SCOTT *Antiq.* xxxii, It was an unco thing to bid a mother leave her ain house wi' the tear in her ee. **1871** W. ALEXANDER *Johnny Gibb* xliv. 306 Buyin' a twa three rigs o' grun' an' sittin' doon wi' a' thing unco aboot's.

b. Weird, uncanny.

1828 MOIR *Mansie Wauch* x, It was an unco thought, and garred all my flesh creep. **1893** STEVENSON *Catriona* xv, It was an unco place by night, unco by day.

2. Remarkable, notable, great, large.

1724 *Ramsay's Tea-t. Misc.* (1733) I. 25, I had amaist forgot My mistress and my song to boot, And that's an unco faut I wate. **1786** BURNS *The Calf* 4 There's yoursel just now, God knows, an unco Calf! **1815** SCOTT *Guy M.* xi, [The boy's disappearance] made an unca noise ower a' this country. **1820** —— *Monast.* xxxiii, It would be an unco task to mend the yetts. **1869** A. MACDONALD *Love, Law & Theol.* viii. 133 She thinks an unco heep o' Mr. Ochtertyre.

B. *adv.* Extremely, remarkably, very.

1724 *Ramsay's Tea-t. Misc.* (1733) I. 26, I hate to live; but O I'm wae And unko sweer to die. **1786** BURNS *Twa Dogs* 116 Whyles twalpennie-worth o' nappy Can mak the bodies unco happy. **1816** SCOTT *Antiq.* xi, Though you're near enough, yet Miss Grizel has an unco close grip. **1869** C. GIBBON *R. Gray* iv, Ye're getting unco fine in your ways.

b. ***the unco guid***, those who are professedly strict in matters of morals and religion.

1786 BURNS (*title*), Address to the Unco Guid, or the Rigidly Righteous. **1859** *Habits of Gd. Society* iv. 160 Indifference and consequent inattention to dress,..extolled by the 'unco gude' as a virtue. **1887** *Daily Tel.* 12 Mar. 5/2 The absurdities initiated by the 'unco' guid' in their futile attempts to promote public morality by legislation.

C. *sb.* **1.** A strange or unusual thing or tale; a novelty or piece of news. Usu. *pl.*

1785 BURNS *Cotter's Sat. Nt.* v, Each tells the uncos that he sees or hears. **1822** GALT *Steam-Boat* xvii. 359, I.. was thankful for being returned in safety among my friends, after seeing such uncos. **1886** B. BRIERLEY *Cast upon World* xi. (E.D.D.), Jone knew all the 'uncos' that were afloat.

2. A stranger.

1800 ADAIR in Currie *Burns' Wks.* I. 172 She gave as her first toast after dinner, *Awa, Uncos*, or, away with the strangers. **1821** GALT *Ann. Parish* xx, We had advised her, by course of post, of our coming, and intendment to lodge with her, as uncos and strangers.

un'coach, *v.* (UN-2 5.)

1615 CHAPMAN *Odyss.* VI. 124 These (here arriv'd) the Mules vncoacht, and draue Vp to the gulphie riuers shore. **1630** DAVENANT *Cruel Brother* III, Watch my Lords comming from the Duke, and bring Me word, before he is vncoach'd.

unco'acted, *ppl. a.* [UN-1 8 and 5 b.]

1. Not compelled or constrained.

1545 *St. Papers Hen. VIII*, V. 485 Donald Maclane of Kengerloch, wncoakit or incompulsit. **1567** TURBERV. *Epit.*, etc. 4 b, With free and vncoacted minde. **1577** tr. *Bullinger's Decades* III. ix. 470 Such an vncoacted affection, voluntarie loue, and free goodwill as children.. beare to their parents.

2. Not forced together.

1642 H. MORE *Song of Soul* To Rdr., All homogeneall, simple, single,.. unknotted, uncoacted.

unco'agulable, *a.* (UN-1 7 b and 5 b.)

1669 W. SIMPSON *Hydrol. Chym.* 103 This wild uncoagulable spirit we call wind. **1809** *Phil. Trans.* XCIX. 333 It appeared that.. it might be dissolved in alcohol, and thereby became uncoagulable. **1836–9** *Todd's Cycl. Anat.* II. 152/1 The animal matters thus mixed with the blood.. constitute the.. uncoagulable animal matter of the blood.

unco'agulated, *ppl. a.* (UN-1 8.)

1770 *Phil. Trans.* LX. 408 A part of the blood.. was found uncoagulated thirteen hours after death. **1845** TODD & BOWMAN *Phys. Anat.* I. 39 Not a particle of caseine.. will remain uncoagulated. **1873** ROLFE *Phys. Chem.* 153 Place in it 5 ounces of fresh uncoagulated blood.

unco'agulating, *ppl. a.* (UN-1 10.)

1822–7 GOOD *Study Med.* (1829) IV. 402 The blood itself was black, uncoagulating, and of an oily appearance.

†un-coalcarrying, *ppl. a. Obs.*-1 (See UN-1 10 and COAL *sb.*1 12.)

1611 CHAPMAN *May Day* III, Now sir he (being of an vncole-carrying spirit) fals foule on him, cals him gull openly.

un'coat, *v.* (UN-2 4.)

1571 GOLDING *Calvin on Ps.* l. 1 To bee uncoted out of that their masking garment of holynesse, whereof they vaunted themselves.

un'coated, *ppl. a.* [UN-1 8.]

1. Not covered with a coating of some substance.

1663 BOYLE *Usef. Exp. Nat. Philos.* II. App. 351 Put it into a strong glasse retort uncoated. **1798** *Phil. Trans.* LXXXVIII. 577 When the flints appeared perfectly uncoated, and in their usual state, I decanted the liquor. **1800** *Ibid.* XC. 339 A piece of the polished or uncoated red coral was now taken. **1878** ABNEY *Photogr.* 26 If the plate be exposed.. with the uncoated side next the image.

2. Not wearing a coat.

1853 G. JOHNSTON *Nat. Hist. E. Bord.* I. 106 You must add life to the landscape:.. the uncoated ploughman [etc.].

un'cock, *v.*1 [UN-2 3.]

†1. *trans.* To take (the match) out of the cock of the old matchlock gun. Also *absol.*, and with *piece* as obj. *Obs.*

1598 BARRET *Theor. Warres* 32 Let him vncocke his match, clap his musket vpon his shoulder, and so retire. **1639** *Verney Papers* (Camden) 240 Charles Price.. bedd them uncock theyr peeces. **1650** R. ELTON *Military Art* (1659) 192 Uncock, and return your Match.

2. To lower the cock or hammer of (a fire-arm) in order to prevent accidental discharge.

[**1775** ASH.] **1804** tr. *La Martelier's Three Gil Blas* I. 30 One of my pistols, which.. I had forgot to uncock, went off. **1818** SCOTT *Br. Lamm.* xxxiii, Ravenswood.. uncocked and returned his pistol to his belt. **1824** W. IRVING *T. Trav.* (1849) 422 The pistol was uncocked; the burden was resumed.

un'cock, *v.*2 (UN-2 3. Cf. COCK *v.*4)

1745 W. ELLIS *Mod. Husbandman* VII. II. 80 Then this Nobleman thought it high time to uncock all the wheat again. **1844** J. T. HEWLETT *Parsons & W.* v, To uncock and toss about Farmer Read's hay.

un'cocked, *ppl. a.*1 [UN-1 8.] Of a hat: Not cocked or turned up.

1721 RAMSAY *Morning Interview* 13 The sons of Bacchus stagger home to rest, With tatter'd wigs, foul shoes, and uncock'd hats. **1751** JOHNSON *Rambler* No. 109 ¶6 With.. my hair unpowdered, and my hat uncocked. **1785** GROSE *Dict. Vulgar T.*, *Zouch*, or *Slouch*, a slouched hat; a hat with its brims let down, or uncocked.

un'cocked, *ppl. a.*2 [UN-1 8.] Of crops: Not put up in cocks.

1641 BEST *Farm. Bks.* (Surtees) 58 If theire come any great raines, then they [pease] are better uncocked then cocked.

un'cocted, *ppl. a.* [UN-1 8 and 5 b.] Not properly prepared or digested by heat, etc.; crude.

1598 SYLVESTER *Du Bartas* II. i. III. *Furies* 481 An impotence for Generation's-deed, And lust-lesse Issue of th' uncocted seed. **1601** HOLLAND *Pliny* II. 476 [Vermilion] uncocted and crude is.. brought to Rome in the masse as it lay within the veine. **1622** DONNE *Serm.* xvi. 157 In a devotion perchance indigested, uncocted, and retaining yet some crudities.

†uncod, obs. var. UNCOUTH *a.* or UNKED *a.*

1399 *Pol. Poems* (Rolls) I. 364 Her eldest bryd his taken her fro, into an uncod place.

un'codified, *ppl. a.* (UN-1 8.)

1867 *Nation* 12 Sept. 205 The uncodified regulations required by public opinion.

†un-'codpieced, *a. Obs.*-1 (UN-1 9.)

1580 G. HARVEY *Let. to Spenser* S.'s Wks. (1912) 625/2 Largebelled Kodpeasd Dublet, vnkodpeased halfe hose.

unco'erced, *ppl. a.* (UN-1 8.)

1791–2 BENTHAM *Anarchical Fallacies* Wks. 1843 II. 505 The liberty which the law ought to.. leave uncoerced, unremoved. **1802–12** —— *Ration. Judic. Evid.* (1827) V. 657 Gain or loss.. from the uncoerced conduct of individuals. **1864** SIR F. PALGRAVE *Norm. & Eng.* III. 363 The first community which had made a formal and uncoerced submission of their own free will.

un'coffer, *v.* [UN-2 5.] *trans.* To take out of a coffer.

c **1412** HOCCLEVE *De Reg. Princ.* 4245 þe bagged gold by þe marchaunt hym lent He hath vncofred. *a* **1470** HARDING *Chron.* CXXII. i, Then went he furth to Duram wher he offred, And to the Churche he gaue great good vncoffred.

un'coffered, *ppl. a.* (UN-1 8.)

1870 BARING-GOULD *In Exitu Israel* I. viii. 118 There remained still one of Gabrielle's dresses uncoffered.

un'coffined, *ppl. a.*1 [UN-1 8.] Not enclosed in a coffin.

1648 HEXHAM II, *Ongekist*, Vnchested, or Vncoffined. *a* **1680** GLANVILL *Sadducismus* II. (1681) 218 An uncoffined body being laid in a ground exposed to wet [etc.]. **1742** BLAIR *Grave* 152 A Dungeon-Slave, that's bury'd In the High-way, unshrouded and uncoffin'd. **1855** [J. R. LEIFCHILD] *Cornwall* 30 A small ancient dungeon, wherein were found the uncoffined bones of a large man. **1884** *Athenæum* 16 Aug. 203/3 This is the last instance we remember of a body being buried uncoffined when laid in consecrated ground with the rites of the Church.

un'coffined, *ppl. a.*2 [UN-2 8.] Taken out of a coffin.

1836 F. MAHONY *Rel. Father Prout* 164 A newly uncoffined mummy (warranted of the era of Sesostris).

un'coft, *ppl. a. Sc.* [UN-1 8 b. Cf. MDu. and Du. *ungekocht.*] Unbought.

1536 BELLENDEN *Descr. Alb.* iv. in *Cron. Scot.* (1541) B ij b, Thay mycht.. haif all necessaris within thaym self vncoft. **15..** J. BALNAVIS '*O Gallandis all*' 15 (Maitland MS.), With stufe oncoft, set vpone loft, Aneuch is ewin a feist. **1721** KELLY *Sc. Prov.* 388 You strive about uncoft Gait [*i.e.* goats]. **1737** RAMSAY *Sc. Prov.* xliii. 116 Ye cangle about uncoft kids.

un'cogged, *ppl. a.*1 [UN-1 8 + COG *v.*1] Not blocked or stopped.

1637 GILLESPIE *Eng. Pop. Cerem.* Ep. A ij b, Those who are wealthy and well at ease, and mounted aloft upon the uncogged wheeles of prosperous fortune.

un'cogged, *ppl. a.*2 [UN-1 8 + COG *v.*3] Of dice: Not cogged or loaded.

1870 LOWELL *Among my Bks.* Ser. I. (1873) 230 Honest dice, uncogged by those three hoary sharpers, Prerogative, Patricianism, and Priestcraft.

†un'cogible, *a. Obs.*-1 [UN-1 7 + L. *cōg-ĕre* to compel.] Incapable of being constrained.

1646 S. BOLTON *Arraignm. Err.* 314 Those acts of conscience which are internall, are free and uncogible; they fall not under mans cognizance.

†un'cogitable, *a. Obs.* (UN-1 7 b and 5 b.)

1529 MORE *Suppl. Souls* 43 But [they] haue in them selfe a farre more excellent syght,.. by meanys vncogitable to man. **1534** —— *Comf. agst. Trib.* III. xxvi. (1553) Uvj, Ye Ioys of heauen are.. to mannes hearte vncogitable.

un'cognisant, *a.* (UN-1 7.) Also uncognizant. So **un'cognizantly** *adv.*

1843 Uncognizantly [see *pigeon-pie* s.v. PIGEON *sb.* 5 a]. **1860** GOSSE *Rom. Nat. Hist.* 153 There exists a world of animated beings.. of which our senses are altogether uncognisant.

uncog'nizable, *a.* (UN-1 7 b and 5 b.)

1720 WELTON *Suffer. Son of God* I. iii. 39 Constrain'd to continue in that Covert, and Uncognisable State,.. many Years. **1827** *Perils & Captivity* in *Constable's Misc.* 326 Until he came to the spot where their corpses laid, already putrid and uncognizable. **1849** HERSCHEL *Outl. Astron.* 590 This displacement, however, is.. uncognizable by any phænomenon, so long as the solar motion remains invariable.

uncog'nized, *ppl. a.* (UN-1 8.)

1877 BLACKIE *Wise Men* 216 So all in all, believe me, Lies hidden, uncognised.

uncognosci'bility. (UN-1 12 and 5 b.)

1802–12 BENTHAM *Ration. Judic. Evid.* (1827) IV. 152 Making more and more rubbish, with the help of factitious and groundless diversification, thence uncognoscibility, uncertainty, and so forth. **1865** MILL *Exam. Hamilton* 56 Our author has merely proved the uncognoscibility of a being which is nothing but infinite.

uncog'noscible, *a.* (UN-1 7 and 5 b.)

1810 BENTHAM *Packing* (1821) 23 Rendering the subject.. as incomprehensible, or.. as uncognoscible as possible. **1840** POLSON *Law & Lawyers* (1858) 197 Perhaps abstractedly speaking law phrases are not one whit more barbarous and uncognoscible than those of any other science.

†unco'herent, *a. Obs.* (UN-1 7 and 5 b.)

1588 FRAUNCE *Lawiers Log.* Ded., Neyther himselfe can well understand his unjoynted discourse, nor the hearers conceave his uncoherent jangling. **1611** FLORIO, *Incoherente*, vncoherent.

un'coif, *v.* (UN-2 3.)

1598 FLORIO, *Dischiomare*, to vnhaire, to vncoiffe, to disheuell, to touze ones haire. **1611** COTGR., *Descoeffer*, to vncoife; to disarray,.. vncouer, the head. *c* **1714** POPE, etc. *Mem. M. Scriblerus* vi. Wks. 1797 VI. 109 Yonder are two Apple-women scolding, and just ready to uncoif one another. **1876** F. K. ROBINSON *Whitby Gloss.* 205.

un'coifed, *ppl. a.* (UN-1 8 and UN-2 8.)

1611 COTGR., *Descoeffé*, vncoifed. **1727** BAILEY (vol. II). **1742** YOUNG *Nt. Th.* VIII. 601 Lorenzo! thou, her majesty's renown'd, Tho' uncoift, counsel, learned in the world! **1870** [see UNCHAPLETED].

un'coil, *v.* [UN-2 3.]

1. *trans.* To unwind; to take out of a coiled state.

1713 DERHAM *Phys.-Theol.* x. (1727) 406 *note*, Between which [great fibres], may be seen the Spiral Air-Vessels (like Threads of Cobweb) a little uncoiled. **1811** *2nd Rep. Records Irel.* 26 The Parliament Rolls.. often extend many perches in length; actually requiring a machine to uncoil and wind them up. **1839** DARWIN *Voy. Nat.* i. 19 Where the stream uncoils into long streaks the froth collected in the eddies. **1860** TYNDALL *Glac.* I. xi. 73 We.. paused while our guide uncoiled a rope and tied us all together.

refl. **1824** DIBDIN *Libr. Comp.* 742 His muse.. is capable of uncoiling and rousing herself, as it were, for attacks of tremendous severity. **1859** TENNYSON *Vivien* 738 The snake of gold slid from her hair, the braid Slipt and uncoil'd itself.

2. *absol.* To become uncoiled.

1854 OWEN in *Orr's Circ. Sci.*, *Org. Nat.* I. 195 The constrictor slowly uncoils. **1870** HOOKER *Stud. Flora* 472 Elaters, which are coiled round the spore when moist, and uncoil when dry.

Hence **un'coiled** *ppl. a.*; **un'coiling** *vbl. sb.*

1839 URE *Dict. Arts*, etc. 1284 The coiling and uncoiling of the cord. **1844** W. UPTON *Physioglyphics* 176 The English capital represents it uncoiled, but still quiescent. **1856** EMERSON *Eng. Traits*, *Result*, Who would see the uncoiling of that tremendous spring.

†un'coin, var. of (or error for) UNCOINED *ppl. a.*

1640 SHIRLEY *Arcadia* II. i, Be there a myne Of Coyne or vncoyne mettall, it is mine.

un'coin, *v.* (UN-2 3.)

1833 HT. MARTINEAU *Berkeley* I. ii. 33 Every week uncoins what was coined the week before. **1875** JEVONS *Money* viii. 81 These are the people who frequently uncoin money, either by melting it, or by exporting it.

un'coined, *ppl. a.* (UN-1 8.)

1423 *Rolls of Parlt.* IV. 256/2 Silver is bought and soold unkoyned atte pris of xxxii *s.* the pound of troie. *c* **1550** R. BIESTON *Bayte Fortune* A vj, That tyme was I vncoyned, therfore man chaunge thy mynde To blame me of all euylles. **1555** EDEN *Decades W. Ind.* (Arb.) 290 The Ruthenians vse money vncoyned. **1625** T. GODWIN *Moses & Aaron* (1641) 269 Though at last they used coined money, yet at first they weighed their money, uncoined. **1696** *Lond. Gaz.* No. 3238/3 A free Exportation of Gold and Silver, both coined and uncoined. **1715** LEONI *Palladio's Archit.* (1742) II. 80 The first Money in Rome, was of Brass, and uncoined. **1790** in *Nairne Peerage Evidence* (1874) 99 Gold & silver coined & uncoined. **1862** *Lond. Rev.* 23 Aug. 175 All the mentions of money in the Bible before the Babylonian captivity may be explained as of uncoined money. **1886** *Pall Mall G.* 12 June 9/2 The scarcity of the supply both of the coined and uncoined metal.

fig. **1599** SHAKS. *Hen. V*, V. ii. 164 While thou liu'st, deare Kate, take a fellow of plaine and vncoyned Constancie.

un'coked, *ppl. a.* (UN-1 8.)

1868 JOYNSON *Metals* 24 Uncoked coal—that is,.. coal in its ordinary condition.

'unco-like, *a.* and *adv. Sc.* [f. UNCO *a.*]

a. *adv.* In a strange manner. **b.** *adj.* Strange; abnormal.

1636 RUTHERFORD *Lett.* (1836) I. 126 He looked fremed and unco-like upon me when I came first here. **1842** D. VEDDER *Poems* 139 Rax doon the nuts, ye uncolike loon. **1891** H. JOHNSTON *Kilmallie* I. iii, It's an unco-like suspicion, I'm sure.

un'collar, *v.* (UN-2 4 b.)

1611 COTGR., *Escolleté*, vncollered; whose coller is taken off, or pulled away. **1613** PURCHAS *Pilgr.* (1614) 702 Then they are vncollared, freed, and dignified with the Title of Souldiours. **1755** *Mem. Capt. P. Drake* II. i. 2, I.. unbridled and [un]collared my Horse, and put the Hay before him.

unco'llated, *ppl. a.* (UN-1 8.)

[**1775** ASH.] **1787** WHITAKER *Mary Q. Scots Vind.* I. 62 They thus condemn the Queen.. upon letters unauthenticated by the producers, uncollated by themselves. **1885** *Athenæum* 2 May 566/3 The text of various MSS. of the Septuagint unknown or uncollated in Montfaucon's time.

unco'llected, *ppl. a.* (UN-1 8.)

a. Of persons, the mind, etc.: (see COLLECT *v.* 3).

1611 BEAUM. & FL. *Maid's Trag.* IV. ii, What a wild beast is uncollected man! **1613–6** BROWNE *Brit. Past.* I. i, Fearing lest those often idle fits Might clean expel her uncollected wits. **1639** BP. REYNOLDS *Lord's Supper* xviii, Sudden, uncomposed, & uncollected thoughts. **1718** PRIOR *Solomon* II. 291 Asham'd, confus'd I.. to my Soul yet uncollected said: Into Thy self, fond Solomon, return. **1833** MARRYAT *P. Simple* lxiii, My mind was so uncollected.. that I could not feel assured of it for a minute.

b. Of things: (see COLLECT *v.* 1, 1 b).

1730 THOMSON *Autumn* 731 As when of old.., Light, uncollected, thro' the Chaos urg'd Its infant way. **1828–32** WEBSTER s.v., Uncollected taxes; debts uncollected. **1847** L. HUNT Title-p., Men, Women, and Books. A Selection.. from his uncollected Prose Writings.

unco'llegiate, *v.* (UN-² 6 c.)

1851 HANNA *Chalmers* III. 446 The uncollegiating of the five parishes which enjoyed a double ministry. **1867** BLACK *Hist. Brechin* (ed. 2) xi. 278 There is a talk of uncollegiating the parish church.

unco'lloquial, *a.* (UN-¹ 7.)

1840 *London & Westminster Rev.* XXXIII. 113 It is impossible that the impression made upon the audience of the native story-tellers can be of the same uncolloquial and semi-scriptural sort.. as that which [etc.].

unco'lonial, *a.* (UN-¹ 7.)

1861 DICKENS *Gt. Expect.* xlv. III. 92 A certain person not altogether of uncolonial pursuits.

un'colonize, *v.* (UN-² 6 c.)

1824 MEDWIN *Convers. Byron* I. 96 When once she obtained a footing inside my door, .. I had great difficulty in uncolonizing her.

un'colourably, *adv.* (UN-¹ 11.)

1541 WYATT *Decl.* in *Poems* (1913) II. 265 Syncearely and vncolourably from tyme to tyme to declare the trouthe.

un'coloured, *ppl. a.* [UN-¹ 8.]

1. Not having a colour or colours.

1538 ELYOT, *Abaphus*, vndied or vncoloured. **1541** R. COPLAND *Galyen's Terap.* 2 C iij, The partye of the vlcere that is stony and harde and vncoloured ought to be cut. **1667** MILTON *P.L.* v. 189 Whether to deck with Clouds the uncolourd skie, Or wet the thirstie Earth with falling showers. *a* **1684** LEIGHTON *Com. 1 Pet.* (1693) 184 When you look.. through pure uncolour'd glass, you receive the clear light. **1784** COWPER *Task* VI. 178 All this uniform, uncolour'd scene, Shall.. flush into variety again. **1843** PRICHARD *Nat. Hist. Man* 89 When the light.. shone through the transparent texture uncoloured. **1876** O. C. STONE in *Jrnl. R. Geog. Soc.* XLVI. 42 The substitution of a yellow-stained belt for a plain uncoloured one.

2. *fig.* **a.** Not invested with any specious or deceptive appearance or quality; open, undisguised; not influenced or affected *by* something.

1585 ABP. SANDYS *Serm.* 21 Without trecherie and deceit, .. in naked simplicitie, in trueth vncoloured. **1775** BURKE *Corr.* (1844) II. 65 The insolent and uncoloured act of injustice which has been done to my brother. **1827** CARLYLE *Misc.* (1840) I. 30 Such, seen through no uncoloured medium,.. are some features of.. Richter and his works. **1868** FARRAR *Seekers* I. ii. (1875) 32 They have been even entirely uncoloured by his teaching.

b. Plain, simple.

? **1845** DE QUINCEY *Ess., J. Foster* Wks. (1858) 292 The uncoloured style of his general diction.

Hence **un'colouredly** *adv.*; **un'colouredness**.

1561 T. NORTON *Calvin's Inst.* III. 216 They saw themselues to be openly and uncoloredly scorned of the Pope and his Bulbearers. **1660** H. MORE *Myst. Godl.* I. x. 30 *marg.*, The invisibility and uncolouredness of the Air is called Hades or Hell.

un'colted, *a.* [UN-² 8.] Deprived of a horse.

1596 SHAKS. *1 Hen. IV*, II. ii. 41 *Falstaff.* What a plague meane ye to colt me thus? *Prince.* Thou ly'st, thou art not colted, thou art vncolted.

un'combated, *ppl. a.* (UN-¹ 8.)

1649 LOVELACE *Poems* 102 Captive they in Triumph lead each eare and eye, Claiming uncombated the Victorie. **1796** MME. D'ARBLAY *Camilla* III. 65 The uncombated sway of an unavailing, however well-placed attachment.

un'combed, *ppl. a.* Also 6 vncomde, vncomed, 7 vnkombt; *Sc.* and *north.* 7 unkamed, 9 unkaimed. [UN-¹ 8. Cf. UNKEMPT *ppl. a.* and Sw. *okammad*, Du. *ongekamd.*]

1. Not combed; not dressed or smoothed with a comb: **a.** Of hair (or of persons in this respect).

1561 T. NORTON *Calvin's Inst.* IV. xii. §17. 79 Accused men.. with long hanging beard, with vncombed heare. **1591** SPENSER *Daphnaida* 43 His carelesse locks, vncombed and vnshorne, Hong long adowne. **1606** DANIEL *Queen's Arcadia* 2509 Worthier people too, of subtler spirits, Then these vnfashion'd and vncomb'd rude swaines. **1648** CRASHAW *Steps to Temple, Sospetto* ix, Their lockes are beds of uncomb'd snakes. **1745** MRS. MONTAGU *Corr.* (1906) I. 203 The doctor's man, whose uncombed hair so resembled the mane of the horse he rode. **1809–11** COMBE *Syntax* XXIII. 98 My uncomb'd wig,—my suit of black. **1849–50** ALISON *Hist. Eur.* XII. lxxix. §43. 37 The rustic air and uncombed locks of these Scandinavian warriors. **1883** *Sword & Trowel* July 355 All these ragged, unwashed, uncombed children.

b. Of wool.

1642 *Bk. Rates Merchandizes* H 2 b, Irish wooll uncomb'd the hundred weight, .. £2. 16s. **1844** H. STEPHENS *Bk. Farm* III. 894 Combed and uncombed wool of different varieties.

2. *fig.* Rude, inelegant. (Cf. INCOMPT *a.*)

1633 P. FLETCHER *Purple Isl.* III. iii, How may I hope to quit your strong desires, In verse uncomb'd such wonders comprehending?

uncom'binable, *a.* (UN-¹ 7 b.)

1791 WALKER *Pronouncing Dict.* s.v. *Chamber*, *mb* being uncombinable consonants, we cannot end the first syllable with *a.* **1871** BROWNING *Pr. Hohenstiel-Schw.* Wks. 1896 II. 307 Health, strength, beauty,.. uncombinable with flesh and blood.

uncom'bine, *v.* [UN-² 3.] *trans.* To disunite.

1595 DANIEL *Civ. Wars* III. vi, When out-breaking vengeance vncombines The ill-ioyn'd plots so fairly ouercast. **1847** DICKENS *Haunted Man* i, Some of these phantoms trembling at heart like things that knew his power to uncombine them.

uncom'bined, *ppl. a.* (UN-¹ 8.)

1611 FLORIO, *Incombinato*, vncombined. **1803** WELLESLEY in Owen *Desp.* (1877) 222 Uncombined with the power of Scindiah, Holkar will not probably venture to resist the Peishwa. **1858** H. BUSHNELL *Nat. & Supernat.* ix. (1864) 251 Nature, unapplied or uncombined by our wills, could do no such thing.

b. *spec.* in chemical or technical use.

1785 *Phil. Trans.* LXXV. 293 There was never any sensible quantity of uncombined fixed air mixed with the inflammable air. **1825** J. NICHOLSON *Operat. Mechanic* 708 The specific gravity of the alloy is greater than that of the two metals in an uncombined state. **1876** TAIT *Rec. Adv. Phys. Sci.* vii. (ed. 2) 161 There may be.. enormous masses of as yet uncombined iron and uncombined sulphur.

uncom'bining, *ppl. a.* (UN-¹ 10.)

1643 MILTON *Divorce* 18 To sowe the furrow of mans nativity with seed of two incoherent and uncombining dispositions. **1651** JER. TAYLOR *Serm. for Year* II. ii. 22 His purposes untwist, as easily as the rude conjuncture of uncombining cables, in the violence of a Northern tempest.

Hence **uncom'biningness**.

1850 *Tait's Mag.* XVII. 735/1 The very same characteristics of inertia, unintellectuality, and uncombiningness.

†**uncom'bust**, *ppl. a. Obs.* (UN-¹ 8 b.)

a **1568** in *Bannatyne MS.* (Hunter. Club) 110/43 Thow, Moyses busk remanyng vncombust. **1673** HICKERINGILL *Greg. F. Greyb.* 34 Jove being uncombust and free.

uncom'bustible, *a.* (UN-¹ 7.)

1576 G. BAKER tr. *Gesner's Jewell of Health* 191 An oyle of Naphta, that is of Brimstone uncombustible or never burned.

†**uncome**, *sb. Obs.* [Of obscure formation: see ONCOME *sb.* and ANCOME.]

1. = ONCOME *sb.* 1.

1538 ELYOT, *Aduentitius morbus*, syckenes that cometh without our defaute, and of some menne is called an vncome.

2. = ANCOME, INCOME *sb.*²

1542–3 *Act 34 & 35 Hen. VIII*, c. 8 § 1 Vncomes of handes .. & such other like diseases. **1562** BULLEIN *Bulwarke, Dial. Sorenes & Chir.* 10 b, Apostumacions that spryng of blood, or choller, be diuersly termed by sundrie names as botches, .. uncomes. **1597** GERARDE *Herbal* 362 An impostume in the ioints of the fingers (called among the vulgare sort a fellon or vncome). **1601** HOLLAND *Pliny* II. 188 The seed [of the tamarisk].. is singular good for any uncom or fellon. **1697** *View Penal Laws* 208 It is lawful for persons skilful in the Nature of Herbs.. to Practise and Minister to any outward Sore, Uncom, Wound.

un'come, *ppl. a.* Now *north. dial.* Also *Sc.* 6 uncum, vncuming, 7 oncum. [UN-² 8 b. Cf. ON. and Icel. *ú-*, *ókominn* (Norw. *ukomen*, MSw. *okomin*).] Not (yet) arrived.

1512 *Acc. Ld. High Treas. Scot.* IV. 295 The Kingis schippis boght and as ȝit uncum to Scotland. **1535** STEWART *Cron. Scot.* (Rolls) III. 441 The lordis.. Quhilk in England vncuming hame war than. **1649** I. BASIRE *Corr.* (1831) 98 A bill of 50 *l* which should have come in August last, is yet uncome. **1659** *Knaresb. Wills* (Surtees) II. 240 Yeares of a lease.. which are yet uncome and unexpired. *a* **1670** SPALDING *Troub. Chas. I* (1851) II. 343 He mist sum of Strathbogie men oncum thair. **1828** *Craven Gloss.*, *Uncome*, not come. **1877** *Holderness Gloss.* 151 He's uncome yit.

uncome-'at-able, *a.* (Freq. unhyphened.) Also 7 uncomatible, 8–9 -able. [UN-¹ 7 b.] Unattainable; inaccessible.

Characterized by Johnson as 'a low, corrupt word'.

α. **1694** CONGREVE *Double-Dealer* II. v, My Honour is infallible and uncomatible. **1706** E. WARD *Wooden World Diss.* (1708) 69 It's an uncomatable Mark, that's certain. **1726** *Adv. Capt. R. Boyle* (1768) 231 The Juice of the Grape is very uncomatable there. **1822** SCOTT *Nigel* xxxii, To whom, I doubt, he awes an uncomatable sum.

β. **1709** STEELE *Tatler* No. 12 ¶ 18 He has a perfect Art in being unintelligible in Discourse, and uncomeatable in Business. **1732** *Hist. Litteraria* III. 549 Some have asserted .. that Truth was absolutely uncomeatable. **1818** MISS MITFORD in L'Estrange *Life* (1870) II. 35 He is un-come-at-able. One never knows where to catch him. **1847** *Illustr. Lond. News* 4 Sept. 158, I have never seen so uncomeatable a place. **1890** D. C. MURRAY *John Vale's Guardian* xv, The hidden uncomeatable parts of his purchase.

Hence **uncome-'at-ableness**.

1727 BAILEY (vol. II).

†**un'comelily**, *adv. Obs.* (UN-¹ 11.)

c **1420** *Anturs of Arth.* 106 (Thornton MS.), Bare was hir body, and.. Alle by-claggede in claye, vn-comlyly clede. **1561** T. NORTON *Calvin's Inst.* IV. v. §17. 31 The dignitie of the Church is by that magnificence not vncomlily vpholden. **1658** GURNALL *Chr. in Arm.* II. (1669) 50/1 He walks not haltingly and uncomelily.

un'comeliness. [f. next.]

1. The quality of being uncomely; want of comeliness (†or seemliness); an uncomely feature.

1542 BECON *Potation for Lent* G iij, To make clene yᵉ face of our hart, from all fylthinesse of synnes & from the vncomelynes of trespasse. **1589** PUTTENHAM *Eng. Poesie* III. xxiv. (Arb.) 297 In euery vncomlinesse there must be a certaine absurditie and disproportion to nature. **1624** HEYWOOD *Gunaik.* II. 64 They raysed a kind of uncomelinesse and deformitie in the faces of such as playd upon them. **1670** MILTON *Hist. Brit.* II. 60 Her own Subjects, who detested.. the uncomeliness of thir Subjection to the Monarchie of a Woeman. **1711** STEELE *Spect.* No. 52 ¶ 3 The native and unaffected Uncomeliness of her Person. **1795** BURKE *Abridgm. Eng. Hist.* Wks. 1842 II. 509 He has joined to these powers of living existence uncomeliness, want of strength, want of distinction. **1865** M. ARNOLD *Ess. Crit.* iv. (1875) 164 That brick-and-mortar image of English Protestantism, representing it in all its prose, all its uncomeliness.

†**2.** Unruliness. *Obs.*⁻¹

1607 MARKHAM *Cavel.* v. 22 If you finde his [a horse's] vncomelinesse onelye proceedes from ticklishnesse.

un'comely, *a.* [UN-¹ 7.]

1. Not pleasing or agreeable to the moral sense or to notions of propriety; unbecoming, improper, unseemly.

c **1230** *Hali Meid.* 25 As tah ha nefden wit in ham ne tweire schead as mon haueð, ba of god & of uuel, of cumelich & of uncumelich [*v.r.* vnkumelich]. **1362** LANGL. *P. Pl.* A. x. 180 Hit is an vn-Comely Couple.. To ȝeuen a ȝong wenche to an old feble Mon. *a* **1400** *Sir Degrev.* 1638 The body syttys opon the hors, Hyt was uncomely to the cors. **1538** STARKEY *England* 52 He.. began to persuade the rest.. to forsake that rudnes & vncomly lyfe. **1583** BABINGTON *Commandm.* (1590) 271 Whereunto for an other inticement to vncleannes, wee may referre all vndecent and vncomely pictures. **1622** in *Harl. Misc.* (Malh.) III. 459 All such reasons are uncomely and unchristian to be objected. **1653** A. WILSON *Jas. I*, 39 If any man speaks any thing uncomely there, the Chancellour.. interrupts him. *a* **1683** OWEN *Two Discourses Holy Spirit* II. iv. (1693) 169 Uncomely Artifices of intreiguing Secular Courts. **1759** ROBERTSON *Hist. Scot.* App. x, To avoid broad and uncomely speech.

2. Not pleasing or agreeable to the senses; not comely or fair to look upon. Also *absol.*

a **1400** *Octavian* 884 Clement broght forthe schylde and spere, That were uncomely for to were, Alle sutty, blakk, and unclene. **1513** MORE *Hist. Rich. III*, Wks. 36/2 In hys later dayes with ouer liberall diet, sommewhat corpulente and boorelye, and nathelesse not vncomelye. **1531** ELYOT *Gov.* I. xi, We se, that therof.. the childrens personages do waxe uncomely and lasse growe in stature. **1607** MARKHAM *Cavel.* IV. (1617) 36 To make horses amble without either marring their mouthes, vnsetling their heads, or breeding any other vncomely disorders. **1611** BIBLE *1 Cor.* xii. 23 Our vncomely parts haue more abundant comlinesse. **1710** STEELE *Spect.* No. 17 ¶ 1 Since our Persons are not of our own Making, when they are such as appear Defective or Uncomely, it is, methinks, an honest and laudable Fortitude to dare to be Ugly. **1824** BYRON *Def. Transf.* I. i, Your aspect is Dusky, but not uncomely. **1847** BRONTË *J. Eyre* xvi, Mrs. Poole's square, flat figure, and uncomely, dry, even coarse face. **1866** WHITTIER *Margaret Smith's Jrnl.* 12 Nov. 1678, Charity.. maketh the weak strong and the uncomely beautiful.

†**un'comely**, *adv. Obs.* [UN-¹ 11.] In an uncomely manner; unsuitably, unbecomingly.

c **1375** *Cursor M.* 891 (Fairf.), Worme þou sal be vncumly diȝt, mare þan any oþer wiȝt. *c* **1420** *Anturs of Arth.* 106 (Douce MS.), Bare was þe body, and.. Al bi-clagged in clay, vncomly cladde. *c* **1510** BARCLAY *Mirr. Gd. Manners* (1570) A ij, A man with hoare heres vncomely doth incline To misframed fables or gesture feminine. **1542** UDALL *Erasm. Apoph.* 300 Will noman chastice this feloe here uncomely demeanyng hymself? **1605** BACON *Adv. Learn.* I. iii. §9 The great Ladie.. would needs haue him carie her little Dogge, which he doing officiously, and yet vncomely, the Page scoffed. **1619** FLETCHER & MASS. *False One* III. i, 'Tis most uncomely spoken.

un'comfort, *sb.* (UN-¹ 12.)

1805 MISS BERRY *Jrnls. & Corr.* (1865) II. 297 No uncomforts of situation, no sufferings, shall ever tempt me to any step [etc.]. **1853** G. J. CAYLEY *Las Alforjas* I. 154 Getting tired of.. the uncomfort of our rude, straw-stuffed pads.

un'comfort, *v. rare*⁻¹. (UN-² 3.)

1637 WHITING *Albino & Bell.* 22 The gods.. have ravel'd thy content, Sorrowes uncomfort will thy virgine yeares.

un'comfortable, *a.* [UN-¹ 7 b and 5 b.]

1. Not comforting; causing or involving discomfort or uneasiness; disquieting.

1592 SHAKS. *Rom. & Jul.* IV. v. 60 Vncomfortable time, why cam'st thou now To murther, murther our solemnitie? **1615** G. SANDYS *Trav.* 92 The lightning ministring uncomfortable light, intermixed with thunder and tempests. **1653** W. RAMESEY *Astrol. Restored* To Rdr. 8 But pass we these five troublesome, uncomfortable years also. **1680** W. ALLEN *Peace & Unity* Pref. p. iii, To put an end to our dishonourable and uncomfortable contentions. **1711** ADDISON *Spect.* No. 159 ¶ 8 The Genius.. bid me quit so uncomfortable a Prospect. **1785** BURNEY in *Parr's Wks.* (1828) VII. 397, I lament.. the uncomfortable account which you give of your health. **1843** PRESCOTT *Mexico* III. i. (1850) I. 347 They were to sanguine to allow such uncomfortable surmises long to dwell in their minds. **1873** TRISTRAM *Moab* i. 16 The Jehalin look.. most uncomfortable ruffians to meet in an unfriendly way.

†**2.** Incapable of being comforted; inconsolable.

1592 R. D. *Hypnerotomachia* 22 b, The uncomfortable and still mourning Cyparissus. **1611** COTGR., *Inconsolable*,

inconsolable, vncomfortable, not to be comforted. **1667** MARVELL *Corr.* Wks. (Grosart) II. 402 On a private loss,.. to be impatient, to be uncomfortable, would be to dispute with God.

3. Feeling discomfort; ill at ease; uneasy.

1796 MME. D'ARBLAY *Camilla* IV. 427 [She was] impelled by this notion, yet wavering, dissatisfied and uncomfortable. **1825** J. NEAL *Bro. Jonathan* I. 3 The whole family were afraid of him;..felt uncomfortable, if he looked into their eyes. **1841** HELPS *Ess., Aids Contentm.* (1842) 16 They are most uncomfortable if their little projects do not turn out according to their fancy. **1887** *Spectator* 20 Aug. 1115 One of them wanting the window open and the other wanting it shut, one of them must be uncomfortable.

un'comfortableness. [f. prec.]

†**1.** Inconsolableness. *Obs.*$^{-1}$

a **1639** W. WHATELEY *Prototypes* I. xxi. (1640) 267 Isaac outlived Josephs selling into Egypt, and was afflicted in Jacobs uncomfortablenesse under that crosse. **1727** BAILEY (vol. II), *Inconsolableness*, a State of uncomfortableness, or that will not admit of Comfort.

2. The quality or state of causing or involving discomfort.

1677 MIÉGE, Uncomfortableness, *l'état triste, ou fâcheux de quēque chose.* **1727** BAILEY (vol. II), *Uncomfortableness*, Uneasiness, Unpleasingness. **1743** BULKELEY & CUMMINS *Voy. S. Seas* 82 Add to our Uneasiness, the Uncomfortableness of the Climate. **1795** FRANCES DILLON in *Jerningham Lett.* (1896) I. 83 The Uncomfortableness of y[ou]r long absence. **1853** KANE *Grinnell Exp.* xxix. (1856) 240 Our abiding-place below has a smoky atmosphere of lamplit uncomfortableness. **1856** HAWTHORNE *Eng. Note-bks.* (1879) I. 379 The vile uncomfortableness of a military life.

3. The fact of feeling uncomfortable.

1828 LYTTON *Pelham* II. xxv, There is such a certain uncomfortableness always occasioned to the mind by stillness and mystery united, that [etc.]. **1847** MRS. SHERWOOD *Fairchild Family* III. ii. 24 Ready to cry from fatigue, sleep, and uncomfortableness. **1872** HUXLEY *Physiol.* viii. 188 Such are the sensations of uncomfortableness.

un'comfortably, *adv.* [f. as prec.] In an uncomfortable manner; with discomfort or uneasiness, disagreeably; †inconsolably.

c **1425** *St. Mary of Oignies* II. iii. 13 in *Anglia* VIII. 158 þe holy man..made dule vncomfortabely for defoylynge of chirches. *a* **1548** HALL *Chron., Hen. V*, 60 b, This miserable people vncomfortably forsaken & vnnaturally dispised of their owne nacion. **1594** DRAYTON *Matilda* xxxvi, Thus in my closet being left alone, Vpon the floore vncomfortably lying. **1612** T. TAYLOR *Comm. Titus* iii. 6 Water is so necessarie a creature, as nothing can be more dangerously or vncomfortably wanting to the life of man. **1643–5** MILTON *Divorce* II. viii, Rather then to live uncomfortably and unhappily both to himself and to his wife,..he might dismisse her. **1719** DE FOE *Crusoe* I. (Globe) 112, I wander'd about very uncomfortably. **1796** MRS. M. ROBINSON *Angelina* I. 104, I felt most uncomfortably, and would have given anything I possess to have been out of the carriage. **1856** KANE *Arct. Expl.* II. ix. 96 Long and uncomfortably have I pondered over these opposing calls. **1879** *Cassell's Techn. Educ.* IV. 236/1 The native article becomes uncomfortably sticky in the heat of tropical climates.

un'comforted, *ppl. a.* (UN-^{1} 8.)

1583 BABINGTON *Commandm.* (1590) 344 It is very barbarous crueltie to leaue them vtterly vncomforted, with any portion of that which was taken about them. *a* **1586** SIDNEY *Arcadia* I. xvii. (1912) 110 So (uncomforted therein) [he] sent him away. *a* **1625** BEAUM. & FL. *Laws of Candy* III. i, Let me yet by these Awake your love to my uncomforted Brother. **1797** COLERIDGE *Dungeon* 12 And this is their best cure! uncomforted And friendless solitude. **1832** TENNYSON *Œnone* 256 Lest their shrill happy laughter come to me Walking the cold and starless road of Death Uncomforted. **1835** TRENCH *Justin Martyr* 130 Our great Father, when he sat Uncomforted on Ararat.

un'comforting, *ppl. a.* (UN-^{1} 10.)

1798 *Monthly Mag.* IV. 47, I wander And look upon the busy Danaids Alike uncomforting, uncomforted.

†**un'comfortless,** *a. Obs.* (UN-^{1} 5 a.)

1598 YONG *Diana* 235 Wofull man vncomfortlesse, and sad.

†**un'coming,** *vbl. sb. Obs.*$^{-1}$ (UN-^{1} 13.)

1593 T. MATHEWS in Tytler *Hist. Scotl.* (1864) IV. 199 Mr. Lock, whom these two days he hath looked for, and mervaileth not a little at his uncoming.

†**unco'mmand,** *v. Obs.*$^{-1}$ [UN-^{2} 3.] *trans.* To countermand, to abrogate.

c **1430** *Pilgr. Lyf Manhode* II. xxi. (1869) 83 Wolt thou hold the gospel at fable and lesinge? thou seist it vncomanded that that god hath ordeyned.

unco'mmanded, *ppl. a.* [UN-^{2} 8.]

1. Not ordered to be done or observed.

14.. *Chaucer's Parl. Foules* 518 (Camb. MS.), For office vncommaundet full ofte anoyth. **1538** BALE *Thre Lawes* 1682 In vayne offer yow that vncommaunded seruyce. **1594** HOOKER *Eccl. Pol.* IV. vii. §5 Except the one doe auoid whatsoeuer Rites and Ceremonies vncommanded of God the other doth embrace. **1643** *Let. from Grave Gentleman* 3 The People, engaged..under Pretence of an uncommanded protestation. **1692** SOUTH *Serm.* (1697) I. 39 Those affected, uncommanded, absurd Austerities,..exercised by some of the Romish Profession. **1723** ATTERBURY *Serm.* (1726) I. x. 352 They were, I say, Uncommanded Instances of Virtue. **1794** MRS. PIOZZI *Synon.* II. 323 Such uncommanded seclusion is evil for society.

2. Not ordered to do something.

1534 MORE *Comf. agst. Trib.* III. Wks. 1224/1 That they maye..commaunde and controlle other menne, and liue vncommaunded them selfe. *a* **1586** SIDNEY *Arcadia* V. (1598) 449 Pardon me most honoured Iudge, saith he, that vncommaunded I begin my speech vnto you. **1646** EARL MONM. tr. *Biondi's Civil Warres* VI. 54 Lewis after this commanded his men to retire; and Edwards men forthwith withdrew uncommanded. *a* **1667** COWLEY *On Death W. Hervey* i, My eyes with Tears did uncommanded flow. *a* **1716** BLACKALL *Wks.* (1723) I. 133 If any private Soldier quits his Station, and runs himself uncommanded upon a dangerous Adventure, he deserves Reproof.

3. Not dominated or overlooked (*by* something).

1693 *Mem. Ct. Teckely* III. 56 Being seated upon an inaccessible Rock uncommanded,..a few Men might be able to defend it against a great Army. **1821** BYRON *Sardanap.* V. i, The river's broad and swoln, and uncommanded..by these besiegers. **1829** SCOTT *Anne of G.* xv, It was in a corner,..uncommanded by any of the angles of the fortification.

Hence **unco'mmandedness.**

1646 HAMMOND *Tracts* Pref., Perswading themselves and others..that the uncommandednesse of any thing induces that excesse.

unco'mmander-like, *a.* (UN-^{1} 7 c.)

1644 MILTON *Divorce* II. xi. 53 What more un-Judge-like, more un-Magistrate-like, and..more un-commander-like?

unco'mmendable, *a.* (UN-^{1} 7 b and 5 b.)

1509 BARCLAY *Shyp of Folys* (1570) 228 It is thing lawfull and not vncommendable. **1548** UDALL *Erasm. Par. Luke* Pref. C j b, It is vncommendable thorough vain arrogancie to take vpon vs that we haue not. **1603** BRETON *Dial. Pith & Pleas.* Wks. (Grosart) II. 9/2 The most dishonourable, and vncommendable of all creatures in the world. **1697** JOS. WOODWARD *Relig. Soc.* i. (1701) 15, I know no worldly, sinister, or uncommendable design proposed or prosecuted thereby. **1758** WALPOLE *Catal. Roy. Authors* (1759) II. 172 This is the only uncommendable performance of our Author's life. **1959** I. & P. OPIE *Lore & Lang. Schoolch.* xviii. 377 Almost any group of 12-year-olds, asked what are their favourite after-dark games, will name doorbell-ringing, and similar uncommendable activities. **1983** T. DE VERE WHITE *Johnnie Cross* i. 12 The public had shown uncommendable restraint in the book shops.

Hence **unco'mmendably** *adv.*

1589 PUTTENHAM *Eng. Poesie* II. xii[i]. (Arb.) 126 As he that translated certaine bookes of Virgils Eneydos in such measures and not vncommendably. **1882** *Academy* 16 Dec. 433/3 He dipped a little into scholarship, too, and not uncommendably.

unco'mmended, *ppl. a.* (UN-^{1} 8.)

1570 LEVINS *Manip.* 50 Vncommended, *illaudatus.* **1645** WALLER *'Goe lovely Rose'* ii, Hadst thou sprung In deserts where no men abide, Thou must have uncommended dy'd.

†**unco'mmensurate,** *a. Obs.* (UN-^{1} 7 and 5 b.)

1676 GLANVILL *Ess.* i. 18 Our Senses are short, imperfect, and uncommensurate to the vastness and profundity of things. **1702** S. PARKER tr. *Cicero's De Finibus* IV. 237 Upon what Account therefore is Man so singular as to..take up with a *Summum Bonum* uncommensurate to the whole of his Person?

unco'mmented, *ppl. a.* (UN-^{1} 8.)

1751 J. BROWN *Shaftesb. Charac.* 318 The only method.. is to search for them in the uncommented pages of the Gospel. **1877** BROWNING *La Saisiaz* 359 T'aversed heart must tell its story uncommented on.

unco'mmerciable, *a.* (UN-^{1} 7 b.)

1787 JEFFERSON *Writ.* (1859) II. 189 By prohibiting all his Majesty's subjects from dealing in tobacco, one third of the exports of the United States are rendered uncommerciable here.

unco'mmercial, *a.* (UN-^{1} 7.)

1768 PENNANT *Brit. Zool.* I. 23 The uncommercial genius of the people. **1796** H. HUNTER tr. *St.-Pierre's Stud. Nat.* (1799) III. 116 There reigned at that time so much honesty and simplicity in this un-commercial island, that [etc.]. **1860** DICKENS (*title*), The Uncommercial Traveller. **1892** E. REEVES *Homeward Bound* 271 Cordova..is the quiet, uncommercial centre of an excellent wheat and olive country.

unco'mmingled, *ppl. a.* (UN-^{1} 8.)

1861 S. WILBERFORCE *Ess.* (1874) I. 181 Both natures being uncommingled, though both eternally united in the person of the Son.

un'comminuted, *ppl. a.* (UN-^{1} 8.)

1757 *Phil. Trans.* L. 156 This part will be retained, after long trituration,..uncomminuted by the pestle.

unco'mmiserated, *ppl. a.* (UN-^{1} 8.)

1611 SPEED *Hist. Gt. Brit.* IX. xvi. §45. 831/2 Thus Sommerset, and the English, are compelled to quit Normandy, not onely inglorious, but also in England it selfe vncommiserated.

unco'mmiserating, *ppl. a.* (UN-^{1} 10.)

1679 *Establ. Test* 41 Oh Injustice and uncomiserating Cruelty!

unco'mmissioned, *ppl. a.* [UN-^{1} 8.]

1. Not commissioned or authorized.

1659 FULLER *App. Inj. Innoc.* (1840) 618 Commissioned plunder begun with the war, but uncommissioned plunder was before it. *a* **1711** KEN *Anodynes* Poet. Wks. 1721 III. 460 Whose Voice I labour to suppress; While she my State bemoans, In uncommission'd Sighs and Groans. **1738** WARBURTON *Div. Legat.* I. 168 A little Priest's bringing the Mysteries into Etruria, on his own head; uncommissioned by his Superiors. **1802–12** BENTHAM *Ration. Judic. Evid.* (1827) I. 533 Uncommissioned inspecting judges. **1842** PUSEY *Crisis Eng. Ch.* 107 The one holds Ordination to be derived from the Apostles; the other, that Presbyters, uncommissioned, may confer it.

2. Of ships: = NON-COMMISSIONED *a.* 2.

1822 M. EDGEWORTH *Let.* 12 June (1971) 407 The Nelson —just finished but uncommissioned a first rate man of war 120 guns. **1863** *Lond. Rev.* 10 Jan. 7 The order of Earl Russell to detain her at Nassau must have been made under the impression that she would have reached that port uncommissioned.

unco'mmitted, *ppl. a.* [UN-^{1} 8.]

1. Not entrusted or delegated.

c **1381** CHAUCER *Parl. Foules* 518 Whoso hyt doth full fowle hymsylf accloyeth For offyce vncommyttyd oft anoyeth.

2. Not committed or perpetrated; (left) undone.

1598 BARRET *Theor. Warres* 11 Gracelesse fellowes which do leaue no kinde of rauening crueltie vncommitted. **1607** HIERON *Wks.* I. 183 He would haue giuen a world, if he had beene able, that the fact of betraying Christ had beene vncommitted. **1643** HAMMOND *Lent Serm. at Oxford* Wks. 1683 IV. 511 Because he hath..no strength to maintain, no injury to provoke the uncommitted sin. **1814** BYRON *Corsair* II. xi. 22 She scarce had left an uncommitted crime. **1891** MEREDITH *One of our Conq.* xxxiv, To have the forgiveness for her uncommitted sin dashed in her face.

3. Not referred to a committee.

1807 JEFFERSON *Writ.* (1830) IV. 95 We propose..to leave the question of war, non-intercourse, or other measures, uncommitted, to the legislature.

4. Not pledged to any particular course. Also *absol.*

1814 CHALMERS *Let.* in Hanna *Life* (1849) I. 444, I trust you will concede to me the right of bringing a free and uncommitted mind to this matter. **1826** DISRAELI *Viv. Grey* III. i, A young man, uncommitted in political principles. **1884** *Manch. Exam.* 28 Oct. 5/3 Up to the present..the deputation..prefer to regard themselves as uncommitted. **1956** BALL & KILLOUGH *International Relations* xxiii. 494 The Arabs had rejected association with the West and insisted on maintaining a 'neutral' position. Many Arab leaders regarded the Middle Eastern states as likely to be safer from Soviet attack if they remained uncommitted to the West. **1958** *Listener* 6 Mar. 390/2 It brings in not only countries committed to Western alignment, like the Philippines, Siam, and Pakistan, but also uncommitted countries of the neutral bloc, like India, Burma, and Indonesia. **1958** *Spectator* 22 Aug. 259/2 The key..lies..in a transformation of American relations with the uncommitted world. **1959** *Oxf. Mag.* 11 June 469/2 Islam is likely to gain far more of the uncommitted than is Christianity. **1959** *News Chron.* 10 July 4/2 The uncommitted voter. **1961** *Daily Tel.* 31 Aug. 10 Neutralism, Mr Foster Dulles once declared, is immoral. Nowadays, when the 'uncommitted' constitute a decisive, if not solid, phalanx in the United Nations, Western statesmen eschew such language.

unco'mmixed, *ppl. a.* (UN-^{1} 8 and 5 b.)

c **1611** CHAPMAN *Iliad* x. 369 The Thracian quarter lies Utmost of all and uncommix'd with Trojan regiments. **1660** J. H[ARDING] *Basil. Valent. Chariot Antim.* 3 The Chaff being separated from the uncommix'd and undefiled Corn. **1814** SOUTHEY *Roderick* xv. 250 A feeling uncommixed with sense of guilt Or shame..thrill'd through the King.

†**unco'mmoded,** *ppl. a. Obs.* (UN-^{1} 8 and 5 b.)

1683 MOXON *Mech. Exerc., Printing* ii. ⁋1 A Window..on the North-side the Room, that the Press-men..may be the less uncommoded with the heat of the Sun.

†**unco'mmodious,** *a. Obs.* (UN-^{1} 7 and 5 b.)

1539 ELYOT *Cast. Helthe* (1541) 54 b, If any grefe hapneth of the heade, vomite is than uncommodious. **1597** BEARD *Theatre God's Judgem.* (1612) 463 How hurtfull and vncommodious the desire..was vnto them. **1643–5** MILTON *Divorce* II. xxi, To forbid dislike..were indeed an uncommodious rudenesse, not a just power. **1680** MOXON *Mech. Exerc.* x. 184 To tire it [the leg] quickly with bringing it down again, after it is raised to so uncommodious a position.

So †**unco'mmodiously** *adv. Obs.*

1545 ELYOT, *Incommode*,..vncommodiously, ylle fauouredly. **1647** HEXHAM I, Vncommodiously, *ongerievelick.*

un'common, *a.* (and *adv.*). [UN-^{1} 7.]

1. Not possessed in common. *rare*$^{-1}$.

1548 UDALL, etc., *Erasm. Par. John* xiv. 85 b, Betwene vs two is no vnlykenes, or any thyng vncommon as touchyng the hier, and our diuine nature.

2. Not commonly (to be) met with; not of ordinary occurrence; unusual, rare.

1611 COTGR., *Incommune*, vncommon; or, not common. **1665** BOYLE *Occas. Refl.* VI. vi. 209 'Tis so uncommon a thing to see Tulips last till Roses come to be blown. **1676** GLANVILL *Ess.* vi. 28 To give us some general notice of those uncommon Events which they foresee. **1712** ADDISON *Spect.* No. 421 ⁋2 Whatever is New or Uncommon is apt to delight the Imagination. **1732** BERKELEY *Alciphr.* v. §20 Nor is it an uncommon thing to behold ignorance and zeal united in men. **1770** *Junius Lett.* xli. (1788) 227 Yours is not an uncommon character. **1818** BYRON *Juan* I. i, I want a hero: an uncommon want, When every year and month sends forth a new one. **1884** THOMPSON *Tumours of Bladder* 1 There is little doubt that these growths are by no means uncommon.

absol. **1806** SURR *Winter in Lond.* II. 58 He was compelled to admit, that the uncommon is nevertheless the possible.

3. Unusual in amount, extent, or degree; remarkably great; above the ordinary.

1700 PRIOR *Carm. Sec.* xxiii, She, from the noble Precipices thrown, Comes rushing with uncommon Ruin down. **1736** BERKELEY *Disc.* Wks. III. 427 Such bad notions have..been propagated with uncommon industry in these kingdoms. **1774** J. BRYANT *Mythol.* II. 100 Semiramis, a woman of uncommon endowments, and great personal charms. **1825** COBBETT *Rur. Rides* 450 He seems to have taken uncommon pains in the execution of this work. **1864** FROUDE *Short Stud.* (1867) I. 2 He was a man of uncommon power.

4. Of an unusual type or character; exceptional in kind or quality. Also *absol.*

1705 ADDISON *Italy* Pref., His masterly and uncommon Observations on the Religion and Governments of Italy. **1758** S. HAYWARD *Serm.* xvii. 550 We could not but value so uncommon a friend. **1819** SHELLEY *Peter Bell 3rd* IV. xvi, The Devil was no uncommon creature. **1882** W. SHARP *Rossetti* iii. 105 The spiritual is ever foreign to the material, the *un*common to the common.

5. *Mus.* (See quot.)

c **1833** *Encycl. Metrop.* (1845) V. 778 *Uncommon chord*, the chord of the sixth, not so called because unusual or improper, but in contradistinction to the common chord.

6. As *adv.* = UNCOMMONLY *adv.* 2. *colloq.* or *dial.*

1784 *New Spectator* No. 15. 1 To hear another of austere gravity, burst into an uncommon loud fit of laughter at a trifling incident. **1818** LADY MORGAN *Autobiog.* (1859) 190 He was uncommon afraid of the custom-house officers. **1851** KINGSLEY *Yeast* ix, He consorts with them poachers, sir, uncommon. I hope he ben't one himself. **1891** 'J. S. WINTER' *Lumley* i, They're an uncommon thirsty lot to-night.

un'commonable, *a.* (UN-[1] 7 b.)

1768 BLACKSTONE *Comm.* III. 237 In case..the uncommonable cattle of a commoner be found upon the land.

un'commonly, *adv.* [Cf. UNCOMMON *a.* and UN-[1] 11.]

1. *not uncommonly*, not rarely; pretty frequently.

1747 J. SMITH *Mem. Wool* Pref. a j *note*, A Person more than ordinarily concerned, and not uncommonly employed. **1883** STUBBS *Med. & Mod. Hist.* xv. (1886) 343 We are not uncommonly told that Henry VII. had not in his own person the shadow of hereditary right.

2. In an uncommon or unusual degree; unusually, remarkably.

1751 EARL ORRERY *Remarks Swift* (1752) 10 Otherwise it was thought impossible, that he could be so uncommonly munificent to a young man, no ways related to him. **1794** MRS. RADCLIFFE *Myst. Udolpho* liv, There was something in his countenance uncommonly interesting. **1840** R. H. DANA *Bef. Mast* xxiv, He wrote an uncommonly handsome hand. **1885** *Truth* 28 May 847/2 The high-priced nobodies who.. do so uncommonly little.

un'commonness. [f. UNCOMMON *a.*] The quality or state of being uncommon; unusualness.

1705 ADDISON *Italy* 225 Our admiration of 'em does not so much arise out of their Greatness as Uncommonness. **1730** GAY *Let. to Swift* 6 Dec., For the uncommonness of the thing, I fansy, your curiosity will prevail over your fear. **1830** CARLYLE *Misc.* (1840) II. 365 Some features of originality, as well as of uncommonness. **1882** *Pall Mall G.* 8 April, This..presents the common with due uncommonness and suggestiveness.

un'commonplace, *a.* (UN-[1] 7.)

1873 HELPS *Anim. & Mast.* i. (1875) 23 Everything seems clever and uncommonplace in a language of which you know but little. **1887** LD. GRANVILLE in Fitzmaurice *Life* (1905) II. 497 The charm of your..uncommonplace character.

unco'mmunicable, *a.* [UN-[1] 7 b and 5 b.]

1. That cannot or may not be communicated; incommunicable.

1382 WYCLIF *Wisd.* xiv. 21 The vncomunycable name to stones and trees thei putten. **1555** EDEN *Decades* (Arb.) 297 The diuine prouidence hath made nothynge vncommunicable. **1587** GOLDING *De Mornay* vi. (1592) 70 Men were forbidden to vtter the vncommunicable name of God. **1612** SELDEN *Illustr. Drayton's Poly-olb.* xiii. 269 A perfect and uncommunicable power royall. **1650** COWLEY *Let.* 9 July, Wks. (Grosart) II. 348/2 Their hopes of an uncommunicable Victory. **1742** WARBURTON in *Pope's Wks.* (1788) VI. 135 His having no Delight in any thing uncommunicated or uncommunicable. **1780** BURKE *Sp. at Bristol* Wks. 1808 III. 369 The peculiar, reserved, uncommunicable rights of England. **1833** LD. HOUGHTON *Mem. Many Scenes, To Landor* (1844) 144 The power of uncommunicable Art.

†2. Uncommunicative. *Obs.*[−1]

1628 FELTHAM *Resolves* II. vii. 16 Neither [master nor servant] can haue comfort, where both are vncommunicable.

Hence **unco'mmunicably** *adv.*

1817 SHELLEY *To Constantia Singing* 12 A breathless awe, ..Wild, sweet, but uncommunicably strange.

†**unco'mmunicant.** *Obs.*[−1] [UN-[1] 12.] = NON-COMMUNICANT.

1600 *Vestry Bks.* (Surtees) 278 Our certificate concerninge the recusantes and uncommunicantes.

†**unco'mmunicate**, *a. Obs.*[−1] [UN-[1] 7 and 5 b.] = next.

1664 H. MORE *Antid. Idolatry* ii. 34 If it be not, we give an uncommunicate Excellency to the Creature, and rob God of his Right and Honour.

unco'mmunicated, *ppl. a.* (UN-[1] 8 and 5 b.)

1597 HOOKER *Eccl. Pol.* v. liii. §1 Whatsoeuer is naturall to Deitie, the same remaineth in Christ vncommunicated vnto his Manhood. **1647** CLARENDON *Contempl. Ps.* Tracts (1727) 438 Whose uncommunicated prerogative it is, to discern clearly the thoughts and inclinations of all hearts. **1720** WATERLAND *Eight Serm.* 224 Supreme Power, whether communicated or uncommunicated, is supreme Power. **1826** SOUTHEY *Vind. Eccl. Angl.* 278 Disposed to uphold the[ir] ascendancy..by uncommunicated knowledge, and unrelenting severity.

unco'mmunicating, *ppl. a.* (UN-[1] 10, 5 b.)

1650 JER. TAYLOR *Funeral Serm. C'tess Carbery* 5 There are exterminating Angels that fly wrapt up in the curtains of immateriality and an uncommunicating nature. **1765** BLACKSTONE *Comm.* I. 95 From a diversity of practice in two large and uncommunicating jurisdictions. **1801** SOUTHEY *Thalaba* IV. xxv, In uncommunicating misery Silent they stood. **1821** LAMB *Elia* I. *Quakers' Meeting*, The uncommunicating muteness of fishes.

unco'mmunicative, *a.* (UN-[1] 7 and 5 b.)

1691 NORRIS *Pract. Disc.* 297 To be selfish and strait-laced, niggardly and covetous, reserved and uncommunicative. **1730** SWIFT *Dean's Reasons* 43 Whose uncommunicative heart Will scarce one precious word impart. **1756** COWPER *Wks.* (1837) XV. 285 Our nation has, indeed, been generally supposed to be of a sullen and uncommunicative disposition. **1807** G. CHALMERS *Caledonia* I. Pref. p. vii, The scholars of Scotland remained inert, and uncommunicative of what they did not know. **1865** W. G. PALGRAVE *Arabia* II. 296 We made sail..in company with some islanders, silent uncommunicative men.

Hence **unco'mmunicativeness.**

1748 RICHARDSON *Clarissa* (1811) IV. 291, I might justify my secrecy and uncommunicativeness by her own. **1829** DISRAELI in Monypenny *Life* (1910) I. 122 Though generally accused of uncommunicativeness, I like a gentle chat with a friend. **1851** GALLENGA *Italy* i. 22 The Italians had given him blame for a dark simulation—which proceeded from sheer timidity and uncommunicativeness.

unco'mmuted, *ppl. a.* (UN-[1] 8.)

1870 W. R. GREG *Polit. Problems* 151 He believes (correctly) that his fair share, uncommuted and unadvanced, would be 23*s.* in good years. **1872** GEO. ELIOT *Middlem.* v, Such a lady gave a neighbourliness to both rank and religion, and mitigated the business of uncommuted tithe.

uncom'pact, *a.* (UN-[1] 7 and 5 b.)

1705 ADDISON *Italy* 237 How could a Liquid, that lay hardening by degrees, settle in such a furrow'd uncompact Surface?

uncom'pacted, *ppl. a.* (UN-[1] 8 and 5 b.)

1661 FELTHAM *Resolves* (ed. 8) II. xxiii. 230 He catches at that which is not yet in his reach; which seems to unfold but an uncompacted mind. **1781** JOHNSON *L.P., Lyttelton*, Lord Lyttelton..had a slender uncompacted frame, and a meagre face. **1793** W. ROBERTS *Looker-on* No. 36 (1794) II. 31 Democracies were all either loose and uncompacted, or violent and distorted. **1863** DANA *Man. Geol.* 49 Whether solid or uncompacted earth.

†**uncompanable**, *a. Obs.* Also 6 vncompaignable. [UN-[1] 7 b.] Uncompanionable.

1555 WATREMAN *Fardle Facions* II. iv. 143 Thei ware sterne men, and vncompaignable. **1611** COTGR., *Insociable*, vnsociable, vncompanable.

†**uncompane**, *v. Obs.*[−1] [UN-[1] 14 or UN-[2] 7.] *intr.* To avoid or shun society.

1589 WARNER *Alb. Eng.* VI. xxix. 128 She vncompaned, To flie He bids her solitarie moodes.

un'companied, *ppl. a.* [UN-[1] 8.] Unaccompanied.

a **1547** SURREY *Æneid* IV. (1557) F ij b, And still her thought, that she was left alone Vncompanied great viages to wende. **1570** LEVINS *Manip.* 50 Vncompanied, *incomitatus.* **1600** FAIRFAX *Tasso* I. xlviii, Yet thence she fled, uncompaned, unsought. **1791** COWPER *Odyss.* v. 38 Our fixt resolve, that brave Ulysses thence Depart, uncompanied by God or man. **1814** SOUTHEY *Roderick* III. 161 The daughters of the land..to the Mosque Holding uncompanied their jealous way.

uncom'panionable, *a.* [UN-[1] 7 b.]

1. Of persons: Not companionable; unsociable.

1748 RICHARDSON *Clarissa* VII. 149 Uncompanionable poor creatures. **1796-7** JANE AUSTEN *Pride & Prej.* xxvii, With such a mother and such uncompanionable sisters, home could not be faultless. **1819** SHELLEY *Cyclops* 425 Do you desire, or not, to fly This uncompanionable man? **1873** HELPS *Anim. & Mast.* viii. 177 But any thing more uncompanionable than the society of London cannot well be imagined.

2. Of things: Not fitted to go together.

1855 [J. D. BURN] *Autobiog. Beggar Boy* (1859) 121 Philosophy and hungry bellies are as uncompanionable as they were at the siege of Jerusalem!

uncom'panioned, *ppl. a.* [UN-[1] 8.]

1. Unmatched, unequalled.

1608 MACHIN *Dumbe Knight* I. i, Dost thou not thinke She is..Vnparalleld, and vncompanioned?

2. Not provided with a companion; not accompanied by any other (person or thing).

1809 CAMPBELL *Gert. Wyom.* I. xii, All uncompanioned else her heart had gone. *a* **1851** MOIR *Poems, Tombless Man* iii, With uncompanion'd step, measured and slow,..Up a long vista'd avenue I wound. **1863** LD. LYTTON *Ring Amasis* I. II. I. v. 264 Now, completely uncompanioned, he had withdrawn himself from his retinue.

b. Characterized by the absence or want of a companion or companionship.

1822 J. WILSON *Lights & Shadows Sc. Life* 229 In his hours of uncompanioned darkness. **1860** LD. LYTTON *Lucile* II. iii. §5. 18 A sense Of his own uncompanion'd, remote, and intense Isolation. **1885** M. ARNOLD *Poor Matthias*, Fare for ever well, nor fear..to stray Down the uncompanion'd way!

un'comparable, *a.* [UN-[1] 7 b and 5 b.]

†1. = INCOMPARABLE *a. Obs.*

1382 WYCLIF *Judith* x. 4 That she aperede to the eȝen of alle men with fairnesse vncomparable. **1483** CAXTON *Cato* e iv b, I consydere and suppose that god is so ouer souerayn and uncomparable and unlyke. **1548** GESTE *Pr. Masse* A v b, What an vnspeakable and vncomparable vyce is thee Pryuee Masse. **1586** F. GREVILLE in Sidney *Poems* (1873) I. p. xix, Sir Philip's uncomparable judgement. **1634** P. SMITH in Fuller *Abel Rediv.* (1867) II. 316 Had that father been born and lived in Italy or France, his wit, though uncomparable, had been much more refined.

2. Incapable of being compared (to anything else).

1826 SOUTHEY *Vind. Eccl. Angl.* 177 An unexpressible, uncomparable, unimaginable stench.

Hence **un'comparably** *adv.*

1548 GESTE *Pr. Masse* E v b, By reason wherof thee priest sacryfyce as it most hyghly empayrethe christes honoure & maiestie so vncomperablely offendeth god.

uncom'paratively, *adv.* [UN-[1] 11.]

†Absolutely, positively.

1702 S. PARKER tr. *Cicero's De Finibus* III. 174 What-ever touches not upon the Confines of Vertue or Vice is in its own Nature Uncomparatively Indifferent.

uncom'pared, *ppl. a.* (UN-[1] 8.)

1755 YOUNG *Centaur* ii. Wks. 1757 IV. 146 Come you..to make these young criminals appear more innocent, than they could appear uncompared with superior indiscretion?

un'compassable, *a.* (UN-[1] 7 b.)

c **1530** tr. *Erasmus' Serm. Ch. Jesus* (1901) 7 He abydeth in hymselfe vncompassable and vnmeasurable. **1611** FLORIO s.v. *Incircondéuole.* **1644** DIGBY *Nat. Soul* Concl. 456 So extreme must the rauenous inclemency..be of such an vncompassable desire gnawing eternally vpon the soule.

un'compassed, *a.* [UN-[1] 9.] Not provided with a compass.

1827 POLLOK *Course T.* II. 242 Choosing, thus unshipped, Uncompassed, unprovisioned, and bestormed, To swim a sea of breadth immeasurable. *a* **1844** CAMPBELL *Napoleon & Brit. Sailor* 35 A wherry..Untarr'd, uncompass'd, and unkeel'd, No sail, no rudder.

un'compassed, *ppl. a.* [UN-[1] 8.] Not bounded or circumscribed; unlimited.

1577 tr. *Bullinger's Decades* Preface, The Churche in this time is like lande that hath lyen..vnmanured, vncompassed, vntilled. **1602** J. DAVIES (Heref.) *Mirum in Modum* i. Wks. (Grosart) I. 5/1 Center of true Rest, Compass'd with glory, and vncompass'd blisse. **1642** H. MORE *Song of Soul* II. III. iv. 27 Why not dispred The world withouten bounds, endlesse uncompassed? **1665** CODRINGTON *Life Earl Essex* 11 When the ambition and the excesse of the Bishops did swell them up to such an uncompassed greatnesse.

uncom'passionate, *a.* [UN-[1] 7 and 5 b.] Wanting in compassion; unfeeling.

1591 SHAKS. *Two Gent.* III. i. 231 Neither bended knees, ..nor siluer-shedding teares Could penetrate her vncompassionate Sire. *a* **1663** SANDERSON *Serm., Ad Magist.* (1681) 80 To wrestle with the unjust and bitter upbraidings of unreasonable and uncompassionate men. **1671** MILTON *Samson* 818 If thou in strength all mortals dost exceed, In uncompassionate anger do not so. **1792** G. WAKEFIELD *Mem.* (1804) II. 392 Nor can a single syllable in support of such uncompassionate persuasions be produced from the Christian Scriptures. **1871** ALABASTER *Wheel of Law* 61 This is uncompassionate and wicked. **1877** WALLACE *Russia* iii. 39 The personification of uncompassionate, inflexible law.

absol. **1688** COLLIER *Several Disc.* (1725) 351 The Designing, the Parsimonious and Uncompassionate.

Hence **uncom'passionately** *adv.*; **-ness.**

1608 HIERON *Wks.* I. 743 The vncompassionatenesse which I finde among the men of this yron age. **1612** SHELTON *Quix.* I. III. x. 225 Catching hold of one anothers beards, and be-fisting themselues..vncompassionately. **1862** F. HALL *Hindu Philos. Syst.* 124 Cruelty is uncompassionateness.

uncom'passionated, *ppl. a.* (UN-[1] 8.)

1867 'OUIDA' *Idalia* xxix, Those..uncompassionated millions who are the prey alike of despot and of demagogue. **1882** FARRAR *Early Christianity* I. 159 Once not a people, but now a people of God; once uncompassionated, but compassionated now.

uncom'passionating, *ppl. a.* (UN-[1] 10.)

a **1711** KEN *Edmund* Poet. Wks. 1721 II. 279 They..with an uncompassionating Eye Into their panting Breasts began to pry.

uncom'passioned, *ppl. a.* (UN-[1] 8.)

1827 POLLOK *Course T.* III. 597 A cold..Forsaken thing, that wandered on, forlorn, Undestined, uncompassioned, unupheld.

uncom'peered, *ppl. a.* (UN-[1] 8.)

1602 WARNER *Alb. Eng.* XII. lxxviii. (1612) 321 For Good must God be vncompeer'd.

uncom'pellable, -ible, *a.* (UN-[1] 7, 7 b.)

1613 DRUMM. OF HAWTH. *Cypress Grove* Wks. (S.T.S.) II. 91 Thy Will is vncompellable [**1711** uncompellible], resisting Force, daunting Necessitie, despising Danger. **1661** FELTHAM *On Luke* xiv. 20 in *Resolves* (ed. 8) 386 A noble Courtesie..conquers the uncompellable mind, and disinterests Man of himself.

uncom'pelled, *ppl. a.* (UN-[1] 8.)

1470-1 *Rolls of Parlt.* VI. 233/1 The other pety Capytaynes affermed to be trewe at their Dethes, uncompelled, unstured or undesired soo to doo. **1548** PATTEN *Exped. Scot.* O j b, Thear wear but fewe of Lordes ..and gentlemen in the feld, but..did thearin right willyngly & vncompeld their partes. **1549** COVERDALE, etc. *Erasm. Par. 1 Tim.* 4 b, They..runne vncompelled, and doe more than al the whole law requireth. **1621** G. SANDYS *Ovid's Met.* I. 3 The Golden Age was first; which vncompeld, And without rule, in Faith and Truth exceld. **1648** BOYLE *Seraph. Love* xxv. (1700) 152 The amorous Needle, once joyn'd unto the Load-stone, would never uncompell'd forsake the inchanting Mineral. **1725** POPE *Odyss.* II. 420 But..swear To keep my voyage from the royal ear, Nor uncompelled the dang'rous truth betray. **1816** BYRON *Childe Harold* III. xii, Still uncompell'd, He would not yield dominion of his mind. **1856** MRS. BROWNING *Aur. Leigh* IV. 544 Of course the people came in uncompelled.

uncom'pensable, *a.* (UN-[1] 7 b and 5 b.)
1734 WATTS *Reliq. Juv.* 121 The Destruction of such a rare Piece of Workmanship would have been an uncompensable Loss.

un'compensated, *ppl. a.* [UN-[1] 8.]
1. Not compensated by any gain or good.
1774 BURKE *Sp. Amer. Tax.* 23 To join together the restraints of an universal..monopoly, with an universal..taxation, is an unnatural union; perfect uncompensated slavery. **1787** *Ann. Reg., Hist. Eur.* 81/1 Mr. Fox inferred that the revenue of this country would suffer a very serious and uncompensated loss. **1802–12** BENTHAM *Ration. Judic. Evid.* (1827) III. 484 The vexation and expense incident to the production of it, is uncompensated. **1898** *Educat. Rev.* Oct. 277 Their story is one of almost universal and uncompensated disappointment.
2. Not balanced or made up for.
1789 *Phil. Trans.* LXXIX. 283 The uncompensated electricity which is as essential to the charge as that which is in equilibrio. **1835** MRS. SOMERVILLE *Connex. Phys. Sci.* iii. (ed. 2) 22 An uncompensated portion of the direct motion.
3. Unrecompensed.
1830 COBBETT *Rur. Rides* 163 That gentleman remains uncompensated for his sufferings. **1882** *Amer. Missionary* (N.Y.) Apr. 100 The House of Refuge,..to whose interest he gave untiring and uncompensated time and attention.

†**un'competence**. *Obs.*[−1] [UN-[1] 12 and 5 b.] Want of fittingness.
1541 R. COPLAND *Galyen's Terap.* 2 E j b, In Ametrie, that is to saye, in vncompetence and immoderacyon.

†**un'competent**, *a. Obs.* [UN-[1] 7 and 5 b.] Incompetent.
1563 FOXE *A. & M.* 721 Him that is conuented before an vncompetente and suspecte iudge. **1659** *Gentl. Calling* (1696) 45 All, whose value and wishes of a Mahometan Paradise render them not uncompetent to estimate these purer and refined pleasures.

†**uncompetible**, *a. Obs.*[−1] (UN-[1] 7 and 5 b.)
a **1628** LD. BROOKE *Alaham* II. ii, He first despiseth thee, Then triumphs in thy once forsaken loue; Proclaimes deceipt to be thy state of mind, Vncompetible, vnpossible to finde.

uncom'petitive, *a.* (UN-[1] 7.)
1885 RUSKIN in *Pall Mall G.* 2 Mar. 4/2 An English officer,..totally inexperienced in war,..uncompetitive in any manner of examination. **1886** HISSEY *On Box Seat* 242 The shops are uncompetitive of course, and..provokingly uninteresting.

uncom'placent, *a.* (UN-[1] 7.)
1805 FOSTER *Ess.* (1806) I. 189 This new desire must have been a very uncomplacent associate for them.

uncom'plained, *ppl. a.* (UN-[1] 8.)
1648 HEXHAM II, *Onbeklaeght*, Vncomplained. **1691** T. H[ALE] *Acc. New Invent.* f 7 Instances of Complaints.., and observation of a greater number of Ships resting uncomplained of.

uncom'plaining, *ppl. a.* (UN-[1] 10.)
1744 THOMSON *Spring* 390 The bleeding Breast Of the weak, helpless, uncomplaining Wretch. **1816** SHELLEY *Sunset* 48 Whether the dead..are the uncomplaining things they seem. **1848** DICKENS *Dombey* iii, The child..was so gentle, so quiet, and uncomplaining. **1873** SYMONDS *Grk. Poets* 295 The uncomplaining submission of Iphigeneia and Polyxena.
Hence **uncom'plainingly** *adv.*; **-ness**.
[**1847** WEBSTER.] **1861** WHYTE MELVILLE *Good for Nothing* I. 68 Ada bore with it all, sadly, but uncomplainingly. **1876** SMILES *Sc. Natur.* xiii. (ed. 4) 252 Edward's perseverance, self-denial, and uncomplainingness.

un'complaisance. (UN-[1] 12.)
1707 NORRIS *Treat. Humility* vii. 311 Pride is hated..as an uncomplaisance, as something that opposes and hinders, and stands in the way.

un'complaisant, *a.* (UN-[1] 8.)
1693 LOCKE *Educ.* §143 A natural Roughness, which makes a Man uncomplaisant to others. **1704** CIBBER *Careless Husb.* IV. 73 This is very Uncomplaisant to Engross so Agreeable a Part of the Company to yourself. *a* **1734** NORTH *Lives* I. 93 His lordship, of one that was not morose and uncomplaisant, was the most sober that [etc.]. **1802** *Phil. Trans.* XCI. 154 This metal is so uncomplaisant as to retain the white colour.
Hence **un'complaisantly** *adv.*
1766 BLACKSTONE *Comm.* II. xiv. 213 Thus sons shall be admitted before daughters; or, as our male lawgivers have somewhat uncomplaisantly expressed it, the worthiest of blood shall be preferred.

un'complemental, *a.* (UN-[1] 7. Cf. COMPLEMENTAL *a.* 6.)
1673 CAVE *Prim. Chr.* II. iii. 61 The severe and uncomplemental man..bluntly entertained her with this discourse.

†**uncom'plete**, *a. Obs.* (UN-[1] 7 and 5 b.)
1398 TREVISA *Barth. De P.R.* XIX. lxxix. (1495) ll v b/2 Wynde egges..ben lesse in quantite for they ben vncomplete. *c* **1430** *Art of Nombryng* 19 The last ternary other uncomplete nombre. **1611** COTGR., *Imperfaict*, imperfect, vncompleat. **1725** POPE *Odyss.* I. p. xii, These various incidents..are only uncompleat and unfinish'd parts of one and the same Action and Fable.

uncom'pleted, *ppl. a.* (UN-[1] 8 and 5 b.)
1513 DOUGLAS *Æneid* VII. Prol. 148, I..wolx ennoyit.., Thair restit vncompleittit so gret ane part. **1661** FELTHAM *On Luke* xiv. 20 in *Resolves*, etc. (ed. 8) 393 Marriage is Creations perfectness, barren Virginity is but uncompleted Man. **1681** BURNET *Hist. Ref.* II. 363 The other more pressing things that were still uncompleted. *a* **1771** GRAY *Dante* 44 In low and uncompleated Sounds I heard 'em wail for Bread. **1858** LONGF. *M. Standish* IX. 67 Each with his plan for the day, and the work that was left uncompleted. **1875** J. P. HOPPS *Princ. Relig.* xiv. 46 The salvation that is left uncompleted here will be continued in the brighter world beyond.

†**uncom'pletely**, *adv. Obs.*[−1] (UN-[1] 11 and 5 b.)
c **1380** WYCLIF *Sel. Wks.* II. 197 And þes blasfemes out of bileve, þat seien þat Crist spekiþ here falsely or uncompletly.

un'complex, *a.* (UN-[1] 7 and 5 b.)
1702 S. PARKER tr. *Cicero's De Finibus* v. 292 The Six Uncomplex Acceptations of *Summum Bonum* I have now laid before you. **1854** MILL *Lett.* (1910) II. 368 Small things, or at least things uncomplex and composed of few parts.

uncom'pliable, *a.* (UN-[1] 7 b and 5 b.)
1626 in *Cosin's Corr.* (Surtees) I. 95 The disposition of some men..who will not be won, but are uncompliable and intractable. **1687** H. MORE *Answ. Psychop.* (1689) 127 How uncompliable this Difference is with History.
Hence **uncomplia'bility**, **-ableness**.
1687 H. MORE *Contn. Remark. Stor.* (1689) 427 His displeasure against her uncompliableness. **1880** BURTON *Reign Anne* I. ii. 62 Their uncompliability was neutral, not active.

uncom'pliant, *a.* (UN-[1] 7 and 5 b.)
1659 GAUDEN *Tears Ch.* III. xv. 305 By which you and they must needs be so well informed, as to be justly opposite and uncompliant to those Errours. **1678** CUDWORTH *Intell. Syst.* I. v. 672 When..the stubborn necessity of matter proves uncompliant. **1768–74** TUCKER *Lt. Nat.* (1834) II. 581 They generate a stiffness and preciseness.., rendering men troublesome and uncompliant. **1828** D'ISRAELI *Chas. I*, I. viii. 259 The King, in despair, dissolved this uncompliant Parliament. **1860** W. L. COLLINS *Luck of Ladysmede* (1862) I. 320 A miserable wife, as some said,—an uncompliant mistress, according to others.

un'complicated, *ppl. a.* (UN-[1] 8.)
[**1775** ASH.] **1792** BURKE *Let. Sir H. Langrishe* Wks. VI. 369 You may leave that deliberation of a parliamentary reform..uncomplicated and unembarrassed with the other question. **1879** SPENCER *Data of Ethics* viii. §51. 139 Observing, in their uncomplicated forms, what are the negative conditions to harmonious social life. **1881** *Macm. Mag.* XLIII. 359/2 The worship..in its primitive form, and uncomplicated with elements of later mythic growth.
b. *spec.* in *Path.*
1835–6 *Todd's Cycl. Anat.* I. 456/1 In a simple and uncomplicated case [of necrosis] recovery is nearly certain. **1871** A. MEADOWS *Man. Midwifery* (ed. 2) 418 Thus what was originally simple uncomplicated local inflammation may become a specific contagious disease.

uncompli'mentary, *a.* (UN-[1] 7.)
1842 J. S. MILL *Let.* 25 Nov. in *Wks.* (1963) XIII. 558 People call you by various uncomplimentary names indicative of self-conceit. **1846** WORCESTER (citing *Qu. Rev.*). **1861** MILL *Repr. Govt.* (1865) 88/1 If he forms an uncomplimentary opinion of their part in the affair. **1878** *Masque Poets* 228 With Robert Lorne's Florinda's name was coupled In terms uncomplimentary to both.
Hence ˌ**uncompli'mentarily** *adv.*
1909 'MARK TWAIN' *Is Shakes. Dead?* xi. 127 It would grieve me to know that any one could think so injuriously of me, so uncomplimentarily, so unadmiringly of me.

uncom'plying, *ppl. a.* (UN-[1] 10 and 5 b.)
1643 MILTON *Divorce* 11 When he shall find himselfe bound fast to an uncomplying discord of nature. *a* **1661** FULLER *Worthies, Carmarthen.* IV. (1662) 27 A man not unlearned, but somewhat indiscreet, or rather uncomplying, which procured him much trouble. **1724** SWIFT *Verses Whitshed's Motto on Coach* 14 To shew my Fury Against an uncomplying Jury. **1777** ROBERTSON *Hist. Amer.* VI. (1778) II. 234 He was endowed only with integrity and courage; the former harsh and uncomplying. **1834** DE QUINCEY in *Tait's Mag.* I. 21/2 His sturdy and uncomplying morality. **1862** S. LUCAS *Secularia* 197 Others of the company..incurred the Protector's displeasure by too uncomplying principles.

uncom'posable, *a.* (UN-[1] 7 b.)
1640 LD. DIGBY *Sp. Triennial Parl.* 14 All the rest of the world at the same time in Tempest, in Combustions, in uncomposable Warres. *a* **1734** NORTH *Exam.* I. ii. §63 A Difference..at length flamed so high as to be uncomposeable.

uncom'posed, *ppl. a.* [UN-[1] 8 and 5 b.]
1. Not composed or made up; not composite.
1570 BILLINGSLEY *Euclid* VII. def. xii. 186 Numbers vncomposed, haue no part to measure them, but onely vnitie. **1644** DIGBY *Nat. Soul* i. §3. 358 We can not diuide the actions of mans mind, further then into apprehensions; and therefore we called them simple and vncomposed.
2. Not put together in proper form.
1598 FLORIO, *Discomposto*, vncomposed, shapelesse, formelesse. *c* **1610** *Women Saints* 189, I haue sett downe her life in playne and vncomposed wordes. **1753** HOGARTH *Anal. Beauty* ii. 17 Variety uncomposed, and without design, is confusion and deformity. **1838** CARLYLE *Misc.* (1857) IV. 140 Scott's Biography if uncomposed, lies..here, in the elementary state, and can at any time be composed, if necessary.
3. Not reduced to an orderly or tranquil state; disordered, excited.
1601 B. JONSON *Ev. Man in Hum.* (Qo.) V. i. 526 It is a vertue that persues Any saue rude and vncomposed spirites. **1639** BP. REYNOLDS *Lord's Supper* xviii, Sudden, uncomposed, & uncollected thoughts. **1691** HARTCLIFFE *Virtues* 205 The Scum of an empty Mind, the very froth of an unsetled and uncomposed Spirit.
b. Unregulated; disorderly.
1631 BRATHWAIT *Whimzies, Traveller* 93 Not an irregular haire about him, nor an unset looke to attend him, nor an uncomposed cringe to accoutre him. **1649** *Alcoran* 411 The uncomposed gestures of the drunkard.
4. Not brought into a state of concord.
1650 R. STAPYLTON *Strada's Low C. Wars* V. 133 In his Letters to the Governess, the Emperour promised her his endeavours, if any thing was yet uncomposed. **1651** C. CARTWRIGHT *Cert. Relig.* I. 87 Whilst the Catholicks have no jars undecided, no differences uncomposed.

†**uncom'pound**, *a. Obs.* (UN-[1] 7 and 5 b.)
1539 ELYOT *Cast. Helthe* (1541) 1 b, The Elementes be those originall thinges unmyxt and uncompounde, of whose ..myxture all other thynges be compacte. **1557** RECORDE *Whetst.* A iij b, 2. is accompted truely an euen number, originall, and vncompounde.

uncom'poundable, *a.* (UN-[1] 7 b.)
1691 E. TAYLOR *Behmen's Theos. Philos.* 66 Tin and silver ..coming of different Properties are uncompoundable.

uncom'pounded, *ppl. a.* [UN-[1] 8 and 5 b.]
1. Not compounded; not made up of various elements; unmixed: a. Of the Deity or his essence.
1587 GOLDING *De Mornay* iv. 45 By these conclusions we come to another, which is, that God is not compounded. [*marg.*] God is single and vncompounded. **1602** WARNER *Alb. Eng.* XIII. lxxix. 326 Sufficeth vs to know he is.. Vnpassiue, vnmateriall, vncompounded. *a* **1619** FOTHERBY *Atheom.* II. x. §3 (1622) 304 His vncompounded simplicitie, is the true matter of his Vnitie. *a* **1676** HALES *Prim. Orig. Man.* I. i. (1677) 11 Though he is but one, and one most simple uncompounded Being. **1720** WATERLAND *Eight Serm.* 200 The proof of the Father's being..one simple, uncompounded, undivided, intelligent Agent. *a* **1751** BOLINGBROKE *Philos.* Wks. 1754 V. 77 Various manifestations of the infinite wisdom of one simple uncompounded being. **1867** BP. FORBES *Explan. 39 Art.* i. 10 If God is absolutely, He is simple and uncompounded.
b. Of material things, their nature or qualities.
1615 H. CROOKE *Body of Man* I. xx. 32 Aristotle calleth them..Simple and vncompounded Parts, because they are not compounded of other parts. **1665** HOOKE *Microgr.* 1 We must endevour to follow Nature in the more plain and easie ways she treads in the most simple and uncompounded bodies. **1742** H. BAKER *Microsc.* I. Introd. 12 In the School of Nature we must begin with..the smallest and most uncompounded Parts. **1794** HUTTON *Philos. Light*, etc. 212 The antiphlogistic theory maintains, that sulphur and metals are simple substances, or to us uncompounded bodies. **1808** J. WEBSTER *Nat. Philos.* 171 The divisions of the uncompounded colours on the spectrum. **1875** E. WHITE *Life in Christ* I. viii. (1878) 72 That the soul of man is an uncompounded substance, or indivisible essence, has never been proved.
fig. *a* **1633** W. AUSTIN *Medit.* (1635) 103 Alwaies, in secret, Men are most direct, plaine, and uncompounded: when (often) in publike they play the Hypocrites. **1703** MRS. CENTLIVRE *Stolen Heiress* IV, It was her single uncompounded self, her self without addition that I lov'd.
c. Of ideas, abstractions, etc.
1650 EARL MONM. tr. *Senault's Man bec. Guilty* 115 Christian Eloquence is uncompounded. **1690** LOCKE *Hum. Und.* II. ii. §1 Those simple Ideas; which being each in itself uncompounded, contains in it nothing but one uniform Appearance. **1713** BERKELEY *Hylas & Phil.* I. Wks. 1871 I. 267 Fire affects you only with one simple, or uncompounded idea. **1785** REID *Intell. Powers* 234 To consider them as one uncompounded operation. **1822–7** GOOD *Study Med.* (1829) IV. 16 The sensorial power in its simplest and uncompounded state. **1862** MARSH *Lect. Eng. Lang.* iii. 62 It is, however, rarely the case that a simple uncompounded word so well repays the labour of investigation.
d. Const. *with*.
a **1633** W. AUSTIN *Medit.* (1635) 33 They were simple men, uncompounded with the world. **1803** W. BLACKBURNE in *Med. Jrnl.* X. 463 Accumulated human effluvia.. uncompounded with limose or paludous gas.
†2. = UNCOMPOSED *ppl. a.* 3. *Obs.*
1659 RUSHWORTH *Hist. Coll.* I. 2 To keep his Majesty from declaring himself opposite to Spain in the business of Cleves and Juliers, which still remained uncompounded.
Hence **uncom'poundedly** *adv.*; **-ness**.
1628 T. SPENCER *Logick* 163 It is a simple Axiome: because one thing barely, and *vncompoundedly, is referred to another. **1683** [see UNCLOTHEDLY *adv.*]. **1653** BLITHE *Eng. Improver Impr.* xxi. 136 The description of it [*sc.* marl] is not so much in Colour..as in the Purity and *uncompoundedness of it. **1835** *Blackw. Mag.* XXXVIII. 751 There is a oneness, a wholeness, an uncompoundedness of character in these elect instruments.

uncom'pounding, *ppl. a.* (UN-[1] 10.)
1782 J. BROWN *Comp. View Nat. & Rev. Relig.* IV. i. 298 It is an uncompounding union, both the united natures retaining their distinct essential properties. **1821** *Tales Landlord, Fair Witch of Glas Llyn* II. 191 His wanton cruelty was accepted as the pledge of uncompounding sincerity.

uncompre'hend, *v.* (UN-[1] 14.)
1602–3 DANIEL *Musophilus* 656 If this grosse spirit.. Neglect, distaste, vncomprehend, disdaine.

uncompre'hended, *ppl. a.* (UN-[1] 8 and 5 b.)
1598 FLORIO, *Incompreso*, vncomprehended, incomprehensible. **1829** LYTTON *Devereux* III. vii, What wonder that ye should have gleaned from the uncomprehended earth an answer to the enigmas of Fate! **1866** GEO. ELIOT *F. Holt* xi, A large experience in the effect of uncomprehended words.

uncompre'hending, *ppl. a.* (UN-¹ 10, 5 b.)
1838 MRS. BROWNING *Song agst. Singing* iv, Thou.. Wouldst.. Upturn thy bright uncomprehending eyes And bid me play instead. **1871** FARRAR *Witn. Hist.* ii. 64 The light which..shone quietly in the uncomprehending darkness.

Hence **uncompre'hendingly** *adv.*
1858 MISS MULOCK *Th. ab. Wom.* 260 Tell her this, and the chances are she will stare at you uncomprehendingly.

†**uncompre'hensible**, *a. Obs.* [UN-¹ 7 and 5 b.] = INCOMPREHENSIBLE *a.*
1388 WYCLIF *Jer.* xxxii. 19 Greet in councel, and vncomprehensible in thouȝt. *c* **1532** DU WES *Introd. Fr.* in *Palsgr.* 1057 [The soul] is uncomprehensyble. **1567–9** JEWEL *Def. Apol.* 239 It is vntoucheable, and vncomprehensible vnto our senses. **1587** GOLDING *De Mornay* xxiv. (1592) 370 The matters of God which are vncomprehensible to man. **1740** CHEYNE *Regimen* 185 An uncomprehensible and inexplicable Mystery.

uncompre'hension. (UN-¹ 12 and 5 b.)
1862 MRS. OLIPHANT *Last of Mortimers* II. 27 The child looked up..with an amazed uncomprehension of any order issued to her.

uncompre'hensive, *a.* [UN-¹ 7 and 5 b.]
†**1.** That cannot be comprehended. *Obs.*
1606 SHAKS. *Tr. & Cr.* III. iii. 198 The prouidence that's in a watchfull State..Findes bottome in th' vncomprehensiue deepes.
2. Lacking in comprehension.
1667 SOUTH *Serm.* (1697) II. 46 Some narrow-spirited, Uncomprehensive Zealots, who know not the world.
3. Not sufficiently comprehensive or inclusive.
1862 HELPS *Org. Daily Life* 21 Great efforts will be made in a scattered, uncomprehensive, and unbusiness-like way.

uncom'pressed, *ppl. a.* (UN-¹ 8.)
1666 BOYLE *Orig. Forms & Qual.* (1667) 17 The Learned Horstius..ascribes the Indolence of the Part, whil'st uncompress'd, to some slimy Juice. **1713** DERHAM *Phys.-Theol.* 5 *note*, I shall leave the ingenious Reader to judge what the cause was of both the Birds living longer in compressed, than uncompressed Air. **1808** J. WEBSTER *Nat. Philos.* 77 It produces considerable pain in the part which is uncompressed. **1863** TYNDALL *Heat* ii. 24 The uncompressed lead they said had a greater capacity for heat than the compressed substance.

uncom'prized, *ppl. a.* (UN-¹ 8.)
1598 DRAYTON *Heroical Ep.* xii. 31 Whose vncomprised wisedomes did fore-see, That you in marriage should be linck'd to mee. **1610** HEALEY *St. Aug. Citie of God* 213 It is no way credible that he would leave the kingdomes of men ..uncomprized in..his eternall providence. **1652** BENLOWES *Theoph.* v. lxxiii, Thou all-comprizing, uncompriz'd!

un'compromised, *ppl. a.* (UN-¹ 8.) Hence **un'compromisedness.**
[**1775** ASH.] **1851** H. MELVILLE *Moby Dick* III. xxi. 145 This strange uncompromisedness in him. **1882** MISS BRADDON *Mt.-Royal* I. iv. 105 He might..ride off at the last uncompromised.

un'compromising, *ppl. a.* [UN-¹ 10.] Not willing or seeking to compromise; unyielding, unbending; stiff, stubborn: **a.** Of persons.
1828 LYTTON *Pelham* II. i, We must pursue the same course—stern and uncompromising. **1849** MACAULAY *Hist. Eng.* v. I. 541 The most honest, fearless, and uncompromising republican of his time. **1863** 'OUIDA' *Held in Bondage* vi, Among uncompromising patriots as among poor foreigners.
b. Of feelings, attitudes of mind, etc.
1830 *Forrester* III. 89 [He was] aroused..to a full sense of the danger he had incurred by his uncompromising hostility. **1885** 'MRS. ALEXANDER' *At Bay* vii, Whose uncompromising sincerity might convince the hardest skeptic of its reality.
c. *fig.* Of things.
1875 LADY BARKER *Year's Housekeeping S. Africa* i. (1877) 7 The 'Devil's Peak' is uncompromising enough for any one's taste. **1889** HISSEY *Tour in Phaeton* 363 A square house 'with no nonsense about it',..an uncompromising square house.

Hence **un'compromisingly** *adv.*; **-ness.**
1834 J. S. MILL in *Monthly Repos.* VIII. 527 The military tribunals..Mr. Abercromby..steadily and *uncompromisingly opposed. **1837** PUSEY *Let.* in Liddon *Life* (1894) I. 388 However uncompromisingly they maintain the maxim. **1888** MISS BRADDON *Fatal Three* I. iv, The dressmaker sent home three new frocks, all uncompromisingly ugly. **1865** PUSEY *Eiren.* 284 The *uncompromisingness of the Church of England in maintaining Catholic truth. **1894** *Fortn. Rev.* May 690 Even her uncompromisingness is preferable to the ostentatious abandonment of principles.

†**un'compt**, *a. Obs.* [UN-¹ 7 and 5 b.]
1. Of persons: Not neat in dress or appearance.
a **1641** BP. MOUNTAGU *Acts & Mon.* (1642) 247 The cited to appeare in Court, came in humble manner,..attired in black, uncompt, undrest. **1647** N. BACON *Disc. Govt. Eng.* I. xli. 104 Nor was this the originall trick of the rude and uncompt Germans, or Barbarous Britons, but of the wise Greeks.
2. Of style: Incompt, inelegant, unpolished.
1633 PRYNNE *Histriomastix* 925 Whenever I fell to read the Prophets after I had beene reading Tully and Plautus,.. their uncompt stile became irkesome to me.

uncom'pulsory, *a.* (UN-¹ 7.)
1567 in Tytler *Hist. Scot.* (1864) III. 271, I asked him what freewill there might be, or uncompulsory consent, for a prisoner.

uncom'putable, *a.* (UN-¹ 7 b and 5 b.)
1678 CUDWORTH *Intell. Syst.* I. iv. §14. 241 Proclus contends..that the world had lasted such a length of time, as was in a manner inestimable to us, or uncomputable by us. **1906** SOMERVILLE & 'ROSS' *Some Irish Yesterdays* 51 Large statements as to her uncomputable value had not her tail in youth been shut into a stable door and given a double angle like a bayonet. **1979** *Sci. Amer.* Nov. 30/2 Consider a more traditional way of encoding the halting problem in an uncomputable irrational number.

uncom'puted, *ppl. a.* (UN-¹ 8.)
[**1775** ASH.] **1885** *Leeds Mercury* 31 Jan. 7/2 The millions of dollars..required to provide these Civil War pensions seem to have been uncomputed.

†**un'conable**, *a. Obs.* [UN-¹ 7 b.] Improper, unbefitting.
a **1340** HAMPOLE *Psalter* lxxii. 9 Þair bostus speche, sua vncunable was, þat it passed in[to] þe earth. *Ibid., Cant. Marie* 1 Þat soul worshippys god, þe whilk..vnkonnabil beryng heghis not. *c* **1440** *Jacob's Well* 294 Vnconable ioye of ony wordly vanyte.

Hence †**un'conableness; -ablety; -ably** *adv.*
a **1340** HAMPOLE *Psalter* xxxviii. 1 Þe haly man..thynkis ..to be still, þat he say nathynge vnconabilly. *Ibid.* lxxii. 14 If god war nought wytand al things, or punyscht not synne, þere vnconabiltes folouid. *Ibid.* cv. 31 Moyses wes for þe mykil vnconabilnes of þe folk lettid in thoght.

unconand, obs. f. UNCUNNING.

†**uncon'catenable**, *a. Obs.* (UN-¹ 7 b. Cf. CONCATENATE *v.*)
1654 GAYTON *Pleas. Notes* III. viii. 117 His Auditory smiling at..what an irreconcileable piece of Scripture they had proposed, and unconcatenable to his usuall subject.

uncon'cealable, *a.* (UN-¹ 7 b.)
Also, in recent use, ***unconcealably*** adv.
1809–14 WORDSW. *Excurs.* VI. 158 Through his frame it crept With slow mutation unconcealable. **1860** EMERSON *Cond. Life, Behaviour* Wks. (Bohn) II. 380 The power of manners is incessant,—an element as unconcealable as fire. **1879** H. GEORGE *Progr. & Pov.* VIII. iii. (1881) 375 The immovable and unconcealable character of the land itself.

uncon'cealed, *ppl. a.* (UN-¹ 8.)
[**1775** ASH.] **1839** DE LA BECHE *Rep. Geol. Cornwall*, etc. iii. 71 The whole is unconcealed by more modern deposits. **1860** TRISTRAM *Gt. Sahara* iv. 62 The nests which are.. unprotected and unconcealed among the mud and grass.

uncon'cealing, *ppl. a.* (UN-¹ 10.)
1804 *Ann. Rev.* II. 289 To what dire resources the alarmists at length had to recur, is thus related by this unconcealing writer. *a* **1822** SHELLEY *Matilda* 30 This [water], whose unconcealing dew, Dark, dark, yet clear, moved under the obscure Eternal shades.

uncon'ceded, *ppl. a.* (UN-¹ 8.)
1674 BOYLE *Excell. Theol.* II. v. 229, I should have forborn to make use of divers of the arguments I have employed, as fetched from unconceded topicks.

uncon'ceited, *a.* (UN-¹ 9.)
[**1775** ASH.] **1838** LD. COLERIDGE in E. H. Coleridge *Life* (1904) I. 50, I pray God I may be humble and unconceited like you.

uncon'ceitedly, *adv.* (UN-¹ 11.)
1812 *Examiner* 24 Aug. 541/1 You..(very unconceitedly to be sure) boast that you do not condescend to read it.

uncon'ceivable, *a.* [UN-¹ 7 b and 5 b.] Inconceivable. (Common in 17–18th c.)
1611 COTGR., *Incomprehensible*, incomprehensible, vnconceiueable. **1612** T. TAYLOR *Comm., Titus* ii. 14 Christ ..willingly suffered such torments as are vnconceiuable. **1647** TRAPP *Comm. Rev.* ii. 17 The feast of a good conscience, which is unconceivable and full of glory. **1705** STANHOPE *Paraphr.* II. 203 Many and great Pleasures, yet hidden from our Eyes, unutterable, unconceivable. **1768** *Woman of Honor* II. 133 The effect this had..would be unconceivable but for one just reflexion. **1838** [see UNCONCEIVED *ppl. a.* 1]. **1867** PUSEY *Eleven Addresses* xi. (1908) 143 The souls of those, who are departed hence in the grace of God, are in unconceivable bliss.

Hence **uncon'ceivableness.**
1611 COTGR., *Incomprehensibilité*, incomprehensiblenesse, vnconceiuablenesse. **1655** H. MORE *App. Antid. Ath.* (1712) 185 The unconceivableness of that line that is produced by the Motion of a Globe on a Plane. **1704** NORRIS *Ideal World* II. vii. 337 The unconceivablenesse of supposing that a body ..should always send forth from itself species on all sides. **1854** HALLAM *Hist. Lit.* (ed. 4) III. iii. §119 *marg.*, Unconceivableness of infinity.

uncon'ceivably, *adv.* [f. prec.] = INCONCEIVABLY *adv.*
1630 BP. HALL *Serm., Hypocrite* Wks. 1837 V. 381 How then? what is their case? Surely inexplicably, unconceivably fearful. **1683** E. HOOKER *Pref. Pordage's Mystic Div.* 67 Imperceptibl subtilities of unconceivably profound Contemplators. *a* **1711** KEN *Hymnotheo* Poet. Wks. 1721 III. 45 Yet curs'd Abaddon's Diabolick Crew, Death's Terrors unconceivably outdo. **1861** PAGE *Past & Pr. Life of Globe* 239 The divine idea of moral perfection..[is] unconceivably unattainable by created existences.

uncon'ceived, *ppl. a.* [UN-¹ 8.]
1. a. Not conceived or thought of; unimagined.
1434 MISYN *Mending of Life* 126 God truly is infinit.., of all wroght kyndes vnconsauyd. **1591** SYLVESTER *Du Bartas* I. iii. 949 Renowned Load-stone, which on Iron acts,.. Attracts it strangely..With unknow'n cords, with unconceived hooks. **1598** BP. HALL *Sat.* Postscr., Sith.. that is almost unseene which is unconceived. **1648** J. BEAUMONT *Psyche* XIV. lxii, Judas who neer this place did frying lie With unconceived anguish gnash'd his teeth. **1710** BERKELEY *Princ. Hum. Knowl.* §23 It is necessary that you conceive them existing unconceived or unthought of. **1742** YOUNG *Nt. Th.* I. 111 They live! they greatly live a life on earth Unkindl'd, unconceiv'd. **1838** POE *A. G. Pym* Wks. 1864 IV. 89 Events..of the most unconceived and unconceivable character. **1871** MORLEY *Vauvenargues* in *Crit. Misc.* Ser. I. (1878) 9 The Encyclopædia was yet unconceived.
†**b.** Uncomprehended; not understood. *Obs.*⁻¹
1619 PURCHAS *Microcosmus* lxix. 689 In the meane while, sometimes without dores, on Horse-backe, they heare their vn-conceiued Liturgie.
2. Not brought into being; not properly formed or developed.
1599 MARSTON *Sco. Villanie* III. ix. G viij b, Whilst I.. abuse chast virgin time, Deflowring her with unconceiued rime. **1848** BAILEY *Festus* (ed. 3) 205 All the forms Of plant, fish, brute, bird, insect, and the lives Insensible and unconceived.

uncon'ceiving, *ppl. a.* [UN-¹ 10.] Not apprehending or understanding; dull-witted.
1593 NASHE *Strange Newes* Wks. (Grosart) II. 253 Art thou so innocent & vnconceiuing that thou shouldst ere hope to dash mee quite out of request? **1614** R. TAILOR *Hog hath lost Pearl* III. E j b, Why should I teach them, and go beate my braines, To instruct vnapt, and vnconceauing dolts? **1740** CIBBER *Apol.* (1756) I. 124 A broad laughing voice,..round shoulders, an unconceiving eye.

uncon'cern, *sb.* [UN-¹ 12.] Lack of concern, anxiety, or solicitude; indifference, equanimity.
1711 STEELE *Spect.* No. 75 ¶5 He..is in a fair way of doing all things with a graceful Unconcern, and Gentleman-like Ease. **1769** E. BANCROFT *Guiana* 326 Their unconcern for futurity..is by no means singular. **1849** EASTWICK *Dry Leaves* 93 Their faces were pale with terror and they vainly attempted to simulate unconcern. **1865** W. G. PALGRAVE *Arabia* I. 116 We put on an appearance of great ignorance and unconcern.

†**uncon'cern**, *v.*¹ *Obs.* [UN-¹ 14.] *refl.* Not to concern or interest (oneself) *in* a thing.
1670 PENN *Tracts* Wks. 1726 I. 488, I might here overlook his abusive reflections upon me..by unconcerning my self in the Matter. **1682** GREW *Anat. Plants* 220, I also know, that Your Lordship unconcerneth Your self..in what I even now spake.

uncon'cern, *v.*² *rare.* [UN-² 3.] *trans.* To free from concern or anxiety.
1653 SHIRLEY *Court Secret* II. iv, I was taking pains to unconcern the jealousie Of Antonio, and find him my own Rivall.

uncon'cerned, *ppl. a.* [UN-¹ 8.]
1. Devoid of concern or interest; uninterested, indifferent, unmoved.
? *c* **1635** WALLER *Misc., On Lady Isabella* 2 Such moving sounds from such a careless touch! So unconcern'd her self, and we so much! **1659** *Gentl. Calling* (1696) 2, I have been no unconcerned..Spectator of the Depression the Gentry have fallen under. **1725** POPE *Odyss.* XXIII. 169 Canst thou, oh cruel! unconcern'd survey Thy lost Ulysses, on this signal day? **1796** MME. D'ARBLAY *Camilla* III. 81 See but how he smiles..in defiance of all his efforts to look unconcerned! **1822** SCOTT *Peveril* xxxiii, Had Peveril come thither as an unconcerned visitor, his heart would have sunk within him.
b. Const. *about, at, in.*
1659 PEARSON *Creed* vii. 614 If there were no other judge beside our own soules, we should be..wholly unconcern'd in our own condemnations. **1697** COLLIER *Ess. Mor. Subj.* I. (1709) 155 To suppose that he has made the Nature of Man such, that..he should be unconcerned about the Happiness of his Neighbour. **1749** FIELDING *Tom Jones* IV. xiii, He was not unconcerned at the accident. **1822** LAMB *Elia* I. *Artificial Comedy*, A passing pageant, where we should sit as unconcerned at the issues,..as at a battle of the frogs and mice.
c. Of feeling, conduct, etc.
1658 PHILLIPS, *Indifference*, a carelesse, general, and unconcerned affection. **1702** ECHARD *Eccl. Hist.* (1710) 617 The holy man gave him an unconcern'd answer. **1820** HAZLITT *Lect. Dram. Lit.* 14 The same strength and depth and richness,..poured out in unconcerned profusion from the lap of nature. **1853** R. S. SURTEES *Sponge's Sp. Tour* xxxvii, He saw Soapey Sponge's preparations for departure with an unconcerned air.
2. Not affected by concern or anxiety; free from solicitude; undisturbed.
1660 COWLEY *Ode his Majesty's Restoration* xv, Methoughts I saw the three Judæan Youths..In the Chaldæan Furnace walk; How chearfully and unconcern'd they talk! **1685** DRYDEN *Thren. August.* i, We liv'd as unconcern'd and happily As the first Age in Natures golden Scene. **1747** HERVEY *Medit., Contempl. Night* (1740) 226 To be utterly unconcerned, where it is the truest wisdom to take the alarm. **1800** MRS. HERVEY *Mourtray Fam.* II. 226 If I had been cool and unconcerned..; but I was in a fright. **1897** MARY KINGSLEY *W. Africa* 351, I attempted to look as unconcerned as possible.
3. Indifferent or uninterested between two parties; disinterested, impartial.
1664 ATKYNS *Orig. Printing* Ded. C ij b, I have so far prevailed upon your Royal Goodness, as to ask unconcern'd Councel what is best to be done. **1697** DRYDEN *Æneis* x. 166 Each to his proper fortune stand or fall; Equal and unconcern'd I look on all. *a* **1718** PRIOR *Poems, Democritus & Heraclitus* 5 Between You both I unconcern'd stand by. **1748** SMOLLETT *R. Random* xxx, I begged to be examined by some unconcerned person on board.
4. Not concerned or involved, having no part or share, *in* something.
1647 CLARENDON *Hist. Reb.* II. §7 They believed there was no part of their Civil Government, uninvaded by them, and

no Persons of what Quality soever unconcerned and.. unhurt in them. **1683** *Apol. Prol. France* i. 9 The two Successors of Henry the Fourth look'd not upon themselves as unconcern'd in this Edict. **1764** HARMER *Observ.* iv. §14. 163 The robb of grapes..is, I should think, unconcerned in this enquiry.

b. Not concerned or occupied *with* something.

1667 MILTON *P.L.* XI. 174 The Morn, All unconcern'd with our unrest, begins Her rosie progress smiling. **1732** BERKELEY *Alciphr.* IV. §16 They were indolent gods, unconcerned with human affairs.

c. Without const. Also *ellipt.*, not affected by drink; sober. (Cf. CONCERNED *ppl. a.* 2.)

1668 HOWE *Bless. Righteous* 5 Not..as an unconcern'd circumstance, that hath nothing to do with the businesse spoken of. **1699** BENTLEY *Phal.* Pref. p. lxxvi, It's a very difficult thing, for a person unconcern'd and out of the reach of Harm, to be a fair Arbitrator there. **1748** RICHARDSON *Clarissa* VII. 373 Mowbray and Tourville grew very noisy. .. As to myself, the little part I had taken in their gaiety kept me unconcerned.

uncon'cernedly, *adv.* [f. prec. + -LY[2].] In an unconcerned manner; without anxiety or concern; with indifference.

1636 *Destr. Troy* I Not the most cruel of Our conquering Foes So unconcern'dly can relate our woes, As not to lend a tear. **1679** EVERARD *Popish Plot* 12, I unconcernedly expected a speedy enlargement. *a* **1721** SHEFFIELD (Dk. Buckhm.) *Wks.* (1723) II. 81 To discourse about the serving of the Tide..as coolly, and unconcernedly, as if it had been only a common journey. **1768–74** TUCKER *Lt. Nat.* (1834) I. 603 We shall never do it..unconcernedly, but as an unavoidable means for attaining some greater good. **1828** LYTTON *Pelham* III. i, Thrusting the miniature in my bosom, and turning unconcernedly away. **1872** BLACK *Adv. Phaeton* xv. 208 We were unconcernedly having luncheon.

uncon'cernedness. [f. as prec. + -NESS.] The quality or state of being unconcerned; freedom from anxiety; indifference.

1647 CLARENDON *Hist. Reb.* I. §46 So little dejected with it, that he answered the Articles with great steddyness, and unconcernedness. **1675** WYCHERLEY *Country Wife* v. i, To shew my unconcernedness, I'll come to your wedding. **1738** GRAY *Let.* Poems (1775) 36 My resolution and unconcernedness in the midst of evils. **1768–74** TUCKER *Lt. Nat.* (1834) II. 65 To attain a perfect unconcernedness at everything past,..is more plausible in theory, than feasible in practice. **1800** MRS. HERVEY *Mourtray Fam.* I. 9 He possessed great equanimity of temper, and a quiet unconcernedness of mind. **1860** PUSEY *Min. Proph.* 290 This union of inherent strength and unconcernedness about foreign aid is an adequate test of days anterior to Ahaz.

uncon'cerning, *ppl. a.* [UN-[1] 10 and 5 d.] Not concerning or affecting one; unconnected with one's affairs or interests; having no importance or relevance.

1612 DONNE *Progr. Soule, 2nd Anniv.* 285 To know but Catechismes and Alphabets Of unconcerning things, matters of fact. **1651** FULLER *Abel Rediv., Jerome* (1867) I. 29 They vexed him with trivial objections about unconcerning matters. **1742** MELMOTH *Fitzosborne Lett.* (1763) 438 With other topics of the same unconcerning kind. *a* **1779** WARBURTON *Unpubl. Papers* (1841) 568 It will teach him to distinguish real from imaginary knowledge,..useful from unconcerning. **1821** COLERIDGE *Lett., Convers.*, etc. II. 22 Lonely in an unconcerning crowd of human figures. **1833** LAMB *Elia* II. *Barrenness Imag. Faculty in Modern Art*, As if unconscious of Bacchus, or but idly casting her eyes as upon some unconcerning pageant,..Ariadne is still pacing the.. shore.

†**b.** Const. *to*, or with direct object. *Obs.*

1647 L. HAWARD *Charges Crown Rev.* Ded., Having medled with the publishing of such a Subject so unconcerning my own quality. **1654** WHITLOCK *Zootomia* 87 They will satisfie the Patients thirst with cooling Juleps, be they never so improper for the Malignity Nature hath to struggle with, or unconcerning her assistance to resist. **1667** *Decay Chr. Piety* v. ¶10. 228 Those things that are either impossible in their nature, or unconcerning to us, cannot beget it.

uncon'cernment. [UN-[1] 12.] The fact of not concerning oneself; unconcern.

1660 STANLEY *Hist. Philos.* IX. (1687) 507/1 This happened from two Causes, as well by reason of the unconcernment of the Cities..as by reason of the Death of the most excellent persons. **1676** GLANVILL *Ess.* I. 31 If there be any repose attainable by the Methods of Reason, there is nothing so like to afford it, as unconcernment in doubtful Opinions. **1716–7** BENTLEY *Serm.* xi. 383 The Seat of Selfishness and of Unconcernment for all about him. **1832** W. STEPHENSON *Gateshead Local Poems* 69 No matter where these daring souls have been, They always are in unconcernment seen. **1892** *Nation* (N.Y.) 12 May 364 They show the scholar among his books, handling his thoughts with a certain unconcernment.

†**uncon'cernness.** *Obs.*[−1] = prec.

1700 BLACKMORE *Job* xix. 80 Job in Affliction you refuse to know, And a shy Stranger's unconcernness show.

uncon'certed, *ppl. a.* (UN-[1] 8.)

1594 CAREW *Huarte's Exam. Wits* (1616) 215 The Stoicks held opinion, that..there was another [cause] vnwise and vnconcerted, whose workes prooued without order. **1711** SHAFTESB. *Charac.* III. 325 A Company where alternate Discourse is carry'd on, in un-concerted Measure, and un-premeditated Language. **1793** *Monthly Rev.* X. 376 In so much that the unconcerted composition of the gospels..is with some difficulty to be proved.

uncon'cessible, *a.* (UN-[1] 7.)

1643 HUNTON *Treat. Mon.* II. vii. 69 It is strange to see, how in this Epidemicall division of the Kingdome, the Abettors of both parts claime this unconcessible Judgement.

†**uncon'ciliable.** *a. Obs.*[−1] (UN-[1] 7 b, 5 b.)

1610 J. MELVILL *Diary* (Wodrow Soc.) 554 Peace betwixt the unconciliabill natiounes of Scottis and English.

uncon'ciliated, *ppl. a.* (UN-[1] 8.)

1828–32 WEBSTER. **1868** *Once a Week* 18 Jan. 66/2 But the company was unconciliated.

uncon'ciliating, *ppl. a.* (UN-[1] 10.)

1807 COXE *House of Austria* I. v. 72 He offended the natives by his stern and unconciliating manners. **1855** MACAULAY *Hist. Eng.* xv. III. 578 His clemency was peculiar to himself... It was cold, unconciliating, inflexible.

uncon'ciliatory, *a.* (UN-[1] 7.)

1789 JEFFERSON *Writ.* (1859) II. 572 Ternant will see that his predecessor is recalled for unconciliatory conduct. **1861** TROLLOPE *Tales All Countries* I. 4 She was..unconciliatory when any change even for a day was proposed to her. **1873** SYMONDS *Grk. Poets* iii. 90 We may gather..that his friend Cyrnus was of a rash and haughty and unconciliatory temper.

uncon'cludable, *a.* (UN-[1] 7 b.)

1642 J. BALL *Answ. to Can.* I. 131 To reason from the effect of things (you say) is unsound and unconcludable. **1653** H. MORE *Conject. Cabbal.* A 4, Nor does it at all follow, because a truth is delivered by way of Tradition, that it is unconcludable by Reason.

uncon'cluded, *ppl. a.* (UN-[1] 8.)

1564 PALFREYMAN *Baldwin's Mor. Philos.* 146 So many matters laid aside and left vnconcluded. *a* **1633** AUSTIN *Medit.* (1635) 73 But this (as well as the rest) stands unconcluded, since (peradventure) God would not have it certainely knowne. **1822** RANKEN *Hist. France* IX. x. ii. 241 The court pronounced the business unconcluded. **1837** LYTTON *Athens* I. 103 Yet he wrote in an age when the struggle was still unconcluded. **1886** A. WEIR *Hist. Basis Mod. Europe* (1889) 165 When the peace of Amiens was yet unconcluded.

†**uncon'cludency.** *Obs.*[−1] (UN-[1] 12 and 5 b.)

1654 HAMMOND *Answ. Animadv. Ignat.* iv. §1. 91 Produced by me as an argument to convince the unconcludency of Blondel's collection.

†**uncon'cludent**, *a. Obs.* (UN-[1] 7 and 5 b.)

1634 JACKSON *Creed* VII. xv. §3 It was then an allegation unconcludent and impertinent..to say [etc.]. **1647** HAMMOND *Power of Keys* iv. 80 The arguments..being utterly unconcludent against us. *a* **1676** HALE *Prim. Orig. Man.* I. vi. (1677) 116 All our Argumentations touching them are inevident and unconcludent.

uncon'cludible, *a.* (UN-[1] 7.)

1647 H. MORE *Song of Soul* Notes 352 Endeavouring..to comprehend and conclude that which is so unconcludible and incomprehensible.

†**uncon'cluding**, *ppl. a. Obs.* [UN-[1] 10 and 5 b.] Inconclusive.

a **1643** LD. FALKLAND, etc. *Infallibility* (1646) 200 You are to wise to claime by *Tu es Petrus* or any other so unconcluding an argument. **1662** H. MORE *Philos. Writ.* Pref. Gen. p. iii, The Author's Excuse for his omitting..to confute the unconcluding Reasons some use for the proof of a God. **1713** E. CALAMY *Life R. Baxter* xiii. 356 He shews his arguments both *ad Rem* and *ad Hominem* to be unconcluding.

Hence †**uncon'cludingness.** *Obs.*

1647 JER. TAYLOR *Lib. Proph.* vi. 110 The uncertainty of the truth of its decrees, by reason of the unconcludingnesse of the Arguments brought to attest it. **1661** BOYLE *Scept. Chym.* IV. (1680) 440 The unconcludingness of the Analytical Experiments vulgarly Relyed on.

†**uncon'clusive**, *a. Obs.* (UN-[1] 7 and 5 b.)

1640 HAMMOND *Poor Man's Tithing* Wks. 1684 IV. 554 Had the Promises been of any other sort,..the Apostles illation..had been utterly unconclusive, if not impertinent. **1672** H. DODWELL *Two Lett.* Pref. C iij, There being no more politick way for betraying the Truth..than to offer to defend it by unconclusive arguments.

Hence †**uncon'clusively** *adv.*, **-ness.** *Obs.*

1660 COKE *Justice Vind.* 13 When a man talks unconclusively, they say he talks not sense. **1723** MATHER *Vind. Bible* 209 The appearing unconclusiveness of the reasoning used in Scripture.

†**uncon'coct**, *a.* [UN-[1] 7 and 5 b.] = next.

1591 SYLVESTER *Du Bartas* I. ii. 132 Too-much Moist, which (unconcoct within) The Liver spreads betwixt the flesh and skin. **1625** HART *Anat. Ur.* II. i. 53 A great agitation and stirring of crude and vnconcoct humours.

uncon'cocted, *ppl. a.* [UN-[1] 8 and 5 b.]

1. Not digested in the stomach.

1611 FLORIO, *Indigesto*, vndigested, vnconcocted. **1615** CROOKE *Body of Man* 110 The stomacke..receyueth the meate when it is harder and vnconcocted. **1651** WITTIE tr. *Primrose's Pop. Err.* III. 150 The meat..being unconcocted doth encrease the disease, and the symptomes thereof. **1774** GOLDSM. *Nat. Hist.* V. 244 The red-beaked toucan..feeds chiefly upon pepper,..gorging itself in such a manner that it voids it crude and unconcocted. **1802** LAMB *John Woodvil* IV. i. 2 A weight of wine lies heavy on my head, The unconcocted follies of last night.

2. Not brought to a proper state or condition; crude, immature.

1649 E. REYNOLDS *Hosea* iii. 12 Those fruites..are sowre, unsavoury, and unconcocted. **1693** SIR T. P. BLOUNT *Nat. Hist.* 250 Erastus affirms..that in Germany there hath been Unripe and Unconcocted Silver found in Mines. **1726** LEONI *Alberti's Archit.* I. 34 When it [*sc.* lime] is used too soon.., there will be some small unconcocted Stones in it. **1770** LANGHORNE *Plutarch* (1879) II. 792/1 The fruits were so crude and unconcocted, that they pined away and decayed.

3. *fig.* Not properly worked up or elaborated.

c **1628** DONNE *Serm.* (1640) 599 Ever more there will be some things raw and unconcocted in every church. **1658** OSBORN *Adv. Son* Wks. (1673) 89 Such unconcocted Rebellions turn seldom to the hurt of any, but the Parties that promote them. **1745** WESLEY *Wks.* (1872) XII. 68 Such frothy, unconcocted trifles, such undigested crudities, as a man of learning..would have been ashamed to set his name to. **1846** LANDOR *Imag. Conv.* Wks. I. 201/2 The smoky, verminous, unconcocted doctrine of passive obedience.

†**uncon'coction.** *Obs.*[−1] (UN-[1] 12 and 5 b.)

1662 J. CHANDLER *Van Helmont's Oriat.* 199 Because the one only ignorance of ferments hath caused digestions, and the remedies of unconcoction to be unknown.

uncon'current, *a.* (UN-[1] 7 and 5 b.)

1613–8 DANIEL *Coll. Hist. Eng.* (1626) 49 A league, consisting of seuerall Nations, emulous and vnconcurrent in their courses.

uncon'curring, *ppl. a.* (UN-[1] 10 and 5 b.)

1639 FULLER *Holy War* v. xiii. 251 The confluence of Princes otherwise unconcurring in their severall courses. **1728** SAVAGE *Bastard* 36 While your backward Will retrench'd Desire, And unconcurring Spirits lent no Fire.

uncon'demnable, *a.* (UN-[1] 7 b.)

1643 PRYNNE *Sov. Power Parl.* III. 121 Therefore our Opposites must grant all Bishops, Priests, Ministers,..as irresistible, uncensurable, undeprivable, uncondemnable, for any crimes whatsoever, as they say kings are.

uncon'demned, *ppl. a.* (UN-[1] 8.)

1526 TINDALE *Acts* xxii. 25 Ys it laufull for you to scourge a Romain vncondempned? *c* **1545** BRINKLOW *Compl.* xii. (1874) 27 To put a man to death vncondemnyd is to commyt murder. **1600** [see UNCONFUTED]. **1680** BAXTER *Answ. Stillingfl.* xxxvii. 62 How few were there un-Cursed, and un-Condemned in the Roman World? **1842** MANNING *Serm.* xvi. (1848) I. 236 Set side by side..your rules and your acts; and who shall go uncondemned? **1861** STANLEY *East. Ch.* p. l, See..what evils are left uncondemned.

uncon'densable, *a.* (UN-[1] 7 b and 5 b.)

1846 WORCESTER (citing Turner). **1857** MILLER *Elem. Chem., Org.* ix. 555 A large amount of volatile matter is expelled, partly in the form of uncondensable gases.

uncon'densed, *ppl. a.* [UN-[1] 8.]

1. Not condensed or compressed.

a **1711** KEN *Hymnotheo* Poet. Wks. 1721 III. 212 By Manna uncondens'd, and Heav'nly Dew. **1859** GREGORY *Egypt* I. 330 The clouds, the centre of which furrowed by uncondensed lightnings, reflected a silvery light.

2. *spec.* (See CONDENSED *ppl. a.* 2.)

1810 HENRY *Chem.* (ed. 6) I. 43 The gas passes, uncondensed, through the second right-angled tube. **1838** GRANVILLE *Spas Germ.* 255 The steam, at such a temperature, must differ little from that of uncondensed distilled water. **1862** MILLER *Elem. Chem., Org.* (ed. 2) ix. 638 The remaining portion of the distillate, consisting of uncondensed gases.

†**unconde'scendable**, *a. Obs.*[−1] [UN-[1] 7 b.] Incapable of coming down.

1683 E. HOOKER *Pref. Pordage's Mystic Div.* 67 These Sublimities in Religion,..uncondescendabl to the meerly Rational, or uncompliabl with the Rules of Syllogism.

unconde'scending, *ppl. a.* (UN-[1] 10.)

1660 GAUDEN *God's Gt. Demonstr.* 16 Who will carry himself..with an uncondescending height, and divine stiffness against those that are not humble in his sight. **1969** *Guardian* 31 July 2/3 A performance that was obviously pleasing and uncondescending.

unconde'scension. (UN-[1] 12.)

1681 J. KETTLEWELL *Meas. Chr. Obed.* II. iv. 165 The Law..against uncourteousness, against stiffness or uncondescension. *Ibid.* II. vi. 197 Stateliness or difficulty of access and uncondescension.

†**unconde'scensive**, *a. Obs.*[−1] (UN-[1] 7.)

1681 J. KETTLEWELL *Meas. Chr. Obed.* v. iii. 633 Has any man..been surprized into rash words and censures,..or uncandid, or uncondescensive behaviour?

†**uncon'dited**, *ppl. a. Obs.*[−1] [UN-[1] 8.] Unseasoned, unflavoured.

a **1667** JER. TAYLOR *Suppl. Serm. for Year* (1678) 86 While he estimates the secrets of Religion by such Measures, they must needs seem as insipid as..the uncondited Mushroom.

†**uncon'ditionable**, *a. Obs.*[−1] = next.

1642 *View Print. Bk. int. Observat.* 7 The King hath in nothing appertaining to His Crown, an unconditionable Property.

uncon'ditional, *a.* [UN-[1] 7 and 5 b.]

Not limited by or subject to conditions or stipulations; absolute, unlimited, complete.

1666 DRYDEN *Ann. Mirab.* cclxix, O pass not, Lord, an absolute Decree, Or bind thy Sentence unconditional. **1726** AYLIFFE *Parergon* 19 Our Saviour left a Power in his Church to absolve men from their Sins; but this was not an absolute or unconditional Power. **1776** ADAM SMITH *W.N.* II. ii. I. 399 The obligation of an immediate and unconditional payment of such bank notes as soon as presented. **1830** HAZLITT *Life Napoleon Buonaparte* IV. l. 119 We will have more, namely the original stake we played for; unconditional surrender of the right of nations to chuse their own government. **1839** JAMES *Louis XIV*, I. 404 The chamber of accounts leaned towards unconditional obedience, and prepared to quit Paris. **1844–8** H. H. WILSON *Brit. India* II. 351 He pretended that he had come to offer an unconditional surrender of the fortress. **1885** 'MRS. ALEXANDER' *At Bay* viii, There must be nothing about possibility... Give me an unconditional promise, or I shall not leave you! **1901** H. CAMPBELL-BANNERMAN in *Hansard Commons* 14 Feb. 89 Unconditional surrender was our first and last word. **1930** G. B. SHAW *Apple Cart* II. 69 In plain terms we require from you an unconditional surrender. **1949** *New Statesman* 30 July 115/2 The sharp argument about 'unconditional surrender' in the House of Commons last week revealed much that was of more than historical significance... He [*sc.* Mr. Bevin] had not protested when Mr. Churchill brought back this fatal slogan from Casablanca. **1956** A. HUXLEY *Adonis & Alphabet* 81 The only completely unconditional surrender will come when everybody—but *everybody*—is a corpse. **1974** *Times* 20 Dec. 1/2 The Kuwait authorities insisted that the [hijackers'] surrender was 'unconditional'.

Hence **uncon'ditionalness**.

1843 MILL *Logic* I. 372 If there be any meaning which confessedly belongs to the term necessity, it is unconditionalness. **1884** *Expositor* Feb. 151 The unconditionalness of God's election.

unconditio'nality. [f. prec. Cf. UNCONDITIONALITY.] The quality of being unconditional.

a **1714** M. HENRY *Treat. Baptism* ii. Wks. 1853 I. 509/1 Those who speak so much of free grace, and the unconditionality of the gospel covenant. **1811–31** BENTHAM *Univ. Gram.* Wks. 1843 VIII. 355/2 The verb at large, considered independently of..conditionality and unconditionality. **1870** J. H. NEWMAN *Gram. Assent* iv. 38 The reality of the thesis is almost a condition of its unconditionality.

uncon'ditionally, *adv.* [UN-^{1} 11.] Without conditions.

a **1660** HAMMOND *Serm. 2 Cor. vii. 1* Wks. 1684 IV. 503 We are the special Favorites to whom those Promises are unconditionally consign'd. **1743** WESLEY *Jrnl.* 23 Aug., That God before the foundation of the world, did unconditionally elect certain persons to do certain works. **1791** BOSWELL *Johnson* July 1762, Thus, then,..there was nothing inconsistent..in Johnson's accepting of a pension so unconditionally and so honourably offered to him. **1837** HT. MARTINEAU *Soc. Amer.* III. 287 That faith which would lead them..to appropriate all truth, fearlessly and unconditionally. **1882** FARRAR *Early Chr.* II. 469 Yet Christ prayed unconditionally for his murderers.

uncon'ditionate, *a.* [UN-^{1} 7 and 5 b.] Not subject to or limited by conditions.

1642 *Answ. to Printed Bk.* 11 So unconditionate and high a propriety in all the Subjects lives. **1668** H. MORE *Div. Dial.* I. xx. 84 The Divine Decrees, when they finde not men fitting Tools, make them so, where Prophecies are peremptory or unconditionate.

So **uncon'ditionated** *ppl. a.*

1836 F. MAHONY *Reliques Father Prout, Painter, Barry* (1859) 503 He claimed..unconditionated pedigree, ascending..to the ancient masters of the world.

uncon'ditionately, *adv.* [UN-^{1} 11.] Unconditionally.

1670 CUDWORTH *Serm. 1 Cor. xv.* 57, 234 The Divine Spirit of Grace doth not work absolutely, unconditionately, and irresistibly in the Souls of men. **1695** KENNETT *Par. Antiq.* ix. 607 All Ecclesiastical dues are to be voluntarily and unconditionately paid. **1820** MILNER *Suppl. Mem. Eng. Cath.* 28 In those times..no orthodox Catholic could unconditionately swear that [etc.].

uncon'ditioned, *ppl. a.* [UN-^{1} 8.]

1. Not subject to, or dependent upon, conditions or stipulations.

a **1631** DONNE *Serm.* xxxix. (1640) 391 Thou must stay out that time,..and by no practice, no not so much as by a deliberate wish, or unconditioned prayer, seeke to be delivered of it. **1692** BEVERLEY *Disc. Dr. Crisp* 10 Therein it must needs be, as unconditioned, as Election is. **1712** BERKELEY *Pass. Obed.* Wks. 1871 III. 139, I speak of non-resistance as an absolute, unconditioned, unlimited duty. **1776** GIBBON *Decl. & F.* xi. I. 301 With the choice only of submitting to his unconditioned mercy, or waiting the utmost severity of his resentment. **1852** BAILEY *Festus* (ed. 5) 491 Who thus pour forth Unmeasured, unconditioned, your divine Riches of works and words. **1864** R. A. ARNOLD *Cotton Famine* 477 They had grown used to 'th' relief', and regarded it as their unconditioned right.

2. a. Not dependent upon, or determined by, an antecedent condition.

1796 F. A. NITSCH *Gen. View Kant's Princ. concerning Man* 127 Reason..produces the idea of an unconditioned Limitation. **1829** SIR W. HAMILTON in *Edin. Rev.* L. 204 We are..inspired with a belief in the existence of something unconditioned beyond the sphere of all comprehensible reality. **1846** LEWES *Hist. Philos.* IV. 205 An entirely unconditioned Thought. **1862** H. SPENCER *First Princ.* I. iii. §15 (1875) 50 If Space and Time are the conditions under which we think, then when we think of Space and Time themselves, our thoughts must be unconditioned.

b. ***unconditioned reflex***, an inborn, instinctual reflex or reflex action (cf. CONDITIONED *ppl. a.* 7 b). So ***unconditioned stimulus***.

1906, 1927 [see CONDITIONED *ppl. a.* 7 b]. **1937** *Discovery* Jan. 17/2 Its instincts, or, to use Pavlov's expression, its unconditioned reflexes. **1972** *New Yorker* 26 Aug. 32/3 In the vocabulary that Pavlov adopted to describe his findings, the meat powder was labelled an 'unconditioned stimulus'.

3. *absol.* That which is not subject to the conditions of finite existence and cognition.

1829 SIR W. HAMILTON in *Edin. Rev.* L. 198 The first of these ideas..is variously expressed, under the terms unity, identity, substance, absolute cause, the infinite, pure thought, &c.; we would briefly call it the *unconditioned*. **1836** —— *Metaph.* xxxviii. (1859) II. 373 The Conditioned is that which is alone conceivable or cogitable; the Unconditioned, that which is inconceivable or incogitable. **1877** E. CAIRD *Philos. Kant* iii. 45 The form of time, in which we always find condition beyond condition, cause beyond cause, and never reach the unconditioned, the *causa sui*.

Hence **uncon'ditionedness**.

1854 GEO. ELIOT tr. *Feuerbach's Essence Christianity* iv. 54 The metaphysical attributes of eternity, unconditionedness, ..and the like abstractions. **1860** J. YOUNG *Prov. Reason* 47 Only through and on account of this undefinedness (unconditionedness) is Being Non-Being. **1903** *Edin. Rev.* July 71 Nor is the test of this unconditionedness arbitrary.

uncon'doled, *ppl. a.* (UN-^{1} 8.)

a **1711** KEN *Hymns Evang.* Poet. Wks. 1721 I. 102 Bless'd are the Merciful,..Who uncondol'd pass no one's Sorrow by.

uncon'ducing, *ppl. a.* (UN-^{1} 10.)

1660 JER. TAYLOR *Duct. Dubit.* I. iv. Wks. IX. 209 The affairs of the world..are..unconducing to the affairs of the spirit. **1675** E. PHILLIPS *Theat. Poet.* Pref. 4 b, I judged it a Work in some sort not unconducing to a public benefit.

uncon'ducive, *a.* (UN-^{1} 7 and 5 b.)

1661 BOYLE *Style Script.* (1675) 79 Those volumes, which ..must contain nothing unconducive to those designs. **1776** S. JENYNS *Internal Evid. Chr. Relig.* 33 A religion..totally unconducive to any worldly purpose. **1802–12** BENTHAM *Ration. Judic. Evid.* (1827) IV. 435 A short experiment will be found not unconducive to his purpose. **1984** *Times Lit. Suppl.* 25 May 593/4 A number of local CIA men do seem to have taken steps unconducive to the success of Kennedy liberalism.

uncon'ducted, *ppl. a.* (UN-^{1} 8.)

a **1677** BARROW *Serm. Jer. li.* 15 Wks. 1686 II. 96 An undisciplined and unconducted troop of atoms rambling up and down confusedly.

'unconess. *Sc.* [f. UNCO *a.*] Strangeness.

1637 RUTHERFORD *Lett.* (1836) I. 330 Our Lord loveth not niceness and dryness and unconess in friends. **1652** WARISTON *Diary* (S.H.S.) II. 164 My awen mynd found an uncounesse and deadnesse of my sprite in exercises.

uncon'fected, *ppl. a.* (UN-^{1} 8.)

1650 BULWER *Anthropomet.* 119 If it carry the unconfected meat, it works nothing upon the meat.

uncon'federated, *ppl. a.* (UN-^{1} 8.)

[**1775** ASH.] **1802–12** BENTHAM *Ration. Judic. Evid.* (1827) V. 118 If..it be necessary for the acquirer to have recourse to an ordinary and unconfederated dealer.

uncon'ferred, *ppl. a.* (UN-^{1} 8).

1645 MILTON *Tetrach.* Introd., Who..hath not forborn to scandalize him, unconferr'd with, unadmonisht, undealt with by any Pastorly or brotherly convincement.

uncon'fess, *v.* (UN-^{2} 3.)

1749 LAVINGTON *Enthus. Meth. & Papists* II. Pref. (1754) p. xxvi, Whether..I have not in some measure unconfessed my confessions.

uncon'fessed, *ppl. a.* Also 6 *Sc.* **wnconfessyt**, 7–8 **unconfest**. [UN-^{1} 8.]

1. Not confessed or avowed; unacknowledged. †Also const. *of*.

a **1500** in *Ratis Raving*, etc. 3 He bryngis to his mynd..the synis that he has done, wnconfessyt of or rapentyt. **1509** FISHER *Wks.* (1876) 86, I shall..thynke on my synne that no thynge of it be vncontryte & vnconfessed. **1526** *Pilgr. Perf.* (W. de W. 1531) 227 b, Leuyng no mortall synne vnconfessed. **1648** HEXHAM II, *Ongebiecht*, Vnconfessed. **1863** JULIA KAVANAGH *Q. Mab* II. 306 It was love mutual —unconfessed, but ardent and impassioned. **1871** R. H. HUTTON *Ess.* I. 4 All unconscious and unconfessed acts of surrender to the divine influence.

b. Of persons: Not self-avowed.

1742 YOUNG *Nt. Th.* v. 817 Like princes unconfest in foreign courts, Who travel under cover. **1898** A. MACKENNAL in *Life* xix. (1905) 314, I think that unconfessed Christians..must have brought the gospel into Britain.

2. Not having confessed; unshriven.

1607 J. CARPENTER *Plaine Mans Plough* 205 For want of Confession, thou shalt be damned, as unconfest. **1638** *Penit. Conf.* xii. (1657) 331 He came into the Forest to hunt, and there was wounded with an arrow; and forthwith died impenitent and unconfessed. **1808** SCOTT *Marm.* I. Introd. 267 A sinful man, and unconfess'd, He took the Sangreal's holy quest. **1810** —— *Lady of L.* III. v, Alice..lock'd her secret in her breast, And died in travail, unconfess'd. **1889** 'MARK TWAIN' *Yankee at Crt. K. Arthur* xvii, It were peril to my own soul to let him die unconfessed and unabsolved.

uncon'fessing, *ppl. a.* (UN-^{1} 10.)

1641 MILTON *Animadv.* 57 Because hee may not as a Judge sit out the wrangling noyse of litigious Courts to shreeve the purses of unconfessing and unmortify'd sinners.

un'confidence. (UN-^{1} 12 and 5 b.)

a **1670** HACKET *Abp. Williams* I. (1692) 124 In all his employments for this [the Spanish] match,..he never raised his style higher when he wrote than with Ifs and suppositive unconfidence.

un'confident, *a.* (UN-^{1} 7 and 5 b.)

Also, in recent use, ***unconfidently*** adv.

a **1652** A. WILSON *Jas. I* (1653) 51 The Jesuits unconfident of him (inclining more to the hot zeal of Spain) one of their Instruments stab'd him into the mouth with a knife, without much hurt. **1869** *Athenæum* 13 Feb. 242/1, I mean, us unconfident lovers. **1871** RUSKIN *Fors Clav.* ix. 8 [He] turned to me with an anxious, yet not unconfident expression.

unconfi'dential, *a.* (UN-^{1} 7.)

1772 BURKE *Corr.* (1844) I. 384 As I have stated this matter so much at large,..it is not necessary to say more by this unconfidential conveyance. **1834** LYTTON *Pompeii* I. vi, Why is it to me thou art thus unconfidential? **1839** *John Bull* 15 Apr., Showing however unconfidential they may be, that they are at any rate confident men. **1847** MRS. GORE *Castles in Air* I. xi. 227 The unconfidential terms on which we lived.

uncon'fiding, *ppl. a.* (UN-^{1} 10.)

1820 MRS. OPIE *Tales of Heart* IV. 344 Rash unconfiding boy! **1870** J. BRUCE *Life Gideon* xx. 368 Gideon's for long unconfiding and undutiful because unbelieving demeanour.

uncon'finable, *a.* (UN-^{1} 7 b and 5 b.)

1598 SHAKS. *Merry W.* II. ii. 21 You stand vpon your honor: why, (thou vnconfinable basenesse), it is as much as I can doe to keepe the termes of my honor precise. **1669** EARL ORRERY *Parthen.* (1676) 771 Your pity is so great and unconfinable. **1794** G. ADAMS *Nat. & Exp. Philos.* (1806) I. 523 [Light and caloric] being of too subtile a nature to be confined in any vessel that we possess, have..been termed unconfinable bodies. **1815** J. SMITH *Panorama Sci. & Art* II. 291 Light and caloric, those unconfinable powers which so many of these manipulations elicit or require. **1820** W. IRVING *Sketch Bk.* (1821) I. 152 It is the divine attribute of the imagination, that it is irrepressible, unconfinable.

Hence **uncon'finably** *adv.*

a **1657** R. LOVEDAY *Lett.* (1663) 161 But I outrun the Constable: Dear Brother, Unconfinably yours to serve you, R. L.

uncon'fine, *v.* [UN-^{2} 4 b.] *trans.* To release from restraint; to give free course to.

1651 STANLEY *Poems* 16 Yet there's a way to unconfine thy heart. *a* **1711** KEN *Hymnotheo* Poet. Wks. III. 35 Curs'd Infidelity to reinstil, Unfix the Mind, and unconfine the Will. **1820** KEATS *Isabella* xxi, Each unconfines His bitter thoughts to other.

uncon'fined, *ppl. a.*^{1} [UN-^{1} 8.]

1. Not restrained or restricted in respect of freedom of action. Also const. *to*.

1607 BEAUM. & FL. *Woman Hater* III. i, Were we not made our selves, free, unconfin'd Commanders of our own affections? **1624** MASSINGER *Renegado* I. ii, It is his pleasure .., provided (For so far I am unconfined) that I Affect and like your person. **1694** *Gracian's Courtier's Orac.* 49 Never to be too forward nor passionate, is the sign of a free and unconfined heart. **1709** POPE *Ess. Crit.* 639 Blest with a taste exact, yet unconfin'd. **1711** STEELE *Spect.* No. 2 ¶1 His being unconfined to Modes and Forms. **1784** COWPER *Task* III. 713 Pure is the nymph, though lib'ral of her smiles, And chaste, though unconfin'd, whom I extol. **1808** SCOTT *Marm.* IV. Introd. 163 Oft our talk its topic chang'd, And.. Rang'd, unconfin'd, from grave to gay. **1820** J. P. NEALE *Views Seats Eng.*, etc. III. *Porkington* 2 To the east the eye roams unconfined over the rich and highly ornamented plains of Shropshire.

b. Unlimited, unbounded.

1626 MASSINGER *Roman Actor* I. ii, As his rule is infinite, his pleasures Are unconfined. **1662** BP. HOPKINS *Serm.* (1685) 26 We begin to grow more unconfined in our knowledge, as well as our being. *a* **1672** STERRY *Freed. Will* (1675) 109 As an heavenly Marriage eternally established in its own unconfined Unity. *a* **1721** PRIOR *Ess. Opinion* Wks. 1907 II. 202 However our Vanities or desires are unconfined. **1738** GLOVER *Leonidas* XII. 82 Now devastation, unconfin'd, involves The Malian fields. **1818** CRUISE *Digest* (ed. 2) IV. 279 The former was subject to some restraint..; the latter consisting in general and unconfined dominion.

2. Not kept in confinement; not shut up or enclosed; not secured or kept in place.

1649 LOVELACE *To Althea* i, When Love with unconfined wings Hovers within my Gates. *a* **1711** KEN *Psyche* Poet. Wks. IV. 299 The Soul in Vision seem'd from Flesh unloos'd To fly abroad, and spatiate unconfin'd. **1739** 'R. BULL' tr. *Dedekindus' Grobianus* 5 Thy Hairs, uncut and unconfin'd, With loose Disorder wanton in the Wind. **1762** R. GUY *Pract. Obs. Cancers* 30 The Matter having a free and unconfined Discharge. **1808** SCOTT *Marm.* III. Introd. 22 Then, wild as cloud, or stream, or gale, Flow on, flow unconfin'd, my Tale! **1832** HT. MARTINEAU *Ella of Gar.* i. 9 Her hair [was] unconfined by any cap. **1892** GREENER *Breech Loader* 163 Unconfined wood powder..may be ignited without obtaining a third of the available explosive force.

Hence **uncon'finedly** *adv.*; **uncon'finedness**.

1654–66 EARL ORRERY *Parthen.* (1676) 598 Sorrow, to which they so justly and unconfinedly abandon'd themselves. **1673** A. WALKER *Lees Lachrymans* 3 The healthful Vigour, the agile Unconfinedness,..of his Youth. **1687** DRYDEN *Hind & P.* II. 617 Prove any Church, oppos'd to this our head, So one, so pure, so unconfin'dly spread. **1899** *Macm. Mag.* LXXIX. 455/2 The sense of the desert was upon me, the embracing, soothing spirit of unconfinedness.

uncon'fined, *ppl. a.*^{2} [UN-^{2} 8.] Released from confinement.

1833 TENNYSON *Two Voices* 371 And men,..From cells of madness unconfined, Oft lose whole years of darker mind.

uncon'fining, *ppl. a.* (UN-^{1} 8.)

1846 WORCESTER (citing Chesterfield).

uncon'firm, *v.* (UN-^{2} 3.)

1550 BALE *Eng. Votaries* II. 66 Anselme intreated for hys dysgraded abbottes and vnconfirmed prelates, whyche was graunted foorthwith, and they restored to their dygnytees. **1598** FLORIO, *Disconfermare*, to vnconfirme, to disestablish. **1843** CARLYLE *Past & Pr.* II. ix, Long ages of..entirely confirmed Valethood—which will have to *un*confirm itself again.

uncon'firmed, *ppl. a.* [UN-^{1} 8 and 5 b.]

1. Not having received the rite of confirmation.

1565 CALFHILL *Answ. Martiall* 99, I besech you, how many be suffered to dye, vnconfirmed. **1920** *Conference of Bishops of Anglican Communion* 30 The irregularity of admitting to Communion the baptized but unconfirmed Communicants of the non-episcopal congregations. **1977** R. L. WOLFF *Gains & Losses* II. ii. 122 Danger besets the unconfirmed girls... They find their own vicar crusty and aloof.

2. a. Not strengthened or fortified; not yet made firm or sure.

c **1592** MARLOWE *Jew of Malta* III. iii, Then were my thoughts so fraile And vnconfirm'd, and I was chain'd to follies of the world. **1609** DANIEL *Civ. Wars* IV. xxxvi, In th' unconfirmed troupes, much fear did breed. **1706** ROWE *Ulysses* IV, A boy!..feeble in Infancy, Essaying the first Rudiments of Manhood, With Strength unpractis'd yet, and unconfirm'd. **1750** *Phil. Trans.* XLVI. 399 As I observed the Callus to be unconfirmed, I re-applied the Bandage. **1795** SOUTHEY *Joan of Arc* I. 98 Thoughts of politic craftiness arose Within him, and his faith, yet unconfirm'd, Determin'd to prompt action.

†**b.** Uninstructed, ignorant. *Obs.*

1588 SHAKS. *L.L.L.* IV. ii. 19 After his..vntrained, or rather vnlettered, or ratherest vnconfirmed fashion. **1599** —— *Much Ado* III. iii. 120 *Con.* I wonder at it. *Bor.* That shewes thou art vnconfirm'd.

c. Not supported or established by further evidence; uncorroborated.

1671 MILTON *P.R.* I. 29 Nor was long His witness unconfirm'd. **1781** V. KNOX *Liberal Education* Concl. 359 Their [*sc.* French] recent histories are destitute of dignity, both of diction and sentiment, and unconfirmed by authorities. **1897** *Westm. Gaz.* 26 Aug. 2/1 The report that 300 of these brave fellows have been cut to pieces is unconfirmed.

3. Not formally confirmed or sanctioned.

1656 BRAMHALL *Replic.* ii. 105 Therefore we give the same priviledges to a Councell unconfirmed..and to a Councell confirmed by the Pope.

†**uncon'form**, *a. Obs.* [UN-[1] 7 and 5 b.]

1. = INCONFORM *a.*

1653 GAUDEN *Hierasp.* 14 How unscriptural, how unconform to the examples of all ancient Churches,..do they seem to many judicious and gracious Christians? **1667** MILTON *P.L.* V. 259 From hence..he sees, Not unconform to other shining Globes, Earth and the Gard'n of God.

2. = NON-CONFORM *a.*

1653 R. BAILLIE *Dissuas. Vind.* (1655) 74 Not only the Separatists but the unconform ministers. **1676** JOHN ROW *Contin. Blair's Autobiog.* viii. (1848) 113 The preaching of the Word by honest unconform and anti-prelatic men.

unconforma'bility. [UN-[1] 12. Cf. next.] The state or quality of being unconformable. Chiefly *Geol.*

1833 LYELL *Princ. Geol.* III. 30 The frequent unconformability in the stratification of the inferior and overlying formation. **1865** LIVINGSTONE *Zambesi* ii. 54 A picture of dislocation or unconformability which would gladden a geological lecturer's heart. **1873** EARLE *Philol. Eng. Tongue* (ed. 2) §6 One important cause of unconformability is the introduction of foreign words.

uncon'formable, *a.* [UN-[1] 7 b and 5 b.]

1. Not conformable or correspondent *to* something. Also without const.

1594 HOOKER *Eccl. Pol.* III. vii. §4 Vnto those generall rules..we doe not defend that we may hold any thing vnconformable. **1598-9** E. FORDE *Parismus* II. (1672) 73 So far is this Picture unconformable to the perfect description of her cælestial perfections, as far as is black from white. *a* **1688** CUDWORTH *Immut. Mor.* (1731) 157 This must not be granted, that the Modes of Conception in the Understanding..are disagreeable to the Reality of the Things conceived by them; and so being unconformable, are therefore False. **1711** STEELE *Spect.* No. 145 ¶7 We retain still a Quilted one [*sc.* petticoat] underneath, which makes us not altogether unconformable to the Fashion. **1726** LEONI *Alberti's Archit.* I. 11 The..Parts may not be unconformable to the Rules of Art. **1802-12** BENTHAM *Ration. Judic. Evid.* (1827) I. 156 In so far as it is the will..of the witness, that his testimony..be in any respect unconformable to the real state of the case. **1883** M. PATTISON *Mem.* (1885) 299 He wanted to get me out as an unconformable element.

b. Of persons: Unwilling to conform. (Cf. next.)

1647 CLARENDON *Hist. Reb.* I. § 173 That People..would not appear unconformable to his Majesty's wish in any particular. **1728** MORGAN *Algiers* I. iv. 76 His libidinous and unconformable Proselytes.

2. *spec.* in *Eng. Hist.* Not conforming to the usages of the Church of England, in later use esp. as prescribed by the Act of Uniformity of 1662. Also const. *to.* (Cf. NON-CONFORMABLE *a.*)

1611 A. STAFFORD *Niobe* 175 These men, whose puritie hath made them vnconformable to the present Discipline of the Church. **1647** CLARENDON *Hist. Rep.* IV. §10 The recommending some seditious, Unconformable Ministers, to be Lecturers in Churches about London. **1672** BAXTER *Bagshaw's Scand.* iii. 32 Could you wish..that the.. Protestant Religion were kept up by none but the unconformable Ministers in private? **1732** NEAL *Hist. Purit.* I. 307 Many ministers of his diocese being returned unconformable, were suspended. **1736** CHANDLER *Hist. Persec.* 358 A warrant from the Council..to stop all ministers unconformable to the discipline and ceremonies of the Church. **1861** W. S. PERRY *Hist. Ch. Eng.* I. xvi. 591 Unconformable clergy could be reduced..into a sullen outward compliance.

3. *Geol.* Not having the same direction or plane of stratification. Also const. *to.*

1813 BAKEWELL *Introd. Geol.* (1815) 76 Granite is sometimes met with not under the slate rocks, but resting upon them in an unconformable position. **1830** LYELL *Princ. Geol.* I. 201 The travertin is unconformable to the lacustrine beds. **1882** GEIKIE *Text-bk. Geol.* IV. x. 601 Wherever one series of rocks is found to rest upon a highly denuded surface of an older series, the junction is unconformable.

Hence **uncon'formableness.**

1711 *Phil. Trans.* XXVII. 329 The unconformableness that the Figure of the compounded Globe had to a perfect Sphere.

uncon'formably, *adv. Geol.* [UN-[1] 11.] In an unconformable manner or position.

1839 MURCHISON *Silur. Syst.* I. xxxiv. 451 In the former district, it has just been shown to lie unconformably upon the coal measures and more ancient strata. **1875** DAWSON *Dawn of Life* ii. 9 The crumpled..strata..are seen to underlie unconformably.

uncon'formed, *ppl. a.* [UN-[1] 8.]

†**1.** Not conforming; nonconformist. *Obs.*

a **1631** DONNE *Lett.* (1651) 36 That more single [duellism], and almost self-homicide, between the unconformed Ministers, and Bishops. **1676** ROW *Contn. Blair's Autobiog.* xii. (1848) 454 All the unconformed ministers were summoned..to come to their meeting.

2. *Geol.* (Cf. UNCONFORMABLE *a.* 3.)

1833-4 J. PHILLIPS *Geol.* in *Encycl. Metrop.* (1845) VI. 656/2 A little appearance of the chalk is observable North of the coal of Elberfeld, to which it is unconformed. **1876** PAGE *Adv. Text-bk. Geol.* 325 Where any beds of the oolitic system are really unconformed to others of the same system below them.

Hence **uncon'formedly** *adv.*

1833-4 J. PHILLIPS *Geol.* in *Encycl. Metrop.* (1845) VI. 590/1 The Northern and Southern portion of this great tract ..agree in being..covered unconformedly by the magnesian limestone.

uncon'forming, *ppl. a.* [UN-[1] 10.] Failing or refusing to conform; *spec.* = NONCONFORMING.

1641 *Vind. Smect.* xiii. 131 There is one practice of our Bishops he is something more laborious to justifie: That is, their casting out unconforming brethren. **1656** SANDERSON *Serm.* (1689) 13 Unconforming Ministers have no cause to complain. **1680** *Dial. Pope & Phanatick* 7 We post within the Establish'd Church as many Unconforming Ministers as we can. **1753** CHESTERF. in *World* No. 29. 256 To be plagued ..by the unconforming obstinacy, the low vulgar excesses, ..of my son. **1821** WORDSW. *Eccl. Sonn.*, *Clerical Integrity* 2 Nor shall the eternal roll of praise reject Those Unconforming; whom one rigorous day Drives from their Cures. **1825** *Monthly Rev.* CVI. 513 Calvinistic laymen are seldom tolerant, their women less unconforming.

†**uncon'formist.** *Obs.* [UN-[1] 12 and 5 b.] = NONCONFORMIST.

1640 R. BAILLIE *Canterb. Self-convict.* 117 Since by severe punishment the number of the unconformists have decayed, ..their cause can not bee from God. **1653** —— *Dissuas. Vind.* (1655) 15 This no meer unconformists had ever done. **1688** C'TESS OF CLARE in *Buccleuch MSS.* (Hist. MSS. Comm.) I. 348 Mr. Gilbert, an unconformist minister.

†**uncon'formitable**, *a. Obs.*[−1] [UN-[1] 7 b: cf. next.] = UNCONFORMABLE *a.* 2.

1647 CLARENDON *Hist. Reb.* III. §15 (1888) I. 232 *note*, Many preachers, whom he named and who he knew were of precious memory with the unconformitable party.

†**uncon'formitant.** *Obs. rare.* [UN-[1] 12.] = NONCONFORMITANT.

1605 HIERON *Short Dial.* 43 The vnconformitant and the not subscriber for just reasons perswading his conscience. **1629** W. SCLATER *Exp. 2 Thess.* 82 What one Separatist, or but vnconfor[mi]tant, hath the contrary course wonne?

uncon'formity. [UN-[1] 12 and 5 b.]

1. Lack of conformity (*to* something).

a **1600** HOOKER *Eccl. Pol.* VII. xxiii. §11 So odiously to be upbraided with unconformity unto the pattern of our Lord and Saviour's estate. *a* **1716** SOUTH *Serm.* (1717) III. 435 The Moral Goodness or Evil of men's Actions, which consist in their Conformity, or Unconformity to Right Reason. **1728** R. MORRIS *Ess. Anc. Archit.* 69 In a direct Unconformity to the Rules. **1781** M. MADAN *Thelyphthora* III. Pref. p. vii, He..has been at the pains to shew its unconformity to the Divine system, in the former parts of this work. **1982** K. SMIDT (*title*) Unconformities in Shakespeare's history plays.

†**2.** = NONCONFORMITY. *Obs.*

1635 BP. OF PETERBOROUGH in *Buccleuch MSS.* (Hist. MSS. Comm.) I. 275 No man's learning and piety shall excuse, with me, his unconformity. **1657** J. SERGEANT *Schism Dispach't* 580 To wit, distractions, dissentions, Unconformity, with a perpetually-fleeting Changeablenes of their tenet. *a* **1677** MANTON *Serm. John xvii. 11* Wks. 1872 X. 330 Every modest dissent and unconformity is branded with the name of schism.

3. *Geol.* **a.** The fact of being unconformable or unconformed; difference of plane.

1829 J. PHILLIPS *Geol. Yorks.* I. 125 Proving the great unconformity of strata beneath the Yorkshire wolds. **1880** HAUGHTON *Phys. Geogr.* iii. 81 The general unconformity of the Permian and Triassic rocks.

b. With *a* and pl. An instance of this.

1863 J. G. MURPHY *Com., Gen.* i. 12-13 The stratifications of the earth's crust with all their slips, elevations, depressions, unconformities. **1895** J. W. POWELL in *Nat. Geog. Monogr.* I. i. 18 Ore deposits are often found in unconformities.

uncon'found, *v.* [UN-[2] 3.] *trans.* To free from confusion.

1648 MILTON *Tenure Kings* (1649) 40 His people..now.. against thir own disciplin,..absolve him, unconfound him, though unconverted, unrepentant.

uncon'founded, *ppl. a.* (UN-[1] 8.)

1577 tr. *Bullinger's Decades* 677 The selfe same sonne is.. true God and man..abideing in two vnconfounded natures. **1612** W. SCLATER *Ministers Portion* 36 Alienation of possessions..was flatly forbidden..that Christs linage and descent might bee kept vnconfounded. **1676** BOYLE in *Phil. Trans.* XI. 783 As if some odd subtile matter..interposed, to keep them unconfounded. **1758** WARBURTON *Div. Legat.* IV. §6 II. 414 The only place where they could remain, for so long a time, safe and unconfounded with the natives. **1836** I. TAYLOR *Phys. The. Another Life* (1858) 113 Then does the mind hold each of these sets of signs.. unconfounded and distinct. **1856** G. WILSON *Gateways Knowl.* (1859) 50 Music forms the universal language which ..the confusion of Babel left unconfounded.

Hence **uncon'foundedly** *adv.*

1664 H. MORE *Myst. Iniq.* Apol. 525 Son, Lord, onely-begotten, acknowledged to be unconfoundedly, immutably, indivisibly and inseparably in two natures.

uncon'fronted, *ppl. a.* (UN-[1] 8.)

a **1656** USSHER *Ann.* vi. (1658) 555 To provide, that they should die free women and unconfronted. **1802-12** BENTHAM *Ration. Judic. Evid.* (1827) II. 141 If these several modes..were to be left altogether unconfronted and uncompared. **1891** *Pall Mall G.* 9 Nov. 6/2 Are these by no means ineffectual tactics to go on unconfronted, unchecked?

uncon'fused, *ppl. a.* (UN-[1] 8 and 5 b.)

1609 J. DAVIES *Holy Roode* G 3 b, Ye vnconfused orders Angellick In order come to take this Blood effuz'd. **1635** JACKSON *Creed* VIII. vi. §3 The diversity of these two natures might still remaine unconfused without diversity of persons. *a* **1676** HALES *Prim. Orig. Man.* I. ii. (1677) 56 In that it is more distinct and unconfused than the sensitive Memory. **1768-74** TUCKER *Lt. Nat.* (1834) I. 304 When we see qualities affecting our senses, we may have an unconfused idea of something exerting them. **1853** RUSKIN *Stones Ven.* II. vi. §97. 222 A few of the most common forms are represented, unconfused by exterior mouldings. **1882** *Edin. Rev.* Oct. 344 He keeps his eyes open and his senses unconfused by prejudice or sentiment.

Hence **uncon'fusedly** *adv.*

1655 MRQ. WORCESTER *Cent. Inv.* §42 To write..by these three Senses as perfectly, distinctly and unconfusedly, yea as readily as by the sight. **1690** LOCKE *Hum. Und.* IV. vii. §4 He knows them distinctly and unconfusedly one from another. **1709** BERKELEY *Th. Vision* §50 To treat accurately and unconfusedly of vision.

uncon'futable, *a.* (UN-[1] 7 b and 5 b.)

1643 CHAS. I *Treaty at Oxford* Wks. 1662 II. 285 So just and unconfutable a Censure. **1684** CUDWORTH *Let.* in Birch *Life R. Boyle* (1744) 257 Your pieces of natural history are unconfutable. *a* **1849** H. COLERIDGE *Ess.* (1851) I. 259 Though..little beholden to the privileged orders, Mr. Green was a sound unconfutable Tory.

uncon'futed, *ppl. a.* (UN-[1] 8.)

1600 NASHE *Summer's Last Will* D 2, If Enuy vnconfuted may accuse, Then Innocence must vncondemned dye. **1645** MILTON *Tetrach.*, To Parlt. A 4, That what he writes though unconfuted, must therefore be mistrusted. **1720** WATERLAND *Eight Serm.* Pref. p. xxviii, It is in vain to think of any Expedients in this affair, while our Doctrine stands unconfuted. **1760** LAW *Spir. Prayer* II. 60 Till then, the Appeal must, and therefore will for ever, stand unconfuted.

uncon'geal, *v.* [UN-[2] 3 and 7.] *trans.* and *intr.* To unfreeze; to thaw.

1593 NASHE *Christ's T.* Wks. (Grosart) IV. 246 The infected ayre will vncongeale, and the wombes of the contagious Clowdes will be clensed. **1664** POWER *Exp. Philos.* I. 35 When I came again about two or three hours after to uncongeal the Liquor, by keeping the glass in my warm hand. **1833** TENNYSON *Two Voices* 407 Like soften'd airs that blowing steal, When meres begin to uncongeal.

uncon'gealable, *a.* (UN-[1] 7 b and 5 b.)

1611 COTGR., *Incongelable*, vncongealable, not to bee congealed. **1794** R. J. SULIVAN *View Nat.* I. 191 Air..being uncongealable, or incapable of being fixed by any known method. **1799** SOUTHEY *Nondescripts, Cool Reflect.* 22 A road whose white intensity Would now make platina uncongealable Like quicksilver.

uncon'gealed, *ppl. a.* (UN-[1] 8.)

1646 SIR T. BROWNE *Pseud. Ep.* II. i. 51 The aqueous parts will freeze, but the spirit retyre and be found uncongealed in the center. *a* **1700** EVELYN *Diary* 3 Feb. 1645, A quantity of uncongealed water. **1816** BYRON *Parisina* xx, Those tears.. in its depth endure, Unseen, unwept, but uncongeal'd. **1883** *Standard* 31 Aug. 3/6 Congealed or uncongealed milk.

uncon'genial, *a.* [UN-[1] 7 and 5 b.]

1. Not congenial or kindred; unsympathetic.

[**1775** ASH.] **1813** SCOTT *Rokeby* II. iv, And small the intercourse, I ween, Such uncongenial souls between. **1846** TRENCH *Mirac.* xxix. (1862) 402 The disturbing influences of that uncongenial circle. **1884** BLACK *Jud. Shakes.* xiii, Refusing to harbor such uncongenial guests.

2. Unsuited to the nature of the thing mentioned or under consideration.

1788 V. KNOX *Winter Even.* xxx. (1790) II. 202 In England, a cold northern country, where I imagine its growth is impeded by an uncongenial climate. **1830** LYELL *Princ. Geol.* III. vii. (1835) III. 86 Insects..can readily spread themselves wherever their progress is not opposed by uncongenial climates. **1846** J. BAXTER *Libr. Pract. Agric.* (ed. 4) I. 67 The stratum beneath,..if uncongenial to the growth of the tree, will assuredly cause it to canker. **1873** SYMONDS *Grk. Poets* v. 136 Into the Æolian style Anacreon introduced a new and uncongenial element.

3. Not suited or agreeable to one's temperament; not to one's taste.

1805 *Ann. Rev.* III. 58 This is best resisted by uncongenial employment during youth. **1860** MRS. CARLYLE *Lett.* (1883) III. 20 The reading of that book will be an even more uncongenial job. **1905** 'GUY THORNE' *Lost Cause* iii, He felt that he was in a thoroughly uncongenial atmosphere.

b. Const. *to, with.* †Also as *adv.*, in disagreement, at variance *with.*

1799 SICKELMORE *Agnes & Leonora* II. 190 They trusted ..that their father..would..relinquish his intention of marrying his daughter uncongenial with her wishes. **1812** SHELLEY in Dowden *Life* (1887) I. 221 Oxonian society was insipid to me, uncongenial with my habits of thinking. **1839** HALLAM *Hist. Lit.* III. ii. §25 This..important book..must have been very uncongenial to the ruling party. **1871**

JOWETT *Plato* I. 66 The good is congenial, and the evil uncongenial to every one.

uncongeni'ality. [Cf. prec. and UN-[1] 12.] The quality or state of being uncongenial.

1805 FOSTER *Ess.* IV. ii. 129 This feeling of uncongeniality. **1848** DICKENS *Dombey* xxx, Dombey found no uncongeniality in an air of scant and gloomy state that pervaded the room. **1873** MORLEY *Rousseau* II. 298 The vicious excess..in his character..was irritated into further activity by the uncongeniality of the surrounding medium.

† **uncon'gruity.** *Obs.* (UN-[1] 12 and 5 b.)

c **1449** PECOCK *Repr.* II. xviii. 255 And thei ordeyneden.. certein figuris..forto excuse tho spechis fro vncongruyte of gramer. **1587** GOLDING *De Mornay* xi. (1592) 155 There starts me vp a whole world of Grammarians, which inforce their wittes..to finde some elegancie in thine vncongruities.

† **un'congruous,** *a. Obs.* (UN-[1] 7 and 5 b.)

1709 in Hardiman *O'Flaherty's Iar Connaught* (1845) 441 Hanmer,..to rectify that as uncongruous, must invent that they were consecrated by the Archbishops of Canterbury.

uncon'jecturable, *a.* (UN-[1] 7 b.)

1806 J. WILSON *Let.* in *Mem.* iv. (1879) 78, I have long been conjecturing the reason of your unconjecturable silence. **1829** BENTHAM *Justice & Cod. Petit.* 88 Not to speak of an unconjecturable variety of other circumstances. **1863** LYTTON *Caxtoniana* I. 308 Thus Faith..loses itself no more among the phantom shadows of the Unknown and Unconjecturable.

So **unconjectura'bility.**

1802-12 BENTHAM *Rationale* (1827) IV. 37 From this unconjecturability, two..advantages accrue to the partnership.

uncon'jectured, *ppl. a.* (UN-[1] 8.)

a **1647** BOYLE in Birch *Life* (1744) 27 The true cause.. remained long unconjectured, until the effects betrayed it. **1850** TENNYSON *In Mem.* xciii, Therefore from thy sightless range With gods in unconjectured bliss,..Descend, and touch, and enter. **1862** LYTTON *Str. Story* I. 165, I imagined that..the discovery might lead to some sublime and unconjectured secrets of science.

un'conjugal, *a.* (UN-[1] 7.)

1644 MILTON *Divorce* I. i, What hinders that more then the unfitnes and defectivenes of an unconjugal mind. **1671** —— *Samson* 979 My name..may stand defam'd, With malediction mention'd, and the blot Of falshood most unconjugal traduc't. **1809** MALKIN *Gil Blas* IV. iv. ¶18 An unconjugal and litigious defence of her insulted virtue. **1877** BLACKMORE *Cripps* xxi, Unconjugal, perhaps, is what I mean; unuxorial, or what it may be.

un'conjugated, *a. Med.* and *Gram.* [UN-[1] 8 a.] Not conjugated.

1909 in WEBSTER (undefined). **1963** *Jrnl. Clin. Endocrinol.* XXIII. 820/2 Measurement of unconjugated cortisol in the urine affords a reliable index of the biologically active fraction of circulating cortisol. **1964** *Language* XL. 277 The description of pronoun position with verbal constructs..is simple and clear: where the unconjugated form precedes the conjugated, it is equated with the other elements that cause anteposition. **1977** *Proc. R. Soc. Med.* LXX. 598/2 Some patients do have an increase in biliary unconjugated bilirubin.

uncon'junctive, *a.* (UN-[1] 7.)

1644 MILTON *Divorce* II. xvi, Parted from each other, as two persons unconiunctive and unmariable together.

un'conjured, *ppl. a.* [UN-[1] 8.]

† Unconsecrated.

1546 *Wyckliffe's Wycket* (1828) p. xii, Then makest thou to worshyppe a false god in the chalyce, whych is unconjured when ye worshyp the breade.

unco'nnect, *v.* [UN-[2] 3.] *trans.* To disconnect.

1796 LAMB *Lett.* (1904) I. 36, I can unconnect myself with him, and shall manage all my father's moneys in future myself.

unco'nnected, *ppl. a.* [UN-[1] 8 and 5 b.]

1. a. Not connected or associated *with* something.

1736 BUTLER *Anal.* I. i. 13 There would be no apprehension that any other power or event unconnected with this of death would destroy these faculties. **1796** MORSE *Amer. Geog.* I. 471 The colony of New Haven, though unconnected with the colony of Connecticut. **1842** SEDGWICK in *Hudson's Guide Lakes* (1843) 191 We find.. great masses of alluvial drift, entirely unconnected with any erosion of the existing rivers. **1885** *Law Times* 10 Jan. 183/1 A surveyor..who is entirely unconnected with the neighbourhood.

ellipt. **1813** SHELLEY *Q. Mab* IV. 74 This is no unconnected misery, Nor stands uncaused, and irretrievable.

b. Not physically joined *with* something.

1829 T. CASTLE *Introd. Bot.* 150 The flowers have upwards of twenty-five stamens, all unconnected with the calyx.

2. Characterized by want of connexion.

1745 HUME *Let. from Gentleman* (1967) 32 Suppose Mankind, in some primitive unconnected State [etc.]. **1762** GIBBON *Misc. Wks.* (1814) V. 250 His epistles,..translated in a very bad style, and unconnected method. **1824** L. MURRAY *Eng. Gram.* (ed. 5) I. 193 As the fashionable mode of unconnected composition is less improving to the mind of the reader. **1886** WILLIS & CLARK *Cambridge* III. 249 His buildings are disposed in an unconnected manner about a quadrangular court.

3. Not joined together in order or sequence; disunited, isolated.

1777 RICHARDSON *Pers. Dict.* 1925 Incongruous, unconnected speech. **1791** BOSWELL *Johnson* (1831) I. 180 Addison's note was a fiction, in which unconnected fragments of his lucubrations were purposely jumbled together. **1809-10** COLERIDGE *Friend* (1865) 9 These short and unconnected sentences are easily and instantly understood. **1889** GRETTON *Memory's Harkb.* 55, I simply record unconnected anecdotes and disjointed facts.

4. Not having personal connexions; not related by family ties, common aims, etc.

1802 MAR. EDGEWORTH *Moral T., A Summons,* An individual in society who has friends..and a home, is in a more desirable situation than an unconnected being. **1822** BYRON *Werner* IV. i. 516, I could only guess at one, And he to me a stranger, unconnected. **1846** MRS. GORE *Eng. Char.* I. 40 But without this..what would become of the vapid, unmeaning, unconnected Lady P——?

unco'nnectedly, *adv.* [f. prec.] In an unconnected manner; disconnectedly.

1778 TOOKE *Let. to Dunning* ad fin., He thought the best way to make his zany talk unconnectedly and nonsensically, was [etc.]. **1799** V. KNOX *Lord's Supper* xvii. Wks. 1824 VII. 423 This petition therefore comes in very abruptly and unconnectedly. **1817** J. SCOTT *Paris Revisit.* (ed. 4) 389 Enabling them to regard it unconnectedly with circumstances of humiliation. **1841** MARRYAT *Poacher* xxxix, They..would talk unconnectedly, running from one subject to another. **1877** RAYMOND *Statist. Mines & Mining* 192 Twenty-six mining districts are distributed irregularly over the county, occupying unconnectedly the various mountain-ranges.

unco'nnectedness. [f. as prec.] The quality or state of being unconnected.

1772 MACKENZIE *Man World* I. xxix, She relapsed into her former unconnectedness. **1780** M. MADAN *Thelyphthora* (1781) I. 146 The marriage destroys their unconnectedness, distinctness, and independency on each other. **1837** LANDOR *Pentameron, 4th Day's Interv.* Wks. 1853 II. 339/2 The loose and shallow foundation of so vast a structure; its unconnectedness. **1877** 'H. A. PAGE' *De Quincey* II. xix. 168 Hence the unconnectedness, the obtrusive digressions and rangings from date to date.

unco'nnection. (UN-[1] 12 and 5 b.)

a **1756** CHANDLER *Life of David* (1766) I. 113 There is a force and elegance in the very unconnection of the expressions. **1794** *Monthly Rev.* XIV. 320 English ode-writers..seem..to have considered eccentricity and unconnection as the very characteristics of their task. *a* **1834** COLERIDGE *Notes & Lect.* (1849) I. 14 That unconnection by contradictions of the inward being, to which all folly is owing. **1876** MRS. WHITNEY *Sights & Ins.* xiii, [These ideas] rushed through my thought in a connected unconnection.

un'conned, *ppl. a.* (UN-[1] 8.)

1742 SHENSTONE *School-mistr.* ii, They..oft-times on vagaries idly bent, For unkempt hair, or task unconn'd, are sorely shent.

† **unco'nnexed,** *ppl. a. Obs.*[−1] (UN-[1] 8.)

1716 M. DAVIES *Athen. Brit.* II. 304 In the unconnex'd heaping of Texts in that and most of his Sermons.

unconning, obs. f. UNCUNNING *sb.* and *a.*

unco'nniving, *ppl. a.* (UN-[1] 10.)

1671 MILTON *P.R.* I. 363 To that hideous place not so confin'd By rigour unconniving.

un'conquerable, *a.* [UN-[1] 7 b and 5 b.]

1. Of persons, places, etc.: That cannot be overcome by conquest or force of arms; not yielding to superior force; invincible.

1598 FLORIO, *Inuincibile,* inuincible, vnconquerable. **1608** J. KING *Serm. 24 Mar.* 10 Whose priuiledge and right vnquestionable, is, *per me reges regnant,* and his might vnconquerable. **1632** LITHGOW *Trav.* I. 40 There is neither out-going nor in-comming, without a Pylot, which maketh the Citty vnconquerable. **1649** MILTON *Eikon.* ix. 76 So farr was any man..from esteeming him unconquerable. **1760** PITT in Ellis *Orig. Lett.* Ser. II. IV. 421 To give stability and happiness to the fortunes of this unconquerable Monarch. **1798** PENNANT *Hindoostan* II. 196 The most unconquerable fort in the world. **1855** SINGLETON *Virgil* II. 360 The buckler, which the Lord of Fire himself Vouchsafed, unconquerable. **1878** BOSW. SMITH *Carthage* 315 They forgot now that..Hannibal was still in Italy, still unconquered, and, as far as they knew, unconquerable.

b. Of the mind, feelings, etc., with similar implication.

(*a*) **1667** MILTON *P.L.* I. 106 All is not lost; the unconquerable Will, And study of revenge, immortal hate. **1702** ROWE *Tamerl.* III. i, But to subdue th' unconquerable Mind,..Impossible! **1754** GRAY *Progr. Poesy* 65 Th' unconquerable Mind, and Freedom's holy flame. **1802** WORDSW. *Poems Independence & Liberty* I. viii. 14 Man's unconquerable mind. **1875** HENLEY *Life & Death* iv, *Bk. Verses* (1888) 56, I thank whatever gods may be For my unconquerable soul.

(*b*) **1776** GIBBON *Decl. & F.* xii. I. 339 Their unconquerable love of freedom, rising against despotism, provoked them into hasty rebellions. **1797** MRS. RADCLIFFE *Italian* xvi, He fought with unconquerable audacity and fierceness. **1825** SCOTT *Talism.* ii, Animated by a zeal as fiery as their own, and possessed of as unconquerable courage, address, and success in arms. **1881** JOWETT *Thucyd.* I. 154 The unconquerable quality which is inherent in our minds.

2. Incapable of being overcome, mastered, brought under control, etc.

1642 FULLER *Holy & Prof. St.* II. viii. 78 Nothing was unconquerable to his pains, who had a golden wit in an iron body. **1654** COKAINE *Dianea* I. 53 That there was nothing more unconquerable than love. **1695** LD. PRESTON *Boeth.* IV. 166 By this almost unconquerable Bent and Help of Nature. **1771** BEATTIE *Minstrel* I. i, Check'd by the scoff of pride, by envy's frown, And poverty's unconquerable bar. **1781** GIBBON *Decl. & F.* xviii. II. 118 Yet he mentions with admiration the unconquerable fertility of the soil. **1828** D'ISRAELI *Chas. I,* I. i. 7 Something of pity and terror must blend with the story of a noble mind wrestling with unconquerable Fate. **1846** TRENCH *Mirac.* Introd. (1862) 72 His argument is..unconquerable so long as it is permitted to rest upon the earth out of which it sprung. *a* **1881** A. BARRATT *Phys. Metempiric* (1883) 17 As this assumption..is perhaps not wholly unconquerable, it will be wise not to lay too much stress on it.

b. Of feelings. (Cf. INVINCIBLE *a.* 1 b.)

1727 DE FOE *Hist. Appar.* x. I. 73 An unconquerable aversion to any restraint. **1767** WILKES *Corr.* (1805) III. 217 The same fixed and unconquerable hatred to the enemies of freedom. **1798** S. & HT. LEE *Canterb. T.* II. 492 Actuated by an unconquerable curiosity. **1828** TYTLER *Hist. Scot.* (1864) I. 49 His unconquerable thirst of vengeance against the English influenced their choice. **1863** GEO. ELIOT *Romola* III. vi, Romola..shrank with unconquerable disgust from the shrill excitability of those illuminated women.

un'conquerableness. [f. prec. + -NESS.] The quality or state of being unconquerable.

1647 SPRIGG *Anglia Rediv.* To Englishmen, We would least of all be thought..to fixe unconquerablenesse..upon this Army. **1652** HEYLIN *Cosmogr.* II. 254 When all the Persians soothed the King in the unconquerableness of his forces; Artabanus told him [etc.]. **1866** RUSKIN *Eth. Dust* 182 Some real notion of the extent and the unconquerableness of our ignorance. **1901** 'LINESMAN' *Words by Eyewitness* (1902) 75 The greatest of the three failures which..nerved her retreating soldiers to a pitch of absolute unconquerableness.

un'conquerably, *adv.* [f. as prec. + -LY[2].] In an unconquerable manner or degree; invincibly.

1654 COKAINE *Dianea* 220 Which..obtained more hearts which gave up their Liberties to it, than it met with eyes that unconquerably could behold it. **1725** POPE *Odyss.* XI. 356 Wild, furious herds, unconquerably strong! **1797** FRERE in *Anti-Jacobin* 25 Dec. (1852) 26 True to herself unconquerably bold. **1826** MISS MITFORD *Village* Ser. II. (1863) 342 But it would not do: she was unconquerably stupid. **1849** MACAULAY *Hist. Eng.* vi. II. 103 His temper acrimonious, turbulent, and unconquerably stubborn.

un'conquered, *ppl. a.* [UN-[1] 8.] Not conquered or vanquished: **a.** Of persons, places, etc.

1549 UDALL, etc. *Erasm. Par. 1 John* ii. 47 A mynde that is vnbroken and vnconquered agaynst al wanton enticementes, agaynst all iniuries, sheweth a man to be a Christian. **1591** SHAKS. *1 Hen. VI,* IV. ii. 32 Loe, there thou standst a breathing valiant man Of an inuincible vnconquer'd spirit. **1618** J. TAYLOR (Water P.) *Penniless Pilgr.* Wks. (1630) 129/2, I haue seene many Straights and Fortresses.., but they must all giue place to this vnconquered Castle, both for strength and scituation. **1684** BURNET tr. *More's Utop.* 1 Henry the 8th, the unconquered King of England. **1715** POPE *Iliad* I. 378 That imperious, that unconquer'd soul, No laws can limit, no respect control. **1765** BLACKSTONE *Comm.* I. 93 Wales had continued independent of England, unconquered and uncultivated. **1813** BYRON *Corsair* III. i, The mountain shadows kiss Thy glorious gulf, unconquer'd Salamis! **1867** 'OUIDA' *C. Castlemaine's Gage* 3 So she would put them all aside..and go on her own way, proud, peerless,..conquering and unconquered.

b. Of things, in various applications.

1651 WITTIE *Primrose's Pop. Err.* I. viii. 30 Wood annointed with Alome remaines unconquered of the fire. *a* **1718** PRIOR *Henry & Emma* 22 While my Notes to future Times proclaim Unconquer'd Love. **1750** tr. *Leonardus' Mirr. Stones* 63 The diamond..had its name from the Greek interpretation, which is, an unconquered virtue. **1813** SHELLEY *Q. Mab* III. 97 The unconquered powers Of precedent and custom interpose Between a king and virtue. **1860** TYNDALL *Glac.* I. xi. 78 The chief difficulties remained unconquered. **1887** *Spectator* 5 Nov. 1497 Saint Elias,..the still unconquered peak of Alaska.

† **un'conquest,** *ppl. a.* [UN-[1] 8 b.] = prec.

1584 HUDSON *Du Bartas' Judith* v. 30 But now..his minde doth frame To conquer this most chast vnconquest Dame. *a* **1600** MONTGOMERIE *Sonn.* viii. 5 The hundreth saxt, by lyne, vnconqueist king.

un'conscienced, *a.* (UN-[1] 9.)

1833 TENNYSON in *Mem.* (1897) I. 130 That luxurious, eye-glass-wearing, unconscienced fellow. **1888** *Andover Rev.* Oct. 363 The riot of unconscienced power.

† **un'consciencely,** *adv. Obs.* [UN-[1] 11.] = UNCONSCIENTIOUSLY *adv.*

1450 *Rolls of Parlt.* V. 206/1 The seid late predecessours have made divers Releses, Obligacions, and other Suertees unconciensly. **1485** *Rolls of Parlt.* VI. 322/1 The said Morgan..unconsciencely causyd theym to fynde by their Verdyt, that [etc.].

unconsci'entious, *a.* [UN-[1] 7.] Not conscientious; not scrupulous or careful: **a.** Of actions, etc.

[**1775** ASH.] **1791** BOSWELL *Johnson* (1831) III. 183 Johnson was shocked at this unconscientious conduct. **1803** MACKINTOSH *Def. Peltier* Wks. 1846 III. 246 An immoderate and unconscientious exercise of power. **1818** SCOTT *Rob Roy* xvii, This base and unconscientious scheme of plundering his benefactor. **1884** *Law Times* 11 Oct. 382 The Act supposes that the real owner is actuated by unconscientious motives.

b. Of persons.

1827 SCOTT *Napoleon* v, This unconscientious tribunal found the prisoner guilty. **1827** —— *Surg. Dau.* xii, An able and active, but unconscientious man. **1884** H. SPENCER in *Pop. Sci. Monthly* XXIV. 732 Representatives are unconscientious enough to vote for bills [etc.].

Hence **unconsci'entiousness.**

1860 FROUDE *Hist. Eng.* V. 256 The Earl of Warwick himself was untroubled with religious convictions of any kind, and might take either side with equal unconscientiousness. **1879** SPENCER *Data Ethics* xii. 210 Not in large ways only..does each suffer from the general unconscientiousness.

unconsci'entiously, *adv.* [f. prec. + -LY^2.] In an unconscientious manner; unscrupulously.

1649 [see UNCASUISTLY *adv.*]. **1780** *Ann. Reg., Chron.* 208/2 The attorney had acted very unconscientiously. **1855** PUSEY *Doctr. Real Presence* Note S. 428 In that, unconscientiously and unprofitably,.. he approacheth thanklessly to such a mystery, he bringeth on him the judgment of slothfulness. **1898** G. W. STEEVENS *Egypt* xix. 219 The Chicago colonel.. unconscientiously copies them.

un'conscionable, *a.* (*sb.*, *adv.*). [UN-^{1} 7 b, 5 b.]

1. Of persons: Having no conscience; not controlled by conscience; unscrupulous; unreasonably grasping, extortionate, harsh, etc.

1570 ABP. PARKER *Corr.* (Parker Soc.) 374 Christ's holy religion,.. as it may be choked with overmuch in unconscionable men's hands, so it will fall to ground amongst beggars. **1583** STUBBES *Anat. Abus.* II. (1882) 51 Least these cunning barbers might seeme vnconscionable in asking much for their paines. **1611** SPEED *Hist. Gt. Brit.* IX. iii. §20 None were rich but Treasurers and Collectors, none in fauour but vnconscionable Lawyers. **1667** WATERHOUSE *Fire Lond.* 31 Occupancy is judged by men unconscionable, the best title. **1681** DRYDEN *Abs. & Achit.* To Rdr., You cannot be so Unconscionable, as to charge me for not Subscribing of my Name. **1708** MRS. CENTLIVRE *Busy Body* II, Can you be so unconscionable, Madam, to let me say all these fine things to you without one single Compliment in return? **1765** STERNE *Tr. Shandy* VII. xvii, How can that unconscionable coachman talk so much bawdy to that lean horse? **1824** W. IRVING *T. Trav.* I. 242 Sometimes the unconscionable editors will clip our paragraphs. **1865** DICKENS *Mut. Fr.* I. viii, I am not so unconscionable as to think it likely. **1885** 'MRS. ALEXANDER' *Valerie's Fate* i, What an unconscionable old slave-holder!.. Why do you submit to such an imposition?

absol. **1623** HALL *Contempl., O.T.* XIX. ii, The unconscionable will know no other law, but their profit, their pleasure.

b. With depreciatory terms, as an intensive.

1597 BEARD *Theatre God's Judgem.* (1612) 457 Barnabe, Vicount of Milan,.. was an vnconscionable oppressor of his subjects and tenants. **1609** W. M. *Man in Moone* (1849) 27 He is an insatiable cormorant,.. a mercilesse mony-monger, .. and unconscionable extortioner. **1655** FULLER *Ch. Hist.* I. v. §30 Unconscionable Liars, though they most hurt them-selves, do the least harm others. **1687** M. CLIFFORD *Notes Dryden* ii. 7 You are therefore a strange unconscionable Thief. **1732** FIELDING *Miser* v. xviii, I am an unconscionable beggar. **1755** SMOLLETT *Quix.* (1803) IV. 93 Your excellency may perceive what a shameless and unconscionable rogue he is.

c. As *sb.* An arrant rogue.

1825 KNAPP & BALDWIN *Newgate Cal.* III. 496/1 One of the trading unconscionables.

2. Of actions, etc.: Showing no regard for conscience; not in accordance with what is right or reasonable.

1565 CALFHILL *Answ. Martial* 79 Was not thys a goodly councell then? The cause so vnlawfull?.. The order so vnconscionable? Brag, as ye please, of your Nice councell. **1586** J. HOOKER *Hist. Irel.* in *Holinshed* II. 106/2 Which he rather of pleasure vttered, than of anie vnconscionable meaning purposed to haue doone. **1628** WITHER *Brit. Rememb.* VI. 1251 Ev'n in our Court of Conscience, some things are Unconscionable. **1653** PRYNNE *Gospel-plea* 14 It must needs be most unjust, unreasonable, unconscionable, and against the common rules of war. **1656** H. PHILLIPS *Purch. Patt.* (1676) 145 The errour.. is so much the more unconscionable, because it gives the buyer so much less than his due. **1738** A. HILL *Let. to Pope* 29 Aug., When I remember'd you had read it four times, I found not enough of the Poet, within me, to presume the unconscionable fifth. **1796** MME. D'ARBLAY *Camilla* III. 425 So difficult was even this, in an affair so dark and unconscionable. **1828** KEIGHTLEY *Fairy Mythol.* (1850) 95 They plundered their pantries in a most unconscionable manner. **1890** *Spectator* 19 July, St. Kevin's behaviour on a famous occasion was not quite so unconscionable as that attributed to him by Moore.

b. Unreasonably excessive.

a **1586** SIDNEY *Arcadia* I. xv. (1912) 99 She tooke the advauntage one daye uppon Phalantus unconscionable praysinges of her. **1598** B. JONSON *Ev. Man in Hum.* I. ii, Draw your bill of charges, as unconscionable as any Guildhall verdict will give it you. **1601** F. GODWIN *Bps. of Eng.* 295 That wrongfull and vnconscionable raunsome. **1654** WHITELOCKE *Jrnl. Swed. Emb.* (1772) II. 264 Such is their unconscionable exaction uppon strangers. **1671** MILTON *Samson* 1245 His Giantship is gone somewhat crestfall'n, Stalking with less unconsci'nable strides, And lower looks. **1760** STERNE *Tr. Shandy* III. xxxiii, What an unconscionable jointure, my dear, do we pay out of this small estate of ours! **1785** MARTYN *Lett. Bot.* x. (1794) 108 This letter not being of so unconscionable a length as the former. **1818** SCOTT *Hrt. Midl.* xii, We are out unconscionable sums just for barkened hides and leather. **1849** MACAULAY *Hist. Eng.* iv. I. 439 He had been, he said, a most unconscionable time dying. **1871** 'HOLME LEE' *Miss Barrington* II. xiii. 203 He had stayed an unconscionable time—had made her quite a visitation.

c. As an intensive: Egregious, arrant.

1593 *Tell-Troth's N.Y. Gift* (1876) 14 To blabb such vnconscionable vntrothes. **1603** H. CROSSE *Vertues Commw.* (1878) 43 Tearing out the bowelles of his brethren, with vsurie, extortion, and vnconscionable brokerie. **1650** FULLER *Pisgah* v. i. 143 It seems not onely an ungentile harshness, but an unconscionable injustice. *a* **1734** NORTH *Exam.* III. ix. §14 (1740) 657 A due Reward of unconscionable Cheating. **1782-3** W. F. MARTYN *Geog. Mag.* I. 308 Which sum he consented to abate in favour of those who were called upon to make up the amount of this unconscionable imposition.

3. As *adv.* = UNCONSCIONABLY *adv.* 2.

1596 NASHE *Saffron Walden* F ij, Tis an vnconscionable vast gorbellied Volume. **1807-8** W. IRVING *Salmag.* (1824) 272 One of Christopher's unconscionable long stories. **1847** ROBB *Squatter Life* (Bartlett), 'That's an unconscionable slick gal of your'n,' says I.

un'conscionableness. [f. prec.] The quality or state of being unconscionable; unscrupulousness, unreasonableness.

1607 HIERON *Defence* I. 179 Observe further, his unconscionablenes and whether.. he hath not sold himselfe to speake he careth not what. **1657** G. STARKEY *Helmont's Vind.* 173 A cover-slut of idleness, ignorance, and unconscionableness. **1670** BAXTER *Cure Ch. Div.* 380 Are not the most conscientious, necessary helpers of the Ministry, by their example, to cure the unconscionableness of the rest?

un'conscionably, *adv.* [f. as prec.]

1. In an unconscionable manner; without regard for conscience; unreasonably.

1583 GOLDING *Calvin on Deut.* ii. 65 If a poore man deale vnconscionably when he hath not wherewith to liue,.. yet shall he bee condemned. **1589** *Acts Privy Council* (1898) XVII. 19 He was verie unconscionablie dealte and proceeded withall by his credytours. **1631** T. POWELL *Tom All Trades* (1876) 161 To a good old Vsurer, or one that had got his great estate together vnconscionably. **1646** P. BULKELEY *Gospel Covt.* IV. 298 Such as live loosely, carnally, unconscionably, doe but deceive themselves. **1705** HICKERINGILL *Priest-cr.* II. v. 56 The.. Avarice and Ambition of some Highflyers, have.. most Unchristian like and Unconsionably.. endeavoured to monopolize by Law all Places of Honour, Profit, Trust.

2. To an unconscionable extent or degree; inordinately.

1583 STUBBES *Anat. Abus.* II. (1882) 37 For whereas the others inhanse the price of their hides excessiuely, these felowes racke it very vnconcionably. **1602** in Moryson *Itin.* II. (1617) 265 Her Subiects.., by the excessiue rates in the sale of all commodities, haue beene vnconscionably ouercharged. *a* **1661** FULLER *Worthies, Cheshire* I. (1662) 171 Some have Flesh, Salt,.. but so unconscionably dear, that Common people have little comfort therein. **1672** MARVELL *Reh. Transp.* I. 270 The Fanaticks.. made them pay for it most unconscionably and through the nose. **1771** MME. D'ARBLAY *Early Diary* Aug., His visit was unconscionably long, and.. I had the whole weight of it. **1787** BECKFORD *Italy*, etc. (1834) II. 54, I felt no inclination to prolong a walk which already had been prolonged unconscionably. **1863** *N. & Q.* 3rd Ser. IV. 214 Having trespassed unconscionably on your valuable space, I will now conclude at once. **1884** A. BIRRELL *Obiter Dicta* Ser. I. 183 The age has remained transitional so unconscionably long.

un'conscious, *a.* and *sb.* [UN-^{1} 7 and 5 b.]

A. *adj.* **1. a.** Not conscious or knowing within oneself; unaware, regardless, heedless.

1712 BLACKMORE *Creation* VI. 646 Unconscious we these motions never heed, Whether they err, or by just laws proceed. **1848** DICKENS *Dombey* xiii, As he stood.. surveying his (of course unconscious) clerk, from head to foot. **1889** *Anthony's Photogr. Bull.* II. 202, I mean the unconscious model, i.e., one taken unawares with a detective camera.

b. Const. *of*, *that*, etc.

1712 BLACKMORE *Creation* VII. 632 Through every dark recess [they] pursue their flight, Unconscious of the road. **1789** BURNS *Kirk's Alarm* vii, Are ye huirdin' the penny, Unconscious what evils await? **1820** SCORESBY *Acc. Arctic Reg.* II. 172 Never having been disturbed, these animals were unconscious of danger. **1841** CARLYLE *Heroes* i. (1904) 33 Silent, with closed lips, as I fancy them, unconscious that they were specially brave. **1863** KINGLAKE *Crimea* I. 158 All this time he was unconscious of exercising any ascendancy.

2. a. Not characterized by, or endowed with, the faculty or presence of consciousness.

1712 BLACKMORE *Creation* III. 266 Unconscious causes only still impart Their utmost skill, their utmost power exert. **1744** AKENSIDE *Pleas. Imag.* I. 527 For what are all The forms which brute, unconscious matter wears, Greatness of bulk, or symmetry of parts? **1802** PALEY *Nat. Theol.* iv. §1. 55 Can any distinction be assigned.. between the producing watch, and the producing plant? both passive, unconscious substances. **1890** W. JAMES *Princ. Psych.* I. 199 Sleep, fainting, coma, epilepsy, and other 'unconscious' conditions.

absol. **1843** CARLYLE *Past & Pr.* II. xv, The Unconscious is the alone Complete. **1876** *Westm. Review* XLIX. 512 Those who are acquainted with the 'pessimist' conclusions of the 'philosophy of the Unconscious'. **1884** COUPLAND (*title*), Philosophy of the Unconscious, by Eduard von Hartmann.

b. Temporarily devoid of consciousness.

1860 O. W. HOLMES *Elsie Venner* xxvi. (1861) 302 A man is stunned by a blow with a stick on the head. He becomes unconscious. **1890** *Retrospect Med.* CII. 118 The patient had a temperature of 105·8° for thirty-six hours, and was unconscious for twenty-four hours.

c. *Psychol.* Applied to mental or psychic processes of which a person is not aware but which have a powerful effect on his attitudes and behaviour, *spec.* in Freud's psychoanalytic theory, processes activated by desires, fears, or memories which are unacceptable to the conscious mind and so repressed; also designating that part of the mind or psyche in which such processes operate.

1912 FREUD in *Proc. Soc. Psychical Res.* XXVI. LVI. 315 The term *unconscious*, which was used in the purely descriptive sense before, now comes to imply something more. It designates not only latent ideas in general, but especially ideas with a certain dynamic character, ideas keeping apart from consciousness in spite of their intensity and activity. **1925** C. E. M. JOAD *Mind & Matter* iv. 111 This greater part is known as the unconscious mind, or simply as 'the unconscious'. The theory of the unconscious is based mainly on the work of.. Freud. **1946** *Mind* LV. 21 Perhaps further investigation following Wisdom's hint that philosophical views are the vehicles for expressing 'unconscious fantasies', will lead to an understanding of this point. **1956** R. F. C. HULL tr. *Jung's Symbols of Transformation* in *Coll. Wks.* V. ix. 443 The Miller case is a classic example of the unconscious manifestations which precede a serious psychic disorder.

3. Not realized or known as existing in oneself.

1800 COLERIDGE *Christabel* II. xxvii, Still picturing that look askance With forced unconscious sympathy Full before her father's view. **1870** L'ESTRANGE *Miss Mitford* I. vi. 166 And is not the sunny felicity of childhood in itself unconscious virtue? **1890** 'R. BOLDREWOOD' *Col. Reformer* (1891) 150 [She] rode.. extremely well, and with an unconscious grace.

absol. **1817** COLERIDGE *Biogr. Lit., Poesy or Art*, In every work of art there is a reconcilement of the external with the internal; the conscious is so impressed on the unconscious as to appear in it.

4. Not attended by, or present to, consciousness; performed, employed, etc., without conscious action.

unconscious cerebration: see CEREBRATION.

1820 LAMB *Elia* I. *Oxford in Vacation*, He has long taken up his unconscious abode, amid an incongruous assembly of attorneys, attorneys' clerks [etc.]. **1836** C. WORDSWORTH *Athens* xxiii. (1855) 156 It may be considered as an unconscious emblem of the consecration of earthly history and glory and majesty to the Cross. **1866** J. MARTINEAU *Ess.* I. 133 It is wrong to punish an unconscious act. **1878** S. BUTLER *Life & Habit* ii. 26 In like manner, the most perfect humour and irony is generally quite unconscious.

B. *absol.* as *sb. Psychol.* The unconscious mind (see A. 2 c). Cf. *collective unconscious* s.v. COLLECTIVE *a.* 2 e; ID^2.

a **1884** M. PATTISON *Mem.* (1885) vii. 329, I cannot help observing the remarkable force with which the Unconscious —*das Unbewusste*—vindicated its power. *Ibid.* 330 By whatever name you call it, the Unconscious is found controlling each man's destiny without, or in defiance of, his will. **1912** FREUD in *Proc. Soc. Psychical Res.* XXVI. LVI. 318 The system revealed by the sign that the single acts forming part of it are unconscious we designate by the name 'The Unconscious', for want of a better and less ambiguous term. .. And this is the third and most significant sense which the term 'unconscious' has acquired in psychoanalysis. **1914** [see CO-CONSCIOUS *a.* and *sb.*]. **1959** N. MAILER *Advts. for Myself* (1961) 216 To put it crudely, I would think I was dropping people when they were dropping me. And of course my unconscious knew better. **1977** A. SHERIDAN tr. *J. Lacan's Écrits* iii. 50 The unconscious is that chapter of my history that is marked by a blank or occupied by a falsehood: it is the censored chapter.

un'consciously, *adv.* [f. prec.] In an unconscious manner; without conscious action or effort.

1779 JOHNSON *L.P., Milton* Wks. II. 119, I cannot but remark a kind of respect, perhaps unconsciously, paid to this great man by his biographers. **1813** SHELLEY *Q. Mab* III. 234 Man, like these passive things, Thy will unconsciously fulfilleth. **1856** FROUDE *Hist. Eng.* (1858) I. v. 422 The populace of England were unconsciously on the rapid road to protestantism. **1887** W. P. FRITH *Autobiog.* I. xx. 243 Pretty groups of ladies were to be found.. unconsciously forming themselves into very paintable compositions.

un'consciousness. [f. as prec.]

1. The state or fact of being mentally unconscious or unaware *of* something.

1779-81 JOHNSON *L.P., Addison* Wks. III. 51 The work did not suffer much by his unconsciousness of its commencement. **1794** PALEY *Evid.* I. ix. §1 We perceive also in Clement a total unconsciousness of doubt whether these were the real words of Christ. **1837** HT. MARTINEAU *Soc. Amer.* II. 336 In a society where things like these are said and done.. there is a prevalent unconsciousness of the existing wrong. **1870** J. H. NEWMAN *Gram. Assent* II. vi. 181 Our unconsciousness of those innumerable acts of assent, which we are incessantly making.

b. Without const.

1828 LYTTON *Pelham* III. xx, It was Dawson who shut the door, through utter unconsciousness. **1882** FARRAR *Early Chr.* I. 264 Josephus.. falsifies and colours... Philo on the other hand wrote with far greater unconsciousness.

2. The fact of being devoid of consciousness.

1759 JOHNSON *Rasselas* xlvii, All the notices of sense and investigations of science concur to prove the unconsciousness of matter.

3. The state of being unconscious; loss of consciousness; insensibility.

1849 FROUDE *Nemesis of Faith* 223 When he came he found her in a state of almost unconsciousness. **1868** MORRIS *Earthly Par.* (1870) II. III. 135 The peace of dull unconsciousness His wild torn heart at last did bless. **1890** *Retrospect Med.* CII. 160 A longer or shorter period of continued unconsciousness, without convulsion.

un'consecrate, *v.* [UN-^{2} 3.] *trans.* To render unconsecrated; to desecrate or profane.

1598 FLORIO, *Disconsecrare*, to degrade, to profane, to vnconsecrate. *a* **1660** HAMMOND *Serm.*, *2 Cor. vii. 1* (1664) 86 Heaven must be unconsecrated by such violence. **1667** SOUTH *Serm., Ps. lxxxvii. 2* (1715) I. 258 The Sins of Israel had even unconsecrated and prophaned that Sacred Edifice. **1711** *Brit. Apollo* III. No. 143. 3/1 To Unconsecrate his Dust. **1768-74** TUCKER *Lt. Nat.* (1834) II. 450, I should apprehend it might by natural effect prove an unconsecrating the place with respect to myself.

un'consecrate, *ppl. a.* [UN-^{1} 8 b.] = next.

1529 MORE *Dyaloge* I. xiv. Wks. 134/2 Diuers times she was houseled.. with an host vnconsecrate. *Ibid.* II. 193/1 If we worshippe an host in the masse which percase the neglygence or malice of some lewde priest hath left vnconsecrat. **1607** G. WILKINS *Miseries Enforced Marr.* K iij b, Here wil I seale the children that are born, From wombes vnconsecrate. **1673** [R. LEIGH] *Transp. Reh.* 13 Except only this unconsecrate Lay-Clergy. **1850** J. MARTINEAU *Misc.* (1852) 330 The heroes of modern fiction and biography are unconsecrate according to the measure of theology.

un'consecrated, *ppl. a.* (UN-[1] 8.)
1579 FULKE *Heskins' Parl.* 99 It was better then yᵉ vnconsecrated bread and wine. **1641** MILTON *Ch. Govt.* II. iii. 54 They fear religion..and think..that any uncleannesse is more sutable to their unconsecrated estate. **1684** BUNYAN *Pilgr.* II. 159 One questioned if it was lawful to go upon unconsecrated Ground. **1790** PENNANT *London* 116 A chapel was erected, well-pewed, well-warmed, dedicated, unendowed, unconsecrated. **1816** BYRON *Parisina* xix, No tomb, no memory had they; Theirs was unconsecrated clay. **1848** THACKERAY *Van. Fair* xxxv, There the young officer was laid by his friend, in the unconsecrated corner of the garden.

unconsen'taneous, *a.* (UN-[1] 7.)
1818 T. L. PEACOCK *Nightmare Abbey* iv, The results are unconsentaneous, and their respective necessitated volitions clash.

uncon'sented, *ppl. a.* (UN-[1] 8 and 8 c.)
1631 FULLER *David's Punishm.* xvi. in *Joseph's Coat*, etc. (1867) 233 Sins unconsented to no souls impair. **1643** MILTON *Divorce* Pref., Not that licence and levity and unconsented breach of faith should herein be countenanc't. **1668** CLARENDON *Vind.* Tracts (1727) 79 He read all the articles..which remained undetermined and unconsented to. **1800** *Monthly Mag.* VIII. 601 From Scandinavia have poured the only barbarians who ever achieved an unconsented conquest of the British isles.

uncon'senting, *ppl. a.* (UN-[1] 10.)
a **1693** T. YALDEN *Rape of Theutilla* 42 Vanquish'd by that repose from which he flies, Now slumbers close his unconsenting eyes. **1713** ROWE *Jane Shore* v. i, Tho' the King by Force possest her Person, Her unconsenting Heart dwelt still with you. **1725** POPE *Odyss.* xv. 221 Let not Pisistratus in vain be prest, Nor unconsenting hear his friend's request. *a* **1859** DE QUINCEY *Posth. Wks.* (1891) I. 192 Blood, lawless blood—a horrid Moloch..revelling in a thousand unconsenting women. **1889** *Anthony's Photogr. Bull.* II. 20 The right to photograph unconsenting strangers.

unconse'quential, *a.* [UN-[1] 7 and 5 b.]
1. Not properly or necessarily following or ensuing; inconsequential.
1769 BLACKSTONE *Comm.* IV. 37 A, though accessory to the burning, is not accessory to the robbery, for that is a thing of a distinct and unconsequential nature. **1779–81** JOHNSON *L.P.*, *Waller* Wks. II. 261 Some applications may be thought too remote and unconsequential: as in the verses on the *Lady dancing*. *a* **1849** POE *F. S. Osgood* Wks. 1865 III. 90 The 'situations' of Elfrida are improbable or ultra-romantic, and its incidents unconsequential. **1885** *Athenæum* 19 Dec. 804/3 Her punishment is..too unconsequential to be accepted as a natural transcript from every-day life.
2. Of no consequence; insignificant.
1782 I. REED *Baker's Biog. Dram.* I. 187/2 Notwithstanding an unconsequential figure and uncommon timidity, he says, he succeeded beyond his most sanguine expectations. **1789** MRS. PIOZZI *Journ. France* I. 146 [It] is ..crowded with small unconsequential figures.

†**un'consequently**, *adv. Obs.* (UN-[1] 11 and 5 b.)
1565 COOPER *Thesaurus*, *Insequenter*,..vnconsequently: not to the purpose. **1647** HEXHAM I, Vnconsequently, *niet ten propooste.*

uncon'servative, *a.* (UN-[1] 7.)
1877 D. M. WALLACE *Russia* I. i. 11 Even in unconservative Russia customs outlive the conditions that created them.

uncon'siderable, *a.* [UN-[1] 7 b.]
= INCONSIDERABLE *a.*
1643 PRYNNE *Sov. Power Parl.* II. 43 Better then either the King himselfe, his Cabinet-Counsell, or any unconsiderable Privadoes, Courtiers, Favorites. **1654–66** EARL ORRERY *Parthen.* (1676) 501 My Crime..merited a higher punishment than these unconsiderable wounds. **1668** CRESSY *Ch. Hist. Brit.* Errata, Unconsiderable ones [*sc.* errors] which have hapned by mistake of single Letters resembling one the other. **1914** W. J. LOCKE *Fortunate Youth* i. 19 Sky and grass and trees and white mass of ladies ..and unconsiderable men and boys became a shimmering blur. **1976** *Brit. Jrnl. Sociol.* XXVII. 109/2 The rank and file of British Educationalists, sociologists of education and educational psychologists have concentrated their considerable energies and occasionally some not unconsiderable talents on devising arguments to legitimate the equalization of opportunity on moral grounds and to support it on scientific grounds.

†**uncon'siderance.** *Obs.*[−1] (UN-[1] 12 and 5 b.)
1546 BALE *1st Exam. Anne Askewe* Concl. 44 b, If I shuld holde my peace,..my conscyence wolde both accuse me and condempne me of vnconsyderaunce of my lorde God.

†**uncon'siderate**, *a. Obs.* (UN-[1] 7 and 5 b.)
1594 DANIEL *Cleopatra* I. I vij, Thus much beguiled haue Poore vnconsiderat wights These momentary pleasures, fugitiue delights. **1612** COTTA (*title*), A Short Discouerie of the Vnobserued Dangers of seuerall sorts of ignorant and vnconsiderate Practisers of Physicke in England.
Hence †**uncon'siderately** *adv.*; **-ness**. *Obs.*
1570 T. NORTON tr. *Nowel's Catech.* III. 56 They that come rashly and vnconsiderately to prayer. **1611** FLORIO, *Inconsideranza*, vnconsideratenesse. **1621** G. SANDYS *Ovid's Met.* III. (1626) 56 [He] Admireth all;..And vnconsiderately himselfe desir'd.

†**unconside'ration.** *Obs.* (UN-[1] 12 and 5 b).
c **1449** PECOCK *Repr.* I. xvi. 89 The vnconsideracion of this ..hath be a greet cause of the wickidli enfectid scole of heresie among the lay peple in Ynglond. *Ibid.* IV. ix. 474.

uncon'sidered, *ppl. a.* [UN-[1] 8 and 5 b.]
1. Not considered or thought of; not taken into consideration.
1587 GOLDING *De Mornay* xii. (1592) 167 Those that haue the distributing of goods and honors, are blamed for leauing them vnconsidered. **1611** SHAKS. *Wint. T.* IV. iii. 26 A snapper-vp of vnconsidered trifles. **1613** —— *Hen. VIII*, I. ii. 17 That you would..Not vnconsidered leaue your Honour,..is the poynt Of my Petition. **1619** DONNE *Serm.* 139 This is the unexpected and unconsidered strangenesse of that day. **1729** YOUNG *Merchant* Contents, The unconsidered benefits of liberty. **1826** MISS MITFORD *Village* Ser. II. (1863) 454 The gift of some unconsidered trifles. **1856** FROUDE *Hist. Eng.* I. 152 There was a third party in the country, unconsidered as yet, who [etc.]. **1873** PROCTOR *Expanse Heav.* viii. 86 A different opinion has long been entertained, owing to the details of the matter being left unconsidered.
2. Unaccompanied by, not done with, consideration or intention.
1876 T. HARDY *Ethelberta* xxv, She got up in an unconsidered and unusual impulse to seek relief. **1877** MRS. OLIPHANT *Makers Flor.* iii. 82 The cruel levity of these probably unconsidered jests.

†**uncon'siderer.** *Obs.*[−1] (UN-[1] 12)
c **1456** PECOCK *Bk. of Faith* (1909) 122 Which favour, peraventure, sum hasty unconsidere(r)s schulen not aspie.

uncon'sidering, *ppl. a.* (UN-[1] 10 and 5 b.)
1660 *Rope for Pol* To Rdr., 'Tis incredible what influence they had upon numbers of unconsidering persons. **1682** T. FLATMAN *Heraclitus Ridens* No. 79 (1713) II. 237 They take up with the unconsidering People who admire their Wealth. **1700** BLACKMORE *Paraphr.*, *Moses' Song* 246 O that these unconsidering tribes were wise! **1710** SWIFT *Jrnl. to Stella* 13 Oct., I'll never do it again, though all mankind should persuade me, unconsidering puppies!
absol. **1691** LOCKE *Tolerat.* III. viii. 172 Some of the ignorant and unconsidering that are in the National Church.

uncon'signed, *ppl. a.* (UN-[1] 8.)
1647 JER. TAYLOR *Lib. Proph.* xviii. 227 This mercy which appertaines to Infants is so secret and undeclar'd and unconsign'd. **1891** M. COLE *Cy Ross* 142 The ship sped on, bearing its unconsigned merchandise of sin to a haven of safety.

†**uncon'sistent**, *a. Obs.* (UN-[1] 7 and 5 b.)
1638 CHILLINGW. *Relig. Prot.* I. ii. §65. 76 Nor lyable to any such exception, as is unconsistent with due Intention in giving the Sacrament of Orders.

uncon'sociable, *a.* [UN-[1] 7 b: cf. CONSOCIATE *v.*] Incapable of being united.
1697 J. SERGEANT *Solid Philos.* 90 To clap these most unconsociable Things, Light and Darkness, into one Dusky Compound.

uncon'solable, *a.* (UN-[1] 7 b and 5 b.)
a **1618** RALEIGH *Son's Advice* Rem. (1664) 115 Oh how unconsolable were your case, your friends being fled. **1654–66** EARL ORRERY *Parthen.* (1676) 598 This relation.. had a resembling operation on the unconsolable Emilia. **1731** FIELDING *Mod. Husb.* v. ix, What an unconsolable creature would you be if [etc.].
Hence **uncon'solably** *adv.*
1895 W. PLATT *Women*, etc. 61 She went off and wept unconsolably.

uncon'solatory, *a.* (UN-[1] 7.)
1760 STERNE *Lett.* (1775) I. 91 The consolation you give me..is very unconsolatory. **1803** MARY CHARLTON *Wife & Mistress* III. 73 Laura, wearied by this unconsolatory nonsense, shook her head.

uncon'soled, *ppl. a.* (UN-[1] 8.)
1814 WORDSW. *Excurs.* IV. 310 Therefore, not unconsoled, I wait. **1860** ELLICOTT *Life Our Lord* viii. 384 Standing weeping by the tomb, unconsoled and inconsolable. **1879** B. TAYLOR *Stud. Germ. Lit.* 82 Tristan is wandering alone and unconsoled.

uncon'solidated, *ppl. a.* (UN-[1] 8.)
[**1775** ASH.] **1802** PLAYFAIR *Illustr. Hutton. Th.* 49 The opposite sides of the rock..have the interval between them filled with soft and unconsolidated earth. **1851** CARPENTER *Man. Phys.* (ed. 2) 263 Having the fibrous element of the shell..unconsolidated by the intervening deposit of chalky particles. **1874** STUBBS *Const. Hist.* I. iii. 41 They are not only unconquered, but unconsolidated.

uncon'soling, *ppl. a.* (UN-[1] 10.)
1846 WORCESTER (citing Buckminster).

un'consonancy. (UN-[1] 12.)
1665 J. SERGEANT *Sure Footing* 216 Not to note the unconsonancy of this carriage, I shall yeild him the honour [etc.].

un'consonant, *a.* [UN-[1] 7.] = INCONSONANT *a.*
a. Const. *to* or *with*.
1535 STEWART *Cron. Scot.* (Rolls) III. 33 Vnconsonand is to the veritie To do to ws so greit inormitie. *a* **1600** HOOKER *Serm. on Pride* IV. §1 If..it be a thing most unequal and unconsonant unto justice. **1657** TOMLINSON *Renou's Disp.* Pref., Which is not altogether unconsonant to reason. *a* **1676** HALE *Prim. Orig. Man.* III. ii. (1677) 260 As his Supposition of these *Semina*, thus casually produc'd, seems unconsonant both to the Reason and Course of Nature. **1805** FOSTER *Ess.* IV. v. 183 A certain order of opinions unconsonant, or at least not identical, with the principles of that religion. **1843** in J. Hawthorne *N. Hawthorne & Wife* (1885) I. vi. 273 It was a magnificent comedy to watch him,..so unconsonant to what was about him.
b. Without const.
1597 HOOKER *Eccl. Pol.* v. li. §3 It seemeth a thing vnconsonant that the world should honor any other as the Sauiour but him whom it honoreth as the creator of the world. **1658** MANTON *Exp. Jude 4* Wks. 1871 V. 167 To observe..whether we embrace it upon undue grounds, or match it with unconsonant practices. **1665** J. SERGEANT *Sure Footing* 241 If he does, he must hold it was Eternal; If not, how unconsonant is his parallel?
Hence **un'consonantly** *adv.*
1863 COWDEN CLARKE *Shaks. Char.* v. 128 He is gradually led on to act unconsonantly with his real nature.

uncon'spicuous, *a.* (UN-[1] 7 and 5 b.)
1802–12 BENTHAM *Ration. Judic. Evid.* (1827) V. 659 Latent and unconspicuous the single force of a pecuniary interest is capable of rising. **1816** —— *Chrestom.* 187 These properties are..recondite and unconspicuous. **1861** MILL *Utilit.* ii. 22 A part however small and unconspicuous, in the endeavour. **1874** MICKLETHWAITE *Mod. Par. Churches* 216 Placing ventilators in some unconspicuous positions in the walls.

uncon'spiringness. (UN-[1] 12.)
1661 BOYLE *Style of Script.* 76 A Harmony whose Dissonances serve but to manifest the Sincerity and Unconspiringnesse of the Writers.

†**unconsta'bility.** [UN-[1] 12. Cf. late L. *inconstābilītio*.] Want of stability; changeableness.
1611 SPEED *Hist. Gt. Brit.* VI. xlviii. §2. 166 Gregory Nazianzen charging him with..vnconstability, sayth; That by..his vnsteady and halting pace [etc.].

†**un'constance.** *Obs.* (UN-[1] 12 and 5 b.)
c **1449** PECOCK *Repr.* II. vii. 177 Forto remove..al vnstable vnconstaunce and variaunce and vnperseueraunce. **1603** HOLLAND *Plutarch's Mor.* 1034 So great unconstance and repugnance of words, as to affirme one and the same nature to be created and uncreated.

†**un'constancy.** *Obs.* [UN-[1] 12 and 5 b.]
1. = INCONSTANCY 1.
1548 ELYOT, *Instabilitas*, vnconstancie, instabilitee. **1583** GOLDING *Calvin on Deut.* i. 2 Because he saw the lightnes and unconstancy of the people. **1605** BACON *Adv. Learn.* I. v. §2 We see..the leuitie and vnconstancie of mens iudgements. **1652** J. WRIGHT tr. *Camus' Nat. Paradox* II. 45 The thoughts of them..who are not Reeds of the Desart in unconstancy, but Pillars of the Temple of Stability. **1699** BURNET *39 Art.* xxviii. 335 The scandalous Unconstancy of the Councils of those Ages.
2. = INCONSTANCY 2.
1587 GOLDING *De Mornay* xi. (1592) 162 The vnmoouable decree of his euerlasting Prouidence, which.. directeth all the vnconstancies of this world to one certeine end. **1627** in Rushw. *Hist. Coll.* (1659) I. 485 The Frame of other States are subject, some to Unconstancy, some to Faction..and to many Distempers. **1650** BAXTER *Saints' R.* I. vii. (1662) 95 But there is none of this unconstancy, nor mixtures in Heaven.

†**un'constant**, *a. Obs.* [UN-[1] 7 and 5 b.]
1. = INCONSTANT *a.* 1.
c **1480** HENRYSON *Test. Cres.* 570 Traisting in vther als greit vnfaithfulnes, Als vnconstant, and als vntrew of fay. **1483** CAXTON *Cato* c vj, And by the contrarye the man unconstaunt..falleth in to many vyces and synnes. **1564** PALFREYMAN *Baldwin's Mor. Philos.* 45 All men are ignorant, and as fraile and vnconstant as ye shadow of smoke. **1581** PETTIE tr. *Guazzo's Civ. Conv.* I. (1586) 26 b, To some, stout hardinesse, and deuout holinesse, haue been alwaies proper and naturall, who neuerthelesse are worldlings and vnconstant. **1602** FULBECKE *Pandects* 89 For the Ægyptians as others report of them, are men vnconstant, raging, proude,..desirous of nouelties. **1647** N. BACON *Disc. Govt. Eng.* I. lxvi. 229 They found the King either wilfull or unconstant. **1693** *Mem. Ct. Teckely* IV. 25 The Will of the Soveraign, which is as unconstant as his Passions. **1712** ARBUTHNOT *John Bull* I. v, Bull..was..of a very unconstant temper.
Comb. **1653** R. SANDERS *Physiogn.* 194 A mutable, wavering, unconstant-minded person.
b. *spec.* Unfaithful in love or wedlock.
1561 *Chaucer's Wks.* 340 A balade whiche Chaucer made agaynst women vnconstaunt. **1593** MARLOWE *Edw. II*, v. i, My vnconstant Queene, Who spots my nuptiall bed with infamie. **1611** BEAUM. & FL. *King & No King* IV, She lives to tell thee thou art more unconstant, Than all ill women ever were together. **1676** D'URFEY *Mme. Fickle* IV. i, I am grown jealous of my Mistriss, several Reports declare she is unconstant. **1757** W. WILKIE *Epigon.* VII. 196 To reclaim The hero's love,..If e'er, devoted to a stranger's charms, He stray'd, unconstant, to her widow'd arms.
c. Of actions, conduct, etc.
1549 *Compl. Scot.* xii. 100 Thai culd nocht meruel aneucht of his onconstant ansuer. **1563** B. GOOGE *Eglogs* vii. (Arb.) 59 Men do smarte not through your words but your vnconstant deeds. **1609** DANIEL *Civ. Wars* VIII. lxxxvii, Without which, nor his Greatnes, nor his Wits, Could ward him from the Kings vnconstant fits. **1621** QUARLES *Hadassa* Introd., Bleare-eyd mortals,..with vnconstant frailty,.. vary From what is good, to what is cleane contrary. **1694** KETTLEWELL *Comp. Penitent* 66 My good Thoughts are unconstant and Changeable.
2. = INCONSTANT *a.* 2.
1574 HYLL *Conject. Weather* ii, The winter shall be windie and unstable, the Spring windy, and unconstant of weather. **1592** tr. *Junius on Rev.* xvii. 15 As unconstant and variable as are the waters. *a* **1619** FOTHERBY *Atheom.* II. viii. §2 (1622) 284 Error is alwayes vnconstant, and neuer true vnto it selfe. **1645** QUARLES *Sol. Recant.* III. 21 Vnconstant earth! what can thy treasure show, That is not, like thy self, unconstant too? **1691** T. H[ALE] *Acc. New Invent.* 79 An unconstant and unequal decay. **1703** R. NEVE *City & C. Purchaser* 3 Being kept in an unconstant Temper, it decays in a little time. **1721** RAMSAY *Keitha* 93 The powers..dinna like to gie o'er meikle trust To this unconstant earth, with what's divine.
b. = INCONSTANT *a.* 2 b.
1610 FLETCHER *Faithf. Sheph.* II. i, Ne'r did my unconstant eye yet greet That beauty.

†**un'constantly**, *adv. Obs.* [f. prec.] = INCONSTANTLY *adv.*
a **1542** WYATT *Sonnet*, *'Alas the greefe'* iii, in *Anglia* XVIII. 275 O cruell causer of vndeserued chaunge, by

greatt desire vnconstantly to raunge. **1586** T. B. *La Primaud. Fr. Acad.* I. 121 Philosophie is..not a plaie or prittle prattle, unconstantlie uttered to obtaine honor onelie. **1607** MIDDLETON *Fam. Love* I. ii, As chaff, which when our nourishing grains Are winnow'd from them, unconstantly they fly. **1650** HOBBES *Hum. Nat.* v, Consider..how unconstantly names have been settled, and how subject they are to equivocation. **1714** FORTESCUE-ALAND *Pref. Fortescue's Abs. & Lim. Mon.* 7 The others have only Names and Words, and such as some-times are unconstantly used.

† **un'constantness.** [f. as prec.] Inconstancy.
1551 BIBLE *2 Cor.* i. *note*, Yea, yea, Nay, nay;..in this place they are taken for vnconstauntenes of mynde, as to say both yea, and naye to one thynge. **1581** T. HOWELL *Deuises* (1879) 175 Which change full oft hath falne through her vnconstantnesse. **1600** SIR W. CORNWALLIS *Ess.* i. Bj b, So much haue I hated this giddy vnconstantnesse.

† **un'constanty,** variant of UNCONSTANCY.
1563 *Wills & Inv. N.C.* (Surtees) 213, I..knowing the constantie of Death & ye vnconstantie of ye houre & time.

un'constellated, *ppl. a.* (UN-[1] 8.)
1782–3 W. F. MARTYN *Geog. Mag.* I. Introd. 13 Observations on the unconstellated bodies. **1866** J. B. ROSE tr. *Ovid's Met.* 230 The great brother twins, not yet on high, Unconstellated yet.

un'constituted, *ppl. a.* (UN-[1] 8.)
1660 WATERHOUSE *Arms* 186 Whatever is new, unconstituted, and of a spurious birth.

unconsti'tutional, *a.* [UN-[1] 7.]
1. Not in harmony with, or authorized by, the political constitution; at variance with the recognized principles of the state.
1734 *Country Jrnl.* 16 Nov. 1/2 Lest all other Provisions should be ineffectual to keep the Members of the House of Commons out of this unconstitutional Dependency..the Wisdom of our Constitution hath thought fit that the Representatives of the People should not have Time to forget that they are such; that they are empowered to act for the People, not against them. **1765** BLACKSTONE *Comm.* I. 245 Whenever the unconstitutional oppressions, even of the Sovereign power,..threaten desolation to a State. **1770** *Junius Lett.* xxxix. (1778) 220 The unconstitutional employment of the military. **1849** MACAULAY *Hist. Eng.* vii. II. 210 That the Declaration of Indulgence was unconstitutional is a point on which both the great English parties have always been entirely agreed. **1893** *Times* 29 Apr., Lord S. described such a step as in the highest degree unconstitutional.
2. Not inherent in, or in accordance with, a person's constitution.
1794 GODWIN *Caleb Williams* 198 The keeper once more made his appearance..with his former unconstitutional and ambiguous humanity.
Hence **unconsti'tutionalism; unconsti'tutionally** *adv.*
1791 *Gentl. Mag.* Jan. 32, I am concerned..to see you unconstitutionally adopting a French word when there is no occasion. **1845** LD. CAMPBELL *Chancellors* (1857) IV. lxxxix. 215 The bill had been unconstitutionally got rid of. **1889** SIR S. WALPOLE *Life Ld. J. Russell* xxiv. II. 202 It was..asserted ..that the Prince was interfering unconstitutionally both in foreign and domestic affairs. **1920** *Glasgow Herald* 11 Dec. 7 It is the first area of dry land which has shown itself after the deluge of unconstitutionalism in that part of the country [*sc.* Ireland]. **1949** ST. J. ERVINE *Craigavon* II. lxxvi. 344 He might have made an effective debating retort to the Ulstermen about unconstitutionalism.

unconstitutio'nality. [f. prec.] The quality of being unconstitutional.
1795 WASHINGTON *Let.* Writ. 1892 XIII. 73 The unconstitutionality of the measure. **1850** GROTE *Greece* II. lxii. VIII. 48 Indictment on the score of informality, illegality, or unconstitutionality. **1890** HOSMER *Anglo-Sax. Freedom* 215 A popular explanation of the unconstitutionality of government acts.

uncon'strainable, *a.* (UN-[1] 7 b.)
1659 MILTON *Civil Power* Wks. 1851 V. 319 Both our beleef and practise..flow from faculties of the inward man, free and unconstrainable of themselves by nature.

uncon'strained, *ppl. a.* [UN-[1] 8.]
1. Not constrained or forced; not acting under constraint or compulsion.
c **1386** CHAUCER *Doctor's T.* 61 And of hir owene vertu vnconstreyned She hath ful ofte tyme syk hire feyned. **1513** DOUGLAS *Æneid* VII. v. 25 Vnconstrenyt, nocht be law bound thairtill, Bot be our inclinatioun and fre will Just and equale. **1548** UDALL, etc. *Erasm. Par. John* xix. 108 b, The luste to reuenge was so greate, that vnconstrayned they adiudged themselues to perpetuall bondage. *a* **1614** DONNE *Βιαθανατος* (1664) 201 He dyed, as the same man sayes, with the same zeale as Christ, unconstrained. **1665** GLANVILL *Def. Van. Dogm.* 27 A free and unconstrained will. *a* **1704** T. BROWN *Sat. agst. Woman* Wks. 1730 I. 56 Unconstrain'd by want of choice they lie Wallowing in all the filth of boundless luxury. **1827** POLLOK *Course T.* II. 145 Making His soul an offering for sin,..By doing, suffering, dying, unconstrained. **1831** SCOTT *Ct. Rob.* xxviii, Let me find my way to the grave, unnoticed, unconstrained.
† b. Without exertion. *Obs.*[-1]
1539 ELYOT *Cast. Helthe* (1541) 55 b, If he whiche oftentymes unconstrayned hath had great sieges [= evacuations], be sodeynly stopped.
2. Not done, made, given, etc., under constraint or compulsion; free, spontaneous.
1535 *Act 27 Hen. VIII*, c. 25 The voluntary and vnconstreined almes & charitie of the parishens. *a* **1600** HOOKER *Two Serm. Jude* i. § 12 What meaneth this Apostasie and vnconstrained departure? Why doe His seruants so willingly forsake him? **1632** LITHGOW *Trav.* I. 7 Thy voluntary wandring, and vnconstrayned exyle. **1656** BRAMHALL *Replic.* iii. 116 These Acts were unconstrained. *a* **1704** T. BROWN *Let. Dissent. Preacher* Wks. 1711 IV. 191 Thanks must be Voluntary; not only unconstrain'd, but unsolicited. **1770** GIBBON *Misc. Wks.* (1814) IV. 504 The unconstrained workings of nature.
3. Free from constraint or embarrassment; natural.
1704 *Moderat. Displ.* iv, So Free, so Unconstrain'd in his Address. **1707** SIR W. HOPE *New Method Fencing* vii. 205 In a Good Guard, the whole Body should be easy, and as much unconstrain'd as possible. **1759** STERNE *Tr. Shandy* II. xvii, He looked frank,—unconstrained,—something assured,—but not bordering upon assurance. **1818** SCOTT *Rob Roy* ix, Dismissing from his countenance some part of the hypocritical affectation of humility..and saying, with a more frank and unconstrained air [etc.].
4. Not subject to restraint; unrestrained.
1796 MME. D'ARBLAY *Camilla* IV. 278 The unconstrained freedom with which he was empowered to have more books upon the table. **1891** FARRAR *Darkn. & Dawn* xlvii, The intercourse which the prisoner could hold with any who came to visit him was unconstrained.
Hence **uncon'strainedness.**
1656 EARL ORRERY *Parthen.* III. IV. 12 He acquitted himselfe with so much grace and unconstrainednesse in the dance.

uncon'strainedly, *adv.* [f. prec.] In an unconstrained manner; without constraint.
1561 T. NORTON *Calvin's Inst.* I. 16 b, Vnconstrainedly publishing..that the principall auncester of the familie.. was an abhominable doer. **1594** HOOKER *Eccl. Pol.* IV. vii. § 6 To thinke..that..wee did vnconstrainedly those things, for which conscience was pretended. **1686** PLOT *Staffordsh.* 14 Some of the Witches..unconstrainedly confest, that the Devil appeared to them like a short black Man. **1854** FABER *Hymn*, '*The Eternal Years*' xiv, Keep unconstrain'dly in this thought, Thy loves..and tears. **1875** GLADSTONE *Glean.* (1879) VI. 107 So long..as it naturally and unconstrainedly bears some sense not entailing such a consequence.

uncon'straining, *ppl. a.* (UN-[1] 10.)
1644 MILTON *Areop.* (Arb.) 51 Those unwritt'n, or at least unconstraining laws of vertuous education. **1691** NORRIS *Pract. Disc.* 80 When the Allurements to Vice were strong, and the ingagements to Duty but weak and unconstraining.

uncon'straint. (UN-[1] 12.)
1711 H. FELTON *Classicks* (1718) 56 Dryden..wanted that Easiness,..that Air of Freedom and Unconstraint,..which is more sensibly to be perceived, than described. **1851** D. COLERIDGE *H. Coleridge's Ess.*, etc. II. 268 The characteristic unconstraint and naïveté of the style carries with it an air of genuineness. **1865** MRS. WHITNEY *Gayworthys* xxviii, It was so hard for him with..his habits of unconstraint, to remember the traditional sanctities of the place.

uncon'struable, *a.* (UN-[1] 7 b and 5 b.)
1856 DOVE *Logic Chr. Faith* IV. i. § 1 Nothing and infinity are equally unconstruable to human thought. **1896** *Law Times* CII. 125/1 He pourtrays the Legislature passing unconstruable statutes.

uncon'structive, *a.* (UN-[1] 7.)
1859 R. F. BURTON *Centr. Afr.* in *Jrnl. Geog. Soc.* XXIX. 45 The unconstructive African..loves his hut, and has a superstitious horror of stone walls.

uncon'strued, *ppl. a.* (UN-[1] 8.)
1755 YOUNG *Centaur* ii, Does this yet unconstrued, undecyphered creature consider himself as an immortal being?

uncon'sultable, *a.* (UN-[1] 7 b and 5 b.)
1843 E. FORBES *Let.* in Wilson & Geikie *Mem.* xi. (1861) 330 The Zoological Society's collection is boxed up and unconsultable in an old warehouse. **1887** H. G. HEWLETT in *Academy* 26 Mar. 220/1 The preparation of trustworthy calendars and indexes to records previously unconsultable.

uncon'sulted, *ppl. a.* [UN-[1] 8 and 5 b.]
† 1. Unconselled, unadvised. *Obs.*[-1]
1567 *Reg. Privy Council Scot.* I. 515 Quhat is abill to be objectit that evir hir Majestie tuke on hand unconsultit be the nobill men, hir Counsall.
2. Not consulted (*with*) or referred to.
1619 SIR J. SEMPIL *Sacrilege Handled* Ded., God was vnconsulted;..his Church spoyled; the Commons oppressed. **1642** MILTON *Apol. Smect.* 7 A suspicion that in setting forth this pamphlet the Remonstrant was not unconsulted with. **1829** CASSAN *Lives Bps. of Bath & Wells* 268 He left no history or chronicle of this nation unconsulted. **1847** DE QUINCEY *Milton* Wks. 1857 VII. 318 The reasons assigned to Labienus for passing the oracle of the Libyan Jupiter unconsulted. **1884** *St. James' Gaz.* 4 Apr. 5/2 Our feelings having been entirely unconsulted in the matter.

uncon'sulting, *ppl. a.* [UN-[1] 10 and 5 d.]
1. Taking no counsel; inconsiderate, rash.
a **1586** SIDNEY *Arcadia* II. xxii. (1912) 290 It was the faire Zelmane,..whom unconsulting affection..had made borrowe so much of her naturall modestie, as [etc.].
2. With object: Without consulting (something).
1848 LYTTON *Harold* XI. vii, The oath that would bestow on a stranger the fates of a nation, against its knowledge, and unconsulting its laws.

uncon'sumable, *a.* [UN-[1] 7 b and 5 b.]
1. That cannot be consumed; inexhaustible.
1571 GOLDING *Calvin on Ps.* xviii. 17 From whence the rivers have so unconsumable store and abundance of waters. **1586** T. B. *La Primaud. Fr. Acad.* I. 418 The wealth which proceedeth from liberalitie is unconsumeable. **1615** G. SANDYS *Trav.* 127 [Arms and legs] from the Mummes (whereof there are an vnconsumeable number).
2. Incapable of being destroyed by fire.
1670 BROOKS *Wks.* (1867) VI. 207 How will an unconsumable soul and body be able to endure the scorching flames of hell for ever? **1859** SALA *Tw. round Clock* (1861) 381 It was..suggested that he was unconsumable, made of asbestos. **1870** MEREDITH *Odes Fr. Hist.* (1898) 57 Ever invoking fire from heaven, the fire Has grasped her, unconsumable.

uncon'sumed, *ppl. a.* (UN-[1] 8 and 5 b.)
1549 *Compl. Scot.* vi. 46 Of this sort the art of astronomie suld ay remane onconsumit. **1627** MAY *Lucan* VIII. P vij, The bones halfe-burnt, not yett dissolu'd hee takes, Stil full of nerues, and vnconsumed marrow. **1697** CONGREVE *Mourn. Bride* II. v, The poor remains..Yet fresh and unconsum'd by time and worms. **1724** RAMSAY *Health* 86 Long unconsum'd the oak can bear the beams. **1818** CRUISE *Digest* (ed. 2) V. 91 Every such fine..should be of the same force and effect, as if it had still remained upon record unconsumed or not lost. **1857** MILLER *Elem. Chem., Org.* 329 A charred mass remains, consisting of carbonate of potash and unconsumed carbon.

uncon'suming, *ppl. a.* (UN-[1] 10.)
1628 FELTHAM *Resolves* II. xxv. 80 Though pleasure merries the Sences for a while: yet horror after vultures the vnconsuming heart. [**1718** *Entertainer* No. 15. 97 No sooner shall the enjoyment be over, when Horrour will..act the Promethean Vulture upon the unconsuming Conscience.] **1836** KEBLE in *Lyra Apost.* (1849) 204 God of the unconsuming fire, On Horeb seen of old. **1851** TRENCH *Sonnet* Poems (1865) 92 It straightway kindled then, and was afire, And with the unconsuming radiance blended.

uncon'summate, *ppl. a.* [UN-[1] 8 b and 5 b. Cf. next.] Not consummated; uncompleted.
1609 BIBLE (Douay) *Deut.* xxiv. *comm.*, Nothing..can loose the band of Mariage..unconsummate, but death, or solemne vow in an approved rule of religion. *a* **1643** W. CARTWRIGHT *Siege* III. i, I cannot then retire me from the sin, Though I do leave the action unconsummate. **1702** S. PARKER tr. *Cicero's De Finibus* III. 196 Whatever Action bears the Name of a Compleat Good one is a Duty perform'd, as there is also Duty Unconsummate. **1868** BROWNING *Ring & Bk.* IX. 421 The unconsummate blow, Adroitly baulked by her.

un'consummated, *ppl. a.* (UN-[1] 8.)
1813 T. BUSBY *Lucretius* I. III. 1138 Joys unconsummated round thee play. **1852** IS. WILLIAMS *Apocalypse* 119 The unnumbered company [intimates] the gathering in as yet unconsummated.

uncon'tagious, *a.* (UN-[1] 7.)
1822 GOOD *Study Med.* II. 71 The production of uncontagious intermittent fever.

uncon'tainable, *a.* (UN-[1] 7 b.)
1618 T. ADAMS *Generat. Serpents* Wks. (1629) 890 His vncontainable poyson would soone burst him. **1681** RYCAUT tr. *Gracian's Critick* 40 Pythagoras calls it a Tuned-Harp, whose measure and harmony wraps up our Contemplations and Thoughts with uncontainable Ravishments. **1883** *Harper's Mag.* Jan. 284/2 Jim had an awkward expression of uncontainable happiness.

uncon'tained, *ppl. a.* (UN-[1] 8.)
c **1611** CHAPMAN *Iliad* I. 93 This still will empty in our hearts His deathful quiver, uncontain'd till to her loved sire The black-eyed damsel be resign'd. **1836** EMERSON *Nature* 13, I am the lover of uncontained and immortal beauty.

uncon'taminable, *a.* (UN-[1] 7 b and 5 b.)
1657 EARL MONM. tr. *Paruta's Pol. Disc.* 52 So well disposed towards the good of their Country, and so uncontaminable by any other affection.

uncon'taminate, *ppl. a.* (UN-[1] 8 b and 5 b.)
1675 COCKER *Morals* 24 A Conscience uncontaminate. **1784** COWPER *Task* VI. 789 The pure and uncontam'nate blood. **1842** R. I. WILBERFORCE *Rutilius & Lucius* 164 The corrupted traditions..flowed from a source which originally was clear and uncontaminate. **1876** LOWELL *Among my Bks.* Ser. II. 249 Abstinence, exercise, and uncontaminate air.

uncon'taminated, *ppl. a.* (UN-[1] 8 and 5 b.)
1611 COTGR., *Incontaminé*, vncontaminated, vnpolluted. **1774** GOLDSM. *Nat. Hist.* II. xvi. 375 Nature has providently stopped the fruitfulness of these ill-formed productions, in order to preserve the form of every animal uncontaminated. **1832** MISS MITFORD *Village* Ser. v. 7 Our village, though in the centre of the insurgents, continued uncontaminated. **1879** FROUDE *Cæsar* ii. 19 Whose minds were still uncontaminated, in whom the ancient habits of life still survived.

uncon'temned, *ppl. a.* (UN-[1] 8.)
1613 SHAKS. *Hen. VIII*, III. ii. 10 Which of the Peeres Haue vncontemn'd gone by him? **1634** HABINGTON *Castara* II. *Wife*, Shee is so true a friend, her Husband may to her communicate even his ambitions, and if successe Crowne not expectation, remaine neverthelesse uncontemned.
Hence **uncon'temnedly** *adv.*
1628 FELTHAM *Resolves* II. 296, I beg no more, then may keepe mee vncontemnedly, and vnpittiedly-honest.

uncontemplated, *ppl. a.* (UN-[1] 8.)
1709 SHAFTESB. *Charac.* (1711) II. 424 Never can the Form be of real force where it is uncontemplated,.. unexamin'd. **1837** LYTTON *Athens* II. 268 So do the most important results arise from causes uncontemplated by the providence of statesmen. **1860** DICKENS *Uncomm. Trav.* x, He may be seen..haling the blind man away on expeditions wholly uncontemplated by..the man.

uncontempo'raneous, *a.* (UN-[1] 7.)
1859 G. WILSON *Mem. E. Forbes* i. (1861) 26 The uncontemporaneous events which are recorded in the same page of an almanac. **1870** LOWELL *Among my Bks.* Ser. I. 6 Unless, like Goethe, he is of a singularly uncontemporaneous nature.

uncon'tended, *ppl. a.* (UN-^{1} 8.)
1697 DRYDEN *Æneis* v. 510 Permit me, Chief, permit without Delay, To lead this uncontended Gift away.

uncon'tending, *ppl. a.* (UN-^{1} 10.)
1748 RICHARDSON *Clarissa* (1811) III. 248 Thou knowest my generosity to my uncontending Rosebud. **1881** RUSKIN *Lett. to Faunthorpe* (1895) I. 43 The recognition of uncontending and natural worth.

uncon'tent, *sb.* [UN-^{1} 12.] Absence of content; dissatisfaction.
1873 MISS BROUGHTON *Nancy* II. 131 Over all the landscape there is a look of plaintive uncontent.

uncon'tent, *a.* [UN-^{1} 7.] = next.
1502 ARNOLDE *Chron.* (1811) 125 And so wolde leue dyuers persones that I am in dett to vncontent. **1591** *Troub. Raigne K. John* (1611) A 2, Yet Iohn your Lord, contented vncontent, Will (as he may) sustaine the heauy yoke Of pressing cares. **1885** L. OLIPHANT *Sympneumata* 167 The records of the intellect..cannot evince a perfect understanding..of this vast subject, so long as..its moral whole is uncontent.

uncon'tented, *ppl. a.* [UN-^{1} 8. Cf. DISCONTENTED.] Not contented; unsatisfied.
1568 T. HOWELL *Newe Sonets* (1879) 124 Mewsing how I best might ease mine vncontented minde. **1586** T. B. *La Primaud. Fr. Acad.* I. 31 Perturbations..which fill the soule with endlesse trouble and disquietnes, causing man to live alwaies uncontented. **1605** DANIEL *Philotas* Ded. A iv, When your iudgment shal ariue so far, As t' ouerlooke th' intricate designes Of vncontented man. **1675** *Art Contentm.* I. xii, The torture which every repining uncontented spirit provides for its self. **1718** G. SEWELL *Proclam. Cupid* 4 Thus uncontented with a private Wrong, He spreads his Baseness with a busie Tongue. **1861** MILL *Repr. Govt.* (1865) 24/1 Nothing is more certain, than that improvement in human affairs is wholly the work of the uncontented characters.
Hence **uncon'tentedness.**
a **1660** HAMMOND *Fundamentals* xi. Wks. 1674 I. 298 Contentedness is most eminently one of these specialties,.. as it is opposed to ambition, covetousness, injustice, uncontentedness.

uncon'tenting, *ppl. a.* (UN-^{1} 10.)
1698 NORRIS *Pract. Disc.* IV. 357 His Future Expectations shall prove every whit as vain and uncontenting as his past Fruitions.

uncon'tentingness. (UN-^{1} 12.)
1648 BOYLE *Seraph. Love* viii. (1700) 51 The decreed uncontentingness of all other goods.

uncon'tentious, *a.* (UN-^{1} 7.)
Also, in recent use, ***uncontentiousness.***
1828 PUSEY *Hist. Eng.* I. 66 Either pupils of Calixtus, or of the same uncontentious disposition. **1868** E. EDWARDS *Ralegh* I. iv. 63 [He] proposed that all difficulty..should be referred to lawyers for uncontentious decision. **1884** *Manch. Exam.* 25 June 6/1 A comparatively uncontentious measure.

uncon'testable, *a.* (UN-^{1} 7 b and 5 b.)
1681 *Whole Duty Nations* 13 Religion..being a most uncontestable duty and obligation in those lesser Kingdoms, Families. **1714** SWIFT *Pres. St. Aff.* Wks. 1755 II. I. 217, I must therefore lay it down as an uncontestable truth. **1725** *Fam. Dict.* s.v. *Vegetation,* As to what is said concerning the heat of the Sun, it is uncontestable. **1826** *Westm. Rev.* Oct. 483 The arrangement, which Mr. Humphreys, and with uncontestable reason, proposes. **1831** LD. PALMERSTON in *Westm. Rev.* July (1855) 60 *note,* The will of a sovereign whose rights are uncontestable.
Hence **uncon'testably** *adv.*
1709 (*title*), An Exact Narrative of the many Surprizing Matters of Fact uncontestably wrought by an Evil Spirit. **1740–1** *Johnson's Parliamentary Debates* (1787) I. 201 That where this maxim is not..adhered to, rights and liberties are empty sounds, is uncontestably evident.

uncon'tested, *ppl. a.* (UN-^{1} 8 and 5 b.)
1678 OLDHAM *On Wks. B. Jonson* x, Poems (1684) 81 Thou thy own Works didst strictly try By known and uncontested Rules of Poetry. **1692** NORRIS *Curs. Reflect.* 14, I affirm that there are..as uncontested Propositions in Morality as in any other Science. **1750** JOHNSON *Rambler* No. 45 ¶2 You seem..to have allowed as an uncontested principle, that marriage is generally unhappy. **1800** *Misc. Tr.* in *Asiat. Ann. Reg.* 248/1 The Goosaigns maintained an uncontested authority, till the arrival of about 12 or 14,000 Seik horsemen. **1855** MACAULAY *Hist. Eng.* xvii. IV. 47 A government of which the title was uncontested. **1874** DISRAELI in Froude *Carlyle's Life in Lond.* xxxiii. (1884) II. 429, I see only two living names which..stand out in uncontested superiority.
Hence **uncon'testedly** *adv.*
1699 T. BAKER *Refl. Learn.* ii. 10 As for the Greek [tongue], which is uncontestedly Learned, most know, how copious it is. **1719** J. T. PHILLIPS tr. *Thirty-four Confer.* 298 These sorts of Beads had been for some thousand Years uncontestedly an efficacious Medecine for Souls.

†**un'continent,** *a. Obs.* [UN-^{1} 7 b.] = INCONTINENT *a.* Also †**un'continently** *adv.*
1382 WYCLIF *2 Tim.* iii. 2 Men schulen be..fals blameris, vncontynent, vnmylde. *a* **1420** *Wycliffite Bible* (1850) III. 12 *marg.,* He that is vncontynent, ether a lecchour, renneth in to the snare of synne. **1565** COOPER *Thesaurus, Incontinens,* ..vncontinent. *Ibid., Incontinenter,*..vncontinently. **1598** FLORIO, *Incontinente,* vncontinent, vncleane of life.

†**uncontinent,** var. INCONTINENT *adv.*
1506 in *Charters,* etc. *Edinb.* (1871) 189 We charge you straitlie and commandis vncontinent [etc.].

un'continented, *a.* (UN-^{1} 9.)
1847 EMERSON *Poems, Monadnoc,* The bullet of the earth Whereon ye sail, Tumbling steep In the uncontinented deep.

uncon'tinued, *ppl. a.* (UN-^{1} 8.)
1576 ABP. SANDYS *Serm.* (1585) 171 Their seruice was vnrewarded, because it was vncontinued.

uncon'tinuous, *a.* (UN-^{1} 7 and 5 b.)
1846 MOZLEY *Ess.* (1878) II. 154 A succession of momentary, uncontinuous, fragmentary impulses, ideas, and feelings. **1863** COWDEN CLARKE *Shaks. Char.* x. 257 He is light-minded, being inconsequent and uncontinuous, which is very French.

uncon'torted, *ppl. a.* (UN-^{1} 8.)
1834 FOSTER in Ryland *Life & Corr.* (1846) II. 248 If.. the diction be perspicuous, natural, and uncontorted.

uncon'tract, *v.* [UN-^{2} 3.] To relax, unbend.
1628 FELTHAM *Resolves* II. lvi. 162 The best way is, to vncontract the brow, and let the worlds mad spleene fret.

uncon'tracted, *ppl. a.* [UN-^{1} 7 b and 5 b.]
†**1.** Not affianced or betrothed. *Obs.*
1527 [see UNAFFIED]. **1564–5** *Reg. Privy Council Scot.* I. 325 He sould..keip the said Jane..as fre woman uncontractit or mariit..for the space of ane yeir. *c* **1625** [see UNAFFIED].
2. Not brought into smaller compass.
1758 JOHNSON *Idler* No. 9 ¶2 To give the smooth feature and the uncontracted muscle. **1864** PUSEY *Lect. Daniel* i. 49 In the Biblical Chaldee the older uncontracted forms prevail. **1877** RAYMOND *Mines & M.* 116 This serpentine belt..extending its course southeasterly with uncontracted dimensions.

uncontra'dictable, *a.* (UN-^{1} 7 b and 5 b.)
1707 *Curios. in Husb. & Gard.* 134 We know by uncontradictable Experiments, that Nitre..attracts.. Humidity. **1825** BENTHAM *Offic. Apt. Maximized, Indicat.* (1830) 70 That confidence-commanding and uncontradictable hand.
Hence **uncontra'dictably** *adv.*
1862 T. A. TROLLOPE *Marietta* I. iv. 64 The means by which one moral nature speaks..uncontradictably to another.

uncontra'dicted, *ppl. a.* (UN-^{1} 8.)
1606 WARNER *Alb. Eng.* xv. xcvi. 383 And new Rome,.. Vncontradicted, for that Plot from Hell the Palme doth win. **1651** HOBBES *Leviath.* I. xvi. 83 The excesse of Negatives, standing uncontradicted, are the onely voyce the Representative hath. **1748** HARTLEY *Observ. Man* II. ii. §21. 92 The People..let it pass uncontradicted. **1815** J. SMITH *Panorama Sci. & Art* II. 71 The inference drawn by the Florentines, remained uncontradicted by any experiment, till about 1762. **1885** *Law Rep. 14 Q.B. Div.* 248 There was uncontradicted evidence given at the trial that [etc.].
Hence **uncontra'dictedly** *adv.*
1652 GAULE *Magastrom.* 129 So they may (more easily and uncontradictedly) resist the truth.

uncontra'dictory, *a.* (UN-^{1} 7.)
In quot. = uncontradictable.
1698 NORRIS *Pract. Disc.* (1707) IV. 231 He need not deny it because it is an uncontradictory Truth.

uncontrite, *a.* (UN-^{1} 7.)
c **1440** *Jacob's Well* 167 Sche wolde noȝt leve here synne & dyed vncontrite. **1509** [see UNCONFESSED 1]. **1646** HAMMOND *Pract. Catech.* I. iii. (ed. 2) 28 [The priest] by absolving an uncontrite sinner, cannot sure make him contrite. **1861** LYTTON & FANE *Tannhäuser* 96 Even though unabsolved, not uncontrite.

uncon'trived, *ppl. a.* (UN-^{1} 8.)
1612 W. PARKES *Curtaine-Dr.* (1876) 49 If he shall practise vncontriued conclusions vpon our liues. **1646** SIR T. BROWNE *Pseud. Ep.* I. xi. 44 Thus hath he deluded many Nations..from casuall and uncontrived contingences divining events succeeding. **1790** PALEY *Horæ Paul.* iv. §8 A species of confirmation..evidently uncontrived.

uncon'triving, *ppl. a.* (UN-^{1} 10.)
1774 GOLDSM. *Nat. Hist.* I. xxii. 401 To the savage uncontriving man the earth is an abode of desolation.

uncon'trol. (UN-^{1} 12.)
1861 MRS. H. WOOD *East Lynne* I. xvi, She burst forth in passionate uncontrol.

uncontrollability. (UN-^{1} 12.)
1909 *Chambers's Jrnl.* June 342/2 Wherever horses are there must be unsanitary filth, and sometimes uncontrollability born of nerves or vice. **1980** *New Scientist* 31 Jan. 341/2 The uncontrollability of medical costs.

uncon'trollable, *a.* [UN-^{1} 7 b and 5 b.]
†**1.** Incontrovertible, indisputable, irrefutable.
1577 tr. *Bullinger's Decades* III. ix. 460 That diuine saying of Saint Peter remaineth for euer vncomptroleable. **1602** WARNER *Alb. Eng.* Epit. (1606) 362 It is to be noted, as warranted out of vncontrowlable authours, that [etc.]. **1646** SIR T. BROWNE *Pseud. Ep.* VI. i. 273 His labours are rationall, and uncontroulable upon the grounds assumed. **1673** CAVE *Prim. Chr.* III. iii. 304 He makes it an uncontrolable Argument of the Truth. **1701** SWIFT *Contests Nobles & Comm.* i, The error of those, who think it an uncontrollable maxim, that power is always safer lodged in many hands than in one. **1738** —— *Pol. Conversat.* Introd. 74.
2. Not subject to control from a higher authority; absolute.
1593 G. HARVEY *Pierce's Super.* Wks. (Grosart) II. 180 Armed with that supreme & Vncontrowlable authoritie, which they affect in causes Ecclesiasticall. **1630** *R. Johnson's Kingd. & Commw.* 526 His sentence in matters of Law and Religion is uncontrollable. **1672** MARVELL *Reh. Transp.* I. 140 He had vested them with an..unlimited power, and uncontroulable in the Government of Religion. **1711** STEELE *Spect.* No. 167 ¶3, I have grasped imaginary Scepters, and delivered uncontroulable Edicts. **1752** HUME *Ess. & Treat.* (1777) I. 39 Authority..can never..become quite entire and uncontroulable. **1809** MAR. EDGEWORTH *Manœuvring* xv, She had an uncontroulable right to marry as she thought proper. **1836** J. GILBERT *Chr. Atonem.* ii. 49 The power of the Creator over all his creatures is entirely uncontrollable.
b. In quasi-adverbial use.
a **1704** T. BROWN *Praise Drunkenness* Wks. 1730 I. 35 Consider whether 'tis not the Drunkard, that..acts so uncontroulable as the Gods themselves.
3. That cannot be controlled or restrained.
1648 R. JOSSELIN *Diary* (1908) 54 The wofull uncontroulable encrease of all manner of wickedness. **1665** SIR T. HERBERT *Trav.* (1677) 262 Cardarigas..fancies to himself that they were brought thither by some uncontroulable destiny to be destroyed. **1748** RICHARDSON *Clarissa* (1811) I. i. 2 His natural imperiousness and fierce and uncontroulable temper. **1823** SCOTT *Quentin D.* ix, His horse, seizing the bit with his teeth, went forth at an uncontrollable gallop. **1846** MCCULLOCH *Acc. Brit. Empire* (1854) II. 629 Poverty and misery produced by accidental and uncontrollable causes. **1879** H. C. WOOD *Therap.* 570 Hydrophobia is a perfectly uncontrollable disease.
absol. **1754** RICHARDSON *Corr.* (1804) IV. 89 Dr. Young is another uncontrollable, therefore unaccountable. **1819** SHELLEY *Ode West Wind* 47 The impulse of thy strength, only less free Than thou. O uncontrollable!

uncon'trollableness. [f. prec.] The state or quality of being uncontrollable.
1634 BP. HALL *Contempl., N.T.* IV. vii, Vices,..when they grow inveterate, have a strong plea for their abode and uncontroulableness. **1673** CAVE *Prim. Chr.* III. ii. 243 The Uncontroulableness of the Miracles performed in his Name. **1748** RICHARDSON *Clarissa* (1811) II. xxx. 192 My charge upon him of unpoliteness and uncontroulableness. **1833** CARLYLE *Misc. Ess., Diderot* (1888) 62 With vehemence enough, with even a female uncontrollableness. **1862** MILL *Syst. Logic* (ed. 5) II. 416 [It] cannot fail..to create a feeling of uncontrollableness in the former also.

uncon'trollably, *adv.* [f. as prec. Cf. INCONTROLLABLY *adv.*]
†**1. a.** As if uncontrovertible. *Obs.*
1629 PRYNNE *Ch. Eng.* 52 Being alwayes..unanimously, professedly and uncontrollablie entertained. **1646** SIR T. BROWNE *Pseud. Ep.* VI. viii. 312 Hereof uncontroulably and under generall consent many opinions are passant, which not-withstanding..do admit of doubt.
†**b.** Incontrovertibly, indisputably. *Obs.*
1676 HALE *Contempl.* I. 222 Abundantly and uncontrollably convincing the reality of our Saviour's death and true Resurrection. **1678** JONES *Heart & Right Sov.* 134 Our Brittish Churches appear to be uncontrollably of apostolical descent.
2. Without submission to control or restraint; absolutely; unrestrainedly.
1637 *Declar. Pfaltzgrave's Faith* 34 In which Commandement God hath forbidden two things vncontroleably. **1672** [H. STUBBE] *Rosemary & Bayes* 22, I conceive it is uncontroulably settled by law. **1768** TUCKER *Lt. Nat.* III. 311 Though it be certain God may uncontrolably and lawfully deal with his creatures as he pleases. **1809** MAR. EDGEWORTH *Manœuvring* xv, He became uncontroulably impatient to declare his own attachment. **1873** SYMONDS *Grk. Poets* i. 26 Pericles governed the most uncontrollably free of nations by Reason.

uncon'trolled, *ppl. a.* [UN-^{1} 8 and 5 b.]
1. Not subjected to control; unrestrained, ungoverned, unchecked: **a.** In predicative use.
1513 MORE *Hist. Rich. III,* Wks. 56 To rule..ye realm at their pleasure, & therbi to pil and spoil whom thei list vncontroled. **1595** SPENSER *Col. Clout* 662 Happie..I him hold, That may that blessed presence still enioy, Of fortune and of enuy vncomptrold. **1614** GORGES *Lucan* IV. 147 The coasts on both sides shall behold Valour vn-vanquisht vn-controld. **1655** *Nicholas Papers* (Camden) II. 311 To suffer so greate a prodigy of baseness to goe vncontrolld, were an injury to humane society. *a* **1718** PRIOR *Cloe Jealous* x, Fall uncontroll'd my Tears, and free. **1755** YOUNG *Centaur* i, Thus the sluices are set open for all sensuality..to pour in uncontrouled. **1844** H. H. WILSON *Brit. India* III. 541 The whole of India would fall under the dominion of one Governor, unassisted and uncontrolled. **1890** 'R. BOLDREWOOD' *Col. Reformer* (1891) 332 Possessing no very near relatives, she was uncontrolled as to her..mode of life.
b. In attributive use.
c **1586** C'TESS PEMBROKE *Ps.* (1823) LXXV. ii, Then [will I] denounce my uncontrolled pleasure. *a* **1592** GREENE *Selimus* 961 Or have the uncontrolled Christians Unsheath'd their swords to make more war on us? **1614** MARKHAM *Cheap Husb.* I. i. 2 He withstandeth all effects of sickness, with vncontroled constancy. **1660** *Gentl. Calling* 46 The Affections..will have as free and uncontrolled a sway in men, as they have in meer animals. **1742** RICHARDSON *Pamela* IV. 56 An Example to all who know him and his uncontrouled Temper. **1777** ROBERTSON *Hist. Amer.* II. (1778) I. 156 They flattered themselves that now they should enjoy an uncontrouled liberty. **1824** DIBDIN *Libr. Comp.* 745 *note,* The spleen..broke out with uncontrolled bitterness in..the Third Canto. **1875** JOWETT *Plato* (ed. 2) III. 112 The uncontrolled licence and freedom of the democrat.
†**2.** Not checked by comparison with facts; untested as to accuracy. *Obs.*
1529 MORE *Suppl. Souls* Wks. 297/2 Sith he knoweth hys tale false: it is wisdome to leue the time vnknowen, that hys lye may bee vncontrolled. **1584** in *Cath. Rec. Soc. Publ.* V. 81 To make this slaunder more probable, Or at the lest to be the longer uncontrowled.
†**3.** Not called in question; not gainsaid or disproved; undisputed. *Obs.*
1534 MORE *Comf. agst. Trib.* III. Wks. 1223/2 If he perceyued that they sayde but the trouthe, he would lette it passe by, vncontrolled. **1591** *Troub. Raigne K. John* II. (1611) 86 Faire Lewis of Fraunce..Hath title of an vncontrouled strength To England. **1672–5** COMBER *Comp.*

Temple (1702) 44 The main part of them is genuine, as the uncontrouled Tradition of the Eastern Church assures us. **1724** SWIFT *Drapier's Lett.* 14 Dec., I ever thought it the most uncontrouled and universally agreed maxim. **1731** —— *Let. to Ventoso* 28 Apr., It is an uncontrolled truth.

Hence **uncon'trolledly** *adv.*

1579 KNEWSTUB *Confut.* To Rdr., The sinnes of our Countrey..are done so openly and so vncontrolledly in the sight of the Lord. **1667** FLAVEL *Saint Indeed* (1754) 17 To let thy heart habitually and uncontrouledly wander from God. **1768–74** TUCKER *Lt. Nat.* (1834) II. 559 Men commonly place it in a license to do uncontrolledly whatever their desires..shall prompt them to. **1855** DORAN *Queens of Eng.* I. ix. 400 Uncontrolledly exercising the power she had attained.

†uncontro'versable, *a. Obs.* (UN-^{1} 7 b.)

1617 HALES *Gold. Rem.* I. (1673) 18 The litteral, plain, and uncontroversable meaning of Scripture.

†un'controversed, *ppl. a. Obs.* (UN-^{1} 8.)

1634 JACKSON *Creed* VII. iii. §3 The deduction of Mathematicall conclusions from the uncontrovers'd Maximes of the same Art.

uncontro'versial, *a.* (UN-^{1} 7.)

1861 J. G. SHEPPARD *Fall Rome* vii. 359 Races of uncontroversial warriors, such as were the Vandals and the Goths. **1870** J. H. NEWMAN *Gram. Assent* I. v. 144 Foreign, strange, and hard to the pious but uncontroversial mind.

So **uncontro'versially** *adv.*

1847 PUSEY *Paradise Chr. Soul* v. Advert. p. viii, No one can look uncontroversially at such occasional addresses.

†uncontro'versory, *a. Obs.* [UN-^{1} 7.] = prec.

1641 BP. HALL *Def. Humble Remonstr.* ii. 10 The Devotion of it yeeldeth no cause of offence to a very Popes eare, as onely ayming at an uncontroversory Piety.

†uncontro'vertably, *adv. Obs.* [UN-^{1} 11.] = UNCONTROVERTIBLY.

a **1658** DURHAM *Comm. Rev.* xvii. (1660) 660 These things being..uncontrovertably applicable to Rome.

uncontro'verted, *ppl. a.* (UN-^{1} 8.)

1654 WARISTON *Diary* (S.H.S.) II. 250 They..wer angrye to heare of the acts of uncontraverted assemblies. *a* **1674** CLARENDON *Surv. Leviath.* (1676) 63 His speculation is contradicted by constant and uncontroverted practice. **1712** ADDISON *Spect.* No. 529 ¶6 A standing and uncontroverted Principle. **1771** *Junius Lett.* xlviii. (1788) 264 The resolutions..stand upon your Journals, uncontroverted and unrepealed. **1800** *Med. Jrnl.* III. 527 It is uncontroverted that the original author intended to destroy contagious matter.

Hence **uncontro'vertedly** *adv.*

1644 BP. MAXWELL *Prerog. Chr. Kings* ii. 31 By Thrones, Dominions, Principalities and Powers, uncontrovertedly Angels are meant. **1705** CLARKE *Disc. Nat. Relig.* xiv. (1738) 445 Most of the Books were uncontrovertedly written by the Apostles themselves.

uncontro'vertible, *a.* (UN-^{1} 7 and 5 b.)

1664 H. MORE *Myst. Iniq.* 350, I mean the latter end of his real and uncontrovertible reign,..not that imaginary one. **1693** *Humours Town* 62 A good Assurance dubs any one an uncontrovertible Critick. **1742** *Johnson's Parliamentary Debates* II. 251 Even the positions..which are laid down as uncontrovertible, are generally false. **1794** R. J. SULIVAN *View Nat.* xliv. II. 253 This is a position, uncontrovertible in some points, but in others..much to be doubted. **1818** BENTHAM *Ch. Eng.* Introd. 13 May not then this position be stated as uncontrovertible? **1894** H. GARDENER *Unoff. Patriot* 24 The watchwords and uncontrovertible basis of belief for the succeeding generation.

Hence **uncontro'vertibly** *adv.*

1755 JOHNSON, *Incontestably*,..indisputably; uncontrovertibly. **1770** —— *False Alarm* (ed. 2) 24 It is uncontrovertibly certain, that [etc.]. **1818** BENTHAM *Ch. Eng.* p. xli, Shew me..that proposition in Euclid which is more uncontrovertibly demonstrated than is this one.

†uncon'tunded, *ppl. a. Obs.*$^{-1}$ (UN-^{1} 8 and 5 b.)

1599 A. M. tr. *Gabelhouer's Bk. Physicke* 125/1 Take Horsedung, as much as an Egge,..& half a drag. of vncontundede Safferne.

†unconva'lesced, *ppl. a. Obs.*$^{-1}$ (UN-^{1} 8.)

1590–1 *Reg. Privy Council Scot.* IV. 578 He wes lyand bed-fast,..unconvalesitt of the said woundis.

un'convenable, *a. Obs.*$^{-1}$ (UN-^{1} 7.)

1542 UDALL *Erasm. Apoph.* 256 b, Yt there was nothyng more unconvenable for a perfecte good Capitaine, then over muche hastyng.

uncon'vened, *ppl. a.* (UN-^{1} 8.)

[**1775** ASH.] **1855** GROTE *Greece* II. lxii, [The conspirators'] design was to appropriate the powers of government..; leaving this body of Five-thousand not merely unconvened, but non-existent.

†uncon'venience. *Obs.* (UN-^{1} 12 and 5 b.)

1535 in *Lett. Suppress. Monast.* (Camden) 56 We shall not be drevyn be necessyte nether to begge, nor to fall to no other unconveniynce. **1635** FELTHAM *Resolves* II. ii. 325 If I must have one, give me an unconvenience, not a mischiefe.

uncon'venient, *a.* and *sb. Obs.* exc. *dial.* [UN-^{1} 7, 5 b, and 12.]

A. *adj.* = INCONVENIENT *a.* (in various senses).

1450–80 tr. *Secreta Secret.* 8 The name of skarste is vnconvenient to a kyng. **1523** FITZHERB. *Husb.* §154 It shoulde seme vnconuenient for a temporall man to take vpon hym to shewe or teache any suche spirytuall matters. **1551** ROBINSON tr. *More's Utopia* II. (1895) 278 It were an vnconuenient thinge, that the blessed shoulde not be at libertye to goo whether they wold. **1590** *Disc. Span. Invasion* in *Harl. Misc.* (1809) II. 158 It seemed unconvenient that he should in every thing be inferior to the Englishmen. **1683** MOXON *Mech. Exerc., Printing* p. iii, A Low Case is unconvenient for a Compositer to work at. **1880–** in dial. glossaries.

†B. *sb.* = INCONVENIENT *sb.* 3. *Obs.*

?*c* **1536** in Ellis *Orig. Lett.* Ser. III. III. 43 It was thoght.. the matter..wolde have growen to forther vnconueniaunts.

Hence **uncon'veniently** *adv.*

1538 ELYOT, *Indecore*, vnhonestly, vnconueniently. **1548** UDALL, etc. *Erasm. Par. John* xix. 108 b, That it myght appeare howe vnconueniently the cryme of any cruell auctoritie..was layd agaynst hym. **1561–6** *Child-Marriages* 112 She..had sene the said Custance Wade and Robert Rile ..unconvenientlie together in the..chambre.

uncon'ventional, *a.* [UN-^{1} 7.] Not limited or bound down by convention; free and easy.

Also, in recent use, ***unconventionally*** adv.

1839 G. DARLEY *Beaumont & Fletcher's Wks.* I. Introd. p. xxxii, The unsettled and unconventional state of our language at that period. **1861** [H. S. CUNNINGHAM] *Wheat & Tares* 387 His views as to grammar were entirely unconventional. **1884** E. DREW *Elocutionist* Nov. 3/1 The book..is entirely unconventional.

Hence **uncon'ventionalism.**

1868 *Round Table* No. 202. 374 The freedom and unconventionalism in such writing. **1883** *Nonconf. & Indep.* 28 Dec. 1167 The work needs freshness and unconventionalism.

uncon,ventio'nality. (UN-^{1} 12. Cf. prec.)

1854 H. SPENCER *Ess.* I. 153 Such of his unconventionalities as can be attributed only to eccentricity, he has no qualms about. **1866** G. MACDONALD *Ann. Q. Neighb.* xxii. (1878) 396 The fact of his unconventionality and justice in leaving his property to my sister.

uncon'ventioned, *a.* (UN-^{1} 9.)

1876 WHITTIER *June on Merrimac* 77 What cares the unconventioned wood For pass-words of the town?

uncon'versable, *a.* Also -ible. [UN-^{1} 7 b, 7, and 5 b.] Unfit or unsuitable for social converse.

α. **1593** NASHE *Strange Newes* Ep. Ded., I loue and admire thy pleasant wittie humor, which no care or crosse can make vnconuersable. **1681** J. SCOTT *Chr. Life* I. iii. §3 In what a miserable state shall we be, when every Member of our Society shall be of the same unconversable Temper with our selves. **1697** COLLIER *Ess. Mor. Subj.* I. (1703) 79 What a rugged, tempestuous, unconversable mortal was Achilles. **1728** SWIFT *Let. to Carteret* 18 Jan., If I had not been confined to my chamber by the continuance of my unconversable disorder [*i.e.* deafness]. **1803** LAMB *Let. to Manning* in *Final Mem.* vii. 69 Among nasty, unconversable, horse-belching, Tartar-people.

β. **1674** *Govt. Tongue* 158 Nothing rendering a man so unconversible [as pride]. **1687** *Lond. Gaz.* No. 2302/2 The Ignorance or unconversible Humor of the Turks. **1736** H. WALPOLE *Lett.* (1861) I. 9 Great mathematicians have been of great use, but the generality of them are quite unconversible.

Hence **uncon'versableness.**

1684 H. MORE *Answer* 315 Contemptuousness, Malepertness against their Betters,..Unconversableness. **1702** S. PARKER tr. *Cicero's De Finibus* I. 45 The many.. Dangers and Frights that go along with Unconversableness and Solitude.

un'conversant, *a.* (UN-^{1} 7 and 5 b.)

a **1674** CLARENDON *Surv. Leviath.* (1676) 57 If Mr. Hobbes were not strangely unconversant with the transactions of those times. **1708** T. MADOX *Exchequer* Pref. p. xvi, Persons who are haply unconversant in disquisitions of this kind. **1813** T. BUSBY *Lucretius* I. III. Comm. p. xxxiii, A being, unconversant with its own existence. **1853** *Topographer & Geneal.* II. 6 Though this may sound marvellous to those unconversant with the subject.

unconversible: see UNCONVERSABLE.

uncon'versing, *ppl. a.* (UN-^{1} 10.)

1643–5 MILTON *Divorce* I. iii, How preposterous [it is] in the Canon Law..to have had no care about the unconversing inability of minde.

uncon'version. (UN-^{1} 12, 5 b.)

1846 WORCESTER (citing *Ch. Ob.*). **1861** F. W. ROBINSON *No Church* I. viii. 169 He might never wake again, but die.. in his brutal ignorance and unconversion.

uncon'vert, *v.* [UN-^{2} 3.]

1. *trans.* To transform.

1654 GAYTON *Pleas. Notes* IV. xvii. 258 Who with head full addle, Would unconvert his Pannell from a saddle.

2. To undo the conversion of.

1825 R. P. WARD *Tremaine* II. xv. 146 As he indeed wished to convert Monsieur Dupuis, so the valet..thought it but a fair return of kindness to endeavour to unconvert her. **1887** *Advance* (Chicago) 1 Dec. 760 We are not suffering so much from disturbing methods of converting people, as we are from the influences which un-convert them.

uncon'verted, *ppl. a.* [UN-^{1} 8 and 5 b.]

1. That has not been brought over to a religious faith or profession; not changed from one faith or opinion to another.

1648 [see UNCONFOUND *v.*]. **1685** BAXTER *Paraphr. N.T.* Matt. xxv. 7 Self-love, and fear, will make them cry for Mercy, with some kind of Repentance, though they be unconverted. **1745** WESLEY *Answ. Ch.* 35 Our Lord commanded those very Men who were then unconverted,.. to do this in Remembrance of Him. **1825** SCOTT *Talism.* viii, There is no doubt that the primitive Christians used the services of the unconverted heathen. **1865** B. NORTH *Ourselves* 7 These are solemn statements, and surely they should make every unconverted man who hears them, Think.

transf. *a* **1864** FERRIER *Grk. Philos.* (1866) I. xii. 340 The ignorant and unconverted soul supposes that its knowledge of sensible objects is due to the impressions which it receives.

absol. **1657** BAXTER *Treat. Conversion* (title-p.), The lamentable State of the Unconverted. **1672** ALLEINE *Alarm* iv. 88 Some of the Unconverted carry their marks in their fore-heads, more openly. *a* **1805** PALEY *Serm. Several Subjects* vii, It has been usual to divide all mankind into two classes, the converted and the unconverted. **1828** CARLYLE *Misc.* (1857) I. 239 They are in the camp of the Unconverted.

2. 'Not turned or changed from one form to another' (Webster, 1828–32).

3. *Law.* (See CONVERT *v.* 15.)

1884 V. R. SMITH in *Law Times Rep.* LI. 83/2 The premises..were taken improperly, and are therefore unconverted.

uncon'vertible, *a.* [UN-^{1} 7 and 5 b.] Incapable of conversion (in various senses); inconvertible.

1695 CONGREVE *Love for L.* IV. xii, Ill stars, and unconvertible ignorance attend him! **1805** *Ann. Rev.* III. 622 The Mohammedans have been found unconvertible for this plain reason. **1864** BOWEN *Logic* v. 139 Unconvertible are A and B.

Hence **unconverti'bility.**

1804 SOUTHEY *Lett.* (1856) I. 285 That the common opinion of the unconvertibility of this people is ill-founded.

uncon'veyed, *ppl. a.* (UN-^{1} 8 and 8 c.)

14.. *Chaucer's Parl. Foules* 518 (MS. St. John's, Oxf.) For office vnconveyid offt tym Anoyithe. **1696** STANHOPE *Chr. Pattern* (1711) 218 No property or claim any longer remaining unconveyed over.

†uncon'vict, *ppl. a. Obs.* [UN-^{1} 8 b.] = next.

a **1618** SYLVESTER *Job* IV. 12 Against Job began his wrath to flame,..And..his Foe-friends, for so strict Condemning Job, untry'd and unconvict.

uncon'victed, *ppl. a.* (UN-^{1} 8.)

1675 OTWAY *Alcibiades* IV. iii, The basest wretch not unconvicted dies. **1760** STERNE *Tr. Shandy* IV. *Slawkenb.'s Tale*, Am I to be the sport of Fortune and Slander—destined to be driven forth unconvicted—unheard—untouched? **1828** P. CUNNINGHAM *N.S. Wales* (ed. 3) II. 135, I see no reason whatever for excluding a man who has been once convicted, from any office the unconvicted now enjoy here. **1858** MERIVALE *Rom. Emp.* lii. (1865) VI. 286 He did not venture to command his execution, unarraigned and unconvicted. **1894** H. NISBET *Bush Girl's Rom.* 20 To personate the dead but unconvicted criminal.

uncon'vince, *v.* (UN-^{2} 3.)

1815 *Zeluca* II. 42 Mrs. Delvayne said she would.. unconvince herself if possible.

unconvincea'bility. (UN-^{1} 12.)

1868 W. R. GREG *Lit. & Soc. Judgm.* 390 A match for bureaucratic immovability and (to coin a word) unconvinceability.

uncon'vinceable, *a.* (UN-^{1} 7 b.)

1875 RUSKIN *Fors Clav.* lii. 100 [The bees] knocking themselves..again and again, unconvinceable of their fallacy. **1887** RIDER HAGGARD *Jess* xiv, Sturdy, determined, unconvinceable Englishmen.

uncon'vinced, *ppl. a.* [UN-^{1} 8.]

†1. Undisproved, unrefuted. *Obs.*$^{-1}$

1643–5 MILTON *Divorce* II. xv, He lets go that sophistry unconvinc't, for that had bin to teach them else.

2. Not convinced or persuaded.

1675 J. OWEN *Indwelling Sin* xiii. (1732) 175 God is pleased to leave no Generation unconvinced of this Truth. **1681** FLAVEL *Meth. Grace* iv. 73 Never was there one tear of true repentance seen to drop from the eye of an unconvinced sinner. **1797** MRS. RADCLIFFE *Italian* ii, Vivaldi quitted her unconvinced by her arguments, and unmoved in his designs. **1819** LADY MORGAN *Autobiog.* (1859) 313 The man retired, satisfied at not losing his place, but unconvinced of his error. **1897** MARY KINGSLEY *W. Africa* 426 The official is unconvinced and goes up the ladder to see other officers about it.

Hence **uncon'vincedly** *adv.*; **-con'vincedness.**

1642 D. ROGERS *Naaman* 847 Another let is unconvincedness of heart. **1850** F. W. NEWMAN *Phases* iv. 120 The soul..has to learn from, and unconvincedly submit to, some external authority.

unconvinci'bility. (UN-^{1} 12 and 5 b.)

1883 *Blackw. Mag.* Apr. 534/1 The obdurate unconvincibility of a fool.

uncon'vincible, *a.* (UN-^{1} 7 and 5 b.)

a **1747** J. WESLEY *Wks.* (1829) V. xxxvii. 476 An unadvisable and unconvincible spirit. **1787** tr. *Klopstock's Messiah* III. 102 Of an unconvincible mind. *a* **1921** N.E.D. In recent use. **1979** C. MCCARRY *Better Angels* II. vii. 119 He made his argument to her, knowing that Patrick..was unconvincible.

uncon'vincing, *ppl. a.* (UN-^{1} 10.)

1653 MILTON *Hirelings* Wks. 1851 V. 357 To heap such unconvincing Citations as these in Religion,..argues not much Learning nor Judgment. **1885** W. S. GILBERT *Mikado* II. 41 A bald and unconvincing narrative.

Hence **uncon'vincingly** *adv.*

1891 F. W. NEWMAN *Cdl. Newman* 18 He quoted Scripture unconvincingly.

un'convoluted, *ppl. a.* (UN-^{1} 8.)

c **1842** *Todd's Cycl. Anat.* III. 291/2 In the Phalangers.., the surface of the cerebral hemispheres is..unconvoluted.

uncon'vulsed, *ppl. a.* (UN-^{1} 8.)

1794 G. ADAMS *Nat. & Exp. Philos.* I. ii. 59 The liquor will flow out steadily and unconvulsed.

un'cooked, *ppl. a.* [UN-[1] 8. Cf. Du. *ongekookt*, G. *ungekocht*, Sw. *okokt*, Da. *ukogt*.]

1. Not cooked for eating.

[**1775** ASH.] **1846** SOYER *Cookery* 381 Half a pound of lean uncooked ham. **1856** KANE *Arct. Expl.* II. i. 21 Fire would ruin the..vitality which belongs to its uncooked juices. **1870** N. F. HELE *Aldeburgh* vii. 78 They would eat freely of birds and uncooked liver.

2. *fig.* Not altered to suit a purpose.

1860 GEN. P. THOMPSON *Audi Alt.* III. clxxx. 223 The earliest reports..(which are always most to be depended on, as being un-cooked). **1865** BUCKSTONE in *Morn. Star* 13 Apr., We always present an uncooked balance-sheet.

uncooled, *ppl. a.* Also 6 *Sc.* onculyt. (UN-[1] 8.)

1513 DOUGLAS *Æneid* XI. v. 65 And ȝit all warm, onculyt, sone thai have Bedelvyn thame, and in the erd begrave. **1648** HEXHAM II, *Ongekoelt*, vncooled. **1894** F. A. STEEL *Potter's Thumb* iii, Insipid as uncooled water on a summer's day.

un'coopered, *ppl. a.* (UN-[1] 8.)

1757 W. THOMPSON *R.N. Adv.* 36 Your Memorialist.. Prevented many hundred of Casks fresh packed, from being many Weeks uncoopered.

unco-'ordinated, *ppl. a.* (UN-[1] 8.)

1892 *Spectator* 30 Apr. 612/2 There is plenty of imagination in the story, but it is uncoördinated.

un'cope, *v.* (UN-[2] 3: see COPE *sb.*[1] 9.)

1703 R. NEVE *City & C. Purchaser* 19 To remove the Earth over the Stones, or uncope it, as Workmen call it. *Ibid.* 256 The Stone..lay almost level with the Ground, and requir'd but very little uncopeing.

un'coped, *ppl. a.* (UN-[1] 8 c.)

1594 NASHE *Unfort. Trav.* Wks. (Grosart) V. 58 Those that beholding him at the stake yet vncoapte with, wisht him a sutable death to his vgly shape. **1972** J. G. VERMANDEL *Last Seen in Samarra* xii. 81 Wearing a housecoat, and with her red hair curlier than he'd ever seen it before. Uncoped with. **1981** E. NORTH *Dames* i. 4 They..think back over life uncoped with.

un'copiable, *a.* (UN-[1] 7 b.)

1846 WORCESTER (citing Ware). **1856** RUSKIN *Mod. Paint.* III. IV. ix. §17 His [*sc.* Turner's] finish is so delicate as to be nearly uncopiable. **1870** LOWELL *Among my Bks.* Ser. I. (1873) 226 This country tradesman's son..could set high-bred wits..uncopiable lessons in drawing gentlemen.

un'copied, *ppl. a.* (UN-[1] 8.)

1737 W. KNOWLER in *Camden Misc.* IX. (1895) p. ix, There is four or five times the number of Letters uncopied for one transcribed. **1859** LADY MORGAN *Autobiog.* p. vii, The auto-graph letters, from which uncopied they have been printed.

†**uncoqued,** *ppl. a. Obs.* [UN-[1] 8.] Uncooked.

1617 AINSWORTH *Annot. Exod.* xvi. 31 As it was gathered, and uncoqued, [it] was like honey wafers.

unco'quettish, *a.* (UN-[1] 7.)

Also, in recent use, *uncoquettishness.*

1798 JANE AUSTEN *Northang. Abb.* vii, So pure and uncoquettish were her feelings. **1876** *Daily News* 8 Nov. 5/6 With a not uncoquettish shrug of the shoulders.

un'cord, *v.* [UN-[2] 4 b.] *trans.* To unstring (a bow); to free or disengage from a cord or cords.

c **1430** *Pilgr. Lyf Manhode* IV. lviii. (1869) 204 þe corde [with] which þe bowe was corded, and þat j haue vncorded. **1611** COTGR. s.v. *Desencordé*. **1622** MABBE tr. *Aleman's Guzman d'Alf.* II. 73 His servants punctually performed that, which his Master had commanded him; vn-cording.. the very selfe-same Trunke. ?**1712** *Dangerous Present* 4 If the Box had been uncorded, and the Cords drawn leisurely. **1754** G. K. in *Connoisseur* No. 33. 198 Pinning baskets, and cording trunks; as again..in unpinning, uncording, locking up foul linnen. **1842** BORROW *Bible in Spain* viii, The fellow ..began to pull the trunks off the sumpter mule and commenced uncording them.

un'cordial, *a.* Also 5 *Sc.* -uall. [UN-[1] 7.]

†**1.** *Sc.* Uncongenial. *Obs.*[−1]

c **1470** HENRY *Wallace* IX. 430 Still in to pes he couth nocht lang endur; Wncorduall it was till his natur.

2. Not cordial; lacking in heartiness.

1643 PRYNNE *Sov. Power Parl.* III. 150 In which to be.. cold, uncordiall, or timerous.., demerits a perpetuall brand of infamy. **1797** JANE AUSTEN *Sense & Sens.* xxxiv, A little proud-looking woman of uncordial address. **1824** SCOTT *St. Ronan's* xxv, We were bundled off to Scotland, coupled up like two pointers in a dog-cart, and.. with much the same uncordial feeling towards each other. **1871** MEREDITH *H. Richmond* xxxvii, I took upon myself to be..always courteous, deliberate in my replies, and not uncordial.

Hence **un'cordially** *adv.*

1811 *Ora & Juliet* 50 She begged his forgiveness, which he granted, though somewhat uncordially.

†**un'core,** *ppl. a. Obs.*[−1] [UN-[1] 8 b.] Unchosen; not employed.

13.. *St. Gregory* (Vernon MS.) 530 Be stille, dame, and hold þi pes, let suche wordus ben vnkore.

un'core, *v.* (UN-[2] 3.)

1611 FLORIO, *Dis-callire*, to suple, to vnharden, to vncore. **1615** CHAPMAN *Odyss.* XVII. 194 Your son..knows clearly nothing more, Hear me yet speak, that can the truth uncore.

‖**uncore prist.** *Obs.* [AF. *uncore* (F. *encore*) still + *prist* (F. *prêt*) ready.] (See quot. 1607.)

1607 COWELL *Interpr.*, *Vncore prist*, is a plee for the Defendant, being siewed for a debt due at a day past, to saue the forfeiture of his bond; saying, that he tendered the dept at the time and place, and that there was none to receiue it, and that he is now also readie to pay the same. *a* **1613** OVERBURY *Characters, Meere Common Lawyer* (1615) E 4 His loue letters..are stuft with Discontinuances, Remitters, and *Vncore prists*. **1685** J. KEBLE *Rep. K.B.* II. 178 He pleaded a tender by the Stranger and did not say *uncore prist*, for which cause the Plaintiff demurred. **1768** BLACKSTONE *Comm.* III. 303.

un'cork, *v.* [UN-[2] 3.]

1. *trans.* To draw the cork of (a bottle, etc.).

1727 POPE, etc. *Art of Sinking* 113 Uncork the bottle. **1784** *Phil. Trans.* LXXIV. 375 The funnel was taken out,.. and uncorked over a weighed cup. **1848** THACKERAY *Van. Fair* vi, He made the salad; and uncorked the Champagne. **1894** H. NISBET *Bush Girl's Rom.* 222 Timothy..brought out a fresh bottle of brandy. This he uncorked cautiously.

b. *transf.* and *fig.*

1749 FIELDING *Tom Jones* XVII. iv, The froth bursting forth from his lips the moment they were uncorked. **1892** ZANGWILL *Childr. Ghetto* I. x, In the ferment of freethought he had uncorked his soul, and it had run over with much froth. **1894** A. ROBERTSON *Nuggets*, etc. 17 Their courage had been uncorked.., and they felt as limp as a wet rag.

2. To draw out, withdraw (a cork, etc.).

1740 CHEYNE *Regimen* p. xlix, To uncork the Plugs, and concreted Recrements, that stop the Mouths of the perspiratory Glands.

Hence **un'corker; un'corking** *vbl. sb.*

1855 OWEN in R. Owen *Life* (1894) ii. 8 The uncorker uncorks the bottle. **1881** MISS BRADDON *Asphodel* I. 250 She sat..sipping her lemonade, half of which had been lost in the process of uncorking.

un'corked, *ppl. a.* [UN-[1] 8 and UN-[2] 8.] Not fitted or stopped with a cork; also, having the cork removed.

1791 O'KEEFFE *Wild Oats* I. i, You found the tenth bottle uncorked. **1835** *Wilson's Tales Borders* I. 305/1 Dead as uncorked small beer that has stood an hour in the sun. **1854** P. B. ST. JOHN *Amy Moss* 206 The whiskey bottle stood before him uncorked. **1878** ABNEY *Photogr.* 148 The water ..should stand in an uncorked bottle for twenty-four hours.

†**un'corn.** [UN-[1] 4 b.] Evil grain; 'wild oats'.

1513 DOUGLAS *Æneid* IV. Prol. 13 Quhar schame is lost, thair..Ripis ȝour perellus frutis and oncorn. **1710** RUDDIMAN *Gloss. Douglas' Æneis* s.v., In some places of Scotland they say, that one hath sown his uncorn.

un'coronated, *a.* (UN-[1] 8. Cf. next.)

1802 H. MARTIN *Helen of Glenross* III. 162 If an uncoronated cloathing was put on any one of these ducal steeds, he would kick it to pieces.

un'coroneted, *a.* (UN-[1] 8.)

1817 BENTHAM *Parl. Reform* Introd. 19 Great Landholding, and as yet uncoroneted Commoners, styled Country Gentlemen. **1852** ROBERTSON *Lect.* (1858) 159 That daring warrior..who has been laid aside uncoroneted and almost unhonoured.

un'corporal, *a.* ? *Obs.* (UN-[1] 7 and 5 b.)

1565 GOLDING *Ovid's Met.* Epist. (1567) b j b, God the father..made first of all Both heauen and earth vncorporall. **1570** T. NORTON tr. *Nowel's Catech.* 25 b, God..made..the vncorporall spirites whom we call Angels. **1590** SWINBURN *Testaments* 218 All the goods, & cattels,..whether they bee moueable or immoueable, corporal or vncorporall.

un'corpulent, *a.* (UN-[1] 7.)

1827 POLLOK *Course T.* VIII. 70 The man Of tithes,.. ungowned, unbeneficed, Uncorpulent.

unco'rrect, *ppl. a.* and *a.* [UN-[1] 8 b, 7, 5 b.]

†**1.** = UNCORRECTED *ppl. a. Obs.*

1502 ATKYNSON tr. *De Imitatione* I. xvi. (1893) 165 We wolde that other that offendeth shulde be straitly correcte & our selfe more coulpable vncorrecte. **1553** *Respublica* Prol. 51 That yls whiche long tyme have reigned vncorrecte shall nowe foreuer bee redressed with effecte.

2. = INCORRECT *a.*

1568 CHARTERIS *Pref. Lyndesay's Wks.* A j b, Quhat difference is betuix..correct and vncorrect Imprenting, salbe cleirlie sene. **1669** DRYDEN *Wild Gallant* Pref. A 2 b, You have..receiv'd with Applause, as bad, and as uncorrect Playes from other Men. **1702** *Eng. Theophrast.* 23 The Ancients, tho' generally uneven and uncorrect, have yet here and there some fine touches. **1752** SALMON *Universal Trav.* I. viii. 20 Before the Missionaries taught them, their tables of eclipses were very uncorrect.

unco'rrectable, *a.* Also -ible. (UN-[1] 7 b.)

1560 WHITEHORNE *Arte Warre* 6 b, Parte of theim are wonte to bee enemies of warre, parte vncorrectable. **1902** A. H. BUCK *Ref. Handbk. Med. Sci.* (ed. 2) IV. 528/2 Finally the deformity becomes permanent and uncorrectible. **1952** G. SARTON *Hist. Sci.* I. xxi. 546 Superstition is of necessity more conservative than science, because it is uncorrectible and unprogressive. **1970** *New Yorker* 30 May 26 A regularly scheduled airliner..radioed..to report..an undiagnosed and uncorrectable loss of power. **1970** *Time* 21 Sept. 57 For many years, facial paralysis has been uncorrectable.

unco'rrected, *ppl. a.* [UN-[1] 8 and 5 b.]

1. Not freed from error or inexactness; not revised or emended.

1387 TREVISA *Higden* (Rolls) III. 73 He putte Ianeuer and Feuerrer to þe bygynnynge of þe ȝere, and so þe ȝere lefte among þe Romayns vncorrected anon to Iulius Cesar his tyme. **1548** ELYOT, *Incorrectus*,..vncorrected. **1598** FLORIO, *Scorretto*, vncorrected, vnpolished, rude, rough. **1699** BENTLEY *Phalaris* 251 Whole Lines were omitted by the Stone-Cutter, and pass'd uncorrected. **1711** G. HICKES *Two Treat. Chr. Priesth.* (ed. 3) I. 170 If these holy Men's Notion..be..a Mistake, it..stood uncorrected for almost sixteen hundred Years. **1798** SOUTHEY *Lett.* (1856) I. 55 They are, I know, hastily written and uncorrected. **1819** SHELLEY *Let.* Pr. Wks. 1888 II. 299 You are to write me uncorrected letters, just as the words come. **1837** GORING & PRITCHARD *Microgr.* 77 Perfectly direct day-light also gives apparent achromatism with any common uncorrected lenses.

2. Not chastised or punished.

1475 *Bk. Noblesse* (Roxb.) 56 So many wrecchid synnes as among us dailie uncorrectid hathe reigned. **1513** MORE *Hist. Rich. III*, Wks. 40/1 Robbers and riuers walking at libertie vncorrected. **1548** ELYOT, *Incastigatus*,..not chastised: vncorrected. **1647** HEXHAM I, Vncorrected, *ongestraft*. **1670** BAXTER *Cure Ch. Div.* 338 Parents must not be so patient with sin as to leave their children uncorrected.

3. Not improved by training or discipline; not guided into the proper course.

1599 SHAKS. *Hen. V*, v. ii. 50 The freckled Cowslip, Burnet and greene Clouer, Wanting the Sythe, withall vncorrected, ranke; Conceiues by idlenesse. **1718** *Freethinker* No. 23 ¶6 Amongst the many Abuses, of which we stand uncorrected. **1750** CARTE *Hist. Eng.* II. 790 A fine youth, but..having too much of his mother's spirit, uncorrected as yet by reflection and experience. **1865** FROUDE *Short Stud.* (1867) I. 161 Submissiveness, humility, obedience produce if uncorrected in politics a nation of slaves.

4. Not counteracted or neutralized.

1694 SALMON *Bate's Dispens.* (1713) 373/2 If any of the kinds of Flowers be used uncorrected, it is much better to use their Infusion in Wine. **1825** SCOTT *Betrothed* xxi, During slumber, when Imagination, uncorrected by the organs of sense, weaves her own fantastic web. **1899** *Allbutt's Syst. Med.* VI. 829 Such consequences may be produced in uncorrected hypermetropia.

†**unco'rrectly,** *adv. Obs.* (UN-[1] 11, 5 b.)

1706 STEVENS *Span. Dict.* I, *Incorrectamente*, uncorrectly. **1716** M. DAVIES *Athen. Brit.* III. *Diss. Physick* 32 It had been printed long before uncorrectly, at Norimberg 1532.

†**unco'rrectness.** *Obs.* (UN-[1] 12, 5 b.)

1669 DRYDEN *Wild Gallant* Pref., I doubt not but you will see in it the uncorrectness of a young writer. **1711** SHAFTESB. *Charac.* III. 274 Their Remis[s]ness, Uncorrectness, Insipidness, and downright Ignorance of all literate Art.

un'correlated, *ppl. a.* (UN-[1] 8.)

1881 *Med. Rev.* II. 43 Occurring at haphazard, or as uncorrelated coincidences.

uncorre'spondency. (UN-[1] 12, 5 b: cf. next.)

1659 GAUDEN *Tears Ch.* IV. xi. 459 This uncorrespondency, to which I am upon those grounds compelled.

uncorre'spondent, *a.* (UN-[1] 7 and 5 b.)

a **1631** SIR W. CORNWALLIS *Ess.* II. lii. (1632) 334 Wee must offer the eyes of men nothing vncorrespondent to the peculiar grace of our callings. **1659** GAUDEN *Tears Ch.* III. xxviii. 363 Vicious extremes..are contrary to each other, and yet uncorrespondent with that vertue from which they are divided. **1784** J. POTTER *Virtuous Villagers* I. 43 Nothing can be more preposterous or uncorrespondent. **1844** ELLIOTT *Horæ Apoc.* (1862) IV. 14 Very much as in a famous, and probably not uncorrespondent, prophecy of Ezekiel.

uncorre'sponding, *ppl. a.* (UN-[1] 10 and 5 b.)

1826 LAMB *Elia* II. *Pop. Fallacies* xiii, His insufferable procerity of stature, and uncorresponding dwarfishness of observation. **1885** RUSKIN *Præterita* I. x. 307 Most [forces] act irregularly, or else at uncorresponding periods.

†**un'corrigible,** *a. Obs.* (UN-[1] 7 and 5 b.)

a **1420** *Wycliffite Bible* (1850) III. 39 *marg.*, Stryue thou not..with vncorrigible men bi word of blamyng. *c* **1440** *Gesta Rom.* xxxvii. 151 We vncorrigible wrecchis conne not sece of oure synnynge. **1539** ELYOT *Cast. Helthe* 69 Either for vncorrigible vices, or infortunate chances. **1583** GOLDING *Calvin on Deut.* xiii. 77 To blinde the reprobates and such as are vncorrigible. **1655** GURNALL *Chr. in Arm.* I. (1669) 62/1 We wrestle against Providence, when uncorrigible under the..dispensations of God towards us. **1692** SOUTH *Serm.* (1697) I. 489 Such is the peculiar Insolence of this sort of Men, such the uncorrigible Vileness of all slavish Spirits.

unco'rroborated, *ppl. a.* (UN-[1] 8.)

[**1775** ASH.] **1911** CRAIK *Clarendon* I. 100 He found a 'copy' of a paper which supported his father's uncorroborated evidence.

unco'rroded, *ppl. a.* (UN-[1] 8.)

1685 BOYLE *Salubr. Air* 65 It will leave all the rest uncorroded, and fall onely upon the Gold.

un'corrugated, *ppl. a.* (UN-[1] 8.)

1863 COWDEN CLARKE *Shaks. Char.* ix. 228 How the velvets would have escaped with uncorrugated pile!

†**unco'rrumped,** *ppl. a. Obs.* [UN-[1] 8.] Uncorrupted.

a **1400-50** *Alexander* 4334 For þe aire within oure habitacle is ai vn-corumpid.

unco'rrupt, *a.* [UN-[1] 7 and 5 b.]

1. = INCORRUPT *a.* 1.

1382 WYCLIF *1 Cor.* ix. 25 Thei [strive]..that thei take a coruptible crowne, we forsothe vncorupt. *a* **1425** tr. *Arderne's Treat. Fistula*, etc. 43 It is certayne þat bones shul noȝt be corrupte wiþ in a fourtniȝt if þai war vncorrupte afore þat tyme. *c* **1450** CAPGRAVE *Life St. Gilbert* 75 Ther was bred kept sextene ȝere aftir his deth, on-corupte, on-mouled. *a* **1513** FABYAN *Chron.* V. cxxvii. 108 Thou shalt fynde our thre bodyes hoole & vncorrupte. **1555** EDEN *Decades* (Arb.) 264 If it [*sc.* ruby] coomme owt of the fyer vncorrupte, it be-commeth of the coloure of a burnynge cole. **1600** SURFLET *Countrie Farme* III. xliii. 509 The leaues of the Bay tree doe preserue, keepe vncorrupt and make faster the fish that is fried. **1692** RAY *Disc.* II. iv. (1693) 127 The real Shells them-selves..remaining still entire and uncorrupt. **1733** TULL *Horse-Hoeing Husb.* viii. 82 The Seeds..are so hardy, as to lie sound and uncorrupt for many Years..in the Earth. **1794** R. J. SULIVAN *View Nat.* I. 254 So that several substances may be preserved in it uncorrupt for a considerable time.

2. = INCORRUPT *a.* 2.

c **1440** *Alph. Tales* 344 Sho sent hur one þat was a maydyn and vncorrupte. **1535** COVERDALE *Wisd.* vi. 19 The kepinge of yᵉ lawes is perfeccion & an vn corrupte life. **1561** T. NORTON *Calvin's Inst.* III. 269 Honest in dede and of vncorrupt maners. **1597** HOOKER *Eccl. Pol.* v. lvi. §8 That which in him made our nature vncorrupt. **1638** JUNIUS *Paint. Ancients* 6 Such Artificers..carry in their mind an uncorrupt image of perfect beautie. **1670** COTTON *Espernon* II. VII. 304, I have..preserv'd my Hands clean, my Conscience uncorrupt. **1725** BERKELEY *Proposal*, etc., Wks. 1871 III. 215 The pure un-corrupt doctrine of the gospel. **1784** COWPER *Task* II. 400, I would express him simple, grave, sincere; In doctrine uncorrupt. *c* **1814** SOUTHEY *Ode War Amer.* vi, Thy martyrs purchased at the stake Faith uncorrupt for thine inheritance. **1871** MEREDITH *H. Richmond* liv, History, like the air we breathe, must be in motion to keep us uncorrupt.

b. Of language, texts, etc.

1596 DALRYMPLE tr. *Leslie's Hist. Scot.* (S.T.S.) I. 95 Mair than 2 thowsand ȝeirs thay haue keipet the toung hail vncorrupte. **1600** E. BLOUNT tr. *Conestaggio* 1 An enimie to the vncorrupt writing of Historiographers. **1693** J. EDWARDS *Author. O. & N. Test.* 53 These Masoretick Doctors have kept it [*sc.* the Hebrew text] undepraved and uncorrupt. **1845** KITTO *Cycl. Bibl. Lit.* I. 377/1 That..their writings.. should be preserved entire and uncorrupt.

3. = INCORRUPT *a.* 3.

1651 HOBBES *Leviath.* I. x. 42 A learned and uncorrupt Judge. **1656** EARL MONM. tr. *Boccalini's Advts. fr. Parnass.* I. v. (1674) 9 The eternal glory of the uncorrupt Venetian Justice. **1724** SWIFT *Drapier's Lett.* Wks. 1755 V. II. 114 The greatest, the wisest, and the most uncorrupt minister I ever conversed with. **1774** J. READE in *Buccleuch MSS.* (Hist. MSS. Comm.) I. 416 A respectable, unshaken, uncorrupt majority. **1841** BORROW *Zincali* I. xii. I. 192 Pure and uncorrupt justice has never existed in Spain.

unco'rrupted, *ppl. a.* [UN-^{1} 8 and 5 b.]

1. Of organic matter: Not corrupted or decomposed.

c **1400** *Destr. Troy* 8724 The body..may not long vpon loft ly vncorruppit. **1555** EDEN *Decades* (Arb.) 131 Only one remayned vncorrupted, the other being putrified by reason of the longe vyage. **1610** HOLLAND *Camden's Brit.* (1637) 541 His hand remained heere uncorrupted many hundred yeeres after. **1615** G. SANDYS *Trav.* 134 The iuyce of Cedars ..preserued them vncorrupted. **1707** MORTIMER *Husb.* (1721) I. 286 It keepeth all things uncorrupted which are put into it. **1734** tr. *Rollin's Anc. Hist.* XVI. i. (1827) VI. 344 The body continued uncorrupted all that time. **1870** BRYANT *Iliad* XIX. II. 230 The body shall remain Even more than uncorrupted.

2. Of persons: Not rendered morally unsound; not debased or depraved; not influenced by bribes.

1565 COOPER *Thesaurus*, *Integri testes*, witnesses vncorrupted. **1570** T. NORTON tr. *Nowel's Catech.* 41 b, Their life, which..shalbe examined by the vncorrupted and seuere iudge according to the truth. **1599** *Life Sir T. More* in Wordsw. *Eccl. Biog.* (1853) II. 185 John More his father a civill man,..just, and uncorrupted. **1620** MIDDLETON & ROWLEY *World Tost at Tennis* 826 Thou, uncorrupted Lawyer, Virtue's great miracle. **1732** POPE *Epit. on Gay* 6 Above Temptation, in a low Estate, And uncorrupted, ev'n among the Great. **1754** WILKES *Corr.* (1805) I. 26 Gentlemen, I come here uncorrupting, and I promise you I shall ever be uncorrupted. **1849-50** ALISON *Hist. Eur.* VIII. li. §8. 231 Calamities..draw forth the energy of the uncorrupted portion of mankind. **1875** JOWETT *Plato* (ed. 2) I. 367 Not the corrupted youth only,..but their uncorrupted elder relatives.

b. Of personal attributes, actions, etc.

1571 GOLDING *Calvin on Ps.* lxvi. 245 He expresseth trew and uncorrupted woorshippinge. *a* **1586** SIDNEY *Arcadia* III. (1912) 401 Glad to receyve an uncorrupted libertie. **1615** G. SANDYS *Trav.* 8 The nuptiall sheetes..are..preserued.. as a testimonie of their vncorrupted virginities. **1697** DRYDEN *Æneis* VIII. 548 Thus frugally they earn their children's bread, And uncorrupted keep their nuptial bed. **1713** BERKELEY *Guardian* No. 49 ¶5 It is this alone that makes them desirable to an uncorrupted taste. **1797** S. & HT. LEE *Canterb. T.* (1799) I. 303 The lad, whose good-nature was yet uncorrupted by the world, greeted her with cordiality. **1847** HELPS *Friends in C.* I. i. 7 To do that, he must have an uncorrupted judgment.

3. Unadulterated.

1539 ELYOT *Cast. Helthe* (1541) 57 So true a poticary, that hath always drowges uncorrupted. **1683** *Roxb. Ball.* (1885) V. 564 Springs and Streams that still run pure, Nature's uncorrupted Goods.

Hence **unco'rruptedly** *adv.*; **-'ruptedness**.

1570 T. NORTON tr. *Nowel's Catech.* 2 b, How godlynesse, holynesse, and Religion, are to be purely and vncorruptedly yelded to God. **1611** FLORIO, *Incorrottibilita*, vncorruptednesse. **1644** MILTON *Areop.* (Arb.) 48 The grace of infallibility, and uncorruptednesse. **1783** BLAIR *Lect. Rhet.* xxviii. II. 97 The purity and uncorruptedness of their morals. **1882** MAYNE REID in *N.Y. Tribune* 19 July, Even when the contest is conducted..uncorruptedly.

unco'rruptible, *a.* [UN-^{1} 7 and 5 b.]

1. = INCORRUPTIBLE *a.* 1.

1382 WYCLIF *John* Prol., Bigynnynge the work of an vncorruptible word, other Goddis sone. **1382** —— *Rom.* i. 23 The glorie of God vncorruptible. **1535** COVERDALE *1 Peter* v. 4 Ye shal receaue the vncorruptible crowne of glory. **1594** CAREW *Huarte's Exam. Wits* (1616) 49 One of the greatest arguments..that the reasonable soule is vncorruptible. **1611** BIBLE *Rom.* i. 23 The glory of the vncorruptible God.

2. = INCORRUPTIBLE *a.* 2.

1843 tr. *Custine's Empire of Czar* II. 316 It was to the advice of these uncorruptible men that he owed much of his glory. **1897** OLIVE SCHREINER *Trooper P. Halket* Ded., An uncorruptible justice and a broad humanity.

Hence **uncorrupti'bility**; **-'ruptibleness**.

1382 WYCLIF *1 Pet.* iii. 4 The ilke that is the hid man of herte, in vncoruptibilite of quyete..and mylde spirit. **1579** FULKE *Heskins' Parl.* 186 This corruptible nature..could not..be brought to vncorruptiblenesse and life. **1645** PAGITT *Heresiogr.* (1661) 150 They that teach this, do thereby deny the uncorruptibleness of that divine seed.

unco'rrupting, *ppl. a.* (UN-^{1} 10.)

a **1711** KEN *Hymns Festiv.* Poet. Wks. 1721 I. 223 For uncorrupting Myrrh, an Heart sincere I'll bring. **1754** [see UNCORRUPTED *ppl. a.* 2].

unco'rruption. [UN-^{1} 12 and 5 b.] Absence of corruption; uncorrupt character or condition.

1382 WYCLIF *Rom.* ii. 7 Glorie, and honour, and vncoripcioun, to hem sekynge euerelasting lyf. *a* **1420** *Wycliffite Bible* Wisd. vi. 19 *marg.*, That is, of goostly vncorrupcioun, bi eschewing of synne. **1526** TINDALE *Titus* ii. 7 Shew vncorrupcion, honestie, and the wholsome worde which cannot be rebuked. **1542** UDALL *Erasm. Apoph.* 74 b, Onely in the children remained the aunciente integritee & uncorrupcion. **1802-12** BENTHAM *Ration. Judic. Evid.* (1827) IV. 56 That perfect purity and uncorruption which has so long been regarded as a characteristic..of an English judge. **1824** —— *Bk. Fallacies* IV. vii. 284.

unco'rruptive, *a.* (UN-^{1} 7 and 5 b.)

1737 R. GLOVER *Leonidas* VII. 412 Those other climes of uncorruptive joy, Which Heav'n in dark futurity conceals.

unco'rruptly, *adv.* [UN-^{1} 11 and 5 b.] In an uncorrupt manner; genuinely; correctly.

1553 BRENDE *Q. Curtius* VII. 57, I shall declare vncorruptly the sayinges which the eldest of those embassadours dyd speake. **1565** COOPER *Thesaurus* s.v. *Integre*, To bestow his time vncorruptely and honestly. **1647** HEXHAM I, Vncorruptly, *onverderflick*. *a* **1700** EVELYN *Diary* 8 Feb. 1678, The Conte de Castel Mellor..had behaved himselfe..uncorruptly in all his ministrie. **1736** BUTLER *Anal.* I. vi. 164 Whether the revelation itself be uncorruptly handed down.

unco'rruptness. [UN-^{1} 12 and 5 b.] The quality of being uncorrupt; incorruptness.

1583 GOLDING *Calvin on Deut.* xlviii. 287 Wee must.. worshippe him with such vncorruptnesse, as all ydoles bee vtterly cast downe. **1611** BIBLE *Titus* ii. 7 In doctrine shewing vncorruptnesse, gravity, sinceritie. **1671** E. CHAMBERLAYNE *Pres. St. Eng.* I. (ed. 5) 194 These are the Principal Judges,..persons for Knowledge, Courage, Uncorruptness, &c., equal..to any other in former Kings Raigns. *c* **1728** EARL OF AILESBURY *Mem.* (1890) 705 He makes amends by the high stock he hath of zeal, industry and uncorruptness. [**1860** S. WILBERFORCE *Addr. Cand. Ordination* 124 Gravity, sincerity, uncorruptness and habitual soundness of speech.]

†**un'corsayed**, *ppl. a. Obs.*$^{-1}$ (UN-^{1} 8. Sense doubtful.)

a **1400-50** *Alexander* 3775 Sone as þai wist of his will þai wiȝtly him sente Ten vncorsayd coltis.

†**un'corse**, *v. Obs.* Also 5 vncorce. [UN-^{2} 5.] *trans.* To remove from the body.

c **1470** HARDING *Chron.* XCV. x, This Audry..In Ely bode ..To tyme hir soule were lesed and vncorced. *Ibid.* CV. xv, Before his soule was passed and vncorced.

un'corseted, *ppl. a.* (UN-^{1} 8.)

1856 P. H. GOSSE *Tenby* ii, The busy bathing-women— uncouth, uncorseted figures.

†**un'corven**, *ppl. a.* [UN-^{1} 8 b. Cf. MDu. *ongecorven*, Du. *ongekorven*.] Unpruned.

c **1380** CHAUCER *Former Age* 14 Vn-koruen [*v.r.* Vncaruyn] and vn-grobbed lay the vyne.

†**un'cost**^{1}. *Obs.*$^{-1}$ [UN-^{1} 4 b + COST *sb.*^{1}] Bad disposition, evil nature.

c **1220** *Bestiary* 192 in *O.E. Misc.* 7 Oc walke..mildelike among men; no mod ðu ne cune,..ne mannes vncost.

†**uncost**^{2}. *Obs.* [ad. MDu. (also mod.Du.) *onkosten* pl., f. *on-* UN-^{1} 4 b + *kost* COST *sb.*^{2} So G. *unkosten*.] Additional or incidental expenses. (Cf. ONCOST.)

c **1480** *Howard Househ. Bks.* (Roxb.) 285 Paid for the aparayll of a chymeny... Item, for uncostes of the same to brynge it to the water syde, .xd. **1488** *Acta Dom. Audit.* (1839) 117/1 þe Custemez, fraucht & vncostis maid be the said george of þe said malt. **1511-2** *Acc. Ld. High Treas. Scot.* IV. 334 For fraucht of sex kistis of sukkoure,..and for the uncostis of thame fra the Feir to Leith. **1581** *Burgh Rec. Edinb.* (1882) IV. 217 The pryce he gaif thairfor with all vncostes maid thairon to be payit to him.

un'cost^{3}. [UN-^{1} 12.] Lack of cost.

1868 PUSEY *Serm. Pharisaism* 9 Such acts..cost us individually little,..and may give evidence of their valuelessness by their uncost.

un'costly, *a.* [UN-^{1} 7. Cf. MDu. *oncostelijc*, *-lic*, Du. *onkostelijk*, MLG. *unkostlik*.] Inexpensive.

1638 JUNIUS *Paint. Ancients* 52 Making a very fine and uncostly shew. **1651** JER. TAYLOR *Serm. for Year* I. xv. 186 A mans spirit is naturally carelesse of baser and uncostly materials. **1798** *Poetry Anti-Jacobin* No. 15. 76 Uncostly cabbage springs from cabbage seed. **1837** LOCKHART *Scott* (1839) VII. 384 A volume every second month in this new and uncostly form. **1893** J. W. BARRY *Stud. Corsica* 204 The simple, primitive, and uncostly type that one sees at Pompeii.

Hence **un'costliness.**

1861 MILL *Utilit.* ii. 11 The greater permanency, safety, uncostliness,..of the former [pleasures].

un'couch, *v.* [UN-^{2} 5 and 7.]

1. *trans.* To raise up from a couch.

c **1430** *Pilgr. Lyf Manhode* II. xxxv. (1869) 154 It is a god that..wole that men cowchen him ofte and vncowche him. **1611** FLORIO, *Dislettare*, to vnbed, to vncouch.

2. To drive (an animal) out of its lair. Also *fig.*

a **1562** G. CAVENDISH *Wolsey* (1893) 89 The kyng.. commaunded the hunts to oncouche the boore. **1609** T. JACKSON *Londons New Yeeres Gift* 14 b, They are resembled vnto Foxes, whom we are now to vncouch. *Ibid.* 20 b, In the next place, we are to vncouch the Foxes Ecclesiasticall.

b. *intr.* Of an animal: To come out of its lair.

1860 LD. LYTTON *Lucile* II. iv. §11. 4 As a young fawn uncouches..from the fern where some hunter approaches.

Hence **un'couched** *ppl. a.*, **un'couching** *vbl. sb.*

1609 T. JACKSON (*title*), Londons New-Yeeres Gift, or the Vncovching of the Foxe. *Ibid.* Ded. A ij b, My selfe [shall] remaine the safer from the teeth of vncouched Foxes, if [etc.].

un'counsellable, *a.* [UN-^{1} 7 b, 5 b.]

1. Of persons: Not open to counsel.

Very common in the 17th century.

a **1578** LINDESAY (Pitscottie) *Chron. Scot.* (S.T.S.) I. 266 Takand no thocht as ane man wncons[al]able. **1646** J. WHITAKER *Uzziah* 28 Pride..makes the soul unconsellable. **1680** C. NESSE *Ch. Hist.* 60 Those sturdy rebels were uncounsellable. **1825** JAMIESON, *Unbiddable*, unadvisable, uncounselable.

†**2.** Of things: Inadvisable. *Obs.*

a **1674** CLARENDON *Hist. Reb.* (J.), It would have been uncounsellable to have march'd to any distance, and have left such an enemy at their backs.

un'counselled, *ppl. a.* (UN-^{1} 8.)

c **1400** *Rom. Rose* 6868 Wher so they clad or naked be Vncounceiled goth ther noon fro me. *a* **1500** *Voc.* in *MS. Harl.* 2257 fol. 69 b, *Inconsultus*, vnconsiled. **1648** HEXHAM II, *Onberaden*, Vncouncelled. **1786** *Francis the Philanthropist* III. 110 Parentless, uncounselled, and unguided, I yielded to his solicitations. **1796** BURKE *Let. Noble Lord* Wks. VIII. 17 When it appeared, nothing to subdue it was left uncounselled, nor unexecuted, as far as I could prevail. **1818** SCOTT *Br. Lamm.* xxix, Alone and uncounselled, I involved myself in these perils. **1887** BOWEN *Æneid* III. 452 Pilgrims depart uncounselled, and bear no love to the shrine.

un'countable, *a.* and *sb.* [UN-^{1} 7 b.]

A. *adj.* **1.** = UNACCOUNTABLE *a.* 2 b. *Obs.*$^{-1}$

a **1400-50** *Bk. Curtasye* 544 in *Babees Bk.*, The Countrollour shalle wryte to hym,..Vncountabulle he is, as y ȝou say.

2. a. Too numerous to be counted; innumerable. *spec.* in *Math.*, infinite and incapable of being put into a one-to-one correspondence with the integers. Opp. COUNTABLE *a.* 2 c.

1582 STANYHURST *Æneis*, etc. (Arb.) 142 But toe what eend labor I..Thee stars too number, poincts playnely vncounctabil opning. **1586** W. WEBBE *Eng. Poetrie* (Arb.) 36 The vncountable rabble of ryming Ballet makers. **1614** RALEIGH *Hist. World* I. i. §11. 15 So were not those vncountable glorious bodies set in the firmament, to no other end, than to adorne it. **1829** MARRYAT *F. Mildmay* xix, Nests in numbers uncountable. **1876** MRS. WHITNEY *Sights & Ins.* xxi, Millions of little uncountable, inseparable threads. **1952** R. L. WILDER *Introd. Foundation Math.* iv. 88 Some mathematicians do not admit the existence of an uncountable set of real numbers as a legitimate consequence of the argument. **1964** T. O. MOORE *Elem. Gen. Topology* i. 16 The set *R* of all real numbers is uncountable. **1971** *Sci. Amer.* Dec. 98/1 If the final destination of the bird is not specified, an uncountable infinity of such graphs can start at *C* and end anywhere on the track between *A* and *B*.

b. Of the pulse, etc.: Too rapid to be counted.

1823 GR. KENNEDY *Father Clement* x. (1824) 293 Ernest gave his hand, and Dormer pressed it on his temples. The full throb seemed uncountable. **1897** *Allbutt's Syst. Med.* III. 623 The tongue soon becomes dry, the pulse is uncountable.

3. Inestimable, immense.

1858 CARLYLE *Fredk. Gt.* III. viii. I. 263 Which has been of uncountable advantage to Brandenburg. **1860** *Cornh. Mag.* 134 To give uncountable happiness and delight to the world.

4. *Gram.* That cannot be counted; invariable in number; *spec.* of a noun: that cannot form a plural or be used with the indefinite article.

1924 [see B below]. **1948** A. S. HORNBY et al. *Learner's Dict. Current Eng.* p. x, The sign [U] is a warning that the noun..stands for a material, quality, etc. that is uncountable. The noun..may not be used with the indefinite article and must not be used in the plural. **1961** R. B. LONG *Sentence & its Parts* ix. 225 There is a tendency to assign uncountable-plural status and *mumps are dangerous to adults* is heard alongside the preferred *mumps is dangerous to adults*. **1966** J. DERRICK *Teaching Eng. to Immigrants* ii. 71 Foreign learners may misuse these 'uncountable' nouns by analogy with 'countable' ones and say such things as 'I want two milks', 'This is a rice', 'These are moneys', 'This is an ink', etc. **1980** *Chambers Universal Learners' Dict.* p. viii, *nu* This is short for *noun uncountable* and means that a noun (or a particular meaning) labelled in this way may not be used in the plural form.

B. *sb. Gram.* An uncountable noun or its referent.

1924 O. JESPERSEN *Philos. Gram.* xiv. 188 There is a class of 'things' to which words like one, two are inapplicable; we may call them uncountables, though dictionaries do not recognize this use of the word *uncountable*, which is known to them only in the relative sense 'too numerous to be (easily) counted'. **1965** K. SCHIBSBYE *Mod. Eng. Gram.* ii. 100 Though uncountables are normally in the singular, some of these (nearly) always appear in the plural: *oats*, *riches*. **1981** *Fremdsprachen* XXV. 236 Modern grammarians often divide nouns according to their capacity to be used with numerical values into: countables and uncountables.

Hence **ˌuncounta'bility**, the property of being uncountable; **un'countably** *adv.*

1599 NASHE *Lenten Stuffe* 27 Her Maiesties tributes and customes.. augmenteth and enlargeth vncountably. **1952** R. L. WILDER *Introd. Foundation Math.* iv. 88 The proof of the uncountability of *R*. **1955** J. L. KELLEY *Gen. Topology* iv. 122 The product of uncountably many topological spaces does not generally satisfy the first axiom of countability. **1977** *Sci. Amer.* Jan. 115/3 Conway's proof of the uncountability of Penrose patterns.. can be outlined as follows. **1981** *Ibid.* Nov. 29/1 Their number, however, will be uncountably infinite.

un'counted, *ppl. a.* (UN-¹ 8.)
a **1500** in *Makculloch & Gray MSS.* (S.T.S.) 55 Kingis & knichtis in company Vncountit curiously vp I kest. **1597** SHAKS. *2 Hen. IV*, Induct. 18 The blunt Monster, with vncounted heads, The still discordant, wauering Multitude. **1611** COTGR. s.v. *Brebis*, The wolfe eats counted, as well as uncounted, sheepe. **1677** SIR T. HERBERT *Trav.* (ed. 3) 375 Above threescore millions of Men, Women being uncounted. **1782** JOHNSON *Ode Death Levet* viii, The busy day—the peaceful night, Unfelt, uncounted, glided by. **1802–12** BENTHAM *Ration. Judic. Evid.* (1827) V. 700 A mass of uncounted money. **1837** CARLYLE *Misc.* (1840) V. 17 How they lay, for uncounted ages and æons,.. Silently imbedded in the rock. **1868** MORRIS *Earthly Par.* (1870) I. II. 511 Upon the floor uncounted medals lay.

un'countenanced, *ppl. a.* (UN-¹ 8.)
1776 MICKLE *Camoens' Lusiad* Introd. 129 Fanshaw's Lusiad, where.. there are puns, conceits, and low quaint expressions, uncountenanced by the original. **1820** T. MITCHELL *Aristoph.* I. 159 Desertion, uncountenanced as yet by the example of the unprincipled Alcibiades, was held in strong and merited abhorrence.

uncounte'racted, *ppl. a.* (UN-¹ 8.)
1809–10 COLERIDGE *Friend* (1818) III. 256 Some general law by the untempered and uncounteracted action of which both would be prevented. *a* **1864** FERRIER *Grk. Philos.* (1866) I. x. 217 All the.. difficulties.. would continue uncounteracted.

uncounter'balanced, *ppl. a.* (UN-¹ 8.)
1780 BENTHAM *Princ. Legisl.* xii. §23 In proportion to that part of the primary [mischief] which remains unexcluded or uncounterbalanced. **1862** LYTTON *Str. Story* II. 226 Power infinitely greater, and, when uncounterbalanced, infinitely more dangerous than that which superstition exaggerates in magic.

un'counterfeit, *a.* (UN-¹ 7.)
a **1542** WYATT in *Anglia* (1896) XIX. 186 And as it is it doeth appeare Vncontrefaict mistrust to barr. *c* **1585** [R. BROWNE] *Answ. Cartwright* 24 They are true and vncounterfaite sacraments. *a* **1626** BP. ANDREWES *Serm.* (1629) 64 If it be true, and vncounterfeit, a first degree it is, and not lightly to be accompted of. **1669** COKAINE *Poems* 150 Her breath was sweet as Venus bower of bliss, Her joyes uncounterfeit; and not remiss. **1834** DE QUINCEY *Autob. Sk.* Wks. 1853 I. 98 These proportions are best measured from the fathoming ground of a real uncounterfeit sympathy.

un'counterfeit, *v.* (UN-² 3.)
1580 T. LUPTON *Sivqila* 10 Sivqila. Alas, they counterfaite themselues, vntyll they get in. *Omen.* And when they vncounterfeite themselues agaìne, why are they not thrust out?
Hence **un'counterfeiting** *ppl. a.*
1912 [see *uncounterfeitable* s.v. UN-¹ 7 b (a)].

un'counterfeited, *ppl. a.* (UN-¹ 8.)
1571 GOLDING *Calvin on Ps.* Ep. Ded. 2 If your vertues be uncounterfayted. **1613** SIR W. ALEXANDER in Sidney *Arcadia* (1622) 343 Hee went with an vncounterfeited reuerence. **1625** K. LONG tr. *Barclay's Argenis* v. xiv. 383 All that were present honoured this reall and uncounterfeited vertue.

uncounter'mandable, *a.* (UN-¹ 7 b.)
1846 WORCESTER (citing M. Hale).

un'countrified, *ppl. a.* (UN-¹ 8.)
1839 HOOD *Rur. Felicity* 86 So one isn't so very uncountrified in the very heart of the town.

uncountry: see UN-¹ 12 b.

un'couple, *v.* [UN-² 4 b. Cf. MDu. *ontcoppelen*, *-copplen*, Du. *ontkoppelen*.]
1. a. *trans.* To release (dogs) from being fastened together in couples; to set free for the chase.
13.. *Guy Warw.* (A.) 2512 A gret bore þai founden, y-wis, & hij uncopled her houndis. **1390** GOWER *Conf.* I. 119 The houndes weren in a throwe Uncoupled and the hornes blowe. *c* **1410** *Master of Game* (MS. Digby 182) xiii, þe firste bolde houndes hunteth alle manere of beestes þat his maister will vncouple hym to. *a* **1450** *Knt. de la Tour* (1868) 43 The houndes were uncoupeled on hem, and chaced and bote hem spitously bi the eeres and thies. **1555** *Instit. Gentl.* H vj b, Likewise huntyng in his kinde, as to fleshe a dogge, to vncupple houndes, to followe them [etc.]. **1576** TURBERV. *Venerie* 102 They shall place their houndes in some faire place.., forbidding the varlet that he uncouple them not without their knowledge. **1600** SURFLET *Countrie Farme* VII. xxv. 847 He must not vncouple any of his dogs; but onely marke the way that the Hart runneth. **1821** SCOTT *Kenilw.* xii, Ere we had uncoupled the hounds, he.. turns bridle.. and leaves us to hunt at leisure by ourselves. **1842** MRS. GORE, etc. *Fascination* xi, Order the hounds to be uncoupled, and I will beat the underwood with three or four of the surest.
b. *absol.* (Also in fig. use.)
c **1386** CHAUCER *Monk's T.* 512 He maked hym so konnyng and so sowple That longe tyme it was er tirannye Or any vice dorste on hym vncowple. *c* **1410** *Master of Game* (MS. Digby 182) xxxv, þe herte houndes.. þat before haue be ladde by somme forster or parker þedur as þei shull vncouple. **1596** *Edward III*, I. ii. 91 What, are the stealing Foxes fled and gone, Before we could vncupple at their heeles? **1599** SHAKS. *Mids. N.* IV. i. 112 My Loue shall heare the musicke of my hounds. Vncouple in the Westerne valley.
2. To unfasten, disconnect, detach.
a **1533** LD. BERNERS *Gold Bk. M. Aurel.* (1546) N nj b, How far is our vnderstandyng vncoupled for thy thoughtes. **1548** UDALL, etc. *Erasm. Par. John* xiv. 87 b, That shall so couple you and vs together, that neyther lyfe nor death can vncouple vs. **1581** MULCASTER *Positions* xxxv. (1887) 124 Being so neare companions in linke, and not to be vncoupled in learning. **1685** DRYDEN *Lucretius* III. 10 When our mortal frame shall be disjoyn'd, The lifeless Lump uncoupled from the mind, From sense of grief and pain we shall be free. **1786** JEFFERSON *Writ.* (1859) II. 23 Congress have desired those States to uncouple the grants, so that each may come into force separately. **1858** O. W. HOLMES *Aut. Break.-t.* viii, Will nobody block those wheels, uncouple that pinion, cut the string that holds those weights? **1884** *Harper's Mag.* July 273/1 The locomotive is uncoupled from the cars.
3. a. *Biochem.* To separate the processes of (phosphorylation) *from* those of oxidation.
1948 *Jrnl. Biol. Chem.* CLXXIII. 808 These results indicate that DNP [*sc.* dinitrophenol] reversibly uncouples phosphorylation from oxidation. **1977** D. E. METZLER *Biochemistry* vii. 366/1 Arsenate is said to uncouple phosphorylation from oxidation.
b. *Physics.* To cause to cease to interact; to decouple (sense 2 a).
1980 *Chem. in Brit.* XVI. 456/2 This excited state may return to groundstate or undergo a chemical reaction or may uncouple two electron spins (intersystem crossing) to yield a triplet state.
Hence **un'coupled** *ppl. a.*¹; **un'coupler**: *spec.* in *Biochem.*, any agent that causes the uncoupling of oxidative phosphorylation.
1687 DRYDEN *Pal. & Arc.* II. 236 Th' appointed Place In which th' uncoupl'd Hounds began the Chace. **1705** STEVENS II, An Uncoupler, *desuñidor*. **1728** CHAMBERS *Cycl.*, *Decouple*, in Heraldry, the same as *Uncoupled*, i.e. parted or sever'd. **1803** SCOTT *Cadyow Castle* x, Steeds snort; uncoupled stag-hounds bay. **1954** *Proc. Nat. Acad. Sci.* XL. 919 Mitochondria suspensions taken from thyroxine-treated animals remain uncoupled. **1956** *Science* 22 June 1107/1 The factor specifically inhibits phosphorylation without affecting the oxidation of β-hydroxybutyrate and thus simulates the action of 2,4-dinitrophenol and other known uncouplers. **1976** *Sci. Amer.* June 44/3 Then we tried uncouplers: agents that allow electron transport to proceed but that in effect disconnect it from phosphorylation and thus from the ATP synthesis it usually accomplishes. **1979** *Nature* 8 Feb. 486/1 We have found that the rapid efflux of Ca^{2+} brought about by collapse of the membrane potential by uncouplers or antimycin A.. is not affected by tetracaine. **1981** *Plant Physiol.* LXVIII. 1485/1 The light saturated rate of photosystem I-dependent electron transport.. was increased by a high concentration of DCMU added to broken and uncoupled chloroplasts.

un'coupled, *ppl. a.*² [UN-¹ 8. Cf. MDu. *ongecoppelt*, Du. *ongekoppeld*.]
a. Not coupled or joined; left detached or separate.
1377 LANGL. *P. Pl.* B. Prol. 162 Vncoupled þei wenden Boþe in wareine & in waste where hem leue lyketh. *Ibid.* 206 Coupled & vncoupled. *c* **1430** LYDG. *Min. Poems* (Percy Soc.) 32 Thouhe she be yong, yet wol she wele abide, Uncoupled to a fresshe man of iunesse. **1589** PUTTENHAM *Eng. Poesie* II. x. (Arb.) 102 There is a band to be giuen euery verse in a staffe, so as none fall out alone or vncoupled. **1625** MILTON *On Death of Fair Infant* 13 Th' infamous blot, Of long-uncoupled bed, and childless eld. **1659** CHAMERLAYNE *Pharonnida* (T.), Vows, whose harsh events must be Uncoupled cold virginity. **1818** COLEBROOKE *Obligations* 55 Exorbitancy of price too, uncoupled with fraud. **1869** COLBURN in *Eng. Mech.* 19 Mar. 579/2 There was not.. an engine.. having.. uncoupled driving-wheels.
b. *Physics.* Not physically interacting.
1965 W. T. THOMSON *Vibration Theory & Applications* vi. 167 The two pendulums behave as if they were uncoupled and independent of each other. **1981** *Sci. Amer.* July 56/1 Wiesel's computer simulations of the evolution of the resonance begin with Io, Europa and Ganymede in uncoupled orbits and with Io driven outward by its tidal interaction with Jupiter.

un'coupling, *vbl. sb.* [f. UNCOUPLE *v.*]
a. The action of the verb.
c **1369** CHAUCER *Dethe Blaunche* 377 With a grete horne [he] blewe thre mote At the vncoupylynge of hys houndys. *c* **1410** *Master of Game* (MS. Digby 182) xxxv, He shulde blowe iii. longe moot to þe vncoupelynge. **1470–85** MALORY *Arthur* x. lii. 500 To the vncoupelynge, to the sekynge, to the rechate [etc.]. **1611** COTGR., *Descouple*, the vncoupling of houndes, or loossing them after their game. **1954** *Proc. Nat. Acad. Sci.* XL. 919 As much thyroxine was carried down by rat mitochondria which did not show any appreciable uncoupling. **1983** *Nature* 10 Feb. 512/1 A progressive uncoupling of [bacterial] growth and H_2S production was observed during approach to the stationary state.
b. *attrib.* and *Comb.*, as ***uncoupling chain***, ***lever***, ***pole***, ***rod***; **uncoupling agent** *Biochem.*, = UNCOUPLER.
1879 *Car-Builder's Dict.* 172/1 *Uncoupling-chain*, a chain by which the uncoupling lever of a Miller-coupler is connected with the coupling-hook or draw-bar. *Ibid.*, *Uncoupling-lever, for Miller-coupler*, a lever attached to the platform of a car, and connected by a chain with a Miller coupling-hook or draw-bar to disengage or uncouple it from the one on the adjoining car. **1895** *Ibid.* (ed. 3) 139/2 *Uncoupling-rod*,.. a rod connecting the uncoupling-lever with the lock of an automatic coupler. **1956** *Jrnl. Biol. Chem.* CCXXII. 338 Certain uncoupling agents such as thyroxine and Ca^{++} caused rapid swelling of the mitochondria. **1976** A. WHITE *Long Silence* ix. 88 Two trains were being worked... I counted five men walking about the yard with long uncoupling poles. **1981** *Arch. Microbiol.* CXXIX. 94/1 Inhibition was relieved by low concentrations of uncoupling agent.

uncou'rageous, *a.* (UN-¹ 7.)
1878 DOWDEN *Stud. Lit.* 123 Wordsworth's.. uncourageous elder years.

un'coursed, *a.* [UN-¹ 9.] Of masonry: Not laid or set in courses.
1825 J. NICHOLSON *Operat. Mechanic* 537 In uncoursed rubble the stones are placed promiscuously in the wall. **1886** WILLIS & CLARK *Cambridge* I. 17 Its wall.. is of rough uncoursed rubble work.

un'courted, *ppl. a.* (UN-¹ 8.)
1595 DANIEL *Civ. Wars* II. lii, Uncourted, unrespected, unobeyed. **1640** HABINGTON *Castara* III. (Arb.) 117 While I my life of fame beguile And under my owne vine uncourted sit. **1714** MANDEVILLE *Fab. Bees* (1733) II. 224 No female of twelve would be refractory, if applied to; or remain long uncourted, if there were men. **1796** MME. D'ARBLAY *Camilla* V. 295 Devotion paid straight forward, and uncourted.

un'courteous, *a.* [UN-¹ 7.] Wanting in courtesy; discourteous: **a.** Of persons.
α. **1303** R. BRUNNE *Handl. Synne* 6798 þys ryche man, as þe gospel seys, Was but to o man vncurteys. *a* **1352** MINOT in *Pol. Poems* (Rolls) I. 79 Unkind he was and uncurtayse. *a* **1400–50** *Bk. Curtasye* 128 in *Babees Bk.*, Dip not þi thombe þy drynke into, þou art uncurtayse yf þou hit do. **1470–85** MALORY *Arthur* IV. xxiii. 151 Yf syre Pelleas had ben as vncurteis to yow as ye haue ben to hym ye hadde bene a dede knyghte. **1533** MORE *Apol.* ix. Wks. 865/2 Were not a manne.. worthye to bee compted vncourteyse, that woulde [etc.]. **1548** ELYOT, *Inclemens*,.. vngentil: vncurteis.
β. **13..** *E.E. Allit. P.* A. 303, I halde þat iueler lyttel to prayse,.. & much to blame & vn-cortoyse. **1530** PALSGR. 328 Uncourtoyse, *ingrat*. **1552** HULOET, Vncurtoyse, *illiberalis*.
γ. **1426** AUDELAY *Poems* (Percy Soc.) 14 He is unkynd and uncurtes. **1456** SIR G. HAYE *Law Arms* (S.T.S.) 222 Quhasa did the contrair he war ungentill, uncurtas, and unconnand. ? *a* **1500** *Chester Pl.* II. 105 God forbyde that we were So uncurtise to you heare. **1542** UDALL *Erasm. Apoph.* 264 b, Hymselfe remained prisoner emong the most uncourtise Silicians. **1575** LANEHAM *Let.* 41 Yoor only prezens shallbe matter sufficient of abandoning this vncurtess knight.
δ. **1535** COVERDALE *Bar.* iv. 15 An vncurteous people, and of a straunge language. **1551** RECORDE *Pathw. Knowl.* Pref., If I were as vncurteous as you vnkind, I shuld vtterly refuse to do them any good. **1652** J. TAYLOR (Water P.) *Short Relat. Long Journ.* (Spenser Soc.) 23 Then most uncurteous Mistris, quoth I, I doubt I must bee necessitated to take up my lodging in the Field. **1801** *Lusignan* II. 49 Strangers, you seem not uncourteous. **1858** TROLLOPE *Dr. Thorne* xxxiii, She was more than ordinarily anxious not to appear uncourteous or unkind to him.
b. Of actions, speech, etc.
c **1490** *Plumpton Corr.* (Camden) 71, I besech you speake to my master, that no uncurtes dealing be had with none of his servants. *a* **1548** HALL *Chron.*, *Hen. IV*, 19 He beyng netteled with these uncurteous ye unvertuous prickes & thornes, serched out the authours. **1594** HOOKER *Eccl. Pol.* IV. xiii. §10 They ease us of that vncourteous burden. **1601** SHAKS. *Twel. N.* v. i. 369 Vpon some stubborne and vncourteous parts We had conceiu'd against him. **1828** SCOTT *F.M. Perth* xxiv, It would be, therefore, uncourteous to leave my readers under any doubt concerning the agency. **1875** W. S. HAYWARD *Love agst. World* 11, 'I know what I am doing,' was the uncourteous reply.

un'courteously, *adv.* [f. prec. + -LY². Cf. ON. *úkurteisliga* and INCOURTEOUSLY.] In an uncourteous manner; discourteously, uncivilly.
α. **1338** R. BRUNNE *Chron.* (1810) 143 Loke how kyng Philip said vncurteisly, Daþet haf his lip, & his nose þerby. **1393** LANGL. *P. Pl.* C. XIV. 172 Ich took kepe How vncorteisliche þe cok hus kynde forth strenede. **1477** EARL RIVERS *Dictes* (1877) 56 b, If he demaunde ony thing he shal axe it vncurtaisly. **1565** COOPER *Thesaurus* s.v. *Inclementer*, To speake vncourteisly or churlishly to his father.
β. *c* **1485** *Digby Myst.* (1882) IV. 655 He & I com both of your kyn, And that ye kithe vn-curteslye. **1523** LD. BERNERS *Froiss.* I. cccxxii. 131 b/1 They be men of warr, suche as can nat lyue, but by pyllage & robbery: and haue vncurtesly ouer ryden oure countrees. **1548** CRANMER *Catech.* 49 b, Beware good children yᵗ you depise not your parentes, or vncurtesely entreat them.
γ. **1535** COVERDALE *1 Esdras* vi. 33 To deale vncurteously with the house of the Lorde at Ierusalem. **1575** VAUTROLLIER *Luther on Ep. Gal.* 25 Paul might have handled the Galatians more uncurteously. **1632** SHERWOOD, Vncourteously, *incivilement*. **1849** EASTWICK *Dry Leaves* 118 They were.. at last dismissed uncourteously with a refusal. **1856** KANE *Arct. Expl.* II. ix. 94 A cordial meal it is. I am sorry to hurry over it so uncourteously.

un'courteousness. [f. as prec. + -NESS.] The quality of being uncourteous; discourtesy.
1530 PALSGR. 285/1 Uncourtesnesse, *ingratitude*. **1531** TINDALE *Exp. 1 John* (1537) 99 Al blameth his vncourteousnesse. **1597** J. KING *On Jonas* (1618) 598 The time inuiting mee thereunto,.. and the vncurteousnes of these our times, requiring no less. **1681** [see UNCONDESCENSION]. **1843** *Florist's Jrnl.* (1846) IV. 95 He accuses us of 'uncourteousness' and 'partiality'.

† **un'courtesy.** *Obs.* [UN-¹ 12. Cf. ON. *úkurteisi*.] Discourtesy, incivility.
c **1380** *Sir Ferumb.* 2058 'Mahoun,' quaþ sche, 'ȝyue þe schame for þyn oncortesye!' *c* **1400** *Rom. Rose* 3587, I wole in no wise.. Denye that ye haue asked heere; It were to gret uncurtesie. *c* **1449** PECOCK *Repr.* II. iii. 151 Thou art to be excusid of vncurtesie bi thi greet folie and madnes. **1523** LD. BERNERS *Froiss.* I. cvii. 129 Certaynly cosyn, ye haue done me great vncourtesy, to fight with our ennemyes without me. **1569** NEWTON *Cicero's Olde Age* 4 Unbrideled insolencie, and blunt uncurtesie. **1605** *1st Pt. Jeronimo* II. iii. 97 Your wife condemns you of a vncurtesie.

un'courtierlike, *a.* (UN-[1] 7 c.)
1786 MME. D'ARBLAY *Diary* (1842) III. 103 Here we had new court scenery, in which I acted but an uncourtier-like part. **1812** R. H. in *Examiner* 23 Nov. 747/2 Excuse my.. uncourtier like language. **1857** LD. GRANVILLE in Ld. Fitzmaurice *Life* (1905) I. ix. 224 He talked of the advantages and disadvantages of being Prince of Wales in a very uncourtierlike manner.

un'courting, *ppl. a.* (UN-[1] 10 and 5 d.)
1744 ELIZA HEYWOOD *Female Spect.* No. 3 (1748) I. 133 Uncourting, unindebted to favour, a native greatness shines through his whole deportment. **1887** C. C. R. *Minora Carmina* 303 She came.., Uncourting gaze of curious men.

un'courtlike, *a.* (UN-[1] 7 c.)
1659 FULLER *App. Inj. Innoc.* III. 21 The roughnesse of his uncourt-like nature, sweetned many men when they least looked for it. **1733** LD. CHESTERF. in *Lett. C'tess Suffolk* (1824) II. 63 Your letter..I must look upon as a most uncommon and uncourtlike piece of friendship. **1865** STOPFORD BROOKE in *Life & Lett.* (1917) I. x. 179 He is—they say on account of this uncourtlike manner—a great favourite with the Queen.

un'courtliness. [f. next.] Lack of courtliness; uncourtly behaviour.
1668 H. MORE *Div. Dial.* v. xxi. (1713) 474 A great piece of roughness, rudeness and uncourtliness. **1710** ADDISON *Whig Exam.* No. 5 ¶11 Notwithstanding the uncourtliness of their phrases the sense was very honest. **1748** RICHARDSON *Clarissa* (1811) I. v. 34 Our sex perhaps expect to hear a little—uncourtliness shall I call it? from the husband.

un'courtly, *a.* [UN-[1] 7.]
1. Not adapted or suited to the Court; *esp.* not sufficiently polished or refined: **a.** Of persons, their attributes, etc.
1598 CHAPMAN *Contn. Marlowe's Hero & Leander* III. 251 This euent vncourtly Hero thought Her inward guilt would in her lookes haue wrought. **1632** MASSINGER & FIELD *Fatal Dowry* III. i, You will find it safer Rather to be uncourtly than immodest. *a* **1662** HEYLIN *Laud* (1668) 57 A man of independent Fortune..but otherwise of an uncourtly disposition. **1759** STERNE *Tr. Shandy* II. ix, A little squat, uncourtly figure. **1838** EMERSON *Misc. Papers, Milton* Wks. (Bohn) III. 294 Lord Bacon..shrinks and falters before the absolute and uncourtly Puritan. **1876** BANCROFT *Hist. U.S.* IV. xxiv. 491 The retired and uncourtly scholar.
b. Of things or actions.
1640 HABINGTON *Q. of Arragon* I. i. B ij b, His Garbe was so uncourtly. **1727** POPE *Let. to Gay* 16 Oct., I can only add a plain, uncourtly Speech. **1775** ADAIR *Amer. Ind.* 341 The uncourtly leave he took of our gallant, and faithful old friends. **1827** POLLOK *Course T.* IX. 653 No longer hid by coarse uncourtly garb.
2. Not subservient to, not seeking to please, the Court.
1712 SWIFT *Cond. Allies* Wks. 1751 II. 127 The present Lord Treasurer,..not entering into those refinements of paying the public money upon private considerations, hath been so uncourtly as to stop it. **1821** W. H. LYTTELTON in *Corr. Lady Lyttelton* ix. (1912) 237 The Archbishop's sermon [at the Coronation].., on the whole uncourtly enough to..diplease the courtiers. **1855** MACAULAY *Hist. Eng.* xx. IV. 476 Two eminent orators, who had, during some years, been on the uncourtly side of every question.

'uncous, *a. rare.* [f. L. *unc-us* hook, or *unc-us* adj., hooked.] Hooked, curved.
1658 SIR T. BROWNE *Gard. Cyrus* iii. 124 The calicular shafts [of the teasel] and uncous disposure of their extremities. *a* **1682** —— *Pseud. Ep.* (1686) v. i. 191 The uncous and pointed extremity of their Bill.

uncouth (ʌnˈku:θ), *a.* and *sb.* Forms: α. 1 uncuþ, 1–3 uncuð (3 vn-), 2 unkuþ, 3 -kuð, 4 un-, vncuth (-cut), 5 vnchut; 3 vnecouþ, 3–4 onecouþ, 4 vnkouþ; 4–7 vn-, 4– uncouth (5–6 *Sc.* wn-, 6 on-), 4–6 vnkouth (5 -koud, 6 *Sc.* wn-, onkouth), 6 *Sc.* oncoutht, 6–8 uncooth, 7 uncough; 4 oncouþe, 4–5 vn-, unkouþe, 4–6 vn-, uncouthe (4 -kouthe, 5 *Sc.* wncou(y)the, 6 vncovthe); 3–5 vncowþe, -the (5 -k(u)owthe), 4 vnkowth (6 on-), 5 oncowth, 6 oncowght. β. 2 uncoð-, 3 vncoþ-, vnekoþ-, 4 vnchoþe, 5 -koth, 5–6 -cothe, 6–7 vn-, uncoth. (See also UNQUOD, -QUOTH, and UNCO.) [OE. *uncúþ* (f. *un-* UN-[1] + *cúþ* COUTH *a.*), = MDu. *oncont* (Du. *onkond*), OHG. *unkund*, *-chunt* (MHG. *unkunt*), ON. *úkunnr* (obs. Da. *ukund*), Goth. *unkunþs*. In many examples from the 17th and 18th centuries the exact sense is difficult to determine.]
A. *adj.* †**1.** Of facts or matters of knowledge: Unknown; also, not certainly known, uncertain. *Obs.*
c **897** K. ÆLFRED *Gregory's Past. C.* Pref. ad fin., Uncuð [hit is] hu longe ðær swæ ȝelærede biscepas sien. *c* **900** tr. *Baeda's Hist.* II. xiii. (1890) 134 To wiðmetenesse þære tide, þe us uncuð is. **971** *Blickl. Hom.* 51 Us is swiþe uncuþ hwæt ure yrfeweardas..don willon æfter urum life. *c* **1000** ÆLFRIC *On Old Test.* (Gr.) 4 God..sealde heora ælcum synderlice spræce, þæt heora ælcum wæs uncuð, hwæt oðer sæde. *a* **1200** *Vices & Virtues* 23 Ic bliðeliche ðine rad wile hlesten,..ȝif ðu me ðin uncuðe name woldest kyðen. **1303** R. BRUNNE *Handl. Synne* 4296 Ful fewe bedys are yn hys mouþe, He vsyþ none; þey are vncouthe. **1423** JAS. I *Kingis Q.* lxiii, Quhen all ȝour merci rew vpon ȝour man, Quhois seruice is ȝit vncouth vnto ȝow? **1447** BOKENHAM *Seyntys* Introd. (Roxb.) 4 Wych story is no thyng unkouwthe At mownt Flask. **1533** BELLENDEN *Livy* I. viii. (S.T.S.) I. 48 This ordour of preisthede was..nocht vncouth to þe pepill of albane. *a* **1577** GASCOIGNE *Dan Barth.* Wks. (1587) 101 With stopping sobs..he sought To utter that which was to one uncouth. **1616** BOYS *Wks.* (1622) 871 Now the whole superficies of the earth as well vncouth as discouered, is but a little point. **1650** R. GELL *Serm.* 8 Aug. 2 A kind of attestation not uncouth among the Poets.
2. With which one is not acquainted or familiar; unfamiliar, unaccustomed, strange: **a.** Of ways, paths, etc. (frequently passing into sense 5).
α. *Beowulf* 1410 Ofereode þa æþelinga bearn..enge anpaðas, uncuð ȝelad. *a* **1000** *Boeth. Metr.* xiii. 58 Merecondel scyfð on ofdæle, uncuðne weȝ nihtes ȝeneðeð. **1387–8** T. USK *Test. Love* II. xi. (Skeat) l. 45 Folisshe ignoraunce mis-ledeth wandring wrecches by uncouth wayes that shulden be forleten. *c* **1450** *Merlin* xx. 314 Ride euer be nyght and by the moste vn-cowth weyes that ye may. **1582** STANYHURST *Æneis* II. (Arb.) 67, I wandred through streets and passages vncooth. **1611** FLORIO, *Inuio sentiere*, an vngone, vntroden or vncouth path or way. **1667** MILTON *P.L.* x. 475 But I Toild out my uncouth passage, forc't to ride Th' untractable Abysse. **1691** SWIFT *Athenian Soc.* Wks. 1755 IV. I. 231 To grope her uncouth way After a mighty light that leads her wand'ring eye. **1704** —— *T. Tub* xi, They would make choice of the..most uncouth rounds ..that they might be sure to avoid one another.
β. **1579** FENTON *Guicciard.* XIV. 829 Frauncis Sforce taking a straunge and vncothe waye, was receyued at Sesto by Prospero. **1588** GREENE *Alcida* Wks. (Grosart) IX. 55 Wandring awhile by many vncoth paths, at last wee came into a faire place. **1600** J. LANE *Tom Tel-troth* 69 Nature.. Is now inforc'd in vncoth walkes to stray.
b. Of lands or places.
α. *c* **960** *Rule St. Benet* lxi. 109 Se utancumena munuc, þe of uncuðum eardum cymð. *c* **1175** *Lamb. Hom.* 157 Wume nu..þet ic scal wunien in unkuþe londe. *c* **1200** *Trin. Coll. Hom.* 53 Hu muȝe we singen godes loft song in uncuðe londe? *c* **1290** *S. Eng. Leg.* I. 325 þus feor in one-couþe londe Mit deol and soruwe ich habbe i-leoued. **13..** *Guy Warw.* (A.) 1192 Time it is þat ich fond To winne priis in vncouþe lond. *c* **1400** *Destr. Troy* 12510 The sea..Depertid the pepull, pyne to be-hold, In costes vnkowthe. *a* **1450** *Le Morte Arth.* 851 She it yaff to the scottisshe knight, For he was of an vnkouth stede. *a* **1470** HARDING *Chron.* CCXLI. vii, Who hath power to make you resistence In any wise, in any vncouth lande? **1534** MORE *Comf. agst. Trib.* III. Wks. 1237/2 Whan they shall..cary vs farre from home into a straunge vncouth lande. **1632** RUTHERFORD *Lett.* (1862) I. xxvi. 97 The silly stranger in an uncouth country must take with a smoky inn. **1671** MILTON *Samson* 333 Brethren and men of Dan, for such ye seem, Though in this uncouth place. **1722** DE FOE *Plague* (1840) 97 [They] wandered into fields and woods, and into secret uncouth places. **1824** SCOTT *Redgauntlet* let. xi, Ye see, birkie, it is nae chancy thing to tak a stranger traveller for a guide, when you are in an uncouth land.
β. **1297** R. GLOUC. (Rolls) 6445 þat he hom to deþe broȝte So ver in vnekoþe lond, þat no mon of hom ne roȝte. *c* **1400** *Destr. Troy* 531 A sure knyghte..ayres into vnkoth lond auntres to seche.
c. Of persons.
For the early legal use see HOGHENHINE. For the phrase *uncouth, unkissed*, see UNKISSED.
c **893** K. ÆLFRED *Oros.* VI. xxxi. 286 þa com him onȝean an uncuð mon, & ofstong Iulianus. *c* **1000** *Ags. Gosp.* John x. 5 Ne fyliað hiȝ uncuþum,..forþam þe hiȝ ne ȝecneowon uncuþra stefne. *c* **1000** ÆLFRIC *Saints' Lives* xxiii. 613 þæt þær ȝelæht wære binnan þære byriȝ an uncuð ȝeong man. *a* **1175** *Cott. Hom.* 231 Scewie we þes uncoðe mæn ur ȝefo. *c* **1205** LAY. 7107 Seoððen her com vncuð folc faren in þessere þeode. *a* **1225** *Ancr. R.* 54 A meiden..eode vt uor to biholden uncuðe wummen. *a* **1300** *Cursor M.* 5495 þar ras an vncut king þat had to ioseph na knauing. **1362** LANGL. *P. Pl.* A. VIII. 141 Vnkouþe knihtes schul come þi kingdam to clayme. *c* **1400** *Ywaine & Gaw.* 501 Unkowth men wele may he shende, That to his felows es so unhende. **1446** LYDG. *Nightingale Poems* ii. 44 From the god of love To me was sent an vnkouth messangier. **1470–85** MALORY *Arthur* III. vi. 105 Vncouth men ye shold debate with al & no broder with broder. **1596** WARNER *Alb. Eng.* XI. lxii. (1612) 272 They, seeing vncouth Men and Ships, weare wondringly agaste.
d. Of peoples or nations.
c **1000** ÆLFRIC *Deut.* xxviii. 36 Drihten sent uncuðe þeode ofer eow, þa þe ȝe ne cunnon. *a* **1300** *Cursor M.* 1171 In vncuth lede sal end mi wa. *Ibid.* 4177 þan sagh þai cumand be þe stret Marchands of an vncuth thede. *c* **1400** *St. Alexius* (Trin.) 258 Tydynges none hy ne broȝte Of his sone, þat him soȝte In vncouþe þede. *c* **1450** LYDG. *Secrees* 219 In Rethoryk he hadde experyence Of euery strange, unkouth nacyoun.
†**e.** *Sc.* Pertaining to other nations; foreign. *Obs.*
1533 BELLENDEN *Livy* II. xv. (S.T.S.) I. 187 How beit þe ciete was in quiet þis ȝere but ony vncouth or domestic weris. *Ibid.* v. xxiv. II. 232 Nocht standing oure neir þe sey to resaif dammaige be perell of oncouth flotis.
3. Of an unknown or unfamiliar character; unusual, uncommon, strange; marvellous. Now *rare.*
Very common *c* 1590–1700. In later use passing into 6.
Beowulf 876 Secg..welhwylc ȝecwæð, þæt he fram Siȝemunde secgan hyrde ellendædum uncuþes fela. *c* **900** tr. *Baeda's Hist.* II. xii. (1890) 128 þa ȝeseah he..sumne mon wið his gongan..uncuðes ȝegyrlan. *c* **1000** *Sax. Leechd.* I. 194 ðif men þæt heafod berste, oððe uncuð swyle onȝesitte. *a* **1122** *O.E. Chron.* an. 1106, Hiȝ ma on þison timon uncuðra steorra ȝesawon. *c* **1200** ORMIN 228 þeȝȝ wisstenn þatt himm wass þatt daȝȝ Summ unncuþ sihhþe shæwedd. *a* **1300** *Cursor M.* 22494 Efter þe tua fules þe þrid, An uncuth dai þan es it kidd. **1340–70** *Alisaunder* 683 Queme yee me might, Of this unkouth case too karp þe soothe. *c* **1384** CHAUCER *H. Fame* I. 1279 Ther saugh I Colle tregetour Vpon a table of Sygamour Pley an vncouthe thynge to telle. *c* **1386** —— *Sqr.'s T.* 284 Who couþe telle you þe forme of daunces So vncouthe. *c* **1430** LYDG. *Min. Poems* (Percy Soc.) 25 The tragedies divers and unkouth Of morall Senec. **1430–40** —— *Bochas* IX. xxxiii. 34 b, His vncouth story breuely to compyle. **1448–9** METHAM *Amoryus & Cl.* 1278 The venym owte off hys tayle in-to hys mowth He drawyth anone..; Thow yt gretly be meruulus and oncowth. *a* **1513** FABYAN *Chron.* v. lxxxiii. 61 The Kynge had maryed a woman of vncowght beleue. **1548** UDALL, etc. *Erasm. Par. Matt.* xxi. 101 Moued with this uncouthe syght. **1582** STANYHURST *Æneis* III. (Arb.) 80, I through pangs vncoth vnhabled,.. thus fumbled an aunswer. **1603** B. JONSON *Sejanus* III. iii, It is no uncouth thing To see fresh buildings from old ruines spring. **1648** *Hunting of Fox* 24 Saint Bridgit her selfe, the mother of so many uncouth Revelations. **1693** N. MATHER in Owen *Holy Spirit* Pref., Novel and uncouth Terms foreign to the Things of God. **1710** BERKELEY *Princ. Hum. Knowl.* I. §1 We are insensibly drawn into uncouth paradoxes. **1748** HARTLEY *Observ. Man* I. iii. 350 The Speculations may seem uncouth to those who are not conversant in Mathematical Inquiries. **1801** tr. *Gabrielli's Myst. Husb.* III. 173 When James's uncouth story was absolutely confirmed. **1847** G. HARRIS *Ld. Hardwicke* II. viii. 237 To gaze on the uncouth, unaccustomed spectacle presented by the Highlanders. **1864** BOWEN *Logic* v. 136 It would certainly be accounted a forced and uncouth assertion.
†**b.** Alien or foreign *to* something. *Obs. rare.*
c **1374** CHAUCER *Boeth.* II. pr. ii. (1868) 34 Syn þat stedfastnesse is vnkouþ to my maneres. **1697** J. SERGEANT *Solid Philos.* 273 Any other and higher Points, especially such as are Uncouth to..Natural Reason.
†**c.** Unrecognizable. *Obs.*[−1]
1390 GOWER *Conf.* II. 318 So what with blod and what with teres..He made hire faire face uncouth.
†**4.** Of a strange and unpleasant or distasteful character. *Obs.*
c **1380** WYCLIF *Sel. Wks.* III. 242 þis unkouþe discencioun þat is bitwixe þes popes. **1430–40** LYDG. *Bochas* II. xxviii. (1554) 64 Atwene them, there was an uncouth strife. **1586** DAY *Eng. Secretorie* I. (1625) 46 The sight became so vncouth, as all men shamed, each one feared, and none durst abide it. **1641** BROME *Joviall Crew* I. (1652) B iv, I hop'd thou hadst abjur'd that uncough practice. **1696** WHISTON *The. Earth* (1722) 7 An uncouth and incredible system. **1719** DE FOE *Crusoe* II. (Globe) 382 The Sight, you may be sure, was something uncouth to our Spaniards. **1785** BURKE *Nabob Arcot* Wks. IV. 320 To some the subject is strange and uncouth; to several harsh and distasteful. **1797** GODWIN *Enquirer* I. vi. 43 They will not accept an uncouth and disgustful lesson.
†**b.** Of smells, sounds, etc. *Obs.*
1600 HOLLAND *Livy* XXI. lv. 425 The Elephants..frighted the horses especially, & not onely with the straunge sight, but also with as uncouth a sent and savor. **1658** ROWLAND tr. *Moufet's Theat. Ins.* 909 Poysoned Honey..hath a strange and uncouth smell. **1665** SIR T. HERBERT *Trav.* (1677) 29 Toddy..tasts like Rhenish; at first draught it is uncouth, but every draught tasts better than other. **1720** DE FOE *Capt. Singleton* xv. (1840) 257 A strange noise more uncouth than any they had ever heard.
†**c.** Unseemly, indecorous. *Obs.*
1589 GREENE *Menaphon* (Arb.) 40 Samela meruailed at such an vncouth banquet. **1600** FAIRFAX *Tasso* I. xviii. 4 Nor sweld his brest with vncouth pride therefore, That heau'n on him aboue this charge had laide. **1659** BROME *Eng. Moor* I. iii, Which uncouth Policie to sorrow leads Thousands a thousand wayes.
5. Of places: Not commonly known or frequented; solitary, desolate, wild, rugged, rough.
α. *a* **1542** WYATT in *Anglia* (1897) XX. 432 So close the Cave was and unkouth Y[t] none but God was record off his payne. **1600** SHAKS. *A.Y.L.* II. vi. 6 If this vncouth Forrest yeeld any thing sauage, I wil either be food for it, or bring it for foode to thee. **1633** T. STAFFORD *Pac. Hib.* I. xviii. (1821) 191 Lurking in desart, uncouth, and unknowen places. **1653** H. COGAN *Diod. Sic.* 256 Wandring alone through desert and uncouth places, he died with sorrow. **1728** MORGAN *Algiers* I. iii. 72, I have met with the Ruins of several stately Buildings..in uncouth Mountains. **1748** *Anson's Voy.* I. vii. 73 This uncouth and rugged coast. **1814** SCOTT *Wav.* lxiii, He soon pursued a very uncouth path. **1830** J. G. STRUTT *Sylva Brit.* 119 The Prior of St. Mary's at York was chosen Abbot by the Monks; with whom they withdrew into this uncouth desert.
β. **1582** STANYHURST *Æneis* IV. (Arb.) 99 When they toe thee mountayns and too layrs vncoth aproched. **1595** *Locrine* III. vi. 7 Where may I finde some hollow vncoth rocke, Where I may..ban my fill?
b. Of life, surroundings, etc.: Unattractive, unpleasant, uncomfortable. *Obs.* or *arch.*
1611 CORYAT *Crudities* 409 Duke Iohn..liued a most vncouth and solitary life in the desert forrests. *a* **1627** MIDDLETON *Witch* II. i, 'Tis so uncouth Living i' th' country, now I'm us'd to th' city. **1670** CLARENDON *Hist. Reb.* XII. §130 [He] order'd his other small Troops to contain themselves in those uncouth Quarters, in which they were. **1685** in *Verney Mem.* (1907) II. 404 This place is very uncouth to me now you are gone out of it! **1888** STEVENSON *Black Arrow* III. iv, The pair were left to their uncouth reflections for the night.
†**c.** Strange; uneasy; at a loss. *Obs.*[−1]
1660 PEPYS *Diary* 26 May, All the great company being gone, I found myself very uncouth all this day for want thereof.
6. Of an unfamiliar or strange appearance or form; *spec.*, having an odd, uncomely, awkward, or clumsy shape or bearing.
1513 DOUGLAS *Æneid* XI. xv. 12 In brovne sangwane weill dycht Abuf hys onkouth armour blomand brycht. **1600** FAIRFAX *Tasso* II. 38 In vncouth armes yclad and strange disguise. **1613** PURCHAS *Pilgrimage* 685 An vncouth Idoll, great and hollow, fastened in the wall with lime. **1653** H. MORE *Antid. Ath.* II. ii. §14 The Frost and Wind will draw upon Doors and glass-Windows pretty uncouth streaks like feathers and other fooleries. **1713** POPE *Windsor For.* 403 Then ships of uncouth form shall stem the tide. **1770** COOK *Voy. round World* II. ix. (1773) III. 453 The dress of a New Zealander is certainly..the most uncouth that can be imagined. **1838** LYTTON *Leila* I. v, A profusion of strange and uncouth instruments and machines. **1845** FORD *Handbk. Spain* I. 53 The ponies of Gallicia, although ugly and uncouth, are admirably suited to the wild hilly country.

1879 H. PHILLIPS *Notes Coins* 12 A heavy and uncouth gold British coin of remote antiquity.

b. Of persons: Awkward and uncultured in appearance or manners. Also *transf.*

1732 SIR C. WOGAN *Let. to Swift* 27 Feb., The very name of Irish carries so uncouth an idea along with it. **1740** SOMERVILLE *Hobbinolia* I. 165 The jocund Troop.. incessant shake Their uncouth brawny Limbs. **1798** S. & HT. LEE *Canterb. T.* II. 64, I have never seen this redoubtable, troublesome, uncouth cousin of mine. **1825** MACAULAY *Ess., Milton* (1851) I. 24 People saw nothing of the godly but their uncouth visages. **1828** LYTTON *Pelham* iii, A raw, uncouth sort of young man, with a green coat and lank hair. **1868** FARRAR *Seekers* I. vi. (1875) 75 He dragged out an uncouth panic-stricken mortal.

Comb. **1809** W. IRVING *Knickerb.* (1861) 57 Several uncouth-looking beings seated on rocks. **1869** TOZER *Highl. Turkey* I. 292 The shepherds were an uncouth-looking set.

c. Of language, style, etc.

1694 PENN *Rise & Progr. Quakers* v, Though that side of his understanding which lay next to the world, and especially the expression of it, might sound uncouth and unfashionable to nice ears. **1699** GARTH *Dispens.* IV. 50 Harsh words, tho' pertinent, uncouth appear. **1717** LADY MONTAGU *Let. to Pope* 1 Apr., An expression in an ancient author.. may be extremely fine with them, when at the same time it looks low or uncouth to us. **1762** FALCONER *Shipwr.* I. 82 Tho' terms uncouth shou'd strike th' offended ear, For sake of truth the uncouth measures bear. **1773** MRS. CHAPONE *Improv. Mind* (1774) II. 128 Buried in obsolete words and uncouth constructions. *a* **1834** COLERIDGE *Shaks. Notes* (1875) 145 The scholastic and uncouth words homogeneity, proportionateness. **1870** LOWELL *Among my Bks.* 162 Where it does not make Shakespeare write bad sense, uncouth metre, or false grammar.

absol. **1737** POPE *Hor., Ep.* II. ii. 174 Prune the luxuriant, the uncouth refine, But show no mercy to an empty line.

d. Of manners, actions, etc.

1740 JOHNSON *Life Drake* Wks. IV. 426 Nor were their other customs less wild or uncouth. **1763** J. BROWN *Poetry & Music* iii. 27 Their Gestures are uncouth and horrid. **1837** W. IRVING *Capt. Bonneville* I. 274 It was a day of uncouth gambols, and frolics, and rude feasting. **1860** ADLER *Prov. Poet.* ii. 29 The uncouth heroism of the barbarous times. **1868** NETTLESHIP *Ess. Browning* ii. 62 This uncouth mind, so cramped.. by the exigencies.. of rhythm and rhyme.

†**7.** Unknowing, ignorant. Also *absol. Obs. rare.*

c **1220** *Bestiary* 112 in *O.E. Misc.* 4 His muð is ȝet wel unkuð wið pater noster and crede. *Ibid.* 512 Ðer-fore oðre fisses to him draȝen;.. of his swike he arn uncuð. *c* **1340** HAMPOLE *Prose Tr.* 25 For he taght the vn-couthe and vn-kunnynge by his prechynge. **1624** in *Abbotsford Club Misc.* 4 *margin*, The pannell denyet not, bot scho said scho was vncouth, and wist not quhat to say.

B. 1. *absol.* An unknown person; a stranger.

a **1225** *Ancr. R.* 348 Ich halsie ou.. alse unkuðe & pilegrimes, þet ȝe wiðholden ou from vlesliche lustes. *a* **1300** *Cursor M.* 6835 To pilgrime and to vncuth þou ber þe wit þi dedis cuth. **1340** *Ayenb.* 37 Þe priue þyeues byeþ þo þet ne steleþ naȝt of oncouþe ac of priues. **14..** *Sir Beues* (C.) 2134 'What þow?' sche seyde, 'þou onkowth?'

2. *sb. pl.* Things not commonly known; news.

a **1529** SKELTON *Col. Clout* 1054 The people.. wyl talke of such vncouthes. **1684** G. MERITON *Yorks. Dial.* 42 What uncuths hes ta brought Come tell me seaun? *c* **1746** J. COLLIER (Tim Bobbin) *View Lanc. Dial.* Wks. (1775) 33 I'd ash him.. whot Uncoth's he heard sturrink. **1828** *Craven Gloss.*

†**3.** *spec.* (See quot.) *Obs.*$^{-1}$

1589 PUTTENHAM *Eng. Poesie* III. xxii. (Arb.) 262 Ye haue another vicious speech which the Greekes call *Acyron*, we call him the vncouthe, and is when we vse an obscure and darke word.

un'couthie, *a. Sc.* [UN-[1] 7.] Dreary; uncomfortable; unfriendly.

1768 ROSS *Helenore* II. 68 Tyn heart, tyn a'; we'll even tak sic bield, As thir uncouthy heather hills can yield. **1835** D. WEBSTER *Orig. Sc. Rhymes* 25 (E.D.D.), Think ye the auld uncouthie byke Wad wish them parted?

un'couthly, *a.* [f. UNCOUTH *a.*] Awkward.

1821 CLARE *Vill. Minstr.* I. 19 A more uncouthly lout was hardly seen Beneath the shroud of ignorance than he.

un'couthly, *adv.* [f. as prec. + -LY[2].] In a strange, unfamiliar, or uncouth manner.

c **900** *Laws K. Ælfred* c. 47 (Liebermann), Þam elðeodeȝan & utancumenan ne læt ðu no uncuðlice wið hine. *c* **1200** ORMIN 14341 Þatt he spacc till hiss moderr þær þuss unncuþliȝ wiþþ worde. *a* **1300** *Cursor M.* 4818 Cuth þai wit him na kything tak, And vncuthli to þam he spak. ? *a* **1366** CHAUCER *Rom. Rose* 584 She hadde no thought.. but if it were oonly To graythe hir wel and vncouthly. **1423** JAS. I *Kingis Q.* ix, Is non estate nor age Ensured, more the prince nor than the page: So vncouthly hir werdes sche deuidith. *c* **1440** *Promp. Parv.* 511/1 Vncowthly, *extranee.* **1535** STEWART *Cron. Scot.* (Rolls) II. 396 Out throw the horne ilkone that tyme tha spak Richt vncouthlie, and with sic awfull sound. **1703** ROWE *Fair Penit.* v. i. Hiij, What Charnel has been rifl'd for these Bones? Fye! this is Pageantry; they look uncouthly. **1777** SHERIDAN *Sch. Scand., Portrait* 50 She,.. Not stiff with prudence, nor uncouthly wild. **1784** COWPER *Task* IV. 276 The shadow.. Dancing uncouthly to the quiv'ring flame. **1834** J. FOSTER *Ess. Evils Pop. Ignorance* 246 These are still further and most uncouthly confounded by the admixture of the ancient heathen notion of fate. **1881** FOWLER *Bacon* 160 What are, somewhat uncouthly, called the Idealists, the Materialists, and the Dualists.

un'couthness. [f. as prec.] The quality or condition of being uncouth, in various senses.

1435 MISYN *Fire of Love* 2 For vncuthnes of slike helefull habundance oft-tymes haue I gropyd my breste. **1442** *Rec. Coldingham Priory* (Surtees) I. 138 The unkouthness at is lyke to ryss be[tween] S[r] Alex[r] Howme & S[r] David Howme. **1600** *Gowrie's Conspir.* in *Select. fr. Harl. Misc.* (1793) 192 His hienes being stricken in great admiration.. of the vncouthnes of the tale. **1628** *World Encomp. by Sir F. Drake* 13 Notwithstanding the vncouthnes of the way. **1654–66** EARL ORRERY *Parthen.* (1676) 267 My Prince, by the uncouthness of the ground, advanced slowly with his Battalion. **1672** MARVELL *Reh. Transp.* I. 220 A peculiar uncouthness and obscurity of stile. **1712** STEELE *Spect.* No. 514 ¶4 Some in the Habit of Laplanders,.. notwithstanding the Uncouthness of their Dress, had lately obtained a Place upon the Mountain. **1778** [W. H. MARSHALL] *Minutes Agric., Digest* 47 The uncouthness of the Yoke and Goad. **1815** JANE AUSTEN *Emma* iv, The uncouthness of a voice, which I heard to be wholly unmodulated. **1871** FREEMAN *Norm. Conq.* IV. xviii. 154 The building whose combined uncouthness of outline and perfection of detail makes it unique among English churches.

un'couthsome, *a. rare.* [UN-[1] 7.] Unfavourable, unpleasant.

1684 tr. *Bucaniers Amer.* I. i. 3 This uncouthsom weather being spent, we had again the use of very favourable gales. **1824** J. TELFER *Border Ball.* 65 The witches.. grinded with their mucke-rake teeth, Uncouthsome to the view.

†**un'covenable**, *a. Obs.* [UN-[1] 7b.]

1. Inappropriate, unsuitable, unfitting.

In the first quot. rendering L. *importuna.*

c **1374** CHAUCER *Boeth.* IV. pr. vi. (1868) 141 Perauenture þe nature of som man is so ouerþrowyng to yuel and so vncouenable [etc.]. **1382** WYCLIF *1 Tim.* iv. 7 Forsothe schonye thou vncouenable fablis and veyn. *a* **1425** tr. *Arderne's Treat. Fistula*, etc. 47 Oon aposteme come to a man.. þat was hard to breke for vncouenable emplastres putte þer-to first. *c* **1450** tr. *De Imitatione* I. xxi. 26 Yeue not þiself to uncouenable gladnes. **1477** EARL RIVERS *Dictes* 41 Do not vncouenable werkis, take compaynie with wyse men and studie in their bookis.

2. Unseasonable.

c **1380** WYCLIF *Sel. Wks.* II. 121 We mai lerne, over þis, to fede not uncovenable axingis. **1382** —— *1 Kings* iii. 20 Risynge with silence of the vnkouenable niȝt, she took my sone fro myn syde.

Hence †**un'covenably** *adv. Obs.*

1382 WYCLIF *Ecclus.* xxxii. 6 Vncouenabli wile thou not ben enhauncid in thi wisdam. **1387** TREVISA *Higden* (Rolls) VI. 473 Sche was þerfore i-blamed of seint Ethelwold, and sche answerede noþer unkovenabeliche noþer ful curteisliche.

un'covenant, *v.* (UN-[2] 3.)

1643 W. GREENHILL *Axe at Root* 8 Now the Lord did un-covenant them, un-church them, un-power them. **1679** C. NESSE *Antid. agst. Popery* 102 The Jews.. did apostatize,.. unchurching and uncovenanting themselves. **1881** *Edin. Rev.* Apr. 483 There it was that, so to speak, Carlyle un-covenanted himself.

un'covenanted, *ppl. a.* [UN-[1] 8.]

1. Not promised or secured by a (*spec.* a Divine) covenant.

1648 HEXHAM II, *Onbevoorwaerdet*, Vncovenanted. **1689** SHERLOCK *Death* iii. §7 (1731) 207 They must be saved by uncovenanted Grace and Mercy. *a* **1711** KEN *Hymnarium* Poet. Wks. 1721 II. 133 Since we the Grace that we obtain, By Supereffluence uncovenanted gain. *a* **1806** BP. HORSLEY *Serm.* (1816) III. xxxviii. 165, I will cast me on his free un-covenanted mercy. **1887** S. COX *Expositions* Ser. III. xiii. 177 On the testimony of the Bible itself.. his uncovenanted mercies are just as sure as his covenanted mercies.

b. Lying outside of any Divine covenant.

1858 J. MARTINEAU *Stud. Chr.* 114 Many a parable did Jesus utter, proclaiming his Father's intended mercy to the uncovenanted nations. **1860** BP. S. WILBERFORCE *Addr. Ordination* 41 Men who lay in the uncovenanted darkness of a fallen nature.

2. Not sanctioned by, not in accordance with, a covenant or agreement.

1727 E. LAWRENCE *Duty of Steward* 55, I have known Instances of Gentlemen's Estates sinking very much by irregular and uncovenanted practices.

3. Not bound by a covenant; *spec.* in the Indian Civil Service (cf. COVENANTED *ppl. a.* 4).

1790 BURKE *Fr. Rev.* 88 The first fundamental right of uncovenanted man, that is, to judge for himself, and to assert his own cause. **1845** STOCQUELER *Handbk. Brit. India* (1854) 105 The uncovenanted servants, the East Indians, and the natives themselves. **1884** *Truth* 13 Mar. 386/2 A member of the uncovenanted service of India.

b. Not having subscribed the Covenant.

1818 SCOTT *Hrt. Midl.* xviii, The present government, which, however mild and paternal, was still uncovenanted. **1855** MACAULAY *Hist. Eng.* III. 706 These men continued.. to disclaim all allegiance to an uncovenanted Sovereign. **1889** LOWELL *Latest Lit. Ess., Walton* (1891) 74 Some foraging party from Leslie's army which would not have spared his uncovenanted chickens.

un'covenanter. (UN-[1] 12.)

1640–1 *Kirkcudbr. War-Comm. Min. Bk.* (1855) 131 Johne Cutlar.. declares no.. uncovenanters within his bounds.

un'cover, *v.* Also 4–5 vnkeuer(e, 5 oncowyr, 5–6 vncouere, etc. [UN-[2] 3, 5, 7.]

1. *fig.* To disclose, lay bare, make known.

a **1300** *Cursor M.* 27425 And sua his rede ask he þat naman scrift vn-couer[d] be. **1628** FELTHAM *Resolves* II. xvii. 52 In our demaunds, we vncouer our owne desires. **1649** MILTON *Eikon.* xxviii. 238 Neither was it to cover thir perjury as he accuses, but to uncover his perjury to the Oath of his Coronation. **1674** JEAKE *Arith.* (1696) 405, I now come to review them in their common nature.. and uncover their Comparative Elements. **1891** HARDY *Tess* xlix, The terrible evening over the hearth, when her simple soul uncovered itself to his.

2. To lay open or bare by the removal of some covering thing or matter.

a **1375** *Joseph Arim.* 559 Eualac.. vn-keuered his scheld & on þe cros biholdes. *c* **1400** *Brut* I. 125 Þis Hardiknoght.. lete vncouere his broþer Harolde, and smote of his Heuede.. at Westmynstr. **14..** *Three Kings Cologne* 28 (Camb. MS.), Whan hit [the snow] is vncouered oute of þe chaf, anoone hit dissolueþ and wasteþ awey. *c* **1430** *Pilgr. Lyf Manhode* I. xxxv. (1869) 22 It is bettere the keyes.. ben hid than vnhyd, For al bi times may men come to vnkeuere both that oon and that oother. **1553** BRENDE *Q. Curtius* IV. 56 The teares yet distilling downe his chekes [he] vn-couered his face. **1597** A. M. tr. *Guillemeau's Fr. Chirurg.* 9/2 Which we can not certaynlye espye, without makinge denudatione of the Cranium, and to our sight vncover it. **1603** [see UNBAR *v.* a]. **1779** *Mirror* No. 64, That mental feast with which I was to be regaled when the table should be uncovered. **1796** MME. D'ARBLAY *Camilla* V. 276 Weeping always, and never.. uncovering her face. **1839** YEOWELL *Anc. Brit. Ch.* xii. (1847) 133 Human bones, which from time to time have been uncovered by the winds, and lie bleaching on the sand. **1892** *Photogr. Ann.* II. 414 It really does uncover the inches set forth below, whereas many other patterns only uncover about two-thirds.

b. To make bare or naked by removal of clothing; to expose unclothed or unveiled.

1530 PALSGR. 767/1 Uncover this man, take awaye the clothes. **1560** BIBLE (Genev.) *Isaiah* xlvii. 2 Vncouer y[e] legge, & passe through the floods. **1609** —— (Douay) *Ibid.*, Discouer the shoulder, vncouer the thighes. **1769** COOK *Voy. round World* I. xix. (1773) 242 When an Indian is about to worship at the Morai, or brings his offering to the altar, he always uncovers his body to the waste. **1815** J. SMITH *Panorama Sci. & Art* II. 200 On uncovering the foot, at that part was found a blue mark. **1875** JOWETT *Plato* (ed. 2) I. 167 Uncover your chest and back to me that I may have a better view.

refl. **1535** COVERDALE *2 Sam.* vi. 20 The kynge.. hath vn-couered himselfe before the maydens of his seruauntes. **1734** in Sale *Koran* 291 *note*, It being reckoned.. indecent, for a woman.. to uncover her self before one who is an infidel.

absol. **1713** ADDISON *Guard.* No. 109 ¶3 We were forced to uncover after them, being unwilling to give out so soon.

c. To drive (a fox) out of cover.

1812 *Sporting Mag.* XXXIX. 185 Proceeding to Minting Wood, they uncovered a fox. **1824** MACTAGGART *Gallovid. Encycl.* 414 The hounds could not uncover him, so the ron was set in flames about his lugs.

3. To remove a cover or covering from, to take the cover or top off (something).

c **1400** *Beryn* 3935 The Cup was vncoverid, þe swerd was out i-brayid. *c* **1410** *Sir Cleges* 364 Sir Cleges oncowyrd the panyere, And schewed.. the cheryse. **1507** *Coventry Leet Bk.* 609 That on Joh. a Woode, mercer, let on-couere the Redde diche, which renneth throwgh his gardeyn. **1534** TINDALE *Mark* ii. 4 They vncovered the rofe of the housse where he was. **1586** J. HOOKER *Hist. Irel.* in *Holinshed* II. 114/1 The churches for the most part were all destroied & vncouered. **1699** DAMPIER *Voy.* II. 47 A long Pole or Bambo.. with a Cutting-hook at the end of it, purposely for uncovering the houses. **1737** CHALLONER *Cath. Chr. Instr.* (1753) 220 Our Altars we also uncovered and stript of all their Ornaments.

4. To remove the hat from (the head), as a mark of reverence, respect, or courtesy.

1530 PALSGR. 767/1 Why do you thus, I pray you, be nat uncovered for me. **1535** COVERDALE *Lev.* x. 6 Ye shall not vncouer youre heades, ner rente youre clothes. **1608** *Yorkshire Trag.* iii. 60, I that neuer could abide to vncouer my head ith Church. **1699** DAMPIER *Voy.* II. 129 None of the Eastern people use the Complement of uncovering their Heads when they meet, as we do.

b. *absol.*

1627 MAY *Lucan* IX. S 3 b, Thus hauing spoke Straight hee vncouers, and presents the head. **1841** MACAULAY *Ess., W. Hastings* (1851) 595 The House of Commons which un-covered and stood up to receive him. **1889** F. E. GRETTON *Memory's Harkb.* 37 He stopped short, reverentially un-covered, and stood bare-headed till the line of mourners had passed.

5. *Mil.* **a.** To expose, leave open, by the moving or manœuvring of men. **b.** To leave unprotected by withdrawal of troops.

1796 *Instr. & Reg. Cavalry* (1813) 122 As soon as the rear division is uncovered, it receives the word, *March!* **1802** JAMES *Milit. Dict.* s.v., The different leading companies or divisions, &c. successively uncover those in their rear. **1832** *Prop. Reg. Instr. Cavalry* III. 72 The Troop.. advances till its right uncovers the left of the Base Troop. **1899** *Daily News* 27 Mar. 7/4 The old battle lines surrounding the city are maintained, and the city cannot be safely uncovered.

un'coverable, *a.* (UN-[1] 7b.)

1837 CARLYLE *Fr. Rev.* III. II. v, To stretch out the old Formula.., so that it may cover the new, contradictory, entirely *un*coverable Thing?

un'covered, *ppl. a.* [UN-[1] 8.]

1. Not roofed or closed in overhead; not sheltered by a roof.

c **1400** *Destr. Troy* 11667 The walles were wroght to þe wale rofe, All clanly by course vncouert aboue. **1563** GOLDING *Cæsar* VII. (1565) 192 Bycause they saw the penthouses of our turrettes burned downe, and that oure men could not with ease go vncouered to saue them. **1587** *Southampton Court Leet Rec.* (1906) II. 255 The wollon hawle is vncovered and decayed which wee desier maye be amended. **1600** J. PORY tr. *Leo's Africa* III. 125 The middle part of the house is alwaies open or uncouered. **1697** DRYDEN *Æneis* II. 700 Uncovered but by heaven, there stood in view An altar.

2. Not covered by clothing; bare, naked.

c **1400** T. CHESTRE *Launfal* 291 For hete her clothes down sche dede, Almest to her gerdyl stede, Than lay sche un-covert. **1535** COVERDALE *Gen.* ix. 21 Noe.. was dronken, and laye vncouered in his tente. **1560** BIBLE (Genev.) *Isaiah* xx. 4 Bothe yong men and olde men,.. with their buttockes vncouered. **1605** SHAKS. *Lear* III. iv. 106 Thou wert better in a Graue, then to answere with thy vncouer'd body, this extremitie of the Skies. **1827** Faraday *Chem. Manip.* ii. (1842) 54 It is requisite that the bottle should not be handled by uncovered hands. **1851** Longf. *Gold. Leg.* v. *At Foot of Alps*, A band of pilgrims, moving slowly On their long journey, with uncovered feet.

b. Not wearing a hat; bareheaded.

1570 in W. H. Turner *Select. Rec. Oxford* (1880) 331 Every man..spekeyng within the same Counsell howse, shall stand upp bare headed or uncovered. **1593** Shaks. *2 Hen. VI*, iv. i. 128 Rather let my head..dance vpon a bloody pole, Then stand vncouer'd to the Vulgar Groome. **1611** Bible *1 Cor.* xi. 13 It is comely that a woman pray vnto God vncouered? *a***1656** Bp. Hall *Rem. Wks.* (1660) 242 The French Divines preach with their hats on, ours uncovered. **1710** Addison *Tatler* No. 253 ¶3 The Censor, who continued hitherto un-covered, put on his hat with great dignity. **1831** Scott *Ct. Rob.* ix, Sitting stationary..when so many noble knights..stand uncovered around. **1884** *Manch. Exam.* 26 Nov. 5/1 The members of the House of Commons stand uncovered, the peers sit and wear their hats.

c. Of women: Unveiled.

1585 T. Washington tr. *Nicholay's Voy.* i. viii. 8b, The wiues of the Turkes..are not seene goe vncouered.

3. Having no covering; left open or exposed; not covered *by* or *with* (also †*of*) something.

1530 Palsgr. 840/1 Oncovered, *a descouuert*. **1563** Hyll *Art Garden*. (1593) 12 They wil also that those furrowes so lie all the winter open and vncouered. **1638** Mayne *Lucian* (1664) 24 Let's finde out some eminent place, un-covered with Snow, where we may the firmelier chain him. **1650** Earl Monm. tr. *Senault's Man bec. Guilty* 368 Whilst any mountains were yet uncovered with water, the remainders of man-kind were fixed there. **1692** Ray *Disc.* ii. (1693) 65 He sent forth Birds, that he might try whether they could espy any Land uncovered of Water. **1793** Cowper *A Tale* 17 The heaths uncover'd, and the moors, Except with snow. **1807** Wordsw. *White Doe* vi. 144 One of the Norton Tenantry Espied the uncovered Corse. **1819** Scott *Ivanhoe* iii, The board was uncovered by a cloth. **1827** Faraday *Chem. Manip.* iv. (1842) 93 The sand being cleared off.. leaves the metal uncovered. **1875** W. S. Hayward *Love agst. World* i, The polished oak flooring, uncovered by carpet.

b. Not furnished with the usual covering.

1565 in Hay Fleming *Reform. Scotl.* (1910) 610 Item, in the lauche chalmer, four stullis oncoverit. **1907** E. Glyn *3 Weeks* xiv, The bed unmade and piled with uncovered hotel pillows.

†**4.** Not having a cover laid for meals. *Obs.*

1494 in *Househ. Ord.* (1790) 116 For all manner of estates that are to bee uncovered.

5. Not protected or screened by another or others. (See cover *v.*^{1} 8 and 12.)

*a***1795** Philidor *Studies of Chess* (1817) 98 It would be scarcely possible to prevent the uncovered king..from doubling on the same line. **1832** *Prop. Reg. Instr. Cavalry* ii. 17 If the numbers are uneven, the last man but one..must remain uncovered.

6. Not covered by insurance.

1892 *Pall Mall G.* 22 Aug. 2/1 The building only was insured, and all the furnishings were uncovered.

Hence **un'coveredly** *adv.*

1683 E. Hooker *Pref. Pordage's Mystic Div.* 67 Where, unclothedly, uncoveredly, nakedly,..Hee stood.

un'covering, *vbl. sb.* [f. uncover *v.*] The action of the verb, in various senses.

1495 *Trevisa's Barth. De P.R.* v. xxvii. 137 [In acute fevers] vncouerynge and puttynge out of bare armes is token of deth. **1598** Florio, *Scomiglio*, an vncouering, an vnhilling. **1611** Cotgr., *Descouvrement*, a discouering, vncouering, detecting, disclosing. **1647** T. Moore (*title*), A Uncovering of Mysterious Deceits. **1817** J. Scott *Paris Revisit.* (ed. 4) 70 The uncovering of the established and fruitful face of things. **1855** Macaulay *Hist. Eng.* xiv. III. 414 That the sitting and rising, the covering and the uncovering, should have been regulated by exactly the same etiquette. **1895** *Athenæum* 5 Oct. 460/2 To carry out a complete uncovering of the immense accumulations of rubbish.

†**un'covert,** *a.* [un-^{1} 7.] = discovert *a.*

1485 *Rolls of Parlt.* VI. 285 To vest and be in her sole.., as she were sole and uncovert. **1487** *Act 4 Hen. VII*, c. 24 Five years next after that they..be..uncovert, and of whole Mind.

un'covery. [f. uncover *v.*, after *discovery*, *recovery*, etc.: see -ery.] The action of uncovering or bringing to light.

1963 *Listener* 12 Sept. 377/2 When we indulge in.. deduction..the theorem contains the discovery (or, more exactly, the uncovery of something which was there in the axioms and postulates, though it wasn't actually evident). **1977** *Times Lit. Suppl.* 25 Mar. 336/1 Dr Ray's uncovery of a dusty trove of illustrated books in the basement of a London dealer recalls the accidental discovery of the golden bowl.

un'coveted, *ppl. a.* (un-^{1} 8.)

1760–72 H. Brooke *Fool of Quality* xiv. (1792) III. 45 Uncoveted wealth came pouring in upon me. **1833** Mrs. Browning *Prometh. Bound* 163, I..keep An uncoveted watch o'er the world and the deep. **1882** 'F. Anstey' *Vice Versâ* v. 92 He had contrived..to evade the uncoveted wooden spoon by just two places.

un'covetingly, *adv.* (un-^{1} 11.)

1862 R. H. Patterson *Ess. Hist. & Art* 47 To beg for the rose, yet look uncovetingly on the dandelion.

un'covetous, *a.* (un-^{1} 7.)

*a***1500** *Ratis Raving* i. 624 Scho is louand in kind lawtee, Vncouatice, of gyftys free. **1648** Hexham ii, *Onbegeerigh*, Vncovetous. **1871** Ruskin *Fors Clav.* v. 22 An uncalculating and uncovetous wisdom. *Ibid.* x. 7 The healthy delight of uncovetous admiration.

uncow, obs. f. unco.

un'cowed, *ppl. a.* (un-^{1} 8.)

1891 Miss Dowie *Girl in Karp.* 127 The children sharp, clever, and uncowed.

un'cowl, *v.* (un-^{2} 4.)

1611 Cotgr., *Descapuchonner*, to vnhood, vncowle, vncouer. **1812** Coleridge *Remorse* i. ii. 260, I pray you, think us friends—uncowl your face. **1829** I. Taylor *Enthus.* ix. 242 Let him uncowl his ears, and cover his naked feet. **1840** Browning *Sordello* vi. 348 One blood-drop to the bowl Which brimful tempts the sluggish asp uncowl At last.

un'cowled, *ppl. a.* (un-^{1} 8.)

1728 Pope *Dunc.* iii. 114 Behold yon' Isle, by Palmers, Pilgrims trod, Men bearded, bald, cowl'd, uncowl'd, shod, unshod. **1868** Geo. Eliot *Sp. Gypsy* iii. 301 To work the will of a more tyrannous friend Than any uncowled father.

un'cracked, *ppl. a.* (un-^{1} 8.)

1581 Bp. Aylmer in Nicolas *Mem. Sir C. Hatton* (1847) 240 If you will have..your credit kept uncracked for commending me. **1623** Middleton & Rowley *Sp. Gipsy* iv. i, The un-crack'd diamond of my faith shall hold. **1648** Sanderson *Serm.* (1681) II. 226 The ice..is of that firmness, that it will bear a loaden cart uncrackt. **1763** Churchill *Ghost* iv. 1397 Good men..With names uncrack'd, and credit sound. **1826** Lamb *Lett.* (1886) II. 228 Heaven send him his jars un-crack'd. **1891** Kipling *Light that Failed* (1900) 244 The person who demanded muffins and an uncracked teapot.

un'craftily, *adv.* [un-^{1} 11.] †Unskilfully.

1519 Horman *Vulg.* 42b, Woundis..yf they be touchyd vncraftelye out of season,..waxe angry and rauncleth. **1538** Elyot, *Infabre*, vnkunningly, vncraftily.

un'craftiness. [un-^{1} 12.] †Unskilfulness.

*c***1520** Barclay *Jugurth* 88 They dispyse my..vnnoble lynage, and I dyspyse the vncraftynesse and slouthe of them.

un'crafty, *a.* [un-^{1} 7. Cf. (with the sense of 'weak, feeble') OS. *unkrahtag*, MDu. *oncrachtich*, *-crechtich*, *-creftich* (older Du. *onkrachtig*), MLG. *unkrechtich*, OHG. *unchreftic* (MHG. *unkreftig*, G. *unkräftig*), MDa. *ukraftig*.]

†**1.** Not dexterous or ingenious; unskilful. *Obs.*

1483 *Cath. Angl.* 80/1 Vn Crafty, *inartificiosus*. *c***1520** Barclay *Jugurth* 47 Whiche armye was vncraftie, sluggishe and feble. **1533** Bellenden *Livy* i. iii. (S.T.S.) I. 23 þe rude and vncrafty pepill of þat regioun.

2. Not crafty or cunning; guileless.

1647 Hexham i, Vncraftie, *sonder schalckheyt*. **1660** Jer. Taylor *Ductor* Pref. (1676) p. vii, By the new methods, a Simple and Uncrafty Man cannot be wise unto salvation.

un'cramp, *v.* (un-^{2} 3.)

1851 Sir F. Palgrave *Norm. & Eng.* I. 353 Uncramping or shattering the pedestals supporting the idols. **1860** Miss Yonge *Stokesley Secr.* viii, Susie extended each hand to its broadest stretch to uncramp them. **1937** V. Woolf *Diary* 21 Apr. (1984) V. 80 What a mercy to use this page to uncramp in! after squeezing drop by drop into my 17 minute BBC. **1952** E. Hemingway *Old Man & Sea* 70 His left hand was still..tight... It will uncramp though, he thought.

un'cramped, *ppl. a.* (un-^{1} 8.)

1797 *Monthly Rev.* XXIV. 194 Providing him with the means of pursuing his inquiries uncramped and at leisure. **1860** Pusey *Min. Proph.* 519 An unconfined, uncramped population, spreading itself freely, without restraint of walls. **1899** Rodway *Guiana Wilds* 109 Their broad backs were quite unaffected by burning sun or pouring rain, and their limbs uncramped by sitting on the bottom of the canoe.

Hence **un'crampedness.**

1882 *Academy* 18 Nov. 358 The free handling and absolute uncrampedness of the landscape.

un'crannied, *ppl. a.* (un-^{1} 8.)

?*a***1625** Webster *Appius & Virg.* i. iii, Trust my bosom To be the closet of your private griefs: Believe me, I am uncrannied. *a***1627** Drayton *Sheph. Sirena* 70 There is nothing to that friend, To whose close vncranied brest, We our secret thoughts may send. **1649** G. Daniel *Trinarch.*, *Hen. V*, cxxix, Where Loyaltie vncranied, doth keepe out The Subtle Flame, the Fæces, cannot doe't.

uncra'vatted, *ppl. a.* (un-^{1} 8.)

1847 Helps *Friends in C.* i. ii. 31 A great, unhatted, uncravated, bearded man.

un'cravingly, *adv.* (un-^{1} 11.)

1849 M. Arnold *Resignation* 161 Beautiful eyes meet his; and he Bears to admire uncravingly.

un'crazed, *ppl. a.* (un-^{1} 8.)

1608 Heywood *Lucrece* iv. iv, So I keep unstain'd The un-craz'd honour I have yet maintain'd. **1613–8** Daniel *Coll. Hist. Eng.* (1626) 119 Who in that broken time, onely held vncrased..the part of an euen Counsellour and Officer.

uncre'atable, *a.* (un-^{1} 7b.)

1846 Worcester (citing Tillock). **1883** H. Drummond *Nat. Law in Spir. W.* 297 Matter is uncreatable and indestructible.

Hence **uncreata'bility; uncre'atableness.**

1878 Newcomb *Pop. Astron.* iv. iii. 502 The uncreatableness and indestructibility of matter. **1883** *Glasgow Weekly Her.* 6 Oct. 8/2 The incontrovertibility of matter and energy..and their consequent indestructibility and uncreatability.

uncre'ate, *ppl. a.* [un-^{1} 8b and 5b.] = uncreated *ppl. a.*

1548–9 *Bk. Com. Prayer, Quicunque vult*, The father uncreate, the sonne uncreate, and the holy gost uncreate. **1608** L. Machin *Dumbe Knight* iii. i, A creature vncreate in paradise, And one thats onely of a womans making. **1807** Opie in *Lect. Paint.* i. (1848) 240 All that poets yet have feigned..of uncreate or unembodied being. **1842** Manning *Serm.* (1848) I. i. 3 We talk of powers, and qualities,..and the like; but..they do not exist apart from beings, create or uncreate. **1870** Myers *Poems* 120 Then in scorn My lips are silent; uncreate, unborn, Evanishes the visionary lay.

absol. **1851** Kingsley *Yeast* xvii, You can only see the Uncreate in the Create—the Infinite in the Finite.

uncre'ate, *v.* [un-^{2} 3.] *trans.* To undo the creation of; to unmake. Also *refl.*

1633 Prynne *Histrio-m.* 172 Is this a light, a despicable effeminacie, for men..thus purposely..to vnman, vn-christian, vncreate themselves? **1640** Habington *Edw. IV*, 37 It was as easie for him to uncreate as to create a King. **1690** C. Nesse *O. & N. Test.* I. 2 When we are once created in Christ, we can, indeed, do something to uncreate our selves. **1760–72** H. Brooke *Fool of Qual.* (1809) III. 107 Could I have had my wish, creation would again have been uncreated. **1847** Bushnell *Chr. Nurt.* viii. (1861) 209 One religion was creating and the other uncreating manhood. **1894** *Fallen Angels* xxi. 112 God himself could not preserve the unfilial from suffering, save by uncreating them.

absol. *a***1634** Chapman & Shirley *Chabot* v. i. 89 With one breath they uncreate. **1651** Stanley *Poems* 74 Thus thy diviner Muse a power 'bove Fate May boast, that can both make and uncreate. **1744** Young *Nt. Th.* vii. 1221 But tho' you can deform, you can't destroy; To curse, not uncreate, is all your pow'r.

uncre'ated, *ppl. a.* [un-^{1} 8 and 5b.]

1. Not brought into existence by a special act of creation; of a self-existent or eternal nature.

1548–9 *Bk Com. Prayer, Quicunque vult*, As also there be not..three uncreated; but one uncreated. **1587** Golding *De Mornay* ix. (1592) 118 If it were created after the example of a thing vncreated, can it come to passe that it should be euerlasting? *a***1633** W. Austin *Medit.* (1635) 246 Certaine Hereticks held them [*sc.* angels] to be uncreated, and Co-ëternall with God. **1667** Milton *P.L.* ii. 150 To perish.. in the wide womb of uncreated night. **1704** Clarke *Attributes* iii. (1738) 22 Original Being, Uncreated, Independent, and of it self Eternal. **1777** Priestley *Matt. & Spir.* (1782) I. xix. 225 Uncreated light could not be seen by mortal eyes. **1801** Southey *Thalaba* iv. ix, Of these Angels' fate Thus in the uncreated book is written. **1860** Pusey *Min. Proph.* 481 Love, joy, peace..are created in man. Only in God they exist, undivided, uncreated.

absol. **1678** Cudworth *Intell. Syst.* Pref., The Pagan Polytheism and Idolatry consisted not in worshipping Many Creators, or Uncreateds, but [etc.]. **1805** Wordsw. *Prelude* ii. 413 Every form of creature..looked Towards the Un-created with a countenance Of adoration. **1877** Sparrow *Serm.* vi. 78 What we are as creatures we never can know, as we ought, but by studying the uncreated.

2. Not created; not brought into being.

1607 Beaum. & Fl. *Woman-Hater* ii. i, Nor will I Wish my self uncreated for this evil. **1667** Milton *P.L.* vi. 268 How hast thou..into Nature brought Miserie, uncreated till the crime Of thy Rebellion? **1890** *Spectator* 18 Oct., In the case of an uncreated book, of course the argument is infinitely stronger.

uncre'atedness. [f. prec.] The quality or state of being uncreated.

1648 Hexham ii, *Ongeschapenheydt*, Vncreatednesse, or Vnshapennesse. **1678** Cudworth *Intell. Syst.* i. iv. §6. 197 Some Modern Sects..do also assert the Vncreatedness of the Matter. *a***1740** Waterland *Wks.* (1823) II. 326 Making a distinction between derived uncreatedness, and underived uncreatedness. **1857** Susanna Winkworth tr. *Life Tauler* 288 God..is equal to the soul as touching freedom, and unequal as touching uncreatedness, for the soul is created. **1877** W. Bright in *Dict. Chr. Biog.* I. 181/2 When Arius.. expressly denied..the uncreatedness of the Son of God.

uncre'ating, *ppl. a.* [f. uncreate *v.*] Destroying; reducing to nonentity.

1742 Pope *Dunc.* iv. 654 Light dies before thy uncreating word. **1820** Shelley *Naples* 138 The Anarchs of the North lead forth their legions Like Chaos o'er creation, uncreating.

uncre'ation. [un-^{2} 8: cf. prec.] The action of uncreating.

1884 *Edin. Rev.* Oct. 334 The famous lines on the uncreation of the world by 'Chaos old'. **1885** G. Macdonald *Book of Strife* 16 Dec., A thing..Which uncreation can alone release.

uncre'ative, *a.* (un-^{1} 7 and 5b.)

1855 Milman *Lat. Chr.* xiv. viii. VI. 566 The East.. settled down in unprogressive, uncreative acquiescence, and went on copying that type.

uncre'ativeness. (un-^{1} 12.)

1855 Lewes *Goethe* I. iii. viii. 291 The contempt of Prometheus for the idleness, the uncreativeness of the Gods.

un'creatural, *a.* (un-^{1} 7.)

1649 J. Ellistone tr. *Behmen's Epistles* 30 We our selves are the property of the foure Elements, and they are in Us creaturall; and without us they are uncreaturall.

un'creaturely, *a.* [un-^{1} 7.] Not belonging, natural, or proper to creatures.

1668 Howe *Bless. Righteous* (1825) 89 That diabolical un-creaturely pride that is long since banished heaven. **1707** Norris *Treat. Humility* vii. 295 Hatred of God..is strictly an uncreaturely sin. **1877** Sparrow *Serm.* 334 The proud, selfish, ungrateful, rebellious, impious, uncreaturely temper.

†**un'credible,** *a. Obs.* [un-^{1} 7 and 5b.]

1. = incredible *a.* 1. (Common *c* 1550–1650.)

*c***1440** *Wycliffite Bible* Judg. xx. 5 (MS. Bodl. 277), þei han traueilid my wijf wiþ vncredible wodnesse of leccherie. **1482** *Monk of Evesham* xlix. (Arb.) 98 An oncredyble and inestymable conforte of ioye and plesure. **1560** Daus tr.

Sleidane's Comm. 424 b, It is vncredible, with what rebukes and railinges ye people receiued hym. **1605** BACON *Adv. Learn.* I. iv. § 10 Rarities and reports, that seeme vncredible. **1653** HOLCROFT *Procopius, Vandal Wars* II. 47 A thing seeming difficult, and uncredible to such as have not seen our former actions. **1680** MORDEN *Geog. Rect., Turkey* 356 Taken by.. Mustapha.. with an uncredible Slaughter.

2. Incredulous. *rare.*

1553 *Douglas's Æneid* IV. 87 Quhy dois he refuse my wourdis and prayers To lat entyr in hys dul vncredyble [*Small* vntretable] eris?

Hence †**uncredi'bility**; †**un'credibly** *adv.*

1486 *Bk. St. Albans* f vj b, An vncredibilitie of Cocoldis. **1565** STAPLETON tr. *Bede's Hist. Ch. Eng.* Pref. 9 We see as much vncredibilitie.. in the one as in the other. **1565** COOPER *Thesaurus, Incredibiliter*,.. vncredibly: meruaylously.

†**un'credit,** *v. Obs.* [UN-^{1} 14 and UN-^{2} 3.] *trans.* To distrust; to discredit.

1615 DANIEL *Hymens Triumph* II. ii, Such meanes can wit deuise To make mens mindes vncredit their owne eies. **1628** FELTHAM *Resolves* II. xxi. 70 Affirmations are apter to winne beliefe, then Negatiues to vncredit them. **1655** FULLER *Ch. Hist.* XI. ii. §82. 156 Then was it Kilvert his designe to uncredit the Testimony of Pregion, by charging him with several accusations.

un'creditable, *a.* [UN-^{1} 7 b and 5 b.] Discreditable; disreputable.

1643 HAMMOND *Serm.* Wks. 1684 IV. 511 He.. that abstains only from uncreditable or unfashionable, from branded or disused sins. **1688** COLLIER *Several Disc.* (1725) 2 The Design.. being to make all Injustice and Encroachment an uncreditable, as well as an unprofitable Practice. **1710** PALMER *Proverbs* 342 A brawl, in which both parties use a hundred impertinent and uncreditable expressions. **1782** PALEY *Serm.* 21 Sept., The vocation in time comes to be thought mean and uncreditable. **1818** BENTHAM *Ch. Eng., Catech. Exam.* 427 No need has he of any such uncreditable and hazardous practice. **1866** *Illustr. Lond. News* 1 Dec. 526 The credit which Mr... has received .. is very uncreditable to the English nation.

Hence **un'creditableness.**

1667 *Causes Decay Chr. Piety* xix. 419 To all other disswasives we may add this of the Uncreditableness.

un'credited, *ppl. a.* (UN-^{1} 8 and 5 b.)

1586 WARNER *Alb. Eng.* II. ix. (1592) 36 It cannot weepe, nor wring the handes, but say that she did so: And saieth so vncredited. **1607** CHAPMAN *Rev. Bussy D'Ambois* Plays 1873 II. 140 God (said she) Would haue me vtter things vn-credited. **1670** CLARENDON *Contempl. Ps.* Tracts (1727) 532 Who.. does render.. their virulent suggestions against our reputations ineffectual and uncredited. **1777** *Ann. Reg., Antiq.* 134/2 This opinion remained.. uncredited by all skilful medallists. **1828** *Lights & Shades* II. 133 Being at the same time.. unmannered, uncredited, unwitted. **1959** *Times* 17 Aug. 12/6 This version (adapter uncredited) concentrated on the two main conflicts in the book. **1977** *Rolling Stone* 30 June 102/3 The uncredited musicians play sparely but with enough fire to make their presence, and this entire album, memorable.

un'creeping, *ppl. a.* (UN-^{1} 10.)

1727 *Fam. Dict.* s.v. *Dog's Cawl*, The uncreeping *Apocynon* shoots forth great Twigs of an ill Scent.

un'creolized, *ppl. a.* [UN-^{1} 8.] Of a language or dialect: not creolized; that has not undergone creolization.

1980 *English World-Wide* I. I. 50 The greater contact with uncreolized English on the American mainland had altered the identity of this speech. **1982** D. SUTCLIFFE *Brit. Black Eng.* I. 23 And English—that is, uncreolized English—is also the official language in Jamaica.

un'crested, *ppl. a.*^{1} [UN-^{1} 8.] Not adorned or furnished with a crest.

1655 MOUFET & BENNET *Health's Improv.* 103 Some of each sort are high crested like a lapwing, others un-crested. **1757** DYER *Fleece* IV. 436 Soldier, and statesman, and uncrested chief. **1888** GUNTER *Mr. Potter* ix. 117 Plain letter paper and uncrested envelope.

un'crested, *ppl. a.*^{2} [UN-^{2} 8.] Deprived of a crest.

1611 COTGR., *Ecreté*, topped, vncrested; whose top or crest is taken off. **1834** DE QUINCEY *Autob. Sk.* Wks. 1853 I. 181 *note*, Supposing the city to be uncrested, as it were; its upper tiers to be what the sailors call unshipped.

un'cribbed, *ppl. a*: see UNCABINED *a.*

un'cried, *ppl. a.* [UN-^{1} 8 c.] ***uncried up***, not extolled or praised.

1630 B. JONSON *New Inn* IV. ii, *Huf.* So you will name no Spaniard, I will pledge you. *Tip.* I rather choose to thirst, .. Then leaue that creame of nations vncry'd vp.

un'criminal, *a.* (UN-^{1} 7.)

1864 CARLYLE *Fredk. Gt.* XVI. xi. IV. 432 With other the like uncriminal fancies. **1881** *Daily News* 25 Jan. 3/1 The uncriminal but powerful organization of the Land League.

un'criminally, *adv.* (UN-^{1} 11.)

a **1864** HAWTHORNE *S. Felton* (1883) 258 A human life, taken (however uncriminally) by his own hands.

un'crinkle, *v.* [UN-^{2} 7, 3.] **a.** *intr.* To lose crinkles, to become less crinkled. **b.** *trans.* To remove crinkles from.

1904 G. A. B. DEWAR *Glamour of Earth* viii. 173 The tiny leaves will be uncrinkling in a day or two about the dark twiggy bole. **1911** W. DE MORGAN *Likely Story* v. 136 He uncrinkled a result of the shape of that letter-box. **1935** E. BOWEN *House in Paris* II. vii. 165 No one with him to smile and make his face uncrinkle.

un'crippled, *ppl. a.* (UN-^{1} 8.)

a **1800** COWPER *Odyss.* (ed. 2) XX. 437, I have eyes and ears, Two feet uncrippled. **1812** CARY *Dante, Purgat.* XXV. 2 It was an hour, when he who climbs, had need To walk un-crippled. **1894** *Daily News* 11 June 8/2 Love of beauty and of uncrippled happiness.

un'crisp *v.* (UN-^{2} 3.)

1598 FLORIO, *Discrespare*, to vncurle, to vnfrizle, to vncrispe, to vnwrinkle.

un'crisped, *ppl. a.* (UN-^{2} 8.)

1827 HOOD *Hero & Leander* lxiii, His uncrispt locks uncurling in the brine.

un'critical, *a.* [UN-^{1} 7. Cf. Du. *onkritisch*, G. *unkritisch*, Da. *ukritisk*.]

1. Not critical; lacking in judgement; not addicted to criticism.

1659 GAUDEN *Tears Church* I. i. 24 We are not so rude understanders, or uncriticall speakers. **1767** STERNE *Tr. Shandy* X. xxiv, A most uncritical fever which attacked me at the beginning of this chapter. **1826** MISS MITFORD *Village* Ser. II. (1863) 361 She discovered none of the imputed sublimity; her uncritical eye could only scan the tremendous number of pages. **1854** MAURICE *Mor. & Met. Philos.* (ed. 2) 20 It has been the ungrateful fashion of some modern historians to speak of him as an uncritical retailer of anecdotes. **1890** 'R. BOLDREWOOD' *Col. Reformer* xx, He played.. well enough to satisfy the uncritical audience.

absol. **1874** SPENCER *Study Sociol.* v. 81 Statements.. readily accepted by the uncritical who believe all they see in print.

2. Showing lack of criticism or critical exactness; not in accordance with critical methods.

1846 J. KENRICK *Ess. Primæval Hist.* Pref. p. xii, An arbitrary and uncritical preference of the Septuagint to the Hebrew. **1855** J. PHILLIPS *Man. Geology* 420 A perverse and uncritical application of the Mosaic narrative. **1874** MAHAFFY *Soc. Life Greece* vii. 215 It is uncritical to judge an age by its greatest men.

Hence **un'critically** *adv.*

1807 G. CHALMERS *Caledonia* I. 402 Huntington, however, copies it, uncritically. **1858** SPENCER in *Westm. Rev.* July 195 We see that the notion, of late years idly repeated and uncritically received,.. involves us in sundry absurdities. **1895** *Blackw. Mag.* Nov. 634/1 You took with you a temperament uncritically alert to fresh impressions.

un'criticizable, *a.* (UN-^{1} 7 b.)

1858 HAWTHORNE *Fr. & It. Note-bks.* (1872) II. 137 Pictures.. cold, proper, and uncriticisable.

un'criticized, *ppl. a.* (UN-^{1} 8.)

1846 WORCESTER (citing Scott). **1884** *Pall Mall G.* 9 Dec. 3/1 The most intolerable government in the world—an absolute and uncriticized bureaucracy.

un'criticizingly, *adv.* (UN-^{1} 11.)

1850 F. W. NEWMAN *Phases* vi. 212 The claims.. implied .. the duty of all to sit at his feet uncriticizingly.

un'crooked, *ppl. a.* (UN-^{1} 8.)

1611 FLORIO, *Inobliquo*, vncrooked, straight. **1618** FLETCHER *Loyal Subj.* III. ii, Now you have moulded us.. To easie and obedient ways, uncrooked, Where the fair mind can never lose nor loiter. **1776** S. J. PRATT *Pupil of Pleas.* (1777) I. 184 Plain, clear, clean, uncrooked honesty.

un'cropped, *ppl. a.* [UN-^{1} 8.]

1. Of flowers, etc.: Not cut or plucked; not eaten by cattle. Also *fig.*

1601 SHAKS. *All's Well* V. iii. 328 If thou beest yet a fresh vncropped flower, Choose thou thy husband, and Ile pay thy dower. **1610** FLETCHER *Faithf. Sheph.* I. i, If I keep My Virgin Flower uncropt, pure, chaste, and fair. **1667** MILTON *P.L.* IV. 731 Where thy abundance wants Partakers, and uncropt falls to the ground. **1825** J. NEAL *Bro. Jonathan* III. 396 A bright circle of uncropped herbage was about the root. **1835** E. JESSE *Glean. Nat. Hist.* Ser. III. 228 Nature has given them a distaste for several flowers which are.. left uncropped.

2. Not cropped or cut; left uncut.

1802 COLEMAN *Br. Grins, Knt. & Friar* (1819) 101 Uncropp'd his ears, undock'd his flowing tail. **1895** *Westm. Gaz.* 7 June 3 Nineteen black-and-tans with uncropped ears. *Ibid.*, The first prize.. was won by.. an uncropped dog.

3. Of land: Not used for cropping.

1857 MILLER *Elem. Chem., Org.* xiii. § 1. 733 Allowing the land to lie uncropped for a year.

un'cross, *v.* [UN-^{2} 3.] *trans.* To take out of, change back from, a crossed position.

1599 G. SILVER *Paradoxes Def.* 4 He shal haue great disaduantage, both in making of a strong crosse, and also in vncrossing againe. **1611** COTGR., *Descroiser*, to vncrosse; to open,.. lay, or set straight a thing which standeth acrosse. **1760** STERNE *Tr. Shandy* IV. *Slawkenb. Tale*, Having uncrossed his arms with the same solemnity with which he crossed them. **1815** SCOTT *Guy M.* iii, The Dominie groaned deeply, uncrossed his legs. **1871** 'M. LEGRAND' *Cambr. Freshm.* ix. 169 Mr. Samuel uncrossed the knives, and let the salt lie, in a reckless manner.

un'crossable, *a.* (UN-^{1} 7 b.)

1882 R. H. PATTERSON *New Gold. Age* I. 112 The hardly known region beyond the almost uncrossable mountain wall.

un'crossed, *ppl. a.* [UN-^{1} 8.]

1. Not wearing or invested with a cross.

1560 BECON *Jewel of Joy* Pref., What a swarme of popyshe shauelyngs brought he forth,.. some crossed, some vncrossed. **1858** BAILEY *Age* 78 Unstarred, uncrossed, uneagled, pure of mind.

†**2.** Not obliterated or cancelled. (See CROSS *v.* 4.)

1611 SHAKS. *Cymb.* III. iii. 26 Such gaine the Cap of him, that makes him fine, Yet keepes his Booke vncros'd. **1640** *Wand. Jew telling Fortunes* C 2, These rich clothes cost me nothing, the Mercers uncrost booke shall sweare for me. **1690** NORRIS *Beatitudes* Ep. Ded., I am got too far in your Accounts..; some part of them I must ever leave uncrossed as a standing Hold upon me.

3. *fig.* Not thwarted or opposed.

a **1634** CHAPMAN *Rev. for Honour* III. i. 118 With as secure as ease 'T shall be accomplish'd as the blest desires Of uncross'd lovers. **1833** WORDSW. *Sonn.*, '*Desire we past*' 8 Conquering Reason, if self-glorified, Can nowhere move uncrossed by some new wall Or gulf of mystery. **1899** *Allbutt's Syst. Med.* VI. 516 An uncrossed influence arising somewhere above the lower end of the fourth ventricle.

absol. **1846** LANDOR *Imag. Conv.* I. 249/2 The studious.. the unhardened in politics, the uncrossed in literature.

4. Of a cheque: (see CROSS *v.* 7 c).

1882 [see *open cheque* s.v. OPEN *a.* 22 c]. **1884** *Law Times* 29 Nov. 79/2 Three.. were crossed generally 'and Co.', and three were uncrossed.

uncross-e'xaminable, *a.* (UN-^{1} 7 b), **uncross-e'xamined,** *ppl. a.* (UN-^{1} 8.)

1802-12 BENTHAM *Ration. Judic. Evid.* (1827) V. 285 Unsanctioned and uncross-examinable evidences. *Ibid.* III. 563 The evidence unsanctioned, and the author uncross-examined. *a* **1873** MILL *Ess. Relig.* (1874) 236 The uncross-examined testimony of extremely ignorant people.

un'crossly, *adv.* [UN-^{1} 11.] Not adversely.

1615 *Marr. & Wiving* in *Harl. Misc.* (Malh.) III. 253 That the joy their forward youth hath sought, Uncrossly matched, may come more near their thought.

un'crowded, *ppl. a.* (UN-^{1} 8.)

1701 ADDISON *Let. Italy* 76, Wks. 1721 I. 49 An amphitheater's amazing height.. That on its publick shows Unpeopled Rome, And held Uncrowded nations in its womb. **1732** J. WHALEY *Poems* 162 There roll your River's wide extended Waves, That on its Side uncrouded Fleets receives. **1791** COWPER *Yardley Oak* 55 The numerous flock That graz'd it stood beneath that ample cope Uncrowded. *a* **1817** T. DWIGHT *Trav. New Eng.*, etc. (1821) II. 412 The situation is.. at a sufficient distance from the Green Mountains to furnish a fine, uncrowded view of them. **1899** A. WRIGHT *Depopulation* 124 Strong for what? For the crowded millions, or for their uncrowded masters only?

un'crown, *v.* [UN-^{2} 4. Cf. Du. *ontkroonen* (Sewel), G. *entkrönen*.]

1. *trans.* To take the crown from (a ruler); to deprive of royalty.

a **1300** *Cursor M.* 9084 'Tas of,' he said, 'mi kinges croun þat i na langer agh to bere... I will þat yee vncroun me'. **1593** SHAKS. *3 Hen. VI*, III. iii. 232 He hath done me wrong, And therefore Ile vn-Crowne him, er't be long. **1605** SYLVESTER *Du Bartas* II. iii. II. 85 The voyce which made all things, Which sceptereth Shepheards, and un-croweneth Kings. **1645** E. CALAMY *Indictm. Eng.* 18 They seeke his life, and would uncrowne Him and his Posteritie. **1705** HICKERINGILL *Priest-cr.* (1721) I. 39 The insulting Priest.. let him know, that he that Crown'd him could Uncrown him. **1747** W. HORSLEY *Fool* (1748) II. 222 Where an Inquisitor-General.. is uncrowning the Monarchy. **1855** MACAULAY *Hist. Eng.* XI. III. 7 They had meant to obtain from him some guarantee.., but not to uncrown and banish him.

fig. **1638** FORD *Lady's Trial* II. iv, Prepare a welcome to uncrown the greatness Of his prevailing fates.

refl. **1846** *Literary Gaz.* Oct. 842 Francis II uncrowned himself, declaring that the holy Roman empire was at an end.

2. To remove a crown from (the head); to divest *of* (a crown).

1598 FLORIO, *Disghirlandare*, to vngarlande, to vncrowne. *a* **1658** LOVELACE *Poems* (1864) 167 Of the wet pearls uncrown thy hair. **1697** DRYDEN *Æneis* XII. 449 The Italians strip the dead Of his rich armour, and uncrown his head.

b. *fig.* To uncover; to display.

1849 M. ARNOLD *Shakespeare* 4 The loftiest hill That to the stars uncrowns his majesty.

Hence **un'crowning** *vbl. sb.*

1611 SPEED *Hist. Gt. Brit.* IX. viii. §45. 499/1 That the mindes of the vulgar should not bee vnpossessed with like expectation of Iohns vn-crowning. **1862** R. H. PATTERSON *Ess. Hist. & Art* 357 The uncrowning of the Seven-Hilled Queen by the barbarians of the North.

un'crowned, *ppl. a.* [UN-^{1} 8. Cf. MDu. *ongecroont*, Du. *ongekroond*, G. *ungekrönt*.]

†**1.** Untonsured. *Obs.*$^{-1}$

1393 LANGL. *P. Pl.* C. VI. 62 Hit by-comeþ for clerkus crist for to seruen, And knaues vncrouned to cart and to worche.

2. a. Not invested with a crown.

1634 BP. HALL *Contempl. N.T., Faithful Canaanite*, Never did such grace goe away uncrowned. **1810** CRABBE *Borough* xi. 58 Unlike the nobler beast, the Bear is bound, And with the Crown so near him, scowls uncrown'd. **1889** R. BRIDGES *Sonn.* lxvii, And Autumn with a sad smile fled uncrown'd From fruitless orchards and unripen'd grain.

b. ***uncrowned king*** (***queen***), a man (woman) exerting autocratic influence over a specified sphere; a dominant man (woman). Const. *of.*

1917 J. W. GERARD *My Four Years in Germany* ii. 22 Heydebrand, is known as the 'Uncrowned King of Prussia'. *a* **1940** in *Harper's Bazaar* (1969) Oct. 36/3 Lady Dashwood, uncrowned Queen of Diabolo. **1978** 'S. WOODS' *Exit Murderer* 154 The uncrowned King of the diamond smugglers. **1981** I. BOLAND tr. *Ginzburg's Within Whirlwind* II. iv. 226 Old General Nikishov.. had this handsome lady living with him.. the uncrowned Queen of Kolyma.

3. Not consummated or perfected.

1742 BLAIR *Grave* 731 The glad Soul Has not a Wish uncrown'd.

un'crucified, *ppl. a.* (UN-[1] 8.)
1528 TINDALE *Obed. Chr. Man* 87 b, Yf Christe had not rebuked the Phareses..he mighte haue be vncrucified vnto this daye.

†un'crud, *v. Obs.* [UN-[2] 3.] = UNCURD *v.*
1398 TREVISA *Barth. De P.R.* XIX. li. (Bodl. MS.), It is tempred wiþ a litel hony and salte and þan it cruddeþ neuer but vncruddeþ [**1495** vncurdyth] ʒif it bigynneþ to crudde in þe stomake. **1598** FLORIO, *Squagliare*, to..vncrud milk.

un'crudded, *ppl. a.* [UN-[1] 8.] = UNCURDLED.
1594 SPENSER *Epithal.* 175 Her brest like to a bowle of creame vncrudded.

un'crude, *a.* (UN-[1] 7.)
1574 NEWTON *Health Mag.* 31 b, Hippocrates commaundeth vs to minister Phisicke to those thinges that be concoct and to mooue the vncrude. **1675** EVELYN *Terra* 161 Mingle the residue with the grosser Compost.. frequently moistned with uncrude water.

un'cruel, *a.* (UN-[1] 7.)
1611 FLORIO, *Incrudele*, vncruell, milde. **1720** MRS. MANLEY *Power of Love* (1741) 272 If this Gentleman..had pressed her to make Him happy,..the uncruel fair One would not have been so hard-hearted to deny him. **1863** COWDEN CLARKE *Shaks. Char.* xiv. 363 Such a destiny would have been a sorry climax to thy uncruel misdemeanours.

un'crumbled, *ppl. a.* (UN-[1] 8.)
[**1775** ASH.] **1878** B. TAYLOR *Deukalion* I. iii. 30 There the sun Sheds..hoary splendor on uncrumbled stone.

un'crumple, *v.* [UN-[2] 3.]
1. *trans.* To restore from a crumpled state.
1611 COTGR., *Deffroncer*, to vnfrounce, vnwrinckle, vncrumple. *Ibid.*, *Desplissure*, an vnfoulding, vnplaiting, vnwrinkling, vncrumpling. **1863** LYTTON *Caxtoniana* I. vii. 92 No hand save his own could uncrumple the rose-leaf that chafed him. **1887** BROWNING *Parleyings, G. de Lairesse* v, Crisp buds a struggling bee Uncrumples.
2. *intr.* To become free from crumples.
1866 M. ARNOLD *Thyrsis* 84 Next year he will return,.. With whitening hedges, and uncrumpling fern.

un'crumpled, *ppl. a.* (UN-[1] 8.)
1854 CDL. WISEMAN *Fabiola* (1855) 39 The same scarf streams out, like a pennant, unruffled and uncrumpled by the breeze. **1873** BROWNING *Red Cott. Nt.-cap* 37 The varech limit-line, Burnt cinder-black with brown uncrumpled swathe Of berried softness.

un'crushable, *a.* (UN-[1] 7 b.)
1873 MISS BRADDON *Str. & Pilgr.* I. xiii, 'I have more sense of the fitness of things,' replied the uncrushable youngest. **1894** *Westm. Gaz.* 22 Feb. 3/3 Its good wearing and uncrushable habit recommend it still more. **1929** *Daily Mail* 20 July 8/3 What are our scientists and inventors doing that they have not yet invented uncrushable linen? **1935** C. ELLIS *Chem. Synthetic Resins* I. xxx. 641 Natural or artificial textile fibers can be given an uncrushable finish by the use of urea-formaldehyde resins condensed with alkalies. **1954** M. STEWART *Madam, will you Talk?* x. 78, I..shook out the green dress, thanking heaven and the research chemists for uncrushable materials. **1983** 'E. ANTHONY' *Company of Saints* i. 16 She..put on one of the long, uncrushable shifts that are a godsend to travellers.

un'crushed, *ppl. a.* (UN-[1] 8.)
1626 JACKSON *Creed* VIII. xxxi. §6 The adoration of this serpent, whilst it stood uncrusht, was..the most preposterous idolatry. **1759** STERNE *Tr. Shandy* II. xix, Provided all goes right after, and his cerebellum escapes uncrushed. **1856** MRS. BROWNING *Aur. Leigh* I. 457 Her head uncrushed by that round weight of hat. **1875** HUXLEY & MARTIN *Elem. Biol.* (1877) 8 Note the..solid and uncrushed transparent sacs; the soft crushed stained protoplasm.

un'crusted, *ppl. a.* (UN-[1] 8.)
[**1775** ASH.] **1880** *Contemp. Rev.* Feb. 210 An incandescent, uncrusted molten ball.

†uncry, *v.* [UN-[2] 3.] *trans.* To countermand.
1594 CAREW *Tasso* (1881) 66 Who in his name their ouerhardinesse Vncries, and straight to turne doth straight impose.

un'crystalled, *ppl. a.* (UN-[1] 8.)
1796 KIRWAN *Elem. Min.* (ed. 2) I. 446 The adherence of some uncrystalled substance.

un'crystalline, *a.* (UN-[1] 7.)
1833–4 J. PHILLIPS *Geol.* in *Encycl. Metrop.* (1845) VI. 702/1 The exterior of most uncrystalline rocks..seems to be slowly eaten away. **1875** RUSKIN *Fors Clav.* lx. 329, Such uncrystalline termination must now happen to all my work.

uncrysta'llizable, *a.* (UN-[1] 7 b.)
1791 W. HAMILTON *Berthollet's Dyeing* I. I. I. xii. 37 The uncrystallizable residue of the alum. **1812** SIR H. DAVY *Chem. Philos.* 496 This body is strongly acid and uncrystallizable. **1839** URE *Dict. Arts* 398 The small quantity of uncrystallizable sugar present in them. **1887** A. M. BROWN *Anim. Alkaloids* 142 Azotized uncrystallizable substances.
Hence **uncrystalliza'bility**.
1841 BRANDE *Chem.* (ed. 5) 1077 The uncrystallizability of molasses is partly referable to a similar cause.

un'crystallized, *ppl. a.* (UN-[1] 8.)
1759 STERNE *Tr. Shandy* I. xxiii, A dark covering of uncrystalized flesh and blood. **1794** R. J. SULIVAN *View Nat.* I. 467 The spherical..masses called geodes, are also crystaline, though they are, as it were, externally uncrystalized. **1830** HERSCHEL *Study Nat. Phil.* 242 The division of bodies into crystallized and uncrystallized, or imperfectly crystallized. **1874** GARROD & BAXTER *Mat. Med.* 277 Amorphous quinine, which bears the same relation to the crystallized alkaloid as uncrystallized syrup does to ordinary sugar.

†unct, *v.* Chiefly *Sc. Obs.* Also 5–6 vnt-, 5 vynte. [f. L. *unct-*, ppl. stem of *ungĕre*, *unguĕre* to smear, etc.] *trans.* To anoint.
14.. *Voc.* in Wr.-Wülcker 577/44 *Delibutus*, bebawdyd or vntyd. *c* **1425** WYNTOUN *Cron.* VIII. xxii. 2930 All kingis of Scotland Suld be sa vnctit befor regnand. *c* **1500** KENNEDY *Passion of Christ* 358 Thai laithly lippis vntit with fals tressoun. **1549** *Compl. Scot.* iv. 30 Osias vas bot aucht ʒeir of aige quhen he vas vnctit kyng. **1596** H. CLAPHAM *Briefe Bible* I. 75 [David] having raigned..33 yeares in Ierusalem, where he was the third time vncted.
Hence **†'uncting** *vbl. sb. Obs.*
1551 HAMILTON *Catechism* 131 Quhen the uncting is completit, yair followis ane Catechisme.

†'uncteous, obs. var. UNCTIOUS *a.*
1601 HOLLAND *Pliny* II. 510 The same also in the bruising will..be uncteous or fattie. **1603** —— *Plutarch's Mor.* 659 That sea water is uncteous, Aristotle..beareth witnesse.

unction (ˈʌŋkʃən). Forms: 4–5 vnccioun, 5–6 vnccion (5 -ione, 6 -yon); 5 unxioun; 5–6 uncion (5 ovncion); 5 unctioun, 6–7 vnction (6 vun-), 6– unction. [ad. L. *unctiōn-*, *unctio*, noun of action f. *unct-*, *ung(u)ĕre*: see UNCT *v.* So F. *onction* (12th c.), It. *unzione*, Sp. *uncion*, Pg. *unção*.]
1. The action of anointing with oil as a religious rite or symbol; occas. *ellipt.* = b.
1387 TREVISA *Higden* (Rolls) I. 113 Seynt Austyn..clepeþ it [*sc.* Mount Olivet] þe hulle of crisma and of vnccioun. *c* **1400** MAUNDEV. (Roxb.) iii. 10 þai make bot ane vnccioun, when þai christen childer. *c* **1430** LYDG. *Min. Poems* (Percy Soc.) 253 The hooly unctioun, shrift, hosyl, repentaunce. ? *a* **1500** *Chester Pl.* VIII. 289 Then both vnctions, sacrafices, and rites Ceremoniall Of the old Testament..shall vtterly cease. **1560** DAUS tr. *Sleidane's Comm.* 24 Then [he] treateth also of the other foure [sacraments], confirmation, order, matrimonye and Unction. **1697** J. POTTER *Antiq. Greece* II. ii. (1715) 196 The Act of Consecration chiefly consisted in the Unction, which was a ceremony derived from the most primitive Antiquity. **1745** BUTLER *Lives Saints* (1821) XI. 169 The ancient councils order them [*sc.* altars] to be consecrated by the unction of chrism, and the blessing of priests. **1768–74** TUCKER *Lt. Nat.* (1834) II. 414 The primitive fathers..practised exorcisms, unctions, signatures of the cross, and lustrations by holy water. **1856** R. A. VAUGHAN *Mystics* (1860) I. 94 The three sacraments.—Baptism, the Eucharist, and Unction. **1879** R. T. SMITH *Basil Gt.* x. 121 We bless both the water of baptism and the oil of unction.
personif. *c* **1425** LYDG. *Assembly of Gods* 1444 Then came to the fylde the mynystre fynall, Called Holy Vnccion, with a crysmatory.
b. ***extreme unction***: see EXTREME *a.* 3.
1513 *Life Hen. V* (1911) 182 After he had receaued the Sacraments of the Alter, and of extreame vunction. **1558** BP. WATSON *Sev. Sacram.* xxx. 193 To remoue these twoo euils, God hath ordeyned this Sacrament of extreme Unction to bee ministred. **1579** [see EXTREME *a.* 3]. **1602** J. COLVILLE *Parænese* uj, Dispysing the Sacrament of the altar, Celibat and extrem Vnction as many do nou a dayis. **1663** DRYDEN *Rival Ladies* v. ii, 'Tis like giving the extream Unction In the beginning of a Sickness. **1734** in *Cath. Rec. Soc. Publ.* (1914) XIV. 122 Her last Sickness..only left time for ye Extrem unction. **1783** W. THOMSON *Watson's Philip III* (1839) 373 The blessed sacrament was administered to him about midnight. He received the extreme unction at two o'clock in the morning. **1871** MISS MULOCK *Fair France* vii. 218 He told us a woman lay dying, and the priest was administering extreme unction.
2. The action of anointing as a symbol of investing with a certain office, esp. that of kingship.
c **1400** *Three Kings Cologne* (1886) 32 þe Iewes..seyden þat longe tyme aftir þe Natiuite of crist her vnccioun cesyd noʒt, but þey had many kyngis aftir. *a* **1500** *Cov. Corpus Christi Pl.* ii. 204 Of that kyng that I ma haue a syght,..At whose cumyng the tru ovncion of Juda schall seyse. **1626** D'EWES in Ellis *Orig. Lett.* Ser. I. III. 218 The Archbishop performed the unction, which I doubted hee should not. **1690** BOYLE *Chr. Virtuoso* II. 30 The Heavenly Coronation has a Virtue like that of the Unction of Saul. **1757** BURKE *Abridgm. Eng. Hist.* Wks. X. 430 He proceeded..to London to be crowned, and to sanctify by the solemnity of the unction the choice of the people. **1761** HUME *Hist. Eng.* I. ii. 43 Leo III gave Alfred the royal unction. **1845** SARAH AUSTIN *Ranke's Hist. Ref.* I. 19 Otho could receive the unction without scruple. **1869** FREEMAN *Norm. Conq.* (1875) III. xi. 41 The hands of Stigand might not administer an unction which was held to confer some-what of sacramental grace.
3. *fig.* A spiritual influence acting upon a person.
Chiefly in renderings and echoes of 1 John ii. 20 and of the hymn *Veni, Creator spiritus* 8.
1382 WYCLIF *1 John* ii. 20 But ʒe han vnccioun of the Holy Goost, and han knowe alle thinges. **1526** *Pilgr. Perf.* (W. de W. 1531) 154 They can not leaue & forsake the delectable wyne of contemplacyon & swete vnccyon of oyle of the holy goost. **1549** (Mar.) *Bk. Com. Prayer, Order. Priests*, Thou art the very comforter..and Unction spirituall. **1597** HOOKER *Eccl. Pol.* v. lv. §6 There is no other way how it should grow but either by the grace of vnion with deitie, or by the grace of vnction receiued from deitie. **1627** COSIN '*Veni Creator*,' Thou the anointing Spirit art;..Thy blessed vnction from aboue Is comfort, life, and fire of loue. **1663** BP. PATRICK *Parab. Pilgr.* xxxvi, When he felt those distillations on his head, he could think of nothing else but the Vnction from above. **1693** DRYDEN '*Creator Spirit*' ii, Come, and thy Sacred Unction bring To Sanctifie us, while we sing! **1763** J. PAYNE tr. *Imit. Christ* III. xix. 214 Give me, instead of all worldly comfort, the Divine Unction of Thy Holy Spirit. **1858** NEALE *Bernard de M.* (1865) 26 The mention of thy glory Is unction to the breast. **1869** FREEMAN *Norm. Conq.* III. xi. 46 So now the oil poured on the head of God's servant might be a true sign of the inner unction of the heart.
b. Deep spiritual feeling, or the manifestation of this in language and utterance; a manner suggestive of religious earnestness or appreciation of spiritual things.
In later use freq. in depreciative sense, implying that the feeling or manner is superficial or assumed, or is tinged with obvious self-complacency.
1692 BURNET *Past. Care* Pref. p. xxxiv, I began my Studies in Divinity with reading these, and I never yet grew weary of them; they..carry so much of unction and life in them, that [etc.]. **1817** LADY MORGAN *France* (1818) I. 85 The peasantry..were seen..chaunting the office with as much faith and unction as if they had been paid. **1830** COLERIDGE *Table-t.* 1 June, There is a great decay of devotional unction in the numerous books of prayers put out now-a-days. **1870** LOWELL *Among my Bks.* 235 That clerical unction which in a vulgar nature so easily degenerates into greasiness.
c. *transf.* A manner of utterance or address showing real appreciation or enjoyment of the subject or situation.
1815 SCOTT *Guy M.* xvi, I have heard you too often describe the scene with comic unction. **1849** C. BRONTE *Shirley* vi, He delivered the haughty speech of Caius Marcius to the starving citizens with unction. **1886** *Pall Mall G.* 7 Dec. 4/2 Is an actor subject to dismissal..because he does not 'throw enough unction' into his part?
4. The action of anointing or rubbing with an ointment or oil as a lubricating or preserving substance.
1580 HESTER tr. *Fioravanti's Disc. Chirurg.* 21 The first thing is to euacuate the stomacke, the second to sweate, the thirde vnccion. **1605** B. JONSON *Volpone* II. i, Applying onely a warme napkin to the place, after the vnction and fricace. **1632** LITHGOW *Trav.* (1906) 235 We saw..the place of Unction, which is a foure squared stone;..on which (say they) the dead body of our Saviour lay, and was embalmed. **1726** POPE *Odyss.* XIX. 590 The bath renew'd, she ends the pleasing toil With plenteous unction of ambrosial oil. **1740** JOHNSON *Life Drake* Wks. IV. 425 In hot countries,..the natives only use unction to preserve them from the other extreme of weather. **1887** D. MAGUIRE *Art Massage* iii. (ed. 4) 39 Unction does not, properly speaking, form part of the manipulations classified amongst frictions.
5. Any soft composition used for anointing or lubricating; an unguent or ointment.
1580 HESTER tr. *Fioravanti's Disc. Chirurg.* 26 b, Glisters, Vomittes, Purgations, and Vnctions;..the vnctions dissolue the winde. **1602** SHAKS. *Ham.* IV. vii. 142, I bought an Vnction of a Mountebanke. **1631** MABBE *Celestina* VI. 78 Clothing them [*sc.* their faces] with diuers colourings, glisseninngs, paintings, vnctions, oyntments. **1760** R. JAMES *Canine Madness* 132 He must..get a considerable quantity of the unction rubbed into the arm-pits. **1860** FROUDE *Hist. Eng.* VI. 101 The next day, Arras having sent the necessary unction, the ceremony was performed at the Abbey. **1884** F. J. BRITTEN *Watch & Clockm.* 202 The unction or paste obtained by rubbing two blue stones together.
fig. **1657** TRAPP *Comm. Esther* ii. 12 Let women learn and labour to smell of Christ, who is the royal Unction.
b. *fig.* A soothing influence or reflection.
1602 SHAKS. *Ham.* III. iv. 145 Lay not a flattering Vnction to your soule, That not your trespasse, but my madnesse speakes. **1836** HOR. SMITH *Tin Trump.* I. 7 The stings of conscience would be intolerable, could we not lay some flattering unction to our souls. **1877** FARRAR *Days of Youth* 108 Think not to lay to your diseased conscience the flattering unction that your sin was the result of circumstance.

'unctional, *a.* [f. prec. 3 b.] Full of spiritual unction; deeply religious.
1849 TWEEDIE *Life J. Macdonald* iv. 398 The discourse.. is rich, unctional, and full. **1864** *Mem. G. Paterson* 31 There was..no glib use of a sweet unctional phraseology.

'unctionless, *a.* [f. as prec.] Devoid of spiritual unction.
1842 *Blackw. Mag.* LI. 163 Tillotson and Burnet..show it in all the unctionless elegance..of its philosophic good sense.

†'unctious, *a. Obs.* Also 5–6 vnctius, vnctyous, 6–7 vnctious. [f. L. *unct-um* ointment: see -IOUS.]
= UNCTUOUS *a.* 1. (Common *c* 1600–1725).
1477 NORTON *Ord. Alch.* v. (MS. Ashm. 1445) fol. 67 þe same degrees..Vnctius sapor engender euer shall. **1542** BOORDE *Dyetary* xiii. (1870) 265 Euery thyng that is vnctious..doth swymme aboue in the brynkes of the stomacke. **1594** CAREW *Huarte's Exam. Wits* vi. 84 That [moisture] which springs from the aire maketh them to prooue vnctious and ful of oyle and fat. **1639** T. DE GRAY *Expert Farrier* 274, I will never use any other oyle or vnctious matter in any medicine. **1697** TRYON *Way to Health* vi. (ed. 3) 100 Whereby it is made more Spirituous than other Waters, and of a fat unctious Quality. **1764** HARMER *Observ.* 408 Lamps that are supplied with more than ordinary quantities of oyl, or other unctious substances.
fig. **1645** QUARLES *Sol. Recant.* VI. 66 Or is she gone to oyle the wings of Time With unctious pleasures in some foraine Clime? **1646** —— *Judgem. & Mercy* Wks. (Grosart) I. 69 Steepe thy stupid senses in unctious, in delightful sports.
Hence **†'unctiousness.** *Obs.*
1560 WHITEHORNE *Ord. Souldiours* 27 So that nothinge else be burnte but..certaine grosse vnctiousnes of the saltepeter. *a* **1661** FULLER *Worthies, Warwick.* III. (1662) 115 It burneth..clear and bright, as if the Sappe thereof had a fire-feeding Unctiousness therein.

unctment, obs. Sc. f. OINTMENT.

†**unctu·ose**, *a. Obs. rare.* [ad. med.L. *unctuōsus.*] = UNCTUOUS *a.*

c **1400** *Lanfranc's Cirurg.* 137 Also y seye þat oyle of roses ..is noȝt vnctuose, but is dreyȝe. **1471** RIPLEY *Comp. Alch.* I. vi. (MS. Ashm. 1445), And we make calxes vnctuose both white & red.

unctuosity (ʌŋktjuːˈɒsɪtɪ). Forms: 4–5 vnctuosite, 6 -yte, 6–7 -itie, 7 -ity; 6 vnctuositee, 7 unctuositie, -ocity, 7– unctuosity. [a. OF. *unctuosite* (F. *onctuosité*), or ad. med.L. *unctuōsitas*, f. *unctuōs-us* UNCTUOUS: see -ITY. Cf. It. *untuosità, untosità*, Sp. *untuosidad*, Pg. *unctuosidade.*]

1. Unctuousness; oiliness, greasiness.

1398 TREVISA *Barth De P.R.* XIX. xxxiii. (Bodl. MS.), For vnctuosite leide to þe tunge openeþ swiþe & dissolueþ, & sotel substaunce entreþ ful swiþe. c **1400** tr. *Secreta Secret., Gov. Lordsh.* 98 Swetnesse, bitternesse, saltnesse, & vnctuosite. **1539** ELYOT *Cast. Helthe* (1541) 37 Whay,..by the vnctuositee of the butter,..is both moist and norishing. **1562** BOORDE *Dyetary* xiii. Ej, The vnctuosyte of it doth.. augmente the heate of the lyuer. **1601** HOLLAND *Pliny* II. 558 A certaine unctuositie or fattinesse it carrieth with it. **1644** DIGBY *Nat. Bodies* xix. §8. 173 They haue a high degree of aqueous humidity ioyned with their vnctuosity. **1712** tr. *Pomet's Hist. Drugs* I. 102 The more nitrous and fossile the Salts are, the more Unctuosity they have. **1756** C. LUCAS *Ess. Waters* II. 58 The gentlemen who talk of.. unctuosity in sea water. **1805** SAUNDERS *Min. Waters* 487 Inhabitants of hot climates, protected by the greater unctuosity of their skin,..are enabled to lead an almost amphibious life. **1873** *Beeton's Dict. Comm., Musk*..comes to us dry, with a kind of unctuosity.

2. *fig.* Unctuous religiosity or complacency.

1884 TENNYSON *Becket* III. iii, From whence there puffed out such an incense of unctuosity into the nostrils of our Gods of Church and State. **1885** *Spectator* 22 Aug. 1114/4 The author's style,..its well-known grace, and its at least equally well-known unctuosity.

unctuous (ˈʌŋktjuəs), *a.* Also 4–7 vnctuous, 6 ounctuous; 5, 7 vnctuos. [ad. med.L. *unctuōs-us*, f. L. *unct-um* ointment, f. *unct-*, ppl. stem of *ung(u)ĕre* to anoint. Cf. OF. *unctueus* (F. *onctueux*), It. and Sp. *untuoso*, Pg. *unctuoso.*]

1. Of the nature or quality of an unguent or ointment; oily, greasy.

1387 TREVISA *Higden* (Rolls) I. 113 þe fruit of olyue is ful of liȝt, likynge, and vnctuous. **1528** PAYNELL *Salerne's Regim.* b ij b, The vnctuous fleme whiche is engendred by mynglynge, of vnctuous bloud and fleme. **1555** EDEN *Decades* (Arb.) 293 Gummes..and other vnctuous frutes and trees growing in hotte regions. **1604** F. HERING *Mod. Defence* 22 Sallet oile, butter, or any other vnctuous things. a **1691** BOYLE *Hist. Air* (1692) 202 As if all the unctuous parts that were wanting in the dried portion of the cheese had retired thither. **1733** *Phil. Trans.* XXXVIII. 64 When this Operation succeeds rightly, there comes forth, First, a thick unctuous Oil. **1818** *Art Preserv. Feet* 105 The unctuous matter which exudes from excretory vessels. **1875** C. C. BLAKE *Zool.* 152 The poison itself is an unctuous gelatinous fluid.

b. Of meat: Greasy, fat, rich. Now *arch.*

1495 *Trevisa's Barth. De P.R.* XIX. xlv. 888 Vnctuous meete fletyth aboue for the lyghtnesse therof. **1539** ELYOT *Cast. Helthe* (1541) 18 b, Meates..fatte and vnctuous, nourisheth, and maketh soluble. **1555** EDEN *Decades* (Arb.) 147 When their fingers are imbrued with any ounctuous meates. **1610** B. JONSON *Alch.* II. ii, The swelling vnctuous paps Of a fat pregnant sow. **1650** BULWER *Anthrop.* 241 They feed upon unctuous and sweet meats. **1821** LAMB *Elia* I. *Grace before Meat*, Those unctuous morsels of deer's flesh. *transf.* **1675** GREW *Disc. Tastes Plants* i. §13 Contrary to an Unctuous Taste, are Astringent and Pungent. **1879** *Cassell's Techn. Educ.* IV. 162/2 The exquisite and unctuous taste which this excellent mollusk gives.

c. Characterized by the presence of oil or fat.

1641 MILTON *Reform.* II. Wks. 1851 III. 66 Warming their Palace Kitchins, and from thence their unctuous and epicurean paunches, with the almes of the blind. **1768** [see 1 d]. **1791** COWPER *Iliad* II. 664 Pallas rear'd him: her own unctuous fane She made his habitation. **1837** DICKENS *Pickw.* iv, There was something in the sound of the last word, which roused the unctuous boy. **1856** EMERSON *Eng. Traits, Charac.* Wks. (Bohn) II. 62 English day-labourers.. are of an unctuous texture.

d. *unctuous sucker*: (see quot.).

1768 PENNANT *Brit. Zool.* (1776) III. 135 Unctuous Sucker. This fish takes the name of sea snail from the soft and unctuous texture of its body, resembling that of the land snail.

2. Of ground or soil: Of a soft adhesive nature; fat, rich.

1555 EDEN *Decades* (Arb.) 227 As fat and vnctuous groundes..yelde a fast and firme moysture. **1675** EVELYN *Terra* (1676) 30 Good and excellent Earth should be..not too unctuous nor too lean. **1693** —— *De la Quint. Compl. Gard.* I. 18 Some [soils] are Unctuous and Sticking together. **1707** MORTIMER *Husb.* 68 A soft unctuous Chalk, which is the best for Lands. **1777** ROBERTSON *Hist. Amer.* (1778) I. 474 Their hunger is so great as compels them to eat ..a kind of unctuous earth. **1813** BAKEWELL *Introd. Geol.* (1815) 297 When the matrix, or the substance which principally fills veins, is a soft unctuous clay. **1839** MURCHISON *Silurian System* 435 A layer of unctuous shale or fuller's earth. **1867** D. G. MITCHELL *Rural Studies* 293 There are farms I know, unctuous with an accumulated fertility.

3. Of vapours, etc.: Partaking of the nature of oil or grease.

1606 N. B[AXTER] *Sydney's Ourania* D 3 b, For Shepheards fayne..That from Bodyes buried in Summer season, An vnctuos vapour, hot and dry, doth rise. **1610** B. JONSON *Alch.* II. iii, A humide exhalation, which we call *Materia liquida*, or the vnctuous water. **1635–56** COWLEY *Davideis* III. Note xl, Lambent fire is, A thin unctuous exhalation made out of the Spirits of Animals. **1712** BLACKMORE *Creation* IV. 173 Evening trains of unctuous vapours. **1774** GOLDSM. *Nat. Hist.* I. 390 Falling stars, which are thought to be no more than unctuous vapours, raised from the earth to small heights. **1812** SIR H. DAVY *Chem. Philos.* Introd. 19 Unctuous or inflammable gas. **1820** SHELLEY *Sensit. Pl.* III. 74 Unctuous meteors from spray to spray..flitted in broad noonday Unseen. **1840** DICKENS *Old C. Shop* xviii, And an unctuous steam came floating out.

4. Having an oily or greasy feel or appearance. Also of feel, touch, etc.

1668 WILKINS *Real Char.* 82 Being of an unctuous touch, and used for Sallets. **1804** ABERNETHY *Surg. Obs.* 44 But it is not at all unctuous to the touch. **1828** J. E. SMITH *Eng. Flora* II. 9 Pubescence mealy, friable, and unctuous. **1863** HAWTHORNE *Our Old Home* (1879) 96 Excellently carved in oak, now black with time and unctuous with kitchen-smoke. **1876** DUHRING *Dis. Skin* 17 To the touch the skin has a soft, smooth, somewhat unctuous feel.

5. Characterized by spiritual unction (in later use *esp.* of an assumed or superficial nature); complacently agreeable or self-satisfied: **a.** Of persons.

1742 CHEYNE in *Byrom's Rem.* (1857) 331, I think him.. more plain,..luminous, and unctuous, than any I ever met with. **1854** *Poultry Chron.* I. 292/2 Bland, unctuous, and rosy as they appear, they are nevertheless excessively fastidious. **1882** J. ASHTON *Soc. Life Reign Q. Anne* II. 138 A Quaker could not be drawn without being caricatured into an unctuous rogue. **1896** 'IAN MACLAREN' *Kate Carnegie* 171 A certain class of smug, self-contented, unctuous men.

b. Of speech, conduct, etc.

1822 LAMB *Elia* I. *Chimney-Sweepers*, It was a pleasure to see the sable younkers lick in the unctuous meat, with *his* more unctuous sayings. **1848** DICKENS *Dombey* iv, Laying an unctuous emphasis upon the words. **1871** MORLEY *Carlyle* in *Crit. Misc.* Ser. I. 217 In the corrupt and unctuous forms of a mechanical religious profession.

ˈ**unctuously**, *adv.* [f. prec. + -LY².] In an unctuous manner; with unction.

1864 WEBSTER. **1872** GOLDW. SMITH in *Fortn. Rev.* Mar. 246 The [religious] faith in the name of which the aristocracy had unctuously stolen the property of the nation. **1888** MISS BRADDON *Fatal Three* I. v, 'I think hers is about the best case,' answered the Doctor unctuously.

ˈ**unctuousness.** Also 4 vnctuosnes. [f. as prec. + -NESS.] The quality or state of being unctuous.

1398 TREVISA *Barth. De P.R.* XIX. xxxiii. (Bodl. MS.), Somme vnctuous þinges greueþ þe breste wᵗ drynes þᵗ is þerin, as it fareþ in oile of nottes, for suche haue not pure vnctuosnes. **1644** DIGBY *Nat. Bodies* xxix. (1658) 316 Softnesse, unctuousnesse, and viscousnesse, encreaseth blacknesse. **1682** T. GIBSON *Anat.* (1697) 25 Whilst Nature takes care that it..besmear both the Stomach and Intestines with its Unctuousness. **1705** ADDISON *Italy* (1733) 140 Its Unctuousness will make it heavy. **1758** REID tr. *Macquer's Chym.* I. 23 We shall afterwards see that, bating this unctuousness, it has none of the properties of oils. **1891** W. A. JAMIESON *Dis. Skin* (ed. 3) i. 11 The office of the coil glands is to impart unctuousness to the skin.

fig. **1866** *Pall Mall G.* 3 Jan., The coarse, self-exhibiting unctuousness with which his book overflows.

†**uncture.** *Obs.* [a. OF. *uncture* (*ungture, ointure*), or ad. L. *unctūra*, f. *unct-, ung(u)ĕre.* So Sp. and Pg. *untura.*] Ointment.

c **1400** *Lanfranc's Cirurg.* 41 For þys vncture ratefieþ & efenyþ þo placys by whom akþe goth to þe brayn. *Ibid.* 103 þenne y dede efte sonys þe same medycine & þe same vncture. c **1440** *Pallad. on Husb.* VI. 128 For sheep yshorn make vncture of lupynys.

un'cuckold, *v.* (UN-² 3.)

1789 J. MOORE *Zeluco* xxi, I never yet heard of any method by which a man can be uncuckolded.

un'cuckolded, *ppl. a.* (UN-¹ 8.)

1606 SHAKS. *Ant. & Cl.* I. ii. 76 It is a deadly sorrow, to beholde a foule Knaue vncuckolded.

un'cudgelled, *ppl. a.* (UN-¹ 8.)

1682 SHADWELL *Medal* 1 The fool uncudgell'd, for one Libel swells.

ˈ**uncular**, *a. rare*⁻¹. [f. UNCLE *sb.*, after *avuncular.*] Belonging to an uncle.

1847 DE QUINCEY *Span. Nun* vi. Misc. (1854) 12 The grave Don..clasped the hopeful young gentleman..to his *uncular* and rather angular breast.

un'culled, *ppl. a.* (UN-¹ 8.)

1667 MILTON *P.L.* XI. 436 A sweatie Reaper from his Tillage brought First Fruits,..Uncull'd, as came to hand. **1820** WORDSW. *River Duddon* VII. 12 There are whose calmer mind it would content To be an unculled floweret of the glen. **1826** GALT *Last of Lairds* i. 7 She was neither particular in her attire, nor methodical in her work, and her words were unculled.

†**un'culpable**, *a. Obs.* [UN-¹ 7 b, 5 b.] Not culpable or blameworthy; free from fault or blame.

1382 WYCLIF *Num.* xxxii. 22 Thanne ȝe shulen be vnculpable anentis God, and anentis Irael. **1532** MORE *Confut. Tindale* Wks. 355/1 For then is the fayth of the church in that point infallyble, or at yᵉ lest vnculpable. **1594** HOOKER *Eccl. Pol.* III. vii. §2 Which the Iewes obseruing as yet vn-written,..are notwithstanding in that respect vnculpable. **1613** JACKSON *Creed* II. vii. §11 We vpon inuincible or vnculpable ignorance, did not apprehend it for such. **1659** STANLEY *Hist. Philos.* XIII. (1687) 912 It behoves us..not to suffer wickedness to escape unculpable. **1748** RICHARDSON *Clarissa* VII. 55 You shall set over me, instead of my poor obliging, but really unculpable Hannah, your Betty Barnes.

†**un'cult**, *a. Obs.* [UN-¹ 7, 5 b.] Uncultured.

1675 J. SMITH *Chr. Relig. App.* II. i. 4 The Gallick Druides (that most uncult Tribe of Divines).

†**un'culted**, *ppl. a.* [UN-¹ 8.] Uncultivated.

1548 *Act 2 & 3 Edw. VI*, c. 13 §16 The saide Countrey of Wales was throughe civile dissencion unculted. **1685** R. BURTON *Eng. Emp. Amer.* vii. 107 Whatever wast or unculted Country is the Discovery of any Prince, it is the Right of that Prince.

un'cultivable, *a.* (UN-¹ 7 b.)

1663 HEATH *Flagellum* (1672) 12 Which like Weeds, sprung out of his rank and uncultivable nature. **1849** *Florist* 185 This interesting class of plants..a few years ago were thought uncultivable by common people. **1869** RUSKIN *Q. of Air* §79 The sedges are essentially the clothing of waste, and more or less poor or uncultivable soils.

Hence **uncultiva'bility**.

1880 A. GRAY *Struct. Bot.* iii. §1. 38 This occurs in species of Gerardia and other plants of the same family, the uncultivability of which is thereby explained.

un'cultivatable, *a.* (UN-¹ 7 b.)

1870 *Putnam's Mag.* Sept. 290/1 The land..is..perfectly uncultivatable.

un'cultivate, *ppl. a.* [UN-¹ 8 b, 5 b.] = next.

1659 H. MORE *Immort. Soul* III. x. 428 The greatest part of the Universe..would lye as it were uncultivate, like a desart of sand. **1694** ADDISON *Acc. Eng. Poets* 19 An age that yet uncultivate and rude, Where-e'er the poet's fancy led, pursu'd..the unfrequented floods. **1732** J. WHALEY *Poems* 286 A pleasing Wildness.., That seems uncultivate and rude to lie. **1785** ANNA SEWARD *Lett.* (1811) I. 36 Uncultivate minds are always in extremes respecting those high abilities whose elevation they cannot clearly discern.

un'cultivated, *ppl. a.* [UN-¹ 8 and 5 b.]

1. *fig.* Of persons, their faculties, etc.: Not improved by education or training; uncultured.

1646 SIR T. BROWNE *Pseud. Ep.* I. iii. 8 Whereof their uncultivated understandings scarce holding any theory, they are but bad discerners of verity. **1746** HERVEY *Medit.* (1818) 145 Such are the usual products of savage nature! such, the furniture of the uncultivated soul! **1796** MME. D'ARBLAY *Camilla* III. 146 Mr. Dennel was a man as unfavoured by nature as he was uncultivated by art. **1864** MRS. CARLYLE *Lett.* (1883) III. 224 He was a coarse, uncultivated man. **1898** J. ARCH *Story of Life* 247 Their uncultivated minds were like dark lanterns with a rushlight inside.

b. Of nations, times, etc.: Not improved by culture; uncivilized.

1725 BERKELEY *Proposal* Wks. 1871 III. 227 They shew as much natural sense as other uncultivated nations. **1779** *Mirror* No. 13, The rude and uncultivated age in which the poet is supposed to have lived. **1817** JAS. MILL *Brit. India* Pref. p. xiii, Tacitus..was certainly not acquainted with the language of our uncultivated ancestors.

2. Of land: Not cultivated or laboured; untilled.

1683 BURNET tr. *More's Utopia* 90 A part of their Soil, of which they make no use, but let it lie idle and uncultivated. **1697** DRYDEN *Æneis* I. 425 It looked a wild uncultivated shore. **1719** SWIFT *Hist. Engl.* Wks. 1841 I. 555/1 The fields lay uncultivated, all the arts of civil life were banished. **1781** GIBBON *Decl. & F.* xviii. II. 95 A more numerous band.. were easily admitted to share a superfluous waste of uncultivated land. **1849** MACAULAY *Hist. Eng.* iii. I. 313 How many square miles, which were formerly uncultivated or ill cultivated, have..been fenced and carefully tilled. **1869** TOZER *Highl. Turkey* I. 340 The open country extends in a sea of green vegetation, which gives way..to uncultivated land.

fig. **1693** *Ladies Petit.* in *Harl. Misc.* (1809) IV. 329 Will you not provide that so many longing young ladies shall not lie unploughed, unharrowed, and uncultivated? **1738** WOLLASTON *Relig. Nat.* (ed. 6) §3. 55, I believe many more [things] will in time be cleard, which..are yet in their dark and uncultivated estate. **1828** B. WHITE in Liddon *Life Pusey* (1893) I. 166 The growth of some weeds which were breaking out in the long uncultivated ground of my mind.

b. Of plants: Not produced or improved by cultivation; growing without tillage or care.

1697 DRYDEN *Virg. Georg.* II. 601 Trees of Nature, and each common Bush, Uncultivated thrive. **1809** W. IRVING *Knickerb.* I. v, The roots and uncultivated fruits of the earth. **1871** GARROD *Met. Med.* (ed. 3) 286 The uncultivated plant is stated to be preferable to the cultivated.

3. Not attended to or practised; not properly trained or developed.

1684–5 BOYLE *Min. Waters* 110 A First essay upon so difficult and uncultivated a Subject as I have ventur'd to treat of. **1712** STEELE *Spect.* No. 334 ¶3 The Art [of dancing]..lies altogether uncultivated. **1751** EARL ORRERY *Remarks Swift* (1752) 50 Swift indeed has left no weapon of sarcasm untried, no branch of satyr uncultivated. **1796** MME. D'ARBLAY *Camilla* IV. 93 The superior force of goodness, even where most simple and uncultivated. **1837** HALLAM *Hist. Lit.* I. iv. §11 He became..a comic writer.. in the same vein of uncultivated genius.

Hence **un'cultivatedness**.

1764 HARMER *Observ.* Pref., There is a sameness in human nature every where, under the like degree of uncultivatedness.

unculti'vation. [UN-¹ 12 and 5 b.] Lack of cultivation; want of culture.

1796 J. MOSER *Hermit of Caucasus* I. 52 The disorder and uncultivation that reigned in it. **1829** CARLYLE *Misc.* (1857) II. 112 It is the sign of uncultivation to wonder. **1840** MILL *Diss. & Disc.* (1859) I. 94 The question often is, which is least prejudicial.., uncultivation or malcultivation?

†**un'cultived,** *ppl. a. Obs.* [UN-^{1} 8.] = UNCULTIVATED *ppl. a.* 2.

1605 VERSTEGAN *Dec. Intell.* ix. 292 Leyland, [so named] of the lying *legh* or empty thereof, to wit, vncultyued. **1614** RALEIGH *Hist. World* II. xvii. 484 Hee had now both horse and chariots good store to cary his prouisions through those vncultived places.

un'culturable, *a.* [UN-^{1} 7 b and 5 b.] Incapable of receiving culture or cultivation.

1860 I. TAYLOR *Spir. Hebrew Poetry* (1873) 118 The endeavour to find your way to the mind and heart of untutored and of unculturable and sanguinary savages. **1881** *Athenæum* 10 Sept. 329/2 The existence of large areas of forest, mountain, and unculturable waste in each province.

un'culture. [UN-^{1} 12, 5 b.] Lack of culture.

c **1624** BP. HALL *Serm.* Wks. 1837 V. 205 Idleness, ill-husbandry, in mistiming, neglect of meet helps, unculture, ill choice of seeds. **1812** SHELLEY *Let. to E. Hitchener* 6 June, Might not your father,..led on by the unculture of his mind, form conclusions of the utmost asperity? **1896** *Daily News* 10 Mar. 6/4 The humiliation of western culture before Russian unculture and Turkish fanaticism.

un'cultured, *ppl. a.* [UN-^{1} 8.]

1. Of soil or plants: Not cultivated or subjected to cultivation.

1555 EDEN *Decades* (Arb.) 299 By reason of so many marisshes,..it is yet rude vncultured, and lyttle knowen. **1607** J. CARPENTER *Plaine Mans Plough* 197 Brambles and tares, such as naturally spring of evill and uncultured fields. **1633** BP. HALL *Hard Texts* 85 Some obscure valley that lies ..utterly uncultured. **1762–9** FALCONER *Shipwr.* III. 247 A sanguine train, With midnight ravage, scour the uncultured plain. **1804** CHARLOTTE SMITH *Conversations*, etc. I. 150 Blushing, the uncultured Rose Hangs high her beauteous blossoms there. **1872** STOPFORD BROOKE in L. P. Jacks *Life & Lett.* (1917) I. xiii. 267 The uncultured breast of Blackford and the Pentlands.

2. *fig.* Not developed or improved by education; not characterized by culture; unrefined.

1777 T. SWIFT *Gamblers* I. 56 At school half brute, the self-same passions roll, And stamp for life his low, uncultur'd soul. **1796** MME. D'ARBLAY *Camilla* II. 369 Those who unite native hardness with uncultured minds and manners. **1840** CARLYLE *Heroes* ii. (1904) 67 The man [Mahomet] was an uncultured semi-barbarous Son of Nature. **1878** BOSW. SMITH *Carthage* 277 He was a rough soldier, uncultured as Marius and hardly less cruel.

un'cumber, *v.* [UN-^{2} 3.] *trans.* To free from encumbrance; to disencumber. Also *refl.*

c **1440** *Pallad. on Husb.* VI. 51 Haue up this stones; storne [*sic*] vnto the wallis, They may thy feeld vnkomber & defende. **1529** MORE *Dyaloge* II. x. 60 b/2 For a pek of otys she wyll not fayle to vncumber theym of theyr husbondys. **1571** GOLDING *Calvin on Ps.* xviii. 37 When he was browght to utter despayre, he was uncombered agein by the help of God. **1620** SHELTON *Quix.* II. lviii. 385 When Don Quixote saw himselfe in open field, free and vn-cumbred from Altisidora's wooing. **1876** *Whitby Gloss.* 205.

un'cumbered, *ppl. a.* [UN-^{1} 8. Cf. MSw. *okumbradh.*] Not encumbered.

1551 RECORDE *Pathw. Knowl.* To Rdr., For neither is..mi laiser so quiet and vncombered, that I maie perform iustlie so learned a laboure. **1600** HAKLUYT *Voy.* III. 64 But a seruant,..a good footman, and vncombred with any furniture..ouertooke one of them. **1699** DRYDEN *To J. Driden* 18 Lord of your self, uncumber'd with a Wife. **1738** POPE *Epil. Sat.* I. 31, I have..Seen him, uncumber'd with the Venal tribe, Smile without Art. **1748** THOMSON *Cast. Indol.* II. xxii, Unless..mighty patrons the coy sisters call Up to the sun-shine of uncumber'd ease. **1823** J. BADCOCK *Dom. Amusem.* 210 He is..uncumbered with the concealment sometimes practised, of bushes or sprigs hung about his person. **1870** BRYANT *Iliad* VIII. I. 261 The Trojans,..In a clear space uncumbered by the slain, Held council.

†**un'cunning,** *sb. Obs.* Forms: (see CUNNING *sb.*). [UN-^{1} 12.] Lack of knowledge; ignorance. Common in 14–15th c.

c **1290** *Beket* 1028 in *S. Eng. Leg.* I. 136 For euere ich dradde for oncunninge mi soule forto spille. **1338** R. BRUNNE *Chron.* (1810) 256, I wite þis no man, Bot myn vnconyng, þis folie my self bigan. *c* **1380** WYCLIF *Sel. Wks.* II. 394 þerfore trewe men in þis cheef shulden be wel paied of þis vncunnyng. *c* **1412** HOCCLEVE *De Reg. Princ.* 325 Myn vnkonyng of þat me schal excuse, Of whiche matere knowleche haue I non. *c* **1449** PECOCK *Repr.* II. iv. 156 At whiche men mowe lawȝe and take bourde for her symplenes or her vnkunnyng as of folis. *a* **1470** H. PARKER *Dives & Pauper* (W. de W. 1496) I. lvii. 99/1 They wolde excuse them by unconnynge yf they dyde amys.

un'cunning, *a.* Now *arch.* Forms: (see CUNNING *a.*). [UN-^{1} 10. Cf. OHG. *unchunnênti*, Goth. *unkunnands.*]

1. Of persons: Ignorant, unlearned, unskilful.

α. **1340** *Ayenb.* 59 Hi..ziggeþ þet hi byeþ..zuo zenuol and zuo onconnynde. *c* **1340** HAMPOLE *Pr. Consc.* 152 Bot som men has wytte to understand, And yhit þai er ful unkunand. *c* **1400** *Rowland & O.* 293 Unconnande Sarazene,..in þis place þi wykkednes es ȝare. **1456** SIR G. HAYE *Law Arms* (S.T.S.) 222 Quhasa did the contrair he war ungentill, uncurtas, and unconnand.

β. *c* **1374** CHAUCER *Boeth.* I. pr. i. (1868) 7 Any vnkonnyng and vnprofitable man. *c* **1420** *Chron. Vilod.* 4 þys werke, þat y, so vnconnynge, Presumpswysly haue vndere-take. *c* **1450** *Mirk's Festial* 213 Lest any vnconyng man take on for anoþir, I will tell you þes woymen. **1483** CAXTON *Gold. Leg.* 287/1 The bisshop repreuyd hym sore as unconnyng and an ydeote. **1549** CHALONER *Erasm. on Folly* F iv, The rasher, the uncunnynger, and lesse circumspect,..the more yet is he regarded. *a* **1577** SIR T. SMITH *Commw. Eng.* III. viii. (1584) 112 Some vncunning Lawyers that would make a newe barbarous Latine worde to betoken lande giuen *in fidem.* **1601** MUNDAY & CHETTLE *Death Earl Huntington* V. ii, Thus is Matildaes story showne in act, And rough heawen out by an vncunning hand.

[**1791** WOLCOT (P. Pindar) *Ode to my Ass* ix, But I'm a modest, not unconnyinge elf. **1792** —— *Odes Kien Long* V. ii, This to my simple and unconnying mind Seems œconomical.] **1826–7** K. DIGBY *Broadst. Hon.* II, *Tancredus* (1828) 280 A theme which requires a far less earthly and uncunning tongue than mine.

b. *absol.* (chiefly as pl.).

1338 R. BRUNNE *Chron.* (1810) 244 Wardeyns gode he sette,..Justise þat þe lawe gette to vnkonand þei kende. **1477** EARL RIVERS *Dictes* (1877) 36 b, A wyseman ought not to exalte him self byfore the vnconning. **1495** *Festivall* 186 b, The fyrst is teche the vnconnynge that he sauour rightfully. **1511–2** *Act 3 Hen. VIII*, c. xi, Many of the Kynges liege people..cannot descerne the uncunnyng from the cunnyng.

c. Const. *in*, *of*, or with inf.

a **1340** HAMPOLE *Psalter* cxviii. 92 He is vnkunand in gastly batayle. **1357** *Lay Folks Catech.* (Lamb. MS.) 1146 To teche men þat be vncunnynge of goddys lawe. **1377** LANGL. *P. Pl.* B. XII. 185 Person or parisch prest,.. Vnconnynge to lere lewed men. *c* **1440** *Gesta Rom.* xliii. 170 (Harl. MS.), They coude fynde noon, but that they wer corrupte,..or vncunnynge in the mystery. *a* **1450** *Knt. de la Tour* (1868) 159 That is gret pite, as in youthe to be vncunnynge and vnknowynge of hym selff. [**1888** DOUGHTY *Arabia Deserta* I. 278 But ye be also uncunning in many things, which the Aarab ken.]

2. Of actions, etc.: Arising from, indicative of, ignorance or unskilfulness.

1387 TREVISA *Higden* (Rolls) VII. 245 William put þat knyȝt out of þat chivalrie, for he hadde i-doo an unkonnynge dede. *c* **1449** PECOCK *Repr.* I. x. 51 The wanton and vnkunnyng bering of hem whiche wolen not allowe eny gouernaunce to be the lawe..of God. **1549** COVERDALE, etc. *Erasm. Par. Titus* iii. 31 b, Folyshe and vnconnyng questions, and entangled genealogies. *a* **1652** BROME *City Wit* I. i. Wks. 1873 I. 284 If my uncunning Disposition be my only vice.

So †**un'cunninghead, -ship.** *Obs.*

a **1300** *Cursor M.* 26306, I wat not quar-on it es lang, Queþer on mi plight or on þin,..Or min vnconanscipe [*v.r.* unkunnandeshepe], mai fall. **1340** *Ayenb.* 33 Efterward comþ slacnesse;..hit comþ of onconnyndehede, and of fole hete. *Ibid.* 40 Be hare kueadnesse, oþer uor onconynghede.

un'cunningly, *adv.* [f. prec.] In an uncunning manner; ignorantly, unskilfully.

a **1340** HAMPOLE *Psalter* lxxiv. 2 For many fals breþere vnconandly demes, crist says.., i sall deme rightwisnes. **1397** *Rolls of Parlt.* III. 379/1, I dede evyll and unkunnyngelych. **1408** tr. *Vegetius' De re milit.* (MS. Digby 233) fol. 185/2 Long tyme of pees haþ maad vs to chese vnkonnyngliche oure knyȝtes. *c* **1440** *Pallad. on Husb.* IV. 87 Vnconnyngly they do right as they are. **1519** HORMAN *Vulg.* 218 b, This mater was vncunnyngly or indiscretly handled. **1550** BALE *Eng. Votaries* II. 88 b, And whan she had vnconnyngly perfourmed that acte, they toke vp the peces. **1632** SHERWOOD, Vncunningly, *lourdement.*

un'cunningness. [f. as prec.] Ignorance; unskilfulness.

a **1325** *Prose Psalter* lxxxi. 5 Hii ne wyst nouȝt ne vnderstode nowit, and hii ne gon in vnconandnes [*v.r.* vncunnyngnes]. *c* **1375** *Cursor M.* 27571 (Fair.), Oft be-tidis þat man I-wis be-comis proude for vn-kunningnes. **1408** tr. *Vegetius' De re milit.* (MS. Digby 233) fol. 186/2 Vnkonnyngnesse of swymmynge. **1422** YONGE tr. *Secreta Secret.* 235 Ful smale leggis tokenyth vnconyngnesse. *c* **1475** *Partenay* 12 By lachesse, Or..by vnconyngnesse. **1513** DOUGLAS *Æneid* VIII. Prol. 87 Clerkis for oncunnandnes mysknawis ilk wycht.

†**uncunyed,** *ppl. a. Sc. Obs.* [UN-^{1} 8.] Uncoined.

1513 DOUGLAS *Æneid* X. ix. 53 Ane huge wecht of fynast gold tharby, Oncunȝeit ȝit. *a* **1572** KNOX *Hist. Ref.* Wks. 1846 I. 173 Silver, gold, and mettall, alsweill cunȝeit as uncunȝeit.

un'cup, *v.* (UN-^{2} 5.)

1857 HEAVYSEGE *Saul* (1869) 222 This victory's new-risen splendour Hath gathered and uncupped itself, as if An ocean were condensed there to a drop.

un'cupidate, *a.* [UN-^{1} 8 b.] Divested of the form of Cupid.

1631 P. FLETCHER *Sicelides* III. iv, Now must I be vncupidate, & shortly appeare here Cosmafied.

un'cupped, *ppl. a.* (UN-^{2} 8.)

1861 MORRIS *Jason* x. 328 On their heads fell down The uncupped acorn, and the long leaves brown.

†**un'curable,** *a. Obs.* [UN-^{1} 7 b and 5 b. Cf. MDu. *oncurable.*]

1. = INCURABLE *a.* 1. (Common *c* 1400–1650.)

a. Of wounds, diseases, etc.

1382 WYCLIF *Deut.* xxxii. 33 Venym of eddres vncurable. **1388** —— *Isaiah* xiv. 6 The ȝerde of lordis, that beet puplis ..with vncurable wounde. *a* **1425** tr. *Arderne's Treat. Fistula*, etc. 4, I afferme noȝt that I miȝt hele al ffistulae in ano, ffor som ben vncurable. *c* **1450** LYDG. *Secrees* 1425 The tyme dyuerse..sodeynly men schent, be seknessys which be unkurable. **1526** *Pilgr. Perf.* (W. de W. 1531) 82 Lepry, fransy, & suche other, whiche be in maner vncurable. **1562** TURNER *Baths* Pref., Many sore and otherwyse uncurable syknesses. **1593** SHAKS. *2 Hen. VI*, III. i. 286 Send Succours (Lords) and stop the Rage betime, Before the Wound doe grow vncurable. **1622** GATAKER *Spirituall Watch* 86 Decay of nature, old age, and some vncureable diseases. **1650** TRAPP *Comm. Exod.* xv. 26 To an Almightie Physician no diseas is uncurable.

fig. **1652** HEYLYN *Cosmogr.* IV. 22 Of all Surfeits this of Forraign supplies is most uncurable.

b. Of persons. Also *fig.*

a **1425** tr. *Arderne's Treat. Fistula*, etc. 1 Sir Adam..made for to aske counsel at all the lechez and cirurgienz that he myȝt fynde... And all forsoke hym for vncurable. *c* **1440** *Gesta Rom.* xxxvii. 152 (Add. MS.), Yit he dothe many synnes ayenst god, and so he is vncurable. **1560** DAUS tr. *Sleidane's Comm.* 36 b, As al those Romish be utterly uncurable. **1609** BIBLE (Douay) *Deut.* xxviii. 35 Be thou uncurable from the sole of thy foote unto the toppe of thy head. **1657** SPARROW *Bk. Com. Prayer* 138 Malice or revenge which makes us unpardonable and uncurable. **1775** ASH.

2. *transf.* and *fig.* = INCURABLE *a.* 2.

a **1340** HAMPOLE *Psalter* cxxxix. 3 Thai hafe..malice vncurabil in þaire hert. *c* **1545** H. RHODES *Bk. Nurture* B iiij, An olde man & a yonge woman, to satysfye is vncurable. **1626** in Foster *Eng. Factories India* (1909) III. 136 Her leake prooved uncureable. **1650** BAXTER *Saints' R.* III. iii. (1662) 325 An eternal, absolute, tormenting, uncurable despair. *a* **1676** HALE *Prim. Orig. Man.* I. iv. (1677) 103 The absurdities and incongruities..are infinite and uncurable.

Hence †**un'curableness**; †**un'curably** *adv.*

a **1425** tr. *Arderne's Treat. Fistula*, etc. 38 Whiche.. makeþ euermore pronosticacion..als wele of deþ as of vncurablenes. **1548** UDALL *Erasm. Par. Luke* v. 59 b, Wheras theim selfes wer euen for this verai poynte vncurably wicked enemies of God. **1643** MILTON *Divorce* vii. *heading*, A matrimony found to be uncurably unfit. **1651** BIGGS *New Disp.* ¶ 61 The uncurablenesse of diseases.

un'curb, *v.* [UN-^{2} 4 b.] *trans.* To free (a horse) from a curb. Also *fig.*

1580 HOLLYBAND *Treas. Fr. Tong*, *Desgourmer vn cheval*, to vncurbe a horse. **1684** T. GODDARD *Plato's Demon* 160, It is like uncurbing, or laying the Reins upon the Necks of headstrong Horses. **1729** YOUNG *Merchant* v. ix, Who curbs the tide, Uncurbs, extends, throws wide Britannia's reign.

un'curbable, *a.* (UN-^{1} 7 b.)

1606 SHAKS. *Ant. & Cl.* II. ii. 67 So much vncurbable, her Garboiles (Cæsar) Made out of her impatience.

un'curbed, *ppl. a.* [UN-^{1} 8.]

1. Not curbed; unchecked, unrestrained.

1599 SHAKS. *Hen. V*, I. ii. 243 Therefore with franke and with vncurbed plainnesse, Tell vs the Dolphins minde. **1621** QUARLES *Div. Poems, Esther* Med. 19 True 'tis, the Law of God's the rule and squire, Whereby to limit Man's vncurb'd desire. **1660** H. MORE *Myst. Godl.* v. xvii. 207 Their death conducing so much to the uncurbed fruition of all worldly and carnal enjoyments. **1734** tr. *Rollin's Anc. Hist.* (1827) I. 120 So licentious and uncurbed a liberty. **1821** KEATS *Sonn., On Peace* 13 Give thy kings law—leave not uncurbed the great. **1879** DIXON *Windsor* I. vii. 67 Uncurbed by scruple, she gave orders to employ material force.

2. Free from a curb.

1680 C. NESSE *Church-Hist.* 143 Absaloms mule..runs from under him with the reins uncurbed. **1801** SOUTHEY *Thalaba* VI. iv, But when he saw the mouth Uncurb'd, the unbridled neck, Then his heart leapt. **1825** LONGF. *Burial of Minnisink* 38 Leading the war-horse of their chief,.. Uncurbed, unreined, and riderless.

Hence **un'curbedly** *adv.*

1685 H. MORE *Illustr.* 150 The King of Pride, or Anti-christ, reigneth uncurbedly for a time.

un'curd, *v.* (UN-^{2} 3.)

1495 [see UNCRUD *v.*] **1598** FLORIO, *Disquagliare*, to vncurd as milk is. **1611** COTGR., *Se Descailler*, to resolue, vncurd, fall asunder.

un'curdled, *ppl. a.* (UN-^{1} 8.)

[**1775** ASH.] **1823** BYRON *Juan* IX. xliii, White stockings drawn uncurdled as new milk O'er limbs whose symmetry set off the silk. **1894** H. NISBET *Bush Girl's Rom.* 11 His coming disciples were still in long clothes,..being satisfied then with their milk uncurdled.

un'curdling, *vbl. sb.* (UN-^{2} 8.)

1673 *Phil. Trans.* VIII. 6169 The Secretion of the Serum from the blood is ingeniously cleared up by the curdling and un-curdling of Milk.

†**un'cure,** *v. Obs.* [UN-^{2} 3 + CURE *v.*^{2}] *trans.* To uncover; to disclose.

c **1440** *Promp. Parv.* 364/2 Oncuryn, or on-hyllyn, *detego*, *discooperio.* *c* **1450** LYDG. & BURGH *Secrees* 2347 Swyfft massageerys..To whoom thou mayst thy wyl also vncure. *c* **1485** *Digby Myst.* (1882) III. 769 He hath oncuryd þe therknesse of þe clowdy nyth.

un'cured, *ppl. a.* [UN-^{1} 8.]

1. Not healed or restored to health; not remedied.

a. Of wounds, diseases, etc.

1548 ELYOT, *Incuratus*,..vncured, vnhealed. **1597** A. M. tr. *Guillemeau's Fr. Chirurg.* 30 b/1 The perforation of the artery tarrieth vncured and open. **1676** HOBBES *Iliad* 119 Let them imbark at least in haste, and bear Along with them their wounds uncured home. **1819** SCOTT *Ivanhoe* xliii, Thy wounds are uncured—Meet not that proud man. **1879** *St. George's Hosp. Rep.* IX. 742 The mother had milk-fever and abscess of breast. This last remained uncured.

fig. **1598–9** B. JONSON *Case is Altered* v. iv, I am ashamed That my extreame affection to my sonne Should giue my honour so vncur'd a maine. **1642** FULLER *Holy & Prof. St.* II. xxiv. 152 Thus..the Wounds to the Commonwealth (in the breach of the Laws) are left uncured. *a* **1683** OWEN *Two Disc. Holy Spirit* (1693) 74 The uncured Darkness of their Minds. **1793** COWPER *Stanza for Year* 33 That want, uncur'd.., Speaks him a criminal, assur'd Of everlasting death. **1884** SIR C. S. C. BOWEN in *Law Rep. 12 Q.B.D.* 170 The blot in the proceedings of the respondent still remains uncured.

b. Of persons. Also *fig.*

1601 Sir W. Brown in Collins *Lett. & Mem. State* (1746) II. 228 The hurt Men that lye in the Streets, vncured, for Want of Surgins, make..a noysom Smell. **1674** R. Godfrey *Inj. & Ab. Physic* 150 Many times..they go uncured through deficiency in Medicine. **1757** Burke *Abridgm. Eng. Hist.* III. iv. Wks. 1812 X. 432 Uncured by his misfortunes of a loose generosity,..he..mortgaged every branch of his revenue. **1825** Scott *Talism.* xiv, We physicians are sworn not to send away a patient uncured. **1899** *Allbutt's Syst. Med.* VII. 683 It does not appear that there is any material difference in the percentage of cured and uncured cases.

2. Not dressed or prepared for keeping.

1622 in Foster *Eng. Factories Ind.* (1908) II. 103 [4000 pieces of cloth,] most partt uncurd, but ours are all cured. **1770** *Phil. Trans.* LX. 304 The certain consequence..will be, that maggots will be generated in such uncured parts [of stuffed birds]. **1828** Spearman *Brit. Gunner* (ed. 2) 77 Cartridges, uncured. **1883** Day *Indian Fish* 3 (Fish. Exhib. Publ.), Inland places having no special facilities for carriage do not receive uncured sea fish in a wholesome condition.

†**3.** Of land: Not cleared for cultivation. *Obs.*

1719 De Foe *Crusoe* I. 37, I purchased as much Land that was uncur'd, as my Money would reach.

un'curious, *a.* [un-[1] 7 and 5 b.]

1. Of persons: = incurious *a.* 2.

1570 Levins *Manip.* 226 Uncuriouse, *incurius, ignauus.* **1621** Quarles *Div. Poems, Esther* To Rdr., It is enough for an vncurious questioner to know it was indited by the Spirit of God. **1641** —— *Enchyridion* IV. lxxxviii, If thou art not worth more than the world can make thee, thy Redeemer had a bad pennyworth, or thou an uncurious Redeemer. **1712** Steele *Spect.* No. 340, That I have not been so uncurious a Spectator, as not to have seen Prince Eugene. **1716-7** in *Collect. Hist. Aberdeen & Banff* (Spalding Club) I. 39 A most elegant and powerfull preacher,..uncurious of politeness, save in the pulpit.

†**2.** = incurious *a.* 5. *Obs.*

1598 Sylvester *Du Bartas* II. i. IV. *Handycrafts* Argt., The praise of Peace, the miserable states Of Eden's Exiles: their un-curious Cates: Their simple habit, silly habitation.

†**3.** = incurious *a.* 6. *Obs.*

1601-3 Daniel *Ep. Sir T. Egerton* 54 The state of truth.. dwells free in the open plaine, Vncurious, Gentle, easie of accesse.

4. = incurious *a.* 7.

1684-5 Boyle *Min. Waters* 69 This Glass was judged capable of holding Water enough for not uncurious Tryals. **1712** Steele *Spect.* No. 546 ¶1 He added very many Particulars not uncurious concerning the Manner of taking an Audience. **1768** *Woman of Honor* I. 96, I was by chance witness to a not uncurious scene. **1846** Thackeray *Crit. Rev.* Wks. 1886 XXIII. 97 A not uncurious specimen of the biography of a literary man. *a* **1860** H. H. Wilson *Ess. & Lect.* (1862) I. 136 It is not an uncurious feature..that the veneration paid to their Gosáins is paid solely to their descent.

un'curiously, *adv.* [un-[1] 11; cf. prec.]

†**1.** In a plain or unelaborate manner. *Obs.*

1490 Caxton *Eneydos* ii. 15 Ensiewed creusa his wyf, vncuryously aourned, Nothyng appertenaunt to thestate Royall. **1611** Cotgr., *Incurieusement*, vncuriously, plainely, after a homely manner. **1716-20** *Lett. fr. Mist's Jrnl.* (1722) I. 284 Handling the Subject uncuriously and unpolitely.

2. Without curiosity. Cf. incuriously *adv.*

1667 G. Digby *Elvira* I. 15, I should have thought you strangely chang'd in humour Should you have gone away so uncuriously. **1862** 'Shirley' (J. Skelton) *Nugæ Crit.* xi. 483, I began, not uncuriously, to peruse these latest products of the English imagination.

un'curl, *v.* [un-[2] 7 and 3.]

1. *intr.* To come out of curl; to unfold from a curved or spiral form.

1588 Shaks. *Tit. A.* II. iii. 34 My fleece of Woolly haire, that now vncurles, Euen as an Adder when she doth vnrowle. **1601** B. Jonson *Poetaster* Introd. 8 Cling to my necke, and wrists, my louing wormes, And cast you round, in soft and amorous foulds, Till I doe bid, vncurle. **1697** Dryden *Virg. Georg.* IV. 693 The Furies harken, and their Snakes uncurl. **1827** Hood *Hero & Leander* lxiii, His uncrispt locks uncurling in the brine. **1873** 'Ouida' *Pascarel* II. 162 The green corn uncurling underneath the blossoming vines.

2. *trans.* To take out of curl; to untwist.

1598 Florio, *Discrespare*, to vncurle, to vnfrizle, to vncrispe. **1687** Dryden *Hind & P.* III. 270 He sheathes his paws, uncurls his angry mane. **1697** —— *Æneis* v. 167 The raging billows..Uncurl their ridgy backs, and at his foot appear. **1816** Scott *Bl. Dwarf* xvi, On the other side sate Isabella,..her long hair uncurled by the evening damps. **1848** Thackeray *Van. Fair* i, A black servant, who reposed on the box beside the fat coachman, uncurled his bandy legs. **1887** M. Arnold *Kaiser Dead* x, I see the tail,..In moments of disgrace uncurl'd, Then at a pardoning word refurl'd.

refl. **1606** Dekker *Seuen Deadly Sinnes* 32 The vgliest Serpent hath not vncurld himselfe. **1884** *Nonconf. & Indep.* 5 June 545/1 The bracken has not yet uncurled itself.

un'curled, *ppl. a.* [un-[1] 8, or f. prec.]

1. Of hair: Not formed into, or growing in, curls or ringlets; out of curl.

1596 Spenser *F.Q.* IV. vii. 40 His faire lockes..He let to grow and griesly to concrew, Vncomb'd, vncurl'd, and carelesly vnshed. **1611** L. Barry *Ram Alley* II. i, Thy head, Which is with greasy hair orespred, And being vncurld and black as cole [etc.]. **1693** Congreve in *Dryden's Juvenal* XI. (1697) 291 Two home-bred Youths..With honest Faces, tho' with uncurl'd Hair. **1712-4** Pope *Rape Lock* v. 26 Curl'd or uncurl'd, since Locks will turn to gray. **1796** Morse *Amer. Geog.* I. 72 Their black hair, long and uncurled. **1828** Scott *Tapestr. Chamb.* ¶25 His hair..was dishevelled, uncurled, void of powder, and dank with dew. **1848** Lytton *Harold* I. i, His forehead shaded with short thick hair, uncurled, but black..as the wings of a raven.

b. Not adorned with curls or ringlets.

1799 in *Spirit Pub. Jrnls.* III. 322 Leave me uncurl'd, undinner'd, here to mourn.

2. Not disposed in coils or spiral convolutions; also, relaxed from a spiral form.

1597 Middleton *Wisd. Solomon* iii. 1 The adder is not always seen uncurl'd. **1708** Pope *Ode St. Cecilia's Day* iv, The Furies sink upon their iron beds, And snakes uncurl'd hang list'ning round their heads. **1820** Keats *Hyperion* II. 46 A serpent's plashy neck; its barbed tongue Squeez'd from the gorge, and all its uncurl'd length Dead. **1841** T. R. Jones *Anim. Kingd.* 259 When not in use, the proboscis is coiled up ..; but when uncurled, its structure is readily examined.

un'curling, *ppl. a.* (un-[1] 10.)

1728 Thomson *Spring* 185 Th' uncurling Floods, diffus'd In glassy Breadth, seem, thro' delusive Lapse Forgetful of their Course. **1800** *Monthly Mag.* VIII. 726 When on the tea's uncurling leaves it lies, With golden hues the porcelain vases flow. **1854** Whyte Melville *Gen. Bounce* (1855) 119 None..would have thought the long golden brown hair spoiled by hanging down in those rich, uncurling clusters. **1883** Dixon *Mano* I. ii. 5 A heavy fall Of dark uncurling hair flowed either side.

un'current, *a.* [un-[1] 7.]

1. Of money: Not current; not in circulation.

1601 Shaks. *Twel. N.* III. iii. 16, I can no other answer make, but thankes, And thankes: and euer oft good turnes, Are shuffel'd off with such vncurrant pay. **1639** S. Du Verger tr. *Camus' Admir. Events* a 3 It is a strange thing, that reasonable spirits can be payd with such counterfeit and uncurrant coyne. **1655** tr. *Sorel's Com. Hist. Francion* II. 39 My neighbours..cryed me down more than uncurrent Money. **1855** W. Irving *Washington* lxii. II. 497 Paper money issued by Congress which was uncurrent among the Canadians. **1883** *Encycl. Brit.* XVI. 484 After a certain amount of wear a gold coin..loses weight and becomes legally uncurrent.

fig. **1618** Fletcher *Loyal Subj.* II. v, Thou crackt uncurrant Lord. **1646** G. Daniel *Poems* Wks. (Grosart) I. 201 Such for vncurrant Knights or new-coyn'd Squire Might suite. **1827** Pollok *Course T.* VIII. 597 Honour.. Bearing the signature of Time alone, Uncurrent in Eternity, and base!

2. Not commonly accepted or recognized.

1611 Shaks. *Wint. T.* III. ii. 50 Since he came, With what encounter so vncurrant, I Haue strayn'd t'appeare thus. **1639** Ld. Digby, etc. *Lett. conc. Relig.* (1651) 77 Conceits of their own, and other uncurrent doctrines. **1665** Boyle *Occas. Refl.* II. xiii. 233 'Tis hard..to be sure, that his present Repentance is not of the same ignoble and uncurrent kind.

3. Of a warrant: Having no legal force; invalid.

1647 Clarendon *Hist. Reb.* v. §156 The Messenger would scarce have return'd to have reported how uncurrent such Warrants were like to be in York.

Hence **un'currentness.**

1641 Sir T. Roe *Sp.* in *Harl. Misc.* (Malh.) IV. 457 Another cause of scarcity of coin, may be the over-strict rule of the uncurrentness of any good coin.

un'curried, *ppl. a.* (un-[1] 8.)

c **1616** Fletcher *Thierry & Theod.* v. i, Out upon you, you uncurried colts. **1734** *Prompter* 29 Nov. 2/2 Stray'd,.. a lean, ragged, uncurried creature, call'd Common Sense. **1888** Doughty *Arabia Deserta* I. vii. 198 We saw the Prince's gift-mare standing,..weak, and uncurried.

un'curse, *v.* (un-[2] 3.)

1593 Shaks. *Rich. II*, III. ii. 137 Againe vncurse their Soules; their peace is made With Heads, and not with Hands. *c* **1831** H. Coleridge *Ess.* (1851) I. 180 Old Prynne and Jeremy Collier, if their hearts were in the right place,.. would have uncursed the stage.

un'cursed, un'curst, *ppl. a.* (un-[1] 8.)

a **1628** F. Grevil *Cælica* cii, All things vncurst, nothing yet done amisse, And so in him no base of his defection. **1680** Baxter *Answ. Stillingfl.* xxxvii. 62 How few were there un-Cursed, and un-Condemned in the Roman World? **1759** Young *Conject. Orig. Composition* 60 What we mean by Blank verse, is verse unfallen, uncurst. **1827** Pollok *Course T.* VII. 497 That morn When first they met in Paradise, unfallen, Uncursed. **1843** Ld. Cockburn *Jrnl.* (1874) II. 5, I see no ground for expecting that..we can even be uncursed by these heartrending visitations.

un'cursing, *ppl. a.* (un-[1] 10.)

1806 Wolcot (P. Pindar) *Tristia* Wks. 1812 V. 317 How thou..with uncursing breath Couldst see Saint Paul.. Stoned,..a second time, to death.

uncur'tailed, *ppl. a.* (un-[1] 8.)

1741 Richardson *Pamela* II. 21 Will you,..on your Honour, let me see them uncurtail'd, and not offer to make them away? **1820** T. Mitchell *Aristoph.* I. 25 To our share Fell some fine oxen—whole, sirs,—uncurtail'd. **1856** Froude *Hist. Eng.* (1858) I. iv. 288 Making use of their yet uncurtailed powers of persecution. **1861** W. S. Perry *Hist. Ch. Eng.* I. iv. 171 The ancient canon law was still in force, uncurtailed by the Reformation.

un'curtain, *v.* [un-[2] 4.] *trans.* To remove a curtain or veil from; to disclose or reveal. Also *refl.*

1628 Feltham *Resolves* II. l. 147 The honest man will rather be a graue to his neighbours failes, then any way vncurtaine them. **1659** W. Chamberlayne *Pharonnida* III. 186 She in these words uncurtains mystick Fate. **1817** Moore *Lalla Rookh, Veiled Prophet* 766 Now thou seest my soul's angelic hue, 'Tis time these features were uncurtain'd too. **1858** Carlyle *Fredk. Gt.* IX. x. II. 499 Watching the great War-theatre uncurtain itself in this manner, from Dantzig down to Naples. **1887** Bowen *Æneid* IV. 120 When Phœbus at earliest morn..with radiant light uncurtains the land.

absol. **1897** 'O Rhoscomyl' *White Rose Arno* 242 The tender smile of Night's white queen uncurtained to the world.

un'curtained, *a.* (un-[1] 8.)

[**1775** Ash.] **1804** J. Grahame *Sabbath* 49 The toil Of ministering around th' uncurtain'd couch Of pain and poverty. **1842** Dickens *Amer. Notes* (1850) 49/2 A blazing fire shone through the uncurtained windows. **1865** Miss Braddon *Eleanor's Vict.* ii, Broad uncurtained open windows.

‖**uncus** ('ʌŋkəs). *Zool.*, etc. Pl. unci ('ʌnsaɪ). [L. *uncus* hook.] A hook or hook-like process.

1826 Kirby & Sp. *Entomol.* III. 390 *Unci* (the *Unci*), two pair of robust organs..with which the anus of *Locusta*..is furnished. **1888** Rolleston & Jackson *Anim. Life* 158 A stout decurved pointed process terminating in two hooks, the *uncus* of Gosse or *tegumen* of White. **1899** *Allbutt's Syst. Med.* VII. 324 Smell was impaired on the side of the lesion, by a tumour which caused erosion of the uncus.

un'cushioned, *ppl. a.* (un-[1] 8.)

[**1775** Ash.] **1852** H. W. Dulcken tr. *Pfeiffer's Visit to Holy Land, Egypt, & Italy* i. 23 Uncushioned benches serve for seats by day and for beds by night. **1873** Mrs. Whitney *Other Girls* xxvii, There were window-seats in the two windows, uncushioned.

un'cusped, *a.* (un-[1] 9.)

1859 Ruskin *Perspective* 116 A square niche of good Veronese Gothic, with an uncusped arch.

†**un'custom,** *sb. Sc. Obs.* [un-[1] 4 b.] An improper or illegal tax.

1569 *Reg. Privy Council Scot.* Ser. I. I. 672 He hes send his officiaris to tak up uncustomes sic as ane cott hen..from every cottar.

†**un'custom,** *v.* [un-[2] 3.] To disaccustom.

1530 Palsgr. 767/1, I uncustume, I leave of a thyng that I was wonte to use, *je desacoustume.* *Ibid.*, I coulde shoote with any man that came, but nowe I am uncustomed. **1570** Levins *Manip.* 162 To Vncustome, *desuefacere.*

un'customable, *a.* [un-[1] 7 b.]

†**1.** Not according to custom; unusual. *Obs.*

1387 Trevisa *Higden* (Rolls) VIII. 241 þe pope greved þe chirches of Engelond wiþ taxes..undewe and uncustemable. **1570** Levins *Manip.* 4 Vncustomable, *inconsuetus.*

2. Of goods: Not liable to pay custom.

1727 Bailey (vol. II).

un'customary, *a.* [un-[1] 7.] Not according to custom; unusual, unwonted.

1650 H. Brooke *Conserv. Health* 115 Meats also that are uncustomary..must very sparely be fed upon. **1744** T. Birch *Life R. Boyle* 296 In such private meetings it was not uncustomary for any one of the hearers, who was unsatisfied about any matter then uttered, to give in his objections. **1798** Pennant *Hindoostan* I. 173 A female reign in these parts is not uncustomary. **1802-12** Bentham *Ration. Judic. Evid.* (1827) I. 11 If the lamb were to be cut up into uncustomary joints. **1871** Alabaster *Wheel of Law* 208 Such is not uncustomary among the higher classes.

Hence ˌ**un'customarily** *adv.*

1909 Webster, Uncustomarily, adv. **1966** *Punch* 2 Mar. p. viii/2 Functional, even austere decor, and uncustomarily fast service don't mark this splendid Chelsea restaurant as unluxurious. **1982** *Nature* 25 Feb. 642/1 Your uncustomarily superficial and misleading article.

†**un'customate,** *ppl. a. Sc. Obs.* [un-[1] 8 b.] Not having paid duty.

1510 *Reg. Privy Seal Scotl.* I. 326/2 With power to eschaete all custumable gudis passand furth of the realme uncustumate. **1565** *Reg. Privy Council Scot.* I. 332 Certane malivolus personis..fraudulentlie transportis thair gudis and marchandices, sumtymes uncustumat.

un'customed, *ppl. a.* [un-[1] 8.]

1. Of merchandise: On which no custom or duty has been paid. †Also, not charged with or liable to duty.

1393 *Rec. Elgin* (New Spald. Cl. 1903) I. 19 Al ye wol, ye clathe and al vthir thyngis yt gais be schipe owte of wre hafine of Spee vncustomyt. **1427** *Rolls of Parlt.* IV. 318/1 To passe oute of this Royaume be way of Marchandise, un-custumed. **1487** *Naval Acc. Hen. VII* (1896) 32, vij hausers forfetted..in bringyng the same on land uncustumed. *a* **1548** Hall *Chron., Hen. VIII*, 65 A great nombre of rascal & pedlers..brought ouer hattes and cappes, and diuerse merchaundise vncustomed. **1594** J. Dickenson *Arisbas* (1878) 48 Hee had aboord certayne vnlawfull and vncustomed wares. **1631** Heywood *Fair Maid of West* v, An Englishman Hath forfeited his ship for goods uncustom'd. **1669** Sturmy *Mariner's Mag., Penalties & Forfeit.* 7 Liberty to go on board and take out Prohibited and Uncustomed Goods. **1718-9** *Act 5 Geo. I*, c. 11 (*title*), An Act against clandestine running of uncustomed Goods. **1733** *Gentl. Mag.* May 266/2 The Watchmen..seized 1100 Weight of uncustom'd Tea. *c* **1820** Hogg *Tales & Sk.* (1836) I. 304 Uncustomed wine and spirits. **1887** *Times* 10 Sept. 4/4 Dealing with uncustomed goods—i.e., tobacco—with intent to defraud Her Majesty's Customs.

2. Unaccustomed *to* something. *Obs.* or *arch.*

c **1520** Barclay *Jugurth* (1557) 41 b, Other vncustomed to suche busynesse of batayle..fered the losse of their libertie. **1607** C. Lever *A Crucifix* cxv, To adulation they vncustomd are. **1791** Cowper *Odyss.* VIII. 553 Glad he beheld The steaming vase, uncustom'd to its use E'er since his voyage from the isle of fair Calypso. **1877** Blackie *Wise Men* 179 They show like moles uncustomed to the light.

3. Not customary; unusual. *Obs.* or *arch.*

1552 Huloet, Vncustomed or out of vse, *disuetus.* **1565** Stapleton tr. *Bede's Hist. Ch. Eng.* 79 An Abbat..to whom ..the bishops them selues ought after a straunge and vn-customed order to be subiect. **1581** Marbeck *Bk. of Notes* 730 A Miracle is a worke, hard and vncustomed by the power of God. **1603** Florio *Montaigne* I. xxv. 85 My father purposed to make mee learne it [*sc.* Greek] by arte; But by new and vncustomed meanes. **1872** Blackie *Lays Highl.* 35, I feel the keen, uncustomed temper of the thin, clear air.

un'cut, *ppl. a.* Also 5 unkyt. [UN-[1] 8 b, 8 c.]

1. a. Not cut, gashed, or wounded with a sharp-edged instrument; not having received a cut.

1426 Audelay *Poems* (Percy Soc.) 12 Who mai kepe hym unkyt fro a kene knyfe, ȝif he boldly that blad touche in his tene. **1615** *Work for Cutlers* 4 Ile make a Capon of you before I haue done with you, you shall nere come home vncut Ile warrant you. **1623** Massinger & Field *Bondman* iv. ii, *Gracculo.* [We'll] not leave One house unfired. *Cimbrio.* Or throat uncut of those We have in our power. **1834** M. Scott *Cruise Midge* (1863) 236 An open book, the leaves kept down .. by a most enticing uncut pine apple. **1840** Eliza Cook *To Favourite Pony* v, Thy knees uncut, my bones unshatter'd.

b. Without being operated on.

a **1548** Hall *Chron., Edw. V*, 1 b, Shee could not be delivered of hym uncut.

2. a. That has not been subjected to cutting; not severed by cutting; not mown, lopped, etc.

1548 Udall, etc. *Erasm. Par. John* xix. 110 Therfore the souldiers thought good that it should be kept whole unkut. **1583** Greene *Mamillia* Wks. (Grosart) II. 49 The grasse looketh better being vncut, then that which withereth with the sieth. *a* **1593** Marlowe *Ovid's Elegies* iii. i. 1 An old wood, stands vncut of long yeares space. **1639** Horn & Rob. *Gate Lang. Unl.* lxi. §641 Heathenish Priests in their Temples & uncut groves, dedicated presents. **1745** *Transl. & Paraphr. Sc. Ch.* xxiv. i, Say, grows the Rush without the Mire?.. Green and Uncut, it quickly fades. **1841** Elphinstone *Hist. Ind.* I. 27 Clad in bark, .. with his hair and nails uncut. **1846** J. Baxter *Libr. Pract. Agric.* (ed. 4) II. 323 Keep these branches uncut till you arrive at the season of grafting. **1885** *Times* (weekly ed.) 25 Sept. 13/4 A few of the fields being still uncut.

b. With *down* or *up*.

1546 J. Heywood *Prov.* (1867) 27 He that hangth him selfe a sondaie Shall hang still vncut downe a mondaie for mee. **1607** Beaum. & Fl. *Woman Hater* i. ii, Great, cumbersom, un-cut-up pies .. to make a shew with.

3. Not fashioned or shaped by cutting.

uncut diamond, velvet, etc.: cf. cut *ppl. a.*

1596 *Acc. Bk. W. Wray* in *Antiquary* XXXII. 281, j li. cut and uncut fringe, iiij s. **1605** Drayton *Poems* 69 b, Which being now but in so meane a bed, Is like an vncut diamond in lead. *a* **1700** Evelyn *Diary* 22 Oct. 1644, With a terrace at each side having rustic uncut balustrades. **1771** Mme. D'Arblay *Early Diary* (1889) I. 121 She fixed upon a suite of dark blue, uncut velvet. **1875** Knight *Dict. Mech.* 695/2 Until 1476 .. the diamond was worn uncut. **1902** Marshall *Metal Tools* 41 Most flat files are provided with one plain, uncut edge.

4. a. Of books: Not having the leaves cut open.

1828 Macaulay *Misc. Writ.* (1860) I. 273 The new novel lies uncut. **1850** Mrs. Carlyle *Lett.* (1883) II. 125 The new 'Copperfield' .. to this hour remains uncut. **1893** Liddon, etc. *Life Pusey* I. xii. 276 The copy of the published sermon which was sent him 'from the author' is still uncut.

b. Not having the margins cut down.

1809 Dibdin *Bibliomania* 60 Uncut Copies, .. books of which the edges have never been sheared by the binder's tools. *Ibid.* 61 An uncut first Shakspeare, as well as an uncut first Homer. **1863** Hotten *Hand-bk. Topogr.* 95/1 Fine uncut copy (sells at £4 5s.) 35s. **1888** Jacobi *Printers' Vocab.*, *Uncut edges*, books not cut down, but not necessarily 'unopened'.

c. *transf.* Given to collecting 'uncut' books.

1862 Burton *Bk. Hunter* (1882) 19 He was not a black letter man or a tall copyist or an uncut man.

5. Not curtailed or shortened. Also, without excisions or omissions.

1896 *Westm. Gaz.* 7 Dec. 3/2 The uncut 'first night' is apt to cause great injustice to the performers. **1946** *Partisan Rev.* Nov.—Dec. 577 O'Neill's new play .. is guaranteed to last two-and-a-half hours longer than any other play, with the exception of the uncut *Hamlet*. **1953** K. Reisz *Technique Film Editing* xii. 193 The documentary or story-film editor's job .. requires a subtler understanding and interpretation of the shades of meaning in the uncut shots. **1960** *News Chron.* 15 Mar. 8/3 His film 'India 1958', so far only seen in the uncut version at private showings. **1967** *Guardian* 9 May 5/3 (*heading*) Film director defends uncut 'Ulysses'. *Ibid.*, 'Ulysses' is due to be shown uncut at the Academy Cinema in London from June 1.

6. Undiluted, unadulterated.

1967 C. Drummond *Death at Furlong Post* vii. 104 All six of the Dancer's gaffs have been taken to pieces. Four ounces of uncut heroin. **1978** T. Williamson *Technicians of Death* vi. 43 They can produce very large amounts of uncut heroin.

†un'cut, *v. Obs.* [UN-[2] 9.] *trans.* To sever by cutting.

1611 Speed *Hist. Gt. Brit.* ix. xvi. 13 Behold how God began to vncut the knot of those bands with which the English held France bound. **1622** *Prosopopoeia* in *Phœnix Brit.* (1732) I. 314 You see it is of a greater Consequence than to uncut a Gordian Knot.

†un'cuted, *a. Obs.*[−1] [UN-[1] 9 + *cute* cuit.] Not converted into cuit or sweet wine.

1615 G. Sandys *Trav.* 224 Wines that seldome come vnto vs vncuted, but excellent where not.

uncweme, var. unqueme *a. Obs.*

un'cynical, *a.* (UN-[1] 7.)

1824 Byron *Juan* xvi. xliii. *note*, A table-cloth, or some other expensive and uncynical piece of furniture.

un'cynically, *adv.* (UN-[1] 11.)

1895 Meredith *Amazing Marr.* xxxviii, Must we be proxy if we are profoundly, uncynically sincere?

un'cypressed, *a.* (UN-[1] 9.)

1799 in *Spirit Pub. Jrnls.* III. 105 Slow to th' uncypress'd church-yard he was borne.

†und. *Obs. rare.* Also 2 unde, 6 vnd. [a. OF. *unde*, or ad. L. *unda* wave.] A wave; *Her.*, a wave-like marking. (Cf. undee *a.*)

c **1200** *Trin. Coll. Hom.* 177 Ðe water stremes on-heueden up here undes [L. *fluctus*]. **1490** Caxton *Eneydos* ii. 15 By troblous reuolucyons of the vndes or wawes [they] were broughte into the Ile of Anchandron. **1592** Wyrley *Armorie* 12 John Basset of new place .. left the Labell, and charged the blacke vnds with manie besants dispersed all ouer them. [**1694** Motteux *Rabelais* 249 Lute, Unds and Sands did long our March oppose.]

†undade, -adie, *a. Obs.* [Cf. prec.] *Her.* = undated *a.*, undee *a.*

1562 Leigh *Armorie* 137 He beareth Or, and Tenne, parted per Saltier Vndade, which is as much to say as watried with a flood. **1572** Bossewell *Armorie* iii. 9 b, These bendes sinister vndadie or waterie, maye foreshowe some .. enterprise done by force, violence, or rage of the waters.

†un'daftiness. *Obs.*[−1] [UN-[1] 12.] Untidiness.

1555 Watreman *Fardle Facions* ii. iv. I vj b, As for checkes or reuilinges, was to them muske and Honie, and slouenly vndaftinesse, a greate comelinesse.

†un'dainteous, *a. Obs.*[−1] [UN-[1] 7.] Not dainty through rarity.

c **1449** Pecock *Repr.* ii. viii. 184 Tho ymagis .. schulde be vndeinteose for the grete plente of hem; .. plente is no deinte.

un'dam, *v.* [UN-[2] 3.]

1. *trans.* To release from a dam. Also *fig.*

1697 Dryden *Virg. Georg.* i. 160 The wary Ploughman, on the Mountain's Brow, Undams his watry Stores. **1885** *Pall Mall G.* 27 Oct. 5/1 A stream of impertinent chatter such as the most voluble sciolist would hesitate to undam.

2. To deprive of a protective dam.

a **1713** A. Pitcairne in *N. & Q.* Ser. v. VIII. 498/1 Amphibious wretches, Sudden be your fall! May man undam you, And God damn you all! (Cf. undamn *v.*)

un'damageable, *a.* (UN-[1] 7 b.)

1648 Hexham ii, *Ondeerlick*, vndammageable. **1884** *Stubbs' Mercantile Circular* 30 Jan. 94/1 Iron wire declared to be undamageable.

un'damaged, *ppl. a.* (UN-[1] 8.)

1648 Hexham ii, *Onbeschadight*, Vndammaged, or Vnharmed. **1708** J. Philips *Cyder* i. 305 Thou'lt find that Plants will frequent Changes try, Undamag'd, and their marriageable Arms Conjoin with others. **1859** Geo. Eliot *A. Bede* xxvii, So long as there was hope of gathering in their own corn undamaged. **1897** Mary Kingsley *W. Africa* 604 The only point I congratulate myself on is having got my men up so high, and back again, undamaged.

un'damasked, *a.* (UN-[1] 9.)

1838 Eliza Cook *Old Water-Mill* vi, Our seats were undamasked, our partners were rough.

un'dammed, *ppl. a.* (UN-[1] 8.)

a **1849** Poe *Monos & Una* Wks. 1865 II. 278 Holy, august and blissful days, when blue rivers ran undammed, between hills unhewn. **1896** *Fortn. Rev.* LIX. 632 The undammed stream of sarcasm, invective and calumny.

un'damn, *v.* (UN-[2] 3. Also a punning variant of undam *v.* 2.)

1719 T. Gordon *Cordial for Low Spirits* (1763) 90 The most gross sinners are now innocent, being undamned by the priest. **1741** *Pol. Ballads* (1860) II. 267 Let France damn the Germans, and undamn the Dutch. **1809** in *Spirit Pub. Jrnls.* XIII. 206 Turned-in to my cot; muttered a short prayer; d——nd the French; *und*——d the Dutch.

un'damned, *ppl. a.* (UN-[1] 8.)

1382 Wyclif *Acts* xxii. 25 If it is leefful to ȝou, for to scourge a man Romayn, and vndampned? *a* **1400** *New Test.* (Paues) Acts xvi. 37 þei hauen beten vs vnrightly ande vn-dampned. *c* **1450** *Mirk's Festial* 89 þen schall non scape vndampned. **1631** Dekker *Match me in London* iii, A Broaker that's vndamn'd for halfe a dram For halfe a scruple. **1852** James *Pequinillo* III. 125 'I hope my blood will remain und——d,' replied Doctor Pequinillo. **1862** T. A. Trollope *Marietta* II. xi. 191 Thus the work dragged on —undamned—to the end of the first act.

†un'damnified, *ppl. a. Obs.* [UN-[1] 8.] Undamaged, unimpaired.

1576 Fleming *Panopl. Epist.* 199 Returne I pray thee, returne, in hope to be saued harmelesse and undamnified. **1658** Earl Monm. tr. *Paruta's Wars Cyprus* 140 He .. past through the midst of our Fleet with some 30 gallies, un-damnified. **1686** *Lond. Gaz.* No. 2197/3 There remains not one Beam undamnified. **1709** T. Robinson *Vind. Mosaick Syst.* 31 To keep undamnify'd his .. beloved Hypothesis.

un'damped, *ppl. a.* [UN-[1] 8.]

1. Of persons, their spirits, etc.: Not discouraged or checked; undepressed.

1742 Young *Nt. Th.* ii. 693 Undampt by doubt, undarken'd by despair, Philander, thus, augustly rears his head. **1792** S. Rogers *Pleas. Mem.* i. 301 Undamped by time, the generous Instinct grows. **1834** Wordsw. *Lines Album C'tess Lonsdale* 62 They, who mark thy course, .. See cheerfulness undamped by stealing Time. **1863** *N. & Q.* 3rd Ser. III. 506 With ardour undamped, and obstinacy undrowned.

b. *spec.* (See quots. and damp *v.* 1 c.)

1883 A. J. Hipkins in Grove *Dict. Mus.* III. 636 In the edition of 1797 he remarks that the undamped register of the Fortepiano is the most agreeable. **1906** *Westm. Gaz.* 28 Nov. 5/2 He obtained a million or more vibrations per second, and .. produced continuous or undamped waves.

2. Not damped or made wet.

1898 *Westm. Gaz.* 10 Sept. 8/2 Having a surface undamped by rain.

un'dancing, *ppl. a.* (UN-[1] 10.)

1633 Prynne *Histrio-m.* 249 If this be true, how many happy Husbands are there now, when there are so few undancing wives?

un'dangered, *ppl. a.* (UN-[1] 8.)

c **1400** *Beryn* 2410 For, had ye dwellid within yeur shippis, .. Then had yee been vndaungerid, & quyt of al hir wrong. **1816** J. Scott *Visit Paris* (ed. 5) 245 Undangered and inevitable duration can be promised to nothing in this world.

un'dangerous, *a.* (UN-[1] 7.)

1727 Thomson *Britannia* 205 Then cherish this, this unexpensive power, Undangerous to the public. **1818** Bentham *Ch. Eng.*, *Catech. Exam.* 113 To which these modern effusions .. are but inadequate, and not altogether undangerous, substitutes. **1831** Gen. P. Thompson *Exerc.* (1842) I. 423 The charge .. was not more futile, .. and it may be added undangerous, than that advanced against the Radicals.

Hence **un'dangerousness.**

1817 Bentham *Parl. Reform* Introd. p. i, The necessity, —and .. the undangerousness,—of a Parliamentary Reform.

un'dared, *ppl. a.* (UN-[1] 8.)

1587 Hughes *Misfort. Arth.* i. ii, O wrong content with no reuenge; seeke out Vndared plagues. **1611** Florio, *Inauso*, vndaring, vndared. **1936** Auden *Look, Stranger!* 12 And into the undared ocean swung north their prow.

un'daring, *ppl. a.* (UN-[1] 10.)

Also *undaringness* (Florio s.v. *Inaudacia*).

1611 Florio, *Inaudace*, vndaring, cowardly. **1650** Lluellyn *Elegie* in *J. Gregory's Posthuma*, Graie Customs, which our dead dismettled Sloth Gave up, to surfet the undaring Moth. **1815** J. Cormack *Abol. Fem. Infanticide Guzerat* xii. 219 We might be excused .. for cherishing hopes of a very un-daring nature. **1877** Lanier, *Poems, Florida Sunday* 57 Mine thy dole Of shut undaring wings.

un'dark, *a.* (UN-[1] 7.)

1876 Morris *Sigurd* i. 4 On Mid-Summer Even ere the undark night began.

un'dark, *v.* (UN-[2] 6 a.)

1644 Quarles *Sheph. Oracles* v, How each spark Contends for greater brightnes, to undark The shades of night.

un'darken, *v.* (UN-[2] 3.)

1598 Florio, *Stenebrare*, to .. cleare vp, to vndarken. **1866** W. Stokes in Meyer *Voy. Bran* (1895) I. 222 Chief lights irradiating and un-darkening the City.

un'darkened, *ppl. a.* (UN-[1] 8.)

1742 [see undamped 1]. **1818** Shelley *Marenghi* 20 Reconciling factions .. swear to keep each spirit Undarkened by their country's last eclipse. **1847** J. Martineau *Chr. Life* 130 A heaven undarkened by a doubt. **1889** Ruskin *Præterita* III. 181 Fireflies .. shone fitfully in the still undarkened air.

un'darned, *ppl. a.* (UN-[1] 8.)

1797 Brydges *Hom. Trav.* I. 337 His dear Nelly, who had scarce An undarn'd smicket. **1880** Lee *Church under Q. Eliz.* I. 317 His lawn-sleeves perfectly clean and undarned. **1894** Eliz. Banks *Camp. Curiosity* 29 Basket upon basket of gentlemen's undarned socks.

un'dashed, *ppl. a.* [UN-[1] 8.]

1. Not discouraged or dismayed; undaunted.

1601 Daniel *Civ. Wars* vi. lxxviii, Yet standes he stiffe, vndasht, vnterrifi'd. **1616** R. Weldon in B. Holyday *Persius* A vij, I thinkt'a taske too great for humane sleights, Vn-graueld or vndasht to passe those streights. **1896** C. Allen *Papier Mâché* 12 'But who plays on them now?' asked Paul, undashed by this dismal possibility of a future.

2. Not mingled *with*, or affected *by*, something.

1803 *Edwin* III. vii. 125 And may the tide of friendship gently glide undashed with sorrow. **1868** Milman *St. Paul's* xi. 267 Whose creed was therefore in a continual state of change, not undashed with doubt. **1885** *Athenæum* 2 May 565/1 The same quaint humour not undashed by pathos.

3. Not provided with a dash or dashes.

1879 *Encycl. Brit.* X. 401/2 Replacing the dashed letters by those undashed ones which denote the same points.

un'datable, *a.* (UN-[1] 7 b.)

1882 *Schaff's Encycl. Relig. Knowl.* 74 A momentous but undatable event.

'undated, *a.* Now *rare* or *Obs.* [f. med.L. *undāt-us*, f. L. *unda* wave.]

1. *Her.* = undee *a.*, wavy *a.*

1486 *Bk. St. Albans, Her.* 94 Palyt armys oftyme ar founde vndatyt, that is to say watteri. *Ibid.*, They be called barrit vndatit for they be made of ij colouris metyng togedre by the maner of a floyng watre. **1572** Bossewell *Armorie* ii. 31 b, These pales may be borne vndated, whiche is as moche as to saye, as watered with a floode.

2. *Ornith.* Having wavy markings.

Also *Bot.*, waved (Webster, 1828, citing Lee).

1783 Latham *Gen. Synop. Birds* IV. 391 Undated L[ark]. *Ibid.* 477 Undated W[arbler].

un'dated, *ppl. a.* [UN-[1] 8. Cf. G. *undatirt*, Du. *ongedateerd*, Sw. *odaterad.*]

1. Not furnished or marked with a date; left without indication of date.

1570 Foxe *Acts & Mon.* (ed. 2) 383/1 The certein tyme .. I cannot searche out, neyther may it be [in] his epistles vndated, easly found out. **1658** Sir T. Browne *Hydriot.* 24 The undated ruines of winds, flouds or earthquakes. **1710** H. Bedford *Vind. Ch. Eng.* 177 The Latin Edition .. is without Numbers, as well as his undated English one. **1824** Miss Mitford *Village* Ser. i. 159 The precious epistle was undated. **1856** Froude *Hist. Eng.* I. 383 This letter is undated, but it was written..some time in the year 1532. **1886** Willis & Clark *Cambridge* II. 104 The Statement is undated. *Ibid.* 578 The list..is unfortunately undated.

2. Having no fixed date or limit; unending.

In quot. 1637 misused for 'dated'.

1624 Quarles *Sion's Elegies* II. xxii, Yet my vndated Euills, no time will minish, Though Yeers, and Months, though Daies and Howers, finish. **1637** D. Digges *Elegy* in *Jonsonus Viribus* (1638) 23 They did receive new life from you; Which shall not be undated, since thy breath Is able to immortall, after death.

3. Marked by no striking events.

1878 W. C. Smith *Hilda* 184 A wild, black night of tempest, such as men remember long In the dull undated life of a sleepy country town.

un'dation. [ad. L. type **undātio*, f. L. *undāre* to rise in waves. Cf. OF. *undation, -acion.*] A waving; an undulation. *Obs. rare* exc. in b.

1656 Blount *Glossogr.*, *Undation*, a flowing or rising of waves. **1668** Culpepper & Cole *Barthol. Anat.* II. vi. 101 A certain Undation or waving towards one side according to the carriage of the right Ventricle.

b. undation theory *Geol.* [tr. Du. *undatietheorie* (1932)], the theory that selective internal heating of the earth's mantle causes large wave-like folds to appear in the crust.

1932 R. W. van Bemmelen in *Natuurk. Tijdschr. Nederlandsch. Indië* XCII. 93 The geologic history of the western part of the Sunda arc has been examined according to the Undation Theory. **1950** P. H. Kuenen *Marine Geol.* ii. 146 In his undation theory, van Bemmelen (1939) postulates a primary salsima layer formerly enveloping the whole earth and now forming the floor of the oceans. **1975** *Nature* 3 Apr. 386/1 The..hypothesis bears some resemblance to the minority view of Van Bemmelen..and others, whose 'undation theory' proposes that selective high radioactive heating in the mantle produces warping of the overlying crust followed by lateral spreading under gravity.

un'daub, *v.* (UN-[2] 3.)

1611 Cotgr., *Desenduire*, to vndawbe; to bare; to pull the dawbing off. **1620** Brinsley *Virgil* 129 If..you will emptie (Vndaube or vncouer) their stately seate [*sc.* the honeycombs].

un'daubed, *ppl. a.* (UN-[1] 8.)

1648 Hexham II, *Ongemortert*, Vnplaistered, or Vndawbed. **1885** *Harper's Mag.* Dec. 136 Within the rude stable of unhewn logs, all undaubed.

un'daughterly, *a.* (UN-[1] 7.)

1748 Richardson *Clarissa* VII. 149 Any-thing undaughterly, unsisterly, or unlike a kinswoman. **1886** *Academy* 6 Mar. 162 It was at least ungenerous and undaughterly for Capri to expose all the seamy side of his nature to her friend.

un'dauntable, *a.* [UN-[1] 7 b.] That cannot be daunted; indomitable. (Freq. in 17th c.)

1587 Harmar tr. *Beza* 381 The vndauntable insolencie of Pharao. **1593** G. Harvey *Pierce's Super.* Wks. (Grosart) II. 112 He will welcome me with a fierce reioynder:..and so forth *in infinitum*, with an vndauntable courage. **1611** Speed *Hist. Gt. Brit.* IX. xxiv. §222 Their enemies no lesse fierce and vndauntable, then fortunate. **1631** Weever *Anc. Funeral Mon.* 589 Of an haughtie and vndauntable spirit. *a* **1670** Hacket *Life Abp. Williams* I. (1693) 181 That heroick and undauntable Boldness. **1848** Dickens *Dombey* liv, She was resolute, he saw; undauntable.

un'daunted, *ppl. a.* [UN-[1] 8.]

†**1.** Of horses: Not broken in; untamed. *Obs.*

1422 Yonge tr. *Secreta Secret.* 168 Hit happid, that Traiane his Sonne rode an hors vndauntid. *c* **1560** A. Scott *Poems* (S.T.S.) xxx. 11 Thay rin lyk wyld vndantit hors, But brydillis, to and fro.

†**b.** *transf.* Unbridled, unrestrained. *Obs.*

Chiefly used by Sc. writers of the 16th cent.

1513 Douglas *Æneid* VI. iv. 82 The felloun Hungir with hir vndantit rage. **1535** Stewart *Cron. Scot.* (Rolls) I. 103 This king he wox rycht vile;..Drokkit and dull throw vndantit delyte. *c* **1550** Rolland *Crt. Venus* I. 341 Weill I knaw thy vndantid barnage Will haif ane May. **1683** D. A. *Art Converse* 21 Nothing [is] more destructive than an undaunted passion.

†**c.** *Sc.* Undisciplined; disorderly. *Obs.*

1533 Bellenden *Livy* III. v. (S.T.S.) I. 261 Ane cumpanye of ȝoung vndantit men. **1549** *Compl. Scot.* xv. 128 Rustical and inciuile, ondantit, ignorant, dullit slauis.

†**2.** Unsubdued, unconquered. *Obs. rare.*

1513 Douglas *Æneid* IV. i. 84 Heir the vndantit folk of Numyda duell. *a* **1547** Surrey *Æneid* IV. 52 Eke the vndaunted Numides compasse thee.

3. Of persons: Not daunted or discouraged; undismayed; intrepid.

1587 Turberv. *Trag. T.* (1837) 126 The tone Rossilion calde, a bold undaunted knight. **1594** *Selimus* D ij, They are strong vndanted enemies. **1635–56** Cowley *Davideis* III. 125 Th' undaunted Prince, though thus well guarded here, Yet his stout Soul durst for his Parents fear. **1671** Clarendon *Dial.* Tracts (1727) 290 They are undaunted when it may be we look pale. **1697** Dryden *Virg. Georg.* IV. 113 To War they follow their undaunted King. **1708** J. Philips *Cyder* I. (1728) 31 Where shall we find Men more undaunted,..More prodigal of Life? **1781** Cowper *Table-t.* 366 Undaunted still, though wearied and perplex'd. **1828** D'Israeli *Chas. I*, I. xii. 325 The courtly patriot was disconcerted; the undaunted Duke was facing his accuser. **1891** Farrar *Darkn. & Dawn* vii, If he had been a Regulus or a Fabricius he could not have been more undaunted.

transf. **1820** Wordsw. *River Duddon* IV. 9 Starts from a dizzy steep the undaunted Rill.

b. Of courage, spirit, etc.

1591 Sylvester *Du Bartas* I. ii. 806 Th' vndaunted strength of the Diuine right-hand. **1631** Gouge *God's Arrows* III. Ep. Ded. p. iv/1 Joshua, a Generall of an undaunted spirit. **1663** Bp. Patrick *Parab. Pilgr.* xviii, I have known many Pilgrims of great courage and undaunted Resolution. **1727** Gay *Fables* I. x. 1 The man who with undaunted toils Sails unknown seas. **1759** Robertson *Hist. Scot.* III. Wks. 1813 I. 167 The spirit of Knox, however, still remained undaunted and erect. **1855** Macaulay *Hist. Eng.* xvii. IV. 54 With undaunted courage, with considerable talents.., he was emphatically a bad man. **1868** Milman *St. Paul's* 306 Norfolk's..undaunted mendacity..was unknown to Nowell.

un'dauntedly, *adv.* [f. prec.] In an undaunted manner; without fear; boldly.

1598 Florio, *Strenuamente*, valiantly, stoutly,.. vndantedly, courageouslie. **1610** Healey *St. Aug. Citie of God* 326 Our martyrs..bore all tortures undantedly. **1653** Gataker *Vind. Annot. Jer.* 51 The Roman Souldiery.. undauntedly and cheerfully addressed themselves to encounter with the enemy. **1694** Kettlewell *Comp. Persecuted* 145 Give me Courage..to behave myself undauntedly. *a* **1720** Sewel *Hist. Quakers* (1795) I. 3 He had preached the gospel undauntedly. **1742** Fielding *J. Andrews* IV. xiv, She walked undauntedly to Slipslop's room. **1852** Miss Yonge *Cameos* I. xxx. 259 The princes undauntedly strove to collect their shattered forces. **1894** Baring-Gould *Deserts S. France* II. 270 He stood upright, proudly and undauntedly facing the soldiers.

un'dauntedness. [f. as prec.] The quality or state of being undaunted. (Freq. in 17th c.)

1598 Florio, *Strenuita*, valiancie,..courage, vndantednes. **1626** Gouge *Serm. Dignity Chivalry* §6 Stoutnesse and courage of mind, Vndauntednesse in danger, Discretion mixed with passion. *a* **1656** Ussher *Ann.* (1658) 300 Antigonus..stood amazed at this bold attempt of his, and undauntednesse of his high courage. **1709** S. Clarke *Serm. Vict. near Mons* 16 'Tis by his blessing..that generals are inspir'd with wisdom, and troops with undauntedness and bravery. **1879** S. Brooke *Milton* 12 He moved so that men said he had courage and undauntedness.

un'daunting, *ppl. a.* [UN-[1] 10.] Not quailing.

1786 Burns *Ep. to Young Friend* 84 May Prudence, Fortitude and Truth, Erect your brow undaunting!

†**un'dauntless,** *a. Obs.*[−1] (UN-[1] 15.)

1654 Earl Monm. tr. *Bentivoglio's Wars Flanders* 106 Death will come the more welcome, when sought..with undauntless valour.

†**un'dauntoned,** *ppl. a. Sc. Obs.* [UN-[1] 8.] Not tamed or broken in; unsubdued.

1609 Skene *Reg. Maj.* 5 That..he may breake downe the proudnes of the vnreulie and vndantoned people. *a* **1653** Binning *Serm.* (1743) 564 To tame and danton that undantoned wild beast. **1678** *Geneal. Campbells* in *Highland Papers* (S.H.S.) II. 77 He was a wild undauntoned person.

un'dawned, *ppl. a.* (UN-[1] 8.)

1854 J. S. C. Abbott *Napoleon* (1855) I. xxx. 472 The gloom of the yet undawned morning. *a* **1860** D. Gray *Luggie*, etc. (1862) 9 The light Quickens in the undawned east.

un'dawning, *ppl. a.* (UN-[1] 10.)

1784 Cowper *Task* IV. 130 Thou hold'st the sun A pris'ner in the yet undawning east.

un'dazed, *ppl. a.* (UN-[1] 8.)

1757 W. Thompson *Hymn to May* xvi. 13 He who undaz'd can wander o'er her face, May gain upon the solar-blaze at noon. **1868** Adah I. Menken *Infelicia* 101 The Eagle's gray eyes..Undazed by the sun. **1871** B. Taylor *Faust* (1875) II. III. 198 Her glance Gods only bear undazed.

un'dazzle, *v.* (UN-[2] 3 and 7.)

1611 Florio, *Sbarbagliare*,..to vndazle. **1833** Tennyson *Dream Fair Wom.* xlv, Slowly my sense undazzled.

un'dazzled, *ppl. a.* (UN-[1] 8.)

1644 Milton *Areop.* (Arb.) 72 Kindling her undazl'd eyes at the full midday beam. **1665** Boyle *Occas. Refl.* IV. iii. 16 Ev'n upon such bright Eyes..I could gaze undazel'd enough to approve my self a right Eagle. **1743** Francis tr. *Hor., Odes* II. ii. 28 To him..Who can a treasur'd Mass of Gold With firm, undazzled Eye behold. **1799** Campbell *Pleas. Hope* II. 270 As the spirit eyes, with eagle gaze, The noon of Heaven undazzled by the blaze. **1834** A. F. Tytler *Univ. Hist.* (1850) II. 278 Undazzled by the splendor of so high an object of ambition. **1875** Jowett *Plato* (ed. 2) III. 137 There too he may remain undazzled by wealth or the allurements of evil.

un'dazzling, *ppl. a.* (UN-[1] 10.)

1601–3 Daniel *Ep. Ld. H. Howard* 80 They carry things assuredlie Vndazling of theire owne or others sight. **1814** in *Orr's Circ. Sci., Pract. Chem.* (1856) 498[The light was] soft and undazzling as moonlight. **1846** Keble *Lyra Innoc.* (ed. 3) 347 To His Sight Heaven's secrets are undazzling light. **1855** W. Irving *Washington* xviii. I. 151 The sterling, enduring, but undazzling qualities of Washington.

unde, undé, varr. UNDEE *a.*

un'dead, *a.* [UN-[1] 7. Cf. ON. *údauðr.*] Not dead; alive. Also, not quite dead but not fully alive, dead-and-alive. In vampirism, clinically dead but not yet at rest. Also *absol.* as *sb.*

a **1400–50** *Alexander* 158 And many was þe bald berne at banned þar quile, þat euer he dured þat day vndede opon erthe. *c* **1475** *Rauf Coilȝear* 855 Ane of vs sall neuer hine Vndeid in this place. **1548** Udall, etc. *Erasm. Par. John* vi. 41 b, Where as all men did eat therof, they neuertheles dyed, nether did any one of so great a number remain vndead. **1592** Warner *Alb. Eng.* VII. xxxiv. 149 The same..That thought he liued not because his Neeces weare vndead. **1897** B. Stoker *Dracula* xxvii. 381 There remain one more victim in the Vampire fold; one more to swell the grim and grisly ranks of the Un-dead. *Ibid.* 382 This then was the Un-Dead home of the King-Vampire. **1920** H. G. Wells *Outl. Hist.* 286/2 Presently by some amazing miracle he would become undead again and return, and set up his throne with much splendour and graciousness in Jerusalem. **1936** Dylan Thomas *Twenty-Five Poems* 4 They suffer the undead water where the turtle nibbles. **1949** D. L. Sayers tr. *Dante's Divine Comedy* I. viii. 118 Why walks this man, Undead, the kingdom of the dead? **1956** C. S. Lewis *Till we have Faces* xiv. 169 Shadow and monster in one, may be, a ghostly, undead thing. **1959** *Twentieth Cent.* Dec. 427 The vampire or 'undead' can only move about freely..between sunset and sunrise. **1972** P. H. Kocher *Master of Middle-Earth* (1973) iv. 62 They still inhabit their original bodies, but these have faded and thinned in their component matter until they can no longer be said to exist in the dimension of the living. Their flesh is not alive, not dead, but 'undead'. **1981** J. Sutherland *Bestsellers* v. 59 The good old folkloric remedies for killing the undead.

un'deadened, *ppl. a.* (UN-[1] 8.)

1813 T. Busby *Lucretius* I. III. 119 While o'er the soul undeadened transports steal. **1856** R. A. Vaughan *Mystics* x. i. II. 172 That heaven, where..glorious powers shall be gloriously developed, undeadened by any lethargy. **1895** *Outing* XXVI. 70/1 The noises, which wide-open windows admitted undeadened.

†**un'deadliness.** [f. next.] Immortality.

c **1000** Ælfric *Hom.* II. 484 Ure æhta sind ece on heofenum, þær ðær undeadlicnys ricsað. *a* **1225** *Leg. Kath.* 1119 He ne losede na lif, onont þet he godd wes, ne undedlichnesse onont his drihtnesse. *c* **1380** *Lay Folks' Catech.* (L.) 1115 He wyle cloþe oure sowlys..with þe stole of vndedlynesse and blysse of heuyn. *c* **1420** *Prose Life Alexander* 73 'Gyffe vs,' quoþ þay, 'vndedlynesse, so þat we mow noȝte dye'. **1481** Botoner *Tulle on Old Age* (Caxton) H v, It nedith not also that I speke euir of the undedlynesse of the soules, but I holde..that the soules of men be undedly.

un'deadly, *a.* [UN-[1] 7. OE. had both *undéadlic* and *undéaþlic* (see UN-[1] 3), corresponding to OHG. *untôdlîh* (MHG. *untôtlîch*, G. *untödtlich*), ON. *údauðligr* (Sw. *odödlig*, Da. *udødelig*).]

†**1.** Not subject to death; immortal. *Obs.*

c **950** *Rit. Eccl. Dunelm.* (Surtees) 169 Haliȝ God,.. strong, haliȝ, & vndeadlic. *c* **1000** Ælfric *Hom.* I. 150 He.. wunað..undeadlic, se þe ær his ðrowunge wæs deadlic. *c* **1000** —— *Saints' Lives* iv. 385 þær bið æfre ece fyr and undeadlic wyrm. *a* **1200** *St. Marher.* 10 Keiser of kinges, drihtin undedlich. *a* **1225** *Leg. Kath.* 390 Hwen þu forcweðest, for þi Crist, ure undedliche godes. *c* **1230** *Hali Meid.* 39 Eadi is te were..hwas streon is undeadlich. *a* **1340** Hampole *Psalter* xxiii. 4 He..feland his saule vndedly, enterly gaf him til godis luf. **1382** Wyclif *1 Tim.* i. 17 To the kyng of worldis, vndeedly and invisyble God aloone, honour and glorie. *c* **1425** *St. Christina* iii. in *Anglia* VIII. 120/45 To suffre peynes of an vndeedly soule by a deedly body. *c* **1449** Pecock *Repr.* II. xvi. 243 Tho spiritis were vnmade and vndeedli withoute bigynnyng or eending in tyme. ? **1554** Coverdale *Hope of Faithful* xxiv. 169 Vndeadlye or immortall is it called, because it neuer ceaseth to lyue. **1612** T. James *Corrupt. Scripture* III. 8 For rightfulnes is euerlasting and vndeadlie.

2. Not causing death; not mortal.

c **1611** Chapman *Iliad* XI. 390 Ulysses knowing well The wound undeadly..Thus spake to Socus.

un'deaf, *v.* (UN-[2] 6 a.)

1593 Shaks. *Rich. II*, II. i. 16 Though Richard my liues counsell would not heare My deaths sad tale, may yet vndeafe his eare. **1933** W. de la Mare *Fleeting* 53 Fame with trump and drum Cannot undeaf the dumb.

un'dealt, *ppl. a.* [UN-[1] 8 b. Cf. OFris. *unideld, ondeld*, MDu. *ongedeelt* (Du. *-deeld*), OHG. *unchideilit* (G. *ungeteilt*), ON. *údeildr* (Da. *udelt*, Sw. *odelad*) undivided, unshared.]

1. Undivided. (OE. *undǽled.*)

a **1300** *Cursor M.* 9761 An-fald godd vndelt es he.

2. Not dealt *with.*

1645 Milton *Tetrach.* Introd., Unadmonisht, undealt with by any Pastorly or brotherly convincement. **1648** Hexham II, *Ongehandelt*, Vnhandled, or Vndealt withall. **1870** Proctor *Other Worlds* xiii. 319 *note*, Certain difficulties suggest themselves which must not be left undealt with.

un'dean, *v.* (UN-[2] 6 b.)

1857 Trollope *Barchester T.* xlvi, Thorne gave him a look which undeaned him completely.

un'dear, *a.* [OE. *undeore* (see UN-[1] 7 and DEAR *a.*[1]), = MDu. *ondiere, -dure, -duyr* (older Du. *ondier*), OHG. *undiuri, -tiuri* (MHG. *untiure*), ON. *údýrr* (Icel. *ódýr*).]

†**1.** Of little value or estimation; worthless, cheap. *Obs.*

c **897** K. Ælfred *Gregory's Past. C.* lvii. 439 He nemde ða undiorestan wyrta ðe on wyrttunum weaxe. *c* **1000** Ælfric *Gloss.* in Wr.-Wülcker 130 *Uile ualet*, undeor hit is. *a* **1225** *Ancr. R.* 408 Vndeore he makeð God, & to unwurð mid alle, þet for eni worldliche luue his luue trukie. *a* **1300** *Cursor M.* 16034 Parfai, pilate, wel þou aght to hald him ful vn-dere.

2. Not dear; not regarded with affection.

1748 Richardson *Clarissa* (1811) IV. 168 So hasty, dearest Madam—And so slow, undearest Sir, I could have said. **1790** Mme. D'Arblay *Diary* V. IV. 182 Adieu, my dear friends! Adieu—undear December! **1881** Mrs. A. R. Ellis *Sylvestra* II. 76 One art Sylvestra gained, not undear to her, ..the getting-up of 'small linen'.

un'deathlich, *a.*, etc.: see UN-[1] 3.

unde'barred, *ppl. a.* (UN-[1] 8.)

1595 Daniel *Civ. Wars* v. v, For warelesse insolence whilst vndebard Of bounding awe, runnes on to such excesse. **1852** M. Arnold *Summer Night* 59 Awhile he [*sc.* Man] holds some false sway, undebarr'd By thwarting signs.

unde'based, *ppl. a.* (UN-[1] 8.)
1753 GLOVER *Boadicea* I. ad fin., We can shew.. Firm hearts, and manners undebased by fraud. **1768–74** TUCKER *Lt. Nat.* (1834) II. 24 So.. gold is pure when undebased by any alloy. **1825** SOUTHEY *Tale Paraguay* IV. v, A peaceful lot ..By Avarice undebased, exempt from care. **1846** *P. Parley's Ann.* VII. 191 The lama seems to be the only animal that is undebased by being subjected to man.

unde'batable, *a.* (UN-[1] 7 b.)
Also, in recent use, ***undebatably*** *adv.*
1869 F. W. NEWMAN *Misc.* 200 Seas, Desarts or great Mountain ranges have always been the chief arbiters in this undebateable question. **1898** *Mission. Herald* (Boston) Mar. 104/2 The pastors settled it by saying it was undebatable.

unde'bated, *ppl. a.* (UN-[1] 8.)
1620 DONNE *Serm.* Wks. 1839 IV. 551 It must not be a rash, a sudden, an undebated Resolution. **1648** MILTON *Observ. Art. Peace* Wks. 1851 IV. 563 Men whose serious consideration thereof hath left no certain precept, or example undebated. **1897** *Daily News* 15 Mar. 5/1 The undebated clauses of the Home Rule Bill.

unde'bauched, *ppl. a.* (UN-[1] 8.)
a **1656** BP. HALL *Rem. Wks.* (1660) 255 He sends us for the determination of decency, to the judgment of our right reason, undebauched nature, and approved custome. **1693** DRYDEN *Juvenal* VI. 17 For when the World was bucksom, fresh, and young, Her Sons were undebauch'd, and therefore strong. **1710** *Tatler* No. 191 ¶2 There are some that preserve their Relish undebauched with common Impressions. **1784** COWPER *Task* III. 744 Were England now What England was; plain, hospitable, kind, And undebauch'd.

unde'bilitated, *ppl. a.* (UN-[1] 8.)
[1775 ASH.] **1879** SPENCER *Data of Ethics* vi. 89 Those who are undebilitated by voluntary or enforced submission to actions injurious to the organism.

unde'bilitating, *ppl. a.* (UN-[1] 10.)
1811 ABERNETHY *Surg. Obs.* II. 208 Unirritating and undebilitating doses.. were given.

† **undebo'nairty.** *Obs.*[−1] [UN-[1] 12.] Ungraciousness.
13.. *Prose Psalter* lxxii. 6 Hij ben couerd wyþ her wickednes and vndeboneerte [*v.r.* vnbonerte].

† **un'debted**, *ppl. a. Obs.*[−1] [UN-[1] 8.] Not due as a debt or obligation.
a **1564** BECON *Art. Chr. Relig.* iv, The goodnesse of God, ..which by the vndebted death of the same hys sonne, had chosen them into the inherytaunce of euerlasting life.

undeca- (ʌn'dɛkə), before a vowel **undec-**, comb. form of L. *undecim* eleven, as in UNDECAGON; cf. HENDECA-. In *Chem.* and *Biochem.* used to form the names of molecules that contain eleven carbon atoms or consist of eleven of the second element, as **un'decane**, any of a series of isomeric hydrocarbons $C_{11}H_{24}$, *esp.* the liquid unbranched member $CH_3(CH_2)_9CH_3$; ˌ**undeca'peptide**, any polypeptide composed of eleven amino-acids; ˌ**undecy'lenic acid**, a yellow, water-insoluble carboxylic acid, CH_2: $CH(CH_2)_8COOH$, which is used as an antifungal agent.
1899 *Jrnl. Chem. Soc.* LXXVI. I. 816 The same substances were also detected in neutral creosote from paraffin oil; in this, *undecane was found. **1971** E. O. WILSON *Insect Societies* xii. 237/1 Undecane and the mandibular gland substances.. evoke the alarm response at concentrations of 10^9–10^{12} molecules per cubic centimeter. **1960** *Jrnl. Biol. Chem.* CCXXXV. 3645/2 Imidazole-heme *undecapeptide exhibits a more complex behavior. **1979** *Nature* 8 Feb. 480/2 Several lines of evidence suggest that the undecapeptide, substance P, is involved in synaptic transmission in various areas of the central nervous system. **1879** *Jrnl. Chem. Soc.* XXXVI. 306 Undecylic acid, $C_{11}H_{22}O_2$, prepared by heating *undecylenic acid with red phosphorus and hydriodic acid.., is a colourless transparent substance. **1952** S. SPENDER *Learning Laughter* xiii. 179 Castor oil plants can also be broken down into eneanthol and undecylenic acid. **1979** *Jrnl. Pharm. Sci.* LXVIII. 384/1 The antifungal activity of products containing undecylenic acid and its salts was demonstrated some time ago.

undecagon (ʌn'dɛkəgən). *Geom.* [Irreg. f. L. *undec-im* eleven, after *decagon* (cf. HENDECAGON). So Sp. and Pg. *undecágono*, F. *ondécagone.*] A plane figure having eleven sides and angles.
1728 CHAMBERS *Cycl., Undecagon*, is a regular Polygon of eleven Sides. **1798** HUTTON *Course Math.* (1806) I. 271. **1879** *Cassell's Techn. Educ.* I. 251.

unde'cayable, *a.* (UN-[1] 7 b.)
1534 MORE *Treat. Passion* Introd., Wks. 1270/2 The infinite perfection of their.. vndecayable glory. **1586** DAY *Eng. Secretorie* I. (1595) 145 Feruent and assured loue grounded vpon the vndecaiable staie and prop of your vertues. *c* **1610** *Women Saints* 78 Let vs liue.. that.. we may receyue in heauen vnmeasurable and vndecayable ioyes. **1872** HAWTHORNE *S. Felton* (1883) 318 Safe against disease, and undecayable by age.

unde'cayed, *ppl. a.* Also 6 *Sc.* ondekeyt. [UN-[1] 8.]
1. Not decayed or impaired; not reduced in quality or condition.
1513 DOUGLAS *Æneid* X. xiv. 71 Hys stalwart hart And curage ondekeyt was gude in neyd. **1697** DRYDEN *Æneis* X. 860 How fierce in fight, with courage undecay'd; Judge if such warriors want immortal aid. **1815** BYRON *Hebrew Mel.*, '*When coldness wraps*' ii, Eternal, boundless, undecay'd, A thought unseen, but seeing all. **1869** DK. ARGYLE *Primeval Man* IV. 158 Accidents which did not happen to civilized nations so long as their civilization was yet undecayed.
2. That has not begun to crumble or fall in pieces; not physically wasted.
1632 W. LITHGOW *Trav.* III. 86 The Temple.. is a worke ..as yet vndecayed. *a* **1682** SIR T. BROWNE *Tracts* (1683) 39 Coffins of this Wood, which he found yet fresh and undecayed. **1799** KIRWAN *Geol. Ess.* 198 We find the quantity of iron much the same as in undecayed basalts. **1826** KIRBY & SP. *Entomol.* IV. xlviii. 469 The one in a putrescent and the other in an undecayed state. **1864** J. RAINE *Hexham* (Surtees) I. Pref. p. lv, In the grave were.. a chasuble, a tunic, and a napkin uninjured and undecayed.
Hence **unde'cayedness.**
1650 TRAPP *Comm. Num.* xi. 7 This might be some cause of Moses his undecayedness.

unde'caying, *ppl. a.* (UN-[1] 10.)
1599 DANIEL *Musoph.* Wks. (1602) A vj, These Lines are ..the arteries, And vndecaying life-strings of those harts That stil shall pant. **1641** MILTON *Prel. Episc.* 11 The intire, the spotlesse, and undecaying robe of Truth. **1725** POPE *Odyss.* IX. 239 Unmingled wine, Mellifluous, undecaying, and divine! **1810** SOUTHEY *Kehama* X. vii, Every amaranthine flower Its deathless blossom interweaves With bright and undecaying leaves. **1868** W. CORY *Lett. & Jrnls.* (1897) 128, I don't care for Henri Deux and the undecaying Diane.

unde'ceased, *ppl. a.* (UN-[1] 8.)
a **1585** MONTGOMERIE *Cherry & Slae* (1597) 272 Like to ane fische fast in the nette, In dead-thraw vndeceist. **1589** WARNER *Alb. Eng.* VI. xxix. 127 For often Vprores did ensue for him, as vndeceast. *c* **1611** CHAPMAN *Iliad* XIII. 679 Of whom, some were not to be found unhurt, or undeceas'd.

unde'ceitful, *a.* (UN-[1] 7.) Also **-fully** *adv.*
1571 GOLDING *Calvin on Ps.* xviii. 31 God helpeth his seruants vndeceytfully. **1682** GREW *Anat. Roots* iv. §14 Undeceitful and accurate Observation of both their Number, and Size, must be made by the Microscope. **1744** AKENSIDE *Pleas. Imag.* I. 383 Where is.. the seal of undeceitful good, To save your search from folly?

unde'ceivable, *a.* [UN-[1] 7 b.]
†**1.** Incapable of deceiving; undeceptive; certain, sure. *Obs.*
1534 MORE *Comf. agst. Trib.* II. xvi. (1553) I vj, Shall you not lacke to enquyer, by what sure & vndeceiuable tokens, a man maye descerne yᵉ true reuelacions from yᵉ false illusions? **1581** J. BELL *Haddon's Answ. Osor.* 453 b, Where be those irreproveable Testimonyes, and undeceiveable examples, whereupon you crake so lustely? **1650** BAXTER *Saints' R.* II. iv. (1662) 220 The way that this Testimony hath come down to us is a certain and undeceivable way. **1669** STURMY *Mariner's Mag.* V. viii. 26 These Rules are undeceivable with Authority.
2. Incapable of being deceived.
1608 BP. HALL *Epist.* I. i, Shame not to haue the weake eyes of the world see that, which once your vndeceiuable Iudge shall see. **1687** BOYLE *Martyrd. Theodora* ii. 20 They look on Sufferers for truth with His undeceiveable Eyes. **1827** POLLOK *Course T.* VIII. 290 His votaries, who left the earth Secure of bliss, around him, undeceived, Stood, undeceivable till then. **1860** RUSKIN *Mod. Paint.* V. VI. ix. §14 An undeceivable common sense, and an obstinate rectitude.
Hence **unde'ceivableness; unde'ceivably** *adv.*
1560 BECON *New Catech.* Wks. 1564 I. 314 b, Tokens or markes, whereby we may truely and vndeceaueably knowe the true Catholyke and Apostolyke church. **1685** H. MORE *Paralip. Prophet.* Pref. p. xii, To acknowledge the Autority and Undeceivedness.. though not Undeceivableness or Infallibility of the ancient Catholick Church.

unde'ceive, *v.* [UN-[2] 3.]
1. *trans.* To free (a person) from deception or mistake; to deliver from an erroneous idea.
1598 FLORIO, *Disingannare*, to vndeceiue, to cleare, to free or resolue from any doubt. **1651** BAXTER *Let. to Ch. at Bewdley* 9 If this much will not undeceive the misled, let them for me be deceived still. **1687** T. BROWN *Saints in Uproar* Wks. 1730 I. 83, I am resolved to undeceive mankind. **1712** tr. *Pomet's Hist. Drugs* I. 215, I think my self oblig'd to undeceive the Publick. **1769** *Junius Lett.* xxxv. (1788) 182 Nothing less than your own misfortunes can undeceive you. **1839** ALISON *Hist. Eur.* liv. VII. 305 No sooner was he undeceived in this particular, than he despatched the most pressing orders. **1875** W. S. HAYWARD *Love agst. World* 45, I will very soon undeceive his lordship.
refl. **1687** MIÈGE II, To undeceive himself, *se desabuser.* **1708** J. HUGHES tr. *Fontenelle's Dial.* I. v. 21 Undeceive yourself, I beseech you. **1829** LYTTON *Devereux* II. vii, It is hard to undeceive ourselves. **1890** 'R. BOLDREWOOD' *Miner's Right* ii, My heart had only now undeceived itself.
b. Const. *of* (an error, etc.).
1653 W. RAMESEY *Astrol. Restored* To Rdr. 1 To undeceive my Country men of such Calumnies as are cast upon this.. study. **1710** J. CLARKE tr. *Rohault's Nat. Philos.* (1729) I. Pref., A Man who had undeceived the World of an ancient Errour. **1823** SOUTHEY *Hist. Penins. War* I. 427 He was undeceived of both errors in the Peninsula.
2. To instruct by removal of error.
1649 MILTON *Eikon.* i. 13 Thus much be said in general to his Prayers;.. anough to undeceive us what esteem we are to set upon the rest.

unde'ceived, *ppl. a.* [UN-[1] 8.] Not deceived or imposed upon.
c **1400** *Apol. Loll.* 15 To haue þe more clere and vndeceyuid knowyng of þis mater. **1529** MORE *Dyaloge* II. Wks. 186/2 It may well.. happen, that the good men wel beleuing & vndeceiued, be those that beleue the worship of ymages & praying to saintes to be ydolatry. **1747** LD. LYTTELTON *Monody* xii, A prudence undeceiving, undeceiv'd, That nor too little, nor too much believ'd. **1799** WORDSW. *Ruth* 148 Deliberately, and undeceived, Those wild men's vices he received. **1827** [see UNDECEIVABLE *a.* 2].
absol. **1832** WORDSW. *Rural Illusions* 29 The World's illusive shows.. For the undeceived.. Are melancholy things.
Hence **unde'ceivedness.**
1685 [see UNDECEIVABLENESS].

unde'ceiver. [f. UNDECEIVE *v.*] One who or that which undeceives.
1643 (*title*), The Vn-Deceiver. **1668** R. L'ESTRANGE *Vis. Quev.* (1708) 114 Some call me the Plain-Dealer; others, the Undeceiver General. **1825** LYTTON *Falkland* 20 My manhood has been the undeceiver of my youth.

unde'ceiving, *vbl. sb.* [f. as prec.] The action of the verb.
1648 [P. HEYLYN] (*title*), The Undeceiving of the People in point of Tithes. **1652** T. NICOLS *Lapidary* Title-p., Cautions for the undeceiving of all those that deal with Pretious Stones. *a* **1708** BEVERIDGE *Thes. Theol.* (1711) III. 331 Godliness is profitable for the soul.. in its will, by undeceiving of it. **1886** HALL CAINE *Son of Hagar* I. ii, The undeceiving came at length, and then the Laird Fisher was old and poor.

unde'ceiving, *ppl. a.* (UN-[1] 10.)
a **1586** SIDNEY *Arcadia* III. x. (1912) 403 In paying the tribute of undeceyving skill. **1607** HIERON *Wks.* I. 319 Who would not esteeme such vndeceiuing engagements of Gods vnchanging loue? **1704** NORRIS *Ideal World* II. iii. 170 The undeceiving answers of Truth itself,.. whose instructions are faithful and unerring. **1747** [see UNDECEIVED].

un'decency. Now *Obs.* or *rare.* [UN-[1] 12 and 5 b: cf. UNDECENT *a.*] = INDECENCY I.
1589 PUTTENHAM *Eng. Poesie* III. xxiii. (Arb.) 271 Diuers points, in which the wise and learned men of times past haue noted much decency or vndecencie. **1656** *Clarke Papers* (Camden) III. 75 Upon a motion against blackpatches used by women on their faces, all undecency in apparrell was also moved again. **1692** SOUTH *Serm.* (1697) I. 482 From this springs the Notion of Decency or Undecency; that which becomes or mis-becomes.
b. = INDECENCY I b.
1624 GATAKER *Transubst.* 189 It should be subject to many undecencies, as corruption, putrefaction, mice-eating. **1660** JER. TAYLOR *Worthy Commun.* Introd. 5 A disproportionate instrument is an undecency, and makes the effect impossible. *a* **1716** SOUTH *Serm.* (1744) VII. 30 Every vacuity is (as it were) the hunger of the creation, both an undecency, and a torment.

unde'cennary, *a. rare.* [f. L. *undec-im* eleven, after *decennary.*] Given, occurring, or observed every eleventh year, or once in every eleven years.
a **1847** E. STILES (Webster), It appears from an undecennary account laid before Parliament.
So **unde'cennial** *a.* (1864 WEBSTER.)

un'decent, *a. Obs.* exc. *dial.* Also 5 vndesent, 7, 9 *dial.*, ondecent. [UN-[1] 7 and 5 b.]
1. Unfitting, unbecoming, improper; = INDECENT *a.* I. Now *arch.*
1546 *Supplic. Poore Commons* (1871) 72 That it were farre vndesent to musell the oxe that trauaylleth all the daye. **1576** FLEMING *Panopl. Epist.* 177, I thincke it undecent, that I writing of mine owne matters, should, in yours, shewe mee selfe negligent. **1608** D. T[UVILL] *Ess. Pol. & Mor.* 51 b, As beeing a thing altogether vndecent, that one of her composition should any way intermeddle with Armes. **1658** T. WALL *Charact. Enemies Ch.* Ded. 1 To entitle a Book to the name of a Brother, is neither unusual or undecent. **1703** R. NEVE *City & C. Purch.* 86 It would be undecent to see a great Fabrick, consist of little Apartments. *a* **1721** SHEFFIELD (Dk. Buckhm.) *Wks.* (1723) II. 208 'Tis surely not undecent to mention one's self when 'tis rather with censure than approbation. **1823** LAMB *To Southey* Wks. 1908 I. 290, I have endeavoured there to rescue a voluntary duty.. from the charge of an undecent formality.
b. Const. *for* (a person).
1559 MORWYNG *Evonym.* 196 All the use of Cosmetical.. thinges oughte to be taken for unhonest and undecent for a man that is.. godly minded. **1581** PETTIE *Guazzo's Civ. Conv.* III. (1586) 159 It is an undecent thinge for a woman to resemble a man. **1604** T. WRIGHT *Passions* IV. ii. §1. 127 Such passions are.. vndecent for graue persons. **1660** N. INGELO *Bentiv. & Ur.* II. (1682) 113 [No more] than it is undecent for a man to stand upon two Feet. **1685** SOUTH *Serm.* (1727) V. i. 28 It is very undecent for a Master to jest or play with his Scholars.
†**2.** Uncomely, unhandsome, unbecomingly mean; = INDECENT *a.* 2. *Obs.*
1622 WITHER *Philarete* (1633) F 5 b, 'Twixt the Eyes, no hollow place, Wrinkle nor undecent space, Disproportions her in ought. **1637–8** in Willis & Clark *Cambridge* (1886) I. 118 Fairer accesse to their Chappell, wᶜʰ is now most undecent. **1670** DRYDEN *2nd Pt. Conq. Granada* I, *Ozym.* I cast it from me, like a Garment torn, Ragged, and too undecent to be worn.
3. Offensive to propriety or moral feeling; = INDECENT *a.* 3. Now *dial.*
1563 *Homilies* II. *Excess of Apparel* ¶10 Thou.. makest of thy vndecent apparell of thy body, the deuilles nette. **1573–80** G. HARVEY *Letter-bk.* Wks. (Grosart) I. 135 What Stoick or Eremite will bar them of any merriments and iestes that are not ether merely undecent or simple unhonest? **1654** GATAKER *Disc. Apol.* 77 Away with all undecent, unwashed and defiled langage. **1693** *Dryden's Juvenal* XIV. (1697) 342 Much more is it their Duty to their Children, that nothing appear corrupt or undecent in their Family. **1711** E. WARD *Quix.* 111 He spy'd her stretch'd out in an undecent Manner on the Ground. **1717** *Entertainer* No. 8. 48 Shocking Sentences and Undecent Dialogues. **1810** S. GREEN *Reformist* I. 86 Aren't you ashamed, you undecent fellow, to be appearing on the stair-case in that there

manner? **1861** J. BARR *Poems* 108 (E.D.D.), 'Twas a shamefu' undecent remark.

†**un'decently,** *adv. Obs.* [Cf. UN-[1] 11 and 5 b, and prec.]

1. Unbecomingly, unsuitably, improperly; = INDECENTLY *adv.*

1563 *Homilies* II. *Sacrament* I. ¶2 Lest..this comfortable medicine of the soule vndecently receaued, tende to our greater harme. **1577** tr. *Bullinger's Decades* (1592) 637 Hee ought to be free, least the image of God should seeme to bee bond vndecently. **1628** T. SPENCER *Logick* 171 We may not thinke, that he hath omitted it: for that is to charge him vndecently:..and against reason. **1671** GREW *Anat. Plants* iii. App. §4 The Branches whereof..must needs by their own weight, and that of their Fruit, undecently fall. **1716** M. DAVIES *Athen. Brit.* II. 96 He made early Applications to King Henry's Queen Dowager, who comply'd with him a little undecently.

2. Unhandsomely, inelegantly.

1587 *Presentmt.* in *Essex Rev.* XV. 43 The church is undecently and unsemely and filthily kept. **1644** LAUD *Hist. Troub. & Trials* (1695) xxxii. 310, I say so too, or else my Chappel must lye more undecently than is fit to express. **1664** J. WEBB *Stone-Heng* (1725) 38 They are most undecently high, saith Scamozzi. **1673** *Lady's Call.* I. v. §32 Shall she take no care how sordidly, how undecently she appear when the King of Kings gives audience?

3. With impropriety or indecency.

1589 PUTTENHAM *Eng. Poesie* III. xxiii. (Arb.) 275 It was not vndecently spoken.., for it was the cleaneliest excuse he could make. **1603** FLORIO *Montaigne* III. v. 522, I know a hundred Cuckolds, which are so, honestlie and little vndecently. **1655** STANLEY *Hist. Philos.* III. (1687) 92/2 Another time she offered to go to a publick show attired undecently. **1689** BURNET *Trav.* iii. (1750) 140 The great Libertinage that is so undecently practised by most Sorts of People at Venice.

unde'ception. [UN-[2] 8.] The action of undeceiving or the fact of being undeceived.

1694 *Gracian's Courtier's Orac.* 191 At present undeception is politick, it goes commonly betwixt two lights. **1820** C. R. MATURIN *Melmoth* xxix. IV. 309 Oh Margaret—that undeception plants a dagger in the heart. **1870** R. BLACK tr. *Guizot's France* I. xiii. 301 Length of life brings, in the soul of the ambitious, days of hearty undeception.

undeceptious, -titious: see UN-[1] 7.

unde'ceptive, *a.* (UN-[1] 7.)

1846 WORCESTER (citing Foster). **1883** D. C. MURRAY *Hearts* i. (1885) 2 With an undeceptive pretence of gaiety.

unde'cidable, *a.* [UN-[1] 7 b.] **a.** Incapable of being decided.

1640 BP. HALL *Episc.* III. v. 244 Things so utterly undetermined, that they are indeed altogether undecidable. **1683** MOXON *Mech. Exerc., Printing* 1 An undecidable Controversie about the original Contriver..remains on foot. **1737** L. CLARKE *Hist. Bible* (1740) II. 224 The question being undecidable among themselves, they appeal to Jerusalem. **1845** CARLYLE *Cromwell* (1872) V. 16 As this matter of the Kingship is to me even now, very 'dark' and undecidable!

b. *Logic* and *Math.* Of a proposition, theorem, etc.: incapable of being either proved or disproved.

1937 *Mind* XLVI. 60 Gödel has shown that the particular sentence in question is undecidable, *i.e.*, neither it nor its negation is demonstrable. **1966** S. BEER *Decision & Control* x. 208 The network language which spans the gap between a problem situation and its conceptual model also contains undecidable sentences. **1979** *Sci. Amer.* Feb. 5/1 Logicians have been able to show that even simple and mathematically interesting statements may be undecidable.

Hence ˌ**undecida'bility**, the property of being undecidable.

1942 *Mind* LI. 260 It therefore raises the issue of undecidability in the arithmetical as well as in the linguistic realm. **1967** S. C. KLEENE *Math. Logic* v. 279 By the essential undecidability of S, S_2 is undecidable. **1971** *Sci. Amer.* Aug. 99/1 In contrast, the Platonists, who count among their number even Gödel himself, believe (like Einstein) that the undecidability in mathematics is a statement about the inherent limitations of our present axiomatic mode of investigation and not about the mathematical objects themselves.

unde'cide, *v.* (UN-[2] 3 and 7.)

1601 DANIEL *Civ. Wars* VI. xc, To vndiscide The late concluded Act they held for vaine. **1853** MRS. GASKELL *Ruth* xxi, She was weary of hearing all the..deciding, and undeciding, and re-deciding, before it was possible for her to go.

unde'cided, *ppl. a.* and *sb.* [UN-[1] 8.]

A. *adj.* **1. a.** Not decided; unsettled; uncertain.

1540 in *Charters*, etc. *Edinb.* (1871) 212 The pley beand.. as yet ondecidit, na innovatioun suld be maid. **1588** LAMBARDE *Eiren.* III. i. 330, I find it both doubted and undecided. **1603** FLORIO *Montaigne* I. xxvi. 89 Glory.. forbids vs to leaue any thing vnresolued or vndecided. **1651** HOBBES *Leviath.* I. xv. 78 For else the question is undecided, and left to force. **1697** DRYDEN *Virg. Georg.* IV. 132 A Cast of scatter'd Dust will..undecided leave the Fortune of the Day. **1731** *Hist. Litteraria* III. 762 Finding, that notwithstanding the great pains he had taken, many Controversies remained still undecided. **1782** MISS BURNEY *Cecilia* II. vi, If any thing is yet undecided, it will not, perhaps, be amiss that I should be consulted. **1825** J. NICHOLSON *Operat. Mechanic* 671 It appears to us that this point still remains in a very undecided state. **1853** RUSKIN *Stones Ven.* (1874) II. vi. §91. 217 This is not an unimportant distinction, nor an undecided one.

b. Lacking in decision or definiteness.

1828 LYTTON *Pelham* III. vii, To engage a certain rather than a doubtful and undecided support. **1864** TREVELYAN *Compet. Wallah* (1866) 292 To have..an undecided opinion on the question of Eternal Punishment.

c. *Coursing.* Not decided between the competing dogs; indecisive.

1839 in Youatt *Dog* (1845) 261 In running a match the judge may declare the course to be undecided. **1856** 'STONEHENGE' *Brit. Sports* 206, etc.

2. Irresolute, hesitating.

1779 *Mirror* No. 66, He knows..that the undecided mind, without choice or active sense of propriety, is equally accessible to the next [feelings] that occur. **1791** COWPER *Iliad* I. 242 So doubted he, and undecided yet Stood drawing forth his faulchion huge. **1860** TYNDALL *Glac.* I. xi. 71 The man..stood beside the chasm manifestly undecided as to whether he should take the step. **1875** JOWETT *Plato* (ed. 2) III. 173 When action above all things is required he is undecided.

B. *sb.* **1.** *Coursing.* An indecisive course.

1876 *Coursing Calendar* 5 Miss Steel and No More ran a short undecided. *Ibid.* 222 We did not make the anticipated headway, only getting thirty courses, including the two undecideds.

2. An undecided person, one who has not made up his mind.

1968 *Listener* 31 Oct. 568/2 Who can decide what an undecided is going to do? **1974** *Times* 7 Oct. 4/4 The Labour Party is picking up more support from the undecideds than any other party.

Hence **unde'cidedly** *adv.*

[**1847** WEBSTER.] **1856** OLMSTED *Slave States* 19 They seem to move very awkwardly, slowly, and undecidedly. **1885** SIR J. F. STEPHEN in *Law Q. Rev.* Jan. 8 Their language hovers undecidedly between two meanings.

unde'ciding, *ppl. a.* (UN-[1] 10.)

1802 WOLCOT (P. Pindar) *Gt. Cry & Little Wool* IX. ii, A certain Law Lord of our days, A great *un*-deciding decider. **1846** WORCESTER (citing Burke).

unde'ciduous, *a.* (UN-[1] 7 and 5 b.)

1851 MRS. BROWNING *Casa Guidi Wind.* II. 380 From bole to bole Of immemorial, undeciduous trees. **1893** W. H. HUDSON *Patagonia* 136 The grey undeciduous foliage of the tree and shrub vegetation.

un'decimal, *a.* [f. L. *undecim* eleven.] Characterized in some way by the number eleven.

1804 SHAW *Gen. Zool.* V. I. 24 Undecimal Silure... Silure with single dorsal fin of eleven rays. **1845** *Encycl. Metrop.* XXV. 1397/1 The numeration [of the New Zealanders] is undecimal by successive multiples of eleven.

un'deciman, *a.* [f. as prec.] Connected with eleven o'clock. Also **undeci'marian** *a.*

1883 *Ch. Times* 27 Apr. 293 The service began at ten instead of eleven. After this revolt from the true *Undeciman Faith [etc.]. **1874** MICKLETHWAITE *Mod. Par. Churches* 308 But, says *undecimarian respectability, we should go to church to say our prayers and be preached to.

undecimar'ticulate, *a. Zool.* [f. L. *undecim* eleven + *articul-us* joint.] Having eleven sections.

1856 W. CLARK *Van der Hoeven's Zool.* I. 340 Antennæ undecimarticulate, perfoliate.

‖**unde'cimvir.** *Gr. Antiq.* Also **undecem-**. [f. L. *undecim* eleven + *vir* man, after Gr. οἱ ἕνδεκα.] *pl.* The body of eleven magistrates in ancient Athens. Hence **unde'cimvirate**.

1728 CHAMBERS *Cycl.* s.v., The Functions of the *Undecimviri* at Athens, were much the same as those of the *Prevots de Marechaussee* in France. **1775** ASH, *Undecemvirate*.., the office or dignity of the undecemviri.

unde'cipher, *v.* [UN-[2] 9.] *trans.* **a.** To decipher. **b.** To make undecipherable.

1654 GAYTON *Pleas. Notes* I. ii. 6 It were very good policy in times of warre, suites, or jealousie, to learne to undecipher mouths, lookes, and gates. **1764** D. E. BAKER *Compan. to Play-house* II. s.v. *Denham*, All his Letters..were constantly decypher'd [= ciphered] and undecyphered by Mr. Cowley. **1856** E. FITZGERALD *Salámán* Prelim., Oh distracted Lover! writing What the Sword-wind of the Desert Undeciphers so that no one After you shall understand.

unde'cipherable, *a.* [UN-[1] 7 b and 5 b.] That cannot be deciphered or made out; indecipherable: **a.** Of writings, inscriptions, etc.

1758 H. WALPOLE *Lett. to Mann* 23 Feb. (1846) III. 346 Your copyist or his original have made undecypherable mistakes. *a* **1827** MISS BENGER in *Literary Souvenir* 39 This paper..being in many parts almost undecypherable. **1862** STANLEY *Serm. in East* (1863) 136 In another fifty years it is probable that many of them will be almost undecypherable. **1877** 'H. A. PAGE' *De Quincey* II. xviii. 128 The rest of this letter is so mutilated as to be undecipherable.

b. *transf.*

1757 CHESTERF. *Let.* in *Misc. Wks.* (1777) II. 435 Public matters have been long, and are still, too undecypherable for me to understand, consequently to relate. **1822–56** DE QUINCEY *Confess.* (1862) 272 Its cause, its nature, and its undecipherable issue. **1850** GROTE *Greece* VIII. 574 In settling the undecipherable portions of the problem. **1876** T. HARDY *Ethelberta* This deep undecipherable habit sometimes suggested..Ethelberta's busy brain to her sisters.

Hence **undeciphera'bility; -ably** *adv.*

1847 WEBSTER, *Undecipherably*. **1881** RUSKIN *Morn. Florence* 35 The whole landscape is quite undecipherably changed and spoiled. **1890** *Standard* 17 Jan. 5/3 Owing to the undecipherability of many of the signatures.

unde'ciphered, *ppl. a.* [UN-[1] 8.] Not deciphered or made out.

a **1668** DAVENANT *Philos. Disquisition* Wks. (1673) 326 She steals to Natures Closet, and from thence, Brings nought but undecypher'd Characters. **1755** YOUNG *Centaur* ii. Wks. 1757 IV. 153 Does this yet unconstrued, undecyphered creature consider himself as an immortal being? **1827** HOOD *Hero & Leander* lvii, As one, who pores on undecypher'd books, Strains vain surmise. **1897** P. WARUNG *Tales Old Régime* 231 The fear that..any written message from their friend..might remain undeciphered.

†**unde'cised,** *ppl. a.* [UN-[1] 8.] Undecided.

1528 in *Lett. Suppress. Monast.* (Camden) 3 For the tryall of certen laundes and rightus which lately did depende..in contraversie, and yet doith depende undecised.

unde'cision. (UN-[1] 12 and 5 b.)

1611 COTGR., *Indecision*, an vndecision; a doubtfull, vndetermined, or vncleered state of things. **1795** *Jemima* I. 56 This state of torturing undecision shall terminate. **1930** W. FAULKNER *As I lay Dying* 13, I mislike undecision as much as ere a man.

unde'cisive, *a.* [UN-[1] 7 and 5 b.]

1. = INDECISIVE *a.* 1.

1661 GLANVILL *Van. Dogm.* 132 The two Nations differing about the antiquity of their Language, made appeal to an undecisive experiment. **1769** *Junius' Lett.* xxxv. (1788) 178 Undecisive qualifying measures will disgrace your government still more than open violence. **1796** KIRWAN *Elem. Min.* (ed. 2) I. 24 The analyses..present different results, and consequently are undecisive. **1807** G. CHALMERS *Caledonia* I. 291 At Air-Gialla..an undecisive conflict was fought. **1855** SINGLETON *Virgil* I. 278 When a bull..from his neck Hath shaken out the undecisive axe.

2. = INDECISIVE *a.* 2.

1780 *Mirror* No. 104, My poor friend, naturally of an undecisive temper,..had accustomed himself to deliberate on every trifle. **1802** WOLCOT (P. Pindar) *Pitt & Statue* Wks. 1812 IV. 510 So very undecisive in decision, Leaving for future Chancery-traps provision.

Hence **unde'cisively** *adv.*; **unde'cisiveness**.

1771 MACPHERSON *Introd. Hist. Gt. Brit.* 174 Their law-giver and prophets..speak very obscurely, as well as undecisively, upon the subject. **1778** *Ann. Reg., Hist.* 30/2 The undecisiveness of the campaign had..occasioned a prodigious desertion on both sides.

un'deck, *v.* (UN-[2] 3.)

1593 SHAKS. *Rich. II*, IV. i. 250, I haue giuen here my Soules consent T' vndeck the pompous Body of a King. **1598** FLORIO, *Disornare*, to disadorne, to vndeck.

un'decked, *ppl. a.* [UN-[1] 8.]

1. Not decked, adorned, or embellished.

1570 LEVINS *Manip.* 50 Vndecked, *incultus*. **1596** *Edward III*, I. ii. 150 The ground, vndect with natures tapestrie, Seemes barrayne. **1621** G. SANDYS *Ovid's Met.* XI. (1626) 225 A Fane, vndeckt with gold or marble stone Adioynes. **1667** MILTON *P.L.* v. 380 Eve Undeckt, save with her self.., Stood to entertain her guest from Heav'n. **1740** DYER *Ruins Rome* 247 Those piles undeck'd, capacious, vast. **1811** WILLAN in *Archaeol.* XVII. 162 *Undight*, undressed, or undecked.

2. Not furnished with a deck or decks.

1769 FALCONER *Dict. Marine* (1780) s.v. *Couloirs*, The sides of undecked vessels. **1824** SMYTH *Mem. Sicily*, etc. iv. 123 The undecked boats of the Rhegians. **1841** EMERSON *Ess., Self-reliance* Wks. (Bohn) I. 37 Columbus found the New World in an undecked boat. **1894** C. N. ROBINSON *Brit. Fleet* 202 Large, undecked row-boats.

unde'clarable, *a.* (UN-[1] 7 b and 5 b.)

c **1449** PECOCK *Repr.* II. xvi. 245 Of the spirit and of the ymage to gidere in an vndeclarable maner schulde be maad a sensible God. **1675** PENN *Summons to Christendom* Wks. 1782 III. 319 Oh the peace, the joy, the pleasure and the undeclarable comfort!

unde'clared, *ppl. a.* (UN-[1] 8.)

1526 *Pilgr. Perf.* (W. de W. 1531) 172 b, Here we may perceyue that we touched in the first peticyon, & lefte vndeclared. *a* **1548** HALL *Chron., Hen. VI*, 185 The breaches whereof, he neither forgat, nor omitted vndeclared. **1599** *Life Sir T. More* III. in Wordsw. *Eccl. Biog.* (1818) II. 180 Seeing to declare the causes is so dangerous, then to leave them undeclared is no obstinacie. **1647** JER. TAYLOR *Lib. Proph.* xviii. 227 This mercy which appertaines to Infants is so secret and undeclared and unconsign'd. *a* **1665** J. GOODWIN *Filled w. the Spirit* (1867) 487 If we consider God..as undeclared unto the world in that covenant and word. **1751** SMOLLETT *Per. Pic.* lxviii, Pickle's intention..was still dubious and undeclared. **1840** THACKERAY *Shabby-genteel Story* v, He was allowed to remain in the house, an undeclared but very assiduous lover. **1884** *American* IX. 182 A war nearly unprovoked and entirely undeclared.

unde'clinable, *a.* [UN-[1] 7 b and 5 b.]

1. *Gram.* = INDECLINABLE *a.* 3.

1530 PALSGR. 77 Any other of the partes that be undeclynable. **1775** ASH, *Undeclinable*.., not admitting a change of termination.

2. Unswerving; = INDECLINABLE *a.* 1.

1610 HEALEY *St. Aug. Citie of God* XXII. xxx. 919 An vndeclinable and sted-fast delight of not sinning.

3. Unavoidable; = INDECLINABLE *a.* 2.

1652 CHARLETON *Darkn. Atheism Dispelled* 242 The malignant impressions of the Stars, epidemick contagions, or other undeclinable Accidents. *a* **1670** HACKET *Abp. Williams* I. (1693) 107, I have shewn how blameless the Lord Keeper was, and that the Offence on his Part was undeclinable. *a* **1711** KEN *Hymnotheo* Poet. Wks. 1721 III. 90 At ev'ry Sense..Shall Horrors undeclinable rush in.

4. That cannot be refused.

1641 SIR E. DERING *Carmelite* 20, I offer you a fair tryall, and Iudges undeclinable.

Hence **unde'clinably** *adv.*, †unswervingly.

1662 STILLINGFL. *Orig. Sacræ* III. iii. §15 Speaking of those souls which are undeclinably good.

†unde'cline, *v.* [UN-^{1} 14.] = DESCEND *v.* 7b. **1651** CLEVELAND *Poems* 5 Were the note I sing Above heavens *Ela*, should I undecline, And with a deep-mouth'd Gammut sound agen.., I could not reach her worth.

unde'clined, *ppl. a.* [UN-^{1} 8.]
1. *Gram.* Having no cases marked by variations in the termination.
In the following quot. the meaning is not clear:—**1509** FISHER *7 Penit. Ps.* xxxviii. ee vij, This verbe morior after saynt Augustyne is vndeclyned.
1530 PALSGR. 77 Partes that be undeclyned. *nous* and *vous* remayne undeclyned. **1565** COOPER *Thesaurus* (*) 4 This varietie of construction is not onely to be considered in the diuersity of cases, but also of other partes vndeclined. **1612** BRINSLEY *Lud. Lit.* vi. (1627) 56 The other foure last are undeclined; that is, such as cannot be so turned, and have but onely one ending. *a* **1721** PRIOR *Dial. Dead, Chas. & Clenard* ¶2 Adverb, Conjonction, Preposition, Interjection undeclined. **1733** J. BRAMSTON *Man of Taste* 6 Good Parts are better than Eight Parts of Speech: Since these declin'd those undeclin'd they call, I thank my Stars, that I declin'd 'em all.
†2. Not turned aside. *Obs.*$^{-1}$
1638 G. SANDYS *Paraphr. Job* 31 For in his tract my wary feet have stept; His undeclined wayes precisely kept.

unde'clining, *ppl. a.* (UN-^{1} 10.)
1820 SHELLEY *Prometh. Unb.* I. 281 [I] thus devote to sleepless agony, This undeclining head.

†unde'coct, *a. Obs.* [UN-^{1} 7.] Undigested.
1542 BOORDE *Dyetary* xi. (1870) 261 Hote breade is vnholsome.., haustyng vndecoct humours.

unde'cocted, *ppl. a.* [UN-^{1} 8.] †Uncooked.
1542 BOORDE *Dyetary* xiii. (1870) 267 Rawe crayme undecocted, eaten with strawberyes or hurtes.

undecom'posable, *a.* [UN-^{1} 7b and 5b.] = INDECOMPOSABLE *a.* Also const. *by*.
1807 SOUTHEY *Espriella's Lett.* III. 363 Nothing will vegetate upon it, and it is undecomposable by the weather. **1865** MILL *Exam. Hamilton* 13 Many of our intellectual ideas are regarded by him as ultimate and undecomposable facts. **1870** JEVONS *Elem. Logic* ii. 15 A simple undecomposable substance called by chemists an element.

undecom'posed, *ppl. a.* [UN-^{1} 8.] Not decomposed: **a.** Of chemical or mineral substances.
1758 REID tr. *Macquer's Chym.* I. 248 If the Fixed Alkali be desired perfectly free from any mixture of undecomposed Nitre. **1789** *Phil. Trans.* LXXIX. 307 The volatile alkali.. will frequently pass over in great quantities undecomposed. **1849** D. CAMPBELL *Inorg. Chem.* 49 Sometimes there is a very small quantity of undecomposed matter remaining undissolved. **1880** J. LOMAS *Man. Alkali Trade* 277 Large quantities of undecomposed manganese.
b. Of substances liable to organic decay.
a **1835** MCCULLOCH *Attributes* (1837) III. xlii. 120 The fallen wood in particular is useless to future vegetation while it is undecomposed. **1855** *Orr's Circ. Sci., Inorg. Nat.* 64 The flesh having been preserved in a sufficiently undecomposed state to serve as food for wild animals.

undecom'posible, *a.* [UN-^{1} 7 and 5b.] = UNDECOMPOSABLE *a.* Also **undecomposi'bility.**
1866 ODLING *Anim. Chem.* 126 Its undecomposibility save by oxidation. *Ibid.* 129 Without this additional oxygen it has hitherto proved undecomposible. **1879** *Cassell's Techn. Educ.* I. 211 The other colours of the spectrum are due to simple or undecomposible rays.

undecom'pounded, *ppl. a.* (UN-^{1} 8.)
1795 *Phil. Trans.* LXXXV. 340 Wrought iron is to be considered as a simple or undecompounded body. **1804** *Edin. Rev.* IV. 126 A number of substances which are still undecompounded. **1843** *Civil Eng. & Arch. Jrnl.* VI. 420/1 The earths being classed as undecompounded bodies.

un'decorated, *ppl. a.* (UN-^{1} 8.)
a **1763** SHENSTONE *Ess., Gardening* Wks. 1777 II. 113 A sufficient quantity of undecorated space is necessary to exhibit such decorations to advantage. **1844** MARY HOWITT *My Own Story* ix. 84 His horn, undecorated with ribands. **1874** LUBBOCK *Mod. Savages* 107 If in the very low races the women are often wholly undecorated [etc.]. **1897** J. R. TANNER in *Eng. Hist. Rev.* XII. 31 The Commons found the undecorated facts alarming enough.

un'decorative, *a.* (UN-^{1} 7.)
1881 *Athenæum* 16 July 86/3 An inappropriate, undecorative stamp on the cover. **1886** RUSKIN *Præterita* II. v. 162 The undecorative structural arrangement, Swiss to the very heart.. of it.

unde'creasing, *ppl. a.* (UN-^{1} 10.)
1587 GOLDING *De Mornay* vi. 72 To be short, he calleth him ye myndly speech,..vncorruptible, vnincreasing, vndecreasing,..and firstbeknowne after God.

unde'cree, *v.* (UN-^{2} 3.)
1667 WATERHOUSE *Fire Lond.* 182 Be that Judgment, O Lord, undecreed by thee. **1691** DRYDEN *K. Arthur* III. ii, As if eternal doom Could be reversed, and undecreed for me. **1898** B. GREGORY *Side Lights* 205 He..cannot possibly afford to undecree his own infallibility.

unde'cried, *ppl. a.* (UN-^{1} 8.)
[**1775** ASH.] **1868** H. BUSHNELL *Serm. Living Subj.* 292 They fall into their places, unenvied, undecried.

undecylenic: see UNDECA-.

un'dedicated, *ppl. a.* (UN-^{1} 8.)
1661 BOYLE *Style of Script.* Ep. Ded. 2 That I should let this Book come forth Undedicated. **1675** HAN. WOOLLEY *Gentlewom. Comp.* 100 You would not let one minute pass undedicated to some good employment. **1794** W. TINDAL *Hist. Evesham* 31 It is difficult to conceive..that it should have remained long undedicated after being built. **1881** *Times* 20 Dec. 4/1 With the intention of walking over the defendant's undedicated land.

undee, undé(e, *a. Her.* Also 6–7 (9) unde. [a. OF. *unde, -ee* (F. *ondé, -ée*), f. L. *unda* (F. *onde*) wave, UND.] Having the form of waves; wavy. (Cf. UNDY *a.*, OUNDY *a.*, UNDATED *a.*, UNDADE *a.*)
1513 in Glover *Hist. Derby* (1829) I. App. 61, 3 barrs upon his nek, sabul unde or wave. **1572** BOSSEWELL *Armorie* 26 Crosses,..vairee, vndee, nebulee, cordee [etc.]. *Ibid.* II. 28 G. beareth Or and Gules, parted per Pale, vndee. It is termed Vndee, because two colors are caried one into an other, by the maner of water troubled with ye wind. **1611** GUILLIM *Heraldry* II. v. 50 This is termed a Bend Vnde. **1688** R. HOLME *Armoury* I. 19/1 Wavee, or Wavey, or Waved, or Unde, or Surged. *c* **1828** BERRY *Encycl. Her.* I. Gloss., *Unde, Undée*..is applied to charges, the edges of which curve and recurve, like the waves of water. **1863** BOUTELL *Her. Hist. & Pop.* xxi. 287 Barry undée of six, arg. and az. **1868** CUSSANS *Her.* (1893) 47 The lines by which a shield is divided..may assume any of the..forms:..Undé, or Wavy. Nebulé [etc.].

†un'deeded, *a. Obs.*$^{-1}$ (UN-^{1} 9.)
1605 SHAKS. *Macb.* V. vii. 20 Either thou Macbeth, Or else my Sword with an vnbattered edge I sheath againe vndeeded.

un'deemed, *ppl. a.* [UN-^{1} 8.]
†1. Not judged or condemned; uncensured. *Obs.*
c **1200** ORMIN 16725 Wha se lefeþþ upponn himm, þatt mann iss all unndemedd. *Ibid.* 17045 Ec off þatt, tatt illc an mann Iss all þwerrt ut unndemedd. *c* **1460** *Towneley Myst.* xxi. 230 Sir, the law will not he gang on nokyn wyse Vndemyd. **1500–20** DUNBAR *Poems* xviii. 50 Do weill, and sett not by demying, For no man sall vndemit be.
2. Unsuspected, unimagined.
1845 BAILEY *Festus* (ed. 2) 152 The words of gods, And fragments of the undeemed tongues of Heaven. **1856** VAUGHAN *Mystics* VI. vi. I. 394 The consciousness that all possessed is but a drop of the illimitable undeemed Perfection yet beyond.

un'deemous, *a. Sc.* and *†north.* Forms: 4 vndemes, 6 vndemus, -ous, 9 undeemous, -deemis, ondeemas, etc. [ad. ON. *údǿmis*, gen. of *údǿmi* (Norw. *udøme*, MSw. *odome*) an unexampled or monstrous thing or deed, f. *ú-* UN-^{1} + *dǿmi* example, instance, related to DEEM *v.*, DOOM *sb.* The ending has partly been taken as -OUS.] Unexampled, unparalleled, extraordinary, remarkable.
a **1300** *Cursor M.* 23235 (Gött.), The fiȝft [pain] es vndemes of dint [*Cott.* vndemnes dint; *Edinb.* vndemenes of dint], þat þa wreches þar sal hint. **1536** BELLENDEN *Cron. Scot.* I. vii. (1541) 6b/2 Suppone we be vincust (quhilk may nocht succeid but vndemus murdir of ȝow) then sall ye be ane facyll pray to ȝour ennymes. *Ibid.* VI. xvi. 76b/2 Thay ruschit..on the said Romanis; and maid sic vndemus slauchter on thaym, that [etc.]. **1596** DALRYMPLE tr. *Leslie's Hist. Scot.* I. 349 Edward..gathiris..ane armie vndemous. **1808** JAMIESON s.v., *Undeemis..money*, a countless sum. **1871** W. ALEXANDER *Johnny Gibb* x, An ondeemas thing o'siller.
Hence **un'deemously** *adv. Sc.*
1846 W. CROSS *Disruption* xiv, It's groun just undeemously since we cam' to Embro'.

undeep, *sb.* [f. next.] A shoal, shallow place.
1513 DOUGLAS *Æneid* V. iv. 114 First Sergest behind sone left hes he, Wreland on skelleis and wndepis of the see. **1847** G. LEE tr. *Hist. Ceylon* 6 Some of their vessels were driven into the undeeps near the place..called Chilaw.

un'deep, *a.* [OE. *undéop* (see UN-^{1} 7 and DEEP *a.*), = WFris. *ûn-, ondjip*, Du. and Flem. *ondiep*, G. *untief*.] Not deep; shallow.
c **897** K. ÆLFRED *Gregory's Past. C.* lxv. 469 Nis ðæt rædlic ðing, ȝif swa hlutor wæter hlud and undiop tofloweð æfter feldum. *Ibid.* lxiii. 459 On ðæt undiope mod. **1154** *O.E. Chron.* (Laud MS.) an. 1137, Sume hi diden in crucethus, ðæt is in an cæste þat was scort & nareu & undep. **1597** A. M. tr. *Guillemeau's Fr. Chirurg.* 4/2 Smalle and vndiepe woundes. **1671** *Phil. Trans.* VI. 3074 These Galleys are of great use both in Rivers and Un-deep Seas.

unde'faceable, *a.* (UN-^{1} 7b.)
1587 in T. Norton *Calvin's Inst.* Table XX x 6, Of the undelible character or undefaceable marke of the oyle where-with popish Priestes are annointed at their creation. **1611** COTGR., *Ineffaçable*, vneffaceable, vndefaceable.

unde'faced, *ppl. a.* [UN-^{1} 8.]
1. Not defaced or disfigured; not destroyed.
c **1400** *Destr. Troy* 8730 He fraynet..How the korse might be keppit..Fresshe, vndefacede, & in fyne hew. **1537** *Lett. Suppr. Monast.* (Camden) 164 The churche and house remenythe as yet undefacede. **1566** *Eng. Ch. Furniture* (Peacock, 1866) 115 John hyxon haythe ij candelstickes & sensors vndefased. **1582** *Wills & Inv. N.C.* (Surtees, 1860) 100 The chamber, as yt now standeth, vndefaced. **1631** WEEVER *Anc. Funeral Mon.* To Rdr., Such memorials..as were remaining yet vndefaced. **1676** HOBBES *Iliad* 374 Yet is his body uncorrupt,..And..doth whole remain And undefac'd, the bloud all washt away. **1772** [SHRUBSOLE & DENNE] *Hist. Rochester* 63 The monuments of the dead.. escaped undefaced. **1839** DARWIN *Voy. Nat.* xxiii. 604 The primeval forests undefaced by the hand of man. **1863** WHYTE MELVILLE *Gladiators* III. 165 Never again would she lie in the moonlight, beautiful and gracious and undefaced.
2. Not obliterated or blotted out; uneffaced.
1565 *MS. Cott. Cal. B. 10.* fol. 270 Which charters remain still undefaced. *a* **1619** FOTHERBY *Atheom.* I. iii. §3 (1622) 19 There is a sense of God still vndefac't. **1633** T. NASHE *Quaternio* (1636) 224 Both he and shee are branded with infamie, and the stigmaticall characters remaine as yet vndefaced in them. **1709** *Brit. Apollo* II. No. 15. 1/2 Undefac'd Impressions of our Maker's Image. **1818** SCOTT *Br. Lamm.* xxi, The softer substances, when they receive an impression, retain it undefaced. **1873** W. CORY *Lett. & Jrnls.* (1897) 333 The undefaced cross and bull on the door-post.

unde'falcated, *ppl. a.* [UN-^{1} 8.] Not curtailed or reduced; undiminished.
a **1745** SWIFT *Wks.* 1841 II. 223/2 A real undefalcated income of 600 *l.* a-year. **1802–12** BENTHAM *Ration. Judic. Evid.* (1827) V. 187 A perfect and undefalcated interest in the establishment of the will.

†unde'fame, irreg. var. of next. *Obs.*
1560 ROLLAND *Seven Sages* 10 Lord, I am auld, and neuer [*sic*] vndefame On ȝour counsall, and hes bene mony ȝeir.

unde'famed, *ppl. a.* (UN-^{1} 8.)
a **1450** *Knt. de la Tour* (1868) 36 Ther she might abide atte home with her worshippe saued, vndefamed of her good name. **1530–1** *Act 22 Hen. VIII*, c. 14 Whiche appertayne to the libertie of the kynges subiectes undefamed. **1578** *Reg. Privy Council Scot.* III. 60 He is ane trew man, knawin honest and undefamit sen he was borne. **1623** tr. *Favine's Theat. Hon.* III. vi. 374 That the Order may remaine pure and vndefamed, according as it ought to doe. **1648** HEXHAM II, *Onbefaemt*, Vndefamed.

†unde'fatigable, *a. Obs.* (UN-^{1} 7b and 5b.)
1630 tr. *Camden's Hist. Eliz.* IV. 89 Meane while, the Lord Deputy with vndefatigable paynes prosecuteth Mac-Hugh. **1662** GURNALL *Chr. in Arm.* III. xx. §1 Men, furnished by the blessing of God on their undefatigable labours and studies.

†unde'faulting, *ppl. a.* [UN-^{1} 10.] Unfailing.
a **1440** *Found. St. Bartholomew's* (E.E.T.S.) 45 He preyid the vndefawtynd mercy of criyst.

†unde'feased, *ppl. a. Sc. Obs.* [UN-^{1} 8.] Undischarged.
1492 *Acta Dom. Conc.* (1839) 273/1 þat þe said James sall content & pay to þe said Johne þe somme of v li contenit in þe said sentence arbitrale & vndefesit tharintill.

†unde'feasible, *a. Obs.* Also -able. [UN-^{1} 7, 7b.] = INDEFEASIBLE *a.* (Freq. in 17th c.)
1461 *Rolls of Parlt.* V. 465/2 By auncient maters of.. notable recorde undefaisible. **1548** UDALL *Erasm. Par. Luke* xxii. 165 And the said victorie consisteth in the vndefeasable scriptures of ye olde and newe testament. **1650** ELDERFIELD *Tythes* 38 Foundation of dominion cannot but have settled me a sufficient title and undefeasible. **1695** TRYON *Dreams* vii. 117 This great and undefeazable Law of the Creator.

unde'feat, *v.* (UN-^{2} 3.)
1746 GRAY *Let. to Walpole* 3 Feb., Our defeat to be sure is a rueful affair..; but the Duke is gone it seems..to undefeat us again.

unde'featable, *a.* (UN-^{1} 7b and 5b.)
a **1640** JACKSON *Creed* X. iv. §2 Either by the power of their almighty Creator, or by the undefeatable contrivance of his wisdom. **1938** J. W. DAY *Dog in Sport* xvi. 218 Of great heart and wisdom, with great courage undefeatable. **1943** —— *Farming Adventure* xvii. 192 All bids were overtopped by the undefeatable broad Norfolk of an aircraftman who bought recklessly.
Hence **unde'featably** *adv.*
1980 *Oxf. Diocesan Mag.* Mar. 19/2 A power which will work unceasingly and undefeatably until the kingdoms of the world become the Kingdom of God.

unde'feated, *ppl. a.* (UN-^{1} 8.)
[**1775** ASH.] **1818** SHELLEY *Rosalind* 701 Faith, the Python, undefeated, Even to its blood-stained steps dragged on her foul and wounded train. **1875** WHYTE-MELVILLE *Katerfelto* ii, Game-cocks, of which he owned a choice and undefeated breed. [Common in recent use.]
Hence **unde'featedly** *adv.*
1897 QUILLER-COUCH in Stevenson *St. Ives* xxxiii, He was pale, but undefeatedly voluble.

un'defecated, *ppl. a.* (UN-^{1} 8.)
1812 *Dramatic Censor 1811* 325 We have not met with any thing on the stage, more abounding in pure, unalloyed, undefecated absurdity, than the '*Wood Dæmon*'. **1817** GODWIN *Mandeville* II. vi. 115 Mine was pure, simple, undefecated rage, that did not dream of controling itself.

unde'fective, *a.* (UN-^{1} 7, 5b.)
1599 SANDYS *Europæ Spec.* (1632) 45 The most heavenly order reaching from the heighth of al power to the very lowest of all subjection, with admirable harmony and undefectiue corespondence.

unde'fectiveness. (UN-^{1} 12.)
1702 S. PARKER tr. *Cicero's De Finibus* V. 318 As certainly as our Nature is desirous of Consummation and Undefectiveness.

†unde'fenced, *ppl. a. Obs.* [UN-^{1} 8.]
1. = UNDEFENDED *ppl. a.* 2.
1451 CAPGRAVE *Life St. Gilbert* 94 So was our old man eke disposed þat he wold not leue þe church on-defensed. **1544** BETHAM *Precepts War* II. li. Lijb, Let hym beware that he leaue not his campe vndefenced and vnmanned. **1586** DAY *Eng. Secretorie* II. (1595) 100 The nature of the Dolphin is not to suffer the yong ones of her kind to straggle vndefenced. **1609** BIBLE (Douay) *Gen.* xlii. 12 You came to consider the undefensed partes of this land. **1652** HEYLYN

Cosmogr. 4 God sends man into the world..naked, and weak, and undefenced against all violences and dangers.

2. Unfenced.

1607 J. NORDEN *Surv. Dial.* v. 239 It is common..where men sow their corne, in undefenced grounds, there they make a dead hay..to keepe the cattle from the corne.

unde'fendable, *a.* [UN-[1] 7 b.] **a.** Of a place: that cannot be defended.

1931 W. S. CHURCHILL *World Crisis* VI. viii. 126 Belgrade, the capital, stood actually upon the Danube at the frontier and was undefendable.

b. Of a person = DEFENCELESS, DEFENSELESS *a.* 1.

1938 E. BOWEN *Death of Heart* I. vi. 109 Her tears were like a flag lowered at once: she felt herself to be undefendable. **1977** W. M. SPACKMAN *Armful of Warm Girl* 114, I never felt so undefendable and I didn't even know who you were.

unde'fended, *ppl. a.* [UN-[1] 8.]

†**1.** Not forbidden. *Obs.*

1399 GOWER *Praise of Peace* 223 We..soeffrin every lond To slen ech other as thing undefendid. **1598** FLORIO, *Indiffeso*, vndefended, not forbidden.

2. Not defended or guarded; unprotected.

1564 DORMAN *Proofe Cert. Articles Relig.* 28 b, Why haue they left him so long vndefended, who did no other thing then whereof them selues wer the authors. **1660** JER. TAYLOR *Ductor* I. iv. rule 2 §22 If a sober man shall stand alone unarm'd, undefended, or unprovided, and shall tell that he will make the Sun stand still. **1687** DRYDEN *Hind & P.* III. 626 The rest were strugling still with death, and lay The Crows and Ravens rights, an undefended prey. **1795** BURKE *Let. to W. Elliot* Wks. VII. 363 Property, left undefended by principles, became a repository of spoils to tempt cupidity. **1810** CRABBE *Borough* I. 136 There stands a cottage with an open door, Its garden undefended blooms before. **1869** TOZER *Highl. Turkey* I. 200 [A] bridge..with a single lofty arch undefended by a parapet.

3. *Law.* **a.** Not defended; not assisted by legal defence.

1607 COWELL *Interpr., Informatus non sum*, is a formall aunswer or of course made by an atturney,..by the which he is deemed to leaue his client vndefended. **1832** MISS MITFORD *Village* v. (1863) 323 The judge..hearing that he was a voluntary witness for the undefended prisoner, proceeded to question him. **1900** *Daily News* 4 May 5/5 The accused is undefended.

b. Against which no defence is raised.

1898 *Daily News* 26 July 8/7 The undefended petition of Major..for a divorce. **1899** *Ibid.* 4 May 8/4 Action was brought against him..and was undefended.

unde'fending, *ppl. a.* (UN-[1] 10.)

1651 JER. TAYLOR *Serm. for Year* I. xx. 253 Birds, sheep, and bevers, who..have not the foresight to avoid a snare, but by their fear and undefending follies are driven thither. **1888** O. CRAWFURD *Sylvia Arden* 329 Having to slay an undefending man in cold blood.

†**unde'fensable,** *a. Obs.* Also 7 -ceable. [UN-[1] 7 b.] **a.** = next 2. **b.** Unpreventable.

c **1412** HOCCLEVE *De Reg. Princ.* 2619 We armes bere A-geyn the armed men, hem for to dere, And naght a-geyn children vndefensable. *c* **1440** *Jacob's Well* 194 A knyȝt wyth-outen armoure, or armoure wyth-outen a knyȝt, is vndefensable. **1622** CALLIS *Stat. Sewers* (1647) 114 Things which happen extraordinarily by the Sea or great waters.. are counted inevitable and undefenceable.

unde'fensible, *a.* [UN-[1] 7 and 5 b.]

1. = INDEFENSIBLE *a.* 2.

1529 MORE *Dyaloge* IV. Wks. 256/2 Luther hath bee fayne for the defence of his vndefencible errours, to..forsake al yᵉ maner of profe & trial. **1830** *Westm. Rev.* July 85 Perhaps it is to a little undefensible latitude this way..that he owes a portion of the affected contempt of Pope, Swift, and Co.

2. Incapable of defence. Also *absol.*

1616 SURFL. & MARKH. *Country Farme* v. v. 531 To take away the stones were to impouerish the ground, and make it bare and vndefensible both against the wind, heat, and cold. **1661** J. DAVIES *Civ. Warres* 87 He..enters the unarmed and undefencible Town without resistance. **1661** FELTHAM *Resolves* (ed. 8) II. i. 174 How below the gallantry of man is it, to tyrannize upon the undefensible and senselesse?

†**unde'fensive,** *a. Obs.* (UN-[1] 7 and 5 b.)

1587 A. DAY *Daphnis & Chloe* (1890) 16 Loue..had.. prepared a secrete ambush wherewith to frame some notable breache into the vndefensiue imaginations of these..louers.

undefe'rentially, *adv.* (UN-[1] 11.)

1876 RUSKIN *Fors Clav.* lxix. 291, I looked at him, in one sense, not undeferentially.

unde'ficient, *a.* (UN-[1] 7, 5 b.)

1854 PATMORE *Angel in Ho., Betrothal* 71 And therefore in herself she stands Adorn'd with undeficient grace.

†**unde'fied,** *ppl. a.*[1] *Obs.* [UN-[1] 8.] Undigested; unconcocted.

1398 TREVISA *Barth. De P.R.* IV. ix. (Tollem. MS.), Aristotel sayeþ þat flemme is an undefied superfluite of mete. *Ibid.* v. xxxix. (Bodl. MS.), If þe blood is vndefied þe body þat is ifed þerewith swelleþ and strecchiþ. *c* **1440** *Promp. Parv.* 364/2 On-defyyd, *indigestus.* *c* **1450–80** tr. *Secreta Secret.* 25 That mete dwellith vndefied in þe bottom of the stomak.

unde'fied, *ppl. a.*[2] (UN-[1] 8.)

1590 SPENSER *F.Q.* II. viii. 31 Miscreant, thou broken hast The law of armes, to strike foe vndefide. **1670** DRYDEN *1st Pt. Conq. Granada* I, Tarifa..Chang'd his blunt Cane for a Steel-pointed Dart, And..basely threw it at him, undefy'd.

unde'filable, *a.* (UN-[1] 7 b.)

1855 CDL. WISEMAN *Fabiola* xvi. 99 Simple as light is His nature, one and the same every where, indivisible, undefilable.

unde'filed, *ppl. a.* [UN-[1] 8.]

1. Not rendered morally foul or impure; unpolluted, untainted.

13.. *E.E. Allit. P.* A. 725 He com þyder ryȝt as a chylde, Harmlez, trwe & vnde-fylde. *c* **1440** CAPGRAVE *Life St. Kath.* v. 576 He offred hym-selue on-to the fadyr of blis An oste ful clene, ondefiled with synne. **1504** C'TESS RICHMOND tr. *De Imitatione* IV. ii. (1893) 263 Lorde, kepe my herte and my body vndefyled. **1561** T. NORTON *Calvin's Inst.* I. 13 The law of the Lord (sayth he) is vndefiled, conuerting soules. **1628** SIR W. MURE *Spir. Hymne* 16 That I may spreade thy praise, thy might, With heart pure, vndefyl'de. **1662** STILLINGFL. *Orig. Sacræ* III. iii. §7 He had a pure and undefiled soul. **1784** COWPER *Task* III. 260 Immortal Hale! ..fam'd For sanctity of manners undefil'd. *a* **1839** PRAED *Legend of Drachenfels* Poems 1864 I. 150 Thou, in whose all-searching sight No human thing is undefiled. **1851** FROUDE *Short Stud.* (1867) I. 379 To..keep themselves if possible undefiled by so much as one corrupt thought.

absol. **1611** BIBLE *Ps.* cxix. 1 Blessed are the vndefiled in the way. MONSELL *Hymn, 'God of that glorious gift'* v, Make him and keep him Thine own child, Meek follower of the Undefiled!

b. Sexually pure or unpolluted; chaste.

c **1450** *Cov. Myst.* (Shaks. Soc.) 141 A mayd undefyled I hope he xal me preve. *c* **1470** *Pol., Rel., & L. Poems* (1903) 4 Thove vergyne knight of whom we synge, Vn-Deffiled sithe thy begynnyng. **1531** ELYOT *Gov.* III. xviii, But whan he knewe that they were of noble lignage, he sent them undefiled to their parentes and kynnes folke. **1539** CRANMER *Heb.* xiii. 4 Wedlocke is to be had in honoure among all men, and the bed vndefyled. **1611** BIBLE *Wisd.* xiv. 24 They kept neither liues nor mariages any longer vndefiled. **1667** MILTON *P.L.* IV. 761 Perpetual Fountain of Domestic sweets, Whose Bed is undefil'd and chast pronounc't. **1710** STEELE *Tatler* No. 210 ¶6, I have lived a pure and undefiled Virgin these Twenty seven Years. **1793** COWPER *A Tale* 6 Husband..and wife may boast Their union undefil'd. **1816** BYRON *Siege Corinth* xxvii, She is safe..In heaven;..Far from thee, and undefiled.

†**2.** Undefaced, unimpaired. *Obs. rare.*

1432–50 tr. *Higden* (Rolls) I. 185 That mownte..in whom letters wryten [in dust] were founde vndefilede [L. *illibatæ*] at the end of the yere. *c* **1460** *Oseney Reg.* 14 And what-so-euer thyng..may be i-purchased, to þem or to þere successours..vnbroke and undefylyd [L. *illibata*] abyde.

3. Not rendered foul or dirty. Also *fig.*

1590 SPENSER *F.Q.* IV. ii. 32 Dan Chaucer, well of English vndefyled. **1660** J. H[ARDING] *Basil. Valent. Chariot Antim.* 3 The Chaff being separated from the uncommix'd and undefiled Corn. **1718** LADY M. W. MONTAGU *Verses written in the Chiosk at Pera* 34 The streams still murmur, undefil'd with rain. **1821** WORDSW. *Mem. Tour Continent* XXXIII. 35 A sea-green river,..With current swift and undefiled. **1826** SCOTT *Woodst.* ii, Perhaps it is a punishment on me, who thought the loyalty of my house was like undefiled ermine.

4. Not violated or desecrated.

1586 J. MUSH *Life Margt. Clitherow* in Morris *Troub. Cath. Forefathers* Ser. III. (1877) 363 Insomuch as now not one Religious house standeth, not one altar unrased and undefiled. **1715** ROWE *Lady Jane Grey* II, Merciful, great Defender! Preserve thy holy Altars undefil'd. **1818** BYRON *Ch. Har.* IV. cliv, In this eternal ark of worship undefiled. **1865** MISS YONGE *Clever Woman of Family* I. ix. 225 He did think he had one lawn in the world undefiled by those horrible [croquet] hoops!

Hence **unde'filedly** *adv.*; **unde'filedness.**

1548 UDALL, etc. *Erasm. Par. Matt.* v. 24 But I wyll haue Matrimonye obserued more holyly and *vndefyledly amonge them that professe the new lawe. **1583** GOLDING *Calvin on Deut.* xxxiv. 200 Wee cannot serue him vndefyledly, except wee bee separated from the defylings that are contrarie to him. **1868** NETTLESHIP *Ess. Browning* 215 Here only could he be led to yearn undefiledly..after truths. **1571** GOLDING *Calvin on Ps.* li. 8 God requireth *undefylednesse in the inward partes. ? **1657** FARINDON *Serm.* xiii. (1672) I. 274 The colours and Beauty of it [*sc.* religion]; first, in its Purity..; secondly, its Vndefiledness, having no pollution.

unde'finable, *a.* and *sb.* (UN-[1] 7 b, 5 b.)

1694 LOCKE *Hum. Und.* (ed. 2) III. iv. §4 *marg.*, Names of simple Ideas undefinable. **1750** CHESTERF. *Lett.* (1774) 49 That is the occasion in which manners, dexterity, address, and the undefineable *je ne sçais quoi*, triumph. **1780** BURKE *Œcon. Reform* Wks. III. 306 Other persons meriting as little as they do, might be put upon it to an undefinable amount. **1827** DISRAELI *V. Grey* v. xv, When he was experiencing emotions, which, though undefinable, he felt to be new. **1884** CHURCH *Bacon* viii. 201 The undefinable but very real character of greatness.

sb. **1809** MALKIN *Gil Blas* x. xii. ¶23, I had no mind to meddle any more with the dish of undefinables.

Hence **unde'finableness; unde'finably** *adv.*

? **1705** BERKELEY in Fraser *Life* (1871) 437 There may be another cause of the undefinableness of certain ideas,..viz. the want of names. **1796** F. BURNEY *Camilla* V. x. xi. 470 This reverie, poignantly agitating, yet undefinably soothing. **1886** W. J. TUCKER *E. Europe* 127 Every village one passes through has..something undefinably characteristic about it.

unde'fined, *ppl. a.* [UN-[1] 8.] Not defined or clearly marked; indefinite.

1611 FLORIO, *Indefinito*, vndefined. **1658** PHILLIPS, *Indefinite*, not limited, undefined, undetermined. **1716** ADDISON *Freeholder* No. 31 ¶5 The Terms which the Author makes use of are loose, general, and undefined. **1797** GODWIN *Enquirer* I. xii. 105 A sort of floating and undefined reverie. **1844** KINGLAKE *Eothen* viii, The prestige created by the rumours of her high and undefined rank. **1875** JOWETT *Plato* (ed. 2) IV. 156 Theology..is full of undefined terms which have distracted the human mind for ages.

Hence **unde'finedly** *adv.*; **unde'finedness.**

1827 MONTGOMERY *Pelican Isl.* IX. 190 His soul explored immensity, In search of something undefinedly great. *a* **1832** BENTHAM *Language* Wks. 1843 VIII. 304/1 Clearness, as opposed to: 1. Obscurity, 2. Ambiguity, 3. Undefinedness. **1860** J. YOUNG *Prov. Reason* 47 Only through and on account of this undefinedness..is Being non-Being.

†**un'definite,** *a.* [UN-[1] 7.] = INDEFINITE *a.*

1589 NASHE *Anat. Absurd.* Epistle, The vndefinite desire to be suppliant vnto you in some subiect of witte. **1603** FLORIO *Montaigne* I. ix. 17 The opposite of truth hath many many shapes, and an vndefinite field.

unde'flected, *ppl. a.* (UN-[1] 8.)

1852 BAILEY *Festus* (ed. 5) 475 The sun-sire and the death-world too, And undeflected spirit, pure from Heaven. **1882** GEIKIE *Text-bk. Geol.* IV. VII. i. §3. 554 The dykes may be traced undeflected across some of the largest faults.

†**undeflore,** *a. Obs.* [UN-[1] 7.] = INDEFLORE *a.*

a **1568** BELLENDEN *Benner of Pietie* 138 (Bann. MS.), The secund wes ane richt excellent thing, Quhen moderfull wes the Virgin, vndefloir.

unde'flowered, *ppl. a.* (UN-[1] 8.)

(*a*) *a* **1533** LD. BERNERS *Gold. Bk. M. Aurel.* ii. (1535) 101 b, They leaue no cattayle vnslayne, no gardeyne vnrobbed, no wyld beest vnchased, nor no mayde vndefloured. **1602** DEKKER *Satirom.* Wks. 1873 I. 225 A charme, that shall lay downe the spirit of lust, and keep thee undeflowerd. **1641** EARL MONM. tr. *Biondi's Civil Wars* II. 83 No maidenhood was undeflowred, nor marriage bed unviolated.

(*b*) **1641** MILTON *Reform.* II. Wks. 1851 III. 65 Much more may a King injoy his rights, and Prerogatives undeflowr'd, untouch'd. **1678** CUDWORTH *Intell. Syst.* I. v. 728 The Atomick Philosophy [has been] restored, as it was in its first genuine and virgin state, undeflowred as yet by Atheists. **1746** YOUNG *Nt. Th.* IX. 1210 Minds elevate.. alone obtain Full relish of existence un-deflower'd. *a* **1861** D. GRAY *Poet. Wks.* (1874) 23 He feels As one newborn to being undeflowered.

†**unde'foiled,** *ppl. a. Obs. rare.* (UN-[1] 8. Cf. *defoil* DEFOUL *v.*)

a **1325** *Prose Psalter* (1891) 193 Þe which bot ȝif ichon kepe hole & nouȝt de-fouled [*v.r.* vndefoylid],..he shal peris wyþ-outen ende. [**1859** J. T. STATON *Song Sol.* vi. 9 Ma dove, ma undefoilt, is but one.]

†**unde'foiling,** *vbl. sb. Obs.* (UN-[1] 13; cf. prec.)

c **1425** *St. Mary of Oignies* II. iii. 26 in *Anglia* VIII. 158 Vndefoylynge of þe forseyde holy virgyns.

unde'formed, *ppl. a.* (UN-[1] 8.)

1672–3 GREW *Anat. Roots* I. v. §8 To be chosen, while the Plant is yet growing; at which time, it may be often found dry, yet undeformed. *c* **1714** POPE *Let.* Wks. 1751 VII. 127 The sight of so many gallant fellows, with all the pomp and glare of war, yet undeform'd by battles,..may possibly invite your curiosity. **1812** BRACKENRIDGE *Views Louisiana* (1814) 34 Those clean smooth meadows,..covered with a short sweet grass.., undeformed by a single weed! **1886** E. WARD *Dress Problem* v. 84 Strong, healthy lungs and an undeformed pelvis.

†**unde'fouled,** *ppl. a. Obs.* (UN-[1] 8.)

Common from *c* 1380 to 1450.

13.. *Propr. Sanct.* (Vernon MS.) 95 in Herrig's *Archiv* LXXXI. 86 He him kneuh for Innocent And vndefoulet. *c* **1374** CHAUCER *Boeth.* II. pr. iv. (1868) 40 Yif þat þilke þing ..be kept to þe..vnwemmed and vndefouled. *c* **1410** HOCCLEVE *Mother of God* 1 Modir of god and virgyne vndeffouled! *a* **1450** *Knt. de la Tour* (1868) 157 She that hathe atte al tymes putte her payne in trauaile to kepe her body vndefouled and in clennesse. **1483** CAXTON *Gold. Leg.* 392/1 That I may haue the prepucye vndefouled.

†**unde'foulingness.** (UN-[1] 12.)

c **1400** *Wycliffite Bible* 1 Pet. iii. 4 The hid man of herte, in vncoruptibilite [*MS. New Coll. 67* vndefoulingnesse] of quyete..and mylde spirit.

unde'frayed, *ppl. a.* (UN-[1] 8.)

1611 COTGR., *Insolu*, vnpayed, vndischarged, vndefrayed. **1727** BAILEY (vol. II). **1817** *Monthly Rev.* LXXXIV. 520 The expences of alterations at Osmanstadt were still undefrayed. **1842** MADDEN *United Irishmen* I. x. 325 No expenses of these gentlemen were left undefrayed.

unde'generacy. (UN-[1] 12.)

1793 HOLCROFT tr. *Lavater's Physiog.* xxxv. 180 Much has been said of the openness, undegeneracy, simplicity and ingenuousness of a childish and youthful countenance.

unde'generate, *a.* (UN-[1] 7.)

1743 BLAIR *Grave* 470 Fantastic schemes, which the long livers In the world's hale and undegenerate days Could scarce have leisure for. **1822** CAMPBELL *'Men of England'* i, Men whose undegenerate spirit Has been proved on land and flood. **1854** H. MILLER *Sch. & Schm.* xiii. (1860) 135/1 While the as yet undegenerate plant had merely borne atop a few florets. **1870** RUSKIN *Lect. Art* i. 27 We are still undegenerate in race. **1897** *Allbutt's Syst. Med.* VII. 229 The quick normal response of the undegenerate muscle-fibres to the negative closure.

unde'generated, *ppl. a.* (UN-[1] 8.)

1794 MRS. PIOZZI *Synon.* I. 354, I believe large oxen..do no more work..than beasts of the common undegenerated size. **1897** *Trans. Amer. Pediatric Soc.* IX. 168 A constant and potent factor in..maintaining the type undegenerated.

unde'generating, *ppl. a.* (UN-[1] 10.)

1606 in Nichols *Progr. Jas. I* (1828) II. 51 We of hereditary and fee-simple blood, and undegenerating valour. **1693** EVELYN tr. *De la Quint. Compl. Gardener, Melons* I The most Undegenerating sort of Melons are..of a middling Size. **1753** WEST *Odes Pindar, Nemean Odes* xi, Him, whose undegenerating Breast Swells with a Tide of Spartan Blood.

†**unde'grade,** obs. Sc. var. of next.

c **1560** A. Scott *Poems* (S.T.S.) xiv. 13 In lykwayis dois hir bewty vndegraid Transcend all vþiris, wyfe, wedow, or maid.

unde'graded, *ppl. a.* (UN-[1] 8.)

[**1775** Ash.] **1821** V. Knox *Rem. Grammar Schools* 24 The intention of a founder in preserving grammar studies undegraded ought to be held sacred. **1825** Scott *Talism.* xv, It is King Richard's pleasure that you die undegraded. **1853** Ruskin *Stones Ven.* II. vi. 179 It can shrink into a turret,.. or spring into a spire, with undegraded grace.

un'deified, *ppl. a.* [f. next.] Reduced from the position of a deity.

1643–5 Milton *Divorce* I. vi, That originall and firie vertue giv'n him by Fate, all on a sudden goes out and leaves him undeifi'd and despoil'd of all his force. **1858** Froude *Hist. Eng.* III. xv. 287 The undeified images passed by a swift transition to the flames.

un'deify, *v.* [UN-[2] 6 c.] *trans.* To deprive of the status, character, or qualities of a deity.

1637 R. Ashley tr. *Malvezzi's David Persecuted* 119 All sinners in regard of themselves doe undeifie him. **1664** H. More *Myst. Iniq.* vi. 121 It is plainly to un-deify him, if I may so speak, and to declare him to be no God at all. **1711** Addison *Spect.* No. 73 ¶11 An Idol may be Undeified by many accidental Causes. **1789** J. White *Earl Strongbow* I. 93 Modern Nobles who employ their pens in writing down religion, and undeifying their Redeemer. **1845** R. Wardlaw in *Ess. Chr. Union* vi. 307 The acknowledgement of Him undeified all else besides. **1871** Macduff *Patmos* 161 Let us not dethrone and undeify the great Maker and Sustainer. *refl.* **1675** J. Smith *Chr. Relig. App.* I. 15 They must undeifie themselves, and become no Gods of other Cities, before they are allowed to be Gods in that. **1700** Asgill *Argument* 36 God cannot lie without undeifying himself. **1709** *Brit. Apollo* II. No. 44. 2/1 To act contrary to his own .. Eternal Essence, and Consequently to Un-Deify himself. *absol.* **1718** Wodrow *Corr.* (1843) II. 353 This would infer a superior excellency in the First, and undeify.

Hence **un'deifying** *vbl. sb.* and *ppl. a.*

1637 R. Ashley tr. *Malvezzi's David Persecuted* 4 It is an undeifying of God. *a* **1680** Charnock *Attrib. God* (1834) I. 201 When we come before him with undeifying thoughts of him. **1864** Pusey *Lect. Daniel* 271 *note*, The whole boasted theory then..was at stake, and, with it, the whole undeifying of prophecy.

unde'istical, *a.* (UN-[1] 7.)

1755 Young *Centaur* 218, I, therefore, drop this dispute, not only as Unchristian, but Undeistical too.

unde'jected, *ppl. a.* (UN-[1] 8.)

1613 Wither *Abuses Stript* Ep. Ded. A v, In despight of outward Destinies haue a care to keepe an vndeiected heart still free for Vertue. **1645** Quarles *Sol. Recant.* vii. 19 Wisdome affords more strength, more fortifies The undejected courage of the wise. **1729** Congreve *Epist. to Ld. Cobham* 6 Not so robust in Body, as in Mind, And always undejected, tho' declin'd. **1782** V. Knox *Ess.* iv. I. 19 We shall indeed often fall; but let us rise again undejected. **1862** Lytton *Str. Story* ii, My children would have entered on manhood..undejected by the charity of strangers.

unde'lated, *ppl. a.* (UN-[1] 8.)

1597 in *Maitland Cl. Misc.* (1840) I. 129 That na eldar.. suffir ane singill woman..to dwell hir allane in ane hous undelaited to the sessioune of the kirk.

unde'layable, *a.* (UN-[1] 7 b.)

1628 Feltham *Resolves* II. xxii. 72 With what vndelayable heate, does the lime-twig'd Louer court a deseruing Beautie? **1887** Lowell *Democr.*, etc. 6 The undelayable year has rolled round.

unde'layed, *ppl. a.*[1] [UN-[1] 8 + DELAY *v.*[1]] Not delayed or deferred; unretarded; immediate.

1439 in *Fenland N. & Q.* July (1905) 221 Hasty and undelaied provision of gret and notable puissance. **1472** *Paston Lett.* III. 64 The Kynge hathe specially doon for me in thy case,..that iff thys fayle..I shalle have on-delayed justyce. **1540** *Act 32 Hen. VIII*, c. 48 More redy & vndelaied paimentes herafter shalbe had and made to all officers. **1591** in Picton *L'pool Munic. Rec.* (1883) I. 82 The first buier of the same shall..geve undelaied notice..hereof to Mr. Maior. **1611** Speed *Hist. Gt. Brit.* IX. xxiv. §190 The demand of the Queene was, to haue..a present and vndelayed truce. **1667** in *10th Rep. Hist. MSS. Comm.* App. V. 40 It may please your Grace to require the said Christopher..to make your petitioner undelayed satisfaction. *a* **1711** Ken *Serm.* Wks. (1838) 204, I earnestly exhort you to a serious and undelayed repentance. **1818** Scott *Rob Roy* x, He wished to get back to his own country, undelayed and unembarrassed by any..judicial inquiries.

b. quasi-*adv.* Without delay.

1470 Harding *Chron.* CXIX. iv, Vpon the holy euangelis sworne vndelayed, The kyng graunted hym his grace. **1653** Milton *Ps.* vii. 59 His ill trade Of violence will undelay'd Fall on his crown with ruine steep.

Hence **unde'layedly** *adv.*

1534 Hen. VIII in Froude *Hist. Eng.* (1858) II. 231 We.. command you that you do make, undelayedly, and with all speed and diligence,..advertisement to us. **1603** Florio *Montaigne* II. v. 213 All the assemblie, and even his accuser himselfe did vndelayedly follow him towards the temple.

†**unde'layed,** *ppl. a.*[2] *Obs.* [UN-[1] 8 + DELAY *v.*[2]] Undiluted; not weakened by dilution.

1600 Surflet *Countrie Farme* VI. xxii. 780 The learned.. haue alwaies reiected and disallowed pure and vndelaied wine. **1601** Holland *Pliny* II. 174 The same being vsed with pure vndelaied wine, is singular for the prick of scorpions.

unde'laying, *ppl. a.* (UN-[1] 10.)

1791 Cowper *Iliad* XXIII. 163 Undelaying each Complied, and in bright arms stood soon array'd. **1820** Shelley *Prometh. Unb.* III. iii. 157 Trampling the..glassy lakes With feet unwet, unwearied, undelaying. **1882** Myers *Renewal of Youth* 76 Yon unhurrying undelaying star.

unde'lectable, *a.* (UN-[1] 7 b and 5 b.)

1610 Healey *St. Aug. Citie of God* IX. xv. 352 The diuels immortality is miserable: But Christs mortality hath nothing vndelectable. **1760** Sterne *Tr. Shandy* IV. xxvii, The genial warmth..was not undelectable for the first twenty or five-and-twenty seconds.

un'delegated, *ppl. a.* (UN-[1] 8.)

1790 Burke *Fr. Rev.* Wks. V. 398 It is one instance, among many indeed, of your assumption of undelegated power. **1815** *Monthly Rev.* LXXVII. 468 [He] would never have usurped an undelegated authority.

unde'liberate, *a.* (UN-[1] 7 and 5 b.)

15.. [see UNDELIVERED *ppl. a.*[2]]. **1593** Nashe *Christ's T.* 91 b, Let not worldlings iudge thee inconstant, or vndeliberate in thy choyse. **1753** Richardson *Grandison* (1781) V. xxxviii. 237 It was not a request made on undeliberate motives. **1874** Lowell *Agassiz* III. i, With no pedant blindness to the worth Of undeliberate mirth. **1876** Ruskin *Fors Clav.* lxviii. 271 The difference between deliberate and undeliberate heartlessness..is for God to judge.

Hence **unde'liberateness.**

1817 Coleridge *Biog. Lit.* (1907) II. 41 With due allowances for the undeliberateness, and less connected train, of thinking natural and proper to conversation.

unde'liberated, *ppl. a.* (UN-[1] 8 and 5 b.)

a **1674** Clarendon *Hist. Reb.* VIII. §87 The strange manner of the Prince's coming, and undeliberated throwing himself and all the King's hopes into that suddain and unnecessary Engagement. **1874** Pusey *Lent. Serm.* 352 Our undeliberated close-cleaving weaknesses.

unde'liberating, *ppl. a.* (UN-[1] 10.)

a **1763** Shenstone *Economy* II. 78 It much avails to seize the present hour, And, undeliberating, call around Thy hungry creditors. **1768** Sterne *Sent. Journ.* (1782) II. 10 She did it of herself with..undeliberating simplicity.

†**un'delible,** *a.* [UN-[1] 7.] = INDELIBLE *a.*

1534 More *Treat. Passion* Wks. 1316/2 The caracter and spirituall token, by baptisme imprinted in the soule, is vndelible and neuer canne be putte out. **1587** [see UNDEFACEABLE *a.*]. **1679** Jenison *Popish Plot* 13 Which I knew would undergo an undelible blot. **1747** Carte *Hist. Eng.* I. 213 That army composed of their followers, was branded with an undelible mark of reproach.

unde'licious, *a.* [UN-[1] 7.] †**a.** Not dainty or delicate. *Obs.* **b.** Not pleasant or agreeable.

a **1618** Sylvester tr. *Mathieu's Mem. Mortalitie* II. xcvii, Little sufficeth Life in th' un-delicious. **1829** I. Taylor *Enthus.* ix. 246 The spiritual Monk..there passed his hours, not uncheered, not undelicious, in prayer and meditation.

unde'light. [UN-[1] 12.] Lack of delight.

1821 Shelley *Ginevra* 20 The weary glare..Vexing the sense with gorgeous undelight. **1835** Trench *Poems* 176 If at seasons this world's undelight oppressed him.

unde'lighted, *ppl. a.* (UN-[1] 8.)

1667 Milton *P. L.* IV. 286 From this Assyrian Garden, where the Fiend Saw undelighted all delight. **1713** *Guardian* No. 68 ¶2 If she has no Relish for rural Views, but is undelighted with Streams, Fields and Groves. *a* **1763** Shenstone *Ess.* Wks. 1765 II. 228, I love painting and statuary so well, as to be not undelighted with moderate performances. **1805** Wordsw. *Prelude* III. 217 Could I behold.., with undelighted heart, So many happy youths? **1852** M. Arnold *Empedocles* II. 296 Uncaring and undelighted.

unde'lightful, *a.* (UN-[1] 7.)

Frequently used with preceding negative.

1585 Bullokar *Æsopz Fablz* 155 Go-away henc' with a mischef, with that thy vn-deliht-ful howsband. **1599** Daniel *Let. Octavia* xli, Wretched Mankind, wherfore hath nature made The lawfull vndelightfull? **1616** Breton *Good & Bad* Wks. (Grosart) II. 5/2 Hee is..an vndelightfull friend, and a tormentor of himselfe. **1662** J. Davies tr. *Olearius' Voy. Ambass.* 274 The Dancing of the Women.. was not undelightfull. **1682** Sir T. Browne *Chr. Mor.* III. §22 In such an Age Delights will be undelightful and Pleasures grow stale unto him. **1742** Richardson *Pamela* IV. 221, I am now..quitting this undelightful Town, as it has been, and is, to me. **1775** S. J. Pratt *Liberal Opin.* xcviii. (1783) III. 215, I never felt such feverish, yet not undelightful attacks before. *c* **1819** Shelley *Ess. & Lett.* (1887) 305 Tacitus, or Livius,..are.. undelightful and uninstructive in translation. **1876** Mrs. Oliphant *Curate in Charge* viii, The odour of this very undelightful feature in the scene.

Hence **unde'lightfully** *adv.*; **-fulness.**

1653 *Cloria & Narcissus* I. (1665) 79 They soon retired, with the undelightfulness of the prospect, into their own Lodgings. **1749** J. Cleland *Mem. Woman Pleasure* I. 86 The extreme whiteness of her skin was not undelightfully contrasted by the smooth glossy brown of her lover's. **1783** Johnson *Let. to Mrs. Thrale* 13 Aug., Ovid says that the sun is undelightfully uniform. **1893** Swinburne *Stud. Prose & Poetry* (1894) 32 In this..his real..kinship to his beloved Dr. Johnson..was not undelightfully manifest.

unde'lighting, *ppl. a.* [UN-[1] 10.]

1. Taking no delight or pleasure (*in* something).

1570 Foxe *A. & M.* (ed. 2) 37/1 The vndelityng wil of man to God and hys word. **1798** *Monthly Mag.* VI. 556 Undelighting in so artificial a deception, he would have fallen off in the courage to persevere.

2. Affording no delight or pleasure.

1768–74 Tucker *Lt. Nat.* (1834) II. 546 What keeps them in slavery under an undelighting habit, but because it would cost them pains to break it? **1984** *Times Lit. Suppl.* 27 Apr. 449/4 Trakl himself, whose cold, undelighting, unhuman speech, with its small, select and poisoned vocabulary, is like no other in German.

unde'lightsome, *a.* (UN-[1] 7.)

c **1586** C'tess Pembroke *Ps.* CXXXIX. iv, O whither might I take my way?.. To dead mens undelightsome stay? There is thy walk.

unde'lineable, *a.* (UN-[1] 7 b.)

1767 Mrs. S. Pennington *Lett.* I. 122 The utter impossibility of expressing what they feel to be equally true and undelineable.

unde'liverable, *a.* (UN-[1] 7 b.)

In recent use esp. of postal matter, as in quot. 1862.

1843 Carlyle *Past & Pr.* II. xvii, Fix thyself in Dandyhood, undeliverable: it is thy doom. **1862** Trollope *N. Amer.* II. 388 The task of returning to their writers undelivered and undeliverable letters.

†**unde'liverance.** [UN-[1] 12.] Non-delivery.

a **1578** Lindesay (Pitscottie) *Chron. Scot.* (S.T.S.) II. 313 The erle of argyle vas put to the horne for ondelyuerance of certaine jowallis.

unde'livered, *ppl. a.*[1] [UN-[1] 8 + DELIVER *v.*[1]]

1. Not handed over or transferred to another's possession; not delivered or distributed.

1472–3 *Rolls of Parlt.* VI. 5/2 [The money] there to be kept, undelyvered by eny mean unto You, Soverayn Lord. **1561–2** *Reg. Privy Council Scot.* I. 203 To keip the samyn in his handis and keping undeliverit to George Dowglas. *a* **1600** Hooker *Eccl. Pol.* VII. xxiv. §17 To withdraw any mite of that..bequeathed, though as yet undelivered into the sacred treasure of God. **1640–1** *Kirkcudbr. War-Comm. Min. Bk.* (1855) 79 We resolve to keip the commissione undelyverit till we heir from you. **1767** in *Nairne Peerage Evidence* (1874) 169 These presents shall be habit and repute a valid & delivered evident albeit found..undelivered the time of my death. **1775** Sheridan *Duenna* I. iii, I must slip out to seal it up, as undelivered. **1842** Tytler *Hist. Scot.* (1864) IV. 29 If he found the fortress..undelivered, he was to remonstrate loudly against its being surrendered. **1887** *Daily News* 6 Oct. 2/8 Discovery of undelivered letters.

2. Not set free or released. Also const. *from.*

a **1513** Fabyan *Chron.* VII. 382 The prynce..remayned longe after vndelyuered wt many other prysoners. **1653** Milton *Hirelings* Wks. 1851 V. 339 To deliver us the only People of all Protestants left still undeliver'd from the Oppressions of a simonious decimating Clergy. **1721** Strype *Eccl. Mem.* III. xliii. 355 He..did as much as possible he might to see them undelivered. **1837** Wordsw. *White Doe* Introd., The soul..from mortal bonds Yet undelivered.

†**3.** Not dispatched or disposed of. *Obs.*[−1]

1535 Stewart *Cron. Scotl.* (Rolls) II. 240 The Saxone herald thair remaning maid, ȝit wndeliuerit on his answer baid.

4. Of a child: Not brought forth or born.

1595 Daniel *Civ. Wars* II. xcvii, This mighty burthen wherewithall they goe Dies vndeliuered, perishes vnborne.

5. Of a woman: Not disburdened of offspring.

1799 *Med. Jrnl.* II. 434 It is not improbable that..the poor woman..survived as long as she would have done, if she had been permitted to perish undelivered. **1871** A. Meadows *Man. Midwifery* (ed. 2) 242 Rather than see the mother die undelivered, I used the perforator and extracted.

6. Not made or attempted.

1895 *Review of Rev.* Aug. 148 An attack, which now, alas, must remain for ever undelivered.

†**unde'livered,** *ppl. a.*[2] *Obs.*[−1] [UN-[1] 8 + DELIVER *v.*[2]] Unconsidered, unwise.

c **1425** Wyntoun *Cron.* v. xi. 3172 Off þare counsall and assent, And vndeliuerit [**15..** *Lansdowne MS.* vndeliberait] avisment, Thare estait þai renunsit haill.

unde'livery. [UN-[1] 12.] Non-delivery.

1679 in W. M. Morison *Dict. Decis.* (1807) 16178 The defences, for Lothian, which resolved into two, the incompleteness, and undelivery [etc.].

unde'ludable, *a.* (UN-[1] 7 b.)

1839 J. Sterling *Ess.*, etc. (1848) I. 365 Those who hold themselves undeludable.

unde'lude, *v.* [UN-[2] 3.] *trans.* To free from delusion or deception; to undeceive.

1654 Earl Orrery *Parthen.* (1676) 77 All things had contributed to undelude you. *a* **1711** Ken *Hymnotheo* Poet. Wks. 1721 III. 325 She..Would not consult her Adam first, lest she Should by his Counsel undeluded be.

unde'luded, *ppl. a.* (UN-[1] 8.)

1746 Young *Nt. Th.* IX. 1022 There..she [the soul] can rove at large;..And, undeluded, grasp at something great. **1756** *Demi-Rep* 22 Ye undeluded shun the flow'ry shore, Nor split, where thousands have been wreck'd before! **1816** Byron *A Sketch* 20 That high Soul..panted for the truth it could not hear, With longing breast and undeluded ear.

un'deluged, *ppl. a.* (UN-[1] 8.)

1791 Cowper *Odyssey* XXIV. 621 Peace, O ye men of Ithaca! while yet The field remains undeluged with your blood. **1819** Campbell *Rainbow* 21 When o'er the green, undeluged earth, Heaven's covenant thou didst shine.

unde'lusive, *a.* (UN-[1] 7.)

1817 Bentham *Parl. Reform* Introd. 104 Sound, dispassionate, and undelusive information. **1829** Wordsw. *Humanity* 14 Inviting..ears and eyes To watch for undelusive auguries.

un'delve, *v.* [UN-[2] 9.] *trans.* To dig up.

1340 *Ayenb.* 61 Þet is þe felliste best þet me clepeþ hyane, þet ondelfþ þe bodies of dyade men and hise eteþ.

un'delved, *ppl. a.* (UN-[1] 8.)

1602 *Kyd's Sp. Trag.* III. xii. A 84 All the undelued mynes cannot buy An ounce of iustice. **1623** Lisle *Ælfric on O. &*

N. Test. Ded. xviii, This three-cornered Ile,..Unfens'd, undelv'd, ungardined, unset. **1794** SOUTHEY *Botany Bay Ecl.* i, Welcome, ye wild plains Unbroken by the plough, undelved by hand Of patient rustic.

unde'magnetizable, *a.* (UN-[1] 7 b.)
1876 *S. Kensington Mus. Catal.* No. 1703, Pair of Undemagnetisable Coils, designed in 1866. **1882** *Crystal Palace Internat. Electric Exhib. Catal.* 17 Brittan's Undemagnetizable Needle.

unde'manded, *ppl. a.* (UN-[1] 8.)
1513 DOUGLAS *Æneid* VI. viii. 46 Vndemandit, with freyndly wordis and soundis Enee hym grat, sayand [etc.]. *a* **1652** BROME *Mad Couple* III. i, Will you never..receive that onely fit for you to understand, which I deliver to you undemanded? **1748** THOMSON *Cast. Indol.* I. xxxiv, Some hand unseen these silently display'd, Even undemanded by a sign or sound. **1796** MME. D'ARBLAY *Camilla* V. 409 To present herself..undemanded and unforgiven at Etherington, she thought impossible. **1860** FORSTER *Gr. Remonstr.* 28 With new conditions of restraint and constitutional safeguards before undemanded, assistance is rendered again.

unde'manding, *ppl. a.* [UN-[1] 10.] Not rigorous or exacting; tolerant; easy. So **unde'mandingness**.
1939 'A. BRIDGE' *Four-Part Setting* xi. 143 'She..is the most unexacting person I ever met... She *asks* less of you than anyone I know.'..Rose Pelham..had not hit on that peculiar undemandingness. **1940** W. FAULKNER *Hamlet* III. ii. 180 [She] was loyal, discreet, undemanding, and thrifty with his money. **1958** *Times* 18 Dec. 14/1 An undemanding public can be blamed in these cases for spoiling art. **1971** HINDELL & SIMMS *Abortion Law Reformed* v. 122 His publishing activities were fairly undemanding.

†**unde'merited**, *ppl. a. Obs.* [UN-[1] 8.] Unmerited; undeserved.
1629 PRYNNE *God no Impostor* 13 Pulling downe many vndemerited blessings, vpon Reprobates and Castawayes. **1644** —— *Check to Britannicus* 4 His undemerited free Pardon.

†**un'demnified**, *ppl. a. Obs. rare.* [UN-[1] 8: cf. INDEMNIFY *v.*[2]] Uninjured, unhurt.
1576 NEWTON *Lemnie's Complex.* 15 b, Hee therefore that woulde preserue his spirites vndemnifyed..must endeuour ..to keepe his body in right good plight. **1608** WILLET *Hexapla Exod.* 487 How much should he remaine vndemnified,..which goeth to the bosome of his mother the Church?

undemo'cratic, *a.* (UN-[1] 7.)
1839 T. MITCHELL *Frogs of Aristoph.* Introd. p. cv, Æschylus, young, ardent, and at that time not undemocratic in his politics. **1856** OLMSTED *Slave States* 183 Through a similar undemocratic, uneconomical and unjust..exercise of power. **1895** *Thinker* VIII. 252 All assumptions of sacerdotal superiority and sanctity are undemocratic.
Hence **undemo'cratically** *adv.*
1865 E. BURRITT *Walk to Land's End* 363 How we glory in the humble origin, as it is most undemocratically called, of our great men!

unde'molishable, *a.* (UN-[1] 7 b.)
1837 CARLYLE *Fr. Rev.* II. v. xii, Will jingle and fanfaronade demolish the Veto; or will the Veto..remain undemolishable by these?

unde'molished, *ppl. a.* (UN-[1] 8.)
1571-2 *Reg. Privy Council Scot.* Ser. I. II. 121 For sauftie of the houssis..being within the same unbrint and [un]dimolissit. **1610** J. HEALEY *St. Aug. Citie of God* 82 This Nasica would haue Carthage stand stil vndemolished. **1634** SIR T. HERBERT *Trav.* 117 A stately Palace, which remayned vndemolisht for many ages. **1708** J. PHILIPS *Cyder* I. 182 Then also, tho' to foreign Yoke submiss, She undemolish'd stood, and even 'till now Perhaps had stood. **1837** CARLYLE *Fr. Rev.* II. III. v, Vincennes stands undemolished, reparable.

undemonstrable, *a.* (UN-[1] 7 b and 5 b.)
1594 HOOKER *Eccl. Pol.* III. ix. §2 Out of the precepts of the lawe of nature as out of certaine common & vndemonstrable principles. **1865** *Reader* 14 Oct. 420/2 The theological or undemonstrable part of the question.

undemonstrated, *ppl. a.* (UN-[1] 8.)
1648 HEXHAM II, *Onbetoont*, Vnshowne, or Vndemonstrated. **1657** HOBBES *Absurd Geom.* Wks. 1845 VII. 378 Your first forty-one propositions are undemonstrated. **1794** *Monthly Rev.* XIV. 285 We seek in vain for the facts that should disprove..this undemonstrated but very possible circumstance. **1833** HAMPDEN *Bampt. Lect.* 433 He professes also not to rest the proof of his point on mere undemonstrated faith, but on exact argument. **1870** J. H. NEWMAN *Gram. Assent* II. viii. 334 We are bound to give heed to the undemonstrated sayings and opinions of the experienced and aged.

unde'monstrative, *a.* [UN-[1] 7.]
1. Not given to, or characterized by, outward expression (of the feelings, etc.).
1846 *Edin. Rev.* Jan. 48 That type of an undemonstrative Englishwoman, Cordelia. **1847** C. BRONTE *Jane Eyre* xxix, 'You *shall*,' repeated Mary, in the tone of undemonstrative sincerity which seemed natural to her. **1880** MRS. ROLLINS *New Eng. Bygones* (1883) 87 Repulsive spectacles..on the surface of its pure, calm, undemonstrative life.
2. *Gram.* (Cf. DEMONSTRATIVE *a.* 3.)
1871 EARLE *Philol. Eng. Tongue* 457 Two or three very undemonstrative conjunctions, such as *if, but, for, that,* &c.
Hence **unde'monstratively** *adv.*; **-iveness**.
1858 MISS MULOCK *Th. ab. Wom.* 167 Its total absence of sentimentality, its undemonstrativeness, depth, and power. **1864** W. HANNA *Earlier Years our Lord's Life* vi. 133 Living so naturally, unostentatiously, undemonstratively.

unde'mure, *a.* (UN-[1] 7.)
1538 BALE *Thre Lawes* II. A viij b, The beastes oft vndemure, Whych were left to mannys cure, Wyll hym sumtyme deuoure.

un'den, *v.* (UN-[2] 5.)
1598 FLORIO, *Scopare*,..to rouze, to vndenne, to vnkenell. **1613** HEYWOOD *Braz. Age* II. ii, Some plant the toiles, others brauely mount To unden this sauadge.

unde'niable, *a.* [UN-[1] 7 b and 5 b.]
1. That cannot be denied or refuted; incontrovertible, indisputable.
1547 COVERDALE *Old Faith* E viij b, Now is it certayne and vndenyable, that he which speaketh, & he to whom ought is spoken, are not one, but two personnes. **1594** HOOKER *Eccl. Pol.* II. vii. §9 If there be either vndeniable appearance that so it doth [avouch], or reason such as cannot deceiue. **1631** GOUGE *God's Arrows* I. Ded. p. vii, This ancient, undeniable aphorisme. **1651** BAXTER *Inf. Bapt.* 229, I will name some undeniable Arguments. **1727** DE FOE *Hist. Appar.* ii. (1840) 19 These apparitions of angels..are undeniable on other occasions. **1794** R. J. SULIVAN *View Nat.* I. 455 The fact is undeniable. **1809-10** COLERIDGE *Friend* (1865) 118 The system commences with an undeniable truth, and an important deduction therefrom equally undeniable. **1880** SWINBURNE *Stud. Shaks.* 301 What he did say was undeniable by any but those who trusted only to their ear.
b. Of witnesses: Irrefragable.
1619 MRQ. BUCKHM. in *Fortescue Papers* (Camden) 78 You were accused of nothing that was not proved by oath of divers witnesses alltogither undeniable. **1663** BP. PATRICK *Parab. Pilgr.* xxviii, Together with the testimony of many undeniable Witnesses. **1855** MILMAN *Lat. Chr.* IX. v. IV. 111 *note*, The historians, all ecclesiastics, are undeniable witnesses. **1883** *Contemp. Rev.* June 774 Karema is there as an undeniable witness of the success of these efforts.
2. Incapable of being refused; admitting or accepting no denial.
1549 OLDE *Erasm. Par. Peter* Dedication, I toke it in hande for none other ende, but only to doe at my hartie frendes vndenyable request. **1649** JER. TAYLOR *Gt. Exemp.* II. xii. 42 The multitude found him out, imprisoning him in their circuits and undeniable attendances. *Ibid.* III. xiv. 42 The seeming denial made her importunity more bold and undenyable. **1839** LADY LYTTON *Cheveley* (ed. 2) III. vi. 150 Thoughts, those..undeniable visitors, *will* intrude.
3. Not open to objection; unexceptional, excellent.
1793 SMEATON *Edystone L.* Contents p. ix, Moorstone being undeniable. **1799** H. MITCHELL *Scotticisms* 87 His public character is undeniable. **1808** *Times* 2 Mar. 4/1 Nursery Maid..; can have an undeniable character from the Lady she last served. **1861** WHYTE-MELVILLE *Market Harb.* viii, Her foot and ankle were undeniable, and her hands white and well-shaped. **1884** *Graphic* 9 Aug. 134/1 Italian fruits..are open to much criticism, but the grapes and green figs are undeniable.
absol. **1861** WHYTE MELVILLE *Market Harb.* xx, A dry biscuit and a magnum of the undeniable make their appearance.
Hence **unde'niableness**.
1654 WHITLOCK *Zootomia* 254 What Author so ever denyeth the undeniablenesse of any of our received Tenets. **1677** GILPIN *Demonol.* (1867) 463 The plainness and undeniableness of this inference. **1889** *19th Cent.* Sept. 404 The undeniableness of the facts he adduces.

unde'niably, *adv.* [f. prec.]
1. In an undeniable manner; so that denial (of the fact) is impossible; incontrovertibly.
1646 SIR T. BROWNE *Pseud. Ep.* VI. viii. 314 It is undeniably rejected by the Modernes, and must be warily received by any. **1679** BEDLOE *Popish Plot* Ep. A 2 b, By this Letter..the Witnesses evidence..is undeniably confirmed. **1758** MRS. DELANY *Life & Corr.* (1861) III. 483 My present situation is undeniably an anxious one. **1825** MCCULLOCH *Pol. Econ.* II. ii. 135 It is undeniably certain we shall have to export ten or twenty millions worth..to pay them. **1848** DICKENS *Dombey* i, The son was an undeniably fine infant. **1881** JOWETT *Thucyd.* I. 47 The event proved undeniably that the fate of Hellas depended on her navy.
2. Without heeding any denial, refusal, or protest.
1705 tr. *Bosman's Guinea* 74 Some Negroes are so unreasonable that they will undeniably take back all their pure Gold.

unde'nied, *ppl. a.* Also 7 -denayed. (UN-[1] 8.)
1621 QUARLES *Div. Poems, Esther* ii, Perhaps (Asuerus) Vashti might haue stayed Vnsent for, and thy selfe been vndenayed. **1660** *Trial Regic.* 11, I think it is an undenied consequence, He must needs be Superiour over them. **1760** LAW *Spir. Prayer* I. 63 If self is undenied, if thou livest to thine own will,..thou art dead whilst thou livest. **1887** *Pall Mall G.* 1 July 1/1 This is undenied and undeniable.
Hence **unde'niedly** *adv.*
1837 G. S. FABER *Prim. Doctr. Justif.* 226 For there, undeniedly and undeniably in the case of the regenerated and converted, the Apostle says: The Flesh [etc.].

un'denizened, *ppl. a.* (UN-[1] 8.)
1635 HEYWOOD *Hierarchie* IV. 208 Words at which th' Ignorant laugh, but the Learn'd smile, Because Adulterate and Vndenizen'd. **1887** G. M. HOPKINS *Poems* (1967) 103 Undenizened, beyond bound Of earth's glory, earth's ease, all.

un'denizing, *vbl. sb.* (UN-[2] 3, 8.)
1716 M. DAVIES *Athen. Brit.* II. To Rdr. p. v, To give the Athenian Law..a new Vigour and Sanction, under the Forfeiture and Penalty of Undenizing and Expulsion.

unde,nomi'national, *a.* [UN-[1] 7.] Not belonging to any particular religious denomination.
Freq. in 19th cent. use in connexion with religious education in elementary schools.
1871 *Athenæum* 15 Apr. 465 It has ruled that the new Board schools are to be strictly undenominational. **1885** *Manch. Exam.* 20 Mar. 8/5 The..advantage of an undenominational system of education.
Hence **undenomi'nationalism**, **-alist**, **-alize** *v.*, **-ally** *adv.*
1883 *Christian* 1 Nov. 12/2 His strong protest against *undenominationalism..does not appear to us well-timed. **1879** T. LEGGE in A. Peel *Lett. to Victorian Editor* (1929) 323 Somerville Hall will belong to the *undenominationalists. **1884** *Pall Mall G.* 14 Aug. 4/2 The most animated debate of the whole Conference was that between Churchmen and undenominationalists. **1895** *Forum* (N.Y.) June 435 Our own scattered colleges, now '*undenominationalized', if not secularized, can be gathered into groups and unified. **1906** *Westm. Gaz.* 8 Feb. 2 How this is to be done *undenominationally I do not know.

unde'noted, *ppl. a.* (UN-[1] 8.)
1859 CORNWALLIS *New World* I. 52 Many a lifeless tenant of an undenoted grave. **1882** STEVENSON *Mem. & Portraits* iii. (1887) 41 Among the thousand undenoted countenances of the city street.

unde'nounced, *ppl. a.* (UN-[1] 8.)
[**1775** ASH.] **1837** CARLYLE *Fr. Rev.* III. II. vi, Let him withdraw again; not undenounced. **1896** LD. ROSEBERY in *Daily News* 10 Oct. 2/5 There is a much more drastic instrument in existence undenounced, unrepealed.

unde'nuded, *ppl. a.* (UN-[1] 8.)
1872 W. S. SYMONDS *Rec. Rocks* xi. 406 An outlier of undenuded rocks.

†**unde'partable**, *a. Obs.* [UN-[1] 7 b and 5 b.] Inseparable; indivisible.
c **1374** CHAUCER *Boeth.* IV. pr. iii. (1868) 120 No wise man ne may doute of þe vndepartable peyne of shrewes. **1382** WYCLIF *Luke* 1st Prol., Bi the entringe of the generacioun of vndepartable God. *c* **1450** tr. *De Imitatione* III. xxvii. 97 Ioyne me to þe wiþ an undepartable bonde of loue. **1483** *Cath. Angl.* 96 Vn Departiabylle, *indiuisibilis, indiuiduus.*
Hence **unde'partableness**; **unde'partably** *adv.*
c **1449** PECOCK *Repr.* I. iii. 15 Tweyne pointis of matrimonie, which ben vndepartabilnes and fleischli vce of bodies into childe bigeting. *c* **1456** —— *Bk. of Faith* (1909) 245 Oon man to have bi the lawe oon wyf undepartabili. *a* **1470** H. PARKER *Dives & Pauper* (W. de W. 1496) VI. viii. 244/2 There wolde no man knytte hym undepartably to ony woman.

unde'parted, *ppl. a.* [UN-[1] 8 and 5 b.] †Not parted or separated; undivided.
1430-40 LYDG. *Bochas* I. viii. (1544) 13 b, And, undeparted, [I] yeue to you mine herte. **1453** *Rolls of Parlt.* V. 231/2 Kept hole, undepartid, undevided and unsevered. *a* **1470** HARDING *Chron.* CCVI. iv, Twenty strokes with euery wepen smyten, Vndeparted without any mote. **1610** HEALEY *St. Aug. Citie of God* 475 Thus is hee..not yet in death, because the soule is vndeparted.

unde'parting, *vbl. sb.* [UN-[1] 13.] †Absence of separation.
c **1400** tr. *Secreta Secret., Gov. Lordsh.* 90 In þe whilk we sall determyn of singuleryte, and vndepartyng of some planetis vegetablez.

unde'parting, *ppl. a.* (UN-[1] 10.)
1581 *Reg. Privy Council Scot.* III. 436 He hes..kepit the said burgh, undeparting as yit thairfra. **1587** *Ibid.* IV. 195 The Senatouris to remane undepairting oute of the burgh. **1842** WORDSW. *Poems of Fancy* XXIX. 23 Each stood companionless and eyed This undeparting Flower in crimson dyed.

unde'pendable, *a.* [UN-[1] 7 b.] Not to be depended upon; unreliable, untrustworthy.
1860 *Sat. Rev.* 10 Mar. 303/2 The praises of the official world are, from obvious reasons, quite undependable. **1865** W. G. PALGRAVE *Arabia* I. 193 The fickle and undependable Bedouins. **1894** 'J. S. WINTER' *Red-Coat* 63 Just a fickle, changeable thing,..an undependable nothing.

unde'pending, *ppl. a.* [UN-[1] 10 and 5 b.]
1. Not depending *from* or *on* something.
1649 MILTON *Eikon.* x. Wks. 1851 III. 414 If the power of the Sword were any where separate and undepending from the power of Law. **1659** —— *Hirelings* Ibid. V. 387 While they are thus upheld undepending on the Church, on which alone they anciently depended.
2. Not dependent; independent.
1649 MILTON *Observ. Peace Ormond* Wks. 1851 IV. 569 [To] claim an absolute and undepending Jurisdiction. **1712** [P. METCALFE] *Life St. Winefride* 19 That with an undepending Freedom, they might be more absolute Masters of short time. **1724** SWIFT *Drapier's Lett.* Wks. 1755 V. II. 60 But the landed undepending men..will never receive it.

†**unde'phlegmated**, *ppl. a. Obs.* (UN-[1] 8.)
1664 BOYLE *Exp. Colours* III. xl. 309 Common and undephlegmated Aqua-fortis. **1758** *Elaboratory laid Open* 161 The undephlegmated spirit may be used.
So †**unde'phlegmed** *ppl. a. Obs.*
1673 *Phil. Trans.* VIII. 6002 Not when 'tis undephlegmed, but when highly rectified.

unde'plored, *ppl. a.* (UN-[1] 8.)
Chiefly in renderings of Greek and Latin originals.
c **1611** CHAPMAN *Iliad* XXII. 330 Dead, vndeplor'd, Vnsepulcherd, he lies at fleete, vnthought on. **1621** G. SANDYS *Ovid's Met.* XI. (1626) 232 Arise, weepe, put on black: nor vndeplor'd Forpitie send me to the Stygian Ford. **1654** OWEN *Doctr. Saints' Persev.* 17 With these Garlands.. doth he surround the Head of the Sacrifice,..that so it may fall an undeplored Victim. **1791** COWPER *Odyss.* XI. 60 But we had left his corse In Circe's palace, tombless, undeplored. **1818** BYRON *Ch. Har.* IV. xliii, Then might'st thou,..less desired, Be homely and be peaceful, undeplored

For thy destructive charms. **1855** SINGLETON *Virgil* II. 442 We, despicable souls, A rout unsepulchred and undeplored.

undeˈposable, *a.* (UN-[1] 7 b and 5 b.)
1669 E. CHAMBERLAYNE *Pres. St. Eng.* 83 England is an Hereditary Paternal Monarchy, governed by one Supreme, Independent, and Undeposable Head. **1855** [see next].

undeˈposed, *ppl. a.* (UN-[1] 8.)
1624 BEDELL *Lett.* i. 43 They are Martyrs that are executed for plotting to blow him vp with Gun-powder, though vndeposed. **1855** MILMAN *Lat. Chr.* VII. iii. (1864) IV. 115 The actual, undeposed, undeposable King.

undeˈposited, *ppl. a.* (UN-[1] 8.)
1646 HAMMOND *Tracts* 37 The hypocrisy of him which keeps any one close undeposited sin upon his soul.

undeˈpraved, *ppl. a.* [UN-[1] 8.]
1. Not morally depraved or corrupted; not lowered in character or tone.
1646–7 J. HALL *Poems* 95 There did he loose his snowy Innocence, His undepraved will. **1660** STANLEY *Hist. Philos.* XIII. (1687) 909/2 Thus doth every undepraved animal, its own nature judging incorruptly and entirely. **1697** COLLIER *Ess. Mor. Subj.* I. (1703) 152 If we hearken to the undepraved suggestions of our minds. **1782** V. KNOX *Ess.* (1819) II. lxxi. 67 Who possess all the faculties of perception, in a state undepraved by artificial refinement. **1784** COWPER *Task* I. 124 The palate, undeprav'd By culinary arts. **1826** *Q. Rev.* XXXIII. 283 Men whose sense of right and wrong is undepraved.
2. Not vitiated textually.
1686 W. HOPKINS tr. *Ratramnus* Dissert. ii. (1688) 33 Whether it [a book] be come pure and undepraved to our hands, I shall enquire in the next chapter. **1693** J. EDWARDS *Author. O. & N. Test.* 53 These Masoretick Doctors..have kept it [*sc.* the Hebrew text] undepraved and uncorrupt.
Hence **undeˈpravedness**.
1723 MATHER *Vind. Bible* 337 The sense of the place pleads for the undepravedness of the Hebrew in this verse.

undeˈpreciated, *ppl. a.* (UN-[1] 8.)
1818 COLEBROOKE *Obligations* 30 Movables..of small account and such as could not be preserved undepreciated. **1845** McCULLOCH *Taxation* II. xii. 369 Loans and engagements..[to] be made good in an undepreciated currency.

undeˈpressed, -ˈprest, *ppl. a.* [UN-[1] 8.]
1. Not depressed in spirit; not dejected.
1697 D. F. *Char. Dr. S. Annesley* 6 When Griefs come threatning on, or Comfort flows, He was undepress'd by these, unrais'd by those. **1782** D. E. BAKER *Biog. Dram.* I. 222 He maintained his wit and good humour undepressed by misfortunes. **1813** BYRON *Corsair* II. viii, 'Tis he indeed—disarm'd but undeprest. **1880** McCARTHY *Own Times* III. 225 Undepressed by early poverty, unspoiled by later and almost unequalled success.
2. Not pressed down or bent; not hollowed or sunken.
1807 WORDSW. *White Doe* III. 146 A stature undepressed in size, Unbent, which rather seemed to rise. **1819** SCOTT *Ivanhoe* xxxv, His gait, undepressed by age and toil, was erect. **1879** *St. George's Hosp. Rep.* IX. 314 The depressed bone was much driven in, and the margins of the surrounding undepressed portions formed..irregular edges.

undeˈprivable, *a.* (UN-[1] 7 b, 5 b.)
1643 [see UNCONDEMNABLE *a.*]. **1860** READE *8th Commandm.* 15 He could not give me any undeprivable possession of his work.

undeˈprived, *ppl. a.* (UN-[1] 8.)
1564 HAWARD *Eutropius* To Rdr. 7 Worthy to be..un-depryved of theyr wel deserved prayse. **1655** FULLER *Ch. Hist.* VIII. i. §20 Only two Protestant Bishops..found the favour to be last undone, as remaining un-deprived at the beginning of the Parliament. **1700** DRYDEN *Fables, Gd. Parson* 126 Much to himself he thought; but little spoke: And, Undepriv'd, his Benefice forsook. **1709** STRYPE *Ann. Ref.* I. xii. 154 Papers wherein..are shewn, who were dead, who deprived, and who were yet alive and undeprived.

under, *sb. rare.* [f. UNDER *adv.* and UNDER- *prefix*[1].]
1. a. A state of lowness or inferiority. In phr. *to be at a great under.* Now *dial.*
1600 HOLLAND *Livy* XXII. lxi. 471 They were unwilling..that Annibal (who as the voyce went, was at a very great under for money) should be inriched thereby. **1869** *Lonsdale Gloss.* 89/2 *To be at a girt under*, to be in a state of thraldom, subdued.
b. *dial.* An undervalue.
1828 CARR *Craven Gloss.* s.v.
2. *pl.* Underclothes, underwear.
1731 FIELDING *Letter-writers* Wks. 1775 II. 158 He'll make us pope [= pawn] our unders for the reckoning: we'll not go with him. **1905** 'E. NESBIT' *Amulet* vii, Let's..get into flannels. We can't go in our unders.

under, obs. var. UNDERN *sb.*

ˈunder, *a.* [f. UNDER- *prefix*[1], detached from compounds on the analogy of OVER *a.*
There is no clear distinction between the prefix and the adj. when immediately preceding a noun, beyond the writing of the latter as a separate word.]
1. Having a lower or underlying place or position; lying beneath or at a lower level: **a.** Of places, their contents or inhabitants.
a **1300** *Cursor M.* 541 Þe ouer fir gis man his sight, þat ouer air of hering might; þis vnder wynd him gis his aand. **1597** BEARD *Theatre God's Judgem.* (1612) 222 He first remoued his lodging..to a base vnder roome. *c* **1611** CHAPMAN *Iliad* XIX. 2 The Morne arose, and..Gaue light to all, As well to gods, as men of th' vnder globe. **1632** LITHGOW *Trav.* II. 49 The Sunne had imparted his brightnesse to our vnder neighbours. **1874** SWINBURNE *Bothwell* IV. i, For look where yonder..Comes up to usward from the under field One with a flag of message. **1897** *Daily News* 15 Oct. 5/2 He took to the water, disappeared, leaving it on the low under bank of the stream.
b. Of things (esp. one of a pair).
1648 [see SUB- 10]. **1669** STURMY *Mariner's Mag.* VII. iii. 7 The Wyre at the under end at D. **1704** *Dict. Rust.* (1726) s.v. *Cart*, The under pieces which keep the bottom of the Cart together. **1723** CHAMBERS tr. *Le Clerc's Treat. Archit.* I. 89 The upper Order must always be less Massive than the under. **1774** GOLDSM. *Nat. Hist.* II. v. 91 Those [adults] whose upper and under row of teeth are equally prominent. **1839** URE *Dict. Arts* 765 The upper stopcock is closed, and the under is opened to run off the liquor. **1859** TENNYSON *Geraint & Enid* 675 At this he turn'd all red.., Now gnaw'd his under, now his upper lip.
2. a. Lying under (so as to be covered).
1547 in Feuillerat *Revels Edw. VI* (1914) 12 Twoo vnder ffrockes without sleves. **1611** BIBLE *2 Esdras* xii. 19 The eight small vnder feathers sticking to her wings. **1611** FLORIO, *Sottocoperta*, an vnder couerlet. **1872** [see UNDER-GARMENT].
b. Facing downwards.
1731 P. MILLER *Gard. Dict.* s.v. *Leaves*, The upper and under Surfaces of the two Leaves. **1738** [see UNDERSIDE β]. **1839** URE *Dict. Arts* 999 The under face of the licker-up is made rough like a rasp. **1892** *Photogr. Ann.* II. 267 This lever is sunk into the under surface of D.
c. Of sound: Low, subdued.
1806 WOLCOT (P. Pindar) *Tristia* Wks. 1812 V. 319 Tones in the Minor Key, so sweet, so under. **1834** WORDSW. *Lines in Album of C'tess Lonsdale* 33 Those self-solacing, those under, notes Trilled by the redbreast.
3. Inferior, subordinate; of lower rank or position.
1580 *Brief Disc. why Cath. refuse to goe to Ch.* 41 b, For that they haue not receaued the vnder Orders, which they should haue done before Preisthoode. **1611** COTGR., *Soubzacazement*, a dead Fief, rent secke, mesne, or vnder rent. **1693** *Humours Town* 86 The under classes of them, Attorneys, Sollicitors, and Pettifoggers. **1727** POPE, etc. *Art of Sinking* 120 For the under characters, gather them from Homer and Virgil, and change the names as occasion serves. **1823** EGAN *Grose's Dict. Vulgar T.*, *Under dubber*, a turnkey. **1890** R. C. LEHMANN *H. Fludyer* 33 The poor dear servants ..going in batches to the pantomime—at least, the under ones.
4. Below the proper standard, amount, etc.; defective, insufficient.
1673 *Essex Papers* (Camden) 103 Getting a long Lease of it at an under rent from yᵉ Citty. **1710** PALMER *Proverbs* 294 Men..rarely fail of over-measure in the return of an injury, and under in the acknowledgment of a kindness. **1737** BRACKEN *Farriery Impr.* (1757) II. 258 'Tis best to begin rather with an under than over Dose. **1817** KEATINGE *Trav.* I. 9 Flat tracts of hungry pasture ground in under proportion to the tillage.

under (ˈʌndə(r)), *prep.* Forms: 1– under (3 *Orm.* unnderr), 3–7 vnder (5–7 wnder), 4–5 vndere, undere (undre), vndire, 4–6 vn-, wn-, undir, 4–5 vn-, undur, 4–5 vndyr (5 hun-, 6 wn-); 4 vnþer, 5 vnther, vnþur; 4–6, 7 *Sc.*, onder (4 honder), 5 ondre, ondyr, 5–6 ondir; 5 onþer, onther; *Sc.* 8 oner, 9 oonder, oon'er, unner. [Common Teutonic: OE. *under*, = OFris. *under, onder* (WFris. *ûnder, onder*, NFris. *onner, önner*), OLFr. *under, undir* (MDu. and Du. *onder*), OS. *undar* (MLG. *under*, LG. *under, unner*), OHG. *untar, untir, undar, undir* (MHG. and G. *unter*), ON. and Icel. *undir* (Norw., Sw., Da. *under*), Goth. *undar*. The stem is regarded as identical with that of Skr. *ádharas* lower, inferior (*adhamás* lowest, *adhás* below, down), and L. *infrā*.]
I. In senses denoting position beneath or below something, so as to have it above or overhead, or to be covered by it.
1. With reference to: **a.** The heavens or heavenly bodies. (See also HEAVEN *sb.* 1, SUN *sb.*[1] 1 e, COPE *sb.*[1] 7, CANOPY *sb.* 2 b.)
Beowulf 8 He..weox under wolcnum. *Ibid.* 51 Hæleð under heofenum. *a* **900** CYNEWULF *Elene* 13 (Gr.), Æðelinges weox rice under roderum. *c* **1000** ÆLFRIC *Gen.* i. 7 þa wæteru þe wæron under þære fæstnisse. *c* **1175** *Lamb. Hom.* 151 Ure drihten him solf..seide þet under houene ne [wes] nan his ilike. *c* **1205**– [see SUN *sb.* 1 e]. **1340–70** *Alex. & Dind.* 219 We weren tauht..þat non haþel vndur heuene so holi is founde. *a* **1400–50** *Alexander* 247 þare enhabetis in þat erd..þe wisest wees in þis werd þe welken vndire. *c* **1400** *Destr. Troy* 3873 Was neuer kyng vnder cloude his knightes more louet. **1458** AGNES PASTON in *P. Lett.* I. 423 The blyssyng of all seyntes undir heven. *a* **1542** WYATT in *Tottel's Misc.* (Arb.) 64 Thinke not alone vnder the sunne Vnquit to cause thy louers plaine. **1555** [see FIRMAMENT 1]. **1609** BIBLE (Douay) *Deut.* xxix. 20 Our Lord abolish his name vnder heauen. **1644** MILTON *Educ.* 7 They are by a sudden..watch word, to be call'd out to their military motions, under skie or covert, according to the season. **1712** BERKELEY *Pass. Obed.* Wks. 1871 III. 108 In every kingdom or society of men under heaven. **1766** GOLDSM. *Vicar* xiv, The greatest rascal under the canopy of heaven. **1821** WORDSW. *Three Cottage Girls* 56 Gay vision under sullen skies! **1885** *Manch. Exam.* 29 June 5/3 They rush off immediately..and bathe under a hot and broiling sun.
†**b.** The Deity as dwelling in heaven. *Obs.*
c **1205** LAY. 27976 Neoðeles heo auered weoren..þat nusten heo under criste nenne ræd godne. *c* **1320** *Cast. Love* 225 þat vche þing vnder heuene-driht So muche les of strengþe and miht. *c* **1400** *Destr. Troy* 11776 There is no greuaunce so grete vndur god one, As the glemyng of gold.
c. Special parts of the heavens, esp. as indicating terrestrial locality.
c **1391** CHAUCER *Astrol.* I. §21 Whan the planetes ben vnder thilke signes, þei causen vs..effectes lik to the operaciouns of bestes. *c* **1400** [see PLANET *sb.*[1] 1 b]. **1432–50** [see POLE *sb.*[2] 1]. *c* **1450** HOLLAND *Howlat* 31 Under the Cirkill solar thir sauorus seidis War nurist be dame Natur. **1559** W. CUNNINGHAM *Cosmogr. Glasse* 82 There be some that suppose..Paradise to be situated vnder th' Equinoctiall. **1590** SPENSER *F.Q.* III. iii. 6 The learned Merlin well could tell, Vnder what coast of heauen the man did dwell. **1611** R. JOHNSON *Kingd. & Commw.* 437 Authours affirme, that vnder the very pole lyeth a black and high rocke. **1634** HERBERT *Trav.* 186 This day we were under nine degrees fifteene minutes North. **1679** MOXON *Math. Dict.* 162 Under the Sun Beams. **1728** CHAMBERS *Cycl.* s.v. *Current*, Under the Equator, where the Motion of the Earth is the greatest. **1783** JUSTAMOND tr. *Raynal's Hist. Indies* (ed. 3) I. 3 A man living under the equator or under the pole.
d. The stars as having influence on persons.
1583 STUBBES *Anat. Abus.* II. 14, Whether all the host of Pharao were borne vnder one and the same starre and planet. **1590** SPENSER *F.Q.* II. ii. 2 Ah lucklesse babe, borne vnder cruell starre. **1601** [see STAR *sb.* 3]. *a* **1715** BURNET *Own Time* (1724) I. 525 Great applications were made to the Duke for saving his life: But he was not born under a pardoning planet. **1823** SCOTT *Quentin D.* xii, This..youth has his destiny under the same constellation with mine. **1837** [see PLANET *sb.*[1] 1 b].
2. With reference to the surface of the earth or water. (Cf. UNDERGROUND *adv.*)
In early use without *the* before the noun.
Beowulf 1656 Ic þæt unsofte ealdre ᵹediᵹde, wiᵹᵹe under wætere. *Ibid.* 2415 Goldmaðmas heold eald under eorðan. *a* **900** CYNEWULF *Elene* 218 (Gr.), Hwær se wuldres beam haliᵹ under hrusan hyded wære. *a* **1300** *Cursor M.* 1079 Þe bodi moght he nan-gat hide, For vnder erth most it not rest. *c* **1330** R. BRUNNE *Chron. Wace* (Rolls) 2068 He didde hure kepe Vnder erthe in a seler depe. **1398** TREVISA *Barth. De P.R.* VI. ii. (Bodl. MS.), He is iputte aside and iberied vndur þe erthe. *c* **1400** *Gamelyn* 68 A-none as he was dede and vnder gras grave. **1477** EARL RIVERS (Caxton) *Dictes* 22 But nowe they may not be perceyued for they ar hidde vnther the erthe. *c* **1511** *1st Eng. Bk. Amer.* Introd. (Arb.) 28/1 There dwellyng is vnder the erthe. **1530** PALSGR. 328/1 Under the grounde, *soubzterraine*. **1555** EDEN *Decades* (Arb.) 142 They had certeyne dyuers or fysshers exercised..in swymmynge vnder the water. **1601** HOLLAND *Pliny* II. 408 Anon it is swallowed up within a hole under the ground. **1721** [see TURF *sb.*[1] 2]. **1790** [see EARTH *sb.*[1] 2]. **1818** CRUISE *Digest* (ed. 2) V. 21 In cases of copyholds, a lord may have a right under the soil of the copyholder. **1880** R. M. BALLANTYNE (*title*), Under the Waves; or, Diving in Deep Waters.
3. a. With words denoting natural or artificial structures or means of shelter; freq. = beneath the cover or shelter of.
See also GLASS *sb.*[1] 3 b, HATCH *sb.*[1] 3, 4, ROOF *sb.* 1 b. For examples with abstract terms see COVER *sb.*[1] 3 c, COVERT *sb.* 2 c, SHADE *sb.* 8, UMBRAGE *sb.* 2 b.
a **900** CYNEWULF *Elene* 653 (Gr.), ðe þa byrᵹenna under stanhleoðum..on ᵹewritu setton. **971** *Blickl. Hom.* 209 Under þæm stane wæs niccra eardung & wearᵹa. *c* **1000** ÆLFRIC *Gen.* xxi. 15 Heo þa alede þone sunu under sumum treowe. *a* **1310** in Wright *Lyric P.* xiii. 44 Wormes woweth under cloude [= clod]. **1338** R. BRUNNE *Chron.* (1810) 14 Sibriht, þat I of told,..þat a suynhird slouh vnder a busk of thorn. **1340–70** *Alex. & Dind.* 435 We ne han none hous bote holus in þe holou cauus Vndur hillus ful hie. *c* **1374** CHAUCER *Anel. & Arc.* 19 Thow..Syngest with voice memorial in þe shade Vndir the laurier. *c* **1400** MAUNDEV. (Roxb.) iii. 9 Vnder þe stages er stables. **1422** YONG tr. *Secreta Secret.* 192 Lik as a man ne restith not well vndir a dropping hous. *c* **1470** *Gol. & Gaw.* 356 Thus with trety ye cast yon trew vndre tyld. **1508** DUNBAR *Tua Mariit Wemen* 11, I hard, vnder ane holyn.., Ane hie speiche at my hand. **1571** CAMPION *Hist. Irel.* II. ix. (1633) 115 You are served under a Canopy. **1585** T. WASHINGTON tr. *Nicholay's Voy.* II. vi. 36 [He] giueth vnto the inhabitants..these trees..vpon condition that euery one..shall trim them & keep the ground cleane that is vnder them. **1662** *Extr. St. Papers Friends* Ser. II. (1911) 148 These Anabaptist..meete..privately vnder hedges at vnseasonable houres in the night. **1693** *Humours Town* 43 If they had kept under their own Vine in the Country. **1711** STEELE *Spect.* 82 ¶1 Passing under Ludgate the other Day, I heard a Voice bawling for Charity. **1761** MRS. F. SHERIDAN *Sidney Bidulph* I. 319 Whatever your designs may be, it will be less to my dishonour if you prosecute them from under your husband's roof. **1843** *Fraser's Mag.* XXVIII. 649 Under this canopy was the coffin. **1891** FARRAR *Darkn. & Dawn* lxiv, They reached the green level under the trees.
fig. **1711** *Spect.* No. 67 ¶5, I love to shelter my self under the Examples of Great Men.
b. *Sc.* With reference to the cover or shelter of darkness. ***under night***, during the night, by night.
under cloud of night: see CLOUD *sb.* 9.
1434 *Extr. Aberd. Reg.* (1844) I. 391 That na fischar of sawmound..house nane bot thai be tane vndir nycht, and on the morn brocht to the markete. **1508** KENNEDIE *Flyting w. Dunbar* 428 And ondir nycht quhyle stall thou staggis & stirkis. **1567** *Reg. Privy Council Scot.* I. 592 The said Oliver ..come to the said Androis dwelling hous..under silence of nycht. **1725** RAMSAY *Gentle Sheph.* II. iii, He brought east the howdy under night. **1730** T. BOSTON *Mem.* xi. (1899) 371 Under night we lost the way again. **1824** MACTAGGART *Gallovid. Encycl.* 450 To sing undernight for 'bawbees' in the large towns on their way. **1844** H. STEPHENS *Bk. Farm* I. 129 Some mares..are known to drop their foals under night in the stable.
4. a. In general use.
In some phrases with development of figurative senses: see FOOT *sb.* 33, NOSE *sb.* 7 b, ROSE *sb.*[1] 7, WING *sb.* ***under metal***: see METAL *sb.* 7; ***under the counter***: see COUNTER *sb.*[3] 4 b; ***under the table***: see TABLE *sb.* 5 e and 6 d. In quot. 1553 the reference is app. to relative position on the map.
c **825** *Vesp. Ps.* ix. 28 Under tungan his [bioð] ᵹewin & sar. *c* **950** *Lindisf. Gosp.* Mark iv. 21 Hueðer cuom leht-fæt

..þætte under mitta..ȝesetted bið *vel* under bed. *a* **1000** *Kent. Gloss.* in Wr.-Wülcker 82 *Sub ascella sua*, under his oxne. *a* **1250** *Owl & Night.* 86 Þe were icundere to one frogge þat sit at Mulne vnder cogge. *c* **1320** *Sir Tristr.* 1947 A siue he fond tite And bond vnder his fete. *c* **1386** CHAUCER *Knt.'s T.* 1727 Ant in that selue moment Palamon Is vnder Venus Estward in the place. *a* **1400** *Octouian* 1851, I fond my chyld lye yn oo place, Onther a lyone..With whelpys tweyne. *c* **1430** *Art of Nombryng* (E.E.T.S.) 15 Therfor vnder the last in an od place sette me most fynde a digit. **1508** KENNEDIE *Flyting w. Dunbar* 364 Thou wald be fayn to gnaw,..Wnder my burd, smoch banis behynd doggis bakkis. **1523** FITZHERB. *Husb.* §27 If it be a newe house, they thacke it vnder theyr fote. **1553** EDEN *Treat. New Ind.* (Arb.) 8 The situation of the cytie of Saba in Ethiopia vnder Egipt. **1669** STURMY *Mariner's Mag.* v. xii. 72 If the said Work be under the Platform, Substract the Difference found by your Quadrant. **1683** MOXON *Mech. Exerc., Printing* xi. ¶23 The Stoking-hole lying far under the Caldron. **1727** BAILEY (vol. II), To *Chuck* one under the Chin. **1762** MILLS *Syst. Pract. Husb.* I. 265 The share will be more inclined..if the wedge under the beam is loosened. **1815** J. SMITH *Panorama Sci. & Art* II. 525 Here the bracket..denotes, that these two substances..form the compound written under it. **1862** THACKERAY *Philip* xxvii, Those scratches or dashes under her words, by which some ladies are accustomed to point their satire. **1888** 'J. S. WINTER' *Bootle's Childr.* vii, A goodly crop of curly brown hair which he held under the pump..almost every morning.

b. Denoting the relationship of a horse to the rider, of a ship to a person on board, or of a motor-cycle to the rider.

a **900** CYNEWULF *Elene* 1192 (Gr.), þæs cyninges sceal mearh under modeȝum midlum ȝeweorðod. **1338** R. BRUNNE *Chron.* (1810) 183 Fightand on a gate, vndir him þei slouh his stede. **1485** CAXTON *Chas. Gt.* 210 Also that same day the hors of charles was slayn under hym. **1709** STEELE *Tatler* No. 17 ¶4 My Lord Galway had his Horse shot under him in this Action. **1720** DE FOE *Capt. Singleton* iii. (1840) 46 We might have some better vessels under us. **1795** *Ann. Reg., Hist.* 30 Three horses were killed under him. **1806** A. DUNCAN *Nelson* 15 His ship sunk under him. **1841** *Penny Cycl.* XXI. 492/1 Having had a horse shot under him. **1942** [see NIP *v.*[1] 4c]. **1980** *Dirt Bike* Oct. 57/1 If you're a specialist, you must think long and hard about the MAG 3. Especially if one knifes under you on a flat corner.

c. = At a point just below (a part of the body).

c **1275** *Passion of our Lord* 388 in *O.E. Misc.* 48 Seþþe hi knowede and seyde, hayl gywene king, And smyten vnder þat ere, ne sparede hi no þing. *c* **1400** *Rom. Rose* 2097 He touchide me Vndir the side full softly. *c* **1475** *Rauf Coilȝear* 150 He..hit him vnder the eir with his richt hand. **1539** BIBLE *2 Sam.* iii. 27 Joab..smote hym vnder ye short rybbes y^t he dyed. **1585** T. WASHINGTON tr. *Nicholay's Voy.* III. x. 86 Breaches..gathered and made fast vnder the knee. **1604** SHAKS. *Oth.* I. ii. 5 Nine, or ten times I had thought t' haue yerk'd him here vnder the Ribbes. **1611-** [see FIFTH *a.* 1 a]. **1653** URQUHART *Rabelais* I. xxvii. 128 With a sound bounce under the hollow of their short ribs, he overturned their stomachs. **1886** ELWORTHY *W. Somerset Word-bk.* 500 I'll gi thee a nap under the ear.

d. Denoting position between the arm, etc., and the body.

1377 LANGL. *P. Pl.* B. xv. 119 A peyre bedes in her hande and a boke vnder her arme. *c* **1480** HENRYSON *Fables, Lion & Mouse* 37 Ane Roll of paper in his hand he bair; Ane Swannis pen stikand vnder his eir. **1485** in *Yorkshire Deeds* (1909) 3 Lawrence..brought with him a small coferet under his arme and bar it hens. **1596** SPENSER *F.Q.* IV. vii. 24 And now he her away with him did beare Vnder his arme. **1602** *2nd Pt. Return fr. Parnass.* Prol., Stage Direction, Stagekeeper carrieth the boy away vnder his arme. **1721** KELLY *Scot. Prov.* 319 She is welcome that brings some Present under her Arm. **1820** KEATS *Cap & Bells* lxviii, Under one arm the magic book he bore. *c* **1850** *Arab. Nts.* (Rtldg.) 741 She shut the box, put it under her arm, and returned to the house.

e. Passing into the sense of 'in'.

1812 SIR H. DAVY *Chem. Philos.* 285 It may be purified by ..passing it under water through shamois leather. **1827** FARADAY *Chem. Manip.* xv. (1842) 343 The transference of gas from vessel to vessel under mercury. **1855** *Orr's Circ. Sci., Inorg. Nat.* 215 The resulting lime..sets rapidly in a damp atmosphere, and even under water.

5. Denoting the relationship of persons: **a.** To something worn on the head. (In ME. esp. in conventional phrases.)

Beowulf 342 Word æfter spræc, heard under helme. *Ibid.* 1163 Þa cwom Wealhþeo forð gan under gyldnum beaȝe. *a* **1310** in Wright *Lyric P.* xvi. 52 With browen blysfol under hode. *c* **1400** *Emare* 303 Ther was noþer olde ny ȝynge, That kowþe stynte of wepynge, For þat comely vnþer kelle. **1508** DUNBAR *Poems* iv. 22 He takis the knythis in to feild, Anarmit vnder helme & scheild. *Ibid.* v. 4 Scho wes lik a caldrone cruke cler vnder kellis. **1550** [see HOOD *sb.*[1] 7]. **1667** MILTON *P.L.* III. 640 Under a Coronet his flowing haire In curles on either cheek plaid. **1825** BENTHAM *Offic. Apt. Maximized, Indic.* (1830) 38 Think now of the scene;.. culprit and judge under one hood. **1846** G. E. CORRIE in Holroyd *Mem.* (1890) xi. 241 There may be..more pride and hypocrisy under a close plain bonnet, than under a veil of silk. **1853** THACKERAY *Eng. Hum.* i. 17 What small men they must have seemed under these enormous periwigs.

b. To something carried or raised above the head, as a standard, etc. Hence in pregnant sense, denoting military service, nationality, etc.

Beowulf 1205 Siðþan he under seȝne sinc ealȝode. *c* **1500** [see STANDARD *sb.* 1 b]. **1517** *Reg. Privy Seal Scotl.* I. 451/1 William Turnbule..deit under umquhile our soverane lordis baner. *a* **1548** HALL *Chron., Edw. IV*, 243 Therle of Northumberlande, vnder whose standerd were..sixe thousande and seuen .c. men. **1552** [see BANNER *sb.*[1] 1 b]. **1596** DALRYMPLE tr. *Leslie's Hist. Scot.* (S.T.S.) I. 277 Wndir this croce, scotis men ar sure. **1611** COTGR. s.v. *Subhastation*, The auncient Romans vsed..to hold their Outcries [= auctions] vnder a kind of speare, or iauelin. **1667** MILTON *P.L.* VI. 533 Him soon they met Under spred Ensignes moving nigh. **1725** DE FOE *Voy. round World* (1840) 213 A small frigate-built vessel, under Spanish Colours. **1750** BEAWES *Lex Mercat.* (1752) 9 Very soon all the commerce of those parts was only carried on under French colours. **1769** [see BANNER *sb.*[1] 1]. **1852** [see STANDARD *sb.*[1] 1 b]. **1869** in *Cornh. Mag.* June (1918) 635 Some of the Colonies..may in process of time find themselves under the Stars and Stripes of the Flag of the United States.

c. *Naut.* Of ships, with reference to the sails, etc.

c **893**, **1508-** [see SAIL *sb.*[1] 3 d]. **1669** STURMY *Mariner's Mag.* I. ii. 17 Thus have you the Ship a trije under a Mizen. *Ibid.* 18 Thus you have the Ship..steering under all her Canvas. **1707** *Lond. Gaz.* No. 4380/3 The Firebrand.. forc'd in under a Fore-course for the Light of St. Agnes. **1719** D'URFEY *Pills* III. 306 She lies a try under her Mizen. **1780** COXE *Russ. Disc.* 130 Drove 24 hours under bare poles. **1840** R. H. DANA *Bef. Mast* ix. 22 A large ship under top-gallant sails. **1885** *Law Times' Rep.* LIII. 54/1 The J. M. Stevens was proceeding under all sail close-hauled on the port tack.

6. a. With reference to something which covers, clothes, envelops, or conceals; passing into the sense of 'within'.

In ME. freq. in phrases: see quots. and GORE *sb.*[2] 2, LACE *sb.* 3, LINE *sb.*[1] 2 b, SHIELD *sb.* 1 b. ***under arms*** (see ARM *sb.*[2] 5) is prob. an extension of this sense. For the fig. sense of *under a cloud* see CLOUD *sb.* 10 b. ***under water*** (= flooded): see WATER *sb.*

Beowulf 1209 He under rande ȝecranc. *a* **1122** *O.E. Chron.* (Laud MS.) an. 688, He syððan..forðferde..under Cristes claðum. *a* **1225** *Leg. Kath.* 809 Schome ow is to schuderin lengre under schelde. **1382** WYCLIF *Jude* i. 6 Sothliche aungels..he reseruede..in euerelastinge boondis vndir derknesse. *c* **1386** CHAUCER *Frankl. T.* 381 Þis matere.. Vnder his brest he baar it moore secree Than euere dide Pamphilus for Galathee. *c* **1400** *Emare* 250 Then sayde þat wordy vnþer wede. *Ibid.* 501 That semely vnþer serke. *c* **1402** LYDG. *Compl. Bl. Knt.* 64, I sawe ther Daphne closed under rynde. *c* **1450** HOLLAND *Howlat* 82 That is the plesant Pacok..Constant and kirklyk vnder his cler cape. **1579** W. WILKINSON *Confut. Fam. Love* Ep. Ded. *ij b, While the watchmen slept, many..vnder Lambes skinnes craftely crept into the sheepfold. **1599** GREENE *Orpharion* Wks. (Grosart) XII. 33 And vnder a faire face resteth a faithfull hart. **1621** T. WILLIAMSON tr. *Goulart's Wise Vieillard* 26 Our life may be compared to..the Moone,..often ecclipsed and vnder a cloud. **1775** FRANKLIN *Let.* in *Europ. Mag.* (1804) XLV. 349/2 Please to send your letters to him, under cover, directed to Mr. Alderman Lee. **1791** COWPER *Odyssey* VII. 357 There, under wither'd leaves, forlorn, I slept All the long night. **1798**, **1804** [see COVER *sb.*[1] 2 d]. **1817** BOWDICH *Mission to Ashantee* ix. 375 It proceeds by ulcerating under the skin. **1859** *Habits of Gd. Society* 50 If you do not wear silk stockings under your boots. **1872** *Routledge's Ev. Boy's Ann.* 185/2 All addressed..to him under cover to the agents of his regiment.

fig. **1500-20** DUNBAR *Poems* xiii. 5, I tell ȝow this vndir confessioun.

b. Denoting the relationship of land to crops grown, or animals reared, on it: Planted, sowed or stocked with; used for growing or rearing.

(*a*) **1569** *Reg. Privy Council Scot.* I. 676 Peciabill possessioun of the landis and stedingis of Cullard and Conege, under crop as it is. **1795** VANCOUVER *Agric. Essex* 53 The marshes which were formerly under grass, are now very generally under the plough. **1806** [see CROP *sb.* 8 b]. **1845** *Jrnl. R. Agric. Soc.* VI. II. 524, I put the ground..under early potatoes. **1868** *Ibid.* Ser. II. IV. II. 322 This field has been laid under grass. **1890** STANLEY *Darkest Africa* I. x. 232 The Manyuema had..five acres under rice, and as many under beans.

(*b*) **1799** [A. YOUNG] *Agric. Lincoln* 194 [The pasture] that had been under sheep [was] so greatly superior. **1891** *Pall Mall G.* 24 Aug. 2/2 Again, in Ross-shire, the area under deer has advanced..to a little more than one-half.

7. a. Denoting position at the bottom or foot of something, or beside it but at a lower level: By the side of, close by (a wood, town, etc.). Sometimes with implication of shelter or protection.

Also with abstract terms, esp. LEE *sb.*[1] 1, SHELTER *sb.* 2. ***under the wind***: see WIND *sb.*

Beowulf 211 Flota wæs on yðum, bat under beorȝe. *Ibid.* 710 Ða com of more under misthleoþum Grendel gongan. **971** *Blickl. Hom.* 211 Þæt wæter wæs sweart under þæm clife neoðan. *c* **1205** LAY. 27163 Þa he com in ane dale vnder ane dune, þer he gon at-stonden. *c* **1305** *Judas Iscariot* 70 in *E.E.P.* (1862) 109 So þat þis tuei schrewen..Adai ȝeode alone pleye vnder an orchard. *c* **1386** CHAUCER *Knt.'s T.* 1123 And dounward from an hille vnder a bente Ther stood the temple of Mars Armypotente. **1387** TREVISA *Higden* (Rolls) V. 329 Þat ryver renneþ under the citee of Wygan. *c* **1402** LYDG. *Compl. Bl. Knt.* 77, I sawe a litel welle, That had his course..Under a hille. **1495** *Cov. Leet Bk.* 563 Such grounde as the seid Maister had vnder the parke syde. *a* **1548** HALL *Chron., Edw. IV*, 201 So vnder a wooddes side, thei couertly espied them passe forward. **1585** T. WASHINGTON tr. *Nicholay's Voy.* II. i. 31 b, [We lay] seuen daies vnder the castle and fortresse called Capsali. *Ibid.* II. x. 44 b, The castle,..vnder which lieth a vallie very fertile. **1600** *1st Pt. Sir J. Oldcastle* IV. iv. 75 Hard vnder Islington wait you my comming. **1662** STILLINGFL. *Orig. Sacræ* III. iv. §12 That part of Thessaly which lyes under the mountains Ossa and Olympus. **1720** DE FOE *Capt. Singleton* xi. (1840) 185 We were obliged to come to an anchor under a little island. **1751** LABELYE *Westm. Bridge* 28 The Carpenters began to make and erect, under the Surry Shore, 12 Frames of Timber. **1806** *Gazetteer Scotl.* (ed. 2) 402/2 Under the rock where the fowls build they row their boat. **1840** ALISON *Hist. Eur.* VIII. lxii. 365 Seeking refuge under any projecting ground from the intolerable musketry. **1842** LOUDON *Suburban Hort.* 625 Either in the open garden,..or under a wall.

b. In military and naval use.

1677 *Lond. Gaz.* No. 1237/2 The slaughter would have been much greater, but that by the favor of the night they got under the Cannon of the Fort of Kiel. **1710** *Ibid.* No. 4731/2 The Duke of Anjou was encamped..under the Cannon of Lerida. **1805** in Nicolas *Disp. Nelson* (1846) VII. 167 *note*, At 2.5 The French Admiral's Ship under our Quarter had lost her foremast.

8. With verbs of motion, impulsion, etc., denoting change of place to a position below or beneath something.

Beowulf 403 Þa secg wisode under Heorotes hrof. *Ibid.* 820 Scolde Grendel þonan..fleon under fenhleoðu. *c* **888** K. ÆLFRED *Boeth.* xxxix. §3 Hwa ne wundrað ðæs þæt sume steorran ȝewitað under þa sæ. *c* **1000** *Ags. Gosp.* Luke vii. 6 Ne eom ic wyrðe þæt ðu ga under mine þecene. *c* **1200** ORMIN 1551 And þurrh þatt tatt tu fullhtnesst hemm & unnderr waterr dippesst. *c* **1205** LAY. 8406 Tweien scalkes ..scriðen under bordes & skirmden mid mæine. **13..** *E.E. Allit. P.* C. 179 A lodes-mon lyȝtly lep vnder hachches. **1382** WYCLIF *Luke* vii. 6, I am not worthi, that thou entre vndir my roof. **1585** T. WASHINGTON tr. *Nicholay's Voy.* II. xxiv. 65 The arcenal..hath neare an hundreth arches or vaultes to builde and hale the gallies vnder couert and drye. **1617** MORYSON *Itin.* I. 210 All which, at the ringing of this bell to prayer, went vnder the hatches. **1648** HEXHAM II, *Onderduycken*, to Dive vnder water, as in swimming. **1697** DRYDEN *Virg. Georg.* IV. 72 When Golden Suns appear, And under Earth have driv'n the Winter Year. **1702** ADDISON *Dial. Medals* (1726) 102 She thrusts a lighted torch under a heap of armour that lies by an Altar. **1806** *Med. Jrnl.* XV. 275 He admits that various active substances may be introduced under the cuticle. **1827** *Mirror* II. 254/1 Chance ..led him under an apple-tree. **1892** *Photogr. Ann.* II. 251 Rude Boreas, who likes to let daylight under the focussing cloth.

II. In senses denoting subordination or subjection.

9. a. With reference to persons acting in a certain capacity, considered in relation to one holding a superior position or office.

c **893** K. ÆLFRED *Oros.* III. xi. 142 Þa þe under Alexandre fyrmest wæron. *c* **1000** *Rule of Chrodegang* vi, Se bisceop oððe se ðe under him ealdor is. *a* **1300** *Cursor M.* 16026 Þai ..sent to pilate þair procuratur,..For he sett vte-ouer þam Vnder cesar þe king. *c* **1380** WYCLIF *Serm.* Sel. Wks. I. 316 So Syryne, þat was þere cheef undur þe emperour, bigan to make þis discripcion. *c* **1420** LYDG. *Assembly of Gods* 1259 Then made Vertu Frewyll baylle vndyr Reson. *c* **1425** *Eng. Conq. Ireland* 6 In that tym was prince in wales, Rys, Gryffynes son, onþer the kyng of england. **1473** *Rental Bk. Cupar-Angus* (1879) I. 166 We hafe grantyt hym..to mak tenandis onder hym. **1531** *Dial. on Laws Eng.* II. xxxvi. 75 The pope is the vycar generall vnder god. **1546** *Yorks. Chantry Surv.* (Surtees) 348 The same prebendaries have vj vicars inducted under them. **1611** COTGR., *Soubcurateur*,.. one that hath the..charge of a thing vnder another. **1667** MILTON *P.L.* V. 695 Hee together calls..the Regent Powers, Under him Regent. **1761** *List Officers Army* 195/2 Capt. Sir Duncan Campbell, Bt. Staff-offi. la. under L. G. St. Clair. **1820** LAMB *Elia* I. *South-Sea House*, Deputy, under Evans, was Thomas Tame. **1849** MACAULAY *Hist. Eng.* i. I. 55 The King was, under Christ, sole head of the Church. **1854** R. S. SURTEES *Handley Cr.* vii, Betsey, a maid of all work, and a girl under her. **1891** E. PEACOCK *N. Brendon* I. 133 He had worked under Clark.

b. ***under God, Heaven***, etc., in parenthetic use. (Cf. GOD *sb.* 9 d.)

1544 *Star Chamb. Cases* (Selden) II. 279 The ship.. wherof one John Goodlade..then vndir god was master. **1616** R. COCKS *Diary* (Hakl. Soc.) I. 199 Of his arivall there in our junck,..he under God saveing her. *a* **1704** LOCKE *Ess. Underst. St. Paul's Epist.* (1707) 17 This is the only safe Guide (under the Spirit of God..) that can be rely'd on. **1719** DE FOE *Crusoe* II. (Globe) 332 He..thank'd me that had, under God, given him and so many miserable Creatures their Lives. **1841** LYTTON *Night & Morn.* III. xi, The husband and wife..looked up to her as the author, under Heaven, of their happiness. *Ibid.* v. xix, It is from you, under Providence, that [etc.].

†**c.** = In addition to; besides. *Obs.*

c **1400** T. CHESTRE *Launfal* 48 For the lady bar..swych word, That sche had lemannys unther her lord. *c* **1440** *Gesta Rom.* i. 1 (Harl. MS.), Þis woman lovid by wey of synne an oþer knyȝt, vndir hire husbond. *Ibid.* v. 12 There was a knyȝt hadde a faire wife, þat tooke an oþer vndir him.

d. With reference to derivative rights or claims.

1818 CRUISE *Digest* (ed. 2) II. 505 As to the grantee of the rent-charge, he was in under the first joint tenant who released. **1896** *Law Times* C. 410/1 The acts or defaults of any person other than himself and those claiming under him.

10. a. Denoting subordination to, or control by, a person or persons having or exercising recognized authority or command; occas. = in the service of.

c **950** *Lindisf. Gosp.* Matt. viii. 9 Ic..hæfo under mec ðeignas. *c* **1000** ÆLFRIC *Num.* iii. 9 Beon hiȝ þenas under Aarone and his sunum. *a* **1225** *Leg. Kath.* 223 He ane is to herien, þurh hwam & under hwam alle kinges rixleð. *c* **1230** *Hali Meid.* 31 For, beo hit nu, þat..[þu] habbe monie under þe, hirdmen in halle. **1382** WYCLIF *Matt.* viii. 9 For whi and I am a man..hauynge vndir me kniȝtis. *c* **1400** MAUNDEV. (Roxb.) xxx. 133 Prestre Iohn has vnder him many kynges. *c* **1450** HOLLAND *Howlat* 133 For all statis of kirk that wnder Crist standis. **1495** *Act 11 Hen. VII*, c. 22 §1 A maister Ship Carpenter taking the charge of the werke havyng men undre hym. **1538** STARKEY *England* I. i. 24 Now also vse your tyme, vnder so nobul a prynce, to the mayntenance..of the same. *a* **1548** HALL *Chron., Hen. V*, 38 While all was vnder one [king], no nacion durste..attempte warre against the Britons. **1639** A. WHEELOCKE in *Lett. Lit. Men* (Camden) 157, I could wish that our learned gentrie..would imploy some scholars to be under them..to compile a body of our Divinity. **1726** SWIFT *Gulliver* IV. iv, In my last voyage I was commander of the ship, and had about fifty Yahoos under me. **1779** *Mirror* No. 4, An uncle of my wife, who..had obtained a very considerable office under government. **1838** W. BELL *Dict. Law Scot.* 168 The society is now under the keeper of the signet. **1849** MACAULAY *Hist. Eng.* i. I. 141 Favourable to the plan of reviving the old civil constitution under a new dynasty.

b. *spec.* Denoting relation to military commanders or political leaders: Led or commanded by; in the forces or following of.

1297 R. GLOUC. (Rolls) 1332 Vor þe maistrie nis noȝt a kinges.. Ac kniȝtes þat vnder him viȝteþ & ssedeþ hor blod. **1564** STAPLETON tr. *Staphylus' Apol.* Pref. 11 His wisedom ..he well declared..in the like seruice vnder the Catholike and vertuous Duke of Bauaria. **1599** SHAKS. *Hen. V*, IV. vii. 154 *King.* Who seru'st thou vnder? *Will.* Vnder Captaine Gower. **1612** T. TAYLOR *Comm. Titus* ii. 6 Let them now serue as voluntaries vnder the Captaine Iesus Christ. **1718** PRIOR *Poems Sev. Occas.* Ded., In the first Dutch War He went a Voluntier under the Duke of York. **1816** SCOTT *Old Mort.* xxxvi, I made my first campaigns under him. **1839** *Penny Cycl.* XIV. 347/2 On the 18th May, 1565, the Turks, under Mustapha Pacha,..landed on the island of Malta. **1855** MACAULAY *Hist. Eng.* xii. III. 204 He..had fought bravely under Monmouth on the Continent. **1861** M. PATTISON *Ess.* (1889) I. 45 The great communistic uprising under Wat Tyler in 1381.

c. Denoting relation to teachers or instructors: Subject to the instruction, direction, or guidance of.

to sit under (a preacher): see SIT *v.* 30. See also STUDY *v.* 1 c.

1524 *Reg. Mag. Sig. Scot.* 200 The said M. Hary..has maid under him gude and perite scolaris now laitlie the tyme that he was maister of our scule. **1691** WOOD *Ath. Oxon.* II. 693 His first education in Grammar learning was under one Thom. Sibley. **1711** STEELE *Spect.* No. 154 ¶2, I..had the finishing Part of my Education under a Man of great Probity. **1724** H. BEDFORD tr. *Life J. Barwick* App. 362 Under this Instructor he learnt the Art of blurting out crude Sermons. **1749** FIELDING *Tom Jones* VII. xii, There were likewise two Ensigns,..one of whom had been bred under an Attorney. **1808** SCOTT in Lockhart *Life* I. i. 43, I made some progress in Ethics under Professor John Bruce. **1837** K. H. DIGBY *Mores Cath.* VIII. vi. (1846) II. 594/2 He studied under Albert at Cologne and Paris. **1900** D. C. TOVEY in *Gray's Lett.* I. 3 *note*, Birkett was the tutor under whom Gray was admitted a Pensioner at Peterhouse.

d. = As a tenant of.

1754 in *Nairne Peerage Evidence* (1874) 51 She lived under said lord Nairn very near his house.

e. = In the hands of (a doctor).

1846 S. MAGOFFIN *Diary* 19 Sept. in *Down Santa Fé Trail* (1926) 135 He has been under the Doctor for some time. **1898** *Hutchinson's Arch. Surg.* IX. 382, I go once a week to Dr. Brown, but whether I am under him or he is under me I never can quite tell.

f. *Mus.* = Conducted by.

1887 E. DANNREUTHER tr. *Wagner's On Conducting* 63 Fancies of this sort, however, were not permitted during the strictly classical performance, under the veteran Capellmeister, at the Munich Odeon. **1910** G. B. SHAW *How to become a Musical Critic* (1960) 278 A performance under Manns of a Mozart symphony. **1943** *N.Y. Times* 9 May II. 5/5 The City Amateur Symphony Orchestra, under Judge Leopold Prince, will give its annual series of Summer concerts. **1962** *Listener* 12 Apr. 661/2 The BBC Northern Orchestra under Jacques-Louis Monod. **1976** Y. MENUHIN *Unfinished Journey* (1977) xvi. 342 During Sir Thomas Beecham's sponsorship of it, I performed the Viotti A Minor Concerto with him—the last time I played under Sir Thomas's baton.

11. a. With names or designations of rulers, passing into the sense of 'during the reign or administration of', 'in the time or period of'.

c **888** K. ÆLFRED *Boeth.* i, He þa ȝemunde..þara ealdrihta þe hi under þam caserum hæfdon. ?*a* **900** *O.E. Chron.* (Parker MS.) an. 653, Her Middel-Seaxe onfengon under Peadan aldormen ryhtne ȝeleafan. *c* **950** *Lindisf. Gosp.* Luke iv. 27 Moniȝo hreafo weron..under [Helisaeo] ðæne witȝo. **1340** *Ayenb.* 12 þe uerþe article belongeþ to his passion, þet is to zigge, þet he þolede dyaþ onder pouns pilate. *c* **1375** *Sc. Leg. Saints* ii. (*Paul*) 28 Quhen he come to rome, Wndir fell nero tholit dowme, And ded wes. **1445** in *Anglia* XXVIII. 277 What so evir we loste toforne vndir our princis fele By thi comforte..may soon be yolden ageyn. **1548–9** (Mar.) *Bk. Com. Prayer, Communion*, [He] was crucified also for vs vnder Pontius Pilate. **1565** HARDING *Answ. to M. Ivelles Challenge* 41 b, Soter Byshop of Rome..who suffred martyrdom vnder Antoninus Verus the Emperour. **1618** BOLTON *Florus* Ep. Ded. A 3 b, An heathen man, and living under Trajan the Emperour. **1756–9** BUTLER *Lives of Saints* (1821) XI. 105 Bishop Fisher, who was put to death for his religion under Henry VIII. **1807** SYD. SMITH *Lett. Catholics* i. ¶12 There were as many persons put to death for religious opinions under the mild Elizabeth as under the bloody Mary. **1849** MACAULAY *Hist. Eng.* iii. I. 280 The national wealth..was greater under the Tudors than under the Plantagenets. **1891** FARRAR *Darkn. & Dawn* xxvi, He would have lost his head under Caligula.

b. Similarly with other nouns.

a **1400** *New Test.* (Paues) Heb. vii. 11 For vnder þat presthod þe pepel vnderfong þe lawe. **1641** J. JACKSON *True Evang. T.* II. 89 They are such beasts as while the Law was up,..furnished Gods Altar with Sacrifices, and now under the Gospell, our tables with meate. **1662** STILLINGFL. *Orig. Sacræ* II. vi. §8 The Prophets under the old Testament, when they speak of things to come to pass in the New. **1688** DRYDEN tr. *Life Francis Xavier* I. 39 Overjoy'd, that under his Pontificate, a gate shou'd be open'd to the Gospel, in the Oriental Indies. **1807** SYD. SMITH *Lett. Catholics* i. ¶8 Under the reign of his present Majesty. **1826** LAMB *Popular Fallacy* Wks. 1908 I. 368 But who can show it?.. Under what king's reign is it pretended?

12. a. Denoting subjection to power or force exercised by some person or persons: Beneath the rule or domination of; subject to.

a **950** *O.E. Chron.* (Parker MS.) an. 942, Burȝa fife.. Dæne wæran ær, under Norðmannum nyde ȝebeȝde. *a* **1225** *Leg. Kath.* 1092 He is godd seolf, þe duste deað under him. **1297** R. GLOUC. (Rolls) 9873 Hii..gret raunson him ȝeue, In þraldom as vnder him þere to bileue. *a* **1340** HAMPOLE *Psalter* xvii. 43 þou supplantid rysand in me vndire me. *c* **1400** MAUNDEV. (Roxb.) xxix. 132 Cristen men schall be vnder þaim. **1517** TORKINGTON *Pilgr.* (1884) 63 The havyn of Corfewe, whiche Cite and yle ys vnder the Venycianns. **1526** TINDALE *1 Cor.* xv. 27 It is manifest that he is excepted, which did putt all thynges vnder him. **1610** HEALEY *St. Aug. Citie of God* 122 What liues the citizens lastly led, vnder so huge a bed-roll of gods Guardians!

b. ***under the sea*** (see quots.).

under the weather (*dial.* and *U.S.*): see WEATHER *sb.*

1627 CAPT. SMITH *Seaman's Gram.* ix. 40 When they would lie obscurely in the Sea, or stay for some consort, [they] lash sure the helme a lee, and so a good ship will lie at ease vnder the Sea as wee terme it. **1867** SMYTH *Sailor's Word-bk.* 706 *Under the sea*, a ship lying-to in a heavy gale, and making bad weather of it.

13. a. With abstract or other sbs. denoting authority or control, with or without specification of the person or persons exercising it.

Cf. COMMAND *sb.* 3 d. Also in fig. phrases with HAND *sb.* 35 a, FOOT *sb.* 30 c and 33, THUMB *sb.* 5 a *f, g*, EYE *sb.*[1] 6.

(*a*) *c* **888** K. ÆLFRED *Boeth.* xxxvi. §1 Ðætte æfre swylc yfel ȝeweorðan sceolde under ðæs ælmihtȝan Godes anwalde. *c* **910** *O.E. Chron.* (Parker MS.) an. 901, Se wæs cyning ofer eall Ongelcyn butan ðæm dæle þe under Dena onwalde wæs. **971** *Blickl. Hom.* 99 Eaþmodȝiaþ eow sylfe under þære mihte Godes handa. *c* **1175** *Lamb. Hom.* 13 Murðhe sculen wunian on londe þet bið on griðe and on friðe under mire onwalde. *c* **1200** ORMIN Introd. 35 To ben unnderr deofless þeowwdom. *c* **1340** HAMPOLE *Pr. Consc.* 5884 Prelats..Sal acount yhelde in sere degre Of þair suggets undir þair powere. **1390** GOWER *Conf.* I. 18 So that under the clerkes lawe Men sen the Merel al mysdrawe. **1399** —— *Praise of Peace* 39 Of all the world to winne the victoire, So that undir his swerd it myht obeie. *c* **1450** *Merlin* xxviii. 576 The xix kynges..comaunded alle hem that were vnther theire Iustice that [etc.]. **1457** HARDING *Chron.* in *Eng. Hist. Rev.* Oct. (1912) 744 Compleyntes of wrong alway in general Refourmed were, so vndyr his yerde egall. **1512** *Act 4 Hen. VIII*, c. 19 §4 Every alien & stranger nott borne under the Kynges allegiance & not made Denyzen. *a* **1533** LD. BERNERS *Gold. Bk. M. Aurel.* Z 5 b, Thou shalte tourne to be bonde to theim that are nowe under thy bondage. **1667** MILTON *P.L.* III. 242 Under his gloomie power I shall not long Lie vanquisht. **1754** A. MURPHY *Gray's-Inn Jrnl.* No. 95, In all Ages the Managers of Play-houses have acquiesced under the Gallery-Jurisdiction. **1781–** [see SUPERVISION 1]. **1817** JAS. MILL *Brit. India* II. v. iii. 412 He proposed that it should no longer act under the orders of that Presidency. **1850** *Tait's Mag.* XVII. 366/1 Banking operations come necessarily under its sphere. **1888** *Contemp. Rev.* July 36 A person who is under the direction of amateurish clerks.

(*b*) *c* **950** *Lindisf. Gosp.* Matt. viii. 9 Ic monn amm under mæht. [*c* **1000** *Ags. Gosp.* ibid., Soðlice ic eom man under anwealde.] *a* **1000** *Colloq. Ælfric* in Wr.-Wülcker 102 Forðam cild ic eom under gyrda drohtniende. *a* **1300** *Cursor M.* 12117, þou est vnder [lagh] and þar-in bunden, Bot i am ar þe lagh was funden. *c* **1400** *Rom. Rose* 4923 That he may er he hennes pace Conteyne vndir obedience Thurgh the vertu of pacience. **1565** COOPER *Thesaurus, Subiugo*,..to bryng vnder yoke. **1615** JACKSON *Creed* IV. III. ix. § 1. 348 In the Fort..of the soule, where it hath euery..desire as it were vnder shot, or at..command. **1667** MILTON *P.L.* II. 322 To remaine In strictest bondage,..Under th' inevitable curb. **1682** DRYDEN *Medal* Ep. Whigs, Laws under which we were born. **1784** P. WRIGHT *New Bk. Martyrs* 806/1 He ..was at last taken..by three Moss-troopers, under no discipline. **1832** HT. MARTINEAU *Life in Wilds* Pref. 3 How the universe was formed and under what rules its movements proceed. **1846** RAIKES *Life of Brenton* 125 The Santa Dorothea frigate, then under orders for England. **1890** LD. ESHER in *Law Times Rep.* LXIII. 734/1 Whenever that official acts under the rules ordinarily regulating his duties. **1892** *Photogr. Ann.* II. 397 It must be obvious how much the light is under control.

b. With words denoting guidance or direction.

under correction: see CORRECTION 1 b.

a **1575** tr. *Pol. Verg. Eng. Hist.* (Camden) I. 108 Thei camen home under the conduite of their lodesmanne Fergusius. **1598** HAKLUYT *Voy.* Ep. Ded. ¶3 As..our skill in Nauigation hath hitherto bene very much betterd.. vnder the Admiraltie of your Lordship. **1632–** [see CONDUCT *sb.*[1] 1 *β*]. *a* **1700** in *Cath. Rec. Soc. Publ.* (1911) IX. 336 She was both loved & fear'd by those y[t] had y[e] happines to be under her conduct. **1711** *Spect.* No. 67 ¶6 My eldest Daughter..has for some time been under the Tuition of Monsieur Rigadoon. **1794** MRS. RADCLIFFE *Myst. Udolpho* xxxi, She saw herself at the approach of night under his guidance, among wild and solitary mountains. **1827** FARADAY *Chem. Manip.* xxi. 546 Unless this be done by the experimenter, or under his particular directions, it should be left untouched. **1885** *Law Times* 23 May 63/1 A fourth edition..has just appeared under the editorship of Mr. Charles Burney.

c. With words denoting or implying subjection to, or being the subject of, (*a*) some form of handling or treatment, (*b*) consideration, trial, or notice.

(*a*) **1535**, **1659** [see HAND *sb.* 35 c]. *a* **1670** HACKET *Abp. Williams* II. (1693) 28 The Subject which is now under the Quill is the Bishop of Lincoln. **1706** E. WARD *Wooden World Diss.* (1708) 61 He may with Justice boast, that very few die under his hands. *a* **1719** ADDISON *Virg. Georg.* Wks. 1721 I. 258 That Poem, which lay so long under Virgil's correction, and had his last hand put to it. **1792** COWPER *Let.* 26 Jan., But no laurels are to be won by sitting patiently under the knife of a surgeon. **1837** DISRAELI *Venetia* I. xvi, As the Doctor was under the operation of the barber. **1843** *Blackw. Mag.* LIV. 616, I left him under the hands of his valet. **1884** *Marshall's Tennis Cuts* 234 He is..now under medical treatment.

(*b*) **1652** NEEDHAM tr. *Selden's Mare Cl.* 2 As to what concerns the point of Law, this Question falls chiefly under debate. **1664** *Extr. St. Papers Friends* Ser. III. (1912) 214, I have had them thrice under private examination. **1677** EARL ESSEX in *E. Papers* (Camden) II. 112 The throwing ye man overboard, for w[hi]ch ye Master..of the ship will be brought under question. **1737** *Gentl. Mag.* VII. 660/2 Let me next suppose the Payment now under our Consideration to be made to the Bank. **1780** *Mirror* No. 102, It is not the character itself that falls under my observation. **1827** FARADAY *Chem. Manip.* xii. 278 Any number of parts by volume of the acid under trial. **1849** *Tait's Mag.* XVI. 163/2 The first judge who comes under our notice is William Fitz-Osborne. **1892** *Photogr. Ann.* II. 198 The subject under discussion has nothing to do with chemicals.

d. ***under the plough***, employed as arable land. So ***under cultivation, tillage***, etc.

1795 [see 6 b]. **1805** R. W. DICKSON *Pract. Agric.* I. 296 Land..under an arable system of cultivation. *Ibid.* 314 Soils ..under tillage. **1833** HT. MARTINEAU *Brooke Farm* iv, Lands that have been under the plough for hundreds of years. **1862** ANSTED *Channel Isl.* I. iii. (ed. 2) 37 Of this area, about 10,000 acres are under cultivation.

e. ***under steam***, etc. (Cf. 5 c.)

1839 *Civil Eng. & Arch. Jrnl.* II. 475/2 She can scarcely fail to attain an uncommon speed under steam. **1860**, **1873** [see STEAM *sb.* 7 d]. **1883** *Law Times Rep.* XLIX. 332/1 About to round Blackwall Point under a port helm.

f. *Math.* With sbs. denoting an operation performed.

1901 L. E. DICKSON *Linear Groups* II. xi. 252 *G* contains ..such conjugate cyclic subgroups, all of whose substitutions are conjugate under *G*. **1940** E. T. BELL *Devel. Math.* xx. 394 The constancy of the cross ratio of four collinear points under projection. **1956** E. M. PATTERSON *Topology* iv. 84 y_0 is the image of x_0 under the homeomorphism. **1974** *Encycl. Brit. Macropædia* XI. 657/1 A conic has a central projection that is another conic, but some properties are not preserved under projection.

14. a. With words denoting or implying restraint, confinement, or safe keeping.

a **900** CYNEWULF *Elene* 485 (Gr.), In byrȝenne [he] bidende wæs under þeosterlocan. *a* **1300–** [see LOCK *sb.*[2] 1 b]. **13..–** [see KEY *sb.*[1] 1 b]. *c* **1386–** [see ARREST *sb.*[1] 9 b, 10]. **1495** *Cov. Leet Bk.* 569 þat they be putte vnder suertie fro session vnto session. **1611** FLORIO, *Sottogardia*, vnder guard, keeping or custody. **1629** WADSWORTH *Pilgr.* viii. 90 He left mee alone.., lockt vnder seuen doores. **1645** HOWELL *Twelve Treat.* (1661) 338 Their faculties have a kind of ubiquitary freedom, though the body be never so under restraint. **1689** *Sc. Acts Parlt.* (1875) XII. 50/2 The petitioner was sent for to be brought to the meeting under a gaurd [*sic*]. **1737** in *10th Rep. Hist. MSS. Comm.* App. I. 488 While he was Under confinement He liv'd very magnificently. **1799** *Hull Advertiser* 17 Aug. 2/4 No officer could be landed, the ship being under quarantine. **1841** DICKENS *B. Rudge* 4 Sent under a strong guard to the tower. **1847** [see RESTRAINT *sb.* 2 d].

b. With words denoting an obligation, compact, or formal engagement: Subject to, bound or constrained (legally or morally) by.

1456 SIR G. HAYE *Law Arms* (S.T.S.) 103 Cristin men that ar duelland in the mistrowand menis housis under malis suld be lele to thair malaris. **1538** STARKEY *England* I. iv. 115 Certayn landys were gyuen out..to inferyor personys.. vnder such condycyon that [etc.]. *a* **1548** HALL *Chron., Hen. VI*, 98 b, My Lorde of Winchester..hath subscribed with his awne hande, under the worde of priestehod, to stande at the aduise..of the persones abouesaied. **1626** C. POTTER tr. *Sarpi's Hist. Quarrels* 185 He had particular Commandement from the King his Master, to oblige him vnder the Word of a King, to a neere Vnion with the Republique. **1712** STEELE *Spect.* No. 362 ¶1 All who vend Wines should be under oaths in that behalf. **1790** PALEY *Horæ Paul.* xi. §1 As he was also under a promise to the church of Philippi to see them. **1818** CRUISE *Digest* (ed. 2) IV. 488 A covenant to renew a lease, under the same rent and covenants as those contained in the original lease. **1834** DICKENS *Sk. Boz, Steam Excurs.*, Mr. Samuel, the eldest, was an attorney, and Mr. Alexander, the youngest, was under articles to his brother. **1848** MRS. CARLYLE *Lett.* (1883) II. 26 This time I am under engagement to go. **1861** M. PATTISON *Ess.* (1889) I. 47 Every master was under an obligation..to keep an iron helmet and harness.

15. a. With reference to physical weight or pressure. (Orig. in literal sense.) Also in fig. context.

a **1300** *Cursor M.* 6830 If þou find..Vnder birthin his beist ligand, Help him. *a* **1400** *New Test.* (Paues) 2 Peter ii. 16 He spak not as resonable man, but as a doume beste þat vnder synne was ȝoked. **1591** SPENSER *Ruins of Rome* 161 Th' earth vnder her childrens weight did grone. **1611** BIBLE *Exod.* vi. 6, I will bring you out from vnder the burdens of the Egyptians. **1667** MILTON *P.L.* XII. 539 So shall the World goe on,..Under her own waight groaning. **1714** ADDISON *Spect.* No. 559 ¶7 They wandered up and down under the Pressure of their several Burthens. **1794** MRS. RADCLIFFE *Myst. Udolpho* xxvi, Her reason seemed to totter under the intolerable weight. **1827** FARADAY *Chem. Manip.* xv. 374 The glass vessels intended to retain gases under pressure. **1842** LOUDON *Suburban Hort.* 346 The health of the tree must decline under the load of..imperfectly nourished fruit. **1891** T. HARDY *Tess* iii, The cradle-rockers, ..under the weight of so many children,..were worn nearly flat.

b. With words denoting pains, penalties, or similar consequences: Subject to the risk or certainty of incurring or suffering. Sometimes *ellipt.*

c **1449** [see PAIN *sb.*[1] 1 b]. **1560** [see PENALTY 2 d]. **1599** SANDYS *Europæ Spec.* (1632) 112 Whom they charge under an high degree of mortall sinne and damnation..to appeach even their neerest and dearest friends. **1632** LITHGOW *Trav.* II. 49 Neither may they stay..all night vnder the paine of imprisonment. **1635** PAGITT *Christianogr.* I. iii. 56 Vndoubted verities, and to be believed under the Popes curse. **1665** in *Extr. St. Papers Friends* Ser. III. (1912) 231 [They] shalbe vnder such penalties as the law may inflict vpon them. **1711** STEELE *Spect.* No. 66 ¶5 Under Pain of never having an Husband. **1737** CHALLONER *Cath. Chr. Instr.* (1753) 123 Which is the Case of all who refuse..to comply with any Part of their Duty, to which they are obliged under mortal Sin. **1756** C. LUCAS *Ess. Waters* I. 154 Of these, no subject was permitted to drink under severe penalties. **1820** MILNER *Suppl. Mem. Eng. Cath.* App. 305 An obligation..under the guilt of a grievous sin. **1845** LINGARD *Anglo-Saxon Ch.* II. ix. 67 He..forbade his sons, under their father's malediction, to molest them.

c. With words denoting something oppressive, distressing, or restrictive of free action: In the condition of suffering from, being afflicted or distressed by, etc.

Cf. the use of OE. *under* with words meaning 'grip' or 'grasp'. With somewhat weakened force, the sense occurs frequently with certain words, as *contribution, difficulty, disadvantage, necessity, sentence.*

1382 WYCLIF *Gal.* iii. 10 Who euere ben of the workis of lawe, ben vndir curs. **1512** *Reg. Privy Seal Scotl.* I. 365/2 Thai stand now under accusatioun for crime of tresoun. **1569** *Reg. Privy Council Scot.* I. 682 [He] ressavit fra ilk ane ..the sowme of thre pundis, and yit hes thame under danger of the rest. **1644-** [see CONTRIBUTION 1 b]. **1663** J. SPENCER *Prodigies* (1665) 335 The more modern Rabbins were under a despair of..equalling the Traditional..Commentators upon their Law. **1688** COLLIER *Several Disc.* (1725) 369 The Publishers of it..lay under Discountenance and Persecution from the civil Powers. **1711** *Spect.* No. 116 ¶7 If I was under any Concern, it was on the Account of the poor Hare. *Ibid.* ¶8 A noble Soul struggling under innumerable Pains and Distempers. **1750** JOHNSON *Rambler* No. 6 ¶6 Those that suffer under the dreadful symptom of canine madness. **1779** *Mirror* No. 8, It was with regret that the Editor found himself under the necessity of abridging the following letter. **1806-7** J. BERESFORD *Miseries Hum. Life* II. x, If..it may afford you any consolation under the recollection of a calamity so dreadful. **1849** MACAULAY *Hist. Eng.* v. I. 612 *note*, Wade was writing under the dread of the halter. **1869** FREEMAN *Norm. Conq.* III. xiv. 360 Harold was under the ban of Rome.

d. With reference to mental impressions: Possessed, swayed, or affected by.

1667 MILTON *P.L.* I. 313 Under amazement of their hideous change. **1683** [see MISTAKE *sb.* 2 a]. **1759** [see IMPRESSION 6 b]. **1779** *Mirror* No. 16, A man under the impressions I have described, will be led to look into himself. **1842** LOVER *Handy Andy* xlvi, That Tom wouldn't hurt a fly, only 'under a mistake'. **1849** MACAULAY *Hist. Eng.* v. I. 662 Evidence was produced which proved that Goodenough was also under the influence of personal enmity. **1875** JOWETT *Plato* (ed. 2) I. 395 Are you under the impression that they will be better cared for..here? **1885** [see MISAPPREHENSION].

e. *ellipt.* = Under the influence of.

1884 THOMPSON *Tumours of Bladder* 95 Some phosphatic deposits, which were removed..under ether. **1889** *Science-Gossip* XXV. 220/1 A fixed oil..is obtained from the seeds by expression under heat. **1892** HUGH LANE *Differ. Rheum. Dis.* (ed. 2) 72, I have seen these cases frequently treated.. under chloroform.

III. In senses implying that one thing is covered by, or included in, another.

16. a. Denoting that a thing is presented or observed in a certain form or aspect.

See also KIND *sb.* 13 b, SPECIES 2.

a **1000** *Guthlac* 682 (Gr.), Eom ic þara twelfa sum, þe he ʒetreoweste under monnes hiw mode ʒelufade. *c* **1320** *Cast. Love* 657 Oþer God nis þen he þat..vnder vre wede vre kynde nom. *c* **1450** *Myrr. our Ladye* 189 This hympne ys spoken vnder ful fayre and darke examples. **1561** RASTELL *Confut. Ivelles Serm.* (1565) 128 The people receiued under both kindes. **1586** in *Cath. Rec. Soc. Publ.* (1911) IX. 171 At wch time vi or vii of the said company did communicate..by receaving the sacrament under one kind only. **1659** PEARSON *Creed* xii. 780 Life eternall may be looked upon under three considerations; as Initiall, as Partial, and as Perfectional. **1663** BP. PATRICK *Parab. Pilgr.* xxxvii, Bidding him to take great heed lest under the guise of this Humility..he proved unthankful for Gods favours. **1712** ADDISON *Spect.* No. 419 ¶7 When the Author represents any Passion, Appetite, Virtue or Vice, under a Visible Shape. **1713** —— *Guard.* No. 101, The painter has represented his most Christian Majesty under the figure of Jupiter. **1774** GOLDSM. *Nat. Hist.* VIII. 26 Some insects continue under the form of an aurelia not above ten days. **1817** JAS. MILL *Brit. India* II. v. vii. 608 Under the ignominious light in which imprisonment is regarded by the Indians. **1870** J. H. NEWMAN *Gram. Assent* II. viii. 307 We must contemplate the God of our conscience as a Living Being..under the aspect of this or that attribute. **1879** E. WATERTON *Pietas Mariana Brit.* 225 The several types under which our Ladye was represented in England.

b. With words implying a specious or deceptive appearance. Also *ellipt.* = 'under the pretence of'.

See COLOUR *sb.*¹ 12 d, COVER *sb.* 3 d, COVERT *sb.* 2 c, GUISE *sb.* 5 b, PRETENCE *sb.* 3 b, 4, 6, PRETEXT *sb.*¹, SEMBLANT *sb.* 2, SHOW *sb.*¹ 7 c, VEIL *sb.*¹ 5.

1607 SHAKS. *Timon* III. iii. 33 Like those that vnder hotte ardent zeale, would set whole Realmes on fire.

c. With suggestion of one thing being hidden or disguised beneath another: Beneath the form, guise, or concealment of.

a **1340** HAMPOLE *Psalter* cxxxix. 5 þe snare is endles pyne, þat þai hid vndire delit of syn. **1382** WYCLIF *Pref. St. Jerome* vii. (1850) 70/1 Vndir name of Nynyue, [he] tellith helthe to Gentils. *c* **1400** *Destr. Troy* 11489 He thoght his falshed to feyne, vndur faire wordes. **1592** KYD *Sp. Trag.* III. x. 22 Vnder fained iest Are things concealde that els would breed vnrest. **1723** *Pres. St. Russia* II. 46 The Vagulitzes..have their own Language, and worship the Devil under their Idols. **1779** *Mirror* No. 27, A..friend of mine, whose real name I shall conceal under that of Wentworth. **1854** MRS. JAMESON *Commonpl. Bk.* (1877) 1 Extreme vanity sometimes hides under the garb of ultra modesty. **1857** PUSEY *Doctr. Real Presence* i. 156 A sacramental invisible presence of the Body and Blood of Christ, under the Bread and Wine.

d. *under the name* (etc.) *of*, = by the name of. (See NAME *sb.* 13.)

1641-2 LAUD *Diary* 20 Feb., There came a tall man to me, under the name of Mr. Hunt. **1662** *Extr. St. Papers Friends* Ser. II. (1911) 150 Seuerall Persons who are under the names of Quakers and other names of separacion now in the Goales of London and Middlesex. **1744** BERKELEY *Siris* §268 The Egyptians..had..even deified her under the name of Isis. **1780** *Mirror* No. 80, The authors of those little essays which appear in the learned world under the title of *Advertisements.* **1817** JAS. MILL *Brit. India* II. v. ix. 704 Under the stile and title of a commutation, an additional window tax..was imposed. **1843** PEREIRA *Food & Diet* 120 Hard confectionary, sold under the names of Lozenges, Brilliants, Pipe, Rock, Comfits, Nonpareils. **1876** *Beneden's Anim. Parasites* 75 Naturalists had recognized some crustaceans under the name of *Ancei.*

†**e.** = In (a manner or fashion). *Obs. rare.*

1523 in *Gentl. Mag.* (1785) II. 939/1 I..dyd christen the same childe under this manner. **1532** TINDALE *Exp. Matt.* v. (1550) 22 With greate payne they can suffry their grosse synnes to be rebuked vnder a fassion, as in a parable.

17. a. Denoting inclusion in a group, category, class, etc. †*under (them) all*, in all, altogether.

c **960** ÆTHELWOLD *Rule St. Benet* xvii. (Schröer) 40 Ælc [psalm] on sundron and nan under anum gloria. *a* **1225** *Ancr. R.* 222 þe oðer, & te ueorðe [temptation], ulleð under þe uttre. *c* **1290** *S. Eng. Leg.* I. 59/176 [Francis, Giles, and Bernard] and sethþe oþur þreo, So þat vnder heom alle sixe freres to-gadere weren i-brouȝt. **1297** R. GLOUC. (Rolls) 6998 þe king..ȝef al so Tueie gode maners sein swithin þer to, þat wolde be tuenty vnder al. **1576** FLEMING *Panopl. Epist.* 352 *margin*, Under that word: lightening, thunder,.. mysts, fogges, earthquakes, &c. are to be understoode. **1585** T. WASHINGTON tr. *Nicholay's Voy.* IV. iii. 115 b, The Persians..whiche went vnder the armie of Darius. **1635** PAGITT *Christianogr.* I. ii. (1636) 43 Under these eight provinces all France is conteined. *a* **1662** HEYLYN *Cosmogr.* III. (1674) 173/2 Principal Cities of the whole at this present time under the notion of Cathay, are [etc.]. **1676** *Office Clerk of Assize* F iij, They shall speak without Oath unless the Fact be under Felony. **1711** ADDISON *Spect.* No. 21 ¶2 The rest are comprehended under the Subalterns. **1756** P. BROWNE *Jamaica* p. xxxiii, I have..distributed the species under their proper genera. **1793** SMEATON *Edystone L.* §291 The fitting or adapting the parts of matter together, comes under no calculation in point of time. **1853** *Our Coal-Fields & Coal-Pits* 221 Many matters which would come under this head have already been incidentally mentioned. **1885** *Times* 6 Apr. 7 The owners of travelling booths and circuses come strictly under the class.

b. Denoting occurrence in a particular section or article of a literary work.

1589 HAKLUYT *Voy.* To Rdr. ¶6 Vnder this title thou shalt first finde the old northerne Nauigations of our Brittish Kings. **1728** CHAMBERS *Cycl.* s.v. *Substraction*, Write the less Number under the greater,..as we have directed under *Addition.* **1783** *Encycl. Brit.* (ed. 2) X. 8307/2 Under the article Natural History, Sect. I. it is observed, that [etc.]. **1823** SCORESBY *Jrnl.* 280 The day of the present voyage under which these remarks are introduced. **1846** *Penny Cycl.* Suppl. II. 431 As explained under *House*,..it is frequently necessary [etc.]. **1879** E. WATERTON *Pietas Mariana Brit.* 221 As I have mentioned in the Series under Stowe.

c. *under one*, in one, united(ly), conjointly, together, at one time. *Obs.* exc. *dial.*

Cf. Du. *ondereen*, together, pell-mell.

1596 NASHE *Saffron Walden* Ep. Ded. B ij b, And so [I] leave them..outright to hang, draw, and quarter them al vnder one. **1611** COTGR. s.v. *Chemin*, *Tout d'un chemin*, all vnder one. **1642** D. ROGERS *Naaman* 170 So that he seeks his owne and his Masters advantage both under one. *a* **1667** C. HOOLE *School-Colloquies* (1688) 105 Come, I pray you, and you shall sup with us all under one. **1839-** in *Eng. Dial. Dict.* s.v. *Under* 2.

d. Of figures or angles in relation to the lines determining their size.

1570 BILLINGSLEY *Euclid* II. def. i. 61 Rectangle parallelogrammes which are comprehended vnder equal lines are equal the one to the other. **1660** BARROW *Euclid* I. prop. xlviii, The angle comprehended under those two other sides of the triangle. **1764** [see COMPREHEND *v.* 10]. **1798** HUTTON *Course Math.* II. 124 The rectangles under the sum and difference of the ordinates. **1854** TOMLINSON *Arago's Astron.* 167 The angle under which we see objects.

18. With words denoting protection, care, or benevolent interest.

See also AUSPICE 3, PROTECTION 1 b. To this sense may be assigned the apologetic phrases *under favour* (FAVOUR *sb.* 3 a), *leave, pardon.*

971 *Blickl. Hom.* 41 Ne þurfon ʒe wenan þæt ʒe þæt orceape sellon, þæt ʒe under Drihtnes borh syllaþ. *c* **1230** *Hali Meid.* 7 Se seli sikernesse as ha was in, & mahte beon under Godes warde. *c* **1375** *Sc. Leg. Saints* iii. (*Andrew*) 943 Vndir ȝour proteccione to luf in contemplacione. *c* **1400** [see CARE *sb.*¹ 4]. **1470-85** [see SAFE-CONDUCT *sb.* 1]. **1550** *Reg. Privy Council Scot.* I. 84 Thair is diverse assurit personis.. sittis under assurance duelland within the boundes of the Merse. **1596** *Edward III*, v. i. 111 Vnder safe conduct of the Dolphins seale. **1692** E. WALKER tr. *Epictetus' Mor.* xxxvii, Methinks they've given enough, in that you live Under their prudent Care. **1711** ADDISON *Spect.* No. 106 ¶4 My worthy Friend has put me under the particular Care of his Butler. **1768** [W. DONALDSON] *Life Sir B. Sapskull* I. x. 105 To.. institute an independant academy, under the auspices of that great name. **1803** SCOTT *Let.* in *Lockhart* (1837) I. xi. 392 The *mode* of telling the story approved by the French minstrel, under the authority of his Tomas. **1844** MRS. BROWNING *Drama of Exile* 32, I hold that Eden is impregnable Under thy keeping. **1866** [see PATRONAGE 3]. **1885** *Law Rep.* 14 *Q.B.D.* 867 Even if the plaintiff succeeds the action may have been defended under good advice.

19. a. Denoting a state or condition (frequently one imposed by implied circumstances).

In later use common with *circumstances* (see CIRCUMSTANCE *sb.* 4) and *conditions.* In parenthetical phrases, as *under these circumstances*, the sense passes into 'having regard to', 'taking account of'. For *under way* or *weigh* see the sbs.

c **1200** ORMIN Ded. 9 Þurrh þatt witt hafenn takenn ba An reȝhellboc to follȝhenn, Unnderr kanunnkess had & lif. *Ibid.* 10530 Unnderr Crisstenndom, & unnderr læfe o Criste. *c* **1205** LAY. 395 Assaracus heuede enne broþer, þe wes under wedlac iboren. **1428** *Munim. de Melros* (Bann. Cl.) 519, I wes requerit..for to wytnes vnder wryt þe thyng at wes determynyt befor me in iugement. **1490** CAXTON *Eneydos* xxvi. 93 Thou haste deliuerde me my traytour & peruerse enmye, vnder hope of loue & benyuolence. **1564** *Reg. Privy Council Scot.* I. 276 James Barry..quha allegeit him to be undir the King of Denmarkis wageis. **1581** RICH *Farew.* (1846) 58 She beyng under covert barne, your obligation is unpleadable. **1662** STILLINGFL. *Orig. Sacræ* II. v. §1 A meer seducer was to be stoned to death under sufficient testimony. **1668** PEPYS *Diary* 7 July, Because of Fleet Bridge being under rebuilding. **1689** in *Sc. Acts Parlt.* (1875) XII. 76/1 Such persones as he hes already put under baile. **1712** ADDISON *Spect.* No. 349 ¶7 He died under a fixed and settled Hope of Immortality. **1720** WELTON *Suffer. Son of God* I. viii. 200 All things here are under a perpetual vicissitude and alteration. **1780** M. MADAN *Thelyph.* II. 61 Augustus rejected the testament of a man who died under a state of celibacy. **1817** JAS. MILL *Brit. India* II. v. vii. 607 He knew, under the sentiments which prevailed at home, by what a slender and precarious tenure he enjoyed his place. **1855** BAIN *Senses & Int.* II. i. §11 The physical state of a muscle under contraction may be inferred from the details already given. **1884** DUNCKLEY in *Manch. Exam.* 26 May 6/2 Under the ballot it is as easy to vote as to pay a morning call.

b. *under trust*, in a state of supposed safety. *Obs.* exc. *arch.*

1545 in Tytler *Hist. Scot.* (1864) II. 349 The Lord Maclanis fader was cruellie murdressit under traist, in his bed. **1589** R. ROBINSON *Gold. Mirr.* (1851) 5 Then Mischief calde for treason vndertrust; Helpe now (quoth he) or els I am o'rethrowen. **1609, 1818** [see TRUST *sb.* 5 a].

20. a. Denoting participation in the authoritative or confirmatory effect of a seal, signature, etc.: Authorized, warranted, or attested by.

See also HAND *sb.* 35 d, SEAL *sb.*² 1 c, SIGNET *sb.* 2, 3, SIGN-MANUAL 1.

1338 R. BRUNNE *Chron.* (1810) 288 He kept his castels, his vitaile, his mone, Undere þe kyng seales. *a* **1400-50** *Alexander* 1845, I send to ȝowe my sawe vndir my sele wreten. **1417** [see SIGNET *sb.* 3]. **1460** in *Rec. City of Norwich* (1910) II. 94 If þe cloth be tokened and founde defauty under þe tokene. **1471** K. EDW. IV in *Rep. Hist. MSS. Comm., Var. Coll.* IV. 209 Yeven undir oure signet at oure Paleis of Westminster the xixth day of December. **1546** LANGLEY tr. *Pol. Verg. de Invent.* VII. iv. 135 b, Gregorie the nynth..canonised Dominicke, and by his Bulle vnder Lead, allowed him for a sainct. **1551** in Feuillerat *Revels Edw. VI* (1914) 62 A warrante vnder the kinges Maiesties owne handes. **1592** in J. Morris *Troub. Cath. Forefathers* (1877) 23 And this averred by writing under all or most of his neighbours' hands. **1613** PURCHAS *Pilgrimage* (1614) 215 The bill of diuorce is..deliuered to the woman before three credible witnesses, vnder their hands and seales. **1687** *Assur. Abby Lands* 120 Altho' we have empowered thee..by divers of our Letters, as well made under-Lead as in the Form of Breves. **1765-8** [see SIGNATURE *sb.* 1]. **1838** W. BELL *Dict. Law Scot.* 889 Under this seal commissions of tutory, gifts of bastardy,..are passed.

†**b.** *under (the) name of*, = in the name of. (See NAME *sb.* 11 c.) *Obs.*

1445 tr. *Claudian* in *Anglia* XXVIII. 265 His shrewde seruauntis..Pretendyng evir the Kyngis title..vndir his name þe wrongid. **1535** COVERDALE *Zech.* xiii. 3 Thou shalt dye, for thou speakest lyes vnder the name off the Lorde. **1585** T. WASHINGTON tr. *Nicholay's Voy.* I. x. 12 b, [He] coyned money vnder his name. **1596** SHAKS. *Tam. Shr.* IV. iii. 12 He does it vnder name of perfect loue.

c. Implying a statement or suggestion as to the authorship of a work.

1662 STILLINGFL. *Orig. Sacræ* II. i. §3 Who would ever undertake to prove..that Euclide was the undoubted Author of the *Geometry* under his name? **1712** P. METCALFE *Life St. Winefride* (1917) 5 Altho' the mention'd Author publish'd his Tomes under the Borrow'd Names of Alford, alias Griffith. **1802** MAR. EDGEWORTH *Moral T., Forester* xvi, Our hero..inserted his compositions, under a fictitious signature, in his master's newspaper.

d. = In accordance with (some regulative power or principle).

1779 *Ann. Reg., Chron.* 216/2 Numbers of them had been long supersedable, or intitled to their discharges under insolvent acts. **1867** FROUDE *Short Stud.* Ser. I. I. 47 Under this edict.. more than fifty thousand human beings..were deliberately murdered. **1874** *Nairne Peerage Evidence* 169 That is the lady who was examined under a commission from this House? **1884** *Manch. Exam.* 16 Feb. 4/6 The first contested county election under the provisions of the Corrupt Practices Act.

IV. In senses which imply falling below a certain standard or level.

21. a. Beneath or below in point of worth or dignity.

c **888** K. ÆLFRED *Boeth.* xxxiii. §5 Under hire selfre hio bið þonne, ðonne hio lufað þas eorðlican þing. *Ibid.* xxxvii. §4 Hiora yfelnes awirpð hi under þa menniscan ʒecynd. *a* **1340** HAMPOLE *Ps.* xvii. 40 Til þa þat ere vndire me, ill men vndire me in merit bifor god. **1548** UDALL, etc. *Erasm. Par. Matt.* 100 b, This they thought a goodly prayse, although that it was farre vnder his maiestie. **1598** GRENEWEY *Tacitus, Ann.* III. i. 63 Tiberius and Augusta abstained from mourning in publicke: iudging it a thing vnder their maiestie.

b. Below the rank, standing, or level of.

1610 B. JONSON *Alch.* II. vi, No, sir, shee'll neuer marry Vnder a knight. **1632** MASSINGER & FIELD *Fatal Dowry* IV. i, Fight with Romont? No, I'll not fight under a lord. **1650** FULLER *Pisgah* IV. vii. 123 Nothing under an Infinite can expleat and satiate the immortall minde of man. **1711** ADDISON *Spect.* No. 122 ¶9 It was too great an Honour for any Man under a Duke. **1822** LAMB *Elia* I. *Distant Correspondents*, No person, under a diviner, can..conduct a correspondence at such arm's length. **1847** L. HUNT *Men, Women, & B.* II. vii. 96 He uttered nothing under a gentility or a dulcitude.

22. a. Below, less, or fewer than (a specified number or amount).

c **1380** WYCLIF *Last Age Ch.* (1840) 30 Þat we ben undir þe hundrid ȝeere of .x. lettre I schewe schortly by Bede. **1530** TINDALE *Pract. Prelates* H iij, The Emperours host was vnder xx. thousande. **1557** NORTH *Gueuara's Diall Pr.* II. xi. 95 b, There was a lawe amongeste them, that no man should marye under three wiues. **1590** SIR J. SMYTH *Disc. Weapons* 6 b, In case they should compose smaller bands of 300 to an Ensigne, or vnder that number. **1601** R. JOHNSON *Kingd. & Commw.* (1603) 154 They receiue, some 1000. some 80. rubles a yeare, none vnder 70. **1664** P. HENRY *Diaries & Lett.* (1882) 155 That interdict lasted under 5. yeares. **1699** R. L'ESTRANGE *Erasm. Colloq.* (1725) 174 Sometimes ten, sometimes twelve, but never under six. **1745** H. WALPOLE *Lett.* (1857) I. 406 Repeated accounts make them under five thousand. ? **1800** WORDSW. *Andrew Jones* 28 Under half a-crown, What a man finds is all his own. **1832** MACAULAY in Trevelyan *Life* (1876) I. 287 The voters are under 4,000 in number. **1855** —— *Hist. Eng.* iv. IV. 624 The weight.. proved to be under one hundred and fourteen thousand ounces.

b. Below, not having attained to (a specified age).

c **1400** MAUNDEV. (1839) xxvii. 278 The faireste Damyseles, that myghte ben founde undir the Age of 15 Zere. **1565** COOPER *Thesaurus* s.v. *Minor*, Vnder .xxv. yeres of age. **1570–4** BP. COX *Injunct.* in *2nd Rep. Ritual Comm.* (1868) 406/2 Their chyldren and seruauntes.. beyng of sixe yeres of age, and vnder twentie. **1658** HARRINGTON *Prerog. Pop. Govt.* Wks. (1700) 335 It is provided.. that no man under thirty years of Age be capable of Magistracy. **1692** O. WALKER *Grk. & Rom. Hist.* 9 Then was Augustus under nineteen years old. **1729** JACOB *Law Dict., Nonage*,.. is all the Time of a Person's being under the Age of One and twenty; and, in a special Sense, where one is under Fourteen, as to Marriage, &c. **1825** T. HOOK *Sayings* Ser. II. II. 247 He is *under* fifty-seven. **1885** *Law Rep. 10 P.D.* 189 Till their only child should attain twenty-one, or die under that age.

(*b*) Hence prefixed to a number and used as a *sb. pl.* (usu. with *the*) to denote the class of persons who have not yet attained that particular age. Cf. OVER- 13 b.

1937 E. GARNETT *Family from One End Street* v. 98 John was hopping along.. in a sack race for 'under tens'. **1939** E. R. BOYCE *Infant School Activities* 201 As much provision as possible should be made for the sort of period suggested for the 'under-fives'. **1941** [see CROSS-SECTIONAL *a.*]. **1953** K. TENNANT *Joyful Condemned* xii. 100 He added her to the other two under-sixteens, Else and Violet. **1968** *Catholic Herald* 15 Mar. 12/5 The Cenacle, Grayshott... Retreat for the Under Thirties. **1973** M. AMIS *Rachel Papers* 153 But then, you see, we did the sort of lyrically zany thing that the under-twenties do fairly often.

c. At or for a less sum or lower price than (that specified).

c **1430** LYDG. *Min. Poems* (Percy Soc.) 107 'Thou scapst not here,' quod he, 'under ij. pence'. **1496** *Act 12 Hen. VII*, c. 6 They be sold far under the Price that they be worth. **1583** STUBBES *Anat. Abus.* II. M i, You will not sell a sermon vnder a roiall, or a noble. **1592** *Arden of Feversham* II. ii. 76 But, were my consent to giue againe, we would not do it vnder ten pound more. **1712** STEELE *Spect.* No. 362 ¶1 They can have no advice for him under a Guinea. **1733** TULL *Horse-Hoeing Husb.* 142 *note*, Wheat was under Three Shillings a Bushel. **1831** JAMES *Phil. Augustus* III. i, I should suppose they would never free a knight of his renown under a ransom of ten thousand crowns.

d. In less time than (that specified).

1632 J. HAYWARD tr. *Biondi's Eromena* 114 Great Fleets, which cannot be rigg'd under a great deale of time. **1639** W. MOUNTAGU in *Buccleuch MSS.* (Hist. MSS. Comm.) I. 280 We.. can get none, neither can any be made under three weeks' time. **1711** ADDISON *Spect.* No. 102 ¶4 Flirts and Vibrations [of the fan].. that are seldom learned under a Month's Practice. **1726** LEONI *Alberti's Archit.* I. 29 Cato advises to dig the Stone in Summer.., and not to use it under two Years. **1728** FIELDING *Love in Sev. Masques* I. v, I shall hardly reduce it to any tolerable consistency under a fortnight's course of acids.

e. With less than; of less size, depth, etc., than.

1570 FOXE *A. & M.* (ed. 2) I. 321/2 For commonly he neuer rode vnder a 1500 horses of Chaplaynes, Priestes, and other seruyng men waytyng vpon hym. **1702** *Eng. Theophrast.* 15 They will scarce believe that two and two make four, under a demonstration from Euclid. **1719–20** SWIFT *To Yng. Clergym.* Wks. 1727 II. II. 12, I remember several young men in this town, who could never leave the pulpit under half a dozen conceits. **1795** *Act 35 Geo. III*, c. 20 Sch. A, Ufers.. under eight Inches square. **1867** SMYTH *Sailor's Word-bk., Hand-lead*, a small lead.. for sounding in rivers or harbours under 20 fathoms. **1883** *Rep. Channel Tunnel Comm.* App. Case li. 546 Barbarous orders.. to sink every Spanish ship under 100 tons.

f. *ellipt.*, esp. in ***and under, or under***, placed after statements of size, price, etc.

1482 in *Eng. Hist. Rev.* XXV. 122 The firste and leeste soorte is of vj. ynchesse in lenghte and vndre. **1495** *Act 11 Hen. VII*, c. 61 §1 To lette and demyse fermes ther for the terme of vij yere and undir. **1526** TINDAL *Matt.* ii. 16 All the chyldren,.. as many as were two yere old and vnder. **1576** *Act 18 Eliz.* c. 6 In good Wheate after vjs. viijd. the Quarter or under. *c* **1580** in *Eng. Hist. Rev.* July (1914) 521 Yf you will by 100 Ballettes of woade together they will asshewre it to be good; yf you by under you shall bye it at your owne adventure. **1644** G. PLATTES in *Hartlib's Legacy* (1655) 211 When Barley is at two shillings the bushel, or under. **1670** in *12th Rep. Hist. MSS. Comm.* App. V. 15 Courser [hangings].. your Honour may be served with from Flanders, att 18*s.* per stick or under. **1708** *Lond. Gaz.* No. 4422/7 The Commodore appear'd to be a Ship of 50 Guns, ..and the rest of 20 and under. **1797** *Encycl. Brit.* (ed. 3) XVII. 432/1 Courses and topsails.. for 44 gun ships and under. **1803** BEDDOES *Hygeia* XI. 40 Dr. C... estimates the infecting distance of patients in the plague at a foot or under. **1911** JACQUES in *36th Prov. Meeting Law Soc.* 263 Leaving property worth only £500 or under.

23. a. ***under age*** (or †***years***), below the (legal) age of majority.

1590 SPENSER *F.Q.* II. x. 64 Three sonnes he dying left, all vnder age. **1603** G. OWEN *Pembrokeshire* (1892) 22 William, who was then onder age. **1617** MORYSON *Itin.* I. 274 The Lords of Eriskin.. vse to haue the keeping of the Prince of Scotland, being vnder yeeres. **1632** SHERWOOD, Under-yeares, *mineur, en bas age*. **1765–8** ERSKINE *Inst. Law Scot.* I. vii. §1 But minority.. includes all under age, whether pupils or *puberes*. **1821** KEATS *Cap & Bells* xxi, This was his page, ..Sent as a present, while yet under age, From the Viceroy of Zanguebar. **1843** JARMAN *Wills* (1881) I. xiv. 446 Under the old law.. personalty was.. disposable by the will of a person under age.

b. Below (a certain standard).

See also MARK *sb.*[1] 12 c, PAR *sb.*[1] 3 b, PROOF *sb.* 11.

1615 W. LAWSON *Country Housew. Gard.* (1623) 30 Your graffe.. will grow but to small purpose,.. and lightly it will be vnder growth. **1661** WALTON *Angler* (ed. 3) ii. 52 So many Nets and Fish, that are under the Statute size. **1748** [see PROOF *sb.* 11]. **1799** COLERIDGE *Lett.* (1895) 271 The frost.. was 20 degrees under the freezing point. **1825** J. NEAL *Bro. Jonathan* I. 364 Poor fatty! you know he's rather under par. **1857** MILLER *Elem. Chem., Org.* 121 If the spirit burned off and left the powder damp, it was considered under proof. **1875** E. C. STEDMAN *Victorian Poets* 275 The statement of Bulwer's preface is under the truth.

c. ***under*** (one's) ***breath***, in a low voice, in a whisper.

1832 [see BREATH *sb.* 9 b]. **1883** WHITELAW *Sophocles, Oedipus Col.* 489 Pray, under breath, not lifting up thy voice. **1898** 'MERRIMAN' *Roden's Corner* xv. 155 'Oh, hang!' she added,.. under her breath.

V. †24. Among. *Obs. rare.*

c **893** K. ÆLFRED *Oros.* IV. x. 196 Þa ne mehton þa senatus nænne consul under him findan þe dorste on Ispanie ..ȝefaran. *c* **1205** LAY. 915 Wet speke ȝe kempen vnder eou alle?

†25. a. During; in the time of. *Obs.*

Also *Sc.* †***under ane time***, at the same time.

c **893** K. ÆLFRED *Oros.* I. x. 46 Þa under þæm ȝewinne hie ȝenamon friþ wið þa wæpnedmen. **971** *Blickl. Hom.* 35 Þæt we sceolan under þæm feowertiȝeoþan ȝerime.. syllan þone teoþan dæl ure worldspeda. *c* **1205** LAY. 32028 Vnder þissen uare-coste he sumnede ferde of alle þane monne þat he bi-ȝeten mihte. *c* **1425** *Eng. Conq. Ireland* 8 Vnder that tyme, Robert Steunes-son hym dyght to wend in-to Irland. **1533** BELLENDEN *Livy* I. ix. (S.T.S.) I. 51 Legatis war send on athir side vnder ane tyme desiring redres of all displeseris. **1597** J. PAYNE *Royal Exch.* 5 Now ys the tyme vnder lyfe to help one another; but when.. breathe ys gon, neyther angells nor Apostles can geve any help. **1662** STILLINGFL. *Orig. Sacræ* II. vi. §8 Not that these things should really be under Gospell times. *a* **1670** SPALDING *Troub. Chas. I* (1851) II. 396 Wnder speiking this Williame Forbes schootis the gentilman with ane pistoll deid.

†b. With demonstrative pronouns: During this or that time; meantime, meanwhile. *Obs.*

c **893** K. ÆLFRED *Oros.* II. ii. 66 He.. him ȝehet ðæt he his rice wið hiene dælan wolde, & hiene under ðæm ofsloȝ. *a* **900** *O.E. Chron.* (Parker MS.) an. 876, Hie þa under þam hie nihtes bestælon.. into Escanceaster. *a* **1122** *Ibid.* (Laud MS.) an. 1046, Ða wearð hit under þam þet þam cynge com word [etc.]. *c* **1205** LAY. 6433 Wnder þon hær com tidinde. *Ibid.* 9660 Vnder þan comen tiðende. *a* **1225** *Leg. Kath.* 1858 Under þis com þe þurs Maxence.. aȝein to his kineburh. **1297** R. GLOUC. (Rolls) 2503 Þer come out of germaynie vnder þat.. ssipes eiȝtetene. *a* **1300** *Floriz & Bl.* 635 The children awoken under thon.

under ('ʌndə(r)), *adv.* Forms: 1– **under**, 3–7 **vnder** (6 *Sc.* **wnder**), 4–5 **vndyr**, 5 **vn-**, **undir**, **-dre**, **undur**, **owndir**. [OE. *under*, = OS. *undar* etc.: see prec.]

1. a. Below, down below, beneath.

Beowulf 1417 Wæter under stod, dreoriȝ and ȝedrefed. *Ibid.* 2213 Stiȝ under læȝ eldum uncuð. *a* **900** *O.E. Martyrol.* 5 May 76 Se dæl þære ciricean.. þær þæs hælendes fotlastas sindon under. *c* **1000** ÆLFRIC *Saints' Lives* iv. 393 He.. het þa.. fyr under betan. *c* **1250** *Gen. & Ex.* 3188 Moyses it folwede ðider it flet, And stod ðor ðe graue under let [= lay]. **13..** *Cursor M.* 377 (Gött.), He wroȝt.. þe sky.. wid watir schinand als cristall, þat es on hey, þat es vnder. **1390** GOWER *Conf.* I. 173 And under al aboute he seth The faire lusti floures springe. *c* **1400** MAUNDEV. (Roxb.) iv. 12 Men may see þare þe erthe of þe toumbe.. stirre and moue, as þer ware a qwikke thing vnder. **1422** YONGE tr. *Secreta Secret.* 241 Yf the lyght mettis vndyr be, whan hit is defiet. **1535** COVERDALE *Gen.* xlix. 25 Helped ..with blessynges of heauen from aboue, with blessinges of ye depe y[t] lyeth vnder. **1591** SPENSER *Vis. World's Vanity* 65 A sword-fish.. in his throat him pricking softly vnder. **1648** CRASHAW *Poems* (1904) 152 Storme and Thunder Would sit under, And keepe silence round about thee. **1819** W. TENNANT *Papistry Storm'd* (1827) 48 At anes the bells baith up and under Begoud to rattle on like thunder. **1820** SHELLEY *The Cloud* 10, I wield the flail of the lashing hail, And whiten the green plains under.

b. With verbs expressing or implying movement.

†***to look under***, to look down (LOOK *v.* 44).

a **1120** *O.E. Chron.* (Laud MS.) an. 1083, Þa wreccan munecas laȝon onbuton þam weofode & sume crupon under. *c* **1400** *Destr. Troy* 1297 Þen the Troiens.. Gird euyn to the Grekes with a grym fare,.. Wondit of þe wightist, warpide hom vnder. **1539** BIBLE *1 Kings* xviii. 23 Let them.. laye hym on wodd, and put no fyre vnder. **1608** SYLVESTER *Du Bartas* II. iv. *Schism* 1012 Like as a Roach, or Ruff, or Gudgeon.. Frisks to and fro, aloft and under dives. **1818** BYRON *Juan* I. cliii, There is the closet, there the toilet, there The antechamber—search them under, over. **1846** SOYER *Cookery* 176 Saw the rib bones asunder in the middle; pass your knife under.

2. In special senses: **a.** Beneath the rider.

c **1100** *O.E. Chron.* (MS. D) an. 1079, His hors wearð under of-scoten.

b. Lower down on a page, etc.

Chiefly in combs., as ***under-mentioned, -named, -specified***; cf. also HEREUNDER *adv.* †***to seal under***: see SEAL *v.*[1] 4.

c **1362** [see UNDERWRITTEN *ppl. a.*]. **1474** *Cov. Leet Bk.* 390 These ben the names vnder folowyng of the Collectours. **1786** BURNS *Inventory* 74 This list,.. I wrote it, Day an' date as under notit. **1892** *Photogr. Ann.* II. 257, I have designed a slide as under.

c. Below the garments; on the inner side of a garment.

c **1400** *Brut* clxxviii. 199 He.. smote him wyþ a knyf; but þe false traitoure was armed vnder, so þat þe stroke myght done him none harme. **1457** *Sc. Acts Jas. II*, c. 13 Þat na woman weir.. talys of vnsittande lenthe nor furryt vnder bot on þe haliday.

d. Of the sun, etc.: Below the horizon; set.

c **1489** CAXTON *Sonnes of Aymon* i. 46 Nyghe was the sonne vnder, and it was well aboute complyn tyme. *Ibid.* xiv. 346 Whan reynawd sawe all redy that ye sonne was goon vndre, & that the nyght cam fast on. **1609** SKENE *Reg. Maj.* 104 He may cast the Proces, saying, that.. it was made vnlawfullie vnder Sunne. **1850** R. G. CUMMING *Hunter's Life S. Afr.* (1902) 93/2 The sun was under before I laid him low. *Ibid.* 118/2 The moon was now under, and it was very dark. **1859** MEREDITH *R. Feverel* xxxiv, The sun was under.

e. Under water; submerged.

1830–1873 [see GUNWALE b]. **1890** *Cent. Dict.* s.v. *Rail*, The vessel sailed rail under.

f. ***down under***, in the Antipodes.

1899 *Westm. Gaz.* 1 June 5/1 He had once made 74 for Australia against England 'down under'.

3. a. Into a position or state of subjection or submission. (See also BRING *v.* 26, GET *v.* 79.)

c **1250** *Gen. & Ex.* 4041 Of ðe sal risen.. a wond ðe sal smiten riȝt Moab kinges, and under don Al sedes kin ðis werld up-on. *a* **1300** *K. Horne* 1420 (Camb.), To schupe we mote draȝe; Fikenhild me haþ i-don vnder. **1390** GOWER *Conf.* I. 5 Love, which doth many a wonder And many a wys man hath put under. *Ibid.* 117, I that lawe obeie Of which the kinges ben put under. **1509** HAWES *Past. Pleas.* VI. (Percy Soc.) 26 It is alwaye at mannes pleasaunce To take the good and caste the evyll under. **1567** MAPLET *Gr. Forest* 1 Wherefore the Greekes call it Fickleforce, for that it can not be brought under. **1646** DRUMM. OF HAWTH. *Answ. to Objections* Wks. (1711) 214 We are not brought to such a Nonplus, and so under,.. but that we dare both say and maintain, They proceed unjustly with us. **1723** *Lockhart Papers* (1817) II. 112 Both the contending partys did desire to promote unity and peace, provyded their opponents would knock under. **1791** *Ann. Reg., Chron.* 4* The fire was got under. **1852** MRS. STOWE *Uncle Tom's C.* xxix, I've begun now to bring them under. **1882** [see KNUCKLE *v.* 2].

b. In subjection or submission; in a subordinate or inferior position.

13.. *K. Alis.* 3054 (Laud MS.), For no power, ne for no wonder, ȝitt ne weren we neuer vnder. *c* **1460** *Oseney Reg.* 19 Know he hym-selfe gilty,.. And be he vndur to þe streyte veniaunce in þe last dome. **1463** G. ASHBY *Prisoner's Refl.* 292 The ryche slepeth, the pore laboreth vnder. **1480** *Robt. Devyll* 341 Nowe the people dyd wonder To se that all knyghtes to hym wer vnder. **1568** GRAFTON *Chron.* II. 330 Why should we then be so kept vnder lyke beastes and slaues? **1598** R. BERNARD tr. *Terence, Andria* I. i, How couldst thou know his nature,.. whilst.. awe and his master kept him vnder? **1611** BIBLE *1 Cor.* ix. 27 But I keepe vnder my body, and bring it into subiection. **1647** N. BACON *Disc. Govt. Eng.* I. xvii. 54 The new stemme of Kingly power.. sucked much from them, and kept them under. *a* **1700** EVELYN *Diary* 15 Aug. 1687, The King keeps them under by an army of 40,000 men.

c. ***to go under***: see GO *v.* 95.

d. In a state of unconsciousness; below the level of consciousness; *spec.* under anaesthetic, in a trance. Also, under the influence of alcohol. *colloq.*

a **1936** 'G. ORWELL' *Shooting Elephant* (1950) 28 Doctors ..thinking it funny to start operating before you were properly 'under'. **1946** K. TENNANT *Lost Haven* (1947) xix. 332 Well, one night when I was down at the pub, this cove ..is beside me and he's well under. **1960** M. SPARK *Bachelors* vii. 98 He attempted to question me while I was under the other night. **1979** D. ANTHONY *Long Hard Cure* xxvii. 207, I.. stretched out on my bed, and let the music take me under.

4. With preps. **†a.** ***at under***, in an inferior place or position; in subjection. *Sc. Obs.*

1375 BARBOUR *Bruce* VII. 365 For he ves put at vndir swa, That he ves left all hym allane. *c* **1425** WYNTOUN *Cron.* V. x. 2396 Dycius.. held þaim euer at vnder ay. **1456** SIR G. HAYE *Law Arms* (S.T.S.) 36 Sum men wenis to be at outhe and abune that is at undir. **1500–20** DUNBAR *Poems* l. 23 He hes att warslingis beine ane hunder, ȝett lay his body nevir at wnder. **1573** J. TYRIE in *Cath. Tract.* (S.T.S.) 3 Sufficient to put at vnder the euill foundet fortres my aduersar hes builded. **1652** URQUHART *Jewel* 197 The cruelty of whose perverse zeal, will keep the effects of his vertue still at under. **1677** GILPIN *Dæmonol.* (1867) 153 They kept them at under, as captives in a dungeon.

b. ***from under***, from below.

1535 COVERDALE *Amos* ii. 9, I destroyed his frute from aboue, and his rote from vnder. **1611** BIBLE *Ezek.* xlvii. 1 The waters came downe from vnder from the right side of the house.

c. ***to get out*** (***stand***, etc.) ***from under***, to escape or get away from a dangerous or awkward situation. *colloq.* (orig. *U.S.*).

[**1857** *Chicago Times* 6 Oct., To enable me to stand from under the present crash, I shall offer my entire stock for the next 30 days at a great sacrifice.] **1861** *Cincinnati* (Ohio) *Commercial* 24 Apr. (*heading*) Stand from under. **1875** *Scribner's Monthly* Nov. 124/2 The system is rotten.. and, if the nation cares for its life, the quicker it gets 'out from under' the better. **1916** *Lit. Digest* (N.Y.) 8 Jan. 88/2 The next to 'get from under'. **1916** 'TAFFRAIL' *Pincher Martin* iii. 35 Shouts of 'stand from under!' and empty bags came from the deck above. **1938** *New Statesman* 20 Aug. 298/2 The extension of anti-Semitic persecution in the business field [in Germany] has probably led to a certain amount of 'getting out from under' sales by Jews. **1951** H. McCLOY *Alias Basil Willing* xiv. 178 I'll get out from under by going to the police myself before anyone else. **1966** 'H. Calvin' *Italian Gadget* ix. 143 Maybe you'll come some day... If I ever get from under Count Capucci. **1974** 'J. Ross' *Burning of Billy Toober* xvi. 157 I'll buy you a dinner when I get out from under.

5. Less in amount, etc.; lower in price.

1574 W. Bourne *Regiment for Sea* ii. (1577) 9b, The Epacte sheweth the age of the Moone or chaunge day, within 12 houres under or over. **1632** Lithgow *Trav.* iv. 137 The price of a virgin was too deare for him,..and widdowes were farre vnder.

6. ***under and over***, a gambling game with dice.

1890 *Newcastle Even. Chron.* 26 Dec. 3/1 Fined..on a charge of playing 'under and over' with the dice and box.

†**'under**, *v. Obs.*$^{-1}$ [f. under *adv.*] *trans.* To cast down, depress.

1502 Atkynson tr. *De Imitatione* iii. xxxviii. 227 As longe as the symple entent of his soule amonge all suche varyacyons is nat vndered, but dyrecte to me contynually.

under- ('ʌndə(r)), *prefix*[1], representing OE. *under-*, = OS. *undar-*, OHG. *untar-*, ON. *undir-*, etc. (see under *prep.*). In OE. about eighty words with this prefix are recorded, but only fifteen or sixteen of these are of frequent occurrence. Of the total number about fifty are verbs, and twenty-five nouns, the adjectives being few and rare. In OHG. there are also many examples both of verbs and nouns, in ON. of nouns only; on the other hand there are few recorded examples in OS., and none in Gothic.

2. In OE. (as in OHG.) a considerable number of the compounds with *under-* were clearly suggested by Latin forms with *sub-* (*suc-*, etc.) and occur only as renderings of these, e.g. *underberan*, supportare, sustinere; *underbéᵹed*, subjectus; *underbrǽdan*, *-breᵹdan*, substernere; *undercerrende*, subvertens; *undercuman*, subvenire. The frequency of such forms no doubt contributed greatly to establish the vogue of the prefix in ordinary use. The practice of rendering L. *sub-* by *under-* is extensively followed in the earlier Wycliffite version of the Bible, and gives rise to a large number of unique or unusual forms, as *underburn*, *-cry*, *-drench*, *-grow*, *-heave*, *-hile*, *-join*, *-laugh*, *-lead*, *-minister*, *-mow*, etc., which are illustrated below, together with some others occurring in the anonymous translation of the Pauline Epistles. Similar examples are occasionally found in other ME. translated texts, as *underorn*, *-slake* (q.v.), after L. *subornare*, *summitigare*.

1382 Wyclif *Nahum* ii. 13 And Y shal *vndre brenne [L. *succendam*] thi cartis of foure horsis. —— *Gen.* xxxix. 14 Whanne Y hadde *vndercried [L. *succlamassem*],..he forsoke the mantil that I heelde. —— *Luke* xxiii. 21 Thei vndircryeden [L. *succlamabant*], seyinge, Crucifie, crucifie him. —— *Exod.* xv. 10 The see couerde hem; and thei ben *vnder dreynt [L. *submersi*] as leed in hidows watris. *a* **1400** *Pauline Ep.* (Powell) Gal. ii. 4 þe false breþerene þe whyche *vndyrentredyn [L. *subintroierunt*] to spye oure freenesse þat we hafe in iesu crist. **1382** Wyclif *Gen.* xxvi. 13 He ȝede profytynge and *vndurgrowynge [L. *succrescens*] to the tyme that he was maad hugeli greet. —— *Exod.* xxiii. 5 If thow se an asse of hym that hatith thee lye vnder the charge,..thow shalt *vnderheue [L. *sublevabis*] with hym. —— *Num.* xii. 14 Whether shulde she not..seuen days with reednes be *vnder-hilid [L. *suffundi*]? —— *Ps.* Prol., Heer also is taȝt.. what bi penaunce be purchasid, whan he *vnderioyneth, 'I shal teche wicke men thi weies'. —— *Ecclus.* xiii. 7 And *vnder laȝhende [L. *subridens*] hope he shal ȝyue, tellende to thee alle goodes. —— *Ezek.* xxiii. 3 There the breestis..of hem ben *vndirled [L. *subacta*]. —— *Ecclus.* xxxix. 39 Alle the werkes of the Lord [are] good; and ech werk in his hour shal *vndermynestren [L. *subministrabit*]. —— *1 Tim.* v. 10 If she vndirmynistride to men suffringe tribulacioun. *a* **1400** *Pauline Ep.* (Powell) Eph. iv. 16 On whom alle þe body is.. knyt to gydere by alle þe ioynture of *vndermynystracion [L. *subministrationis*]. **1382** Wyclif *Ps.* xxxiv. 16 Thei *vndermouwiden [L. *subsannaverunt*] me with vndermouwing. —— *Rom.* Prol., He writeth therfore to the Romaynes, the whiche..wolden with proud contencioun *vnderpoten either other. —— *Gen.* xxvii. 36 Now secounde he hath *vnder rauyshide [L. *surripuit*] my benysoun. —— *1 Sam.* ii. 7 The Lord..mekith, and *vndurrerith [L. *sublevat*]. —— *Acts* xxvii. 4 We *vndirsaileden [L. *subnavigavimus*] to Cypre, for that wyndis weren contrarie. —— *Acts* xxvii. 17 The vessel *vndirsent [L. *summisso*], so thei were borun. *a* **1400** *Pauline Ep.* (Powell) Col. ii. 19 þe hed, of whom alle þe body is bildid in to one þurgh coniunccions and *vnderseruyd [L. *subministratum*] þurgh þe bondys of charite. **1382** Wyclif *Eph.* iv. 16 Al the body sett to gidere, and boundyn to gidere by ech ioynture of *vndir-seruyng [L. *subministrationis*]. —— *Deut.* xxxii. 22 Fier is *vndurtent [L. *succensus*] in my woodnes. —— *Ps.* xvii. 9 Colis ben vndertend of hym. —— *Dan.* viii. 3 Oo wether..hauynge heeȝ horns, and oon heeȝer than an other, and *vndrewexinge [L. *succrescens*]. —— *1 Sam.* Prol., Fro thens thei *vndurweuyden Sophym, that is, the book of Jugis. —— *Gen.* xxvii. 37 Alle his britheren I haue *vndir ȝockid [L. *subjugavi*] to the seruyce of hym. —— *Nehemiah* v. 5 We han vnder ȝokid our sonus and oure doȝtris in to seruage.

3. In combination both with verbs and with nouns various senses of the prefix were already developed in OE., and further variations have arisen in the later language, the starting-point for new developments being usually the Elizabethan period. In most of its senses *under-* can be freely employed to form new compounds, the meaning of which is obvious except when they are used in some special or technical connexion. In some of these general types *under-* is correlative to over-, and not infrequently the actual compound in *under-* is entirely due to the previous use of one in *over-*.

In the following sections a number of the more casual formations are given by way of illustration; those which have a more permanent character, or which for some reason require special treatment, are entered in their alphabetical places as main words. The uses which are most capable of giving rise to new formations, of which complete enumeration is impossible, are 4 a, 5, 6, 9, 10 a, b. Altogether the senses of the prefix may be classed under four heads:—

I. Denoting local position.

4. With verbs. The following variations are found in OE. and in the later language: **a.** Denoting action (or continuance of a state) carried on under or beneath something, as OE. *underberan* to support from below, *underdelfan* to dig beneath, *underetan* to eat away, to sap, *underiernan* to run beneath, etc., ME. *undercut*, *-dig*, *-grow*, *-hole*, *-mine*, *-pitch*, *-shore*, *-strew*, and the later *underbind*, *-brace*, *-build*, *-gird*, *-hew*, etc. **b.** Denoting the action of moving so as to be or to get under something, as OE. *underflówan* to flow under, *underhníᵹan* to descend beneath, *underscéotan* to pass under; ME. *undercreep*; also with causative force, as OE. *underbreᵹdan* to spread under, *underdón* to put under, *understingan*, to thrust under, ME. *underput*, *-set*. Additions to this group are not frequent in the later language, but occur in *undercrawl*, *-dive*, *-run*, *-work*, and with slight variation of sense in *underpeep*, *-peer*. **c.** Rarely, the sense of 'from below' is found, as in *underpeep*, *redden*, *-shine*.

In the dictionaries of Florio (1611) and Hexham (1647), *under-* is used in the above senses to form a number of compounds which are merely suggested by Italian forms in *sog-*, *sop-*, *sot(to)-* and Dutch in *onder-*, as *underbend*, *-knit*, *-loft*, *-mark*, *-note*, *-roof* (Florio), *underfume*, *-gripe*, *-lift*, *-press*, *-smoke* (Hexham). In addition to verbs, the following miscellaneous examples include instances of the ppl. adj. and agent-noun.

c **1900** *Buck's Handbk. Med. Sci.* VIII. 142 (Cent. Suppl.), The building is very solidly built, but *undercellared only. **1890** Nasmith *Cotton Spinning Mach.* x. 148 The '*under clearer' spring is attached to the roller beam. **1892** —— *Students' Cotton Spinning* ix. 329 An underclearer D', is sustained below the bottom front rollers. **1883** A. Dobson *Old-World Idylls, Dead Letter* iii, Bonzes with squat legs *undercurled. **1828–32** Webster, **Underditch*, v.t., to form a deep ditch or trench to drain the surface of land. **1904** *Nature* 13 Oct. 593/2 An *underfolded and underthrust knot of younger strata. *a* **1825** Forby *Voc. E. Anglia*, **Under-grub*, to undermine. **1808** Coleridge *Lett.*, *to T. Jeffrey* (1895) 537 When I first wrote it I *undermarked it. **1839** *Q. Rev.* LXIII. 415 No accuracy in *underpiling the platform is thus practicable. **1846** tr. *Port Royal Method Grk. Tongue* 8 The three *under-pointed [Greek vowels], ᾳ, ῃ, ῳ. **1866** G. M. Hopkins *Jrnls. & Papers* (1959) 138 The meadows yellow with buttercups and *under-reddened with sorrel. **1864** Kingsley *Roman & T.* p. liv, We shall believe not merely in an over-ruling Providence, but (if I may dare to coin a word) in an *under-ruling one. **1800** Hurdis *Fav. Village* 132 Behold! where now he *undersaps the sward. **1846** Landor *Imag. Conv.* Wks. I. 472/2 One hath fallen the moment when he had reached the last step of the ladder, having *undersawed it for him who went before. **1877** Blackie *Wise Men* 119 The hidden working of the travelling fire That *underscoops the earth. **1879** Lanier *Poems, To B. Taylor* 2 To range, deep-wrapt, along a heavenly height, O'erseeing all that man but *undersees. **1885** W. K. Parker *Mammalian Descent* vii. 169 We have a..ploughshare bone large and long in proportion to the..beam which it *undersplices. **1889** *Voice* (N.Y.) 28 Nov., A pure serious aim *undersweeps his work and comes out in it like a transfiguration. **1893** *Amer. Jrnl. Sci.* XLV. 306 (*heading*), *Underthrust Folds and Faults.

d. A noun of action with *under-* may have the same form as the verb, as *undercut*, *-gnaw*, *-hang*, *-lay*, *-lie*, *-lift*, *-mine*, *-run*, *-score*, *-spin*, *-thrust*.

1895 J. J. Raven *Hist. Suffolk* 1 The coast line has suffered, and still suffers, from the constant undergnaw of the German Ocean.

5. With nouns: **a.** In names of garments worn under other articles of clothing, found in OE. *underhwítel*, *-syrc*, but not common till the 16th century, when *undercap*, *-forebody*, *-frock*, *-garment*, *-girdle*, *-sleeve* occur. The following are examples of recent or less usual compounds.

Contrasted with over 8 c, and in modern use sometimes replaced by sub- 3.

1873 *Young Englishwoman* Apr. 194/1 (*heading*) *Under-bodice of jaconet, insertion, and lace. **1895** *Daily News* 24 Dec. 6/3 The chiffon under-bodice being visible between the two sides. **1611** Florio, *Sottomanto*, an *vnder-cloake, a Cassocke. **1894** 'G. Egerton' *Keynotes* 177 They [*sc.* trousers] ruck up at the knees, and show the end line of his *under-drawers quite plainly. **1859** *Habits of Gd. Society* iii. 144, I should like to know how often the advocates of linen change their own *under-flannel. **1960** 'E. McBain' *See them Die* (1963) iii. 28 Murchison..tugged at his *undershorts, and wondered if it was any cooler upstairs. **1978** W. F. Buckley *Stained Glass* xii. 129 She had opened the door, exhilarated at the prospect of seeing Paul lying there as she so regularly came on him, dressed only in his undershorts. **1922** Joyce *Ulysses* 321 The bride..looked exquisitely charming in a creation carried out in green mercerised silk, moulded on an *underslip of gloaming grey. **1968** B. Hines *Kestrel for Knave* 23 His mother was standing in her underslip, a lipstick poised at her mouth. **1857** in A. V. G. Allen *Life Phillips Brooks* (1900) I. vi. 209 Thick winter *underwaists and socks. *a* **1911** D. G. Phillips in *Hearst's Mag.* (1916) Feb. 137/1 She bought a pair of shoes for a dollar,..two underwaists for a quarter.

b. Denoting that the thing specified is either placed below something else, or is the lower in position of two similar things; the two cases are only clearly distinguishable when it is usual for the things to go in pairs. The use is very rare in OE. and ME., but begins to extend in the 16th century and is common from the 17th. When pairs of things are contrasted, *under-* becomes equivalent to *lower* (as *over-* to *upper*), and readily assumes an adjectival function: see under *a.* 1 b.

1878 P. H. Carpenter in *Quart. Jrnl. Microsc. Sc.* XVIII. 366, I shall shortly show that these second or *under basals are also present in the calyx of *Pentacrinus briareus*. **1889** *Science-Gossip* XXV. 261/1 A starling was found..having its *under-beak evidently shot off. **1611** Cotgr., *Soupoultreau*, an *vnder-beame. **1862** in Veness *El Dorado* (1866) App. 140 An *under-box for a pump. **1707** Mortimer *Husb.* 363 To rub off all the *Under-buds, leaving only a few near the top to draw up the Sap. **1738** Chambers *Cycl.* s.v. *Letter*, Printers distinguish their letters into capital..or upper-case letters,..and minuscule, small, or *under-case letters. **1890** Nasmith *Cotton Spinning Mach.* Index, *Undercasings for carding machine. **1892** —— *Students' Cotton Spinning* iv. 112 The relative position of the..knives and undercasing. **1690** C. Nesse *O. & N. Test.* I. 23 If the outside and the *underceiling..of this glorious room be so glittering. **1875** W. McIlwraith *Guide Wigtownshire* 7 Many of these smugglers had *under-cellars in their houses of concealment. **1611** Florio, *Sotto camera*, an *vnder-chamber. **1906** Galsworthy *Man of Property* I. iii. 44 Between the points of his stand-up collar,..the pale flesh of his *underchin remained immovable. **1978** J. A. Michener *Chesapeake* 19 The geese [had]..jet-black head and neck, snow-white under-chin. **1805** Wordsw. *Prel.* vi. 227 Her exulting outside look of youth And placid *under-countenance. **1852** Mrs. Craik *Agatha's Husb.* xx. 281 He took out a paper,..tore it open—tore likewise an *under-cover addressed to his wife. **1845** M. Pattison *S. Langton* in *Lives Eng. Saints* vii. 124 A more honourable place..than the damp and dark *undercrypt. **1611** Florio, *Sottotazza*, an *vnder-cup of essay. **1897** *Daily News* 1 Jan. 6/6 After a diver has been down to examine the *under-fittings of the Delta. **1611** Cotgr., *Beisle*, th' Orelop, or *vnder-hatches, of a ship. **1867** Augusta Wilson *Vashti* xxxv, There were tears hanging..on the long jet *under-lashes. **1841** *Florist's Jrnl.* (1846) II. 266 They are natives of the table land of Mexico,..wholly below the *underlimit of frost. **1611** Florio, *Sopalco*, an *vnder-loft, or sellar, or seeling. **1895** *Archæol. Æliana* XVII. ii. 287 It has apparently been moved..for use as an *underpacking when the Early English arcade was built. **1855** *Poultry Chron.* II. 498 How again can they avoid mistakes when half the birds are hidden in dark *under-pens? **1730** A. Gordon *Maffei's Amphith.* 402 The Pedestal or *Under-Pilaster. **1871** tr. *Schellen's Spectr. Anal.* xxv. 87 This micrometer consists..of a sliding-plate,..[and] an *under-plate on which the first plate travels. **1598** Florio, *Sopportico*, an *vnderporch. **1839** Carlyle *Lett.* (1904) I. 158 Chorley's under jaw went like the hopper or *under-riddle..of a pair of fanners. **1883** Gresley *Gloss. Coal-m.* 234 **Under-rope* [= S-rope, the winding rope which passes round the under side of the drum]. *Ibid.* 268 **Under-seams*, lower or deeper coal seams. **1733** W. Ellis *Chiltern & Vale Farm.* 128 The Drip of their Heads falling upon their *Under-shoots. **1883** F. Day *Indian Fish* 28 Where large *under-sluices are present, fish can pass up such when open. **1843** *Civil Eng. & Arch. Jrnl.* VI. 265/2 A cross sheth..to be bolted down to the *undersole. **1877** Ruskin *St. Mark's Rest* iv. (1894) 49 With such solid *under-support that, from 1480 till now, it stands rain and frost! **1902** *Westm. Gaz.* 29 Jan. 9/2 A large Government order for 20 *undertrucks and 150 complete wagons. **1822** J. Parkinson *Outl. Oryctol.* 150 *note*, Attached to an operculum, or *undervalve.

c. Denoting position below a surface or covering, or at a depth. Examples of this occur from the 17th century, but are not common until the 19th.

1856 Kane *Arct. Expl.* II. i. 26, I hope that the *under-bottom ice exceeds that height. **1892** Meredith *Poet. Wks.* (1912) 325 There chimed a bubbled *underbrew With witch-wild spray of vocal dew. **1894** Crockett *Raiders* (ed. 3) 286 The rippling tide..swirling in the smooth places with an oily *underbubble. **1930** *Engineering* 15 Aug. 197/3 The [U.S.] War Department..imposed the limiting conditions of 100 feet *under-clearance above the level of mean high water. **1967** *Jane's Surface Skimmer Systems 1967–68* 64/1 Riser bars may be used, depending on load underclearance. **1869** J. Martineau in *Life* (1902) I. 446 How curiously the religious tendency..finds an *under-course, and breaks out at unexpected points! *a* **1930** D. H. Lawrence *Last Poems* (1932) 7 As if any Mind could have imagined a lobster dozing the *under-deeps. **1858** Caswall *Poems* 192 Up from the *underdepth unsearchable of primal Being. **1897** Mary Kingsley *W. Africa* 257 Hour after hour..we passed on, in the *under-gloom of the great forest. **1885** Mabel Collins *Ld. Vanecourt's Dan.* I. vi. 80 The light..brought out a warm *underglow in her hair. *a* **1825** Forby *Voc. E. Anglia*, **Under-grup*, an under-drain; a concealed water course in wet soils. **1611** Florio, *Sotto-stanza*, an *vnder-lodging. **1913** —— *Love Poems & Others* 27 And even in the watery shells that lie Alive within the oozy *under-mire, A grain of this same fire I can descry. **1943** *Mind* LII. 135 These instincts or reflexes are the second point of contact where behaviour science, factually though not methodologically, rests upon its biological *understructure.

1980 *Dædalus* Spring 99 Stories about dreams..often deliberately obfuscate the understructure of common sense. **1856** Ruskin *Mod. Paint.* IV. v. xv. §2 The most fantastic.. curves, governed by some grand *under-sweep like that of a tide. **1899** B. Capes *Lady of Darkness* xviii. 151 There must be *underwarmth somewhere for the surface so to flower into colour.

d. Denoting something which is either covered (completely or partially) by, or is subordinate to, something of the same kind. An early example of this is *underwood* (1325), followed by *undergrowth*, *-shrub* (*c* 1600). Other examples are mostly of recent date, and show considerable extension of the usage, as in *underfleece*, *-fur*, *-marking*, etc.

1873 E. Spon *Workshop Receipts* Ser. I. 420/1 The colour should be a trifle darker than the undergraining. **1901** *Smithsonian Rep.* 405 Where sheep have been allowed to graze..the under-vegetation is destroyed. **1909** Mrs. Smith Lewis *Codex Climaci Rescr.* Introd. p. xiii, The under-script of a palimpsest is seldom homogeneous. **1914** D. H. Lawrence in *Eng. Rev.* Feb. 305 And lamps like venturous glow-worms steal among The shadowy stubble of the under-dusk. **1916** —— *Amores* 137 Bright blue crops Surge from the under-dark to their ladder-tops. **1917** —— *Look! We have come Through!* 48 Over there is Russia—Austria, Switzerland, France, in a circle! I here in the undermist on the Bavarian road. *Ibid.* 120 Where the seed sinks in To the earth of the under-night Where all is silent. **1922** —— in *Eng. Rev.* June 509 Fishes, with their gold-red eyes, and green-pure gleam, and under-gold. **1923** —— *Kangaroo* i. 8 It..was like a whole country with towns and bays and darknesses. And all lying mysteriously within the Australian underdark, that peculiar lost, weary aloofness of Australia. **1929** —— *Pansies* 17 Twilight thick underdusk.. While darkness submerges the stones. **1934** T. S. Eliot *Elizabethan Essays* 190 What distinguishes poetic drama from prosaic drama is a kind of doubleness... The drama has an under-pattern, less manifest than the theatrical one.

e. With the sense of 'situated on the under side'.

1888 *Century Mag.* XXXVI. 703/1 Its head and back are blue, its throat and breast red, and its underfeathering white. **1902** Cornish *Naturalist Thames* 45 The parti-coloured grey and yellow under-colouring of their wings.

II. Denoting inferiority in rank or importance.

6. a. With designations of persons, esp. of subordinate officers or officials. This use occurs in OE. in *undercyning*, *-diacon*, *-ȝeréfa*, *-ládtéow*, *-þéow*, becomes common in ME., and is extensively employed from the latter part of the 16th century. The meaning is however as frequently expressed by sub- 5 a and 6.

Examples of *under-* prefixed to a term of general import are rare, but *underman* occurs in the 14th cent., *underbeing*, *underfellow* in the 16th, *underswain* in the 17th.

1751 *Eng. Gazetteer* s.v. *Preston*, It..is governed by a mayor, recorder, 8 aldermen, 4 *under-aldermen. **1942** M. Harcourt *Parson in Prison* 20 The whole school was assembled before the *underbosses. **1964** *Amer. Speech* XXXIX. 305 Over each [Mafia] family presides a boss... Beneath the boss are an underboss, also known as *sotto capo*, and a *consiglieri*. **1972** *N.Y. Times Mag.* 4 June 95 In the restructured family on which Joe Colombo solidified his hold as boss, another tantalizing figure emerged, Charles (Charlie Lemons) Mineo... Mineo has become a unique kind of underboss. **1687** Miége *Gt. Fr. Dict.* II, *Under-Brigadier, *Sou-Brigadier*. **1611** Cotgr., *Soubchantre*, an *vnder-chaunter..inferiour to the head Chaunter. **1857** Livingstone *Trav.* (1861) 189 An imposing embassy from Masiko. It consisted of all his *underchiefs. **1888** 'J. S. Winter' *Bootle's Childr.* ii, All the 'lads'..had gone home for the night, with the exception of the *under-coachman. **1708** J. Chamberlayne *St. Gt. Brit.* (1710) 569 A Chief-Crier, Two *Under-Criers, Two Ushers. **1846** Etheridge *Syrian Churches* 200 After which is read the Gospel in Syriac; an *underdeacon reading it in the vernacular Arabic. **1854** *Poultry Chron.* I. 265/1 Some competent feeder to look after the whole, and see that the *under-feeders..are constantly at work. **1891** *Daily News* 30 Nov. 6/6 The first footman..had an altercation with..an *under-footman. **1611** Cotgr., *Subministrateur*,..an *vnder-furnisher, an inferior officer. **1876** E. A. Abbott in *Contemp. Rev.* June 141 To serve him as *under-gamekeeper. **1708** J. Chamberlayne *St. Gt. Brit.* (1710) 707 Edinburgh-Castle: ..Master-Gunner,..6 *Under-Gunners. **1820** Scott *Abbot* iv, The famous university of Leyden, where they lack an *underjanitor. **1611** Florio, *Sequestratore*,..an *vnder-iudge, an arbitrator. **1898** *Atlantic Monthly* LXXXII. 474 The cooks and the under-cooks, the laundresses, the *under-laundress. **1852** Bailey *Festus* (ed. 5) 338 The more We feel of poesie do we become Like God in love and power,—*under-makers. **1818** Mrs. Shelley *Frankenst.* ii. (1897) 6 Twice I actually hired myself as an *under-mate in a Greenland whaler. **1976** 'W. Trevor' *Children of Dynmouth* ii. 42 The *under-matron, Miss Tomm, had come into the dormitory and asked him to come with her to the study. **1839** J. Rogers *Antipopopr.* x. §2. 253 We read nothing in Holy Scripture about the submediation or the *undermediators. **1868** Holme Lee *B. Godfrey* xxiii. 122 Rebecca was the *under-nurse. **1771** Ledwich *Antiq. Sarisb.* 223 He joined himself to..a tallow-chandler, as an *underpartner with him in the business. **1648** Hexham II, *Een Onder-Prioor*, an *Vnder-Priour. **1818** Moore *Fudge Fam. Paris* vi. 32 Friends, whom his Lordship keeps in store, As *under-saviours of the nation. **1614** Selden *Titles Honor* 267 Earle, Churl, Thane, and *Underthane. **1559** Aylmer *Harborowe* L 2 b, Then must the hyghe Shrife be his frende: And the *vnderthefe (vndershrife I should saye) his man. **1748** Melmoth *Fitzosborne Lett.* lvi. (1749) II. 79 All that numerous *undertribe in the commonwealth of literature. **1818** Scott *Hrt. Midl.* xiii, Just the post of *under-turnkey, for I understand there's a vacancy. **1706** Phillips (ed. Kersey), *Sub-vicar*, an *Under-Vicar. **1611** Cotgr., *Arriere-vasseur*, an vnder-vassall; or, an *vnder-villaine. **1657** J. Watts *Vind. Ch. Eng.* 125 The ministers are Christs *under-vine-dressers. **1854** *Poultry Chron.* I. 388/1 Abounding with game..which, by game-keepers and '*under-watchers', was..rigorously preserved. **1880** *Under-waiter [see landlord *sb.* 4]. **1921** E. M. Forster *Let.* 17 May in *Hill of Devi* (1953) 81 He worked like an under-waiter in a Soho restaurant.

b. With other nouns, in the sense of 'subordinate, subsidiary, minor'. An early instance of this is *underhelp* (1579); others, such as *underaccident*, *-action*, *-cause*, *-ministry*, etc., occur in the 17th cent. In later use the tendency is to employ either *sub-* (see sub- 5 b, c, d) or an adjective, but A. Tucker *Light Nat.* (1768) has *under-aim*, *-plan*, *-scheme*, *-society*, *-species*, *-stage*.

1598 Florio, *Sottodistintione*, an *vnder-distinction, or subdistinction. **1711** Swift *Jrnl. Stella* 28 Apr. (1901) 203 All the *under-hints there are mine too. **1691** Norris *Pract. Disc.* 205 The Desire of Happiness..governs all the *under-motions of the Man. **1874** Stubbs *Const. Hist.* I. v. 100 The Lathe and the Rape may represent the *undershires of the Heptarchic kingdom. **1648** Hexham II, *Onder-vooght*, *Under-tuterage, or *Under-wardship.

7. With verbs, denoting reduction to (or acceptance of) an inferior or subordinate standing. Chiefly OE., as *underbieȝan* to subject, *underbúȝan* to submit, *underþéodan* to subject, subjugate; and ME., as *undercast*, *-put*, *-thew*. See also *undershining*, *-sphere*, *-study*, *-sweat*, *-thrown*.

Under- is rarely employed in the sense of sub- 9 (*b*); Florio (1611) has *under-appoint* rendering It. *sottodelegare*.

III. In figurative senses.

8. With verbs. **a.** In OE., various secondary meanings of *under-* are represented by such verbs as *under(be)ȝinnan* to begin or attempt, *underfón* to receive, *underȝietan*, *-niman*, *-standan* to understand, *undersécan* to investigate. Several of these survive in ME., as *underfo*, *underȝete*, *-nim*, *-stand*, *underseche*; and a few more are added, as *underfind*, *-grope*, *-take*. In later examples the sense is usually that of (secret) investigation, as *underfeel*, *-look*, *-search*, *-watch*, or of unobserved action, as *underhear*. In addition to the verbs some agent-nouns occur, as *under-dealer*, *-plotter*, *-puller*.

Florio (1611) renders It. *sottosapere*, *-ridere* by *underknow*, *-smile*.

b. From the end of the 16th cent. *under-* is used with verbs in the sense of 'below (= at a lower rate than) another person', as in *underbid*, *-buy*, *-sell*, *-spend*, *-work*.

c. Occasionally the sense is 'to a point or degree below what is normal or customary', as in *undercooled*, *-hew*.

d. Very rarely, subordinate action is implied, as in *underlet* = sublet.

9. With nouns, denoting actions, etc., which lie or are kept beneath the surface or in the background. An early instance is *undercraft* (*c* 1400); others occur from the 17th cent., as *underdealing*, *-thought*. Modern instances are chiefly of an individual character.

1857 Heavysege *Saul* (1869) 421 Thine eyeballs roll, As if from some great *under-agitation. **1830** Coleridge *Church & State* (1839) 274 A sort of *under-consciousness blends with our dreams. **1876** T. Hardy *Ethelberta* xix, Simply an *underfeeling I have that [etc.]. **1863** Bp. S. Wilberforce in *Life* (1882) III. 100 The curious *under-history of Trench's appointment to the archbishopric. **1817** Coleridge *Biog. Lit.* (1907) II. 207 There is a dull *underpain that survives the smart which it had aggravated. **1876** Mrs. Whitney *Sights & Ins.* II. iii. 362 To me, who felt an *underpulse in all these things, there was a plain perception [etc.]. **1890** W. James *Princ. Psychol.* I. viii. 206 Barring a certain common fund of information, like the command of language, etc., what the upper self knows the *under self is ignorant of, and *vice versa*. **1914** W. De Morgan *When Ghost meets Ghost* II. xvi. 662 This underself of hers may have vibrated in response to the strange hints he had thrown out. **1732** Sir C. Wogan *Let. to Swift* 27 Feb., A very grave phiz that carried a wicked *undersneer. **1893** *Nation* (N.Y.) 29 June 475/3 The effect is artistic, while the *undersuggestion is scientific. **1908** H. James *Spoils of Poynton* p. xxiii, An air of comedy comparatively free from sharp *under-tastes. **1980** R. B. Kitaj *Artist's Eye* (Nat. Gallery) 3 Their lives at the sinister heart of the Baudelairean city, the spell its compelling undertaste cast on them. **1805** Wordsw. *Prel.* vi. 558 Something of stern mood, an *under-thirst Of vigour seldom utterly allayed.

b. With words denoting sound of a subdued or subordinate character, esp. when produced or perceived at the same time as a louder or more distinct sound. (See also underbreath, -song, -strain, -tone, -tune, -voice.)

1904 E. Rickert *Reaper* 10 He could hear the *underbeat of the surf on the rocks. **1863** Is. Williams *Baptistery* II. xxiv. (1874) 102 Or deep Gregorian chaunt of plaintive *underchime. **1893** E. H. Barker *Wand. Southern Waters* 43 That continuous *undercry of the iron tongues. **1815** Scott *Guy M.* iv, She answered in the same tone of *under-dialogue. **1832** J. P. Kennedy *Swallow B.* xxi, Ducks and geese,..with a sedate *under-gabble, like that of old burghers in conversation. **1892** Meredith *Poems, Spring* 134 But now the common life has come;..The grasses one vast *underhum. **1859** Mrs. Craik *Romantic Tales* 182 The low, woman's voice, whose *under-melody,..lost amidst the tempests of life, was now needed to soothe its ending. *a* **1835** Mrs. Hemans *Poems, Flowers & Music* (1875) 572, I ..caught an *under-music of lament in the stream's voice. **1876** Meredith *Beauch. Career* I. iii. 39 He quoted sayings ..in which neither his ear nor Wilmore's detected the *underring Stukely was famous for. **1874** Lanier *Poems, Corn* 28 Fragmentary whispers, blown From *undertalks of leafy souls unknown. **1872** T. Hardy *Under Greenw. Tree* I. i, Dick Dewy..continued his tune in an *under-whistle.

IV. Denoting insufficiency or defect.

10. a. With verbs. From the latter part of the 16th cent., by contrast with over- 27, *under-* is prefixed to verbs to imply that the action falls below the usual or proper standard, and thus acquires the sense of 'at too low a rate', 'too low', 'too little', 'insufficiently'. Early instances are *underprize*, *-value*, others of slightly later date are *underbuy*, *-charge*, *-rate*, *-reckon*, *-sell*, etc. Subsequently the use becomes extremely common, especially in the sense of 'insufficiently, not enough', as *under-calculate*, *-emphasize*, *-fulfil*, *-graze*, *-react*, *-recover*, etc., and occurs frequently with pa. pples. and ppl. adjs., as *under-endowed*, *-equipped*, *-financed*, *-fulfilled*, *-funded*, *-garrisoned*, *-grazed*, *-gunned*, *-industrialized*, *-informed*, *-policed*, *-powered*, *-publicized*, *-researched*, *-stained*, *-stressed*, etc. Examples of vbl. sbs. (cf. b), as *under-funding*, *-grazing* etc. are also included in the following illustrations.

1885 *Pall Mall G.* 14 Feb. 3/2 The..over-worked and *under-accommodated class of reporters. **1862** *Lond. Rev.* 16 Aug. 141 Another baker will make his loaves originally of short weight, and will then *underbake them. **1901** *Scotsman* 5 Mar. 7/8 *Under-ballasted vessels were..a source of danger to themselves. *Ibid.*, Accidents to British ships..due to *under-ballasting. **1882** *St. James' Gaz.* 3 Apr. 5/2 The Cantabs were slightly *underboated this year. **1725** *Fam. Dict.* s.v. *Brewing*, This is generally attributed to their *under-boiling their strong Worts. **1836** Dickens *Let.* 8 Oct. (1965) I. 181 There really is not time, unless Hansard's people, have greatly *under-calculated the quantity sent. **1910** *Practitioner* Feb. 152 Cough..is one of the..most significant symptoms of pulmonary tuberculosis. .. It is too often undercalculated by the patient and his friends. **1983** *Platt's Oil Marketing Bull.* 15 Aug. 1/1 It has been undercalculating its Windfall Tax payments. **1889** *Boy's Own Paper* 3 Aug. 700/2 My boat being considerably *under-canvassed, the weather was rarely too bad for me to make a start. **1866** *Ecclesiologist* XXVII. 220 The reproach usual in French provincial towns, of being lamentably *under-churched. **1737** Waterland *Eucharist* 202 But there may be danger of *under-commenting, as well as of interpreting too high. **1861** Mrs. Beeton *Bk. Househ. Managem.* xxxviii. 893 If the patient be allowed to eat vegetables, never send them up *undercooked. **1889** *Anthony's Photogr. Bull.* II. 155 We lose the strength..by over-timing and *under-developing. **1778** [W. H. Marshall] *Minutes Agric., Digest* 134 Whose Farm is for ever under-stocked, *under-dunged, and under-tilled! **1856** Miss Yonge *Daisy Chain* II. vi. 393 He has been *under-educated,..and is not very brilliant. **1964** *Amer. Psychologist* XIX. 14/2 If I have seemed to *underemphasize the importance of inner capacities..it is because I believe that this part of the story is given by the nature of man's evolution. **1909** H. G. Wells *Ann Veronica* xvii. 344, I remarked that science was disgracefully *under-endowed, and confessed I'd had to take to more profitable courses. **1969** N. W. Pirie *Food Resources* viii. 191 They are almost all under-endowed while money is squandered on projects with little bearing on the world's real needs. **1960** *Times Lit. Suppl.* 2 Sept. 553/4 Our teenagers are cast out into the world with boredom as the only memory of their ill-disciplined, *under-equipped schooldays. **1923** *Daily Mail* 30 Jan. 4 This Department is under-staffed, *under-financed, unprovided with many of the safeguards it has itself demanded. **1977** M. Edelman *Political Lang.* v. 100 An under-financed and uncoordinated reaction to widespread destitution becomes a 'war on poverty'. **1950** A. Lee *Soviet Air Force* 77 Unlike the later Five Year Plans, the target for the first was '*underfulfilled'. **1964** *Ann. Reg. 1963* 230 According to Premier Široký..the plan as a whole had been underfulfilled by 1·2 per cent. **1982** T. J. Binyon *Swan Song* v. 32 The professor..accused me..of consistently underfulfilling the department's norms in teaching, research and administration. **1970** *Nature* 8 Aug. 551/2 It also suggests, perhaps intentionally, that the project is grossly *underfunded. **1963** *Economist* 27 Apr. 342/1 Over-funding last year could be compensated by *under-funding this year. **1981** *Daily Tel.* 17 Oct. 12/3 The continual underfunding of the Royal Shakespeare Company..was endangering its ability to..retain its talented staff. **1936** Auden & Isherwood *Ascent of F6* I. ii. 24 We're *under-garrisoned and under-policed and..we're in a blue funk that the Ostnians will come over the frontier. **1977** J. L. Harper *Population Biol. of Plants* xiv. 438 Swards were overgrazed in winter and spring and *undergrazed in summer and autumn. **1960** *Farmer & Stockbreeder* 8 Mar. 71/1 Those swards which needed improvement were the *undergrazed type. **1933** *Jrnl. R. Agric. Soc.* XCIV. 24 This plot was subjected to overstocking in winter and early spring, followed by gross *undergrazing during the summer and autumn. **1974** *Times* 7 Jan. 12/3 To tear up large areas at once has led too often to undergrazing, drainage difficulties, [etc.]. **1648** T. Hill *Spring of Grace* 11 We are apt to overgrieve or *undergrieve at crosses. **1928** C. F. S. Gamble *Story North Sea Air Station* xiii. 214 As a fighting machine the H.12 was *under-gunned for her size. **1944** *Return to Attack* (Army Board, N.Z.) 8/1 The armoured brigades.. were equipped with..both types [of tank] fast-moving but under-gunned compared with the German tanks. **1964** I. L. Horowitz *New Sociol.* 33 We cannot examine demography without basing our analysis on some definite correlation of ..*underindustrialized and overpopulated. **1968** *Punch* 31 July 141/1 The *under-informed voter. **1866** Odling *Anim. Chem.* 144 Strongly suggestive of these animals being, so to speak, *under-lunged. **1778** [W. H. Marshall] *Minutes Agric., Digest* 66 Re-load *under-made Hay. **1847** Helps

Friends in C. I. iv. 67 An ugly phantom of a caricature.. which..*under-mimics its wisdom, over-acts its folly. **1936** *Under-policed [see *under-garrisoned* above]. **1978** *N.Y. Times* 30 Mar. A20/5 Underpoliced and unkempt, [the bus terminal]..serves as headquarters for an ominous army of hookers, muggers and pimps. **1884** *Spectator* 4 Oct. 1298/2 If..only the pure Milesian race should own the soil..the country would be *under-populated. **1882** *Garden* 25 Feb. 135/3 Use manure water freely..to all [ferns] that are *under-potted. **1905** KIPLING *Actions & Reactions* (1909) 128 *Under-powered craft..can ascend to the limit of their lift. **1980** 'M. HARRIS' *Treasure of Sainte Foy* i. 4 The small Renault is underpowered and rather cheaply built. **1971** H. WILSON *Labour Govt.* xxxvi. 739 One of the *under-publicised achievements of comprehensive secondary education. **1965** *Under-react [see OVERREACT *v.*] **1982** *Economist* 5 June 37/2 The markets may, on average, have underreacted to the publication of the money figures. **1849** MAURICE *Let.* in *Life* (1884) II. 9 A misunderstanding, contraction or *under-realising of the truths of God's Absolute, Fatherly Love. **1776** ADAM SMITH *W.N.* I. x. I. (1869) I. 105 In point of pecuniary gain..they..are generally *under-recompensed. **1967** *Under-recover [see *over-recovered* s.v. OVER- 27 b]. **1884** *Manch. Exam.* 16 Oct. 5/1 We are told that the counties are enormously *under-represented. **1942** M. MCCARTHY *Company she Keeps* v. 239 [He] went back to the public library; perhaps..the material was *under-researched. **1982** *Pol. Sci. Q.* XCVII. 474 Rawlings's intervention, so sadly underresearched. **1881** *Daily Tel.* 20 Oct., An absurdly *under-rigged steamer. **1844** H. STEPHENS *Bk. Farm* II. 673 The *under-ripened seed of the bad season of 1841 produced the good crop of potatoes of 1842. **1832** *Nat. Philos., Electric.* ii. §49. 13 (L.U.K.), In a deficiency of fluid, or in matter *under-saturated. **1786** *Trans. Soc. Arts* IV. 102 The land was *under seeded. **1872** H. W. BEECHER *Lect. Preach.* iv. 109 Some men *under-sleep, and some over-sleep; some eat too much, and some too little. **1941** *Understained [see HETEROCHROMATIN]. **1956** Under-stained [see HETEROCHROMATIC *a.* 2]. **1900** *Christian* 15 Nov. 9/1 We frequently have to pay.. excess on delivery of *understamped letters. **1778** *Under-tilled [see *under-dunged* above]. **1900** *Phil. Mag.* L. 132 A lower factor of safety might..be used in such cases, where there is a large reserve of *understressed material. **1928** *Observer* 17 June 8 It is a curious book. Colloquial and offhand, deliberately understressed in feeling and description, [etc.]. **1969** *Harper's Bazaar* Sept. 27/1 An expensive car must be one hundred per cent reliable, and this..means an under-stressed engine of the simplest possible kind. **1889** *Anthony's Photogr. Bull.* II. 227 The negative was so badly *undertimed as to be useless. **1861** O. W. HOLMES *Pages fr. Old Vol. Life* (1891) 9 They are very commonly pallid, *undervitalized, shy, sensitive creatures. **1832** *Prop. Reg. Instr. Cavalry* III. 99 The Troop Leaders may know whether to over-wheel or *under-wheel.

ellipt. **1628** FELTHAM *Resolves* II. xxviii. 89, I hold it a greater iniurie to bee ouer-valued, then vnder. **1847** C. BRONTE *Jane Eyre* vii, The under..or the over dressing of a dish.

b. With nouns, in the sense of 'insufficient, deficient, defective', contrasted with OVER- 29. Examples occur in the 17th cent. in *underprice*, *-rate*, *-value*, *-wages*, and are not uncommon in later use, though less frequent than the verbal forms. Recent examples include *under-capacity*, *-emphasis*, *-fulfilment*, *-population*, *-recovery*, *-registration*.

1962 E. SNOW *Other Side of River* (1963) lxxxvi. 725 The American problem of abundance or overcapacity to produce commodities and *undercapacity to consume them. **1916** E. POUND *Let.* 17 Apr. (1971) 76 In 'Impression', I don't think 'dissolved' is just the right word, though I recognize that you may have been aiming at a sort of restraint or *under-emphasis which *can* be effective. **1977** M. EDELMAN *Political Lang.* v. 83 Hess and Torney found a repetitive emphasis in the schools on the values of loyalty, authority, and law, and an underemphasis on citizens' rights. **1895** *Pop. Sci. Monthly* July 380 The result is always over-eating and *under-exercise. **1962** E. SNOW *Other Side of River* (1963) vii. 58, I can't recall visiting any mine or factory where '*underfulfillment' was predicted. **1861** M. ARNOLD *Pop. Educ. France* 11, I shall proceed to point out..some inconveniences of *under-government. **1899** PATTEN *Developm. Eng. Th.* vi. 382 Overnutrition as well as *undernutrition weakens the body. **1922** *Daily Mail* 29 Nov. 8/4 The absurd *underpopulation of the country parts. **1966** *Times* 28 Mar. (Austral. Suppl.) p. xii/6 Faced with the difficulties of isolation and under-population, managements argue that secondhand top name overseas packages are a cheaper..investment. *c* **1900** *Buck's Handbk. Med. Sci.* VI. 158 (Cent. Suppl.), The foul air..makes a direct escape,.. providing..it meets or passes no compartment on its way in which *under-pressure exists. **1887** *Pall Mall G.* 28 Feb. 1/2 Over production may exist in manufactures owing to *under production of crops. **1961** *Ann. Reg. 1960* 511 The Sugar Board..revealed a loss..; the deficit brought the Board's total '*under-recovery' to £7·1 million. **1952** C. P. BLACKER *Eugenics* 160 Lorimer gives good reasons for thinking that this discrepancy arose from *under-registration of deaths, especially of infantile deaths, in the intervening period. **1894** *Westm. Gaz.* 14 Sept. 1/3 More important..is the *under-representation of the big societies. **1864** RUSKIN in *Daily Tel.* 31 Oct., An *under-supply of wages and an over-supply of labourers. **1883** GRESLEY *Gloss. Coal-m.* 268 **Under ventilation*, too little air circulating in a mine.

c. With adjectives *under-* is rarely employed as the opposite of OVER- 28, except when directly suggested by the latter, e.g. *under-scrupulous* as the converse of *over-scrupulous*; *underhonest* (Shaks.) in contrast to *overproud*; *under-ripe*, etc.

1971 *Nature* 23 Apr. 517/1 With this value..Fig. 1 suggests that the primary is grossly underluminous for its mass.

11. In words formed with *under-* the stress is variable. Normally it falls on the stem in verbs (including participles in predicative use) and on the prefix in nouns, adjectives, and attributive participles, with a secondary stress on prefix or stem respectively, whenever form or sense makes a double stressing natural or necessary. Even in verbs, however, the prefix naturally takes either the main or an equal stress whenever it becomes emphatic through contrast either with the simple verb or with a compound in OVER-.

12. Compounds in which the two parts are not felt to be distinct are written as one word without a hyphen. In other formations the use of the hyphen is variable, and depends to a great extent on the form or the frequency of the word. Complete separation of the prefix, common in older usage, is now restricted to instances in which *under* may be taken as an adjective. Examples of these have been included under the compounds, as no clear distinction can be drawn between the two.

under- ('ʌndə(r)), *prefix*², originating in the coalescence of the preposition UNDER with a following noun, the compound being then usually employed as an adj. or adv., as UNDERFOOT, -GROUND, -HAND, -STAIRS, -WATER. In attributive use these compounds have the stress on the prefix.

Purely adjectival formations, as *under-celestial* (Florio), *-natural* (1642), *-proficient* (1703), are rare. An unusual type occurs in UNDERGRADUATE.

1892 *Daily News* 1 Feb. 2/3 The Indian season being.. dull in consequence of *under-average grain crops. **1886** *Pall Mall G.* 24 Aug. 4/2 The substitution for the old *under-guard lever of the 'snap', or spring action for opening the breech. **1876** T. HARDY *Ethelberta* ii, Everything turned upon whether the postmaster..would be in his *under-government manner. **1966** *Times* 28 Feb. (Canada Suppl.) p. xvi/6, The submarine freighter..must have an *under-ice capacity of 800 to 1,000 miles. **1976** *Jrnl. R. Soc. Arts* CXXIV. 638/2 BAS has undertaken surface sledge traverses for major anomalies and to interpret the under-ice rocks and principal structural features such as George VI Sound. **1887** MEREDITH *Ballads & P.* 149 Some *undermountain narrative he tells. **1894** *Daily News* 3 Sept. 4/1 The work of real difficulty is..the *under-river portion of the tunnel. **1897** MARY KINGSLEY *W. Africa* 301 A bridge across an *under-swamp river. **1959** *Encounter* Nov. 17/2, 175 divisions in the Red Army..as against 14 *under-strength divisions in the U.S. army. **1971** R. PETRIE *Thorne in Flesh* ix. 117 An understrength police force was at full stretch.

'under-a,byss. (UNDER-¹ 5 c.)

1662 GLANVILL *Lux Orient.* xiv, They are disposed of into those black under-abysses.

'under-,accident. (UNDER-¹ 6 b.)

c **1630** H. R. *Mythomystes* A 3, Nor in the vnder-Accidents, but in the Essentiall Forme, of true Poesy.

under-a'chiever. *Psychol.* Also as one word without hyphen. [UNDER-¹ 10 b.] Someone whose actual performance consistently fails to reach the level predicted by intelligence tests or other measures of ability. Cf. OVER-ACHIEVER.

1953 *Jrnl. Abnormal Psychol.* XLVIII. 533/2 If his grades fell a full rank below prediction he was labelled an 'underachiever'. **1962** 'I. ROSS' *Old Students Never Die* viii. 105 Nowadays we have a name for them: the kids with the high potential and the low grades. We call them 'under-achievers'. **1968** D. LAWTON *Social Class, Lang. & Educ.* i. 6 For a number of reasons working-class children tend to be under-achievers. **1973** E.-J. BAHR *Nice Neighbourhood* v. 47, I identify with the underachievers of this world. **1975** *Kingston* (Ontario) *Whig-Standard* 6 Sept. 27/6 The survey also found that those not using seat belts also were under-achievers in school.

So **under-a'chievement; under-a'chieve** *v. intr.*, **under-a'chieving** *ppl. a.* and *vbl. sb.*

1951 *School Rev.* LIX. 472 (*title*) Factors related to over-achievement and under-achievement in school. **1953** Underachieving *vbl. sb.* [see OVERACHIEVING *vbl. sb.*]. **1954** *Jrnl. Educ. Psychol.* Oct. 322 It is virtually impossible for a pupil at or near the..first percentile [on an intelligence test] to 'under-achieve'. **1965** in M. Kornrich *Underachievement* 553 A role for the counselor may be to help the underachieving student. **1972** *Guardian* 21 July 12/5 Parents who want their children to go to a popular school may..encourage them to underachieve. **1982** *Secondary Educ. Jrnl.* XII. III. 1/2 Underachievement is not confined to pupils in secondary schools. *Ibid.*, Many of these pupils are..not achieving their full potential—in other words they are underachieving.

under'act, *v.* [UNDER-¹ 10 a.] *trans.* To perform inefficiently or inadequately; *spec.* to act (a part) insufficiently.

a **1623** BUCK *Rich. III*, I. (1646) 9 Faulconbridge was appointed Admirall, with Commission to take or sinke all Ships he met;..who did not under act it, but made many depredations on the Coasts. **1775** ASH, *Underact*.., to perform in a manner below what is required or expected. **1847** MACREADY *Remin., Diary & Lett.* (1875) II. 293 The play was so under-acted by the people engaged in it, that it broke down under their weight. **1899** *Daily News* 4 Dec. 6/6 It was reserved for Mr. Coghlan to underact the part.

'under-,action. [UNDER-¹ 6 b, 10 b.]

1. Subordinate or subsidiary action, as in the plot of a play or poem.

1697 DRYDEN *Æneis* Ded. ¶1 The least and most trivial episodes, or under-actions, which are interwoven in it, are parts either necessary or convenient to carry on the main design.

2. Insufficient or defective action; less than normal activity.

1887 *Buck's Handbk. Med. Sci.* IV. 656 Correction of underaction and overaction of muscles, nerves, and their central reflex apparatus.

'under-,actor. [UNDER-¹ 6 a.] A subordinate actor or agent.

1723 BLACKMORE *Alfred* Pref. 46 The chaste, discreet, and honourable Characters of the chief Heroe and other under-Actors. **1771** GOLDSM. *Hist. Eng.* IV. 79 Some of the under actors, seized with fear or remorse, resolved to prevent the execution by a timely discovery. *a* **1797** H. WALPOLE *Mem. Geo. II* (1822) I. 199, I take leave of the reader, to add this person's portrait to those of the under-actors.

'under-,admiral. (UNDER-¹ 6 a: cf. Du. *onder-admiraal*, G. *unteradmiral*.)

16.. *Black Bk. Admiralty* (Rolls) I. 17 If hee hath an under-admirall (or rear-admirall). **1729** JACOB *Law Dict.*, *Vice-Admiral*, an under Admiral at Sea.

'under-ad,venturer. (UNDER-¹ 6 a.)

1607 in *E. India Co. Crt. Bks.* II. 48 (MS.), Any man coming in as an under-adventurer under any of the forenamed 50 adventurers.

under-'age, *a.* and *sb.* [See UNDER *prep.* 22 b and UNDER-².]

1. *adj.* Not of full age; youthful, immature.

1594 NASHE *Unfort. Trav.* Wks. (Grosart) V. 52 Farre bee it my vnder-age argumentes should intrude themselues as a greene weake prop to support so high a building. **1612** WEBSTER *White Devil* I. ii, I myself have loved a lady, and pursued her with a great deal of under-age protestation. **1876** T. HARDY *Ethelberta* xli, As secret as if I were some under-age heiress to an Indian fortune.

2. Carried on by someone below the legal age (for the activity).

1978 *Morecambe Guardian* 14 Mar. 19/8 He went on, about supervision on the rally site, and the danger of under-age drinking. **1983** *Sun* 8 June 15/3 He persuaded her to pose nude and sing about under-age sex.

†**3.** *sb.* The time during which a person is under age; minority. *Obs.*

1613-8 DANIEL *Coll. Hist. Eng.* (1626) 28 The Duke.. recouers his peace, and the Castle of Thuilliers taken from him in his vnder-age. **1641** EARL MONM. tr. *Biondi's Civil Wars* III. 147 The underage and weaknesse of his succeeding sonne. **1649** BP. HALL *Cases Consc.* IV. i. (1654) 289 Neither do the Roman doctors generally hold otherwise this day in case of an under-age.

So **under'agedness.** *rare*⁻⁰.

1648 HEXHAM II, *Onbejaertheyt*, Vnder-agednesse.

'under-,agency. [UNDER-¹ 6 b.] The office of an under-agent.

1856 LEVER *Martins of Cro' M.* xxviii, I told him I'd hold the under-agency till he named some one to succeed me.

'under-,agent. [UNDER-¹ 6 a.] A sub-agent.

1677 GILPIN *Demonol.* (1867) 191 The woman Jezebel.. was Satan's under-agent. **1679** EVERARD *Popish Plot* 2, I askt her..who were the leading-men in the contrivance, and who the Under-agents to carry it on? **1711** ADDISON *Spect.* No. 225 ¶3 Discretion..is like an Under-Agent of Providence, to guide and direct us in the ordinary Concerns of Life. **1733** T. STEWARD *Ordination Charge*, You [*sc.* clergymen] are made Ministers of Christ, and, as I may say, his Under-Agents. **1805** WORDSW. *Prelude* XIII. 273 Words are but under agents in their souls. **1883** *Manch. Guard.* 15 Oct. 5/3 The Earl of Dalhousie was driving near Carnoustie with his under agent.

'under-aid, *sb.* (UNDER-¹ 6 b.)

1579 TOMSON *Calvin's Serm. Tim.* 212/2 The woman is rather giuen to the man for an vnder ayde. **1611** COTGR., *Soubs-aide*, an vnder Aid; the Aid which tenants pay vnto their mesne Lord [etc.].

under-'aid, *v.* (UNDER-¹ 4 a.)

1613-8 DANIEL *Coll. Hist. Eng.* (1626) 23 Robert..is said to have under-aided Roul secretly, of purpose to make him friend his designes.

'under-air. (UNDER-¹ 5 b.)

1833 TENNYSON *Miller's Dau.* xix, I heard,.. When all the under-air was still, The low voice of the glad new year. **1905** *Westm. Gaz.* 16 Jan. 1/3 A dust of snow is in the under-air of the streets.

'under-and-'over, *adj.* (and *sb.*) *phr.* Also unhyphened. [UNDER *adv.* I.] = OVER-AND-UNDER *a.* Also *absol.* as *sb.*

1881 W. W. GREENER *Gun & its Development* 380 (*caption*) Under and over Wedge-fast Gun. **1911** *Encycl. Brit.* XXIII. 336/1 There is also Greener's 'under and over', the rifle barrel being topmost (usually 16-bore shot-gun barrel and ·450 rifle barrel). **1931** G. BURRARD *Modern Shotgun* I. ix. 235 (*heading*) The Woodward 'under and over' gun. **1958** *Spectator* 1 Aug. 163/1 The 'professionals'..tended to shoot with under-and-over guns. **1969** C. CHEVENIX TRENCH *Shooter & his Gun* viii. 97 (*caption*) Double-barrelled under and over.

unde'ranged, *ppl. a.* (UN-¹ 8.)

1817 KIRBY & SP. *Entomol.* xxiii. II. 353 The wings of many male butterflies..are distinguished by a remarkable apparatus..for keeping them steady and underanged in their flight.

under'arch, *v.* [UNDER-¹ 4 a.] *trans.* To lie under, or support, as an arch; to span with an inverted arch.

1611 FLORIO, *Subbarcare*, to bow vnder as a bow, to vnder arch, to vnder vault. **1827** MONTGOMERY *Pelican Isl.* I. 148

One sevenfold circle, That spanned the horizon, meted out the heavens, And underarched the ocean.

†**under-a'rear**, *v.* [UNDER-[1] 4 a.] *trans.* To suborn.

1502 ARNOLDE *Chron.* 174 Also al thei..whiche such false witnesse in-bryng or vnder-areren in cause of matrimony.

ˌ**under-'argue**, *v.* (UNDER-[1] 10 a.)

1645 RUTHERFORD *Tryal & Tri. Faith* (1845) 55 We are not either to over-argue or to under-argue, neither to faint nor despise.

'**under-arm**, *a.* [UNDER-[2].]

1. a. *Cricket.* = UNDERHAND *a.* 1 c, d.

1816 in Box *Cricket* (1877) 33 The ball may be twisted by the usual mode of under-arm bowling. **1882** *Daily Tel.* 19 May, This brought on Humphreys, slow under-arm bowler.

b. In other sporting contexts. Also as *adv.*

1929 W. E. COLLINSON *Spoken Eng.* 90 I'll have to serve underarm, I've strained my wrist. **1960** E. W. SWANTON *West Indies Revisited* 230 An under-arm throw by Smith. **1974** MILLS & BUTLER *Tackle Badminton* v. 39 Take a good underarm swing, turning your left shoulder towards the net. **1976** *Times* 3 Feb. 9/4 When one recalls that most women of the period [*sc.* 1909] would have added a hat to the recommended [tennis] ensemble one can see why they had to serve under-arm.

2. *Swimming.* Of a stroke: Made with the arm below the level of the body. Also *ellipt.*

1905 *Times* 10 Aug. 10/4 Burgess,..using his favourite under-arm stroke,..went off at a good pace. **1906** *Westm. Gaz.* 18 Aug. 9/2 After the second hour he varied his stroke for a while to the underarm.

3. *Dressmaking.* Of a seam: that edges the lower half of the arm-hole of a garment, or that joins the underside of a sleeve or the side of a bodice.

1908 M. E. MORGAN *How to dress Doll* (1973) v. 43 Put the seam of the sleeve a little to the front of the under-arm seam. **1941** L. I. WILDER *Little Town on Prairie* ix. 85 Laura sewed the whalebone stays onto the underarm seams. **1964** *McCall's Sewing* xi. 161/1 Pin the underarm seam of bodice and sleeve. *Ibid.* 162/1 On the pattern there will be a slash marking at the curve of the underarm.

4. Of a bag or case: carried under the arm.

[**1925** *T. Eaton & Co. Catal.* Spring & Summer 279/1 Under-the-arm bag.] **1927** *Glasgow Herald* 21 Jan. 8 Whatever she carries about with her she keeps in an attaché case, an 'under-arm bag', or some other receptacle. **1974** *Harrod's Christmas Catal.* 19 Under-arm document case £27.50.

5. Applied to various items of personal care used on the armpit, as ***under-arm deodorant, razor***. Also ***under-arm odour***.

1947 H. M. MCLUHAN in *Horizon* Oct. 132 The means of defeating under-arm odour. **1968** A. DIMENT *Great Spy Race* viii. 122 At twelve, showered, shaved with her small under-arm razor..we were on the coast road. **1976** J. WAINWRIGHT *Walther P. 38* 21 You use under-arm deodorant.

under-'arming, *a.* [UNDER-[2].] Worn under the armour.

c **1611** CHAPMAN *Iliad* VIII. 341 Then put she on her ample breast her under-arming tire, And on it her celestial arms.

'**underback.** *Brewing.* [UNDER-[1] 5 b.] A vessel placed below the mash-tub or mash-tun to receive the raw wort when let out from this. (See also UNDERBECK.)

1635 *Toke* (Kent) *Estate Acc.* (MS.) fol. 178 Underbacks in the bruehouse. **1686** in *Essex. Rev.* (1906) XV. 173 One mashing tubb, and underback. **1725** *Fam. Dict.* s.v. *Brewing*, When all is run out into the Receiver, or Under-Back, lade or pump out your second Liquor. **1763** *Museum Rust.* I. 203 The first wort is then let out in a small stream into the under-back. **1830** M. DONOVAN *Dom. Econ.* I. 159 When the tap has been set, and the worts are allowed to run from the mash-tun, the transparent liquor is received into a large vessel called the underback. **1887** *Pall Mall G.* 25 Oct. 6/1 A huge display of saccharometers, hydrometers,..false bottoms, copper underbacks, and live steam injectors.

b. (See quot.)

1875 KNIGHT *Dict. Mech.* 2679/2 The name *underback* is also applied to a similar vessel in a vinegar factory.

'**under-ˌbailiff.** (UNDER-[1] 6 a: cf. MDu. *onder-bailliu*, Du. *-baljuw.*)

1621 ELSING *Debates Ho. Lords* (Camden) 33 The undersheriff knewe not that he was the Kinges servaunte; nor the underbaylliffes. **1631** *Star Chamb. Cases* (Camden) 118 The underbayliffes come into the roome.

'**underˌbalance.** (UNDER-[1] 10 b: cf. Da. *underbalance*, Sw. *-balans* deficit.)

1641 *Decay of Trade* 1 The profit or losse which is made by the over or underbalance of our Forraigne Trade.

'**under-ˌbarber.** (UNDER-[1] 6 a.)

1666 HARRISON in Bedloe *Popish Plot* (1679) 16 He answered, The King's Under-Barber, Phillips.

'**under-bark**, *a.* (and *adv.*). [UNDER-[2].]

Measured or taken without including the bark of a tree trunk. Also as *adv.* Cf. OVER-BARK.

1911 C. L. HANSON *Forestry for Woodmen* xiv. 192 If it [*sc.* a log] is 16 inches over bark it will be taken as 15 inches under bark. **1927** *Forestry* I. 8 Sample plots..gave the age as 123 years..and the underbark quarter girth volume per acre over 8,000 cubic feet. **1953** H. L. EDLIN *Forester's Handbk.* xiv. 215 Under-bark measure is strictly the volume of the log as measured after the bark has been peeled off it; but in practice it is often taken as the over-bark measure less the customary bark allowance. **1967** SCOTT & PALMER *Hiley's Woodland Managem.* (ed. 2) ix. 130 Prices which are quoted for timber nearly always apply to the under-bark measurement.

'**under-ˌbeadle.** (UNDER-[1] 6 a.)

1679 BEDLOE *Popish Plot* 9 The under Beadle of White-Chappel-Parish. **1755** JOHNSON, *Subbeadle*, an under beadle.

under'bear, *v.* Now *rare.* [OE. *underberan*: see UNDER-[1] 4 a, and BEAR *v.*]

1. *trans.* To sustain, suffer, endure. Also *absol.*

c **950** *Rit. Eccl. Dunelm.* (Surtees) 13 *Subportantes invicem*, vnderbearað bitvien. *a* **1050** *Liber Scintill.* v. (1889) 24 Mid geþylde underberende [L. *supportantes*] ᵹemænelice & forgyfende eow sylfum. **1340** *Ayenb.* 84 Uirtue makeþ wynne heuene..and alle þe kueades of þe wordle onderbere and gledliche þolye. **1382** WYCLIF *Ecclus.* xii. 14 If forsothe thou bowe doun, he shal not vnderbern [L. *supportabit*]. *a* **1400** *Pauline Ep.* (Powell) Col. iii. 13 Onderberande oþþer oþer and forgifande. *Ibid.* Heb. xiii. 22, I preye ȝou..þat ȝee vndyrbere [L. *sufferatis*] pacyently þe woord of solace. **1595** SHAKS. *John* III. i. 65 Get thee gone, And leaue those woes alone, which I alone Am bound to vnder-beare. *a* **1634** CHAPMAN *Alphonsus* IV. i. 183, I am not able for to underbear The weight of sorrow which doth bruise my soul. **1697** CONGREVE *Mourn. Bride* IV. vii, All pains and tortures That..dire revenge can think Shall he accumulated under-bear. **1888** G. YOUNG tr. *Sophocles* 265 My misery No mortal but myself can underbear.

2. To sustain, support, bear up.

1382 WYCLIF *Ezra* vi. 3 Cirus the king demede..that thei putte groundis vnderberende [L. *supportantia*] the heiȝte of sixti cubitus. **1593** NASHE *Christ's T.* F iij, I will corroborate my Crosse Giant-like, to vnder-beare the Atlas burthen of her insolences. **1595** PEELE *Anglorum Feriæ* 202 Show the way To help to underbear with grave advice The weighty beam whereon the state depends. *a* **1618** RALEIGH *Rem.* (1644) 154 The first would soon be broken from their bodies, were they not underborn by many branches.

†**3.** To introduce, apply. *Obs.*[−1]

1382 WYCLIF *2 Peter* i. 5 Forsothe ȝe vndir beringe, or ȝeuynge, al cure [L. *curam omnem subinferentes*], mynistre in ȝoure feith vertu.

4. To trim round the lower part.

1599 SHAKS. *Much Ado* III. iv. 20 Cloth a gold..set with pearles,..and skirts, round vnderborn with a blewish tinsel.

Hence **under'bearing** *vbl. sb.*

1593 SHAKS. *Rich. II*, I. iv. 29 Wooing poore Craftes-men, with the craft of soules, And patient vnder-bearing of his Fortune. **1598** FLORIO, *Sopportatione*, a toleration,..a suffring, a supporting, an vnderbearing. **1600** SURFLET *Countrie Farme* VI. vi. 737 To vines so planted there neede no propping or vnderbearing.

†'**underbeard.** *Obs.*[−1] (UNDER-[1] 5 b: cf. BEARD *sb.* 8.)

1753 *Chambers' Cycl.* Suppl., *Beard*, or under-beard, called also *chuck*, of a horse.

under'bearer. Now *dial.* and *U.S.* [UNDER-[1] 4 a. Cf. BEARER *sb.* 1 c.] One who assists in carrying the coffin at a funeral.

1700 S. SEWALL *Diary* 23 Mar., She is buried... The under-bearers were honest men. **1755** JOHNSON, *Underbearer*, in funerals, those that sustain the weight of the body, distinct from those who are bearers of ceremony, and only hold up the pall. **1777** BRAND *Pop. Antiq.* iii. 35 St. Jerom..informs us, that Bishops were what in modern Language we call Under-bearers at her Funeral. **1859** GEO. ELIOT *A. Bede* xl, All th' under-bearers and pall-bearers as I'n picked for my funeral are i' this parish and the next to't. **1885** *Century Mag.* July 394/1 The 'underbearers', who carried the coffin,..were provided with plain gloves.

'**underˌbearing**, *ppl. a.* [UNDER-[1] 8 a.] Unassuming.

1802 R. MANT *Mem. Warton* in *W.'s Poet. Wks.* I. p. ci, He was, as a friend of his once described him to me, the most under-bearing man existing.

underbeck, var. of UNDERBACK.

1764 *Museum Rust.* II. xcviii. 326 Large fats, or vats, (containing..wood ashes) with under-becks. **1828** *Hull Rockingham* 14 June 84/2 Three large guile tubs, several mash tubs and under becks. **1839** *Hist. Chesterfield Antiq.* 274 The instrument used in brewing, which is now called by some a betony, and by others an underbeck.

'**underbed.** (UNDER-[1] 5 b: cf. Du. *onderbed*, G. *unterbett*, Sw. *underbädd.*)

1648 HEXHAM II, *Onder-bedde*, an Vnder-bed. **1725** in F. Kidder *Exped. Capt. Lovewell* (1865) 93 A feather bed and under bed and bed furniture. **1778** *New Hampsh. Hist. Soc. Coll.* (1889) IX. 108 We have cut up all the sheets, table cloths, underbeds, towels, &c. **1827** STEUART *Planter's G.* (1828) 275 The thickness of the mass of roots and earth together, from the upper part of the collar, to the underbed of the roots. **1868** G. G. CHANNING *Recoll. Newport* 254 The bed or under-bed of straw was laid on cords, and the feather bed above. **1978** *Morecambe Guardian* 14 Mar. 6/5 You can buy beds already fitted with underbed drawers. **1982** *Habitat Catal. 1982/83* 122 Sturdy underbed storage on fixed nylon castors.

'**under-ˌbeing.** (UNDER-[1] 6 a.)

1587 GOLDING *De Mornay* v. 65 As we can not imagine God without his actions, so can wee not consider..any other underbeeings that proceede from thence.

†**under'beit**, *v. Obs.* [UNDER-[1] 4 a.] *trans.* To work under. Hence †**underbeiting** *vbl. sb.*

1670 PETTUS *Fodinæ Reg.* 88 And if any Miner of his own underbeit his Neighbours Meer, that then he shall fill his Underbeitings with such as he got out.

'**under-ˌbelly.** Also underbelly. [UNDER-[1] 5 c.]

1. a. A pouch or bag under the belly of an animal; the belly or underside of an animal.

1607 TOPSELL *Four-f. Beasts* 20 Vnderneath the common belly, there was a skinne like a bagge or scrip, wherin she keepeth..her young ones,..so that the same vnderbelly is her best remedie..to preserue her young ones. **1963** *Listener* 10 Jan. 65/2, I creep along on my cat's underbelly Nursing the floor for smells.

b. *transf.*, esp. of motor vehicles. Cf. UNDERBODY 2, 3 b.

1960 *Times* 3 Mar. 8/6 Both propellers were buckled and the front underbelly was severely dented. **1964** S. BELLOW *Herzog* 327 The great car got up the hill slowly, scraping its underbelly on rocks.

2. *fig.* **a.** A vulnerable part, esp. in phr. ***soft underbelly***.

1942 W. S. CHURCHILL in *Hansard Commons* 11 Nov. 28 We make this wide encircling movement in the Mediterranean..having for its object the exposure of the under-belly of the Axis, especially Italy, to heavy attack. **1949** *Life* 31 Oct. 36/2 An all-out attack on the 'soft under-belly' of socialism. **1959** E. H. CLEMENTS *High Tension* vii. 130 The educational organisation..attacked the soft under-belly of the nation: the children. **1976** J. CROSBY *Snake* (1977) x. 45 She was..sticking her knife into the disgusting underbelly of male chauvinism, and..into the soft underbelly of capitalism. **1980** *Encounter* May 86/2 The plan was to..punch their way through the soft, unsuspecting underbelly of Iran.

b. The underside or inferior part of something, which is often unnoticed or concealed.

1962 *Listener* 6 Dec. 957/2 It is a picaresque language from the under-belly of a culture, the speech of people on the move..of the wagon, railroad, and camp. *Ibid.* 27 Dec. 1106/3 The many programmes of popular music, the under-belly, so to speak, of the broadcast structure. **1976** *National Observer* (U.S.) 21 Aug. 16/3 What we're seeing is the underbelly of some of the great legends of American history. **1981** 'D. JORDAN' *Double Red* ix. 97 The seamy underbelly of American capitalism.

'**under-ˌbevelling.** [UNDER-[1] 5 b.] (See quots.)

1754 [see STANDING *ppl. a.* 6]. **1846** A. YOUNG *Naut. Dict.* 33 The bevelling of a timber implies the angle contained between two of its adjacent sides: if an acute angle, it is termed an under bevelling (or bevel). **1875** KNIGHT *Dict. Mech.* 278/2 A *standing* beveling is made on the outside; an *under* beveling is one on an inner surface of a frame of timber.

under'bid, *v.* [UNDER-[1] 8 b, 10 a. Cf. Da. *underbyde*, Sw. *-bjuda.*]

†**1.** *trans.* To value at a lower rate; to undervalue.

1593 NASHE *Christ's T.* 67 When hee hath resolued to prize himselfe..so great, and some man (as proude as himselfe) comes and vnderbids him. **1645** RUTHERFORD *Tryal & Tri. Faith* (1845) 99 Oh, we under-bid, and undervalue that Prince of love, who did overvalue us.

2. *intr.* To make too low an offer.

1611 COTGR., *Mesoffrir*, to vnderbid; to offer lesse for a thing then its worth. **1679** DRYDEN *Limberham* II. i, Before George, Son Limberham, you'll spoil all, if you under-bid so.

3. a. *trans.* To outbid (a person); to supplant by making a better offer.

1677 MIÉGE *Fr. Dict.* II, To under-bid one. **1694** CONGREVE *Double Dealer* III. v, 'Tis only an inhancing the price of the Commodity, by telling you how many Customers have under-bid her. **1864** LOWELL *Study Wind.* (1886) 124 Strepsiades striving to underbid him in demagogism.

b. *spec.* To supplant by making a lower offer; to offer services, labour, or goods at lower wages or prices than (another).

1825 J. NEAL *Bro. Jonathan* II. 78 A pauper, who[m]..the Major had got for a coachman by underbidding everybody else. **1871** MILL *Pol. Econ.* IV. vii. §7 II. 378 It is also to be protected against being underbid for employment by a less highly paid class of labourers. **1878** JEVONS *Prim. Pol. Econ.* 131 No tradesman or manufacturer likes to see himself underbid by those who offer better goods at lower prices.

4. *Bridge.* To bid less on (a hand) than its strength warrants. Also *intr.*

1908 R. F. FOSTER *Auction Bridge* 29 It is a mistake to underbid the hand. **1945** 'S. J. SIMON' *Why you lose at Bridge* 58 The average player overbids his big hands and underbids his small ones. **1969** A. TRUSCOTT *Gt. Bridge Scandal* xii. 159 He had decided to underbid his hand. **1974** *Times* 16 Feb. 13/3 He did not wish to deny diamonds..nor could he afford to underbid by signing off in Three No Trumps.

Hence **under'bidding** *vbl. sb.* and *ppl. a.*

1642 D. ROGERS *Naaman* 142 That we might bee dispensed within our underbidding of the price which God calls for. *Ibid.* 146 To take out of thine heart this slavish, base, and unbeteaming and underbidding nature. **1900** *Contemp. Rev.* July 128 We must abolish competition, preventing under-bidding by fixing prices.

'**under-bid**, *sb.* *Bridge.* [f. the vb.] **a.** A bid of a number of tricks insufficient to surpass the previous bid. *rare.* **b.** A lower bid than is warranted by the strength of a hand or of a partnership's combined hands.

1923 *Daily Mail* 6 Oct. 6/4 The under-bid of 2 spades is automatically raised to 3 spades by the fact of one of the opponents calling attention to it. **1945** 'S. J. SIMON' *Why you lose at Bridge* 96 Most of the time I make what seems to me the best bid in the circumstances, whether it is an overbid, an underbid, or even an anti-system bid. **1977** *Times* 10 Dec. 13/6 The response which is outstanding is a gross underbid of One No Trump.

ˈunderˌbidder. [UNDER-[1] 10 b.] **1.** One who offers a price next below the highest bid.

1883 *Daily News* 13 July 3/6 Mr. H. Stevens..in this case was the underbidder at 600*l.*, the book being bought by Mr. Quaritch for 605*l.*

2. *Bridge.* A player who under-bids.

1923 [see OVERBID *v.* 2 c]. **1945** 'S. J. SIMON' *Why you lose at Bridge* 58 On the cancelled hands, both overbidder and underbidder remain oblivious of their enormities.

underˈbill, *v. U.S.* [UNDER-[1] 10 a.] *trans.* To bill or enter (goods) at less than the actual amount or value. Also **underˈbilling** *vbl. sb.*

1888 *Boston* (Mass.) *Jrnl.* 13 Apr. 3/3 The Interstate Commerce Commission has been investigating..the matter of underbilling. **1889** *Advance* (Chicago) 17 Jan., The bribing of a railroad servant to underbill goods or in some other way to give an advantage to a shipper.

ˈunder-ˌbillow. (UNDER-[1] 5 c.)

1608 CHAPMAN *Byron's Consp.* IV. i. 29 His high spirit That stoops to fear, less than the poles of heaven, Should doubt an under-billow of the sea.

† **underˈbind,** *v. Obs.* [UNDER-[1] 4 a. Cf. MDu. and Du. *onderbinden*, MHG. and G. *unterbinden* (OHG. *untarpintan*), MSw. and Sw. *underbinda*, Da. *underbinde.*] *trans.* To bind by a fastening placed beneath; also, to bind down, keep down firmly.

1538 ELYOT, *Subligo*, to vnderbynde. **1600** FAIRFAX *Tasso* XIX. xviii, But the good prince his hand more fit for blowes With his huge weight the Pagan vnderbound. **1647** HEXHAM I, To Vnderbind, *onder-binden.* [Also in Bailey and Ash.]

ˈunder-ˌbishop. (UNDER-[1] 6 a. Cf. MDu. and Du. *onderbisschop*, OIcel. *undirbiskup*, G. *unterbischof.*) **-ˌbishopric.** (UNDER-[1] 6 b.)

1574 *Life 70th Abp. Canterb.* To Rdr. D 2 Then followeth the Lorde suffraganes, which euery vnder-bishoppe may haue vnder him. *Ibid.* C 8 Somwhat they strained at the vnderbishoprikes.

ˈunderbit. *U.S.* [UNDER-[1] 5 b.] An earmark to indicate ownership, made on the lower part of the ear of cattle. Cf. UNDER-BITTED *ppl. a.*, UNDERKEEL.

1837 *Knickerbocker* X. 408 The young bridegroom boasted that he had taken an 'under bit out of his left ear'. **1869** *Overland Monthly* III. 126 A red mulley cow, with a crop and an underbit in the right [ear]. **1915** *Dialect Notes* IV. 185 *Under-bit*, a triangular cut from the lower side.

underˈbite, *v.* (UNDER-[1] 10 a.)

1876 P. G. HAMERTON *Etching & Etchers* 427 It is better to underbite a plate in the darks than to overbite it, because if underbitten in these lines it is easily darkened afterwards by rebiting.

ˈunderbite, *sb.* [UNDER-[1], after OVERBITE.] The projection of the lower jaw or the lower incisors beyond the upper.

Not a term used in Dentistry.

1976 M. MACHLIN *Pipeline* xlvi. 484 Coutts was a big lantern jawed man with a pronounced underbite that gave his chin an appearance something like an Arctic ice-breaker. **1982** *Guardian* 26 Oct. 8/6 You stick your jaw way out until it's almost as if you have an underbite.

under-ˈbitted, *ppl. a. north. dial.* [UNDER-[1] 4 a.] Earmarked in a special manner.

Cf. mod. U.S. UNDERBIT, and *under-bitten* ppl. a.

1555 *Knaresb. Wills* (Surtees) I. 69 To my doughter..a browne rigged cowe, under bytted of bothe eyres. **1899** in *Cumbld. Gloss.* 381/2 Cheviot ewe, under bitted both ears.

† **under-blade-lurker.** *Obs.* [UNDER-[2].] The subscapular muscle.

1683 SNAPE *Anat. Horse* IV. xviii. (1686) 180 The second Puller or Drawer back of the shoulder is the *subscapularis*, the under-blade-lurker.

ˈunder-blanket. Also as one word. [UNDER-[1] 5 b and UNDER *a.* 2 a.] A blanket laid under the bottom sheet, as opp. to one used as a covering; now often an electric blanket.

[**1746** *Exmoor Scolding* (E.D.S.) 30 That wan tha liv'st up to tha Cot, tha wart the Old Rager Hill's Under Bedblonket.]**1819** S. BUTLER in *Life & Lett.* (1896) I. 164 One under and one good upper blanket. **1930** *Daily Express* 6 Oct. 9/7 (Advt.), Under blankets. **1971** *Guardian* 12 July 3/1 (Advt.), Electric underblanket. Single size approx. 50″ × 26″. **1979** *Daily Tel.* 24 Jan. 14 A simple pin magnet together with a bag of corks placed between the under sheet and the underblanket has made me immune [from cramp].

ˈunder-board, *sb.* [UNDER-[1] 5 b and UNDER *a.* 1 b.] The lower of two boards forming an organ bellows or wind-chest.

1781 *Encycl. Brit.* (ed. 2) VIII. 5747/1 [In] the church-organ..the sound-board..is composed of two parts, the upper board..and the under board. **1845** STIMPSON *Gt. Organ B'ham* 8 Directly over the under-board is situated the upper-board, which is perforated with holes to correspond with those in the under-board.

† **ˈunderboard,** *adv. Obs.* [UNDER-[2].]

1. a. Under the table. Also *fig.*

a **1548** HALL *Chron., Hen. VI*, 99 b, When the greate fire of this discencion..was thus..vtterly quenched out, and laied vnder boord. **1620** GATAKER *Marriage Duties* 46 Like those that climbe and take paines to get nuts, which hauing crackt and eaten the kernell out of, they cast the shels vnderbord. **1642** D. ROGERS *Naaman* 309 [They will] be idle otherwise, as they were at their worke never well, till they have drunk themselves underboord.

b. Under deck.

1588 PARKE tr. *Mendoza's Hist. China* 118 They do make their dwellings in ships,..where they haue their..families under borde to defende them from the sunne and rayne.

2. In an underhand or secret manner; clandestinely; not openly or honestly. (Opposed to *above-board.*)

1581 GOSSON *Plaies Confuted* F 5, [Thus] to shake off the yoake of seuerer discipline..is to iuggle vnder boarde. **1590** NASHE *Pasquil's Apol.* I. B iij b, My Reformer doth nothing but play the Iugler, he packs vnder-boord, and shewes not how farre forth the Archb. hath affirmed it. *a* **1603** T. CARTWRIGHT *Confut. Rhem. N.T.* (1618) 641 The better to discouer your ligier-demain and your playing vnder-board. **1664** H. MORE *Myst. Iniq.* 445 Then shall that Wicked one be revealed (who has dealt under-board hitherto with his Conspirators). **1703** *Secr. Policy of Jansenists* 6 It play'd now no more underboard.

ˈunderˌbody. Also **under-body.** [UNDER-[1] 5 b, c.]

1. † **a.** The lower part of a woman's dress. *Obs.*

1621 BRATHWAIT *Times Curtaine Drawne* D 4, About the May pole while she tripps, Downe fell her vnder-bodie from her hipps. **1621** —— *Nat. Embassie* 204.

b. *U.S. dial.* A corset-cover; underwaist. Also, any undergarment for the body, esp. an under-bodice or under-shirt.

1873 in *Mag. Albemarle County* (Va.) *Hist.* (1963) XX. 57 She gave me some mighty pretty nansook to make an underbody. **1936** E. GLASGOW *Vein of Iron* I. i. 12 She hoped the minister couldn't see the top of her red flannel underbody, which would poke up at the neck, though it was sewed to her petticoat.

2. The underside of an animal's body.

1879 J. BURROUGHS *Locusts & W. Honey* 128 A dog..will manœuvre round the porcupine till he..fastens on his quill-less underbody.

3. a. *Naut.* The part of a ship's hull which is below the water-line.

1895 *Westm. Gaz.* 6 Sept. 7/2 A coat of black composition ..has been given to the underbody of Valkyrie.

b. The under portion of the body of a vehicle. Freq. *attrib.*, with reference to rust protection.

1904 *Daily Chron.* 6 Sept. 6/7 The wagons..were lifted bodily at the end of a trace of chains, hooked to the under-body of the vehicle. **1956** *Autocar* 19 Oct. 596/1 Underbody sealing and sound-deadening compound. **1976** *Sci. Amer.* Feb. 77 (*caption*) Spot-welding robots..are used in assembling the underbodies of Chevrolet Novas, Pontiac Venturas and Buick Skylarks at the General Motors plant. **1976** *Time* 20 Dec. 56/2 (Advt.), The entire underbody is sealed against the elements. **1977** *R.A.F. News* 8–21 June 5/3 (Advt.), Like fitted front seat belts, full underbody seal and servo-assisted front disc brakes.

ˈunder-ˌbonnet, *a.* [UNDER-[2].] Pertaining to, situated, or occurring beneath the bonnet of a motor vehicle (i.e. in or of the engine).

1962 *Times* 24 Apr. 16/2 Oil supply, from an under-bonnet tank. **1973** *Times* 3 May 35/2 A few pounds worth of sound damping material would probably work wonders in suppressing underbonnet and underfloor noise. **1977** *Custom Car* Nov. 13/3 Presumably, Ford believe that customers in that price bracket leave under-bonnet checks to a garage.

ˈunderborn, *ppl. a.* [UNDER-[1] 10 a.] Born with insufficient development.

1884 D. GRAY *Homesick* in *Home in Poetry* (N.Y.) 162 The winter is decrepit, underborn.

ˈunder-bough. [UNDER-[1] 5 b.] One of the lower boughs or branches of a tree. Also *fig.*

1523 FITZHERB. *Husb.* §135 And than the vnder bowes wolde be cutte awaye. **1626** BACON *Sylva* §532 It is certain that timber trees in Coppice-woods grow more upright and more free from under-boughs, than those that stand in the fields. **1642** FULLER *Holy & Prof. St.* II. xxii. 143 These under-boughs grow from the same root with the top-branches. *a* **1661** —— *Worthies, Wilts.* III. (1662) 153 His father,..a fortunate Gentleman in all his Children,..some of his under-boughs out-growing the top-branch. **1814** WORDSW. *Excurs.* v. 148 The roof upheld By naked rafters intricately crossed, Like leafless underboughs, in some thick wood.

ˈunder-ˌbowser. [UNDER-[1] 6 a.] An under-bursar.

a **1659** CLEVELAND *Rustick Ramp.* Wks. (1687) 458 The Under-Bowser's House, standing over against the Fish-market.

ˈunder-boy. [UNDER-[1] 6 a.] A boy belonging to the lower or under-school.

1843 THACKERAY *Fitz-Boodle P., Mr. & Mrs. Berry* i, Here, under-boy, take my coat. **1856** J. RICHARDSON *Recoll.* I. iv. 96 If the under boy refuses or declines to obey, he is punished by blows at the discretion of his tyrant.

underˈbrace, *v.* [UNDER-[1] 4 a.] *trans.* To fasten together underneath.

1791 COWPER *Iliad* III. 440 The broider'd band That under-braced his helmet at the chin.

ˈunderbreath, *sb.*, *a.*, and *adv.* [UNDER-[1] 9 b and UNDER-[2].]

1. *sb.* A low subdued tone; a whisper.

1844 MRS. BROWNING *Rime Duchess May* III. x, I said in underbreath,—All our life is mixed with death. **1884** H. R. HAWEIS *Musical Life* 175 All the point was taken out of it [a story] because I had to hurry over it and end in a guilty kind of underbreath.

b. Whispered rumour.

1880 MEREDITH *Tragic Com.* ii, She heard things related of Alvan by the underbreath.

2. *adj.* Low-toned, whispered.

1853 H. LUSHINGTON *Italian War* (1859) 259 Rather extravagant in his liberalism, and given to underbreath confessions of conspiracy. **1874** AYLWARD in Manning *Ess. Relig. & Lit.* III. 106 The audience was greatly excited, and under-breath communications were made.

3. *adv.* In an undertone or whisper.

1865 SWINBURNE *Chastelard* v. i. 177 Small broken oaths ..And underbreath some praise of Ashtaroth Sighed laughingly.

ˈunder-ˌbreathing, *ppl. a.* (UNDER-[1] 4 a. Cf. prec.)

1760–72 H. BROOKE *Fool of Qual.* (1792) IV. 26 A kind of under-breathing bustle, and whispering commotion.

[In the earlier Wycliffite version of 2 Macc. vii. 5 *vndirbrethinge* is used to render L. *spirantem*; the translator probably read *suspirantem* (cf. UNDER-[1] 2).]

underbred (-ˈbrɛd, older ˈʌndə-), *ppl. a.* and *sb.* [UNDER-[1] 10 a.]

1. Of inferior breeding or upbringing; wanting in polish or refinement; vulgar: **a.** Of persons.

1650 B. *Discolliminium* 50 Our late..under-bred Committee-men. **1706** FARQUHAR *Recruiting Officer* v, Pray, Sir, dunna be offended at my Sister, she's something underbred. **1771** GOLDSM. *Haunch Venison* 37 An under-bred, fine-spoken fellow was he. **1825** T. HOOK *Sayings* Ser. II. III. 154 The boisterous mirth of the under-bred village belle. **1885** *Spectator* 30 May 715/1 All the gentlemen and ladies he has to do with are just a little underbred.

Comb. **1824** SCOTT *Redgauntlet* ch. vi, Behind a long table ..sat a smart, underbred-looking man.

b. Of manners or conduct.

1796 MME. D'ARBLAY *Camilla* III. 209 The under-bred positiveness of her father. **1840** WILLIS *Loiterings* II. 161 His underbred politeness of insisting on following his host. **1849** C. BRONTE *Shirley* vii, His somewhat underbred manner and aspect.

2. Of animals: Not pure bred; of inferior strain.

1890 'R. BOLDREWOOD' *Col. Reformer* (1891) 337 Australian horses..seem wretched underbred creatures.

b. *sb.* An underbred animal (esp. a horse).

1880 *Encycl. Brit.* XII. 198/1 When the thoroughbred is but cantering, the underbred will be doing his utmost. **1897** *Times* 11 Mar. 12/2 At recent shows in Ireland he thought there were more under-breds than 15 or 20 years ago.

ˈunder-ˌbreeding, *vbl. sb.* (UNDER-[1] 10 b. Cf. prec.)

1673 *Ess. Educ. Gentlewom.* 22 Doubtless this under-breeding of Women began among Heathen and Barbarous People. **1850** *Bentley's Misc.* Sept. 234 Some of the lords and ladies..used to..ridicule Mrs. Rawlings before her face, and when they were gone, criticise her underbreeding.

ˈunder-bridge. Also *dial.* -brigg. [UNDER-[1] 5 c.] A bridge spanning an opening beneath a road or railway.

1828 CARR *Craven Gloss.*, *Under-brigg*, an arch under a road to open a communication between two fields. **1876** *Encycl. Brit.* IV. 284/2 The over and under bridges of railways. **1891** *Daily News* 19 June 6/1 The state of the under-bridges throughout the [railway] system.

ˈunder-bright. [UNDER-[1] 5 c.] (See quots.)

1824 CARR *Craven Gloss.* 119 *Under-breet*, a bright light appearing under the clouds in the horizon. **1867** SMYTH *Sailor's Word-bk.* 705 *Under-bright*,..the strong light which sometimes appears below clouds near the horizon.

ˈunderbrim. [UNDER-[1] 5 e.] The underside of the brim of a hat; a trimming or lining attached to this.

1908 *Sears, Roebuck Catal.* 1036/1 This child's hat is.. made on wire frame with the entire upper and under brim very closely covered with shirred pink milliners' mull. **1922** JOYCE *Ulysses* 344 A hat of wide-leaved nigger straw contrast trimmed with an underbrim of eggblue chenille. **1923** *Daily Mail* 5 Mar. 15 A pretty girl's hat is a mushroom shape of rough biscuit straw with a flower-covered underbrim. **1935** BRAND & MUSSARED *Millinery* viii. 64 Tack the underbrim to the interlining at the headline, work from the centre-front in either direction.

† **underˈbring,** *v. Obs.* [UNDER-[1] 4 b and 8. Cf. Du. *onderbrengen*, G. *unterbringen.*]

1. *trans.* To bring into subjection.

c **1320** *Cast. Love* 1316 For whon þe world was furst wrouȝt, He haþ him vnder-i-brouȝt [*v.r.* underbrowght]. *c* **1440** *Eng. Conq. Irel.* 91 Smyrte agayn the bolde, meke wyth ham that weryn vndyr-broght.

2. To bring in surreptitiously.

1382 WYCLIF *Gal.* ii. 4 For false britheren vndirbrouȝt yn, the whiche priuely entriden for to aspie oure liberte.

ˈunderbrush, *sb.* [UNDER-[1] 5 c.]

a. Shrubs and small trees forming the undergrowth in a forest.

Originally and chiefly *U.S.*; common from *c* 1845.

1775 J. JEFFREY *Jrnl.* 3 Apr. in *Essex Inst. Hist. Coll.* (1914) L. 107 The fire ran among the leaves & dry underbrush for upwards of a mile. *a* **1813** A. WILSON *Foresters* Poet. Wks. (1846) 256 Here piles of logs like furnaces appear, The rows of underbrush rage far and near. **1840** R. H. DANA *Bef. Mast* xix, The next thing was to clear away the underbrush, and have fair play at the trees. **1888** STEVENSON *Black Arrow* vi, It was a tall grove of oaks, firm under foot and clear of underbrush.

b. *fig.*

1888 *Kansas State Hist. Soc. Trans.* (1890) IV. 274 The underbrush of forgetfulness has so grown that but few in

Kansas know that Joel K. Goodin ever lived. **1927** *Bulletin* (Glasgow) 6 Apr. 16/1 Taking up a tarnished knife and fork, he pushed aside the underbrush of onions and came face to face with his steak. **1938** [see PRETRIAL *sb.*]. **1968** *Med. World News* 20 Sept. 86/2 It drags the reader through dense verbal underbrush.

Hence **'underbrush** *v. trans.*, to clear of underwood; **'underbrushing** *vbl. sb.*; also *fig.*

1824 *Canad. Mag.* III. 246 Every year we..have a quantity of wood land under-brushed. **1838** *Six Years in Bush* 80 Underbrushing consists in cutting and removing all the young trees and brushwood. **1863** Under-brushing [see LINE *sb.*[2] 26 e]. **1865** P. B. ST. JOHN *Snow Ship* vi, A thorough good chopper, after the land is underbrushed, will, in eight days, on an average, fell the trees. **1896** *Home Missionary* (N.Y.) Jan. 461 The minister..begins to underbrush and cut down the giant sins that have grown on such fat soil. **1933** D. G. CAMERON *Twigs from Oak* 124 That process..called 'underbrushing', was continued over a space about twenty yards wide. **1964** E. C. GUILLET *Pioneer Days Upper Canada* (ed. 2) 122 After underbrushing the piece of land the workers proceeded with logging.

under'build, *v.* [UNDER-[1] 4 a, 10 a.]

1. *trans.* To build under, as a means of strengthening or supporting; to underpin. Also *intr.*

1610 HOLLAND *Camden's Brit.* 185 In the underbuilding, pinning and propping up of their pits. **1653** BLITHE *Eng. Improver Impr.* To Rdr., I shall a little by way of Reparation in some parts underbuild, and some lean-to, or less necessary, quite pull down of the old work. **1828** OWEN & BLAKEWAY *Hist. Shrewsbury* II. 245 A stone-mason.. proposed to cut away the lower parts of the pirm pier, and to underbuild it with free stone. **1861** SMILES *Engineers* II. 322 Directing him to cut away the injured part of the pillar, in order to underbuild it.

2. To build or pile up under one.

1627 MAY *Lucan* VIII. P 6 b, Fire brought, not vnderbuilt great Pompey takes.

3. To fall below in respect of building.

1847 DISRAELI *Tancred* I. iv, It was built by the first duke of the second dynasty, who was always afraid of underbuilding his position.

'under-,builder. [UNDER-[1] 6 a.] An assistant or subordinate builder. Also *fig.*

1651 JER. TAYLOR *Holy Dying* Ded. (1719) A viij b, It is enough for me to be an under-builder in the House of God. **1658–9** SIR H. VANE in *Burton's Diary* (1828) III. 177 Now shall we be under-builders to supreme Stuart? **1841** TRENCH *Parables* 185 The great master builder was about to take down the temporary scaffolding.., and this..the under builders were setting themselves to resist.

'under-buoy. (UNDER-[1] 5 b.)

1793 SMEATON *Edystone L.* §152 He..proposed to fix an under-buoy..nine fathoms under the surface of the sea.

†**underburn,** *v.*[1] (See UNDER-[1] 2.)

,under'burn, *v.*[2] [UNDER-[1] 10 a.] *trans.* To burn insufficiently. Also **'underburnt** *ppl. a.*

1841 *Civil Eng. & Arch. Jrnl.* IV. 341/2 The loss from over-burning, from under-burning and other accidents [to bricks]. **1844** H. STEPHENS *Bk. Farm.* I. 555 An under-burnt as well as an over-burnt tile is bad.

,under'bury, *v.* [UNDER-[1] 8 b.] *trans.* To bury for lower charges than (another).

1753 H. WALPOLE *Lett.* (1857) II. 337 G——d d——n the bishops... So they will hinder my marrying... I'll be revenged! I'll buy two or three acres of ground, and.. underbury them all!

'underbush, *sb.* [UNDER-[1] 5 c.] Underwood, underbrush.

1849 S. C. BREES *Panorama N.Z.* 27 Crawling along the ground, among the underbush and trees. **1867** tr. *Guéranger's Life St. Austin* x. 97 Others grafting fruit trees, or thinning the underbush. **1891** STEVENSON *South Seas* IV. ii, Smoke rose in the green underbush. **1897** MARY KINGSLEY *W. Africa* 114 Pretty trailing lycopodium climbing..over the cardamoms which abound in the under-bush.

Hence **'underbush** *v. trans.*, = UNDERBRUSH *v.*

1886 *Nature* 21 Jan. 269/2, I was watching a coolie under-bushing in the bush.

'under-,butler. (UNDER-[1] 6 a.)

1611 COTGR., *Soubscelerier*, an vnder Butler. **1708** J. CHAMBERLAYNE *St. Gt. Brit.* (1710) 651 The Establishment of..the said Hospital [of Chelsea includes]..2 Under-Butl[ers] at 5*l.* each. **1821** C. BUTLER *Hist. Mem. Cath.* III. xxxvi. 238 He himself was, for some time, under-butler in Gray's-inn. **1887** MISS BRADDON *Like & Unlike* i, The under-butler was over fifty.

,under'buy, *v.* [UNDER-[1] 8 b, 10 a.] *trans.* To buy at less than the actual value, or for less than another. Hence **under'buying** *vbl. sb.*

a **1614** FLETCHER *Valentinian* II. iv, Madam ye have a witty woman. *Mar.* Two Sir, Or else ye underbuy us. *c* **1630** SANDERSON *Serm.* (1681) II. 274 The underbuying of commodities far below the worth.

'undercap. [UNDER-[1] 5 a.] A cap worn under another; ? a night-cap.

1531 *Rec. St. Mary at Hill* 43 Item, two olde Caps and two ondercaps, x d. **1547** in Feuillerat *Revels Edw. VI* (1914) 11, vij vnder Cappes or nyght Cappes to the same of Crymsin Satten. **1651** in *Verney Mem.* (1907) I. 480, 6 serge undercapps and 6 Browne callico under-capps. **1825** JAMIESON *Suppl.*, *Hoomet*,..a child's under cap.

under'capitalize, *v.* [UNDER-[1] 10 a.] *trans.* To furnish with insufficient capital (to achieve a desired result). Chiefly as **under'capitalized** *ppl. a.*

1934 WEBSTER, Undercapitalize. **1962** E. SNOW *Other Side of River* (1963) lxvii. 509 The vicious paradox of China's undercapitalized economy. **1976** *Broadcast* Dec. 4/2 The External Services of both the BBC and these other broadcasting organisations are under-capitalised. **1982** J. FOX *White Mischief* i. 15 The early settlers..most of them were chronically undercapitalised.

,under-'capitalled, *ppl. a.* [UNDER-[1] 10 a.] Not furnished with sufficient capital.

1794 *Monthly Rev.* XV. 185 Many facts here stated fully prove that the country is under-capitalled. **1804** *Crit. Rev.* Ser. III. I. 382 An habitually lower rate of profit than can be accepted by the merchants of under-capitaled countries.

†**'under-,captain.** *Obs.* [UNDER-[1] 6 a.] A captain subordinate to another.

In quots. 1526 = 'centurion'.

1442 *Rolls of Parlt.* V. 60/1 All these saide Shippes..to obey suche rewle..as be their Capitayne and undre Capitayns shall to hem be ordeyned. *c* **1450** *Harl. Contin. Higden* (Rolls) VIII. 453 That he delyvered..the castell.., when he was undercapiten, to the kynge of Fraunce. **1526** TINDALE *Acts* xxi. 32 The hye captayne..toke soudiers and vndercaptynes. [*Ibid.* 33 When they sawe the vpper captayne, etc.] *Ibid.* xxvii. 11 The vndercaptayne beleved the gouerner..better then..Paul. **1550** CROWLEY *Way to Wealth* 641 He woulde not harken to the right aduice of Achior hys vndercaptaine. **1614** RALEIGH *Hist. World* III. 112 He lost fame and high reputation as easily againe, by meanes of some sleight injury done to them by his under-Captaines. **1648** GAGE *West Ind.* x. (1655) 35 Also there were other Gentlemen, that were Under-captains, but a small number.

'under,carriage. Also under-carriage. [UNDER-[1] 5 b.]

a. The part of a carriage or wagon, etc. underneath the body.

1794–6 W. FELTON *Carriages* (1801) I. 49 The fore or under carriage, united to the upper carriage by the perch-bolt. **1886** ELWORTHY *W. Somerset Word-bk.* 813 The under-carriage [of a wagon]..includes all the framework which supports the body.

b. The landing-gear of an aircraft.

1911 HARPER & FERGUSON *Aerial Locomotion* 92 The under-carriage was formed of wheels alone. **1922** *Aerial Age* Aug. 420/2 A shock-absorbing type of under-carriage. **1935** C. G. BURGE *Compl. Bk. Aviation* 160/2 In addition to the undercarriage, alighting gear includes subsidiary items such as tail skids, wing-tip skids, and floats. **1946** *Happy Landings* July 7/1 A characteristic fault of this aircraft made it necessary to operate the undercarriage lever two or three times. **1969** G. MACBETH *War Quartets* 71 One clutched the under-carriage Of a packed hospital-plane. **1977** D. BEATY *Excellency* vi. 80 The three green undercarriage lights, the two white engine lights, the red inverter lights.

'under,carry. [UNDER-[1] 5 c.] The movement of water beneath the surface.

1894 CROCKETT *Raiders* x. 94 The Seahorse..came swiftly, swaying with the undercarry of the sea into the harbour mouth.

'undercart. *slang.* [UNDER-[1] 5 b; cf. UNDER-CARRIAGE.] = UNDER-CARRIAGE b.

1934 *Popular Flying* Sept. 295 (*caption*) The British Klemm 'Eagle'..going great guns, with undercart out of the way. **1939** J. L. RHYS *World owes me Living* xvi. 244 We've got de-icers, variable pitch airscrews, retractable undercart. **1948** 'N. SHUTE' *No Highway* v. 127 Honey had ruined a Reindeer at Gander by pulling up its under-cart. **1958** 'CASTLE' & HAILEY *Flight into Danger* vii. 103 Look, Janet, I think you'd better work the under-cart lever and call off the air-speed as the wheels come down. *a* **1963** J. LUSBY in 'B. James' *Austral. Short Stories* (1963) 225 Do remember that release-tit on the undercart-lever.

under-'carve, *v.* [UNDER-[1] 4 a.] *trans.* To cut away from below or from behind.

1904 LETHABY *Mediæval Art* i. 15 At Baalbec the frieze.. has become a band of carving..under-carved so that the light falls through it as through a trellis.

'under-,carved, *ppl. a.* [UNDER-[1] 4 a.] Carved below or lower down.

1616 B. JONSON *Forest, To C'tess of Rutland* 85 There like a rich and golden pyramede, Borne up by statues, shall I reare your head, Aboue your vnder-carued ornaments.

'undercast, *sb. Mining.* (UNDER-[1] 5 c.)

1883 GRESLEY *Gloss. Coal-m.* 266 *Undercast*, an air course or wind road carried underneath a wagon way or other road. **1886** J. BARROWMAN *Sc. Mining Terms* 69 *Undercast*, the lower of two air courses at an air crossing.

under'cast, *v.* [UNDER-[1] 5 b, 7, 8, 10 a. Cf. MDa. and Da. *underkaste*, MSw. *undir-*, Sw. *underkasta*.]

†**1.** *Obs.* **a.** *trans.* To cast down; to make subject, subdue.

a **1340** HAMPOLE *Psalter* viii. 7 All thyngis þou vndirkast vndir his fete. **1382** WYCLIF *Wisd.* xviii. 22 In wrd hym that ouertrauailede hym, he vndircaste. *a* **1395** HYLTON *Scala Perf.* II. xxxvii. (W. de W. 1494), Thenne forsakyth he vtterly hymself & vndercastyth hym holy to Jhesu. **1483** *Cath. Angl.* 259/2 To Ondyr cast, *subicere, subiectare*. *a* **1618** SYLVESTER *Mysterie of Myst.*, *The Father* 7 Under All things, not under-cast: Over all things, not over-plac't.

b. To subject *to* a penalty.

1382 WYCLIF *Exod.* xxi. 21 If..he [*sc.* a servant] lyue over a day, or two, he shal not be vndurcast to that peyne.

†**2.** To cast under or below. *Obs.*

c **1440** *Pallad. on Husb.* III. 1155 Of vines that forwepe,.. the fattest roote away they tere,..And aisel kene is vnderkest in ground.

†**3.** To consider, reflect. *Obs.*

1489 *Barbour's Bruce* v. 552 (Edin. MS.), Till he..Intill hys hart gan undercast [*Camb. MS.* vmbecast] That the King had in custome ay For to ryss arly ilk day.

4. *Theatr.* To allot (a part) to an inadequate player; to cast (a player) in an insufficient role.

1827 J. BOADEN *Mem. Mrs. Siddons* II. xiii. 66 The Anna, by Miss Wheeler, was rather under-cast. **1920** G. B. SHAW *Let.* in *Bernard Shaw & Mrs. Patrick Campbell* (1952) 206 Overcasting a part means undercasting an artist. **1957** *Observer* 12 May 15/2 [The part] is admittedly under-written; that is no reason why it should have been undercast. **1970** *New Yorker* 22 Aug. 59 Rossellini deliberately undercasts him, as he does every-one else. Colbert is made to look uninteresting and rather bourgeois. **1977** *Times* 9 July 10 The play was woefully undercast.

'under-cause. [UNDER-[1] 6 b.] A subordinate or secondary cause.

1645 RUTHERFORD *Tryal & Tri. Faith* (1845) 385 In regard of irresistible efficacy and success, under-causes..are but idol-causes. **1768–74** TUCKER *Lt. Nat.* (1834) I. 591 No more than a declaration or record of the causes in act, and operations of under-causes flowing from them.

†**under-ce'lestial,** *a. Obs.*[−1] [UNDER-[2].] Subcelestial.

1640 BP. REYNOLDS *Passions* xl. (1647) 529 Creeping alwayes like those under-cælestial Orbes into another motion.

'under-,chamberlain. (UNDER-[1] 6 a.)

13.. *K. Alis.* 246 (Laud MS.), She clepeþ to hir ane sweyn, þat is hire vnder chaumberleyn. **1607** COWELL *Interpr.* s.v., Vnder-chamberlaine of the Exchequer. **1642** C. VERNON *Consid. Exch.* 44 The two Vnder-Chamberlaines bee both the Chamberlaines Deputies for the Recept. **1729** JACOB *Law Dict.* s.v. *Chamberlain*, There are also Under Chamberlains of the Exchequer, who make Searches for all Records in the Treasury.

'under-,chambress. (UNDER-[1] 6 a.)

c **1450** in Aungier *Syon* (1840) 292 The sexteyne, and undersexteyn, the treseres and undertreseres, the chambres and under-chambresse.

'under-,chancellor. (UNDER-[1] 6 a.)

1707 *Lond. Gaz.* No. 4382/3 They write from Lemberg, That the Primate and the Under-Chancellor of the Crown arrived..last Month.

'underchange. [UNDER-[1] 2.] (See quot.)

1589 PUTTENHAM *Eng. Poesie* III. xv. (Arb.) 183 The Greekes call this figure *Hipallage* the Latins *Submutatio*, we in our vulgar may call him the vnderchange but I had rather haue him called the Changeling.

'under-chap. [UNDER-[1] 5 b.] The lower jaw.

1607 TOPSELL *Four-f. Beasts* 29 Their vnderchappe doeth in a deformed manner stretch foorth it selfe beyond the vpper, as it is in many fishes. *a* **1608** DEE *Relat. Spir.* I. (1659) 78 He striketh him with an yern,..griping his brain and underchaps, and so he fell down and disappeared. **1774** GOLDSM. *Nat. Hist.* V. 382 The stork..produces no other noise than the clacking of its under chap against the upper. **1802** PALEY *Nat. Theol.* xxiii, The skin which lies between the under chaps.

under'characterize, *v.* [UNDER-[1] 10 a.] *trans.* To depict or play with insufficient characterization or subtlety. So **under'charac-terized** *ppl. a.*; **,undercharacteri'zation.**

1960 *Times* 13 Jan. 6/6 Minor characters, either under-characterized..or over-characterized, but in both cases quite lifeless. **1963** *Times* 14 Feb. 8/1 The outer movements ..sounded mechanical and under-characterized. **1968** *Time* 26 Apr. 50 *Couples* is flawed by overwriting and undercharacterization. **1970** *Times* 16 Dec. 11 In the wry second movement..the players needed more detailed help with phrasing, and the work as a whole was under-characterized. **1977** *Gramophone* Feb. 1270/1 Impressive as his playing is, in the last resort it is a degree under-characterized.

'undercharge, *sb.* [UNDER-[1] 10 b.] An insufficient charge. Also, an adjustment made to correct an account (see quot. 1861).

1861 E. B. IVATTS *Handbk. Railway Station Managem.* 86 The undercharges or amounts that are afterwards added when the proper charge has not been made,—(when a charge has been once made on an invoice, the figures in English accounts are never altered, errors being corrected by undercharge or overcharge). **1864** WEBSTER, *Under-charge*, a charge less than is usual or suitable. **1920** *Rep. Departmental Comm. Industrial Assurance Companies* 3 If there is under-payment,..it is not due to any undercharge on the assured.

,under'charge, *v.* [UNDER-[1] 10 a.]

Florio (1611) has *Sottocaricare*, to vnder-charge.

1. *trans.* To impose insufficient charges on; to charge (a person, etc.) too little; to make an inadequate charge for (a thing).

1633 STRAFFORD *Lett. & Disp.* (1739) I. 223 They have swallowed down this Maxim, that the Revenue of this Crown must ever be rather over than undercharged. **1712** PRIDEAUX *Direct. Ch.-wardens* (ed. 4) 57 If any be over-charged, or others undercharged, the Ordinary will condemn the Wrong done. **1747** *Gentl. Mag.* 99/1 Any defraud in houses undercharg'd, the persons, &c. to pay double rates. **1864** WEBSTER s.v., To undercharge goods or services. **1895** *Daily News* 15 Mar. 5/6 He affirmed that so far from over-charging India, India was undercharged.

2. To fill or furnish with less than the average charge.

1794 R. J. SULIVAN *View Nature* II. 23 A body that has lost part of its natural quantity, is said to be undercharged, or negatively electrified. **1881** J. C. MAXWELL *Electr. & Magn.* I. 40 If the quantity of fluid in the body is.. less [than that required], the body is said to be Undercharged.

Hence **undercharged** *ppl. a.*

1815 J. SMITH *Panorama Sci. & Art* II. 180 There is an attraction exerted between the overcharged extremity of one magnetic body, and the undercharged extremity of the other. **1834** J. S. MACAULAY *Field Fortif.* 193 When it is required to determine the charge of an undercharged mine, the same rule may be followed.

'under-chord. [UNDER-[1] 5 b.] (See quot.)

1890 *Cent. Dict.* s.v. *Major*, According to this view, the major triad of C is called the *over-chord* of C, and the minor triad of F is called the *under-chord* of C, etc.

'under-chosen, *a. Sociology.* [UNDER-[1] 10 a.] Denoting those who, in a sociometric group study, are chosen by others as companion, fellow-worker, etc., significantly fewer times than average. Cf. OVER-CHOSEN *a.*

1943, 1956 [see OVER-CHOSEN *a.*]. **1968** LINDZEY & BYRNE in Lindzey & Aronson *Handbk. Social Psychol.* (ed. 2) II. xiv. 467 Persons who receive significantly more choices than would be expected by chance may be.. pooled for comparison with a similarly selected group of under-chosen persons.

under'circle, *v.* [UNDER-[1] 4 a.] *trans.* To pass round below.

1668 CULPEPPER & COLE *Barthol. Anat.* I. xiv. 34 A broad Membranous and thin Ligament,.. arising from the Peritonæum which the Midriff undercircles.

'under-,citizen. (UNDER-[1] 6 a.)

1711 ADDISON *Spect.* No. 179 ⁋7 The next that mounted the Stage was an Under-Citizen of the [city of] Bath.

,under'clad, *ppl. a.* [UNDER-[1] 10 a.] Insufficiently clad or clothed. Also *fig.*

1622 T. SCOTT *Belg. Pismire* 81 With vs the only glory is to be gay, and the greatest shame to be under-clad. **1647** N. WARD *Simple Cobler* 77 Not long since, I met with a book, the best to mee I ever saw;.. yet under favour, it was somewhat underclad. **1896** *Voice* (N.Y.) 27 Aug. 4/6 The underfed, underclad, and needy millions.

'underclass. [UNDER-[1] 5 b.] A subordinate social class; *spec.* [ad. Sw. *underklass*] the lowest social stratum in a country or community, consisting of the poor and the unemployed.

1918 J. MACLEAN in 'H. MacDiarmid' *Company I've Kept* (1966) iv. 124 The whole history of Society has proved that Society moves forward as a consequence of an under-class overcoming the resistance of a class on top of them. **1963** G. MYRDAL *Challenge to Affluence* iii. 40 Less often observed.. is the tendency of the changes under way to trap an 'underclass' of unemployed and, gradually, unemployable persons and families at the bottom of a society. **1964** *Observer* 12 Jan. 10/7 The Negro's protest today is but the first rumbling of the 'underclass'. **1966** *New Statesman* 19 Aug. 247/2 The national economic growth has been bought at the expense of industrial workers and the poor (largely Negro) under-class. **1977** D. M. SMITH *Human Geogr.* x. 299 While in South Africa the black proletariat is large enough radically to change society on its own, the American under-class is in a minority and has much less potential power. **1981** D. G. GLASGOW (*title*) The Black underclass: poverty, unemployment and entrapment in ghetto youth. **1981** *New Statesman* 17 July 14 Many people... have warned of trouble if we went on creating a permanent underclass, and typing it by colour. **1982** *N.Y. Rev. Bks.* 12 Aug. 15/2 The distinctive feature of any under-class is that its members do not conform to the conduct expected of the poor. **1985** *Times* 11 Jan. 5/1 Modern Britain is fostering an underclass of unemployed and unskilled workers.

'under,classman. *U.S.* [UNDER-[1] 6 a.] A junior student; a sophomore or freshman.

1896 F. COHEN & ELIZ. BOYD *Vassar* 53 Other much prized delicacies which tantalize the underclassmen as they pass by.

'underclay. [UNDER-[1] 5 b.] A bed of clay beneath a stratum, now *spec.* under a seam of coal.

1661 J. CHILDREY *Brit. Baconica* 58 The rains that fall, wash by degrees the uppermost mould down into the Valleys,.. but leaves the underclay behind. **1840** [see UNDERCLIFT]. **1845** LYELL *Trav. N. Amer.* I. 84, I was curious to know whether the *Stigmariæ* would be found here in the under-clays. **1867** SMYTHE *Coal* 25 The floor, thill, or seat.. of the coal is an underclay, generally good for fire-brick.

'under-clerk. (UNDER-[1] 6 a. Cf. MDu. *onderclerc*, Du. *-klerk.*)

1393 *Test. Ebor.* (Surtees) I. 185 To the paresch clerk xijd, and to the onder clerk vj d. **1426-7** *Rec. St. Mary at Hill* 64 þe rode lofte & þe vndir clerkes chambre. **1450** *Rolls of Parlt.* V. 195/1 John Browne, undir Clerk of oure Kechyn. **1516** *Will R. Peke of Wakefield* 4 June (MS.), To the clarke iiij d, to the under-clarke ij d. **1611** COTGR., *Soub-despensier*, an vnder Cater, or an vnder Clerke of a kitchin. **1670** CLARENDON *Hist. Reb.* XIV. §73 An Under-Clerk for writing Letters and Commissions. **1708** J. CHAMBERLAYNE *St. Gt. Brit.* (1710) 573 Clerks of the Jurat, or Under-Clerks of the Treasury. **1779** *Mirror* No. 37, Certain concurring circumstances.. placed him as an under-clerk in a counting-house. **1837** B. D. WALSH *Aristoph., Knights* IV. i, I'll ask but ..to.. serve you as your under-clerk in actions. **1841** THACKERAY *Gt. Hoggarty Diamond* ii, We under-clerks all thought it was a fine thing to sit at a desk by oneself.

'undercliff. [UNDER-[1] 5 b or UNDER-[2].]

1. A terrace or lower cliff formed from landslips caused by the action of rain and sea.

[**1781** WORSLEY *Isle of Wight* 211 The country below this range of cliffs, is called, by the inhabitants, Under Cliff, or Under Way.] **1829** PHILLIPS *Geol. Yorks.* 89 A very extensive slip of the superior heights, forming an 'undercliff'. **1865** J. H. BENNET *Winter Medit.* (ed. 3) I. iv. 60 A small amphitheatre, formed on the coast-line or undercliff of the mountains of southern Europe. **1880** *Daily Tel.* 23 Sept., The gradual movements along the undercliffs in the Isle of Wight.

2. (See quot. and next.)

1883 GRESLEY *Gloss. Coal-m.* 267 *Undercliff*, argillaceous shale forming the floor of many coal seams in this coal-field.

'underclift. (UNDER-[1] 5 b.)

1840 W. LOGAN in *Trans. Geol. Soc.* Ser. II. VI. 491 In South Wales, immediately below every regular seam of coal, .. lies a bed of clay, which is commonly called underclay, underclift, understone.

under'close, *v.* (UNDER-[1] 5 a.)

c **1440** *Pallad. on Husb.* II. 94 The first is good ij fote & half or thre Feet depe to turne vp alle, but diligent Thou be lest balkis vndirclosed be [L. *ne crudum solum.. fossor includat*].

'undercloth. (UNDER-[1] 5 b. Cf. MDu. *ondercleet*, Du. *-kleed*; MHG. *underkleit*, G. *unterkleid.*)

c **1440** *Promp. Parv.* 511/1 Vnder clothe, of a bedde, *lodix*. **1452** *Maldon* (Essex) *Court Rolls* Bundle 31, No. 2v (MS.), An olde materas, two pilewys, A vnder clothe of old towylle. **1532-3** *Durham Househ. Bk.* (Surtees) 157, 16 ulnæ pro 2 mappis vocatis underclothez pro tabula domini. **1552-3** *Inv. Ch. Goods, Staffs.*, It[e]m ij underclothes for alters, on cope, ij corporases with a case. **1570** *Bury Wills* (Camden) 156 One bed.. withe a vndercl othe, and my best coverlet.

'underclothe, *v.* [f. UNDERCLOTH-ING.] *trans.* To provide with underclothing.

1857 *Putnam's Monthly Mag.* Mar. 244/1 We were, one and all, stoutly underclothed with flannel. **1904** G. B. SHAW *Comm. Sense Municipal Trading* 70 If you have to choose between underclothing your daughter comfortably [etc.].

,under'clothed, *ppl. a.* [UNDER-[1] 10 a.] Insufficiently clothed.

1890 *Lancet* 17 May 1056/1 No one was either underfed, underclothed,.. or overworked. **1895** P. HEMINGWAY *Out of Egypt* I. i. 9 Women, underclothed and overpainted.

'underclothes. (UNDER-[1] 5 a.)

1835 R. M. BIRD *Hawks* I. 19 Under-clothes of some white summer-stuff. **1855** D. G. MITCHELL *Fudge Doings* I. 47 She supplies her cook with cast-off under-clothes. **1884** MAY CROMMELIN *Brown-Eyes* xviii, Letters A. H. embroidered on the little underclothes I wore.

'under,clothing. [UNDER-[1] 5 a.] Clothing worn below the upper or outer garments, esp. next to the skin. Also *fig.*

1835 T. MITCHELL *Acharn. of Aristoph.* 1061 *note*, Used also of veils, and women's underclothing. **1866** ROGERS *Agric. & Prices* I. xxii. 572 Linen for two purposes—for under-clothing, and for the table. **1878** SPURGEON *Treas. Dav.* Ps. cix. 29 Where sin is the underclothing, shame will soon be the outer vesture.

under'club, *v. Golf.* [UNDER-[1] 10 a.] *refl.* To select (for oneself) a club which will not satisfactorily strike the ball the required distance. Also *intr.* and **under'clubbed** *ppl. a.*, **under'clubbing** *vbl. sb.*

1900 H. HILTON in *Outing* Sept. 654 A besetting sin of nearly all golfers is to what may be termed 'underclub themselves'. **1923** *Daily Mail* 8 May 12 When in doubt underclub yourself and hit hard. **1931** T. H. COTTON *Golf* vii. 56 There are more shots lost through underclubbing than anything else. **1936** P. A. VAILE *Short Game* 33 At least ninety-five per cent. of those that swing putters are grievously under-clubbed. **1955** *Times* 2 May 4/1 Burgess underclubbed at the 11th. **1961** *Times* 28 Mar. 4/2 Underclubbing at the 16th caused their opponents to take three putts. *Ibid.* 8 Sept. 4/1 Wolstenholme under-clubbed himself. **1975** D. LANGDON *How to talk Golf* 78 *Under-clubbing*, a drive which falls short of reaching the green at a short hole. **1979** *Tucson Mag.* Jan. 38/3 Every-body underclubs.

'undercoat. [UNDER-[1] 5 a, c.]

1. A coat worn beneath another. Also *fig.*

1648 HEXHAM II, *Een Onder-rock*, an Vnder-coate. *a* **1680** BUTLER *Rem.* (1759) II. 449 A Pettifogger is an under-Coat to the Long-robe, a Kind of a coarse Jacket, or dirty daggled Skirt and Tail of the long-Robe. **1683** *Lond. Gaz.* No. 1797/4 In a new-fashion'd Campaign Coat of sad colour'd Frize,.. his under-Coat of grey Stuff turned. **1723** *Ibid.* No. 6150/3 His Under-Coat of a fine light Colour.

†2. A woman's underskirt; a petticoat. *Obs.*

1741 RICHARDSON *Pamela* (ed. 3) I. 50, I bought two Flanel Under-coats, not so good as my.. fine Linen ones. **1759** *Ann. Reg., Chron.* 73/2 She was stript of all her cloaths to her shift and under-coat. **1858** H. BAIRD *Poet. Lett.* Ser. I. 52 (Devon dial.).

3. The under layer of hair or down in certain long-haired animals.

1840 DALLAS *Syst. Nat. Hist.* II. 447 The hair [of the goat] covers an undercoat of fine soft woolly down. **1884** *Field* 6 Dec. (Cassell's), The dog looked fresh and well.. though lacking undercoat.

4. a. *Painting* and *Decorating*. A layer or layers of paint applied before the finishing or top coat; the paint used for this. Also *transf.* in electro-plating, cementing, etc.

1873 [see PRIMING *vbl. sb.*[1] 4]. **1901** *Decorators' & Painters' Mag.* I. 1. 45 It is a rather risky experiment to use red lead as an undercoat for vermilion. **1927** W. DEEPING *Kitty* xxvi. 329 'The next job will be to paint 'em.' 'Couldn't I do that?' 'Don't see why you shouldn't, sir. Two good coats over an undercoat.' **1930** FIELD & WEILL *Electro-Plating* 90 The copper is soft and easily buffed, and this is required of the copper which forms the undercoat for nickel. **1958** [see PRIMER *sb.*[2] 3]. **1960** *Farmer & Stockbreeder* 23 Feb. 76/2 Marley Mix is available.. in the following mixes; fine concrete, bricklaying mortar, cement mortar, internal rendering, undercoat mix 1:2:4 concrete. **1976** *Handyman Which?* May 47/1 You'll get a better result by using two coats of primer/sealer beneath the gloss instead of one coat of the primer/sealer and one of undercoat.

b. = UNDERSEAL *sb.*

1960 *Motor* 13 July 21 The Flintkote under-coat service is available in many countries. **1968** *Globe & Mail* (Toronto) 15 Jan. 19/7 (Advt.), Automatic transmission, power disc brakes, undercoat, [etc.].

Hence as *v. trans.*, (*a*) to apply an undercoat of paint to; (*b*) to coat the underside of (something, esp. a motor vehicle) with paint, sealant, or the like; **'undercoated** *ppl. a.*, **'undercoating** *vbl. sb.*

1922 *Decorator* Feb. p. xii (Advt.), Dixon's white paint inside glossy and flat undercoating. *Ibid.* Apr. p. xx (Advt.), The new semi-liquid flat white oil paint for undercoating paint or enamel. **1947** *Automobile Topics* Dec. 20/2 The future of the automobile undercoating business largely rests upon.. a proper job of spraying. **1953** *Ibid.* Mar. 26/1 More than half of the nation's postwar automobiles have been undercoated. **1960** *Farmer & Stockbreeder* 23 Feb. 117/1 It can be brushed or sprayed—one coat being sufficient on suitably.. primed surface—no undercoating being required. **1978** *Detroit Free Press* 5 Mar. C22/2 (Advt.), BMW 2002, red,.. undercoated, 57,000 mi. **1979** P. WALLAGE *Restoration Post-War Cars* ii. 25/2, I once had to tackle one which had been undercoated and painted so well it was almost a shame to scrape it off.

undercoat(e, varr. UNDERCOT *v.*

'under-co,llector. (UNDER-[1] 6 a.)

1475 *Rolls of Parlt.* VI. 152/1 The Collectours.. deputed and ordeyned the maire and Aldermen.. to be their under-collectours. **1570** FOXE *A. & M.* (ed. 2) I. 10/1 Which Sanction was also practised.. agaynst the Popes collectors and vnder-collectors. **1572** *Act 14 Eliz.* c. 7 *Preamble*, Great Deceits done.. by Under-Collectors of the Tenths and Subsidies of the Clergy.

'under-,colour. (UNDER-[1] 5 c.)

1611 FLORIO, *Sotto colore*, vnder-colour. **1891** *Cent. Dict.*, *Under-color*, color beneath the exterior or surface color [as in feathers or fur].

'under-,coloured, *ppl. a.* (UNDER-[1] 10 a.)

1777 H. WALPOLE *Let. to R. Jephson* 17 Oct., In landscape-painting some parts must be under-coloured to give the higher relief to the rest. **1870** *Spectator* 20 Aug. 993 We have steadily asserted that France was outnumbered, and now believe that our statements were under-coloured.

'under-co,mmander. (UNDER-[1] 6 a.)

1617 PURCHAS *Pilgrimage* (ed. 3) 588 The Gouvernour was an Abassine, with Seuen other vnder-Commanders, all renegado-Mahumetanes.

'under-con,dition. [UNDER-[1] 6 b.] A subordinate condition or estate.

1681 *Whole Duty Nations* 23 The Messiah then.. must rest in a very low and under-condition of small, private, and particular Assemblies of his servants.

†**'under-conduct.** *Obs.*[−1] [UNDER-[1] 5 c.] A subterranean conduit.

1624 WOTTON *Archit.* 24 Wee should.. Digge Wels and Cesternes, and other vnder-conducts and conueiances.

'under-,constable. (UNDER- 6 a.)

1647 HAWARD *Crown Rev.* 38 Deputy to the under Constable. Fee *per diem*, 12.d.

underconstumble, var. UNDERCUMSTUMBLE *v.*

under-con'sumption. *Econ.* [UNDER-[1] 10 b.] Insufficient consumption; a demand for goods and services exceeded by supply or insufficient to call forth the full potential supply. Cf. OVER-PRODUCTION.

1895 *Westm. Gaz.* 8 Aug. 2/1 What the world is suffering from is under-production of everything and under-consumption. **1906** J. A. HOBSON *Evolution Mod. Capitalism* xi. 288 When the disease is at its worst, the activity of producer and consumer at its lowest, we have the functional condition of under-production due to the pressure of a quantity of over-supply, and we have a corresponding state of under-consumption. **1931** *Times Lit. Suppl.* 14 May 374/3 They are thus on the way, not only to disentangling the mesh of popular theory connected with the words 'over-production' and 'under-consumption' but to destroying the presupposition.. that.. over-production.. may.. occur. **1961** *Economist* 22 Apr. 348/1 'Under-consumption' at the bottom of the social scale was apparent to a slight extent in dental and ophthalmic care. **1974** B. PEARCE tr. *Amin's Accumulation on World Scale* I. i. 112 After a certain level of development has been reached, possibilities of saving become greater than investment needs (governed by the volume of consumption). We have here a general theory of underconsumption.

Hence **undercon'sumptionist**, an advocate of a theory of underconsumption; also *attrib.* or as *adj.*

1936 A. L. ROWSE *Mr Keynes & Labour Movement* 41 In sympathy.. with the attitude of the under-consumptionists all along. **1948** G. CROWTHER *Outl. Money* (ed. 2) v. 149 'Under-consumptionist' theories. **1974** M. B. BROWN *Economics of Imperialism* ix. 216 Some neo-Marxists.. have accepted an underconsumptionist interpretation of Marx and therefore see the increase of surplus value and the search for its disposal as the main source of the continuing expansionism.

'under-cook. (UNDER-[1] 6 a. Cf. MDu. *ondercoc*, Du. *-kok*, G. *unterkoch*, Da. *underkok*, Sw. *-kock*.)

1598 FLORIO, *Sotto cuoco*, an vnder-cooke. **1620** (*title*), The Historie of Frier Rush: how he came to a house of Religion to seeke seruice, and.. was first made vnder Cooke. **1660** BLOUNT *Boscobel* 35 Col. Carlis the while being but Under-cook.. made the fire and turn'd the Collops in the pan. **1734** BERKELEY in Fraser *Life* (1871) vi. 227 On breaking up of the Duke's kitchen, one of his under-cooks may be got. **1809** MALKIN *Gil Blas* x. iii. ¶ 10 The cook, the under-cook, and the scullion. **1900** *Daily News* 9 Oct. 5/1 An under-cook, aged 55, who had served 39 years in a boys' orphanage.

under'cool, *v.* **1.** [UNDER-[1] 8 c.] **a.** *trans.* = SUPERCOOL *v.* a.

1895 C. S. PALMER tr. *Nernst's Theoret. Chem.* I. iii. 65 Probably the two curves would intersect asymptotically at abs. zero, if one could under-cool a liquid so far. **1962** *Zeitschr. f. Metallkunde* LIII. 600/2 Many molten metals slagged in Pyrex glass can be highly undercooled irrespective of the amount. **1977** *Scripta Metall.* XI. 253 Ingots.. were under-cooled and solidified under increasing gravity-levels.

b. *intr.* = SUPERCOOL *v.* b.

1969 *Cast Metals Research Jrnl.* V. 137/1 Cooling curves for ductile iron showed no distinct eutectic arrest but undercooled during eutectic solidification. **1977** *Scripta Metall.* XI. 253 The prepared boules were heated to 230°C, and allowed to undercool.

2. [UNDER-[1] 10 a.] *trans.* To cool insufficiently.

1983 *New Scientist* 13 Jan. 83/2 The continued loss of core-cooling water.. meant that the reactor's core was seriously undercooled.

Hence **under'cooled** *ppl. a.*; **under'cooling** *vbl. sb.*

1895 C. S. PALMER tr. *Nernst's Theoret. Chem.* I. iii. 65 The dotted line is the pressure curve of the under-cooled liquid substance, and forms the continuation of the pressure curve of the liquid. **1913** *Engineering* 10 Oct. 510/3 The under-cooled liquid phase can in many cases be retained in the metastable condition at temperatures far below the normal freezing-point by a process of under-cooling. **1936** *Forestry* X. 128 The point at which ice formation begins may be still further lowered by under-cooling. If water is kept absolutely still, it is possible to lower its temperature below the freezing point without ice formation... This undercooling often takes place in plants. **1980** *Sci. Amer.* Apr. 84/3 Above the glass temperature, in the undercooled liquid phase, the atoms are free to make extensive translational movements.

'undercooled, *ppl. a.* [UNDER-[1] 8 c.] (See quot.)

1902 *Encycl. Brit.* XXVIII. 568/1 It is generally possible to cool a liquid several degrees below its normal freezing-point without a separation of crystals... A liquid in this state is said to be 'undercooled', or 'superfused'.

'under-,cooper. (UNDER-[1] 6 a.)

1745 in W. Thompson *R.N. Advoc.* (1757) 5 Mr. William Thompson (now an under Cooper in your Office).

,under-co'rrect, *v.* (UNDER-[1] 10 a.)

1831 BREWSTER *Optics* xliii. 368 In which the flint lens either over corrects or under corrects the colours of the crown glass lens.

† under'cot, *v. Sc. Obs.* Also -coat(e. [UNDER-[1] 5 a, with obscure second element: cf. QUAT *sb.*[1]] *intr.* To suppurate or fester inwardly.

1584 HUDSON *Du Bartas' Judith* II. 182 To Medciners, the medcine vailed not; So sore the poisond plague did vndercot. **1591** R. BRUCE *Serm.* T ij b, The outwarde scroofe, suppose it appeareth to be whole when the inward is festered auaileth nothing, bot maketh it to vndercoate again. **1637** RUTHERFORD *Lett.* I. cxl. (1664) 275 These.. cannot have but such a peace with God, as will undercot and break the flesh again. **1669** R. FLEMING *Fulfilling Script.* I. (1726) 77 Too soon letting out of a sore may cause it undercot and gather new matter. **1727** P. WALKER *Biog. Presbyt.* (1827) I. 226 A slight Way of Healing indeed, which now is undercotted, and seems to be incurable.

Hence **† under'cotted, under'cotting** *ppl. adjs.*

1636 RUTHERFORD *Lett.* (1664) 315, I finde old sores bleeding of new; so dangerous.. is an undercotted conscience. **1637** *Ibid.* 222 My dumb sabbaths are undercotting wounds.

'undercount. *Statistics.* [UNDER-[1] 10 b.] An incomplete enumeration; *spec.* the amount by which the number enumerated in a census falls short of the actual number in the group.

1955 *Population Studies* (United Nations) No. 23. 11/2 Is there a possibility of an under-count in the 1950 census in the Vega Alta? **1964** *New Statesman* 13 Mar. 390/3 Allowing for a 5 per cent undercount in 1952 and for a 2 per cent increase per annum,.. the Northern total was just about what had been expected. **1981** *Sci. Amer.* Apr. 70/1 Preliminary study of the raw census data now suggests that the 1980 census was remarkably complete: the undercount is turning out to be much smaller than had been projected.

Hence as *v. trans.*, to enumerate incompletely; **'undercounting** *vbl. sb.*

1955 *Population Studies* (United Nations) No. 23. 11/1 There was serious under-counting in the Southern States at the time of the 1870 census. **1970** *Daily Tel.* 22 Aug. 3/6 Mayor Lindsay is convinced that New York will be seriously undercounted in the 1970 census figures. **1978** *Guardian Weekly* 30 Apr. 17/1 In the United States, the Mexican-American population, which may have been severely undercounted in the 1970 census, is growing steadily.

† 'under-,counter. *Fencing. Obs.* (UNDER-[1] 5 b + COUNTER *sb.*[5])

1692 SIR W. HOPE *Fencing-Master* (ed. 2) 73 The contraries to the parade and slipping of under-counter. *Ibid.* 78 The second way is just done as you play under-counter.

'under-,courtier. (UNDER-[1] 6 a.)

1709 STEELE *Tatler* No. 78 ¶ 5 This Gentleman seems to have the true Spirit, without the Formality of an Under-Courtier.

under-cover (-'kʌvə(r), 'ʌndə-), *a.* (and *sb.*). Also undercover. [UNDER-[2].] **A.** *adj.* **1.** That is situated or occurs under cover; sheltered.

1854 *Poultry Chron.* I. 288/2 It is obvious that.. an 'under-cover show' has.. manifest advantages over an exposed one. **1959** *News Chron.* 14 July 4/4 A good fun-fair and some under-cover amusements. **1971** *Engineering* Apr. 61/1 The first mentioned can be very useful when under-cover storage is not available.

2. a. Of a person: operating in secret within a community or organization, esp. as a detective or spy. Freq. as ***under-cover agent, man***. Also applied to organizations or agencies.

1920 U. B. SINCLAIR *100%* 266 [Mrs. Godd] had written in a large, bland, girlish hand her opinion of 'under cover' men and those who hired them. **1932** W. FAULKNER *Light in August* ii. 41 Whiskey can be bought from Brown almost on sight, and the town is.. waiting for him to.. produce from his raincoat and offer to sell it to an under-cover man. **1933** *B'nai B'rith Mag.* XLVIII. 108/1 German steamship lines were 'in the front ranks of Nazi-ism—active under-cover nests of conspiracy'. **1951** E. PAUL *Springtime in Paris* iii. 67 An undercover worker for the Party. **1958** *Spectator* 20 June 809/3 The Providence Island Company.. which served as undercover organisation for the opposition to Charles I. **1970** *Toronto Daily Star* 24 Sept. 12/8 The undercover agent is the surest way of handling narcotics problems in factories.

b. Surreptitious, covert. Of an activity: conducted or existing in secret.

1933 *Light* Nov. 3/1 That undercover atheism which disguises itself under other names... The undercover atheism which so often sneaks by in the clothing of religion itself. **1935** R. MCKAY *'Intelligence' Game* 169 Perhaps they were made careless because they had an undercover 'tip' about the coming of the Austrian. **1953** M. MCCARTHY *Groves of Academe* iii. 50, I have been useful to them from time to time in various little under-cover jobs. **1960** *Times* 27 Aug. 7/3 The menace of recruitment to under-cover prostitution on a large scale cannot be ignored. **1979** N. MAILER *Executioner's Song* (1980) I. xvii. 285 Years ago, when a patrolman, Nielsen did some under-cover work in narcotics.

B. *sb.* An undercover agent. *slang.*

1962 'K. ORVIS' *Damned & Destroyed* vii. 50 The Horsemen have sneaked plants, undercovers, right inside here. **1972** J. MILLS *Rep. to Commissioner* p. x, She was a very good detective. She was a narcotics undercover.

'under-,covering. (UNDER-[1] 5 a, c.)

1483 CAXTON *Gold. Leg.* 131/2 Of hys skynne was made to the kyng of Perses a vndercoueryng. **1902** HANNAN *Textile Fibres of Commerce* 213 The downy under-covering of the Cashmere goat.

'under-,covert. [UNDER-[1] 5 b, c.]

1. A covert of undergrowth.

1805 WORDSW. *Prelude* III. 433 A primeval grove,.. [Not] indigent of songs warbled from crowds In under-coverts.

2. *Ornith.* One of the small close feathers on the under-side of the wing or tail.

1817 STEPHENS in Shaw *Gen. Zool.* X. I. 259 Tail like the wing-coverts, with its under-coverts white. **1895** *Funk's Standard Dict.* s.v. *Wing-covert*, Feathers.. of the lining of the wing are called *under-coverts*.

† 'undercraft. *Obs.* [UNDER-[1] 9 and 6 b.]

1. Hidden or secret craft or cunning.

c **1400** *Pilgr. Sowle* I. xxii. (1859) 27 If thou be vnwise how that thy sowle asayled is with synne and vndercraft.

2. A sly, underhand trick.

1691 NORRIS *Pract. Disc.* 11 Are not.. the little Undercrafts of the Plebeian all put into Motion by this Spring? **1765** STERNE *Tr. Shandy* VII. xix, 'Tis an undercraft of authors to keep up a good understanding amongst words, as politicians do amongst men.

3. *attrib.* Belonging to inferior crafts.

1723 DK. WHARTON *True Briton* No. 59. 23 Dec. 2/1 The Under-Craft Traders; such as Tide-waiters, Tidesmen, and Supernumeraries.

under-'crawl, *v.* (UNDER-[1] 4 b.)

1844 MRS. BROWNING *Lost Bower* xvii, Under-crawling, overleaping Thorns that prick and boughs that bear, I stood suddenly astonied.

under'creep, *v. Obs.* exc. *dial.* [UNDER-[1] 4 b and 8 b. Cf. OE. *undercrēopan*.]

1. *intr.* To creep in (stealthily).

1382 WYCLIF *Deut.* xv. 9 Be war lest perauenture vndur crepe [L. *subrepat*] to thee a wickid thouзt. *c* **1407** LYDG. *Reson & Sens.* 6226 For age, or thy taken kepe, Lyche a thefe wil vnderkrepe, And appallen the beaute.

2. *trans.* To creep in beneath. Also *fig.*

a **1440** *Found. St. Bartholomews* (E.E.T.S.) 40 And now hath vndircrept them necligence, charite chyllith. **1558** PHAER *Æneid* VI. Q j b, That seat, men say, do Fansies keepe, And Dreames vncertaine dwell, and euery leafe they vndercreepe. *c* **1597** HARINGTON *On Play* in *Nugæ Ant.* (1804) I. 227 The olde wall standes by the helpe of that ivey that was the first cawse of rottinge and undercreepinge the fowndacion thearof. **1615** CHAPMAN *Odyss.* IX. 587, I then, Choosing myself the fairest of the den, His fleecy belly under-crept. **1642** H. MORE *Song of Soul* III. iii, When we that stately wall had undercrept, We straightway found our selves in Dizoie.

b. *fig.* To subvert secretly; to outdo by craft or stealth; to undersell in trade.

1592 in R. W. Cochran-Patrick *Records Mining in Scotl.* (1878) 59 And thairby sum persones seikand thair avin commoditie myndis to vndercrepe my rycht and tytill. *Ibid.* 61. **1602** in H. Foley *Rec. Eng. Prov. Soc. Jesus* (1875) I. i. 10 He approved it for better policy to undercreep the Scottish agents here. **1623** SIR J. ELIOT in Forster *Life* (1864) I. 169 Now, for the price, others under-creep us, and so fore-stall our markets.

c. To evade, escape.

a **1618** RALEIGH *Prerog. Parl.* (1628) 34 Surely my Lord, it is a greater treason (though it vndercrepe the law) to teare from the Crowne the ornaments thereof.

Hence **under'creeping** *vbl. sb.* and *ppl. a.*

1398 TREVISA *Barth. De P.R.* XIII. xix. (Bodl. MS.), Bi vndercreping and.. preuey rennynge of water erþe is ywasted somme and somme. **1847** HALLIWELL, *Undercreeping*, mean; pitiful; in an underhand way. *Somerset.* (Also 1863- in south-western glossaries.) **1893** W. RAYMOND *Gentleman Upcott's Dau.* ix. (E.D.D.), Above everything he hated undercreeping.

under'crest, *v.* [UNDER-[1] 4 a.] *trans.* To support as on a crest.

1607 SHAKS. *Cor.* I. ix. 72, I meane to stride your Steed; and at all times To vnder-crest your good Addition, To th' fairenesse of my power.

'undercroft. [UNDER-[1] 5 b or c + CROFT *sb.*[2]] The crypt of a church; an underground vault or chamber.

In early use app. limited to the crypt of Canterbury Cathedral.

1395 in Legg & Hope *Inventories* (1902) 99 Prope altare beate Marie dicte ecclesie Cant. in Criptis que under croft vulgariter nuncupatur. **1601** F. GODWIN *Bps. of Eng.* 50 The monkes.. buried it [the body] immediately in the vnder-craft. **1631** WEEVER *Anc. Funeral Mon.* 202 This murdered Bishop was buried first in the vndercroft of the Church. *Ibid.* 213. **1640** SOMNER *Antiq. Canterb.* 175 Let me now leade you to the Undercroft. A place fit.. to keepe in memory the subterraneous Temples of the Primitives in the times of persecution. **1772** S. DENNE *Hist. Rochester* 61 From this chapel you descend into the under croft. **1790** PENNANT *London* 330 This undercroft, as these sort of buildings were called, had in it several chauntries and monuments. **1839** *Civil Eng. & Arch. Jrnl.* II. 250/1 The body of the church might be made to stand upon an undercroft. **1865** MORRIS *Jason* xv. 1021 Now went those maids, groping with outstretched hand Betwixt the pillars of the undercroft. **1869** FREEMAN *Norm. Conq.* III. xiii. 292 A vaulted undercroft supported the hall.

† under'crop, *v. Obs.* [UNDER-[1] 8 a.] *trans.* To question stealthily; to sound.

1596 FORMAN *Diary* (Halliw.) 27 When I com home, Henry Pepper cam to me craftely to undercrop me.

'undercrust. (UNDER-[1] 5 b.)

1738 SWIFT *Pol. Conversat.* 158 If you please, my Lord, a Bit of Undercrust. **1764** FOOTE *Mayor of G.* I, I don't think I have eat a bit of under-crust since we have been married.

fig. **1893** *Advance* (Chicago) 13 July, The real teacher knows that shallowness is often due to a second 'undercrust' which he must break.

undercum'stand, *v. dial.* [Alteration of *understand*.] To understand.

1824 CARR *Craven Dial.* 39. **1840** HALIBURTON *Clockm.* Ser. III. iii. 39 Six bottles of iced champaigne,.. then two dollars for tickets, makes a total of twenty-five dollars; do you undercumstand? **1869-** in northern dial. glossaries.

undercum'stumble, *v. dial.* Also -con-. [Alteration of prec.] To understand.

1854 MISS BAKER *Northampt. Gloss.* 368. **1865** MISS BRADDON *Sir Jasper* xxx, Why the gentleman required a boat and a bark is more than I can underconstumble.

undercure (stress variable), *v.* [UNDER-[1] 10.] *trans.* To cure (plastic or rubber) for less than the optimal period.

1916 [see OVERCURE *v.*]. **1965** *Encycl. Polymer Sci. & Technol.* II. 53 To increase the bending capacity still more, the laminated sheets are usually slightly under-cured.

So **'undercured** *ppl. a.*, **under'curing** *vbl. sb.* Also **'undercure** *sb.*, the process or result of undercuring.

1912 *Jrnl. Soc. Chem. Industry* 16 Dec. 1100/1 Nos. (1) and (2) [*sc.* specimens of rubber] were distinctly under-cured at 35 lb. **1915** *Ibid.* 15 Oct. 990/2 In the case of undercures the curve often breaks off too soon for this to be apparent. **1916** *Ibid.* 31 Aug. 872/2 If the impulse is insufficient.. we have the condition of undercuring and the rod falls back, corresponding with a gradual deterioration of the vulcanised product. **1940** J. OSBORNE *Dental Mech.* xi. 128 Under-cured vulcanite is soft and weak, and permeable to mouth fluids and bacteria. **1952** [see *over-cured* ppl. adj. s.v. OVERCURE *v.*]. **1965** *Encycl. Polymer Sci. & Technol.* II. 53 This undercure slightly reduces the quality of the surface, but other advantages are gained so that today a substantial fraction of the total production of decorated, laminated sheet stock is plasticised. **1968** *SPE Jrnl.* Nov. 47/1 Undercured resins are inferior.. but long cure times are uneconomical. **1969** *Jrnl. Paint Technol.* XLI. 702 (*heading*) Effect of undercuring on durability of siliconized polyester enamels with hexakis(methoxymethyl) melamine.

'under,current, *sb.* and *a.* [UNDER-[1] 5 b or c.]

1. a. A stream or current of water, air, etc., flowing beneath the upper current, or below the surface. Also *fig.* of Time.

1683 T. SMITH in *Phil. Trans.* XIV. 565 My conjecture is, that there is an under-current, whereby as great a quantity of water is carried out, as comes flowing in. **1687** NORRIS *Coll. Misc.* (1699) 110 Time shall no more her undercurrent know, But one with great Eternity shall grow; Their streams shall mix. **1762** *Phil. Trans.* LII. 448 Recourse is had to the notion of an under-current. **1830** LYELL *Princ. Geol.* I. 181 The descending water sinks down and forms an under-current. **1878** HUXLEY *Physiogr.* xx. 346 Part of this air then returns as an undercurrent.

b. In hydraulic gold-mining, a settling-box additional to the main sluice.

1877 RAYMOND *Statist. Mines & Mining* 95 The company has this season added a series of under-currents near the point where the washings empty into the river.

2. *fig.* An activity, force, tendency, etc., of a suppressed or underlying character.

1792 [see REACTION 4 a]. **1817** COLERIDGE *Biog. Lit.* I. i. 23 Our genuine admiration of a great poet is a continuous under-current of feeling. **1860** TYNDALL *Glac.* I. xvi. 115 That undercurrent of emotion which surrounds the question of one's personal safety. **1878** BOSW. SMITH *Carthage* 371 That gift of humour, that genuine under-current of the soul.

3. *attrib.* or as *adj.* That runs or flows out of sight; concealed, hidden; suppressed.

1855 TENNYSON *Maud* I. XVIII. viii, My heart more blest than heart can tell, Blest, but for some dark undercurrent woe. **1896** *Daily News* 9 Apr. 3/2 There was a good deal of under-current protest.

'undercut, *sb.* [UNDER-^{1} 5 b and 4 d.]

1. The under-side of a sirloin of beef.

1859 *Habits of Gd. Society* v. 223 The sirloin has an upper and an under cut, about which tastes differ. **1890** MRS. BEETON *Cookery Bk.* 165 The undercut, or fillet of a sirloin, is best eaten when hot.

2. a. *U.S.* A cut made in the trunk of a tree on the side towards which it is intended to fall.

Several other technical senses are recorded in modern American dictionaries.

1883 *Harper's Mag.* Jan. 201/1 In about an hour the undercut had approached the heart of the tree.

b. *Dentistry.* A horizontal cut at the base of a tooth cavity; *esp.* one made to anchor a filling more securely.

1892 R. OTTOLENGUI *Methods of filling Teeth* i. 6 Many fillings have failed through the well-meant but unwise efforts of the operator to give great retentive strength to his cavity by deep undercuts. **1923** J. B. PARFITT *Operative Dental Surgery* (ed. 2) x. 87 The condition for retention, namely, some kind of 'undercut', has already been fulfilled. **1980** J. R. GRUNDY *Conservative Dentistry* vii. 41/1 Minor undercuts should be removed during cavity preparation.

c. *Mining.* A long, thin cut made under a vein of ore or a face of coal. Cf. OVERCUT *sb.* c.

1892 *Trans. Federated Inst. Mining Engineers* I. 130 (*table*) Depth of undercut. **1902** A. S. E. ACKERMANN *Coal-Cutting by Machinery in Amer.* ii. 31 They hole about 2in. in the clay, and partly because of this and partly because of two dirt bands at the bottom, they got practically the whole of the coal taken out of the undercut. **1939** B. L. COOMBES *These Poor Hands* vii. 109 With such a large undercut there was the likelihood of it [*sc.* the roof] falling any second. **1959** G. D. MITCHELL *Sociol.* viii. 136 Gummers..clean out the undercut so that when the shot is fired the coal will have space in which to fall.

d. *gen.* A space formed by the removal or absence of material from the lower part of something.

1914 [see INTERFERENCE 5 b (i)]. **1964** F. O'ROURKE *Mule for Marquesa* iii. 58 Fardan found an under-cut in the south wall two miles from the mouth. **1971** *Country Life* 15 July 141/3 Some sickness has made them lie out of sight in one of those undercuts that sheep rub for themselves in an eroding bank of light soil. **1977** *Design. Engin.* July 54/2 In load bearing applications, undercuts, knurls, lugs, and dovetails are used to provide the component with surfaces onto which the molten metal can lock as it shrinks.

3. A projection on a pattern corresponding to an undercut portion of the mould.

1909 in *Cent. Dict.* Suppl. **1935** *Die-Casting* (Machinery's Yellow Back Series No. 4) i. 10 To provide the undercut a collapsible core is necessary.

under'cut, *v.* [UNDER-^{1} 4 a and 8 b.]

†**1.** *trans.* To cut down or cut off. *Obs.*

1382 WYCLIF *Isaiah* xxxviii. 12 Kut of is as of a weuere my lif; whil ȝit I weuede, he under kutte me.

2. a. To cut (away) below or beneath.

1598 FLORIO, *Sottotagliare*, to vnder-cut. **1725** *Fam. Dict.* s.v. *Turfing Spade*, Its of very great Use to some to undercut the Turf, after it is mark'd out with the Trenching Plough. **1881** J. GEIKIE *Prehist. Europe* 71 Cliffs of homogeneous composition are often undercut by streams.

b. *spec.* To cut or carve so as to leave the upper or exposed portion larger than the under or hidden part.

1874 RUSKIN *Val D'Arno* (1886) 141 He has undercut his Madonna's profile..too delicately for time to spare. **1875** SIR T. SEATON *Fruit-Cutting* 61 You must now commence to back carve the whole; that is to say, to undercut the leaves, stems, and branches.

c. *Golf.* To strike (a ball) below the centre, causing it to rise high in the air. Also in *Lawn Tennis*, to impart backspin to (the ball) by slicing down on it below the centre (in quot. *absol.*, to play a stroke which would have this effect).

1891 *Cent. Dict.* **1926** E. BOWEN *Ann Lee's* 86 Mr. Barlow ..walked springily about..hacking, slashing, and under-cutting with his racquet at the air.

d. *Mining.* To cut away the under-part of (a vein of ore or a face of coal); to obtain (coal, etc.) in this way.

1883 GRESLEY *Gloss. Coal-m.* 135 *Hole*, to undercut a seam of coal, &c., by chipping away the coal, &c., with a *pick*. **1892** *Trans. Federated Inst. Mining Engineers* I. 130 The function of all these machines is to undercut the coal in the same way as has hitherto been done by hand labour. **1939** B. L. COOMBES *These Poor Hands* vii. 108 It [*sc.* the coal-cutter] undercut the coal to the depth of the jib. **1945** D. H. ROWLANDS *Coal* xiii. 172 The very first coal-cutter was patented in the eighteenth century, and since then hundreds of inventors have worked on the problem of undercutting the coal-face. **1982** *Sci. Amer.* Sept. 66/1 By the end of World War II 90 percent of the coal mined in the U.S. was undercut by machine.

3. a. To supplant by working for lower wages or payment, or by selling at lower prices.

1884 *Manch. Exam.* 30 July 5/2 We do not want the Post Office to 'undercut' private agencies at the expense of the national taxpayer. **1886** MRS. LYNN LINTON in *Fortn. Rev.* Oct. 500 They are able to undercut the men, and can afford to work for less.

b. *fig.* To render unstable; to render less firm, to undermine.

1955 W. J. BATE *Achievement Sam. Johnson* ii. 81 In the very activity or process of wishing, there are inherent liabilities that are able to undercut the wish itself. **1976** *National Observer* (U.S.) 13 Nov. 1/3 Many vowed that their children would not grow up with the same sort of expectations and handicaps that had so undercut their own self-reliance. **1977** L. GORDON *Eliot's Early Years* iii. 63 The wry, derisive note..undercuts the posturing of Saint Narcissus. **1981** R. HAYMAN *K.* xi. 146 He was aware of undercutting all his gestures towards healthy living by starving himself of sleep.

'undercut, *ppl. a.* [f. prec.] **1.** Cut or carved so as to have material removed from beneath the surface. (Cf. prec. 2 b.)

1793 SMEATON *Edystone L.* §39 The hole was somewhat under-cut; so that, when the lead was poured in, the whole together would make a sort of dovetail engraftment. **1853** ROCK *Ch. of Fathers* III. I. 111 Their slight open skreen-work looks but a frame for the deeply undercut thin foliage roving every where about it. *a* **1878** SIR G. SCOTT *Lect. Archit.* (1879) II. 187 They are most wonderfully carved, the leaves being so much undercut as in places to be quite detached.

2. In *Lawn Tennis*, applied to a stroke which undercuts or imparts backspin to the ball.

1920 [see CHOP *sb.*^{1} 4 e]. **1977** *New Yorker* 10 Oct. 152/2 He shifted from his usual top-spin backhand to a sliced undercut backhand—a stroke that many of us had seen him use only rarely.

3. *Mountaineering.* Of a handhold: cut from below, and used esp. to maintain balance when climbing.

1950 tr. *Mountaineering Handbk.* (Assoc. Brit. Members Swiss Alpine Club) vi. 46 Hand and footholds make progress possible... They can be horizontal, oblique, vertical or undercut. **1965** A. BLACKSHAW *Mountaineering* vi. 161 Side-holds and undercut holds are valuable for maintaining balance or for moving 'in opposition'. **1975** W. UNSWORTH *Encycl. Mountaineering* 120/1 An undercut hold is one that is upside down, but it can be useful.

under'cutter. [f. UNDERCUT *v.*] One who undercuts; a tool or machine for undercutting.

1891 *Engineer* 16 Jan. 59/3 [Patent for] An expanding reversible Undercutter.

under'cutting, *vbl. sb.* [f. UNDERCUT *v.*] The action of the verb in various senses; the result of cutting away below.

1613–39 I. JONES in Leoni *Palladio's Archit.* (1742) II. 45 The under cutting of the Corona too, is simple. *Ibid.*, Many times the Ancients did carve the Undercutting of the Corona, with Leaves. **1836** PALGRAVE *Cal. & Inv. Exchequer* I. p. xxi, The ground [of the seal] is grained, and the under-cutting and fillagree are so deep [etc.]. **1853** RUSKIN *Stones Ven.* III. ii. 89 Elaborate backgrounds,..together with useless undercutting, and over-finish in subordinate parts. **1877** RAYMOND *Statist. Mines & Mining* 37 This will allow an undercutting of the old works from 800 to 1,000 feet.

under'damped, *a.* [UNDER-^{1} 10 a.] Of a physical system: incompletely damped; damped to the extent of allowing only a few oscillations after a single disturbance. So **under'damping** *vbl. sb.* Cf. OVERDAMPED *a.*

1934 W. V. HOUSTON *Princ. Math. Physics* iv. 45 Write the expression for the work done by an under-damped oscillator against the damping force. **1951** [see HUNT *v.* 7 b]. **1952** D. E. CHRISTIE *Intermediate College Mech.* xii. 297 We shall limit our discussion to what is called underdamping. **1976** *Water Resources Res.* XII. 71/1 In the underdamped case the water level oscillates about the equilibrium level.

'underdamper. [UNDER-^{1} 5 b.] Any of the set of dampers in an upright piano of a type in which the dampers are placed below the hammers. Freq. *attrib.*

1870 E. BRINSMEAD *Hist. Pianoforte* 74 Square piano action, with under dampers, and a screw in each key. **1909** *Northampton Independent* 30 Oct. 29/2 (Advt.), A magnificent overstrung underdamper, upright iron grand. **1933** R. E. M. HARDING *Piano-Forte* iv. 56 The under damper is also found in connection with the Single Action. **1980** *Early Music* Apr. 241 (Advt.), After John Broadwood, 1801, a simple under-damper square fortepiano.

†**under-dark,** *a. Obs.* [UNDER-^{1} 2, after L. *subobscurus*.] Somewhat dark; darkish.

1382 WYCLIF *Lev.* xiii. 26 If..thilke spice of lepre were vnder derk, he shal recluse hym seuen daies.

†**under-datary.** *Obs.*$^{-1}$ (UNDER-^{1} 6 a.)

1670 G. H. *Hist. Cardinals* III. III. 320 He confirm'd Monsignor the Under-Datary likewise.

under-dauber. (UNDER-^{1} 6 a.)

1667 JER. TAYLOR *Dissuas. Popery* II. I. ii. 64 That truth.. will..cast down this new mud-wall, thrown into a dirty heap by M. W. and his under-dawber M. S.

under-dead. (UNDER-^{1} 5 c.)

1648 HERRICK *Hesper.*, *Death of Sparrow*, Are not here.. all flowers,..Met in one Hearce-cloth, to ore-spred The body of the under-dead?

†**'underdeal.** *Obs.*$^{-1}$ [UNDER-^{1} 6 b.] Discomfiture.

1553 ASCHAM *Germany* Wks. (1904) 144 He..should haue had that countrey his onely refuge, if that in warre he had come to any vnderdele.

†**under'dealer.** *Obs.*$^{-1}$ [UNDER-^{1} 8 a.] An underhand dealer or agent.

1682 SOUTHERNE *Loyal Brother* v, All underdealers, as procurers, and retailers of pleasure.

†**under'dealing,** *vbl. sb. Obs.* [UNDER-^{1} 9.] Underhand or secret action.

1649 MILTON *Eikon.* xii. 122 He..mentions not that by his underdealing to debaush Armies heer at home..hee had brought the Parlament into..a diffidence of him.

under-debauchee. (UNDER-^{1} 6 a.)

1676 ETHEREDGE *Man of Mode* IV. i, A dozen such good men as you would be enough to atone for..all the under-debauchees of the town.

'under-deck. [UNDER-^{1} 5 b. Cf. Du. *onderdek*, G. *unterdeck*, Da. *underdæk*, Sw. *-däck*.] The lower deck of a vessel. Also *attrib.*

1826 SCOTT *Provinc. Antiq. Scot.* 73 Each inhabitable space was crowded like the underdeck of a ship. **1867** SMYTH *Sailor's Word-bk.* 705 *Under deck*, the floor of a cabin, or 'tween decks. **1872** TALMAGE *Serm.* 43 Allow your appetites and passions only an under-deck passage.

'under-de,greed, *a.* [UNDER-^{1} 6 b.] Of lower degree; of inferior rank.

1748 RICHARDSON *Clarissa* (1811) IV. 48 The reputation of persons of birth must not lie at the mercy of every under-degreed sinner.

†**under'delve,** *v. Obs.* [UNDER-^{1} 4 a, after L. *suffodĕre*. Cf. Du. *onderdelven*.] *trans.* To dig under; to undermine by digging.

c **1000** ÆLFRIC *Saints' Lives* xxxii. 204 Sum eac underdealf þa duru mid spade. *c* **1000** *Ags. Gosp.* Luke xii. 39 He wacode, and ne ȝeþafode þæt man his hus underdulfe. **1382** WYCLIF *Gen.* xlix. 6 In her owne wil thei vndurdelueden the wal. *a* **1400** *Pauline Ep.* (Powell) Rom. xi. 3 Lord þey haue slayn þi prophetis; þey haue vndyrdolue þyn auteris. *c* **1440** *Promp. Parv.* 511/1 Vnder delvyn, *suffodio*.

Hence †**under'delving** *vbl. sb.*, **under'dolven** *ppl. a. Obs.*

1382 WYCLIF *Ps.* lxxix. 17 The tend vp thingis with fyr, and the vnder doluen. *c* **1440** *Promp. Parv.* 511/1 Vnder deluynge,..*subfossura, subfossio*.

underde'termine, *v.* [UNDER-^{1} 10 a.] *trans.* To account for (a theory or phenomenon) with less than the amount of evidence needed for proof or certainty. Freq. as *pa. pple.* Cf. OVERDETERMINE *v.*

1966 J. J. KATZ *Philos. of Lang.* ii. 11 As in other sciences, the evidence underdetermines a generalization. **1977** A. GIDDENS *Stud. in Social & Polit. Theory* 11 Even in the most developed areas of the natural sciences, theories are underdetermined by facts. **1979** A. R. PEACOCKE *Creation & World of Science* ii. 73 It is salutary to remember that most cosmological theories are underdetermined by the facts. **1984** *Times Lit. Suppl.* 14 Dec. 1453/3 Early exploratory models will be drastically underdetermined by the data.

Also **,underdetermi'nation**, the state or quality of being underdetermined; **under-de'termined** *ppl. a.*

1966 J. J. KATZ *Philos. of Lang.* iv. 114 Such underdetermination means that the slack must be taken up by considerations that have to do with the simplicity and generality of the hypotheses. **1977** A. GIDDENS *Stud. in Social & Polit. Theory* 11 The underdetermination of theories by facts in social science is certainly greater than in natural science. **1978** HOOKWAY & PETTIT *Action & Interpretation* p. xi, The argument is that with underdetermined theories as to someone's beliefs and desires, there is no language-independent realm of meanings in regard to which the theories differ.

under-de'veloped, *a.* [UNDER-^{1} 10 a.]

a. Incompletely developed, in various senses of the vb.

1892 *Photogr. Ann.* II. 259 It might have been printed from a much under-developed negative. **1910** H. G. WELLS *Hist. Mr. Polly* vii. 165 Mr. Polly felt himself the faintest under-developed simulacrum of man that had ever hovered on the verge of non-existence. **1944** *Ann. Reg. 1943* 328 A creed of this kind [*sc.* Fascist] will appeal to certain types of under-developed Europeans. **1975** *Gen. Systems* XX. 107/1 Anthropology is disorganized and crisis-ridden, yet vastly underdeveloped.

b. *spec.* designating a country or other region in which economic and social conditions fail to reach their potential level or an accepted standard. Cf. DEVELOPING *ppl. a.* and THIRD WORLD.

1949 H. S. TRUMAN in *Congressional Record* 20 Jan. 478/1 Fourth, we must embark on a bold new program for making the benefits of our scientific advances and industrial progress available for the improvement and growth of underdeveloped areas. **1950** *U.S. Dept. State Bull.* 25 Sept. 497 (*title*) Methods of financing economic development of underdeveloped countries. **1956** T. Balogh in A. Pryce-Jones *New Outl. Mod. Knowl.* 519 The typical under-developed country even in the more recent past has only attracted capital for the exploitation of primary products. **1964** Auden in *Listener* 1 Oct. 525/2 It's heartless to forget about the under-developed countries. **1977** P. Johnson *Enemies of Society* xix. 253 Among the so-called underdeveloped countries, the group most likely to carry through industrialization are those which have profited from the 'energy crisis' which has given them truly gigantic quantities of investment capital. **1984** *Guardian* 5 Nov. 12/2 Few people begrudge the aid we send to the starving or merely under-developed regions of the earth.

Also ˌ**underde'velopment**, incomplete development.

1891 *Lancet* 14 Mar. 624/2 Cases..of under-growth, and underdevelopment. **1892** *Photogr. Ann.* II. 59 When from.. under-development, only a poor slide results. **1927** H. G. Wells in *Sunday Express* 20 Feb. 12/6 The development of Soviet flying is retarded by comparative poverty and the economic underdevelopment of the huge regions concerned. **1958** *Listener* 21 Aug. 274/1 It has for too long been.. assumed that inserting a technical skill into a different society will automatically overcome that aspect of underdevelopment to which it is applied. **1969** A. G. Franks *Latin Amer.* (1970) i. 3 Most studies of development and underdevelopment fail to take account of the economic and other relations between the metropolis and its economic colonies.

'under-ˌdevil. (under-[1] 6 a.)

1659 R. Wilde *Poems* (1870) 8 He raised of armed sprites —Elves, goblins, fairies, Quakers, and new lights,—To be his under-devils. **1801** Strutt *Sports & Past.* iii. ii. 118 Beelzebub seems to have been the principal comic actor, assisted by his merry troop of under-devils.

ˌunderdiag'nosis. *Med.* [under-[1] 10 b.]

Failure, on a significant scale, to detect or correctly diagnose all the cases of a disease examined.

1966 *Gastroenterology* LI. 1074 (*heading*) Under-diagnosis of biliary tract disorders? **1971** *Brit. Med. Bull.* XXVII. 14/1 Under-diagnosis has also contributed to the apparently low incidence. **1982** *Brit. Med. Jrnl.* 29 May 1585/1 This low figure for Britain is unlikely to represent underdiagnosis.

So **under'diagnose** *v. trans.*, **under'diagnosed** *ppl. a.*

1974 *Med. Jrnl. Austral.* 12 Jan. 49/1 (*heading*) Cœliac disease: an underdiagnosed disorder with important implications. **1975** *Gut* XVI. 81 The condition may have been underdiagnosed in Britain. **1979** *Brit. Med. Jrnl.* 15 Dec. 1582/3 Surely this does not show general practitioners to be disgracefully underdiagnosing or under-treating hypertension, especially with regard to detection, as a great number of these people had not seen their doctor for some considerable time. **1983** *Ibid.* 17 Sept. 827/1 He considers the disorder to be seriously underdiagnosed.

ˌunder-differenti'ation. *Linguistics.* [under-[1] 10 b.] The incomplete differentiation of phonemic elements in a language, esp. in loanwords taken from a language in which certain phonemic distinctions do not correspond to those in the receiving language. Cf. differentiation 1 b.

1953 U. Weinreich *Languages in Contact* ii. 18 Under-differentiation of phonemes occurs when two sounds of the secondary system whose counterparts are not distinguished in the primary system are confused. **1962** *Canadian Jrnl. Linguistics* VII. 82 These three types of substitution have been variously called..under-differentiation, over-differentiation, and reinterpretation. **1976** *Amer. Speech 1973* XLVIII. 220 Underdifferentiation is the failure to distinguish two or more sounds of the donor language because of the existence of a single counterpart in the recipient language. **1983** *English World-Wide* IV. 53 The orthography gives near maximum representation of significant sounds but allows for underdifferentiation in spelling.

†**under'dig**, *v. Obs.* [under-[1] 4 a.] *trans.* = underdelve *v.*

1382 Wyclif *Ezek.* xxxvi. 35 Citees desert and destitute and vndirdiggid. **1548** Patten *Exped. Scot.* B vj, Yᵉ Castel, whose walles were so thick..that it was not an easy matter sone to vnderdig them. **1580** Hollyband *Treas. Fr. Tong*, *Sarfouir*,..to vnderdig or vndermine. **1600** Surflet *Countrie Farme* iii. iv. 430 So soon as they growe, they must be..clensed from weedes, and vnderdigd.

'under-dip, *a. Mining.* [under-[1] 5 c.] Lying below the level of the bottom of the engine-pit. Also const. *of*.

1839 Ure *Dict. Arts* 975 What is not included, is termed the under-dip coal. *Ibid.* 994 Under-dip workings have been already executed more than an English mile under-dip of the engine-pit bottom. **1886** J. Barrowman *Sc. Mining Terms* 69 Under-dip coals.

'under-dish. (under-[1] 5 b.)

1653 Greaves *Seraglio* 111 A deep Purcelain dish covered, standing upon a flat under-dish of the same mettal.

ˌunder-di'spersion. [under-[1] 10 b.] A reduced degree or amount of dispersion; *spec.* in *Ecol.*, a greater evenness in the distribution of individuals than would be expected on purely statistical grounds. Cf. over-dispersion. Also ˌ**under-di'spersed** *ppl. a.*

1935 *Ann. Bot.* XLIX. 794 There is significant under-dispersion or aggregation among the individuals of the population. **1940** *Proc. Linnean Soc. N.S.W.* LXV. 135 The distribution of individual species in the areas examined must be either random, or over- or under-dispersed. **1946**, **1957** [see over-dispersion]. **1962** D. R. Cox *Renewal Theory* iii. 42 Expression..is less than one, so that there is apparent under-dispersion relative to the Poisson distribution. **1964** K. A. Kershaw *Quantitative & Dynamic Ecol.* vi. 98 Several species showed either 'overdispersion' or 'underdispersion'. **1982** G. A. F. Seber *Estimation of Animal Abundance* (ed. 2) xii. 479 The classification into overdispersed and underdispersed is not sufficiently fine.

'under-diˌstributor. (under-[1] 6 a.)

1708 J. Chamberlayne *St. Gt. Brit.* (1710) ii. iii. 512 There are also several Under-Distributors employ'd [by the distributors of stamped vellum].

under'dive, *v.* [under-[1] 4 b.] *trans.* To dive down into.

1615 Chapman *Odyss.* ii. 198 How is it, O my son, that you alive This deadly-darksome region underdive?

ˌunder'do, *v.* [under-[1] 10 a.]

1. *intr.* **a.** To refrain from full action.

1611 B. Jonson *Catiline* ii. iii, You ouer-act when you should vnder-doe.

b. To do less than is requisite or necessary.

1622 F. Markham *Bk. War* ii. vii. 67 He [*sc.* the corporal] must equally vnderstand both how to obey and how to command, and therwithal it must be mixt with such a temperance, that he must neither ouerdoe nor vnderdoe, lest he utterly undoe. **1642** W. Price *Serm.* 8 We would not cry, that Preacher overdoes, this underdoes, and that goes too farre, this falls short. **1681** Grew *Musæum* i. iv. iv. 79 Nature is so intent upon finishing her Work, that she may be observ'd much oftener to over do, than under do. **1710** Prideaux *Orig. Tithes* ii. 121 He may either overdoe, and give too much,..or he may underdoe and give too little. **1739** J. Trapp *Righteous Over-much* 5 We may..under-doe, and be defective.

2. *trans.* To do, or deal with, insufficiently or imperfectly.

1716 Derham *Phys.-Theol.* To Reader A vij, In the former of which I fear he will think I have as much under-done, as in the latter over-done, the Matter. **1776** Adam Smith *W.N.* i. v. (1869) I. 47 They sometimes overdo the business, and sometimes underdo it. **1886** Mrs. Hungerford *Mental Struggle* iii, Once or twice..it struck me that you were rather under-doing it. **1888** Rickaby *Mor. Philos.* 77 Doing right is opposed to overdoing the thing, and to underdoing it.

b. To act (a part) inadequately. Also used *attrib.*

1748 Richardson *Clarissa* VII. 401 Thou must, however, own a good deal of blunder of the over-do and under-do kind, with respect to the part thou actedst. **1754** —— *Grandison* I. xv. 95 Can I do it, if I place him in the light of a Lover, and not..underdo his character as such? *a* **1770** Jortin *Serm.* (1771) I. v. 87 A disposition and behaviour which may be overdone as well as underdone.

c. *spec.* To cook insufficiently. (Cf. underdone *ppl. a.*)

1864 Webster. **1894** *Westm. Gaz.* 1 Jan. 7/2 An adept at underdoing the meat and overdoing the potatoes.

Hence ˌ**under'doer.**

1753 Richardson *Grandison* V. ix. 45 These overdoers, my dear, are wicked wretches. What do they, but make religion look unlovely, and put underdoers out of heart?

'under-ˌdoctor. (under-[1] 6 a.)

1639 Drumm. of Hawth. *Consid. to Parl.* Wks. (1711) 187 That it shall be lawful for the school-boys..to take the schools against their masters,..and in their places appoint new doctors, under-doctors, masters, for the space of twenty days.

under'doctored. *a.* [under-[1] 10 a.] Chiefly of an area: insufficiently supplied with doctors; short of doctors.

1960 *New Left Rev.* May–June 23/2 There were..more than 3,500 people per doctor..and, in some under-doctored areas, many more. **1976** *Lancet* 9 Oct. 778/1 Too few graduates from British medical schools are willing to work in underdoctored areas. **1980** *Brit. Med. Jrnl.* 29 Mar. 951/2 Its working party's report on underdoctored areas.

'underdog. Orig. *U.S.* [under-[1] 5 b; cf. *top-dog* s.v. top *sb.*[1] 34.] The beaten dog in a fight; *fig.* the party overcome or worsted in a contest; one who is in a state of inferiority or subjection.

1887 *Daily Tel.* 30 Apr. 3/3 There is an indefinable expression in his face and figure of having been vanquished, of having succumbed, of having been 'under-dog' as the saying is. **1892** *Daily Chron.* 23 June 5/2 The mission of the Democratic party is to fight for the under-dog.

Hence **'underdogger**, one who supports the underdog in a contest; **under'doggery**.

1938 H. Belloc in *Tablet* 1 Jan. 8/1 Anyhow, the difficulty and injustice of under-doggery is softened in all sorts of ways by the virtues of charity and humility. **1969** D. Thomson *Aims of Hist.* 68 It was no doubt natural, perhaps inevitable, that the approach of early enthusiasts for economic history should be strongly tinged with under-doggery. **1970** *N.Y. Times* 17 Aug. 26/4 'We under-doggers have to try harder,' he [*sc.* Governor Rockefeller] explained to reporters. **1977** *Time* 3 Oct. 54 After three crushing defeats, *Australia's* loyal underdoggers were busy recalling all the old familiar whiny excuses. **1978** *Times* 2 Sept. 7 The angel with the perfect smell, the innocent, the do-gooder, the outsider, the perfect stranger. I was a great underdogger. **1981** *London Rev. Bks.* 2–15 July 24/3 He bore a grudge for not getting the Nobel prize... Reviews..have made much of O'Hara's under-doggery.

underdone, *ppl. a.* (Stress var.) [under-[1] 10 a, or f. underdo *v.*] Of meat: Insufficiently cooked; left slightly raw after cooking.

1683 Tryon *Way to Health* 111 That it [*sc.* roast flesh] be neither over nor under-done, but of the two, it is better that it be under-done. **1798** *Spirit Public Jrnls.* (1799) II. 202, I shall give an account of every dinner I eat,..whether under or over-done. **1807** Jane Austen *Lett.* (1884) I. 315 A boiled leg of mutton, underdone even for James. **1842** Dickens *Amer. Notes* x, A plate of underdone roast-beef. **1874** H. W. Pullen *Mod. Christianity* (1876) 65 You..make quite as much fuss, if the mutton is under-done.

transf. **1837** Barham *Ingol. Leg.* Ser. i. *Spectre of Tappington*, A little ferret-faced woman with underdone eyes.

'under-dose, *sb.* (under-[1] 10 b.)

1822–7 Good *Study Med.* (1829) IV. 592 Given in a full dose, they destroy the life instantly; but, in an under-dose, the circulation is continued feebly.

ˌunder'dose, *v.* [under-[1] 10 a.]

1. *trans.* To dose (a person) insufficiently; to administer too small a dose to.

1740 Cheyne *Regimen* p. liv, Nature will,..by acute and intolerable Pains from Hunger, apprize him at least in some time, if he has under-dos'd her.

2. To give in insufficient doses.

1744 *Phil. Trans.* XLIII. 216 On the contrary, I was rather induced to think, that it had..been usually under-dosed.

under'dotted, *ppl. a.* [under-[1] 4 a.] Marked with a dot or dots beneath.

1874 *Ripon Ch. Acts* (Surtees) 68 *note*, These three words under-dotted. **1897** Anne Page *Afternoon Ride* 96 The message conveyed by letters under-dotted in a newspaper.

†**'under-ˌdouble.** *Obs.* [under-[1] 6 b: cf. *subdouble* s.v. sub- 10.] = subduple. Also †**under-doubled** *ppl. a. Obs.*

c **1430** *Art of Nombryng* (E.E.T.S.) 16 It shewithe that a nombre componede was the quadrat, and his rote a digit last founde with vnder-double other vndirdoubles. *Ibid.*, Neper to sette the doublede forwarde nether the vnder doublede.

'under-down. [under-[1] 5 c.] The down below the outer feathers of birds.

1842 J. B. Fraser *Mesopot. & Assyria* xv. 363 Cold winters..have every where the effect of lengthening the hair or fleece of animals, or of supplying them with an under-down. **1857** Dufferin *Lett. High Lat.* (ed. 3) 42 Where the eider ducks..build nests with the soft under-down plucked from their own bosoms.

'under-drain, *sb.* [under-[1] 5 c.]

An underground drain.

1805 R. W. Dickson *Pract. Agric.* I. 151 Where under-drains are formed for taking off the water below the footways. **1868** *Rep. U.S. Commissioner Agric.* (1869) 354 The longitudinal underdrains are to be made of broken stones, and are to be filled up to the level of the surface.

under'drain, *v.* [under-[1] 4 a.] *trans.* To drain by means of underground trenches.

1805 [implied at *underdraining* below]. **1832** *Scoreby Farm Rep.* 13 in *Husb.* III (L.U.K.), The land was..completely underdrained with tiles. **1898** *Yearbk. U.S. Dept. Agric.* 318 If it is not underdrained in all wet spots, [surface draining] should be the first work done.

Hence **under'drainer**; **under'draining** *vbl. sb.*

1805 R. W. Dickson *Pract. Agric.* I. 13 Those clayey soils where water stagnates on the surface of the ground, and.. cannot be removed by the more general modes of under-draining. **1832** *Scoreby Farm Rep.* 25 in *Husb.* III (L.U.K.), The great enemy to underdrainers, the mole. **1879** *Harper's Mag.* June 135/2 Other minor improvements have been made, such as the under-draining of a low tract. **1969** G. E. Evans *Farm & Village* ii. 27 This is under-draining, sometimes called thorough-draining, the technique by which a hollow drain is made under the soil into which excess water can soak and be taken off.

'under-ˌdrainage. [under-[1] 5 c.]

Underground drainage.

1810 *Sporting Mag.* XXXV. 23 The System of under-drainage..in the neighbourhood of Edgwarebury. **1898** *Yearbk. U.S. Dept. Agric.* 504 A proper system of under-drainage.

'under-draught. [under-[1] 5 c.]

An undercurrent.

1853 Kane *Grinnell Exp.* xxxvi. (1856) 330 Our log-line.. showed still a marked under-draught toward the south.

under'draw, *v.* (ʌndə-, ˌʌndə-). [under-[1] 4 a, 10 a.]

1. *trans.* To mark by lines drawn underneath.

1799 Anna Seward *Lett.* (1811) V. 195 The motto you will find underdrawn in the lines which suggested my design.

2. To cover (the inside of a roof or the under-side of a floor) with boards or with lath and plaster.

Hence dial. *underdrawing*, a ceiling.

1843 Wordsw. *Prose Wks.* (1876) III. 201 The interior of it has been..made warmer by underdrawing the roof, and raising the floor. **1865** *Spectator* 22 Apr. 435 The mud walls bulging in here and out there; the roof of thatch, and not underdrawn.

3. To represent or depict inadequately.

1865 Mrs. H. Wood *M. Arkell* I. xvi. 282 The sufferings described..were underdrawn rather than the contrary. **1890** *Academy* 3 May 300/2 One seems to be overdrawn, while the other is underdrawn.

4. To draw from a bank-account so as to leave a reserve. Also *absol.*

1898 *Times* 12 July 13/4, I..generally underdrew so as to leave a margin.

ˈunder-drawing. [UNDER-[1] 5 b.] A preliminary sketch, subsequently covered by layers of paint.
1934 *Burlington Mag.* Feb. 85/2 In the latter picture the under-drawing is done for effect and lacks entirely the astounding precision of Holbein's portraiture. **1968** *New Scientist* 3 Oct. 37/2 Mediaeval European paintings.. were made on wood... Preliminary designs were sketched.. with bone black or carbon black.. and this under-drawing was then.. covered with paint layers.

†underdrawn, *ppl. a. Obs.*[−1] (Meaning obscure; perhaps an error for *undrawn.*)
1581 *Knaresb. Wills* (Surtees) I. 141, I give to Henry Pott seaven kie,.. one oxe,.. and fower stottes under drawen.

ˈunderdress, *sb.* [UNDER-[1] 5 a.]
1. Underclothes; a set of underclothing.
1785 BURNS *Mauchline Wedding* 17 But modest Muses only *think* What ladies' underdress is On sic a day. **1856** KANE *Arct. Expl.* II. xvii. 181 Each man had a woollen underdress.
2. A dress or gown worn beneath another; a part of a gown so made as to present the appearance of being worn in this way.
1806 E. WYNNE *Diary* 22 July (1940) III. viii. 291 My bridal array consisted of a white satin under dress and a patent net over it, with a long veil. **1861** *Archaeologia* XXXIX. 250 The sleeves of his doublet are cloth of gold; the under-dress is of a lavender gray. **1897** *Daily News* 23 Jan. 6/3 The under-dress, which showed in front, had three slashes of velvet at the sides.

ˌunderˈdress, *v.* [UNDER-[1] 10 a.] *intr.* To dress too plainly.
1908 R. BAGOT *A. Cuthbert* xxvi. 339 Miss Cuthbert assured her that there was no greater mistake than to under-dress on occasions such as this.

underdressed, *ppl. a.* (Stress variable.) [UNDER-[1] 10 a.] Too plainly dressed.
a **1784** JOHNSON in Mrs. Piozzi *Anecd.* (1786) 109 No person (said he one day) goes under-dressed till he thinks himself of consequence enough to forbear carrying the badge of his rank upon his back. **1853** MRS. GORE *Dean's Daughter* xxvii, [She] ventured to whisper that Mrs. Hargreave had a sadly provincial air—that she was under-dressed, and a dowdy. **1861** MRS. BEETON *Bk. Househ. Managem.* 10 As a general rule.. it is better to be under-dressed than overdressed.

ˈunderdrift. [UNDER-[1] 5 c.] An undercurrent; *fig.* a tendency beneath the surface of things.
1849 CUPPLES *Green Hand* xiv, Either she [the ship] stood still, or she'd caught some eddy or under-drift. **1891** *Daily News* 12 Jan. 215 Thus the underdrift of things is in favour of an easier money market.

ˈunderdrive. [UNDER-[1] 10 b.] An auxiliary speed-reducing gear in a motor vehicle which may be brought into operation in addition to the ordinary gears to provide an additional set of gear ratios.
1929 [see OVERDRIVE *sb.* 1 a]. **1941** *Automobile Engineer* XXXI. 48/1 Chrysler's new 'underdrive' transmission, when coupled with the fluid drive and conventional clutch, is one of the outstanding mechanical innovations of the year. **1981** *Sunday Express* (Colour Suppl.) 4 Oct. /4 (Advt.), The only car with underdrive.

ˈunder-ˌdrudgery. (UNDER-[1] 6 b.)
1624 MIDDLETON *Game at Chess* III. i, I'd make him do all under-drudgery.

ˈunder-earth, *sb.* [UNDER-[2].]
1. a. The earth or soil lying below the surface.
1765 *Museum Rust.* IV. 157 To defend the roots of my young trees from the damp, raw under-earth.
b. *Mining.* (See quot.)
1883 GRESLEY *Gloss. Coal-m.* 267 *Underearth*, a hard bastard fireclay forming the floor of a seam of coal.
2. The regions below the earth.
1878 GLADSTONE *Homer* iv. 56 Tartaros.. standing to the Under-earth as the heaven stands to the Upper.. world-surface. **1896** *Boston* (Mass.) *Youth's Companion* 10 Dec. 659/2 The economical resources of the underearth were the goals of the first practical studies of the rocks.

ˈunder-ˌearth, *a.* [UNDER-[2].] Subterranean, underground.
1592 NASHE *P. Penilesse* K 3, The vnder-earth spirits, are such as lurk in dens and little cauernes of the earth. **1613** PURCHAS *Pilgrimage* II. i. 104 Philip the Tetrarch.. first found out this under-earth passage. **1662** J. CHANDLER *Van Helmont's Oriat.* 322 Paracelsus reducing all things into an under-earth off-spring. **1816** BYRON *'Could I remount'* 23 The under-earth inhabitants—are they But mingled millions decomposed to clay?

†under-earthly, *a. Obs.* = prec.
1598 SYLVESTER *Du Bartas* II. ii. I. *Ark* 281 No hoorded waues Of ayrie clouds or vnder-Earthly caues.

under-ˈeaten, *ppl. a.* [UNDER-[1] 4 a.] Eaten away or eroded below.
1877 TENNYSON *Harold* I. ii, The sea may roll Sand.., not the living rock Which guards the land,.. Except it be a soft one, And undereaten to the fall.

ˈunder-edge. (UNDER-[1] 5 b.) Also *attrib.* The lower edge; also *spec.* in *Cricket*, the inside- or bottom edge of the bat.
1683 MOXON *Mech. Exerc., Printing* xxiv. ¶19 With the under-edge of the bottom of the Brayer. **1733** TULL *Horse-hoeing Husb.* xxiv. 394 Its Under-edge.. will stand upon the prick'd Line *ef.* **1797** *Encycl. Brit.* (ed. 3) XVII. 395/1 The under edge of the false keel. **1883** GRESLEY *Gloss. Coal-m.* 267 *Underedge stone*, the floor of an iron-stone mine. **1960** E. W. SWANTON *West Indies Revisited* 143 He.. dragged the ball into his stumps off the under-edge. **1977** *Sunday Times* 30 Jan. 30/4 Willis bowled Kirmani off the under-edge.

under-emˈployed, *a.* [UNDER-[1] 10 a.] Insufficiently employed, not used to the optimum capacity. Chiefly of persons or machinery.
1908 W. S. CHURCHILL in R. S. Churchill *Winston S. Churchill* (1969) II. Compan. II. xii. 852 We cannot distinguish between the unemployed and the under-employed. **1941** *Economist* 22 Feb. 241/1 The existence of idle or under-employed machinery—and labour—is sheer waste to the war effort. **1962** *Daily Tel.* 15 June 14/2 There is ample evidence of a progressively under-employed industry and of a turn to export business to employ spare capacity. **1980** *Jrnl. R. Soc. Arts* Feb. 150/2 No sensible organization keeps an expensive designer under-employed.

under-emˈployment. [UNDER-[1] 10 b.] Insufficient use of resources; *spec.* a situation in which the number of the unemployed exceeds the number of job vacancies, producing a labour surplus.
1909 S. & B. WEBB *Public Organization of Labour Market* (Minority Rep. Poor Law Commission II) iv. 185 The evil of Under-employment is shown in its most common form in the great class of Casual Labourers. **1926** GALSWORTHY *Silver Spoon* II. i. 112 To free the country from.. under-employment, and over-population. **1944** A. L. ROWSE *Eng. Spirit* xxxii. 225 Carlyle [in *Past & Present*].. went on to point to the dilemma of over-production and under-employment which is a recurrent trouble of *laissez-faire* capitalism. **1961** *Times* 1 Dec. 13/6 This kind of underemployment is to be seen in many sectors of the economy. **1979** *Dædalus* Spring 90 Under-employment does exist, though, and.. there are strategies to pay certain categories of women to take time off or to leave the labor market early.

ˈunder-enˌgraver. (UNDER-[1] 6 a.)
1656 CROMWELL in *Antiq. Rep.* (1808) II. 408 Thomas Symon, Sole chiefe Engraver,.. by his sufficient deputy or under-engraver [etc.].

ˌunder-ˈenter, *v.* [UNDER-[1] 10 a.] *trans.* To enter at less than the actual quantity.
1692 in Picton *L'pool Munic. Rec.* (1883) I. 300 All salt.. shall be measured, and a reasonable proporcion thereof taken.. if y[e] entrey be right, but if underentred, then y[e] town officers to take so much of y[e] said salt.

†ˈunderer. *Obs.*[−1] [f. UNDER *adv.*] An inferior; one of lower rank.
c **1449** PECOCK *Repr.* III. xvii. 393 How ellis my3te.. haue be ordeyned.. suche statis in the church to be in subordinacioun of vndrers and ouerers.

ˈunder-esˌcheator. (UNDER-[1] 6 a.)
1543 tr. *Acts, 5 Edw. III*, c. 4 B ij, Item it is enacted that no shyriffe, vnder-eschetour, baylyffe of fraunchises,.. shall [etc.].

ˈunder-eˌspial. (UNDER-[1] 6 a.)
1820 SCOTT *Abbot* xxiv, His loyal and faithful service as under-espial.

ˈunder-ˌestimate, *sb.* [UNDER-[1] 10 b.] Too low an estimate (of value, expense, etc.).
1882 *Cornh. Mag.* Feb. 169 He sets a high value on wealth, combating.. the stoical underestimate of its importance. **1895** *Bible Soc. Record* (N.Y.) Dec. 178/2 The statements.. are underestimates rather than overestimates.

ˌunder-ˈestimate, *v.* [UNDER-[1] 10 a.]
1. *trans.* To estimate at too low an amount, quantity, number, etc.
1812 *Q. Rev.* VIII. 329 He states the annual consumption.. at.. from three to four hundred, evidently with no disposition to under-estimate the amount. **1869** TOZER *Highl. Turkey* II. 24 [He] seems to have greatly under-estimated the height.
2. To rate or rank too low; to undervalue.
a **1850** CALHOUN *Wks.* (1874) I. 73 It is not my aim.. to underestimate the great power and influence [of the press]. **1882** FARRAR *Early Chr.* II. 96 Exactly as St. James neither ignores nor underestimates faith, so neither does St. Paul ignore nor underestimate the value.. of good works.
Hence **ˌunder-estiˈmation.** (1891–.)

ˌunder-exˈpose, *v. Photogr.* [UNDER-[1] 10 a.] *intr.* and *trans.* To give too little exposure (to).
1890 *Anthony's Photogr. Bull.* III. 287 The best negatives are not those taken the quickest; sooner over expose, than under expose.

under-exposed (stress var.), *ppl. a. Photogr.* [UNDER-[1] 10 a.] Of a sensitized plate or film: Having received too short an exposure to light.
1861 in *Wylde's Circ. Sci.* (1865) I. 162 This is an.. advantage when the picture is under-exposed. **1878** ABNEY *Photogr.* 81 An under-exposed picture will develop very slowly.

under-exposure (stress variable). *Photogr.* [UNDER-[1] 10 b.] Insufficient exposure to light.
1873 E. SPON *Workshop Receipts* Ser. I. 255 If the negative is deficient in density,.. it is the result of under-exposure. **1892** *Photogr. Ann.* II. 90 Rodinal.. gives much softer negatives than quinol, especially in cases of under-exposure.

†underf, *a.*: see UN-[1] 3.

ˈunder-face. (UNDER-[1] 5 b.)
1869 SWINBURNE *Ess. & Stud.* (1875) 346 A large priestly head,.. a heavy lax lustful under-face.

ˈunder-ˌfaction. (UNDER-[1] 6 b.)
1642 FULLER *Holy & Prof. St.* v. xi. 405 Thus is it given to all Heresies to break out into under-factions. **1667** *Decay Christian Piety* xi. ¶4 'Tis abundant evidence how much Christianity loses by these contests of under factions.

ˈunder-ˌfactor. (UNDER-[1] 6 a.)
1623 *St. Papers, Col.* 168 A purser's mate or underfactor.

ˈunder-ˌfaculty. (UNDER-[1] 6 b.)
a **1628** PRESTON *Serm. bef. His Maj.* (1630) 81 How many impediments doth he finde in the vnder-faculties? *a* **1685** OTWAY *Epist. to Duke* 101 And there methinks, Fancy sits Queen of all; While the poor under Faculties resort, And to her sickly Majesty make Court.

ˈunder-ˌfalconer. (UNDER-[1] 6 a.)
1660 FULLER *Mixt Contempl.* (1841) 252 He was preferred one of the King's underfalconers. **1825** SCOTT *Betrothed* xxiii, Blaming alternately the carelessness of the under-falconer, and the situation of the building.

ˈunderfall, *sb.* [UNDER-[1] 5 b.] A foot-hill slope.
1857 *Smith's Dict. Grk. & Rom. Geog.* II. 1274/2 The underfalls of the Alps that are thrust forward towards the plain. **1883** *Standard* 8 May 4/8 The last 'underfalls' of the.. plateau terminate to the North of Tonquin.

under-ˈfall, *v.* (UNDER-[1] 4 b.)
Prob. *trans.*, to fall under (the hands, etc.).
1614 RALEIGH *Hist. World* IV. i. §1. 157 It commonly falleth out with euery man of marke.. that they vnder-fall, and perish, by the hands and harmes, which they least feare.

underfang, var. UNDERFONG *v. Obs.*

ˈunder-ˌfarmer. (UNDER-[1] 6 a.)
1609 T. COCKS *Diary* (1901) 77/5 Rec' of the vnderfermer of Bramblinge,.. ijs vjd. *a* **1751** BOLINGBROKE *Refl. St. Nation* Wks. 1754 III. 160 All who served, cheated the public,.. from the commissioners of the treasury down to the under-farmers and the under-treasurers. **1890** SETON-KARR *Cornwallis* vi. 131 A law.. defining the extent of the legal coercion which landholders might exercise over under-farmers.

ˈunder-ˌfeature. [UNDER-[1] 6 b.] A minor feature in a landscape; a small elevation.
1879 *Cassell's Techn. Educ.* IV. 115/2 All the small outlying features, such as hillocks or ridges;.. the details of these 'under-features' [are] sketched in. **1900** *Daily News* 10 Mar. 5/6 The whole.. Division, which was lying in front of the enemy's left, concealed by an underfeature.

underfed, *a.* and *sb.* (Stress var.) [UNDER-[1] 10 a.] Insufficiently fed or nourished.
1835 SIR J. ROSS *Narr. 2nd Voy.* xli. 545 We were often far underfed. **1868** M. COLLINS *Sweet Anne Page* I. 67 The boys were not starved, but certainly under-fed.
transf. **1893** *Month* July 326 Places.. overstocked with labour or underfed with orders.
b. As *sb.* An underfed person.
1893 *Advance* (Chicago) 1 June, And Growler's so stuffed now he needs to divide his rations with under-feds.

†ˈunder-fee. *Obs.* (UNDER-[1] 6 b + FEE *sb.*[2])
1594 R. ASHLEY tr. *Loys le Roy* 56 Wherehence are come the termes of fees and vnderfees, of vassals and vndervassals. *Ibid.* 117 b, The Nobilitie of the countrie are bound to go to the warre, by the fees, and vnderfees which they possesse.

ˈunderfeed, *a.* [Cf. next, 2.] Of furnaces: Fed with fuel from below. (In recent use.)

ˌunderˈfeed, *v.* [UNDER-[1] 10 a, 4 a.]
1. *trans.* To feed insufficiently; to stint in food.
1659 GAUDEN *Tears Ch.* III. xxviii. 363 The Fanaticks strive to underfeed and starve it to a despicable feeblenesse. **1842** A. COMBE *Physiol. Digest.* ix. (1845) 75 Underfeeding and great mortality of the poor. **1861** GOLDW. SMITH *Inaugural Lect.* 32 The folly of overworking and underfeeding the labourer.
2. To feed with fuel from below.
1904 *Jrnl. Franklin Inst.* Dec. 439 He was convinced that the fundamental principle of underfeeding was a success.

†underˈfeel, *v. Obs.* [UNDER-[1] 8 a.] *trans.* To examine, pry into, quietly or secretly.
1600 HOLLAND *Livy* 639 The young man.. practised secretly to underfeele and sound his mind. **1630** J. TAYLOR (Water P.) *Bawd* Wks. II. 92/1 The Priest.. wil know her disposition,.. and craftily vnderfeele her policies. **1654** GATAKER *Disc. Apol.* 81 Emissaries, who,.. to underfeel and undermine men, repair to them with counterfeit errands.

underfeet: see UNDERFOOT *adv.*

ˈunder-ˌfellow. (UNDER-[1] 6 a.)
a **1586** SIDNEY *Arcadia* II. viii, A principall officer.. Who with no more civilitie (though with much more busines then those under-fellowes had shewed) beganne.. to put interrogatories unto him.

ˈunderfelt. [UNDER-[1] 5 b.] Felt used as an underlay, esp. beneath a carpet.
1895 *Harrod's Catal.* 1487 Paper and felt for laying under carpets—.. Underfelts.. 0/10 and 1/1 per yard. **1907** *Army & Navy Stores Catal.* 270/4 Electric Illuminating Table Cloth. Is used as an underfelt and covered with a white table cloth. **1934** *Discovery* June 155/2 Carpets are much more effective as absorbents [of sound] at the lower frequencies when they are used with underfelts. **1975** N. LUARD *Robespierre Serial* xiii. 119 Carswell slept.. in the hall, on a roll of underfelt which had been accidentally left behind.

under-fiend. [UNDER-[1] 5 b.] One of the fiends under the earth.
1607 SHAKS. *Cor.* IV. v. 98, I will fight Against my Cankred Countrey, with the Spleene Of all the vnder Fiends.

ˈunderfill, *sb. Metallurgy.* [f. UNDER-[1] 10 b, after OVERFILL *sb.*] The condition of there being insufficient metal to fill the aperture between rolls, the impression of a die, etc., so that the desired shape is not taken; a bar or the like that is too small for the rolling it is to undergo.

1924 F. W. DENCER *Detailing & fabricating Struct. Steel* xxvii. 355 Underfills.—A defect of this kind may result from cobbling, and generally is cause for rejection of the pieces affected. **1929, 1957** [see OVERFILL *sb.*]. **1970** *Welding Engineer* July 24/2 With three of four tetra axis welds inclined to the bottom plane, weld underfill would make conventional welding difficult without a special positioner.

under-filling, *vbl. sb.*

1. *Arch.* (Stressed *'under-filling.*) [UNDER-[1] 5 c.] The under-structure of a building.

1624 [see SUBSTRUCTION 1].

2. *Metallurgy.* (Stressed *under'filling* and written without a hyphen.) [UNDER-[1] 10 a.] The action or result of causing an underfill.

1953 [see OVERFILLING *vbl. sb.*]. **1968** R. N. PARKINS *Mech. Treatm. Metals* ii. 78 In designing a sequence of passes the critical factor is to ensure that each groove in turn is just filled with metal so that its form is accurate... Underfilling will produce an imperfect shape.

So **under'fill** *v. trans.*

1968 [see OVERFILL *v.*].

under'find, *v.* Now *dial.* [UNDER-[1] 8 a. Cf. Du. *ondervinden.*] *trans.* To perceive, understand.

c **1200** *Vices & Virtues* 99 3if hie cumeð fram mannen, hie cann hwatliche underfinden, an hwos half he is icumen. *a* **1300** *Cursor M.* 3664 If mi fader þat es now blind Mai mi fallace oght vnderfind, I dred me sare, for benison He sal me giue his malison. **1320–30** *Horn Ch.* 623 Þe kniȝt toke a schaft in hand, & horn wele vnder-fand, þat he couþe ride. *a* **1800** PEGGE *Suppl. Grose, Underfind,* to understand. Derb. **1877** *N.W. Linc. Gloss.* 263 He was here last neet, I underfind.

'under-fired, *ppl. a.* [UNDER-[1] 4 a, 10 a.]

1. Supplied with fuel from below.

1890 D. K. CLARK *Steam Engine* I. 74 The furnace of an egg-end stationary boiler, under-fired, burning coal.

2. Insufficiently fired or baked.

1891 *Cent. Dict.*

'underfit, *a. Physical Geogr.* [f. UNDER-[1] 10 c, after *misfit.*] Pertaining to or designating a stream which, if its average flow in the past was at present-day levels, would be expected to have eroded a smaller valley than it has done. Cf. OVERFIT *a.*

1913 W. M. DAVIS in *Ann. Assoc. Amer. Geographers* III. 3 Underfit Rivers.—The chief object of this paper is to call attention to an explanation recently suggested for the peculiar relation that is frequently observed between the small-curved meanders of a river and the larger-curved meanders of its valley, a relation that has been called 'underfit'. **1939** A. K. LOBECK *Geomorphology* vi. 199 The beheaded stream, having lost much of its volume, acquires mature characteristics. It develops small meanders not suited to the size of the valley. It becomes a misfit, or an underfit, stream. **1964, 1968** [see MISFIT *sb.* 2]. **1970** R. J. SMALL *Study of Landforms* ii. 46 In post-glacial times, the old channels have been choked with alluvium, and the meandering valleys are now followed by 'under-fit' streams, possessing insufficient power to effect further erosion.

Hence **under'fitness,** the property or state of being underfit.

1913 *Ann. Assoc. Amer. Geographers* III. 24 The lower Seine in Normandy shows a slight underfitness. **1964** *Prof. Papers U.S. Geol. Survey* No. 452-A. 29/2 The underfitness of streams in incised meandering valleys can no longer be denied.

'under-flame. (UNDER-[1] 5 b, 6 b.)

1631 SIR L. CARY *Elegy on Donne* 44 To make us know the Crosse, and value it, (Although we owe that reverence to that name Wee should not need warmth from an under flame.) **1830** TENNYSON *Arab. Nts.* 91 Dark-blue the deep sphere overhead.. Grew darker from that under-flame.

'underflood. (UNDER-[1] 6 b.)

1615 CHAPMAN *Odyss.* XVII. 606 But every fountain hath his underfloods.

under-'floor, *v.* [UNDER-[1] 4 a.] *trans.* To provide with, or form, a floor or under-floor.

1778 *Phil. Trans.* LXVIII. 890 The method of under-flooring I have also applied.. to a wooden stair-case. **1884** COUES *Key N. Amer. Birds* (ed. 2) 155 The basitemporal and parasphenoid bones which underfloor the whole skull.

'underfloor, *a.* [UNDER-[2].] That occurs or is situated below floor level; also, operating below the surface of the floor, as ***underfloor heating*** (often by an electrical element embedded in a concrete floor).

1899 KIPLING *Stalky* 83 By some accident of under-floor drafts. **1934** H. M. VERNON *Princ. Heating & Ventilation* v. 92 The scheme adopted took the form of under-floor heating by means of a pipe running round each room at a distance of about 4 in. from the walls. **1953** D. J. WARBURTON *ABC Commercial Vehicles* 8 An under-floor-engine passenger chassis. **1977** M. DRABBLE *Ice Age* I. 61 The flat she'd lived in with Len had had the lot: de luxe washing machine,.. underfloor central heating, two bathrooms, shower... The lot.

'underflow, *sb.* [UNDER-[1] 5 c.] **1.** An undercurrent. Also *fig.*

1854 S. DOBELL *Balder* xxiv. 169 That underflow and substance wherein the future heaves. **1875** CROLL *Climate & T.* viii. 133 An underflow of polar water south into the Atlantic.

2. The (more or less horizontal) flow of water through the ground, *spec.* underneath a river bed.

1890 *Rep. Secretary of Agric. 1890* (U.S. Dept. Agric.) 472 Papers on underflow and subterranean water. *Ibid.* 475 Mr. [J. W.] Gregory became convinced of the existence at moderate depths below the surface.. of an almost continuous drainage supply, which he has termed the under-sheet or under-flow water. **1905** *U.S. Geol. Survey Water-Supply & Irrigation Papers* No. 140. 85 Such wells, several hundred feet in depth, with perforations opposite the best water-bearing material, would utilize a large part of the underflow which now escapes to the sea. **1951** H. E. THOMAS *Conservation of Ground Water* iii. 138 Underflow is the only method of movement in certain reaches of some streams, where the surface channel is dry. **1970** W. C. WALTON *Groundwater Resource Evaluation* vi. 375 Water leaving basins includes streamflow, evapo-transpiration, and subsurface underflow.

3. *Computing.* [After OVERFLOW *sb.* 2 d.] The generation of a number that is too small to be represented in the device meant to store it.

1959 E. M. MCCORMICK *Digital Computer Primer* xi. 155 A number which is too small (yet is not 0) will cause an 'underflow'. **1970** O. DOPPING *Computers & Data Processing* vi. 102 In machines with automatic floating-point arithmetic.. there may also be indicators for overflow and underflow in the characteristic. **1985** *Personal Computer World* Feb. 182/2 Computer users pay far less attention to underflow than they do to overflow or rounding.

under'flow, *v.* [UNDER-[1] 4 a, b. Cf. OE. *underflówan.*]

1. *intr.* To flow beneath.

1610 HOLLAND *Camden's Brit.* II. 45 It looketh downe to the underflowing sea. **1647** HEXHAM I.

2. *trans.* To flow in under (something).

1872 DIXON *Switzers* v. 45 The waters.. underflowed the beams, and lifted the strong habitations.

3. *intr. Computing.* Usu. *'underflow.* [Cf. prec., sense 3.] Of the result of an arithmetical operation: to become too small for the device meant to store it.

1965 *IBM Systems Jrnl.* IV. 32 If the exponent underflows or the result fraction is zero, the result should be treated as 'zero'. **1973** C. W. GEAR *Introd. Computer Sci.* ii. 73 Give examples of pairs of numbers A and B in internal form such that.. A × B underflows in floating-point arithmetic.

†underfo, *v. Obs.* Pa. t. 1–4 (5) **-feng** (4 **-fenge**), 3–4 **-ueng,** 4 **-uinge,** 5 **-fynge;** 4 **-fang, -vong,** 4–5 **-fong**(e. Pa. pple. 1–2 **-fangen,** 4–5 **-fongen** (4 **-un, -yng**), 3–6 **-fonge,** 4 **-uonge, -venge.** [OE. *underfón,* = MDu. *ondervaen,* OHG. *untarfâhan,* MHG. *undervâhen.* See UNDER-[1] 8 a and FANG *v.*[1]]

1. *trans.* To receive (a thing); to have (something) given to one; to come to have or possess.

c **888** K. ÆLFRED *Boeth.* xiv. §3 Eala þæt hit is god.. þæt mon micelne welan hæbbe, nu se næfre ne wyrð orsorȝ þe hine underfehð. **962–3** *Laws Edgar* Suppl. 1 Þa Godes þeowas, þe þa sceattas underfoð þe we Gode syllað. *c* **1040** *Bidding Prayer* in *Eng. Hist. Rev.* Jan. (1912) 10 For ealle þa saula þe fulluht under-fengan. *c* **1200** *Trin. Coll. Hom.* 97 Þis dai is bicumelich time husel to underfon. *c* **1275** *Sinners Beware* 317 in *O.E. Misc.* 82 To day ye schuleþ y-frede And vnder-fo luþre mede. **1340** *Ayenb.* 101 Alle oure broþren.. þet byeþ children of holy cherche, þe byleaue þet hi onderuinge ine cristnynge. *c* **1400** *Brut* 13 And Guentolen.. vndirfonge feautes & homages of all þe men of þe land. *a* **1513** FABYAN *Chron.* 4 Of the peas that hath been vnder-fonge, Both by great othes, and eke by maryage.

b. To receive willingly; to accept.

c **1000** *Ags. Psalter* (Spelman) vi. 9 Drihten ȝebed min he underfeng. *c* **1175** *Pater Noster* in *Lamb. Hom.* 65 God wule hit underfon, Wenne ic forȝeue min hating. *c* **1205** LAY. 10141 For þe king wolde wel don, & Cristes laȝen vnderfon. *a* **1225** *Leg. Kath.* 982 Þu.. underfest þe an half & dustest adun þe oðere. *a* **1300** *Cursor M.* 2700 His fader [was] nineti and nine þat day þai vnder-fang þis neu lai.

c. To admit into a receptacle; to conceive.

a **1100** in Napier *O.E. Glosses* I. 3819 [*Cadaver*] *receptet,*.. underfo. *c* **1175** *Lamb. Hom.* 77 Þu scald underfon an child in þi wombe. *c* **1275** *XI Pains of Hell* 236 in *O.E. Misc.* 153 Vurþer, þer his on oþer put... Seoue duren þer beoþ on, þe saulen for to under-fon. **1379** *Glouc. Cath. MS. 19* No. 1, Lib. I. iii. fol. 2 Whenne thy duodene hath vnder-fongyng & receyved the fode out froo the mawe gutte.

d. To have understanding of or skill in.

a **1300** *Cursor M.* 1519 Cubal [*v.r.* Tobal] þer broþer first vnderfang Music, þat es þe sune o sang.

2. To take in hand; to undertake.

c **893** K. ÆLFRED *Oros.* II. ii. 66 Romulus æfter þiosan under-feng Cirinensa ȝewinn. *c* **897** —— *Gregory's Past. C.* xxi. 161 Ðonne hie ðara eorðlicra monna heortan underfoð to læronne. *c* **1000** ÆLFRIC *Numb.* xi. 17 Hiȝ underfoð þis folc mid þe, þæt þu ne si ana ȝehefeȝod. **1399** GOWER *Praise of Peace* 264 The heved above hem hath noght undirfongen To sette pes, bot every man sleeth other.

3. To receive (a person); to admit to one's presence, society, or friendship; to accept.

924–5 *Laws Edward* 10 Ne underfo nan man oðres mannes man butan þæs leafe þe he ær fyliȝde. *c* **1000** *Ags. Gosp.* Matt. x. 40 Se þe eow underfehð, he underfehð me. *c* **1200** ORMIN 12936 Þatt Godd iss rædiȝ tunnderrfon þatt follc þatt rihht himm follȝheþþ. *c* **1250** *Gen. & Ex.* 1679 And a maiden was hire bi-tagt, Zelfa bi name... Iacob gan hire under-fon. **13..** *K. Alis.* 7046 (Laud MS.), Þise vnderfongen þe Emperoure, And duden to hym al honoure. **1382** WYCLIF *Rom.* 1st Prol., The Lord.. not onli ȝee wolden not resceyuen, but also ȝee slowen; whom we vnderfongen.

b. To receive in a specified manner.

a **1122** *O.E. Chron.* (Laud MS.) an. 1022, Æðelnoð biscop for to Rome & wæs under-fangen þær fram Benedicte.. myd mycclum wurðscipe. *c* **1200** *Trin. Coll. Hom.* 141 Ure drihten underfeng eadmodliche ane sinfulle wimman and forgiaf hire hire sinnen. *c* **1230** *Hali Meid.* 41 He vnderfeð bliðeliche, & bicluppeð swoteluche, þe alre laðlukest. *c* **1290** *Beket* 1367 in *S. Eng. Leg.* I. 145 Þo seint thomas to Rome cam, faire he was onder-fonge. *a* **1330** *Roland & V.* 87 Þemperour was glad y-wis, & vnderfenge wiþ miche blis Sir charls þe king. **1387** TREVISA *Higden* (Rolls) I. 239 At his comynge he schulde wiþ þre manere worschippe be vnder-fonge. *c* **1400** *Brut* 9 And when Brut wyste whens þei were, he þo vndirfong hem with mychel ioy in-to his Shepys. *c* **1425** *Eng. Conq. Ireland* 8 Þe bisshop well wyrshipfully vndre-fynge [*v.r.* vndyrfonge] Macmorgh.

c. *spec.* To receive at baptism.

1362 LANGL. *P. Pl.* A. I. 74 Holi church Icham... Ich þe vndurfong furst and þi feiþ þe tauȝte. **1377** *Ibid.* B. XI. 113 On holicherche I þouȝte, þat vnderfonge me atte fonte.

4. To receive by way of hurt or harm; to undergo, suffer.

c **1000** ÆLFRIC *Numb.* xiv. 34 On feowertiȝum ȝearum ȝe underfoð eowere unrihtwisnissa, þæt ȝe witon mine wrace. *c* **1175** *Lamb. Hom.* 119 Vre drihtnes.. þrowunge þe he for moncunne underfeng. *a* **1225** *Leg. Kath.* 2234 Streche forð þine swire scharp sweord to underfonne. *c* **1250** *Gen. & Ex.* 480 Lamech droȝe is arwe ner, And letet fleȝen of ðe streng, Caim unwarde it under-feng. *a* **1325** *MS. Rawl. B. 520* fol. 53 Þat he þat hat vnderfonge þe harmes habbe bref of wast.

5. To reprove, rebuke. *rare*[−1].

c **1400** *Brut* 138 Þe Erchebisshope.. vnderfonge [*v.r.* vndir-toke] him of his Wickednesse.

under'focus. [UNDER-[1] 10.] The situation in which the beam of an electron microscope is focused to a point somewhat short of the specimen. So **under'focused** *ppl. a.*, **-'focusing** *vbl. sb.*

1953 C. E. HALL *Introd. Electron Microsc.* x. 268 The pattern appearing at the screen is an underfocused image. **1971** *Jrnl. Physics A* IV. 806 These large phase shifts can be exactly cancelled by underfocus of the objective lens. *Ibid.*, This underfocusing will produce a large chromatic aberration. **1979** *Nature* 17 May 227/1 The contrast of the images taken from very thin parts of crystal at about 700 Å underfocus is known to reflect approximately the projection of the structure; the dark dots show the sites of Re ions.

'underfold, *sb.* (UNDER-[1] 5 c.)

a **1618** SYLVESTER *Job Triumph.* III. 286 Earths surface yeelds him corn & fruits for food, Her under-folds, some burning Sulphury flood.

under'fold, *v.* [UNDER-[1] 8 a.] *trans.* To wrap up, hide, conceal.

1612 W. PARKES *Curtaine-Dr.* (1876) 42 Thou hast often fingered my Curtaine, and beene content therewith to shadow and vnderfold many black and vgly disguises.

†underfollow *v.* (UNDER-[1] 2.) *Obs.* So **underfollowing** *ppl. a.*

1382 WYCLIF *Ps.* xxii. 6 Thi mercy shal vnderfolewe [L. *subsequetur*] me alle the daȝis of my lif. *a* **1400** *Pauline Ep.* (Powell) 1 Tim. v. 24 Þe synnus of summe men ar schewyd opyn goande bifore to þe dome and of summe forsoþe þei vnderfolewyn [L. *subsequuntur*]. **14..** *Acta Parlt. Scot.* (1844) I. 711/2 And sa of vnder-followand [L. *de subsequentibus*], that is to say of subarmigeris.. [etc.].

†under'fong, *v. Obs.* Pa. t. 4 **-fanged, -id, -fonged.** [UNDER-[1] 8 a + FANG *v.*[1] Cf. UNDERFO *v.* and MDu. and Du. *ondervangen,* MLG. *undervangen,* G. *unterfangen.*]

1. *trans.* = UNDERFO *v.* 1.

c **1175** *Lamb. Hom.* 51 Hwenne þu scrift underuongest of þe sunnen þe þu idon hauest. *c* **1200** ORMIN 11112 Forr tunnderrfanngenn Crisstenndom & fulluhht unnderr Criste. *a* **1300** *K. Horn* 345 (Harl. MS.), Shame þe mote by shoure, Ant euel hap to vnderfonge. *c* **1350** *Will. Palerne* 5259 To vnder-fonge in fee al þat faire reaume. *c* **1400** *St. Alexius* (Trin.) 44 Þo þis child to cherche com, To vnderfonge cristendom. *c* **1430** *Syr Gener.* (Roxb.) 3075 At the last we shal vndirfong For oure reward grete maugre. **1553** BECON *Reliques of Rome* (1563) 253 Al y[t].. giuen or vnderfongen in way of simonie. **1579** SPENSER *Sheph. Cal.* Nov. 22 If thou.. lust light virelayes, And looser songs of loue to vnderfong.

b. = UNDERFO *v.* 1 b.

a **1225** *Ancr. R.* 38 Swete lefdi seinte Marie,.. vnderuong mine gretunge mid ten ilke Aue. **13..** *Guy Warw.* (A.) 1015 Ich vnder-fong þis present, & þonke hir þat it hider sent; Hir druerie ich vnder-fong. **1362** LANGL. *P. Pl.* A. III. 208 Þe pope and his prelates presentes vnderfongen. *c* **1400** *Prymer* in Maskell *Mon. Rit.* (1846) II. 107 God, to whom it is propre to be merciful,.. vndirfonge oure preieris.

c. To comprehend; to conceive.

a **1300** *Cursor M.* 1542 For-þi lete god þam lijf sua lang þat þai moght seke and vnderfang þe kynd o thinges þat þan were dern. *Ibid.* 10354 A maiden child noght þar-to lang O þe þi wijf sal vnder-fang.

2. = UNDERFO *v.* 3.

a **1175** *Cott. Hom.* 239 Þer beoð anu ȝeredie þe wereȝede gastes, þe hine uniredlice underfangeð mid stiarne swupen. *a* **1225** *Ancr. R.* 190 Nedlunge ȝe moten underuongen me... Hwose underuongeð me gledliche, & makeð me ueire chere [etc.]. **13..** *Coer de L.* 743 The kyng comaunded.. In strong presoun they schuld be done. His jayler hem gan underfong, And took Kyng Rychard be the hond. *a* **1400–50** *Alexander* 2793 (Dublin MS.), And erls of our empire.. Karyn þaim to sir Alexander,.. And he þaim fair vnderfongez & feffys þaim in Landes. *c* **1440** *Gesta Rom.* I. 226 (Harl. MS.), Be thow tornid to me, thow synfulle soule, and I shalle vnderfonge the. **1553** BECON *Reliques of Rome* (1563) 253 That no man vndirfong or take any folke into his house.

3. = UNDERFO *v.* 2.

c **1330** *Amis & Amil.* 1255 Yif thou this bataile vnderfong, Thou schalt haue an euentour strong. *c* **1400** *Rom. Rose* 5710

He vndirfongith a gret peyne That vndirtakith to drynke vp seyne. **1430–40** LYDG. *Bochas* Prol. 35 To under-fong this labour they him prey. *a* **1500** MEDWALL *Nature* (Brandl) II. 32 Hard yt wyll be for vs.. Agayn them warre or batayll to vnderfong. ? **1525** *La Conusaunce Damours* (Pynson) cj, Our ornate Chaucer other bokes amonge In his lyfe dayes dyd vnderfonge To translate.. the sayd story.

4. = UNDERFO *v.* 4. *rare*$^{-1}$.

1382 WYCLIF *Rev.* Prol., What sche [*sc.* the church] schal suffre in this present tyme, and what sche schal vndurfonge in tyme to come.

5. To seduce, entrap, overcome.

1579 SPENSER *Sheph. Cal.* June 103 Thou.. that by trecheree Didst vnderfong my lasse, to wexe so light. **1596** —— *F.Q.* v. ii. 7 With his powre he.. makes them subiect to his mighty wrong; And some by sleight he eke doth vnderfong. **1614** J. DAVIES (Heref.) *Eclogue* 117 For, time will vnderfong vs; and our voice Woll woxon weake.

6. To surround, enclose. *rare*$^{-1}$.

1599 NASHE *Lenten Stuff* 14 They haue towres vpon them sixteene: mounts vnderfonging and enflancking them.

Hence †**under'fonging** *vbl. sb. Obs.*

1340 *Ayenb.* 37 Þe ontrewe reuen.. þet.. rekeneþ more ine dedes and ine spendinge an lesse ine onderuonginge and ine rentes. *c* **1400** LOVE *Bonavent. Mirr.* (1908) xiv. 90 His souereyn mekenes in the vnderfongynge of his baptisme.

'underfoot, *a.* [Attrib. use of UNDERFOOT *adv.*]

1. Lying under the foot or feet. Also *spec.* (see quots. 1824, 1844), and applied to the state of the going in *Horse-racing*.

1596 NASHE *Saffron Walden* K 4, The strange vntraffiqu't phrases,.. as of incendarie for fire,.. an vnder foote abiect for a shooe or a boote. **1824** MACTAGGART *Gallovid. Encycl.* 454 *Underfit* peats, peat turf, digged beneath the foot not in the common way of cutting them of a *breest*. **1844** H. STEPHENS *Bk. Farm* II. 318 In the under-foot wheel, the horses draw by means of trace-chains and swing-tree. **1976** *Eastern Even. News* (Norwich) 9 Dec., Underfoot conditions at Chelmsford made it difficult for everyone. **1979** *Oxford Times* (City ed.) 5 Jan. 6 They [*sc.* postmen] begin their round in darkness before underfoot conditions have a chance to improve.

2. Inferior, abject, low, downtrodden.

1594 NASHE *Unfort. Trav.* B 1 b, Euerie vnder-foot souldior had a distenanted tun, as Diogenes had his tub to sleepe in. **1641** MILTON *Reform.* II. 90 The most dejected, most underfoot and downe-trodden Vassals of Perdition. **1645** —— *Tetrach.* 17 What a stupidnes then is it, that.. wee should deject our selvs to such a sluggish and underfoot Philosophy. **1831** CARLYLE *Sart. Res.* II. iii, My Schoolmaster, a downbent, brokenhearted, underfoot martyr.

under foot, under'foot, *adv.* Also underfeet. [UNDER *prep.* 4 (cf. FOOT *sb.* 33), UNDER-². Cf. MDu. *ondervoet(e*.]

1. Beneath the foot or feet; on the ground:

a. With vbs., esp. *tread*. (Also in fig. use: cf. 2.)

α. *c* **1200** ORMIN 2561 Forr ȝho tradd deofell unnderrfot þwerrt ut onn alle wise. *c* **1400** *Hymns Virg.* (1867) 12 To felle oure foomen vndir foote. *c* **1475** *Mankind* 199 in *Macro Plays* 8 Yt doth my soull myche yll, To se þe flesch prosperouse, & þe soull trodyn wnder fote. **1560** DAUS tr. *Sleidane's Comm.* 30 b, Yet is not theyr authoritie so decaied herby that euery man may treade it vnder foote. **1596** SHAKS. *Tam. Shr.* v. ii. 122 Katerine, that Cap of yours becomes you not, Off with that bable, throw it vnderfoote. **1603** DEKKER *Wonderfull Yeare* Wks. (Grosart) I. 107 His lockes that hang wantonly dangling, troden in durt vnderfoote. **1678** WANLEY *Wonders Little World* IV. viii. 374 His Wife.. overthrew the Table, and tumbled down all the Provision under-foot. **1708** T. WARD *Eng. Ref.* IV. (1815) 429 [He] Stamp'd underfoot a crucifix, As Hollanders are wont to do When on Japonian shore they go. **1802** MRS. GUTHRIE *Tour through the Taurida* 64 Instead of effecting this adhesion by the pressure of cylinders, it is done.. by treading them underfoot for a few hours. **1868** MORRIS *Earthly Par.* (1870) I. I. 349 A fair ivory image of the god That underfoot a golden serpent trod.

β. **1539** BIBLE (Great) *Isaiah* xiv. 19 As a dead coarse that is troden vnder fete. *c* **1620** MORYSON *Itin.* IV. (1903) 496 The Empire.. of the Greekes.. hath beene vtterly abolished, and the people haue beene troden vnderfeete. **1641** BURROUGHS *Sions Joy* 33 They sought to cast shame upon the Saints,.. trampling them underfeete as dirt. **1760** *Impostors Detected* II. ii. I. 170 Sacred relicks trampled under feet! **1857** HOLLAND *Bay Path* xxix, Her memory.. trodden under feet by malice, prejudice, and superstition.

b. In other constructions.

1599 E. WRIGHT *Voy. Earl Cumbld.* 22 in *Cert. Errors Navig.*, Some licked with their tongues.. the boardes vnder feete. **1603** HOLLAND *Plutarch's Mor.* 1225 Lysitheus mounting upon the boord, laied him along on the floore, and there under-foot dispatched him. **1667** MILTON *P.L.* IV. 700 Underfoot the Violet, Crocus, and Hyacinth with rich inlay Broiderd the ground. **1802** MRS. GUTHRIE *Tour through the Taurida* 203 They [*sc.* skins] are next worked under-feet in an infusion of oak-leaves in warm water. **1850** TENNYSON *In Mem.* xcv, By night we linger'd on the lawn, For under-foot the herb was dry. **1880** L. WALLACE *Ben-Hur* I. i, Dried leaves in occasional beds rustled underfoot.

c. *Naut.* (See FOOT *sb.* 33 b.)

d. Down below; underneath; underground.

1840 CARLYLE *Heroes* iii. (1904) 96 The obscure sojourn of dæmons and reprobate is underfoot. **1886** STEVENSON *Kidnapped* xxvi, Coming to the edge of the hills [we] saw the whole Carse of Stirling underfoot.

2. *fig.* In (to) a state of subjection or inferiority.

c **1205** LAY. 11693 For þis lond.. he hit hæ fde al vnder fot. *a* **1225** *Ancr. R.* 40 ȝif me worpen mid him al þe world under vet. *c* **1290** *Beket* 1995 in *S. Eng. Leg.* I. 163 Ake nolde it god þat holi churche onder fote were so. **1340** *Ayenb.* 85 Ac uirtue arereþ þane man an heȝ, and him deþ þe wordle onderuot. **1390** GOWER *Conf.* I. 7 Tho was the vertu sett above And vice was put under fote. **1422** YONGE tr. *Secreta Secret.* 172 He ne holdyth hym not y-lowet ne vndyrfote of the dyssayses whyche he hathe escapid. **1508** FISHER 7 *Penit. Ps.* xxxviii. Wks. (1876) 52 She enhaunced herselfe ferre aboue the derknes of synne puttynge vnderfote thoccasyon of it. **1583** GOLDING *Calvin on Deut.* cxxxvi. 833, I sawe that that man was nothing vnder foote, and as for myselfe I was in extreeme neede. **1891** MEREDITH *One of our Conq.* xxxiii, No, not he the man to have pity of women underfoot!

†3. Below the real or current value. *Obs.*

1594 *Death of Usurie* 12 The man beeing driuen to distresse, sels his corne farre vnder foote. **1600** HOLLAND *Livy* 591 The very same plot of ground whereon hee was encamped, happened at the same time to be sold: not under-foot, but at the full price. *a* **1654** SELDEN *Table-T.* (Arb.) 64 When men did let their Land underfoot, the Tenants would fight for their Landlords.

4. Quietly, secretly. *rare*$^{-1}$.

1860 GEN. P. THOMPSON *Audi Alt.* III. cxxxiv. 102 But it is not the same with the minor martyrdoms. A store of these is cherished under foot.

5. Of a person or persons: about one's feet, constantly (and irritatingly) present; 'in the way'. *colloq.*

1891 *Harper's Mag.* June 62/1 He muttered something about children being underfoot and staring at such times. **1922** S. LEWIS *Babbitt* xviii. 230 Kenneth Escott and she were always under foot. **1959** M. SCOTT *White Elephant* i. 3 It has been a trying month for her too, with Deryk always underfoot. **1981** 'S. WOODS' *Dearest Enemy* i. 38 It's really too much of a nuisance having him always underfoot when I'm trying to prepare my own meals.

under'foot, *v.* [UNDER-¹ 4 a.] *trans.* To provide with (new) footings or bases.

1870 *Baines' Hist. Lancs.* II. 27 In 1815 some of the pillars of the N. aisle having given way,.. they were all skilfully underfooted and restored.

'underfoot, *sb. rare.* [f. the adv.] The surface of the ground at the foot of a tree.

1910 W. DE MORGAN *Affair of Dishonour* iv. 50 This morning was no time for breakfast under the cedar trees. For all the underfoot, where grass grew, was no better than a sponge. **1959** E. COLLIER *Three against Wilderness* xxiv. 248 No flame could lick far into the forests so long as their underfoot was moist.

under'footing. [f. UNDER FOOT *adv.*: see -ING¹.]

1. *Ir.* In turf-cutting: (see quots.).

1942 E. E. EVANS *Ir. Heritage* xv. 136 In breast-work the digger stands facing the turf bank, and thrusts his spade horizontally, whereas in underfooting he stands on the bank and cuts vertically. **1957** —— *Ir. Folk Ways* xiv. 189 There are two methods of cutting, vertically or 'underfooting' and horizontally or 'breasting', and they tend to be used respectively on thin upland and deep lowland bogs. **1979** *Country Life* 27 Sept. 963/3 In some areas the [peat] turf is cut horizontally, known as breasting, but most turf is cut vertically, which is termed 'underfooting'.

2. The ground under foot, esp. with regard to its condition. Cf. FOOTING *vbl. sb.* 5.

1948 *Sun* (Baltimore) 29 Apr. 19/1 Shivaree.. was timed in 1.12 3–5, which was excellent in the sloppy underfooting. **1961** L. MUMFORD *City in History* x. 309 Some three centuries before wheeled vehicles became common, the street lost its natural underfooting. **1976** M. & G. GORDON *Ordeal* (1977) xviii. 125 He slowed only when he encountered rough underfooting.

†**under-forebody.** *Obs.*$^{-1}$ (UNDER-¹ 5 a.)

1547 in Feuillerat *Revels Edw. VI* (1914) 10 Longe garmentes narrowe of clothe of golde,.. vnderforebodyes, colers & vnder-sleves of clothe of syluer.

'under-form. (UNDER-¹ 6 b.)

1637 C. DOW *Answ. to H. Burton* 203 Vulgar Christians and the under-forme or ranke of Professors.

†**'under-foud.** *Obs.* (UNDER-¹ 6 a.)

1576–7 in Balfour *Oppressions in Orkney & Shetl.* (1859) 58 The Underfowde (quhilk is the baillie of the parochin or yle).

'under-frame. [UNDER-¹ 5 b.] **a.** The substructure of a railway-carriage, forming the frame on which the body rests; the substructure of a motor vehicle. Cf. *sub-frame* (*b*) s.v. SUB- 3 a.

1855 D. K. CLARK *Railway Mach.* I. 266 The underframe is the foundation of the vehicle, as the frame is that of the locomotive. **1889** G. FINDLAY *Eng. Railway* 105 The underframes of these carriages are constructed of steel. **1903** *Lanchester Motor & Carriage Descriptive Man.* I. 9 The transmission from the car frame to the front under-frame. **1954** D. J. WARBURTON *ABC Brit. Lorries & Road Services* 28 The underframe is also available for the construction of other lightweight bodies.

b. *Furnit.* The framework supporting a seat or table-top.

1934 *Burlington Mag.* Nov. 201/2 The armchair[s] of walnut.. show in the carving on the top-rail and under-frame.. that they are closely connected with the Indian high-back chairs. **1952** HOARD & MARLOW *Cabinetmaker's Treasury* 266/2 *Underbracing*, arrangement of stretchers to brace the legs of chairs, tables... Also *Underframe*. **1982** *Habitat Catal. 1982/83* 53/1 The under-frame and legs of the tables are in solid timber.

So **'under-ˌframing.**

1862 *Chambers's Encycl.* III. 93 The body of the Coach is made by one set of workmen, the under-framing by another. **1898** *Daily News* 11 Oct. 8/1 We have acquired a sufficient store in our own reservoirs, stowed away in the under-framing. **1902** *Carpet & Upholstery Trade Rev.* 1 Sept. 73/1 The chair.. is of a different type... The underframing begins to resemble rather closely the style known as 'Louis Quatorze'. **1969** E. H. PINTO *Treen* xv. 218, I think that the underframing was cut down to support the top, which originally was a loose board.

under-'freight, *v.* (UNDER-¹ 8 d.)

1769 FALCONER *Dict. Marine* (1776), *Sousfréter*, to under-freight a ship, or hire her out to a second person, after having contracted for her freight with the proprietor.

'under-fringe. (UNDER-¹ 5 b.)

1859 TENNYSON *Geraint & Enid* 544 Broad-faced with under-fringe of russet beard.

'under-frock. (UNDER-¹ 5 a.)

1547 in Feuillerat *Revels Edw. VI* (1914) 11, viij vnderfrockes.. of blewe Satten.

'underfug. *Schoolboys' slang.* [UNDER-¹ 5 a + FUG *sb.*] An undervest; also, underpants.

1924 H. DE SÉLINCOURT *Cricket Match* ii. 32 'I do hope you'll be sensible and wear your nice, warm undervest, John.'.. 'I'm not vain, Maria.. But.. I heard one of the toffs say.. 'My God! Look, he's wearin' an underfug.' **1946** B. MARSHALL *George Brown's Schooldays* iv. 18 The matron kept everybody's spare shirts, underfugs and towels and dished clean ones out once a week. **1967** *Listener* 2 Mar. 299/3 Felsted School calls radiators *fugs* and underpants *under-fugs*.

under'function, *sb.* Chiefly *Med.* [UNDER- 10.] = *hypofunction* s.v. HYPO-. Hence as *v. intr.*, to exhibit underfunction; to have a diminished capacity for acting and responding; **under'functioning** *vbl. sb.*

1941 *Trans. Assoc. Amer. Physicians* LVI. 51 The adrenal cortex is underfunctioning because of pituitary disease. *Ibid.*, The term 'hypoleydigism' is defined as underfunction of the cells of Leydig of the male gonad. **1964** M. ARGYLE *Psychol. & Social Probl.* vi. 74 The person suffering from a behaviour disorder is usually ineffective, underfunctioning in his work and social relations. **1979** *Brit. Med. Jrnl.* 15 Dec. 1582/2 It is not uncommon to diagnose pathological underfunctioning in the presence of values which may be above average for the population but which are known.. to fall below the norm for that particular individual. **1981** *Pharmacopsychiatria* XIV. 3 An underfunction of nonadrenergic synaptic transmission in depression.

under-fur, *a. Sc.* [UNDER-².] (See quot. and FURROW *sb.* 1 *a*, quot. 1523.)

1743 MAXWELL *Sel. Trans. Soc. Improv. Agric. Scot.* 34 Sow the Rye above the Dung, plow it down with an ebb Fur, (which is termed under-fur Sowing).

'underfur, *sb.* [UNDER-¹ 5 d.] An inner layer of shorter fur on an animal.

[**1892** H. POLAND *Fur-Bearing Animals* 200 The under fur of this Seal is long compared with other species.] **1895** *Funk's Standard Dict.* **1898** *Guide Mammalia* 70 A thick woolly under-fur. **1904** *Ann. & Mag. Nat. Hist.* XIII. 424 Underfur of back about 15 mm. in length. **1968** [see OVERFUR]. **1971** *Nature* 4 June 331/1 The fur was very spiny with virtually no soft underfur.

ˌunder-'furnish, *v.* (UNDER-¹ 8 a.)

1697 R. COLLIER *Ess. Mor. Subj.* I. (1703) 158 Can we suppose that God would underfurnish man for the state he designed him?

under'gang, *v. Obs.* exc. *dial.* [OE. *undergangan*, = MDa. *undergange*, Sw. *-ganga*.] = UNDERGO *v.* (in various senses).

c **1000** ÆLFRIC *Gram.* xxxvii. (Z.) 217 Ic undergange, *subeo*. *c* **1200** ORMIN 10661 Me birrþ beon fullhtnedd att tin hannd, þin blettsinng tunnderrganngenn. **1425** *Munim. de Melros* (Bann. Cl.) 544 Tyll wndirgang asyse of purale of þe marchis debatabil. *a* **1470** HARDING *Chron.* CXLII. xii, His defautes all to mend.. And vndirgange all his punycioun. **1743** RELPH *Poems* (1747) 94 Fie, Roger, fie—a sairy lass to wrang, And let her aw this trouble undergang. **1855–** in Yorks. and Lancs. dial. glossaries.

Hence **under'ganging** *vbl. sb. Obs.* exc. *dial.*

a **1300** *E.E. Psalter* xl. 10 For man of mi pees.. In wham mikel hoped I,.. Mikled vndergangingе [*v.rr.* -gange, under-going] ouer me. **1855–** in Yorks. dial. glossaries.

'under-ˌgaoler. (UNDER-¹ 6 a.)

1534 MORE *Comf. agst. Trib.* III. Wks. 1246 We forget with our foly, both ourselfe and our gayle, and our vnder gaylers, aungelles and deuilles both, and our chief gayler god. **1627** R. BERNARD *Isle of Man* 111 Now the Chiefe Gaoler.. hath with him three Vnder-Gaolers to looke well to the Prisoners.

'under-ˌgardener. (UNDER-¹ 6 a.)

1687 NORRIS *Coll. Misc.* 112 So 'tis in Eden, let me but have An under-gardener's place, 'tis all I crave. **1710** SWIFT *Mem. Change Q. Anne's Ministry* ¶20 The letter.. was delivered him by an under-gardener. **1830** MISS MITFORD *Village* Ser. IV. III. 109 His elder brother, Tom, could take an under-gardener's place directly. **1865** J. H. INGRAHAM *Pillar of Fire* xiv. 170 This venerable man.. was followed by not less than fifty under-gardeners.

'under-ˌgarment. (UNDER-¹ 5 a.)

1530 PALSGR. 285/2 Undergarment for a woman, *seurcot*. **1547** in Feuillerat *Revels Edw. VI* (1914) 11 Gownes or vndergarmentes of playne clothe of Syluer. **1615** G. SANDYS *Trav.* 68 Their vnder-garments (which within doores are their vppermost) do little differ from those that be worne by the men. **1831** SCOTT *Ct. Rob.* xiv, Over these under-garments was flung a rich velvet cloak. **1864** MRS. CARLYLE *Lett.* (1883) III. 207 A good supply of woollen under-garments. **1872** EARL PEMBROKE & G. H. KINGSLEY *S. Sea Bubbles* i. 29 Every kind of sail being hoisted, from new white canvas to the under garments of the lady passengers.

'under-ˌgarnished, *ppl. a.* (UNDER-¹ 4 a.)

1596 *Edw. III*, I. ii. 159 These ragged walles,.. like a cloake, doth hide From weathers Waste the vnder garnisht pride.

'under-gear. (UNDER-[1] 5 a.)
1883 *Atlantic Monthly* Sept. 365/1 Their undergear hanging out on a pole from an upper window, in full sight of passers-by.

'under-,general. (UNDER-[1] 6 a.)
1698 *Lond. Gaz.* No. 3367/2 His Majesty has appointed the General of Great Poland, and the Under-General of Lithuania as his Commissioners. **1702** LUTTRELL *Brief Rel.* (1857) V. 162 The under general of Lithuania has cut in peices 500 Suedish horse.

'under-,gentleman. (UNDER-[1] 6 a.)
1766 GOLDSM. *Vicar* ix, We found our land-lord, with a couple of under-gentlemen and two young ladies.

†**under-get,** *v. Obs.* [UNDER-[1] 4 b.] *trans.* To catch up with, overtake.
1390 GOWER *Conf.* I. 197 Hire Schip..stinte noght, er it ..hath the vessell undergete, Which Maister was of al the Flete.

under'gird, *v.* [UNDER-[1] 4 a. Cf. Flem. *ondergorden* 'subcingere' (Kilian).] *trans.* To secure or fasten from the under-side, as by a rope or chain passed underneath. Freq. *fig.* (now the dominant use).
In actual use chiefly in renderings or echoes of Acts xxvii. 17 ὑποζωννύντες τὸ πλοῖον.
1526 TINDALE *Acts* xxvii. 17 We..had moche worke to come by a boote, which they toke vppe, and vsed helppe vndergerdynge the shippe. **1611** FLORIO, *Soccingere*, to vnder-guirt, or guird. **1702** ECHARD *Eccl. Hist.* (1710) 325 They undergirt the ship to secure it from splitting. **1857** DUFFERIN *Let. High Lat.* 20 By undergirding the ship with chains, St. Paul fashion, the leaks were partially stopped. *fig.* **1848** H. ROGERS *Ess.* (1874) I. vi. 292 The infirmity of human nature requires to be 'undergirded' by all sorts of supports. **1874** HOLLAND *Mistr. Manse* 3 Its fragments build and undergird The songs and stories we rehearse. **1973** *Times* 30 July 20/6 It involves an understanding of the variety of sub-systems which undergird community life, health, education, welfare, [etc.]. **1975** *Church Times* 15 Aug. 16/5 Dr. Taylor believes that such smaller groups as these are going to become the essential sub-structure of Church life that is needed to undergird the larger congregation in the parish church. **1981** *Dædalus* Spring 19 'Why shouldn't people have these rights?' was the question that undergirded these laws. **1983** *Salisbury Rev.* Spring 18/1 The same instinct directing a man to preserve his life, undergirds his attachment to the institutions which inform his life as a participant in the historical stream of the national culture.
Hence **under'girding** *vbl. sb.* and *ppl. a.*
1868 H. BUSHNELL *Serm. Living Subj.* (1872) 218 That which is the undergirding import and reality of second death. **1895** *Advance* (Chicago) 17 Oct. 546/2 The preacher himself needs them..for the undergirding of his own convictions.

'under-,girder. (UNDER-[1] 5 b.)
1875 JOWETT *Plato* (ed. 2) III. 148 The undergirders of a trireme.

'under-,girdle. (UNDER-[1] 5 a.)
c **1532** DU WES *Introd. Fr.* in *Palsgr.* 906 The under gyrdell, *le demy chaint.* **1648** HEXHAM II, *Een Onder-gordel*, an Vnder-girdle.

'under-glaze, *a.* and *sb.* [UNDER-[2].]
1. a. ***under-glaze painting***, the process of painting on pottery before the application of the glaze. Also in other collocations, as ***under-glaze design, work***, etc.
1879 J. C. L. SPARKES *Pottery Painting* 28 Oil mediums may be used for over-glaze and for under-glaze work. **1883** *Harper's Mag.* July 259/1 The underglaze painting of pottery. **1885** *Encycl. Brit.* XIX. 643/2. **1925** *Heal & Son Catal.: Table Wares*, A simple brushwork under-glaze design in blue and red. **1967** M. CHANDLER *Ceramics in Mod. World* ii. 49 (*caption*) Chinese porcelain bowl with blue underglaze design.
b. *absol.* as *sb.* in the same sense.
1882 *Worcester Exhib. Catal.* iii. 4 Plaques painted in under-glaze. **1884** *American* VII. 217 The mysteries of 'overglaze' and 'underglaze'.
2. Of colours: Used in, adapted for, this method of decoration.
1879 J. C. L. SPARKES *Pottery Painting* 45 An under-glaze flesh tint may be made of claret brown. **1883** *American* VII. 119 The good effects of underglaze colors depend so essentially upon the firing. **1885** *Encycl. Brit.* XIX. 643/2 The soft subdued colours of the under-glaze pigments. **1947** J. C. RICH *Materials & Methods of Sculpture* ii. 49 An under-glaze color is a concentrated pigmenting agent that depends upon the glaze subsequently applied over it for 'life' or gloss and brilliance. **1980** R. ADAMS *Girl in Swing* i. 11, I took out the Copenhagen plate, with its under-glaze blue wave mark.

'undergo, *sb.* [UNDER-[1] 5 a.] (See quot.)
1876 HOLLAND *Seven Oaks* x. 123 They were blue undergoes—in other words blue flannel shirts.

undergo (ʌndə'gəʊ), *v.* [Late OE. *undergán* (f. *under-* UNDER-[1] 4 b + *gán* GO *v.*), = MDu. *ondergaen* (Du. *-gaan*), OHG. *untarkân* (MHG., MLG., LG. *undergân*, G. *untergehen*), Da. *undergaa*, Sw. *undergå*.]
†**1.** *trans.* To work under, so as to impair or destroy; to undermine. *Obs.*
c **1000** *Sax. Leechd.* III. 444 Ne sy la nan eorðcund cyning mid ȝitsunge to þæm swiþe undergan. *a* **1300** *E.E. Psalter* xvi. 14 Ris vp, lauerd; forcome him swa, And als-swa him vnderga [L. *subverte*]. *c* **1315** SHOREHAM VII. 622 Ac þo þe deuel hyt aspyde þat man hym scholde þer abyde..He þouȝte gyle al onder-go. **1642** D. ROGERS *Naaman* 146 Be [thou] affraid lest thou shouldest undergo thy selfe in purchasing the pearle.
†**b.** To deceive, get the better of. *Obs.*
c **1250** *Gen. & Ex.* 1147 Ðis maidenes redden sone on-on ..Hu he miȝten vnder-gon Here fader, ðat he ne wore ðor gon. *a* **1380** *St. Paula* 479 in Horstm. *Altengl. Leg.* (1878) 33 þou hast me gyled and vndur-gone [L. *circumvenisti*].
†**c.** To get under, search below. *Obs.*[−1]
1605 VERSTEGAN *Dec. Intell.* Verses by Author, That all men seeke all what they may to know; Yea Tyme in his own cours to vndergo.
†**2.** To submit *to* (do something). *Obs.*[−1]
c **1200** ORMIN 2527 þatt ȝho wass rædiȝ tunnderrgan Drihhtiness will to follȝhenn.
†**b.** To accept, admit, allow. *Obs.*[−1]
c **1315** SHOREHAM VII. 187 Ȝet oure by-leaue wole ondergon þat þyse þre beþ ryȝt al on.
c. To be subject to, to serve. *rare.*
1586 G. WHITNEY *Emblems* 223 Here, man who first should heauenlie thinges attaine,..First, vndergoes the worlde with might, and maine. **1864** BROWNING in *Mem. Tennyson* (1897) II. i. 16 The new metre is admirable, a paladin's achievement... So have you made our language undergo you.
†**3.** To go or pass under. *Obs.*
c **1220** *Bestiary* 691 in *O.E. Misc.* 22 And tus adam he under-ȝede, reisede him up, and al mankin. *a* **1575** tr. *Pol. Verg. Eng. Hist.* (Camden No. 29) 37 Howbeit, hoping eyther to winne it by assault, or compell it to yeelde, they undergoe the wall. *c* **1611** CHAPMAN *Iliad* VI. 444 Better my shoulders underwent the earth, than thy decease. **1627** MAY *Lucan* v. I 4, That day the sea seem'd mountaines topps t' oreflow, And yeilding earth that deluge t' vndergoe.
†**b.** To sink below (one's sight). *Obs.*
1614 GORGES *Lucan* IX. 386 Thy sight the North-starre vndergoes,..And each starre, that is most of light, Seemes (by the sea) hid from thy sight.
†**4.** To occupy oneself with; to investigate. (Also with *of.*) **b.** To get knowledge of. *Obs.*
c **1250** *Gen. & Ex.* 1160 Nv bi-oueð us to wenden a-gen And of abraham song under-gon. *c* **1290** *S. Eng. Leg.* I. 353/273 His lettre he sende, þat he scholde of swuche þingue onder-go [*v.r.* scholde such þing vndergo]. *c* **1330** *Amis & Amil.* 603 Yif..ani wight of all þi kinne. Might it vndergo, Al our ioie and worldes winne We schuld lese. *a* **1400** *Sir Beues* (MS. S.) 1514 That hors wel ȝerne vnder-ȝede That Beues nas not on is rigge.
5. To bear, endure, sustain, suffer, go through (pain, suffering, danger, etc.).
a **1300** *Cursor M.* 9748 And thol on me þe dom i sal, þat he suld vnder-ga, yon thral. *c* **1375** *Sc. Leg. Saints* xxxviii. (*Adrian*) 243 For-þi mare ardent wes his wil hard martirdome til vndirga. *c* **1400** *Apol. Loll.* 39 We wel þat þe bischops þat are necligent in þis, vndir go þe same peyn. **1595** SHAKS. *John* IV. i. 135 Silence, no more; go closely in with mee, Much danger do I vndergo for thee. **1609** TOURNEUR *Funeral Poem Sir F. Vere* 216 If some were still so bold to undergoe his doome. **1666** in *Verney Mem.* (1907) II. 259 In that or other disappointments or crosses that your sister and I have undergone. **1711** *Spect.* No. 161 ¶5 They were..fit to undergo any Fatigues of bodily Labour. *a* **1770** JORTIN *Serm.* (1771) VII. xiii. 270 What security hath our Church from undergoing the same fate? **1832** HT. MARTINEAU *Weal & Woe* ix. 124 His fine spirit was broken by the anxieties he had undergone. **1887** P. MCNEILL *Blawearie* 121 Soon all speculation anent the punishment we had to undergo was at an end.
absol. **1842** TENNYSON *Godiva* 10 She Did more, and under-went, and overcame.
†**b.** To bear, sustain (a burden, etc.). *Obs.*
c **1460** *Oseney Reg.* 162 All charges to þe saide tithis longyng we..schalle bere and schall vndergoo for euer. *a* **1618** J. DAVIES *Witte's Pilgr.* II. xvii, Though Atlas on him Heau'n impose, He that huge Burden, staidly under-goes! **1656** H. PHILLIPS *Purch. Patt.* (1676) B 4 b, There may be an equality in the loss and charges, that so the burden may be the more easily undergone by both parties.
6. a. To subject or submit oneself, to be subjected, to (a law, inspection, examination, etc.).
a **1300** *Cursor M.* 9114 It semes wel..þat he wan merci of his mis..for þe scrift he vnder-yede. *c* **1315** SHOREHAM v. 152 Ope þe heȝe eȝtynde day He onder-ȝede þe gywen lay, And was ycircumcysed. *a* **1425** *Cursor M.* 12755 (Trin.), In watir baptized he alle þo þat wolde bapteme vndir go. **1594** CAREW *Tasso* (1881) 18 They all agree to vnder go his lawes. *a* **1704** T. BROWN *Two Oxford Scholars* Wks. 1730 I. 4, I must undergo an Examination. **1721** STRYPE *Eccl. Mem.* II. xxvi. 215 The Book of Public and Common Prayer, which about this time underwent a diligent inspection and reformation, by some of the bishops. **1817** JAS. MILL *Brit. India* II. v. v. 479 The danger to which this event might expose the expedition..underwent deliberation in the Council. **1844** H. H. WILSON *Brit. India* I. 547 On the 1st July several clauses again underwent examination.
b. To come or fall under, to experience; to have imposed on one.
1599 SHAKS. *Much Ado* v. ii. 57 Claudio vndergoes my challenge, and either I must shortly heare from him, or I will subscribe him a coward. *a* **1641** BP. MOUNTAGU *Acts & Mon.* (1642) 22 Those Elders, who..had seen and undergone the wars of Canaan. **1650** EARL MONM. tr. *Senault's Man bec. Guilty* 145, I foresee I cannot condemn this Action without under-going the jealousie of such. **1668** HALE *Rolle's Abridgm.* Pref. 2 It is a Posthumous work, which never underwent the last Hand or Pensil of the judicious Author. **1717** LADY M. W. MONTAGU *Let. to Miss S. Chiswell* 1 Apr., Every year thousands undergo this operation. **1774** PENNANT *Tour Scotl. in 1772* 96 The castle has under-gone its different sieges. **1827** D. JOHNSON *Ind. Field Sports* 155 The Hindoos every morning..undergo ablution. **1840** DICKENS *Old C. Shop* xvi, It wouldn't do to let 'em see the present company undergoing repair. **1873** C. M. DAVIES *Unorth. London* (1876) 81, I made up my mind to undergo a Sunday morning service at one of these churches.
c. To experience, pass through (a change or alteration).
1634 MILTON *Comus* 841 She reviv'd And underwent a quick immortal change. **1711** HEARNE *Collect.* (O.H.S.) III. 225, I know not what Alterations the Stone may have underwent. **1765** *Museum Rust.* IV. 339 After this has undergone a strong fermentation. **1825** J. NEAL *Bro. Jonathan* I. 23 Seeing the error of his ways he had undergone a conversion. **1844** H. H. WILSON *Brit. India* III. 116 The situation of the British forces..had undergone a rapid improvement. **1884** L. J. JENNINGS *Croker Papers* I. iv. 116 His views underwent a very thorough change in course of time.
†**d.** To partake of, enjoy. *Obs. rare.*
1603 SHAKS. *Meas. for M.* I. i. 24 If any in Vienna be of worth To vndergoe such ample grace, and honour, It is Lord Angelo. **1604** —— *Ham.* I. iv. 34 (Q 2), His vertues els be they..As infinite as man may vndergoe, Shall in the generall censure take corruption From that particular fault.
†**7.** To expose oneself to (risk). *Obs.*[−1]
c **1315** SHOREHAM I. 288 Ȝet gret peryl hy vndergoþe þat cristneþ twyes enne.
8. To take in hand; to undertake. Now *rare.*
1601 SHAKS. *Jul. C.* I. iii. 123, I haue mou'd already Some certaine of the Noblest minded Romans To vnder-goe, with me, an Enterprize. **1605** SYLVESTER *Du Bartas* III. ii. *Law* 291 Make me no excuse On thy..unworthinesse To undergoe so great a Businesse. **1655** STANLEY *Hist. Philos.* I. 108 Since him a perfect Agent we may call, Who first considers what he undergoes. **1739** TULL *Horse-Hoeing Husb.* (1740) 252 [They] gave me such an Embarras, that if I had foreseen, I would not have underwent. **1817** JAS. MILL *Brit. India* II. v. viii. 670 Responsibility, thus limited, he had no objection to undergo.
†**b.** To perform or discharge (an employment, office, etc.). *Obs.* (Common in 17th c.)
1609 DANIEL *Civ. Wars* IV. xvii. 91 Having the chiefest actions undergone Both foreign and domestical of late. **1631** MAY tr. *Barclay's Mirr. Mindes* II. 38 Few they are..able to undergoe perpetuall employment, and not confounded with the different face of businesse. **1667** PEPYS *Diary* 11 Sept., [He is] a very young man to undergo that place. **1726** AYLIFFE *Parergon* 266 It has been a Question among the Doctors, Whether an Executor may be compelled to undergo this Office?
†**9.** To go under or by, to bear (a name). *Obs.*
1605 *Gunpowder Plot* in *Harl. Misc.* (Malh.) III. 26 Mr. Fawkes underwent the name of Mr. Percy's man. **1809** MALKIN *Gil Blas* VII. xiv. ¶6 A large ape, which underwent the name of Cupid.
Hence **'under,going** *ppl. a.*
1610 SHAKS. *Temp.* I. ii. 159, I haue..Vnder my burthen groan'd, which rais'd in me An vndergoing stomacke.

'under-god. (UNDER- 6 a. Cf. Du. *ondergod*, G. *untergott*, Sw. *undergud.*)
1583 GOLDING *Calvin on Deut.* xlv. 270 As soone as we fall to bringing in of vndergoddes we forsake the liuing God. **1593** NASHE *Christ's T.* 20 The High-priest (the vnder-god of your Cittie). **1605** A. WOTTON *Answ. Popish Pamph.* 47 You Papists..make our Sauiour, as it were an vnder God. **1712** BLACKMORE *Creation* v. 235 Of his own Substance does he Parts convey, Whose Motive Force the Under-Gods obey. **1891** F. W. NEWMAN *Early Hist. Cdl. Newman* 20 This Power is an under-god... If we have no awe for this under-god, why [etc.].

under'goer. *rare.* [f. UNDERGO *v.*]
1. One who endures or is subjected.
1601 SIR W. CORNWALLIS *Ess.* II. xxxviii. A a 7 b, Dracoes lawes [were] very good for the behoulders, whatsoeuer they were for the vndergoers.
2. ? An assailant.
1612 R. DABORNE *Christian turn'd Turke* 869 All religious lawes Must suffer violence, your wife be exposed Vnto all vndergoers.

under'going, *vbl. sb.* [f. UNDERGO *v.*]
1. The action of the verb, in various senses.
c **1380** *E.E. Psalter* xl. 10 [see UNDERGANGING *vbl. sb.*]. *c* **1440** *Promp. Parv.* 511 Vndergoynge, *submeatus.* **1608** D. T[UVILL] *Ess. Pol. & Mor.* 119 The prayse of hauing well conducted the course of one, is a bayte, which drawes them on to the vnder-going of another. **1612** W. SCLATER *Christian's Strength* 9 What avails it..whether on the right hand, or on the left; by overgoing or undergoing; we be deprived of salvation? **1645** BP. HALL *Rem. Discontents* Pref. 4 A meek undergoing of those sufferings. **1712** BERKELEY *Pass. Obed.* Wks. 1871 III. 136 The undergoing an execution is worse than the hazard of a battle.
2. = HOLING *vbl. sb.* 2.
1883 GRESLEY *Gloss. Coal-m.* 135.

under-'gore, *v.* (UNDER-[1] 4 a.)
c **1611** CHAPMAN *Iliad* XIV. 408 The dart did undergore His eye-lid, by his eye's dear roots, and out the apple fell.

'under-,governess. (UNDER-[1] 6 a.)
1669 E. CHAMBERLAYNE *Pres. St. Eng.* I. 317 Governess, Lady Francis Villiers, 400*l.* Under-governess, Mrs. Mary Kilbert, 150*l.* **1688** *Lond. Gaz.* No. 2355/4 The Lady Marchioness of Powis was Sworn by the Lord Chamberlain .., Lady Governess of their Majesties Children; And the Lady Strickland Under-governess.

'under-,governor. (UNDER-[1] 6 a.)
1579 J. STUBBES *Gaping Gulf* D j b, By referring you to the proconsulates of Rome vnder that Empire: to the vndergouernors in the former monarchies. **1587** GOLDING *De Mornay* iii. 29 To be short, hee setteth downe some Gods as principall, some as meane, and othersome as vndergouernours.

'undergown. (UNDER-[1] 5 a.)
1819 SCOTT *Ivanhoe* iv, Her dress was an under-gown and kirtle of pale sea-green silk.

under'grad, abbrev. of UNDERGRADUATE.

1827 *Brasenose Ale* 16 Why, Undergrads, dine ye so early? **1853** 'C. BEDE' *Verdant Green* vii. 63 The temporary sojourn that any undergrad has been forced to make there. **1884** ORNSBY *Mem. J. R. Hope-Scott* I. 34 A brilliant Oxford undergrad of nineteen.

'undergrade, *a.* [UNDER-[2].] (See quot.)

1884 KNIGHT *Dict. Mech.* Suppl. 911/1 *Undergrade*, a term as applied to bridges synonymous with *deck* bridge, in which the track is above the truss.

under'graduacy. *rare.* [f. UNDERGRADUA(TE *sb.* + -CY.] The state or position of (being) an undergraduate in a university.

1927 C. CONNOLLY *Let.* 21 Apr. in *Romantic Friendship* (1975) 295 This sense of living in a sequel tends to be the canker gnawing at the heart of undergraduacy. **1964** *Economist* 11 Jan. 89/2 The rather unworldly cloister of undergraduacy.

under'graduate, *sb.* and *a.* Also formerly **under-graduate** and (rarely) **under graduate**. [UNDER-[2].]

A. *sb.* **1.** A student in a university who has not yet taken a degree, and thus is still below the academical standing of a graduate.

1630 LAUD *Wks.* (1854) V. 29, I think fourteen years is little enough for a bachelor of arts or undergraduate abroad. *a* **1670** HACKET *Abp. Williams* I. (1692) 20 He was an assiduous overseer and interlocutor at the afternoon disputations of the under graduates. **1721** AMHERST *Terræ Filius* No. 33, The Thesis pitch'd upon by the excluding doctors for the undergraduates to moralize upon. **1850** KINGSLEY *A. Locke* I. xiii. 199 They have no influence over the rest of the under-graduates. **1882** MISS BRADDON *Mt. Royal* I. i. 18 The traditionary college misdemeanours handed down from generation to generation of undergraduates.

2. *fig.* One imperfectly instructed, or as yet inexpert (*in* something).

a **1659** OSBORNE *Charac.* Wks. (1673) 624 Which is but the single and wild Opinion of some under-graduates in the Arts of Liveing. **1693** *Humours Town* 97 Thus far I myself have proceeded (that am yet an Under-graduate) in this admirable Science. **1748** RICHARDSON *Clarissa* VII. lxxviii. 258 Now-and-then flitted in.. subordinate sinners, under-graduates, younger than some of the chosen phalanx. **1795** VANCOUVER *Agric. Essex* 110 Here the under graduates in iniquity commence their career with deer stealing. **1832** *Edin. Rev.* LVI. 163 That Mr. Johnson.. is still an under-graduate in modern German, will.. be sufficiently apparent. **1897** P. WARUNG *Tales Old Régime* 88 The Three who were undergraduates [in crime] muttered assent to the spokesman of the Three graduates.

B. *adj.* †**1.** Of lower degree; of inferior importance. *Obs.*

1654 H. L'ESTRANGE *Chas. I* (1655) 119 Sir Giles Allington fell also under censure for a sin of grand, though under-graduate abomination. **1659** —— *Alliance Div. Off.* 437 It is.. to be supposed that in this consecration set forms were used, considering withal that they were assigned to under-graduate concernments.

2. Having the standing of an undergraduate; that is an undergraduate. Also *fig.*

1685 in *Roxb. Ball.* (1885) V. 602 See here the minor Under-graduate Tool Takes his degree i' th' Doctor's flogging school. **1687** W. SHERWIN in *Magd. Coll.* (O.H.S.) 216 There was a Cloth laid in the Hall for the undergraduate Fellow.

3. Of or belonging to an undergraduate; characteristic of undergraduates.

1854 FABER *Growth in Holiness* xix. (1872) 387 There is something undergraduate about this levity. **1889** GRETTON *Memory's Harkb.* 241 In my undergraduate days, one Ash Wednesday, there came down.. a tornado of the tropics.

4. Consisting of undergraduates.

1868 M. PATTISON *Academ. Org.* iv. 109 The discipline of the undergraduate body is usually administered by the vicegerent.

Hence **under'graduatedom**, the body of undergraduates.

1893 *Westm. Gaz.* 1 Mar. 3/3 He became an absentee, so as to remove the voice of undergraduatedom from the jurisdiction of the University.

under'graduateship. [f. UNDERGRADUATE *sb.* 1.] The condition or status of an undergraduate.

1815 WHEWELL in Todhunter *Acc. Writ.* (1876) II. 12 Behold the end of my undergraduateship is at hand. **1850** THACKERAY *Pendennis* lxx, Time, I think, has.. rendered him a more accomplished rascal than he was during your under-graduateship. **1885** *Q. Rev.* Jan. 12 Mansel was rewarded for his laborious undergraduateship with a 'double-first'.

under'graduatish, *a.* [f. UNDERGRADUATE *sb.* + -ISH[1].] Characteristic of an undergraduate; undergraduate-like. Cf. UNDERGRADUATE *a.* 3.

1925 [see FLOATER 5]. **1931** *Times Lit. Suppl.* 10 Dec. 1001/3 He seems, for example, to give way to an undergraduatish melancholy at Cambridge. **1980** W. ASH *Incorporated* iii. 33 You're more interested in undergraduatish cleverness than in pursuing an interest which.. unites us.

undergradu'ette. *colloq.* (now *rare*). [Altered f. UNDERGRADUATE *sb.*: see -ETTE.] A female undergraduate.

1919 *Observer* 23 Nov. 17/4 The audience was chiefly composed of under-graduates and under-graduettes. **1926** *Spectator* 23 Oct. 677/1 There are too many undergraduettes at Oxford. **1934** W. GERHARDIE *Resurrection* xcv. 355 A professor, a don, an undergraduette in black cotton stockings, a green-grocer's boy—all move on bicycles. **1940** GRAVES & HODGE *Long Week-End* viii. 123 The subject of the duel was reported in the London Press to be an 'undergraduette of Somerville'. **1972** J. POTTER *Going West* 70 He ostentatiously walked out arm-in-arm with the prettiest undergraduettes. **1980** *Listener* 23 Oct. 549/2 In the Oxford of 1939.. I remember a red-headed 'undergraduette' (as we then rather quaintly would have called her).

'undergrass. (UNDER-[1] 5 c.)

1838 MRS. BROWNING *Seraphim* I. 144 The yew-tree bows its melancholy head, And all the undergrasses kills and seres.

†**under'grind**, *v. Obs.* [UNDER *adv.*] *trans.* To grind by pressing on (something placed below).

1598 SYLVESTER *Du Bartas* II. i. III. *Furies* 731 Like falling Towers o'rturned by the winde, That break themselves on that they under-grinde. **1608** *Ibid.* iv. IV. *Decay* 847 As with his weight, a hollow Rocky-Hill.. Shivers it selfe on stones it under-grindes.

'undergrip. [UNDER-[1] 5 b.] **a.** *Gymnastics.* A hold in which the hands pass beneath the horizontal bar, with the palms facing the gymnast. **b.** *Mountaineering.* = UNDERHOLD *sb.*

1920 NAYLOR & TEMPLE *Mod. Physical Education* 109 The starting position is reached as in Exercise 90, the hands being in 'under-grip'. **1955** J. E. B. WRIGHT *Technique of Mountaineering* iv. 76 (*caption*) An under grip. **1976** T. & J. COUSMINER tr. *Kaneka's Olympic Gymnastics* 214 Hang straight from the horizontal bar... If your palms face backwards, you are using the *reverse grip* (also called the *undergrip*). **1977** D. LAW *Starting Mountaineering & Rock Climbing* vi. 67 In the *under grip* [hold] the hand is turned over, fingers pointing upwards; it is quite sufficient to maintain balance.

under-'groan, *v.* (UNDER-[1] 4 a.)

c **1611** CHAPMAN *Iliad* II. 693 Earth under-groaned their high-raised feet.

†**under'grope**, *v. Obs.* [UNDER-[1] 8 a.] *trans.* To search into, to investigate; to learn.

?*a* **1412** LYDG. *Two Merch.* 351 And whan his freend the sothe gan vndirgrope Of this myscheef. **1412–20** —— *Chron. Troy* IV. 4644 But he anon.. Gan vndergrope, pleinly, what þei ment. **1447** BOKENHAM *Seyntys* (Roxb.) 28 The secunde yer of the forseyd pope, As be cronyculers I vndyrgrope, Fel a ful greuows dissencyoun. **1678** LITTLETON *Lat. Dict.*, *Subtento*, to assay or try underhand, to under-grope.

underground (-'graʊnd, occas. 'ʌndə-), *adv.* Also **under-ground** and **under ground**. [UNDER-[2].]

1. a. Below the surface of the ground.

1571 [see GROUND *sb.* 8]. **1598** FLORIO, *Sotteraneo*, of or pertaining to things vnderground. *c* **1615** SYLVESTER *Job Triumphant* III. 273 Mines and veinlings (vnder ground) Whence Silver's fetcht. **1684** T. BURNET *Theory Earth* I. 259 The.. passage of the paradisiacal rivers under-ground or under-sea, from one continent into another. **1728** CHAMBERS *Cycl.* s.v. *River*, Some Rivers bury themselves under Ground in the middle of their Course. **1780** COXE *Russ. Disc.* 68 Their dwellings underground are similar to those of the Kamtchadals. **1850** THACKERAY *Pendennis* xlvi, He.. wished that lady.. underground rather than there. **1878** HUXLEY *Physiography* 31 The laws which regulate the flow of water underground.

Comb. *c* **1720** C. PLACE in *Mem. W. Stukeley* (Surtees) I. 157 The old Giants are represented to us as underground-livers all of them. **1857** HENFREY *Bot.* §634 They are Truffles, or underground-fruiting Fungi.

b. Governed by *from.* (Cf. FROM *prep.* 15 a.)

1612 *Two Noble K.* Prol. 18 How will it shake the bones of that good man, And make him cry from under ground. **1697** DRYDEN *Virg. Georg.* III. 820 Tisiphone, let loose from under Ground. **1872** TENNYSON *Gareth & Lynette* 1386 Then sprang the happier day from underground.

2. *fig.* **a.** In secrecy or concealment; in a hidden or obscure manner.

1632 *Star Chamb. Cases* (Camden) 104 If he had medled with St. Austin and the Fathers, and not medled so much with these workes underground, he might have knowen the difference betweene the Church of Rome and us. **1679** *Animadv. Sp. Five Jesuits* 16 Since they may still work under-ground, and not be discovered. **1709** SHAFTESB. *Charac.* (1711) II. 269 Supplanting and Undermining may, in other Cases, be fair War: But in Philosophical Disputes, 'tis not allowable to work underground. **1820** HAZLITT *Lect. Dram. Lit.* 308 [Jeremy Taylor] does not dig his way under-ground, but slides upon ice. **1875** J. H. NEWMAN *Let.* 29 Oct., The pains and achievements of an editor are emphatically underground and out of sight.

b. Into hiding or surreptitious activity, esp. in phr. *to go underground*: applied chiefly to political organizations and their representatives which continue to operate in secret (and often subversively) after becoming officially unacceptable.

1935 *Ann. Reg. 1934* II. 198 The Socialist leaders.. decided that it was best to accept defeat: those leaders who were known made for the frontier, the others 'went underground' and began at once the organising of an illegal party. **1949** 'M. INNES' *Journeying Boy* xxiii. 285 There was nothing for it but a quick get-away and a going underground for good. **1960** E. BOWEN *Time in Rome* iv. 118 Like Resistance workers in the occupied countries, long-ago Christians, from time to time, strategically 'went underground'. **1977** *Times* 15 June 1/5 The crucial factor was the subsequent move underground by a handful of those people [*sc.* Soviet sympathizers], and the covers they assumed to mask their new role as agents.

'underground, *a.* and *sb.* Also occas. **under-ground**. [f. prec.]

A. *adj.* = SUBTERRANEAN *a.*

1. a. Found below the surface of the ground.

1610 HOLLAND *Camden's Brit.* 745 Vnder-grownd trees, or which haue lien a long time buried there. **1673** RAY *Journ. Low C.* 6 In Friesland.. there are great numbers of these under-ground Trees found.

b. Growing, living, or developed underground.

1757 *Phil. Trans.* L. 404 A compressed pod of the.. Under-ground-Pea. **1807** SOUTHEY *Lett.* (1856) I. 417 Some Jerusalem or under-ground artichokes. **1842** LOUDON *Suburban Hort.* 113 The most injurious of all underground larvæ. *Ibid.* 279 Tubers, or underground stems. **1875** BENNETT & DYER tr. *Sachs' Bot.* 673 The buds on underground rhizomes.

c. Dwelling underground or in the underworld.

1833 KEIGHTLEY *Fairy Mythol.* I. 314 A treasure which the underground-people must redeem at any price. **1866–7** BARING-GOULD *Myths Mid. Ages* (1872) 216 The underground folk seek union with human beings.

d. ***underground mutton***, a rabbit; rabbit meat. *Austral. slang.*

1946 A. J. HOLT *Wheat Farms of Victoria* viii. 129 'Underground mutton' (rabbit) is almost always available for those who like it. **1965** E. LAMBERT *Long White Night* xv. 138, I thought a feed of underground mutton would go all right for my tea. **1979** D. R. STUART *Crank Back on Roller* 151 Maybe a rabbit, though I was never what y' could call over fond of the ole underground mutton meself.

2. a. Situated below the surface of the ground.

1611 COTGR., *Hypogee*, a vault, celler, or such like vnder-ground roome. **1664** INGELO *Bentiv. & Ur.* II. VI. 172 An under-ground Temple consecrated to Melancholy. **1665–6** *Phil. Trans.* I. 109 The Divine Structure of the under-ground World. **1774** GOLDSM. *Nat. Hist.* VII. 353 The Mole-Cricket.. at night.. ventures from its under-ground habitation. **1823** P. NICHOLSON *Pract. Build.* 353 If a projected building is to have cellars, or under-ground kitchens. **1846** MRS. A. MARSH *Father Darcy* II. i. 8 One of those long underground passages, used for communication between the different houses. **1878** HUXLEY *Physiogr.* 31 After slowly trickling through a long dark underground course.

b. In fig. context. (Cf. 4.)

1675 OWEN *Indwelling Sin* vi. (1732) 51 It will increase.. until it.. makes it self an underground-passage, by some secret Lust that shall give a full Vent unto it. **1822** DE QUINCEY *Confess.* 48 The stream of London charity flows in a channel.. noiseless and underground.

c. ***underground railroad, railway***, (*a*) a railway running under the surface of the ground, esp. beneath the streets and buildings of a city; also in other collocations, as ***underground line, service***, etc. (now often *attrib.* uses of the sb.); (*b*) *U.S.* the secret system by which slaves were enabled to escape to the Free States and Canada; also ***underground line***; also *fig.*

(*a*) **1834–6** P. BARLOW in *Encycl. Metrop.* (1845) VIII. 240/1 The under-ground Railways.. in Newcastle, and its immediate vicinity. **1883** [see METROPOLITAN *a.* 2 b]. **1885** C. E. PASCOE *London of To-day* xiii. 137 The stuffy underground railway journey to Baker Street. **1926** *Times* 6 May 3/1 In London most of the tube and underground services were in force or others were expected to be to-day. **1926** *Daily Express* 11 May 1/3 The Underground trains yesterday showed no difference from any ordinary Monday morning. **1975** J. SYMONS *Three Pipe Problem* xviii. 204 He lost his way to the Underground station. **1982** G. LYALL *Conduct of Major Maxim* vii. 62 With the Under-ground map in his diary he worked out a route that involved two changes of train.

(*b*) **1852** MRS. B. STOWE *Uncle Tom's C.* viii. 43 Till the gal's been carried on the underground line up to Sandusky or so. **1856** —— *Dred* II. xxx. 318 An indefinite yet very energetic institution, known as the *underground railroad*. **1868** C. M. YONGE *Chaplet of Pearls* I. xviii. 251 There was what in later times has been termed an under-ground railway amid the persecuted Calvinists. **1875** *N. Amer. Rev.* CXX. 67 More fugitives than ever came from the slave states, and the underground railroad was in fuller activity than before. **1940** *Sun* (Baltimore) 14 Oct. 2/3 A so-called 'underground railway' delivering prominent scholars and writers from Nazi-dominated parts of Europe. **1979** R. LAIDLAW *Lion is Rampant* xviii. 137, I could probably have got you smuggled to the Border via my 'Underground Railway'.

3. a. Carried on, taking place, underground.

1709 T. ROBINSON *Nat. Hist. Westmoreld.* Pref. A vj, The Inspection of Under-ground Projects of several Kinds. **1795** EARL DUNDONALD *Connex. Agric. w. Chem.* 171 The clay.. may be wrought by shafting and under-ground mining. **1831** T. HOPE *Ess. Orig. Man* II. 73 The earth-worm,.. to whom a body dense and rigid.. would only impede his underground progress. **1872** YEATS *Techn. Hist. Comm.* 218 The abandonment of ridges will render underground drainage even more necessary.

b. Worn while underground.

1827 *Q. Rev.* XXXVI. 89 As soon as the men come to grass they repair to the engine-house, where they generally leave their underground clothes to dry. **1888** F. HUME *Mme. Midas* I. v, They arrayed themselves in underground garments.

c. Working, having control, underground.

1852 *Eng. & Foreign Mining Gloss.* (1860) 60 *Overman*, an underground overlooker. **1871** *Daily News* 21 Sept., The underlookers, and the underground manager [of the colliery]. **1879** MISS JACKSON *Shropshire Word-bk.* 348 *Reeve*, the underground overlooker of the pits.

d. Adapted for use underground.

1884 KNIGHT *Dict. Mech.* Suppl. 911/1 Stevens's under-ground engine.

4. *fig.* **a.** Hidden, concealed, secret.

1677 GILPIN *Demonol.* (1867) 250 This is their help, that some secret underground hopes which they espy not, do revive, at least sometimes. **1848** KEBLE *Serm.* Pref. p. xlv, There may be an unseen, underground unity. **1886**

GURNEY, etc. *Phantasms of Living* I. 538 We have already had numerous..instances of what may be called 'underground telepathy'.

b. Not open or public; concealed from or avoiding general notice.

1820 J. W. CROKER *Diary* 12 Apr. in *C. Papers*, Brougham ..I believe has been for some time in underground communication with Carlton House. **1883** tr. *Kravchinsky's Underground Russia* 49 The inner life of Underground Russia.

c. Designating (the activities of) a group, organization, or its representatives, working covertly to subvert the aims of a ruling (often occupying) power. Cf. RESISTANCE I c.

1939 [see RESISTANCE I c]. **1939** *War Illustr.* 9 Dec. 392/3 Even in the completely occupied territory there was underground activity. **1944** *Times* 18 July 2/3 An exhibition of the underground press of Europe. **1950** G. BRENAN *Face of Spain* v. 118 Until recently people suspected of Underground activity had been arrested and court-martialed. **1965** J. A. MICHENER *Source* (1966) 784 The night in the Belgian port when another English underground operative had called, 'One more place in the lorry. Look lively.' **1974** J. WHITE tr. *Poulantzas's Fascism & Dictatorship* IV. ii. 186 The KPD's underground apparatus turned out to be non-existent.

d. Of or pertaining to a subculture which seeks to provide radical alternatives to the socially accepted or established mode; *spec.* manifested in its literature, music, press, etc.

1953 *Observer* 13 Sept. 9/3 Its detached picture of barren tragic love..in a furtive fantastic 'underground' sector of London. **1962** *Movie* Dec. 4/2 Fuller is not an 'underground' director whose films actually *do* the opposite of what they overtly *say*. **1969** *Oz* May 36/1 He talked solidly for nearly forty-five minutes—he'd said it all before .. to all the underground papers in the States. **1970** A. TOFFLER *Future Shock* xii. 248 The underground movie..is flourishing even more than the underground press. **1977** *New Yorker* 9 May 126/3 He is attracted to buying *Mainline* because of its history as a radical underground weekly.

e. ***underground economy***, the economic sector of private business deals in which tax liability is not reported; the 'black' economy. Cf. BLACK *a.* 11 c. *U.S.*

1978 *Business Week* 13 Mar. 74 Neither the government nor labour unions seem to have any control over the underground economy. **1980** *Economic Rev.* (Fed. Reserve Bank of Atlanta) Jan.-Feb. 8/2 It suggests increasing activity in the 'underground economy' (gambling, bartering, and other unreported income). **1982** *Christian Sci. Monitor* 1 July B-4/1 Local custom means heavy traffic in illegal drugs and prostitution, an underground economy that is left alone as long as there is no trouble. **1983** *Chicago Sun-Times* 9 Sept. 38/2 The 30 cents a pound is essentially tax-free, part of the underground (or curbside) economy.

B. *sb.* **1. a.** The region below the earth; the lower regions or underworld.

1590 T. WATSON *Poems* (Arb.) 159 That..they may lament with guosts of vnder-ground. **1592** KYD *Sp. Trag.* I. vi. 1 Come we for this from depth of vnder ground? *a* **1618** SYLVESTER *Job Triumph.* III. 278 Beyond the bounds of Darkness Man hath pry'd And th' excellence of underground descry'd. **1887** *Scribner's Mag.* II. 449 The open spaces of the underground may..be divided into several distinct classes.

b. An underground space or passage.

1594 KYD *Cornelia* II. i. 377 Those seas..Returne to springs by vnder-grounds. *c* **1611** CHAPMAN *Iliad* XV. 176 This Jupiter, and I, And Pluto, God of under-grounds. **1884** *Daily News* 24 Sept. 3/2 The financial success..had not been such as to encourage costly exploration in unknown under-grounds.

2. a. Underlying ground or soil; subsoil.

So Du. *ondergrond*, G. *untergrund*.

1812 SIR J. SINCLAIR *Syst. Husb. Scot.* I. 231 A dry, free soil, on a sound under-ground or bottom. **1897** *Allbutt's Syst. Med.* III. 10 The underground of houses in certain localities being infiltrated with the virus [of rheumatic fever].

b. Ground lying at a lower level or below trees.

1842 *Proc. Berw. Nat. Club* II. 7 Rushes and..marsh thistles filled up the under ground. **1878** MRS. OLIPHANT *Primrose P.* II. 124 The mossy underground beneath the firs.

3. An underground railway, esp. the one in London. Usu. with capital initial.

1866 J. R. PLANCHÉ *Orpheus in Haymarket* III. 32 For Tartarus I happened to be bound, And was just starting by the Underground. **1875** L. TROUBRIDGE *Life amongst Troubridges* (1966) 123 Set off from Victoria Station by the Underground for Shepherd's Bush. **1887** DOYLE *Study in Scarlet* (1892) 28 A third class carriage on the Underground.

4. *fig.* **a.** A group or movement organized secretly to work against an existing regime, often by violent means; *spec.* an 'underground' resistance movement. Usu. with *the*.

1946 KOESTLER *Thieves in Night* 277 The Hebrew underground began as a purely political movement. **1946** AUDEN *Nones* (1952) 61 By night our student Underground At cocktail parties whisper round From ear to ear. **1958** L. URIS *Exodus* I. xii. 72 The Danes, by the middle of 1941, had established a small but determined little underground. **1966** A. SACHS *Jail Diary* iii. 30 With her husband Dennis on trial for his life for supporting the underground, she was hoping for some peace. **1973** T. PYNCHON *Gravity's Rainbow* I. 96 Captain must allow for the real chance she's a British spy, or member of the Dutch underground.

b. Any unofficial group or movement which seeks to provide alternatives to the forms of expression and action sanctioned by the society in which it exists.

1959 [see TRANS-WORLD *a.*]. **1969** *Oz* Apr. 27/2 The underground's a great crowd really. We enjoy them as people..just being what they are. **1970** *Guardian* 28 Feb. 9/2 We are going to try..to establish a definition of the underground... The word applies to a life-style, to a group of people who live..outside the constraints of ordinary society..and who largely..have come to the realisation of this new life-style through the use of cannabis and LSD. **1974** M. C. GERALD *Pharmacol.* i. 13 On the one hand, he has been enticed by 'notes from the underground', exalting the wonders of 'acid';..simultaneously, he has often been subjected to..the lies and half-truths of the well-meaning establishment.

Hence **'under,grounder, -,groundling.**

1868 *Once a Week* 18 Jan. 66/1 The Metropolitan railway (the undergroundlings). **1882** *Belgravia* July 67 That the aëronauts had the advantage of the undergrounders. **1954** L. MACNEICE *Autumn Sequel* xv. 94 The hole becomes..a wide Doorway; the undergrounders burst and spout. **1974** K. MILLETT *Flying* IV. 380 This patron saint of all undergrounders.

'underground, *v.* [f. the adv.] *trans.* To lay (electricity or telephone cables) below ground level. So **'under,grounding** *vbl. sb.*

1889 in *Cent. Dict.* **1961** *Times Rev. Industry* Jan. 40/1 In ..transmitting power, there are only two alternatives—the overhead and underground..and it's 16 times as dear to run [cables] underground... I think undergrounding is out of the question. **1964** *Times* 2 Sept. 11/6 We were recently obliged to underground three and a half miles of the Thorpe Marsh-Stalybridge line. **1971** P. GRESSWELL *Environment* 71 In the case of a line of pylons..he [*sc.* the citizen] needs to be told not simply how much undergrounding would cost ..but how this relates to the total capital expenditure. **1977** *New Scientist* 27 Jan. 188/2 The CEGB spent £220,000 undergrounding 2 km..cable..to preserve the view of Oxford as seen from Elsfield.

'under-grove. (UNDER-[1] 5 b, 5 d.)

1731 J. TRAPP tr. *Virg., Eclogues* I. 35 But that above all other Citys tow'rs, As the tall Cypress o'er the Under-Grove. **1798** WORDSW. *'A Whirlblast'* 6, I sat within an undergrove Of tallest hollies. **1820** KEATS *Isabella* xiii, Though Dido silent is in under-grove. *a* **1851** MOIR *Birth of Flowers* xiii, The undergrove Glow'd bright with rhododendron flowers.

undergrowe, obs. var. UNDERGROWN.

under'growing, *ppl. a.* [UNDER-[1] 4 a, 8 a.]

Undergrowing should prob. be read in the gloss. (*a* 1400) in *Rel. Ant.* I. 6 *Frutex*, undirglowyng.

†**1.** Arising, occurring. *Obs.*[-1]

a **1440** *Found. St. Bartholomew's* (E.E.T.S.) 16 But dyuerse vndirgrowynge ympedymentys, and, at the last, lettyng the Article of deith, that he wold had fulfillid he myght nat.

2. Growing beneath trees, etc.; growing up from below.

1598 *Sidney's Arcadia* III. 349 Sitting her downe vnder one of them, and making a posie of the fayre vndergrowing flowers. **1616** W. BROWNE *Brit. Past.* II. i. 17 On his legs Like fetters hang the vnder growing Segs.

'undergrowl. (UNDER-[1] 9 b.)

c **1848** J. KEEGAN *Leg. & Poems* (1907) 480 'Och, you thief of the world!' cried the woman, in a kind of under growl. **1895** MEREDITH *Amazing Marriage* xxxii, The shaking of her gown and the snarl in the undergrowl sounded insatiate.

under'grown, *ppl. a.* [UNDER-[1] 4 a, 10 a.]

1. Imperfectly grown or developed.

c **1386** CHAUCER *Prol.* 156 She hadde a fair forheed. It was almoost a spanne brood I trowe, For hardily she was nat vndergrowe.

†**2.** Showing signs of puberty. *Obs.*

1601 HOLLAND *Pliny* I. 345 As well men as women-kind, ..when they are come to fourteene yeares of age, and be under-growne. **1609** —— *Amm. Marcell.* XXVI. iii. 287 He had put forth a sonne of his, scarce undergrowne, unto a Sorcerer.

3. Furnished with an undergrowth.

1895 *Westm. Gaz.* 14 Aug. 3/1 A thicket of thorn trees, undergrown with long dried-up grass.

'undergrowth. [UNDER-[1] 5 d, 10 b.]

1. A growth of plants or shrubs under trees or other tall vegetation; brushwood, underwood.

1600 SURFLET *Countrie Farme* VI. x. 744 There must good regard be taken euery where, what plants of branches or vndergrowth are dead. **1667** MILTON *P.L.* IV. 175 The undergrowth Of shrubs and tangling bushes. **1794** VANCOUVER *Agric. Cambridge* 117 In this parish is found some very good woodland..; the undergrowth is cut once in fourteen years. **1822** SHELLEY tr. *Calderon's Mag. Prodig.* I. 3 This intricate wild wilderness of trees..and undergrowth of odorous plants. **1884** Q. VICTORIA *More Leaves* 308 The tangled undergrowth of fern, &c. is almost like a jungle.

b. The shorter stems of certain cultivated plants.

1765 *Museum Rust.* IV. 457 What is commonly called under-growth [of flax], may be neglected as useless. **1865** *Pall Mall G.* 3 July 5/2 Much of what farmers call the under-growths or under-stems of wheat are not coming into ear at all.

2. A growth of (shorter and finer) hair or wool underlying the outer fur or fleece.

1641 BEST *Farm. Bks.* (Surtees) 20 Such sheepe as have their wooll thus risen, have, without question, a goode under-growth. **1879** *Encycl. Brit.* X. 709/1 This undergrowth [of the Cashmere goat]..is beautifully soft and silky.

3. The condition of being undergrown or undersized; imperfect growth.

1891 *Lancet* 14 Mar. 624/2 Cases of heart disease,..of undergrowth, and underdevelopment.

'under-,guardian. (UNDER-[1] 6 a.)

1554 *Dial. on Laws Eng.* II. xlii. 135 The sherif shal make such vndergardeins for the which they will aunswere. **1611** COTGR., *Soubcurateur*, an vnder Gardian.

'under-,habit. (UNDER-[1] 5 a.)

1771 *Ann. Reg., Chron.* App. 216/2 The Knights companions in the full habit of the order,..the Knights elect in the under-habits of their order.

†**under-'hale,** *v. Obs.*[-1] [UNDER-[1] 4 a.] *trans.* To under-run.

1615 *Admiralty Court of Oyer & Terminer* 76 No. 10, Underhale the cable.

'under-,hammer. [UNDER-[1] 5 b.] In a pianoforte: (see quot. 1860).

1840 [see HOPPER[1] 9]. **1845** G. DODD *Brit. Manuf.* IV. 160 The key acts on the 'grasshopper', and the 'grasshopper' on the 'under-hammer'. **1860** RIMBAULT *Pianoforte* 396 *Under-hammer*, a hinged lever..to which the hopper is adjusted; used in upright pianofortes.

under'hand, *adv.* [UNDER-[2]. Cf. MDu. *onderhande(n)* by degrees, slowly; Du. *onderhandsch* secret, private; Da. *underhaanden* secretly, privately.]

†**1. a.** In (or into) subjection; under rule or command. *Obs.*

a **900** *Daniel* 71 Hie..ȝelæddon..Israela cyn on eastweȝas ..under hand..hæðenum deman. *a* **1000** in Thorpe *Laws* (1840) II. 218 *note*, Æȝhwæðer ȝa bisceope underhand. *a* **1300** *Cursor M.* 6442 þis ilk folk was vntelland, þat moyses had vnder hand. *Ibid.* 7057 Labdon þan had þam vnder-hand, Was ouerman aght yeir lastand.

†**b.** In (one's) possession or power. *Obs.*

a **1200** in Kemble *Codex Dipl.* (1846) IV. 268 Ðat lond ðat Berric hauede under hande. *c* **1200** in Thorpe *Dipl. Angl. Sax.* (1865) 581 Alle þinge þe hi under honde habben buten þat lond. **1297** R. GLOUC. (Rolls) 2984 þo he adde þe luþer king agag vnder honde, He let him hewe to peces.

†**c.** In hand; in course of doing. *Obs.*

c **1400** *Ywaine & Gaw.* 3478 This batayl wil he undertake, And he haves yit in other land Ful felle dedes underhand. **1693** *Mem. Ct. Teckely* IV. 26 Which made the People have a suspicion that there was a Design under hand, but it could not be discovered.

.†**2. a.** *Archery.* (Meaning uncertain.) *Obs. rare.*

1545 ASCHAM *Toxoph.* II. (Arb.) 126 Those that be lytle brested and big toward the hede..be fit for them whiche shote vnder hande. *Ibid.* 164 A byg brested shafte [is bad] for hym that shoteth vnder hande..: a little brested shafte for him yat shoteth aboue ye hande. ?**15..** *Robin Hoode & Qu. Kath.* xxix. (Percy MS.), Loxly puld forth a broad arrowe, He shott it vnder hand.

b. (See quot. 1834.)

1721 S. SEWALL *Diary* 18 Nov., Went to the Funeral... The Sight was awfull to see the Father, and then the daughter underhand by four. **1834** MRS. BRAY *Warleigh* xx, The coffin..was borne 'underhand', as it is called in Devonshire, that is, carried by bearers, about a foot from the ground, by napkins passed through the coffin-rings.

c. (See quot.)

1771 LUCKOMBE *Hist. Print.* 502 The Light and Easy, or Heavy and Hard Running in of the Carriage. Thus.., the Press goes light and easy under Hand, or it goes heavy or hard under Hand. **1888** JACOBI *Printers' Vocab.* s.v.

d. With the hand held below; *spec.* in *Cricket* (see UNDERHAND *a.* 1 c).

1828 in Box *Cricket* (1868) 77 The ball must be bowled.. and delivered underhand with the hand below the elbow. **1885** *Graphic* 14 Feb. 166/1 He..drew out a pair of steel handcuffs, which he..threw up and caught underhand in the air.

3. In a secret, covert, or stealthy manner; by secret means; quietly or unobtrusively.

Common from *c* 1580; formerly often written as two words (β), or with hyphen (γ).

α. **1538** ELYOT, *Suppilo*, to steale vnderhand [**1545** vnder hande] or craftily. **1580** CAMPION in Allen *Martyrdom* (1908) 22 Neither can I tell who altered his determination saving God, to whom vnderhand I then humbly praied. **1615** G. SANDYS *Trav.* 215 The rest being put to the sword, saue those that were vnderhand saued by the Sidonians. **1654** GATAKER *Disc. Apol.* 44 Being underhand backed and fed with money by two Tenants. **1684** W. HEDGES *Diary* (Hakl. Soc.) I. 148 He told me that Mr. Richard Frenchfeild was, underhand, a great favorer of ye Interlopers. **1733** NEAL *Hist. Purit.* II. 605 His Majesty was underhand preparing for war. **1792** BURKE *Corr.* (1844) III. 375, I should not be surprised if he did all he could, underhand, to lessen you in the opinion..of those who employ you. **1814** SCOTT *Wav.* lxiv, Bailie Macwheeble provided Janet underhand with meal for their maintenance. **1894** STEVENSON & L. OSBOURNE *Ebb Tide* vii, Approaching that island underhand like eaves-droppers and thieves.

β. **1545** [see α]. **1577** HOLINSHED *Chron.* II. 305/1 The same Stigand was an helper vnder hande for king William to atteyne the Crowne. **1611** TOURNEUR *Ath. Trag.* III. iii, He does it under hand, out of a reseru'd disposition to doe thee good without ostentation. **1653** H. COGAN tr. *Pinto's Trav.* x. 31 He..used the interposure of a Man born in the country, who under hand went to the fishermen. **1726** CAVALLIER *Mem.* I. 103 Commonly we liv'd by the Assistance of our Friends, who under Hand supplied us in our Marches, with Bread and other Necessaries.

γ. **1583** BOWES & DAVISON in *B.'s Corr.* (Surtees) 336 He laboureth under-hand to work a peace between the duke and Gowrie. **1639** S. DU VERGER tr. *Camus' Admir. Events* 221 Meane time he under-hand advertises Appollinaire to go always well accompanied. **1683** *Lond. Gaz.* No. 1807/3 They begin very much to suspect that..he does under-hand encourage the Turks to the War. **1705** tr. *Bosman's Guinea* 362 These Gentlemen..agree under-hand with those who sell the Slaves. **1748** *Anson's Voy.* II. iii. 148 In appearance to acquiesce in this resolution, whilst he endeavoured under-hand to give it all the obstruction he could. **1818** SCOTT *Br. Lamm.* xx, That friend.. was labouring hard under-hand to consolidate a band of patriots.

†**4.** = UNDERFOOT *adv.* 3. *Obs.*⁻¹

1617 MORYSON *Itin.* III. 55 If he bring his Horse thither, those that are to buy him, are such crafty knaues,.. as he shall be forced to sell his Horse vnder hand.

'underhand, *a.* and *sb.* [f. prec.]

A. *adj.* (In predicative use often *under'hand.*)

1. †**a.** *Archery.* Used in shooting 'under hand'. (Cf. UNDERHAND *adv.* 2 a.)

1545 ASCHAM *Toxoph.* II. (Arb.) 126 Thus the vnderhande [shaft] must haue a small breste, to go cleane awaye oute of the bowe.

b. Made with the hands kept below the level of the body.

1705 tr. *Bosman's Guinea* 129 Paddling the Water with an under-hand stroke.

c. *Cricket.* Of bowling: Performed with the hand held under the ball and lower than the shoulder or (formerly) the elbow. (Cf. UNDER-ARM *a.* 1 and UNDERHAND *adv.* 2 d.)

1850 'BAT' *Cricket Man.* 33 By the underhand method of bowling, the ball.. went directly to the wicket. **1867** *Lillywhite's Cricketers' Comp.* 8 Underhand bowling is almost extinct. **1905** *F. Sugg's Cricket Annual* 47 It is very essential that he should cultivate the under-hand throw.

d. Using underhand bowling.

1848 W. N. HUTCHINSON *Dog-breaking* ii. 13 Similar to the swing of an under-hand bowler at cricket. **1851** LILLYWHITE *Guide to Cricketers* 68 He is a capital under-hand bowler and a dangerous bat.

2. Secret, clandestine, surreptitious. Also *absol.*

1592 NASHE *P. Penilesse* G ij b, All under-hand cloaking of bad actions with Common-wealth pretences. **1621** ELSING *Debates Ho. Lords* App. (Camden) 149 It was ordered.. that .. the sollicitor should goe with the officer, whoe had the warrant, and showlld searche all underhand workers' howsses. **1649** *Nicholas Papers* (Camden) 139 The former endeavouring by underhand treaties to undermyne him. **1678** WANLEY *Wond. Lit. World* v. ii. §59. 471/1 Manuel.. was an underhand enemy to the Western Christians, and an open enemy to the Turks. **1712** ADDISON *Spect.* No. 550 ¶ 1 Several indirect and underhand Practices. **1823** SCOTT *Quentin D.* i, These turbulent cities.. never failed to find underhand countenance at the Court of Louis. **1868** FREEMAN *Norm. Conq.* (1877) II. ix. 366 Their influence must have been exercised in a purely underhand way. **1892** STEVENSON & L. OSBOURNE *Wrecker* x, A new element of the uncertain, the underhand, perhaps even the dangerous.

b. Of persons: Not straightforward.

1842 J. H. NEWMAN *Lett.* (1891) II. 393, I am often accused of being underhand and uncandid. **1858** LYTTON *What will He do?* I. xvi, You could not mean to be sly and underhand.

3. Not open or obvious; unobtrusive; quiet.

1600 SHAKS. *A.Y.L.* I. i. 142, I had my selfe notice of my Brothers purpose heerein, and haue by vnder-hand meanes laboured to disswade him from it. **1656** EARL MONM. tr. *Boccalini's Advts. fr. Parnass.* I. xxxviii. (1674) 50 By this handsom under-hand dealing, I have reduced the formerly ruinous.. State.. into the condition that now it is. **1824** MISS FERRIER *Inher.* xxiv, For, as she observed, in an underhand way, there was no disputing with a man who held the key of the post-bag. **1856** RUSKIN *Mod. Paint.* IV. v. iv. §14 The most subtle moves of a game of chess,.. which are, in dim, underhand, wonderful way, bringing out their foreseen and inevitable result.

4. Held in, manipulated by, the hand.

1706 BAYNARD in Sir J. Floyer *Hot & Cold Bath* II. 274 He went.. with Crutches, and was in six or eight times Bathing so much reliev'd as to walk with an underhand Stick. **1786** ABERCROMBIE *Gard. Assist.* 136 Ridge out melons in under-hand glasses.

5. *Mining.* Worked from above downwards.

1877 RAYMOND *Statist. Mines & M.* 226 Fifteen men were engaged in underhand stoping from the top of winze No. 3.

B. *sb.* **1.** An underhand ball; underhand bowling.

1866 LE FANU *All in Dark* I. xxxiii. 282 He handles the willow pretty well, and would treat you to a tolerably straight, well pitched slow underhand. **1885** FINCH-HATTON *Advance Australia!* 338 All display a precocious talent for round-hand bowling, very different to the sneaking underhand affected by the uneducated youth of Great Britain.

2. A position of inferiority.

1886 STEVENSON *Kidnapped* xii, I paid the less attention to this, for I knew it was usually said by those who have the underhand.

under'handed, *adv.* and *a.* [f. prec.]

A. *adv.* **1.** = UNDERHAND *adv.* 3.

1825 COBBETT *Rur. Rides* (1830) I. 342 The Quakers have been urging it on, underhanded. **1857** DICKENS *Little Dorrit* II. xx, You are reproaching me, under-handed, with having nobody but you to look to.

2. (Cf. UNDERHAND *a.* 1 c.)

c **1822** *Laws of Cricket* in *Q. Rev.* (1884) CLVIII. 471 The ball must be delivered underhanded, not thrown or jerked.

B. *adj.* (In attributive use *'under,handed.*)

1. = UNDERHAND *a.* 2.

1806 [implied in UNDERHANDEDLY *adv.*]. **1853** DICKENS *Bleak House* xxxvii, Under-handed charges against John Jarndyce. **1865** —— *Mut. Fr.* I. ix, Dark deep underhanded plotting. **1884** *Harper's Mag.* Feb. 395/2 Life seemed to go on in an underhanded, secret way.

b. = UNDERHAND *a.* 2 b.

1865 DICKENS *Mut. Fr.* II. vii, That's an underhanded mind, Sir. **1899** MRS. F. H. BURNETT *Willoughby Claim* vi, You confounded, sneaking, underhanded little thief!

2. Short of 'hands'; undermanned.

1834 COLERIDGE *Table-t.* 4 Jan., If that country could be brought to maintain a million more of inhabitants, Norway might defy the world:.. but it is much under-handed now. **1858** FROUDE *Hist. Eng.* III. 143 He was still underhanded, and entreated assistance. **1874** S. WILBERFORCE *Ess.* II. 97 The clergy are utterly underhanded.

3. *dial.* Undersized.

1856 P. THOMPSON *Hist. Boston* 728 A little, underhanded fellow. **1868-** in Yks. and Cumb. glossaries.

4. Placed or printed below.

1884 *American* VIII. 347 Many of the caricatures were originally published in connection with the 'poem', which is underhanded.

Hence **,under'handedly** *adv.*; **-'handedness.**

1806 *Feltham's Resolves* I. 106 To applaud virtue would procure us far more honour, than underhandedly seeking to disparage her. **1884** TENNYSON *Becket* Prol., All left-handedness and under-handedness. **1886** *Athenæum* 11 Sept. 335/1 A great deal of indirectness—not to say underhandedness. **1891** H. C. HALLIDAY *Someone must Suffer* III. xii. 213 You had acted underhandedly and deceived him.

†**under'handing,** *vbl. sb. Obs.* [UNDER-².] The action of taking in hand.

1639 T. DE GRAY *Expert Farrier* To Rdr., Thou wilt be much bettered and enabled in thy underhanding.

'underhang, *sb.* (UNDER-¹ 4 d. Cf. UNDERHANGING *vbl. sb.*)

1903 *Smart Set* IX. 8/2 He was a short man,.. with the underhang of jaw which tells of indomitable perseverance.

†**under'hang,** *v. Obs.*⁻¹ [UNDER-¹ 4 a.] *trans.* To hang, suspend.

1603 HOLLAND *Plutarch's Mor.* 1064 This saying of Antisthenes,.. that a man is to be provided either of wit to under-stand, or else of a with to under-hang himselfe.

'under,hanging, *vbl. sb.* [UNDER-¹ 4 a. Cf. UNDERHUNG *ppl. a.*] Projection, protrusion (of the lower jaw).

1842 YOUATT *Dog* iv. (1845) 99 A second cross considerably lessens the underhanging of the lower jaw. **1876** T. BRYANT *Pract. Surg.* (ed. 2) I. 545 In some cases complete under-hanging of the jaw is present.

'under,hanging, *ppl. a.* [Cf. prec.] Having a prominent lower jaw.

1865 MRS. CRAIK *Christian's Mistake* ii. 41 Her full-lipped, underhanging mouth.

'under-,hangman. (UNDER-¹ 6 a.)

1611 SHAKS. *Cymb.* II. iii. 135 Thou wert dignified enough .. to be stil'd The vnder Hangman of his Kingdome.

†**under-hat.** *Obs.*⁻¹ [UNDER *prep.*] Some gambling game.

1629 *Maldon* (Essex) *Documents* Bundle 210, No. 3, They went to plaie at a game with shillings and testers called vnder hatt.

'underhead. [UNDER-¹ 6 a.]

1. A subordinate official.

1599 LEWKENOR *Contarini's Commw. Venice* 163 These heads & vnderheads are all elected by lot. **1876** *Whitby Gloss.* 205/2 *Underheeads*, minor officials.

†**2.** A person of inferior intelligence. *Obs.*

1643 SIR T. BROWNE *Relig. Med.* I. §55 Wiser discretions .. offend without a pardon; whereas under heads may stumble without dishonour. **1686** W. DE BRITAINE *Hum. Prud.* xix. 86, I find by experience, that under Heads and narrow Souls by Industry.. work Wonders.

So †**'under-,headed** *a.*, of inferior intellect or parts. *Obs.*⁻¹

1646 *Crashaw's Steps to Temple* Pref. A 4 It were prophane but to mention here.. those under-headed Poets, Retainers to seven shares and a halfe.

†**under'hear,** *v. Obs.* [UNDER-¹ 8 a, after obs. It. *sottoudire* (cf. L. *subaudire*).] To overhear.

c **1570** *The Bugbears* v. ii. 4, I wold not that the maydes.. In theis so waightie matters shold hap to vnderhear vs. [**1598** FLORIO, *Sottoudire*.., to vnderheare, or as we say to ouerheare.]

†**underheave:** see UNDER-¹ 2.

'under,heaven. (UNDER-¹ 5 b.)

1598 CHAPMAN *Contn. Marlowe's Hero & Leander* v. 173 The yellow issue of the skie Came trouping forth, ielous of crueltie To their bright fellowes of this vnder heauen. **1719** OLDISWORTH *Callipædia* I. 117 When from the Azure Summit awful Jove Beheld this Under-heav'n and World of Love.

†**under'heild,** *a. Obs.*⁻¹ [UNDER-¹ 7; the second element is related to HIELD *v.*] Subject.

a **1300** *Cursor M.* 907 And þou, womman,.. sal be to man vnder-heild, To him þi buxumnes to yeild.

'underhelp. (UNDER-¹ 6 b.)

1579 TOMSON *Calvin's Serm. Tim.* 927/2 If we say I haue a wise teacher,.. all this is but an vnder help.

under'hew, *v. rare.* [UNDER-¹ 4 a and 8 c.]

1. *trans.* To undercut, undermine.

1523 LD. BERNERS *Froiss.* I. 675 They.. myned and vnder hewed the walles. [**1611** FLORIO, *Sottotagliare*, to vnder-cut or hew.]

2. *U.S.* To hew (timber) in such a manner that it contains less than the proper number of cubic feet.

1847 WEBSTER (citing S. S. Haldeman).

underhid, *ppl. a.* (UNDER-¹ 4 a.)

1387-8 T. USK *Test. Love* I. vi. (Skeat) l. 72 The under-hidde malice and the rancour of purposing envye.

'under-hill. *rare.* [UNDER-¹ 6 b.]

1. A lower hill.

1687 NORRIS *Coll. Misc.* (1699) 52 Say sacred Mount, what meant thy Trance, And you small under-hills, why did you skip and dance?

2. *attrib.* (Meaning uncertain.)

a **1722** LISLE *Husb.* (1757) 332 He had lost many a pound by not buying coarse or under-hill hay at the first hand of the year for their ewes.

,under'hive, *v.* [UNDER-¹ 10 a.] *trans.* To place (bees) in too small a hive.

1634 C. BUTLER *Fem. Mon.* 86 The Bees may doo wel enough in a middle-sized Hive: for beeing under-hived, they will cast soomwhat the sooner. **1707** MORTIMER *Husb.* 207 Rather under-hive a Swarm, than over-hive them.

'underhold, *sb.* [UNDER-¹ 5 b.] The hold obtained by a wrestler who gets his arms below those of his opponent.

1895 *Funk's Stand. Dict.*

†**under'hold,** *v. Obs.*⁻¹ [UNDER-¹ 8 d.] *intr.* To hold land by a sub-tenure.

1594 R. ASHLEY tr. *Loys le Roy* 55 b, The Gentlemen in France possesse, in high, base, and meane iustice,.. Principalities, and Peereships patrimoniall: with vassalls holding, and vnderholding of them, bound by faith, and homage.

So †**'under,holder,** a subtenant. *Obs.*

1605 CAMDEN *Rem.* 94 Noted.. as men of least account, and as all, or most vnderholders specified in that Booke.

'under-hold, *sb. Mountaineering.* [UNDER-¹ 5 b.] A hold in which the hand grasps a down-turned edge or point from beneath with the palm upwards, used esp. to maintain balance. Cf. UNDER-GRIP b.

1920 G. W. YOUNG *Mountain Craft* iv. 162 A cling 'under'-hold keeps body and eyes free at the length of our arms, bent or straight according to our convenience. **1948** 'MOUNTAINEERS' *Mountaineers' Handbk.* ix. 68 In a cling under hold.. the hands pull upward and exert a tension through the body against the feet, pressing them into the rock. **1965** A. BLACKSHAW *Mountaineering* vi. 175 (*caption*) Note the use of the under-hold.. to permit a high reach with left hand.

under'hole, *v.* [UNDER-¹ 4 a.] *trans.* or *intr.* To undermine; *spec.* (in coal-mining), to undercut. Also **under'holing** *vbl. sb.*

1398 TREVISA *Barth. De P.R.* XIII. xix. (Bodl. MS), Vnder hoolinge and vnder crepinge and wastinge vnder brymmes .. is icleped Alluuio. **1891** *Cent. Dict.* (as U.S. mining term).

under-honest, *a.* (UNDER-¹ 10 c.)

1606 SHAKS. *Tr. & Cr.* II. iii. 133 You shall not sinne, If you doe say, we thinke him ouer proud, And vnder honest.

,under'horsed, *a.* (UNDER-¹ 10 a.)

1860 *Cornh. Mag.* Dec. 689 Why won't he get something able to carry him?.. It's the stupidest thing in the world to be under-horsed. **1887** *Illustr. Lond. News* 24 Sept. 360/2 That such an institution [*sc.* the fire-brigade].. should.. be underhorsed and undermanned.

,under-'horsing, *vbl. sb.* (UNDER-¹ 10 b.)

1839 LEVER *H. Lorrequer* xiv. 108 The dreadful state of the roads,.. the frequency of accidents latterly from under-horsing, &c.

'under-,housemaid. (UNDER-¹ 6 a.)

1796 MME. D'ARBLAY *Camilla* III. 44 Nanny, the under house-maid, now joining them. **1862** MRS. CRAIK *Mistress & Maid* xxii, The only face.. that she was honestly glad to see.. was the under-housemaid. **1896** MRS. CAFFYN *Quaker Grandmother* 131 She returned sadly and fell on the under-housemaid.

under'hung, *ppl. a.* [UNDER-¹ 4 a.] (In attrib. use *'underhung.*)

1. Having the lower jaw projecting beyond the upper, or coming unusually far forward.

1683 *Lond. Gaz.* No. 1800/4 Lost.., a red fallow Colour'd dun Bull-Bitch,.. with a black Muzle under-hung. **1774** GOLDSM. *Nat. Hist.* II. v. 91 Those whose upper and under row of teeth are equally prominent, and strike directly against each other, are what the painters call under-hung. *c* **1815** JANE AUSTEN *Persuas.* xv, He.. must lament his being very much under-hung, a defect which time seemed to have increased. **1861** HUGHES *Tom Brown at Oxf.* ii, [He] had got the trick which many underhung men have of compressing his upper lip.

b. Projecting beyond the upper jaw.

1809 MALKIN *Gil Blas* XI. iv. ¶ 4 Wagging his under-hung jaw in a paroxysm of humour-stricken ecstasy. **1868** DARWIN *Anim. & Pl.* I. i. 38 Bull-dogs.. after two or three generations.. lose the under-hung character of their lower jaws. **1899** *Allbutt's Syst. Med.* VIII. 235 The jaw heavy and sometimes underhung.

2. *Mech.* Suspended on an underlying support; *spec.* of a sliding-door which moves on a rail placed below it. (Opposed to OVERHUNG *ppl. a.* 3.)

1855 D. K. CLARK *Railway Mach.* I. 207/1 Engine Cylinders underhung, castings in two pieces bolted together.

unde'rided, *ppl. a.* (UN-¹ 8.)

1603 KNOLLES *Hist. Turks* (1621) 37 The Turkes attending vpon the Sultan could not walke in the streets vnderided. **1611** FLORIO, *Inderiso*, vnderided, not mocked.

† **un'deringness.** *Obs.* [UN-[1] 10, 12: see DERE *v.*] Harmlessness, innocence.

a **1300** *E.E. Psalter* xxv. 11 In min underandnesse gane am I. *Ibid.* xl. 13, etc.

'under-instrument. (UNDER-[1] 6 b.)

1673 [R. Leigh] *Transp. Reh.* 70 Those who were but accessaries and under-instruments of our late troubles.

under-in'surance. [UNDER-[1] 10 b.] Insurance (of goods, property, etc.) at less than their real value.

1893 *Standard* (Boston) 20 May 518/1 Mr. Goodwin considers the tendency toward under-insurance of safe risks as the cause of the general requirement of the 80 per cent coinsurance clause. **1930** F. E. Wolfe *Princ. Property Insurance* ix. 147 Underinsurance is ignored if the practice is followed by fixing rates from time to time. **1949** R. S. Sharma *Insurance Princ. & Pract.* xxiv. 268 One of the difficulties in arriving at a scientific basis of rating in fire insurance is of under-insurance. **1976** *Business Week* 5 July 24 The hazards of underinsurance.. exploded in Mississippi as a massive liquidity crisis triggered the.. 'bank holiday'.

under-in'sure, *v.* [UNDER-[1] 10 a.] *trans.* To insure at less than the real value. Also *intr.* or *absol.* Cf. OVER-INSURE *v.*

1911 *Rep. Labour & Social Conditions in Germany* (Tariff Reform League) III. 145 If a person.. under-insured to avoid the rates he would lose in case of fire. **1921** W. N. Bament *Co-Insurance* 3 The natural inclination.. is to under-insure and take the chance of not having a total loss. **1982** *Economist* 18 Sept. 25 The problem is that the less well-off might underinsure.

So **under-in'sured** *ppl. a.* (also *absol.* as *sb.*).

1893 *Standard* (Boston) 20 May 518/2 The sufferers of slight and partial losses are able.. to draw their full damage without reference to the insurance carried, which, in the case of small insurance in proportion to value carried, enables a person who is thus under-insured to draw more than an equitable portion. **1909** W. J. Graham *Romance of Life Insurance* v. 66 Life, the great creator and conservator of the world's wealth, is grossly underinsured when compared with fire insurance. **1912** E. R. Hardy in H. P. Dunham *Business of Insurance* I. x. 179 In case of important properties where mortgage loans have to be protected.. all such, although their property may not be subject to any greater loss than the under insured, are paying for the under insured property. **1947** P. Gordis *How to buy Insurance* i. 8 We have established the inadvisability of being under-insured. **1962** A. Lurie *Love & Friendship* iv. 69 A regular firetrap the whole house. Oh they're wild about it now... Underinsured, that's what it was. **1981** M. Duffy *Gor Saga* II. 102 He was underinsured... His capital had been in his stock.

unde'rivable, *a.* [UN-[1] 7 b.]

1. That cannot be derived (*from* a source).

1640 Torriano (*title*), The Italian Tutor, With an Alphabet of primative and originall Italian words, underiveable from the Latin. **1884** tr. *Lotze's Logic* 24 Red and yellow seem to be still more essentially different and underivable one from the other.

† **2.** Not transferable. *Obs.*[−1]

1643 Prynne *Sov. Power Parl.* III. 78 Whose personall Prerogatives.. being incommunicable, underivable to any other, and peculiar to himself alone, he can transferre no such protection to others.

unde'rivative, *a.* (UN-[1] 7 + DERIVATIVE *a.* 2.)

1656 Jeanes *Fuln. Christ* 116 The fulnesse agreeable to Christ, as God, is underivative, without a cause. **1856** Dove *Logic Chr. Faith* 258 Truths which are original and underivative.

unde'rived, *ppl. a.* [UN-[1] 8.] Not derived or drawn *from* a source; primary, original.

c **1630** Sanderson *Serm.* (1681) II. 307 Because of the eternity of His own being, and that from Himself, and underived from any other. **1660** R. Coke *Justice Vind.* 5 If it be absolute and underived, then how can it be rational? **1719** Waterland *Vind. Christ's Div.* 289 To be able to distinguish between a delegated, and a supreme underived Power. **1799** Kirwan *Geol. Ess.* 485 It must have had calcareous earth underived from shell fish. **1850** McCosh *Div. Govt.* III. i. 289 Suppose that man had been a self-existent underived being like God. **1860** Pusey *Min. Proph.* 468 Life specially belongs to God, since He alone is Underived Life.

b. Of words. (See DERIVE *v.* 10 b.)

1668 Wilkins *Real Char.* 303 That kind of word.. is stiled an Adverb; which may be distinguished into Derived and Vnderived. **1827** *Q. Rev.* XXXV. 191 This not more useful than abused verb,.. underived as it is from any parent or adjunct dialect. **1841** Latham *Eng. Lang.* 261 All, in respect to Verbs in general, which the Etymologist has to determine, is whether they be Derived or Underived.

Hence **unde'rivedly** *adv.*; **unde'rivedness.**

1644 Bp. Maxwell *Prerog. Chr. Kings* i. 19 It is underivedly, primarily, and natively in the Communitie. **1850** F. W. Newman *Phases* ii. 51 This derivation of the Son and Spirit and the underivedness of the Father alone. **1886** *Mind* Jan. 39 What is that subjective necessity..? It is.. not its underivedness in any one's mind, not its priority in time.

'under-jaw. [UNDER-[1] 5 b.] The lower jaw or mandible.

1687 A. Lovell tr. *Thevenot's Trav.* I. 22 Mahomet the second having taken Constantinople,.. beat off the under jaw of one of those heads. **1762** Sterne *Tr. Shandy* V. xxxviii, Touching his under-jaw with the thumb. **1774** Goldsm. *Nat. Hist.* II. v. 91 The under jaw in a Chinese face falls greatly more backward than with us. **1802** Paley *Nat. Theol.* xii. §2. 238 The retired under jaw of a swine. **1868** *Rep. U.S. Commissioner Agric.* (1869) 329 [The female trout] has a less-projecting under-jaw.

underjawed (stress var.), *ppl. a.* [f. prec.] Having a protruding lower jaw; underhung.

1772 Lady Mary Coke *Jrnl.* 25 Jan., He is under jaw'd and his chin advances a considerable way. **1812** Shaw *Gen. Zool.* II. 495 Under-jawed Mysticete. **1864** *Realm* 2 Mar. 1 Her mouth, which, slightly underjawed, loses in softness what it gains in piquancy.

'under-ˌjobbing, *ppl. a.* [UNDER-[1] 6 b.] Doing subordinate work.

1697 Bentley *Phal.* (1699) 329 Some under-jobbing Assistant, of a low sordid Spirit.

'underkeel. *U.S.* ? *Obs.* [UNDER-[1] 5 b, with obscure second element.] 'A cut on the under side' of an animal's ear as a mark of ownership.

1783 *Maryland Jrnl.* 4 Feb. (Thornton), A crop in [a cow's] left ear, and an underkeel in her right. **1784** *Ibid.* 27 Jan., The right ear a crop and slit, the left a slit and underkeel.

† **under'keep,** *v. Obs.* [UNDER-[1] 4 a.] *trans.* To keep under or in subjection.

1590 Spenser *F.Q.* III. vii. 33 He lightly lept Vpon the beast, that with great cruelty Rored, and raged to be vnder-kept. **1591** —— *Tears Muses* 77 Learned Impes.. They vnder-keep, and with their spredding armes Doo beat their buds.

'underˌkeeper. [UNDER-[1] 6 a.]

1. An assistant keeper of a forest, park, etc.; an under-gamekeeper.

1502 *Privy Purse Exp. Eliz. York* (1830) 29 To the undre-keper of Swalowfeld for the bringing of iij bukkes. **1589** in *Essex Rev.* (1906) XV. 65 [Another deer was] given away by the underkeeper to his freends. **1622** Ld. E. Mountagu in *Buccleuch MSS.* (Hist. MSS. Comm.) I. 257 The Forest of Rockingham.. where Sir Francis Fane is under-keeper. **1682** *Secr. Serv. Money Chas. & Jas.* (Camden) 58 Henry Lowin, underkeeper of New Lodge Walk within Waltham Forrest. **1826** Scott *Woodst.* xxxii, The horses are at the under-keeper's hut. **1891** C. James *Rom. Rigmarole* 172 One of the under-keepers carried a little bamboo arrangement.

2. A subordinate custodian or warder.

1598 Florio, *Sotto custode*, an vnder-keeper. **1612** Sir T. Bodley in Macray *Ann. Bodleian* (1880) 408 Ye keeper of the vniversitie Library, with his vnderkeeper. **1637** *Documents agst. Prynne* (Camden) 69 The Keeper or Under-Keeper of the Castle of Lancaster. **1679** *Hist. Jetzer* 37 He waited till the Under-keeper [of the jail] came in. **1710** *Douglas' Æneis* Pref., Under-Keeper of the Advocates Library. **1760–72** H. Brooke *Fool of Qual.* (1809) II. 119 Sir, said the under-keeper [of the jail], there are few men now at liberty, near so wealthy as this gentleman.

'underkill. *colloq.* (orig. *U.S.*). [f. UNDER-[1] 10 a, after *overkill.*] (The mobilization of) insufficient capacity, esp. of nuclear weapons, to kill and effect destruction to the level of strategic requirements. Freq. *fig.*

1964 *New Scientist* 10 Sept. 647/2 Mr Goldwater has engaged in a press war.. over the future strength of United States' strategic retaliatory force—what for lack of a better description might be called the question of underkill. **1971** *Time* 5 July 13 Harvard's Paul A. Freund maintained that 'risk for risk, the law has opted for underkill in duels over publication'. **1984** *Financial Times* 20 Jan. 21/1 There is no limit to the silliness resulting when that director goes over the top and weds visual overkill to narrative and dramatic underkill.

† **'under-kind.** *Obs.* [UNDER-[1] 6 b.] A subspecies; an inferior or lower kind.

1571 Golding *Calvin on Ps.* lxxii. 1 It is expedient to descende from the general kynd to the underkynd. **1587** —— *De Mornay* 15 We reduce the particulars to an vnderkind, the vnderkinds to an vpperkind. **1671** Dryden *Even. Love* I. i, I would use thee like an under kind of Chymist, to blow the coals.

'under-king. [UNDER-[1] 6 a. Cf. Du. *onderkoning*, G. *unterkonig*, ON. *undirkonungr* (Sw. *underkonung*, Da. *-konge*).] A prince or ruler subordinate to a chief king.

c **950** *Lindisf. Gosp.* Matt. x. 18 Hia ȝesellas forðon iuih in ȝemotum.. & to under-cyningum.. fore meh. *c* **1060** *O.E. Chron.* (MS. C) an. 1056, Swa þæt Griffin swor aðas þæt he wolde beon Eadwarde kinge hold underkingc. *c* **1175** *12th Cent. Hom.* (1909) 22 Underkyng is ihaten þe under þam casere rixæð. *c* **1205** Lay. 31340 Cadwalan.. nom him to rede.. þat he aȝain wolde.. and bi-teche Penda, þe wes his under-kinge, folc and his ferde. **1387** Trevisa *Higden* (Rolls) VI. 275 He put out Egbertus þe sone of Alcmundus þe underkyng. *a* **1513** Fabyan *Chron.* v. cxl. 125 This kyngedome.. and the kynges therof, namyd vnder-kynges. **1587** Golding *De Mornay* viii. 110 From the great Monarks we come to the Kings of seuerall Nations, and from them to vnderkings of Prouinces. **1867** Freeman *Norm. Conq.* I. ii. 26 Each having its own Ealdorman or Under-King, though united under one supreme chief. **1874** Green *Short Hist.* i. §3 (1882) 18 The under-kings of Essex and East-Anglia received the creed of their overlord.

'under-ˌkingdom. (UNDER-[1] 6 b.)

1581 Sidney *Apol. Poetrie* (Arb.) 63 Where you shal haue Asia of the one side, and Affrick of the other, and so many other vnder-kingdoms. **1859** Tennyson *Merlin & V.* 581 Thro' all The hundred under-Kingdoms that he sway'd. **1877** Freeman *Norm. Conq.* I. App. 774 Cnut, like Charles, established a system of under-kingdoms.

'under-ˌlabourer. (UNDER-[1] 6 a.)

a **1667** Jer. Taylor *Serm.* Wks. 1831 IV. 140 You are the ministers of Christ's priesthood, under-labourers in the great work of mediation and intercession. **1690** Locke *Hum. Und.* To Rdr., 'Tis Ambition enough to be employed as an Under-Labourer in clearing the Ground a little. **1704** Norris *Ideal World* II. vii. 350 The proper office of this agent intellect, to serve as an under-labourer to that which is patient. **1836** Keble *Serm.* viii. (1848) 219 We, indeed, as Priests of the second order, are but under-labourers in that most holy cause.

under'laid (stress var.), *ppl. a.* [UNDER-[1] 4 a. Cf. UNDERLAY *v.*]

1. Laid or placed under or below.

a **1100** in Napier *O.E. Gloss.* I. 3518 *Suppositis.. torribus*, of under ledum.. brandum. **1552** Huloet, Vnder layed, *suffundatus*. **1598** Florio, *Soffondato*, vnderlaide or laid vnder. **1647** Hexham I.

2. Furnished with an under layer or support; strengthened from below; fitted or supplied underneath (*with* something). Chiefly *fig.*

c **1530** *Hickscorner* D iv, Therwith can you cloute me a payre of botes?.. I wolde haue them well vnderlayd and easlye. **1618** Bp. Hall *Contempl.*, *O.T.* XII. viii, That mans faith is well underlaid, that upholds it selfe by the Omnipotency of God. **1650** Trapp *Comm. Deut.* iii. 6 Surely, every man in his best estate, or when best underlaid, is altogether vanity. **1658** J. Harrington *Oceana* 91 If a Common-wealth have been introduced at once,.. you are certain to find her under-lay'd with this as the main foundation. **1712** Budgell *Spect.* No. 379 ¶ 12 The Floor of the Vault was all loose, and under-laid with several Springs. **1820** Shelley *Witch Atl.* liii, They framed the imperial tent.. Of woven exhalations, underlaid With lambent lightning-fire.

b. Const. *by* (what underlies).

1850 Ansted *Elem. Geol., Min.*, etc. §906 Seams of coal.. underlaid by a seam or bed of fire-clay. **1893** Sir H. Howorth *Glacial Nightmare* II. 463 That the coal-beds.. are overlaid by drift I have no doubt; that they are also underlaid by it seems to be most doubtful.

3. *Printing.* Of type, etc.: Raised by means of an underlay.

1771 Luckombe *Hist. Print.* 362 These Underlaid Words standing higher than the rest of the Matter. **1880** *Scribner's Mag.* May 42/2 This addition to the plate springs it up in every part underlaid, so that the surface fairly meets the inking rollers.

† **4.** Of a horse: ? Strong-limbed. *Obs.*

1674 *Lond. Gaz.* No. 892/4 A strong underlaid Brown Bay Nag. *Ibid.* No. 909/4 A truss well underlaid Horse.

'under-land. (UNDER-[1] 5 b, c.)

1874 Holland *Mistr. Manse* v, Down in to wonderland —Down to the under-land Go, oh go! **1877** A. Dobson *Prov. Porcelain, To Greek Girl*, From under-lands of Memory.

under'lap, *v.* [UNDER-[1] 4 a.] To extend some way beneath. Hence **under'lapping** *ppl. a.*

1867 Dk. Argyll *Reign of Law* iii. 141 The feathers of a bird's wing are made to underlap each other. *c* **1900** *Buck's Handbk. Med. Sci.* IV. 680 (Cent. Suppl.), The margin of the underlapping side is sutured to the deep surface of the overlapping side.

'underlap, *sb.* [UNDER-[1] 5 b, after *overlap.*]

† **1.** *Geol.* The fact or state of underlapping. *Obs. rare*[−1].

1883 J. G. Goodchild in *Geol. Mag.* Decade II. X. 226 Overlap, and its correlative Underlap, as it is here suggested to employ them, thus denote the stratigraphical relations of one part of a formation to another where the original extent of the lower part occupied a smaller area than that of the next higher members of the same series.

2. a. In warp knitting, the lateral movements of the guide bar made on the side of the needle remote from the hook.

1926 J. Chamberlain *Hosiery Yarns & Fabrics* vii. 170 The underlap may be at the back of any convenient number of needles. **1952** D. F. Paling *Warp Knitting Technol.* i. 4 The first movement is applied to the guide bars, and consists of a lateral motion in front of the needles.. known as the *underlap*. **1971** D. G. B. Thomas *Introd. to Warp Knitting* iii. 24 In most modern machines, the underlap takes place when the needles are down. The underlap is sometimes called a *shog*.

b. A piece of material that extends beneath another fold or pleat.

1943 I. R. Duncan *Needles & Pins* xiv. 284 Stitch the two pieces together at the top and bottom for a dress.. to form an over and under lap for the placket. **1964** *McCall's Sewing* ii. 33/1 *Underlap*, a part of a garment that extends or laps under another pleat. **1979** *Tucson* (Arizona) *Citizen* 20 Sept. 2B/1 Put the coat on over a skirt or dress and button it closed. Place a pin at the desired new hem length at center front on both the over-lap and underlap.

'under-ˌlawyer. (UNDER-[1] 6 a.)

1638 T. Nabbes *Covent Garden* I. ii, What's his profession? An under-Lawyer, an Attourney.

'underlay, *sb.* [UNDER-[1] 4 d.]

† **1.** (See quot.) *Obs.*

1589 Puttenham *Eng. Poesie* III. xix. (Arb.) 211 Ye haue another sort of repetition... The Greeks call him *Epizeuxis*, the Latines *Subiunctio*, we may call him the *vnderlay*.

2. a. A piece added to the sole of a shoe.

1612 *Pasquil's Night-cap* (1877) 25 She could line her shoes with vnder-laies, So cunningly, that few the fault did spie.

b. = EKE *sb.*[1] 2 b.

1641 Best *Farm. Bks.* (Surtees) 63 They will or within a monethes space worke downe to the bottome of the hive, and then must yow give them an underlay. There is in an underlay usually five wreathes, viz., one for the hive to stand within, and fower belowe; yow are to putte in an underlay two spelles.

c. A piece inserted as a prop or support, esp. so as to make one part level with another.

1683 Moxon *Mech. Exerc., Printing* ii. ¶ 1 Presses [should] have.. an even Horizontal Floor to stand on, That when the Presses are set up their Feet shall need no Underlays. *Ibid.* xxiv. ¶ 1 The aforesaid Battens will also keep these Underlays from working out.

d. *Printing.* A piece of paper or cardboard placed under type, cuts, or plates, to raise these to the required level.

1683 MOXON *Mech. Exerc., Printing* xxiv. 291 He tries thicker or thinner Vnder-lays till he have evened the Vnder-lay with the Face of the Letter. **1688** HOLME *Armoury* III. 118/2 Underlays, are small slips of Scabbord put under letters. **1824** J. JOHNSON *Typogr.* II. xv. 521 They will be found to sink a little from the repeated impressions, consequently the cuts will require an additional underlay. **1880** *Scribner's Mag.* May 43/1 He puts a proper underlay under every cut..that contains much black surface, and fairly braces it to resist hard impression.

e. *gen.* A layer which underlies another; a substratum. Also as *fig.* use of next sense.

1876 W. WHITMAN *Jrnl.* 10 June in *Specimen Days* (1883) 87, I write..here by the creek.. For underlay, trees in fulness of tender foliage—liquid reedy, long-drawn notes of birds. **1964** *Listener* 15 Oct. 572/1 The main characteristic of the new popular manner is an aggressive surface over a soft underlay; it is noisy..about minor issues, but takes good care not to tread any..controversial ground. **1977** C. MCCULLOUGH *Thorn Birds* (1978) II. vii. 174 'I do not intend to make a long eulogy,' he said in his clear, almost Oxford diction with its faint Irish underlay.

f. *spec.* (sheets of) material laid beneath a carpet (usu. felt or paper, or as an integral rubberized backing) or a mattress, for protection and support.

1907 *Army & Navy Stores Catal.* 275/2 Moth proof Cotton underlay to go between wire bottom of bed and mattress..4/8. **1923** *Daily Mail* 21 Feb. 8 (Advt.), Cedar Felt is an improved paper felt underlay for carpets. **1929** W. DEEPING *Roper's Row* xxi. 233 They'll do for underlays on the beds. I shan't waste them. **1959** *Spectator* 7 Aug. 165/2 Underlay adds to the life of a carpet, absorbs pressure from furniture and footsteps and acts as a sound absorber and insulator. **1980** D. ADAMS *Restaurant at End of Universe* xx. 117 The thin tufted nylon floor covering was black, and when they had lifted up a corner of it they had discovered that the foam underlay also was black.

3. *Mining.* = DIP *sb.* 5, HADE *sb.*[2] (See quots. 1831–55, and cf. UNDERLIE *sb.*)

1831–3 *Encycl. Metrop.* (1845) VIII. 203/1 The underlay of a lode is a term used to denote the direction of its inclination with regard to the horizon. **1855** [J. R. LEIFCHILD] *Cornwall* 101 The dip of a lode..being its inclination from a perpendicular line, or its underlay. **1880** C. C. ADLEY *Rep. to Pioneer Mining Co., Lim.* 2 Oct. 1 A small shaft will also be sunk,..following the underlay of the lode.

attrib. **1850** WEALE *Dict. Terms, Underlay shaft,* a shaft sunk on the course of a lode. **1882** *U.S. Rep. Prec. Met.* 461 The mine is entered by an underlay or inclined shaft 150 feet deep.

4. *Early Mus.* The placing of text in relation to music. Cf. sense 1 e of the vb.

1969 G. REANEY in Reese & Snow *Essays in Musicology in Honor of Dragan Plamenac* xvi. 250 The most difficult type of underlay consists of a moderately large group of notes with rather fewer syllables. **1974** *Times Lit. Suppl.* 14 June 642/2 When Petrarch's lines are restored to their proper shape and order and deployed in reasonable fashion below the notes of the vocal part, most if not all of the problems of underlay disappear. **1980** *Early Music* Jan. 21/1 Directions for tempo and dynamics, and frequently for underlay also, are absent from manuscript and printed sources alike.

under'lay, *v.* [OE. *underlecgan* (see UNDER-[1] 4 a and LAY *v.*), = MDu. and Du. *onderleggen,* MHG. *underlegen* (G. *unter-*), MSw. *undirlaggia* (Sw. *underlagga*), MDa. and Da. *underlægge.*]

1. a. *trans.* To support by placing something beneath; to furnish *with* something laid below. Also *fig.*

c **897** K. ÆLFRED *Gregory's Past. C.* xix. 143 Ðonne bið se elnboga underled mid pyle & se hnecca mid bolstre. *c* **1000** ÆLFRIC *Hom.* II. 144 Þa bæd he hi anre sylle, þæt he mihte þæt hus on ða sæ healfe mid þære underlecgan. *c* **1250** *Gen. & Ex.* 3388 He is under-leiden wið an ston, Til sunne him seilede in ðe west. **1555** EDEN *Decades* (Arb.) 327 They vnderlaye them with grasse. **1577** B. GOOGE *Heresbach's Husb.* II. (1586) 60 They vse to set the heads vnderlaying them with a Tileshard. **1658** A. FOX *Würtz' Surg.* II. xiv. 110 You ought not to stitch any wounded Finger,..but underlay it with little splinters. **1679** MOXON *Mech. Exerc.* ix. 157 If the Board be too thin, they underlay that Board upon every Joyst with a Chip. **1726** LEONI *Alberti's Archit.* II. 10 b, Another way of making the weight slip along..is by underlaying it cross-ways with Rollers. **1851** *Athenæum* Oct. 1049/1 Their project of underlaying the sea with electric wires.

b. To furnish with a lining or backing.

1502 *Acc. Ld. High Treas. Scot.* II. 302 Franch tanne to be ane cote to Jacob..v quartaris demy ostad to underlay the bordoring of it.

†**c.** To furnish (shoes) with additional soling-pieces or heel-plates. Also in fig. context. *Obs.*

c **1530** [see UNDERLAID *ppl. a.* 2]. **1583** STUBBES *Anat. Abus.* II. F 4, If the sooles be naught (as they be indeede) yet must they be vnderlaied with other peeces of leather, to make them seeme thicke. **1587** TURBERV. *Epit.* 190 b, The heeles they vnderlay With clouting clamps of steele. **1632** HOLLAND *Cyrupædia* 181 The Medes use..such a kind of shooes, as they might underlay closely and out of sight. **1661** K. W. *Conf. Charac.* To Rdr. (1860) 1 Should I, like an vnthrifty cobler, haue vnderlayed the rotten soles of these now worn out buskings, with the new and costly leather of applause. **1681** W. ROBERTSON *Phraseol. Gen.* 1272 To underlay a shoe, *suppingere.*

fig. **1592** NASHE *Four Lett. Confut.* 7 Then wil I bind my selfe prentise to a Cobler, and fresh vnderlay all those writings of mine that haue trodde awrie. **1603** DEKKER *Wonderfull Yeare* E 3 b, Being a pollitike cobler, and remembring what peece of work he was to vnderlay. ? **1622** FLETCHER *Love's Cure* v. iii, Our souls have trode awry in all mens sight, We'll underlay 'em, till they go upright.

d. *Printing.* To place paper or cardboard under (type, etc.) in order to raise to the required level for printing.

1683 MOXON *Mech. Exerc., Printing* xxiv. 291 If any Wooden Letters..are too Low, (as they generally be) he Vnder-lays them. **1880** *Scribner's Mag.* May 42/2 The pressman underlays the plate, by pasting on its under side bits of paper of suitable size. **1888** JACOBI *Printers' Vocab., Underlay,* the process of making-ready under type or cuts.

e. *Early Mus.* To place (the text of a song, etc.) in relation to the music.

1934 A. HUGHES *Anglo-French Sequelae* 7 Is there any satisfactory reason adducible to explain why the music of the Verba-passages should be underlaid with a text, and not the rest? **1949** W. APEL *Notation of Polyphonic Music 900–1600* (ed. 4) II. ii. 118 This composition also serves to illustrate the problem of text-underlaying in early music... The original frequently leaves considerable room for doubt..as to the 'correct' placing of the words. **1960** D. STEVENS *Hist. Song* 88 The text does not fit the ligatures of the tenor part... But it makes good sense when underlaid to the soprano part.

2. a. To place (something) beneath.

c **1000** ÆLFRIC *Gram.* xxviii. (Z.) 167 *Subpono,* ic underlecge. *c* **1440** *Promp. Parv.* 511/1 Vnderleyyn, *idem quod* underputtyn. **1573** TWYNE *Æneid* XII. N n j, A tower stronge ..the prince..had built alone, And choules [? *read* roules] had vnderlayd [L. *subdideratque rotas*]. **1683** MOXON *Mech. Exerc., Printing* xxii. ¶ 10 If a Page be too big for his Grasp, he underlays the Slice of a Galley.

b. To put underground, to bury.

Used punningly with allusion to sense 1 c.

1639 *Conceits, Clinches,* etc. (1860) 40 If any aske why this same stone was made? (Know) for a cobler newly underlayd Here for his overboasting.

†**3.** To make subject; to submit. *Obs.*

a **1300** *E.E. Psalter* viii. 7 Þ ou vnderlaide [L. *subjecisti*] alle pinges Vnder his fete. *a* **1300** *Cursor M.* 18266 Sin þou þe king o blis werraid And sua þi-self has vnder-laid. **1382** WYCLIF *Jer.* xxvii. 12 Vnderleith [L. *subjicite*] ȝoure neckus vnder the ȝoc of the king of Babyloyne.

4. To lie under or beneath; = UNDERLIE *v.* 3.

1591 SPENSER *Virg. Gnat* 99 Ne cares he if the..glistering of golde, which vnderlayes The summer beames, doe blinde his gazing eye. **1611** COTGR., *Haulse,* the vnderlaying of a shooe, or peece of leather that vnderlayes it. **1799** KIRWAN *Geol. Ess.* 178 In the south of France it occurs reposing on granite, and underlaying basalt. *Ibid.,* In the Altaischan mountains it sometimes underlays argillite. **1826** E. IRVING *Babylon* II. VII. 227 Our brethren and friends, who still under-lay the curse. **1861** DASENT *Burnt Njal* I. Introd. p. xxviii, [The right of duel] underlaid all their early legislation.

5. *intr. Mining.* To slope, incline from the perpendicular; = UNDERLIE *v.* 5.

1728 *Phil. Trans.* XXXV. 403 The Sides of the Load.. constantly underlay either to the North or South. **1802** J. MAWE *Min. Derby* Gloss. s.v., When a vein *hades,* or inclines from a perpendicular line, it is said to underlay. **1855** [J. R. LEIFCHILD] *Cornwall* 101 A lode which underlays towards the north.

under'layer[1]. [f. prec. Cf. Du. *onderlegger,* G. *unterleger.*]

†**1.** An underlying part or thing; a base or support. *Obs.*

In quot. 1609 applied allusively to a woman.

a **1592** GREENE & LODGE *Looking Gl.* I. ii. 255 The Nutmeg..is, saith one Ballad,..an vnderlayer to the braines. **1609** *Ev. Woman in Hum.* I. i, Ist not some vnderlayer, some she Cammell that will beare as much of her belly, as three beastes on their backes? **1702** BOYER *Dict. Royal* II, Under-layer,..(a piece of Wood to shore up any thing,) *une Etaye, un Etançon.* **1775** ASH, *Underlayer*.., that which is laid under to bear up any thing.

†**2.** A cobbler. *Obs.*[−1]

1692 R. L'ESTRANGE *Fables* I. cccci. 375 How many Under-layers,..when they could not live upon their Trade, have rais'd themselves from Cobbling to Fluxing?

3. *Mining.* 'A perpendicular shaft sunk to cut the lode at any required depth.'

1850 WEALE *Dict. Terms.*

'under,layer[2]. [UNDER-[1] 5 b.] A lower layer; a substratum.

1896 *Daily News* 15 Dec. 2/2 The carpets are of heavy velvet pile on an underlayer of elastic felt and cork. **1904** W. P. KER *Dark Ages* 198 Rodulphus represents the permanent underlayer of medieval absurdity above which Gerbert rises so eminently.

under'laying, *vbl. sb.* [f. UNDERLAY *v.*] The action of the verb, or the result of this.

1611 [see UNDERLAY *v.* 4]. **1648** HEXHAM II, *Ondersetsel van pileernen,* the Vnderlaying or the Ground-worke of pillars. **1683** MOXON *Mech. Exerc., Printing* xxiv. ¶ 1, I am loath to name the Vnder-laying of the Feet, because at the best it is but a Botch, and Subjects the whole Press to an unstable position. **1802** J. MAWE *Min. Derby* Gloss., *Hade,* the underlaying or inclination of the vein. **1882** SOUTHWARD *Pract. Printing* (1884) 429 In underlaying we put a piece of paper..under the type.

'underlayment. *U.S.* [f. UNDERLAY *v.* + -MENT.] Carpet underlay; material laid beneath roofing tiles, etc.

1956 *Study of Installation Wood Block Finish Flooring* (U.S. Nat. Res. Council) 17 The sub-floor should be covered with an underlayment of 15 lb. asphalt impregnated felt. **1975** 'E. LATHEN' *By Hook or by Crook* x. 97 You'll be sure that the men have instructions about the underlayment.

'underlead. [UNDER-[1] 4 d.] *Bridge.* The lead of a low card in a suit of which a higher card is held by the player.

1934 E. CULBERTSON *Contract Bridge Red Bk. on Play* xli. 531 An Ace underlead not only has the advantage of the surprise effect on the enemy but it retains the control of the suit. **1947** C. H. GOREN *Better Bridge* ii. 101 This is one of the rare cases in which the under lead of an Ace is recommended. **1964** *Official Encycl. Bridge* 650/2 Another motive for an underlead is an urgent desire to get a particular lead from partner.

Also **under'lead** *v. trans.,* to lead with a card of lower value than (another card of the suit held).

1945 PHILLIPS & REESE *How to play Bridge* III. 111 It is dangerous to underlead Aces against suit contracts. **1962** *Listener* 26 July 154/3 The question was whether East would risk underleading his queen of diamonds, to put partner in with the jack for a spade lead. **1973** *Daily Tel.* 13 Jan. 9/5 West should therefore underlead his ♡ A (assuming he has it) for a second club ruff.

'underleaf. [UNDER-[1] 5 b.]

1. A variety of cider-apple. Also *attrib.*

1707 MORTIMER *Husb.* 540 The Underleaf..is a very plentiful bearer, hath a Rhenish Wine flavour. *Ibid.* 575 The best sorts for Cyder are found to be..the Olive Under-leaf Apple [etc.]. **1786** ABERCROMBIE *Arrangem.* p. xi. in *Gard. Assist.,* Apples valued principally for Cyder..[include] Underleaf.

2. The under surface of a leaf. Also, a lower leaf.

1873 TRISTRAM *Moab* xviii. 353 The charm of the silvery [poplar] underleaf twinkling in the breeze. **1922** JOYCE *Ulysses* 220 The lychgate..showed Father Conmee breadths of cabbages, curtseying to him with ample underleaves. **1969** F. E. ROUND *Introd. Lower Plants* viii. 99 Yet another feature of this group is the basic conservatism of the organs; they differ in detail but vegetatively there are only three basic growth forms, (*a*)..(*b*) a dorsiventral leafy thallus with two rows of lateral leaves and a third modified row of 'underleaves'.

'under-lease, *sb.* [UNDER-[1] 6 b.] A lease granted by a lessee; a sub-lease.

1702 BOYER *Dict. Royal* I, *Soubail,*..an under-lease. **1730** *Act 4 Geo. II,* c. 28 §6 Those Leases cannot by Law be renewed without a Surrender of all the Under-Leases. **1803** *Act 43 Geo. III,* c. 75 §4 It may be for the Benefit of such Persons that Leases, or Under-Leases, should be made of such Estates. **1839** *Penny Cycl.* XIII. 378/2 Where the property is transferred for a part of the original term only, the transfer is called an under-lease, and the under-lessee is not liable to the original lessor. **1885** *Law Times* 7 Mar. 335/2 The underlease contained a covenant that if the under-lessee..should..assign the underlease [etc.].

under'lease, *v.* [UNDER-[1] 8 d.] *trans.* To sublet by an underlease. Also *absol.*

1819 REES *Cycl.* XXXV. s.v. *Tenure,* The takers having the liberty..to under-lease to other tenants. **1885** *Law Times* LXXIX. 233/1 A large plot of ground is leased for a term of 999 years. A part of this is underleased for 990 years.

'under-,leather. (UNDER-[1] 5 b. Cf. MDu. *onderleder,* G. *unterleder,* Sw. *underlader.*)

1569 *Wills & Inv. N.C.* (Surtees, 1835) 307 Eleuen dakers of vnderleathers xxvj *l,* ij daker of soles x *l,* vij dakers of ouerlethers xvj *l* x *s.* **1611** COTGR., *La sollette d'un esperon,* the vnder leather of a spurre. **1845** G. DODD *Brit. Manuf.* IV. 100 The shoes may have scarcely any 'under-leathers' to keep the 'uppers' together.

'under-,legate. (UNDER-[1] 6 a.)

1426 LYDG. *De Guil. Pilgr.* 2752 Seyn Peter..Hath mad yow..Hys vnderlegatys, ther to stonde, To kepe the passage.

†**,under'legged,** *a. Obs.*[−1] [UNDER-[1] 10 a.] = UNDERLIMBED *a.*

1681 *Lond. Gaz.* No. 1566/4 A Brown Bay Gelding,..his neather-lip a little falling, and under-Legg'd behind.

†**underlegger.** *Obs.* [UNDER-[1] 5 b + *legger* LEDGER *sb.*] Some kind of oar.

1405 *For. Acc.* 39 last membr., ij orys vocat' underleggers. **1406** *Exch. Acc.* 44/9 Remi vocati underleggers.

'underle,ssee. (UNDER-[1] 6 a.)

1730 *Act 4 Geo. II,* c. 28 §6 The Under-Lessees shall hold and enjoy the Messuages. **1839, 1885** [see UNDERLEASE *sb.*].

'under,let, *ppl. a.* [UNDER-[1] 4 a.] Let in or inserted beneath.

1884 *Harper's Mag.* Aug. 347/2 Window-curtains of pale greenish-white satin, with underlet appliqués of other pale-hued silks.

under'let, *v.* [UNDER-[1] 8 c, d.]

1. *trans.* To let at an amount or rental below the true or full value.

1677 CAPELL in *Essex Papers* (Camden) II. 128 Ormond.. abusing King in underletting the excise to the value of 300,000 lbs. per annum. **1751** JOHNSON *Rambler* No. 103 ¶ 14 He..knows how much one man's cellar is robbed by his butler, and the land of another underlet by his Steward. **1791** *Rep. Comm. Thames-Isis Navig.* 24 The Two Pound Locks, Tolls, &c. at Ifley and Sandford..were previously much under-let. **1868** ROGERS *Pol. Econ.* xiii. 181 Agricultural land in England is rather under than over let. **1874** GREEN *Short Hist.* vi. §5 (1876) 320 The land indeed had been greatly underlet.

2. To let to a sub-tenant; to sublet.

1819 REES *Cycl.* XXXVII. s.v. *Underletting,* That tenants should have the power of underletting or assigning the farms. **1841** *Penny Cycl.* XXI. 400/1 The merchant may load with his own goods or those of others, or he may underlet the ship altogether. **1872–4** in Jefferies *Toilers Field*

(1892) 253 No allotment, or any part thereof shall be underlet or exchanged.

Hence **under'letter** (Smart, 1836); **under'letting** *vbl. sb.*

1819 REES *Cycl.* XXXVII. s.v., By a subset or underletting there, the principal tenant or tacksman is not changed. **1883** *Law Times* 27 Oct. 433/1 Covenants against assignments and underlettings without the landlord's consent.

'under-ˌlevel. [UNDER-^{2}.] (See quots.)

1852 *Eng. & Foreign Mining Terms* (1860) 66 *Underlevel drift*, a drift driven from the pumping-pit to un-water dip workings. **1883** GRESLEY *Gloss. Coal-m.* 267 *Under-level*, winning the ironstone by driving drifts into the hill-sides, &c., instead of sinking shafts.

'under-ˌlever, *a.* (UNDER-^{1} 5 c.)

1892 GREENER *Breech-Loader* 68 Guns.. with under-lever snap action.

'under-lid. [UNDER-^{1} 5 b.]

1. The lower lid of the eye.

1611 COTGR., *Soucille*, th' vnder-lid of the eye. **1859** MEREDITH *R. Feverel* xxxix, Her underlids worked. **1903** *Smart Set* IX. 12 His under-lids were puffy and discolored.

2. A lid placed under another.

1907 J. H. PATTERSON *Man-Eaters of Tsavo* xi. 122 Opening a tin of biscuits.., and not being able to pull off the under-lid with his fingers.

'underlie, *sb. Mining.* [UNDER-^{1} 4 d.] = UNDERLAY *sb.* 3. Also *attrib.*

1778 W. PRYCE *Min. Cornub.* 80 The underlie or inclination of the Lode. **1818** W. PHILLIPS *Geol.* 106 When the underlie is towards the north, the strata are universally elevated on that side. **1855** [J. R. LEIFCHILD] *Cornwall* 100 The curvatures and irregularities in the underlie of lodes. **1875** J. H. COLLINS *Metal Mining* 36 The chief advantage of an underlie shaft.

under'lie, *v.* [OE. *underlicgan* (f. UNDER-^{1} 4 a + *licgan* LIE *v.*^{1}), = MDu. and Du. *onderliggen*, MHG. *underligen*, G. *unterliegen*, MSw. *undirliggia*, Da. *underligge*.]

†**1.** *trans.* To be subject or subordinate to (a person or thing); to submit to or be controlled by.

Also (quot. 1382) const. *to* in place of earlier dative.

c **897** K. ÆLFRED *Gregory's Past. C.* xxviii. 189 Ða underðieddan mon sceal læran.. ðæt hi him [*sc.* their superiors] eaðmodlice underlicgen. *c* **1000** ÆLFRIC *Saints' Lives* i. 155 Heo [*sc.* the soul] bið atelic þurh leahtras ʒif he him underlið. *c* **1375** *Sc. Leg. Saints* xxvii. (*Machor*) 807 Mony printeise þat redy were Til vndirly his dyscypline. **1382** WYCLIF *Heb.* xiii. 17 Obeye ʒe to ʒoure prouostis, or prelatis, and vndirligge [L. *subjacete*] to hem. *a* **1500** in *Ratis Raving*, etc. 16 All elyk wnder-lyis vanite, and drawis till a law place downwart. **1536** BELLENDEN *Cron. Scot.* (1821) I. 205 The king.. condiscendit to thir desiris; sa the said Donald come.. at Dounstafage to underly his will. **1594** CAREW *Tasso* (1881) 92 But mongst our selues,.. [I say] That others vnderly you, [who] safely might Cull out some ten to patronize her right.

2. To submit or be subjected to; to have (or allow to be) imposed on one; to undergo or suffer under: **a.** a punishment, penalty, accusation, etc.

Very common in older Sc. use: cf. next. Also (quot. 1382) const. *to* in place of dative.

c **960** *Rule St. Benet* xxxii. 56 ʒif he betan nele, underlicgge he rihtlicre þreale. *a* **1300** *Cursor M.* 6691 Qua smites his thain wit a wand,.. If he liue ouer a dai or tuin, þe lauerd sal vnderli na pain. *Ibid.* 22206 þan sal all þaa.. underli sa waful wrake. **1382** WYCLIF *Exod.* xxi. 31 The sone forsothe and the douʒter if it smyte with horn, to the lijk sentence he shal vnderligge. *c* **1400** *Apol. Loll.* 19 þus it semiþ al onli in effect an heretik schuld vnderly þe curse of þe kirk. **1442** *Reg. Mag. Sig.* 64/1 Till underly the charge of ath breking. **1456** SIR G. HAYE *Law Arms* (S.T.S.) 275 Sa that.. the accusour be oblist to underly the payne of talyoun. **1540** *Rec. Elgin* (1903) I. 52 [He] is content to vnderlie the sentence of the bailzeis. **1593** G. HARVEY *Pierce's Super.* Answ. Let., They that would rather vnderly the reproche of obscuritie, than ouercharge their mediocritie. **1612** J. DAVIES (Heref.) *Muse's Sacr.* Wks. (Grosart) II. 66/2 Praying for patience still to vnder-ly The heauie waight of this Worlds iniurie. **1678** SIR G. MACKENZIE *Crim. Laws Scot.* I. xxi. §4 (1699) 112 [He] shall incur and underly the pain and punishment of death. **1819** SCOTT *Ivanhoe* xxvii, This defiance hath already been sent to thee by thy sewer; thou underliest it, and art bound to answer me. **1857** J. W. DONALDSON *Chr. Orthod.* 259 He underlies also the graver charge of intentional misrepresentation. **1882** O'DONOVAN *Merv Oasis* I. xv. 254 Since my last visit to the Russian lines I had underlain a ban.

b. *Sc.* the law. (Common 16–17th c.)

1453 *Extr. Aberd. Reg.* (1844) I. 403 To ansueir and under-lie the law. **1507** *Reg. Privy Seal Scotl.* 205/2 To underly the law for the said slauchter. *a* **1578** LINDESAY (Pitscottie) *Chron. Scot.* (S.T.S.) I. 51 To underly the law for sic crymes. **1678** SIR G. MACKENZIE *Crim. Laws Scot.* I. xi. §16 (1699) 67 His Forefaulture could not fall to the King, upon a simple Denunciation for not appearing to underly the Law. **1752** J. LOUTHIAN *Form of Process* (ed. 2) 37 There to underly the Law for the Crime foresaid. **1838** W. BELL *Dict. Law Scot.* 489 To appear and underlie the law.

†**c.** *Sc.* (and *north.*) a charge or burden. *Obs.*

c **1400** *Rule St. Benet* (Verse) 1012 Who salbe meke,.. Bus hald þam-self vile & worthy Al maners of charch to vnderly. **1473** *Reg. Cupar Abbey* I. 183 Tha sal gane to the monk myre of Coupergrange, and thar tak thar feuale, vndyrlyand al chargis of the wenyng of the myre. **1475** *Ibid.* 203 He sal ondyrly and kep our conyngar fra all scath and peryl. **1565** in Hay Fleming *Mary Q. of Scots* (1897) 495 He onderlyis charge and expensis for the keping of the said Castell. **1622** BRUCE in *Serm.*, etc. (1843) 131 To show.. how unable I am to undertake and underly such a journey and charge.

3. To lie under or beneath; to subtend.

Esp. in *Geol.* of strata lying under others.

a **1600** HOOKER *Eccl. Pol.* VIII. i. §2 In a figure triangle.. the self same Line is both a Base and also a Side;.. a Base if it chance to be the bottom and underly the rest. **1830** LYELL *Princ. Geol.* I. 398 These deep-seated igneous formations must underlie all the strata containing organic remains. **1861** L. L. NOBLE *Icebergs* 139 The dark-blue inland hills.. underlie a sky of unutterable beauty. **1881** *Nature* XXIV. 497 They must be everywhere underlain by the.. Middle Coal Measures.

b. *fig.* To form a basis or foundation to; to exist beneath the surface-aspect of.

In common use from *c* 1860.

1856 KINGSLEY *Misc.* (1859) II. 13 Let the details go for what they are worth; the idea, the spirit which underlies them, is still invaluable. **1866** J. MARTINEAU *Ess.* I. 46 Must a false postulate underlie the whole fabric? **1873** SYMONDS *Grk. Poets* x. 308 Theocritus.. fully felt the charm which underlies the facts of rustic life.

†**4.** *intr.* To lie below ground; to be buried.

1648 HERRICK *Hesper., Death of Sparrow*, She.. for this dead which under-lies, Wept out her heart. **1739** in J. O. Payne *Rec. Eng. Cath.* (1889) 54 Here underlyes William Plowden honourably and very anciently descended.

5. *Mining.* = UNDERLAY *v.* 5.

1778 W. PRYCE *Min. Cornub.* 80 Some Fissures do not alter much from a perpendicular; and some do underlie a fathom in a fathom. **1800** *Ann. Reg., Chron.* 436 It dips or underlies south, one foot in a fathom. **1855** [J. R. LEIFCHILD] *Cornwall Mines* 100 Instances.. in which veins of almost every description dip or underlie in almost every direction. **1899** *Daily News* 3 Nov. 2/6 The vein underlies west 10 degrees from the vertical.

underlie, obs. Sc. var. WONDERLY *a.*

'underˌlier. [f. UNDERLIE *v.*]

1. Something that lies under.

1542 *Acc. Ld. High Treas. Scot.* VIII. 74 Deliverit to him to be underlyaris laid dowbill under the jeit of velvet, thre elnis blak sating. **1640** G. ABBOTT *Job Paraphr.* 522 The weight of which burthen he is not well advised who seeketh not to support by some firme under-lyer.

2. *Mining.* (See quot.)

1778 W. PRYCE *Min. Cornub.* 144 They sink the same Shaft deeper in the body of the Lode, upon its inclination or underlie; whence the Shaft becomes, and bears the name of, an Underlier.

'under-lieuˌtenant. (UNDER-^{1} 6 a. Cf. Du. *onderluitenant*, G. *unterlieutenant*.)

1691 *Lond. Gaz.* No. 2700/3 One under Lieutenant, one Aid-Major.. killed. **1730** BAILEY (fol.), *Sublieutenant*, an under Lieutenant.

'underlife. [UNDER-^{1} 5 c.] A life beneath the surface or on a lower level.

1847 *Edin. Rev.* Jan. 32 On looking more closely into Hume's underlife. **1865** MRS. WHITNEY *Gayworthys* xxiii, The underlife that never had been spoken—that lay between these three. **1878** STEWART & TAIT *Unseen Univ.* vii. §242. 245 What we are driven to is not an under-life resident in the atom but rather a Divine overlife. **1888** *Harper's Mag.* Apr. 753/2 Paris; and the university, with its wild under-life,—some debts, some follies.

'underlift. [UNDER-^{1} 4 d.] A raising (or rising) from below.

1867 H. BUSHNELL *Mor. Uses Dark Th.* (1869) 367 The tremendous underlift of its humble, once dejected people.

'underlight. (UNDER-^{1} 5 c.)

1876 GLADSTONE in Morley *Life* (1903) II. 550, I see that eastward sky of storm and of underlight.

'underˌliking, *vbl. sb.* (UNDER-^{1} 10 b.)

1581 MULCASTER *Positions* xxxix. 215, I feare nothing so much, as the ouerliking of forreine, and so consequently some vnderliking at home, which will neuer let them staye.

ˌunder'limbed, *a.* [UNDER-^{1} 10 a.] Having legs too slender in proportion to the body.

1686 *Lond. Gaz.* No. 2142/4 A blackish brown Gelding.., long straight Legs, somewhat under-limbed. **1695** *Ibid.* No. 3091/4 A red Roan,.. under Limb'd,.. and flat Rib'd. **1751** GIBSON *Dis. Horses* 18 When he happens to be under-limb'd, it is reckoned a great fault. **1833** M. SCOTT *Tom Cringle* xvi, A pair of well polished hessian boots,.. which by adhering close to his legs gave him.. the appearance of being underlimbed. **1835** BURNES *Trav. Bokhara* (ed. 2) I. 132 All the horses appeared to be under-limbed.

'underline, *sb.* [UNDER-^{1} 5 b, c.]

1. The line of the lower part of the body (of an animal).

1886 C. SCOTT *Sheep-farming* 173 The back should be level and evenly covered with meat,.. the underline straight. **1899** *Jrnl. R. Agric. Soc.* Mar. 18 Her back and underline were nearly parallel.

2. a. A line drawn below words printed or written. **b.** *pl.* A set of ruled guiding-lines placed under paper that is being written on.

1888 E. M. GALLAUDET *Life T. M. Gallaudet* 23 It is written on unruled paper, with a most careful regard for lines and margins, suggesting the use of underlines.

3. A line at the bottom of a play-bill announcing the piece to be performed next.

1891 *Cent. Dict.* s.v.

4. The caption or text beneath a picture, esp. in a book, newspaper, etc.

1924 N. J. RADDER *Newspaper Make-Up & Headlines* vi. 109 Practice varies with respect to the underline below the cut... When the underline is brief it is much like the second deck of a headline and the copyreader must.. avoid repetition of words.. in the overline. **1947** A. E. DAVIES in J. G. Herzberg *Late City Edition* xxii. 206 The editor writes captions to run above the picture, and the more detailed underlines to run below them. **1956** H. WILLIAMSON *Methods Bk. Design* p. xiii, In order to simplify the text pages, the underlines of the illustrations refer only to the specific points which are illustrated. **1971** BASKETTE & SISSORS *Art of Editing* x. 203 Picture texts are known by many names—cutlines, captions, underlines (or overlines), legends.

†**'underline,** obs. var. UNDERLING *a.* 1.

1750 ELLIS *Country Housew.* 2 Such Underline small Kernels make more Bran and less Flower than better Wheat does. *Ibid.*, The Underline or Blighted, or other Wheat Ears.

under-line, *adv. rare*$^{-1}$. [UNDER-^{2}.] Below the level of the sea.

1605 CHAPMAN, etc. *Eastward Hoe* II, Tost from one waue to another; Now vnder-line; Now ouer the house.

under'line, *v.*^{1} [UNDER-^{1} 4 a + LINE *v.*^{1}] *trans.* To furnish with an underlining; to form an underlining to. Also *fig.*

1545 RAYNALD *Byrth Mankynde* 8 This ryme vnderlyneth all the hole cauyte,.. or amplytude of the belly. *a* **1639** WOTTON *Reliq.* (1651) 86 By a meer chance, in appearance, though under-lined with a providence, they had a full sight of the Queen Infanta. **1834** WRANGHAM *Homerics* 9 So quick his raft Ulysses made; And floor'd the deck, by spars combined, And with long battens under-lined.

under'line, *v.*^{2} [UNDER-^{1} 4 a + LINE *v.*^{2} Cf. Du. *onderlijnen*.]

1. a. *trans.* To mark (words, etc.) with a line or lines drawn underneath; to underscore. (Cf. ITALICIZE *v.*)

1721 STRYPE *Eccl. Mem.* (1822) II. xi. 579 There is also another memorial.. with lines drawn under many of the words and sentences, and a note of Secretary Cecyl's hand, that what was so underlined was to be put in cypher. **1771** LUCKOMBE *Hist. Print.* 361 A Proof sheet printed Black, with the words to be printed Red under lined. **1856** DICKENS *Lett.* (1880) I. 423, I find myself underlining words constantly. **1901** *Athenæum* 24 July 119/1 Titles of books are printed in italics, though not underlined in the MS.

b. *fig.* To emphasize, esp. in utterance.

1880 *Times* 10 Nov. 9/1 A passage that was not intended by the speaker to refer to Ireland.. was seized upon and underlined by an appreciative audience. **1887** *Daily News* 15 Nov. 5/7 Madame Chaumont's tendency to 'underline' everything.. is certainly no less apparent now than it was in former years.

2. To announce (a play) by an underline.

1825 P. EGAN *Life of Actor* ii. 67 A file of old play bills which might do to bind, With only the play for next night —underlined. **1838** *Actors by Daylight* I. 5 A new burletta is underlined for this week. **1895** *Funk's Stand. Dict.* s.v., Faust is underlined for Thursday. **1900** *Westm. Gaz.* 27 Oct. 1 Mr. Stephen Phillips's historical play.. is underlined for production.

Hence **'underlined** *ppl. a.*

1866 MEREDITH *Vittoria* xxvii, He wrote a few underlined words entreating Vittoria to grant an immediate interview. **1888** HON. MORTEN *Sk. Hosp. Life* 35 An underlined note of warning.

underline'ation. [f. prec., after *interlineation*.] The action or result of underlining.

a **1814** *Masquerade* I. i. in *New Brit. Theatre* I. 223 It is like Italics in print, or underlineation in writing, and always means more than meets the ear. **1864** *Realm* 17 Feb. 2 This extract Mr. Cobden copied, with the due amount of underlineation.

'underˌlinen. [UNDER-^{1} 5 a.] Underwear, underclothing made of linen or similar material.

1862 *Eng. Wom. Dom. Mag.* IV. 237/1 Talking of underlinen, we must not forget the pretty white petticoats. **1882** CAULFEILD & SAWARD *Dict. Needlework* 506 Underlinen is made of a variety of materials. **1883** 'ANNIE THOMAS' *Mod. Housewife* 66 A 'set of underlinen' for children.

'underling, *sb.* and *a.* Forms: 2– underling (3–7 vnder-, 4 vndir-); 2 undur-, 4–6 vnderlyng (5 vndir-, vndyr-); 4 undur-, 4–6 underlynge; 3–4 onderling, -lyng. [Early ME., f. UNDER *adv.* 3 + -LING.]

A. *sb.* **1.** One who is subject or subordinate to another; in later use *esp.* a subordinate agent or official, an understrapper.

c **1175** *Leg. Nathan* in *E.E. Hom.* (1917) 89 Heo.. ʒet synden underlinges, for þan þe heo heora hlaford belæwden. *c* **1200** *Trin. Coll. Hom.* 179 þe riche þe ben louerdinges struien þe wrecche men, þe ben underlinges. *a* **1225** *Ancr. R.* 198 þet child þet ne buhð nout his eldre; vnderling, his prelat; paroschian, his preost. *c* **1275** LAY. 22472 Alcus hehte þe king: he hadde mani onderlyng. *c* **1315** SHOREHAM *Poems* III. 176 þou ne a-nourest god aryʒt, Ac dest is onderlynges. **1390** GOWER *Conf.* III. 128 The sterres.. worchen manye sondri thinges To ous, that ben here underlinges. *c* **1400** *Laud Troy Bk.* 2640 My lord,.. I am ʒoure knyght and ʒoure vndirlyng. *a* **1470** HARDING *Chron.* XXXIX. iv, Emman.. reigned in all kynde of tiranny, For whiche he was deposed, as an vnderlyng. **1553** T. WILSON *Rhet.* Pref. A iv, What manne.. would not rather loke to rule like a lord, then to lyve lyke an underlynge? **1576** FLEMING *Panopl. Epist.* 226 The seruice that an underling.. oweth to his Lord.. is neither greeuous nor tedious. **1619** W. SCLATER *Exp. 1 Thess.* (1630) 259 Compare thy selfe with superiours, rather then with vnderlings in Grace. **1693** *Apol. Clergy Scot.* 102 In the next Paragraph he mentions Mr. Cant, whom he names underling to Mr. Hamilton. **1727** DE FOE *Prot. Monast.* 9 To hear the Daughter.. take up her Father in his Discourse, as if he had been an Idiot or an Underling. **1796** LD. SHEFFIELD in *Ld. Auckland's Corr.* (1862) III. 357 What chance have we.. when the House of Commons is filled with moneyed men, speculators, and underlings in office? **1847** EMERSON *Repr. Men, Napoleon*, He undoubtedly felt..an impatience of fools and underlings. **1878** STUBBS *Const. Hist.* III. xviii. 136 The work of an underling who hoped to secure his own promotion.

transf. **1614** RALEIGH *Hist. World* I. III. xii. 153 Epaminondas..gaue vnto Thebes, which had euer-more beene an vnderling,..the highest command in Greece.

b. A branch, plant, etc., growing under, or less strongly than, another; a small or weakly plant, animal, or child. Now *dial.*

1688 R. HOLME *Armoury* II. 84/2 The Cyons..are underlings, or small twigs of a years growth. **1787** W. H. MARSHALL *Norfolk* II. 148 When one of them has got the superiority so far as to overhang the other, it is generally right to take the underling away. **1842** C. W. JOHNSON *Farmer's Encycl.* 1255 Of the Weeds called Underlings, or such as never rise in the Crop:..These are groundsel [etc.]. **1854** MISS BAKER *Northampt. Gloss.* s.v., The least thriving in a litter of pigs, or brood of chickens, is frequently called 'a poor little underling'. Fruit or vegetables smaller than the rest of the crop are called underlings.

2. In predicative use, passing into *adj.*: Subject, subordinate (*to* a person, etc.).

? **1370** *Robt. Cisyle* 55 He was to alle men undurlynge, So lowe was never ȝyt no kynge! *c* **1440** *Promp. Parv.* 511/1 Vnderlynge, *subditus, infimus.* *c* **1450** *Mirk's Festial* 187 þeras he was befor..prowde of hert, aftyr he was lowe and vndyrlyng to al Godys seruantys. **1549** COVERDALE, etc. *Erasm. Par. 1 Cor.* xi. 3 b, Albeit the husbande be the wiues gouernour, yet is he vnderlyng and subiect to Christe his lorde and maister. **1598** MARSTON *Sco. Villanie* VIII, Can our Soule Be underling to such a vile controule? **1613** PURCHAS *Pilgrimage* (1614) 187 Lilis..would not be vnderling, and Adam would not endure her his equall. **1647** N. BACON *Disc. Govt. Eng.* I. xlvii. 124 A league of cohabitation should be made between the two Swords, though the spirituall were for the present underling.

b. Similarly in attributive use.

1615–6 BOYS *Wks.* (1629) 135 The Lord of all submitted himselfe to the gouernment of his supposed father, and vnderling mother. **1657** J. WATTS *Vind. Ch. Eng.* 265 We underling Shepheards and Pastours may imitate our Paramount Shepheard and Pastour. **1693** *Apol. Clergy Scot.* 104 The underling Pedlars amongst the Presbyterians may write what they please. **1714** POPE *Lett.* (1735) I. 205 There are indeed, a Sort of underling Auxiliars to the Difficulty of a Work, call'd Commentators and Critics. **1764** FOOTE *Patron* I, By..underling bards, that he feeds; and broken book-sellers, that he bribes. **1802–12** BENTHAM *Ration. Judic. Evid.* (1827) IV. 577 The underling sort of lawyer whom the judge punishes every day without scruple.

B. *adj.* **1.** Undersized, small, weak. (Cf. UNDERLINE *a.*)

a **1722** LISLE *Husb.* (1757) 410 The underling hog put up with the rest, is longest a fatting. **1742** *Lond. & Country Brewer* III. (ed. 2) 172 Seven Quarters of these underling Kernels. **1788** W. H. MARSHALL *Yorks.* II. 72 [The flax] remains weak, short, and underling. **1840** in *Jrnl. R. Agric. Soc.* (1841) II. I. 120 Many short or underling straws, as they are here [*sc.* Pusey, Berks.] called.

2. Low-growing.

1830 MACGILLIVRAY *Withering's Brit. Plants* II. 548 In gardens and other cultivated lands, it often proves a most troublesome underling weed.

3. Trivial, unimportant.

1804 SOUTHEY in Robberds *Mem. W. Taylor* (1843) 481 While they can employ me more to their own advantage in little underling works.

'under,lining, *sb.* [UNDER-[1] 5 c.] A lining placed under something; the inner lining of a garment. Also *fig.*

1580 HOLLYBAND, *Vn haulse*, the vnderlining of a shoe. **1631** BRATHWAIT *Eng. Gentlew.* 176 When the Moath shall be your vnderlining, and the Worme your couering. **1897** *Daily News* 16 Jan. 6/5 An underlining of fine soft flannel makes them suitable for even the coldest weather.

under'lining, *vbl. sb.* [f. UNDERLINE *v.*[2]] The action of drawing lines below words, etc.; a line or lines so drawn.

1838 L. HUNT *Let.* July in *Lett. C. Dickens* (1965) I. 685, I have marked..my *most* favourite passages... The underlinings imply admiration. **1864** WILLIAMS & SIMMONDS *Engl. Commerc. Corresp.* 1 Underlinings too are frequent,..so as to catch the eye more readily. **1891** MEREDITH *One of our Conq.* xxxi, She begged Captain Dartrey, in double under-linings of her brief words, to mount the stairs.

'underlip. [UNDER-[1] 5 b. Cf. Du. *onderlip*, G. *unterlippe*, Sw. *underläpp*, Da. *underlæbe.*]

1. The lower lip of a person, animal, or insect.

1669 HOLDER *Elem. Speech* 25 The Tongue and under-Lip..are moveable. *a* **1735** ARBUTHNOT *State Learn. Lilliput* Misc. Wks. 1751 I. 145 At that..he put out his Under-Lip. **1737** CHALLONER *Cath. Chr. Instr.* (1753) 71 His Tongue a little advanced on his Under-lip. **1826** KIRBY & SP. *Entomol.* III. xxx. 124 These maxillæ of larvæ were regarded..as parts of the under-lip, on each side of which they are situated. **1855** TENNYSON *Maud* I. ii. 9 An underlip, you may call it a little too ripe, too full. **1882** 'F. ANSTEY' *Vice Versâ* i, His big underlip drooped rather weakly.

b. *spec.* (See quot.)

1908 *Animal Managem.* 32 'Upperlip' and 'underlip' are the names used to denote white skin at the edges of the lips [of horses].

2. In an organ-pipe: (see quots.).

1852 SEIDEL *Organ* 78 The under lip, on the foot, and immediately below the language. **1875** KNIGHT *Dict. Mech.* 1709 The *foot* is an inverted cone, formed in a similar manner, and having a corresponding indentation, called the *under lip.*

† **,under'live**, *v.* *Obs.* [UNDER-[1] 8 b.] *refl.* To live in a manner unworthy of oneself.

1655 FULLER *Ch. Hist.* III. vi. §37 No wonder then, if easily they did over-grow others in wealth, who basely did under-live themselves in all convenient accommodations. **1682** SIR T. BROWNE *Chr. Mor.* I. §24 They who are merely carried on by the Wheel of such Inclinations are..rather lived than living, or at least underliving themselves.

underloaded (stress variable), *a.* [UNDER-[1] 10 a, after *overloaded.*] Not loaded or burdened to capacity; *spec.* in *Geomorphol.* of a stream: carrying less than the maximum amount of sediment for the given conditions, and eroding its bed.

1898 I. C. RUSSELL *River Development* iv. 68 But if the bottom current is underloaded, the material is carried slowly forward. **1942** O. D. VON ENGELN *Geomorphol.* xii. 234 A stream may be underloaded in which case it will ordinarily be downcutting, or it may be loaded to capacity. **1964** K. G. LOCKYER *Introd. Critical Path Analysis* viii. 70 When too much work is required of a work source, the work source is said to be *Overloaded*, whilst if too little is needed it is said to be *Underloaded.* **1970** R. J. SMALL *Study of Landforms* ii. 57 At some times streams erode vertically (because they are underloaded), at others they erode laterally (because they are graded), at others they deposit (when they change from a graded to an overloaded condition).

Hence **'underload**, an occurrence or state of being incompletely loaded.

1964 K. G. LOCKYER *Introd. Critical Path Analysis* viii. 76 With experience, a great facility is obtained in viewing a histogram and..assessing whether a 'peak' (i.e. an overload) can be toppled into a 'valley' (i.e. an under-load) in order to 'smooth out' the loading. **1971** *Cabinet Maker & Retail Furnisher* 24 Sept. 535/1 Unless the home market improves ..APV could have..an underload position in some of their factories. **1981** *N.Y. Times Mag.* 8 Feb. 12/2 Conservatives are foolishly worrying about lithosphere underload.

'underlook, *sb.* [UNDER-[1] 9.] A covert look or glance.

1821 T. MOORE *Diary* 2 July, She said it was..the peculiarity of a sort of under look he used to give that produced this effect upon her. **1889** HOWELLS *Hazard New Fort.* IV. viii, She said, with an underlook at her husband.

under'look, *v.* [UNDER-[1] 4 b.]

1. *trans.* To look at, or inspect, from beneath.

1682 HICKERINGILL *Black Non-Conf.* iii. 14 They would be Shepherds and feed his Sheep, and anoint them for the Scab, and underlook them. **1873** MRS. WHITNEY *Other Girls* xviii, The place where they could lean in between the trees, and overlook and underlook the shining tumult.

2. To miss seeing by looking too low.

1802 BEDDOES *Hygëia* II. 56 Do they not *underlook* that sole essential condition to happiness, the inward state?

'under,looker. [UNDER-[1] 6 a.]

1. *Mining.* A subordinate to the manager, who has the superintendence of the miners and workings.

1871 *Daily News* 21 Sept., Amongst the number were.. the underlookers, and the underground manager. **1885** *Law Times* LXXIX. 119/2 No person was..to blast coal without the charge having been inspected by the underlooker.

2. A subordinate overseer.

1885 *Manch. Exam.* 9 Jan. 5/1 An underlooker..being struck by a shuttle which flew out of a loom.

'underlord. [UNDER-[1] 6 a.] A subordinate or lesser lord; one in authority below another (opp. *overlord*).

1929 BELLOC *Joan of Arc* ii. 39 The Kingdom was held in fealty from God alone of Whom Charles was Vassal and Under-Lord. **1937** F. L. PACKARD *Dragon's Jaws* 251 And if the old temple is the secret meeting place..and Fan Chao-tao and his underlords..are to be there—what then? **1969** *Daily Tel.* 29 Oct. 16 In the sphere of the other main new overlord (Mr Benn) one nominated underlord has already resigned, presumably because he thinks it won't work. **1985** *Financial Times* 1 Feb. 21/5 The appointment of Lord Young..to the Cabinet as what he calls a kind of 'underlord' responsible for training matters.

Hence **'underlordship** *rare.*

1937 BELLOC *Crusade* ii. 38 The title King meant that he had no overlord. He was the summit in a pyramid of overlordships and underlordships.

'underlout, *a.* and *sb.* *Obs.* exc. *dial.* Forms: 3–5 **underloute** (4–5 **-lowte**), 4–6 **underlout** (4–5 **-lowt**), 4 **underlote, -lut(te**, 4–6 **-lute.** (Also 3–5 **vnder-**, 4–5 **vndir-, vndyr-**, etc.) [Related to OE. *underlútan*: see UNDER-[1] 4 a and LOUT *v.*[1] The second element may be a. ON. *lútr* adj., bending, stooping.]

†**A.** *adj.* Subject, subservient, submissive. Freq. const. *to.* *Obs.*

a **1300** *Cursor M.* 678 þe bestes boud him all aboute, Als to þair lauerd vnderloute. *c* **1325** *Metr. Hom.* 109 Underlout til thaim was he, Als god child au til elderes be. *a* **1340** HAMPOLE *Psalter* xvii. 11 He made aungels vndirelout til man kynd. **1434** MISYN *Mending of Life* 117 In þe flesch if þou be tempyd, make it sugett, þat þe spiryt be not vndir-lowt. *c* **1450** *Mirour Saluacioun* 787 Sho was..devoute To fulfille gods wille all gyven and vnderloute. **1513** DOUGLAS *Æneid* XIII. iii. 71 The chance of kyngis standis onderlout, To mekill dreid ay subiect. **1583** MELBANCKE *Philotimus* Aa iv b, Barbulas..was now at the checke of his vnderlout vassaile.

B. *sb.* **1.** One who is subject or subordinate to another; an underling or servant; an inferior. Now *dial.* (see later quots.).

a **1300** *Cursor M.* 3705 þi breþer be þin vnderlute [*Gött.* -lout], And alle þat wonnes þe a-boute. *Ibid.* 18206 þe erthis werld..has been ai Vr vnderlut als to þis dai. *c* **1340** HAMPOLE *Pr. Consc.* 3877 Yhit may þai graunt Of þair power pardon aparty Til þair hawen underloutes anly. *c* **1400** *Apol. Loll.* 2 To wham Austeyn, Jerom, and Gregor tak awey þe name of þe bischop, or heldarman, þat he may be correctid of wnderlowtis. *c* **1440** *Alph. Tales* 223 Sho made hur selfe ..so grete ane vnderlowte, þat ilkone vggid with hur. *a* **1470** HARDING *Chron.* XXX. viii, Then stande he moste in parell to bee slain, Or els putte doune right by his vnderloute. **1684** MERITON *Yorks. Dial.* 61 Thou's nut think that Ile be thy Underlout. **1790** GROSE *Prov. Gloss.*, *Under-lout*, a drudge in an inferior capacity. **1877** PEACOCK *N.W. Linc. Gloss.* 264 *Underlout*, (1) a lazy servant-boy. (2) The least boy on a farm. (3) The weakest beast in a herd. **1886** COLE *S.W. Linc. Gloss.* 158 *Underlout*,..the weaker pig in a sty,..the smaller and weaker trees in a plantation.

†**2.** Some part of a ship. *Obs. rare.*

1295–6 *Acc. Exch. K.R.* 5/20 m. 1 In vno ligno ad vnderloute cum quatuor aliis lignis ad scalmas..ix. s. vj. d. **1546** *Acc. High Treas. Scot.* VIII. 486 Quhilk he debursit upoun the calfating, dok casting, putting in of the underlute of the said Lyoun and outred of hir to the raid.

† **under'lout**, *v.* *Obs. rare.* [(1) = OE. *underlútan*; cf. prec. (2) f. prec.] **a.** *intr.* To be subject, to submit. **b.** *trans.* To make subject.

a **1400** *Pauline Ep.* (Powell) Heb. xiii. 17 Obesche ȝee to ȝoure prouostis and vndyrloute ȝee [L. *subjacete*] to þem. *c* **1440** *Promp. Parv.* 511/1 Vnderlowton, *subjicio, subjecto.*

'underlow. [UNDER-[1] 6 b.] One of the lower classes at Ushaw College, Durham.

1837 in *Ushaw Mag.* Dec. (1904) 262 The Catechism Exam. of the High and Low Fig. and Underlows. **1896** *Ibid.* Mar. 33 All the classes, from Divinity to Underlow.

† **'underly**, *a.* *rare.* *Obs.* [f. UNDER *a.* or *adv.*]

1. Subordinate; inferior, low.

1648 SYMMONS *Vind. Chas. I*, 3 Themselves were then but poor fellows of an underly condition. **1674** N. FAIRFAX *Bulk & Selv.* Ep. Ded., Such an underly Shrub in Knowledge, and unthrifty Sucker in Philosophy as I am.

2. In a low state of health.

1715 STORY *Life*, etc. (1747) 502 Her Brother..was still very weak and underly.

† **'underly**, *adv.* *Obs.* [f. UNDER *adv.* + -LY[2].] At a lower level.

1671 GREW *Anat. Plants* vii. §17 The Seed-Branch..is presently divided into two main Branches, and those two into other less; whereof some underly, others aloft, run along the Coat.

'underlye. (UNDER-[1] 5 b.)

1887 *Encycl. Brit.* XXII. 203/2 It may be skimmed off the underlye.

under'lying, *vbl. sb.* *Mining.* [f. UNDERLIE *v.* 5.] Declination from the perpendicular.

1778 W. PRYCE *Min. Cornub.* 80 This underlying varies much in different Lodes.

under'lying, *ppl. a.* [UNDER-[1] 4 a, or f. UNDERLIE *v.*] **1.** Lying under or beneath.

1611 COTGR., *Subiacent*, subiacent, vnder-lying. **1615** G. SANDYS *Trav.* 289 This appeared more warlike, to behold from aboue the vnderlying country. **1616** W. BROWNE *Brit. Past.* II. ii. 42 Thence they beheld an vnderlying Vale. **1850** TENNYSON *In Mem.* ii, The stones That name the under-lying dead. **1865** LUBBOCK *Preh. Times* 303 In the pits at Amiens this bed is generally distinct from the under-lying gravels. **1884** *Leisure Hour* June 345/2 They were stripping the tough hide and underlying blubber.

fig. **1852** MRS. STOWE *Uncle Tom's C.* xxxvi, A deep underlying spirit of cautiousness. **1882** FARRAR *Early Chr.* I. 321 The identity of phraseology does but serve to bring into prominence the underlying differences.

2. *Linguistics.* Applied to a significant feature of a linguistic unit or structure which needs to be represented in its derivational or syntactic analysis, but which may not be apparent from the standard written or spoken form. Cf. *deep structure* s.v. DEEP *a.* IV. c.

1933 L. BLOOMFIELD *Language* xiii. 210 By a feature of modulation common to nearly all constructions of English morphology, the underlying form keeps its stress, and the bound form is unstressed. **1958** C. F. HOCKETT *Course in Mod. Linguistics* xxviii. 241 If the underlying form in a secondary derivative is not a single morpheme, its structure is also covered by the classification. Thus the underlying form of *actress-* is the secondary derivative *actor-.* **1970** J. LYONS *Chomsky* 67 This system of phrase structure rules will generate a large (but finite) number of what we may call *underlying strings.* **1978** *Language* LIV. 387 Actually, rather than 'deep structure' we should think in terms of the 'underlying structure' of Generative Semantics, a highly abstract and universal level that is much more closely akin to the Freudian unconscious than is the 'deep structure' of classical transformational grammar.

Hence **under'lyingly** *adv.*

1973 A. H. SOMMERSTEIN *Sound Pattern Anc. Greek* i. 2 There is underlyingly a system of five short..and five corresponding long vowels. **1982** J. C. WELLS *Accents of English* i. 76 It is possible to argue..that an occurrence of the phoneme /r/ is present underlyingly in the critical environments, but that it is obligatorily vocalized or deleted by rule so that it is not present phonetically.

'under,man. [UNDER-[1] 6 a. Cf. ON. *undirmaðr* (Norw. *undermann*, Da. *-mand*), G. *untermann*, a subject, vassal.] **1.** An inferior or subordinate man. *rare.*

13.. *Peter & Paul* 65 in Horstm. *Altengl. Leg.* (1881) 77 Prelates and maisters þat þaire vndirmen so felli faisters Wiþ chidinge. *a* **1661** HOLYDAY *Juvenal* (1673) 152 You undermen (say'st thou) are our base rout, Whose parents country no man can find-out. **1905** *N. & Q.* 9th Ser. III. 273 These [heralds] were so expensive, .. that a set of under-men arose, who acted in their stead.

2. [tr. G. *untermensch.*] *spec.* opp. OVERMAN *sb.* 4; a person with sub-human attributes.

1910 T. COMMON tr. *Nietzsche's Joyful Wisdom* III. 179 The inventing of Gods, heroes and supermen of all kinds, as well as co-ordinate men and undermen—dwarfs, fairies, .. devils—was the inestimable preliminary to the justification of the selfishness .. of the individual. **1936** A. N. FIELD *All these Things* vi. 206 Planned Economy calls for Supermen to control and Undermen to submit. **1963** L. TRILLING in N. Frye *Romanticism Reconsidered* 92 *More life*: perhaps it was this boast of the Underground Man that Nietzsche recalled when he said, 'Dostoevsky's Underman and my Overman are the same person.' **1974** W. KAUFMAN tr. *Nietzsche's Gay Science* III. 192 *Untermensch* (underman, for a subhuman man) is not rare.

3. *Railways.* A subordinate member of a gang of platelayers.

1921 *Dict. Occup. Terms* (1927) §577 *Underman*.., a worker in a permanent way gang supervised by ganger. **1928** *Daily Express* 18 Feb. 7/3 Sidney Coleman, an underman platelayer, said he was one of the gang which was 'packing' sleepers on the down main line. **1931** *Cambridge Daily News* 5 Sept. 5/2 Andrew White, an underman .. said he shouted as hard as he could to warn the men that a train was approaching.

'under-,manager. (UNDER-¹ 6 a.)

1748 RICHARDSON *Clarissa* VII. Concl. 419 They were compelled, for subsistence-sake, to enter themselves as under managers at .. another house. **1894** *Northumberland Gloss.* 517 The manager or under-manager of a pit.

,under'manned, *ppl. a.* [UNDER-¹ 10 a.] Not furnished with a sufficient number of men; short-handed; under-staffed.

1867 SMYTH *Sailor's Word-bk.* 706 *Under-manned*, when a ship has an insufficient complement. **1889** *Boston Mission. Herald* June 236 These are all wide-reaching centers, and every one is undermanned. **1900** [see UNDERMASTED].

,under'manning, *vbl. sb.* [UNDER-¹ 10 a.] The fact of furnishing, or being furnished with, too few men or 'hands'.

1890 *Nature* 3 April 520/2 [They] cannot get on with their work on account of the undermanning of the Department. **1901** *Empire Rev.* I. 431 Caused by faults of organisation, rather than by undermanning.

'under-,marshal. (UNDER-¹ 6 a.)

1670 BLOUNT *Law Dict.* (1691), *Submarshal*, is an Officer in the Marshalsea... He is otherwise called Vnder-Marshal. **1753** HANWAY *Trav.* VI. lxxxii. (1762) I. 373 Monsieur Nariskin, .. now under-marshal to the empress, had a coach.

'under-,marshalman. (UNDER-¹ 6 a.)

1763 *Ann. Reg., Chron.* 70/1 Four king's under-marshalmen on horseback.

'undermass. *Geol.* [UNDER-¹ 5 c.] An older, deformed body of rock overlain by younger, undeformed strata.

1942 O. D. VON ENGELN *Geomorphol.* ix. 168 The geomorphic significance of the abrupt, commonly marked in kind, transition between the materials above and below a plane of angular unconformity is indicated by the introduction of the terms cover mass and undermass. **1956** D. L. LINTON *Sheffield* ii. 35 We .. interpret it as the product of the cycle(s) of erosion which stripped away the presumed chalk cover, removed some hundreds of feet of the undermass, and saw the first group of adjustments of the superimposed streams to the underlying structures. **1966** [see *plate tectonics* s.v. PLATE *sb.* 21].

,under'masted, *ppl. a.* [UNDER-¹ 10 a.] (See quot. 1841.)

1594 DOWNTON in Hakluyt *Voy.* (1599) II. II. 201 She was much vndermasted, and vndersailed, yet she went well for a ship that was so foule. **1627** CAPT. SMITH *Seaman's Gram.* ii. 15 If either too small or too short, she is vnder masted or low masted. **1674** PETTY *Disc. Dupl. Proportion* 29 The chief cause why short, bluff, undermasted Vessels sail cheaper than others. **1841** TOTTEN *Naval Text-book* (1862) 437 *Under-masted*, or *under-sparred*, .. applied to vessels which have masts under the usual dimensions. **1867** SMYTH *Sailor's Word-bk.* 706. **1900** SIR W. KENNEDY *Life Sailor* xiii. 202 She was nothing else than an undermasted, undermanned coal-hulk.

'under,master. [UNDER-¹ 6 a. Cf. MDu. and Du. *ondermeester*, MLG. *undermêster*, MHG. *undermeister.*]

1. A subordinate instructor; esp. in schools, a master or teacher below the head-master.

By Wyclif used to render L. *pædagogus*.

1388 WYCLIF *Gal.* iii. 24 And so the lawe was oure vndirmaister in Crist. *Ibid.* 25 Aftir that bileue cam, we ben not now vndur the vndurmaistir. **1561** in H. B. Wilson *Hist. Merchant Taylors' Sch.* (1814) 14 The high maister .. shall say to the ussher, .. I have chosen you to be the chief ussher or under maister of this schoole. **1598** FLORIO, *Sottomaestro*, an vnder master, an vsher of a schoole. **1709** *Ir. Act 8 Anne* c. 3 §16 Several protestant school-masters .. do entertain such persons .. to be ushers, under-masters, or assistants. **1784** JOHNSON 13 June in *Boswell*, They were written by one Lewis, who was either under-master or an usher of Westminster-school. **1862** MRS. H. WOOD *Mrs. Hallib.* I. iv, [He] was earning his own living as an under-master in a school. **1875** JOWETT *Plato* (ed. 2) I. 250 Masters and under-masters of choruses.

2. A subordinate director or supervisor. *rare.*

1668 *Lond. Gaz.* No. 2322/3 The Under-Master of the Horse. **1703** *Ibid.* No. 3914/4 The Earl of Marr served as Carver, .. and Sir William Enstruther, Baronet, as under Master Houshold.

†'undermatch, *sb. Obs.* [UNDER-¹ 10 b.] One who is no match for another; an inferior rival.

a **1661** FULLER *Worthies, Denbigh* (1662) 34 He was no contemptible Historian, but I confesse an under-match to Doctor Hackwell. **1769** GOLDSM. *Hist. Rome* (1786) I. 281 Claudius Nero .. appearing an under-match for the cunning of the Carthaginian general.

under'match, *v.* [UNDER-¹ 10 a.]

1. *trans.* To undervalue by comparison.

1571 GOLDING *Calvin on Ps.* lx. 10 He passeth foorth to the forreiners, whom hee far undermatcheth to his owne people.

2. To unite or bestow in marriage below the proper rank or condition.

1639 S. DU VERGER tr. *Camus' Admir. Events* 39 There is none that so jealously preserve their Nobility, as the German, nor more feare to undermatch themselves. **1708** CIBBER *Lady's Last Stake* III, Dispose of the Child as soon as you can; rather under-match her, than not at all. **1831** SCOTT *Ct. Rob.* xviii, A damsel .. would think herself heinously undermatched, if wedded to a gallant whose fame in arms was yet unknown.

†under'matched, *ppl. a. Obs.* [UNDER-¹ 10 a.] Not equal to another; inferior.

1642 FULLER *Holy & Prof. St.* II. iv. 60 He tyrannizeth not over a weak, and undermatched Adversary. **1765** JOHNSON *Shakespeare's Cymb.* II. iii. *note*, His argument is just and well enforced... As for rudeness, he seems not to be much undermatched.

'undermath. [UNDER-¹ 5 c: cf. *aftermath.*] An undergrowth of grass, etc.

1881 G. ALLEN *Vignettes* xii. 119 Ferns .. grow in the tangled shady undermath of the banks and thickets.

†'undermeal. *Obs.* Forms: 1 undernmæl, 4–5 vnder-, undermele (5 -mel), 6–7 vndermeale. [OE. *undernmǽl*: see UNDERN *sb.* and MEAL *sb.*²]

1. The time of undern; in later use esp. the early part of the afternoon. Also *attrib.*

Beowulf 1428 Ðesawon .. on næshleoðum nicras licgean, ða on undernmæl oft bewitiȝað sorhfulne sið. *c* **1000** ÆLFRIC *Saints' Lives* xxx. 319 Þa an undern-mæl spræcon hi betwux him þær-inne. *c* **1386** CHAUCER *Wife's T.* 875 Ther walketh now the lymytour hym self In vndermeles and in morwenynges. *c* **1400** *Trevisa's Higden* V. 373 Rosamunda in an undermele tyde [L. *meridiano tempore*] bonde .. faste þe kynges swerd þat was on slepe. *c* **1440** *Promp. Parv.* 511/1 Vndermele, *postmeridies, postmesimbria.*

b. An afternoon nap; a siesta. Also *attrib.*

1426 LYDG. *De Guil. Pilgr.* 9044 To leyn hym softely On Fether beddys, mad ful wel, For to slepe hys vndermel. **1589** NASHE *Greene's Menaphon* Pref. (Arb.) 15 The blacke pot; which makes our Poets vndermeale Muses so mutinous, as euerie stanzo they pen after dinner, is full poynted with a stabbe. **1599** —— *Lenten Stuffe* Ep. Ded., Hee hath dinde at a tauerne, and slept his vnder-meale at a bawdy house. *Ibid.* 11 The forty yeares vndermeale of the seauen sleepers.

2. An afternoon meal.

c **1440** *Promp. Parv.* 511/1 Vndermele, .. *merarium.* **1530** PALSGR. 285/2 Under mele, *ressigner.* **1586** *Withals' Dict.* (1599) 57/2 Another greater supper or vndermeale was made redie for them. **1614** B. JONSON *Barth. Fair* IV. ii, I thinke I am furnish'd for Catherne peares, for one vnder-meale.

'under,meaning. (UNDER-¹ 9.)

1841 RUSKIN *Let.* 12 Feb. in *Lett. to College Friend* (1894) vii. 87 Rhyme and rhythm are .. thoroughly injurious where there is no mystery, when there is not some undermeaning. **1846** TRENCH *Mirac.* xxxiii. 455 We must continue to see an under-meaning .. in all this. **1865** RUSKIN *Sesame* ii. §93 Have you ever considered what a deep undermeaning there lies .. in our custom.

'under-,measure, *sb.* (UNDER-¹ 10 b.)

1596 [see UNDERWEIGHT *sb.*].

,under-'measure, *v.* [UNDER-¹ 10 a.] *trans.* To measure insufficiently or not to the full amount.

1672 GREW *Idea Philos. Hist. Plants* §4 It is impossible to Measure, what we See not. And since we are most likely to under-measure [etc.]. **1845** DISRAELI *Sybil* III. i, Many's the morn we work for nothing, .. and many's the good stint they undermeasure.

,under-'meated, *ppl. a.* [UNDER-¹ 10 a.] Underfed.

1653 J. TAYLOR (Water P.) *Journ. Wales* (1859) 6 He was a beast, had beaten been and cheated; Too much hard over rid and under meated.

under-'mentioned, *ppl. a.* [UNDER *adv.* 2 b.] Named or noted below or in a place beneath.

1640–1 *Kirkcudbr. War-Comm. Min. Bk.* (1855) 10 The Commissioners undermentionit are appoyntit in ilk paroche. **1683** in Picton *L'pool Munic. Rec.* (1883) I. 330 We present the persons undermentioned for absenting from divine service. **1818** THOMSON *Lond. Disp.* 644 Oil of rosemary .. is chiefly used in the under-mentioned preparations. **1875** CROLL *Climate & T.* xx. 332 The number of years required by the undermentioned rivers.

under-metal: see METAL *sb.* 7.

'under-,miller. (UNDER-¹ 6 a.)

1825 JAMIESON, *Gude-will*, .. the proportion of meal .. which is due to the under-miller. **1843** *Rep. Trial by Jury, Magistrates Jedburgh*, etc. 37 The under-miller always drew the multure.

under'minable, *a.* [f. UNDERMINE *v.*] Capable of being undermined.

1622 DONNE *Serm.* Wks. 1839 VI. 228 So underminable is the love of this world which determines every minute. **1679** C. NESSE *Antid. agst. Popery* Ded. 2 Seated upon a rock that is unaccessible and not underminable.

'undermine, *sb.* [UNDER- 4 d, 5 c. Cf. next.]

†1. An underground excavation. *Obs.*

1599 HAKLUYT *Voy.* II. 86 They put fire in the vndermines, weening to haue cast downe the wall. **1610** HOLLAND *Camden's Brit.* I. 650 Under-mines or caves of very great widenesse. **1629** *Descr. S'hertogenbosh* 36 We made an vnder-mine through the walls of the Towne.

†2. A submerged mine. *Obs.*

1682 *Roxb. Ball.* (1885) V. 519 But thou, buoy'd up with Providence Divine, Shall float above, and fear no undermine.

3. An undermining movement.

1898 *Daily News* 12 May 8/4 The Bishop .. said there was a very strong undermine of disloyalty to the Church.

under'mine, *v.* Forms: α. 4–6 undermyne, 5– -mine, 7 -moine (also 4–6 vnder-, 4–5 vndir-, 5 vndyr-). β. 5 vndermynden, 6 -mynde, 6–7 vnder-, underminde, 7–8 (9 *dial.*) undermind. [UNDER-¹ 4 a + MINE *v.* Cf. Du. *ondermijnen*, older Da. *undermine*; also MDu. *ondermineren*, Da. *underminere*, Sw. *-era*, G. *unterminiren.*

In 15th cent. texts *undermyne* or *-mine* is occasionally miswritten for *undernim.*]

1. *trans.* To dig or excavate beneath, to make a passage or mine under (a wall, etc.), esp. as a military operation; to sap.

α. **13..** *Coer de L.* 4721 The Crystene the walles undermyne. **1382** WYCLIF *Jer.* li. 58 The wal of Babilon .. with vndermynyng shal be vndermyned. *c* **1450** *Contin. Brut* 577 And after, [they] vndermynet þe walles and þe toures, and sette shores vndernethe. *a* **1548** HALL *Chron., Hen. V*, 45 Knowyng that their walles were vndermyned and shortely like to fal. **1582** N. LICHEFIELD tr. *Castanheda's Conq. E. Ind.* I. ix. 22 It is a verye great Citie, placed .. so that it cannot be undermined. **1616** J. LANE *Contn. Sqr.'s T.* VII. 397 To lead his men safe to the walled towne, which vndermoine hee shoold. **1618** BOLTON *Florus* (1636) 181 Undermining their port Pireus, and more than six Walls of theirs. **1726** LEONI *Alberti's Archit.* I. 68 When the foundation is .. on a rock, it will be in vain to think of undermining it. **1776** G. SEMPLE *Building in Water* 40 We had no other Way to break it, but by undermining it, and then break it off in Pieces. **1834** MARRYAT *P. Simple* xxi, We must under-mine the gate, O'Brien; we must pull up the pavement until we can creep under. **1848** DICKENS *Dombey* vi, Buildings that were undermined and shaking, [were] propped by great beams of wood.

β. *c* **1440** *Promp. Parv.* 511/1 Vndermyndyn, *idem quod* vnderdelvyn. **1513** DOUGLAS *Æneid* VIII. xi. 38 Sum vndermyndand the ground with a hoill. **1571** LESLIE *Hist. Scot.* (Bann. Cl.) 101 [They] under myndit the neddir sole of the yett of Dunbartane. *a* **1644** *Spottiswoode Misc.* (1844) I. 146 In the late warrs .. the churches [were] undermynded and fired. **1828–** in dial. glossaries (Yks., Linc., Surrey).

b. *absol.* To make excavations or mines.

1382 WYCLIF *Exod.* xxii. 2 If a theef brekynge an hows, or were foundun vndurmynynge. **1412–20** LYDG. *Chron. Troy* II. 6335 Þei .. turnen vp so doun Boþe wal & tour .. Þat no þing stood, so þei vnder-myne. **1601** HOLLAND *Pliny* II. 467 Necessarie it is .. to undermine a great way by candle-light, & to make hollow vaults under the mountains. **1646** H. P. *Medit. Seige* 60 It is an usuall practice to under-mine, and when they have brought the Mine unto the Works, to blow it up with powder. **1685** TRAVESTIN *Siege Newheusel* 34 This day we began to undermine on the side attackt by the Troops of Brunswick.

c. In fig. context.

c **1400** *Beryn* 3480 Ye wend .. þat ye had hym engyned; But yee shul fele in every veyn þat ye be vndirmyned, And I-brouȝt at ground. **1559** AYLMER *Harborowe* C ij b, These .. be .. the pik-axes to vnder mynde the state. **1601** SHAKS. *All's Well* I. i. 130 Man setting downe before you, will vndermine you, and blow you vp. **1668** DRYDEN *Tyrannic Love* III. i, Yet fierceness suits not with her gentle kind; They brave assaults, but may be undermined. **1794** BURKE *Corr.* (1844) IV. 254 As yet, the house is not fallen; but it is completely undermined. **1855** MOTLEY *Dutch Rep.* VI. i. III. 409 Religious fanaticism had undermined the bulwark almost as soon as reared. **1875** JOWETT *Plato* (ed. 2) V. 363 The fair superstructure falls because the old foundations are undermined.

2. a. Of water: To work under and wash away (ground, etc.).

1398 TREVISA *Barth. De P.R.* xv. lxxxii. (Bodl. MS.), þe parties of ilondes beþ ywasted, & vndermyned wiþ betinge of watres. **1562** PILKINGTON *Expos. Abdyas* Pref. 5 A strong heady streame, undermining great hygh bankes. **1610** HOLLAND *Camden's Brit.* 676 The riveret Alen .. undermineth the ground and once or twice hideth himselfe. **1707** MORTIMER *Husb.* 5 Alder makes an extraordinary Fence against Rivers and Streams, and preserves the Banks from being undermined by the Water. **1784** *Cook's Voy.* IV. ix. II. 464 By undermining and washing away those parts that lie exposed to the surge of the sea. **1855** *Orr's Circ. Sci., Inorg. Nat.* 155 The stream .. relieving the gloom of the naked rocks, and at the same time tending to undermine them. **1860** TYNDALL *Glac.* I. xv. 101 The glacier .. is incessantly undermined, .. till at length the projecting mass .. tumbles into the lake.

absol. **1858** MACDONALD *Phantastes* xiii. 148 The springing waters were dammed back into his soul, where, finding no utterance, they .. swelled, and undermined.

b. Of animals: To burrow under or in; to make insecure, to cause to fall, through burrowing; also, to form (a passage) by burrowing.

1526 *Pilgr. Perf.* (W. de W. 1531) 55 Catche these lytell foxes, which with dyggynge of theyr dennes vndermyndeth our vynes. **1567** MAPLET *Gr. Forest* 92 He hath his cabbage [= den] in the yearth with two contrary wayes vndermined to enter into it. **1579** LYLY *Euphues* (Arb.) 109 In a shorte space, there was a Towne in Spayne vndermined with Connyes. **1629** DAVENANT *Albovine* III. i, When she [*sc.* the mole] undermines the earth. **1697** DRYDEN *Virg. Georg.* IV. 355 Lizards .. a dark Retreat Have found in Combs, and undermin'd the Seat. *a* **1704** T. BROWN *Declam. Adverbs*

Wks. 1720 I. 45 All Thessaly had in the twinkling of a Shoeing-horn been certainly undermin'd by Lobsters.

c. *Path.* To erode beneath the surface.

1879 *St. George's Hosp. Rep.* IX. 254 Hip-joint.. surrounded with œdema and undermined by sinuses. **1898** *Hutchinson's Arch. Surg.* IX. 111 The chronic infective inflammations.. which ulcerate to a slight extent whilst they undermine widely.

3. *fig.* (Cf. 1 c.) To work secretly or stealthily against (a person); to overthrow or supplant by underhand means.

α. **1430–40** LYDG. *Bochas* IV. Prol. (1554) 99 b, Fortune could him vndermine That al hys wisedome stode in none auayle. **1535** COVERDALE *Gen.* xxvii. 36 He maye well be called Iacob, for he hath vndermined me now two tymes. **1561** T. NORTON tr. *Calvin's Inst.* IV. xviii, To beguile and vndermine an other man, al men know to be vnlawfull. **1633** P. FLETCHER *Purple Isl.* II. xviii, Whose pleasing sweetnesse .. Doth oft the Prince himself with witch'ries under-mine. **1678** WANLEY *Wond. Lit. World* V. i. §100. 468/1 Rodolphus .. being undermined by his brother Matthias, was forced to surrender to him.. Hungary and Bohemia. **1759** ROBERTSON *Hist. Scot.* III. Wks. 1851 I. 237 Some of his rivals he secretly undermined. **1775** ADAIR *Amer. Ind.* 91 The religious advantages and arguments by which the French used to undermine us with the Indians. **1849** MACAULAY *Hist. Eng.* ii. I. 197 Those who had assailed and undermined him began to struggle for the fragments of his power. **1876** HOLLAND *Seven Oaks* xiv. 200 Are you to sit tamely down and be undermined?

β. **1530** PALSGR. 767/1 Medyll nat with hym,.. for surely he wyll undermynde the. **1596** SPENSER *F.Q.* v. vi. 32 He was nothing valorous, But with slie shiftes and wiles did vnderminde All noble Knights. **1613** JACKSON *Creed* II. vii. §7 Yet are they easily to be underminded by Sathan. **1663** GERBIER *Counsel* 103 If he be a Master workman, whom they will.. suspect to have a design to underminde and supplant them. **1869–** in *Eng. Dial. Dict.* (Yks., Lanc., Linc.).

absol. **1584** LYLY *Sappho* I. iii. 26 Where we suspect, we vndermine. **1712** BLACKMORE *Creation* VII. 349 The ambitious statesman labours dark designs, Now open force employs, now undermines.

†**4.** To underlie and spoil. *Obs.*⁻¹

1430–40 LYDG. *Bochas* I. x. (1544) 21 b, Some fresh floures haue a full bitter rote And lothsom gal can suger eke vnder-mine.

5. To persuade or win over, to tamper with or pervert, by subtle means. Also *absol.*

1457 HARDING *Chron.* in *Eng. Hist. Rev.* Oct. (1912) 747 His language.. so benygne was and trewe it vndyrmyned Thair hertes hole to loue hym at thair myght. **1522** SKELTON *Why not to Court?* 434 So he dothe vndermynde, And suche sleyghtes dothe fynde, That the kynges mynde By hym is subuerted. **1579** LYLY *Euphues* (Arb.) 85 Ferardo.. desired him to kepe silence, vntil he had vndermined hir by subtiltie. **1664** DRYDEN *Rival Ladies* IV. iii, She undermin'd my Soul With Tears. **1671** MILTON *P.R.* I. 179 The Father ..Ventures his filial Vertue, though untri'd, Against whate're may.. Allure, or terrifie, or undermine.

†**6. a.** To ascertain, or inquire, in a secret or underhand manner. *Obs.*

a **1575** tr. *Pol. Verg. Eng. Hist.* (Camden No. 36) 56 Cæsar undermining their counsels throughe his Captives. *Ibid.* 80 When as Agricola hadd.. undermined the purpose of his adversaries. **1596** NASHE *Saffron Walden* 82 He hath been noted.. very suspitiously to vndermine, whither any man knew such a fellow.

†**b.** To question (a person) guilefully. *Obs.*

1581 [A. GILBY] *Test. 12 Patriarchs* 58 b, He wil talke guilefully with thee, and vndermine thee to doe thee a shrewde turne. **1599** HAKLUYT *Voy.* II. I. 266 There was a Dutch Jesuite.. sent vnto them, to vndermine and examine them.

7. To weaken, injure, destroy or ruin, surreptitiously or insidiously.

α. **1569** (*title*), A Bull graunted by The Pope.. to vndermyne.. Allegeance to the Quene. *a* **1596** *Sir T. More* I. ii. 69, I pray ye,.. Goe not aboute to vndermine my life. **1641** J. JACKSON *True Evang. T.* II. 146 It is no fault.. to under-mine fraud with fraud. **1699** BURNET *39 Art.* xviii. 174 Which strikes at the Foundation, and undermines the Truth of all Revealed Religion. **1732** BERKELEY *Alciphr.* i. §2 A dangerous sort of men that would undermine received principles and opinions. **1771** *Junius' Lett.* lix. 272 Who is he, that has made it the study.. of his life, to undermine and alter the whole system of jurisprudence? **1850** MERIVALE *Rom. Emp.* ix. (1865) I. 384 The authority of the nobles as a class had been completely undermined. **1884** RUSKIN *Pleas. Eng.* 16 These controversies vexed and shook, but never undermined, the faith they strove to purify.

β. **1565** STAPLETON tr. *Staphylus' Apol.* 152 To vnderminde Christendom. **1694** R. BURTHOGGE *Reason* 110 The Ground of this underminded, and the nature of the Divine Omnipresence represented. **1726** CAVALLIER *Mem.* Ded. p. iv, Their Civil and Religious Liberties, which after having been artfully underminded by several preceding Princes, were at last totally subverted.

b. To weaken or destroy (the health or constitution) by degrees; to sap.

1812 CRABBE *Tales* II. 417 Augmented pay procured him decent wealth, But years advancing undermined his health. **1843** R. J. GRAVES *Syst. Clin. Med.* xxv. 319 Mercury may be given.. in such a manner as gradually to undermine the constitution. **1860** J. M. CARNOCHAN *Operat. Surg.* 61 The constitution became.. undermined [by ostitis].

Hence **undermined** *ppl. a.*

1844 *P. Parley's Ann.* V. 13 The undermined bank of some river. **1899** *Allbutt's Syst. Med.* VIII. 801 On examination of the undermined skin and granulations.

under'miner. [f. UNDERMINE *v.* So Du. *ondermijner.*]

1. One who undermines; a sapper.

1519 HORMAN *Vulg.* 257 b, Vndermynars ouerthrewe the walle. **1556** WITHALS *Dict.* (1562) 79/1 An vnderminer, *cunicularius.* **1610** HOLLAND *Camden's Brit.* I. 400 A frame or engin.. under which the pioners and underminers had their ingresse and egresse. **1658** OSBORNE *Jas. I,* 34 These underminers.. intended in their calculation the destruction of the house of Lords. **1802** JAMES *Milit. Dict., Underminer,* a sapper.

fig. **1601** SHAKS. *All's Well* I. i. 131 Blesse our poore Virginity from vnderminers and blowers vp. **1654** 'PALAEMON' *Friendship* 28 He that is an underminer of the Foundation must of necessity ruine the Superstructure.

2. A secret or insidious assailant, subverter, destroyer, etc.

1564 PALFREYMAN *Baldwin's Mor. Philos.* (1600) 129 b, The whole broode of.. secret vnderminers, hipocrits, and double dealers. **1571** GOLDING *Calvin on Ps.* xxvi. 4 Neyther will I come in company with undermyners. **1608** D. T[UVILL] *Ess. Pol. & Mor.* 60 b, There are another kinde of cunning vndermyners. **1656** BAXTER *Reformed Pastor* III. ii. §4 Nor suffer underminers or persecutors to scatter them. **1693** SOUTH *Serm.* 96 No one is bound to look upon.. his under-miner.. as his friend. *a* **1734** NORTH *Lives* (1826) I. 386 At court there are always a sort of underminers who [etc.]. **1838** LYTTON *Calderon* i, To.. his foes, his underminers—he assumed a yet greater frankness.

b. Const. *of* (the thing or person assailed).

1598 DALLINGTON *Meth. Trav.* B ij, The Iesuites, vnder-minders and inveiglers of greene wits. **1650** HUBBERT *Pill Formality* 70 In all ages there have been underminers of the power of godliness in a secret way. *a* **1674** CLARENDON *Surv. Leviath.* (1676) 113 The neglect of Justice is an infallible underminer.. of that security. *a* **1715** BURNET *Own Time* (1766) I. 403 A secret enemy to their interest and an underminer of it. **1768–74** TUCKER *Lt. Nat.* (1834) 412 A concealed infidel, a secret underminer of things sacred. **1802** MME. D'ARBLAY *Let.* 14 Mar., Depression, that cruel under-miner of every faculty that makes life worth sustaining. **1879** JOS. COOK *Marriage* 8 Do you stand here, underminers of the family life, and gaze into the eyes of these women!

under'mining, *vbl. sb.* [f. as prec.]

1. The action of digging under, excavating, eroding, etc. Also in fig. contexts.

c **1380** WYCLIF *Serm.* Sel. Wks. I. 277 Þis housebondis hous is his bodi, þat his soule is kept ynne; and undirmynyng of þis hous mai be don on two maneres. *c* **1440** *Promp. Parv.* 511/1 Vnder myndynge (*P.* vndermynynge), *idem quod* vnderdeluynge, *supra.* **1598** BARRET *Theor. Warres* v. i. 124 Fortes are wonne.. by battery,.. by vndermining, and such like. **1629** PRYNNE *Anti-Armin.* 78 By the vndermining of which alone, the whole superstruction.. [is] vtterly subuerted. **1679** C. NESSE *Antichrist* 37 Their worshipping of saints [is].. no better then real underminings of the sacred foundation. **1692** BENTLEY *Boyle Lect.* 271 The banks.. jagged and torn by.. the silent underminings of waves. **1726** CAVALLIER *Mem.* IV. 342 They came by underminding as far as the brink of the Ditch. **1833–4** J. PHILLIPS *Geol.* in *Encycl. Metrop.* (1845) VI. 705/1 The most characteristic effect of a cascade, is that ceaseless undermining of its base and sides. **1897** *Allbutt's Syst. Med.* II. 765 There are ulcers with but slight under-mining of their edges.

†**b.** An excavation or mine. *Obs.*⁻¹

1572 R. H. tr. *Lauaterus' Ghostes* 73 These [spirits] wander vp and down in caues and vnderminings.

2. The action of insidiously plotting, assailing, subverting, etc.; an instance of this.

1433 LYDG. *St. Fremund* 559 By vndirmynyng, this was his menyng; Affter Fremund he to be crownyd kyng. **1530** PALSGR. 285 Undermyndyng, *subornation.* **1571** GOLDING *Calvin on Ps.* iii. 5 He had.. betrayed the giltlesse Preestes by treason and undermyning. **1600** NASHE *Summer's Last Will* F 3 b, Familiaritie and conference, That were the sinewes of societies, Are now for vndermynings onely vsde. **1667** *Decay Chr. Piety* ii. ⁋5 The frauds and underminings, the busie scramblings for little parcels of earth. **1709** [see UNDERGROUND *adv.* 2]. **1841** DICKENS *Barn. Rudge* xxiv, We can't bear the plotting and undermining that takes place. **1904** *Brit. Med. Jrnl.* 17 Sept. 638 An undermining of strength that lessens resisting power.

under'mining, *ppl. a.* [f. as prec.]

1. That excavates or erodes beneath a surface.

1617 MORYSON *Itin.* III. 160 Ireland hath neither singing Nightingall,.. nor vndermining Moule. **1664** INGELO *Bentiv. & Ur.* VI. 219 Those great Hills.. would have been worn away.. and.. their high Tops would have been levell'd by the undermining Streams. **1853** KANE *Grinnell Exp.* viii. (1856) 57 The glacier, thus exposed to a saline water base.. and to an undermining wave action,.. is of course speedily detached. **1882** FLOYER *Unexpl. Baluchistan* 121 It has now probably been carried away piecemeal, for it was then perilously near the undermining river.

b. In fig. contexts.

1661 COWLEY *Cromwell* Wks. 1906 II. 352 No Guards can oppose assaulting Ears, Or undermining Tears. *a* **1665** J. GOODWIN *Filled w. the Spirit* xiv. (1670) 412 The Gospel.. hath cast down.. many a strong hold..; it is of an under-mining nature. **1711** ADDISON *Spect.* No. 124 ⁋7 There are others who are Moles through Envy... I have already caught two or three of these dark undermining Vermin. **1858** J. MARTINEAU *Stud. Chr.* 271 Huge piles of curious learning,.. which.. may detain men from search after the living rock, or notice of the undermining flood.

2. Insidiously subversive or destructive.

1583 MELBANCKE *Philotimus* R iv b, Vndermining easinge droppers.. haue wroughte this estraungment betwene vs. **1616** R. C. *Times' Whistle* (1871) 44 Honours now are purchased by stealth Of vndermining bribes. **1679** *Roxb. Ball.* (1883) IV. 552 The Malice, and the restless Hate, Of Under-mining Foes. **1709** STANHOPE *Paraphr.* IV. 35 Undermining Arts of Disputers and Deceivers. **1849** CLARIDGE *Cold Water Cure* 173 There are many sufferers from this under-mining malady. **1860** GEO. ELIOT *Mill on Floss* v. ii, Instead o' whispering in corners, in that plotting, underminding way.

Hence **under'miningly** *adv.*

c **1590** LADY BACON in J. Spedding *Bacon's Lett.* (1862) III. v. 113 He commonly opened underminingly all letters sent to you from counsel or friends. **1601** DEACON & WALKER *Spirits & Divels* To Rdr. 8 Which these men.. vndermingly haue publisht in print, without any.. authenticall priuiledge. **1832** F. BURNEY *Mem. Dr. Burney* III. 176 The accumulation of the whole had, slowly and underminingly, brought him into the state that has been described.

'under-,minister, *sb.* [UNDER-¹ 6 a.] †An underling, subordinate, assistant.

1543 tr. *Act 2 Edw. III,* c. 7 To enquire of shiriffes,.. constables, and all other ministers.., and of their vnder-mynysters. **1633** T. STAFFORD *Pac. Hib.* II. iv. 155 All Fees .. needfull for any of the sayd Officers, or Vnder-ministers.

†**under-minister,** *v.*: see UNDER-¹ 2.

'under-,ministry. [UNDER-¹ 6 b.] Subordinate service or office.

1651 JER. TAYLOR *Serm. for Year* II. xxi. 272 That we should do all the under-ministeries we can in this great work. **1660** —— *Ductor* III. iv. rule 5 §2 The division of Ecclesiastical charges, the appointment of under-ministeries in the Church.

'undermirth. [UNDER-¹ 9.] A comic underplot.

1635 SHIRLEY *Coronation* Prol., There doth flow No under-mirth, such as doth lard the scene For course delight.

,undermodu'lation. *Radio* and *Cinemat.* [UNDER-¹ 10 b.] Modulation that is less than it need be, so that the available capacity of a transmitter or medium is underused or the signal is too weak. So **under'modulate** *v. trans.*, **-'modulated** *ppl. a.*

1940 *Chambers's Techn. Dict.* 877/1 Undermodulation. **1962** A. NISBETT *Technique Sound Studio* v. 94 Programme meters... Its uses are:.. (ii) to provide indications of levels which would result in under- or over-modulation at the recorder or transmitter. *Ibid.* 100 Reducing the effective service area of the transmitter by undermodulating a whole programme. **1974** *Listener* 2 May 573/3 Why are the transmissions on Radio 3 invariably under-modulated?

under'money, *v.* [UNDER-¹ 4 a.] *trans.* To take by means of bribery.

a **1661** FULLER *Worthies, Suffolk* III. (1662) 65 He took the two Forts,.. but whether they were undermined or under-monied it is not decided.

'under-,moral. (UNDER-¹ 6 b.)

1712 ADDISON *Spect.* No. 369 ⁋15 Besides this great Moral,.. there are an Infinity of Under-Morals which are to be drawn from the several parts of the Poem.

'undermost, *a.* and *adv.* [UNDER *adv.* + -MOST.]

1. a. *adj.* Holding the lowest place or position.

1555 EDEN *Decades W. India* Contents (Arb.) 45 The Antipodes whiche inhabite the vndermost halfe of the baule of the earth. *a* **1586** SIDNEY *Arcadia* III. ii, The fall is greater from the first to the second, then from the second to the vndermost. **1665** BUNYAN *Holy Citie* 171 This Jasper is said to be one of the Foundations, and that too the first and undermost. **1771** *Encycl. Brit.* III. 46 The advantage gained will be always equal to twice the number of pulleys in the moveable or undermost block. **1797** HOLCROFT tr. *Stolberg's Trav.* II. xlvii, The scenes were of three partitions: the undermost of marble,.. and the upper of.. wood. **1838** T. THOMSON *Chem. Org. Bodies* 986 A force sufficient to counter-balance this attraction of the undermost film.

b. *absol.* The bottom.

1822 D. WORDSWORTH *Jrnl.* 22 Sept. (1941) II. 367 A girl, bare-legged, petticoats kilted to her undermost, of white flannel. **1876** MRS. WHITNEY *Sights & Ins.* II. xiii. 429 Living.. with keen, conscious pain at the undermost of everything.

2. Predicative, or as *adv.* In the lowest or lower place or position.

1617 J. TAYLOR (Water P.) *Obs. & Trav. fr. Lond. to Hamburgh* Wks. (1630) 85/2 A good featherbed vndermost, with cleane sheets,.. another featherbed vppermost. **1665** *Phil. Trans.* I. 45 These Crucibles are laid sloaping, eight under-most, and seven above them. **1709** BERKELEY *Th. Vision* §115 It is inverted, because the heels are uppermost and the head undermost. **1781** *Phil. Trans.* LXXI. 391 Upon.. holding it with the snow undermost, the whole of it adhered. **1825** SCOTT *Talism.* iii, The assailant.. flung himself above the struggling Saracen, and.. kept him undermost. **1855** MACAULAY *Hist. Eng.* xiv. III. 396 The party indeed which had then been undermost was now uppermost.

†**undermow,** *v.*: see UNDER-¹ 2.

†**undermye,** *v. Obs.*⁻¹ [UNDER-¹ 4 a.] *trans.* To undermine.

The second element, which rhymes with *sleye* 'sly', may be MYE *v.* in a forced sense.

c **1330** R. BRUNNE *Chron. Wace* (Rolls) 3432 Mynours þey hadde ynowe, & sleye, þe wal to perce & undermye.

undern ('ʌndən), *sb. Obs.* exc. *arch.* and *dial.* Forms: *α.* 1–5, 9 **undern** (2 **unnderrn-**), 3 **vn-**, 4 **ondarne**, 3, 5 **on-**, 4–5 **underne**, 4 **undirne**, 5 **-dyrne**, 4–5 **undorne**, 5 **-dorn**, 4 **undurn**, 4–5 **undurne**, 7 *dial.* **aandorn**, 9 *dial.* **andern**; 4–5 **onderen**, 4–5 (9) **underen** (4–5 **-on**); 2–5 **undren**, 4 **undrin**, **-on**, **-un**, 5 **oundron**, **undrone**, 9 *dial.* **andren**; *Sc.* **ontron**, **auntrin**, **antrum**, **andrum**, etc. *β.* 1–5 **under** (4 **undur**, 4–5 **-yr**), 4–5 **vndre**; 4 **ondre**, **honder-**, 6 **ander-**; *dial.* 7 **oneder**, 7, 9 **aunder**, **ownder**, 9 **ounder**, **oander** (**ōnder**), **andra**, etc.; 8–9 **oandurth**. [Common Teutonic: OE. *undern*, = OFris. *unden*, *ond* (older NFris. *undern*; mod. *unnern-e*, *ünjern*, *onner-n*, *önner*), OS. *undorn*, *undern* (MLG. *undern*, LG. *unden*, *unner*; MDu. *onderen*, *-ern*, *-er*, Du. dial. *onder*),

OHG. *untarn*, *-orn*, *undorn* (MHG. *undarn*, *-ern*, G. dial. *undern*, *untern*, *unnern*, *onnern*, etc.), ON. *undorn*, *undarn* (Norw. dial. *undonn*, *ondaan*, *undaal*, etc., Sw. dial. *undarn*, *-dun*, Da. dial. *unden*, *unnen*), Goth. *undaurn-* (in *undaurnimats* ἄριστον); the relationships of the stem are doubtful. In all the Germanic languages the meaning shows a parallel development to that traceable in English; where the word survives it usually denotes either midday or afternoon or a meal taken at these times.

With some variation of form, *undern* is common in OE. and ME. down to the 15th cent.; in later use it is restricted to dialects of the north-midland and northern counties and the south-west of Scotland. In addition to the forms given above, some northern dialects exhibit (from the 17th c.) variants with a prefixed *d-*, as *downdrens*, *daundren*, *downder*, etc. (*Eng. Dial. Dict.* s.v. *Downdrins*). The OE. *ær undern* also survived in dialect use, and appears as *earnder*, *eender*, etc. (see YEENDER), while OE. *ofer undern* appears in the 15th c. as *orendron*, *ornedrone*, in the 17th as *orndorn*, *arndern*, and later as *ournder*, *orntren*, etc. (*Eng. Dial. Dict.* s.v. *Undern*). Both of these have equivalents in mod.N. Fris. (dialect of Sylt), viz. *irönner*, *irner* forenoon and *aurönner*, *aurner* afternoon.]

†**1.** The third hour of the day; the time at or about 9 o'clock in the morning. In ecclesiastical use = tierce. *Obs.*

α. *a* **900** *O.E. Martyrol.* 3 May 72 On þa þriddan tid dæȝes, þæt is on undern. *c* **1000** *Sax. Leechd.* II. 140 Sele drincan on þreo tida, on undern, on middæȝ, on non. *c* **1200** *Trin. Coll. Hom.* 117 Riht to-genes þe undrene;..þo com a dine of heuene. *c* **1250** *Kent. Serm.* in *O.E. Misc.* 33 Þat ferst uut-yede bi þe Moreghen;..so ha dede at undren and at midday also. **13..** *Sir Beues* (A.) 4168 Þus to gederes þai gonne dinge Fram prime til vnderne gan to ringe. **1338** R. BRUNNE *Chron.* (1810) 18 Bituex vnderon & noen was þe feld alle wonnen. **1382** WYCLIF *Acts* ii. 15 Whanne it is the thridde our of the day, or vndirne. **1470-85** MALORY *Arthur* XI. ii. 574 They lay to gyders vntyl vndorne on the morn. [**1855** ROCK in *N. & Q.* XI. 150/1 The high mass..for Sunday was celebrated immediately after undern or tierce.]

β. *a* **1122** *O.E. Chron.* (Laud MS.) an. 540, Steorran heo ætewdon ful neh healfe tid ofer under. *a* **1225** *Leg. Kath.* 2496, I Nouembres moneð, þe fif & twentuðe dei, & Fridei, onont te under. *a* **1310** in Wright *Lyric P.* xii. 41 In marewe men he sohte, At under mo he brohte. *c* **1315** SHOREHAM II. 72 Crucyfige! crucifige! Gredden hy at ondre. **13..** *E.E. Allit. P.* A. 513 Aboute vnder, þe lorde to marked tos & ydel men stande he fyndez þer-ate. *c* **1450** *Mirk's Festial* 66 A husband-man ȝede..at pryme, and eftsones at vndyr, and efte at myddày,..and hyryd men to his vyneȝorde.

†**b.** ***high undern*** (see HIGH *a.* 11). Also ***half***, ***whole undern*** (see quot. *c* 1440). *Obs.*

c **960** *Rule St. Benedict* xlviii. 74 From ærmorȝenne oð heane undern [L. *ad tertiam plenam*]. *c* **1275** *Passion of our Lord* 657 in *O.E. Misc.* 56 At þon heye vndarne a witsuneday. **1303** R. BRUNNE *Handl. Synne* 4059 Come þou home at hygh vndurne, And no lenger yn þe felde soiurne. **13..** *Floriz & Bl.* 555 Bi þat hit was undern hiȝ, Floris was þe brigge niȝ. **1390** GOWER *Conf.* II. 250 He..lay..Til it was undren hih and more. *c* **1440** *Pallad. on Husb.* VI. 226 Half vndron hath but ix [feet]; High vndron vj. *Ibid.* VII. 254 Half vndern viij, hool vndern v. [= L. *hora tertia* and *hora quarta*].

†**c.** With addition of *dayes* (also *day*) or *of the day*. *Obs.*

c **1122** *O.E. Chron.* (Laud MS.) an. 1122, Þa wearð swiðe mycel wind fram þa undern dæies to þa swarte nihte. *a* **1225** *Ancr. R.* 24 Seoue psalmes..siggeð abuten undern deies. *c* **1290** *Beket* 2445 in *S. Eng. Leg.* I. 176 A-boute onderne of þe daie to þis holi bones heo come. *c* **1386** CHAUCER *Nun's Pr. T.* 402 Stille he lay Til it was passed vndren of the day. *c* **1400** MAUNDEV. (Roxb.) xxxiii. 149 Þai will hyde þam in þe erthe fra vndrun of þe day til efter noone. *c* **1425** *Cast. Persev.* 138 in *Macro Plays* 81 Loke þat ȝe be þere be-tyme, ..for we schul be onward be vnderne of þe day. *a* **1500** *E.E. Misc.* (Warton Cl.) 10 At under day to skole I was i-sete.

†**2.** The sixth hour of the day; midday. *Obs.*

a **1300** *Cursor M.* 16741 Bi þis was vndren [*Laud MS.* vnder] on þe dai, þat mirckend al þe light. **13..** *Gosp. Nicodemus* 657 At vnderon was þis done, omang þam wex it mirk. *c* **1380** WYCLIF *Wks.* (1880) 41 Late lewid freris seie.. for prime, tierce, vndren & noon, for eche of hem seuene pater nostris. **1382** —— *John* iv. 6 Sothli the our was, as the sixte, or vndurn. *c* **1440** *Promp. Parv.* 511/1 Vnderne ..*submeridianum*, *submesimbria*. **1493** *Festivall* 7 An husbounde man went in to his gardeyn or vyne yerde at pryme and ayen at vndren or myddaye. (Cf. *Mirk's Festial* 66.)

3. The afternoon or evening. Now *dial.*

α. **1470-85** MALORY *Arthur* VII. xix. 242 Vpon the morowe he took his hors and rode vn-tyl vnderne,..and bitoke his hors to the dwarf, and commaunded hym to watche al nyghte. **1811** W. AITON *Surv. Ayrs.* Gloss. 693 *Ontron*, evening. **1858** MORRIS *Def. Guenevere*, etc. 206 Summer cometh to an end; Undern cometh after noon.

β. *c* **1480** *Childe of Bristowe* 235 in Hazl. *E.P.P.* I. 119 Betwene mydday and under ther cam a blast of lightnyng and dunder. **1674** RAY *N. Co. Words*, *The Aunder*, or as they pronounce it in Cheshire, Oneder; The afternoon. **1684** MERITON *Yorks. Dial.* 46 To Morn ith' Ownder we mun dod our Sheep. *c* **1746** J. COLLIER (Tim Bobbin) *View Lanc. Dial.* (1775) 16 Th' last oandurth boh one me Measter had lik't o killt meh. **1820** R. WILBRAHAM *Cheshire Gloss.* 49 *Ownder*, or *Aunder*, the afternoon. **1828** CARR *Craven Gloss.* I. 13 *Aunder*, afternoon. Nearly extinct in Craven. **1841** HARTSHORNE *Salop. Ant.* 525 *Ownder*, the evening... A word in general acceptation on the banks of the Severn, betwixt Shrewsbury and Bridgenorth. **1879-81** MISS JACKSON *Shropsh. Word-bk.* 309 In places where this term obtains the day is divided into morning, middle of the day, *ōnder*, and night.

4. *dial.* A light or intermediate meal, esp. one taken in the afternoon. (Cf. ANDERS-MEAT.)

1691 NICOLSON in Ray *N. Co. Words* 139 Aandorn, Merenda. **1866-86** in Lincolnsh. glossaries (in forms *andern*, *andren*, *andra*, *andrew*). **1880** C. H. POOLE *Gloss. Stafford* 17 *Ounder*,..an afternoon tea. **1887** DARLINGTON *S. Chesh. Gloss.* 278 *Oanders*, the afternoon meal, often sent out in harvest time to the labourers in the fields. **1887** *Suppl. Jamieson* s.v. *Andrum* and *Antrum*.

5. *attrib.*, as ***undern-bell***, ***-song*** [OE. *-sang*, *-song*].

See also UNDER-MEAL, UNDERN-TIDE, -TIME.

a **1400** *Sir Beues* 2250 So stod Beues in þat þring, Til noun [*v.r.* vndern] belle be-gan to ring. **1478-9** in Peck *Desiderata Curiosa* (1732) I. VI. 36 That no Person..set ther Corn to sale afore the Hour of Ten of the Bell, or els the Undernone [*sic*] Bell be rongyng. [**1853** ROCK *Ch. of Fathers* III. II. 180 Every Sunday before undern-song or tierce.]

†**un'dern**, *a.* *Obs.* [OE. *undyrne*: see DERN *a.*] Not hidden; open.

a **1225** *Juliana* 75 Ȝe schulen..reopen ripe of þat sed þat ȝe her seowen, þat is underne ȝeld of wa, oðer of wunne.

under'name, *v.* [UNDER *adv.* 2 b.] *trans.* To name or specify below.

1632 W. LITHGOW *Trav.* III. 101 These Cities seuen (I undername) did striue, Who first brought Homer to the world aliue.

under'named, *ppl. a.* [UNDER *adv.* 2 b.] Named or specified below.

1599 HAKLUYT *Voy.* I. 162 The declaration of the rest is proroged vntill a certayne terme vndernamed. **1603** *Philotus* F 4 b, The printer..hes..printit sindrie vther delectabill Discourses vndernamit. **1660** in *Buccleuch MSS.* (Hist. MSS. Comm.) I. 312 The persons undernamed. *c* **1770** *Rolls of Parlt.* II. 433/1 Which of the ancestors of the said William had the Woods undernamed.

under-'natural, *a.* [UNDER-².] Falling below what is natural.

1647 N. WARD *Simple Cobler* 49 Peoples prostrations of these things..are..under-naturall noddaries.

under'neath, *prep.*, *adv.*, *a.*, and *sb.* Forms: 1 **underneoðan**, **-nyðan**, 2 **-næðen**, 4 **-neþen**, 5 **undernethen**, **-nethyn**; 4 **underneþe**, **-nueþe**, **-neyþe**, 4-6 **undernethe**, **-neth**, 6- **underneath**. (Also 4-7 **vnder-**, 5 **vndir-**, **vndur-**, **vndyr-**, 5-6 **undre-**, 6 *Sc.* **wndir-**). [OE. *underneoðan* (f. UNDER *prep.* and *adv.* + NETHEN *adv.*), = older Da. *underneden*.]

A. *prep.* **1.** Beneath or below (in local position).

c **893** K. ÆLFRED *Oros.* III. ix. 134 Ðær wearð Alexander þurhscoten mid anre flan underneoðan oþer breost. *a* **1122** *O.E. Chron.* (Laud MS.) an. 1070, Hi..namen þa þet fot-spure þe wæs undernæðen his fote. *c* **1375** *Cursor M.* 2380 (Fairf.), Abraham..come and lendid..vnder-neyþe a faire valay. *c* **1400** MAUNDEV. (Roxb.) xiii. 57 Vnderneth it es a well. *c* **1450** LOVELICH *Grail* xlvi. 129 Whanne that he say kyng Mordrayn On the Erthe liggen..vnder-nethen here hors feet. **1470-85** MALORY *Arthur* IV. xvi. 362 Vndernethe that castel they sawe a knyghte standynge. *a* **1533** LD. BERNERS *Huon* lix. 203 Vnderneth it was the porte. **1591** SPENSER *Mother Hubberd* 1322 The wicked weed..From vnderneath his head he tooke away. **1678** BUTLER *Hud.* III. i. 1116 He..Insconc'd himself as formidable As could be underneath a Table. **1697** DRYDEN *Virg. Georg.* III. 597 If a swarthy Tongue Is underneath his humid Palate hung, Reject him. **1728** YOUNG *Love Fame* III. 118 Tho' Phoebus and the nine for ever mow, Rank folly underneath the scythe will grow. **1817** SHELLEY *Rev. Islam* V. 2185 Underneath thy feet writhe Faith, and Folly, Custom, and Hell, and mortal Melancholy. **1879** S. C. BARTLETT *Egypt to Pal.* xx. 436 The immense quarries directly underneath the city.

b. *fig.* Under the form, cover, protection, authority, etc., of (something).

1390 GOWER *Conf.* I. 258 Bot undernethe such a jape He hath so for himselve schape, That [etc.]. *a* **1470** HARDING *Chron.* Pref. (1812) p. vii, Vndirnethe ȝoure fadirs magnificence He durste nought so haue lette hys righte fall doun. **1495** *Rolls of Parlt.* VI. 465/1 Dyvers Leesses..hath be made..undrenethe the Seales in these parties of old tyme used. **1560** DAUS tr. *Sleidane's Comm.* 437 Whether Christ is to be worshipped vnder the forme of bread and wine, whether Christ be wholly vnderneath either kinde. **1845** MAURICE *Mor. Philos.* in *Encycl. Metrop.* II. 627/1 The truths which lay underneath its false worship.

2. In subordination or subjection to; under the power or control of.

1375 BARBOUR *Bruce* v. 475 Schir amery..That wes vardane of þe land Vnder-neth þe Ynglis kyng. *c* **1440** *Alph. Tales* 88 A virtuos man..had vndernethe his gouernance in a monasterie ccc wommen. *Ibid.* 514 He had many servandis vnder-nethe hym. **1538** BALE *God's Promises* II, Beynge thy subject, he is undreneth thy cure, Correct hym thu mayest. **1546** *Yorks. Chantry Surv.* (Surtees) 348 The chantor.. hath a vicare indowyd underneth hym. **1597** SHAKS. *2 Hen. IV*, IV. iv. 10 Till these Rebels..Come vnderneath the yoake of Gouernment. **1651** N. BACON *Disc. Govt. Eng.* II. xxvii. 205 A man underneath many Passions, but above fear. **1667** DRYDEN & DAVENANT *Tempest* III. iii, When underneath my power my foes have truckl'd. **1822** SHELLEY tr. *Calderon's Mag. Prodig.* II. 34 Philosophy, thou canst not even Compel their causes underneath thy yoke.

b. Below the level of; inferior to.

1587 GOLDING *De Mornay* Pref. 6 The least creatures which lie farre vnderneath man.

†**3.** Subject to, under (a condition). *Obs.*

c **1440** *Alph. Tales* 333, I will grawnt þe a plyte of my gown vnder-nethe a condicion, at þou sall not hurte me.

†**4.** Below, less than (in amount.) *Obs.*

1455 *Paston Lett.* I. 355 Ther can noon be gete here.. undernethe the iijs. the yerde at the lowest price. **1528** in W. H. Turner *Select. Rec. Oxford* (1880) 57 Above the somme of vjˢ, and..under nethe the seyd somme.

B. *adv.* **1.** Down below; at an underlying or lower point or level.

c **1000** ÆLFRIC *Exod.* xxix. 12 And þu nymst cealfes blod mid þinum fingre,..and ȝitst þæt oðer undernyðan. *a* **1325** *MS. Rawl. B.* 520 fol. 32 b, So þat þis statut ne portenez noȝt to..grete troen [= trees], ware fore [*sic*] hit be cler vnder nueþe. *c* **1375** *Sc. Leg. Saints* I. (*Peter*) 526 Þe hound..schot on symeon..And to þe ȝerde hym vndirnethe Ruschit. **1387** TREVISA *Higden* (Rolls) V. 123 Constantine..made peynte the signe and tokene of þe crosse.., and he made write undirneþe, 'þis is þe signe and tokene' [etc.] *c* **1400** *Destr. Troy* 9998 Till the sun in his sercle set vndernethe. **1489** CAXTON *Faytes of A.* I. xvii. 27 Wher the watre is lest and most low,..there in trauers ought to be sett a route of folke wel horsed and another in like wyse vndrenethe. **1526** *Pilgr. Perf.* (W. de W. 1531) 268 Lyke as they yᵗ wrestleth be somtyme aboue, & somtyme vnderneath. **1560** DAUS tr. *Sleidane's Comm.* 24 b, The floore vnderneth was covered with clothe of Arras. **1615** G. SANDYS *Trav.* 259 The streetes are..vaulted vnderneath for the conueiance of the sulledge. **1657** R. LIGON *Barbadoes* 43 Leaving it hollow underneath for Ventiducts. **1747** WESLEY *Prim. Physick* (1762) 118 If they heal too soon, and a Matter gather underneath. **1791** COWPER *Odyss.* XIX. 552 So thick it was, and underneath, the ground With litter of dry foliage strew'd profuse. **1850** TENNYSON *In Mem.* c, I climb the hill: from end to end Of all the landscape underneath [etc.]. **1860** TYNDALL *Glac.* II. i. 232 The lines of light converged by the ripples upon the sand underneath.

fig. *c* **1374** CHAUCER *Boeth.* III. pr. v. (1868) 75 Ryȝt on þat same side nounpower entriþ vndirneþ þat makeþ hem wreches. **1390** GOWER *Conf.* II. 232 Bot undernethe he was bethoght In what manere he mihte aspie Achilles fro Deïdamie. **1509** HAWES *Past. Pleas.* XI. (Percy Soc.) 40 In an example..the poetes do wryte; And underneth the trouth doth so shroude. **1659** MILTON *Lett. Ruptures Commonw.* Wks. 1851 V. 404 If such a Union as this be not accepted on the Army's part, be confident there is a single Person underneath. **1674** CAMPION *Art Descant* I. 4 A fourth above is the same that a fifth is underneath, and a fourth underneath is as a fifth above.

b. Below or beneath other clothing.

c **1386** CHAUCER *Can. Yeom. Prol.* 5 A man that clothed was in clothes blake And vnder-nethe he wered a white surplys. *c* **1394** *P. Pl. Crede* 695 Ȝif he haue vnder-neþen whijt, þanne he aboue wereþ Blak. **1596** SPENSER *F.Q.* V. ix. 10 On his backe [was] an vncouth vestiment,..And vnderneath his breech was all to torne. **1856** tr. *Vehse's Mem. Court of Austria* I. 124 He wore a suit of black armour, ..and underneath a shirt of close mail.

c. Lower down on a sheet of paper, etc.

1389 in *Eng. Gilds* (1870) 3 Eche of hem had sworen on þe bok to perfourme þe pointz vndernethe wryten. *c* **1550** in Feuillerat *Revels Q. Mary* (1914) 250 Certayne sutes of apparell as be heare vndernethe mentyoned. *a* **1577** SIR T. SMITH *Commw.* II. xxv. (1589) 102 He..deliuereth vp the examination which he tooke of him, and vnderneath the names of those whom he hath bound to giue euidence. **1653** W. RAMESEY *Astrol. Restored* 106 On the head of the fourth column you find *magnitude*, intimating that by the Figures underneath..is shewn the magnitude of each star. **1743** W. EMERSON *Fluxions* 33 Then I take the Sum of the Terms.. and set this Sum..underneath.

2. On the under side.

1776 WITHERING *Bot. Arr. Vegetables* I. 697 Leaves.. with little scales and fringed appendages underneath. **1812** *New Bot. Garden* I. 7 The leaves..not shining or hoary underneath. **1820** SHELLEY *Prometh. Unb.* I. 442 They come Blackening the birth of day with countless wings, And hollow underneath, like death.

C. *adj.* **1.** Underhand; secret. *rare.*

1747 *Mem. Nutrebian Crt.* II. 118 This..causes him to determine, by a sly, underneath cunning, to work that virtuous youth ruin. **1899** in *Eng. Dial. Dict.* (Leeds dial.).

2. Situated below.

1894 *Daily News* 9 Mar. 5/4 In an underneath room, printers..will be seen printing some..newspapers.

D. *sb.* That which is in the lowest place; the under part or side.

1676 MOXON *Print Lett.* 33 You must make up the Top and Underneath with straight lines. **1855** tr. *Labarte's Arts Mid. Ages* viii. 310 The underneath of his dishes. **1887** RUSKIN *Præterita* II. 159 For all other rivers there is a surface, and an underneath. **1889** MRS. LYNN LINTON *Thro' Long Night* II. 215 She read the underneath of the cards.

'underness. [f. UNDER *adv.*] The state or condition of being below a given mark or limit.

1864 RUSKIN in *Daily Tel.* 31 Oct., An under-supply of wages and an over-supply of labourers... On what do this underness and overness of supply depend?

'under-,niceness. (UNDER-¹ 10 b.)

1748 RICHARDSON *Clarissa* VI. xxx. 107 Over-niceness may be under-niceness. Have you not such a proverb?

†**under'nim**, *v.* *Obs.* Forms: (see UNDER-¹ 8 a and NIM *v.*). [OE. *underniman* (f. *under-* UNDER-¹ 8 + *niman* NIM *v.*), = OS. *undarniman* (to interrupt), MDu. and Du. *ondernemen*, OHG. *untarneman* (MHG., MLG. *undernemen*, G. *unternehmen*).]

1. *trans.* To take into the mind (or sense):

a. To understand, comprehend, perceive; to feel. Also const. *that*.

c **1000** *Ags. Gosp.* Matt. xix. 12 Ne underfoð ealle menn þis word... Undername, se þe undernyman mæȝe. *a* **1023** WULFSTAN *Hom.* lviii. (1883) 305 Man mæȝ swiðe eaðe witan, se ðe hit underniman wile, þæt hit eallunga riht nis [etc.]. *c* **1200** *Trin. Coll. Hom.* 11 Ac ich wile seȝen, undernimeð hit, hwat makeð swilch letten. *c* **1230** *Hali Meid.* 19 Ne underneomeð nawt, quoð he, þis ilke word alle. *c* **1250** *Gen. & Ex.* 1553 Quan ysaac it under-nam ðat esau to late cam. **13..** *E.E. Allit. P.* C. 213 He ossed hym by vnnynges þat þay vnder-nomen, þat he was flawen fro þe face of frelych dryȝtyn. *c* **1386** CHAUCER *Sec. Nun's T.* 243 Whan that he the sauour vndernoom, Which that the Roses and the lilies caste. *c* **1400** *St. Alexius* (Laud 463) 199 Sone he it vnder-nom, þat he to a borugh com, þat mychel was.

b. To receive by instruction; to learn.

c **1000** ÆLFRIC *Saints' Lives* xxix. 76 He..folȝode paule.. and deoplice under-nam drihtnes lare æt him. *c* **1200** *Trin. Coll. Hom.* 83 For þat þe hie undernomen þe wise lore of ionan þe prophete. *a* **1225** *Leg. Kath.* 117 Hire feder hefde iset hire earliche to lare, & heo..undernom hit se wel þet nan nes hire euening.

2. To take upon oneself; to undertake.

c **1000** ÆLFRIC *Hom.* I. 590 Ȝif þu leornian wille hu þæt ȝewurðan mæȝe, þonne undernim ðu leorning-cnihtes hiw. *c* **1175** *Lamb. Hom.* 55 Bute weo hes [= them] halden we doð sunne, and uwilc mon hes undernim to halden wel. *c* **1205** LAY. 26734 We..þis feht habbeoð under-numen buten Arðures rede. *a* **1225** *Ancr. R.* 202 Pusillanimitas, þet is, to poure iheorted..eni heih þing to undernimen. **1340** *Ayenb.* 83 Non ne is aryȝt preus..þet ne ys hardy and zyker to greate þinge ondernime. *c* **1425** *Seven Sages* (P.) 2858, I am comen For were that thou havest undirnome, For to helpe the.

b. *absol.* To undertake a journey; to travel.

c **1205** LAY. 8067 Al þat freoliche folc..þene daie heo vnder-nomen, & to Lundene heo comen. *c* **1325** *Orfeo* 441 With ryght gode wille they can out gon... So long they have undernome, That to Crassens they were ycome.

3. To reprove, rebuke.

Occas. miswritten or misprinted *undermyn(e, -mine.*

c **1250** *Gen. & Ex.* 2727 Ðis on wulde don ðe toðer wrong; And moyses nam ðer-of kep,..And vndernam him ðat it aȝte awold. *a* **1325** *Prose Psalter* xxxiv. 19 Hij vndernimmeden me wyþ vnder-nyminge, & gnaisted vp me wyþ her teþe. *c* **1380** WYCLIF *Wks.* (1880) 292 Ech man schulde bi þe lawe of þe gospel vndirnyme ech broþer þat synneþ aȝens him. *c* **1425** *Orolog. Sapient.* vi. in *Anglia* X. 373/21 Wheþer þy seruaunte..dorste be so bolde forto reprehende & vndirnime..his lorde. *c* **1449** PECOCK *Repr.* I. xvii. 97 He comith not to liȝt, that hise werkis ben not vndernome.

absol. *a* **1400** *New Test.* (Paues) 2 Tim. iv. 2 Vndernyme þou, & byseche, & blame þou in eferich pacyence & in techynge. *c* **1449** PECOCK *Repr.* Prol. 2 Wherbi he canne schewe and proue it to be a defaute for which he vndirnymeth and blameth.

b. Const. *of* (a fault, etc.).

c **1320** *Cast. Love* 1420 He among hem com, And of misbileue he hem vndernom. **1377** LANGL. *P. Pl.* B. v. 115 Who-so vndernymeth me here-of I hate hym dedly after. **14..** HOCCLEVE *Min. Poems* 126/455 What art thow now presumptuous become, And list nat of thy mis been vndirnome? *a* **1450** *Knt. de la Tour* (1868) 87 As the wiff of Amon, that undernam not her husbonde of his foly. *a* **1470** H. PARKER *Dives & Pauper* (W. de W. 1496) IV. vii. 169/1 Byfore all the monkes he undername the cellerer of his pryde.

c. *refl.* To convict (oneself).

1502 ARNOLDE *Chron.* (1811) 208 If otherwise he can not the lawe of the Lorde he reproueth and vndernymeth himself to be noo priest of his Lorde.

4. To take or catch, esp. secretly or unawares; to surprise.

c **1175** *Lamb. Hom.* 151 Monie kunnes men foleȝeden ure drihten,..summe to kunnen if heo mihten him mid sunne undernime. *a* **1225** *Leg. Kath.* 122 Modie meistres & feole fondeden hire ofte..for to underneomen hire. *c* **1250** *Gen. & Ex.* 2135 Ic rede ðe..To..gaderen coren, ðat ðin folc ne wurð vnder-numen, Quan ðo hungri ȝere ben forð-cumen. **13..** *Guy Warw.* (A.) 613 And he of mi loue vnder-nome were..Me þenke y no myȝt it him nouȝt werne. **1340** *Ayenb.* 173 Þe dyeaþ ssel come þet ofte ondernimþ þane zeneȝere huer he ne nimþ none hede.

b. To take away by stealth. (Also OE.)

1483 CAXTON *Gold. Leg.* 45 He supplanted me of my patrymonye and now..he hath undernome from me my blessyng.

5. To receive into one's hands or charge.

13.. *St. Gregory* 174 in Herrig's *Archiv* LVII. 61 Þe kniȝt þat leuedi vnder nom And ladde hire forþ wiþ moche honour. *c* **1325** *Orfeo* 306 To his owne lady wel ny he come, And hur wel ny had undernome;..His owe lady, dam Erodysse.

†**under'nimmer.** *Obs.* [f. prec.]

1. A taker-up or supporter.

a **1400** in *Eng. Gilds* (1870) 350 Non of þe for-seyde fowre and twenty ne shal..be tellere ne vndurnemere of wordes in harmynge of þe fraunchyse of þe town.

2. One who reproves or rebukes.

1382 WYCLIF *Prov.* xiii. 18 Who forsothe assenteth to the vndernymere, shal ben glorified. *c* **1449** PECOCK *Repr.* IV. vi. 452 These vndirnymers and blamers beren an hond to the clergie, that [etc.]. *Ibid.* v. xv. 565 Alle the seid ouer myche vndirnemers and blamers.

†**under'nimming,** *vbl. sb.* [f. as prec.] The action of reproving or rebuking; a reproof, rebuke.

a **1325** *Prose Psalter* xliii. 16 Þou settest vs..vndernimyng and scorne to hem þat ben in our cumpas. **1382** WYCLIF *Ps.* xxxvii. 15, I am maad as a man not herende; and not havende in his mouth aȝen vndernemyngus. *c* **1449** PECOCK *Repr.* II. xvii. 253 Se ȝe that in ȝoure vndirnymyng ȝe bere ȝou discreetli.

†**undernone:** see UNDERN *sb.* 5.

'undernote. [UNDER-[1] 9 b.] A subdued note; an undertone or suggestion.

1820 SHELLEY *Prometh. Unb.* IV. 189 Listen too, How every pause is filled with under-notes. **1857** W. COLLINS *Dead Secret* III. iii, There was an under-note of pleasure running through its tones. **1873** SYMONDS *Grk. Poets* viii. 257 The deep under-note of good sense and wisdom which gives eternal value to the jests of Aristophanes.

under-'noted, *pa. pple.* (UNDER *adv.* 2 b.)

1891 *Cent. Dict.* **1902** *Trans. Glasgow Archæol. Soc.* IV. II. 303 Collation of certain identities of line and alliteration between the poems as undernoted.

under-'nourished, *a.* [UNDER-[1] 10 a.] Having had insufficient nourishment, esp. over a sustained period; in a state of semi-starvation. Also *fig.*

1910 GALSWORTHY *Justice* IV. 98 He's under-nourished. It's very trying to go without your dinner. **1928** *Manch. Guardian Weekly* 10 Aug. 110/1 Most of the Indian children are badly under-nourished. *a* **1942** B. MALINOWSKI *Sci. Theory of Culture* (1944) viii. 80 When African labour is drafted into European enterprise, whether mines, plantations, or factories, it is usually found that the workers are undernourished with reference to the efforts which they will have to put into their performances. **1962** E. SNOW *Other Side of River* (1963) xxxix. 289, I asked one how he explained his fine white teeth if he had been undernourished. **1972** *Computer Jrnl.* XV. 200/1 The element of black magic in it satisfies one of our most under-nourished psychological needs.

Also ˌ**under-'nourishment.**

1920 H. G. WELLS *Outl. Hist.* 575/2 Scores of millions were suffering and enfeebled by undernourishment and misery. **1944** M. LASKI *Love on Supertax* v. 62 Never before had he been brought into direct contact with undernourishment. **1971** *Sci. Amer.* Oct. 20/1 A child who has suffered undernourishment very early and for an appreciable length of time will never reach normal size for his age.

†**undern-tide.** *Obs.* Also undertide. [OE. *underntid*: see UNDERN *sb.* and TIDE *sb.*]

1. = UNDERN *sb.* 1.

α. *c* **900** tr. *Bæda's Hist.* IV. xxii. (1890) 328 Oftost his bendas..onlesde wæron from underntide, þonne mon mæssan oftost singeð. *c* **1000** *Ags. Gosp.* Matt. xx. 3 Þa he ut-eode embe undern-tide. *a* **1300** *Cursor M.* 985 Adam..was wroght at vndern tide, At middai eue draun of his side. *c* **1350** *Lybeaus Disc.* 810 Than seyde Gyfroun,..To all thys y graunte well, Thys day at underne-tyde.

β. *a* **1075** *Rule of Chrodegang* xviii, To þære undertide se halȝa gast com ofer þa apostolas. *c* **1160** *Hatton Gosp.* Matt. xx. 3 Þa he ut-eode ymbe under-tide [etc.]. *c* **1175** *Lamb. Hom.* 91 Hit is undertid, hu mihte we on þissere tide beon fordrencte? *a* **1225** *Ancr. R.* 400 Þe soðe sunne iðe undertid was forði istien on heih. *a* **1300** *Cursor M.* 21931 It sal him last ful littel quil. For if it be at vnder tide, It sal noght to þe none abide. **13..** *Sir Beues* (A.) 1756 Þus þai leide on in boþe side Be-twene midmorwe & vndertide. *c* **1325** *Orfeo* 74 The maydenes..lete hur slepe tyl after none, That the undertyde was agone. *a* **1513** FABYAN *Chron.* VII. ccxxvii. 256 At Notyngham from the morne to the vndertyde, the ryuer of Trent was so fordryd..yt men went ouer drye. [Cf. Trevisa *Higden* (Rolls) VII. 446–7.]

2. = UNDERN *sb.* 2.

a **1300** *Cursor M.* 19830 Þan was it vnderntide [*Trin. MS.* vndirtide] o þe dai,..þat petre went him for to prai. **1387** TREVISA *Higden* (Rolls) VII. 23 In an underentyde [*v.rr.* under-, hondertyde; L. *hora meridiana*], while kyng Edgar lay on his bed. **1398** —— *Barth. De P.R.* VIII. xxviii. (Tollem. MS.), The sonne is red in þe dawnynge, þen he schineþ in þe morow tide, and he is hoot in þe undornetide [L. *in meriaie*] and pale at even.

undern-time. *Obs.* exc. *dial.* and *arch.* Also 4–6 vnder-, 5 vndyrtime. [OE. *underntíma*: see UNDERN *sb.* and TIME *sb.*] = prec.

α. *c* **1000** in Bouterwek *Cædmon* (1854) p. ccxiv, On undern-timan Crist wæs þurh þara Iudea dom to deaþe fordemed. *c* **1200** ORMIN 19458 An daȝȝ att unnderrn time I fir þeȝȝ sæȝhenn Godess Gast. *c* **1250** *Gen. & Ex.* 2269 It was vndren time or more, Om cam ðat riche louerd ðore. *a* **1300** *Cursor M.* 25538 Suet iesu, at vndrin time [*c* **1375** vnder-time]..Sufferd..Dintes sare and smert. **1387** TREVISA *Higden* (Rolls) VII. 421 In þat book he radde priveliche in þe underne tymes [L. *meridianis horis*].

1853 ROCK *Ch. of Fathers* III. x. 473 St. Beda died a little after undern-time or tierce-song hour. **1887** *Suppl. Jamieson* s.v. *Andrum*, The afternoon or early evening repast;..called also..*anterin-time*.

β. *c* **1375** [see *a* 1300 above]. *a* **1450** *Le Morte Arth.* 2807 Hys strength shulld wex in suche a space, From the vndyrtyme tylle none. **1495** *Trevisa's Barth. De P.R.* XVIII. xxiv. 783 Whan gete ben meuyd after the vnder tyme they drynke the more water. **1590** SPENSER *F.Q.* III. vii. 13 He comming home at vndertime, there found The fairest creature, that he euer saw.

ˌ**under-occu'pation.** [UNDER-[1] 10 b.] The occupation of a dwelling or dwellings by fewer people than had been planned; *spec.* applied to local authority accommodation that is considered to be under-used.

1961 *Guardian* 6 Nov. 2/4 There is a good deal of under-occupation. **1966** [see *one-person* s.v. ONE B. IX. 34 a]. **1977** *Jrnl. R. Soc. Arts* CXXV. 116/2 Parallel with the so-called scandal of empty homes, we also hear of the scandal of under-occupation. It is all wrong, the critics say, for an elderly council tenant to occupy a three bed-room house, when she could be living in a one-room new council flat.

Also **under-'occupy** *v. trans.*, **under-'occupied** *ppl. a.*

1961 *Guardian* 28 Nov. 8/2 From the point of view of a local authority housing official a house with spare bed-rooms is 'under-occupied'. **1966** J. TUNSTALL *Old & Alone* xiv. 281, 52.3 per cent of old people under-occupying housing were owner-occupiers, against 38.5 per cent who paid rent. **1970** *Times* 23 Mar. 5/1 To find room in this way for the elderly and others needing small homes would release seriously underoccupied large houses for bigger families. *a* **1974** R. CROSSMAN *Diaries* (1975) I. 75 The interesting thing at Leicester..was the admirable way they are trying to deal with the problem of the people who grow elderly on their huge housing estates and then under-occupy their three-room council houses.

'under-ˌofficer. [UNDER-[1] 6 a. Cf. Du. *onderofficier*, G. *unterofficier*, *-offizier*, Da., Norw., and Sw. *underofficer*.] A sub-officer.

c **1400** *Pilgr. Sowle* (Caxton, 1483) III. iv. 53 Confedered and entendyd with other suche brybours, whiche that were your vnder offycers. ? *c* **1425** *Lucidarie* (1909) 29 Hedes & vndirofficeres of hooly chirche. **1555** EDEN *Decades* (Arb.) 112 He spake to al the vnder officers sharplye. **1598** BARRET *Theor. Warres* II. i. 22 Vnto whom the souldiers and vnder-officers are to obey. **1626** JACKSON *Creed* VIII. xxix. §5 Whether Pilate himselfe did write this title, or caused it to be written by some under-officer of the court. **1658–9** LD. FALKLAND in *Burton's Diary* (1828) IV. 154 Major-general Overton might have been committed by the general as an under-officer. **1708** *Lond. Gaz.* No. 4472/1 Bezeredi, with several of his Under-Officers,..divulged it to the common Soldiers. **1796** *Instr. & Reg. Cavalry* (1813) 121 Two under officers are sent from the rear division. **1876** BANCROFT *Hist. U.S.* V. xiii. 470 All officers and under-officers were obliged to appear at his head-quarters.

Hence **'under-ˌofficered** *a.*[1], furnished with under-officers.

1844 THACKERAY *B. Lyndon* vi, The Prussian army..was officered and under-officered by native Prussians.

ˌ**under-'officered,** *a.*[2] [UNDER-[1] 10 a.] Insufficiently furnished with officers.

1856 *Tracts on Increase of Episcopate in Eng. & Wales* I. 3 In respect to her Bishops, the Church of England is, so to speak, under-officered. **1887** in *Gladden's Parish Probl.* 368 Most schools are under-officered. **1897** *Daily News* 19 May 5/6 The Greek regiments are much under-officered.

un'derogating, *pres. pple.* [UN-[1] 10.] Without losing dignity.

1808 SCOTT *Marm.* VI. Introd. 44 The heir..That night might village partner choose; The Lord, underogating, share The vulgar game of 'post and pair'.

unde'rogatory, *a.* (UN-[1] 7.)

1648 BOYLE *Seraph. Love* (1659) 132 The Apostle,..to create in us Apprehensions, underogatory from what we shall possesse,..removes our thoughts from all we Do Enjoy.

'under-oˌpinion. [UNDER-[1] 10 b.] Too low an estimate of a person.

1629 EARLE *Microcosm.* (Arb.) 79 Nothing threatens him so much as great expectation, which he thinks more prejudiciall, then your vnder-opinion.

'under-orb. (UNDER-[1] 6 b.)

1591 SYLVESTER *Du Bartas* I. iv. 350 Th' under-Orbs.. Each by himselfe an oblique course doth slide.

†**under'orn,** *v.* *Obs.*[−1] [UNDER-[1] 2.] *trans.* To suborn.

a **1325** *MS. Rawl. B.* 520 fol. 31 Þe schirreue..þoru his frendes..procurez þe contreie ant underornez.

†**under-over man.** *Coal-mining.* *Obs.* = VIEWER 1 b.

1708 [see VIEWER 1 b].

ˌ**under'paid,** *ppl. a.* (UNDER-[1] 10 a.)

1817 LD. COLCHESTER *Diary* 17 Feb. (1861) II. l. 604 This was objectionable, as giving currency to the vulgar opinion that public men..were overpaid, whereas, they were notoriously underpaid. **1846** *Mechanic's Mag.* 4 July 7 Services..so notoriously underpaid by the government. **1866** W. COLLINS *Armadale* I. ii, The shopman gave warning on the ground that he was underfed as well as underpaid.

'underpainting. *Art.* [UNDER-[1] 5 d.] (The application of) a layer of paint subsequently overlaid by another painted surface; a painting underlying a finished work. Cf. OVERPAINTING *vbl. sb.*

1866 SARTORIS *Week in French Country Ho.* (1902) 33 Working like a galley-slave in order to get the underpainting of my picture done before coming over. **1905** *Spectator* 25 Feb. 287/2 In much of his painting..Whistler seems to have begun with a cool grey underpainting. **1937** *Discovery* July 212/1 Constable himself did not disdain the use of a warm monochromatic under-painting. **1951** E. PAUL *Springtime in Paris* iii. 63 There must have been an under-painting of that tone, because it showed also around the edges of the canvas. **1979** LD. CLARK in *Hist. Today* Nov. 725/1, I had it X-rayed, and there appeared an under-painting that was unquestionably the work of Filippino.

Also **'underpaint,** a layer of paint applied before another coat or finish.

1934 *Burlington Mag.* Jan. 19/2 There are indications of a dark grey underpaint. **1976** D. FRANCIS *In Frame* ii. 38 A gloss on the lips..which one couldn't do until the under paint was dry.

'underpan. [UNDER-[1] 5 b.] The protective metal covering fitted beneath the engine, clutch, and transmission of a motor vehicle.

1913 A. C. CLOUGH *Dict. Automobile Terms* 275 *Sod pan*, a protective covering, fitted under the engine..and other parts of an automobile... Syn.: Pan, underpan. **1934** WEBSTER *Under pan*, in automotive vehicles, a protective metal covering fitting under the engine, clutch, and transmission case. **1968** *Jane's Freight Containers 1968–69* 530/1 Hi-tensile pressed steel bottom rail with cross-members pressed into all welded leak proof underpan of great strength. **1977** *Drive* Mar.–Apr. 57/3 Opel's anti-rust measures include..a wax spray in box sections and over the underpan.

'underpants, *sb. pl.* [UNDER-[1] 5 a.] An undergarment covering the lower part of the body (and part of the legs); short knickers, briefs. Cf. PANTS *sb. pl.* 1 b.

1931 R. CAMPBELL *Georgiad* I. 15 The living image of a country lover, In woolly underpants, a sort of Faun. **1955** J. MORRISON in B. James *Austral. Short Stories* (1963) 144 Without having removed shirt or underpants, he shuffled down between the blankets. **1961** M. BEADLE *These Ruins* *are Inhabited* iii. 37 The Salesman spread out an impressive ..array of undershirts, underpants, knee-high wool socks.. and red Rugby shirts. **1979** R. JAFFE *Class Reunion* I. xi. 105 Chris yanked off her..slip and bra and underpants.

'underpart, *sb.* [UNDER-¹ 5 b, 6 b. Also UNDER *a.* 1 b.]

1. A lower part or portion.

1662 WASE *Lat. Dict.*, *Subtundo*, to knock, or beat the under-part of any thing. **1731** P. MILLER *Gard. Dict.* s.v. *Leaves*, Their Leaves..have shot out young Plants from their under-Parts. **1797** *Encycl. Brit.* (ed. 3) XVII. 394/2 From the upper part of the lower deck to the under part of the main rail. **1825** JAMIESON, *Fair-grass*,..said to be [so] denominated from the whiteness of the under part of the leaf.

b. *spec.* A part of the under-side of the body (of a bird or animal).

1783 LATHAM *Gen. Synop. Birds* II. 362 The under parts wholly white. **1815** STEPHENS in *Shaw's Gen. Zool.* IX. I. 21 The rest of the under parts dirty yellow. **1873** J. E. TAYLOR *Half-hours in Green Lanes* iv. 126 You could see their..black breasts and white underparts.

2. A subordinate part in action, esp. a minor rôle in a play; one who acts a subordinate part.

1679 DRYDEN *Troilus & Cress.* Pref. ¶20 Making Œdipus the best and bravest person, and even Jocasta but an under-part to him. **1693** —— *Juvenal* (1697) p. lxxix, In the famous Pastoral of Guarini,..where Corisca and the Satyre are the Under-parts. **1711** ADDISON *Spect.* No. 7 ¶ 1 My Friend, I found, acted but an under Part at his Table. **1746** FRANCIS tr. *Hor.*, *Sat.* I. ix. 98 You should have a Man of Art; One who might act an under-part. **1780** J. BERINGTON *State Eng. Catholics* 66 Plot was set up against plot, all of them under-parts of the same grand drama. **1822–7** GOOD *Study Med.* (1829) V. 490 The kidneys play merely an under-part, and are only secondarily affected.

3. A subordinate part or portion; a subdivision.

1711 SHAFTESB. *Charac.* III. 113 Our religious Pastors.. have quitted their substantial Service, and uniform Division into Parts and Under-Parts. **1715** POPE *Iliad* Pref. ¶9 Nor is this..only in the principal Quality which constitutes the Main of each Character, but even in the Under-parts of it.

†under-'part, *v.* *Obs.*⁻¹ [UNDER-¹ 8 c.] *trans.* To subdivide.

1626 B. JONSON *Staple of N.* I. v, The foure Emissaries.. haue full parts: and then one part Is vnder-parted to a couple of Clarkes; And there's the iust diuision of the profits.

under-'parted, *a.* *rare.* [UNDER-¹ 10 a: cf. UNDERPART *sb.* 2.] Of an actor: cast in an insufficient role. Cf. UNDERCAST *v.* 4.

1890 G. B. SHAW in *Star* 2 May 2/3 Mr Coffin, being a handsome young man, and considerably under-parted to boot, had an easy time of it. **1898** —— *Our Theatres in Nineties* (1932) III. 290 Miss May Harvey..is almost dangerously underparted. **1984** *Daily Tel.* 14 Aug. 7/8 Only the underparted Andrew Cruickshank as the Abbot, with his hissed cry of 'heresy!' in a superb scene of denunciation, strikes the right balance between malevolence and outrageousness.

'underpass. orig. *U.S.* [UNDER-¹ 5 b.] A (section of) road providing passage beneath another road or a railway; a subway. Cf. OVERPASS *sb.*

1904 *Springfield* (Mass.) *Weekly Republ.* 16 Sept. 8 The need of an underpass at the union railroad station in this city. **1929** [see OVERPASS *sb.*]. **1943** *Sun* (Baltimore) 29 Oct. 4/3 The Ponca-Lombard street bypass, is designed to bypass the Eastern underpass. **1959** *Manch. Guardian* 26 June 8/7 A four-lane underpass..would run under Euston Road. **1973** [see RINGWAY].

'under-,passion. (UNDER-¹ 9 and 6 b.)

1711 STEELE *Spect.* No. 208 ¶1 The Under-Passion (as I may so call it) of a noble Spirit, Pity. **1818** KEATS *Endym.* III. 179 Thy starry sway Has been an under-passion to this hour.

'under-pay, *sb.* (UNDER-¹ 10 b.)

1851 MAYHEW *Lond. Labour* II. 304/1 Over-work makes under-pay and under-pay makes over-work.

,under-'pay, *v.* (UNDER-¹ 10 a.)

1861 LD. BROUGHAM *Brit. Const.* xix. 316 There can be no worse economy..in any State than underpaying such functionaries as judges. **1899** *Daily News* 1 Feb. 5/1 The Post Office is having much trouble with people who under-pay their letters.

Also **under'payment**.

1848 MILL *Pol. Econ.* II. III. xiii. 87 There was an under-payment to one set of persons, and an overpayment to another. **1920** [see UNDERCHARGE *sb.*]. **1972** *Accountant* 26 Oct. 507/3 He received eight changes of code number within ..five months. He also received a notice alleging £42.67 underpayment of tax.

under'peep, *v.* [UNDER-¹ 4 b, c.] **a.** *trans.* To peep under. **b.** *intr.* To peep from under.

1611 SHAKS. *Cymb.* II. ii. 20 The Flame o' th' Taper Bowes toward her, and would vnder-peepe her lids, To see th' inclosed Lights. **1827** HOOD *Hero & Leander* lxi, Yet you might gaze twice Ere Death it seem'd, and not his cousin, Sleep, That through those creviced lids did underpeep.

under-'peer, *v.* [UNDER-¹ 4 b.] *trans.* and *intr.* To peer under.

1589 PUTTENHAM *Eng. Poesie* III. vi. 128 Within they are stuffed full of browne paper and tow, which the shrewd boyes vnderpeering, do guilefully discouer and turne to a great derision. **1614** B. JONSON *Barth. Fair* II. v, Are you under-peering, you Baboon? up off my Hose, an you be Men.

under-peopled (-'pi:p(ə)ld, older 'ʌndə-), *ppl. a.* (UNDER-¹ 10 a.)

a **1687** PETTY *Pol. Arith.* Pref. (1690) a 1 b, There is no Trade nor Employment for the People, and yet..the Land is under-peopled. **1707** ARBUTHNOT *Serm. on Union* 8 This is the chief Cause why Scotland..is underpeopled. **1776** ADAM SMITH *W.N.* I. ix. (1904) I. 102 A new colony must always, for some time, be..more underpeopled..than the greater part of other countries. **1834** HT. MARTINEAU *Moral* I. 24 The question is not now, as it was when the country was underpeopled. **1862** *Q. Rev.* Apr. 510 A valuable acquisition to any underpeopled colony.

underper'form, *v.* [UNDER-¹ 10 a.] **1.** *intr.* To perform in a manner which falls below expectation.

1976 *Business Week* 26 Jan. 71/1 Institutions..under-perform over the all-important long term. **1977** *Daily Mail* 17 Mar. 6/1 What's wrong with comprehensive schools..is ..not that they fail to teach children properly... They just 'underperform'. **1984** *Observer* 26 Feb. 27/2 Our shares have underperformed since 1977. But this time we have performed.

2. *trans.* Of shares, etc.: to perform less well than (the general market).

1975 *Dun's Rev.* June 92/3 A company that fits the criteria ..might underperform the market for several years before somebody wants to acquire it. **1979** *Daily Tel.* 18 July 21 The shares of Midland Bank have under-performed in an astonishing way..those of its rivals. **1984** *Amer. Banker* 14 Mar. 13/4 Further doubts could make bank stocks underperform even a downward moving stock market.

Hence **underper'formance**; **underper'former**.

1975 *Forbes* 15 Aug. 82/3 Stocks like International Flavors, IBM..have all been underperformers in this bull market. **1976** *Business Week* 29 Mar. 86/2 The Japanese economy shows signs of continued underperformance. **1977** *Daily Mail* 17 Mar. 6/1 What's wrong with comprehensive schools, according to the Ministry inspectors, is 'widespread underperformance'. **1981** *Times* 18 May 18/6 Phillips & Drew has put it [*sc.* a named share] on its list of expected underperformers.

'under-,petticoat. (UNDER-¹ 5 a.)

1625 K. LONG tr. *Barclay's Argenis* I. xv. 41 She..herselfe comes, having onely put on an under-petticoate. **1670** in *12th Rep. Hist. MSS. Comm.* App. V. 21 Plaine black skirts, ..and the under pettycoat very richly laced. **1716** LADY MONTAGU *Let. to C'tess of Bristol* 22 Aug., Like a poor town lady of pleasure..with..a ragged under-petticoat. **1762** STERNE *Tr. Shandy* v. vii, Her bed-gowns, and comfortable under-petticoats. **1865** DICKENS *Our Mutual Fr.* II. IV. xvi. 295 Why one should go out to dine with one's own daughter ..as if one's under-petticoat was a backboard. **1924** R. MACAULAY *Orphan Island* xiii. 156 Flora looked with interest at Rosamond's cami-knickers, Rosamond at Flora's under-petticoat of scarlet-dyed cocoa-nut cloth.

Hence **'under-,petticoated** *a.*

1748 RICHARDSON *Clarissa* VII. lxxviii. 257 They were all slip-shoed; stockenless some; only under-petticoated all.

†under'pight, *pa. t.* and *pa. pple.* *Obs.* [UNDER-¹ 4 a: see PITCH *v.*¹] Supported from below; propped up. Also *fig.*

c **1375** *Cursor M.* 7495 (Fairf.), Here-til þou art ful ȝing; ȝone mon wiþ strenght is vnder-piȝt and þou lered neuer atte fiȝt. **1377** LANGL. *P. Pl.* B. XVI. 23 Pieres..bad me toten on þe tree... With þre pyles was it vnder-piȝte I perceyued it sone. **14..** LYDGATE in *MS. Soc. Antiq.* 134 (Halliwell), And undirpyȝte this mancyoun ryalle, With seven pileris. **1549** COVERDALE, etc. *Erasm. Par. Rom.* 11 Nor yet repent we our glory, with hope wherof we for this present tyme are aduaunced & vnderpyght. *Ibid.*, *Gal.* 12 By the obseruaunce of this lawe then were menne so long stayed and vnderpyght.

under'pin, *v.* [UNDER-¹ 4 a + PIN *v.* 3.]

1. *trans.* To support or strengthen (a building or other structure) from beneath, *spec.* by laying a solid foundation below the ground-level, or by substituting stronger or more solid for weaker or softer materials.

1533 *MS. Rawl. D.* 776 fol. 131 Vnder pynnyng the Grownde plattes of the said wharff. **1583–4** in Willis & Clark *Cambridge* (1886) III. 22 To Mr. Stokes..for stone, and vnderpynnyng the whalles of the schooles. *c* **1700** in *Essex Rev.* (1906) XV. 170, I underpinned the side of the dwelling house. **1776** G. SEMPLE *Building in Water* 65 We under-pinned that West End of it, where we found that there was nothing supporting the upper Work, but the Bond of the Stones. **1833** LOUDON *Encycl. Archit.* §234 All the window and door frames to be properly bedded..and the sills under-pinned. **1886** WILLIS & CLARK *Cambridge* I. 24 A facing added to the decayed clunch by way of under-pinning it.

b. *fig.* To support, corroborate.

1522 MORE *De Quat. Noviss.* Wks. 76/1 It is better to.. thinke on some better thing the while, than to geue eare therto & vnder pinne the tale. *a* **1619** FOTHERBY *Atheom.* Pref. p. vi, I am called to vnder-pinne those foure maine Corner-stones. **1646** SALTMARSH *Groanes for Liberty* 9 Was it unlawfull..to underpin Episcopacy with some Texts of Scripture? **1866** DE MORGAN in *Athenæum* 2 Sept. 312/3 If so, away goes free will for good and all; unless, indeed, we underpin our system with the hypothesis [etc.]. **1884** *American* VIII. 294 These powers..might underpin the first lien on the property.

2. To form a base or support to.

1878 BOSW. SMITH *Carthage* 148 Above the precipitous cliffs that underpinned the mountain was a broad plateau.

'under-,pinner¹. [UNDER-¹ 6 a + PINNER².] A subordinate pound-keeper.

1599 *George a Greene* E 4, I am vnder pinner of a towne, And..I shall be turned out of mine office.

under-'pinner². [f. UNDERPIN *v.*] A support or prop; *fig.* a leg.

1859 BARTLETT *Dict. Amer.* (ed. 2) 493 *Underpinners*, the legs, which in English flash language are called pins. **1861** READE *Cloister & H.* xliii, The underpinners gave way, and the tower suddenly sank away from the walls.

under'pinning, *vbl. sb.* [f. as prec.]

1. The action of supporting or strengthening a building, etc., from beneath. (See UNDERPIN *v.* 1.)

1489 in Dugdale *Monast.* (1821) III. 359/2 Paid for a grounsell for the kechyn wall and for underpynnyng and leiyng in of the same, xv d. **1493–4** *Rec. St. Mary at Hill* 198 Payd for vndyrpynyng of Mastres Atclyffe ys pewe, vj d. *Ibid.*, Payd..for vndyrpynny[n]g of þe newe pewys. **1528** *MS. Acc. St. John's Hosp., Canterb.*, Paid to a tyler for stanchonyng, dobyng, & vnderpynnyng of the store house. **1707** MORTIMER *Husb.* 304 Underpinning for the Bricklayer to dig the Foundation..is a Penny a foot. **1842** GWILT *Archit.* Gloss. 1049. **1883** GRESLEY *Gloss. Coal-m.* 267 *Underpinning*, building up the walling of a pit-shaft to join that above it.

2. a. The materials or structure used for giving support to a building from beneath.

1538 ELYOT, *Substructio*, vnderpynnynge or groundyng of a house. **1601** HOLLAND *Pliny* II. 575 When Cambyses.. burnt all before him, as farre as to the very foundation and underpinning of the Obeliske. **1668** WILKINS *Real Char.* 256 Foundation,..Base, Bottom, fundamental, underpinning. **1741** *Phil. Trans.* XLI. 852 [The houses] were all, in a manner, rocked quite off from their Underpinnings. **1789** *Massachusetts Spy* 16 July 3/4 A new frame of a barn, uncovered,..was taken by a whirlwind from its underpinning. **1894** HOWELLS *Traveller fr. Altruria* 112 The sod was backed up against the wooden under-pinning.

b. *fig.* A support or prop.

1589 R. HARVEY *Pl. Perc.* 3 They are like to daunce after his pipe, and set themselues vpon a miry pinne,..till his vnderpinning will faile him, I doubt. **1656** *Artif. Handsom.* 71 Those grosse Solœcismes of Art, which by unseasonable ..affectations (as so many pitifull props and underpinnings) strive in vain to skrew and set up lapsed and tottering age. **1774** BURKE *Sp. Amer. Tax.* Wks. 1842 I. 160 That this house..is itself held up only by the treacherous under-pinning and clumsy buttresses of arbitrary power. *a* **1894** in *Sunday Reform Leaflets* (Columbus) Sept. 6 The moral underpinning requisite to sustain the superstructure of man's rights.

c. *spec.* (*U.S. slang*), the legs. Chiefly in *pl.* Cf. UNDERPINNER².

1848 E. BENNET *Mike Fink* 9/2 Nothing like long under-pinins fur travel. **1895** *N.Y. Dramatic News* 5 Oct. 6/1 Do cigarette girls at work wear their dresses decollete at the bottom and show their underpinning? **1934** A. WOOLLCOTT *While Rome Burns* 48 There he was at last with his underpinnings shot from under him. **1974** R. B. PARKER *God save Child* (1975) xiii. 95, I learned Vic's technique for developing 'sinewy and shapely under-pinnings'.

'underpitch, *a.* *Arch.* (See quot.)

1875 *Encycl. Brit.* II. 466 When the main longitudinal vault of any groining is higher than the cross or transverse vaults which run from the windows, the system of vaulting is called underpitch groining.

,under'pitched, *ppl. a.* (Also *'under,pitched.*) [UNDER-¹ 10 a.]

1. Set at an insufficient angle; having too little pitch.

1677 PLOT *Oxfordsh.* 274 Roofs..whereof some are flat or under-pitched,..others due proportion'd, or over-pitched.

2. *Cricket.* Of a ball: pitched short of a length; = SHORT *a.* 16.

1927 *Daily Tel.* 14 June 6/1 Allen..began to pull Larwood's slightly under-pitched one—a manoeuvre which showed..that he meant to get close to the ball. **1963** *Times* 14 Feb. 3/1 Knight, it is true, is a disappointing fielder and looks vulnerable to the under-pitched ball.

under'plant, *v.* [UNDER-¹ 2, 4 a.] *trans.* †**a.** To supplant. *Obs. rare.*

In OE., other senses of L. *supplantare* are rendered by *underplantian*.

c **1200** *Trin. Coll. Hom.* 151 Iacob on boc leden is icleped on englisse under-plantere of fule custumes [L. *supplantator viciorum*],..and rithliche.., for he under-plantede [L. *supplantavit*] fule custumes..mid his clenliche liflode. **1538** ELYOT, *Supplantare*,..to vnderplante or set a tree or vyne. **1598** FLORIO, *Sotto piantare*, to vnder-plant, to vnderset, to vnderprop.

b. To plant or cultivate the ground about (a tall plant) *with* smaller ones. Chiefly as **underplanted** *pa. pple.* and *ppl. a.*

1891 W. SCHLICH *Man. Forestry* II. iv. 244 Oak woods should be underplanted when the process of opening out has set in. **1909** *Cent. Dict.* Suppl., *Underplant*,..to plant (young trees) under an existing stand. **1959** *Geogr. Rev.* XLIX. 29 Clumps and spinneys were underplanted with evergreens. **1962** R. PAGE *Educ. of Gardener* iii. 101 There were a few old trees which Duchêne had underplanted with yews. *Ibid.* xi. 302 The cypresses are underplanted with sheets of the bright gentian blue echium. **1971** *Guardian* 17 Apr. 7/7 We plan..to underplant a bush of *Spirea arguta*.. with the pale lemon tulip. **1980** *Amat. Gardening* 25 Oct. 24/2 Transform a corner into a mini-woodland garden with light foliage trees, such as silver birch, underplanted with small flowered daffodil varieties.

Hence **†under'planter**, a supplanter. *Obs.*

c **1200** [see *underplant v.* above].

'underplanting, *vbl. sb.* [f. prec.] The planting or cultivation of smaller plants in between taller ones; a plant so grown; *spec.* in *Forestry*, the process of growing shade-bearing trees among taller ones which they may eventually replace.

1914 G. JEKYLL *Colour in Flower Garden* (ed. 3) ix. 86 [Variegated mint] is one of the prettiest things as an underplanting to anything of white or yellow colour. **1928** R. S. TROUP *Silvicultural Systems* xv. 170 Underplanting of the thinned coppice and standards should be carried out with shade-bearers only. **1953** H. L. Edlin *Forester's Handbk.* vii. 108 As a rule the purpose of underplanting is to raise a successor crop, to supersede the present main one, which will gradually be eliminated. **1962** R. Page *Educ. of Gardener* iii. 99 The Shablikine roses share a terrace with an underplanting of agapanthus. **1978** *Country Life* 10 Aug. 367/1 There is an extensive pinetum in which the trees are sufficiently widely spaced to allow generous underplanting.

ˈunderplay, *sb.* [under-¹ 9.]

1. An underlying or hidden motion or action.

1845 J. Martineau *Ess.* (1890) I. 63 The under-play of a living enthusiasm beneath the dry matter of the composition. **1862** R. Vaughan *Eng. Nonconformity* 224 The king was a party to this underplay.

2. *Card-playing.* (See quot. 1863.)

1850 *Bohn's Handbk. Games* 21. **1863** 'Cavendish' *Whist* (ed. 5) 42 Underplay is keeping up the winning card, generally in the second round of a suit, by leading a low card, though holding the best.

ˌunderˈplay, *v.* [under-¹ 8 b, 10 a.]

1. *refl.* To play below one's ability.

1733 Ld. Harvey in *Craftsman* No. 376, No person is ever known to flatter at this game [*sc.* chess], by underplaying himself.

2. *intr.* To play a low card, though holding a high one of the same suit, in hope of later advantage. (Also used *trans.*)

1850 *Bohn's Handbk. Games* 21 To underplay, he wins the trick with the ace, and returns the small one. **1863** 'Cavendish' *Whist* (ed. 5) 42 Experienced players frequently endeavour to obtain the entire command of their suit by underplaying.

3. *Theatr.* To underact (a part); to perform with deliberate restraint. Also *fig.* **a.** *intr.*

1896 G. B. Shaw *Let.* 16 Mar. (1965) I. 612 Waring.. will not exactly fail: he will only underplay, and all the papers will treat him with great politeness. **1962** *Movie* Dec. 10/2 In *Dawn Patrol* we underplayed, dispensing with the emoting and ham-acting. **1975** *New Yorker* 17 Nov. 159/1 Tiant.. did not have full command of his breaking stuff and was forced to underplay.

b. *trans.*

1897 [see routine *v.*]. **1941** B. Schulberg *What makes Sammy Run?* xi. 208 He came in quietly, under-playing the scene. **1976** *Daily Tel.* 11 Aug. 9/8 Whatever happened.. to the amazing gift Mr Williams showed here for underplaying his lines?.. In the Hancock world.. he let the character.. speak.

4. *fig.* To play down the importance of (something); to present less emphatically than usual.

1949 M. Mead *Male & Female* v. 124 So among the Arapesh the six-year-olds are treated gently, their sex underplayed. **1965** *New Statesman* 16 Apr. 599/3 They slowly start approaching the peasants, buying provisions at high prices and.. underplaying their communist identity. **1973** C. Bonington *Next Horizon* iii. 60 The others had tried to underplay my narrow escape, but she had heard them talk about it amongst themselves. **1980** *Amer. Speech* LV. 120 Scargill's book underplays, to some extent, the influence of America on Canadian English. **1983** R. Scruton *Aesthetic Imagination* ii. 15 The point of underplaying intention is to insist on the public character of the aesthetic object.

Hence **underˈplayed** *ppl. a.*, **underˈplaying** *vbl. sb.*

1896 G. B. Shaw *Let.* 16 Mar. (1965) I. 612 XYZ's underplaying will not hurt Janet. **1951** T. Sterling *House without Door* iii. 26 It was not much different from any other bar.. but it had a kind of underplayed elegance which he liked. **1962** *Listener* 13 Dec. 1025/1 Kenneth More's easy underplaying adapts to the television screen much better than one might have thought. **1973** J. J. McKelvey *Man against Tsetse* ii. 83 Davies' analysis of the controversy stressed the underplayed contributions of Nabarro and Baker.

ˈunderplot. [under-¹ 6 b and 9.]

1. A (dramatic or literary) plot subordinate to the principal plot, but connected with it.

1668 Dryden *Dram. Poesy* ¶24 There may be many actions in a play..; but they must all be subservient to the great one, which our language happily expresses in the name of under-plots. **1684** T. Burnet *Theory Earth* I. 146 Such affairs are but the little under-plots in the tragicomedy of the world. **1711** Addison *Spect.* No. 40 ¶3 The skilful Choice of an Under-Plot. **1779** Sheridan *Critic* II. ii, I have laid my under-plot in low life. **1847** *Westm. Rev.* XLVII. 62 The greater part of the underplot was by the inferior writer. **1873** Symonds *Grk. Poets* ix. 300 The under-plots of many plays ..are not sufficiently subordinated to the main design.

2. An underhand scheme or trick.

1668 Etheredge *She wou'd if she cou'd* III. i, We cannot be long without some Underplots in this Town. **1711** Addison *Spect.* No. 170 ¶12 They still suspect an Under-Plot in every female Action. *a* **1845** Hood *Lamia* vi. 62 Canst swear she is.. No cheating underplot—no covert shape, Making a filthy masquerade of nature?

ˈunder-ˌplotter. [under-¹ 8 a.] An underhand schemer.

1728 Ramsay *Bonnie Lass & Looking-Glass* 36 If you're opprest By Parasites with fause Design, Then will sic faithfu' Mirrors best These Underplotters countermine.

ˈunderply. [under-¹ 5 b.] (See quot.)

1883 Gresley *Gloss. Coal-m.* 267 *Underply*, a band or division of the upper portion of a thick seam of coal.

†**underˈpoise**, *v. Obs.*⁻¹ [under-¹ 10 a.] *trans.* To underweigh, undervalue.

1602 Marston *Ant. & Mel.* Induct., His worth being much underpoised by the uneven scale, that currants all thinges by the outwarde stamp of opinion.

ˌunder-ˈpoled, *ppl. a.* [under-¹ 10 a.]

1. Provided with poles of insufficient height.

1707 Mortimer *Husb.* 136 If.. you find a Hop over or under-poled, you may.. place another Pole in its place.

2. Not stirred sufficiently. Cf. pole *v.*¹ 7.

1881 Raymond *Mining Gloss.*, *Under-poled copper*, copper not poled enough to remove all sub-oxide.

ˈunderposed, *ppl. a.* [under-¹ 4 a.] Placed beneath for support.

a **1656** Ussher *Power Princes* II. (1661) 172 The power doth not depart from the Lord; but he useth it by an under-posed hand.

ˈunder-poˌssessor. (under-¹ 6 a.)

1653 Jer. Taylor *Serm. for Year* I. xvii. 230 The disposing them into portions of inheritance, the assignation of charges and governments,.. are the reserves of the superior right, and not to be invaded by the under-possessors.

ˈunder-ˌpower. (under-¹ 6 b.)

1805 Wordsw. *Prelude* I. 152 General Truths, which are themselves a sort Of.. Under-powers, Subordinate helpers of the living mind.

ˌunderˈpraise, *v.* (under-¹ 10 a.)

1698 Dryden *Ep. to Motteux* 52 In underpraising thy Deserts, I wrong. **1842** Mrs. Browning *Bk. of Poets* ii. ¶7 We must not underpraise Surrey to balance the overpraise we murmur at.

ˈunder-ˌprentice. (under-¹ 6 a.)

1632 Massinger *City Madam* I. i, Emploiment.. Fitting an under-prentice, or a footman.

ˈunder-price, *sb.* [under-¹ 10 b. Cf. Sw. *underpris.*] A price below the standard or usual price; an inadequate payment.

1611 Cotgr., *Non-prix*, an vnder value, or vnderprice. **1727** Bailey (vol. II), To *Under-work*, to work for an Under-price. **1770** Langhorne *Plutarch* III. 268 He was selling a considerable estate, which he wanted a friend to have at an under-price. **1771** W. Evans tr. *Welshman's Candle* 399 At under-price men's lands I often bought. **1807** Southey *Espriella's Lett.* II. 354 To advertise in newspapers which.. insert their notices at an under-price. **1862** Mayhew *Lond. Labour* II. 344/2 The employers of these cab-drivers are as willing to receive it at an underprice.

ˌunder-ˈprice, *v.* [under-¹ 8 b, c.]

1. *trans.* To price lower than the value.

1756 H. Walpole *Let. to Montagu* 14 Oct., If you had offered ten pounds for a set of Pelhams, perhaps I should not have thought you had underpriced them.

2. To undercut (one) in price.

1890 *Daily News* 31 Dec. 7/2 Brown, in answer to the charge, said the prosecutor had underpriced him.

ˈunderpriced, *ppl. a.* [under-¹ 10 a.] Selling at less than the usual price(s).

1851–61 Mayhew *Lond. Labour* III. 210/2, I next went to work at a under-priced hatter's,.. but I was disgusted with the price paid for labour.

ˈunderpriest. (under-¹ 6 a. Cf. ON. *undirprestr*, Du. *onderpriester.*)

c **1200** Ormin 1146 Forr bisscopp & forr unnderrpreost, & forr þe follkess nede. *Ibid.* 10882.

underˈprint, *v.* [under-¹ 4 a, 10 a.]

1. *trans.* To print or stamp from below or on the under side.

1598 Florio, *Soppresso*,.. beaten vnder, drowned, boulged, vnder-printed. **1626** *Impeachm. Dk. Buckhm.* (Camden) 62 Subscribed per me,.. and.. sealed with a seale of reade wax, under-printed upon.

2. To print (an engraving or photograph) with insufficient depth or distinctness.

c **1865** *Wylde's Circ. Sci.* I. 154/1 It is better that the positive should be over, rather than under-printed. **1885** *Longm. Mag.* VI. 490 A series of book-illustrations that were over-printed in Paris and under-printed in London.

underˈprivilege. [f. next.] The state of being underprivileged; lack of what are considered the normal amenities of life.

1937 *Nation* 25 Sept. 324/2 The greater part of the book deals with the factors that underlie the spread and control of syphilis, its relation to poverty, underprivilege, [etc.]. **1966** P. Scott *Jewel in Crown* v. 207 He.. had so obviously set his heart on lifting himself by his bootstraps from the state of underprivilege into which he had been born. **1976** *Times* 8 Nov. 3/2 The probation service.. has a duty to oppose policies which intensify underprivilege.

underˈprivileged, *a.* (and *sb.*) [under-¹ 10 b.]

1. Less privileged than others; *spec.* experiencing a standard of living which falls short of an accepted norm, socially disadvantaged. Chiefly applied to persons.

1896 J. Barnes *Princetonian* xxxiii. 380 It was very quiet in the little square that was filled with nurse-maids and children moving about inside the railings—several little underprivileged ones peering in at them from the outside. **1935** Z. N. Hurston *Mules & Men* 18 These people, being usually under-privileged, are the shyest. **1939** C. R. Cooper *Designs in Scarlet* ii. 27 Don't try to say that the problem is one of 'underprivileged districts', and not of such surroundings as yours. **1948** 'J. Tey' *Franchise Affair* xiii. 140 He wrote a.. letter about her.. pointing out how under-privileged she had been. **1960** M. Spark *Bachelors* viii. 109, I was definitely under-privileged by birth.. though not delinquent. **1978** K. Hudson *Jargon of Professions* iv. 96 Writers and speakers on education... refer.. to ..'underprivileged children'.

2. *absol.* as *sb.* with *the.*

1935 A. P. Herbert *What a Word!* iii. 46 She had spent a long time persuading one of the 'underprivileged' to go to hospital to have an operation. **1945** 'L. Lewis' *Birthday Murder* (1951) iii. 36 Not infrequently he got drunk, coming home late from some revel with the under-privileged. **1977** M. Drabble *Ice Age* I. 34 They did not read novels, or go to good films, or read the arts pages of newspapers, or listen to music or discuss the problems of the underprivileged.

ˌunderˈprize, *v.* [under-¹ 10 a.] *trans.* To prize too little; to undervalue.

1596 Shaks. *Merch. V.* III. ii. 129 How farre The substance of my praise doth wrong this shadow In vnderprising it, so farre [etc.]. **1598–9** B. Jonson *Case is Altered* III. iii, If I mistake not, He scorns to have his worth so underprised. **1647** H. More *Cupid's Conflict* l, Nor while I live, heed I what man doth praise Or underprize mine unaffected layes. **1665** Wither *Lord's Prayer* 116 How is it neglected and underprized, as a Form of Prayer fitting none but Ideots and Children! **1889** Skrine *Mem. Thring* 52 Boys thought their own genius under-prized.

ˌunder-proˈficient. (under-².)

1703 S. Parker tr. *Eusebius' Eccl. Hist.* VI. 103 Such Crowds of Scholars daily throng'd to his Lectures.. that he was at last oblig'd to assign the Instruction of the Under-Proficients to Heraclas.

underˈprompt, *v.* (under-¹ 4 a.)

a **1548** Hall *Chron., Edw. V*, 2 b, Slipper youthe [must be] vnderprompted with elder counsaill.

ˈunder-ˌprompter. (under-¹ 6 a.)

1779 Sheridan *Critic* Dram. Pers., Under Prompter: Mr. Phillimore. *Ibid.* II. i, [Stage direction.] Enter Under Prompter.

under-proof: see under *prep.* 23 b.

ˈunderprop, *sb.* [under-¹ 5 b.] A prop or support placed under a thing. Usu. *fig.*

1579 Tomson *Calvin's Serm. Tim.* 45/1 The Monkes, &.. all those iolly vnderprops of that Romish Antichrist. **1602** Breton *Mother's Blessing* D 3, Faiths strong pillars need no vnderprops. **1629** H. Burton *Truth's Triumph* 264 An vnder-proppe or basis supporting and sustaining vs. **1826** W. E. Andrews *Crit. Rev. Fox's Bk. Mart.* II. 204 Cranmer, ..this pillar and underprop of the reformation.

underˈprop, *v.* [under-¹ 4 a.]

1. *trans.* To support with a prop or props; to keep firm or upright with some form of material support. (Common in 17th c.)

1534 More *Comf. agst. Trib.* I. Wks. 1162/2 Some haue I sene euen in their last sicknes set vp in their death bed vnderpropped with pillous. **1591** Harington *Orl. Fur.* XXVII. lxix, One took him napping,.. And underprop't his saddell with foure stakes And so from under him his courser takes. **1637** Heywood *Pleas. Dial.* ii. Wks. 1874 VI. 124 Had you not rather.. To see the trees full branches vnderpropt Laden with ripe fruit? **1699** J. Potter *Antiq. Greece* III. xx. II. 161 It was frequent also for Sea-men, underpropping their Ships with their Shoulders, to thrust them forwards into the Sea. **1726** Leoni *Alberti's Archit.* II. 129 Underprop the Architrave with a strong arch. **1810** Crabbe *Borough* xi. 100 A mirror crack'd, With table underpropp'd, and chairs new-back'd. **1851** C. L. Smith tr. *Tasso* XI. lxxxv, They who guided it their force applied To underprop it.

b. In fig. context.

1532 More *Confut. Tindale* III. Wks. 473/1 But Tyndall perceiuing.. howe fieble hys building is that he setteth therupon, hath therfore.. vndershoren, & vnderpropped it with certayn strong postes made of rotten redes. **1581** J. Bell *Haddon's Answ. Osor.* 34 b, Our deepe Devine doth underproppe his lazie Monckerie upon these pillars. **1633** T. Stafford *Pac. Hib.* (1821) I. xi. 75 The effect thereof was, to implore ayde of that Egyptian Reed, to underprop their ruinous and almost rotten Building. **1645** Rutherford *Tryal & Tri. Faith* 23 This doctrine is a.. Pillar, to under prop the Chamber in Hell, which they call Purgatory.

2. *fig.* To support or sustain; to maintain. (Very common *c* 1550–1675.)

1513 More *Rich. III*, Wks. 39/1 Childehood must be maintained by mens authoritye, & slipper youth vnderpropped with elder counsayle. **1561** T. Norton *Calvin's Inst.* III. 255 To vnderprop and strengthen this faith with yᵉ signes of the good wil of God towarde it selfe. **1593** Shaks. *Lucr.* 53 Within whose face Beautie and Vertue striued, Which of them both should vnderprop her fame. **1647** Digges *Unlawf. Taking Arms* §2. 22 This art.. of underpropping their reputation. **1695** Blackmore *Pr. Arth.* VI. 360 He could th' unstable People's Tumults stop, And a declining Kingdom underprop. **1738** Warburton *Div. Legat.* I. 47 He though fit to underprop it with his earthly God, the Leviathan. **1773** Berridge *Chr. World Unmasked* (1805) 199 Moses is called in hastily to underprop his master Jesus. **1827** Pollok *Course T.* v. 882 Leagues.. on purpose made to underprop Iniquity, and crush the sacred truth. **1849** Thoreau *Week Concord River* Wedn. 300 Let such pure hate still underprop our love.

refl. **1571** Golding *Calvin on Ps.* iii. 3 Assone as he hath underpropped himselfe with assurance of comfort.

absol. **1596** *Edward III*, III. v. 78 Yet marble courage still did vnderprop.

3. To form a prop or support to (something).

c **1590** Marlowe *Faustus* vii. 32 Know that this Citie stands vpon seuen hilles That vnderprops the groundworke of the same. *a* **1661** Holyday *Juvenal* (1673) 56 He had yet forsooth a statue or two, particularly one of Cheiron, which underpropp'd his table. **1672** Marvell *Reh. Transp.* I. 133 There is nothing more natural than for the Ivy to be of opinion.. that the Church cannot hold up longer than It underprops the Walls. **1794** G. Adams *Nat. & Exp. Philos.*

III. xxxi. 261 One considerable use of the wedge, is to raise up the beam of a house, to underprop it, when a floor gives way. **1830** TENNYSON *Arab. Nts.* 145 Six columns..underpropt a rich Throne of the massive ore. **1836** BUCKLAND *Geol. & Min.* xv. §5 (1837) I. 360 The transverse plates..underpropping their flattest and weakest part.

Hence **underpropped, -propping** *ppl. adjs.*
1614 D. DYKE *Myst. Self-Deceiving* 45 There is no sinne, but we may..fall into, if Gods vnderpropping hand withdraw it selfe. **1632** LITHGOW *Trav.* I. 6 O heauy vnderprop'd wrongs. **1655** FULLER *Ch. Hist.* IX. vi. §1 The old under-propped Scaffolds overladen with people, suddenly fell down.

ˌunder-proˈportion, *v.* (UNDER-^{1} 10 a.)
1813 SOUTHEY *Nelson* I. 129 That fatal error of under-proportioning the force to the service.

ˌunder-proˈportioned, *ppl. a.* (UNDER-^{1} 10 a.)
1697 COLLIER *Ess. Mor. Subj.* I. (1703) 26 To make scanty and under-proportioned returns of civility. **1813** G. EDWARDS *Meas. True Pol.* 86 It is underproportioned to the capacity..and abilities of the nation.

ˈunder-propoˌsition. (UNDER-^{1} 6 b.)
1691 NORRIS *Pract. Disc.* 113 Taking the argument for, I shall think my-self further concern'd only to justify the Under-Proposition.

underˈpropper. [f. UNDERPROP *v.*] One who or that which supports or sustains. †Also *spec.* (see SUPPORTASSE).
1532 MORE *Confut. Tindale* Wks. 473/1 This vnderpropper is not very proper for to beare vp his bilding. **1583** MELBANCKE *Philotimus* K ij, The strongest vnderproppers of her princely state. **1655** CROMWELL *Let. to Goodson* Oct. (Carlyle), That Roman Babylon, of which the Spaniard is the great underpropper. **1664** H. MORE *Myst. Iniq.* I. i. 1 For which reason they..style the chief Authour and under-propper thereof..by the name of Antichrist. **1740** CIBBER *Apol.* (1756) I. 43, I had a third chance..of becoming an under-propper of the state.

underˈpropping, *vbl. sb.* [f. as prec.] The action of supporting with props, etc.; also *concr.*, that which serves to underprop.
1586 T. B. *La Primaud. Fr. Acad.* I. 391 Mauger all the power and under-propping, which he receiveth from the wicked. **1592** NASHE *P. Penilesse* 17, I will not, by the vnderpropping of confutation, seeme to giue the idle witted aduersary so much encouragement. **1628** FELTHAM *Resolves* II. xix. 61 [The soul] rests full, in her owne approuement, without the weake Worlds reedy vnder-propping. **1658** A. FOX *Würtz' Surg.* II. xiv. 107 Such Wounds must be helped with underproppings and bolsters. **1726** LEONI *Alberti's Archit.* II. 129 Let this underpropping be run up as fast as possible.

ˈunder-ˌprospect. (UNDER-^{1} 5 b.)
a **1586** SIDNEY *Arcadia* I. x, A pleasant valley (of either side of which high hils lifted up their beetle-browes, as if they would over looke the pleasantnes of their under-prospect).

underˈpry, *v.* (UNDER-^{1} 4 b.)
1600 HOLLAND *Livy* 1073 Two Embassadors..sent rather as spies to under-prie and to learne somwhat as touching those points.

†**underˈpull**, *v. Obs.* [UNDER-^{1} 8 a.] *intr.* To work secretly; to act in matters without appearing to do so.
1697 COLLIER *Ess. Mor. Subj.* II. (1703) 142 Covetousness ..engages honour in the most scandalous intrigues, and makes it under-pull to cheats and sharpers. *a* **1734** NORTH *Life Ld. Guilford* (1742) I. 24 His Lordship,..during his Incapacity to practise aboveboard, was contented to under-pull, as they call it, and managed diverse Suits for his Country Friends and Relations.

under-ˈpuller. [Cf. prec.] A secret agent.
1682 T. FLATMAN *Heraclitus Ridens* No. 69, But 'tis great pity this Scribler be not made an Under-puller in the Work of defending the City-Charter against the King. **1698** FRYER *Acc. E. India & P.* 388 Underpullers to these are the Shop-keepers, whose Mercurial Parts are fitted to put off the worst Wares. *a* **1734** NORTH *Examen* II. iv. §138 For the King is this..Ridiculer, and this Fellow, Fitzharris, his Underpuller.

†**ˈunderput**, *sb. Obs.*$^{-1}$ [UNDER-^{1} 4 d.] A mistress.
1607 MIDDLETON *Michaelmas Term* III. i, Is she but your underput, master Lethe? *Let.* No more, of my credit;..when all comes to all, 'tis but a plain pung.

†**underˈput**, *v. Obs.* [UNDER-^{1} 4 b, 7.]
1. *trans.* To put (one thing) under (another); to place or set beneath.
c **1220** *Bestiary* 669 Rennande cumeð a ȝungling, raðe to him luteð, his snute him under puteð. **1382** WYCLIF *Gen.* xxviii. 18 [Jacob] took the stoon, the which he hadde vnder-put to his heed. —— *Exod.* xxvi. 21 Two stakis to eche table shulen be vnderput. *c* **1480** HENRYSON *Orpheus & Eurydice* 630 (Bann. MS.), Now pray we god..That he wald vndirput his haly hand Of mantenans, and gife ws forss to stand.
b. To furnish with something placed under, esp. as a support.
1387-8 T. USK *Test. Love* II. vii. (Skeat) I. 72 Hadden they ben underput with any helpes, they had not so lightly falle. *c* **1475** *Promp. Parv.* (K.) 511/2 Vnder puttyn, or beryn up,..*suffulcio.* *c* **1611** CHAPMAN *Iliad* XXI. 342 As a caldron, underput with store of fire,..up leapes his wave aloft.
2. To put under the power or control of; to place in subjection; to subject. Const. *to.*
c **1374** CHAUCER *Boeth.* I. pr. vi. (1868) 28 þat þou byleuest þat þe gouernynge of it nis nat subgit ne vnderput to þe folie of þise happes auenterouses. *a* **1400-50** *Alexander* 5402 Synches I hiȝt; And to my powere vndire-putt is all þe playn werd. *c* **1456** PECOCK *Bk. of Faith* (1909) 217 If it like to oure Lord God that he submitte and undirputte alle Cristen personys to resoun and fre wil. **1559** *Mirr. Mag., Hen. VI*, xiv, Wheron the rest depende and vnderput remayne.
b. To lower (the voice).
1382 WYCLIF *Prov.* xxvi. 25 Whan he shal vndirputte [L. *submiserit*] his vois, ne ȝiue thou credence to hym.
3. a. To put or take fraudulently. **b.** To substitute.
c **1400** in Trevisa *Higden* (Rolls) VII. 133 Som men seiþ ..þat sche underput [L. *supposuisse*] to hir self lyenge in childebedde þe forseide Swane. *Ibid.* 137. *Ibid.* 149 He was ..deposed, and anoþer i-ordeyned and underput [L. *subrogatus*].
Hence †**underˈputting** *vbl. sb. Obs.*
1387-8 T. USK *Test. Love* I. ix. (Skeat) l. 62 Though thou be put to serve the ilke jewel duringe thy lyfe, yet is that no servage of underputtinge, but a maner of travayling plesaunce. *c* **1440** *Promp. Parv.* 511/2 Vnder puttynge, ..*subposicio.* **1611** FLORIO, *Supposta*, an vnderputting or setting.

underˈputter. [f. UNDERPUT *v.*] †A pander, a procurer.
1608 *Yorksh. Trag.* I. ii, My second sonne must be a promooter, and my third a theefe, or an vnderputter, a slaue pander.

ˌunderˈqualified, *ppl. a.* (UNDER-^{1} 10 a.)
1624 HEYWOOD *Gunaik.* III. 119 Each heroick and well disposed Ladie, or woman lower degreed and underqualified. **1847** H. BUSHNELL *Chr. Nurt.* II. ii, They are almost all disqualified, or under-qualified.

ˈunder-queen. (UNDER-^{1} 6 a.)
1839 BAILEY *Festus* 186, I am but here the under-queen of beauty.

underˈquote, *v.* [UNDER-^{1} 8 b.] *trans.* To quote a lower price than.
1891 *Engineer* 20 Feb. 156 In some instances merchants have been underquoting makers to the extent of 2s. 6d. to 5s. a ton. **1897** *Westm. Gaz.* 9 Sept. 8/1 The American competitors..are always ready to underquote the official prices.

ˈunder-ˌranger. (UNDER-^{1} 6 a.)
1685 *Secr. Serv. Money Chas. & Jas.* (Camden) 104 To.. Lieut. of Waltham forrest,..for the underkeepers and underrangers within the said forest. **1738** BIRCH *Milton* M.'s Wks. I. p. i, Our Author's Grandfather..was an Under-ranger or Keeper of the Forest of Shotover.

ˈunder-rate, *sb.* [UNDER-^{1} 10 b.] A rate lower than the true or proper one.
1631 WEEVER *Anc. Funeral Mon.* 240 Being valued..at a fauourable and farre vnder-rate. **1693** G. STEPNEY in *Dryden's Juvenal* viii. (1697) 195 The worthless Brute is from New-Market brought, And at an under-rate in Smith-Field bought. **1712** HEARNE *Collect.* (O.H.S.) III. 477, I highly commend your Resolution of not letting Copies go at Under-Rates. **1748** RICHARDSON *Clarissa* VI. 255 Tho' her conscience permitted her to take them [clothes] at such an under-rate.

ˈunder-rate, *a.* [UNDER-^{2}.] Inferior, subordinate.
1709 SWIFT *Let. to Hunter* 12 Jan., The Whigs carry all before them, and how far they will pursue their victories we underrate Whigs can hardly tell. **1776** BENTHAM *Fragm. Govt.* Wks. 1843 I. 282 This deficiency is no other than what an underrate workman might easily supply.

ˌunderˈrate, *v.* [UNDER-^{1} 10 a.]
†**1.** *trans.* To depreciate, lower. *Obs. rare.*
a **1623** BUCK *Rich. III*, III. (1646) 90 Dispatching Doctor William Warkam..to under-rate his credit with those Princes. **1649** LOVELACE *Poems* 69 He..under-rates himself below mankinde.
2. To assess or tax (†lower or) too low.
1641 *Rates for Poll-money*, Such as are under-rated of what they were in the former Subsidies. **1753** *Act 26 Geo. II*, c. 17 §14 As often as they shall find any Person..to have been under-rated.
3. To rate or estimate at too low a value or worth; to undervalue.
1650 E. WILLIAMS *Virgo Triumphans* 3 Though Mr. Bullocke be pleased to under-rate it [*sc.* wheat] at halfe the crowne the bushell. **1712** STEELE *Spect.* No. 272 ¶1 [She] so over-valued her self and under-rated all her Pretenders. **1774** JEFFERSON *Autobiog.* App., Wks. 1859 I. 126 We do not, however, mean to underrate those aids. **1831** D. E. WILLIAMS *Life & Corr. Sir T. Lawrence* II. 393 In the following passage, Sir Thomas..greatly under-rates his own talents. **1869** TOZER *Highl. Turkey* II. 337 [They have] underrated the views of their opponents.
refl. **1854** WHATELY *Common-pl. Bk.* (1864) 150 And one condition, I think, of forgiveness is to appear, or at least pretend to underrate yourself. **1863** COWDEN CLARKE *Shaks. Char.* x. 246 Helena's affection prompts her to *over*rate the man she loves, and to *under*rate herself.
4. To under-estimate in amount or extent.
1691 NORRIS *Pract. Disc.* 35 He made an interest with his Lord's Debtors, by under-rating their Accounts. **1802** PLAYFAIR *Illustr. Hutton. Th.* 348 If we call it one fourth of the whole surface, its extent is certainly not under-rated. **1844** KINGLAKE *Eothen* iii, I had enormously misjudged its distance and underrated its height. *a* **1862** BUCKLE *Misc. Wks.* (1872) I. 358 Nearly every author I have seen, underrates the consumption of wheat in England during the middle ages.
Hence **ˌunderˈrating** *vbl. sb.* and *ppl. a.* Also **ˌunderˈratement.**
1599 DANIEL *Musoph.* Wks. (1602) C ij b, Bring not downe the prizes of the minde With vnder-rating of your selues so base. **1708** *Brit. Apollo* No. 76. 1/1 Affront him not by an Under-ratement of his Merits. **1721** E. ERSKINE *Wks.* (1791) 78/1 It implies low and under-rating thoughts of ourselves.

underˈreach, *v.* [UNDER-^{1} 4 a, 8 a.]
†**1.** *trans.* To stretch below. *Obs.*
1578 BANISTER *Hist. Man* VII. 90 [The] Membran to all the ribbes..and to the whole brest bone vnderreached, and coueryng the bodyes of the Vertebres.
2. To entrap or defraud by stealth. *rare*$^{-1}$.
a **1652** BROME *Mad Couple* II. i, Your hopes are vaine..in seating mee here to overreach or underreach any body.

under-ˈread, *v.* [UNDER-^{1} 10 a.] **a.** *trans.* (See quot. 1934.) **b.** *intr.* Of a gauge, dial, etc.: to show a reading lower than the true one. **c.** *trans.* Of the reading public: to read (an author, a book, etc.) with less than normal frequency or with less than due appreciation.
1934 WEBSTER, *Underread*,..to take a reading below the correct reading of (a test); to read (a temperature, measurement, weight, etc.) as lower than that actually registered. **1975** *Daily Tel.* 7 May 12/4 Under an EEC directive..it would be illegal for speedometers to under-read at all. **1977** *Lancet* 30 Apr. 952/1 The device over-read the systolic pressure by an average of 2.7 mm Hg (S.D. 5.2) and under-read the diastolic pressure by an average of 2.4 mm Hg (S.D. 9.3). **1982** E. DIPPLE *Iris Murdoch* p. ix, Although the role of critic as evangelist may seem questionable, it strikes me as necessary, given the current tendency to under-read and underestimate Murdoch's work. **1984** *N. & Q.* June 274/2 Some progress is made towards consolidating that concept through isolating characteristic aspects of fiction by under-read, minor, and 'popular' novelists as well as by those more familiar names later accorded their separate chapters.

ˈunder-ˌreader. (UNDER-^{1} 6 a.)
1706 PHILLIPS (ed. Kersey), *Sub-Reader*, an Under-Reader in one of the Inns of Court.

ˈunder-realm. (UNDER-^{1} 6 b.)
1591 SYLVESTER *Yvry* 481 When Nile and Euphrate, as her under-Realms, Through fruitfull Plains roul'd tributary streams.

ˈunderreamer. *Oil Industry.* [UNDER-^{1} 5 b.] A drilling bit that can be used to drill a hole below the casing, of sufficient size for the casing to be lowered further. So **ˈunderreaming** *vbl. sb.*
1912 Under-reamer [see ROTARY *a.* 2 c]. **1922** D. T. DAY *Handbk. Petroleum Industry* I. 246 Underreaming is accomplished through the medium of an ingeniously designed bit (termed an 'underreamer' because it reams under the casing). **1939** D. HAGER *Fund. Petroleum Industry* viii. 186 If for any reason the hole has been cased at a certain depth and it is necessary to carry the same diameter of hole deeper without removing the casing, an underreamer is used.

ˈunder-reˌceiver. (UNDER-^{1} 6 a.)
1579 *Reg. Privy Council Scot.* III. 143 Collectour-generall of the thriddis of benefices.., and..his under ressaver. **1651** in Peterkin *Orkney & Zetl.* (1822) I. 104 One to be chamberlain thereof and another to be under receiver of the rents.

ˌunder-ˈreckon, *v.* (UNDER-^{1} 10 a.)
1629 BP. HALL *Serm.* Wks. 1837 V. 354 So Suidas under-reckons it by seven years. **1655** STANLEY *Hist. Philos.* I. 29 Laertius under-reckons him to have lived but eighty seven yeares. *Ibid.* 35 This lustration of the Citty, Eusebius under-reckons. **1876** *Whitby Gloss.* 205 *Under-reckon'd*, pp. undervalued.

under-reˈcord, *v.* [UNDER-^{1} 10 a.] *trans.* **a.** To make too few recordings of (a work or performer). Chiefly *pass.* **b.** To record using too low a signal, so that the sound is obscured by other sounds or by instrument noise. **c.** To record (data, information, etc.) insufficiently or inadequately. So **under-reˈcorded** *ppl. a.*, **under-reˈcording** *vbl. sb.*
1958 P. GAMMOND *Decca Bk. Jazz* xv. 183 There was Teddy Weatherford, a most able but under-recorded musician. **1962** *John o' London's* 18 Jan. 66/3 Nobody can complain that Britain's favourite oratorio is under-recorded. **1968** P. OLIVER *Screening Blues* iii. 122 Though Sunnyland Slim's stentorian voice was under-recorded, his shouting style of blues could be heard outlining the vocal line with its exaggerated rise. **1971** H. WILSON *Labour Govt.* (1974) xxxv. 911 It became clear that for four or five years our national export figures had been increasingly under-recorded. *Ibid.* 913 In the autumn of 1970 the statisticians had discovered that the 1970 figures were still subject to substantial under-recording. **1977** *Gramophone* Mar. 1481/2 One can under-record to a peak of a few dB below zero on the VU meter. **1980** *Times Lit. Suppl.* 31 Oct. 1232/4 Such crucial problems as how to compensate for the under-recording of the activities of the poorer inhabitants of Halesowen.

ˈunder-ˌregion. (UNDER-^{1} 5 b.)
1727 WATTS '*Eternal Wisdom*' iv, Those Under-regions of the Skies Thy num'rous Glories show.

under-reˈhearsal. [UNDER-^{1} 10 b.] Insufficient rehearsal of a play, piece of music, etc., for performance. Hence **under-rehearsed** *a.*
1900 G. B. SHAW *Let.* 30 Dec. (1972) II. 215 The second performance has all the flatness of a second night plus the effects of under rehearsal. **1937** *Discovery* Nov. 331/1 The major difficulty with the B.B.C. transmissions is under-rehearsal. **1960** *Times* 24 Nov. 8/5 The performance itself had an air of under-rehearsal. **1963** *Times* 7 Mar. 15/5 Those under-rehearsed in the intrigues of the narratives can suck

them out from his obliquities. **1982** J. SHERWOOD *Shot in Arm* vi. 51 The show was badly under-rehearsed.

ˌunder-ˈrented, *ppl. a.* (UNDER-¹ 10 a.)
1801 *Farmer's Mag.* Nov. 448 A small piece of ground may serve as an object of convenience, seldom of profit, unless it is under-rented. **1898** *Westm. Gaz.* 17 Mar. 2/3 An independent valuer..reported that Mr. Morris was under-rented to the extent of £82 a year!

ˌunder-ˈrenting, *vbl. sb.* (UNDER-¹ 10 b.)
a **1635** NAUNTON *Fragm. Reg.* (Arb.) 22 One Carwarden.. presented her with a paper, shewing how she was abused in the under-renting of her Customes.

under-reˈport, *v.* [UNDER-¹ 10 a.] To fail to report (income, events, information, etc.) fully. So **under-reˈported** *ppl. a.*, **under-reˈporting** *vbl. sb.*
1959 *Washington Post* 12 Nov. A2/1 Harrington..made public Tuesday night that new steps are needed to deal with the 'shocking' problem of under-reporting of income. *Ibid.*, Americans 'under-reported' their 1957 income by about $24 billion. **1972** *Science* 26 May 857/2 He found that people underreported both their use and knowledge of contraceptives. **1976** A. GREY *Bulgarian Exclusive* v. 35 Bulgaria's the most under-reported, unnoticed East European country of 'em all. **1980** *Sci. Amer.* Oct. 70/2 The actual total was surely higher, not only because of countries not included in the survey but also because of underreporting in the records of those countries that were included.

underˈride, *v.* [UNDER-¹ 4 b.] **a.** *trans.* To form the basis on which (something) occurs; cf. OVERRIDE *v.* 3 a. *rare.*
1956 M. DUGGAN in C. K. Stead *N.Z. Short Stories* (1966) 84 It underrode everything and was to him no more than suspected.
b. *Geol.* Of a mass of rock, water, etc.: to move underneath (another mass).
1970 *Bull. Geol. Soc. Amer.* LXXXI. 1665/1 The seismically active zone of movement..between the moving oceanic crust and upper mantle, and the relatively stationary material that it underrides. **1977** A. HALLAM *Planet Earth* 54/2 Sediment-charged rivers spread material out over the lake floor by under-riding the lake water.

ˌunder-ˈripe, *a.* (UNDER-¹ 10 c.)
1707 MORTIMER *Husb.* 127 You must be very cautious.. that neither the Stalk nor Seed be under-ripe. **1778** [W. H. MARSHALL] *Minutes Agric.* 22 Aug. 1776, As I mean..to sow pea-beans for the sake of the halm,..I will, at all events, cut them under-ripe.

ˈunder-ˌroarer. (UNDER-¹ 6 a.)
1713 *Guardian* No. 124 ¶2 'Tis my Request, that I may be instituted his Under-roarer in this University, Town, and County of Cambridge.

ˌunder-ˈroast, *v.* (UNDER-¹ 10 a.)
1584 COGAN *Haven Health* 116 Mutton, contrarie to veale, should be rather vnder rosted than ouer. **1732** MANDEVILLE *Enq. Origin Honour* p. viii, It is wrong to under-roast Mutton for People who love to have their Meat well done. **1899** *Westm. Gaz.* 24 July 3/1 If it tastes of the raw berry (as Egyptian coffee generally does), it is under-roasted.

ˈunder-robe. (UNDER-¹ 5 a.)
1725 POPE *Odyss.* v. 297 An under robe, unbound, In snowy waves flow'd glitt'ring on the ground. **1797** HOLCROFT tr. *Stolberg's Trav.* (ed. 2) IV. xci. 37 He.. appeared in his underrobe. *a* **1802** *Duel of Wharton & Stuart* I. iii. in Scott *Minstrelsy*, Say, have you got no armour on? Have you no under robe of steel? **1907** *Westm. Gaz.* 6 Sept. 10/2 An under-robe of very rich purple cloth.

ˈunder-rogue. (UNDER-¹ 6 a.)
1706 E. WARD *Wooden World Diss.* (1708) 58 Were it not for this Under-Rogue, and his Superiors, he would be a very rich Fellow.

ˈunder-ˌrolling, *ppl. a.* [UNDER-¹ 4 a.] Having an underswell.
1745 P. THOMAS *Jrnl. Anson's Voy.* 114 We found a large under-rolling sea.

ˈunder-roof. (UNDER-¹ 5 b.)
1611 FLORIO, *Sotto cielo*, an vnder-roofe or testerne. **1830** TENNYSON *Dying Swan* i, The plain was..open to the air, Which had built up everywhere An under-roof of doleful gray.

ˈunder-room. (UNDER-¹ 5 b.)
1597 [see UNCHILDLY *a.*] **1603** DANIEL *Def. Rhime* H 3 b, My ignorance, that hath set me in so lowe an vnder-roome of conceipt with other men.

under-ˈrooted, *ppl. a.* (UNDER-¹ 4 a.)
1485 CAXTON *Chas. Gt.* 210 The bowes & leues, wyth whyche the leues [? *read* speres] were planted and vnder-roted.

ˈunder-ˌrower. [UNDER-¹ 6 a, after Gr. ὑπηρέτης, f. ὑπό under + ἐρέτης rower.] (See quots.)
1647 TRAPP *Comm. 1 Cor.* iv. 1 *Ministers of Christ* Gr. *Under-rowers* to Christ the Master pilot. **1655** FULLER *Ch. Hist.* IX. vii. §23. **1796** J. BENSON in R. Treffry *Mem.* (1840) 221 The ministers of the Gospel..are under-rowers in that vessel of which Christ is the Pilot.

under-ˈruff, *v. Bridge.* [UNDER-¹ 10 a, b.] *intr.* To undertrump. Also as *sb.*
1945 'S. J. SIMON' *Why You lose at Bridge* 151 He made a gallant attempt to avert the impending squeeze by under-ruffing with the seven of Hearts. **1960** T. REESE *Play Bridge with Reese* 185 The under-ruff to preserve possibilities is uncommon but worth noting. *Ibid.*, I under-ruff with the 5 of spades. **1964** R. L. FREY *Official Encycl. Bridge* 651/5 In the following deal an underruff was necessary at the third trick, because East could not spare any cards in the side-suits. *Ibid.*, East had a discard problem which he solved by underruffing with the diamond deuce. **1979** *Country Life* 4 Oct. 1127/3 The Rabbit..underruffed with his Eight. *Ibid.*, Without the under-ruff the contract would have been secure.

ˈunder-ˌruler. (UNDER-¹ 6 a.)
1625 SANDERSON *Serm.* I. 120 At His command Moses striketh the rulers; and at Moses his command, the under-rulers must strike..those that had offended.

ˈunderrun, *sb.* **1.** [UNDER-¹ 5 b.] An undercurrent.
1894 *Pall Mall Mag.* Nov. 381 You may..watch her little shape soar to the underrun of a billow. **1898** *Geogr. Jrnl.* March 291 The discovery of the underrun of the Hudson.
2. [UNDER-¹ 10 b: see sense 4 of the vb.] (An instance of) underrunning; the extent to which a programme, project, etc., underruns.
1941 *B.B.C. Gloss. Broadcasting Terms* 34 *Underrun*, extent by which a programme falls short of its allotted time. **1967** A. BATTERSBY *Network Analysis* (ed. 2) xiv. 238 An example is shown in Fig. 14.2, which displays the extent to which the project is ahead of schedule or behind it, referred to respectively as 'over-run' and 'under-run'.
3. [UNDER-¹ 4 d] The act of running under something, *spec.* (of a vehicle) under the back of the vehicle in front. Used *attrib.* and in *Comb.*, as **underrun bar, bumper,** etc., a guard attached to the back of a large-wheeled vehicle to prevent other vehicles running underneath.
1969 *Jane's Freight Containers 1968–69* 532/1 *Under-run bar*, at the rear of the chassis a massive bumper bar is provided. **1970** *Daily Tel.* 27 May 11/4 What are needed are under-run bumpers or similar protective structures at the rear of lorries, intended to catch a car that might run into them. **1973** *Care on Road* (RoSPA) Feb. 9/1 Referring to under-run accidents on motorways, the report says: 'There were severe and multiple fractures of skull and face with associated brain damage.' **1974** *Ibid.* Oct. 7/2 Some trailer-manufacturers do fit under-run bumpers. **1980** *Daily Tel.* 24 May 30/4 Under-run accidents are one of the most lethal types of collisions, particularly on motorways.

underˈrun, *v.* [UNDER-¹ 4 a, b; in sense 4, UNDER-¹ 10 a. Cf. OE. *underirnan.*]
1. *trans.* To run, flow, or pass beneath.
1594 KYD *Cornelia* IV. ii. 47 Those braue Germains.. Beheld the swift Rheyn vnder-run mine Ensignes. **1681** T. FLATMAN *Heraclitus Ridens* No. 13 (1713) I. 86 These fruitful Meadows came to be stock'd and under-run with those subterranean Inhabitants, vulgarly called Moles. **1799** W. TOOKE *View Russian Emp.* I. 157 The granite is under-run by schistose earth. **1855** MAURY *Phys. Geog. Sea* i. §14 One part of it underruns the Gulf Stream. **1880** BLACKMORE *Mary Anerley* III. vii. 94 A scowl of dark vapour came over the headlands, and under-ran the solid snow-clouds.
fig. **1882** W. B. WEEDEN *Soc. Law Labor* 68 The principle ..underran all these modifications.
2. *Naut.* **a.** To overhaul or examine (a cable, etc.) on the under side, *spec.* by drawing a boat along under it.
1547 *Admiralty Crt. Oyer & Terminer* 73 No. 21, They toke yᵉ kabyll in the botts hed and under rynned yᵉ kabyll tyll yt was a pyke. **1633** T. JAMES *Voy.* 79 We vnder-run our small Cable. **1667** LD. BROUNCKER *Let. to Pepys* 3 July, Not only in my own opinion is the chain broke,..yet we could nether spare hands nor lighter to underrunn it. **1745** P. THOMAS *Jrnl. Anson's Voy.* 156 They..underran the Cables by which..[the ship] rode. **1798** *Hull Advertiser* 25 Aug. 3/2 The harbour..is..very rocky, the bottom so much so as to make it necessary to under-run every cable. **1834** MARRYAT *P. Simple* viii, Oblige me by under-running the guess warp. **1867** SMYTH *Sailor's Word-bk.* 706.
b. (See quot.)
1769 FALCONER *Dict. Marine* (1780), *To under-run a tackle*, is to separate the several parts of which it is composed, and range them in order, from one block to the other.
c. To pull in (a net or trawl) in order to clear it of the catch and reset it.
1883 JONCAS *Fisheries Canada* 30 As soon as the seals are caught in the meshes, the men under-run the nets. **1897** KIPLING *Capt. Cour.* 101 Underrunning a trawl means pulling it in on one side of the dory, picking off the fish, rebaiting the hooks, and passing them back to the sea again.
3. In *pa. pple.* (See quot. 1855.)
1855 *Jrnl. R. Agric. Soc.* XVI. I. 9 Cut away all hoof that is separated from the sensitive parts, or, as a shepherd would say, as much as is 'under-run'. **1908** *Animal Managem.* 337 Any horn [of an ox-hoof] which is underrun should be removed.
4. *intr.* Of a broadcast programme, item, etc.: to run for less than its allotted time.
1941 *B.B.C. Gloss. Broadcasting Terms* 34 *Underrun*, to fall short of the allotted time (of a programme). **1962** [see OVERRUN *v.* 10 d].
5. Of a car: to run under a larger vehicle in front. Cf. UNDERRUN *sb.* 3.
1972 *Care on Road* (RoSPA) Sept. 9/4 A carefully designed bumper is essential at the rear of every truck. It must be large enough to prevent the car under-running.

ˈunder-ˌrunner. [UNDER-¹ 4 a, b, 10 b.]
1. *Printing.* (See quot. 1888.)
1882 SOUTHWARD *Pract. Printing* (1884) 249 Underrunners..are very unsightly and should be avoided. **1888** JACOBI *Printers' Vocab.*, *Under runners*, continuation of side-notes run under the foot of the page in a similar manner to a foot-note.
2. *Cricket.* A batsman who makes too few runs for his hits.
1903 *Windsor Mag.* Sept. 394/1 Marshall, a confirmed under-runner at the best, was so nervous..that he crawled between the wickets.
3. A subterranean stream. *N.Z.*
1921 H. GUTHRIE-SMITH *Tutira* v. 34 At last there is created a subterranean stream, or, in shepherd's phrase, an 'under-runner'. **1949** F. SARGESON *I saw in my Dream* II. xiv. 211 It had been one of those under-runners, with the opening all grown over with biddy-bid. **1959** *Mother Earth* Jan. 428 On the down (lower) country, the problem is one of water retention rather than erosion, though there are some bad cases of the latter, consisting mainly of 'under-runners'.

ˈunder-ˌrunning, *ppl. a.* (UNDER- 4 a.)
a **1586** SIDNEY *Arcadia* II. xvii, Her teares falling into the water, one might have thought, that she began meltingly to be metamorphosed to the under-running river.

† under-sail, *v.*: see UNDER-¹ 2.

ˌunder-ˈsailed, *ppl. a.* (UNDER-¹ 10 a.)
1594 [see UNDERMASTED *ppl. a.*].

† ˈunder-ˌsaker. *Obs.*⁻¹ [UNDER-¹ 6 b.] A small variety of cannon.
1678 EARL ORRERY in *Cal. Ormonde MSS.* (N.S.) IV. 104 The lesser guns, as sakers and under-sakers.

under-salley: see SALLY *sb.*², quot. 1688.
1668 [STEDMAN] *Tintinnalogia* (1671) 3 Next, that he [a young ringer] know how to Ring Round, or Under-Sally.

ˈunder-satisˌfaction. (UNDER-¹ 6 b.)
1748 RICHARDSON *Clarissa* (1811) II. 65 That a person who has any over-ruling passion, will compound by giving up twenty secondary or under-satisfactions,..in order to have that gratified. **1871** MRS. WHITNEY *We Girls* v. 96 The work was getting on; that was such an undersatisfaction.

underˈsaturated, *ppl. a.* [UNDER-¹ 10 a.]
a. Not saturated, falling short of being saturated; *spec.* (of a solution) not containing as much solute as is possible in equilibrium conditions.
1832 *Nat. Philos.* (Libr. Useful Knowl.) II. v. ii. 13/1 In a deficiency of fluid, or in matter under-saturated [with electric fluid]. **1957** G. E. HUTCHINSON *Treat. Limnol.* I. ix. 592 It appears that the surface of the lake is significantly undersaturated throughout the spring months. **1961** L. MARTIN *Clinical Endocrinol.* (ed. 3) ii. 56 The arterial blood is chronically under-saturated with oxygen. **1973** *Sci. Amer.* Jan. 105/2 When the bases of the clouds are fairly high and there is a thick layer of warm, undersaturated air below them.
b. *Petrol.* Of a rock or magma: containing insufficient free silica (or some other specified oxide) to saturate all the bases present; consisting wholly or partly of undersaturated minerals. Of a mineral: unable to form in the presence of free silica; unsaturated.
1913 S. J. SHAND in *Geol. Mag.* Decade V. x. 510 An undersaturated magma (i.e. one which on solidifying would give rise to a partsaturated or unsaturated rock) is capable of entering into chemical combination with the silica of invaded rock masses. **1947**, etc. [see OVERSATURATED *ppl. a.*]. **1965** G. J. WILLIAMS *Econ. Geol. N.Z.* xi. 168/2 A very fine-grained phonolite or undersaturated trachyte of high soda content. **1983** D. S. BARKER *Igneous Rocks* xi. 259 All xenoliths for which a mantle origin seems likely have been found in silica-undersaturated rocks.

ˌundersatuˈration. [UNDER-¹ 10 b.] The state of being undersaturated.
1913 S. J. SHAND in *Geol. Mag.* Decade V. X. 510 It will also be desirable to distinguish partsaturated rocks..from wholly unsaturated ones; as a general term to cover both partsaturation and unsaturation we may employ *undersaturation.* **1957** G. E. HUTCHINSON *Treat. Limnol.* I. ix. 595 Both supersaturations and undersaturations are likely to be recorded at the time of vernal circulation. **1978** *Nature* 19 Oct. 639/1 Magmas with increasing degrees of undersaturation can be produced only by progressively decreased amounts of partial melting of a peridotitic upper mantle if H_2O is the only volatile component present. **1981** *Jrnl. Chem. Physics* LXXIV. 5243/2 The theory predicts evaporation rates at any degree of undersaturation.

ˈunder-ˌsawyer. [UNDER-¹ 6 a.] A subordinate or inferior person. (Cf. TOP-SAWYER.)
1865 DICKENS *Mut. Fr.* I. xii, There were no top-sawyers, every passenger was an under-sawyer.

† underˈsay, *v. Obs.* [UNDER-¹ 8 a.] *trans.* To say by way of answer.
1579 SPENSER *Sheph. Cal.* Sept. 91 They saye they con to heauen the high way, But by my soule I dare vndersaye, They neuer sette foote in that same troade.

ˈunder-school. [UNDER-¹ 6 b. Cf. MDu. *onderscole.*] A (or the) lower or junior school.
1629 WADSWORTH *Pilgr.* iii. 15 After which time..the Students of the three vnder schooles go vp to those of the vpper. *a* **1633** W. AUSTIN *Medit.* (1635) 226 Such Societies are not Separations from the great Congregation, but parts of it, and as it were so many Vnder-schooles. **1843** THACKERAY *FitzBoodle P., Mr. & Mrs. Berry* i, It was agreed that it [*sc.* the combat] should take place behind the under-school in the shade.

ˈunderscore, *sb.* [UNDER-¹ 4 d.] A line drawn below (a word, etc.).
1901 *Phonetic Jrnl.* 4 May 288/1 The correct way of representing italicized words..is to use the underscore.

under'score, *v.* [UNDER-[1] 4a.] **a.** *trans.* To draw a score or line beneath; to underline.

1771 LUCKOMBE *Hist. Print.* 249 [They] either underscore the word, or make some other token, which may inform the Compositor of the Author's intention. **1838** LYTTON *Alice* XI. v, The notice to Howard, with the name of Vargrave underscored, was still on the panels. **1874** BLACKIE *Self-Cult.* 35 Underscore these distinctly with pen or pencil.

b. *fig.* To point up, to emphasize, to reinforce; = UNDERLINE *v.*[2] 1 b.

1891 W. S. GILBERT *Rosencrantz & G.* III, He who doth so mark, label, and underscore his antic speeches. **1939** *Sun* (Baltimore) 17 Apr. 8/2 A look at the gold statistics underscores the fears which are so often expressed on this score. **1952** S. KAUFFMANN *Philanderer* (1954) iv. 58 He could feel the stupidity of what he was writing being underscored by the stupidity of what was being written in the editorial rooms next door. **1966** D. F. GALOUYE *Lost Perception* iv. 37 Headquarters would not be caught unawares. And, in the interest of underscoring that point, the International Guard detail had been tripled. **1979** *Nature* 13 Sept. 98/1 The near catastrophe this year at the nuclear plant at Three Mile Island, Pennsylvania, has underscored dangers which could arise even in the absence of war. **1984** *Toronto Star* 28 Mar. A 3/1 The report.. underscores the common complaint made by several groups about institutional racism.

Hence **under'scored** *ppl. a.*, **-'scoring** *vbl. sb.*

1751 RICHARDSON *Clarissa* (ed. 3) VII. xcix. 386 You will perhaps, Mr. Walton, wonder at the meaning of the lines drawn under many of the words and sentences (*underscoring* we call it). **1847** KINGLAKE *Eothen* viii. 101 *note*, The underscoring of the word 'ancient', is by the writer of the letter. **1865** *Sat. Rev.* 4 Mar. 243 The underscored passages in the favourite sermon. **1871** LOWELL *Study Wind.* (1886) 165 An emphasis out of place.. reminds one of the underscorings in young ladies' letters. **1941** [see PURPLE *a.* 3]. **1983** *N. & Q.* Apr. 100/2 The use of an emboldening effect for titles makes the volume easier on the eye than does the usual method of underscoring.

'under-scribe. (UNDER-[1] 6a.)

1610 B. JONSON *Alch.* I. ii, No cheating Clim-o' the-Clovghs,.. Nor any melancholike vnder-scribe, Shall tell the Vicar.

†**under'scriber.** *Obs.* [Cf. UNDER-[1] 4a, and older Du. *onderschrijver.*] One whose name is written or given below; a subscriber to a document.

1681 in Grant *Burgh Sch. Scot.* (1876) II. iii. 136 We under-scribers, keepers of Latin Schools, bind and oblige ourselves, that [etc.]. **1687** *Lond. Gaz.* No. 2270/3 In Testification hereof, we Underscribers.. Subscribed as followeth. *c* **1785** J. BROWN (Haddington) *Sel. Rem.* (1807) 235 We under-scribers having formed ourselves into a Society.

'underscrub. [UNDER-[1] 5d.]

1. An undergrown or insignificant person.

1822 *Blackw. Mag.* XI. 362* The less you have to do with the Cockney underscrubs the better.

2. Undergrowth; brushwood.

1870 S. F. PRENTICE *Tale of N.Z.* (MS.) 56 To force a passage through lighter underscrub. **1891** [see FALL *v.* 51 c]. **1894** J. GEIKIE *Gt. Ice Age* (ed. 3) 455 The underscrub being composed chiefly of hazels and occasional birches. **1895** *Daily News* 21 May 6/3 They had been unable to commence cultivation until a clearance had been made of the underscrub.

Hence **'under,scrubbery**, a collection of underscrubs; **'underscrubbing** *vbl. sb. N.Z.*, the cutting down of underscrub.

1851 G. W. CURTIS *Nile Notes* xxv. 116, I saw the Commander assisting the confused crowd of under-scrubbery out of the boat, with his kurbash or whip. **1935** N. R. MCKENZIE *Gael fares Forth* vi. 79 To the younger boys was assigned the task of 'under-scrubbing' or cutting the small trees, shrubs, vines.. and other plants which grow so luxuriantly on the forest floor. **1948** D. L. G. MUNDY *There's Gold in Hills* ix. 83 The under-scrubbing in New Zealand would be done for about 4s. to 5s.

'under-sea, *sb. rare*[−1]. [UNDER-[1] 5b.] An underlying sea.

1621 G. SANDYS *Ovid's Met.* XI. (1626) 220 High Tmolus with a steepe ascent vnfolds His rigid browes, and vnder-seas beholds.

'under-sea, *a.* [UNDER-[2]. Cf. Du. *onderzee-*, G. *untersee-(boot).*]

1. Situated or lying below the sea or the surface of the sea; submarine.

1613 PURCHAS *Pilgrimage* V. xiii. 511 The saltnesse of the sea some ascribe.. to vnder-earth or under-sea fires of bituminous nature. **1851** *Chamb. Jrnl.* 27 Dec. 411 Mr. Wheatstone first conceived the possibility of an under-sea telegraph in 1837. **1861** L. L. NOBLE *Icebergs* 256 The noises of the waves at play in the long, concealed, under-sea piazzas.

2. Intended for use below the surface of the sea.

1901 *Westm. Gaz.* 27 Aug. 5/3 The new submarines will be as good as.. any under-sea vessel yet constructed.

under'sea, *adv.* [UNDER-[2].] Below the sea or its surface.

1684 [see UNDERGROUND *adv.* 1]. **1890** R. BRIDGES *Achilles in Scyros* 2 This rocky isle, That far from undersea riseth to crown Its flowery head above the circling waves.

'underseal, *sb.* Also Underseal. [UNDER-[1] 4d.] A waterproofing material for use as a protective coating on the under-parts of motor vehicles; in the *U.S.*, a proprietary term for a particular brand of this.

1948 *Official Gaz.* (U.S. Patent Office) 14 Sept. 307/2 Minnesota Mining & Manufacturing Company... *Underseal* for rust, corrosion and abrasive resistant rubberized coating material. **1964** *Times* 7 Feb. p. iii/4 The wise motorist, for example, protects his new car with Underseal. **1968** BUSBY & HOLTMAN *Main Line Kill* v. 45 The professionals.. bring it in pasted on the underneath of their cars with underseal. Jacks would never think of stripping off underseal looking for junk. **1973** *Sci. Amer.* Dec. 138/3 (Advt.), Underbody, wheel arches, longitudinal members and the underside of the luggage-compartment floor carry a thick coating of underseal.

'underseal, *v.* [f. prec.: see UNDER-[1] 4a.] *trans.* To coat (the underbody of a vehicle) with waterproof material. Also *absol.* So **'under-sealed** *ppl. a.*, **'undersealing** *vbl. sb.*

1958 *Autocar* 24 Oct. 658/1 Undersealing of cars. **1960** *Farmer & Stockbreeder* 12 Jan. 108/1 Unitary all-steel construction with undersealed bodies gives extra strength and durability. **1961** *Economist* 21 Oct. 252/2 The body is undersealed. **1963** N. FREELING *Gun before Butter* III. 141 He liked to get a car in good condition; he cursed the cheap peeling chrome.. the corner-cutting factories that did not underseal. **1976** *Horse & Hound* 3 Dec. 66/1 (Advt.), These ex-Army Land-Rovers are undersealed from new and have heavy duty chassis, springs and suspension. **1980** *Motoring Which?* July 388/2 *'Rustproofed', 'undersealed'* and 'Ziebarted' were the terms cropping up most frequently.

under'search, *v. rare.* [UNDER-[1] 4a, b, 8a.] To search or seek under or into; to investigate.

1609 DANIEL *Civ. Wars* III. iv, Whil'st th' vnder-searching water, working-on, Beares (proudly) downe, all that was idly don. **1648** HEXHAM II, *Ondertasten*, to Examine, or Vndersearch.

'under-,seated, *ppl. a.* (UNDER-[1] 4a.)

c **1611** CHAPMAN *Iliad* XV. 208 All The under-seated Deities that circle Saturn's fall, Had heard of me.

'under-,secretary. (UNDER-[1] 6a. Cf. G. *untersecretär*, Sw. *undersekreter.*)

Used esp. as the specific title of a secretary immediately subordinate to, or ranking below, a principal secretary of state. ***Parliamentary Under-Secretary (of State)***, a member in a department of State, ranking below a minister: see PARLIAMENTARY *a.* 1; ***Permanent Under-Secretary***: see PERMANENT *a.* 1 d; also used for various other ranks in the administrative civil service, esp. as a title next below *Deputy Secretary*.

1687 MIÈGE I, *Sou-Secretaire*, an Vnder-Secretary. **1692** LUTTRELL *Brief Rel.* (1857) II. 372 Said, Mr. Poultney goes undersecretary to Ireland. **1764** in *10th Rep. Hist. MSS. Comm.* App. I. 376, I have known a great many under-secretaries. **1841** *Penny Cycl.* XXI. 176/2 Each [secretary] is assisted by two under-secretaries of state. **1876** BANCROFT *Hist. U.S.* III. xiii. 191 Consulted through the under-secretaries, Franklin gave advice on the conduct of the.. war. **1904** *Rep. War Office Committee* in *Parl. Papers* 9 (Cd. 1932) VIII. 101 The Council should consist of seven members—four military and three civil—with the Permanent Under-Secretary as Secretary. **1917** G. BELL *Let.* 20 July (1927) II. xvi. 420, I wish you would go and see Sir A. Hirtzel, the Permanent Under-Secretary. **1959** C. DIXON *Civil Service* v. 47 The Administrative Class is the top Class of the Civil Service. Direct entrants come in as Assistant Principals and then proceed by promotion to Principal; the next grades are Assistant Secretary and Under-Secretary (or Assistant Under-Secretary in some departments). **1980** KELLNER & CROWTHER-HUNT *Civil Servants* vii. 167 By the time a civil servant is ripe to join the highest ranks of the Service—Under Secretary, Deputy Secretary and Permanent Secretary—he needs to have acquired certain qualities. *Ibid.* 170 Where Assistant Secretaries handle the details of specific issues, Under Secretaries supervise wide areas of policy.

Hence **'under-,secretaryship.**

1687 MIÈGE *Gt. Fr. Dict.* II. **1859** LEVER *Dav. Dunn* lxiii, He might.. mayhap have held some Lordship of This or Under-Secretaryship of That.

'under-sect. (UNDER-[1] 6b.)

1653 JER. TAYLOR *Serm. for Year* I. xxii. 277 The whole religion which.. hath been rent into innumerable sects, and under-sects. **1682** T. FLATMAN *Heraclitus Ridens* No. 65, What the Under-sects might have claim'd upon the score of their wanting Opportunity only.. to do Mischief.

'under-,seedman. (UNDER-[1] 6a.)

1615-6 BOYS *Wks.* (1622) 203 The Preacher is not properly the sower, but the seedcod, at most an vnderseedman.

†**under'seek**, *v. Obs.* Also 4 onderzeke. [OE. *undersécan* (see UNDER- 8a and SEEK *v.*), = OLFrank. *undersuocan* (Du. *onderzoeken*), MHG. *undersuochen* (G. *untersuchen*), Sw. *undersöka*, Da. *-søge.*] *trans.* To search into; to investigate; to seek out.

c **897** K. ÆLFRED *Gregory's Past. C.* xiii. 79 Ðæt is ðæt hie ðara ðing ðe him underðiodde bioð.. inweardlice undersece. **13..** *Guy Warw.* (A.) 1838 Wiþ þat come Sadok prikeing, þe douke Segyn vnder-secheing. **1340** *Ayenb.* 184 Huo þet heþ þise yefþe, he onderzekþ þe redes þet me him yefþ, and þengþ mid greate beþenchinge.. yef me him ret wel.

under'sell, *v.* [UNDER-[1] 8b, 10a. Cf. Da. *undersælge*, Sw. *-sälja.*]

1. *trans.* To sell at a lower price than (another person); to cut out by selling at a lower rate.

1622 MALYNES *Anc. Law-Merch.* 230 The striuing of making commodities, and to vndersel one another, are dangerous. **1677** YARRANTON *Eng. Improv.* 115 Whereby the Manufacture is always cheaply done, and thereby hath the advantage of sending it to foreign Markets, and under-sell others. **1713** *Mercator* No. 9/1 The French being able to Underwork us will also Undersell us. **1799** J. ROBERTSON *Agric. Perth* 213 The price of labour will become so enormous that we shall soon be undersold in every market. **1849-50** ALISON *Hist. Eur.* XIV. xcv. §96. 192 England, which can easily undersell India in cotton manufacture,.. finds its cultivators undersold by Poland and America with grain. **1884** *Law Times Rep.* 31 May 421/1 The defendants are selling cheaper materials and underselling the plaintiffs.

b. *transf.* (Said of the thing sold.)

1757 *Refl. Importation Bar-Iron* 12 The American Iron will always greatly undersell the British at Market. **1792** A. YOUNG *Trav. France* 262 England buys the French cotton, and works it into fabrics that undersell those of France.

2. To sell (a commodity) at too low a price. Also *fig.*

1647 N. WARD *Simple Cobler* 47 Just it is that such as undersell them, should not re-inherit them in haste. **1662** PETTY *Taxes* 20 The farmer for haste is forced to under-sell his corn. **1692** LYTTELTON in *Hatton Corr.* (Camden) II. 169 As to my pictures,.. I doubt those of more esteeme will not be very ready money, unlesse mitily undersold. **1817** MILL *Brit. India* II. v. iv. 469 They accused the Presidency of underselling the lands. **1854** PATMORE *Angel in Ho., Betrothal* 99 But lofty honours undersold Seller and buyer both disgrace.

Hence **under'seller**; **under'selling** *vbl. sb.* and *ppl. a.*

1672 PETTY *Pol. Anat.* (1691) 75 The Interest must enflame the price of Irish Commodities, and consequently give to other Nations the means of underselling. **1842** J. F. WATSON *Ann. Pennsylv.* (1877) I. 242 All prices were alike; ..there was no motive to run about town to seek out undersellers. **1863** WYNTER *Subtle Brains*, etc. 377 The under-seller, however, manages to turn out from ninety-four to ninety-six [loaves]. **1899** *Westm. Gaz.* 16 Feb. 2/3 We doubt if the underselling foreigner could be kept out by such artificial manipulations of the market.

'under-sense. (UNDER-[1] 9.)

1805 WORDSW. *Prelude* VII. 735 To him who looks In steadiness, who hath among least things An under-sense of greatest. **1859** D. MASSON *Brit. Novelists* i. 60 Apart from the allegoric undersense.. the romance is praised as a really interesting story.

'under-,sequence. (UNDER-[1] 6b.)

1863 'CAVENDISH' *Whist* (ed. 5) 19 Sequences which do not head a suit in a hand are called under sequences. *Ibid.* 24 When an under sequence is formed by intermediate cards.

'under-,servant. (UNDER-[1] 6a.)

1548 ELYOT, *Subministrator*, an vnder seruaunt. **1630** tr. *Camden's Hist. Eliz.* IV. 132 One of the ordinary sort of men, ..hauing beene.. an vnder-seruant in the Queenes stable. **1679** BP. CROFT *Coll. Jesuits* 3 The remaining Dwellers in the House.. were but Under-Servants. **1768** *Phil. Trans.* LIX. 10 An under-servant in a gentleman's kitchen. **1809** MALKIN *Gil Blas* III. iii. ¶4 The steward.. loves to see the under-servants creeping and crawling at his feet. **1871** W. ALEXANDER *Johnny Gibb* xlv, I ken my place better nor be forespoken by ony oon'er-servan'.

under'serve, *v.* [UNDER-[1] 8a, 10a. Cf. *underserve* s.v. UNDER-[1] 2.]

†**1.** To be subservient (to). *Obs.*

1611 SPEED *Hist. Gt. Brit.* IX. vii. §1 Things which did but onely vnder-serue, and conduce to the.. principall end.

2. To serve insufficiently.

1710 PALMER *Proverbs* 147 He, that over-works a servant to day, must be content to be under-serv'd to morrow.

'under-,service. [UNDER-[1] 6b.] Service of an inferior kind; subordinate service.

1598 FLORIO, *Sumministratione*, a subministration,.. an vnderseruice. **1641** MILTON *Ch. Govt.* II. Wks. 1851 III. 149 But were it the meanest under-service, if God by his Secretary conscience injoyn it, it were sad for me if I should draw back. **1760-72** H. BROOKE *Fool of Qual.* (1809) III. 4 Will you not suffer a sister.. who may assist in the under-services to the servants of our Master?

'underset, *sb.* [UNDER-[1] 5b, 6a.]

†**1.** *Sc.* = UNDERSETTLE. *Obs. rare.*

1509 *Reg. Privy Seal Scotl.* 285/1 To be haldin and to be had to him and his assignais,.. subtenentis and undersettis under thaim in all or in parte. *Ibid.* 288/1.

2. *Mining.* A lower vein of ore.

1747 HOOSON *Miner's Dict.* S 2 b, These Levells are called Sets, as the first is the Top-Set, the second which is found out by Sinking through the Deadness, is called the Under-Set.

3. An undercurrent. (See first quot.)

1815 BURNEY *Falconer's Marine Dict.*, *Under-set*, a motion of the water beneath the surface, produced by the wind impelling the upper part directly upon the shore of a bay, whereby the water.. necessarily takes a direction contrary to the wind,.. below the surface. **1867** SMYTH *Sailor's Word-bk.* 706 The *resaca*, or underset, is particularly dangerous on those beaches where heavy surf prevails.

under'set, *v.* [UNDER-[1] 4a, etc. Cf. MDu. *ondersetten* (Du. *-zetten*), MLG. *undersetten*, MHG. *undersetzen* (G. *unter-*), MDa. *undersætte.*]

1. *trans.* To support or strengthen by means of something (esp. of the nature of a post or prop) placed beneath; to prop up.

c **1220** *Bestiary* 640 Ðe hunte haueð biholden ðis,.. Saȝeð ðis tre and under-set, o ðe wise ðat he mai bet. *a* **1225** *Ancr. R.* 254 A treou þet wule uallen, me underset hit mid on oðer treou, & hit stont feste. **13..** *Seuyn Sages* (W.) 2101 We schulle the ymage so undersette, That we ne schal hit nothing lette. **1398** TREVISA *Barth De P.R.* XVII. clxiv. (Bodl. MS.), Ofte it nedeþ to vndersette it wiþ a pelere or a poste. *c* **1425** *St. Eliz. of Spalbeck* in *Anglia* VIII. 115/28 Hir sistres.. lifte vp and vndir-sette hir.. wiþ two piloues.

1477–9 *Rec. St. Mary at Hill* (1905) 90, ij postes of tymbir to vndirsette the kechyng. **1513** MORE *Rich. III* (1883) 9 The kynge liftinge vppe himself and vndersette with pillowes. **1555** WATREMAN *Fardle Facions* II. x. 214 Thei make theim..rounde cotages of wickres, or of Felte vndersette with smothe poles. **1600** SURFLET *Countrie Farme* I. x. 48 He shall prepare props..to vnder set his vines. **1678** [BP. J. WILLIAMS] *Hist. Gunp. Treason* 22 A Bag of Powder..that they underset the Pan with. **1841** *Civil Eng. & Arch. Jrnl.* IV. 379/1 The base..has been underset with two pillars of solid masonry. **1842** FRANCIS *Dict. Arts* s.v., The Custom House, London, was underset some years ago, a new foundation having been made to it without the superstructure being disturbed.

absol. **1538** in *Lett. Suppression Monast.* (Camden) 181, x of them hewed the walles abowte, amonge the whych ther were 3 carpentars: thiese made proctes to undersette wher the other cutte away.

b. To serve as a support to. Also *absol. rare.*

c **1330** R. BRUNNE *Chron. Wace* (Rolls) 284 Þe hil was so hey, as men hit leet [*v.r.* lette], þat heuen (men seye) hit vnder-feet [*v.r.* vnder sette]. *c* **1400** *Lanfranc's Cirurg.* 110 Þo boonys þat vndir setten ben clepid ossa mendosa. **1609** DANIEL *Civ. Wars* VIII. xxvi, She had of fatall Lancaster Seene all the pillars crusht and ruined, That vnder-set it.

†**c.** To support or sustain by assistance. *Obs.*

1388 WYCLIF *Eccl.* iv. 10 If oon fallith doun, he schal be vndurset [L. *fulcietur*] of the tothere. **1398** TREVISA *Barth. De P.R.* XII. ix. (Tollem. MS.), Whan þe fader and þe moder wexeþ olde and feble, þan þe ȝonge crowes under-setteþ hem and rereþ hem with hire owen wynges.

d. To act upon, furnish, fasten, etc., with something placed beneath. *rare.*

a **1547** SURREY *Æneid* II. 50 Capys..wild it to drown, or vnderset with flame The suspect present of the Grekes deceit. **1599** *Minutes Archdeaconry Colchester* (MS.) fol. 238 He and they did vndersett the churchdore. *c* **1618** MORYSON *Itin.* IV. 381 The ringe of her dore is all Couered with tape or linnen cloth (and in some places vndersett with a small sticke).

2. *fig.* To support, sustain, or strengthen.

1395 PURVEY *Remonstr.* (1851) 86 Bi here owne statute,.. vndirset with ful strong oth and peynis. *a* **1470** H. PARKER *Dives & Pauper* (W. de W. 1496) A v b/2 Whan youth is vndersette with richesse, & is at his owne rule without drede of punysshyng. **1538** TINDALE *Exp. 1st Ep. John* v. 72 Yf oure soules be truely vnderset wyth sure hope. **1579** W. WILKINSON *Confut. Fam. Love* 38 Vnles the Lord vnderset them, their fall is..greeuous. **1605** RALEIGH *Introd. Hist. Eng.* (1693) 74 Our most renowned Kings have been best underset with Counsel. **1670** CUDWORTH *Serm. 1 John* ii. 3–4 (ed. 2) 185 If we would but vnderset it [truth] with the Holinesse of our Hearts. **1871** L. MORRIS *Songs Two Worlds, Wand. Soul* xxxiii, The archetypes which underset the world With one broad perfect Law.

3. To set or place (a thing) under something else.

a **1340** HAMPOLE *Psalter* xxxvi. 25 When a rightwis has fallen he sall not be hurt, for lord vndirsettis his hand. **1388** WYCLIF *Gen.* xlix. 15 Isachar..vndirsettide his schuldre to bere. **1535** COVERDALE *1 Kings* vii. 30 Vpon the foure corners there were proppes molten,..vnderset vnto the kettell. **1587** GOLDING *De Mornay* xxi. 376 Iulian the Apostata did vnderset his shoulder, to shore vp the seruice of the false Gods. **1611** SPEED *Hist. Gt. Brit.* VI. xxiii. §9. 113 His monyes, whereon he sometimes formed a Trophy.. vndersetting the word Vict. Brit. **1898** E. GLANVILLE *Kloof Bride* xvii, While Miles pressed the rock forward, Hans kept it from swinging back by undersetting a stone.

†**b.** To place in subjection. *Obs.*[−1]

1422 YONGE *Secreta Secret.* 146 If þou wilt submyt or vndreset al thyngis to the, submyt thy-selfe to reysone.

†**4.** *Sc.* To beset. *Obs.*[−1]

c **1470** HENRY *Wallace* IX. 796 With Sotheroun sone we sall be wndirset.

5. To sublet.

1804 MAR. EDGEWORTH *Ennui* viii, These middle-men will underset the land, and live in idleness.

Hence **'underset** *ppl. a.*

1833–4 J. PHILLIPS *Geol.* in *Encycl. Metrop.* (1845) VI. 588 In Swaledale the united thickness of the underset chert and underset lime..is nearly constant. **1865** LIVINGSTONE *Zambesi* xvii. 344 It contrives to pop its underset mouth directly over the unlucky victim.

under'setter. [f. UNDERSET *v.*] One who or that which supports or upholds. Also *fig.*

c **1400** *Lanfranc's Cirurg.* 110 Þe whiche þat beþ vndire-setterys to þo bonys þat beþ y-clepyde *nerualia.* *c* **1430** *Pilgr. Lyf Manhode* II. cxxvi. (1869) 123 J am to orguill an vnder-settere and a susteynour by especial. **1537** BIBLE (Matthew's) *1 Kings* vii. 30 In yᵉ foure corners were vndersetters vnder the lauatorye. **1651** N. BACON *Disc. Govt. Eng.* II. vi. 60 Outward Power, and Honourable places, are but under-setters, or props to this Gourd of Prelacy. **1697** JOS. WOODWARD *Relig. Soc.* ii. (1701) 28 Undersetters, whom gain and the promises of court-favour had brought over to their party.

under'setting, *vbl. sb.* [f. as prec.]

1. A support or prop; a supporting or sustaining structure. Also *fig.*

1388 WYCLIF *Ezek.* xli. 26 In the litle vndursettyngis of the porche. *c* **1440** *Promp. Parv.* 448/1 Schore, undur settynge of a thynge þat wolde falle, *suppositorium.* **1587** GOLDING *De Mornay* ix. 149 Their opinion was, that God was afore the World, howbeit not in time, but in order and by way of vndersetting only. **1624** WOTTON *Archit.* 32 They haue all their Vnder-settings, or Pedistals, in height a third part of the whole Columne. **1841** *Penny Cycl.* XIX. 253/1 The rock was supported by an under-setting of masonry.

2. The action of placing under, or of supporting by something placed under; underpinning.

c **1440** *Promp. Parv.* 511/2 Vndersettynge, *idem quod* vnderputtynge. **1598** FLORIO, *Soggiontione*, an vndersetting or ioining vnderneath. **1842** FRANCIS *Dict. Arts, Under-setting*, the supporting a wall or edifice..after the lower part has been removed.

'under,settle. *Obs.* exc. *Hist.* Also 3 -setle, 5 *Sc.* undirsettill, -sedell, wndersedyll, 6 *Sc.* vndersittell. [f. UNDER-[1] 6 a + *-settle, -setle*, repr. OE. *-setla* (see COTSETLA), f. *set-*, root of SIT *v.*] One who occupies a house (or part of one) held by another; a subtenant.

1235–52 *Rentalia Glaston.* (Somerset Rec. Soc.) 108 Si famulus vel famula vel undersetles venerint, quisque dabit ob. per diem. **1326** in *Court Baron* (Selden Soc.) 146 [Strangers coming from without, who hire houses from divers persons and hold nothing of the lord,..called] Undersettles. **1476** *Peebles Burgh Rec.* (1872) 178 Grantand to..George Robyson fwll power to mak rasonabyll tenandis and wnder-sedyllis. **1480** *Exchequer Rolls Scotl.* IX. 30 De dicto loco de Farnele de anno elapso pro uno undirsettill,.. xx s. **1510** in C. Rogers *Coldstream Chartul.* (1879) 58 With power to mak subtenentis and vndersittellis. **1607** *N. Riding Rec.* (1884) I. 95 Leon. Marshall of Ravensworth [presented] for keeping an undersettle for the space of a moneth. **1612** *Ibid.* 266 John Herdman..for keeping an undersettle in the house wherein one Will. Dynnis now dwelleth. **1781–** *Parish Terriers, Welton* (Yks.), For every messuage or cottage.. six pence and for every under-settle three pence.

So **'under,settler; 'under,settling** *vbl. sb.* and *ppl. a.*

1576 *E. Worsely's MS. Surv. Mannor of Felsted, Essex* 47 It was granted to one John Lord..by vertue of a coppy of undersetling made thereof to the said John. *Ibid.* 147 Every tenant customary commonly called an Undersetling tenant. **1794** W. HUTCHINSON *Hist. Cumbld.* I. 163 *note*, The tenants are subject to pains..for taking in inmates or undersettlers.

'under-,sewer. (UNDER-[1] 6 a.)

1669 *Lond. Gaz.* No. 414/2 Segnior Potoski the under Sewer to the Crown.

under-'sexed, *a.* [UNDER-[1] 10 a.] Having a lesser degree of sexual desire than the average; lacking in sexual feelings or desire, uninterested in sexual gratification.

1931 J. S. HUXLEY *What dare I Think?* ii. 61 Grafts and extracts of the reproductive glands have been used successfully in under-sexed cases. **1947** 'N. BLAKE' *Minute for Murder* ix. 207 Alice simply wouldn't understand the feeling of all-for-love. She's madly civilised. And she's under-sexed. **1965** *Mod. Law Rev.* XXVIII. v. 606 To use the words of the learned judge, 'the husband was undersexed'. **1972** H. J. EYSENCK *Psychology is about People* ii. 88 The introvert..is slightly 'under-sexed', but again not unhealthily so.

'under-,sexton. (UNDER-[1] 6 a.)

c **1450** [see UNDER-CHAMBRESS]. **1722** DE FOE *Plague* (1756) 105 Under-Sexton of the Parish of St. Stephen... By Under-Sexton, was understood at that Time Grave-digger and Bearer of the Dead. **1829** LYTTON *Devereux* II. ii, I was ..the under-sexton of St. Paul's, Covent-Garden.

†**undershad,** *pa. pple. Obs.* [UNDER-[1] 4 a; the second element may be *shod.*] Faced at the bottom.

1528 *Lett. & Pap. Hen. VIII*, IV. II. 2228 The brayes about the towne [Calais] to be mended and heythed and under shadd with stone or brike.

'under,shapen, *ppl. a.* [UNDER-[1] 10 a.] Insufficiently or imperfectly formed.

1859 TENNYSON *Enid* 412 His dwarf, a vicious under-shapen thing, Struck at her with his whip.

'under-,shepherd. (UNDER-[1] 6 a.)

1636 MASSINGER *Bashful Lover* III. i, I am no glutton, but an under-shepherd. **1669** PENN *No Cross* xii. §8 [The Clergy] could be but Ministers, Stewards, and Under-Shepherds. *a* **1711** KEN *Hymnotheo* Poet. Wks. 1721 III. 385 Each Pastor,..Choice Under-Shepherds carefully ordain'd. **1826** MISS MITFORD *Village* Ser. III. (1863) 468 He had a pet sheep-dog, (for..he occasionally acted as under-shepherd). **1876** S. C. J. INGHAM *White Cross*, etc. xlvii, [The rector] had little idea of the true motive power which sustained his under-shepherd.

'under,sheriff. Forms: (see SHERIFF). [UNDER-[1] 6 a: cf. SHERIFF 2.] A deputy sheriff.

α. **1431** in Raine *Scriptores tres* (Surtees) App. p. ccxxi, Ye shall noon hafe to be your undershireve or clerk that was undershyreve or any of the Shyreves clerkes the last yere passed. **1452–3** *Paston Lett.* Suppl. (1901) 48 He schall non undirshireve, ne non othir officer make. **1535** COVERDALE *1 Esdras* vi. 7 The vnder shreue in Syria and Phenices. **1558** in Strype *Eccl. Mem.* (1721) III. lxii. 457 The officers of this town..and the undershereve. **1631** LENTON *Charact.* G 3 b, An Vndershriefe..is the feare and terror of all debtors. *a* **1658** CLEVELAND *Poems, Young Man to Old Wom.* 35 Like Aldermen, or Under-shrieves With Canvas Backs, and Velvet-Sleeves.

β. **1444** *Rolls of Parlt.* V. 108/1 No Sherryff, ne Under Shereff, ne Clerk of the Sherryff. **1501** *Plumpton Corr.* (Camden) 159 Which Inpanell the sayd William Rossell had of the underschereffe of Nottingham. **1589** R. PAYNE *Briefe Descr. Ireland* 5 There is a sheriffe of euerie countie, with vndersheriffes. **1632** MASSINGER *City Madam* V. ii, An Under-sheriffe,..being well paid, will serve An extent on Lords or Lowns land. **1665** *Extr. St. Papers Friends* Ser. III. (1912) 240 The Bishop of Durham..nominates both high sheriffs and under sheriffs. **1723** in Harris *Life Ld. Hardwicke* (1847) I. 130 He made a speech at the gallows, and delivered a paper to the undersheriff. **1769** WESLEY *Jrnl.* 13 July, The Under-Sheriff had promised the use of the Town-hall. **1835** *App. Munic. Corpor. Rep.* III. 1991 (Nottingham), Officers of the corporation..[include] Two Sheriffs. An Under-Sheriff, who is also Steward. **1877** BURROUGHS *Taxation* 327 The under-sheriff cannot perform the duties of collector.

Hence **undersheriffry, undersheriffship, undersheriffwick,** the office of an undersheriff.

a **1613** OVERBURY *A Wife*, etc. (1638) M 7 b, His honesty and learning bring him to Under-Shriveship. **1620** J. WILKINSON *Coroners & Sherifes* 50 All emoluments..to the office of sherifwicke or undersherifwicke belonging. **1625** BACON *Ess., Praise* (Arb.) 357 The Cardinals of Rome..call all Temporall..Emploiments, *Sbirrerie*; which is, Vnder Sheriffries;..Though many times, those Vndersheriffieries doe more good, then their High Speculations. [**1666** BP. PARKER *Platonic Philos.* 17 Being raised above the little concernments and under-Shreiveries of this life (as the Cardinals of Rome are pleased to stile all secular employments).] **1782** BURKE *Let. Penal Laws Rom. Cath.* Wks. 1792 III. 527 The exclusion from the law,..from sheriff-ships, and under-sheriff-ships. **1845** LD. CAMPBELL *Chancellors* I. 512 He declined a handsome pension.., which he could not hold without resigning his under-sheriffship.

under'shine, *v.* [UNDER-[1] 4 c.] *trans.* To shine from below.

1844 MRS. BROWNING *A Portrait* 11 A forehead fair and saintly, Which two blue eyes undershine.

'under,shining, *ppl. a.* [UNDER-[1] 7.] Of inferior brightness.

1581 MULCASTER *Positions* xxxviii. 174 We haue besides her highnes as vndershining starres, many singuler ladies.

'undershirt. (UNDER-[1] 5 a. Cf. NFris. *onnersjürt*, Da. *underskjorte*, Sw. *-skjorta*.)

1648 HEXHAM II, *Een Onder-hemde*, an Vnder-shirt. **1856** EMERSON *Eng. Traits, Aristocr.*, Older than all epics and histories, which clothe a nation, this undershirt sits close to the body. **1903** S. BROWN in F. W. H. Myers *Hum. Personality* I. 38 There was a sum of money in an inside pocket of his undershirt.

undershoe(ing: see UNDERSOLING.

†**undershoot,** *a. Obs. rare.* = UNDERSHOT *a.* 1.

1602 CAREW *Surv. Cornwall* I. 26 b, So the imprisoned water payeth the ransome of dryuing an vnder-shoote wheele for his enlargement. **1678** *Patent Office* No. 208. 1 To Retayne Back Water of all sorts of Mills and..to make Vndershoote to serve Overshoote Mills.

,under'shoot, *v.* [UNDER-[1] 10 a.] **1.** *trans.* and *intr.* To shoot short (of) or too low (for). Also *fig.*, esp. of financial performance.

a **1661** FULLER *Worthies, Lincoln.* II. (1662) 151, I believe they overshoot the Mark, who make it a Miracle, they undershoot it who make it Magick. **1874** J. W. LONG *Amer. Wild-fowl.* i. 24 The rib should be..sufficiently elevated at breech to prevent under-shooting. **1883** *Cent. Mag.* Aug. 492/1 The sportsman of unsteady nerve..is apt to undershoot. **1885** HORNADAY *2 Yrs. in Jungle* xviii. 199, I.. fired at his temple... Fool that I was, I undershot the brain because the elephant was below me. **1977** *Daily Tel.* 10 Mar. 21 Evidence that the public sector borrowing requirement is still firmly under control with only a month of the current financial year to go has added to signs that the money supply is also going to undershoot even the lower end of the target range. **1982** *Times* 23 Apr. 21/3 The public sector borrowing requirement in the financial year just ended undershot the Government's original estimate.

2. *trans.* and *intr.* Of an aircraft or pilot: to fail to reach (a designated landing-point) while attempting to land. Cf. OVERSHOOT *v.* 1 d.

1918 W. G. MCMINNIES *Pract. Flying* v. 79 If he sees that he is going to undershoot, it is a good plan to make another circuit. **1938** *Sun* (Baltimore) 8 Jan. 3/2 He undershot storm-swept Newark airport. **1947** A. C. DOUGLAS *Gliding & Adv. Soaring* 68 If you are still high, wait a bit before turning round into wind, but it is always better to come in slightly high and then do gentle S turns into wind, than undershoot. **1969** *Gloss. Aeronaut. & Astronaut. Terms (B.S.I.)* II. 4 *Undershoot*, to land, or to follow an approach path which would cause an aircraft to land, short of the intended area.

Hence **under'shooting** *vbl. sb.*

1928 B. STUDLEY *Pract. Flight Training* xxiv. 293 Undershooting is always to be avoided. **1982** *Age* (Melbourne) 3/1 The Treasurer..also outlined 'savings' of $361 million made by the Government on earlier appropriation bills..because of normal undershooting of Budget outlay targets.

'undershoot, *sb.* [f. the vb.: cf. OVERSHOOT *sb.*] The action or result of the vb.; *spec.* in *Electronics*, a small variation in signal immediately before, and in the opposite direction to, a sudden (larger) change.

1934 in WEBSTER. **1938** [see *power approach* s.v. POWER *sb.*[1] 18]. **1956** AMOS & BIRKINSHAW *Television Engin.* II. i. 26 (*caption*) Waveform of a pulse with undershoot of the leading and trailing edges. **1959** *Listener* 26 Feb. 371/1 The score now stands at two undershoots by the United States to one powerful drive by the Russians. **1969** [see OVERSHOOT *sb.*]. **1978** *Nature* 12 Oct. 550/1 One of them is a progressive rise in time of the overshoot and under-shoot (for spikes following the first) amplitudes with nearly constant firing level. **1982** *Times* 23 Apr. 23/7 When one allows for the adverse impact on Government resources of the civil servants' dispute, the undershoot is larger still.

under'shore, *v.* [UNDER-[1] 4 a. Cf. Du. and Flem. *onderschoren.*]

1. *trans.* To prop up; to support or strengthen with shores. Also in fig. context.

1393 LANGL. *P. Pl.* C. XIX. 47 Ne were hit vnder-shored, certes hit sholde nat stande. *c* **1440** *Promp. Parv.* 511/1 Vndersettyn, or vnderschoryn, *fulcio, suffulcio.* **1532** MORE *Confut. Tindale* III. Wks. 473/2 He sheweth himself as wise, as one that lest hys rotten house should fall, wold..pull vp ye groundsel to vndershore the sides with the same. **1583** H.

HOWARD *Defensative* B iij b, A sillye proppe to vndershore the ruines of olde Adams walles. **1608** TOPSELL *Serpents* 72 To vnder-shore the ruinous walls. **1726** LEONI *Alberti's Archit.* II. 129 Undershore it with Levers made of strong beams. **1867** SMYTH *Sailor's Word-bk.* 706 *To undershore*, to support or raise a thing by putting a spar or prop under it.

2. *fig.* To support, strengthen, sustain.

c **1500** MEDWALL *Nature* (Brandl) 327 Yf ye wyll vndershore Hys croked old age. **1571** GOLDING *Calvin on Ps.* xxxvii. 34 The faithful..being undershored by him should not suffer themselves too bee drawen hither and thither. **1610** HEALEY *St. Aug. Citie of God* XVIII. xl. 729 The cittizens of Babilon..know not which to beleeue. But we haue a diuine historie to vnder-shore vs. **1665** BUNYAN *Holy Citie* Pref. p. iv, Here is neither paint to adorn thy wrinkled face, nor Crutch to uphold or undershore thy shaking, tottering, staggering Kingdom of Rome.

'under-ˌshortening, *vbl. sb.* (UNDER-[1] 4 a.)

1814 *Monthly Mag.* XXXVIII. 212 The higher the eye above the level of the mirror, the greater is the under-shortening. **1815** *Ibid.* LXXVI. 120 Under-shortening is to be acquired only by fatiguing discipline.

'undershot, (*ppl.*) *a.* (and *sb.*). [UNDER-[1] 4 a.]

1. Driven by water passing under.

undershot wheel, a water-wheel turned by force of water acting on the lower part of the wheel. ***undershot mill***, a mill worked by an undershot wheel.

1610 R. VAUGHAN *Water-Workes* P 3, To plant an vnder-shot-mil vpon a Riuer. **1660** R. D'ACRES *Art Water-drawing* 28 The close bucketted wheels..are of three sorts, the close bucketted under-shot, which receive their charge below [etc.]. **1759** *Phil. Trans.* LI. 125 The undershot-wheel was taken off the axis, and..an overshot wheel..was put into its place. **1805** BREWSTER *Ferguson's Lect.* I. 81 Water mills are divided into breast mills, undershot mills, and overshot mills. **1872** H. W. BEECHER *Lect. Preaching* viii. 149 If you have a great, full strong stream,.. then the wheel is made under-shot.

b. *sb.* An undershot wheel or mill.

1705 S. CARPENTER *Let.* in Penn & Logan *Corr.* (1870) I. 233 After it has passed through the saw-mill it comes to the corn-mill, an undershot, and grinds very well. **1759** *Phil. Trans.* LI. 137 All those that receive the impulse or shock of the water, whether in an horizontal, perpendicular, or oblique direction, are to be considered as undershots.

2. Having the lower jaw or teeth projecting beyond the upper; underhung.

1881 V. SHAW *Bk. Dog* 39 *Undershot*, the lower incisor teeth projecting beyond the upper, as in Bulldogs. **1884** *Live Stock Jrnl.* Aug. 130 The second prize-winner is leggy, with straight shoulders, not good face, and is undershot.

† under'shred, *v. Obs.*$^{-0}$ [UNDER-[1] 4 a.] *trans.* To cut away below.

1545 ELYOT, *Subluco*, to vndershreade boughes, that the lyght may come vnder the tree.

'under,shrievalty. [UNDER-[1] 6 b.] The office of an undersheriff; undersheriffship.

1836 SMART. (Hence in later Dicts.)

undershrieve(ry, varr. UNDERSHERIFF(RY.

'undershrub. [UNDER-[1] 5 d.] A small or low-growing shrub; *spec.* in *Bot.*, a plant having a shrubby base. (Cf. SUBSHRUB.)

1598 FLORIO, *Soffrutice*, any maner of vndershrub. **1633** FORD *'Tis Pity* v. iii, If I must totter like a well-growne Oake, Some vnder shrubs shall in my weighty fall Be crusht to splitts. **1658** ROWLAND tr. *Moufet's Theat. Ins.* 1086 Indeed every shrub and under-shrub is eaten by Worms. **1718** OZELL tr. *Tournefort's Voy.* I. 173 The Stalk..is full of Branches from the very bottom, ligneous, and comes to be an Under-Shrub. **1731** MILLER *Gard. Dict.* s.v. *Abrotanum*, It is used in Gardens as an Under-shrub. **1794** G. ADAMS *Nat. & Exp. Philos.* I. x. 429 At last the under-shrubs and trees put forth in their order. **1830** LINDLEY *Nat. Syst. Bot.* 57 *Halorageæ*... Herbaceous plants or under-shrubs, often growing in wet places. **1897** J. E. WILLIS *Flower. Pl. & F.* I. 165 Such low-growing shrubby plants as heather..are termed undershrubs.

Hence **'under,shrubby** *a.* (Cf. SUBSHRUBBY.)

1777 S. ROBSON *Brit. Flora* 117 Wild-thyme Cistus. Stem undershrubby, leaves oblong. **1786** ABERCROMBIE *Gard. Assist.* 189 The young side shoots of under-shrubby evergreens.

undershut, *ppl. a.* [UNDER-[1] 4 a, 10 a.]

† 1. Imperfectly shut. *Obs.*$^{-1}$

1632 J. HAYWARD tr. *Biondi's Eromena* 17 So vigilant was the villanous Prodotima, who (expecting him, with the doore under-shut) suddenly leade him the way in.

2. *Mech.* (See quot.)

1875 KNIGHT *Dict. Mech.* 2680/2 *Under-shut-valve*, one placed beneath the sole-plate of a pump or other object, and not upon it; shutting underneath by an upward motion.

'underside. Also under-side, under side. [UNDER-[1] 5 b and UNDER *a.* 2 b. Cf. Du. *onderzijde*, Da. *underside*, G. *unterseite*.]

1. The under or lower side or surface.

α. **1680** MOXON *Mech. Exerc.* x. 190 A Seat..having an Iron Pin fastned on either end the underside of it. **1704** *Phil. Trans.* XXV. 1625 The back or underside of the Leaves. **1768–74** TUCKER *Lt. Nat.* (1834) II. 459, I cannot conceive that surface separated from the table without an underside distinguishable from the upper. **1802** JAMES *Milit. Dict.* s.v. *Gun-carriage*, The underside of the gun. **1890** *Science-Gossip* XXVI. 215/1 The under-side of the wings was a blackish-brown.

fig. **1866** GEO. ELIOT *Ess.* (1884) 321 Comfort, which is the under-side or lining of all pleasure. **1876** *Fortn. Rev.* Jan. 108 Fear is the underside or wrong side of zeal.

β. **1738** CHAMBERS *Cycl.* s.v. *Subscapularis*, Spreading itself under the whole convex, or under side of it. **1794** W. CURTIS in *Bot. Mag.* VIII. 272 The blossoms have been of a sulphur colour, shaded..especially on the under side. **1835** J. DUNCAN *Beetles* 169 The legs and under side of the abdomen are reddish yellow. **1884** BOWER & SCOTT *De Bary's Phaner.* 476 At a greater distance from the stem the under side usually has the advantage.

2. *Comb.* **underside-couching,** a form of couching (COUCH *v.* 4 b) in which the couched thread is drawn through the fabric to the underside by each of the couching stitches (cf. *surface couching* s.v. SURFACE *sb.* 6 d); also **underside-couched** *a.*

1936 *Burlington Mag.* Oct. 182/1 Underside-couching is used for the metal threads, and also for some of the silk ones. *Ibid.* 187/1 The heraldic shields..are underside-couched throughout. **1964** tr. *A. Geijer's Textile Treasures Uppsala Cathedral* 24 Embroidery of multicoloured silk, in split stitch, and gold in underside couching forming a herringbone pattern.

'undersight. (UNDER-[1] 10 b.)

1894 H. DRUMMOND *Ascent Man* 13 The reason..is not oversight, but undersight.

under'sign, *v.* [UNDER-[1] 4 a.] *trans.* To sign one's name below (a writing).

1580 HOLLYBAND *Treas. Fr. Tong*, *Soubsigner*, to vndersigne. **1770** SCRAFTON *Indostan* (ed. 2) 80 These words were written in his own hand, at the beginning of the Treaty, and were undersigned by him.

Hence **undersigner, undersigning** *vbl. sb.*

1611 FLORIO, *Sottoscrittione*, a subscription, an vnder signing or writing. **1753** *Scots Mag.* XV. 19/1 The undersigner has the honour to present..copies of the decrees. **1800** COLERIDGE *Piccolom.* II. ii, All rests upon his undersigning.

under'signed, *ppl. a.* [Cf. prec. and SUBSIGNED *ppl. a.*] Whose signature is appended to a document, etc. Freq. *absol.* (in sing. or pl.).

1643 in J. M. Stone *Faithf. unto Death* (1892) 174, I, the undersigned,..am about to-day to lay down my life..in defence of the Roman Catholic Church. **1824** SYD. SMITH *Sp.* Wks. 1859 II. 201/1 We, the undersigned, being clergymen of the Church of England. **1845** in Claridge *Cold Water Cure* (1849) 12 We, the undersigned British and Americans,..deem it our duty [etc.]. **1868** DICKENS *Lett.* (1880) II. 384 The undersigned is in his usual brilliant condition.

'under-ˌsinging, *vbl. sb.* (UNDER-[1] 9 b.)

1382 WYCLIF *Ps.* 3rd Prol., Eiȝtety and eiȝte forsothe seiden the salmys, and two hundrid the vndersinging. **1886** *Good Words* 308 A lark—a hundred larks are in the sky, A myriad birds an undersinging make.

'under-ˌsinner. (UNDER-[1] 6 a.)

1684 OTWAY *Atheist* I, Good, pretty, little, Under-sinners,..that a Man may fool away an Hour or two withal very comfortably.

†'under-ˌsitter. *Obs.* [UNDER-[1] 6 a. Cf. UNDERSETTLE.] One occupying part of another's house; a sub-tenant or lodger. Also *fig.*

1580 *Procl. Q. Eliz.* 7 July, For the offences in this part of increase of many indwellers, or as they be commonly termed Inmates, or vndersitters. **1607** *Proclamations Jas. I* (1609) 162 The letting of part of Houses and Chambers to Inmates and Undersitters. **1609** TUVILL *Vade-mecum* (1629) 18 Vertue cannot endure to be an vnder-sitter to any.

'under-size, *sb.* (UNDER-[1] 10 b.)

1791 W. GILPIN *Forest Scenery* II. 236 If such a distance as this..were painted on a larger scale than common,..we might be tempted to forget it's under-size.

'under-size, *a.* [UNDER-[2].] = next 2.

1820 SCORESBY *Acc. Arctic Reg.* II. 254 Seldom more than two harpoons are struck into an under-size whale. *Ibid.* 419 The diminished value of under-size bone.

ˌunder'sized, *ppl. a.* (In attrib. use '*under-sized*) [UNDER-[1] 10 a.]

† 1. Inadequately employed. *Obs.*$^{-1}$

1657 GAUDEN *J. Watts' Scribe & Let. Answ.* Pref. ¶j, His great abilities..were indeed much under-sized as to his auditory and employment.

2. Below the proper or ordinary size.

1706 *Lond. Gaz.* No. 4244/3 Each undersiz'd [Galloway] to be allow'd half a Stone for every Inch under. **1747** *Frauds & Abuses Coal Trade* (ed. 3) 20 The like Abuse, practised.. by undersized Sacks. **1825** T. HOOK *Sayings* Ser. II. I. 319 Mr. Abberly's undersized man-servant..delivered a note to Louisa. **1851** KINGSLEY *Yeast* xiii, The ill-looks of the young girls surprised him much;..the majority seemed under-sized, under-fed. **1884** T. F. R. CARR in *Fish. Exhib. Lit.* XI. 425 Fishermen..should be compelled to riddle the mussels..and return the undersized to the scalps.

'under-skin. (UNDER-[1] 5 b.)

1653 R. SANDERS *Physiogn.* a 4 b, Open it [*sc.* a peony], and take the flowers forth from that rinde or underskin, which represents the brain-pan.

†'under-ˌskinker. *Obs.* (UNDER-[1] 6 a: see SKINKER I.)

1596 SHAKS. *1 Hen. IV*, II. iv. 26 This peniworth of Sugar, clapt euen now into my hand by an vnder Skinker. **1631** HEYWOOD *2nd Pt. Fair Maid of West* IV, Ile see and I can be entertained to my old trade of drawing wine: if't be but an under skinker, I care not. [**1867** SMYTH *Sailor's Word-bk.* 706 *Under-skinker*, assistant to the purser's steward.]

'under-skirt. [UNDER-[1] 5 a.] A skirt worn under another, a petticoat; also, a foundation over which drapery or an overskirt is disposed.

1861 MRS. RIDDELL *City & Suburb* (1862) 90 (H.), She.. affected flounces and many petticoats, wearing as many as eight or ten underskirts. **1883, 1884** [see OVERSKIRT]. **1907** H. WYNDHAM *Flare of Footlights* xix, Nearly all the latter.. displayed a greater amount of silk underskirt than seemed altogether necessary.

'under-sky. (UNDER-[1] 5 b.)

1830 TENNYSON *Dying Swan* iii, Floating about the under-sky,..the coronach stoll..afar. **1870** MORRIS *Earthly Par.* III. IV. 87 From this dull rainy under-sky and low.

under'slake, *v.* (UNDER-[1] 2.)

c **1440** *Pallad. on Husb.* II. 434 As oyl lauryne is lentiscyne of take, Whos rigour hoot water most vnderslake [gl. *summitigare*].

'under-sleeve. [UNDER-[1] 5 a.] A sleeve, esp. one of light material, worn below another.

1547 in Feuillerat *Revels Edw. VI* (1914) 10 Longe garmentes of playne clothe of Syluer,..thupper & nether Baces & thunder sleves of clothe of golde. **1560** —— *Revels Q. Eliz.* (1908) 21 Undersleves of Damaske Bawdekyn. **1631** A. TOWNSHEND *Alb. Triumph* 13 The Labells of the sleeues, ..the vnder sleeues. **1861** *Archaeologia* XXXIX. 250 The under-sleeve is grey puffed with white. **1893** GEORGIANA HILL *Hist. Eng. Dress* II. 257 Fastening on with elastic or tape those uncomfortable undersleeves.

under'slept, *ppl. a.* [UNDER-[1] 10 a: cf. *undersleep* vb.] Having had insufficient sleep; suffering from or characterized by lack of sleep.

1943 *Our Towns* (Women's Group on Public Welfare) ii. 23 It has become a commonplace to say that the town child is underslept. **1966** K. AMIS *Anti-Death League* III. 340 Lucy took an illustrated magazine to Churchill's bed-side, but she too was underslept, and in a few minutes she nodded off. **1981** P. SHEA *Voices & Sound of Drums* ii. 14 A neglected, underslept appearance.

†'underslops. *Obs.* (UNDER-[1] 5 a.)

1737 OZELL *Rabelais* II. 72 Drawers or Under-slops are worn now by some.

'underslung, *ppl. a.* [UNDER-[1] 4 a.] **a.** *Mech.* That is slung under (another part, etc.), or from the under part of (something).

1909 in WEBSTER. **1920** *Sci. Amer.* 30 Oct. 453/1 Those who have had to do with the handling of lumber have.. discovered that..shapes long and narrow..are frequently best manipulated by the aid of an underslung carriage. **1924** S. R. ROGET *Dict. Electr. Terms* 282/1 Underslung Monorail Railway. See Suspended Railway. **1932** S. C. H. DAVIS *Motor Racing* v. 74 The whole of the front axle had parted from its underslung spring on one side. **1951** *Engineering* 14 Sept. 329/1 A marine Diesel engine has an under-slung crankshaft. **1968** *Gloss. Terms Materials Handling (B.S.I.)* IV. 8 *Under-slung crane*, a crane in which the travelling end carriage wheels run on the lower flanges of the gantry beams. **1982** *Daily Tel.* 24 May 5/6 Helicopters..hover to lift underslung loads.

b. In various *transf.* and *fig.* uses.

1931 'D. STIFF' *Milk & Honey Route* 216 *To get underslung*, means to ride under a train and have the *shacks* [brakemen] throw things at you, or to have them drag a piece of iron on a string under the car so that, bounding up and down, it will punish you plenty. **1931** F. L. ALLEN *Only Yesterday* vi. 130 Charles G. Dawes..entranced the newspaper-reading public with his picturesque language, his underslung pipe, and his broom-waving histrionics. **1940** *Amer. Speech* XV. 248 Though his figure is somewhat *underslung*, he is by way of being a sportsman. **1978** S. SHELDON *Bloodline* xii. 163 She had a tiny potbelly, and her derrière seemed—this was the only word Elizabeth could think of—underslung.

† undersmall, *a.* *Obs.*$^{-1}$ [? UNDER-[1] 2 or WONDER *adv.*] Extremely small.

c **1530** *Judic. Urines* III. xviii. 60 b, They be bodys vndersmall as duste.

†'undersock. *Obs.* [UNDER-[1] 5 a.] A stocking.

1556 *Richmond. Wills* (Surtees) 190 One payr of sloppes of crayncoloryde fustyane, and the vndersokes belongynge the sayme.

'undersoil. [UNDER-[1] 5 b.] Subsoil.

1707 MORTIMER *Husb.* 315 A Planter or Raiser of Trees ought to consider the under Soil, as well as the superficies of the Earth. **1863** BATES *Nat. Amazon* I. 25 The difference in colour from the superficial soil..is owing to their being formed of the undersoil, brought up from a considerable depth.

'under-ˌsoling. (UNDER-[1] 5 b.)

c **1440** *Promp. Parv.* 184/2 Galache, or galoche, vndyr solynge of mannys fote (..*K.* vndirshone, *H.* vnderschoyinge), *crepita*.

'under-ˌsomething. (UNDER-[1] 6 a.)

a **1718** PARNELL *Allegory on Man* 18 Jove talk'd of breeding him on high, An under-something of the sky.

'undersong. [UNDER-[1] 9 b.]

1. A subordinate or subdued song or strain, esp. one serving as an accompaniment or burden to another. Freq. *transf.* of natural sounds.

1579 SPENSER *Sheph. Cal.* Aug. 128 And Willye is not greatly ouergone, So weren his vndersongs well addrest. **1593** DRAYTON *Ecl.* ix. G 3 b, When now at last..Was poynted who the Roundelay should singe And who againe the vnder-song should beare. **1613–6** W. BROWNE *Brit. Past.* II. iii. 1028 He thus began..To prayse his love; his hasty waves among The frothed rockes, bearing the under-song. **1697** DRYDEN *Virg., Past.* III. 86 The challenge to Damœtas shall belong: Menalcas shall sustain his under-song. **1710** PHILIPS *Pastorals* vi. 8 As eldest, Hobbinol, begin; And Languet's Under-Song by Turns come in. **1795** COLERIDGE *To J. Cottle* 24 Th'unceasing rill..Murmurs sweet undersong 'mid jasmin bowers. **1820** KEATS *Lamia* II. 200 While fluent Greek a vowel'd undersong Kept up among the guests. **1885** Runciman *Skippers* 196 The hoarse undersong from the dim distance.

2. *fig.* An underlying meaning; an undertone. **1631** R. H. *Arraignm. Whole Creature* xviii. 326 Which is still as the conclusive undersong to the discanting of my larger Ditty. **1641** J. Jackson *True Evang. T.* iii. 183 Iobs sorrowfull Messengers make it their under song of sad tidings. **1818** Keats *Let.* Wks. 1889 III. 141 If there is any fault in the Preface it is not affectation, but an undersong of disrespect to the public. **1886** Hall Caine *Son of Hagar* ii. xv, Beneath the chorus of their hearts' joy there was an undersong of discord.

ˈunder-ˌsorcerer. (under-^{1} 6 a.) **1678** Butler *Hud.* iii. i. 300, I..Prepar'd..His Under-Sorcerer t' ingage.

ˈunder-sort. (under-^{1} 6 b.) **1655** T. White *Grounds Obed. & Govt.* viii. 48 Of the Authority given to an absolute Governour; and of under-sorts of Governement. **1697** Collier *Ess. Mor. Subj.* i. 116 What if the under Sort of People should take the Hint, and practice upon it. **1828** Carr *Craven Gloss.*, *Undersort*, the vulgar.

ˈundersoul. (under-^{1} 6 b.) **1888** H. Bushnell *Mor. Uses Dark Th.* (1869) 350 The under-soul, the man, the everlasting, divinely moral personality. **1887** H. R. Haweis *Christ & Chr.*, *Light of Ages* i. i. 4 The Oversoul, which is Divine Mind or God, embraces the Undersouls in all flesh.

ˈundersound. (under-^{1} 9 b.) **1847** C. Bronte *Jane Eyre* xxv, The gale still rising, seemed to my ear to muffle a mournful undersound. **1860** Ruskin *Unto this Last* iv. §82 No air is sweet that is silent; it is only sweet when full of low currents of under sound.

ˈunder-ˌsovereign. (under-^{1} 6 a.) *a* **1680** Charnock *Attrib. God* (1834) II. 582 All under-sovereigns are..to be obedient to his orders.

underˈsow, *v.* **1.** [under-^{1} 10 a.] To sow too little seed on (a piece of ground). **1650** W. Brough *Sacr. Princ.* (1659) 73 Let me prudently observe what each parcell of ground will best bear, that I may not over-cloy some, and undersow others.

2. [under-^{1} 4 a.] **a.** To sow (a later-growing crop) on land already seeded with another crop. **b.** To sow land already seeded with (one crop) *with* a second, later-growing crop. Also *absol.* **1950** *N.Z. Jrnl. Agric.* Aug. 145/1 In arable farming districts many spring-sown pastures are established with a cover crop, usually by undersowing the grass mixture on land which is carrying an autumn- or winter-sown cereal. **1951** P. Oyler *Feeding Ourselves* vii. 65 If the wheat has not been under-sown with ryegrass and clover..the stubble will either be scarified..or it will be shallow ploughed. **1960** *Farmer & Stockbreeder* 5 Jan. 102/3 Also include (or undersow) 15lb per acre Westerwolths rye-grass. **1963** *Times* 10 June 7/2 High Mowthorpe..has grown barley for nine successive years, comparing the effects of giving additional nitrogen, undersowing with trefoil and ploughing in straw. **1981** *Daily Tel.* 21 Sept. 10/8 Partridges..lost a major source of food when the practice of undersowing barley with grass was abandoned from the mid-1960s onwards.

So **underˈsowing** *vbl. sb.*, **underˈsown** *ppl. a.* **1943** H. J. Massingham *Men of Earth* viii. 142 There was hardly a crop in the garden that was not undersown to another. **1960** *Farmer & Stockbreeder* 12 Jan. 107/2 What is your opinion of sowing seeds along with corn when undersowing is practised? *Ibid.* 1 Mar. 106/2 (Advt.), Particularly recommended for undersown crops. **1963** *Times* 10 June 7/1 Undersown cereals can be difficult to deal with in a wet year where the corn is slow to ripen. **1972** *Nature* 21 Jan. 135/2 Field experiments..using various types of undersowing on the levels of pest insects and their enemies.

†**underˈspar,** *v. Obs.* [under-^{1} 4 a.] *trans.* To force up by means of a spar thrust underneath. **1577** Stanyhurst *Descr. Ireland* in *Holinshed* I. 14/2 Vndersparring the gates, and bearing vp the dormitorie doore, they stabbed the adulterer.

ˌunder-ˈsparred, *ppl. a.* [under-^{1} 10 a.] Of vessels: Inadequately furnished with spars. **1841** [see undermasted].

†**ˌunderˈspeak,** *v. Obs.*$^{-1}$ [under-^{1} 10 a.] *trans.* To come short in speaking of. **1635** A. Stafford *Fem. Glory* 119 If in this rude speech of mine I have over-talked my selfe, or under-spoken thee, impute it to my..doting yeares.

underˈspecified, *ppl. a.* (under *adv.* 2 b.) **1544** *Extr. Aberd. Rec.* (1844) I. 209 The ressett of this woll vnderwrittin, fra the personis vnderspecifeit. **1561** *Reg. Privy Council Scot.* I. 188 The quhilk day..comperit the gentilmen underspecifit. **1682** *Papers rel. Scots in Poland* (1915) 136, I resaved..all as here underspecified.

under-ˈspend, *v.* **1.** [under-^{1} 8 b.] (See quot.) *a* **1661** Fuller *Worthies, Lincoln* (1662) 168 When his friend [called] for half a pint of Wine, Mr. Sutton for a Gill, under-spending him a Moity.

2. [under-^{1} 10 a.] To spend less than (an estimate or budget). Hence **underˈspending** *vbl. sb.*; **underˈspent** *ppl. a.* **1890** Webster, Underspend. **1963** [see *overspending* vbl. sb. s.v. overspend *v.*]. **1977** *Lancet* 14 May 1065/2 One of the big London authorities for instance, the North West Thames region, underspent its budget by £2.7 million. **1980** *Chem. in Brit.* XVI. 540/2 Sometimes sums of money are available at short notice—maybe several thousands of pounds of an underspent budget have to be allocated quickly. **1982** *Daily Tel.* 24 Mar. 2/7 Council leaders will seek to reassure Mr Heseltine by saying that they traditionally underspend budgets.

ˈunderspend, *sb.* [f. the vb.] An amount (of a budget, etc.) unspent; a shortfall in the amount expected to be spent. **1982** *Jrnl. R. Soc. Arts* Apr. 269/1 The ability to seek to have certain categories of 'underspend' and excess receipts revoted into the following year. **1982** *Sunday Times* 25 Apr. 49/1 The underspend emerged suddenly, at the last moment. **1983** *Hansard Commons* 27 Apr. 868 It looks as though Sheffield might end up with an under-spend this year.

ˈunder-sphere, *sb.* (under-^{1} 5 b.) **1630** Drumm. of Hawth. *Shadow of Judgem.* 4 The..Raine-bow-sparkling Arch of Diamond cleare Which crownes the azure of each vnder spheare. *c* **1631** Sir L. Cary *Elegy on Donne* 86 He conquer'd rebell passions, rul'd them so, As under-spheares by the first Mover goe.

underˈsphere, *v.* (under-^{1} 7.) **1652** Urquhart *Jewel* 162 The imputation, which they deserve for having been in so bad company, and undersphering themselves to the bodies of those vaster orbs.

ˈunderspin. [under-^{1} 4 d.] A backward spin on a ball while in motion. **1901** *Westm. Gaz.* 13 Aug. 2/3, I do not see that photographs..'prove decisively that a golf ball, truly hit, develops underspin'.

†**underˈspore,** *v. Obs.*$^{-1}$ [under-^{1} 4 a + *spore* spur *sb.*^{1} 8.] *intr.* (cf. underspar *v.*). *c* **1386** Chaucer *Miller's T.* 279 Get me a staf, that I may vnderspore, Whil þat thou, Robyn, heuest of the dore.

underˈspread, *v.* (under-^{1} 4 a.) **1609** Holland *Amm. Marcell.* 131 By that time it grew to be faire day-light, the skie all over was under-spread with a feeling, as it were, of yron harneis. **1857** Emerson *Monadnoc* 296 Every morn I lift my head, See New England under-spread.

ˈunderspring. [under-^{1} 5 c.]

1. *attrib.* Having springs beneath. **1837** W. B. Adams *Carriages* 84 The simplest kind of four-wheeled spring vehicle for one horse is called an Underspring Phaeton.

2. An underlying fountain. **1851** Mrs. Browning *Casa Guidi Wind.* i. 956, I feel how nature's ice-crusts keep the dint Of undersprings of silent Deity.

underˈsprout, *v.* (under-^{1} 4 a.) **1584** Hudson *Du Bartas' Judith* iv. (1608) 58 As the painefull plowman..crops his hedge to make it vnder-sprout.

under-spurleather: see spur-leather 2.

ˌunderˈstaff, *v.* (under-^{1} 10 a.) **1894** *Westm. Gaz.* 12 Sept. 2/2 The way in which the employers..had overworked him and understaffed his station.

ˌunderˈstaffed, *ppl. a.* (under-^{1} 10 a.) **1891** *Sat. Rev.* 7 Nov. 516 The country abounds with small churches understaffed.

underˈstaffing, *vbl. sb.* [under-^{1} 10 a.] Inadequate staffing; employment of an insufficient number of staff. **1957** *Economist* 28 Dec. 1142/1 The strong feeling that understaffing lay at the root of the Windscale accident..is confirmed by the report. **1963** *Times* 17 Apr. 5/2 One of the reasons for the present difficulties was the extreme understaffing in the Home Office forensic science laboratory. **1981** R. D. Edwards *Corridors of Death* xi. 48 The problems caused by new legislation, under-staffing and all those other obstacles to achievement.

ˈunderstair(s. [under-^{2}.]

1. *attrib.* Situated below stairs; humble. **1616** T. Adams *Soul's Sickness* 61 Liuing in some vnder-staire office, when he would visite the countrey, he borrowes some Gallants cast sute of his seruant.

2. A space below a staircase. Also *attrib.* **1730** A. Gordon *Maffei's Amphith.* 290 There are two Under-stairs, which form Rooms. **1976** *Cumberland & Westmorland Herald* 4 Dec. 16/3 (Advt.), Understairs cupboard. **1977** *36 Home Handyman Projects* (Austral. Home Jrnl.) 62 Understairs storage is invaluable, so..why not make use of it by modifying these ideas.

†**underˈstand,** *sb. Obs. rare.* [f. the vb.]

1. Understanding; knowledge. *a* **1300** *Cursor M.* 9326 'Ne i herd neuer,' he said, 'in land Men sua herd of vnder-stand'. **1444** *Extr. Aberd. Rec.* (1844) I. 10 It was cum til his vnderstand that Marioune..hes complaynit to the lorde of Erole that [etc.].

2. Support, basis. **1580–90** J. Stewart *Poems* (S.T.S.) II. 149 Flie Sir, from sic, and lerne to vnderstand. Stand quhair ȝe vill, firm be ȝour vnderstand.

underˈstand, *v.* Forms: (see stand *v.*). [OE. *understondan, -standan* (under-^{1} 8 a), = OFris. *understonda*, MDa. *understande*, MSw. *undi(r)standa*, OIcel. (as a foreign word) *undirstanda*. Cf. MLG. *understân* to understand, to step under, MDu. *onderstaen* (Du. *-staan*), MHG. *understân, -stên* (G. *unterstehen*), to take upon oneself, to venture, presume, etc. With a different prefix, the same use of *stand* appears in OE. *forstandan*, OS. *farstandan*, OHG. *far-*, *firstantan* (*firstân*), and MHG. *verstân, -stên* (G. *verstehen*), MDu. *verstaen* (Du. *-staan*).

In the 15th and 16th cents. three forms of the past pple. were current, viz. (*a*) the original *understanden* (also *-stonden*), in use till about 1550; (*b*) the reduced form of this, *understande* (*-stonde*), *-stand* (*-stond*), common till about 1575, and surviving into the 17th cent.; (*c*) the new form *understanded* (*-stonded*), very common from about 1530 to 1585. The occurrence of *understanded* in the Thirty-Nine Articles, xxxv, in the phrase 'understanded of the people', has given rise to recent echoes of it, especially in journalistic use. The modern form *understood* came into use in the latter part of the 16th cent., and was usual by 1600.]

I. *trans.* **1.** To comprehend; to apprehend the meaning or import of; to grasp the idea of. *c* **888** K. Ælfred *Boeth.* xxxix. §8 Se godcunda foreþonc hit understent eall swiðe rihte, þeah..we ne cunnon þæt riht understandan. *c* **1000** Ælfric *Hom.* I. 188 Wæs seo ealde æ swiðe earfoðe and diȝle to understandenne. *a* **1225** *Leg. Kath.* 1013 Liht to ure lare, þet tu mahe stihen to under-stonden in him godes muchele strencðe. *c* **1290** *S. Eng. Leg.* I. 11/343 Þe Aumperour þis onder-stod, þei he heþene were. **1340–70** *Alex. & Dind.* 609 Ȝe ne vndurstonde nouht þat stounde þe storie of þis wordus. **1387–8** T. Usk *Test. Love* iii. iii. (Skeat) l. 77 If these thinges be wel understonde, I wene that non inconvenient shalt thou fynde betwene goddes forweting and liberte of arbitrement. *a* **1450** *Mirk's Festial* 3 Whech noyse God hymselfe schall know and vndyrstond. **1523** [Coverdale] *Old God* (1534) P v, The multytude of dyuerse ceremonyes..not being vnderstanded nor perceyued of the comen sorte..of people. **1548** R. Hutten *Sum of Diuinitie* E 4 b, The sentence shal be better understande if it be changed into a comparyson to an other. **1600** J. Pory tr. *Leo's Africa* iii. 155 A man may much more easily vnder-stand the text then the exposition thereof. **1667** Milton *P.L.* xii. 376 Now clear I understand What oft my steddiest thoughts have searcht in vain. **1733** Berkeley *Th. Vision* §27, I have considered and endeavoured to understand your remarks. **1815** Jane Austen *Emma* ix, One half of the world cannot understand the pleasures of the other. **1891** Farrar *Darkn. & Dawn* xxi, The young prince saw that they were in possession of something more divine than the world could understand.

refl. *c* **1275** in *O.E. Misc.* 45/297 Peter a-non þer-after hyne vnderstod Hwat his louerd hedde iseyd.

b. To be thoroughly acquainted or familiar with (an art, profession, etc.); to be able to practise or deal with properly. **1533** Elyot *Cast. Helthe* (1541) A ij, The science of phisicke,..beyng well vnderstande, truely experienced, and discretely ordred. **1622** J. Taylor (Water P.) *Farew. Tower-bottles* A 4, When Vpland Trades-men thus dares take in hand A wat'ry buis'nesse, they not vnderstand. **1681** Chetham *Angler's Vade-m.* xxxix. (1689) 252, I will not deny but that (as the times phrase it) I understand something of eating. **1727** A. Hamilton *New Acc. E. Ind.* II. 93 He..understood a small Sword excellently well, but [was] not much versed in Merchandize or foreign Commerce. **1768** Earl Carlisle in Jesse *Selwyn & Contemp.* (1843) II. 292 Get somebody who understands it to taste it [*sc.* claret] for you. **1823** Scott *Quentin D.* xxvi, Galeotti..understood his own profession too well to let that ignorance be seen. **1859** *Habits Gd. Society* v. 221 Thomas, bring that fowl to me; Mr. Jones [who is trying to carve it] seems not to understand it.

c. To apprehend clearly the character or nature of (a person). Also *refl.* **1587** Golding *De Mornay* v. 57 God then conceyued and vnderstood himselfe; and it must needes be that he vnder-stood himselfe seeing that the chiefest wisedome is to know ones selfe. **1588** Kyd *Househ. Philos.* Wks. (1901) 267 So that the seruaunt, if you will rightly vnderstand him, is..a liuely and seueral instrument of action. **1846** Mrs. A. Marsh *Father Darcy* II. viii. 137 It is my misfortune to be little understood; but our praise is not of men, but of God. **1876** Parker *Paraclete* i. ix. 142 We cannot understand Christ until we understand Moses, nor can we understand the spirit until we understand Christ.

†**d.** *refl.* (*a*) To know one's place, or how to conduct oneself properly. (*b*) To be in possession of one's senses or faculties. *Obs.* (*a*) **1602** Shaks. *Ham.* i. iii. 96 You doe not vnderstand your selfe so cleerely, As it behoues my Daughter, and your Honour. **1687** Miége, To understand himself, to know how to carry himself, *savoir se conduire*. **1745** J. Mason *Self-Knowledge* i. iii. (1758) 32 Nothing is more common than to say, when a Person does not behave with due Decency towards his Superiors, such a one does not understand himself.

(*b*) **1696** Aubrey *Misc.* 136 He was an Hundred Years old when my Friend was with him; and yet, did understand himself very well.

2. To comprehend by knowing the meaning of the words employed; to be acquainted with (a language) to this extent. *a* **1000** *Colloq. Ælfric* in Wr.-Wülcker 100 Sprec us æfter urum andȝyte þæt we maȝon understandan þa þing þe þu specst. *c* **1250** *Gen. & Ex.* 2210 Wende here non it on his mod, Oc Iosep al it under-stod. *c* **1275** in *O.E. Misc.* 56/668 Eueruych þer vnderstod his icunde speche. *a* **1300** *Cursor M.* 232 Þis ilk bok es translate..For the loue of Inglis lede..For the commun at understand. *a* **1384** Chaucer *H. Fame* ii. 2 Now herkeneth, euery maner man That englissh under-stonde kan. *c* **1400** *Maundev.* (Roxb.) xxix. 131 Neuer þe latter þai wate noȝt whare þai myght aryfe, and also þai schuld noȝt vnderstand þer langage. **1535** Coverdale *Gen.* xi. 7 Let vs..confounde their tonge euen there, yᵗ one vnder-stonde not what another saieth. *c* **1595** Capt. Wyatt *Dudley's Voy.* (Hakluyt Soc.) 40 All theire conference was in the Indian tounge, which our Captaine nor anie of his companie did understande. **1613** Purchas *Pilgrimage* (1614) 250 The Arabike I understand not. **1659** in *Burton's Diary* (1828) IV. 6 Seeing we all understand not French, let us take his word; that is English. **1716** Hearne *Collect.* (O.H.S.) V. 314 He does not understand Latin. **1719** De Foe *Crusoe* ii. (Globe) 351 The Spaniards, two of whom understood

English well enough. **1842** TENNYSON *Vision of Sin* v. 16 An answer peal'd.., But in a tongue no man could understand.

b. To grasp the meaning or purport of the words (or signs) used by (a person).

a **1225** *Leg. Kath.* 1641 Beo nu þenne, Porphire, stille & understont me. *a* **1300** *Cursor M.* 2260 Bot sua he mengud þam þair mode, þat naman oþer vndirstode. *c* **1386** CHAUCER *Man of Law's T.* 520 A maner latyn corrupt was hir speche, But algates ther by was she vnderstonde. *a* **1533** LD. BERNERS *Huon* lx. 208 Thus they compleynyd them one to another, and Huon, who was nere them, vnderstode them well. **1566** STAPLETON *Ret. Untr. Jewell* III. 110 b, To praie, it was not requisit he should be vnderstanded, For that was done..by sighynges. **1595** SHAKS. *John* IV. ii. 237 Thou didst vnder-stand me by my signes. **1667** MILTON *P.L.* XII. 58 Forthwith a hideous gabble rises loud Among the Builders; each to other calls Not understood. **1687** A. LOVELL tr. *Thevenot's Trav.* I. 61 When he eats he speaks to no body, but makes himself be understood by signs to the mute Buffoons. **1838** LYTTON *Leila* II. i, 'Thou understandest me, father?' 'I do. I know your pious heart and well-judging mind.' **1848** THACKERAY *Van. Fair* lvi, Pretending to understand little George when he spoke regarding them.

refl. *c* **1395** *Plowman's T.* 792 Yet he jangleth as a jaie, And understont him selfe no thing. **1618** FLETCHER *Woman Pleas'd* IV. i, What Treason's that? does this fellow understand Himself?

c. ***to understand each other***, to be in agreement or collusion; to be confederates.

1663 *Extr. St. Papers Friends* Ser. II. (1911) 171 The Quakers..with all other Sects are fully agreed in this business and doe perfectly understand each other. **1675** *Essex Papers* (Camden) 24 Its so apparent..that they understand one another. **1853** R. S. SURTEES *Sponge's Sp. Tour* vii, 'You trust me,' replied Leather,..with a look as much as to say, 'we understand each other'.

3. To comprehend as a fact; to grasp clearly, to realize. Chiefly with clause as object.

c **1000** ÆLFRIC *Saints' Lives* xxv. 178 Under-stand be ðam hu se ælmihtiga god hi ealle ȝesceop..of nahte. *c* **1012** WULFSTAN *Hom.* (1883) 156 Understandað eac.. þæt deofol þas þeode nu fela ȝeara dwelode. *a* **1200** *Vices & Virtues* 19 Vnderstandeþ, alle ðe ðis radeþ oðer ihereð,..þe muchele ðolemodnesse of us on ðese liue. *a* **1225** *Ancr. R.* 66 So þe ueond, þurh hire word, understod anonriht hire wocnesse. *a* **1300** *Cursor M.* 4249 Sir putifar wel vndirstod þat ioseph was o gentil blod. *Ibid.* 14874 Quat he was þai noght vnderstode. *c* **1315** SHOREHAM I. 652 Nou onderstand: þe signe her Fourme hys of wyne and brede. **1390** GOWER *Conf.* I. 140 And understond that al this peine..Is schape al only for thi pride. *c* **1425** LYDG. *Assembly of Gods* 2040, I cowde nat vndyrstande Where he became, but sodenly As he came, he went. **1486** *Bk. St. Albans* d ij, Understonde ye that a Goshawke shulde not flie to any fowle. **1535** COVERDALE *John* viii. 27 Howbeit they vnderstode not, that he spake of the father. **1558** BP. WATSON *Seven Sacram.* xxi. 132 He hath often tymes with his reason vnderstande..what God hath commaunded and the goodnes of it. **1597** HOOKER *Eccl. Pol.* v. lxvii. §4 Thus much they knewe, although as yet they vnderstoode not perfectly to what effect or issue the same would come. **1710** ADDISON *Whig Exam.* 14 Sept. ¶3 This Œdipus, you must understand,..was son to a King of Thebes. **1781** COWPER *Expost.* 159 They..could not understand That sin let loose speaks punishment at hand. **1819** SHELLEY *Cenci* IV. i. 101 Tell her to come; yet let her understand Her coming is consent. **1867** H. SPENCER *First Princ.* (ed. 2) I. iv. §23. 70 You now understand..what has disabled the partridge.

†**b.** With reflexive pronoun. *Obs. rare.*

c **1175** *Lamb. Hom.* 35 For-þi leofemen understondet eouseluen þa hwile ȝe mahten: Nis þas weorld nawiht. *c* **1320** *Cast. Love* 1131 A! Mon, nim ȝeme and vnderstond þe Hou fynliche in herte God loueþ þe.

†**c.** To ascertain the purport of (a letter, etc.) by perusal and consideration. *Obs.*

1389 *Eng. Gilds* (1870) 50 We fulliche vndirstondend ȝour lettres sent to vs,..do ȝow openliche to wetyn [etc.]. *c* **1400** *Brut* II. 318 The which lettres, whan þe kyng..had seyn & vndirstonden, he had grete compassioun. **1430–40** LYDG. *Bochas* VIII. xxv. (1558) 16 b, Your letters red and plainly vnderstande. **1502** ARNOLDE *Chron.* (1811) 14 We haue understand the charter the whiche the Lorde Herry..made to yᵉ citezens of London in thes wordes. **1523** LD. BERNERS *Froiss.* I. xiv. 14 Whan all the cases and dedis that the kyng had done..were red, and wel understand.

4. a. To grasp as a fixed or established fact or principle; to regard as settled or implied without specific mention.

c **1055** *Byrhtferth's Handboc* in *Anglia* VIII. 304 þis ylce understand be þam oðrum daȝum. *c* **1400** LOVE *Bonavent. Mirr.* (1908) 9 It is to vndirstonde..as for a principal and general rule, that [etc.]. **1523** FITZHERB. *Husb.* §156 Than it is to be vnderstande, what goodes a man shall take with hym. **1553** EDEN *Treat. New Ind.* (Arb.) 8 The lyke is to be vnderstande of Popingiayes and spyces. **1667** MILTON *P.L.* I. 662 Warr then, Warr Open or understood must be resolv'd. **1854** *Poultry Chron.* II. 363 It must be also understood that no alteration can be made in the prices.

b. To have knowledge of, to know or learn, by information received. (Now merged in next.)

Freq. in *to give* or †*do* (one) *to understand*: see DO *v.* 22 c, GIVE *v.* 29 c.

a **1131** [see DO *v.* 22 c]. ? *a* **1200** in Kemble *Cod. Dipl.* IV. 218, I do ȝowe to understonden ðat I wolle ðat ðe prestes.. haue euere soke and sake ouere alle heore men. *a* **1300** *Cursor M.* 12342 To þe leones coue he yod, þar he þe quelpes vnder-stod. *Ibid.* 19919 Quen þai..vnderstod His cuming, son gain him þai yod. *c* **1350** *Will. Palerne* 5262 Whan þe worþi william..hade vnderston[d] þe tidinges to þende, to þe menskful messageres he made glad chere. *c* **1385** CHAUCER *L.G.W.* Prol. 470 Now wole I seyn what penaunce thow schalt do For thyn trespace, & vndyrstonde it here. **1423** JAS. I *Kingis Q.* cxxvii, My son, I..vnderstond, Be thy reherse, the matere of thy gref. **1482** *Cely Papers* (Camden) 128, I wndyrstonde be Robard Eryke that ȝe hafe ij fayr hawkes. **1560** DAUS tr. *Sleidane's Comm.* 401 b, I require you that you wyll make a direct aunswer..and let me under-stande it tomorrowe. **1585** T. WASHINGTON tr. *Nicholay's Voy.* I. xv. 16 b, The great displeasure he would take, when he should vnderstand the great dammage which the Turks had done. **1611** B. JONSON *Catiline* IV. iv, I vnderstand by Quintus Fabius Sanga,..you haue beene lately Sollicited against the Common-wealth. **1664** MRS. HUTCHINSON *Mem. Col. Hutchinson* (1806) 428 When the colonell's wife under-stood her husband's bad accommodation.

c. To take or accept as a fact, without positive knowledge or certainty; to get as an impression or idea; to believe. Chiefly with obj. clause.

1751 PALTOCK *P. Wilkins* II. x. 112 As I understand your great Ancestor would have come into it,..but for the Ragams. **1788** COWPER *Let. to Lady Hesketh* 6 May, The General, I understand by his last letter, is in town. **1825** T. HOOK *Sayings* Ser. II. I. 217, I understood from Mr. Abberly..that I should find him, if I called at this time of the day. **1829** SCOTT *Anne of G.* xxxiv, They understood it was his wish to observe incognito. **1858** *Congressional Globe* 18 Feb. 752/1, I understand the gentleman from Illinois to give way. *The Chairman.* The Chair understands not. **1885** 'MRS. ALEXANDER' *At Bay* vii, It was understood she had made an engagement to go to India.

5. To take, interpret, or view in a certain way.

c **1000** *Ags. Psalter* xxi. 2 Ne understand þu hit me to unrihtwisnesse. *c* **1000** ÆLFRIC *Saints' Lives* xxv. 472 Æwfestlice understandende be ure ealra æriste. *c* **1175** *Lamb. Hom.* 75 þis word..mon mei understonden on þro wise. *a* **1300** *Cursor M.* 337 Bot þou sal noght vndirstand þat he wroght al his werc wit hand. *c* **1340** HAMPOLE *Pr. Consc.* 4425 þe dragon es understanden þe fende..And þe thred part of þe sternes bright Er cristen men undirstanden right. *c* **1425** WYNTOUN *Cron.* VIII. xi. 1928 (Cott. MS.), þir wordis in to propyrte Al þus may vndirstandyn be. ? *a* **1533** FRITH *Answ. More* (1548) A 2 b, I shewed hym that it was not necessary, that the words shulde so be vnderstonde as they sownde. **1566** *Pasquine in Traunce* 107 That which Christ speaketh..of many false Prophets..may be vnderstand to be the sundry sectes of Monkes and Fryers. **1581** J. BELL *Haddon's Answ. Osorius* 188 b, The Major must be understanded, that Paule treated not of the cause..but of the execution and effect of predestination. **1645** *Docq. Lett. Pat. at Oxf.* (1837) 257 Which Forces shalbe vnderstoode to be in the nature of Posse Comitatus. **1662** STILLINGFL. *Orig. Sacræ* II. iv. §8 Some understand the first words..that he was not born a Prophet. **1772** *Lett. Junius* lxviii. (1788) 343 You, Lord Mansfield, did not understand me so. **1835** T. MITCHELL *Acharn. of Aristoph.* 339 *note*, Elmsley understands this word in its legal sense. **1860** WARTER *Seaboard* II. 492, I do not quite know how Miss Bremer.. intended these words to be understood.

b. Const. *by*. (In passive passing into the sense of 'is signified'.)

c **1340** HAMPOLE *Pr. Consc.* 1681 Bi þe name of ded may be tane, And understanden ma dedes þan ane. **1377** LANGL. *P. Pl.* B. XII. 257 By þe po feet is vnderstonde..Excecutoures, fals frendes. *c* **1400** *Apol. Loll.* 69 By þis man is vnderstondyn feynar þat is fals, and lufiþ his synne. **1456** SIR G. HAYE *Law Arms* (S.T.S.) 10 All the cristin men that war undirstandin be the grene blude. **1484** CAXTON *Fables of Æsop* I. i, By the cok is to vnderstond the fool whiche retcheth not of sapyence. **1502** *Ord. Crysten Men* (W. de W. 1506) I. iii. 34 By the coniuracyon the whiche is made unto the lefte ere is understande that he ought to put out of us all euyl thoughtes. **1561** DAUS tr. *Bullinger on Apoc.* (1573) 123 b, We read..that there was an Aungell of Grece, and an Aungell of Persia, and that by them pᵉ whole people are vnderstand. **1578** BANISTER *Hist. Man* I. 19 You shall heare what space is to be vnderstanded by the name of Necke. **1600** SHAKS. *A.Y.L.* IV. iii. 95 *Ros.* What must we vnderstand by this? *Oli.* Some of my shame. **1651** C. CARTWRIGHT *Cert. Relig.* I. 296 Estius..saith that Chrysostome and his followers by sacrifice then understand ..Baptisme. **1727** DE FOE *Syst. Magic* I. i. (1840) 24 After this story no man need inquire what the world understood by the magicians and astrologers and wise men of those days. **1758** tr. *Juan & Ulloa's Voy.* (1772) I. 440 The llama, to which the Indians added the name of runa, to denote an India sheep; that beast being now under-stood by the *runa-llama*. **1865** RUSKIN *Sesame* i. §3 We do not understand by this advancement, in general, the mere making of money.

c. Const. *of*.

1549 LATIMER *1st Serm. bef. Edw. VI* (Arb.) 22 The forsayd words of Paul are not to be vnderstande of all scriptures. **1581** J. BELL *Haddon's Answ. Osor.* 43 b, He demaundeth of us, what is to be understanded of those Sacramentes which we doe reteine. **1705** ADDISON *Italy* 110 Which is true, if understood only of the Rivers of Italy. **1861** PALEY *Æschylus* (ed. 2) *Prometh.* 898 *note*, This is to be literally understood of the gadfly's sting.

†**d.** ***to understand***, to wit, namely. *Obs.*

1579 J. DEE *Diary* (Camden) 5 To my heires and assignes for ever, to understand, Mr. Bullok and Mr. Taylor.

†**e.** To mean, to imply. (Cf. 12 b.) *Obs.*⁻¹

1617 MORYSON *Itin.* I. 227 Distant from Ierusalem some fiue miles, (in Turky I alwaies vnderstand Italian miles).

†**6. a.** To give heed to, attend to. *Obs.*

c **1000** ÆLFRIC *Saints' Lives* xxiii b 186 þæt ȝeswinc his syðfætes ne understandende..[he] arn. *c* **1275** *O.E. Misc.* 90/8 þu ert help in engelaunde. Vre stephne vnderstonde. *c* **1320** *Cast. Love* 953 ȝif þou wole me louen and vnderstonde, I chul þe bringe in-to þin owne londe. *c* **1400** tr. *Secreta Secret., Gov. Lordsh.* 48 Gouerne hem wyth goodnesse, and vnderstonde hem wyth debonertee.

†**b.** To receive, accept. *Obs.*

c **1200** *Trin. Coll. Hom.* 99 Ech þe understandeð þat holi husel unwurðliche, he understant him seluen eche pine. *Ibid.* 167 þis holie maiden..steȝ þis dai..in to þan heuenliche bure, þar heo was wurðliche understonden. *c* **1250** *Gen. & Ex.* 2275 Al ðo briðere..bedden him riche present... And he leuelike it under-stod. *c* **1275** *O.E. Misc.* 90/3 Haly thomas of heoueriche Alle apostles eueliche þe Martyrs þe vnder-stonde. *c* **1300** *Havelok* 2814 And siþen shal ich under-stonde Of you..Manrede, and holde oþes boþe. *c* **1375** *Cursor M.* 2432 (Fairf.), þe king..comanded þorou-out his lande men sulde him mensk and vnderstande.

†**c.** To conceive. *Obs.*⁻¹

c **1200** *Trin. Coll. Hom.* 21 þu shalt understonde [*Lamb. Hom.* 77, underfon] child on þine innoðe.

7. To recognize or regard as present in thought, though not expressly stated or mentioned; to supply mentally. Chiefly *Gram.*

1530 PALSGR. 342 Whan we use 'they' or 'them', understandyng femynin substantyves, they use ever *elles*. **1533** MORE *Answ. Poysoned Bk.* Wks. 1057/2 Though those wordes wer out, yet they be such as the sentence wold well require to repete and vnderstande. *a* **1704** T. BROWN *Sat. Ancients* Wks. 1720 I. 15 The Ancient Romans said *Saturam* under-standing *Lancem*. **1861** PALEY *Æschylus* (ed. 2) *Seven agst. Thebes* 249 *note*, Understand χαρίζοιο ἄν, or something to that effect, suppressed by aposiopesis.

b. In pa. pple.: Implied, though not expressed.

1580 LYLY *Euphues* (Arb.) 419 You resemble in your sayings the Painter Tamantes, in whose pictures there was euer more vnderstoode then painted. **1581** J. BELL *Haddon's Answ. Osor.* 200 Admit this also that god's name is not expressed, yet have ye not taught us that it is not understanded here. **1631** GOUGE *God's Arrows* v. §1. 410 Circumstantiall words, which are as bonds to knit word to word, it leaveth to be understood. **1669** MILTON *Acced. Grammar* 59 A Noun and Pronoun with a Participle exprest or understood. **1754** R. NEWTON *Char. Theophrastus* 238 Here is an ellipsis of the substantive; which Lambert Bos hath not supply'd, and therefore I will venture to do it by ὁδὸν understood. **1817** MILL *Brit. India* II. IV. v. 192 An exception in favour of the Nabob was, from standing usage, so much understood, that to express it had appeared altogether useless. **1835** T. MITCHELL *Acharn. of Aristoph.* 675 *note*, The verb σκόπει or ὅρα is here understood. **1872** *Punch* 13 July 19/2 In order that any matter of business should be perfectly intelligible, nothing should be 'understood'.

fig. **1858** HOGG *Shelley* II. 417 There was an ellipsis of his waistcoat; it was not expressed, but understood.

†**8. a.** In passive: To be informed, advised, or (so) minded. *Obs.*

c **1275** *O.E. Misc.* 52/518 We beoþ vnderstonde þes ilke swike seyde..Ich wile þene þridde day aryse from deþe to lyue. **1297** R. GLOUC. (Rolls) 9300 ȝif þou seist it vor noble kunne, þou nart noȝt wel vnderstonde, Vor ich was þe kinges sone, þou wost wel, of þis londe. *c* **1440** *Pallad. on Husb.* III. 196 Tho thre wol multiplie, As semeth me, in euery maner lond; Yet Columelle is so not understonde.

†**b.** To plan, devise. With refl. dative. *Obs.*⁻¹

1297 R. GLOUC. (Rolls) 8877 þe king vor ire eritage him gan vnderstonde To bringe roberd is sone..in is warison þere.

9. To stand under. †Also *spec.*, to support or assist; to prop up.

13.. *Northern Passion* 1751 (Addit. MS.), Sayne Iohn hir body [*v.r.* Cristis word wel] vndir stude. [**1591** SHAKS. *Two Gent.* II. v. 31 Why, stand-vnder: and vnder-stand is all one. **1601** —— *Twel. N.* III. i. 90 My legges do better vnder-stand me sir, then I vnderstand what you meane.] *a* **1611** CHAPMAN *Iliad* v. 687 Alcander, and a number more, he slew, and more had slain, If Hector had not understood. **1615** —— *Odyss.* IV. 346 To let him reach the shore Of ships and tents before Troy understood. **1632** HEYWOOD *1st Pt. Iron Age* v. i, Thy rude hand Would lift a shield, thou canst not vnder stand. **1883** *Academy* 16 June 419/2 A full set of collations 'understands' the text.

II. *intr.* **10.** To have comprehension or understanding (in general or in a particular matter).

c **1000** ÆLFRIC *Hom.* I. 302 [þam men] is ȝemæne mid nytenum, þæt he ȝefrede; mid englum, þæt he understande. *c* **1012** WULFSTAN *Hom.* (1883) 161 Eall þæt syndon micle and eȝeslice dæda, understande se ðe wille. **1297** R. GLOUC. (Rolls) 2221 Sire king,..ȝif þou wolt understonde, Deol þou miȝt abbe in þin herte of þin kunde londe. **1340** *Ayenb.* 56 Huanne þe glotoun geþ in to þe tauerne..he..specþ wel and onderstant; huan he comþ ayen, he heþ al þis uorlore. *c* **1380** WYCLIF *Serm.* Sel. Wks. II. 13 ȝit ȝe knowun not, ne undirstonden; ȝit ȝour herte is blyndid. **1456** SIR G. HAYE *Law Arms* (S.T.S.) 13 The quhilk lettis to have perfyte resoun.. to understand rychtwisly. **1530** PALSGR. 767/2 For as farre as I can understande, it is so. **1587** GOLDING *De Mornay* v. 55 Albeit that of the things which are in this world, some vnderstand, and some vnderstand not;..all of them are appoynted to some certeyne end. **1613** FLETCHER, etc. *Hon. Man's Fort.* v. i, All women that on earth do dwell thou lov'st, Yet none that understand love thee again. **1648** MILTON *Ps.* lxxxii. 17 They know not nor will understand, In darkness they walk on. **1746** FRANCIS tr. *Horace, Epist.* I. xiv. 64 By my Advice, let each with chearful Heart, As best he understands, employ his Art. **1781** COWPER *Conversat.* 430 Man's heart had been impenetrably seal'd,..Had not his Maker's all bestowing hand Giv'n him a soul, and bade him understand. **1850** TENNYSON *In Mem.* xcvii. 36 She dwells on him with faithful eyes, 'I cannot understand: I love'.

b. Const. *about*, †*of*. †Also with refl. dative.

c **1000** ÆLFRIC *Hom.* I. 10 Englas..ne maȝon fulfremedlice understandan ymbe God. *a* **1225** *Ancr. R.* 210 Nis..no mon þet ne mei understonden him of his sunnen nomeliche. *c* **1375** [see 10 c]. *c* **1477** CAXTON *Jason* 42 b, Certes gentil knight I knowe wel my self & vnderstonde of this marchandyse. **1860** W. COLLINS *Woman in White* I. xv. 187 You quite understand about that little matter of business being safe in my hands? **1892** J. H. MCCARTHY *1001 Days* II. 7, I under-stood about precious stones, and I had reason to hope that I should not do badly in the business.

†**c.** To know how *to* do something. *Obs.*

a **1300** *Cursor M.* 24792 Willam basterd..conquerur was gode, And for to warray [*c* **1375** of þe were he] vnderstode. **1723** *Pres. St. Russia* I. 337 A Hatchet, which their Carpenters understand to handle with more Skill than those of any Nation whatsoever.

†**11.** To have knowledge or information, to learn, *of* something. *Obs.*

13.. *Cursor M.* 19919 (Gött.), Quen he of his comming vnderstode, Sone he ras and gain þaim him ȝode. *a* **1400** *Octouian* 1589 Anoon the kyng..dede hem alle to vnther-stonde Of the Soudanes fyght. **1401** in Ellis *Orig. Lett.* Ser. II. I. 22 We do yow to understonde of tydynges the weche we have yherd of Owein Glyndor. **1509** *Mem. Hen. VII* (Rolls) 435 Howbe that ye wold mervel in case that ye understode of al the maters that hathe passyd. **1573** L. LLOYD *Marrow of Hist.* (1653) 116 The Philosopher.. having under-stood of his mothers death. **1629** in Ellis *Orig. Lett.* Ser. II. III. 256, I was gladde to understande of your life and health, which this bearer.. made knowen unto me. **1661** *Reg. Privy Counc. Scot.* Ser. III. I. 5, I shall not know nor understand of any maner of thing.. against his Majesties persone.. bot I shall lett and withstand the same.

†**b.** To get news, receive intelligence. *Obs.*$^{-1}$

1574 HELLOWES *Gueuara's Fam. Ep.* (1577) 58 Pyrrhus.. was the first that inuented Currers or Posts: and in this case he was so vigilant, that.. in one day he vnderstood from Rome,.. and in five out of Asia.

12. a. In parenthetic use (chiefly *I understand*): To believe or assume, on account of information received or by inference.

1297 R. GLOUC. (Rolls) 133 Þe kyng of norþhomberlond was king, ich vnderstonde, Of al þe lond biȝonde homber. *a* **1352** MINOT *Poems* vii. 92 Þe teres he lete ful rathly ren Out of his eghen, I vnderstand. **1390** GOWER *Conf.* I. 10 For thilke tyme, I understonde, The Lumbard made non eschange. *c* **1440** *Generydes* 16 Hire fader was a man of grete powre. And kyng of aufrike as I vnderstonde. *c* **1460** *Merita Missæ* 197 Thow ned the to fyght, I vndeyrstonde, With youre flesche, and with the fende. **1508** KENNEDIE *Flyting w. Dunbar* 345 Thow lufis nane Irische, elf, I vnderstand, Bot it suld be all trew Scottis mennis lede. **1592** *Arden of Feversham* IV. iv. 4 He is coming from Shorlow as I vnderstand. **1642** H. MORE *Song of Soul* I. ii. 52 You are Heavens Privy-Counsellour I understond. **1898** 'MERRIMEN' *Roden's Corner* xii. 124 Mr. Wade.. was, he understood, distantly related to the mother.

†**b.** To speak *of* (= to mean) something. *Obs.*$^{-1}$

c **1425** *Craft Nombrynge* (E.E.T.S.) 4 Neuer-þe-les wen he say *Prima significat vnum &c.*,.. he vndirstondes noȝt of þe first figure of euery rew.

†**13.** To be subject *to* one. *Obs. rare.*

?*a* **1200** in Kemble *Cod. Dipl.* IV. 193 Icc hate.. ðæt alcc ða ðeȝnes of ðam landen hinnenforð understande to ðan abbod. *c* **1320** *Cast. Love* 246 He is þorw riht þeuwe and þral, To whos seruise he vnderstod with-al.

†**14.** To give heed, attend, listen, *to* one. *Obs.*

a **1200** *Moral Ode* 227 Vnderstondeð nu to me, edi men and arme, Ich wulle tellen of helle pin. **13..** *Guy of Warw.* 1292 Lordinges, þan seyd þe douk Otoun, Under-stond to mi resoun. *a* **1325** *Prose Psalter* liv. 1 Here myn oreisoun, and ne despise þou nouȝt my praiere, vnder-stonde to me, and here me. *c* **1450** *Merlin* xxxii. 633 Vndirstonde to me, and I shall telle the thy dreme.

under'standable, *a.* Also 5 ondirstandabille. [f. UNDERSTAND *v.* + -ABLE.]

1. That can be understood; intelligible.

c **1475** *Cath. Angl.* 260/1 (MS. A), Ondirstandabille, *jntelligibilis.* **1577** HOLINSHED *Chron.* II. 735/1 Their language was vnknowne, and not vnderstandable to any man that coulde bee brought to talke with them. **1584** R. SCOT *Discov. Witchcr.* XII. xxi. 228 Whether the words of the charme be understandable or not, it skilleth not. **1625** A. GILL *Sacr. Philos.* Pref., Faith is a supplie of reason in things understandable, as the imagination is of sight in things that are visible. **1651** BAXTER *Inf. Baptism* 82 Otherwise we might pervert all Scripture, and none of it would be understandable. *a* **1670** SPALDING *Troub. Chas. I* (1851) II. 294 This vncouth act, scarss wnderstandabill, bred gryte feir and perturbatioun. **1799** SOUTHEY in *Life* (1850) II. 34, I suffer a good deal from illness, and in a way hardly understandable by those in health. **1832** *Examiner* 84/2 Putting the law in a readable and understandable shape. **1870** RUSKIN *Lect. Art* (1875) 73 There are two of the Puritans, whose work if I can succeed in making clearly understandable to you.., it is all I need care to do.

†**2.** Able to understand; capable of understanding.

1382 WYCLIF *Ecclus.* iii. 32 The wis herte and vnderstandable shalabstenen hymself from synnes. **1587** GOLDING *De Mornay* vi. 93 Theodorus.. hath termed them, the substantiall Vnderstanding, the Vnderstandable substance, and the Fountayne of Soules. **1654** GAYTON *Pleas. Notes* IV. 197 The daughters of those mothers.. are forward and understandable of womens matters, sooner than other children.

Hence **under'standableness, understanda'bility.**

1656 tr. *T. White's Peripat. Inst.* 198 The Understandablenesse of a thing, or the quiddity, the whatnesse. **1934** WEBSTER, understandability. **1947** [see IDEAL *a.* 1 b]. **1976** *Economist* 31 July 4 Perhaps such a system would not be as statistically fair as some other suggestions but fairness would not be bought at the expense of understandability.

under'standably, *adv.* [f. UNDERSTANDABLE *a.*: see -ABLY.] For understandable reasons; in a manner that can be understood.

a **1921** in *N.E.D.* s.v. UNDERSTANDABLE *a.* **1928** *Daily Tel.* 10 Jan. 10/6 The members of the Fascist Militia.. might understandably display an aggressive consciousness of their position and power. **1964** *Times* 11 Feb. 11/6 Though it is understandably difficult to find direct evidence, Mr. Wood and officials of both B.R.S. and the major haulage firms are certain that large-scale abuses of the existing laws and trade union agreements are taking place. **1979** A. MCCOWEN *Young Gemini* 75 There was a seventy-five year-old character man in the company who sulked understandably at having to play my son.

†**under'standant.** *Obs.*$^{-1}$ [f. as UNDERSTANDABLE *a.* + -ANT.] An understanding person.

c **1400** *Secreta Secret., Gov. Lordsh.* 51 God.. make his riches to abounde largely in the soules of wyse men, & gif graces to vnderstondantz & studiauntz.

under'stander. [f. as prec. + -ER.]

1. One who understands; one who has knowledge or comprehension (*of* something).

c **1430** *Pilgr. Lyf Manhode* II. xxi. (1869) 84 To good vnderstonderes it is the more gracious and the more plesaunt. **1456** SIR G. HAYE *Law Arms* (S.T.S.) 13 The third part of the understandaris of the faith. **1502** ATKYNSON tr. *De Imitatione* III. xlviii. 236, I am the inwarde techer of trouth, sercher of mannes hert, the vnderstander of mannes thought. **1577** FULKE *Confut. Purg.* 413 If you have not a better vnderstander, then you are a rule giuer, your rule is false. **1613** HEYWOOD *Braz. Age* II. ii, In Greece springs The fountaines of Diuine Phylosophy, They are all vnderstanders. **1677** GILPIN *Dæmonol. Sacra* II. 214 Some are pleased to be accounted Vnderstanders by others, and rest in such high words, as a badge of Knowledge. **1721** R. BALLE *Let.* in *Athenæum* 5 April (1902) 435/1 By th' understanders of sculpture, t'was att Florence esteemed next to the Duke's Veneri. **1855** PUSEY *Doctr. Real Presence* Note S. 527 Those among you who are yet called Catechumens or hearers, could be hearers, when it was being read: could they be understanders too?

†**2. a.** A leg or foot. **b.** A boot or shoe. *Obs.*

1583 MELBANCKE *Philotimus* U iij, She leuieth her army of huge boisterous hobs, wel beseming for their vnderstanders to bee the offspringe of Giauntes. **1749** J. RAY *Hist. Reb.* (1758) 135 They also borrow'd all the Shoes and Boots they could meet with; so that many were depriv'd of their Understanders.

†**3.** A spectator standing on the ground or floor, *spec.* in a theatre. *Obs.*

1633 SHIRLEY *Contention Honour & Riches* C, When you .. make the understanders in Cheapside wonder to see ships swimme upon mens shoulders. **1646** —— *Doubtful Heir* Prol., No shews, no dance, and what you most delight in, Grave understanders, here's no target fighting.

4. *poet.* A supporter, upholder.

1875 BROWNING *Aristoph. Apol.* 113 Strong understander of our common life, Staple sustainment of morality.

†**under'standible**, var. UNDERSTANDABLE *a.*

1638 CHILLINGW. *Relig. Prot.* I. ii. §103. 91 As to be understandible is a condition requisite to a Judge, so is not that alone sufficient to make a Judge.

under'standing, *vbl. sb.* [f. the vb. + -ING^1. Cf. MSw. *undirstandning*, Icel. *-staðning.*]

1. a. (Without article.) Power or ability to understand; intellect, intelligence. Sometimes spec. = c.

a **1050** *Liber Scintill.* lxxxi. (1889) 221 Se þe þa on andȝyte inran understandincge [L. *intelligentiæ*] onfehþ. *a* **1300** *Cursor M.* 320 Minning es to [*v.r.* þe] fader cald, þe sune es vnderstanding tald. *c* **1340** HAMPOLE *Pr. Consc.* 605 Man when he is til worshepe broght Right understandyng has he noght. **1393** LANGL. *P. Pl.* C. XII. 300 Ac þese lewede laborers of lytel vnderstondynge Selde fallen so foule and so deepe in synne As clerkes of holy churche. **1422** tr. *Secreta Secret., Priv. Priv.* 135 By witte and connynge of vndyrstondynge a man may well chese the goode and lewe the ewill. *c* **1460** *Wisdom* 245–6 in *Macro Plays* 43 The iij^{de} parte of þe soule ys 'wndyrstondynge'; For by wndyrstondyng I be-holde wat Gode ys In hym selff. **1531** ELYOT *Gov.* III. xxiv, To perceyue more playnly, what thinge it is that I call understandynge. It is the principall part of the soule. **1587** GOLDING *De Mornay* v. 55 The beginner of all ends is vnderstanding, and in the most of these there is no vnderstanding. **1621** BURTON *Anat. Mel.* I. i. II. x. 40 Vnderstanding is a power of the Soule, by which we perceiue, know, remember, and Iudge. **1667** MILTON *P.L.* IX. 1127 For Understanding rul'd not, and the Will Heard not her lore. **1716** HEARNE *Coll.* (O.H.S.) V. 338 This Nibb is a man of so little understanding that he was never known to laugh. **1759** ROBERTSON *Hist. Scot.* III. Wks. 1813 I. 245 Darnley was not superior to his father in understanding. **1779** *Mirror* No. 64, I found a perfect equality of understanding and of importance. **1821** SHELLEY *Epipsych.* 162 Love is like understanding, that grows bright, Gazing on many truths. **1894** A. BIRRELL *Ess.* xi. 131 He had not enough understanding to obfuscate it by drink.

b. *of understanding*, intelligent, capable of judging with knowledge. Similarly *of some, of no, understanding.*

1428 *Munim. de Melros* (Bann. Club) 520 At þe quhilk day þe saide assis askyt mar help of men of vndirstandyng. **1535** COVERDALE *1 Kings* iii. 12 Beholde, I haue geuen the an hert of wyszdome and vnderstondynge. **1537** BIBLE (Matthew) *Wisd.* xii. 24 They wente astraye.. as chyldren of no vnderstandynge. **1600** HAKLUYT *Voy.* III. 21 And what danger that were,.. each man of reason or vnderstanding may iudge. **1613** SHAKS. *Hen. VIII*, v. III. 135 Men of some vnderstanding, And wisedome. **1772** *Boston Gazette* 3 Aug. 2/2 Men of understanding.. view the Governor's Speech.. as an impertinent sophistical Piece of Toryism.

c. With *the*: The faculty of comprehending and reasoning; the intellect.

1388 WYCLIF *Mark* xii. 33 That he be loued.. of al the vndur-stondynge, and of al the soule. **1620** T. GRANGER *Div. Logike* 108 The Vniuersall notions of the vnderstanding. **1663** BP. PATRICK *Parab. Pilgrim* (1687) 180 It cannot exercise the Understanding without provoking the passions. **1690** LOCKE *Hum. Und.* I. i. §1 The Understanding, like the Eye,.. takes no notice of it self. **1701** NORRIS *Ideal World* II. iii. (1704) 128 The business of the understanding can be no other than to understand. **1754** EDWARDS *Freed. Will* I. ii. 12 Then the Understanding must be taken in a large Sense, as including the whole Faculty of Perception or Apprehension. *a* **1859** DE QUINCEY *Knocking at Gate in Macb.* Wks. 1860 XIV. 192 The mere understanding.. is the meanest faculty in the human mind, and the most to be distrusted. **1872** MORLEY *Voltaire* 5 Manifold ways, of all of which the emotions can give good account to the understanding.

†**d.** Mind, purpose, intent. *Obs. rare.*

1382 WYCLIF *1 Pet.* iii. 8 Alle of oon vndirstondinge, or wille [L. *unanimes*]. **1531** ELYOT *Gov.* III. iv. (1883) II. 220 In euery couenaunt, bargayne, or promise aught to be.. one playne understandinge or meaning betwene the parties.

2. The intellectual faculty as manifested in a particular person or set of persons.

1382 WYCLIF *Phil.* iv. 7 The pees of God.. kepe ȝoure hertis and vndirstondingis in Crist Jhesu. **1387–8** T. USK *Test. Love* I. Prol. (Skeat) I. 31 Right so.. the understanding of Englishmen wol not strecche to the privy termes in Frenche. *c* **1400** MAUNDEV. (1839) xvii. 186 So moche hathe the Erthe in roundnesse.. aftre myn opynyoun and myn undirstondynge. *c* **1450** *Mirk's Festial* 228 Here ys no mencyon of our lady by semyng to mony mennys vndyrstondyng. **1535** COVERDALE *2 Macc.* ii. 30 He that begynneth to wryte a story for the first, must with his vnderstondinge gather the matter together. **1576** FLEMING *Panopl. Epist.* 190 Haue these stately aduauncements of flourishing fortune, so blinded thine understanding? **1615** G. SANDYS *Trav.* 59 Auicen.. reproueth.. that saying of our Sauiour.. as being weake and ill fitted to vulgar vnderstandings. **1666** BP. PARKER *Free & Impart. Censure* (1667) 77 A huge lushious stile.. rather loaths and nauceats a discreet understanding, than informs and nourishes it. **1726** SWIFT *Gulliver, Brobdingnag* vii, It gave him.. a very mean opinion of our understandings. **1769** ROBERTSON *Chas. V*, I. Wks. (1813) V. 167 Her understanding, always weak, was often disordered. **1815** SCOTT *Guy M.* xv, The idea of parting from Miss Lucy.. had never once occurred to the simplicity of his understanding. **1874** CARPENTER *Ment. Phys.* I. ii. §88. 98 Those who have obtained most influence over the understandings of others.

†**3. a.** Signification, meaning, sense. *Obs.*

13.. *Cursor M.* 14753 (Gött.), Vr lauerd Iesus þaim gaue ansuer, Bot þai ne wist quat vnderstanding it bar. **1340** *Ayenb.* 222 Huo þet ine þo onderstondinge yelt oþer acseþ zuiche dette, he ne zeneȝeþ naȝt. **1375** BARBOUR *Bruce* IV. 236 [Fiends] mak ay thair ansuering In-till dowbill vndir-standing, Till dissaf thame that will thame trow. *c* **1400** tr. *Secreta Secret., Gov. Lordsh.* 51 When ȝe haue fully þe vnderstondynges of þe sentences,.. þanne shal ȝe pursewe fully.. ȝoure purpos desiryd. **1424** *Paston Lett.* I. 13 Billes .. makyng mension and bering this undyrstondyng that the seyd William.. schuld be slayn. *c* **1500** *Melusine* 364 There were ryche pictures where as were fygured many a noble hystory, and the wrytyng vndernethe that shewed the vnder-standyng of it. **1538** CROMWELL in Merriman *Life & Lett.* (1902) II. 152 As they be taught euery sentence of the same by rote ye shall expounde.. the understandyng of the same vnto them. **1589** PUTTENHAM *Engl. Poesie* (Arb.) 189 Single words haue their sence and vnderstanding altered and figured many wayes. **1613** PURCHAS *Pilgrimage* (1614) 259 He and his fellowes were sent by.. the Iewes, to learne the vnder-standing of some obscurer places of their law. **1635** *Gram. Warre* C 10 b, *Pasco* receiued two vnderstandings, 'to feed' and 'to bring vp'. **1728** CHAMBERS *Cycl.*, *Intendment of Law*, the Understanding, Intention, and true Meaning of the Law.

†**b.** Reference or application (*to* something).

1433 *Rolls of Parlt.* IV. 451/2 Þat þis said worde Cloth.. have relation and understondyng to hole Clothes.

4. †**a.** Intelligence, information. *Obs.*

1473 WARKW. *Chron.* 7 [He] had understondynge that Kynge Edwarde was in a vilage. *a* **1562** G. CAVENDISH *Wolsey* (1893) 242 His servaunts.. havyng understondyng of my lord's departyng awaye,.. began to grudge. **1585** T. WASHINGTON tr. *Nicholay's Voy.* I. xvii. 19 b, The day before he had vnderstanding, that the Frigate.. was of Malta.

b. Comprehension *of* something. *rare.*

1548 ELYOT s.v. *Intellectus*, To atteyn to the knowlage or vnderstandyng of a thyng.

5. a. *a good* (or †*right*) *understanding*, amicable or friendly relations (between persons).

1649 CROMWELL *Let.* 8 March (Carlyle), I trust there will be a right understanding between us, and a good conclusion. **1703** STEELE *Tender Husb.* v. i, I love to promote among my Clients a good Understanding. **1725** DE FOE *Voy. round World* (1840) 213 We came.. to a better understanding about the frigate. **1762** in *10th Rep. Hist. MSS. Comm.* App. I. 323 To cultivate a good understanding between the two countries. **1833** HT. MARTINEAU *Loom & Lugger* I. iii. 37 The little hope there was of establishing a good understanding between the Coast Guard and the people. **1868** E. EDWARDS *Ralegh* I. xii. 230 Ralegh strove to bring about a good understanding between Essex and Cecil.

transf. **1765** STERNE *Tr. Shandy* VII. xix, 'Tis an under-craft of authors to keep up a good understanding amongst words, as politicians do amongst men.

b. A mutual arrangement or agreement of an informal but more or less explicit nature.

1803 G. COLMAN *John Bull* III. ii. 37 Sit down, and compose yourself, my love; the gentleman and I shall soon come to an understanding. **1812** LADY GRANVILLE *Lett.* (1894) I. 43 They have, I hear, what is called, come to an understanding. **1860** TYNDALL *Glac.* I. xxiii. 164 With this understanding we parted for the night. **1876** BLACK *Madcap Violet* xv, I think it is better we should have a distinct understanding about that.

c. *spec.* (See quot.)

1826 *Oxberry's Dram. Biog.* V. 97, 20 guineas per week and an understanding at Covent-garden. [*Note*] By this is meant, certain emoluments.. that shall increase the real amount of her salary.

6. *slang* or *colloq.* **a.** *pl.* Foot-wear; boots or shoes.

1789 G. PARKER *Life's Painter of Variegated Characters* v. 36 He [*sc.* a cobbler] had frequently furnished men of the first rank (bishops not excepted) with *understandings* of the best sort. **1822** MRS. NATHAN *Langreath* I. 29 They have been seen in the act of adapting their nethermost understandings to the costume of the more wealthy. **1838** JAS. GRANT *Sk. Lond.* 87 His toes began to peep out between the soles and uppers of his 'understandings'—as he sometimes facetiously called his boots. **1874** *Slang Dict.* 333

Men who wear exceptionally large or thick boots, are said to possess good understandings.

b. *pl.* Legs or feet.

1828 *Lancet* 22 March 920/1 His plump, well-formed, little 'understandings' twinkling in the lustre of black silk hose. **1844** 'Jonathan Slick' *High Life N. York* II. 58 She had on a short petticoat that showed a.. considerable chunk of understandings. **1856** 'Stonehenge' *Brit. Rur. Sports* 381/2 Discount was.. the perfection of a strong, well-bred horse,.. if only his understandings had been sound.

under'standing, *ppl. a.* [f. as prec. + -ING[2].]

1. a. Of persons (or animals): Possessed of understanding; having knowledge and judgement; intelligent.

Very common in the 17th century.

c **1200** *Trin. Coll. Hom.* 121 Ðe man is understondinde, þe him seluen cnoweð and gode leueð. **1338** R. Brunne *Chron.* (1810) 35 He was boþe gode & wys in alle his dedis, & right vnderstandyng, to help at alle nedis. **1382** Wyclif *Deut.* iv. 6 A wise puple and an vndirstondynge! *c* **1440** *Promp. Parv.* 511 Vnderstondynge, or wytty, *intelligens.* **1535** Coverdale *Deut.* iv. 6 What a wyse and vnderstondinge folke is this? **1613** Wither *Abuses Stript* II. ii. O 5 b, A selected Crew,.. the Wisest, The Vnderstanding'st, yea, and the Precisest Of a whole Empire. **1634** Sir T. Herbert *Trav.* 29 A modest and vnderstanding Gentleman. *Ibid.* 90 An Elephant (an vnderstanding beast). **1681** Otway *Soldier's Fort.* v. i, Aristotle.. was an understanding fellow. **1711** Addison *Spect.* No. 42 ¶6 The more understanding Part of the Audience immediately see through it and despise it. **1772** Priestley *Inst. Relig.* (1782) I. 377 There were among them many.. understanding persons. **1817–8** Cobbett *Resid. U.S.* (1822) 167 One of the most understanding and most worthy men I ever had the honour to be acquainted with. **1875** Jowett *Plato* (ed. 2) I. 132 The Athenians are an understanding people.

absol. **1650** Gentilis *Considerations* 194 So that.. we may say, that the understandingest doth command by cunning, the most rash by violence.

b. Const. *in* (a matter, etc.). Now *rare* or *Obs.*

1612 Bacon *Ess.*, *Of Judicature* (Arb.) 458 An ancient Clearke, skilful in presidents,.. and vnderstanding in the businesse of the Court. *c* **1643** Ld. Herbert *Autobiog.* (1824) 35 Howsoever he was very understanding in all other things, he was noted yet to be of a very high mind. **1732** Lord Tyrawly in *Buccleuch MSS.* (Hist. MSS. Comm.) I. 381 My Captain, who is a very understanding fellow in these matters. **1755** *Mem. Capt. P. Drake* I. ii. 19 A very understanding Man in the Business of Cow-stealing.

2. a. Of the mind, etc.: Endowed with intelligence; intellectual.

1382 Wyclif *1 Kings* iii. 12 I haue.. ȝeuen to thee a wise herte and an vndurstondynge [L. *sapiens et intelligens*]. **1398** Trevisa *Barth. De P.R.* v. xxviii. (Bodl. MS.), Kinde ȝeueþ to man vndirstonding instrumentes according to his vertues. **1539** Bible (Great) *1 Kings* iii. 9 Geue therfore vnto thy seruaunt an vnderstandyng hert. **1581** J. Bell *Haddon's Answ. Osor.* 141 Mans will and the understandyng parte of his soule. **1662** H. More *Antid. Ath.* III. i. §2 Some free subtile understanding Essence distinct from the brute Matter. **1681** Flavel *Meth. Grace* xxiii. 401 The understanding faculty like a dial is enlightened with the beams of divine truth shining upon it. **1827** Pollok *Course T.* III. 636 Be wise, Ye fools! be of an understanding heart. **1853** F. D. Maurice *Proph. & Kings* v. 78 The understanding heart of Solomon led him to revere as well as to suspect himself.

b. Of speech: Displaying intelligence. *rare*[−1].

1635 J. Taylor (Water P.) *Very Old Man* C, Loves Company, and Vnderstanding talke.

†**3.** Capable of being understood; intelligible. *Obs.*

1387–8 T. Usk *Test. Love* I. Prol. (Skeat) l. 56 By thilke thinges that ben made understonding here to our wittes. *c* **1400** tr. *Secreta Secret., Gov. Lordsh.* 93 All þare-by is vnderstandant, and neghys negh, þat þat ys remued of farre.

4. Of a person, etc.: displaying sympathetic tolerance; of a forgiving nature or temperament.

1913 E. C. Bentley *Trent's Last Case* xiii. 251, I felt that.. I must speak to you about this... Because you seemed to me an understanding person. **1929** E. Bowen *Last September* xviii. 228 You had always been so understanding. **1959** G. Freeman *Jack would be Gentleman* v. 100 Oh thank you... You are understanding. **1974** 'R. Tate' *Birds of Bloodied Feather* iii. 64 Thank you for writing such an understanding note to me about my sister.

under'standingly, *adv.* [f. prec. + -LY[2].] In a comprehending or intelligent manner; with understanding. †Also, so as to be understood.

a **1340** Hampole *Psalter* xlviii. 12 For he wroght not vndir-standan[d]ly he is likynd.. til vnwise bestis in vnwisdome. *c* **1400** tr. *Secreta Secret., Gov. Lordsh.* 101 Besily and vnderstandandly y amonest þe, and gyues þe good conseill. **1580** Hollyband *Treas. Fr. Tong, Entendiblement*, vnderstandingly, learnedly. **1602** Fulbecke *Pandects* 55 It is more plainlie and understandinglie opened by him in these wordes. **1649** F. Roberts *Clavis Bibl.* 46 Still fix your thought upon the Occasion and Scope of every Book, when you would peruse them understandingly. **1697** Humfrey *Righteousn. God* I. 6 This Learned Man hath.. understandingly exprest the very thing as it is. **1754** Edwards *Freedom Will* IV. viii. 248 A Work of his almighty Power,.. upheld understandingly, and on Design, as much as if no other had been made but that. **1833** *New Monthly Mag.* XXXVIII. 154 His was one of those clear eyes which see beauty understandingly. **1850** *Fraser's Mag.* XLI. 524 The young people began to look very understandingly at each other. **1890** Mary E. Wilkins *Far-away Melody* 16 They had studied the Bible faithfully, if not understandingly.

†**under'standingness.** *Obs.* [f. as prec. + -NESS.] The state or condition of having understanding; the faculty of understanding.

a **1628** F. Greville *Poems* (1633) 60 In Mans youth, perchance, Fame multiplies Courage, and actiue vnderstandingnesse. **1662** J. Chandler *Van Helmont's Oriat.* 25 In the understandingness of the understanding.

,under'state, *v.* [UNDER-[1] 10 a.] *trans.* To state below what is correct or warrantable. Also *absol.*, to make an understatement.

1824 Mackintosh *Sp. Ho. Comm.* 1 June, Wks. 1846 III. 430 A pious and amiable woman,.. anxious rather to understate facts. **1850** Grote *Greece* II. lxiv. VIII. 252 *note*, I have understated the number of lives in danger. **1874** Gladstone in *Contemp. Rev.* Oct. 673 In commenting on over-statement, I do not seek to understate.

†**,under-'stated,** *a. Obs.* [UNDER-[1] 10 c.] Of too low or poor an estate.

a **1661** Fuller *Worthies, Bedford.* I. (1662) 118 Sir Henry, though heir to his Brother Richard after his death; yet perceiving himself over-titled or rather under-stated, for so high an honour,.. declined the assuming thereof.

understated (stress variable), *ppl. a.* [UNDER-[1] 10 a. Cf. UNDERSTATE *v.*] **a.** Stated below what is adequate or sufficient; that understates the truth.

1937 E. Ambler *Uncommon Danger* xviii. 275 Zaleshoff gave a brief and, Kenton thought, grossly understated account of their night's adventure. **1978** *Language* LIV. 158 This is most clearly exemplified in his chapter on social class and language, where he discusses criticisms of the work of Bernstein (under the somewhat understated subheading, 'A small misunderstanding?'). **1982** Barr & York *Official Sloane Ranger Handbk.* 10/2 The royal family are pretty good here with their understated asides about 'living above the shop' and 'family business'.

b. Of clothes, appearance, etc.: unemphasized, modest; designed not to attract undue attention. Cf. QUIET *a.* 2 b.

1957 *Punch* 6 Feb. 224/1 The clothes.. were in good taste, wearable and, to borrow a word much in vogue, *understated*—or, to use one's own word, dull. **1963** *Harper's Bazaar* Feb. 41 Catching up with fashion.. in this era of understated looks. **1967** Mrs. L. B. Johnson *White House Diary* 8 Oct. (1970) 578, I changed again into another quiet understated outfit. **1979** R. Jaffe *Class Reunion* (1980) 15 Emily had longed for a camel's hair coat like Daphne's—understated, sophisticated, collegiate.

understatement. [UNDER-[1] 10 b. Cf. UNDERSTATE *v.*] **a.** (*,under-'statement.*) A statement which falls below the truth or fact.

1799 *Monthly Rev.* XXVIII. 528 Stating at the lowest its own populousness and produce, and.. favouring a similar understatement by its neighbours. **1877** Morley *Crit. Misc.* Ser. II. 330 Mr. Mill's remarks.. involve a distinct understatement.

b. (Stress variable.) The quality of being understated (sense b) or modest in design.

1967 *Guardian* 21 July 7/4 The kind of subtly simple dress.. that 'Vogue' would call understated... Under-statement is the thing. **1977** 'J. Fraser' *Hearts Ease in Death* xiii. 142 Her simple Hardy Amies dresses, designed with all the understatement.. that had become the Queen's dressmaker's hallmark.

'understater. [f. UNDERSTATE *v.* + -ER[1].] One who understates or avoids overstatement.

1957 *New Yorker* 2 Nov. 114/3 Mr. Sinatra.. is probably not a natural-born understater. **1977** P. Ustinov *Dear Me* vii. 96 Britain had already supplied Hollywood with a whole battalion of elegant understaters, immaculate actors of the Du Maurier school, who.. were able to play anything.. without their assumed characters.. being allowed to affect their performances.

'understay, *sb.* (UNDER-[1] 5 b.)

a **1603** T. Cartwright *Confut. Rhem. N.T.* (1618) 729 That prop and vnderstay of our faith.. is cleane ouerthrown.

under'stay, *v.* (UNDER-[1] 4 a.)

1679 A. Lovell *Indic. Univ.* 39 To prop or understay the Vine.

understeer, *v.* **1.** (*under'steer.*) [UNDER-[1] 4 b.] To steer under something.

1573 Twyne *Æneid* x. E ej, In sight she deare apeerd With left hand coutching waues, and smoth herself she vndersteerd [L. *subremigat*].

2. (Chiefly *'understeer.*) [UNDER-[1] 10 a.] *intr.* To exhibit understeer. Hence **'understeering** *vbl. sb.* and *ppl. a.*

1936 *Proc. Inst. Automobile Engineers* XXX. 730 If a car under-steers, more rudder is required at the higher speeds. *Ibid.*, The under-steering of the parallel front road springs is.. due to the lack of cornering power. **1948** R. Dean-Averns *Automobile Chassis Design* ii. 49 Under-steering vehicles,.. when put into a turn, endeavour to straighten up and require constant *increase* of lock as the speed on the bend is increased. **1966** J. Miles in T. Wisdom *High-Performance Driving* v. 47 If the wheels are pointing exactly round the line of the circle some cars will actually travel in a wider circle. These are under-steering cars. **1970** *Motoring Which?* Apr. 45/1 Both tended to understeer (run wide of the corners). **1972** *Sci. Amer.* Aug. 20/2 Of the three characteristics understeering is the most desirable.

'understeer, *sb.* [UNDER-[1] 10 b.] A tendency in a motor vehicle to take too wide a turn when made to deviate from the straight.

1936 [see OVERSTEER *sb.*]. **1957** S. Moss *In Track of Speed* xii. 149, I.. watched Castellotte sorting out his Ferrari, the front wheels on full understeer with the inside one off the ground. **1964** *Which?* Apr. 36/2 The *Bedford Romany* had light steering and very little under-steer—it was hardly necessary to turn the steering wheel more when going faster round a bend. **1971** *Daily Tel.* 31 Mar. 11/5 A disadvantage of the bigger engine is the heavier steering and even more marked understeer, made worse by the steep roll angles in fast cornering. **1981** G. G. Hilditch *Further Look at Buses* i. 8/2 You make your approach run perhaps changing down.. and then wind on a bit of lock. The bus doesn't notice thanks to a wonderful degree of understeer so you add a few more degrees.. and the resulting oversteer runs away with you.

'under-stem. (UNDER-[1] 5 b.)

1853 Ruskin *Stones Ven.* II. ii. §6. 17 It is delightful to see how he has rooted the whole leaf in the strong rounded under-stem. **1868** *Rep. U.S. Commissioner Agric.* (1869) 94 The European species.. is found upon low plants, gnawing the under-stems.

'understep, *sb.* (UNDER-[1] 5 b.)

1610 J. Robinson *Justif. Separat.* iii. 10 That by it, as by an understep, he might climb up.. into the throne of iniquity.

under'step, *v.* (UNDER-[1] 10 a.)

1843 *Blackw. Mag.* LIV. 652 Were such phraseology allowable, we should say that the sphere has understepped itself.

'under-,steward. (UNDER-[1] 6 a.)

1472–3 *Rolls of Parlt.* VI. 35/1 Depute and understeward to John Erle of Wilteshire. **1483** *Act 1 Rich. III*, c. 6 §1 No Steward, Under-Steward,.. nor other Minister of such Courts of Pipowders. **1667** in Pettus *Fodinæ Reg.* (1670) 39 One Vnder-Steward to recide at the Mines. **1708** J. Chamberlayne *St. Gt. Brit.* (1710) 226 The Under-Steward of Westminster is likewise an Officer of great Note.

Hence **'under-,stewardship.**

1472–3 *Rolls of Parlt.* VI. 35/1 The said Office of under-stewardshipp.

†**under'stipre,** *v. Obs.*[−1] [UNDER-[1] 4 a: see STIPER.] *trans.* To prop up, support.

The variant *understipen* corresponds to WFris. *stypje*.

a **1225** *Ancr. R.* 142 Heo wuneð under þe chirche, ase uorte understipren [*v.r.* understipen] hire, ȝif heo wolde uallen.

'under-stock, *sb. arch.* (UNDER-[1] 5 b.)

1821 Scott *Kenilw.* xxxi, His shoes being of white velvet; his under-stocks (or stockings) of knit silk.

,under'stock, *v.* (UNDER-[1] 10 a: cf. next.)

1765 *Museum Rust.* IV. 267 The same ill consequences attend either over or under-stocking a farm with all other cattle. **1771** A. Young *Northern Tour* IV. 272 If it be asked, why farmers.. so much understock themselves.

,under'stocked, *ppl. a.* (UNDER-[1] 10 a.)

1670 Sir T. Culpepper *Necess. Abating Usury* 32 His farme is understocked, ill fenced, and out of heart. **1733** Tull *Horse-Hoeing Husb.* xiv. 166 The Ground may be.. understock'd with Plants. **1792** A. Young *Trav. France* 489 For the country.. to import so immensely, shews how wretchedly they are understocked with sheep. **1846** McCulloch *Acc. Brit. Empire* (1854) I. 561 Farms in all parts of Britain are decidedly understocked.

'under-,stockings. (UNDER-[1] 5 a.)

1605 *Knaresb. Wills* (Surtees) I. 252 One paire of white under stockines. **1648** Hexham II, *Onder-koussen*, Vnder or Nether-stockins.

understone: see quot. s.v. UNDERCLIFT.

under'stood, *pa. pple.* and *ppl. a.* [f. UNDERSTAND *v.*]

†**1.** Being made known or patent. *Obs.*[−1]

1576 Lambarde *Peramb. Kent* 152 This done and vnder stoode to the Archbishop, she was by him appointed to S. Sepulcres.

2. Comprehended; thoroughly known.

1605 Shaks. *Macb.* III. iv. 124 Augures, and vnderstood Relations, haue.. brought forth The secret'st man of Blood. **1661** Boyle *Style of Script.* 48 By the light of understood Scriptures to penetrate the sense of the obscurer ones. *a* **1700** Evelyn *Diary* 12 Oct. 1677, The gardens are large,.. and the husbandry part made very convenient and perfectly understood.

3. Agreed upon; assumed as known or fixed.

1607 in W. H. Hale *Prec. in Causes of Office* (1841) 9 He doth now confesse that it was an understood part of his therein. **1833** Ht. Martineau *Fr. Wines & Pol.* iii. 33 There had been established a tolerably steady rate of understood value. **1853** Mrs. Gaskell *Ruth* xxiii, It was an understood thing that no one was to be ill or tired.. without leave asked. **1897** Mary Kingsley *W. Africa* 317 Each chief takes a certain understood value in goods as a commission for himself.

4. *Gram.* Implied though not expressed.

1848 J. T. White *Xenophon's Anab.* Notes 38 Observe the adverb between the article and the understood noun, supplying the place of an adjective.

'understorey. Also -story. [UNDER-[1] 5 d.] The (layer of) vegetation growing beneath the level of the tallest trees in a forest. Cf. UNDERWOOD 1. Also *attrib.*

1945 *Ecology* XXVI. 280/1 The setback in growth for the dominant trees.. may occur because of too dense a hardwood understory. **1958** *New Biol.* XXV. 62 The removal of the dense shrub understorey of rhododendron and laurel from another catchment increased the yield of water. **1970** *New Scientist* 30 Apr. 212/1 The total removal of herb and scrub understory removes a habitat diversity which makes young conifer plantations so attractive to wildlife. **1975** W. Condry *Pathway to Wild* xi. 191 A woodland bird reserve needs a wealth of understorey shrubs for birds to nest in. **1983** M. Gee *Sole Survivor* xxi. 224

Although the sun spreads a watery light in the understoreys of the bush the cold stays on.

'understrain. (UNDER-^{1} 9 b.)
? **1802** COLERIDGE *Happy Husband* 22 A more precipitated vein Of notes, that.. leave their sweeter understrain, Its own sweet self.

'under,strapper. [f. UNDER-^{1} 6 a + STRAP *v.* Cf. STRAPPER^{1} 2.] An underling; a subordinate agent; an assistant. (In common use from *c* 1710.)
a **1704** T. BROWN *Walk round Lond., Thames* Wks. 1709 III. III. 60 Every Wapping Understrapper, that has but a Congregation of old Women to hold himself forth to. **1753** SMOLLETT *Ct. Fathom* xxix, I desire you will order him and this barbar, who is his understrapper, to be examined on the spot. **1842** THACKERAY *Fitz-Boodle's Conf.* Wks. 1869 XXII. 211 Let one of your understrappers correct the spelling and the grammar of my papers. **1894** BLACKMORE *Perlycross* 297 The meanest.. understrapper of the 'Private Enquiry Firm'.

'under,strapping, *a.* [Cf. prec.] Of a subordinate or inferior character or standing.
1762 STERNE *Tr. Shandy* VI. xvii, I.. have as great a share ..of that under-strapping virtue of discretion as the best of you. **1793** J. WILLIAMS *Calm Exam.* 45 The understrapping and base members of the awful mystery [of the law].

'under,stratum. [UNDER-^{1} 5 c.] An underlying stratum or layer; a substratum.
1733 TULL *Horse-Hoeing Husb.* xx. 290 These Drags draw them sometimes into larger Heaps, leaving the Under-Stratum bare betwixt them. **1783** *Encycl. Brit.* (ed. 2) X. 8307/1 However great differences there may be among the under strata. **1807** VANCOUVER *Agric. Devon* (1813) 19 The soil and understrata of Little Torrington. **1886** *19th Cent.* Sept. 421 There is a vast and virtuous understratum in society which really loves the right.

'understream. (UNDER-^{1} 5 c.)
1830 TENNYSON *Poems* 125 The glistering sands that robe The understream. **1883** *Pall Mall G.* 26 July 7/1 As the understreams formed by the Horseshoe Falls rise to the surface.

under'strew, *v.* [UNDER-^{1} 4 a.] *trans.* To strew or spread beneath; *fig.* to cast under foot.
1382 WYCLIF *Luke* xix. 36 Thei vndir strewiden [L. *substernebant*] her clothis in the weye. **1471** RIPLEY *Comp. Alch.* Ep. i. in Ashm. (1652) 109 So that old ranckors under-strewed, Tempestuous troubles and wretchednes shall cease. **1589** FLEMING *Virg. Georg.* III. 46 T' vnderstrew or spread the bare ground with.. Handfuls of ferne.

'understrife. *poet.* [UNDER-^{1} 5 b.] Strife carried on upon the earth.
c **1611** CHAPMAN *Iliad* xx. 138 We soon shall.. send them to heaven, to settle their abode With equals, flying under-strifes.

under'strike, *v.* [UNDER-^{1} 4 a, b.]
†**1.** *trans.* To let down (the sails of a ship). *Obs.*
1615 CHAPMAN *Odyss.* XVI. 474 Amphinomus in port display'd The ship arrived, her sails then under-stroke.
2. To strike (from) below.
1844 MRS. BROWNING *Lady Geraldine's Courtship* xlvii, For the root of some grave earnest thought is understruck so rightly As [etc.].
Hence **'under,striking** *ppl. a.*
1880 A. J. HIPKINS in Grove *Dict. Mus.* II. 647/1 For understriking grand pianos.. and for upright pianos. *Ibid.* 712/1 Both overstriking and understriking apparatus.

'understroke, *sb.* (UNDER-^{1} 5 b.)
1837 WHEELWRIGHT tr. *Aristophanes, Birds* III. i, By their feet the geese with understrokes As 'twere with shovels, threw it in the hods.

under'stroke, *v.* [UNDER-^{1} 4 b. Cf. G. *unterstreichen,* Da. *understrege.*] *trans.* To underline, underscore.
1732 SWIFT *Let. to Duchess of Queensbury* 20 Mar., You have understroaked that offensive word, to shew that it should be printed in italic.

'under,study, *sb.* [f. next.] An actor or actress who studies a superior performer's part in order to be able to take it if required; also, the study of a part of this purpose. Also *transf.*
1882 *Society* 7 Oct. 13/2 His place during his absence.. having been filled by his understudy. **1884** G. MOORE *Mummer's Wife* xv, The girl who.. had been entrusted with the understudy. **1887** LANG *Myth, Ritual & Relig.* I. 336 There is a.. tendency for gods to double their parts, or rather,.. for each part to have its 'under-study'.

understudy ('ʌndə-, older -'stʌdɪ), *v.* [UNDER-^{1} 7.]
1. *trans.* To study (a part or character) in order to be able to take the place of a principal actor or actress if necessary.
1874 *Slang Dict.* 333 Some actors of position.. have always other and inferior.. artists understudying their parts. **1880** *Theatre* Oct. 207 She was selected to understudy the characters of the stars.
2. To act as understudy to (a principal actor or actress).
1884 G. MOORE *Mummer's Wife* xv, Some one must under-study Serpolette. **1894** CROCKETT *Play Actress* ix, She has to understudy Rose Sargeant and play her parts when that lady's temper is out of order.
transf. **1893** *Westm. Gaz.* 23 June 5/2 (Racing), Water-cress had no difficulty in understudying La Flêche last week.
3. *intr.* To act as an understudy.
1909 in WEBSTER. **1939** W. FORTESCUE *There's Rosemary* x. 74 He was very kind and encouraging, but assured me that I should only waste my time in London, understudy and playing small parts. **1962** J. MCCABE *Mr. Laurel & Mr. Hardy* i. 26 He went on as a single again.. and understudied for *Home from the Honeymoon.*
Hence **'under,studied** *ppl. a.*
1880 *Temple Bar* March 321 An under-studied Part.

under'stuffed, *ppl. a.* (UNDER-^{1} 4 a.)
1573 *Arte of Limning* A iij, A litle borde.. couered with a calues skin raysed or vnderstuffed with wolle or floxe or else vnstuffed.

†**under'stumble,** *v. colloq. Obs.* [Alteration of UNDERSTAND *v.*, after STUMBLE *v.* Cf. UNDERCUMSTUMBLE *v.*] *trans.* To understand.
c **1681** HICKERINGILL *Trimmer* vi. Wks. 1716 I. 386 Oh! ho! I begin to understumble you, Edad, I will not tell you. **1738** SWIFT *Polite Conv.* 105, I understumble you, Gentlemen.

†**undersub'scribe, -'scrive,** *v. Sc. Obs.* [UNDER-^{1} 4 a.] *intr.* To subscribe to a document.
α. **1565** *Reg. Privy Council Scot.* I. 363 We, the Erlis.. and Baronis undirsubscrivand. **1605** in *Abst. Protocols Town Cleks of Glasgow* (1896) II. 115 With expres consent.. of the counsall and deikinis of the said burght wndirsubscriveand. **1644** *Reg. Privy Counc. Scotl.* Ser. II. VIII. 97 In presence of me, notar publict undersubscryvand, and witnesses efternamet.
β. **1573** *Reg. Privy Council Scot.* II. 310 We undersubscriband to be bundin and obleist [etc.]. **1642** *Declar. Lords & Comm., To Gen. Assemb. Ch. Scot., Lond.* 12 Divers other undersubscribing. **1708** *Lond. Gaz.* No. 4430/6 We,.. the Noblemen.. of the Shire of Ayr undersubscribing.
Hence †**undersub'scriber.** *Obs.*
1681 W. KER, etc. (*title*), A Blasphemous and Treasonable Paper emitted by the Phanatical Under-subscribers. **1726** SHELVOCKE *Voy. round World* 39 We under subscribers, Officers, seamen and others. **1799** MITCHELL *Scotticisms* 88 We the under subscribers; Sc.—Subscribers, undersigned.

'under-,sucking, *ppl. a.* [UNDER-^{1} 4 a, b.]
a. Sucking from below. **b.** Sucking down.
1611 SPEED *Hist. Gt. Brit.* VII. xxxvii. §2. 335 Y^{e} blossoms of vnder-sucking plants. *a* **1886** CHR. G. ROSSETTI *Poems* (1904) 144/2 Who sinks, uplift from the undersucking silt To set him on Thy rock.

'under-suit. (UNDER-^{1} 5 a.)
1598 *Sidney's Arcadia* III. 361 Hauing.. first put on a sleight vnder-sute of mans apparell. *a* **1661** FULLER *Worthies, Hampsh.* II. (1662) 8 He.. put off his Robes of State, resigning his Office:.. no danger of catching cold, his own Under-suit was well lined, having gotten a fair Estate.. in Sussex. **1696** *Lond. Gaz.* No. 3204/3 The Knight Elect.. being in his Under-Suit of the Order, of Cloth of Silver,.. was.. conducted.. to the Chapter-house.

'under-,surface. (UNDER-^{1} 5 b.)
Also freq. as two words: see UNDER *a.* 2 b.
1733 TULL *Horse-Hoeing Husb.* xxv. 404 The Under-surface of the Limbers.. parallel.. to the Upper-surface.. of the Beam. **1836-9** *Todd's Cycl. Anat.* II. 861/2 The pro-sternum or under-surface of the prothorax. **1853** MARKHAM *Skoda's Auscult. & Percuss.* 214 Murmurs are produced at the aortic valves, when their under-surfaces are roughened.

†**undersusten'tation.** *Obs.* (UNDER-^{1} 5 c.)
1650 ELDERFIELD *Tythes* 180 The bottome foundation fails, and the whole frame must be left to sink and ruine with it for want of sustenance, or undersustentation.

'under-swain. (UNDER-^{1} 6 a.)
1644 QUARLES *Sheph. Orac.* iii, She.. Cast am'rous eyes on every under-swaine.

'undersward. (UNDER-^{1} 5 c.)
1883 G. ALLEN *Colin Clout's Cal.* 182 Stiff wiry knot-grass forming.. a ragged undersward.

'under,swearer. [UNDER-^{1} 6 a.] One who supports another by oath.
1724 SWIFT *Drapier's Lett.* iv. Wks. 1761 III. 77 The infamous Coleby, one of his under-swearers at the Committee of Council.

under'sweat, *v.* (UNDER-^{1} 7 + SWEAT *v.* 6 b.)
1888 *Times* (weekly ed.) 18 May 7/4 The English Jews complain that they are 'undersweated'. **1896** *Globe* 15 Dec., The German toy-makers who undersweat the world.

'underswell. [UNDER-^{1} 5 c.] A swell below the surface; an undercurrent.
1849 *Tait's Mag.* XVI. 760 This placid springtime of life had a strong underswell of sorrow. **1894** *Cycl. Rev. Current Hist.* (Buffalo, N.Y.) IV. 733 A certain insistence of tone which gives note of a strong underswell of feeling and purpose.

†**under-swordfish.** *Obs.* = HALF-BEAK.
1681 GREW *Musæum* I. v. i. 87 The Head of the Under-Sword-Fish.

under'takable, *a.* [f. UNDERTAKE *v.* + -ABLE.] Capable of being undertaken.
1638 CHILLINGW. *Relig. Prot.* Ded., It was undertakable by a man of very mean.. abilities.

†**'undertake,** *sb. Obs.* [f. next.] An undertaking, enterprise.
1647 SPRIGGE *Anglia Rediv.* IV. ix. 295 The spoyle of the Castle, which cannot be avoyded in extreame undertakes against it. **1676** *Doctrine of Devils* To Rdr., I shall say no more in vindication of the undertake.

undertake (ʌndə'teɪk), *v.* [f. UNDER-^{1} 8 a + TAKE *v.*, after UNDERNIM *v.* Cf. MSw. *undertaka.*]
I. *trans.* †**1. a.** To take by craft, to entrap; to overtake, seize upon. *Obs.*
c **1200** ORMIN 10314 Forrþi þatt teʒʒ haffdenn niþ Wiþþ himm.. & wolldenn unnderrtakenn himm Off summwhatt, ʒiff þeʒʒ mihhtenn. **1470-85** MALORY *Arthur* IX. xxxvii. 400 So sire Tristram endured there grete payne, for sekenesse had vndertake hym.
†**b.** To reprove, rebuke, chide. *Obs.*
1377 LANGL. *P. Pl.* B. XI. 89 'Wher-of serueth lawe,' quod lewte, 'if no lyf vndertoke it, Falsenesse ne faytrye'. **1387** TREVISA *Higden* (Rolls) II. 133 He wente to Scotlonde wiþ grete indingnacioun, for Wilfrede vndertook hym for he hylde vnlawfulliche Esterday. *c* **1400** *Pilgr. Sowle* I. xix. (1859) 19, I haue ful oftymes for thy mysdedys undertake the. *c* **1440** *Gesta Rom.* lxv. 290 Whan he was come, the Emperour vndirtoke hym of the cryme that he did to Guy. **1480** CAXTON *Chron. Eng.* cliii, And he wold dysherite the good erle.. for encheson that he undertoke hym of his wikkedness. **1691** tr. *Emiliane's Frauds Rom. Monks* (ed. 3) 53 When he was in the company of Monks, who were not Reformed,.. he would undertake them in a high manner, yea, with Insolence it self.
†**2. a.** To accept, receive willingly. *Obs.*
a **1250** *Ancr. R.* 114 He.. underueng [*Titus MS.* undertoc] hit edmodliche. *a* **1300** *Cursor M.* 917 And þou, man, þat has vndertaken þi wijf red, and min for-saken, Ne sal þou nawight þar wit win. *Ibid.* 9064 Yee rede me nu, for drightin sake, Your consail wil i vndertak. **1303** R. BRUNNE *Handl. Synne* 9984 For he wulde nat men hyt forsoke, But þat alle men hyt vndyrtoke. **1338** —— *Chron.* (1810) 60 þe barons said,.. þare trespas we vndertake opon alle our fee.
†**b.** To receive; to have given. *Obs.*
13.. *Cursor M.* 4642 (Gött.), I will þat he here vndir-take All þe worschip of mi land. **1393** LANGL. *P. Pl.* C. I. 98 And boxes ben broght forþ i-bounden with yre, To vndertake þe tol of vntrewe sacrifice In menynge of miracles. **1623** LISLE *Ælfric on O. & N. Test.* Introd., Moses,.. who wrote as God himself directed.. while he abode with God upon Mount Sinai.. & undertook [OE. orig., *underfeng*] his law.
†**c.** To receive into the mind; to hear. *Obs.*
13.. *St. Alexius* 54 in Horstm. *Altengl. Leg.* (1881) 175 His fadir sette him sone to boke And wele clergie he vndir-toke. **1382** WYCLIF *Ecclus.* ii. 2 Bowe in thyn ere, and vndertac [L. *suscipe*] the wrdis of vndirstonding. **1596** SPENSER *F.Q.* V. iii. 34 Whose voice so soone as he did vndertake, Eftsoones he stood as still as any stake.
†**3.** To understand. *Obs.*
a **1300** *Cursor M.* 307 And be þe hette þou vnderta þa hali gost comms of hem tua. *Ibid.* 2050 Noe wit þat mantil woke, His sun hething he vnder-toke. *a* **1400-50** *Alexander* 2967 Sone þis gouernour of grece is of þis gaude ware,.. & vndire-take he touched of him-selfe. *c* **1440** *York Myst.* xxiii. 23 ʒe cowde noght vndyr-take The tales þat I ʒou tolde. *c* **1510** MORE *Picus* Wks. 10/1 While she spake of the seconde death and euerlasting: & he vndertoke her of the first death & temporal.
4. To take upon oneself; to take in hand.
Sometimes contextually 'to enter upon, begin'.
a **1300** *Cursor M.* 4644, I wil him do at vnder-tak þe wardanscipp of al mi land. *Ibid.* 4795, I am all redi bun Our aller nedes vnder ta. *a* **1340** HAMPOLE *Psalter* xxiv. 7 A ʒoungman dredis noght to vndirtake þe peril þat he is slane in. *c* **1374** CHAUCER *Troylus* II. 807 He which þat no þyng vnder-taketh No þyng ne acheueth. **1404** in Ellis *Orig. Lett.* Ser. II. I. 20 The same cuntrees have undertake the seges of hem til thei ben wonnen. *c* **1489** CAXTON *Sonnes of Aymon* xxvi. 549 Telle me.. what he sayeth of this quarell that ye have vndertake. **1597** HOOKER *Eccl. Pol.* V. liv. §6 The.. offices of that mysticall administration.. which he voluntarily vnder-tooke. *a* **1628** PRESTON *Effectual Faith* (1630) 8 There-fore they vndertake the businesse, they goe about the enterprize, and it comes to naught. **1654** GATAKER *Disc. Apol.* 53 [They] are readie to undertake more than they are able to undergo, or to go through with. **1717** LADY M. W. MONTAGU *Let. to Pope* 1 April, I have gone a journey not undertaken by any Christian for some hundred years. **1781** COWPER *Table-T.* 284 They, that fight for freedom, undertake The noblest cause mankind can have at stake. **1831** SCOTT *Ct. Rob.* xviii, What is the enterprise too bold to be undertaken on such a condition! **1847** MARRYAT *Childr. N. Forest* xvii, I hope you will undertake the post which I now offer you. **1874** GREEN *Short Hist.* vi. §4 (1882) 306 Colet.. was the first to undertake the reform of the Church.
ellipt. **1605** CAMDEN *Rem.* 3 If any one would vndertake the honour and precedence of Britaine before other Realmes in serious manner. **1655** STANLEY *Hist. Philos.* III. 37 His friends.. desired him to æstimate it at 30. minæ, promising to undertake the sum.
b. Const. *to* with *inf.* (Sometimes implying a solemn pledge or promise: cf. next.)
a **1300** *Cursor M.* 3409 Now es god at vnder tak þe store tell [*Gött.* stori to tell] of ysaac. *c* **1385** CHAUCER *L.G.W.* Prol. 71, I ne haue nat vndyr-take As of the lef a-gayn the flour to make. **1390** GOWER *Conf.* I. 151 He.. seith that he wol undertake Upon hire wordes forto stonde. *c* **1440** *Generydes* 3175 Among your knyghtez all that ther is on Shall vnder take to Answer for this lande. **1494** in *Lett. Rich. III & Hen. VII* (Rolls) I. 389 Diuers noble personnes hanne enterprised and undertaked to hold a justis roiall: **1560** DAUS tr. *Sleidane's Comm.* 259, I wold first vndertake to geue ye charge vpon thennemy w^{t} ii legions. **1591** SHAKS. *Two Gent.* III. ii. 38 Then you must vndertake to slander him. **1637** W. SALTONSTALL *Eusebius' Constantine* 26 Constantine had undertooke.. to free the Christians from his tyranny. **1667** MILTON *P.L.* IV. 935, I alone first undertook To wing the desolate Abyss. **1712** BLACKMORE *Creation* v. 281 That matter.. in the immense from endless ages strove, The Stagyrite thus undertakes to prove. **1754** SHEBBEARE *Matrimony* (1766) II. 259 Without this Power the Mother-in-Law would scarce have undertook to have trafficed in the commerce of a Son committed to her care. **1821** SCOTT *Kenilw.* xxvi, Wayland and she followed in silence the deputy-usher, who undertook to be their conductor. **1860** TYNDALL *Glac.* I. xxi. 150 A porter.. undertook to conduct me to one of the adjacent glaciers.

c. To give a formal promise or pledge *that*; to take upon oneself to promise or affirm; to venture to assert.

c **1375** *Sc. Leg. Saints* vii. (*Jacob*) 606 Wil þu vndirta þat I and þai þat are with me, In gud fath sal vnschait be? **1393** LANGL. *P. Pl.* C. XXI. 20 Loue haþ vndertake That þis iesus of hus gentrise shal Iouste in peers Armes. *c* **1450** *Mirk's Festial* 13 He wold vndyrtake þat þay schuld want ryght noght of hor mette. **15..** *Adam Bel* cxxx, I dare vndertake for them That true men they shal be. **1530** PALSGR. 767/2, I dare undertake that he hath sayd nothynge but he wyll parforme it. *a* **1548** HALL *Chron., Edw. IV*, 230, I..undertake, that this communicacion shal sorte, and come to suche an effecte, that [etc.]. **1617** MORYSON *Itin.* II. 63 Sir Richard Moryson (..whom he would vndertake to be as worthy in his profession, as any of his time). *a* **1649** WINTHROP *New Eng.* (1825) I. 145 Mr. Maverick came and undertook that the offenders should be forthcoming. *a* **1715** BURNET *Own Time* (1766) II. 49 He undertook to me, that the King should ask me no question. **1829** SCOTT *Anne of G.* xxxi, I have ridden..to present you with this letter,..having undertaken to your father that it should be delivered without delay. **1895** *Funk's Stand. Dict.* s.v., I'll undertake I can run faster than you.

d. *I (dare) undertake*, added to a statement.

1362 LANGL. *P. Pl.* A. XI. 108 þei two, as Ich hope.., Schul wisse þe to Dowel, I dar vndertake. ? *a* **1366** CHAUCER *Rom. Rose* 175 Wel coude he peynte, I vndirtake, That sich ymage coude make. *a* **1400** *Pistill of Susan* 208 3it schal trouþe hem a-taynt, I dar vnder-take. **1447** BOKENHAM *Seyntys* (Roxb.) 18 The fals goddys doth ye forsake,..Wych be not ellys, I undyrtake, But gold or sylvyr, stonys or tre. *c* **1480** HENRYSON *Fables, Lion & Mouse* 128 Thy fals excuse ..Sall not auaill ane myte, I vnderta. **1821** SCOTT *Kenilw.* i, You have gallants among you, I dare undertake, that have made the Virginia voyage.

e. With ellipse of inf. or obj. clause.

c **1440** *Generides* 7006 A rich woman I shal you make, That dar I wel vndretake. **1638** *Hamilton Papers* (Camden) 2 They [were] injoyned to dou ther best, and to goe presentely home, which they undertuck. **1651** *Nicholas Papers* (Camden) 257 Hee himselfe goes into Plimouth till all the articles be confirmed by Act of Parliament, which they have under-taken.

†**f.** To guarantee to cure. *Obs.*

1479 *Stonor Lett.* (1919) II. 88 And [= if] he may kepe him alive till Tuesday none, he will undertake him. **1480** *Ibid.* 100 The ffesisicion wolle do his cunnyng uppon me, but undertake me he wol not.

†**g.** To be surety for. *Obs.*$^{-1}$

1597 SHAKS. *Lover's Compl.* 280 Lending..credent soul to that strong-bonded oath That shall prefer and undertake my troth.

5. To take in charge; to accept the duty of attending to or looking after.

c **1300** *Havelok* 377 [They] seyden, he moucthe hem [*sc.* the children] best loke, Yif þat he hem vndertoke. *c* **1330** R. BRUNNE *Chron. Wace* (Rolls) 13112 þe kyng dide his prisons loke Wiþ wardeyns þat hem vndertoke. **1382** WYCLIF *Ps.* iii. 6, I sleep, and was a slepe, and ful out ros; for the Lord vndertoc me. *c* **1440** *Gesta Rom.* lxi. 251 (Harl. MS.), Thow shalt bid me..to kepe welle thi suster... And I shalle thenne vndir-take hir. **1613** SHAKS. *Hen. VIII*, II. i. 97 To th' water side I must conduct your Grace: Then giue my Charge vp to Sir Nicholas Vaux, Who vndertakes you to your end. **1629** DONNE *Serm.* 308 The Holy Ghost undertakes every man amongst us and would make every man fit for Gods service. **1658** *Whole Duty Man* Pref. A 8, If a Physician should undertake a patient that were in some desperate disease, and by his skill bring him..out of it. **1795** *Jemima* I. 60 Mrs. Wellon declared her readiness to undertake her. **1814** BYRON *Lett.* (1875) 436, I am going to be married... Miss Milbanke is the good-natured person who has undertaken me. **1846** TRENCH *Mirac.* xiii. (1862) 240 He was rather chasing away diseases..than Himself undertaking them. **1892** 'H. S. MERRIMAN' *Slave of Lamp* xv, It fell to Hilda's lot to undertake the Frenchman.

b. To engage with, enter into combat with.

1470-85 MALORY *Arthur* XIX. x. 788 Syre Vrre..and sir Alphegus..encountred to gyders for veray enuy, and soo eyther vndertook other to the Vtteraunce. **1616** B. JONSON *Cynthia's Rev.* v. iv, Sir, he shall yeeld you all the honor of a competent aduersarie, if you please to vnder-take him. **1667** DENHAM *Direct. Paint.* I. xvi. 4 As if in our reproach, the Wind and Seas Would undertake the Dutch, while we take ease.

c. To take in hand to deal with (a person).

1601 SHAKS. *Twel. N.* I. iii. 61 By my troth I would not vndertake her in this company. Is that the meaning of Accost? **1655** FULLER *Ch. Hist.* IV. iv. §32 The King casually coming thither.., undertook the Priest himself, though we never read before of his Majesties disputing. **1683** CAVE *Ecclesiastici, Athanasius* 58 An ancient Confessor,.. unskill'd in the Tricks and Methods of disputing,..offered himself to undertake him.

†**6.** To assume, take to oneself. *Obs.*

1596 SHAKS. *Tam. Shr.* IV. ii. 106 You are like to Sir Vincentio. His name and credite shal you vndertake. **1596** WARNER *Alb. Eng.* x. lv. (1602) 243 Whilst she, in France, did vndertake our royall Armes and Stile. **1608** TOPSELL *Serpents* 115 It changeth..alwayes into the colour of that which is next it, except red and white, which colours it cannot easily vndertake.

7. To conduct the funeral of.

1900 *Blackw. Mag.* Jan. 97/1 Urijah..gave a notable proof of his filial affection, by gracefully and successfully 'under-taking' his father.

II. *intr.* †**8.** To enter upon, commit oneself to, an enterprise. *Obs.*

c **1386** CHAUCER *Prol.* 405 Hardy he was and wys to vndertake. *c* **1470** HENRY *Wallace* v. 532 He was the man that pryncipall wndirtuk, That fyrst compild in dyt the Latyne buk. **1603** B. JONSON *Sejanus* IV. iii, No ill should force the subject undertake Against the sovereign. **1639** S. DU VERGER tr. *Camus' Admir. Events* 215 The sonne-in-law undertakes against the father in law, and the brothers are at division.

9. To give a pledge or promise; to enter into a compact or contract.

c **1475** *Rauf Coilȝear* 572 Schir Rolland..left the Coilȝear to cum, as he had vndertane. **1608** [see UNDERWRITE *v.* 2 *absol.*]. **1667** MILTON *P.L.* x. 74 The worst on mee must light,..for so I undertook Before thee. **1671** —— *P.R.* II. 129, I, as I undertook,..Have found him.

10. To become surety or security, to make oneself answerable or responsible, *for* a person, fact, etc.

1548 ELYOT, *Spondere pro aliquo*, to vndertake for one. **1586** J. HOOKER *Irel.* in *Holinshed* II. 131/1 He brought also his two other brethren, for whome he had vndertaken. **1588** SHAKS. *Tit. A.* I. i. 436 But on mine honour dare I vndertake For good Lord Titus innocence in all. **1607** TOPSELL *Four-f. Beasts* 323 He..confessed hee would vndertake for the Wolfe, if they would set him at liberty. **1655** M. CASAUBON *Enthus.* (1656) 294 It shall not trouble me, who undertake not for the truth of it. **1690** LOCKE *Toleration* ii. Wks. 1727 II. 277 You undertake for the Success of this method, if rightly used. **1713** ARBUTHNOT *John Bull* III. v, She.. undertook for her brother John's good behaviour. **1770** LANGHORNE *Plutarch* (1879) II. 865/2 It was he who had principally undertaken for the obedience of the Argives. **1817** JAS. MILL *Brit. India* II. IV. v. 162 Clive undertaking for his security, Dooloob Ram joined the camp. **1880** FROUDE *Bunyan* 69 His friends undertook for his appearance when he should be required.

b. To engage oneself in a promise *for.*

a **1715** BURNET *Own Time* I. 393 As there was no reason that..any discontents could be carried so far as to a general rising, which these men undertook for. **1790** BRUCE *Source Nile* I. 260, I sailed with..three passengers, instead of one, for whom only I had undertaken. **1827** HALLAM *Const. Hist.* vi. I. 367 Bacon..laughed at the chimerical notion, that private men should undertake for all the commons of England.

11. *colloq.* To carry on the business of a funeral undertaker. (Cf. 7.)

1891 *Cent. Dict.*

†**under'takement.** *Obs. rare.* [f. prec. + -MENT.] An undertaking.

1678 GALE *Crt. Gentiles* (ed. 2) IV. III. iii. 48 For what is the Psalmists intent and undertakement, but to demonstrate Gods infinite prescience. **1681** FLAVEL *Meth. Grace* xxiv. 419 In all..undertakements the people of God so earnestly beg direction and counsel from him.

under'taken, *ppl. a.* [f. UNDERTAKE *v.*]

†**1.** Attended to, made safe. *Obs.*$^{-1}$

c **1440** *Pallad. on Husb.* I. 203 Eke as the grape is grene and wol not shake, Vpbynde hit softe, and hit is vndirtake.

2. Taken in hand; enterprised.

a **1592** GREENE *Selimus* 2354 With willing heart great Tonombey hath left..my father's court, To aid thee in thy undertaken war. **1608** *Relat. Trav. W. Bush* C 2 b, Where he had so great a wager, as the venture of his life, in the performance of his vndertaken voyage. **1661** BAXTER *Last Work Believer* Wks. 1830 XVIII. 35 May we not trust Him in his undertaken office? **1782** J. BROWN *Nat. & Rev. Relig.* v. i. 383 God was constantly preparing to demand his undertaken satisfaction from his Son.

undertaker ('ʌndəteɪkə(r)). [f. UNDERTAKE *v.*]

†**1.** One who aids or assists; a helper. *Obs.*

In early quots. rendering L. *susceptor*.

1382 WYCLIF *Ps.* iii. 4 Thou forsothe, Lord, art myn vndir-takere. *Ibid.* liii. 6 The Lord is vndertakere of my soule. *c* **1450** tr. *De Imitatione* III. xviii. 85 In God, þe consolacion of poure & þe undertaker of meke men. **1612** *Two Noble K.* I. i. 78, I hope..some God hath put his mercy in your manhood Whereto hee'l infuse powre, and presse you forth Our undertaker. **1634** SIR T. HERBERT *Trav.* 223 Columbus..repaires to some Christian Princes for his vndertakers. **1645** RUTHERFORD *Tryal & Tri. Faith* 56 If believers have not Christ for their undertaker to bring them to glory, to intercede for them.

†**2.** A rebuker, reprover. *Obs.*$^{-1}$

c **1430** *Pilgr. Lyf Manhode* II. civ. (1869) 114, I wole haue noon vndertakere [F. *repreueur*], no maister ne techere.

3. One who undertakes a task or enterprise. Also const. *of* (the thing attempted).

c **1400** *Destr. Troy* 3789 He was..falsest in his fare, and full of disseit, Vndertaker of treyne. **1500-20** DUNBAR *Poems* lxxxi. 87 Schir Johne Kirkepakar, Off many cures ane michtie vndertaker. **1595** RALEIGH *Discov. Guiana* (1596) 21 Neither could any of the forepassed vndertakers, nor Berreo himselfe discover the country. **1603** DANIEL *Def. Ryme* H 3, May wee not..suspect these great vndertakers, lest they haue conspired with enuy to betray our proceedings. **1647** N. BACON *Disc. Govt. Eng.* I. xvii. 55 That was like some enterprises that owe more to extremity of occasion, then to the courage of the undertaker. *a* **1680** BUTLER *Rem.* (1759) I. 236 The Devil was the first o' th' Name,..Who was the first bold Undertaker Of bearing Arms against his Maker. **1712** E. COOKE *Voy. S. Sea* 251 All Attempts fail'd, either by the Death of the Undertakers, or some other Accidents. **1779** JOHNSON *L.P., Pope* Wks. IV. 28 Perhaps no extensive and multifarious performance was ever effected within the term originally fixed in the undertaker's mind.

†**b.** Const. *to* with inf. *Obs.*

1601 HOLLAND *Pliny* II. 594 Wee find it expressely set downe, That the undertaker to build a house at a certaine price, shall use no mortar under three yeers of age. **1634** RAINBOW *Labour* (1635) 40 Let the..Constables..be the undertakers to draine..this fenny..ground. **1684** T. BURNET *Theory Earth* I. 214 Those projectors of immortality, or undertakers to make men live to the age of Methusalah.

†**c.** One who takes up a challenge. *Obs.*

1601 SHAKS. *Twel. N.* III. iv. 349 Nay, if you be an vndertaker, I am for you.

4. *Hist.* **a.** One who undertook to hold crown lands in Ireland in the 16th and 17th centuries.

1586 *Acts Privy Counc.* (N.S.) 208 A letter to the Lord Deputie of Irelande..in the favor of Mr. Smithwicke,..that he might be accepted into the nomber of those that were Undertakers for landes in that Realme. **1589** R. PAYNE *Descr. Irel.* 10 The worsser sorte of vndertakers which haue seignories of her Maiestie, haue done much hurt in the countrie. **1617** MORYSON *Itin.* II. 26 The hatred which the Geraldines bare to those English Vndertakers..which possessed their Ancestors lands. **1633** T. STAFFORD *Pac. Hib.* I. x. (1821) 121 A Castle..appertaining to Master Edward Gray, an Vndertaker. **1642** in Rushw. *Hist. Coll.* (1692) I. III. 417 The Cities of London-Derry, and Coleraign,..and some other places and Castles which were for the present gallantly defended by the British undertakers. **1778** *Phil. Surv. S. Irel.* 311 The occupier of the ground..was unable to pay the fines, and therefore dispossessed by the wealthy undertaker. **1827** HALLAM *Const. Hist.* xviii. II. 738 These lands in the counties of Cork and Kerry..were parcelled out among English undertakers at low rents. **1888** E. LAWLESS *Ireland* xxxiii. 229 Something like a regular stampede of men ambitious to call themselves undertakers, began to cross over from the larger to the smaller island.

b. One of those who in the reigns of Jas. I, Chas. I, and Chas. II undertook to influence the action of Parliament, esp. with regard to the voting of supplies.

1620 JAS. I *Sp.* in Rushw. *Hist. Coll.* (1659) I. 23, I was in my first Parliament a Novice; and in my last there was a kind of beasts called Undertakers, a dozen of whom under-took to govern the last Parliament. **1668** PEPYS *Diary* 14 Feb., The House is..quite mad at the Undertakers, as they are commonly called,..that are brought over to the Court, and did undertake to get the King money. **1670** MARVELL *Corr.* Wks. (Grosart) II. 314 His Majesty, fortified by some undertakers of the meanest of our House, threw up all as nothing. *a* **1734** NORTH *Examen* III. vi. §38 At such Times, a Sort of People stept in, called Undertakers, who would answer that all should be smooth and well in Parliament. **1738** BOLINGBROKE *Patriot., Idea of Patriot King* (1749) 180 Let our great doctors in politics..compare the conduct of Elizabeth in this respect with that of her successor, who endeavoured..to manage his parliament by undertakers. **1827** HALLAM *Const. Hist.* vi. I. 365 Neville, and others who, like him, professed to understand the temper of the commons, and to facilitate the king's dealings with them, were called undertakers.

c. One of those Lowland Scots who attempted to colonize the Island of Lewis towards the end of the 16th century.

1819 SCOTT *Leg. Montrose* ix, He mentioned the celebrated settlement of the Fife Undertakers, as they were called, in the Lewis.

5. One who undertakes to carry out work or business for another; a contractor; †a collector or farmer of taxes. Now *rare.*

1602 in Moryson *Itin.* (1617) II. 242 So soone as any contract is made with the vndertakers, wee send an abstract thereof vnto your Lordship. **1612** in *10th Rep. Hist. MSS. Comm.* App. I. 604 One y[t] that hath inritched himselfe..by having been one of the principall undertakers of y[e] greate farme of salte. **1670** EACHARD *Cont. Clergy* 118 An ordinary bricklayer, or carpenter (I mean not your great undertakers and master-workmen). **1688** in *Cal. Treas. Papers* 28 The further answer of the present undertakers for the Tynne Farme. **1710** *Lond. Gaz.* No. 4651/2 An Agreement is concluded with Undertakers for furnishing the Magazines ..with Forage. **1751** M[c]DOUALL *Inst. Laws Scot.* 393 If one give Commission to demolish a house, which the undertaker believes to belong to him. **1778** PRYCE *Min. Cornub.* 237 The halvans of halvans are mostly dressed by an undertaker for so much in the pound sterling of the money they produce. **1817** SCOTT in *Lockhart* (1839) V. 226 The other point is, to take care that the undertakers in their anxiety for employment do not take the job too cheap. **1833** *1st Rep. Comm. Employment Childr., Western District* 2 There is a class of workmen [in Birmingham] called undertakers, who receive the material from the master manufacturer, and undertake to get it wrought up.

b. One who makes a business of carrying out the arrangements for funerals.

1698 *Pres. St. Trade* in Chester Waters *Parish Reg.* (1883) 52 The furnishing of funerals by a small number of men called undertakers. **1706** PHILLIPS (ed. Kersey), *Pollinctor*, an Embalmer of Dead Bodies..; an Undertaker. **1708** SWIFT *Wks.* (1755) II. I. 164, I was sent, sir, by the company of undertakers,..and they were employed by the honest gentleman, who is executor. **1728** YOUNG *Love of Fame* v. 505 While rival undertakers hover round, And with his spade the sexton marks the ground. **1768** GOLDSM. *Good-n. Man* I. i, His appearance has a stronger effect on my spirits than an undertaker's shop. **1822** BYRON *Vis. Judgem.* xii, He's buried; save the undertaker's bill, Or lapidary scrawl, the world is gone For him. **1884** F. M. CRAWFORD *Rom. Singer* I. 55 You must look as solemn as an undertaker.

6. †**a.** One who engages in the serious study of a subject or science. *Obs.*

1605 BACON *Adv. Learn.* I. iv. §7 Those [School-men].., as they are,..are great undertakers indeed, and fierce with darke keeping. **1654** HOBBES *Lib., Necess., & Chance* (1841) 250 He who will speak with some of our great under-takers about the grounds of learning, had need either to speak by an interpreter, or to learn a new language. **1682** WHELER *Journ. Greece* v. 356 There is another Greek,..an Undertaker in Physick too, who understands Scholastick Greek a little. **1695** WOODWARD *Nat. Hist. Earth* II. 71 To free the Enquiry from the Perplexities that some Undertakers have encumber'd it withall.

b. One who embarks on, or takes part in, some business enterprise. Now *rare.*

1615 E. S. *Britaines Buss* E 2, I confesse the private gaine to euery Vndertaker before propounded may seeme too great to be hoped for. *a* **1661** FULLER *Worthies, Cumb.* I. (1662) 228, I understand two small manufactures are lately set up therein;..and I wish that the Undertakers may not be disheartned with their small encouragement. **1677** W. HUBBARD *Narrative* II. 5 Some of the first Undertakers were encouraged once more to try the verity of their hopes. **1752** *Phil. Trans.* XLVII. 500 The mine, which was formerly wrought on,..yielded vast profit to the under-takers. **1776**

ADAM SMITH *W.N.* IV. ii. (1904) II. 52 The undertaker of a great manufacture. 1799 YOUNG *Agric. Lincoln.* 149 It has long been the common practice for the undertakers of this culture to hire grass land. 1828 *Act 9 Geo. IV*, c. 98 (*title*), The Undertakers of the Navigation of the Rivers Aire and Calder. 1848 MILL *Pol. Econ.* 479 The difference between the interest and the gross profit remunerates the exertions and risks of the undertaker.

†c. One who undertakes the preparation of a literary work. *Obs.*

1685 DRYDEN *Sylvæ* Pref., Ess. (ed. Ker) I. 269, I hope it will not be expected from me, that I should say anything of my fellow undertakers in this Miscellany. 1704 SWIFT *T. Tub* Auth. Pref. ¶3 The undertaker himself will publish his proposals with all convenient speed. 1787 J. ADAMS *Wks.* (1854) IX. 552, I was told by a bookseller that he was about getting it translated into Dutch. But I doubt whether any of these undertakers will proceed. 1800 *Monthly Mag.* VIII. 878 It seems natural to expect..some patronage of a translation, which must else be a mere sacrifice of toil and time to the English undertaker.

†d. A book-publisher. *Obs.*

1697 EVELYN *Numism.* p. lxxiii, Finding it so miserably deformed through the confident undertakers, the phrase was expunged at Bentley's request. 1707 HEARNE *Collect.* (O.H.S.) II. 31 Mr. Wasse..has so swell'd his Salust..y[t] the undertaker is quite weary. 1762 H. WALPOLE *Vertue's Anecd. Paint.* (1782) V. 261 His performances by no means deserved to be condemned as they were by the undertakers, and the performer laid aside. 1823 J. BADCOCK *Dom. Amusem.* p. iv, The duty of rapid revision was imposed upon the Editor..by the undertakers.

†e. A producer of an opera or play; a manager, impresario. *Obs.*

1711 ADDISON *Spect.* No. 5 ¶7 The undertakers [of the opera] being resolved to spare neither Pains nor Mony, for the Gratification of the Audience. c1720 in *Buccleuch MSS.* (Hist. MSS. Comm.) I. 367 The undertaker..has treated me ill..; I never heard a sound of his trifling songs till Monday se'nnight last. 1740 CIBBER *Apol.* III, I laid it down as a settled Maxim, that no Company could flourish while the chief Actors and Undertakers were at variance.

†7. One who acts as security or surety *for* another.

1601 B. JONSON *Poetaster* Ded., I send you this peece of what may liue of mine; for whose innocence, as for the Authors, you were once a noble and timely vndertaker. a1652 BROME *Eng. Moor* Epil., Now let me be a modest undertaker For us the players, the play and the play-maker. 1677 J. OWEN *Justif.* xi. 349 Considering the Person and Grace of this Undertaker or Surety. 1706 PHILLIPS (ed. Kersey), *Sponsor*, Surety, an Undertaker for another.

†b. *spec.* A baptismal sponsor. *Obs.*

1645 USSHER *Body Div.* (1647) 422 Of the vowes and promises which we in our child-hood made by those who were undertakers for us. 1673 CAVE *Prim. Chr.* I. x. 326 A venerable old Deacon who had been the Undertaker for him at his Baptism. 1697 BURGHOPE *Disc. Relig. Assemb.* 126 We are brought to Christ by the charitable help of our parents and undertakers.

Hence (from 5b) **'undertakerish, -takerlike, -takerly** *adjs.* Also **'undertakery.**

1861 WYNTER *Soc. Bees* 136 An attendant in sable habiliments..and with an *undertakerish eye and manner. 1857 DICKENS *Dorrit* I. v, One *undertaker-like Cupid had swing round on his own axis. 1876 MEREDITH *Beauch. Career* xix, You introduced me..to that *undertakerly old Tomlinson. 1869 G. J. CHESTER *Transatl. Sk.* 240, I had also a side-ways view of a large patent-coffin shop... Americans, generally, are great in the matter of *undertakery.

'undertaking, *vbl. sb.* (Also **,under'taking.**) [f. as prec. + -ING[1].]

1. †a. Enterprise, energy. *Obs.*

1375 BARBOUR *Bruce* IX. 484 Bot he wes outrageous hardy, And of so hye vndirtaking, That he neuir had none abasing Of multitude of men. c1400 tr. *Secreta Secret., Gov. Lordsh.* 111 Þe Persiens & þe Turkeys..er right coraious men, and of gret vndertakynge.

b. An action, work, etc., undertaken or attempted; an enterprise.

c1425 WYNTOUN *Cron.* VIII. 3138 Þat þai brocht sone till ending Be sum tressonable vndirtaking. 1598 FLORIO, *Suscettione*, an enterprise, a taking of a thing in hand, an vndertaking. 1602 SHAKS. *Ham.* II. i. 104 This is the very extasie of Loue, Whose violent property..leads the will to desperate Vndertakings. 1647 CLARENDON *Hist. Reb.* I. §23 He did not upon the Suddain comprehend the consequences, which would naturally attend such a rash undertaking. 1669 STURMY *Mariner's Mag.* I. ii. 3 Disastrous Periods have ended their Undertakings. 1707 MORTIMER *Husb.* 148 The Farmer is to consider..the Cost and Charges of such a Stock: that so he may suit his Undertaking to his Purse. 1780 S. J. PRATT *Emma Corbett* (ed. 4) I. 196, I am engaged in a very unthrifty undertaking. 1809 COLERIDGE *Friend* (1865) 8 In the preceding number I named the present under-taking an experiment. 1841 W. SPALDING *Italy & It. Isl.* I. 383 Not unfit preparatives for such extravagant under-takings. 1880 L. STEPHEN *Pope* iii. 62 Both sides took a pride in supporting the great literary undertaking which he [*sc.* Pope] had now announced.

c. The action of taking in hand.

1600 HAKLUYT *Voy.* III. 185 They, who..are well able to spare that which is required of each one towardes the vndertaking of this aduenture. 1634 W. TIRWHYT tr. *Balzac's Lett.* 108 The time of the yeare being as yet somewhat troublesome, for the undertaking thereof, you will rather reserve it. 1640 BP. HALL *Episc.* Ep. Ded. 2 I sate downe, and waited for the undertaking of some abler pen.

d. *spec.* The business or occupation of a funeral undertaker. Also *attrib.*

1843 DICKENS *Mart. Chuz.* (1844) v. 52 There's other businesses. Undertaking, now. That's gloomy. 1850 THACKERAY *Pendennis* xlvii, So Pen..asked about the undertaking business and how many mutes went down with Lady Estrich's remains. 1862 *Macm. Mag.* June 150 In the way of business..nothing seems stirring, except it be the undertaking trade.

†2. a. The action of lifting up; support. *Obs.*

1382 WYCLIF *Ps.* cvii. 9 Myn is Manasses; and Effraym the vndertaking [L. *susceptio*] of myn hed.

†b. Reproof, rebuke. *Obs.*

c1430 *Pilgr. Lyf Manhode* I. iv. (1869) 3 Bi whiche cloumben wel swiftliche in to þilke citee þilke þat weren of hise folke,..with oute vndertakinge of any. c1440 *Promp. Parv.* 461/2 Synbbynge, or vndyrtakynge, *deprehencio*.

3. A pledge or promise; a guarantee or surety.

?a1400 *Morte Arth.* 3187 Of this vndyrtakynge ostage are comyne. 1702 C. MATHER *Magn. Chr.* I. v. (1852) 75 All who dare not submit their children to be baptized by the undertaking of god-fathers. c1800 PEGGE *Anecd. Eng. Lang.* (1814) 338 'Give an Undertaking,' i.e. a Security. 1848 THACKERAY *Van. Fair* lxiv, Three hundred pounds a year, which he proposed to pay to her on an undertaking that she would never trouble him. 1879 M. PATTISON *Milton* 91 In each successive pamphlet he reiterates his undertaking to redeem his pledge of a great work.

'undertaking, *ppl. a.* Now *rare.* [f. as prec. + -ING[2].]

†1. Ready to undertake an enterprise, task, etc., esp. one involving some danger or risk; enterprising, bold. *Obs.*

?a1400 *Morte Arth.* 2723 In ȝone okene wode an oste are arrayede, Vndir-takande mene of thiese owte londes. c1410 *Master of Game* (MS. Bodl. 546) Prol., Men ben bettre rydyng,..and more vndirtakynge, and bettir knowynge of alle contreys and of alle passages. 1456 SIR G. HAYE *Law Arms* (S.T.S.) 60 His men war bathe wys, and hardy, and undertakand. 1614 RALEIGH *Hist. World* v. iii. §12. 486 A thousand men, vnder..an vndertaking and expert Captaine. 1655 FULLER *Ch. Hist.* IX. iii. §41 Rome..entertaining, and rewarding him as a man of a daring, and undertaking spirit. 1671 tr. *Palafox's Conq. China* xiii. 261 The General, who was very ambitious, undertaking, and successful. 1713 STEELE *Englishm.* No. 24. 157 Daring and undertaking Fellows have ever been the Darlings of the Populace.

transf. 1561 T. HOBY tr. *Castiglione's Courtyer* III. Hh iij b, Inventions, merry conceites, vndertaking enterprises, sports [etc.].

†b. ? Engaged in literary work. (Cf. UNDERTAKER 6c.) *Obs.*

1761 STERNE *Tr. Shandy* IV. xx, See!—if he has not galloped full among the scaffolding of the undertaking critics!

†c. Prepared to act as publishers. *Obs.*

1822 SCOTT *Nigel* Introd. Epist., Their power of annoying the public will be soon limited by the difficulty of finding undertaking booksellers.

2. Pledged, bound by promise.

1786 A. GIB *Sacred Contemplations* I. II. i. 85 For these he became an undertaking Surety as their Covenant-head.

Hence **'under,takingly** *adv.*, responsibly.

1665 J. SERGEANT *Sure Footing* 39 What Certainty can we undertakingly promise to weaker heads, that is, to the Generality of Mankind?

,under'talk, *v.* (UNDER-[1] 10a.)

1736 HERVEY *Mem.* (1848) I. 109 Those..used to say he undertalked his capacity, that his conception was much superior to his utterance.

,under'taxed, *ppl. a.* (UNDER-[1] 10a.)

1706 ARBUTHNOT *Serm. Edinb.* Wks. 1751 II. 184 The Party of the North and West, who are under-tax'd.

'under,teacher. (UNDER-[1] 6a.)

1581 MULCASTER *Positions* xl. 230 Prouided that he..hasard not..his childrens profit vpon any absolute vnder-teacher. 1607 in *Hist. Wakefield Gram. Sch.* (1892) 67 A fitt underteacher or usher to be chosen. 1847 C. BRONTË *J. Eyre* v, She looked, indeed, what I afterwards found she really was, an under-teacher. 1878 B. HARTE *Man on Beach* 75 At last..the underteachers..revealed themselves in their true colours.

'under,teller. (UNDER-[1] 6a.)

1694 LUTTRELL *Brief Rel.* (1857) III. 368 Mr. Squibb, an underteller [in the Exchequer], is also dead.

'under-,tenancy. (UNDER-[1] 6b: cf. next.)

1766 BLACKSTONE *Comm.* II. viii. 136 The widow is immediate tenant to the heir, by a kind of subinfeudation or under-tenancy.

'under-,tenant. [UNDER-[1] 6a.] A tenant holding land or premises from another tenant; a subtenant.

1546 in W. H. Turner *Select. Rec. Oxford* (1880) 185 Yf the undertenant be honest. 1582 *Ibid.* 422 Undertenants commonly called inmakes. 1612 DAVIES *Why Ireland*, etc. 276 To settle and secure the Under-Tennants; to the End, there may be a repose and establishment of euery Subiects Estate; Lord and Tenant. 1666 in *10th Rep. Hist. MSS. Comm.* App. V. 23 The said Henry and his undertenants had been in peaceable possession thereof for four yeares. 1704 *Lond. Gaz.* No. 3990/4 The Manor of Lizard,..in the Possession of George Caning Esq., or his Under-Tenants. 1766 BLACKSTONE *Comm.* II. viii. 123 A third incident to estates for life relates to the under-tenants or lessees. 1804 MAR. EDGEWORTH *Ennui* v[iii], These fellows..live in idleness, whilst they *rack* a parcel of wretched under-tenants. 1872 FROUDE *Short Stud.* (1878) II. 556 He had no intention that the under-tenant should be protected against himself.

transf. 1809 MALKIN *Gil Blas* x. v. ¶7 They..exalted him to a level with the under-tenants of Olympus.

†**undertend** (to kindle): see UNDER-[1] 2.

'under,tenure. (UNDER-[1] 6b.)

1611 COTGR., *Subinfeudation*, a subinfeoffing; the creating of an vnder tenure, or tennancie in fee. 1775 JOHNSON *West. Isl.* Wks. X. 476 We were told of a particular mode of under-tenure. The tacksman admits some of his inferior neighbours to the cultivation of his grounds, on condition that [etc.].

'under-te,rrestrial, *a.* [UNDER-[1] 10c; rendering F. *soubterrain.*] Below what is earthly.

1603 [see SUPERCELESTIAL *a.* 2b].

†**'under-thaw.** (UNDER-[1] 5b.)

1726 WOODWARD *Nat. Hist. Earth* Introd. 151 The Thaw underneath is frequently considerably advanc'd..before any Thing like a Liquation or Thaw is perceived, above, at the Surface. This the Country People call a Ground, or Under-Thaw.

†**'under-,thesaurer.** *Obs.* [UNDER-[1] 6a.] An under-treasurer.

1534 CROMWELL in Merriman *Life & Lett.* (1902) I. 373 Suche patenttes and grauntys as your highnes and..your father..haue grauntyd vnto..your undertesawrer of your exchequer. 1536-7 *Act* in Bolton *Stat. Irel.* (1621) 104 So as the said underthesaurer be one.

†**underthew,** *v. Obs.*[−1] [UNDER-[1] 7: cf. THEW *v.*] *trans.* To subject, subdue.

13.. *K. Alis.* 1406 (Laud MS.), Me þinkeþ wel grete wondre þat he miȝth, wiþ so fewe, Al þe werlde hym vnder þewe.

'underthing. [UNDER-[1] 6b.]

1. A lower or inferior thing.

1611 BEAUM. & FL. *Philaster* I. i, My womans strength Is so o'recharg'd with danger..that these under-things Dare not abide in such a troubled sea.

2. *pl.* Under-clothing.

1864 E. A. PARKES *Pract. Hygiene* 354 If..woollen under-things are worn, the perspiration is sufficiently absorbed.

,under'think, *v.* [UNDER-[1] 10a, 4b.]

†1. *trans.* To think too little of, to underestimate.

a1623 BUCK *Rich. III* (1646) 52 Charles..was so..over-weening of his owne..judgement, that he under-thought all mens else.

2. *intr.* To think insufficiently.

1711 SHAFTESB. *Charac.* III. 301 They might rather thank themselves, for having under-thought, or reason'd short, so as to rest satisfy'd with a very superficial Search.

3. *trans.* To penetrate under by thinking.

1886 A. WEIR *Hist. Basis Mod. Europe* (1889) 491 Man..can to some degree return upon his thought, can to some extent underthink the conditions of cognition.

'under-,thorough, *adv.* [See UNDER *prep.* and THOROUGH *sb.* 3.] Under furrow.

1733 W. ELLIS *Chiltern & Vale Farm.* 223 This is half Under-thorough, and half Over, and exceeds all others except Drilling.

'underthought. (UNDER-[1] 9.)

1601 B. JONSON *Poetaster* IV. i, Carrie not too much vnder-thought betwixt your selfe and them. 1886 *Athenæum* 6 Feb. 192 Without any disturbing underthought. 1898 WEYMAN *Castle Inn* i, Until he had put it beyond question that she had no underthought.

†**under'thrast,** *pa. pple. Obs.*[−1] [UNDER-[1] 4a: see THREST *v.*] Suppressed.

?1402 QUIXLEY *Ballade* xi. in *Yorks. Archæol. Jrnl.* (1908) XX. 45 Who euil doth, he mon be vnderthrast.

†**under'thrown,** *pa. pple. Obs.*[−1] [UNDER-[1] 7.] Subjected, made subject.

1387-8 T. USK *Test. Love* III. viii. (Skeat) l. 151 Thus fil man un-to lykenesse of unresonable bestes; and with hem to corrupcion and unlusty apetytes was he under-throwen.

under'thrust, *v. Geol.* [UNDER-[1] 4b.] *trans.* To be forced underneath. Chiefly as **under'thrust** *ppl. a.*, **'underthrusting** *vbl. sb.*

1893 E. A. SMITH in *Amer. Jrnl. Sci.* CXLV. 306, I..suggest the following terms, *under fault, faulted under fold, underthrust fault*, as applicable to this type of structure. 1908 H. B. C. SOLLAS tr. *Suess's Face of Earth* III. ix. 396 Holmquist concludes that, owing to the continuous subsidence of the eastern part (i.e. of the shield or foreland) the overthrusting practically becomes an underthrusting. 1931 *Geol. Mag.* LXVIII. 39 The front of the underthrust mass will be concave towards the direction of underthrusting. 1965 G. J. WILLIAMS *Econ. Geol. N.Z.* xix. 350/1 The south-east flank is steep and in places faulted or underthrust. 1971 I. G. GASS et al. *Understanding Earth* xix. 286 The major mountain chains..occur where moving plates collide and one underthrusts the other. 1977 [see RICHTER].

undertide, var. UNDERN-TIDE *Obs.*

'undertide. (UNDER-[1] 5b.)

1851 MRS. BROWNING *Casa Guidi Wind.* I. 56 The arrowy undertide Shoots on and cleaves the marble as it goes. 1883 in Butler *Bible Work* I. 597 The undertide that bears all up and sweeps all along.

'under,tided, *a.* (UNDER-[1] 4a.)

1855 BAILEY *Mystic* 95 The bells may clang, Still pendulous in those undertided towers.

under'tie, *v.* [UNDER-[1] 4a.] *trans.* To tie beneath. Also *spec.* (see quot. 1894).

1552 HULOET, Vndertye, *subligo*. 1648 HEXHAM II, *Onderbinden*, to Vndertye. 1894 *Outing* XXIV. 258/2 The wings are under-tied, as are all our home-made flies; that is, the wings cover the point of the hook.

under-time, var. UNDERN-TIME.

'undertint. (UNDER-[1] 5 c.)
1885 RUSKIN *Præterita* I. ii. 48 It was done..in grey under-tints of Prussian blue and British ink. **1889** *Athenæum* 12 Jan. 56/3 These clear golden and rosy undertints and sub-tones of grey.

under'tip, *v.* [f. UNDER- 10 a + TIP *v.*[4]] To give an inadequate or insufficient gratuity to (one who has been of service). Hence **under'tipped** *ppl. a.*
1975 'A. HALL' *Mandarin Cypher* iv. 64, I got out and paid and under-tipped..but..he went away happy..with a Hong Kong dollar. **1979** *Guardian* 4 Aug. 19/3 The undertipped taxi-driver who returned his passenger's gratuity. **1984** *New Yorker* 24 Dec. 37/1 My twenty-five-year-old daughter undertipped the airline porter.

'under-,title. (UNDER-[1] 5 b.)
1687 NORRIS *Coll. Misc.* (1699) 166 A Picture that..wants an under-title to discover whose it is.

undertoe, erron. var. UNDERTOW.

'undertone, *sb.* Also under-tone, under tone. [UNDER-[1] 5 c, 9, 9 b, 10 c.]
1. A low or subdued tone: **a.** of utterance.
1762 D. GARRICK *Let.* 24 Jan. (1831) I. 135 It naturally gives him a slow tremulous under-tone of voice. **1806** SURR *Winter in Lond.* II. 44 "Tis very strange!' said Edward in an under tone of voice. **1819** KEATS *Lamia* II. 281 'Fool!' said the sophist, in an under-tone, Gruff with contempt. **1853** KINGSLEY *Hypatia* xv, All this was uttered rapidly, and in a wheedling undertone. **1886** W. J. TUCKER *E. Europe* 79 Hearing a low, monotonous..voice chanting a dirge in an undertone.
b. of sound. Also *attrib.*
1833 [see UNBLISSFUL *a.*]. **1853** KANE *Grinnell Exp.* vii. (1856) 52 With it came a strange undertone accompaniment, a not discordant drone. **1855** KINGSLEY *Westw. Ho!* xxiii, If beyond the silence we listen for the faintest undertones, we detect a stifled, continuous hum of insects.
2. *fig.* **a.** An underlying tone (*of* feeling, etc.); a subordinate or unobtrusive element; an undercurrent.
1861 TULLOCH *Eng. Purit.* II. 211 The undertone of sentiment in the Elizabethan Church. **1879** FARRAR *St. Paul* II. 180 Throughout all these high reasonings..there runs an undertone of controversy.
b. A subdued or underlying tone of colour.
1891 *Cent. Dict.* s.v., There was a subtle undertone of yellow through the picture.
c. The general basis of Exchange or market dealings in any stock or commodity.
1897 *Daily News* 2 Feb. 3/7 Stocks were irregular... The undertone was firm. **1902** *Times* 29 July 11/2 Maize has had a weak undertone during the entire session.
3. A tone (of health, etc.) below the normal.
1872 H. W. BEECHER *Yale Lect. Preaching* viii. 220, I have sometimes had a whole month of undertone, because I let go and ran clear down.
Hence **'undertone** *v. trans.*, to accompany as an undertone; **'undertoned** *ppl. a.*[1], expressed in an undertone.
1861 MEREDITH *Evan Harrington* xxx, His hasty undertoned questions. **1873** W. S. MAYO *Never Again* xi. 145 Low harmonics Undertone the music's roll. **1876** GEO. ELIOT *Dan. Der.* VII. lvi, She uttered this with the same undertoned decision.

,under'toned, *ppl. a.*[2] [UNDER-[1] 10 a.] Defective in tone.
1849 *Athenæum* 3 Nov. 1114/1 Its production appeared to be of an extemporaneous character,—much in it was under-toned. **1888** G. WILSON *Centen. Confer. Missions* I. 96 The influence of a faithless under-toned Missionary on the Church at home is appalling.

'undertow. [UNDER-[1] 5 c.] A sea-current below the surface of the water, moving in a contrary direction to that of the surface current.
1817 *Sporting Mag.* L. 221 A current,..at times counteracted by means of a strong opposing 'undertow', as it is called. **1829** MARRYAT *F. Mildmay* xix, The recoil of the sea, and what is called by sailors the undertow, carried him back again. **1877** HUXLEY *Physiogr.* xi. 172 The water bursts with great force upon the land, and then sweeps back, as a powerful 'undertow' to the sea.
transf. and *fig.* **1840** GEN. P. THOMPSON *Exerc.* (1842) V. 232 There is always a strong 'under-tow', as the Americans would call it, of honest and well-disposed men in such situations. **1879** JEFFERIES *Wild Life* 41 The weathercock will sometimes point in precisely the opposite direction, obeying the 'undertow' of the gale.

'under-,trader. (UNDER-[1] 6 a.)
1677 OTWAY *Cheats of Scapin* I. i, The great Rooks and Cheats allow'd by publick authority ruin such little Under-traders as I am.

†under'tranch, *v. Obs.* [UNDER-[1] 4 a: see TRANCH *v.*] *trans.* To carve (a porpoise).
1508 *Bk. Keruynge* (W. de Worde) A 1 b, Vndertraunche y[t] purpos. [Hence in later works.]

†'under-,traverse. *Obs.*$^{-1}$ (UNDER-[1] 5 b: see TRAVERSE *sb.* 16 β.)
1598 BARRET *Theor. Warres* v. i. 125 The place or roome for the artillery in the vnder Travesse or flanker.

under'tread, *v.* [UNDER-[1] 4 a. Cf. MDu. *ondertreden*, MLG. *undertreden*, MDa. *undertræde*, MHG. *under-*, G. *untertreten.*] *trans.* To tread under foot; to subdue or subjugate.
1525 in Ellis *Orig. Lett.* Ser. III. II. 75, I doubte not but that he will assist..to vndre treade them that they shall not nowe lift vppe their hedds. **1558** PHAER *Æneid* I. A 4 b, Great warre in Italy haue he shall, ere he the people wyld May vndertread. *a* **1618** SYLVESTER *Mem. Mortalitie* II. lv, Wasps break the Web, Flies are held fast and hurt: The Guilty quit, the Guiltlesse under-trod. **1859** WHITTIER *Rock in El Ghor* iv, Unchanged the awful lithograph Of power and glory undertrod.

'undertread, *sb.* [UNDER- 5 d.] A layer of reinforcement in a rubber tyre.
1968 *Wall St. Jrnl.* (Eastern ed.) 29 Jan. 11 The new tire is made with a rubber impregnated mat of steel wire under the tread. Called a reinforced undertread, the mat contains about 80,000 pieces of wire. **1971** *Flying* Apr. 7/1 (Advt.), A deep undertread adds muscle... Next time you buy tires, ask for Goodyear's Flight Custom. **1982** *Coal Age* Apr. 140/2 An undertread or protective cushion of rubber can also be placed on all three tire designs between the tread..and body ply.

'under-,treasurer. (UNDER-[1] 6 a.)
Chiefly as the designation of the officer immediately subordinate to the Lord High Treasurer of England (TREASURER 1 b): see also CHANCELLOR 3.
1447 *Shillingford Lett.* (Camden) 7 There was myche peeple, lordes and other, my Lord Tresorer, under Tresorer,..and many strangers. **1521** WOLSEY in *St. Papers Hen. VIII*, I. 74 Sir Thomas More, your Undre Treasourer. **1610** HOLLAND *Camden's Brit.* I. 283 William Essex, Vnder-treasurer of England under King Edward the Fourth. **1642** C. VERNON *Consid. Exch.* 33 The Vnder-Treasurer or Vice-Treasurer [of the Exchequer] was not knowne till the time of King Hen. 7. **1710** in *Lond. Gaz.* No. 4668/3 They shall receive an Order, signed by the Treasurer and Under-Treasurer of the Exchequer. **1764** GOLDSM. *Hist. Eng. in Lett.* (1782) IV. 109 Harley..was appointed chancellor of the exchequer, and under-treasurer. **1823** *Gentl. Mag.* Feb. 176/1 Chancellor and Under Treasurer of his Majesty's Exchequer. **1863** H. COX *Instit.* III. vii. 696 He now holds..the office of Under-Treasurer.
So **'under-,treasuress.** *rare.*
c **1450** [see UNDER-CHAMBRESS].

under'treat, *v.* [UNDER-[1] 10 a.] *trans.* To treat with too little respect. Also, to provide with insufficient (medical, etc.) treatment.
1721 CIBBER *Refusal* II. i, She that has no Resentment at all, may be under-treated as long as she lives, I find. **1908** H. JAMES *Portrait of a Lady* I. p. xxi, So early was to begin my tendency to overtreat, rather than undertreat..my subject. **1979** [see *underdiagnose* vb. s.v. UNDERDIAGNOSIS].

†under-treble. *Obs.* [UNDER-[1] 6 b.] = SUBTRIPLE. So **†under-triplat, -triple.** *Obs.*
1430 *Art of Nombryng* (E.E.T.S.) 17 That triplat is to be put under the .3 next figure..And the vnder-trebille vnder the trebille. *Ibid.*, And than most thow fynde a digit..the whiche withe his vnder-triplat..sittethe away all that is ouer his hede. *Ibid.* 18 It is open that the nombre proposede was a cubike nombre, And his rote a digit founde last with the vnder-triples.

'undertrial. *India.* [UNDER-[2].] A person held in custody awaiting trial.
1966 *Times of India* 5 May 9/4 An infuriated group of about 50 undertrials tore down the walls of the judicial lock-up. **1979** V. L. PANDIT *Scope of Happiness* xv. 102 The Allahabad District Jail..was used for under-trials or for those prisoners about to be released after completion of their term in other parts of the province.

'undertrick. *Bridge.* [UNDER-[1] 10 b.] A trick required to make up the number of the bid or contract, but not taken. Also *attrib.*
1908 *Laws of Auction Bridge* §50 When he fails, his adversaries score, above the line, 50 points for each undertrick, *i.e.*, each trick short of the number declared. **1929** M. C. WORK *Compl. Contract Bridge* i. 4 Vulnerable..seems appropriate enough when it increases the losses for undertricks. **1952** J. B. PICK *Phoenix Dict. Games* 266 Undertrick points—that is, penalty points when declarer fails to fulfil his contract—are scored by opponents above the line. **1981** REESE & DORMER *Bridge Player's Alphabetical Handbk.* III. 220 (*heading*) Penalties for undertricks. *Ibid.*, Not vulnerable, 50 a trick. Doubled, 100 for the first undertrick, 200 for each subsequent one.

'under,trodden, *ppl. a.* [f. UNDERTREAD *v.*] Downtrodden.
1594 NASHE *Unfort. Trav.* C j b, I was no common squire, no vndertrodden torchbearer.

under'trump, *v.* [UNDER-[1] 10 a.] *trans.* and *intr.* To follow one's partner in trumping, but with a lower card.
1863 'CAVENDISH' *Whist* (ed. 5) 61, I should throw away a small trump, undertrumping *y*, in order to keep two winning queens.

under'truss, *v.* (UNDER-[1] 4 a.)
1703 S. PARKER tr. *Eusebius' Eccl. Hist.* VIII. 157 Some planted Face to Face with their Feet off the Ground, and their Bodies undertruss'd with Chains.

'under-tub. (UNDER-[1] 5 b.)
1606 SYLVESTER *Du Bartas* II. iv. II. *Magnificence* 1139 As in Grape-Harvest..A willing Troup.., dancing in the Must, To th' under-Tub a flowry showr doe thrust.

'undertune. (UNDER-[1] 9 b.)
1865 SWINBURNE *Poems & Ball.*, *August* 26 In the mute August afternoon They trembled to some under-tune Of music. **1897** KIPLING *Capt. Cour.* 49 A steady undertune to the 'click-nick' of the knives in the pen.

'under-,tunic. (UNDER-[1] 5 a.)
1819 SCOTT *Ivanhoe* iv, An under tunic of dark purple silk. **1880** L. WALLACE *Ben-Hur* 379 An undertunic not unlike those of the enemy.

'underturf, *a.* [UNDER-[2].] Of earth or soil: Situated or found below the turf.
1675 EVELYN *Terra* (1676) 14 The fatness of this Under-turf Mould. **1695** WOODWARD *Nat. Hist. Earth* I. 12 That blackisk Layer of Earth or Mould which is called by some Garden-Earth, by others Vnder-turf-Earth. **1765** *Museum Rust.* IV. 156 A tree..round the roots of which some under-turf earth was piled.

under'turn, *v.* [UNDER-[1] 4, 7.]
†1. *trans.* To overturn, overthrow. *Obs.*
1382 WYCLIF *Deut.* vii. 5 The auters of hem vndurturneth [L. *subvertite*], and brekith togidres the ymagis. —— *Ezek.* xxvi. 12 Thei shulen vndirturne thi..housis.
2. To turn under ground; to bury.
1600 SURFLET *Countrie Farme* v. viii. 670 Those..doe presently thereupon bestow an earing vpon such ground, and so vnderturne the said stubble and weedes.

'under-,tutor. (UNDER-[1] 6 a.)
1702 BOYER *Fr. Dict.*, *Sou-gouverneur*,..an Vnder-tutor. **1843** J. BOUVIER *Law Dict. U.S.* s.v., In every tutorship, there shall be an under-tutor, whom it shall be the duty of the judge to appoint.

'under-twig. (UNDER-[1] 5 b.)
1768–74 TUCKER *Lt. Nat.* (1834) II. 319 The impulse of covetousness or lust of fame, and that under twig of it, vanity. **1805** R. W. DICKSON *Pract. Agric.* I. 135 To make the side of the hedge to slope inwards a little above, which gives to the under-twigs a freshness they could not otherwise be made to attain.

'under-,tyrant. (UNDER-[1] 6 a.)
1648 HEYLIN *Relat. & Observ.* I. 25 Our Generall and Army, with their under-Tyrants the Grandees.

under-'use, *sb.* [UNDER-[1] 10 b.] Insufficient use (of a facility, etc.); use below the optimum level.
1960 *Guardian* 26 Nov. 2/7 There might, in some places, be a considerable 'under-use' of [parking] meters. **1971** *Country Life* 18 Feb. 348/2 Under-use leads to poor maintenance of roofs, gutters and party walls. **1975** *Physics Bull.* Sept. 411/3 A current wastage of communication in research (due to underuse of existing services) of the order of 9%.

under-'use, *v.* [UNDER-[1] 10 a.] *trans.* To make insufficient use of (a facility, etc.); to use (something) below the optimum level. So **under-'used** *ppl. a.*
1960 *Farmer & Stockbreeder* 8 Mar. 51/2 Farming can have no overwhelming case to retain all its present land while it is so obvious that some of it is still under-used. **1970** *Guardian* 9 Nov. 10/2 A country can never recover by persistently under-using its resources, as Britain has done for too long. **1976** *Field* 18 Nov. 948/1 The substantial amount of derelict and under-used land which exists in urban areas..indicates that these transfers could be reduced to not more than 29,700 acres per year.

'under-,usher. (UNDER-[1] 6 a.)
1561 in H. B. Wilson *Hist. Merchant-Taylors' Sch.* (1814) 15 Ther shalbe also in the said schoole two underusshers.

under-'utilize, *v.* [UNDER-[1] 10 a.] *trans.* To make use of (equipment, resources, etc.) insufficiently or below the optimum level; to under-use. So **,under-utili'zation** *sb.*, **under-'utilized** *ppl. a.*
1954 *Newsweek* 29 Nov. 89/1 Underutilization of capacity in some lines is inevitable for some time. **1958** *Economist* 18 Oct. 204/1 Mr Amory may go on living down to his..nickname of Derick-or-little-by-little this winter (when industrial capacity may be unnecessarily under-utilised). **1964** K. G. LOCKYER *Introd. Critical Path Anal.* viii. 83 To increase utilization it is common practice to employ the under-utilized resources on another project. **1977** *Lancet* 2 July 26/2 The cause of the lactic acidosis is almost certainly both underutilisation of lactic acid as well as overproduction. **1978** *N.Y. Times* 30 Mar. A 15/1 The small-boat mariners have turned to the 'junk-fish', or underutilized species like perch and pollock, while waiting out the 12-day Federal ban on cod.

'undervalu,ation. [UNDER-[1] 10 b.] The action of undervaluing.
1. †**a.** Reduction or decline in value. *Obs.*$^{-1}$
1622 MALYNES *Anc. Law-Merch.* 482 The vnderualuation of our moneys, causeth no more commodities to be brought into the Realme than is carried out.
b. Valuation at too low a figure; inadequate monetary valuation.
1653 in Somers *Tracts* I. 523 That the said Inventory doth contain all the Goods.., without any wilful Omission or Undervaluation. **1825** HONE *Every-day Bk.* I. 1461 Another person said he was willing to give three hundred for it. This undervaluation was decisive. **1885** *Manch. Exam.* 22 July 5/1 Suggestions as to the best mode of preventing undervaluations.
2. Insufficient appreciation or estimation; depreciation, disparagement.
1626 JACKSON *Creed* VIII. xxviii, In this their undervaluation of his person and paines, they did portend their posterities disesteeme of..the Lord himself. **1681** *No Protestant-Plot* 6 Having been so unhappy as to have heard him spoken of with too much disregard, and undervaluation. **1851** DE QUINCEY *Ld. Carlisle on Pope* Wks. 1859 XIII. 20 The first error was..no more than an undervaluation of the truth.

ˈunderˌvalue, *sb.* [UNDER-[1] 10 b.]

1. Insufficiency in worth. *rare*$^{-1}$.

1605 BACON *Adv. Learn.* I. To King §3 What defects and vndervalewes I finde in such particular actes.

2. An inadequate monetary value; an amount or price below the real value.

1611 COTGR., *Non-prix*, an vnder value, or vnderprice. **1631** T. POWELL *Tom All Trades* 3 Poverty sells all at an vnder value. **1690** CHILD *Disc. Trade* 101 We shall buy Ships..for half their cost, which under value in purchase will be a present clear profit to England. **1737** LD. HARDWICKE in Harris *Life & Lett.* (1847) I. 362 A bishop.. calling in his tenants to fill up leases at an undervalue. **1769** WARBURTON *Lett. to Hurd* (1809) 438 The magnificent set of Chelsea China..she took care should not go at an under-value. **1829** SOUTHEY *Sir T. More* (1831) II. 163 Persons who buy..because they are tempted by the undervalue at which it is offered. **1885** *Law Times Rep.* LII. 648/2 Shaw knew that he was buying at an undervalue.

†**3.** An under-estimate of worth or importance; = UNDERVALUATION 2. *Obs.*

1615 A. STAFFORD *Heav. Dogge* 35 Diogenes knew his owne deserts, and was neerer the ouer then the undervalew of himselfe. **1654** WHITLOCK *Zootomia* 345 That gentlewoman that inverted the undervalue of Marriages Maxime, 'next to no wife a good wife the best'. **1680** J. AUBREY *Brief Lives* (1898) I. 302 He did not care for chymistrey, and was wont to speake against them with undervalue.

ˌunderˈvalue, *v.* [UNDER-[1] 10 a.]

†**1.** *trans.* To rate as inferior in value *to*. *Obs.*

1596 SHAKS. *Merch. V.* II. vii. 53 Or shall I thinke in Siluer she's immur'd Being ten times vndervalued to tride gold. **1612** in *10th Rep. Hist. MSS. Comm.* App. I. 602 Which entertainment they could not afford him, for that thei would not undervalewe themselves to yᵉ Spanishe greatenes.

2. To rate at too low a monetary value. Also *fig.*

1599 *Minutes Archdeaconry Colchester* fol. 257 b (MS.), Dominus, eo quod constat that the goods ar vndervalued, dyd appoynt the same goods to be again appriced. **1619** FLETCHER *Knt. Malta* v. i, How much you undervalue your own price, To give your unbought self, for a poor woman? **1765** *Museum Rust.* IV. 68 In your note..I observe you think the price of the corn undervalued. **1885** *Law Times* 7 Feb. 269/1 There was a strong reason why Mr. Thomas should over-value rather than under-value the goods.

b. To reduce or diminish in value; to make of less value or worth.

1622 MALYNES *Anc. Law-Merch.* 385 It followeth that the Siluer is vnderualued, and the Gold aduanced. **1692** C. O'K[ELLY] in *Irish Narr.* (Camden) 69 What undervalued it [*sc.* the coinage] most was the little esteem the great ones about court shewed for it. **1709** STEELE *Tatler* No. 61 ¶4 'Tis such silly Starts and Incoherences which undervalue the beauteous Sex. **1866** ROGERS *Agric. & Prices* I. xi. 179 The currency has been undervalued by the fraudulent issue.

†**c.** To fall short of in value. *Obs.*

1657 J. SERGEANT *Schism Dispach't* 182 What follows is such pittiful stuff, as would under-value the worth of a piece of paper to vouchsafe it a confute.

3. To estimate or esteem too low; to value or appreciate insufficiently; to depreciate.

1611 FLORIO, *Sottostimare*, to vnder-value or esteeme. **1620** GATAKER *Spirituall Watch* 114 These that so highly ouer-prize their owne priuate deuotions, as thus to vnder-value the publike assemblies of Gods Saints. **1653** W. RAMESEY *Astrol. Restored* To Rdr. 17 Vertue..wanting preferment, and truth riches, shall be disrespected and undervalued. **1713** ARBUTHNOT *John Bull* III. i, Extolling their own good qualities, and undervaluing those of others. **1771** *Junius Lett.* lv. (1788) 302 A vain man does not usually compare himself to an object which it is his design to undervalue. **1824** MISS MITFORD *Village* Ser. I. 210 We shall have a fine sunshiny day to-morrow,—a blessing not to be undervalued. **1884** CHURCH *Bacon* iii. 59 He was no mere idealist or recluse to undervalue or despise the real grandeur of the world.

refl. **1621** BURTON *Anat. Mel.* I. ii. III. xv, Schollers..haue store of gold, but know not the worth of it, they vnder-value themselues. **1822** HAZLITT *Table-T.* Ser. II. 341 He who undervalues himself is justly undervalued by others.

Hence **undervalued** (stress variable) *ppl. a.*

1628 QUARLES *Argalus & P.* I. 30 So rare a Branch, whose undervalued worth Brings greater glory to the Arcadian Land, Then can the dull Arcadians understand. **1661** BOYLE *Style of Script.* (1675) 89 His so much undervalued Parables ..comprise important prophecies.

ˌunderˈvaluer. [f. the vb.] One who undervalues or esteems too lightly; a depreciator.

1651 BAXTER *Inf. Bapt.* 258 What judgements have befaln the undervaluers of God's works. **1690** C. NESSE *O. & N. Test.* I. 361 All our under-valuers shall in time know it. **1804** *Ann. Rev.* II. 233 What was called the jacobinism of Great Britain, that is the confederacies of undervaluers of church and king. **1824** *New Monthly Mag.* XI. 465 The civic classes, no undervaluers of good cheer.

ˌunderˈvaluing, *vbl. sb.* [f. as prec.] The act of estimating at too low a value.

1636 SANDERSON *Serm.* (1681) II. 65 Your under-valuing of me..hath made that glorying now necessary for me. **1661** LOWTHER in *Extr. St. Papers Friends* Ser. II. (1911) 117 To the undervalewing of his Majesties Authorety. **1697** BURGHOPE *Disc. Relig. Assemb.* 167 A manifest undervaluing of Christ. **1831** E. IRVING *Exp. Rev.* I. 85 Against all such undervaluings I present these words of the Eternal and Unchangeable. **1871** R. H. HUTTON *Ess.* I. 129 Even in the highest of the prophetic strains there is perhaps an under-valuing of Nature.

ˌunderˈvaluing, *ppl. a.* [f. as prec.] That undervalues; depreciatory.

1639 SALTMARSH *Policy* I. cxi. 93 If any have had a poore and undervaluing conceit of you. **1648** JENKYN *Blind Guide* iv. 88 Those undervalewing expressions. **1691** tr. *Emiliane's Frauds Rom. Monks* (ed. 3) 412 This Notion..of the Protestants was so far from giving me an undervaluing Conceit of them [etc.]. **1863** COWDEN CLARKE *Shaks. Char.* vi. 148 To write a flippant, undervaluing word of one of Shakespeare's characters.

Hence **underˈvaluing-like** *a.*; **-ˈvaluingly** *adv.*

1637 HENSHAW *Medit.* (1639) 18 Not slightly and undervaluingly to speake of other mens vertues. **1707** NORRIS *Treat. Humility* vi. 289 To lessen and vilify himself, and speak..very undervaluingly of his own worth. **1782** J. BROWN *Nat. & Rev. Relig.* II. i. 117 He uttered several undervaluing like words to his mother.

ˈunderˌvassal. (UNDER-[1] 6 a.)

1594 [see UNDERFEE]. **1611** COTGR., *Arriere-vassal*, an vnder-vassall. **1918** *Times' Lit. Suppl.* 21 Mar. 135/2 Legal reforms which protected the under-vassals from the arbitrary use of seignorial jurisdictions.

underˈvaulted, *ppl. a.* (UNDER-[1] 4 a.)

1843 *Civil Eng. & Arch. Jrnl.* VI. 127/1 If not undervaulted, it may be freed from damp by..furnace slag.

ˈunderˌvaulting. (UNDER-[1] 5 c.)

1823 BUCKLAND *Reliq. Diluv.* 115 These undervaultings have for the most part been entirely filled up.

ˈunderverse. (UNDER-[1] 5 b.)

1579 E. K. *Gloss. to Spenser's Sheph. Cal.* Aug., Perigot maketh hys song in prayse of his loue, to whom Willy answereth euery vnder verse.

ˈunder-vest. (UNDER-[1] 5 a.)

1813 SCOTT *Trierm.* III. xviii, With nought to fence his dauntless breast But the close gipon's vnder-vest. **1883** LD. LYTTON *Life Lytton* I. 47 A delicate pink silk kerchief, carelessly folded to answer the purpose of our modern undervest.

ˈunderˌviewer. *Mining.* [UNDER-[1] 6 a.] An underlooker.

1881 *Instr. Census Clerks* (1885) 84 Miner: Viewer, Under-Viewer, Underlooker. **1885** *Manch. Exam.* 6 Aug. 4/7 The houses of the underviewer and of one of the men.

un-ˈdervished, *a.* (UN-[1] 9.)

1884 BROWNING *Ferishtah, Eagle* 1 Dervish—(though yet un-dervished, call him so No less beforehand).

ˈundervoice. (UNDER-[1] 9 b.)

1810 SHELLEY *Zastrozzi* vii. Pr. Wks. 1881 I. 42 'Ah!' replied Matilda, in an under-voice, 'look in that bed'. **1836** R. HOWITT *Gipsy King* III. lxv, Whilst many an undervoice is soft From many a talking dame.

ˈunderˌwages. (UNDER-[1] 10 b.)

1669 STURMY *Mariner's Mag.* I. ii. 15 Lame and decrepit Fellows preferred..by Serving for Under-Wages. **1835** URE *Philos. Manuf.* 327 Volunteering to work at under-wages from necessity.

ˈunder-ˌwaistcoat. (UNDER-[1] 5 a.)

1794 MRS. OPIE in Brightwell *Memorials*, etc. (1854) 42 His green coat and crimson under-waistcoat. **1826** SOUTHEY *Vind. Eccl. Angl.* 251 The blessed Arnulph of the hedgehog skin underwaistcoat. **1838** LYTTON *Alice* II. ii, His black coat neatly relieved in the evening by a white underwaistcoat. **1863** *N. & Q.* 3rd Ser. III. 50 In some parts of Yorkshire.. an underwaistcoat or 'Jersey' is called a 'singlet'.

ˈunder-walk. (UNDER-[1] 6 b.)

1651 DAVENANT *Gondibert* Pref. ¶29 Those compositions of second beauty I observe in the Drama to be the under-walks. **1673** BP. S. PARKER *Reproof Reh. Transp.* 10 Plots, and Scenes, and Walks, and under-walks.

ˈunder-ward. (UNDER-[1] 5 b.)

1826 SCOTT *Woodst.* viii, Wildrake passed through the under-ward or court.

ˈunder-ˌwarden. (UNDER-[1] 6 a.)

1375 BARBOUR *Bruce* IV. 400 The vndirwardane arivit was With thre batis. **1611** COTGR., *Sou[b]gardien*, an vnder Warden, vnder Keeper. **1819** SCOTT *Leg. Montrose* xiii, A lackey of the Marquis of Argyle, and occasionally acting as under-warden.

ˈunder-warp. (UNDER-[1] 5 b.)

1668 CULPEPPER & COLE *Barthol. Anat.* Introd., Others said that the Groundwork or under-warpe of the Parts is Seed.

underˈwash, *v.* (UNDER-[1] 4 a.)

1538 ELYOT, *Subluere*, to vnderwashe, as water, whyche runneth lowe vnder a banke or hylle.

under-ˈwatch, *v.* (UNDER-[1] 8 a.)

1654 GAYTON *Pleas. Notes* IV. xi. 244 Every step being under-watch'd with Dragons.

ˈunderˌwater, *sb.* [UNDER-[1] 5 c, 5 b.]

1. Water below the surface of the ground. Also *fig.*

1637 RUTHERFORD *Lett.* cxl. (1664) 275 False under-water not seen in the ground of an enlightned conscience, is dangerous. **1703** BP. NICOLSON *Misc. Acc.* (1877) 6 The Church-yard strangely (considering the Discents on each hand of it) infested with Under-water. **1805** R. W. DICKSON *Pract. Agric.* II. 296 Where the under stratum is clay, and there is no under water. **1866** GREGOR *Banffshire Gloss.* 203.

2. Water entering a vessel from beneath.

1645 RUTHERFORD *Tryal & Tri. Faith* 229 The Anchor is broken, or she taketh in under-water, or the Sail is torn.

3. = UNDERTOW. (*Cent. Dict.* citing Herschel.)

ˈunderˌwater, *a.* (Also *ˌunderˈwater*.) [Attrib. use of the phr. *under water*: see UNDER *prep.* 2, UNDER-[2].]

1. Placed, situated, carried on, etc., under water.

1627 MAY *Lucan* IV. G ij b, Some from the rocke, some from the shore oppose, Vulteius found this vnder-water traine. **1674** PETTY *Disc. Dupl. Proportion* 117 The further Truth whereof doth appear in the Under-water-Air within the Vessels of Water-Divers. **1832** *Planting* 109 in *Husb.* (L.U.K.) III, The wood..is esteemed for under-water-work, as piles, pipes, pumps, sluices. **1886** *Pall Mall G.* 7 Sept. 2/1 It is not sufficient to lay down the finest system of under-water mines. **1894** *Westm. Gaz.* 21 Feb. 6/1 A new under-water vessel which might be either a gunboat or an ordinary cargo steamer.

2. *spec.* In ships: Situated below the water-line.

1882 *Nature* XXV. 261 The ships would be secured against sinking by an under-water deck. **1889** WELCH *Text Bk. Naval Archit.* i. 8 The under-water part of the hull.

ˈunderwave. (UNDER-[1] 5 b.)

1838 MRS. BROWNING *Soul's Travelling* viii, When you hearken to the grave Lamenting of the underwave. **1895** A. NUTT in Meyer tr. *Voy. Bran* I. 232 An under- instead of a cross-wave locale appearing for the first time.

†**underwax**, *v.*: see UNDER-[1] 2.

underˈway, *adv.* [The phr. *under way* s.v. WAY *sb.*[1] 38 taken as one word.] **a.** *Naut.* Of a vessel: under way; having begun to move through the water.

1934 W. NELSON *Seaplane Design* vi. 67 The depth of the step affects..the moment to change trim when underway near the planing speed. **1940** P. V. H. WEEMS *Marine Navigation* (1941) v. 82 Before getting underway the navigator should determine by azimuth or by a known true bearing of a prominent object whether any error exists in the compass reading. **1978** *Sunday Mail* (Brisbane) *Boating Suppl.* 26 Nov. 16/6 Technically a vessel is underway when not moored, at anchor or aground.

b. *transf.* Of a process, project, activity, etc.: having begun, in progress, being done or carried out. Of a person: having started doing something.

1935 *Sci. Amer.* Apr., 198/1 Uncle Sam now has underway one of his greatest construction projects. **1950** *Chem. Engin. Progress* XLVI. 112/1 Construction should be underway by 1952. **1955** [see PROGRAM, PROGRAMME *sb.* 2 b]. **1973** M. AMIS *Rachel Papers* 23 Once underway, though, Gloria would have been able to detect few noteworthy points of contrast between sexual arousal and rabies. **1976** *New Scientist* 16 Dec. 660/2 Experiments..with an electro-optically q-switched neodymium-glass laser are underway. **1981** W. BOYD *Good Man in Africa* II. ix. 124 They walked arm-in-arm into the club where the dance was underway.

ˈunderˌweapon. (UNDER-[1] 6 b.)

1646 H. LAWRENCE *Comm. Angells* 109 Unlesse this stone and sling, these underweapons, be mannaged by the name of God.

ˈunderwear. [UNDER-[1] 5 a.] Underclothing; also, the fact of wearing, or of being worn, as underclothing.

1872 *Picayune* (New Orleans) 2 Apr. 6/1 (Advt.), Ladies' underwear... Best Merino Undershirts, fine finish;..fine French corsets. **1875** *Cassell's Family Mag.* I. 113/2 It will scarcely be necessary to give the address where the patterns of hygiene 'under-wear' are to be obtained. It would be more to the purpose to tell how the so-called 'under-wear' is made and trimmed in Paris. **1880** *Scribner's Mag.* 213 The general want of underwear was not so cruelly felt as had been feared. **1885** T. M. COAN *Ounces of Prevention* (1888) 10 Robust persons will get along well enough with the ordinary 'mixed underwear'.

†**underweave**, *v.*: see UNDER-[1] 2.

†**ˌunderˈweening.** *Obs.* [UNDER-[1] 10 b.] Under-estimation (of self or *of* something).

1574 tr. *Marlorat's Apocalips* 16 The words that he [*sc.* St. John] set here..sauor of a certayne singular vnderweening. **1682** SIR T. BROWNE *Chr. Mor.* III. §25 But the greatest underweening of this Life is to undervalue that, unto which this is but exordial.

underˈweigh, *v.* [f. the phr. *under weigh*: see WEIGH *sb.*] *intr.* To get under weigh.

1891 *Times* 25 Nov. 12/5 Witness at once underweighed and went to the rescue.

ˈunderweight, *sb.* [UNDER-[1] 10 b; UNDER *prep.* 23 b. Cf. Da. *undervægt*, Sw. *-vigt*, Du. *onderwigt*, G. *untergewicht*.] **1.** Insufficient weight; deficiency in weight.

1596 BACON *Max. & Use Com. Law* II. (1635) 8 Tradesmen of all sorts, selling with under weights or measures. **1647** N. WARD *Simple Cobler* 30 They never complain of me for giving them hard measure, or under-weight. **1864** R. A. ARNOLD *Cotton Fam.* 470 The underweight of these bales made the stock seem larger than it really was. **1894** *Boston Arena* June 44 The minutest difference of overweight or underweight in the coin.

attrib. **1890** *Daily News* 22 Feb. 5/4 The first cost of the restoration of all underweight coins.

2. a. The condition or quality of being lighter than average for one's height and build.

1935 H. S. DIEHL *Textbk. Healthful Living* x. 143 Both underweight and overweight are handicaps to employment, ..for women overweight is a greater handicap than underweight. **1952** R. MACAULAY *Let.* 16 May (1961) 313, I suspect that thinness and under-weight may be a physical quality that you and I share.

b. [Absol. use of adj.] An underweight person.

1910 A. Bryce *Laws of Life & Health* vii. 247 It is quite a common thing for underweights to live to eighty, ninety, or even a hundred. **1935** H. Roberts *Everyman in Health & Sickness* II. iv. 152 The longest lived are found among the underweights.

under'weight, *a.* Also under-weight. [UNDER-².]

a. Not sufficiently heavy, lacking in weight; *spec.* of a person: lighter than average for one's height and build; too thin.

1899 [see OVER-WEIGHT *a.*]. **1925** C. E. Turner *Personal & Community Health* ii. 53 The underfed person drags himself about—underweight, pale,.. and pessimistic. **1971** 'D. Halliday' *Dolly & Doctor Bird* i. 5 He was a tall, underweight man in his early thirties. **1979** *Irish Times* 28 Sept. 3/6 Two British boats had been found to be underweight but no action was taken.

b. *fig.*

1960 T. Reese *Play Bridge with Reese* 15 Partner is sufficiently pleased with the result not to notice that I was under-weight for my medium no-trump. **1977** *Time* 26 Sept. 42/1 The plot of *Annie Hall* has the two underweight egos twine together, rose and briar. **1985** *Times* 11 Jan. 17/6 With many institutional investors still underweight, the price is set to move up.

under'whelm, *v. joc.* [f. UNDER-¹ 10 a, after OVERWHELM *v.*] *trans.* To leave unimpressed, to arouse little or no interest in. Chiefly as **under'whelmed** *pa. pple.* and *ppl. a.*, and **under'whelming** *ppl. a.*

1956 T. K. Quinn *Giant Corporations* viii. 61 He wrote.. commending the action of one of the giant corporations for a.. price reduction at a time when prices were rising. I was underwhelmed, and investigated. **1968** *Punch* 17 July 81/2, I agree that the wretched parents are not to be penalised till 1969 and I'm sure they are under-whelmed with gratitude. **1970** *Daily Colonist* (Victoria, B.C.) 3 July 47/1 Victoria Fair got off to a quite underwhelming start.. with a concert in the University of Victoria gym. **1972** *Times Lit. Suppl.* 29 Dec. 1569/4 Both the prose and the play are underwhelming. **1978** *Ottawa Citizen* 2 Mar. 3/3 The Sparks Street post office ran out of applications.. but a survey of other post offices.. showed the public was generally underwhelmed. **1984** *Observer* 15 Jan. 9/3 He was.. fluent in speech and crashingly dull. If there was an opportunity to be underwhelming, he unfailingly seized it.

†**'underwind.** *Obs.* (UNDER-¹ 5 b.)

1726 Woodward *Nat. Hist. Earth* Introd. 129 The North of England, where the Natives are wont to ascribe these Phænomena to what they call an Under-Wind, or Vapour ascending from the Bottom.

'underwing. [UNDER-¹ 5 b and UNDER-².]

1. a. A wing placed under, or partly covered by, another.

1535 Coverdale *2 Esdras* xii. 29 Thou sawest two vnderwinges vpon the heade that is on the right syde. **1801** Southey *Thalaba* III. xxxiii, The admiring girl survey'd His out-spread sails of green; His gauzy underwings. **1826** Kirby & Sp. *Entomol.* III. 380 The part.. in many cases is connected with the posterior basal margin of the underwings.

b. The part of a bird's body concealed when the wings are folded.

1956 G. Durrell *Drunken Forest* vi. 110 Two jacanas bathing, their underwings flashing buttercup yellow. **1977** C. McCullough *Thorn Birds* iv. 75 Big pale-grey parrots with brilliant purplish-pink breasts, underwings and heads.

2. a. Used *attrib.*, with adjs. of colour, to designate various species of moths.

1749 Wilkes *Eng. Moths & Butterflies* 2 The great yellow-underwing moth. *Ibid.* 17 The willow red-underwing moth. *Ibid.* 23, 33. **1826** Kirby & Sp. *Entomol.* III. xxxi. 272 A red under-wing-moth (*Noctua pacta*). **1882** *Proc. Berw. Nat. Club* IX. 559 One captured a Yellow Underwing Moth.

b. *ellipt.* = Underwing moth.

1819 Samouelle *Entomol. Compend.* 418 *Noctua Myrtilli.* The beautiful yellow Underwing. **1832** Rennie *Consp. Butterfl. & M.* 51 The Pearl Underwing (*Agrotis æqua*). **1871** Darwin *Desc. Man* II. xi. I. 394 The common yellow under-wings (Triphæna).

3. *attrib.* Situated beneath the wings (of a bird, etc.). Also, situated or occurring beneath the wing of an aeroplane.

1896 *Daily News* 10 Jan. 6/7 The brightly-tinted varieties, ..lined like the underwing feathers of tropical birds. **1946** Taylor & Allward *Spitfire* 27 (*caption*) The Spitfire's eye —the underwing camera installation. **1947** *Shell Aviation News* No. 106 23/1 Underwing or integral fuelling of aircraft is receiving a great deal of attention in the United States and Great Britain. **1949** *Gloss. Aeronaut. Terms (B.S.I.)* II. 14 *Under-wing radiator*, a radiator fitted below a wing. **1979** J. Garnett *Backfire is Hostile* xiii. 143 Aircraft are.. carrying underwing stores.

'underwit. [UNDER-¹ 6 a, 10 b.]

1. A poor or inferior kind of wit.

1655 Shirley *Politician* Ded., Some abuses of the common theatres (which were not so happily purged from scurrility and under-wit—the only entertainment of vulgar capacities).

2. A person of defective understanding; a half-witted person.

Used as a surname in the Duke of Newcastle's *Country Captain* (1649).

1682 T. Flatman *Heraclitus Ridens* No. 52 (1713) II. 75 Having often met with some of the Under-wits of that Panel, who threatened what their Foreman could have done. **1900** *Everybody's Mag.* III. 513/2 He was a single man, and many said an underwit.

'under-witch. (UNDER-¹ 6 a.)

1678 Butler *Hud.* III. I. 282, I found th' Infernal Cunning-man, And th' Under-witch, his Caliban.

,under-'witted, *a.* [UNDER-¹ 10 a.] Of inferior or defective understanding; half-witted.

1683 Kennett *Erasm. on Folly* 18 Cupid.. is an underwitted whipster. *Ibid.* 125 The Athenian Commander.. was a little underwitted. **1856** Hawthorne *Eng. Note-bks.* (1870) I. 424, I rather think it [*sc.* a child] was under-witted, and could not talk.

'underwood. [UNDER-¹ 5 d. Cf. MSw. *undirvidh.*]

1. Small trees or shrubs, coppice-wood or brush-wood, growing beneath higher timber trees.

a **1325** *MS. Rawl. B. 520* fol. 32 b, þat te heiwes [= highways].. ben.. ilargiste, þer ase is wode, hegges oþer buskes ore vnderwode. *c* **1380** *Antecrist* in Todd *Three Treat. Wyclif* (1851) 119 His taile is likenyd to a cedre, [þat] wexyng in to heȝþe passiþ oþer vnderwod. **1467–8** *Rolls of Parlt.* V. 575/2 Every persone or persones, which have bought eny Tymbre, Woode or Underwode. **1480** *Cov. Leet Bk.* 445 The people.. throwen down & beren away the vnderwode of þe seid Priour. **1512** *Act 4 Hen. VIII*, c. 18 §17 Underwode growyng uppon the seid landes. *a* **1596** *Sir T. More* (Malone Soc.) Add. i. 65 Thinke when an oake fals, vnderwood shrinkes downe, And yet may liue, though brusd. **1642** Fuller *Holy & Prof. St.* II. xiii. 100 This underwood serves for supplies to save timber from burning. **1669** Worlidge *Syst. Agric.* (1681) 93 In a few years you may observe many fair Trees to steal up amongst the Underwood. **1733** W. Ellis *Chiltern & Vale Farm.* 128 The Underwood will be fit to fell in.. fifteen Years. **1794** Mrs. Radcliffe *Myst. Udolpho* xliv, At a deep recess of the forest, ..so overgrown with underwood that they proceeded with difficulty. **1827** O. W. Roberts *Voy. Centr. Amer.* 64 Our way.. was nearly free from underwood or any material impediment. **1882** 'Ouida' *Maremma* I. 46 She made her way through the dense underwood.

attrib. **1796** W. H. Marshall *Planting* II. 51 Its branches ..very much resemble those of the Beech:.. especially in the shrubby underwood state.

b. *fig.*

a **1637** B. Jonson *Underwoods* To Rdr., I am bold to entitle these lesser poems, of later growth, by this [name] of Underwood, out of the analogie they hold to the Forest in my former booke. **1693** Dryden *Juvenal* Ded. (1697) p. xxxiv, But these are the Under-Wood of Satire, rather than the Timber-Trees. **1863** Cowden Clarke *Shaks. Char.* ix. 230 It is from among the underwood of these stately productions.. that we bring to remembrance gems of practical wisdom.

2. With *a* and pl. A quantity or stretch, a special kind, of woody undergrowth.

1541 *Act 33 Hen. VIII*, c. 39 All woodes and vnderwoodes, belonging to your office. **1581–2** *Catal. Anc. Deeds* (1906) V. 484 Breers, brembles, bushes and underwoodes. **1607** J. Norden *Surv. Dial.* III. 140 Therefore must the Surueyor be heedful.. to note what trees are among the underwoods. **1646** J. Hall *Horæ Vac.* 101 Great Oakes breake their own branches and neighbouring underwoods. **1708** *Lond. Gaz.* No. 4475/3 Posting the.. Granadiers among the Thickets of an Underwood. **1766** Goldsm. *Vicar* iv, Our little habitation was.. sheltered with a beautiful underwood behind. **1847** Emerson *Poems, Humble-bee* 29 Rover of the underwoods. **1867** Lady Herbert *Cradle L.* i. 5 Enormous groves of date-palms.., with an underwood of poinsettias.

fig. a **1637** B. Jonson (*title*), Underwoods; consisting of divers poems. [Cf. 1 b.]

3. The wood underlying a veneer.

1862 *Catal. Internat. Exhib., Brit.* II. No. 3411, The veneering.. will bear an immense amount of heat or damp before it will strip from the underwood.

Hence **'under,wooded** *a.*

1811 [see *oak barren* s.v. OAK 9]. **1861** Rossetti in Ruskin *Life* (1899) 277 A rich sweet country, beautifully wooded, underwooded, and sloped.

'underwool. [UNDER-¹ 5 a, d.] **1.** Wool used to make underwear; woollen undergarments. *rare*⁻¹.

1910 W. de la Mare *Private View* (1953) 223 The typical Englishman.. a scorner of great-coats and underwool.

2. A layer of wool lying beneath the outer layer on an animal.

1939 J. S. Huxley in *Geogr. Mag.* Dec. 78/2 They [*sc.* Soay sheep] have.. the same general colouration.. with dense underwool. **1965, 1968** [see QIVIUT].

'underwork, *sb.* [UNDER-¹ 5 c, 9, 10 b.]

†**1.** An under-current. *Obs.*⁻¹

1610 G. Fletcher *Christ's Vict.* I. lvi, So curiously the underworke did creepe,.. That afar off the waters seem'd to sleepe.

2. A structure placed under or supporting something; a substructure.

1624 Wotton *Elem. Archit.* 79 The Couer, or Roofe, ..[if] too heauy,.. will suffer a vulgar obiection of pressing too much the vnder-worke. **1772** T. Simpson *Vermin-Killer* Introd., The rain forces its way through, and rots the underwork [of the thatch]. **1776** G. Semple *Building in Water* 18 The Under-work of the second Pier. **1890** W. J. Gordon *Foundry* 158 As packed for export, it goes into a flat case.. and takes up little more room than its underworks.

3. †**a.** Work done at lower rates. *Obs.*⁻¹

1624 T. Scott *Belgic Souldier* E 3, There are so many of all Trades, who confound one another by vnderworke and indirect abuses, that [etc.].

b. Subordinate or inferior work.

1645 Milton *Colast.* 26 To bee put to this under-work of scowring and unrubbishing the low and sordid ignorance of such a presumptuous lozel. **1708** Addison *Pres. State War* 20 You will find most of those that are proper for War absolutely necessary for.. carrying on the Underwork of the Nation.

c. Underhand or secret work.

1814 D'Israeli *Quarrels Auth.* III. 294 The Tyrant himself had an openness, quite in contrast with the dark under-works of his Satellites.

under'work, *v.* [UNDER-¹ 8 a, 8 b, 10 a.]

†**1. a.** *intr.* To work secretly; to take clandestine measures. *Obs.*

1504 *Plumpton Corr.* (Camden) 186 It is sayd that ye be lesse forward, & they underworketh falsly. **1603** B. Jonson *Sejanus* Argt., He raiseth in private a new instrument,.. and by him underworketh, discovers the other's counsels.

†**b.** *trans.* To work against secretly; to seek to undermine or overthrow. *Obs.*

1595 Shaks. *John* II. i. 95 But thou from louing England art so farre, That thou hast vnder-wrought his lawfull King. **1613–8** Daniel *Coll. Hist. Eng.* (1626) 45 His delay yeelds the King time to.. vnder-worke his enemies. **1627** Abp. Abbot *Narr.* in Rushworth *Hist. Collect.* (1659) I. 440 He will underwork any man in the World, so that he may gain by it. **1659** Rushw. *Ibid.* 4 He did first under-work his Voyage to Guienna.

2. †**a.** To spend too little work on; to leave unfinished. *Obs.*

1691 Norris *Pract. Disc.* 228 There is no Artist, but will perform to the utmost of his Skill, provided it be as easy for him to make his Piece compleat, as to under-work it.

b. To impose too little work upon.

1882 Miss Braddon *Mt. Royal* I. iii. 78 Besides, he is not underworked.

c. *intr.* To do too little work.

1869 H. Sidgwick *Let.* 8 Mar. in A. & E. M. Sidgwick *Henry Sidgwick* (1906) 191, I am rather underworking. **1902** G. Howell *Labour Legislation* xlii. 499 The man that under-works is as bad as the man that under-pays.

3. *trans.* To work for less wages than (another).

1695 *Whether Preserving Protest. Relig. was Motive of Revolution* 17 Who by their frugal and parsimonious Living would be able.. to underwork and undersell them. **1713** *Mercator* No. 9/1 The French being able to Underwork us, will also Undersell us.

'under-,worker. [UNDER-¹ 6 a.] An assistant or subordinate worker.

1701 Swift *Contests Nobles & Comm.* iv, An usurping populace is.. a meer underworker, and a purchaser in trust for some single tyrant. **1709** Sacheverell *Serm.* 15 Aug. 10 There must be Co-operators, Partners, and Under-workers in it. **1744** Young *Nt. Th.* VII. 415 Want and convenience, under-workers, lay The basis, on which love of glory builds.

,under'working, *sb.* [UNDER-¹ 9 a.] Action of a secret or unapparent nature.

1613–8 Daniel *Coll. Hist. Eng.* (1621) 26 Skornes, conspiracies and vnder-workings. **1679** Everard *Prot. Princes Europe* 20 The Emissaries of Rome have been the Instruments of the underworkings which have raised this War. **1811** Mrs. Grant in *Mem. & Corr.* (1844) I. 286 The underworkings of petty envy and malignity. **1833** Mill *Lett.* (1910) I. 45 Men who are now gaining.. a considerable and increasing influence.. over the underworkings of our government.

'under,working, *ppl. a.* [UNDER-¹ 8 a, 4 a.] Working or acting in a secret or unapparent manner; also *lit.*, working beneath.

1605 Daniel *Philotas* II. iii. *Chorus* C vj, There dost thou struggle.. Against some underworking pride that must Supplanted be. **1679** C. Nesse *Antid. agst. Popery* 87 He gives them up to the strong delusions of this under-working beast. **1818** Milman *Samor* 283 Deep echoed out From th' underworking caverns. **1883** *Century Mag.* XXVI. 373/2 As a strong character in underworking motive, Squire Gaylord seems to be his best.

'under-,workman. (UNDER-¹ 6 a.)

1608 Willet *Hexapla Exod.* 724 The chiefe workeman doth the principall worke himselfe, and the other by his ministers and vnderworkemen. **1651** C. Cartwright *Cert. Relig.* I. 142 As an Architect, or the like chiefe workman, doth.. appoint under-workmen where they shall imploy themselves. **1708** Swift *Sent. Ch. Eng. Man* Wks. 1755 II. I. 78 Under-workmen, who are expert enough at making a single wheel in a clock, but are utterly ignorant how to adjust the several parts. **1771** Luckombe *Hist. Print.* 8 An Under-workman in the Printing-House at Harlem.

'underworld. [UNDER-¹ 5 b, c. Cf. Du. *onderwereld*, G. *unterwelt*, Da. *underverden.*]

1. The sublunary or terrestrial world.

1609 Daniel *Civ. Wars* VIII. xxx, The glory of that Mightinesse.. That ouer-spreds.. This vnder-world. *a* **1616** Beaum. & Fl. *Bonduca* III. ii, Loud Fame calls ye, Pitch'd on the topless Apenine, and blows To all the underworld. **1700** Rowe *Amb. Step-Mother* I. i, Thou, like the God thou serv'st, shall shine aloft, And with thy influence rule the under world. *a* **1719** Addison tr. *Virgil's Fourth Georgic* Wks. 1721 I. 19 When th' under-world is seiz'd with cold and night. **1822** Shelley *Chas. 1st* II. 140 For a king bears the office of a God To all the under world.

fig. **1694** Atterbury *Serm.* (1726) I. 173 Their Way was.. to look down with Pity and Contempt upon a poor deluded Under-World. **1795** Wolcot (P. Pindar) *Liberty's last Squeak* III. Wks. 1812 III. 425 Our Lords on high, Who call the under-world of man, An assish, mulish, packhorse clan.

2. a. The abode of the departed, imagined as being under the earth; the nether world.

1608 Day *Hum. out of Br.* I. i, Since proud Anthonio.. Is in his iourney towards th' vnderworld. **1713** C'tess Winchelsea *Misc. Poems* 18 When to the Under-world despis'd he goes, A pamper'd carcase on the Worms bestows. **1858** Birch *Anc. Pottery* I. 365 Few Argive representations, except that of the Danaids in the underworld,..are given on vases. **1871** TYLOR *Prim. Cult.* I. 311 The western Hades, the underworld of night and death.

b. A region below the surface of the earth; a subterranean or underlying area.

1885 *Daily News* 4 Nov., The extent to which the underworld in the Potteries is honeycombed with coal mines. **1886** WINCHELL *Walks Geol. Field* 56 Shall we venture among the dangers of the oceanic under-world?

3. The Antipodes; also, the part of the earth beyond the horizon.

1847 TENNYSON *Princ.* IV. 27 Fresh as the first beam glittering on a sail, That brings our friends up from the under-world. **1868** KINGSLEY *Christmas Day* 34 New patriarchs of the new-found underworld. **1890** 'R. BOLDREWOOD' *Col. Reformer* (1891) 154 A shining sail came from the under-world and swept placidly towards the city.

4. a. A sphere or region lying or considered to lie below the ordinary one. Hence also (*fig.*), a lower, or the lowest, stratum of society, etc.

1859 MISS A. B. EDWARDS *Hand & Glove* vi. 54 Slowly I sank away, lower and lower, into the under-world of darkness and dreams. **1894** *Harper's Mag.* Mar. 630 The mysterious processes which go on under the influence of the bacteria in this underworld of life. **1899** F. T. BULLEN *Way Navy* 25 The begrimed company of toilers..in the underworld of engines and boilers [in a ship]. **1903** J. LONDON in *Ainslie's Mag.* Oct. 76/1 And with-out a word, when his *wanderlust* gripped him, he was off and away into that great mysterious underworld he called 'The Road'. **1913** C. J. HOGARTH (*title*) Dostoyevsky's Letters from the underworld. **1929** *Amer. Speech* IV. 337 The following word-list..does..record representative words and phrases commonly used by 'knights of the road', 'migratory workers', and denizens of the so-called 'underworld'. **1972** F. FITZGERALD *Fire in Lake* iii. 126 They managed to create an underworld of warlords, secret societies, and bandit groups.

b. *spec.* The world of criminals or of organized crime (usu. with *the*); hence, the inhabitants of this region.

1900 *McClure's Mag.* Aug. 356 (*heading*) True stories from the Underworld. *Ibid.*, Their life amongst them [*sc.* the criminal classes] is not to break laws, but to understand as thoroughly as possible the motives and methods of that great part of the community which they describe as 'The Under-World'. **1903** 'J. FLYNT' *Rise of R. Clowd* iv. 136 Susan was the accepted Queen of the local Under World. **1926** *Westm. Gaz.* 22 Mar., Four of the most dangerous women in London's underworld began long terms of imprisonment during the weekend. **1956** H. KURNITZ *Invasion of Privacy* xxiii. 146 Remember the code of the underworld and what happens to a squealer. **1977** *Time* 8 Aug. 16/2 He..was presumably executed by the underworld. **1981** M. MOORCOCK *Byzantium Endures* ix. 235 Through an acquaintance in the Podol under-world, I had two copies of my passport printed, complete with photographs.

c. The slang of the criminal underworld. *rare.*

1927 *Vanity Fair* (N.Y.) Nov. 132 'Taking him for a ride' is underworld for enticing a person to death.

5. *attrib.* and as *adj.* (esp. in sense 4b).

1929 D. H. LAWRENCE *Pornography & Obscenity* 12 Genuine pornography is almost always underworld. **1955** D. W. MAURER in *Publ. Amer. Dial. Soc.* XXIV. 12 Perhaps the fact that underworld areas have not been traditionally considered 'respectable' for academic research has discouraged some investigators. **1977** *Time* 4 July 8/2 Widely believed to have underworld as well as high society connections, Riachi was found murdered in his apartment.

Hence **'under,worldling**, a member of an underworld.

1928 *Tablet* 21 Jan. 89/1 One of the points on which Protestant Underworldlings have agreed to blacken the Church. **1962** N. MARSH *Hand in Glove* v. 157 'What can I do for you, Super?' Moppett asked him with the slight smile of the film underworldling.

underwrite ('ʌndə-, older -'raɪt), *v.*[1] [UNDER-[1] 4a, after L. *subscrībere* SUBSCRIBE *v.* Cf. OE. *underwritan*.]

In Langl. *P. Pl.* A. XI. 255 *vndirwriten* is apparently an error for the variant *vnwriten*.

1. a. *trans.* To write (words, figures, etc.) below something, esp. after other written matter.

c **1430** *Art Nombryng* 3 The nombre to be addede is that þat sholde be addede therto, and shalle be vnderwriten. *Ibid.*, It is convenient that the lesse nombre be vnderwrit, and the more addede. **1578** LYTE *Dodoens* 310 Euphorbium prepared in manner as shalbe vnder written, purgeth..slymie flegmes. **1611** SPEED *Hist. Gt. Brit.* IX. xiv. 614/2 The said Author, obseruing the scope of those lines,..doth vnderwrite and annex this Stanza. **1670** G. H. *Hist. Cardinals* I. III. 86 His business is to under-write answers to all Petitions. **1709** *Tatler* No. 74 ⁋11 Each Subscriber should underwrite his Reason for the Place he allots his Candidate. **1753** RICHARDSON *Grandison* VI. xlix. 298, I will entreat her to vnderwrite her mind on this subject. **1882** *Act 45 & 46 Vict.* c. 61 Sched. 1 The bill..should be annexed, or a copy of the bill and all that is written thereon should be underwritten.

†**b.** To write, subscribe, sign (one's name) below, or at the end of, a document, etc. *Obs.*

1569 in Strype *Ann. Ref.* (1709) I. lv. 566 That we, whose names are by ourselves underwritten, do acknowledge [etc.]. *a* **1593** MARLOWE *Edw. II*, v. ii, Our behoofe will beare the greater sway When as a kings name shall be vnder writ. **1616** B. JONSON *Devil an Ass* III. iii, I haue enough on't! for an hundred pieces? Yes, for two hundred, vnder-write me, doe. Your man will take my bond? **1682** SCARLETT *Exchanges* 61 The Acceptant, when he accepts, must underwrite his Name. **1793** GIBBON *Misc. Wks.* (1814) II. 493 When the subscription is proposed, I shall underwrite my name for, at least, six copies.

†**c.** *absol.* To become surety. *Obs.*

c **1650** HIGFORD *Instit.* (1658) 17 For the most part the borrowers of money..are engaged one for another... Those that stand engaged for you; you must underwrite for them also.

†**2. a.** To subscribe (a document) with one's name.

1557 *Order of Hospitals* C7b, Warrants..underwritten by the Thresorer..what shall be paid to any such Pencioner wekly. **1623** in Foster *Eng. Factories Ind.* (1908) II. 320 The agreement mad betwixt us was underwrytten and sealed. **1655** FULLER *Ch. Hist.* VIII. i. §4 No importunity could prevail with him to underwrite this will. **1682** in *Lond. Gaz.* No. 1782/1 One part thereof Signed by such Servant, and also Under-written or Endorsed with the Name and Hand-writing of such Magistrate. **1713** *Guard.* No. 39, I shall not retract any advertisement till I see those verses, and I'll choose what to believe then, except they are under-written by his nurse. **1748** RICHARDSON *Clarissa* (1811) VI. 365 A letter..signed by his Lordship,..and underwritten by myself.

absol. **1608** in Birch *Crt. & Times Jas. I* (1848) I. 84 His brother, whom..he hath now sent for up to undertake and underwrite with him.

b. *spec.* To subscribe (a policy of insurance) thereby accepting the risk of insurance. Also *absol.*

1622 MALYNES *Anc. Law-Merch.* 102 If one be bound, and two or more do put their hand and seale, and vnderwrite, and seale the said Bill as Principals. *Ibid.* 166 The custome..doth impose the losse vpon those Assurors which did first vnderwrite. **1703** *Lond. Gaz.* No. 3940/4 Whosoever..hath underwrittten any Policy of Insurance on the Ship Samuel. **1755** MAGENS *Insurances* I. 7 If this be declared when the Insurance is made, the Insurers..will never refuse to under-write. **1766** W. GORDON *Gen. Counting-ho.* 21 If you under-write a policy mentioning..the sum underwrote. **1809–11** COMBE *Syntax* XXV. 417 The Policies remain'd secure, Waiting for arms of signature; For what brave spirit e'er would fight 'em When nobody would underwrite 'em. **1876** F. MARTIN *Hist. Lloyd's* 365 Both non-underwriting members and annual subscribers are..forbidden to underwrite any policy of insurance.

c. *absol.* To carry on the business of insurance.

1784 LD. MACARTNEY in *Burke's Corr.* (1844) III. 27 The impossibility of men's fairly acquiring great wealth, in a short time, who neither lend, trade, play, nor under-write.

3. a. To set one's name to, subscribe to (a decision, statement, etc.); to agree to or confirm by signature. Also *fig.*, to support or reinforce (an idea, quality, etc.); to lend support to (a party, etc.).

1606 SHAKS. *Tr. & Cr.* II. iii. 137 Worthier then him selfe.., vnder write in an obseruing kinde His humorous predominance. **1633** G. HERBERT *Temple, Ch. Porch* xxiv, Man is a shop of rules, a well-truss'd pack, Whose every parcell under-writes a law. **1656** EARL MONM. tr. *Boccalini's Advts. fr. Parnass.* I. lxxvii. 161 All the Assembly had already underwritten the reformation, when Thales put them in mind [etc.]. **1678** BUTLER *Hud.* III. iii. 148 All which they took in Black and White, And cudgel'd me to underwrite. *a* **1853** MRS. OPIE in Brightwell *Life* (1854) 49, I could, with a safe conscience, underwrite all that he there relates. **1938** *Sun* (Baltimore) 5 Sept. 6/3 This sectional purpose in the bill was in effect underwritten by the new Adminstrator. **1962** *Listener* 15 Mar. 480/1 The fact that Hirst was at the Royal College of Art..at the time of that journalistically stimulated style known as 'New Realism', to some extent underwrites this basic quality of factualness in his work. **1965** *Ibid.* 10 June 851/2 We must not always find ourselves underwriting the regimes of yesterday while our opponents support those of tomorrow. **1978** *Jrnl. R. Soc. Arts* CXXVI. 439/1 Their sponsors (usually governments) underwrote the belief that an exhibition's ultimate social and economic benefits would outweigh its immediate costs.

†**b.** *intr.* To subscribe or agree *to* something.

1643 QUARLES *Loyal C.* 16 In case Papists should largely under-write to your Propositions,..would you not accept it?

4. †**a.** To guarantee to subscribe or contribute (a certain sum of money, etc.). *Obs.*

1623 HERIOT in *Mem.* App. III. (1822) 72 All my stock and adventures in the East India Company,..wherein I did under-write one thousand pounds. **1642** *Lanc. Tracts Civ. War* (Chetham Soc.) 62 Such moneyes and plate as Mr. Thomas Case..shall underwrite for the defence of Lancashire. *a* **1692** POLLEXFEN *Disc. Trade* (1697) 99 The last Stock was under-writ by Vertue of a Charter granted Anno 1657. **1705** R. BEVERLEY *Virginia* I. iv. (1722) 90 The Subscription-Money did not come in with the same readiness, with which it had been underwritten.

absol. **1680** R. L'ESTRANGE *Citt & Bumpkin* (ed. 3) 3 Masters underwrit for their Children, and Servants, Women for their Husbands.

b. *spec.* To agree to take up, in a new company or new issue (a certain number of shares if not applied for by the public).

1889 LINDLEY *Company Law* 761 A promoter of a company who had agreed to underwrite 10,000 shares. **1896** *Times Law Rep.* (1897) XIII. 570 The Globe Company shall under-write, or procure to be underwritten,..the first issue of 250,000 shares.

c. To support by a guarantee of funds. Also *transf.*, to guarantee by military or other power.

1890 *Spectator* 22 Nov., Many of the usual holders of great sums of money have of late been 'underwriting' great industrial enterprises. **1964** *Ann. Reg. 1963* 224 A free West Berlin could have its social system underwritten by the United Nations, and foreign troops could remain there 'for a certain period' under the U.N. flag. **1979** T. BENN *Arguments for Socialism* ii. 50 Big business..underwrote the cost of the campaign to keep Britain in the Common Market at the time of the 1975 referendum.

†**5. a.** To undertake or guarantee in writing *to* do something. *Obs.*

1621 in Foster *Eng. Factories Ind.* (1906) I. 346 The Ballochs..whoe underwrot to carry the last yeares caphila to Mando. **1642** *Propos. conc. Rais. Horse*, etc. 5 Whosoever..shall underwrite to furnish and maintain any number of Horse. **1644** VICARS *God in Mount* 163 Persons..who had..under-written to lend horse, and moneyes.

†**b.** To guarantee or promise *that*. *Obs.*

1838 CALHOUN *Wks.* (1874) III. 237 Pass the bill, and I underwrite that we shall never have again to complain of a surplus.

Hence **'under,writing** *ppl. a.*

1876 F. MARTIN *Hist. Lloyd's* 364 All underwriting members pay..an entrance fee of £100.

,under'write, *v.*[2] *rare.* [UNDER-[1] 10a.]

1. *trans.* To describe in too low an aspect.

1723–4 DK. WHARTON *True Briton* No. 69 II. 589 Who has under-wrote his Character, and represented him in faint and unbecoming Colors.

2. *refl.* To fall below (oneself) in writing.

1766 *Monthly Rev.* XXXIV. 407 An author capable of so strangely under-writing himself.

'under,writer. [f. UNDERWRITE *v.*[1]]

†**1.** A subscriber to, or shareholder in, a mercantile venture. *Obs.*

1616 in *Buccleuch MSS.* (Hist. MSS. Comm.) I. 250 For your venture in the East India Company I know not what to say... It's thought the King might do well to call to all the underwriters for a supply.

2. One who underwrites an insurance policy; *spec.* one who carries on an insurance business, esp. of shipping.

1622 MALYNES *Anc. Law-Merch.* 166 The later vnderwriters of the Assurors do not beare any part of the losse, but make restitution of the *Premio.* **1713** STEELE *Englishm.* No. 53, An Abuse crept into the World for the Advantage of the Under-writers. **1791** BENTHAM *Panopt.* 71 He would get underwriter's profit by me; but let him get that and welcome. **1833** MARRYAT *P. Simple* (1863) 281 The plate presented me by the merchants and underwriters of Lloyd's. **1874** BURNAND *My Time* vii. 65 The fearful gales..had resulted in serious losses to the underwriters.

†**3.** One who appends his name to a writing; a subscriber. *Obs.*

a **1639** WOTTON in *Reliq.* (1651) 458, I have now no more to say, but that while the foresaid report shall be false, The under-writer is Truly yours H. Wotton.

4. A subordinate writer or clerk.

1654 TAYLOR *Real Pres.* 288 Part of these words which Bellarmine, and from him the under-writers object. *c* **1710** CELIA FIENNES *Diary* (1888) 262 Under them is the 60 Clerks and other under writers.

5. One who engages to take up a certain number of company shares (see UNDERWRITE *v.*[1] 4b.)

1889 LINDLEY *Company Law* Index s.v., Difference between underwriter and person agreeing to place shares. **1897** *Times Law Rep.* XIII. 570 If..underwriter substitutes could not be procured, the Globe Company remained underwriter.

underwriting ('ʌndə-, older -'raɪtɪŋ), *vbl. sb.*[1] [f. as prec.]

1. The action of writing beneath, *esp.* of appending one's name to a document; also, that which is so written.

1598 FLORIO, *Sottoscrittione*, a subscription, a signing, an vnderwriting. **1622** MALYNES *Anc. Law-Merch.* 166 The later vnderwriters of the Assurors..reserue onely..10s. for their vnderwriting in the policie of Assurance. **1642** (*title*), That Great Expedition for Ireland By way of underwriting proposed by both Houses of Parliament..is heere Vindicated.

2. *spec.* **a.** The action or practice of (marine) insurance; the business of an underwriter. Also *attrib.*

1775 ASH, *Underwriting*, the act of insuring by writing the name under certain conditions. **1887** *Daily News* 26 Jan. 6/4 The Union Marine Insurance Company show an underwriting income of 172,133*l.* **1905** *Times* 13 Sept. 2/6 One of the blackest years in the history of underwriting.

b. The action of agreeing to take up shares (see UNDERWRITE *v.*[1] 4b). Freq. *attrib.*

1895 in *Times Law Rep.* (1897) XIII. 156 Underwriting letter for ordinary shares. **1897** *Ibid.* 569 An underwriting agreement..between the two companies.

underwriting, *vbl. sb.*[2] *rare*[−1]. [f. UNDERWRITE *v.*[2]] Writing with less than acceptable power or fervour, 'low-key' writing.

1938 O. SITWELL *Trio* 69 These days of 'under-writing', as of 'under-acting'.

'under,writing, *sb.* [UNDER-[1] 5b.] Writing lying below other writing; the first writing in a palimpsest.

1858 WISEMAN *Last Four Popes, Gregory XVI*, v. 305 It was this underwriting that Mai scanned with a sagacious eye.

under'written, *ppl. a.* [UNDER-[1] 4a: cf. UNDERWRITE *v.*[1]]

1. Of words, statements, etc.: Written (out), expressed in writing, below or beneath; following upon, coming after, what is already written.

1389 in *Eng. Gilds* (1870) 22 Deuouteliche we begynnen þis fraternite by þes ordynaunces vnderwriten. **1450–80** tr. *Secreta Secret.* Prol. 3 On of his Epistelis is here vndir writene, which he sent to Alexandre. **1483** *Rolls of Parlt.* VI. 240/1 All things said..and remembred in the said Rolle, and in the tenour of the same underwritten. **1568** GRAFTON *Chron.* II. 352 And al these Justices were commaunded to set to their handes to the questions under written. *a* **1586** SIDNEY *Arcadia* I. xix, Lalus..was by him answered in the underwritten sort. **1656** EARL MONM. tr. *Boccalini's Advts. fr. Parnass.* II. vi. (1674) 142 These under-written Articles were..penned..and sworn unto. **1667** *Protests Lords* I. 37, I, whose name is underwritten, do [etc.]. **1721** STRYPE *Eccl. Mem.* II. xviii. 389 She..writ English very well, as appears by her letter under-written. **1769** WESLEY *Wks.* (1831) XIII. 211 We, whose names are under-written,..are resolved [etc.]. **1874** SWINBURNE *Bothwell* IV. iv, His young child kneeling,..And the word under-written of his prayer. *absol.* **1683** W. HEDGES *Diary* (Hakl. Soc.) I. 113 The underwritten is Coppy of Capt. Minchin's affirmation. **1712** STEELE *Spect.* No. 431 ¶2, I was sent for to see the Lady who sends you the Underwritten.

2. Of things or matters: Specified or set down in writing below, etc.

1423 *Coventry Leet Bk.* 48 Ric. Hyckelyng & his felows.. sayn, þat thes ffeldys vndurwryton owtȝ to be comyn from Lammas. **1455** *Rolls of Parlt.* V. 295/2 In certayn sommes of money undrewreten. **1497** *Naval Acc. Hen. VII* (1896) 309 The Stuff takle..and Abillamentes of warre vndre-wrytyn. **1512** *Act 4 Hen. VIII*, c. 19 §9 The Collectoures..in maner underwritten to be..appoynted. **1545** *Reg. Privy Council Scot.* I. 3 To be sauld to the Franche army upoun the prices underwrittin. **1617** MORYSON *Itin.* III. 12 Let a Traueller obserue the vnderwritten things. **1669** STURMY *Mariner's Mag.* II. 115 These Years in the first Column under-written ..are all Leap-years. **1747** in *Nairne Peerage Evidence* (1874) 81 The debts and sums of money underwritten viz. **1829** COOPER *Good's Study Med.* (ed. 3) IV. 268 Mr. Buchanan also directs the underwritten injection to be used. **1883** PICTON *L'pool Munic. Rec.* I. 10 From the date of the grant of this deed..you may take the underwritten tolls, that is to say [etc.].

3. Of persons: Whose names are written or signed below, etc.

1425 *Munim. Melros* (Bann. Cl.) 544 Þe qwylke assyse was thir personis wnder wrytyn. **1483** in *Somerset Med. Wills* (1901) 238 The sadde discrecion of myn executours underwretyn. **1552–3** in Feuillerat *Revels Edw. VI* (1914) 94 Those persones be alredy furnyshed so yt yt nedyth not to provyde but only for these vnderwrytten. **1772** *Ann. Reg., Chron.* 74/2 We the underwritten liverymen.

absol. *a* **1704** T. BROWN *Let. Oxford Taylor* Wks. 1711 IV. 253 We the under-written.., having maturely considere'd the Purport of your Charge [etc.]. **1809** BAWDWEN *Domesday Bk.* 413 The under-written have not paid the King's tax as they ought.

† **under'wroot,** *v. Obs.* [UNDER-[1] 4 b.] *trans.* To burrow under; to undermine.

a **1272** *O.E. Misc.* 97/123 Hit stont vppon a treowe mote. .. Ne may no Mynur hire vnderwrote, ne neuer false þene grundwal. *a* **1300** *Cursor M.* 23281 Þar wormes sal þaim vnder wrote In bale wit-vten hope and bote.

† **underyawde,** app. for *-yode*, gone or passed under. *Obs.*[−1]

c **1557** ABP. PARKER *Ps.* I iv b, Ungodlynes in folyshnes, his tong hath under yawde.

† **under'yete,** *v. Obs.* Forms: 1 -ȝytan, 3 -ȝiten; 2 -ȝeite, 3–4 -ȝete; *3rd sing.* 2–3 -ȝit. *Pa. t.* 1 -ȝeat, -ȝet, 3 -ȝeat, -ȝæt, 3–4 -ȝat, -ȝet, 5 -yate, -gat; *pl.* 1 -ȝeaton, -ȝeton, 3–4 -ȝete(n. *Pa. pple.* 1 -ȝiten, 3–4 -ȝite, -ȝete. [OE. *underȝietan*: see UNDER-[1] 8 a and GET *v.*]

1. *trans.* To get to know, to become aware of, to ascertain, to observe (a fact).

c **893** K. ÆLFRED *Oros.* III. vii. 112 Þa Crece þæt þa underȝeaton,..hie þa ealle wið hiene ȝewin up ahofan. *c* **1066** *O.E. Chron.* (MS. C) an. 1066, Þa Eadwine eorl and Morkere eorl þæt underȝeaton, þa coman hi þyder. *a* **1250** *Owl & Night.* 1055 Þe louerd þat sone vnderȝat. *c* **1290** *Beket* 1194 in *S. Eng. Leg.* I. 140 Seint thomas it vnder-ȝat and ȝare-with ne paid him nouȝt. *a* **1300** *Floriz & Bl.* (Camb. MS.) 556 Ac longe ne miȝte hi hem wite þat hi neren vnderȝete. *a* **1330** *Otuel* 1351 Þo garsie it vnder-ȝat, He was swiþe sori for þat.

b. With clause as object.

c **1000** ÆLFRIC *Saints' Lives* xxxi. 762 Þa underȝet se halȝa wer þurh haliȝne gast þæt hit se sylfa deofol wæs. *a* **1175** *Cott. Hom.* 231 Him a þance befell to underȝeite wa..him were frend oðer fend. *c* **1200** *Trin. Coll. Hom.* 197 Wanne þe neddre hit underȝit þat hie sechen after hire, hie warneð hire wið hem. *c* **1205** LAY. 15028 Nu vnder-ȝat Uortimer his sune, þet he hefde atter inomen. **1297** R. GLOUC. (Rolls) 2227 Þe londes abouten vs abbeþ wel under ȝite þat þer nis no volc bileued þat lond vor to wite. **13..** *Sir Beues* (A.) 1514 Þat hors wel sone vnder-ȝit, Þat Beues has nouȝt vpon is rigge.

2. To perceive, observe (a person or thing); to catch sight of.

c **1000** ÆLFRIC *Judges* xvi. 3 Hwæt, þa Samson heora syrwunga underȝeat. *c* **1205** LAY. 1811 Brutus & his gode folc under-ȝeten þeos feondes. *a* **1225** *Ancr. R.* 150 Helle muchares, þat robbeð al þe gold-hordes þet heo muwen underȝiten. *c* **1305** *Pilate* 200 in *E.E.P.* (1862) 116 Whan þu vnderȝete..þe gywene falshede, Whi naddestou ispeke þer aȝe? **13..** *Sir Beues* (A.) 4354 Beues at þe mete sat. He beheld and vnder-ȝat Al is fon, þat were þer oute.

3. To learn or know the character of; to understand the meaning of.

c **1000** *Ags. Gosp.* Matt. vii. 16 Fram hyra wæstmun ȝe hi underȝytað. *a* **1240** *Lofsong* in *O.E. Hom.* I. 215 Me ne hit underȝit nout er þen me hit leose. **13..** *Seven Sag.* (P.) 3151 The child was wys,..And hadde wyt of the Holy Gost, And wat they sayden he undirgat.

† **underyoke,** *v.*: see UNDER-[1] 2.

'under-zeal. (UNDER-[1] 10 b.)

1841 CARLYLE *Heroes* i. (1904) 40 King Olaf has been harshly blamed for his over-zeal;..I should have blamed him far more for an under-zeal!

'under-,zealot. (UNDER-[1] 6 a.)

1682 T. FLATMAN *Heraclitus Ridens* No. 70 (1713) II. 181 Those crafty Knaves..do usually drop their Under-Zealots, when the success does not answer expectations.

undescanted, *ppl. a.* (UN-[1] 8 c.)

1573–80 TUSSER *Husb.* (1878) 23 Leaue Princes affaires undeskanted on.

unde'scendable, *a.* (UN-[1] 7 b.)

1877 TENNYSON *Harold* I. i, Steam'd upward from the undescendable Abysm.

unde'scended, *a.* [UN-[1] 8.]

1. Of a person: not in the line of descent.

1701 DE FOE *Trueborn Eng.* I. 169 Yet who the Heroe was, no Man can tell... The silent Record Blushes to reveal Their Undescended Dark Original.

2. *Med.* Applied to a testis that has not descended into the scrotum from its fœtal position in the abdominal cavity.

1897 in *Lippincott's Med. Dict.* **1901** *Ann. Surg.* XXXIV. 234 The undescended testicle is an extremely interesting organ. **1908**, etc. [see MALDESCENDED *a.*]. **1964** [see MALDESCENT]. **1980** *Amer. Jrnl. Roentgenol.* CXXXV. 211/2 Until recently, localization of the undescended testicle has remained a clinical urologic problem.

unde'scribable, *a.* (UN-[1] 7 b and 5 b.)

1728 ELIZA HEYWOOD tr. *Mme. de Gomez's Belle A.* (1732) II. 201, I have heard it reported, resumed the Marquis with an undescribable Agitation, that he was..in love with a Spanish Lady. **1768** STERNE *Sent. Journ.* 217, I felt such undescribable emotions within me. **1818** BYRON *Ch. Har.* IV. liii, Let these describe the undescribable. **1860** EMERSON *Cond. Life* v. (1861) 116 Graces and felicities not only unteachable, but undescribable.

Hence **unde'scribably** *adv.*

1792 CHARLOTTE SMITH *Desmond* II. 149 She is in love! —Oh! undescribably in love. **1818** MAR. EDGEWORTH *Let.* 8 Apr., You..will understand..how undescribably and exquisitely it is mixed with pain and pleasure.

unde'scribed, *ppl. a.* [UN-[1] 8.]

1. Not described; not expressed in words.

1575 T. CARTWRIGHT *2nd Reply to Whitgift* 446 As the Lord set forth the one, so he left nothing vndescribed in the other. **1600** PORY *Leo's Africa* 11 A description of places vndescribed by John Leo. **1697** COLLIER *Ess. Mor. Subj.* I. (1703) 32, I had rather leave it undescribed, than be forced to give it its proper character. **1837** CARLYLE *Fr. Rev.* III. II. i, It is a change such as History must beg her readers to imagine, undescribed. **1851** RUSKIN *Stones Ven.* (1874) I. Pref. p. vi, The reader will find..that the buildings..have been hitherto undescribed.

b. *spec.* Not yet scientifically described. (Cf. NONDESCRIPT *a.* 1.)

c **1680** *Enquiries* 2/1 Have you any undescribed Plants, or others of special note? **1768** PENNANT in *Phil. Trans.* LVIII. 94 We believe this species to have been undescribed. **1817** KIRBY & SP. *Entomol.* xxi. II. 221 Two or three Brazilian species in my cabinet, that seem undescribed. **1890** *Science-Gossip* XXVI. 76/2 A very beautiful species of Metopidia, which I believe to be undescribed.

2. Not marked off or delineated.

1852 BAILEY *Festus* (ed. 5) 475 The Atlantean axis of the world And all the undescribed circumference.

unde'scried, *ppl. a.* (UN-[1] 8.)

1595 DANIEL *Civ. Wars* III, xl, Within rests more of feare, More dread of sad euent yet vndiscride, Than..I would there were. **1611** SHAKS. *Wint. T.* IV. iv. 669 Muffle your face,..that you may..to Ship-boord Get vndescry'd. **1642** SLINGSBY *Diary* (1836) 83 He comes close up to ye town undiscry'd. **1722** WOLLASTON *Relig. Nat.* iii. 49 Who can tell at what undescried fields of knowledge even men may at length arrive? **1830** TENNYSON *Isabel* 22 Right to the heart and brain, tho' undescried. **1855** BROWNING *Men & Wom.* II. *In Three Days* iv, But years must teem with change untried,..With an end somewhere undescried.

unde'scriptive, *a.* (UN-[1] 7.)

1744 *Essay on Acting* 16 The Sentiment is languid, unintelligible and undescriptive. **1827** *Westm. Rev.* Oct. 431 The title..is altogether undescriptive of the contents..of the work. **1883** *Fortn. Rev.* July 42 It is undescriptive of such limitations..as were imposed by the Treaty of Paris.

† **unde'scrived,** *ppl. a. Obs.* [UN-[1] 8.] Undescribed.

1435 MISYN *Fire of Love* 86 Þat lyght vndescryuyd with qwos fayrnes þa ar rauischyd.

un'desecrated, *ppl. a.* (UN-[1] 8.)

1865 *Sat. Rev.* 21 Oct. 527/1 They..will leave nothing undesecrated by their ribald impertinence. **1884** F. HARRISON *Choice Bks.* (1886) 250 Conventual edifices still.. undestroyed and undesecrated.

unde'sert. (UN-[1] 12 and 5 b.)

1587 GOLDING *De Mornay* xxvii. 492 This infinite Godhead is not to recompence..our vndesert otherwise than with desert. **1841** HOR. SMITH *Moneyed Man.* III. vii. 180, I felt..my own total undesert, my inexcusable presumption.

unde'serted, *ppl. a.* (UN-[1] 8.)

[**1775** ASH.] **1792** WORDSW. *Descr. Sk.* 146 The mazes of a wood In which a cabin undeserted stood. **1892** LD. LYTTON *King Poppy* Prol. 32 That undeserted garden of the gods.

unde'serve, *v.* [UN-[1] 14.] *trans.* To fail to deserve. Also *absol.*

1621 QUARLES *Div. Poems, Esther* vii, The blaze of Honour, Fortune's sweet excesse, Doe vndeserue the name of Happinesse. **1650** GENTILIS *Considerations* 73 Where they doe not undeserve wanting the use of reason, wee should merit in rightly using it. **1721** CIBBER *Heroic Daughter* II. Sp. 23 Let us not..undeserve the Grace by new false Fears. **1757** MRS. GRIFFITH *Lett. Henry & Frances* (1767) II. 277 There are certain base natures, which not deserving favours before hand, are sure to undeserve the more they receive. **1894** LD. ROSEBERY in *Daily News* 3 May 6/6, I am inclined to think that..Government have done nothing so far to undeserve that welcome.

unde'served, *ppl. a.* [UN-[1] 8.]

† **1.** Without having deserved it; undeserving.

c **1374** CHAUCER *Troylus* III. 1021 O were it leful þat I pleyne of þe, That vndeserued suffrest Ialousie. **1390** GOWER *Conf.* III. 13 Some comen to the dole In happ, and ..Drinke undeserved of the beste. **1412–20** LYDG. *Chron. Troy* I. 2407 And vndeserued [*sc.* of me] ben to me so trewe, Þat I ensure vpon my feith [etc.]. *a* **1536** *Calisto & Melib.* A vj b, Yet vndeseruyd now thou comyst hydyr. **1593** KYD *Let. to Puckering* Wks. (1901) p. cviii, Atheisme,..which I was vndeserved chargd withall.

† **b.** Without reason; unjustly. *Obs.*[−1]

? *c* **1570** *Bugbears* III. iv. 8 Vnderservde [*sic*] a thowsand tymes I wysh to see hym deade.

2. Not deserved or merited (*a*) as a reward, favour, etc., (*b*) as a punishment, harm, etc.

(*a*) **1390** GOWER *Conf.* I. 43 Bot as the whiel aboute went He yifth his graces undeserved. *c* **1450** *Myrr. our Ladye* 132 That was hys othe, to gyue hymselfe to vs, A greate gyfte and vndeserued. **1551** ROBINSON tr. *More's Utopia* I. (1895) 20 Your great gentlenes to me, of my part vndeserued. **1596** SHAKS. *Merch. V.* II. ix. 40 Let none presume To weare an vndeserued dignitie. **1631** GOUGE *God's Arrows* I. §33. 54 The whole cause therfore resteth in God; even in his free grace, and undeserved love. **1722** WODROW *Corr.* (1843) II. 681 The undeserved kindness you have heaped on me. **1825** SCOTT *Talism.* xxiii, Permit me rather to express..my gratitude for..this undeserved generosity. **1855** MACAULAY *Hist. Eng.* IV. 459 He was widely known by the very undeserved appellation of Honest Tom.

(*b*) **1513** MORE *Rich. III*, Wks. 62 What speke we of losse, his vtter spoile and vndeserued distruccyon. **1590** SPENSER *F.Q.* I. ii. 26 Hart of flint would rew The vndeserued woes and sorrowes, which ye shew. **1644** MILTON *Areop.* (Arb.) 61 The removal of an undeserved thraldom upon lerning. **1777** SHERIDAN *Sch. Scand.* IV. i, He was a merchant in Dublin, but has been ruined by a series of undeserved misfortunes. **1849** EASTWICK *Dry Leaves* 63 The undeserved injuries and insults which had been heaped on the Amirs. **1896** W. K. LEASK *H. Miller* ii. 39 Undeserved denunciations of the dangers of Chartism.

unde'servedly, *adv.* [UN-[1] 11; cf. prec.]

1. Without having deserved (to suffer); without contributory fault or demerit; unjustly.

In group (*a*) referring to the subject of the clause or concept, in (*b*) to the object of the action.

(*a*) **1549** COVERDALE, etc. *Erasm. Par. 1 Pet.* i. 3 Where you suffre suche thynges vndeseruedly, you shall..receyue a great fruyte of your fayth. **1583** MELBANCKE *Philotimus* U iv b, With these daungers vndeseruedlye was noble Bellerophon distreste. **1652** GAULE *Magastrom.* 289 Iulian ..so died,..cursing..the Star-gazers and himselfe, for adhering to them, not undeservedly. **1712** STEELE *Spect.* No. 474 ¶6 A yearly Relief of my undeservedly necessitious Neighbours. **1809–10** COLERIDGE *Friend* (1865) 29 That I may have attracted notice to a writer undeservedly forgotten. **1877** E. VENABLES in *Dict. Chr. Biog.* I. 291/1 Whose reputation for orthodoxy was not undeservedly low.

(*b*) **1560** DAUS tr. *Sleidane's Comm.* 264 [He] therfore ascribeth vnto vs Tyranny, extortion and disturbaunce of the Clergie, but vndeseruedly. **1597** A. M. tr. *Guillemeau's Fr. Chirurg.* 51/1 Oftentimes Princes vndeseruedlye punishe theire Chyrurgians. **1625** HART *Anat. Ur.* I. iv. 43 He had wrongfully and vndeseruedly bene offended with me. **1656** EARL MONM. tr. *Boccalini, Pol. Touchstone* (1674) 269 A perfect Braggadochio, [they]..do not undeservedly personate..by a Spaniard. **1901** *Athenæum* 27 July 115/1 This curt reference makes undeservedly light of Mr. Langley's immense labours.

2. Without desert or merit; in an unmerited degree.

In (*b*) referring to the object of the action.

(*a*) **1610** HEALEY *St. Aug. Citie of God* 620 There were kings in Israel, for some..predictions of theirs, may not undeservedly be called Prophets. **1651** HOBBES *Govt. & Soc.* iv. §1. 58 The same Law..is also wont to be called Divine, nor undeservedly. **1712** STEELE *Spect.* No. 302 ¶5 Many of the prevailing Passions of Mankind do undeservedly pass under the Name of Religion. **1771** LUCKOMBE *Hist. Print.* 464 The great number of Boxes which they undeservedly occupy. **1835** *Court Mag.* VI. 55/1 S. Filippo Neri has a high character, and not undeservedly.

(*b*) **1603** FLORIO *Montaigne* I. li. 167 Vnworthily and vndeseruedly to bestow on whom we list the..loftiest titles. **1700** DRYDEN *Fables* Ded., One of those Athletick Brutes whom undeservedly we call Heroes.

unde'servedness. [UN-[1] 12.] **a.** The quality of being undeserved. **b.** Want of desert.

1611 SPEED *Hist. Gt. Brit.* IX. xix. 713/2 The reuerence of the man, or vnderseruednesse of his wrongs, moued so the affection of the Oxford Academians, that [etc.]. **1646** JENKYN *Remora* 16 Ponder it in the..unexpectednesse, undeservednes, manner of bestowing it. **1711–2** R. NEWTON *Serm.* (1784) 458 If much be due..on account of the Greatness of our Blessing, how much more is due when we consider the Undeservedness of it? *a* **1834** J. MARTIN *Disc.* iv. 54 That consciousness of sin and undeservedness which every one feels.

unde'server. [UN-[1] 12.] One who is not deserving (*of* something); an unworthy person.

1597 SHAKS. *2 Hen. IV*, II. iv. 406 The vndeseruer may sleepe, when the man of Action is call'd on. **1630** MASSINGER *Picture* IV. i, Too great an honour For such an undeserver. **1709** MRS. MANLEY *Secret Mem.* (1720) III. 247 Since her Widowhood, she has been the perpetual Mark of..a Croud of Undeservers. **1721** CIBBER *Cæsar* v. Sp. 12 Hence,..Ye undeservers of Pharsalian Honour!

undeˈserving, *vbl. sb.* [UN-¹ 13.] Want of desert or merit.

1598 FLORIO, *Immerito*, vnworthines, vndeseruing. *a* **1635** SIBBES *Confer. Christ & Mary* (1656) 24 When any temptation cometh for our unworthinesse, and our undeserving. **1711** M. HENRY *Hope & Fear Balanced* 14 Let us keep up an humble Sense of our own Vndeservings and Ill-deservings. **1906** QUILLER-COUCH *Mayor of Troy* xi, They came contritely, conscious of their undeserving.

undeˈserving, *ppl. a.* [UN-¹ 10, 5 d.]

1. Not deserving (something good); lacking desert or merit; unworthy. Also const. *of*.

1549 COVERDALE, etc. *Erasm. Par. Jas.* ii. 30 b, He yᵗ hath..preferred the vndeseruing rich man before the deseruing pore man. **1591** SHAKS. *Two Gent.* III. i. 7 When I call to minde your gracious fauours Done to me (vndeseruing as I am). **1647** COWLEY *Mistr., Discovery* iv, One would give with lesser grief, To an undeserving Beggar than a Thief. **1725** POPE *Odyss.* xv. 335 Mingling with the suitors' haughty train, Not undeserving, [I may] some support obtain. **1748** G. WHITE *Serm.* (MS.), So should we love others, though undeserving of our Love. **1796–7** JANE AUSTEN *Pride & Prej.* xlix, Wickham is not so undeserving, then, as we have thought him. **1821** SHELLEY *Adonais* xxiv, Whose sacred blood..Paved with eternal flowers that undeserving way. **1847** HARRIS *Life Ld. Hardwicke* I. 8 Such influences..certainly were not..undeserving of attention.

absol. **1713** *Guardian* No. 4 ¶1 Fame..promiscuously bestowed on the Meritorious and Undeserving. **1749** FIELDING *Tom Jones* II. v, We are liable..to confer our choicest favours often on the undeserving.

b. With direct object.

1603 DANIEL *Panegyric Congratulatory* xxv, There is no accesse By grosse corruption, bribes cannot effect For th' vndeseruing any offices. **1796** MME. D'ARBLAY *Camilla* V. 515 [It] makes me..feel undeserving my own hopes! **1860** MRS. CLIVE *Why Paul Ferroll killed his Wife* xii, Creatures undeserving respect, incapable of goodness.

2. Not deserving (harsh treatment, etc.); guiltless, innocent. Also with direct object.

a **1586** SIDNEY *Arcadia* II. x, I was caried..to doo my best to destroy this sonne..undeserving destruction. **1598** R. BERNARD tr. *Terence, Phormio* I. v, I hard you long since accuse vs all vndeseruing. **1697** DRYDEN *Æneis* VIII. 763 If your hard decrees..Have doomed to death his undeserving head. **1796** MME. D'ARBLAY *Camilla* III. 59 Unused to, because undeserving control. *Ibid.* 404 Thou must linger on, then, in captivity, thou poor little undeserving sufferer! **1865** CONINGTON tr. *Horace, Odes* I. xvii. (ed. 3) 21 Lest Cyrus..His passion on your chaplet wreak, Or spoil your undeserving dress.

†**3.** Undeserved, unmerited. *Obs.*⁻¹

1588 SHAKS. *L.L.L.* v. ii. 366 My Ladie..In curtesie giues vndeseruing praise.

undeˈservingly, *adv.* [UN-¹ 11.]

1. Without possessing desert or merit; unworthily.

1552 HULOET, Vndeseruyngelye, *immerito*. **1611** COTGR., *Indignement*, vnworthily, vndeseruingly,..without merit. **1653** *Nissena* 118 Abusing the authority wherewith he was undeservingly intrusted. **1695** LD. PRESTON *Boeth.* III. 116 For they who are praised & applauded undeservingly, must needs..be ashamed.

2. Without having done wrong; innocently.

1645 MILTON *Tetrach.* 56 He suffer'd..in his comon wealth some to bee undeservedly rich, others to bee undeservingly poore. **1781** G. JOHNSTON *Hist. J. Juniper* II. 43 That state of happiness, from which she had so undeservingly fallen.

undeseuered, obs. var. UNDISSEVERED.

†**undesiccable**, *a.* (UN-¹ 7 b; see DESICCATE *v.*)

a **1425** tr. *Arderne's Treat. Fistula*, etc. 13 A fistule is noȝt ellez þan ane vlcus vndesiccable, and for it is vndesiccable, þerfore by consequens it is vncurable.

unˈdesignated, *ppl. a.* (UN-¹ 8.)

1795 SEWARD *Anecd.* (ed. 2) II. 183 The miseries of an idle and undesignated life. **1875** WHITNEY *Life Lang.* iii. 44 Linguistic changes..produced for the designation of conceptions before undesignated.

undeˈsigned, *ppl. a.* [UN-¹ 8.] Not designed or intended; unintentional.

1654 EARL ORRERY *Parthen.* (1676) 9 Having begg'd Ambixules pardon for an undesign'd wrong. **1745** FIELDING *Tom Jones* XI. vii, The most undesigned word, the most accidental look,..will be misconstrued. **1790** PALEY *Horæ Paul.* ii §2 Such coincidences may fairly be stated as undesigned. **1847** J. J. BLUNT *Undesigned Coincidences* III. iii. 235 Confirmed as a matter of fact..by an undesigned coincidence. **1872** YEATS *Growth Comm.* 40 A result undesigned but of great moment followed the policy.

undeˈsignedly, *adv.* [UN-¹ 11: cf. prec.] Without design or intention; unintentionally.

1687 BOYLE *Martyrd. Theodora* xi. 120 Having been, though undesignedly, so..accessory to the early loss of a life. **1768–74** TUCKER *Lt. Nat.* (1834) II. 679 It is better they should do good undesignedly..than not to do it at all. **1829** I. TAYLOR *Enthus.* x. 299 Insensibly and undesignedly and from the operation of various causes. **1884** *Law Times* 20 Sept. 345 It is this aspect..on which 'W. B.' seems, perhaps not altogether undesignedly, to have thrown most light.

undeˈsignedness. [f. UNDESIGNED *ppl. a.*] The quality of being undesigned.

1768–74 TUCKER *Lt. Nat.* (1834) II. 87 The very essence of chance consists in undesignedness, and deviation from rule. **1794** PALEY *Evid.* II. vii, The undesignedness of the agreements..demonstrates that [etc.].

undeˈsigning, *ppl. a.* [UN-¹ 10.]

1. Not designing or planning. *rare.*

1673 *Remarques Humours Town* 4 That careless and undesigning way of living now in use. **1685** BOYLE *Enq. Notion Nat.* vii. 260 What..happens to deliberating or designing, and..to inanimate or undesigning beings.

2. Having no ulterior or selfish designs; free from designing or underhand motives.

1697 COLLIER *Ess. Mor. Subj.* II. (1703) 164 Children..believe others as kind and undesigning as themselves. **1748** RICHARDSON *Clarissa* (1811) II. xix. 130 An undesigning, open heart. **1796** MME. D'ARBLAY *Camilla* III. 316 Unsuspicious as she was undesigning, [she] thanked the Baronet for his message. **1866** GEO. ELIOT *Ess.* (1844) 336 The undesigning ignorant poor.

b. *transf.* Of things.

1709 in *Lady M. W. Montagu's Lett.* (1887) I. 47 'Tis a plain undesigning truth, your friendship is the only happiness of my life. **1779** J. MOORE *View Soc. Fr.*, etc. (1789) II. liv. 44 An open manner, and undesigning civility, distinguish the German character. **1860** DICKENS *Uncom. Trav.* xvi, Of such undesigning aspect is his guileless yard now.

undesiraˈbility. (UN-¹: cf. next.)

1870 MISS BROUGHTON *Red as Rose* I. 22 Quite affected by her lover's description of his own undesirability. **1885** *Manch. Exam.* 25 Feb. 5/2 The undesirability of leaving Berber in his rear.

undeˈsirable, *a.* and *sb.* [UN-¹ 7 b.]

a. *adj.* Not to be desired; objectionable.

1667 MILTON *P.L.* IX. 824 So to..render me more equal, and perhaps, A thing not undesireable, sometime Superior. *a* **1768** SECKER *Serm.* (1770) I. v. 113 It will provoke the better Part of their Inferiors to think ill of them, which is a very undesirable Thing. **1813** LAMB in *Gentl. Mag.* June 618/1 A little excess in that article is not undesirable in youth. **1887** RUSKIN *Præterita* II. 142 A porter's lodge, where undesirable visitors could be stopped.

b. *sb.* An undesirable thing or person.

1883 *Athenæum* 20 Jan. 81/3 Why not, then, connect..'glanders' and 'gluttony' as undesirables, at once? **1900** *Daily News* 12 Nov. 7/5 Having among her passengers 42 'undesirables', deported from Capetown.

Hence **undeˈsirableness.**

1675 OWEN *Indwelling Sin* xi. (1732) 137 It casts Death and undesirableness upon them all. *c* **1815** JANE AUSTEN *Persuas.* ii, The undesirableness of any other house..for Sir Walter. **1886** *Athenæum* 20 Feb. 267/2 The doctrine of the utter unreality and undesirableness of all life.

undeˈsirably, *adv.* (UN-¹ 11.)

1890 *Restrospect Med.* CII. 36 An undesirably large amount of glycerin.

undeˈsire, *sb.* (UN-¹ 12.)

1880 W. S. BLUNT *Love Sonnets of Proteus* xciv, One winter's discontent..[has] brought me to this pass of undesire.

†**undeˈsire**, *v. Obs.* (UN-² 3.)

a **1395** HYLTON *Scala Perf.* II. xli. (W. de W. 1494), He that hath ones sothfastly feled it,..he maye not vndesyre it.

undeˈsired, *ppl. a.* [UN-¹ 8.]

1. Not asked or requested; uninvited.

1470–1 *Rolls of Parlt.* VI. 223/1 Uncompelled, unstirred or undesired soo to doo. **1509** FISHER *Funeral Serm. C'tess Richmond* Wks. (1876) 302 He prayed vndesyred of ony. **1598** FLORIO, *Ingerire*,..to offer himselfe vndesired. **1634** SIR T. HERBERT *Trav.* 123 Mahomet-Ally-beg vndesired, bolted out, that he knew his Master..stood more affected to no one Prince..then to our King.

2. Not desired or wished for; unsought.

1599 T. M[OUFET] *Silkwormes* 38 Striuing no lesse to be deliuered Than Thisbe did from vndesired life. **1617** MORYSON *Itin.* III. 45 As the Poet saith, *Ignoti nulla Cupido*: Unknowne, undesired. **1697** DRYDEN *Æneis* II. 902 Your gift was undesired, and came too late. **1751** JOHNSON *Rambler* No. 175 ¶2 The knowledge of crimes intrudes uncalled and undesired. **1850** MRS. CARLYLE *Lett.* (1883) II. 112 Walked in Mrs. N——, of all undesired people! **1877** MRS. OLIPHANT *Makers Flor.* v. 133 Filippo set his active mind to work to get rid of his undesired partner.

Hence **undeˈsiredly** *adv.*

1845 T. W. COIT *Puritanism* 276 Those who are undesiredly tender of Puritan reputation.

undeˈsirer. *poet. rare.* (? UN-¹ 12.)

1945 DYLAN THOMAS in *Horizon* Jan. 13 In the name of the unborn And the undesirers Of midwiving morning's Hands or instruments.

undeˈsiring, *ppl. a.* (UN-¹ 10.)

1693 DRYDEN *Persius* v. 161 Money to despise, And look on Wealth with undesiring Eyes. **1728–46** THOMSON *Spring* 676 Away they fly, Affectionate, and undesiring bear The most delicious morsel to their young. **1880** MEREDITH *Tragic Com.* (1881) 88 The convalescent is receptive and undesiring, or but very faintly desiring.

undeˈsirous, *a.* (UN-¹ 7.)

Chiefly const. *of* (also *that*, *to*).

1654–66 EARL ORRERY *Parthen.* (1676) 289 That vice would render me as unworthy, as undesirous to live. **1670** *Devout Commun.* (1688) 15 The qualms of undesirous Communicants. **1787** JEFFERSON *Writ.* (1859) II. 230 This hasty measure has embarrassed England, undesirous of war if it can be avoided. **1860** RUSKIN *Mod. Paint.* V. IX. i. §11 To a being undesirous of it, and hating it, revelation is impossible. **1879** *Athenæum* 13 May, Forcing the crude productions of his mind on an undesirous world.

undeˈsirously, *adv.*, **-ness.** (UN-¹ 11, 12; cf. prec.)

1587 FLEMING *Contn. Holinshed* III. 1320/2 Therefore these knights by the authoritie of darkenes verie vndesirouslie are compelled to depart from whence they came. **1668** HOWE *Bless. Righteous* (1825) 261 An undesirousness or indifferency of spirit towards the eternal glory.

undesolved, obs. var. UNDISSOLVED.

undeˈspaired, *ppl. a.* (UN-¹ 8.)

1412–20 LYDG. *Chron. Troy* IV. 3323 Þis was hir hope, fully deuoide of drede, Vndispeired in ther oppinioun.

undeˈspairing, *ppl. a.* (UN-¹ 10.)

1730 THOMSON *Sophonisba* I. i, Mean time the dauntless, undespairing youth Lay in a cave conceal'd. **1757** DYER *Fleece* IV. 601 'Twas there Perils and conflicts inexpressible Anson, with steady undespairing breast, Endur'd. **1824** CARLYLE in Froude *Life* (1882) I. 233 Who is it that has struggled for me..with undespairing diligence? **1847** FR. A. KEMBLE in *Rec. Later Life* (1882) III. 313 That faith which alone can bear us undespairing over the earth.

undeˈspised, *ppl. a.* (UN-¹ 8.)

c **1550** *Vertuous Scholehous* H iij b, He wyll haue wedlock kept pure and vndespised. **1579** FULKE *Heskins' Parl.* 76 That they may haue a principall and vndespised sanctification.

undeˈspising, *vbl. sb.* [UN-¹ 13.] †Lack of (self-)depreciation.

c **1400** LOVE *Bonavent. Mirr.* (1908) 304 They that dreden not god..thoruȝ her owne wickednesse and vndespisynge in soule taken hit and eten hit.

undeˈspoiled, *ppl. a.* (UN-¹ 8.)

1846 WORCESTER (citing Scott). **1881** JOWETT *Thucyd.* I. 53 Their fields will be still untouched, and their goods undespoiled.

undeˈspondent, *a.* (UN-¹ 7.)

1876 LOWELL *Among my Bks.* Ser. II. 119 Such a life as his through all those sorrowing but undespondent years.

undeˈsponding, *ppl. a.* (UN-¹ 10.)

1818 HALLAM *Mid. Ages* (1872) II. 271 The appearance of a Nero so undesponding.

undeˈspotic, *a.* (UN-¹ 7.)

1820 BENTHAM *Lib. Press* Wks. 1843 II. 286/2 The difference between a despotic government and an undespotic one. **1888** BRYCE *Amer. Commw.* I. 343 So undespotic an instrument as the Federal Constitution of 1789.

unˈdestined, *ppl. a.* (UN-¹ 8.)

1827 [see UNCOMPASSIONED *ppl. a.*].

undeˈstroyable, *a.* (UN-¹ 7 b.)

a **1420** *Wycliffite Bible* Wisd. ii. 23 For whi God made man [vnable to be distried; *margin*] vndistriable. **1533** GAU *Richt Vay* 67 Of it cummis ane ondistroyabil power and heil in ye body. **1678** CUDWORTH *Intell. Syst.* 70 The substance of matter and body..is the only thing in the world that is uncorruptible and undestroyable. **1846** RUSKIN *Mod. Paint.* III. I. iv. §9 A trace of feeling..undestroyable by any reasoning.

undeˈstroyed, *ppl. a.* (UN-¹ 8.)

c **1450** LOVELICH *Merlin* 9886 Al the Lordschepis..That this Lond defenden schal evere with-al Vndistroyed. **1523** [COVERDALE] *Old God* (1534) Cj, Beel contynued afterwardes in babylon..as long as that proud kyngdom dyd stonde vndestroied. **1598** DRAYTON *Heroical Ep.* 31 How can that beauty yet be vndestroyd, That yeares haue wasted? **1637–50** ROW *Hist. Kirk* (Wodrow Soc.) 54 A principal act wes concluded, and also remains undestroyed in the Books..of this Kirk. **1758** *Elaboratory laid Open* 273 The leaving too much [sulphur] undestroyed. **1826** MISS MITFORD *Village* Ser. I. II. 245 The shrubs and flowering trees are undestroyed. **1886** WILLIS & CLARK *Cambridge* II. 383 The original windows..with the cusps still undestroyed, may still be seen.

undeˈstructible, *a.* (UN-¹ 7, 5 b.)

[**1775** ASH.] **1807** *Ann. Rev.* V. 589 All good is progressive, prolific, and undestructible. **1872** W. R. GREG *Enigmas of Life* iv. 157 Men in whose nature Love is as undestructible as Thought.

undeˈtachable, *a.* (UN-¹ 7 b.)

1871 MRS. WHITNEY *Real Folks* xvii, [He] attached himself to her forthwith in a most undetachable and determined manner. **1898** *Harper's Mag.* XCVI. 681 Every machine also must have a maker's number stamped on some undetachable part.

undeˈtached, *ppl. a.* (UN-¹ 8.)

[**1775** ASH.] **1877** RAYMOND *Mines* 449 The particles showed plainly..these grayish colors undetached from the more white quartz.

undeˈtainable, *a.* (UN-¹ 7 b.)

1630 DONNE *Serm.* 249 Christ was and I am..undetainable in the state of Death.

undeˈtained, *ppl. a.* (UN-¹ 8.)

1795 COLERIDGE *Æolian Harp* 39 Full many a thought uncall'd and undetain'd..traverse my indolent and passive brain.

undeˈtectable, *a.* (UN-¹ 7 b, 5 b.)

1863 *Cornh. Mag.* VII. 345 Substances which may cause death and yet be undetectable, with certainty, in the body.

Hence ˌ**undetectaˈbility**, **undeˈtectably** *adv.*

1960 *Jrnl. Amer. Chem. Soc.* LXXXII. 673/1 No step corresponding to equation 10 is included because of the undetectability of an uncatalyzed term. **1978** J. MCDOWELL in Hookway & Pettit *Action & Interpretation* 141 How can one derive, from confrontation with a detectable circumstance, an idea of what it would be for a circumstance of some kind to which it belongs to obtain undetectably? **1981** M. SPARK *Loitering with Intent* vi. 108 The point..was undetectably lost in a web of multisyllabic words.

undeˈtected, *ppl. a.* (UN-¹ 8.)

a **1593** MARLOWE *Ovid's Elegies* III. v. 84 But woods and groues keepe your faults vndetected. **1663** BOYLE *Usef. Exp. Nat. Philos.* II. v. ii. 124 Undetected properties might in many others..be discovered. **1749** JOHNSON *Irene* III. ii, Strange! that this gen'ral fraud from day to day Should fill the world with wretches undetected. **1825** LD. COCKBURN *Mem.* (1856) 206 Which show how much inaccuracy may sometimes pass undetected. **1862** LYTTON *Str. Story* I. 194 The gift..is stored, unknown to the possessor, undetected by the common observer.

unde'tectible, *a.* (UN-^{1} 7, 5 b.)
1802–12 BENTHAM *Ration. Judic. Evid.* (1827) IV. 16 On a variety of undetectible, though false, pretences. **1877** LE CONTE *Elem. Geol.* (1879) 239 In the strata the quantity is so small as to be undetectible.

unde'teriorated, *ppl. a.* (UN-^{1} 8.)
1856 RUSKIN *Mod. Paint.* IV. v. xi. §2. 130 The most delicate sculptures if executed in good marble will remain for ages undeteriorated.

unde'terminable, *a.* [UN-^{1} 7 b and 5 b.]
†**1.** Incapable of being terminated; unending. *Obs.*
1581 J. BELL *Haddon's Answ. Osor.* 444 Albeit the thing it selfe..be past, and ye tyme thereof determined: yet doth the power..thereof remaine unmoveable, sure, and undeterminable beyond all ages. **1605** CHAPMAN *All Fools* v. ii. 358 Lastly, for continuance of the horne, it is undeterminable till death. **1622** DONNE *Serm.* xvi. (1640) 160 He..considers farther..the inevitable, the irreparable, and for all that, undeterminable torments of hell.
†**b.** = INDETERMINABLE *a.* 1. *Obs.*
1633 EARL MANCH. *Al Mondo* (1636) 32 An undeterminable desire of more than present life can yeeld. **1653** H. MORE *Conject. Cabbal.* (1713) 12 This vast Capability of things was unsettled, fluid, and, of it self, undeterminable as Water.
2. = INDETERMINABLE *a.* 3 and 3 b.
1588 J. HARVEY *Disc. Probl.* 44 The certaine Locall region ..lurketh stil undetermined, yea, and undeterminable to, in my poore conceite. **1644** MILTON *Divorce* (ed. 2) II. xxi. 78 It doth all one as if it sent back the matter undeterminable at law, and intractable by rough dealing [etc.]. **1692** RAY *Disc.* III. ix. (1732) 397 This is absolutely uncertain and undeterminable. **1754** GOODALL *Exam. Lett. Mary Q. Scots* Introd. 28 More might have been expected from so high a pretender to reason..than to conclude the question to be undeterminable. **1872** W. S. SYMONDS *Rec. Rocks* viii. 301 The fish remains are scanty and undeterminable.
†**3.** = INDETERMINABLE *a.* 2. *Obs.*
a **1639** WOTTON in Gutch *Coll. Cur.* I. 217 The fight was ..surely undeterminable without the death of one of the chiefest. **1670** G. H. *Hist. Cardinals* I. II. 54 Profound and undeterminable Disputes.

unde'terminate, *a.* [UN-^{1} 7 and 5 b.]
†**1.** = INDETERMINATE *a.* 2. *Obs.*
1603 HOLLAND *Plutarch's Mor.* 768 Thus would not he admit, or leave any thing..infinit and undeterminate; but adorne nature with proportion, measure, and number. **1690** LOCKE *Hum. Und.* II. xvii. §10 As if this line of number were extended both ways to an unconceivable, undeterminate, and infinite length.
†**2.** = INDETERMINATE *a.* 2 b. *Obs.*
1649 JER. TAYLOR *Gt. Exemp.* Disc. vi. II. §9 He, under an undeterminate reproof, intended those that were such. **1664** H. MORE *Myst. Iniq.* 213 Any determinate conception does more vigorously..affect the mind than what is more general and undeterminate. **1736** BUTLER *Anal.* II. viii. 276 Owing to Half-views,..and to undeterminate Language.
†**3.** = INDETERMINATE *a.* 5. *Obs.*
1668 H. MORE *Div. Dial.* I. xx. (1713) 42 To know a free Agent, which is undeterminate to either part, to be so undeterminate, and that he may choose which part he will.
4. = INDETERMINATE *a.* 3 and 4. Now *rare.*
1767 A. YOUNG *Farmer's Lett. to People* 162 This undeterminate provision for the poor makes them depend on the parish for all. **1813** T. BUSBY *Lucretius* I. I. Comm. p. xxii, The argument is derived from that which is undeterminate. **1863** D. WILSON *Preh. Ann.* (ed. 2) I. iv. 128 Caverns..of undeterminate age.

†**unde'terminated**, *ppl. a.* (UN-^{1} 8; cf. prec.)
1641 EARL MONM. tr. *Biondi's Civil Wars* III. 156 Betweene two and three thousand; an undeterminated number. **1653** H. MORE *Antid. Ath.* II. v. §6 Changing the fluid and undeterminated Matter into shapes so comely and symmetrical.

unde'terminately, *adv.* (UN-^{1} 11 and 5 b.)
1571 GOLDING *Calvin on Ps.* lv. 10 The name of (citie) is put undeterminately, too the intente [etc.] **1588** FRAUNCE *Lawiers Log.* I. iv. 33 b, If the generall bee but indefinitely, simply, or undeterminately put downe. **1670** H. STUBBE *Plus Ultra* 95 When we speak undeterminately of the Sinus, we understand those of the brain. **1681** H. MORE *Exp. Dan.* iv. 112 What was spoke more at large and more undeterminately..may here..be more punctually defined.

unde'terminateness. (UN-^{1} 12 and 5 b.)
1653 H. MORE *Conject. Cabbal.* (1713) 184 What Moses may mean by the mobility of the Waters, Plotinus has expressed by..the Indefiniteness or Undeterminateness of Matter. **1656** tr. *T. White's Peripat. Inst.* 232 Quantity implying a kind of undeterminatenesse and confusion.

†**undetermi'nation.** *Obs.* (UN-^{1} 12 and 5 b.)
a **1631** DONNE *Serm.* Wks. 1839 IV. 289 Though I do with-draw myself from the woeful uncertainties and irresolutions and undeterminations of the Court. *a* **1676** HALE *Prim. Orig. Man.* (1677) 61 The undetermination, incertainty, and unsteadiness of the operation of his Faculties.

unde'termined, *ppl. a.* [UN-^{1} 8 and 5 b.]
1. Not authoritatively decided or settled; not brought to an end by decision.
1442 in *Proc. King's Council Irel.* (Rolls) 275 Many grete tresons..stonde yet vndetermyned. *a* **1513** FABYAN *Chron.* VII. ccxxviii. 257 The pope gaue suche a defuse sentence in this mater y^t^ he left ye stryfe vndetermyned and vnassoyled. **1541** *Act 33 Hen. VIII*, c. 39 Thinges nowe..dependinge before them vndiscussed and vndetermined. **1628** COKE *On Litt.* (1629) 40 b, Hanging the voucher and vndetermined, the wife of the feoffee brings her action of dower. **1698** LUTTRELL *Brief Rel.* (1857) IV. 396 To leave the points undetermined to the arbitration of King William. **1771** LUCKOMBE *Hist. Print.* 1 It long remained an undetermined point..concerning the place. **1826** *Art Brewing* (ed. 2) 127 The question, therefore, still remains undetermined. **1885** SIR L. W. CAVE in *Law Rep.* 15 *Q.B.D.* 327 The question.. was discussed and left undetermined in the case of Reg. *v.* Robson.
b. Not definitely settled or fixed; still subject to alteration or uncertainty.
1668 [see UNCONSENTED]. **1697** DRYDEN *Virg. Georg.* I. 30 Thou, whose undetermin'd State Is yet the Business of the Gods' Debate. **1736** BUTLER *Anal.* I. iv. (1834) 88 Which miseries are, beforehand, just as contingent and undetermined as their conduct, and left to be determined by it. **1779** FORREST *Voy. N. Guinea* 171 All the charts..leave the north coast of Waygiou undetermined by a dotted line. **1831** SCOTT *Ct. Rob.* xxxiii, I vow..that the combat was yet within the undetermined doom of Providence, when [etc.]. **1862** SPENCER *First Princ.* I. v. §29 (1875) 102 That conception of disorder, or undetermined order, which underlies every superstition.
2. Not definitely ascertained or identified; uncertain, doubtful.
1588 [see UNDETERMINABLE *a.* 2]. **1697** BENTLEY *Phal.* (1699) 191 Though the date be undetermined, it might fairly be presumed to be more recent than He. **1794** R. J. SULIVAN *View Nat.* I. 435 Onyx, an undetermined transparent gem. **1839** DE LA BECHE *Rep. Geol. Cornw.* etc. viii. 223 A few casts of one or two undetermined species. **1884** HIGGS *Magn. Dyn. Electr. Mach.* 269 Where ρ, the only quantity remaining unexplained, represents the undetermined factor.
3. Not definitely limited or restricted in meaning or application; indefinite, vague.
1611 FLORIO *World of Words* Rules 640 The Preterpluperfect or vndetermined tence. **1656** tr. *Hobbes' Elem. Philos.* 21 Some names are of certain and determined, others of uncertain and undetermined signification. **1705** BERKELEY *Cave of Dunmore* Wks. 1871 IV. 506 Such undetermined expressions as wide, narrow, deep. **1769** SIR J. REYNOLDS *Disc.* ii. (1778) 47 By precepts only, which will always be fleeting, variable and undetermined.
4. Not restrained within limits; left free or open.
1627 MAY *Lucan* Ep. Ded., The vast strength and forces of the Prince gaue him too absolute and vndetermined a power. **1697** CONGREVE *Mourn. Bride* II. viii, Not so the mind, whose undetermined view Revolves, and to the present adds the past. **1712** ADDISON *Spect.* No. 412 ¶2 Such wide and undetermined Prospects are..pleasing to the Fancy. **1818** SHELLEY *Let. to Peacock* 5 June, The mountains are wide and wild, and the whole scenery broad and undetermined.
5. Not determined or fixed in respect of character, action, etc.
a **1676** HALE *Prim. Orig. Man.* (1677) 74 Possibly Matter it self undetermined to any particular form, or under any particular constitution. **1712** ADDISON *Spect.* No. 458 ¶2 False Modesty..is only a general undetermined Instinct. **1754** EDWARDS *Freed. Will* II. ix. 83 A Self-determining Power in the Understanding,..independent, undetermined by any Thing prior to its own Acts and Determinations.
6. Undecided, irresolute.
1718 POPE *Iliad* xv. 595 How long on these cursed confines will ye lie, Yet undetermined or to live or die? **1796** MME. D'ARBLAY *Camilla* III. 110 Perceiving him undetermined, [she] called forth all her artillery of eloquence. **1862** BORROW *Wales* I. 1 We were undetermined for some time with respect to where we should go.

unde'terred, *ppl. a.* (UN-^{1} 8.)
1607 TOPSELL *Four-f. Beasts* 203 If their rage proceede vndeterred,..forth they go into the woods. *c* **1765** FALCONER *Demagogue* 55 The fearless muse..True to herself, advances, undeterr'd By the rude clamours. **1814** WORDSW. *Excurs.* VI. 321 Who, by humiliation undeterred, Sought for his weariness a place of rest. **1846** TRENCH *Mirac.* xviii. 306 Step by step he had advanced,.. undeterred by opposition.

unde'testing, *ppl. a.* (UN-^{1} 10.)
1736 THOMSON *Liberty* v. 293 Who these indeed can undetesting see?—But who unpitying?

unde'thronable, *a.* (UN-^{1} 7 b.)
1835 in H. Martineau *Soc. in America* (1837) III. 69 Like an Asian monarch,..unimpeachable, undethronable. **1848** LOWELL *Biglow P.* I. v, Justice, venerable with the undethronable majesty of countless æons.

unde'tractingly, *adv.* (UN-^{1} 11.)
1661 BOYLE *Style of Script.* (1675) 156 As little..as the water of a diamond can be undetractingly painted.

unde'veloped, *ppl. a.* [UN-^{1} 8.] That has not developed or been developed.
1736 THOMSON *Liberty* IV. 224 Where undevelop'd lay The future wonders that enrich'd mankind. **1817** LADY MORGAN *France* VIII. (1818) II. 381 Those profounder feelings..remained cold and undeveloped. **1850** GROTE *Greece* II. lxvii. VIII. 459 Of all this, the undeveloped germ doubtless existed in the previous epic..composition. **1870** DICKENS *Edwin Drood* iii. 18 Triumphs of engineering skill ..are to change the whole condition of an undeveloped country. **1897** MARY KINGSLEY *W. Africa* 659 A black man is no more an undeveloped white man than a rabbit is an undeveloped hare. **1911** H. F. HOWARD *India & Gold Standard* p. iii, Conditions in India, as in other undeveloped countries, differ from those in the more advanced countries.
2. *spec.* of a film.
1939 EMANUEL & DASH *All-in-One Camera Bk.* 133 Once they have been exposed, colour films should not be left undeveloped too long. **1959** W. S. SHARPS *Dict. Cinematogr.* 137/2 *Undeveloped*, the term applied to film that has not yet passed through the development stage of processing. **1983** D. FRANCIS *Danger* iii. 39 It was..routine to send the undeveloped films..to the London office.

un'deviated, *ppl. a.* (UN-^{1} 8.)
1889 *Anthony's Photogr. Bull.* II. 40 The undeviated ray DE, drawn parallel to SA.

un'deviating, *ppl. a.* [UN-^{1} 10.] Showing no deviation; maintaining the same course; steady, constant: **a.** Of conduct, character, etc.
1732 ARBUTHNOT in Aitken *Life & Wks.* (1892) 138 The undeviating pravity Of his Manners. **1763** GOLDSM. *Misc. Wks.* (1836) I. 526 Rational entertainment and undeviating candour. **1808** SCOTT in *Lockhart* I. i. 59 Stern, steady, and undeviating industry. **1841** MISS MITFORD in L'Estrange *Life* (1870) III. viii. 123 Whose kindness is, and has been, constant and undeviating.
b. In other applications.
1784 COWPER *Task* v. 37 With such undeviating and even force He severs it away. *Ibid.* VI. 127 The race Of the undeviating and punctual sun. **1826** *Art Brewing* (ed. 2) 7 Undeviating and powerful causes of destruction or fermentation. **1874** SAYCE *Compar. Philol.* i. 11 Language.. obeys undeviating laws of its own.

un'deviatingly, *adv.* (UN-^{1} 11; cf. prec.)
1812 J. HENRY *Camp. agst. Quebec* 10 A simple tale of truth, which he undeviatingly throughout his book adheres to. **1854** W. OSBURN *Mon. Hist. Egypt* I. i. 7 Its [*sc.* the Nile's] course is undeviatingly from south to north. **1894** *Educat. Rev.* June 77 Their demands agree substantially, though not undeviatingly.

un'devil, *v.* [UN-^{2} 4 b and 6.]
1. *trans.* To free from demoniacal possession.
1632 QUARLES *Div. Fancies* I. xi, Whenas our blessed Saviour did un-devill The Man possest, the Spirits.. Entred the Swine. **1655** FULLER *Ch. Hist.* x. iv. §55 The Boy ..would not be undeviled by their Exorcisms. **1890** TALMAGE *From Manger to Throne* 81 Mouth of cavern, where mad-man was undevilled.
2. To deprive of the qualities of a devil.
1726 DE FOE *Hist. Devil* II. iii. (1840) 199 If we should take away his invisibility too, we should undevil him quite.
Hence **un'devilling** *vbl. sb.*
1653 A. WILSON *Jas. I*, 108 Some Romish Priests.. tampering with their Exorcisms, to the undevilling of the boy.

un'devious, *a.* (UN-^{1} 7.)
1777 MELMOTH *Cato* (ed. 2) I. 206 So shall thy steps.. Undevious tread in virtue's paths divine. **1804** EUGENIA DE ACTON *Tale without Title* III. 206 He is not so impertinent as to put them out of their undevious path.

un'deviously, *adv.* (UN-^{1} 11; cf. prec.)
1813 T. BUSBY *Lucretius* I. II. 256 But did they undeviously descend, Nor contact nor concussion would ensue.

unde'visable, *a.* (UN-^{1} 7 b.)
1858 CARLYLE *Fredk. Gt.* III. xiv, Quirks did not prove undevisable on behalf of the Kaiser.

unde'vised, *ppl. a.* [UN-^{1} 8.]
1. Not assigned by will.
1766 BLACKSTONE *Comm.* II. xxxii. 515 The undevised surplus of the estate shall go to the next of kin. **1875** POSTE *Gaius* II. (ed. 2) 239 The undevised or lapsed portion..goes ..to the devisee..of the remainder of the heritage.
2. Not planned or intended.
1894 H. GARDENER *Unoff. Patriot* 37 With long and undevised breaks in the continuity of sound and sense.

†**undevote**, obs. var. UNDEVOUT *a.*
a **1300** *Cursor M.* 28368 Vn-deuote in my praier Seruid i haue a-but þe autere. *a* **1340** HAMPOLE *Psalter* xlix. 17 Whi þou vndeuot, takis my haly testament thurght þi filed mouth?

unde'voted, *ppl. a.* (UN-^{1} 9, 5 b.)
1647 CLARENDON *Hist. Reb.* II. §36 The lords Say and Brook (two popular men, and most undevoted to the Church, and in truth to the whole Government).

†**unde'votely**, obs. var. UNDEVOUTLY *adv.*

†**unde'votion.** *Obs.* (UN-^{1} 12 and 5 b.)
c **1340** HAMPOLE *Prose Treat.* (1876) 10 Of new prechynge þat es vanyte and vndevocyone. *c* **1386** CHAUCER *Pars. T.* ¶649 Thanne comth vndeuocion thurgh which a man is blent. **1502** *Ord. Crysten Men* (W. de W. 1506) II. xv. 122 Undeuocyon and foulenes of spyryte unto us is foreboden. **1565** JEWEL *Repl. Harding* 14 Priuate Masse..came in afterwarde by the negligence and vndeuotion of the people.

unde'voured, *ppl. a.* (UN-^{1} 8.)
1661 *Peacham's Compl. Gent.* 235 The only Baron that is left undevoured by time of those eight. **1827** POLLOK *Course T.* v. 79 Undevoured By spurious appetites, she found enough.

unde'vout, *a.* (UN-^{1} 7 and 5 b.)
a **1395** HYLTON *Scala Perf.* II. xlii. (W. de W. 1494), It is bothe olde & drye, vndeuoute & vnsauery in itselfe. *c* **1430** *Hymns Virgin* (1867) 89 þan þi bodi þat was rank & Vndeuout, Of alle men is bihatid. **1502** ATKYNSON tr. *De Imitatione* I. xxv. 178 So vndeuout & remysse in the seruyce of god. **1575** FENTON *Gold. Epist.* (1582) 96 No other thing is the religious man vndeuout, than a candel dead. **1656** JEANES *Fuln. Christ* 70 Men come with as..undevout thoughts and affections to a sermon, as to a play. *a* **1701** MAUNDRELL *Journ. Jerus.* (1707) 136 The Greeks being seemingly the most undevout..of any sort of People in the Christian World. **1746** YOUNG *Nt. Th.* IX. 771 An undevout astronomer is mad. **1829** CARLYLE *Misc.* (1857) II. 48 Destitute of Religious reverence,..undevout both in heart and head. **1874** H. R. REYNOLDS *John Bapt.* v. §1. 301 Sceptical and supercilious, frivolous and undevout.
absol. **1561** T. NORTON *Calvin's Inst.* III. 309 If he had willed, of the vndeuout he mighte haue made deuoute.

†**unde'vout,** *v. Obs.* (UN-^{2} 6.)
c **1440** *Jacob's Well* 283 Abraham kecche awey flyes fro þe sacryfyse; Ryȝt so, kacche out flyes þat vndeuoutyth thouȝt.

unde'voutly, *adv.* (UN-^{1} 11.)
1377 LANGL. *P. Pl.* B. Prol. 98 Here messe and here matynes and many of here oures Arn don vndeuoutlych [C. I. 126 vndeuotlich]. *c* **1380** WYCLIF *Wks.* (1880) 167 Be þe masse seide..schortly & vndewoutly, litel sauour of holynesse schal men fynden wiþ hem. *c* **1440** *Jacob's Well* 281 Whanne þou slawly, & vndeuoutly, & heuyly,..doost ony good dede. **1509** BARCLAY *Shyp of Folys* 203 In prayeng thou bokest vnmanerly Spuynge vp thy prayers: god wot vndeuoutly. **1647** HEXHAM I, Vndevoutely, *ongodtsdienstelick.*

unde'voutness. (UN-^{1} 12; cf. prec.)
c **1440** *Jacob's Well* 294 Þe synnes of þe herte arn..dulhed, vndeuowtnesse, wanhope [etc.].

un'dewed, *ppl. a.* (UN-^{1} 8.)
c **1440** *Pallad. on Husb.* VII. 237 Now flouring grapes wilde vndewed [L. *sine rore*] strie In sunnne.

un'dewy, *a.* (UN-^{1} 7.)
c **1440** *Pallad on Husb.* V. 139 To x sester old wyn, v pound inslake Of violet vndewy. **1771** *Ann. Reg., Poetry* 242 O may thy sun..Parch with unusual heat th' undewy ground.

un'dexterous, -trous, *a.* (UN-^{1} 7 and 5 b.)
1688 MRQ. HALIFAX *Lady's New-years Gift* (ed. 2) 59 You must be very undextrous if when your Husband shall resolve to be an Ass, you do not take care he may be your Ass. **1781** JUSTAMOND *Priv. Life Lewis XV*, I. 162 This was not surely undextrous management. **1840** CLOUGH *Dipsychus* II. iv. 63 If the occasion coming should find us undexterous, incapable.

un'dexterously, *adv.* (UN-^{1} 11; cf. prec.)
1848 THACKERAY *Van. Fair* lxv, 'She hasn't a friend in the world,' Jos went on, not undexterously.

un'diademed, *a.* (UN-^{1} 9.)
1846 WORCESTER (citing Milman). **1879** MEREDITH *Egoist* II. 109 Movements of similarity..in crowned and undiademed ladies.

undiag'nosed, *ppl. a.* (UN-^{1} 8.)
1864 E. A. PARKES *Pract. Hygiene* 426 Many of the diseases of nutrition, which..are yet undiagnosed.

undi'aphanous, *a.* (UN-^{1} 7.)
1666 BOYLE *Orig. Forms* 231 Swarms of little Metalline and Undiaphanous Bodies, shining in the water.

undic'tated, *ppl. a.* (UN-^{1} 8.)
a **1797** H. WALPOLE *Mem. Geo. II* (1847) I. xi. 361 Undictated by religion as those Bills were,..they breathed the very essence of it. **1804** *Ann. Rev.* II. 275 These letters have not so unaffected, uninspired, undictated an appearance as the earlier. **1873** MOZLEY *Univ. Serm.* viii. (1876) 189 It is..His own free and undictated choice.

undies ('ʌndɪz), *sb. pl. colloq.* [f. UNDER- in UNDERGARMENT, UNDERWEAR, etc.] Articles of girls' or women's underclothing.
1906 *Punch* 30 May 384/3 She'd blouses for Sundays, And marvellous 'undies' Concocted of ribbons and lace. **1920** A. BENNETT *Our Women* i. 35 You have only to reflect..upon the astonishing public importance given to what are delicately known as 'undies'. **1939** A. RANSOME *Secret Water* xxvii. 321 Go on, Bridgie. Off with your things. Undies too. **1967** N. FREELING *Strike out where not Applicable* 107 Arlette..knows I'm not just belting off for the afternoon because of the black undies.

un'dieted, *ppl. a.* (UN-^{1} 8.)
1649 *Markham's Country Contentm.* (ed. 6) I. xix. 109 The best cock undyeted, not being able to encounter with the worst cock that is dyeted. **1855** SMEDLEY *Occult Sciences* 128 Undieted by ambrosia and nectar.

†**undi'ffaded,** *ppl. a.* (UN-^{1} 8: cf. DEFADE *v.*)
c **1430** LYDG. *Min. Poems* (Percy Soc.) 178 Roosys reede, Medlyd with lilies..Fresshe undiffadid.

†**un'difference,** *v. Obs.*$^{-1}$ (UN-^{1} 14, 15; app. for DIFFERENCE *v.* 4.)
1654 GAYTON *Pleas. Notes* III. xi. 144 Whether a man may abdicate his reason..for a time, and discover..no reasonable Acts, whereby a man should not undifference him from a Beast.

un'differenced, *ppl. a.* (UN-^{1} 8.)
1859 SIR W. HAMILTON *Lect.* (1877) II. xxxv. 295 Abstracting from differences, and attending to resemblances, we arrive at naked or undifferenced existence. **1865** *Edin. Rev.* Apr. 346 The transgressors included..cadets bearing their arms undifferenced.

un'differencing, *ppl. a.* (UN-^{1} 10.)
1624 CHAPMAN *Homer's Hymn Hermes* 1006 Thus..Hermes lived, Who truly help'd but few, but all deceived With an undifferencing respect. *a* **1661** FULLER *Worthies, Essex* I. (1661) 320 Some Sciolists will boast to distinguish bones of Beasts from Men by their Porosity, which the learned deride as an undifferencing difference.

†**un'differency.** *Obs.*$^{-1}$ (UN-^{1} 12, 15; app. misused for 'partiality'.)
1583 GOLDING *Calvin on Deut.* cii. 627 A continuall holding on so as no vndifferencie may be perceiued nor any diuersitie of weightes and ballances nor any respect of persons.

†**un'different,** *a. Obs.*$^{-1}$ [UN-^{1} 7, 5 b.] = INDIFFERENT *a.*^{1} I.
c **1400** *Destr. Troy* 3915 The fourme of þo freikes was..Right suche as the syre,..Vndifferent to deme fro þere dere fader.

undiffe'rentiated, *ppl. a.* (UN-^{1} 8 and 5 b.)
In very common use from *c* 1875.
1862 H. SPENCER *First Princ.* I. iv. §26 (1867) 96 That undifferentiated substance of consciousness which is conditioned anew in every thought. **1879** G. ALLEN *Colour Sense* iii. 27 Simple undifferentiated animal tissue.

un'dig, *v.* [UN-^{2} 5 b.] *trans.* To exhume or open again, by digging.
1641 *Termes de la Ley* 87 Neverthelesse the Coroner ought to undigge the body out of the ground. **1824** MISS MITFORD *Village* Ser. I. I. 165 One is tempted to send for the sexton and the undertaker, to undig the grave.

un'digenous, *a. rare*$^{-1}$. [f. L. *und-a* wave.] Produced by aqueous action.
1799 KIRWAN *Geol. Ess.* 221 All stratified mountains were considered as secondary, and called undigenous (flotzgebirge).

†**undi'gest,** *ppl. a. Obs.* [UN-^{1} 8 b and 5 b.] Undigested. Also *fig.*
1398 TREVISA *Barth. De P.R.* XVII. i. (Bodl. MS.) fol. 186 b/2, Leues springeþ sone for moche watry humoure vndigeste. **1456** SIR G. HAY *Gov. Princes* Wks. (S.T.S.) II. 126 Quhen it ressavis mare na it was wont to, that remaynis in the stomak undegest and rawe. **1513** DOUGLAS *Æneid* XI. iv. 63 This haisty deid [= death], sa ondegest. *Ibid.* vii. 104 A man nocht indegest [*v.r.* vndegest], bot wys and cald. **1570** LEVINS *Manip.* 92 Vndigest, *inconcoctus.* **1590** BARROUGH *Meth. Physick* I. x. (1596) 13 If the wine be yet vndigest, and do flow in the stomacke. **1623** HART *Arraignm. Ur.* I. iv. 17 The urine may be thin, crude, and undigest or raw.

undi'gestable, *a.* (UN-^{1} 7 b and 5 b.)
1612 SELDEN *Illustr. Drayton's Poly-olb.* xvii. 271 He was so besieged with continuall & vndigestable incentiues of the Clergy.

undi'gested, *ppl. a.* [UN-^{1} 8 and 5 b.]
1. Not brought to a mature or proper condition by natural physical change.
1528 PAYNELL *Salerne's Regim.* b j b, Fleme is vndigested bloudde. *Ibid.* B iv b, The vndigested & rawe humours are yᵉ cause of opilations. **1586** T. B. *La Primaud. Fr. Acad.* I. 201 When we behold the sunne through thicke clouds and undigested vapors, we see it not cleere. **1634** SIR T. HERBERT *Trav.* 168 Vpon Mount Taurus, where wee exposed our heated bodies to vndigested vapours which easily penetrated vs. **1700** BLACKMORE *Job* 10 Deform'd he lay, disfigur'd, cover'd o'er With running boyls and undigested gore. **1738** GRAY *Tasso* 58 Further they pass, where ripening minerals flow, And embryon metals undigested glow.
2. Of food, etc.: Not digested in the stomach.
1597 A. M. tr. *Guillemeau's Fr. Chirurg.* 27 b/2 When as the stomacke is burthened with anye cruditye of vndigested meat or drincke. **1620** VENNER *Via Recta* viii. 166 It is the hurtfullest thing to the body, to ingest meat vpon meat vndigested. **1693** DRYDEN, etc. *Juvenal* IV. (1697) 60 Thy own third Story smoaks, while thou, supine, Art drench'd in Fumes of undigested Wine. **1808** *Med. Jrnl.* XIX. 22 She then took an emetic, which brought up some green undigested stuff. **1892** H. LANE *Differ. Rheum. Dis.* (ed. 2) 87 Undigested food giving rise to acute gastritis.
fig. *c* **1610** *Women Saints* 122 Verie bitter speaches..such as swelling and vndigested discord is wonte to belke oute. **1855** MACAULAY *Hist. Eng.* xiv. III. 460 His reading, too, though undigested, was of immense extent. **1890** *Daily News* 2 June 5/5 Trusts have found favour with the public, and have relieved financiers of much undigested stock.
3. Not reduced to order or harmony; not properly arranged or regulated; chaotic; confused.
1598 FLORIO, *Indigésto*, vndigested, vnpollished. **1621** SANDYS tr. *Ovid's Met.* I. (1626) 1 One face had Nature, which they Chaos nam'd: An vndigested lump. **1633** P. FLETCHER *Purple Isl.* I. xxxix, When that great Power..Brought into act this undigested Ball. **1665** in *Surtees Misc.* (1860) 263 The Treasury and Registry are undigested into order. **1866** J. B. ROSE tr. *Ovid's Met.* 1 One dull unvaried face Of matter undigested. **1884** *Manch. Exam.* 17 Sept. 4/6 A crude and undigested mass of useless rubbish.
b. Of discourse, ideas, etc.
1655 *Nicholas Papers* (Camden) II. 282 Thus haue I made you a most broken vndigiested discourse. **1692** WASHINGTON tr. *Milton's Def. People* Pref., M.'s Wks. 1851 VIII. 11 The undigested and immethodical bulk of his Book. **1742** WEST *Let.* in *Gray's Poems* (1775) 147 At least a volume of undigested observations. **1792** BURKE *Corr.* (1844) IV. 35 What signifies their sputtering out a few hasty and undigested invectives? **1839** HALLAM *Lit. Eur.* II. i. II. 35 *note*, The whole was published in an undigested, incoherent, and some-times self-contradictory paragraph.

†**undi'gestible,** *a. Obs. rare.* (UN-^{1} 7 and 5 b.)
1611 COTGR., *Indigestible*, vndisgestible; which cannot, or will not, be disgested. **1613** PURCHAS *Pilgrimage* (1614) 696 The chaine holding him..and by his vndigestible nature deuouring the deuourer.

undi'gesting, *ppl. a.* (UN-^{1} 10.)
1725 *Fam. Dict.* s.v. *Nicotiana*, The Indians use it to comfort a weak and undigesting Stomach. **1865** KINGSLEY *Lett.* (1878) II. 215 Not a mere formula to be swallowed by the undigesting reason.

†**undi'gestion.** *Obs.* (UN-^{1} 12, 5 b.)
c **1450** LYDG. *Secrees* 1252 That vndigestion..Causith ofte sithe by processe that they deye. **1650** W. D. tr. *Comenius' Gate Lat. Unl.* §292 Of rawness or undigestion com belchings, hickoping and windie rumbling.

un'digged, *ppl. a.* (UN-^{1} 8.)
1580 LUPTON *Sivqila* 25 For what is it to sowe seede uppon the..greene swarde, unplowed or undigged? **1633** SALTONSTALL tr. *Ovid's Tristia* III. xii. (1637) F j b, I see the snow melt with the Sunne, The undigged waters now begin to run.

†**un'dight,** *v. Obs.* [UN-^{2} 4, 4 b.]
1. *trans.* To divest (of clothing, armour, etc.); to disarray, strip. Also *refl.* and with *of.*
a **1400** *Sir Beues* (E.) 2064 Beues anon þo doun lyȝte, And þe palmere hym vndyȝte. *c* **1400** *Laud Troy Bk.* 7030 The stedis..ar vndight and set in stable. *Ibid.* 10348 Ector..wolde not him vndyght Off his armure & his a-tire. **1611** FLORIO, *Disornare*, to disadorne, to vndight.
2. To unfasten, undo; to unclench or open.
1590 SPENSER *F.Q.* I. iii. 4 From her faire head her fillet she vndight, And laid her stole aside. *Ibid.* III. v. 31 His mayled haberieon she did vndight. **1633** P. FLETCHER *Purple Isl.* x. xxxvi, When she deignes those precious bones undight, Soon heav'nly notes from those divisions flow.

un'dight, *ppl. a. dial.* or *arch.* [UN-^{1} 8 b.]
1. Not adorned, decked, or put in order.
1555 *Richmond. Wills* (Surtees) 86, xxxvij dight dishes viijᵈ; xviij undight dishes viijᵈ. **1558** PHAER *Æneid* VI. Q ij, His hoary bushe and beard both ouergrown and foule vndight. **1593** DRAYTON *Ecl.* viii. 98 Sayth she, I may not stay till night, And leaue my summer hall vndight. **1811** WILLAN in *Archaeol.* XVII. 162 *Undight*, undressed, or undecked. **1817** SHELLEY *Rev. Islam* IX. xxxvi, Her dark deep eyes, her lips,..her locks undight.
2. *Sc.* Unwinnowed. (See DIGHT *v.* 14 e.)
1574 *Reg. Privy Council Scot.* II. 341, xvi bollis of beir or thairby undicht in the said Archibaldis barne.

un'dighted, *ppl. a.* (UN-^{1} 8.) Undressed.
1673 WEDDERBURN *Voc.* 21 (Jam.), *Lana rudis*, undighted wool.

†**un'digne,** *a. Obs.* [UN-^{1} 7, 5 b.] Unworthy.
c **1315** SHOREHAM I. 425 Þi bileaue of ihesu crist His nou al weuerinde, Vndigne. **1340–70** *Alex. & Dind.* 745 For þe dedus undingne þat ȝe don alle..ȝe schulle be..put in paine for euere. *c* **1400** *Rule St. Benet* (Prose) vii. 13 Þu sal þinke in þi herte þat tu es vndinge to gode dede. *a* **1470** HARDING *Chron.* CXIII. xvii, His barons, for cause he was vndigne, Made hym his crowne for to resigne.
Hence †**un'dignely** *adv.*, unworthily. *Obs.*
c **1315** SHOREHAM I. 601 For, wo þat hyȝt takeþ ondygneliche, Hys iugement he gnaȝeþ.

un'dignified, *ppl. a.* [UN-^{1} 8.]
1. Of clergy: Not holding a position of dignity; not ranking as a dignitary. ? *Obs.*
1689 *Apol. Fail. Walker's Acc.* 24 All this by the Service..attributed to one of their undignify'd Clergy. **1776** ENTICK *London* I. 95 A great number of the undignified clergy. **1833** ALISON *Hist. Eur.* I. iii. 125 The great body of the undignified ecclesiastics.
2. Not dignified *by* or *with* something; undistinguished.
1716 SWIFT *Further Acc. E. Curll* Wks. 1755 III. I. 154 An undignified scribler of a sheet and half. **1744** J. HARRIS *Coll. Voy. & Trav.* I. Ded., I have also chosen the greatest..Body of Men undignified with Titles. **1779–81** JOHNSON *L.P., Prior* Wks. III. 134 Through the reigns of William and Anne no prosperous event passed undignified by poetry. *a* **1821** [see UNBENEFITED].
3. Lacking in dignity of manner, etc.
1782 V. KNOX *Ess.* iii. (1819) I. 18 The undignified vivacity of nations which have been taught by their philosophy to degrade human nature. **1836** HOR. SMITH *Tin Trump.* I. 14 Deep and genuine emotion..is never undignified, never ungraceful. **1880** MᶜCARTHY *Own Times* xli. III. 233 He sometimes ran the risk of seeming undignified.
Hence **un'dignifiedly** *adv.*
1856 FABER *Creator & Creature* I. ii. (1858) 70 Facts which seem so undignifiedly familiar. **1859** F. FRANCIS *Newton Dogvane* xxx, Sneaking,..undignifiedly, out of the gate.

un'dignify, *v.* [UN-^{2} 6 c.] *trans.* **a.** To deprive of ecclesiastical dignity. ? *Obs.* **b.** To make undignified.
1702 DE FOE *Reform. Manners* Pref. 1 All our Clergy are undignified and suspended at a Blow. **1768** *Woman of Honor* I. 224 Selfishness, which not only undignifies them, but endangers their..interest. **1840** MILMAN *Hist. Chr.* I. 185 His father's humble station..had..still farther undignified the person of Jesus to the mind of his fellow-townsmen. **1867** HOWELLS *Ital. Journ.* iii. 33 Modern civilization has not crossed the castle moat, to undignify its exterior with any visible touch of the present.

un'diked, -dyked, *ppl. a.* (UN-^{1} 8, 9.)
c **1611** CHAPMAN *Iliad* XV. 311 The Greeks found time to get Beyond the dike and th' undik'd pales. **1870** MORRIS *Earthly Par.* IV. 261 Woodbine, and the odorous virgin's-bower, Hung in great heaps about that undyked tower.

undi'lapidated, *ppl. a.* (UN-^{1} 8.)
1830 SCOTT *Demonol.* viii. 229 Their comparatively undilapidated revenue.

undi'latable, *a.* (UN-^{1} 7 b, 5 b.)
1862 MEADOWS *Man. Midwifery* 173 The os [uteri]..is still very undilatable. **1863** BATES *Nat. Amazon* iii. I. 102 The undilatable jaws..also distinguish them from other snakes.

undi'lated, *ppl. a.* (UN-^{1} 8.)
[**1775** ASH.] **1858** R. BARNES *Placenta Praevia* iii. 96 At the same time undilated and rigid. **1862** A. MEADOWS *Man. Midwifery* 243 If the parts are undilated and unyielding.

un'dilatory, *a.* (UN-^{1} 7, 5 b.)
1802–12 BENTHAM *Ration. Judic. Evid.* (1827) I. 471 This undilatory, unexpensive..mode of redress.

un'diligent, *a.* (UN-[1] 8 and 5 b.)
1547 BALDWIN *Mor. Philos* 111 Those which be vndiligent, carelesse, and sluggish. **1570** LEVINS *Manip.* 69 Vndiligent, *incurius*. **1649** JER. TAYLOR *Gt. Exemp.* I. Disc. iv. 122 He that is apt to be angry.. may at some time or other be surprized when his guards are undiligent. *a* **1684** LEIGHTON *Comm.* I Pet. iii. 19–21 Why wear you out the day of grace.. as uncertain of Christ, yea, as undiligent after Him, as you were long ago? **1886** RUSKIN *Præterita* II. ix. 330 Though perfectly well-behaved, he was undiligent and effectless.
Hence **un'diligently** *adv.*
1645 MILTON *Tetrach.* Wks. 1851 IV. 209 Cameron.., commenting this place not undiligently, affirmes that [etc.].

†**undi'lucidated**, *ppl. a. Obs.* (UN-[1] 8.)
1635 PERSON *Varieties* I. 23 Ferdinando Oviedes.. leaveth that question undilucidated. **1638** SIR T. HERBERT *Trav.* (ed. 2) 14 The mountaines, without doubt, abound with.. mineralls, which for want of search are yet undilucidated.

undi'lute, *ppl. a.* [UN-[1] 8 b.] = next.
1876 BRISTOWE *The. & Pract. Med.* (1878) 657 Undilute liquid extract of opium.

undi'luted, *ppl. a.* (UN-[1] 8.)
1756 F. HOME *Exper. Bleaching* 89 If.. the oil of vitriol remains, in some parts, undiluted, the cloth is corroded into holes. **1791** COWPER *Odyss.* IX. 343 When thus the Cyclops ..had quaff'd Much undiluted milk. **1860** PIESSE *Lab. Chem. Wonders* 14 An atmosphere of undiluted oxygen. **1873** ROLFE *Phys. Chem.* 159 A concentrated solution of.. undiluted blood.

un'dim, *a.* (UN-[1] 7.)
c **1838** MRS. BROWNING *An Island* xxvii, The undim Unsetting Godlight.

undi'minishable, *a.* (UN-[1] 7 b and 5 b.)
1653 H. MORE *Conject. Cabbal.* 145 It being no object of sense but of intellect, and being also impassible and undiminishable. **1661** RUST *Origen's Opin.* 43 By an unchangeable and undiminishable necessity of Nature. **1817** SHELLEY *Pr. Athan.* II. ii. 12 Sharing that undiminishable store. **1844** EMERSON *Ess., Character* ¶ 1 Character is of.. undiminishable greatness. **1893** R. T. JEFFREY *Visits Calvary* 436 Out of His.. undiminishable fulness, thou mayest receive.
Hence **undi'minishableness.**
1653 H. MORE *Antid. Ath.* III. xvi. *heading*, By reason of the undiminishableness of their magnitude.

undi'minished, *ppl. a.* (UN-[1] 8.)
1587 GOLDING *De Mornay* iii. 34 He.. should be fayne to set downe his whole treatises vndiminished. **1641** MILTON *Ch. Govt.* II. 64 While he keeps them about him undiminisht and unshorn. **1693** DRYDEN *Juvenal* x. 443 Sergius, who a bad Cause bravely try'd, All of a Piece, and undiminish'd Dy'd. **1762** FALCONER *Shipwr.* II. 485 Now the sounding cord, Updrawn, an undiminish'd depth explor'd. **1820** C. R. MATURIN *Melmoth* xxx, With fading sight but undiminished feeling. **1891** FARRAR *Darkn. & Dawn* xlix, Thrasea.. set out on his return to Rome with undiminished cheerfulness.

undi'minishing, *ppl. a.* (UN-[1] 10.)
[**1828** WEBSTER.] **1882** H. S. HOLLAND *Logic & Life* (1885) 291 A permanent and undiminishing gladness of soul.

un'dimmed, *ppl. a.* (UN-[1] 8.)
1723 A. HILL *Hen. V*, III. i. 26 When Your great Father shall perceive Your Flame, Burning, undimm'd. **1839** BAILEY *Festus* 187 Thou art as the cloudless moon, Undimmed and unarrayed. **1871** MACDUFF *Mem. Patmos* xiv. 186 The strong frame, the vigorous pulse, and undimmed eye.

un'dimpled, *ppl. a.* (UN-[1] 8.)
[**1775** ASH.] **1821** SCOTT *Pirate* x, The little lake lay in profound quiet; its surface undimpled. *c* **1872** G. H. KINGSLEY *Sp. & Trav.* v. (1900) 110 The clear brown water, ..undimpled by the sign of a fish.

†**undimy.** *Obs.*[−1] [ad. med.L. *undimia, udimia*, ad. Gr. οἴδημα ŒDEMA.] An impostume.
1562 BULLEIN *Bulwarke, Dial. Sorenes & Chir.* 10 b, Apostumacions, of Fleume or Melancholie, have ioined unto them these names, as undimies, knottes.

undine ('ʌndiːn). Also **ondine.** [ad. mod.L. *Undina* (Paracelsus *De Nymphis* etc., Wks. 1658 II. 391), f. L. *unda* wave. Hence also G. *undine*, F. *ondine* (whence the α-forms), *ondin*.] A supernatural female being, imagined as inhabting the water; a nymph. Also *attrib.*
(The following early instance is based upon the variant *Undena* also employed by Paracelsus:—**1657** PINNELL tr. Crollius *Philos. Reformed* i. 26 To the Water there belongs Nimphs, Undens, Melosyns.)
α. **1821** *Tales Landlord, Fair Witch Glas Llyn* III. 207 The ondines rich in the spoils of pearls and coral from the deep bed of ocean. **1865** LECKY *Ration.* (1878) I. i. 42 The Cabalists believed in the existence of spirits of nature, embodiments.. of the four elements, sylphs, salamanders, gnomes, and ondines.
β. **1837** HALLAM *Hist. Lit.* I. vii. §19 Nature.. is peopled with spiritual beings,.. the silvains (sylphs), undines, or nymphs, gnomes and salamanders. **1867** AUGUSTA WILSON *Vashti* vi, Their foaming cataracts braided glittering spray into spectral similitude of Undine tresses and Undine faces.

un'dined, *ppl. a.* (UN-[1] 8.)
1500–20 DUNBAR *Poems* xxii. 14 The gentill goishalk gois vndynd. **1544** BETHAM *Precepts War* I. lxxvii. Ej b, His souldiours whych were wyllynge to fyght, fastyng and vndyned. **1596** DANETT tr. *Comines* (1614) 35 Neuer was so plentifull a marriage feast, but some departed vndined. **1602** L. LLOYD *Confer. Lawes* 55 They should goe away vndined for that day. **1837** CARLYLE *Fr. Rev.* I. VII. v, Dined or undined, they march with one heart. **1865** —— *Fredk. Gt.* XIX. iv. VIII. 146 This gallop home of the undined Generals.

‖**unding** ('ʊndɪŋ). [Ger., = absurdity.] A non-thing, vague abstraction, or concept having no properties.
1932 H. H. PRICE *Perception* v. 132 It turns out to be a mere *Unding*, in short, to be nothing at all. **1941** *Mind* L. 249 The *bringing about*.. is non-existent, an *Unding*. **1950** *Ibid.* LIX. 477 An object without properties is assuredly an *Unding*. **1955** C. S. LEWIS *Surprised by Joy* xiii. 199, I did believe (so far as one can believe in an *Unding*) in the Absolute.

Undinism ('ʌndiːnɪz(ə)m). *Psychol.* [f. UNDINE (see also Baron F. H. C. La Motte Fouqué *Undine, eine Erzählung* 1811) + -ISM.] (A term proposed for) a strong interest in water and in the urinary function (see quots. 1928 and 1934). Now usu. = UROLAGNIA.
1928 H. H. ELLIS *Stud. in Psychol. of Sex* VII. vii. 409 The peculiarities of those human water-folk with whom I am here concerned I propose to call by the rather arbitrary but convenient name of *Undinism*. **1933** —— *Psychol. of Sex* iv. 142, I have been accustomed to apply the term Undinism to the frequent presence of an early interest in water in general, and the urinary function in particular, persisting in later life. This interest, not amounting to a definite deviation of the sexual impulse.. is common, especially in women. **1959** *Times Lit. Suppl.* 6 Feb. 65/4 Mr. Collis also avoids the question of the earlier Undinism and Urolagnia. **1977** *Ibid.* 13 May 584/3 Ellis was not homosexual. His 'germ of a perversion' was Undinism (ie watching women pee).

un'dinnered, *ppl. a.* (UN-[1] 8.)
1799 *Spirit Pub. Jrnls.* III. 322 Leave me uncurl'd, undinner'd, here to mourn.

un'dinted, *ppl. a.* (UN-[1] 8.)
1606 SHAKS. *Ant. & Cl.* II. vi. 39 To part with vnhackt edges, and beare backe Our Targes vndinted. **1636** R. DURHAM in *Ann. Dubrensia* (1877) 56 With what nimble pace Your coursers poasted, ore th' undinted face O' th' earth. **1863** BARING-GOULD *Iceland* 231 To our right lay.. the undinted snow.

un'diocesed, *a.* (UN-[1] 9.)
1641 MILTON *Reform.* I. 22 He that will mould a modern Bishop into a primitive, must yeeld him to be.. undiocest, unrevenu'd, unlorded.

undi'plomaed, *a.* (UN-[1] 9.)
1790 J. WILLIAMS *Shrove Tuesday* 28 Authoritative Oafs combine to teize Unhappy Oaflings—undiploma'd Curs.

undiplo'matic, *a.* (UN-[1] 7. Cf. G. *undiplomatisch*.)
1831 CARLYLE *Sart. Res.* III. iii, The most undiplomatic and unstrategic of these [men.] **1853** LYTTON *My Novel* II. ii, The dark eyes.. went right into Frank's unprotected and undiplomatic heart.
Hence **undiplo'matically** *adv.*
1961 R. B. LONG *Sentence & its Parts* 479 He makes his points too undiplomatically. **1969** 'E. LATHEN' *When in Greece* xi. 118 Bill Riemer undiplomatically interrupted.

un'dipped, *ppl. a.* [UN-[1] 8.]
1. Not dipped (in a liquid).
1648 G. DANIEL *Eclog* ii. 160 A Qvill soe low, soe yet vndipt, to cope with these well-mention'd worthyes. **1692** DRYDEN *Cleomenes* IV. i, Like Achilles, Thou hadst a soft Egyptian heel undipt, And that has made thee mortal. **1868** GEO. ELIOT *Sp. Gipsy* 18 A fountain near,.. Where timorous birds alight,.. And fly away again with undipped beak. **1886** *Daily News* 13 Oct. 3/4 They will during the dipping season guard the undipped sheep.
2. *spec.* Unbaptized.
1693 (*title*), Semper idem:.. Dedicated to undipt John [*sc.* Tillotson]. **1821** LAMB *Elia* I. *Valentine's Day*, The consigner of undipt infants to eternal torments. **1880** RUSKIN *Fathers have told us* I. i. 28 That undipped people may be as good as dipped if their hearts are clean.
3. Of (the beams of) a headlight of a vehicle: not lowered.
1960 *Guardian* 12 Sept. 2/3 One glaring, undipped.. headlight. **1969** 'A. HALL' *Striker Portfolio* ix. 112 My undipped heads catching the Mercedes full across the screen. **1983** *Times* 23 Dec. 3/6 Once the ignition is switched on the choice will be between dim-dip (dipped headlights with reduced light), full dip and undipped.

†**undi'rect**, *a. Obs.* [UN-[1] 7.] = INDIRECT *a.*
a **1592** GREENE *Selimus* 929 His brethren both.. Do seeke the Empire while your grace doth liue, And that by vndirect sinister meanes. **1614** LATHAM *Falconry* (1633) 80 When through our disorder & vndirect courses, we haue wrought their vnsoundnes, we forget to looke backe. **1652** J. WRIGHT tr. *Camus' Nat. Paradox* II. 45 Those, who by oblique and undirect wayes do seek to accomplish their pretensions.

undi'rect, *v.* [UN-[1] 14.] *trans.* To misdirect, lead astray.
1647 FULLER *Gd. Th. in Worse T.* 100 Some English People on the Sea side.. who make false fires to undirect Seamen in a Tempest.

undi'rected, *ppl. a.* (UN-[1] 8 and 5 b.)
1596 SPENSER *St. Irel.* Wks. (Globe) 617/1 The realme was left, like a shipp in a storme,.. unruled, and undirected of any. **1692** BENTLEY *Boyle Lect.* 103 To make out, how matter by undirected motion could.. fall.. into such a curious formation of humane bodies. **1762** STERNE *Tr. Shandy* VI. xxxv, Listlessness, with her lax fibre and undirected eye, sat quietly down beside him. **1822** LAMB *Elia* I. *On Some Old Actors*, A veering undirected goodness of purpose. **1882** MINCHIN *Unipl. Kinemat.* 108 Any quantity which has merely magnitude but not direction is called an undirected, or scalar, quantity.

†**undi'rectly**, *adv. Obs.* (UN-[1] 11, 5 b.)
1535 in Strype *Eccl. Mem.* (1721) I. App. lxiv. 158 That neither of both parties shal give any help.. against the other, directly or undirectly, secretly or openly, to the invasor. **1550** BALDWIN *Mor. Philos.* II. v. Kij, Lyfe iudgeth vndirectly of deathe.

undis'abled, *ppl. a.* (UN-[1] 8.)
1705 J. COLLIER *Ess. Mor. Subj.* III. *Pain* 6 Why then should we suppose the Touch continues entire and undisabled? **1875** KINGLAKE *Crimea* (1877) V. i. 237 The survivors of the first line who remained undisabled.

undisa'ppointable, *a.* (UN-[1] 7 b.)
1871 RUSKIN *Fors Clav.* v. 15 The straightforward and undisappointable effort to advance.

undisa'ppointed, *ppl. a.* (UN-[1] 8.)
1750 *Rambler* No. 3 *motto*, Undisappointed in designs, With native honours virtue shines.

undis'armed, *ppl. a.* (UN-[1] 8.)
1648–9 *Eikon Bas.* 130 Nor shall they be long undisarmed and undestroyed. **1879** FROUDE *Cæsar* 349 Pompey was still undisarmed.

undis'banded, *ppl. a.* (UN-[1] 8.)
1641 *Nicholas Papers* (Camden) 32 If any soldiours be kept together.. undisbanded, it will rayse jelousies. **1649** MILTON *Eikon.* x. 92 There were 8000 Irish Papists which he refus'd to disband,.. and so kept them undisbanded [etc.]. *a* **1754** CARTE *Hist. Eng.* (1755) IV. 373 There was at that time a body of 5000 foot, part of their army undisbanded. **1810** *Monthly Rev.* LXII. 495 Some events are too complex to be wholly transacted in the presence of an undisbanded chorus. **1860** FORSTER *Grand Remonstr.* 166 The pay of the five undisbanded troops of the Northern army.

undis'burdened, *ppl. a.* (UN-[1] 8.)
1659 O. WALKER *Oratory* 11 The mind travelling with many conceptions at once (undisburdened of any) must needs be much surcharged.

†**undi'scernable**, *a. Obs.* [UN-[1] 7 b and 5 b.] = UNDISCERNIBLE *a.* (Common in 17th c.)
1586 HOOKER *Disc. Justif.* §23, I doe not meane.. that building vndiscernable by mortall eyes,.. but I speake of the visible Church. *a* **1633** W. AUSTIN *Medit.* (1635) 139 Let us (then) not will, or strive to ascend to Honour.. by secret and undiscernable meanes. **1656** JEANES *Fuln. Christ* 229 If we take but a drop of the sea, it makes some diminution, though it be unsensible, and undiscernable. **1710** *Tatler* No. 205 ¶ 5 How undiscernable [is] the Transition from one to the other! **1794** G. ADAMS *Nat. & Exp. Philos.* IV. xliii. 169 The primordial threads, or first principles of the texture, are utterly undiscernable.
Hence †**undi'scernableness.** *Obs.*
1645 HAMMOND *View Infallibility* (1646) 141 Your answer to the undiscernablenesse of errours. **1654** WHITLOCK *Zootomia* 536 Compared with which.. the Stateliest Pallaces lessen into undiscernablenesse.

†**undi'scernably**, *adv. Obs.* (UN-[1] 11: cf. prec.)
1594 NASHE *Unfort. Trav.* Hij b, By the mathematicall experimentes of long siluer pipes.. vndiscerneablie conuaid ..into their small throats. **1642** MILTON *Apol. Smect.* 54 If they for lucre use to creepe into the Church undiscernably. **1690** LOCKE *Hum. Und.* II. xxxi. §15 The sensible Ideas.. are most commonly very near and undiscernably alike.

undi'scerned, *ppl. a.* (UN-[1] 8 and 5 b.)
1529 MORE *Dyaloge* II. ix. 57 b/2 Standyng as they do vnknowen and vndyscerned. *a* **1625** FLETCHER *Captain* IV. iv, Bring me to a place Where undiscerned of her self I may Feed my desiring eyes. **1653** HOLCROFT *Procopius, Vand. Wars* II. 41 The plot was undiscerned by any: For though many were engaged in it, yet none.. revealed it. **1703** ROWE *Ulysses* II. i, Warriors from my Fleet Who undiscern'd.. and by Stealth Late came ashore. **1784** COWPER *Task* III. 242 If his word.. reveal Truths undiscern'd but by that holy light, Then all is plain. **1819** SHELLEY *Peter Bell 3rd* v. iii, But he in shadows undiscerned Trusted.
absol. **1898** MEREDITH *Odes Fr. Hist.* 16 She had.. Forgot her faith in the Great Undiscerned.
Hence **undi'scernedly** *adv.*
1660 N. INGELO *Bentiv. & Ur.* (1682) II. 61 The traiterous dispositions.. in their own breasts; which though they might lurk more undiscernedly before, will then be sure to shew what they are. **1665** BOYLE *Occas. Refl.* V. x. 185 Death has undiscernedly stoll'n upon them, and unawares intruded into their Studies. **1734** FALLE *Jersey* (ed. 2) vi. 243 Others lavish theirs [*sc.* grants] out so wantonly and undiscernedly, that to be ev'n loaded with them is no argument of Merit.

undi'scernible, *a.* [UN-[1] 7 and 5 b: cf. UNDISCERNABLE *a.*] = INDISCERNIBLE *a.*
1624 GATAKER *Transubst.* 162 Not by running into a corner.. but by becoming undiscernible by them. **1706** STANHOPE *Paraphr.* III. 384 Albeit the manner of working be undiscernible yet the Work it self can be none but God's. **1768–74** TUCKER *Lt. Nat.* (1834) I. 618 Minute particles, undiscernible with a microscope. **1837** HT. MARTINEAU *Soc. Amer.* III. 18 Where men, knowing how undiscernible consequences are,.. abide them without fear. **1873** PROCTOR *Expanse Heaven* 270 Those other stars separately undiscernible, which produce the milky light of the galaxy.
Hence **undi'scernibleness.**
1646 HAMMOND *Sinnes* 4 The levity and undiscerniblenesse of the matter. **1743** J. ELLIS *Knowl. Div. Things* ii. 84 Because of their Remoteness, Subtilty, and Undiscernibleness, it cannot know them adequately.

undi'scernibly, *adv.* [UN-[1] 11 and 5 b: cf. UNDISCERNABLY *adv.*] = INDISCERNIBLY *adv.*
1655 JER. TAYLOR *Repentance* v. §5 Disc. (1674) 685 While one habit lessens, another may undiscernibly increase. **1681** FLAVEL *Right Man's Ref.* 183 The angels.. working secretly and undiscernibly, but very effectually. **1802** *Eng. Encycl.*

VI. 118/2 The ideas..are very near, and undiscernibly like. **1862** GEO. ELIOT *Romola* II. v, It is probable that his imperious need of ascendancy had burned undiscernibly.

undi'scerning, *sb.* [UN-[1] 13.] Want of discernment.

1711 STEELE *Spect.* No. 157 ¶1 The Ignorance and Undiscerning of the Generality of Schoolmasters. **1850** BROWNING *Christmas Eve* VII. 14 Far alike from thriftless learning And ignorance's undiscerning.

undi'scerning, *ppl. a.* (UN-[1] 10 and 5 b.)

1589 NASHE *Pref.* in Greene *Menaphon* (Arb.) 8 Which being the effect of an vndescerning iudgement, makes drosse as valuable as gold. **1643–5** MILTON *Divorce* II. xii, That power the undiscerning Canonist hath improperly usurpt. **1673** *Lady's Calling* I. ii. §5 These sophisticators of divinity desire the most undiscerning auditors. **1711** POPE *Temple of Fame* 297 Thus..fickle Fortune.., undiscerning, scatters crowns and chains. **1751** JOHNSON *Rambler* No. 164 ¶6 He is on one side censured by undiscerning malice,..and idolized on the other by ignorant admiration. **1812** CRABBE *Tales* x. 132 All are appropriate—bog, and marsh, and fen, Are only poor to undiscerning men. **1849** MACAULAY *Hist. Eng.* vii. II. 240 Intemperate and undiscerning as was his zeal for the Declaration.

Hence **undi'scerningly** *adv.*

1707 W. CAROLL *Let. Dr. Prat* 10 Not upon the 10th Chap. of that Essay, as this Gentleman very undiscerningly has it.

undis'chargeable, *a.* (UN-[1] 7 b.)

1587 GOLDING *De Mornay* xx. 354 These are so farre off from amounting to a discharge, that they turne to a huge heape of worse and more vndischargeable bonds.

undis'charged, *ppl. a.* [UN-[1] 8.]

1. Unpaid; not cleared off or settled.

1585 ABP. SANDYS *Serm. Rom. xiii. 8–13* xi. 181 What should we say but..confesse that wee haue left that debt of loue..vndischarged? **1611** COTGR., *Insolu*, vnpayed, vndischarged, vndefrayed. *a* **1639** SPOTTISWOOD *Hist. Ch. Scot.* (1655) 336 Some private accounts, that rested undischarged at his parting forth of the Countrey. **1723** *Lond. Gaz.* No. 6183/2 The said four Exchequer Bills (which are all that are now standing out and undischarged). **1800** *Misc. Tr.* in *Asiat. Ann. Reg.* 34/2 The arrears have accumulated..and the claims of the government remain undischarged. **1908** ATTON & HOLLAND *King's Customs* 16 The long-standing claims of the Aquitaine mayors were still undischarged.

2. Not set free or dismissed; not released from office, liability, etc.

1603 B. JONSON *Sejanus* v. iii, Those [cohorts] we must Hold still in readiness and undischarged. *a* **1671** LD. FAIRFAX *Mem.* (1699) 125 Being yet undischarged of my place, they set my name in way of course to all their papers. **1834** COLERIDGE *Let.* in *Sotheby's Sale Catalogue* 20 Nov. (1899) 17, I know myself an undischarged debtor. **1888** *Pall Mall G.* 6 Mar. 2/1 He was duly adjudicated a bankrupt;.. he paid nothing.., and is at present undischarged.

3. Not relieved *of* something.

1670 *Devout Commun.* (1688) 27 An unfixed heart, undischarged of worldly thoughts.

4. Not accomplished or carried out.

c **1705** POPE *Jan. & May* 473 For whate'er work was undischarg'd a-bed, The duteous knight in this fair garden sped. **1881** *Atlantic Monthly* XLVIII. 380 Fulfilling important..functions which would otherwise go undischarged.

5. Not fired off.

1798 S. & HT. LEE *Canterb. T.* II. 46 Throwing down the remaining pistol undischarged. **1812** J. HENRY *Camp. agst. Quebec* 130 A drunken sailor returned to his gun swearing he would not forsake it while undischarged.

6. Not unloaded (*from* a vessel).

1864 WILLIAMS & SIMMONDS *Engl. Commerc. Corresp.* 225 Tincal undischarged from the country steamer at the Ghat.

un'disciplinable, *a.* (UN-[1] 7 b and 5 b.)

a **1652** J. SMITH *Sel. Disc.* VI. i. (1821) 183 God..would not make us so undisciplinable in divine things. **1676** HALE *Contempl.* II. (1677) 97 Such [boys] as are undisciplineable, are after some years of probation sent away to Mechanical Imployments. **1749** SMOLLETT *Gil Blas* XII. vi, I imagined that the pedagogues..would find their Latin thrown away, believing one at his age undisciplinable. **1815** SIMOND *Tour Gt. Brit.* I. 371 How can you expect to succeed with this undisciplinable spirit. **1860** PUSEY *Min. Proph.* 52 The.. wild ass of the east, is heady, unruly, undisciplinable.

un'discipline. (UN-[1] 12 and 5 b.)

1827 SCOTT *Napoleon* Introd., Amidst debauchery and undiscipline. **1840** ALISON *Hist. Europe* (1859) VIII. 668 The undiscipline of part of the Hungarian force. **1889** GORE *Rom. Cath. Claims* x. 162 This undiscipline in doctrine is at least no worse than undiscipline in morals.

un'disciplined, *ppl. a.* [UN-[1] 8. Cf. G. *undisciplinirt*, Sw. *odisciplinerad*.]

1. Not subjected to discipline; untrained.

1382 WYCLIF *Wisd.* xvii. 1 For these the vndisciplyned soulis erreden. —— *Ecclus.* v. 14 Lest thou be take in an vndisciplyned wrd, and thou be confoundid. **1596** SPENSER *F.Q.* VI. v. 1 Like this wyld man, being vndisciplynd. **1602** WARNER *Alb. Eng.* Epit. (1612) 357 The Warr-intricated Romaines vtterly left Britaine to the vndisciplind Britons. **1665** J. SPENCER *Vulg. Proph.* 46 Their undisciplin'd mind is unable to disabuse it self by an appeal to some sober and enduring principles. **1736** BERKELEY *Disc.* Wks. 1871 III. 415 The savage state of undisciplined men, whose minds are nurtured to no doctrine. **1796** COLERIDGE *Destiny of Nations* 137 She was quick to mark The good and evil thing, in human love Undisciplined. **1841** W. SPALDING *Italy & It. Isl.* I. 19 The passions of the people were then nearly as undisciplined. **1892** WESTCOTT *Gospel of Life* 285 The fancies of undisciplined enthusiasm.

2. *spec.* Not properly subjected or submissive to military discipline.

1718 PRIOR *Solomon* II. 728 Loose and undisciplin'd the Soldier lay. **1792** GOUV. MORRIS in Sparks *Life & Writ.* (1832) II. 177 The French troops are extremely undisciplined. **1846** H. W. TORRENS *Rem. Milit. Hist.* 240 The army..as yet wholly undisciplined by those to whom.. new and unwonted authority had been delegated. **1878** BOSW. SMITH *Carthage* i. 37 The discipline which he enforced on the most undisciplined of his army.

Hence **un'disciplinedness.**

1661 BOYLE *Style of Script.* 55 Generous Horses, [acting] ..not out of Undisciplinednesse, but purely out of Metall. **1888** ABP. BENSON in *Life* (1899) II. 209 The undisciplinedness of the spirit which despised 'the day of small things'.

†undisciplinous, *a. Obs.* (UN-[1] 7.)

1382 WYCLIF *Ecclus.* xxiii. 17 To the vndisciplynous speche [L. *indisciplinatæ loquelæ*] vse not thi mouth.

undis'close, *v.* [UN-[1] 14.] *trans.* To keep concealed.

1601 DANIEL *Delia* xxxvi, The halfe blowne Rose,.. Whilst yet her tender bud doth vndisclose That full of beautie, tyme bestowes vpon her.

undis'closed, *ppl. a.* [UN-[1] 8.]

1. Not revealed or made known.

1571 GOLDING *Calvin on Ps.* vi. 6 The grace of God being yet undisclosed before the comming of Christ. **1648** HEXHAM II, *Ongeopenbaert*, Vnrevealed, Vndiscovered, or Vndisclosed. **1814** BYRON *Lara* I. xxiii, Whate'er there be between you undisclosed, This is no time [etc.]. **1880** MUIRHEAD tr. *Ulpian* xxv. §17 *note*, It is doubtful whether he could take under a secret and undisclosed trust.

2. Unhatched. (Cf. DISCLOSE *v.* 1 b.)

1581 T. HOWELL *Deuises* H j, Counte not the byrds that vndisclosed bee. **1744** THOMSON *Summer* 260 The sweet task,..where to wrap In what soft beds their young, yet undisclos'd, Employs their tender care. **1817** KIRBY & SP. *Entomol.* xxvii. II. 503 They place a guard over the cells of those [bees yet] undisclosed.

undis'coloured, *ppl. a.* (UN-[1] 8.)

1666 BOYLE *Orig. Forms & Qual.* 318 An undiscolour'd mixture of syrup of Violets. **1814** WORDSW. *Excurs.* v. 164 Fixed aloft A faded hatchment hung, and one by time Yet undiscoloured. **1847** H. ROGERS *Ess.* (1874) I. v. 237 The severest raillery..flows on in a stream undiscoloured by one particle of malevolence. **1876** MISS BROUGHTON *Joan* xxvii, A face unswollen, undiscoloured by any tears.

undis'comfitable, *a.* (UN-[1] 7 b.)

a **1555** PHILPOT in *Exam. & Writ.* (Parker Soc.) 351 But those things are so undisconfitable..that for want of good argument [etc.].

undis'comfited, *ppl. a.* Also 4–5 *Sc.* **vndisconfit, wndiscumfyt.** (UN-[1] 8.)

c **1374** CHAUCER *Boeth.* I. met. iv. (1868) 12 He may holde hys chiere vndiscomfited. **1375** BARBOUR *Bruce* III. 274 Thai that wald Thar hartis wndiscumfyt hald. **1523** LD. BERNERS *Froiss.* I. cclix. 384 They..fought..and so helde themselfe vndiscomfitted the space of ii. houres. **1856** MRS. BROWNING *Aur. Leigh* I. 775 That..undiscomfited Look steadfast truths against Time's changing mask.

undiscon'tinued, *ppl. a.* (UN-[1] 8.)

1629 DONNE *Serm.* (1839) V. 253, I shall have..an unintermitted, an undiscontinued Sight of God. **1702** S. PARKER tr. *Cicero's De Finibus* II. 125 For a true Blessedness of Life..is as Lasting and as Undiscontinu'd as Wisdom. **1719** JAS. THE PRETENDER *Let.* in *Pearson's Catal.* (1894) 33, I hope God will bless at last my undiscontinued efforts. **1818** BENTHAM *Ch. Eng.* 47 The test above brought to view ..consisting of the undiscontinued assortment of quotations.

undi'scordant, *a.* (UN-[1] 7.)

1819 WORDSW. *'Departing Summer'* 21 Wide is the range, and free the choice Of undiscordant themes.

undi'scording, *ppl. a.* (UN-[1] 10.)

c **1630** MILTON *At a Solemn Musick* 17 That we..with undiscording voice May rightly answer that melodious noise. **1742** G. WEST *Inst. Order of Garter* (1807) 109 Attuning to the sweet harmonious spheres Their undiscording lyres.

undi'scourageable, *a.* (UN-[1] 7 b.)

1571 GOLDING *Calvin on Ps.* xxii. 2 Such an one as was undiscourageable in undertaking troubles. **1684** *Gilby's Test. 12 Partriarchs* B 8 b, My heart was stout, my mind unmoveable, and my stomach undiscourageable. **1865** H. BUSHNELL *Vicar. Sacr.* II. iv, His..upright, impartial, passionless, undiscourageable rule. **1882** H. C. MERIVALE *Faucit of B.* III. II. xv. 94 She had watched..the fair Emily's patient and undiscourageable angling.

undi'scouraged, *ppl. a.* (UN-[1] 8.)

a **1628** F. GREVIL *Life Sidney* xiv. (1652) 167 My yet undiscouraged Genius. **1642** in *Chas. I's Wks.* (1662) II. 201 Your Parliament, whose constant and undiscouraged Endeavours..have passed through Difficulties unheard-of. **1773** *Cook's 1st Voy.* I. Introd. p. xii, Mr. Banks however returned, undiscouraged, from his first expedition. **1859** H. KINGSLEY *G. Hamlyn* xiv, He, nevertheless, held on his way undiscouraged. **1898** G. W. STEEVENS *Egypt in 1898* xvii. 203 The practical, undiscouraged Englishman.

undi'scoursed, *ppl. a.* (UN-[1] 8.)

a **1670** HACKET *Abp. Williams* I. (1693) 130 We would submit to all with indefinite and undiscoursed Obedience. *Ibid.* II. 217.

undi'scoverable, *a.* (UN-[1] 7 b and 5 b.)

1642 QUARLES *Observ. Princes & States* lxxvi, It is the height of a provident Commander..to keepe his owne designes undiscoverable to the Enemy. **1688** BOYLE *Final Causes Nat. Things* II. 79 Among the ends of God, which he thought undiscoverable by us. **1768–74** TUCKER *Lt. Nat.* (1834) II. 79 The multitude of events..produced by the concurrence of undiscoverable causes. **1841** MYERS *Cath. Th.* IV. §36 What..portion of such Plan it is, is at present undiscoverable by us. **1885** *Law Times* 11 Apr. 420/2 The undiscoverable flaw constituted a breach of such warranty.

Hence **undi'scoverableness.**

1656 JEANES *Fuln. Chr.* 383 His riches are said to be unsearchable,..which Epithet denoteth the undiscoverablenesse of them by the light of nature.

undi'scoverably, *adv.* (UN-[1] 11 and 5 b.)

1645 MILTON *Tetrach.* Wks. 1851 IV. 228 He..permitted by accident the evil of them who divorc't against the laws intention undiscoverably. **1680** COTTON *Compl. Gamester* (ed. 2) 12 How neatly and undiscoverably he managed his tricks. **1892** ZANGWILL *Bow Mystery* 171 To assassinate secretly, mysteriously, unintelligibly, undiscoverably.

undi'scovered, *ppl. a.* [UN-[1] 8 and 5 b.]

†1. Uncovered, exposed. *Obs.*[-1]

1542 BOORDE *Dyetary* viii. (1870) 247 When..you do slepe, let not..your handes, nor fete,..lye bare vndyscouered.

2. Undisclosed, unrevealed; not cleared up.

a **1542** WYATT *Psalm, 'Oh happy ar they'* 20 As adder freshe new stryppid from his skin, nor in his sprite is owght vndiscoverd. **1576** FLEMING *Panopl. Epist.* 64 All your loue is apparant and manifest unto me.., and neuer a part or parcel thereof left undiscouered. **1611** SHAKS. *Wint. T.* v. ii. 130 This Mysterie remained vndiscouer'd. **1697** TUTCHIN *Search Honesty* v, In whose Bigg Bellies undiscover'd lye The Fate of Kings. **1867** M. ARNOLD *A Wish* vii, The future and its viewless things—That undiscover'd mystery.

3. Not discovered, found, or come upon.

1555 EDEN *Decades* (Arb.) 285 What parts of the baul of the earth remained yet vndiscouered. **1602** SHAKS. *Haml.* III. i. 79 The vndiscouered Countrey, from whose Borne No Traueller returnes. **1676** GLANVILL *Ess.* VII. 1 In that immense undiscover'd Abyss, that was beyond both the Old World, and the New. **1769** E. BANCROFT *Guiana* 2 If we may be allowed to form an idea of things undiscovered, by the immense variety..of its Animal and Vegetable Productions. **1806** LAMB *Mr. H——* ii. Wks. 1908 II. 758 Some yet undiscovered Otaheite. **1850** TENNYSON *In Mem.* xl, My paths are in the fields I know, And thine in undiscover'd lands. **1894** H. NISBET *Bush Girl's Rom.* 171 They were not so pleased to hear that their cash was as yet undiscovered.

b. Not ascertained or made out.

1707 MORTIMER *Husb.* A 2 b, The detecting of specious and prevailing Errors,..so as to clear the way to what remains undiscovered. **1793** BEDDOES *Calculus* 273 The grasses (of which the product is variable from undiscovered causes). **1855** BREWSTER *Newton* II. xxvii. 408 Those inspired doctrines which alone can throw a light over the dark ocean of undiscovered truth.

4. Not found out; unobserved, undetected.

1593 SHAKS. *2 Hen. VI*, III. i. 369 Full often Hath he conuersed with the Enemie, And vndiscouer'd, come to me againe. **1669** STURMY *Mariner's Mag., Penalties & Forfeit.* 4 Goods..that shall be Exported, and escape undiscovered unto the Officers of the Customs. **1697** C. LESLIE *Snake in Grass* (ed. 2) 308 The Quakers take it very ill to suppose that Jesuits cou'd Preach among them undiscover'd. **1725** DE FOE *Voy. round World* (1840) 63 A little cape which kept us perfectly undiscovered. **1798** S. & HT. LEE *Canterb. T.* II. 101 Let me fly undiscovered. **1890** *Retrospect Med.* CII. 310 In order to guard against the possibility of leaving a perforation undiscovered.

undi'scovering, *ppl. a.*: see UN-[1] 5 d.

†undi'screet, *a. Obs.* [UN-[1] 7 and 5 b. Cf. MDu. *ondiscreet*.] = INDISCREET *a.* (Common *c* 1400–1650.) **a.** Of persons.

1382 WYCLIF *Ecclus.* xxxi. 23 Waking, and colere, and anguysh to an vndiscreet man. *c* **1400** tr. *Secreta Secret., Gov. Lordsh.* 116 He þat hauys a greet wombe, ys vndiscreet, foltysch, proud. **1482** *Monk of Evesham* (Arb.) 97 He was lyght of behauyng and ondyscrete as in eatyng and drynkyng. **1549** LATIMER *3rd Serm. bef. Edw. VI* (Arb.) 77 We are noted to be rassh, and vndiscrete in our preachynge. **1584** R. SCOT *Discov. Witchcr.* XIV. viii. (1886) 311 Into what follie and madnes vaine hope may drive undiscreete and unexpert men. **1676** HOBBES *Iliad* 308 What need we, like two women in the street,..to rail and scoff? Who, say they true or false, are undiscreet. *a* **1704** T. BROWN *Wks.* (1709) III. II. 116 My Despair proceeded not from the same Motive, as that of the undiscreet Lucretia.

absol. **1535** COVERDALE *Ecclus.* xxvii. 12 Yf thou be amonge the vndiscrete. **1595** DANIEL *Civ. Wars* I. l, This publique course..compassion drawes; Especially in cases of the great, Which worke much pitty in the undiscreat.

b. Of actions, conduct, etc.

c **1340** HAMPOLE *Prose Tr.* 17 He..by vndiscrete trauellynge turnes þe braynes in his heuede. **1420–2** LYDG. *Thebes* III. 3114 Thorgh vndiscret and hasty gredynesse. *c* **1440** *Jacob's Well* 99 Be-cause of þin vndyscret dyspysing it doth hym vnworschip. **1529** MORE *Dyaloge* IV. Wks. 276/2 Some of them may haue som time either ouer feruent mynd or vndiscrete zele. **1579** LYLY *Euphues* (Arb.) 133 By which their vndiscreet dealing, they are like those sicke men which reiect the..cunning Phisition. **1640** FULLER *Joseph's Coat* 182 The flames of ill-tempered and undiscreet zeal. **1694** *Gracian's Courtier's Orac.* 50 Blind passion, undiscreet engagement, imprudent haste, fool-hardiness.

†undi'screetly, *adv.* [UN-[1] 11: cf. prec.] = INDISCREETLY *adv.* (Common *c* 1450–1650.)

c **1380** WYCLIF *Sel. Wks.* III. 362 For ȝif þei cursen undiscretly,..þanne þei cursen hemsilf first. *c* **1440** *Jacob's Well* 262 Whanne þou behotyst myche thyng vndyscretly, and doost noȝt þi behest. *c* **1491** *Chast. Goddes Chyld.* 21 Suche men unresonably and undyscretly encline to the rest and commodyte of the body. **1539** ELYOT *Cast. Helthe* 63 Put to the heed vndiscretely, it hurteth both the heed and the eies. **1579** FULKE *Heskins' Parl.* 201 Dionyse the Charterhouse Monke, whom he matcheth vndiscretely with Cyrill. **1618** *Barnevelt's Apol.* G ij b, Seeing both the words and meaning thereof are much different from that which they vndiscreetely coyne. **1698** *Phil. Trans.* XX. 75 'Tis very necessary for them to forbear much drinking undiscreetly. **1704** *Collect. Voy.* (Churchill) III. 680/2 Heated with strong Liquor, [he] reply'd undiscreetly.

†undi'screetness. *Obs.* [UN-¹ 12: cf. prec.] = INDISCREETNESS.
1542 UDALL *Erasm. Apoph.* 295 b, He gravely restreigned and staied the heddie undiscretenesse of the oratours. **1587** GOLDING *De Mornay* xi. 181 The fault is in thyne owne vndiscreetnesse, and not in their nature. **1647** HEXHAM I. s.v.

undi'screte, *a.* (UN-¹ 7, 5 b.)
1862 BEVERIDGE *Hist. Ind.* II. IV. iv. 119 Eternal matter, undiscrete, destitute of parts.

†undi'scretion. *Obs.* [UN-¹ 12 and 5 b.] = INDISCRETION.
a **1395** HYLTON *Scala Perf.* I. xxviii. (W. de W. 1494), Therfor they by undescrecion oft sithes ouertraueyle her witts. **1420–2** LYDG. *Thebes* III. 3449 ȝoure-silf to drowne in torment & in woo..Is gret foly and vndiscrecciioun. **1563** HARDING *Answ. to M. Ivelles Challenge* To Rdr. (1565) 4 b, The note of vndiscretion shall remaine to them.

undi'scriminated, *ppl. a.* [UN-¹ 8 and 5 b.] Not discriminated; also with *against*.
1768 GIBBON *Misc. Wks.* (1814) V. 569 All M. de Buffon's witnesses appear levelled by an undiscriminated equality. **1883** F. H. BRADLEY *Princ. Logic* 422 We begin here with a vague and undiscriminated unity. **1890** W. JAMES *Princ. Psychol.* II. xx. 146 All our sensations (however as yet unconnected and undiscriminated) are of extensive objects. **1981** *Observer* 27 Sept. 36/5 Those of my generation and younger who found ourselves undiscriminated against in our respective faculties. **1984** *Times Lit. Suppl.* 23 Mar. 306/3 A recurring topic was the inchoate, undiscriminated bulk of information and misinformation now being stored.

undi'scriminating, *ppl. a.* (UN-¹ 10, 5 b.)
a **1800** COWPER *Odyss.* (ed. 2) XXII. 298 Hurl the spear At once with undiscriminating aim Against them all. **1844** H. H. WILSON *Brit. India* III. 440 The undiscriminating nature of their outrages. **1871** FREEMAN *Hist. Ess.* Ser. I. iv. 87 Morris writes in a spirit of undiscriminating admiration.
Hence **undi'scriminatingly** *adv.*, **-ness.**
1866 GEO. ELIOT *F. Holt* xvi, They encourage a coarse undiscriminatingness. **1894** *Athenæum* 27 Oct. 574/1 The bookworm swallows all printed matter undiscriminatingly.

†undi'scurrent, *a.* *Obs.* (UN-¹ 7.)
a **1529** SKELTON *Bk. 3 Fools* Wks. 1843 I. 200 Shee is so debylyte, colde,..vnnaturall, and vndyscurrente, for the coldenes that is in her.

undi'scursive, *a.* (UN-¹ 7.)
1633 T. ADAMS *Exp. 2 Peter* ii. 2 It is an inconsiderate, undiscoursive applyment of them-selves to anothers will, without waighing the goodnesse or fitnesse of the action. **1874** LEWES *Probl. Life & Mind* I. 141 Enough here to define it [*sc.* knowledge] as lapsed or undiscursive Intelligence.

undi'scussable, *a.* (UN-¹ 7 b and 5 b.)
1861 DICKENS *Gt. Expect.* viii, She said it finally and in.. an undiscussable way.

undi'scussed, *ppl. a.* (UN-¹ 8 and 5 b.)
In older use (15–17th c.) chiefly in the sense of 'undecided, unsettled': see DISCUSS *v.* 4.
c **1340** HAMPOLE *Pr. Consc.* 5697 Þe lest thoghtes þat thurgh use had yhe In þe dome sal noght undiscussed be. **1439** *Rolls of Parlt.* V. 17/1 Which Assise hangyng undiscussed, ye same Phelip desired often tymes [etc.]. *a* **1513** FABYAN *Chron.* v. cxvi. 90 Not without great stryfe had atwene hym and his sayde vncle,..whereof at this day some deale was vndiscussyd. **1567–9** JEWEL *Def. Apol.* (1611) 458 This matter notwithstanding it had beene much beaten thorow the world, yet lay still vndiscussed. **1610** HEALEY *St. Aug. Citie of God.* 561 This question wee touched at in our third booke, but left it undiscussed. **1643** PRYNNE *Sov. Power Parl.* I. (ed. 2) 31 That the Parliament should not depart so long as any Petition..hangeth undiscussed or undecided.
[**1775** ASH.] **1818** COBBETT *Resid. U.S.* (1819) 294 There remains a very important part of the subject yet undiscussed. **1898** S. EVANS *Holy Graal* 30 The question was left undiscussed and unsettled.

undi'seased, *ppl. a.* [UN-¹ 8.]
†1. Free from discomfort or trouble. *Obs. rare.*
c **1450** *Life St. Cuthbert* (Surtees) 6881 Þar was nane wery, alde ne ȝyng,..þai come to Rypoun all vndyseesed. **1535** COVERDALE *Dan.* vi. 2 Aboue these he set thre prynces,.. that the lordes might geue accomptes vnto them, and the kynge to be vndiseased.
2. Not affected by or suffering from disease.
1746 YOUNG *Nt. Th.* IX. 1804 Where reason (un-diseas'd with you) runs mad, And nurses folly's children as her own. **1807** SOUTHEY *Espriella's Lett.* (1808) II. 322 Undiseased parts will not convey any ramarkable impression to the examiner. **1879** H. SPENCER *Data of Ethics* xv. 277 Scientific knowledge of organic actions that are undiseased.

undis'figured, *ppl. a.* (UN-¹ 8.)
1720 POPE *Iliad* XXIV. 509 Yet undisfigured, or in limb or face, All fresh he lies. *a* **1873** LYTTON *Pausanias* i, Severe and early training..had left, undisfigured by superfluous flesh, the grand proportions [etc.]. **1897** MISS KINGSLEY *W. Africa* 223 Their teeth..undisfigured by filing.

undisful'filled, *ppl. a.* (UN-¹ 8.)
1823 BENTHAM *Not Paul* 285 So long as the predictor lived, it [*sc.* the prediction] would remain good and undisfulfilled.

undis'graced, *ppl. a.* (UN-¹ 8 and 5 b.)
1748 CHESTERF. *Lett.* cxlvii. (1792) II. 24 If Shakespeare's genius had been cultivated, those beauties..would have been undisgraced by those extravagancies. **1812** BYRON *Ch. Harold* II. xciii, So may our country's name be undisgraced. **1820** KEATS *Hyperion* II. 344 Hyperion, Our brightest brother, still is undisgraced.

undis'guisable, *a.* (UN-¹ 7 b.)
1673 R. HEAD *Canting Acad.* 89 Their speech is undisguisable. **1804** SOUTHEY in Robberds *Mem. W. Taylor* (1843) I. 501 Your language is as undisguisable as my face. **1862** MRS. OLIPHANT *Last of Mortimers* IV. v, Blushing in the most violent undisguisable way.

undis'guise, *sb.* (UN-¹ 12.)
1804 *Europ. Mag.* XLV. 339/2 He told her with equal undisguise, but more warmth, that [etc.]. **1869** *Pall Mall G.* 9 Aug. 11 The bitter candour and reckless undisguise of Heine.

undis'guise, *v.* [UN-² 4.] *trans.* To strip of, or free from, a disguise. Also *refl.* and *absol.*
1638 MAYNE *Lucian* (1664) A iv, Who stopt the mouthes of Oracles,..undisguised their Delusions [etc.]. *Ibid.* 390 As soon as I undisguise him, I shall know the truth. **1655** tr. *Sorel's Com. Hist. Francion* III. 60 You promis'd..to undisguise your selfe, and give me a real account of your more particular Adventures. **1671** CROWNE *Juliana* v, Madam, undisguize, and let the Duke affront you if he dares. **1700** MOTTEUX *Quix.* I. IV. iv, The Curate advis'd him to return it, telling him that he might now undisguise himself. **1871** B. TAYLOR *Faust* (1875) I. iii. 53 Now, to undisguise thee, Hear me exorcise thee.

undis'guised, *ppl. a.* (UN-¹ 8.) **a.** Of things.
a **1500** *Chaucer's Dreme* 1450 The prince,..in plaine English undisguised, Hem shewed hole his journeye. **1656** [see UNARTIFICIAL *a.* 2]. **1663** BP. PATRICK *Parab. Pilgr.* vii, The naked and undisguised practice of real Godliness. **1697** COLLIER *Ess. Mor. Subj.* I. (1709) 165 By parity of Reason, we may court undisguised Ruin. **1726** POPE *Odyss.* XVII. 18 The very truth I undisguised declare. **1828** LYTTON *Pelham* III. iii, A friendly dinner, a family meal, are things from which I fly with undisguised aversion. **1873** HOLLAND *A. Bonnic.* i. 19 With ingenuous and undisguised wonder.
b. Of persons.
1671 MILTON *P.R.* I. 357 Whom thus answer'd th' Arch Fiend now undisguis'd. **1727** DE FOE *Syst. Magic* I. iii. (1840) 79 He did not walk about in person, undisguised and open,..and acting like himself. **1796** MME. D'ARBLAY *Camilla* III. 383 The declared and undisguised pursuer of her favour. **1827** POLLOK *Course T.* VIII. 137 Each,.. undisguised, was what his seeming showed.
Hence **undis'guisedness.**
1814 SHELLEY in Hogg *Life* (1858) II. 494 It proves..the sincerity, undisguisedness, of your passion.

undis'guisedly, *adv.* (UN-¹ 11; cf. prec.)
1611 in *10th Rep. Hist. MSS. Comm.* App. I. 548, I desire your Lo[rdship] should undisguisedly bee informed of yᵉ truthe how things heere passe. **1805** *Ann. Rev.* III. 308 This corn-bill undisguisedly..undertakes to increase the price of necessary food. **1875** POSTE *Gaius* I. (ed. 2) 154 All power was undisguisedly absorbed by the emperor.

undis'guising, *ppl. a.* (UN-¹ 10.)
1813 SHELLEY *Q. Mab* v. 187 Those duties..Are bought and sold as in a public mart Of undisguising selfishness. *Ibid.* IX. 42 Crime..Unblushing, undisguising.

undis'gusting, *ppl. a.* (UN-¹ 10.)
1755 YOUNG *Centaur* i. Wks. 1757 IV. 115 Rendering them..undisgusting, and palateable to all the rational part of mankind.

undis'heartened, *ppl. a.* (UN-¹ 8.)
1827 HALLAM *Const. Hist.* xiv. II. 432 To this one object ..the whole of his heroic life was directed with undeviating, undisheartened firmness. **1877** W. R. COOPER *Egyptian Obelisks* xx. (1878) 104 Undisheartened by this want of success, he waited till the fall of the Nile.

undis'honested, *ppl. a.* (UN-¹ 8.)
1631 T. POWELL *Tom All Trades* 5 While your Land is of virgin reputation, while it is chast, and vndishonested.

undis'honoured, *ppl. a.* (UN-¹ 8.)
1590 SHAKS. *Com. Err.* II. ii. 148 I liue distain'd, thou vndishonoured. **1613** BEAUM. & FL. *Honest Man's Fort.* I. i, Then you were So noble, that I durst have trusted your Embraces.., And yet come from you—undishonor'd. **1638** BROME *Antipodes* III. vii, In money I tender him double satisfaction, With his own wares again unblemished, undishonor'd. **1726** POPE *Odyss.* XXII. 350 Still undishonour'd or by word or deed Thy house, for me, remains. **1850** THACKERAY *Pendennis* lviii, The name of Pendennis..was left undishonoured behind us. **1881** SWINBURNE *Mary Stuart* III. i, I had rather die Thus undishonoured.

undisin'heritable, *a.* (UN-¹ 7 b.)
a **1631** DONNE *Sermons* i. (1634) 35 The undisinheritable sonnes of God.

undis'joined, *ppl. a.* (UN-¹ 8.)
a **1800** COWPER *Odyss.* (ed. 2) v. 431 While yet the planks sustain This tempest undisjoin'd, I will abide A suff'rer on the raft.

undis'jointed, *ppl. a.* (UN-¹ 8.)
1631 WEEVER *Anc. Funeral Mon.* 778 An ashie dry carkasse.., whole and vndisioynted.

un'dislocated, *ppl. a.* (UN-¹ 8.)
[**1775** ASH.] **1876** MRS. WHITNEY *Sights & Ins.* xxix. 286 The wonder was that she..had come off with undislocated vertebræ.

undis'lodged, *ppl. a.* (UN-¹ 8.)
[**1775** ASH.] *a* **1847** CHALMERS *Bridgewater Treat.* (1853) I. i. 64 Moral rectitude still undislodged from its empire.

undis'mantled, *ppl. a.* (UN-¹ 8.)
[**1775** ASH.] **1830** WORDSW. *Elegiac Musings* 28 Oh! severed too abruptly,..Rapt in the grace of undismantled age. **1871** BROWNING *Pr. Hohenst.* 117 The fort which caps the crag, All undismantled of a turret-stone.

undis'mayable, *a.* (UN-¹ 7 b.)
a **1586** SIDNEY *Arcadia* III. viii, Neither could danger be dreadfull to Amphialus his undismayable courage. **1940** W. FAULKNER *Hamlet* III. ii. 187 The face.., bent, in profile or three-quarters, sober and undismayable.

undis'mayed, *ppl. a.* (UN-¹ 8.)
1615 G. SANDYS *Trav.* 83 His body (hers) she imbrac't: and undismaide, Betweene his lips, her cleauing soule conuaide. **1667** MILTON *P.L.* II. 432 With reason hath deep silence and demurr Seis'd us, though undismaid. **1712** BLACKMORE *Creation* III. 227 But undismay'd we face the intrepid foe. **1798** MATHIAS *Purs. Lit.* 7 England is still prepared, and alert..and bold, and undismayed. **1823** SCOTT *Quentin D.* xxii, His look was composed and undismayed. **1855** SINGLETON *Virgil* II. 402 He undismayed remains, His high-souled foe awaiting.

undis'membered, *ppl. a.* (UN-¹ 8.)
1758 J. DALRYMPLE *Ess. Feudal Property* (ed. 2) 50 The extent of the residue of the fief remaining undismembered.

undis'missed, *ppl. a.* (UN-¹ 8.)
a **1800** COWPER *Iliad* (ed. 2) XXIII. 5 Their valiant band Still undismiss'd Achilles thus bespake.

undiso'bliging, *ppl. a.* [UN-¹ 10 + DISOBLIGE *v.* 1 b.] †Not causing disconnexion.
1715 BROOME in Pope *Iliad* I. 235 *note*, All this he would have expatiated upon with Connexions of the Discourses,.. and the most easy,..undisobliging Transitions.

undisonant, *a.* *rare*⁻¹. [f. It. *undisono*, ad. L. *undisonus*.] Making the noise of waves.
1592 R. D. *Hypnerotomachia* 3 b, Their current..still augmented by other undissonant [It. *undisoni*] torrents.

undis'ordered, *ppl. a.* (UN-¹ 8.)
1805 WORDSW. *Prelude* III. 154 If things viewed By poets in old time..May in these tutored days no more be seen With undisordered sight. **1847** DE QUINCEY *Sp. Mil. Nun* Wks. 1853 III. 13 Spanish diet and youth leave the digestion undisordered.

undi'sparaged, *ppl. a.* (UN-¹ 8.)
1636 HEYWOOD *Love's Mistress* III. i, Thus undisparag'd, Phœbus leaves the place. **1770** LANGHORNE *Plutarch* (1879) II. 905/2 Demosthenes..left none of the actions of the King of Macedon undisparaged.

undi'spatchable, *a.* (UN-¹ 7 b.)
1853 MRS. GORE *Dean's Daughter* II. vi. 143 Devoting weeks and months to despatch of undespatchable business.

undi'spatched, *ppl. a.* [UN-¹ 8.]
†1. Not having one's business completed. *Obs.*
c **1610** SIR J. MELVIL *Mem.* (Bann. Cl.) 101 Being yet at Paris on dispatched, I rasauit wretingis to com in Scotland. **1684** *Col. Rec. Pennsylv.* I. 109 They have been soe long un-Dispacht of the Business proposed.
2. Not settled or disposed of.
1614 RALEIGH *Hist. World* II. (1634) 435 This..had caused many men's private businesses to lie undispatched. **1628** in *Buccleuch MSS.* (Hist. MSS. Comm.) I. 267 Your wardenship when I found undispatched I would not let longer to stick. **1721** STRYPE *Eccl. Mem.* II. I. xvi. 134 Which [bill] was..sent up to the lords' house, where it lay undispatched.
3. Not deprived of life; not killed outright.
1589 WARNER *Alb. Eng.* VI. xxxii. 142 But not long His Father moned vndispatcht alike for death and wrong. **1888** STEVENSON *Black Arrow* 71 Here and there..horse or man rolled, undespatched, in his agony.

undi'spatching, *ppl. a.* (UN-¹ 10.)
1648 *Petit. Eastern Assoc.* 4 The tedious Suspensions of the undispatching Parliament.

undi'spellable, *a.* (UN-¹ 7 b, 5 b.)
1839 LADY LYTTON *Cheveley* viii, All of which plunged his wife into an undispellable fit of sulk.

undi'spelled, *ppl. a.* (UN-¹ 8.)
[**1775** ASH.] **1860** BP. S. WILBERFORCE *Addr. Ordination* 105 Delusion on our part and undispelled darkness on theirs. **1877** *In Mem. J. M. Charlton* 2 The shadows of the grave remained undispelled.

†undi'spended, *ppl. a.* (UN-¹ 8.)
a **1483** *Liber Niger* in *Househ. Ord.* (1790) 82 The chaundelers truelye..to bringe to the pantrey the remanentes undispended.

†undi'spensable, *a.* *Obs.* [UN-¹ 7 b, 5 b.]
1. = INDISPENSABLE *a.* 2.
1559 BP. COX in Strype *Ann. Ref.* (1709) I. App. xxii. 51 Your Majesty's learned and godly clergy..do think this commandment of God to be undispensable. *a* **1600** HOOKER *Eccl. Pol.* VII. xiv. §4 Things whereunto everlasting, immutable, and undispensable observation did belong. **1651** HOBBES *Leviath.* II. xxviii. 164 The Punishment of the transgression of a Law undispensable. **1672** H. MORE *Brief Reply* Pref. a 3 This..could never affright me into the neglect of so undispensable a duty.
2. = INDISPENSABLE *a.* 1.
1609 BIBLE (Douay) *Gen.* xvi. comm., The Catholique doctrin..sheweth how pluralitie of wives was..especially since Christ altogether unlawful and undispensable. **1649** MILTON *Eikon.* ix. 84 He was bound..by a most strict and undispensable Oath to preserve that Order.
3. = INDISPENSABLE *a.* 3.
1658 T. WALL *Charact. Enemies Ch.* 27 Religion being.. the undispensable prop of States.
So **†undi'spensably** *adv.* *Obs.*

a **1676** HALE *Prim. Orig. Man.* I. iii. (1677) 81 Some determinate *ubi* or *situs*..is undispensably necessary to every created individual Body.

undi'spensed, *ppl. a.* [UN-^{1} 8.] Not absolved or released by dispensation. Also *absol.*

a **1300** *Cursor M.* 28367 In dedly sin i tok vnscriuen Myn orders.., And..vn-despensed sang i messe. **1604** TOOKER *Fabrique Ch.* 47 He..doth not onely seeke being vnqualified and vndispensed with to procure vnto himselfe two diuerse Ecclesiasticall dignities. **1863** BP. WILBERFORCE in *Life* (1882) III. 87 Then the undispensed are bound, because the dispensed are released. **1902** *Academy* 24 May 526/1 Even undispensed, such [convent] vows do not invalidate a marriage subsequently contracted.

undi'spensing, *ppl. a.* [UN-^{1} 10.] Not giving dispensation.

1643-5 MILTON *Divorce* II. iv, Under such an undispencing covenant as Moses made with them,..[this] cannot give quiet to the brest of any intelligent man.

undi'spersed, *ppl. a.* (UN-^{1} 8, 5 b.)

c **1586** C'TESS PEMBROKE *Ps.* (1823) LXXXIX. iv, What one thy foe did undisperst abide? **1621** QUARLES *Div. Poems, Esther* Medit. xviii. M 3 b, The Sunne (whose beames so bright And vndispers'd, are too-too much refin'd For view). **1673** HICKERINGILL *Greg. F. Greyb.* 284 There is or at least was such a nation undispersed. **1860** ELLICOTT *Life Our Lord* vii. 327 Still followed by the yet undispersed Eleven, our Lord now leaves that upper room.

undi'spersing, *ppl. a.* (UN-^{1} 10.)

1837 CARLYLE *Fr. Rev.* II. I. ii, To..serve any undispersing Assemblage with musket-shot, or whatever shot will disperse it.

†**undi'spiteous,** *a. Obs.*$^{-1}$ (UN-^{1} 7.)

a **1500** *Chaucer's Dreme* 676 Save onely a looke piteous Of womanhead undispiteous That she shewed in countenance.

undis'placed, *ppl. a.* (UN-^{1} 8.)

1802-12 BENTHAM *Ration. Judic. Evid.* (1827) I. 570 The audience in the court remaining undisplaced. **1881** LD. RAYLEIGH in *Nature* XXV. 66 An eye applied to the prism sees the disks undisplaced as a whole.

undi'splayed, *ppl. a.* (UN-^{1} 8.)

1822 BYRON *Heaven & Earth* I. iii, Their flashing banners,..Yet undisplay'd, Save to the Spirit's all-pervading eye.

undis'pleased, *ppl. a.* (UN-^{1} 8.)

a **1500** *Chaucer's Dreme* 925 He would forgive all old trespace And undispleased be of time past. **1631** A. TOWNSHEND *Alb. Triumph* 13 Sit not secure, nor thinke in ease Still vndispleas'd, your selues to please.

†**undi'sponed,** *ppl. a. Sc. Obs.* (UN-^{1} 8.)

1488 *Acta Dom. Conc.* (1839) 93/1 Gif þar be ony of þar gudis in place ondisponit apoun. **1530** *Reg. Privy Seal Scot.* II. 66/1 The tua merk land and ane half..wer in his handis ..undisponit to ony personis. *a* **1651** CALDERWOOD *Hist. Kirk* (1843) II. 299 The reteaning of them in her owne hands, undispouned to qualifeid persouns, is ungodlie.

†**undi'spose,** *v. Obs.* [UN-^{1} 14 and 5 b.] *trans.* = INDISPOSE *v.* (in various senses).

c **1380** WYCLIF *Sel. Wks.* I. 218 But make we no general reule to undispose men on þe dai, whanne þei shulden do workes of liȝt. *c* **1400** *Apol. Loll.* 14 Þat is dedely synne, bi þe wilk a man..vndisposiþ himsilf to tak part of þe merits of þe kirk. *c* **1430** LYDG. *Min. Poems* (Percy Soc.) 23 The wolf ..Saide he maade his water unholsom, His tender stomake to hinder and undispose. **1777** POTTER *Æschylus, Persians* Introd. 458 The poet..indirectly undisposing his countrymen to a continuation of the war.

undi'sposed, *ppl. a.* [UN-^{1} 8, 8 c, 5 b.]

†**1.** Unfitted; unprepared; unqualified. *Obs.*

c **1380** WYCLIF *Wks.* (1880) 191 To maken men wery & vndisposid to studie goddis lawe. **1421** HOCCLEVE *Min. Poems* xxiii. 546 He mischeeueth Where as he wende han recouered be; Vndisposid to dye, steruetb he. *c* **1449** PECOCK *Repr.* III. v. 308 If eny man be..vndisposid vnscapabili, lete him abstene and forbere that he come not into prelacie endewid.

†**2.** Disordered; out of condition. *Obs.*

c **1380** WYCLIF *Sel. Wks.* I. 104 Þus þis lond is undisposid bi þree enemyes of a man. *Ibid.* II. 348 Man þat þus contrarieþ himsilf mut nedis be undisposid bi synne. **1599** DAVIES *Immort. Soul* II. ccclxxvii, The Soule to such a body knit, Whose inward senses vndisposed bee. **1645** QUARLES *Sol. Recant.* xii. 6 Then shall the sinews silver cord be los'd ..: The undispos'd And idle liver's ruby fountain dri'd.

†**3.** Of death: For which one is not prepared.

1421 HOCCLEVE *Min. Poems* xxiii. 474 Lest þat heere-aftir y..In-to lyke peril haaste may and hye Of vndisposid sodein deeth. *c* **1425** *Orolog. Sapient.* v. in *Anglia* X. 359/23, I wepe for þe harmes of vndisposed dethe.

†**4.** Ill-disposed; unfriendly; adverse. *Obs.*

1456 *Rolls of Parlt.* V. 451/1 Your said Besecher, by the untrewe synfull procuryng of the said undisposed persones, ..was endited of Treason. **1472** *Coventry Leet Bk.* 384 If eny mysdoers, or persones vndisposid, be the occasion of eny supportacion. **1621** QUARLES *Div. Poems, Esther* xvii, Some curse Fate, Others blaspheme the name of heau'n, and rate Their vndisposed Starres.

5. Not disposed of; not put to any purpose.

1483 *Rolls of Parlt.* VI. 260/2 The residue of the said money, goodes, and catalles..undistributed and undisposed. **1653** HARTLIB *Discov. Divis. Land* (title-p.), The Fens and other Waste and undisposed Places in England and Ireland. **1711** *Lond. Gaz.* No. 4946/3 The several Quantities of Tin..remaining undisposed. **1827** HALLAM *Const. Hist.* xviii. II. 770 The house took care..to prevent the recurrence of an undisposed surplus.

b. With *of.* (Now usual; cf. DISPOSE *v.* 8.)

1626 B. JONSON *Staple of N.* I. ii, Emissarie Westminster's vndispos'd of yet. **1667** in *10th Rep. Hist. MSS. Comm.* App. V. 29 Other lands undisposed of, now remaining in his Majestie's disposall. **1743** POPE *Last Will* Wks. 1751 IX. 270 All the residue and remainder to be considered as undisposed of, and to go to my next of kin. **1803** tr. *P. Le Brun's M. Botte* III. 124 That preference which would have made him..choose her, if her heart had been undisposed of. **1893** *Bailey's Mag.* Oct. 282/2 Finding himself with some undisposed-of stock.

6. Not inclined or willing, indisposed (*to* or *to do* something).

1590 SHAKS. *Com. Err.* I. ii. 80, I shall breake that merrie sconce of yours That stands on tricks, when I am vndispos'd. **1597** HOOKER *Eccl. Pol.* v. lxviii. § 10 Because the greater part is carelesse and vndisposed to ioine with them. **1650** BAXTER *Saints' R.* I. vii. (1662) 86 That I conceive the reason also, why we are more undisposed to those secret duties.

Hence **undi'sposedness.**

1600 SURFLET *Countrie Farme* III. xxxviii. 504 There hapneth..vnto it [*sc.* the plum-tree] an vndisposednes, through the fault of the gardener. **1658** A. FOX tr. *Würtz' Surg.* II. xii. 95 A rottenness, which you may know by the Patients breath,..and his daily undisposedness. **1675** BAXTER *Cath. Theol.* II. I. 114 Can no man,.. notwithstanding the undisposedness of his Will, yet so far.. prevail against his undisposedness, as [etc.]?

undi'sposing, *ppl. a.* (UN-^{1} 10.)

c **1400** LOVE *Bonavent. Mirr.* (1908) 132 He that taketh mete or drynke wilfully knowynge that it is contrarie to hym and vndisposynge to bodily hele.

†**undispo'sition.** *Obs.* (UN-^{1} 12, 5 b.)

c **1400** *Apol. Loll.* 28 Wan Crist..may not..hele þe folk for þer..vndisposicoun, and vnabilitie to reseyue. *c* **1449** PECOCK *Repr.* III. v. 308 In indisposid persoones bi her vndisposicioun oonli thei ben..occasiouns of vicis.

undis'privacied, *ppl. a.* (UN-^{1} 8.)

1869 LOWELL *Cathedral* 224 He can find a fireside..By throngs of strangers undisprivacied.

undis'proved, *ppl. a.* (UN-^{1} 8.)

1579 J. STUBBES *Gaping Gulf* A iij, I will aunswere such.. peruerse reasons as shall be lefte vndisproued in thys my proofe. **1614** JACKSON *Creed* III. v. § 3 Arguments unrefuted, and probable pledges of God's Spirit undisproved. **1838** MRS. BROWNING *The Sleep* iii, What do we give to our beloved? A little faith all undisproved. **1841** WISEMAN *Remarks on Lett. fr. Palmer* 84, I therefore..consider it to stand as yet undisproved.

†**undi'spunged,** *ppl. a. Obs.* (UN-^{1} 8.)

a **1670** HACKET *Abp. Williams* II. (1693) 120 The Court did all vote..that the Defence should remain undispunged.

undi'sputable, *a.* Now *rare.* [UN-^{1} 7 b and 5 b.] = INDISPUTABLE *a.* I.

1598 SYLVESTER *Du Bartas* II. ii. IV. *Columnes* 218 Undisputable Art, and fruitfull skill, Which with new wonders all the World shall fill. **1650** BULWER *Anthropomet.* 254 Whereof there passe for current many undisputable examples. **1699** BURNET *39 Art.* i. 40, I think it is upon such undisputable grounds. **1886** *New Princeton Rev.* Sept. 156 A wealth of undisputable evidence is at hand.

undi'sputably, *adv.* (UN-^{1} 11 and 5 b.)

1706 E. WARD *Wooden World Diss.* (1708) 107 Our Ships of War are undisputably the best in the World. **1762** [see UNDISPUTEDLY.]

undi'sputed, *ppl. a.* [UN-^{1} 8 and 5 b.]

1. Not disputed or argued *with. rare*$^{-1}$.

1570 FOXE *A. & M.* (ed. 2) 2034/2 So in the end, the bishop making to our ambassadours good countenaunce,.. dismissed them vndisputed wythall.

2. Not disputed or called in question.

a **1625** FLETCHER *Nice Valour* IV. i, That if my anger chance let fall a stroke,..Yet it may pass unmurmur'd, undisputed. *a* **1698** TEMPLE *Ess. Pop. Discontents* Wks. 1720 I. 261 This Moral Principle..is certainly the most undisputed. **1732** BERKELEY *Alciphr.* VI. § 5 If a man assent to the undisputed books, he is no longer an infidel. **1781** COWPER *Truth* 527 Let heathen worthies..Possess, for me, their undisputed lot. **1844** KINGLAKE *Eothen* viii, Her superiority over all others..remained undisputed. **1866** GEO. ELIOT *F. Holt* Introd., A man who..held a position of easy, undisputed authority.

undi'sputedly, *adv.* [UN-^{1} 11: cf. prec.] Without dispute or question.

1778 HUME *Hist. Eng.* (new ed.) I. 200 The reigning prince, provided he be of the royal family, passes undisputedly [**1762** undisputably] for the legal sovereign. **1821** BYRON *Let. to Murray* 7 Feb., The Georgics are indisputably, and, I believe, undisputedly, even a finer poem than the Æneid. **1896** *Cent. Mag.* Feb. 590 He is undisputedly one of the first Latinists of our time.

undi'sputing, *ppl. a.* (UN-^{1} 10.)

1827 POLLOK *Course T.* IX. 49 Inquiring still..to know their duty, When known, with undisputing trust.. performing.

undis'quieted, *ppl. a.* (UN-^{1} 8.)

1627 MAY *Lucan* VIII. O v b, If you, O Parthians, vndisquieted I euer left. **1649** *Test. conc. F. Boehme* ii. 7 The two..witnesses..have remained in their Graves undisquieted by the Babylonians. **1863** H. ALLON *Mem. J. Sherman* Introd. 6 He..spake with the power and passion of full and undisquieted conviction.

undi'ssembled, *ppl. a.* [UN-^{1} 8.]

1. Not feigned or pretended; genuine.

1651 BAXTER *Inf. Bapt.* 97 A reall undissembled Faith. **1697** COLLIER *Ess. Mor. Subj.* I. (1703) 170 An infallible proof of a natural and undissembled goodness. **1748** MELMOTH *Fitzosborne Lett.* lv. (1749) II. 73 Tell me then, with the same undissembled sincerity [etc.]. **1804** LARWOOD *No Gun Boats* 10 Caparisoned for undissembled Field-of-Battle contest.

2. Not disguised or concealed; evident.

1671 MILTON *Samson* 400 She purpos'd to betray me, and (which was worse Then undissembl'd hate) with what contempt [etc.]. **1751** SMOLLETT *Per. Pic.* lxxvi, Emilia.. listened to his protestations with undissembled pleasure. **1814** SCOTT *Wav.* xxix, Callum..enjoyed, with undissembled glee, the ridiculous figure of Mr. Cruickshanks. **1850** HAWTHORNE *Scarlet L.* xi, The anguish in his inmost soul, and the undissembled expression of it in his aspect.

Hence **undi'ssembledness.**

1681 KETTLEWELL *Chr. Obed.* III. viii. 301 The sincerity and undissembledness of our faculties.

undi'ssembling, *ppl. a.* (UN-^{1} 10.)

1613 ZOUCHE *Dove* 28 Helen in her undissembling glasse, Viewing the wrinckles which her age had wrought. **1727** THOMSON *Summer* 904 The Heart Of Innocence, and undissembling Truth. **1788** COWPER *Let. to S. Rose* 29 March, Be assured of an undissembling welcome. **1830** E. E. CROWE *Hist. France* I. 259 The same frank and undissembling temper..made speedy enemies of those whom he disliked.

undi'ssemblingly, *adv.* (UN-^{1} 11; cf. prec.)

1585 CARTWRIGHT in R. Browne *Answ.* 87 If there were but in euery church one truely and vndissemblingly faithfull. **1607** HIERON *Wks.* I. 296 To professe truely and vndissemblingly a dependance onely vpon Christ. **1621** SANDERSON *Serm.* I. 184 Hadst thou not a faithful counsellour.., if thou wouldst but have conferred with him ..undissemblingly?

undi'ssevered, *ppl. a.* (UN-^{1} 8.)

α. **1521** FISHER *Wks.* (1876) 332 Though all theyr workes be vndiuyded & vndeseuered one from another. **1598** STOW *Surv.* 164 They found..the Corps of a woman, whole of skin, and of bones vndeseuered.

β. **1548** PATTEN *Exped. Scot.* G iv b, If they doo assaile vndisseuered, no force can well withstond them. **1556** OLDE *Antichrist* 45 A constant vndisseuered faithe.

†**undi'ssimulate,** *a. Obs.*$^{-1}$ (UN-^{1} 7.)

1652 COTTERELL tr. *Calprenède's Cassandra* I. 21 That warlike, franck, and undissimulate people.

undi'ssimulated, *ppl. a.* (UN-^{1} 8.)

1776 S. J. PRATT *Pupil of Pleas.* (1777) I. 189 Real, undissimulated love. **1779** G. KEATE *Sketches fr. Nat.* (ed. 2) II. 27 All tenderness and undissimulated nature.

un'dissipated, *ppl. a.* (UN-^{1} 8.)

1661 BOYLE *Scept. Chem.* I. 41 That it may not appear absurd to conceive, that such little primary Masses..may remain undissipated. **1733** *Phil. Trans.* XXXVIII. 7 Capable of..conveying the tender medullary Substance.. safe, unhurt, and undissipated to the several Organs. **1779** *Ann. Reg., Hist.* 52/2 If the reduction..of France was the object, the war against her might be pursued with undissipated force. **1830** LD. GRANVILLE in *Life* (1905) I. i. 17 Although you say that it is such an undissipated season.

undi'ssociated, *a. Chem.* [UN-^{1} 8 a.] Of a molecule: whole, not split into oppositely charged ions.

1899 *Jrnl. Physical Chem.* III. 284 The properties of this acid are therefore to be attributed almost solely to the undissociated molecule, $CH_3 \cdot COOH$. **1930** FIELD & WEILL *Electro-Plating* i. 14 The undissociated copper sulphate.. takes no direct part in the plating process. **1965** PHILLIPS & WILLIAMS *Inorg. Chem.* I. vii. 237 At pressures around 1 atmosphere I_2 is largely undissociated at 1000 °K, but largely dissociated at 2000 °K. **1976** *Electrochimica Acta* XXI. 280/1 The activity coefficient of the undissociated acid is taken as unity.

†**un'dissoluble,** *a. Obs.*$^{-1}$ (UN-^{1} 7 and 5 b.)

1587 GOLDING *De Mornay* xv. 264 Now..the Soule of Man is very like the Godhead;..Vniforme, Vndissoluble, and euer-more of one sorte.

undisso'lution. (UN-^{1} 12.)

1662 J. C. CHANDLER *Van Helmont's Oriat.* 267 Under the co-resemblance of immortality, and undissolution.

undi'ssolvable, *a.* [UN-^{1} 7 b and 5 b.] = INDISSOLUBLE *a.*

(*a*) **1611** COTGR., *Indissoluble*, indissoluble,.. vndissolueable. **1622** T. SCOTT *Belg. Pismire* 64 God hath bound vs together by an vndissolueable band of necessitie. **1656** OSBORNE *Adv. Son* 57 This requires Love to be ushered into this undissolveable noose, by Discretion. **1702** ROWE *Tamerl.* III. i, That holy Knot, which ty'd once, all Mankind Agree to hold Sacred, and Undissolvable.

(*b*) **1705** T. GREENHILL *Art Embalming* 153 The Sands.. over-whelm Passengers.., who..are thro' the power of the hot Sun..so dry'd, they become..for ever undissolvable. **1756** F. HOME *Exper. Bleaching* 268 There remained half a grain of powder that was undissolvable by the spirit.

undi'ssolved, *ppl. a.* [UN-^{1} 8.]

1. Not dissolved by loosening, undoing, annulling, dismissing, etc.

1535 *Act 27 Hen. VIII*, c. 26 § 15 Every suche celle shalbe ..ondyssolvyd..as yf this Acte had never be made. **1598** DRAYTON *Heroical Ep.* 23 b, By that firme and vndissolued knot, Betwixt the neighboring French, and bordering Scot. **1649** MILTON *Eikon.* v. 45 As necessity of affaires call'd them, so the same necessity should keep them undissolv'd, till that were fully satisfi'd. **1833** KEBLE *Serm.* vi. (1848) 127 Those members of the Church also believe..the oaths and obligations..undissolved and indissoluble. **1856** FROUDE *Hist. Eng.* I. 166 By the law he could not have formed a second engagement so long as the first was undissolved.

2. Not broken up; not dissolved by natural decay.

1603 KNOLLES *Hist. Turks* (1621) 54 [Andronicus' body] is yet there vndissolued to be seene. **1615** CHAPMAN *Odyss.*

XII. 594 The mast torn down Tore her up piece-meal, and for me to drown Left little undissolved. **1759** JOHNSON *Rasselas* xlvii, It is commonly supposed that the Egyptians believed the soul to live as long as the body continued undissolved.

3. Not reduced to a soft or liquid state; unmelted.

1674 tr. *Scheffer's Lapland* iii. 8 The snows which as well in Summer as Winter continue undissolved. **1694** SALMON *Bate's Dispens.* (1713) 150/1 That which remains undissolv'd..is the acid or saline Part of the Sulphur. **1765** A. DICKSON *Treat. Agric.* (ed. 2) 377 Some things are digested..by some animals, that pass thro' others sound and undissolved. **1807** T. THOMSON *Chem.* (ed. 3) II. 461 The dissolved portion having the properties of a resin; the undissolved, of asphaltum. **1868** *Amer. Naturalist* I. 39 Ice accumulates..during the winter, and lies undissolved until late in spring.

undi'ssolving, *ppl. a.* (UN-¹ 10.)

1712 BLACKMORE *Creation* v. 351 A coherent, undissolving chain Of causes and effects. **1726** THOMSON *Winter* 657 Where undissolving from the first of time Snows swell on snows amazing to the sky. **1805** WORDSW. *Waggoner* IV. 105 A moving shroud To form, an undissolving cloud.

undi'stained, *ppl. a.* (UN-¹ 8.)

1565 COOPER *Thesaurus* s.v. *Incolumis*, To keepe his good name vndisteyned. **1622** WITHER *Philarete* G ij b, I know her Maker will Keepe her vndistained still. **1625** QUARLES *Sion's Sonn.* xvii. 3 Vnblemisht, vndistayned with a spot.

†**undis'tasted,** *ppl. a. Obs.* (UN-¹ 8; cf. DISTASTED *ppl. a.* 2.)

1607 DANIEL *Introd. Poems* Wks. (Grosart) I. 14 There will be found therein, that which..will sufficiently allow T' an vndistasted iudgement fit delight.

undi'stempered, *ppl. a.* (UN-¹ 8.)

c **1589** *Theses Martinianæ* 4 Hee might sitte long enough vndistempered in his chaire for vs. **1634** SIR T. HERBERT *Trav.* 79 See how mischiefe appeares in a louely and vndistempered Scene. *a* **1698** TEMPLE *Ess. Pop. Discontents* Wks. 1720 I. 266 Some Parliament that..shall be cool and undistemper'd from those Heats of Faction. **1814** WORDSW. *Excurs.* v. 487 With undistempered and unclouded spirit.

undi'stend, *v.* (UN-² 3.)

1868 BROWNING *Ring & Bk.* II. 1502 Had Guido..Cloven each head..In one clean cut..—Bidding, who pitied, undistend the skulls.

undi'stilled, *ppl. a.* (UN-¹ 8.)

1600 SURFLET *Countrie Farme* III. lxix. 593 The very water of the vine alone vndistilled doth the like. **1652** FRENCH *Yorksh. Spa* vii. 67 The two first spoonfuls, which were distilled, and the rest undistilled that remained. **1771** *Phil. Trans.* LXI. 125, I found, that..tin distilled or sublimed..would produce finer colours than any solution..of tin, unsublimed or undistilled.

undi'stinct, *a.* [UN-¹ 7 and 5 b.]

1. = INDISTINCT *a.* 3.

1495 *Trevisa's Barth. De P.R.* v. xxiii. h vij/1 Men that ben kyndely dombe ben deef, and they haue voys & all vndystyncte. **1555** EDEN *Decades* (Arb.) 367 Sum yelowe, and sum of vndistinct colours. **1853** MISS MULOCK *Avillon*, etc. II. 274 The image of a dim and undistinct divinity.

†**2.** = INDISTINCT *a.* 1. *Obs.*

1534 MORE *Treat. Passion* Introd., One vndiuisable & vndistinct infinit almighty god. **1610** HEALEY *St. Aug. Citie of God* 13 It doth not proue the persons vndistinct, because so they both do joyntly indure like pains. **1631** WEEVER *Anc. Funeral Mon.* 74 The Church will haue them to be of an vndistinct excellence.

undi'stinction. (UN-¹ 12, 5 b.)

1647 HEXHAM I, Vndistinction, *onverscheydenheydt.* **1662** J. CHANDLER *Van Helmont's Oriat.* Prayer, Tis true indeed, that thou wilt be worshipped by men in the Spirit, but not in such a manner that it may remain in the undistinction of the first object.

undi'stinctive, *a.* (UN-¹ 7, 5 b.)

c **1860** DICKENS *Reprinted Pieces* (1866) 220 As undistinctive Death will come here, one day, sleep comes now. **1888** STOPFORD BROOKE in *Life & Lett.* (1917) II. 398 Undistinctive praise and blame.

†**undi'stinctly,** *adv. Obs.* [UN-¹ 11, 5 b.] = INDISTINCTLY *adv.* 1.

1548 ELYOT, *Indistincté*, vndistinctely. **1597** HOOKER *Eccl. Pol.* v. lxviii §9 To consider..their sundry ouer-sights, first, in equalling vndistinctly crimes with errours. **1602** FULBECKE *1st Pt. Parall.* 100 Yet our law punisheth undistinctly and without difference, the immature eiecting of any of these. **1706** STEVENS I, *Indistintamente*, undistinctly.

†**undi'stingued,** *ppl. a. Obs.*⁻¹ [UN-¹ 9.] Undistinguished.

1398 TREVISA *Barth. De P.R.* VIII. xvi. (1495) v. vij/2 Shappes of thynges whiche ben vnknowen in derknesse and vndystyngued.

undi'stinguish, *v. rare*⁻¹. [UN-² 3.] *trans.* To make undistinguishable.

1690 NORRIS *Refl. Hum. Life* (1695) 132 One Glance whereof shall..undistinguish the greatest Doctor from the most ignorant Peasant.

undi'stinguishable, *a.* [UN-¹ 7 b and 5 b.]

1. Incapable of being made out or discerned; imperceptible.

1590 SHAKS. *Mids. N.* II. i. 100 The queint Mazes in the wanton greene, For lacke of tread are vndistinguishable. **1645** MILTON *Tetrach.* 19 The Form by which the thing is what it is, is oft so slender and undistinguishable. **1768** H. WALPOLE *Hist. Doubts* 92 One does not learn any language..with a good, nay, undistinguishable accent, between Christmas and Easter. **1816** SCOTT *Old Mort.* xxxvi, The city and port..became undistinguishable in the distance. **1872** BLACK *Adv. Phaeton* xii. 171 Two almost undistinguishable figures pacing along.

2. Incapable of being distinguished or discriminated; of which the different elements cannot be distinguished or recognized; inseparably alike.

1679 DRYDEN *Troil. & Cress.* Pref. ⁋26 It has been prov'd already that confus'd passions make undistinguishable characters. **1693** *Humours Town* 128 Drunken Rakes, and dirty Beau's,..besides a number of undistinguishable Mob. **1794** GISBORNE *Walks Forest* III. 9 Where sunk the parting orb, and with the sky In undistinguishable splendor join'd. **1802–12** BENTHAM *Ration. Judic. Evid.* (1827) V. 662 Hope and fear..run into one another and are undistinguishable. **1860** PUSEY *Min. Proph.* 124 The locust [-swarm]..becomes in a few hours one undistinguishable, putrifying, heaving mass.

b. Const. *from.* (Common in recent use.)

1686 PLOT *Staffordsh.* 380 Altogether undistinguishable from the best French wines. **1833–4** J. PHILLIPS *Geol.* in *Encycl. Metrop.* (1845) VI. 674/2 The badger (probably undistinguishable from the common European species). **1870** J. H. NEWMAN *Gram. Assent* I. v. 112 That apprehension..may become almost undistinguishable from an inferential acceptance of the great truth.

†**3.** Indiscriminate. *Obs. rare.*

1702 *Eng. Theophrast.* 86 An undistinguishable Facility shall never fail of meeting with an undistinguishable Infidelity.

Hence **undi'stinguishableness.**

1727 BAILEY (vol. II). **1843** MILL *Logic* I. iii. §11. 93 Resemblance, when it exists in the highest degree of all, amounting to undistinguishableness, is often called identity. **1878** E. WHITE *Life in Christ* (ed. 3) III. xx. 289 The undistinguishableness of generic difference in character.

undi'stinguishably, *adv.* [UN-¹ 11 and 5 b.]

†**1.** Without distinction or difference. *Obs.*

1671 BARROW *Serm.* Wks. 1687 I. 427 So that righteousness and mercifulness..are in Scripture-expression..undistinguishably put one for the other. **1710** *Tatler* No. 270 ⁋5 Gold and silver galloon upon hats..being undistinguishably worn by Soldiers, Esquires [etc.].

2. So as to be undistinguishable.

a **1691** BOYLE *Hist. Air* (1692) 248 Whilst the liquor was hot..they would swim together undistinguishably in the liquor. **1705** T. GREENHILL *Art Embalming* 138 The Humour..assumes no visible Body, but undistinguishably mixes with the pure Air. **1780** BENTHAM *Princ. Legisl.* x. §27 In many instances the desire of pleasure and the sense of pain run into one another undistinguishably. **1869** MᶜLAREN *Serm.* Ser. II. xii. 213 A faint ethereal echo..which blends undistinguishably with its parent sound.

undi'stinguished, *ppl. a.* [UN-¹ 8 and 5 b.]

1. Not separated or kept distinct.

1598 FLORIO, *Indistinto*, vndistinct, vndistinguished, confused. **1647** COWLEY *Mistress, Bathing* v, Her Beauties..will mixt and undistinguisht ly, With all the meanest things that dy. **1760** STERNE *Serm. Yorick* vii. (1784) 197 The undistinguished offers of his services. **1792** WORDSW. *Descrip. Sketches* 161 Where afar rich orange lustres glow Round undistinguished clouds, and rocks. **1879** J. TODHUNTER *Alcestis* 10 If Zeus arms to smite thee,..let us stand one undistinguished mark For his stern thunder!

b. In which no distinction is made or can be observed.

1608 SHAKS. *Lear* IV. vi. 278 (Q 2), O vndistinguish't space of womans wit. **1666** BOYLE *Orig. Forms & Qual.* 30 Nor must we look upon the Universe that surrounds us as upon a moveless and undistinguish'd Heap of Matter. **1727** THOMSON *Summer* 347 A dazling deluge reigns; and all From pole to pole is undistinguish'd blaze. **1814** BYRON *Address Caledonian Meeting* 17 The lowly brave,..Who sleep beneath the undistinguish'd sod. **1851** TRENCH *Poems* 155 Like undistinguished Night, darkening the skirts of Eve.

c. Not distinguished *from* or *by* something.

1612 CHAPMAN *Rev. Bussy d'Ambois* IV. i. 86, I grieve that virtue lives so undistinguish'd From vice in any ill. **1693** DRYDEN *Juvenal* III. 291 Their Habits (undistinguish'd by Degree) Are plain, alike. **1784** COWPER *Task* I. 592 Blest he, though undistinguish'd from the crowd By wealth or dignity, who dwells secure. **1823** SCOTT *Quentin D.* xxxvii, The noise..was of a character so undistinguished by any peculiar or precise sound, that [etc.]. **1882** FARRAR *Early Chr.* I. 491 The majority are only known to us as names, sometimes undistinguished by a single incident.

2. Not made distinct to perception:

a. Indistinct, confused. Now *rare.*

1595 DANIEL *Civ. Wars* II. lxviii, Where diuers-speaking zeale, one murmure findes In vndistinguisht voice to tell their mindes. **1611** FLORIO, *Inarticolata voce*, an vndistinguished voice. **1678** DRYDEN *All for Love* v. i, Some undistinguish'd Words she inly murmur'd. **1781** J. RIPLEY *Sel. Orig. Lett.* 62 Standing upon the bank of a river, muttering undistinguished prayers. **1814** SCOTT *Lord of Isles* II. xxx, Flush'd is his brow,..And undistinguish'd accents broke The awful silence ere he spoke.

b. Not clearly perceived or discerned.

1814 JANE AUSTEN *Mansfield Park* xxxviii, Finding herself undistinguished in the dusk. **1821** SCOTT *Kenilw.* xxxvii, Mixing with the crowd, [he] stood in some degree an undistinguished spectator..of the masque.

3. Not marked by any distinction; not noted or elevated above others.

1600 E. BLOUNT tr. *Conestaggio* 6 Being vndistinguished, and allyed for money with some Noblemen of the country. *a* **1643** W. CARTWRIGHT *Poems, No Drawing of Valentines* Wks. (1651) 242 Cast not in Chloe's Name among the Common undistinguish'd Throng. **1693** CONGREVE in *Dryden's Juvenal* XI. (1697) 283 Who..tho' a Knight, 'mongst common Slaves now stands Begging an Alms, with undistinguisht hands. **1757** W. WILKIE *Epigon.* II. 31 Hissing amidst the Spartan ranks it came, And struck a youth of undistinguish'd name. **1800** *Asiatic Ann. Reg.* 26/2 He remained undistinguished for any thing, except the infamous action, in which [etc.]. **1875** JOWETT *Plato* (ed. 2) I. 140 Would not their sons grow up to be distinguished or undistinguished according to their own natural capacities?

undi'stinguishing, *ppl. a.* [UN-¹ 10.]

1. Making no distinction or difference; not discriminating: **a.** Of persons, personal attributes, etc.

1599 SANDYS *Europæ Spec.* (1629) 229 The blunt and undistinguishing witts of the vulgar. **1641** 'SMECTYMNUUS' *Answ.* §16 (1653) 67 If it be a fault in the impetuous, and undistinguishing Vulgar. **1712** ADDISON *Spect.* No. 291 ⁋7 A sower undistinguishing Critick. **1776** GIBBON *Decl. & F.* vi. I. 160 *note*, The undistinguishing compiler has buried these interesting anecdotes under a load of trivial and unmeaning circumstances. **1836** J. GILBERT *Chr. Atonem.* iii. 102 There is still addressed to undistinguishing minds another objection. **1871** BLACKIE *Four Phases* i. 129 The superficial undistinguishing eye of the general public of Athens.

b. *transf.* Of things.

1665 MANLEY *Grotius' Low C. Wars* 205 There was none of them so imprudent, as to trust their Lives and Fortunes to the undistinguishing Sword of a Forreign Conquerour. **1753** W. ROBERTS *Looker-On* No. 36, These furious advocates..are at issue with all governments..and would involve them all in one undistinguishing ruin. **1821** SOUTHEY *Vis. Judgem.* XI. 19 In undistinguishing battle, Or by pestilence stricken, they fell. **1847** G. HARRIS *Life Ld. Hardwicke* II. 230 Numbers of people..were sacrificed to the undistinguishing vengeance of the victorious army.

c. Const. *of.*

1811 *Henry & Isabella* I. 259 Our..dog.., haply undistinguishing of crimes and evils, kindly fawned upon me.

2. Of actions, etc.: Marked by want of distinction or discrimination; indiscriminate.

a **1677** BARROW *Serm.* xxxvi. Wks. 1686 III. 403 Benefits would not be scattered among the crowd of men with so promiscuous and undistinguishing a freeness. **1710** STEELE *Tatler* No. 204 ⁋7 An undistinguishing Application of Sounds of Honour. **1782** ELIZ. BLOWER *Geo. Bateman* II. 60 But don't you think the ridicule rather too undistinguishing? **1853** RUSKIN *Stones Ven.* III. 104 That opposition was..intemperate, undistinguishing and incautious. **1892** LOUNSBURY *Stud. Chaucer* III. vii. 201 We need not make it an object of undistinguishing depreciation.

undi'stinguishingly, *adv.* [UN-¹ 11: cf. prec.] Without distinction or discrimination.

1665 J. SERGEANT *Sure Footing* 159 To alledge Authorities undistinguishingly..is such a wild proceeding. **1725** *Fam. Dict.* s.v. *Mixing Colours*, 'Till you see it perfectly and undistinguishingly mix'd together. **1780** MRS. COWLEY *Belle's Stratagem* II. i, Her behaviour is undistinguishingly polite to her husband, and all mankind. **1830** MACKINTOSH *Eth. Philos.* Wks. 1846 I. 89 For a time the work was admired more undistinguishingly than its literary character warrants. *a* **1871** GROTE *Eth. Fragm.* v. (1876) 139 No man can blindly and undistinguishingly follow every immediate impulse.

undi'storted, *ppl. a.* (UN-¹ 8.)

1647 H. MORE *Song of Soul* To Rdr. B 3 b, The undistorted suggestions of his own heart. **1662** STILLINGFL. *Orig. Sacræ* III. i. §15 Those more refined..spirits who went only upon principles of pure and undistorted reason. **1814** *Monthly Rev.* LXXIII. 480 In a series of plays which imprint the leading events on the memory in an..undistorted manner. **1881** C. A. YOUNG *Sun* 33 If the planet's edge were..sharp and definite, and the sun's limb undistorted.

undi'storting, *ppl. a.* (UN-¹ 10.)

1823 *Monthly Rev.* CI. 513 A mirror so sincere and so undistorting.

undi'stracted, *ppl. a.* [UN-¹ 8.]

†**1.** Not drawn apart by dissension. *Obs.*⁻¹

a **1649** DRUMM. OF HAWTH. *Hist. Jas. V*, Wks. (1711) 100 To turn the Imperial Crown Hereditary to his own House, which, Germany being all of one Mind and undistracted, he could never have brought to pass.

†**2.** Not drawn aside or perverted; genuine, real.

1656 STANLEY *Hist. Philos.* v. ii. 149 That there is a credible undistracted concurrence, is manifest from Menelaus. *Ibid.*, Such is undistracted phantasy. *a* **1659** OSBORNE *Charac.*, etc. (1659) 126 Valour and Cowardice, both strangers, if not Contrary to the Practice of undistracted Nature.

3. Not diverted or interrupted by other occupations or interests.

1648 BOYLE *Seraph. Love* (1659) 106 He was pleas'd..to admit him to a yet Closer, more Immediate, and more Undistracted Communion with himself. **1683** *Brit. Spec.* 121 By undistracted Prayers to renew their Courage and Patience in their Apostolical Employment. **1817** COLERIDGE *Biogr. Lit.* ii. (1907) I. 30 In order to devote himself, an entire and undistracted man, to the instruction..of his fellow-citizens. **1871** LIDDON in *Life & Lett.* (1904) 155, I..require an amount of undistracted thought which I never get here.

b. Const. *by.*

1759 ROBERTSON *Hist. Scot.* II. Wks. 1813 I. 112 Undistracted by those cares..which occupy and oppress other men. **1852** M. ARNOLD *Self-Depend.* v, Undistracted by the sights they see, These demand not [etc.].

4. Not drawn aside or away *from* something.

1833 LAMB *Elia* II. *Barrenness Mod. Art*, [With] her soul undistracted from Theseus—Ariadne is still pacing the solitary shore. **1862** LYTTON *Str. Story* I. 87 Some one..by whom your thoughts would have been undistracted from the channels into which your calling should concentrate their flow.

Hence **undi'stractedness.**
1660 BOYLE *New Exp. Phys. Mech.* Pref. p. viii, That calmness of Minde, and undistractedness of Thoughts, that are wont to be requisite to Happy Speculations. **1886** *Athenæum* 7 Aug. 166/3 The impression.. as a whole is one of undistractedness and elegance.

undi'stractedly, *adv.* [UN-[1] 11: cf. prec.] Without distraction.
1648 BOYLE *Seraph. Love* iv. (1663) 26 The affections of one being at liberty, to devote themselves more undistractedly to God. **1687** —— *Martyrd. Theodora* iv. (1703) 56 The great advantage of serving God more undistractedly. **1806** A. DUNCAN *Nelson* 66 The attention of every captain could almost undistractedly be paid to the condition of his.. ship. **1872** BENSON in A. C. Benson *Life* (1899) I. 349 The work in God's Church to which I should devote myself undistractedly.

undi'stracting, *ppl. a.* (UN-[1] 10.)
a **1684** LEIGHTON *Exp. Lect. Psalm xxxix*, iii. Wks. 1805 II. 375 It were good we used more easy and undistracting diligence, for increasing of these treasures.

undi'strained, *ppl. a.* (UN-[1] 8.)
a **1400-50** *Alexander* 2779 It semed noȝt ȝoure seruand sire, vndistreyned Vn-to ȝour mekill maieste þis mater to write. **1475** *Aberdeen Reg.* (1844) I. 34 The said Johne his landis and gudis.. to be vncompellit, vndistrengeit.. be ony juge.

undi'straught, *ppl. a.* (UN-[1] 8b.)
1773 J. ROSS *Fratricide* IV. 528 (MS.), His senses Yet undistraught remain. **1874** J. THOMSON *City Dreadf. Nt.* XXI. iii, The keen wolf-hound sleeping undistraught.

undi'stressed, *ppl. a.* (UN-[1] 8.)
1582 in J. H. Pollen *Acts Eng. Martyrs* (1891) 28 He sought for honours uncorrupt, and undistressed joys. **1591** HARINGTON *Orl. Fur.* XXV. lxxiv, He.. sweares that when his Prince were undistrest, The siege quite raised [etc.]. **1614** SYLVESTER *Parlt. Vertues Royall* 191 When for som pretence Hee hath betraid.. his Prince Or yeelded-up som un-distressed Place. **1772** *Test Filial Duty* I. 122 She was sensible an undistressed heroine would make a very uninteresting figure. **1807** WORDSW. *White Doe* VII. 205 She .. Received the memory of old loves, Undisturbed and undistrest. **1897** *Westm. Gaz.* 9 Mar. 2/2 Thousands of pounds go to the relief of undistressed land.

undi'stributed, *ppl. a.* [UN-[1] 8.]
Not distributed. **a.** *gen.*
1483 [see UNDISPOSED *ppl. a.* 5]. **1802-12** BENTHAM *Ration. Judic. Evid.* (1827) II. 508 The keeping of the rule of action .. in one immense and unorganic mass, undistributed. **1869** GLADSTONE *Juv. Mundi* viii. 280 Their journeys are usually undistributed and instantaneous. They set out, and.. arrive.
b. *Logic.* (See DISTRIBUTE *v.* 6.)
1827 WHATELEY *Logic* (ed. 2) 93 You will then have either the middle Term undistributed, or an illicit process. *Ibid.* 96 Another.. is an allowable mood in the third Figure; but in the first it would have an undistributed middle. **1864** BOWEN *Logic* vii. 193 It is a Negative with an undistributed Predicate.

†**undi'stroubled**, *ppl. a. Sc. Obs.* (UN-[1] 8.)
1456 SIR G. HAYE *Law Arms* (S.T.S.) 29 The quhilkis has maid trouble that was clere undistroublit. **1466** *Acta Dom. Audit.* (1839) 5/1 To kepe & defend þe saide elisabeth vndistrublit.. in tyme tocum. **1561** *Reg. Privy Council Scot.* I. 183 To be unharmit, unvexit, unmolestit, and undistrublit.

undis'trustful, *a.* (UN-[1] 7.)
1654 R. CODRINGTON tr. *Iustine* II. 44 [They] had not only undistrustful but delightful feastings together. **1865** MRS. WHITNEY *Gayworthys* xxiii, There were hearts weary often, but undistrustful.

undi'sturbable, *a.* (UN-[1] 7b, 5b.)
1577 KNEWSTUB *Confut.* (1579) 61b, An everlasting fast standing Jerusalem,.. the which is the very true vndisturbable Kingdome. **1883** T. M. HEALY in *Pall Mall G.* 28 Dec. 2/1 Then in turn the new Act becomes perfect, final, and undisturbable.

undi'sturbed, *ppl. a.* [UN-[1] 8, 5b.] Not disturbed or interfered with.
1. In predicative use.
It is doubtful whether *vndistrobbed* in *Alexander* 3418 (see UNDISTURBLED *ppl. a.*) belongs here, or is an error for *vndistrobled* = UNDISTROUBLED *ppl. a.*
a **1610** HEALEY *Epictetus* (1636) 70 So shall thy thoughts remaine undisturbed. **1622** in Foster *Eng. Factories Ind.* (1908) II. 73 Wee shall not be undisturbed till the one or other of us have given some kind of sattisfaxione. **1712** ADDISON *Spect.* No. 381 ¶4 His Imagination is always clear, and his Judgment undisturbed. **1794** S. WILLIAMS *Vermont* 90 When undisturbed, this animal is without any ill scent. **1807** [see UNDISTRESSED]. **1876** BANCROFT *Hist. U.S.* I. Introd. 2 Even the enemies of the state.. have liberty to express their opinions undisturbed.
b. Const. *by*, †*with*.
1635-56 COWLEY *Davideis* I. 80 Where their vast Court the Mother-waters keep, And undisturb'd by Moons in silence sleep. **1674** *Jackson's Recant.* D4, On that day the Roads are most quiet, being undisturbed with great quantities of People. **1796** MME. D'ARBLAY *Camilla* IV. 258 Undisturbed by the various noises around him. **1827** LYTTON *Falkland* I. 36, I am undisturbed by a single intruder. **1875** JOWETT *Plato* (ed. 2) I. 373 Like the sleep of him who is undisturbed even by the sight of dreams.
2. In attrib. use: **a.** Of things, places, or persons.
1627 MAY *Lucan* V. H4b, Shee vtters from an vndisturbed brest Fain'd words with no confused murmure flowing. **1692** BENTLEY *Boyle Lect.* 108 All the parts of an undisturb'd fluid. **1728** ELIZA HEYWOOD tr. *Mme. de Gomez's Belle A.* (1732) II. 272 To retire from Court; and in some safe and undisturb'd Retreat.. pass the remainder of my days. **1819** KEATS *Fame* 12 The undisturbed lake has crystal space. **1898** J. T. FOWLER *Durh. Cath.* 33 The undisturbed grave-covers of the bishops buried beneath.
b. Of conditions, courses of action, etc.
1647 CLARENDON *Hist. Reb.* I. §162 A full, entire, and undisturbed Peace. **1728** ELIZA HEYWOOD tr. *Mme. de Gomez's Belle A.* (1732) II. 105 This Night was pass'd.. in all the Charms of an undisturbed Tranquillity. **1765** BLACKSTONE *Comm.* I. 197 By a long and undisturbed descent from his ancestors. **1862** ANSTED *Channel Isl.* IV. xxiii. (ed. 2) 538 Undisturbed possession during thirty years is a good title. **1884** *Manch. Exam.* 17 May 4/7 The volumes .. are left to undisturbed repose on the shelves of our public libraries.
Hence **undi'sturbedness.**
1649 RAINBOW *Funeral Serm. 29 May* 25 They have health, leisure and undisturbedness of understanding. **1718** *Entertainer* No. 34. 229 None has given us a truer idea of.. Moderation, Calmness and Undisturbedness.

undi'sturbedly, *adv.* [UN-[1] 11: cf. prec.] Without being disturbed; tranquilly, quietly.
1647 H. MORE *Song of Soul* Notes 350 For infinite animadversion can discern all things unmixtly and undisturbedly. **1683** CAVE *Ecclesiastici* Introd. p. lxxi, The Gentiles undisturbedly brought their Sacrifices.. to their Images. **1768-74** TUCKER *Lt. Nat.* (1834) I. 517, I expect.. that the healed will accompany me as undisturbedly as the unwounded along our future progress. **1842** F. E. PAGET *Milford Malvoisin* 94 She.. slept as calmly and undisturbedly as the infant at her breast. **1877** LADY BRASSEY *Voy. Sunbeam* xix, Ravens croak, and pigeons coo, as undisturbedly as if.. in the deepest woodland solitude.

undi'sturbing, *ppl. a.* (UN-[1] 10.)
1607 MARKHAM *Cavel.* II. (1617) 123 Letting him goe and come continuall with easie, soft, and vndisturbing mouings. **1814** WORDSW. *Excurs.* VIII. 161 The punctual stars.. in the firmament of heaven Glitter—but undisturbing, undisturbed. *a* **1851** MOIR *Poems, Angler* ii, At his feet.. An undisturbing spaniel lay.

†**undi'sturbled**, *ppl. a. Obs.* (UN-[1] 8.)
a **1400-50** *Alexander* 3418 The passage shall.. plane be & opyn, þe Comers oute of athir coste to cayre vndistourblett [*v.r.* vndistrobbed].

†**un'dit**, *v. Obs.* [UN-[2] 3.] *trans.* To open (up). Also *fig.*
a **1225** *Leg. Kath.* 1821 Ne we nusten hwet we duden aðet he undutte us, & tahte us treowe bileaue. *c* **1275** in *O.E. Misc.* 153/234 Vurþer þer his on oþer put þat ne cumeþ neuer vndut. *c* **1300** *Childhood Jesus* 1038 Þo Jhesu crist was i gon, vndut was þe Ouene a non.

un'ditch, *v.* [UN-[2] 5.] *trans.* To get (a vehicle, etc.) out of a ditch (by hauling, levering, or the like). So **un'ditching** *vbl. sb.* (usu. *attrib.*).
1920 *Blackw. Mag.* Feb. 272/1 The unditching beam could not be used. **1928** *Daily Tel.* 6 Mar. 9/7 All [the tanks] were either repaired or unditched. **1971** 'D. RUTHERFORD' *Clear Fast Lane* 40 In the [car's] boot were the spares and.. a couple of unditching mats.

undi'urnal, *a.* (UN-[1] 7.)
1832 LYTTON *Eugene A.* IV. vii, The solemn and undiurnal mood.. was reflected back in hues so gentle. **1837** —— *E. Maltrav.* IX. v, The novel glow of Ernest's undiurnal and stately thoughts.

undi'verging, *ppl. a.* (UN-[1] 10.)
1795 COLERIDGE *Lett.* (1895) 139 The wisdom of making Self an undiverging Centre.

†**undi'versificated**, *ppl. a. Obs.* (UN-[1] 8.)
1659 H. MORE *Immort. Soul* I. ii. 11 The Idea of a meer Undiversificated Substance.

undi'versified, *ppl. a.* (UN-[1] 8.)
1684 T. BURNET *Theory Earth* I. 291 To conceive it [*sc.* matter] undivided, undiversified, and unmov'd. **1862** *Mem. R. Craig* ix. 170 The life.. is generally of a very uniform and undiversified character.

undi'verted, *ppl. a.* [UN-[1] 8.]
1. Not turned aside.
1665 BOYLE *Occas. Refl.* IV. ix. 57 Though these Grounds have not any patent Passages, whereby to derive Water and Fatness from the River, and therefore must suffer the greatest part of it to run by them undiverted. *a* **1711** KEN *Psyche* Poet. Wks. 1721 I. 205, I was ambitious of that Height, To gain of Heav'n an undiverted Sight. **1794** MATHIAS *Purs. Lit.* (1798) 313 By a patient continuance and undiverted attention to academical studies. **1859** MISS MULOCK *Dom. Stories* (1862) 124 Her mind, undiverted from the past by any charms of the present, became dead to all outward impressions. **1859** I. TAYLOR *Logic in Theol.* 308 Such persons find it difficult to read their Bible in undiverted remembrance of what it is.
2. Not entertained or amused.
1792 G. WAKEFIELD *Mem.* 8 The reader, however, may not be undiverted with its unaffected simplicity and pathos.

undi'vertible, *a.* (UN-[1] 7, 5b.)
1856 MRS. BROWNING *Aur. Leigh* VI. 21 Even so direct, So sternly undivertible of aim, Is this French people. **1880** *Daily Tel.* 4 Mar., The true and undivertible highroads of Eastern traffic.

undi'vertibly, *adv.* (UN-[1] 11, 5b.)
1865 BUSHNELL *Vicar. Sacrif.* V. 81 A few of the passages that persist most undivertibly in this kind of testimony.

undi'verting, *ppl. a.* (UN-[1] 10.)
1697 COLLIER *Ess. Mor. Subj.* II. (1703) 195 The charms of authority made Cato aver that old age was none of the most undiverting periods of life. **1754** SHEBBEARE *Matrimony* (1766) II. 260 These accounts might furnish out a Novel not undiverting and certainly useful. **1859** *Sat. Rev.* 12 Mar. 293/1 A character not altogether undiverting.

undi'vested, *ppl. a.* (UN-[1] 8.)
1753 RICHARDSON *Grandison* (1781) V. xxxvi. 223, I cannot be so great, so undivested,.. as you can be! **1853** MRS. MOODIE *Life in Clearings* 154 The animals undivested of their harness were browsing peacefully.

undi'vestedly, *adv.* (UN-[1] 11, 15.)
1748 RICHARDSON *Clarissa* (1811) II. x. 64 As undivestedly as possible of favour or resentment.

undi'vidable, *a.* (and *sb.*). Now *rare.* [UN-[1] 7b, 5b.] Incapable of being divided; indivisible.
1548 R. HUTTEN *Sum of Diuinitie* I 3b, A person is an undeuidable substaunce in vnderstandyng. **1594** CAREW *Huarte's Exam. Wits* 97 In respect of which selfe qualitie, Galen tearmeth them vndiuidable. **1617** HIERON *Wks.* II. 215 Hee knew iustification and sanctification to be vndiuidable. **1650** EARL MONM. tr. *Senault's Man bec. Guilty* 82 Eternity.. in it's undividable unity. **1831** T. HOPE *Ess. Orig. Man* I. 48 Since mere space is undividable in parts separate from each other.
b. As *sb.* An indivisible thing.
a **1739** JARVIS *Quix.* II. IV. viii. (1749) 351 Reducing the undivideables into money, he shared it among his company.

undi'vidably, *adv. rare.* (UN-[1] 11: cf. prec.)
1611 COTGR., *Indivisiblement*, indiuisibly, vndiuidably. *a* **1641** BP. MOUNTAGU *Acts & Mon.* (1642) 472 Schisme and heresie are not the same thing, nor ever incident individably to the same parties.

undi'vided, *ppl. a.* [UN-[1] 8 and 5b.]
1. Not divided, separated, or broken up into parts.
c **1412** HOCCLEVE *De Reg. Princ.* 4469 The blessid trinite, Whiche þat euery man of cristen byleeue Knoweth an vndyuyded vnite. **1480** *Cov. Leet Bk.* 442 And so ye togeder, as on holy body vndevided, to sewe for the redresse therof. **1553** EDEN *Treat. New Ind.* (Arb.) 16 Theyr fete.. hauing fyue toes like hoeues vndeuided. *c* **1620** ROBINSON *Mary Magd.* 952 A robe hee wore, like to his essence, pure; That vndiuided; vndeuided hee. **1662** STILLINGFL. *Orig. Sacræ* III. ii. §18 Some of them [*sc.* particles] are more undivided then others are. **1780** *Mirror* No. 100, One great undivided impression, or an uninterrupted chain of congenial events. **1837** P. KEITH *Bot. Lex.* 374 The feet.. are single and undivided, as in the horse. **1869** TOZER *Highl. Turkey* II. 152 One unbroken level, which.. presents an undivided area of dry and yellow soil.
b. Not separated or parted from each other.
1521 [see UNDISSEVERED *ppl. a.*]. *c* **1600** SHAKS. *Sonn.* xxxvi, We two must be twaine, Although our vndeuided loues are one. **1626** BACON *Sylva* §752 There have been some Men, that have had their Teeth undivided, as of one whole Bone. **1760-72** H. BROOKE *Fool of Qual.* (1809) IV. 34 In death we will be undivided. **1822** SHELLEY *Epitaph* I These are two friends whose lives were undivided.
2. Not divided by disagreement or dissension.
c **1440** LYDG. *Hors, Shepe & G.* 510 Vndevided with herte, will & thouht To doon her office as nature hath hem wrouht.
3. Not divided between persons; shared or held jointly or in common. Also quasi-*adv.*, jointly.
1544 tr. *Littleton's Tenures* 67 They ought by the lawe to occupy suche landes and tenementes in comon, and vndeuyded to take the profytes in comon. **1660** R. COKE *Power & Subj.* 1 To suppose.. all men to be equal, and to have a common and undivided Right to all things. **1713** C'TESS WINCHELSEA *Misc. Poems* 243 Your unentailed, your undivided Air, Where no Proprietor was ever known. **1817** SHELLEY *Rev. Islam* IX. xxix, Let those.. Insult with careless tread, our undivided tomb. **1877** RAYMOND *Statist. Mines & Mining* 247 It.. is owned by Lewis Reese and Co.,.. who hold an undivided half interest.
b. Not divided between different objects; concentrated on, devoted to, directed towards, one object; whole, entire.
1746 HERVEY *Refl. on Flower Garden* 81 Be it thy one undivided Aim to glorify Him! **1779** *Mirror* No. 13, Where the undivided attention has leisure to brood over the few.. objects which surround him. **1856** *N. Brit. Rev.* XXVI. 261 A course of study.. sufficient to occupy the undivided time of the longest life. **1876** BANCROFT *Hist. U.S.* I. Pref., The present revision, to which a solid year of close and undivided application has been devoted.
c. Not shared by others; confined to one person.
1867 PEARSON *Hist. Eng.* I. 39 The success of Agricola, showed that the country was not too large for an undivided command. **1878** BOSW. SMITH *Carthage* 177 On his own undivided responsiblity, he crossed the straits.
Hence **un'dividedness.**
1889 ABP. BENSON in *Life* (1899) II. 283 To illustrate the undividedness of the Church of Wales and England.

undi'videdly, *adv.* [UN-[1] 11: cf. prec.] In an undivided manner; without division.
1539 *Act 31 Hen. VIII*, c. 1 §1 Dyuers.. haue lyke righte .. in the same maners,.. jointly or in common undevidedly togither with other. **1624** GATAKER *Transubst.* 107 Under them all and each particle of them undevidedly remaining. **1681** FLAVEL *Meth. Grace* vi. 122 Christ is offered to us in the Gospel, intirely and undividedly, as cloathed with all his offices. **1704** NORRIS *Ideal World* II. xii. 438 This universal nature which so undividedly communicates itself to all that is intellectual. **1848** MILL *Pol. Econ.* II. viii. §1. 347 The case in which the produce of land and labour belongs undividedly to the labourer. **1887** BP. W. HOW in *Mem.* (1898) 225 Pray for me that God will give me grace.. to be more undividedly His.

†**undi'vidible**, obs. var. UNDIVIDABLE *a.*
1569 J. SANFORD tr. *Agrippa's Van. Artes* 65b, Betweene the *Atomi*, that is undiuidible parts.

† **undi'vidual**, *a. Obs. rare.* [UN-[1] 7 and 5 b.] Indivisible; = INDIVIDUAL *a.* 1.

1603 J. DAVIES (Heref.) *Microcosmos* 195 Shee is Prides second selfe, or other name, Monsters distinct, yet vndiuiduall. *a* **1661** FULLER *Worthies, Worc.* III. (1662) 172 Indeed true courage and courtesie, are undividuall Companions.

undi'vinable, *a.* (UN-[1] 7 b, 5 b.)

1611 COTGR., *Indivinable*, vndiuinable, most obscure, not to be ghessed at. **1858** CARLYLE *Fredk. Gt.* VI. iii. (1872) II. 159 He..was complimentary to a degree,—for reasons undivinable to Wilhelmina.

undi'vine, *a.* (UN-[1] 7 and 5 b.)

1685 H. MORE in Norris *Theory of Love* (1688) 191 It were a thing Disangelical, if I may so speak, and undivine. **1732** BERKELEY *Alciphr.* v. §19 If divines are quarrelsome, that is not so far forth as divine, but as undivine and unchristian. **1837** CARLYLE *Misc. Ess.* (1888) V. 161 With force of genius she represses..her Undivine Idea. **1860** RUSKIN *Unto this Last* (1862) 134 All attempt at concealment implies some practice of the opposite, or undivine science.

undi'vined, *ppl. a.* (UN-[1] 8.)

1852 BAILEY *Festus* 500 The sunsmile of Salvation beamed..Unrecognized—unrecked of—undivined. **1880** 'VERNON LEE' *Stud. Italy* III. ii. 122 An obscure youth with undivined talents.

undi'vinelike, *adv.* (UN-[1] 7 c.)

1649 MILTON *Eikon.* xvii. Wks. 1851 III. 465 How undivinelike writt'n, and how like a worldly gospeller.., posterity no doubt will be able to judge.

undi'vinely, *adv.* [UN-[1] 11.]

†**1.** In a manner unbefitting a divine. *Obs.*

1618 DANIEL *Coll. Hist. Eng.* 182 The Bishop of Hereford ..concludes most undevinely, that an aking..Head of a Kingdome was of necessity to be taken of. **1657** J. WATTS *Vind. Ch. Eng.* 110 You not onely inartificially but undivinely say From the University, whereas every good gift is from above, as the Apostle saith.

2. In a manner which is not divine.

1884 *Congregational Year Bk.* 65 There was nothing so undivinely merciless as the divine beauty of Greece.

undi'vining, *ppl. a.* (UN-[1] 5 d.)

1848 LYTTON *Harold* IX. vii, Undivining the solemnity of the appointed snare.

undi'visible, *a.* (UN-[1] 7 and 5 b.)

1495 *Trevisa's Barth. De P.R.* XIX. cxxiii. mm iij/2 That nombre is par that is departyd in euen nombres alwaye vnto one that is vndiuysible. **1533** MORE *Wks.* 1131/2 For he seeth..that the soule is vndiuisible and is in euery part of the body, and in euery part it is whole. **1561** T. NORTON *Calvin's Inst.* I. 7 Let Epicure answer me, what meting of vndiuisible bodies..bringeth to passe [etc.]. **1907** G. B. SHAW *John Bull's Other Island* Pref. p. xix, A supporter of Church and State one and undivisible.

undi'vorceable, *a.* (UN-[1] 7 b.)

1825 COLERIDGE *Aids Refl.* (1848) I. 205 From the same reluctance to abandon the too dear and undivorceable Eve. **1884** *Encycl. Brit.* XVII. 86 The musical moiety undivorceable from the literary half.

undi'vorced, *ppl. a.* (UN-[1] 8.)

1744 YOUNG *Nt. Th.* v. 1057 These dy'd together; Happy in ruin! undivorc'd by death! [Also in recent use.]

undi'vorcing, *sb.* (UN-[1] 12.)

1644 MILTON *Divorce* (ed. 2) II. ix. 51 Questionlesse this were a hardheartednesse of undivorcing, worse then that in the Jewes.

undi'vorcing, *ppl. a.* (UN-[1] 7.)

1643 MILTON *Divorce* 13 Made the thrall of heavines and discomfort by an undivorcing Law of God, as he erroneously thinks.

undi'vulged, *ppl. a.* (UN-[1] 8.)

1605 SHAKS. *Lear* III. ii. 52 Tremble thou Wretch, That hast within thee vndivulged Crimes Vnwhipt of Iustice. **1854** J. S. C. ABBOTT *Napoleon* (1855) I. xxxi. 477 He.. listened, with emotions undivulged, to the acclamations of seventy thousand voices. **1883** A. DOBSON *Fielding* vi. 167 A secret that, to this day, remains undivulged.

un'dizened, *ppl. a. rare.* (UN-[1] 8.)

1601 HOLLAND *Pliny* II. 298 The peasants..forbid their wives..to carie their rockes and distaves undizened or bare.

undo (ʌn'duː), *v.* [OE. *an-*, *on-*, *undón* (see UN-[2] 3 and DO *v.*), = OFris. *un(d)dua* (WFris. *ont-*, *ûntdwaen*), MDu. and Du. *ontdoen*, OS. *an(t)dôn*, *-duan* (MLG. *entdôn*), OHG. *anttoan*, *in(t)duon*, etc. (MHG. *entuon*).

The absence or scarcity of material illustrating senses 1 and 3 in the 17th and 18th centuries is remarkable; the evidence suggests that, in these senses, the word was revived or reintroduced into literary use by Scott.]

I. 1. *trans.* To unfasten and open: **a.** A door, gate, or window.

c **893** K. ÆLFRED *Oros.* VI. i. 254 Þa wearð eft Ianes duru andon,..þeh þær nan ȝefeoht þurhtoȝen ne wurde. *c* **1000** *Ags. Psalter* (Thorpe) xxiii. 7 Undoð nu eowre ȝeatu,..and onhlidað þa ecan ȝeata. **11..** *Grave* 20 in *Anglia* V. 290 Nefst ðu nenne freond..Ðæt æfre wndon ðe wule ða dure. *c* **1175** *Lamb. Hom.* 5 Þet faire ȝet me hat hit, &..nefre ouer xii monþe nis hit undon bute to dei. *c* **1250** *Gen. & Ex.* 603 Arches windoȝe undon it is, ðe Rauen ut-fleȝ. *c* **1325** *Lai le Freine* 183 The porter of the abbay aros,..The chirche dore he vndede. *c* **1386** CHAUCER *Miller's T.* 541 The wyndow she vndoth, and that in haste. **1412–20** LYDG. *Chron. Troy* IV. 4691 We for fer dar nat issen oute, Nor be so bolde to vndone a gate. **1520** in *Collect.* (O.H.S.) I. 100 Vndo your dore. **1581** A. HALL *Iliad* VI. 114 The dores of gold she doth vndoe, vnfolded, rich and large. **1801** SCOTT *Eve St. John* xvii, The door she'll undo, to her knight so true. **1821** —— *Kenilw.* xxxii, The Earl undid the lattice, and stepped out. **1841** DICKENS *Barn. Rudge* ix, Undo the shop window, that I may get in that way. **1880** MRS. PARR *Adam & Eve* II. 63 She undid the gate, and held it half open.

absol. *a* **1300** *K. Horn* 1069 (Camb. MS.), He com to þe gateward... Horn bad undo softe. **1390** GOWER *Conf.* I. 243 This Geta cam thanne ate laste Unto the dore and seide, 'Undo'. *c* **1425** *Seven Sages* 1410 (P.), At hys dore he wolde inne,..He schof ther-onne and bade undo.

b. A box, sack, bale, etc.

c **1000** ÆLFRIC *Gen.* xlii. 27 Þa undyde hira an his sacc. *a* **1300** *Cursor M.* 5004 Þai..did þair fardels be vndon. *c* **1315** SHOREHAM I. 2148 He seȝ a bok was fast ischet;..Ne myȝte hy no man ondo. *c* **1350** *Will. Palerne* 4846 Þe clerk þanne deliuerli vndede þo letteres. *c* **1412** HOCCLEVE *De Reg. Princ.* 1112 Vn-to his cofre he dressith hym in hye;..He it vndoth, and opneth. *c* **1450** *Mirk's Festial* 85 Then made he men to vndo þe tombe. **1466** *Paston Lett.* II. 293, I sende yow..iij. tracle pottes of Geane;..they weer neuer ondoo syns that they come from Geane. **1535** *Act 27 Hen. VIII*, c. 14 §4 Which packes..be not vndone nor opened at their arriual within the portes. **1573** BARET *Alv.* O 144 To vndooe, or open a letter sealed. **1853** M. ARNOLD *Scholar Gipsy* xxv, [The] Tyrian trader..on the beach undid his corded bales.

fig. *c* **1300** *Sarmun* xxxvi. in *E.E.P.* (1862) 5 Vn-do þin hert þat is iloke wiþ couetise. *a* **1310** in Wright *Lyric P.* xviii. 58 Swete Jhesu,..Undo myn herte ant liht ther-yn. **1596** DRAYTON *Legends* iii. 106 What is that Man, by whom thou art controll'd, Or hath the Key of Reason to vndoe thee?

†**c.** To open by unlocking or uncovering. *Obs.*

a **1122** *O.E. Chron.* (Laud MS.) an. 656, Ȝif hwa hit hælt, S. Petre mid heofne keie undo him heofenrice. *a* **1300** *Cursor M.* 6611 Þaa holes, quen þai þam vndid, þai fand bot wormes creuland emid. *Ibid.* 6725 If animan vndus a pitt, And siþen wil it noght ditt.

†**2.** To open (the mouth or eyes). *Obs.*

a **1000** *Kentish Gloss.* in Wr-Wülcker 62 *Aperientur* [*labia mea*], siont ondone. *c* **1000** ÆLFRIC *Hom.* I. 548 He undyde his muð, and hi lærde. *c* **1055** *Byrhtferth's Handboc* in *Anglia* VIII. 317 Þæt he undo his eaȝan. *c* **1175** *Lamb. Hom.* 121 Imong alle þere pine..ne undude he nefre ene his muð. *c* **1250** *Gen. & Ex.* 3971 Balaam it spureð and smit ðor-on; And god vndede ðis asses muð. **1297** R. GLOUC. (Rolls) 7185 He gan as he awoke of slepe is eyen þo vndo. *c* **1420** *Lay Folks Mass Bk.* 82 Lorde un-do my lyppis. *c* **1430** *Syr Gener.* (Roxb.) 684 Yit a little his eyen he vndede.

3. To unfasten by untying or by releasing from a fixed position; to unfix. Also in fig. context.

c **950** *Lindisf. Gosp.* John i. 27 Ðæs ic ne am wyrðe þætte ic undoe [*Rushw.* ondoe] his ðuong scoes. *c* **1000** ÆLFRIC *Hom.* I. 572 On ðære ylcan nihte Godes engel undyde þa locu ðæs cweartернes. *c* **1250** *Gen. & Ex.* 2114 Ne was non so wis man in al his lond, ðe kude vn-don ðis dremes bond. **13..** *Cursor M.* 17357 (Gött.), [þai] vndid þair lock all wid þe kay. **1382** WYCLIF *Mark* i. 7 Of whom I..am not worthi for to vndo, or vnbynde, the thwong of his schoon. *c* **1440** *Promp. Parv.* 365/1 Ondoon, or ondo lokys or speryngys, *aperio.* *c* **1450** *Mirk's Festial* 248 Oure lady aperet..yn þe prison, and vndyd his bondes. **1542** UDALL *Erasm. Apoph.* 230 b, Writhen..with so diffuse a knotte, that no man could vndooe it. *c* **1586** C'TESS PEMBROKE *Ps.* (1823) LXVIII. ii, The prisoners chaines are by his hands undone. **1605** SHAKS. *Lear* V. iii. 309 Pray you vndo this Button. **1683** MOXON *Mech. Exerc., Printing* iv. 44 The Cheeks may..receive the Head..without un-doing the Cap and Winter. **1805** SCOTT *Last Minstrel* v. xxii, Some friendly hand Undo the visor's barred band! **1818** BYRON *Juan* I. cxxxvii, Do pray undo the bolt a little faster. **1868** MORRIS *Earthly Par.* (1870) I. I. 431 She..turned the box round,..undid The clasp, and fearfully raised up the lid.

b. To unfasten the clothing of (a person).

1633 ROWLEY *Match at Midn.* IV, *Wid*[*ow*]. Alas! you will undo me. *Alex.* No, no, I will undo myself, look ye. **1841** DICKENS *Barn. Rudge* ix, Having undone her mistress, as she phrased it (which means, assisted to undress her). **1899** T. M. ELLIS *3 Cat's-Eye Rings* 90 'Now undo me. I shall get into bed.' 'Yes, my lady.'

†**4.** To unbind; to release or free from a bond, bandage, covering, etc. *Obs.*

c **930** *Laws Athelstan* i. 23 Beon þreo niht, ær mon þa hond undo. *c* **950** *Durham Rit.* 42 From allvm vsiȝ..synnvm.. vndo. *c* **1250** *Gen. & Ex.* 581 Ilc wateres springe here strengðe undede. *c* **1290** *S. Eng. Leg.* I. 34/30 Nov, he seide, we schullen iseo..3weþer he þe mai a-ȝein me vndo. *a* **1300** *Cursor M.* 14970 A moder ass yee sal þar find, And yee hir sal vn-do Vte of hir band. *c* **1380** *Sir Ferumb.* 1310 Oundo þis prysouns on & on;..þey schulleþ out of þis sory won. *c* **1400** *Melayne* 785 The kynge vndid his hede alle bare. **1513** DOUGLAS *Æneid* VI. vi. 45 Sche,..with that word, the branch schew and vndid, That preualie ondir hir clok wes hid.

†**5. a.** To remove, take away; to detach, cut off.

c **1275** LAY. 19205 Merlyn hadde al his craft ondo of þan kinge. **1340** *Ayenb.* 106 Þe yefþe of wysdom, þet uestneþ ..þe herte in god,..þet hi ne may by ondo ne to-deld. **1513** DOUGLAS *Æneid* IV. xii. 117, I man Vndo this hair, to Pluto consecrait.

†**b.** To cut up (an animal). *Obs.*

13.. *Gaw. & Gr. Knt.* 1327 Quykly of þe quelled dere a querre þay maked,..& didden hem derely vndo. *c* **1400** *Master of Game* (MS. Digby 182) xxxiii, Þenne he shulde charge whome hym lyste to vndo þe deere. **1486** *Bk. St. Albans, Hunting* e iii, When ye haue slayn the boore.., Ye shall vndo hym vnflayne when he shall be dight.

†**c.** To cut open; to open with a knife. *Obs.*

c **1440** *Anc. Cookery* in *Househ. Ord.* (1790) 451 Take pykes, and undo hom on the bale. *c* **1440** *Pallad. on Husb.* I. 601 Al esely me may vndo the skyn With prickyng of a nelde or of a pyn. *a* **1450** MYRC *Par. Pr.* 99 Teche the mydwyf that scho hye For to vndo hyre wyth a knyf, And for to saue the chyldes lyf. **1672** WALKER *Paræm.* 34 Undone, as ye would undoe an Oyster. **1688** J. GRUBB in *Roxb. Ball.* (1888) VI. 726 George undid the Dragon just as you'd undo an oyster.

†**6.** *intr.* To go apart; to open; to become unfastened, come undone. *Obs.*

1122 *O.E. Chron.* (Laud MS.), Se wolcne undide on fower healfe and faht þær to ȝeanes. *c* **1300** *Harrow. Hell* 138 (Harl. MS.), Helle gates y come nou to, ant y wole þat heo vndo. *c* **1500** in Hazlitt *E.P.P.* III. 109 At the dore I will assaie, If it will undoe. **1548** in S. Haynes *St. Papers Cecil* (1740) 99 The Lady Elizabeth heryng the Pryvie-Lock undo,..ran out of hir Bed.

II. 7. *trans.* To annul, cancel, rescind (something done, effected, or decided on); to reduce to the condition of not having been done, effected, decided, etc.

c **970** in Birch *Cartul.* (1887) III. 417 Þet hyra nan næ undo þe ic to ðam haliȝum mynstrum binnan þære byrig ȝedon hæbbe. *a* **1122** *O.E. Chron.* (Laud MS.) an. 656, Leidon þa Godes curs..[on him] þe ani þing undyde þæt þær wæs ȝedon. **1123** *Ibid.* an. 1123, He sæde þone cyng þæt hit wæs to ȝeanes riht,..ac se cyng hit nolde undon. *c* **1250** *Gen. & Ex.* 3014 Pharaon wroð herte on hard, And vndede hem ðat forward. **1297** R. GLOUC. (Rolls) 5692 He vndude alle þe luþer lawes þat me huld biuore, & gode lawes broȝte vorþ. *c* **1315** SHOREHAM I. 1669 For þet compleþ þet spoushod..þat hyt ne may be ondon. *c* **1400** *Beryn* 3355 For I have made a bargeyn, þat may nat be vndo. **1495** *Act 11 Hen. VII*, c. 56 §2 Provided alweys that this present acte extend not..to undo eny your lettres patentes. *a* **1533** LD. BERNERS *Gold Bk. M. Aurel.* (1546) B viij, Julius Cesar.. adnulled and vndyd all that Sylla hadde made. **1605** SHAKS. *Macb.* v. i. 75 What's done, cannot be vndone. **1651** HOBBES *Leviath.* II. xix. 96 The diligent appearance of a few of the contrary opinion undoes to day, all that was concluded yesterday. **1680** BAXTER *Answ. Stillingfl.* I. 72 And what Princes do, they have power to undo. **1709** ADDISON *Tatler* No. 108 ¶5 To disappoint and undo what the most refined Spirits have been labouring to advance. **1768** TUCKER *Lt. Nat.* II. I. xiv. 196 Annihilating time and space, undoing past events or producing contrary ones. **1820** SHELLEY *Œd. Tyr.* I. 384 With a little common sense,..Only undoing all that has been done. **1873** DIXON *Two Queens* XXII. viii, No one could recall a case in which the peers had undone the finding of a grand jury.

absol. **1440** *Bone Flor.* 1511 He seyde, Thou haste wychyd me,..Undo or thou schalt abye. **1577–82** BRETON *Floorish upon Fancie* Wks. (Grosart) I. 6/1 To doo, and vndoo too, so that they may obtaine Their mistresse loue. **1593** SHAKS. *3 Hen. VI*, II. vi. 105 Warwicke as our Selfe, Shall do, and vndo as him pleaseth best. **1697** VANBRUGH *Prov. Wife* I. i, Methinks, they do and undo, and make but bad work on't. **1803** WORDSW. *Sonn. Liberty* xxii. 3 One man..Raised up to sway the world, to do, undo.

b. To reverse the doing or making of (some material thing or effect) so as to restore the original form or condition.

1426 LYDG. *De Guil. Pilgr.* 11328 Tel me..Why makestow, & vndost ageyn Thy werk [*sc.* mats] so offte sythe a day? **1606** SHAKS. *Ant. & Cl.* II. ii. 210 Whose winde did seeme To gloue the delicate cheekes which they did coole, And what they vndid did. **1632** SANDERSON *Serm.* I. 309 He never knoweth the end of his work: what he doth now, anon he must undo. **1679** MOXON *Mech. Exerc.* vii. 125 It is sometimes used when Carpenters have committed error in their work, and must undo what they did, to mend it. **1797** *Encycl. Brit.* (ed. 3) XVI. 484/1 It will not stop till it has turned as often as the end *m* has been twisted, and now all the twist will be undone. **1853** *Arab. Nts.* (Rtldg.) 572 He went up..to the workmen, and..made them..undo all they had yet finished. **1866** GEO. ELIOT *F. Holt* i, She liked to insist that work done without her orders should be undone from beginning to end.

8. To destroy; to bring to naught; to do away with; to take away, remove. Now *rare.*

c **950** *Lindisf. Gosp.* Mark xiv. 58 Ic undoe *vel* ic toslito [L. *dissolvam*] tempel. *c* **1175** *Lamb. Hom.* 7 Ne swincke þu nefre swa muchel, a hit bið undon. *c* **1250** *Gen. & Ex.* 3902 Quat stungen man so saȝ ðor-on, ðat werk him sone al was vn-don. *a* **1275** in *O.E. Misc.* 101 Hwenne deþ heom lat to þe murehþe þat neuer ne byþ undon. **13..** *E.E. Allit. P.* B. 562 Hym rwed þat he hem vp-rerde.., & efte þat he hem vndyd, hard hit hym þoȝt. **1382** WYCLIF *Matt.* v. 17, I came not to vndo the lawe, but to fulfille. *c* **1425** *Eng. Conq. Ireland* 94 Thay comen ayeyn hym..for to mak hym turne ayeyne; other, to vndo hym ryght yn the watyr. *c* **1440** *Pallad. on Husb.* I. 284 Vnhusbondynge vndoth fertilite. *c* **1482** J. KAY in Gibbon *Crusades*, etc. (1870) 135 To undoo and subuerte the holy cytee of Rome. **1573** TUSSER *Husb.* (1878) 73 Look daily well to them, least dogs vndoo them. **1638** SIR T. HERBERT *Trav.* (ed. 2) 303 The Bannyan is..so innocent, as not to undoe the silliest vermin. **1669** PEPYS *Diary* 31 May, Having done now so long as to undo my eyes almost every time that I take a pen in my hand. **1703** ROWE *Fair Penit.* I. i, Nor tell him that which will undo his Quiet. **1788** *Trifler* No. 14. 186 This hypothesis however is undone by the manifest design and order displayed through the whole creation. **1871** JOWETT *Plato* I. 499 The love of Aristogeiton and the constancy of Harmodius had a strength which undid their power.

9. To destroy in respect of means or position; to ruin. †Also (*refl.*) with (*out*) *of*.

1390 GOWER *Conf.* I. 193 Thurgh the conseil of you tuo I stonde in point to ben undo. **1477** *Paston Lett.* III. 199, I beseche yow that I maye have an assyngnement of suche dettes..; ffor..I sholde ellys wylfully ondoo myselffe. **1483** CAXTON *G. de la Tour* C v b, For a lytel thynge ye haue vndo yow. **1531** *Star Chamb. Cases* (Selden) II. 187 Extending vtterly to defame, inpouerisshe and vndoo your seid oratours. **1573** TUSSER *Husb.* (1878) 24 The rich it compelleth to paie for his pride; the poore it vndooeth on euerie side. **1612** *Two Noble K.* III. vi. 137 Our Folly has undon us. **1687** A. LOVELL tr. *Thevenot's Trav.* I. 32 It is never heard in Turkie, that a man hath undone himself by House-keeping. **1712** ARBUTHNOT *John Bull* II. iii, A foolish and negligent husband, who..was undone by his wife's elopement from him. **1798** S. & HT. LEE *Canterb. T.* II. 15 A single error undid him. **1852** MISS YONGE *Cameos* I. i. 5 England had been well-nigh undone by them, when the spirit of her greatest king awoke. **1867** MORRIS *Jason* II. 81 For surely mayst thou lean upon me, when..a king with wrong Would fain undo thee.

(*b*) **1621** J. TAYLOR (Water P.) *Unnat. Father* Wks. (1630) 136/2 He was enticed to vndoe himselfe out of all his earthly possessions. **1628** GAULE *Pract. The.* 4 He hath quite vndone himselfe of Money, Wit [etc.].

c. To injure (a person) seriously. *rare.*
1530 PALSGR. 767/2, I undo one by any..hurt done to his person by reason of any stroke. **17..** *Christmas Ba'ing* xxi. in *Skinner's Misc. Poet.* (1809) 130 An't had na been for Davy Mair, The rascals had ondune him.

d. To ruin by seducing. Also *absol.* Now *rare.*
1612 SHELTON *Quix.* I. iii. 16 Doing many wrongs, solliciting many widdowes, vndoing certaine maidens. *a* **1695** PRIOR '*Whither would my passion run*' i, Losing Her I am undone, Yet would not gain Her to undo Her. **1792** WOLCOT (P. Pindar) *More Money* II. ix, As Darkness oft turns Pimp to undo a belle. **1809** MALKIN *Gil Blas* II. vii. ¶14 In my eyes he was created to undo.

9. To explain, interpret, expound. Now *rare.*
Sometimes with suggestion of sense 3.
a **1300** *Cursor M.* 4474 Said ioseph,..I sal vn-do þe wel þi sueuen. *Ibid.* 12206 Vndos me first quat es alpha. ? *a* **1366** CHAUCER *Rom. Rose* 9 Macrobes, That..vndothe vs the auysioun That whilom mette kyng Cipioun. **1393** LANGL. *P. Pl.* C. III. 40 Dauid vn-doþ hit hym-self, as þe doumbe sheweþ. *c* **1450** *St. Cuthbert* (Surtees) 680 Ga in my blissing þi mayster to, He sall þis dreeme þe vndo. **1581** PETTIE *Guazzo's Civ. Conv.* II. (1586) 82, I praie you..vndo me the knot of this Gentrie, which I see to be verie intricate. **1618** FLETCHER *Women Pleas'd* IV. i, Here may be so much wit (though much I fear it) To undo this knotty question. **1654** WHITLOCK *Zootomia* 252 Commend them to such as can undo a Text (as they tearm it) with as much ease as a bow-knot. **1833** TENNYSON *Two Voices* 232 In seeking to undo One riddle, and to find the true.

undo, obs. variant of UNDONE *ppl. a.*

un'doable, *a.* (UN-[1] 7 b.)
1865 CARLYLE *Fredk. Gt.* XVIII. ii. VII. 113 'Difficult, not undoable,' persists the King.

undoch(t: see UNDOUGHT.

†**un'docible**, *a.* [UN-[1] 7, 5 b.] = INDOCIBLE.
1653 R. SANDERS *Physiogn., Moles* 17 He is undocible and stubborn. **1668** H. MORE *Div. Dial.* I. xxxi. (1713) 69 You see..that I am not altogether an undocible Auditor of Metaphysicks. **1702** DE FOE *Reform. Manners* 52 The hardn'd Guilt undocible appears. **1722** —— *Col. Jack* (1840) 157 A negro..perfectly untractable, undocible.

†**un'docile**, *a. Obs.* (UN-[1] 7 and 5 b.)
1656 COWLEY *Pindar. Odes, Plagues Egypt* 241 What Blindness..did there e'er Like this undocil King's appear? **1703** *Secret Policy Jansenists* (ed. 2) 25 They give out they are Undocil, but the truth is, they are not Instructed.

un'dock, *v.* [UN-[2] 5.] *trans.* To take (a ship) out of a dock; sometimes *spec.*, to launch.
1750 *Naval Expos.* 15 On docking and undocking Ships. **1804** *Trans. Soc. Arts* XXII. 277 Enabling large ships to be docked, suspended, and undocked, the same spring tides. **1897** *Westm. Gaz.* 30 Sept. 5/2 Before the *Lynx* could be docked it was necessary to undock..another destroyer.
transf. To separate a lunar module from its command ship; also *absol.*
1966 *Time* 23 Sept. 67 On the third day of the flight, Conrad undocked Gemini and used his thrusters to back slowly away from the Agena. **1969** *Observer* 2 Mar. 2/8 The astronauts..will crawl from the command ship through a tunnel into the LEM. They will then undock and separate the LEM from the command ship. **1970** N. ARMSTRONG et al. *First on Moon* xiii. 324 You can undock at your convenience.
Hence **un'docking** *vbl. sb.*
1966 *Life* 14 Jan. 88 We discussed undocking, but we had to be sure that the tumbling rate at the instant of separation would be low enough to keep us from colliding. **1969** *Daily Tel.* 8 Mar. 1/2 The 'undocking' of the two [modules] was the first step in the dress rehearsal that will have to work equally faultlessly if two Americans are to step on to the moon later this year.

un'docked, *ppl. a.* (UN-[1] 8 + DOCK *v.*[1])
1677 *Lond. Gaz.* No. 1231/4 A light dun Colt,..three years old,..undockt. **1802** [see UNCROPPED 2]. **1859** F. MAHONY *Rel. Father Prout* 375 Remotest posterity..would enjoy thy book undocked of its due proportions.

un'doctor, *v.* (UN-[2] 6 b.)
[**1598** FLORIO, *Disdottorare*, to vndoctor, to degrade a doctor.] **1833** MRS. CARLYLE in Froude *Carlyle, First Forty Years* II. 353 My brother-in-law is a paragon of the class,..but he is so by..undoctoring himself.

un'doctored, (*ppl.*) *a.* (UN-[1] 8, 9.)
1803 in *Spirit Pub. Jrnls.* VII. 370 No diploma did he bring from Jutland, but came undoctored and undubbed. **1882** *Med. Temp. Jrnl.* L. 85 It would be much better to use the spirit undoctored.

un'doctrinal, *a.* (UN-[1] 7.)
1863 GEO. ELIOT *Romola* xxv, Brave undoctrinal lovers of a sober republican liberty, who preferred fighting to arguing.

un'doctrined, *ppl. a.* (UN-[1] 7.)
1869 BLACKMORE *Lorna Doone* i. (1891) 3 Any boy, soever small and undoctrined.

un'documented, *ppl. a.* (UN-[1] 8.) That has not been documented; *spec.* in *U.S.*, not having the appropriate legal document or licence. Also *absol.*
1883 *Boston Herald* 12 May 2 During such undocumented period. **1886** *Navigation Laws U.S.* 456 (Index), *Documents* Of vessels, or undocumented. **1888** *Athenæum* 4 Aug. 153/2 The inexact and undocumented synthesis of the insufficient student. **1919** *Statutes at Large U.S.A.* XL. 602 Every undocumented vessel, operated in whole or in part by machinery,..shall be numbered. **1977** *New Yorker* 23 May 112/3 On the list were, among other things,..undocumented workers (illegal aliens). **1979** *Tucson* (Arizona) *Citizen* 28 Apr. 6 A/3 The bishop..sees it as an effective way to bring about social change for the elderly, undocumented, alcoholics and drug users. **1984** *New Yorker* 28 May 52/2 When undocumented workers are picked up, the Immigration Service encourages them to accept a sort of plea bargain.

un'doer[1]. [f. UNDO *v.* + -ER[1].]
†**1.** An expounder, interpreter. *Obs.*
1382 WYCLIF *Jas.* Prol., So also of interpretouris, or vndoeris, in to Latyn speche thei were turned treuly. *c* **1440** *Promp. Parv.* 365 Ondoar, or expownare, *expositor, interpres.*
2. One who opens or unfastens. *rare.*
c **1440** *Promp. Parv.* 365/1 Ondoare, or opynnare of thyngys schet or closyd.., *apertor.*
3. A destroyer, wrecker, ruiner.
c **1440** *Promp. Parv.* 365/1 Ondoare, or dystroyare, *destructor.* **1456** SIR G. HAY *Gov. Princes* Wks. (S.T.S.) II. 101 Thus ar the tymes of somer and wynter bathe doare and undoare to all erdly thing that growis under the hevyn. **1567** DRANT *Horace, Ep.* I. xv. E vj, Th' vndoer, tempest, and the hell of al the shambles then. **1598** R. BERNARD tr. *Terence, Adelphos* v. iii, Loe heere at hand the common corruption and vndoer of our children. **1633** HEYWOOD *Eng. Trav.* IV, This my customary comming hither, Hath bin to base and sorded purposes: To..be mine owne vndoer. **1796** C. ANSTEY *Pleaders' Guide* (1803) 171 Sure Law was made to be the undoer Of just such Nincompoops as you are! **1844** MRS. BROWNING *Drama of Exile* 423, I now confess myself thy death And thine undoer. **1885** R. L. & F. STEVENSON *Dynamiter* 161 Greed..has been your undoer.
b. *spec.* One who ruins a woman; a seducer.
1703 ROWE *Fair Penit.* IV. i, Think, whom I shou'd devote to Death and Hell, Whom Curse, as my Undoer, but Lothario. **1760–72** H. BROOKE *Fool of Qual.* (1809) II. 49, I awakened..in the arms of my cruel and accursed undoer. **1847** LYTTON *Lucretia* II. xiv, The child of..your betrayer, your undoer, stands between the daylight and your son.

un'doer[2]. *rare*[−1]. [UN-[1] 12.] One who does not act or perform.
1628 FELTHAM *Resolves* II. 232 Hope without Action is a barren vndooer.

un'doffed, *ppl. a.* (UN-[1] 8.)
c **1440** *Alph. Tales* 173 And so [the priest] þe shone lefte vndofte vnto his servand did þaim off. **1854** MISS BAKER *Northampt. Gloss.*, *Undoffed*, undressed. 'He hasn't been undoffed this two days.'

undog'matic, *a.* (UN-[1] 7.)
1857 PUSEY *Doctr. Real Presence* i. 108 Melancthon's mind however was undogmatic. **1894** DRUMMOND *Ascent Man* 9 Of all men the Evolutionist..must be humble, tolerant, and undogmatic.

undog'matical, *a.* (UN-[1] 7.)
1863 *Q. Rev.* CXIV. 571 It was only on the most dogmatic of all sciences..that he lived for the purpose of making all teaching undogmatical.

un'doing, *vbl. sb.*[1] [f. UNDO *v.*]
†**1.** Exposition; interpretation. *Obs.*
a **1330** *Seuyn Sages* (W.) 2352 He scholde..brenge a besaund to offring, And of his sweuen have undoing. **1382** WYCLIF *Gen.* xl. 8 And Joseph seide to hem, Whether not of God is the vndoyng? *c* **1425** WYNTOUN *Cron.* IV. xxvi. 2576 Discripcion is wrytynge In til our propyr vndoynge. *c* **1440** *Promp. Parv.* 365/1 Ondoynge, or expownynge, *exposicio.*
2. The action of opening, unfastening, taking apart, loosening, etc.
c **1375** *Sc. Leg. Saints* vi. (*Thomas*) 477 Of þat ee þe vndoynge Is of oure harte & vndirstandinge. *a* **1400** *Pauline Ep.* (Powell) 1 Cor. vii. 27 If þou art bowndyn to a wif, seeke þou not vndoyng. *c* **1440** *Promp. Parv.* 365/1 Ondoynge, or opynynge of schettellys, or sperellys, *apercio.* **1486** *Bk. St. Albans, Hunting* e iii, Now of thage & undoyng of the boore. **1598** FLORIO, *Disciolare*,..to put off hose and doublet without vndoing of points. **1613** PURCHAS *Pilgrimage* (1614) 484 The heeles of their shoeres are seldome pulled up, to saue labour of vndoing them. **1897** *Allbutt's Syst. Med.* II. 912 They all bring about a loosening of the frame-work of..nervous matter... The muscular system also..shows a like undoing.
3. a. The action of bringing to nought, destroying, or ruining; the fact of being so dealt with; the state of being undone; also (with *a*), an instance of this.
Quotations under (*a*) illustrate the active, those under (*b*) the passive, use of the word.
(*a*) **1398** TREVISA *Barth. De P.R.* x. iii. (Tollem. MS.), It is þe leste party and laste in undoynge of the body. **1423** *Rolls of Parlt.* IV. 198/2 In hy udoyng to the Kynges Liege peple, and ayenis the ordenaunce and statuts. *c* **1440** *Promp. Parv.* 365/1 Ondoynge, or dystroyynge, *dissipacio, destruccio.* *c* **1475** *Golagros & Gaw.* 497 May nane do thame na deir with vndoyng. **1598** FLORIO, *Sfaccimento*, a defacing,..a defeasance, an vndooing. **1617** HIERON *Wks.* II. 358 If thou leauest out the manner of doing, this is an vndoing to thy doing. **1671** FLAVEL *Fount. Life* v. 13 An Undoing to him in point of Reputation.
(*b*) *c* **1400** *Laud Troy Bk.* 9125 The Grekes were in point of vndoyng: Ne hadde ther comen ther riche kyng. **1415** SIR T. GREY in *43rd Rep. Dep. Kpr. Rec.* (1882) 583 Hit has broghte me to þis shame and undoyng. **1503–4** *Plumpton Corr.* (Camden) p. cxiii, Sir Roger Hastings is at the point of undoinge, because hee hath not money to pay where he ought to pay. **1577** tr. *Bullinger's Decades* II. vi. 171/1 Neither doest thou read that the state..of the Israelites was euer at any time in greater daunger and peril of vndooing. **1614** R. TAILOR *Hog hath lost Pearle* IV, How many country Clyents then might rest, Free from vndooing! *a* **1716** SOUTH *Serm.* (1744) XI. viii. 183 He that ventures to be a surety for another, ventures an undoing for his sake.
b. With possessive pronoun or genitive.
Chiefly in passive sense.
1377 LANGL. *P. Pl.* B. xv. 589 Danyel of her vndoynge deuyned and seyde [etc.]. *c* **1440** *Jacob's Well* 127 He took redyly þo ȝiftes, & þat was cause of his vndoyng. **1478** *Paston Lett.* Suppl. (1901) 151 Now he ys uppon hys makyng by vertues governance, or undoyng to the contrarye. **1562** PILKINGTON *Expos. Abdias* Pref. 16 They saved your lyves and goods, not seeking your undoinge when it laye in their handes. **1609** HOLLAND *Amm. Marcell.* 353 For, exposed he was..to the accesse of as manie as sought the undoing of others. **1679** J. GOODMAN *Penit. Pard.* II. i. (1713) 157 His undoing was his making, and his misfortune proved his recovery. **1740** RICHARDSON *Pamela* (1824) I. 64 You see your undoing has been long hatching. **1823** BYRON *Juan* XIV. lxxxv, The latter works its own undoing. **1852** THACKERAY *Esmond* III. ix, He was not the first that has..brought about his own undoing.
c. In the phrase ***to*** (one's) ***undoing.***
? **1456** *Paston Lett.* Suppl. (1901) 59 Thei wuld put alle juparte up on me to myn utter ondoyng. **1526** *Pilgr. Perf.* (W. de W. 1531) 97 b, Lest he gete helpe of thy superyour, & so vanquysshe y[e] to thy vtter vndoynge. *a* **1548** HALL *Chron., Edw. V*, 5 b, Whiche..might abuse the name of his commaundemente to any of our vndoyng. **1621** ELSING *Debates Ho. Lords* (Camden) App. 138 By that meanes all his creditors came upon him to his utter undoinge. **1641** W. HAKEWILL *Libertie of Subject* 83 That desperate motion that had been made against them to all their utter undoings. **1883** WHITELAW *Sophocles, Ajax* 402 But me the child of Zeus..plagues To my undoing.
4. A cause of ruin or destruction.
1390 GOWER *Conf.* III. 229 Which was to him his undoinge. *a* **1450** *Knt. de la Tour* (1906) 60 Adam..beleued his wyff, the whiche was dethe and vndoyng to hym and her, and to us all. **1576** in Feuillerat *Revels Q. Eliz.* (1908) 414 It is an accion of accompt..like to be the vtter vndoinge both of him and his. **1605** CHAPMAN *All Fools* II. i. 197 It had beene her undooing t' have hime seene. **1659** RUSHW. *Hist. Coll.* I. 420 The Soldiers brake out into great disorders..; they were a terror to all, and an undoing to many. **1727** GAY *Begg. Op.* I. iv, Mary-bone and the Chocolate-houses are his Undoing. **1818** SCOTT *Hrt. Midl.* xxiii, She will tell the truth, if it should be the undoing of her. **1871** FREEMAN *Norm. Conq.* (1875) III. xiii. 264 The marriage of Emma had well nigh been the undoing of England.
5. a. The action of reversing, annulling, etc.
1540 *Act 32 Hen. VIII*, c. 30 §1 The said judgementes..shall stande..without any reuersell or vndooyng of the same. **1611** COTGR., *Rompement*,..a cancelling, dissoluing, infringing, vndoing. **1650** B. *Discolliminium* 16 Our Trade of doing, and undoing, will be endlesse. **1866** J. H. NEWMAN *Let. to Pusey* 36 He..became man, that by what way the disobedience arising from the serpent had its beginning, by that way also it might have an undoing. **1891** J. WINSOR *Columbus* ii. 50 When Isabella decreed the undoing of Columbus's kidnapping exploits.
b. *Psychoanal.* The obsessive repetition of a ritualistic action as if to undo some previous event, action, or attitude, or to signify that it never happened, usu. a symptom of obsessional neurosis.
1927 L. P. CLARK tr. *Freud's Inhibition, Symptom & Anxiety* vi. 42 The precautionary measures are rational, the abolitions through undoing are irrational, magical in nature. **1960** HINSIE & CAMPBELL *Psychiatric Dict.* (ed. 3) 770/2 Expiatory acts, counter-compulsions, and some forms of compulsive ceremonials and counting compulsions are among the more frequent expressions of undoing. **1965** ROSEN & GREGORY *Abnormal Psychol.* iv. 75/2 A magical attempt to wipe out a real or fancied guilt is termed undoing. The individual engages in ritualistic behavior. **1972** H. J. EYSENCK *Encycl. Psychol.* III. 366/2 *Undoing*, an (inner) defense mechanism which allows appeasement of a guilt feeling about a forbidden motive gratification that has already occurred.

un'doing, *vbl. sb.*[2] *rare*[−1]. [UN-[1] 12.] The omission or neglect of doing; non-performance.
1587 GOLDING *De Mornay* ii. 25 To speake properly, we must not seeke whence commeth the doing of euill, but whence commeth the vndoing of good.

un'doing, *ppl. a.* [f. UNDO *v.*] Ruinous, destructive.
1654 TUCKNEY *Death Disarmed* 33 It is an undoing gain to break their arm by catching at a feather. **1681** FLAVEL *Meth. Grace* xvi. 305 Little do such men know how..they put an undoing cheat upon their own souls for ever. **1793** ANNA SEWARD *Lett.* (1811) III. 292 The present fashion of head-dress..has an undoing influence upon youth and beauty.

un'doingness. *rare*[−1]. [UN-[1] 12.] Inaction.
1640 O. SEDGWICK *Christs Counsell* 192 Forgetfulnesse keeps us..in an estate of barrennesse and undoingnesse.

undo'mestic, *a.* [UN-[1] 7.]
1. Not caring for, not pertaining to, home life or duties.
1754 RICHARDSON *Grandison* V. lviii. 385 That wives and daughters were never more faulty, more undomestic, than at present. **1806** R. CUMBERLAND *Mem.* (1807) II. 281, I am very rarely called off by avocations of an undomestic kind. **1857** DUFFERIN *Lett. High Lat.* (ed. 3) 5 The undomestic Mr. Ebenezer Wyse.
2. Unlike a home; lacking the character of a home.
1798 COLERIDGE *Lett.* (1895) 265 When the tears rolled out of my eyes, and this naked, undomestic room became again visible. **1883** *Century Mag.* Oct. 859/1 As undomestic a looking pile of brick and mortar as was ever put together.

undo'mesticate, *v.* (UN-[2] 6 a.)
1754 RICHARDSON *Grandison* I. xlvii. 326 The turn our Sex take in *un*-domesticating themselves. **1799** HAN. MORE *Strict. Mod. Syst. Fem. Educ.* XVI, Clubs..generate..every temper and spirit which tends to undomesticate.

undo'mesticated, *ppl. a.* (UN-[1] 8.)
1834 J. S. MILL in *Monthly Repos.* VIII. 411 To remain ..undomesticated and without a home. **1847** WEBSTER (citing Chalmers). **1926** G. B. SHAW *Transl. & Tomfooleries* 9 Mrs Billiter, an elderly housekeeper, has something of the

same undomesticated air as the room. 1972 P. M. North *Mod. Law Animals* ii. 41 The second category is that of more normally peaceful, but undomesticated, animals.

un'done, *ppl. a.*[1] [UN-[1] 8b. Cf. OFris. *ondan* (N.Fris. *ündōn*), MDu. *ongedaen* (Du. *-daan*), MHG. *ungetân* (G. *-than, -tan*).]

1. Not done; unaccomplished, uneffected.

a 1300 *Cursor M.* 13176 His comandment was noght vn-dun, For he was heued and þat als sun. *c* 1380 Wyclif *Wks.* (1880) 90 He mot leue goddis comaundement vndon. *c* 1440 *Jacob's Well* 114 3if.. þou leve vnsayd or vndo þat is nedefull .. þanne is it dedly synne. *a* 1450 Myrc *Par. Pr.* 1187 Hast þou any pylgrimage laft vn-do When þou were i-ioynet þer-to? 1535 *Act 27 Hen. VIII*, c. 25 Euery parishe.. shal lose & forfait .xx.s. for euery moneth, in whiche it is omitted and vndone. 1585 T. Washington tr. *Nicholay's Voy.* III. xxi. 110 [They] goe on such pilgrimage, leauing vndone al other houshold or common affaires. 1678 Butler *Hud.* III. II. 160 The Publick Business is undone, Which still the longer 'tis in doing, Becomes the surer way to Ruine. 1706 Prior *Ode to the Queen* xix, Nought done the Hero deem'd, while ought undone remain'd. 1759 Johnson *Rasselas* xxx, I must not.. leave at last undone what I came hither only to do. 1791 Mrs. Radcliffe *Rom. Forest* iv, They went out of the shop together, leaving my horse's shoe undone. 1847 Helps *Friends in C.* I. 5 If I leave it undone, some one else will do it to my mind. 1871 Macduff *Mem. Patmos* vi. 74 The sword completed what the fire had left undone.

b. As *sb.* That which is not done.

1872 Ruskin *Arrows of Chace* (1880) II. 208 The condemnation.. is all for the *undones* and not for the *dones*.

2. Not done *away*, not removed.

1679 C. Nesse *Antichrist* 204 While this Vail and face of Covering is undone away.

un'done, *ppl. a.*[2] [f. UNDO *v.*]

1. Brought to decay or ruin; ruined, destroyed.

Chiefly predicative, but the attributive use was not infrequent in the 17th and was common in the 18th century.

1340 *Ayenb.* 136 Hueruore his bodi is ondo, and his inwyt uolueld. *a* 1400–50 *Alexander* 1472 We ere dredles vnd one, bot dri3ten vs help. *a* 1450 *Mirk's Festial* 192 He.. 3af hym all to foly aftyr, and laft hit neuer til he wer vndon. 1484 Caxton *Fables of Æsop* II. ix, Many one is vndone and lost for faulte of obedyence. *a* 1542 Wyatt in *Tottel's Misc.* (Arb.) 85 When her store was stroyed with the floode: Then weleaway for she undone was cleane. 1573 Tusser *Husb.* (1878) 91 Keepe hop from sunne, and hop is vndunne. 1608 Middleton *Trick to catch Old One* III. i, That Witgood is a riotous, undone man. 1646 P. Bulkeley *Gospel Covt.* I. 48 The low and undone condition they have brought themselves into by their sins. *a* 1687 Petty *Pol. Arith.* (1690) 89 England commonly beareth the whole burthen, and charge, whereby many in England are utterly undone. 1724 Swift *Drapier's Lett.* ii, We are all undone if Wood's halfpence must pass. 1749 Fielding *Tom Jones* XVII. iv, I am the most miserable undone Wretch upon Earth. 1810 Crabbe *Borough* xiv. 14 Blaney, a wealthy heir at twenty-one, At twenty-five was ruin'd and undone. 1839 Dickens *Nickleby* lvi, I am undone. Whichever way I turn, I am undone. *a* 1864 Ferrier *Grk. Philos.* (1866) I. xii. 348 A soul without justice.. is a soul undone.

2. Unfastened, untied, detached, etc.

1565 Cooper *Thesaurus*, *Vincla resoluta*, loosed or vndoone. 1806–7 J. Beresford *Miseries Hum. Life* VI. xxxvi, The outer bandage of a hurt in your bridle-hand coming undone. 1884 W. S. Gilbert *Princess Ida* II, Let all your things misfit, and yourselves At inconvenient moments come undone.

Hence **un'doneness**. *rare*$^{-1}$.

1835 R. M. McCheyne *Addit. Rem.* (1847) 35 Under a sense of undoneness, to flee for refuge to the Saviour.

un'doomed, *ppl. a.* (UN-[1] 8.)

[1775 Ash.] 1813 Byron *Giaour* xvi, Unfit for earth, undoom'd for heaven. 1821 Scott *Pirate* xix, Visitor bold, .. Who hast hither presumed,—Ungifted, undoom'd, Thou shalt not depart.

un'dose, *a. rare.* [ad. L. *undōs-us*, f. *unda* wave. Cf. Sp. and Pg. *undoso*, It. *ondoso*.]

†1. Of the pulse: Having beats of unequal strength. *Obs.*

1707 Floyer *Physic. Pulse-Watch* 138 Generally an undose Pulse is a degree of slow Pulses from weak Spirits. 1758 *Phil. Trans.* L. 524 The pulse.. was sometimes heavy and undose.

2. *Ent.* (See quot.)

1826 Kirby & Sp. *Entomol.* IV. xlvi. 271 *Undose*, having undulating nearly parallel broader depressions which run into each other.

†**un'dosous**, *a. Obs.*$^{-0}$ (Cf. prec. and -OUS.)

1623 Cockeram I, *Vndosous*, full of surges and waues. 1644 *Vindex Anglicus* 6 [in list of pedantic words].

un'dotted, *ppl. a.* (UN-[1] 8.)

1830 Lindley *Nat. Syst. Bot.* 101 Pinnated resinous undotted leaves. 1891 *Science-Gossip* XXVII. 95/1 The stonechat and whinchat seem to have dotted and undotted eggs with almost equal frequency.

un'double, *v.* [UN-[2] 6.]

1. a. *trans.* To take out of a doubled or folded state; to straighten out. b. *intr.* To become unfolded or straight.

1611 Florio, *Sdoppiare*, to vndouble, to vnfold. 1683 Moxon *Mech. Exerc., Printing* xxiv. ¶15 As he comes to a Token-sheet, he un-doubles that, and smooths out the Crease. 1730 A. Gordon *Maffei's Amphith.* 363 Then undoubling the Rope,.. I extended the Rope with a Pin. 1850 Thackeray *Pendennis* lviii, The dirty fist.. was obliged to undouble itself. 1889 *Advance* (Chicago) 14 Nov., To Jim's surprise, the fists undoubled, and no angry words came.

2. *Chess. trans.* To move (pawns) so that one no longer stands directly in front of the other.

1868 *Illustr. Lond. News* 25 Aug. 187 By this advance Dr. Lange undoubles and consolidates the Pawns on the Q's side, and thus adds greatly to the strength of his game.

un'doubled, *ppl. a.* (UN-[1] 8.)

1598 Barret *Theor. Warres* III. i. 40 The od file or rank which resteth vndoubled, may.. close vp shoulder to shoulder.

un'doubtable, *a.* (and *adv.*). [UN-[1] 7b, 5b.] That cannot be doubted; indubitable.

c 1425 *St. Christina* Prol. 40 in *Anglia* VIII. 119 As wee haue leeryd be ful certeyne and vndoutabil tellynge. 1529 More *Dyaloge* IV. Wks. 265/1 That the gospell he had preached, was the plain, sure and undoubtable trouth. 1611 Cotgr., *Indubitable*, vndoubtable. 1665 J. Sergeant *Sure Footing* 233 How can their Authority ever come to be undoubtable or certain? 1815 Lamb *Lett.* (1888) I. 284 Let me.. mention that my brother.. has picked up an undoubtable picture of Milton. 1870 *Daily News* 21 Oct., The leading facts.. I have.. from an undoubtable source.

†b. As *adv.* = next. *Obs.*

c 1440 *Alph. Tales* 196 þat þou may trow vndowtable at þe rysyng of deade folk sall be trew. 1513 Douglas *Æneid* VI. v. 56 Anchises get!.. Discend vndowtable of the goddis blude.

un'doubtably, *adv.* ? *Obs.* [UN-[1] 11, 5b: cf. prec.] Without doubt; indubitably.

c 1425 *St. Eliz.* in *Anglia* VIII. 107/26 þoos þinges þat I perceyued vndoutably with myn eyen. *c* 1449 Pecock *Repr.* I. v. 26 Hise iij. parties schal conferme vndoutabli al what is seid here. *a* 1513 Fabyan *Chron.* VII. ccxxi. 244 Where thou sayest.. that Gregory myght.. haue confirmed all things vndowtably with this worde,.. that is sothe.

un'doubted, *ppl. a.* and *adv.* [UN-[1] 8, 8c, 5b.]

1. Not held doubtful in respect of fact.

c 1460 Fortescue *Abs. & Lim. Mon.* v. (1885) 119 But we must holde it for vndouted, þat ther mey no reaume prospere.. vndir a poure kynge. 1487 Hen. VII in *Ep. Acad. Oxon.* (1898) II. 514 Yff ye will take hym as fore a scolare, as we hold it undowted ye wyll nott do. 1590 Swinburne *Testaments* 191 If it be certaine and vndoubted, that the testament is written or subscribed with the testators owne hand. 1634 Sir T. Herbert *Trav.* 81 The mighty Army and vndoubted threats of the King. 1757 W. Wilkie *Epigon.* Pref. p. iv, This is his undoubted privilege; and I have no intention to break in upon it. 1791 Cowper *Judgm. Poets* 36 Adorning May.. With June's undoubted right. 1839 T. Mitchell *Frogs of Aristoph.* Introd. p. xci, It is the undoubted business of learned men to profit by those hints.

2. Of persons: Not called in question in respect of status or character.

c 1460 *Brut* II. 514 The general Counsel of Basil deposed Eugeny, which was only Pope & vndoubted. 1568 Grafton *Chron.* II. 643 King Richard the seconde was the true and vndoubted heyre to the valiant Conquerour. 1593 Shaks. *3 Hen. VI*, v. vii. 6 Three Dukes of Somerset, threefold Renowne, For hardy and vndoubted Champions. 1659 Pearson *Creed* (1839) 173 It is true, at first he was subject.. to his reputed father and undoubted mother. *a* 1718 Prior *Power* 464 He made Me to his Crimes undoubted Heir. 1751 Earl Orrery *Remarks Swift* (1752) 14 She was.. the concealed, but undoubted wife of Dr. Swift. 1827 Scott *Surg. Dau.* iv, Mr. Gray is an undoubted judge.. what person will best suit him as a professional assistant.

3. Not affected or impaired by doubt; absolute, complete.

1489 *Cov. Leet Bk.* 536 Wherin ye may be.. ioyous and haue full trust and vndoubted affiance therunto. 1560 Daus tr. *Sleidane's Comm.* 182 Wherof.. the Bisshops legat hath put him into an undoubted hope. 1813 Shelley *Q. Mab* IX. 82 Those delicate and timid impulses.. with undoubted confidence disclosed The growing longings of.. love.

4. About the nature of which no doubt is entertained; accepted as true, certain, or genuine.

1513 More *Rich. III*, Wks. 61/1 This is his own countenance,.. yᵉ sure vndoubted image.. of that noble Duke. 1577 Hanmer *Anc. Eccl. Hist.* 56 The undoubted writings of Clement are apparent. 1665 J. Spencer *Vulg. Proph.* 42 That natural wisdom,.. of which the true prophets of God gave such undoubted evidences. 1710 Berkeley *Princ. Hum. Knowl.* §10 An undoubted truth, which they can demonstrate beyond all exception. 1808 L. Murray *Eng. Gram.* I. 199 An historian of undoubted credit. 1897 J. W. Clark *Barnwell* Intr. 13 Relics of undoubted authenticity.

†b. Similarly with *of. Obs.*

1683 D. A. *Art Converse* 40 'Tis an undoubted of truth, that the greatest swearers are commonly the greatest liars.

†5. As *adv.* = UNDOUBTEDLY *adv.* 1. *Obs.*

Common in the early part of the 16th cent.

a 1500 *Coventry Corpus Chr. Pl.* I. 395 Ondowtid sche ys cum of hy parrage. 1523 Fitzherb. *Husb.* §146 Vndouted a woman can-not gette her lyuynge honestely with spynnynge on the distaffe.

Hence **un'doubtedness**.

1691 W. Nicholls *Answ. Naked Gospel* Pref. Cj, When he has full assurance of the undoubtedness of the Testimony.

un'doubtedly, *adv.* [UN-[1] 11, 5b; cf. prec.]

1. Without or beyond any doubt; indubitably, assuredly, certainly.

? *a* 1500 *Chester Pl.* xiii. 180 Our sonne he is,.. And blynde was borne undowtedlye. 1551 T. Wilson *Logike* (1580) 37 By searchyng euery borough he shall haue his purpose vndoubtedly. 1585 T. Washington tr. *Nicholay's Voy.* IV. xxxv. 158b, They (quoth he) are vndoubtedly condemned by nature. 1662 Stillingfl. *Orig. Sacræ* II. i. §3 The Records under the name of Moses were undoubtedly his. 176. Wilkes *Corr.* (1805) III. 13 This is undoubtedly the handsomest compliment that has been paid to his present majesty. 1838 James *Louis XIV*, I. 164 He was, however, undoubtedly a man of much courage. 1874 Green *Short Hist.* iii. §6 (1882) 147 The influence which the Friars undoubtedly exerted.

b. Used to introduce a sentence.

1521 Wolsey in *St. Papers Hen. VIII*, VI. 85 And ondowgtydly, by all apparance, He shall prove a very wyse man. 1596 *Edward III*, II. ii. 20 Vndoubtedly, then, some thing is a misse. 1663 Cowley *Cutter Coleman St.* II. vii, Undoubtedly they had a Hand in't. 1765 *Museum Rust.* IV. 185 Undoubtedly the farmers will think the charges of this feed too great. 1834 J. H. Newman *Par. Serm.* I. i. 2 Undoubtedly He may prescribe the terms on which He will give it. 1878 Seeley *Stein* II. 160 Undoubtedly this refusal was honourable to him.

†2. In a manner which removes or rejects all doubt; positively, decidedly. *Obs.*

1513 *Life Hen. V* (1911) 182 When this.. Kinge was vndoubtedly acertained of his phisicions that the time of his resolucion approached. 1584 R. Scot *Discov. Witchcr.* III. xix. 56 They affirme undoubtedlie, that the divell plaieth Succubus to the man. 1638 R. Baker tr. *Balzac's Lett.* (vol. II) 36, I.. assure you most undoubtedly, that [etc.]. 1653 H. More *Antid. Ath.* I. ii. §3 The thing that it doth thus resolvedly and undoubtedly reject.

un'doubtful, *a.* [UN-[1] 7.]

†1. Not mixed with or qualified by doubt; firm, sure. *Obs.*

c 1450 *Oseney Reg.* 161 Vndowtefull feith to þese presente writynges to 3eve. 1508 Fisher *7 Penit. Ps.* li. Wks. (1876) 94 He promyseth very true and vndoubtefull hope to hym-selfe of the desyre that he asketh. *a* 1626 W. Sclater *Exp. Rom.* iv. (1650) 134 Sure.. to us, in respect of our apprehension, and undoubtful perswasion.

2. Not admitting of doubt; free from any dubiety; positive, certain.

1533–4 *Act 25 Hen. VIII*, c. 22 §2 The laufull matrimonie .. shall be.. taken for vndoubtfull, trewe, sincere, and perfecte. 1619 W. Sclater *Exp. 1 Thess.* (1630) 22 Is the cleannesse of the outward life an vndoubtfull euidence of the cleannesse of the heart? 1655 tr. *Sorel's Com. Hist. Francion* XII. 25 To render the affair more criminal and undoubtfull, I came hither. 1856 Mrs. Browning *Aur. Leigh* III. 539 A girl of doubtful life, undoubtful birth.

3. Not feeling doubt; certain (*of* something).

1613 Fletcher, etc. *Hon. Man's Fortune* I. i, Our husbands might have lookt into our thoughts, And made themselves undoubtfull. 1773 J. Ross *Fratricide* v. 630 (MS.), And.. Justice bids go on Undoubtful of his patronizing pow'r.

Hence **un'doubtfulness**.

1619 W. Sclater *Exp. 1 Thess.* (1630) 241 Some Foole I haue heard boasting of vndoubtfulnesse for the matter of their owne saluation.

un'doubtfully, *adv.* [UN-[1] 11; cf. prec.] †Without doubt; indubitably.

1628 Verstegan *Dec. Intell.* ii. 51 Such as so persuade themselues are therin vndoubtfully deceiued. 1629 Lynde *Via Tuta* 251 Little can be said of any certainty, or as vndoubtfully true.

un'doubting, *ppl. a.* (and *adv.*). [UN-[1] 10.]

†1. *Sc.* Undoubted; also *adv.*, undoubtedly. *Obs.*

c 1400 *Sc. Trojan War* II. 2887 At his moder he gan Inquere Quho was his fader vndowtand. 1552 Abp. Hamilton *Catech.* (1884) 4 It is undoutand ane synfull.. thing to varie and discord in materis of our faith.

2. Harbouring no doubts; confident.

1735 Berkeley *Free-think. in Math.* §1 Asserting with such undoubting assurance things so easily disproved. 1788 V. Knox *Winter Even.* xi. (1790) II. 71 When any man speaks with the assurance of undoubting conviction. 1810 Scott *Lady of L.* I. xxxiii, Again returned the scenes of youth, Of confident undoubting truth. 1828 Webster s.v., An undoubting believer. 1870 Bryant *Iliad* IV. I. 112 All this I know in my undoubting mind.

Hence **un'doubtingness**.

1857 M. Pattison *Ess.* (1889) II. 404 We can turn the history of a foreign people into doctrine.. with a rapidity and undoubtingness which fail us when we attempt our own. 1871 W. G. Ward *Ess. Philos. Theism* (1884) I. 14 The mere undoubtingness of an assent.. arises from mere accident.

un'doubtingly, *adv.* [UN-[1] 11; cf. prec.]

1. Without harbouring any doubts; unhesitatingly; with confidence.

c 1400 *Sc. Trojan War* II. 788 He lay befor þe gret altere.. Wndoutandly [L. *indubitanter*] þe dede bydand. 1742 Richardson *Pamela* IV. 337, I.. shall then be able to let you know all my Sentiments.. more undoubtingly, as I shall be more improv'd by Years. 1802 Mrs. E. Parsons *Myst. Visit* II. 9 Neither did she consign him over undoubtingly to guilt and shame. 1882 H. S. Holland *Logic & Life* iv. 62 We know undoubtingly what good is, and what evil is.

†2. *Sc.* Undoubtedly. *Obs.*$^{-1}$

1552 Abp. Hamilton *Catech.* (1884) 64 Undoutandly the abhominabil abusioun of the name of God.. bringis apon vs the vengeance of God.

†**un'doubtly**, obs. var. UNDOUBTEDLY *adv.*

1487 Hen. VII in *Ep. Acad. Oxon.* (1898) II. 517 Oure extent in thys partie shalbe undowtly executed. 1539 Taverner *Erasm. Prov.* (1552) 48 Undoutly, nothynge is more hurtfull to a man, then selfe loue is.

†**un'doubtous**, *a. Obs.*$^{-1}$ [UN-[1] 7.] Undoubtful, undoubted.

c 1374 Chaucer *Boeth.* v. pr. i. (1868) 149 Syn it nis nat to douten of þe þinges folwynge whan euery side of þi disputisoun shal be stedfast to me by vndoutous [L. *indubitata*] feiþ.

un'dought. *Sc.* Now *rare* or *Obs.* Forms: 6 wn-, 7 vn-, undought; 6 wn-, vn-, 8 undocht, 7 vndoght; 6 vndoche, 7 undoch. [UN-[1] 12 + DOUGHT *sb.* or *a*. Cf. NFris. *ündöght* worthless person; WFris. *on-*, *ûnducht* corrupt or morbid matter; obs. Flem. *ondocht* a worthless kind of crab (Kilian).] An ineffective worthless person. (Cf. WANDOUGHT.)

1508 KENNEDIE *Flyting w. Dunbar* 508 Tak the a fidill, or a floyt & geste, Wndought [*v.r.* vndocht], thou art ordanyt to not ellis! *a* **1583** MONTGOMERIE *Flyting* 454 (Tullib. MS.), Let nevir þis vndoche [*v.rr.* vndoght, vndought] of evill doing Irk. **1636** W. SCOT *Apol. Narr.* (1846) 239 Mr. George Grahame, the undought of Bishops. **1679** in Wodrow *Hist. Suff. Ch. Scot.* (1828) IV. 501 Mr. Brown being removed, they will have little to do to trample upon the poor undought that is left behind. **1721** RAMSAY *Poems* Gloss., *Undocht*, or *wandocht*, a silly weak person.

†**un'doughty**, *a. Obs.* [UN-[1] 7. Cf. MDu. *onduchtich*, *-dochtich*, MLG. *undochtich*, MHG. *untuchtic* (G. *untüchtig*), MDa. and Da. *udygtig*.] Lacking in good qualities; worthless, bad, vile.

a **1225** *Juliana* 4 (Royal MS.), Maximian þe modi keiser.. wið unmeð muchel hird & unduhti duheðe. *c* **1460** *Towneley Myst.* xxiv. 367 Now thise dyse that ar vndughty for los of this good, here I forswere hertely. **1570** *Satir. Poems Reform.* xxiv. 43 Deir sall ȝe by ȝone foule vnduchtie deid.

†**un'dowed**, *ppl. a. Obs.* [UN-[1] 8 + DOW *v.*[2]] Unendowed.

c **1380** WYCLIF *Sel. Wks.* III. 357 As þis power were in vein ȝif þe Chirche were undowid. **1596** WARNER *Alb. Eng.* XI. lxii. (1597) 288 How seldome Women come vndow'd with.. answerable Faults to these. **1648** HEXHAM II, *Onbegaeft*, Vndowed, or Vngifted.

un'dowered, *ppl. a.* (UN-[1] 8.)

1803 GODWIN *Chaucer* II. xlvi. 378 The other [religion] humble, naked and undowered. **1830** D'ISRAELI *Chas. I*, III. viii. 161 His celebrated but undowered daughter. **1876** MISS BRADDON *Dead Men's Shoes* I. ii. 27 He.., if Nature's bounties are to be counted as a heritage, is not undowered.

un'downed, *a.* (UN-[1] 9 + DOWN *sb.*[2])

1657 LOVELACE *Poems* (1864) 251 When thy undown'd face mov'd the Nine to shake.

un'drag, *v.* (UN-[2] 4 b.)

1809 MAR. EDGEWORTH *Ennui* iii, When we had dragged and undragged, and came up with Paddy, we found him.. mending some of his tackle.

un'dragoned, *a.* (UN-[1] 9.)

1868 BROWNING *Ring & Bk.* VI. 1772 The officious priest would personate Saint George For a mock Princess in undragoned days.

un'drainable, *a.* [UN-[1] 7 b.]

1. Incapable of being drained dry; inexhaustible.

1611 COTGR., *Inespuisable*,.. vndraynable, which cannot be dryed vp, or laden dry. **1627** J. CARTER *Plain Expos.* 108 Your heauenly Father,.. The undrainable Fountaine of all goodnesse. **1652** J. WRIGHT tr. *Camus' Nat. Paradox* I. 6 A very plentiful and almost undrainable source of riches. **1842** TENNYSON *Œnone* 113 Overflowing revenue.. from labour'd mines undrainable of ore.

2. Incapable of being freed from water by means of draining.

1852 HENFREY *Veget. Europe* 181 Parts.. irreclaimable to cultivation.. being either steep arid slopes of the hills or undrainable bogs. **1884** *Harper's Mag.* Apr. 761/1 Undrainable or undrained.. surfaces.

un'drained, *ppl. a.* (UN-[1] 8.)

1573 TUSSER *Husb.* (1878) 114 The fen and the quamire, .. Which yeerelie vndrained.. annoieth the meadowes that thereon doo but. **1697** DRYDEN *Æneis* III. 921 The.. fenny lake, undrained by Fate's decree. **1761** STERNE *Tr. Shandy* IV. xxxi, A fine, large, whinny, undrained, unimproved common. **1812** *Examiner* 11 May 292/1 Ill-cultivated and undrained soils. **1898** *Allbutt's Syst. Med.* V. 350 In some cases of small empyema, even when undrained.

undra'matic, *a.* [UN-[1] 7.]

1. Lacking the essential qualities of drama.

1754 A. MURPHY *Gray's Inn Jrnl.* No. 94, The following Lines.. are certainly very inartificial and undramatic. **1805** *Ann. Rev.* III. 621 As works of literary art, these dialogues are dull and undramatic. **1861** GEO. ELIOT in Cross *Life* (1885) II. 289 These less known undramatic tales of want.

2. Not gifted with or exhibiting dramatic power; not adapted for the production of drama.

1769 *Garrick's Vagary* 10 Procuring the Stage's deliverance from the many undramatic Beasts of Lumber. **1821** BYRON *Let.* Jan., Wks. 194/2 Many people think my talent essentially undramatic. **1870** LOWELL *Among my Bks.* Ser. I. (1873) 205 Goethe affirmed, that.. Shakespeare was too undramatic for the German theatre.

b. Unable to appreciate drama.

1836 T. HOOK *G. Gurney* i, English audiences, who are.. as undramatic in their notions as methodists.

3. Not written in the form of drama.

1840 L. HUNT in *Dram. Wks. Wycherley*, etc. (Rtldg.) p. xxxv, Congreve's undramatic prose writings are few.

So **undra'matical** *a.*, **undra'matically** *adv.*

1829 BEDDOES *Let.* Feb., in *Poems* (1851) p. lxxx, The play is too long;.. the second [act] dull and *undramatical. **1827** SIR H. TAYLOR *Autobiog.* (1885) I. 97 If I were to write another play at this rate, I might die *undramatically before the fifth act. **1901** M. PEMBERTON *Pro Patria* xx. 223, I told him, undramatically, that I was the man.

un'drape, *v.* (UN-[2] 4.)

1869 *Sat. Rev.* 30 Jan. 140/1 Our own women are encouraged to undrape themselves for show and not for comfort.

un'draped, *ppl. a.* [UN-[1] 8.] Not furnished or covered with draperies; nude, naked.

1814 *Monthly Rev.* LXXIII. 531 He observes that those .. intend to incur the contemplation of the undraped figure. **1866** *Athenæum* 24 Nov. 676/3 He made of the little, lively, happy fellow, a joyous, undraped child.

fig. **1870** BURTON *Hist. Scot.* lxii. (1873) V. 373 Although his indulgence in drinking was.. undraped by any outward cover of decorum.

un'draperied, *a.* (UN-[1] 9.)

1802 MME. D'ARBLAY *Diary* 4 May, My feet in their native, undraperied state. **1837** HAWTHORNE *Twice-told T.* (1851) I. vi. 95 The unplastered walls, the naked woodwork, and the undraperied pulpit.

un'draw, *v.* [UN-[2] 3.]

†**1.** *trans.* To draw out, withdraw. *Obs.*

c **1400** *Trevisa's Higden* (Rolls) V. 373 Rosamunda.. bonde so faste þe kynges swerd.. þat it myȝte not be undrawe [*MS. γ.* y-drawe] out of þe scaberke.

2. To draw back (esp. a curtain); to unfasten by pulling.

1677 MIÉGE II, To Undraw the curtains, *ouvrir les rideaux*. **1744** YOUNG *Nt. Th.* VII. 813 Death's inexorable hand Draws the dark curtain close; undrawn no more. *Ibid.* 1107 Angels undrew the curtain of the throne. **1791** MRS. RADCLIFFE *Rom. Forest* iv, The door was held by two strong bolts. Having undrawn these, it disclosed a flight of steps. **1839** LADY LYTTON *Cheveley* (ed. 3) III. iii. 71 He undrew the window curtain, and sat in the window. **1872** J. L. SANFORD *Estimates Eng. Kings, Jas. I*, 324 In the cause of the Palatine.. the purse-strings of the English people would have been willingly undrawn.

3. *intr.* To move back on being pulled.

1794 MRS. RADCLIFFE *Myst. Udolpho* xxxiii, Emily presently heard.. the heavy chain fall, and the bolts undraw of a small postern door. **1845** BROWNING *How they brought the News* 3 'Good speed!' cried the watch, as the gate-bolts undrew.

Hence **un'drawing** *vbl. sb.*

1797 MRS. RADCLIFFE *Italian* xix, She distinguished the undrawing of iron bars.

un'drawn, *ppl. a.*[1] [UN-[1] 8.]

†**1.** ? That has never drawn a plough. *Obs.*

1527 *Lanc. Wills* (Chetham Soc.) I. 32 A heffur in calf and ij bolokks of the best sort undrawen.

2. a. Not disembowelled.

1562 TURNER *Herbal* II. 25 At the tyme of yeare the feldefares fede only of Iuniper berries the people Eate the feldefares undrawen.

b. Unmilked.

1820 SHELLEY *Prometh. Unb.* II. ii. 90 Noontide would come, And thwart Silenus find his goats undrawn.

3. Not drawn from a receptacle; untapped.

a **1595** SOUTHWELL *Christs Bloody Sweat* 3 Fat soil, full spring, sweet olive, grape of bliss,.. Untill'd, undrawn, unstamp'd, untouch'd of press. **1809** BYRON *Bards & Rev.* 636 Beer undrawn, and beards unmown. **1868** R. BUCHANAN *Tragic Dramas, Wallace* I. iii, Even at the first assault,.. A drop of blood undrawn, the dastard fled.

4. a. Not drawn, dragged, or pulled along, out, etc. Also with *forth*.

1667 MILTON *P.L.* VI. 751 Forth rush'd with whirl-wind sound The Chariot of Paternal Deitie,.. Wheele within Wheele undrawn. **1730** *Act 3 Geo. II*, c. 25 §11 The same Names shall be.. returned to the former Box or Glass, there to be kept with the other Names remaining at that Time undrawn. **1760** STERNE *Tr. Shandy* IV. *Slawkenb. T.*, Was there in the great arsenal of chance, one single engine left undrawn forth to torture your curiosities? **1837** LYTTON *Athens* II. 219 Lamenting.. that his sword was as yet undrawn against the invader. **1899** *Westm. Gaz.* 16 June 2/1 The casting-line should be of the finest undrawn gut.

b. Of a lottery: cf. DRAW *v.* 34.

1730 FIELDING *Author's Farce* I. i, A Benefit-Ticket in an un-drawn Lottery.

c. Of curtains, etc.: open, not drawn across the window.

1923 E. BOWEN *Encounters* 153 Here the curtains were undrawn and they could see the lights twinkling out in the windows of the other houses. **1940** M. SADLEIR *Fanny by Gaslight* II. 311 The curtains were undrawn and the daylight dim... She rang for the curtains to be drawn and the gas lit. **1954** 'M. COST' *Invitation from Minerva* 84 The Utrecht hangings of scarlet velvet and gold which.. festooned the lower floor windows.. were undrawn. **1968** J. FLEMING *Kill or Cure* xv. 203 The thick velvet undrawn curtains.

5. Not delineated or depicted.

1742 YOUNG *Nt. Th.* II. 621 The Death-bed of the just! is yet undrawn By mortal hand.

un'drawn, *ppl. a.*[2] [f. UNDRAW *v.*] Drawn back, withdrawn.

1748 RICHARDSON *Clarissa* (1811) III. iii. 30, I have told thee what were my transports, when the undrawn bolt presented to me my long-expected goddess.

un'dreaded, *ppl. a.* (UN-[1] 8.)

1535 *Aberdeen Reg.* (Jam.), And cam nocht to be ondreyd be him thairof. **1647** STANLEY *Poems, Europa* 11 Oh whither sacred Bull? who art thou, say! That through undreaded flouds canst break thy way. **1692** RAY *Disc.* 239 A dreadful indeed, but by these formerly undreaded sentence. **1784** COWPER *Task* II. 811 Vice parries wide Th' undreaded volley with a sword of straw. **1834** *Tait's Mag.* I. 338/2 Death, undreaded, approached; and the spirit departed. *a* **1873** LYTTON *Pausanias* i, The unexpected, and not undreaded, approach of the great Pausanias.

un'dreadful, *a. rare.* [UN-[1] 7.]

†**1.** Having no dread; unapprehensive (*of*). *Obs.*

c **1400** *Comm. Luke* i. 13 (MS. Bodl. 143), þe deuels cruelte is best ouercomon bi vndredeful feiþ. **1648** HERRICK *Hesper.*, *Christian Militant*, A man prepar'd against all ills to come,.. Undreadfull too of courtly thunderclaps.

2. Not causing dread.

1611 FLORIO, *Informidabile*, vndreadfull, not terrible.

So **un'dreadfully** *adv.*, †without dread or fear.

c **1430** *Life St. Katherine* (Roxb. Club) 34 She made vppon hir self þe token of þe crosse and vndredfully went vnto þe paleys. *a* **1440** *Found. St. Bartholomew's* (E.E.T.S.) 55 For cause, yn rycchynge of thy-self othir men thou spoylid vndredfully, now thou begynnyst to nede.

un'dreading, *ppl. a.* (UN-[1] 5 d, 10.)

1745 ELIZA HEYWOOD *Female Spect.* III. 171 By them we sleep securely, undreading all Incursions and foreign Depredations. **1750** COLLINS *Ode Superstit. Highlands* 166 They.., Along th' Atlantic rock, undreading, climb. **1830** TENNYSON *Grasshopper* I. 16 Unknowing fear, Undreading loss.

un'dreamed, -'dreamt, *ppl. a.* [UN-[1] 8, 8 c.]

1. Not apprehended (even) in a dream or dreams; not imagined or thought of.

1611 SHAKS. *Wint. T.* IV. iv. 578 A Course more promising, Then a wild dedication of your selues To vnpath'd Waters, vndream'd Shores. **1827** MOORE *Alciphron* iii. 278 A light Leading to undreamt happiness. **1880** E. WHITE *Cert. Relig.* 48 That Voice which.. lifted up men's thoughts to heights undreamed before.

2. With *of*. (Cf. DREAM *v.*[2] 1.)

1636 PAGITT *Christianography* (ed. 2) II. 40 Ecclesiasticks were unexempted, and deposing of Kings was then undreamed of. **1674** BOYLE *Excell. Theol.* II. v. 213 Even practical inventions.. by undreamed of discoveries may be brought to lose the general reputation they had. **1802** COLERIDGE *Dejection* v, A new Earth.., Undreamt of by the sensual and the proud. **1860** RUSKIN *Unto this Last* ii. (1896) 65 In some far-away and yet undreamt-of hour. **1880** GEO. ELIOT in Cross *Life* (1885) III. 406 The great, once undreamed-of change in my life.

un'dreaming, *ppl. a.* (UN-[1] 10.)

1831 LAMB *Elia* II. *Ellistoniana*, The days when, undreaming of Theatres and Managerships, thou wert a scholar. **1850** L. HUNT *Autobiog.* ii. 41 The most real of all things, and our only undreaming time.

un'dreamy, *a.* (UN-[1] 7.)

1849 LYTTON *Caxtons* II. i, My love for study.. was a vigorous, wakeful, undreamy love.

un'dreggy, *a.* (UN-[1] 7.)

1720 T. BOSTON *Fourfold State* (1784) 12 Man had a life of pure delight and undreggy pleasure in this state.

†**un'dreigh**, *a. Obs. rare.* [UN-[1] 7 + *dreigh* DREE *a.* Cf. ON. *údrjúgr* (Norw. *udrjug*, Sw. *odryg*, Da. *udrøi*) falling short, insufficient.]

1. ? Lacking in diligence; slack.

a **1310** in Wright *Lyric P.* xii. 41 To hem he sayde an heh, That suythe he[m] wes undreh, so ydel forte stonde.

2. Not tedious or tiresome.

a **1400** in *Hampole's Wks.* (1895) I. 80 þi dayes sal be vndregh, þat þe na sorw schende.

un'drenched, *ppl. a.* (UN-[1] 8.)

1627 MAY *Lucan* IX. R 3 b, You slowly seeing Cynosure, suppose Her vndrench'd carre into the Ocean goes. **1794** CAMPBELL tr. *Medea* Antist. II. 16 The blade, undrenched in blood's eternal dye.

'undress, un'dress, *sb.* [UN-[1] 12.]

1. Partial or incomplete dress; dress of a kind not ordinarily worn in public; dishabille. Also (esp. of men), informal or ordinary dress, as distinct from that worn on ceremonial or special occasions.

a. Of women.

The common use during the 18th century.

1685 CROWNE *Sir C. Nice* IV, To-day the beauty lyes ambush'd in undresses, the hair pin'd up in papers. *a* **1704** T. BROWN *Pleasant Lett. to Gent.* Wks. 1709 III. II. 15 How he surpriz'd a famous Miss of the Town, dining at her Lodgings in an Undress. **1767** *Lond. Gaz.* No. 10716. 2/1 The Ladies to wear black Silk or Velvet.. Undress, white or grey Lustrings [etc.]. **1785** SARAH FIELDING *Ophelia* I. viii, The night-gowns and common undresses were grown familiar to me. **1821** SCOTT *Kenilw.* xxii, Where she sat.. adorned with all that Janet's art, and a rich and tasteful undress, could bestow. *a* **1847** [see DISHABILLE 2].

b. Of men.

1683 DRYDEN *Life Plutarch* 94 Here you are led into the private lodgings of the hero; you see him in his undress. *a* **1700** EVELYN *Diary* 4 Feb. 1685, He had ben on the bed, but was now risen and in his undresse. **1767** *Lond. Gaz.* No. 10716. 2/1 The Men to continue in Black full trimmed;.. Undress, light grey Frocks. **1821** SCOTT *Kenilw.* xxxii, Varney.. had changed his splendid attire, and now waited on his patron in a very modest and plain undress. **1853** R. S. SURTEES *Sponge's Sp. Tour* viii, There are few more difficult persons to identify than a huntsman in undress.

c. *Mil.* and *Naval*: Dress or uniform authorized to be worn on ordinary occasions, as distinguished from *full* or *service dress*.

1748 SMOLLETT *R. Random* xx, To get into [Captain] O'Donnell's apartment, while he was abroad in an undress, and examine his sword. **1783** *Ann. Reg., Chron.* 193/2 Undress. Admiral's. A blue cloth frock, with blue cuff and blue lappels. **1829** S. HAIGH *Sk. Buenos Ayres & Chile* 123 The soldiers wore what I supposed was their undress; it consisted of a military cap, a poncho, and sandals of hide. **1849** LEVER *Con Cregan* v, A young officer, in a cavalry undress. **1857** *Dress Regul. Army* 28 Scarlet Undress.. Blue Undress. **1879** *Unif. Reg.* in *Navy List* July (1882) 487/2 Trowsers, without lace.—As in undress.

2. *transf.* and *fig.*

(*a*) **1684** T. BURNET *Theory Earth* I. 141 'Tis very useful .. to look often upon such bare draughts as shew us nature in an undress. **1692** DRYDEN *Cleomenes* IV. i, This famine has a sharp and meagre face: 'Tis death in an undress of skin and bone. *c* **1705** POPE *Imit. Eng. Poets, Cowley's Garden* 6 Where Lilies smile in virgin robes of white, The thin Undress of superficial Light. **1853** IS. WILLIAMS *Baptistery* I. xi. (1874) 138 Such Basil's Pontic home,.. beautiful in nature's stern undress.

(*b*) **1797** *Monthly Mag.* III. 493/1 When we are able to attend the author in the sequestered scenes of life, and contemplate the undress of his mind. **1825** *Examiner* 738/2 We now and then detected a little colloquial undress in the female dialogue. **1886** PATER *Appreciations* (1890) 127 When he writes (still in undress) he does but take the 'friendly reader' into his confidence.

3. *attrib.* Constituting an undress; worn when in undress; *spec.* in *Mil.* and *Naval* use (see 1 c).

1777 P. THICKNESSE *Year's Journey* II. 231 You cannot dine, or visit after dinner, in an undress frock. **1829** MARRYAT *F. Mildmay* vii, The officers in their undress uniform. **1844** *Regul. & Ord. Army* 132 When Officers attend in Uniform as spectators at the Review,.. they are not to appear in Blue Frock-Coats or Undress Jackets. **1894** MRS. DYAN *Man's Keeping* (1899) 238 The Collector of Poggulpore's portly form, in very much undress garb.

fig. **1806** W. TAYLOR In Robberds *Mem.* (1843) II. 135 The simple, idiomatic, undress, conversational tone of Lessing's blank verse.

un'dress, *v.* [UN-² 4.]

1. *refl.* To divest (oneself) of clothing.

1596 SHAKS. *Tam. Shr.* Induct. ii. 119 Madam vndresse you, and come now to bed. **1674** J. B[RIAN] *Harv. Home* iv. 29 T' undress themselves they all see cause, And call'd to come they seldome use to pause. **1712** *Spect.* No. 506 ¶5 A French Woman offering to undress and dress herself before the Lover. **1788** GIBBON *Decl. & F.* l. V. 184 Undress thyself, thy aunt.. is without a garment. **1853** *Arab. Nts.* (Rtldg.) 149 She then undressed herself and went to bed.

b. *intr.* To take off one's clothes.

a **1625** FLETCHER *Noble Gent.* II. ad fin., What are you mad, to make me Dress, and undress,.. Because you find me plyant? *a* **1721** PRIOR *Truth & Falsehood* 25 Falsehood more leisurely undrest, And laying by Her tawdry vest, Trick'd her self out in Truth's array. *c* **1755** in B. Ward *Hist. St. Edmund's Coll.* (1893) 302 It is always one of the Masters Business to be present while they are undressing. **1841** LANE *Arab. Nts.* I. 121 In cold weather, the bather undresses in the former. **1885** *Law Rep. 10 P.D.* 93 She lay down on the bed in her clothes, and for three hours refused to undress.

†**c.** *refl.* and *intr.* To change one's dress. *Obs.*

1760–72 H. BROOKE *Fool of Qual.* (1809) IV. 83 If such a fine gentleman could condescend to undress himself, you might come.. as a person who wanted hire. **1769** LADY MARY COKE *Jrnl.* 15 June, Being engaged to dine at the Imperial Ambassador's at Kensington I undressed and set out at four o'clock.

2. *trans.* To divest or strip (a person) of clothes.

1615 G. SANDYS *Trav.* 67 Women stand prepared to vndresse her. **1732** LEDIARD *Sethos* II. IX. 282 He caus'd him to be undress'd in his presence. **1796** MME. D'ARBLAY *Camilla* V. 453 She resisted being undressed, and was seized with an aguish shivering fit. **1838** [MRS. MAITLAND] *Lett. fr. Madras* (1843) 206 The ayah undressed me as quickly as she could. **1885** R. BUCHANAN *Annan Water* ii, We must undress the child at once and put him to bed.

b. In fig. uses.

1633 P. FLETCHER *Poet. Misc., Ps. lxiii*, ii, Till I slumber, and death shall undresse me, Thus will I sing. **1668** BP. HOPKINS *Serm., Vanity* (1685) 143 It is childish to quarrel at that hand which undresses us.. only to lay us to sleep. *a* **1734** NORTH *Examen* Pref. (1740) p. i, The present Writer hath chosen.. to undress a filthy Libel not long since published. **1883** G. MOORE *Modern Lover* (1887) 75 He was conscious that Lord Seaton was undressing him with a look, and already knew that his clothes had come from Halet's.

c. To strip *of* something.

1641 MILTON *Ch. Govt.* II. Wks. 1851 III. 177 The protestant religion.. must undresse them of all their guilded vanities. *a* **1699** J. BEAUMONT *Psyche* XVI. xvii, Disrobe me of my Beauty, and unty My closest veins; undress me of my skin.

d. To dress scantily or lightly.

1818 *La Belle Assemblée* XVII. 75/1 She shrunk from the gaze on that display which mamma had undressed her in.

†**3.** To undo or disarrange (the hair). *Obs.*

1598 FLORIO, *Scapigliare*,.. to vndresse or vntie ones head or haires. **1601** WEEVER *Mirr. Mart.* B ij b, The baulme-sweet breathing of the aire.. diuides each haire, each plight vndresses. **1652** CRASHAW *Carmen Deo Nostro, Epiphanie* (Close), Thus he undresses His sacred unshorn tres[s]es.

4. To remove the dressing from (a wound).

1651 DAVENANT *Gondibert* I. VI. xxxiv, His hands the duke's worst-order'd wounds undress And gently binde.

Hence **un'dresser**. *rare.*

1611 COTGR., *Desapareilleur*, an vndresser; a maker vnreadie; a disorderer. **1658** COKAINE *Epithalamium* Poems 134 The fearfull Virgin's lead away;.. And her undresse[r]s tell next morn, What she must rise.

un'dressable, *a.* Of a doll: that can be undressed.

1972 *Daily Tel.* 7 Jan. 13 His 6½-year-old sister, longing for a 'mod' but cuddly undressable doll. **1983** *Harrods Mag.* Christmas 194/2 Washable, undressable dolls.

un'dressed, *ppl. a.* [UN-¹ 8, 8 c.]

I. Not dressed by trimming, putting in order, or preparing in some way.

1. Of the hair. (Cf. DRESS *v.* 13 b.)

1445 tr. *Claudian* in *Anglia* XXVIII. 281 Gallia fers with heere vndressid stode with a coler of price, Holdyng in hande ij. dartys to gider. **1598** FLORIO, *Scapigliata*, desheueled, vnkembd, vndrest about the head.

b. *fig.* Inelegant, unkempt.

1588 SHAKS. *L.L.L.* IV. ii. 17 To show as it were his inclination after his vndressed, vnpolished.. fashion.

c. Of a horse: Ungroomed.

1731 FIELDING *Grub St. Op.* I. ix, Have I not left my horses undrest, to whet thy knives?

2. †**a.** Of places (or things) in respect of orderly appearance or arrangement. *Obs.*

1530 *Nottingham Rec.* III. 364 [He] suffreth the merkett places to be vndressed. **1611** COTGR., *Taudis*,.. a foule, sluttish, vnhandsome, or vndressed roome. **1635** *Boston Rec.* (1877) II. 4 That all the wood.. shall bee gathered up, and layd or heaped in pyles,.. upon the forfeyture of 6*s.* for every load left undressed up. **1649** G. DANIEL *Trinarch., Rich. II*, ccxxxix, Ashes flew about The vndrest Hearth, and the ill house-wif'd roome Lay all on heaps.

b. Of a shop-window. (Cf. DRESS *v.* 8.)

1883 MISS BROUGHTON *Belinda* II. vii, In the haberdashers' undressed windows.. are to be seen nothing but bare boards and skeleton stands.

3. a. Of textile fabrics or materials. (Cf. DRESS *v.* 13 g and 11.)

1535 *Act 27 Hen. VIII*, c. 13 §1 Whiche white clothe.. shalbe.. solde for lesse price.. then thei shulde be vndressed. **1557** N. T. (Genev.) *Matt.* ix. 16 No man peceth an olde garment with a pece of new clothe and vndressed. **1617** MORYSON *Itin.* III. 274 Strict Lawes are made.. that the web vndressed be viewed by three skillfull men, and be marked according to the goodnes. **1670** R. COKE *Disc. Trade* 3 The Exportation of our White and Undrest Clothes. **1763** *Act 4 Geo. III*, c. 26 (*heading*), The Importation of.. rough and undressed Flax. **1834** MᶜCULLOCH *Dict. Commerce* (ed. 2) 646, Undressed hemp imported in 1831.

b. Of skins or leather. (Cf DRESS *v.* 13 f.)

1808 SCOTT *Marm.* V. v, The hunted red-deer's undress'd hide Their hairy buskins well supplied. **1853** KANE *Grinnell Exp.* v. (1856) 38 A black-locked Esquimaux, enveloped in an undressed seal-skin. **1898** *Daily News* 2 Dec. 5/1 The bindings in undressed morocco which mellows with age.

c. Of stone or wood. (Cf. DRESS *v.* 11.)

1846 *Hull & Lincoln Railway Bill* 11 All undressed materials for the repair of public roads. **1854** H. MILLER *Sch. & Schm.* (1858) 101 Flat undressed stones lay thick amid the rank grass. **1893** EARL DUNMORE *Pamirs* I. 22 Piers composed entirely of undressed logs.

4. Of wounds or sores. (Cf. DRESS *v.* 10.)

1597 A. M. tr. *Guillemeau's Fr. Chirurg.* 45 b/2 Simple Fractures, we keep sometimes sixe or seaven dayes vndressed. **1669** EARL ORRERY *Parthen.* (1676) 781 Those sleight hurts I had received, were still undrest. **1747** DODDRIDGE *Col. Gardiner* 12 The poor Patient's Wound being still undressed. **1782** J. WARTON *Ess. Pope* II. ix. 102 With their wounds undressed and putrifying. **1848** T. AIRD *Christian Bride* III. xxxii, That I may know if, still his wounds undressed, 'Tis safe to move him farther on his way.

5. Of grounds, trees, etc. (Cf. DRESS *v.* 13 c.)

1611 BIBLE *Lev.* xxv. 5 Thou shalt not.. gather the grapes of thy Vine vndressed. —— *2 Esdras* xvi. 78 Like as a field is.. left vndressed. **1697** DRYDEN *Virg. Past.* II. 104 Thy vineyard lies half-pruned, and half-undressed. **1780** A. YOUNG *Tour Irel.* I. 264 Crossing some of this undressed ground, we came to the point of a hill. **1813** SCOTT *Rokeby* II. xvii, Untrimm'd, undress'd, neglected now, Was alley'd walk and orchard bough.

6. Of food. (Cf. DRESS *v.* 13 a.)

1647 COWLEY *Mistress, Answ. Platonicks* 10 Beasts.. taste those pleasures as they do their food; Undrest they tak't. **1714** *Advt.* in *Westm. Gaz.* 18 Mar. (1909) 2/3 If any.. bring with them their own Provisions for Eating, undressed,.. they may have them dress'd after their own way. **1771** GOLDSM. *Haunch of Venison* 21 So I cut it [*sc.* venison], and sent it to Reynolds undrest. **1806** A. HUNTER *Culina* (ed. 3) 220 A dish, that.. differs very little from the flesh of an undressed lobster. **1832** R. & J. LANDER *Exped. Niger* I. i. 22 The chief was eating an undrest onion.

II. 7. Not covered or invested with clothing; unclothed, naked (or nearly so).

1613 W. BROWNE *Brit. Past.* I. iv. 474 To see misfortune spending Her utmost rage on Truth, dispisde, distressed, Unhappy, unrelieved, yet undressed. **1649** MARVELL in Lovelace *Poems* (1904) 5 The Ladies.. all in mutiny though yet undrest Sally'd. **1749** FIELDING *Tom Jones* I. iii, He.. now.. recollected his being undressed, and put an end to her terrors by desiring her to stay without the door. **1815** L. SIMOND *Tour Gt. Brit.* I. 3 The women highly dressed, or rather highly undressed, in extremely thin draperies. **1892** *Daily Tel.* 28 Apr. 3/2 What I would consider.. indecent is a naked woman which represents an undressed woman.

fig. **1754** WARBURTON *Bolingbroke's Philos.* ii. 102 You catch his First Philosophy.. undressed, and without a rag of form, but flaunting and fluttering in Fragments.

8. Not properly or fully dressed; wearing informal dress or undress.

1605 CHAPMAN *All Fooles* I. i. 73 Undressed, sluttish, nasty, to their husbands, Spung'd up, adorn'd, and painted to their lovers. **1668** PEPYS *Diary* 31 Mar., Took up my wife and Deb., and to the Park, where, being in a hackney, and they undressed, was ashamed to go into the tour. **1693** W. BOWLES in *Dryden's Juvenal* v. (1697) 96 Thus Blest, must Trebius to his Levees run,.. Break off sweet Slumbers, drowsie, and undrest, To shew his Zeal. **1753** RICHARDSON *Grandison* (1781) II. iv. 42 You came, though undressed, with your sword on. **1792** A. YOUNG *Trav. France* 213 The orchestra powerful, yet.. the musicians all so dirty and undressed. **1859** *Habits of Gd. Society* iii. 155 To be 'undressed' is to be dressed for work and ordinary occupations.

b. *transf.* Not of a dressy character; not requiring formal or full dress.

1798 JANE AUSTEN *Northang. Abb.* v, Neither at the upper nor lower rooms, at dressed or undressed balls, was he perceivable. **1809** MALKIN *Gil Blas* I. xv. ¶3 Plain cloths.. I threw aside with contempt, as thinking them too undrest.

un'dressing, *vbl. sb.* [f. UNDRESS *v.*] The action of taking off (one's own or another's) clothes.

1677 MIÉGE *Fr. Dict.* II. s.v., The Undressing of one. **1741–3** WESLEY *Jrnl.* (1749) 60 Our children were always put into a regular method of living,.. as in dressing, undressing, changing their linen, etc. **1789** GOUV. MORRIS *Diary* 27 May, So we have the whole performance of undressing and dressing except the shift. **1824** BYRON *Juan* XVI. xi, But next to dressing for a rout or ball, Undressing is a woe. **1866** KINGSLEY *Herew.* xiv, The queen-countess' chamber, where a solemn undressing of that royal lady.. took place.

attrib. **1697** POTTER *Archæol. Græca* I. 40 The Undressing-room. **1862** E. FALKENER *Ephesus* I. iv. 93 The large room at the back might be the apodyterium, or undressing-room.

undret, obs. variant of HUNDRED.

un'dried, *ppl. a.* (UN-¹ 8.)

c **1440** *Pallad. on Husb.* XII. 454 Elm & asshe ydried beth rigent, And while they beth vndried, so curuable [etc.]. **1565** COOPER, *Insiccatus*,.. vndried. **1683** MOXON *Mech. Exerc., Printing* xxiv. ¶10 Least his Weight pressing it cause the un-dryed Inck to Set-off. **1707** MORTIMER *Husb.* 139 Four pounds of undried Hops, thorough ripe. **1798** S. & HT. LEE *Canterb. T.* II. 372 The tears of apprehension were yet undried on the cheeks of Emily. **1801** *Farmer's Mag.* Apr. 215 An half boll of dried (about 8 pecks and a half of undried) bear.

un'drilled, *ppl. a.* (UN-¹ 8.)

[**1775** ASH.] **1837** CARLYLE *Fr. Rev.* III. I. iv, All Paris shall.. have itself enrolled. Unarmed,.. and undrilled; but desperate. **1864** E. SARGENT *Peculiar* I. 17 A mob of undrilled, uneducated Africans.

†**undrincled,** *ppl. a.*: see UN-¹ 3.

un'drinkable, *a.* (UN-¹ 7 b.)

1611 COTGR., *Imbuvable*, vndrinkable, vnfit to be drunke of. **1826** DISRAELI *V. Grey* VI. i, We.. refrain from refreshing our bodies with that sanctified and most undrinkable fluid. **1880** GEIKIE *Phys. Geog.* iii. 107 Should he taste some of this.. water he would find it salt and undrinkable.

Hence **un'drinkably** *adv.*

1894 *Pall Mall Mag.* Nov. 455 It [*sc.* coffee] was not undrinkably bad.

un'drinking, *vbl. sb.* (UN-¹ 13.)

1692 [see UNEATING *vbl. sb.*].

un'drivable, *a.* (UN-¹ 7 b.)

1873 LYTTON *Ken. Chillingly* I. v, If it be hard to drive a common pig.., a hog in armour is indeed undrivable.

un'driven, *ppl. a.* [UN-¹ 8 b and 15. Cf. OE. *undrifen.*] Not forced on by driving.

1615 BP. HALL *Contempl., O.T.* x. vi, When maintenance and honour calls him, hee goes vndriuen. **1697** DRYDEN *Æneis* x. 499 The doubtful rack of heav'n Stands without motion, and the tyde undriv'n. **1748** RICHARDSON *Clarissa* (1811) I. 214 It shall sooner burst than voluntarily, uncompelled, undriven, dictate a measure that shall cast a slur.. upon them. **1892** M. DODS *John* II. xiii. 195 To stand before life as independent, unfettered, undriven men.

b. Of snow: (App. for DRIVEN *ppl. a.* 2).

1833 DISRAELI *Cont. Flem.* v. xxii, Its [Sunium's] columns against a dark cloud looked like undriven snow. **1865** GOSSE *Land & Sea* 195 The purity of the undriven snow.

un'drooping, *ppl. a.* (UN-¹ 10.)

1736 THOMSON *Liberty* v. 79 Whate'er.. An ample generous Heart, undrooping Soul, And firm tenacious Valour can bestow. **1814** WORDSW. *Excurs.* VI. 1128 Bright garland form they for the pensive brow Of their undrooping Father's widowhood. **1854** J. D. BURNS *Vis. Prophecy* 121 Whose undrooping eye alone can keep Watch over His beloved.

un'dropped, *ppl. a.* (UN-¹ 8.)

1798 COLERIDGE *Nightingale* 105 His fair eyes, that swam with undropped tears.

un'drossy, *a.* (UN-¹ 7.)

1708 J. PHILIPS *Cyder* II. 228 Her wat'ry Skirts are edg'd With lucid Amber, or undrossy Gold. **1716** POPE *Iliad* VIII. 53 Of heaven's undrossy gold the god's array Refulgent, flash'd intolerable day.

un'drowned, *ppl. a.* [UN-¹ 8.] Not drowned, in various senses.

(*a*) **1573** TUSSER *Husb.* (1878) 104 To prouide ye of meadow for hay; if fennes be vndrowned, there cheapest ye may.

(*b*) **1610** SHAKS. *Temp.* II. i. 237 'Tis as impossible that hee's vndrown'd, As he that sleepes heere, swims. *Seb.* I haue no hope That hee's vndrown'd. *a* **1684** LEIGHTON *Com. 1 Pet.* iii. 21 (1849) II. 240 What availed it wicked Ham, to outlive the flood,.. to be kept undrowned in the waters? **1849** ALISON *Hist. Eur.* II. viii. §36 Such.. as were thrown undrowned upon the shore. **1858** CARLYLE *Fredk. Gt.* v. vii. (1872) II. 128 Gundling.. breaks a big hole in the ice, and scarcely.. can be got out undrowned.

(*c*) **1838** [MRS. MAITLAND] *Lett. fr. Madras* (1843) 222, I was in hopes.. I might be able to make out some of their tunes undrowned by their.. accompaniments. **1861** GEO. ELIOT *Silas M.* i, A village where many of the old echoes lingered, undrowned by new voices.

un'drugged, *ppl. a.*¹ (UN-¹ 8.)

1868 BROWNING *Ring & Bk.* VI. 1452 You lay down undrugged, I see. **1874** TYNDALL *Fragm. Sci.* (1879) II. x. 221 Out of the conflict of vanities his words emerge wholesome and strong, because undrugged by dogma.

un'drugged, *ppl. a.*² (UN-² 4 b, 8.)

1868 BROWNING *Ring & Bk.* II. 919 While Guido was left go and get undrugged.

un'drunk, *ppl. a.* [UN-¹ 8 b, c.]

1. Not swallowed by drinking; not drunk.

1637 HEYWOOD *Pleas. Dial.* ii. Wks. 1874 VI. 124 The wine that men At merry meetings jovially downe poure, Is happier far, than what (vndrunke) growes soure. **1796** MME. D'ARBLAY *Camilla* II. 47 Feeling her chagrin almost intolerable, [she] quitted the room with her tea undrunk. **1897** *Daily News* 2 June 7/3 Kaiser's health undrunk. Odd omission at a Hamburg banquet.

2. Not drunk *to*. (Cf. DRINK *v.*[1] 13 b.)

1618 HOLYDAY *Marr. Arts* III. v, These Noune-Adiectiues of the Fœminine gender sit all this while vndrunke to.

un'drunken, *ppl. a.* [UN-[1] 8 b. Cf. (in sense a) ON. *údrukkinn*, (in sense b) MDu. and Du. *ongedronken*, MHG. *ungetrunken*.]

a. Not affected by drinking; not partaking of drink. **b.** = UNDRUNK *ppl. a.* 1.

c **897** K. ÆLFRED *Gregory's Past C.* xl. 295 He..sua micle bet his aȝen dysiȝ oncnew sna he undruncenra wæs. *a* **1275** *Prov. Ælfred* 459 Drunken & vndrunkin, eyþer is wisdome wel god. *a* **1400–50** *Bk. Curtasye* III. 787 in *Babees Bk.*, In þe lordys cupp þat leuys vndrynken, Into þe almesdisshe hit schalle be sonken.

un'dry, *v.* [UN-[2] 7.] *intr.* To lose dryness.

c **1440** *Pallad. on Husb.* XI. 70 Ek there is warm & drie Ablaqueate hem that they may vndrie.

un'drying, *ppl. a.* (UN-[1] 10.)

1541 R. COPLAND *Galyen's Terap.* 2 Bj, The salues that are layde to the sayde vlceres must be more vndryeng than they that are layd to a syngle sore.

‖**und so weiter** (ʊnt zo 'vaɪtər). Also *occas.* as one word. [Ger.] And so forth.

1885 A. EDWARDES *Girton Girl* I. xiv. 277 One gets beastly weather for this sort of thing. Festive gatherings, I mean, *und so weiter*. **1930** E. POUND *XXX Cantos* xii. 54 First lot mortgaged to buy the second lot, undsoweiter. **1972** J. WAIN in Cox & Dyson *20th-Cent. Mind* I. xi. 366 They..held meetings to study European magic and Eastern philosophy, the fourth dimension, Odic force, *und so weiter*.

un'dub, *v.* (UN-[2] 3 + DUB *v.*[3] 2.)

1807 H. TUFTS in E. Pearson *Autobiogr. of Criminal* (1930) II. iv. 293 *Undub the jigger*, unlock the door..*Undub the qua*, unlock the jail. **1812** J. H. VAUX *Flash Dict.*, *Undub*, to unlock, unfasten, &c.

un'dubbed, *ppl. a.* [UN-[1] 8.]

1. Not invested with dignity or title.

1602 [? SIR J. ROE] in *Donne's Wks.* (1912) I. 403, I know What made his Valour, undubb'd, Windmill go, Within a Pintat most. **1803** [see UNDOCTORED]. **1894** STEVENSON *Songs of Travel*, *Woodman* x, I..climb Where no undubbed civilian dares, In my war harness, the loud stairs Of honour.

2. Not having the comb and gills removed.

1855 *Poultry Chron.* III. 429/1 To know whether the game chickens..are to be dubbed or undubbed. **1867** TEGETMEIER *Poultry Bk.* 139 In these combats an undubbed bird is at fearful disadvantage.

un'dubitable, *a.* Now *rare.* [UN-[1] 7 b and 5 b.] = INDUBITABLE *a.*

1643 PRYNNE *Sov. Power Parl.* II. 59 b, This their ancient undubitable oft-enjoyed Right and Priviledge. **1664** H. MORE *Myst. Iniq.* 207 A sense of things..so coherent with undubitable Principles. **1816** BENTHAM *Chrestom.* 208 To judge from the undubitable etymologies of the two words.

un'dubitably, *adv.* Now *rare.* [UN-[1] 11 and 5 b.] = INDUBITABLY *adv.*

1660 R. COKE *Power & Subj.* 38 Extorting it [*sc.* dominion] from their rightful Kings in whom it undubitably was. **1709** MRS. MANLEY *Secret Mem.* (1720) I. 219 That to be well receiv'd, it is undubitably necessary to become useful to those we would recommend ourselves to. **1778** STEEVENS in *Shaks. Wks.*, *Tit. A.* VIII. 561 The performances on which the seal of Shakespeare is undubitably fixed. **1890** *Retrospect Med.* CII. 133 The beneficial effect of the operation was thus undubitably established.

†**un'dubitate**, *a. Obs.* [UN-[1] 7 and 5 b.] = INDUBITATE *a.*

1482 CAXTON *Polycron.* VIII. xiii. 406 b, To depose them that were scysmatykes, and to chose one very heede and vndubytate pope. *a* **1548** HALL *Chron.*, *Hen. IV*, 15 An vndubitate kyng, crouned and anoynted by the spiritualtie. **1590** BARROUGH *Meth. Physick* IV. xi. (1596) 243 This shalbe a great and vndubitate signe to you. **1611** SPEED *Hist.* IX. xix. §26 The vndubitate heire to Richard Plantagenet.

So †**un'dubitately** *adv.* = INDUBITATELY *adv.*

a **1548** HALL *Chron.*, *Edw. IV*, 249 My hope is with a sure anchor grounded, and myne inwarde conceipte vndubitatly resolued. *Ibid.*, *Hen. VII*, 31 b.

un'ducal, *a.* (UN-[1] 7.)

1824 MOORE *Mem.* (1853) IV. 161 The Duke of Montrose's most un-ducal letter.

un'duchess, *v.* (UN-[2] 6 b.) Hence **un'duchessed**, *ppl. a.*

1819 *Metropolis* III. 239 How it would mortify my pride if I was, at a future period, to be un-Duchessed! **1887** BROWNING *Parleyings*, *D. Bartoli* xiv, That a fervid youth..loved, as boyhood can, The unduchessed lady.

undue (ʌn'dju:), *a.* [UN-[1] 7 + DUE *a.*, after OF. *indeu*, L. *indēbitus*.]

1. Not properly owing or payable.

1387 TREVISA *Higden* (Rolls) VIII. 241 For þe pope greved þe chirches of Engelond wiþ taxes and wiþ paiementis undewe and uncustemable. **1818** COLEBROOKE *Obligations* 98 It was not undue, though payment might have been postponed. **1843** CARLYLE *Past & Pr.* II. xii, My Lord of Clare, coming to claim his *un*due 'debt' in the Court at Witham.

2. Not appropriate or suitable; improper. Also of times, etc.: Unseasonable.

1398 TREVISA *Barth. De P.R.* II. xix. (1495) 45 Also in an undewe manere the deuyll coueyted highnes that fell not for hym. **1436** *Pol. Poems* (Rolls) II. 176 Thow this proverbe be homly and undew, Yet be liklynesse it is for soth fulle trew. *c* **1440** *Jacob's Well* 165 Whan playes arn hantyd in vndewe places & in vndewe tyme. **1541** *Act 33 Hen. VIII*, c. 21 §1 Culpeper and she met..at an vndue houre of a leuen a clocke in the night. **1585** T. WASHINGTON tr. *Nicholay's Voy.* I. xvii. 19 Wee woulde not at an vndue houre enter amongest the Turkes armie. **1641** SIR E. DERING *Sp. on Relig.* (1642) 77 Throwing that overboard which is adventitious, borrowed, and undue. **1680** W. ALLEN *Peace & Unity* Pref. p. lx, Our undue separations, and unchristian Contentions. *a* **1716** BP. O. BLACKALL *Wks.* (1723) I. 250 It is a Sin to omit the holy Duty, and it is likewise a Sin to perform it in an undue manner. **1774** J. BRYANT *Mythol.* I. 344 They seem to have been aware, that they were guilty of an undue representation. **1865** KINGSLEY *Herew.* xxi, Men-at-arms.., who would, on due or undue cause shown, hunt men while he hunted game. **1875** JOWETT *Plato* (ed. 2) V. 58 The undue awarding of honours is the ruin of states.

3. Not in accordance with what is just and right; unjustifiable; illegal.

c **1400** *Apol. Loll.* 11 If þe pope..graunt or behiȝt ani swilk þingis..for vndeu seruise, or oþer vndeu cause and vnpertinent. *c* **1440** *Jacob's Well* 99 Ȝif þou do it..wyth exces of vndewe mesure, wyth a strong wyll to sle,..it is dedly synne. **1456** *Coventry Leet Bk.* 293 Diuers subbaillifs of this Cite afore this han made many vndue returnes of preceptes directed..vnto theym. **1598** FLORIO, *Iritto*, vnlawfull, vndue, vnfit, vnright. **1622** BACON *Hen. VII*, 14 Which proceeding being even at that time taxed for vigorous and undue [etc.]. **1660** R. COKE *Justice Vind.* Ep. Ded. 7 Such miscreants..had by undue ways devoured the patrimony of the Church. **1692** LUTTRELL *Brief Rel.* (1857) II. 601 Irish letters say, divers persons were committed for undue practices. **1783** BURKE *Rep. Aff. India* Wks. XI. 149 Complaints against the inferiour collectors of the Landed Revenue, stating their undue and vexatious exactions.

b. In special contexts.

(*a*) **1477** EARL RIVERS (Caxton) *Dictes* iij b, To gadre money..by subtyl extorcion or other undewe meanes. **1534** *Act 26 Hen. VIII*, c. 2 Without gile, fraude, or other vndew meane. **1621** ELSING *Debates Ho. Lords* (Camden) App. 136 Those innes..that have benne lately erected by his undue meanes. **1676** HALE *Contempl.* II. 132 Frauds, and Plots, and Underminings, and Undue Means.

(*b*) **1687** BP. CARTWRIGHT in *Magd. Coll. & Jas. II* (O.H.S.) 134 The Election was undue. **1736** *Gentl. Mag.* VI. 440/1 The Petition..complaining of an undue Election and Return for the City of Coventry. **1764** T. HUTCHINSON *Hist. Mass.* I. (1765) 62 This election was immediately determined..to be undue..[and] a warrant issued for a new.

(*c*) **1735** BOLINGBROKE *On Parties* 122 Thus He acquired an undue Influence over the Elections. **1772** *Junius' Lett.* Ded. p. viii, Long parliaments are the foundation of the undue influence of the crown. **1584** *Act 17 & 18 Vict.* c. 102 (*title*), An Act to..amend the Laws relating to Bribery, Treating, and undue Influence at Elections.

†**c.** Of persons: Acting unjustly. *Obs.*[-1]

a **1400** *Pistill of Susan* 236 Hir domus men vnduwe do hir be withdrawen.

4. Going beyond what is appropriate, warranted, or natural; excessive.

a **1684** LEIGHTON *Comm. 1 Pet.* iv. 8 (1849) II. 350 [Love] delights not in the undue disclosing of brethren's failings. **1739** *Hist. Works of Learned* I. 137 He seems to own they are both chargeable with some Instances of undue Warmth and Zeal. **1780** COWPER *Progr. Error* 269 Pleasure admitted in undue degree, Enslaves the will. **1814** CHALMERS *Evid.* i. 21 An undue advantage has been given to that argument. **1865** TYLOR *Early Hist. Man.* i. 2 An undue confidence in the statements of ancient writers. **1893** TRAILL *Soc. Eng.* Introd. p. xiv, The undue prominence formerly given..to these matters has produced a reaction.

Hence **un'dueness.** *rare.*

1653 W. A[LLEN] (*title*), An Answer..in which..the Undueness of mixt Communion is declared. **1680** —— *Peace & Unity* Pref. p. xxxv, I shall..argue the undueness of their practise that withdraw..upon the foresaid ground.

unduely, obs. f. UNDULY *adv.*

un'dug, *ppl. a.* (UN-[1] 8 b, c.)

1657 W. RAND tr. *Gassendi's Life Peiresc* III. 34 The remainder [of the epitaph] being as yet..undug up. *c* **1730** WALDRON *Descr. Isle of Man* Wks. (1731) 188 Their Turf lay in the Bowels of the Earth undug for. **1775** S. J. PRATT *Liberal Opin.* xliii. (1783) I. 256 There may be still an undug mine of knowledge. **1844** MRS. BROWNING *Drama of Exile* 1149, I feel your steps..strike A sense of death to me, and undug graves! **1894** *Outing* XXIV. 427/2 In the few drills of undug potatoes which the improvident Casey had left.

un'duke, *v.* (UN-[2] 6 b.)

1611 FLORIO, *Sducare*, to vn-duke. **1663** PEPYS *Diary* 12 Dec., He hath letters from France that the King hath unduked twelve Dukes. **1893** *Westm. Gaz.* 10 Mar. 3/2 Is it the Duke of Devonshire un-Duked?

undulant ('ʌndjʊlənt), *a.* [ad. L. **undulant-*, *undulans*: cf. next, and Sp. *undulante*, F. *ondulant*.] **a.** Moving after the manner of waves; rising and falling like waves.

1830 MAUNDER *Dict.* **1834** LD. HOUGHTON *Tour Greece* 138 Whose sweet undulant murmur the homeless mariner hearkened, Over the undulant sapphire. **1862** SIR H. TAYLOR *St. Clement's Eve* II. ii, Sea-spirits..Gliding and lapsing in an undulant dance. **1896** HOWELLS *Impress. & Exp.* 215 The lesser craft that plied upon the many channels of the meadows..seemed to sail upon their undulant grasses.

b. *undulant fever*: a rarely fatal febrile disease, caused by bacteria of the genus *Brucella*, which may be chronic but intermittent or acute and chiefly affects the reticuloendo-thelial system; (human) brucellosis.

1896 M. L. HUGHES in *Lancet* 25 July 239/2 It has occurred to me that the term 'Undulant Fever', by referring to the peculiar pyrexial curve so characteristic of the disease, might prove a serviceable name. **1897** M. L. HUGHES *Medit. Fever* i. 3 *note*, During epidemics of undulant or enteric fevers. **1930** J. T. DUNCAN et al. in *Syst. Bacteriol.* (Med. Research Council) V. ix. 404 There has been much controversy as to whether *Br. abortus*, so commonly found in cattle, is capable of producing undulant fever in man. **1968** PASSMORE & ROBSON *Compan. Med. Stud.* I. xviii. 75/1 *Br. melitensis* causes a similar infection in goats and is common in Mediterranean countries. In man it gives rise to a severe form of undulant fever called Malta fever.

Hence **'undulancy**, wave-like motion.

a **1921** *N.E.D.* s.v. Undulant *a.*

'undular, *a.* [ad. L. type **undulār-is*: cf. next.]

a. Wavy, undulating.

1738 CHAMBERS *Cycl.* s.v. *Muscle*, They contract themselves into an undular kind of surface.

b. Applied to a type of hydraulic jump consisting of a number of waves of diminishing size trailing downstream, with little difference in the water levels on either side of them.

1961 V. L. STREETER *Handbk. Fluid Dynamics* XXIV. 36 On the basis of Froude number..the hydraulic jump may be classified into five types... For F_1 = 1 to 1·7, the flow surface shows undulations; an undular jump is formed. **1982** *Sci. Amer.* June 134/2 Whether a particular bore is breaking or undular depends on the height of the tide, the depth of the river, [etc.].

Hence **'undularly** *adv.*

1805 T. WEAVER tr. *Werner's Ext. Charact. Fossils* 275, 1. Spherically..2. Undularly.

†**'undulary**, *a. Obs.*[-1] [ad. L. type **undulārius*, f. *unda* wave: cf. next.] Coming in waves.

1646 SIR T. BROWNE *Pseud. Ep.* VII. xvii. 377 The blasts and undulary breaths thereof maintaine no certainty in their course.

undulate ('ʌndjʊlət), *a.* [ad. L. *undulāt-us* diversified as with waves, f. *unda* wave. Cf. Sp. *undulado*, F. *ondulé*.]

1. Furnished with wave-like markings.

1658 PHILLIPS, *Undulate*, Chamolet wrought, or painted like waves. **1661** LOVELL *Hist. Anim. & Min.* Isagoge, The cramp-fish,..raie undulate and oculate. **1706** PHILLIPS (ed. Kersey), *Undulate*, or *Undulated*, made in fashion of Waves, as watered Stuffs and the Grain of Wainscot.

2. *Bot.* and *Zool.* = UNDULATED *ppl. a.* 1.

Also comb., as ***undulate-convex***, ***-serrate***, etc.

a. *Bot.* **1760** J. LEE *Introd. Bot.* I. xii. (1765) 28 *Undulate*, waved, as in *Gloriosa*. **1821** W. P. C. BARTON *Flora N. Amer.* I. 91 Leaves..entire, but undulate and irregular on the margin. **1870** HOOKER *Stud. Flora* 305 Margins cartilaginous and undulate when dry.

b. *Zool.* **1826** KIRBY & SP. *Entomol.* IV. 290 *Undulate*,.. when fasciæ, strigæ, lines, &c. curve into alternate sinuses resembling the rise and fall of waves. *Ibid.* 293 *Undulate*,.. when the surface rises and falls obtusely, not in angles. **1846** DANA *Zooph.* (1848) 167 Surface a little undulate.

undulate ('ʌndjʊleɪt), *v.* [ad. L. type **undulāt-* (cf. prec.), ppl. stem of **undulāre*, f. *unda*. Cf. Sp. and Pg. *undular*, It. *ondulare*, F. *onduler*.]

1. *intr.* To move in, or after the manner of, waves; to have a wave-like motion.

1664 POWER *Exp. Philos.* I. 69 The former Experiment of the Snail,..whose Animal Spirits never begin to undulate till she begin to move. **1721** BAILEY, To *Undulate*, to roll as waves do. **1796** H. HUNTER tr. *St.-Pierre's Stud. Nat.* (1799) II. 41 The..swallow is continually skimming along their surface, undulating like the waters of a lake. **1820** SHELLEY *To M. Gisborne* 120 The ripe corn under the undulating air Undulates like an ocean. **1869** J. PHILLIPS *Vesuv.* ix. 253 The water undulates, the land vibrates.

b. *transf.* Of sound, etc.

1760–72 H. BROOKE *Fool of Qual.* (1809) IV. 158 An universal shout..followed and undulated after our company. **1784** COWPER *Task* I. 175 Tall spire, from which the sound of cheerful bells Just undulates upon the list'ning ear. **1818** SHELLEY *Rosalind* 833 The light serene Of smiles, whose lustre bright and soft Beneath lay undulating there.

c. To float *on* waves. Also *fig.*

1813 H. & J. SMITH *Horace in Lond.* 24 He undulates on Ocean's swell. **1891** T. HARDY *Tess* xix, She undulated upon the thin notes [of the harp] as upon billows.

2. *trans.* **a.** To cause to move, esp. to rise and fall, after the manner of waves.

1669 HOLDER *Elem. Speech* 47 It may very well be, that Breath vocalized, i.e. vibrated or undulated, may in a different manner affect the Lips. **1725** *Fam. Dict.* s.v. *Hot-bath*, Like a Fomentation, which..by gently shaking and undulating the Fibres, helps forwards those animal Motions. **1865** *Intell. Observ.* Sept. 84 A snail-leech.. attaching its suckers to the glass vessel in which it is confined, and..undulating the intervening portion of the body. **1873** LELAND *Egypt. Sketch-Bk.* 135 The first dancing of all Ghawâzi is simply moving about to the music and undulating the body.

b. To invest with the form or appearance of a wavy or rippling surface.

1730 A. GORDON *Maffei's Amphith.* 351 The red..and yellow Coverings of the Theatre, reflected back on the Assembly of Spectators,..undulating the whole with their Colours. **1804** SHAW *Gen. Zool.* V. 419 The body is obliquely undulated by twelve lines of the same colour. **1843** tr. *Custine's Empire of Czar* I. 216 It is for man to build mountains, when nature has not undulated the surface of the earth.

3. *intr.* To present a wavy surface or outline.

1833 L. RITCHIE *Wand. by Loire* 255 The vast plain undulates in hills and valleys. **1849** RUSKIN *Sev. Lamps* v. §13. 149 There is not one of the arches the same in height as another; their tops undulate all along the wall. **1866** GEO.

Eliot *F. Holt* i, A..masculine face, with rich brown hair.. undulating beside each cheek.

b. To have the effect of waves to the eye.

1888 H. W. PARKER *Spirit of Beauty* 220 Silks of changing hues that undulate like a purple sunset on a billowy sea.

undulated (ˈʌndjʊleɪtɪd), *ppl. a.* [Cf. prec. and UNDULATE *a.*]

1. Formed into a waved surface or outline; arranged in a series of wave-like curves.

1623 COCKERAM I, *Vndulated*, made like the waues of the Sea. **1673** GREW *Anat. Trunks* I. i. §31 Next there is an undulated Ring of other Lymphæducts. **1753** *Chambers' Cycl.* Supp. s.v. *Leaf, Undulated leaf*, that whose..edges are necessitated to rise and fall in a regular manner. **1783** *Phil. Trans.* LXXIII. 181 The bridge has taken an undulated form, and the rail on each side is curiously scolloped. *a* **1853** PEREIRA *Polarized Light* (1854) 117 A series of rods disposed horizontally in an undulated form, so as to represent a system of plane waves. **1873** J. TOMES *Dental Surg.* (ed. 2) 7 The inferior edge of the lower jaw..is undulated.

b. Of ground, hills, etc. (Cf. UNDULATING 2 b.)

1821 T. NUTTALL *Arkansa* 11 A deeply undulated country. **1845** E. WARBURTON *Crescent & Cross* I. 15 An amphitheatre of finely undulated hills. **1893** SIR H. HOWORTH *Glacial Nightmare* I. 59 A small elevated plain, slightly undulated.

2. Furnished or diversified with wavy markings.

1664 EVELYN *Sylva* xxv. 65 The Roots of this [Box] Tree ..do furnish the..Cabinet-makers with pieces rarely undulated. **1706** PHILLIPS [see UNDULATE *a.* 1]. **1787** [see 2 b]. **1798** *Lond. Gaz.* 20 Nov., A Chief undulated Argent, thereon Waves of the Sea. **1811** SHAW *Gen. Zool.* VIII. 469 Yellowish Green Parrakeet, undulated above with brown.

b. *spec.* In the names of birds or fishes.

1785 LATHAM *Gen. Synop. Birds* III. 333 Undulated Fly-catcher. **1787** *Ibid.* Suppl. 225 Undulated Trumpeter;..the plumage..of a pale reddish brown, beautifully undulated with black. **1803** SHAW *Gen. Zool.* IV. 223 Undulated Coryphene. **1811** *Ibid.* VIII. 469 Undulated Parrakeet.

ˈundulately, *adv.* [f. UNDULATE *a.*] In a wave-like manner.

1872 H. C. WOOD *Fresh-Water Algæ* (1874) 144 End lobes ..sinuately or undulately cut at the apex.

ˈundulating, *ppl. a.* [f. UNDULATE *v.*]

1. Moving after the manner of waves; rising and falling in (or like) waves.

1711 POPE *Temple Fame* 446 Thro' undulating air the sounds are sent. **1758** REID tr. *Macquer's Chym.* I. 268 From these cracks will issue undulating flames. **1816** SIR H. DOUGLAS *Milit. Bridges* 70 The intervals must be considerable, and the balks be laid from boat to boat only, to admit of an undulating motion. **1820** W. IRVING *Sketch Bk.* I. 12 To watch the gently undulating billows, rolling their silver volumes. *a* **1874** in Coues *Birds N.W.* 113 Its flight is in undulating lines, like the Crossbill's.

b. *transf.* Of sounds.

1700 DRYDEN *Ovid's Met.* XII. 60 Whence all Things.. thither bring their Undulating Sound. **1712** BLACKMORE *Creation* VII. 101 Mark how the spirits..Seize undulating sounds, and catch the vocal air. **1844** KINGLAKE *Eothen* i. 6 Those well-undulating tones [of speech] which belong to the best Osmanlees.

c. *fig.* Exhibiting variations comparable to the rising and falling of waves.

1815 BENTHAM *Springs of Action* Wks. 1843 II. 202 The maintenance of discipline among the undulating and tumultuous multitude. **1849** DE MORGAN *Trigonometry & Double Algebra* 1 Trigonometry contains the science of continually undulating magnitude. **1898** P. MANSON *Trop. Diseases* x. 182 Those cases [of Malta Fever] with well-marked waves of fever he calls 'undulating'.

2. Forming a series of wave-like curves.

1728 CHAMBERS *Cycl.* s.v. *Muscle*, The Fibres..contract themselves into a wavy undulating kind of Surface. **1799** KIRWAN *Geol. Ess.* 369 The strata are parallel to each other, horizontal or undulating. **1846** ELLIS *Elgin Marb.* II. 23 The undulating flow given to every part of the drapery. **1884** BOWER & SCOTT *De Bary's Phaner.* 366 The endodermis.. only differs..in the undulating bands on its radial walls.

b. Of grounds, hills, etc.: Presenting a succession of gently rounded heights and hollows.

1794 PIOZZI *Synon.* II. 353 The wavy corn floats very beautifully upon the undulating downs. **1815** ELPHINSTONE *Acc. Caubul* III. i. 351 It is an undulating plain, about twenty-five miles long. **1832** G. DOWNES *Lett. Cont. Countries* I. 451 The luxuriance of the region, into whose leafy and beautifully undulating bosom we were now to be immerged. **1873** MRS. BROOKFIELD *Not a Heroine* II. 162 Soft, undulating distant hills.

Hence **ˈundulatingly** *adv.*

1796 KIRWAN *Elem. Min.* (ed. 2) I. 85 In some places it was dark grey, and undulatingly slaty. **1835** *Blackw. Mag.* XXXVII. 341 The..line of the sky, that..plays undulatingly from and into the..deeper tones of the river's visible bed.

undulation (ʌndjʊˈleɪʃən). [ad. med. or mod.L. **undulātio*: cf. UNDULATE *a.* and *v.*, and Sp. *undulacion* (Pg. *-ação*), F. *ondulation*, It. *ondulazione*.]

1. The action of moving in a wave-like manner; a gentle rising and falling in the manner of waves.

1646 SIR T. BROWNE *Pseud. Ep.* III. xv. 142 Those animals, whose bodies consist of..annulary fibers, and move by undulation, that is, like the waves of the Sea. **1664** POWER *Exp. Philos.* I. 36 Their motion is..restless and constant, with perpetual undulations and wavings, like Eels or Snakes. **1707** FLOYER *Physic. Pulse-Watch* 267 The undulation of the Spirits towards the Brain produces all our Sensations. **1762** FALCONER *Shipwreck* I. 308 Soon this transient undulation o'er The sea subsides. **1820** KEATS *Hyperion* III. 132 His golden tresses..Kept undulation round his eager neck. **1854** OWEN in *Orr's Circ. Sci., Org. Nat.* I. 228 Whales and porpoises progress by bounding movements or undulations in a vertical plane. **1875** MANNING *Mission H. Ghost* iv. 106 We are as unstable as.. the restless undulation of the water.

transf. **1777** JOHNSON *Lett.* I. 389 Mrs. * * grows old, and has lost much of her undulation and mobility.

b. A wave-like motion of the air, 'ether', etc., as in the propagation of sound or light.

1658 PHILLIPS s.v., Undulation of the air. **1672** *Phil. Trans.* VII. 5148 The other Secondary Affections of Winds; as their Undulation,..Opposition, etc. **1728** CHAMBERS *Cycl.* s.v. *Sound*, A Wave or Undulation of Air. **1764** REID *Inquiry* iv. §1. 117 Each undulation must be made up of the advance and recoil of innumerable particles of elastic air. **1802** YOUNG in *Phil. Trans.* XCII. 21 The undulations of green light being nearly in the ratio of 6½. **1870** H. SPENCER *Princ. Psych.* I. I. iii. 47 Those minute agents that terminate the nerves of the retina are acted on by luminiferous undulations.

Comb. **1838** WHEWELL in Todhunter *Acc. Writ.* (1876) II. 269 A curious..paper upon the theory of the rainbow treated undulation-wise.

c. *transf.* Of sound.

1668 DRYDEN *Ess. Dram. Poesy* ¶3 Those little undulations of sound..still seeming to retain somewhat of their first horror. **1705** ADDISON *Italy* 42 Two parallel Walls that beat the Sound back on each other, till the Undulation is quite worn out. **1791** MRS. RADCLIFFE *Rom. Forest* xi, The notes floated on the air in soft undulations. **1851** FROUDE *Short Stud., Homer* (1867) II. 166 The actions of men.. crumble away into the softer undulations of prose.

†**d.** *spec.* (See quot.) *Obs.*⁻¹

1676 GREW *Musæum, Anat. Stomach* vi. 25 Vndulation, is when the Contraction is made in several parts of the Stomach successively.

2. A wave-like curve or a series of these; an undulating curvature or sweep.

1670 EVELYN *Sylva* (ed. 2) 119 The Root of the wilder sort [is] incomparable for its crisped undulations. **1803** SHAW *Gen. Zool.* IV. 497 Scales..edged with yellow, so as to form numerous obliquely transverse undulations over the whole body. **1846** CARPENTER *Man. Phys.* 186 Minute tubuli,.. exhibiting numerous minute undulations, and sometimes more decided curvatures, in their course. **1875** SIR T. SEATON *Fret-Cutting* 36 How..you will turn or bend the stalks, so as to give a natural undulation and appearance to the whole work.

3. The fact of forming or presenting a series of rounded heights and hollows; an undulating rise and fall of level.

1798 S. & HT. LEE *Canterb. T.* II. 441 For many a mile, with graceful undulation, wandered the high road. **1835** WILLIS *Pencillings* I. xxiv. 167 A continual undulation of rock and sand.

b. An instance of this; also, a single rise and fall of this nature.

1823 RUTTER *Fonthill* 86 The undulations of the surface occasionally give a beautiful variety to the scene. **1878** HUXLEY *Physiogr.* 214 Here the strata..have been thrown into a succession of gentle undulations.

unduˈlationist. [f. prec. + -IST.] One who holds the undulatory theory of light.

1834 WHEWELL in Todhunter *Acc. Writ.* (1876) II. 194 We undulationists do not conceive that we are in many points inferior to our adversaries. **1881** *Nature* XXIV. 382/1, I suppose that in the ordinary language of undulationists the velocity of light means..the velocity with which an individual wave travels.

ˈundulative, *a. rare*⁻⁰. = UNDULATORY *a.*

1860 WORCESTER (citing Fletcher).

unduˈlato-, comb. form of UNDULATE *a.*, used in some botanical terms, as ***undulato-rugose***, ***-striate***.

1829 LOUDON *Encycl. Plants* (1836) 1027 *Stromatosphæria deusta*;..rigid spreading thick undulato-rugose. **1866** *Treas. Bot.* 1191/1 Undulato-striate.

undulator (ˈʌndjʊleɪtə(r)). [f. UNDULATE *v.* + -OR.] **1.** *Telegr.* A device for recording Morse signals in which a line is traced on a roll of paper by a pen that is deflected sideways during the transmission of a dot or dash.

1910 *Post Office Electr. Engineers' Jrnl.* II. 312 The undulator is an instrument of considerable sensitiveness working with a current of ·5 milliampères, and is capable of recording 200, or slightly more, words per minute. **1921** *Wireless World* IX. 479/2, I have in addition two picture slides which illustrate the undulator of Messrs. Creed & Co. **1959** K. HENNEY *Radio Engin. Handbk.* (ed. 5) xxiv. 35 Reception..is effected by recording the incoming Morse signal on an ink recorder, or undulator.

2. *Physics.* A device in which a beam of particles is made to describe a sinusoidal path (and so emit radiation) by a series of transverse electric or magnetic fields of alternating polarity.

Orig. introduced as a means of generating microwaves of millimetre and submillimetre wavelength.

1951 H. MOTZ in *Jrnl. Appl. Physics* XXII. 529/2 We want to calculate the energy radiated by an electron riding through a succession of electric or magnetic fields of alternating polarity. We shall call the arrangement an undulator. **1963** A. F. HARVEY *Microwave Engin.* xii. 559 The electrons can be given a transverse motion by passage through an undulator. **1981** *McGraw-Hill Yearbk. Sci. & Technol.* 406/1 Multiperiod wigglers or undulators have also been used recently to make quasi-monochromatic photon beams.

undulatory (ˈʌndjʊlətərɪ), *a.* [ad. mod.L. type **undulātōri-us*: cf. UNDULATE *v.* and -ORY. So Sp. and Pg. *undulatorio*, It. *ondulatorio*, F. *ondulatoire*.]

1. Of motion: Characterized by successive rise and fall after the manner of waves.

1728 CHAMBERS *Cycl.* s.v. *Undulation*, The Undulatory Motion of the Air, is supposed the..Cause of Sound. **1759** *Phil. Trans.* LI. 531 The motion here appeared to be very deep, and was rather undulatory than tremulous. **1832** BREWSTER *Nat. Magic* iv. (1833) 78 A tempest at sea is imitated, by having the sea on one slider, and the ships on other sliders, to which an undulatory movement is communicated. **1879** R. H. ELLIOT *Written on Forehead* xvi, The translator..tells us that breadth across the hips.. would give an undulatory motion to their walk.

b. Exhibiting, or acting with, undulating motion.

1794 R. J. SULIVAN *View Nat.* I. 169 An elastic fluid.. would cause an undulatory diffusion of the luminous particles. **1813** J. THOMSON *Lect. Inflam.* 525 This air.. gives an elastic undulatory sensation to the fingers. **1882** *Gd. Words* June 382 Vast masses of white cumulus clouds.. piled up as in great undulatory breaking billows.

c. ***undulatory theory*** (also ***hypothesis***, †***system***), the theory that light consists in an undulatory movement of an elastic medium pervading space.

1802 YOUNG in *Phil. Trans.* XCII. 13 That prepossession which I before entertained for the undulatory system of light. **1827-8** HERSCHEL in *Encycl. Metrop.* (1845) IV. 449 General Statement of the Undulatory Theory of Light. **1834** MRS. SOMERVILLE *Connex. Phys. Sci.* xxi. 190 These intervals determine the lengths of the waves on the undulatory hypothesis.

2. = UNDULATING *ppl. a.* 2 and 2 b.

1796 MORSE *Amer. Geog.* I. 220 The other moccasin snake is..of a pale grey, sky-coloured ground, with brown undulatory ringlets. **1845** DARWIN *Voy. Nat.* xiv, In wooded undulatory districts. **1853** G. JOHNSTON *Nat. Hist. E. Bord.* I. 51 An undulatory rising ground. **1884** in H. Thompson *Tumours Bladder* 94 The deep limit of the growth is clearly defined, convex, undulatory or lobular in character.

3. *fig.* = UNDULATING *ppl. a.* 1 c.

1897 M. L. HUGHES *Medit. Fever* 99 The remittent..type of pyrexia of the undulatory or malignant varieties.

unˈdull, *a.* (UN-¹ 7.)

c **1400** *Destr. Troy* 13908 To the noise oponone neghit þe kyng..With a dart vndull.

unˈdull, *v.* (UN-² 6 a.)

1654 WHITLOCK *Zootomia* 477 Poetry..is a most musicall Modulator of all Intelligibles,..undulling their Grossenesse.

unˈdulled, *ppl. a.* (UN-¹ 8.)

[**1775** ASH.] **1837** MANGAN *Poems* (1903) 265 His laughing flowers are Undulled by tears. **1899** MACKAIL *Life Morris* II. 337 His own admiration was undulled by their complete ..fraternity.

unˈdullness. (UN-¹ 12.)

1793 T. TWINING in *Recreat. & Stud.* (1882) 180 His admirable sense, and undulness of conversation.

ˈundulose, *a.* [Cf. next and -OSE.] = next. ***undulose extinction***, extinction (sense 1 c(ii)) that occurs in strips which move across the field of view of the microscope as the stage is turned.

1889 *Q. Jrnl. Geol. Soc.* May 342 The curvature of the twin-lamellæ, which is accompanied by..a marked 'undulose' extinction. **1975** *Nature* 10 Apr. 489/1 Granular xenoliths..show various strain effects, including undulose extinction.

undulous (ˈʌndjʊləs), *a.* [ad. mod.L. type **undulōs-us*: cf. UNDULATE *v.* and -OUS. So Sp. and Pg. *unduloso*, F. *onduleux*.] Of an undulating nature. Hence (more recently) **ˈundulously** *adv.*

1728 CHAMBERS *Cycl.* s.v. *Undulation*, The adjoining Liquid..forms the first undulous Circle. **1862** LYTTON *Str. Story* xvii, A vague, dusky vapour, undulous, and coiling like a vast serpent. *Ibid.* lxx, Beyond stretch undulous pastures. **1869** BLACKMORE *Lorna D.* lxv, He felt the undulous readiness of her volatile paces under him.

unduly (ʌnˈdjuːlɪ), *adv.* [UN-¹ 11: cf. UNDUE *a.*]

1. Without due cause or justification; without proper regard to right and wrong; unrightfully, improperly.

1399 LANGL. *Rich. Redeles* II. 124 þus ȝe derid hem vnduly with droppis of anger. **1426** AUDELAY *Poems* (Percy Soc.) 35 Aȝayns the order of holé cherch and Goddys ordenawns This dole is undeulé dalt, hit maketh dystans. **1477** EARL RIVERS (Caxton) *Dictes* 44 b, Nether is nothing so [un]couenable to a king as to coueyte vnduely the goodes of his peple. **1598** FLORIO, *Indebitamente*, vndulie, vnlawfullie. **1657** in Picton *L'pool Munic. Rec.* (1883) I. 214 The same Ley shalbe denyed and not paid, being unduly taxed. **1687** *Reason. Toleration* 33 Unless it can be prov'd that it is for the Common Good,..the Penal Laws are unduly made. **1721** STRYPE *Eccl. Mem.* III. xix. 161 Remitting and relaxing to all persons..all the fruits and profits from the same taken, however unduly. **1796** MME. D'ARBLAY *Camilla* III. 394 She could only feel reproach from a conquest, unduly, unfairly and uningenuously obtained. **1844** MRS. BROWNING *Lost Bower* ix, While beyond,..Malvern hills, for mountains counted Not unduly, loom a-row.

b. Irregularly.

1660 JER. TAYLOR *Ductor* III. iv. rule 16 §4 Alexander the third..was a schismatical Pope,..and unduly elected.

† **2.** Without due care or industry; badly; not in the right way. *Obs.*

1423 *Rolls of Parlt.* IV. 255/2 All the werk of Brauderie so undwely made as above. **1444** *Ibid.* V. 108/1 Divers Sherryffs..unduely and yvell and untruely served the Kyng and his poeple. **1477** EARL RIVERS (Caxton) *Dictes* 35 b, Many erre by cause they seke her [*sc.* Wisdom] vnduely and blame her without cause.

3. More than is due or proper; excessively.

a **1779** WARBURTON *Serm.* Wks. 1788 V. 431 The mechanism of the body,..when unduly agitated either by sensation or reflection. **1841** MYERS *Cath. Th.* IV. §19. 276 Unquestionably External evidences..have been unduly magnified. **1869** FREEMAN *Norm. Conq.* (1875) III. xiii. 281 On such mere backslidings William had never been unduly harsh.

un'dumpish, *v.* (UN-² 6; see DUMPISH *a.*)

a **1661** FULLER *Worthies, Stafford.* III. (1662) 47 When Queen Elizabeth was serious..and out of good humour, he could un-dumpish her at his pleasure.

un'dunged, *ppl. a.* (UN-¹ 8.)

c **1440** *Pallad. on Husb.* II. 152 Vndonged sleck wole make hem lene, as preue is. **1733** TULL *Horse-hoeing Husb.* 73 Wider and narrower Spaces, more or less Hoed, dung'd and undung'd. **1763** MILLS *Pract. Husb.* II. 351, I perceived no ..difference..between the dunged and the undunged beds.

undur, var. of UNDERN *Obs.*

un'durable, *a.* (UN-¹ 7 b and 5 b.)

c **1550** COVERDALE *Bk. Death* I. viii. 28 Among all thinges, most vndurable and most frayle is mannes lyfe. **1600** SURFLET *Countrie Farme* III. xlix. 530 A rawe, weake,.. vndurable, and soone souring licour. **1650** ARNWAY *Tablet* 107 All unmeasurable vice is undurable. **1721** R. KEITH tr. *T. à Kempis, Vall. Lillies* xxx. 93 All temporal Things are defective and undurable. **1886** DICEY *England's Case* 65 As undurable as Grattan's Constitution of 1782.

Hence **un'durableness.**

1648 HEXHAM II, *Ongeduerigheyt*, Vndurablenesse. **1691** T. H[ALE] *Acc. New Invent.* 7 Its undurableness and doubtful efficacy.

† **un'dure**, *v. Obs.*⁻¹ [f. UN-² 6 a + L. *dūr-us* hard.] *trans.* To crumble, break up.

c **1440** *Pallad. on Husb.* III. 1174 And pocion forsayd in sum mesure Half ful be don, quik erthe among vndure [L. *resolvas*] As ly is made.

undurn(e, varr. UNDERN *Obs.*

un'dust, *v.* [UN-² 4 b.] *trans.* To clear from dust; to wipe clean.

1611 FLORIO, *Dispolueráre*, to vndust. **1654** W. MONTAGUE *Dev. Ess.* II. vi. §3. 121 When we frequently dress up the Altar of our hearts, and undust it from all these little foulnesses. **1884** in *N. & Q.* 14 June 466/1 The piece [a play] has been unearthed, or rather undusted, by Mr. Thicke.

un'dusted, *ppl. a.* [UN-¹ 8.]

1. Not sprinkled with dust.

1648 HEXHAM II, *Onbestoven*, Vndusted.

2. Not freed from dust; left dusty.

1862 THORNBURY *Turner* I. 308 The old Greek books, long undusted, are brought out. **1868** *Dublin Univ. Mag.* Aug. 124/2 Dr. Johnson wrote a tragedy, but..suffered it to moulder on his undusted shelves.

un'duteous, *a.* (and *adv.*). [UN-¹ 7.]

1. Undutiful; also *adv.*, undutifully.

1598 SHAKS. *Merry W.* v. v. 240 This deceit looses the name of craft, Of disobedience, or vnduteous title. **1645** MILTON *Tetrach.* Wks. 1851 IV. 260 Perpetually unsociable, unpeacefull, or unduteous. **1694** DRYDEN *Love Triumph.* I. i, I..must condemn This carriage, as unduteous to your father. **1745** *Matrimony pro & con* 7 What! teach a Child unduteous to behave? **1848** LYTTON *Harold* XI. viii, Why this dispute?—why this unduteous discord?

2. *spec.* = INOFFICIOUS *a.* 1 b. *rare*⁻¹.

1861 MAINE *Anc. Law* vii. 215 A new remedy..called ..'The Plaint of an Unduteous Will,' directed to the reinstatement of the issue in inheritances, from which they had been unjustifiably excluded.

un'dutiful, *a.* [UN-¹ 7.]

1. Contrary to the spirit of duty.

1582 (*title*), A Particular Declaration..of the undutifull and traiterous Affection borne against her Maiestie by Edmond Campion. **1647** CLARENDON *Hist. Reb.* II. §58 The Old Man..with some bitterness put his Son in mind of his Undutyful carriage towards him. **1697** LUTTRELL *Brief Rel.* (1857) IV. 169 Undutifull words, which were..spoken by him of the King. **1870** J. BRUCE *Life Gideon* xx. 368 Gideon's ..undutiful because unbelieving demeanour.

2. Lacking in the observance of duty.

1593 SHAKS. *3 Hen. VI*, v. v. 33, I know my dutie, you are all vndutifull. **1623** GOUGE *Serm. Extent God's Provid.* §7 Such undutifull servants as take occasion from their masters ..weaknesse. **1641** TATHAM *Distracted State* II. i, And y'ave proved The most undutiful'st of all her children. **1700** T. BROWN *Amusem. Ser. & Com.* viii. (1709) 81 Many Citizens Wives had hard Hearts, Undutiful Husbands, and Disobedient Children. **1748** RICHARDSON *Clarissa* (1811) I. xli. 312 Come not near us, if you resolve to be undutiful. **1831** *Society* I. xii. 178 She..begged him to remonstrate with the undutiful girl. **1849** MACAULAY *Hist. Eng.* vi. II. 117 The King in reply sharply reprimanded his undutiful Councillors.

un'dutifully, *adv.* (UN-¹ 11: cf. prec.)

1583 BABINGTON *Commandm.* (1590) 216 These boiling hearts not bearing iust reproofe, vnduetyfullie haue often.. repined at their authoritie. **1643-5** MILTON *Divorce* II. xvi, It justifies a man in so doing, that nothing is done undutifully to father or mother. **1693** *Dryden's Juvenal* IV. (1697) 79 The Fish had long in Cæsar's Ponds been fed, And from its Lord undutifully fled. **1824** SCOTT *St. Roman's* xviii, He had a son who most undutifully laughed at all this. **1849** MACAULAY *Hist. Eng.* iv. I. 457 The guilt of having acted undutifully and disrespectfully towards France.

un'dutifulness. (UN-¹ 12.)

1549 CHEKE *Hurt Sedit.* (1569) F iv b, The haie..hath bene by mens ydlenesse and vndutifulnesse, let alone vntouched. **1571** DK. NORFOLK in *14th Rep. Hist. MSS. Comm.* App. IV. 574, I confesse my unduetifullnes nowe hath blotted the same. **1662** HIBBERT *Body Divinity* I. 278 Not to answer when called, is incivility in most, and it is undutifulness in some. **1742** FIELDING *J. Andrews* II. vi, He had seen such examples of undutifulness happen from the too early generosity of parents. **1825** T. HOOK *Sayings* Ser. II. I. 168 The extraordinary undutifulness of his child. **1876** MISS YONGE *Womankind* xvi, Opposition or undutifulness are fatal blots in a Christian character.

un'duty. *rare.* (UN-¹ 12.)

1594 H. WALPOLE in *Cath. Rec. Soc. Publ.* V. 266 For which my vndutye I humbly crave pardon. *Ibid.* 267.

un'dwellable, *a.* (UN-¹ 7 b.)

1382 WYCLIF *Jer.* vi. 8 Be taȝt, Jerusalem,..lest par auenture I sette thee desert, a lond vndwellable. **1611** FLORIO, *Inhabitabile*, vnhabitable, vndwellable.

un'dwelt, *ppl. a.* [UN-¹ 8 b, c.] Not dwelt *in*; †uninhabited.

c **1550** CHEKE *Matt.* xii. 44 He commeth and findeth it vndwelt in, swept, and trimmd. **1613** W. BROWNE *Brit. Past.* I. i. 635 If beautie wanting lovers long should stay, It like an house undwelt in would decay. **1674** MARVELL *Ball. Ld. Mayor & Aldermen* ii, Whilst their churches [are] unbuilt, And their houses undwelt.

'undy, *a. Her.* [Anglicized f. UNDEE *a.*] Wavy.

1592 WYRLEY *Armorie* 9 The sonne of Thomas went away with his ancestors marke without distinction (being vndie golde and red). **1611** COTGR., *Vndé*,..in Blason, vndie, or wauie. **1728** CHAMBERS *Cycl.*, *Undee*, or Undy, in Heraldry. See *Wavy.* **1780** *Encycl. Brit.* (ed. 2) V. 3588/1 Vert, a Chief undy Or. **1880** *Encycl. Brit.* XI. 694/1 A bend undy or wavy is not a mere bend with a wavy edge, but the whole bend is in waves.

un'dye, *v.* (UN-² 3.)

14.. LYDG. in *MS. Soc. Antiq.* 134 fol. 1 (Halliwell), Blakke into white may not be undyed, Ne blood infecte with corrupcioun.

un'dyed, *ppl. a.* (UN-¹ 8.)

1538 ELYOT, *Abaphus*, vndied or vncoloured. **1570** LEVINS *Manip.* 50 Undyed, *non tinctus.* **1603** J. DAVIES (Heref.) *Extasie* Wks. (Grosart) I. 91/2 Thou shalt haue powre to crush the crownes of kings.., and yet thy hands vndide. *a* **1618** RALEIGH *Rem.* (1661) 191 About fourscore thousand undrest and undied cloaths. **1807** WORDSW. *White Doe* VII. 58 A hood of mountain-wool undyed. **1880** L. WALLACE *Ben-Hur* 32 An unbleached, undyed blanket.

un'dying, *ppl. a.* [UN-¹ 10.] That does not die; immortal.

a **1300** *Cursor M.* 18620 He ras..Bath godd and man als he was ar, Vndeiand [*Trin.* Vndyinge] nu for euermar. **1608** BEAUM. & FL. *Four Plays in One* III. Wks. 1912 X. 337 And [I] wish heartily, That firm affection.. May take as deep undying root..Betwixt my Daughter Casta, and your goodness. **1667** MILTON *P.L.* VI. 739 Driven down To chains of Darkness, and th' undying Worm. **1816** BYRON *Siege Cor.* xv, They fell devoted, but undying. **1887** MORRIS *Odyss.* XI. 133 Unto the Gods undying of the widespread heavenly home.

absol. **1821** [see UNBORN *ppl. a.* 3]. **1891** MORRIS (*title*), The Story of the Glittering Plain,..or the Acre of the Undying.

b. *transf.* Of feelings, etc.

c **1765** FALCONER *Occas. Elegy* 31 No more..Shall.. hopeless Love impart undying pain. **1816** BYRON *Ch. Har.* III. c, By heavenly feet thy paths are trod,—Undying Love's. **1885** 'MRS. ALEXANDER' *Valerie's Fate* v, The undying interest ever felt by kindly women in a question of love or marriage.

Hence **un'dyingly** *adv.*, **un'dyingness.**

a **1864** HAWTHORNE *Septimius* (1872) 33 That strange idea of undyingness which had recently taken possession of him. **1881** MISS BRADDON *Asph.* II. 282 He remembered how devotedly,..undyingly, he had once loved..Madeline.

une, obs. Sc. var. OVEN.

† **une**, *v. Obs.* [ad. L. *ūnīre* (= It. *unire*, OF. and mod.F. *unir*, Sp. and Pg. *unir*), f. *ūn-us* one.] *trans.* To unite.

c **1400** *Beryn* 3724 The hole science of al surgery Was vnyd, or the chaunge was made of both hir eye, With many sotill enchauntours. *c* **1450** *Myrr. Our Ladye* 104 So..had yt bene vnpossyble that thys worde..shulde haue bene touched.. but yf yt had bene vned to mannes body. **1526** *Pilgr. Perf.* (W. de W. 1531) 295 This is how the hole ymage of god, memory, vnderstandynge and wyll, be vned and ioyned to god. **1534** MORE *Treat. Passion* Wks. 1348/2 He is not by the spirite of god vnyd with holy saintes as a liuely membre of Christes..body. **1538** BALE *God's Promises* III. C ij, O most myghtye gouernour of thy people,..that of two maketh one, vnynge the Jewes with the gentyles in one churche.

refl. **1533** tr. *Erasmus' Com. Crede* 69 b, It vned or dyd knytte itselfe into one hypostase or persone.

b. In Sc. use in pa. pple.

Perh. in some instances ad. L. *ūnīt-us*: see UNITE *ppl. a.*

1456 SIR G. HAY *Gov. Princes* Wks. (S.T.S.) II. 133 Than is the naturale hete unyt in the body. **1529** *Reg. Privy Seal Scot.* II. 49/2 The barony of Wester Ferny with certane uther landis and officis annexit and unit thairto. **1568** *Peebles Burgh Rec.* (1872) 73 The said prebendarie of the Rude and Halie Bludealtare, baith vnit in ane. **1615** *Reg. Great Seal Scot.* 543/1 Quhilk deanrie is unit and incorporat to the patrimonie of the said colledge.

Hence † **'uning** *vbl. sb. Obs.*

1545 DOUGLAS in *St. Papers Hen. VIII*, V. 418, I sal..be glade to set fordvart the uneing off thir two Relmis.

† **une**, app. an obs. var. of EVEN *adv.*

c **1400** *Destr. Troy* 1545 The walles vp wroght..Fro the vrthe vpward vne of a mesure. *Ibid.* 5529 He was made as a mon fro þe myddell vp, And fro the nauyll by-neithe, vne an abill horse.

un'eager, *a.* (UN-¹ 7.)

1819 KEATS *Lamia* I. 218 Like a young Jove with calm uneager face. **1844** LD. HOUGHTON *Mem. Many Scenes* 186 A youth..with dull, uneager face.

Hence **un'eagerness.**

c **1867** HARDY *Time's Laughingstocks* (1909) 83 Your intention seemed Converted by my false uneagerness To putting off for ever the caress.

un'eagled, *a.* (UN-¹ 9.)

1858 [see UNCROSSED 1].

uneais, Sc. var. UNEATHS. *adv. Obs.*

un'eared, *ppl. a. Obs.* exc. *arch.* [UN-¹ 8 + EAR *v.*¹] Unploughed, untilled.

c **1000** ÆLFRIC *Gloss.* in Wr.-Wülcker 147 *Rus*, unered land. *c* **1440** *Pallad. on Husb.* II. 15 The balkis that they calle vnered lond. **1558** *Reg. Cupar Abbey* (1890) II. 268 [He] sall ere.. Robertsonis land for this instant crope, safar as is vnerit. *c* **1600** SHAKS. *Sonn.* iii, Where is she so faire whose vn-eard wombe Disdaines the tillage of thy husbandry? **1922** JOYCE *Ulysses* 200 When he wants to do for him, and for all other and singular uneared wombs, the holy office an ostler does for the stallion.

un'earned, *ppl. a.* [UN-¹ 8.]

1. Not earned by merit or desert; unmerited or undeserved (as reward or punishment).

c **1200** *Trin. Coll. Hom.* 33 Deflen..bireueden him [Adam] alle his riche weden, þat waren unerned giue, and undeð-licnesse. **1599** SHAKS. *Mids. N.* v. i. 439 If we haue vnearned lucke, Now to scape the Serpents tongue, We will make amends ere long. **1796** MME. D'ARBLAY *Camilla* II. 383 The sufferings, so utterly unearned by fault or by folly, of a sister so dear to her. **1805** WORDSW. *Prelude* VI. 168 Such dispositions then were mine unearned By aught, I fear, of genuine desert.

2. a. Not earned by labour; not worked for.

1667 MILTON *P.L.* IX. 225 Casual discourse..intermits Our dayes work brought to little,..and th' hour of Supper comes unearn'd. **1708** J. PHILIPS *Cyder* I. 374 Wilt thou.. rather chuse To lye supinely, hoping Heav'n will..give thee Bread unearn'd? **1799** COLERIDGE *Ode to Duchess of Devonsh.* 17 Rich viands..Were yours unearned by toil. **1850** GROTE *Greece* II. lxii. VIII. 53 This anticipation of an unearned salary. **1873** HAMERTON *Intell. Life* I. iii. 11 One of the unearned gifts of nature.

b. ***unearned increment***, such increase in the value of land or property as takes place without labour or expenditure on the part of the owner.

1871 *Scotsman* 10 Aug. 3/7 But there is no doubt that the touch of his [*sc.* Scott's] pen does in many places form an important element of that unearned increment of value—that, I believe, is the scientific term—which Mr Stuart Mill and friends propose shortly to transfer from the lords of the soil to the Lords of the Treasury. **1873** J. S. MILL in *Dissert. & Discuss.* (1875) IV. 299 The detention by the State of the unearned increment of rent. **1884** in A. Cawston *Street Improv. London* (1893) 115 The increased value, the unearned increment of this property.

c. ***unearned income***, (an) income derived from property, interest payments, etc., as opposed to one from a wage, a salary, or from fees.

1889 G. B. SHAW *Fabian Essays in Socialism* 189 A growing disposition to impose a tax of twenty shillings in the pound on obviously unearned incomes. **1912** P. SNOWDEN *Living Wage* xiii. 148 Even if the enforcement of a living wage lessened the spending power of the people who live on 'unearned incomes', that, too, would be for the national good. **1935** *Planning* 15 Jan. 5 In the case of a married couple the first 30s of unearned income is not taken into account. **1965** AUDEN *About House* (1966) 15 No unearned income Can buy us back the gait and gestures To manage a baroque staircase. **1970** *Times* 29 Jan. 27/5 Is it not about time that the starting point for the imposition of surtax on 'unearned' income be raised above £2,000 per annum?

un'earnest, *a.* (UN-¹ 7.)

1542 UDALL *Erasm. Apoph.* 332 Alyᵉ whyle [he] pronounced suche an hainous matier wᵗ an unearnest countenaunce. **1548** —— *Erasm. Par. Luke* xii. 105 Except that euen those veraie thinges..be possessed of vs after an vnearnest sorte. **1611** FLORIO, *Disferuorare*, to make vnearnest, to coole. **1877** ABP. BENSON in *Life* (1899) I. 435 The state of things in which she wrote was..very unearnest in many ways.

un'earth, *v.* [UN-² 5 and 6.]

1. *trans.* To dig out of the earth, to exhume; to disclose by the removal of earth.

c **1450** *Mirour Saluacioun* (Roxb.) 7 When he his fadirs body efter deth vnherthid. **1626** T. H[AWKINS] *Caussin's Holy Ct.* 67 As Diamonds buryed in a Dunghill, which if once you vn-earth,..will set the sunne before your eyes. **1798** WORDSW. *Simon Lee* 75, I chanced to see This old Man doing all he could To unearth the root of an old tree. *a* **1845** BARHAM *Ingol. Leg.* Ser. III. *Knight & Lady*, His cane,.. which he used..when unearthing his worms and his grubs. **1877** HUXLEY *Physiogr.* 209 When the ruins were first unearthed, the upper floor stood much higher.

b. To force out of a hole or burrow.

1622 MABBE tr. *Aleman's Guzman d' Alf.* I. 48 Hee was jealous, that the Foxe was now vn-earthed. **1730** THOMSON *Autumn* 475 The sly destroyer of the flock..from his craggy winding haunts unearth'd. **1818** SCOTT *Rob Roy* xii, We will join the rest..and see their luck at unearthing the badger. **1844** H. H. WILSON *Brit. India* III. 39 One man..dug a hole in the ground deep enough to give him shelter,..[but] he was speedily unearthed.

transf. **1841** LEVER *C. O'Malley* cxii, Oh, it's you, is it?—at last! so I've unearthed you, have I?

c. To free from, to clear by removal of, earth. **1663** DAVENANT *Siege of Rhodes* I. 31 Away! unchain the Streets, unearth the Ports! Pull down each barracade!

2. *fig.* To bring to light; to disclose, reveal, discover, etc. (Freq. from *c* 1860.)

1820 BYRON *Blues* ii, *Scamp*. They have merit, I own.. *Ink*. Then why not unearth it in one of your lectures? **1863** COWDEN CLARKE *Shaks. Char.* xii. 308 You may trust a woman to unearth a plot. **1883** STEVENSON *Silverado Sq.* 114 What would I not have given to unearth a letter..?

3. *fig.* To free from earthly qualities.

1765 J. BROWN *Chr. Jrnl.* 286 O to be unearthed, unselfed, that I may be like him!

Hence **un'earthed** *ppl. a.*[1]; **un'earthing** *vbl. sb.* and *ppl. a.*

1612 *Two Noble K.* v. i. 58 Thou mighty one,..whose havocke in vaste Feild Vnearthed skulls proclaime. **1870** MORRIS *Earthly Par.* III. IV. 21 An unearthed blind mole.. Was wandering there. **1876** FOX BOURNE *Locke* II. xv. 527 To invent,..with much..material of his own unearthing, the art of logic. **1897** *19th Cent.* Aug. 276, I got to regard a resurrection man as..an unearthly because unearthing demon.

un'earthed, *ppl. a.*[2] [UN-[1] 8.] Not buried; not carried into the ground.

1513 DOUGLAS *Æneid* VI. ii. 145 Vnerdit lyis of new the deid body. *Ibid.* v. 62. **1905** *Elect. World & Engin.* 18 Feb. 339 (Cent. Suppl.), Giving over 14,000 volts between the unearthed conductors.

un'earthliness. (UN-[1] 12; cf. next.)

(*a*) **1860** PUSEY *Min. Proph.* 569 A picture of our Lord's humility and of the unearthliness of His kingdom. **1896** G. A. SIMCOX in *Academy* 22 Feb. 150/3 The world..liked him all the better for the elegant unearthliness of his aspect.

(*b*) **1867** H. MACMILLAN *Bible Teach.* ii. 33 There was a coldness and unearthliness about it..which repelled..me.

un'earthly, *a.* [UN-[1] 7.]

1. Rising above what is characteristic of earth; exalted, sublime; celestial.

1611 SHAKS. *Wint. T.* III. i. 7 O, the Sacrifice. How ceremonious, solemne, and vn-earthly It was i' th' Offring? **1795** COLERIDGE *Refl. Place of Retirem.* 24 The inobtrusive song of Happiness, Unearthly minstrelsy! **1855** BRIMLEY *Ess.* (1858) 304 [An] almost unearthly intensity of faith, love, and resignation. **1876** H. W. PULLEN *Mod. Christianity* 73 Having made choice of an unearthly Guide, you should be content to follow Him along unearthly paths.

2. Not belonging to this earth; supernatural, mysterious, ghostly. (Cf. Sc. *wanearthly*.)

a **1802** *Tamlane* xxxv. in Scott *Minstrelsy*, How shall I thee knaw Amang so many unearthly knights? **1828** LYTTON *Pelham* II. x, A mysterious and unearthly communion of the soul with the beings of another world. **1871** L. STEPHEN *Playgr. Eur.* ii. 82 There is something almost unearthly in the sight of enormous spaces of hill and plain.

b. Of sounds or voices.

1808 SCOTT *Marm.* II. Introd., In the bittern's distant shriek, I heard unearthly voices speak. **1846** MRS. A. MARSH *Father Darcy* II. xi. 183 The unearthly sound.. immediately ceased. **1890** 'R. BOLDREWOOD' *Col. Reformer* (1891) 150 The half-heard music is full of unearthly cadences.

c. *colloq.* Not appropriate to anything earthly; absurdly early or inconvenient.

1865 MRS. CARLYLE *Lett.* (1883) III. 267 Your starting from the Gill at an unearthly hour. **1891** MRS. RIDDELL *Mad Tour* 63 In the streets of Cologne at that unearthly hour in the morning.

un'ease, *sb.* [UN-[1] 12. Cf. WANEASE *sb.*] Want or lack of ease; discomfort; uneasiness.

App. not in use in the 18th cent., and not common in the 19th till about 1880.

a **1300** *Cursor M.* 29091 Discipline..in askes and in hare, And weping and vneses lair. *c* **1400** *Rom. Rose* 3102 Thanne seide I, ser, not you displease To knowen of myn gret vnnese. *a* **1450** *Knt. de la Tour* (1906) 152 That none other creatoure aught not to be ameruailed to suffre displesaunce and vnese, whanne so high a lady suffered..so gret sorw and tribulacion. **1523** LD. BERNERS tr. *Froiss.* I. cxlvi. 174 We haue endured moche payne and vnease. **1593** NASHE *Christ's Tears* 13 More and more thou addest to my vnease. **1632** LITHGOW *Trav.* VII. 327 In this unease Of tackling Boards, we so the way make short. **1676** HOBBES *Iliad* Pref. (1686) 3 Such unease, as in a Coach a man unexpectedly finds in passing over a furrow. **1828** CARR *Craven Gloss.*, *Unease*, uneasiness. **1857** SIR F. PALGRAVE *Norm. & Eng.* II. 458 The unease thereby occasioned was exceedingly enhanced ..when general belief superadded [etc.]. **1894** J. KNIGHT *D. Garrick* vii. 109 A tendency to self-consciousness with a consequent unease was a fault of his style.

†**un'ease**, *v.* *Obs.* [UN-[2] 4.] *trans.* To incommode, trouble, distress.

c **1400** *Laud Troy Bk.* 14481 Vnnethes of vs is any That we nare wounded or vnhesed. *c* **1440** *Pallad. on Husb.* III. 562 Cannetes old ek tyme is now to wede, And of to kytte hit that their roote vneseth. **1464** *Rolls of Parlt.* V. 568/1 The comon people..is gretely uneased therby. *c* **1590** J. STEWART *Poems* (S.T.S.) II. 195 Not, Sir, til vneis ȝow, Bot mening to meis ȝow.

un'easeful, *a.* (UN-[1] 7.)

1515 in Ellis *Orig. Lett.* Ser. II. I. 266 Forsomuche as the Quene-is lyeng here is uneasfull and costelye, by occasion of farre cariage of every thing. **1567** DRANT *Horace, Ep.* xii. E iij, For thou this drosse, vneasefull drosse, doste sette but little by. **1840** LOWELL *The Moon* 28 Howe'er its waves above May toss and seem uneaseful.

Hence **un'easefulness**.

1661 RUST *Origen's Opin.* 74 If this gentler smart and uneasefulness will not reclaim them.

un'easily, *adv.* [UN-[1] 11.]

†**1. a.** With difficulty on account of discomfort; only with pain or suffering. *Obs.*

c **1290** *Beket* 2211 in *S. Eng. Leg.* I. 170 With luytel aise he miȝte sitte, and ful on-aisi-liche ride, And on-aisiliche ligge also. **1535** STEWART *Cron. Scot.* (Rolls) II. 534 Vneselie thocht that he mycht ryde or go,..Than vp he rais rycht fraklie on his feit. **1600** HAKLUYT *Voy.* III. 54 It was.. counted a place very hardly and vneasily to be inhabited for the great colde.

†**b.** Not in any easy or simple manner; with difficulty or trouble. *Obs.*

1600 E. BLOUNT tr. *Conestaggio* 232 Where (although vneasily)..they might imbarke and descend. **1669** STURMY *Mariner's Mag.* A. 4, I might haply appear..monstrous to the eye of the World, and uneasily escape submersion. **1725** SLOANE *Jamaica* II. 17 They are uneasily kept from apes and squirrels.

2. In an uneasy or uncomfortable manner; in such a way as to cause discomfort.

In older use (*a*) of physical uneasiness.

(*a*) **1377** LANGL. *P. Pl.* B. XIV. 232 He goth to cold beddynge, And his heued vn-heled vn-esiliche I-wrye. *a* **1425** tr. *Arderne's Treat. Fistula*, etc. 38 þai slepe vnesely; þai ar made heuy als wele in mynde as in body. **1550** THOMAS *Ital. Dict.*, *Distretto*, straictly or vneasilie. **1621** J. TAYLOR (Water P.) *Sir G. Nonsence* Wks. (1630) Aa 1 b, Resting vneasily on a banke of Sicamores. **1822–7** GOOD *Study Med.* (1829) I. 211 Concentrated jellies..sit more uneasily on a weak stomach, than meat..in a solid form.

(*b*) **1863** MRS. OLIPHANT *Salem Chapel* iv. 30 Mr. Vincent stood uneasily at a corner when he was brought into the apartment. **1887** MISS BETHAM-EDWARDS *Next of Kin Wanted* II. xi. 140 He..hemmed and ha'd uneasily.

†**3.** Without ease; awkwardly. *Obs.*—[0]

1611 COTGR., *Inhabilement*,..vnweldily, vneasily, vnhandsomely.

un'easiness. [UN-[1] 12.]

†**1.** The quality of being troublesome. *Obs.*

1387 TREVISA *Higden* (Rolls) VII. 331 He commaundede to put out Lanfranc out of Normandye for his unesynes [L. *pro sua importunitate*]. **1712** in J. J. Vernon *Par. & Kirk Hawick* (1900) 100 The s[ai]d day compeared Bessie Pasley ..for her uneasiness among her nighbours.

†**2.** Difficulty; difficult nature or character.

1594 R. ASHLEY tr. *Loys le Roy* 73 b, The vneasinesse of the places where he made his Conquests. **1645** USSHER *Body Div.* 271 Frowardnesse, and uneasinesse to be intreated. **1691** T. H[ALE] *Acc. New Invent.* 38 Very apt to gather Filth, and of no less uneasiness when fouled to be thoroughly cleansed again.

†**b.** Unwillingness, reluctance. *Obs.*

a **1715** BURNET *Own Time* II. viii. (1897) I. 374 The king.. charged him to tell him the truth. The other did it, though not without some uneasiness. **1737** WHISTON *Josephus, Hist.* IV. iii. §3 The Roman garrisons,..partly out of their uneasiness to take such trouble,..did little or nothing.

†**c.** Unpleasantness; ill feeling. *Obs.*

a **1734** NORTH *Lives* (1826) III. 366, I mentioned before some uneasinesses between the doctor and his seniors about elections. **1771** LEDWICH *Antiq. Sarisb.* 42 The Prelate stiffly refused, and thereby created much uneasiness between Henry and Pope Paschal.

3. Discomfort, trouble, or anxiety, as affecting one's circumstances or welfare. Also (with pl.), an instance of this.

1599 SHAKS. *Hen. V*, II. ii. 27 There's not I thinke a subiect That sits in heart-greefe and vneasinesse Vnder the sweet shade of your gouernment. **1658** *Whole Duty Man* vii. §9 An abundant amends for all the uneasiness and hardship thou canst suffer in the way. **1681** J. SCOTT *Chr. Life* I. i. 8 Short intermissions of the pains and uneasinesses of a wretched Life. **1740** RICHARDSON *Pamela* I. 13 But, may-be, without these Uneasinesses to mingle with these Benefits, I might be too much puffed up. **1805** A. KNOX *Rem.* (1834) I. 29 When we wish to rise above worldly uneasiness.

b. Physical discomfort (falling short of actual or definite pain).

1665 BOYLE *Occas. Refl.* II. xiv. 235 Having sadly Experienc'd the uneasiness of Sickness. **1709** *Phil. Trans.* XXVI. 491 The Cause of this Peeping in the Shell, I take to be from some Uneasiness the young Bird may find there. **1774** GOLDSM. *Nat. Hist.* (1776) II. 55 The infant's cries are sufficient indications of the uneasinesses it must at every interval endure. **1815** J. SMITH *Panorama Sci. & Art* II. 446 With nearly all persons who have breathed this gas, not the least uneasiness or languor subsequently remains. **1862** A. MEADOWS *Man. Midwifery* 220 Pain in the seat of injury, followed by a general sense of uneasiness and distension.

c. Mental discomfort; anxiety, apprehension.

1682 NORRIS *Hierocles* 60 There is a necessity therefore of Impatience and Uneasiness, and that our misery be augmented from the ignorance of our selves. **1709** LADY M. W. MONTAGU *Let. to Miss A. Wortley* 8 Aug., Till then I shall be in terrible uneasiness. **1756** COWPER *Wks.* (1837) XV. 291, I have lately been under some uneasiness at your silence. **1844** KINGLAKE *Eothen* xviii, My coming from an infected city did not cause him the least uneasiness. **1885** 'MRS. ALEXANDER' *At Bay* iv, The next day brought Glynn a few lines..which struck him as expressing more uneasiness than was intended.

un'eastern, *a.* (UN-[1] 7.)

1760–2 GOLDSM. *Cit. W.* li, Unnatural, un-Eastern,.. would be the whole cry. **1838** THACKERAY *Major Gahagan* iv, The phraseology peculiar to my own country..is so uneastern.

un'easy, *a.* [UN-[1] 7.]

1. Not conducing to ease or comfort; productive of physical discomfort. Also in fig. context. †Occas. const. *to* (a person).

c **1290** *Beket* 1446 in *S. Eng. Leg.* I. 148 Swiþe on-aisi [*v.r.* unese] was is brech a-boute for-to ride. **1398** TREVISA *Barth. De P.R.* XVII. clxix. (Bodl. MS.), Whete þat groweth in vnmoderat tyme & vnesy wedre & tyme is vnperfite. **1601** HOLLAND *Pliny* II. 265 If the skin be newly fretted off by wearing some uneasie shoes. **1660** N. INGELO *Bentiv. & Ur.* II. (1682) 21 Golden fetters are as uneasie as those of Iron. **1713** *Guardian* No. 32 ¶7 [He] appeared in Cloths, that were so strait and uneasy to him, that he seemed to move with Pain. **1748** *Anson's Voy.* II. v. 183 The heat in..the tropics must be much more troublesome and uneasy. **1820** KEATS *Hyperion* II. 64 Above her, on a crag's uneasy shelve,.. Shadow'd Enceladus. **1860** HAWTHORNE *Marb. Faun* viii, A minute's walk will transport the visitor from the small, uneasy lava stones.

†**b.** Causing mental discomfort for disquietude; unpleasant, disagreeable. *Obs.*

Very common in 18th cent., freq. with *to*.

1483 *Gower's Conf.* (Caxton) v. 459 Wherof it is y[t] he conceyueth That ylke vnesy [*orig.* unsely] maladye, The which is cleped jelousye. **1669** EARL ORRERY *Parthen.* (1676) 790 Till I knew my Fate..I should be in Horrors, whose visible Effects were the least uneasie part of them. **1691** STILLINGFLEET *Charge* 52 Nothing will be more uneasie to me, than to be forced to make use of any Severity against you. **1744** JOHNSON *Let. to J. Levett* 3 Jan., Not to have the satisfaction of waiting upon [you]..will be a great and uneasy disappointment. **1788** CHARLOTTE SMITH *Emmeline* (1816) IV. 240 The anxiety of Delamere..is uneasy even to me. **1798** —— *Yng. Philos.* IV. 209 My mother,..I thought, wished..to conceal something from me; that something then must be uneasy.

c. Characterized by absence of ease or comfort; suggesting or manifesting want of ease in body or mind.

a **1513** FABYAN *Chron.* VI. clxxii. 167 Alurede, beynge thus ouerset in multytude of enemyes,..ladde an vncertayne lyfe, and vneasy. **1590** SPENSER *F.Q.* I. v. 36 Where was a Caue..Deepe, darke, vneasie, dolefull, comfortlesse. **1647** CLARENDON *Hist. Reb.* II. §55 They..made the residence of any amongst them very uneasy, and very insecure, who were but suspected by them not to wish well to their Proceedings. **1667** MILTON *P.L.* I. 295 His Spear..He walkt with to support uneasie steps Over the burning Marle. **1748** *Anson's Voy.* II. v. 184 That uneasy and suffocating sensation. **1780** *Mirror* No. 88, I soon found my situation at the university a very hard and uneasy one. **1846** MRS. A. MARSH *Father Darcy* II. iii. 75 He sank into an uneasy slumber. **1893** TOUT *Edw. I*, 54, The surgeons exchanged uneasy whispers.

†**2.** Of persons: Troublesome, annoying, disagreeable, unaccommodating (*to* others). *Obs.*

1387 TREVISA *Higden* (Rolls) I. 87 Euere þei beeþ vnesi [L. *inquieti*] to hir owne neiheboures oþer to strong [= strange] men. *c* **1400** *Pilgr. Sowle* (Caxton, 1483) IV. xxxiv. 83 Shirreues shold speke for the peple, so that they be nought mysfaren ne ouercharged with ouer sore seruyce ne by vnesy lordes. **1652** *Nicholas Papers* (Camden) 291, I am much afraid that Mr. Attorney will be very unquiet with his associates and uneasy to the K[ing] in council. **1678** DRYDEN *All for Love* II. i. 26, I kept you far from an uneasie Wife. *a* **1715** BURNET *Own Time* II. xii. (1897) I. 481 He was cynical in the whole administration, and uneasy to the king in every thing. **1737** WHISTON *Josephus, Antiq.* I. xviii. §4 Not caring to be uneasy to his son,..he resolved to be silent.

†**b.** Unfriendly; on bad terms. *Obs.*—[1]

1725 P. WALKDEN *Diary* (1866) 15, I..discoursed them concerning the division that is among them, and they both own they had been uneasy, but were now reconciled.

†**c.** Displeased, dissatisfied. *Obs.*

a **1715** BURNET *Own Time* III. vii. (1900) II. 125 The king was uneasy at this, and sent them several very angry messages. *Ibid.* xvii. 449 The king seemed to be so uneasy with him, that he was glad to send him away from the court.

d. Uncompromising, rigid.

1819 BYRON *Juan* I. lxii, Ladies even of the most uneasy virtue Prefer a spouse whose age is short of thirty.

3. Not easy or simple; difficult, hard, troublesome. Now *rare*. (Common in 17th c.)

In first quot. = 'having difficulty'.

1398 TREVISA *Barth. De P.R.* V. vi. (Tollem. MS.), The thycker and more trowbled spirite that a man hathe, the unneasyer [L. *tanto difficilior*] and the feblier of syghte he is. *Ibid.* VI. xx. (Bodl. MS.), In olde menne abstinence of mete is eth and esy, and in ȝonge menne & children hard and vnesye. **1570** LEVINS *Manip.* 108 Vneasy, *difficilis*. **1591** SAVILE *Tac. Hist.* I. xxi. 50 By lewdenesse and craft (a matter not vneasy) [he] bare it away from good men. **1614** RALEIGH *Hist. World* I. III. 139 About this time the Spartans beganne to perceive how uneasie a thing it would bee to maintaine the warre against men as good as themselves. **1663** BOYLE *Consid. Usef. Nat. Philos.* II. (1664) 348 To keep the rectified Spirit..is more uneasie, than any thing but trial would make one think. *a* **1724** in *Ramsay's Tea-t. Misc.* (1733) I. 22 If I can but get it [*sc.* a sword] drawn, Which will be right uneasy. **1851** HELPS *Comp. Solit.* iii. 37 By a not uneasy diversion of mind, I turned to another branch. **1900–1** in *Eng. Dial. Dict.*

b. Const. with inf. (active or passive).

(*a*) *a* **1548** HALL *Chron.*, *Edw. IV*, 241 The kyng of England answered, that the tounes of Flanders were..verie uneasie to bee kepte when they were conquered. **1603** H. CROSSE *Vertues Commw.* (1878) 45 A way vneasie to be trackt, hard to finde. **1666** BOYLE *Orig. Forms & Qual.* 268 Much more elaborate, and therefore more uneasie to be restored, then that of many other Concretes.

(*b*) **1570** BUCHANAN *Admonitioun* Wks. (S.T.S.) 26 It is not vneasie to persave..that yai meane..ye deid of ye King. **1594** SYLVESTER *Monodia* 82 Till time..had worne away Her sorrowe's edge, uneasie to allay. **1621** QUARLES *Div. Poems, Esther* Wks. (Grosart) II. 58/2 To him there's nought vneasie to atchieue. **1690** T. BURNET *Theory Earth* II. 163 It will be very uneasie to give a satisfactory account ..of the regeneration. **1819** SCOTT *Ivanhoe* ii, 'The road will be uneasy to find,' answered Gurth.

†**c.** Of ways, etc.: Difficult to traverse on account of ruggedness, steepness, or other obstacles. *Obs.*

1550 T. HOBY *Trav.* (1902) 46 It is a very uneasie waye by the reason of the great quantitie of great and sharpe stones that are upon yt. **1604** E. G[RIMSTONE] *D'Acosta's Hist. Indies* IV. vi. 221 As he strived to gette vp a way which was somewhat rough and vneasie, hee was forced to lay holde vpon a braunch. **1697** DRYDEN *Æneis* XI. 458 The flood, constrained within a scanty space, Roars horrible along the uneasy race. **1756** NUGENT *Gr. Tour, Italy* III. 38 Gentlemen..are in the wrong to choose to travel there in winter, for the ways are uneasy at that time, and dangerous.

†**d.** Difficult to handle. *Obs.*—⁰

1611 COTGR., *Inhabile*,.. vnweldie, vneasie, vnhandsome.

4. Uncomfortable or disturbed in mind; anxious, apprehensive.

1680 BURNET *Rochester* Pref. A 5 b, He..seemed not uneasie at my frequent Visits. **1693** in *Verney Memoirs* (1907) II. 486 Nothing but the want of your blessing can make me uneasie, for otherwise I am perfectly happy. **1719** DE FOE *Crusoe* II. (Globe) 362 The Spaniard..found himself very uneasy in the Night, and could by no Means get any Sleep. **1748** *Anson's Voy.* II. ix. 230 We began to be uneasy for her safety. **1782** MISS BURNEY *Cecilia* V. i, It contributed to render her thoughtful and uneasy. **1832** HT. MARTINEAU *Ireland* 38 His countenance brightened,..but he still seemed uneasy till he had put one question. **1859** W. COLLINS *Q. of Hearts* I. 117, I was..as anxious and as uneasy as our guest.

b. Suffering physical discomfort.

1725 N. ROBINSON *Th. Physick* 276 If he be very restless and uneasy, let the following Prescriptions be exhibited.

c. Of animals: Restless, unsettled.

1855 *Poultry Chron.* II. 449/2 Should they not be fed at regular intervals, it will tend to make them uneasy and discontented. **1897** 'MRS. RAYNER' *Type-writer Girl* xix, Like..restless Spanish sheep in spring, when they herd and leap, uneasy to be driven to their pastures in the mountains.

d. *transf.* Of things: Moving in a disturbed or unquiet manner.

1816 L. HUNT *Rimini* III. 61 Scattering smiles on this uneasy earth. *c* **1860** H. STUART *Seaman's Catech.* 62 Weights at the extremities cause a ship to be uneasy in a seaway. **1894** CROCKETT *Raiders* 103 The upper arch of the cave is not less than forty feet above the floor of uneasy water.

5. Quasi-*adv.* Uneasily.

1596 MASCALL *Govt. Cattle* 120 Let your axeltrees..fill close the nathes of the wheeles, for when they gaggle or shake, they goe vneasie. **1597** SHAKS. *2 Hen IV*, III. i. 31 Vneasie lyes the Head, that weares a Crowne. **1684** *Contempl. St. Man* II. viii. (1699) 226 You..will perswade your self, that you never laid so uneasie in your whole Life before. **1807** SOUTHEY *Espriella's Lett.* I. 176 The farmer told him it was but an uneasy-going beast. **1862** THACKERAY *Philip* xxviii, [So] thinks the general, rolling uneasy on the midnight pillow.

un'eatable, *a.* (UN-¹ 7 b.)

1611 COTGR., *Immangeable*, vneatable, vnfit to be fed on. **1775** ADAIR *Amer. Ind.* 16 The..Indians..formerly reckoned it [*sc.* opossum] as..uneatable an animal, as a hog. **1798** W. BLAIR *Soldier's Friend* 16 Biscuits would..be preferable: a loaf becomes mouldy and uneatable in a few days. **1861** MUSGRAVE *By-roads* 12 A dreary breadth of sand hills, dotted with tufts of uneatable herbage and rank weeds. **1876** MRS. WHITNEY *Sights & Ins.* xviii, We got an uneatable dinner (having blundered upon a wrong hotel).

Hence **un'eatableness**.

1869 *Trans. Entom. Soc.* I. 21 Thus showing that the spines were not the cause of the uneatableness of the larvæ.

un'eaten, *ppl. a.* [UN-¹ 8 b. Cf. ON. *ú-etinn*, MDu. *ongeëten* (Du. *-gegeten*), MLG. *ungegeten*, MHG. *ungeëzzen*, *-gëzzen* (G. *ungegessen*).] Not eaten; left undevoured.

c **1290** *St. Brendan* 301 in *S. Eng. Leg.* I. 227 Al ore couent nis nouȝt here, ake muche it hath vn-ete [*v.r.* for moche del is un-y-ete]. *c* **1375** *Sc. Leg. Saints* vii. (*James Min.*) 682 For nothire wes lewit in þat towne hwnde, na catte,..vn-hetyne, be þis wes done. *c* **1450** *Bk. Hawking* in *Rel. Ant.* I. 307 Of thees fleschys loke that she have good plente ech day, so that shce leve sum what uneton. **1611** BEAUM. & FL. *King & No King* III, Therefore I will out-swear him and all his followers, that this is all that's left uneaten of my sword. **1630** J. TAYLOR (Water P.) *Siege Jerus.* Wks. 15/1 From out their throats they tear the meat in haste, Halfe eaten, halfe vneaten. **1791** COWPER *Odyss.* VIII. 582 A huge brawn, of which uneaten still Large part and delicate remain'd. **1868** *Rep. U.S. Commissioner Agric.* (1869) 297 The remains of the uneaten leaves must be carefully taken away.

u'neath, *a. Obs.* or *arch.* Forms: (see quots.) [OE. *unéaðe*, *-íeðe*, etc.: see UN-¹ 7 and EATH *a.*] Difficult, hard, troublesome, distressing.

a **900** *Andreas* 205 Nis þæt uneaðe eallwealdan gode to ȝefremmanne on foldweȝe. *c* **1000** ÆLFRIC *Saints' Lives* xiii. 247 Þa cwæð dauid him to: Uneaðe me is ðis. *c* **1050** *Voc.* in Wr.-Wülcker 444 *Molestus*, unyþe. *a* **1200** *Moral Ode* 181 Nis na sullic þech hom bo wa and hom be uneaðe [*v.r.* uneaðe]. *c* **1205** LAY. 2259 Corineus wes un-eðe, & wa on his mode.

1570 LEVINS *Manip.* 213 Vneathe, *difficilis*. **1590** SPENSER *F.Q.* IV. x. 39 An altar of some costly masse, Whose substance was vneath to vnderstand. **1629** H. BURTON *Truth's Triumph* 210 The..hare..makes many doubles,.. that vneath it is for the most sagacious pursuer to..finde her out. **1647** H. MORE *Song of Soul* II. liii, But what's within, uneath is to convey to narrow vessels that are full afore. *Ibid.* lxxxv. **1714** CROXALL *Another Orig. Canto Spenser* xii, Where Freres and Monks swarm round, that it uneath May seem 'mongst them to live. **1767** MICKLE *Concubine* II. xxxvii, Uneath it is long Habits to expell. **1799** SCOTT *Covenanter's Fate* xxii, 'I fear me,' quoth he, 'uneath it will be To match thy word with deed'.

uneath (ʌ'niːθ), *adv.* Now only *arch.* Forms: *α.* 1–3 uneaðe (3 -æðe), 2–3 uneðe (2 -ieþe), 3 on-, 4 uneþe, 4–6 unethe (4–5 on-), 6 *Sc.* on-, uneith, 6– uneath. *β.* 3–5 unneþe (3 -eæþe, -eðe, onneþe), 4–6 (9) unnethe (5 onnethe, unnythe); 3 unneaðe, -eaþe, 4 onn(y)eaþe, 6–7 unneath, 7 unneeth. *γ.* 4–7 uneth (5–6 oneth), 4 unneþ, 4–7 unneth. (Also 3–7 vn-.) [OE. *unéaðe*, f. *un-* UN-¹ 11 b + *éaðe* EATH *adv.*]

1. Not easily; (only) with difficulty; scarcely, hardly.

In very common use from *c* 1300 to *c* 1600. Usually denoting limitation of the power to act in the way desired or intended, so that the sense of 'scarcely' becomes the prominent one.

c **888** K. ÆLFRED *Boeth.* v. §3 Uneaþe ic mæȝ forstandan þine acsunga. *Ibid.* xxxix. §4 Uneaðe hire cymð ænig mon of, ȝif he ærest an cemð. *c* **950** *Lindisf. Gosp.* Matt. xix. 23 Forðon wlonc uneaðe *vel* hefiȝ innȝeongas in ric heofna. *a* **1000** *Colloq. Ælfric* in Wr.-Wülcker 96 Hwylon forlidenesse ic þolie.., uneaþe cwic ætberstende. ? *a* **1050** *O.E. Chron.* (MS. C) an. 1040, He..astealde þa swiðe strang ȝyld, þæt man hit uneaðe acom. *c* **1205** LAY. 31438 Mucchel del heo sloȝen of þan mon-weorede, and þe king Penda uneðe gon anwende. *a* **1250** *Owl & Night.* 1605 Þu me hauest sore igremed..þat ic may vnneþe speke. **13..** *Sir Beues* (A.) 884 So mani arwes to him þai sende, Unneþe a miȝte him self defende. *c* **1369** CHAUCER *Dethe Blaunche* 712 As I yow telle Vnnethe myght y lenger duelle. **1382** *Pol. Poems* (Rolls) I. 267 Unnethe may prestes seculers Gete any service for thes frers. *c* **1440** *Generydes* 977 So sorowfull he was That he onnethe myght speke to the kyng. *Ibid.* 4946 [He] was..sore for-bled that vnnethe myght he stonde. *a* **1450** *Knt. de la Tour* (1906) 9 Making suche noise that unnethe thei might haue herde the thundre. **1542** UDALL *Erasm. Apoph.* 338 b, Whiche did asmuche benefite to the commen-weale, as uneth any penne maye wryte. **1578** LYTE *Dodoens* v. lxxiv. 641 The blades are cut almost euery day harde by the grounde,..and therefore it can vnethe or scarsely growe vp. **1601** HOLLAND *Pliny* II. 90 Thyme seed lyeth so close, that unneth or hardly it can be found. **1631** GOUGE *God's Arrows* I. §70. 117 There was so grievous a mortality of people, as the quicke might unneath burie the dead. *a* **1656** USSHER *Ann.* (1658) 395 His army grew so loaden with the spoile..that they were unneeth able to march above five mile a day. **1739** G. WEST *Abuse Trav.* xliii, A small river, that full slow did glide, As it uneath mote find its watry path For stones and rubbish. **1805** SCOTT *Last Minstrel* VI. xxix, The standers-by might hear uneath, Footstep, or voice,..Through all the lengthen'd row. **1834** HARE *Guesses* (1848) 346 Man's hard, clencht mouth, whence words uneath do slip.

b. Scarcely, hardly, barely (in respect of extent, amount, degree, etc.).

c **1200** *Trin. Coll. Hom.* 33 Þeues..wundeden him swiðe sore, and forleten him unneðe liues. **1297** R. GLOUC. (Rolls) 1421 After him was gayus [emperor] vif ȝer vnneþe. *c* **1300** *Seyn Julian* (Ashm. MS.) 178 Þat led þat bolynde was, vnneþe it þoȝte hire warm. *c* **1374** CHAUCER *Ancl. & Arc.* 135 On him is al hir thought, þat wele vnneþe of mete tooke she keepe. **1390** GOWER *Conf.* I. 364 The remenant of folk aboute Unethe stonden eny doute To werre ech other and to slee. *c* **1430** *Two Cookery-bks.* 44 Put hem in a panne.., & vnneþe ony grece in þe panne. **1484** CAXTON *Fables of Alfonce* i, I haue lyued lenger than thy self haste & vnnethe I haue gete half a frend. **1542** UDALL *Erasm. Apoph.* 296 Uneth any tree [is] more goodly to beholde afarre of then the cypres tree. **1596** FITZ-GEFFREY *Sir F. Drake* (1881) 58 Honour enmoves her to attempt the flight, And wave her feathers (unneath taught to flie). **1606** N. BAXTER *Sidney's Ourania* D ij, Ignorant, lewde, Uneth with one drop of Nectar bedewde.

†**c.** With accompanying negative. *Obs.*

13.. *Guy Warw.* (A.) 254 He no dar his loue keþe, No sen hir wel vnneþe. **1362** LANGL. *P. Pl.* A. v. 100 Al my breste bolleþ for bitter of my galle; May no suger so swete aswagen hit vnneþe. *c* **1400** MAUNDEV. (1919) xxii. 128 Fissches.. casten hem self to the see banke of þat yle, so gret plentee ..þat noman may vnnethe see but fissch. **1412–20** LYDG. *Chron. Troy* I. 3392 Wel onethe he ne myȝt endure Hym to dismembre. **1477** *Paston Lett.* III. 175 The causey..is so over flowyn that ther is no man that may onethe passe it. **1559** *Primer* in *Priv. Prayers* (1851) 90, I dare not unneth make my prayers unto thee, for thou art angry with me. **1600** FAIRFAX *Tasso* V. xxxiv, And further ads,..That none offence could greater be vneath, And yet the place the fault did aggrauate.

†**d.** *ellipt.* with *but.* (Cf. BUT *conj.* 7.) *Obs.*

1601 WEEVER *Mirr. Mart.* C 2 b, A vile contagious mist which can vnneath But pestilence or worse diseases breede.

†**e.** *erron.* Almost. *Obs. rare.*

1590 SPENSER *F.Q.* I. xi. 4 A roaring hideous sound That ..seemd vneath to shake the stedfast ground. **1600** FAIRFAX *Tasso* IV. lix, Thus causelesse hatred, endlesse is vneath.

†**2. a.** Reluctantly, unwillingly. *Obs.*

c **900** tr. *Baeda's Hist.* II. ii. 100 Þa ȝeðafodan þæt uneaðe þa his ȝesacan. *c* **1000** ÆLFRIC *Gen.* xxxii. 11 Ic bidde þe, þæt þu onfo þissa laca... Þa underfeng he hiȝ uneaðe. *a* **1200** *Moral Ode* 189 We ȝeueð uneðe [*v.r.* uneaðe] for his luue a stuche of ure brede. **1382** WYCLIF *Gen.* xxxiii. 11 Vnneth, the brother compellynge, takynge [he] seith, Goo we togideres.

†**b.** In difficult circumstances; in hardship. *Obs.*

1591 SPENSER *F.Q.* I. ix. 38 Is then uniust to each his due to giue?.. Or let him die at ease, that liueth here vneath? *a* **1592** GREENE *Selimus* I. 375 The gray-beard..liu'd at ease, while others liu'd vneath.

†**3.** Scarcely, in respect of time; only just. *Obs.*

c **1000** ÆLFRIC *Gen.* xxvii. 30 Uneaðe Isaac ȝeendode þas spræce, þa Iacob ut eode. *c* **1205** LAY. 16397 Vn-neæðe [*c* 1275 onneþe] wes þis spel isæid to þan ende, þa iseȝen heo Hængest halden ouer dune. *a* **1225** *Leg. Kath.* 1993 Þis wes uneaðe iseid, þet an engel ne com. *a* **1300** *Cursor M.* 11685 Vnnethe had he said þe sune, Quen þe tre it boghed dune. **1382** WYCLIF *Gen.* xxvii. 30 Vnneth Ysaac had fulfillid the word, and Jacob goon out, Esau com. *a* **1400–50** *Alexander* 4185 Vnneth his prayer was past, quen purid all þe cloudis. **1513** BRADSHAW *St. Werburge* I. 1227 Whan kynge Vulfer approched his castell And vnneth was entred into his hall. **1556** J. HEYWOOD *Spider & Fly* lxxiv. 83, I was no soner returnd vnneth, Ere I had..iudgement of deth.

†**u'neaths**, *adv. Obs.* Forms: *α.* 3 uneðes, 4 uneþes, 4–6 unethes (5–6 -is), 5 onethes (-ys), anedes, 6 uneathes. *β.* 2–3 unneðes, 4 unneþes (-is, -ys, -us), 4–6 unnethes (4–5 -is, 5 -ys), 5 onnethis. *γ.* 4 uneths, 4–5, 7 unneths. *δ. north.* and *Sc.* 4 unees, 4–5 un(n)ese, 5 onnese, un(h)es, unnes, wnes, 5–6 uneis, 6 uneais. [f. prec. + -S¹.]

1. = UNEATH *adv.* 1.

α, β, γ. *c* **1200** *Trin. Coll. Hom.* 179 Unneðes hie winnen ȝiet here louerdes rihttes. *c* **1220** *Bestiary* 134 He..nimeð vnneðes ðuræ, for his fel he ðer leteð. *c* **1250** *Gen. & Ex.* 2341 He dede halle ut ðe toðere gon, And spac un-eðes, so e gret. *a* **1300** *Cursor M.* 12686 Hes knes war bolnd sua þat he ne moght vnnethes ga. *Ibid.* 20982 Vneths he bar lif a-way. *c* **1330** R. BRUNNE *Chron. Wace* (Rolls) 1176 Byhinde, bifore, on þeym þei cam, Vneþes any a-wey þer nam. *c* **1380** WYCLIF *Wks.* (1880) 22 Þei wolen travaile..so bisily þat vnneþis may þei at reste seie metenes or masse. **1450** *Paston Lett.* I. 124, I..have soo wesshe this litel bille with sorwfulle terys, that on-ethes ye shalle reede it. **1482** *Monk of Evesham* iv. (Arb.) 23 In a voyce onethys audybille and noo thyng intelligibille. *c* **1520** BARCLAY *Jugurth* (1557) 7 b, Vnnethes coude he with moche paine induce him therto. *c* **1530** LD. BERNERS *Arth. Lyt. Bryt.* (1814) 135 Rockes..of suche heyght, that..the toppe of them myght vnnethes be sene. **1590** SPENSER *F.Q.* II. vi. 1 Vneathes it can refraine From that, which feeble nature couets faine. **1621** BP. MOUNTAGU *Diatribæ* 22 For unneths shall we finde a man..but hath a tang one of these two wayes. **1635** HEYWOOD *Hierarchy* IX. 579 He lifts at juggs.., but they..Had been so well fill'd, that he vnneths may Aduance them..to his head.

δ. *a* **1300** *Cursor M.* 1648 Al ar þai worthþi for to wite, vnnes es ani funden quite. *c* **1375** *Sc. Leg. Saints* xix. (*Christopher*) 247 Þe lytil barne..wox [h]euiare mare & mare, þat vnese oure þe watir he wane. *c* **1400** *Ywaine & Gaw.* 342 There sal cum slik slete and rayne, That unnese sal thou stand ogayne. *c* **1450** *St. Cuthbert* (Surtees) 282 Þar was a grete clernes of lyght,..Vnnes þar on men luke myght. *c* **1475** *Rauf Coilȝear* 157 He start vp stoutly agane—vneis micht he stand. **1500–20** DUNBAR *Poems* lxxii. 45 Vueis with lyf he mycht sustene That croune.

2. = UNEATH *adv.* 2 a.

1388 WYCLIF *Gen.* xxxiii. 11 Vnnethis, while the brothir compellide, he resseyuede, and seide, Go we to gidere.

3. = UNEATH *adv.* 3.

a **1300** *Cursor M.* 8159 Vnnethes [*Gött.* vnese] had he monid his mode, þat a lem fra þe wandes stode. *c* **1340** HAMPOLE *Pr. Consc.* 476 For unnethes es a child born fully þat it ne bygynnes to..cry. **1388** WYCLIF *Gen.* xxvii. 30 Vnnethis Isaac hadde fillid the word, and..Esau cam.

un'eating, *vbl. sb.* (UN-¹ 13.)

1692 R. L'ESTRANGE *Fables* I. 51 They..that take Eating and Drinking, and Un-Eating, and Un-Drinking,..to be the Great Bus'ness of Mankind.

un'ebbing, *ppl. a.* (UN-¹ 10.)

1652 BENLOWES *Theoph.* VII. xc, Flouds of unebbing joyes from Thee do rowl. **1822** BYRON *Juan* VII. lxviii, Oh, glorious laurel! since for one sole leaf,..Of blood and tears must flow the unebbing sea.

un'ebriate, *a.* [UN-¹ 7, 5 b.] **a.** Unintoxicating. **b.** Unintoxicated.

1853 LYTTON *My Novel* IV. xvii, There were..unebriate liquors, pressed from cooling fruits. *Ibid.* VI. xxii, Forth, unebriate, unpolluted, he came from the orgy.

unecclesi'astical, *a.* (UN-¹ 7.) Also **-ally** (UN-¹ 11).

1766 STERNE *Tr. Shandy* IX. iv, Most un-ecclesiastically did the Corporal do it. **1834** MOZLEY *Lett.* (1885) 40 Newman and all his party declare it to be quite unecclesiastical. **1870** F. R. WILSON *Ch. Lindisf.* 41 Carham Church is another of the unecclesiastical buildings.

un'echoed, *ppl. a.* (UN-¹ 8.)

1601 SIR W. CORNWALLIS *Ess.* II. xlii, Speach and reason ..loue trafficke and exercise, the former of which is vnecchoed without company.

un'echoing, *ppl. a.* (UN-¹ 10.)

1817 MOORE *Lalla R.*, *Veiled Proph. Khorassan* 486 The.. Priestess, whose light bound Came like a spirit o'er th' unechoing ground. **1823** J. WILSON *Marg. Lyndsay* ix. 66 There was..no sound in the misty and unechoing air.

une'clipsed, *ppl. a.* (UN-¹ 8.)

1649 RAWLINS in Lovelace *Poems* (1904) 8 More bright Then the first day in 's uneclipsed light, Is thy Lucasta. *a* **1657** R. LOVEDAY *Lett.* (1663) 180 Till the uneclipsed Sun shall chase keen winter before his victorious rayes. **1764** *Phil. Trans.* LIV. 106 A full digit of the Sun, or more, remained uneclipsed. **1827** POLLOK *Course T.* VI. 357 The moon..grew black and dark, Unclouded, uneclipsed. **1882** *Nature* XXV. 573 Various phenomena observed on the uneclipsed sun.

fig. **1675** tr. *Camden's Hist. Eliz.* III. 269 Her Glory..she retained intire to herself and uneclipsed. **1683** in *Lond. Gaz.* No. 1856/5 An uninterrupted, uneclips'd Monarchy. **1824** GALT *Rothelan* IV. vii, Increasing the lustre of your own hitherto unclouded and uneclipsed renown.

uneco'nomical, *a.* (UN-¹ 7.) Also **-ally** *adv.*, **-alness**.

1816 BENTHAM *Chrestom.* Wks. 1843 VIII. 117 As to uneconomicalness. **1840** HERSCHEL *Ess.* (1857) 109 The abandonment of ancient methods as comparatively inefficient and uneconomical. **1881** *Nature* XXIV. 137 It would work..not so uneconomically as to be..fatal to the proposed use.

un'edge, *v.* [UN-² 4.] *trans.* To take the edge off; to blunt. Also *fig.*

a **1614** FLETCHER *Valentinian* I. iii, Here our weapons And bodies..Are both unedg'd and old with ease and women. **1638** MAYNE *Lucian* (1664) 71 Least despaire should lessen their flame, or unedge their desires. **1718** D'URFEY *Grecian*

Heroine v. i, About good Kings, I grant there is a..sacred Virtue That would unedge the Sword of Treachery. **1893** F. THOMPSON *Poems* 37 It seemed corrival of the world's great prime, Made to un-edge the scythe of Time.

un'edged, *a.* (UN-¹ 9.)
1799 LAMB *J. Woodvil* in *Lett.* (1837) I. 126 To instruct raw youth in..practice of the unedg'd players' foils.

un'edible, *a.* (UN-¹ 7 and 5 b.)
1884 *Imp. Dict.* (citing H. Miller). **1894** *19th Cent.* XXXVI. 421 We reposed under a spreading tree, a wild unedible fig.

un'edified, *ppl. a.* (UN-¹ 8.)
1618 FLETCHER *Women Pleas'd* IV. i, This un-edified ambling, hath brought a scourge upon us. **1644** MILTON *Areop.* (Arb.) 59 Our Ministers..frequented with such an unprincipl'd, unedify'd, and laick rabble. **1740** SOMERVILLE *Hobbinolia* II. 261 In Shoals they come, Neglected, feeless Clients, nor return Unedify'd. **1815** LAMB *Lett.* (1888) I. 298 My zeal is great against the unedified heathen. **1859** SALA *Tw. round Clock* (1861) 58 Not wholly, I trust, unedified by the cursory view we have taken of Babylon the Great.

un'edifying, *ppl. a.* (UN-¹ 10, 5 b.)
Also *unedifyingly* adv. (Webster, 1847).
1641 BP. HALL *Answ. Vind. Smect.* ii. 19 Bringing in loud Musick; uncouth, and unedifying Anthems. **1698** NORRIS *Pract. Disc.* (1707) IV. 2 Those that think and know most, being remarkable for speaking least, which makes their conversation so insignificant and unedifying. **1722** WODROW *Corr.* (1843) II. 649 Matters are yet before sub-committees, and tedious, unedifying debates cast up. **1834** BECKFORD *Italy* II. 309 It was not unedifying to witness the solemnity ..with which these devotions were performed. **1881** W. R. SMITH *Old Test. in Jew. Ch.* i. 10 Finding much that seems .., at first sight, positively unedifying.

un'edited, *ppl. a.* (UN-¹ 8, 5 b.)
1829 *Q. Rev.* XXXIX. 368 The unedited Poem on the Superstitions of the North. **1834** J. AKERMAN (*title*), Descriptive Catalogue of Rare and Unedited Roman Coins.

un'educable, *a.* (UN-¹ 7 b, 5 b.)
1884 *Contemp. Rev.* May 685 The sufferer, unless utterly uneducable, is directed to a suitable dietary.

un'educate, *a.* *Obs.* exc. *Sc.* [UN-¹ 8 b.] Uneducated.
1592 KYD *Sol. & Pers.* I. iii. 141 O harsh, vn-edicate, illiterate pesant. **1871** W. ALEXANDER *Johnny Gibb* xxxv, An inhaudin, unedicat taupie chiel.

un'educate, *v.* (UN-² 3.)
1838 R. MUDIE *Man his Phys. Struct.* ii. 66 That system which uneducates the physical powers of the child. **1851** SPENCER *Soc. Stat.* xxvi. §10. 355 A government can educate in one direction only by *un*educating in another.

un'educated, *ppl. a.* (UN-¹ 8.)
1588 SHAKS. *L.L.L.* IV. ii. 17 After his vndressed, vnpolished, vneducated..fashion. *a* **1676** M. HALE *Prov. for Poor* Pref., The multitude of Poor, and necessitous, and uneducated persons. **1780** *Mirror* No. 106, His mind was as empty and uneducated as that of Drexelius. **1847** PRESCOTT *Peru* (1850) II. 348 His uneducated mind had no relish for ..intellectual recreation. **1879** B. TAYLOR *Stud. Germ. Lit.* 87 He was wholly uneducated, could not read and write.
Hence **un'educatedness.**
1825 BENTHAM *Offic. Apt. Maximized, Indic.* (1830) 59 Uneducatedness..operating in extenuation of moral guilt.

un'eerily, *adv.* *Sc.* [UN-¹ 11.] † Fearlessly.
c **1375** *Sc. Leg. Saints* xliii. (*Cecilia*) 379 þai brethire þane vnerely Sad to þe prefet opynly [etc.].

† **un'effable,** *a.* [UN-¹ 7, 5 b.] = INEFFABLE *a.*
c **1400** *Comm. Luke* i. 20 (MS. Bodl. 143), þe heuenly & vneffable natiuyte of crist. **1548** UDALL, etc. *Erasm. Par. John* 26 Therfore there is felt an vneffable strength & efficacie. **1575–85** ABP. SANDYS *Serm.* 264 Yea, inestimable & vneffable was the loue of our gratious Lord. **1614** RALEIGH *Hist. World* I. i. 1 God, whom the wisest men acknowledge to be a Power vneffable. **1689** *Contempl. St. Man.* II. iv. (1699) 160 The Joy and Happiness of God, must needs be infinite and uneffable.

une'ffaceable, *a.* (UN-¹ 7 b and 5 b.)
1611 [see UNDEFACEABLE *a.*]. **1851** [J. B. HUME] *Poems Early Years* 169 A fragment of a sculptur'd stone..; there it lies Apart and uneffaceable.

une'ffaced, *ppl. a.* (UN-¹ 8.)
[**1775** ASH.] **1792** V. KNOX *Serm.* ii. 46 If we have received a good impression, let us bear it away uneffaced to our graves. **1816** BYRON *Siege Cor.* iv, Unnamed accusers.. Within the 'Lion's mouth' had placed A charge against him uneffaced. **1864** PUSEY *Lect. Daniel* 564 Its own unchanging brightness..uneffaced, undimmed, uninjured.

une'ffected, *ppl. a.* (UN-¹ 8.)
1592 KYD *Span. Trag.* III. iv. 80 One onely thing is vneffected yet, And thats to see the Executioner. **1653** WHITELOCKE *Jrnl. Swed. Emb.* (1772) I. 75 Butt the busines was delayed, and uneffected, to Whitelocke's great discouragement. **1846** WORCESTER (citing C. B. Brown).

une'ffectible, *a.* (UN-¹ 7.)
1646 EARL MONM. tr. *Biondi's Civil Wars* IX. 167 Moved by her womanish anger to practise uneffectible Chimæra's, she lost her Honour.

une'ffective, *a.* (UN-¹ 7 and 5 b.)
1670 C. GATAKER in *Gataker's Antid. Errour* Ep. Ded. A iij, The Stars, Skie, Air, or other Elements, which are all ..uneffective upon the wills of men. *a* **1676** HALE *Prim. Orig. Man.* IV. vii. (1677) 351 Yet a Law or Rule or Order is a dead, unactive, uneffective thing of itself.

une'ffectless, *a.* [UN-¹ 7.] Not ineffective.
1607 TOPSELL *Four-f. Beasts* 347 This I haue proued vneffectlesse for this disease, and also much auaileable for any other inward sicknesse.

† **une'ffectual,** *a.* *Obs.* [UN-¹ 7 and 5 b.] = INEFFECTUAL *a.* (Common *c* 1550–1660.)
1548 UDALL, etc. *Erasm. Par. John* i. 7 Moses..brought a lawe vneffectuall, sharpe, and hard. **1590** SWINBURNE *Testaments* 240 The testament made by feare is vneffectuall. **1620** GATAKER *Mariage Praier* 13 The vndue manner of the repairing euen of such to Gods board, maketh those holy things vnfruitfull and vneffectuall vnto them. **1668** R. STEELE *Husbandman's Calling* v. 117 They shall go to Hell for their uneffectual knowledge.
So † **une'ffectually** *adv.*, † **une'ffectualness.**
1661 BAXTER *Mor. Prognost.* II. xxxiii. 55 Nor [shall] an uncertain Evil be *uneffectually resisted by a certain greater Mischief. **1598** FLORIO, *Inefficacia*, *vneffectualnes. **1651** BAXTER *Inf. Bapt.* 319 His..reasons of the uneffectualness of baptism to some. **1663** BOYLE *Usef. Exp. Nat. Philos.* II. 228 Having found the uneffectualness of ordinary Remedies,..he resolved to try a sympathetick Medicine.

† **une'ffectuous,** *a.* *Obs.* (UN-¹ 7.)
1549 W. WYCHERLEY in *Lansd. MS. 2*, fol. 63 b, About two monethes past he vsed..a sworde vnconsecrated, and therefor vneffectuouse.

une'ffeminate, *a.* (UN-¹ 7.)
1606 DRUMM. OF HAWTH. *Answ. Chall. Knts.* Wks. (1711) 233 Men, overcome with Women, are made..far inferior to the Valour of uneffeminate Knights.

une'ffeminate, *v.* (UN-² 6 a.)
1631 QUARLES *Samson* Wks. (Grosart) II. 144/2 That strength of Nature..with her manly bounty did begin To uneffeminate his smoother chin.

une'ffeminated, *ppl. a.* (UN-¹ 8.)
[**1775** ASH.] **1813** T. BUSBY *Lucretius* II. v. p. xxvii, Uneffeminated by luxury, his naked body braved the boisterous winds.

† **unefferyde** (= *un-yfurred*), obs. var. UNFURRED *ppl. a.*
1531 *Rec. St. Mary at Hill* (1905) 44 Item, iiij parteletes of velvett,..two feryd with Cony and two vnefferyde.

uneffi'cacious, *a.* (UN-¹ 7 and 5 b.)
1742 *Johnson's Debates* (1787) II. 264 Mocking her calamities with unefficacious friendship.

une'ffigiated, *ppl. a.* (UN-¹ 8: cf. EFFIGIATE *v.*)
1747 CARTE *Hist. Eng.* I. 44 A great unshapen uneffigiated pillar or obelisk.

une'ffused, *ppl. a.* (UN-¹ 8.)
[**1775** ASH.] **1827** G. S. FABER *Sacr. Calend. Prophecy* (1844) III. 236 The contents of the still uneffused seventh vial.

† **un'egall,** *a.* *Obs.* [UN-¹ 7, 5 b: cf. WFris. *on-, ûnegael*, and UNEQUAL *a.*] Unequal. Also † **un'egally** *adv.*, † **un'egalness.**
1508 FISHER *7 Penit. Ps.* li. Wks. (1876) 104 Is not my waye good and egall, & yours shrewed nought & more *vnegall [L. *prava*]. **1589** PUTTENHAM *Eng. Poesie* I. xx. (Arb.) 57 Not onely because mens estates are vnegall, but for that also vertue it selfe is not in euery respect of egall value. **1541** R. COPLAND *Galyen's Terap.* 2 D ij b, After the pustule is broken there commeth an vlcere dyscoloured with fretyng *vnegally. **1589** PUTTENHAM *Eng. Poesie* II. iii. (Arb.) 81 He must be sometimes swift, sometimes slow, sometime vnegally marching. **1561** T. NORTON *Calvin's Inst.* IV. 98 It behoued that he shoulde shewe that there is no *vnegalnesse betwene vs and them in those good thinges.

une'gested, *ppl. a.* (UN-¹ 8.)
1616 T. ADAMS *Serm.* Wks. (1629) 1053 The former crudities vndigested, vnegested, hauing the greater force, turne the good nutriment into themselues.

unego'tistically, *adv.* (UN-¹ 11.)
1854 E. G. HOLLAND *Mem. Badger* vii. 91 Unegotistically do I record the simple fact.

† **un'egual(ly,** varr. UNEGAL(LY.
1542 UDALL *Erasm. Apoph.* 48 b, Thou and I do carke & feare for a..life of *vnegual valour [= value]. **1553** T. WILSON *Rhet.* 101 b, UnegualI examples commende muche the matter. **1548** UDALL, etc. *Erasm. Par. Luke* xiv. 127 b, To tryе the hasarde of battayle with powers..*vnegually matched.

une'laborate, *a.* (UN-¹ 7 and 5 b.)
1663 BOYLE *Usef. Exp. Nat. Philos.* II. v. vi. 159 Either simples, or cheap, or unelaborate Galenical mixtures. **1688** —— *Final Causes Nat. Things* ii. 44 Most of them..are of such easy and unelaborate contextures. **1747** WARBURTON in *Shakespeare's Wks.* VII. 349 The work of brief nature, i.e. of hasty, unelaborate nature. **1819** WORDSW. *To Rev. Dr. Wordsw.* 34 Whether the rich man's sumptuous gate Call forth the unelaborate sounds [etc.]. **1853** RUSKIN *Stones Ven.* III. ii. 106 The comparatively Hebraized and unelaborate idiom.

une'laborated, *ppl. a.* (UN-¹ 8 and 5 b.)
1817 COLERIDGE *Biog. Lit.* xvii. (1907) II. 38 Simple and unelaborated expressions. **1850** CARLYLE *Latter-day Pamph.* ii. (1872) 21 The materials of human virtue..lie yet unelaborated and stagnant in..[their] souls.

une'lapsed, *ppl. a.* (UN-¹ 8.)
1805 *Ann. Rev.* III. 307 The average unelapsed term of a lease being three years and a half.

une'lastic, *a.* (UN-¹ 7 and 5 b.)
1728 CHAMBERS *Cycl.* s.v. *Elasticity*, The Difference between Elastic and Unelastic Bodies. **1764** REID *Inquiry* vi §21 Are the small vessels distended with some redundant elastic or unelastic fluid? **1826** KIRBY & SP. *Entomol.* IV. xlvi. 259 A hard unelastic substance like wood. **1861** BERESF. HOPE *Eng. Cathedr. 19th C.* 14 An unelastic law of parochial subdivision and endowment.
Hence **unela'sticity.** (Webster, 1847.)

une'lated, *ppl. a.* (UN-¹ 8.)
1710 PALMER *Prov.* 236 How happy shou'd we be, if we cou'd..bear prosperity with a steady unelated mind. **1758** JOHNSON *Idler* No. 11 ¶10 To make man unshaken by calamity, and unelated by success. **1885** *Soc. in London* 285 Unelated by the memory of past successes.

un'elbowed, *ppl. a.* (UN-¹ 8.)
1732 POPE *Ep. Bathurst* 242 Is there a Lord..Whose table, Wit, or modest Merit share, Unelbow'd by a Gamester, Pimp, or Play'r? **1814** WORDSW. *Excurs.* IX. 130 Unelbowed by such objects as oppress Our active powers. **1866** SEELEY *Ecce Homo* xii. 135 When the Roman cannot walk the Via Sacra unelbowed by Greeks and Syrians.

† **un'eld.** *Obs.*$^{-1}$ [UN-¹ 4 b.] Weak or miserable old age.
a **1300** *E.E. Psalter* lxx. 18 Til in un-elde and alder-elde, God, ne forlete me in un-welde.

une'lect, *v.* *rare*$^{-1}$. (UN-² 3.)
1570 FOXE *A. & M.* (ed. 2) 362/2 One Iohn Blund was elected, who..was also repealed and vnelected agayne.

une'lected, *ppl. a.* (UN-¹ 8.)
1581 SIDNEY *Apol. Poetrie* (Arb.) 20 In these my not old yeres.., hauing slipt into the title of a Poet, [I] am prouoked to say somthing vnto you in the defence of that my vnelected vocation. **1607** SHAKS. *Cor.* II. iii. 207 You should haue ta'ne th' aduantage of his Choller, And pass'd him vnelected. **1621** G. SANDYS *Ovid's Met.* v. (1626) 97 Then, vnelected, rudely stept forth one, Who sung the Giants warre. **1836** E. HOWARD *R. Reefer* vi, The agonies of a new-born infant, under the torture of eternal fire, because it had died unelected. **1866** *Sat. Rev.* 8 Sept. 286/1 The privilege of.. telling the unelected many [etc.].

une'lective, *a.* (UN-¹ 7.)
1666 BP. S. PARKER *Free & Impart. Censure* (1667) 161 The Issues of a necessary and unelective cause. *a* **1676** HALE *Prim. Orig. Man.* III. v. (1677) 274 An ignorant, unknowing, unelective Principle.

une'lectric, *a.* (UN-¹ 7.)
[**1775** ASH.] **1876** BLACKMORE *Cripps* xxvii, To do all this required some hours with a mind so unelectric.

une'lectrified, *ppl. a.* (UN-¹ 8.)
1747 *Gentl. Mag.* 200/2 Six being addled eggs, among which was one unelectrified egg. **1771** *Phil. Trans.* LXI. 654 A small unelectrified ball. **1867** NOAD *Text Bk. Electricity* 207 In its natural or unelectrified state the natural electricities..are in equilibrium.

une'lectrify, *v.* (UN-² 6 c.)
1760 *Phil. Trans.* LI. 900 After unelectrifying the bottle, it was set again upon the stand of wood.

une'lectrized, *ppl. a.* (UN-¹ 8.)
1761 *Phil. Trans.* LIII. 84, I placed myself on an electric stand, and, being well electrised, threw my hat to an unelectrised person.

† **u'neled,** *ppl. a.* *Obs.* [f. UN-¹ 8 + OE. *ǣlan* to burn: cf. ANNEAL *v.*] Unbaked.
c **1440** *Pallad. on Husb.* IX. 103 A potters potte vneled wol alete..Yf eny sprynge of water ther wole rise.

† **un'elegant,** *a.* *Obs.* [UN-¹ 7 and 5 b.] = INELEGANT *a.*
1570 LEVINS *Manip.* 26 Vnelegant, *inelegans.* **1611** FLORIO, *Ineleganté*, vnelegant, without grace. **1666** DRYDEN *Ann. Mirab.* Pref., I hope they are neither improper nor altogether unelegant in Verse. **1711** *Spect.* No. 67 ¶8 Concluding..that the Person who collected them is a Man of no unelegant Taste. *a* **1768** SECKER *Serm.* (1771) VII. xv. 343 Possibly in some of these Books you meet with Expressions..which appear unelegant and singular.
So † **un'elegantly** *adv.* *Obs.*
1603 HOLLAND *Plutarch's Mor.* 517 Neither seemeth he unelegantly and besides the purpose..to have expressed as much in this verse. **1659** O. WALKER *Oratory* 23 Transitions ..are not unelegantly ushered in, by the Orators making Interrogations himself. **1758** JORTIN *Erasm.* I. 142 It was no wonder if they wrote it ill and unelegantly.

unele'mentary, *a.* (UN-¹ 7.)
a **1706** EVELYN *Hist. Relig.* (1850) I. 185 Things unelementary, incorporeal, and consequently immortal.

† **un'elementated,** *ppl. a.* (UN-¹ 8.)
a **1706** EVELYN *Hist. Relig.* (1850) I. 156 That they could tell us how to unite an unelementated substance with corporeal matter.

un'elevated, *ppl. a.* (UN-¹ 8.)
1627 W. SCLATER *Exp. 2 Thess.* (1629) 243 Nature, I mean, vneleuated aboue itselfe, and vnaltered by grace. **1690** SHADWELL *Am. Bigot* I, Thou hast a gross unelevated fancy. **1774** *Trinket* 198 A soul unelevated by nature, or

worn down by art. **1877** F. H. LAING *Bacon's Philos. Exam.* 7 So unelevated a philosopher as the materialist Mill.

†**un'eligible**, *a. Obs.* [UN-[1] 7 and 5b.] = INELIGIBLE *a.*

1690 LOCKE *Hum. Und.* I. iii. §13 Unavoidable punishment, great enough to make the transgression very uneligible. **1709** SHAFTESB. *Charac.* (1711) II. 141 He himself may..endeavour the utmost Prolongment of his own un-eligible State. **1775** ADAIR *Amer. Ind.* xx. 187 [The] state of celibacy; which to many of them is as uneligible, as it was to the Hebrew ladies.

une'liminable, *a.* (UN-[1] 7b and 5b.)

1876 *Contemp. Rev.* XXVIII. 800 The uneliminable element of dualistic relation and difference.

un'eloquent, *a.* (UN-[1] 7 and 5b.)

1565 COOPER *Thesaurus* s.v. *Incolo*, A rude style without eloquence: vneloquent. **1603** FLORIO *Montaigne* III. x. 605 If they once conceive a hatred against an Orator.., the next day he becommeth barbarous and vneloquent. **1642** GAUDEN *Serm.* 63 Innocence is often timorous, uneloquent, unexpert. **1885** PENNELL *Fishing* 241 The foregoing description, however uneloquent, may give..a faint idea of what every lover of the sport feels on rising and hooking a salmon.

un'eloquently, *adv.* (UN-[1] 11, 5b; cf. prec.)

1611 COTGR., *Indisertement*, vneloquently. **1792** A. YOUNG *Trav. France* (1794) I. I. 124 He speaks ungracefully, and uneloquently. **1836** J. GILBERT *Chr. Atonem.* ix. 412 We give many of you credit..for kindly deeds, and for recommending them not uneloquently.

une'lucidated, *ppl. a.* (UN-[1] 8.)

[**1775** ASH.] **1845** *Encycl. Metrop.* II. 742/1 The most diligent research has left many things obscure and unelucidated.

DOMI MINA
NVS TIO
ILLV MEA